The Oxford College Dictionary

SECOND EDITION

SPARK PUBLISHING

New York

First published 2002 (as the *Oxford American College Dictionary*)

This second edition published by Spark Publishing, a division of
Barnes & Noble, Inc., by arrangement with Oxford University Press, Inc.

ISBN-13: 978-1-4114-0500-4
ISBN-10: 1-4114-0500-5

Library of Congress Cataloging-in-Publication Data available

This book includes some words that are, or are asserted to be, proprietary names or trademarks. Their inclusion does not imply that they have acquired for legal purposes a nonproprietary or general significance, nor is any other judgment implied concerning their legal status. In cases where the editor has some evidence that a word is used as a proprietary name or trademark, this is indicated by the designation trademark, but no judgment concerning the legal status of such words is made or implied thereby.

Printed and bound in the United States of America

3 5 7 9 10 8 6 4 2

The Oxford College Dictionary

SECOND EDITION

Contents

Staff

FOR THE FIRST EDITION

Managing Editor
Christine A. Lindberg

Staff Project Editors
Suzanne Stone Burke
Joseph M. Patwell

Editors
Orin Hargraves
Alan Hartley
Archie Hobson
Nancy LaRoche
Martha Mayou
Sue Ellen Thompson

Production Coordinator
Karen A. Fisher

Illustrators
Debra Argosy
Marta Cone
Elizabeth Gaus
Matthew Hansen
Mike Malkovas
Susan Van Winkle

Type Compositor
Stephen Perkins,
dataformat.com

Pronunciation Editors
Linda M. Costa
John Bollard
Sharon Goldstein
Anne Marie Hamilton
Katherine Isaacs
Ellen Johnson
William Kretzschmar
Rima McKinzey
Katherine Sietsema
Susan Tamasi
Matthew Zimmerman

Proofreaders
Joan Carlson
Joseph Colpibene
Adrienne Makowski

Keyboarders
Martin Coleman
JoAnn Magyarik
Kimberly Roberts

Technical Support
Elizabeth J. Jewell
Erin McKean
James Marra

FOR THE SECOND EDITION

Publishing Manager
Judy Pearsall

Project Manager
Catherine Soanes

Senior Editor
Christine A. Lindberg

Editor
Benjamin G. Zimmer

Editorial Support
Orin K. Hargraves
Erin McKean

Pronunciation Editors
Constance Baboukis
Katherine Sietsema

Keyboarding
Elizabeth J. Jewell

Data Processing and Technical Support
James McCracken
Orion Montoya

Preface to the First Edition

(first published as the *Oxford American College Dictionary*)

The *Oxford American College Dictionary* is a new kind of college dictionary, written on new principles. It builds on the excellence of the lexicographical traditions of scholarship and analysis of evidence as set down by the *Oxford English Dictionary* over a century ago, but it is also a new, specifically American, departure. The *Oxford American College Dictionary* is a dictionary of current American English, based on currently available evidence and current thinking about language and cognition. It is an inventory of the words and meanings of present-day English, both those in actual use and those found in the literature of the past. The compilers have gone to the heart of the traditional practices of dictionary making and reappraised the principles on which lexicography is based. In particular, the focus has been on a different approach to an understanding of "meaning" and how this relates to the structure, organization, and selection of material for the dictionary.

Linguists, cognitive scientists, and others have been developing new techniques for analyzing usage and meaning, and the *Oxford American College Dictionary* has taken full advantage of these developments. Foremost among them is an emphasis on identifying what is "central and typical," as distinct from the time-honored search for "necessary conditions" of meaning (that is, a statement of the conditions that would enable someone to pick out all and only the cases of the term being defined). Past attempts to cover the meaning of all possible uses of a word have tended to lead to a blurred, unfocused result, in which the core of the meaning is obscured by many minor uses. In the *Oxford American College Dictionary,* meanings are linked to central norms of usage as observed in the language. The result is fewer meanings, with sharper, crisper definitions.

The style of definition adopted for the *Oxford American College Dictionary* aims in part to account for the dynamism, imaginativeness, and flexibility of ordinary American usage. The *Oxford American College Dictionary* records and explains all normal meanings and uses of well-attested words, but also illustrates transferred, figurative, and derivative meanings, insofar as these are conventional within the language.

The layout and organization of each entry in the dictionary reflect this new approach to meaning. Each entry has at least one core meaning, to which a number of sub-senses, logically connected to it, may be attached. The text design is open and accessible, making it easy to find the core meanings and so to navigate the entry as a whole.

At the heart of this dictionary lies the evidence. This evidence forms the basis for everything that we, as lexicographers, are able to say about the language and the words within it. In particular, the large databank of searchable electronic texts collected by Oxford gives, with its 100 million words, a selection of real, modern, and everyday language, equivalent to an ordinary person's reading over ten years or more. Using computational tools to analyze this databank and other corpora, the editors have been able to look at the behavior of each word in detail in its natural contexts, and so to build up a picture for every word in the dictionary.

Databank analysis has been complemented by analysis of other types of evidence: the *Oxford American College Dictionary* makes extensive use of the citation database of the Oxford North American Reading Program, a collection of citations (currently standing at more than 69 million words and growing at a rate of about 4.5 million words a year) taken from a variety of sources from all the English-speaking countries of the world. In addition, a specially commissioned reading program targeted previously neglected specialist fields as diverse as computing, alternative medicine, antique collecting, and sports.

The general approach to defining in the *Oxford American College Dictionary* has particular application for specialist vocabulary. Here, in the context of dealing with highly technical information that may be unfamiliar to the nonspecialist reader, the focus on clarity of expression is of great importance. Avoidance of over-technical terminology and an emphasis on explaining and describing as well as defining are balanced by the need to maintain a high level of technical information and accuracy.

The *Oxford American College Dictionary* views the language from the perspective that English, though a world language, is now centered in the United States, and that American vocabulary and usage deserve special attention. Although the focus is on American English, a network of consultants throughout the English-speaking world has enabled us to ensure excellent coverage of world English, from the United Kingdom and Canada to the Caribbean, India, South Africa, Australia, and New Zealand. We have been indebted to the opportunities provided for communication by the Internet; lively discussions by e-mail across the oceans have formed an everyday part of the dictionary-making process.

Preface to the Second Edition

This new dictionary is an updated, revised, and redesigned edition of the *Oxford American College Dictionary* (2002). It contains hundreds of extra entries for words and senses which have entered the English language since the publication of that first edition and also benefits from an attractive new design, ensuring that finding the right meaning is easy to do.

The dictionary's new words and senses illustrate the influence of certain fast-moving subject areas on the generation of new vocabulary: for example, the world of food and drink has provided *edamame*, *Manchego*, *potsticker*, and *EVOO*, while the Internet, computing, and telecommunications have given us *folksonomy*, *moblog*, *adbot*, and *malware*. The source for all this new material was the 1.5-billion word Oxford English Corpus, an unrivaled database made up of a balanced selection of texts from around the world and from a huge range of subject fields, providing lexicographers with an extensive picture of current English as an international language.

Also new to the dictionary are thousands of word origins, giving the fascinating histories of words as old as *game* (Old English) and as recent as *sudoku* (21st century).

How to Use This Dictionary

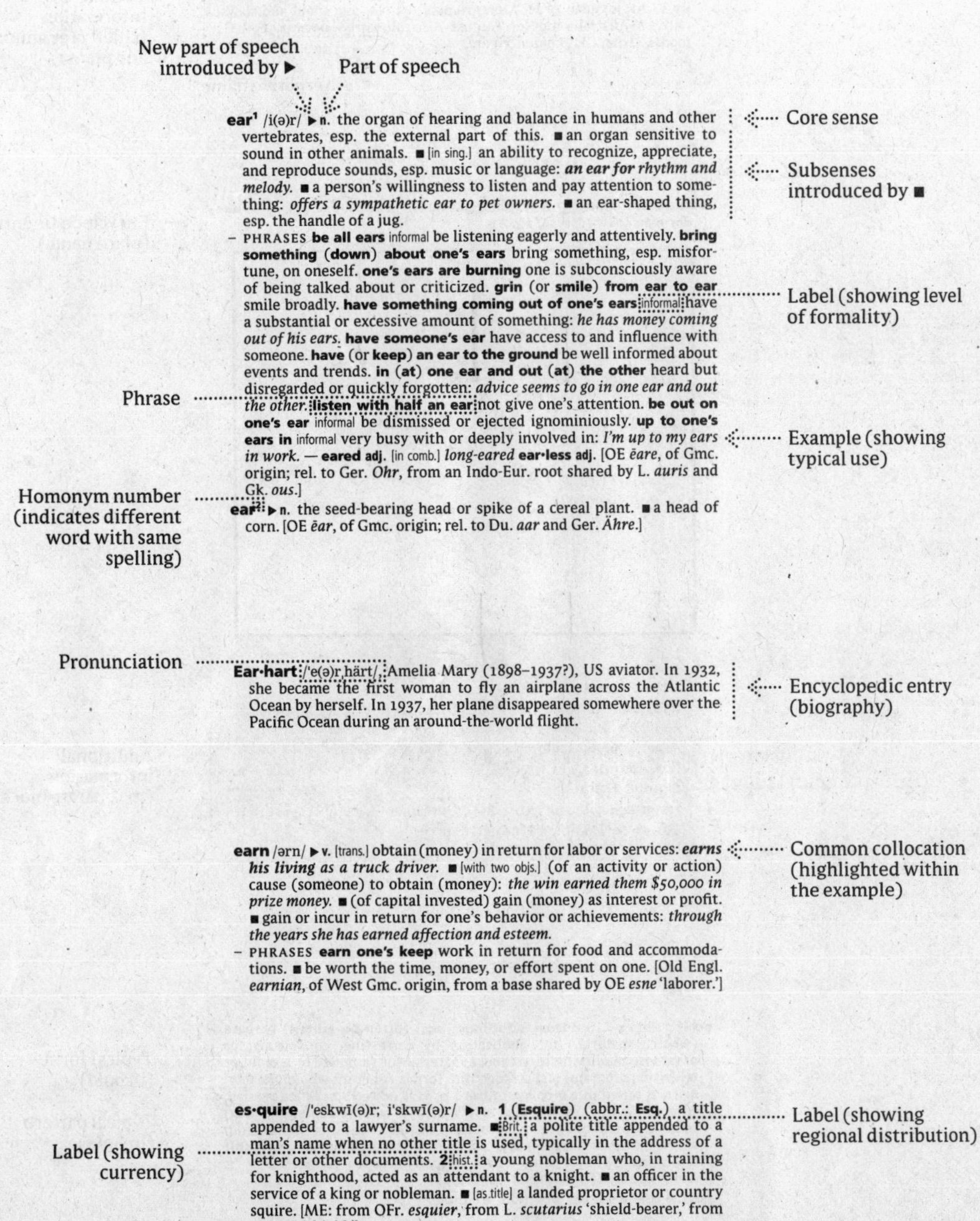

Subject label

ec·dy·sis /ˈekdəsis/ ▶ **n.** *Zool.* the process of shedding the old skin (in reptiles) or casting off the outer cuticle (in insects and other arthropods). — **ec·dys·i·al** /ekˈdizēəl/ **adj.** [19th C.: from Gk. *ekdusis*, from *ekduein* 'put off,' from *ek-* 'out, off' + *duein* 'put.']

Syllabic break

e·chid·na /iˈkidnə/ ▶ **n.** a spiny insectivorous egg-laying mammal (family Tachyglossidae, order Monotremata) with a long snout and claws, native to Australia and New Guinea. Also called SPINY ANTEATER. [19th C.: mod. L., from Gk. *ekhidna* 'viper.']

Technical information (chiefly for animals and plants)

Alternative name

Ec·ua·dor /ˈekwəˌdôr/ a republic in South America. *See box.* — **Ec·ua·dor·e·an** /ˌekwəˈdôrēən/ **adj. & n.**

Encyclopedic entry (place name)

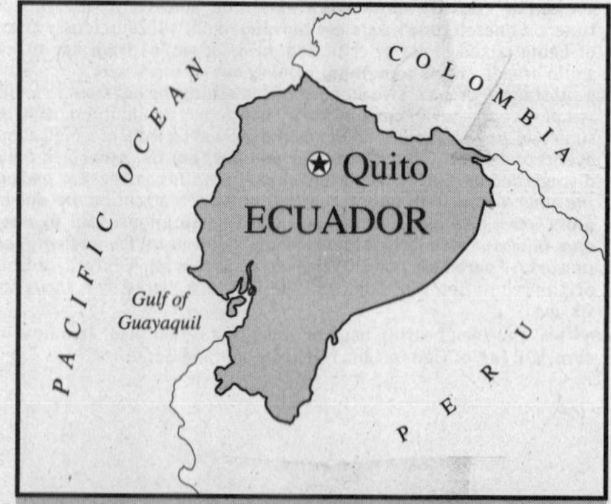

Ecuador

Official name: Republic of Ecuador
Location: northwestern South America, between Colombia and Peru, bordered on the west by the Pacific Ocean
Area: 106,900 square miles (276,800 sq km)
Population: 13,212,700
Capital: Quito
Languages: Spanish (official), Quechua
Currency: US dollar (formerly sucre)

Additional information (in separate block)

Verb inflections

ed·it /ˈedit/ ▶ **v.** (**ed·it·ed, ed·it·ing**) [trans.] (often **be edited**) prepare (written material) for publication by correcting, condensing, or otherwise modifying it. ■ choose material for (a movie or a radio or television program) and arrange it to form a coherent whole: *the footage was edited into broadcast form* | [as adj.] (**edited**) *an edited version.* ■ be editor of (a newspaper or magazine). ■ (**edit something out**) remove unnecessary or inappropriate words, sounds, or scenes from a text, movie, or program. ▶ **n.** a change or correction made as a result of editing. [18th C.: partly a back-form. from EDITOR, reinforced by Fr. *éditer* 'to edit' (from *édition* 'edition').]

Typical form (in bold)

Typical pattern (in bold)

edit. ▶ **abbr.** ■ edited. ■ edition. ■ editor.

Plural form

elf /elf/ ▶ **n.** (pl. **elves** /elvz/) a supernatural creature of folk tales, typically represented as a small, elusive figure in human form with pointed ears, magical powers, and a capricious nature. — **elf·ish** **adj.** **elv·en** /ˈelvin/ **adj.** (literary) **elv·ish** /ˈelvisн/ **adj.** [OE, of Gmc. origin; rel. to Ger. *Alp* 'nightmare.']

Derivatives (in alphabetical order)

en·large /enˈlärj/ ▶ **v.** make or become bigger or more extensive. ■ [trans.] (often **be enlarged**) develop a bigger print of (a photograph).
– PHRASAL VERBS **enlarge on/upon** speak or write about (something) in greater detail: *I would like to enlarge on this theme.* [ME: from OFr. *enlarger*, from *en-* + *large* 'large.']

Phrasal verbs

Grammatical information (in square brackets)

e·o·hip·pus /ˌē-ōˈhipəs/ ▶ **n.** (pl. **-pus·es**) another term for **HYRACOTHERIUM**. [19th C.: from Gk. *ēōs* 'dawn' + *hippos* 'horse.']

Cross reference entry

Variant spelling

ep·i·cen·ter /ˈepiˌsentər/ (Brit. **ep·i·cen·tre**) ▶ **n.** the point on the earth's surface vertically above the focus of an earthquake. ■ fig. the central point of something, typically a difficult or unpleasant situation. — **ep·i·cen·tral** /ˌepiˈsentrəl/ **adj.** [19th C.: from Gk. *epikentros* 'situated on a center,' from *epi* 'upon' + *kentron* 'center.']

Es·ki·mo /ˈeskəˌmō/ ▶ **n.** (pl. same or **-mos**) **1** a member of an indigenous people inhabiting northern Canada, Alaska, Greenland, and eastern Siberia, traditionally living by hunting (esp. of seals) and by fishing. **2** either of the two main languages of this people (Inuit and Yupik), forming a major division of the Eskimo-Aleut family. ▶ **adj.** of or relating to the Eskimos or their languages. [from Fr. *Esquimaux*, possibly from Sp. *esquimao*, *esquimal*, from Montagnais *ayasˇkimew* 'netter of snowshoes.']
– USAGE **1** In recent years, **Eskimo** has come to be regarded as offensive because of one of its possible etymologies (Abnaki *askimo* 'eater of raw meat'), but this descriptive name is accurate since Eskimos traditionally derived their vitamins from eating raw meat. This dictionary gives another possible etymology above, but the etymological problem is still unresolved. **2** The peoples inhabiting the regions from northwestern Canada to western Greenland call themselves **Inuit** (see usage at **INUIT**). Since there are no Inuit living in the US, **Eskimo** is the only term that can be properly applied to all of the peoples as a whole, and it is still widely used in anthropological and archaeological contexts. The broader term **Native American** is sometimes used to refer to Eskimo and Aleut peoples. See usage at **NATIVE AMERICAN**.

Word origin (in square brackets)

Usage note

Key to the Abbreviations

abbr.	abbreviation
adj.	adjective
adv.	adverb
Aeron.	Aeronautics
Afr.	African
Afrik.	Afrikaans
alt.	alteration/altered
Amer.	American
Amer. Ind.	American Indian
Amer. Sp.	American Spanish
Anat.	Anatomy
Anglo-Ind.	Anglo-Indian
Anthropol.	Anthropology
appar.	apparently
Arab.	Arabic
Archaeol.	Archaeology
Archit.	Architecture
Astrol.	Astrology
Astron.	Astronomy
attrib.	attributive
Austral.	Australian
aux.	auxiliary
back-form.	back-formation
Biochem.	Biochemistry
Biol.	Biology
Bot.	Botany
Brit.	British
C	Celsius
C.	century
c.	circa
Canad. Fr.	Canadian French
cent.	century
cents.	centuries
cf., Cf.	compare with
Chem.	Chemistry
Chin.	Chinese
Christian Ch.	Christian Church
Christian Theol.	Christian Theology
cl	centiliter, centiliters
cm	centimeter, centimeters
colloq.	colloquial
comb.	combination
compar.	comparative
Comput.	Computing
contr.	contraction
Crystallog.	Crystallography
cu m	cubic meter, cubic meters
Dan.	Danish
deriv.	derivative
derog.	derogatory
dial.	dialect
dimin.	diminutive
Du.	Dutch
e.g.	for example (*exempli gratia*)
eccles.	ecclesiastical
Ecol.	Ecology
Econ.	Economics
Electron.	Electronics
Embryol.	Embryology
Engin.	Engineering
Engl.	English
Entomol.	Entomology
esp.	especially
euphem.	euphemistic
exclam.	exclamation
F	Fahrenheit
fem.	feminine
fig.	figurative
Finn.	Finnish
fl.	flourished
fl. oz.	fluid ounce, fluid ounces
Fr.	French
ft.	foot, feet
Gael.	Gaelic
Genet.	Genetics
Geog.	Geography
Geol.	Geology
Geom.	Geometry
Ger.	German
Gk.	Greek
Gk. Mythol.	Greek Mythology
Gmc.	Germanic
Gram.	Grammar
Heb.	Hebrew
hist.	historical
I.	Island
i.e.	that is (*id est*)
Immunol.	Immunology
imper.	imperative
Ind.	Indian
Indo-Eur.	Indo-European
infin.	infinitive

intrans.	intransitive
Ital.	Italian
kg	kilogram, kilograms
km	kilometer, kilometers
Kor.	Korean
L.	Lake
L.	Latin
l	liter, liters
L. Amer. Sp.	Latin American Spanish
late L.	late Latin
lb.	pound, pounds
Ling.	Linguistics
lit.	literally
Lith.	Lithuanian
m	meter, meters
masc.	masculine
Math.	Mathematics
MDu.	Middle Dutch
ME	Middle English
Mech.	Mechanics
Med.	Medicine
med.	medieval
med. L.	medieval Latin
Meteorol.	Meteorology
Mex. Sp.	Mexican Spanish
mi.	mile, miles
Microbiol.	Microbiology
Mid. High Ger.	Middle High German
Mid. Low Ger.	Middle Low German
Mil.	Military
Mineral.	Mineralogy
ml	milliliter, milliliters
mm	millimeter, millimeters
mod.	modern
mod. L.	modern Latin
mph	miles per hour
Mythol.	Mythology
n.	noun
N. Amer.	North American
N. Irish	Northern Irish
Naut.	Nautical
NE	northeast(ern)
neut.	neuter
north. Engl.	northern English
Norw.	Norwegian
NW	northwest(ern)
NZ	New Zealand
obj.	object
obs.	obsolete
Oceanog.	Oceanography
OE	Old English
offens.	offensive
OFr.	Old French
Old North. Fr.	Old Northern French
ON	Old Norse
orig.	originally
Ornithol.	Ornithology
oz.	ounce, ounces
Paleontol.	Paleontology
part.	participle
perh.	perhaps
Pers.	Persian
Philos.	Philosophy
Phonet.	Phonetics
Photog.	Photography
phr.	phrase
phrs.	phrases
Physiol.	Physiology
pl.	plural
Pol.	Polish
pop.	population
pop. L.	popular Latin
Port.	Portuguese
poss.	possessive
predic.	predicate
prep.	preposition
pres.	present
pres. part.	present participle
Print.	Printing
prob.	probably
pron.	pronoun
pronunc.	pronunciation
Pros.	Prosody
Psychoanal.	Psychoanalysis
Psychol.	Psychology
R.	River
ref.	reference
rel.	related
rel.	relative
Relig.	Religion
Rhet.	Rhetoric
Rom. Mythol.	Roman Mythology
rpm	revolutions per minute
Russ.	Russian
Scand.	Scandinavian
Scand. Mythol.	Scandinavian Mythology
Scot.	Scottish
Scot. Gael.	Scottish Gaelic
SE	southeast(ern)
sing.	singular
Sociol.	Sociology
Sp.	Spanish
sq km	square kilometer, square kilometers
sq m	square meter, square meters
Stat.	Statistics
Stock Ex.	Stock Exchange
Str.	Strait
Surg.	Surgery
SW	southwest(ern)
Swed.	Swedish
symb.	symbol

tech.	technical
Telecom.	Telecommunications
Theol.	Theology
trans.	transitive
Turk.	Turkish
UK	United Kingdom
ult.	ultimately
UN	United Nations
uncert.	uncertain
US	United States
USSR	Union of Soviet Socialist Republics (Soviet Union)
usu.	usually
v.	verb
var.	variant
vars.	variants
Vet.	Veterinary
W. Ind.	West Indian
Zool.	Zoology

Key to the Pronunciations

This dictionary uses a simple respelling system to show how entries are pronounced, using the symbols listed below. Generally, only the first of two or more identical headwords will have a pronunciation respelling. Where a derivative simply adds a common suffix such as *-less*, *-ness*, or *-ly* to the headword, the derivative may not have a pronunciation respelling unless some other element of the pronunciation also changes.

a as in **hat** /hat/, **fashion** /'fasHən/, **carry** /'karē/
ā *as in* **day** /dā/, **rate** /rāt/, **maid** /mād/, **prey** /prā/
ä *as in* **lot** /lät/, **father** /'fäTHər/, **barnyard** /'bärnyärd/
b *as in* **big** /big/
CH *as in* **church** /CHərCH/, **picture** /'pikCHər/
d *as in* **dog** /dôg/, **bed** /bed/
e *as in* **men** /men/, **bet** /bet/, **ferry** /'ferē/
ē *as in* **feet** /fēt/, **receive** /ri'sēv/
e(ə)r *as in* **air** /e(ə)r/, **care** /ke(ə)r/
ə *as in* **about** /ə'bout/, **soda** /'sōdə/, **mother** /'məTHər/, **person** /'pərsən/
f as *in* **free** /frē/, **graph** /graf/, **tough** /təf/
g *as in* **get** /get/, **exist** /ig'zist/, **egg** /eg/
h *as in* **her** /hər/, **behave** /bi'hāv/
i *as in* **fit** /fit/, **guild** /gild/, **women** /'wimin/
ī as in **time** /tīm/, **guide** /gīd/, **hire** /hīr/, **sky** /skī/
i(ə)r *as in* **ear** /i(ə)r/, **beer** /bi(ə)r/, **pierce** /pi(ə)rs/
j *as in* **judge** /jəj/, **carriage** /'karij/
k *as in* **kettle** /'ketl/, **cut** /kət/, **quick** /kwik/
l *as in* **lap** /lap/, **cellar** /'selər/, **cradle** /'krādl/
m *as in* **main** /mān/, **dam** /dam/
n *as in* **need** /nēd/, **honor** /'änər/, **maiden** /'mādn/
NG *as in* **sing** /siNG/, **anger** /'aNGgər/
ō *as in* **go** /gō/, **promote** /prə'mōt/
ô *as in* **law** /lô/, **thought** /THôt/, **lore** /lôr/
oi *as in* **boy** /boi/, **noisy** /'noizē/
o͝o *as in* **wood** /wo͝od/, **football** /'fo͝ot,bôl/, **sure** /SHo͝or/
o͞o *as in* **food** /fo͞od/, **music** /'myo͞ozik/
ou *as in* **mouse** /mous/, **coward** /'kou(-ə)rd/
p *as in* **put** /po͝ot/, **cap** /kap/
r *as in* **run** /rən/, **fur** /fər/, **spirit** /'spirit/
s *as in* **sit** /sit/, **lesson** /'lesən/, **face** /fās/
SH *as in* **shut** /SHət/, **social** /'sōSHəl/, **action** /'akSHən/
t *as in* **top** /täp/, **seat** /sēt/
TH *as in* **thin** /THin/, **truth** /tro͞oTH/
TH *as in* **then** /THen/, **father** /'fäTHər/
v *as in* **never** /'nevər/, **very** /'verē/
w *as in* **wait** /wāt/, **quit** /kwit/
(h)w as *in* **when** /(h)wen/, **which** /(h)wiCH/
y *as in* **yet** /yet/, **accuse** /ə'kyo͞oz/
z *as in* **zipper** /'zipər/, **musician** /myo͞o'ziSHən/
ZH *as in* **measure** /'meZHər/, **vision** /'viZHən/

Foreign Sounds

KH as in **Bach** /bäKH/
A fricative consonant pronounced with the tongue in the same position as for /k/, as in German *Buch* and *ich*, or Scottish *loch*.

N as in **en route** /äN'ro͞ot/, **Rodin** /rō'daN/
The /N/ does not represent a consonant; it indicates that the preceding vowel is nasalized, as in French *bon* (bon voyage) and *en* (en route).

œ as in **hors d'oeuvre** /ôr 'dœvrə/, **Goethe** /'gœtə/
A vowel made by rounding the lips as with /ô/ while saying /e/ or /ā/, as in French *boeuf and feu,* or German *Hölle* and *Höhle.*

Y as in **Lully** /lY'lē/, **Utrecht** /'Y,treKHt/
A vowel made by rounding the lips as with /o͝o/ or /o͞o/ while saying /i/ or /N/, as in French *rue* or German *fühlen.*

Stress Marks

Stress (or 'accent') is represented by marks placed before the affected syllable. The primary stress mark is a short, raised vertical line /'/ which signifies that the heaviest emphasis should be placed on the following syllable. The secondary stress mark is a short, lowered vertical line /, / which signifies a somewhat weaker emphasis than on the syllable with primary stress.

Variant Pronunciations

There are several ways in which variant pronunciations are indicated in the respellings. Some respellings show a pronunciation symbol within parentheses to indicate a possible variation in pronunciation; for example, in **sandwich** /'san(d)wiCH/ sometimes the /d/ is pronounced, while at other times it is not.

Variant pronunciations may be respelled in full, separated by semicolons. The more common pronunciation is listed first, if this can be determined, but many variants are so common and widespread as to be of equal status.

Variant pronunciations may be indicated by respelling only the part of the word that changes. A hyphen will replace the part of the pronunciation that has remained the same. These 'cutback' respellings will occur primarily in three areas:

a) where the headword has a variant pronunciation:
quasiparticle /ˌkwāzīˈpärtəkəl; ˌkwäzē-/

b) in derivative forms:
dangle /ˈdaNGgəl/
dangler /-glər/
dangly /-glē/

Note: Cutbacks in derivatives always refer back to the headword respelling, not the preceding derivative.

c) at irregular plurals:
parenthesis /pəˈrenTHəsis/
parentheses /-ˌsēz/

Note: A hyphen sometimes serves to separate syllables where the respelling might otherwise look confusing, as at **reinforce** /ˌrē-inˈfôrs/.

Aa

A[1] /ā/ (also **a**) ▶ **n.** (pl. **As** or **A's**) **1** the first letter of the alphabet. ■ denoting the first in a set of items, categories, sizes, etc. ■ denoting the first of two or more hypothetical people or things: *suppose A had killed B.* ■ the highest class of academic mark. ■ (usu. *a*) the first fixed quantity in an algebraic expression. ■ **(A)** the human blood type (in the ABO system) containing the A agglutinogen and lacking the B. **2** a shape like that of a capital A: [in comb.] *an A-shape.* See also **A-FRAME, A-LINE. 3** Music the sixth note of the diatonic scale of C major. ■ a key based on a scale with A as its keynote.
– PHRASES **from A to B** from one's starting point to one's destination: *most road atlases will get you from A to B.* **from A to Z** over the entire range; completely: *make sure you understand the subject from A to Z.*

A[2] ▶ **abbr.** ■ ace (used in describing play in bridge and other card games): *you cash AK of hearts.* ■ ampere(s). ■ **(Å)** ångstrom(s). ■ answer: *Q: What's the senator's zodiac sign? A: He's a Leo.* ■ (in personal ads) Asian. ■ a dry cell battery size.

a /ā; ə/ (**an** before a vowel sound) [called the indefinite article] ▶ **adj. 1** used when referring to someone or something for the first time in a text or conversation: *a man came out of the room | it has been an honor to have you.* Compare with **THE.** ■ used with units of measurement to mean one such unit: *a hundred | a quarter of an hour.* ■ [with negative] one single; any: *I haven't a thing to wear.* ■ used when mentioning the name of someone not known to the speaker: *a Mr. Smith telephoned.* ■ someone like (the name specified): *you're no better than a Hitler.* **2** used to indicate membership of a class of people or things: *he is a lawyer.* **3** used when expressing rates or ratios; in, to, or for each; per: *typing 60 words a minute.* [ME: from OE *ān* 'one.']

a-[1] ▶ **prefix** not; without: *atheistic | atypical.* [from Gk.]

a-[2] ▶ **prefix** to; toward: *aside | ashore.* ■ in a specified state or manner: *asleep | aloud.* ■ in the process of (an activity) *a-hunting.* ■ on: *afoot.* ■ in: *nowadays.* [OE, from **ON.**]

a-[3] ▶ **prefix** var. of **AD-** assimilated before *sc, sp,* and *st* (as in *ascend, aspire* and *astringent*).

a-[4] ▶ **prefix 1** of: *anew.* [from **OF**] **2** utterly: *abash.* [from Anglo-Norman Fr., from L. *ex.*]

-a[1] ▶ **suffix** forming: **1** ancient or Latinized modern names of animals and plants: *primula.* **2** names of oxides: *baryta.* **3** geographical names: *Africa.* **4** ancient or Latinized modern feminine forenames: *Lydia.* **5** nouns from Italian, Portuguese and Spanish: *duenna | stanza.* [from Gk., L., or Romance fem. sing.]

-a[2] ▶ **suffix** forming plural nouns: **1** from Greek or Latin neuter plurals corresponding to a singular in *-um* or *-on* (such as *addenda, phenomena*). **2** in names (often from modern Latin) of zoological groups: *Protista | Insectivora.*

-a[3] ▶ **suffix** informal **1** of: *coupla.* **2** have: *mighta.* **3** to: *oughta.* [casual pronunc.]

A1 ▶ **adj.** informal very good or well; excellent. ■ Naut. (of a vessel) equipped to the highest standard, esp. as certified by a classification society; first-class.

AA ▶ **abbr.** ■ Alcoholics Anonymous. ■ antiaircraft. ■ administrative assistant. ■ Associate of Arts. ■ a dry cell battery size.

aa /'ä,ä/ ▶ **n.** Geol. basaltic lava forming very rough jagged masses with a light frothy texture. Often contrasted with **PAHOEHOE.** [19th C.: from Hawaiian *'a-'a.*]

AAA /'tripəl 'ā/ ▶ **abbr.** American Automobile Association. ■ Baseball see **TRIPLE A.** ■ a 1.5 volt dry cell battery size.

AAAS ▶ **abbr.** American Association for the Advancement of Science.

Aa·chen /'äKHən/ a city in western Germany; pop. 244,440. French name **AIX-LA-CHAPELLE.**

Aal·borg /'ôl,bôr(g)/ (also **Ål·borg**) a city in northern Jutland, Denmark; pop. 155,000.

Aal·to /'ältō/, Alvar (1898–1976), Finnish architect and designer; full name *Hugo Alvar Henrik Aalto.* He invented bent plywood furniture.

AAM ▶ **abbr.** air-to-air missile.

A&M ▶ **abbr.** Agricultural and Mechanical (college).

A&R ▶ **abbr.** artist(s) and repertory.

aard·vark /'ärd,värk/ ▶ **n.** a nocturnal burrowing African mammal (*Orycteropus afer,* family Orycteropidae) with long ears, a tubular snout, and a long extensible tongue, feeding on ants and termites. Also called **ANT BEAR.** [18th C.: from South Afr. Du., from *aarde* 'earth' + *vark* 'pig.']

aard·wolf /'ärd,wo͝olf/ ▶ **n.** (pl. **-wolves**) a nocturnal black-striped African mammal (*Proteles cristatus*) of the hyena family, feeding mainly on termites. [19th C.: from South Afr. Du., from *aarde* 'earth' + *wolf* 'wolf.']

aargh /är(g)/ ▶ **exclam.** used as an expression of anguish, horror, rage, or other strong emotion, often with humorous intent. [18th C.: imitative of a cry, from **AH.**]

Aar·hus /'ôr,ho͞os/ (also **År·hus**) a city on the coast of eastern Jutland, Denmark; pop. 261,440.

Aar·on[1] /'e(ə)rən; 'ar-/ (in the Bible) brother of Moses and traditional founder of the Jewish priesthood.

Aar·on[2], Hank (1934–), US baseball player; full name *Henry Louis Aaron.* He set the all-time career record of 755 home runs.

AARP /ärp; 'ā'ā,är 'pē/ ▶ **abbr.** American Association of Retired Persons.

AAU ▶ **abbr.** Amateur Athletic Union.

AB[1] ▶ **n.** a human blood type (in the ABO system) containing both the A and B agglutinogens.

AB[2] ▶ **abbr.** ■ able seaman; able-bodied seaman. ■ Bachelor of Arts. ■ airman basic. ■ Baseball at bat. ■ Alberta (in official postal use).

Ab[1] /äb; äv/ (also **Av**) ▶ **n.** (in the Jewish calendar) the eleventh month of the civil year and the fifth month of the religious year, usually coinciding with parts of July and August. [from Heb. *'āḇ.*]

Ab[2] Biol. ▶ **abbr.** antibody.

ab- (also **abs-**) ▶ **prefix** away; from: *abaxial | abominate.* [from L.]

ABA ▶ **abbr.** ■ American Bar Association. ■ American Basketball Association. ■ American Bankers Association. ■ American Booksellers Association.

a·ba·ca /,abə'kä/ ▶ **n.** a large herbaceous Philippine plant (*Musa textilis*) of the banana family that yields Manila hemp. ■ Manila hemp. [18th C.: via Sp. from Tagalog *abaká.*]

a·back /ə'bak/ ▶ **adv. 1** archaic toward or situated to the rear. **2** Sailing with the sail pressed backward against the mast by a headwind.
– PHRASES **take someone aback** shock or surprise someone. [OE *on bæc.*]

ab·a·cus /'abəkəs/ ▶ **n.** (pl. **-cus·es**) **1** an oblong frame with rows of wires or grooves along which beads are slid, used for calculating. **2** Archit. the flat slab on top of a capital, supporting the architrave. [ME: from L., from Gk. *abax, abak-* 'slab,' of Semitic origin; prob. akin to Heb. *'āḇāq* 'dust.']

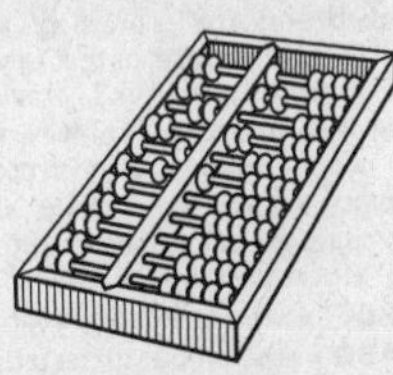

abacus 1

A·ba·dan /,äbə'dän; ,abə'dan/ a city in western Iran; pop. 308,000.

A·bad·don /ə'badn/ (in the Bible) the Devil; hell. [ME: via Gk. from Heb. *ăḇaddōn* 'destruction.']

a·baft /ə'baft/ Naut. ▶ **adv.** in or behind the stern of a ship. ▶ **prep.** nearer the stern than; behind. [ME: from **A-**[2] + *baft* 'in the rear.']

A·ba·kan /,äbə'kän; ,əbə-/ a city in south central Russia, capital of the republic of Khakassia; pop. 154,000.

ab·a·lo·ne /,abə'lōnē/ ▶ **n.** an edible mollusk (genus *Haliotis,* family Haliotidae) of warm seas that has a shallow ear-shaped shell lined with mother-of-pearl and pierced with respiratory holes. [19th C.: via L. Amer. Sp. from *aulun,* from an Amer. Ind. language of Monterey Bay, California.]

a·ban·don /ə'bandən/ ▶ **v.** [trans.] **1** give up completely (a course of action, a practice, or a way of thinking). ■ discontinue (a scheduled event) before completion. **2** cease to support or look after (someone); desert. ■ leave (a place, typically a building) empty or uninhabited, without intending to return. ■ leave (something, typically a vehicle or a vessel) decisively, esp. as an act of survival. ■ **(abandon someone/something to)** condemn someone or something to (a specified fate) by ceasing to take an interest in them. **3** **(abandon oneself to)** allow oneself to indulge in (a desire or impulse). ▶ **n.** complete lack of inhibition or restraint.
– PHRASES **abandon ship** leave a ship because it is sinking. — **a·ban·don·ment n.** [ME: from OFr. *abandoner,* from *a-* 'at') + *bandon* 'control,' based on late L. *bannus, bannum* (see **BAN**[1]).]

a·ban·doned /ə'bandənd/ ▶ **adj. 1** (of a person) having been deserted or cast off. **2** (of a building or vehicle) remaining empty or unused; having been left for good. **3** unrestrained; uninhibited: *a wild, abandoned dance.*

a·base /ə'bās/ ▶ **v.** [trans.] behave in a way so as to belittle or degrade (someone). — **a·base·ment n.** [ME: from OFr. *abaissier,* from *a-* 'to' +

baissier 'to lower,' based on late L. *bassus* 'short.']

a·bash /ə'basн/ ▶ **v.** [trans.] [usu. as adj.] (**abashed**) cause to feel embarrassed, disconcerted, or ashamed. — **a·bash·ment n.** [ME: from Anglo-Norman Fr. *abaïss-*; akin to OFr. *esbaïr*, from *es-* 'utterly' + *baïr* 'astound.']

a·bate /ə'bāt/ ▶ **v.** [intrans.] (of something perceived as hostile or negative) become less intense or widespread. ■ [trans.] cause to become smaller or less intense. ■ [trans.] Law lessen, reduce, or remove (esp. a nuisance): *this action would abate the odor nuisance.* [ME: from OFr. *abatre* 'to fell,' from *a-* 'to') + *batre* 'to beat' (from L. *battuere.*]

a·bate·ment /ə'bātmənt/ ▶ **n.** (often in legal use) the ending, reduction, or lessening of something.

ab·at·toir /'abə,twär/ ▶ **n.** a slaughterhouse. [19th C.: from Fr., from *abattre* 'to fell.']

ab·ax·i·al /ab'aksēəl/ ▶ **adj.** Bot. facing away from the stem of a plant (esp. denoting the lower surface of a leaf).

Ab·ba /'äbä; 'abä/ ▶ **n.** (in the New Testament) God. ■ (in the Syrian Orthodox and Coptic churches) a title given to bishops and patriarchs. [via Gk. from Aramaic *abbā* 'daddy.']

ab·ba·cy /'abəsē/ ▶ **n.** (pl. **-cies**) the office or period of office of an abbot or abbess. [ME: from eccles. L. *abbacia.*]

Ab·bas, Mahmoud (1935–), Palestinian statesman; also known as **Abu Mazen**. Appointed prime minister of the Palestinian Authority in 2003, he was elected president in 2005, following the death of Yasser Arafat.

Ab·bas·id /'abəsid; ə'basid/ ▶ **adj.** of or relating to a dynasty of caliphs who ruled in Baghdad 750–1258. ▶ **n.** a member of this dynasty.

ab·ba·tial /ə'bāsнəl/ ▶ **adj.** of or relating to an abbey, abbot, or abbess. [17th C.: from med. L. *abbatialis.*]

ab·bé /a'bā/ ▶ **n.** (in France) an abbot or other cleric: *the abbé was his confessor* | [as title] *Abbé Pierre.* [16th C.: Fr., from eccles. L. *abbas, abbat-* (see **ABBOT**).]

ab·bess /'abis/ ▶ **n.** a woman who is the head of an abbey of nuns. [ME: from OFr. *abbesse*, from eccles. L., ult. *abbas, abbat-* (see **ABBOT**).]

Abbe·vill·i·an /,ab(ə)'vilēən/ (also **Abbe·vil·l·ean**) ▶ **adj.** Archaeol., dated of, relating to, or denoting the first Paleolithic culture in Europe. It is now usually referred to as the Lower Acheulean. ■ [as n.] (**the Abbevillian**) the Abbevillian culture or period. [1930s: from Fr. *Abbevillien* 'from *Abbeville*,' town in France.]

ab·bey /'abē/ ▶ **n.** (pl. **-beys**) the building or buildings occupied by a community of monks or nuns. [ME: from OFr. *abbeïe*, from med. L. *abbatia* 'abbacy,' from *abbas, abbat-* (see **ABBOT**).]

ab·bot /'abət/ ▶ **n.** a man who is the head of an abbey of monks. [OE *abbod*, from eccles. L. *abbas, abbat-*, from Gk. *abbas* 'father,' from Aramaic *abbā* (see **ABBA**).]

Ab·bott /'abət/ Berenice, (1898–1991), US photographer. Her documentation of New York City was published in *Changing New York* (1939).

abbr. ▶ **abbr.** abbreviation.

ab·bre·vi·ate /ə'brēvē,āt/ ▶ **v.** [trans.] (usu. **be abbreviated**) shorten (a word, phrase, or text). [ME: from late L. *abbreviat-* 'shortened,' from v. *abbreviare*, from L. *brevis* 'short.']

ab·bre·vi·a·tion /ə,brēvē'āsнən/ (abbr.: **abbr.**) ▶ **n.** a shortened form of a word or phrase. ■ the process or result of abbreviating.

ABC[1] ▶ **n.** the alphabet. ■ (also **ABCs**) the rudiments of a subject. ■ an alphabetical guide: *an ABC of Civil War battlefields.*
– PHRASES **easy** (or **simple**) **as ABC** extremely easy or straightforward.

ABC[2] ▶ **abbr.** American Broadcasting Company.

ABD ▶ **abbr.** all but dissertation, used to denote a student who has completed all other parts of a doctorate.

ab·di·cate /'abdi,kāt/ ▶ **v.** [intrans.] (of a monarch) renounce one's throne: *in 1918 Kaiser Wilhelm abdicated as German emperor* | [trans.] *Ferdinand abdicated the throne in favor of the emperor's brother.* ■ [trans.] fail to fulfill or undertake (a responsibility or duty): *the government was accused of abdicating its responsibility* | [intrans.] *the secretary of state should not* **abdicate from** *leadership on educational issues.* — **ab·di·ca·tion** /,abdi'kāsнən/ **n.** [16th C.: from L. *abdicat-* 'renounced,' from the v. *abdicare*, from *ab-* 'away' + *dicare* 'declare.']

ab·do·men /'abdəmən; ab'dō-/ ▶ **n.** the part of the body of a vertebrate containing the digestive organs; the belly. In mammals it is bounded by the diaphragm and the pelvis. ■ Zool. the posterior part of the body of an arthropod, esp. the segments of an insect's body behind the thorax. — **ab·dom·i·nal** /ab'dämənl/ **adj.** [16th C.: from L.]

ab·du·cens nerve /ab'd(y)o͞osənz/ ▶ **n.** Anat. each of the sixth pair of cranial nerves, supplying the muscles concerned with the lateral movement of the eyeballs. [19th C.: *abducens* (mod. L., 'leading away'), from L. v. *abducere.*]

ab·duct /ab'dəkt/ ▶ **v.** [trans.] **1** take (someone) away illegally by force or deception; kidnap. **2** Physiol. (of a muscle) move (a limb or part) away from the midline of the body or from another part. [17th C.: from L. *abduct-* 'led away,' from *abducere*, from *ab-* + *ducere* 'to lead.']

ab·duct·ee /,abdək'tē/ ▶ **n.** a person who has been abducted.

ab·duc·tion /ab'dəksнən/ ▶ **n. 1** the action or an instance of forcibly taking a person or persons away against their will. ■ (in legal use) the illegal removal of a child from parents or guardians. **2** Physiol. the movement of a limb or other part away from the midline of the body, or from another part. The opposite of **ADDUCTION** (see **ADDUCT**[1]).

ab·duc·tor /ab'dəktər/ ▶ **n. 1** a person who abducts another person. **2** (also **abductor muscle**) Anat. a muscle whose contraction moves a limb or part away from the midline of the body, or from another part. ■ any of a number of specific muscles in the hand, forearm, or foot: [followed by Latin genitive] *abductor pollicis.*

Ab·dul-Jab·bar /ab'do͞ol jə'bär/ Kareem, (1947–), US basketball player; former name *Lewis Ferdinand Alcindor.* He played for the Milwaukee Bucks 1960–75 and the Los Angeles Lakers 1975–89.

Ab·dul·lah ibn Hus·sein /,äbdo͝ol'ä ,ibən ho͞o'sān/ (1882–1951), king of Jordan 1946–51. He was assassinated in 1951.

Ab·dul Rah·man /äb'do͝ol 'rämən; 'räкнmän; räкн'män/, Tunku (1903–90), prime minister of Malaya 1957–63 and of Malaysia 1963–70.

a·beam /ə'bēm/ ▶ **adv.** on a line at right angles to a ship's or an aircraft's length. ■ (**abeam of**) opposite the middle of (a ship or aircraft): *she was lying almost abeam of us.*

a·be·ce·dar·i·an /,ābēsē'de(ə)rēən/ ▶ **adj. 1** arranged alphabetically. **2** rudimentary; elementary. ▶ **n.** a person who is just learning; a novice. [17th C.: from late L. *abecedarius* 'alphabetical,' *a, b, c, d.*]

a·bed /ə'bed/ ▶ **adv.** archaic in bed.

A·bel[1] /'ābəl/ (in the Bible) the second son of Adam and Eve, murdered by his brother Cain.

A·bel[2] /'äbəl/, Niels Henrik (1802–29), Norwegian mathematician.

Ab·e·lard /'abə,lärd/, Peter (1079–1142), French theologian and philosopher. He is famous for his tragic love affair with his student Héloïse. See also **HÉLOÏSE**.

a·bele /ə'bēl/ ▶ **n.** the white poplar. [ME: ult. from med. L. *albellus*, dimin. of *albus* 'white.']

A·be·li·an /ə'bēlēən; -yən/ ▶ **adj.** Math. (of a group) having members related by a commutative operation (i.e., $a \times b = b \times a$). [19th C.: named after N. H. *Abel* (see **ABEL**[2]).]

A·be·na·ki /,abə'nakē; ,äbə'nä-/ ▶ **n.** var. of **ABNAKI**.

A·be·o·ku·ta /ä'bā-ōko͞o,tä/ a city in southwestern Nigeria, capital of the state of Ogun; pop. 308,800.

Ab·er·deen /,abər'dēn; 'abər,dēn/ a city in northeastern Scotland; pop. 201,100.

Ab·er·deen An·gus ▶ **n.** an animal of a Scottish breed of hornless black beef cattle. Also called **BLACK ANGUS**.

Ab·er·nath·y /'abər,naтнē/, Ralph David (1926–90), US civil rights activist. He was president of the Southern Christian Leadership Conference (SCLC) 1968–1977.

ab·er·rant /'abərənt; ə'ber-/ ▶ **adj.** departing from an accepted standard. ■ esp. Biol. diverging from the normal type. — **ab·er·rance n. ab·er·ran·cy** /-ənsē/ **n. ab·er·rant·ly adv.** [16th C.: from L. *aberrant-* 'wandering away,' from v. *aberrare*, from *ab-* + *errare* 'to stray.']

ab·er·ra·tion /,abə'rāsнən/ ▶ **n.** a departure from what is normal, usual, or expected, typically one that is unwelcome. ■ a person whose beliefs or behavior are unusual or unacceptable. ■ a departure from someone's usual moral character or mental ability, typically for the worse. ■ Biol. a characteristic that deviates from the normal type. ■ Optics the failure of rays to converge at one focus because of limitations or defects in a lens or mirror. ■ Astron. the apparent displacement of a celestial object from its true position, caused by the relative motion of the observer and the object. — **ab·er·ra·tion·al** /-sнənl/ **adj.** [16th C.: from L. *aberratio(n-)*, from *aberrare.*]

Abertawe /,abər'tou-ē/ see **SWANSEA**.

a·bet /ə'bet/ ▶ **v.** (**a·bet·ted, a·bet·ting**) [trans.] encourage or assist (someone) to do something wrong, in particular, to commit a crime or other offense. ■ encourage or assist someone to commit (a crime). — **a·bet·ment n. a·bet·tor** /ə'betər/ (also **a·bet·ter**) **n.** [ME: from OFr. *abeter*, from *a-* 'to') + *beter* 'urge on.']

a·bey·ance /ə'bāəns/ ▶ **n.** a state of temporary disuse or suspension. ■ Law the position of being without, or waiting for, an owner or claimant. — **a·bey·ant** /ə'bāənt/ **adj.** [16th C.: from OFr. *abeance* 'aspiration to a title,' from *abeer* 'aspire after,' from *a-* + *beer* 'to gape.']

ab·hor /ab'hôr/ ▶ **v.** (**-horred, -hor·ring**) [trans.] formal regard with disgust and hatred. — **ab·hor·rer n.** [ME: from L. *abhorrere*, from *ab-* 'away' + *horrere* 'to shudder.']

ab·hor·rence /ab'hôrəns; -'här-/ ▶ **n.** a feeling of repulsion; disgusted loathing.

ab·hor·rent /ab'hôrənt; -'här-/ ▶ **adj.** inspiring disgust and loathing; repugnant.

a·bide /ə'bīd/ ▶ **v. 1** [intrans.] (**abide by**) accept or act in accordance with (a rule, decision, or recommendation): *I would abide by their decision.* **2** [trans.] (**can/could not abide**) informal be unable to tolerate (someone or something): *I cannot abide a lack of discipline.* **3** [intrans.] (of a feeling or a memory) continue without fading or being lost. ■ archaic live; dwell. [OE *ābīdan* 'wait,' from *ā-* 'onward' + *bīdan* (see **BIDE**).]

a·bid·ing /ə'bīdiɴɢ/ ▶ **adj.** [attrib.] (of a feeling or a memory) lasting a long time; enduring. — **a·bid·ing·ly adv.**

Ab·i·djan /,abi'jän/ the chief port of the Ivory Coast, the capital 1935–83; pop. 1,850,000.

Abi·lene /'abə,lēn/ **1** a city in east central Kansas; pop. 6,242. It was the first end of the Chisholm Trail. **2** a city in north central Texas; pop. 106,654.

a·bil·i·ty /ə'bilitē/ ▶ **n.** (pl. **-ties**) **1** [in sing., with infin.] the capacity to do something. **2** talent that enables someone to achieve a great deal. ■ (in the context of education) a level of mental power. ■ a special talent or skill. [ME: from OFr. *ablete*, from L. *habilitas*, from *habilis* 'able.']

-abil·i·ty /ə'bilitē/ ▶ **suffix** forming nouns of quality corresponding to adjectives ending in *-able* (such as *suitability* corresponding to *suitable*). [from Fr. *-abilité* or L. *-abilitas*, n. endings.]

Ab·ing·ton /'abiNGtən/ a township in southeastern Pennsylvania, north of Philadelphia; pop. 56,103.

ab in·i·ti·o /,ab ə'nisHē,ō/ ▶ **adv.** from the beginning. [17th C.: L.]

a·bi·o·gen·e·sis /,ābī-ō'jenəsis/ ▶ **n.** technical term for **SPONTANEOUS GENERATION.** [19th C.: from **A-**[1] + Gk. *bios* 'life.']

a·bi·ot·ic /,ābī'ätik/ ▶ **adj.** physical rather than biological; not derived from living organisms. ■ devoid of life; sterile.

ab·ject /'ab,jekt; ab'jekt/ ▶ **adj. 1** [attrib.] (of a situation or condition) extremely bad, unpleasant, and degrading. ■ (of an unhappy state of mind) experienced to the maximum degree. ■ (of a failure) absolute and humiliating. **2** (of a person or their behavior) completely without pride or dignity; self-abasing. — **ab·jec·tion** /ab'jeksHən/ **n. ab·ject·ly adv. ab·ject·ness n.** [ME: from L. *abjectus*, past part. of *abjicere* 'reject,' from *ab-* 'away' + *jacere* 'to throw.']

ab·jure /ab'jŏŏr/ ▶ **v.** [trans.] formal solemnly renounce (a belief, cause, or claim). — **ab·ju·ra·tion** /,abjə'rāsHən/ **n.** [ME: from L. *abjurare*, from *ab-* 'away' + *jurare* 'swear.']

Ab·khaz /äb'käz; ab'kaz; əb'KHäz/ (also **Ab·kha·zi·an** /ab'kazHən; -zēən; äb'kä-/) ▶ **adj.** of or relating to Abkhazia, its people, or their language. ▶ **n. 1** a member of a Caucasian people living in Abkhazia. **2** a Northwest Caucasian language.

Ab·kha·zi·a /äb'käzēə; ab'käzH(ē)ə/ an autonomous territory in northwestern Georgia, on the Black Sea; pop. 537,500; capital, Sokhumi. In 1992, Abkhazia unilaterally declared itself independent, sparking ongoing armed conflict with Georgia.

ab·la·tion /ə'blāsHən/ ▶ **n. 1** the surgical removal of body tissue. **2** the removal of snow and ice by melting or evaporation, typically from a glacier or iceberg. ■ the erosion of rock, typically by wind action. ■ the loss of surface material from a spacecraft or meteorite through evaporation or melting caused by friction with the atmosphere. — **ab·late** /ə'blāt/ **v.** [ME: from late L. *ablatio(n-)*, from L. *ablat-* 'taken away,' from *ab-* + *lat-* 'carried' (from v. *ferre*).]

ab·la·tive /'ablətiv/ ▶ **adj.** [attrib.] **1** Gram. relating to or denoting a case (esp. in Latin) indicating separation or an agent, instrument, or location. **2** (of surgical treatment) involving ablation. **3** of, relating to, or subject to ablation through melting or evaporation. ▶ **n.** Gram. a word in the ablative case. ■ (**the ablative**) the ablative case.

ab·la·tive ab·so·lute ▶ **n.** a construction in Latin that consists of a noun and participle or adjective in the ablative case and that is syntactically independent of the rest of the sentence.

ab·laut /'ab,lout/ ▶ **n.** a change of vowel in related words or forms, e.g., in Germanic strong verbs (e.g., in *sing, sang, sung*). [19th C.: from Ger., from *ab* 'off' + *Laut* 'sound.']

a·blaze /ə'blāz/ ▶ **adj.** [predic.] burning fiercely. ■ very brightly colored or lighted. ■ made bright by a strong emotion: *eyes ablaze with anger.*

a·ble /'ābəl/ ▶ **adj.** (**a·bler, a·blest**) **1** [with infin.] having the power, skill, means, or opportunity to do something. **2** having considerable skill, proficiency, or intelligence. [ME: from OFr. *hable*, from L. *habilis* 'handy,' from *habere* 'to hold.']

-able /əbəl/ ▶ **suffix** forming adjectives meaning: **1** able to be: *calculable.* **2** due to be: *payable.* **3** subject to: *taxable.* **4** relevant to or in accordance with: *fashionable.* **5** having the quality to: *suitable* | *comfortable.* [from Fr. *-able* or L. *-abilis*, adjectival endings.]

a·ble-bod·ied ▶ **adj.** fit, strong, and healthy; not physically disabled.

a·ble-bod·ied sea·man (also **a·ble sea·man**) ▶ **n.** a merchant seaman qualified to perform all routine duties.

a·bloom /ə'blōōm/ ▶ **adj.** [predic.] covered in flowers.

ab·lu·tion /ə'blōōsHən/ ▶ **n.** (usu. **ablutions**) the act of washing oneself. ■ a ceremonial act of washing parts of the body or sacred containers. — **ab·lu·tion·ar·y** /-sHə,nerē/ **adj.** [ME: from L. *ablutio(n-)*, from *abluere*, from *ab-* 'away' + *luere* 'wash.']

a·bly /'āblē/ ▶ **adv.** skillfully; competently.

-ably /əblē/ ▶ **suffix** forming adverbs corresponding to adjectives ending in *-able* (such as *suitably* corresponding to *suitable*).

ABM ▶ **abbr.** antiballistic missile.

Ab·na·ki /ab'nakē; äb'nä-/ (also **Ab·e·na·ki** /,abə-; ,äbə-/) ▶ **n.** (pl. same or **-kis**) **1** a member of a North American Indian people of Maine on the Atlantic coast to southern Quebec. **2** either or both of two Algonquian languages, **Eastern Abnaki** and **Western Abnaki**, now nearly extinct. ▶ **adj.** of or relating to this people or their language. [from Fr. *Abénaqui*, from Eastern Abnaki.]

ab·ne·gate /'abni,gāt/ ▶ **v.** [trans.] rare renounce or reject (something desired or valuable). — **ab·ne·ga·tor** /-,gātər/ **n.** [17th C.: from L. *abnegat-* 'renounced,' from v. *abnegare*, from *ab-* 'away' + *negare* 'deny.']

ab·ne·ga·tion /,abni'gāsHən/ ▶ **n.** the act of renouncing or rejecting something. ■ self-denial.

ab·nor·mal /ab'nôrməl/ ▶ **adj.** deviating from what is normal or usual, typically in a way that is undesirable. — **ab·nor·mal·ly adv.** [19th C.: alt. of *anormal*, from Fr., ult. from Gk. *anōmalos* (see **ANOMALOUS**).]

ab·nor·mal·i·ty /,abnôr'malitē/ ▶ **n.** (pl. **-ties**) an abnormal feature, characteristic, or occurrence. ■ the quality or state of being abnormal.

A·bo /'abō/ (also **a·bo**) Austral. informal, offens. ▶ **n.** (pl. **A·bos**) an Aborigine. ▶ **adj.** Aboriginal.

Å·bo /'ôbōō/ Swedish name for **TURKU.**

a·board /ə'bôrd/ ▶ **adv. & prep.** on or into (a ship, aircraft, train, or other vehicle): [as adv.] *welcome aboard, sir* | [as prep.] *aboard the yacht.* ■ on or onto (a horse): [as adv.] *with Migliore aboard, he won the cup.* ■ fig. into an organization or team as a new member: [as adv.] *coming aboard as IBM's new chairman.* ■ Baseball on base as a runner: *putting their first batter aboard.*
– PHRASES **all aboard!** a call warning passengers to get on a ship, train, or bus that is about to depart.

a·bode[1] /ə'bōd/ ▶ **n.** formal or literary a place of residence; a house or home. ■ archaic a stay; a sojourn. [ME from **ABIDE.**]

a·bode[2] ▶ **v.** archaic past of **ABIDE.**

a·bol·ish /ə'bälisH/ ▶ **v.** [trans.] formally put an end to (a system, practice, or institution). — **a·bol·ish·er n. a·bol·ish·ment n.** [ME: from OFr. *aboliss-*, from *abolir*, from L. *abolere* 'destroy.']

ab·o·li·tion /,abə'lisHən/ ▶ **n.** the action or an act of abolishing a system, practice, or institution. [16th C.: from L. *abolitio(n-)*, from *abolere* 'destroy.']

ab·o·li·tion·ist /,abə'lisHənist/ ▶ **n.** a person who favors the abolition of a practice or institution, esp. capital punishment or (formerly) slavery. — **ab·o·li·tion·ism n.**

ab·o·ma·sum /,abə'māsəm/ ▶ **n.** (pl. **-sa** /-sə/) Zool. the fourth stomach of a ruminant, which receives food from the omasum and passes it to the small intestine. [17th C.: mod. L., from *ab-* 'away' + *omasum* (see **OMASUM**).]

A-bomb ▶ **n.** short for **ATOM BOMB.**

Ab·o·mey /,abə'mā; ə'bōmē/ a town in southern Benin; pop. 54,400.

a·bom·i·na·ble /ə'bäm(ə)nəbəl/ ▶ **adj.** causing moral revulsion. ■ informal very unpleasant. — **a·bom·i·na·bly adv.**

A·bom·i·na·ble Snow·man ▶ **n.** (pl. **-men**) another term for **YETI.**

a·bom·i·nate /ə'bämə,nāt/ ▶ **v.** [trans.] formal detest; loathe. — **a·bom·i·na·tor** /-,nātər/ **n.** [17th C.: from L. *abominat-* 'deprecated,' from v. *abominari*, from *ab-* 'away' + *omen, omin-* 'omen.']

a·bom·i·na·tion /ə,bämə'nāsHən/ ▶ **n.** a thing that causes disgust or hatred. ■ a feeling of hatred.

ab·o·ral /ab'ôrəl/ ▶ **adj.** Zool. relating to or denoting the side or end that is furthest from the mouth. ■ moving or leading away from the mouth. — **ab·o·ral·ly adv.**

ab·o·rig·i·nal /,abə'rijənl/ ▶ **adj.** inhabiting or existing in a land from the earliest times; indigenous. ■ (**Aboriginal**) of or relating to the Australian Aboriginals or their languages. ▶ **n.** an aboriginal inhabitant of a place. ■ (**Aboriginal**) a person belonging to one of the indigenous peoples of Australia.

ab·o·rig·i·ne /,abə'rijənē/ ▶ **n.** a person, animal, or plant that has been in a country or region from earliest times. ■ (**Aborigine**) an aboriginal inhabitant of Australia. [19th C.: back-form. from pl. *aborigines*, from L. *ab origine* 'from the beginning.']

a·born·ing /ə'bôrniNG/ ▶ **adv.** while being born or produced. ▶ **adj.** [predic.] being born or produced. [1930s: from *a-* 'in the process of' + *borning*, from *born* (North Amer. dial.) 'to be born.']

a·bort /ə'bôrt/ ▶ **v.** [trans.] **1** carry out or undergo the abortion of (a fetus). ■ [intrans.] (of a pregnant woman or female animal) have a miscarriage. ■ [intrans.] Biol. (of an embryonic organ or organism) remain undeveloped. **2** bring to a premature end because of a problem or fault. ▶ **n.** informal or tech. an act of aborting a flight, space mission, or other enterprise: *there was an abort because of bad weather.* [16th C.: from L. *aboriri* 'miscarry,' from *ab-* 'away' + *oriri* 'be born.']

a·bor·ti·fa·cient /ə,bôrtə'fāsHənt/ Med. ▶ **adj.** (chiefly of a drug) causing abortion. ▶ **n.** an abortifacient drug.

a·bor·tion /ə'bôrsHən/ ▶ **n. 1** the deliberate termination of a human pregnancy. ■ a miscarriage. ■ Biol. the arrest of the development of an organ, typically a seed or fruit. **2** an object or undertaking regarded as unpleasant or badly made or carried out.

a·bor·tion·ist /ə'bôrsHənist/ ▶ **n.** a person who carries out abortions, esp. illegally.

a·bor·tion pill ▶ **n.** informal a drug that can induce abortion, esp. mifepristone.

a·bor·tive /ə'bôrtiv/ ▶ **adj. 1** failing to produce the intended result. **2** Biol., dated (of an organ or organism) rudimentary; arrested in development. ■ Med. (of a virus infection) failing to produce symptoms. **3** [attrib.] rare causing or resulting in abortion. — **a·bor·tive·ly adv.**

ABO system ▶ **n.** a system of four basic types (A, AB, B, and O) into which human blood may be classified, based on the presence or absence of certain inherited antigens.

a·bou·li·a /ə'bōōlēə/ ▶ **n.** var. of **ABULIA.**

a·bound /ə'bound/ ▶ **v.** [intrans.] exist in large numbers or amounts. ■ (**abound in/with**) have in large numbers or amounts. [ME: ult. from L. *abundare* 'overflow,' from *ab-* + *undare* 'surge' (from *unda* 'wave').]

a·bout /ə'bout/ ▶ **prep. 1** on the subject of; concerning: *I was thinking about you.* ■ so as to affect: *there's nothing we can do about it.* ■ (**be about**) be involved or to do with; have the intention of: *it's all about having fun.* **2** used to indicate movement within a particular area: *she looked about the room.* **3** used to express location in a particular place: *rugs strewn about the hall.* ■ used to describe a quality apparent in a

person: *there was a look about her that said everything.* ▶ **adv.** **1** used to indicate movement in an area: *finding my way about.* **2** used to express location in a particular place: *there was a lot of flu about.* **3** (used with a number or quantity) approximately: *he's about 35.*
– PHRASES **about to do something** intending to do something or close to doing something very soon. **be not about to do something** be unwilling to do something. **how about** see HOW[1]. **just about** see JUST. **know what one is about** informal be aware of the implications of one's actions or of a situation, and of how best to deal with them. **up and about** see UP. **what about** see WHAT. [OE *onbūtan*, from *on* + *būtan* 'outside of.']

a·bout-face ▶ **n.** (chiefly in military contexts) a turn made so as to face the opposite direction. ■ informal a complete change of opinion or policy. ▶ **v.** [intrans.] turn so as to face the opposite direction. ▶ **exclam.** (**about face!**) (in military contexts) a command to make an about-face. [19th C.: shortening of *right-about face.*]

a·bove /ə'bəv/ ▶ **prep.** **1** in extended space over and not touching: *a display of fireworks above the town.* ■ extending upward over: *her arms above her head.* ■ higher than and to one side of; overlooking: *on the wall above the altar.* **2** at a higher level or layer than: *bruises above both eyes.* ■ higher in grade or rank than: *at a level above the common people.* ■ considered of higher status or worth than; too good for: *above reproach.* ■ in preference to: *they chose profit above safety.* ■ at a higher volume or pitch than: *above a whisper.* **3** higher than (a specified amount, rate, or norm): *above average.* ▶ **adv.** at a higher level or layer: *place a quantity of mud in a jar with water above.* ■ higher in grade or rank: *an officer of the rank of superintendent or above.* ■ higher than a specified amount, rate, or norm: *boats of 31 ft. or above.*
– PHRASES **above all (else)** more so than anything else. **above oneself** conceited; arrogant. **from above** from overhead. ■ from a position of higher rank or authority. **not be above** be capable of stooping to (an unworthy act). **over and above** see OVER. [OE *abufan* (adv.), from *a-* 'on' + *bufan* (from *bi* 'by' + *ufan* 'above').]

a·bove·board /ə'bəv,bôrd/ ▶ **adj.** legitimate, honest, and open. ▶ **adv.** legitimately, honestly, and openly: *the accountants acted completely aboveboard.*

ab o·vo /ab 'ō,vō; äb/ ▶ **adv.** from the very beginning. [18th C.: L., lit. 'from the egg.']

ab·ra·ca·dab·ra /,abrəkə'dabrə/ ▶ **exclam.** a word said by magicians when performing a magic trick. ▶ **n.** informal the implausibly easy achievement of difficult feats. ■ language, typically in the form of gibberish, used to give the impression of arcane knowledge or power. [17th C. (word engraved and used as charm to ward off illness): from L., from Gk. base.]

a·brade /ə'brād/ ▶ **v.** [trans.] scrape or wear away by friction or erosion. — **a·brad·er n.** [17th C.: from L. *abradere*, from *ab-* 'away' + *radere* 'to scrape.']

A·bra·ham /'ābrə,ham/ (in the Bible) the Hebrew patriarch from whom all Jews trace their descent (Gen. 11:27–25:10).

A·bra·ham, Plains of see PLAINS OF ABRAHAM.

a·bra·sion /ə'brāzʜən/ ▶ **n.** the process of scraping or wearing away. ■ an area damaged by scraping or wearing away. [17th C.: from L. *abrasio(n-)*, from *abradere* (see ABRADE).]

a·bra·sive /ə'brāsiv; -ziv/ ▶ **adj.** (of a substance or material) capable of polishing or cleaning a hard surface by rubbing or grinding. ■ tending to rub or graze the skin. ■ fig. (of sounds or music) rough to the ear; harsh. ■ fig. (of a person or manner) showing little concern for the feelings of others; harsh. ▶ **n.** a substance used for grinding, polishing, or cleaning a hard surface.

ab·re·act /,abrē'akt/ ▶ **v.** [trans.] Psychol. release (an emotion) by abreaction. ■ cause (someone) to undergo abreaction. [20th C.: back-form. from ABREACTION.]

ab·re·ac·tion /,abrē'akshən/ ▶ **n.** Psychol. the expression and consequent release of a previously repressed emotion, achieved through reliving the experience that caused it (typically through hypnosis or suggestion). — **ab·re·ac·tive adj.** [20th C.: from AB- + REACTION, translating Ger. *Abreagierung.*]

a·breast /ə'brest/ ▶ **adv.** **1** side by side and facing the same way: *they were riding three abreast.* **2** alongside or even with something. ■ fig. up to date with the latest news, ideas, or information.

a·bridge /ə'brij/ ▶ **v.** [trans.] (usu. **be abridged**) **1** shorten (a book, movie, speech, or other text) without losing the sense. **2** Law curtail (rights or privileges). — **a·bridg·er n.** [ME: from OFr. *abregier*, from late L. *abbreviare* (see ABBREVIATE).]

a·bridg·ment /ə'brijmənt/ (also **a·bridge·ment**) ▶ **n.** **1** a shortened version of a larger work. **2** Law a curtailment of rights.

a·broad /ə'brôd/ ▶ **adv.** **1** in or to a foreign country or countries. ■ dated or humorous out of doors: *few people ventured abroad from their warm houses.* **2** in different directions; over a wide area. ■ (of a feeling or rumor) widely current. ■ freely moving about. **3** archaic wide of the mark; in error. ▶ **n.** foreign countries considered collectively.

ab·ro·gate /'abrə,gāt/ ▶ **v.** [trans.] formal repeal or do away with (a law, right, or formal agreement). — **ab·ro·ga·tion** /,abrə'gāshən/ **n.** [16th C.: from L. *abrogat-* 'repealed,' from v. *abrogare*, from *ab-* 'away' + *rogare* 'propose a law.']

ab·rupt /ə'brəpt/ ▶ **adj.** **1** sudden and unexpected. **2** brief to the point of rudeness; curt. ■ (of a style of speech or writing) not flowing smoothly; disjointed. **3** steep; precipitous. — **ab·rupt·ly adv.** **ab·rupt·ness n.** [16th C.: from L. *abruptus* 'broken off,' past part. of *abrumpere*, from *ab-* + *rumpere* 'break.']

ab·rup·tion /ə'brəpshən/ ▶ **n.** tech. the sudden breaking away of a portion from a mass. ■ (also **placental abruption**) Med. separation of the placenta from the wall of the uterus.

ABS ▶ **abbr.** ■ acrylonitrile-butadiene-styrene, a composite plastic used to make car bodies and cases for computers and other appliances. ■ anti-lock braking system (for motor vehicles).

abs /abz/ informal ▶ **n.** the abdominal muscles.

abs- ▶ **prefix** var. of AB- before *c*, *q*, and *t* (as in *abscond, abstain*).

ab·scess /'ab,ses/ ▶ **n.** a swollen area within body tissue, containing an accumulation of pus. [16th C.: from L. *abscessus* 'a going away,' from v. *abscedere*, from *ab-* + *cedere* 'go.']

ab·scise /ab'sīz/ ▶ **v.** [trans.] cut off or away. ■ [intrans.] Bot. separate by abscission; fall off.

ab·scis·sa /ab'sisə/ ▶ **n.** (pl. **-scis·sae** /-'sisē/ or **-scis·sas**) Math. (in a system of coordinates) the *x*-coordinate, the distance from a point to the vertical or *y*-axis measured parallel to the horizontal or *x*-axis. Compare with ORDINATE. [17th C.: from mod. L. *abscissa (linea)* 'cutoff (line),' fem. past part. of *abscindere* (see ABSCISSION).]

ab·scis·sion /ab'sizʜən/ ▶ **n.** Bot. the natural detachment of parts of a plant, typically dead leaves and ripe fruit. ■ any act of cutting off. [17th C.: from L. *abscissio(n-)*, from *abscindere*, from *ab-* 'off' + *scindere* 'to cut.']

ab·scond /ab'skänd/ ▶ **v.** [intrans.] leave hurriedly and secretly, typically to avoid detection or arrest. ■ (of someone on bail) fail to surrender oneself for custody at the appointed time. ■ (of a person kept in detention or under supervision) escape. — **ab·scond·er n.** [16th C.: from L. *abscondere* 'hide,' from *ab-* 'away' + *condere* 'stow.']

ab·seil /'äp,zīl; 'ab,sāl/ ▶ **n. & v.** another term for RAPPEL. — **ab·seil·er n.**

ab·sence /'absəns/ ▶ **n.** the state of being away from a place or person. ■ an occasion or period of being away from a place or person. ■ (**absence of**) the nonexistence or lack of. [ME: from OFr., from L. *absentia*, from *absens, absent-* (see ABSENT).]

ab·sent ▶ **adj.** /'absənt/ **1** not present in a place or at an occasion. ■ (of a part or feature of the body) not forming part of a creature in which it might be expected. **2** (of an expression or manner) showing that someone is not paying attention to what is being said or done: *an absent smile.* ▶ **v.** /ab'sent/ (**absent oneself**) stay or go away. ▶ **prep.** /'absent/ formal without: *employees could not be fired absent other evidence.* — **ab·sent·ly adv.** (in sense 2). [ME: ult. from L. *absens, absent-* 'being absent,' from v. *abesse*, from *ab-* 'away' + *esse* 'to be.']

ab·sen·tee /,absən'tē/ ▶ **n.** a person who is expected or required to be present at a place or event but is not.

ab·sen·tee bal·lot ▶ **n.** a ballot completed and mailed before an election by a voter unable to be present at the polls.

ab·sen·tee·ism /,absən'tē,izəm/ ▶ **n.** the practice of regularly staying away from work or school without good reason.

ab·sent·mind·ed /'absənt,mīndid/ ▶ **adj.** (of a person or a person's behavior or manner) having or showing a habitually forgetful or inattentive disposition. — **ab·sent·mind·ed·ly adv.** **ab·sent·mind·ed·ness n.**

ab·sinthe /'ab,sinтн/ (also **ab·sinth**) ▶ **n.** **1** the shrub wormwood. ■ an essence made from this. **2** a potent green aniseed-flavored liqueur prepared from wormwood, now largely banned because of its toxicity. [ME: from Fr., ult. from Gk. *apsinthion* 'wormwood.']

ab·so·lute /'absə,lo͞ot; ,absə'lo͞ot/ ▶ **adj.** **1** not qualified or diminished in any way; total: *absolute secrecy.* ■ used for general emphasis when expressing an opinion: *the policy is absolute folly.* ■ (of powers or rights) not subject to any limitation; unconditional: *absolute authority* ■ (of a ruler) having unrestricted power: *absolute monarch.* ■ Law (of a decree) final: *the decree of nullity was made absolute.* **2** viewed or existing independently and not in relation to other things. ■ Gram. (of a construction) syntactically independent of the rest of the sentence, as in *dinner being over, we left the table.* ■ Gram. (of a transitive verb) used without an expressed object (e.g., *guns kill*). ■ Gram. (of an adjective) used without an expressed noun (e.g., *the brave*). ▶ **n.** Philos. a value or principle regarded as universally valid or viewed without relation to other things. ■ (**the absolute**) Philos. that which exists without being dependent on anything else. ■ (**the absolute**) Theol. ultimate reality; God. — **ab·so·lute·ness n.** **ab·so·lut·ize** /'absəlo͞o,tīz/ **v.** [ME: from L. *absolutus* 'freed,' past part. of *absolvere* (see ABSOLVE).]

ab·so·lute·ly /,absə'lo͞otlē; 'absə,lo͞otlē/ ▶ **adv.** **1** with no qualification, restriction, or limitation; totally. ■ used to emphasize the truth or appropriateness of a very strong or exaggerated statement: *he absolutely adores that car.* ■ [with negative] none whatsoever: *she had absolutely no idea what he was talking about.* ■ [as exclam.] informal used to express and emphasize one's assent. **2** independently; not viewed in relation to other things or factors: *white-collar crime increased both absolutely and in comparison with other categories.* ■ Gram. (of a verb) without a stated object.

ab·so·lute mag·ni·tude ▶ **n.** Astron. the magnitude (brightness) of a celestial object as it would be seen at a standard distance of 10 parsecs. Compare with APPARENT MAGNITUDE.

ab·so·lute ma·jor·i·ty ▶ **n.** a majority over all rivals combined; more than half.

ab·so·lute mu·sic ▶ **n.** instrumental music composed purely as music, and not intended to represent or illustrate something else. Compare with PROGRAM MUSIC.

ab·so·lute pitch ▶ **n.** Music the ability to recognize the pitch of a note or produce any given note; perfect pitch. ■ pitch according to a fixed standard defined by the frequency of the sound vibration.

ab·so·lute tem·per·a·ture ▶ **n.** a temperature measured from absolute zero in kelvins. (Symbol: **T**)

ab·so·lute val·ue ▶ **n.** **1** Math. the magnitude of a real number without regard to its sign. The absolute value of a complex number $a^2+ ib$ is the positive square root of $a^2+ b^2$. Also called MODULUS. **2** tech. the actual magnitude of a numerical value, irrespective of its relation to other values.

ab·so·lute ze·ro ▶ **n.** the lowest temperature theoretically possible, at which the motion of particles that constitutes heat would be minimal. It is zero on the Kelvin scale (−273.15°C or −459.67°F).

ab·so·lu·tion /ˌabsəˈlo͞osʜən/ ▶ **n.** formal release from guilt, obligation, or punishment. ■ an ecclesiastical declaration of forgiveness of sins. [ME: ult. from L. *absolutio(n-)*, from *absolvere* (see ABSOLVE).]

ab·so·lut·ism /ˈabsəlo͞oˌtizəm/ ▶ **n.** the acceptance of or belief in absolute principles in political, philosophical, ethical, or theological matters. — **ab·so·lut·ist n. & adj.**

ab·solve /əbˈzälv; -ˈsälv/ ▶ **v.** [trans.] declare (someone) free from blame, guilt, or responsibility. ■ Christian Theol. give absolution for (a sin). [ME: from L. *absolvere* 'set free,' from *ab-* 'from' + *solvere* 'loosen.']

ab·sorb /əbˈzôrb; -ˈsôrb/ ▶ **v.** [trans.] **1** take in or soak up (energy, or a liquid or other substance) by chemical or physical action, typically gradually. ■ take in and assimilate (information, ideas, or experience). ■ take control of (a smaller or less powerful entity), making it a part of oneself by assimilation. ■ use or take up (time or resources): *arms spending absorbs 2 percent of the national income.* ■ take up and reduce the effect or intensity of (sound or an impact). **2** engross the attention of (someone). — **ab·sorb·a·bil·i·ty** /əbˌzôrbəˈbilitē; -ˌsôr-/ **n.** **ab·sorb·a·ble adj.** **ab·sorb·er n.** [ME: from L. *absorbere*, from *ab-* 'from' + *sorbere* 'suck in.']

ab·sorb·ance /əbˈzôrbəns; -ˈsôr-/ ▶ **n.** Physics a measure of the capacity of a substance to absorb light of a specified wavelength.

ab·sorbed /əbˈzôrbd; -ˈsôrbd/ ▶ **adj.** [predic.] intensely engaged; engrossed. — **ab·sorb·ed·ly** /-bidlē/ **adv.**

ab·sorbed dose ▶ **n.** Physics the energy of ionizing radiation absorbed per unit mass by a body.

ab·sorb·ent /əbˈzôrbənt; -ˈsôr-/ ▶ **adj.** (of a material) able to soak up liquid easily. ▶ **n.** a substance or item that soaks up liquid easily. — **ab·sorb·en·cy n.**

ab·sorb·ent cot·ton ▶ **n.** fluffy wadding of a kind originally made from raw cotton, used for cleansing wounds, removing cosmetics, etc.

ab·sorb·ing /əbˈzôrbiɴɢ; -ˈsôr-/ ▶ **adj.** intensely interesting: *an absorbing account of their marriage.* — **ab·sorb·ing·ly adv.**

ab·sorp·tion /əbˈzôrpsʜən; -ˈsôrp-/ ▶ **n.** **1** the process or action by which one thing absorbs or is absorbed by another: *shock absorption.* ■ Physics the process or action by which neutrons are absorbed by the nucleus. **2** the fact or state of being engrossed in something. — **ab·sorp·tive adj.** [16th C.: from L. *absorptio(n-)*, from *absorbere* (see ABSORB).]

ab·sorp·tion spec·trum ▶ **n.** Physics a spectrum of electromagnetic radiation transmitted through a substance, showing dark lines or bands due to absorption of specific wavelengths.

ab·squat·u·late /abˈskwäcʜəˌlāt/ ▶ **v.** [intrans.] humorous leave abruptly: *some overthrown dictator who had absquatulated to the USA.* — **ab·squat·u·la·tion** /abˌskwäcʜəˈlāsʜən/ **n.** [19th C.: blend, simulating L., of *abscond, squattle* 'depart,' and *perambulate*.]

ab·stain /abˈstān/ ▶ **v.** [intrans.] **1** restrain oneself from doing or enjoying something. ■ refrain from drinking alcohol. **2** formally decline to vote either for or against a proposal or motion. — **ab·stain·er n.** [ME: ult. from L. *abstinere*, from *ab-* 'from' + *tenere* 'hold.']

ab·ste·mi·ous /abˈstēmēəs/ ▶ **adj.** not self-indulgent, esp. when eating and drinking. — **ab·ste·mi·ous·ly adv.** **ab·ste·mi·ous·ness n.** [17th C.: from L. *abstemius*, from *ab-* 'from' + word akin to *temetum* 'strong drink'.]

ab·sten·tion /abˈstensʜən/ ▶ **n.** **1** an instance of declining to vote for or against a proposal or motion. **2** the fact or practice of restraining oneself from indulging in something; abstinence. — **ab·sten·tion·ism n.** [16th C.: from late L. *abstentio(n-)*, from *abstinere* (see ABSTAIN).]

ab·sti·nence /ˈabstənəns/ ▶ **n.** the fact or practice of restraining oneself from indulging in something. — **ab·sti·nent adj.** **ab·sti·nent·ly adv.** [ME: ult. from L. *abstinentia*, from *abstinere* (see ABSTAIN).]

ab·stract ▶ **adj.** /abˈstrakt; ˈabˌstrakt/ existing in thought or as an idea but not having a physical or concrete existence. ■ dealing with ideas rather than events. ■ not based on a particular instance; theoretical. ■ (of a word, esp. a noun) denoting an idea, quality, or state rather than a concrete object. ■ of or relating to abstract art. ▶ **v.** /abˈstrakt/ [trans.] **1** consider (something) theoretically or separately from something else: *to **abstract** science and religion **from** their historical context can lead to anachronism.* ■ [intrans.] form a general idea in this way. **2** extract or remove (something). ■ used euphemistically to say that someone has stolen something: *his pockets contained all he had been able to **abstract from** the apartment.* ■ (**abstract oneself**) withdraw. **3** make a written summary of (an article or book). ▶ **n.** /ˈabˌstrakt/ **1** a summary or statement of the contents of a book, article, or formal speech. **2** an abstract work of art. **3** (**the abstract**) that which is abstract; the theoretical consideration of something.
– PHRASES **in the abstract** in a general way; without reference to specific instances. — **ab·stract·ly adv.** **ab·strac·tor** /-ˈstraktər/ **n.** (in sense 3 of the **verb**). [ME: from L. *abstractus* 'drawn away,' from v. *abstrahere*, from *ab-* + *trahere* 'draw.']

ab·stract art ▶ **n.** art that does not attempt to represent external, recognizable reality but seeks to achieve its effect using shapes, forms, colors, and textures.

ab·stract·ed /abˈstraktid/ ▶ **adj.** showing a lack of concentration on what is happening around one. — **ab·stract·ed·ly adv.**

ab·stract ex·pres·sion·ism ▶ **n.** a development of abstract art that originated in New York in the 1940s and 1950s and aimed at subjective emotional expression with particular emphasis on the creative spontaneous act (e.g., action painting). — **ab·stract ex·pres·sion·ist n.**

ab·strac·tion /abˈstraksʜən/ ▶ **n.** **1** the quality of dealing with ideas rather than events. ■ something that exists only as an idea. **2** freedom from representational qualities in art. ■ an abstract work of art. **3** a state of preoccupation. **4** the process of considering something independently of its associations, attributes, or concrete accompaniments. **5** the process of removing something, esp. water from a river or other source.

ab·strac·tion·ism /abˈstraksʜəˌnizəm/ ▶ **n.** the principles and practice of abstract art. ■ the presentation of ideas in abstract terms. — **ab·strac·tion·ist n.**

ab·stract of ti·tle /ˈabˌstrakt/ ▶ **n.** Law a summary giving details of the title deeds and documents that prove an owner's right to dispose of land, together with any encumbrances that relate to the property.

ab·struse /abˈstro͞os/ ▶ **adj.** difficult to understand; obscure. — **ab·struse·ly adv.** **ab·struse·ness n.** [16th C.: from L. *abstrusus* 'hidden,' from *abstrudere* 'conceal,' from *ab-* 'from' + *trudere* 'to push.']

ab·surd /əbˈsərd; -ˈzərd/ ▶ **adj.** (of an idea or suggestion) wildly unreasonable, illogical, or inappropriate: *so you think I'm a spy? How absurd!* | [as n.] (**the absurd**) *he had a keen eye for the absurd.* ■ (of a person or a person's behavior or actions) foolish; unreasonable. ■ (of an object or situation) arousing amusement or derision; ridiculous. — **ab·surd·ly adv.** [16th C.: from L. *absurdus* 'out of tune,' akin to *surdus* 'deaf.']

ab·surd·ism /əbˈsərdˌizəm; -ˈzərd-/ ▶ **n.** the belief that human beings exist in a purposeless, chaotic universe. — **ab·surd·ist adj. & n.**

ab·surd·i·ty /əbˈsərditē; -ˈzərd-/ ▶ **n.** (pl. **-ties**) the quality or state of being ridiculous or wildly unreasonable.

A·bu Dha·bi /ˌäbo͞o ˈᴛʜäbē; ˈdäbē/ the largest of the seven member states of the United Arab Emirates, lying between Oman and the Gulf coast; pop. 670,125. ■ the capital of this state; pop. 242,975. It is also the federal capital of the United Arab Emirates.

A·bu·ja /äˈbo͞oyä/ a new city in central Nigeria, designated in 1982 as the national capital; pop. 378,670.

a·bu·li·a /əˈbo͞olēə/ (also **a·bou·li·a**) ▶ **n.** an absence of willpower or an inability to act decisively, as a symptom of mental illness. [19th C.: from A-[1] + Gk. *boulē* 'the will.']

a·bun·dance /əˈbəndəns/ ▶ **n.** a very large quantity of something. ■ the quantity or amount of something, e.g., a chemical element or an animal or plant species, present in a particular area, volume, sample, etc. ■ the state or condition of having a copious quantity of something; plentifulness. ■ plentifulness of the good things of life; prosperity.

a·bun·dant /əˈbəndənt/ ▶ **adj.** existing or available in large quantities; plentiful. ■ [predic.] (**abundant in**) having plenty of something. [ME: from L. *abundant-* 'abounding,' from *abundare* (see ABOUND).]

a·bun·dant·ly /əˈbəndəntlē/ ▶ **adv.** in large quantities. ■ [as submodifier] extremely.

a·buse ▶ **v.** /əˈbyo͞oz/ [trans.] **1** use (something) to bad effect or for a bad purpose; misuse. ■ make excessive and habitual use of (alcohol or drugs, esp. illegal ones). **2** treat (a person or an animal) with cruelty or violence, esp. regularly or repeatedly. ■ assault (someone, esp. a woman or child) sexually. ■ use or treat in such a way as to cause damage or harm. ■ speak in an insulting and offensive way to or about (someone). ▶ **n.** /əˈbyo͞os/ **1** the improper use of something. ■ unjust or corrupt practice. **2** cruel and violent treatment of a person or animal. ■ violent treatment involving sexual assault, esp. on a repeated basis. ■ insulting and offensive language. [ME: ult. from L. *abus-* 'misused,' from the v. *abuti*, from *ab-* + *uti* 'to use.']

a·bus·er /əˈbyo͞ozər/ ▶ **n.** [usu. with adj.] someone who regularly or habitually abuses someone or something, in particular: ■ someone who makes excessive use of alcohol or illegal drugs. ■ someone who sexually assaults another person, esp. a woman or child.

A·bu Sim·bel /ˌäbo͞o ˈsimbəl/ the site of two huge rock-cut temples in southern Egypt, built during the reign of Ramses II in the 13th century BC.

a·bu·sive /əˈbyo͞osiv; -ziv/ ▶ **adj.** **1** extremely offensive and insulting. **2** engaging in or characterized by habitual violence and cruelty. **3** involving injustice or illegality. — **a·bu·sive·ly adv.** **a·bu·sive·ness n.**

a·but /əˈbət/ ▶ **v.** (**a·but·ted**, **a·but·ting**) [trans.] (of an area of land or a building) be next to or have a common boundary with: *gardens abutting Great Prescott Street* | [intrans.] *a park **abutting on** an area of wasteland.* ■ touch or lean upon: *masonry may crumble where a roof abuts it.* [ME: 'be next to" from Anglo-L. *abuttare*, from *a-* 'at' + Old Fr. *but* 'end'; 'lean upon' (16th C.) from OFr. *abouter*, from *a-* 'at') + *bouter* 'to strike,' from Gmc.]

a·bu·ti·lon /əˈbyo͞otlˌän/ ▶ **n.** a herbaceous plant or shrub (genus *Abutilon*) of the mallow family, native to warm climates and typically bearing showy yellow, red, or mauve flowers. [mod. L., from Arab. *ūbūṭīlūn* 'Ind. mallow.']

a·but·ment /ə'bətmənt/ ▶ **n.** a structure built to support the lateral pressure of an arch or span, e.g., at the ends of a bridge. ■ the process of supporting something with such a structure. ■ a point at which something abuts against something else.

a·but·ter /ə'bətər/ ▶ **n.** the owner of property that abuts (touches on) another.

a·bysm /ə'bizəm/ ▶ **n.** a literary or poetic term for ABYSS: *the abysm from which nightmares crawl.* [ME: ult. from med. L. *abysmus*, alt. of late L. *abyssus* 'bottomless pit.']

a·bys·mal /ə'bizməl/ ▶ **adj. 1** informal extremely bad; appalling. **2** literary very deep. — **a·bys·mal·ly adv.**

a·byss /ə'bis/ ▶ **n.** a deep or seemingly bottomless chasm: *a rope led down into the dark abyss* | fig. *I was stagnating in an abyss of boredom.* ■ fig. a wide or profound difference between people; a gulf: *the abyss between the two nations.* ■ fig. the regions of hell conceived of as a bottomless pit. ■ **(the abyss)** fig. a catastrophic situation seen as likely to occur. [ME: ult. from Gk. *abussos* 'bottomless,' from *a-* + *bussos* 'depth.']

a·byss·al /ə'bisəl/ ▶ **adj.** esp. tech. relating to or denoting the depths or bed of the ocean, esp. between about 10,000 and 20,000 feet (3,000 and 6,000 m) down. ■ Geol. another term for PLUTONIC (sense 1).

Ab·ys·sin·i·a /,abə'sinēə/ former name for ETHIOPIA.

Ab·ys·sin·i·an /,abə'sinēən/ ▶ **adj.** hist. of or relating to Abyssinia or its people. ▶ **n. 1** hist. a native of Abyssinia. **2** (also **Abyssinian cat**) a domestic cat of a breed having long ears and short brown hair flecked with gray.

Ab·zug /'ab,zo͝og/, Bella Savitsky (1920–98), US politician and civil rights activist. She served in Congress as a Democrat from New York 1971–77.

AC ▶ **abbr.** ■ (also **ac**) alternating current: ■ (also **ac**) air conditioning. ■ before Christ. ■ appellation contrôlée. ■ athletic club. ■ **(ac.)** acre: *a 22-ac. site.*

Ac ▶ **symb.** the chemical element actinium.

a/c ▶ **abbr.** ■ account. ■ (also **A/C**) air conditioning.

ac- ▶ **prefix** var. of AD- assimilated before *c* and *q* (as in *accept*, *acquit*, and *acquiesce*).

-ac ▶ **suffix** forming adjectives that are also often (or only) used as nouns, such as *maniac*. Compare with -ACAL. [from Gk. *-akos* via L. *-acus* or Fr. *-aque*.]

a·ca·cia /ə'kāshə/ (also **acacia tree**) ▶ **n.** a tree or shrub (genus *Acacia*) of the pea family that bears spikes or clusters of yellow or white flowers and is frequently thorny. ■ see FALSE ACACIA. [ME: via L. from Gk. *akakia*.]

ac·a·deme /,akə'dēm; 'akə,dēm/ ▶ **n.** the academic environment or community; academia. [16th C.: from L. *academia* (see ACADEMY).]

ac·a·de·mi·a /,akə'dēmēə/ ▶ **n.** the environment or community concerned with the pursuit of research, education, and scholarship. [1950s: from L. (see ACADEMY).]

ac·a·dem·ic /,akə'demik/ ▶ **adj. 1** of or relating to education and scholarship. ■ of or relating to an educational or scholarly institution or environment. ■ (of an institution or a course of study) placing a greater emphasis on reading and study than on technical or practical work. ■ (of a person) interested in or excelling at scholarly pursuits and activities. ■ (of an art form) conventional, esp. in an idealized or excessively formal way. **2** not of practical relevance; of only theoretical interest. ▶ **n.** a teacher or scholar in a university or institute of higher education. — **ac·a·dem·i·cal·ly** /-ik(ə)lē/ **adv.**

ac·a·de·mi·cian /,akədə'mishən; ə,kadə-/ ▶ **n. 1** an academic; an intellectual. **2** a member of an academy.

ac·a·dem·i·cism /,akə'demə,sizəm/ (also **a·cad·e·mism** /ə'kadə,mizəm/) ▶ **n.** adherence to formal or conventional rules and traditions in art or literature.

ac·a·dem·ic year ▶ **n.** the period of the year during which students attend an educational institution, usually from September to June. Also called SCHOOL YEAR.

a·cad·e·my /ə'kadəmē/ ▶ **n.** (pl. **-mies**) **1** a place of study or training in a special field. ■ hist. a place of study. ■ a secondary school, typically a private one. ■ **(the Academy)** the teaching school founded by Plato. **2** a society or institution of distinguished scholars, artists, or scientists, that aims to promote and maintain standards in its particular field. ■ the community of scholars; academe. [ME (denoting the garden where Plato taught): ult. from L. *academia*, from Gk. *akadēmeia*, from *Akadēmos*, hero after whom Plato's garden was named.]

A·cad·e·my A·ward ▶ **n.** any of a series of awards of the Academy of Motion Picture Arts and Sciences in Hollywood given annually since 1928 for achievement in the movie industry in various categories; an Oscar.

A·ca·di·a /ə'kādēə/ a former French colony established in 1604 in the territory that now forms Nova Scotia in Canada.

A·ca·di·an /ə'kādēən/ esp. hist. ▶ **adj.** of or relating to Acadia or its people. ▶ **n.** a native or inhabitant of Acadia. ■ esp. Canadian a French-speaking descendant of the early French settlers in Acadia. ■ a Cajun.

ac·a·jou /'akə,zho͞o; -jo͞o/ ▶ **n. 1** the wood of certain tropical timber-yielding trees, esp. mahogany. **2** another term for CASHEW. [16th C.: from Fr., via Port. from Tupi *acajú*.]

-acal ▶ **suffix** forming adjectives such as *maniacal*, often making a distinction from nouns ending in *-ac* (as in *maniacal* compared with *maniac*).

a·cal·cu·li·a /,ākal'kyo͞olēə/ ▶ **n.** Med. loss of the ability to perform simple arithmetic calculations, typically resulting from disease or injury of the parietal lobe of the brain. [20th C.: from A-[1] + L. *calculare* 'calculate.']

acantho- (also **acanth-** before a vowel) ▶ **comb. form** having thornlike characteristics. [from Gk. *akantha* 'thorn.']

A·can·tho·ceph·a·la /ə,kanthō'sefələ/ Zool. a small phylum of parasitic invertebrates that comprises the thorny-headed worms. — **a·can·tho·ceph·a·lan adj. & n. a·can·tho·ceph·a·lid** /-lid/ **adj. & n.** [mod. L., from ACANTHO- + Gk. *kephalē* 'head.']

a·can·thus /ə'kanthəs/ ▶ **n. 1** a herbaceous plant or shrub (genus *Acanthus*, family Acanthaceae) with bold flower spikes and spiny decorative leaves, native to Mediterranean regions. **2** Archit. a representation of an acanthus leaf, used as a decoration for Corinthian column capitals. [via L. from Gk. *akanthos*, from *akantha* 'thorn,' from *akē* 'point.']

acanthus 2

a cap·pel·la /,ä kə'pelə/ ▶ **adj. & adv.** (with reference to choral music) without instrumental accompaniment. ■ [as adj.] relating to or concerned with such music: *the English a cappella tradition.* [Ital., lit. 'in chapel style.']

A·ca·pul·co /,äkə'po͞olkō; ,ak-/ a city in southern Mexico, on the Pacific coast; pop. 592,290. Full name ACAPULCO DE JUÁREZ.

Ac·a·ri /'akə,rī/ (also **Ac·a·ri·na** /akə'rīnə/) Zool. a large order (or subclass) of small arachnids that comprises the mites and ticks. — **ac·a·rid** /-rid/ **n. & adj. ac·a·rine** /-,rīn; -,rēn/ **n. & adj.** [mod. L. (pl.), from *acarus*, from Gk. *akari* 'mite.']

a·car·i·cide /ə'karə,sīd; 'akərə-/ ▶ **n.** a substance poisonous to mites or ticks. [19th C.: from Gk. *akari* 'mite'.]

ac·a·rol·o·gy /,akə'räləjē/ ▶ **n.** the study of mites and ticks. — **ac·a·rol·o·gist** /-jist/ **n.** [20th C.: from Gk. *akari* 'mite.']

a·cat·a·lec·tic /,ā,katl'ektik/ Pros. ▶ **adj.** (of a line of verse) having the full number of syllables. ▶ **n.** a line of verse of such a type.

Ac·ca·di·an /ə'kādēən/ ▶ **n.** var. of AKKADIAN.

ac·cede /ak'sēd/ ▶ **v.** [intrans.] formal **1** assent or agree to a demand, request, or treaty. **2** assume an office or position. ■ become a member of a community or organization. [ME: from L. *accedere*, from *ad-* 'to' + *cedere* 'yield.']

ac·cel·er·an·do /äk,selə'rändō; ak-; ä,chelə-/ (pl. **-dos** or **-di** /-dē/) Music ▶ **adj. & adv.** with a gradual increase of speed (used chiefly as a direction). [Ital.]

ac·cel·er·ant /ak'selərənt/ ▶ **n.** a substance used to aid the spread of fire. ▶ **adj.** accelerating or causing acceleration.

ac·cel·er·ate /ak'selə,rāt/ ▶ **v.** [intrans.] (of a vehicle or other physical object) begin to move more quickly: *the car accelerated toward her.* ■ increase in amount or extent. ■ Physics undergo a change in velocity. ■ [trans.] cause to go faster: *the key question is whether stress accelerates aging.* — **ac·cel·er·a·tive** /-ərətiv; -,rātiv/ **adj.** [16th C.: from L. *accelerat-* 'hastened,' from v. *accelerare*, from *ad-* 'toward' + *celer* 'swift.']

ac·cel·er·a·tion /ak,selə'rāshən/ ▶ **n.** increase in the rate or speed of something. ■ Physics the rate of change of velocity per unit of time. ■ a vehicle's capacity to gain speed within a short time.

ac·cel·er·a·tor /ak'selə,rātər/ ▶ **n.** something that brings about acceleration, in particular: ■ the device, typically a foot pedal, that controls the speed of a vehicle's engine. ■ Physics an apparatus for accelerating charged particles to high velocities. ■ a substance that speeds up a chemical process. ■ Comput. short for ACCELERATOR BOARD.

ac·cel·er·a·tor board (also **accelerator card**) ▶ **n.** an accessory circuit board that can be plugged into a small computer to increase the speed of its processor or input/output operations.

ac·cel·er·om·e·ter /ak,selə'rämitər/ ▶ **n.** an instrument for measuring acceleration, typically that of an automobile, ship, aircraft, or spacecraft. [20th C.: from ACCELERATE.]

ac·cent ▶ **n.** /'aksent/ **1** a distinctive mode of pronunciation of a language, esp. one associated with a particular nation, locality, or social class. ■ the mode of pronunciation used by native speakers of a language. **2** a distinct emphasis given to a syllable or word in speech by stress or pitch. ■ a mark on a letter or word to indicate pitch, stress, or vowel quality. ■ Music an emphasis on a particular note or chord. **3** [in sing.] a special or particular emphasis. ■ a feature that gives a distinctive visual emphasis to something. ▶ **v.** /'aksent; ak'sent/ [trans.] emphasize (a particular feature). ■ Music play (a note, a beat of the bar, etc.) with an accent. — **ac·cen·tu·al** /ak'sencho͞oəl/ **adj.** [ME: from L. *accentus* 'tone' from *ad-* 'to' + *cantus* 'song.']

ac·cen·tu·ate /ak'sencho͞o,āt/ ▶ **v.** [trans.] make more noticeable or prominent. [18th C.: from med. L. *accentuat-* 'accented,' from the v. *accentuare*, from *accentus*.]

ac·cen·tu·a·tion /ak,sencho͞o'āshən/ ▶ **n.** the action of emphasizing something. ■ the prominence of a thing relative to the normal. ■ the manner in which accents are apparent in pronunciation, or indicated in writing.

ac·cept /ak'sept/ ▶ **v.** [trans.] **1** consent to receive (a thing offered). ■ agree to undertake (an offered position or responsibility). ■ give an affirmative answer to (an offer or proposal); say yes to: *he would accept their offer* | [intrans.] *Damien offered Laura a lift home and she accepted.* ■ dated say yes to a proposal of marriage from (a man): *Ronald is a good match and she ought to accept him.* ■ receive as adequate, valid, or suitable: *credit cards are widely accepted.* ■ regard favorably or with approval; welcome: *the literati accepted him as one of them.* ■ agree to meet (a draft or bill of exchange) by signing it. ■ (of a thing) be designed to allow (something) to be inserted or applied: *vending machines accept 100-yen coins for cans of beer.* **2** believe or come to recognize (an opinion, explanation, etc.) as valid or correct: *this explanation came to be accepted.* ■ be prepared to subscribe to (a belief or philosophy): *accept the tenets of the Episcopalian faith.* ■ take upon oneself (a responsibility or liability); acknowledge: *Jenkins is willing to accept his responsibility.* ■ tolerate or submit to (something unpleasant or undesired): *they accepted the need to cut expenses.* — **ac·cept·er** n. [ME: from L. *acceptare*, frequentative of *accipere* 'take something to oneself,' from *ad-* + *capere* 'take.']

ac·cept·a·ble /ak'septəbəl/ ▶ **adj.** **1** able to be agreed on; suitable. ■ adequate; satisfactory. ■ pleasing; welcome. **2** able to be tolerated or allowed. — **ac·cept·a·bil·i·ty** /-ˌseptə'bilitē/ **n.** **ac·cept·a·ble·ness** **n.** **ac·cept·a·bly** /-blē/ **adv.**

ac·cept·ance /ak'septəns/ ▶ **n.** **1** the action of consenting to receive or undertake something offered. ■ agreement to meet a draft or bill of exchange, effected by signing it. ■ a draft or bill so accepted. **2** the action or process of being received as adequate or suitable, typically to be admitted into a group. **3** agreement with or belief in an idea, opinion, or explanation. ■ approval or favorable regard. ■ willingness to tolerate a difficult or unpleasant situation.

ac·cept·ant /ak'septənt/ ▶ **adj.** (**acceptant of**) rare willingly accepting.

ac·cep·ta·tion /ˌaksep'tāsʜən/ ▶ **n.** a particular sense or the generally recognized meaning (**common acceptation**) of a word or phrase.

ac·cep·tor /ak'septər/ ▶ **n.** a person or thing that accepts something, in particular: ■ a person or bank that accepts a draft or bill of exchange. ■ Chem. an atom or molecule that is able to bind to or accept an electron or other species. ■ Physics such an atom forming a positive hole in a semiconductor.

ac·cess /'akˌses/ ▶ **n.** **1** a means of approaching or entering a place. ■ the right or opportunity to use or benefit from something: *do you have access to a computer?* ■ the right or opportunity to approach or see someone: *we were denied access to our grandson.* ■ the action or process of obtaining or retrieving information stored in a computer's memory: *this prevents unauthorized access to the file.* ■ the condition of being able to be reached or obtained. ■ [as adj.] denoting noncommercial broadcasting produced by local independent groups, rather than by professionals: ***public-access television.*** **2** [in sing.] an attack or outburst of an emotion. ▶ **v.** [trans.] (usu. **be accessed**) **1** Comput. obtain, examine, or retrieve (data or a file). **2** approach or enter (a place): *single rooms have private baths accessed via the balcony.* [ME: from L. *accessus*, from *accedere* (see ACCEDE).]

ac·cess charge (also **access fee**) ▶ **n.** a charge made for the use of computer or local telephone-network facilities.

ac·ces·si·ble /ak'sesəbəl/ ▶ **adj.** **1** (of a place) able to be reached or entered. ■ (of an object, service, or facility) able to be easily obtained or used. ■ easily understood. ■ able to be reached or entered by people in wheelchairs. **2** (of a person, typically one in a position of authority or importance) friendly and easy to talk to; approachable. — **ac·ces·si·bil·i·ty** /-ˌsesə'bilitē/ **n.** **ac·ces·si·bly** /-blē/ **adv.**

ac·ces·sion /ak'sesʜən/ ▶ **n.** **1** the attainment or acquisition of a position of rank or power, typically that of monarch or president. ■ the action or process of formally joining or being accepted by an association, institution, or group. **2** a new item added to an existing collection of books, paintings, or artifacts. ■ an amount added to an existing quantity of something. **3** the formal acceptance of a treaty or agreement. ▶ **v.** [trans.] (usu. **be accessioned**) record the addition of (a new item) to a library, museum, or other collection.

ac·ces·so·rize /ak'sesəˌrīz/ ▶ **v.** [trans.] provide or complement (a garment) with fashion accessories. ■ serve as a fashion accessory to (a garment).

ac·ces·so·ry /ak'ses(ə)rē/ (also **ac·ces·sa·ry**) ▶ **n.** (pl. **-ries**) **1** a thing that can be added to something else in order to make it more useful, versatile, or attractive. ■ a small article or item of clothing carried or worn to complement a garment or outfit. **2** Law someone who gives assistance to the perpetrator of a crime, without directly committing it, sometimes without being present. ▶ **adj.** [attrib.] esp. tech. contributing to or aiding an activity or process in a minor way; subsidiary or supplementary.

– PHRASES **accessory before** (or **after**) **the fact** Law, dated a person who incites or assists someone to commit a crime (or knowingly aids someone who has committed a crime).

ac·ces·so·ry nerve ▶ **n.** Anat. each of the eleventh pair of cranial nerves, supplying certain muscles in the neck and shoulder.

ac·cess time ▶ **n.** Comput. the time taken to retrieve data from storage.

ac·ciac·ca·tu·ra /äˌcʜäkə'to͝orə/ ▶ **n.** (pl. **-tu·ras** or **-tu·re** /-'to͝orā; -'to͝orē/) Music a grace note performed as quickly as possible before an essential note of a melody, and falling before the beat. [Ital., from *acciaccare* 'to crush.']

ac·ci·dence /'aksidəns/ ▶ **n.** the part of grammar that deals with the inflections of words. [16th C.: from late L. *accidentia*, neut. pl. of the pres. part. of *accidere* (see ACCIDENT).]

ac·ci·dent /'aksidənt/ ▶ **n.** **1** an unfortunate incident that happens unexpectedly and unintentionally, typically resulting in damage or injury. ■ a crash involving road or other vehicles, typically one that causes serious damage or injury. ■ informal used euphemistically to refer to an incidence of incontinence, typically by a child or an animal. **2** an event that happens by chance or that is without apparent or deliberate cause. ■ the working of fortune; chance. **3** Philos. (in Aristotelian thought) a property of a thing that is not essential to its nature.

– PHRASES **an accident waiting to happen** **1** a potentially disastrous situation, typically caused by negligent or faulty procedures. **2** a person certain to cause trouble. **accidents will happen** however careful you try to be, it is inevitable that some unfortunate or unforeseen events will occur. **by accident** unintentionally; by chance. [ME: via OFr. from L. *accident-* 'happening,' from v. *accidere*, from *ad-* 'to' + *cadere* 'to fall.']

ac·ci·den·tal /ˌaksi'dentl/ ▶ **adj.** **1** happening by chance, unintentionally, or unexpectedly. **2** incidental; subsidiary. **3** Philos. (in Aristotelian thought) relating to or denoting properties not essential to a thing's nature. ▶ **n.** **1** Music a sign indicating a momentary departure from the key signature by raising or lowering a note. **2** Ornithol. another term for VAGRANT. — **ac·ci·den·tal·ly** **adv.**

ac·ci·dent-prone ▶ **adj.** tending to be involved in a greater than average number of accidents.

ac·ci·die /'aksidē/ ▶ **n.** acedia. [ME: ult. from med. L. *accidia*, alt. of ACEDIA.]

ac·cip·i·ter /ak'sipitər/ ▶ **n.** Ornithol. a hawk (*Accipiter* and related genera) of a group distinguished by short, broad wings and relatively long legs, adapted for fast flight in wooded country. [19th C.: L., 'hawk.']

ac·cip·i·trine /ak'sipitrin; -ˌtrīn/ ▶ **adj.** [attrib.] Ornithol. of or relating to birds of a family (Accipitridae) that includes most diurnal birds of prey other than falcons, New World vultures, and the osprey. [19th C.: from Fr., from L. *accipiter* 'bird of prey.']

ac·claim /ə'klām/ ▶ **v.** [trans.] (usu. **be acclaimed**) praise enthusiastically and publicly. ▶ **n.** enthusiastic and public praise. [17th C.: from L. *acclamare*, from *ad-* 'to' + *clamare* 'to shout.']

ac·cla·ma·tion /ˌaklə'māsʜən/ ▶ **n.** loud and enthusiastic approval, typically to welcome or honor someone or something.

– PHRASES **by acclamation** (of election, agreement, etc.) by overwhelming vocal approval and without ballot. [16th C.: from L. *acclamatio(n-)*, from *acclamare* (see ACCLAIM).]

ac·cli·mate /'akləˌmāt; ə'klīmit/ ▶ **v.** [intrans.] (usu. **be acclimated**) become accustomed to a new climate or to new conditions. ■ Biol. respond physiologically or behaviorally to a change in a single environmental factor. Compare with ACCLIMATIZE. ■ [trans.] Bot. & Horticulture harden off (a plant). — **ac·cli·ma·tion** /ˌaklə'māsʜən/ **n.** [18th C.: from Fr. *acclimater*, from *a-* 'to' + *climat* 'climate.']

ac·cli·ma·tize /ə'klīməˌtīz/ ▶ **v.** [intrans.] acclimate. ■ Biol. respond physiologically or behaviorally to changes in a complex of environmental factors. ■ [trans.] Bot. & Horticulture harden off (a plant). — **ac·cli·ma·ti·za·tion** /əˌklīmətə'zāsʜən/ **n.**

ac·cliv·i·ty /ə'klivitē/ ▶ **n.** (pl. **-ties**) an upward slope. — **ac·cliv·i·tous** /-itəs/ **adj.** [17th C.: from L. *acclivitas*, from *acclivis*, from *ad-* 'toward' + *clivus* 'slope.']

ac·co·lade /'akəˌlād; -ˌläd/ ▶ **n.** **1** an award or privilege granted as a special honor or as an acknowledgment of merit. ■ an expression of praise or admiration. **2** a touch on a person's shoulders with a sword at the bestowing of a knighthood. [17th C.: from Fr., from Provençal *acolada*, lit. 'embrace around the neck,' from L. *ad-* + *collum* 'neck.']

ac·com·mo·date /ə'käməˌdāt/ ▶ **v.** [trans.] **1** (of physical space, esp. a building) provide lodging or sufficient space for. **2** fit in with the wishes or needs of: *it's hard to accommodate the new management style.* ■ [intrans.] (**accommodate to**) adapt to. — **ac·com·mo·da·tive** /-ˌdātiv/ **adj.** [16th C.: from L. *accommodat-* 'made fitting,' from v. *accommodare*, from *ad-* 'to' + *commodus* 'fitting.']

ac·com·mo·dat·ing /ə'käməˌdātiɴɢ/ ▶ **adj.** fitting in with someone's wishes or demands in a helpful way. — **ac·com·mo·dat·ing·ly** **adv.**

ac·com·mo·da·tion /əˌkämə'dāsʜən/ ▶ **n.** **1** an action of accommodating or the process of being accommodated. ■ (usu. **accommodations**) a room, group of rooms, or building in which someone may live or stay. ■ (**accommodations**) lodging; room and board. ■ the available space for occupants in a building, vehicle, or vessel. ■ the provision of a room or lodging. **2** a convenient arrangement; a settlement or compromise. ■ the process of adapting or adjusting to someone or something. ■ the automatic adjustment of the focus of the eye by flattening or thickening of the lens.

ac·com·mo·da·tion·ist /əˌkämə'dāsʜənist/ ▶ **n.** a person who seeks compromise with an opposing point of view, typically a political one.

ac·com·mo·da·tion lad·der ▶ **n.** a ladder or stairway up the side of a ship allowing access, esp. to and from a small boat, or from a dock.

ac·com·pa·ni·ment /ə'kəmp(ə)nimənt/ ▶ **n.** **1** a musical part that supports or partners a solo instrument, voice, or group. ■ music played to complement or as background to an activity. **2** something that is supplementary to or complements something else, typically food.

ac·com·pa·nist /ə'kəmpənist/ ▶ **n.** a person who provides a musical accompaniment to another musician or to a singer.

ac·com·pa·ny /ə'kəmpənē/ ▶v. (-nies, -nied) [trans.] 1 go somewhere with (someone) as a companion or escort. 2 (usu. **be accompanied**) be present or occur at the same time as (something else). ■ provide (something) as a complement or addition to something else. 3 play a musical accompaniment for. [ME: from OFr. *accompagner*, from *a-* 'to' + *compagne, compaignon* 'companion.']

ac·com·plice /ə'kämplis/ ▶n. a person who helps another commit a crime. [16th C.: alt. of ME *complice* 'an associate,' via OFr. from late L. *complex, complic-* 'allied.']

ac·com·plish /ə'kämplish/ ▶v. [trans.] achieve or complete successfully. [ME: from OFr. *acompliss-*, from *acomplir*, based on L. *ad-* 'to' + *complere* 'to complete.']

ac·com·plished /ə'kämplisht/ ▶adj. highly trained or skilled. ■ dated having a high level of education and good social skills.

ac·com·plish·ment /ə'kämplishmənt/ ▶n. something that has been achieved successfully. ■ the successful achievement of a task. ■ an activity that a person can do well, typically as a result of study or practice. ■ skill or ability in an activity.

ac·cord /ə'kôrd/ ▶v. 1 [trans.] give or grant someone (power, status, or recognition): *the powers accorded to the head of state.* 2 [intrans.] (**accord with**) (of a concept or fact) be harmonious or consistent with. ▶n. an official agreement or treaty. ■ agreement or harmony.
– PHRASES **of its own accord** without outside intervention: *the rash may go away of its own accord.* **of one's own accord** voluntarily: *he would not seek treatment of his own accord.* [OE, from OFr. *acorder* 'reconcile,' from L. *ad-* 'to' + *cor, cord-* 'heart.']

ac·cord·ance /ə'kôrdns/ ▶n. (in phrase **in accordance with**) in a manner conforming with: *the product is disposed of in accordance with federal regulations.*

ac·cord·ant /ə'kôrdnt/ ▶adj. [predic.] archaic agreeing or compatible.

ac·cord·ing /ə'kôrding/ ▶adv. 1 (**according to**) as stated by or in. ■ in a manner corresponding or conforming to. ■ in proportion or relation to. 2 (**according as**) depending on whether.

ac·cord·ing·ly /ə'kôrdinglē/ ▶adv. 1 in a way that is appropriate to the particular circumstances. 2 [sentence adverb] consequently; therefore.

ac·cor·di·on /ə'kôrdēən/ ▶n. a portable musical instrument with metal reeds blown by bellows, played by means of keys and buttons. ■ [as adj.] folding like the bellows of an accordion. — **accor·di·on·ist** n. [19th C.: from Ger. *Akkordion*, from Ital. *accordare* 'to tune.']

accordion

ac·cost /ə'kôst; ə'käst/ ▶v. [trans.] approach and address (someone) boldly or aggressively. ■ approach (someone) with hostility or harmful intent. ■ approach and address (someone) with sexual intent. [16th C.: from Fr. *accoster*, based on L. *ad-* 'to' + *costa* 'rib, side.']

ac·couche·ment /,äkōōsh'män; ə'kōōshmənt/ ▶n. archaic the action of giving birth to a baby. [18th C.: Fr., from *accoucher* 'act as midwife,' from *a-* 'to' + *coucher* 'put to bed' (see COUCH).]

ac·cou·cheur /,äkōō'shər/ ▶n. a male midwife. [18th C.: Fr.]

ac·count /ə'kount/ ▶n. 1 a report or description of an event or experience. ■ an interpretation or rendering of a piece of music. 2 (abbr.: **acct.**) a record or statement of financial expenditure or receipts relating to a particular period or purpose. ■ the department of a company that deals with such records. 3 (abbr.: **acct.**) an arrangement by which a body holds funds on behalf of a client or supplies goods or services to the client on credit. ■ the balance of funds held under such an arrangement. ■ a client having such an arrangement with a supplier. ■ a contract to do work periodically for a client. 4 importance. ▶v. [with obj. and complement] consider or regard in a specified way: *her visit could not be accounted a success*
– PHRASES **by** (or **from**) **all accounts** according to what one has heard or read. **call** (or **bring**) **someone to account** require someone to explain a mistake or poor performance. **give a good** (or **bad**) **account of oneself** make a favorable (or unfavorable) impression through one's performance. **keep an account of** keep a record of. **leave something out of account** fail or decline to consider a factor. **on someone's account** for a specified person's benefit. **on account of** because of. **on no account** under no circumstances. **on one's own account** with one's own money or assets, rather than for an employer or client. **settle** (or **square**) **accounts with** pay money owed to (someone). ■ have revenge on: *the dirty business of settling accounts with former Communists.* **take something into account** (or **take account of**) consider a specified thing along with other factors before reaching a decision or taking action. **turn something to (good) account** turn something to one's advantage.
– PHRASAL VERBS **account for** 1 give a satisfactory record of (something, typically money, that one is responsible for). ■ provide or serve as a satisfactory explanation or reason for. ■ (usu. **be accounted for**) know the fate or whereabouts of (someone or something), esp. after an accident. ■ succeed in killing, destroying, or defeating. 2 supply or make up a specified amount or proportion of. [ME: from OFr. *acont* (n.), *aconter* (v.), based on *conter* 'to count.']

ac·count·a·ble /ə'kountəbəl/ ▶adj. 1 (of a person, organization, or institution) required or expected to justify actions or decisions; responsible. 2 explicable; understandable. — **ac·count·a·bil·i·ty** /ə,kountə'bilitē/ n. **ac·count·a·bly** adv.

ac·count·an·cy /ə'kount(ə)nsē/ ▶n. the profession or duties of an accountant.

ac·count·ant /ə'kount(ə)nt/ (abbr.: **acct.**) ▶n. a person whose job is to keep or inspect financial accounts.

ac·count ex·ec·u·tive ▶n. a business executive who manages the interests of a particular client, typically in advertising.

ac·count·ing /ə'kounting/ ▶n. the action or process of keeping financial accounts.

ac·counts pay·a·ble ▶plural n. money owed by a company to its creditors.

ac·counts re·ceiv·a·ble ▶plural n. money owed to a company by its debtors.

ac·cou·tre /ə'kōōtər/ (also **ac·cou·ter**) ▶v. (-tred, -tring; -tered, -ter·ing) [trans.] (usu. **be accoutred**) clothe or equip, typically in something noticeable or impressive. [16th C.: from Fr. *accoutrer*, from OFr. *acoustrer*, from *a-* 'to' + *cousture* 'sewing' (see COUTURE).]

ac·cou·tre·ment /ə'kōōtərmənt; -trə-/ (also **ac·cou·ter·ment**) ▶n. (usu. **accoutrements**) additional items of dress or equipment, carried or worn by a person or used for a particular activity. ■ a soldier's outfit other than weapons and garments.

Ac·cra /'äkrə; 'akrə; ə'krä/ the capital of Ghana, a port on the Gulf of Guinea; pop. 867,460.

ac·cred·it /ə'kredit/ ▶v. (-it·ed, -it·ing) [trans.] (usu. **be accredited**) 1 give credit (to someone) for. ■ attribute (an action, saying, or quality) to. 2 (of an official body) give authority or sanction to (someone or something) when recognized standards have been met. 3 give official authorization for (someone, typically a diplomat or journalist) to be in a particular place or to hold a particular post. — **ac·cred·i·ta·tion** /ə,kredi'tāshən/ n. [17th C. (sense 2): from Fr. *accréditer*, from *a-* (from L. *ad* 'to, at') + *crédit* 'credit.']

ac·cred·it·ed /ə'kreditid/ ▶adj. (of a person, organization, or course of study) officially recognized or authorized: *an accredited chiropractic school.*

ac·crete /ə'krēt/ ▶v. [intrans.] grow by accumulation or coalescence: *ice that had accreted grotesquely into stalactites.* ■ [trans.] form (a composite whole or a collection of things) by gradual accumulation: *the collection of art he had accreted was to be sold.* ■ Astron. (of matter) come together under the influence of gravitation; (of a body) be formed from such matter: *the gas will cool and then accrete to the galaxy's core.* ■ [trans.] Astron. cause (matter) to come together in this way. [18th C.: from L. *accret-* 'grown,' from v. *accrescere*, from *ad-* 'to' + *crescere* 'grow.']

ac·cre·tion /ə'krēshən/ ▶n. the process of growth or increase, typically by the gradual accumulation of additional layers or matter. ■ a thing formed or added by such growth or increase. ■ Astron. the coming together and cohesion of matter under the influence of gravitation to form larger bodies. — **ac·cre·tive** /ə'krētiv/ adj.

ac·crue /ə'krōō/ ▶v. (-crues, -crued, -cru·ing) [intrans.] (of sums of money or benefits) be received by someone in regular or increasing amounts over time: *financial benefits will accrue from restructuring.* ■ [trans.] accumulate or receive (such payments or benefits). ■ [trans.] make provision for (a charge) at the end of a financial period for work that has been done but not yet invoiced. — **ac·cru·al** /ə'krōōəl/ n. [ME: from OFr. *acreue*, past part. of *acreistre* 'increase,' from L. *accrescere* (see ACCRETE).]

acct. ▶abbr. ■ account. ■ accountant.

ac·cul·tur·ate /ə'kəlchə,rāt/ ▶v. assimilate or cause to assimilate a different culture: [intrans.] *those who have acculturated to the United States* | [trans.] *the next weeks were spent acculturating the field staff.* — **ac·cul·tur·a·tion** /ə,kəlchə'rāshən/ n. **ac·cul·tur·a·tive** /-ərətiv; -ə,rātiv/ adj. [20th C.: from AC- + CULTURE.]

ac·cum·bent ▶adj. Bot. (of a cotyledon) lying edgewise against the folded radicle in the seed. [19th C.: from L. *accumbent-* 'reclining,' from *accumbere*, from *ad-* 'to' + v. akin to *cubare* 'to lie.']

ac·cu·mu·late /ə'kyōōmyə,lāt/ ▶v. [trans.] gather together or acquire an increasing number or quantity of. ■ gradually gather or acquire (a resulting whole): *her goal was to accumulate a huge fortune.* ■ [intrans.] gather or build up: *the toxin accumulated in their bodies.* [15th C.: from L. *accumulat-* 'heaped up,' from v. *accumulare*, from *ad-* 'to' + *cumulus* 'a heap.']

ac·cu·mu·la·tion /ə,kyōōmyə'lāshən/ ▶n. the acquisition or gradual gathering of something. ■ a mass or quantity of something that has gradually gathered or been acquired. ■ the growth of a sum of money by the regular addition of interest.

ac·cu·mu·la·tive /ə'kyōōmyələtiv; -,lātiv/ ▶adj. [attrib.] gathering or growing by gradual increases.

ac·cu·mu·la·tor /ə'kyōōmyə,lātər/ ▶n. a person or thing that accumulates things. ■ Comput. a register used to contain the results of an arithmetical or logical operation.

ac·cu·ra·cy /'akyərəsē/ ▶n. (pl. -cies) the quality or state of being correct or precise. ■ the ability to perform a task with precision. ■ tech. the degree to which the result of a measurement, calculation, or specification conforms to the correct value or a standard.

ac·cu·rate /'akyərit/ ▶adj. 1 (of information, measurements, statistics, etc.) correct in all details; exact. ■ (of an instrument or method) capable of giving such information. ■ (of a piece of work) meticulously careful and free from errors. ■ faithfully or fairly representing the truth about someone or something. 2 (of a weapon or the person using it) capable of reaching the intended target. ■ (of a shot or throw, or the person making it) successful in reaching a target. — **ac·cu·rate·ly** adv. [16th C.: from L. *accuratus* 'done with care,' past part. of *accurare*, from *ad-* 'toward' + *cura* 'care.']

ac·curs·ed /ə'kərst; ə'kərsid/ ▶ **adj. 1** literary under a curse. **2** [attrib.] informal, dated used to express strong dislike of or anger toward someone or something. [ME: past part. of obs. *accurse*, from *a-* (intensive) + CURSE.]

ac·cu·sal /ə'kyōōzəl/ ▶ **n.** another term for ACCUSATION.

ac·cu·sa·tion /,akyə'zāsʜən; ,akyōō-/ ▶ **n.** a charge or claim that someone has done something illegal or wrong. ■ the action or process of making such a charge or claim.

ac·cu·sa·tive /ə'kyōōzətiv/ Gram. ▶ **adj.** relating to or denoting a case that expresses the object of an action or the goal of motion. ▶ **n.** a word in the accusative case. ■ **(the accusative)** the accusative case. [ME: from L. *(casus) accusativus*, lit. 'of the nature of accusation.']

ac·cu·sa·to·ri·al /ə,kyōōzə'tôrēəl/ ▶ **adj.** [attrib.] Law (esp. of a trial or legal procedure) involving accusation by a prosecutor and a verdict reached by an impartial judge or jury. Often contrasted with INQUISITORIAL.

ac·cu·sa·to·ry /ə'kyōōzə,tôrē/ ▶ **adj.** indicating or suggesting that one believes a person has done something wrong: *he pointed an accusatory finger in her direction.*

ac·cuse /ə'kyōōz/ ▶ **v.** [trans.] (often **be accused**) charge (someone) with an offense or crime. ■ claim that (someone) has done something wrong. — **ac·cus·er n.** [ME: from OFr. *acuser*, from L. *accusare* 'call to account,' from *ad-* + *causa* 'reason, lawsuit.']

ac·cused /ə'kyōōzd/ ▶ **n.** [treated as sing. or pl.] **(the accused)** a person or group of people who are charged with or on trial for a crime.

ac·cus·ing /ə'kyōōziɴɢ/ ▶ **adj.** (of an expression, gesture, or tone of voice) indicating a belief in someone's guilt or culpability: *she stared at him with accusing eyes.* — **ac·cus·ing·ly adv.**

ac·cus·tom /ə'kəstəm/ ▶ **v.** [trans.] make (someone or something) accept something as normal or usual. ■ **(be accustomed to)** be used to: *my eyes gradually became accustomed to the darkness.* [ME: from OFr. *acostumer*, from *a-* 'to') + *costume* 'custom.']

ac·cus·tomed /ə'kəstəmd/ ▶ **adj.** [attrib.] customary or usual: *his accustomed route.*

AC/DC ▶ **adj.** alternating current/direct current. ■ informal bisexual.

ace /ās/ ▶ **n. 1** a playing card with a single spot on it, ranked as the highest card in its suit in most card games. ■ Golf, informal a hole in one. **2** [often with adj.] informal a person who excels at a particular sport or other activity. ■ a pilot who has shot down many enemy aircraft, esp. in World War I or World War II. **3** (in tennis and similar games) a service that an opponent is unable to return and thus wins a point. ▶ **adj.** informal very good. ▶ **v.** [trans.] informal (in tennis and similar games) serve an ace against (an opponent). ■ Golf, score an ace on (a hole) or with (a shot). ■ get an A or its equivalent in (a test or exam). ■ **(ace someone out)** outdo someone in a competitive situation.

– PHRASES **an ace up one's sleeve** (or **in the hole**) a plan or piece of information kept secret until it becomes necessary to use it. **hold all the aces** have all the advantages. **play one's ace** use one's best resource. **within an ace of** very close to. [ME: via OFr. from L. *as* 'unity, a unit.']

-acea ▶ **suffix** Zool. forming the names of zoological groups: *Crustacea.* Compare with -ACEAN. [from L., neut. pl. adjectival ending.]

-aceae ▶ **suffix** Bot. forming the names of families of plants: *Liliaceae.* [from L., fem. pl. adjectival ending.]

-acean ▶ **suffix** Zool. forming adjectives and nouns from taxonomic names ending in *-acea* (such as *crustacean* from *Crustacea*). [from L. *-aceus*, adjectival ending.]

a·ce·di·a /ə'sēdēə/ ▶ **n.** spiritual or mental sloth; apathy. [17th C.: late L., from Gk. *akēdia* 'listlessness,' from *a-* + *kēdos* 'care.']

a·cel·lu·lar /ā'selyələr/ ▶ **adj.** Biol. not consisting of, divided into, or containing cells. ■ (esp. of protozoa) consisting of one cell only.

-aceous ▶ **suffix 1** Bot. forming adjectives from nouns ending in *-aceae* (such as *ericaceous* from *Ericaceae*). **2** esp. Biol. & Geol. forming adjectives describing similarity, esp. in shape, texture, or color: *arenaceous* | *olivaceous.* [from L. *-aceus* 'of the nature of,' adjectival ending.]

a·ceph·a·lous /ā'sefələs/ ▶ **adj.** no longer having a head. ■ Zool. not having a head. ■ having no leader or chief. [18th C.: ult. from Gk. *akephalos* 'headless,' from *a-* + *kephalē* 'head.']

a·cerb /ə'sərb/ ▶ **adj.** another term for ACERBIC. [17th C.: from L. *acerbus.*]

a·cer·bic /ə'sərbik/ ▶ **adj. 1** (esp. of a comment or style of speaking) sharp and forthright. **2** archaic or tech. tasting sour or bitter. — **a·cer·bi·cal·ly** /-ik(ə)lē/ **adv. a·cer·bi·ty** /-bitē/ **n.** [19th C.: from L. *acerbus* 'sour-tasting.']

acet- ▶ **prefix** var. of ACETO- shortened before a vowel (as in *acetaldehyde*).

ac·e·tab·u·lum /,asi'tabyələm/ ▶ **n.** (pl. **-la** /-lə/) Anat. the socket of the hipbone, into which the head of the femur fits. ■ Zool. any cup-shaped structure, esp. a sucker. [ME: from L., from *acetum* 'vinegar' + *-abulum* 'container.'']

ac·e·tal /'asi,tal/ ▶ **n.** Chem. an organic compound, $R_1CH(OR_2)_2$, formed by the condensation of two alcohol molecules with an aldehyde molecule. [19th C.: from ACETIC + *-al* from *alcohol, aldehyde.*]

ac·et·al·de·hyde /,asi'taldə,hīd/ ▶ **n.** Chem. a colorless volatile liquid aldehyde, CH_3CHO, obtained by oxidizing ethanol. Alternative name: ethanal.

a·cet·am·ide /ə'setə,mīd/ ▶ **n.** Chem. the crystalline amide of acetic acid, CH_3CONH_2. [19th C.: from ACETYL.]

a·ce·ta·min·o·phen /ə,sētə'minəfən/ ▶ **n.** an analgesic drug, $C_8H_9NO_2$, used to treat headaches, arthritis, etc., and also to reduce fever, often as an alternative to aspirin.

ac·et·an·i·lide /,asi'tanə,līd/ ▶ **n.** Chem. a crystalline solid, $C_6H_5NHCOCH_3$, prepared by acetylation of aniline, used in dye manufacture. [19th C.: from *acet(yl)* + *anil(ine).*]

ac·e·tate /'asi,tāt/ ▶ **n. 1** Chem. a salt or ester of acetic acid, containing the anion CH_3COO- or the group $-OOCCH_3$. **2** cellulose acetate, esp. as used to make textile fibers or plastic. ■ a transparency made of cellulose acetate film. ■ a recording disk coated with cellulose acetate. [18th C.: from ACETIC.]

a·ce·tic /ə'sētik/ ▶ **adj.** of or like vinegar or acetic acid. [18th C.: from Fr. *acétique*, from L. *acetum* 'vinegar.']

a·ce·tic ac·id ▶ **n.** Chem. the acid, CH_3COOH, that gives vinegar its characteristic taste. The pure acid is a colorless viscous liquid or glassy solid.

ace·tic an·hy·dride ▶ **n.** Chem. the anhydride of acetic acid. It is a colorless pungent liquid, $(CH_3CO)_2O$, used in making synthetic fibers.

aceto- (also **acet-** before a vowel) ▶ **comb. form** Chem. representing ACETIC or ACETYL.

a·ce·to·bac·ter /ə,sētə'baktər; ,asitə-/ ▶ **n.** bacteria (genus *Acetobacter*) that oxidize organic compounds to acetic acid, as in vinegar formation. [mod. L., from ACETO- + BACTERIUM.]

ac·e·tone /'asi,tōn/ ▶ **n.** Chem. a colorless volatile liquid ketone, CH_3COCH_3, made by oxidizing isopropanol, used as an organic solvent and synthetic reagent. [19th C.: from ACETIC.]

a·ce·to·ne·mi·a /ə,sētə'nēmēə; ,asitə-/ ▶ **n.** another term for KETONEMIA.

ac·e·tous /ə'sētəs; 'asitəs/ ▶ **adj.** producing or resembling vinegar. [ME: from late L. *acetosus* 'sour,' from L. *acetum* 'vinegar.']

a·ce·tyl /ə'sētl; 'asitl/ ▶ **n.** [as adj.] Chem. the acyl radical $-C(O)CH_3$, derived from acetic acid. [19th C.: from ACETIC.]

a·cet·y·late /ə'setl,āt/ ▶ **v.** [trans.] Chem. introduce an acetyl group into (a molecule or compound). — **a·cet·y·la·tion** /ə,setl'āsʜən/ **n.**

a·ce·tyl·cho·line /ə,sētl'kō,lēn; ,asitl-/ ▶ **n.** Biochem. a compound that occurs throughout the nervous system, in which it functions as a neurotransmitter.

a·ce·tyl·cho·lin·es·ter·ase /ə'sētl,kōlə'nestə,rās; -,rāz; 'asitl-/ ▶ **n.** Biochem. an enzyme that causes rapid hydrolysis of acetylcholine.

a·ce·tyl-co·en·zyme A ▶ **n.** Biochem. the acetyl ester of coenzyme A, involved as an acetylating agent in many biochemical processes.

a·cet·y·lene /ə'setlən; -,ēn/ ▶ **n.** Chem. a colorless pungent-smelling hydrocarbon gas (C_2H_2), which burns with a bright flame, used in welding and formerly in lighting. [19th C.: from ACETIC + -YL.]

a·ce·tyl·sal·i·cyl·ic ac·id /ə,sētl,sali'silik/ ▶ **n.** systematic chemical name for ASPIRIN.

A·chae·a /ə'kēə; ə'kāə/ a region of ancient Greece on the north coast of the Peloponnesus.

A·chae·an /ə'kēən/ ▶ **adj.** of or relating to Achaea in ancient Greece. ■ literary (esp. in Homeric contexts) Greek. ▶ **n.** an inhabitant of Achaea. ■ literary (esp. in Homeric contexts) a Greek.

A·chae·me·nid /ə'kēmənid/ (also **A·chae·me·ni·an** /,akə'mēnēən/) ▶ **adj.** of or relating to the dynasty ruling in Persia from Cyrus I to Darius III (553–330 BC). ▶ **n.** a member of this dynasty. [from Gk. *Akhaimenēs* 'Achaemenes,' the reputed ancestor.]

A·cha·tes /ə'kātēz/ Greek Rom. Mythol. a companion of Aeneas. His loyalty to his friend was so exemplary as to become proverbial.

ache /āk/ ▶ **n.** a continuous or prolonged dull pain in a part of one's body. ■ [in sing.] fig. an emotion experienced with painful or bittersweet intensity. ▶ **v.** [intrans.] **1** (of a person) suffer from a continuous dull pain. ■ (of a part of one's body) be the source of such a pain. ■ fig. feel intense sadness or compassion: *she sat still and silent, her heart aching.* **2** feel an intense desire for. — **ach·ing·ly adv.** [OE *æce* (n.), *acan* (v.). The mod. spelling is due to a mistaken assumption that the word is derived from Gk. *akhos* 'pain.']

A·che·be /ä'ᴄʜābā/, Chinua (1930–), Nigerian writer; born *Albert Chinualumgu.* He wrote *A Man of the People* (1966) and *Anthills of the Savannah* (1988). Nobel Prize for Literature (1989).

a·chene /ā'kēn/ ▶ **n.** Bot. a small, dry, one-seeded fruit that does not open to release the seed. [19th C.: from mod. L. *achaenium*, from *a-* 'not' + Gk. *khainein* 'to gape.']

A·cher·nar /'akər,när; 'äk-/ Astron. the ninth brightest star in the sky, and the brightest in the constellation Eridanus (the River). [from Arab., 'end of the river (i.e., Eridanus).']

Ach·er·on /'akə,rän; -rən/ Gk. Mythol. one of the rivers of Hades. ■ literary hell. [16th C.: L., from Gk. *Akherōn.*]

Ach·e·son /'acʜəsən/, Dean Gooderham (1893–1971), US secretary of state 1949–53. He was instrumental in the formation of NATO and implemented the Marshall Plan and the Truman Doctrine.

A·cheu·le·an /ə'sʜōōlēən/ (also **A·cheu·li·an**) ▶ **adj.** Archaeol. of, relating to, or denoting the main Lower Paleolithic culture in Europe, represented by hand-ax industries, and dated to about 1,500,000–150,000 years ago. [20th C.: from Fr. *Acheuléen*, from *St-Acheul* France.]

a·chieve /ə'cʜēv/ ▶ **v.** [trans.] reach or attain (a desired objective, level, or result) by effort, skill, or courage: *he achieved his ambition to become* *a journalist* | [intrans.] *people striving to achieve.* ■ accomplish or bring about. — **a·chiev·a·ble** adj. **a·chiev·er** n. [ME: from OFr. *achever* 'come to a head,' from *a chief* 'to a head.']

a·chieve·ment /ə'CHēvmənt/ ▶ n. **1** a thing done successfully, typically by effort, courage, or skill. **2** the process or fact of achieving something. ■ a child's or student's progress in a course of learning, typically as measured by standardized tests or objectives. **3** Heraldry a representation of a coat of arms with all the adjuncts to which a bearer of arms is entitled.

ach·il·le·a /ə'kilēə/ ▶ n. a plant (genus *Achillea*) of the daisy family, including yarrow, typically with heads of small white or yellow flowers and fernlike leaves. [via L. from Gk. *Akhilleios*, a plant supposedly used medicinally by Achilles.]

A·chil·les /ə'kilēz/ Gk. Mythol. a hero of the Trojan War, son of Peleus and Thetis and killer of Hector.

Achil·les heel ▶ n. a weakness or vulnerable point. [19th C.: after ACHILLES, whose heel was the only vulnerable part of his body.]

Achil·les ten·don ▶ n. the tendon connecting calf muscles to the heel.

a·chlor·hy·dri·a /,āklôr'hīdrēə/ ▶ n. Med. absence of hydrochloric acid in the gastric secretions.

a·chon·dro·pla·sia /ā,kändrə'plāZH(ē)ə/ ▶ n. a hereditary condition in which the growth of long bones by ossification of cartilage is retarded, resulting in very short limbs and sometimes a face that is small in relation to the (normal-sized) skull. — **a·chon·dro·plas·tic** /-'plastik/ adj. [19th C.: from A-[1] + Gk. *khondros* 'cartilage.']

ach·ro·mat /'akrə,mat/ ▶ n. another term for ACHROMATIC LENS.

ach·ro·mat·ic /,akrə'matik; ,ākrə-/ ▶ adj. [attrib.] **1** relating to, employing, or denoting lenses that transmit light without separating it into constituent colors. **2** literary without color.

ach·ro·mat·ic lens ▶ n. a lens that transmits light without separating it into constituent colors.

ach·y /'ākē/ ▶ adj. [predic.] suffering from continuous dull pain: *she felt tired and achy.*

a·cic·u·lar /ə'sikyələr/ ▶ adj. tech. (chiefly of crystals) needle-shaped. [18th C.: from late L. *acicula*, dimin. of *acus* 'needle.']

ac·id /'asid/ ▶ n. a chemical substance (typically, a corrosive or sour-tasting liquid) that neutralizes alkalis, dissolves some metals, and turns litmus red. ■ fig. bitter or cutting remarks or tone of voice. ■ informal the drug LSD. ■ Chem. a molecule or other entity that can donate a proton or accept an electron pair in reactions. ▶ adj. **1** containing acid or having the properties of an acid; in particular, having a pH of less than 7. ■ Geol. (of rock, esp. lava) containing a relatively high proportion of silica. ■ Metallurgy relating to or denoting steelmaking processes involving silica-rich refractories and slags. **2** sharp-tasting or sour. ■ (of a person's remarks or tone) bitter or cutting. ■ (of a color) intense or bright. — **ac·id·y** adj. [17th C.: from L. *acidus*, from *acere* 'be sour.']

ac·id·head /'asid,hed/ ▶ n. informal a habitual user of the drug LSD.

a·cid·ic /ə'sidik/ ▶ adj. **1** having the properties of an acid, or containing acid; having a pH below 7. ■ Geol. (of rock, esp. lava) relatively rich in silica. ■ Metallurgy relating to or denoting steelmaking processes involving silica-rich refractories and slags. **2** sharp-tasting or sour. ■ (of a person's remarks or tone) bitter or cutting. ■ (of a color) intense or bright. **3** of or relating to acid rock or acid house music.

a·cid·i·fy /ə'sidə,fī/ ▶ v. (**-fies, -fied**) make or become acid: [trans.] *pollutants can acidify surface water* | [intrans.] *the paper was acidifying.* — **a·cid·i·fi·ca·tion** /ə,sidəfi'kāSHən/ n.

ac·i·dim·e·try /,asi'dimitrē/ ▶ n. measurement of the strengths of acids.

a·cid·i·ty /ə'siditē/ ▶ n. **1** the level of acid in substances such as water, soil, or wine. ■ such a level in the gastric juices, typically when excessive and causing discomfort. **2** the bitterness or sharpness of a person's remarks or tone.

ac·id·ly /'asidlē/ ▶ adv. with bitterness or sarcasm.

a·cid·o·phil /ə'sidə,fil; 'asidə-/ ▶ n. Biol. an acidophilic white blood cell.

a·cid·o·phil·ic /ə,sidə'filik; ,asidə-/ ▶ adj. Biol. **1** (of a cell or its contents) readily stained with acid dyes. **2** (of a microorganism or plant) growing best in acidic conditions. [20th C.: from ACID + *-philic* (see -PHILIA).]

ac·i·doph·i·lus /,asi'däfələs/ ▶ n. a bacterium (*Lactobacillus acidophilus*) that is used to make yogurt and to supplement the intestinal flora. [1920s: mod. L., lit. 'acid-loving.']

ac·i·do·sis /,asi'dōsis/ ▶ n. Med. an excessively acid condition of the body fluids or tissues. — **ac·i·dot·ic** /-'dätik/ adj.

ac·id rad·i·cal ▶ n. Chem. a radical formed by the removal of hydrogen ions from an acid.

ac·id rain ▶ n. rainfall made sufficiently acidic by atmospheric pollution that it causes environmental harm, typically to forests and lakes.

ac·id re·flux ▶ n. a condition in which gastric acid is regurgitated.

ac·id rock ▶ n. a type of rock music associated with or inspired by the use of hallucinogenic drugs.

ac·id test ▶ n. [in sing.] a conclusive test of the success or value of something. [orig. a test for gold using nitric acid.]

a·cid·u·late /ə'sijə,lāt/ ▶ v. [trans.] [usu. as adj.] (**acidulated**) make slightly acidic. — **a·cid·u·la·tion** /ə,sijə'lāSHən/ n. [18th C.: from L. *acidulus*, from *acidus*.]

a·cid·u·lous /ə'sijələs/ ▶ adj. sharp-tasting or sour. ■ (of a person's remarks or tone) bitter or cutting. [18th C.: from L. *acidulus*, from *acidus* 'sour.']

ac·i·nus /'asənəs/ ▶ n. (pl. **-ni** /-,nī/) Anat. **1** a small saclike cavity in a gland, surrounded by secretory cells. **2** a region of the lung supplied with air from one of the terminal bronchioles. [18th C.: L., 'kernel.']

-acious ▶ suffix (forming adjectives) inclined to; having as a capacity: *audacious* | *capacious.* [from L. ending *-ax, -acis* + -OUS.]

-acity ▶ suffix forming nouns of quality or state corresponding to adjectives ending in *-acious* (such as *audacity* corresponding to *audacious*). [from Fr. *-acité* or L. *-acitas*, n. endings.]

ack-ack /'ak ,ak/ Mil., informal ▶ n. an antiaircraft gun or regiment. ■ antiaircraft gunfire. [World War II: signalers' name for *AA*.]

ac·kee ▶ n. var. of AKEE.

ac·knowl·edge /ak'nälij/ ▶ v. [trans.] **1** accept or admit the existence or truth of. **2** (of a body of opinion) recognize the fact or importance or quality of. ■ express or display gratitude for or appreciation of. ■ accept the validity or legitimacy of. **3** show that one has noticed or recognized (someone) by making a gesture or greeting. ■ confirm (receipt of something). [15th C.: from obs. v. *knowledge*.]

ac·knowl·edg·ment /ak'nälijmənt/ (also **ac·knowl·edge·ment**) ▶ n. **1** acceptance of the truth or existence of something. **2** the action of expressing or displaying gratitude or appreciation for something. ■ the action of showing that one has noticed someone or something. ■ a letter confirming receipt of something. **3** (usu. **acknowledgments**) an author's or publisher's statement of indebtedness to others, typically one printed at the beginning of a book.

a·clin·ic line /ā'klinik/ ▶ n. another term for MAGNETIC EQUATOR. [19th C.: from Gk. *aklinēs*, from *a-* 'not' + *klinein* 'to bend.']

ACLU ▶ abbr. American Civil Liberties Union.

ac·me /'akmē/ ▶ n. [in sing.] the point at which someone or something is best, perfect, or most successful. [16th C.: from Gk. *akmē* 'highest point.']

Ac·me·ist /'akmē-ist/ ▶ adj. denoting or relating to an early 20th century movement in Russian poetry that rejected the values of symbolism in favor of formal technique and clarity of exposition. ▶ n. a member of this movement. — **Ac·me·ism** /-,izəm/ n.

ac·ne /'aknē/ ▶ n. the occurrence of inflamed or infected sebaceous glands in the skin; in particular, a condition characterized by red pimples on the face. — **ac·ned** adj. [19th C.: ult. from Gk. *aknas*, misreading of *akmas*, accusative pl. of *akmē* 'peak.']

ac·o·lyte /'akə,līt/ ▶ n. a person assisting the celebrant in a religious service or procession. ■ an assistant or follower. [ME: ult. from eccles. L. *acolytus*, from Gk. *akolouthos* 'follower.']

A·con·ca·gua /,akən'kägwə; ,äkôNG-/ an extinct volcano in the Andes, between Chile and Argentina, rising to 22,834 feet (6,960 m). It is the highest mountain in the western hemisphere.

ac·o·nite /'akə,nīt/ ▶ n. a poisonous plant (genus *Aconitum*) of the buttercup family, including monkshood. Native to temperate regions of the northern hemisphere, it bears hooded pink or purple flowers. ■ an extract of such a plant, used as a poison or in medicinal preparations. [16th C.: ult. from Gk. *akoniton*.]

a·corn /'ā,kôrn/ ▶ n. the fruit of the oak, a smooth oval nut in a rough cuplike base. [OE *æcern*, from Gmc.; akin to Du. *aker*.]

a·corn bar·na·cle ▶ n. a stalkless barnacle (genus *Balanus*, family Balanidae). Large numbers may attach themselves to a ship, forming a heavy encrustation that can impede the ship's progress.

a·corn squash ▶ n. a winter squash, typically of a dark green variety, with a longitudinally ridged rind.

a·cot·y·le·don /,ākätl'ēdn/ ▶ n. a plant with no distinct seed-leaves, esp. a fern or moss. — **a·cot·y·le·don·ous** /-'ēdn-əs/ adj.

a·cous·tic /ə'kōōstik/ ▶ adj. [attrib.] **1** relating to sound or the sense of hearing. ■ (of building materials) used for soundproofing or modifying sound. ■ (of an explosive mine or other weapon) able to be set off by sound waves. **2** (of music or musical instruments) not having electrical amplification. ■ (of a person or group) playing such instruments. ▶ n. **1** (usu. **acoustics**) the properties or qualities of a room or building that determine how sound is transmitted in it. ■ (**acoustic**) the acoustic properties or ambience of a sound recording or of a recording studio. **2** (**acoustics**) [treated as sing.] the branch of physics concerned with the properties of sound. **3** a musical instrument without electrical amplification, typically a guitar. — **a·cous·ti·cal** adj. **a·cous·ti·cal·ly** /-ik(ə)lē/ adv. [17th C.: from Gk. *akoustikos*, from *akouein* 'hear.']

ac·ous·ti·cian /,akōō'stiSHən/ ▶ n. a physicist concerned with the properties of sound.

ac·quaint /ə'kwānt/ ▶ v. [trans.] (**acquaint someone with**) make someone aware of or familiar with. ■ (**be acquainted**) be an acquaintance. [ME: from OFr. *acointier* 'make known,' ult. from L. *accognoscere*, from *ad-* 'to' + *cognoscere* 'come to know.']

ac·quaint·ance /ə'kwāntns/ ▶ n. **1** a person's knowledge or experience of something. ■ one's slight knowledge of or friendship with someone. **2** a person one knows slightly, but who is not a close friend. ■ such people considered collectively.

– PHRASES **make the acquaintance of** (or **make someone's acquaintance**) meet someone for the first time and become only slightly familiar. — **ac·quaint·ance·ship** n.

ac·quaint·ance rape ▶ n. rape by a person who is known to the victim.

ac·qui·esce /,akwē'es/ ▶ v. [intrans.] accept something reluctantly but without protest. — **ac·qui·es·cence** /-'esəns/ n. [17th C.: from L. *acquiescere*, from *ad-* 'to' + *quiescere* 'to rest.']

ac·qui·es·cent /,akwē'esənt/ ▶ adj. (of a person) ready to accept something without protest, or to do what someone else wants.

ac·quire /ə'kwī(ə)r/ ▶ v. [trans.] buy or obtain (an asset or object) for oneself. ■ learn or develop (a skill, habit, or quality). ■ achieve (a particular reputation) as a result of one's behavior or activities.

– PHRASES **acquired taste 1** a thing that one has come to like only through experience. **2** a liking of this kind. —**ac·quir·a·ble** adj. **ac·quir·er** n. [ME *acquere*, based on L. *acquirere* 'get in addition,' from *ad-* 'to' + *quaerere* 'seek.']

ac·quired char·ac·ter·is·tic (also **ac·quired char·ac·ter**) ▶ n. Biol. a modification or change in an organ or tissue during the lifetime of an organism due to use, disuse, or environmental effects, and not inherited.

ac·quired im·mune de·fi·cien·cy syn·drome see **AIDS**.

ac·quire·ment /ə'kwī(ə)rmənt/ ▶ n. the action of acquiring. ■ something acquired, typically a skill.

ac·qui·si·tion /,akwə'zisHən/ ▶ n. **1** an asset or object bought or obtained, typically by a library or museum. ■ an act of purchase of one company by another. ■ buying or obtaining an asset or object. **2** the learning or developing of a skill, habit, or quality. [ME (in the sense 'act of acquiring something'): from L. *acquisitio(n-)*, from the v. *acquirere* (see ACQUIRE).]

ac·quis·i·tive /ə'kwizitiv/ ▶ adj. excessively interested in acquiring money or material things. —**ac·quis·i·tive·ly** adv. **ac·quis·i·tive·ness** n. [19th C.: ult. from late L. *acquisitivus*. from L. *acquisit-* 'acquired,' from *acquirere* (see ACQUIRE).]

ac·quit /ə'kwit/ ▶ v. (**-quit·ted, -quit·ting**) **1** [trans.] (usu. **be acquitted**) free (someone) from a criminal charge by a verdict of not guilty. **2** (**acquit oneself**) conduct oneself or perform in a specified way. ■ (**acquit oneself of**) archaic discharge (a duty or responsibility). [ME: from OFr. *acquiter*, from med. L. *acquitare* 'pay a debt,' from *ad-* 'to' + *quitare* 'set free.']

ac·quit·tal /ə'kwitl/ ▶ n. a judgment that a person is not guilty of the crime with which the person has been charged: *the trial resulted in an acquittal.*

ac·quit·tance /ə'kwitns/ ▶ n. Law, dated a written receipt attesting the settlement of a fine or debt.

A·cre /'äkrə; 'äkər; 'ākər/ **1** a city in Israel; pop. 39,100. Also called **AKKO**. **2** /'äkrə; 'äkrā/ a state in western Brazil; capital, Rio Branco.

a·cre /'ākər/ ▶ n. a unit of land area equal to 4,840 square yards (0.405 hectare). ■ (**acres of**) informal a large extent or amount of something. [OE *æcer* (denoting the amount of land a yoke of oxen could plow in a day), of Gmc. origin.]

a·cre·age /'āk(ə)rij/ ▶ n. an area of land, typically when used for agricultural purposes, but not necessarily measured in acres: *a 35% increase in net acreage.*

a·cre-foot ▶ n. (pl. **a·cre-feet**) a unit of volume equal to the volume of a sheet of water one acre (0.405 hectare) in area and one foot (30.48 cm) in depth; 43,560 cubic feet (1233.5 cu m).

ac·rid /'akrid/ ▶ adj. having an irritatingly strong and unpleasant taste or smell. ■ angry and bitter. —**a·crid·i·ty** /ə'kriditē/ n. **ac·rid·ly** adv. [18th C.: from L. *acer, acri-* 'sharp' + -ID[1].]

ac·ri·dine /'akri,dēn/ ▶ n. Chem. a colorless solid compound, $C_{13}H_9N$, obtained from coal tar, used in the manufacture of dyes and drugs.

ac·ri·fla·vine /,akrə'flāvēn/ ▶ n. a bright orange-red dye derived from acridine, used as an antiseptic. [20th C.: formed irregularly from ACRIDINE.]

Ac·ri·lan /'akrə,lan/ ▶ n. trademark a synthetic acrylic textile fiber. [1950s: from ACRYLIC + L. *lana* 'wool.']

ac·ri·mo·ni·ous /,akrə'mōnēəs/ ▶ adj. (typically of speech or a debate) angry and bitter. —**ac·ri·mo·ni·ous·ly** adv.

ac·ri·mo·ny /'akrə,mōnē/ ▶ n. bitterness or ill feeling. [16th C.: ult. from L. *acrimonia*, from *acer, acri-* 'pungent.']

ac·ro·bat /'akrə,bat/ ▶ n. an entertainer who performs gymnastic feats. [19th C.: ult. from Gk. *akrobatēs*, from *akrobatos* 'walking on tiptoe,' from *akron* 'tip' + *bainein* 'to walk.']

ac·ro·bat·ic /,akrə'batik/ ▶ adj. performing, involving, or adept at spectacular gymnastic feats. —**ac·ro·bat·i·cal·ly** /-ik(ə)lē/ adv.

ac·ro·bat·ics /,akrə'batiks/ ▶ plural n. [usu. treated as sing.] gymnastic feats.

ac·ro·meg·a·ly /,akrō'megəlē/ ▶ n. Med. abnormal growth of the hands, feet, and face, caused by overproduction of growth hormone by the pituitary gland. —**ac·ro·me·gal·ic** /-mə'galik/ adj. [19th C.: coined in Fr. from Gk. *akron* 'tip' + *megas, megal-* 'great.']

ac·ro·nym /'akrə,nim/ ▶ n. a word formed from the initial letters of other words (e.g., *radar, laser*). [1940s: from Gk. *akron* 'end, tip' + *onuma* 'name,' on the pattern of *homonym*.]

a·crop·e·tal /ə'kräpitl/ ▶ adj. Bot. (of growth or development) upward from the base or point of attachment. ■ (of the movement of dissolved substances) outward toward the shoot and root apexes. —**a·crop·e·tal·ly** adv. [19th C.: from Gk. *akron* 'tip' + L. *petere* 'seek.']

ac·ro·pho·bi·a /,akrə'fōbēə/ ▶ n. extreme or irrational fear of heights. —**ac·ro·pho·bic** /-'fōbik/ adj. & n. [19th C.: from Gk. *akron* 'summit.']

a·crop·o·lis /ə'kräpəlis/ ▶ n. a citadel or fortified part of an ancient Greek city, typically built on a hill. ■ (**the Acropolis**) the ancient citadel at Athens, containing the Parthenon and other notable buildings. [Gk., from *akron* 'summit' + *polis* 'city.']

a·cross /ə'krôs; ə'kräs/ ▶ prep. & adv. from one side to the other of (something). ■ expressing movement over a place or region: *I ran across the street.* ■ expressing position or orientation: *the bridge across the river.* ■ [as adv.] used with an expression of measurement: *can grow to 4 feet across.* ■ [as adv.] with reference to a crossword puzzle answer that reads horizontally: *19 across.*

– PHRASES **across the board** applying to all. ■ (in horse racing) denoting a bet in which equal amounts are staked on the same horse to win, place, or show in a race. [ME (adv.): from OFr. *a croix, en croix* 'in or on a cross.']

a·cros·tic /ə'krôstik; ə'kräs-/ ▶ n. a poem, word puzzle, or other composition in which certain letters in each line form a word or words. [16th C.: from Fr. *acrostiche*, from Gk. *akrostikhis*, from *akron* 'end' + *stikhos* 'row.']

A·crux /'ā,krəks/ the brightest star in the Southern Cross (Crux). It is the twelfth brightest star in the sky. [from *A* for alpha + CRUX.]

a·cryl·ic /ə'krilik/ ▶ adj. (of synthetic resins and textile fibers) made from polymers of acrylic acid or acrylates. ■ of, relating to, or denoting paints based on acrylic resin as a medium. ▶ n. **1** an acrylic textile fiber. **2** (often **acrylics**) an acrylic paint. [19th C.: from *acrolein* (from L. *acer, acri-* 'pungent' + *ol(eum)* 'oil' + -IN[1]) + -YL.]

a·cryl·ic ac·id ▶ n. Chem. a pungent liquid organic acid, $CH_2CH{=}COOH$, that can be polymerized to make synthetic resins.

ac·ry·lo·ni·trile /,akrəlō'nītril; -trēl; -trīl/ ▶ n. Chem. a pungent, toxic liquid, $CH_2{=}CHCN$, used in making artificial fibers and other polymers.

ACT ▶ abbr. American College Test.

act /akt/ ▶ v. [intrans.] **1** take action; do something: *they urged Washington to act.* ■ (**act on**) take action according to or in the light of. ■ (**act for**) take action in order to bring about. ■ (**act for/on behalf of**) represent (someone) on a contractual, legal, or paid basis. ■ (**act from/out of**) be motivated by: *you acted from greed.* **2** [with adverbial] behave in the way specified: *he acts as if he owned the place.* ■ (**act as/like**) behave in the manner of: *try to act like civilized adults.* **3** (**act as**) fulfill the function or serve the purpose of: *they need volunteers to act as foster parents.* ■ have the effect of: *a five-year sentence will act as a deterrent.* **4** take effect; have a particular effect: *bacteria act on proteins and sugar.* **5** perform a fictional role in a play, movie, or television production: *she acted in her first professional role at the age of six.* ■ [trans.] perform (a part or role): *he acted the role of the dragon.* ■ [with complement] behave so as to appear to be; pretend to be: *I acted dumb at first.* ■ [trans.] (**act something out**) perform a narrative as if it were a play. ■ [trans.] (**act something out**) Psychoanal. express repressed or unconscious feelings in overt behavior. ▶ n. **1** a thing done; a deed: *a criminal act.* **2** [in sing.] a pretense: *she was **putting on an act**.* ■ [with adj.] a particular type of behavior or routine: *he did his Sir Galahad act.* **3** Law a written ordinance of Congress, or another legislative body; a statute: *the act to abolish slavery.* ■ a document attesting a legal transaction. ■ (often **acts**) dated the recorded decisions or proceedings of a committee or an academic body. **4** a main division of a play, ballet, or opera. ■ a set performance: *her one-woman poetry act.* ■ a performing group: *an act called the Apple Blossom Sisters.*

– PHRASES **act of God** an instance of uncontrollable natural forces in operation (often used in insurance claims). **act of grace** a privilege or concession that cannot be claimed as a right. **catch someone in the act** (usu. **be caught in the act**) surprise someone in the process of doing something wrong. **clean up one's act** behave in a more acceptable manner. **get one's act together** informal organize oneself in the manner required in order to achieve something. **get** (or **be**) **in on the act** informal become or be involved in a particular activity, in order to gain profit or advantage. **in the act of** in the process of. **read the Riot Act** see RIOT ACT. **a tough** (or **hard**) **act to follow** an achievement or performance that sets a standard regarded as being difficult for others to measure up to.

– PHRASAL VERBS **act up** (of a thing) fail to function properly. ■ (of a person) misbehave. —**act·a·bil·i·ty** /,aktə'bilitē/ n. (in sense 5 of the verb). **act·a·ble** adj. (in sense 5 of the verb). [ME: from L. *actus* 'event,' *act-* 'done,' from the v. *agere*.]

Ac·tae·on /ak'tēən/ Gk. Mythol. a hunter who, because he accidentally saw Artemis bathing, was changed into a stag and killed by his own hounds.

ACTH Biochem. ▶ abbr. adrenocorticotropic (or adrenocorticotrophic) hormone.

ac·tin /'aktin/ ▶ n. Biochem. a protein that forms (with myosin) the contractile filaments of muscle cells. [1940: from Gk. *aktis, aktin-* 'ray.']

act·ing /'aktiNG/ ▶ n. the art or occupation of performing in plays, movies, or television productions. ▶ adj. [attrib.] temporarily doing the duties of another person.

ac·tin·i·an /ak'tinēən/ ▶ n. Zool. a sea anemone. [18th C.: from mod. L. *Actinia*, from Gk. *aktis, aktin-* 'ray.']

ac·tin·ic /ak'tinik/ ▶ adj. [attrib.] (of light) able to cause photochemical reactions through having a significant short wavelength or ultraviolet component. ■ relating to or caused by such light. —**ac·tin·ism** /'aktə,nizəm/ n. [19th C.: from Gk. *aktis, aktin-* 'ray.']

ac·ti·nide /'aktə,nīd/ ▶ n. Chem. any of the series of fifteen metallic elements from actinium (atomic number 89) to lawrencium (atomic number 103) in the periodic table. [1940s: from ACTINIUM.]

ac·tin·i·um /ak'tinēəm/ ▶ n. the chemical element of atomic number 89, a radioactive metallic element of the actinide series. It is rare in nature, occurring as an impurity in uranium ores. (Symbol: **Ac**) [20th C.: from Gk. *aktis, aktin-* 'ray.']

ac·ti·nom·e·ter /,aktə'nämitər/ ▶ n. Physics an instrument for measuring the intensity of radiation, typically ultraviolet radiation. [19th C.: from Gk. *aktis, aktin-* 'ray.']

ac·tin·o·mor·phic /ˌaktənō'môrfik/ ▶**adj.** Biol. characterized by radial symmetry, such as a starfish or the flower of a daisy. — **ac·tin·o·mor·phy** /ak'tinəˌmôrfē/ **n.** [19th C.: from Gk. *aktis, aktin-* 'ray' + *morphē* 'form.']

ac·tin·o·my·cete /ˌaktənō'mīˌsēt; -mī'sēt/ ▶**n.** a bacterium (order Actinomycetales) of an order of typically nonmotile filamentous form. Formerly regarded as fungi, they include the economically important streptomycetes. [1920s (plural): mod. L., from Gk. *aktis, aktin-* 'ray' + *mukētes*, pl. of *mukēs* 'fungus.']

ac·tion /'akshən/ ▶**n.** **1** the fact or process of doing something, typically to achieve an aim: *demanding tougher action against terrorism.* ■ the way in which something such as a chemical has an effect or influence. ■ armed conflict. ■ a military engagement: *a rearguard action.* ■ the events represented in a story or play. ■ informal exciting or notable activity: *the nonstop action of mountain biking.* ■ informal betting. ■ [as exclam.] used by a movie director as a command to begin: *lights, camera, action!* **2** a thing done; an act: *she frequently questioned his actions.* ■ a legal process; a lawsuit: *an action for damages.* ■ a gesture or movement. **3** [usu. with adj.] a manner or style of doing something, typically the way in which a mechanism works or a person moves: *a high paddle action in canoeing.* ■ the mechanism that makes a machine or instrument work: *a piano with an escapement action.*

– PHRASES **go into action** start work or activity. **in action** engaged in a certain activity; in operation. **out of action** temporarily unable to engage in a certain activity; not working. **put into action** put into effect; carry out. [ME: ult. from L. *actio(n-)*, from *agere* 'act.']

ac·tion·a·ble /'akshənəbəl/ ▶**adj.** Law giving sufficient reason to take legal action.

ac·tion com·mit·tee (also **action group**) ▶**n.** a body formed to campaign politically.

ac·tion paint·ing ▶**n.** a technique and style of abstract painting in which paint is randomly splashed, thrown, or poured on the canvas.

ac·tion po·ten·tial ▶**n.** Physiol. the change in electrical potential associated with the passage of an impulse along the membrane of a muscle cell or nerve cell.

Ac·ti·um, Bat·tle of /'akshēəm; -tē-/ a naval battle that took place in 31 BC off the promontory of Actium in western Greece, in the course of which Octavian defeated Mark Antony.

ac·ti·vate /'aktəˌvāt/ ▶**v.** [trans.] make (something) active or operative. ■ convert (a substance, molecule, etc.) into a reactive form: [as adj.] (**activated**) *activated chlorine.* — **ac·ti·va·tion** /ˌaktə'vāshən/ **n.** **ac·ti·va·tor** /-ˌvātər/ **n.**

ac·ti·vat·ed car·bon (also **activated charcoal**) ▶**n.** charcoal that has been heated or otherwise treated to increase its adsorptive power.

ac·ti·va·tion a·nal·y·sis /ˌaktə'vāshən/ ▶**n.** Chem. a technique of analysis in which atoms of a particular element in a sample are made radioactive, and their concentration is then determined radiologically.

ac·tive /'aktiv/ ▶**adj.** **1** (of a person) engaging or ready to engage in physically energetic pursuits. ■ moving or tending to move about vigorously or frequently. ■ characterized by energetic activity: *an active social life.* ■ (of a person's mind or imagination) alert and lively. **2** doing things for an organization, cause, or campaign, rather than simply giving it one's support: *she was an active member of the church.* ■ (of a person) participating or engaged in a particular sphere or activity. ■ [predic.] (of a person or animal) pursuing their usual occupation or activity, typically at a particular place or time: *tigers are active mainly at night.* **3** working; operative. ■ (of a bank account) in continuous use. ■ (of an electrical circuit) capable of modifying its state or characteristics automatically in response to input or feedback. ■ (of a volcano) currently erupting, or that has erupted within historical times. ■ (of a disease) in which the symptoms are manifest; not in remission or latent: *active colitis.* ■ having a chemical or biological effect on something: *350 active ingredients have been banned from pesticides.* **4** Gram. relating to or denoting the voice that attributes the action of a verb to the person or thing from which it logically proceeds (e.g., of the verbs in *guns kill* and *we saw him*). The opposite of PASSIVE. ▶**n.** Gram. an active form of a verb. ■ (**the active**) the active voice. — **ac·tive·ly** **adv.** [ME: from L. *activus*, from *act-* 'done,' from v. *agere*.]

ac·tive du·ty ▶**n.** full-time service in the police or armed forces.

ac·tive im·mu·ni·ty ▶**n.** Physiol. the immunity that results from the production of antibodies in response to an antigen.

ac·tive serv·ice ▶**n.** direct participation in warfare as a member of the armed forces.

ac·tive site ▶**n.** Biochem. a region on an enzyme that binds to a protein or other substance during a reaction.

ac·tive trans·port ▶**n.** Biol. the movement of ions or molecules across a cell membrane into a region of higher concentration, assisted by enzymes and requiring energy.

ac·tive·wear /'aktivˌwe(ə)r/ ▶**n.** clothing designed to be worn for sports, exercise, and outdoor activities.

ac·tiv·ism /'aktəˌvizəm/ ▶**n.** the policy or action of using vigorous campaigning to bring about political or social change. — **ac·tiv·ist** **n.**

ac·tiv·i·ty /ak'tivitē/ ▶**n.** (pl. **-ties**) **1** the condition in which things are happening or being done. ■ busy or vigorous action or movement. **2** (usu. **activities**) a thing that a person or group does or has done. ■ a recreational pursuit or pastime. ■ (**activities**) actions taken by a group in order to achieve their aims: *the police were investigating anarchist activities.* **3** the degree to which something displays its characteristic property or behavior: *liver enzyme activities.* ■ Chem. a thermodynamic quantity representing the effective concentration of a particular component in a solution or other system, equal to its concentration multiplied by an **activity coefficient**.

ac·to·my·o·sin /ˌaktə'mīəsin/ ▶**n.** Biochem. a complex of actin and myosin of which the contractile protein filaments of muscle tissue are composed. [1940s: from ACTIN + MYOSIN.]

ac·tor /'aktər/ ▶**n.** a person whose profession is acting on the stage, in movies, or on television. ■ a person who behaves in a way that is not genuine. ■ a participant in an action or process. [ME: from L., 'doer, actor,' from *agere* 'do.']

ac·tress /'aktris/ ▶**n.** a female actor.

ac·tress·y /'aktrisē/ ▶**adj.** characteristic of an actress; stereotypically being self-consciously theatrical or emotionally volatile.

Acts /akts/ (also **Acts of the Apostles**) a New Testament book immediately following the Gospels and relating the history of the early Church.

ac·tu·al /'akchōōəl/ ▶**adj.** **1** existing in fact; typically as contrasted with what was intended, expected, or believed. ■ used to emphasize the important aspect of something: *the book could be condensed into half the space, but what of the actual content?* **2** existing now; current: *actual income.* [ME: from OFr. *actuel* 'active,' from late L. *actualis*, from *actus* (see ACT).]

ac·tu·al·i·ty /ˌakchōō'alitē/ ▶**n.** (pl. **-ties**) actual existence, typically as contrasted with what was intended, expected, or believed. ■ (**actualities**) existing conditions or facts.

ac·tu·al·ize /'akchōōəˌlīz/ ▶**v.** [trans.] make a reality of. — **ac·tu·al·i·za·tion** /ˌakchōōələ'zāshən/ **n.**

ac·tu·al·ly /'akchōōəlē/ ▶**adv.** **1** as the truth or facts of a situation; really: *the time actually worked on a job.* **2** [as sentence adverb] used to emphasize that something someone has said or done is surprising: *he actually expected me to be pleased about it!*

ac·tu·ar·y /'akchōōˌerē/ ▶**n.** (pl. **-ar·ies**) a person who compiles and analyzes statistics and uses them to calculate insurance risks and premiums. — **ac·tu·ar·i·al** /ˌakchōō'e(ə)rēəl/ **adj.** **ac·tu·ar·i·al·ly** /ˌakchə'werēəlē/ **adv.** [16th C.: from L. *actuarius* 'bookkeeper,' from *actus* (see ACT).]

ac·tu·ate /'akchōōˌāt/ ▶**v.** [trans.] **1** cause (a machine or device) to operate. **2** (usu. **be actuated**) cause (someone) to act in a particular way; motivate: *the defendants were actuated by malice.* — **ac·tu·a·tion** /ˌakchōō'āshən/ **n.** **ac·tu·a·tor** /-ˌātər/ **n.** [16th C.: from med. L. *actuat-* 'carried out,' from v. *actuare*, from L. *actus* (see ACT).]

a·cu·i·ty /ə'kyōōitē/ ▶**n.** sharpness or keenness of thought, vision, or hearing. [ME: ult. from med. L. *acuitas*, from L. *acuere* (see ACUTE).]

a·cu·le·ate /ə'kyōōlēit; -ˌāt/ ▶**adj.** **1** (of an insect) having a sting. **2** Bot. sharply pointed; prickly. ▶**n.** a stinging insect of a group (section Aculeata, suborder Apocrita, order Hymenoptera) that includes the bees, wasps, and ants. [17th C.: from L. *aculeatus*, from *aculeus* 'a sting,' dimin. of *acus* 'needle.']

a·cu·men /ə'kyōōmən; 'akyə-/ ▶**n.** the ability to make good judgments and quick decisions, typically in a particular domain: *business acumen.* [16th C.: from L., 'sharpness,' from *acuere* (see ACUTE).]

a·cu·mi·nate /ə'kyōōmənit; -ˌnāt/ ▶**adj.** Biol. (of a plant or animal structure, e.g., a leaf) tapering to a point. [16th C.: from late L. *acuminatus*, based on L. *acuere* 'sharpen'.]

ac·u·pres·sure /'akyəˌpreshər/ ▶**n.** another term for SHIATSU. [1950s: blend of ACUPUNCTURE and PRESSURE.]

ac·u·punc·ture /'akyəˌpəngkchər/ ▶**n.** a system of complementary medicine that involves pricking the skin or tissues with needles, used to alleviate pain. Originating in ancient China, acupuncture is now widely practiced in the West. — **ac·u·punc·tur·ist** **n.** [17th C.: from L. *acu* 'with a needle.']

a·cute /ə'kyōōt/ ▶**adj.** **1** (of a bad, difficult, or unwelcome situation or phenomenon) present or experienced to a severe or intense degree. ■ (of a disease or its symptoms) of short duration but typically severe. ■ denoting or designed for patients with such conditions. **2** having or showing a perceptive understanding or insight: shrewd. ■ (of a physical sense or faculty) highly developed; keen. **3** (of an angle) less than 90°. See illustration at ANGLE[1]. ■ having a sharp end; pointed. ■ (of a sound) high; shrill. ▶**n.** short for ACUTE ACCENT. — **a·cute·ly** **adv.** **a·cute·ness** **n.** [ME (sense 2): from L. *acutus*, past part. of *acuere* 'sharpen,' from *acus* 'needle.']

a·cute ac·cent ▶**n.** a mark (´) placed over certain letters in some languages to indicate an alteration of a sound, as of quality, quantity, or pitch, e.g., in *risqué*.

-acy ▶**suffix** forming nouns of state or quality: *celibacy* | *lunacy.* [a branch of the suffix -CY, from L. *-atia* (med. L. *-acia*), or from Gk. *-ateia*, n. suffixes.]

a·cy·clic /ā'sīklik; ā'sik-/ ▶**adj.** not displaying or forming part of a cycle. ■ Chem. (of a compound or molecule) containing no rings of atoms.

a·cy·clo·vir /ā'sīkləˌvi(ə)r/ ▶**n.** Med. an antiviral drug used esp. in the treatment of herpes and AIDS.

ac·yl /'asəl/ ▶**n.** [as adj.] Chem. a radical of general formula $-C(O)R$, where R is an alkyl group, derived from a carboxylic acid: *acyl groups.* [19th C.: formed in Ger. from L. *acidus* (see ACID).]

ac·yl·ate /'asəˌlāt/ ▶**v.** [trans.] Chem. introduce an acyl group into (a molecule or compound). — **ac·yl·a·tion** /ˌasə'lāshən/ **n.**

AD ▶**abbr.** ■ Anno Domini (used to indicate that a date comes the specified number of years after the accepted date of Christ's birth).

■ Mil. active duty. ■ athletic director.

ad[1] /ad/ ▸ n. informal an advertisement.

ad[2] ▸ n. Tennis short for ADVANTAGE.

ad- ▸ prefix denoting motion or direction to: *advance* | *adduce.* ■ reduction or change into: *adapt* | *adulterate.* ■ addition, increase, or intensification: *adjunct* | *adhere* | *admixture.* [from L. *ad* 'to.']

-ad[1] ▸ suffix forming nouns: **1** in collective numerals: *pentad* | *triad.* ■ in groups, periods, or aggregates: *Olympiad.* **2** in names of females in classical mythology, such as *Dryad* and *Naiad.* ■ in names of districts such as *Troad.* **3** in names of poems and similar compositions: *Iliad* | *jeremiad.* **4** forming names of members of some taxonomic groupings: *bromeliad.* [from Gk. *-ad-.*]

-ad[2] ▸ suffix forming nouns such as *ballad, salad.* Compare with -ADE[1]. [from Fr. *-ade.*]

A·da /'ādə/ ▸ n. a high-level computer programming language used esp. in real-time computerized control systems, e.g., for aircraft navigation. [1980s: *Ada* Lovelace (1815–52), who designed a mechanical computer with Charles Babbage.]

ad·age /'adij/ ▸ n. a proverb or short statement expressing a general truth. [16th C.: ult. from L. *adagium* 'saying,' akin to *aio* 'I say.']

a·da·gio /ə'däjō; ə'däzhē,ō/ Music ▸ adj. & adv. (esp. as a direction) in slow tempo. ▸ n. (also **A·da·gio**) (pl. **-gios**) a movement or composition marked to be played adagio. [Ital., from *ad agio* 'at ease.']

Ad·am /'adəm/ (in the Bible) the first man, created by God as the progenitor of the human race and the husband of Eve.
– PHRASES **not know someone from Adam** not know or be completely unable to recognize the person in question. [from Heb. *ādām* 'man.']

ad·a·mant /'adəmənt/ ▸ adj. refusing to be persuaded or to change one's mind. ▸ n. archaic a legendary rock or mineral, formerly associated with diamond or lodestone. — **ad·a·mance** n. **ad·a·man·cy** n. **ad·a·mant·ly** adv. [OE (n.), ult. from Gk. *adamas, adamant-*, 'untamable'.]

ad·a·man·tine /,adə'man,tīn; -tin-; -,tēn/ ▸ adj. literary unbreakable.

Ad·ams[1] /'adəmz/, Abigail Smith (1744–1818), US first lady 1797–1801; wife of President John Adams; mother of President John Quincy Adams. She is noted for her letters that gave an insider's view of the era.

Ad·ams[2], Alice (1926–99), US writer. Her novels include *Superior Women* (1984) and *Southern Exposure* (1995).

Ad·ams[3], Ansel Easton (1902–84), US photographer noted for his black-and-white photographs of American landscapes.

Ad·ams[4], John (1735–1826), 2nd president of the US 1797–1801. A Massachusetts Federalist, he was a delegate to the Continental Congress 1774–78 and helped draft the Declaration of Independence in 1776. With John Jay and Benjamin Franklin, he negotiated the Treaty of Paris, which ended the American Revolution in 1783. Adams was minister to Great Britain 1785–88 before becoming the first vice president of the US 1789–97.

Ad·ams[5], John Quincy (1767–1848), 6th president of the US 1825–29; eldest son of President John Adams. A Massachusetts Democratic-Republican, Adams served as minister to the Netherlands 1794–96, Germany 1796–1801, St. Petersburg 1809–11, and Great Britain 1815–17. He held a seat in the US Senate 1803–08 and helped negotiate the Treaty of Ghent 1814, which ended the War of 1812. As President Monroe's secretary of state 1817–24, he was chief architect of the Monroe Doctrine.

Ad·ams[6], Samuel (1722–1803), US patriot; cousin of President John Adams. A leader of the Boston Tea Party in 1773, he was active in pre-Revolution anti-British activities. He served in the First and Second Continental Congresses 1774–75 and was a signer of the Declaration of Independence 1776.

Ad·am's ap·ple ▸ n. the projection at the front of the neck formed by the thyroid cartilage of the larynx, often prominent in men.

Ad·am's Bridge a line of shoals between Sri Lanka and Tamil Nadu in India.

Ad·am's nee·dle ▸ n. a frost-hardy yucca (*Yucca filamentosa*) native to the eastern US, with long leaves that are edged with white threads.

Ad·am's Peak a mountain in south central Sri Lanka, rising to 7,360 feet (2,243 m). It is regarded as sacred by Buddhists, Hindus, and Muslims.

A·da·na /,ädə'nä/ a town in southern Turkey, capital of a province of the same name; pop. 916,150.

a·dapt /ə'dapt/ ▸ v. [trans.] make (something) suitable for a new use or purpose; modify. ■ [intrans.] become adjusted to new conditions. ■ alter (a text) to make it suitable for filming, broadcasting, or the stage. — **a·dap·tive** adj. [ME: ult. from L. *adaptare*, from *ad-* 'to' + *aptare* (from *aptus* 'fit').]

a·dapt·a·ble /ə'daptəbəl/ ▸ adj. able to adjust to new conditions. ■ able to be modified for a new use or purpose. — **a·dapt·a·bil·i·ty** /ə,daptə'bilitē/ n. **a·dapt·a·bly** adv.

ad·ap·ta·tion /,adap'tāshən; ,adəp-/ ▸ n. the action or process of adapting or being adapted. ■ a movie, television drama, or stage play that has been adapted from a written work, typically a novel. ■ Biol. a change by which an organism or species becomes better suited to its environment. ■ the process of making such changes.

a·dapt·er /ə'daptər/ (also **a·dap·tor**) ▸ n. **1** a device for connecting pieces of equipment that cannot be connected directly. **2** a person who adapts a text to make it suitable for filming, broadcasting, or the stage.

a·dap·tion /ə'dapshən/ ▸ n. another term for ADAPTATION.

a·dap·tive ra·di·a·tion ▸ n. Biol. the diversification of a group of organisms into forms filling different ecological niches.

A·dar /ä'där; 'ä,där/ ▸ n. (in the Jewish calendar) the sixth month of the civil and twelfth of the religious year, usually coinciding with parts of February and March. It is known in leap years as **Second Adar.** ■ an intercalary month preceding this in leap years, also called **First Adar.** [from Heb. *'ăḏār.*]

ad·ax·i·al /ad'aksēəl/ ▸ adj. Bot. facing toward the stem of a plant (esp. denoting the upper surface of a leaf). The opposite of ABAXIAL.

ad·bot /'ad,bät/ ▸ n. a computer program that caches advertising on personal computers from an Internet-connected server and then displays the advertising when certain linked programs are being used. [blend of *ad(vertising)* and *(ro)bot.*]

ADC ▸ abbr. ■ aide-de-camp. ■ analog-to-digital converter. ■ Aid to Dependent Children. ■ Air Defense Command.

ADD ▸ abbr. ■ attention deficit disorder.

add /ad/ ▸ v. [trans.] **1** join (something) to something else so as to increase the size, number, or amount. ■ [intrans.] (**add up**) increase in amount, number, or degree. ■ put or mix (an ingredient) together with another as one of the stages in the preparation of a dish. ■ put (something) in or on something else so as to improve or alter its quality or nature. ■ contribute (an enhancing quality) to something. **2** put together (two or more numbers or amounts) to calculate their total value. ■ [intrans.] (**add up to**) amount to: *this adds up to 400 calories* | fig. *these incidents don't add up to a true picture of the situation.* ■ [intrans.] [usu. with negative] (**add up**) informal seem reasonable or consistent; make sense: *many things in her story didn't add up.* **3** say as a further remark. [ME: from L. *addere*, from *ad-* 'to' + base of *dare* 'put.']

Ad·dams[1] /'adəmz/, Charles Samuel (1912–88), US cartoonist noted for his macabre characters. The television series "The Addams Family" (1964–66) and two later movies were based on his work.

Ad·dams[2], Jane (1860–1935), US social activist. In 1889 she founded Hull House, a center for Chicago's poor. Nobel Peace Prize (1931).

ad·dax /'ad,aks/ ▸ n. a large antelope (*Addax nasomaculatus*) with a mainly grayish and white coat, native to the deserts of North Africa. [17th C.: from L., from an African word.]

ad·den·dum /ə'dendəm/ ▸ n. (pl. **-da** /-də/, **-dums**) **1** an item of additional material, typically omissions, added at the end of a book or other publication. **2** Engin. the radial distance from the pitch circle of a cogwheel, worm wheel, etc., to the crests of the teeth or ridges. [17th C.: L., gerundive of *addere* (see ADD).]

ad·der /'adər/ ▸ n. a small Eurasian viper (*Vipera berus*) that has a dark zigzag pattern on its back and bears live young. ■ used in names of similar or related snakes, e.g., **puff adder.** [OE *nædre* 'serpent, adder,' of Gmc. origin; rel. to Du. *adder* and Ger. *Natter.* The initial *n* was lost in ME by wrong division of *a naddre*; cf. APRON, AUGER, and UMPIRE.]

ad·der's tongue (also **ad·der's-tongue**) ▸ n. **1** a widely distributed atypical fern (genus *Ophioglossum*, family Ophioglossaceae) that has a single pointed oval leaf and a straight unbranched spore-bearing stem. **2** another term for DOGTOOTH VIOLET, esp. a trout lily.

ad·dict /'adikt/ ▸ n. a person who is addicted to a particular substance, typically an illegal drug. ■ [with adj.] informal an enthusiastic devotee of a specified thing or activity. [20th C.: from obs. v. *addict*, back-form. from ADDICTED.]

ad·dict·ed /ə'diktid/ ▸ adj. physically and mentally dependent on a particular substance, and unable to stop taking it without incurring adverse effects. ■ enthusiastically devoted to a particular thing or activity. [16th C.: ult. from L. *addict-* 'assigned,' from v. *addicere*, from *ad-* 'to' + *dicere* 'say.']

ad·dic·tion /ə'dikshən/ ▸ n. the fact or condition of being addicted to a particular substance, thing, or activity: *he committed the theft to finance his drug addiction.*

ad·dic·tive /ə'diktiv/ ▸ adj. (of a substance, thing, or activity) causing or likely to cause someone to become addicted to it. ■ of, relating to, or susceptible to the fact of being or becoming addicted to something.

Ad·dis A·ba·ba /,adəs 'ababə; ,ädəs 'äbəbə/ (also **A·dis A·be·ba**) the capital of Ethiopia, in the central part of the country; pop. 2,113,000.

Ad·di·son /'adəsən/, Joseph (1672–1719), English writer. In 1711 he founded the *Spectator* magazine with Sir Richard Steele.

Ad·di·so·ni·an /,adə'sōnēən/ ▸ adj. **1** of, relating to, or characteristic of the works or style of Joseph Addison. **2** Med. of, relating to, or characterized by Addison's disease.

Ad·di·son's dis·ease ▸ n. a disease characterized by progressive anemia, low blood pressure, great weakness, and bronze discoloration of the skin. It is caused by inadequate secretion of hormones by the adrenal cortex. [19th C.: Thomas *Addison* (1793–1860), English physician.]

ad·di·tion /ə'dishən/ (abbr.: **addn.**) ▸ n. **1** the action or process of adding something to something else. ■ a person or thing added or joined, typically in order to improve something. **2** (abbr.: **addn.**) the process or skill of calculating the total of two or more numbers or amounts. ■ Math. the process of combining matrices, vectors, or other quantities under specific rules to obtain their sum.
– PHRASES **in addition** as an extra person, thing, or circumstance. [ME: from L. *additio(n-)*, from *addere* (see ADD).]

ad·di·tion·al /əˈdisʜənl/ ▸ **adj.** added, extra, or supplementary to what is already present or available.

ad·di·tion·al·ly /əˈdisʜənl-ē/ ▸ **adv.** as an extra factor or circumstance.

ad·di·tion re·ac·tion ▸ **n.** Chem. a reaction in which one molecule combines with another to form a larger molecule with no other products.

ad·di·tive /ˈaditiv/ ▸ **n.** a substance added to something in small quantities, typically to improve or preserve it. ▸ **adj.** characterized by, relating to, or produced by addition: *an additive process.*

ad·dle /ˈadl/ ▸ **v.** [trans.] esp. humorous make unable to think clearly; confuse. ▸ **adj.** archaic (of an egg) rotten. [ME: from OE *adela* 'liquid filth,' from Gmc.; akin to Ger. *Adel* 'mire.']

ad·dle·brained /ˈadl,brānd/ (also **ad·dle·head·ed** /-ˌhedid/, **ad·dle·pat·ed** /-ˌpātid/) ▸ **adj.** lacking in common sense; having a muddled mind.

addn. ▸ **abbr.** addition.

add-on ▸ **n.** something that has been or can be added to an existing object or arrangement.

ad·dress /əˈdres; ˈadres/ ▸ **n.** **1** the particulars of the place where someone lives or an organization is situated. ■ the place itself. ■ Comput. a binary number that identifies a particular location in a data storage system or computer memory. ■ Computing a string of characters that identifies a destination for e-mail messages. **2** a formal speech delivered to an audience. ■ archaic a person's manner of speaking to someone else. ■ (**addresses**) archaic courteous or amorous approaches to someone. **3** dated skill, dexterity, or readiness. ▸ **v.** [trans.] **1** write the name and address of the intended recipient on (an envelope, letter, or package). **2** speak to (a person or an assembly), typically in a formal way. ■ (**address someone as**) name someone in a specified way when talking or writing. ■ (**address something to**) say or write remarks or a protest to (someone). **3** think about and begin to deal with (an issue or problem). **4** Golf take up one's stance and prepare to hit (the ball). —**ad·dress·er** **n.** [ME: from OFr., based on L. *ad-* 'toward' + *directus* (see DIRECT).]

ad·dress·a·ble /əˈdresəbəl/ ▸ **adj.** Comput. relating to or denoting a memory unit in which all locations can be separately accessed by a particular program.

ad·dress·ee /ˌadreˈsē; əˌdreˈsē/ ▸ **n.** the person to whom something, typically a letter, is addressed.

Ad·dres·so·graph /əˈdresəˌgraf/ ▸ **n.** trademark a machine for printing addresses on envelopes.

ad·duce /əˈd(y)o͞os/ ▸ **v.** [trans.] cite as evidence. —**ad·duc·i·ble** **adj.** [ME: from L. *adducere*, from *ad-* 'toward' + *ducere* 'to lead.']

ad·duct[1] /əˈdəkt/ ▸ **v.** [trans.] (of a muscle) move (a limb or other part of the body) toward the midline of the body or toward another part. —**ad·duc·tion** /əˈdəksʜən/ **n.** [19th C.: ult. from late L. *adductio(n-)* 'bringing forward,' from *adducere*.]

ad·duct[2] ▸ **n.** Chem. the product of an addition reaction between two compounds. [1940s: from Ger. *Addukt* (blend of *Addition* and *Produkt*).]

ad·duc·tor /əˈdəktər/ (also **adductor muscle**) ▸ **n.** Anat. a muscle whose contraction moves a limb or other part of the body toward the midline of the body or toward another part. ■ any of a number of specific muscles in the hand, foot, or thigh: [followed by Latin genitive] *adductor hallucis.* [17th C.: mod. L., from L. *adduct-* 'brought in,' from *adducere*.]

-ade[1] ▸ **suffix** forming nouns: **1** denoting an action that is completed: *barricade* | *blockade.* **2** denoting the body concerned in an action or process: *brigade* | *cavalcade.* **3** denoting the product or result of an action or process: *arcade* | *lemonade* | *marmalade.* [from Fr. ult. from L. *-atus* (past participial suffix).]

-ade[2] ▸ **suffix** forming nouns such as *decade.* Compare with -AD[1]. [from Fr. *-ade*, from Gk. *-ada*.]

-ade[3] ▸ **suffix** forming nouns: **1** equivalent to -ADE[1]: *brocade.* **2** denoting a person: *renegade.* [from Sp. or Port. *-ado*.]

Ad·e·laide /ˈadlˌād/ a city in southern Australia, the capital of the state of South Australia; pop. 1,050,000.

A·dé·lie Land /əˈdālē/ (also **Adélie Coast**) a part of Antarctica south of the 60th parallel.

A·dé·lie pen·guin /əˈdālē/ ▸ **n.** a gregarious and territorial penguin (*Pygoscelis adeliae*) of Antarctica, perhaps the most familiar of all the penguins. The adults have a distinctive white ring around the eye.

Adélie penguin

A·den /ˈädn; ˈādn/ a city in Yemen at the mouth of the Red Sea; pop. 417,370. It was the capital of former South Yemen 1967–90.

A·den, Gulf of a part of the eastern Arabian Sea that lies between the southern coast of Yemen and the Horn of Africa.

A·de·nau·er /ˈadnˌou(ə)r/, Konrad (1876–1967), chancellor of the Federal Republic of Germany 1949–63.

ad·e·nine /ˈadnˌēn; -ˌīn/ ▸ **n.** Biochem. a compound, $C_5H_5N_5$, that is one of the four constituent bases of nucleic acids. A purine derivative, it is paired with thymine in double-stranded DNA. [19th C.: coined in Ger. from Gk. *adēn* 'gland.']

adeno- ▸ **comb. form** relating to a gland or glands: *adenocarcinoma.* [from Gk. *adēn* 'gland.']

ad·e·no·car·ci·no·ma /ˌadn-ōˌkärsəˈnōmə/ ▸ **n.** (pl. **-mas** or **-ma·ta** /-mətə/) Med. a malignant tumor formed from glandular structures in epithelial tissue.

ad·e·noids /ˈadnˌoidz/ ▸ **plural n.** a mass of enlarged lymphatic tissue between the back of the nose and the throat, often hindering speaking and breathing in young children. —**ad·e·noi·dal** /ˌadnˈoidl/ **adj.** [19th C.: from Gk. *adēn* 'gland.']

ad·e·no·ma /ˌadnˈōmə/ ▸ **n.** (pl. **-mas** or **-ma·ta** /-mətə/) Med. a benign tumor formed from glandular structures in epithelial tissue. [19th C.: from L., from Gk. *adēn* 'gland.']

a·den·o·sine /əˈdenəˌsēn; -sin/ ▸ **n.** Biochem. a compound consisting of adenine combined with ribose, one of four nucleoside units in RNA. [20th C.: blend of ADENINE and RIBOSE.]

a·den·o·sine mon·o·phos·phate /ˌmänōˈfäsˌfāt/ (abbr.: **AMP**) ▸ **n.** Biochem. a compound consisting of an adenosine molecule bonded to one acidic phosphate group, present in most DNA and RNA.

a·den·o·sine tri·phos·phate /trīˈfäsˌfāt/ (abbr.: **ATP**) ▸ **n.** Biochem. a compound consisting of an adenosine molecule bonded to three phosphate groups, present in all living tissue. The breakage of one phosphate linkage (to form **adenosine diphosphate, ADP**) provides energy for physiological processes such as muscular contraction.

ad·e·no·vi·rus /ˌadn-ōˈvīrəs/ ▸ **n.** Med. any of a group of DNA viruses first discovered in adenoid tissue, most of which cause respiratory diseases.

a·den·yl·ate cy·clase /əˈdenlˌāt ˈsīˌklās; -ˌklāz; əˈdenl-it/ (also **ad·en·yl cy·clase** /ˈadn-il/) ▸ **n.** Biochem. an enzyme that catalyzes the formation of cyclic adenylic acid from adenosine triphosphate.

ad·e·nyl·ic ac·id /ˌadnˈilik/ ▸ **n.** another term for ADENOSINE MONOPHOSPHATE. [19th C.: *adenylic* from ADENINE]

a·dept ▸ **adj.** /əˈdept/ very skilled or proficient at something. ▸ **n.** /ˈadept; əˈdept/ a person who is skilled or proficient at something. —**a·dept·ly** **adv.** **a·dept·ness** **n.** [17th C.: from L. *adeptus*, past part. of *adipisci* 'obtain.']

ad·e·quate /ˈadikwit/ ▸ **adj.** satisfactory or acceptable in quality or quantity. —**ad·e·qua·cy** /-kwəsē/ **n.** **ad·e·quate·ly** **adv.** [17th C.: from L. *adaequatus* 'made equal to,' past part. of *adaequare*, from *ad-* + *aequus* 'equal.']

à deux /ä ˈdœ/ ▸ **adv.** for or involving two people. [19th C.: Fr.]

ad fin. ▸ **adv.** at or near the end of a piece of writing. [17th C.: from L. *ad finem* 'at the end.']

ADH Biochem. ▸ **abbr.** antidiuretic hormone.

ADHD ▸ **abbr.** attention deficit hyperactivity disorder.

ad·here /adˈhi(ə)r/ ▸ **v.** [intrans.] (**adhere to**) stick fast to (a surface or substance). ■ believe in and follow the practices of. ■ represent truthfully and in detail. [15th C.: from L. *adhaerere*, from *ad-* 'to' + *haerere* 'to stick.']

ad·her·ent /adˈhi(ə)rənt; -ˈher-/ ▸ **n.** someone who supports a particular party, person, or set of ideas. ▸ **adj.** sticking fast to an object or surface. —**ad·her·ence** **n.**

ad·he·sion /adˈhēzʜən/ ▸ **n.** **1** the action or process of adhering to a surface or object. ■ the frictional grip of wheels, shoes, etc., on a road, track, or other surface. ■ Physics the sticking together of particles of different substances. ■ faithfulness to a particular person, party, or set of ideas. **2** Med. an abnormal union of membranous surfaces due to inflammation or injury. [15th C.: ult. from L. *adhaesio(n-)*, from *adhaerere*.]

ad·he·sive /adˈhēsiv; -ziv/ ▸ **adj.** able to stick fast to a surface or object; sticky. ▸ **n.** a substance used for sticking objects or materials together; glue. —**ad·he·sive·ly** **adv.** **ad·he·sive·ness** **n.**

ad·hib·it /adˈhibit/ ▸ **v.** (**-it·ed, -it·ing**) [trans.] formal apply or affix (something) to something else. —**ad·hi·bi·tion** /ˌad(h)əˈbisʜən/ **n.** [16th C.: from L. *adhibit-* 'brought in,' from v. *adhibere*, from *ad-* + *habere* 'have.']

ad hoc /ˈad ˈhäk; ˈhōk/ ▸ **adj. & adv.** formed, arranged, or done for a particular purpose only. [16th C.: L., lit. 'for this.']

ad·hoc·ra·cy /adˈhäkrəsē/ ▸ **n.** a flexible, adaptable, and informal organizational structure without bureaucratic policies or procedures. [1970s: blend of AD HOC and -CRACY.]

ad ho·mi·nem /ˈad ˈhämənəm/ ▸ **adv. & adj.** **1** (of an argument or reaction) arising from or appealing to the emotions and not reason or logic. ■ attacking an opponent's motives or character rather than the policy or position they maintain. **2** relating to or associated with a particular person. [16th C.: L., lit. 'to the person.']

ad·i·a·bat·ic /ˌādīəˈbatik; ˌadēə-/ Physics ▸ **adj.** relating to or denoting a process or condition in which heat does not enter or leave the system concerned. —**ad·i·a·bat·i·cal·ly** /-ik(ə)lē/ **adv.** [19th C.: from Gk. *adiabatos* 'impassable,' from *a-* + *dia* 'through' + *batos* 'passable' (from *bainein* 'go.')]

a·dieu /əˈd(y)o͞o; äˈdyœ/ esp. literary ▸ **exclam.** another term for GOODBYE. ▸ **n.** (pl. **a·dieus** or **a·dieux** /əˈd(y)o͞oz; äˈdyœ/) a goodbye. [ME: from OFr., from *à* 'to' + *Dieu* 'God.']

ad in·fi·ni·tum /ˌad infəˈnītəm/ ▸ **adv.** again and again in the same way; forever. [17th C.: L., lit. 'to infinity.']

ad·i·os /ˌädēˈōs; ˌadē-/ ▸ **exclam. & n.** Spanish term for GOODBYE. [Sp. *adiós*, from *a* 'to' + *Dios* 'God.']

ad·i·po·cere /ˈadəpōˌsi(ə)r/ ▸ **n.** a grayish waxy substance formed by the decomposition of soft tissue in dead bodies subjected to moisture. [19th C.: from French *adipocire*, from L. *adeps, adip-* 'fat' + Fr. *cire* 'wax.']

ad·i·po·cyte /ˈadəpōˌsīt/ ▶ **n.** Biol. a cell specialized for the storage of fat, found in connective tissue. [1930s: from **ADIPOSE**.]

ad·i·pose /ˈadəˌpōs/ ▶ **adj.** tech. (esp. of body tissue) used for the storage of fat. — **ad·i·pos·i·ty** /ˌadəˈpäsitē/ **n.** [18th C.: from mod. L. *adiposus*, from *adeps, adip-* 'fat.']

Ad·i·ron·dack chair /ˌadəˈränˌdak/ ▶ **n.** an outdoor wooden armchair constructed of wide slats. The seat typically slants downward toward the sloping back.

Adirondack chair

Ad·i·ron·dack Moun·tains (also **the Ad·i·ron·dacks**) a range of mountains in New York, source of the Hudson and Mohawk rivers.

A·dis A·be·ba var. of **ADDIS ABABA**.

ad·it /ˈadit/ ▶ **n.** a horizontal passage leading into a mine for the purposes of access or drainage. [17th C.: from L. *aditus* 'entrance,' from *adit-* 'approached,' from v. *adire*, from *ad-* + *ire* 'go.']

adj. ▶ **abbr.** ■ adjective. ■ adjustment. ■ adjunct. ■ (**Adj.**) adjutant.

ad·ja·cent /əˈjāsənt/ ▶ **adj.** **1** next to or adjoining something else: *adjacent rooms.* **2** Geom. (of angles) having a common vertex and a common side. — **ad·ja·cen·cy n.** [ME: from L. *adjacent-* 'lying near to,' from *adjacere*, from *ad-* + *jacere* 'lie down.']

ad·jec·tive /ˈajiktiv/ ▶ **n.** Gram. a word or phrase naming an attribute, added to or grammatically related to a noun to modify or describe it. — **ad·jec·ti·val** /ˌajikˈtīvəl/ **adj. ad·jec·ti·val·ly** /ˌajikˈtīvəlē/ **adv.** [ME: from OFr. *adjectif, -ive*, from L. *adject-* 'added,' from the v. *adjicere*, from *ad-* 'toward' + *jacere* 'throw.']

ad·join /əˈjoin/ ▶ **v.** [trans.] be next to and joined with (a building, room, or piece of land). [ME: from OFr. *ajoindre*, from L. *adjungere*, from *ad-* 'to' + *jungere* 'to join.']

ad·journ /əˈjərn/ ▶ **v.** [trans.] (usu. **be adjourned**) break off (a meeting, legal case, or game) with the intention of resuming it later. ■ [no obj., with adverbial] (of people who are together) go somewhere else, typically for refreshment: *they adjourned to a local bar.* ■ put off or postpone (a resolution or sentence). — **ad·journ·ment n.** [ME: from OFr. *ajorner*, from *a jorn (nome)* 'to an (appointed) day.']

ad·judge /əˈjəj/ ▶ **v.** [with obj. and complement] (usu. **be adjudged**) consider or declare to be true or the case: *she was adjudged guilty.* ■ (**adjudge something to**) (in legal use) award something judicially to (someone). ■ (in legal use) condemn (someone) to pay a penalty. — **ad·judg·ment** (also **ad·judge·ment**) **n.** [ME: ult. from L. *adjudicare*, from *ad-* 'to' + *judicare*, from *judex, judic-* 'a judge.']

ad·ju·di·cate /əˈjo͞odiˌkāt/ ▶ **v.** [intrans.] make a formal judgment or decision about a problem or disputed matter: *the committee **adjudicates on** all disputes* | [trans.] *the case was adjudicated in court.* ■ act as a judge in a competition: *we asked him to adjudicate at the local flower show.* ■ [trans.] pronounce or declare judicially: *he was adjudicated bankrupt.* — **ad·ju·di·ca·tion** /əˌjo͞odiˈkāsʜən/ **n. ad·ju·di·ca·tive** /-ˌkātiv/ **adj. ad·ju·di·ca·tor** /-ˌkātər/ **n.** [18th C.: from L. *adjudicat-* 'awarded judicially,' from *adjudicare* (see **ADJUDGE**).]

ad·junct /ˈajəɴɢkt/ ▶ **n.** **1** a thing added to something else as a supplementary rather than an essential part. ■ a person who is another's assistant or subordinate. **2** Gram. a word or phrase used to amplify or modify the meaning of another word or words in a sentence. ▶ **adj.** [attrib.] connected or added to something, typically in an auxiliary way: *alternative or adjunct therapies.* ■ (of an academic post) attached to the staff of a college in a temporary or assistant capacity. — **ad·junc·tive** /əˈjəɴɢ(k)tiv/ **adj.** [16th C.: from L. *adjunctus*, past part. of *adjungere* (see **ADJOIN**).]

ad·jure /əˈjo͝or/ ▶ **v.** [with obj. and infin.] formal urge or request (someone) solemnly or earnestly to do something: *I adjure you to tell me the truth.* — **ad·ju·ra·tion** /ˌajəˈrāsʜən/ **n. ad·jur·a·to·ry** /-əˌtôrē/ **adj.** [ME: from L. *adjurare*, from *ad-* 'to' + *jurare* 'swear' (from *jus, jur-* 'oath').]

ad·just /əˈjəst/ ▶ **v.** **1** [trans.] alter or move (something) slightly in order to achieve the desired fit, appearance, or result. | ■ [intrans.] permit small alterations or movements so as to allow a desired fit, appearance, or result to be achieved: *a harness that **adjusts to** the correct fit.* ■ [intrans.] adapt or become used to a new situation: *his eyes had **adjusted to** semi-darkness.* **2** [trans.] assess (loss or damages) when settling an insurance claim. — **ad·just·a·bil·i·ty** /əˌjəstəˈbilitē/ **n. ad·just·a·ble adj. ad·just·er n. ad·just·ment n.** [17th C. ult. from OFr. *ajoster* 'to approximate,' based on L. *ad-* 'to' + *juxta* 'near.']

ad·ju·tant /ˈajətənt/ ▶ **n.** **1** a military officer who acts as an administrative assistant to a senior officer. ■ a person's assistant or deputy. **2** (also **adjutant stork** or **adjutant bird**) a large black-and-white stork (genus *Leptoptilos*) with a massive bill and a bare head and neck, found in India and Southeast Asia. — **ad·ju·tan·cy n.** [17th C.: from L. *adjutant-* 'being of service to,' from *adjutare*, frequentative of *adjuvare* (see **ADJUVANT**).]

ad·ju·tant gen·er·al ▶ **n.** (pl. **ad·ju·tants gen·er·al**) the adjutant of a unit having a general staff. ■ (**the Adjutant General**) (in the US Army) the chief administrative officer. ■ the senior officer in the National Guard of a US state.

ad·ju·vant /ˈajəvənt/ ▶ **adj.** Med. (of therapy) applied after initial treatment for cancer, esp. to suppress secondary tumor formation. ▶ **n.** Med. a substance that enhances the body's immune response to an antigen. [16th C.: from L. *adjuvant-* 'helping toward,' from v. *adjuvare*, from *ad-* + *juvare* 'to help.']

Ad·ler /ˈadlər; ˈäd-/, Alfred (1870–1937), Austrian psychiatrist. He introduced the concept of the inferiority complex.

ad lib /ˈad ˈlib/ ▶ **v.** (**ad libbed, ad lib·bing**) [intrans.] speak or perform in public without previously preparing one's words: *Charles had to ad lib because he'd forgotten his script.* ▶ **n.** something spoken or performed in such a way. ▶ **adv. & adj.** **1** spoken or performed without previous preparation. **2** as much and as often as desired. **3** Music (in directions) in an improvised manner with freedom to vary tempo and instrumentation. [19th C.: abbrev. of **AD LIBITUM**.]

ad lib·i·tum /ad ˈlibitəm/ ▶ **adv. & adj.** more formal term for **AD LIB** (sense 2). [17th C.: L., lit. 'according to pleasure.']

ad li·tem /ad ˈlītəm/ ▶ **adj.** Law (esp. of a guardian) appointed to act in a lawsuit on behalf of a child or other person incapable of representing themselves. [18th C.: L., lit. 'for the lawsuit.']

ad loc. ▶ **abbr.** to or at that place.

Adm. ▶ **abbr.** Admiral.

ad·man /ˈadˌman/ ▶ **n.** (pl. **-men**) informal a person who works in advertising.

ad·min·is·ter /ədˈminəstər/ ▶ **v.** [trans.] **1** manage and be responsible for the running of (a business, organization, etc.). ■ be responsible for the implementation or use of (law or resources). **2** dispense or apply (a remedy or drug). ■ deal out or inflict (punishment). ■ (of a priest) perform the rites of (a sacrament, typically the Eucharist). ■ archaic or Law direct the taking of (an oath): *the chief justice will administer the oath of office.* **3** give help or service: *we must selflessly administer to his needs.* — **ad·min·is·tra·ble** /-əstrəbəl/ **adj.** [ME: via OFr. from L. *administrare*, from *ad-* 'to' + *ministrare* (see **MINISTER**).]

ad·min·is·trate /ədˈminəˌstrāt/ ▶ **v.** [trans.] less common term for **ADMINISTER** (sense 1). [16th C.: from L. *administrat-* 'managed,' from *administrare*.]

ad·min·is·tra·tion /ədˌminəˈstrāsʜən/ (abbr.: **admin.**) ▶ **n.** **1** the process or activity of running a business, organization, etc. ■ (**the administration**) the people responsible for this, regarded collectively. ■ the management of public affairs; government. ■ Law the management and disposal of the property of an intestate, deceased person, debtor, or other individual; or of an insolvent company, by a legally appointed administrator: *the company **went into administration.*** **2** the officials in the executive branch of government under a particular chief executive. ■ the term of office of a political leader or government. ■ a government agency. **3** the action of dispensing, giving, or applying something.

ad·min·is·tra·tive /ədˈminiˌstrātiv; -strətiv/ ▶ **adj.** of or relating to the running of a business, organization, etc. — **ad·min·is·tra·tive·ly adv.**

ad·min·is·tra·tor /ədˈminəˌstrātər/ ▶ **n.** a person responsible for running a business, organization, etc. ■ Law a person legally appointed to manage and dispose of the estate of an intestate, deceased person, debtor, or other individual, or of an insolvent company. ■ a person who performs official duties in some sphere, esp. dealing out punishment or giving a religious sacrament: *administrators of justice.*

ad·min·is·tra·trix /ədˌminəˈstrātriks/ ▶ **n.** Law a female administrator of an estate.

ad·mi·ra·ble /ˈadmərəbəl/ ▶ **adj.** arousing or deserving respect and approval. — **ad·mi·ra·bly adv.**

ad·mi·ral /ˈadmərəl/ ▶ **n.** **1** a commander of a fleet or naval squadron, or a naval officer of very high rank. ■ a commissioned officer of very high rank in the US Navy or Coast Guard, ranking above a vice admiral. ■ short for **VICE ADMIRAL** or **REAR ADMIRAL**. **2** [with adj.] a butterfly (subfamilies Limenitidinae and Nymphalinae, family Nymphalidae) that has dark wings with bold colorful markings. See also **RED ADMIRAL, WHITE ADMIRAL**. — **ad·mi·ral·ship n.** [ME: from OFr. *amiral, admirail*, via med. L. from Arab. *amīr* 'commander'.]

Ad·mi·ral of the Fleet ▶ **n.** the highest rank of admiral in the Royal Navy. Compare with **FLEET ADMIRAL**.

ad·mi·ral·ty /ˈadmərəltē/ ▶ **n.** (pl. **-ties**) **1** the rank or office of an admiral. **2** Law the jurisdiction of courts of law over cases concerning ships or the sea and other navigable waters (maritime law). **3** (**Admiralty**) the department of the British government that once administered the Royal Navy.

Ad·mi·ral·ty Is·lands /ˈadmərəltē/ a group of about 40 islands in the western Pacific, part of Papua New Guinea.

ad·mi·ra·tion /ˌadməˈrāsʜən/ ▶ **n.** respect and warm approval. ■ (**the admiration of**) the object of such feelings: *her house was the admiration of everyone.* ■ pleasurable contemplation (of something).

ad·mire /ədˈmī(ə)r/ ▶ **v.** [trans.] regard (an object, quality, or person) with respect or warm approval. ■ look at with pleasure. — **ad·mir·ing·ly adv.** [16th C.: from L. *admirari*, from *ad-* 'at' + *mirari* 'wonder.']

ad·mir·er /ədˈmī(ə)rər/ ▶ **n.** someone who has a particular regard for someone or something. ■ a man who is attracted to a particular woman or a woman who is attracted to a particular man.

ad·mis·si·ble /ədˈmisəbəl/ ▶ **adj.** **1** acceptable or valid, esp. as evidence in a court of law. **2** having the right to be admitted to a place. — **ad·mis·si·bil·i·ty** /-ˌmisəˈbilitē/ **n.** [17th C.: from med. L. *admissibilis*, from L. *admittere*.]

ad·mis·sion /əd'misHən/ ▶ **n.** **1** a statement acknowledging the truth of something: *an admission of guilt.* **2** the process or fact of entering or being allowed to enter a place, organization, or institution: *the country's admission to the UN* | [as adj.] **(admissions)** *the university admissions office.* ■ the money charged for allowing someone to enter a public place. ■ **(admissions)** the number of people entering a place: *hospital admissions decreased nearly 65 percent.*

ad·mit /əd'mit/ ▶ **v.** (**-mit·ted, -mit·ting**) **1** [trans.] confess to be true or to be the case, typically with reluctance. ■ [trans.] confess to (a crime or fault, or one's responsibility for it). ■ acknowledge (a failure or fault): [intrans.] *he admits to having lied.* **2** [trans.] allow (someone) to enter a place. ■ (of a ticket) give (someone) the right to enter a place. ■ carry out the procedures necessary for (someone) to be received into a hospital for treatment. ■ allow (a person, country, or organization) to join an organization or group. ■ allow (someone) to share in a privilege. ■ [trans.] accept as valid: *the courts can refuse to admit police evidence which has been illegally obtained.* **3** [intrans.] **(admit of)** allow the possibility of: *the need to inform him was too urgent to admit of further delay.* [ME: from L. *admittere*, from *ad-* 'to' + *mittere* 'send.']

ad·mit·tance /əd'mitns/ ▶ **n.** **1** the process or fact of entering or being allowed to enter a place or institution. **2** Physics a measure of electrical conduction, numerically equal to the reciprocal of the impedance.

ad·mit·ted·ly /əd'mitidlē/ ▶ **adv.** [sentence adverb] used to introduce a concession or recognition that something is true or is the case.

ad·mix /ad'miks/ ▶ **v.** [trans.] esp. tech. mix (something) with something else. [ME: ult. from L. *admixtus* 'mixed together,' past part. of *admiscere*, from *ad-* + *miscere* 'to mix.']

ad·mix·ture /ad'miksCHər/ ▶ **n.** a mixture. ■ something mixed with something else, typically as a minor ingredient. ■ the action of adding such an ingredient. [17th C.: from AD- + MIXTURE.]

ad·mon·ish /əd'mänisH/ ▶ **v.** [trans.] warn or reprimand someone firmly. ■ advise or urge (someone) earnestly. ■ archaic warn (someone) of something to be avoided. — **ad·mon·ish·ment** **n.** [ME *amonest* 'urge, exhort,' from OFr. *amonester*, based on L. *admonere* 'urge by warning.']

ad·mo·ni·tion /ˌadmə'nisHən/ ▶ **n.** an act or action of admonishing; authoritative counsel or warning. [ME: ult. from L. *admonitio(n-)* (see ADMONISH).]

ad·mon·i·to·ry /əd'mänəˌtôrē/ ▶ **adj.** giving or conveying a warning or reprimand.

ad·nate /'adˌnāt/ ▶ **adj.** Bot. joined by having grown together. [17th C.: from L. *adnatus*, var. of *agnatus* (see AGNATE).]

ad nau·se·am /ad 'nôzēəm/ ▶ **adv.** referring to something that has been done or repeated so often that it has become annoying or tiresome. [18th C.: L., lit. 'to sickness.']

ad·nex·a /ad'neksə/ ▶ **plural n.** Anat. the parts adjoining an organ. — **ad·nex·al** **adj.** [19th C.: L., neut. pl. of *adnexus* 'joined,' from *adnectere* 'fasten to.']

a·do /ə'do͞o/ ▶ **n.** trouble or difficulty. ■ fuss, esp. about something that is unimportant. [ME: from northern ME *at do* 'to do,' from ON *at* (infinitive marker) and DO[1].]

-ado ▶ **suffix** forming nouns such as *bravado, desperado.* Compare with -ADE[3]. [representing Spanish and Port. n. ending *-ado* or refashioning of Ital. *-ata*, Sp. *-ada*, based on L. *-atus* (past participial suffix).]

a·do·be /ə'dōbē/ ▶ **n.** a kind of clay used as a building material, typically in the form of sun-dried bricks. ■ a brick of such a type. ■ a building constructed from such material. [18th C.: from Sp., from *adobar* 'to plaster,' from Arab. *aṭ-ṭūb*, from *al* 'the' + *ṭūb* 'bricks.']

ad·o·les·cence /ˌadl'esəns/ ▶ **n.** the period following the onset of puberty during which a young person develops from a child into an adult.

ad·o·les·cent /ˌadl'esənt/ ▶ **adj.** (of a young person) in the process of developing from a child into an adult. ■ relating to or characteristic of this process: *his adolescent years.* ▶ **n.** an adolescent boy or girl. [ME: via Fr. from L. *adolescent-* 'coming to maturity,' from *adolescere*, from *ad-* + *alescere* 'grow,' from *alere* 'nourish.']

A·do·nai /ˌädō'nī; -'noi/ ▶ **n.** a Hebrew name for God. [from Heb. *ăḏōnāy*; see also JEHOVAH.]

A·don·is /ə'dänis/ Gk. Mythol. a beautiful youth loved by both Aphrodite and Persephone. ■ [as n.] **(an Adonis)** an extremely handsome young man.

a·dopt /ə'däpt/ ▶ **v.** [trans.] legally take another's child and bring it up as one's own. ■ take up or start to use or follow (an idea, method, or course of action): *this approach has been adopted by many banks.* ■ take on or assume (an attitude or position): *he adopted a patronizing tone.* ■ formally approve or accept (a report or suggestion). ■ choose (a textbook) as standard or required for a course of study. ■ choose (an animal) to become a house pet. — **a·dopt·a·ble** **adj.** **a·dopt·ee** /əˌdäp'tē/ **n.** **a·dopt·er** **n.** [15th C.: via Fr. from L. *adoptare*, from *ad-* 'to' + *optare* 'choose.']

a·dop·tion /ə'däpsHən/ ▶ **n.** the action or fact of adopting or being adopted. [as adj.] *an adoption agency.*

a·dop·tive /ə'däptiv/ ▶ **adj.** [attrib.] as a result of the adoption of another's child: *adoptive parents.* ■ denoting a country or city to which a person has moved and in which they have chosen to make their permanent place of residence. — **a·dop·tive·ly** **adv.**

a·dor·a·ble /ə'dôrəbəl/ ▶ **adj.** inspiring great affection; delightful; charm-ing. — **a·dor·a·bil·i·ty** /əˌdôrə'bilitē/ **n.** **a·dor·a·ble·ness** **n.** **a·dor·a·bly** **adv.**

a·dore /ə'dôr/ ▶ **v.** [trans.] love and respect (someone) deeply. ■ worship; venerate. ■ informal like (something or someone) very much. — **ad·o·ra·tion** /ˌadə'rāsHən/ **n.** **a·dor·er** **n.** **a·dor·ing·ly** **adv.** [ME: via OFr. from L. *adorare* 'to worship,' from *ad-* 'to' + *orare* 'speak.']

a·dorn /ə'dôrn/ ▶ **v.** [trans.] make more beautiful or attractive. — **a·dorn·er** **n.** **a·dorn·ment** **n.** [ME: via OFr. from L. *adornare*, from *ad-* 'to' + *ornare* 'add luster.']

ADP ▶ **abbr.** ■ Biochem. adenosine diphosphate. ■ automatic data processing.

ADR ▶ **abbr.** ■ American depositary receipt.

A·drar des I·fo·ras /ä'drär dāz ˌēfôr'ä/ a massif region in the central Sahara.

ad rem /'ad 'rem/ ▶ **adv. & adj.** formal relevant to what is being done or discussed at the time. [16th C.: L., lit. 'to the matter.']

ad·re·nal /ə'drēnl/ ▶ **adj.** of, relating to, or denoting a pair of ductless glands situated above the kidneys. Each consists of a core region (**adrenal medulla**) secreting epinephrine and norepinephrine, and an outer region (**adrenal cortex**) secreting corticosteroids. ▶ **n.** (usu. **adrenals**) an adrenal gland. [19th C.: from AD- + RENAL.]

a·dren·al·ine /ə'drenl-in/ (also **a·dren·al·in**) ▶ **n.** another term for EPINEPHRINE. ■ **(Adrenalin)** trademark the hormone epinephrine extracted from animals or prepared synthetically for medicinal purposes. [20th C.: from ADRENAL.]

ad·ren·er·gic /ˌadrə'nərjik/ ▶ **adj.** Physiol. relating to or denoting nerve cells in which epinephrine (adrenaline), norepinephrine (noradrenaline), or a similar substance acts as a neurotransmitter. [1930s: from ADRENALINE + Gk. *ergon* 'work.']

a·dre·no·cor·ti·co·trop·ic hor·mone /ə'drēnōˌkôrtikō'träpik; -'trōpik/ (also **a·dre·no·cor·ti·co·troph·ic hor·mone** /-'träfik; -'trōfik/) (abbr.: **ACTH**) ▶ **n.** Biochem. a hormone secreted by the pituitary gland and stimulating the adrenal cortex. [1930s: from *adreno-* and *cortico-* (from ADRENAL, CORTEX).]

ad·re·no·cor·ti·co·tro·pin /ə'drēnōˌkôrtikō'trōpin/ (also **a·dre·no·cor·ti·co·tro·phin** /-'trōfin/) ▶ **n.** another term for ADRENOCORTICOTROPIC HORMONE.

A·dri·an IV /'ādrēən/ (*c.*1100–59), pope 1154–59; born *Nicholas Breakspear.* He is the only person from England to have held the office of pope.

A·dri·at·ic /ˌādrē'atik/ ▶ **adj.** of or relating to the region comprising the Adriatic Sea and its coasts and islands. ▶ **n.** **(the Adriatic)** the Adriatic Sea or its coasts and islands.

A·dri·at·ic Sea an arm of the Mediterranean Sea between the Balkans and the Italian peninsula.

a·drift /ə'drift/ ▶ **adj. & adv.** (of a boat or its passengers) floating without being either moored or steered. ■ fig. (of a person) without purpose or guidance; lost and confused: *adrift in a strange country.*

a·droit /ə'droit/ ▶ **adj.** clever or skillful in using the hands or mind. — **a·droit·ly** **adv.** **a·droit·ness** **n.** [17th C.: from Fr., from *à droit* 'according to right.']

ad·sci·ti·tious /ˌadsi'tisHəs/ ▶ **adj.** rare forming an addition or supplement; not integral or intrinsic. [17th C.: from L. *adscit-* 'admitted,' from *adsciscere.*]

ad·sorb /ad'zôrb; -'sôrb/ ▶ **v.** [trans.] (of a solid) hold (molecules of a gas or liquid or solute) as a thin film on the outside surface or on internal surfaces within the material. — **ad·sorb·a·ble** **adj.** **ad·sorp·tion** **n.** **ad·sorp·tive** **adj.** [19th C.: blend of AD- + ABSORB.]

ad·sorb·ate /ad'zôrbit; -ˌbāt; -'sôr-/ ▶ **n.** a substance adsorbed.

ad·sorb·ent /ad'zôrbənt; -'sôr-/ ▶ **n.** a substance that adsorbs another. ▶ **adj.** able to adsorb substances.

ad·su·ki /ad'so͞okē; -'zo͞o-/ ▶ **n.** var. of ADZUKI.

ad·u·late /'ajəˌlāt/ ▶ **v.** [trans.] praise (someone) excessively or obsequiously. — **ad·u·la·tor** /-ˌlātər/ **n.** **ad·u·la·to·ry** /-ləˌtôrē/ **adj.** [18th C.: from L. *adulat-* 'fawned on,' from v. *adulari.*]

ad·u·la·tion /ˌajə'lāsHən/ ▶ **n.** obsequious flattery; excessive admiration or praise.

a·dult /ə'dəlt; 'adˌəlt/ ▶ **n.** a person who is fully grown or developed. ■ a fully developed animal. ■ Law a person who has reached the age of majority. See MAJORITY (sense 2). ▶ **adj.** (of a person or animal) fully grown or developed. ■ of or for adult people: *adult education.* ■ emotionally and mentally mature. ■ sexually explicit or pornographic (used euphemistically to refer to a movie, book, or magazine). — **a·dult·hood** **n.** [16th C.: from L. *adultus*, past part. of *adolescere* 'grow to maturity' (see ADOLESCENT).]

a·dul·ter·ant /ə'dəltərənt/ ▶ **n.** a substance used to adulterate another. ▶ **adj.** used in adulterating something.

a·dul·ter·ate ▶ **v.** /ə'dəltəˌrāt/ [trans.] render (something) poorer in quality by adding another substance, typically an inferior one. — **a·dul·ter·a·tion** /əˌdəltə'rāsHən/ **n.** **a·dul·ter·a·tor** /-ˌrātər/ **n.** [16th C.: from L. *adulterat-* 'corrupted,' from v. *adulterare.*]

a·dul·ter·er /ə'dəltərər/ ▶ **n.** a person who commits adultery.

a·dul·ter·ess /ə'dəlt(ə)ris/ ▶ **n.** a female adulterer.

a·dul·ter·ine /ə'dəltəˌrēn; -ˌrīn/ ▶ **adj.** (of a child) born as the result of an adulterous relationship. ■ archaic & hist. illegal, unlicensed, or spurious.

a·dul·ter·ous /ə'dəlt(ə)rəs/ ▶ **adj.** of or involving adultery: *an adulterous affair.* — **a·dul·ter·ous·ly** **adv.**

a·dul·ter·y /ə'dəlt(ə)rē/ ▶ **n.** voluntary sexual intercourse between a married person and a person who is not his or her spouse. [15th C.: from obs. n. *adulter*, from L. *adulter* 'adulterer.']

ad·um·brate /'adəm,brāt; ə'dəm-/ ▶**v.** [trans.] formal report or represent in outline. ■ indicate faintly. ■ foreshadow or symbolize. ■ overshadow. — **ad·um·bra·tion** /,adəm'brāsHən/ **n.** **ad·um·bra·tive** /ə'dəmbrətiv; 'adəm,brā-/ **adj.** [16th C.: from L. *adumbrat-* 'shaded,' from v. *adumbrare*, from *ad-* 'to' + *umbrare* 'cast a shadow' (from *umbra* 'shade').]

Ad·vai·ta /əd'vītə/ ▶**n.** Hinduism a Vedantic doctrine that identifies the individual self (atman) with the ground of reality (brahman). [Sanskrit, lit. 'nonduality.']

ad va·lo·rem /,ad və'lôrəm/ ▶**adv. & adj.** (of the levying of tax or customs duties) in proportion to the estimated value of the goods or transaction concerned. [17th C.: L., lit. 'according to the value.']

ad·vance /əd'vans/ ▶**v. 1** [intrans.] move forward, typically in a purposeful way: *the troops **advanced on** the capital.* ■ make progress: *our knowledge is advancing all the time.* ■ [trans.] cause (an event) to occur at an earlier date than planned: *I advanced the date of the meeting.* ■ [trans.] promote or help the progress of (a person, cause, or plan): *it was a chance to advance his own interests.* ■ put forward (a theory or suggestion): *the hypothesis I wish to advance.* ■ (esp. of shares of stock) increase in price. **2** [with two objs.] lend (money) to (someone): *the bank advanced them a loan.* ■ pay (money) to (someone) before it is due: *he advanced me a month's salary.* ▶**n. 1** a forward movement: *the rebels' advance on Madrid* | fig. *the advance of civilization.* ■ a development or improvement: *great scientific advance.* ■ an increase or rise in amount, value, or price. **2** an amount of money paid before it is due or for work only partly completed: *the author was paid a $250,000 advance.* ■ a loan: *an advance from the bank.* **3** (usu. **advances**) an approach made to someone, typically with the aim of initiating a sexual encounter. ▶**adj.** done, sent, or supplied beforehand: *advance notice.*
– PHRASES **in advance** ahead in time. **in advance of** ahead of in time or space; before. — **ad·vanc·er n.** [ME: from OFr. *avance* (n.), *avancer* (v.), from late L. *abante* 'in front,' from *ab* 'from' + *ante* 'before.']

ad·vanced /əd'vanst/ ▶**adj.** far on or ahead in development or progress. ■ new and not yet generally accepted.

ad·vance di·rec·tive ▶**n.** a written statement of a person's wishes regarding medical treatment, often including a living will, made to ensure those wishes are carried out should the person be unable to communicate them to a doctor.

ad·vanced place·ment (abbr.: **AP**) ▶**n.** the placement of a student in a high school course that offers college credit if successfully completed.

ad·vance guard ▶**n.** a body of soldiers preceding and making preparations for the main body of an army.

ad·vance man ▶**n.** a person who visits a location before the arrival of an important visitor to make the appropriate arrangements.

ad·vance·ment /əd'vansmənt/ ▶**n.** the process of promoting a cause or plan. ■ the promotion of a person in rank or status. ■ development or improvement.

ad·van·tage /əd'vantij/ ▶**n.** a condition or circumstance that puts one in a favorable or superior position. ■ the opportunity to gain something; benefit or profit: *you could learn something **to your advantage**.* ■ a favorable or desirable circumstance or feature; a benefit. ■ Tennis a player's score in a game when they have won the first point after deuce (and will win the game if they win the next point). ▶**v.** [trans.] put in a favorable or more favorable position.
– PHRASES **take advantage of 1** make unfair demands on someone who cannot or will not resist; exploit or make unfair use of for one's own benefit. ■ euphem. seduce. **2** make good use of the opportunities offered by (something). **turn something to one's advantage** handle or respond to something in such a way as to benefit from it. — **ad·van·ta·geous** /,advən'tājəs; -van-/ **adj.** **ad·van·ta·geous·ly** /,advən'tājəslē; -van-/ **adv.** [ME: from OFr. *avantage*, from *avant* 'in front,' from late L. *abante* (see ADVANCE).]

ad·vec·tion /ad'veksHən/ ▶**n.** the transfer of heat or matter by the flow of a fluid, esp. horizontally in the atmosphere or the sea. — **ad·vect** /-'vekt/ **v.** **ad·vec·tive adj.** [20th C.: from L. *advectio(n-)*, from *advehere* 'bring,' from *ad-* 'to' + *vehere* 'carry.']

ad·vent /'ad,vent/ ▶**n.** [in sing.] the arrival of a notable person, thing, or event. ■ (**Advent**) the first season of the church year, leading up to Christmas and including the four preceding Sundays. ■ (**Advent**) Christian Theol. the coming or Second Coming of Christ. [OE, from L. *adventus* 'arrival,' from *advenire*, from *ad-* 'to' + *venire* 'come.']

Ad·vent·ist /'ad,ventist/ ▶**n.** a member of any of various Christian sects emphasizing belief in the imminent Second Coming of Christ. — **Ad·vent·ism** /-,tizəm/ **n.**

ad·ven·ti·tia /,adven'tisH(ē)ə/ ▶**n.** the outermost layer of the wall of a blood vessel. — **ad·ven·ti·tial adj.** [19th C.: from mod. L. *(tunica) adventitia* 'additional (sheath).']

ad·ven·ti·tious /,adven'tisHəs/ ▶**adj.** happening or carried on according to chance rather than design or inherent nature. ■ coming from outside; not native. ■ Biol. formed accidentally or in an unusual anatomical position. ■ Bot. (of a root) growing directly from the stem or other upper part of a plant. — **ad·ven·ti·tious·ly adv.** [17th C.: from L. *adventicius*.]

Ad·vent Sun·day ▶**n.** the first Sunday in Advent, falling on or near November 30.

ad·ven·ture /ad'vencHər; əd-/ ▶**n.** an unusual and exciting, typically hazardous, experience or activity. ■ daring and exciting activity calling for enterprise and enthusiasm: *a sense of adventure.* ■ archaic a commercial speculation. ▶**v.** [intrans.] dated engage in hazardous and exciting activity, esp. the exploration of unknown territory: *they had **adventured into** the forest.* ■ [trans.] dated put (something, esp. money or one's life) at risk: *he adventured $3,000 in the purchase of land.* [ME: from OFr. *aventure* (n.), *aventurer* (v.), based on L. *adventurus* 'about to happen,' from *advenire* 'arrive.']

ad·ven·ture game ▶**n.** a type of computer game in which the participant plays a fantasy role in an episodic adventure story.

ad·ven·tur·er /ad'vencHərər; əd-/ ▶**n.** a person who enjoys or seeks adventure. ■ a person willing to take risks or use dishonest methods for personal gain: *a political adventurer.* ■ archaic a financial speculator. ■ archaic a mercenary soldier.

ad·ven·ture·some /ad'vencHərsəm; əd-/ ▶**adj.** given to adventures or to running risks; adventurous. — **ad·ven·ture·some·ness n.**

ad·ven·tur·ess /ad'vencHəris; əd-/ ▶**n.** a woman who enjoys or seeks adventure. ■ a woman who seeks social or financial advancement by dishonest or unscrupulous methods.

ad·ven·tur·ism /ad'vencHə,rizəm; əd-/ ▶**n.** the willingness to take risks in business or politics (esp. in the context of foreign policy); actions, tactics, or attitudes regarded as daring or reckless. — **ad·ven·tur·ist n. & adj.**

ad·ven·tur·ous /ad'vencHərəs; əd-/ ▶**adj.** willing to take risks or to try out new methods, ideas, or experiences. ■ involving new ideas or methods. ■ full of excitement. — **ad·ven·tur·ous·ly adv.** **ad·ven·tur·ous·ness n.**

ad·verb /'ad,vərb/ ▶**n.** Gram. a word or phrase that modifies or qualifies an adjective, verb, or other adverb or a phrase, expressing a relation of place, time, circumstance, manner, cause, degree, etc. (e.g., *gently, quite, then, there*). [ME: from L. *adverbium*, from *ad-* 'to' + *verbum* 'word.']

ad·ver·bi·al /ad'vərbēəl/ Gram. ▶**adj.** like or relating to an adverb. ▶**n.** a word or phrase functioning like an adverb. — **ad·ver·bi·al·ly adv.**

ad·ver·sar·i·al /,advər'se(ə)rēəl/ ▶**adj.** involving or characterized by conflict or opposition. ■ opposed; hostile. ■ Law (of a trial or legal procedure) in which the parties in a dispute have the responsibility for finding and presenting evidence. — **ad·ver·sar·i·al·ly adv.**

ad·ver·sar·y /'advər,serē/ ▶**n.** (pl. **-sar·ies**) one's opponent in a contest, conflict, or dispute. ■ (**the Adversary**) the Devil. ▶**adj.** another term for ADVERSARIAL.

ad·ver·sa·tive /əd'vərsətiv/ ▶**adj.** Gram. (of a word or phrase) expressing opposition or antithesis.

ad·verse /ad'vərs; 'advərs/ ▶**adj.** preventing success or development; harmful; unfavorable: ***adverse** weather conditions.* — **ad·verse·ly adv.** [ME: from OFr. *advers*, from L. *adversus* past part. of *advertere*.]

ad·ver·si·ty /ad'vərsitē/ ▶**n.** (pl. **-ties**) difficulties; misfortune.

ad·vert[1] /'ad,vərt/ ▶**n.** Brit., informal an advertisement.

ad·vert[2] /ad'vərt/ ▶**v.** [intrans.] (**advert to**) formal refer to in speaking or writing. [ME: from OFr. *avertir*, from L. *advertere*, from *ad* 'to' + *vertere* 'to turn.']

ad·ver·tise /'advər,tīz/ ▶**v.** [trans.] describe or draw attention to (a product, service, or event) in a public medium in order to promote sales or attendance: *a billboard advertising beer* | [intrans.] *we had a chance to advertise on television.* ■ seek to fill (a vacancy) by putting a notice in a newspaper or other medium: *for every job we advertise we get a hundred applicants* | [intrans.] *he **advertised for** dancers in the trade papers.* ■ make (a quality or fact) known. ■ archaic notify (someone) of something. — **ad·ver·tis·er n.** [ME: from OFr. *advertiss-*, from *advertir*.]

ad·ver·tise·ment /'advər,tīzmənt; əd'vərtiz-/ ▶**n.** a notice or announcement in a public medium promoting a product, service, or event or publicizing a job vacancy.

ad·ver·tis·ing /'advər,tīziNG/ ▶**n.** the activity or profession of producing advertisements for commercial products or services.

ad·ver·to·ri·al /,advər'tôrēəl/ ▶**n.** a newspaper or magazine advertisement giving information about a product in the style of an editorial or objective journalistic article. [1960s: blend of ADVERTISEMENT and EDITORIAL.]

ad·vice /əd'vīs/ ▶**n.** guidance or recommendations concerning prudent future action, typically given by someone regarded as knowledgeable or authoritative. ■ archaic information; news. [ME: from OFr. *avis*, based on L. *ad* 'to' + *visum*, past part. of *videre* 'to see.']

ad·vis·a·ble /əd'vīzəbəl/ ▶**adj.** [often with infin.] (of a course of action) to be recommended; sensible: *it is advisable to carry one of the major credit cards.* — **ad·vis·a·bil·i·ty** /-,vīzə'bilitē/ **n.** **ad·vis·a·bly adv.**

ad·vise /əd'vīz/ ▶**v.** offer suggestions about the best course of action to someone: [trans.] *he advised caution.* ■ [trans.] recommend (something): *sleeping pills are not advised.* ■ [trans.] inform (someone) about a fact or situation, typically in a formal or official way: *you will be advised of the requirements.* [ME: from OFr. *aviser*, based on L. *ad-* 'to' + *visere*, frequentative of *videre* 'to see.']

ad·vised /əd'vīzd/ ▶**adj.** behaving as someone, esp. the speaker, would recommend; sensible; wise.

ad·vis·ed·ly /əd'vīzidlē/ ▶**adv.** deliberately and after consideration (used esp. of what might appear a mistake or oversight): *I've used the term "old" advisedly.*

PRONUNCIATION KEY ə *ago, up*; ər *over, fur*; a *hat*; ā *ate*; ä *car*; e *let*; ē *see*; i *fit*; ī *by*; NG *sing*; ō *go*; ô *law, for*; oi *toy*; o͝o *good*; o͞o *goo*; ou *out*; TH *thin*; T͟H *then*; ZH *vision*

ad·vi·see /ad,vī'zē; ,advī-/ ▸ **n.** a person who meets with an adviser.

ad·vise·ment /əd'vīzmənt/ ▸ **n.** careful consideration. ▪ advice or counsel.
– PHRASES **take something under advisement** reserve judgment while considering something.

ad·vis·er /əd'vīzər/ (also **ad·vi·sor**) ▸ **n.** a person who gives advice, typically someone who is expert in a particular field: *the military adviser to the President.* ▪ in a school, college, or university, a teacher or staff counselor who helps a student plan a course of study.

ad·vi·so·ry /əd'vīzərē/ ▸ **adj.** having or consisting in the power to make recommendations but not to take action enforcing them: *an independent advisory committee.* ▪ recommended but not compulsory: *universities may treat the recommendations as advisory.* ▸ **n.** (pl. **-ries**) an official announcement, typically a warning about bad weather conditions: *a frost advisory.*

ad·vo·ca·cy /'advəkəsē/ ▸ **n.** public support for or recommendation of a particular cause or policy. ▪ the profession or work of a legal advocate.

ad·vo·cate ▸ **n.** /'advəkit/ a person who publicly supports or recommends a particular cause or policy. ▪ a person who pleads on someone else's behalf: *advocates for their clients.* ▪ a pleader in a court of law; a lawyer. ▸ **v.** /-,kāt/ [trans.] publicly recommend or support: *they advocated strict adherence to Islam.* — **ad·vo·ca·tion** /,advə'kāsʜən/ **n.** **ad·vo·ca·tor** /-,kātər/ **n.** [ME: from OFr. *avocat*, from L. *advocatus*, past part. of *advocare* 'call (to one's aid),' from *ad-* + *vocare* 'to call.']

ad·vow·son /ad'vouzən/ ▸ **n.** (in English ecclesiastical law) the right to recommend a member of the Anglican clergy for a vacant benefice, or to make such an appointment. [ME: from OFr. *avoeson*, from L. *advocatio(n-)*, from *advocare* 'summon.']

advt. ▸ **abbr.** advertisement.

A·dy·ge·a /,ädə'gāə/ an autonomous republic in southwestern Russia; pop. 432,000; capital, Maikop. Full name **Adygei Autonomous Republic.**

ad·y·tum /'aditəm/ ▸ **n.** (pl. **-ta** /-tə/) the innermost sanctuary of an ancient Greek temple. [L., from Gk. *aduton*, neut. sing. of *adutos* 'impenetrable,' from *a-* + *duein* 'enter.']

adze /adz/ (**adz**) ▸ **n.** a tool similar to an ax with an arched blade at right angles to the handle, used for cutting or shaping large pieces of wood. [OE *adesa.*]

ad·zu·ki /ad'zōōkē/ (also **adzuki bean**) ▸ **n.** **1** a small, round, dark-red edible bean. **2** the bushy leguminous Asian plant (*Vigna angularis*) that produces this bean. [18th C.: from Japanese *azuki.*]

Æ (also **æ**) ▸ **n.** a ligatured letter used in Old English to represent either a long sound like that in modern American English *hair* or the short vowel of *hat;* currently used in some phonetic alphabets to represent the vowel of *hat,* which is symbolized in this dictionary by /a/ (see **ash²**).

-ae ▸ **suffix** forming plural nouns: **1** used in names of animal and plant families and other groups: *Felidae* | *Gymnospermae.* **2** used instead of *-as* in the plural of many nonnaturalized or unfamiliar nouns ending in *-a* derived from Latin or Greek: *alumnae* | *larvae.* [representing L. plural, or the Gk. pl. ending *-ai* of some nouns.]

AEC hist. ▸ **abbr.** Atomic Energy Commission.

ae·dile /'ē,dīl/ ▸ **n.** Roman history either of two (later four) Roman magistrates responsible for public buildings and originally also for the public games and the supply of grain to the city. — **ae·dile·ship** **n.** [16th C.: from L. *aedilis* 'concerned with buildings,' from *aedes* 'building.']

AEF ▸ **abbr.** American Expeditionary Force.

Ae·ge·an /i'jēən/ ▸ **adj.** of or relating to the region comprising the Aegean Sea and its coasts and islands. ▸ **n.** (**the Aegean**) the Aegean Sea or its region. [17th C.: via L. from Gk. *Aigaios.*]

Ae·ge·an Is·lands islands in the Aegean Sea that form a region of Greece. They include Chios, Samos, Lesbos, the Cyclades, and the Dodecanese.

Ae·ge·an Sea a part of the Mediterranean Sea between Greece and Turkey.

ae·gis /'ējis/ ▸ **n.** [in sing.] the protection, backing, or support of a particular person or organization: *negotiations were conducted* ***under the aegis of*** *the UN.* ▪ (in classical art and mythology) an attribute of Zeus and Athena usually represented as a goatskin shield. [17th C.: via L. from Gk. *aigis* 'shield of Zeus.']

Ae·gis·thus /ē'jisтнəs/ Gk. Mythol. the son of Thyestes and lover of Agamemnon's wife Clytemnestra.

Ael·fric /'alfrik/ (*c.*955–*c.*1020) Anglo-Saxon grammarian; called **Grammaticus.** He wrote *Lives of the Saints* (993–996).

-aemia ▸ **comb. form** British spelling of **-emia.**

Ae·ne·as /i'nēəs/ Greek Rom. Mythol. a Trojan leader, legendary ancestor of the Romans, and hero of Virgil's *Aeneid.* When Troy fell to the Greeks he escaped and after wandering for many years eventually reached Italy.

Ae·ne·id /i'nēid/ a Latin epic poem in twelve books by Virgil, that relates the travels and experiences of Aeneas after the fall of Troy.

ae·o·li·an /ē'ōlēən; ā'ō-/ (also **e·o·li·an**) ▸ **adj.** **1** Gk. Mythol. of or relating to Aeolus. ▪ literary characterized by a sighing or moaning sound as if produced by the wind. **2** esp. Geol. see **eolian.**

ae·o·li·an harp ▸ **n.** a stringed instrument that produces musical sounds when a current of air passes through it.

Ae·o·li·an Is·lands /ē'ōlēən; ā'ō-/ ancient name for **Lipari Islands.**

Ae·o·lus /'ēələs/ Gk. Mythol. the god of the winds. [from Gk. *Aiolos*, from *aiolos* 'swift.']

ae·on ▸ **n.** Brit. var. of **eon.**

ae·py·or·nis /,ēpē'ôrnis/ ▸ **n.** another term for **elephant bird.** [19th C.: mod. L., from Gk. *aipus* 'high' + *ornis* 'bird.']

aer·ate /'e(ə)rāt/ ▸ **v.** [trans.] introduce air into (a material). — **aer·a·tion** /e(ə)'rāsʜən/ **n.** **aer·a·tor** /'e(ə)rātər/ **n.**

aer·i·al /'e(ə)rēəl/ ▸ **adj.** [attrib.] existing, happening, or operating in the air. ▪ coming or carried out from the air, esp. using aircraft. ▪ (of part of a plant) growing above ground: *knobby sections of aerial roots.* ▪ insubstantial and hard to grasp or define: *fine and aerial distinctions.* ▸ **n.** **1** another term for **antenna** (sense 2). **2** (**aerials**) a type of maneuver in gymnastics, skiing, or surfing involving freestyle jumps or somersaults. — **aer·i·al·ly** **adv.** [16th C.: via L. *aerius* from Gk. *aerios* (from *aēr* 'air.')]

aer·i·al·ist /'e(ə)rēəlist/ ▸ **n.** a person who performs acrobatics high above the ground on a tightrope or trapezes.

aer·i·al lad·der ▸ **n.** a long extension ladder, esp. on a fire engine, used to reach high places.

aer·ie /'e(ə)rē; 'i(ə)rē/ (also **eyr·ie**) ▸ **n.** a large nest of a bird of prey, esp. an eagle, typically built high in a tree or on a cliff. [15th C.: from med. L. *aeria, aerea, eyria,* prob. from OFr. *aire,* from L. *area* 'level piece of ground.']

aero- ▸ **comb. form** **1** of or relating to air: *aerobe* | *aerobics.* **2** of or relating to aviation: *aerodynamics* | *aeronautics.* [from Gk. *aēr* 'air.']

aer·o·bat·ics /,e(ə)rə'batiks/ ▸ **plural n.** [usu. treated as sing.] feats of spectacular flying performed in one or more aircraft to entertain an audience on the ground. — **aer·o·bat·ic** **adj.** [World War I: from **aero-** + **acrobatics.**]

aer·obe /'e(ə)r,ōb/ ▸ **n.** a microorganism that grows in the presence of air or requires oxygen for growth. [19th C.: coined in Fr. from Gk. *aēr* 'air' + *bios* 'life.']

aer·o·bic /ə'rōbik; e(ə)'rō-/ ▸ **adj.** Biol. relating to, involving, or requiring free oxygen: *simple aerobic bacteria.* ▪ relating to or denoting exercise that improves the efficiency of the body's cardiovascular system in absorbing and transporting oxygen. — **aer·o·bi·cal·ly** **adv.**

aer·o·bics /ə'rōbiks; e(ə)'rō-/ ▸ **plural n.** [often treated as sing.] vigorous exercises, such as swimming or walking, designed to strengthen the heart and lungs.

aer·o·bi·ol·o·gy /,e(ə)rōbī'äləjē/ ▸ **n.** the study of airborne microorganisms, pollen, spores, and seeds, esp. as agents of infection.

aer·o·brake /'e(ə)rō,brāk/ ▸ **v.** [intrans.] tech. cause a spacecraft to slow down by flying through a planet's rarefied atmosphere to produce aerodynamic drag. ▸ **n.** a mechanism for aerobraking.

aer·o·drome /'e(ə)rə,drōm/ ▸ **n.** Brit. a small airport or airfield.

aer·o·dy·nam·ic /,e(ə)rōdī'namik/ ▸ **adj.** of or relating to aerodynamics: *aerodynamic forces.* ▪ of or having a shape that reduces the drag from air moving past: *the plane has a more aerodynamic shape.* — **aer·o·dy·nam·i·cal·ly** /-ik(ə)lē/ **adv.**

aer·o·dy·nam·ics /,e(ə)rōdī'namiks/ ▸ **plural n.** [treated as sing.] the study of the properties of moving air, and esp. of the interaction between the air and solid bodies moving through it. ▪ [treated as pl.] these properties insofar as they result in maximum efficiency of motion. — **aer·o·dy·nam·i·cist** /-'naməsist/ **n.**

aer·o·dyne /'e(ə)rə,dīn/ ▸ **n.** any heavier-than-air aircraft that derives its lift principally from aerodynamic forces.

aer·o·e·las·tic·i·ty /,e(ə)rō-i,la'stisitē; -,ēla-/ ▸ **n.** the science of the interaction between aerodynamic forces and nonrigid structures. — **aer·o·e·las·tic** /-i'lastik/ **adj.**

aer·o·foil /'e(ə)rə,foil/ ▸ **n.** British term for **airfoil.**

aer·o·gel /'e(ə)rə,jel/ ▸ **n.** a solid material of extremely low density, produced by removing the liquid component from a conventional gel.

aer·o·gramme /'e(ə)rə,gram/ (also **aer·o·gram**) ▸ **n.** a sheet of light paper folded and sealed to form a letter for sending by airmail.

aer·o·lite /'e(ə)rə,līt/ ▸ **n.** a stony meteorite, composed mainly of silicates.

aer·ol·o·gy /e(ə)'räləjē/ ▸ **n.** dated the study of the atmosphere, esp. away from ground level. — **aer·o·log·i·cal** /,e(ə)rə'läjikəl/ **adj.**

aer·o·mag·net·ic /,e(ə)rōmag'netik/ ▸ **adj.** relating to or denoting the measurement of the earth's magnetic field using airborne instruments.

aer·o·med·i·cal /,e(ə)rō'medikəl/ ▸ **adj.** of or relating to the use of aircraft for medical purposes such as transporting patients to a hospital.

aer·o·med·i·cine /,e(ə)rō'medəsən/ ▸ **n.** a branch of medicine relating to conditions specific to flight.

aer·o·naut /'e(ə)rə,nôt/ ▸ **n.** esp. hist. a traveler in a hot-air balloon, airship, or other flying craft. [18th C.: from Fr. *aéronaute*, from Gk. *aēr* 'air' + *nautēs* 'sailor.']

aer·o·nau·tics /,e(ə)rə'nôtiks/ ▸ **plural n.** [treated as sing.] the science or practice of travel through the air. — **aer·o·nau·tic** **adj.** (rare) **aer·o·nau·ti·cal** /-ikəl/ **adj.**

ae·ron·o·my /e'ränəmē/ ▸ **n.** the science of the upper atmosphere, esp. those regions where there is significant ionization of gases.

aer·o·pha·gia /,e(ə)rə'fājə; -jēə/ ▸ **n.** Med. the swallowing of air, whether deliberately to stimulate belching, accidentally, or as an involuntary habit.

aer·o·plane /'e(ə)rə,plān/ ▸ **n.** British term for **airplane.** [19th C.: from Fr. *aéroplane*, from *aéro-* 'air' + Gk. *-planos* 'wandering.']

aer·o·sol /'e(ə)rə,sôl; -,säl/ ▸ **n.** a substance enclosed under pressure and able to be released as a fine spray, typically by means of a propellant gas. ▪ a container holding such a substance. ▪ Chem. a colloidal suspension of particles dispersed in air or gas.

aer·o·space /'e(ə)rō,spās/ ▶ **n.** the branch of technology and industry concerned with both aviation and space flight.

aer·o·stat /'e(ə)rə,stat/ ▶ **n.** an airship or hot-air balloon, esp. one that is tethered. [18th C.: from Fr. *aérostat*, from Gk. *aēr* 'air' + *statos* 'standing.']

Aes·chy·lus /'eskələs/ (*c.*525–*c.*456 BC), Greek playwright. His trilogy, the *Oresteia* (458 BC) consists of the tragedies *Agamemnon, Choephoroe*, and *Eumenides*.

Aes·cu·la·pi·an /,esk(y)ə'lāpēən/ ▶ **adj.** archaic of or relating to medicine or physicians. [16th C.: from L. *Aesculapius*, Roman god of medicine.]

Ae·sir /'āzir; 'āsir/ Scand. Mythol. the Norse gods and goddesses collectively, including Odin, Thor, and Balder.

Ae·sop /'ē,säp; 'ēsəp/ (6th century BC), Greek slave and storyteller noted for his moralized fables featuring personified animals.

aes·thete /'es,THēt/ (also **es·thete**) ▶ **n.** a person who has or affects to have a special appreciation of art and beauty. [19th C.: from Gk. *aisthētēs* 'person who perceives,' or from AESTHETIC.]

aes·thet·ic /es'THetik/ (also **es·thet·ic**) ▶ **adj.** concerned with beauty or the appreciation of beauty. ■ giving or designed to give pleasure through beauty; of pleasing appearance. ▶ **n.** [in sing.] a set of principles underlying and guiding the work of a particular artist or artistic movement. — **aes·thet·i·cal·ly** /-ik(ə)lē/ **adv.** **aes·thet·i·cism** /-'THeti,sizəm/ **n.** [18th C.: from Gk. *aisthētikos*, from *aisthēta* 'perceptible things,' from *aisthesthai* 'perceive.']

aes·the·ti·cian /,esTHə'tisHən/ (also **es·the·ti·cian**) ▶ **n.** **1** a person who is knowledgeable about the nature and appreciation of beauty, esp. in art. **2** a beautician.

aes·thet·i·cize /es'THetə,sīz/ ▶ **v.** [trans.] represent (something) as being beautiful or artistically pleasing.

aes·thet·ics /es'THetiks/ (also **es·thet·ics**) ▶ **plural n.** [usu. treated as sing.] a set of principles concerned with the nature and appreciation of beauty, esp. in art. ■ the branch of philosophy that deals with the principles of beauty and artistic taste.

aes·ti·val ▶ **adj.** var. of ESTIVAL.

aes·ti·vate ▶ **v.** var. of ESTIVATE.

aes·ti·va·tion ▶ **n.** var. of ESTIVATION.

aet. (also **aetat.**) ▶ **abbr.** aetatis.

ae·ta·tis /ī'tätis; ē'tätis/ ▶ **adj.** of or at the age of. [19th C.: L.]

ae·ther ▶ **n.** var. of ETHER (senses 2 and 3).

AF ▶ **abbr.** ■ air force. ■ audio frequency. ■ autofocus.

af- ▶ **prefix** var. of AD- assimilated before *f* (as in *affiliate, affirm*).

a·far /ə'fär/ ▶ **adv.** esp. literary at or to a distance. [ME *of feor* 'from far.']

A·fars and Is·sas, French Territory of the /'äfärz and ē'säz/ former name (1946–77) of DJIBOUTI.

AFB ▶ **abbr.** Air Force Base.

AFC ▶ **abbr.** ■ American Football Conference. ■ automatic frequency control.

AFDC ▶ **abbr.** Aid to Families with Dependent Children, a welfare benefit program of the federal government.

a·feard /ə'fi(ə)rd/ (also **a·feared**) ▶ **adj.** archaic or dialect afraid. [OE, from *āfǣran* 'frighten,' from *ā-* (intensive) + *fǣran*.]

a·fe·brile /ā'febrəl; -'fē-/ ▶ **adj.** Med. not feverish.

af·fa·ble /'afəbəl/ ▶ **adj.** friendly, good-natured, or easy to talk to. — **af·fa·bil·i·ty** /,afə'bilitē/ **n.** **af·fa·bly** **adv.** [ME: via OFr. from L. *affabilis*, from v. *affari*, from *ad-* 'to' + *fari* 'speak.']

af·fair /ə'fe(ə)r/ ▶ **n.** **1** an event or sequence of events of a specified kind or that has previously been referred to. ■ a matter that is a particular person's concern or responsibility. ■ (**affairs**) matters of public interest and importance. ■ (**affairs**) business and financial dealings. ■ [with adj.] informal an object of a particular type: *her dress was a black low-cut affair.* **2** a love affair. [ME: from OFr. *afaire*, from *à faire* 'to do.']

af·faire /ə'fe(ə)r; ä'fer/ (also **af·faire de** or **du cœur** /də 'kœr/) ▶ **n.** a love affair. [19th C.: Fr., lit. 'affair (of the heart).']

af·fect[1] /ə'fekt/ ▶ **v.** [trans.] have an effect on; make a difference to: *the dampness began to affect my health.* ■ touch the feelings of (someone); move emotionally. ■ (of an illness) attack or infect: *people who are affected by AIDS.* — **af·fect·ing·ly** **adv.** [ME: from Fr. *affecter* or L. *affect-* 'affected,' from *afficere* (see AFFECT[2]).]

af·fect[2] /ə'fekt/ ▶ **v.** [trans.] pretend to have or feel (something): *as usual I affected a supreme unconcern.* ■ use, wear, or assume (something) pretentiously or so as to make an impression on others: *an American who had affected a British accent.* [ME: from Fr. *affecter* or L. *affectare* 'aim at,' frequentative of *afficere* 'work on,' from *ad-* 'to' + *facere* 'do.']

af·fect[3] /'afekt; ə'fekt/ ▶ **n.** Psychol. emotion or desire, esp. as influencing behavior or action. — **af·fect·less** **adj.** **af·fect·less·ness** **n.** [19th C.: coined in Ger. from L. *affectus* 'disposition,' from *afficere*.]

af·fec·ta·tion /,afek'tāsHən/ ▶ **n.** behavior, speech, or writing that is artificial and designed to impress. ■ a studied display of real or pretended feeling: *an affectation of calm.*

af·fect·ed /ə'fektid/ ▶ **adj.** **1** influenced or touched by an external factor: *apply moist heat to the affected area.* **2** artificial, pretentious, and designed to impress: *the gesture appeared both affected and stagy.* — **af·fect·ed·ly** **adv.** (in sense 2).

af·fec·tion /ə'feksHən/ ▶ **n.** **1** a gentle feeling of fondness or liking. ■ physical expressions of these feelings. **2** archaic the act or process of affecting or being affected. ■ a condition of disease: *an affection of the skin.* ■ a mental state; an emotion. — **af·fec·tion·al** /-sHənl/ **adj.**

af·fec·tion·ate /ə'feksHənit/ ▶ **adj.** readily feeling or showing fondness or tenderness. ■ expressing fondness. — **af·fec·tion·ate·ly** **adv.**

af·fec·tive /ə'fektiv/ ▶ **adj.** esp. Psychol. relating to moods, feelings, and attitudes: *affective disorders.* — **af·fec·tive·ly** **adv.** **af·fec·tiv·i·ty** /,afek'tivitē/ **n.**

af·fen·pin·scher /'äfən,pincHər/ ▶ **n.** a dog of a small breed resembling the griffin. [20th C.: from Ger., from *Affe* 'monkey' + *Pinscher* 'terrier.']

af·fer·ent /'af(ə)rənt/ ▶ **adj.** Physiol. conducting or conducted inward or toward something (for nerves, the central nervous system; for blood vessels, the organ supplied). ▶ **n.** an afferent nerve fiber or vessel. [19th C.: from L. *afferent-* 'bringing toward', from v. *afferre*, from *ad-* + *ferre* 'bring.']

af·fi·ance /ə'fīəns/ ▶ **v.** (**be affianced**) literary be engaged to marry. [15th C.: from OFr. *afiancer*, from *afier* 'entrust,' from med. L. *affidare* 'declare on oath,' from *ad-* + *fides* 'trust.']

af·fi·ant /ə'fīənt/ ▶ **n.** Law a person who swears to an affidavit. [19th C.: from Fr., pres. part. of *afier*, from med. L. *affidare*.]

af·fi·da·vit /,afi'dāvit/ ▶ **n.** Law a written statement confirmed by oath or affirmation, for use as evidence in court. [16th C.: from med. L., lit. 'he has stated on oath,' from *affidare*.]

af·fil·i·ate ▶ **v.** /ə'filē,āt/ [trans.] (usu. **be affiliated with**) officially attach or connect (a subsidiary group or a person) to an organization: *the college is **affiliated with** the University of Wisconsin.* ■ [intrans.] officially join or become attached to an organization. ▶ **n.** /-it/ a person or organization officially attached to a larger body. — **af·fil·i·a·tive** /-ətiv; -,ātiv/ **adj.** [18th C.: from med. L. *affiliat-* 'adopted as a son,' from v. *affiliare*, from *ad-* 'toward' + *filius* 'son.']

af·fil·i·a·tion /ə,filē'āsHən/ ▶ **n.** the state or process of affiliating or being affiliated: *his political affiliations.*

af·fine /ə'fīn; 'afīn/ ▶ **adj.** Math. allowing for or preserving parallel relationships. ▶ **n.** Anthropol. a relative by marriage. [16th C.: from OFr. *afin* or L. *affinis*.]

af·fined /ə'fīnd/ ▶ **adj.** archaic related or connected. [16th C.: from L. *affinis*).]

af·fin·i·ty /ə'finitē/ ▶ **n.** (pl. **-ties**) (often **affinity between/for/with**) a spontaneous or natural liking or sympathy for someone or something. ■ a similarity of characteristics suggesting a relationship, esp. a resemblance in structure between animals, plants, or languages. ■ relationship, esp. by marriage as opposed to blood ties. ■ esp. Biochem. the degree to which a substance tends to combine with another: *the affinity of hemoglobin for oxygen.* [ME: via OFr. from L. *affinitas*, from *affinis* 'rel.,' from *ad-* 'to' + *finis* 'border.']

af·firm /ə'fərm/ ▶ **v.** state as a fact; assert strongly and publicly. ■ [trans.] declare one's support for; uphold or defend. ■ [trans.] Law accept or confirm the validity of (a judgment or agreement); ratify. ■ [intrans.] Law make a formal declaration rather than taking an oath (e.g., to testify truthfully). ■ Law (of a court) uphold (a decision) on appeal. — **af·firm·er** **n.** [ME: via OFr. from L. *affirmare*, from *ad-* 'to' + *firmus* 'strong.']

af·firm·a·tion /,afər'māsHən/ ▶ **n.** the action or process of affirming or being affirmed. ■ Law a formal declaration by a person who declines to take an oath for reasons of conscience.

af·firm·a·tive /ə'fərmətiv/ ▶ **adj.** agreeing with a statement or to a request. ■ (of a vote) expressing approval or agreement. ■ supportive, hopeful, or encouraging. ■ active or obligatory: *an affirmative duty.* ■ Gram. & Logic stating that a fact is so; making an assertion. ▶ **n.** a statement of agreement with an assertion or request: *he accepted her reply as an affirmative.* ■ (**the affirmative**) a position of agreement or confirmation. ■ Gram. a word or particle used in making assertions. ■ Logic a statement asserting that something is true of the subject of a proposition. ▶ **exclam.** expressing agreement with a statement or request; yes.

– PHRASES **in the affirmative** so as to accept or agree to a statement or request. — **af·firm·a·tive·ly** **adv.**

af·firm·a·tive ac·tion ▶ **n.** an action or policy favoring those who tend to suffer from discrimination, esp. in relation to employment or education; positive discrimination.

af·fix ▶ **v.** /ə'fiks/ [trans.] stick, attach, or fasten (something) to something else. ▶ **n.** /'a,fiks/ Gram. an additional element placed at the beginning or end of a root, stem, or word, or in the body of a word, to modify its meaning. See also INFIX, PREFIX, SUFFIX. — **af·fix·a·tion** /,afik'sāsHən/ **n.** [ME: from OFr. *affixer* or med. L. *affixare*, frequentative of L. *affigere*, from *ad-* 'to' + *figere* 'to fix.']

af·fla·tus /ə'flātəs/ ▶ **n.** formal a divine creative impulse or inspiration. [17th C.: from L., from v. *afflare*, from *ad-* 'to' + *flare* 'to blow.']

af·flict /ə'flikt/ ▶ **v.** [trans.] (of a problem or illness) cause pain or suffering to; affect or trouble. — **af·flic·tive** **adj.** (archaic). [ME: from L. *afflictare* 'injure,' or from *afflict-* 'weakened,': from v. *affligere*, from *ad-* 'to' + *fligere* 'to strike.']

af·flic·tion /ə'fliksHən/ ▶ **n.** something that causes pain or suffering. ■ pain or suffering.

af·flu·ent /'aflōōənt; ə'flōō-/ ▶ **adj.** **1** (esp. of a group or area) having a great deal of money; wealthy: *the affluent societies of the western* *world* | [as pl. n.] **(the affluent)** *only the affluent could afford to travel abroad.* **2** archaic (of water) flowing freely or in great quantity. ▶ **n.** archaic a tributary stream. — **af·flu·ence n. af·flu·ent·ly adv.** [ME: via OFr. from L. *affluent-* 'flowing toward,' from v. *affluere*, from *ad-* + *fluere* 'to flow.']

af·flux /'aˌfləks/ ▶ **n.** archaic a flow of something, esp. water or air. [17th C.: from med. L. *affluxus*, from *affluere*.]

af·ford /ə'fôrd/ ▶ **v.** [trans.] **1 (can/could afford)** have enough money to pay for. ■ have (a certain amount of something, esp. money or time) available or to spare. ■ [with infin.] be able to do something without risk of adverse consequences: *kings could afford to be wrathful.* **2** provide or supply (an opportunity or facility): *the rooftop terrace affords beautiful views.* [OE *geforthian*, from *ge-* + *forthian* 'to further,' from FORTH.]

af·ford·a·ble /ə'fôrdəbəl/ ▶ **adj.** inexpensive; reasonably priced: *affordable housing.* — **af·ford·a·bil·i·ty** /əˌfôrdə'bilitē/ **n.**

af·for·est·a·tion /əˌfôrə'stāsʜən; əˌfär-/ ▶ **v.** [trans.] the conversion (of land) into forest, esp. for commercial use. — **af·for·est** /ə'fôrist; ə'fär-/ **v.** [16th C.: from med. L. *afforestare*, from *ad-* 'to' + *foresta* 'forest.']

af·fran·chise /ə'franˌᴄʜīz/ ▶ **v.** [trans.] archaic release from servitude. [15th C.: from OFr. *afranchiss-*, stem of *afranchir*, from *a-* + *franc* 'free.']

af·fray /ə'frā/ ▶ **n.** Law, dated an instance of group fighting in a public place that disturbs the peace. [ME: from Anglo-Norman Fr. *afrayer* 'disturb,' based on Gmc. word akin to OE *frithu* 'peace."]

af·fri·cate /'afrikit/ ▶ **n.** Phonet. a phoneme that combines a plosive with an immediately following fricative or spirant sharing the same place of articulation, e.g., *ch* as in *chair* and *j* as in *jar*. [19th C.: from L. *affricatus*, past part. of *affricare*, from *ad-* 'to' + *fricare* 'to rub.']

af·fright /ə'frīt/ archaic ▶ **v.** [trans.] frighten (someone). ▶ **n.** fright. [ME: from *āfyrhted* 'frightened" in OE.]

af·front /ə'frənt/ ▶ **n.** an action or remark that causes outrage or offense. ▶ **v.** [trans.] (usu. **be affronted**) offend the modesty or values of: *she was affronted by his familiarity.* [ME: from OFr. *afronter* 'to insult,' based on L. *ad frontem* 'to the face.']

Af·ghan /'afˌgan/ ▶ **n. 1** a native or national of Afghanistan, or a person of Afghan descent. **2** another term for PASHTO. **3 (afghan)** a woolen blanket or shawl, typically one knitted or crocheted in strips or squares. **4** short for AFGHAN HOUND. ▶ **adj.** of or relating to Afghanistan, its people, or their language. [from Pashto *afghānī*.]

Afghan hound

Af·ghan hound ▶ **n.** a tall hunting dog of a breed with long silky hair.

af·ghan·i /af'ganē; -'gä-/ ▶ **n.** (pl. **-ghan·is**) the basic monetary unit of Afghanistan, equal to 100 puls. [from Pashto *afghānī*.]

Af·ghan·i·stan /af'ganəˌstan/ a country in central Asia. *See box.*

a·fi·ci·o·na·do /əˌfisʜ(ē)ə'nädō; əˌfisyə-/ ▶ **n.** (pl. **-dos**) a person who is very knowledgeable and enthusiastic about an activity, subject, or pastime. [19th C.: from Sp., 'amateur,' past part. of *aficioner* 'become fond of' based on L. *affectio(n-)* (see AFFECTION).]

a·field /ə'fēld/ ▶ **adv. 1** to or at a distance. **2** in the field (usually in reference to hunting).

a·fire /ə'fī(ə)r/ ▶ **adv. & adj.** esp. literary on fire; burning: [as predic. adj.] *the whole mill was afire.*

a·flame /ə'flām/ ▶ **adv. & adj.** in flames; burning: [as adv.] *pour brandy over the steaks and then set aflame.*

af·la·tox·in /ˌaflə'täksən/ ▶ **n.** Chem. any of a class of toxic compounds that are produced by fungi of the *Aspergillus flavus* group. Found esp. in moldy grains, they can cause liver damage and cancer. [1960s: from elements of the mod. L. taxonomic name (see above) + TOXIN.]

AFL-CIO ▶ **abbr.** American Federation of Labor and Congress of Industrial Organizations.

a·float /ə'flōt/ ▶ **adj. & adv.** floating in water; not sinking. ■ on board a ship or boat. ■ fig. out of debt or difficulty: [as adv.] *I contrived to stay afloat in self-employment.* ■ in general circulation; current: [as predic. adj.] *the rumor has been afloat.*

a·foot /ə'fo͝ot/ ▶ **adv. 1** in preparation or progress; happening or beginning to happen. **2** on foot.

a·fore /ə'fôr/ ▶ **prep.** archaic or dialect before. [OE *onforan* (see A-[2], FORE).]

afore- ▶ **prefix** before; previously.

a·fore·men·tioned /ə'fôrˌmensʜənd/ ▶ **adj.** denoting a thing or person previously mentioned.

a·fore·said /ə'fôrˌsed/ ▶ **adj.** another term for AFOREMENTIONED.

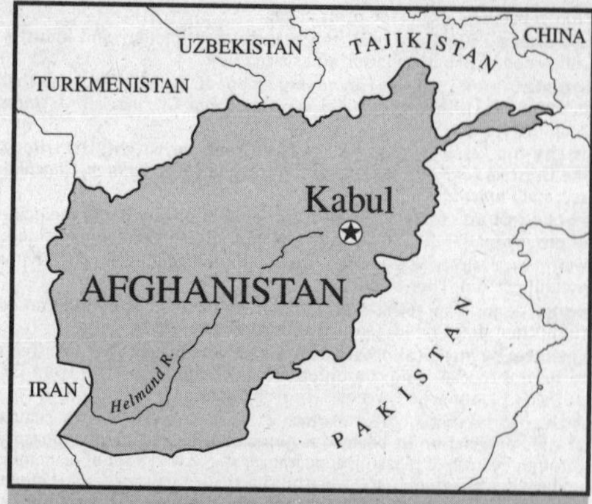

Afghanistan

Official name: Islamic State of Afghanistan
Location: central Asia, north and west of Pakistan
Area: 250,100 square miles (647,500 sq km)
Population: 16,600,000
Capital: Kabul
Languages: Pashto, Dari (local form of Persian)
Currency: afghani

a·fore·thought /ə'fôrˌᴛʜôt/ ▶ **adj.** see MALICE AFORETHOUGHT.

a for·ti·o·ri /'ä ˌfôrtē'ôrē; 'ā ˌfôrtē'ôrī/ ▶ **adv. & adj.** used to express a conclusion for which there is stronger evidence than for a previously accepted one. [17th C.: L., from *a fortiori argumento* 'from stronger argument.']

a·foul /ə'foul/ ▶ **adv.** into conflict or difficulty with.
– PHRASES **fall afoul of** see FALL. **run afoul of** see RUN.

a·fraid /ə'frād/ ▶ **adj.** [predic.] feeling fear or anxiety; frightened. ■ worried that something undesirable will occur or be done: *she was afraid of antagonizing him.* ■ unwilling or reluctant to do something for fear of the consequences. ■ **(afraid for)** anxious about the well-being or safety of someone or something: *William was suddenly afraid for her.*
– PHRASES **I'm afraid** [with clause] used to express polite or formal apology or regret: *I'm afraid I don't understand.* [ME: past part. of obs. v. *affray*, from Anglo-Norman Fr. *afrayer* (see AFFRAY).]

A-frame

A-frame ▶ **n.** a frame shaped like a capital letter A. ■ a house built around such a timber frame.

af·reet /'afrēt; ə'frēt/ (also **af·rit**) ▶ **n.** (in Arabian and Muslim mythology) a powerful jinn or demon. [18th C.: from Arab. *ifrīt*.]

a·fresh /ə'fresʜ/ ▶ **adv.** in a new or different way.

Af·ri·ca /'afrikə/ the second largest continent (11.62 million square miles; 30.1 million sq km), a southward projection of the Old World landmass divided roughly in half by the equator and surrounded by sea except where the Isthmus of Suez joins it to Asia. *See box on next page.*

Af·ri·can /'afrikən/ ▶ **n.** a person from Africa, esp. a black person. ■ a person of black African descent. ▶ **adj.** of or relating to Africa or people of African descent. [from L. *Africanus*, from *Africa (terra)* '(land) of the *Afri*,' ancient people of North Africa.]

Af·ri·can A·mer·i·can ▶ **n.** a black American. ▶ **adj. (African-American)** of or relating to black Americans.
– USAGE **African American** is the currently accepted term in the US, having first become prominent in the 1980s. See also usage at BLACK.

Af·ri·can buf·fa·lo ▶ **n.** another term for CAPE BUFFALO.

Af·ri·can dai·sy ▶ **n.** a plant of the daisy family (*Arctotis, Gerbera*, and other genera), sometimes cultivated for its bright flowers.

Af·ri·can el·e·phant ▶ **n.** the elephant (*Loxodonta africana*) native to Africa. Larger than the Indian elephant, it has larger ears and a two-lipped trunk. See illustration at ELEPHANT.

Af·ri·can·ism /'afrikəˌnizəm/ ▶ **n. 1** a feature of language or culture

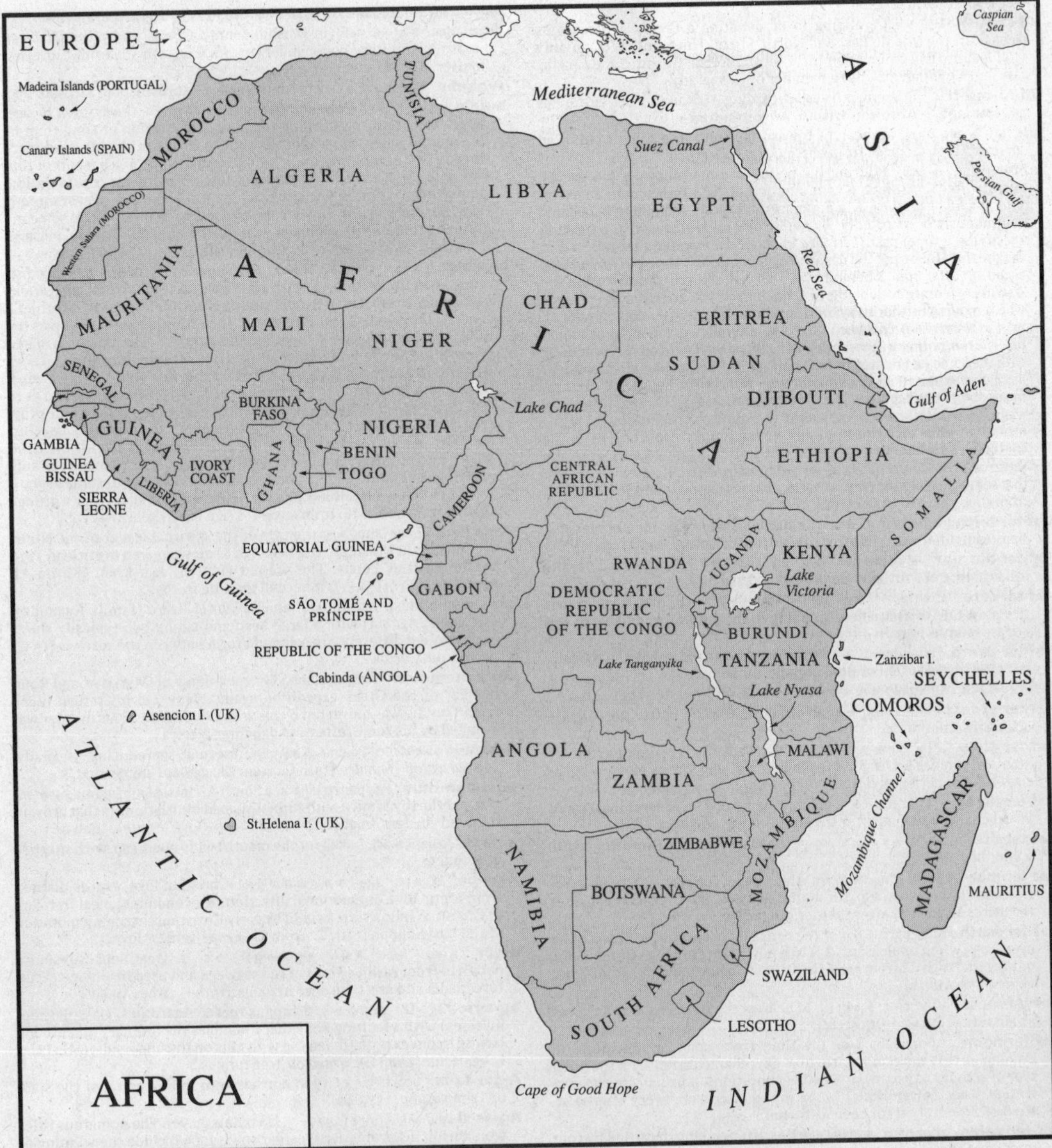

regarded as characteristically African. **2** the belief that black Africans and their culture should predominate in Africa.

Af·ri·can·ist /ˈafrikənist/ ▶ **n.** **1** someone who studies the culture, history, and languages of Africa. **2** someone who espouses a belief in Africanism.

Af·ri·can·ize /ˈafrikəˌnīz/ ▶ **v.** [trans.] **1** make African in character. ■ (in Africa) restructure (an organization) by replacing white employees with black Africans. **2** [usu. as adj.] (**Africanized**) hybridize (honeybees of European stock) with bees of African stock, producing an aggressive strain. In recent years hybrids have spread from Brazil to the US, where they have become known colloquially as "killer bees." — **Af·ri·can·i·za·tion** /ˌafrikənəˈzāshən/ **n.**

Af·ri·can Na·tion·al Con·gress (abbr.: **ANC**) a South African political party and black nationalist organization. Having been banned by the South African government 1960–90, the ANC was victorious in the country's first democratic elections in 1994 and its leader, Nelson Mandela, became the country's president.

Af·ri·can vi·o·let ▶ **n.** a small East African plant (genus *Saintpaulia*, family Gesneriaceae) with heart-shaped velvety leaves and violet, pink, or white flowers, widely cultivated as a houseplant.

Af·ri·kaans /ˌafriˈkänz/ ▶ **n.** a language of southern Africa, derived from the form of Dutch brought to the Cape by Protestant settlers in the 17th century, and an official language of South Africa. ▶ **adj.** relating to the Afrikaner people, their way of life, or their language. [Afrik., from Du., lit. 'African.']

Af·ri·ka Korps /ˈafrikə ˌkôr; ˈäfrēkä/ a German army force sent to North Africa in 1941 under General Rommel.

Af·ri·kan·der /ˌafriˈkandər/ ▶ **n.** an animal of a South African breed of sheep or longhorn cattle. [19th C. (an early form of **Afrikaner**, having the same senses): via Afrik. from South Afr. Du.]

Af·ri·ka·ner /ˌafriˈkänər/ ▶ **n.** an Afrikaans-speaking person in South Africa, esp. one descended from the Dutch and Huguenot settlers of the 17th century. [Afrik., based on Du. *Afrikaan* 'an Afr.' + personal suffix *-der*.]

af·rit ▶ **n.** var. of **afreet**.

Af·ro /ˈafrō/ ▶ **n.** a thick hairstyle with very tight curls that sticks out all around the head, like the natural hair of some black people. [1930s: from **Afro-**, or abbrev. of **African**.]

Afro- ▶ **comb. form** African; African and ...: *Afro-Asiatic* | *Afro-Belizean*. ■ relating to Africa: *Afrocentric*. [from L. *Afer, Afr-* 'Afr.']

Af·ro-A·mer·i·can ▶ **adj. & n.** another term for **African American**.
– USAGE The term **Afro-American**, first recorded in the 19th century and popular in the 1960s and 1970s, has now largely given way to **African American** as the current accepted term in the US for black American.

See also usage at **BLACK**.

Af·ro-A·si·at·ic ▶ **adj.** relating to or denoting a family of languages spoken in the Middle East and North Africa. The family is commonly divided into five groups: Semitic, Omotic, Berber, Cushitic, and Chadic. Ancient Egyptian was also a member of this family.

Af·ro·cen·tric /ˌafrōˈsentrik/ ▶ **adj.** regarding African or black culture as preeminent. — **Af·ro·cen·trism** n. **Af·ro·cen·trist** n.

aft /aft/ ▶ **adv. & adj.** at, near, or toward the stern of a ship or tail of an aircraft. [17th C.: prob. from obs. *baft* (see **ABAFT**).]

af·ter /ˈaftər/ ▶ **prep. 1** during the period of time following (an event): *shortly after Christmas.* ■ with a period of time rather than an event: *after a while he returned.* ■ in phrases indicating something happening continuously or repeatedly: ***day after day*** *we kept studying.* ■ (used in specifying a time) past: *I strolled in about ten minutes after two.* ■ during the time following the departure of (someone): *she cooks for him and cleans up after him.* **2** behind: *she went out, shutting the door after her.* ■ (with reference to looking or speaking) in the direction of someone who is moving further away: *she stared after him.* **3** in pursuit or quest of: *most of them are after money.* **4** next to and following in order or importance: *x comes after y in the series.* **5** in allusion to (someone or something with the same or a related name): *they named her Pauline, after Barbara's mother.* ■ in imitation of: *a drawing after Millet's* The Reapers. **6** concerning or about: *she has asked after Iris's mother.* ▶ **adj.** [attrib.] **1** archaic later: *he was sorry in after years.* **2** Naut. nearer the stern: *the after cabin.*

– PHRASES **after all** in spite of any indications or expectations to the contrary. **after hours** after normal working or opening hours, typically those of licensed premises. **after you** a polite formula used to suggest that someone goes in front of or takes a turn before oneself. [OE *æfter*, from Gmc.; akin to Du. *achter*.]

af·ter·birth /ˈaftərˌbərTH/ ▶ **n.** the placenta and fetal membranes discharged from the uterus after the birth of offspring.

af·ter·burn·er /ˈaftərˌbərnər/ ▶ **n.** an auxiliary burner fitted to the exhaust pipe of a turbojet engine to increase thrust.

af·ter·care /ˈaftərˌke(ə)r/ ▶ **n.** subsequent care or maintenance, in particular: ■ care of a patient after a stay in the hospital or of a person on release from prison.

af·ter·damp /ˈaftərˌdamp/ ▶ **n.** choking gas, rich in carbon monoxide, left after an explosion of firedamp in a mine.

af·ter·deck /ˈaftərˌdek/ ▶ **n.** an open deck toward the stern of a ship.

af·ter·ef·fect /ˈaftəriˌfekt/ ▶ **n.** an effect that follows after the primary action of something.

af·ter·glow /ˈaftərˌglō/ ▶ **n.** [in sing.] light or radiance remaining in the sky after the sun has set. ■ good feelings remaining after a pleasurable or successful experience: *basking in the afterglow of victory.*

af·ter·im·age /ˈaftərˌimij/ ▶ **n.** an impression of a vivid sensation (esp. a visual image) retained after the stimulus has ceased.

af·ter·life /ˈaftərˌlīf/ ▶ **n.** [usu. in sing.] **1** (in some religions) life after death. **2** later life.

af·ter·mar·ket /ˈaftərˌmärkit/ ▶ **n.** the market for spare parts, accessories, and components, esp. for motor vehicles. ■ Stock Market the market for shares and bonds after their original issue.

af·ter·math /ˈaftərˌmaTH/ ▶ **n. 1** the consequences or aftereffects of an event, esp. when unpleasant. **2** Farming new grass growing after mowing or harvest. [15th C.: from **AFTER** (adj.) + dial. *math* 'mowing,' from Gmc.; akin to Ger. *Mahd*.]

af·ter·most /ˈaftərˌmōst/ ▶ **adj.** [attrib.] nearest the stern of a ship or tail of an aircraft. [18th C.: from **AFTER**.]

af·ter·noon /ˌaftərˈno͞on/ ▶ **n.** the time from noon or lunchtime to evening. ■ this time on a particular day, characterized by a specified type of activity or particular weather conditions: *it was an afternoon of tension.* ▶ **adv.** (**afternoons**) informal in the afternoon; every afternoon. ▶ **exclam.** informal short for **GOOD AFTERNOON**.

af·ter·pains /ˈaftərˌpānz/ ▶ **plural n.** pains after childbirth caused by contraction of the uterus.

af·ters /ˈaftərz/ ▶ **plural n.** Brit., informal dessert.

af·ter·shave /ˈaftərˌSHāv/ ▶ **n.** an astringent, typically scented lotion for applying to the skin after shaving.

af·ter·shock /ˈaftərˌSHäk/ ▶ **n.** a smaller earthquake following the main shock of a large earthquake.

af·ter·taste /ˈaftərˌtāst/ ▶ **n.** a taste, typically an unpleasant one, remaining in the mouth after eating or drinking something.

af·ter-tax ▶ **adj.** relating to income that remains after the deduction of taxes due.

af·ter·thought /ˈaftərˌTHôt/ ▶ **n.** an item or thing that is thought of or added later.

af·ter·touch /ˈaftərˌtəCH/ ▶ **n.** a facility on an electronic music keyboard by which an effect is produced by the player depressing a key after striking it.

af·ter·ward /ˈaftərwərd/ (also **af·ter·wards**) ▶ **adv.** at a later or future time; subsequently. [OE *æftewearde*, from *æftan* (see **AFT**) + **-WARD**.]

af·ter·word /ˈaftərˌwərd/ ▶ **n.** a concluding section in a book, typically by a person other than the author.

af·ter·world /ˈaftərˌwərld/ ▶ **n.** a world supposedly entered after death.

AG ▶ **abbr.** ■ adjutant general. ■ attorney general.

Ag[1] ▶ **symb.** the chemical element silver. [from L. *argentum*.]

Ag[2] Biochem. ▶ **abbr.** antigen.

ag informal ▶ **adj.** short for **AGRICULTURAL**. ▶ **n.** short for **AGRICULTURE**.

ag- ▶ **prefix** var. of **AD-** assimilated before *g* (as in *aggravate, aggress*).

a·ga /ˈägə/ ▶ **n.** esp. hist. (in Muslim countries, esp. under the Ottoman Empire) a military commander or official. [16th C.: from Turk. *ağa* 'master' from Mongolian *aqa*.]

A·ga·dir /ˌägəˈdi(ə)r/ a city in southwestern Morocco; pop. 110,500.

a·gain /əˈgen; əˈgān/ ▶ **adv.** another time; once more: *it was great to meet old friends again.* ■ returning to a previous position or condition: *he rose and sat down again.* ■ in addition to what has already been mentioned: *the wages were low, but they made half as much again in tips.* ■ [sentence adverb] used to introduce a further point for consideration, supporting or contrasting with what has just been said: *I never saw any signs, but* ***then again****, maybe I wasn't looking.* ■ used to ask someone to repeat something: *what was your name again?* [OE *ongēan, ongægn*, from Gmc.; akin to Ger. *entgegen* 'opposite.']

a·gainst /əˈgenst; əˈgānst/ ▶ **prep. 1** in opposition to: *the fight against crime.* ■ in opposition to, with reference to legal action: *allegations against police officers.* ■ in opposition to, with reference to an athletic contest: *the game against Virginia.* ■ (in betting) in anticipation of the failure of: *the odds were 5–1 against Pittsburgh.* **2** in anticipation of and preparation for (a problem or difficulty): *insurance against sickness.* ■ in resistance to; as protection from: *he turned up his collar against the wind.* ■ in relation to (an amount of money owed or due) so as to reduce or cancel it: *money was advanced against the value of the property.* **3** in conceptual contrast to: *the benefits must be weighed against the costs.* ■ in visual contrast to: *he was silhouetted against the light.* **4** in or into physical contact with (something), typically so as to be supported by or collide with it: *she stood with her back against the door.*

– PHRASES **have something against someone** dislike or bear a grudge against someone. [ME: from **AGAIN** + *-s* (adverbial genitive) + *-t*.]

A·ga Khan /ˌägə ˈkän/ ▶ **n.** the title of the spiritual leader of the Nizari sect of Ismaili Muslims. The first Aga Khan was given his title in 1818 by the shah of Persia. The present (fourth) Aga Khan (Karim Al-Hussain Shah (1937–)) inherited the title in 1957.

ag·a·ma /əˈgāmə; ˈagəmə/ ▶ **n.** an Old World lizard (family Agamidae, esp. genus *Agama*) with a large head and a long tail, typically showing a marked difference in color and form between the sexes. [18th C.: perh. from Carib.]

Ag·a·mem·non /ˌagəˈmemˌnän/ Gk. Mythol. king of Mycenae and commander of the Greek expedition against Troy. On his return home from Troy, he was murdered by his wife Clytemnestra; his murder was avenged by his son Orestes and daughter Electra.

a·gam·ic /āˈgamik; əˈgam-/ ▶ **adj.** Biol. asexual; reproducing asexually: *winged agamic females.* [19th C.: from Gk. *agamos* 'unmarried.']

ag·a·pan·thus /ˌagəˈpanTHəs/ ▶ **n.** a South African plant (genus *Agapanthus*) of the lily family, with funnel-shaped bluish flowers that grow in rounded clusters. [mod. L., from Gk. *agapē* 'love' + *anthos* 'flower.']

a·gape[1] /əˈgāp/ ▶ **adj.** [predic.] (of the mouth) wide open, esp. with surprise or wonder.

a·ga·pe[2] /äˈgäˌpā; ˈägə-/ ▶ **n.** Christian Theol. Christian love, esp. as distinct from erotic love or emotional affection. ■ a communal meal in token of Christian fellowship, as held by early Christians in commemoration of the Last Supper. [17th C.: from Gk. *agapē* 'selfless love.']

a·gar /ˈäˌgär; ˈāˌgär/ (also **a·gar-a·gar**) ▶ **n.** a gelatinous substance obtained from various kinds of red seaweed and used in biological culture media and as a thickener in foods. [19th C.: from Malay.]

ag·a·ric /ˈagərik; əˈgar-/ ▶ **n.** a fungus (order Agaricales, class Basidiomycetes) with a fruiting body that resembles the ordinary mushroom, having a convex or flattened cap with gills on the underside. [ME: from L. *agaricum*, from Gk. *agarikon* 'tree fungus.']

A·gar·ta·la /ˌəgərtəˈlä/ a city in northeastern India, capital of the state of Tripura; pop. 157,640.

Ag·as·si /ˈagəsē/, André (1970–), US tennis player. The numerous titles won during his professional career 1986–2006 include the winning of all four Grand Slam singles events.

Ag·as·siz /ˈagəsē/, Jean Louis Rodolphe (1807–73), US zoologist, geologist, and paleontologist; born in Switzerland. In 1837, he proposed that much of Europe had once been in the grip of an ice age.

Ag·as·siz, Lake /ˈagəsē/ a lake that covers parts of Minnesota and North Dakota in the US and Manitoba and Ontario in Canada.

ag·ate /ˈagit/ ▶ **n.** an ornamental stone consisting of a hard variety of chalcedony, typically banded in appearance. ■ a colored toy marble resembling a banded gemstone. [15th C.: from Fr., via L. from Gk. *akhatēs*.]

a·ga·ve /əˈgävē/ ▶ **n.** a succulent plant (genus *Agave*, family Agavaceae) with rosettes of narrow spiny leaves and tall flower spikes, native to the southern US and tropical America. [L., from Gk. *Agauē*, a daughter of Cadmus, from *agauos* 'illustrious.']

AGC Electron. ▶ **abbr.** automatic gain control.

age /āj/ ▶ **n. 1** the length of time that a person has lived or a thing has existed: *he died at the age of 51.* ■ a particular stage in someone's life: *children of primary school age.* ■ the latter part of life or existence; old age: *with age this gland can become sluggish.* **2** a distinct period of history: *a child of the television age.* ■ Geol. a division of time that is a subdivision of an epoch, corresponding to a stage in chronostratigraphy. ■ archaic a lifetime taken as a measure of time; a generation. ■ (**ages/an age**) informal a very long time: *I haven't seen her for ages.* ▶ **v.** (**ag·ing**) [intrans.] grow old or older, esp. visibly and obviously so: *you haven't aged a lot.* ■ [trans.] cause to grow, feel, or appear older: *he tried aging*

the painting with coffee. ■ (esp. with reference to an alcoholic drink) mature or allow to mature. ■ [trans.] determine how old (something) is: *we didn't have a clue how to age these animals.*
– PHRASES **act** (or **be**) **one's age** [usu. in imper.] behave in a manner appropriate to someone of one's age and not to someone much younger. **come of age** (of a person) reach adult status. ■ (of a movement or activity) become fully established. **through the ages** throughout history. [ME: from OFr., based on L. *aetas, aetat-*, from *aevum* 'age, era.']

-age ▶ suffix forming nouns: **1** denoting an action: *leverage* | *voyage.* ■ the product of an action: *spillage* | *wreckage.* ■ a function; a sphere of action: *homage* | *peerage.* **2** denoting an aggregate or number of: *mileage* | *percentage* | *signage.* ■ fees payable for; the cost of using: *postage* | *tonnage.* **3** denoting a place or abode: *vicarage* | *village.* [from OFr., based on L. *-aticum*, neut. of adjectival ending *-aticus.*]

aged /ājd/ ▶ adj. **1** [predic. or postpositive] having lived for a specified length of time; of a specified age: *he died aged 60.* **2** /ˈājid/ having lived or existed for a long time; old.

A·gee /ˈājē/, James Rufus (1909–55), US writer. He wrote *Let Us Now Praise Famous Men* (1941).

age group ▶ n. a number of people or things classed together as being of similar age.

age·ing /ˈājiNG/ ▶ adj. & n. var. of AGING.

age·ism /ˈāj,izəm/ (also **ag·ism**) ▶ n. prejudice or discrimination on the basis of a person's age. — **age·ist** (also **ag·ist**) adj. & n.

age·less /ˈājlis/ ▶ adj. never growing or appearing to grow old: *the town retains an ageless charm.* — **age·less·ness** n.

age-long ▶ adj. [attrib.] having existed for a very long time.

a·gen·cy /ˈājənsē/ ▶ n. **1** [often with adj.] a business or organization established to provide a particular service, typically one that involves organizing transactions between two other parties. ■ a department or body providing a specific service for a government or similar organization. **2** action or intervention, esp. such as to produce a particular effect: *a belief in supernatural agency.* ■ a thing or person that acts to produce a particular result.

a·gen·da /əˈjendə/ ▶ n. a list of items of business to be considered and discussed at a meeting. ■ a list or program of things to be done or problems to be addressed. [17th C.: from L., neut. pl. of *agendum*, gerund of *agere* 'do.']

a·gent /ˈājənt/ ▶ n. **1** a person who acts on behalf of another, in particular: ■ a person who manages business, financial, or contractual matters for an actor, performer, or writer. ■ a person or company that provides a particular service, typically one that involves organizing transactions between two other parties: *a travel agent.* ■ a person who obtains information for a government or other official body, typically in secret. **2** a person or thing that takes an active role or produces a specified effect: *agents of change* | *bleaching agents.* ■ Gram. the doer of an action, typically expressed as the subject of an active verb or in a *by* phrase with a passive verb. [ME: from L. *agent-* 'doing,' from v. *agere.*]

a·gent noun ▶ n. a noun denoting someone or something that performs the action of a verb, typically ending in *-er* or *-or*, e.g., *worker, accelerator.*

A·gent Or·ange ▶ n. a defoliant chemical used by the US in the Vietnam War.

a·gent pro·vo·ca·teur /ä,ZHän(t) prə,väkəˈtər/ ▶ n. (pl. **a·gents pro·vo·ca·teurs** pronunc. same or /-ˈtərz/) a person who induces others to break the law so that they can be convicted. [19th C.: Fr., lit. 'provocative agent.']

age of con·sent ▶ n. the age at which a person's, typically a girl's, consent to sexual intercourse is valid in law.

age of dis·cre·tion ▶ n. the age at which someone is considered able to manage their own affairs or take responsibility for their actions.

age-old ▶ adj. having existed for a very long time.

ag·glom·er·ate ▶ v. /əˈglämə,rāt/ collect or form into a mass or group. ▶ n. /-rit/ a mass or collection of things. ■ Geol. a volcanic rock consisting of large fragments bonded together. ▶ adj. /-rit/ collected or formed into a mass. — **ag·glom·er·a·tion** /ə,gläməˈrāSHən/ n. **ag·glom·er·a·tive** /-ə,rātiv; -ərətiv/ adj. [17th C.: from L. *agglomerat-* 'added to,' from v. *agglomerare*, from *ad-* + *glomerare* (from *glomus* 'ball').]

ag·glu·ti·nate /əˈglo͞otn,āt/ ▶ v. firmly stick or be stuck together to form a mass. ■ Biol. (with reference to bacteria or red blood cells) clump together. ■ [trans.] Ling. combine (simple words or parts of words) without change of form to express compound ideas. — **ag·glu·ti·na·tion** /ə,glo͞otnˈāSHən/ n. [16th C.: from L. *agglutinat-* 'caused to adhere,' from v. *agglutinare*, from *ad-* 'to' + *glutinare* (from *gluten* 'glue').]

ag·glu·ti·na·tive /əˈglo͞otn-ətiv/ ▶ adj. Ling. (of a language) forming words predominantly by agglutination.

ag·glu·ti·nin /əˈglo͞otn-in/ ▶ n. Biol. an antibody, lectin, or other substance that causes agglutination. [19th C.: from AGGLUTINATE.]

ag·glu·tin·o·gen /əˈglo͞otn-əjən/ ▶ n. Biol. an antigen that stimulates the production of an agglutinin.

ag·gra·da·tion /,agrəˈdāSHən/ ▶ n. the deposition of material by a river, stream, or current. [19th C.: from AG- + *(de)gradation.*]

ag·gran·dize /əˈgran,dīz/ ▶ v. [trans.] increase the power, status, or wealth of. ■ enhance the reputation of (someone) beyond what is justified by the facts. — **ag·gran·dize·ment** /-,dīzmənt; -diz-/ n. **ag·gran·diz·er** n. [17th C.: from Fr. *agrandiss-*, from *agrandir*, prob. from Ital. *aggrandire*, from L. *grandis* 'large.']

ag·gra·vate /ˈagrə,vāt/ ▶ v. [trans.] **1** make (a problem, injury, or offense) worse or more serious. **2** informal annoy or exasperate (someone), esp. persistently. — **ag·gra·vat·ing·ly** adv. **ag·gra·va·tion** /,agrəˈvāSHən/ n. [16th C.: from L. *aggravat-* 'made heavy,' from v. *aggravare*, from *ad-* 'to' + *gravis* 'heavy.']

ag·gra·vat·ed /ˈagrə,vātid/ ▶ adj. [attrib.] (of an offense) made more serious by attendant circumstances (such as frame of mind): *aggravated burglary.*

ag·gre·gate ▶ n. /ˈagrigit/ **1** a whole formed by combining several (typically disparate) elements. **2** a material or structure formed from a loosely compacted mass of fragments or particles. ■ pieces of broken or crushed stone or gravel used to make concrete. ▶ adj. [attrib.] /-git/ formed or calculated by the combination of many separate units or items; total: *the aggregate amount of grants made.* ■ Bot. (of a group of species) comprising several very similar species formerly regarded as a single species. ■ Econ. denoting the total supply or demand for goods and services in an economy at a particular time: *aggregate demand.* ▶ v. /-,gāt/ form or group into a class or cluster.
– PHRASES **in (the) aggregate** in total; as a whole. — **ag·gre·ga·tion** /,agriˈgāSHən/ n. **ag·gre·ga·tive** /-,gātiv/ adj. [ME: from L. *aggregat-* 'herded together,' from v. *aggregare*, from *ad-* + *grex, greg-* 'a flock.']

ag·gre·gate fruit ▶ n. Bot. a fruit formed from several carpels derived from the same flower, e.g., a raspberry.

ag·gre·ga·tor /ˈagri,gātər/ ▶ n. **1** Computing an Internet company that collects information about competing products and services and distributes it through a single Web site: *a travel insurance aggregator.* **2** a wholesale buyer or broker of a utility service, such as electricity or long-distance telephone service, who packages it and sells it to consumers.

ag·gres·sion /əˈgreSHən/ ▶ n. hostile or violent behavior or attitudes toward another; readiness to attack or confront. ■ the action of attacking without provocation, esp. in beginning a quarrel or war: *the dictator resorted to armed aggression.* ■ forceful and sometimes overly assertive pursuit of one's aims and interests. [17th C.: from L. *aggressio(n-)*, from *aggredi* 'to attack,' from *ad-* 'toward' + *gradi* 'proceed.']

ag·gres·sive /əˈgresiv/ ▶ adj. ready or likely to attack or confront; characterized by or resulting from aggression. ■ pursuing one's aims and interests forcefully, sometimes unduly so: *an aggressive businessman.* — **ag·gres·sive·ly** adv. **ag·gres·sive·ness** n.

ag·gres·sor /əˈgresər/ ▶ n. a person or country that attacks another first.

ag·grieved /əˈgrēvd/ ▶ adj. feeling resentment at having been unfairly treated. — **ag·griev·ed·ly** /əˈgrēvidlē/ adv. [ME: past part. of *aggrieve*, from OFr. *agrever* 'make heavier,' based on L. *aggravare* (see AGGRAVATE).]

ag·gro /ˈagrō/ ▶ n. Brit., informal aggressive, violent behavior. ■ problems and difficulties. [1960s: abbrev. of *aggravation* or AGGRESSION.]

a·ghast /əˈgast/ ▶ adj. [predic.] filled with horror or shock: *when the news came out they were aghast.* [ME: past part. of the obs. v. *agast, gast* 'frighten,' from OE *gǣsten.*]

ag·ile /ˈajəl/ ▶ adj. able to move quickly and easily: *as agile as a monkey* | fig. *an agile mind.* — **ag·ile·ly** /ˈajə(l)lē/ adv. **a·gil·i·ty** /əˈjilitē/ n. [ME: via Fr. from L. *agilis*, from *agere* 'do.']

a·gin /əˈgin/ ▶ prep. dialect form of AGAINST. [19th C.: var. of obs. *again* 'against.']

Ag·in·court, Bat·tle of /ˈajin,kôrt; äZHänˈko͝or/ a battle in northern France in 1415 during the Hundred Years War, in which the English under Henry V defeated a large French army.

ag·ing /ˈājiNG/ (also **age·ing**) ▶ n. the process of growing old. ■ the process of change in the properties of a material occurring over a period, either spontaneously or through deliberate action. ▶ adj. (of a person) growing old; elderly.

ag·i·tate /ˈaji,tāt/ ▶ v. [trans.] make (someone) troubled or nervous. ■ [intrans.] campaign to arouse public concern about an issue in the hope of prompting action: *they agitated for a reversal.* ■ stir or disturb (something, esp. a liquid) briskly. — **ag·i·tat·ed·ly** adv. [ME: from L. *agitat-* 'agitated,' from *agitare*, frequentative of *agere* 'do.']

ag·i·ta·tion /,ajiˈtāSHən/ ▶ n. **1** a state of anxiety or nervous excitement. ■ the action of arousing public concern about an issue and pressing for action on it. **2** the action of briskly stirring or disturbing something, esp. a liquid.

a·gi·ta·to /,ajiˈtätō/ ▶ adv. & adj. Music (esp. as a direction after a tempo marking) in an agitated manner. [Ital., lit. 'agitated.']

ag·i·ta·tor /ˈaji,tātər/ ▶ n. **1** a person who urges others to protest or rebel. **2** an apparatus for stirring liquid, as in a washing machine or a photographic developing tank.

ag·it·prop /ˈajit,präp/ ▶ n. political (originally communist) propaganda, esp. in art or literature: [as adj.] *agitprop painters.* [1930s: Russ., blend of *agitatsiya* 'agitation' and *propaganda* 'propaganda.']

a·gleam /əˈglēm/ ▶ adj. [predic.] gleaming.

ag·let /ˈaglit/ ▶ n. a metal or plastic tube fixed tightly around each end of a shoelace. [ME: from Fr. *aiguillette*, dimin. of *aiguille* 'needle.' (see AIGUILLE).]

a·gley /əˈglā; əˈglē/ ▶ adv. Scot. askew; awry. [18th C.: from A-[2] + Scots *gley* 'squint.']

a·glow /əˈglō/ ▶ adj. [predic.] glowing.

ag·ma /ˈagmə/ ▶**n.** the speech sound represented by *ng* as in *thing*, a velar nasal consonant. ■ represented by ŋ in the International Phonetic Alphabet. [1950s: ult. from Gk., 'fragment.']

ag·nail /ˈagˌnāl/ ▶**n.** another term for HANGNAIL.

ag·nate /ˈagˌnāt/ esp. Law ▶**n.** a person descended from the same male ancestor as another specified or implied person, esp. through the male line. ▶**adj.** descended from the same male ancestor as a specified or implied subject, esp. through the male line. ■ of the same clan or nation. — **ag·nat·ic** /agˈnatik/ **adj.** **ag·na·tion** /agˈnāsHən/ **n.** [15th C. (n.): from L. *agnatus*, from *ad-* 'to' + *gnatus*, *natus* 'born.']

Ag·na·tha /ˈagnəTHə/ Zool. a group of primitive jawless vertebrates (superclass Agnatha) that includes the lampreys, hagfishes, and many fossil fishlike forms. — **ag·na·than** **n. & adj.** [from mod. L. *Agnatha*, from A-[1] + Gk. *gnathos* 'jaw.']

Ag·nes, St.[1] /ˈagnəs/ (died c.304), Roman martyr. She is the patron saint of virgins.

Ag·ni /ˈagnē; ˈəg-/ the Vedic god of fire, the priest of the gods and the god of the priests.

ag·no·sia /agˈnōzH(ē)ə/ ▶**n.** Med. inability to interpret sensations and hence to recognize things, typically as a result of brain damage. [20th C.: ult. from Gk. *agnōsia* 'ignorance.']

ag·nos·tic /agˈnästik/ ▶**n.** a person who believes that nothing is known or can be known of the existence or nature of God or of anything beyond material phenomena; a person who claims neither faith nor disbelief in God. ▶**adj.** of or relating to agnostics or agnosticism. — **ag·nos·ti·cism** /-təˌsizəm/ **n.** [19th C.: from A-[1] + GNOSTIC.]

Ag·nus De·i /ˈägnəs ˈdāˌē; ˈdēˌī; ˈänyo͞os/ ▶**n.** **1** a figure of a lamb bearing a cross or flag, as an emblem of Christ. **2** Christian Church an invocation beginning with the words "Lamb of God" forming a set part of the Mass. ■ a musical setting of this. [ME: from L., 'Lamb of God.']

a·go /əˈgō/ ▶**adv.** (used after a measurement of time) before the present; earlier: *he went five minutes ago.* [ME *ago*, *agone*, past part. of the obs. *ago* 'to pass.']

a·gog /əˈgäg/ ▶**adj.** [predic.] very eager or curious to hear or see something: *I'm all agog to see London.* [16th C.: from OFr. *en gogues*, from *en* 'in' + pl. of *gogue* 'fun.']

a go·go /ə ˈgōˌgō/ ▶**adj.** [postpositive] informal in abundance; galore: *Gershwin a gogo—all the hits.* [1960s: from Fr. *à gogo*, from OFr. *gogue* 'fun.']

a·gon·ic line /āˈgänik/ ▶**n.** an imaginary line around the earth passing through both the north pole and the north magnetic pole, at any point on which a compass needle points to true north. [19th C.: from Gk. *agōnios*, *agōnos*, from *a-* 'without' + *gonia* 'angle.']

ag·o·nist /ˈagənist/ ▶**n.** **1** Biochem. a substance that initiates a physiological response when combined with a receptor. **2** Anat. a muscle whose contraction moves a part of the body directly. **3** another term for PROTAGONIST. — **ag·o·nism** /-ˌnizəm/ **n.** [20th C.: from Gk. *agōnistēs* 'contestant,' from *agōn* 'contest.']

ag·o·nis·tic /ˌagəˈnistik/ ▶**adj.** combative; polemical. ■ Zool. (of animal behavior) associated with conflict. ■ Biochem. of, relating to, or acting as an agonist. — **ag·o·nis·ti·cal·ly** /-ik(ə)lē/ **adv.**

ag·o·nize /ˈagəˌnīz/ ▶**v.** [intrans.] undergo great mental anguish through worrying about something. ■ [trans.] cause mental anguish to (someone). [16th C.: from Fr. *agoniser* or late L. *agonizare*, from Gk. *agōnizesthai* 'contend,' from *agōn* 'contest.']

ag·o·nized /ˈagəˌnīzd/ ▶**adj.** manifesting, suffering, or characterized by great physical or mental pain.

ag·o·niz·ing /ˈagəˌnīziNG/ (also **ag·o·nis·ing**) ▶**adj.** causing great physical or mental pain. — **ag·o·niz·ing·ly** **adv.** [as submodifier] *agonizingly slow steps.*

ag·o·ny /ˈagənē/ ▶**n.** (pl. **-nies**) extreme physical or mental suffering. ■ [with adj.] the final stages of a difficult or painful death: *his last agony.* [ME: ult. from Gk. *agōnia*, from *agōn* 'contest.']

ag·o·ny col·umn ▶**n.** Brit., informal a column in a newspaper or magazine offering advice on personal problems to readers who write in.

ag·o·ra[1] /ˈagərə/ ▶**n.** (pl. **-rae** /-rē/ or **-ras**) (in ancient Greece) a public open space used for assemblies and markets.

a·go·ra[2] /əˈgôrə; ˌägōˈrä/ ▶**n.** (pl. **a·go·rot** /əˈgôrōt; ˌägōˈrōt/ or **a·go·roth** /əˈgôrōt; ˌägōˈrōt/) a monetary unit of Israel, equal to one hundredth of a shekel. [from Heb. *ăgōrāh* 'small coin.']

ag·o·ra·pho·bi·a /ˌagərəˈfōbēə/ ▶**n.** extreme or irrational fear of crowded spaces or enclosed public places. — **ag·o·ra·pho·bic** /-ˈfōbik/ **adj. & n.** **ag·o·ra·phobe** /ˈagərəˌfōb/ **n.** [19th C.: from Gk. *agora* 'marketplace.']

a·gou·ti /əˈgo͞otē/ ▶**n.** (pl. same or **-tis**) a large, long-legged burrowing rodent (genera *Agouti* and *Dasyprocta*, family Dasyproctidae) related to the guinea pig, native to Central and South America. ■ fur in which each hair has alternate dark and light bands, producing a grizzled appearance. ■ a rodent, esp. a mouse, having fur of this type. [16th C.: via Fr. or from Sp. *aguti*, from Tupi *akutí*.]

A·gra /ˈägrə/ a city in northern India, on the Jumna River, in Uttar Pradesh state; pop. 899,000. It is the site of the Taj Mahal.

a·gran·u·lo·cy·to·sis /āˌgranyəˌlōsīˈtōsis/ ▶**n.** Med. a deficiency of granulocytes in the blood, causing increased vulnerability to infection.

a·grar·i·an /əˈgre(ə)rēən/ ▶**adj.** of or relating to cultivated land or the cultivation of land. ■ relating to landed property. ▶**n.** a person who advocates a redistribution of landed property. [17th C.: from L. *agrarius*, from *ager*, *agr-* 'field.']

a·gree /əˈgrē/ ▶**v.** (**a·grees, a·greed, a·gree·ing**) [intrans.] **1** have the same opinion about something; concur: *I completely agree with your recent editorial* | [with clause] *the authors agree that Jerusalem must remain united.* ■ (**agree with**) approve of (something) with regard to its moral correctness: *I'm not sure I agree with abortion.* **2** (**agree to** or **to do something**) consent to do something that has been suggested by another person: *agreed to go.* ■ [intrans.] reach agreement about (something), typically after a period of negotiation. **3** (**agree with**) be consistent with. ■ Gram. have the same number, gender, case, or person as: *the verb must agree with the subject.* ■ [usu. with negative] be healthy or appropriate for someone: *she's eaten something that did not agree with her.*

– PHRASES **agree to differ** see DIFFER. [ME: from OFr. *agreer*, based on L. *ad-* 'to' + *gratus* 'pleasing.']

a·gree·a·ble /əˈgrēəbəl/ ▶**adj.** **1** enjoyable and pleasurable; pleasant. **2** [predic.] willing to agree to something: *they were agreeable to its publication.* ■ (of a course of action) acceptable. — **a·gree·a·ble·ness** **n.** **a·gree·a·bly** /-blē/ **adv.** [as submodifier] *an agreeably warm day.*

a·greed /əˈgrēd/ ▶**adj.** [attrib.] discussed or negotiated and then accepted by all parties: *the agreed time.* ■ [predic.] (of two or more parties) holding the same view on something: *all the republics are agreed on the policy.*

a·gree·ment /əˈgrēmənt/ ▶**n.** harmony or accordance in opinion or feeling; a position or result of agreeing. ■ a negotiated and typically legally binding arrangement between parties as to a course of action: *a trade agreement.* ■ the absence of incompatibility between two things; consistency: *agreement between observations and theory.* ■ Gram. the condition of having the same number, gender, case, or person.

a·gres·tic /əˈgrestik/ ▶**adj.** esp. poetic or literary of or relating to the country; rural; rustic. [17th C.: from L. *agrestis*, from *ager*, *agr-* 'field' + -IC.]

agri- ▶**comb. form** var. of AGRO-: *agriculture* | *agribusiness.*

ag·ri·busi·ness /ˈagrəˌbiznis/ ▶**n.** **1** agriculture conducted on commercial principles, esp. using advanced technology. ■ an organization engaged in this. **2** the group of industries dealing with agricultural produce and services required in farming. — **ag·ri·busi·ness·man** /ˌagrəˈbiznismən/ **n.** (pl. **-men**). [1950s (US): blend of AGRICULTURE and BUSINESS.]

A·gric·o·la /əˈgrikələ/, Gnaeus Julius (AD 40–93), Roman general; governor of Britain 78–84.

ag·ri·cul·tur·al /ˌagriˈkəlCHərəl/ ▶**adj.** of or relating to agriculture. — **ag·ri·cul·tur·al·ist** /-ist/ **n.** **ag·ri·cul·tur·al·ly** **adv.**

ag·ri·cul·ture /ˈagriˌkəlCHər/ ▶**n.** the science or practice of farming, including cultivation of the soil for the growing of crops and the rearing of animals to provide food, wool, and other products. — **ag·ri·cul·tur·ist** /-rist/ **n.** [ME: from L. *agricultura*, from *ager*, *agr-* 'field' + *cultura* 'cultivation.']

ag·ri·mo·ny /ˈagrəˌmōnē/ ▶**n.** (pl. **-nies**) a plant (genus *Agrimonia*) of the rose family bearing slender flower spikes and spiny fruits. [ME: ult. from L. *agrimonia*, alt. of *argemonia*, from Gk. *argemōnē* 'poppy.']

A·grip·pa /əˈgripə/, Marcus Vipsanius (63–12 BC), Roman general. He played an important part in the naval victories over Mark Antony.

agro- (also **agri-**) ▶**comb. form** agricultural: *agro-industry* | *agrobiology* | *agribusiness.* ■ agriculture and ...: *agroforestry.* [from Gk. *agros* 'field.']

ag·ro·bi·ol·o·gy /ˌagrōbīˈäləjē/ ▶**n.** the study of soil science and plant nutrition and its application to crops. — **ag·ro·bi·o·log·i·cal** /-ˌbīəˈläjikəl/ **adj.** **ag·ro·bi·ol·o·gist** **n.**

ag·ro·chem·i·cal /ˌagrōˈkemikəl/ ▶**n.** a chemical used in agriculture, such as a pesticide or a fertilizer.

ag·ro·for·est·ry /ˌagrōˈfôrəstrē; -ˈfär-/ ▶**n.** agriculture incorporating the cultivation and conservation of trees.

ag·ro·in·dus·try ▶**n.** industry connected with agriculture. ■ agriculture developed along industrial lines. — **ag·ro·in·dus·tri·al** **adj.**

a·grol·o·gy /əˈgräləjē/ ▶**n.** Canadian the application of science to agriculture. — **a·grol·o·gist** **n.**

a·gron·o·my /əˈgränəmē/ ▶**n.** the science of soil management and crop production. — **ag·ro·nom·ic** /ˌagrəˈnämik/ **adj.** **ag·ro·nom·i·cal** /ˌagrəˈnämikəl/ **adj.** **a·gron·o·mist** **n.** [19th C.: from Fr. *agronomie*, based on Gk. *agros* 'field' + *-nomos* 'arranging' (from *nemein* 'arrange').]

Agro Pontino Italian name for PONTINE MARSHES.

ag·ros·tol·o·gy /ˌagrəˈstäləjē/ ▶**n.** the branch of botany concerned with grasses. [19th C.: from Gk. *agrōstis* (a grass).]

a·ground /əˈground/ ▶**adj. & adv.** (with reference to a ship) on or onto the bottom in shallow water.

a·guar·dien·te /ˌägwärˈdyentā/ ▶**n.** (in Spanish-speaking regions) a distilled liquor resembling brandy, esp. as made in South America from sugar cane. [from Sp., from *agua* 'water' + *ardiente* 'fiery.']

A·guas·ca·lien·tes /ˌägwäsˌkälˈyentās/ a state in central Mexico. ■ its capital, noted for its hot springs; pop. 506,000.

a·gue /ˈāˌgyo͞o/ ▶**n.** archaic malaria or some other illness involving fever and shivering. ■ a fever or shivering fit. — **a·gued** **adj.** **a·gu·ish** **adj.** [ME: ult. from med. L. *acuta (febris)* 'acute (fever).']

A·gul·has, Cape /əˈgələs/ the most southern point of the continent of Africa, in South Africa.

A·gul·has Cur·rent an ocean current in the Indian Ocean that flows south along the east coast of Africa.

AH ▶**abbr.** in the year of the Hegira; of the Muslim era. [from L. *anno Hegirae.*]

ah /ä/ ▶**exclam.** used to express a range of emotions including surprise, pleasure, sympathy, and realization. [ME: from OFr.]

AHA ▶ abbr. ■ American Heart Association. ■ alpha-hydroxy acid.

a·ha /ä'hä/ ▶ exclam. used to express satisfaction, triumph, or surprise: *Aha! So that's your secret plan!* [ME: from AH + HA[1].]

a·head /ə'hed/ ▶ adv. further forward in space; in the line of one's forward motion. ■ further forward in time; in advance; in the near future: *plan ahead.* ■ onward so as to make progress. ■ in the lead: *he was ahead on points.* ■ higher in number, amount, or value than previously: *profits were slightly ahead.*
– PHRASES **ahead of** in front of or before. ■ in store for; awaiting. ■ earlier than planned or expected. **ahead of one's** (or **its**) **time** innovative and radical by the standards of the time; more characteristic of a later age. **ahead of the curve** see CURVE.

a·hem /ə'hem; ə'hm/ ▶ exclam. used to represent the noise made when clearing the throat, typically to attract attention or express disapproval or embarrassment. [18th C.: extension of HEM[2].]

a·hi /'ähē/ noun Japanese name for YELLOWFIN.

a·him·sa /ə'him,sä/ ▶ n. (in the Hindu, Buddhist, and Jain tradition) the principle of nonviolence toward all living things. [Sanskrit, from *a* 'without' + *hiṃsā* 'violence.']

a·his·tor·i·cal /,āhi'stôrikəl; -'stär-/ ▶ adj. lacking historical perspective or context.

Ah·mad·a·bad /'ämədə,bäd/ (also **Ah·med·a·bad**) a city in western India; pop. 2,873,000.

a·ho·le·ho·le /ə'hōlē'hōlē/ ▶ n. a small silvery fish (*Kuhlia sandvicensis*, family Kuhliidae) occurring only in the shallow waters around the Hawaiian islands, where it is a food fish.

-aholic (also **-oholic**) ▶ suffix denoting a person addicted to something: *shopaholic* | *workaholic.* [from *(alc)oholic*.]

a·hoy /ə'hoi/ ▶ exclam. Naut. a call used in hailing. [18th C.: from AH + HOY[1].]

Ah·ri·man /'ärimən/ the evil spirit in the doctrine of Zoroastrianism, the opponent of Ahura Mazda.

A·hu·ra Maz·da /ə,hŏŏrə 'mäzdə/ the creator god of Zoroastrianism, the force for good and the opponent of Ahriman. Also called ORMAZD. [Avestan, lit. 'wise deity.']

Ah·vaz /ä'väz/ (also **Ah·waz** /ä'wäz/) a town in western Iran; pop. 725,000.

Ah·ve·nan·maa /'ävə,nän,mä/ Finnish name for ÅLAND ISLANDS.

AI ▶ abbr. ■ Amnesty International. ■ artificial insemination. ■ artificial intelligence.

AID ▶ abbr. Agency for International Development.

aid /ād/ ▶ n. help, typically of a practical nature. ■ financial or material help given to a country or area in need: *700,000 tons of food aid* | [as adj.] *aid convoys.* ■ a person or thing that is a source of help or assistance: *a teaching aid.* ■ hist. a grant of subsidy or tax to a king. ▶ v. [trans.] help, assist, or support (someone or something) in the achievement of something. ■ promote or encourage (something): *diet and exercise aid healthy skin.*
– PHRASES **aid and abet** see ABET. [ME: from OFr. *aïde* (n.), *aïdier* (v.), based on L. *adjuvare*, from *ad-* 'toward' + *juvare* 'to help.']

aide /ād/ ▶ n. an assistant to an important person, esp. to a political leader. ■ short for AIDE-DE-CAMP.

aide-de-camp /'ād də 'kamp/ ▶ n. (pl. **aides-de-camp** pronunc. same or /'ādz/) a military officer acting as a confidential assistant to a senior officer. [17th C.: from Fr., 'camp adjutant.']

aide-me·moire /'ād mem'wär/ ▶ n. (pl. **aides-me·moires** or **aides-me·moire** pronunc. same) an aid to the memory, esp. a book or document. ■ an informal diplomatic message. [19th C.: from Fr. *aide-mémoire*, from *aider* 'to help' and *mémoire* 'memory.']

AIDS /ādz/ ▶ n. acquired immune deficiency syndrome, a disease in which there is a severe loss of the body's cellular immunity, greatly lowering the resistance to infection and malignancy. The cause is a virus (the human immunodeficiency virus, or HIV) transmitted in blood and in sexual fluids. [1980s: acronym.]

AIDS-re·lat·ed com·plex ▶ n. the symptoms of a person who is infected with HIV but does not necessarily develop the disease.

ai·grette /ā'gret/ ▶ n. a head ornament consisting of a white egret's feather or other decoration. [18th C.: Fr., lit. 'egret.']

ai·guille /ā'gwēl/ ▶ n. a sharp pinnacle of rock in a mountain range. [18th C.: Fr., lit. 'needle.']

ai·guil·lette /,āgwə'let/ ▶ n. an ornament on some military and naval uniforms, consisting of braided loops hanging from the shoulder. [16th C.: from Fr., dimin. of *aiguille* 'needle.']

ai·ki·do /,īkē'dō; ī'kēdō/ ▶ n. a Japanese form of self-defense and martial art that uses locks, holds, throws, and the opponent's own movements. [1950s: from Japanese *aikidō*, from *ai* 'unify' + *ki* 'spirit' + *dō* 'way.']

ail /āl/ ▶ v. [trans.] trouble or afflict (someone) in mind or body: *exercise is good for whatever ails you.* [OE *eglian, eglan*, from *egle* 'troublesome,' from Gmc.; akin to Gothic *agls* 'disgraceful.']

ai·lan·thus /ā'lanTHəs/ ▶ n. a tall large-leaved deciduous tree (genus *Ailanthus*, family Simaroubaceae), native to Asia and Australasia and widely grown elsewhere. [mod. L., ult. from Amboinese *ailanto*, lit. 'tree of heaven.']

aiguillette

ai·ler·on /'ālə,rän/ ▶ n. a hinged surface in the trailing edge of an airplane wing, used to control lateral balance. [20th C.: Fr., lit. 'small wing.']

Ai·ley /'ālē/, Alvin (1931–89), US dancer and choreographer. He founded the Alvin Ailey Dance Theater in 1958.

ail·ing /'āliNG/ ▶ adj. in poor health.

ail·ment /'ālmənt/ ▶ n. an illness, typically a minor one.

ai·lur·o·phile /ī'lŏŏrə,fīl; ā'lŏŏr-/ ▶ n. a cat lover.

ai·lu·ro·pho·bi·a /ī,lŏŏrə'fōbēə; ā,lŏŏr-/ ▶ n. extreme or irrational fear of cats. — **ai·lu·ro·phobe** /ī'lŏŏrə,fōb; ā'lŏŏr-/ n. [20th C.: from Gk. *ailuros* 'cat.']

AIM /ām/ ▶ abbr. American Indian Movement.

aim /ām/ ▶ v. **1** [trans.] point or direct (a weapon or camera) at a target. ■ direct (an object or blow) at someone or something: *she had aimed the bottle at his head.* ■ (**aim something at**) direct information or an action toward (a particular group): *the TV campaign is aimed at the 16–24 age group.* **2** [intrans.] have the intention of achieving: *new French cooking aims at producing clear, fresh flavors* | [with infin.] *we aim to give you the best possible service.* ▶ n. **1** a purpose or intention; a desired outcome. **2** [in sing.] the directing of a weapon or object at a target. [ME: from OFr. *amer* (based on L. *aestimare* 'assess'), reinforced by *aemer, aesmer* (based on *aestimare*).]

aim·less /'āmlis/ ▶ adj. without purpose or direction. — **aim·less·ly** adv. **aim·less·ness** n.

ain't /ānt/ informal ▶ contr. ■ am not; are not; is not: *if it ain't broke, don't fix it.* ■ has not; have not: *they ain't got nothing to say.* [from dial. *hain't*.]

Ain·tab /īn'täb/ former name (until 1921) of GAZIANTEP.

Ai·nu /'ī,nŏŏ/ ▶ n. **1** (pl. same or **-nus**) a member of an aboriginal people of Japan, physically distinct from the majority population. **2** the language of this people, of unknown affinity. ▶ adj. of or relating to this people or their language. [19th C.: the name in Ainu, lit. 'man, person.']

ai·o·li /ī'ōlē; ā'ō-/ (also **aï·o·li**) ▶ n. mayonnaise seasoned with garlic. [Fr., from Provençal *ai* 'garlic' + *oli* 'oil.']

air /e(ə)r/ ▶ n. **1** the invisible gaseous substance surrounding the earth, a mixture mainly of oxygen and nitrogen. ■ this substance regarded as necessary for breathing: *the air was stale.* ■ the free or unconfined space above the surface of the earth: *he celebrated by tossing his hat high in the air.* ■ [as adj.] used to indicate that something involves the use of aircraft: *air travel.* ■ the earth's atmosphere as a medium for transmitting radio waves. ■ air considered as one of the four elements in ancient philosophy and in astrology (associated with the signs of Gemini, Aquarius, and Libra). ■ a breeze or light wind. See also LIGHT AIR. **2** (**air of**) an impression of a quality or manner given by someone or something: *a faint air of boredom.* ■ (**airs**) an annoyingly affected and condescending manner: *he began to put on airs and boss us around.* **3** Music a tune or short melodious composition, typically a song. ▶ v. **1** [trans.] (often **be aired**) express (an opinion or grievance) publicly: *grievances were aired.* ■ broadcast (a program) on radio or television. **2** [trans.] expose (a room) to the open air in order to ventilate it.
– PHRASES **in the air** noticeable all around; becoming prevalent. **on** (or **off**) **the air** being (or not being) broadcast on radio or television. **up in the air** (of a plan or issue) still to be settled; unresolved. **walk on air** feel elated. [ME: from OFr. *air*, from L. *aer*, from Gk. *aēr*, denoting the gas; sense 2 prob. from OFr. *aire* 'site, disposition.']

air bag ▶ n. a safety device fitted inside a road vehicle, consisting of a cushion designed to inflate rapidly in the event of a collision to protect passengers.

air ball ▶ n. Basketball, informal a shot that misses the backboard, rim, and net entirely.

air·base /'e(ə)r,bās/ ▶ n. a base for the operation of military aircraft.

air blad·der ▶ n. an air-filled bladder or sac found in certain animals and plants. ■ another term for SWIM BLADDER.

air·boat /'e(ə)r,bōt/ ▶ n. a shallow-draft boat powered by an aircraft engine, for use in swamps.

air·borne /'e(ə)r,bôrn/ ▶ adj. transported by air. ■ (of an aircraft) in the air after taking off.

air brake ▶ n. a brake worked by air pressure. ■ a movable flap or other device on an aircraft to reduce its speed.

air·brush /'e(ə)r,brəsH/ ▶ n. an artist's device for spraying paint by means of compressed air. ▶ v. [trans.] paint with an airbrush. ■ alter or conceal (a photograph) using an airbrush: *wings airbrushed onto her shoulders.* ■ represent or describe as better or more attractive than in reality:

airbrush

air·burst /'e(ə)r,bərst/ ▶ n. an explosion in the air, typically of a nuclear bomb or large meteorite.

air·bus /'e(ə)r,bəs/ ▶ n. trademark an aircraft designed to carry a large number of passengers economically, esp. over relatively short routes.

air com·mand ▶ n. a high-level organizational unit in the US Air Force.

air con·di·tion·ing ▶n. a system for controlling the humidity, ventilation, and temperature in a building or vehicle, typically to maintain a cool atmosphere. — **air con·di·tioned** adj. **air con·di·tion·er** n.

air-cooled ▶adj. cooled by means of a flow of air.

air cor·ri·dor ▶n. a route to which aircraft are restricted, esp. over a foreign country.

air cov·er ▶n. protection from aircraft for land-based or naval operations in war situations.

air·craft /ˈe(ə)r,kraft/ ▶n. (pl. same) an airplane, helicopter, or other machine capable of flight.

air·craft car·ri·er ▶n. a warship that serves as a base for aircraft to take off from and to land on.

air·crew /ˈe(ə)r,kro͞o/ ▶n. (pl. **-crews**) [treated as sing. or pl.] the crew manning an aircraft.

air cush·ion ▶n. **1** an inflatable cushion. **2** the layer of air supporting a hovercraft or similar vehicle.

air date ▶n. the date on which a recorded program is to be broadcast.

air·drop /ˈe(ə)r,dräp/ ▶n. an act of dropping supplies, troops, or equipment by parachute from an aircraft. ▶v. (**-dropped, -drop·ping**) [trans.] drop (such things) by parachute.

air-dry ▶v. make or become dry through contact with unheated air. ▶adj. not giving off any moisture on exposure to air.

Airedale

Aire·dale /ˈe(ə)r,dāl/ ▶n. a large terrier of a rough-coated black and tan breed. [19th C.: from *Airedale*, a district in Yorkshire, England, where the dog was bred.]

air·fare /ˈe(ə)r,fe(ə)r/ ▶n. the price of a passenger ticket for travel by aircraft.

air·field /ˈe(ə)r,fēld/ ▶n. an area of land set aside for the takeoff, landing, and maintenance of aircraft.

air fil·ter ▶n. a device for preventing dust, dirt, etc., from entering the air inlet of an internal combustion engine.

air·flow /ˈe(ə)r,flō/ ▶n. the flow of air, esp. that encountered by a moving aircraft or vehicle.

air·foil /ˈe(ə)r,foil/ ▶n. a structure with curved surfaces designed to give the most favorable ratio of lift to drag in flight, used as the basic form of the wings, fins, and horizontal stabilizers of most aircraft.

air force ▶n. (often **the air force** or **the Air Force**) the branch of a nation's armed services that conducts military operations in the air.

Air Force One the designation (when the president of the US is aboard) of any of several specially equipped jetliners maintained by the US Air Force.

air·frame /ˈe(ə)r,frām/ ▶n. the body of an aircraft as distinct from its engine.

air·freight /ˈe(ə)r,frāt/ ▶n. the transportation of goods by aircraft. ■ goods in transit, or to be carried, by aircraft. ▶v. [trans.] carry or send (goods) by aircraft.

air·glow /ˈe(ə)r,glō/ ▶n. a glow in the night sky caused by radiation from the upper atmosphere.

air gui·tar ▶n. informal used to describe the actions of someone playing an imaginary guitar.

air gun ▶n. a gun that fires pellets using compressed air.

air·head[1] /ˈe(ə)r,hed/ ▶n. Mil. a base secured in enemy territory where supplies and troops can be received and evacuated by air. [World War II: on the pattern of *bridgehead*.]

air·head[2] ▶n. informal a silly or foolish person.

air·ing /ˈe(ə)riNG/ ▶n. [in sing.] **1** an exposure to warm or fresh air, for the purpose of ventilating. **2** a public expression of an opinion or subject. ■ a transmission of a television or radio program.

air-kiss ▶v. [trans.] purse the lips as if kissing (someone), without making contact. ▶n. (**air kiss**) a simulated kiss, without physical contact.

air lane ▶n. a path or course regularly used by aircraft.

air lay·er·ing ▶n. Horticulture a form of layering in which the branch is potted or wrapped in a moist growing medium to promote root growth.

air·less /ˈe(ə)rlis/ ▶adj. stuffy; not ventilated. ■ without wind or breeze; still: *a hot, airless night.* — **air·less·ness** n.

air let·ter ▶n. another term for AEROGRAMME.

air·lift /ˈe(ə)r,lift/ ▶n. an act of transporting supplies by aircraft, typically in a blockade or other emergency. ▶v. [trans.] transport (troops or supplies) by aircraft, typically when transportation by land is difficult.

air·line /ˈe(ə)r,līn/ ▶n. **1** an organization providing a regular public service of air transportation on one or more routes. ■ (usu. **air line**) a route that forms part of a system regularly used by aircraft. **2** (usu. **air line**) a pipe supplying air.

air·lin·er /ˈe(ə)r,līnər/ ▶n. a large passenger aircraft.

air·lock /ˈe(ə)r,läk/ (also **air lock**) ▶n. **1** a blockage of the flow in a pump or pipe, caused by an air bubble. **2** a compartment with controlled pressure and parallel sets of doors, to permit movement between areas at different pressures.

air·mail /ˈe(ə)r,māl/ ▶n. a system of transporting mail by aircraft, typically overseas. ■ a letter carried by aircraft. ▶v. [trans.] send (mail) by aircraft.

air·man /ˈe(ə)rmən/ ▶n. (pl. **-men**) a pilot or member of the crew of an aircraft, esp. in an air force. ■ a member of the US Air Force of the lowest rank, below sergeant. ■ a member of the US Navy whose general duties are concerned with aircraft.

air·man·ship /ˈe(ə)rmən,SHip/ ▶n. skill in flying an aircraft.

air mass ▶n. Meteorol. a body of air with horizontally uniform levels of temperature, humidity, and pressure.

air mat·tress ▶n. an inflatable mattress.

air mile ▶n. a nautical mile used as a measure of distance flown by aircraft.

air·mo·bile /ˈe(ə)r,mōbəl/ ▶adj. (of troops) moved about by helicopters.

air pis·tol ▶n. a pistol that fires pellets using compressed air.

air·plane /ˈe(ə)r,plān/ ▶n. a powered flying vehicle with fixed wings and a weight greater than that of the air it displaces.

air plant ▶n. a typically epiphytic tropical American plant (genus *Tillandsia*, family Bromeliaceae) with grasslike or fingerlike leaves through which nutrients are absorbed.

air·play /ˈe(ə)r,plā/ ▶n. broadcasting time devoted to a particular record, performer, or musical genre.

air pock·et ▶n. a cavity containing air. ■ a region of low pressure causing an aircraft to lose height suddenly.

air·port /ˈe(ə)r,pôrt/ ▶n. a complex of runways and buildings for the takeoff, landing, and maintenance of civil aircraft, with facilities for passengers. ■ [as modifier] relating to or denoting light popular fiction such as is offered for sale to travelers in airports: *another airport thriller.*

air pow·er ▶n. airborne military forces.

air pump ▶n. a device for pumping air into or out of an enclosed space.

air raid ▶n. an attack in which bombs are dropped from aircraft onto a ground target.

air ri·fle ▶n. a rifle that fires pellets using compressed air.

air sac ▶n. a lung compartment containing air; an alveolus. ■ an extension of a bird's lung cavity into a bone or other part of the body.

air shaft ▶n. a straight, typically vertical passage admitting air into a mine, tunnel, or building.

air·ship /ˈe(ə)r,SHip/ ▶n. a power-driven aircraft that is kept buoyant by a body of gas that is lighter than air.

air show ▶n. a show at which aircraft perform aerial displays.

air·sick /ˈe(ə)r,sik/ ▶adj. affected with nausea due to travel in an aircraft. — **air·sick·ness** n.

airship

air·side /ˈe(ə)r,sīd/ ▶n. the side of an airport terminal from which aircraft can be observed; the area beyond security checks and passport and customs control. ▶adv. on or to this side of an airport terminal.

air·space /ˈe(ə)r,spās/ ▶n. space available in the atmosphere immediately above the earth. ■ the air available to aircraft to fly in, esp. the part subject to the jurisdiction of a particular country. ■ Law the right of a private landowner to the space above his land and any structures on it, which he can use for ordinary purposes such as the erection of signposts or fences. ■ space left to be occupied by air for purposes of insulation.

air·speed /ˈe(ə)r,spēd/ ▶n. the speed of an aircraft relative to the air through which it is moving. Compare with GROUNDSPEED.

air sta·tion ▶n. an airfield operated by a navy or marine corps.

air·stream /ˈe(ə)r,strēm/ ▶n. a current of air.

air strike ▶n. an attack made by aircraft.

air·strip /ˈe(ə)r,strip/ ▶n. a strip of ground set aside for the takeoff and landing of aircraft.

air sup·port ▶n. assistance given to ground or naval forces in an operation by their own or allied aircraft.

air·tight /ˈe(ə)r,tīt/ ▶adj. not allowing air to escape or pass through. ■ having no weaknesses; unassailable: *an airtight alibi.*

air·time /ˈe(ə)r,tīm/ ▶n. time during which a broadcast is being transmitted. ■ time during which a cellular phone is in use, including calls made and received.

air-to-air ▶adj. [attrib.] directed or operating from one aircraft to another in flight.

air-to-ground ▶adj. directed or operating from an aircraft in flight to the land surface.

air-to-sur·face ▶ adj. directed or operating from an aircraft in flight to the surface of the sea or other body of water.

air traf·fic con·trol ▶ n. the ground-based personnel and equipment concerned with controlling and monitoring air traffic within a particular area. — **air traf·fic con·troll·er** n.

air·waves /'e(ə)r,wāvz/ ▶ plural n. the radio frequencies used for broadcasting.

air·way /'e(ə)r,wā/ ▶ n. **1** the passage by which air reaches a person's lungs. ■ a tube for supplying air to a person's lungs in an emergency. ■ a ventilating passage in a mine. **2** a recognized route followed by aircraft.

air·wor·thy /'e(ə)r,wərTHē/ ▶ adj. (of an aircraft) safe to fly. — **air·wor·thi·ness** n.

air·y /'erē/ ▶ adj. (**airier, airiest**) **1** (of a room or building) spacious, well lit, and well ventilated. ■ delicate, as though filled with or made of air. ■ fig. giving an impression of light gracefulness and elegance: *her airy presence filled the house.* **2** giving an impression of being unconcerned or not serious, typically about something taken seriously by others. — **air·i·ly** /-əlē/ adv. (in sense 2) **air·i·ness** n.

aisle /īl/ ▶ n. a passage between rows of seats in a building such as a church or theater, an airplane, or a train. ■ a passage between shelves of goods in a supermarket or other building. ■ Archit. (in a church) a lower part parallel to and at the side of a nave, choir, or transept, from which it is divided by pillars. — **aisled** /īld/ adj. [ME *ele, ile*, from OFr. *ele*, from L. *ala* 'wing;' confused with *isle*.]

aitch /āCH/ ▶ n. the name of the letter H. [16th C.: from OFr. *ache*.]

aitch·bone /'āCH,bōn/ ▶ n. the buttock or rump bone of cattle. ■ a cut of beef lying over this. [15th C.: from dial. *nache* 'rump,' from OFr., based on L. *natis* 'buttock(s).' The initial *n* in *a nache-bone* was lost by wrong division.]

Aix-en-Pro·vence /,eks än prō'väNs; ,āks/ a city in Provence in southern France; pop. 126,850.

Aix-la-Cha·pelle /,eks lä SHä'pel; ,āks/ French name for **Aachen**.

Ai·zawl /ī'zoul/ a city in northeastern India, capital of the state of Mizoram; pop. 154,000.

A·jac·cio /,ä,ZHäk'syō/ a port on the western coast of Corsica; pop. 59,320.

a·jar[1] /ə'jär/ ▶ adv. & adj. (of a door or other opening) slightly open. [17th C.: from **a-**[2] + obs. *char (cerr)* 'a turn.']

a·jar[2] ▶ adv. archaic out of harmony. [19th C.: from **a-**[2] + **jar**[2].]

A·jax /'ā,jaks/ Gk. Mythol. **1** a Greek hero of the Trojan war, son of Telamon, king of Salamis. He was proverbial for his size and strength. **2** a Greek hero, son of Oileus, king of Locris.

Aj·man /aj'män; -'man/ the smallest of the seven emirates of the United Arab Emirates; pop. 64,320. ■ its capital city.

Aj·mer /,əj'mi(ə)r/ a city in northwestern India; pop. 402,000.

a·ju·ga /'ajəgə/ ▶ n. a plant (genus *Ajuga*) of the mint family, esp. bugle. [mod. L., from med. L. *ajuga*.]

AK ▶ abbr. Alaska (in official postal use).

AK-47 ▶ n. a type of assault rifle, originally manufactured in the Soviet Union. [acronym for Russ. *Avtomat Kalashnikova 1947*, designed in 1947 by Mikhail T. Kalashnikov (1919–).]

aka ▶ abbr. also known as.

A·kan /'ä,kän/ ▶ n. **1** (pl. same) a member of a people inhabiting southern Ghana and adjacent parts of Ivory Coast. **2** the Kwa language spoken by this people. ▶ adj. of or relating to this people or their language. [Akan.]

A·ka·shi /ä'käSHē/ a city in west central Japan, on southwestern Honshu Island; pop. 271,000.

Ak·bar /'äk,bär; 'akbər/, Jalaludin Muhammad (1542–1605), Mogul emperor of India 1556–1605; known as **Akbar the Great**. He expanded the Mogul empire to northern India.

AKC ▶ abbr. American Kennel Club.

a·ke·bi·a /ə'kēbēə/ ▶ n. a climbing shrub (*Akebia quinata*, family Lardizabalaceae) with purplish flowers, deeply divided leaves, and purple berries. [1837: mod. L., from Japanese *akebi*.]

a·kee /a'kē; 'akē/ (also **ac·kee**) ▶ n. a West African tropical tree (*Blighia sapida*) of the soapberry family that is cultivated for its fruit. ■ the fruit of this tree, widely eaten as a vegetable, but which can be poisonous unless cooked. [18th C.: from Kru *ākee*.]

A·khe·na·ten /,äk(ə)'nätn/ (also **A·khe·na·ton** or **Ikh·na·ton** /ik'nätn/) (14th century BC), Egyptian pharaoh of the 18th dynasty; reigned 1379–1362 BC as *Amenhotep IV*.

Akh·ma·to·va /äKH'mätəvə/, Anna (1889–1966), Russian poet; pen name of *Anna Andreevna Gorenko*.

A·ki·hi·to /,äkē'hētō/, (1933–), emperor of Japan 1989–; full name *Tsugu Akihito*; son of Hirohito.

a·kim·bo /ə'kimbō/ ▶ adv. with hands on the hips and elbows turned outward. [ME: from *in kenebowe*, prob. from ON.]

a·kin /ə'kin/ ▶ adj. of similar character: *genius and madness are akin.* ■ related by blood. [16th C.: from *of kin*.]

a·ki·ne·sia /,āki'nēZHə; ,ākī-/ ▶ n. Med. loss or impairment of the power of voluntary movement. — **a·ki·net·ic** /-'netik/ adj. [19th C.: from Gk. *akinēsia* 'quiescence,' from *a-* 'without' + *kinēsis* 'motion.']

A·ki·ta[1] /ä'kētə/ a city in northeastern Japan, on northern Honshu Island; pop. 302,000.

Akita[2]

A·ki·ta[2] ▶ n. a spitz (dog) of a Japanese breed. [20th C.: from *Akita*, district in Japan.]

Ak·kad /'ak,ad; 'äk,äd/ the capital city that gave its name to an ancient kingdom in north central Mesopotamia.

Ak·ka·di·an /ə'kādēən; ə'kä-/ ▶ adj. of or relating to Akkad in ancient Babylonia or its people or their language. ▶ n. **1** an inhabitant of Akkad. **2** the Semitic language of Akkad.

Ak·ko /ä'kō/ another name for **Acre** 1.

Ak-Me·chet /,äk mi'CHet/ former name for **Simferopol**.

a·kra·sia /ə'kräZH(ē)ə/ (also **a·cra·sia**) ▶ n. esp. Philos. the state of mind in which someone acts against their better judgment through weakness of will. — **a·krat·ic** /ə'kratik/ (also **a·crat·ic**) adj. [19th C.: from Gk., from *a-* 'without' + *kratos* 'power.']

Ak·ron /'akrən/ a city in northeastern Ohio; pop. 217,074.

Ak·sai Chin /'ak,sī 'CHin/ a region of the Himalayas occupied by China since 1950, but claimed by India as part of Kashmir.

Ak·sum /'äk,so͝om/ (also **Ax·um**) a town in northern Ethiopia. It was the capital of the Axumite kingdom 1st–6th centuries AD. — **Ak·sum·ite** /'äkso͞o,mīt/ adj. & n.

ak·va·vit /'äkvə,vēt/ ▶ n. var. of **aquavit**.

AL ▶ abbr. ■ Alabama (in official postal use). ■ Baseball American League. ■ American Legion.

Al ▶ symb. the chemical element aluminum.

al- ▶ prefix var. of **ad-** assimilated before *-l* (as in *alleviate, allocate*).

-al ▶ suffix **1** (forming adjectives) relating to; of the kind of: ■ from Latin words: *annual | infernal* ■ from Greek words: *historical.* ■ from English nouns: *tidal.* **2** forming nouns chiefly denoting verbal action: *arrival | transmittal.* [sense 1 from French *-el* or Latin *-alis*; sense 2 from Fr. *-aille* or L. *-alis*.]

Ala. ▶ abbr. Alabama.

à la /'ä ,lä; 'ä lə/ ▶ prep. (of a dish) cooked or prepared in a specified style or manner: *cooked à la meunière.* ■ informal in the style of: *afternoon talk shows à la Oprah.* [Fr., from **à la mode**.]

Al·a·bam·a /,alə'bamə/ a state in the southeastern US, on the Gulf of Mexico; capital, Montgomery; statehood, Dec. 14, 1819 (22). Visited by Spanish explorers in the mid 16th century and later settled by the French, it passed to Britain in 1763 and to the US in 1783. — **Al·a·bam·an** adj. & n.

Al·a·bam·a Riv·er a river in southern Alabama that flows for 315 miles (507 km) to meet the Mobile River.

al·a·bas·ter /'alə,bastər/ ▶ n. a fine-grained, translucent form of gypsum, often carved into ornaments. ▶ adj. made of alabaster. ■ literary like alabaster in whiteness and smoothness. [ME: via OFr. from, ult., Gk. *alabastos, alabastros*.]

à la carte /,ä lä 'kärt; lə/ ▶ adj. (of a menu or restaurant) listing or serving food that can be ordered as separate items, rather than part of a set meal. ■ (of food) available on such a menu. ▶ adv. as separately priced items from a menu, not as part of a set meal. [19th C.: Fr., lit. 'according to the (menu) card.']

a·lac·ri·ty /ə'lakritē/ ▶ n. brisk and cheerful readiness. [ME: from L. *alacritas*, from *alacer* 'brisk.']

A·lad·din /ə'ladn/ the hero of a story in the *Arabian Nights*, who finds an old lamp that, when rubbed, summons a genie who obeys the will of the owner. [from Arab. *'Alā' al-dīn*.]

Alain-Four·nier /ä'laN fo͞orn'yā/ (1886–1914), French writer; pen name of *Henri-Alban Fournier*.

à la king /,ä lə 'kiNG; ,al ə/ ▶ adj. (of a dish) with diced meat in a cream sauce, usually with green peppers and pimientos.

Al·a·me·da /,alə'mēdə; -'mādə/ a city in western California, on San Francisco Bay; pop. 72,300.

al·a·me·da /,alə'mādə/ ▶ n. (in Spain and Spanish-speaking regions) a public walkway or promenade shaded with trees.

A·la·mein /,alə'mān/ see **El Alamein, Battle of**.

Al·a·mo /'alə,mō/ (**the Alamo**) a mission in San Antonio, Texas, site of a siege in 1836 by Mexican forces, in which all 180 defenders were killed.

à la mode /,ä lä 'mōd/ ▶ adv. & adj. **1** in fashion; up to date. **2** served with ice cream. [16th C.: Fr., lit. 'in the fashion.']

Al·a·mo·gor·do /,aləmə'gôrdō/ a city in southern New Mexico; pop. 35,582. White Sands is nearby.

Å·land Is·lands /'ôlənd/ a group of Finnish islands in the Gulf of Bothnia; capital, Mariehamn (known in Finnish as Maarianhamina). Finnish name AHVENANMAA.

al·a·nine /'alə,nēn/ ▶ **n.** Biochem. an amino acid, $CH_3CH(NH_2)COOH$, that is a constituent of most proteins. [19th C.: from Ger. *Alanin*, from ALDEHYDE + *-an* + -INE[4].]

Al-A·non /'al ə,nän/ a mutual support organization for the families and friends of alcoholics, esp. those of members of Alcoholics Anonymous.

A·lar /'ā,lär/ ▶ **n.** trademark for DAMINOZIDE.

a·lar /'ālər/ ▶ **adj.** esp. Zool. of or relating to a wing or wings. ■ Anat. winglike or wing-shaped. ■ Bot. another term for AXILLARY. [19th C.: from L. *alaris*, from *ala* 'wing.']

A·lar·cón /,älär'kôn/, Pedro Antonio de (1833–91), Spanish writer. His works include *The Three-Cornered Hat* (1874).

A·lar·cón y Men·do·za see RUIZ DE ALARCÓN Y MENDOZA.

Al·a·ric /'alərik/ (*c.*370–410), king of the Visigoths 395–410. He captured Rome in 410.

a·larm /ə'lärm/ ▶ **n.** an anxious awareness of danger. ■ [in sing.] a warning of danger. ■ a warning sound or device: *a burglar alarm.* ■ an alarm clock. ▶ **v. 1** [trans.] cause (someone) to feel frightened, disturbed, or in danger. **2** (**be alarmed**) be fitted or protected with an alarm: *this door is locked and alarmed between 11 p.m. and 6 a.m.* — **a·larm·ing·ly adv.** [ME: from OFr. *alarme*, from Ital. *allarme*, from *all' arme!* 'to arms!']

a·larm clock ▶ **n.** a clock with a device that can be made to sound at the time set in advance, used to wake someone up.

a·larm·ist /ə'lärmist/ ▶ **n.** someone who is considered to be exaggerating a danger and so causing needless worry or panic. ▶ **adj.** creating needless worry or panic. — **a·larm·ism n.**

a·lar·um /ə'lärəm; ə'lar-/ ▶ **n.** archaic term for ALARM.

– PHRASES **alarums and excursions** humorous confused activity and uproar.

Alas. ▶ **abbr.** Alaska.

a·las /ə'las/ ▶ **exclam.** esp. literary or humorous an expression of grief, pity, or concern. [ME: from OFr. *a las, a lasse*, from *a* 'ah' + *las(se)* (from L. *lassus* 'weary').]

A·las·ka /ə'laskə/ the largest state in the US, in northwestern North America, with coasts on the Arctic and North Pacific oceans and on the Bering Sea, separated from the contiguous 48 US states by Canada; pop. 626,932; capital, Juneau; statehood: Jan. 3, 1959 (49). The territory was purchased from Russia in 1867. After oil was discovered in 1968, a pipeline was completed in 1977 to carry the oil from the North Slope to Valdez. — **A·las·kan adj. & n.**

A·las·ka, Gulf of a part of the northeastern Pacific Ocean between the Alaska Peninsula and the Alexander Archipelago.

A·las·kan mal·a·mute /ə'laskən/ (also **A·las·kan mal·e·mute**) ▶ **n.** a powerful dog of a breed with a thick, gray coat, bred by the Inuit and typically used to pull sleds. [19th C.: from Inuit *malimiut*, a people of Kotzebue Sound, Alaska.]

A·las·ka Pen·in·su·la a peninsula on the south coast of Alaska, extending south-westward into the northeastern Pacific Ocean.

A·las·ka Range a mountain chain in southern Alaska, rising to 20,320 feet (6,194 m) at Mt. McKinley.

a·late /'ā,lāt/ ▶ **adj.** Bot. & Entomol. (chiefly of insects or seeds) having wings or winglike appendages. [17th C.: from L. *alatus*, from *ala* 'wing.']

alb /alb/ ▶ **n.** a white vestment worn by clergy and servers in some Christian Churches. [OE *albe*, from L. *albus* 'white.']

alb

al·ba /'albə/ ▶ **n.** a shrub rose of a variety with gray-green leaves and pinkish-white, sweet-scented flowers. [19th C.: from L. *alba*, fem. of *albus* 'white,' from *rosa alba*, a rose.]

Al·ba·ce·te /,älvä'sātā/ a city in Albacete Province in southeastern Spain; pop. 134,600.

albacore tuna

al·ba·core /'albə,kôr/ (also **albacore tuna**) ▶ **n.** a tuna that travels in large schools and is of commercial importance as a food fish. Its two species are *Thunnus alalunga* and the **false albacore** (*Euthynus alletteratus*). [16th C.: from Port. *albacora*, from Arab. *al-bakūra*, perh. from *al* 'the' + *bakūr* 'premature.']

Albania

Official name: Republic of Albania
Location: southeastern Europe, on the Adriatic Sea
Area: 10,600 square miles (27,400 sq km)
Population: 3,500,000
Capital: Tirana
Languages: Albanian (official), Greek
Currency: lek

Al·ba Iu·lia /,älbə 'yoolyə/ a city in west central Romania, north of the Transylvanian Alps; pop. 72,330.

Al·ban, St. /'ôlbən; 'al-/ (3rd century), the first English Christian martyr. He was put to death for sheltering a fugitive priest.

Al·ba·ni·a /al'bānēə; ôl-/ a republic in southeastern Europe. *See box.*

Al·ba·ni·an /al'bānēən; ôl-/ ▶ **adj.** of or relating to Albania or its people or their language. ▶ **n. 1** a native or national of Albania, or a person of Albanian descent. **2** the language of Albania, a separate branch of Indo-European.

Al·ba·ny /'ôlbənē/ **1** a city in southwestern Georgia; pop. 76,939. **2** the capital of New York, in the eastern part, on the Hudson River; pop. 95,658. **3** a city in northwestern Oregon; pop. 40,852.

al·ba·tross /'albə,trôs; -,träs/ ▶ **n.** (pl. **-tross·es**) a large oceanic bird (genera *Diomedea* and *Phoebetria*, family Diomedeidae) whose long narrow wings may span greater than 10 feet (3.3 m). Several species include the **Laysan albatross** (*D. immutablis*). ■ a source of frustration; an encumbrance (in allusion to Coleridge's *The Rime of the Ancient Mariner*). [17th C.: alt. (influenced by L. *albus* 'white') of 16th-cent. *alcatras*, applied to various seabirds, from Sp. and Port. *alcatraz*, from Arab. *al-ġaṭṭās* 'the diver.']

Laysan albatross

al·be·do /al'bēdō/ ▶ **n.** (pl. **-dos**) esp. Astron. the proportion of the incident light or radiation reflected by a surface, typically that of a planet or moon. [19th C.: eccles. Latin, 'whiteness,' from L. *albus* 'white.']

Al·bee /'ôlbē; 'albē/, Edward Franklin (1928–), US playwright. He wrote *Who's Afraid of Virginia Woolf?* (1962).

al·be·it /ôl'bē-it; al-/ ▶ **conj.** although: *he was making progress, albeit rather slowly.* [ME: from *all be it* 'although it be (that).']

Al·be·marle Sound /'albə,märl/ an inlet of the Atlantic Ocean in northeastern North Carolina.

Al·bert, Lake /'albərt/ a lake in eastern central Africa, between the Democratic Republic of the Congo (formerly Zaire) and Uganda. Also called LAKE MOBUTU SESE SEKO.

Al·bert, Prince /'albərt/ (1819–61), consort to Queen Victoria and prince of Saxe-Coburg-Gotha; full name *Albert Francis Charles Augustus Emmanuel*.

Al·ber·ta /al'bərtə/ a province in western Canada; capital, Edmonton; pop. 2,545,553.

Al·ber·ti /äl'bertē/, Leon Battista (1404–72), Italian painter and critic. He wrote *On Painting* (1435), which was the first account of the theory of perspective.

Al·bert Nile the upper part of the Nile River that flows through northwestern Uganda.

Al·ber·tus Mag·nus, St. /al'bərtəs 'magnəs/ (*c.*1200–80), Dominican theologian, philosopher, and scientist; known as **Doctor Universalis.** He was a pioneer in the study of Aristotle.

Al·bi·gen·ses /,albi'jensēz/ ▶ **plural n.** the members of a heretical sect in southern France in the 12th–13th centuries, identified with the

Cathars. — **Al·bi·gen·si·an** /-'jensēən; -SHən/ **adj.** [med. L., from *Albiga*, the L. name of Albi in Southern France.]

al·bi·no /al'bīnō/ ▶**n.** (pl. **-nos**) a person or animal having a congenital absence of pigment in the skin and hair (which are white) and the eyes (typically pink). ■ informal an abnormally white animal or plant. — **al·bi·nism** /'albə,nizəm/ **n.** [18th C.: from Port., Sp., from *albo*, from L. *albus* 'white.']

Al·bi·nus /'albīnəs/ see **ALCUIN**.

Al·bi·on /'albēən/ ▶**n.** literary Britain or England (often used in referring to ancient times). [OE, from Latin, prob. of Celtic origin and rel. to L. *albus* 'white' (in allusion to the white cliffs of Dover).]

al·bite /'al,bīt/ ▶**n.** a sodium-rich mineral of the feldspar group, typically white, occurring widely in igneous rocks. [19th C.: from L. *albus* 'white.']

al·biz·zi·a /al'bizēə; -'bitsēə/ (also **al·biz·i·a**) ▶**n.** a leguminous tree or shrub (genus *Albizia*) with feathery leaves and densely clustered plumelike flowers. [mod. L., after Filippo degli *Albizzi*, 18th-cent. Tuscan nobleman.]

Ål·borg /'ôl,bôrg/ var. of **AALBORG**.

Al·bright /'ôl,brīt/, Madeleine Korbel (1937–), US secretary of state 1997–2001; born in Czechoslovakia. She was the first woman to head the US Department of State.

al·bum /'albəm/ ▶**n.** **1** a blank book for the insertion of photographs, stamps, or pictures. **2** a collection of recordings, on long-playing record, cassette, or compact disc, issued as a single item. [17th C.: from L., 'a blank tablet,' neut. of *albus* 'white.']

al·bu·men /al'byo͞omən/ ▶**n.** egg white, or the protein contained in it. [16th C.: from L., 'egg white,' from *albus* 'white.']

al·bu·min /al'byo͞omən/ ▶**n.** Biochem. a simple form of protein, soluble in water and coagulable by heat, such as that found in egg white, milk, and blood serum. [19th C.: from Fr. *albumine*, based on L. *albumen*, *albumin-* (see **ALBUMEN**).]

al·bu·mi·noid /al'byo͞omə,noid/ ▶**n.** another term for **SCLEROPROTEIN**.

al·bu·mi·nous /al'byo͞omənəs/ ▶**adj.** consisting of, resembling, or containing albumen.

Al·bu·quer·que[1] /'alb(y)ə,kərkē/ a city in central New Mexico, on the Rio Grande; pop. 448,607.

Al·bu·quer·que[2], Alfonso de (1453–1515), Portuguese statesman. He conquered Goa (1510) and made it the capital of the Portuguese empire in the east.

Al·cae·us /al'sēəs/ (*c.*620–*c.*580 BC), Greek poet. He invented a new form of lyric meter called the alcaic.

al·ca·ic /al'kā-ik/ Pros. ▶**adj.** a four-line verse stanza in the meter invented by the Greek poet Alcaeus. ▶**n.** (usu. **alcaics**) alcaic verse. [17th C.: ult. from Gk. *alkaikos*, from *Alkaios* (see **ALCAEUS**).]

Al·ca·lá de He·na·res /,älkə'lä dā ā'näräs/ a city in central Spain, on the Henares River; pop. 162,780.

al·cal·de /äl'käldē; al-/ ▶**n.** a magistrate or mayor in a Spanish, Portuguese, or Latin American town. [16th C.: Sp., from Arab. *al-ķāḍī* 'the judge' (see **CADI**).]

Al·ca·traz /'alkə,traz/ a rocky island in San Francisco Bay, California, site of a federal penitentiary 1934–63.

al·ca·zar /,alkə'zär; al'kazər/ (often **Al·ca·zar**) ▶**n.** a Spanish palace or fortress of Moorish origin. [17th C.: from Sp. *alcázar*, from Arab. *al-ķaṣr* 'the castle.']

Al·ces·tis /al'sestis/ Gk. Mythol. wife of Admetus, king of Pherae in Thessaly, whose life she saved by consenting to die on his behalf.

al·che·my /'alkəmē/ ▶**n.** the medieval forerunner of chemistry, based on the supposed transformation of matter, esp. that of base metals into gold. ■ fig. a process by which paradoxical results are achieved or incompatible elements combined with no obvious rational explanation. — **al·chem·ic** /al'kemik/ **adj.** **al·chem·i·cal** /al'kemikəl/ **adj.** **al·che·mist** /-mist/ **n.** **al·che·mize** /-,mīz/ **v.** [ME: via OFr. from, ult., Arab. *alkīmiyā'*, from *al* 'the' + *kīmiyā'* (from Gk. *khēmia*, *khēmeia* 'art of transmuting metals').]

Al·ci·bi·a·des /,alsə'bīə,dēz/ (*c.*450–404 BC), Athenian general and statesman, who held commands during the Peloponnesian War.

al·cid /'alsid/ ▶**n.** Ornithol. a bird of the auk family (Alcidae); an auk or puffin. [19th C.: mod. L. *Alcidae*, from *Alca* based on ON *álka* 'razorbill.']

Al·cin·dor /al'sindər/, Lewis Ferdinand, see **ABDUL-JABBAR**.

al·co·hol /'alkə,hôl; -,häl/ ▶**n.** a colorless volatile flammable liquid, C_2H_5OH, that is the intoxicating constituent of wine, beer, spirits, and other drinks, and is also used as an industrial solvent and as fuel. ■ drink containing this. ■ Chem. any organic compound whose molecule contains one or more hydroxyl groups attached to a carbon atom. [16th C.: Fr. (earlier form of *alcool*), or from med. L., from Arab. *al-kuḥl* 'the kohl.']

al·co·hol·ic /,alkə'hôlik; -'häl-/ ▶**adj.** containing or relating to alcoholic liquor. ■ caused by the excessive consumption of alcohol: *alcoholic liver disease.* ■ suffering from alcoholism. ▶**n.** a person suffering from alcoholism.

Al·co·hol·ics A·non·y·mous (abbr.: **AA**) a self-help organization for people fighting alcoholism, founded in the US in 1935.

al·co·hol·ism /'alkəhô,lizəm; -hä-/ ▶**n.** an addiction to the consumption of alcoholic liquor or the mental illness and compulsive behavior resulting from alcohol dependency.

Al·cott[1] /'ôlkət; -,kät; 'al-/, Bronson (1799–1888), US educator; full name *Amos Bronson Alcott*; father of Louisa May Alcott. He advocated racial integration in the classroom and created the first parent-teacher association.

Al·cott[2], Louisa May (1832–88), US writer. Her novels include *Little Women* (1868–69).

al·cove /'al,kōv/ ▶**n.** a recess, typically in the wall of a room or of a garden. [16th C.: from Fr. *alcôve*, from Sp. *alcoba*, from Arab. *al-ķubba* 'the vault.']

Al·cuin /'alkwin/ (*c.*735–804) English scholar and theologian; also known as **Albinus**. He transformed Charlemagne's court into a cultural center.

Al·dab·ra /al'dabrə/ a coral island group in the Indian Ocean, northwest of Madagascar.

Al·dan Riv·er /əl'dän/ a river in eastern Russia that rises in the Stanovoy Khrebet Mountains and flows for 1,400 miles (2,240 km) into the Lena River.

Al·deb·a·ran /al'debərən/ the brightest star in the constellation Taurus. It is a binary star of which the main component is a red giant. [Arab., 'the follower (of the Pleiades).']

al·de·hyde /'aldə,hīd/ ▶**n.** Chem. an organic compound containing the group –CHO, formed by the oxidation of alcohols. Typical aldehydes include methanal (formaldehyde) and ethanal (acetaldehyde). — **al·de·hy·dic** /,aldə'hīdik/ **adj.** [19th C.: shortened from L. *alcohol dehydrogenatum* 'alcohol deprived of hydrogen.']

al den·te /äl 'dentā; al/ ▶**adj. & adv.** (of food, typically pasta) cooked so as to be still firm when bitten. [Ital., lit. 'to the tooth.']

al·der /'ôldər/ (also **alder tree**) ▶**n.** a widely distributed tree (genus *Alnus*) of the birch family that has toothed leaves and bears male catkins and woody female cones. [OE *alor*, *aler*, from Gmc. akin to Ger. *Erle*.]

al·der·fly /'ôldər,flī/ (also **alder fly**) ▶**n.** (pl. **-flies**) a brownish flylike insect (family Sialidae, order Neuroptera) that lives near water and has predatory aquatic larvae.

al·der·man /'ôldərmən/ ▶**n.** (pl. **-men**) an elected member of a municipal council. — **al·der·man·ic** /,ôldər'manik/ **adj.** **al·der·man·ship** /-,SHip/ **n.** [OE *aldormann*, from *aldor*, *ealdor* 'chief,' from *ald* 'old' + **MAN**.]

Al·der·ney /'ôldərnē/ an island in the English Channel, to the northeast of Guernsey; pop. 2,130.

al·der·wom·an /'ôldər,wo͝omən/ ▶**n.** (pl. **-wom·en**) an elected female member of a municipal council.

al·di·carb /'aldi,kärb/ ▶**n.** a systemic agricultural pesticide used particularly against some mites, insects, and nematodes. [1970s: blend of **ALDEHYDE** and *carbamide* (from **CARBO-** + **AMIDE**).]

al·dol /'al,dôl; -,däl/ ▶**n.** Chem. a viscous liquid, $CH_3CH(OH)CH_2CHO$, obtained when acetaldehyde dimerizes in dilute alkali or acid. [19th C.: from *ald(ehyde)* + **-OL**.]

al·dos·te·rone /al'dästə,rōn/ ▶**n.** Biochem. a corticosteroid hormone that stimulates absorption of sodium by the kidneys and so regulates water and salt balance. [1950s: blend of **ALDEHYDE** and **STEROID**, + **-ONE**.]

al·do·ster·on·ism /,aldō'stərə,nizəm; al'dästərə-/ ▶**n.** Med. a condition in which there is excessive secretion of aldosterone. This disturbs the balance of sodium, potassium, and water in the blood and so leads to high blood pressure.

Al·drin /'ôldrin/, Buzz (1930–), US astronaut; full name *Edwin Eugene Aldrin*. He walked in space for 5 hours and 37 minutes during the 1966 Gemini 12 mission, and in the 1969 Apollo 11 mission he was the second person to set foot on the moon.

al·drin /'ôldrin/ ▶**n.** a toxic synthetic insecticide, $C_{12}H_8Cl_6$, now generally banned. [1940s: from K. *Alder* (1902–58), German chemist.]

ale /āl/ ▶**n.** a type of beer with a bitter flavor and higher alcoholic content. [OE *alu*, *ealu*, from Gmc.; akin to ON *ǫl*.]

a·le·a·tor·ic /,ālēə'tôrik; ,al-/ ▶**adj.** another term for **ALEATORY**. [1960s: from L. *aleatorius*, from *aleator* 'dice player,' from *alea* 'die,' + **-IC**.]

a·le·a·to·ry /'ālēə,tôrē; 'al-/ ▶**adj.** depending on the throw of a die or on chance; random. ■ relating to or denoting music or other forms of art involving elements of random choice during their composition, production, or performance. [17th C.: from L. *aleatorius* (see **ALEATORIC**).]

A·lec·to /ə'lektō/ (also **Al·lec·to**) Gk. Mythol. one of the Furies.

a·lee /ə'lē/ ▶**adv. & adj.** [predic.] on the side of a ship that is sheltered from the wind. [ME: from **A-**[2] + **LEE**.]

ale·house /'āl,hous/ ▶**n.** dated a tavern.

A·lei·chem /ə'lāKHəm; -kəm/ see **SHOLOM ALEICHEM**.

a·lem·bic /ə'lembik/ ▶**n.** a distilling apparatus, now obsolete, consisting of a rounded, necked flask and a cap with a long beak for condensing and conveying the products to a receiver. [ME: from med. L. *alembicus*, from Arab. *al-'anbīķ*, from *al-* 'the' + *'anbīķ* 'still' (from Gk. *ambix*, *ambik-* 'cup').]

alembic

a·leph /'älif; 'älef/ ▶**n.** the first letter of the Hebrew alphabet. [ME: from Heb. *ālep*, lit. 'ox.']

A·lep·po /ə'lepō/ a city in northern Syria; pop. 1,355,000.

a·lert /ə'lərt/ ▶ **adj.** quick to notice any unusual and potentially dangerous or difficult circumstances; vigilant. ■ able to think clearly; intellectually active. ▶ **n.** the state of being watchful for possible danger. ■ an announcement or signal warning of danger. ■ a period of vigilance in response to such a warning. ▶ **v.** [trans.] warn (someone) of a danger, threat, or problem, typically with the intention of having it avoided or dealt with.
– PHRASES **on the alert** vigilant and prepared. — **a·lert·ly** adv. **a·lert·ness** n. [16th C.: from Fr. *alerte*, from Ital. *all' erta* 'to the watchtower.']

-ales ▶ **suffix** Bot. forming the names of orders of plants: *Rosales*. [from pl. of L. *-alis* (see -AL).]

A·letsch·horn /'älicH,hôrn/ a mountain in Switzerland that rises to 13,763 feet (4,195 m).

al·eu·rone /'alyə,rōn; ə'lo͝orōn/ ▶ **n.** Bot. protein stored as granules in the cells of plant seeds. [19th C.: from Gk. *aleuron* 'flour.']

Al·eut /ə'lo͞ot; 'alē,o͞ot/ ▶ **n.** **1** a member of a people inhabiting the Aleutian Islands, other islands in the Bering Sea, and parts of western Alaska. **2** the language of this people, related to Eskimo. ▶ **adj.** of or relating to this people or their language. [from Russ.]

A·leu·tian Is·lands /ə'lo͞osHən/ (also **the A·leu·tians**) a chain of US volcanic islands that extend southwest from the Alaska Peninsula.

A·leu·tian Range an extension of the Coast Ranges in southwestern Alaska.

ale·wife /'āl,wīf/ ▶ **n.** (pl. **-wives**) a northwestern Atlantic fish (*Alosa pseudoharengus*) of the herring family that swims up rivers to spawn. [17th C.: possibly from *alewife* 'woman who keeps an alehouse,' with ref. to the fish's large belly.]

Al·ex·an·der[1] /,alig'zandər/ (356–323 BC), king of Macedon 336–323; known as **Alexander the Great**; son of Philip II. He conquered Persia, Egypt, Syria, Mesopotamia, Bactria, and the Punjab; in Egypt he founded the city of Alexandria.

Al·ex·an·der[2] three kings of Scotland: ■ Alexander I (*c.*1077–1124), son of Malcolm III; reigned 1107–24. ■ Alexander II (1198–1249), son of William I of Scotland; reigned 1214–49. ■ Alexander III (1241–86), son of Alexander II; reigned 1249–86.

Al·ex·an·der[3] three tsars of Russia: ■ Alexander I (1777–1825), reigned 1801–25. ■ Alexander II (1818–81), son of Nicholas I; reigned 1855–81; known as **Alexander the Liberator**. ■ Alexander III (1845–94), son of Alexander II; reigned 1881–94.

Al·ex·an·der Ar·chi·pel·a·go a group of more than 1,000 US islands off the coast of southeastern Alaska.

Al·ex·an·der Nev·sky, St. /'nefskē/ (also **Nevski**) (*c.*1220–63), prince of Novgorod 1236–63; born *Aleksandr Yaroslavich*. He defeated the Swedes on the banks of the Neva River in 1240.

Al·ex·an·dret·ta /,aligzan'dretə/ former name for ISKENDERUN.

Al·ex·an·dri·a /,alig'zandrēə/ **1** the chief port of Egypt; pop. 2,893,000. Founded in 332 BC by Alexander the Great, it was a center of Hellenistic culture, renowned for its library and for the Pharos lighthouse. **2** a city in central Louisiana; pop. 46,342. **3** a city in northern Virginia, across from Washington, DC; pop. 128,283.

Al·ex·an·dri·an /,alig'zandrēən/ ▶ **adj.** of or relating to Alexandria in Egypt. ■ (of a writer) derivative rather than creative; fond of recondite learning.

al·ex·an·drine /,alig'zandrin; -,drēn/ Pros. ▶ **adj.** (of a line of verse) having six iambic feet. ▶ **n.** (usu. **alexandrines**) an alexandrine line. [16th C.: from Fr. *alexandrin*, from *Alexandre* (see ALEXANDER[1]), subject of an OFr. poem.]

al·ex·an·drite /,alig'zan,drīt/ ▶ **n.** a gem variety of chrysoberyl that appears green in daylight and red in artificial light. [19th C.: Tsar *Alexander* II of Russia (see ALEXANDER[3]).]

al·fal·fa /al'falfə/ ▶ **n.** a leguminous plant (*Medicago sativa*) with cloverlike leaves and bluish flowers. Native to southwestern Asia, it is widely grown for fodder. [19th C.: from Sp., from Arab. *al-fașfașa*, a green fodder.]

Al Fa·tah /,äl fə'tä/ see FATAH, AL.

Al·fon·so XIII /al'fänsō; äl'fônsō/ (1886–1941), king of Spain 1886–1931.

Al·fred /'alfrəd/ (849–99), king of Wessex 871–899; known as **Alfred the Great**. His military resistance saved southwestern England from Viking occupation.

Al·fre·do /al'frädō/ ▶ **n.** a sauce for pasta incorporating butter, cream, garlic, and Parmesan cheese. [*Alfredo* di Lelio, Ital. restaurateur.]

al·fres·co /al'freskō; äl-/ ▶ **adv. & adj.** in the open air. [18th C.: from Ital. *al fresco* 'in the fresh (air).']

Alf·vén /äl'vān/, Hannes Olof Gösta (1908–95), Swedish theoretical physicist. His work was important for controlled thermonuclear fusion. Nobel Prize for Physics (1970, shared with Louis Néel 1904–2000).

al·ga /'algə/ ▶ **n.** (usu. in pl. **-gae** /-jē/) a large group of simple nonflowering plants containing chlorophyll but lacking true stems, roots, leaves, and vascular tissue, e.g. the seaweeds and many single-celled forms. — **al·gal** /-gəl/ adj. [16th C.: from L., 'seaweed.']

al·ge·bra /'aljəbrə/ ▶ **n.** the part of mathematics in which letters and other symbols are used to represent numbers and quantities in formulae and equations. ■ a system of this based on given axioms. — **al·ge·bra·ist** /-,brā-ist/ n. [ME: from Ital., Sp., and med. L., from Arab. *al-jabr* 'the reunion of broken parts,' 'bone setting,' from *jabara* 'reunite, restore.']

al·ge·bra·ic /,aljə'brā-ik/ ▶ **adj.** relating to or involving algebra. ■ (of a mathematical expression or equation) in which symbols are combined using only arithmetic operations and exponentiation with constant rational exponents. Compare with TRANSCENDENTAL. — **al·ge·bra·i·cal** adj. **al·ge·bra·i·cal·ly** /-ik(ə)lē/ adv.

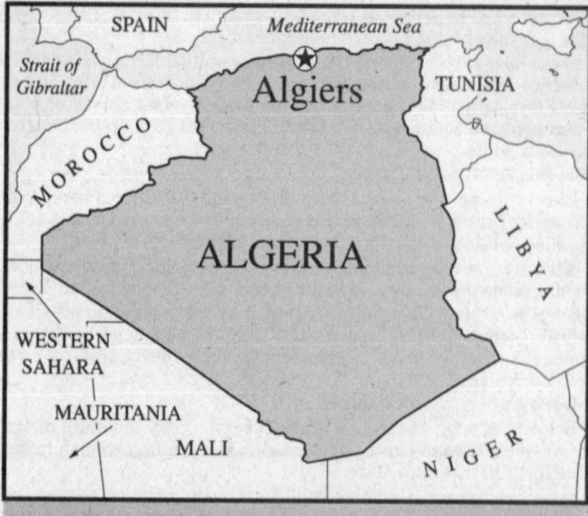

Algeria

Official name: Democratic Republic and Popular of Algeria
Location: northwestern Africa, on the Mediterranean coast, between Morocco and Libya
Area: 919,800 square miles (2,381,700 sq km)
Population: 32,100,000
Capital: Algiers
Languages: Arabic (official), French, Berber dialects
Currency: Algerian dinar

Al·ge·ci·ras /,älkHä'THēräs; -'sēräs/ a port and resort in southern Spain; pop. 101,365.

Al·ger /'aljər/, Horatio, Jr. (1832–99), US writer. His novels include *Ragged Dick* (1867).

Al·ge·ri·a /al'ji(ə)rēə/ a republic in northwestern Africa. *See box.* — **Al·ge·ri·an** adj. & n.

-algia ▶ **comb. form** denoting pain in a specified part of the body: *neuralgia* | *myalgia*. — **-algic** comb. form in corresponding adjectives. [from Gk. *algos* 'pain.']

al·gi·cide /'aljə,sīd/ ▶ **n.** a substance that is poisonous to algae.

Al·giers /al'ji(ə)rz/ port city and capital of Algeria; pop. 1,722,000.

al·gin·ic ac·id /al'jinik/ ▶ **n.** Chem. an insoluble gelatinous carbohydrate found (chiefly as salts) in many brown seaweeds. The sodium salt is used as a thickener in foods and many other materials. — **al·gi·nate** /'aljə,nāt/ n. [19th C.: from ALGA + -IN[1].]

Al·gol[1] /'al,gôl; -,gäl/ Astron. a variable star or star system in the constellation Perseus, regarded as the prototype of eclipsing binary stars. [from Arab. *al gūl* 'the ghoul.']

Al·gol[2] ▶ **n.** one of the early high-level computer programming languages that was devised to carry out scientific calculations. [1950s: from *algo(rithmic)* + LANGUAGE.]

al·gol·o·gy /al'gäləjē/ ▶ **n.** the study of algae. — **al·go·log·i·cal** /,algə'läjikəl/ adj. **al·gol·o·gist** /-jist/ n.

Al·gon·qui·an /al'gäNGk(w)ēən/ (also **Al·gon·ki·an** /-kēən/) ▶ **adj.** denoting, belonging to, or relating to a family of North American Indian languages formerly spoken across a vast area from the Atlantic seaboard to the Great Lakes and the Great Plains. ▶ **n.** **1** this family of languages. **2** a speaker of any of these languages. [from ALGONQUIN + -IAN.]

Al·gon·quin /al'gäNGk(w)in/ (also **Al·gon·kin** /-kin/) ▶ **n.** **1** a member of a North American Indian people living in Canada along the Ottawa River and its tributaries and westward to the north of Lake Superior. **2** the dialect of Ojibwa spoken by this people. ▶ **adj.** of or relating to this people or their language. [Fr., contr. of obs. *Algoumequin*, prob. from Malecite *elægómogwik* meaning 'they are our relatives or allies.']

al·go·rithm /'algə,riTHəm/ ▶ **n.** a process or set of rules to be followed in calculations or other problem-solving operations, esp. by a computer. — **al·go·rith·mic** /,algə'riTHmik/ adj. **al·go·rith·mi·cal·ly** /,algə'riTHmik(ə)lē/ adv. [17th C.: var. of ME *algorism*, via OFr. from med. L. *algorismus*, from Arab. *al-Ḵwārizmī* 'the man of Ḵwārizm' (now Khiva), which was the cognomen of 9th-cent. mathematician Abū Ja'far Muhammad ibn Mūsa.]

Al·ham·bra /al'hambrə/ a city in southwestern California; pop. 82,106.

Al·ham·bra, the /al'hambrə/ a Moorish palace and citadel near Granada, Spain, built between 1248 and 1354.

Al-Hu·day·da Arabic name for HODEIDA.

A·li[1] /ä'lē/, Muhammad, see MUHAMMAD ALI[1].

A·li[2] /ä'lē; 'älē/, Muhammad (1942–), US boxer; born *Cassius Marcellus Clay*. He won the world heavyweight title in 1964, 1974, and 1978.

a·li·as /'ālēəs/ ▶ **adv.** used to indicate that a named person is also known or more familiar under another specified name. ■ informal indicating another term or synonym: *the catfish—alias bullhead—is mighty tasty.* ▶ **n.** a false or assumed identity. ■ Comput. an alternative name or label that refers to a file, command, address, or other item, and can be used to locate or access it. [ME: from L., 'otherwise.']

a·li·as·ing /'ālēəsiNG/ ▶ **n.** Comput. in computer graphics, the jagged or saw-toothed appearance of curved or diagonal lines on a low-resolution monitor.

A·li Ba·ba /,älē 'bäbə/ the hero of a story supposed to be from the *Arabian Nights*, who discovered the magic formula ("Open Sesame!") that opened a cave where forty robbers kept their treasure.

al·i·bi /'alə,bī/ ▶ **n.** (pl. **-bis**) a claim or piece of evidence that one was elsewhere when an act, typically a criminal one, is alleged to have taken place. ■ informal an excuse or pretext. ▶ **v.** (**-bis**, **-bied**, **-bi·ing**) [trans.] informal offer an excuse or defense for (someone), esp. by providing an account of their whereabouts at the time of an alleged act: *her friend agreed to alibi her.* ■ [intrans.] make excuses: *he never alibied.* [17th C. (adv.): from L., 'elsewhere.']

Al·i·can·te /,ali'kantē; ,älə'käntā/ a seaport in southeastern Spain; pop. 270,950.

Al·ice Springs /'alis/ a railroad terminus and supply center in Northern Territory, Australia; pop. 20,450.

al·i·cy·clic /,alə'sīklik; -'sik-/ Chem. ▶ **adj.** relating to or denoting organic compounds that combine cyclic structure with aliphatic properties, e.g., cyclohexane. Compare with AROMATIC. ▶ **n.** (usu. **alicyclics**) an alicyclic compound. [19th C.: blend of ALIPHATIC and CYCLIC.]

a·li·en /'ālyən; 'ālēən/ ▶ **adj.** belonging to a foreign country or nation. ■ unfamiliar and disturbing or distasteful: *bossing anyone around was alien to him.* ■ [attrib.] relating to or denoting beings supposedly from other worlds; extraterrestrial. ■ (of a plant or animal species) introduced from another country and later naturalized. ▶ **n.** a foreigner, esp. one who is not a naturalized citizen of the country where they are living ■ a hypothetical or fictional being from another world. ■ a plant or animal species originally introduced from another country and later naturalized. — **al·ien·ness** **n.** [ME: ult. from L. *alienus* 'belonging to another,' from *alius* 'other.']

al·ien·a·ble /'ālēənəbəl; 'ālyənə-/ ▶ **adj.** Law able to be transferred to new ownership. — **a·lien·a·bil·i·ty** /,ālēənə'bilitē; ,ālyən-/ **n.**

al·ien·age /'ālēənij; 'ālyə-/ ▶ **n.** the state or condition of being an alien.

al·ien·ate /'ālēə,nāt; 'ālyə-/ ▶ **v.** [trans.] **1** cause (someone) to feel isolated or estranged. ■ cause (someone) to become unsympathetic or hostile: *the association alienated its members.* **2** Law transfer ownership of (property rights) to another.

al·ien·a·tion /,ālēə'nāSHən; ,ālyə-/ ▶ **n.** isolation from a group or an activity to which one should belong or in which one should be involved. ■ loss or lack of sympathy; estrangement: *public alienation from bureaucracy.* ■ Psychiatry a state of depersonalization or loss of identity in which the self seems unreal. ■ Law the transfer of the ownership of property rights.

al·ien·ist /'ālēənist; 'ālyə-/ ▶ **n.** former term for PSYCHIATRIST. ■ a psychiatrist who assesses the competence of a defendant in a court of law.

a-life /'ā,līf/ ▶ **n.** short for ARTIFICIAL LIFE.

al·i·form /'alə,fôrm; 'ālə-/ ▶ **adj.** wing-shaped. [18th C.: from mod. L. *aliformis*, from L. *ala* 'wing' + *-formis* (see -FORM).]

A·li·ghie·ri /,aləg'yerē/, Dante, see DANTE.

a·light¹ /ə'līt/ ▶ **v.** [intrans.] (of a bird) descend from the air and settle: *a blue swallow alighted on a branch.* ■ descend from a train, bus, or other form of transportation.

– PHRASAL VERBS **alight on** find by chance; notice. [OE *ālīhtan*, from *ā-* (intensive) + *līhtan* 'descend' (see LIGHT³).]

a·light² ▶ **adv. & adj.** on fire; burning. ■ shining brightly. [ME: prob. from *on a light* (= lighted) *fire*.]

a·lign /ə'līn/ ▶ **v. 1** [trans.] place or arrange (things) in a straight line. ■ put (things) into correct relative positions. ■ [intrans.] lie in a straight line, or in correct relative positions. **2** (**align oneself with**) give support to (a person, organization, or cause). ■ [intrans.] come together in agreement or alliance. [17th C.: from Fr. *aligner*, from *à ligne* 'into line.']

a·lign·ment /ə'līnmənt/ ▶ **n. 1** arrangement in a straight line, or in correct relative positions. ■ the act of aligning parts of a machine: *wheel alignments.* ■ the route or course of a road or railroad. **2** a position of agreement or alliance.

a·like /ə'līk/ ▶ **adj.** [predic.] (of two or more subjects) similar to each other: *the brothers were very much alike.* ▶ **adv.** in the same or a similar way: *the girls dressed alike.* ■ used to show that something applies equally to a number of specified subjects: *he talked in a friendly manner to staff and patients alike.* [OE *gelīc*, from Gmc. akin to Ger. *gleich*.]

al·i·men·ta·ry /,alə'ment(ə)rē/ ▶ **adj.** of or relating to nourishment or sustenance. [16th C.: from L. *alimentarius*, from *alimentum* 'nourishment.']

al·i·men·ta·ry ca·nal ▶ **n.** the passage (including the esophagus, stomach, and intestines) along which food passes through the body from mouth to anus.

al·i·men·ta·tion /,aləmen'tāSHən/ ▶ **n.** formal the provision of nourishment or other necessities of life.

al·i·mo·ny /'alə,mōnē/ ▶ **n.** a husband's or wife's court-ordered provision for a spouse after separation or divorce. [17th C.: from L. *alimonia* 'nutriment,' from *alere* 'nourish.']

A-line /'ā,līn/ ▶ **adj.** (of a garment) slightly flared from a narrow waist or shoulders: *A-line skirts.*

al·i·phat·ic /,alə'fatik/ Chem. ▶ **adj.** relating to or denoting organic compounds in which carbon atoms form open chains (as in the alkanes), not aromatic rings. Compare with ALICYCLIC. ▶ **n.** (usu. **aliphatics**) an aliphatic compound. [19th C.: from Gk. *aleiphar, aleiphat-* 'fat' + -IC.]

al·i·quot /'alikwət/ ▶ **n.** a portion of a larger whole, esp. a sample taken for chemical analysis. ■ (also **aliquot part** or **portion**) Math. a quantity that can be divided into another an integral number of times. [16th C.: ult. from L. *aliquot* 'some, so many,' from *alius* 'one of two' + *quot* 'how many.']

A-list /'ā ,list/ (or **B-list** /'bē ,list/) ▶ **n.** a real or imaginary list of the most (or, for B-list, second-most) celebrated or sought-after individuals, especially in show business: [as modifier] *an A-list celebrity.*

a·lit·er·ate /ā'litərit/ ▶ **adj.** unwilling to read, although able to do so. ▶ **n.** an aliterate person. — **a·lit·er·a·cy** /-əsē/ **n.**

A·li·to /ə'lētō/, Samuel Anthony, Jr. (1950–), US Supreme Court associate justice 2006–.

a·live /ə'līv/ ▶ **adj.** [predic.] **1** (of a person, animal, or plant) living, not dead. ■ (of a feeling or quality) continuing in existence: *keeping hope alive.* ■ continuing to be supported or in use. **2** (of a person or animal) alert and active; animated. **3** (**alive to**) aware of and interested in; responsive to. **4** (**alive with**) swarming or teeming with.

– PHRASES **look alive** another term for LOOK LIVELY (see LIVELY). [OE *on līfe*, lit. 'in life.']

a·li·yah /,älē'ä/ ▶ **n.** (pl. **a·li·yoth** /,älē'ōt/) Judaism **1** immigration to Israel. **2** the honor of being called upon to read from the Torah. [from Heb. *'ălīyāh* 'ascent.']

a·liz·a·rin /ə'lizərin/ ▶ **n.** Chem. a red pigment, $C_{14}H_8O_4$, present in madder root, used in dyeing. ■ [as adj.] denoting dyes derived from or similar to this pigment: *alizarin crimson.* [19th C.: from Fr. *alizarine*, from *alizari* 'madder,' from Arab. *al-iṣāra* 'pressed juice.']

Al Ji·zah /äl 'jēzə/ var. of GIZA.

al·ka·li /'alkə,lī/ ▶ **n.** (pl. **-lis**) a chemical compound that neutralizes or effervesces with acids and turns litmus blue; typically, a caustic or corrosive substance of this kind such as lime or soda. Often contrasted with ACID; compare with BASE¹. [ME: from med. L., from Arab. *al-ḳalī* 'calcined ashes,' from *ḳalā* 'fry, roast.']

al·kal·ic /al'kalik/ ▶ **adj.** Geol. (of a rock or mineral) richer in sodium and/or potassium than is usual for its type.

al·ka·li feld·spar ▶ **n.** Geol. any of the group of feldspars rich in sodium and/or potassium.

al·ka·li met·al ▶ **n.** Chem. any of the highly reactive elements lithium, sodium, potassium, rubidium, cesium, and francium, occupying Group IA (1) of the periodic table.

al·ka·line /'alkəlin; -,līn/ ▶ **adj.** having the properties of an alkali, or containing alkali; having a pH greater than 7. Often contrasted with ACID or ACIDIC; compare with BASIC. — **al·ka·lin·i·ty** /,alkə'linitē/ **n.**

al·ka·line earth (also **alkaline earth metal**) ▶ **n.** any of the reactive elements beryllium, magnesium, calcium, strontium, barium, and radium, occupying Group IIA (2) of the periodic table.

al·ka·lize /'alkə,līz/ (also **al·ka·lin·ize** /'alkəli,nīz/) ▶ **v.** [trans.] [usu. as adj.] (**alkalized** or **alkalizing**) treat with alkali. — **al·ka·li·za·tion** /,alkələ'zāSHən/ **n.** **al·ka·liz·er** **n.**

al·ka·loid /'alkə,loid/ ▶ **n.** Chem. any of a class of nitrogenous organic compounds of plant origin that have pronounced physiological actions on humans, including morphine, quinine, atropine, and strychnine. [19th C.: coined in Ger. from ALKALI.]

al·ka·lo·sis /,alkə'lōsis/ ▶ **n.** Med. an excessively alkaline condition of the body fluids or tissues that may cause weakness or cramps.

al·kane /'al,kān/ ▶ **n.** Chem. any of the series of saturated hydrocarbons having the general formula C_nH_{2n+2}, including methane, ethane, and propane [19th C.: from ALKYL.]

al·kene /'al,kēn/ ▶ **n.** Chem. any of the series of unsaturated hydrocarbons containing a double bond and having the general formula C_nH_{2n}, including ethylene and propylene.

al·ky /'alkē/ (also **al·kie**) ▶ **n.** (pl. **-kies**) informal an alcoholic.

al·kyd /'alkid/ ▶ **n.** Chem. any of a group of synthetic polyester resins derived from various alcohols and acids, used in varnishes, paints, and adhesives. [1920s: blend of ALKYL and ACID.]

al·kyl /'alkəl/ ▶ **n.** [as adj.] Chem. of or denoting a hydrocarbon radical derived from an alkane by removal of a hydrogen atom. [19th C.: Ger., from *Alkohol* 'alcohol.']

al·kyl·ate /'alkə,lāt/ ▶ **v.** [trans.] [usu. as adj.] (**alkylating** or **alkylated**) Chem. introduce an alkyl radical into (a compound): *alkylating agents.* — **al·kyl·a·tion** /,alkə'lāSHən/ **n.**

al·kyne /'al,kīn/ ▶ **n.** Chem. any of the series of unsaturated hydrocarbons containing a triple bond and having the general formula C_nH_{2n-2}, including acetylene. [20th C.: from ALKYL.]

all /ôl/ ▶ **predeterminer, adj., & pron.** used to refer to the whole quantity or extent of a particular group or thing: [as predeterminer] *all the people I met* | [as adj.] *10% of all cars sold* | [as pron.] *four bedrooms, all with balconies.* ■ [adj.] any whatever: *he denied all knowledge.* ■ [adj.] used to emphasize the greatest possible amount of a quality: *with all due respect.* ■ informal dominated by a particular feature or characteristic: *an eleven-year-old* *string bean, all elbows and knees.* ■ [pron.] [with clause] the only thing (used for emphasis): *all I want is to be left alone.* ■ [pron.] (used to refer to surroundings or a situation in general) everything. ■ informal used to indicate more than one person or thing. ▶ **adv.** **1** used for emphasis: ■ completely: *dressed all in black.* ■ consisting entirely of: *all leather varsity jacket.* **2** (in games) used after a number to indicate an equal score: *after extra time it was still two all.* ▶ **n.** the whole of one's possessions, energy, or interest: *giving their all for what they believed.*

– PHRASES **all along** all the time; from the beginning. **all and sundry** everyone. **all around** (Brit. also **all round**) **1** in all respects: *a bad day all around.* **2** for or by each person: *drinks all around.* **all but 1** very nearly: *the subject was all but forgotten.* **2** all except: *all but one of the networks.* **all comers** esp. informal anyone who chooses to take part in an activity, typically a competition. **all for** informal strongly in favor of. **all in** informal exhausted. **all in all** everything considered; on the whole. **all kinds** (or **sorts**) **of** many different kinds of. **all manner of** see MANNER. **all of** as much as (typically used ironically of a quantity considered small by the speaker): *the show lasted all of six weeks.* **all of a sudden** see SUDDEN. **all one to someone** making no difference to someone: *simple cases or hard cases, it's all one to me.* **all out** using all one's strength or resources. **all over 1** completely finished: *it's all over between us.* **2** informal everywhere: *there were bodies all over.* ■ with reference to all parts of the body: *I was shaking all over.* **3** informal typical of the person mentioned. **4** informal effusively attentive to (someone): *James was all over her.* **all over the place** (or **map**) informal everywhere ■ in a state of disorder. **all sorts of** see *ALL KINDS OF* above. **all that** —— see THAT. **all the same** see SAME. **all the** —— see THE (sense 6). **all there** [usu. with negative] informal in full possession of one's mental faculties. **all the time** see TIME. **all together** all in one place or in a group; all at once. Compare with ALTOGETHER. **all told** in total. **all very well** informal used to express criticism or rejection of a favorable or consoling remark. **all the way** informal without limit or reservation. See also *GO ALL THE WAY* at WAY. —— **and all** used to emphasize something additional that is being referred to: *she threw her coffee over him, mug and all.* ■ informal as well: *it must hit him hard, being so young and all.* **at all** [with negative or in questions] (used for emphasis) in any way; to any extent: *I don't like him at all.* **be all up with** see UP. **for all** —— in spite of ——: *for all its clarity and style, the book is not easy reading.* **in all** in total number; altogether. **of all** see OF. **on all fours** see FOUR. **one and all** see ONE. [OE *all, eall*, from Gmc. akin to Ger. *all.*]

al·la bre·ve /ˌälə ˈbrev(ā)/ ▶ **n.** Music a time signature indicating 2 or 4 half-note beats in a bar. [Ital., lit. 'according to the breve.']

Al·lah /ˈälə; ˈalə/ the name of God among Muslims (and Arab Christians). [from Arab. *ʾallāh*, contr. of *al-ʾilāh* 'the god.']

Al·lah·a·bad /ˈäləhəˌbäd; ˈaləhəˌbad/ a city in Uttar Pradesh state, in north central India; pop. 806,000.

all-A·mer·i·can ▶ **adj.** **1** possessing qualities characteristic of American ideals, such as honesty, industriousness, and health. **2** having members or contents drawn only from America or the US. ■ involving or representing the whole of America or the US. ■ (also **all-America**) (of a sports player) honored as one of the best amateur competitors in the US. ▶ **n.** (also **all-America**) a sports player honored as one of the best amateurs in the US.

al·lan·to·in /əˈlantō-in/ ▶ **n.** Biochem. a crystalline compound, $C_4H_6N_4O_3$, formed in the nitrogen metabolism of many mammals (excluding primates). [19th C.: from ALLANTOIS.]

al·lan·to·is /əˈlantō-is/ ▶ **n.** (pl. **al·lan·to·i·des** /ˌalənˈtō-idēz/) the fetal membrane lying below the chorion in many vertebrates, formed as an outgrowth of the embryo's gut. — **al·lan·to·ic** /ˌalənˈtō-ik/ **adj.** **al·lan·toid** /-toid/ **adj.** [17th C.: mod. L., based on Gk. *allantoeidēs* 'sausage-shaped.']

all-a·round (Brit. **all-round**) ▶ **adj.** having many uses or abilities; versatile: *an all-around artist.* ■ in many or all respects: *his all-around excellence.* ■ comprehensive; extensive. *an all-around education.*

al·lay /əˈlā/ ▶ **v.** [trans.] diminish or put at rest (fear, suspicion, or worry). ■ relieve or alleviate (pain or hunger). [OE *ālecgan* 'lay down.']

all clear ▶ **n.** a signal that danger or difficulty is over.

all-day ▶ **adj.** lasting or available throughout the day.

al·lée /äˈlā/ ▶ **n.** an alley in a formal garden or park, bordered by trees or bushes. [18th C.: Fr.]

al·le·ga·tion /ˌaliˈgāsʜən/ ▶ **n.** a claim or assertion that someone has done something illegal or wrong, typically one made without proof. [ME: from L. *allegatio(n-)*, from *allegare* 'allege.']

al·lege /əˈlej/ ▶ **v.** claim or assert that someone has done something illegal or wrong, typically without proof that this is the case. ■ (usu. **be alleged**) suppose or affirm to be the case. [ME: from OFr. *esligier*, based on Latin *lis, lit-* 'lawsuit'; confused in sense with L. *allegare* 'allege.']

al·leged /əˈlejd/ ▶ **adj.** [attrib.] (of an incident or a person) said, without proof, to have taken place or to have a specified illegal or undesirable quality. — **al·leg·ed·ly** /-idlē/ **adv.**

Al·le·ghe·ny Moun·tains /ˌaləˈgānē; -ˈgenē/ (also **the Al·le·ghe·nies**) part of the Appalachian mountain range that extends from West Virginia through Pennsylvania.

Al·le·ghe·ny Riv·er a river of southwestern New York and western Pennsylvania that flows for 325 miles (523 km), joining the Monongahela at Pittsburgh to form the Ohio.

al·le·giance /əˈlējəns/ ▶ **n.** loyalty or commitment of a subordinate to a superior or of an individual to a group or cause. [ME: from Anglo-Norman Fr., var. of OFr. *ligeance*, from *lige, liege* (see LIEGE).]

al·le·gor·i·cal /ˌaliˈgôrikəl; -ˈgär-/ ▶ **adj.** constituting or containing allegory: *an allegorical painting.* — **al·le·gor·ic adj.** **al·le·gor·i·cal·ly** /-ik(ə)lē/ **adv.**

al·le·go·rize /ˈaligəˌrīz/ ▶ **v.** [trans.] interpret or represent symbolically. — **al·le·go·ri·za·tion** /ˌaliˌgôrəˈzāsʜən/ **n.**

al·le·go·ry /ˈaləˌgôrē/ ▶ **n.** (pl. **-ries**) a story, poem, or picture that can be interpreted to reveal a hidden meaning, typically a moral or political one. ■ the genre to which such works belong. ■ a symbol. — **al·le·go·rist n.** [ME: ult. from Gk. *allēgoria*, from *allos* 'other' + *-agoria* 'speaking.']

al·le·gro /əˈlegrō/ Music ▶ **adj. & adv.** (esp. as a direction) at a brisk tempo. ▶ **n.** (pl. **-gros**) a passage or movement in an allegro tempo. [Ital., lit. 'lively.']

al·lele /əˈlēl/ ▶ **n.** Genet. one of two or more alternative forms of a gene that arise by mutation and are found at the same place on a chromosome. Also called ALLELOMORPH. — **al·lel·ic** /əˈlēlik; əˈlel-/ **adj.** [1930s: from Ger. *Allel*, abbrev. of ALLELOMORPH.]

al·le·lo·morph /əˌlēləˈmôrf; əˌlel-/ ▶ **n.** another term for ALLELE. — **al·le·lo·mor·phic** /-ˈmôrfik/ **adj.** [20th C.: from Gk. *allēl-* 'one another' + *morphē* 'form.']

al·le·lop·a·thy /əlēˈläpəтнē; ˌalə-/ ▶ **n.** the chemical inhibition of one plant (or other organism) by another, due to the release into the environment of substances acting as germination or growth inhibitors. [1950s: from Gk. *allēl-* 'one another.']

al·le·lu·ia /ˌaləˈlo͞oyə/ ▶ **exclam.** var. of HALLELUJAH. [OE, from Gk. *allēlouia*, from Heb. *hallĕlūyāh* 'praise ye the Lord.']

al·le·mande /ˈaləˌmand; -ˌmänd/ ▶ **n.** any of a number of German dances. ■ the music for any of these, esp. as a movement of a suite. ■ a figure in square dancing in which adjacent dancers link arms or join or touch hands and make a full or partial turn. [16th C.: from Fr., 'Ger. (dance).']

all-em·brac·ing ▶ **adj.** including or covering everything or everyone; comprehensive.

Al·len /ˈalən/, Ethan (1738–89), American soldier. He fought the British in the American Revolution and led the Green Mountain Boys in their campaign to gain independence for the state of Vermont.

Al·len·de /äˈyenˌdā/, Salvador (1908–73), Chilean statesman; president 1970–73. The first avowed Marxist to win a presidency in a free election, he was overthrown and killed in a military coup.

Al·len·town /ˈalənˌtoun/ a city in eastern Pennsylvania, on the Lehigh River; pop. 106,632.

Al·len wrench (also **al·len wrench**) ▶ **n.** an L-shaped metal bar with a hexagonal head at each end, used to turn bolts and screws having hexagonal sockets. [1960s: *Allen* Manufacturing Company, of Hartford, Connecticut.]

al·ler·gen /ˈalərjən/ ▶ **n.** a substance that causes an allergic reaction. — **al·ler·gen·ic** /ˌalərˈjenik/ **adj.** **al·ler·ge·nic·i·ty** /ˌalərjəˈnisitē/ **n.** [20th C.: blend of ALLERGY and -GEN.]

al·ler·gic /əˈlərjik/ ▶ **adj.** caused by or relating to an allergy. ■ having an allergy to (a substance). ■ (**allergic to**) informal having a strong dislike for: *I'm allergic to his sister.*

al·ler·gist /ˈalərjist/ ▶ **n.** a medical practitioner specializing in the diagnosis and treatment of allergies.

al·ler·gy /ˈalərjē/ ▶ **n.** (pl. **-gies**) a damaging immune response by the body to a substance, esp. pollen, fur, a particular food, or dust, to which it has become hypersensitive. ■ informal an antipathy: *their allergy to free enterprise.* [20th C.: from Ger. *Allergie*, from Gk. *allos* 'other.']

Al·le·rød /ˈaləˌro͝od; -ˌrœd/ ▶ **n.** (**the Allerød**) Geol. the second climatic stage of the late-glacial period in northern Europe (about 12,000 to 10,800 years ago). It was an interlude of warmer weather marked by the spread of birch, pine, and willow. [1920s: Allerød, Denmark.]

al·le·vi·ate /əˈlēvēˌāt/ ▶ **v.** [trans.] make (suffering, deficiency, or a problem) less severe. — **al·le·vi·a·tion** /əˌlēvēˈāsʜən/ **n.** **al·le·vi·a·tor** /-ˌātər/ **n.** [ME: from late L. *alleviat-* 'lightened,' from the v. *alleviare*, based on L. *ad-* 'to' + *levare* 'raise.']

al·ley[1] /ˈalē/ ▶ **n.** (pl. **-leys**) a narrow passageway between or behind buildings. ■ a path lined with trees, bushes, or stones. Compare with ALLÉE. ■ [with modifier] a long, narrow area in which games such as bowling are played. ■ Tennis either of the two areas of the court between the doubles sideline and the singles or service sideline. ■ Baseball the area between the outfielders in left center or right center field.

– PHRASES **up one's alley** (or **right up one's alley**) informal well suited to one's tastes, interests, or abilities. [ME: from OFr. *alee* 'passage,' from *aler* 'go,' from L. *ambulare* 'to walk.']

al·ley[2] (also **al·ly**) ▶ **n.** (pl. **-leys**) a toy marble made of marble, alabaster, or glass. [18th C.: perh. dimin. of ALABASTER.]

al·ley cat ▶ **n.** a cat that lives wild in a town.

al·ley-oop /ˌalēˈo͞op/ ▶ **exclam.** used to encourage or draw attention to the performance of some physical, esp. acrobatic, feat. ▶ **n.** (also **alley-oop pass**) Basketball a high pass caught by a leaping teammate who tries to dunk the ball before landing. [20th C.]

al·ley·way /ˈalēˌwā/ ▶ **n.** another term for ALLEY[1].

all-fired informal ▶ **adv.** extremely. ▶ **adj.** extreme.

All Fools' Day ▶ **n.** another term for APRIL FOOL'S DAY.

All Hal·lows ▶ **n.** another term for ALL SAINTS' DAY.

all·heal /ˈôlˌhēl/ ▶ **n.** any of a number of plants, esp. valerian, used in herbal medicine.

al·li·a·ceous /ˌalēˈāsʜəs/ ▶ **adj.** Bot. of, relating to, or denoting plants of a group that comprises the onions and other alliums. [18th C.: from L. *allium* 'garlic.']

al·li·ance /ə'līəns/ ▶ n. a union or association formed for mutual benefit, esp. between countries or organizations. ■ a relationship based on an affinity in interests, nature, or qualities: *an alliance between medicine and morality.* ■ a state of being joined or associated. [ME: from OFr. *aliance*, from *aliere* (see ALLY[1]).]

al·li·cin /'alisin/ ▶ n. Chem. a pungent oily liquid, $(C_3H_5S)_2O$, with antibacterial properties, present in garlic. [from L. *allium* 'garlic.']

al·lied /ə'līd; 'al,īd/ ▶ adj. joined by or relating to members of an alliance. ■ (usu. **Allied**) of or relating to the US and its allies in World War I and World War II and after. ■ (**allied to/with**) in combination or working together with. ■ connected or related.

Al·lier /äl'yā/ a river in central France that flows northwest for 258 miles (410 km) to meet the Loire River.

American alligator

al·li·ga·tor /'ali,gātər/ ▶ n. a large semiaquatic reptile (genus *Alligator*, family Alligatoridae, order Crocodylia) similar to a crocodile but with a broader and shorter head. Its two species are the **American alligator** (*A. mississippiensis*) and the **Chinese alligator** (*A. sinensis*). ■ the skin of the alligator or material resembling it. [16th C.: from Sp. *el lagarto* 'the lizard,' prob. based on L. *lacerta*.]

al·li·ga·tor clip ▶ n. a sprung metal clip with long, serrated jaws, used attached to an electric cable for making a temporary connection to a battery or other component.

al·li·ga·tor pear ▶ n. another term for AVOCADO.

al·li·ga·tor snap·ping tur·tle (also **al·li·ga·tor snap·per**) ▶ n. a large-headed, long-tailed snapping turtle (*Macroclemys temminckii*, family Chelydridae) of the southeastern US, found esp. in the Gulf States. Weighing up to 150 pounds (67.5 kg), it is the largest freshwater turtle in North America.

all-im·por·tant ▶ adj. vitally important; crucial.

all-in·clu·sive ▶ adj. including everything or everyone.

all-in-one ▶ adj. [attrib.] combining two or more items or functions in a single unit.

alligator clip

al·lit·er·ate /ə'litə,rāt/ ▶ v. [intrans.] (of a phrase or line of verse) contain words that begin with the same sound or letter. ■ use words that begin with the same sound or letter. [18th C.: back-form. from ALLITERATION.]

al·lit·er·a·tion /ə,litə'rāsHən/ ▶ n. the occurrence of the same letter or sound at the beginning of adjacent or closely connected words. — **al·lit·er·a·tive** /ə'litərətiv; -,rātiv/ adj. **al·lit·er·a·tive·ly** adv. [17th C.: from med. L. *alliteratio(n-)*, from L. *ad-* + *littera* 'letter.']

al·li·um /'alēəm/ ▶ n. (pl. **-ums**) a bulbous plant (genus *Allium*) of the lily family that includes the onion and its relatives (e.g., garlic, leek, and chives). [19th C.: L., 'garlic.']

all-night ▶ adj. [attrib.] lasting, open, or operating throughout the night: *an all-night party.*

all-night·er /,ôl 'nītər/ ▶ n. informal an event or task that continues throughout the night, esp. a study session before an examination.

allo- ▶ comb. form other; different: *allopatric* | *allotrope.* [from Gk. *allos* 'other.']

al·lo·cate /'alə,kāt/ ▶ v. [trans.] distribute (resources or duties) for a particular purpose. — **al·lo·ca·ble** /-kəbəl/ adj. **al·lo·ca·tor** /-,kātər/ n. [17th C.: from med. L. *allocat-* 'allotted,' from v. *allocare*, from *ad-* 'to' + *locare* (see LOCATE).]

al·lo·ca·tion /,alə'kāsHən/ ▶ n. the action or process of allocating or distributing something. ■ an amount or portion of a resource assigned to a particular recipient.

al·loch·tho·nous /ə'läkTHənəs/ ▶ adj. Geol. denoting a sediment or rock that originated at a distance from its present position. Often contrasted with AUTOCHTHONOUS. [20th C.: from ALLO- + Gk. *khthōn* 'earth.']

al·lo·cu·tion /,alə'kyōōsHən/ ▶ n. a formal speech giving advice or a warning. [17th C.: from L. *allocutio(n-)*, from *alloqui* 'speak to,' from *ad-* + *loqui* 'speak.']

al·log·a·my /ə'lägəmē/ ▶ n. Bot. the fertilization of a flower by pollen from another flower, esp. one on a different plant. Compare with AUTOGAMY. — **al·log·a·mous** /-məs/ adj. [19th C.: from ALLO- + Gk. *-gamia* (from *gamos* 'marriage').]

al·lo·ge·ne·ic /,aləjə'nē-ik/ ▶ adj. Immunol. denoting, relating to, or involving tissues or cells that are genetically dissimilar and hence immunologically incompatible, although from individuals of the same species. [1960s: from ALLO- + Gk. *genea*.]

al·lo·gen·ic /,alə'jenik/ ▶ adj. **1** Geol. (of a mineral or sediment) transported to its present position from elsewhere. **2** Ecol. (of a successional change) caused by nonliving factors in the environment.

al·lo·graft /'alə,graft/ ▶ n. a tissue graft from a donor of the same species as the recipient but not genetically identical. Compare with HOMOGRAFT.

al·lom·e·try /ə'lämitrē/ ▶ n. Biol. the growth of body parts at different rates, resulting in a change of body proportions. ■ the study of such growth. — **al·lo·met·ric** /,alə'metrik/ adj.

al·lo·path /'alə,paTH/ ▶ n. a person who practices allopathy.

al·lop·a·thy /ə'läpəTHē/ ▶ n. the treatment of disease by conventional means, i.e., with drugs having opposite effects to the symptoms. Often contrasted with HOMEOPATHY. — **al·lo·path·ic** /,alə'paTHik/ adj. **al·lop·a·thist** /-THist/ n.

al·lo·pat·ric /,alə'patrik/ ▶ adj. Biol. (of animals or plants, esp. of related species or populations) occurring in separate nonoverlapping geographical areas. Compare with SYMPATRIC. ■ (of speciation) taking place as a result of such separation. — **al·lop·a·try** /'alə,patrē/ n. [1940s: from ALLO- + Gk. *patra* 'fatherland.']

al·lo·phone /'alə,fōn/ ▶ n. Ling. any of the spoken speech sounds that represent a single phoneme, such as the aspirated *k* in *kit* and the unaspirated *k* in *skit*, which are allophones of the phoneme /k/. — **al·lo·phon·ic** /,alə'fänik/ adj. [1930s: from ALLO- + PHONEME.]

al·lo·pu·ri·nol /alə'pyŏŏri,nôl; -,näl/ ▶ n. Med. a synthetic drug that inhibits uric acid formation in the body and is used to treat gout and related conditions. [1960s: from ALLO- + PURINE + -OL.]

all-or-none ▶ adj. another way of saying ALL-OR-NOTHING. ■ Physiol. (of a response) having a strength independent of the strength of the stimulus that caused it.

all-or-noth·ing ▶ adj. having no middle position or compromise available: *an all-or-nothing decision.*

al·lo·saur /'alə,sôr/ (also **al·lo·sau·rus** /,alə'sôrəs/) ▶ n. a large bipedal carnivorous dinosaur (genus *Allosaurus*, suborder Theropoda) of the late Jurassic period. — **al·lo·sau·ri·an** adj. [mod. L., from Gk. *allos* 'other' + *sauros* 'lizard.']

al·lo·ster·ic /,alə'sterik; -'sti(ə)r-/ ▶ adj. Biochem. relating to or denoting the alteration of the activity of a protein through the binding of an effector molecule at a specific site. — **al·lo·ster·i·cal·ly** /-ik(ə)lē/ adv.

al·lot /ə'lät/ ▶ v. (**-lot·ted, -lot·ting**) [trans.] give or apportion (something) to someone as a share or task. [15th C.: from OFr. *aloter*, from *a-* 'to' + *loter* 'divide into lots.']

al·lot·ment /ə'lätmənt/ ▶ n. the amount of something allocated to a particular person. ■ the action of allotting.

al·lo·trope /'alə,trōp/ ▶ n. Chem. each of two or more different physical forms in which an element can exist. Graphite, charcoal, and diamond are all allotropes of carbon. [19th C.: back-form. from ALLOTROPY.]

al·lot·ro·py /ə'lätrəpē/ ▶ n. Chem. the existence of two or more different physical forms of a chemical element. — **al·lo·trop·ic** /,alə'träpik; -'trō-/ adj. [19th C.: from Gk. *allotropos* 'of another form,' from *allo-* 'other' + *tropos* 'manner.']

al·lot·tee /ə,lä'tē/ ▶ n. a person to whom something is allotted, esp. land or shares.

all-ov·er ▶ adj. [attrib.] covering the whole of something.

al·low /ə'lou/ ▶ v. [trans.] **1** admit (an event or activity) as legal or acceptable. ■ give (someone) permission to do something. ■ permit (someone) to have (something): *he was allowed his first sip of wine.* ■ [trans.] permit (someone) to enter a place or go in a particular direction. ■ fail to prevent (something) from happening: *we allowed the opportunity to slip away.* **2** give the necessary time or opportunity for: *they agreed to a cease-fire to allow talks with the government.* ■ [intrans.] (**allow for**) make provision or provide scope for (something): *the house was demolished to allow for road widening.* ■ take (something) into consideration when making plans or calculations. ■ [trans.] provide or set aside (a specified amount of something) for a specific purpose: *allow an hour or so for driving.* **3** admit the truth of; concede. ■ [with clause] informal or dialect assert; be of the opinion: *Lincoln allowed that he himself could never support the man.* — **al·low·a·ble** adj. **al·low·a·bly** /-əblē/ adv. [ME: from OFr. *alouer*, from L. *allaudare* 'to praise,' reinforced by med. L. *allocare* 'to place' (see ALLOCATE).]

al·low·ance /ə'louəns/ ▶ n. the amount of something that is permitted, esp. within a set of regulations or for a specified purpose. ■ a sum of money paid regularly to a person, typically to meet specified needs or expenses. ■ a small amount of money that a parent regularly gives a child. ■ an amount of money that can be earned or received free of tax. ■ a reduction in price, typically for the exchange of used goods.
– PHRASES **make allowance(s) for 1** take into consideration when planning or making calculations. **2** regard or treat leniently on account of mitigating circumstances.

al·low·ed·ly /ə'lou-idlē/ ▶ adv. [sentence adverb] as is generally admitted to be true.

al·loy ▶ n. /'aloi/ a metal made by combining two or more metallic elements, esp. to give greater strength or resistance to corrosion. ■ an inferior metal mixed with a precious one. ▶ v. /'aloi; ə'loi/ [trans.] mix (metals) to make an alloy. ■ fig. debase (something) by adding something inferior. [16th C.: from Old French *aloi* (n.) and Fr. *aloyer* (v.), both from OFr. *aloier, aleier* 'combine,' from L. *alligare* 'bind.']

all-per·vad·ing (also **all-per·va·sive**) ▶ adj. having an effect on everything or throughout something: *the all-pervading excitement.*

all-points bul·le·tin (abbr.: **APB**) ▶ **n.** a radio message sent to every officer on a police force giving details of a suspected criminal or stolen vehicle.

all-pow·er·ful ▶ **adj.** having complete power; almighty.

all-pur·pose ▶ **adj.** having many uses, esp. all that might be expected from something of its type.

all right ▶ **adj.** satisfactory but not especially good; acceptable. ■ (of a person) in a satisfactory mental or physical state: *are you all right?* ■ permissible; allowable. ▶ **adv.** **1** in a satisfactory manner or to a satisfactory extent; fairly well: *everything will turn out all right.* **2** used to emphasize how certain one is about something: *"Are you sure it's him?" "It's him all right."* ▶ **exclam.** expressing or asking for assent, agreement, or acceptance: *all right, I'll tell you.*

all-round ▶ **adj.** esp. Brit. another term for **ALL-AROUND.**

All Saints' Day ▶ **n.** a Christian festival in honor of all the saints, held (in the Western Church) on November 1.

all·seed /'ôl,sēd/ ▶ **n.** any of a number of plants producing a great deal of seed for their size, such as knotgrass and goosefoot.

All Souls' Day ▶ **n.** a festival in some Christian churches with prayers for the souls of the dead, held on November 2.

all·spice /'ôl,spīs/ ▶ **n.** **1** the dried aromatic fruit of a West Indian tree, used whole or ground as a culinary spice. **2** a tree (*Pimenta dioica*) of the myrtle family from which this spice is obtained. Also called **PIMENTO.** **3** an aromatic North American tree or shrub (genus *Calycanthus*, family Calycanthaceae).

all-star ▶ **adj.** [attrib.] composed wholly of outstanding performers or players. ▶ **n.** a member of such a group or team.

All·ston /'ôlstən/, Washington (1779–1843), US painter. The first major artist of the American romantic movement, his paintings exhibit a taste for the monumental, apocalyptic, and melodramatic.

all-ter·rain ve·hi·cle (abbr.: **ATV**) ▶ **n.** a small open motor vehicle with one or two seats and three or more wheels fitted with large tires, designed for use on rough ground.

all-time ▶ **adj.** [attrib.] unsurpassed: *all-time favorite.*

al·lude /ə'lo͞od/ ▶ **v.** [intrans.] **(allude to)** suggest or call attention to indirectly; hint at. ■ mention without discussing at length. ■ (of an artist or a work of art) recall (an earlier work or style) in such a way as to suggest a relationship with it. [15th C.: from L. *alludere*, from *ad-* 'toward' + *ludere* 'to play.']

al·lure /ə'lo͝or/ ▶ **n.** the quality of being powerfully and mysteriously attractive or fascinating. ▶ **v.** [trans.] powerfully attract or charm; tempt. — **al·lure·ment n. al·lur·ing adj. al·lur·ing·ly adv.** [ME: from OFr. *aleurier* 'attract,' from *a-* 'to' + *luere* 'a lure.']

al·lu·sion /ə'lo͞ozHən/ ▶ **n.** an expression designed to call something to mind without mentioning it explicitly; an indirect or passing reference. ■ the practice of making such references, esp. as an artistic device. — **al·lu·sive** /ə'lo͞osiv/ **al·lu·sive·ly adv. al·lu·sive·ness n.** [16th C. from late L. *allusio(n-)*, from *alludere* (see **ALLUDE**).]

al·lu·vi·al /ə'lo͞ovēəl/ ▶ **adj.** of, relating to or derived from alluvium: *rich alluvial soils.*

al·lu·vi·al fan ▶ **n.** a fan-shaped mass of alluvium deposited as the flow of a river decreases in velocity.

al·lu·vi·on /ə'lo͞ovēən/ ▶ **n.** Law the action of the sea or a river in forming new land by deposition. Compare with **AVULSION.** [16th C.: from Fr., from L. *alluvio(n)-*, from *ad-* 'toward' + *luere* 'to wash.']

al·lu·vi·um /ə'lo͞ovēəm/ ▶ **n.** a deposit of clay, silt, sand, and gravel left by flowing streams in a river valley or delta, typically producing fertile soil. [17th C.: L., neut. of *alluvius* 'washed against,' from *ad-* + *luere* 'to wash.']

all-wheel drive ▶ **n.** a transmission system that always operates in four-wheel drive and does not alternate with two-wheel drive.

al·ly[1] /'alī/ ▶ **n.** (pl. **-lies**) a state formally cooperating with another for a military or other purpose, typically by treaty. ■ a person or organization that cooperates with or helps another in a particular activity. ■ **(the Allies)** a group of nations taking military action together, in particular the countries that fought with the US in World War I and World War II. ▶ **v.** **(-lies, -lied)** [trans.] **(ally something to/with)** combine or unite a resource or commodity with (another) for mutual benefit. ■ **(ally oneself with)** side with or support (someone or something). [ME (v.): from OFr. *alier*, from L. *alligare* 'bind together,' from *ad-* 'to' + *ligare* 'to bind.']

al·ly[2] ▶ **n.** (pl. **-lies**) var. of **ALLEY**[2].

-ally ▶ **suffix** forming adverbs from adjectives ending in *-al* (such as *radically* from *radical*).

al·lyl /'alil/ ▶ **n.** [as modifier] Chem. the unsaturated hydrocarbon radical $-CH=CHCH_2$: *allyl alcohol.* — **al·lyl·ic** /ə'lilik/ **adj.** [19th C.: from L. *allium* 'garlic.']

Al·ma-A·ta var. of **ALMATY.**

Al Ma·di·nah /,äl mä'dēnə/ Arabic name for **MEDINA.**

Al·ma·gest /'almə,jest/ ▶ **n.** **(the Almagest)** an Arabic version of Ptolemy's astronomical treatise. [ME: from OFr. *almageste*, based on Arab., from *al* 'the' + Gk. *megistē* 'greatest (composition).']

al·ma ma·ter /'älmə 'mätər; 'almə/ ▶ **n.** **(one's Alma Mater)** the school, college, or university that one once attended. ■ the anthem of a school, college, or university. [17th C.: L., lit. 'bounteous mother.']

al·ma·nac /'ôlmə,nak; 'al-/ (also, esp. in titles, **al·ma·nack**) ▶ **n.** an annual calendar containing important dates and statistical information such as astronomical data and tide tables. ■ a handbook, typically published annually, containing information of general interest or on a sport or pastime. [ME: via med. L. from Gk. *almenikhiaka.*]

al·man·dine /'almən,dēn/ ▶ **n.** a kind of garnet with a violet tint. [ME: from obs. Fr., alt. of *alabandine*, from med. L. *alabandina (gemma)* 'jewel from *Alabanda*,' ancient city in Asia Minor.]

Al·ma·ty /,älmə'tē/ (also **Al·ma-A·ta** /,älmə ə'tä/) a city in southeastern Kazakhstan, formerly the capital (until 1998); pop. 1,515,300.

Al·me·rí·a /,älmä'rēə/ a seaport in southern Spain; pop. 157,760.

al·might·y /ôl'mītē/ ▶ **adj.** having complete power; omnipotent: *God almighty.* ■ **(the Almighty)** a name or title for God. ■ informal very great; enormous: *an almighty roar.* [OE *ælmihtig* (see **ALL, MIGHTY**).]

al·mond /'ä(l)mənd; 'a(l)-/ ▶ **n.** **1** the oval nutlike seed (kernel) of the almond tree, used as food. **2** (also **almond tree**) the widely cultivated Asian tree (*Prunus dulcis*) of the rose family that produces this nut. ▶ **adj.** made of or flavored with almonds. ■ of an oval shape, pointed at one or both ends: *almond eyes.* ■ a pale tan color, as of an almond shell. [ME: from OFr. *alemande*, from med. L. *amandula*, from Gk. *amugdalē.*]

al·mond oil ▶ **n.** oil expressed from bitter almonds, used as a flavoring and in cosmetics and medicines.

al·mond paste ▶ **n.** another term for **MARZIPAN.**

al·mon·ry /'almənrē; 'äm-/ ▶ **n.** (pl. **-ries**) a building or place where alms were formerly distributed.

al·most /ôl'mōst; 'ôl,mōst/ ▶ **adv.** not quite; very nearly: *he almost knocked Georgina over.* [OE *æl mǣst* 'for the most part' (see **ALL, MOST**).]

alms /ä(l)mz/ ▶ **plural n.** (in historical contexts) money or food given to poor people. [OE *ælmysse, ælmesse*, from Christian L. *eleemosyna*, from Gk. *eleēmosunē* 'compassion,' from *eleēmōn* 'compassionate,' from *eleos* 'mercy.']

alms·house /'ä(l)mz,hous/ ▶ **n.** a house built originally by a charitable person or organization for poor people to live in.

al·oe /'alō/ ▶ **n.** **1** a succulent plant (genus *Aloe*) of the lily family, typically having a rosette of toothed fleshy leaves and bell-shaped or tubular flowers on long stems. ■ **(al·oes** or **bitter aloes)** a strong laxative obtained from the bitter juice of various kinds of aloe. ■ (also **American aloe**) another term for **CENTURY PLANT.** **2** **(aloes)** (also **al·oes·wood**) the fragrant heartwood of a tropical Asian tree (genus *Aquilaria*, family Thymelaeaceae). ■ the resin obtained from this wood, used in perfume, incense, and medicine. [OE *alewe, alwe* ('resin or heartwood of certain Oriental trees'), via L. from Gk. *aloē.*]

al·oe ver·a /'alō'verə; 'vi(ə)rə/ ▶ **n.** a gelatinous substance obtained from a particular aloe (*Aloe vera*), used esp. in cosmetics and for the treatment of burns. [20th C.: mod. L., lit. 'true aloe.']

a·loft /ə'lôft/ ▶ **adj.** [predic.] **& adv.** up in or into the air; overhead. ■ up the mast or into the rigging of a sailing vessel. [ME: from ON *á lopt, á lopti*, from *á* 'in' + *lopt* 'air.']

a·log·i·cal /ā'läjikəl/ ▶ **adj.** opposed to or lacking in logic.

a·lo·ha /ə'lō,hä/ ▶ **exclam. & n.** Hawaiian word used when greeting or parting from someone.

a·lo·ha shirt ▶ **n.** a loose, brightly patterned Hawaiian shirt.

a·lone /ə'lōn/ ▶ **adj. & adv.** **1** having no one else present; on one's own. ■ without others' help or participation; single-handed. ■ [as adj.] isolated and lonely: *she was terribly alone and exposed.* ■ having no companions in a particular position or course of action: *they were not alone in dissenting from the advice.* **2** [as adv.] indicating that something is confined to the specified subject or recipient: *it is Congress alone that can declare war.* ■ used to emphasize that only one factor out of several is being considered and that the whole is greater or more extreme: *there were fifteen churches in the town center alone.*

– PHRASES **go it alone** informal act by oneself without assistance. **leave** (or **let**) **someone/something alone 1** abandon or desert someone or something. **2** stop disturbing or interfering with someone or something. **let alone** see **LET**[1]. — **a·lone·ness n.** [ME: from **ALL** + **ONE.**]

a·long /ə'lôNG; ə'läNG/ ▶ **prep.** **1** moving in a constant direction on (a path or any more or less horizontal surface): *soon we were driving along a narrow road.* ■ used metaphorically to refer to the passage of time or the making of progress. **2** extending in a more or less horizontal line on: *the path along the cliff.* ▶ **adv.** in or into company with others. ■ at hand; with one: *take along a camcorder when you visit.*

– PHRASES **along about** informal or dialect around about (a specified time or date): *he generally leaves there along about daylight.* **along the lines (of)** in conformity with. **along with** in company with or at the same time as. **be** (or **come**) **along** arrive: *she'll be along soon.* [OE *andlang*, from West Gmc. akin to **LONG**[1].]

a·long·shore /ə'lôNG'SHôr; ə'läNG-/ ▶ **adv.** along or by the shore: *currents flowing alongshore.*

a·long·side /ə'lôNG'sīd; ə'läNG-/ ▶ **prep.** (also **alongside of**) close to the side of; next to: *she was sitting alongside him* | [as adv.] *the boat came alongside.* ■ together and in cooperation with. ■ at the same time as or in coexistence with.

a·loof /ə'lo͞of/ ▶ **adj.** not friendly or forthcoming; cool and distant. ■ conspicuously uninvolved and uninterested, typically through distaste. — **a·loof·ly adv. a·loof·ness n.** [16th C.: from **A-**[2] + **LUFF.** Originally adv. 'away and to windward!,' i.e., with the ship's head kept close to the wind away from a lee shore, etc.]

al·o·pe·ci·a /,alə'pēSH(ē)ə/ ▶ **n.** Med. the partial or complete absence of hair from areas of the body where it normally grows; baldness. [ME: via L. from Gk. *alōpekia*, lit. 'fox mange,' from *alōpēx* 'fox.']

a·loud /ə'loud/ ▶ **adv.** **1** audibly; not silently or in a whisper: *he read the* *letter aloud.* 2 archaic loudly. [ME: from A-² + LOUD.]

alp /alp/ ▶ n. a high mountain, esp. a snowcapped one. ■ (in Switzerland) an area of green pasture on a mountainside. [ME: sing. of ALPS.]

al·pac·a /al'pakə/ ▶ n. (pl. same or **-pac·as**) a long-haired domesticated South American mammal (*Lama pacos*) of the camel family, related to the llama and valued for its wool. ■ the wool of the alpaca. ■ fabric made from this wool, with or without other fibers. [18th C.: from Sp., from Aymara *allpaca*.]

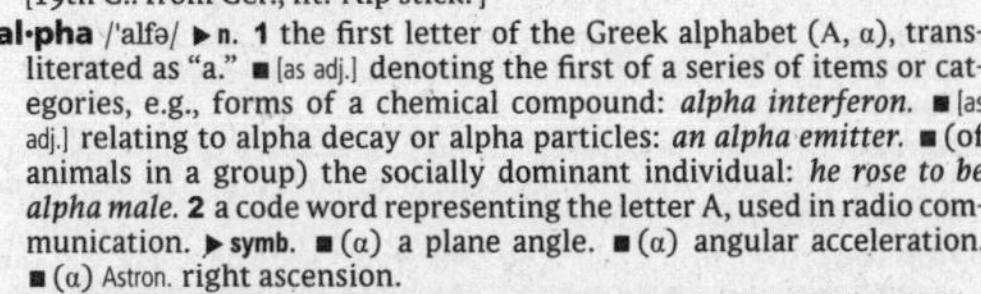

alpaca

al·pen·glow /'alpən,glō/ ▶ n. the rosy light of the setting or rising sun seen on high mountains. [19th C.: partial translation of Ger. *Alpenglühen*, lit. 'Alp glow.']

al·pen·horn /'alpən,hôrn/ (also **alp·horn** /'alp,hôrn/) ▶ n. a valveless wooden horn up to 12 feet (4 m) long, used for signaling in the Alps. [19th C.: from Ger., lit. 'Alp horn.']

al·pen·stock /'alpən,stäk/ ▶ n. a long iron-tipped staff used by hikers and mountain climbers. [19th C.: from Ger., lit. 'Alp stick.']

al·pha /'alfə/ ▶ n. 1 the first letter of the Greek alphabet (Α, α), transliterated as "a." ■ [as adj.] denoting the first of a series of items or categories, e.g., forms of a chemical compound: *alpha interferon.* ■ [as adj.] relating to alpha decay or alpha particles: *an alpha emitter.* ■ (of animals in a group) the socially dominant individual: *he rose to be alpha male.* 2 a code word representing the letter A, used in radio communication. ▶ symb. ■ (α) a plane angle. ■ (α) angular acceleration. ■ (α) Astron. right ascension.

– PHRASES **alpha and omega** the beginning and the end (esp. used by Christians as a title for Jesus). ■ the essence or most important features.

al·pha·bet /'alfə,bet; -bit/ ▶ n. a set of letters or symbols in a fixed order, used to represent the basic sounds of a language; in particular, the set of letters from A to Z. ■ the basic elements in a system which combine to form complex entities: *DNA's 4-letter alphabet.* [16th C.: from late L. *alphabetum*, from Greek *alpha, bēta*, first two letters of the Gk. alphabet.]

al·pha·bet·i·cal /,alfə'betikəl/ ▶ adj. of or relating to an alphabet. ■ in the order of the letters of the alphabet. — **al·pha·bet·ic** adj. **al·pha·bet·i·cal·ly** /-ik(ə)lē/ adv.

al·pha·bet·ize /'alfəbi,tīz/ ▶ v. [trans.] arrange (words or phrases) in alphabetical order. — **al·pha·bet·i·za·tion** /,alfə,betə'zāsʜən/ n.

al·pha·bet soup ▶ n. informal incomprehensible or confusing language, typically containing many abbreviations or symbols. [20th C.: alluding to a clear soup containing pasta in the shapes of letters.]

al·pha block·er ▶ n. Med. any of a class of drugs that prevent the stimulation of the adrenergic receptors responsible for increased blood pressure.

Al·pha Cen·tau·ri /sen'tôrē/ Astron. the third brightest star in the sky, in the constellation Centaurus.

al·pha-fe·to·pro·tein /,fētō'prōtē(ə)n/ ▶ n. Med. a protein produced by a fetus and present in amniotic fluid and the bloodstream of the mother. Levels of the protein can be measured to detect certain defects such as spina bifida and Down syndrome.

al·pha glob·u·lin ▶ n. see GLOBULIN.

al·pha·nu·mer·ic /,alfə,n(y)o͞o'merik/ ▶ adj. consisting of or using both letters and numerals. ▶ n. a character that is either a letter or a number. — **al·pha·nu·mer·i·cal** adj. [1950s: blend of ALPHABETICAL and NUMERICAL.]

al·pha par·ti·cle ▶ n. Physics a helium nucleus emitted by some radioactive substances, originally regarded as a ray.

al·pha ra·di·a·tion ▶ n. ionizing radiation consisting of alpha particles, emitted by some substances undergoing radioactive decay.

al·pha rhythm ▶ n. Physiol. the normal electrical activity of the brain when conscious and relaxed, consisting of oscillations (**alpha waves**) with a frequency of 8 to 13 hertz.

alp·horn /'alp,hôrn/ ▶ n. another term for ALPENHORN.

al·pine /'al,pīn/ ▶ adj. [usu. attrib] of or relating to high mountains: *alpine habitats.* ■ (in the names of plants and animals) growing or found on high mountains: *the alpine forget-me-not.* ■ (**Alpine**) of or relating to the Alps. ■ (also **Alpine**) (of skiing) involving downhill racing. ▶ n. a plant native to mountain districts, often suitable for growing in rock gardens. [ME: from L. *Alpinus*, from *Alpes* (see ALPS).]

al·pin·ist /'alpənist/ ▶ n. a climber of high mountains, esp. in the Alps.

al·pra·zo·lam /al'prazə,lam/ ▶ n. Med. a drug of the benzodiazepine group, used to treat anxiety. [1970s: from *al-* of unknown origin + *p(henyl)* + *(t)r(i)azol(e)* + *(-azep)am*.]

Alps /alps/ a mountain system of southern Europe that extends from the coast of southeastern France through Switzerland to the Balkan Peninsula; highest peak, Mont Blanc, 15,771 feet (4,807 m).

al Qae·da /al 'kīdə; 'kādə; kä'ēdə/ (also **al-Qa'i·dah, al-Qae·da**) an international terrorist organization founded in the late 1980s to combat the Soviets in Afghanistan. Under the control of Osama bin Laden since 1989, its goal is to establish a pan-Islamic caliphate by collaborating with Islamic extremists to overthrow non-Islamic regimes and to expel Westerners and non-Muslims from Muslim countries.

Al Qa·hi·ra /äl 'kähērə/ Arabic name for CAIRO.

al·read·y /ôl'redē/ ▶ adv. 1 before or by now or the time in question: *Anna has suffered a great deal already.* ■ as surprisingly soon or early as this. 2 informal used as an intensive after a word or phrase to express impatience: *enough already with these kids!* [ME: from ALL (adv.) + READY.]

al·right /ôl'rīt/ var. of ALL RIGHT.

ALS ▶ abbr. amyotrophic lateral sclerosis.

Al·sace /al'sas; -'sās/ a region of northeastern France, on the borders with Germany and Switzerland.

Al·sa·tian /al'sāsʜən/ ▶ n. 1 esp. Brit. another term for GERMAN SHEPHERD. 2 a native or inhabitant of Alsace. ▶ adj. of or relating to Alsace or its inhabitants. [from med. L. *Alsatia* 'Alsace.']

al·sike /'al,sik; -,sīk/ (also **alsike clover**) ▶ n. a tall clover (*Trifolium hybridum*) that is widely grown for fodder. [19th C.: *Alsike*, Sweden.]

al·so /'ôlsō/ ▶ adv. in addition; too. [OE *alswā* 'quite so' (see ALL, SO¹).]

al·so-ran ▶ n. a loser in a race or contest, esp. by a large margin. ■ an undistinguished or unsuccessful person or thing. [19th C.: orig. applied to horses in a race that do not get a "place."]

al·stroe·me·ri·a /,alstrə'mi(ə)rēə/ ▶ n. a South American plant (genus *Alstroemeria*) of the lily family, often cultivated for its showy flowers. [18th C.: mod. L., after Klas von *Alstroemer* (1736–96), Swedish naturalist.]

Alt /ôlt/ ▶ n. short for ALT KEY.

alt. ▶ abbr. ■ alternate. ■ altimeter. ■ altitude.

Alta. ▶ abbr. Alberta.

Al·ta·ic /al'tāik/ ▶ adj. 1 of or relating to the Altai Mountains. 2 denoting or belonging to a phylum of languages that includes the Turkic, Mongolian, Tungusic, and Manchu languages. ▶ n. the Altaic family of languages.

Al·tai Moun·tains a mountain system in central Asia that extends from Kazakhstan into western Mongolia and northern China.

Al·tair /'al,te(ə)r; -,tī(ə)r; al'tī(ə)r; -'te(ə)r/ Astron. the brightest star in the constellation Aquila. [Arab., lit. 'flying eagle.']

Al·ta·mi·ra /,altə'mi(ə)rə/ the site of a cave with Paleolithic rock paintings, discovered in Spain in 1879.

al·tar /'ôltər/ ▶ n. the table in a Christian church at which the bread and wine are consecrated in communion services. ■ a table or flat-topped block used as the focus for a religious ritual, esp. for making sacrifices or offerings to a deity.

– PHRASES **lead someone to the altar** marry. [OE *altar, alter*, based on late L. *altar, altarium*, from L. *altus* 'high.']

al·tar boy ▶ n. a boy who acts as a priest's assistant during a service, esp. in the Roman Catholic Church.

al·tar girl ▶ n. a girl who acts as a priest's assistant during a service, esp. in the Roman Catholic Church.

al·tar·piece /'ôltər,pēs/ ▶ n. a work of art, esp. a painting on wood, set above and behind an altar.

alt·az·i·muth /al'tazəməᴛʜ/ ▶ n. (also **altazimuth mount** or **mounting**) Astron. a telescope mounting that moves in azimuth (about a vertical axis) and in altitude (about a horizontal axis). Compare with EQUATORIAL MOUNT. ■ (also **altazimuth telescope**) a telescope on such a mounting. [19th C.: blend of ALTITUDE and AZIMUTH.]

al·ter /'ôltər/ ▶ v. change or cause to change in character or composition, typically in a comparatively small but significant way: [trans.] *Eliot was persuaded to alter the passage* | [intrans.] *our outward appearance alters as we get older.* ■ make structural changes to (a building). ■ [trans.] tailor (clothing) for a better fit or to conform to fashion. ■ [trans.] castrate or spay (a domestic animal). — **al·ter·a·ble** adj. [ME: from OFr. *alterer*, from late L. *alterare*, from L. *alter* 'other.']

al·ter·a·tion /,ôltə'rāsʜən/ ▶ n. the action or process of altering or being altered.

al·ter·cate /'ôltər,kāt/ ▶ v. [intrans.] archaic dispute or argue noisily and publicly. [16th C.: from L. *altercat-* 'wrangled,' from *altercari*.]

al·ter·ca·tion /,ôltər'kāsʜən/ ▶ n. a noisy argument or disagreement, esp. in public.

al·ter e·go ▶ n. a person's secondary or alternative personality. ■ an intimate and trusted friend. [16th C.: L., 'other self.']

al·ter·i·ty /ôl'teritē/ ▶ n. formal the state of being other or different; otherness.

al·ter·nant /'ôltərnənt/ ▶ n. an alternative form of a word or other linguistic unit; a variant. ▶ adj. alternating; changing from one to the other.

al·ter·nate ▶ v. /'ôltər,nāt/ [intrans.] occur in turn repeatedly: *bouts of depression **alternate with** periods of elation.* ■ [trans.] do or perform in turn repeatedly: *some adults who wish to **alternate** work **with** education.* ▶ adj. /-nit/ (abbr.: **alt.**) [attrib.] 1 every other; every second (of a series). ■ (of two things) each following and succeeded by the other in a regular pattern. ■ (of a sequence) consisting of alternate items. ■ Bot. (of leaves or shoots) placed alternately on the two sides of the stem. 2 taking the place of; alternative: *alternate routes.* See usage at ALTERNATIVE. ▶ n. /-nit/ (abbr.: **alt.**) a person who acts as a deputy or substitute. — **al·ter·nate·ly** /-nitlē/ adv. **al·ter·na·tion** /,ôltər'nāsʜən/ n. [16th C.: from L. *alternat-* 'done by turns,' from *alternare*, from *alternus* 'every other,' from *alter* 'other.']

al·ter·nate an·gles ▶ plural n. two angles, not adjoining one another, that are formed on opposite sides of a line that intersects two other lines. If the original two lines are parallel, the alternate angles are equal.

al·ter·nat·ing cur·rent (abbr.: **AC** or **ac**) ▶ n. an electric current that reverses its direction many times a second at regular intervals, typically used in power supplies. Compare with DIRECT CURRENT.

al·ter·na·tion of gen·er·a·tions ▸ n. Biol. a pattern of reproduction occurring in the life cycles of many lower plants and some invertebrates, in which the generations are alternately sexual and asexual (as in ferns) or dioecious and parthenogenetic (as in some jellyfish).

al·ter·na·tive /ôl'tərnətiv/ ▸ adj. [attrib.] (of one or more things) available as another possibility. ■ (of two things) mutually exclusive: *the facts fit two alternative scenarios.* ■ of or relating to behavior that is considered unconventional and is often seen as a challenge to traditional norms: *an alternative lifestyle.* ▸ n. one of two or more available possibilities. — **al·ter·na·tive·ly** adv.

al·ter·na·tive fuel ▸ n. a fuel other than gasoline for powering motor vehicles, such as natural gas, methanol, or electricity.

al·ter·na·tive med·i·cine ▸ n. any of a range of medical therapies that are not regarded as orthodox by the medical profession, such as herbalism, homeopathy, and acupuncture. See also COMPLEMENTARY MEDICINE.

al·ter·na·tor /'ôltər,nātər/ ▸ n. a generator that produces an alternating current.

Al·thing /'ôl,THiNG; 'äl-/ the bicameral legislative assembly of Iceland.

alt·horn /'alt,hôrn/ ▸ n. a musical instrument of the saxhorn family, esp. the alto or tenor saxhorn in E flat. [19th C.: from Ger., from *alt* 'high' + *Horn* 'horn.']

al·though /ôl'THō/ ▸ conj. in spite of the fact that; even though. ■ however; but. [ME: from ALL (adv.) + THOUGH.]

al·tim·e·ter /al'timitər/ (abbr.: **alt.**) ▸ n. an instrument for determining altitude attained, esp. a barometric or radar device used in an aircraft. [20th C.: from L. *altus* 'high.']

al·tim·e·try /al'timitrē/ ▸ n. the measurement of height or altitude. — **al·ti·met·ric** /,altə'metrik/ adj. **al·ti·met·ri·cal·ly** /,altə'metrik(ə)lē/ adv. [ME: from med. L. *altimetria*.]

al·ti·pla·no /alti'plänō/ ▸ n. (pl. **-nos**) the high tableland of central South America.

al·tis·si·mo /al'tisə,mō; äl-/ ▸ adj. Music very high in pitch. [Ital., superlative of *alto* 'high.']

al·ti·tude /'alti,t(y)ōōd/ (abbr.: **alt.**) ▸ n. the height of an object or point in relation to sea level or ground level. ■ great height. ■ Astron. the apparent height of a celestial object above the horizon, measured in angular distance. ■ Geom. the length of the perpendicular line from a vertex to the opposite side of a figure. — **al·ti·tu·di·nal** /,alti't(y)ōōdn-əl/ adj. [ME: from L. *altitudo*, from *altus* 'high.']

al·ti·tude sick·ness ▸ n. illness caused by ascent to a high altitude and shortage of oxygen, characterized by hyperventilation, nausea, and exhaustion.

Alt key /'ôlt/ ▸ n. Comput. a key on a keyboard that when pressed at the same time as another key gives the second key an alternative function.

Alt·man /'ôltmən/, Robert (1925–2006), US director. His movies include *M*A*S*H* (1970) and *A Prairie Home Companion* (2006).

al·to /'altō/ ▸ n. (pl. **-tos**) Music a voice, instrument, or part below the highest range and above tenor, in particular: ■ the highest adult male singing voice; countertenor. ■ the lowest female singing voice; contralto. ■ [as adj.] denoting the member of a family of instruments pitched second or third highest: *alto flute.* ■ an alto instrument, esp. an alto saxophone. [16th C.: from Ital. *alto (canto)* 'high (song).']

al·to clef ▸ n. a clef placing middle C on the middle line of the staff, now used chiefly for viola music.

al·to·cu·mu·lus /,altō'kyōōmyələs/ ▸ n. (pl. **-li** /-,lī/) cloud forming a layer of rounded masses with a level base, occurring at medium altitude, usually 6,500–23,000 feet (2–7 km).

al·to·geth·er /,ôltə'geTHər/ ▸ adv. completely; totally. ■ including everything or everyone; in total: *he had forty-six children altogether.* ■ taking everything into consideration; on the whole: *altogether it was a great evening.*

– PHRASES **in the altogether** informal naked.

al·to-re·lie·vo /'altō rə'lēvō/ ▸ n. (pl. **-vos**) Sculpture another term for *HIGH RELIEF* at RELIEF (sense 4). ■ a sculpture or carving in high relief. [17th C.: from Ital. *alto-rilievo*.]

al·to·stra·tus /,altō'strātəs; -'stratəs/ ▸ n. cloud forming a continuous uniform layer that resembles stratus but occurs at medium altitude, usually 6,500–23,000 feet (2–7 km).

al·tri·cial /al'triSHəl/ Zool. ▸ adj. (of a young bird or other animal) hatched or born in an undeveloped state and requiring care and feeding by the parents. Also called NIDICOLOUS. Often contrasted with PRECOCIAL. ■ (of a particular species) having such young. ▸ n. an altricial bird. [19th C.: from L. *altrix, altric-*, fem. of *altor* 'nourisher,' from *alere* 'nourish.']

al·tru·ism /'altrōō,izəm/ ▸ n. the belief in or practice of disinterested and selfless concern for the well-being of others. ■ Zool. behavior of an animal that benefits another at its own expense. — **al·tru·ist** n. **al·tru·is·tic** /,altrōō'istik/ adj. **al·tru·is·ti·cal·ly** /,altrə'wistik(ə)lē/ adv. [19th C.: from Fr. *altruisme*, from Ital. *altrui* 'somebody else,' from L. *alteri huic* 'to this other.']

ALU Comput. ▸ abbr. arithmetic logic unit.

al·u·del /'alyə,del/ ▸ n. a pear-shaped earthenware or glass pot, open at both ends to enable a series to be fitted one above another, formerly used in sublimation and other chemical processes. [ME: from OFr. *alutel*, via Sp. from Arab. *al-'uṭāl* 'the sublimation vessel.']

al·u·la /'alyələ/ ▸ n. (pl. **-u·lae** /-yə,lē/) technical term for BASTARD WING. [18th C.: mod. L., lit. 'small wing,' dimin. of *ala*.]

a·lum /'aləm/ ▸ n. Chem. a colorless astringent compound, $AlK(SO_4)_2 \cdot 12H_2O$, a hydrated double sulfate of aluminum and potassium, used in solution medicinally and in dyeing and tanning. ■ any of a number of analogous crystalline double sulfates of a monovalent metal (or group) and a trivalent metal.

a·lu·mi·na /ə'lōōmənə/ ▸ n. aluminum oxide, Al_2O_3, a white solid that is a major constituent of many rocks, esp. clays, and is found crystallized as corundum, sapphire, and other minerals.

a·lu·mi·nize /ə'lōōmə,nīz/ ▸ v. [trans.] [usu. as adj.] (**aluminized**) coat with aluminum: *an aluminized reflector.*

a·lu·mi·no·sil·i·cate /ə,lōōmənə'silikit/ ▸ n. Chem. a silicate in which aluminum replaces some of the silicon, esp. a rock-forming mineral such as a feldspar or a clay mineral.

a·lu·mi·nous /ə'lōōmənəs/ ▸ adj. (chiefly of minerals and rocks) containing alumina or aluminum.

a·lu·mi·num /ə'lōōmənəm/ (Brit. **al·u·min·i·um** /,alyə'minēəm/) ▸ n. the chemical element of atomic number 13, a light silvery-gray metal. Aluminum is the most abundant metal in the earth's crust. Its lightness, resistance to corrosion, and strength (esp. in alloys) have led to widespread use in domestic utensils, engineering parts, and aircraft construction. (Symbol: **Al**) [19th C.: from *alumin(a)* + *-(i)um*.]

a·lum·na /ə'ləmnə/ ▸ n. (pl. **-nae** /-nē; -nī/) a female graduate or former student of a particular school, college, or university. [19th C.: from L., fem. of *alumnus*.]

a·lum·nus /ə'ləmnəs/ ▸ n. (pl. **-ni** /-nī; -nē/) a graduate or former student, esp. male, of a particular school, college, or university. [17th C.: from L., 'pupil,' from *alere* 'nourish.']

al·um·root /'aləm,rōōt; -,rŏŏt/ (also **al·um root**) ▸ n. a heuchera, esp. the green-flowered *H. americana* and the white-flowered *H. parvifolia.*

Al Uq·sur /äl 'ŏŏk,sŏŏr/ Arabic name for LUXOR.

al·ve·o·lar /al'vēələr/ ▸ adj. of or relating to an alveolus, in particular: ■ Anat. relating to or denoting the bony ridge that contains the sockets of the upper teeth. ■ Phonet. (of a consonant) pronounced with the tip of the tongue on or near this ridge (e.g., *n, s, t*). ■ Anat. of or relating to an alveolus or the alveoli of the lung. ▸ n. Phonet. an alveolar consonant.

al·ve·o·lus /al'vēələs/ ▸ n. (pl. **-li** /-,lī/) esp. Anat. a small cavity, pit, or hollow, in particular: ■ any of the many tiny air sacs in the lungs where the exchange of oxygen and carbon dioxide takes place. ■ the bony socket for the root of a tooth. ■ an acinus in a gland. — **al·ve·o·late** /-lit; -,lāt/ adj. [17th C.: from L., 'small cavity,' dimin. of *alveus*.]

al·ways /'ôl,wāz; -wēz/ (archaic **al·way**) ▸ adv. **1** at all times; on all occasions. ■ throughout a long period of the past. ■ for all future time; forever. ■ repeatedly and annoyingly: *he's always barking.* **2** as a last resort; failing all else: *if it doesn't work, we can always try Plan B.* [ME: genitive of *all way*.]

a·lys·sum /ə'lisəm/ ▸ n. (pl. **-sums**) a widely cultivated plant (genera *Alyssum* and *Lobularia*) of the cabbage family that bears small flowers in a range of colors, typically white, yellow, or violet. [16th C.: mod. L., from L. *alysson*, from Gk. *alusson*, from *a-* 'without' + *lussa* 'rabies' (from early herbalist use).]

Alz·hei·mer's dis·ease /'älts,hīmərz; 'ôlts-; 'älz-; 'ôlz-/ ▸ n. progressive mental deterioration occurring in middle or old age, due to generalized degeneration of the brain. [20th C.: Alois *Alzheimer* (1864–1915), German neurologist.]

AM ▸ abbr. ■ amplitude modulation. ■ Master of Arts. [L. *artium magister*.]

Am ▸ symb. the chemical element americium.

am /am/ 1st person singular present of BE.

a.m. ▸ abbr. before noon, used with times of day between midnight and noon. [from L. *ante meridiem*.]

AMA ▸ abbr. ■ American Medical Association.

a·mah /'ämə/ ▸ n. a nursemaid or maid in the Far East or India. [from Port. *ama* 'nurse.']

a·mal·gam /ə'malgəm/ ▸ n. a mixture or blend. ■ Chem. an alloy of mercury with another metal, esp. one used for dental fillings.

a·mal·ga·mate /ə'malgə,māt/ ▸ v. combine or unite to form one organization or structure: [trans.] *he amalgamated his company with another* | [intrans.] *numerous small railroad companies amalgamated.* ■ Chem. alloy (a metal) with mercury. — **a·mal·ga·ma·tion** /ə,malgə'māSHən/ n.

Am·al·the·a /,aməl'THēə; ə,mal-/ Astron. satellite V of Jupiter, the third closest to the planet. [from the name of a goat in Greek mythology, which suckled the infant Zeus.]

A·ma·na Col·o·nies /ə'manə/ a Christian religious settlement in east central Iowa, known for the manufacture of appliances.

a·man·dine /,ämən'dēn; ,amən-/ ▸ adj. (of a dish) prepared or garnished with sliced almonds.

a·man·u·en·sis /ə,manyōō'ensis/ ▸ n. (pl. **-ses** /-,sēz/) a literary or artistic assistant, in particular one who takes dictation or copies manuscripts. [17th C.: L., from *(servus) a manu* '(slave) at hand(writing), secretary' + *-ensis* 'belonging to.']

am·a·ranth /'amə,ranTH/ ▸ n. **1** any plant of the genus *Amaranthus* (family Amaranthaceae), typically having small green, red, or purple flowers. Certain varieties are grown for food. **2** an imaginary flower that never fades. **3** a purple color. — **am·a·ran·thine** /,amə'ranTHin; -,THīn/ adj. [16th C.: from Fr. *amarante* or mod. L. *amaranthus*, based on Gk. *amarantos* 'everlasting,' from *a-* 'not' + *marainein* 'wither.']

am·a·ret·ti /,amə'retē/ ▸ plural n. Italian almond-flavored cookies. [Ital., based on *amaro* 'bitter.']

am·a·ret·to /ˌamə'retō; ˌämə-/ ▶ **n.** a sweet, almond-flavored liqueur.

Am·a·ril·lo /ˌamə'rilō/ a city in northwestern Texas; pop. 173,627.

am·a·ryl·lis /ˌamə'rilis/ ▶ **n.** a bulbous plant of the lily family with showy white, pink, or red flowers and straplike leaves, in particular: ■ a South African plant (*Amaryllis belladonna*), also called BELLADONNA LILY. ■ a tropical South American plant that is frequently grown as a houseplant (hybrids of the genus *Hippeastrum*, formerly *Amaryllis*). [mod. L., from L. *Amaryllis* (from Gk. *Amarullis*), a country girl in pastoral poetry.]

a·mass /ə'mas/ ▶ **v.** [trans.] gather together or accumulate (a large amount or number of valuable material or things) over a period of time. ■ [intrans.] archaic (of people) gather together in a crowd or group. — **a·mass·er n.**

A·ma·te·ra·su /ˌämäte'räso͞o/ the principal deity of the Japanese Shinto religion, the sun goddess and ancestor of Jimmu, founder of the imperial dynasty.

am·a·teur /'amətər; -ˌtər; -ˌchŏŏr; -chər/ ▶ **n.** a person who engages in a pursuit, esp. a sport, on an unpaid basis. ■ derog. a person considered contemptibly inept at a particular activity. ▶ **adj.** engaging or engaged in without payment; nonprofessional. ■ derog. inept or unskillful: *it's all so amateur!* — **am·a·teur·ism n.** [18th C.: from Fr., based on L. *amator* 'lover,' from *amare* 'to love.']

am·a·teur·ish /ˌamə'tərish; -'t(y)ŏŏr-; -'chŏŏr-/ ▶ **adj.** derog. unskillful; inept: *amateurish actors.* — **am·a·teur·ish·ly adv. am·a·teur·ish·ness n.**

A·ma·ti /ä'mätē/ a family of Italian violin-makers from Cremona. In the 16th and 17th centuries, three generations, including Andrea (*c.*1520–80), his sons Antonio (1550–1638) and Girolamo (1551–1635), and the latter's son Nicolò (1596–1684), developed the basic proportions of the violin, viola, and cello.

am·a·tol /'aməˌtôl; -ˌtäl/ ▶ **n.** a high explosive consisting of a mixture of TNT and ammonium nitrate. [20th C.: from *am(monium)* + *tol(uene)*.]

am·a·to·ry /'aməˌtôrē/ ▶ **adj.** [attrib.] relating to or induced by sexual love or desire. [16th C.: from L. *amatorius*, from *amator* (see AMATEUR).]

am·au·ro·sis /ˌamô'rōsis/ ▶ **n.** Med. partial or total blindness without visible change in the eye, typically due to disease of the optic nerve, spinal cord, or brain. — **am·au·rot·ic** /-'rätik/ **adj.** [17th C.: from Gk. *amaurōsis*, based on *amauros* 'dim.']

a·maze /ə'māz/ ▶ **v.** [trans.] (often **be amazed**) surprise (someone) greatly; fill with astonishment.

a·maze·ment /ə'māzmənt/ ▶ **n.** a feeling of great surprise or wonder.

a·maz·ing /ə'māzing/ ▶ **adj.** causing great surprise or wonder; astonishing. ■ informal startlingly impressive. — **a·maz·ing·ly adv.**

Am·a·zon[1] /'aməˌzän; -zən/ a river in South America that flows more than 4,150 miles (6,683 km) from the Andes to the Atlantic; the largest river in the world. — **Am·a·zo·ni·an** /ˌamə'zōnēən/ **adj.**

Am·a·zon[2] ▶ **n.** **1** a member of a legendary race of female warriors believed by the ancient Greeks to exist in Scythia (near the Black Sea in modern Russia) or elsewhere on the edge of the known world. ■ (also **amazon**) a tall and strong or athletic woman. **2** (**amazon**) a parrot (genus *Amazona*), typically green and with a broad rounded tail, found in Central and South America. — **Am·a·zo·ni·an adj.**

Am·a·zo·ni·a /ˌamə'zōnēə/ the area around the Amazon River in northern South America, comprising about one third of the world's remaining tropical rain forest.

am·bas·sa·dor /am'basədər; -ˌdôr/ ▶ **n.** an accredited diplomat sent by a country as its official representative to a foreign country. ■ a person who acts as a representative or promoter of a specified activity. — **am·bas·sa·do·ri·al** /amˌbasə'dôrēəl/ **adj. am·bas·sa·dor·ship** /-ˌship/ **n.** [ME: from Fr. *ambassadeur*, based on L. *ambactus* 'servant.']

am·bas·sa·dor-at-large ▶ **n.** an ambassador with special duties, not appointed to a particular country.

am·bas·sa·dress /am'basədris/ ▶ **n.** a female ambassador. ■ archaic an ambassador's wife.

Am·ba·to /äm'bätō/ a city in the Andes of central Ecuador; pop. 229,190.

am·ber /'ambər/ ▶ **n.** hard translucent fossilized resin produced by extinct coniferous trees of the Tertiary period, typically yellowish in color. It has been used in jewelry since antiquity. ■ a honey-yellow color typical of this substance. ■ a yellow light used as a cautionary signal between green for "go" and red for "stop." ▶ **adj.** made of amber. ■ having the yellow color of amber.

AMBER A·lert /'ambər əˌlərt/ (also **Am·ber A·lert**) ▶ **n.** an emergency response system that disseminates information about a missing person (usually a child), by media broadcasting or electronic roadway signs. ■ a public announcement or alert that uses this system. [acronym from America's Missing: Broadcast Emergency Response, named after Amber Hagerman, a child kidnapped in Texas in 1996.]

am·ber·gris /'ambərˌgris; -ˌgrē(s)/ ▶ **n.** a waxlike substance that originates as a secretion in the intestines of the sperm whale, found floating in tropical seas and used in perfume manufacture. [ME: from OFr. *ambre gris* 'gray amber.']

am·ber·jack /'ambərˌjak/ ▶ **n.** a large marine game fish (genus *Seriola*) of the jack family, found in inshore tropical and subtropical waters of the Atlantic and South Pacific. [19th C.: from AMBER (from its yellowish tail) + JACK[1].]

am·bi·ance ▶ **n.** var. of AMBIENCE.

am·bi·dex·trous /ˌambi'dekst(ə)rəs/ ▶ **adj.** (of a person) able to use the right and left hands equally well. ■ (of an implement) designed to be used by left-handed and right-handed people with equal ease. — **am·bi·dex·ter·i·ty** /-dek'steritē/ **n. am·bi·dex·trous·ly adv.** [17th C.: from late L. *ambidexter* (from L. *ambi-* 'on both sides' + *dexter* 'right-handed').]

am·bi·ence /'ambēəns/ (also **am·bi·ance**) ▶ **n.** [usu. in sing.] the character and atmosphere of a place. ■ background noise added to a musical recording to give the impression that it was recorded live. [19th C.: from AMBIENT, or from Fr. *ambiance*, from *ambiant* 'surrounding.']

am·bi·ent /'ambēənt/ ▶ **adj.** [attrib.] of or relating to the immediate surroundings of something: *ambient temperature.* ▶ **n.** (also **ambient music**) a style of instrumental music with electronic textures and no persistent beat, used to create or enhance a mood or atmosphere. [16th C.: from Fr. *ambiant* or L. *ambient-* 'going around,' from *ambire*.]

am·bi·gu·i·ty /ˌambi'gyo͞oitē/ ▶ **n.** (pl. **-ties**) uncertainty or inexactness of meaning in language. ■ a lack of decisiveness or commitment resulting from a failure to make a choice between alternatives.

am·big·u·ous /am'bigyo͞oəs/ ▶ **adj.** (of language) open to more than one interpretation; having a double meaning. ■ unclear or inexact because a choice between alternatives has not been made. — **am·big·u·ous·ly adv.** [16th C.: from L. *ambiguus* 'doubtful' (from *ambigere* 'waver,' from *ambi-* 'both ways' + *agere* 'to drive') + -OUS.]

am·bi·sex·u·al /ˌambi'seksho͞oəl/ ▶ **adj.** bisexual or androgynous. ▶ **n.** an ambisexual person. — **am·bi·sex·u·al·ly adv.** [1930s: from L. *ambi-* 'on both sides.']

am·bit /'ambit/ ▶ **n.** [in sing.] the scope, extent, or bounds of something: *within the ambit of federal law.* [ME: from L. *ambitus* 'circuit,' from *ambire* 'go around.']

am·bi·tion /am'bishən/ ▶ **n.** a strong desire to do or to achieve something, typically requiring determination and hard work. ■ desire and determination to achieve success.

am·bi·tious /am'bishəs/ ▶ **adj.** having or showing a strong desire and determination to succeed. ■ (of a plan or piece of work) intended to satisfy high aspirations and therefore difficult to achieve. — **am·bi·tious·ly adv. am·bi·tious·ness n.**

am·biv·a·lent /am'bivələnt/ ▶ **adj.** having mixed feelings or contradictory ideas about something or someone. — **am·biv·a·lence n. am·biv·a·lent·ly adv.** [20th C.: from Ger. *Ambivalenz*.]

am·bi·vert /'ambəˌvərt/ ▶ **n.** Psychol. a person whose personality has a balance of extrovert and introvert features. — **am·bi·ver·sion** /ˌambi'vərzhən/ **n.**

am·ble /'ambəl/ ▶ **v.** [intrans.] walk or move at a slow, relaxed pace. ▶ **n.** a walk at a slow, relaxed pace, esp. for pleasure. — **am·bler** /-blər/ **n.** [ME: from OFr. *ambler*, from L. *ambulare* 'to walk.']

am·bly·o·pi·a /ˌamblē'ōpēə/ ▶ **n.** Med. impaired or dim vision without obvious defect or change in the eye. — **am·bly·op·ic** /-'äpik/ **adj.** [18th C.: from Gk. *ambluōpia* 'dim-sightedness,' based on *amblus* 'dull' + *ōps*, *ōp-* 'eye.']

am·bo /'amˌbō/ ▶ **n.** (pl. **am·bos** or **am·bo·nes** /am'bōnēz/) (in an early Christian church) an oblong pulpit with steps at each end. [17th C.: ult. from Gk. *ambōn* 'rim.']

Am·boi·na wood /am'boinə/ (also **Am·boy·na wood**) ▶ **n.** the decorative wood of a rapidly growing Southeast Asian tree (*Pterocarpus indicus*) of the pea family, often used for furniture making. [19th C.: *Amboina* (see AMBON).]

Am·boi·nese /ˌamboi'nēz; -'nēs; ˌäm-/ ▶ **adj.** of or relating to the island of Ambon, its people, or their language. ▶ **n.** **1** a native or inhabitant of Ambon. **2** the Indonesian language of this people.

Am·bon /äm'bôn; 'amˌbän/ (also **Am·boi·na** /am'boinə/) an island in the Moluccas, in eastern Indonesia. ■ a port on this island, the capital of the Molucca Islands; pop. 80,000.

Am·brose, St. /'amˌbrōz; -ˌbrōs/ (*c.*339–397), leader of the early Christian Church. He was the bishop of Milan from 374.

am·bro·sia /am'brōzh(ē)ə/ ▶ **n.** Greek & Rom. Mythol. the food of the gods. ■ something very pleasing to taste or smell. ■ a fungal product used as food by ambrosia beetles. ■ a dessert made with oranges and shredded coconut. — **am·bro·sial adj.** [16th C.: via L. from Gk., 'elixir of life,' from *ambrotos* 'immortal.']

am·bro·sia bee·tle ▶ **n.** a small wood-boring beetle (families Platypodidae and Scolytidae), the adults and larvae of which feed on a fungus that they cultivate.

am·bry /'ômbrē/ (also **aum·bry**) ▶ **n.** (pl. **-bries**) a small recess or cupboard in the wall of a church. [ME: from OFr. *armarie*, from L. *armarium* 'closet, chest,' from *arma* 'utensils.']

am·bu·lac·rum /ˌambyə'lakrəm; -'lākrəm/ ▶ **n.** (pl. **-lac·ra** /-'lakrə; -'lākrə/) Zool. (in a starfish or other echinoderm) each of the radially arranged bands, together with their underlying structures, through which the double rows of tube feet protrude. — **am·bu·lac·ral adj.** [19th C.: L., 'avenue,' from *ambulare* 'to walk.']

am·bu·lance /'ambyələns/ ▶ **n.** a vehicle specially equipped for taking sick or injured people to and from the hospital, esp. in emergencies. [19th C.: Fr., from *hôpital ambulant* 'mobile (horse-drawn) field hospital,' from L. *ambulant-* 'walking.']

am·bu·lance chas·er ▶ **n.** derog. a lawyer who specializes in bringing cases seeking damages for personal injury.

am·bu·lant /'ambyələnt/ ▶ **adj.** Med. (of a patient) able to walk around; not confined to bed. ■ (of treatment) not confining a patient to bed.

[17th C.: from L. *ambulant-* 'walking,' from *ambulare*.]

am·bu·late /'ambyə,lāt/ ▶ v. [intrans.] formal or tech. walk; move about. — **am·bu·la·tion** /,ambyə'lāsHən/ n.

am·bu·la·to·ry /'ambyələ,tôrē/ ▶ adj. relating to or adapted for walking. ■ Med. able to walk; not bedridden. ■ Med. relating to patients who are able to walk. ■ movable; mobile. ▶ n. (pl. **-ries**) a place for walking, esp. an aisle around the apse or a cloister in a church or monastery.

am·bus·cade /'ambə,skād; ,ambə'skād/ ▶ n. dated an ambush. ▶ v. [trans.] archaic attack from an ambush. ■ [intrans.] archaic lie in ambush. [16th C.: from Fr. *embuscade*, based on late L. word 'to place in a wood.']

am·bush /'am,bŏosH/ ▶ n. a surprise attack by people lying in wait in a concealed position. ▶ v. [trans.] (often **be ambushed**) make a surprise attack on (someone) from a concealed position. [ME (verb): from OFr. *embusche* (n.), *embuschier* (v.), based on a late L. word 'to place in a wood.']

AME ▶ abbr. African Methodist Episcopal.

a·me·ba /ə'mēbə/ (also **a·moe·ba**) ▶ n. (pl. **-bas** or **-bae** /-bē/) a single-celled animal (phylum Rhizopoda, kingdom Protista) that catches food and moves about by extending fingerlike projections of protoplasm. Amebas are either free-living in damp environments or parasitic. — **a·me·bic** /-bik/ adj. **a·me·boid** /-boid/ adj. [19th C.: mod. L., from Gk. *amoibē* 'change.']

am·e·bi·a·sis /,amə'bīəsis/ (also **am·oe·bi·a·sis**) ▶ n. Med. infection with amebas, esp. as causing dysentery.

a·me·bic dys·en·ter·y /ə'mēbik/ ▶ n. dysentery caused by infection of the intestines by the protozoan *Entamoeba histolytica* and spread by contaminated food and water.

a·me·lio·rate /ə'mēlyə,rāt; ə'mēlēə-/ ▶ v. [trans.] make (something bad or unsatisfactory) better. — **a·me·lio·ra·tion** /ə,mēlyə'rāsHən; ə,mēlēə-/ n. **a·me·lio·ra·tive** /-rətiv; -,rātiv/ adj. **a·me·lio·ra·tor** /-,rātər/ n. [18th C.: alt. of MELIORATE, influenced by Fr. *améliorer*, from *meilleur* 'better.']

a·men /ä'men; ā'men/ ▶ exclam. uttered at the end of a prayer or hymn, meaning 'so be it.' ■ used to express agreement or assent: *amen to that!* ▶ n. an utterance of "amen." [OE, ult. from Gk. *amēn*, from Heb. *'āmēn* 'truth.']

a·me·na·ble /ə'mēnəbəl; ə'men-/ ▶ adj. (of a person) open and responsive to suggestion; easily persuaded or controlled. ■ [predic.] (**amenable to**) (of a thing) capable of being acted upon in a particular way; susceptible. — **a·me·na·bil·i·ty** /ə,mēnə'bilitē; ə,men-/ n. **a·me·na·bly** /-blē/ adv. [16th C.: an Anglo-Norman Fr. legal term, from OFr. *amener* 'bring to,' from *a-* + *mener* 'bring' (from late L. *minare* 'drive (animals),' from L. *minari* 'threaten').]

a·men cor·ner ▶ n. (in some Protestant churches) seats, usually near the preacher, occupied by those who lead responses from the congregation.

a·mend /ə'mend/ ▶ v. [trans.] make minor changes in (a text) in order to make it fairer, more accurate, or more up-to-date. ■ modify formally, as a legal document or legislative bill. ■ make better; improve. ■ archaic put right. — **a·mend·a·ble** adj. **a·mend·er** n. [ME: from OFr. *amender*, based on L. *emendare* (see EMEND).]

a·mend·ment /ə'men(d)mənt/ ▶ n. a minor change in a document. ■ a change or addition to a legal or statutory document. ■ (**Amendment**) an article added to the US Constitution. ■ something that is added to soil in order to improve its texture or fertility.

a·mends /ə'mendz/ ▶ plural n. [treated as sing.] reparation or compensation.
– PHRASES **make amends** do something in order to make up for a wrong inflicted on someone.

a·men·i·ty /ə'menitē; ə'mē-/ ▶ n. (pl. **-ties**) (usu. **amenities**) a desirable or useful feature or facility of a building or place. ■ the pleasantness of a place or a person. [ME: ult. from L. *amoenitas*, from *amoenus* 'pleasant.']

a·men·or·rhe·a /ā,menə'rēə/ (Brit. **a·men·or·rhoe·a**) ▶ n. an abnormal absence of menstruation.

am·ent /'āment; 'am-/ ▶ n. Bot. a catkin.

a·men·tia /ā'mencHēə/ ▶ n. severe congenital mental handicap. [ME: from L., 'madness,' from *amens, ament-* 'mad,' from *a-* 'without' + *mens* 'the mind.']

Am·er·a·sian /,amə'rāzHən/ ▶ adj. having one American and one Asian parent. ▶ n. a person with one American and one Asian parent.

a·merce·ment /ə'mərsmənt/ ▶ n. English Law, hist. a fine. — **a·merce** v. [ME: from Anglo-Norman Fr. *amerciment*, based on *estre amercie* 'be at the mercy of another,' from *a merci* 'at (the) mercy.']

A·mer·i·ca /ə'merikə/ (also **the A·mer·i·cas**) a landmass in the western hemisphere that consists of the continents of North and South America joined by the Isthmus of Panama. ■ used as a name for the United States.

A·mer·i·can /ə'merikən/ ▶ adj. of, relating to, or characteristic of the United States or its inhabitants. ■ relating to or denoting the continents of America. ▶ n. **1** a native or citizen of the United States. ■ [usu. with adj.] a native or inhabitant of any of the countries of North, South, or Central America. **2** the English language as it is used in the United States; American English. — **A·mer·i·can·ness** n.

A·mer·i·ca·na /ə,meri'känə; -'kanə/ ▶ plural n. things associated with the culture and history of America, esp. the United States.

A·mer·i·can al·oe another term for CENTURY PLANT.

A·mer·i·can bald ea·gle ▶ n. another term for BALD EAGLE.

A·mer·i·can cheese ▶ n. a type of mild-flavored semisoft processed cheese.

A·mer·i·can Civ·il War the war between the northern US states (usually known as the Union) and the Confederate states of the South, 1861–65.

A·mer·i·can croc·o·dile ▶ n. a crocodile (*Crocodylus acutus*) with a long tapering head, occurring from southernmost Florida to Ecuador.

American crocodile

A·mer·i·can de·pos·i·tar·y re·ceipt (abbr.: **ADR**) ▶ n. (in the U.S.) a negotiable certificate of title to a number of shares in a non-US company that are deposited in an overseas bank.

A·mer·i·can dream ▶ n. the traditional social ideals of the United States, such as equality, democracy, and material prosperity.

A·mer·i·can ea·gle ▶ n. another term for BALD EAGLE.

A·mer·i·can e·gret ▶ n. another term for GREAT EGRET.

A·mer·i·can Eng·lish ▶ n. the English language as spoken and written in the US.

A·mer·i·can Falls see NIAGARA FALLS.

A·mer·i·can Fed·er·a·tion of La·bor a federation of North American trade unions, merged in 1955 with the Congress of Industrial Organizations to form the American Federation of Labor and Congress of Industrial Organizations (AFL–CIO).

A·mer·i·can In·de·pend·ence, War of British term for AMERICAN REVOLUTION.

A·mer·i·can In·di·an ▶ n. a member of any of the indigenous peoples of North, Central, and South America, esp. those of North America. ▶ adj. of or relating to any of these groups.
– USAGE The term **American Indian** has been steadily replaced, esp. in official contexts, by the more recent term **Native American** (first recorded in the 1950s and becoming prominent in the 1970s). The latter is preferred by some as being a more accurate description (the word *Indian* recalling Columbus's assumption that, on reaching America, he had reached the east coast of India). **American Indian** is still widespread in general use, however, partly because it is not normally regarded as offensive by American Indians themselves. See also NATIVE AMERICAN, AMERINDIAN, and INDIAN.

A·mer·i·can·ism /ə'merikə,nizəm/ ▶ n. a word or phrase peculiar to or originating from the US. ■ the qualities regarded as definitive of America or Americans.

A·mer·i·can·ize /ə'merikə,nīz/ ▶ v. [trans.] make American in character or nationality. — **A·mer·i·can·i·za·tion** /ə,merikəni'zāsHən/ n.

A·mer·i·can League ▶ n. one of the two major leagues in American professional baseball.

A·mer·i·can Le·gion an association of former US servicemen formed in 1919.

A·mer·i·can lo·tus ▶ n. see LOTUS.

A·mer·i·can plan ▶ n. (in hotels) a system of paying a single daily rate that covers the room and all meals.

A·mer·i·can Rev·o·lu·tion the war of 1775–83 in which the American colonists won independence from British rule.

A·mer·i·can Sa·mo·a /sə'mōə/ an unincorporated overseas territory of the US that is composed of a group of islands in the southern Pacific Ocean, east of Western Samoa and south of Kiribati; pop. 57,900; capital, Pago Pago.

A·mer·i·can Sign Lan·guage (abbr.: **ASL**) ▶ n. a form of sign language developed in the US for the use of the deaf, consisting of more than 4,000 signs.

A·mer·i·can Stand·ard Ver·sion (abbr.: **ASV**) ▶ n. an English translation of the Bible published in the US in 1901, based on the Revised Version of 1881–95.

A·mer·i·cas /ə'merikəz/ (**the Americas**) another name for AMERICA.

A·mer·i·ca's Cup an international yachting race held every three to four years.

am·er·i·ci·um /amə'risHēəm/ ▶ n. the chemical element of atomic number 95, a radioactive metal of the actinide series. (Symbol: **Am**) [1940s: from AMERICA.]

Am·er·in·di·an /,amə'rindēən/ (also **Am·er·ind** /'amərind/) ▶ adj. & n. another term for AMERICAN INDIAN, used chiefly in anthropological and linguistic contexts.

Ames /āmz/ a city in central Iowa; pop. 50,731.

Am·e·slan /'am(i),slan/ acronym for AMERICAN SIGN LANGUAGE. [1970s: acronym.]

Ames test /'āmz/ ▶ n. Med. a test to determine the mutagenic activity of chemicals by observing whether they cause mutations in sample bacteria. [1970s: Bruce N. *Ames* (1928–), US biochemist.]

am·e·thyst /ˈaməTHəst/ ▶ **n.** a precious stone consisting of a violet or purple variety of quartz. ▪ a violet or purple color. — **am·e·thys·tine** /ˌaməˈTHistin; -tīn/ **adj.** [ME: ult. from Gk. *amethustos* 'not drunken' (because the stone was believed to prevent intoxication).]

Amex /ˈameks/ ▶ **abbr.** ▪ trademark American Express. ▪ American Stock Exchange.

Am·ha·ra /ämˈhärə/ ▶ **n.** (pl. same or **-ras**) a member of an Amharic-speaking Semitic people of central Ethiopia.

Am·har·ic /amˈharik/ ▶ **n.** the Semitic language descended from Ge'ez that is the official language of Ethiopia. ▶ **adj.** of or relating to this language.

Am·herst[1] /ˈam(h)ərst/ **1** a town in west central Massachusetts, home to several colleges and universities; pop. 35,228. **2** a town in western New York; pop. 116,500.

Am·herst[2] /ˈamərst/, Lord Jeffrey (1717–97), English governor general of British North America 1760–63.

a·mi·a·ble /ˈāmēəbəl/ ▶ **adj.** having or displaying a friendly and pleasant manner. — **a·mi·a·bil·i·ty** /ˌāmēəˈbilitē/ **n.** **a·mi·a·bly** /-blē/ **adv.** **a·mi·a·ble·ness** **n.** [ME (orig. in the senses 'kind' and 'lovely, lovable'): via OFr. from late L. *amicabilis* 'amicable.']

am·i·ca·ble /ˈamikəbəl/ ▶ **adj.** (of relations between people) having a spirit of friendliness; without serious disagreement or rancor. — **am·i·ca·bil·i·ty** /ˌamikəˈbilitē/ **n.** **am·i·ca·bly** /-blē/ **adv.** [ME: from late L. *amicabilis*, from L. *amicus* 'friend.']

am·ice[1] /ˈamis/ ▶ **n.** a white linen cloth worn on the neck and shoulders, under the alb, by a priest celebrating the Eucharist. [ME: from med. L. *amicia, amisia*.]

am·ice[2] ▶ **n.** a cap, hood, or cape worn by members of certain religious orders. [ME: from OFr. *aumusse*, from med. L. *almucia*.]

a·mi·cus /əˈmēkəs; əˈmī-/ (in full **a·mi·cus cu·ri·ae** /ˈkyo͝orēˌī; -ēˌē/) ▶ **n.** (pl. **a·mi·ci** /əˈmēkē; əˈmīkī/, **a·mi·ci cu·ri·ae**) an impartial adviser, often voluntary, to a court of law in a particular case. [17th C.: from mod. L. *amicus curiae*, 'friend of the court.']

a·mid /əˈmid/ ▶ **prep.** surrounded by; in the middle of. ▪ in an atmosphere or against a background of.

am·ide /ˈamīd; -id/ ▶ **n.** Chem. an organic compound containing the group $-C(O)NH_2$, related to ammonia by replacing a hydrogen atom by an acyl group. ▪ a compound derived from ammonia by replacement of a hydrogen atom by a metal, containing the anion NH_2^-.

a·mid·ships /əˈmidˌSHips/ (also **a·mid·ship**) ▶ **adv. & adj.** in the middle of a ship.

a·midst /əˈmidst/ ▶ **prep.** variant of AMID.

Am·i·ens /ˈamēənz; ämˈyeN/ a town in northern France; pop. 136,230.

a·mi·go /əˈmēgō/ ▶ **n.** (pl. **-gos**) informal used to address or refer to a friend, chiefly in Spanish-speaking areas.

A·min /äˈmēn/, Idi (1925–2003), president of Uganda 1971–79; full name *Idi Amin Dada*. He was deposed after a rule characterized by the murder of political opponents.

A·min·di·vi Is·lands /ˌəmənˈdēvē/ a group of islands off the coast of southwestern India in the Arabian Sea.

a·mine /əˈmēn; ˈamēn/ ▶ **n.** Chem. an organic compound derived from ammonia by replacement of one or more hydrogen atoms by organic radicals.

a·mi·no /əˈmēnō/ ▶ **n.** [as adj.] Chem. the group $-NH_2$, present in amino acids, amides, and many amines.

amino- ▶ **comb. form** designating or containing the group $-NH_2$: *aminobutyric*.

a·mi·no ac·id ▶ **n.** Biochem. a simple organic compound containing both a carboxyl (−COOH) and an amino ($-NH_2$) group. They occur naturally in plant and animal tissues and form the basic constituents of proteins.

a·mir /əˈmi(ə)r/ ▶ **n.** an Arab ruler. [16th C.: from Pers. and Urdu, from Arab. *'amīr* 'commander,' from *'amara* 'to command.']

A·mis /ˈāməs/ family of English novelists. Sir Kingsley (1922–95) wrote *Lucky Jim* (1954). His son Martin Louis (1949–) wrote *London Fields* (1989) and *House of Meetings* (2006).

A·mish /ˈämiSH/ ▶ **plural n.** the members of a strict Mennonite sect that established major settlements in Pennsylvania and Ohio from 1720 onward. ▶ **adj.** of or relating to this sect. [19th C.: appar. from Ger. *amisch*.]

a·miss /əˈmis/ ▶ **adj.** [predic.] not quite right; inappropriate or out of place. ▶ **adv.** dated wrongly or inappropriately. [ME: prob. from ON *á mis* 'so as to miss,' from *á* 'on' + *mis* (akin to MISS[1]).]

am·i·tot·ic /ˌāmīˈtätik; ˌamī-/ ▶ **adj.** Biol. relating to the division of a cell nucleus into two parts by constriction with no involvement of a mitotic apparatus. — **am·i·to·sis** /-ˈtōsis/ **n.** **am·i·tot·i·cal·ly** /-ik(ə)lē/ **adv.**

am·i·ty /ˈamitē/ ▶ **n.** a friendly relationship. [ME: from OFr. *amitie*, based on L. *amicus* 'friend.']

Am·man /äˈmän; əˈmän; əˈman/ the capital of Jordan, in the northwestern part of the country; pop. 1,160,000.

am·me·ter /ˈa(m)ˌmētər/ ▶ **n.** an instrument for measuring electric current in amperes.

am·mo /ˈamō/ ▶ **n.** informal term for AMMUNITION.

Am·mon /ˈamən/ Greek and Roman form of AMUN.

am·mo·nia /əˈmōnyə; -nēə/ ▶ **n.** a colorless gas, NH_3, with a characteristic pungent smell. It dissolves in water to give a strongly alkaline solution. ▪ a solution of this gas, used as a cleaning fluid. [18th C.: mod. L., from *sal ammoniacus* (see SAL AMMONIAC).]

am·mo·ni·a·cal /ˌaməˈnīikəl/ ▶ **adj.** of or containing ammonia.

am·mo·ni·at·ed /əˈmōnēˌātid/ ▶ **adj.** combined or treated with ammonia. — **am·mo·ni·a·tion** /əˌmōnēˈāSHən/ **n.**

am·mo·nite /ˈaməˌnīt/ ▶ **n.** an ammonoid that belongs to the order *Ammonitida*, typically having elaborately frilled suture lines.

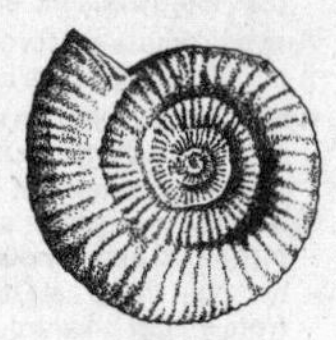
ammonite

am·mo·ni·um /əˈmōnēəm/ ▶ **n.** [as adj.] Chem. the cation NH_4^+, present in solutions of ammonia and in salts derived from ammonia.

am·mo·ni·um car·bon·ate ▶ **n.** Chem. a white crystalline solid, $(NH_4)_2CO_3$, that slowly decomposes, giving off ammonia.

am·mo·ni·um chlo·ride ▶ **n.** Chem. a white crystalline salt, NH_4Cl, used chiefly in dry cells, as a mordant, and as soldering flux. Also called SAL AMMONIAC.

am·mo·ni·um ni·trate ▶ **n.** Chem. a white crystalline solid, NH_4NO_3, used as a fertilizer and as a component of some explosives.

am·mu·ni·tion /ˌamyəˈniSHən/ ▶ **n.** a supply or quantity of bullets and shells. ▪ fig. considerations that can be used to support one's case in debate. [16th C.: from obs. Fr. *amunition*, alt. (by wrong division) of *la munition* 'the munition' (see MUNITION).]

am·ne·sia /amˈnēZHə/ ▶ **n.** a partial or total loss of memory. — **am·ne·si·ac** /amˈnēzēˌak; -ZHēˌak/ **n. & adj.** **am·ne·sic** /-zik; -sik/ **adj. & n.** **am·nes·tic** /amˈnestik/ **adj.** [18th C.: from Gk. *amnēsia* 'forgetfulness.']

am·nes·ty /ˈamnistē/ ▶ **n.** (pl. **-ties**) an official pardon for people who have been convicted of political offenses. ▪ an undertaking by the authorities to take no action against specified offenses or offenders during a fixed period. ▶ **v.** (**-ties, -tied**) [trans.] grant an official pardon to. [16th C.: via L. from Gk. *amnēstia* 'forgetfulness.']

Am·nes·ty In·ter·na·tion·al an independent international organization in support of human rights, esp. for prisoners of conscience. Nobel Peace Prize (1977).

am·ni·o /ˈamnē-ō/ ▶ **n.** (pl. **-os**) informal term for AMNIOCENTESIS.

am·ni·o·cen·te·sis /ˌamnē-ōsenˈtēsis/ ▶ **n.** (pl. **-ses** /-sēz/) Med. the sampling of amniotic fluid using a hollow needle inserted into the uterus, to screen for developmental abnormalities in a fetus.

am·ni·on /ˈamnēˌän; -ən/ ▶ **n.** (pl. - or **-ni·a** /-nēə/) the innermost membrane that encloses the embryo of a mammal, bird, or reptile. [17th C.: from Gk., 'caul,' dimin. of *amnos* 'lamb.']

am·ni·ote /ˈamnēˌōt/ ▶ **n.** Zool. an animal whose embryo develops in an amnion and chorion and has an allantois; a mammal, bird, or reptile.

am·ni·ot·ic flu·id /ˌamnēˈätik/ ▶ **n.** the fluid surrounding a fetus within the amnion.

a·moe·ba ▶ **n.** (pl. **-bas** or **-bae** /-bē/) var. of AMEBA. — **a·moe·bic** **adj.** **a·moe·boid** **adj.**

a·mok /əˈmək; əˈmäk/ (also **a·muck**) ▶ **adv.** (in phrase **run amok**) behave uncontrollably and disruptively. [17th C. (n.): via Port. *amouco*, from Malay *amok* 'rushing in a frenzy.']

a·mo·le /əˈmōlā; -lē/ ▶ **n.** a plant of a group native to Mexico and the southern US whose roots are used as detergent, esp. the soap plant or the lechuguilla. [19th C.: Mex. Sp.]

A·mon var. of AMUN.

a·mong /əˈməNG/ (esp. Brit. also **a·mongst** /əˈməNGst/) ▶ **prep.** **1** surrounded by; in the company of. **2** being a member or members of (a larger set): *he was among the first 29 students enrolled.* **3** occurring in or practiced by (some members of a community): *rooting out abuses among the clergy.* ▪ involving most or all members of a group reciprocally: *they bickered among themselves.* **4** indicating a division, choice, or differentiation involving three or more participants.

a·mon·til·la·do /əˌmäntlˈädō; -təˈyädō/ ▶ **n.** (pl. **-dos**) a medium dry sherry. [Sp., from *Montilla*, town in Spain.]

a·mor·al /āˈmôrəl/ ▶ **adj.** lacking a moral sense; unconcerned with the rightness or wrongness of something. — **a·mo·ral·i·ty** /ˌāməˈralitē/ **n.** **a·mor·al·ism** **n.** **a·mor·al·ist** /-list/ **n.**

am·o·ret·to /ˌaməˈretō/ ▶ **n.** (pl. **-ret·ti** /-ˈretē/) a representation of Cupid in a work of art. [17th C.: Ital., dimin. of *amore* 'love,' from L. *amor*.]

am·o·rist /ˈamərist/ ▶ **n.** a person who is in love or who writes about love. [16th C.: from L. *amor* or Fr. *amour* 'love' + -IST.]

Am·o·rite /ˈaməˌrīt/ ▶ **n.** a member of seminomadic people living in Mesopotamia, Palestine, and Syria in the 3rd millennium BC, founders of Mari on the Euphrates and the first dynasty of Babylon. ▶ **adj.** of or relating to this people. [from Heb. *'ĕmōrī*, from Akkadian *'amurrū* + -ITE[1].]

am·o·rous /ˈamərəs/ ▶ **adj.** showing, feeling, or relating to sexual desire. — **am·o·rous·ly** **adv.** **am·o·rous·ness** **n.** [ME: via OFr. from med. L. *amorosus*, from L. *amor* 'love.']

a·mor·phous /əˈmôrfəs/ ▶ **adj.** without a clearly defined shape or form. ▪ vague; ill-organized; unclassifiable. ▪ (of a group of people or an organization) lacking a clear structure or focus. ▪ Mineral. & Chem. (of a solid) noncrystalline; having neither definite form nor apparent structure. — **a·mor·phous·ly** **adv.** **a·mor·phous·ness** **n.** [18th C.: from mod.

L. *amorphus*, from Gk. *amorphos* (from *a-* 'without' + *morphē* 'form').]

am·or·tize /'amər,tīz/ ▶ **v.** [trans.] reduce or extinguish (a debt) by money regularly put aside. ■ gradually write off the initial cost of (an asset). — **am·or·ti·za·tion** /,amərti'zāshən; ə,môrti-/ **n.** [ME: from OFr. *amortiss-*, from *amortir*, based on L. *ad* 'to' + *mors, mort-* 'death.']

A·mos /'āməs/ a Hebrew minor prophet (*c.*760 BC), a shepherd of Tekoa, near Jerusalem. ■ a book of the Bible containing his prophecies.

a·mount /ə'mount/ ▶ **n.** a quantity of something, typically the total of a thing or things in number, size, value, or extent. ■ a sum of money. ▶ **v.** [intrans.] (**amount to**) come to be (the total) when added together. ■ be the equivalent of. ■ develop into; become.
– PHRASES **any amount of** a great deal or number of. **no amount of** not even the greatest possible amount of. [ME (v.): from OFr. *amunter*, from *amont* 'upward,' lit. 'uphill,' from L. *ad montem*.]

a·mour /ə'mo͝or; ä'mo͝or/ ▶ **n.** a secret or illicit love affair or lover. [ME: via OFr. from L. *amor* 'love.']

a·mour fou /ä'mo͝or 'fo͞o/ ▶ **n.** uncontrollable or obsessive passion. [1970s: Fr., lit. 'insane love.']

a·mour pro·pre /ä,mo͝or 'prôpr(ə)/ ▶ **n.** a sense of one's own worth; self-respect. [18th C.: Fr., lit. 'love of oneself.']

a·mox·i·cil·lin /ə,mäksə'silin/ (also **a·mox·y·cil·lin**) ▶ **n.** a broad-spectrum semisynthetic penicillin, related to ampicillin but better absorbed when taken orally, used esp. for ear and upper respiratory infections.

A·moy /ä'moi/ another name for XIAMEN.

AMP Biochem. ▶ **abbr.** adenosine monophosphate.

amp[1] /amp/ ▶ **n.** short for AMPERE.

amp[2] ▶ **n.** informal short for AMPLIFIER.

am·pe·lop·sis /,ampə'läpsis/ ▶ **n.** (pl. same) either of two bushy climbing plants of the grape family: the **American ampelopsis** (*Ampelopsis cordata*) and the **Asiatic ampelopsis** (*A. brevipedunculata*).

am·per·age /'amp(ə)rij/ ▶ **n.** the strength of an electric current in amperes.

Am·père /äN'per/, André-Marie (1775–1836), French physicist. He analyzed the relationship between magnetic force and electric current.

am·pere /'am,pi(ə)r/ (abbr.: **A**) ▶ **n.** the SI base unit of electric current, equal to a flow of one coulomb per second. [19th C.: A.-M. AMPÈRE.]

am·per·sand /'ampər,sand/ ▶ **n.** the sign & (standing for *and*, as in *Smith & Co.*, or the Latin *et*, as in *&c.*). [19th C.: alt. of *and per se and* '& by itself is *and*.']

am·phet·a·mine /am'fetə,mēn; -min/ ▶ **n.** a synthetic, addictive, mood-altering drug, $C_6H_5CH_2CH(CH_3)NH_2$, used illegally as a stimulant and legally as a prescription drug to treat children with ADD and adults with narcolepsy. [1930s: abbrev. of its chemical name, *a(lpha-)m(ethyl) phe(ne)t(hyl)amine*.]

amphi- ▶ **comb. form 1** both: *amphibian*. ■ of both kinds: *amphipod*. ■ on both sides: *amphiprostyle*. **2** around: *amphitheater*. [from Gk.]

am·phib·i·an /am'fibēən/ ▶ **n.** Zool. a cold-blooded vertebrate animal of a class (Amphibia) that comprises the frogs, toads, newts, and salamanders, distinguished by having an aquatic gill-breathing larval stage followed (typically) by a terrestrial lung-breathing adult stage. ■ a seaplane, tank, or other vehicle that can operate on land and on water. ▶ **adj.** Zool. of or relating to this class of animals. [17th C. (in the sense of dual or doubtful nature): from mod. L. *amphibium* 'an amphibian,' from Gk. *amphibion* (n. use of *amphibios* 'living both in water and on land,' from *amphi* 'both' + *bios* 'life').]

am·phib·i·ous /am'fibēəs/ ▶ **adj.** relating to, living in, or suited for both land and water. ■ (of a military operation) involving forces landed from the sea. ■ (of forces) trained for such operations.

am·phi·bole /'amfə,bōl/ ▶ **n.** any of a class of rock-forming silicate or aluminosilicate minerals typically occurring as fibrous or columnar crystals. [19th C.: from L. *amphibolus* 'ambiguous' from Gk. *amphibolos*, from *amphi-* 'both' + *ballein* 'to throw.']

am·phib·o·lite /am'fibə,līt/ ▶ **n.** Geol. a granular metamorphic rock consisting mainly of hornblende and plagioclase.

am·phi·bol·o·gy /,amfə'bäləjē/ ▶ **n.** (pl. **-gies**) a phrase or sentence that is grammatically ambiguous, such as *she sees more of her children than her husband*. — **am·phib·o·lous** /am'fibələs/ **adj.**

am·phi·brach /'amfə,brak/ ▶ **n.** Pros. a metrical foot consisting of a stressed syllable between two unstressed syllables or (in Greek and Latin) a long syllable between two short syllables. [16th C.: via L. from Gk. *amphibrakhus* 'short at both ends.']

am·phi·mix·is /,amfə'miksis/ ▶ **n.** Bot. sexual reproduction involving the fusion of two different gametes to form a zygote. Often contrasted with APOMIXIS. — **am·phi·mic·tic** /-'miktik/ **adj.** [19th C.: from AMPHI- + Gk. *mixis* 'mingling.']

am·phi·ox·us /,amfē'äksəs/ ▶ **n.** a lancelet (genus *Branchiostoma*, family Branchiostomidae) that is caught for food in parts of Asia.

Am·phip·o·da /am'fipədə/ Zool. an order of crustaceans with a laterally compressed body and a large number of leglike appendages. — **am·phi·pod** /'amfə,päd/ **n.** [mod. L. (pl.), from AMPHI- + Gk. *pous, pod-* 'foot.']

am·phip·ro·style /am'fiprə,stīl; ,amfə'prō-/ ▶ **adj.** (of a classical building) having a portico at each end and no columns along the sides. [18th C.: via L. from Gk. *amphiprostulos*, from *amphi-* 'both'+ *prostulos* 'having pillars in front' (see PROSTYLE).]

Am·phis·bae·ni·a /,amfis'bēnēə/ Zool. a group of reptiles (suborder Amphisbaenia, order Squamata) that comprises the worm lizards. — **am·phis·bae·ni·an** **n.** & **adj.** [mod. L., from Gk. *amphisbaina*, from *amphis* 'both' + *bainein* 'go.']

am·phi·the·a·ter /'amfə,thēətər/ ▶ **n.** (esp. in Greek and Roman architecture) a round building, typically unroofed, with a central space for the presentation of dramatic or sporting events. Tiers of seats for spectators surround the central space. ■ a sloping, semicircular seating gallery. ■ a large circular hollow in rocks or hills. [ME: via L. from Gk. *amphitheatron*, from *amphi* 'both' + *theatron* (see THEATER).]

Am·phi·tri·te /,amfi'trītē/ Gk. Mythol. a sea goddess, wife of Poseidon and mother of Triton.

am·pho·ra /'amfərə/ ▶ **n.** (pl. **-rae** /-,rē/ or **-ras**) a tall ancient Greek or Roman jar with two handles and a narrow neck.

am·pho·ter·ic /,amfə'terik/ ▶ **adj.** Chem. (of a compound, esp. a metal oxide or hydroxide) able to react both as a base and as an acid. [19th C.: from Gk. *amphoteros*, compar. of *amphō* 'both,' + -IC.]

am·pi·cil·lin /,ampi'silin/ ▶ **n.** Med. a semisynthetic form of penicillin used chiefly to treat infections of the urinary and respiratory tracts. [1960s: blend of AMINO and contr. of PENICILLIN.]

am·ple /'ampəl/ ▶ **adj.** (**-pler, -plest**) enough or more than enough; plentiful. ■ large and accommodating. ■ used euphemistically to convey that someone is overweight. — **am·ple·ness** **n.** **am·ply** **adv.** [ME: via Fr. from L. *amplus* 'large.']

am·plex·i·caul /am'pleksi,kôl/ ▶ **adj.** Bot. (of a leaf) embracing and surrounding the stem.

am·plex·us /am'pleksəs/ ▶ **n.** Zool. the mating position of frogs and toads, in which the male clasps the female about the back. [1930s: from L., 'an embrace.']

am·pli·fi·er /'amplə,fīər/ ▶ **n.** an electronic device for increasing the amplitude of electrical signals, used chiefly in sound reproduction. ■ a device of this kind combined with a loudspeaker, used to amplify musical instruments.

am·pli·fy /'amplə,fī/ ▶ **v.** (**-fies, -fied**) [trans.] (often **be amplified**) increase the volume of (sound), esp. using an amplifier. ■ increase the amplitude of (an electrical signal or other oscillation). ■ cause to become more marked or intense. ■ Genet. make multiple copies of (a gene or DNA sequence). ■ enlarge upon or add detail to (a story or statement). — **am·pli·fi·ca·tion** /,ampləfi'kāshən/ **n.** [ME: from OFr. *amplifier*, from L. *amplificare*, from *amplus* 'large.']

am·pli·tude /'ampli,t(y)o͞od/ ▶ **n. 1** Physics the maximum extent of a vibration or oscillation, measured from the position of equilibrium. ■ the maximum difference of an alternating electrical current or potential from the average value. **2** Astron. the angular distance of a celestial object from the true east or west point of the horizon at rising or setting. **3** breadth, range, or magnitude. **4** Math. the angle between the real axis of an Argand diagram and a vector representing a complex number. [16th C.: from L. *amplitudo*, from *amplus* 'large.']

am·pli·tude mod·u·la·tion (abbr.: **AM**) ▶ **n.** the modulation of a wave by varying its amplitude, used chiefly as a means of radio broadcasting, in which an audio signal is combined with a carrier wave. Often contrasted with FREQUENCY MODULATION. ■ the system of radio transmission using such modulation.

am·poule /'am,p(y)o͞ol/ (also **am·pul** or **am·pule** /'ampyo͞ol/) ▶ **n.** a sealed glass capsule containing a liquid, esp. a measured quantity ready for injecting.

am·pul·la /am'po͝olə; -'pələ/ ▶ **n.** (pl. **-lae** /-lē/) a roughly spherical flask with two handles, used in ancient Rome. ■ a flask for sacred uses such as holding holy oil. ■ Anat. & Zool. a cavity, or the dilated end of a duct, shaped like a Roman ampulla. [ME: from L., dimin. of *ampora*, var. of *amphora* (see AMPHORA).]

am·pu·tate /'ampyə,tāt/ ▶ **v.** [trans.] cut off (a limb), typically by surgical operation. — **am·pu·ta·tion** /,ampyə'tāshən/ **n.** [16th C.: from L. *amputat-* 'lopped off,' from *amputare*, from *am-* (for *amb-* 'around') + *putare* 'to prune.']

am·pu·tee /,ampyə'tē/ ▶ **n.** a person who has had a limb amputated.

am·rit /'əmrit/ (also **am·ri·ta** /əm'rētə/) ▶ **n.** a syrup considered divine by Sikhs and taken by them in religious observances. [from Sanskrit *amṛta* 'immortal.']

Am·rit·sar /,əm'ritsər; äm-/ a city in the state of Punjab in northwestern India; pop. 709,000.

Am·ster·dam /'amstər,dam/ a port city and the capital of the Netherlands; pop. 702,440.

am·trac /'am,trak/ (also **am·track, am·trak**) ▶ **n.** an amphibious tracked vehicle used for landing assault troops on a shore. [World War II: blend of AMPHIBIOUS and TRACTOR.]

amu ▶ **abbr.** atomic mass unit.

a·muck /ə'mək/ ▶ **adv.** var. of AMOK.

A·mu Dar·ya /,ämo͞o 'däryə/ a river in central Asia that rises in the Pamirs and flows 1,500 miles (2,400 km) into the Aral Sea. Formerly known as the Oxus.

am·u·let /'amyəlit/ ▶ **n.** an ornament or small piece of jewelry thought to give protection against evil, danger, or disease. [16th C.: from L. *amuletum*.]

A·mun /'ämən/ (also **A·mon**) Egyptian Mythol. a supreme god of the ancient Egyptians, identified with the sun god Ra and in Greek and Roman times with Zeus and Jupiter (under the name **Ammon**).

A·mund·sen /'ämənsən/, Roald (1872–1928), Norwegian explorer. He was the first to navigate the Northwest Passage (1903–06) and in 1911 became the first person to reach the South Pole.

A·mur /ä'mo͝or/ a river of northeastern Asia, 2,737 miles (4,350 km) long, that forms much of the boundary between Russia and China. Chinese name HEILONG.

a·muse /ə'myo͞oz/ ▶ v. [trans.] **1** cause (someone) to find something funny; entertain. **2** provide interesting and enjoyable occupation for (someone). — **a·mus·ed·ly** /ə'myo͞ozidlē/ adv. (in sense 1). [15th C.: from OFr. *amuser* 'entertain, deceive,' from *a-* + *muser* 'stare stupidly.']

a·muse·ment /ə'myo͞ozmənt/ ▶ n. the state or experience of finding something funny. ■ the provision or enjoyment of entertainment. ■ something that causes laughter or provides entertainment.

a·muse·ment park ▶ n. a large outdoor area with fairground rides, shows, refreshments, games of chance or skill, and other entertainments.

a·mus·ing /ə'myo͞oziNG/ ▶ adj. causing laughter or providing entertainment. — **a·mus·ing·ly** adv.

a·myg·da·la /ə'migdələ/ ▶ n. (pl. **-lae** /-lē/) Anat. a roughly almond-shaped mass of gray matter deep inside each cerebral hemisphere, associated with the sense of smell. [ME: via L. from Gk. *amugdalē* 'almond.']

a·myg·da·lin /ə'migdəlin/ ▶ n. Chem. a bitter crystalline compound, found in bitter almonds and the stones of peaches, apricots, and other fruit. [19th C.: from L. *amygdala* 'almond.']

a·myg·da·loid /ə'migdə,loid/ ▶ adj. tech. shaped like an almond. ▶ n. **1** (also **amygdaloid nucleus**) Anat. another term for AMYGDALA. **2** Geol. volcanic rock with amygdules.

a·myg·da·loi·dal /ə,migdə'loidl/ ▶ adj. Geol. relating to or containing amygdules.

a·myg·dule /ə'mig,d(y)o͞ol/ (also **a·myg·dale** /-,dāl/) ▶ n. Geology a vesicle in an igneous rock, containing secondary minerals. [19th C.: from French, from Latin *amygdala* (see AMYGDALA).]

am·yl /'aməl/ ▶ n. [as adj.] Chem. the straight-chain pentyl radical $-C_5H_{11}$. ■ informal short for AMYL NITRITE. [19th C.: from L. *amylum* 'starch.']

am·yl·ase /'amə,lās; -,lāz/ ▶ n. Biochem. an enzyme, found chiefly in saliva and pancreatic fluid, that converts starch and glycogen into simple sugars.

am·yl ni·trate ▶ n. Chem. a colorless synthetic liquid, $C_5H_{11}NO_3$, used as an additive in diesel fuel to improve its ignition properties.

am·yl ni·trite ▶ n. a yellowish volatile synthetic liquid, $C_5H_{11}NO_2$, used medicinally as a vasodilator.

am·y·loid /'amə,loid/ Med. ▶ n. a starchlike protein that is deposited in the liver, kidneys, spleen, or other tissues in certain diseases. ■ another term for AMYLOIDOSIS.

am·y·loi·do·sis /,aməloi'dōsis/ ▶ n. Med. a disorder marked by deposition of amyloid in the body.

am·y·lo·pec·tin /,amələ'pektin/ ▶ n. Biochem. the noncrystallizable form of starch, consisting of branched polysaccharide chains.

am·yl·ose /'amə,lōs; -,lōz/ ▶ n. Biochem. the crystallizable form of starch, consisting of long unbranched polysaccharide chains.

a·my·o·troph·ic lat·er·al scle·ro·sis /,āmīə'träfik; -ə'trō-/ (abbr.: **ALS**) ▶ n. a progressive degeneration of the motor neurons of the central nervous system, leading to wasting of the muscles and paralysis. Also called LOU GEHRIG'S DISEASE.

am·y·ot·ro·phy /,āmī'ätrəfē/ ▶ n. Med. muscular atrophy. — **a·my·o·troph·ic** /,āmīə'träfik; -ə'trō-/ adj.

Am·y·tal /'amə,tôl; -,tal/ ▶ n. trademark a barbiturate drug, $C_{11}H_{18}N_2O_3$, used as a sedative and a hypnotic.

an /an/ ▶ adj. the form of the indefinite article (see A) used before words beginning with a vowel sound.

an-[1] ▶ prefix var. of A-[1] before a vowel (as in *anemia, anechoic*). [from Gk.]

an-[2] ▶ prefix var. of AD- assimilated before *n* (as in *annihilate, annotate*).

an-[3] ▶ prefix var. of ANA- shortened before a vowel (as in *aneurysm*).

-an /ən/ (also **-ean** or **-ian** /ēən/) ▶ suffix **1** forming adjectives and nouns, esp. from: ■ names of places: *Ohioan.* ■ names of systems: *Anglican.* ■ names of zoological classes or orders: *crustacean.* ■ names of founders or leaders when referring to them as sources: *Lutheran.* **2** Chem. forming names of organic compounds, chiefly polysaccharides: *dextran.*

ana- (usu. **an-** before a vowel) ▶ prefix **1** up: *anabasis.* **2** back: *anamnesis.* **3** again: *anabiosis.* [from Gk. *ana* 'up.']

-ana ▶ suffix (forming plural nouns) denoting things associated with a person, place, or field of interest: *Americana* | *Victoriana.* [from neut. pl. of L. *-anus.*]

An·a·bap·tism /,anə'bap,tizəm/ ▶ n. the doctrine that baptism should only be administered to believing adults, held by a radical Protestant sect that emerged during the 1520s and 1530s. — **An·a·bap·tist** n. & adj. [16th C.: ult. from Gk. *anabaptismos*, from *ana-* 'over again' + *baptismos* 'baptism.']

a·nab·a·sis /ə'nabəsis/ ▶ n. (pl. **-ses** /-,sēz/) rare a march from a coast into the interior, as that of the younger Cyrus into Asia in 401 BC, as narrated by Xenophon in his work *Anabasis.* ■ a military advance. [18th C.: Gk., 'ascent.']

an·a·bat·ic /,anə'batik/ ▶ adj. Meteorol. (of a wind) caused by local upward motion of warm air. [20th C.: from Gk. *anabatikos*, based on *anabainein* 'walk up.']

an·a·bi·o·sis /,anəbī'ōsis/ ▶ n. Zool. a temporary state of suspended animation or greatly reduced metabolism. — **an·a·bi·ot·ic** /-'ätik/ adj. [19th C.: from Gk. *anabiōsis*, from *anabioein* 'return to life.']

an·a·bol·ic /,anə'bälik/ ▶ adj. Biochem. relating to or promoting anabolism.

an·a·bol·ic ste·roid ▶ n. a synthetic steroid hormone that resembles testosterone in promoting the growth of muscle. Such hormones are used medicinally to treat some forms of weight loss and (illegally) by some athletes and others to enhance physical performance.

a·nab·o·lism /ə'nabə,lizəm/ ▶ n. Biochem. the synthesis of complex molecules in living organisms from simpler ones together with the storage of energy; constructive metabolism. [19th C.: from Gk. *anabolē* 'ascent,' from *ana-* 'up' + *ballein* 'to throw.']

a·nach·ro·nism /ə'nakrə,nizəm/ ▶ n. a thing belonging or appropriate to a period other than that in which it exists, esp. a thing that is conspicuously old-fashioned. ■ an act of attributing a custom, event, or object to a period to which it does not belong. — **a·nach·ro·nis·tic** /ə,nakrə'nistik/ adj. **a·nach·ro·nis·ti·cal·ly** /-'nistik(ə)lē/ adv. [17th C.: from Gk. *anakhronismos*, from *ana-* 'backward' + *khronos* 'time.']

an·a·clit·ic /,anə'klitik/ ▶ adj. Psychoanal. relating to or characterized by a strong emotional dependence on another or others. [1920s: from Gk. *anaklitos* 'for reclining,' from *anaklinein* 'recline.']

an·a·co·lu·thon /,anəkə'lo͞oTHän/ ▶ n. (pl. **-tha** /-THə/) a sentence or construction that lacks grammatical sequence, such as *while in the garden, the door banged shut.* — **an·a·co·lu·thic** /-THik/ adj. [18th C.: ult. from Gk. *anakolouthon*, from *an-* 'not' + *akolouthos* 'following.']

an·a·con·da /,anə'kändə/ ▶ n. a semiaquatic snake (genus *Eunectes*) of the boa family that may grow to a great size, native to tropical South America. [18th C.: alt. of L. *anacandaia* 'python,' from Sinhalese *henakan̆dayā* 'whipsnake,' from *hena* 'lightning' + *kan̆da* 'stem.']

A·nac·re·on /ə'nakrēən; -,än/ (*c.*570–478 BC), Greek poet. He was noted for his celebrations of love and wine.

a·nac·re·on·tic /ə,nakrē'äntik/ (also **A·nac·re·on·tic**) Pros. ▶ adj. (of a poem) composed in the manner of the Greek poet Anacreon. ▶ n. (usu. **anacreontics**) an anacreontic poem. [17th C. (adj.): from late L. *anacreonticus*, from Gk. *Anakreōn.*]

an·a·cru·sis /,anə'kro͞osis/ ▶ n. (pl. **-ses** /-sēz/) **1** Pros. one or more unstressed syllables at the beginning of a verse. **2** Music one or more unstressed notes before the first bar line of a piece or passage. [19th C.: mod. L., from Gk. *anakrousis* 'prelude,' from *ana-* 'up' + *krousis*, from *krouein* 'to strike.']

an·a·dam·a bread /,anə'damə/ ▶ n. a type of yeast bread typically made with cornmeal and dark molasses.

a·nad·ro·mous /ə'nadrəməs/ ▶ adj. Zool. (of a fish, such as the salmon) migrating up rivers from the sea to spawn. The opposite of CATADROMOUS. [18th C.: from Gk. *anadromos* (from *ana-* 'up' + *dromos* 'running.')]

a·nae·mi·a ▶ n. British spelling of ANEMIA.

a·nae·mic ▶ adj. British spelling of ANEMIC.

an·aer·obe /'anə,rōb/ ▶ n. Biol. an organism that grows without air, or requires oxygen-free conditions to live.

an·aer·o·bic /,ane(ə)'rōbik; ,anə-/ ▶ adj. Biol. relating to, involving, or requiring an absence of free oxygen. ■ relating to or denoting exercise that does not improve or is not intended to improve the efficiency of the body's cardiovascular system in absorbing and transporting oxygen. — **an·aer·o·bi·cal·ly** /-bik(ə)lē/ adv.

an·aes·the·sia, etc. ▶ n. British spelling of ANESTHESIA, etc.

an·a·gen·e·sis /,anə'jenəsis/ ▶ n. Biol. species formation without branching of the evolutionary line of descent. Compare with CLADOGENESIS. — **an·a·ge·net·ic** /-jə'netik/ adj.

an·a·glyph /'anə,glif/ ▶ n. **1** Photog. a stereoscopic photograph with the two images superimposed and printed in different colors, producing a stereo effect when the photograph is viewed through correspondingly colored filters. **2** an object, such as a cameo, embossed or carved in low relief. — **an·a·glyph·ic** /,anə'glifik/ adj. [16th C. (sense 2): from Gk. *anagluphē*, from *ana-* 'up' + *gluphē* (from *gluphein* 'carve').]

an·a·gram /'anə,gram/ ▶ n. a word, phrase, or name formed by rearranging the letters of another, such as *cinema*, formed from *iceman.* ▶ v. (**-grammed, -gram·ming**) another term for ANAGRAMMATIZE. — **an·a·gram·mat·ic** /,anəgrə'matik/ adj. **an·a·gram·mat·i·cal** /,anəgrə'matikəl/ adj. [16th C.: from Fr. *anagramme* or mod. L. *anagramma*, from Gk. *ana-* 'back' + *gramma* 'letter.']

an·a·gram·ma·tize /,anə'gramə,tīz/ ▶ v. [trans.] make an anagram of (a word, phrase, or name). — **an·a·gram·ma·ti·za·tion** /-,gramətə'zāSHən/ n.

An·a·heim /'anə,hīm/ a city in southwestern California, home to Disneyland; pop. 328,014.

a·nal /'ānl/ ▶ adj. involving, relating to, or situated near the anus. ■ (in Freudian psychoanalysis) relating to or denoting a stage of infantile psychosexual development supposedly preoccupied with the anus and defecation. ■ informal anal-retentive. — **a·nal·ly** adv.

an·a·lects /'anl,ek(t)s/ (also **an·a·lec·ta** /,anl'ektə/) ▶ plural n. a collection of short literary or philosophical extracts. [ME: via L. from Gk. *analekta* 'things gathered up,' from *analegein* 'pick up,' from *ana-* + *legein* 'gather.']

an·a·lep·tic /,anə'leptik/ Med. ▶ adj. (chiefly of a drug) tending to restore a person's health or strength; restorative. ▶ n. a restorative drug. ■ a drug that stimulates the central nervous system. [16th C.: via late L. from Gk. *analēptikos* 'restorative.']

an·al·ge·si·a /,anl'jēzēə; -ZHə/ ▶ n. Med. the inability to feel pain. [18th C.: from Gk. *analgēsia* 'painlessness,' from *an-* + *algeein* 'feel pain.']

an·al·ge·sic /ˌanlˈjēzik; -sik/ Med. ▶ **adj.** (chiefly of a drug) acting to relieve pain. ▶ **n.** an analgesic drug.

an·a·log /ˈanlˌôg; -ˌäg/ (also **an·a·logue**) ▶ **n.** a person or thing seen as comparable to another. ■ Chem. a compound with a molecular structure closely similar to that of another. ▶ **adj.** relating to or using signals or information represented by a continuously variable physical quantity such as spatial position or voltage. Often contrasted with DIGITAL (sense 1). ■ (of a clock or watch) showing the time by means of hands rather than displayed digits. [19th C.: from Fr., from Gk. *analogon*, neut. of *analogos* 'proportionate.']

a·nal·o·gize /əˈnaləˌjīz/ ▶ **v.** [trans.] make a comparison of (something) with something else to assist understanding.

a·nal·o·gous /əˈnaləgəs/ ▶ **adj.** (often **analogous to**) comparable in certain respects, typically in a way that makes clearer the nature of the things compared. ■ Biol. (of structures) performing a similar function but having a different evolutionary origin, such as the wings of insects and birds. Often contrasted with HOMOLOGOUS. — **a·nal·o·gous·ly** **adv.** [17th C.: ult. from Gk. *analogos* 'proportionate.']

an·a·log-to-dig·it·al con·vert·er (abbr.: **ADC**) ▶ **n.** a device for converting analog signals to digital form.

an·a·logue ▶ **n. & adj.** var. of ANALOG.

a·nal·o·gy /əˈnaləjē/ ▶ **n.** (pl. **-gies**) a comparison between two things, typically on the basis of their structure and for the purpose of explanation or clarification. ■ a correspondence or partial similarity. ■ a thing that is comparable to something else in significant respects. ■ Logic a process of arguing from similarity in known respects to similarity in other respects. ■ Ling. a process by which new words and inflections are created on the basis of regularities in the form of existing ones. ■ Biol. the resemblance of function between organs that have a different evolutionary origin. — **an·a·log·i·cal** /ˌanlˈäjikəl/ **adj.** **an·a·log·i·cal·ly** /ˌanlˈäjik(ə)lē/ **adv.**

an·al·pha·bet·ic /ˌanalfəˈbetik/ ▶ **adj.** **1** representing sounds by composite signs rather than by single letters or symbols. **2** completely illiterate.

a·nal-re·ten·tive Psychoanal. ▶ **adj.** (of a person) excessively orderly and fussy (supposedly owing to conflict over toilet-training in infancy). ▶ **n.** (also **anal retentive**) a person who is excessively orderly and fussy. — **a·nal re·ten·tion** **n.** **a·nal re·ten·tive·ness** **n.**

a·nal·y·sand /əˈnaləˌsand; -ˌzand/ ▶ **n.** a person undergoing psychoanalysis.

an·a·lyse ▶ **v.** British spelling of ANALYZE.

a·nal·y·sis /əˈnaləsis/ ▶ **n.** (pl. **-ses** /-ˌsēz/) detailed examination of the elements or structure of something, typically as a basis for discussion or interpretation. ■ the process of separating something into its constituent elements. Often contrasted with SYNTHESIS. ■ the identification and measurement of the chemical constituents of a substance or specimen. ■ short for PSYCHOANALYSIS. ■ Ling. the use of separate, short words and word order rather than inflection or agglutination to express grammatical structure. ■ Math. the part of mathematics concerned with the theory of functions and the use of limits, continuity, and the operations of calculus.
– PHRASES **in the final** (or **last**) **analysis** when everything has been considered (used to suggest that a statement expresses the basic truth about a complex situation). [16th C.: ult. from Gk. *analusis*, from *analuein* 'unloose,' from *ana-* + *luein* 'loosen.']

an·a·lyst /ˈanl-ist/ ▶ **n.** a person who conducts analysis, in particular: ■ an investment expert, typically in a specified field. ■ short for PSYCHOANALYST. ■ a chemist who analyzes substances. ■ short for SYSTEMS ANALYST.

an·a·lyt·ic /ˌanlˈitik/ ▶ **adj.** another term for ANALYTICAL. ■ Logic true by virtue of the meaning of the words or concepts used to express it, so that its denial would be a self-contradiction. Compare with SYNTHETIC. ■ Ling. (of a language) tending not to alter the form of its words and to use word order rather than inflection or agglutination to express grammatical structure. Often contrasted with SYNTHETIC. [17th C.: via L. from Gk. *analutikos*, from *analuein* 'unloose.']

an·a·lyt·i·cal /ˌanlˈitikəl/ ▶ **adj.** relating to or using analysis or logical reasoning. — **an·a·lyt·i·cal·ly** /-ik(ə)lē/ **adv.**

an·a·lyt·i·cal ge·om·e·try ▶ **n.** geometry using coordinates.

an·a·lyt·i·cal phi·los·o·phy (also **an·a·lyt·ic phi·los·o·phy**) ▶ **n.** a method of approaching philosophical problems through analysis of the terms in which they are expressed, associated with Anglo-American philosophy of the early 20th century.

an·a·lyt·i·cal psy·chol·o·gy ▶ **n.** the psychoanalytic system of psychology developed by Carl Jung.

an·a·lyze /ˈanlˌīz/ (Brit. **an·a·lyse**) ▶ **v.** [trans.] examine methodically and in detail the constitution or structure of (something, esp. information), typically for purposes of explanation and interpretation. ■ discover or reveal (something) through such examination. ■ psychoanalyze (someone). ■ identify and measure the chemical constituents of (a substance or specimen). ■ Gram. resolve (a sentence) into its grammatical elements; parse. — **an·a·lyz·a·ble** /ˌanəˈlīzəbəl/ **adj.** **an·a·lyz·er** **n.** [16th C.: influenced by Fr. *analyser*, from med. L. *analysis* (see ANALYSIS).]

an·am·ne·sis /ˌanəmˈnēsis/ ▶ **n.** (pl. **-ses** /-sēz/) recollection, in particular: ■ the remembering of things from a supposed previous existence (often used with reference to Platonic philosophy). ■ Med. a patient's account of a medical history. [16th C.: from Gk. *anamnēsis* 'remembrance.']

an·am·nes·tic /ˌanamˈnestik/ ▶ **adj.** Med. denoting an enhanced reaction of the body's immune system to an antigen that is related to an antigen previously encountered.

an·a·mor·pho·sis /ˌanəˈmôrfəsis/ ▶ **n.** **1** a distorted projection or drawing that appears normal when viewed from a particular point or with a suitable mirror or lens. ■ the process by which such images are produced. **2** Biol. a gradual, ascending progression or change of form to a higher type. ■ development of the adult form through a series of small changes, esp. in some arthropods, the acquisition of additional body segments after hatching. — **an·a·mor·phic** /-fik/ **adj.** [18th C.: from Gk. *anamorphōsis* 'transformation,' from *ana-* 'back, again' + *morphosis* 'a shaping' (based on *morphē* 'shape, form').]

a·nan·da /ˈänəndə/ ▶ **n.** (in Hinduism, Buddhism, and Jainism) extreme happiness, one of the highest states of being. [from Sanskrit *ānanda* 'bliss.']

An·a·ni·as /ˌanəˈnīəs/ two figures in the New Testament: ■ the husband of Sapphira, struck dead because he lied. ■ the Jewish high priest before whom St. Paul was brought.

an·a·pest /ˈanəˌpest/ (Brit. **an·a·paest**) ▶ **n.** Pros. a metrical foot consisting of two short or unstressed syllables followed by one long or stressed syllable. — **an·a·pes·tic** /ˌanəˈpestik/ **adj.** [16th C.: via L. from Gk. *anapaistos* 'reversed,' from *ana-* 'back' + *paiein* 'strike' (because it is the reverse of a dactyl).]

an·a·phase /ˈanəˌfāz/ ▶ **n.** Genet. the stage of meiotic or mitotic cell division in which the chromosomes move away from one another to opposite poles of the spindle.

a·naph·o·ra /əˈnafərə/ ▶ **n.** **1** Gram. the use of a word referring to or replacing a word used earlier in a sentence, to avoid repetition, such as *do* in *I like it and so do they*. **2** Rhet. the repetition of a word or phrase at the beginning of successive clauses. — **an·a·phor·ic** /ˌanəˈfôrik/ **adj.** [16th C.: via L. from Gk., 'repetition,' from *ana-* 'back' + *pherein* 'to bear.']

an·aph·ro·dis·i·ac /anˌafrəˈdizēˌak; -ˈdēzē-; -ˈdēzнē-/ Med. ▶ **adj.** (chiefly of a drug) tending to reduce sexual desire. ▶ **n.** an anaphrodisiac drug.

an·a·phy·lax·is /ˌanəfəˈlaksis/ ▶ **n.** (also **anaphylactic shock**) Med. an extreme, often life-threatening, allergic reaction to an antigen (e.g., a bee sting) to which the body has become hypersensitive following an earlier exposure. — **an·a·phy·lac·tic** /-ˈlaktik/ **adj.** [20th C.: mod. L., from Gk. *ana-* 'again' + *phulaxis* 'guarding.']

an·ap·tyx·is /ˌanapˈtiksis/ ▶ **n.** Phonet. the insertion of a vowel between two consonants in pronunciation, as in *filim* for *film*. — **anaptyctic** /-ˈtiktik/ **adj.** [19th C.: mod. L., from Gk. *anaptuxis* 'unfolding,' from *ana-* 'back' + *ptuxis* 'folding.']

an·arch /ˈanˌärk/ ▶ **n.** literary an anarchist. ▶ **adj.** anarchic.

an·ar·chic /aˈnärkik/ ▶ **adj.** with no controlling rules or principles to give order. ■ (of comedy or a person's sense of humor) uncontrolled by convention. — **an·ar·chi·cal** /-kikəl/ **adj.** **an·ar·chi·cal·ly** /-ik(ə)lē/ **adv.**

an·ar·chism /ˈanərˌkizəm/ ▶ **n.** belief in the abolition of all government and the organization of society on a voluntary, cooperative basis without recourse to force or compulsion. ■ anarchists as a political force or movement. — **an·ar·chist** /ˈanərkist/ **n.** **an·ar·chis·tic** /ˌanərˈkistik/ **adj.**

an·ar·chy /ˈanərkē/ ▶ **n.** a state of disorder due to absence or nonrecognition of authority. ■ absence of government and absolute freedom of the individual, regarded as a political ideal. [16th C.: via med. L. from Gk. *anarkhia*, from *anarkhos*, from *an-* 'without' + *arkhos* 'chief.']

A·na·sa·zi /ˌanəˈsäzē/ ▶ **n.** (pl. same or **-zis**) a member of an American Indian people of the southwestern US, who flourished between c.200 BC and AD 1500. [1930s: from Navajo, lit. 'ancestors of our enemies' (the Pueblo peoples).']

an·as·tig·mat /ˌanəˈstigmat/ ▶ **n.** an anastigmatic lens system.

an·as·tig·mat·ic /ˌanəstigˈmatik/ ▶ **adj.** (of a lens system) constructed so that the astigmatism of each element is canceled out.

a·nas·to·mose /əˈnastəˌmōz; -ˌmōs/ ▶ **v.** [intrans.] Med. be linked by anastomosis. ■ [trans.] (usu. **be anastomosed**) link by anastomosis: *the graft is anastomosed to the vein of the recipient.*

a·nas·to·mo·sis /əˌnastəˈmōsis/ ▶ **n.** (pl. **-ses** /-sēz/) tech. a cross-connection between adjacent channels, tubes, or other parts of a network. ■ Med. a connection made surgically between adjacent blood vessels or parts of the intestine, or the operation in which this is constructed. — **a·nas·to·mot·ic** /-ˈmätik/ **adj. & n.** [16th C.: mod. L., from Gk. *anastomōsis*, from *anastomoun* 'provide with a mouth.']

a·nas·tro·phe /əˈnastrəfē/ ▶ **n.** Rhet. the inversion of the usual order of words or clauses. [16th C.: from Gk. *anastrophē* 'turning back,' from *ana-* 'back' + *strephein* 'to turn.']

anat. ▶ **abbr.** ■ anatomical. ■ anatomy.

an·a·tase /ˈanəˌtās; -ˌtāz/ ▶ **n.** one of the tetragonal forms of titanium dioxide, usually found as brown crystals, used as a pigment in paints and inks.

a·nath·e·ma /əˈnaтнəmə/ ▶ **n.** **1** something or someone that one vehemently dislikes. **2** a formal curse by a pope or a council of the Church, excommunicating a person or denouncing a doctrine. ■ literary a strong curse. [16th C.: ult. from Gk. *anathema* 'thing dedicated, accursed thing,' from *anatithenai* 'to set up.']

a·nath·e·ma·tize /əˈnaтнəməˌtīz/ ▶ **v.** [trans.] curse; condemn.

An·a·to·li·a /ˌanəˈtōlēə/ the western peninsula of Asia that forms the greater part of Turkey.

An·a·to·li·an /ˌanəˈtōlēən/ ▶ **adj.** of or relating to Anatolia, its inhabitants, or their ancient languages. ▶ **n.** **1** a native or inhabitant of Anatolia. **2** an extinct branch of ancient Indo-European languages including Hittite, Luwian, Lydian, and Lycian.

an·a·tom·i·cal /ˌanəˈtämikəl/ (abbr.: **anat.**) ▶ **adj.** of or relating to bodily structure. ■ of or relating to anatomy. —**an·a·tom·i·cal·ly** /-ik(ə)lē/ **adv.**

an·a·tom·i·cal·ly cor·rect /ˌanəˈtämik(ə)lē/ ▶ **adj.** (of a doll) having the sexual organs plainly represented.

a·nat·o·mist /əˈnatəmist/ ▶ **n.** an expert in anatomy.

a·nat·o·mize /əˈnatəˌmīz/ ▶ **v.** [trans.] dissect (a body). ■ examine and analyze in detail.

a·nat·o·my /əˈnatəmē/ (abbr.: **anat.**) ▶ **n.** (pl. **-mies**) the branch of science concerned with the bodily structure of humans, animals, and other organisms, esp. as revealed by dissection. ■ the bodily structure of an organism. ■ informal, humorous a person's body. ■ fig. a study of the structure or internal workings of something. [ME: from OFr. *anatomie* or late L. *anatomia*, from Gk., from *ana-* 'up' + *tomia* 'cutting' (from *temnein* 'to cut').]

An·ax·ag·o·ras /ˌanəkˈsagərəs; ˌanak-/ (*c.*500–*c.*428 BC), Greek philosopher. He believed that all matter was infinitely divisible and motionless until animated by mind (*nous*).

A·nax·i·man·der /əˌnaksəˈmandər; əˈnaksəˌmandər/ (*c.*610–*c.*545 BC), Greek scientist. He believed the earth to be cylindrical and poised in space and taught that life began in water.

An·ax·im·e·nes /ˌanakˈsiməˌnēz/ (*c.*546 BC), Greek scientist. He believed the earth to be flat and shallow.

ANC ▶ **abbr.** African National Congress.

-ance /əns; ns/ ▶ **suffix** forming nouns: **1** denoting a quality or state or an instance of one: *allegiance.* **2** denoting an action: *utterance.* [from Fr. *-ance*, from L. *-antia*, *-entia* (from *-ant-*, *-ent-*).]

an·ces·tor /ˈanˌsestər/ ▶ **n.** a person, typically one more remote than a grandparent, from whom one is descended. ■ an early type of animal or plant from which others have evolved. [ME: from OFr. *ancestre*, from L. *antecessor*, from *antecedere*, from *ante* 'before' + *cedere* 'go.']

an·ces·tral /anˈsestrəl/ ▶ **adj.** [attrib.] of, belonging to, inherited from, or denoting an ancestor or ancestors.

an·ces·tress /ˈanˌsestris/ ▶ **n.** a female ancestor.

an·ces·try /ˈanˌsestrē/ ▶ **n.** (pl. **-tries**) [usu. in sing.] one's family or ethnic descent. ■ the evolutionary or genetic line of descent of an animal or plant. ■ fig. the origin or background of something.

An·chi·ses /anGˈkīsēz/ Greek & Rom. Mythol. the father of the Trojan hero Aeneas.

an·cho /ˈancHō; ˈän-/ (also **ancho chili**) ▶ **n.** a large aromatic variety of chili, used (usually dried) in dishes of Mexican origin or style. [from Mex. Sp. *(chile) ancho* 'wide (chili).']

an·chor /ˈaNGkər/ ▶ **n. 1** a heavy object attached to a rope or chain and used to moor a vessel to the sea bottom, typically having a metal shank with a ring at one end for the rope and a pair of flukes at the other. ■ fig. a person or thing that provides stability or confidence in an otherwise uncertain situation. **2** an anchorman or anchorwoman, esp. in broadcasting or athletics. ▶ **v.** [trans.] **1** moor (a ship) to the sea bottom with an anchor. ■ secure firmly in position. ■ provide with a firm basis or foundation. **2** to act or serve as an anchor for (a news program or sporting event).

– PHRASES **at anchor** (of a ship) moored by means of an anchor. **drop anchor** (of a ship) let down the anchor and moor. **weigh anchor** (of a ship) take up the anchor when ready to depart. [OE *ancor, ancra*, via L. from Gk. *ankura*.]

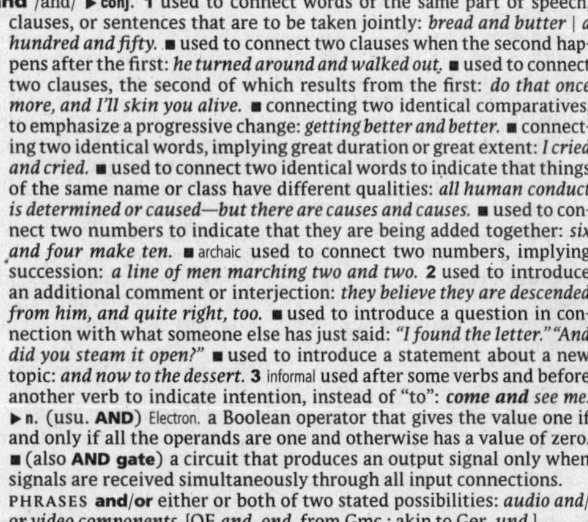
anchor with arm and flukes

mushroom anchor

types of anchors

An·chor·age /ˈaNGk(ə)rij/ a seaport in southern Alaska; pop. 260,283.

an·chor·age /ˈaNGk(ə)rij/ ▶ **n. 1** an area off the coast that is suitable for a ship to anchor. ■ the action of securing something to a base or the state of being secured. **2** hist. an anchorite's dwelling place.

an·cho·ress /ˈaNGkəris/ ▶ **n.** hist. a female anchorite.

an·cho·rite /ˈaNGkəˌrīt/ ▶ **n.** hist. a religious recluse. —**an·cho·rit·ic** /ˌaNGkəˈritik/ **adj.** [ME: ult. from eccles. Gk. *anakhōrētēs*, from *anakhōrein* 'retire,' from *ana-* 'back' + *khōra*, *khōr-* 'a place.']

an·chor·man /ˈaNGkərˌman/ ▶ **n.** (pl. **-men**) a man who presents and coordinates a live television or radio program involving other contributors. ■ a man who plays the most crucial part or is the most dependable contributor. ■ the member of a relay team who runs the last leg.

an·chor·per·son /ˈaNGkərˌpərsən/ ▶ **n.** (pl. **-per·sons** or **-peo·ple**) an anchorman or anchorwoman (used as a neutral alternative).

an·chor·wom·an /ˈaNGkərˌwŏŏmən/ ▶ **n.** (pl. **-wom·en**) a woman who presents and coordinates a live television or radio program involving other contributors.

an·cho·vy /ˈanˌcHōvē; anˈcHōvē/ ▶ **n.** (pl. **-vies**) a small shoaling fish (genus *Engraulis*, family Engraulidae). Commercially important as a food fish, it is strongly flavored and usually preserved in salt and oil. [16th C.: from Sp. and Port. *anchova*.]

an·cien ré·gime /änˈsyaN rāˈzHēm/ ▶ **n.** (pl. **an·ciens ré·gimes** pronunc. same) a political or social system that has been displaced, typically by one more modern. ■ **(Ancien Régime)** the political and social system in France before the Revolution of 1789. [18th C.: Fr., lit. 'old rule.']

an·cient[1] /ˈāncHənt/ ▶ **adj.** belonging to the very distant past and no longer in existence. ■ having been in existence for a very long time. ■ esp. humorous showing or feeling signs of age or wear: *you make me feel ancient.* ▶ **n.** archaic or humorous an old person.

– PHRASES **the ancients** the people of ancient times, esp. the Greeks and Romans of classical antiquity. ■ the classical Greek and Roman authors. —**an·cient·ness n.** [ME: from OFr. *ancien*, based on L. *ante* 'before.']

an·cient[2] ▶ **n.** archaic a standard, flag, or ensign. [16th C.: alt. of **ENSIGN**.]

an·cient his·to·ry ▶ **n.** the history of the ancient civilizations of the Mediterranean and the Near East to the fall of the Western Roman Empire in AD 476. ■ informal something that is already long familiar and no longer new, interesting, or relevant.

an·cient·ly /ˈāncHəntlē/ ▶ **adv.** long ago.

an·cient world ▶ **n.** the region around the Mediterranean and the Near East before the fall of the Western Roman Empire in AD 476.

an·cil·lar·y /ˈansəˌlerē/ ▶ **adj.** providing necessary support to the primary activities or operation of an organization, institution, industry, or system. ■ additional; subsidiary. ▶ **n.** (pl. **-laries**) a person whose work provides necessary support to the primary activities of an organization, institution, or industry. ■ something that functions in a supplementary or supporting role. [17th C.: from L. *ancillaris*, from *ancilla* 'maidservant.']

an·con /ˈaNGˌkän/ ▶ **n.** (pl. **an·co·nes** /ˌaNGˈkōnēz/) Archit. **1** a console or bracket, typically with two volutes, that supports or appears to support a cornice. **2** each of a pair of projections on either side of a block of stone or other material, used for lifting it. [18th C.: via L. from Gk. *ankōn* 'bend, elbow.']

ancon 1

An·co·na /änˈkōnə; äNG-/ a port on the Adriatic coast of central Italy, capital of Marche region; pop. 103,270.

-ancy ▶ **suffix** (forming nouns) denoting a quality or state: *buoyancy* | *expectancy.* Compare with **-ANCE**. [from L. *-antia*.]

an·cy·lo·sto·mi·a·sis /ˌaNGkəˌlōstəˈmīəsis; ˌansə-/ (also **an·ky·lo·sto·mi·a·sis**) ▶ **n.** Med. hookworm infection of the small intestine. [19th C.: from mod. L. *Ancylostoma* (from Gk. *ankulos* 'crooked' + *stoma* 'mouth.')]

An·cy·ra /anˈsīrə/ ancient Roman name for **ANKARA**.

and /and/ ▶ **conj. 1** used to connect words of the same part of speech, clauses, or sentences that are to be taken jointly: *bread and butter* | *a hundred and fifty.* ■ used to connect two clauses when the second happens after the first: *he turned around and walked out.* ■ used to connect two clauses, the second of which results from the first: *do that once more, and I'll skin you alive.* ■ connecting two identical comparatives, to emphasize a progressive change: *getting better and better.* ■ connecting two identical words, implying great duration or great extent: *I cried and cried.* ■ used to connect two identical words to indicate that things of the same name or class have different qualities: *all human conduct is determined or caused—but there are causes and causes.* ■ used to connect two numbers to indicate that they are being added together: *six and four make ten.* ■ archaic used to connect two numbers, implying succession: *a line of men marching two and two.* **2** used to introduce an additional comment or interjection: *they believe they are descended from him, and quite right, too.* ■ used to introduce a question in connection with what someone else has just said: *"I found the letter." "And did you steam it open?"* ■ used to introduce a statement about a new topic: *and now to the dessert.* **3** informal used after some verbs and before another verb to indicate intention, instead of "to": ***come and see me.*** ▶ **n.** (usu. **AND**) Electron. a Boolean operator that gives the value one if and only if all the operands are one and otherwise has a value of zero. ■ (also **AND gate**) a circuit that produces an output signal only when signals are received simultaneously through all input connections.

– PHRASES **and/or** either or both of two stated possibilities: *audio and/or video components.* [OE *and, ond*, from Gmc.; akin to Ger. *und*.]

-and ▶ **suffix** (forming nouns) denoting a person or thing to be treated in a specified way: *analysand.* [from L. gerundive ending *-andus*.]

An·da·lu·sia /ˌandəˈlōōzH(ē)ə; -sH(ē)ə/ the southernmost region of Spain, bordering on the Atlantic Ocean and the Mediterranean Sea; capital, Seville.

An·da·lu·sian /ˌandəˈlōōzH(ē)ən; -sH(ē)ən/ ▶ **adj.** of or relating to Andalusia or its people or their dialect. ▶ **n. 1** a native or inhabitant of Andalusia. **2** the dialect of Spanish spoken in Andalusia.

an·da·lu·site /ˌandlˈōōsīt/ ▶ **n.** a gray to pink aluminosilicate mineral occurring mainly in metamorphic rocks, sometimes of gem quality.

An·da·man and Nic·o·bar Is·lands /ˈandəmən and ˈnikəˌbär; ˈandəˌman/ two groups of islands in the Bay of Bengal that constitute a Union Territory in India; pop. 279,110; capital, Port Blair.

an·dan·te /änˈdäntā/ Music ▶ **adj. & adv.** (esp. as a direction) in a moderately slow tempo. ▶ **n.** a movement or composition marked to be played andante. [Ital., lit. 'going,' from v. *andare*.]

an·dan·ti·no /ˌändänˈtēnō/ Music ▶ **adj. & adv.** (esp. as a direction) more lighthearted than andante, and in most cases quicker. ▶ **n.** (pl. **-nos**) a movement or composition marked to be played andantino. [Ital., dimin. of **ANDANTE**.]

PRONUNCIATION KEY ə *ago, up*; ər *over, fur*; a *hat*; ā *ate*; ä *car*; e *let*; ē *see*; i *fit*; ī *by*; NG *sing*; ō *go*; ô *law, for*; oi *toy*; ŏŏ *good*; ōō *goo*; ou *out*; TH *thin*; T͟H *then*; ZH *vision*

An·de·an /'andēən; an'dē-/ ▶ **adj.** of or relating to the Andes. ▶ **n.** a native or inhabitant of the Andes.

An·der·sen /'andərsən/, Hans Christian (1805–75), Danish writer. He is noted for his fairy tales, such as "The Snow Queen" and "The Ugly Duckling."

An·der·son¹ /'andərsən/ a city in east central Indiana; pop. 59,734.

An·der·son², Carl David (1905–91), US physicist. In 1932 he discovered the positron. Nobel Prize for Physics (1936, shared with Victor F. Hess).

An·der·son³, Marian (1902–93), US opera singer. Initially barred from giving concerts in the US, she toured Europe 1925–35. In 1955, she became the first black singer to perform at the Metropolitan Opera House in New York.

An·der·son⁴, Maxwell (1888–1959), US playwright. His plays include *Anne of the Thousand Days* (1948) and *The Bad Seed* (1954).

An·der·son⁵, Philip Warren (b.1923), American physicist. He investigated magnetism and superconductivity. Nobel Prize for Physics (1977).

An·der·son⁶, Sherwood (1876–1941), US writer. He is noted for *Winesburg, Ohio* (1919), a cycle of stories that explore the loneliness and frustration of small-town life.

An·der·son·ville /'andərsən,vil/ a village in southwestern Georgia, site of a Confederate prison during the Civil War.

An·des /'andēz/ a mountain system that extends more than 5,000 miles (8,000 km) along the Pacific coast of South America; highest peak, Aconcagua.

an·des·ite /'andi,zīt/ ▶ **n.** Geol. a dark, fine-grained, brown or grayish volcanic rock that is intermediate in composition between rhyolite and basalt. — **an·de·sit·ic** /,andi'zitik/ **adj.** [19th C.: ANDES.]

An·dhra Pra·desh /,ändrə prə'dāsh; 'ändrə; prə'desh/ a state in southeastern India, on the Bay of Bengal; capital, Hyderabad.

and·i·ron /'an,dīərn/ ▶ **n.** a metal support, typically one of a pair, that holds wood burning in a fireplace. [ME: from OFr. *andier*.]

An·dor·ra /an'dôrə/ a small autonomous principality in southwestern Europe, between France and Spain; pop. 69,800; capital, Andorra la Vella. — **An·dor·ran adj. & n.**

an·dou·ille /an'do͞o-ē/ ▶ **n.** a spicy pork sausage seasoned with garlic, used esp. in Cajun cooking. [17th C.: Fr.]

andr- ▶ **comb. form** var. of ANDRO- shortened before a vowel (as in *androecium*).

an·dra·dite /'andrə,dīt/ ▶ **n.** a mineral of the garnet group, containing calcium and iron. It occurs as yellow to black crystals, sometimes of gem quality. [19th C.: named after J. B. de *Andrada* e Silva (*c.*1763–1838), Brazilian geologist.]

An·dré /'andrē/, John (1750–80), British soldier. He negotiated with Benedict Arnold for the betrayal of West Point 1779–80. Captured while returning from West Point, he was tried and hanged as a spy.

An·dre·an·of Is·lands /,andrē'anôf; -əf; ,ändrē'änəf/ an island group in southwestern Alaska, part of the Aleutian Islands.

An·dret·ti /an'dretē/, Mario Gabriele (1940–), US race car driver; born in Italy. He won major championships during the 1960s and 1970s.

An·drew, Prince /'andro͞o/, (1960–), British prince; second son of Elizabeth II; full name *Andrew Albert Christian Edward, Duke of York.*

An·drew, St., one of the 12 Apostles; the brother of St. Peter. He is the patron saint of Scotland and Russia.

andro- (usu. **andr-** before a vowel) ▶ **comb. form** man (as opposed to woman): *androcentric* | *androgenize.*

an·dro·cen·tric /,andrō'sentrik/ ▶ **adj.** focused or centered on men.

An·dro·cles /'andrə,klēz/ in a story by Aulus Gellius (2nd century AD), a runaway slave who extracted a thorn from the paw of a lion, which later recognized him and refrained from attacking him in the arena.

an·droe·ci·um /an'drēsh(ē)əm/ ▶ **n.** (pl. **-ci·a** /-sh(ē)ə/) Bot. the stamens of a flower collectively. [19th C.: mod. L., from Gk. *anēr, andr-* 'man' + *oikion* 'house.']

an·dro·gen /'andrəjən/ ▶ **n.** Biochem. a male sex hormone, such as testosterone. — **an·dro·gen·ic** /,andrə'jenik/ **adj.**

an·dro·gen·ize /an'dräjə,nīz/ ▶ **v.** [trans.] [usu. as adj.] **(androgenized)** treat with or expose to male hormones, typically resulting in the production of male sexual characteristics. — **an·drog·e·ni·za·tion** /an,dräjənə'zāshən/ **n.**

an·dro·gyne /'andrə,jīn/ ▶ **n.** an androgynous individual. ■ a hermaphrodite. [16th C.: via L. from Gk. *androgunos*, from *anēr, andr-* 'man' + *gunē* 'woman.']

an·drog·y·nous /an'dräjənəs/ ▶ **adj.** partly male and partly female in appearance; of indeterminate sex. ■ having the physical characteristics of both sexes; hermaphrodite. — **an·drog·y·ny** /-nē/ **n.**

an·droid /'an,droid/ ▶ **n.** (in science fiction) a robot with a human appearance. [18th C.: from mod. L. *androides*, from Gk. *anēr, andr-* 'man.']

An·drom·a·che /an'drämәkē/ Gk. Mythol. the wife of Hector.

An·drom·e·da /an'drämidə/ **1** Gk. Mythol. Ethiopian princess who was rescued from a sea monster by Perseus. **2** Astron. a large northern constellation between Perseus and Pegasus, with few bright stars. It is chiefly notable for the **Andromeda Galaxy** (or **Great Nebula of Andromeda**), a conspicuous spiral galaxy probably twice as massive as our own and located 2 million light years away.

an·drom·e·da /an'drämidə/ ▶ **n.** an evergreen shrub (genera *Andromeda* and *Pieris*) of the heath family, typically with clusters of small bell-like flowers.

An·dro·pov¹ /an'dräpôf; än'drôpəf/ former name (1984–89) for RYBINSK.

An·dro·pov², Yuri Vladimirovich (1914–84), president of the Soviet Union 1983–84. He initiated the reform process that was carried out by his successor, Mikhail Gorbachev.

an·dros·ter·one /an'drästə,rōn/ ▶ **n.** Biochem. a relatively inactive male sex hormone produced by metabolism of testosterone. [1930s: from Gk. *anēr, andr-* 'man' + STEROL.]

-androus ▶ **comb. form** Bot. & Zool. having male organs or stamens of a specified number: *monandrous.* [ult. from Gk. *-andros*, from *andros*, genitive of *anēr* 'man.']

-ane¹ ▶ **suffix** var. of -AN, usually with a distinction of sense (such as *humane* compared with *human*) but sometimes with no corresponding form in *-an* (such as *mundane*).

-ane² ▶ **suffix** Chem. forming names of saturated hydrocarbons: *methane* | *propane.* [on the pattern of words *-ene, -ine.*]

an·ec·dot·age /'anik,dōtij/ ▶ **n. 1** anecdotes collectively. **2** humorous old age, esp. in someone who is inclined to be garrulous. [18th C. (sense 2): sense 1 from ANECDOTE + -AGE; sense 2 blend of ANECDOTE and DOTAGE.]

an·ec·do·tal /,anik'dōtl/ ▶ **adj.** (of an account) not necessarily true or reliable, because based on personal accounts rather than facts or research. ■ characterized by or fond of telling anecdotes. ■ [attrib.] (of a painting) depicting small narrative incidents. — **an·ec·do·tal·ist** /-tl-ist/ **n.** **an·ec·do·tal·ly adv.**

an·ec·dote /'anik,dōt/ ▶ **n.** a short and amusing or interesting story about a real incident or person. ■ an account regarded as unreliable or hearsay. ■ the depiction of a minor narrative incident in a painting. [17th C.: ult. from Gk. *anekdota* 'things unpublished,' from *an-* + *ekdotos*, from *ekdidōnai* 'publish.']

an·e·cho·ic /ane'kō-ik/ ▶ **adj.** tech. free from echo. ■ (of a coating or material) tending to deaden sound.

a·nele /ə'nēl/ ▶ **v.** [trans.] archaic anoint (someone), esp. as part of the Christian rite of giving extreme unction. [ME: from *an-* 'on' + archaic *elien* 'to oil' (from OE *ele*, from L. *oleum* 'oil').]

a·ne·mi·a /ə'nēmēə/ (Brit. **a·nae·mi·a**) ▶ **n.** a condition marked by a deficiency of red blood cells or of hemoglobin in the blood, resulting in pallor and weariness. [19th C.: via mod. L. from Gk. *anaimia*, from *an-* 'without' + *haima* 'blood.']

a·ne·mic /ə'nēmik/ (Brit. **a·nae·mic**) ▶ **adj.** suffering from anemia. ■ fig. lacking in color, spirit, or vitality.

anemo- ▶ **comb. form** wind: *anemometer.*

a·nem·o·graph /ə'nemə,graf/ ▶ **n.** an anemometer that records on paper the speed, duration, and sometimes also the direction of the wind.

an·e·mom·e·ter /,anə'mämitər/ ▶ **n.** an instrument for measuring the speed of the wind, or of any current of gas. — **an·e·mom·e·try** /-trē/ **n.** **an·e·mo·met·ric** /-mə'metrik/ **adj.**

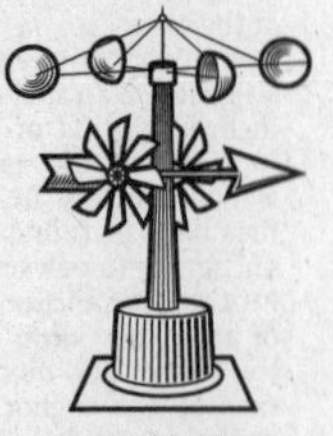
anemometer

a·nem·o·ne /ə'nemənē/ ▶ **n. 1** a widely distributed, often cultivated plant (genus *Anemone*) of the buttercup family, typically bearing brightly colored flowers. **2** short for SEA ANEMONE. [16th C.: said to be from Gk. *anemōnē*, lit. 'daughter of the wind.']

an·e·moph·i·lous /,anə'mäfələs/ ▶ **adj.** Bot. (of a plant) wind-pollinated. — **an·e·moph·i·ly** /-lē/ **n.** [19th C.: from Gk. *anemos* 'wind' + *-philous* (see -PHILIA).]

an·en·ce·phal·ic /,anensə'falik/ Med. ▶ **adj.** having part or all of the cerebral hemispheres and the rear of the skull congenitally absent. ▶ **n.** an anencephalic fetus or infant. — **an·en·ceph·a·ly** /-'sefəlē/ **n.** [19th C.: from Gk. *anenkephalos* 'without brain.']

a·nent /ə'nent/ ▶ **prep.** esp. archaic concerning; about. [OE *on efen* 'in line with.']

-aneous ▶ **suffix** forming adjectives from Latin words: *cutaneous* | *spontaneous.*

an·er·gi·a /a'nərj(ē)ə/ ▶ **n.** Psychiatry abnormal lack of energy. [19th C.: mod. L., from Gk. *an-* 'without' + *ergon* 'work.']

an·er·gy /'anərjē/ ▶ **n. 1** Med. absence of the normal immune response to a particular antigen or allergen. **2** another term for ANERGIA. [20th C.: from Ger. *Anergie*, from Gk. *an-* 'not,' on the pattern of *Allergie* 'allergy.']

an·er·oid /'anə,roid/ ▶ **adj.** relating to a barometer measuring air pressure by the action of the air in deforming the elastic lid of an evacuated box or chamber. ▶ **n.** a barometer of this type. [19th C.: coined in Fr. from Gk. *a-* 'without' + *nēros* 'water.']

an·es·the·sia /,anəs'thēzhə/ (Brit. **an·aes·the·sia**) ▶ **n.** insensitivity to pain, esp. as artificially induced by the administration of gases or the injection of drugs before surgical operations. ■ the induction of this state, or the branch of medicine concerned with it.

an·es·the·si·ol·o·gy /,anəs,thēzē'äləjē/ (Brit. **an·aes·the·si·ol·o·gy**) ▶ **n.** the branch of medicine concerned with anesthesia and anesthetics. — **an·es·the·si·ol·o·gist** /-jist/ **n.**

an·es·thet·ic /,anəs'thetik/ (Brit. **an·aes·thet·ic**) ▶ **n. 1** a substance that induces insensitivity to pain. **2 (anesthetics)** [treated as sing.] the study or practice of anesthesia. ▶ **adj.** inducing or relating to insensitivity to pain. [19th C.: from Gk. *anaisthētos*.]

an·es·the·tist /ə'nesTHitist/ (Brit. **an·aes·the·tist**) ▶ **n.** a medical specialist who administers anesthetics.

an·es·the·tize /ə'nesTHi,tīz/ (Brit. **an·aes·the·tize**) ▶ **v.** [trans.] administer an anesthetic to. ■ fig. deprive of feeling or awareness. — **an·es·the·ti·za·tion** /-THitə'zāSHən/ **n.**

an·eu·rysm /'anyə,rizəm/ (also **an·eu·rism**) ▶ **n.** Med. an excessive localized enlargement of an artery caused by a weakening of the artery wall. — **an·eu·rys·mal** /-,rizməl/ **adj.** [ME: from Gk. *aneurusma* 'dilatation,' from *aneurunein* 'widen out.']

a·new /ə'n(y)o͞o/ ▶ **adv.** esp. literary in a new or different, typically more positive, way. ■ once more; again.

an·frac·tu·ous /an'frakCHo͞oəs/ ▶ **adj.** rare sinuous or circuitous. — **an·frac·tu·os·i·ty** /-,frakCHo͞o'äsitē/ **n.** [16th C.: from late L. *anfractuosus*, from L. *anfractus* 'a bending.']

An·ga·ra Riv·er /,äNGgə'rä; ,əNG-/ a river in southeastern Siberia that flows for 1,039 miles (1,779 km) from Lake Baikal to the Yenisei River.

an·gel /'ānjəl/ ▶ **n. 1** a spiritual being believed to act as an attendant, agent, or messenger of God, conventionally represented in human form with wings and a long robe. ■ an attendant spirit, esp. a benevolent one. See also GUARDIAN ANGEL. ■ informal a financial backer of an enterprise, typically in the theater. ■ in traditional Christian angelology, a being of the lowest order of the celestial hierarchy. ■ informal an unexplained radar echo. **2** a person of exemplary conduct or virtue. ■ used in similes or comparisons to refer to a person's outstanding beauty, qualities, or abilities. ■ used in approval when a person has been or is expected to be kind or willing to oblige. ■ used as a term of endearment. **3** hist. an old English coin minted between 1470 and 1634 and bearing the figure of the archangel Michael killing a dragon. **4** (**angels**) aviation slang an aircraft's altitude (often used with a numeral indicating thousands of feet): *we rendezvous at angels nine.* [OE *engel*, ult. from Gk. *angelos* 'messenger.']

an·gel dust ▶ **n.** informal **1** the hallucinogenic drug phencyclidine hydrochloride. **2** another term for CLENBUTEROL.

An·ge·le·no /,anjə'lēnō/ (also **Los An·ge·le·no, An·ge·li·no**) ▶ **n.** (pl. **-nos**) a native or inhabitant of Los Angeles. [19th C.: from Amer. Sp.]

An·gel Falls /'ānjəl/ the highest waterfall in the world, in southeastern Venezuela, with an uninterrupted descent of 3,210 feet (978 m).

gray angelfish

an·gel·fish /'ānjəl,fiSH/ ▶ **n.** (pl. same or **-fish·es**) any of a number of laterally compressed deep-bodied fish with extended dorsal and anal fins, in particular: ■ the freshwater cichlid *Pterophyllum scalare*, native to the Amazon basin and popular in tropical aquariums. ■ the **grey angelfish** (*Pomacanthus arcuatus*, family Pomacanthidae), a coastal marine fish.

an·gel food cake ▶ **n.** a light, pale, typically ring-shaped sponge cake made with egg whites and no fat.

an·gel hair (also **an·gel's hair**) ▶ **n.** a type of pasta consisting of very fine long strands.

an·gel·ic /an'jelik/ ▶ **adj.** of or relating to angels. ■ (of a person) exceptionally beautiful, innocent, or kind. — **an·gel·i·cal adj. an·gel·i·cal·ly** /-ik(ə)lē/ **adv.**

an·gel·i·ca /an'jelikə/ ▶ **n.** a tall aromatic plant (genus *Angelica*) of the parsley family, with large leaves and yellowish-green flowers.

an·gel·i·ca tree ▶ **n.** another term for *DEVIL'S WALKING STICK* (see HERCULES-CLUB).

An·gel·ic Doc·tor the nickname of St. Thomas Aquinas.

An·ge·li·co /än'jeli,kō/, Fra (*c.*1400–55), Italian painter and monk; born *Guido di Pietro*; monastic name *Fra Giovanni da Fiesole.* He painted the frescos in the convent of San Marco, Florence (*c.*1438–47).

An·ge·li·no ▶ **n.** var. of ANGELENO.

An·gel Is·land an island in San Francisco Bay that was the chief immigration station on the US western coast.

an·gel·ol·o·gy /,ānjə'läləjē/ ▶ **n.** theological dogma or speculation concerning angels. — **an·gel·ol·o·gist** /-jist/ **n.**

An·ge·lou /'anjə,lō; -,lo͞o/, Maya (1928–), US writer and poet; born *Marguerite Johnson.* Her works include the autobiographical *I Know Why the Caged Bird Sings* (1970).

An·ge·lus /'anjələs/ (also **an·ge·lus**) ▶ **n.** [in sing.] a Roman Catholic devotion commemorating the Incarnation of Jesus, said at morning, noon, and sunset. ■ a ringing of church bells announcing this. [17th C.: from L. *Angelus domini* 'the angel of the Lord,' the opening words.]

an·ger /'aNGgər/ ▶ **n.** a strong feeling of annoyance, displeasure, or hostility. ▶ **v.** [trans.] (often **be angered**) fill (someone) with such a feeling; provoke anger in. [ME: from ON *angr* 'grief,' *angra* 'vex.']

An·gers /'anjərz; äN'ZHā/ a town in western France, capital of historical Anjou; pop. 146,160.

An·ge·vin /'anjəvən/ ▶ **n.** a native, inhabitant, or ruler of Anjou. ■ any of the Plantagenet kings of England. ▶ **adj.** of or relating to Anjou. ■ of, relating to, or denoting the Plantaganets.

an·gi·na /an'jīnə/ ▶ **n. 1** (also **an·gi·na pec·to·ris** /'pektəris/) a condition marked by severe pain in the chest, often spreading to the shoulders, arms, and neck, caused by an inadequate blood supply to the heart. **2** [with adj.] any of a number of disorders in which there is an intense localized pain. [16th C.: from Latin, 'quinsy,' from Gk. *ankhonē* 'strangling'; *pectoris* (sense 1): L., 'of the chest.']

angio- ▶ **comb. form** relating to blood vessels: *angiography.* ■ relating to seed vessels: *angiosperm.* [from Gk. *angeion* 'vessel.']

an·gi·o·gen·e·sis /,anjē-ō'jenəsis/ ▶ **n.** Med. the development of new blood vessels. — **an·gi·o·gen·ic adj.**

an·gi·o·gram /'anj(ē)ə,gram/ ▶ **n.** an X-ray photograph of blood or lymph vessels, made by angiography.

an·gi·og·ra·phy /,anjē'ägrəfē/ ▶ **n.** examination by X-ray of blood or lymph vessels, carried out after introduction of a radiopaque substance. — **an·gi·o·graph·ic** /-ə'grafik/ **adj. an·gi·o·graph·i·cal·ly** /-ə'grafik(ə)lē/ **adv.**

an·gi·o·ma /,anjē'ōmə/ ▶ **n.** (pl. **-mas** or **-ma·ta** /-mətə/) Med. an abnormal growth due to the dilatation or new formation of blood vessels.

an·gi·o·plas·ty /'anjēə,plastē/ ▶ **n.** (pl. **-ties**) surgical repair or unblocking of a blood vessel, esp. a coronary artery. See also BALLOON ANGIOPLASTY.

an·gi·o·sperm /'anjēə,spərm/ ▶ **n.** Bot. a plant that has flowers and produces seeds enclosed within a carpel. The angiosperms are a large group and include herbaceous plants, shrubs, grasses, and most trees.

an·gi·o·sta·tin /,anjēō'statn/ ▶ **n** Med. a drug used to inhibit the growth of new blood vessels in malignant tumors.

an·gi·o·ten·sin /,anjē-ō'tensin/ ▶ **n.** Biochem. a protein whose presence in the blood promotes aldosterone secretion and tends to raise blood pressure. [1950s: from ANGIO- + *(hyper)tens(ion)*.]

Ang·kor /'aNGkər; -kôr/ the capital of the ancient kingdom of Khmer in northwestern Cambodia; noted for its temples, esp. the **Angkor Wat** (mid 12th century).

An·gle /'aNGgəl/ ▶ **n.** a member of a Germanic people, originally inhabitants of what is now Schleswig-Holstein, who migrated to England in the 5th century AD and gave their name to England and the English. [from L. *Anglus*, (pl.) *Angli* 'people of *Angul*,' district of Schleswig, akin to ANGLE[2].]

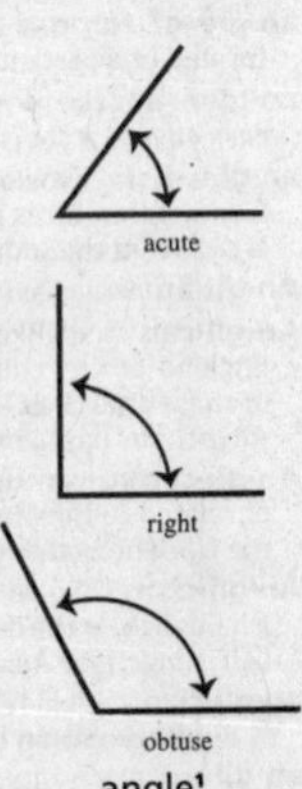

angle[1]

an·gle[1] /'aNGgəl/ ▶ **n. 1** the space (usually measured in degrees) between two intersecting lines or surfaces at or close to the point where they meet. ■ a corner, esp. an external projection or an internal recess of a part of a structure. ■ slope; a measure of the inclination of two lines or surfaces with respect to each other, equal to the amount that one would have to be turned in order to point in the same direction as the other: *an angle of 33° to the horizontal.* ■ a position from which something is viewed or along which it travels or acts, often as measured by its inclination from an implicit horizontal or vertical baseline. **2** a particular way of approaching or considering an issue or problem: *a fresh angle on life.* ■ one part of a larger subject, event, or problem: *she downplayed the racial angle.* ■ a bias or point of view: *he saw the world from an angle that few could understand.* ▶ **v.** [trans.] direct or incline at an angle: *angle the camera toward the tree.* ■ [intrans.] move or be inclined at an angle: *the sun angled into the dining room.* ■ [trans.] present (information) to reflect a particular view or have a particular focus. [ME: from OFr., from L. *angulus* 'corner.']

an·gle[2] ▶ **v.** [intrans.] fish with rod and line: *there are no big fish left to angle for.* ■ seek something desired by indirectly prompting someone to offer it: *Ralph had begun to angle for an invitation.* ▶ **n.** archaic a fishhook. [OE *angul* (n.).]

an·gle brack·et ▶ **n. 1** either of a pair of marks in the form < >, used to enclose words or figures so as to separate them from their context. **2** another term for BRACKET (sense 3).

an·gled /'aNGgəld/ ▶ **adj. 1** placed or inclined at an angle to something else: *a sharply angled flight of stairs.* **2** [in comb.] (of an object or shape) having an angle or angles of a specified type or number. ■ (of information) presented so as to reflect a particular view or to have a particular focus.

an·gle i·ron ▶ **n.** a construction material consisting of pieces of iron or steel with an L-shaped cross-section, able to be bolted together. ■ a piece of metal of this kind.

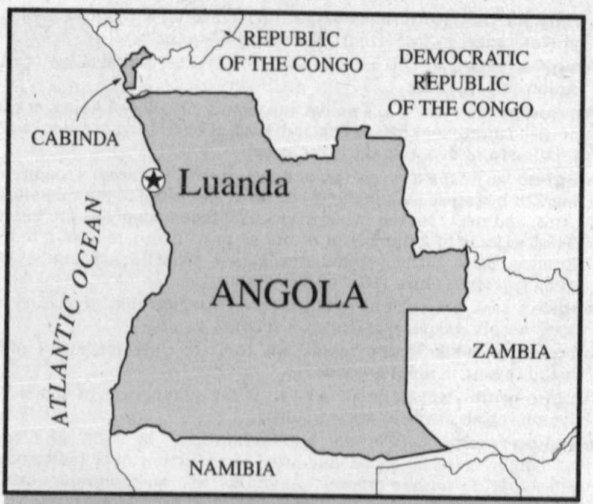

Angola

Official name: Republic of Angola
Location: western coast of southern Africa
Area: 481,500 square miles (1,246,700 sq km)
Population: 10,978,000
Capital: Luanda
Languages: Portuguese (official), Bantu, other African languages
Currency: kwanza

an·gle of at·tack ▶ n. the angle between the chord of an airfoil and the direction of the surrounding undisturbed flow of gas or liquid.

an·gle of in·ci·dence ▶ n. Physics the angle that an incident line or ray makes with a perpendicular to the surface at the point of incidence.

an·gle of re·pose ▶ n. the steepest angle at which a sloping surface formed of a particular loose material is stable.

an·gler /ˈanɢglər/ ▶ n. a person who fishes with a rod and line: [with adj.] *a carp angler.* ■ short for ANGLERFISH.

an·gler·fish /ˈanɢglər,fisн/ ▶ n. (pl. same or **-fish·es**) a fish (order Lophiiformes) that lures prey with a fleshy lobe attached to a filament that arises from the snout and hangs in front of the mouth.

An·gli·an /ˈanɢglēən/ ▶ adj. of or relating to the ancient Angles.

An·gli·can /ˈanɢglikən/ ▶ adj. of, relating to, or denoting the Church of England or any church in communion with it. ▶ n. a member of any of these churches. — **An·gli·can·ism** /-,nizəm/ n. [17th C.: from med. L. *Anglicanus* based on *Angli* (see ANGLE).]

An·gli·can com·mun·ion the group of Christian Churches derived from or related to the Church of England, including the Episcopal Church in the US. The body's primate is the Archbishop of Canterbury.

An·gli·cism /ˈanɢglə,sizəm/ ▶ n. a word or phrase that is peculiar to British English. ■ the quality of being typically English or of favoring English things. [see ANGLE.]

an·gli·cize /ˈanɢglə,sīz/ ▶ v. [trans.] make English in form or character. — **an·gli·ci·za·tion** /,anɢgləsəˈzāsнən/ n.

an·gling /ˈanɢg(ə)linɢ/ ▶ n. the sport or pastime of fishing with a rod and line.

An·glo /ˈanɢglō/ ▶ n. (pl. **-glos**) a white, English-speaking American as distinct from a Hispanic American. [19th C.: from ANGLO-.]

Anglo- ▶ comb. form English: *anglophone.* ■ of English origin: *Anglo-Saxon.* ■ English and ...: *Anglo-Latin.* ■ British and ...: *Anglo-Indian.* [mod. L., from L. *Anglus* 'English.']

An·glo-A·mer·i·can ▶ adj. of or relating to both Britain and the United States. ■ of English descent, but born or living in the United States. ▶ n. an American born in England or of English ancestry. ■ an American whose native tongue is English.

An·glo-Ca·thol·i·cism ▶ n. a tradition within the Anglican Church that is close to Catholicism in its doctrine and worship and is broadly identified with High Church Anglicanism. — **An·glo-Cath·o·lic** adj. & n.

An·glo-Celt ▶ n. a person of British or Irish descent (typically used outside Britain and Ireland). — **An·glo-Celt·ic** adj.

An·glo·cen·tric /,anɢglōˈsentrik/ ▶ adj. centered on or considered in terms of England or Britain.

An·glo-In·di·an ▶ adj. of, relating to, or involving both Britain and India: *Anglo-Indian business cooperation.* ■ (esp. of a person living in the Indian subcontinent) of mixed British and Indian parentage. ■ esp. hist. of British descent or birth but living or having lived long in India. ■ (of a word) adopted into English from an Indian language. ▶ n. an Anglo-Indian person.

An·glo·ma·ni·a /,anɢglōˈmānēə/ ▶ n. excessive admiration of English customs.

An·glo-Nor·man French (also **An·glo-Nor·man**) ▶ n. the variety of Norman French used in England after the Norman Conquest. It has had a strong influence on legal phraseology in English. ▶ adj. of or relating to this language.

An·glo·phile /ˈanɢglə,fīl/ ▶ n. a person who is fond of or greatly admires England or Britain. ▶ adj. fond or admiring of England or Britain. — **An·glo·phil·ia** /,anɢgləˈfilēə/ n.

An·glo·phobe /ˈanɢglə,fōb/ ▶ n. a person who greatly hates or fears England or Britain. ▶ adj. greatly hating or fearing England or Britain. — **An·glo·pho·bi·a** /,anɢgləˈfōbēə/ n.

an·glo·phone /ˈanɢglə,fōn/ ▶ adj. English-speaking. ▶ n. an English-speaking person.

An·glo-Sax·on ▶ adj. relating to or denoting the Germanic inhabitants of England from their arrival in the 5th century up to the Norman Conquest. ■ of English descent. ■ of, in, or relating to the Old English language. ■ informal (of an English word or expression) plain, in particular vulgar. ▶ n. **1** a Germanic inhabitant of England between the 5th century and the Norman Conquest. ■ a person of English descent. ■ any white, English-speaking person. **2** another term for OLD ENGLISH. ■ informal plain English, in particular vulgar slang. [from mod. L. *Anglo-Saxones* (pl.), med. L. *Angli Saxones.*]

An·go·la /anɢˈgōlə; an-/ a republic in southern Africa. *See box.* — **An·go·lan** adj. & n.

An·go·ra /anɢˈgôrə/ former name (until 1930) of ANKARA.

an·go·ra /anɢˈgôrə/ ▶ n. [often as adj.] a cat, goat, or rabbit of a long-haired breed. ■ a fabric made from the hair of the angora goat or rabbit.

an·go·ra wool ▶ n. a mixture of sheep's wool and angora rabbit hair.

An·gos·tu·ra /,anɢgəˈst(y)o͝orə/ former name (until 1846) for CIUDAD BOLÍVAR.

an·gos·tu·ra /,anɢgəˈst(y)o͝orə/ (also **angostura bark**) ▶ n. an aromatic bitter bark taken from the South American trees *Angostura febrifuga* and *Galipea officinalis* (rue family), used as a flavoring, and formerly as a tonic and to reduce fever. ■ short for ANGOSTURA BITTERS.

An·gos·tu·ra bit·ters ▶ n. trademark a kind of tonic first made in Angostura.

an·gry /ˈanɢgrē/ ▶ adj. (**-gri·er, -gri·est**) having a strong feeling of or showing annoyance, displeasure, or hostility; full of anger. ■ fig. (of the sea or sky) stormy, turbulent, or threatening. ■ (of a wound or sore) red and inflamed. — **an·gri·ly** /-grəlē/ adv.

an·gry white male ▶ n. derog. a politically conservative or anti-liberal white man.

an·gry young man ▶ n. a young man dissatisfied with and outspoken against social and political structures. ■ (**Angry Young Men**) a number of British playwrights and novelists of the early 1950s whose work was marked by irreverence toward the Establishment and disgust at the survival of class distinctions and privilege.

angst /anɢ(k)st; änɢ(k)st/ ▶ n. a feeling of deep anxiety or dread, typically an unfocused one about the human condition or the state of the world in general. ■ informal a feeling of persistent worry about something trivial. [1920s: from Ger., 'fear, anxiety.']

Ång·ström /ˈônɢstrəm; ˈanɢ-/, Anders Jonas (1814–1874), Swedish physicist.

ang·strom /ˈanɢstrəm/ (also **ång·ström, angstrom unit**) (abbr.: Å) ▶ n. a unit of length equal to one hundred-millionth of a centimeter, 10–10 meter, used mainly to express wavelengths and interatomic distances. [19th C.: after A. J. ÅNGSTRÖM.]

An·guil·la /anɢˈgwilə; an-/ the northernmost island of the Leeward Islands in the West Indies; pop. 7,020. — **An·guil·lan** adj. & n.

an·guish /ˈanɢgwisн/ ▶ n. severe mental or physical pain or suffering. ▶ v. suffer or cause someone to suffer anguish: *he anguished over how to reply.* [ME: via OFr. from L. *angustia* 'tightness,' (pl.) 'distress,' from *angustus* 'narrow.']

an·guished /ˈanɢgwisнt/ ▶ adj. experiencing or expressing severe mental or physical pain or suffering.

an·gu·lar /ˈanɢgyələr/ ▶ adj. **1** (of an object, outline, or shape) having angles or sharp corners. ■ (of a person or part of their body) lean and having a prominent bone structure. ■ (of a person's way of moving) not flowing smoothly; awkward or jerky. ■ placed or directed at an angle: *angular penmanship.* **2** esp. Physics denoting physical properties or quantities measured with reference to or by means of an angle, esp. those associated with rotation. — **an·gu·lar·i·ty** /,anɢgyəˈlaritē/ n. **an·gu·lar·ly** adv. [ME: from L. *angularis,* from *angulus* (see ANGLE[1]).]

an·gu·lar mo·men·tum ▶ n. Physics the quantity of rotation of a body, which is the product of its moment of inertia and its angular velocity.

an·gu·lar ve·loc·i·ty ▶ n. Physics the rate of change of angular position of a rotating body.

an·gu·late /ˈanɢgyə,lāt/ ▶ v. [trans.] (often **be angulated**) tech. hold, bend, or distort (a part of the body, esp. of an animal) so as to form an angle or angles. — **an·gu·la·tion** /,anɢgyəˈlāsнən/ n.

ang·wan·ti·bo /anɢˈ(g)wäntə,bō/ ▶ n. (pl. **-bos**) a small rare nocturnal primate (*Arctocebus calabarensis,* family Lorisidae) of west central Africa, related to the potto. [19th C.: from Efik.]

an·he·do·ni·a /,anhēˈdōnēə; -hi-/ ▶ n. Psychiatry inability to feel pleasure. — **an·he·don·ic** /-ˈdänik/ adj. [19th C.: from Fr. *anhédonie,* from Gk. *an-* 'without' + *hēdonē* 'pleasure.']

an·he·dral /anˈhēdrəl/ ▶ adj. Crystallog. (of a crystal) having no plane faces. ▶ n. Aeron. downward inclination of an aircraft's wing, or the angle of this. Compare with DIHEDRAL. [19th C.: from AN-[1] 'not' + *-hedral* (see -HEDRON).]

an·hin·ga /an'hiNGə/ ▶ **n.** a long-necked fish-eating bird (genus *Anhinga*, family Anhingidae) related to the cormorants, typically found in fresh water. Anhingas spear fish with their long pointed bills and frequently swim submerged to the neck. Also called **DARTER, SNAKEBIRD.** [18th C.: from Port., from Tupi *áyinga.*]

An·hui /'än'hwā/ (also **An·hwei**) a province in eastern China; capital, Hefei; pop. 59,380,000.

an·hy·dride /an'hī,drīd/ ▶ **n.** Chem. the compound obtained by removing the elements of water from a particular acid. ■ [usu. with adj.] an organic compound containing the group –C(O)OC(O)–, derived from a carboxylic acid.

an·hy·drite /an'hī,drīt/ ▶ **n.** a white mineral consisting of anhydrous calcium sulfate. [see **ANHYDROUS.**]

an·hy·drous /an'hīdrəs/ ▶ **adj.** Chem. (of a substance, esp. a crystalline compound) containing no water. [19th C.: from Gk. *anudros* (from *an-* 'without' + *hudōr* 'water') + **-OUS.**]

a·ni /ä'nē/ ▶ **n.** (pl. **a·nis**) a glossy black long-tailed bird (genus *Crotophaga*) of the cuckoo family, with a large deep bill, found in Central and South America.

an·i·line /'anl-in; -,īn/ ▶ **n.** Chem. a colorless oily liquid, $C_6H_5NH_2$, present in coal tar. It is used in the manufacture of dyes, drugs, and plastics, and was the basis of the earliest synthetic dyes. [19th C.: from *anil* 'indigo,' ult. from Arab. *an-nīl* (from Sanskrit *nīlī*, from *nīla* 'dark blue').]

a·ni·lin·gus /,ānə'liNGgəs/ ▶ **n.** sexual stimulation of the anus by the tongue or mouth. [1960s: from L. *anus* 'anus.']

an·i·ma /'anəmə/ ▶ **n.** Psychol. Jung's term for the feminine part of a man's personality. Often contrasted with **ANIMUS** (sense 3). ■ the part of the psyche that is directed inward, and is in touch with the subconscious. Often contrasted with **PERSONA.** [1920s: from L., lit. 'mind, soul.']

an·i·mad·ver·sion /,anəmad'vərZHən/ ▶ **n.** formal criticism or censure. ■ a comment or remark, esp. a critical one. [16th C.: ult. from L. *animadversio(n-)*, from *animadvertere* (see **ANIMADVERT**).]

an·i·mad·vert /,anəmad'vərt/ ▶ **v.** [intrans.] (**animadvert on/upon/against**) formal pass criticism or censure on; speak out against. [ME: from L. *animadvertere*, from *animus* 'mind' + *advertere* (from *ad-* 'toward' + *vertere* 'to turn').]

an·i·mal /'anəməl/ ▶ **n.** a living organism that feeds on organic matter, typically having specialized sense organs and nervous system and able to respond rapidly to stimuli. ■ any such living organism other than a human being. ■ a mammal, as opposed to a bird, reptile, fish, or insect. ■ a person whose behavior is regarded as devoid of human attributes or civilizing influences, esp. someone who is very cruel, violent, or repulsive. ■ [with adj.] a particular type of person or thing: *a regular party animal.* ▶ **adj.** [attrib.] of, relating to, or characteristic of animals: *animal life.* ■ of animals as distinct from plants. ■ characteristic of the physical and instinctive needs of animals; of the flesh rather than the spirit or intellect: *animal lust.* [ME: ult. from L. *animalis* 'having breath,' from *anima* 'breath.']

an·i·mal·cule /,anə'mal,kyōōl/ ▶ **n.** archaic a microscopic animal.

an·i·mal hus·band·ry ▶ **n.** the science of breeding and caring for farm animals.

an·i·mal·ism /'anəmə,lizəm/ ▶ **n.** behavior that is characteristic of or appropriate to animals, particularly in being physical and instinctive. ■ religious worship of or concerning animals. — **an·i·mal·is·tic** /,anəmə'listik/ **adj.**

an·i·mal·i·ty /,anə'malitē/ ▶ **n.** animal nature or character. ■ physical, instinctive behavior or qualities.

an·i·mal·ize /'anəmə,līz/ ▶ **v.** [trans.] make into or like an animal. — **an·i·mal·i·za·tion** /,anəməli'zāSHən/ **n.**

an·i·mal mag·net·ism ▶ **n. 1** a quality of sexual attractiveness. **2** hist. a supposed emanation to which the action of hypnotism was ascribed.

an·i·mal pole ▶ **n.** Biol. the portion of an egg containing the nucleus and less yolk, opposite the vegetal pole.

an·i·mal rights ▶ **plural n.** rights believed to belong to animals to live free from use in medical research, hunting, and other services to humans.

an·i·mal spir·its ▶ **plural n.** natural exuberance.

an·i·mate ▶ **v.** /'anə,māt/ [trans.] **1** esp. fig. bring to life. ■ give inspiration, encouragement, or renewed vigor to. **2** (usu. **be animated**) give (a movie or character) the appearance of movement using animation techniques. ▶ **adj.** /-mit/ alive or having life (often as a contrast with **INANIMATE**). ■ lively and active. [ME: from L. *animat-* 'instilled with life,' from v. *animare*, from *anima* 'life.']

an·i·mat·ed /'anə,mātid/ ▶ **adj. 1** full of life or excitement; lively. **2** (of a movie) made using animation techniques. ■ moving or appearing to move as if alive. — **an·i·mat·ed·ly adv.**

an·i·ma·tion /,anə'māSHən/ ▶ **n. 1** the state of being full of life or vigor; liveliness. ■ esp. archaic the state of being alive. **2** the technique of filming successive drawings or positions of puppets or models to create an illusion of movement when the movie is shown as a sequence. ■ (also **computer animation**) the manipulation of electronic images by means of a computer in order to create moving images.

a·ni·ma·to /,änə'mätō/ Music ▶ **adj. & adv.** (esp. as a direction) in an animated manner. ▶ **n.** (pl. **-ma·tos** or **-ma·ti** /-'mätē/) a passage marked animato. [Ital.]

an·i·ma·tor /'anə,mātər/ ▶ **n.** a person who animates something, esp. a person who prepares animated movies.

an·i·ma·tron·ics /,anəmə'träniks/ ▶ **plural n.** [treated as sing.] the technique of making and operating lifelike robots, typically for use in film or other entertainment. — **an·i·ma·tron·ic adj.** [1970s: blend of **ANIMATED** and **ELECTRONICS.**]

a·nime /'anə,mā/ ▶ **n.** Japanese movie and television animation, often having a science fiction theme and sometimes including violent or explicitly sexual material. Compare with **MANGA.** [1980s: Japanese.]

an·i·mism /'anə,mizəm/ ▶ **n. 1** the attribution of a living soul to plants, inanimate objects, and natural phenomena. **2** the belief in a supernatural power that organizes and animates the material universe. — **an·i·mist n. an·i·mis·tic** /,anə'mistik/ **adj.** [19th C.: from L. *anima* 'life.']

an·i·mos·i·ty /,anə'mäsitē/ ▶ **n.** (pl. **-ties**) strong hostility. [ME: ult. from late L. *animositas*, from *animosus* 'spirited,' from L. *animus* 'spirit.']

an·i·mus /'anəməs/ ▶ **n. 1** hostility or ill feeling. **2** motivation to do something. **3** Psychol. Jung's term for the masculine part of a woman's personality. Often contrasted with **ANIMA.** [19th C.: from L., 'spirit.']

an·i·on /'an,īən/ ▶ **n.** Chem. a negatively charged ion, i.e., one that would be attracted to the anode in electrolysis. The opposite of **CATION.** — **an·i·on·ic** /,anī'änik/ **adj.** [19th C.: from **ANODE** or **ANA-** + **-ION.**]

an·ise /'anis/ ▶ **n. 1** a Mediterranean plant (*Pimpinella anisum*) of the parsley family, cultivated for its aromatic seeds, used in cooking and herbal medicine. **2** an Asian or American tree or shrub (genus *Illicium*, family Illiciaceae) that bears fruit with an aniseedlike odor, esp. **star anise** (*I. verum*), used in Chinese cooking. [ME: via OFr. from L. *anisum*, from Gk. *anison* 'anise, dill.']

an·i·seed /'anə(s),sēd/ ▶ **n.** the seed of the anise, used in cooking and herbal medicine.

an·i·sette /,ani'set; -'zet/ ▶ **n.** a liqueur flavored with aniseed.

an·i·sog·a·my /,anī'sägəmē/ ▶ **n.** Biol. sexual reproduction by the fusion of dissimilar gametes. Often contrasted with **ISOGAMY.** — **an·i·sog·a·mous** /-məs/ **adj.** [19th C.: from Gk. *anisos* 'unequal' + *-gamy* (from *gamos* 'marriage').]

an·i·so·trop·ic /an,īsə'trōpik; -'träpik/ ▶ **adj.** Physics (of an object or substance) having a physical property that has a different value when measured in different directions. A simple example is wood, which is stronger along the grain than across it. — **an·i·sot·ro·py** /,anī'sätrəpē/ **n.** [19th C.: from Gk. *anisos* 'unequal' + *tropos* 'turn.']

An·jou /'anjōō; äN'ZHōō/ a former province of western France, on the Loire River.

An·ka·ra /'äNGkərə; 'aNG-/ the capital of Turkey since 1923; pop. 2,559,470. Former name (until 1930) **ANGORA.**

ankh /aNGk/ ▶ **n.** an object or design resembling a cross but having a loop instead of the top arm, used in ancient Egypt as a symbol of life. [19th C.: from Egyptian, 'life, soul.']

ankh

an·kle /'aNGkəl/ ▶ **n.** the joint connecting the foot with the leg. ■ the narrow part of the leg between the foot and the calf. ▶ **v.** [trans.] leave: *he ankled the series to do a movie.* [OE *ancleow*, from Indo-Eur.; akin to Ger. *Enkel* and **ANGLE**[1].]

an·kle bone ▶ **n.** the chief bone of the ankle joint; the talus.

an·klet /'aNGklit/ ▶ **n. 1** a sock that reaches just above the ankle. **2** an ornament worn around an ankle.

an·ky·lo·saur /'aNGkəlō,sôr/ (also **an·ky·lo·sau·rus** /,aNGkəlō'sôrəs/) ▶ **n.** a heavily built quadrupedal herbivorous dinosaur (*Ankylosaurus* and other genera, order Ornithischia) primarily of the Cretaceous period, armored with bony plates. — **an·ky·lo·sau·ri·an** /,aNGkəlō'sôrēən/ [20th C.: from mod. L. *Ankylosaurus*, from Gk. *ankulos* 'crooked' + *sauros* 'lizard.']

an·ky·lose /'aNGkə,lōs; -,lōz/ ▶ **v.** (**be/become ankylosed**) Med. (of bones or a joint) be or become stiffened or united by ankylosis. [18th C.: back-form. from **ANKYLOSIS.**]

an·ky·lo·sis /,aNGkə'lōsis/ ▶ **n.** Med. abnormal stiffening and immobility of a joint due to fusion of the bones. — **an·ky·lot·ic** /-'lätik/ **adj.** [18th C.: from Gk. *ankulōsis*, based on *ankuloun* 'crooked.']

an·la·ge /'än,lägə/ ▶ **n.** (pl. **-lag·en** /-,lägən/) Biol. the rudimentary basis of a particular organ or other part, esp. in an embryo. [19th C.: from Ger., 'foundation.']

An·na·ba /a'näbə/ a port of northeastern Algeria; pop. 348,000. Former name **BÔNE.**

An Na·jaf /,an 'najaf/ another name for **NAJAF.**

an·nal·ist /'anl-ist/ ▶ **n.** a person who writes annals. — **an·nal·is·tic** /,anl'istik/ **adj.**

an·nals /'anlz/ ▶ **plural n.** a record of events year by year. ■ historical records. ■ (**Annals**) used in the titles of learned journals: *Annals of Internal Medicine.* [16th C.: from L. *annales (libri)* 'yearly (books),' from *annus* 'year.']

An·nan /ə'nän/, Kofi Atta (1938–), Ghanaian diplomat; secretary-general of the UN 1997–2006. Nobel Peace Prize (2001).

An·nan·dale /'anən,dāl/ a town in northern Virginia, suburb of Washington, DC; pop. 54,994.

An·nap·o·lis /əˈnapəlis/ the capital of Maryland, on Chesapeake Bay, home of the US Naval Academy; pop. 35,838.

An·na·pur·na /ˌanəˈpərnə/ a ridge of the Himalayas, in north central Nepal; highest peak 26,503 feet (8,078 m).

Ann Ar·bor /ˌan ˈärbər/ a city in southeastern Michigan; pop. 114,024.

an·nat·to /əˈnätō/ (also **a·nat·to**) ▶ **n.** (pl. **-tos**) **1** an orange-red dye obtained from the pulp of a tropical fruit, used for coloring foods and fabric. **2** the tropical American tree (*Bixa orellana*, family Bixaceae) from which this fruit is obtained. [17th C.: from Carib.]

Ann, Cape /an/ a peninsula in northeastern Massachusetts, noted for its resorts and scenery.

Anne /an/ (1665–1714), queen of England, Scotland, and Ireland 1702–14; daughter of James II. She was the last of the Stuart monarchs.

Anne, St. traditionally the mother of the Virgin Mary.

an·neal /əˈnēl/ ▶ **v.** [trans.] heat (metal or glass) and allow it to cool slowly, in order to remove internal stresses and toughen it. — **an·neal·er n.** [OE *onǣlan*, from *on* + *ǣlan* 'burn, bake,' from *āl* 'fire.']

Anne Bol·eyn see **Boleyn**.

An·nel·i·da /əˈnelidə/ Zool. a large phylum that comprises the segmented worms, which include earthworms, lugworms, and leeches. — **an·ne·lid** /ˈanlˌid/ **n. & adj. an·nel·i·dan** /əˈnelidn/ **n. & adj.** [mod. L. (pl.), from Fr. *(animaux) annelés* 'ringed (animals),' based on L. *anulus* 'a ring.']

Anne of Cleves /klēvz/ (1515–57), fourth wife of Henry VIII.

an·nex ▶ **v.** /əˈneks; ˈaneks/ [trans.] (often **be annexed**) append or add as an extra or subordinate part, esp. to a document: *the first ten amendments were annexed to the Constitution in 1791.* ■ add (territory) to one's own territory by appropriation. ■ informal take for oneself; appropriate. ▶ **n.** /ˈaneks; -iks/ (esp. Brit. also **an·nexe**) (pl. **-nex·es**) **1** a building joined to or associated with a main building, providing additional space or accommodations. **2** an addition to a document. — **an·nex·a·tion** /ˌanekˈsāsʜən; ˌanik-/ **n. an·nex·a·tion·ist** /ˌanekˈsāsʜənist; ˌanik-/ **n. & adj.** [ME: from OFr. *annexer*, from L. *annectere* 'connect,' from *ad-* 'to' + *nectere* 'to tie.']

an·ni·hi·late /əˈnīəˌlāt/ ▶ **v.** [trans.] destroy utterly; obliterate. ■ defeat utterly. ■ Physics convert (a subatomic particle) into radiant energy. — **an·ni·hi·la·tor** /-ˌlātər/ **n. an·ni·hi·la·tion** /əˌnīəˈlāsʜən/ **n.** [ME (adj.): from late L. *annihilatus* 'reduced to nothing,' from v. *annihilare*, from *ad-* + *nihil* 'nothing.']

an·ni·ver·sa·ry /ˌanəˈvərsərē/ ▶ **n.** (pl. **-ries**) the date on which an event took place in a previous year. ■ the date on which a country or other institution was founded in a previous year. ■ the date on which a couple was married in a previous year. [ME: from L. *anniversarius* 'returning yearly,' from *annus* 'year' + *versus* 'turning.']

An·no Dom·i·ni /ˈanō ˈdämənē; -nī; ˈänō/ ▶ **adv.** full form of **AD**. [16th C.: L., 'in the year of the Lord.']

an·no·tate /ˈanəˌtāt/ ▶ **v.** [trans.] add notes to (a text or diagram) giving explanation or comment. — **an·no·tat·a·ble adj. an·no·ta·tor** /-ˌtātər/ **n.** [16th C.: from L. *annotat-* 'marked,' from v. *annotare*, from *ad-* 'to' + *nota* 'a mark.']

an·no·ta·tion /ˌanəˈtāsʜən/ ▶ **n.** a note by way of explanation or comment added to a text or diagram. ■ the action of annotating a text or diagram.

an·nounce /əˈnouns/ ▶ **v.** [reporting verb] make a public and typically formal declaration about a fact or occurrence or intention: [with clause] *the president's office announced that the state of siege would be lifted* | [trans.] *he announced his retirement.* ■ make known: *these glossy and expensive volumes announce anxiety.* ■ give information about (transportation) in a station or airport via a public address system: *they were announcing her train.* ■ (of a notice, letter, sound, etc.) give information to (someone) via the senses of sight or hearing: *she heard the strains of music announcing her arrival in the church.* ■ make known the arrival or imminence of (a guest or a meal) at a formal social occasion. [15th C.: from Fr. *annoncer*, from L. *annuntiare*, from *ad-* 'to' + *nuntiare* 'declare' (from *nuntius* 'messenger').]

an·nounce·ment /əˈnounsmənt/ ▶ **n.** a public and typically formal statement about a fact, occurrence, or intention. ■ the action of making such a statement. ■ a notice appearing in a newspaper or public place and announcing something such as a birth, death, or marriage. ■ a statement of information given over a public address system.

an·nounc·er /əˈnounsər/ ▶ **n.** a person who announces something, esp. someone who introduces or gives information about programs on radio or television.

an·noy /əˈnoi/ ▶ **v.** [trans.] (often **be annoyed**) irritate (someone); make (someone) a little angry: *your cheerfulness annoyed me* | [intrans.] *rock music loud enough to annoy.* ■ archaic harm or attack repeatedly. [ME: from OFr. *anoier* (v.), *anoi* (n.), based on L. *in odio* in *mihi in odio est* 'it is hateful to me.']

an·noy·ance /əˈnoi-əns/ ▶ **n.** the feeling or state of being annoyed; irritation. ■ a thing that annoys someone; a nuisance.

an·noy·ing /əˈnoi-iɴɢ/ ▶ **adj.** causing irritation or annoyance: *annoying habits.* — **an·noy·ing·ly adv.**

an·nu·al /ˈanyo͞oəl/ ▶ **adj.** occurring once every year. ■ calculated over or covering a period of a year: *his basic annual income.* ■ (of a plant) living only for a year or less, perpetuating itself by seed. ▶ **n.** a book or magazine that is published once a year under the same title but with different contents: *a Christmas annual.* ■ an annual plant. — **an·nu·al·ly adv.** [ME: from OFr. *annuel*, based on L. *annus* 'year.']

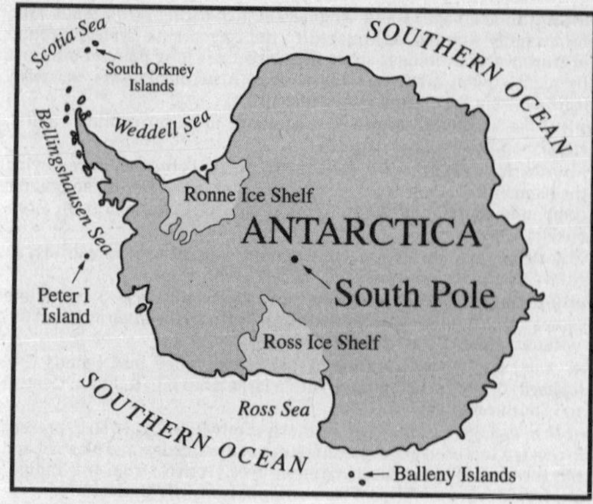

an·nu·al·ized /ˈanyo͞oəˌlīzd/ ▶ **adj.** (of a rate of interest, inflation, or return on an investment) recalculated as an annual rate: *an annualized yield of about 11.5%.*

an·nual ring ▶ **n.** another term for **tree ring**.

an·nu·i·tant /əˈn(y)o͞oitənt/ ▶ **n.** formal a person who receives an annuity.

an·nu·i·ty /əˈn(y)o͞oitē/ ▶ **n.** (pl. **-ties**) a fixed sum of money paid to someone each year, typically for the rest of their life. ■ a form of insurance or investment entitling the investor to a series of annual sums. [ME: ult. from med. L. *annuitas*, from L. *annuus* 'yearly,' from *annus* 'year.']

an·nul /əˈnəl/ ▶ **v.** (**-nulled, -nul·ling**) [trans.] (usu. **be annulled**) declare invalid (an official agreement, decision, or result). ■ declare (a marriage) to have had no legal existence. — **an·nul·ment n.** [ME: ult. from late L. *annullare*, from *ad-* 'to' + *nullum* 'nothing.']

an·nu·lar /ˈanyələr/ ▶ **adj.** tech. ring-shaped. — **an·nu·lar·ly adv.** [16th C.: ult. from L. *annularis*, from *anulus*, *annulus* 'a ring.']

an·nu·lar e·clipse ▶ **n.** an eclipse of the sun in which the edge of the sun remains visible as a bright ring around the moon.

an·nu·late /ˈanyəlit; -ˌlāt/ ▶ **adj.** esp. Zool. having rings; marked with or formed of rings: *an annulate worm.* — **an·nu·lat·ed adj. an·nu·la·tion** /ˌanyəˈlāsʜən/ **n.**

an·nu·let /ˈanyəlit/ ▶ **n. 1** Archit. a small fillet or band encircling a column. **2** Heraldry a charge in the form of a small ring. [ME: from OFr. *anelet*, from L. *anulus*, *annulus* 'ring.']

an·nu·lus /ˈanyələs/ ▶ **n.** (pl. **-li** /-ˌlī/) tech. a ring-shaped object, structure, or region. [16th C.: from L. *anulus*, *annulus*.]

an·nun·ci·ate /əˈnənsēˌāt/ ▶ **v.** [trans.] archaic announce (something). [ME: from med. L. *annunciat-*, var. of L. *annuntiat-* 'announced,' from v. *annuntiare*.]

an·nun·ci·a·tion /əˌnənsēˈāsʜən/ ▶ **n.** (usu. **the Annunciation**) the announcement of the Incarnation by the angel Gabriel to Mary (Luke 1:26–38). ■ the church festival commemorating this, held on March 25 (Lady Day). ■ a painting or sculpture depicting this. ■ formal or archaic the announcement of something.

an·nun·ci·a·tor /əˈnənsēˌātər/ ▶ **n.** a bell, light, or other device that provides information on the state or condition of something by indicating which of several electrical circuits has been activated.

an·nus hor·ri·bi·lis /ˈanəs həˈribəlis/ ▶ **n.** a year of disaster or misfortune. [20th C.: mod. L.]

an·nus mi·ra·bi·lis /ˈanəs məˈräbəlis/ ▶ **n.** a remarkable or auspicious year. [17th C.: mod. L., 'wonderful year.']

a·no·a /əˈnōə/ ▶ **n.** (pl. same or **-as**) a small deerlike buffalo (genus *Bubalus*), native to Sulawesi.

an·ode /ˈanōd/ ▶ **n.** the positively charged electrode by which the electrons leave a device. The opposite of **cathode**. ■ the negatively charged electrode of a device supplying current such as a primary cell. — **an·od·al** /ˈanōdl; āˈnōdl/ **adj. an·od·ic** /anˈädik/ **adj.** [19th C.: from Gk. *anodos* 'way up,' from *ana* + *hodos* 'way.']

an·o·dize /ˈanəˌdīz/ ▶ **v.** [trans.] [usu. as adj.] (**anodized**) coat (a metal, esp. aluminum) with a protective oxide layer by an electrolytic process in which the metal forms the anode. — **an·o·diz·er n.**

an·o·dyne /ˈanəˌdīn/ ▶ **adj.** not likely to provoke dissent or offense; uncontentious or inoffensive, often deliberately so: *anodyne New Age music.* ▶ **n.** a pain-killing drug or medicine. ■ fig. something that alleviates a person's mental distress. [16th C.: via L. from Gk. *anōdunos* 'painless,' from *an-* + *odunē* 'pain.']

a·no·gen·i·tal /ˌānōˈjenitl/ ▶ **adj.** Med. & Anat. of or relating to the anus and genitals.

a·noint /əˈnoint/ ▶ **v.** [trans.] smear or rub with oil, typically as part of a religious ceremony. ■ (**anoint something with**) smear or rub something with (any other substance): *they anoint the tips of their arrows with poison.* ■ ceremonially confer divine or holy office upon (a priest or monarch) by smearing or rubbing with oil. ■ fig. nominate or choose (someone) as successor to or leading candidate for a position.

– PHRASES **Anointing of the Sick** (in the Roman Catholic Church) the sacramental anointing of the ill or infirm with blessed oil; unction. [ME: from OFr. *enoint* 'anointed,' past part. of *enoindre*, from L. *inungere*, from *in*- 'upon' + *ungere* 'smear with oil.']

a·no·le /ə'nōlē/ ▶ **n.** a small, mainly arboreal American lizard (genus *Anolis*, family Iguanidae) with a throat fan that (in the male) is typically brightly colored. Anoles have some ability to change color. Also called CHAMELEON. [18th C.: from Carib.]

a·nom·a·lis·tic year ▶ **n.** a year measured between successive perihelia of the earth (approximately 365 1/4 days).

a·nom·a·lous /ə'nämələs/ ▶ **adj.** deviating from what is standard, normal, or expected. — **a·nom·a·lous·ly** adv. **a·nom·a·lous·ness** n. [17th C.: ult. from Gk. *anōmalos* (from *an*- 'not' + *homalos* 'even.')]

a·nom·a·ly /ə'näməlē/ ▶ **n.** (pl. **-lies**) **1** something that deviates from what is standard, normal, or expected. **2** Astron. the angular distance of a planet or satellite from its last perihelion or perigee.

an·o·mie /'anə,mē/ (also **an·o·my**) ▶ **n.** lack of the usual social or ethical standards in an individual or group. — **a·nom·ic** /ə'nämik; ə'nō-/ **adj.** [1930s: from Fr., from Gk. *anomia*, from *anomos* 'lawless.']

a·non /ə'nän/ ▶ **adv.** archaic soon; shortly. [OE *on ān* 'into one,' *on āne* 'in one.' The original sense was 'in or into one state, course, etc.,' which developed into the temporal sense 'at once.']

anon. ▶ **abbr.** anonymous.

a·non·y·mize /ə'nänə,mīz/ ▶ **v.** [trans.] make anonymous. ■ [usu. as adj.] (**anonymized**) Med. remove identifying particulars from (test results) for statistical or other purposes.

a·non·y·mous /ə'nänəməs/ ▶ **adj.** (of a person) not identified by name; of unknown name. ■ having no outstanding, individual, or unusual features; unremarkable or impersonal. — **an·o·nym·i·ty** /,anə'nimitē/ **n.** **a·non·y·mous·ly** **adv.** [16th C.: via late L. from Gk. *anōnumos* 'nameless' (from *an*- + *onoma* 'name') + -OUS.]

a·non·y·mous FTP ▶ **n.** Comput. part of the File Transfer Protocol (FTP) on the Internet that lets anyone log on to an FTP server, using a general username and without a password.

a·noph·e·les /ə'näfə,lēz/ (also **anopheles mosquito**) ▶ **n.** a mosquito (genus *Anopheles*, family Culicidae) common in warm climates. Its many species include those that transmit the malarial parasite to humans. — **a·noph·e·line** /-,līn; -lin/ **adj. & n.** [19th C.: mod. L., from Gk. *anōphelēs* 'useless.']

An·o·plu·ra /,anə'plōōrə/ Entomol. an order of insects that comprises the sucking lice. See also PHTHIRAPTERA. — **an·o·plu·ran** **n. & adj.** [mod. L. (pl.), from *anoplos* 'unarmed' + *oura* 'tail.']

an·o·rak /'anə,rak/ ▶ **n.** a waterproof jacket, typically with a hood, of a kind originally used in polar regions. [1920s: from Greenland Eskimo *anoraq*.]

an·o·rec·tal /'anə'rektəl/ ▶ **adj.** Med. & Anat. of or relating to the anus and rectum.

an·o·rex·i·a /,anə'reksēə/ ▶ **n.** a lack or loss of appetite for food (as a medical condition). ■ (also **an·o·rex·i·a ner·vo·sa** /nər'vōsə/) an emotional disorder characterized by an obsessive desire to lose weight by refusing to eat. [16th C.: via late L. from Gk., from *an*- 'without' + *orexis* 'appetite.']

an·o·rex·ic /,anə'reksik/ (also **an·o·rec·tic** /,anə'rektik/) ▶ **adj.** relating to or suffering from anorexia. ■ informal extremely thin. ▶ **n.** **1** a person suffering from anorexia. **2** (**anorectic**) a medicine that produces a loss of appetite.

an·or·gas·mi·a /,anôr'gazmēə/ ▶ **n.** Med. persistent inability to achieve orgasm despite responding to sexual stimulation. — **an·or·gas·mic** /-mik/ **adj.**

an·or·thite /an'ôr,THīt/ ▶ **n.** a calcium-rich mineral of the feldspar group occurring in limestones metamorphosed by contact with an igneous intrusion. [19th C.: from AN-[1] + Gk. *orthos* 'straight' + -ITE.]

an·os·mi·a /a'näzmēə; a'näs-/ ▶ **n.** Med. the loss of the sense of smell, either total or partial. — **an·os·mic** /-mik/ **adj.** [19th C.: from AN-[2] + Gk. *osmē* 'smell.']

an·oth·er /ə'nəTHər/ ▶ **adj. & pron.** **1** used to refer to an additional person or thing of the same type as one already mentioned or known about; one more; a further: [as adj.] *have another drink* | [as pron.] *one in the morning and another in the afternoon.* ■ [usu. as adj.] used with a proper name to indicate someone or something's similarity to the person or event specified: *this will not be another Vietnam.* **2** used to refer to a different person or thing from one already mentioned or known about. ■ [adj.] used to refer to someone sharing an attribute in common with the person already mentioned. [ME: as *an other* until the 16th C.]

A·nouilh /ä'nōōē; än'wē/, Jean (1910–87), French playwright. He wrote *Antigone* (1944).

an·ov·u·lant /an'ävyələnt/ Med. ▶ **adj.** (chiefly of a drug) preventing ovulation. ▶ **n.** an anovulant drug.

an·ov·u·la·to·ry /an'ävyələ,tôrē/ ▶ **adj.** Med. (of a menstrual cycle) in which ovulation does not occur.

an·ox·i·a /a'näksēə/ ▶ **n.** tech. an absence of oxygen. ■ Med. an absence or deficiency of oxygen reaching the tissues; severe hypoxia. — **an·ox·ic** **adj.** [1930s: from AN-[1] + *ox(ygen)*.]

An·schluss /'än,SHlōōs/ the annexation of Austria by Germany in 1938. [Ger., from *anschliessen* 'to join.']

An·selm, St. /'an,selm/ (*c.*1033–1109), archbishop of Canterbury 1093–1109; born in Italy.

ANSI /'ansē/ ▶ **abbr.** American National Standards Institute.

an·swer /'ansər/ ▶ **n.** a thing said, written, or done to deal with or as a reaction to a question, statement, or situation. ■ a thing written or said in reaction to a question in a test or quiz. ■ the correct solution to such a question. ■ a solution to a problem or dilemma. ■ [in sing.] (**answer to**) a thing or person that imitates or fulfills the same role as something or someone else: *Britain's answer to Marilyn Monroe.* ■ Law the defendant's reply to the plaintiff's charges. ▶ **v.** **1** [reporting verb] say or write something to deal with or as a reaction to someone or something. ■ [trans.] provide the required responses to (a test or quiz). ■ [intrans.] (**answer back**) respond impudently or disrespectfully to someone, esp. when being criticized or told to do something. ■ [trans.] act in reaction to (a sound such as a telephone ringing or a knock or ring on a door): *David answered the door* | [intrans.] *she called Edward's house, hoping he would answer.* ■ [trans.] act in response to (a stimulus). ■ [trans.] discharge (a responsibility or claim). ■ [trans.] defend oneself against (a charge, accusation, or criticism). ■ [intrans.] (**answer for**) be responsible or to blame for. ■ [intrans.] (**answer to**) be responsible or report to (someone): *I answer to the commissioner.* ■ [intrans.] (**answer to**) be required to explain or justify oneself to (someone): *you will have the police to answer to.* **2** [trans.] be suitable for fulfilling (a need); satisfy. [OE *andswaru* (n.), *andswarian* (v.), from Gmc.; akin to SWEAR.]

an·swer·a·ble /'ansərəbəl/ ▶ **adj.** **1** [predic.] (**answerable to**) required to explain or justify one's actions to; responsible or having to report to. ■ (**answerable for**) responsible for. **2** (of a question) able to be answered.

an·swer·ing ma·chine ▶ **n.** a tape recorder or digital device that supplies a recorded answer to a telephone call and can record a message from the caller.

an·swer·ing serv·ice ▶ **n.** a business that receives and answers telephone calls for its clients.

ant /ant/ ▶ **n.** a small insect (family Formicidae, order Hymenoptera), often with a sting, that usually lives in a complex social colony with one or more breeding queens. It is wingless except for fertile adults, which often form large mating swarms. [OE *ǣmete*, from West Gmc.]

ant- ▶ **prefix** var. of ANTI- before a vowel or *h* (as in *Antarctic*).

-ant ▶ **suffix** **1** (forming adjectives) denoting attribution of an action or state: *arrogant.* **2** (forming nouns) denoting an agent: *deodorant.*

Ant·a·buse /'antə,byōōs/ ▶ **n.** trademark for DISULFIRAM.

ant·ac·id /ant'asid/ ▶ **adj.** (chiefly of a medicine) preventing or correcting acidity, esp. in the stomach. ▶ **n.** an antacid medicine.

An·tae·us /an'tēəs; -'tā-/ Gk. Mythol. a giant who compelled all comers to wrestle with him until he was defeated by Hercules.

an·tag·o·nism /an'tagə,nizəm/ ▶ **n.** active hostility or opposition. ■ Biochem. inhibition of or interference with the action of a substance or organism by another.

an·tag·o·nist /an'tagənist/ ▶ **n.** a person who actively opposes or is hostile to someone or something; an adversary. ■ Biochem. a substance that interferes with or inhibits the physiological action of another. ■ Anat. a muscle whose action counteracts that of another specified muscle. Compare with AGONIST. [16th C.: ult. from Gk. *antagōnistēs*, from *antagōnizesthai* (see ANTAGONIZE).]

an·tag·o·nis·tic /an,tagə'nistik/ ▶ **adj.** showing or feeling active opposition or hostility toward someone or something. ■ Biochem. & Physiol. of or relating to an antagonist or its action. — **an·tag·o·nis·ti·cal·ly** /-ik(ə)lē/ **adv.**

an·tag·o·nize /an'tagə,nīz/ ▶ **v.** [trans.] cause (someone) to become hostile. ■ Biochem. (of a substance) act as an antagonist of (a substance or its action). [18th C.: from Gk. *antagōnizesthai*, from *ant*- 'against' + *agōnizesthai* 'struggle' (from *agōn* 'contest').]

An·ta·kya /,äntäk'yä/ Turkish name for ANTIOCH.

An·tal·ya /,äntäl'yä; ,äntl-/ a port in southern Turkey; pop. 378,200.

An·ta·na·na·ri·vo /,äntə,nänə'rēvō; ,antə,nanə-/ the capital of Madagascar, located in the central plateau; pop. 802,390. Former name (until 1975) TANANARIVE.

Ant·arc·tic /ant'är(k)tik/ ▶ **adj.** of or relating to the south polar region or Antarctica. ▶ **n.** (**the Antarctic**) the Antarctic region. [ME: ult. from Gk. *antarktikos* 'opposite to the north,' from *ant*- 'against' + *arktikos* (see ARCTIC).]

Ant·arc·ti·ca /ant'ärktikə; -'ärtikə/ the ice-covered continent around the South Pole, situated mainly within the Antarctic Circle. *See map on previous page.*

Ant·arc·tic Cir·cle the parallel of latitude 66° 33′ south of the equator.

Ant·arc·tic O·cean the sea surrounding Antarctica, consisting of parts of the southern Atlantic, Pacific, and Indian oceans. Also called SOUTHERN OCEAN.

Ant·arc·tic Pen·in·su·la a peninsula of Antarctica that extends northward toward Cape Horn and the Falkland Islands.

An·tar·es /an'te(ə)rēz; -'tar-/ a red supergiant, binary star, the brightest in the constellation Scorpius. [Gk., lit. 'simulating Mars.']

ant bear ▶ **n.** **1** another term for AARDVARK. **2** the giant anteater.

an·te /'antē/ ▶ **n.** a stake put up by a player in poker and similar games before receiving cards. ▶ **v.** (**-tes, -ted, -te·ing**) [trans.] (**ante something up**) put up an amount as an ante in poker and similar games. ■ informal pay an amount of money in advance. ■ [intrans.] (**ante up**) informal put up

one's money; pay up.
– PHRASES **up** (or **raise**) **the ante** increase what is at stake or under discussion, esp. in a conflict or dispute. [19th C.: from L., 'before.']

ante- ▶ prefix before; preceding: *antecedent*.

ant·eat·er /ˈantˌētər/ ▶ n. a mammal that feeds on ants and termites. It has a long snout and sticky tongue. Most anteaters are edentates of the Central and South American family Myrmecophagidae. See also ECHIDNA, PANGOLIN.

an·te·bel·lum /ˌantēˈbeləm/ ▶ adj. [attrib.] occurring or existing before a particular war, esp. the American Civil War. [19th C.: from L., from *ante* 'before' and *bellum* 'war.']

an·te·ced·ent /ˌantəˈsēdnt/ ▶ n. a thing or event that existed before or logically precedes another. ■ (**antecedents**) a person's ancestors or family and social background. ■ Gram. a word, phrase, clause, or sentence to which another word (esp. a following relative pronoun) refers. ■ Logic the statement contained in the "if" clause of a conditional proposition. ■ Math. the first term in a ratio. ▶ adj. preceding in time or order; previous or preexisting. ■ denoting a grammatical antecedent. — **an·te·ced·ence** n. [ME: from OFr. or from L. *antecedent-* 'going before,' from *antecedere*, from *ante* + *cedere* 'go.']

an·te·cham·ber /ˈantēˌCHāmbər/ ▶ n. a small room leading to a main one. [17th C.: from Fr. *antichambre*, from Ital. *anticamera*, from *anti-* 'preceding' + *camera* (see CHAMBER).]

an·te·date /ˈantiˌdāt/ ▶ v. [trans.] precede in time; come before (something) in date. ■ indicate that (a document or event) should be assigned to an earlier date.

an·te·dat·ing /ˈantiˌdātiNG/ ▶ n. an example or instance of (a sense of) a word, phrase, etc., at a date earlier than previously known or recorded.

an·te·di·lu·vi·an /ˌantēdəˈlo͞ovēən/ ▶ adj. [attrib.] of or belonging to the time before the biblical Flood. ■ esp. humorous ridiculously old-fashioned. [17th C.: from ANTE- + L. *diluvium* 'deluge.']

an·te·lope /ˈantlˌōp/ ▶ n. (pl. same or **-lopes**) a swift-running deerlike ruminant of the cattle family with smooth hair and upward-pointing horns, native to Africa and Asia. ■ another term for PRONGHORN. [ME (name of a mythical creature): via OFr., ult. from late Gk. *antholops*.]

an·te·mor·tem /ˌantēˈmôrtəm/ ▶ adj. & adv. before death. [19th C.: L. *ante mortem*, 'before death.']

an·te·na·tal /ˌantēˈnātl/ ▶ adj. [attrib.] before birth; during or relating to pregnancy; prenatal. ▶ n. informal a medical examination during pregnancy. — **an·te·na·tal·ly** adv.

an·ten·na /anˈtenə/ ▶ n. **1** Zool. (pl. **-ten·nae** /-ˈtenē/) either of a pair of long, thin sensory appendages on the heads of insects, crustaceans, and some other arthropods. ■ (**antennae**) fig. the faculty of instinctively detecting and interpreting subtle signs. **2** (pl. **-ten·nas**) a rod, wire, or other device used to transmit or receive radio or television signals. — **an·ten·nal** /-ˈtenl/ adj. (in sense 1) **an·ten·na·ry** /-ˈtenərē/ adj. (in sense 1). [17th C.: from L., alt. of *antemna* 'yard' (of a ship), used in the pl. to translate Gk. *Keraioi* 'horns (of insects).']

an·ten·nule /anˈtenˌyo͞ol/ ▶ n. Zool. a small antenna, esp. either of the first pair of antennae in a crustacean. [19th C.: dimin. of ANTENNA.]

an·te·par·tum /ˌantēˈpärtəm/ ▶ adj. [attrib.] Med. occurring not long before childbirth. [19th C.: from L. *ante partem* 'before birth.']

an·te·pe·nul·ti·mate /ˌantēpəˈnəltəmit/ ▶ adj. [attrib.] last but two in a series; third last.

an·te·ri·or /anˈti(ə)rēər/ ▶ adj. **1** tech., esp. Anat. & Biol. nearer the front, esp. situated in the front of the body, or nearer to the head or forepart. The opposite of POSTERIOR. ■ Bot. (of a part of a flower or leaf) situated further away from the main stem. **2** formal coming before in time; earlier. — **an·te·ri·or·i·ty** /anˌti(ə)rēˈôritē; -ˈär-/ n. **an·te·ri·or·ly** adv. [16th C.: from Fr. *antérieur* or L. *anterior*, compar. of *ante* 'before.']

antero- ▶ comb. form esp. Anat. representing ANTERIOR.

an·te·room /ˈantēˌro͞om; -ˌro͝om/ ▶ n. an antechamber, typically serving as a waiting room.

an·te·vert·ed /ˈantēˌvərtid/ ▶ adj. Anat. & Med. (of an organ, esp. the uterus) inclined forward. [19th C.: from L. *antevertere*, from *ante* 'before' + *vertere* 'to turn.']

ant·he·li·on /antˈhēlēən; anˈTHē-/ ▶ n. (pl. **-li·a** /-lēə/) a luminous halo around a shadow projected by the sun onto a cloud or fog bank. ■ a parhelion seen opposite the sun in the sky. [17th C.: from Gk. *anthēlion*, neut. of *anthēlios* 'opposite to the sun,' from *anth-* (var. of *anti-*) + *hēlios* 'sun.']

ant·hel·min·tic /ˌant-helˈmintik; ˌanTHel-/ Med. ▶ adj. [attrib.] (chiefly of medicines) used to destroy parasitic worms. ▶ n. an anthelmintic medicine. [17th C.: from *anth-* (var. of *anti* 'against') + Gk. *helmins, helminth-* 'worm' + -IC.]

an·them /ˈanTHəm/ ▶ n. **1** a rousing or uplifting song identified with a particular group, body, or cause. ■ (also **national anthem**) a song officially adopted by a country as an expression of national identity. **2** a choral composition based on a biblical passage, for singing by a choir in a church service. [OE *antefn, antifne*, from late L. *antiphona* (see ANTIPHON).]

an·ther /ˈanTHər/ ▶ n. Bot. the part of a stamen that contains the pollen. [18th C.: ult. from Gk. *anthēra* 'flowery,' from *anthos* 'flower.']

an·ther·id·i·um /ˌanTHəˈridēəm/ ▶ n. (pl. **-ther·id·i·a** /-THəˈridēə/) Bot. the male sex organ of algae, mosses, ferns, fungi, and other nonflowering plants. — **an·ther·id·i·al** /-T͟Həˈridēəl/ adj. [19th C.: mod. L., from *anthera* (dimin.).]

an·ther·o·zo·id /ˌanTHərəˈzō-id; ˈanTHərəˌzoid/ ▶ n. Bot. another term for SPERMATOZOID. [19th C.: from ANTHER + ZOOID.]

an·the·sis /anˈTHēsis/ ▶ n. Bot. the flowering period of a plant, from the opening of the flower bud. [19th C.: from Gk. *anthēsis* 'flowering,' from *anthein* 'to blossom.']

ant·hill /ˈantˌhil/ ▶ n. a moundlike nest built by ants or termites.

antho- ▶ comb. form of or relating to flowers. [from Gk. *anthos* 'flower.']

an·tho·cy·a·nin /ˌanTHəˈsīənin/ ▶ n. Chem. a blue, violet, or red flavonoid pigment found in plants. [19th C.: from Ger. *Anthocyan*, from Gk. *anthos* 'flower' + *kuanos* 'blue.']

an·thol·o·gize /anˈTHäləˌjīz/ ▶ v. [trans.] [usu. as adj.] (**anthologized**) include (an author or work) in an anthology: *the most anthologized of today's poets*.

an·thol·o·gy /anˈTHäləjē/ ▶ n. (pl. **-gies**) a published collection of poems or other pieces of writing. ■ a similar collection of songs or musical compositions issued in one album. — **an·thol·o·gist** /-jist/ n. [17th C.: via Fr. or med. L. from Gk. *anthologia*, from *anthos* 'flower' + *-logia* 'collection.']

An·tho·ny /ˈanTHənē/, Susan Brownell (1820–1906), US social activist who cofounded the National Woman Suffrage Association in 1869.

An·tho·ny of Pad·u·a, St. (also **Antony**) (1195–1231), Portuguese Franciscan friar. His devotion to the poor is commemorated by alms known as St. Anthony's bread; he is invoked to find lost articles.

An·tho·ny, St. /ˈanTHənē/ (also **Antony** /ˈantənē/) (*c.*251–356), Egyptian hermit. He founded monasticism.

An·tho·zo·a /ˌanTHəˈzōə/ Zool. a large class of sedentary marine coelenterates that includes the sea anemones and corals. — **an·tho·zo·an** n. & adj. [mod. L. (pl.), from Gk. *anthos* 'flower' + *zōia* 'animals.']

an·thra·cene /ˈanTHrəˌsēn/ ▶ n. Chem. a colorless crystalline aromatic hydrocarbon, $C_{14}H_{10}$, obtained by the distillation of crude oils and used in chemical manufacture. [19th C.: from Gk. *anthrax, anthrak-* 'coal' + -ENE.]

an·thra·cite /ˈanTHrəˌsīt/ ▶ n. coal of a hard variety that contains relatively pure carbon and burns with little flame and smoke. — **an·thra·cit·ic** /ˌanTHrəˈsitik/ adj. [16th C.: from Gk. *anthrakitēs*, from *anthrax, anthrak-* 'coal.']

an·thrac·nose /anˈTHrakˌnōs/ ▶ n. a mainly fungal disease of plants, causing dark lesions. [19th C.: coined in Fr. from Gk. *anthrax, anthrak-* 'coal' + *nosos* 'disease.']

an·thra·qui·none /ˌanTHrəkwiˈnōn; -ˈkwēnōn/ ▶ n. Chem. a yellow crystalline compound, $C_{14}H_8O_2$, obtained by oxidation of anthracene. It is the basis of many natural and synthetic dyes.

an·thrax /ˈanˌTHraks/ ▶ n. a notifiable bacterial disease of sheep and cattle, typically affecting the skin and lungs. It can be transmitted to humans, causing severe skin ulceration or a form of pneumonia (also called WOOL-SORTERS' DISEASE). [ME: L., 'carbuncle,' from Gk. *anthrax, anthrak-* 'coal, carbuncle.']

anthropo- ▶ comb. form human; of a human being. ■ relating to humankind: *anthropology*. [from Gk. *anthrōpos* 'human being.']

an·thro·po·cen·tric /ˌanTHrəpōˈsentrik/ ▶ adj. regarding humankind as the central or most important element of existence, esp. as opposed to God or animals. — **an·thro·po·cen·tri·cal·ly** /-trik(ə)lē/ adv. **an·thro·po·cen·trism** /-ˌtrizəm/ n.

an·thro·po·gen·ic /ˌanTHrəpōˈjenik/ ▶ adj. (chiefly of environmental pollution and pollutants) originating in human activity. — **an·thro·po·gen·i·cal·ly** /-ik(ə)lē/ adv.

an·thro·poid /ˈanTHrəˌpoid/ ▶ adj. resembling a human being in form. ■ Zool. of or relating to the group of higher primates, which includes monkeys, apes, and humans. ■ Zool. (of an ape) belonging to one of the families of great apes. ■ informal, derog. (of a person) apelike in appearance or behavior. ▶ n. Zool. a higher primate (suborder Anthropoidea), esp. an ape or apeman. ■ informal, derog. a person that resembles an ape in appearance or behavior.

an·thro·pol·o·gy /ˌanTHrəˈpäləjē/ ▶ n. the study of humankind, in particular: ■ (also **cultural** or **social anthropology**) **the comparative study of human societies and cultures and their development.** ■ (also **physical anthropology**) the science of human zoology, evolution, and ecology. — **an·thro·po·log·i·cal** /-pəˈläjikəl/ adj. **an·thro·pol·o·gist** /-jist/ n.

an·thro·pom·e·try /ˌanTHrəˈpämitrē/ ▶ n. the scientific study of the measurements and proportions of the human body. — **an·thro·po·met·ric** /-pəˈmetrik/ adj.

an·thro·po·mor·phic /ˌanTHrəpəˈmôrfik/ ▶ adj. relating to or characterized by anthropomorphism. ■ having human characteristics. — **an·thro·po·mor·phi·cal·ly** /-ik(ə)lē/ adv.

an·thro·po·mor·phism /ˌanTHrəpəˈmôrˌfizəm/ ▶ n. the attribution of human characteristics or behavior to a god, animal, or object. — **an·thro·po·mor·phize** /-ˌfīz/ v.

an·thro·po·mor·phous /ˌanTHrəpəˈmôrfəs/ ▶ adj. (of a god, animal, or object) human in form or nature.

an·thro·poph·a·gi /ˌanTHrəˈpäfəjī; -gī/ ▶ plural n. cannibals, esp. in legends or fables. [16th C.: from L., pl. of *anthropophagus*, from Gk. *anthrōpophagos* 'man-eating,' from *anthrōpos* 'human being' + *phagein* 'eat' (see -PHAGOUS).]

an·thro·poph·a·gy /ˌanTHrəˈpäfəjē/ ▶ n. the eating of human flesh by human beings. — **an·thro·poph·a·gous** /-gəs/ adj.

an·thro·pos·o·phy /ˌanTHrəˈpäsəfē/ ▶ n. a formal educational, therapeutic, and creative system established by Rudolf Steiner (1861–1925) seeking to use natural means to optimize physical and mental health.

— **an·thro·po·soph·i·cal** /-pə'säfikəl/ **adj.** [20th C.: from **ANTHROPO-** + Gk. *sophia* 'wisdom.']

an·thu·ri·um /an'THoorēəm/ ▶ **n.** (pl. **-ums**) a tropical American plant (genus *Anthurium*) of the arum family, often cultivated for its ornamental foliage or brightly colored flowering spathes. [mod. L., from Gk. *anthos* 'flower' + *oura* 'tail.']

an·ti /'antī; 'antē/ ▶ **prep.** opposed to; against. ▶ **n.** (pl. **an·tis**) informal a person opposed to a particular policy, activity, or idea.

anti- /'antē; 'antī/ (also **ant-**) ▶ **prefix** opposed to; against: *antiaircraft.* ■ preventing: *antibacterial.* ■ reversing or undoing: *anticoagulant.* ■ the opposite of: *anticlimax.* ■ Physics the opposite state of matter or of a specified particle: *antimatter.* ■ acting as a rival: *antipope.* ■ unlike the conventional form: *anti-hero.* [from Gk. *anti* 'against.']

an·ti·air·craft /,antē'er,kraft; ,antī-/ (also **an·ti-air·craft**) ▶ **adj.** [attrib.] (esp. of a gun or missile) used to attack enemy aircraft.

an·ti·a·li·as·ing /,antē'ālēəsiNG; ,antī-/ ▶ **n.** (in computer graphics) a technique used to add greater realism to a digital image by smoothing jagged edges on curved lines and diagonals.

an·ti·bac·te·ri·al /,antēbak'ti(ə)rēəl; ,antī-/ ▶ **adj.** [attrib.] active against bacteria.

an·ti·bal·lis·tic mis·sile /,antēbə'listik; ,antī-/ (abbr.: **ABM**) ▶ **n.** a missile designed for intercepting and destroying a ballistic missile while in flight.

an·ti·bi·o·sis /,antēbī'ōsis; ,antī-/ ▶ **n.** Biol. an antagonistic association between two organisms (esp. microorganisms), in which one is adversely affected. See also **SYMBIOSIS.** [19th C.: from **ANTI-** + shortened form of **SYMBIOSIS.**]

an·ti·bi·ot·ic /,antēbī'ätik; ,antī-/ ▶ **n.** a medicine (such as penicillin or its derivatives) that inhibits the growth of or destroys microorganisms. ▶ **adj.** relating to, involving, or denoting antibiotics. [19th C.: from **ANTI-** + Gk. *biōtikos* 'fit for life' (from *bios* 'life').]

an·ti·bod·y /'anti,bädē/ ▶ **n.** (pl. **-bod·ies**) a blood protein produced in response to and counteracting a specific antigen.

an·tic /'antik/ ▶ **adj.** literary grotesque or bizarre. [16th C.: from Ital. *antico* 'antique,' used to mean 'grotesque.']

an·ti·choice /,antē'CHois; ,antī-/ ▶ **adj.** opposed to a pregnant woman's choice of a medically induced abortion.

an·ti·cho·lin·er·gic /,antē,kōlə'nərjik; ,antī-/ Med. ▶ **adj.** (chiefly of a drug) inhibiting the physiological action of acetylcholine, esp. as a neurotransmitter. ▶ **n.** an anticholinergic drug.

An·ti·christ /'antē,krīst; 'antī-/ ▶ **n.** (**the An·ti·christ**) a great personal opponent of Christ who will spread evil throughout the world before being conquered at Christ's Second Coming. ■ a person or force seen as opposing Christ or the Christian Church. [OE, ult. from Gk. *antikhristos*, from *anti* 'against' + *Khristos* (see **CHRIST**).]

an·tic·i·pate /an'tisə,pāt/ ▶ **v.** [trans.] **1** regard as probable; expect or predict. ■ guess or be aware of (what will happen) and take action in order to be prepared. ■ look forward to. ■ use or spend in advance. **2** act as a forerunner or precursor of. ■ come or take place before (an event or process expected or scheduled for a later time). ■ react or respond to (someone) too quickly, without giving them a chance to do or say something. ■ pay (a debt) before it is due. — **an·tic·i·pa·tor** /-,pātər/ **n.** [16th C.: from L. *anticipat-* 'acted in advance,' from *anticipare*, based on *ante-* + *capere* 'take.']

an·tic·i·pa·tion /an,tisə'pāSHən/ ▶ **n.** the action of anticipating something; expectation or prediction. ■ Music the introduction in a composition of part of a chord that is about to follow in full.

an·tic·i·pa·to·ry /an'tisəpə,tôrē/ ▶ **adj.** happening, performed, or felt in anticipation of something. ■ Law (of a breach of contract) taking the form of an announcement or indication that a contract will not be honored.

an·ti·cler·i·cal /,antē'klerikəl; ,antī-/ esp. hist. ▶ **adj.** opposed to the power or influence of the clergy, esp. in politics. ▶ **n.** a person holding such views. — **an·ti·cler·i·cal·ism** /-,lizəm/ **n.**

an·ti·cli·max /,antē'klīmaks; ,antī-/ ▶ **n.** a disappointing end to an exciting or impressive series of events. — **an·ti·cli·mac·tic** /-klī'maktik/ **adj.** **an·ti·cli·mac·ti·cal·ly** /-klī'maktik(ə)lē/ **adv.**

an·ti·cline /'antē,klīn; 'antī-/ ▶ **n.** Geol. a ridge or ridge-shaped fold of stratified rock in which the strata slope downward from the crest. Compare with **SYNCLINE.** — **an·ti·cli·nal** /,antē'klīnl; ,antī-/ **adj.** [19th C.: from **ANTI-** + Gk. *klinein* 'lean.']

an·ti·co·ag·u·lant /,antēkō'agyələnt; ,antī-/ ▶ **adj.** having the effect of retarding or inhibiting the coagulation of the blood. ▶ **n.** an anticoagulant substance.

an·ti·con·vul·sant /,antēkən'vəlsənt; ,antī-/ ▶ **adj.** (chiefly of a drug) used to prevent or reduce the severity of epileptic fits or other convulsions. ▶ **n.** an anticonvulsant drug.

an·tics /'antiks/ ▶ **plural n.** foolish, outrageous, or amusing behavior. [16th C.: from **ANTIC.**]

an·ti·cy·clone /,antē'sīklōn; ,antī-/ ▶ **n.** a weather system with high atmospheric pressure at its center, around which air slowly circulates in a clockwise (northern hemisphere) or counterclockwise (southern hemisphere) direction. — **an·ti·cy·clon·ic** /-sī'klänik/ **adj.**

an·ti·de·pres·sant /,antēdə'presnt; ,antī-/ ▶ **adj.** (chiefly of a drug) used to alleviate depression. ▶ **n.** an antidepressant drug.

an·ti·di·ar·rhe·al /,antē,dīə'rēəl; ,antī-/ ▶ **adj.** (of a drug) used to alleviate diarrhea. ▶ **n.** an antidiarrheal drug.

an·ti·di·u·ret·ic hor·mone /,antē,dīə'retik; ,antī-/ (abbr.: **ADH**) ▶ **n.** another term for **VASOPRESSIN.**

an·ti·dote /'anti,dōt/ ▶ **n.** a medicine taken or given to counteract a particular poison. ■ something that counteracts or neutralizes an unpleasant feeling or situation. — **an·ti·dot·al** /,anti'dōtl/ **adj.** [ME: via L., from Gk. *antidoton*, neut. of *antidotos* 'given against,' from *anti-* + *didonai* 'give.']

an·ti·drom·ic /,anti'drämik/ ▶ **adj.** Physiol. (of an impulse) traveling in the opposite direction to that normal in a nerve fiber. The opposite of **ORTHODROMIC.** [20th C.: from **ANTI-** + Gk. *dromos* 'running' + **-IC.**]

an·ti·es·tab·lish·ment /,antē-i'stablishmənt; ,antī-/ ▶ **adj.** against the establishment or established authority.

An·tie·tam /an'tētəm/ historic site in northwestern Maryland, scene of a major Civil War battle in 1862.

an·ti·foul·ing /,antē'fouliNG; ,antī-/ ▶ **n.** treatment of a boat's hull with a paint or similar substance designed to prevent fouling. ■ an antifouling substance.

an·ti·freeze /'anti,frēz/ ▶ **n.** a liquid, typically one based on ethylene glycol, which can be added to water to lower the freezing point, chiefly used in the radiator of a motor vehicle.

an·ti·g ▶ **adj.** short for **ANTIGRAVITY.**

an·ti·gen /'antijən/ ▶ **n.** a toxin or other foreign substance that induces an immune response in the body, esp. the production of antibodies. — **an·ti·gen·ic** /,anti'jenik/ **adj.**

an·ti·glob·al·i·za·tion /,antē,glōbələ'zāSHən; ,antī-/ ▶ **n.** opposition to the agendas and actions of groups perceived to favor globalization, such as the IMF, the World Trade Organization, and the G8 countries.

An·tig·o·ne /an'tigənē/ Gk. Mythol. daughter of Oedipus and Jocasta. She was sentenced to death for defying her uncle Creon, king of Thebes, but she took her own life before the sentence could be carried out, and Creon's son Haemon, who was engaged to her, killed himself over her body.

an·ti·grav·i·ty /,antē'gravitē; ,antī-/ ▶ **n.** Physics a hypothetical force opposing gravity. ▶ **adj.** [attrib.] (chiefly of clothing for a pilot or astronaut) designed to counteract the effects of high acceleration.

An·ti·gua and Bar·bu·da /bär'boodə/ a country in the western West Indies, in the Leeward Islands, that consists of two main islands (Antigua and Barbuda) and Redonda, a smaller island to the southwest of Antigua; pop. 68,320; capital, St. John's (on Antigua). — **An·ti·guan** **adj. & n.**

an·ti·he·ro /'antē,hi(ə)rō; 'antī-/ ▶ **n.** a central character in a story, movie, or drama who lacks conventional heroic attributes.

an·ti·her·o·ine /'antē,herōin; 'antī-/ ▶ **n.** a female antihero.

an·ti·his·ta·mine /,anti'histəmin; -mēn/ ▶ **n.** [usu. as adj.] a drug or other compound that inhibits the physiological effects of histamine, used esp. in the treatment of allergies.

an·ti-in·flam·ma·to·ry ▶ **adj.** (chiefly of a drug) used to reduce inflammation. ▶ **n.** (pl. **-ries**) an anti-inflammatory drug.

an·ti-in·tel·lec·tu·al ▶ **n.** a person who scorns intellectuals and their views and methods. ▶ **adj.** characteristic of a such a person. — **an·ti-in·tel·lec·tu·al·ism** **n.**

an·ti·knock ▶ **n.** a substance (such as tetraethyl lead) added to gasoline to inhibit preignition.

An·ti-Leb·a·non Moun·tains a range of mountains that run along the border between Lebanon and Syria.

An·til·les /an'tilēz/ a group of islands that form the greater part of the West Indies; the **Greater Antilles** are comprised of Cuba, Jamaica, Hispaniola, and Puerto Rico; the **Lesser Antilles**, include the Virgin, Leeward, and Windward islands. See also **NETHERLANDS ANTILLES.**

an·ti·lock /,antē'läk; ,antī-/ (also **an·ti-lock**) ▶ **adj.** [attrib.] (of brakes) designed so as to prevent the wheels from locking and the vehicle from skidding if applied suddenly.

an·ti·log /'antē,lôg; -,läg; 'antī-/ ▶ **n.** short for **ANTILOGARITHM.**

an·ti·log·a·rithm /,antē'lôgə,riTHəm; -'läg-; ,antī-/ ▶ **n.** the number to which a logarithm belongs.

an·ti·ma·cas·sar /,antimə'kasər/ ▶ **n.** esp. hist. a piece of cloth put over the back of a chair to protect it from grease and dirt or as an ornament.

an·ti·mag·net·ic ▶ **adj.** (esp. of watches) resistant to magnetization.

an·ti·mat·ter /'antē,matər; 'antī-/ ▶ **n.** Physics molecules formed by atoms consisting of antiprotons, antineutrons, and positrons.

an·ti·me·tab·o·lite /,antēmi'tabə,līt; ,antī-/ ▶ **n.** Physiol. a substance that interferes with the normal metabolic processes within cells, typically by combining with enzymes.

an·ti·mo·ny /'antə,mōnē/ ▶ **n.** the chemical element of atomic number 51, a brittle silvery-white metalloid. (Symbol: **Sb**) — **an·ti·mo·ni·al** /,antə'mōnēəl/ **adj.** **an·ti·mo·nic** /,antə'mänik/ **adj.** **an·ti·mo·ni·ous** /,antə'mōnēəs/ **adj.** [ME ('stibnite': from med. L. *antimonium.*]

an·ti·na·tion·al ▶ **adj.** opposed to national interests or nationalism.

an·ti·neu·tron /,antē'n(y)ooträn; ,antī-/ ▶ **n.** Physics the antiparticle of a neutron.

an·ti·node /'anti,nōd/ ▶ **n.** Physics the position of maximum displacement in a standing wave system.

an·ti·noise ▶ **adj.** [attrib.] promoting the suppression or reduction of noise. ▶n. sound generated for the purpose of reducing noise by interference.

an·ti·no·mi·an /,anti'nōmēən/ ▶adj. of or relating to the view that Christians are released by grace from the obligation of observing the moral law. ▶n. a person holding this view. — **an·ti·no·mi·an·ism** /-,nizəm/ n. [17th C.: from med. L. *Antinomi*, 16th-cent. sect in Germany, from Gk. *anti-* 'against' + *nomos* 'law.']

an·tin·o·my /an'tinəmē/ ▶n. (pl. **-mies**) a contradiction between two beliefs or conclusions that are in themselves reasonable; a paradox. [16th C.: from L. *antinomia*, from Gk., from *anti* 'against' + *nomos* 'law.']

an·ti·nu·cle·ar ▶adj. [attrib.] opposed to the development of nuclear weapons or nuclear power.

An·ti·och /'äntē,äk/ **1** a city in southern Turkey near the Syrian border, it was the ancient capital of Syria; pop. 123,871. Turkish name **Antakya**. **2** a city in ancient Phrygia. **3** a city in north central California; pop. 62,195.

An·ti·o·chus /an'tīəkəs/ the name of eight Seleucid kings, including: ■ Antiochus III (c.242–187 BC), reigned 223–187 BC; known as **Antiochus the Great**. ■ Antiochus IV (c.215–163 BC), reigned 175–163 BC; son of Antiochus III; known as **Antiochus Epiphanes**. His attempt to Hellenize the Jews resulted in the revival of Jewish nationalism.

an·ti·ox·i·dant /,antē'äksidənt; ,antī-/ ▶n. a substance that inhibits oxidation, esp. one used to counteract the deterioration of stored food products. ■ a substance such as vitamin C or E that removes potentially damaging oxidizing agents in a living organism.

an·ti·par·ti·cle /'antē,pärtikəl; 'antī-/ ▶n. Physics a subatomic particle having the same mass as a given particle but opposite electric or magnetic properties.

an·ti·pas·to /,antē'pästō; ,än-/ ▶n. (pl. **-pas·ti** /-'pästē/) (in Italian cooking) an appetizer typically consisting of olives, anchovies, cheeses, and meats. [Ital., from *anti-* 'before' + *pasto* (from L. *pastus* 'food').]

an·ti·pa·thet·ic /an,tipə'THetik/ ▶adj. showing or feeling a strong aversion. [19th C.: from **antipathy**.]

an·tip·a·thy /an'tipəTHē/ ▶n. (pl. **-thies**) a deep-seated feeling of dislike; aversion. [16th C.: ult. from Gk. *antipatheia*, from *antipathēs* 'opposed in feeling,' from *anti* 'against' + *pathos* 'feeling.']

an·ti·per·son·nel ▶adj. [attrib.] (of weapons, esp. bombs) designed to kill or injure people rather than to damage buildings or equipment.

an·ti·per·spi·rant /,anti'pərspərənt/ ▶n. a substance that is applied to the skin, esp. under the arms, to prevent or reduce perspiration.

an·ti·phon /'antə,fän/ ▶n. (in traditional western Christian liturgy) a short sentence sung or recited before or after a psalm or canticle. ■ a musical setting of such a sentence or sentences. [ME: via eccles. L. from Gk. *antiphōna* 'harmonies,' neut. pl. of *antiphōnos* 'responsive,' from *anti* 'in return' + *phōnē* 'sound.']

an·tiph·o·nal /an'tifənl/ ▶adj. (in traditional western Christian liturgy) (of a short sentence or its musical setting) sung, recited, or played alternately by two or more groups. — **an·tiph·o·nal·ly** adv.

an·tiph·o·ny /an'tifənē/ ▶n. antiphonal singing, playing, or chanting.

an·tip·o·dal /an'tipədl/ ▶adj. relating to or situated on the opposite side of the earth. ■ (**antipodal to**) diametrically opposed to something.

an·ti·pode /'anti,pōd/ ▶n. the direct opposite of something else. [17th C.: back-form. from **antipodes**.]

an·tip·o·des /an'tipədēz/ ▶plural n. (**the An·tip·o·des**) Australia and New Zealand (used by inhabitants of the northern hemisphere). ■ the direct opposite of something. — **an·tip·o·de·an** /an,tipə'dēən/ adj., n. [ME: ult. from Gk. *antipodes* 'having the feet opposite,' from *anti* + *pous, pod-* 'foot.']

an·ti·pope /'anti,pōp/ ▶n. a person established as pope in opposition to one held by others to be canonically chosen. [ME *antipape*, via Fr. from med. L. *antipapa*.]

an·ti·pro·ton /'antē,prōtän; 'antī-/ ▶n. Physics the negatively charged antiparticle of a proton.

an·ti·psy·chot·ic /,antēsī'kätik; ,antī-/ ▶adj. [attrib.] (chiefly of a drug) used to treat psychotic disorders. ▶n. an antipsychotic drug.

an·ti·py·ret·ic /,antē,pī'retik; ,antī-/ ▶adj. (chiefly of a drug) used to prevent or reduce fever. ▶n. an antipyretic drug.

an·ti·quar·i·an /,anti'kwe(ə)rēən/ ▶adj. relating to or dealing in antiques or rare books. ■ valuable because rare or old. ▶n. a person who studies or collects antiques or antiquities. — **an·ti·quar·i·an·ism** /-,nizəm/ n.

an·ti·quark /'antē,kwôrk; -,kwärk; 'antī-/ ▶n. Physics the antiparticle of a quark.

an·ti·quar·y /'anti,kwerē/ ▶n. (pl. **-quar·ies**) another term for **antiquarian**.

an·ti·quat·ed /'anti,kwātid/ ▶adj. old-fashioned or outdated.

an·tique /an'tēk/ ▶n. a collectible object such as a piece of furniture or work of art that has a high value because of its considerable age. ▶adj. **1** (of a collectible object) having a high value because of considerable age. ■ (of a method of finishing a wooden surface) intended to resemble the appearance of antique furniture. **2** belonging to ancient times. ■ old-fashioned or outdated. ■ often humorous showing signs of great age or wear. ▶v. **1** (**-tiques, -tiqued, -ti·quing**) [trans.] [usu. as adj.] (**antiqued**) make (something) resemble an antique by artificial means. **2** (**go antiquing**) shop in stores where antiques are sold. [15th C.: from L. *antiquus, anticus* 'former, ancient,' from *ante* 'before.']

an·tiq·ui·ty /an'tikwitē/ ▶n. (pl. **-ties**) **1** the ancient past, esp. the period before the Middle Ages. ■ [with adj.] a specified historical period during the ancient past. ■ (usu. **antiquities**) an object, building, or work of art from the ancient past. **2** great age.

an·ti·roll bar ▶n. a rubber-mounted bar fitted in the suspension of a vehicle to increase its stability, esp. when cornering.

an·tir·rhi·num /,anti'rīnəm/ ▶n. (pl. **-nums**) a plant (genus *Antirrhinum*) of the figwort family, with showy two-lipped flowers, in particular the snapdragon. [from L., from Gk. *antirrhinon*, from *anti-* + *rhis, rhin-* 'noselike.']

an·ti·scor·bu·tic /,antēskôr'byōōtik; ,antī-/ Med. ▶adj. (chiefly of a drug) having the effect of preventing or curing scurvy. ▶n. an antiscorbutic food or drug.

an·ti-Sem·i·tism ▶n. hostility to or prejudice against Jews. — **an·ti-Sem·ite** n. **an·ti-Se·mit·ic** adj.

an·ti·sense /'antē,sens; 'antī-/ ▶adj. Genet. having a sequence of nucleotides complementary to a coding sequence, which may be either that of the strand of a DNA double helix that undergoes transcription, or that of a messenger RNA molecule.

an·ti·sep·sis /'anti,sepsis/ ▶n. the practice of using antiseptics to eliminate the microorganisms that cause disease. Compare with **asepsis**.

an·ti·sep·tic /,anti'septik/ ▶adj. of, relating to, or denoting substances that prevent the growth of disease-causing microorganisms. ■ (of medical techniques) based on the use of such substances. ■ fig. scrupulously clean or pure, esp. so as to be bland or characterless. ▶n. an antiseptic compound or preparation. — **an·ti·sep·ti·cal·ly** /-ik(ə)lē/ adv.

an·ti·se·rum /'anti,si(ə)rəm/ ▶n. (pl. **-se·ra** /-,si(ə)rə/) a blood serum containing antibodies against specific antigens, injected to treat or protect against specific diseases.

an·ti·so·cial /,antē'sōSHəl; ,antī-/ ▶adj. **1** contrary to the laws and customs of society; devoid of or antagonistic to sociable instincts or practices. **2** not sociable; not wanting the company of others.

an·ti·spas·mod·ic /,antēspaz'mätik; ,antī-/ ▶adj. (chiefly of a drug) used to relieve spasm of involuntary muscle. ▶n. an antispasmodic drug.

an·ti·stat·ic ▶adj. [attrib] preventing the buildup of static electricity or reducing its effects.

an·tis·tro·phe /an'tistrəfē/ ▶n. the second section of an ancient Greek choral ode or of one division of it. Compare with **strophe** and **epode** (sense 2). [16th C.: ult. from Gk. *antistrophē*, from *antistrephein* 'turn against,' from *anti* + *strephein* 'to turn.']

an·ti·tank ▶adj. [attrib.] for use against enemy tanks.

an·ti·ter·ror·ism /,antē'terə,rizəm; ,antī-/ ▶n. the prevention or abatement of terrorism. — **an·ti·ter·ror·ist** n. & adj.

an·tith·e·sis /an'tiTHəsis/ ▶n. (pl. **-ses** /-,sēz/) a person or thing that is the direct opposite of someone or something else. ■ a contrast or opposition between two things. ■ a figure of speech in which an opposition of ideas is expressed by parallelism of words that are the opposites of each other, such as "hatred stirs up strife, but love covers all sins." ■ (in Hegelian philosophy) the negation of the thesis as the second stage in the process of dialectical reasoning. Compare with **synthesis**. [ME: from late L., from Gk. *antitithenai* 'set against,' from *anti* + *tithenai* 'to place.']

an·ti·thet·i·cal /,antə'THetikəl/ ▶adj. **1** directly opposed or contrasted; mutually incompatible. **2** [attrib.] connected with, containing, or using the rhetorical device of antithesis. — **an·ti·thet·ic** adj. **an·ti·thet·i·cal·ly** /-ik(ə)lē/ adv.

an·ti·tox·in /,antē'täksin/ ▶n. Physiol. an antibody that counteracts a toxin. — **an·ti·tox·ic** adj.

an·ti·trades /'anti,trādz/ (also **an·ti·trade winds**) ▶plural n. steady winds that blow in the opposite direction to and overlie the trade winds.

an·ti·trust /,antē'trəst; ,antī-/ ▶adj. [attrib.] of or relating to legislation preventing or controlling trusts or other monopolies, with the intention of promoting competition in business.

an·ti·type /'anti,tīp/ ▶n. **1** a person or thing that represents the opposite of someone or something else. **2** something that is represented by a symbol. — **an·ti·typ·i·cal** /,anti'tipikəl/ adj. [17th C.: ult. from Gk. *antitupos* 'corresponding to,' from *anti* 'against' + *tupos* 'type.']

an·ti·ven·in /,antē'venin; ,antī-/ ▶n. an antiserum containing antibodies against specific poisons, esp. those in the venom of snakes, spiders, and scorpions. Also called **antivenom**. [19th C.: from **anti-** + *ven(om)*.]

an·ti·vi·ral /,antē'vīrəl; ,antī-/ ▶adj. Med. (chiefly of a drug or treatment) effective against viruses.

an·ti·vi·rus /,antē'vīrəs; ,antī-/ ▶adj. [attrib.] Comput. (of software) designed to detect and destroy computer viruses.

ant·ler /'antlər/ ▶n. one of the branched horns on the head of an adult (usually male) deer, which are made of bone and are grown and cast off annually. ■ one of the branches on such a horn. — **ant·lered** adj. [ME: from Anglo-Norman Fr., var. of OFr. *antoillier*.]

Ant·li·a /'antlēə/ Astron. a small and faint southern constellation (the Air Pump), between Hydra and Vela. [L., from Gk.]

ant li·on ▶n. an insect (family Myrmeleontidae, order Neuroptera) that resembles a dragonfly, with predatory larvae that construct conical pits into which insect prey, esp. ants, fall.

An·to·fa·gas·ta /,äntōfə'gästə/ a port in northern Chile, capital of Antofagasta region; pop. 218,750.

An·to·nine /'antə,nīn/ ▶adj. [attrib] of or relating to the Roman emperors Antoninus Pius and Marcus Aurelius or their rules (AD 137–80). ▶plural n. (**the Antonines**) the Antonine emperors.

An·to·ni·nus Pi·us /ˌantəˈnīnəs ˈpīəs/ (86–161), Roman emperor 138–161.

an·to·no·ma·sia /anˌtänəˈmāzh(ē)ə/ ▶ **n.** Rhet. the substitution of an epithet or title for a proper name (e.g., *the Bard* for Shakespeare). ■ the use of a proper name to express a general idea (e.g., *a Scrooge* for a miser). [16th C.: via L. from Gk., from *antonomazein* 'name instead,' from *anti-* + *onoma* 'a name.']

An·to·ny /ˈantənē; ˈanthənē/, Mark (*c.*83–30 BC), Roman general; Latin name *Marcus Antonius*. Following Julius Caesar's assassination in 44 BC, he took charge of the Eastern Empire.

An·to·ny, St. see Anthony, St.

An·to·ny of Pad·u·a, St. see Anthony of Padua, St.

an·to·nym /ˈantəˌnim/ ▶ **n.** Ling. a word opposite in meaning to another (e.g., *bad* and *good*). — **an·ton·y·mous** /anˈtänəməs/ **adj.** [19th C.: from Fr. *antonyme*, from *ant-* (from Greek *anti-* 'against') + Gk. *onuma* 'a name.']

An·trim /ˈantrim/ one of the Six Counties of Northern Ireland, formerly an administrative area. ■ a town in this county; pop. 21,000.

an·trum /ˈantrəm/ ▶ **n.** (pl. **-tra** /-trə/) Anat. a natural chamber or cavity in a bone or other anatomical structure. ■ the part of the stomach just inside the pylorus. — **an·tral** /-trəl/ **adj.** [19th C.: from L., from Gk. *antron* 'cave.']

ant·sy /ˈantsē/ ▶ **adj.** agitated, impatient, or restless. [19th C.: prob. from *have ants in one's pants.*]

Ant·werp /ˈanˌtwərp/ a port in northern Belgium, on the Scheldt River; pop. 467,520. French name Anvers, Flemish name Antwerpen. ■ a province of Belgium of which Antwerp is the capital.

A·nu·bis /əˈno͞obis/ Egyptian Mythol. the god of mummification, protector of tombs, typically represented as having the head of a jackal.

Anubis

An·u·ra /əˈn(y)o͝orə/ Zool. an order of tailless amphibians that comprises the frogs and toads. Also called Salientia or Batrachia. ■ [as pl. n.] (**anura**) amphibians of this order; frogs and toads. — **an·u·ran** **n.** & **adj.** [mod. L., from an-[1] + Gk. *oura* 'tail.']

an·u·ri·a /əˈn(y)o͝orēə/ ▶ **n.** Med. failure of the kidneys to produce urine. — **an·u·ric** /-ik/ **adj.**

a·nus /ˈānəs/ ▶ **n.** Anat. & Zool. the opening at the end of the alimentary canal through which solid waste matter leaves the body. [ME: from L., orig. 'a ring.']

An·vers /änˈver(s)/ French name of Antwerp.

an·vil /ˈanvil/ ▶ **n.** a heavy steel or iron block with a flat top, concave sides, and typically a pointed end, on which metal can be hammered and shaped. ■ the horizontally extended upper part of a cumulonimbus cloud. ■ Anat. another term for incus. [OE *anfilte*, from Gmc. base of on + a verbal stem meaning 'beat.']

anvil

anx·i·e·ty /angˈzī-itē/ ▶ **n.** (pl. **-ties**) a feeling of worry, nervousness, or unease, typically about an imminent event or something with an uncertain outcome. ■ [with infin.] desire to do something, typically accompanied by unease. ■ Psychiatry a nervous disorder characterized by a state of excessive uneasiness and apprehension, typically with compulsive behavior or panic attacks.

anx·i·o·lyt·ic /ˌangzēəˈlitik/ Med. ▶ **adj.** (chiefly of a drug) used to reduce anxiety. ▶ **n.** an anxiolytic drug.

anx·ious /ˈang(k)shəs/ ▶ **adj.** **1** experiencing worry, unease, or nervousness, typically about an imminent event or something with an uncertain outcome. ■ [attrib.] (of a period of time or situation) causing or characterized by worry or nervousness. **2** [usu with infin.] wanting something very much, typically with a feeling of unease. — **anx·ious·ly** **adv.** **anx·ious·ness** **n.** [17th C.: from L. *anxius* (from *angere* 'to choke') + -ous.]

an·y /ˈenē/ ▶ **adj.** & **pron.** **1** [usu. with negative or in questions] used to refer to one or some of a thing or number of things, no matter how much or many: [as adj.] *I don't have any choice* | [as pron.] *you don't know any of my friends* ■ anyone. **2** whichever of a specified class might be chosen: [as adj.] *any fool knows that* | [as pron.] *the illness may be due to any of several causes.* ▶ **adv.** [usu. with negative or in questions] [as submodifier] (used for emphasis) at all; in some degree: *he wasn't any good at basketball.* ■ informal used alone, not qualifying another word: *I didn't hurt you any.*

– PHRASES **any amount of** see amount. **any old** see old. **any time** (also **anytime**) **1** at whatever time. **2** without exception or doubt. **any time** (or **day** or **minute**, etc.) **now** informal very soon. **hardly any** see hardly. [OE *ǣnig* (see one, -y[1]), from Gmc.; akin to Ger. *einig*.]

an·y·bod·y /ˈenēˌbädē; -ˌbədē/ ▶ **pron.** **1** anyone. **2** a person of any importance.

an·y·how /ˈenēˌhou/ ▶ **adv.** **1** another term for anyway. **2** in a careless way: *suitcases flung anyhow.*

an·y·more /ˌenēˈmôr/ (also **any more**) ▶ **adv.** [usu. with negative or in questions] to any further extent; any longer: *she refused to listen anymore.*

an·y·one /ˈenēˌwən/ ▶ **pron.** **1** [usu. with negative or in questions] any person or people: *there wasn't anyone there.* ■ [without negative] used for emphasis: *anyone could do it.* **2** a person of importance or authority: *they are read by anyone who's anyone.*

– PHRASES **anyone's guess** see guess.

an·y·place /ˈenēˌplās/ ▶ **adv.** informal term for anywhere.

an·y·thing /ˈenēˌthing/ ▶ **pron.** [usu. with negative or in questions] used to refer to a thing, no matter what: *nobody was saying anything* | *have you found anything?* ■ [without negative] used for emphasis: *I was ready for anything.*

– PHRASES **anything but** not at all (used for emphasis): *he is anything but racist.* **anything like —** [with negative] at all like— (used for emphasis): *it doesn't taste anything like wine.* **if anything** see if. **like anything** see like[1].

an·y·time /ˈenēˌtīm/ ▶ **adv.** variant of *any time* at any.

An·y·town /ˈenēˌtoun/ ▶ **n.** (also **Anytown U.S.A.**) any real or fictional place regarded as being typical of American small-town appearance or values.

an·y·way /ˈenēˌwā/ ▶ **adv.** **1** used to confirm or support a point or idea just mentioned: *it's too late now anyway.* ■ used in questions to emphasize the speaker's wish to obtain the truth: *"What are you doing here, anyway?"* **2** used in conversations: ■ to change the subject or to resume a subject after interruption: *How she lives with him is beyond me. Anyway, I really like her.* ■ to indicate that the speaker wants to end the conversation: *"Anyway, Dot, I must go."* **3** used to indicate that something happened or will happen in spite of something else: *nobody invited Miss Honey to sit down so she sat down anyway.*

an·y·ways /ˈenēˌwāz/ ▶ **adv.** informal or dialect form of anyway.

an·y·where /ˈenēˌ(h)we(ə)r/ ▶ **adv.** [usu. with negative or in questions] in or to any place: *he couldn't be found anywhere.* ■ [without negative] used for emphasis: *I could go anywhere in the world.* ■ used to indicate a range: *this iron garden seat dates anywhere from 1890 to 1920.* ▶ **pron.** any place: *he doesn't have anywhere to live.*

an·y·wheres /ˈenēˌ(h)we(ə)rz/ ▶ **adv.** & **pron.** informal or dialect form of anywhere.

An·zac /ˈanˌzak/ ▶ **n.** a soldier in the Australian and New Zealand Army Corps (1914–18). ■ dated a person, esp. a member of the armed services, from Australia or New Zealand. [acronym.]

An·zio /ˈäntsēˌō; ˈanzēō/ a seaport in western Italy, south of Rome, site of Allied landing 1944; pop. 36,000.

AOC ▶ **abbr.** *appellation d'origine contrôlée* (see appellation contrôlée).

ao dai /ˈouˌdī; ˈōˌdī/ ▶ **n.** (pl. **ao dais**) a Vietnamese woman's long-sleeved tunic with ankle-length panels at front and back, worn over trousers.

A-OK (also **A-o·kay**) informal ▶ **adj.** in good order or condition; all right. ▶ **adv.** in a good manner or way; all right. [1960s: from *all systems OK.*]

AOR ▶ **n.** [usu. as adj.] a type of popular music in which a hard rock background is combined with softer or more melodic elements. [1970s: from *album-oriented rock* or *adult-oriented rock.*]

a·o·rist /ˈāərist/ Gram. ▶ **n.** (esp. in Greek) an unqualified past tense of a verb without reference to duration or completion of the action. ▶ **adj.** relating to or denoting this tense. — **a·o·ris·tic** /ˌāəˈristik/ **adj.** [16th C.: from Gk. *aoristos* 'indefinite,' from *a-* + *horizein* 'define, limit.']

a·or·ta /āˈôrtə/ ▶ **n.** the main artery of the body, supplying oxygenated blood to the circulatory system. — **a·or·tic** /-tik/ **adj.** [16th C.: from Gk. *aortē*, from *aeirein* 'raise.']

Ao·te·a·ro·a /ˌoutäəˈrōə/ the Maori name for New Zealand.

a·ou·dad /ˈä-o͞oˌdad/ ▶ **n.** another term for Barbary sheep. [19th C.: from Fr., from Berber *udād.*]

à ou·trance /ˌä o͞oˈträns/ ▶ **adv.** literary to the death or the very end. [17th C.: Fr., lit. 'to the utmost.']

AP ▶ **abbr.** ■ Associated Press. ■ advanced placement.

ap-[1] ▶ **prefix** var. of ad- assimilated before *p* (as in *apposite, apprehend*).

ap-[2] ▶ **prefix** var. of apo- before *h* (as in *aphelion*).

a·pace /əˈpās/ ▶ **adv.** literary swiftly; quickly. [ME: from OFr. *a pas* 'at pace.']

A·pach·e /əˈpachē/ ▶ **n.** **1** (pl. same or **A·pach·es**) a member of a North American Indian people living chiefly in New Mexico and Arizona. **2** the Athabaskan language of this people. ▶ **adj.** of or relating to the Apache or their language. [from Mex. Sp., prob. from Zuni *Apachu*, lit. 'enemy.']

a·pach·e /əˈpash; äˈpäsh/ ▶ **n.** (pl. **a·paches** pronunc. same) a violent street ruffian, originally in Paris.

A·pa·la·chi·co·la Riv·er /ˌapəˌlachiˈkōlə/ see Chattahoochee River.

a·part /əˈpärt/ ▶ **adv.** **1** (of two or more people or things) separated by a distance; at a specified distance from each other in time or space: *his parents live apart.* **2** to or on one side; at a distance from the main body: *Isabel stepped away from Joanna and stood apart.* ■ used after a noun to indicate that someone or something has distinctive qualities that mark them out from other people or things: *wrestlers were a breed apart.* ■ used after a noun to indicate that someone or something has been dealt with sufficiently or is being excluded from what follows: *Alaska apart, America's energy business concentrates on producing gas.* **3** so as to be shattered; into pieces: *the car was blown apart.*

– PHRASES **apart from 1** except for. **2** in addition to; as well as. **tell apart** distinguish or separate one from another. — **a·part·ness** **n.** [ME: from OFr., from L. *a parte* 'at the side.']

a·part·heid /ə'pärt,(h)āt; -,(h)īt/ ▶ **n.** hist. (in South Africa) a policy or system of segregation or discrimination on grounds of race. ■ segregation in other contexts. [1940s: Afrik., lit. 'separateness,' from Du. *apart* 'separate' + *-heid* -HOOD.]

a·part·ment /ə'pärtmənt/ (abbr.: **apt.**) ▶ **n.** a suite of rooms forming one residence, typically in a building containing a number of these. ■ a large building containing such suites; an apartment building. ■ (**apartments**) a suite of rooms in a very large or grand house set aside for the private use of a monarch or noble. [17th C.: from Fr. *appartement*, from Ital. *appartamento*, from *appartare* 'to separate,' from *a parte* 'apart.']

a·part·ment build·ing (also **apartment block** or **apartment house**) ▶ **n.** a large building divided into separate apartments.

ap·a·thet·ic /,apə'THetik/ ▶ **adj.** showing or feeling no interest, enthusiasm, or concern. — **ap·a·thet·i·cal·ly** /-ik(ə)lē/ **adv.**

ap·a·thy /'apəTHē/ ▶ **n.** lack of interest, enthusiasm, or concern. [17th C.: ult. from Gk. *apatheia*, from *apathēs* 'without feeling,' from *a-* + *pathos* 'suffering.']

ap·a·tite /'apə,tīt/ ▶ **n.** a widely occurring pale green to purple mineral, consisting of calcium phosphate with some fluorine, chlorine, and other elements. [19th C.: coined in Ger. from Gk. *apatē* 'deceit' (from the mineral's diverse forms).]

a·pa·to·saur /'apətō,sôr/ (also **a·pa·to·sau·rus** /,apətō'sôrəs/) ▶ **n.** a huge herbivorous dinosaur (genus *Apatosaurus*, infraorder Sauropoda, order Saurischia) of the late Jurassic period, with a long neck and tail. Also called, esp. formerly, BRONTOSAURUS. See illustration at DINOSAUR. — **a·pa·to·sau·ri·an** **adj.** [mod. L., from Gk. *apatē* 'deceit' + *sauros* 'lizard.']

APB ▶ **abbr.** all-points bulletin.

APC ▶ **abbr.** ■ armored personnel carrier. ■ aspirin, phenacetin, and caffeine, used in some analgesics.

ape /āp/ ▶ **n.** a large primate (families Pongidae and Hylobatidae) that lacks a tail, including the gorilla, chimpanzees, orangutan, and gibbons. See also GREAT APE, GIBBON. ■ used in names of macaque monkeys with short tails, e.g., **Barbary ape**. ■ (in general use) any monkey. ■ an unintelligent or clumsy person. ▶ **v.** [trans.] imitate the behavior or manner of (someone or something), esp. in an absurd or unthinking way.
– PHRASES **go ape** informal express wild excitement or anger.

A·pel·doorn /'apəl,dôrn/ a town in the east central Netherlands; pop. 148,200.

ape·man /'āp,man/ ▶ **n.** (pl. **-men**) an extinct apelike primate believed to be related or ancestral to present-day humans.

Ap·en·nines /'apə,nīnz/ a mountain range in Italy that extends for 880 miles (1,400 km) from the northwest to the southern tip of the country.

a·per·çu /,äper'so͞o/ ▶ **n.** (pl. **-çus** pronunc. same) a comment or brief reference that makes an illuminating or entertaining point. [19th C.: from Fr., past part. of *apercevoir* 'perceive.']

a·per·i·ent /ə'pi(ə)rēənt/ Med. ▶ **adj.** (chiefly of a drug) used to relieve constipation. ▶ **n.** an aperient drug. [17th C.: from L. *aperient-* 'opening,' from *aperire*.]

a·pe·ri·od·ic /,āpi(ə)rē'ädik/ ▶ **adj.** tech. not periodic; irregular. ■ Physics denoting a potentially oscillating or vibrating system that is damped to prevent oscillation or vibration. — **a·pe·ri·o·dic·i·ty** /ā,pi(ə)rēə'disitē/ **n.**

a·pe·ri·tif /ä,peri'tēf; -ə,per-/ ▶ **n.** an alcoholic drink taken before a meal to stimulate the appetite. [19th C.: from Fr. *apéritif*, from med. L. *aperitivus*, based on L. *aperire* 'to open.']

ap·er·ture /'apər,CHər/ ▶ **n.** esp. tech. an opening, hole, or gap. ■ a space through which light passes in an optical or photographic instrument, esp. the variable opening by which light enters a camera. [ME: from L. *apertura*, from *apert-* 'opened,' from *aperire* 'to open.']

ap·er·y /'āpərē/ ▶ **n.** archaic the act of imitating the behavior or manner of someone, esp. in an absurd way.

a·pet·al·ous /ā'petl-əs/ ▶ **adj.** Bot. (of a flower) having no petals.

a·pex /'āpeks/ ▶ **n.** (pl. **a·pex·es** or **a·pi·ces** /'āpə,sēz; 'apə-/) the top or highest part of something, esp. one forming a point: *the apex of the roof* | fig. *the apex of his career*. ▶ **v.** [intrans.] reach a high point or climax. [17th C.: from L., 'peak, tip.']

Ap·gar score /'ap,gär/ ▶ **n.** Med. a measure of the physical condition of a newborn infant. It is obtained by adding points (2, 1, or 0) for heart rate, respiratory effort, muscle tone, response to stimulation, and skin coloration; ten represents the best possible condition. [1960s: Virginia *Apgar* (1909–74), US anesthesiologist.]

a·phaer·e·sis /ə'ferəsis/ ▶ **n.** **1** Ling. the loss of a sound or sounds at the beginning of a word, e.g., in the derivation of *adder* from *nadder*. **2** (usu. **a·pher·e·sis**) Med. the removal of blood plasma from the body by the withdrawal of blood, its separation into plasma and cells, and the reintroduction of the cells, used esp. to remove antibodies in treating autoimmune diseases. [16th C.: via late L. from Gk. *aphairesis*, from *aphairein* 'take away,' from *apo* + *hairein* 'take.']

a·pha·sia /ə'fāZHə/ ▶ **n.** Med. loss of ability to understand or express speech, caused by brain damage. — **a·pha·sic** /-zik/ **adj.** & **n.** [19th C.: from Gk., from *aphatos* 'speechless,' from *a-* + *phanai* 'speak.']

a·phe·li·on /ə'fēlyən; ə'fēlēən/ ▶ **n.** (pl. **a·phe·li·a** /ə'fēlyə; ə'fēlēə/ or **a·phe·li·ons**) Astron. the point in the orbit of a planet, asteroid, or comet at which it is furthest from the sun. The opposite of PERIHELION. [17th C.: alt. of mod. L. *aphelium*, from Gk. *aph' hēlion* 'from the sun.']

aph·e·sis /'afisis/ ▶ **n.** Ling. the loss of an unstressed vowel at the beginning of a word (e.g., of *a* from *around* to form *round*). — **a·phet·ic** /ə'fetik/ **adj.** **a·phet·i·cal·ly** /ə'fetik(ə)lē/ **adv.** [19th C.: from Gk., lit. 'letting go,' from *apo* 'from' + *hienai* 'let go, send.']

a·phid /'āfid; 'af-/ ▶ **n.** a minute bug (superfamily Aphidoidea, suborder Homoptera) that feeds by sucking sap from plants. It reproduces rapidly, often producing live young without mating, and may live in large colonies that cause extensive damage to crops. [19th C.: back-form. from *aphides*, pl. of APHIS.]

aphid

a·phis /'āfis; 'af-/ ▶ **n.** (pl. **a·phi·des** /'āfi,dēz; 'afi-/) an aphid, esp. one of the genus *Aphis*. [18th C.: mod. L., from Gk., perh. misreading of *koris* 'bug.']

a·pho·ni·a /ā'fōnēə/ (also **aph·o·ny** /'afənē/) ▶ **n.** Med. loss of ability to speak through disease of or damage to the larynx or mouth. [17th C.: mod. L., from Gk. *aphōnia*, from *aphōnos* 'voiceless,' from *a-* + *phōnē* 'voice.']

aph·o·rism /'afə,rizəm/ ▶ **n.** a pithy observation that contains a general truth. ■ a concise statement of a scientific principle, typically by an ancient classical author. — **aph·o·rist** **n.** **aph·o·ris·tic** /,afə'ristik/ **adj.** **aph·o·ris·ti·cal·ly** /,afə'ristik(ə)lē/ **adv.** **aph·o·rize** /-,rīz/ **v.** [16th C.: ult. from Gk. *aphorismos* 'definition,' from *aphorizein* 'define.']

aph·ro·dis·i·ac /,afrə'dizē,ak; -'dēzē-; -'dēZHē-/ ▶ **n.** a food, drink, or drug that stimulates sexual desire. ■ a thing that causes excitement. [18th C.: from APHRODITE.]

Aph·ro·di·te /,afrə'dītē/ Gk. Mythol. the goddess of beauty, fertility, and sexual love. Roman equivalent VENUS. [Gk., lit. 'foam-born,' from *aphros* 'foam.']

aph·tha /'afTHə/ ▶ **n.** (pl. **-thae** /-THē/) Med. a small ulcer occurring in groups in the mouth or on the tongue. ■ a condition in which such ulcers occur. — **aph·thous** /-THəs/ **adj.** [17th C.: via L. from Gk., akin to *haptein* 'set on fire.']

API ▶ **abbr.** ■ American Petroleum Institute.

A·pi·a /ə'pēə; ä'pēə/ the capital of Samoa; pop. 32,200.

a·pi·an /'āpēən/ ▶ **adj.** [attrib.] of or relating to bees. [19th C.: from L. *apianus*, from *apis* 'bee.']

a·pi·ar·y /'āpē,erē/ ▶ **n.** (pl. **-ar·ies**) a place where bees are kept; a collection of beehives. — **a·pi·ar·i·an** /,āpē'e(ə)rēən/ **adj.** **a·pi·a·rist** /-ə,rist/ **n.**

a·pi·cal /'āpikəl; 'ap-/ ▶ **adj.** tech. of, relating to, or denoting an apex. ■ Phonet. (of a consonant) formed with the tip of the tongue.

a·pi·ces /'āpə,sēz; 'apə-/ plural form of APEX.

a·pi·cul·ture /'āpi,kəlCHər/ ▶ **n.** technical term for BEEKEEPING. — **a·pi·cul·tur·al** /,āpi'kəlCHərəl/ **adj.** **a·pi·cul·tur·ist** /,āpi'kəlCHərist/ **n.**

a·piece /ə'pēs/ ▶ **adv.** (used after a noun or an amount) to, for, or by each one of a group.

A·pis /'āpis/ Egyptian Mythol. a god depicted as a bull, symbolizing fertility and strength in war.

ap·ish /'āpiSH/ ▶ **adj.** of or resembling an ape in appearance. ■ likened to an ape in being foolish or silly. — **ap·ish·ly** **adv.** **ap·ish·ness** **n.**

ap·la·nat /'aplə,nat/ ▶ **n.** Physics a reflecting or refracting surface that is free from spherical aberration. — **ap·la·nat·ic** /,aplə'natik/ **adj.** [19th C.: coined in Ger. from Gk. *aplanētos* 'free from error,' from *a-* 'not' + *planan* 'wander.']

a·pla·sia /ə'plāZHə/ ▶ **n.** Med. the failure of an organ or tissue to develop or to function normally. — **a·plas·tic** /ā'plastik/ **adj.** [19th C.: from A-[1] + Gk. *plasis* 'formation.']

a·plas·tic a·ne·mi·a /ā'plastik ə'nēmēə/ ▶ **n.** Med. deficiency of all types of blood cells caused by failure of bone marrow development.

a·plen·ty /ə'plentē/ ▶ **adj.** [postpositive] in abundance.

a·plomb /ə'pläm; ə'pləm/ ▶ **n.** self-confidence or assurance, esp. when in a demanding situation. [18th C.: from Fr., from *à plomb* 'according to a plummet.']

ap·ne·a /'apnēə; ap'nēə/ (Brit. **ap·noe·a**) ▶ **n.** Med. temporary cessation of breathing, esp. during sleep. [18th C.: mod. L., from Gk. *apnoia*, from *apnous* 'breathless.']

APO ▶ **abbr.** ■ (US) Army Post Office. ■ (US) Air Force Post Office.

apo- ▶ **prefix** **1** away from: *apocrypha* | *apostrophe*. ■ separate: *apocarpous*. **2** Astron. denoting the furthest point in the orbit of a body in relation to the primary: *apolune*. Compare with PERI-. [from Gk. *apo* 'from, away, quite, un-.']

Apoc. ▶ **abbr.** ■ Apocalypse. ■ Apocrypha. ■ Apocryphal.

a·poc·a·lypse /ə'päkə,lips/ ▶ **n.** (often **the Apocalypse**) the complete final destruction of the world, esp. as described in the biblical book of Revelation. ■ an event involving destruction or damage on an awesome or catastrophic scale. ■ (**the Apocalypse**) (esp. in the Vulgate Bible) the book of Revelation. [OE, ult. from Gk. *apokalupsis*, from *apokaluptein* 'uncover, reveal,' from *apo-* + *kaluptein* 'to cover.']

a·poc·a·lyp·tic /ə,päkə'liptik/ ▶ **adj.** describing or prophesying the complete destruction of the world. ■ resembling the end of the world; momentous or catastrophic. ■ of or resembling the biblical Apocalypse. — **a·poc·a·lyp·ti·cal·ly** /-ik(ə)lē/ **adv.** [17th C.: from Gk. *apokaluptikos*, from *apokaluptein*.]

ap·o·car·pous /,apə'kärpəs/ ▶ **adj.** Bot. (of a flower, fruit, or ovary) having distinct carpels that are not joined together. The opposite of SYNCARPOUS. [19th C.: from APO- + Gk. *karpos* 'fruit' + -OUS.]

ap·o·chro·mat /,apə'krōmat/ ▶ **n.** Physics a lens that reduces spherical and chromatic aberration. — **ap•o•chro•mat•ic** /-krō'matik/ **adj.** [20th C.: from APO- + CHROMATIC.]

a•poc•o•pe /ə'päkəpē/ ▶ **n.** Ling. the loss of a sound or sounds at the end of a word, e.g., in the derivation of *curio* from *curiosity*. [16th C.: from late L., from Gk. *apokoptein* 'cut off,' from *apo-* + *koptein* 'to cut.']

ap•o•crine /'apəkrin; -ˌkrīn; -ˌkrēn/ ▶ **adj.** Physiol. relating to or denoting multicellular glands that release some of their cytoplasm in their secretions, esp. the sweat glands associated with hair follicles in the armpits and pubic regions. Compare with ECCRINE. [20th C.: from APO- + Gk. *krinein* 'to separate.']

A•poc•ry•pha /ə'päkrəfə/ ▶ **plural n.** [treated as sing. or pl.] biblical or related writings not forming part of the accepted canon of Scripture. ■ (**apocrypha**) writings or reports not considered genuine. [ME: from eccles. L. *apocrypha (scripta)* 'hidden (writings),' from Gk. *apokruphos*, from *apokruptein* 'hide away.']

a•poc•ry•phal /ə'päkrəfəl/ ▶ **adj.** (of a story or statement) of doubtful authenticity, although widely circulated as being true. ■ (also **Apocryphal**) of or belonging to the Apocrypha.

ap•o•dal /ā'pōdl/ ▶ **adj.** Zool. without feet or having undeveloped feet. ■ (of fish) without ventral fins. [19th C.: from Gk. *apous, apod-* 'footless' (from *a-* + *pous, pod-* 'foot') + -OUS.]

ap•o•dic•tic /ˌapə'diktik/ (also **ap•o•deic•tic** /-'dīktik/) ▶ **adj.** formal clearly established or beyond dispute. [17th C.: via L. from Gk. *apodeiktikos*, from *apodeiknunai* 'show off.']

a•pod•o•sis /ə'pädəsis/ ▶ **n.** (pl. **-ses** /-ˌsēz/) Gram. the main (consequent) clause of a conditional sentence (e.g., *I would agree* in *if you asked me I would agree*). Often contrasted with PROTASIS. [17th C.: via late L. from Gk., from *apodidonai* 'give back.']

ap•o•gee /'apəjē/ ▶ **n.** Astron. the point in the orbit of the moon or a satellite at which it is furthest from the earth. The opposite of PERIGEE. ■ fig. the highest point in the development of something; the climax or culmination of something. [16th C.: from Fr. *apogée* or mod. L. *apogaeum*, from Gk. *apogaion (diastēma)* '(distance) away from earth,' from *apo* + *gaia, gē* 'earth.']

a•po•lit•i•cal /ˌāpə'litikəl/ ▶ **adj.** not interested or involved in politics: *a former apolitical housewife.*

A•pol•lo /ə'pälō/ **1** Gk. Mythol. a god, son of Zeus and Leto and brother of Artemis. He is associated with music, poetic inspiration, archery, prophecy, medicine, pastoral life, and in later poetry with the sun. **2** the American space program for landing astronauts on the moon.

Ap•ol•lo•ni•an /ˌapə'lōnēən/ ▶ **adj. 1** Gk. Mythol. of or relating to the god Apollo. **2** of or relating to the rational, ordered, and self-disciplined aspects of human nature. Compare with DIONYSIAN.

Ap•ol•lo•ni•us[1] /ˌapə'lōnēəs/ (*c.*260–190 BC), Greek mathematician; known as **Apollonius of Perga**. He was the first to use the terms *ellipse, parabola*, and *hyperbola* for types of curves.

Ap•ol•lo•ni•us[2] (3rd century BC), Greek poet; known as **Apollonius of Rhodes**. He wrote *Argonautica*.

A•pol•lyon /ə'pälyən/ a name for the Devil (Rev. 9:11). [from late L. (Vulgate), from Gk. *Apolluōn* 'destroyer' (translating ABADDON), from *apollunai*, from *apo-* 'quite' + *ollunai* 'destroy.']

a•pol•o•get•ic /əˌpälə'jetik/ ▶ **adj.** regretfully acknowledging or excusing an offense or failure. ■ of the nature of a formal defense or justification of something such as a theory or religious doctrine. ▶ **n.** a reasoned argument or writing in justification of something, typically a theory or religious doctrine. — **a•pol•o•get•i•cal•ly** /-ik(ə)lē/ **adv.** [ME: from Fr. *apologétique* or late L. *apologeticus*, from Gk. *apologētikos*, from *apologeisthei* 'speak in one's own defense,' from *apologia* (see APOLOGY).]

a•pol•o•get•ics /əˌpälə'jetiks/ ▶ **plural n.** [treated as sing. or pl.] reasoned arguments or writings in justification of something, typically a theory or religious doctrine. [18th C.: from APOLOGETIC.]

ap•o•lo•gi•a /ˌapə'lōj(ē)ə/ ▶ **n.** a formal written defense of one's opinions or conduct. [18th C.: from L. (see APOLOGY).]

a•pol•o•gist /ə'päləjist/ ▶ **n.** a person who offers an argument in defense of something controversial.

a•pol•o•gize /ə'päləˌjīz/ ▶ **v.** [intrans.] express regret for something that one has done wrong.

ap•o•logue /'apəˌlôg; -ˌläg/ ▶ **n.** a moral fable, esp. one with animals as characters. [16th C.: from Fr., via L. from Gk. *apologos* 'story.']

a•pol•o•gy /ə'päləjē/ ▶ **n.** (pl. **-gies**) **1** a regretful acknowledgment of an offense or failure: *my apologies for the delay.* ■ a formal, public statement of regret, such as one issued by a newspaper, government, or other organization. ■ (**apologies**) used to express formally one's regret at being unable to attend a meeting or social function. **2** (**an apology for**) a very poor or inadequate example of: *we were shown into an apology for a bedroom.* **3** a reasoned argument or writing in justification of something, typically a theory or religious doctrine: *a specious apology for capitalism.* [16th C.: from Fr. *apologie*, or via late L. from Gk. *apologia* 'speech in defense,' from *apo* 'away' + *-logia* (see -LOGY).]

ap•o•lune /'apəˌlo͞on/ ▶ **n.** the point at which a spacecraft in lunar orbit is furthest from the moon. The opposite of PERILUNE. [1960s: from APO- + L. *luna* 'moon.']

ap•o•mict /'apəˌmikt/ ▶ **n.** Bot. a plant that reproduces by apomixis.

ap•o•mix•is /ˌapə'miksis/ ▶ **n.** Bot. asexual reproduction in plants, in particular agamospermy. Often contrasted with AMPHIMIXIS. — **ap•o•mic•tic** /-'miktik/ **adj.** [20th C.: from APO- + Gk. *mixis* 'mingling.']

ap•o•mor•phine /ˌapə'môrfēn; -fin/ ▶ **n.** Med. a white crystalline compound, $C_{17}H_{17}NO_2$. A morphine derivative, it is used as an emetic and in the treatment of Parkinson's disease.

ap•o•neu•ro•sis /ˌapən(y)o͝o'rōsis/ ▶ **n.** (pl. **-ses** /-ˌsēz/) Anat. a sheet of pearly-white fibrous tissue that takes the place of a tendon in sheetlike muscles having a wide area of attachment. — **ap•o•neu•rot•ic** /-'rätik/ **adj.** [17th C.: mod. L., from Gk. *aponeurōsis*, from *apo* 'off' + *neuron* 'sinew' + -OSIS.]

ap•o•phthegm ▶ **n.** British spelling of APOTHEGM.

a•poph•yl•lite /ə'päfəˌlīt; ˌapə'filīt/ ▶ **n.** a mineral occurring typically as white glassy prisms, usually as a secondary mineral in volcanic rocks. It is a hydrated silicate and fluoride of calcium and potassium. [19th C.: from APO- + Gk. *phullon* 'leaf.']

a•poph•y•sis /ə'päfəsis/ ▶ **n.** (pl. **-ses** /-ˌsēz/) Zool. & Anat. a natural protuberance from a bone, or inside the shell or exoskeleton of a sea urchin or insect, for the attachment of muscles. ■ Bot. a swelling at the base of the sporangium in some mosses. ■ Geol. a small offshoot extending from an igneous intrusion into the surrounding rock. — **a•po•phys•e•al** /əˌpäfə'sēəl/ **adj.** [16th C.: mod. L., from Gk. *apophusis* 'offshoot,' from *apo-* 'from' + *phusis* 'growth.']

ap•o•plec•tic /ˌapə'plektik/ ▶ **adj.** informal overcome with anger; extremely indignant. ■ dated relating to or denoting apoplexy (stroke): *an apoplectic attack.* — **ap•o•plec•ti•cal•ly** /-ik(ə)lē/ **adv.** [17th C.: ult. from Gk. *apoplēktikos*, from *apoplēssein* (see APOPLEXY).]

ap•o•plex•y /'apəˌpleksē/ ▶ **n.** (pl. **-plex•ies**) dated incapacity resulting from a cerebral hemorrhage or stroke. ■ informal incapacity or speechlessness caused by extreme anger. [ME: ult. from Gk. *apoplēxia*, from *apoplēssein* 'disable by a stroke.']

a•po•ri•a /ə'pôrēə/ ▶ **n.** an irresolvable internal contradiction in a text, argument, or theory: *the celebrated aporia whereby a Cretan declares all Cretans to be liars.* ■ Rhet. the expression of doubt. [16th C.: via late L. from Gk., from *aporos* 'impassable,' from *a-* + *poros* 'passage.']

ap•o•se•mat•ic /ˌapəsi'matik/ ▶ **adj.** Zool. (of coloration or markings) serving to warn or repel predators. ■ (of an animal) having such coloration or markings. — **ap•o•se•ma•tism** /ˌapə'sēməˌtizəm/ **n.**

ap•o•si•o•pe•sis /ˌapəˌsīə'pēsis/ ▶ **n.** (pl. **-ses** /-sēz/) Rhet. the device of suddenly breaking off in speech. — **ap•o•si•o•pet•ic** /-'petik/ **adj.** [16th C.: via L. from Gk. *aposiōpēsis*, from *aposiōpan* 'be silent.']

a•pos•ta•sy /ə'pästəsē/ ▶ **n.** the abandonment or renunciation of a religious or political belief. [ME: from eccles. L. *apostasia*, ult. from Gk. *apostasis* 'defection.']

a•pos•tate /ə'pästāt; -tit/ ▶ **n.** a person who renounces a religious or political belief or principle. ▶ **adj.** abandoning such a belief or principle. — **ap•o•stat•i•cal** /ˌapə'statikəl/ **adj.** [ME: ult. from Gk. *apostatēs* 'apostate, runaway slave.']

a•pos•ta•tize /ə'pästəˌtīz/ ▶ **v.** [intrans.] renounce a religious or political belief or principle.

a pos•te•ri•o•ri /'ā päˌsti(ə)rē'ôrē; -'ôrī/ ▶ **adj.** relating to or denoting reasoning or knowledge that proceeds from observations or experiences to the deduction of probable causes. Compare with A PRIORI. ■ [sentence adverb] (loosely) of the nature of an afterthought or subsequent rationalization. ▶ **adv.** in a way based on reasoning from known facts or past events rather than by making assumptions. ■ (loosely) with hindsight; as an afterthought. [17th C.: L., 'from what comes after.']

a•pos•tle /ə'päsəl/ ▶ **n.** (often **Apostle**) each of the twelve chief disciples of Jesus Christ. ■ any important early Christian teacher, esp. St. Paul. ■ (**Apostle of**) the first successful Christian missionary in a country or to a people: *Kiril and Metodije, the Apostles of the Slavs.* ■ a vigorous and pioneering advocate or supporter of a particular policy, idea, or cause. ■ a messenger or representative. ■ one of the twelve administrative officers of the Mormon church. — **a•pos•tle•ship n.** [OE *apostol*, ult. from Gk. *apostolos* 'messenger,' from *apostellein* 'send forth.']

A•pos•tles' Creed a statement of Christian belief used in the Western Church, dating from the 4th century and traditionally ascribed to the twelve Apostles.

a•pos•to•late /ə'pästəˌlāt; -lit/ ▶ **n.** (chiefly in Roman Catholic contexts) the position or authority of an Apostle or a religious leader. ■ a group of Apostles or religious leaders. ■ religious or evangelistic activity. [ME: from eccles. L. *apostolatus*, from *apostulus*.]

ap•os•tol•ic /ˌapə'stälik/ ▶ **adj.** Christian Church of or relating to the Apostles. ■ of or relating to the pope, esp. when he is regarded as the successor to St. Peter. [ME: ult. from Gk. *apostolikos*.]

Ap•os•tol•ic Fa•thers ▶ **plural n.** the Christian leaders immediately succeeding the Apostles.

ap•os•tol•ic suc•ces•sion ▶ **n.** (in Christian thought) the uninterrupted transmission of spiritual authority from the Apostles through successive popes and bishops, taught by the Roman Catholic Church.

a•pos•tro•phe[1] /ə'pästrəfē/ ▶ **n.** a punctuation mark (') used to indicate either possession (e.g., *Harry's book; boys' coats*) or the omission of letters or numbers (e.g., *can't; he's; class of '99*). [16th C.: ult. from Gk. *apostrophos* 'accent of elision,' from *apostrephein* 'turn away,' from *apo* + *strephein* 'to turn.']

a•pos•tro•phe[2] ▶ **n.** Rhet. an exclamatory passage in a speech or poem addressed to a person (typically one who is dead or absent) or thing (typically one that is personified). [16th C.: via L. from Gk. *apostrophē* 'turning away,' from *apostrephein*.]

a·pos·tro·phize /ə'pästrə,fīz/ ▶ **v.** [trans.] **1** Rhet. address an exclamatory passage in a speech or poem to (someone or something). **2** punctuate (a word) with an apostrophe.

a·poth·e·car·ies' meas·ure /ə'päTHi,kerēz/ (also **apothecaries' weight**) ▶ **n.** hist. systems of units formerly used in pharmacy for liquid volume (or weight).

a·poth·e·car·y /ə'päTHi,kerē/ ▶ **n.** (pl. **-car·ies**) archaic a person who prepared and sold medicines and drugs. [ME: via OFr. from late L. *apothecarius*, from L. *apotheca*, from Gk. *apothēkē* 'storehouse.']

ap·o·thegm /'apə,THem/ (Brit. **ap·oph·thegm** /'apə,THem/) ▶ **n.** a concise saying or maxim; an aphorism. — **ap·o·theg·mat·ic** /,apəTHeg'matik/ **adj.** [16th C.: from Fr. *apophthegme* or mod. L. *apothegma*, from Gk., from *apophthengesthai* 'speak out.']

ap·o·them /'apə,THem/ ▶ **n.** Geom. a line from the center of a regular polygon at right angles to any of its sides. [19th C.: from Gk. *apotithenai* 'put aside,' from *apo* + *tithenai* 'to place.']

a·poth·e·o·sis /ə,päTHē'ōsis; ,apə'THēəsis/ ▶ **n.** (pl. **-ses** /-,sēz/) [usu. in sing.] the highest point in the development of something; culmination or climax. ■ the elevation of someone to divine status; deification. [16th C.: ult. from Gk. *apotheōsis*, from *apotheoun* 'make a god of,' from *apo* 'from' + *theos* 'god.']

a·poth·e·o·size /ə'päTHēə,sīz; ,apə'THēə-/ ▶ **v.** [trans.] elevate to, or as if to, the rank of a god; idolize.

ap·o·tro·pa·ic /,apətrə'pā-ik/ ▶ **adj.** supposedly having the power to avert evil influences or bad luck. — **ap·o·tro·pa·i·cal·ly** /-ik(ə)lē/ **adv.** [19th C.: from Gk. *apotropaios* 'averting evil,' from *apotrepein* 'turn away.']

app /ap/ ▶ **n.** Comput. short for APPLICATION (sense 5).

Ap·pa·la·chi·a /,apə'lāCH(ē)ə; -SH(ē)ə; -laCH-/ a term for areas in the Appalachian Mountains of the eastern US. — **Ap·pa·la·chi·an adj.**

Ap·pa·la·chi·an dul·ci·mer ▶ **n.** see DULCIMER.

Ap·pa·la·chi·an Moun·tains (also **the Ap·pa·la·chi·ans**) a mountain system in eastern North America that stretches from Quebec to Alabama; highest peak, Mt. Mitchell, 6,684 feet (2,037 m).

Ap·pa·la·chi·an Trail an approximately 2,000-mile (3,200-km) footpath through the Appalachian Mountains from central Maine to northern Georgia.

ap·pall /ə'pôl/ ▶ **v.** (**-palled, -pall·ing**) [trans.] (usu. **be appalled**) greatly dismay or horrify: *bankers are **appalled at** the economic incompetence of some officials.* [ME: from OFr. *apalir* 'grow pale,' from *a-* 'to' + *palir* 'to pale.']

ap·pall·ing /ə'pôliNG/ ▶ **adj.** informal awful; terrible. — **ap·pall·ing·ly adv.**

Ap·pa·loo·sa /,apə'lōōsə/ ▶ **n.** a horse of a North American breed having dark spots on a light background. [1920s: from *Opelousas* in Louisiana, or *Palouse*, river in Idaho.]

ap·pa·nage /'apənij/ (also **ap·a·nage**) ▶ **n.** archaic a gift of land, an official position, or money given to the younger children of kings and princes to provide for their maintenance. ■ a necessary accompaniment. [17th C.: from Fr., based on med. L. *appanare* 'equip' from *ad-* 'to' + *panis* 'bread.']

ap·pa·rat /'äpə,rät; ,apə-/ ▶ **n.** esp. hist. the administrative system of a communist party, typically in a communist country. [1940s: Russ., from Ger., lit. 'apparatus.']

ap·pa·rat·chik /,äpə'räCHik/ ▶ **n.** (pl. **-chiks** or **-chi·ki** /-CHi,kē/) derog. humorous an official in a large organization, typically a political one. ■ esp. hist. a member of a party apparat. [1940s: from Russ., from *apparat*.]

ap·pa·rat·us /,apə'ratəs; -'rātəs/ ▶ **n.** (pl. **-us·es**) **1** the equipment needed for a particular activity or purpose. ■ the organs used to perform a particular bodily function. **2** a complex structure within an organization or system. **3** (also **critical apparatus** or **apparatus criticus**) a collection of notes, variant readings, and other matter accompanying a printed text. [17th C.: from L., from *apparare* 'make ready for,' from *ad-* + *parare* 'make ready.']

ap·par·el /ə'parəl/ ▶ **n.** formal clothing. ▶ **v.** (**-eled, -el·ing**; Brit. **-elled, -el·ling**) [trans.] archaic clothe (someone). [ME: from OFr. *apareillier* 'to clothe, prepare,' based on L. *ad-* 'to' + *par* 'equal.']

ap·par·ent /ə'parənt; ə'pe(ə)r-/ ▶ **adj.** clearly visible or understood; obvious. ■ seeming real or true, but not necessarily so. [ME: ult. from L. *apparent-* 'appearing,' from *apparere* (see APPEAR).]

ap·par·ent ho·ri·zon ▶ **n.** see HORIZON (sense 1).

ap·par·ent·ly /ə'parəntlē; ə'pe(ə)r-/ ▶ **adv.** [sentence adverb] as far as one knows or can see: *the child nodded, apparently content with the promise.* ■ used by speakers or writers to avoid committing themselves to the truth of what they are saying: *foreign ministers met but apparently failed to make progress.*

ap·par·ent mag·ni·tude ▶ **n.** Astron. the magnitude of a celestial object as it is actually measured from the earth. Compare with ABSOLUTE MAGNITUDE.

ap·par·ent so·lar time ▶ **n.** Astron. time as calculated by the motion of the apparent (true) sun. The time indicated by a sundial corresponds to apparent solar time. Compare with MEAN SOLAR TIME.

ap·par·ent time ▶ **n.** another term for MEAN SOLAR TIME.

ap·pa·ri·tion /,apə'riSHən/ ▶ **n.** a ghost or ghostlike image of a person. ■ the appearance of something remarkable or unexpected, typically an image of this type. — **ap·pa·ri·tion·al** /-'riSHənl/ **adj.** [ME: from L. *apparitio(n-)* 'attendance,' from *apparere* (see APPEAR).]

ap·peal /ə'pēl/ ▶ **v.** [intrans.] **1** make a serious or urgent request, typically to the public. **2** Law apply to a higher court for a reversal of the decision of a lower court: *he would **appeal against** the conviction* | [trans.] *they can appeal the decision.* ■ (**appeal to**) address oneself to (a principle or quality in someone) in anticipation of a favorable response. **3** be attractive or interesting: *the range of topics will **appeal to** youngsters.* ▶ **n.** **1** a serious or urgent request, typically one made to the public. ■ an attempt to obtain financial support. ■ entreaty. **2** Law an application to a higher court for a decision to be reversed: *the right of appeal.* ■ an address to a principle or quality in anticipation of a favorable response. **3** the quality of being attractive or interesting. — **ap·peal·er n.** [ME: from OFr. *apel* (n.), *apeler* (v.), from L. *appellare* 'to address,' based on *ad-* 'to' + *pellere* 'to drive.']

ap·peal·ing /ə'pēliNG/ ▶ **adj.** **1** attractive or interesting. **2** (of an expression or tone of voice) showing that one wants help or sympathy: *an appealing look.* — **ap·peal·ing·ly adv.**

ap·peals court ▶ **n.** a court that hears appeals from a lower court.

ap·pear /ə'pi(ə)r/ ▶ **v.** [intrans.] **1** come into sight; become visible or noticeable, typically without visible agent or apparent cause: *smoke appeared on the horizon.* ■ come into existence or use: *the major life forms appeared on earth.* ■ (of a book) be published. ■ feature or be shown: *the symbol **appears in** many paintings of the period.* ■ perform publicly in a movie, play, etc.: *he **appeared on** Broadway.* ■ (of an accused person, witness, or lawyer) make an official appearance in a court of law. ■ informal arrive at a place. **2** seem; give the impression of being. [ME: from OFr. *apareir*, from L. *apparere*, from *ad-* 'toward' + *parere* 'come into view.']

ap·pear·ance /ə'pi(ə)rəns/ ▶ **n.** **1** the way that someone or something looks. ■ an impression given by someone or something, although this may be misleading: *she read it with every appearance of interest.* **2** an act of performing or participating in a public event. **3** [usu. in sing.] an act of becoming visible or noticeable; an arrival: *his sudden appearance startled her.* ■ a process of coming into existence or use.
– PHRASES **keep up appearances** maintain an impression of wealth or well-being, typically to hide the true situation. **make** (or **put in**) **an appearance** attend an event briefly, typically out of courtesy. **to** (or **by**) **all appearances** as far as can be seen: *to all appearances, it had been a normal day.*

ap·pease /ə'pēz/ ▶ **v.** [trans.] **1** pacify or placate (someone) by acceding to their demands. **2** relieve or satisfy (a demand or a feeling): *we give to charity because it appeases our guilt.* — **ap·pease·ment n. ap·peas·er n.** [ME: from OFr. *apaisier*, from *a-* 'to') + *pais* 'peace.']

ap·pel·lant /ə'pelənt/ ▶ **n.** Law a person who applies to a higher court for a reversal of the decision of a lower court. [ME: from Fr. *apelant*, lit. 'appealing,' from the v. *apeler* (see APPEAL).]

ap·pel·late /ə'pelit/ ▶ **adj.** [attrib.] Law (typically of a court) concerned with or dealing with applications for decisions to be reversed. [ME (orig. in the sense 'appealed against, accused'): from L. **appellatus** 'appealed against,' from the v. **appellare** (see APPEAL). The current sense dates from the mid 18th C.]

ap·pel·la·tion /,apə'lāSHən/ ▶ **n.** formal a name or title. ■ the action of giving a name to a person or thing.

ap·pel·la·tion con·trô·lée /äpelä'syôN ,kôNtrô'lā/ (also **ap·pel·la·tion d'ori·gi·ne con·trô·lée** /dôrē'ZHēn/) ▶ **n.** a description awarded to French wine guaranteeing that it was produced in the region specified, using vines and methods that satisfy the regulating body. [20th C.: Fr., lit. 'controlled appellation.']

ap·pel·la·tive /ə'pelətiv/ ▶ **adj.** formal relating to or denoting the giving of a name. ▶ **n.** Gram. a common noun, such as "doctor," "mother," or "sir," used as a vocative. [ME: from late L. **appellativus**, from *appellat-* 'addressed,' from the v. *appellare* (see APPEAL).]

ap·pel·lee /,apə'lē/ ▶ **n.** Law the respondent in a case appealed to a higher court. [16th C.: from Fr. *appelé*, past part. of *appeler* (see APPEAL).]

ap·pend /ə'pend/ ▶ **v.** [trans.] add (something) as an attachment or supplement. [ME: from L. *appendere* 'hang on,' from *ad-* + *pendere* 'hang.']

ap·pend·age /ə'pendij/ ▶ **n.** (often with negative or pejorative connotations) a thing that is added or attached to something larger or more important. ■ Biol. a projecting part of an organism, with a distinct appearance or function.

ap·pend·ant /ə'pendənt/ formal archaic ▶ **adj.** attached or added, typically in a subordinate capacity. ▶ **n.** a subordinate person or thing.

ap·pen·dec·to·my /,apən'dektəmē/ (Brit. also **ap·pen·di·cec·to·my** /ə,pendə'sektəmē/) ▶ **n.** (pl. **-mies**) a surgical operation to remove the appendix.

ap·pen·di·ci·tis /ə,pendə'sītis/ ▶ **n.** a serious medical condition in which the appendix becomes inflamed and painful.

ap·pen·dic·u·lar /,apən'dikyələr/ ▶ **adj.** tech. relating to or denoting an appendage or appendages. ■ Anat. of or relating to a limb or limbs. [17th C.: from L. *appendicula* dimin. of *appendix*.]

ap·pen·dix /ə'pendiks/ ▶ **n.** (pl. **-di·ces** /-di,sēz/; **-dix·es**) **1** Anat. a tube-shaped sac attached to and opening into the lower end of the large intestine in humans and some other mammals. Also called VERMIFORM APPENDIX. **2** a section or table of additional matter at the end of a book or document. [16th C.: from L., from *appendere* (see APPEND).]

ap·per·cep·tion /,apər'sepSHən/ ▶ **n.** Psychol., dated the mental process by which a person makes sense of an idea by assimilating it to the body of ideas he or she already possesses. ■ fully conscious perception. — **ap·per·cep·tive** /-tiv/ **adj.** [18th C.: from Fr. *aperception* or mod. L. *aperceptio(n-)*, from L. *ad-* 'to' + *percipere* 'perceive.']

ap·per·tain /,apər'tān/ ▶ **v.** [intrans.] (**appertain to**) relate to; concern.

ap·pe·stat /ˈapəˌstat/ ▶**n.** Physiol. the region of the hypothalamus of the brain that is believed to control a person's appetite for food. [1950s: from APPETITE.]

ap·pe·ten·cy /ˈapitənsē/ ▶**n.** (pl. **-cies**) archaic a longing or desire. ■ a natural tendency or affinity. [17th C.: from L. *appetentia*, from *appetere* (see APPETITE).]

ap·pe·tite /ˈapiˌtīt/ ▶**n.** [usu. in sing.] a natural desire to satisfy a bodily need, esp. for food. ■ a strong desire or liking for something. [ME: ult. from L. *appetitus* 'desire for,' from *appetere* 'seek after,' from *ad-* + *petere* 'seek.']

ap·pe·ti·tive /ˈapiˌtītiv/ ▶**adj.** characterized by a natural desire to satisfy bodily needs. — **ap·pe·ti·tive·ness** **n.** **ap·pe·ti·tive·ly** **adv.**

ap·pe·tiz·er /ˈapiˌtīzər/ ▶**n.** a small dish of food or a drink taken before a meal to stimulate one's appetite.

ap·pe·tiz·ing /ˈapiˌtīzing/ (also **ap·pe·tis·ing**) ▶**adj.** stimulating one's appetite. — **ap·pe·tiz·ing·ly** **adv.**

Ap·pi·an Way /ˈapēən/ an ancient Roman road, named after Appius Claudius Caecus, who built the section to Capua in 312 BC; it was later extended to Brindisi. Latin name VIA APPIA.

ap·plaud /əˈplôd/ ▶**v.** [intrans.] show approval or praise by clapping: *the crowd whistled and applauded* | [trans.] *his speech was loudly applauded.* ■ [trans.] show strong approval of (a person or action); praise: *Jill applauded the decision.* [15th C.: from L. *applaudere*, from *ad-* 'to' + *plaudere* 'to clap,' reinforced by Fr. *applaudir*.]

ap·plause /əˈplôz/ ▶**n.** approval or praise expressed by clapping: *they gave him a round of applause.* [ME: from med. L. *applausus*, from *applaudere*.]

ap·ple /ˈapəl/ ▶**n.** **1** the round fruit of a tree of the rose family, which typically has thin red or green skin and crisp flesh. ■ [with adj.] an unrelated fruit that resembles this in some way. See also CUSTARD APPLE, THORN APPLE. **2** (also **apple tree**) the tree (genus *Malus*) bearing such fruit. **3** (**the Apple**) short for the BIG APPLE.

– PHRASES **the apple never falls far from the tree** proverb family characteristics are usually inherited. **the apple of one's eye** a person of whom one is extremely fond and proud. **apples and oranges** (of two people or things) irreconcilably or fundamentally different. [OE *æppel*, from Gmc.; akin to Ger. *Apfel*.]

ap·ple but·ter ▶**n.** a paste of spiced stewed apple used as a spread or condiment, typically made with cider.

ap·ple-cheeked ▶**adj.** (of a person) having round rosy cheeks.

ap·ple green ▶**n.** a bright yellowish green.

ap·ple·jack /ˈapəlˌjak/ ▶**n.** an alcoholic drink distilled from fermented cider.

ap·ple pie ▶**n.** [in sing.] used to represent a cherished ideal of comfort and familiarity.

– PHRASES **as American as apple pie** typically American in character.

ap·ple-pie or·der ▶**n.** perfect order or neatness.

ap·ple pol·ish·er ▶**n.** informal a person who behaves obsequiously to someone important. — **ap·ple-pol·ish·ing** **n.**

ap·ple·sauce /ˈapəlˌsôs/ ▶**n.** **1** a purée of stewed apples, typically sweetened. **2** informal nonsense.

Ap·ple·seed /ˈapəlˌsēd/, Johnny (1774–1845), US folk hero; born *John Chapman*. He traveled throughout Ohio and Indiana planting apple orchards.

ap·plet /ˈaplit/ ▶**n.** Comput. a very small application, esp. a utility program performing one or a few simple functions. [1990s: blend of APPLICATION and -LET.]

Ap·ple·ton[1] /ˈapəltən/ a city in east central Wisconsin; pop. 70,087.

Ap·ple·ton[2], Sir Edward Victor (1892–1965), English physicist. He discovered ionized gases (the Appleton layer) in the atmosphere. Nobel Prize for Physics (1947).

ap·pli·ance /əˈplīəns/ ▶**n.** **1** a device designed to perform a specific task, typically a domestic one. ■ an apparatus fitted by a surgeon or a dentist for corrective or therapeutic purpose. **2** Brit the action or process of bringing something into operation: *the appliance of science could increase crop yields.*

ap·pli·ca·ble /ˈaplikəbəl; əˈplik-/ ▶**adj.** relevant or appropriate. — **ap·pli·ca·bil·i·ty** /ˌaplikəˈbilitē/ **n.** **ap·pli·ca·bly** /-blē/ **adv.** [16th C.: ult. from med. L. *applicabilis*, from *applicare* (see APPLY).]

ap·pli·cant /ˈaplikənt/ ▶**n.** a person who makes a formal application for something, typically a job. [19th C.: from APPLICATION.]

ap·pli·ca·tion /ˌapliˈkāsHən/ ▶**n.** **1** a formal request to an authority for something. ■ the action or process of making such a request. **2** the action of putting something into operation. ■ [often with negative] practical use or relevance. **3** the action of putting something on a surface. ■ a medicinal substance put on the skin. **4** sustained effort; hard work. **5** Comput. a program or piece of software designed and written to fulfill a particular purpose of the user. — **ap·pli·ca·tion·al** /-sHənl/ **adj.** [ME: ult. from L. *applicatio(n-)*, from *applicare* (see APPLY).]

ap·pli·ca·tion pro·gram ▶**n.** another term for APPLICATION (sense 5).

ap·pli·ca·tive /ˈapliˌkātiv; əˈplikə-/ ▶**adj.** relating to or involving the application of a subject or idea; practical.

ap·pli·ca·tor /ˈapliˌkātər/ ▶**n.** a device used for inserting something or for applying a substance to a surface. ■ a person who applies a substance.

ap·plied /əˈplīd/ ▶**adj.** [attrib.] (of a subject or type of study) put to practical use as opposed to being theoretical: *applied chemistry.* Compare with PURE.

ap·plied math·e·mat·ics see MATHEMATICS.

ap·pli·qué /ˌapliˈkā/ ▶**n.** ornamental needlework in which pieces of fabric are sewn or stuck onto a large piece of fabric to form pictures or patterns. ▶**v.** (**-qués, -quéd, -qué·ing**) [trans.] (usu. **be appliquéd**) decorate (a piece of fabric) in such a way: *the coat is **appliquéd with** exotic-looking cloth.* ■ sew or stick (pieces of fabric) onto a large piece of fabric to form pictures or patterns. [18th C.: from Fr., past part. of *appliquer* 'apply,' from L. *applicare* (see APPLY).]

ap·ply /əˈplī/ ▶**v.** (**-plies, -plied**) **1** [intrans.] make a formal application or request: *you need to **apply to** the local authorities **for** a grant.* ■ put oneself forward formally as a candidate for a job: *she had **applied for** the position.* **2** [intrans.] be applicable or relevant: *normal rules apply.* **3** [trans.] put or spread (something) on a surface: *the sealer can be **applied to** new wood.* ■ administer: *smooth over with a cloth, applying even pressure.* **4** (**apply oneself**) give one's full attention to a task; work hard. **5** bring or put into operation or practical use: *the oil industry has failed to apply appropriate standards of care.* [ME: from OFr. *aplier*, from L. *applicare* 'fold, fasten to,' from *ad-* + *plicare* 'to fold.']

ap·pog·gia·tu·ra /əˌpäjəˈto͝orə/ ▶**n.** (pl. **-tu·ras** or **-tu·re** /-ˈto͝orā/) Music a grace note performed before a note of the melody and falling on the beat. [Ital., from *appoggiare* 'lean upon, rest.']

ap·point /əˈpoint/ ▶**v.** [trans.] **1** assign a job or role to (someone): *she has been **appointed to** the board.* **2** determine or decide on (a time or a place): *they appointed a day in May for the meeting.* **3** Law decide the disposal of (property of which one is not the owner) under powers granted by the owner. — **ap·point·ee** /əˌpoinˈtē/ **n.** **ap·point·er** **n.**

ap·point·ed /əˈpointid/ ▶**adj.** **1** (of a time or place) decided on beforehand; designated. **2** (of a building or room) equipped or furnished in a specified way or to a specified standard.

ap·poin·tive /əˈpointiv/ ▶**adj.** (of a job) relating to or filled by appointment rather than election.

ap·point·ment /əˈpointmənt/ ▶**n.** **1** an arrangement to meet someone at a particular time and place. **2** an act of appointing; assigning a job or position to someone. ■ a job or position. ■ a person appointed to a job or position. **3** (**appointments**) furniture or fittings.

Ap·po·mat·tox /ˌapəˈmatəks/ a town in central Virginia, site of the former village of Appomattox Court House, where Robert E. Lee's surrender of his Confederate forces in April 1865 ended the Civil War.

ap·por·tion /əˈpôrsHən/ ▶**v.** [trans.] divide and allocate: *voting power will be apportioned according to contribution.* ■ assign: *they did not apportion blame to anyone.* [16th C.: from OFr. *apportionner* or med. L. *apportionare*, from *ad-* 'to' + *portionare* 'divide into portions.']

ap·por·tion·ment /əˈpôrsHənmənt/ ▶**n.** the action or result of apportioning something. ■ the determination of the proportional number of members each US state sends to the House of Representatives, based on population figures.

ap·pose /əˈpōz/ ▶**v.** [trans.] tech. place (something) in proximity to or juxtaposition with something else.

ap·po·site /ˈapəzit/ ▶**adj.** apt in the circumstances or in relation to something. — **ap·po·site·ly** **adv.** **ap·po·site·ness** **n.** [16th C.: from L. *appositus*, past part. of *apponere* 'apply,' from *ad-* 'toward' + *ponere* 'put.']

ap·po·si·tion /ˌapəˈzisHən/ ▶**n.** **1** esp. tech. the positioning of things or the condition of being side by side or close together. **2** Gram. a relationship between two or more words or phrases in which the two units are grammatically parallel and have the same referent (e.g., *my friend Sue*).

ap·po·si·tion·al /ˌapəˈzisHənl/ Gram. ▶**adj.** of or relating to apposition.

ap·pos·i·tive /əˈpäzitiv/ ▶**adj.** & **n.** Gram. another term for APPOSITIONAL.

ap·prais·al /əˈprāzəl/ ▶**n.** an act of assessing something or someone. ■ an expert estimate of the value of something.

ap·praise /əˈprāz/ ▶**v.** assess the value or quality of. ■ (of an official or expert) set a price on; value. — **ap·prais·er** **n.** **ap·prais·ing·ly** **adv.** [ME: alt. of APPRIZE.]

ap·pre·ci·a·ble /əˈprēsH(ē)əbəl/ ▶**adj.** large or important enough to be noticed. — **ap·pre·ci·a·bly** /-blē/ **adv.**

ap·pre·ci·ate /əˈprēsHēˌāt/ ▶**v.** [trans.] **1** recognize the full worth of. ■ be grateful for (something). **2** understand (a situation) fully; recognize the full implications of. **3** [intrans.] rise in value or price: *they expected the house to appreciate in value.* — **ap·pre·cia·tive** /-sH(ē)ətiv/ **adj.** (in sense 1). **ap·pre·cia·tive·ly** /-sH(ē)ətivlē/ **adv.** (in sense 1). **ap·pre·ci·a·tor** /-ˌātər/ **n.** [16th C.: from late L. *appretiat-* from v. *appretiare*, from *ad-* 'to' + *pretium* 'price.']

ap·pre·ci·a·tion /əˌprēsHēˈāsHən/ ▶**n.** **1** the recognition and enjoyment of the good qualities of someone or something. ■ gratitude for something. ■ a piece of writing in which the qualities of a person or the person's work are discussed and assessed. ■ sensitive understanding of the aesthetic value of something. **2** a full understanding of a situation. **3** increase in monetary value: *the appreciation of the franc against the dollar.*

ap·pre·hend /ˌapriˈhend/ ▶**v.** [trans.] **1** arrest (someone) for a crime. **2** understand or perceive. ■ archaic anticipate (something) with uneasiness or fear. [ME: ult. from L. *apprehendere*, from *ad-* 'toward' + *prehendere* 'lay hold of.']

ap·pre·hen·si·ble /ˌapriˈhensəbəl/ ▶**adj.** archaic or literary capable of being understood or perceived.

ap·pre·hen·sion /ˌapriˈhenshən/ ▶ n. 1 anxiety or fear that something bad or unpleasant will happen. 2 understanding; grasp. 3 the action of arresting someone. [ME: from late L. *apprehensio(n-)*, from *apprehendere*.]

ap·pre·hen·sive /ˌapriˈhensiv/ ▶ adj. 1 anxious or fearful that something bad or unpleasant will happen. 2 archaic or literary of or relating to perception or understanding. — **ap·pre·hen·sive·ly** adv. **ap·pre·hen·sive·ness** n.

ap·pren·tice /əˈprentis/ ▶ n. a person who is learning a trade from a skilled employer, having agreed to work for a fixed period at low wages. ■ [usu. as adj.] a beginner at something. ▶ v. [trans.] (usu. **be apprenticed**) employ (someone) as an apprentice. ■ [intrans.] serve as an apprentice. — **ap·pren·tice·ship** /-ˌship/ n. [ME: from OFr. *aprentis*, from *apprendre* 'learn,' from L. *apprehendere* 'apprehend.']

ap·press /əˈpres/ ▶ v. [trans.] (usu. **be appressed**) tech. press (something) close to something else.

ap·prise /əˈprīz/ ▶ v. [trans.] inform or tell (someone). [17th C.: from Fr. *appris, apprise*, past part. of *apprendre* 'learn, teach,' from L. *apprehendere* (see APPREHEND).]

ap·prize /əˈprīz/ ▶ v. [trans.] archaic put a price upon; appraise: *the sheriff was to apprize the value of the lands.* ■ value highly; esteem. [ME: from OFr. *aprisier*, from *a-* 'to') + *prisier* 'to price, prize,' from *pris* (see PRICE).]

ap·proach /əˈprōch/ ▶ v. [trans.] 1 come near or nearer to (someone or something) in distance: *the train approached the main line* | [intrans.] *she heard him approach.* ■ come near or nearer to (a future time or event): *he was approaching retirement.* ■ [intrans.] (of a future time) come nearer: *the time is approaching when you will be destroyed.* ■ come close to (a number, level, or standard) in quality or quantity: *the population will approach 12 million by the end of the decade.* ■ (of an aircraft) descend toward and prepare to land on (an airfield, runway, etc.). 2 speak to (someone) for the first time about something, typically with a proposal or request. 3 start to deal with (something) in a certain way. ▶ n. 1 a way of dealing with something: *we need a whole new approach to the job.* 2 an act of speaking to someone for the first time about something, typically a proposal or request. ■ (**approaches**) dated behavior intended to propose personal or sexual relations with someone. 3 [in sing.] the action of coming near or nearer to someone or something in distance or time. ■ (**approach to**) an approximation to something: *the past is impossible to recall with any approach to accuracy.* ■ the part of an aircraft's flight in which it descends gradually toward an airfield or runway for landing. 4 (usu. **approaches**) a road, sea passage, or other way leading to a place: *the eastern* **approaches** *to the town.* [ME: from OFr. *aprochier, aprocher*, from eccles. L. *appropiare* 'draw near,' from *ad-* + *propius* (compar. of *prope* 'near').]

ap·proach·a·ble /əˈprōchəbəl/ ▶ adj. 1 friendly and easy to talk to. 2 (of a place) able to be reached from a particular direction or by a particular means. — **ap·proach·a·bil·i·ty** /əˌprōchəˈbilitē/ n.

ap·proach shot ▶ n. Golf a stroke that sends the ball from the fairway onto or nearer the green.

ap·pro·bate /ˈaprəˌbāt/ ▶ v. [trans.] rare approve formally; sanction: *a letter approbating the affair.* [ME: from L. *approbat-* 'approved,' from v. *approbare*, from *ad-* 'to' + *probare* 'to try' (from *probus* 'good').]

ap·pro·ba·tion /ˌaprəˈbāshən/ ▶ n. formal approval or praise: *the opera met with high approbation.* — **ap·pro·ba·tive** /ˈaprəˌbātiv; əˈprōbətiv/ adj. **ap·pro·ba·to·ry** /əˈprōbəˌtôrē/ adj.

ap·pro·pri·ate ▶ adj. /əˈprōprē-it/ suitable or proper in the circumstances. ▶ v. /-ˌāt/ [trans.] 1 take (something) for one's own use, typically without the owner's permission. 2 devote (money or assets) to a special purpose: *appropriating funds for legal expenses.* — **ap·pro·pri·ate·ly** /-itlē/ adv. **ap·pro·pri·ate·ness** /-itnis/ n. **ap·pro·pri·a·tor** /-ˌātər/ n. [ME: from late L. *appropriatus*, past part. of *appropriare* 'make one's own,' from *ad-* 'to' + *proprius* 'own.']

ap·pro·pri·a·tion /əˌprōprēˈāshən/ ▶ n. 1 the action of taking something for one's own use, typically without the owner's permission. ■ often derog. the artistic practice or technique of reworking images from well-known paintings, photographs, etc., in one's own work. 2 a sum of money or total of assets devoted to a special purpose.

ap·prov·al /əˈpro͞ovəl/ ▶ n. 1 the action of officially agreeing to something or accepting something as satisfactory. ■ the belief that someone or something is good or acceptable. 2 (usu. **approvals**) Philately stamps sent by request to a collector or potential customer.
– PHRASES **on approval** (of goods) supplied on condition that they may be returned if not satisfactory.

ap·prove /əˈpro͞ov/ ▶ v. [trans.] 1 officially agree to or accept as satisfactory: *the budget was approved by Congress* | [as adj.] (**approved**) *an approved profit-sharing plan.* ■ [intrans.] believe that someone or something is good or acceptable: *I don't* **approve of** *the way she pampers my father and brothers.* 2 archaic prove; show: *he* **approved himself** *ripe for military command.* — **ap·prov·ing·ly** adv. [ME: from OFr. *aprover*, from L. *approbare* (see APPROBATE).]

approx. ▶ abbr. approximate(ly).

ap·prox·i·mate ▶ adj. /əˈpräksəmit/ close to the actual, but not completely accurate or exact. ▶ v. /-ˌmāt/ [intrans.] come close or be similar to something in quality, nature, or quantity: *a leasing agreement approximating to ownership* | [trans.] *reality can be approximated by computational techniques.* ■ [trans.] estimate or calculate (a quantity) fairly accurately: *I had to approximate the weight of my horse.* — **ap·prox·i·mate·ly** adv. **ap·prox·i·ma·tion** /əˌpräksəˈmāshən/ n. [ME: from late L. *approximatus*, past part. of *approximare*, from *ad-* 'to' + *proximus* 'very near.']

ap·prox·i·ma·tive /əˈpräksəˌmātiv/ ▶ adj. (of a method, description, etc.) giving only an approximation to something: *a crudely approximative outline.*

ap·pur·te·nance /əˈpərtn-əns/ ▶ n. (usu. **appurtenances**) an accessory or other item associated with a particular activity or style of living. [ME: from OFr. *apertenance*, based on late L. *appertinere* (see APPERTAIN).]

ap·pur·te·nant /əˈpərtn-ənt/ ▶ adj. belonging; pertinent.

APR ▶ abbr. annual (or annualized) percentage rate, typically of interest on loans or credit.

Apr. ▶ abbr. April.

a·prax·i·a /āˈpraksēə/ ▶ n. Med. inability to perform particular purposive actions, due to brain damage. — **a·prax·ic** /-sik/ adj. [19th C.: from Ger. *Apraxie*, from Gk. *apraxia* 'inaction.']

après- ▶ prefix informal, humorous coming after in time, typically specifying a period following an activity: *a low-fat, après-workout snack.* [20th C.: Fr., lit. 'after.']

a·près-ski /ˌäprāˈskē/ ▶ n. the social activities and entertainment following a day's skiing: [as adj.] *the après-ski disco.* — **a·près-ski·ing** n. [1950s: Fr., lit. 'after skiing.']

ap·ri·cot /ˈapriˌkät; ˈāpri-/ ▶ n. 1 a juicy, soft fruit, resembling a small peach, of an orange-yellow color. ■ an orange-yellow color like the skin of a ripe apricot. 2 (also **apricot tree**) the tree (*Prunus armeniaca*) of the rose family that bears this fruit. [16th C.: from Port. *albricoque* or Spanish *albaricoque*, from Sp. Arab. *al* 'the' + *barḳūḳ* (from late Gk. *praikokion*, based on Latin *praecox* 'early ripe'); influenced by L. *apricus* 'ripe.']

A·pril /ˈāprəl/ ▶ n. the fourth month of the year, in the northern hemisphere usually considered the second month of spring. [OE, from L. *Aprilis*.]

A·pril fool ▶ n. a person who is the victim of a trick or hoax on April 1. ■ a trick or hoax on April 1: [as adj.] *an April fool joke.*

A·pril Fool's Day (also **A·pril Fools' Day**) ▶ n. April 1, in many Western countries traditionally an occasion for playing tricks. Also called ALL FOOLS' DAY.

a pri·o·ri /ˈäprīˈôrī; ˈä prēˈôrē/ ▶ adj. relating to or denoting reasoning or knowledge that proceeds from theoretical deduction rather than from observation or experience: *a priori assumptions about human nature.* ▶ adv. in a way based on theoretical deduction rather than empirical observation. — **a·pri·o·rism** /ˌāprīˈôrizəm; ˌāprē-/ n. [16th C.: L., 'from what is before.']

a·pron /ˈāprən/ ▶ n. 1 a protective or decorative garment worn over the front of one's clothes, either from chest or waist level, and tied at the back. ■ a similar garment worn as part of official dress, as by a Freemason. ■ a sheet of lead worn to shield the body during an X-ray examination. 2 a small area adjacent to another larger area or structure: *a tiny apron of garden.* ■ a hard-surfaced area on an airfield used for maneuvering or parking aircraft. ■ (also **apron stage**) a projecting strip of stage for playing scenes in front of the curtain. ■ a broadened area of pavement at the end of a driveway. ■ the narrow strip of the floor of a boxing ring lying outside the ropes. ■ the outer edge or border of a golf green. ■ Geol. an extensive outspread deposit of sediment, typically at the foot of a glacier or mountain. 3 an object resembling an apron in shape or function, in particular: ■ a covering protecting an area or structure, for example, from water erosion. ■ [often as adj.] an endless conveyor made of overlapping plates. ■ Med. a pendulous fold of abdominal fat that obscures the genital region.
– PHRASES (**tied to**) **someone's apron strings** (too much under) the influence and control of someone. [ME *naperon*, from OFr., dimin. of *nape, nappe* 'tablecloth,' from L. *mappa* 'napkin.' The *n* was lost by wrong division of *a napron*.]

ap·ro·pos /ˌaprəˈpō/ ▶ prep. with reference to; concerning. ▶ adv. [sentence adverb] (**apropos of nothing**) used to state a speaker's belief that someone's comments or acts are unrelated to any previous discussion or situation: *Isabel kept smiling apropos of nothing.* ▶ adj. [predic.] very appropriate to a particular situation: *the composer's reference to child's play is apropos.* [17th C.: from Fr. *à propos* 'to the purpose.']

apse /aps/ ▶ n. 1 a large semicircular or polygonal recess in a church, arched or with a domed roof, typically at the eastern end, and usually containing the altar. 2 another term for APSIS. — **ap·si·dal** /ˈapsidl/ adj. [19th C.: from L. *apsis* (see APSIS).]

ap·sis /ˈapsis/ ▶ n. (pl. **-si·des** /-siˌdēz/) either of two points on the orbit of a planet or satellite that are nearest to or furthest from the body around which it moves. — **ap·si·dal** /ˈapsidl/ adj. [17th C.: via L. from Gk. *apsis, hapsis* 'arch, vault,' perh. from *haptein* 'fasten.']

apt /apt/ ▶ adj. 1 appropriate or suitable in the circumstances. 2 [predic.] (**apt to do something**) having a tendency to do something: *she was apt to confuse the past with the present.* 3 quick to learn. — **apt·ly** adv. **apt·ness** n. [ME: from L. *aptus* 'fitted,' past part. of *apere* 'fasten.']

apt. ▶ abbr. ■ apartment. ■ aptitude.

ap·ter·ous /ˈaptərəs/ ▶ adj. Entomol. (of an insect) having no wings. [18th C.: from Gk. *apteros* (from *a-* + *pteron* 'wing').]

ap·ti·tude /ˈaptiˌt(y)o͞od/ ▶ n. 1 (abbr.: **apt.**) (often **aptitude for**) a natural ability to do something. ■ a natural tendency. 2 archaic suitability or fitness: *aptitude of expression.* [ME: via OFr. from late L. *aptitudo*, from *aptus* (see APT).]

ap·ti·tude test ▶ n. a test designed to determine a person's ability in a particular skill or field of knowledge.

Ap·u·le·ius /ˌapyəˈlēəs/ (*c.* 123–*c.* 179), Roman writer; born in Africa. He wrote *The Golden Ass*.

A·pus /ˈāpəs/ Astron. a faint southern constellation, the Bird of Paradise, close to the south celestial pole. [L., a bird, from Gk. *apous*.]

A·qa·ba /ˈäkəbə; ˈak-/ a port in Jordan; pop. 40,000.

A·qa·ba, Gulf of part of the Red Sea between the Sinai and Arabian peninsulas.

aq·ua /ˈäkwə; ˈak-/ ▶ **n.** a light bluish-green color. [1930s: abbrev. of AQUAMARINE.]

aqua- ▶ **comb. form** relating to water: *aquaculture*. [from L. *aqua* 'water.']

aq·ua·cade /ˈäkwəˌkād; ˈak-/ ▶ **n.** a spectacle involving swimming and diving with musical accompaniment.

aq·ua·cul·ture /ˈäkwəˌkəlCHər; ˈak-/ ▶ **n.** Bot. the cultivation of aquatic animals or plants for food. [19th C.: from L. *aqua* 'water.']

aq·ua·lung /ˈäkwəˌləNG; ˈak-/ ▶ **n.** a portable breathing apparatus for divers. [1950s: from L. *aqua* 'water.']

aq·ua·ma·rine /ˌäkwəməˈrēn; ˌak-/ ▶ **n.** a precious stone consisting of a light bluish-green variety of beryl. ■ a light bluish-green color. [18th C.: from L. *aqua marina* 'seawater.']

aq·ua·naut /ˈäkwəˌnôt; ˈak-/ ▶ **n.** a scuba diver who works underwater. [19th C.: from L. *aqua* 'water' + Gk. *nautēs* 'sailor.']

aq·ua·plane /ˈäkwəˌplān; ˈak-/ ▶ **n.** a board for riding on water, pulled by a speedboat. ▶ **v.** [intrans.] [often as n.] (**aquaplaning**) ride standing on an aquaplane. ■ (of a vehicle) slide uncontrollably on a wet surface: *the plane aquaplaned on the runway.* [20th C. (US): from L. *aqua* 'water.']

aq·ua·relle /ˌäkwəˈrel; ˌak-/ ▶ **n.** a style of painting using thin, typically transparent, watercolors. ■ a painting in such a style. [19th C.: from Fr., from Ital. *acquarella* 'watercolor,' dimin. of *acqua*, from L. *aqua* 'water.']

A·quar·i·an /əˈkwe(ə)rēən/ Astrol. ▶ **n.** a person born under the sign of Aquarius. ▶ **adj.** of or relating to such people. ■ of or relating to the Age of Aquarius or the New Age.

a·quar·ist /əˈkwe(ə)rist/ ▶ **n.** a person who keeps an aquarium.

a·quar·i·um /əˈkwe(ə)rēəm/ ▶ **n.** (pl. **-i·ums** or **-i·a** /-ēə/) a transparent tank of water in which fish and other water creatures and plants are kept. ■ a building containing such tanks for exhibit. [19th C.: from L., neut. of *aquarius* 'of water.']

A·quar·i·us /əˈkwe(ə)rēəs/ **1** Astron. a large constellation, the Water-carrier or Water-bearer, said to represent a man pouring water from a jar. **2** Astrol. the eleventh sign of the zodiac, which the sun enters about January 21. ■ (**an Aquarius**) a person born under this sign.
– PHRASES **Age of Aquarius** an age that the world has just entered or is about to enter, believed by some to signal a period of peace and harmony. [L. *aquarius* 'of water,' also 'water carrier.']

a·quat·ic /əˈkwätik; əˈkwat-/ ▶ **adj.** of or relating to water. ■ (of a plant or animal) growing or living in or near water. ■ (of a sport) played in or on water. ■ (of a shop or dealer) specializing in products for ponds or aquariums. ▶ **n. 1** an aquatic plant or animal. **2** (**aquatics**) sports played in or on water. [15th C.: ult. from L. *aquaticus*, from *aqua* 'water.']

aq·ua·tint /ˈäkwəˌtint; ˈak-/ ▶ **n.** a print resembling a watercolor, produced from a copper plate etched with nitric acid. ■ the technique or process of making such pictures. [18th C.: from Fr. *aquatinte*, from Ital. *acqua tinta* 'colored water.']

aq·ua·vit /ˈäkwəˌvēt; ˈak-/ (also **ak·va·vit** /ˈäkväˌvēt/) ▶ **n.** an alcoholic spirit made from potatoes or other starchy plants. [19th C.: from Norw., Swed., Dan. *akvavit* (see AQUA VITAE).]

aq·ua vi·tae /ˈäkwə ˈvītē; ˈvēˌtī; ˈakwə/ ▶ **n.** strong alcoholic spirit, esp. brandy. [ME: from L., lit. 'water of life.']

aq·ue·duct /ˈäkwəˌdəkt; ˈak-/ ▶ **n.** an artificial channel for conveying water, typically in the form of a bridge supported by tall columns across a valley. ■ Anat. a small canal containing fluid. [16th C.: from obs. Fr., from L. *aquae ductus* 'conduit,' from *aqua* 'water' + *ducere* 'to lead.']

a·que·ous /ˈākwēəs; ˈak-/ ▶ **adj.** of or containing water, typically as a solvent or medium. ■ fig. like water; watery. [17th C.: from med. L. *aqueus*, from L. *aqua* 'water.']

a·que·ous hu·mor ▶ **n.** the clear fluid filling the space in the front of the eyeball between the lens and the cornea. Compare with VITREOUS HUMOR.

aq·ui·fer /ˈäkwəfər; ˈak-/ ▶ **n.** a body of permeable rock that can contain or transmit groundwater. [20th C.: from L. *aqui-* (from *aqua* 'water') + *-fer* 'bearing.']

A·quil·a /əˈkwilə; ˈakwilə/ Astron. a small northern constellation, the Eagle. It contains the bright star Altair. [L.]

aq·ui·le·gi·a /ˌakwəˈlēj(ē)ə/ ▶ **n.** a plant (genus *Aquilegia*) of the buttercup family, bearing showy flowers with backward-pointing spurs. [from med. L., prob. from L. *aquilegus* 'water collecting.']

aq·ui·line /ˈakwəˌlīn; -lin/ ▶ **adj.** like an eagle. ■ (of a person's nose) hooked like an eagle's beak. [17th C.: from L. *aquilinus*, from *aquila* 'eagle.']

A·qui·nas, St. Thom·as /əˈkwīnəs/ (1225–74), Italian philosopher and theologian; known as *the Angelic Doctor*. A Dominican friar, his works include the *Summa Contra Gentiles* and *Summa Theologiae*.

A·qui·no /äˈkēnō; əˈkē-/ Corazon (1933–), president of the Philippines 1986–92; full name *Maria Corazon Sumulong Cojuangco–Aquino*.

Aq·ui·taine[1] /ˈakwəˌtān/ a region and former province in southwestern France, on the Bay of Biscay.

Aq·ui·taine[2], Eleanor of, see ELEANOR OF AQUITAINE.

a·quiv·er /əˈkwivər/ ▶ **adj.** [predic.] quivering; trembling.

AR ▶ **abbr.** ■ (also **A/R**) accounts receivable. ■ Arkansas (in official postal use). ■ Army Regulation.

Ar ▶ **symb.** the chemical element argon.

ar- ▶ **prefix** var. of AD- assimilated before *r* (as in *arrive, arrogate*).

-ar[1] ▶ **suffix** **1** (forming adjectives) of the kind specified; relating to: *molecular*. **2** forming nouns such as *scholar*. [from OFr. *-aire, -ier*, or from L. *-aris*.]

-ar[2] ▶ **suffix** forming nouns such as *pillar*. [from Fr. *-er* or from L. *-ar, -are* (neut. of *-aris*).]

-ar[3] ▶ **suffix** forming nouns such as *bursar, vicar*. [from OFr. *-aire, -ier*, or from L. *-arius, -arium*.]

-ar[4] ▶ **suffix** alteration of -ER[1], -OR[1] (as in *beggar*).

Ar·ab /ˈarəb/ ▶ **n.** a member of a Semitic people inhabiting much of the Middle East and North Africa. ▶ **adj.** of or relating to Arabia and the people of Arabia. [from Fr. *Arabe*, ult. from Arab. *arab*.]

ar·a·besque /ˌarəˈbesk/ ▶ **n. 1** an ornamental design of intertwined flowing lines, originally found in Arabic or Moorish decoration. ■ Music a passage or composition with fanciful ornamentation of the melody. **2** Ballet a posture in which the body is supported on one leg, with the other leg extended horizontally backward. [17th C.: from Fr., from Ital. *arabesco* 'in the Arab. style,' from *arabo* 'Arab.']

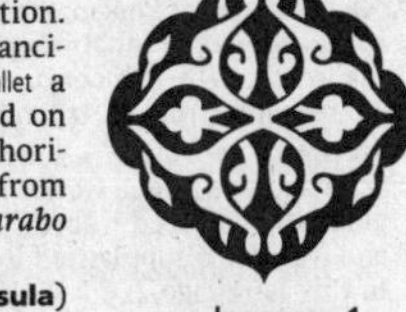
arabesque 1

A·ra·bi·a /əˈrābēə/ (also **Arabian peninsula**) a peninsula in southwestern Asia that lies between the Red Sea and the Persian Gulf. It comprises the states of Saudi Arabia, Yemen, Oman, Bahrain, Kuwait, Qatar, and the United Arab Emirates.

A·ra·bi·an /əˈrābēən/ ▶ **adj.** of or relating to Arabia or Arabs. ▶ **n.** hist. a native or inhabitant of Arabia. ■ (also **Arabian horse**) a horse of a breed originating in Arabia, with a distinctive face and tail.

A·ra·bi·an cam·el ▶ **n.** a domesticated one-humped camel (*Camelus dromedarius*), probably native to the deserts of North Africa and southwestern Asia. See also DROMEDARY.

A·ra·bi·an Des·ert /əˈrābēən/ a desert in eastern Egypt, between the Nile River and the Red Sea. Also called the EASTERN DESERT.

A·ra·bi·an Gulf another name for PERSIAN GULF.

A·ra·bi·an Nights a collection of stories and romances that include the tales of Aladdin and Sinbad the Sailor. Also called the THOUSAND AND ONE NIGHTS.

A·ra·bi·an pen·in·su·la another name for ARABIA.

A·ra·bi·an Sea the northwestern part of the Indian Ocean, between Arabia and India.

Ar·a·bic /ˈarəbik/ ▶ **n.** the Semitic language of the Arabs. Arabic is written from right to left in a characteristic cursive script of twenty-eight consonants, the vowels being indicated by additional signs. ▶ **adj.** of or relating to the literature or language of Arab people. [ME: via L. from Gk. *arabikos*, from *Araps, Arab-* 'Arab.']

a·rab·i·ca /əˈrabikə/ ▶ **n.** a bush (*Coffea arabica*) of the bedstraw family that is the most widely grown kind of coffee plant, native to the Old World tropics. [1920s: from L., fem. of *arabicus* (see ARAB.).]

Ar·a·bic nu·mer·al ▶ **n.** any of the numerals 0, 1, 2, 3, 4, 5, 6, 7, 8, and 9. Arabic numerals replaced Roman numerals by about AD 1200.

a·rab·i·nose /əˈrabəˌnōs; ˈarəbə-/ ▶ **n.** Chem. a sugar of the pentose class that is a constituent of many plant gums. [19th C.: from ARABICA + -IN[1].]

Ar·ab·ism /ˈarəˌbizəm/ ▶ **n. 1** Arab culture or identity. ■ support for Arab nationalism or political interests. **2** an Arabic linguistic usage, word, or phrase.

Ar·ab·ist /ˈarəbist/ ▶ **n.** a person who studies Arabic civilization or language. ■ a supporter of Arab nationalism.

ar·a·ble /ˈarəbəl/ ▶ **adj.** (of land) used or suitable for growing crops. ■ (of crops) able to be grown on such land. ■ concerned with growing such crops. ▶ **n.** land or crops of this type. [ME: ult. from L. *arabilis*, from *arare* 'to plow.']

A·ra·ca·jú /ˌärəkəˈZHOO/ a port in eastern Brazil, on the Atlantic coast; pop. 404,828.

ar·a·chi·don·ic ac·id /ˌarəkiˈdänik/ ▶ **n.** Biochem. a polyunsaturated fatty acid, $C_{19}H_{31}COOH$, present in animal fats. It is important in metabolism, esp. in the synthesis of prostaglandins and leukotrienes, and is an essential constituent of the diet. [20th C.: from *arachidic* + -ONE.]

A·rach·ne /əˈraknē/ Gk. Mythol. a skillful weaver whom Athena changed into a spider after Arachne challenged her to a contest. [from Gk. *arakhnē* 'spider.']

A·rach·ni·da /əˈraknidə/ Zool. a class of chelicerate arthropods that includes spiders, scorpions, mites, and ticks. — **a·rach·nid** **n. & adj.** [mod. L. (pl.), from Gk. *arakhnē* 'spider.']

a·rach·noid /əˈraknoid/ ▶ **adj.** like a spider or arachnid. ▶ **n.** (also **arachnoid membrane** or **arachnoid mater**) Anat. the middle of three membranes that surround the brain and spinal cord. [18th C.: from mod.

L. *arachnoides*, from Gk. *arakhnoeidēs* 'like a cobweb,' from *arakhnē* 'spider.']

a·rach·no·pho·bi·a /ə,raknə'fōbēə/ ▶ **n.** extreme or irrational fear of spiders. — **a·rach·no·phobe** /ə'raknə,fōb/ **n.** **a·rach·no·pho·bic** /-bik/ **adj.** [1920s: mod. L., from Gk. *arakhnē* 'spider.']

Ar·a·fat /'arə,fat/, Yasser (1929–2004), chairman of the Palestine Liberation Organization from 1968 and president of Palestine 1996–2004. Nobel Peace Prize (1994, shared with Yitzhak Rabin and Shimon Peres).

A·ra·fu·ra Sea /,arə'fo͝orə/ a sea bounded by Australia, Indonesia and New Guinea.

A·ra·gon[1] /'arə,gän; -gən/ an autonomous region in northeastern Spain; capital, Saragossa.

A·ra·gon[2], Catherine of, see CATHERINE OF ARAGON.

a·rag·o·nite /ə'ragə,nīt; 'arəgə-/ ▶ **n.** a mineral consisting of calcium carbonate, typically occurring in white seashells. [19th C.: from ARAGON[1].]

ar·ak ▶ **n.** var. of ARRACK.

Ar·al Sea /'arəl/ an inland sea in central Asia, on the border between Kazakhstan and Uzbekistan.

Ar·a·mae·an /,arə'mäən; -'mēən/ ▶ **n.** a member of an ancient Aramaic-speaking people inhabiting Aram (modern Syria) and part of Babylonia in the 11th–8th centuries BC. ▶ **adj.** of or relating to Aram or the Aramaeans. [from L. *Aramaeus* (from Gk. *Aramaios*.]

Ar·a·ma·ic /,arə'māik/ ▶ **n.** a Semitic language, a Syrian dialect of which was used as a lingua franca in the Near East from the 6th century BC. It gradually replaced Hebrew as the language of the Jews in those areas and was itself supplanted by Arabic in the 7th century AD. ▶ **adj.** of or in this language. [19th C.: from Gk. *Aramaios* 'of *Aram*' (the biblical name of Syria).]

ar·a·me /'arə,mā; ə'rä-/ ▶ **n.** an edible Pacific seaweed (*Ecklonia bicyclis*, class Phaeophyceae) with broad brown leaves, used in Japanese cooking.

a·ra·ne·id /ə'rānē-id/ ▶ **n.** Zool. an invertebrate of an order (Araneidae) that comprises the spiders. [19th C.: from mod. L. *Araneida*, from *aranea* 'spider.']

A·rap·a·ho /ə'rapə,hō/ ▶ **n.** **1** (pl. same or **-hos**) a member of a North American Indian people living chiefly on the Great Plains, esp. in Wyoming. **2** the Algonquian language of this people. ▶ **adj.** of or relating to this people or their language. [from Crow *aaraxpéahu*, lit. 'those having many tattoo marks.']

Ar·a·rat, Mount /'arə,rat/ two volcanic peaks in eastern Turkey. The higher peak, which rises to 16,946 feet (5,165 m), is the traditional site of the resting place of Noah's ark after the Flood (Gen. 8:4).

Ar·au·ca·ni·an /,arô'kānēən/ ▶ **n.** **1** a member of a group of South American Indian peoples of Chile and Argentina, of which the only people that has a surviving cultural identity is the Mapuche. **2** the family of languages spoken by this people. ▶ **adj.** relating to or denoting this people or their language. See also MAPUCHE. [from Sp. *Araucania*, region in Chile.]

ar·au·car·i·a /,arô'ke(ə)rēə/ ▶ **n.** an evergreen conifer of a genus (*Araucaria*) that includes the monkey puzzle and the Norfolk Island pine, having stiff sharp leaves. [mod. L., from Sp. *Arauco*, province in Chile.]

Ar·a·wak /'arə,wäk/ ▶ **n.** (pl. same or **-waks**) **1** a member of a native people originally of the Greater Antilles and adjacent South America, now living mainly in Guiana. **2** any of the Arawakan languages of these peoples. ▶ **adj.** designating or relating to this people or their languages.

Ar·a·wak·an /,arə'wäkən/ ▶ **adj.** **1** of or relating to the Arawak people. **2** denoting or belonging to a nearly extinct family of South American Indian languages. ▶ **n.** this family of languages.

ar·ba·lest /'ärbəlist/ ▶ **n.** hist. a crossbow with a mechanism for drawing back and releasing the string. [OE *arblast*, from OFr. *arbaleste*, based on L. *arcus* 'bow' + *ballista* (see BALLISTA).]

ar·bi·ter /'ärbitər/ ▶ **n.** a person who settles a dispute or has ultimate authority in a matter. ■ (usu. **arbiter of**) a person whose views or actions influence social behavior. [ME: from L., 'judge.']

ar·bi·trage /'ärbi,träzн/ ▶ **n.** the simultaneous buying and selling of securities, currency, or commodities in different markets or in derivative forms in order to take advantage of differing prices for the same asset. ▶ **v.** [intrans.] buy and sell assets in such a way. [ME: from Fr., from *arbitrer* 'give judgment,' from L. *arbitrari* (see ARBITRATE).]

ar·bi·tra·geur /,ärbiträ'zнər; 'ärbi,träzнər/ (also **ar·bi·tra·ger** /'ärbi,träzнər/) ▶ **n.** a person who engages in arbitrage. [19th C.: from Fr.]

ar·bi·tral /'ärbitrəl/ ▶ **adj.** [attrib.] relating to or resulting from the use of an arbitrator to settle a dispute.

ar·bi·trar·y /'ärbi,trerē/ ▶ **adj.** based on random choice or personal whim, rather than any reason or system. ■ (of power or a ruling body) unrestrained and autocratic in the use of authority. — **ar·bi·trar·i·ly** /,ärbi'tre(ə)rəlē/ **adv.** **ar·bi·trar·i·ness** **n.** [ME: from L. *arbitrarius*, from *arbiter* 'judge.']

ar·bi·trate /'ärbi,trāt/ ▶ **v.** [intrans.] (of an independent person or body) reach an authoritative judgment or settlement: *the power to arbitrate in disputes* | [trans.] *a commission to arbitrate border tensions.* [16th C.: from L. *arbitrat-* 'judged,' from *arbitrari*, from *arbiter* 'judge.']

ar·bi·tra·tion /,ärbi'trāsнən/ ▶ **n.** the use of an arbitrator to settle a dispute.

ar·bi·tra·tor /'ärbi,trātər/ ▶ **n.** an independent person or body officially appointed to settle a dispute.

ar·bor[1] /'ärbər/ ▶ **n.** an axle or spindle on which something revolves. ■ a device holding a tool in a lathe. [17th C.: from Fr. *arbre* 'tree, axis.']

ar·bor[2] (Brit. **ar·bour**) ▶ **n.** a shady garden alcove formed by trees or climbing plants trained over a wooden framework. [ME: from OFr. *erbier*, from *erbe* 'grass, herb,' from L. *herba*.]

Ar·bor Day ▶ **n.** a day dedicated annually to public tree-planting in the US, Australia, and other countries. [from L. *arbor* 'tree.']

ar·bo·re·al /är'bôrēəl/ ▶ **adj.** (chiefly of animals) living in trees. ■ of or relating to trees. [17th C.: from L. *arboreus*, from *arbor* 'tree.']

ar·bo·res·cent /,ärbə'resənt/ ▶ **adj.** esp. Bot. treelike in growth or appearance. — **ar·bo·res·cence** **n.**

ar·bo·re·tum /,ärbə'rētəm/ ▶ **n.** (pl. **-re·tums** or **-re·ta** /-'rētə/) a botanical garden devoted to trees. [19th C.: from L., 'place with trees,' from *arbor* 'tree.']

ar·bor·i·cul·ture /'ärbəri,kəlcнər; är'bôri-/ ▶ **n.** the cultivation of trees and shrubs. — **ar·bor·i·cul·tur·al** /,ärbəri'kəlcнərəl; är'bôri,kəl-/ **adj.** **ar·bor·i·cul·tur·ist** /,ärbəri'kəlcнərist; är'bôrə,kəl-/ **n.** [19th C.: from L. *arbor* 'tree.']

Ar·bo·ri·o /är'bôrē-ō/ (also **ar·bo·ri·o**) ▶ **n.** a variety of round-grained rice used in making risotto. [Ital.]

ar·bor·i·za·tion /,ärbərə'zāsнən/ ▶ **n.** Anat. a fine branching structure at the end of a nerve fiber.

ar·bor vi·tae /'ärbər 'vītē/ (also **ar·bor·vi·tae**) ▶ **n.** **1** a North American and eastern Asian evergreen coniferous tree (genus *Thuja*) of the cypress family, in particular the northern white cedar (see WHITE CEDAR). **2** the arborescent appearance of the white matter in a vertical section of the cerebellum. [16th C.: from L., lit. 'tree of life.']

ar·bour ▶ **n.** British spelling of ARBOR[2].

ar·bo·vi·rus /'ärbə,vīrəs/ ▶ **n.** Med. any of a group of viruses transmitted by mosquitoes, ticks, or other arthropods. They include encephalitis and yellow fever. [1950s: from *ar(thropod)-bo(rne)*.]

Ar·bus /'ärbəs/, Diane (1923–71), US photographer, best known for her disturbing images of people.

ar·bu·tus /är'byo͞otəs/ ▶ **n.** either of two evergreen plants of the heath family: ■ a tree or shrub of the genus *Arbutus*, which includes the strawberry tree. ■ (in full **trailing arbutus**) a North American trailing plant (Epigaea repens) that bears pink or white flowers. Also called MAYFLOWER. [from L.]

ARC /ärk/ ▶ **abbr.** ■ Med. AIDS-related complex. ■ American Red Cross.

arc /ärk/ ▶ **n.** **1** a part of the circumference of a circle or other curve. See illustration at GEOMETRIC. ■ a curved shape, or something shaped like a curve. ■ a curving trajectory. **2** (also **electric arc**) a luminous electrical discharge between two electrodes or other points. ▶ **v.** (**arced**; **arc·ing**) [intrans.] **1** [with adverbial of direction] move with a curving trajectory: *the ball arced across the room.* **2** [usu. as n.] (**arcing**) form an electric arc.
– PHRASES **minute of arc** see MINUTE[1] (sense 2). **second of arc** see SECOND[2] (sense 2). [ME: via OFr. from L. *arcus* 'bow, curve.']

ar·cade /är'kād/ ▶ **n.** **1** a covered passageway with arches along one or both sides. ■ a covered walk with stores along one or both sides. ■ Archit. a series of arches supporting a wall, or set along it. **2** short for VIDEO ARCADE. — **ar·cad·ed** **adj.** **ar·cad·ing** **n.** [17th C.: from Fr., based on L. *arcus* 'bow.']

Ar·ca·di·a /är'kādēə/ **1** a mountainous district in the Peloponnese of southern Greece. **2** a city in southwestern California, northeast of Los Angeles; pop. 48,290. The Santa Anita racetrack is here.

Ar·ca·di·an /är'kādēən/ ▶ **n.** a native of Arcadia. ■ literary an idealized country dweller. ▶ **adj.** of or relating to Arcadia. ■ literary of or relating to an ideal rustic paradise.

ar·ca·na /är'kānə/ ▶ **plural n.** [treated as sing. or pl.] (sing. **-num** /-nəm/) secrets or mysteries. [16th C.: from L., neut. pl. of *arcanus* (see ARCANE).]

ar·cane /är'kān/ ▶ **adj.** understood by few; mysterious or secret. — **ar·cane·ly** **adv.** [16th C.: from L. *arcanus*, from *arcere* 'to shut up,' from *arca* 'chest.']

Ar·ca·ro /är'karō; -'ke(ə)rō/, Eddie (1916–1997), US jockey; full name *George Edward Arcaro*. He was the first two-time Triple Crown winner (1941, 1948).

Arc de Tri·omphe /'ärk də trē'ônf/ a ceremonial arch standing at the top of the Champs Élysées in Paris.

arc fur·nace ▶ **n.** a furnace that uses an electric arc as a heat source, esp. for steelmaking.

arch[1] /ärcн/ ▶ **n.** a curved symmetrical structure spanning an opening and typically supporting the weight of a bridge, roof, or wall above it. ■ a structure of this type forming a passageway or a ceremonial monument. ■ a shape resembling such a structure or a thing with such a shape. ■ the inner side of the foot. ▶ **v.** **1** [intrans.] have the curved shape of an arch: *a bridge that arched over a canal.* ■ form or cause to form the curved shape of an arch: [intrans.] *her eyebrows arched in surprise.* **2** [trans.] [usu. as adj.] (**arched**) provide (a bridge, building, or part of a building) with an arch. [ME: from OFr. *arche*, based on L. *arcus* 'bow.']

arch[2] ▶ **adj.** deliberately or affectedly playful and teasing. — **arch·ly** **adv.** **arch·ness** **n.** [16th C. (in the sense 'chief, principal'): from ARCH-, because of its association with words such as *rogue*.]

arch- ▶ **comb. form** chief; principal: *archbishop.* ■ preeminent of its kind: *archenemy.* ■ (in unfavorable senses) out-and-out: *arch-scoundrel.* [via L. from Gk. *arkhi-*, from *arkhos* 'chief.']

ar·chae·a /är'kēə/ ▶ **plural n.** another term for ARCHAEBACTERIA. — **ar·chae·an** **adj.** & **n.**

Ar·chae·an ▶ **adj.** British spelling of ARCHEAN.

ar·chae·bac·te·ri·a /ˌärkēbakˈti(ə)rēə/ ▶ **plural n.** (sing. **-te·ri·um**/-ˈti(ə)rēəm/) Biol. microorganisms that are similar to bacteria in size and simplicity of structure but radically different in molecular organization. They are now believed to constitute an ancient intermediate group between the bacteria and eukaryotes. Also called ARCHAEA. — **ar·chae·bac·te·ri·al adj.** [mod. L. (pl.), from Gk. *arkhaios* 'primitive.']

archaeo- (also **archeo-**) ▶ **comb. form** relating to archaeology or prehistoric times: *archaeoastronomy.* [from Gk. *arkhaios* 'ancient,' from *arkhē* 'beginning.']

ar·chae·o·as·tron·o·my /ˌärkēˌōəˈstränəmē/ ▶ **n.** the study of the astronomy of prehistoric cultures. Also called **astroarchaeology**.

ar·chae·ol·o·gy /ˌärkēˈäləjē/ (also **ar·che·ol·o·gy**) ▶ **n.** the study of human history and prehistory through the excavation of sites and the analysis of artifacts. — **ar·chae·o·log·ic** /-əˈläjik/ **adj.** **ar·chae·o·log·i·cal** /-əˈläjikəl/ **adj.** **ar·chae·o·log·i·cal·ly** /-əˈläjik(ə)lē/ **adv.** **ar·chae·ol·o·gist** /-jist/ **n.** [17th C.: from mod. L. *archaeologia*, from Gk. *arkhaiologia* 'ancient history,' from *arkhaios* 'ancient.']

ar·chae·op·ter·yx /ˌärkēˈäptəriks/ ▶ **n.** the oldest known fossil bird (*Archaeopteryx lithographica*, subclass Archaeornithes), of the late Jurassic period. It had feathers, wings, and hollow bones like a bird, but teeth, a bony tail, and legs like a small coelurosaur dinosaur. [from Gk. *arkhaios* 'ancient' + *pterux* 'wing.']

ar·cha·ic /ärˈkāik/ ▶ **adj.** very old or old-fashioned. ■ (of a word or a style of language) no longer in everyday use but sometimes used to impart an old-fashioned flavor. ■ of an early period of art or culture, esp. the 7th–6th centuries BC in Greece. — **ar·cha·i·cal·ly** /-ik(ə)lē/ **adv.** [19th C.: from Fr. *archaïque*, from Gk. *arkhaikos*, based on *arkhē* 'beginning.']

ar·cha·ism /ˈärkēˌizəm; ˈärkā-/ ▶ **n.** a thing that is very old or old-fashioned. ■ an archaic word or style of language or art. ■ the use of old-fashioned styles in language or art. — **ar·cha·is·tic** /ˌärkēˈistik; ˌärkā-/ **adj.**

ar·cha·iz·ing /ˈärkēˌīziNG; ˈärkā-/ ▶ **adj.** consciously imitating a word or a style of language or art that is very old or old-fashioned.

Arch·an·gel /ˈärkˌānjəl/ a port in northwestern Russia, on the White Sea; pop. 419,000. Russian name ARKHANGELSK.

arch·an·gel /ˈärkˌānjəl/ ▶ **n.** an angel of high rank. — **arch·an·gel·ic** /ˌärkanˈjelik/ **adj.** [ME, from Anglo-Norman Fr. *archangele*, from eccles. Gk. *arkhangelos*, from *arkhi-* 'chief' + *angelos* 'angel.']

arch·bish·op /ˌärCHˈbiSHəp/ ▶ **n.** the chief bishop responsible for an archdiocese. [OE, from ARCH- + *biscop* (see BISHOP.]

arch·bish·op·ric /ˌärCHˈbiSHəprik/ ▶ **n.** the office of an archbishop. ■ an archdiocese. [OE *arcebiscopríce* (see ARCH-, BISHOPRIC).]

arch·dea·con /ˈärCHˈdēkən/ ▶ **n.** a senior Christian cleric to whom a bishop delegates certain responsibilities. [OE *arce-*, *ercediacon*, ult. from eccles. Gk. *arkhidiakonos*, from *arkhi-* 'chief' + *diakonos* (see DEACON).]

arch·dea·con·ry /ˌärCHˈdēkənrē/ ▶ **n.** (pl. **-ries**) the office of an archdeacon. ■ the district for which an archdeacon is responsible. ■ the residence of an archdeacon.

arch·di·o·cese /ˌärCHˈdīəsis; -ˌsēz/ ▶ **n.** the district for which an archbishop is responsible. — **arch·di·oc·e·san** /ˌärCHdīˈäsəsən/ **adj.**

arch·duch·ess /ˈärCHˈdəCHis/ ▶ **n.** hist. the wife or widow of an archduke. ■ a daughter of the emperor of Austria.

arch·duke /ˈärCHˈd(y)o͞ok/ ▶ **n.** hist. a son of the emperor of Austria. — **arch·du·cal** /ˌärCHˈd(y)o͞okəl/ **adj.** [16th C.: from OFr. *archeduc*, from Merovingian L. *archidux*, *archiduc-*, from *archi-* 'chief' + *dux*, *duc-* (see DUKE).]

Ar·che·an /ärˈkēən/ (Brit. **Ar·chae·an**) ▶ **adj.** Geol. of, relating to, or denoting the eon that constitutes the earlier (or middle) part of the Precambrian. Also called AZOIC. ■ [as n.] (**the Archean**) the Archean eon or the system of rocks deposited during it. [19th C.: from Gk. *arkhaios* 'ancient.']

ar·che·go·ni·um /ˌärkiˈgōnēəm/ ▶ **n.** (pl. **-ni·a** /-nēə/) Bot. the female sex organ in mosses, liverworts, ferns, and most conifers. [19th C.: mod. L., from Gk. *arkhegonos*, from *arkhe-* 'first' + *gonos* 'race.']

arch·en·e·my /ˈärCHˈenəmē/ ▶ **n.** a person who is extremely hostile or opposed to someone or something. ■ (**the Archenemy**) the Devil.

arch·en·ter·on /ärkˈentəˌrän/ ▶ **n.** Embryol. the rudimentary alimentary cavity of an embryo at the gastrula stage. [19th C.: from Gk. *arkhē* 'beginning' + *enteron* 'intestine.']

archeo- ▶ **comb. form** var. of ARCHAEO-.

ar·che·ol·o·gy ▶ **n.** variant of ARCHAEOLOGY.

arch·er /ˈärCHər/ ▶ **n.** a person who shoots with a bow and arrows, esp. at a target for sport. ■ (**the Archer**) the zodiacal sign or constellation Sagittarius. [ME: from OFr. *archier*, based on L. *arcus* 'bow.']

ar·cher·fish /ˈärCHərˌfiSH/ ▶ **n.** (pl. same or **-fish·es**) a freshwater fish (genus *Toxotes*, family Toxotidae) that knocks insect prey off overhanging vegetation by spitting water at it.

ar·cher·y /ˈärCHərē/ ▶ **n.** the sport or skill of shooting with a bow and arrows, esp. at a target.

ar·che·typ·al /ˌärk(i)ˈtīpəl/ ▶ **adj.** very typical of a certain kind of person or thing. ■ recurrent as a symbol or motif in literature, art, or mythology. ■ of, relating to, or denoting an original that has been imitated. ■ relating to or denoting Jungian archetypes.

ar·che·type /ˈärk(i)ˌtīp/ ▶ **n.** a very typical example of a certain person or thing. ■ an original that has been imitated. ■ a recurrent symbol or motif in literature, art, or mythology. ■ Psychoanal. (in Jungian psychology) a primitive mental image inherited from the earliest human ancestors, and supposed to be present in the collective unconscious. — **ar·che·typ·i·cal** /ˌärk(i)ˈtipikəl/ **adj.** [16th C.: via L. from Gk. *arkhetupon*, from *arkhe-* 'primitive' + *tupos* 'a model.']

arch·fiend /ˈärCHˈfēnd/ ▶ **n.** literary a chief fiend, esp. the Devil.

ar·chi·di·ac·o·nal /ˌärkidīˈakənl/ ▶ **adj.** of or relating to an archdeacon. — **ar·chi·di·ac·o·nate** /-nit/ **n.** [ME: from med. L. *archidiaconalis*, from *archi-* 'chief' + *diaconalis* (see DIACONAL).]

ar·chi·e·pis·co·pal /ˌärkēəˈpiskəpəl/ ▶ **adj.** of or relating to an archbishop. — **ar·chi·e·pis·co·pa·cy** /-əˈpiskəpəsē/ **n.** (pl. **-cies**) **ar·chi·e·pis·co·pate** /-pit; -ˌpāt/ **n.** [17th C.: ult. from Gk. *arkhiepiskopos* 'archbishop' (from *arkhi-* 'chief' + *episkopos* 'bishop.']

Ar·chil·o·chus /ärˈkiləkəs/ (8th or 7th century BC), Greek poet. He invented iambic meter.

ar·chi·man·drite /ˌärkəˈmandrīt/ ▶ **n.** the head of a large monastery or group of monasteries in the Orthodox Church. [17th C.: ult. from eccles. Gk. *arkhimandritēs*, from *arkhi-* 'chief' + *mandra* 'monastery.']

Ar·chi·me·de·an screw /ˌärkəˈmēdēən/ ▶ **n.** a device invented by Archimedes for raising water by means of a spiral within a tube.

Ar·chi·me·des /ˌärkəˈmēdēz/ (*c.*287–212 BC), Greek mathematician and inventor. He is noted for his discovery of Archimedes' principle. — **Ar·chi·me·de·an** /-ˈmēdēən/ **adj.**

Ar·chi·me·des' prin·ci·ple Physics a result stating that a body totally or partially immersed in a fluid is subject to an upward force equal in magnitude to the weight of fluid it displaces.

ar·chi·pel·a·go /ˌärkəˈpeləˌgō/ ▶ **n.** (pl. **-gos** or **-goes**) a group of islands. ■ a sea or stretch of water containing many islands. [16th C.: from Ital. *arcipelago*, from Gk. *arkhi-* 'chief' + *pelagos* 'sea.']

Ar·chi·pen·ko /ˌärkəˈp(y)eNGkō/, Aleksandr Porfirevich (1887–1964), US sculptor; born in Russia. He adapted cubist techniques to sculpture.

Ar·chi·pié·la·go de Co·lón /ˌärCHēˈpyālāˌgō dā kōˈlōn/ official Spanish name for GALAPAGOS ISLANDS.

ar·chi·tect /ˈärkiˌtekt/ ▶ **n.** a person who designs buildings and often supervises their construction. ■ a person who conceives or realizes an idea or project. ▶ **v.** [trans.] (usu. **be architected**) Comput. design and make. [16th C.: from Fr. *architecte*, ult. from Gk. *arkhitektōn*, from *arkhi-* 'chief' + *tektōn* 'builder.']

ar·chi·tec·ton·ic /ˌärkitekˈtänik/ ▶ **adj.** of or relating to architecture or architects. ■ (of an artistic composition or physical appearance) having a clearly defined structure, esp. one that is artistically pleasing. ▶ **n.** (**architectonics**) [usu. treated as sing.] the scientific study of architecture. ■ musical, literary, or artistic structure. — **ar·chi·tec·ton·i·cal·ly** /-ik(ə)lē/ **adv.** [17th C.: via L. from Gk. *arkhitektonikos*, from *arkhitektōn* (see ARCHITECT).]

ar·chi·tec·ture /ˈärkiˌtekCHər/ ▶ **n.** **1** the art or practice of designing and constructing buildings. ■ the style of a building with regard to a specific period, place, or culture. **2** the complex or carefully designed structure of something. ■ the conceptual structure and logical organization of a computer or computer-based system. — **ar·chi·tec·tur·al** /ˌärkiˈtekCHərəl/ **adj.** **ar·chi·tec·tur·al·ly** /ˌärkiˈtekCHərəlē/ **adv.** [16th C.: from L. *architectura*, from *architectus* (see ARCHITECT).]

ar·chi·trave /ˈärkiˌtrāv/ ▶ **n.** **1** (in classical architecture) a main beam resting across the tops of columns, specifically the lower third entablature. **2** the molded frame around a doorway or window. ■ a molding around the exterior of an arch.

ar·chive /ˈärˌkīv/ (usu. **archives**) ▶ **n.** a collection of historical documents or records providing information about a place, institution, or group of people. ■ the place where such documents or records are kept. ▶ **v.** [trans.] place or store (something) in such a collection. ■ Comput. transfer (data) to a less frequently used storage medium such as magnetic tape, typically external to the computer system. — **ar·chi·val** /ärˈkīvəl/ **adj.** [17th C.: from Fr. *archives* (pl.), ult. from Gk. *arkheia* 'public records,' from *arkhē* 'government.']

ar·chi·vist /ˈärkəvist; -ˌkī-/ ▶ **n.** a person who maintains and is in charge of archives.

ar·chi·volt /ˈärkəˌvōlt/ ▶ **n.** a band of molding, resembling an architrave, around the lower curve of an arch. ■ the lower curve itself. [17th C.: from Fr. *archivolte* or Ital. *archivolto*, based on L. *arcus* 'bow, arch' + *volvere* 'to roll.']

ar·chon /ˈärkän/ ▶ **n.** a chief magistrate in ancient Athens. ■ any ruler. — **ar·chon·ship n.** [16th C.: from Gk. *arkhōn* 'ruler,' from *arkhein* 'to rule.']

ar·cho·saur /ˈärkəˌsôr/ (also **ar·cho·sau·rus** /ˌärkəˈsôrəs/) ▶ **n.** Zool. & Paleontol. a reptile of a large group that includes the dinosaurs and pterosaurs, represented today only by the crocodilians. — **ar·cho·sau·ri·an adj.** [1930s: from mod. L. *Archosauria*, from Gk. *arkhos* 'chief' or *arkhōn* 'ruler.']

arch·priest /ˈärCHˈprēst/ ▶ **n.** a chief priest.

arch·way /ˈärCHˌwā/ ▶ **n.** a curved structure forming a passage or entrance.

arc light (also **arc lamp**) ▶ **n.** a light source using an electric arc.

arc min·ute /ˈminit/ ▶ **n.** see MINUTE[1] (sense 2).

arc sec·ond (also **second of arc**) ▶ **n.** see SECOND[2] (sense 2).

Arc·tic /'ärktik; 'ärtik/ ▶ **adj.** **1** of or relating to the regions around the North Pole. ■ (of animals or plants) living or growing in such regions. ■ designed for use in such regions. **2** (**arctic**) informal (of weather conditions) very cold. ▶ **n.** **1** (**the Arctic**) the regions around the North Pole. **2** (**arctics** /'ärtiks/) thick waterproof overshoes. [ME: ult. from Gk. *arktikos*, from *arktos* 'bear, North Star.']

Arc·tic Ar·chi·pel·a·go the name for the islands that lie north of mainland Canada and the Arctic Circle.

Arc·tic char ▶ **n.** see **CHAR**[3].

Arc·tic Cir·cle the parallel of latitude 66° 33′ north of the equator.

Arc·tic fox ▶ **n.** a fox (*Alopex lagopus*) with a thick coat that turns white in winter, found on the tundra of North America and Eurasia.

Arc·tic hare ▶ **n.** a hare (*Lepus arcticus*, family Leporidae) whose coat turns white in winter, found in the arctic areas of North America.

Arc·tic O·cean a sea that surrounds the North Pole and lies within the Arctic Circle.

Arc·tic tern ▶ **n.** a red-billed tern (*Sterna paradisaea*) that breeds in the Arctic and adjacent areas, migrating to Antarctic regions for the winter.

Arc·tu·rus /ärk't(y)o͝orəs/ Astron. the brightest star in the constellation Boötes. [from Gk. *arktos* 'bear' + *ouros* 'guardian.']

ar·cu·ate /'ärkyo͞o-it; -,āt/ ▶ **adj.** tech. shaped like a bow; curved. [ME: from L. *arcuatus*, past part. of *arcuare* 'to curve,' from *arcus* 'bow, curve.']

arc weld·ing ▶ **n.** a technique in which metals are welded using heat generated by an electric arc.

-ard ▶ **suffix** forming nouns such as *wizard*. ■ forming nouns having a depreciatory sense: *drunkard*. [ME and OFr., from Ger. *-hard* 'hard, hardy.']

Ar·den /'ärdn/, Elizabeth (*c.*1880–1966), US businesswoman; born in Canada; born *Florence Nightingale Graham*. She had her own line of cosmetics and beauty salons.

Ar·dennes /är'den/ an upland region in parts of Belgium, France, and Luxembourg. It was the scene of fierce fighting in both world wars.

ar·dent /'ärdnt/ ▶ **adj.** enthusiastic or passionate. — **ar·dent·ly adv.** [ME: ult. from L. *ardens, ardent-*, from *ardere* 'to burn.']

ar·dor /'ärdər/ (Brit. **ar·dour**) ▶ **n.** enthusiasm or passion. [ME: via OFr. from L., from *ardere* 'to burn.']

ar·du·ous /'ärjo͞oəs/ ▶ **adj.** involving or requiring strenuous effort; difficult and tiring. — **ar·du·ous·ly adv. ar·du·ous·ness n.** [16th C.: from L. *arduus* 'steep, difficult.']

are[1] /är/ 2nd person singular present and 1st, 2nd, 3rd person plural present of **BE**.

are[2] /är; e(ə)r/ ▶ **n.** hist. a metric unit of measure, equal to 100 square meters (about 119.6 square yards). [18th C.: from Fr., from L. *area* (see **AREA**).]

ar·e·a /'e(ə)rēə/ ▶ **n.** **1** a region or part of a town, a country, or the world. ■ [with adj.] a space allocated for a specific purpose. ■ a part of an object or surface. ■ a subject or range of activity or interest. **2** the extent or measurement of a surface or piece of land. — **ar·e·al adj.** [16th C.: from L., 'vacant piece of level ground.']

ar·e·a code ▶ **n.** a three-digit number that identifies one of the telephone service regions into which the US, Canada, and certain other countries are divided.

ar·e·a rug ▶ **n.** a rug that covers only a part of a floor.

ar·e·a·way /'e(ə)rēə,wā/ ▶ **n.** a sunken enclosure giving access to the basement of a building. ■ a passageway between buildings.

a·re·ca /ə'rēkə; 'arikə; 'e(ə)r-/ (also **areca palm**) ▶ **n.** a tropical Asian palm (genus *Areca*). [via Port. from Malayalam *áḍekka*.]

a·re·ca nut ▶ **n.** the astringent seed of an areca palm (*Areca catechu*), which is often chewed with betel leaves. Also called **BETEL NUT**.

A·re·ci·bo /,ärə'sēbō/ a city in northwestern Puerto Rico, west of San Juan; pop. 49,545.

a·re·na /ə'rēnə/ ▶ **n.** a level area surrounded by seats for spectators, in which public events are held. ■ a place or scene of activity, debate, or conflict. [17th C.: from L. *harena, arena* 'sand, sand-strewn place of combat.']

ar·e·na·ceous /,arə'nāsнəs/ ▶ **adj.** Geol. consisting of sand or sandlike particles. ■ Biol. (of animals or plants) living or growing in sand.

Ar·endt /'ärənt/, Hannah (1906–75), US philosopher; born in Germany. She proposed that Nazism and Stalinism had common roots.

aren't /är(ə)nt/ ▶ **contr.** ■ are not: *they aren't here.* ■ am not (only used in questions): *I'm right, aren't I?*

a·re·o·la /ə'rēələ/ ▶ **n.** (pl. **-lae** /-,lē/) Anat. a small circular area, in particular the ring of pigmented skin surrounding a nipple. ■ Biol. any of the small spaces between the veins on a leaf or the nervures on an insect's wing. ■ Med. a reddened patch around a spot or papule. — **a·re·o·lar adj. a·re·o·late** /-lit; -,lāt/ **adj.** [17th C.: from L., dimin. of *area* (see **AREA**).]

Ar·e·op·a·gus /,arē'äpəgəs/ (in ancient Athens) a hill on which met the highest governmental council and later a judicial court. [from Gk. *Areios pagos* 'hill of Ares.']

A·re·qui·pa /,ärə'kēpə/ a city in southern Peru, in the Andes; pop. 634,500.

Ar·es /'e(ə)rēz/ Gk. Mythol. the Greek war god, son of Zeus and Hera. Roman equivalent **MARS**.

a·rête /ə'rāt/ ▶ **n.** a sharp mountain ridge. [19th C.: from Fr., from L. *arista* 'spine.']

arf /ärf/ ▶ **exclam.** (usu. **arf arf**) used to imitate or represent a dog's bark.

ar·ga·li /'ärgəlē/ ▶ **n.** (pl. same) the largest wild sheep (*Ovis ammon*), which has massive horns and is found in mountainous areas of Asia. [18th C.: from Mongolian.]

Ar·gand di·a·gram /'ärgənd; -gand/ ▶ **n.** Math. a diagram on which complex numbers are represented geometrically using Cartesian axes, the horizontal coordinate representing the real part of the number and the vertical coordinate the complex part. [20th C.: J. R. *Argand* (1768–1822), French mathematician.]

ar·gent /'ärjənt/ ▶ **adj.** literary silver; silvery white. [ME: via OFr. from L. *argentum* 'silver.']

ar·gen·tif·er·ous /,ärjən'tifərəs/ ▶ **adj.** (of rocks or minerals) containing silver.

Argentina

Official name: Argentine Republic
Location: southern South America, bordered on the west by Chile and the east by the Atlantic Ocean
Area: 1,056,900 square miles (2,736,700 sq km)
Population: 39,144,000
Capital: Buenos Aires
Languages: Spanish (official), English, French, German, Italian
Currency: peso

Ar·gen·ti·na /,ärjən'tēnə/ a republic in South America. *See box.* — **Ar·gen·tine** /'ärjən,tēn; -,tīn/ **adj. & n. Ar·gen·tin·i·an adj. & n.**

ar·gen·tine /'ärjən,tīn; -,tēn/ ▶ **adj.** archaic of or resembling silver. [ME: from OFr. *argentin, argentine*, from *argent* 'silver,' from L. *argentum*.]

ar·gil·la·ceous /,ärjə'lāsнəs/ ▶ **adj.** Geol. (of rocks or sediment) consisting of or containing clay. [17th C.: from L. *argillaceus* (from *argilla* 'clay').]

ar·gil·lite /'ärjə,līt/ ▶ **n.** Geol. a sedimentary rock that does not split easily, formed from consolidated clay. [18th C.: from L. *argilla* 'clay.']

ar·gi·nine /'ärjə,nēn; -,nīn/ ▶ **n.** Biochem. a basic amino acid, $HN{=}C(NH_2)NH(CH_2)_3CH(NH_2)COOH$, that is a constituent of most proteins. It is an essential nutrient in the diet of vertebrates. [19th C.: from Ger. *Arginin*, perh. from Gk. *arginoeis* 'white.']

Ar·give /'är,jīv; -,gīv/ ▶ **adj.** of or relating to the ancient city of Argos. ■ (esp. in Homer) Greek. ▶ **n.** a citizen of Argos. ■ (esp. in Homer) a Greek person. [from L. *Argivus*, from Gk. *Argeios* 'relating to Argos.']

Ar·go /'ärgō/ Astron., hist. a large southern constellation (the ship *Argo*). [L.]

ar·gol /'ärgəl/ ▶ **n.** tartar obtained from wine fermentation. [ME: from Anglo-Norman Fr. *argoile*.]

ar·gon /'ärgän/ ▶ **n.** the chemical element of atomic number 18, an inert gaseous element of the noble gas group. Argon is the most common noble gas, making up nearly one percent of the earth's atmosphere. (Symbol: **Ar**) [19th C.: from Gk., neut. of *argos* 'idle,' from *a-* + *ergon* 'work.']

ar·go·naut /'ärgə,nôt/ ▶ **n.** a small floating octopus (genus *Argonauta*), the female of which has webbed arms like sails and secretes a thin, coiled, papery shell in which the eggs are laid. Also called PAPER NAUTILUS.

Ar·go·nauts /ˈärgəˌnôts/ Gk. Mythol. a group of heroes who accompanied Jason on board the ship *Argo* in the quest for the Golden Fleece. [*argonaut* from Gk. *Argonautēs* 'sailor in the ship *Argo*.']

Ar·gonne /ärˈgän; ˈärgän/ a plateau in northeastern France near the Belgian border; major Allied offensive staged here during World War I; occupied by Germany during World War II.

Ar·gos /ˈärgəs; -gôs/ an ancient city in southern Greece, in the northeastern Peloponnese; pop. 20,702.

ar·go·sy /ˈärgəsē/ ▶n. (pl. **-sies**) literary a large merchant ship. [16th C.: appar. from Ital. *Ragusea (nave)* '(vessel) of *Ragusa*.']

ar·got /ˈärgō; -gət/ ▶n. the jargon or slang of a particular group or class: *teenage argot.* [19th C.: from Fr.]

ar·gu·a·ble /ˈärgyo͞oəbəl/ ▶adj. able to be argued or asserted: *an arguable case for judicial review.* ■ open to disagreement; not obviously correct: *a highly arguable assumption.*

ar·gu·a·bly /ˈärgyo͞oəblē/ ▶adv. [sentence adverb] it may be argued (used to qualify the statement of an opinion or belief): *she is arguably the greatest woman tennis player of all time.*

ar·gue /ˈärgyo͞o/ ▶v. (**-gues, -gued, -gu·ing**) **1** [reporting verb] give reasons or cite evidence in support of an idea, action, or theory, typically with the aim of persuading others to share one's view: [with clause] *defense attorneys **argue that the police lacked "probable cause" to arrest the driver.*** ■ [trans.] (**argue someone into/out of**) persuade someone to do or not to do (something) by giving reasons: *I tried to argue him out of it.* **2** [intrans.] exchange diverging or opposite views in a heated or angry way: *don't **argue with me.*** — **ar·gu·er** n. [ME: from OFr. *arguer*, from L. *argutari* 'prattle,' frequentative of *arguere* 'make clear.']

ar·gu·fy /ˈärgyəˌfī/ ▶v. (**-fies, -fied**) [intrans.] humorous or dialect argue or quarrel, typically about something trivial: *it won't do to argufy, I tell you.* [17th C.: from ARGUE.]

ar·gu·ment /ˈärgyəmənt/ ▶n. **1** an exchange of diverging or opposite views, typically a heated or angry one: *I've **had an argument with** my father.* **2** a reason or set of reasons given with the aim of persuading others that an action or idea is right or wrong: *there is a strong **argument for** submitting a formal appeal.* **3** Math. an independent variable associated with a function and determining the value of the function. ■ another term for AMPLITUDE (sense 4). ■ Comput. a value or address passed to a procedure or function at the time of call. **4** archaic a summary of the subject matter of a book.
– PHRASES **for the sake of argument** as a basis for discussion or reasoning. [ME: via OFr. from L. *argumentum*, from *arguere* 'make clear.']

ar·gu·men·ta·tion /ˌärgyəmənˈtāsʜən/ ▶n. the action or process of reasoning systematically in support of an idea, action, or theory: *lines of argumentation used to support his thesis.*

ar·gu·men·ta·tive /ˌärgyəˈmentətiv/ ▶adj. **1** given to expressing divergent or opposite views: *an argumentative child.* **2** using or characterized by systematic reasoning: *the highest standards of argumentative rigor.* — **ar·gu·men·ta·tive·ly** adv. **ar·gu·men·ta·tive·ness** n.

ar·gus /ˈärgəs/ ▶n. **1** (**Argus**) Gk. Mythol. a monster with a hundred eyes, used by Hera to watch over Io. ■ an alert, watchful guardian. **2** (also **argus pheasant**) either of two long-tailed pheasants with generally brown plumage, found in Southeast Asia and Indonesia: ■ the **great argus** (*Argusianus argus*), the male of which has lengthened secondary wing feathers bearing eyespots, spread during display. ■ the **crested argus** (*Rheinartia ocellata*), with the longest tail feathers of any bird. [ME: from L., from Gk. *Argos*.]

Ar·gus-eyed /ˈärgəs/ ▶adj. literary vigilant.

ar·gy-bar·gy /ˈärjē ˈbärjē/ ▶n. (pl. **-gies**) informal, esp. Brit. noisy quarreling or wrangling. [19th C.: rhyming jingle based on ARGUE.]

ar·gyle /ˈärgīl/ ▶n. [usu. as adj.] a pattern composed of diamonds of various colors on a plain background, used in knitted garments such as sweaters and socks. ■ a sock with such a pattern. [1940s: from *Argyll*, name and former county of Scotland.]

argyle

ar·hat /ˈärhət/ ▶n. (in Buddhism and Jainism) someone who has attained the goal of the religious life. [19th C.: from Sanskrit, lit. 'meritorious.']

År·hus var. of AARHUS.

a·rhyth·mic ▶adj. var. of ARRHYTHMIC.

a·ri·a /ˈärēə/ ▶n. Music a long, accompanied song for a solo voice, typically one in an opera or oratorio. [18th C.: from Ital., from L. *aer* 'air.']

Ar·i·ad·ne /ˌarēˈadnē/ Gk. Mythol. the daughter of King Minos, who helped Theseus to escape from the Minotaur's labyrinth.

Ar·i·an /ˈe(ə)rēən/ ▶n. **1** an adherent of Arianism. **2** a person born under the sign of Aries. ▶adj. **1** of or concerning Arianism. **2** of or relating to a person born under the sign of Aries.

-arian ▶suffix (forming adjectives and corresponding nouns) having a concern or belief in a specified thing: *antiquarian* | *humanitarian* | *vegetarian.* [from L. *-arius*.]

Ar·i·an·ism /ˈe(ə)rēəˌnizəm/ ▶n. Christian Theol. a heresy denying the divinity of Christ, originating with the Alexandrian priest Arius (*c.*250–*c.*336).

ar·id /ˈarid/ ▶adj. (of land or a climate) having little or no rain; too dry or barren to support vegetation: *hot and arid conditions.* ■ fig. lacking in interest, excitement, or meaning: *his arid years in suburbia.* — **a·rid·i·ty** /əˈriditē/ n. **ar·id·ly** adv. **ar·id·ness** n. [17th C.: from Fr. *aride* or L. *aridus*, from *arere* 'be dry.']

Ar·i·el /ˈe(ə)rēəl/ **1** Astron. a satellite of Uranus. **2** a series of satellites devoted to studies of the ionosphere and X-ray astronomy (1962–79). [after a spirit in Shakespeare's *The Tempest*.]

Ar·ies /ˈe(ə)rēz; ˈe(ə)rē-ēz/ **1** Astron. a small constellation (the Ram), said to represent the ram whose Golden Fleece was sought by Jason and the Argonauts. **2** Astrol. the first sign of the zodiac, which the sun enters at the vernal equinox (about March 20). ■ (**an Aries**) (pl. same) a person born when the sun is in this sign. [L.]

ar·il /ˈarəl/ ▶n. Bot. an extra seed covering, typically colored and hairy or fleshy, e.g., the red fleshy cup around a yew seed. — **ar·il·late** /-əlit; -əˌlāt/ adj. [18th C.: from mod. L. *arillus*, perh. akin to med. L. *arilli* 'dried grapestones.']

a·rio·so /ˌärēˈōsō; -zō/ Music ▶adj. & adv. in a melodious, expressive, songlike style. ▶n. (pl. **-sos**) a piece of music to be performed in this way. [Ital., from ARIA.]

A·ri·os·to /ˌärēˈästō; -ˈōstō/, Ludovico (1474–1533), Italian poet. He wrote the epic *Orlando Furioso* (1532).

-arious ▶suffix forming adjectives such as *gregarious, vicarious.* [from L. *-arius* + -OUS.]

a·rise /əˈrīz/ ▶v. (past **a·rose** /əˈrōz/; past part. **a·ris·en** /əˈrizən/) [intrans.] **1** emerge; become apparent: *new difficulties had arisen.* ■ come into being; originate: *the practice arose in the nineteenth century.* ■ (**arise from/out of**) occur as a result of: *most conflicts arise from ignorance or uncertainty.* **2** formal or literary get or stand up: *he arose at 9:30 and went out for a walk.* [OE *ārisan*, from *ā-* 'away' + RISE (v.).]

Ar·is·tar·chus[1] /ˌarəˈstärkəs/ (3rd century BC), Greek astronomer; known as **Aristarchus of Samos**. He founded a school of Hellenic astronomy.

Ar·is·tar·chus[2] (*c.*217–145 BC), Greek scholar; known as **Aristarchus of Samothrace**. He is noted for his editions of the writings of Homer.

A·ri·stide /ärēˈstēd/, Jean-Bertrand (1953–), president of Haiti 1991–96, 2001–04. Exiled 1991 by a military coup, he returned 1994; deposed by coup 2004.

Ar·is·ti·des /ˌarəˈstīdēz/ (5th century BC), Athenian general; known as **Aristides the Just**. He led the Athenian army at the battle of Plataea (479 BC).

Ar·is·tip·pus /ˌarəˈstipəs/ (late 5th century BC), Greek philosopher; known as **Aristippus the Elder (of Cyrene)**. He founded the Cyrenaic school.

a·ris·to /əˈristō/ informal term for ARISTOCRAT.

ar·is·toc·ra·cy /ˌariˈstäkrəsē/ ▶n. (pl. **-cies**) [treated as sing. or pl.] (usu. **the aristocracy**) the highest class in certain societies, esp. those holding hereditary titles or offices. ■ a form of government in which power is held by the nobility. ■ a state governed in this way. ■ fig. a group regarded as privileged or superior in a particular sphere: *high-level technocrats make up a large part of this "technical aristocracy."* [15th C.: from OFr. *aristocratie*, from Gk. *aristokratia*, from *aristos* 'best' + *-kratia* 'power.']

a·ris·to·crat /əˈristəˌkrat/ ▶n. a member of the aristocracy: *an aristocrat by birth.* ■ something believed to be the best of its kind: *the trout is the aristocrat of freshwater fish.*

a·ris·to·crat·ic /əˌristəˈkratik/ ▶adj. of or relating to the aristocracy: *an aristocratic family.* ■ distinguished in manners or bearing: *a stately, aristocratic manner.* ■ grand; stylish: *aristocratic-sounding names* | *a snob with aristocratic aspirations.* — **a·ris·to·crat·i·cal·ly** /-ik(ə)lē/ adv.

Ar·is·toph·a·nes /ˌarəˈstäfəˌnēz/ (*c.*450–*c.*385 BC), Greek playwright. He wrote *The Birds* and *The Frogs*.

Ar·is·to·te·lian /əˌristəˈtēlyən; -lēən; ˌaristə-/ ▶adj. of or relating to Aristotle or his philosophy. ▶n. a student of Aristotle or an adherent of his philosophy.

Ar·is·to·te·lian log·ic ▶n. the traditional system of deductive logic expounded by Aristotle.

Ar·is·tot·le /ˈarəˌstätl; ˌarəˈstätl/ (384–322 BC), Greek philosopher and scientist. A pupil of Plato and tutor to Alexander the Great, he founded a school (the Lyceum) outside Athens. His surviving works cover logic, ethics, metaphysics, politics, natural science, and physics.

a·rith·me·tic ▶n. /əˈriᴛʜməˌtik/ the branch of mathematics dealing with the properties and manipulation of numbers: *the laws of arithmetic.* ■ the use of numbers in counting and calculation: *he could do arithmetic in his head.* ▶adj. /ˌariᴛʜˈmetik/ (also **ar·ith·met·i·cal**) of or relating to arithmetic: *perform arithmetic functions.* — **a·rith·me·ti·cian** /əˌriᴛʜməˈtisʜən/ n. [ME: from OFr. *arismetique*, based on Gk. *arithmētikē (tekhnē)* '(art) of counting,' from *arithmos* 'number.']

a·rith·me·tic mean /ˌariᴛʜˈmetik/ ▶n. the average of a set of numerical values, calculated by adding them together and dividing by the number of terms in the set.

a·rith·me·tic pro·gres·sion /ˌariᴛʜˈmetik/ (also **arithmetic series**) ▶n. a sequence of numbers in which each differs from the preceding by a constant quantity (e.g., 3, 6, 9, 12, etc.; 9, 7, 5, 3, etc.). ■ the relationship between numbers in such a sequence: *the numbers are in arithmetic progression.*

-arium ▶suffix forming nouns usually denoting a place: *planetarium* |

vivarium. [from L., neut. of adjectives in *-arius.*]

Ariz. ▶ abbr. Arizona.

Ar·i·zo·na /,arəˈzōnə/ a state in the southwestern US, on the border with Mexico; pop. 5,130,632; capital, Phoenix; statehood, Feb. 14, 1912 (48). Part of New Spain until 1821, it was organized as a US territory in 1863 from lands ceded by the Treaty of Guadalupe Hidalgo in 1848 and the Gadsden Purchase in 1853. — **Ar·i·zo·nan** n. & adj.

Ar·ju·na /ˈärjənə; ˈər-/ Hinduism a hero prince in the Mahabharata.

Ark. ▶ abbr. Arkansas.

ark /ärk/ ▶ n. **1** (**the ark**) (in the Bible) the ship built by Noah to save his family and two of every kind of animal from the Flood; Noah's ark. ■ fig. a vessel or sanctuary that serves as protection against extinction: *a starship ark built by their android protectors.* ■ archaic a chest or box: *the ark was of Italian walnut.* ■ a large, flat-bottomed boat. **2** short for ARK OF THE COVENANT. ■ (also **Holy Ark**) a chest or cupboard housing the Torah scrolls in a synagogue. [OE *ærc,* from L. *arca* 'chest.']

Ar·kan·sas /ˈärkən,sô/ a state in the southern central US, on the western banks of the Mississippi River; pop. 2,673,400; capital, Little Rock; statehood, June 15, 1836 (25). It seceded from the Union in 1861 to join the Confederacy during the Civil War and rejoined the Union in 1868.

Ar·kan·sas Riv·er /ˈärkən,sô; ärˈkanzəs/ a river rising in the Rockies in Colorado and flowing for 1,450 miles (2,320 km) to the Mississippi River in Arkansas.

Ar·khan·gelsk /ärˈKHängilsk; ärˈkaNG,gelsk/ Russian name for ARCHANGEL.

Ark of the Cov·e·nant the chest containing the tablets of the laws of the ancient Israelites, which was kept in the Temple at Jerusalem.

ar·kose /ˈärkōs/ ▶ n. Geol. a coarse-grained sandstone that is at least 25 percent feldspar. —**ar·ko·sic** /ärˈkōsik/ adj. [19th C.: from Fr., prob. from Gk. *arkhaios* 'ancient.']

Arles /ärl/ a city in southeastern France; pop. 52,590.

Ar·ling·ton /ˈärliNGtən/ **1** a county in northern Virginia, site of the Pentagon and Arlington National Cemetery. **2** a town in eastern Massachusetts, northwest of Boston; pop. 44,630. **3** an industrial city in northern Texas, between Dallas and Fort Worth; pop. 332,969.

Ar·ling·ton Heights a village in northeastern Illinois, northwest of Chicago; pop. 76,031.

arm¹ /ärm/ ▶ n. **1** each of the two upper limbs of the human body from the shoulder to the hand: *she held the baby in her arms.* ■ (in technical use) each of these upper limbs from the shoulder to the elbow. ■ each of the forelimbs of an animal. ■ a flexible limb of an invertebrate animal, e.g., an octopus. ■ a sleeve of a garment. ■ an ability to throw a ball skillfully: *he has a good arm.* ■ an athlete with such an ability: *he wasn't the best arm in the outfield.* ■ used to refer to the holding of a person's arm in support or companionship: *he arrived with a pretty girl on his arm.* **2** a thing resembling an arm in form or function, in particular: ■ a side part of a chair or other seat on which a sitter's arm can rest. ■ a narrow strip of water or land projecting from a larger body. ■ a large branch of a tree. **3** a branch or division of a company or organization: *the political arm of the separatist group.* ■ one of the types of troops of which an army is composed, such as infantry or artillery. [also understood as a figurative use of ARM².]
– PHRASES **arm in arm** with arms linked. **the long arm of the law** used to refer to the criminal justice system as far-reaching: *act now before the long arm of the law catches up with you.* **as long as one's** (or **someone's**) **arm** informal very long: *I have a list of vices as long as your arm.* **cost an arm and a leg** informal be extremely expensive. **give one's right arm** informal used to convey a strong desire to have or do something: *I'd give my right arm to go with them.* **into the arms of** into the possession or control of: *the violin passed into the arms of a wealthy dilettante.* **keep someone/something at arm's length** avoid intimacy or close contact with someone or something. **with open arms** with great affection or enthusiasm: *schools have welcomed such arrangements with open arms.* —**arm·ful** /-,fo͝ol/ n. (pl. **-fuls**) **arm·less** adj. [OE *arm, earm,* Gmc.; akin to Ger. *Arm.*]

arm² ▶ v. [trans.] supply or provide with weapons: *both sides* **armed** *themselves with grenades.* ■ supply or provide with equipment, tools, or other items in preparation or readiness for something: *she* **armed** *them with brushes and mops.* ■ activate the fuse of (a bomb or other device) so that it is ready to explode. ▶ n. see ARMS. [ME: ult. from L. *armare,* from *arma* 'armor, arms.']

ar·ma·da /ärˈmädə/ ▶ n. a fleet of warships. ■ (**the Spanish Armada**) a Spanish naval invasion force defeated by the English fleet in 1588. [16th C.: from Sp., from *armata,* fem. past part. of L. *armare* 'to arm.']

ar·ma·dil·lo /,ärməˈdilō/ ▶ n. (pl. **-los**) a nocturnal omnivorous mammal native to Central and South America, with large claws for digging and a body covered in bony plates. Several genera and species include the **nine-banded armadillo** (*Dasypus novemcinctus,* family Dasypodidae), which has spread into the southern US. [16th C.: from Sp., dimin. of *armado* 'armed man,' from L. *armatus.*]

Ar·ma·ged·don /,ärməˈgedn/ ▶ n. (in the New Testament) the last battle between good and evil before the Day of Judgment. ■ the place where this battle will be fought. ■ a dramatic and catastrophic conflict, typically seen as likely to destroy the world or the human race: *nuclear Armageddon.* [Gk., from Heb. *har mĕgiddōn* 'hill of Megiddo' (Rev. 16:16).]

Ar·magh /ärˈmä; ˈär,mä/ one of the Six Counties of Northern Ireland, formerly an administrative area. ■ the chief town of this county; pop. 12,700.

Ar·mag·nac /,ärmənˈyak; -ˈyäk/ n. a type of brandy, traditionally made in Aquitaine in southwestern France.

ar·ma·ment /ˈärməmənt/ ▶ n. (also **armaments**) military weapons and equipment: *chemical weapons and other unconventional armaments.* ■ the process of equipping military forces for war. ■ archaic a military force equipped for war. [17th C.: from L. *armamentum,* from *armare* 'to arm.']

ar·ma·men·tar·i·um /,ärməmənˈte(ə)rēəm/ ▶ n. (pl. **-tar·i·a** /-ˈte(ə)rēə/) the medicines, equipment, and techniques available to a medical practitioner. ■ the resources available for a certain purpose: *the entire armamentarium of electronic surveillance.* [19th C.: from L., 'arsenal.']

Ar·ma·ni /ärˈmänē/, Giorgio (1935–), Italian fashion designer.

ar·ma·ture /ˈärməCHər; -,CHo͝or/ ▶ n. **1** the rotating coil or coils of a dynamo or electric motor. ■ any moving part of an electrical machine in which a voltage is induced by a magnetic field. ■ a piece of iron or other object acting as a keeper for a magnet. **2** a metal framework on which a sculpture is molded with clay or similar material. **3** Biol. the protective covering of an animal or plant. ■ archaic armor. [ME: from Fr., from L. *armatura* 'armor,' from *armare* 'to arm.']

arm·band /ˈärm,band/ ▶ n. a band worn around the upper arm to hold up a shirtsleeve or as a symbol.

arm can·dy ▶ n. informal a sexually attractive companion accompanying a person, esp. a celebrity, at social events: *the athletes and their arm candy clustered around the bar.*

arm·chair ▶ n. /ˈärm,CHe(ə)r/ a comfortable chair, typically upholstered, with side supports for the arms. ▶ adj. [attrib.] not involving direct experience of a subject or activity: *armchair adventurers.*

armed /ärmd/ ▶ adj. equipped with or carrying a weapon or weapons. ■ involving the use of firearms: *armed robbery.* ■ (of a bomb, alarm, or other device) prepared to activate or explode. ■ fig. supplied with equipment, tools, or other items in preparation or readiness for something: *he is armed with a list of questions.*
– PHRASES **armed to the teeth** see TEETH.

armed camp ▶ n. a town, territory, or group of people fully armed for war.

armed forc·es (also **armed services**) ▶ plural n. a country's military forces, esp. its army, navy, and air force.

Armenia

Official name: Republic of Armenia
Location: southwestern Asia, in the Caucasus
Area: 11,000 square miles (28,400 sq km)
Population: 2,991,000
Capital: Yerevan
Languages: Armenian (official), Russian
Currency: dram

Ar·me·ni·a /ärˈmēnēə/ a country in southwestern Asia. *See box.*

Ar·me·ni·an /ärˈmēnēən; -ˈmēnyən/ ▶ adj. of or relating to Armenia, its language, or the Christian Church established there (*c.* 300). ▶ n. **1** a native of Armenia or a person of Armenian descent. **2** the Indo-European language of Armenia.

arm·guard /ˈärm,gärd/ ▶ n. another term for BRACER².

arm·hole /ˈärm,hōl/ ▶ n. each of two openings in a garment through which the wearer puts their arms.

ar·mi·ger /ˈärmijər/ ▶ n. a person entitled to heraldic arms. —**ar·mig·er·ous** /ärˈmijərəs/ adj. [16th C.: L., lit. 'bearing arms,' from *arma* 'arms' + *gerere* 'to bear.']

ar·mil·lar·y sphere /ˈärmə,lerē/ ▶ n. a model of the celestial globe constructed from rings and hoops representing the equator, the tropics, and other celestial circles, and able to revolve on its axis. [17th C.: from mod. L. *armillaris* 'relating to an *armilla,*' astronomical instrument, from L. *armilla* 'bracelet.']

Ar·min·i·an /är'minēən/ ▶ **adj.** relating to the doctrines of Jacobus Arminius (1560–1609), a Dutch Protestant theologian, who rejected the Calvinist doctrine of predestination. ▶ **n.** an adherent of these doctrines. — **Ar·min·i·an·ism** /-ə,nizəm/ **n.**

ar·mi·stice /'ärməstis/ ▶ **n.** an agreement made by opposing sides in a war to stop fighting for a certain time; a truce. [18th C.: from Fr., or from mod. L. *armistitium*, from *arma* 'arms' + *-stitium* 'stoppage.']

Ar·mi·stice Day ▶ **n.** the anniversary of the armistice of November 11, 1918, now replaced by Veterans Day.

arm·let /'ärmlit/ ▶ **n.** **1** a band or bracelet worn around the upper part of a person's arm. **2** a small inlet of a sea or branch of a river.

arm·load /'ärm,lōd/ ▶ **n.** the amount that can be carried with one arm or in both arms.

arm·lock /'ärm,läk/ ▶ **n.** a method of restraining someone by holding an arm tightly behind their back.

ar·moire /ärm'wär; 'ärm,wär/ ▶ **n.** a wardrobe or movable cabinet, typically one that is ornate or antique. [16th C.: from Fr., from OFr. *armarie* (see AUMBRY).]

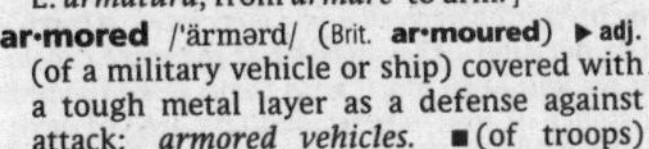

armoire

ar·mor /'ärmər/ (Brit. **ar·mour**) ▶ **n.** metal coverings formerly worn by soldiers to protect the body in battle. ■ (also **armor plate**) the tough metal layer covering a military vehicle or ship to defend it from attack. ■ military vehicles collectively: *the contingent includes infantry, armor, and logistic units.* ■ the protective layer or shell of some animals and plants. ■ a person's emotional, social, or other defenses: *his armor of self-confidence.* ▶ **v.** [trans.] provide (someone) with emotional, social, or other defenses: *the knowledge armored him against her.* — **ar·mor·plat·ed adj.** [ME: from OFr. *armure*, from L. *armatura*, from *armare* 'to arm.']

ar·mored /'ärmərd/ (Brit. **ar·moured**) ▶ **adj.** (of a military vehicle or ship) covered with a tough metal layer as a defense against attack: *armored vehicles.* ■ (of troops) equipped with such vehicles: *the 2nd Armored Division.* ■ (of some animals and plants) having a protective layer or shell: *armored fish.*

ar·mored per·son·nel car·ri·er ▶ **n.** an armored military vehicle used to transport troops.

ar·mor·er /'ärmərər/ (Brit. **ar·mour·er**) ▶ **n.** **1** a maker, supplier, or repairer of weapons or armor. **2** an official in charge of the arms of a military unit.

ar·mo·ri·al /är'môrēəl/ ▶ **adj.** of or relating to heraldry or heraldic devices: *armorial shields.*

ar·mor·y[1] /'ärmərē/ (Brit. **armoury**) ▶ **n.** (pl. **-ies**) **1** a place where arms are kept. ■ a supply of arms: *the most powerful weapon in our armory.* ■ a place where arms are manufactured. ■ [in sing.] fig. an array of resources available for a particular purpose: *his armory of comic routines.* **2** a place where military reservists are trained or headquartered.

ar·mor·y[2] ▶ **n.** [mass noun] heraldry. [ME: from OFr. *armoierie* (see ARMOURY).]

ar·mour ▶ **n.** British spelling of ARMOR.

arm·pit /'ärm,pit/ ▶ **n.** a hollow under the arm at the shoulder; also called AXILLA. ■ informal a place regarded as extremely unpleasant: *they call the region the armpit of America.*

– PHRASES **up to one's armpits** deeply involved in a particular unpleasant situation or enterprise: *the country is **up to its armpits** in drug trafficking.*

arm·rest /'ärm,rest/ ▶ **n.** a padded or upholstered arm of a chair or other seat on which one's arm can rest.

arms /ärmz/ ▶ **plural n.** **1** weapons and ammunition; armaments: *they were subjugated by force of arms* **2** distinctive emblems or devices, forming the heraldic insignia of families, corporations, or countries. See also COAT OF ARMS.

– PHRASES **a call to arms** a call to prepare for confrontation: *a call to arms to defend against a takeover.* **up in arms** protesting vigorously about something: *teachers are up in arms about new school tests.* [ME: from OFr. *armes*, from L. *arma*.]

arms con·trol ▶ **n.** international disarmament or arms limitation, esp. by mutual consent.

arms race ▶ **n.** a competition between nations for superiority in the development and accumulation of weapons, esp. between the US and the former USSR during the Cold War.

Arm·strong[1] /'ärm,strôNG/, Edwin Howard (1890–1954), US engineer. He invented the frequency modulation (FM) system.

Arm·strong[2], Lance (1971–) US cyclist. After surviving advanced testicular cancer, he won the Tour de France seven times (1999–2005).

Arm·strong[3], Louis (1900–71), US musician; known as **Satchmo**; full name *Louis Daniel Armstrong.* A major influence on Dixieland jazz, he was a trumpet and cornet player, as well as a bandleader and a distinctive singer.

Arm·strong[4], Neil Alden (1930–), US astronaut. He was the first man to set foot on the moon (July 20, 1969), during the Apollo 11 mission.

arm-twist·ing ▶ **n.** informal persuasion by the use of physical force or moral pressure: *eight years of arguing and diplomatic arm-twisting.* — **arm-twist v.**

arm-wres·tling ▶ **n.** a trial of strength in which two people sit opposite each other with one elbow resting on a table, clasp each other's hands, and try to force each other's arm down onto the table. — **arm-wres·tle v.**

ar·my /'ärmē/ ▶ **n.** (pl. **-mies**) an organized military force equipped for fighting on land. ■ (**the army** or **the Army**) the branch of a nation's armed services that conducts military operations on land: *an enlisted man in the army* | [as adj.] *army officers.* ■ (**an army of** or **armies of**) a large number of people or things: *an army of photographers* [ME: from OFr. *armee*, from *armata*, fem. past part. of L. *armare* 'to arm.']

ar·my ant ▶ **n.** a blind nomadic tropical ant that forages in large columns, preying chiefly on insects and spiders. Also called DRIVER ANT.

ar·my brat ▶ **n.** informal a child of a career soldier, esp. one who has lived in various places as a result of military transfers.

ar·my is·sue ▶ **n.** [usu. as adj.] equipment or clothing supplied by the army.

ar·my-na·vy ▶ **adj.** denoting the type of store that specializes in military surplus equipment, or the goods sold there.

ar·my worm ▶ **n.** any of a number of insect larvae that occur in large numbers, in particular: ■ the caterpillars of some moths (*Spodoptera* and other genera, family Noctuidae), which feed on cereals and other crops, moving *en masse* when the food is exhausted. ■ the small maggots of certain gnats (genus *Sciara*, family Mycetophilidae) that feed on fungi and move in very large numbers within secreted slime.

Arne /ärn/, Thomas (1710–78), English composer. He wrote the music for "Rule, Brittania."

Arn·hem /'ärnəm; 'ärn,hem/ a town in the eastern Netherlands; pop. 131,700.

Arn·hem Land a peninsula in Northern Territory, Australia.

ar·ni·ca /'ärnikə/ ▶ **n.** a plant (genus *Arnica*) of the daisy family that bears yellow daisylike flowers. ■ a preparation of this plant (chiefly *A. montana* of central Europe) used medicinally, esp. for the treatment of bruises. [18th C.: mod. L.]

Ar·no /'ärnō/ a river that rises in northern Italy and flows west for 150 miles (240 km) to the Ligurian Sea.

Ar·nold[1] /'ärnld/, Benedict (1741–1801), American general who conspired to surrender West Point to the British during the Revolutionary War. His name became synonymous with "traitor."

Ar·nold[2], Matthew (1822–88), English poet and critic. His poetry included "Dover Beach" (1867) and "Westminster Abbey" (1882).

ar·oid /'aroid/ (also **aroid lily**) ▶ **n.** Bot. a plant of the arum family (Araceae). [19th C.: from ARUM.]

a·ro·ma /ə'rōmə/ ▶ **n.** a distinctive, typically pleasant smell: *the tantalizing aroma of fresh coffee.* ■ a subtle, pervasive quality or atmosphere of a particular type: *the aroma of officialdom.* [ME: via L. from Gk. *arōma* 'spice.']

a·ro·ma·ther·a·py /ə,rōmə'THerəpē/ ▶ **n.** the use of aromatic plant extracts and essential oils in massage or baths. — **a·ro·ma·ther·a·peu·tic** /-,THerə'pyo͞otik/ **adj.** **a·ro·ma·ther·a·pist** /-pist/ **n.**

ar·o·mat·ic /,arə'matik/ ▶ **adj.** **1** having a pleasant and distinctive smell. **2** Chem. (of an organic compound) containing a planar unsaturated ring of atoms that is stabilized by an interaction of the bonds forming the ring. ▶ **n.** **1** a substance or plant emitting a pleasant and distinctive smell. **2** (usu. **aromatics**) Chem. an aromatic compound. — **ar·o·mat·i·cal·ly** /-ik(ə)lē/ **adv.** **ar·o·ma·tic·i·ty** /-mə'tisitē/ **n.** (Chem.). [ME: via OFr. ult. from Gk. *arōmatikos*, from *arōma*.]

a·ro·ma·tize /ə'rōmə,tīz/ ▶ **v.** [trans.] **1** Chem. convert (a compound) into an aromatic structure. **2** cause to have a pleasant and distinctive smell. — **a·ro·ma·ti·za·tion** /ə,rōməti'zāSHən/ **n.**

a·rose /ə'rōz/ past of ARISE.

a·round /ə'round/ ▶ **adv.** **1** (Brit. also **round**) located or situated on every side: *the mountains towering all around.* ■ so as to surround someone or something: *everyone crowded around.* ■ with circular motion: *the boats were spun around by waterspouts.* ■ so as to cover or take in the whole area surrounding a particular center: *she paused to glance around admiringly at the décor.* ■ so as to reach everyone in a particular group or area: *he passed a newspaper clipping around.* **2** (Brit. also **round**) so as to rotate and face in the opposite direction: *Jack seized her by the shoulders and turned her around.* ■ so as to lead in another direction: *it was the last house before the road curved around.* ■ used in describing the position of something, typically with regard to the direction in which it is facing or its relation to other items: *the picture shows the pieces the wrong way around.* ■ used to describe a situation in terms of the relation between people, actions, or events: *it was he who was attacking her, not the other way around.* **3** (Brit. also **round**) so as to reach a new place or position, typically by moving from one side of something to the other: *he made his way around to the back of the building.* ■ in or to many places throughout a locality: *his only ambition is to drive around in a sports car.* ■ used to convey an ability to navigate or orient oneself: *I like pupils to find their own way around.* ■ informal used to convey the idea of visiting someone else: *why don't you come around to my office?* ■ randomly or unsystematically; here and

there: *one of them was glancing nervously around.* **4** (Brit. also **round**) in existence, in the vicinity, or in active use: *there was no one around.* **5** approximately; about: *software costs would be around $1,500* | [as prep.] *I returned to my hotel around 3 a.m.* ▶ **prep.** (Brit. also **round**) **1** on every side of: *the palazzo is built around a courtyard* | *the hills around the city.* ■ (of something abstract) having (the thing mentioned) as a focal point: *our entire culture is built around those loyalties.* **2** in or to many places throughout (a locality): *cycling around the village.* ■ on the other side of (a corner or obstacle): *Steven parked the car around the corner.* **3** so as to encircle or embrace (someone or something): *he put his arm around her.* ■ following an approximately circular route: *it can drill around corners.* ■ so as to cover or take in the whole area of (a place): *she went around the house and saw that all the windows were barred.*
– PHRASES **around the bend** see BEND[1]. **have been around** informal have a lot of varied experience and understanding of the world. [ME: from A-[2] 'in, on' + ROUND.]

a·rouse /ə'rouz/ ▶ **v.** [trans.] **1** evoke or awaken (a feeling, emotion, or response): *something about the man aroused the guard's suspicions.* ■ excite or provoke (someone) to anger or strong emotions: *an ability to influence the audience and to arouse the masses.* ■ excite (someone) sexually. **2** awaken (someone) from sleep. — **a·rous·al** /ə'rouzəl/ **n.** [16th C.: from ROUSE.]

Arp /ärp/, Jean (1887–1966), French painter and sculptor; also known as **Hans Arp.** He cofounded the Dada movement.

ar·peg·gi·ate /är'pejē,āt/ ▶ **v.** [trans.] Music play (a chord) as a series of ascending or descending notes. — **ar·peg·gi·a·tion** /är,pejē'āshən/ **n. ar·peg·gi·a·tor** /-,ātər/ **n.**

ar·peg·gi·o /är'pejē,ō/ ▶ **n.** (pl. **-os**) Music the notes of a chord played in succession, either ascending or descending. [Ital., from *arpeggiare* 'play the harp,' from *arpa* 'harp.']

ar·que·bus /'ärk(w)əbəs/ ▶ **n.** var. of HARQUEBUS.

arr. ▶ **abbr.** ■ (of a piece of music) arranged by: *Variations on a theme of Corelli (arr. Wild).* ■ (with reference to the arrival time of a bus, train, or airplane) arrives.

ar·rack /'arək; ə'rak/ (also **ar·ak**) ▶ **n.** an alcoholic liquor typically distilled from the sap of the coconut palm or from rice. [17th C.: from Arab. *arak* 'sweat,' from *arak al-tamr*, 'alcoholic spirit made from dates.']

ar·raign /ə'rān/ ▶ **v.** (often **be arraigned**) call or bring (someone) before a court to answer a criminal charge: *her sister was* ***arraigned on*** *attempted murder charges.* ■ find fault with (someone or something); censure: *the soldiers bitterly arraigned the government for failing to keep its word.* — **ar·raign·ment n.** [ME: from OFr. *araisnier*, based on L. *ad-* 'to' + *ration-* 'reason.']

Ar·ran /'arən/ an island in the Firth of Clyde, in western Scotland.

ar·range /ə'rānj/ ▶ **v.** [trans.] **1** put (things) in a neat, attractive, or required order: *she had just finished arranging the flowers.* **2** organize or make plans for (a future event): *they hoped to arrange a meeting.* ■ [intrans.] reach agreement about an action or event in advance: *I* ***arranged with*** *my boss to have the time off.* **3** Music adapt (a composition) for performance with instruments or voices other than those originally specified: *songs* ***arranged for*** *viola and piano.* — **ar·range·a·ble adj. ar·rang·er n.** [ME: from OFr. *arangier*, from *a-* 'to') + *rangier* 'to range' (see RANGE).]

ar·range·ment /ə'rānjmənt/ ▶ **n. 1** the action, process, or result of arranging or being arranged: *the arrangement of the furniture in the room.* ■ a thing that has been arranged in a neat or attractive way: *an intricate arrangement of gravel paths.* **2** (usu. **arrangements**) plans or preparations for a future event: *all the* ***arrangements for*** *the wedding were made.* ■ an agreement with someone: *the travel agents have an* ***arrangement with*** *the hotel.* **3** Music a composition adapted for performance with different instruments or voices than those originally specified.

ar·rant /'arənt/ ▶ **adj.** [attrib.] dated complete, utter: *what arrant nonsense!* [ME: var. of ERRANT.]

Ar·ras /ä'räs; 'arəs/ a town in northeastern France; pop. 42,700.

ar·ras /'arəs/ ▶ **n.** a rich tapestry, typically hung on the walls of a room or used to conceal an alcove. [ME: ARRAS.]

ar·ray /ə'rā/ ▶ **n. 1** an impressive display or range of a particular type of thing: *a bewildering array of choices.* **2** an ordered arrangement, in particular: ■ an arrangement of troops. ■ Math. an arrangement of quantities or symbols in rows and columns. ■ Comput. an ordered set of related elements. **3** literary elaborate or beautiful clothing: *he was clothed in fine array.* ▶ **v. 1** [trans.] (usu. **be arrayed**) display or arrange (things) in a particular way: *the forces arrayed against him.* **2** [trans.] (usu. **be arrayed in**) dress someone in (the clothes specified): *they were arrayed in Hungarian national dress.* [ME: from OFr. *arei* (n.), *areer* (v.), based on L. *ad-* 'toward' + Gmc. base 'prepare.']

ar·rears /ə'ri(ə)rz/ ▶ **plural n.** money that is owed and should have been paid earlier.
– PHRASES **in arrears** (also esp. Law **in arrear**) behind in paying money that is owed: *two out of three tenants are in arrears.* ■ (of payments made or due for wages, rent, etc.) at the end of each period of work or occupancy: *you will be paid monthly in arrears.* — **ar·rear·age** /ə'ri(ə)rij/ **n.** [ME: from *arrear* (adv.) 'behind' ult. from med. L. *adretro*, from *ad-* 'toward' + *retro* 'backward.']

ar·rest /ə'rest/ ▶ **v.** [trans.] **1** seize (someone) by legal authority and take into custody. **2** stop or check (progress or a process): *the spread of the disease can be arrested.* **3** attract the attention of (someone): *his attention was arrested by a strange sound.* ▶ **n. 1** the action of seizing someone to take into custody: *I have a warrant for your arrest.* **2** a stoppage or sudden cessation of motion: [with adj.] *a cardiac arrest.* [ME: from OFr. *arester*, based on L. *ad-* 'to' + *restare* 'stop.']

ar·rest·ee /ə,res'tē/ ▶ **n.** a person who has been arrested.

ar·rest·er /ə'restər/ (also **ar·res·tor**) ▶ **n.** [usu. with adj.] a device that prevents or stops a specified thing: *a spark arrester* | *a lightning arrester.* ■ a device on an aircraft carrier that slows aircraft after landing by means of a hook and cable.

ar·rest·ing /ə'restiNG/ ▶ **adj. 1** striking; eye-catching: *at 6 feet 6 inches he was an arresting figure.* **2** a person or agency that seizes and detains (someone or something) by legal authority: *the arresting officer.* — **ar·rest·ing·ly adv.**

Ar·rhe·ni·us /ə'rēnēəs; -ə'rā-/, Svante August (1859–1927), Swedish chemist. He worked with electrolytes. Nobel Prize for Chemistry (1903).

ar·rhyth·mi·a /ā'riTHmēə; ə'riTH-/ ▶ **n.** Med. a condition in which the heart beats with an irregular or abnormal rhythm. — **ar·rhyth·mic** /-mik/ **adj.** [19th C.: from Gk. *arruthmia* 'lack of rhythm,' from *a-* + *rhuthmos* (see RHYTHM).]

ar·rhyth·mic /ə'riTHmik/ (also **a·rhyth·mic**) ▶ **adj.** not rhythmic; without rhythm or regularity. ■ Med. of, relating to, or suffering from cardiac arrhythmia. — **ar·rhyth·mi·cal adj. ar·rhyth·mi·cal·ly** /-mik(ə)lē/ **adv.**

ar·rière-pen·sée /ä,ryer päN'sā/ ▶ **n.** a concealed thought or intention; an ulterior motive. [19th C.: Fr., lit. 'behind thought.']

ar·ris /'aris/ ▶ **n.** Archit. a sharp edge formed by the meeting of two flat or curved surfaces. [17th C.: alt. of early mod. Fr. *areste* 'sharp ridge,' earlier form of ARÊTE.]

ar·ri·val /ə'rīvəl/ ▶ **n.** the action or process of arriving: *Ruth's arrival in New York.* ■ a person who has arrived somewhere: *hotel staff greeted the late arrivals.* ■ the emergence or appearance of a new development, phenomenon, or product: *the arrival of democracy.* ■ such a new development, phenomenon, or product: *sociology is a relatively new arrival on the academic scene.*

ar·rive /ə'rīv/ ▶ **v.** [intrans.] reach a place at the end of a journey or a stage in a journey: *we* ***arrived at*** *his house and knocked at the door.* ■ be brought or delivered: *the invitation arrived a few days later.* ■ (**arrive at**) reach (a conclusion or decision): *they arrived at the same conclusion.* ■ happen or come: *we will be in touch with them when the time arrives.* ■ come into existence or use: *microcomputers arrived at the start of the 1970s.* ■ be born: *he will feel jealous when a new baby arrives.* ■ informal achieve success or recognition. [ME: from OFr. *ariver*, based on L. *ad-* 'to' + *ripa* 'shore.']

ar·ri·viste /,ärē'vēst/ ▶ **n.** a self-seeking person who has recently acquired wealth or social status. [20th C.: from Fr., from *arriver* (see ARRIVE).]

ar·ro·gant /'arəgənt/ ▶ **adj.** having or revealing an exaggerated sense of one's own importance or abilities. — **ar·ro·gance n. ar·ro·gant·ly adv.** [ME: ult. from L. *arrogant-* 'claiming for oneself,' from *arrogare* (see ARROGATE).]

ar·ro·gate /'arə,gāt/ ▶ **v.** [trans.] take or claim (something) for oneself without justification: *they* ***arrogate to themselves*** *the ability to divine the nation's true interests.* — **ar·ro·ga·tion** /,arə'gāshən/ **n.** [16th C.: from L. *arrogat-* 'claimed for oneself,' from *arrogare*, from *ad-* 'to' + *rogare* 'ask.']

ar·ron·disse·ment /ə'rändismənt; ärōNdēs,mäN/ ▶ **n.** a subdivision of a department in France. ■ an administrative district of certain large French cities, in particular Paris. [Fr., from *arrondir* 'make round.']

Ar·row /'arō/, Kenneth Joseph (1921–), US economist, noted chiefly for his work on general economic equilibrium and social choice. Nobel Prize for Economics (1972).

ar·row /'arō/ ▶ **n.** a shaft sharpened at the front and with feathers or vanes at the back, shot from a bow as a weapon or for sport. ■ a mark or sign resembling an arrow, used to show direction or position; a pointer. [OE *arewe*, *arwe*, from ON.]

ar·row·head /'arō,hed/ ▶ **n. 1** the pointed end of an arrow, typically wedge-shaped. ■ a decorative device resembling an arrowhead. **2** an aquatic or semiaquatic plant (genus *Sagittaria*, family Alismataceae) with arrow-shaped leaves and three-petaled white flowers. Several species include the common **broad-leaved arrowhead** (*S. latifolia*).

ar·row·root /'arō,rōōt; -,rŏŏt/ ▶ **n.** a West Indian plant (*Maranta arundinacea*, family Marantaceae) from which a starch is prepared. ■ the fine-grained starch obtained from this plant, used in cooking and medicine. [17th C.: alt. of Arawak *aru-aru* (lit. 'meal of meals').]

ar·row worm ▶ **n.** a finned, transparent wormlike marine animal (phylum Chaetognatha) with spines on the head for grasping prey. It commonly feeds on plankton.

ar·roy·o /ə'roi,ō/ ▶ **n.** (pl. **-os**) a steep-sided gully cut by running water in an arid or semiarid region. [19th C.: from Sp.]

ar·roz /ä'rōs/ ▶ **n.** Spanish word for RICE, used in the names of various dishes.

broad-leaved arrowhead

arse /ärs/ British spelling of ASS². [OE *ærs*, Gmc.; rel. to Ger. *Arsch*.]

ar·se·nal /ˈärs(ə)nl/ ▶ **n.** a collection of weapons and military equipment stored by a country, person, or group: *Britain's nuclear arsenal.* ■ a place where weapons and military equipment are stored or made. ■ [in sing.] fig. an array of resources available for a certain purpose: *an arsenal of computers at our disposal.* [16th C.: from Fr., or from obs. Ital. *arzanale*, based on Arab. *dār-aṣ-ṣinā a*, from *dār* 'house' + *al-* '(of) the' + *sinā a* 'art' (from *ṣana a* 'make').]

ar·se·nate /ˈärs(ə)nit; -ˌnāt/ ▶ **n.** Chem. a salt or ester of arsenic acid.

ar·se·nic ▶ **n.** /ˈärs(ə)nik/ the chemical element of atomic number 33, a brittle steel-gray metalloid. (Symbol: **As**) ▶ **adj.** /ärˈsenik/ of or relating to arsenic. [ME: ult. from Gk. *arsenikon* 'yellow orpiment,' from Arab. *al-zarnīk* 'the orpiment,' based on Pers. *zar* 'gold.']

ar·se·nic ac·id /ärˈsenik/ ▶ **n.** Chem. a weakly acidic crystalline solid, H_3AsO_4, with oxidizing properties, formed when arsenic reacts with nitric acid.

ar·sen·i·cal /ärˈsenikəl/ ▶ **adj.** of or containing arsenic. ▶ **n.** (usu. **arsenicals**) an arsenical drug or other compound.

ar·se·nide /ˈärs(ə)ˌnīd/ ▶ **n.** Chem. a binary compound of arsenic with a metallic element.

ar·se·no·py·rite /ˌärsənōˈpīrīt; ärˌsenō-/ ▶ **n.** a silvery-gray mineral consisting of an arsenide and sulfide of iron, chemical formula FeAsS.

ar·sine /ˈärsēn; ärˈsēn/ ▶ **n.** Chem. a poisonous gas, AsH_3, smelling slightly of garlic, made by the reaction of some arsenides with acids. [19th C.: from ARSENIC.]

ar·sis /ˈärsis/ ▶ **n.** (pl. **-ses** /-ˌsēz/) Pros. the unstressed syllable of a metrical foot. [ME: via late L. from Gk., lit. 'lifting,' from *airein* 'raise.']

ar·son /ˈärsən/ ▶ **n.** the criminal act of deliberately setting fire to property: *police are treating the fire as arson.* —**ar·son·ist** /-nist/ **n.** [17th C.: from med. L. *arsio(n-)*, from L. *ardere* 'to burn.']

ars·phen·a·mine /ärsˈfenəmən; -ˌmēn/ ▶ **n.** Med. a synthetic organic arsenic compound formerly used to treat syphilis and other diseases. [20th C.: blend of ARSENIC, PHENYL, and AMINE.]

art¹ /ärt/ ▶ **n. 1** the expression or application of human creative skill and imagination, typically in a visual form such as painting or sculpture, producing works to be appreciated primarily for their beauty or emotional power: *the art of the Renaissance.* ■ works produced by such skill and imagination. ■ creative activity resulting in the production of paintings, drawings, or sculpture: *she's good at art.* **2** (**the arts**) the various branches of creative activity, such as painting, music, literature, and dance. **3** (**arts**) subjects of study primarily concerned with the processes and products of human creativity and social life, such as languages, literature, and history (as contrasted with scientific or technical subjects). **4** a skill at doing a specified thing, typically one acquired through practice: *the art of conversation.* [ME: via OFr. from L. *ars, art-*.]

art² archaic dialect 2nd person singular present of BE.

art. ▶ **abbr.** ■ article. ■ artificial. ■ artillery.

art dec·o ▶ **n.** a decorative style of the 1920s and 1930s, marked by precise and boldly delineated geometric shapes and strong colors, used in household objects and architecture. [1960s: from Fr. *art décoratif* 'decorative art,' from the 1925 *Exposition des Arts décoratifs* in Paris.]

ar·te·fact ▶ **n.** British spelling of ARTIFACT.

ar·tel /ärˈtel/ ▶ **n.** hist. (in prerevolutionary Russia) a cooperative association of craftsmen. [from Russ. *artel'*.]

Ar·te·mis /ˈärtəmis/ Gk. Mythol. a goddess, daughter of Zeus and sister of Apollo. She was a huntress and is typically depicted with a bow and arrows. Roman equivalent DIANA.

ar·te·mis·i·a /ˌärtəˈmēzh(ē)ə/ ▶ **n.** an aromatic or bitter-tasting plant (genus *Artemesia*) of the daisy family that includes wormwood, mugwort, and sagebrush. Several kinds are used in herbal medicine and many are cultivated for their feathery gray foliage. [ME: via L. from Gk., 'wormwood,' after the goddess ARTEMIS.]

ar·te·ri·al /ärˈti(ə)rēəl/ ▶ **adj.** [attrib.] of or relating to an artery or arteries. ■ denoting an important route in a system of roads, railroad lines, or rivers: *one of the main arterial routes from New York.*

ar·te·ri·al·ize /ärˈti(ə)rēəˌlīz/ ▶ **v.** [trans.] [usu. as adj.] (**arterialized**) convert venous into arterial (blood) by reoxygenation, esp. in the lungs. —**ar·te·ri·al·i·za·tion** /ärˌti(ə)rēələˈzāshən/ **n.**

arterio- ▶ **comb. form** of or relating to the arteries: *arteriosclerosis.* [from Gk. *artēria* (see ARTERY).]

ar·te·ri·og·ra·phy /ärˌti(ə)rēˈägrəfē/ ▶ **n.** Med. radiography of an artery, carried out after injection of a radio-opaque substance.

ar·te·ri·ole /ärˈti(ə)rēˌōl/ ▶ **n.** Anat. a small branch of an artery leading into capillaries. —**ar·te·ri·o·lar** /ärˌti(ə)rēˈōlər/ **adj.** [19th C.: from Fr. *artériole*, dimin. of *artère* (see ARTERY).]

ar·te·ri·o·scle·ro·sis /ärˌti(ə)rēˌōskləˈrōsis/ ▶ **n.** Med. the thickening and hardening of the walls of the arteries, occurring typically in old age. —**ar·te·ri·o·scle·rot·ic** /-ˈrätik/ **adj.**

ar·te·ri·o·ve·nous /ärˌti(ə)rēōˈvēnəs/ ▶ **adj.** Anat. of, relating to, or affecting an artery and a vein.

ar·te·ri·tis /ˌärtəˈrītis/ ▶ **n.** Med. inflammation of the walls of an artery.

ar·ter·y /ˈärtərē/ ▶ **n.** (pl. **-ter·ies**) any of the muscular-walled tubes forming part of the circulation system by which blood (mainly that which has been oxygenated) is conveyed from the heart to all parts of the body. Compare with VEIN (sense 1). ■ an important route in a system of roads, rivers, or railroad lines: *the east-west artery.* [ME: from L. *arteria*, from Gk. *artēria*, prob. from *airein* 'raise.']

ar·te·sian /ärˈtēzhən/ ▶ **adj.** relating to or denoting a well bored perpendicularly into water-bearing strata lying at an angle, so that natural pressure produces a constant supply of water. [19th C.: from Fr. *artésien* 'from Artois' (see ARTOIS).]

art film ▶ **n.** an artistic or experimental film.

art form ▶ **n.** a conventionally established form of artistic composition, such as the novel, sonata, or sonnet. ■ any activity regarded as a medium of imaginative or creative self-expression.

art·ful /ˈärtfəl/ ▶ **adj. 1** clever or skillful, typically in a crafty or cunning way. **2** showing creative skill or taste: *an artful photograph.* —**art·ful·ly adv. art·ful·ness n.**

art his·to·ry ▶ **n.** the academic study of the history and development of the visual arts. —**art his·to·ri·an n. art his·tor·i·cal adj.**

art house ▶ **n.** a movie theater that specializes in artistic or experimental films.

ar·thral·gia /ärˈthralj(ē)ə/ ▶ **n.** Med. pain in a joint. [19th C.: from Gk. *arthron* 'joint.']

ar·thri·tis /ärˈthrītis/ ▶ **n.** painful inflammation and stiffness of the joints. —**ar·thrit·ic** /-ˈthritik/ **adj. & n.** [16th C.: via L. from Gk., from *arthron* 'joint.']

arthro- ▶ **comb. form** of a joint; relating to joints. [from Gk. *arthron* 'joint.']

ar·throd·e·sis /ärˈthrädəsis/ ▶ **n.** surgical immobilization of a joint by fusion of the adjacent bones. [20th C.: from ARTHRO- + Gk. *desis* 'binding together.']

Ar·throp·o·da /ärˈthräpədə/ Zool. a large phylum of invertebrate animals that includes insects, spiders, and crustaceans. They have a segmented body, an external skeleton, and jointed limbs. —**ar·thro·pod** /ˈärthrəˌpäd/ **n.** [19th C.: mod. L. (pl.), from Gk. *arthron* 'joint' + *pous, pod-* 'foot.']

ar·thro·scope /ˈärthrəˌskōp/ ▶ **n.** Med. an instrument through which the interior of a joint may be inspected or operated on. —**ar·thro·scop·ic** /ˌärthrəˈskäpik/ **adj. ar·thros·co·py** /ärˈthräskəpē/ **n.**

Ar·thur¹ /ˈärthər/ a legendary king of Britain, historically perhaps a 5th- or 6th-century Romano-British chieftain or general. Stories of his life, his knights, and the Round Table of the court at Camelot were developed by Malory, Chrétien de Troyes, and other medieval writers. —**Ar·thu·ri·an** /ärˈthoorēən/ **adj.**

Ar·thur², Chester Alan (1830–86), 21st president of the US 1881–85. A New York Republican, he became James Garfield's vice president in March 1881, succeeding to the presidency upon the assassination of Garfield six months later.

ar·ti·choke /ˈärtiˌchōk/ ▶ **n. 1** (also **globe artichoke**) a European plant (*Cynara scolymus*) of the daisy family cultivated for its large thistlelike flowerheads. ■ the unopened flowerhead of this, of which the heart and the fleshy bases of the bracts are edible. **2** see JERUSALEM ARTICHOKE. [16th C.: from northern Ital. *articiocco*, from Sp. *alcarchofa*, from Arab. *al-ḳaršūfa*.]

ar·ti·cle /ˈärtikəl/ ▶ **n. 1** a particular item or object, typically one of a specified type: *small household articles.* **2** a piece of writing in a newspaper, magazine, or other publication: *an article about middle-aged executives.* **3** a separate clause or paragraph of a legal document or agreement: [as adj.] *it is an offense under Article 7 of the treaty.* **4** Gram. see DEFINITE ARTICLE, INDEFINITE ARTICLE. ▶ **v.** [trans.] (usu. **be articled**) bind by the terms of a contract, as one of apprenticeship. [ME: from OFr., from L. *articulus*, dimin. of *artus* 'joint.']

Ar·ti·cles of Con·fed·er·a·tion ▶ **n.** the original constitution of the United States, ratified in 1781, which was replaced by the US Constitution in 1789.

ar·tic·u·lar /ärˈtikyələr/ ▶ **adj.** [attrib.] of or relating to a joint or the joints: *articular cartilage.* [ME: from L. *articularis*, from *articulus* (see ARTICLE).]

ar·tic·u·late ▶ **adj.** /ärˈtikyəlit/ **1** (of a person or a person's words) having or showing the ability to speak fluently and coherently. **2** having joints or jointed segments. ▶ **v.** /-ˌlāt/ **1** [trans.] express (an idea or feeling) fluently and coherently: *they were unable to articulate their emotions.* ■ pronounce (something) clearly and distinctly: *he articulated each word with precision* | [intrans.] *people who do not articulate well are more difficult to lip-read.* **2** [intrans.] form a joint: *the mandible is a solid piece articulating with the head.* ■ (**be articulated**) be connected by joints. —**ar·tic·u·la·ble adj. ar·tic·u·la·cy** /-ləsē/ **n. ar·tic·u·late·ly adv. ar·tic·u·late·ness n. ar·tic·u·la·tor** /-ˌlātər/ **n.** [16th C.: from L. *articulatus*, past part. of *articulare* 'divide into joints' from *articulus* (see ARTICLE).]

ar·tic·u·lat·ed /ärˈtikyəˌlātid/ ▶ **adj. 1** having two or more sections connected by a flexible joint. **2** (of an idea or feeling) expressed; put into words: *the lack of a clearly articulated policy.*

ar·tic·u·la·tion /ärˌtikyəˈlāshən/ ▶ **n. 1** the action of putting into words an idea or feeling of a specified type: *it would involve the articulation of a theory of the just war.* ■ the formation of clear and distinct sounds in speech: *the articulation of vowels and consonants.* ■ Music clarity in the production of successive notes: *beautifully polished articulation from the violins.* **2** the state of being jointed: *articulation of the lower jaw.* ■ [with adj.] a specified joint: *the leg articulation.*

ar·tic·u·la·to·ry /ärˈtikyələˌtôrē/ ▶ **adj.** [attrib.] of or relating to the formation of speech sounds.

ar·ti·fact /'ärtə,fakt/ ▶ n. **1** an object made by a human being, typically an item of cultural or historical interest: *gold and silver artifacts.* **2** something observed in a scientific investigation or experiment that is not naturally present but occurs as a result of the preparative or investigative procedure: *widespread tissue infection may be a technical artifact.* — **ar·ti·fac·tu·al** /,ärtə'fakCHōōəl/ adj. [19th C.: from L. *arte* 'by art' + *factum* (neut. past part. of *facere* 'make').]

ar·ti·fice /'ärtəfis/ ▶ n. clever or cunning devices or expedients, esp. as used to trick or deceive others: *artifice and outright fakery.* [ME: from OFr., from L. *artificium*, based on *ars, art-* 'art' + *facere* 'make.']

ar·tif·i·cer /är'tifəsər/ ▶ n. archaic a skilled craftsman or inventor.

ar·ti·fi·cial /,ärtə'fisHəl/ ▶ adj. **1** made or produced by human beings rather than occurring naturally, typically as a copy of something natural: *artificial light | an artificial limb | artificial flowers.* ■ not existing naturally; contrived or false: *the artificial division of people into age groups.* **2** (of a person or a person's behavior) insincere or affected: *an artificial smile.* — **ar·ti·fi·ci·al·i·ty** /-,fisHē'alitē/ n. **ar·ti·fi·cial·ly** adv.

ar·ti·fi·cial ho·ri·zon ▶ n. a gyroscopic instrument or a fluid surface, used to provide a horizontal reference plane for navigational measurement.

ar·ti·fi·cial in·sem·i·na·tion (abbr.: **AI**) ▶ n. the injection of semen into the vagina or uterus other than by sexual intercourse.

ar·ti·fi·cial in·tel·li·gence (abbr.: **AI**) ▶ n. the theory and development of computer systems able to perform tasks that normally require human intelligence, such as visual perception, speech recognition, decision-making, and translation between languages.

ar·ti·fi·cial life ▶ n. the production or action of computer programs or computerized systems that simulate the characteristics of living organisms.

ar·ti·fi·cial res·pi·ra·tion ▶ n. the restoration or substitution of someone's breathing by manual, mechanical, or mouth-to-mouth methods.

ar·til·ler·y /är'tilərē/ ▶ n. (pl. **-ler·ies**) large-caliber guns used in warfare on land: *tanks and heavy artillery.* ■ a military detachment or branch of the armed forces that uses such guns. — **ar·til·ler·ist** n. **ar·til·ler·y·man** n. [ME: from OFr. *artillerie*, from *artiller*, alt. of *atillier* 'equip, arm,' prob. var. of *atirier*, from *a-* 'to') + *tire* 'rank, order.']

Ar·ti·o·dac·ty·la /,ärtē-ō'daktl-ə/ Zool. an order of mammals that comprises the even-toed ungulates. See illustration at EVEN-TOED UNGULATE. — **ar·ti·o·dac·tyl** /-'daktl/ n. & adj. [mod. L. (pl.), from Gk. *artios* 'even' + *daktulos* 'finger, toe.']

ar·ti·san /'ärtizən/ ▶ n. a worker in a skilled trade, esp. one that involves making things by hand. — **ar·ti·san·al** /-zənl/ adj. [16th C.: from Fr., based on L. *artitus*, past part. of *artire* 'instruct in the arts,' from *ars, art-* 'art.']

art·ist /'ärtist/ ▶ n. a person who produces paintings or drawings as a profession or hobby. ■ a person who practices any of the various creative arts, such as a sculptor, novelist, poet, or filmmaker. ■ a person skilled at a particular task or occupation: *a surgeon who is an artist with the scalpel.* ■ a performer, such as a singer, actor, or dancer. ■ informal [with adj.] a habitual practitioner of a specified reprehensible activity: *a con artist | rip-off artists.*

ar·tiste /är'tēst/ ▶ n. a professional entertainer, esp. a singer or dancer: *cabaret artistes.* [19th C.: from Fr. (see ARTIST).]

ar·tis·tic /är'tistik/ ▶ adj. having or revealing natural creative skill: *my lack of artistic ability.* ■ of, relating to, or characteristic of art or artistry. ■ aesthetically pleasing. — **ar·tis·ti·cal·ly** /-tik(ə)lē/ adv.

ar·tis·tic di·rec·tor ▶ n. the person with overall responsibility for the selection and interpretation of the works performed by a theater, ballet, or opera company.

art·ist·ry /'ärtistrē/ ▶ n. creative skill or ability: *the artistry of the pianist.*

art·ist's fun·gus ▶ n. a bracket fungus (*Ganoderma applanatum*, family Ganodermataceae) that has the shape of an artist's palette, with a reddish-brown upper surface, found in both Eurasia and North America.

art·less /'ärtlis/ ▶ adj. without guile or deception. ■ without effort or pretentiousness; natural and simple: *an artless literary masterpiece.* ■ without skill or finesse: *her awkward, artless prose.* — **art·less·ly** adv.

art nou·veau /är(t) nōō'vō/ ▶ n. a style of decorative art, architecture, and design characterized by intricate linear designs and flowing curves based on natural forms (late 19th–early 20th centuries). [20th C.: from Fr., lit. 'new art.']

Ar·tois /är'twä/ a region and former province of northeastern France.

arts and crafts ▶ plural n. decorative design and handicraft.

Arts and Crafts Move·ment a decorative arts movement of the late 19th century that sought to revive craftsmanship in an age of increasing mechanization.

art song ▶ n. Music a song written to be sung in recital, often set to a poem.

art·sy /'ärtsē/ (also **art·y** /'ärtē/) ▶ adj. (**-si·er, -si·est**) informal making a strong, affected, or pretentious display of being artistic or interested in the arts: *the artsy town of Taos | artsy French flicks.* — **art·si·ness** n.

art·sy-craft·sy /'kraftsē/ informal ▶ adj. interested or involved in making decorative objects, typically ones perceived as quaint or homespun: *artsy-craftsy gift shops.*

art·sy-fart·sy /'färtsē/ ▶ adj. informal, derog. associated with or showing a pretentious interest in the arts: *you can wear a turtleneck to join your artsy-fartsy friends.*

art ther·a·py ▶ n. a form of psychotherapy that encourages self-expression through painting or drawing.

art·work /'ärt,wərk/ ▶ n. illustrations, photographs, or other nontextual material prepared for inclusion in a publication. ■ paintings, drawings, or other artistic works.

A·ru·ba /ə'rōōbə/ an island in the Caribbean Sea, close to the Venezuelan coast; pop. 69,539; capital, Oranjestad. It is a self-governing territory of the Netherlands.

a·ru·gu·la /ə'rōōgələ/ (also **ru·co·la, ru·go·la**) ▶ n. the rocket plant, used in salads. [1970s: from Ital. dial., ult. dimin. of L. *eruca* 'down-stemmed plant.']

ar·um /'arəm/ ▶ n. a North American and European plant that has arrow-shaped leaves and a broad leafy spathe enclosing a club-shaped spadix, and that bears bright red berries in late summer. The **arum family** (Araceae) includes jack-in-the-pulpit, cuckoopint, skunk cabbage, philodendrons, and calla lilies. [ME: from L., from Gk. *aron*.]

Aru·na·chal Pra·desh /,ärə'näcHəl prə'däsH; prə'desH/ a state in northeastern India on the border of Tibet to the north and Myanmar (Burma) to the east; capital, Itanagar.

Ar·va·da /är'vadə; -'vädə/ a city in north central Colorado; pop. 102,153.

-ary[1] ▶ suffix **1** forming adjectives such as *budgetary, primary.* **2** forming nouns such as *dictionary, granary.* [from Fr. *-aire* or L. *-arius* 'connected with.']

-ary[2] ▶ suffix forming adjectives such as *capillary, military.* [from Fr. *-aire* or L. *-aris* 'belonging to.']

Ar·ya·bha·ta I /,äryə'bətə/, (476–*c.*550), Indian astronomer and mathematician. His surviving work is *Aryabhatiya* (499).

Ar·y·an /'e(ə)rēən; -yən; 'ar-/ ▶ n. a member of a people speaking an Indo-European language who invaded northern India in the 2nd millennium BC. ■ (in Nazi ideology) a person of Caucasian race not of Jewish descent. ▶ adj. of or relating to this people or their language. [from Sanskrit *ārya* 'noble.']

ar·yl /'arəl/ ▶ n. [as adj.] Chem. of or denoting a radical derived from an aromatic hydrocarbon by removal of a hydrogen atom: *aryl groups.* [20th C.: from AROMATIC.]

ar·y·te·noid /ə'ritn,oid; ,arə'tē,noid/ Anat. ▶ adj. [attrib.] of, relating to, or denoting a pair of cartilages at the back of the larynx. ▶ n. either of these cartilages. [18th C.: from mod. L. *arytaenoides*, from Gk. *arutainoeidēs*, from *arutaina* 'funnel.']

AS ▶ abbr. ■ Anglo-Saxon. ■ Associate in Science. ■ American Samoa.

As ▶ symb. the chemical element arsenic.

as[1] /az/ ▶ adv. (usu. **as —— as**) used in comparisons to refer to the extent or degree of something: *hailstones as big as tennis balls.* ■ used to emphasize an amount: ***as many as*** *twenty-two rare species may be at risk.* ▶ conj. **1** used to indicate that something happens during the time when something is taking place: *Frank watched him as he ambled through the crowd.* **2** used to indicate by comparison the way that something happens or is done: *they can do as they wish.* ■ used to add or interject a comment relating to the statement of a fact: *as you can see, I didn't go after all.* **3** because; since: *I must stop now as I have to go out.* **4** even though: *sweet as he is, he doesn't pay his bills.* ▶ prep. **1** used to refer to the function or character that someone or something has: *he got a job as a cook.* **2** during the time of being (the thing specified): *he had often been sick as a child.*

– PHRASES **as for** with regard to: *as for you, you'd better be quick.* **as if** (or **as though**) as would be the case if: *she behaved as if he weren't there.* **as if!** informal I very much doubt it: *You know how lottery winners always say it won't change their lives? Yeah, as if!* **as (it) is** in the existing circumstances: *I've got enough on my plate as it is.* **as it were** in a way (used to be less precise): *areas that have been, as it were, pushed aside.* **as of** used to indicate the time or date from which something starts: *I'm on unemployment as of today.* **as to** with respect to; concerning: *decisions as to which patients receive treatment.* **as yet** [usu. with negative] until now or a particular time in the past: *the damage is as yet undetermined.* [ME: from OE *alswā* 'similarly' (see ALSO).]

as[2] /as/ ▶ n. an ancient Roman copper coin. [17th C.: L., lit. 'unit.']

as- ▶ prefix var. of AD- assimilated before *s* (as in *assemble, assess*).

ASA ▶ abbr. American Standards Association (esp. in film-speed specification).

a·sa·fet·i·da /,asə'fetidə/ (Brit. **a·sa·foet·i·da**) ▶ n. **1** a fetid resinous gum obtained from the roots of a herbaceous plant, used in herbal medicine. **2** the Eurasian plant (*Ferula assa-foetida*) of the parsley family, from which this gum is obtained. [ME: from med. L. *asafoetida*, from *asa* (from Pers. *azā* 'mastic') + *foetida* (see FETID).]

a·sa·na /'äsənə/ ▶ n. a hatha yoga posture. [from Sanskrit *āsana*.]

A·san·sol /,əsən'sōl/ a city in northeastern India, in West Bengal; pop. 262,000.

A·san·te var. of ASHANTI[1].

ASAP (also **asap**) ▶ abbr. as soon as possible.

as·bes·tos /as'bestəs; az-/ ▶ n. a heat-resistant fibrous silicate mineral that can be woven into fabrics, used in fire-resistant and insulating materials. ■ fabric containing such a mineral. [17th C.: via L. from Gk. *asbestos* 'unquenchable,', from *a-* + *sbestos* (from *sbennumi* 'quench').]

as·bes·to·sis /,asbes'tōsis; ,az-/ ▶ n. a lung disease resulting from the inhalation of asbestos particles.

As·bury Park /'az,berē; -b(ə)rē/ a city in east central New Jersey, long a noted resort; pop. 16,930.

ASCAP ▶ abbr. American Society of Composers, Authors, and Publishers.

as·ca·ri·a·sis /,askə'rīəsis/ ▶ n. Med. infection of the intestine with ascarids.

as·ca·rid /ˈaskərid/ (also **as·ca·ris** /-ris/) ▶ **n.** Zool. a parasitic nematode (family Ascaridae) that typically lives in the intestines of vertebrates. [17th C.: back-form. from Gk. *askarides*, pl. of *askaris* 'intestinal worm.']

as·cend /əˈsend/ ▶ **v. 1** [trans.] go up or climb: *she ascended the stairs* | [intrans.] *new magmas were created and ascended to the surface* ■ climb to the summit of: *the first traveler to ascend the mountain.* ■ move upstream along (a river). **2** [intrans.] rise through the air: *we had ascended 3,000 ft.* ■ (of a road or flight of steps) slope or lead up: *the road ascends to the lake.* ■ move up the social or professional scale: *he took exams to ascend through the ranks.* ■ (of a spiritual being or soul) rise into heaven.
– PHRASES **ascend the throne** become king or queen. [ME: from L. *ascendere*, from *ad-* 'to' + *scandere* 'to climb.']

as·cend·an·cy /əˈsendənsē/ (also **as·cend·en·cy**) ▶ **n.** occupation of a position of dominant power or influence: *the ascendancy of good over evil.*

as·cend·ant /əˈsendənt/ (also **as·cend·ent**) ▶ **adj. 1** rising in power or influence: *ascendant factions in the party.* **2** Astrol. (of a planet, zodiacal degree, or sign) just above the eastern horizon. ▶ **n.** Astrol. the point on the ecliptic at which it intersects the eastern horizon at a particular time, typically that of a person's birth. ■ the point on an astrological chart representing this.

as·cend·er /əˈsendər/ ▶ **n.** a person or thing that ascends, in particular: ■ a part of a letter that extends above the main part (as in *b* and *h*). ■ a letter having such a part. ■ a device used in climbing that can be clipped to a rope to act as a foothold or handhold.

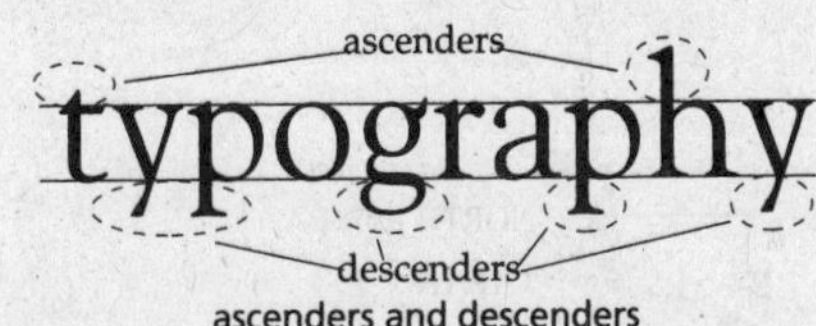

ascenders and descenders

as·cend·ing /əˈsendiNG/ ▶ **adj.** [attrib.] **1** increasing in size or importance. **2** sloping or leading upward.

as·cend·ing co·lon ▶ **n.** Anat. the first main part of the large intestine.

as·cen·sion /əˈsenSHən/ ▶ **n.** [in sing.] the act of rising to an important position or a higher level. ■ (**Ascension**) the ascent of Christ into heaven on the fortieth day after the Resurrection. [ME: via OFr. from L. *ascensio(n-)*, from *ascendere*.]

As·cen·sion Day the fortieth day after Easter, on which Christ's Ascension is celebrated in the Christian Church.

As·cen·sion Is·land /əˈsenSHən/ an island in the South Atlantic Ocean, a dependency of the UK; pop. 1,007.

as·cent /əˈsent/ ▶ **n. 1** a climb or walk to the summit of a mountain or hill. ■ an upward slope or path: *the ascent grew steeper.* **2** [in sing.] an instance of rising through the air: *the first balloon ascent was in 1783.* ■ [in sing.] a rise to an important position or a higher level: *his ascent to power.* [16th C.: from ASCEND.]

as·cer·tain /ˌasərˈtān/ ▶ **v.** [trans.] find (something) out for certain; make sure of: *ascertain the cause of the accident.* — **as·cer·tain·a·ble adj. as·cer·tain·ment n.** [ME: from OFr. *acertener*, based on L. *certus* 'sure.']

as·cet·ic /əˈsetik/ ▶ **adj.** characterized by severe self-discipline and abstention from all forms of indulgence, typically for religious reasons. ▶ **n.** a person who practices such self-discipline. — **as·cet·i·cal·ly** /-ik(ə)lē/ **adv. as·cet·i·cism** /-ˌsizəm/ **n.** [17th C.: from med. L. *asceticus* or Gk. *askētikos*, from *askētēs* 'monk,' from *askein* 'to exercise.']

As·cham /ˈaskəm/, Roger (*c.*1515–68), English humanist scholar and writer, noted for *The Scholemaster* (1570), a tract on education.

asc·hel·minth /ˈask-helˌminTH/ ▶ **n.** (pl. **asc·hel·minths** or **asc·hel·min·thes** /ˌask-helˈminTHēz/) Zool. an invertebrate animal belonging to the phylum Nematoda and about seven minor phyla, distinguished by the lack of a well-developed coelom and blood vessels. Most aschelminths are minute wormlike animals, including the nematodes, rotifers, and water bears. [from mod. L. *Aschelminthes*, from Gk. *askos* 'sac' + *helminth* 'worm.']

as·ci /ˈasī; -kī; -kē/ plural form of ASCUS.

as·cid·i·an /əˈsidēən/ ▶ **n.** Zool. a sea squirt. [19th C.: from mod. L. pl. *Ascidia* (genus name), from Gk. *askidion*, dimin. of *askos* 'wineskin.']

ASCII /ˈaskē/ Comput. ▶ **abbr.** American Standard Code for Information Interchange, a set of digital codes widely used as a standard format in the transfer of text between computers.

as·ci·tes /əˈsītēz/ ▶ **n.** Med. the accumulation of fluid in the peritoneal cavity, causing abdominal swelling. — **as·cit·ic** /əˈsitik/ **adj.** [ME: via late L. from Gk. *askitēs*, from *askos* 'wineskin.']

As·cle·pi·us /əˈsklēpēəs/ Gk. Mythol. god of healing.

as·co·my·cete /ˌaskəˈmīsēt; -mīˈsēt/ ▶ **n.** Bot. a fungus (phylum Ascomycota, class Ascomycetes) whose spores develop within asci. The ascomycetes include most molds, mildews, and yeasts, the fungal component of most lichens, and a few large forms such as morels and truffles. Compare with BASIDIOMYCETE. [19th C.: from mod. L. *Ascomycetes*, from Gk. *askos* 'sac' + *muskētes* 'fungi.']

as·con /ˈaskän/ ▶ **n.** Zool. a sponge of the simplest structure, with a tubelike or baglike form lined with choanocytes. Compare with LEUCON and SYCON. — **as·co·noid** /-kəˌnoid/ **adj.** [19th C.: mod. L., from Gk. *askos* 'bag.']

a·scor·bic ac·id /əˈskôrbik/ ▶ **n.** a vitamin, $C_6H_8O_6$, found particularly in citrus fruits and vegetables. It is essential in maintaining healthy connective tissue, and is thought to act as an antioxidant. Severe deficiency causes scurvy. Also called VITAMIN C. [1930s: from A-[1] + med. L. *scorbutus* 'scurvy.']

As·cot /ˈasˌkät; -kət/ a town in southern England, site of an annual horse race.

ascot

as·cot /ˈaskät; -kət/ ▶ **n.** (also **ascot tie**) a man's broad silk necktie. [20th C.: ASCOT.]

as·cribe /əˈskrīb/ ▶ **v.** [trans.] attribute something to (a cause): *he ascribed Jane's short temper to her upset stomach.* ■ (usu. **be ascribed to**) attribute (a text, quotation, or work of art) to a particular person or period: *a quotation ascribed to Thomas Cooper.* — **a·scrib·a·ble adj.** [ME: from L. *ascribere*, from *ad-* 'to' + *scribere* 'write.']

as·crip·tion /əˈskripSHən/ ▶ **n.** the attribution of something to a cause: *an ascription of effect to cause.* ■ the attribution of a text, quotation, or work of art to a particular person or period. [16th C.: from L. *ascriptio(n-)*, from *ascribere*.]

as·cus /ˈaskəs/ ▶ **n.** (pl. **as·ci** /ˈasī; ˈaskī; -kē/) Bot. a sac in which the spores of ascomycete fungi develop. [19th C.: mod. L., from Gk. *askos* 'bag.']

asdic /ˈazdik/ (also **ASDIC**) ▶ **n.** esp. Brit. an early form of sonar used to detect submarines. [World War II: acronym from *Allied Submarine Detection Investigation Committee*.]

-ase ▶ **suffix** Biochem. forming names of enzymes: *amylase.* [from *(diast)ase*.]

ASEAN /ˈäsēˌän; ˈas-/ ▶ **abbr.** Association of Southeast Asian Nations.

a·seis·mic /āˈsīzmik/ ▶ **adj.** Geol. not characterized by earthquake activity.

a·sep·sis /āˈsepsis/ ▶ **n.** the absence of bacteria, viruses, and other microorganisms. ■ the exclusion of bacteria and other microorganisms, typically during surgery. Compare with ANTISEPSIS.

a·sep·tic /āˈseptik/ ▶ **adj.** free from contamination caused by harmful microorganisms. ■ [attrib.] (of surgical practice) aiming at the complete exclusion of harmful microorganisms.

a·sex·u·al /āˈsekSHo͞oəl/ ▶ **adj.** without sex or sexuality, in particular: ■ Biol. (of reproduction) not involving the fusion of gametes. ■ Biol. without sex or sexual organs: *asexual parasites.* ■ without sexual feelings or associations: *she rested her hand on the back of his head, in a maternal, wholly asexual, gesture.* — **a·sex·u·al·i·ty** /āˌsekSHo͞oˈalitē/ **n. a·sex·u·al·ly adv.**

As·gard /ˈasˌgärd; ˈaz-/ Scand. Mythol. a region in the center of the universe, inhabited by the gods.

ash[1] /asH/ ▶ **n.** the powdery residue left after the burning of a substance. ■ (**ashes**) the remains of something destroyed; ruins: *democracies taking root in the ashes of the Soviet empire.* ■ (**ashes**) the remains of the human body after cremation or burning. ■ the mineral component of an organic substance, as assessed from the residue left after burning: *coal contains higher levels of ash than premium fuels.* [OE *æsce, aexe*, from Gmc.; akin to Ger. *Asche*.]

ash[2] ▶ **n. 1** (also **ash tree**) a tree (genus *Fraxinus*) of the olive family, with silver-gray bark and compound leaves, widely distributed throughout north temperate regions. Its many species include the North American **white ash** (*F. americana*) and the **European ash** (*F. excelsior*). ■ the hard pale wood of this tree. **2** an Old English runic letter (so named from the word of which it was the first letter). ■ the symbol æ or Æ, used in the Roman alphabet in place of the runic letter, and as a phonetic symbol. See also Æ. [OE *æsc*, Gmc.; akin to Ger. *Esche*.]

a·shamed /əˈSHāmd/ ▶ **adj.** [predic.] embarrassed or feeling guilt because of something one has done or a characteristic one has. ■ (**ashamed to do something**) reluctant to do something through fear of embarrassment or humiliation: *I am not ashamed to be seen with them.* — **a·sham·ed·ly** /əˈSHāmidlē/ **adv.** [OE *āscamod*, past part. of *āscamian* 'feel shame,' from *ā-* (intensive) + SHAME (v.).]

A·shan·ti[1] /əˈSHäntē; əˈSHan-/ (also **A·san·te** /əˈsäntē; əˈsan-/) a region in central Ghana. Annexed by Britain in 1902, it became part of the former British colony of the Gold Coast.

A·shan·ti[2] (also **A·san·te**) ▶ **n.** (pl. same) **1** a member of a people of south central Ghana. **2** the dialect of Akan spoken by this people. ▶ **adj.** relating to this people or their language. [Akan.]

ash blond (also **ash blonde**) ▶ **adj.** very pale blond. ▶ **n.** a very pale blond color. ■ a person with hair of such a color.

ash·can /ˈasHˌkan/ ▶ **n.** a metal receptacle for trash or ashes. ■ military slang a depth charge.

Ash·can School /ˈasHˌkan/ a group of American realist painters in the early 1900s who painted scenes from the slums of New York.

Ash·croft /ˈasHˌkrôft/, John David (1942–), US attorney general 2001–05. A Republican, he was governor of Missouri 1985–93 and a US senator 1995–2001.

Ashe /asH/, Arthur Robert (1943–93), US tennis player. He won the US Open championship in 1968 and Wimbledon in 1975, becoming the first black male player to achieve world rankings.

ash·en[1] /ˈasHən/ ▶ **adj.** of the pale gray color of ash: *the ashen morning*

sky. ■ very pale with shock, fear, or illness.

ash·en² ▶ **adj.** archaic made of timber from the ash tree.

Ash·er /'ashər/ (in the Bible) a Hebrew patriarch; son of Jacob and Zilpah. ■ the tribe of Israel traditionally descended from him.

Ashe·ville /'ashvəl; -,vil/ a city in western North Carolina, a mountain resort; pop. 68,889.

Ash·ga·bat /'äshgə,bät; 'ashgə,bat/ (also **Ash·kha·bad** /'äshkə,bäd; 'ashkə,bad/) the capital of Turkmenistan; pop. 517,200. Former name (1919–27) **Poltoratsk**.

a·shine /ə'shīn/ ▶ **adj.** [predic.] literary shining.

Ash·ke·naz·i /,ashkə'näzē; ,äshkə'näzē/ ▶ **n.** (pl. **-naz·im** /-'nazim; -'nä-/) a Jew of central or eastern European descent. More than 80 percent of Jews today are Ashkenazim. Compare with **Sephardi**. — **Ash·ke·naz·ic** /-'nazik; -'nä-/ **adj.** [from mod. Heb., from *Ashkenaz*, son of Japheth, a son of Noah (Gen. 10:3).]

Ash·ke·na·zy /,ashkə'näzē; ,äsh-/, Vladimir Davidovich (1937–), Russian pianist. He left the Soviet Union in 1963, finally settling in Iceland in 1973.

Ash·kha·bad /'äshkə,bäd/ var. of **Ashgabat**.

ash·lar /'ashlər/ ▶ **n.** masonry made of large square-cut stones, used as a facing on walls of brick or stone. ■ a stone used in such masonry. [ME: from OFr. *aisselier*, from L. *axilla*, dimin. of *axis* 'plank.']

Ash·ley /'ashlē/, Laura (1925–85), Welsh fashion designer; known for her use of floral patterns.

Ash·more and Car·ti·er Is·lands /'ash,môr; 'kärtē,ā; ,kärtē'ā/ uninhabited islands in the Indian Ocean, an external territory of Australia.

A·sho·ka var. of **Asoka**.

a·shore /ə'shôr/ ▶ **adv.** to or on the shore from the direction of the sea: *the seals come ashore to breed.* ■ on land as opposed to at sea: *we spent the day ashore.*

ash·ram /'äshrəm/ ▶ **n.** a hermitage, monastic community, or other place of religious retreat for Hindus. ■ a place of religious retreat or community life modeled on the Indian ashram. [from Sanskrit *āśrama* 'hermitage.']

ash·tang·a /ash'tängə/ (also **asth·tang·a; as·tang·a** /as-/) ▶ **n.** a type of yoga based on eight principles and consisting of a series of poses executed in swift succession, combined with deep, controlled breathing. [from Hindi *aṣṭaṅ* or its source, Sanskrit *aṣṭaṅga* 'having eight parts,' from *ashtán* 'eight.']

ash·tray /'ash,trā/ ▶ **n.** a receptacle for tobacco ash and cigarette butts.

A·shur·ba·ni·pal /,äshŏŏr'bäni,päl/, king of Assyria *c.*668–627 BC; grandson of Sennacherib. He was a patron of the arts.

Ash Wednes·day ▶ **n.** the first day of Lent in the Western Christian Church. [from the custom of marking the foreheads of penitents with ashes.]

ash·y /'ashē/ ▶ **adj. 1** of a pale grayish color; ashen. **2** covered with, consisting of, or resembling ashes.

ASI ▶ **abbr.** airspeed indicator.

A·sia /'āzhə/ the largest of the world's continents, constituting nearly one-third of the landmass, lying entirely north of the equator except for some Southeast Asian islands. It is connected to Africa by the Isthmus of Suez and borders Europe (part of the same landmass) along the Ural Mountains and across the Caspian Sea.

A·sia Mi·nor /'mīnər/ a western peninsula in Asia that now constitutes most of modern Turkey.

A·sian /'āzhən/ ▶ **adj.** of or relating to Asia or its people, customs, or languages. ▶ **n.** a native of Asia or a person of Asian descent.
– USAGE See usage at **oriental**.

A·sian A·mer·i·can ▶ **n.** an American who is of Asian (chiefly Far Eastern) descent. ▶ **adj.** of or relating to such people.

A·sian el·e·phant ▶ **n.** another term for **Indian elephant**.

A·sia-Pa·cif·ic ▶ **n.** (also **Asia-Pacific region**) a business region consisting of the whole of Asia as well as the countries of the Pacific Rim.

A·si·at·ic /,āzhē'atik; ,āzē-/ ▶ **adj.** relating to or deriving from Asia: *Asiatic* *cholera* | *Asiatic coastal regions.* ▶ **n.** offens. an Asian person.

– USAGE The standard and accepted term when referring to individual people is **Asian** rather than **Asiatic**, which can be offensive. However, **Asiatic** is standard in scientific and technical use, for example in biological and anthropological classifications. See also usage at **ORIENTAL.**

A-side ▶ **n.** the side of a pop single or album regarded as the main release.

a·side /ə'sīd/ ▶ **adv.** to one side; out of the way: *he pushed his plate aside* | *they stood aside to let a car pass.* ■ in reserve; for future use: *she set aside some money for rent.* ■ used to indicate that one is dismissing something from consideration, or that one is shifting from one topic or tone of discussion to another: *joking aside, I've certainly had my fill.* ▶ **n. 1** a remark by a character in a play intended to be heard by the audience but not by the other characters. ■ a remark not intended to be heard by everyone present: *"Does that make him a murderer?" whispered Alice in an aside to Fred.* **2** a remark that is not directly related to the main topic of discussion: *the recipe book has little asides about the importance of home and family.*

– PHRASES **aside from** apart from. [ME (*on side*): see **A-²**, **SIDE.**]

As·i·mov /'azə,môv; -,môf/, Isaac (1920–92), US writer and scientist; born in Russia. He is noted for his science fiction, his books on science for nonscientists, and his essays.

as·i·nine /'asə,nīn/ ▶ **adj.** extremely stupid or foolish. — **as·i·nin·i·ty** /,asə'ninitē/ **n.** [15th C.: from L. *asininus*, from *asinus* 'ass.']

A·sir Moun·tains /ä'si(ə)r/ a range in southwestern Saudi Arabia that runs parallel to the Red Sea.

-asis (often **-iasis**) ▶ **suffix** forming the names of diseases: *onchocerciasis* | *psoriasis.* [via L. from Gk. in nouns, 'state, condition.']

ask /ask/ ▶ **v. 1** [reporting verb] say something in order to obtain an answer or some information. ■ [intrans.] (**ask around**) talk to various people in order to find something out: *there are fine meals to be had if you ask around.* ■ [intrans.] (**ask after**) inquire about the health or well-being of: *Mrs. Savage asked after Iris's mother.* **2** [trans.] request (someone) to do or give something: *Mary **asked** her father **for** money* | *I asked him to call the manager.* ■ [with clause] request permission to do something: *she **asked if** she could move in.* ■ [intrans.] (**ask for**) request to speak to: *when I arrived, I asked for Catherine.* ■ request (a specified amount) as a price: *he was **asking** $250 **for** the guitar.* ■ expect or demand (something) of someone: *it's asking a lot, but could you look through Billy's things?* **3** [trans.] invite someone to (one's home or a function): *it's about time we **asked** Pam **to** dinner.* ■ (**ask someone along**) invite someone to join one on an outing: *do you want to ask him along?* ■ (**ask someone out**) invite someone out socially, typically on a date. ▶ **n.** [in sing.] the price at which an item, esp. a financial security, is offered for sale: [as adj.] *ask prices for bonds.*

– PHRASES **be asking for it** (or **trouble**) informal behave in a way that is likely to result in difficulty for oneself: *they accused me of asking for it.* **for the asking** used to indicate that something can be easily obtained: *the job was his for the asking.* — **ask·er n.** [OE *āscian, āhsian, āxian*, from West Gmc.]

a·skance /ə'skans/ (also **a·skant** /ə'skant/) ▶ **adv.** with an attitude or look of suspicion or disapproval: *the reformers **looked askance at** the mystical tradition.* [15th C.: origin unknown.]

as·ka·ri /'askərē/ ▶ **n.** (pl. same or **-ris**) (in East Africa) a soldier or police officer. [19th C.: from Arab. *'askarī* 'soldier.']

as·ke·sis /ə'skēsis/ (also **as·ce·sis** /ə'sēsis/) ▶ **n.** the practice of severe self-discipline. [19th C.: from Gk. *askēsis* 'training,' from *askein* 'to exercise.']

a·skew /ə'skyōō/ ▶ **adv. & adj.** not in a straight or level position: [as adv.] *the door was hanging askew on one twisted hinge* | [as predic. adj.] *her hat was slightly askew.* ■ fig. wrong; awry: [as adv.] *the plan went sadly askew* | [as adj.] *outrageous humor with a decidedly askew point of view.* [16th C.: from **A-²** + **SKEW.**]

ask·ing price ▶ **n.** the price at which something is offered for sale.

ASL ▶ **abbr.** American Sign Language.

a·slant /ə'slant/ ▶ **adv.** at an angle or in a sloping direction: *some of the paintings hung aslant.* ▶ **prep.** across at an angle or in a sloping direction: *rays of light fell aslant a door.*

a·sleep /ə'slēp/ ▶ **adj. & adv.** in or into a state of sleep. ■ not attentive or alert; inactive: *the competition was not asleep.* ■ (of a limb) having no feeling; numb: *his legs were asleep.* ■ literary used euphemistically to say that someone is dead.

– PHRASES **asleep at the switch** (or **wheel**) informal not attentive or alert; inactive: *someone must have been asleep at the switch to allow this.*

a·slope /ə'slōp/ ▶ **adv. & adj.** archaic or literary in a sloping position. [ME: origin uncert.]

As·ma·ra /äz'märə/ (also **As·me·ra** /az'merə/) the capital of Eritrea; pop. 400,000.

a·so·cial /ā'sōsHəl/ ▶ **adj.** avoiding social interaction; inconsiderate of or hostile to others: *the cat's independence has encouraged a view that it is asocial.*

A·so·ka /ə'sōkə/ (also **A·sho·ka** /ə'sHōkə/) (died *c.*232 BC), emperor of India *c.*269–232 BC. He established Buddhism as the state religion.

asp /asp/ ▶ **n.** (also **asp viper**) a small southern European viper (*Vipera aspis*) with an upturned snout. ■ another term for **EGYPTIAN COBRA.** [ME: from L. *aspis*, from Gk.]

as·par·a·gine /ə'sparə,jēn; -jin/ ▶ **n.** Biochem. a hydrophilic amino acid, $CONH_2CH_2CH(NH_2)COOH$, that is a constituent of most proteins. [19th C.: from **ASPARAGUS.**]

as·par·a·gus /ə'sparəgəs/ ▶ **n.** a tall plant (*Asparagus officinalis*) of the lily family with fine feathery foliage, cultivated for its edible shoots. ■ the tender young shoots of this plant, eaten as a vegetable. [16th C.: via L. from Gk. *asparagos.*]

as·par·a·gus fern ▶ **n.** a decorative indoor or greenhouse plant (genus *Asparagus*) with feathery foliage, related to the edible asparagus.

as·par·tame /'aspär,tām/ ▶ **n.** a very sweet substance used as an artificial sweetener in low-calorie products. It is a derivative of aspartic acid and phenylalanine.

as·par·tic ac·id /ə'spärtik/ ▶ **n.** Biochem. an acidic amino acid, $COOHCH_2CH(NH_2)COOH$, that is a constituent of most proteins and also occurs in sugar cane. Important in the metabolism of nitrogen in animals, it also acts as a neurotransmitter. [19th C.: *aspartic* from Fr. *aspartique*, from L. *asparagus.*]

ASPCA ▶ **abbr.** American Society for the Prevention of Cruelty to Animals.

as·pect /'aspekt/ ▶ **n. 1** a particular part or feature of something: *the financial aspect can be overstressed.* ■ a specific way in which something can be considered: *from every aspect, theirs was a changing world.* ■ [in sing. with adj.] a particular appearance or quality: *the air of desertion lent the place a sinister aspect.* **2** [usu. in sing.] the positioning of a building or thing in a specified direction: *a greenhouse with a southern aspect.* ■ the side of a building facing a particular direction: *the front aspect of the hotel was unremarkable.* ■ Astrol. a particular position of a planet or other celestial body relative to another. **3** Gram. a grammatical category or form that expresses the way in which time is denoted by the verb. — **as·pec·tu·al** /a'spekCHōōəl/ **adj.** [ME: from L. *aspectus*, from *aspicere* 'look at,' from *ad-* 'at' + *specere* 'to look.']

as·pect ra·tio ▶ **n.** the ratio of two dimensions of something as considered from a specific direction, in particular: ■ the ratio of the width to the height of the image on a television screen. ■ Aeron. the ratio of the span to the mean chord of an airfoil.

As·pen /'aspən/ a city in south central Colorado, a noted ski resort; pop. 5,914.

as·pen /'aspən/ ▶ **n.** a poplar (genus *Populus*) with rounded, long-stalked, and typically coarsely-toothed leaves that tremble in even a slight breeze. Its several species include the North American **quaking aspen** (*P. tremuloides*) and **bigtooth aspen** (*P. grandidentata*). [ME (adj.): from dial. *asp* 'aspen' + **-EN².**]

As·per·ger's syn·drome /'aspərjərz/ ▶ **n.** a rare and relatively mild autistic disorder characterized by awkwardness in social interaction and by the development of restricted interests and activities. [named after Hans *Asperger* (1906–80), the Austrian psychiatrist who described the condition.]

as·per·ges /ə'spərjəz/ ▶ **n.** Christian Church the rite of sprinkling holy water at the beginning of the Mass. [16th C.: L., lit. 'thou shalt purge.']

as·per·gil·lum /,aspər'jiləm/ ▶ **n.** (pl. **-gil·la** /-'jilə/ or **-gil·lums**) an implement for sprinkling holy water. [17th C.: from L.]

as·per·i·ty /ə'speritē/ ▶ **n.** (pl. **-ties**) harshness of tone or manner: *he pointed this out with some asperity.* ■ (**asperities**) harsh qualities or conditions: *the asperities of a harsh and divided society.* ■ (usu. **asperities**) a rough edge on a surface: *the asperities of the metal surfaces.* [ME: from OFr. *asperite*, or L. *asperitas*, from *asper* 'rough.']

as·perse /ə'spərs/ ▶ **v.** [trans.] rare attack or criticize the reputation or integrity of: *he aspersed the place and its inhabitants.* [15th C.: from L. *aspers-* 'sprinkled,' from v. *aspergere*, from *ad-* 'to' + *spargere* 'sprinkle.']

as·per·sion /ə'spərzHən/ ▶ **n.** (usu. **aspersions**) an attack on the reputation or integrity of someone or something: *I don't think anyone is casting aspersions on you.*

as·phalt /'asfôlt/ ▶ **n.** a mixture of dark bituminous pitch with sand or gravel, used for surfacing roads, flooring, roofing, etc. ■ the pitch used in this mixture, sometimes found in natural deposits but usually made by the distillation of crude oil. ▶ **v.** [trans.] cover with asphalt. — **as·phal·tic** /as'fôltik/ **adj.** [ME: from Fr. *asphalte*, based on late L. *asphalton, asphaltum*, from Gk. *asphalton.*]

as·phalt jun·gle ▶ **n.** the modern city, esp. when considered as a place of poverty and crime.

a·spher·i·cal /ā'sferikəl/ ▶ **adj.** (esp. of the surface an optical lens) not spherical. — **a·spher·ic adj.**

as·pho·del /'asfə,del/ ▶ **n. 1** a Eurasian plant (genera *Asphodelus* and *Asphodeline*) of the lily family, typically having long slender leaves and flowers borne on a spike. See also **BOG ASPHODEL. 2** literary an immortal flower said to grow in the Elysian fields. [ME: via L. from Gk. *asphodelos.*]

as·phyx·i·a /as'fiksēə/ ▶ **n.** a condition arising when the body is deprived of oxygen, causing unconsciousness or death; suffocation. — **as·phyx·i·al adj. as·phyx·i·ant** /-sēənt/ **adj. & n.** [18th C.: mod. L., from Gk. *asphuxia*, from *a-* 'without' + *sphuxis* 'pulse.']

as·phyx·i·ate /as'fiksē,āt/ ▶ **v.** [trans.] (usu. **be asphyxiated**) kill (someone) by depriving them of air. ■ [intrans.] die in this way: *they slowly asphyxiated.* — **as·phyx·i·a·tion** /as,fiksē'āsHən/ **n.**

as·pic /'aspik/ ▶ **n.** a jelly made with meat or fish stock, usually set in a mold and used as a garnish. [18th C.: from Fr., lit. 'asp.']

as·pi·dis·tra /ˌaspi'distrə/ ▶**n.** a bulbous plant (genus *Aspidistra*) of the lily family, with broad tapering leaves, native to eastern Asia and often grown as a houseplant. [19th C.: mod. L., from Gk. *aspis, aspid-* 'shield.']

as·pir·ant /'aspərənt; ə'spī-/ ▶**adj.** [attrib.] (of a person) having ambitions to achieve something, typically to follow a particular career: *an aspirant politician.* ▶**n.** a person who has ambitions to achieve something: ***an aspirant to the throne.***

as·pi·rate ▶**v.** /'aspəˌrāt/ [trans.] **1** Phonet. pronounce (a sound) with an exhalation of breath. ■ [intrans.] pronounce the sound *h* at the beginning of a word. **2** (usu. **be aspirated**) Med. draw (fluid) by suction from a vessel or cavity. ■ draw fluid in such a way from (a vessel or cavity). ■ breathe (something) in; inhale: *some drowning victims don't aspirate any water.* ▶**n.** /-rit/ **1** Phonet. an aspirated consonant. ■ the sound *h* or a character used to represent this sound. **2** Med. matter that has been drawn from the body by aspiration: *gastric aspirate | esophageal aspirates.* [16th C.: from L. *aspiratus* 'breathed,' past part. of *aspirare* (see **ASPIRE**).]

as·pi·ra·tion /ˌaspə'rāsʜən/ ▶**n.** **1** (usu. **aspirations**) a hope or ambition of achieving something: *he had nothing tangible to back up his literary aspirations.* ■ the object of such an ambition; a goal. **2** the action of pronouncing a sound with an exhalation of breath. **3** Med. the action of drawing fluid by suction from a vessel or cavity. — **as·pi·ra·tion·al** /-sʜənl/ **adj.** (in sense 1).

as·pi·ra·tor /'aspəˌrātər/ ▶**n.** Med. an instrument or apparatus for aspirating fluid from a vessel or cavity.

as·pire /ə'spī(ə)r/ ▶**v.** [intrans.] direct one's hopes or ambitions toward achieving something: *we never thought that we might **aspire to** those heights.* ■ literary rise high; tower. [ME: from Fr. *aspirer* or L. *aspirare*, from *ad-* 'to' + *spirare* 'breathe.']

as·pi·rin /'asp(ə)rin/ ▶**n.** a synthetic compound, $C_6H_4(OCOCH_3)COOH$, used medicinally to relieve mild or chronic pain and to reduce fever and inflammation. Also called **acetylsalicylic acid.** ■ (pl. same or **-rins**) a tablet containing this. [19th C.: from Ger., from *acetylierte Spirsäure* 'acetylated salicylic acid' (*Spir-* from plant genus *Spiraea*).]

a·sprawl /ə'sprôl/ ▶**adv. & adj.** sprawling.

a·squint /ə'skwint/ ▶**adv. & adj.** with a glance to one side or from the corner of the eyes. [ME: perh. from **A-**[2] + Low Ger. or Dutch word akin to Du. *schuinte* 'slant.']

As·quith /'askwəᴛʜ/, Herbert Henry, 1st Earl of Oxford and Asquith (1852–1928), prime minister of Britain 1908–16.

ass[1] /as/ ▶**n.** **1** a hoofed mammal (genus *Equus*) of the horse family with a braying call, typically smaller than a horse and with longer ears. The two species are *E. africanus* of Africa, which is the ancestor of the domestic ass or donkey, and *E. hemionus* of Asia. ■ (in general use) a donkey. **2** informal a foolish or stupid person.
– PHRASAL VERBS **make an ass of oneself** informal behave in a way that makes one look foolish or stupid. [OE *assa*, from Celtic word akin to Welsh *asyn*, based on L. *asinus*.]

ass[2] ▶**n.** vulgar slang a person's buttocks or anus. ■ a stupid, irritating, or contemptible person. ■ oneself (used in phrases for emphasis): *get your ass in here fast.*
– PHRASES **bust one's ass** try very hard to do something. **kick (some) ass** (or **kick someone's ass**) see **KICK**. **kiss ass** see **KISS**. **you bet your ass** you can be very sure: [with clause] *you can bet your ass I'll go for it every time.*
— **assed** /ast/ **adj.** [in comb.] *fat-assed guys.*

-ass ▶**comb. form** used in slang terms as an intensifier, often with depreciatory reference: *smart-ass | lame-ass.* [see **ASS**[2].]

As·sad /ä'säd; 'äsäd/, Hafiz al- (1928–2000), president of Syria 1971–2000. He supported the coalition forces during the 1991 Gulf War. His son **Bashar al-Assad** (1965–) succeeded him in 2000.

as·sa·gai ▶**n. & v.** var. of **ASSEGAI**.

as·sa·i /ä'sī/ ▶**adv.** Music very: *allegro assai.* [Ital., 'very much.']

as·sail /ə'sāl/ ▶**v.** [trans.] make a concerted or violent attack on. ■ (usu. **be assailed**) (of an unpleasant feeling or physical sensation) come upon (someone) suddenly and strongly: *she was assailed by doubts and regrets.* ■ criticize (someone) strongly. — **as·sail·a·ble adj.** [ME: from OFr. *asaill-*, *asalir*, from L. *assilire*, from *ad-* 'to' + *salire* 'to leap.']

as·sail·ant /ə'sālənt/ ▶**n.** a person who physically attacks another.

As·sam /ä'säm; ə'sam; 'asam/ a state in northeastern India, much of which lies in the valley of the Brahmaputra River; capital, Dispur.

As·sa·mese /ˌäsə'mēz; -'mēs/ ▶**n.** (pl. same) **1** a native or inhabitant of Assam. **2** the Indic language that is the official language of Assam. ▶**adj.** of or relating to Assam, its people, or its language.

as·sas·sin /ə'sasin/ ▶**n.** a murderer of an important person in a surprise attack for political or religious reasons. ■ (**Assassin**) hist. a member of the a branch of Ismaili Muslims (1094–1256), renowned as violent militant fanatics. [16th C.: from Fr., or from med. L. *assassinus*, from Arab. *ḥaššīšī* 'hashish eater.']

as·sas·si·nate /ə'sasəˌnāt/ ▶**v.** (often **be assassinated**) murder (an important person) in a surprise attack for political or religious reasons. — **as·sas·si·na·tion** /əˌsasə'nāsʜən/ **n.**

as·sas·sin bug ▶**n.** a long-legged predatory or bloodsucking bug (family Reduviidae) that occurs chiefly in the tropics and feeds mainly on other arthropods. Some of those that bite humans can transmit Chagas' disease.

As·sa·teague Is·land /'asəˌtēg/ a barrier island off of Maryland and Virginia, noted for its wild ponies.

as·sault /ə'sôlt/ ▶**v.** [trans.] make a physical attack on. ■ fig. attack or bombard (someone or the senses) with something undesirable or unpleasant: *her right ear was assaulted with a tide of music.* ■ carry out a military attack or raid on (an enemy position). ■ rape. ▶**n.** **1** a physical attack: *his imprisonment for an **assault on** the film director | sexual assaults.* ■ Law an act, criminal or tortious, that threatens physical harm to a person, whether or not actual harm is done. ■ a military attack or raid on an enemy position: ■ a strong verbal attack: *the **assault on** the party's tax policies.* **2** a concerted attempt to do something demanding: *a winter **assault on** Mt. Everest.* — **as·sault·er n.** [ME: from OFr. *asaut* (n.), *assauter* (v.), based on L. *ad-* 'to' + *saltare*, frequentative of *salire* 'to leap.']

as·sault and bat·ter·y ▶**n.** Law the crime of threatening a person together with the act of making physical contact with them.

as·saul·tive /ə'sôltiv/ ▶**adj.** tending or likely to commit an assault. ■ extremely aggressive or forcefully assertive: *his loud, assaultive playing style can leave you cowering.*

as·sault ri·fle ▶**n.** a rapid-fire, magazine-fed automatic rifle designed for infantry use.

as·say /'asā; a'sā/ ▶**n.** the testing of a metal or ore to determine its ingredients and quality: *submission of plate for assay.* ■ a procedure for measuring the biochemical or immunological activity of a sample: *each assay was performed in duplicate.* ▶**v.** [trans.] **1** determine the content or quality of (a metal or ore). ■ determine the biochemical or immunological activity of (a sample): *cell contents were **assayed for** enzyme activity.* ■ examine (something) in order to assess its nature: *stepping inside, I quickly assayed the clientele.* **2** archaic attempt: *I assayed a little joke of mine on him.* — **as·say·er n.** [ME: from OFr. *assai* (n.), *assaier* (v.), var. of *essai* 'trial,' *essayer* 'to try' (see **ESSAY**).]

ass-back·wards informal ▶**adv. &adj.** (used disparagingly) backwards or in a contrary way.

as·se·gai /'asəˌgī/ (also **as·sa·gai**) ▶**n.** (pl. **-gais**) **1** a slender, iron-tipped, hardwood spear used chiefly by southern African peoples. **2** (also **assegai wood**) a South African tree (*Curtisia dentata*) of the dogwood family that yields hard timber. [17th C.: from obs. Fr. *azagaie* or Port. *azagaia*, from Arab. *az-zağāyah*, from *az*, *al* 'the' + Berber *zağāyah* 'spear.']

as·sem·blage /ə'semblij/ ▶**n.** a collection or gathering of things or people. ■ a machine or object made of pieces fitted together: *some vast assemblage of gears and cogs.* ■ a work of art made by grouping found or unrelated objects. ■ the action of gathering or fitting things together.

as·sem·ble /ə'sembəl/ ▶**v.** **1** [intrans.] (of people) gather together in one place for a common purpose. ■ [trans.] bring (people or things) together for a common purpose: *he assembled the surviving members of the group for a tour.* **2** [trans.] fit together the separate component parts of (a machine or other object): *a factory that assembled parts for trucks.* ■ Comput. translate (a program) from assembly language into machine code. [ME: from OFr. *asembler*, based on L. *ad-* 'to' + *simul* 'together.']

as·sem·bler /ə'semblər/ ▶**n.** **1** a person who assembles a machine or its parts. **2** Comput. a program for converting instructions written in low-level symbolic code into machine code. ■ another term for **ASSEMBLY LANGUAGE**.

as·sem·bly /ə'semblē/ ▶**n.** (pl. **-blies**) **1** a group of people gathered together in one place for a common purpose: *an assembly of scholars and poets.* ■ a legislative body, esp. the lower legislative house in some US states: *the Connecticut General Assembly.* **2** the action of gathering together as a group for a common purpose: *a decree guaranteeing freedom of assembly.* ■ a regular gathering of the teachers and students of a school. ■ (usu. **the assembly**) esp. hist. a signal for troops to assemble, given by drum or bugle. **3** [often as adj.] the action of fitting together the component parts of a machine or other object: *a car assembly plant.* ■ a unit consisting of components that have been fitted together: *the tail assembly of the aircraft.* ■ [usu. as adj.] Comput. the conversion of instructions in low-level code to machine code by an assembler.

as·sem·bly lan·guage ▶**n.** Comput. a low-level symbolic code converted by an assembler.

as·sem·bly line ▶**n.** a series of workers and machines in a factory by which a succession of identical items is progressively assembled.

as·sem·bly·man /ə'semblēmən/ ▶**n.** a member of a legislative assembly.

as·sem·bly·wo·man /ə'semblēˌwo͝omən/ ▶**n.** a woman who is a member of a legislative assembly.

as·sent /ə'sent/ ▶**n.** the expression of approval or agreement: *a loud murmur of assent.* ■ official agreement or sanction: *the governor has power to withhold his assent from a bill.* ▶**v.** [intrans.] express approval or agreement, typically officially: *Roosevelt assented to the agreement.* — **as·sent·er n.** [ME: from OFr. *as(s)enter* (v.), *as(s)ente* (n.), based on L. *assentiri*, from *ad-* 'toward' + *sentire* 'feel.']

as·sert /ə'sərt/ ▶**v.** [reporting verb] state a fact or belief confidently and forcefully: [with clause] *the company asserts that the cuts will not affect development* | [trans.] *he asserted his innocence.* ■ [trans.] cause others to recognize (one's authority or a right) by confident and forceful behavior: *the good librarian is able to assert authority when required.* ■ (**assert oneself**) behave or speak in a confident and forceful manner: — **as·sert·er n.** [17th C.: from L. *asserere* 'claim,' from *ad-* 'to' + *serere* 'to join.']

as·ser·tion /ə'sərsʜən/ ▶**n.** a confident and forceful statement of fact or belief: [with clause] ***his assertion that** his father had deserted the family.* ■ the action of stating something or exercising authority confidently and forcefully: *the assertion of his legal rights.*

as·ser·tive /ə'sərtiv/ ▶ **adj.** having or showing a confident and forceful personality: *patients should be more assertive with their doctors.* — **as·ser·tive·ly adv. as·ser·tive·ness n.**

as·ses /'asiz/ plural form of AS², ASS¹, ASS².

as·sess /ə'ses/ ▶ **v.** [trans.] evaluate or estimate the nature, ability, or quality of: *the committee must assess the relative importance of the issues.* ■ (usu. **be assessed**) calculate or estimate the price or value of: *the damage was assessed at $5 billion.* ■ (often **be assessed**) set the value of a tax, fine, etc., for (a person or property) at a specified level: *all empty properties will be assessed at 50 percent.* — **as·sess·a·ble adj.** [ME: from OFr. *assesser*, based on L. *assidere* 'sit by', from *ad-* + *sedere* 'sit.']

as·sess·ment /ə'sesmənt/ ▶ **n.** the evaluation or estimation of the nature, quality, or ability of someone or something: *the assessment of educational needs | he made a rapid assessment of the situation.*

as·ses·sor /ə'sesər/ ▶ **n.** a person who assesses someone or something, in particular: ■ a person who calculates or estimates the value of something or an amount to be paid, chiefly for tax or insurance purposes. ■ a person who is knowledgeable in a particular field and is called upon for advice, typically by a judge or committee of inquiry.

as·set /'aset/ ▶ **n.** a useful or valuable thing, person, or quality: *quick reflexes were his chief asset.* ■ (usu. **assets**) property owned by a person or company, regarded as having value and available to meet debts, commitments, or legacies: *growth in net assets.* ■ (**assets**) military equipment employed or targeted in military operations. [16th C.: from OFr. *asez* 'enough,' based on L. *ad* 'to' + *satis* 'enough.']

as·sev·er·a·tion /ə,sevə'rāsHən/ ▶ **n.** the solemn or emphatic declaration or statement of something: *a dogmatic outlook marks many of his asseverations.* — **as·sev·er·ate** /ə'sevə,rāt/ **v.** [16th C.: from L. *asseveratio(n-)*, from v. *asseverare*, from *ad-* 'to' + *severus* 'serious.']

ass·hole /'as,hōl/ ▶ **n.** vulgar slang the anus. ■ an irritating or contemptible person.

as·sib·i·late /ə'sibə,lāt/ ▶ **v.** [trans.] Phonet. pronounce (a sound) as a sibilant or affricate ending in a sibilant (e.g., sound *t* as *ts*). — **as·sib·i·la·tion** /ə,sibə'lāsHən/ **n.** [19th C.: from L. *assibilat-* 'hissed at,' from v. *assibilare*, from *ad-* + *sibilare* 'to hiss.']

as·si·du·i·ty /,asi'd(y)o͞oitē/ ▶ **n.** (pl. **-ties**) constant or close attention to what one is doing.

as·sid·u·ous /ə'sijo͞oəs/ ▶ **adj.** showing great care and perseverance: *she was assiduous in pointing out every feature.* — **as·sid·u·ous·ly adv. as·sid·u·ous·ness n.** [16th C.: from L. *assiduus*, from *assidere* (see ASSESS).]

as·sign /ə'sīn/ ▶ **v.** [trans.] **1** allocate (a job or duty): *Congress* ***assigned*** *the task to the agency.* ■ (often **be assigned**) appoint (someone) to a particular job, task, or organization: *he was assigned to prosecute the case.* **2** designate or set (something) aside for a specific purpose: *assign large sums of money to travel budgets.* ■ (**assign something to**) attribute something as belonging to: *it is difficult to decide whether to assign the victory to Goodwin.* **3** transfer (legal rights or liabilities): *they will ask you to assign your rights against the airline.* ▶ **n.** Law another term for ASSIGNEE (sense 1). — **as·sign·a·ble adj.** (in sense 3 of the **verb**). **as·sign·er n. as·sign·or** /ə'sīnər/ **n.** (in sense 3 of the **verb**). [ME: ult. from L. *assignare*, from *ad-* 'to' + *signare* 'to sign.']

as·sig·na·tion /,asig'nāsHən/ ▶ **n. 1** an appointment to meet someone in secret, typically one made by lovers. **2** the allocation or attribution of someone or something as belonging to something.

as·sign·ee /ə,sī'nē/ ▶ **n.** esp. Law **1** a person to whom a right or liability is legally transferred. **2** a person appointed to act for another.

as·sign·ment /ə'sīnmənt/ ▶ **n. 1** a task assigned as part of a job or course of study: *a homework assignment.* ■ the allocation of a job or task to someone: *the assignment of tasks.* ■ the task or post to which one has been appointed: *I was* ***on assignment*** *for a German magazine.* **2** the attribution of someone or something as belonging: *the assignment of individuals to particular positions.* **3** an act of making a legal transfer of a right, property, or liability: *an assignment of property.* ■ a document effecting such a transfer.

as·sim·i·late /ə'simə,lāt/ ▶ **v.** [trans.] **1** take in (information, ideas, or culture) and understand fully: *assimilate the week's events.* ■ (usu. **be assimilated**) absorb and integrate (people, ideas, or culture) into a wider society or culture: *pop trends are* ***assimilated into*** *the mainstream.* ■ absorb or integrate and use for one's own benefit: *the music business assimilated whatever aspects of punk it could turn into profit.* ■ (usu. **be assimilated**) (of the body or any biological system) absorb and digest (food or nutrients): *sugars in fruit are readily assimilated by the body.* **2** cause (something) to resemble; liken: *philosophers had* ***assimilated*** *thought* ***to*** *perception.* ■ [intrans.] come to resemble: *the churches* ***assimilated to*** *a certain cultural norm.* ■ Phonet. make (a sound) more like another in the same or next word. — **as·sim·i·la·ble** /-ləbəl/ **adj. as·sim·i·la·tion** /ə,simə'lāsHən/ **n. as·sim·i·la·tive** /-,lātiv; -lətiv/ **adj. as·sim·i·la·tor** /-,lātər/ **n.** [ME: from L. *assimilat-* 'absorbed' from v. *assimilare*, from *ad-* 'to' + *similis* 'like.']

as·sim·i·la·tion·ist /ə,simə'lāsHə,nist/ ▶ **n.** a person who advocates or participates in racial or cultural integration.

As·sin·i·boin /ə'sinə,boin/ (also **As·sin·i·boine**) ▶ **n.** (pl. same or **-boins**) **1** a member of an American Indian people in Montana, Alberta, and Saskatchewan. **2** the Siouan language of this people. ▶ **adj.** of or relating to the Assiniboin or their language. [17th C.: from Canad. Fr., from Ojibwa *assini:pwa:n* from *assin* 'stone' + *pwa:n* 'Sioux.']

As·si·ni·boine Riv·er /ə'sinə,boin/ a river rising in eastern Saskatchewan and flowing 590 miles (950 km) to the Red River at Winnipeg.

As·si·si¹ /ə'sēsē; -zē/ a town in the province of Umbria in central Italy; pop. 24,790.

As·si·si² see CLARE OF ASSISI, ST.

As·si·si³ see FRANCIS OF ASSISI, ST.

as·sist /ə'sist/ ▶ **v.** [trans.] help (someone), typically by doing a share of the work. ■ help by providing money or information: *they were assisting police with their inquiries.* ■ [intrans.] be present as a helper or spectator: *midwives who* ***assisted at*** *a birth.* ▶ **n.** an act of help, typically by providing money: *the budget must have an assist from tax policies.* ■ (chiefly in ice hockey, basketball, or baseball) the act of touching the puck or ball in a play in which a teammate scores or an opposing batter is put out: *he led the league with 14 outfield assists.* — **as·sist·er n.** [ME: ult. from L. *assistere* 'take one's stand by,' from *ad-* + *sistere* 'take one's stand.']

as·sis·tance /ə'sistəns/ ▶ **n.** the provision of money, resources, or information to help someone. ■ the action of helping someone with a task: *the work was completed* ***with the assistance of*** *carpenters.*

as·sis·tant /ə'sistənt/ ▶ **n.** a person who ranks below a senior person: *the managing director and her assistant.* ■ [with adj. or modifier] a person who helps in particular work: *a laboratory assistant.*

as·sis·tant pro·fes·sor ▶ **n.** a university teacher ranking immediately below an associate professor.

as·sis·tant·ship /ə'sistənt,sHip/ ▶ **n.** a paid academic appointment made to a graduate student that involves part-time teaching or research.

as·sist·ed liv·ing ▶ **n.** housing for the elderly or disabled that provides nursing care, housekeeping, and prepared meals as needed.

as·sist·ed su·i·cide ▶ **n.** the suicide of a patient suffering from an incurable disease, effected by the taking of lethal drugs provided by a doctor for this purpose.

as·size /ə'sīz/ ▶ **n.** (usu. **assizes**) hist. a court that formerly sat at intervals in each county of England and Wales to administer civil and criminal law. [ME: from OFr. *assise*, fem. past part. of *asseeir* 'sit,' from L. *assidere* (see ASSESS).]

ass-kiss·ing ▶ **n.** vulgar slang the use of compliments, flattery, or similar behavior in order to gain favor. — **ass-kiss·er n.**

assn. ▶ **abbr.** association.

Assoc. ▶ **abbr.** ■ Associate. ■ Association.

as·so·ci·ate ▶ **v.** /ə'sōsē,āt; -sHē-/ [trans.] connect (someone or something) with something else in one's mind: *I* ***associated*** *wealth* ***with*** *freedom.* ■ (usu. **be associated**) connect (something) with something else because they occur together or one produces another: *the environmental problems* ***associated with*** *nuclear waste.* ■ (**associate oneself with**) allow oneself to be connected with or seen to be supportive of: *I cannot associate myself with some of the language used.* ■ (**be associated with**) be involved with: *she has been associated with the project from the first.* ■ [intrans.] meet or have dealings with someone commonly regarded with disapproval: *she began* ***associating with*** *socialists.* ▶ **n.** /-it/ **1** a partner or colleague in business or at work. ■ a companion or friend. **2** a person with limited or subordinate membership in an organization. ■ a person who holds an academic degree conferred by a junior college: *an associate's degree in science.* ▶ **adj.** /-it/ [attrib.] joined or connected with an organization or business: *an associate company.* ■ denoting shared function or membership but with a lesser status: *the associate director of the academy.* — **as·so·ci·a·ble** /ə'sōsH(ē)əbəl; -sHē-/ **adj. as·so·ci·ate·ship n.** [ME: from L. *associat-* 'joined,' from v. *associare*, from *ad-* 'to' + *socius* 'sharing.']

As·so·ci·at·ed Press (abbr.: **AP**) an international news agency based in New York City.

as·so·ci·ate jus·tice ▶ **n.** (the title of) a member of a supreme court who is not the chief justice, notably any of the eight members of the US Supreme Court who sit with the Chief Justice of the US.

As·so·ci·ate of Arts (abbr.: **AA**) (also **Associate's degree**) ▶ **n.** a degree granted after a two-year course of study, esp. by a community or junior college.

as·so·ci·ate pro·fes·sor ▶ **n.** an academic ranking immediately below full professor.

as·so·ci·a·tion /ə,sōsē'āsHən; -sHē-/ ▶ **n. 1** (abbr.: **assn.**) a group of people organized for a joint purpose: *the National Association of Broadcasters.* ■ Ecol. a plant community defined by a characteristic group of dominant plant species. **2** a connection or cooperative link between people or organizations: *the program was promoted* ***in association with*** *the Department of Music.* ■ the action or state of becoming a member of an organization with subordinate status: [as adj.] *Slovenia signed association agreements with the European Union.* ■ Chem. the linking of molecules through hydrogen bonding or other interaction short of full bond formation. **3** (usu. **associations**) a mental connection between ideas or things: *the word bureaucracy has unpleasant associations.* ■ the action of making such a connection: *the association of alchemy with "cabala."* ■ the fact of occurring with something else; co-occurrence: *cases of cancer found* ***in association with*** *colitis.* — **as·so·ci·a·tion·al** /-sHənl/ **adj.**

as·so·ci·a·tion ar·e·a ▶ **n.** Anat. a region of the brain that connects sensory and motor areas, and thought to be concerned with higher mental activities.

PRONUNCIATION KEY ə *ago, up*; ər *over, fur*; a *hat*; ā *ate*; ä *car*; e *let*; ē *see*; i *fit*; ī *by*; NG *sing*; ō *go*; ô *law, for*; oi *toy*; o͝o *good*; o͞o *goo*; ou *out*; TH *thin*; T̲H̲ *then*; ZH *vision*

as·so·ci·a·tion·ism /əˌsōsēˈāsHəˌnizəm; -ˌsōsHē-/ ▶**n.** a theory that regards the simple association or co-occurrence of ideas or sensations as the primary basis of meaning, thought, or learning. —**as·so·ci·a·tion·ist n. & adj.**

As·so·ci·a·tion of South·east A·sian Na·tions (abbr.: **ASEAN**) a regional organization intended to promote economic cooperation.

as·so·ci·a·tive /əˈsōsēˌātiv; -sHē-; -sēətiv; -sHətiv/ ▶**adj.** **1** of or involving the action of associating ideas or things: *an associative, nonlinear mode of thought.* ■ [attrib.] Comput. denoting computer storage in which items are identified by content rather than address. **2** Math. involving the condition that a group of quantities connected by operators gives the same result whatever their grouping, as long as their order remains the same, e.g., $(a \times b) \times c = a \times (b \times c)$.

as·so·ci·a·tive mem·o·ry ▶**n.** Comput. a memory capable of determining whether a given datum (the search word) is contained in one of its addresses or locations.

as·so·nance /ˈasənəns/ ▶**n.** in poetry, the repetition of the sound of a vowel or diphthong in nonrhyming stressed syllables (e.g., *penitence, reticence*). Compare with **ALLITERATION**. —**as·so·nant adj. as·so·nate** /-ˌnāt/ **v.** [18th C.: from Fr., from L. *assonare* 'respond to,' from *ad-* + *sonare* (from *sonus* 'sound').]

as·sort /əˈsôrt/ ▶**v. 1** [intrans.] Genet. (of genes or characters) become distributed among cells or progeny. **2** [trans.] archaic place in a group; classify: *he would assort it with the fabulous dogs as a monstrous invention.* [15th C.: from OFr. *assorter*, from *a-* 'to') + *sorte* 'sort.']

as·sort·ed /əˈsôrtid/ ▶**adj.** [attrib.] of various sorts put together; miscellaneous: *bowls in assorted colors.*

as·sort·ment /əˈsôrtmənt/ ▶**n.** a miscellaneous collection of things or people: *an assortment of clothes.*

ASSR hist. ▶**abbr.** Autonomous Soviet Socialist Republic.

Asst. ▶**abbr.** Assistant.

as·suage /əˈswāj/ ▶**v.** [trans.] make (an unpleasant feeling) less intense: *the letter assuaged the fears of most members.* ■ satisfy (an appetite or desire): *an opportunity occurred to assuage her desire for knowledge.* —**as·suage·ment n.** [ME: from OFr. *assouagier, asouagier*, based on L. *ad-* 'to' + *suavis* 'sweet.']

as·sume /əˈso͞om/ ▶**v.** [trans.] **1** suppose to be the case, without proof: *afraid of what people are going to assume* | [with clause] *reasonable to assume that such changes have social effects.* **2** take or begin to have (power or responsibility): *he assumed full responsibility for all organizational work.* **3** take on (a specified quality, appearance, or extent): *militant activity had assumed epidemic proportions.* ■ adopt falsely: *Oliver assumed an expression of penitence* | [as adj.] (**assumed**) *a man living under an assumed name.* —**as·sum·ed·ly** /əˈso͞omidlē/ **adv.** [ME: from L. *assumere*, from *ad-* 'toward' + *sumere* 'take.']

as·sum·ing /əˈso͞omiNG/ ▶**conj.** used for the purpose of argument to indicate a premise on which a statement can be based: ***assuming*** *that the treaty is ratified, what is its relevance?* ▶**adj.** archaic arrogant or presumptuous.

as·sump·tion /əˈsəm(p)sHən/ ▶**n. 1** a thing that is accepted as true or as certain to happen, without proof: *they made certain assumptions about the market.* **2** the action of taking power or responsibility: *the assumption of an active role in regional settlements.* **3** (**Assumption**) the reception of the Virgin Mary bodily into heaven, a doctrine of the Roman Catholic Church. ■ the feast in honor of this, celebrated on August 15. [ME: ult. from L. *assumptio(n-)*, from *assumere*.]

as·sur·ance /əˈsHo͝orəns/ ▶**n. 1** a positive declaration intended to give confidence; a promise: [with clause] *he gave an assurance that work would not recommence until Wednesday.* **2** confidence or certainty in one's own abilities: *she drove with assurance.* ■ certainty about something: *assurance of faith depends on our trust in God.* **3** esp. Brit. insurance, specifically life insurance.

as·sure /əˈsHo͝or/ ▶**v. 1** [reporting verb] tell someone something positively or confidently to dispel any doubts they may have: [trans.] *Tony assured me that there was a supermarket in the village.* ■ make (someone) sure of something: *you would be assured of a fine welcome.* **2** [trans.] (often **be assured**) make (something) certain to happen: *victory was now assured.* ■ esp. Brit. cover (a person) with life insurance. —**as·sur·er n.** [ME: from OFr. *assurer*, based on L. *ad-* 'to' + *securus* (see **SECURE**).]

as·sured /əˈsHo͝ord/ ▶**adj. 1** confident: *"certainly not," was her assured reply.* **2** [attrib.] protected against discontinuance or change: *an assured tenancy.* —**as·sur·ed·ly** /əˈsHo͝oridlē/ **adv.** [sentence adverb] *if they lose their hold, they will assuredly drown.*

As·syr·i·a /əˈsi(ə)rēə/ an ancient country in what is now northern Iraq; the center of a succession of empires.

As·syr·i·an /əˈsi(ə)rēən/ ▶**n. 1** an inhabitant of ancient Assyria. **2** the language of ancient Assyria, a dialect of Akkadian. **3** a dialect of Aramaic still spoken in northern Iraq, the mountains of Syria, and surrounding regions. ▶**adj. 1** of or relating to ancient Assyria or its language. **2** relating to modern Assyrian or its speakers.

As·syr·i·ol·o·gy /əˌsi(ə)rēˈäləjē/ ▶**n.** the study of the language, history, and antiquities of ancient Assyria. —**As·syr·i·o·log·i·cal** /əˌsi(ə)rēəˈläjikəl/ **adj. As·syr·i·ol·o·gist** /-jist/ **n.**

AST ▶**abbr.** Atlantic Standard Time.

A·staire /əˈste(ə)r/, Fred (1899–1987), US dancer, singer, and actor; born *Frederick Austerlitz*. He starred in a number of movie musicals, including *Top Hat* (1935) and *Shall We Dance?* (1937).

A·sta·na /äsˈtänə/ the capital of Kazakhstan (since 1998); pop. 287,000. Formerly called **Aqmola** and, earlier, **Tselinograd**.

As·tar·te /əˈstärtē/ Mythol. a Phoenician goddess of fertility and sexual love.

a·stat·ic /āˈstatik/ ▶**adj.** not keeping a steady position or direction, in particular: ■ Physics (of a system or instrument) consisting of or employing a combination of magnets suspended in a uniform magnetic field on a single wire or thread in such a way that no torque is present (e.g., to minimize the effect of the earth's magnetic field). [19th C.: from Gk. *astatos* 'unstable.']

as·ta·tine /ˈastəˌtēn; -tin/ ▶**n.** the chemical element of atomic number 85, produced by bombarding bismuth with alpha particles, and occurring in traces in nature as a decay product. (Symbol: **At**) [1940s: from Gk. *astatos* 'unstable.']

as·ter /ˈastər/ ▶**n. 1** a plant (genus *Aster*) of the daisy family that has bright rayed flowers, typically purple or pink. Many species, including the **New England aster** (*A. novae-angliae*), bloom in autumn. **2** Biol. a star-shaped structure formed during division of the nucleus of an animal cell. [17th C.: via L. from Gk. *astēr* 'star.']

New England aster

-aster ▶**suffix** forming nouns: **1** denoting poor quality: *poetaster.* **2** Bot. denoting incomplete resemblance: *oleaster.* [from L.]

as·ter·isk /ˈastəˌrisk/ ▶**n.** a symbol (*) used to mark printed or written text, typically as a reference to an annotation or to stand for omitted matter. ▶**v.** [trans.] [usu. as adj.] (**asterisked**) mark (printed or written text) with an asterisk: *asterisked entries.* [ME: via late L. from Gk. *asteriskos* 'small star,' dimin. of *astēr*.]

– USAGE Avoid pronouncing this word /ˈastəˌriks/, as many regard such pronunciation as uneducated.

as·ter·ism /ˈastəˌrizəm/ ▶**n. 1** Astron. a prominent pattern or group of stars, typically having a popular name but smaller than a constellation. **2** a group of three asterisks (⁂) drawing attention to following text.

a·stern /əˈstərn/ ▶**adv. 1** behind or toward the rear of a ship or aircraft: *the engine rooms lay astern.* **2** (of a ship) backward: *the lifeboat was carried astern by the tide.*

as·ter·oid /ˈastəˌroid/ ▶**n.** a small rocky body orbiting the sun. Large numbers of these, ranging in size from nearly 600 miles (1,000 km) across to dust particles, are found between the orbits of Mars and Jupiter. —**as·ter·oi·dal** /ˌastəˈroidl/ **adj.** [19th C.: from Gk. *asteroeidēs* 'starlike,' from *astēr* 'star.']

As·ter·oi·de·a /ˌastəˈroidēə/ Zool. a class of echinoderms that comprises the starfishes. —**as·ter·oid** /ˈastəˌroid/ **n. & adj.** [mod. L. (pl.), from Gk. *asteroeidēs* 'starlike,' from *astēr* 'star.']

as·the·ni·a /asˈTHēnēə/ ▶**n.** Med. abnormal physical weakness or lack of energy. [18th C.: mod. L., from Gk. *astheneia*, from *asthenēs* 'weak.']

as·then·ic /asˈTHenik/ ▶**adj.** Med. relating to, involving, or suffering from asthenia.

as·then·o·sphere /asˈTHenəˌsfi(ə)r/ ▶**n.** Geol. the upper layer of the earth's mantle, below the lithosphere, in which there is relatively low resistance to plastic flow and convection is thought to occur. —**as·then·o·spher·ic** /asˌTHenəˈsfi(ə)rik; -ˈsferik/ **adj.** [20th C.: from Gk. *asthenēs* 'weak.']

asth·ma /ˈazmə/ ▶**n.** a respiratory condition marked by spasms in the bronchi of the lungs, causing difficulty in breathing. It usually results from an allergic reaction or other forms of hypersensitivity. [ME: from med. L. *asma*, from Gk. *asthma*, from *azein* 'breathe hard.']

asth·mat·ic /azˈmatik/ ▶**adj.** relating to or suffering from asthma. ▶**n.** a person who suffers from asthma. —**asth·mat·i·cal·ly** /-ik(ə)lē/ **adv.**

As·ti /ˈästē/ ▶**n. 1** a white wine from the province of Asti and neighboring parts of Piedmont. **2** a light sparkling wine from this region, also called **Asti Spumante**.

a·stig·ma·tism /əˈstigməˌtizəm/ ▶**n.** a defect in the eye or in a lens caused by a deviation from spherical curvature, which prevents light rays from meeting at a common focus, resulting in distorted images. —**as·tig·mat·ic** /ˌastigˈmatik/ **adj.** [19th C.: from **A-**[1] + Gk. *stigma* 'point.']

a·stil·be /əˈstilbē/ ▶**n.** an Old World plant (genus *Astilbe*) of the saxifrage family, with plumes of tiny white, pink, or red flowers. [mod. L., from Gk. *a-* 'not' + *stilbē*, fem. of *stilbos* 'glittering.']

a·stir /əˈstər/ ▶**adj.** [predic.] in a state of excited movement: *the streets are all astir.* ■ awake and out of bed. [18th C.: from **A-**[2] + **STIR**[1] (n.).]

As·ton /ˈastən/, Francis William (1877–1945), English physicist. He helped to invent the mass spectrograph. Nobel Prize for Chemistry (1922).

as·ton·ish /əˈstänisH/ ▶**v.** [trans.] surprise or impress (someone) greatly. —**as·ton·ish·ing·ly adv.** [as submodifier] *an astonishingly successful program.* [16th C.: from obs. *astone* 'stun,' from OFr. *estoner*, based on L. *ex-* 'out' + *tonare* 'to thunder.']

as·ton·ish·ment /əˈstänisHmənt/ ▶**n.** great surprise.

As·tor[1] /ˈastər/, John Jacob (1763–1848), US merchant; born in Germany. He made a fortune in the fur trade.

As·tor[2], Nancy Witcher Langhorne, Viscountess (1879–1964), British politician; born in the US; the first woman to sit in the House of Commons.

as·tound /əˈstound/ ▶**v.** [trans.] shock or greatly surprise: *her bluntness* *astounded him.* [ME (adj.): from *astoned*, past part. of obs. *astone* (see ASTONISH).]

as·tound·ing /ə'stoundiNG/ ▶ **adj.** surprisingly impressive or notable: *the summit offers astounding views.* — **as·tound·ing·ly adv.** [as submodifier] *an astoundingly good performance.*

a·strad·dle /ə'stradl/ ▶ **prep.** with the legs stretched widely on each side of: *sitting astraddle motorcycles.* ▶ **adj. & adv.** with the legs stretched widely on each side.

as·tra·gal /'astrəgəl/ ▶ **n.** a convex molding or wooden strip across a surface or separating panels, typically semicircular in cross-section. [17th C.: from ASTRAGALUS.]

as·trag·a·lus /ə'stragələs/ ▶ **n.** (pl. **-li** /-,lī/) esp. Zool. another term for TALUS[1] (ankle bone). [16th C.: via L. from Gk. *astragalos* 'ankle bone.']

As·tra·khan /'astrə,kan; -kən/ a city in southern Russia, on the delta of the Volga River; pop. 509,000.

as·tra·khan /'astrəkən; -,kan/ ▶ **n.** the dark curly fleece of young karakul lambs from central Asia. ■ a cloth imitating this. [18th C.: ASTRAKHAN.]

as·tral /'astrəl/ ▶ **adj.** [attrib.] of, connected with, or resembling the stars: *astral navigation.* ■ of or relating to a supposed nonphysical realm of existence in which the physical human body is said to have a counterpart. [17th C.: from late L. *astralis*, from *astrum* 'star.']

a·stray /ə'strā/ ▶ **adv. 1** away from the correct path or direction: *we went astray but a man redirected us.* **2** into error or morally questionable behavior. [ME): ult. from OFr. *estraie*, past part. of *estraier*, based on L. *extra* 'out of bounds' + *vagari* 'wander.']

a·stride /ə'strīd/ ▶ **prep.** with a leg on each side of: *he was sitting astride the bike.* ■ extending across: *the port stands astride an international route.*

as·trin·gent /ə'strinjənt/ ▶ **adj. 1** causing the contraction of body tissues, typically of the cells of the skin: *an astringent skin lotion.* **2** sharp or severe in manner or style: *astringent words.* ■ (of taste or smell) sharp or bitter. ▶ **n.** a substance that causes the contraction of body tissues, typically used to reduce bleeding from minor abrasions. — **as·trin·gen·cy n. as·trin·gent·ly adv.** (in sense 2 of the **adjective**). [16th C.: from Fr., from L. *astringent-* 'pulling tight,' from v. *astringere*, from *ad-* 'toward' + *stringere* 'bind.']

astro- ▶ **comb. form** relating to the stars, celestial objects, or outer space: *astrophysics.* [from Gk. *astron* 'star.']

as·tro·bi·o·lo·gy /,astrōbī'äləjē/ ▶ **n.** the science concerned with life in space.

as·tro·chem·is·try /,astrō'kemәstrē/ ▶ **n.** the study of the chemical substances and species occurring in stars and interstellar space. — **as·tro·chem·i·cal** /-ikəl/ **adj. as·tro·chem·ist** /'astrō,kemist/ **n.**

as·tro·com·pass /'astrō,kəmpəs; -,käm-/ ▶ **n.** an instrument designed to indicate direction with respect to the stars.

as·tro·cyte /'astrə,sīt/ ▶ **n.** Anat. a star-shaped glial cell of the central nervous system. — **as·tro·cyt·ic** /,astrə'sitik/ **adj.**

as·tro·dome /'astrə,dōm/ ▶ **n. 1** a domed window in an aircraft for astronomical observations. **2** (**the Astrodome**) an enclosed stadium in Houston, Texas, with a domed roof.

as·tro·labe /'astrə,lāb/ ▶ **n.** esp. hist. an instrument formerly used to make astronomical measurements, before the development of the sextant. [ME: from OFr. *astrelabe*, ult. from Gk. *astrolabon*, neut. of *astrolabos* 'star-taking.']

as·trol·o·gy /ə'stäləjē/ ▶ **n.** the study of the movements and relative positions of celestial bodies interpreted as having an influence on human affairs. — **as·trol·o·ger** /-jər/ **n. as·tro·log·i·cal** /,astrə'läjikəl/ **adj. as·trol·o·gist** /-jist/ **n.** [ME: from OFr. *astrologie*, ult. from Gk., from *astron* 'star.']

as·trom·e·try /ə'strämitrē/ ▶ **n.** the measurement of the positions, motions, and magnitudes of stars. — **as·tro·met·ric** /,astrō'metrik/ **adj.**

as·tro·naut /'astrə,nôt/ ▶ **n.** a person who is trained to travel in a spacecraft. — **as·tro·nau·ti·cal** /,astrə'nôtikəl/ **adj.** [1920s: from ASTRO-, on the pattern of *aeronaut*.]

as·tro·nau·tics /,astrə'nôtiks/ ▶ **n.** the science and technology of human space travel and exploration.

as·tro·nav·i·ga·tion /,astrō,navi'gāSHən/ ▶ **n.** determination of the position and course of an aircraft or a spacecraft by means of observation of the stars. — **as·tro·nav·i·ga·tor** /-'navi,gātər/ **n.**

as·tron·o·mer /ə'stränəmər/ ▶ **n.** an expert in or student of astronomy.

as·tro·nom·i·cal /,astrə'nämikəl/ ▶ **adj. 1** of or relating to astronomy. **2** informal (of an amount) extremely large: *he wanted an astronomical fee.* — **as·tro·nom·ic adj.** (in sense 2). **as·tro·nom·i·cal·ly** /-ik(ə)lē/ **adv.**

as·tro·nom·i·cal u·nit (abbr.: **AU**) ▶ **n.** Astron. a unit of measurement equal to 149.6 million kilometers, the mean distance from the center of the earth to the center of the sun.

as·tron·o·my /ə'stränəmē/ ▶ **n.** the branch of science that deals with celestial objects, space, and the physical universe as a whole. [ME: ult. from L. *astronomia*, from Gk., from *astronomos* 'star-arranging.']

as·tro·pho·tog·ra·phy /,astrōfə'tägrəfē/ ▶ **n.** the use of photography in astronomy; the photographing of celestial objects and phenomena. — **as·tro·pho·tog·ra·pher n. as·tro·pho·to·graph·ic** /-,fōtə'grafik/ **adj.**

as·tro·phys·ics /,astrō'fiziks/ ▶ **n.** the branch of astronomy concerned with the physical nature of celestial bodies, and the application of the laws of physics to astronomical observations. — **as·tro·phys·i·cal** /-ikəl/ **adj. as·tro·phys·i·cist** /-isist/ **n.**

As·tro·Turf /'astrō,tərf/ ▶ **n.** trademark an artificial grass surface, used for athletic fields. [1960s: from ASTRODOME.]

As·tu·ri·as[1] /ə'st(y)o͝orēəs/ an autonomous region in northwestern Spain; capital, Oviedo.

As·tu·ri·as[2], Miguel Ángel (1899–1974), Guatemalan writer, best known for his experimental novel *The President* (1946). Nobel Prize for Literature (1967).

as·tute /ə'st(y)o͞ot/ ▶ **adj.** having or showing an ability to accurately assess situations or people and turn this to one's advantage: *an astute businessman.* — **as·tute·ly adv. as·tute·ness n.** [17th C.: ult. from L. *astutus*, from *astus* 'craft.']

a·sty·lar /ā'stīlər/ ▶ **adj.** Archit. (of a classical building) lacking columns or pilasters. [19th C.: from A-[1] + Gk. *stulos* 'column.']

A·sun·ción /ä,so͞onsē'ōn; -'syōn/ the capital and chief port of Paraguay, on the Paraguay River; pop. 637,737.

a·sun·der /ə'səndər/ ▶ **adv.** archaic or literary apart; divided. ■ into pieces.

a·su·ra /'əsərə/ Hinduism ▶ **n.** a member of a class of evil divine beings in the Vedic period Compare with DEVA, AHURA MAZDA.

As·wan /as'wän; äs-/ a city on the Nile River in southern Egypt, 10 miles (16 km), north of Lake Nasser; pop. 195,700.

a·swarm /ə'swôrm/ ▶ **adj.** [predic.] crowded; full of moving beings or objects: *streets aswarm with vendors.*

as well as ▶ **conj.** and also; and in addition.

a·swim /ə'swim/ ▶ **adj.** [predic.] swimming: *sardines aswim in oil.*

a·swirl /ə'swərl/ ▶ **adj. & adv.** swirling; covered or surrounded with something swirling: *flowers aswirl with bees.*

a·sy·lum /ə'sīləm/ ▶ **n. 1** (also **political asylum**) the protection granted by a nation to someone who has left their native country as a political refugee: *granting asylum to foreigners persecuted for political reasons* ■ shelter or protection from danger. **2** dated an institution for the mentally ill. [ME: via L. from Gk. *asulon* 'refuge,' from *asulos* 'inviolable,' from *a-* + *sulon* 'right of seizure.']

a·sym·met·ri·cal /,āsə'metrikəl/ ▶ **adj.** having parts that fail to correspond to one another in shape, size, or arrangement; lacking symmetry. ■ having parts or aspects that are not equal or equivalent; unequal in some respect: *the asymmetrical relationship between a landlord and a tenant.* — **a·sym·met·ric adj. a·sym·met·ri·cal·ly** /-ik(ə)lē/ **adv.**

a·sym·me·try /ā'simitrē/ ▶ **n.** (pl. **-tries**) lack of equality or equivalence between parts or aspects of something; lack of symmetry.

a·symp·to·mat·ic /,āsim(p)tə'matik/ ▶ **adj.** Med. (of a condition or a person) showing no symptoms.

as·ymp·tote /'asəm(p),tōt/ ▶ **n.** a line that continually approaches a given curve but does not meet it at any finite distance. — **as·ymp·tot·ic** /,asəm(p)'tätik/ **adj. as·ymp·tot·i·cal·ly** /-ik(ə)lē/ **adv.** [17th C.: from mod. L. *asymptota (linea)* '(line) not meeting,' from Gk. *asumptōtos* 'not falling together,' based on *a-* + *sun* 'together' + *piptein* 'to fall.']

a·syn·chro·nous /ā'siNGkrənəs/ ▶ **adj. 1** Comput. & Telecom. of or requiring a form of computer control timing protocol in which a specific operation begins upon receipt of an indication (signal) that the preceding operation has been completed. **2** not going at the same rate or exactly together with something else. **3** not existing or happening at the same time. — **a·syn·chro·nous·ly adv.**

a·syn·de·ton /ə'sində,tän/ ▶ **n.** (pl. **-de·ta** /-dətə/) the omission or absence of a conjunction between parts of a sentence. — **as·yn·det·ic** /,asən'detik/ **adj.** [16th C.: mod. L., from Gk. *asundeton*, neut. of *asundetos* 'unconnected,' from *a-* + *sundetos* 'bound together.']

At ▶ **symb.** the chemical element astatine.

at[1] /at/ ▶ **prep. 1** expressing location or arrival in a particular place or position: *they live at Conway House.* ■ used in speech to indicate the sign @ in electronic mail addresses. **2** expressing the time when an event takes place: *at nine o'clock.* **3** denoting a particular point or segment on a scale: *prices start at $18,500 | driving at 50 mph.* ■ referring to someone's age: *at fourteen he began to work.* **4** expressing a particular state or condition: *placed them at a serious disadvantage.* ■ expressing a relationship between an individual and a skill: *boxing was the only sport I was any good at.* **5** expressing the object of a look, gesture, thought, action, or plan: *I looked at my watch.* **6** expressing the means by which something is done: *holding an officer at knifepoint.*

– PHRASES **at it** engaged in some activity, typically a reprehensible one: *the guy who faked the Hitler diaries is at it again.* **at that** in addition; furthermore: *it was not fog but smoke, and very thick at that.* **where it's at** informal the fashionable place, possession, or activity. [OE; from Indo-Eur.; akin to ON *at*, L. *ad* 'to.']

at[2] /ät/ ▶ **n.** a monetary unit of Laos, equal to one-hundredth of a kip.

at- ▶ **prefix** var. of AD-.

At·a·brine /'atəbrin; -,brēn/ trade name for QUINACRINE.

A·ta·ca·ma Des·ert /,ätə'kämə; ,atə-/ an arid region in western Chile.

a·tac·tic /ā'taktik/ ▶ **adj.** Chem. (of a polymer or polymer structure) in which the repeating units have no regular stereochemical configuration. [19th C.: from Gk. *ataktos*, from *a-* + *taktos* 'arranged.']

At·a·lan·ta /,ätə'läntə/ Gk. Mythol. a huntress who would marry only someone who could beat her in a foot race. She was beaten when a suitor threw down three golden apples which she stopped to pick up.

at·a·man /'atəmən/ ▶ **n.** (pl. **-mans**) a Cossack leader. See also HETMAN. [19th C.: from Russ.]

at·a·rax·y /ˈatəˌraksē/ (also **at·a·rax·i·a** /ˌatəˈraksēə/) ▶ **n.** a state of serene calmness. — **at·a·rac·tic** /ˌatəˈraktik/ **adj. at·a·rax·ic** /ˌatəˈraksik/ **adj.** [17th C.: from Fr. *ataraxie*, from Gk. *ataraxia* 'impassiveness,' from *a-* + *tarassein* 'disturb.']

A·ta·türk /ˌatəˈtərk/, Kemal (1881–1938), president of Turkey 1923–38; born *Mustafa Kemal*; also called **Kemal Pasha**. He abolished the caliphate and introduced policies designed to modernize Turkey.

at·a·vis·tic /ˌatəˈvistik/ ▶ **adj.** relating to or characterized by reversion to something ancient or ancestral: *atavistic fears and instincts.* — **at·a·vism** /ˈatəˌvizəm/ **n. at·a·vis·ti·cal·ly** /-tik(ə)lē/ **adv.** [19th C.: based on L. *atavus* 'forefather,' via Fr. *atavisme*.]

a·tax·i·a /əˈtaksēə/ (also **a·tax·y** /əˈtaksē/) ▶ **n.** Med. the loss of full control of bodily movements. — **a·tax·ic** /-sik/ **adj.** [19th C.: mod. L., from Gk., from *a-* + *taxis* 'order.']

ATB ▶ **abbr.** all-terrain bike.

at bat Baseball. ▶ **n.** a player's turn at batting, as officially recorded: *O'Neill had three singles in four at bats.* ▶ **adv.** batting.

A·tchaf·a·lay·a Riv·er /əˌCHafəˈlīə/ a river in south central Louisiana that flows south for 170 miles (275 km) to the Gulf of Mexico.

ate /āt/ past of EAT.

-ate[1] ▶ **suffix** forming nouns: **1** denoting status or office: *doctorate* | *episcopate.* **2** denoting a group: *electorate.* **3** Chem. denoting a salt or ester, esp. of an acid with a corresponding name ending in *-ic*: *chlorate* | *nitrate.* **4** denoting a product (of a chemical process): *condensate* | *filtrate.* [OFr. from *-at* or *-é(e)*, or from L. *-atus* (n. or past participial form).]

-ate[2] ▶ **suffix** forming adjectives and nouns such as *associate, duplicate, separate.* [representing Fr. *-é* or its L. source *-atus* (past participial suffix).]

-ate[3] ▶ **suffix** forming verbs such as *fascinate, hyphenate.* [from Fr. *-er* or its L. source *-are.*]

A-team ▶ **n.** a group of elite soldiers or the top advisers or workers in an organization.

at·e·lec·ta·sis /ˌatlˈektəsis/ ▶ **n.** Med. partial or complete collapse of the lung. [19th C.: from Gk. *atelēs* 'imperfect' + *ektasis* 'extension.']

at·el·ier /ˌatlˈyā/ ▶ **n.** a workshop or studio, esp. one used by an artist or designer. [17th C.: from Fr., from OFr. *astelle* 'splinter of wood,' from L. *astula*.]

a tem·po /ä ˈtempō/ ▶ **adv.** Music (esp. as a direction) in the previous or original tempo. [Ital., lit. 'in time.']

a·tem·po·ral /āˈtemp(ə)rəl/ ▶ **adj.** existing or considered without relation to time. — **a·tem·po·ral·i·ty** /āˌtempəˈralitē/ **n.**

a·ten·o·lol /əˈtenəˌlôl; -ˌläl/ ▶ **n.** Med. a beta blocker used mainly to treat angina and high blood pressure. [1970s: perh. from *a(ngina)* + *ten(sion)* + *(propran)olol.*]

ATF ▶ **abbr.** (Federal Bureau of) Alcohol, Tobacco, and Firearms.

Ath·a·bas·ca Riv·er /ˌaTHəˈbaskə/ a river in Canada that flows northeast for 765 miles (1,230 km) from the Rocky Mountains to Lake Athabasca.

Ath·a·bas·kan /ˌaTHəˈbaskən/ (also **Ath·a·pas·kan** /-ˈpas-/) ▶ **adj.** denoting, belonging to, or relating to a family of North American Indian languages including esp. Navajo and various Apache languages of the southwest U.S., several languages of coastal California and Oregon, and many languages of Alaska and northwestern Canada, including Chipewyan. ▶ **n. 1** this family of languages. **2** a speaker of any of these languages. [from *Athabasca*, the name of a lake in western Canada, from Cree *Athap-askaw* 'grass and reeds here and there,' + -AN.]

Ath·a·na·sian Creed /ˌaTHəˈnāZHən/ a summary of Christian doctrine formerly attributed to St. Athanasius, but probably dating from the 5th century.

Ath·a·na·sius, St. /ˌaTHəˈnāSHəs/ (*c.*296–373), Greek theologian. He upheld Christian orthodoxy against the Arian heresy.

a·the·ism /ˈāTHēˌizəm/ ▶ **n.** the theory or belief that God does not exist. — **a·the·ist n. a·the·is·tic** /ˌāTHēˈistik/ **adj. a·the·is·ti·cal** /-ˈistikəl/ **adj.** [16th C.: from Fr. *athéisme*, from Gk. *atheos*, from *a-* + *theos* 'god.']

ath·el·ing /ˈaTHəliNG; ˈaT͟H-/ ▶ **n.** hist. a prince or lord in Anglo-Saxon England. [OE *ætheling*, from West Gmc., from a base meaning 'race.']

Ath·el·stan /ˈaTHəlˌstan/ (895–939), king of England 925–939.

a·the·mat·ic /ˌāTHiˈmatik/ ▶ **adj.** Music (of a composition) not based on the use of themes.

A·the·na /əˈTHēnə/ (also **A·the·ne** /-nē/) Gk. Mythol. the patron goddess of Athens, worshiped as the goddess of wisdom, handicrafts, and warfare. Also called PALLAS. Identified with the Roman goddess MINERVA.

ath·e·nae·um /ˌaTHəˈnēəm/ (also **ath·e·ne·um**) ▶ **n.** used in the names of libraries or institutions for literary or scientific study: *the Boston Athenaeum.* ■ used in the titles of periodicals concerned with literature, science, and art. [18th C.: via L. from Gk. *Athēnaion* 'temple of Athena'.]

Ath·ens /ˈaTHənz/ **1** the capital of Greece, in the southern part of the country; pop. 3,096,775. It was an important cultural center in the 5th century BC. It came under Roman rule in 146 BC, fell to the Goths in AD 267, and the Turks in 1456. Greek name ATHÍNAI. **2** a city in northeastern Georgia, the seat of the University of Georgia; pop. 45,734. — **A·the·ni·an** /əˈTHēnēən/ **adj. & n.**

ath·er·o·ma /ˌaTHəˈrōmə/ ▶ **n.** Med. degeneration of the walls of the arteries caused by accumulated fatty deposits and scar tissue. See also ATHEROSCLEROSIS. ■ the fatty material that forms plaques in the arteries. — **ath·er·om·a·tous** /-ˈrämətəs; -ˈrō-/ **adj.** [16th C.: via L. from Gk. *athērōma*, from *athērē, atharē* 'groats.']

ath·er·o·scle·ro·sis /ˌaTHəˌrōskləˈrōsis/ ▶ **n.** Med. a disease of the arteries characterized by the deposition of plaques of fatty material on their inner walls. See also ATHEROMA and ARTERIOSCLEROSIS. — **ath·er·o·scle·rot·ic** /-ˈrätik/ **adj.** [20th C.: ult. from Gk. *athērē* 'groats.']

ath·e·to·sis /ˌaTHiˈtōsis/ ▶ **n.** Med. a condition in which abnormal muscle contractions cause involuntary writhing movements. — **ath·e·toid** /ˈaTHiˌtoid/ **adj. ath·e·tot·ic** /-ˈtätik/ **adj.** [19th C.: from Gk. *athetos* 'without position.']

A·thí·nai /äˈTHēne/ var. of ATHENS.

a·thirst /əˈTHərst/ ▶ **adj.** [predic.] archaic thirsty. ■ very eager to get something: *she was athirst for news.* [OE *ofthyrst*, shortened from *ofthyrsted*, past part. of *ofthyrstan* 'be thirsty.']

ath·lete /ˈaTHlēt/ ▶ **n.** a person who is proficient in sports and other forms of physical exercise. [ME: from L. *athleta*, from Gk. *athlētēs*, from *athlein* 'compete for a prize,' from *athlon* 'prize.']

ath·lete's foot ▶ **n.** a fungal infection affecting the skin between the toes. It is a form of ringworm.

ath·let·ic /aTHˈletik/ ▶ **adj. 1** [attrib.] of or relating to athletes or athletics: *athletic events* | *an athletic club.* **2** physically strong, fit, and active: *big, muscular, athletic boys.* — **ath·let·i·cal·ly** /-ik(ə)lē/ **adv. ath·let·i·cism** /-iˌsizəm/ **n.**

ath·let·ics /aTHˈletiks/ ▶ **plural n.** [usu. treated as sing.] physical sports and games of any kind. ■ esp. Brit. the sport of competing in track and field events.

ath·let·ic sup·port·er ▶ **n.** another term for JOCKSTRAP.

at-home ▶ **n.** an informal party in a person's home. ▶ **adj.** occurring in or suited to one's home: *at-home athletic equipment.*

Ath·os, Mount /ˈaTHˌäs; ˈāˌTHäs/ a peninsula in northeastern Greece that projects into the Aegean Sea, inhabited by Greek Orthodox monks who ban women and female animals from the peninsula. — **Ath·o·nite** /ˈaTHəˌnīt/ **adj. & n.**

a·thwart /əˈTHwôrt/ ▶ **prep. 1** from side to side of; across: *a counter athwart the entranceway.* **2** in opposition to; counter to: *these statistics run athwart conventional presumptions.* ▶ **adv. 1** across from side to side; transversely. **2** contradictory.

-atic ▶ **suffix** forming adjectives and nouns such as *aquatic, idiomatic.* [from Fr. *-atique* or L. *-aticus*, often based on Gk. *-atikos*.]

-ation ▶ **suffix** (forming nouns) denoting an action or an instance of it: *exploration* | *hesitation.* ■ denoting a result or product of action: *plantation.* [from Fr. *-ation* or L. *-ation-*.]

-ative ▶ **suffix** (forming adjectives) denoting a characteristic or propensity: *pejorative* | *talkative.* [from Fr. *-atif, -ative*, or from L. *-ativus*.]

At·lan·ta /ətˈlantə; at-/ the capital of the state of Georgia in the US, in the northwest central part of the state; pop. 416,474.

at·lan·tes /atˈlantēz/ plural form of ATLAS (sense 3).

At·lan·tic /ətˈlantik; at-/ ▶ **adj.** [attrib.] of or adjoining the Atlantic Ocean: *an Atlantic storm* | *the Atlantic coast of Europe.* ▶ **n.** short for ATLANTIC OCEAN. [ME: via L. from Gk. *Atlantikos*, from *Atlas, Atlant-* (see ATLAS).]

At·lan·tic Cit·y a city in southeastern New Jersey, on the Atlantic Ocean, noted gambling resort; pop. 37,986.

At·lan·tic In·tra·coast·al Wa·ter·way a US water route that allows sheltered boat passage for 1,900 miles (3,100 km) between Boston and Key West.

At·lan·ti·cism /ətˈlantiˌsizəm; at-/ ▶ **n.** belief in or support for a close relationship between western Europe and the US, or particularly for NATO. — **At·lan·ti·cist n. & adj.**

At·lan·tic O·cean the ocean that lies between Europe and Africa on the east and North and South America on the west. It is divided by the equator into the North Atlantic and the South Atlantic.

At·lan·tic Prov·in·ces the Maritime provinces and Newfoundland.

At·lan·tic time the standard time in a zone including the easternmost parts of mainland Canada, Puerto Rico, and the Virgin Islands, specifically: ■ **Atlantic Standard Time** (**Atlantic Standard Time**, abbrev.: **AST**) standard time based on the mean solar time at the longitude 60° W, four hours behind GMT. ■ **Atlantic Daylight Time** (**Atlantic Daylight Time**, abbrev.: **ADT**) standard time based on the mean solar time at the longitude 60° W, four hours behind GMT.

At·lan·tis /ətˈlantis; at-/ a legendary island, beautiful and prosperous, which sank into the sea. — **At·lan·te·an** /ˌatlanˈtēən; atˈlantēən/ **adj.**

At·las /ˈatləs/ Gk. Mythol. one of the Titans, who was forced to support the heavens. — **At·lan·te·an** /ˌatlanˈtēən; atˈlantēən/ **adj.**

at·las /ˈatləs/ ▶ **n. 1** a book of maps or charts: *I looked in the atlas to find a map of Italy* | *a road atlas.* ■ a book of illustrations or diagrams on any subject: *Atlas of Surgical Operations.* **2** (also **atlas vertebra**) Anat. the topmost vertebra of the backbone. **3** (pl. **at·las·es**) Archit. a stone carving of a male figure, used as a column to support the entablature of a Greek or Greek-style building. [16th C.: via L. from Gk. *Atlas* (see ATLAS).]

At·las Moun·tains a range of mountains in North Africa that extends from Morocco to Tunisia in a series of chains.

ATM ▶ **abbr.** ■ Telecom. asynchronous transfer mode. ■ automated (or automatic) teller machine.

atm Physics ▶ **abbr.** atmosphere(s), as a unit of pressure.

at·man /ˈätmən/ (also **At·man**) ▶ **n.** Hinduism the spiritual life principle of the universe, esp. when regarded as inherent in the real self of the individual. ■ a person's soul. [from Sanskrit *ātman*, lit. 'essence.']

at·mos·phere /'atməs,fi(ə)r/ ▶ n. [usu. in sing.] **1** the envelope of gases surrounding the earth or another planet: *part of the sun's energy is absorbed by the earth's atmosphere.* ■ the air in any particular place: *we couldn't breathe in the dusty atmosphere.* ■ (abbr.: **atm**) Physics a unit of pressure equal to mean atmospheric pressure at sea level, 101,325 pascals. **2** the pervading tone or mood of a place, situation, or work of art: *the hotel is famous for its friendly, welcoming atmosphere.* ■ a pleasurable and interesting or exciting mood: *a superb restaurant, full of atmosphere.* [17th C.: from mod. L. *atmosphaera*, from Gk. *atmos* 'vapor' + *sphaira* 'ball.']

at·mos·pher·ic /,atməs'fi(ə)rik; -'ferik/ ▶ adj. **1** of or relating to the atmosphere of the earth or (occasionally) another planet: *atmospheric conditions such as fog.* **2** creating a distinctive mood, as of romance or nostalgia: *atmospheric lighting.* — **at·mos·pher·i·cal** adj. (archaic) **at·mos·pher·i·cal·ly** /-ik(ə)lē/ adv.

at·mos·pher·ic pres·sure ▶ n. the pressure exerted by the weight of the atmosphere, which at sea level has a mean value of 101,325 pascals (roughly 14.6959 pounds per square inch). Also called BAROMETRIC PRESSURE.

at·mos·pher·ics /,atməs'fi(ə)riks; -'feriks/ ▶ plural n. **1** electrical disturbances in the atmosphere due to lightning and other phenomena, esp. as they interfere with telecommunications. **2** effects intended to create a particular atmosphere or mood, esp. in music.

at·oll /'atôl; 'atäl; 'ātôl; 'ātäl/ ▶ n. a ring-shaped reef, island, or chain of islands formed of coral. [17th C.: from Maldivian *atolu*.]

at·om /'atəm/ ▶ n. the basic unit of a chemical element. ■ such particles as a source of nuclear energy: *the power of the atom.* ■ [usu. with negative] an extremely small amount of a thing or quality: *I shall not have one atom of strength left.* [15th C.: ult. from Gk. *atomos* 'indivisible,' based on *a-* + *temnein* 'to cut.']

at·om bomb (also **a·tom·ic bomb**) ▶ n. a bomb that derives its destructive power from the rapid release of nuclear energy by fission of heavy atomic nuclei, causing damage through heat, blast, and radioactivity.

a·tom·ic /ə'tämik/ ▶ adj. of or relating to an atom or atoms: *the atomic nucleus.* ■ Chem. (of a substance) consisting of uncombined atoms rather than molecules: *atomic hydrogen.* ■ relating to, denoting, or using the energy released in nuclear fission or fusion. — **a·tom·i·cal·ly** /-ik(ə)lē/ adv.

a·tom·ic age ▶ n. another term for NUCLEAR AGE.

a·tom·ic clock ▶ n. an extremely accurate type of clock that is regulated by the vibrations of an atomic or molecular system such as cesium or ammonia.

at·o·mic·i·ty /,atə'misitē/ ▶ n. **1** Chem. the number of atoms in the molecules of an element. **2** the state or fact of being composed of indivisible units.

a·tom·ic mass ▶ n. the mass of an atom expressed in atomic mass units. It is approximately equivalent to the number of protons and neutrons in the atom (the mass number).

a·tom·ic mass u·nit (abbr.: **amu**) ▶ n. a unit of mass used to express atomic and molecular weights, equal to one-twelfth of the mass of an atom of carbon-12. It is equal to approximately 1.66 x 10-27 kg.

a·tom·ic num·ber ▶ n. Chem. & Physics the number of protons in the nucleus of an atom, which determines the chemical properties of an element and its place in the periodic table. (Symbol: **Z**)

a·tom·ic phys·ics ▶ plural n. [treated as sing.] the branch of physics concerned with the structure of the atom.

a·tom·ic pile ▶ n. dated term for NUCLEAR REACTOR.

a·tom·ic pow·er ▶ n. another term for NUCLEAR POWER.

a·tom·ic spec·trum ▶ n. the spectrum of frequencies of electromagnetic radiation emitted or absorbed during transitions of electrons between energy levels within an atom.

a·tom·ic the·o·ry ▶ n. the theory that all matter is made up of tiny indivisible particles (atoms). The atoms of each element are effectively identical, but differ from those of other elements, and unite to form compounds in fixed proportions. ■ in any field, a theory that proposes the existence of distinct, separable, independent components: *an atomic theory of heredity.*

a·tom·ic vol·ume ▶ n. Chem. the volume occupied by one gram-atom of an element under standard conditions.

a·tom·ic weight ▶ n. Chem. another term for ATOMIC MASS.

at·om·ism /'atə,mizəm/ ▶ n. esp. Philos. a theoretical approach that regards something as interpretable through analysis into distinct, separable, and independent elementary components. The opposite of HOLISM. — **at·om·ist** n. **at·om·is·tic** /,atə'mistik/ adj.

at·om·ize /'atə,mīz/ ▶ v. [trans.] convert (a substance) into very fine particles or droplets: *the CO2 depressurized, atomizing the paint into a mist of even-size particles.* ■ reduce (something) to atoms or other small distinct units. — **at·om·i·za·tion** /,atəmə'zāshən/ n.

at·om·iz·er /'atə,mīzər/ (Brit. also **at·om·is·er**) ▶ n. a device for emitting water, perfume, or other liquids as a fine spray.

at·om smash·er ▶ n. informal term for PARTICLE ACCELERATOR.

at·o·my /'atəmē/ ▶ n. (pl. **-mies**) archaic a skeleton or emaciated body. [16th C.: from ANATOMY.]

atomizer

a·ton·al /ā'tōnl/ ▶ adj. Music not written in any key or mode. — **a·ton·al·ism** n. **a·ton·al·ist** n. **a·to·nal·i·ty** /,ātō'nalitē/ n.

a·tone /ə'tōn/ ▶ v. [intrans.] make amends or reparation: *he was being helpful, to atone for his past mistakes.* [ME: from *at one*.]

a·tone·ment /ə'tōnmənt/ ▶ n. reparation for a wrong or injury: *she wanted to **make atonement for** her behavior.* ■ Relig. reparation or expiation for sin. ■ (**the Atonement**) Christian Theol. the reconciliation of God and humankind through Jesus Christ.

a·ton·ic /ā'tänik/ ▶ adj. Physiol. lacking muscle tone. — **at·o·ny** /'atn-ē/ n.

a·top /ə'täp/ ▶ prep. on the top of. ▶ adv. on the top.

a·top·ic /ā'täpik/ ▶ n. denoting a form of allergy in which a hypersensitivity reaction may occur in a part of the body not in contact with the allergen. — **at·o·py** /'atəpē/ adj. [20th C.: from Gk. *atopia* 'a being out of place,' from *atopos* 'out of place,' based on *topos* 'place.']

-ator ▶ suffix forming agent nouns such as *agitator.* ■ used in names of implements, machines, etc.: *escalator.* [from L., or Fr. *-ateur*.]

-atory ▶ suffix (forming adjectives) relating to or involving an action: *explanatory* | *predatory.* [from L. *-atorius*.]

ATP ▶ abbr. Biochem. adenosine triphosphate.

at·ra·bil·ious /,atrə'bilēəs; -'bilyəs/ ▶ adj. literary melancholy or ill-tempered. — **at·ra·bil·ious·ness** n. [17th C.: from L. *atra bilis* 'black bile.']

at·ra·zine /'atrə,zēn/ ▶ n. a synthetic compound, $C_8H_{14}N_5Cl$, used as an agricultural herbicide. [1960s: blend of AMINO and TRIAZINE]

a·trem·ble /ə'trembəl/ ▶ adj. [predic.] literary trembling: *the breeze failed to set a single leaf atremble.*

a·tre·sia /ə'trēzh(ē)ə/ ▶ n. Med. absence or abnormal narrowing of an opening or passage in the body. [19th C.: from A-[1] + Gk. *trēsis* 'perforation.']

A·tre·us /ā'trēəs; 'ātrōōs/ Gk. Mythol. the father of Agamemnon and Menelaus. He invited his brother Thyestes to a banquet at which he served him flesh of Thyestes' own children.

a·tri·o·ven·tric·u·lar /,ātrē,ōven'trikyələr/ ▶ adj. Anat. & Physiol. relating to the atrial and ventricular chambers of the heart.

at-risk ▶ adj. vulnerable, especially to abuse or deliquency.

a·tri·um /'ātrēəm/ ▶ n. (pl. **a·tri·a** /'ātrēə/ or **a·tri·ums**) **1** Archit. an open-roofed entrance hall or central court in an ancient Roman house. ■ a central hall or court in a modern building, with rooms or galleries opening off it, often glass-covered. **2** Anat. each of the two upper cavities of the heart from which blood is passed to the ventricles. Also called AURICLE. — **a·tri·al** /'ātrēəl/ adj. [16th C.: from L.]

a·tro·cious /ə'trōshəs/ ▶ adj. horrifyingly wicked: *atrocious cruelties.* ■ of a very poor quality; extremely bad or unpleasant: *atrocious weather.* — **a·tro·cious·ly** adv. **a·tro·cious·ness** n. [17th C.: from L. *atrox, atroc-* 'cruel.']

a·troc·i·ty /ə'träsitē/ ▶ n. (pl. **-ties**) an extremely wicked or cruel act: *war atrocities.* ■ humorous a highly unpleasant or distasteful object: *the house was a split-level atrocity.*

at·ro·phy /'atrəfē/ ▶ v. (**-phies, -phied**) [intrans.] (of body tissue or an organ) waste away, typically due to the degeneration of cells, or become vestigial during evolution: *without exercise, the muscles will atrophy.* ■ fig. gradually decline in effectiveness or vigor due to underuse or neglect: *skills atrophied from lack of use.* ▶ n. the condition or process of atrophying. ■ fig. the gradual decline of effectiveness or vigor due to underuse or neglect. — **a·troph·ic** /ā'trōfik; ā'träfik/ adj. [16th C.: ult. from late L. *atrophia*, from Gk., 'lack of food,' from *a-* + *trophē* 'food.']

at·ro·pine /'atrə,pēn/ ▶ n. Chem. a poisonous alkaloid compound, $C_{17}N_{23}NO_3$, found in deadly nightshade and related plants, and used in medicine. [19th C.: mod. L. *Atropa belladonna* 'deadly nightshade,' from ATROPOS.]

At·ro·pos /'atrə,päs/ Gk. Mythol. one of the three Fates. [Gk., lit. 'inflexible.']

at sign ▶ n. the symbol @, used: ■ to indicate cost or rate per unit. ■ in Internet addresses between the user's name and the domain name: *jscott@oup.com.*

at·ta·boy /'atə,boi/ ▶ exclam. an informal expression of encouragement or admiration, typically to a man or boy. ▶ n. a piece of encouragement or congratulations, esp. a letter: *our boss will write you guys an attaboy.* [20th C.: prob. *that's the boy*.]

at·tach /ə'tach/ ▶ v. [trans.] fasten; join: *he made certain that the trailer was securely **attached to** the van.* ■ fasten (a related document) to another: *I attached a copy of the memo.* ■ include (a condition) as part of an agreement: *the Commission can attach appropriate conditions to the agreement.* ■ used to indicate that someone regards something as important or valuable: *he doesn't **attach** too much importance **to** radical ideas.* ■ (**attach oneself to**) join (someone or something) without being invited: *they were ready to attach themselves to you for the whole day.* ■ Law seize (a person's property) by legal authority: *the court attached his wages for child support.* — **at·tach·a·ble** adj. [ME: from OFr. *atachier* or *estachier* 'fasten, fix,' from Gmc. akin to STAKE[1].]

at·ta·ché /,atə'shā ,ata-/ ▶ n. **1** a person on the staff of an ambassador, typically with a specialized area of responsibility: *military attachés.* **2** short for ATTACHÉ CASE. [19th C.: from Fr., lit. 'attached,' past part. of *attacher*.]

at·ta·ché case ▶n. a small, flat, rectangular case used for carrying documents.

at·tached /ə'tacHt/ ▶adj. **1** joined or fastened to something: *please complete the attached form.* ■ (of a building or room) adjacent to and typically connected with another: *bedroom with bathroom attached.* **2** full of affection or fondness: *Mark became increasingly* ***attached to*** *Tara.* **3** (**attached to**) (of a person) appointed to an organization or group for special or temporary duties: *he was attached to military intelligence.* ■ (of an organization or body) affiliated to another larger organization or body: *an agency attached to the university.*

at·tach·ment /ə'tacHmənt/ ▶n. **1** an extra part that can be attached to something for a particular function: *the food processor comes with a blender attachment.* ■ a computer file appended to an e-mail. **2** the condition of being attached to something or someone, in particular: ■ affection, fondness, or sympathy for someone or something: *she felt a sentimental* ***attachment to*** *the place.* ■ an affectionate relationship between two people: *he formed an attachment with a young widow.* **3** the action of attaching something: *the case has a loop for attachment to your belt.* ■ legal seizure of property.

at·tack /ə'tak/ ▶v. [trans.] take aggressive action against (a place or enemy forces) with weapons or armed force: *in December, the Japanese attacked Pearl Harbor.* ■ (of a person or animal) act against (someone or something) aggressively in an attempt to injure or kill: *a doctor was attacked by two youths.* ■ (of a disease, chemical substance, or insect) act harmfully on: *HIV is thought to attack certain cells in the brain.* ■ criticize or oppose fiercely and publicly: *he attacked the government's defense policy.* ■ begin to deal with (a problem or task) in a determined and vigorous way: *a plan to attack unemployment.* ▶n. an aggressive and violent action against a person or place: *he was killed in an* ***attack on*** *a checkpoint.* ■ destructive action by a disease, chemical, or insect: *the tissue is open to attack by fungus.* ■ a sudden short bout of an illness or stress: *an attack of nausea.* ■ an instance of fierce public criticism or opposition: *a stinging* ***attack on*** *the White House.* ■ a determined attempt to tackle a problem or task: *an* ***attack on*** *inflation.* ■ Music the manner of beginning to play or sing a passage.
– PHRASES **under attack** subject to aggressive, violent, or harmful action. [17th C.: ult. from Ital. *attacco* 'an attack,' *attaccare* 'join battle,' based on Gmc. element.]

at·tack·er /ə'takər/ ▶n. a person or animal that attacks someone or something.

at·ta·girl /'atə,gərl/ ▶exclam. an informal expression of encouragement or admiration to a woman or girl. [1920s: after *attaboy*.]

at·tain /ə'tān/ ▶v. [trans.] succeed in achieving (something that one desires and has worked for): *he attained the rank of admiral.* ■ reach (a specified age, size, or amount): *dolphins can attain remarkable speeds in water.* — **at·tain·a·bil·i·ty** /ə,tānə'bilitē/ n. **at·tain·a·ble** adj. [ME: from OFr. *ateindre*, from L. *attingere*, from *ad-* + *tangere* 'to touch.']

at·tain·der /ə'tāndər/ ▶n. hist. the forfeiture of land and civil rights suffered as a consequence of a sentence of death for treason or felony.
– PHRASES **bill of attainder** an item of legislation inflicting attainder without judicial process. [ME: ult. from OFr. *ateindre* 'convict', (see ATTAIN).]

at·tain·ment /ə'tānmənt/ ▶n. the action or fact of achieving a goal toward which one has worked. ■ (often **attainments**) a thing achieved, esp. a skill or educational achievement: *scholarly attainments.*

at·taint /ə'tānt/ ▶v. [trans.] **1** (usu. **be attainted**) hist. subject to attainder. **2** archaic affect or infect with disease or corruption. [ME: ult. from OFr. *ataint*, *ateint*, past part. of *ateindre* (see ATTAIN.)]

at·tar /'atər/ (also **ot·to** /'ätō/) ▶n. a fragrant essential oil, typically made from rose petals. [17th C.: via Pers. from Arab. *'aṭir* 'fragrant.']

at·tempt /ə'tem(p)t/ ▶v. [trans.] make an effort to achieve or complete (something, typically a difficult task or action): *she attempted a comeback in 1989.* ▶n. an act of trying to achieve something, typically one that is unsuccessful or not certain to succeed: [with infin.] *an attempt to halt the bombings.* ■ an effort to surpass a record or conquer a mountain: *we made an* ***attempt on*** *the southwest buttress.* ■ a bid to kill someone: *Karakozov made an* ***attempt on*** *the czar's life.* ■ a thing produced as a result of trying to make or achieve something: *her first* ***attempt at*** *a letter ended up in the wastebasket.* [ME: ult. from L. *attemptare*, from *ad-* 'to' + *temptare* 'to tempt.']

at·tend /ə'tend/ ▶v. **1** [trans.] be present at (an event, meeting, or function). ■ go regularly to: *all children are required to attend school.* **2** [intrans.] (**attend to**) deal with: *business to attend to.* ■ give practical help and care to; look after: *attend to their wounds.* ■ pay attention to: *Alice hadn't attended to a word of his sermon.* **3** [trans.] (usu. **be attended**) occur with or as a result of: *fear that the switch to a peacetime economy would be attended by a severe slump.* ■ escort or accompany so as to assist; wait on: *Her Royal Highness was attended by two women.* — **at·tend·er** /ə'tendər/ n. [ME: ult. from L. *attendere*, from *ad-* 'to' + *tendere* 'stretch.']

at·tend·ance /ə'tendəns/ ▶n. the action or state of going regularly to or being present at a place or event: *the legal enforcement of school attendance.* ■ the number of people present at a particular event: *reports placed the attendance at 500,000.*

at·tend·ant /ə'tendənt/ ▶n. **1** a person employed to provide a service to the public in a particular place: *a gas station attendant.* ■ an assistant to an important person; a servant or courtier. **2** a person who is present at an event, meeting, or function: ▶adj. occurring with or as a result of; accompanying: *the sea and its attendant attractions.* ■ (of a person or animal) accompanying another as a companion or assistant: *a pair of blind tourists with their attendant dogs.* [ME (as an adj.): from OFr., from *atendre* 'give one's attention to' (see ATTEND).]

at·tend·ee /ə,ten'dē; ,aten-/ ▶n. a person who attends a conference or other gathering.

at·ten·tion /ə'tensHən/ ▶n. **1** notice taken of someone or something; the regarding of someone or something as interesting or important: *he* ***drew attention to*** *mistakes | you've never* ***paid*** *that much* ***attention*** *to her.* ■ the mental faculty of considering or taking notice of someone or something: *he* ***turned his attention to*** *the educational system.* **2** the action of dealing with or taking special care of someone or something: *the business needed her attention.* ■ (**attentions**) a person's actions intended to express interest of a sexual or romantic nature: *she felt flattered by his attentions.* **3** Mil. a position assumed by a soldier, standing very straight with the feet together and the arms straight down the sides of the body. ■ [as exclam.] an order to assume such a position. — **at·ten·tion·al** /-sHənl/ adj. [ME: from L. *attentio(n-)*, from *attendere*.]

at·ten·tion def·i·cit dis·or·der (also **attention deficit hyperactivity disorder**) (abbr.: **ADD** or **ADHD**) ▶n. any of a range of behavioral disorders occurring primarily in children, including such symptoms as poor concentration, hyperactivity, and impulsivity.

at·ten·tion span ▶n. the length of time for which a person is able to concentrate on a particular activity.

at·ten·tive /ə'tentiv/ ▶adj. paying close attention to something: *an attentive audience.* ■ assiduously attending to the comfort or wishes of others: *the hotel has attentive service.* — **at·ten·tive·ly** adv. **at·ten·tive·ness** n.

at·ten·u·ate /ə'tenyo͞o,āt/ ▶v. [trans.] (often **be attenuated**) reduce the force, effect, or value of: *her intolerance was attenuated by an unexpected liberalism.* ■ reduce the amplitude of (a signal, electric current, or other oscillation). ■ reduce in thickness; make thin: *the trees are attenuated from being grown too close together.* — **at·ten·u·a·tion** /ə,tenyo͞o'āsHən/ n. [16th C.: from L. *attenuat-* 'made slender,' from v. *attenuare*, from *ad-* 'to' + *tenuare* 'make thin' (from *tenuis* 'thin').]

at·ten·u·at·ed /ə'tenyo͞o,ātid/ ▶adj. unnaturally thin: *she was a drooping, attenuated figure.* ■ weakened in force or effect: *Roman influence became attenuated.*

at·ten·u·a·tor /ə'tenyo͞o,ātər/ ▶n. a device that reduces the strength of a radio or audio signal.

at·test /ə'test/ ▶v. [trans.] provide or serve as clear evidence of: *his status is attested by his recent promotion.* ■ [intrans.] declare that something exists or is the case: *I can attest to his tremendous energy.* ■ be a witness to; certify formally: *the witnesses must attest and sign the will in the testator's presence.* — **at·tes·ta·tion** /,ate'stāsHən/ n. [16th C.: ult. from L. *attestari*, from *ad-* 'to' + *testari* 'to witness' (from *testis* 'a witness').]

At·tic /'atik/ ▶adj. of or relating to Athens or Attica, or the dialect of Greek spoken there in ancient times. ▶n. the dialect of Greek used by the ancient Athenians, the chief literary form of classical Greek. [16th C.: via L. from Gk. *Attikos*.]

at·tic /'atik/ ▶n. a space or room just below the roof of a building. [17th C.: from Fr. *attique*, from L. *Atticus* 'relating to Athens or Attica.']

At·ti·ca /'atikə/ **1** a triangular promontory in eastern Greece. With the islands in the Saronic Gulf, it forms a department of Greece. **2** a town in western New York, the scene of a 1971 prison uprising; pop. 7,383.

at·ti·cism /'atə,sizəm/ (often **At·ti·cism**) ▶n. a word or form characteristic of Attic Greek.

At·ti·la /ə'tilə; 'atl-ə/ (406–453), king of the Huns 434–453. He ravaged vast areas before being defeated by the joint forces of the Roman army and the Visigoths at Châlons in 451.

at·tire /ə'tī(ə)r/ ▶n. clothes, esp. fine or formal ones: *holiday attire.* ▶v. (**be attired**) be dressed in clothes of a specified kind: ***attired in*** *an evening gown.* [ME: from OFr. *atirier*, *atirer* 'equip,' from *a tire* 'in order,' of unknown origin.]

at·ti·tude /'ati,t(y)o͞od/ ▶n. a settled way of thinking or feeling, typically reflected in a person's behavior: *she took a tough attitude toward other people's indulgences.* ■ a position of the body proper to or implying an action or mental state: *the boy was standing in an* ***attitude of*** *despair.* ■ informal uncooperative behavior; a resentful or antagonistic manner: *I asked the waiter for a clean fork, and all I got was attitude.* ■ informal individuality and self-confidence as manifested by behavior or appearance; style: *she snapped her fingers* ***with attitude.*** ■ the orientation of an aircraft or spacecraft, relative to the direction of travel. — **at·ti·tu·di·nal** /,ati't(y)o͞odn-əl/ adj. [17th C.: ult. from Ital. *attitudine* 'posture,' from late L. *aptitudo*, from *aptus* 'fit.']

at·ti·tu·di·nize /,ati't(y)o͞odn,īz/ ▶v. [intrans.] adopt a particular attitude or attitudes, typically just for effect. — **at·ti·tu·di·niz·er** n. [16th C.: from Ital. *attitudine*.]

At·tle·bor·o /'atl,bərō; -,bərə; -,bə-rō; ,bə-rə/ a city in southeastern Massachusetts; pop. 42,068.

Att·lee /'atlē/, Clement Richard, 1st Earl Attlee (1883–1967), prime minister of Britain 1945–51. His term saw the creation of the modern welfare state and the nationalization of major industries.

attn. ▶abbr. attention (i.e., for the attention of): *attn.: Harold Carter.*

atto- ▶comb. form Math. denoting a factor of 10–18: *attowatt.* [from Dan. or Norw. *atten* 'eighteen.']

at·torn /ə'tərn/ ▶v. [intrans.] Law formally make or acknowledge a transfer of something. ■ [trans.] archaic transfer (something) to someone else. [ME: from OFr. *atorner* 'appoint,' from *a-* 'to') + *torner* 'to turn.']

at·tor·ney /ə'tərnē/ ▶n. (pl. **-neys**) **1** a person appointed to act for another in business or legal matters. 2 a lawyer. — **at·tor·ney·ship** n. [ME: from OFr. *atorne*, past part. of *atorner* (see ATTORN).]

at·tor·ney-at-law ▶ n. a lawyer who is qualified to represent a client in court.

at·tor·ney gen·er·al (abbr.: **AG** or **Atty. Gen.**) ▶ n. (pl. **at·tor·neys gen·er·al**) the principal legal officer who represents a country or a state in legal proceedings and gives legal advice to the government. ■ the head of the US Department of Justice.

at·tract /ə'trakt/ ▶ v. [trans.] cause to come to a place or participate in a venture by offering something of interest, favorable conditions, or opportunities: *a campaign to attract more visitors to Virginia.* ■ evoke (a specified reaction): *I did not want to attract attention.* ■ cause (someone) to have a liking for or interest in something: *I was* ***attracted to*** *the idea of working for a ballet company.* ■ cause (someone) to have a sexual or romantic interest in someone: *her beauty attracted him.* ■ exert a force on (an object) that is directed toward the source of the force: *the negatively charged ions attract particles of dust.* — **at·trac·tor** /ə'traktər/ n. [ME: from L. *attract-* 'drawn near,' from v. *attrahere*, from *ad-* + *trahere* 'draw.']

at·tract·ant /ə'traktənt/ ▶ n. a substance that attracts something (esp. animals): *a sex attractant given off by female moths to attract a mate.*

at·trac·tion /ə'trakshən/ ▶ n. the action or power of evoking interest, pleasure, or liking for someone or something: *the timeless attraction of a good tune.* ■ a quality or feature of something or someone that evokes interest, liking, or desire: *this reform has many* ***attractions for*** *those on the left.* ■ a thing or place that draws visitors by providing something of interest or pleasure: *the town's main tourist attraction.* ■ Physics a force under the influence of which objects tend to move toward each other: *gravitational attraction.*

at·trac·tive /ə'traktiv/ ▶ adj. (of a thing) pleasing or appealing to the senses. ■ (of a person) appealing to look at; sexually alluring: *an attractive, charismatic man.* ■ (of a thing) having beneficial qualities or features that induce someone to accept what is being offered: *the site is close to the high-rent district, which should make it* ***attractive to*** *developers.* ■ of or relating to attraction between physical objects. — **at·trac·tive·ly** adv. **at·trac·tive·ness** n.

at·trib·ute ▶ v. /ə'tribyo͞ot/ [trans.] (**attribute something to**) regard something as being caused by (someone or something): *he attributed the firm's success to the managing director.* ■ ascribe a work or remark to (a particular author, artist, or speaker): *the building was attributed to Frank Lloyd Wright.* ■ regard a quality or feature as characteristic of or possessed by (someone or something): *ancient peoples attributed magic properties to certain stones.* ▶ n. /'atrə,byo͞ot/ a quality or feature regarded as a characteristic or inherent part of someone or something: *flexibility and mobility are the key attributes of our army.* ■ a material object recognized as symbolic of a person, esp. a conventional object used in art to identify a saint or mythical figure. — **at·trib·ut·a·ble** /ə'tribyətəbəl/ adj. **at·tri·bu·tion** /,atrə'byo͞oshən/ n. [15th C.: n. from OFr. *attribut*, verb from L. *attribut-* 'allotted,' both from v. *attribuere*, from *ad-* 'to' + *tribuere* 'assign.']

at·trib·u·tive /ə'tribyətiv/ ▶ adj. Gram. (of an adjective or noun) preceding the word it qualifies or modifies and expressing an attribute, as *old* in *the old dog* (but not in *the dog is old*) and *expiration* in *expiration date* (but not in *date of expiration*). Often contrasted with PREDICATIVE. — **at·trib·u·tive·ly** adv.

at·tri·tion /ə'trishən/ ▶ n. 1 the action or process of gradually reducing the strength or effectiveness of someone or something through sustained attack or pressure: *wear down the opposition by attrition.* ■ the gradual reduction of a workforce by employees' leaving and not being replaced rather than by their being laid off: *with so few retirements since March, the year's attrition was insignificant.* ■ wearing away by friction; abrasion: 2 sorrow, but not contrition, for sin. — **at·tri·tion·al** /-shənl/ adj. [ME: from late L. *attritio(n-)*, from *atterere* 'to rub.']

At·tu /'a,to͞o/ an island in southwestern Alaska, the westernmost of the Aleutian Islands.

At·tucks /'atəks/, Crispus (c.1723–70), American patriot. Either an escaped or freed slave, he was one of five colonists killed in the Boston Massacre in 1770.

at·tune /ə't(y)o͞on/ ▶ v. [trans.] (usu. **be attuned**) make receptive or aware: *a society more* ***attuned to*** *consumerism than ideology.* ■ accustom or acclimatize: *students are not* ***attuned to*** *making decisions.* ■ [intrans.] become receptive to or aware of: *an attempt to attune to the wider audience.* ■ make harmonious: *the interests of East and West are now closely attuned.* [16th C.: from AT- + TUNE.]

Atty. ▶ abbr. Attorney.

Atty. Gen. ▶ abbr. Attorney General.

ATV ▶ abbr. all-terrain vehicle.

a·typ·i·cal /ā'tipikəl/ ▶ adj. not representative of a type, group, or class: *a sample of people who are rather atypical of the target audience.* — **a·typ·i·cal·ly** adv.

AU ▶ abbr. ■ (also **a.u.**) astronomical unit(s). ■ ångström unit(s).

Au ▶ symb. the chemical element gold. [from L. *aurum*.]

au·bade /ō'bäd/ ▶ n. a poem or piece of music appropriate to the dawn or early morning. [17th C.: from Fr., from Sp. *albada*, from *alba* 'dawn.']

au·berge /ō'berzh/ ▶ n. an inn in French-speaking countries. [Fr., from Provençal *alberga* 'lodging.']

au·ber·gine /'ōbər,zhēn/ ▶ n. esp. Brit. another term for EGGPLANT. ■ a dark purple color like that of eggplant.

Au·brey /'ôbrē/, John (1626–97), English writer. He is noted for *Brief Lives* (1898).

au·brie·tia /ô'brēsh(ē)ə/ (also **au·bre·ti·a**) ▶ n. a dwarf evergreen Eurasian trailing plant (*Aubrieta deltoidea*) of the cabbage family, with dense masses of foliage and purple, pink, or white flowers. [19th C.: mod. L., after Claude *Aubriet* (1668–1743), French botanist.]

Au·burn /'ôbərn/ 1 a city in eastern Alabama, home to Auburn University; pop. 42,987. 2 a city in southwestern Maine, on the Androscoggin River; pop. 23,203.

au·burn /'ôbərn/ ▶ adj. (chiefly of a person's hair) of a reddish-brown color. ▶ n. a reddish-brown color. [ME: from OFr. *auborne*, *alborne*, from L. *alburnus* 'whitish,' from *albus* 'white' (the word became associated with *brown* because in the 16th and 17th cents. it was often written *abrune* or *abroun*).]

Au·bus·son /'ōbə,sôn/ ▶ n. a kind of French tapestry or carpet, principally from the 18th century. [*Aubusson*, town in France.]

AUC ▶ abbr. used to indicate a date reckoned from 753 BC, the year of the foundation of Rome: *765* AUC. [from L. *ab urbe condita* 'from the foundation of the city,' or *anno urbis conditae* 'in the year of the founding of the city.']

Au·chin·closs /'ôkən,kläs/, Louis Stanton (1917–), US writer; early pen name *Andrew Lee*. His novels include *The House of Five Talents* (1960) and *East Side Story* (2004).

Auck·land /'ôklənd/ a city and chief seaport in New Zealand, on North Island; pop. 952,600.

au cou·rant /,ō ko͞o'räN/ ▶ adj. aware of what is going on; well informed: ***au courant with*** *the literary scene.* ■ fashionable: *light, low-fat, au courant recipes.* [18th C.: from Fr., lit. 'in the course.']

auc·tion /'ôkshən/ ▶ n. a public sale in which goods or property are sold to the highest bidder: *the books are expected to fetch a six-figure sum at tomorrow's auction.* ■ the action or process of selling something in this way: *the Ferrari sold* ***at auction*** *for $10 million.* ■ Bridge the part of the play in which players bid to decide the contract in which the hand shall be played. ▶ v. [trans.] sell or offer for sale at an auction: *his collection is to be* ***auctioned off*** *tomorrow.* [16th C.: from L. *auction-* 'increase,' from *augere* 'to increase.']

auc·tion bridge ▶ n. an obsolete form of the card game bridge, in which all tricks won count toward the game whether bid or not.

auc·tion·eer /,ôkshə'ni(ə)r/ ▶ n. a person who conducts auctions by accepting bids and declaring goods sold. — **auc·tion·eer·ing** n.

auc·tion house ▶ n. a company that runs auctions.

au·da·cious /ô'dāshəs/ ▶ adj. 1 showing a willingness to take bold risks: *an audacious takeover.* 2 showing an impudent lack of respect: *an audacious remark.* — **au·da·cious·ly** adv. **au·da·cious·ness** n. [16th C.: from L. *audax*, *audac-* 'bold' (from *audere* 'dare').]

au·dac·i·ty /ô'dasitē/ ▶ n. 1 the willingness to take bold risks: *her audacity came in handy during our most recent emergency.* 2 rude or disrespectful behavior; impudence: *she* ***had the audacity to*** *pick up the receiver and ask me to hang up.*

Au·den /'ôdn/, W. H. (1907–73), British poet; full name *Wystan Hugh Auden*. His poetry is collected in volumes such as *The Age of Anxiety* (1947).

au·di·al /'ôdēəl/ ▶ adj. relating to or perceived through the sense of hearing. [20th C.: from L. *audire* 'hear.']

au·di·ble /'ôdəbəl/ ▶ adj. able to be heard: *ultrasound is audible to dogs.* ▶ n. Football a change in the offensive play called by the quarterback at the line of scrimmage. — **au·di·bil·i·ty** /,ôdə'bilitē/ n. **au·di·bly** adv. [15th C.: from late L. *audibilis*, from *audire* 'hear.']

au·di·ence /'ôdēəns/ ▶ n. 1 the assembled spectators or listeners at a public event, such as a play, movie, concert, etc.: *the orchestra was given an ovation from the audience.* ■ the people who watch or listen to a television or radio program. ■ the readership of a book, magazine, or newspaper. ■ the people giving or likely to give attention to something: *there will always be an audience for romantic literature.* 2 a formal interview with a person in authority: *an audience with the pope.* [ME: from OFr., from L. *audientia*, from *audire* 'hear.']

au·dile /'ô,dīl/ ▶ adj. another term for AUDITORY. [19th C.: formed from L. *audire* 'hear.']

au·di·o /'ôdē,ō/ ▶ n. [usu. as adj.] sound, esp. when recorded, transmitted, or reproduced: *audio equipment.* [1930s: from AUDIO-.]

audio- ▶ comb. form relating to hearing or sound. [from L. *audire* 'hear.']

au·di·o·book /'ôdē-ō,bo͝ok/ (also **au·di·o book**) ▶ n. an audiocassette recording of a reading of a book.

au·di·o·cas·sette /,ôdē-ōkə'set/ ▶ n. a cassette of audiotape.

au·di·o fre·quen·cy ▶ n. a frequency of oscillation capable of being perceived by the human ear, generally between 20 and 20,000 Hz.

au·di·o·gram /'ôdēə,gram/ ▶ n. a graphic record produced by audiometry.

au·di·ol·o·gy /,ôdē'äləjē/ ▶ n. the branch of science and medicine concerned with the sense of hearing. — **au·di·o·log·i·cal** /-ə'läjikəl/ adj. **au·di·ol·o·gist** /-jist/ n.

au·di·om·e·try /,ôdē'ämitrē/ ▶ n. measurement of the range and sensitivity of a person's sense of hearing. — **au·di·om·e·ter** /-itər/ n. **au·di·o·met·ric** /-ə'metrik/ adj.

PRONUNCIATION KEY ə *ago, up*; ər *over, fur*; a *hat*; ā *ate*; ä *car*; e *let*; ē *see*; i *fit*; ī *by*; NG *sing*; ō *go*; ô *law, for*; oi *toy*; o͝o *good*; o͞o *goo*; ou *out*; TH *thin*; TH *then*; ZH *vision*

au·di·o·phile /ˈôdē-ōˌfīl/ ▶ **n.** a hi-fi enthusiast.

au·di·o·tape /ˈôdē-ōˌtāp/ ▶ **n.** magnetic tape on which sound can be recorded. ■ a length of this, typically in the form of a cassette. ▶ **v.** [trans.] record (sound) on tape: *each interview was audiotaped and transcribed.*

au·di·o·vis·u·al /ˌôdē-ōˈvizHo͞oəl/ ▶ **adj.** using both sight and sound: *audiovisual presentations.*

au·dit /ˈôdit/ ▶ **n.** an official inspection of an individual's or organization's accounts, typically by an independent body. ■ a systematic review or assessment of something: *a complete audit of flora and fauna at the site.* ▶ **v.** (**-dit·ed, -dit·ing**) [trans.] **1** conduct an official financial examination of (an individual's or organization's accounts). ■ conduct a systematic review of: *auditing obstetrical and neonatal care.* **2** attend (a class) informally, not for academic credit. [ME: from L. *auditus* 'hearing,' from *audire* 'hear.']

au·di·tion /ôˈdisHən/ ▶ **n.** an interview at which a singer, actor, dancer, or musician demonstrates their suitability and skill. ▶ **v.** [intrans.] perform an audition. ■ [trans.] assess suitability by means of an audition. [16th C.: from L. *auditio(n-)*, from *audire* 'hear.']

au·di·tor /ˈôditər/ ▶ **n. 1** a person who conducts an audit. **2** a listener. ■ a person who attends a class informally without working for academic credit. — **au·di·to·ri·al** /ˌôdəˈtôrēəl/ **adj.**

au·di·to·ri·um /ˌôdiˈtôrēəm/ ▶ **n.** (pl. **-to·ri·ums** or **-to·ri·a** /-ˈtôrēə/) **1** the part of a theater, concert hall, or other public building in which the audience sits. **2** a large building or hall used for public gatherings. ■ a large room for such gatherings, esp. in a school. [17th C.: from L., neut. of *auditorius* 'relating to hearing.']

au·di·to·ry /ˈôdiˌtôrē/ ▶ **adj.** of or relating to the sense of hearing: *the auditory nerves.* [16th C.: from L. *auditorius*, from *audire* 'hear.']

Au·du·bon /ˈôdəˌbän/, John James (1785–1851), US naturalist and painter. He wrote and illustrated *The Birds of America* (1827–38).

Au·er·bach /ˈou-ərˌbak; -ˌbäk/, Red (1917–2006), US basketball coach; full name *Arnold Jacob Auerbach.* He won nine NBA titles coaching the Boston Celtics 1950–66, including eight straight 1959–66, the longest string of championships in North American professional sports.

au fait /ˌō ˈfe/ ▶ **adj.** (**au fait with**) having a good or detailed knowledge of something: *you should be au fait with the company and its products.* [18th C.: from Fr., lit. 'to the fact.']

au fond /ˌō ˈfôN/ ▶ **adv.** in essence: *she might be, au fond, quite a pleasant woman.* [18th C.:Fr., lit. 'at bottom.']

Aug. ▶ **abbr.** August.

Au·ge·an /ôˈjēən/ ▶ **adj.** of or relating to Augeas. ■ requiring so much effort to solve as to seem impossible: *Augean amounts of debris to clear.*

Au·ge·as /ôˈjēəs/ Gk. Mythol. a legendary king whose stables had never been cleaned. Hercules cleaned them in a day by diverting a river through them.

au·ger /ˈôgər/ ▶ **n.** a tool with a helical bit for boring holes in wood. ■ a similar larger tool for boring holes in the ground. See illustration at BIT³. [OE *nafogār*, from *nafu* (see NAVE²) + *gār* 'piercer.' The *n* was lost by wrong division of *a nauger.*]

Au·ger ef·fect /ōˈzHā/ ▶ **n.** Physics a process in which an electron in an outer shell of an atom makes a transition to a vacancy in an inner shell. The energy gained is transferred to an electron that escapes from the atom. [1930s: named after Pierre V. *Auger* (1899-1944), Fr. physicist.]

aught¹ /ôt/ (also **ought**) archaic ▶ **pron.** anything at all: *know you aught of this fellow, young sir?* [OE *āwiht* (see AYE², WIGHT).]

aught² ▶ **n.** the digit 0; zero.

au·gite /ˈôˌjīt/ ▶ **n.** a dark green or black mineral of the pyroxene group. It occurs in many igneous rocks. [19th C.: from L. *augites*, a precious stone, from Gk. *augitēs*, from *augē* 'luster.']

aug·ment ▶ **v.** /ôgˈment/ [trans.] make (something) greater by adding to it; increase: *he augmented his income by painting houses.* ▶ **n.** Ling. a vowel prefixed to past tenses of verbs in Greek and other Indo-European languages. [ME: ult. from late L. *augmentare*, from L. *augere* 'to increase.']

aug·men·ta·tion /ˌôgmenˈtāsHən/ ▶ **n.** the action or process of making or becoming greater in size or amount. ■ Music the lengthening of the time values of notes in a melodic part.

aug·ment·a·tive /ôgˈmentətiv/ ▶ **adj.** Gram. (of an affix or derived word) reinforcing the idea of the original word, esp. by meaning 'a large —,' as with the Italian suffix *-one* in *borrone* 'ravine,' compared with *borro* 'ditch.'

aug·ment·ed /ôgˈmentid/ ▶ **adj. 1** having been made greater in size or value: *augmented pensions for those retiring at 65.* **2** Music denoting or containing an interval that is one semitone greater than the corresponding major or perfect interval: *augmented fourths.*

au grat·in /ˌō ˈgrätn; ˈgratn; graˈtaN/ ▶ **adj.** [predic.] sprinkled with breadcrumbs or grated cheese, or both, and browned. [19th C.: Fr., lit. 'by grating.']

Augs·burg /ˈôgzˌbərg; ˈouksˌbo͝ork/ a city in southern Germany, in Bavaria; pop. 259,880.

au·gur /ˈôgər/ ▶ **v.** [intrans.] (**augur well/badly/ill**) (of an event or circumstance) portend a good or bad outcome: *the end of the Cold War seemed to augur well.* ■ [trans.] portend or bode (a specified outcome): *they feared that these happenings augured a neo-Nazi revival.* ■ [trans.] (archaic) foresee or predict. ▶ **n.** hist. (in ancient Rome) a religious official who interpreted natural signs as an indication of divine approval or disapproval of a proposed action. — **au·gu·ral** /ˈôgyərəl/ **adj.** (archaic). [ME: from L., 'diviner.']

au·gu·ry /ˈôgyərē/ ▶ **n.** (pl. **-ries**) a sign of what will happen in the future; an omen: *they heard the sound as an augury of death.* ■ the work of an augur; the interpretation of omens.

Au·gust /ˈôgəst/ ▶ **n.** the eighth month of the year. [OE, from L. *augustus* 'venerable'; named after AUGUSTUS.]

au·gust /ôˈgəst/ ▶ **adj.** respected and impressive: *she was in august company.* — **au·gust·ly adv.** [17th C.: from Fr. *auguste* or L. *augustus* 'venerable.']

Au·gus·ta /əˈgəstə/ **1** a city in eastern Georgia, in the US; pop. 44,640. **2** the capital of Maine, in the southwestern part of the state, on the Kennebec River; pop. 18,560.

Au·gus·tan /ôˈgəstən/ ▶ **adj.** connected with or occurring during the reign of the Roman emperor Augustus. ■ relating to or denoting Latin literature of the reign of Augustus. ■ relating to or denoting 17th- and 18th-century English literature of a style considered refined and classical. ▶ **n.** a writer of the (Latin or English) Augustan age.

Au·gus·tine, St.¹ /ˈôgəˌstēn; əˈgəstən/ (died *c.*604), Italian clergyman; known as **St. Augustine of Canterbury**, where he founded a monastery. Feast day, May 26.

Au·gus·tine, St.² (354–430), a leader of the early Christian Church; known as **St. Augustine of Hippo**. He wrote *Confessions* (400) and *City of God* (412–427).

Au·gus·tin·i·an /ˌôgəˈstinēən/ ▶ **adj. 1** of or relating to St. Augustine of Hippo or his theological doctrines. **2** of or relating to a religious order observing a rule derived from St. Augustine's writings. ▶ **n. 1** a member of an Augustinian order. **2** an adherent of the doctrines of St. Augustine.

Au·gus·tus /əˈgəstəs/ (63 BC–AD 14), Roman emperor; born *Gaius Octavianus*; also called **Octavian**. He gained supreme power by his defeat of Antony in 31 BC.

au jus /ō ˈzHo͞os; ˈzHY/ ▶ **adj.** (of meat) with its own natural juices from cooking. [Fr. 'with the juice.']

auk /ôk/ ▶ **n.** a short-winged diving seabird found in northern oceans, typically with a black head and black and white underparts. The **auk family** (Alcidae) comprises the guillemots, murres, razorbills, puffins, and their relatives. [17th C.: from ON *álka* 'razorbill.']

auk·let /ˈôklit/ ▶ **n.** a small auk (*Aethia* and three other genera) found in the North Pacific, typically with gray underparts.

auld /ôld/ ▶ **adj.** Scottish form of OLD. [OE *ald*, Anglian form of OLD.]

auld lang syne /ˈôld laNG ˈzīn; ˈsīn/ ▶ **n.** times long past.
– PHRASES **for auld lang syne** for old times' sake. [18th C.: Scots (see AULD, LANG SYNE).]

au na·tu·rel /ˌō ˌnacHəˈrel/ ▶ **adj. & adv.** with no elaborate treatment, dressing, or preparation: [as adv.] *I wear my hair au naturel these days.* ■ (humorous) naked. [19th C.: Fr., lit. 'in the natural (state).']

Aung San /ˈouNG ˈsän/ (1914–47), Burmese leader. He negotiated a promise of self-government from the British shortly before his assassination.

Aung San Suu Kyi /ˈouNG ˈsän ˈso͞o ˈcHē/ (1945–), Burmese leader; daughter of Aung San. The ruling military government refused to recognize her party's victory in the 1990 elections. She was held under house arrest 1989–95 and since 2000 has frequently been detained again. Nobel Peace Prize (1991).

aunt /ant; änt/ ▶ **n.** the sister of one's father or mother or the wife of one's uncle. ■ informal an unrelated older woman friend, esp. of a child. [ME: from OFr. *ante*, from L. *amita.*]

aunt·ie /ˈantē; ˈän-/ (also **aunt·y**) ▶ **n.** (pl. **-ies**) informal term for AUNT.

Aunt Sal·ly /ˈsalē/ ▶ **n.** (pl. **Aunt Sal·lies**) a game played in some parts of Britain in which players throw sticks or balls at a wooden dummy. ■ fig. a person or thing that is subjected to much criticism, esp. one set up as an easy target for it.

au pair /ˌō ˈpe(ə)r/ ▶ **n.** a young foreign person, typically a woman, who helps with housework or child care in exchange for room and board. [19th C.: from Fr., lit. 'on equal terms.']

au·ra /ˈôrə/ ▶ **n.** (pl. **au·ras**) the distinctive atmosphere or quality that seems to surround and be generated by a person, thing, or place: *the ceremony retains an aura of mystery.* ■ a supposed emanation surrounding the body of a living creature, viewed as the essence of the individual, and allegedly discernible by people with special sensibilities. ■ any invisible emanation, esp. a scent or odor: *there was a faint aura of disinfectant.* ■ Med. (pl. also **au·rae** /ˈôrē/) a warning sensation experienced before an attack of epilepsy or migraine. [ME: via L. from Gk., 'breeze, breath.']

au·ral /ˈôrəl/ ▶ **adj.** of or relating to the ear or the sense of hearing. — **au·ral·ly adv.** [19th C.: from L. *auris* 'ear' + -AL.]

Au·rang·zeb /ˌôräNGˈzeb/ (1618–1707), Mogul emperor of Hindustan 1658–1707.

au·rar /ˈouˌrär; ˈoi-/ ▶ **n.** plural form of EYRIR.

au·re·ate /ˈôrē-it; -ˌāt/ ▶ **adj.** denoting, made of, or having the color of gold. ■ (of language) highly ornamented or elaborate. [ME: from late L. *aureatus*, from L. *aureus* 'golden,' from *aurum* 'gold.']

Au·re·li·an /ôˈrēlēən/ (*c.*215–275), Roman emperor 270–275; Latin name *Lucius Domitius Aurelianus.*

Au·re·li·us /ôˈrēlēəs/, Marcus (121–180), Roman emperor 161–180; full name *Caesar Marcus Aurelius Antoninus Augustus.* Much of his reign involved wars against invading Germanic tribes.

au·re·ole /'ôrē,ōl/ (also **au·re·o·la** /ô'rēələ/) ▶ **n.** a circle of light or brightness surrounding something, esp. as depicted in art around the head or body of a person represented as holy. ■ another term for CORONA[1] (sense 1, of the sun or moon). ■ another term for AREOLA. [ME: from OFr. *aureole*, from L. *aureola* (*corona*) 'golden (crown),' based on *aurum* 'gold'.)]

au re·voir /,ō rəv'wär/ ▶ **exclam.** goodbye until we meet again. [17th C.: from Fr., lit. 'to the seeing again.']

au·ric[1] /'ôrik/ ▶ **adj.** of or relating to the aura supposedly surrounding a living creature.

au·ric[2] ▶ **adj.** Chem. of gold with a valence of three. [19th C.: from L. *aurum* 'gold.']

au·ri·cle /'ôrikəl/ ▶ **n.** Anat. & Biol. a structure resembling an ear or earlobe. ■ another term for ATRIUM (of the heart). ■ strictly, a small muscular appendage of each atrium. ■ the external part or pinna of the ear. [ME: from L. *auricula* 'external part of the ear,' dimin. of *auris* 'ear.']

au·ric·u·lar /ô'rikyələr/ ▶ **adj.** **1** of or relating to the ear or hearing. **2** of, relating to, or shaped like an auricle. [ME: from late L. *auricularis*, based on *auris* 'ear.']

au·ric·u·late /ô'rikyəlit; -,lāt/ ▶ **adj.** esp. Bot. Zool. having one or more ear-like-shaped structures.

au·rif·er·ous /ô'rifərəs/ ▶ **adj.** (of rocks or minerals) containing gold. [17th C.: from L. *aurifer* 'gold-bearing' (from *aurum* 'gold').]

Au·ri·ga /ô'rīgə/ Astron. a large northern constellation (the Charioteer). [L.]

Au·ri·gna·cian /,ôrig'nāshən; ,ôrin'yā-/ ▶ **adj.** Archaeol. relating to the early stages of the Upper Paleolithic culture. It is dated to about 34,000–29,000 years ago and is associated with Cro-Magnon Man. ■ [as n.] (**the Aurignacian**) the Aurignacian culture or period. [20th C.: from Fr. *Aurignacien*, from *Aurignac* in France.]

au·rochs /'ouräks; 'ô,räks/ ▶ **n.** (pl. same) a large wild Eurasian ox (*Bos taurus*) that was the ancestor of domestic cattle. It was probably exterminated in Britain in the Bronze Age, and the last one was killed in Poland in 1627. Also called URUS. [18th C.: from German, based on Old High Ger. *ūrohso*, from *ūr* + *ohso* 'ox.']

Au·ro·ra[1] /ə'rôrə/ **1** a city in north central Colorado, east of Denver; pop. 276,393. **2** a city in northeastern Illinois; pop. 142,990.

Au·ro·ra[2] /ə'rôrə; ô'rôrə/ Rom. Mythol. goddess of the dawn. Greek equivalent **Eos**.

au·ro·ra /ə'rôrə; ô'rôrə/ ▶ **n.** (pl. **au·ro·ras** or **au·ro·rae** /ô'rôrē/) **1** the northern lights (**aurora borealis**) or southern lights (**aurora australis**), a natural electrical phenomenon characterized by the appearance of streamers of reddish or greenish light in the sky, usually near the earth's magnetic poles. **2** [in sing.] literary the dawn. — **au·ro·ral adj.** [ME: from L., 'dawn.']

AUS ▶ **abbr.** Army of the United States.

Ausch·witz /'oushvits/ a Nazi concentration camp in World War II, near the town of Oświęcim (Auschwitz) in Poland.

aus·cul·ta·tion /,ôskəl'tāshən/ ▶ **n.** the action of listening to sounds from the heart, lungs, or other organs, typically with a stethoscope. — **aus·cul·tate** /'ôskəl,tāt/ **v. aus·cul·ta·to·ry** /ô'skəltə,tôrē/ **adj.** [17th C.: from L. *auscultatio(n-)*, from *auscultare* 'listen to.']

aus·pice /'ôspis/ ▶ **n.** archaic a divine or prophetic token.

– PHRASES **under the auspices of** with the help, support, or protection of: *the delegation's visit was arranged under UN auspices.* [16th C.: from Fr., or from L. *auspicium*, from *auspex* 'observer of birds,' from *avis* 'bird' + *specere* 'to look.']

aus·pi·cious /ô'spishəs/ ▶ **adj.** conducive to success; favorable: *an auspicious moment to hold an election.* ■ giving or being a sign of future success. — **aus·pi·cious·ly adv. aus·pi·cious·ness n.**

Aus·sie /'ôsē/ ▶ **n.** (pl. **-sies**) & **adj.** informal term for AUSTRALIA or AUSTRALIAN.

Aus·ten /'ôstən/, Jane (1775–1817), English writer. Her novels include *Sense and Sensibility* (1811) and *Pride and Prejudice* (1813).

aus·ten·ite /'ôstə,nīt/ ▶ **n.** Metallurgy a solid solution of carbon in a nonmagnetic form of iron, stable at high temperatures. It is a constituent of some forms of steel. — **aus·ten·it·ic** /,ôstə'nitik/ **adj.** [20th C.: named after Sir William Roberts-*Austen* (1843–1902), English metallurgist.]

aus·tere /ô'sti(ə)r/ ▶ **adj.** (**-ter·er, -ter·est**) severe or strict in manner, attitude, or appearance: *an austere man with a puritanical outlook.* ■ (of living conditions or a way of life) having no comforts or luxuries; harsh or ascetic. ■ having an extremely plain and simple style or appearance; unadorned. ■ (of an economic policy or measure) designed to reduce a budget deficit, esp. by cutting public expenditure. — **aus·tere·ly adv.** [ME: via OFr. from L. *austerus*, from Gk. *austēros* 'severe.']

aus·ter·i·ty /ô'steritē/ ▶ **n.** (pl. **-ties**) sternness or severity of manner or attitude. ■ extreme plainness and simplicity of style or appearance. ■ (**austerities**) conditions characterized by severity, sternness, or asceticism: *his austerities had undermined his health.* ■ difficult economic conditions created by government measures to reduce a budget deficit, esp. by reducing public expenditure.

Aus·ter·litz, Bat·tle of /'ôstər,lits; 'oustər-/ a battle in 1805 near the town of Austerlitz (now in the Czech Republic), in which Napoleon defeated the Austrians and Russians.

Aus·tin[1] /'ôstən/ the capital of Texas, on the Colorado River; pop. 656,562.

Aus·tin[2], John (1790–1859), English jurist. His work is significant for its strict delimitation of the sphere of law and its distinction from that of morality.

Aus·tin[3], Stephen Fuller (1793–1836), colonizer of Texas. He founded the first recognized Anglo-American settlement in Texas in 1822.

aus·tral /'ôstrəl/ ▶ **adj.** of or relating to the south, in particular: ■ tech. of the southern hemisphere: *the austral spring.* ■ (**Austral**) of Australia or Australasia. [15th C.: from L. *australis*, from *Auster* 'the south.']

Aus·tral·a·sia /,ôstrə'lāzhə/ the region that consists of Australia, New Zealand, New Guinea, and the neighboring islands of the Pacific Ocean. — **Aus·tral·a·sian adj. & n.**

Australia

Official name: Commonwealth of Australia
Location: southern hemisphere between the southeastern Pacific Ocean and the Indian Ocean
Area: 2,942,000 square miles (7,617,900 sq km)
Population: 19,900,000
Capital: Canberra
Languages: English (official), Aboriginal languages
Currency: Australian dollar

Aus·tral·ia /ô'strālyə; ə'strāl-/ a country and continent in the southern hemisphere. *See box.*

Aus·tral·ian /ô'strālyən; ə'strāl-/ ▶ **n.** a native or national of Australia, or a person of Australian descent. ▶ **adj.** of or relating to Australia. [from Fr. *australien*, from L. *Terra Australis* 'the southern land.']

Aus·tral·ian Ant·arc·tic Ter·ri·to·ry an area of Antarctica that lies between longitudes 142° east and 136° east. It is administered by Australia.

Aus·tral·ian Cap·i·tal Ter·ri·to·ry a federal territory in New South Wales, Australia, that consists of two enclaves—one contains Canberra, the other contains Jervis Bay.

Aus·tral·ian crawl ▶ **n.** esp. Austral. another term for CRAWL (sense 2).

Aus·tral·ian La·bor Par·ty (abbr.: **ALP**) Australia's oldest political party, moderately liberal, founded in 1891.

Aus·tral·ian ter·ri·er ▶ **n.** a wire-haired terrier of a breed originating in Australia.

Aus·tra·loid /'ôstrə,loid/ ▶ **adj.** of or belonging to the division of humankind represented by Australian Aboriginal peoples. ▶ **n.** a person belonging to this division of humankind.

Aus·tra·lo·pith·e·cus /,ôstrəlō'pithikəs; ô,strālō-/ ▶ **n.** a fossil bipedal primate (genus *Australopithecus*, family Hominidae) with both apelike and human characteristics, found in Pliocene and lower Pleistocene deposits (*c.*4 million to 1 million years old) in Africa. — **aus·tra·lo·pith·e·cine** /-,sēn; -,sīn/ **n. & adj.** [mod. L., from L. *australis* 'southern' + Gk. *pithēkos* 'ape.']

Aus·tri·a /'ôstrēə/ a country in central Europe. *See box on next page.* — **Aus·tri·an adj. & n.**

Aus·tri·a-Hun·ga·ry (also **Aus·tro-Hun·gar·i·an em·pire** /'ôstrō/) the dual monarchy established in 1867 by the Austrian emperor Franz Josef.

Aus·tri·an shade /'ôstrēən/ ▶ **n.** a window shade made from fabric shirred in puffy frills or pleats, extending about a third of the way down a window.

Aus·tri·an Suc·ces·sion, War of the a group of several related conflicts (1740–48), triggered by the death of the Emperor Charles VI.

Austro-[1] ▶ **comb. form** Austrian; Austrian and ...: *Austro-Hungarian.*

Austria

Official name: Republic of Austria
Location: central Europe
Area: 31,900 square miles (82,700 sq km)
Population: 8,100,000
Capital: Vienna
Language: German
Currency: euro

Austro-[2] ▶ comb. form Australian; Australian and ...: *Austro-Malayan.* ■ southern: *Austro-Asiatic.* [from L. *australis* 'southern.']

Aus·tro-A·si·at·ic /ˈôstrō ˌāzhēˈatik; -shē-; -zē-/ ▶ adj. of, relating to, or denoting a family of languages spoken in Southeast Asia. ▶ n. this family of languages.

Aus·tro·ne·sian /ˌôstrōˈnēzhən/ ▶ adj. of, relating to, or denoting a family of languages spoken in an area extending from Madagascar to the Pacific islands. Also called MALAYO-POLYNESIAN. ▶ n. this family of languages. [from Ger. *austronesisch*, based on L. *australis* 'southern' + Gk. *nēsos* 'island.']

aut- ▶ prefix var. of AUTO-.

au·tarch /ˈôtärk/ ▶ n. a ruler who has absolute power. [19th C.: from Gk. *autarkhos*, from *autos* 'self' + *arkhos* 'leader.']

au·tar·chy /ˈôtärkē/ ▶ n. (pl. **-chies**) **1** another term for AUTOCRACY. **2** var. of AUTARKY. — **au·tar·chic** /ôˈtärkik/ adj. [17th C.: from mod. L. *autarchia*, from Gk. *autos* 'self' + *-arkhia* (from *arkhein* 'take the lead').]

au·tar·ky /ˈôˌtärkē/ ▶ n. economic independence or self-sufficiency. ■ a country, state, or society that is economically independent. — **au·tar·kic** /ôˈtärkik/ adj. [17th C.: from Gk. *autarkeia*, based on *autos* 'self' + *arkein* 'suffice.']

aut·e·col·o·gy /ôtiˈkäləjē/ (also **au·to·e·col·o·gy**) ▶ n. Biol. the ecological study of an individual organism, or sometimes a particular species. Contrasted with SYNECOLOGY. — **aut·ec·o·log·i·cal** /ˌôtekəˈläjikəl; -ēkə-/ adj.

au·teur /ôˈtər/ ▶ n. a filmmaker who influences their movies so much that they rank as their author. — **au·teur·ism** n. **au·teur·ist** adj. [1960s: Fr., lit. 'author.']

auth. ▶ abbr. ■ authentic. ■ author. ■ authorized.

au·then·tic /ôˈTHentik/ (abbr.: **auth.**) ▶ adj. **1** of undisputed origin; genuine: *authentic 14th-century furniture.* ■ made or done in the traditional or original way: *authentic Italian meals.* ■ based on facts; accurate or reliable: *an authentic depiction.* **2** Music (of a church mode) comprising the notes lying between the principal note or final and the note an octave higher. Compare with PLAGAL. — **au·then·ti·cal·ly** /-ik(ə)lē/ adv. [as submodifier] *the food is authentically Cajun.* **au·then·tic·i·ty** /ˌôTHenˈtisitē/ n. [ME: ult. from late L. *authenticus*, from Gk. *authentikos* 'principal.']

au·then·ti·cate /ôˈTHentiˌkāt/ ▶ v. [trans.] prove or show (something, esp. a claim or an artistic work) to be true or genuine: *they were invited to authenticate artifacts from the Italian Renaissance.* ■ validate: *the nationalist statements authenticated their leadership among the local community.* ■ [intrans.] Comput. (of a user or process) have one's identity verified. — **au·then·ti·ca·tion** /ôˌTHentiˈkāSHən/ n. **au·then·ti·ca·tor** /-ˌkātər/ n.

au·thor /ˈôTHər/ (abbr.: **auth.**) ▶ n. a writer of a book, article, or report. ■ someone who writes books as a profession. ■ the writings of such a person: *I had to read authors I disliked.* ■ fig. an originator or creator of something, esp. a plan or idea: *the authors of the peace plan.* ▶ v. [trans.] be the author of (a book or piece of writing): *she has authored several articles on wildlife.* ■ fig. be the originator of; create: *a concept authored by insurance companies.* — **au·tho·ri·al** /ôˈTHôrēəl/ adj. [ME: from OFr. *autor*, from L. *auctor*, from *augere* 'increase, originate.']

au·thor·ess /ˈôTHəris/ ▶ n. a female author.

au·thor·ing /ˈôTHəriNG/ ▶ n. Comput. the creation of programs and databases for computer applications such as computer-assisted learning.

au·thor·i·tar·i·an /əˌTHôriˈte(ə)rēən; əˌTHär-/ ▶ adj. favoring or enforcing strict obedience to authority at the expense of personal freedom: *the transition from an authoritarian to a democratic regime.* ■ showing a lack of concern for the wishes or opinions of others; domineering; dictatorial. ▶ n. an authoritarian person. — **au·thor·i·tar·i·an·ism** /-ˌnizəm/ n.

au·thor·i·ta·tive /əˈTHôriˌtātiv; əˈTHär-/ ▶ adj. **1** able to be trusted as being accurate or true; reliable: *clear, authoritative information.* ■ (of a text) considered to be the best of its kind and unlikely to be improved upon. **2** commanding and self-confident; likely to be respected and obeyed: *she had an authoritative air.* ■ proceeding from an official source and requiring compliance or obedience: *authoritative directives.* — **au·thor·i·ta·tive·ly** adv. **au·thor·i·ta·tive·ness** n.

au·thor·i·ty /əˈTHôritē; əˈTHär-/ (abbr.: **auth.**) ▶ n. (pl. **-ties**) **1** the power or right to give orders, make decisions, and enforce obedience: *he had absolute* ***authority over*** *his subordinates.* ■ [often with infin.] the right to act in a specified way, delegated from one person or organization to another: *military forces have the legal authority to arrest drug traffickers.* ■ official permission; sanction: *the money was spent without congressional authority.* **2** (often **authorities**) a person or organization having power or control in a particular, typically political or administrative, sphere: *the health authorities.* **3** the power to influence others, esp. because of one's commanding manner or one's recognized knowledge about something: *he spoke* ***with authority*** *on the subject.* ■ the confidence resulting from personal expertise: *he hit the ball with authority.* ■ a person with extensive or specialized knowledge about a subject; an expert: ***an authority on*** *the stockmarket.* ■ a book or other source able to supply reliable information or evidence, typically to settle a dispute.
– PHRASES **have something on good authority** have ascertained something from a reliable source.

au·thor·i·za·tion /ˌôTHərəˈzāSHən/ ▶ n. the action or fact of authorizing or being authorized: *the raising of revenue and the authorization of spending.* ■ a document giving permission or authority.

au·thor·ize /ˈôTHəˌrīz/ ▶ v. [trans.] give official permission for or approval to: *the government authorized further aircraft production.*

Au·thor·ized Ver·sion ▶ n. esp. Brit. another name for KING JAMES BIBLE.

au·thor·ship /ˈôTHərˌSHip/ ▶ n. the fact or position of someone's having written a book or other written work: *an investigation into the authorship of the Gospels.* ■ the occupation of writing.

au·tism /ˈôˌtizəm/ ▶ n. Psychiatry a mental condition, present from early childhood, characterized by great difficulty in communicating and forming relationships, and in using language and abstract concepts. ■ a mental condition in which fantasy dominates over reality, as a symptom of schizophrenia and other disorders. — **au·tis·tic** /ôˈtistik/ adj. & n. [20th C.: from Gk. *autos* 'self.']

au·to /ˈôtō/ ▶ n. (pl. **-tos**) [usu. as modifier] informal an automobile.

auto- (usu. **aut-** before a vowel) ▶ comb. form self: *autoanalysis.* ■ one's own: *autograph.* ■ by oneself or spontaneous: *autoxidation.* ■ by itself or automatic: *autofocusing.* [from Gk. *autos* 'self.']

au·to·an·ti·bod·y /ˌôtōˈantiˌbädē/ ▶ n. (pl. **-bod·ies**) Physiol. an antibody produced by an organism in response to a constituent of its own tissues.

au·to·bahn /ˈôtəˌbän/ ▶ n. a German, Austrian, or Swiss expressway. [1930s: from Ger., from *Auto* 'automobile' + *Bahn* 'road.']

au·to·bi·o·graph·i·cal /ˌôtəˌbīəˈgrafikəl/ ▶ adj. (of a written work) dealing with the writer's own life. — **au·to·bi·o·graph·ic** adj.

au·to·bi·og·ra·phy /ˌôtəbīˈägrəfē/ ▶ n. (pl. **-phies**) an account of a person's life written by that person. ■ such writing as a literary genre. — **au·to·bi·og·ra·pher** n.

au·to·ca·tal·y·sis /ˌôtəkəˈtaləsis/ ▶ n. Chem. catalysis of a reaction by one of its products. — **au·to·cat·a·lyst** /-ˈkatl-ist/ n. **au·to·cat·a·lyt·ic** /-ˌkatlˈitik/ adj.

au·to·ceph·a·lous /ˌôtəˈsefələs/ ▶ adj. (of an Eastern Christian Church) appointing its own head, not subject to an external patriarch or archbishop. [19th C.: from Gk. *autokephalos* (from *autos* 'self' + *kephalē* 'head').]

au·toch·thon /ôˈtäkTHən/ ▶ n. (pl. **-thons** or **-tho·nes** /-THəˌnēz/) an original or indigenous inhabitant of a place; an aborigine. [16th C.: from Gk., from *autos* 'self' + *khthōn* 'earth.']

au·toch·tho·nous /ôˈtäkTHənəs/ ▶ adj. (of an inhabitant of a place) indigenous rather than descended from migrants or colonists. ■ Geol. (of a deposit or formation) formed in its present position. Often contrasted with ALLOCHTHONOUS.

au·to·clave /ˈôtəˌklāv/ ▶ n. a strong, heated container used for chemical reactions and other processes using high pressures and temperatures. ▶ v. [trans.] heat (something) in an autoclave. [19th C.: from Fr., from *auto-* 'self' + L. *clavus* 'nail' or *clavis* 'key.']

au·to·cor·re·la·tion /ˌôtōˌkôrəˈlāSHən/ ▶ n. Stat. correlation between the elements of a series and others from the same series separated from them by a given interval. ■ a calculation of such correlation.

au·toc·ra·cy /ôˈtäkrəsē/ ▶ n. (pl. **-cies**) a system of government by one person with absolute power. ■ a regime based on such a principle of government. ■ a country, state, or society governed in such a way. ■ domineering rule or control: *a boss who shifts between autocracy, persuasion, and consultation.*

au·to·crat /ˈôtəˌkrat/ ▶ n. a ruler who has absolute power. ■ someone who insists on complete obedience from others; an imperious or domineering person. [19th C.: ult. from Gk. *autokratēs*, from *autos* 'self' + *kratos* 'power.']

au·to·crat·ic /ˌôtəˈkratik/ ▶ adj. of or relating to a ruler who has absolute power. ■ taking no account of other people's wishes or opinions; domineering. — **au·to·crat·i·cal·ly** /-ik(ə)lē/ adv.

au·to·cross /ˈôtōˌkrôs; -ˌkräs/ ▶ n. a form of competition in which cars are driven around an obstacle course, typically marked out by cones. [1960s: blend of AUTOMOBILE and CROSS-COUNTRY.]

au·to-da-fé /ˈôtō də ˈfā/ ▶ n. (pl. **au·tos-da-fé**) the burning of a heretic by the Spanish Inquisition. ■ a sentence of such a kind. [18th C.: from Port., lit. 'act of the faith.']

au·to·di·al /ˈôtōˌdī(ə)l/ ▶ n. a function of telephonic equipment that allows for automatic dialing of preprogrammed or of randomly selected numbers: *have a telephone with autodial by your bed.* ▶ v. (**-di·aled, -di·al·ing**; Brit. **-di·alled, -di·al·ling**) automatically dial a telephone number, with or without human prompting: [intrans.] *it had autodialed and been online for over 2 hours* | [trans.] *if the first number is busy the modem autodials the backup number.* — **au·to·di·al·er** n.

au·to·di·dact /ˌôtōˈdīdakt/ ▶ n. a self-taught person. — **au·to·di·dac·tic** /-dīˈdaktik/ adj. [18th C.: from Gk. *autodidaktos* 'self-taught,' from *autos* 'self' + *didaskein* 'teach.']

au·to·e·col·o·gy /ˌôtō-iˈkäləjē/ ▶ n. var. of AUTECOLOGY.

au·to·e·rot·ic /ˌôtō-iˈrätik/ ▶ adj. of or relating to sexual excitement generated by stimulating or fantasizing about one's own body. — **au·to·e·rot·i·cism** /-əˌsizəm/ n.

au·to·e·rot·ic as·phyx·i·a ▶ n. asphyxia that results from intentionally strangling oneself while masturbating, in an attempt to heighten sexual pleasure by limiting the oxygen supply to the brain.

au·tog·a·my /ôˈtägəmē/ ▶ n. Biol. self-fertilization, esp. the self-pollination of a flower. — **au·tog·a·mous** /-məs/ adj. [19th C.: from AUTO- + Gk. *-gamia* (from *gamos* 'marriage').]

au·to·ge·net·ic /ˌôtōjəˈnetik/ ▶ adj. tech. self-generated: *autogenetic succession.*

au·tog·e·nous /ôˈtäjənəs/ ▶ adj. arising from within or from a thing itself.

au·to·gi·ro /ˌôtōˈjīrō/ (also **au·to·gy·ro**) ▶ n. (pl. **-ros**) a form of aircraft with freely rotating horizontal vanes and a propeller. [1920s: from Sp., from *auto-* 'self' + *giro* 'gyration.']

au·to·graft /ˈôtəˌgraft/ ▶ n. a graft of tissue from one point to another of the same individual's body.

au·to·graph /ˈôtəˌgraf/ ▶ n. **1** a signature, esp. that of a celebrity written as a memento for an admirer. **2** a manuscript or musical score in the author's or musician's own handwriting. ▶ v. [trans.] (of a celebrity) write one's signature on (something); sign: *the whole team autographed a shirt for him.* ▶ adj. written in the author's own handwriting: *an autograph manuscript.* [17th C.: ult. from Gk. *autographon*, based on *autos* 'self' + *graphos* 'written.']

Au·to·harp /ˈôtōˌhärp/ ▶ n. trademark a kind of zither with a mechanical device that allows the playing of a chord by damping all the other strings.

au·to·hyp·no·sis /ˌôtōhipˈnōsis/ ▶ n. induction of a hypnotic state in oneself; self-hypnosis. — **au·to·hyp·not·ic** /-ˈnätik/ adj.

au·to·im·mune /ˌôtōəˈmyo͞on/ ▶ adj. Med. of or relating to disease caused by antibodies produced against substances naturally present in the body. — **au·to·im·mu·ni·ty** /-əˈmo͞onitē/ n.

au·to·in·tox·i·ca·tion /ˌôtō-inˌtäksiˈkāsʜən/ ▶ n. Med. poisoning by a toxin formed within the body itself.

au·to·load /ˈôtōˌlōd/ ▶ adj. self-loading; semiautomatic: *24mm film in autoload cartridges.* — **au·to·load·er** n. **au·to·load·ing** n.

au·tol·o·gous /ôˈtäləgəs/ ▶ adj. (of cells or tissues) obtained from the same individual: *autologous bone marrow transplants.*

au·tol·y·sis /ôˈtäləsis/ ▶ n. Biol. the destruction of cells or tissues by their own enzymes. — **au·to·lyt·ic** /ˌôtlˈitik/ adj.

au·to·mat /ˈôtəˌmat/ ▶ n. hist. a cafeteria in which food was obtained from vending machines. [17th C. ult. from L. *automaton* (see AUTOMATON).]

au·to·mate /ˈôtəˌmāt/ ▶ v. [trans.] convert (a process or facility) to largely automatic operation. [1950s: back-form. from AUTOMATION.]

au·to·mat·ed tel·ler ma·chine (also **au·to·mat·ic tell·er ma·chine**) (abbr.: **ATM**) ▶ n. a machine that provides cash and performs other banking services on insertion of a special card.

au·to·mat·ic /ˌôtəˈmatik/ ▶ adj. **1** (of a device or process) working by itself with little or no direct human control: *an automatic kettle that switches itself off.* ■ (of a firearm) self-loading and able to fire continuously until the ammunition is exhausted or the pressure on the trigger is released. ■ (of a motor vehicle or its transmission) using gears that shift by themselves according to speed and acceleration: *a four-speed automatic gearbox.* **2** done or occurring spontaneously, without conscious thought or intention: *automatic physical functions such as breathing.* ■ occurring as a matter of course and without debate: *he is the automatic choice for the team.* ■ (esp. of a legal sanction) given or imposed as a result of a fixed rule or set of circumstances: *he received an automatic one-game suspension.* ▶ n. an automatic machine or device, in particular: ■ a gun that continues firing until the ammunition is exhausted or the pressure on the trigger is released. ■ a vehicle with automatic transmission. — **au·to·mat·i·cal·ly** /-ik(ə)lē/ adv. **au·to·ma·tic·i·ty** /-məˈtisitē/ n. [18th C.: from Gk. *automatos* (see AUTOMATON).]

au·to·mat·ic pi·lot ▶ n. a device for keeping an aircraft on a set course without the intervention of the pilot.

au·to·mat·ic writ·ing ▶ n. writing said to be produced by a spiritual, occult, or subconscious agency rather than by the conscious intention of the writer.

au·to·ma·tion /ˌôtəˈmāsʜən/ ▶ n. the use of largely automatic equipment in a system of manufacturing or other production process.

au·tom·a·tism /ôˈtäməˌtizəm/ ▶ n. the performance of actions without conscious thought or intention. ■ Art the avoidance of conscious intention in producing works of art. ■ an action performed unconsciously or involuntarily.

au·tom·a·tize /ôˈtäməˌtīz/ ▶ v. [trans.] [usu. as adj.] (**automatized**) make automatic or habitual. — **au·tom·a·ti·za·tion** /ôˌtämətiˈzāsʜən/ n.

au·tom·a·ton /ôˈtämətən; -ˌtän/ ▶ n. (pl. **-ta** /-tə/ or **-tons**) a moving mechanical device made in imitation of a human being. ■ a machine that performs a function according to a predetermined set of coded instructions. ■ used in similes and comparisons to refer to a person who seems to act in a mechanical or unemotional way: *she went about her preparations like an automaton.* [17th C.: via L. from Gk., neut. of *automatos* 'acting of itself,' from *autos* 'self.']

au·to·mo·bile /ˌôtəməˈbēl; ˈôtəməˌbēl/ ▶ n. a road vehicle, typically with four wheels, powered by an internal combustion engine or electric motor and able to carry a small number of people. [19th C.: from Fr., from *auto-* 'self' + *mobile* 'mobile.']

au·to·mo·tive /ˌôtəˈmōtiv/ ▶ adj. [attrib.] of, relating to, or concerned with motor vehicles.

au·to·nom·ic /ˌôtəˈnämik/ ▶ adj. [attrib.] esp. Physiol. involuntary or unconscious; relating to the autonomic nervous system.

au·to·nom·ic nerv·ous sys·tem ▶ n. the part of the nervous system responsible for control of the bodily functions not consciously directed, such as breathing, the heartbeat, and digestive processes.

au·ton·o·mous /ôˈtänəməs/ ▶ adj. (of a country or region) having self-government. ■ acting independently or having the freedom to do so: *an autonomous committee of the school board.* — **au·ton·o·mous·ly** adv. [19th C.: from Gk. *autonomos* 'having its own laws,' from *autos* 'self' + *nomos* 'law.']

au·ton·o·my /ôˈtänəmē/ ▶ n. (pl. **-mies**) (of a country or region) the right or condition of self-government, esp. in a particular sphere: *Tatarstan demanded greater autonomy within the Russian Federation.* ■ a self-governing country or region. ■ freedom from external control or influence; independence: *economic autonomy is still a long way off for many women.* — **au·ton·o·mist** /-mist/ n. & adj.

au·to·pi·lot /ˈôtōˌpīlət/ ▶ n. short for AUTOMATIC PILOT.

au·top·sy /ˈôtäpsē/ ▶ n. (pl. **-sies**) a postmortem examination to discover the cause of death or the extent of disease: [as adj.] *an autopsy report.* ▶ v. (**-sies, -sied**) [trans.] perform a postmortem examination on (a body or organ): [17th C.: ult. from Gk. *autopsia*, from *autoptēs* 'eyewitness,' from *autos* 'self' + *optos* 'seen.']

au·to·ra·di·o·gram /ˌôtōˈrādēəˌgram/ ▶ n. another term for AUTORADIOGRAPH.

au·to·ra·di·o·graph /ˌôtōˈrādēəˌgraf/ ▶ n. a photograph of an object produced by radiation from radioactive material in the object and revealing the distribution or location of labeled material in the object. ▶ v. [trans.] make an autoradiograph of. — **au·to·ra·di·o·graph·ic** /-ˌrādēəˈgrafik/ adj. **au·to·ra·di·og·ra·phy** /-ˌrādēˈägrəfē/ n.

au·to·ro·ta·tion /ˌôtōrōˈtāsʜən/ ▶ n. rotation of an object caused by the flow of moving air or water around the shape of the object (e.g., a winged seed). ■ such rotation in the rotor blades of a helicopter that is descending without engine power. — **au·to·ro·tate** /-ˈrōtāt/ v.

au·to·route /ˈôtōˌro͞ot/ ▶ n. a highway in a French-speaking country. [1960s: from Fr., from *auto(mobile)* + *route*.]

au·to·some /ˈôtəˌsōm/ ▶ n. Biol. any chromosome that is not a sex chromosome. — **au·to·so·mal** /ˌôtōˈsōməl/ adj.

au·to·stra·da /ˈôtōˌsträdə/ ▶ n. (pl. **-stra·das** or **-stra·de** /-ˌsträdē/) an Italian highway. [1920s: from Ital., from *auto* 'automobile' + *strada* 'road.']

au·to·sug·ges·tion /ˌôtōsə(g)ˈjescʜən/ ▶ n. the hypnotic or subconscious adoption of an idea that one has originated oneself.

au·to·tel·ic /ˌôtəˈtelik/ ▶ adj. formal (of an activity or a creative work) having an end or purpose in itself. [20th C.: from AUTO- + Gk. *telos* 'end.']

au·tot·o·my /ôˈtätəmē/ ▶ n. Zool. the casting off of a part of the body (e.g., the tail of a lizard) by an animal under threat.

au·to·tox·in /ˈôtōˌtäksin/ ▶ n. a substance produced by an organism that is toxic to the organism itself. — **au·to·tox·ic** /ˌôtōˈtäksik/ adj.

au·to·trans·form·er /ˌôtōtransˈfôrmər/ ▶ n. an electrical transformer that has a single coil winding, part of which is common to both primary and secondary circuits.

au·to·troph /ˈôtəˌträf; -ˌtrōf/ ▶ n. Biol. an organism that is able to form nutritional organic substances from simple inorganic substances such as carbon dioxide. Compare with HETEROTROPH. — **au·to·troph·ic** /ˌôtəˈträfik/ adj. **au·tot·ro·phy** /ôˈtätrəfē/ n.

au·to·work·er /ˈôtōˌwərkər/ ▶ n. a worker in the automobile industry.

au·tox·i·da·tion /ˌôtäksiˈdāsʜən/ ▶ n. Chem. spontaneous oxidation of a substance at ambient temperatures in the presence of oxygen. — **au·tox·i·dize** /ôˈtäksiˌdīz/ v.

au·tumn /ˈôtəm/ ▶ **n.** the third season of the year, between summer and winter, in the northern hemisphere from September to November and in the southern hemisphere from March to May. ■ Astron. the period from the autumnal equinox to the winter solstice. [ME: ult. from L. *autumnus*.]

au·tum·nal /ôˈtəmnəl/ ▶ **adj.** of, characteristic of, or occurring in autumn.

au·tum·nal e·qui·nox ▶ **n.** the equinox in autumn, on about September 22 in the northern hemisphere and March 20 in the southern hemisphere.

au·tumn cro·cus ▶ **n.** a crocuslike Eurasian plant (genus *Colchicum*) of the lily family, cultivated for its autumn-blooming flowers.

au·tun·ite /ôˈtənīt; ˈôtnˌīt/ ▶ **n.** a yellow or pale green mineral occurring as square crystals that fluoresce in ultraviolet light. It is a hydrated phosphate of calcium and uranium. [19th C.: from *Autun*, a town in eastern France.]

Au·vergne /ōˈvern(yə); ōˈvərn/ a region in south central France that was a province of the Roman Empire.

aux·il·ia·ry /ôgˈzilyərē; -ˈzil(ə)rē/ ▶ **adj.** providing supplementary or additional help and support: *auxiliary airport staff.* ■ (of equipment) held in reserve: *the ship has an auxiliary power source.* ■ (of troops) engaged in the service of a nation at war but not part of the regular army, and often of foreign origin. ■ (of a sailing vessel) equipped with a supplementary engine. ▶ **n.** (pl. **-ries**) a person or thing providing supplementary or additional help and support. ■ a group of volunteers giving supplementary support to an organization or institution. ■ (**auxiliaries**) troops engaged in the service of a nation at war but not part of the regular army, and often of foreign origin. ■ Gram. an auxiliary verb. ■ a naval vessel with a supporting role, not armed for combat. [ME: from L. *auxiliarius*, from *auxilium* 'help.']

aux·il·ia·ry verb ▶ **n.** Gram. a verb used in forming the tenses, moods, and voices of other verbs. The primary auxiliary verbs in English are *be, do,* and *have.* See also **MODAL VERB.**

aux·in /ˈôksin/ ▶ **n.** a plant hormone that causes the elongation of cells in shoots and is involved in regulating plant growth. [1930s: coined in Ger. from Gk. *auxein* 'to increase.']

aux·o·troph /ˈôksəˌträf; -ˌtrōf/ ▶ **n.** Biol. a mutant organism (typically a bacterium or fungus) that requires a particular additional nutrient that the normal strain does not. —**aux·o·troph·ic** /ˌôksəˈträfik; -ˈtrō-/ **adj.** [1950s: from L. *auxilium* 'help' + Gk. *trophos* 'feeder.']

AV ▶ **abbr.** ■ audiovisual (teaching aids). ■ Authorized Version.

av·a·da·vat /ˈavədəˌvat/ (also **am·a·da·vat** /ˈam-/) ▶ **n.** a small South Asian waxbill (genus *Amandava*, family Estrildidae) that is often kept as a caged bird. [17th C.: named after the city of **AHMADABAD** in India.]

a·vail /əˈvāl/ ▶ **v. 1** (**avail oneself of**) use or take advantage of (an opportunity or available resource): *she did not avail herself of my advice.* **2** help or benefit: [trans.] *no amount of struggle availed Charles.*
– PHRASES **to little** (or **no**) **avail** with little (or no) success or benefit: *he tried to get his work recognized, but to little avail.* [ME: from obs. *vail* 'be of use' (appar. on the pattern of pairs such as *amount, mount*), from OFr. *valoir*, from L. *valere* 'be strong.']

a·vail·a·ble /əˈvāləbəl/ ▶ **adj.** able to be used or obtained; at someone's disposal: *refreshments will be available all afternoon.* ■ (of a person) not otherwise occupied; free to do something. ■ not currently involved in a sexual or romantic relationship. —**a·vail·a·bil·i·ty** /əˌvāləˈbilitē/ **n.**

av·a·lanche /ˈavəˌlanch/ ▶ **n.** a mass of snow, ice, and rocks falling rapidly down a mountainside. ■ a large mass of any material moving rapidly downhill. ■ fig. a sudden arrival or occurrence of something in overwhelming quantities: *an avalanche of applications.* ■ Physics a cumulative process in which a fast-moving ion or electron generates further ions and electrons by collision. ▶ **v.** [intrans.] (of a mass of snow, ice, and rocks) descend rapidly down a mountainside. ■ [trans.] (usu. **be avalanched**) engulf or carry off by such a mass of material. ■ [intrans.] Physics undergo a rapid increase in conductivity due to an avalanche process. [18th C.: from Fr., alt. of Alpine dial. *lavanche*, influenced by *avaler* 'descend.']

Av·a·lon /ˈavəˌlän/ (in Arthurian legend) the place to which Arthur was conveyed after death.

a·vant-garde /ˈävänt ˈgärd; ˌävän/ ▶ **n.** (usu. **the avant-garde**) new and unusual or experimental ideas, esp. in the arts, or the people introducing them. ▶ **adj.** favoring or introducing such new ideas: *a controversial avant-garde composer.* —**a·vant-gard·ism n. a·vant-gard·ist n.** [ME: from Fr., lit. 'vanguard.']

av·a·rice /ˈavəris/ ▶ **n.** extreme greed for wealth or material gain. [ME: from OFr., from L. *avaritia*, from *avarus* 'greedy.']

av·a·ri·cious /ˌavəˈrishəs/ ▶ **adj.** having or showing an extreme greed for wealth or material gain. —**av·a·ri·cious·ly adv. av·a·ri·cious·ness n.**

a·vast /əˈvast/ ▶ **exclam.** Naut. stop; cease. [17th C.: from Du. *hou'vast, houd vast* 'hold fast!']

av·a·tar /ˈavəˌtär/ ▶ **n.** esp. Hinduism a manifestation of a deity in bodily form on earth. ■ an incarnation, embodiment, or manifestation of a person or idea: *he set himself up as a new avatar of Arab radicalism.* ■ Comput. a movable icon representing a person in cyberspace or virtual reality graphics. [from Sanskrit *avatāra* 'descent,' from *ava* 'down' + *tar-* 'to cross.']

a·vaunt /əˈvônt/ ▶ **exclam.** archaic go away. [ME: ult. from OFr. *avant*, from L. *ab* 'from' + *ante* 'before.']

Ave. ▶ **abbr.** Avenue.

a·ve /ˈävā/ ▶ **exclam.** literary used to express good wishes on meeting or parting. ▶ **n. 1** (**Ave**) short for **AVE MARIA. 2** literary a shout of welcome or farewell. [ME: from L., 'fare well!', imper. of *avere*.]

A·ve Ma·ri·a /ˈävā məˈrēə/ ▶ **n.** a prayer to the Virgin Mary used in Catholic worship. Also called **HAIL MARY.** [ME: from L., lit. 'Hail, Mary!']

a·venge /əˈvenj/ ▶ **v.** [trans.] inflict harm in return for (an injury or wrong done to oneself or another): *his determination to avenge the murder of his brother.* ■ inflict such harm on behalf of (oneself or someone else previously wronged or harmed): *we must avenge our dead.* —**a·veng·er n.** [ME: from OFr. *avengier*, from *a-* 'to') + *vengier*, from L. *vindicare* 'vindicate.']

av·ens /ˈavənz/ ▶ **n.** a plant (genus *Geum*) of the rose family, typically having serrated, divided leaves and seeds bearing small hooks. [ME: from OFr. *avence*.]

a·ven·tu·rine /əˈvenchəˌrēn; -ˌrīn/ ▶ **n.** brownish glass containing sparkling particles of copper or gold. ■ a translucent mineral containing small reflective particles, typically quartz containing mica. [18th C.: from Fr., from Ital. *avventurino*, from *avventura* 'chance.']

av·e·nue /ˈavəˌn(y)o͞o/ ▶ **n. 1** a broad road in a town or city, typically having trees at regular intervals along its sides. ■ [in proper names] a thoroughfare running at right angles to the streets in a city laid out on a grid pattern: *7th Avenue.* ■ a tree-lined road or path, esp. one that leads to a country house or similar building. **2** a way of approaching a problem or making progress toward something: *three possible avenues of research.* [17th C.: from Fr., fem. past part. of *avenir* 'arrive,' from L. *advenire*, from *ad-* 'toward' + *venire* 'come.']

a·ver /əˈvər/ ▶ **v.** (**a·verred, a·ver·ring**) [reporting verb] formal state or assert to be the case: [with clause] *he averred that he was innocent of the allegations.* ■ [trans.] Law allege as a fact in support of a plea. [ME: from OFr. *averer*, based on L. *ad* 'to' + *verus* 'true.']

av·er·age /ˈav(ə)rij/ (abbr.: **avg.**) ▶ **n. 1** the result obtained by adding several quantities together and then dividing this total by the number of quantities; the mean: *the housing prices there are twice the national average.* Compare with **MEAN**[3] (sense 1). ■ an amount, standard, level, or rate regarded as usual or ordinary: *the month's snowfall is below average.* **2** the apportionment of financial liability resulting from loss of or damage to a ship or its cargo. ■ reduction in the amount payable under an insurance policy, e.g., in respect of partial loss. ▶ **adj.** constituting the result obtained by adding together several quantities and then dividing this total by the number of quantities. ■ of the usual or ordinary standard, level, or quantity: *a woman of average height.* ■ having qualities that are seen as typical of a particular person or thing. ■ mediocre; not very good: *an average director who made average movies.* ▶ **v.** [trans.] amount to or achieve as an average rate or amount over a period of time: *annual inflation averaged 2.4 percent.* ■ calculate or estimate the average of (figures or measurements). ■ [intrans.] (**average out**) result in an even distribution; even out: *it is reasonable to hope that the results will average out.* ■ [intrans.] (**average out at/to**) result in an average figure of: *the cost should average out to about $6 per page.* —**av·er·age·ly adv.** [15th C.: from Fr. *avarie* 'damage to ship or cargo,' from Ital. *avaria*, from Arab. *'awār*; the mod. sense arose from the equitable sharing of liability for losses at sea between the owners of the vessel and of the cargo.]

a·ver·ment /əˈvərmənt/ ▶ **n.** formal an affirmation or allegation. ■ Law a formal statement by a party that the party offers to prove or substantiate.

A·ver·ro·ës /əˈverōˌēz; ˌavəˈrō-ēz/ (*c.*1126–98), Islamic philosopher, born in Spain; Arabic name *ibn-Rushd*. He is noted for his commentaries on Aristotle.

a·verse /əˈvərs/ ▶ **adj.** [predic.] [usu. with negative] (**averse to**) having a strong dislike of or opposition to something. [16th C.: from L. *aversus* past part. of *avertere*.]

a·ver·sion /əˈvərzhən/ ▶ **n.** a strong dislike or disinclination: *an aversion to exercise.* ■ someone or something that arouses such feelings. —**a·ver·sive** /-siv; -ziv/ **adj.**

a·ver·sion ther·a·py ▶ **n.** a type of behavior therapy designed to make a patient give up an undesirable habit by causing them to associate it with an unpleasant effect.

a·vert /əˈvərt/ ▶ **v.** [trans.] **1** turn away (one's eyes or thoughts): *she averted her eyes during the more violent scenes.* **2** prevent or ward off (an undesirable occurrence): *talks failed to avert a rail strike.* [ME: from L. *avertere*, from *ab-* 'from' + *vertere* 'to turn.']

A·ves /ˈävāz/ Zool. a class of vertebrates that comprises the birds. [L., pl. of *avis* 'bird.']

A·ves·ta /əˈvestə/ ▶ **n.** the sacred writings of Zoroastrianism, compiled in the 4th century AD. [Pers.]

A·ves·tan /əˈvestən/ ▶ **adj.** of or relating to the Avesta or to the ancient Indo-Iranian language in which it is written, closely related to Vedic Sanskrit. ▶ **n.** the Avestan language.

avg. ▶ **abbr.** average.

av·gas /ˈavˌgas/ ▶ **n.** aircraft fuel. [20th C.: from *av(iation)* + **GAS.**]

a·vi·an /ˈāvēən/ ▶ **adj.** of or relating to birds. ▶ **n.** a bird. [19th C.: from L. *avis* 'bird.']

a·vi·an flu ▶ **n.** formal term for **BIRD FLU.**

a·vi·ar·y /ˈāvēˌerē/ ▶ **n.** (pl. **-ar·ies**) a large cage, building, or enclosure for birds.

a·vi·ate /ˈāvēˌāt/ ▶ **v.** pilot or fly in an airplane: [trans.] *an aircraft that can* *be aviated without effort.* [19th C.: back-form. from AVIATION.]

a·vi·a·tion /ˌāvēˈāSHən/ ▶ n. the flying or operating of aircraft. [19th C.: from Fr., from L. *avis* 'bird.']

a·vi·a·tor /ˈāvēˌātər/ ▶ n. dated a pilot.

a·vi·a·tor glass·es ▶ n. a style of sunglasses with thin wire frames and dark lenses.

a·vi·a·trix /ˌāvēˈātriks/ ▶ n. (pl. **-tri·ces** /-trisēz/) dated a female pilot.

Av·i·cen·na /ˌavəˈsenə/ (980–1037), Islamic philosopher; born in Persia; Arabic name *ibn-Sina.* He influenced the development of scholasticism.

a·vi·cul·ture /ˈāviˌkəlCHər; ˈavi-/ ▶ n. the breeding and rearing of birds. —**a·vi·cul·tur·al** /ˌāviˈkəlCHərəl; ˌavi-/ adj. **a·vi·cul·tur·al·ist** /ˌāviˈkəlCHərəlist; ˌavi-/ n. **a·vi·cul·tur·ist** /-CHərist/ n. [20th C.: from L. *avis* 'bird.']

av·id /ˈavid/ ▶ adj. having or showing keen interest or enthusiasm: *an avid reader of science fiction.* ■ (**avid for**) having an eager desire for something: *avid for information about the murder.* —**av·id·ly** adv. [18th C.: ult. from L. *avidus,* from *avere* 'crave.']

av·i·din /ˈavidin/ ▶ n. Biochem. a protein found in raw egg white, which combines with biotin and hinders its absorption. [1940s: from AVID.]

a·vid·i·ty /əˈviditē/ ▶ n. extreme eagerness or enthusiasm: *he read detective stories with avidity.* ■ Biochem. the overall strength of binding between an antibody and an antigen.

a·vi·fau·na /ˌāvəˈfônə; ˌavə-/ ▶ n. the birds of a particular region, habitat, or geological period. —**a·vi·fau·nal** adj. [19th C.: from L. *avis* 'bird.']

A·vi·gnon /ˌävēnˈyôN/ a city in southeastern France on the Rhone River; pop. 89,440.

a·vi·on·ics /ˌāvēˈäniks/ ▶ plural n. [usu. treated as sing.] electronics as applied to aviation. ■ electronic equipment fitted in an aircraft. [1940s: blend of AVIATION and ELECTRONICS.]

a·vir·u·lent /āˈvir(y)ələnt/ ▶ adj. (of a microorganism) not virulent.

a·vi·ta·min·o·sis /āˌvītəmiˈnōsis/ ▶ n. (pl. **-ses** /-sēz/) Med. a condition resulting from a deficiency of one or more particular vitamins.

av·o·ca·do /ˌavəˈkädō; ˌävə-/ ▶ n. (pl. **-dos**) **1** a pear-shaped fruit with a rough leathery skin, smooth oily edible flesh, and a large stone. Also called ALLIGATOR PEAR. ■ a light green color like that of the flesh of avocados. **2** the tropical evergreen tree (*Persea americana,* family Lauraceae) that bears this fruit. It is native to Central America and widely cultivated elsewhere. [17th C.: from Sp., alt. of *aguacate,* from Nahuatl *ahuacatl.*]

av·o·ca·tion /ˌavəˈkāSHən/ ▶ n. a hobby or minor occupation. —**av·o·ca·tion·al** /-SHənl/ adj. [17th C.: from L. *avocatio(n-),* from *avocare* 'call away,' from *ab-* + *vocare* 'to call.']

av·o·cet /ˈavəˌset/ ▶ n. a long-legged wading bird (genus *Recurvirostra,* family Recurvirostridae) with a slender upturned bill and strikingly patterned plumage. [17th C.: from Fr. *avocette,* from Ital. *avosetta.*]

A·vo·ga·dro /ˌävəˈgädˌrō; ˌävō-/, Amedeo (1776–1856), Italian chemist and physicist. His law stated that equal volumes of gases at the same temperature and pressure contain equal numbers of molecules, and was used to derive both molecular weights and a system of atomic weights.

A·vo·ga·dro's num·ber (also **Avogadro's constant**) Chem. the number of atoms or molecules in one mole of a substance, equal to 6.023×10^{23}.

a·void /əˈvoid/ ▶ v. [trans.] **1** keep away from or stop oneself from doing (something): *avoid excessive exposure to the sun.* ■ contrive not to meet (someone): *boys lined up to meet Gloria, but avoided her bossy sister.* ■ (of a person or a route) not go to or through (a place): *this route avoids downtown Boston.* ■ prevent from happening: *make adjustments to avoid an accident.* **2** Law repudiate, nullify, or render void (a decree or contract). —**a·void·a·ble** adj. **a·void·a·bly** /-əblē/ adv. **a·void·ance** /əˈvoidns/ n. **a·void·er** n. [ME: from OFr. *evuider* 'clear out,' from *vuide* 'empty' (see VOID).]

av·oir·du·pois /ˌävərdəˈpoiz/ ▶ n. a system of weights based on a pound of 16 ounces or 7,000 grains, widely used in English-speaking countries. Compare with TROY. [ME: from OFr. *aveir de peis* 'goods of weight,' from *aveir* 'to have' + *peis* 'weight.']

A·von /ˈāvən; ˈävän/ **1** a river in central England that flows 96 miles (154 km) southwest through Stratford to the Severn River. **2** a river in southwestern England that flows 75 miles (121 km) through Bath and Bristol to the Severn River. **3** a county in southwestern England; county town, Bristol.

A·von·dale /ˈāvənˌdāl/ a city in south central Arizona, a western suburb of Phoenix; pop. 35,883.

a·vouch /əˈvouCH/ ▶ v. [trans.] archaic affirm or assert. —**a·vouch·ment** n. [15th C.: from OFr. *avochier,* from L. *advocare* 'summon in defense,' from *ad-* 'to' + *vocare* 'to call.']

a·vow /əˈvou/ ▶ v. [reporting verb] assert or confess openly: [with clause] *he avowed that he had voted Republican in every election.* | [as adj.] (**avowed**) *an avowed Marxist.* —**a·vow·al** /əˈvouəl/ n. **a·vow·ed·ly** /əˈvou-idlē/ adv. [ME: from OFr. *avouer,* from L. *advocare.*]

a·vul·sion /əˈvəlSHən/ ▶ n. esp. Med. the action of pulling or tearing away. ■ Law the sudden separation of land from one property and its attachment to another, esp. by flooding or a change in the course of a river. —**a·vulse** /əˈvəls/ v. [17th C.: from L. *avulsion-,* from v. *avellere,* from *ab-* 'from' + *vallere* 'pluck.']

a·vun·cu·lar /əˈvəNGkyələr/ ▶ adj. **1** of or relating to an uncle. ■ kind and friendly toward a younger or less experienced person: *an avuncular manner.* **2** Anthropol. of or relating to the relationship between men and their siblings' children. [19th C.: from L. *avunculus* 'maternal uncle,' dimin. of *avus* 'grandfather.']

aw /ô/ ▶ exclam. used to express mild protest, entreaty, commiseration, or disapproval: *aw, Dad, that's not fair.* [19th C.: natural exclamation.]

AWACS /ˈāˌwaks/ ▶ n. (pl.) a long-range airborne radar system for detecting enemy aircraft and missiles and directing attacks on them. ■ an aircraft equipped with this radar system. [1960s: from *airborne warning and control system.*]

a·wait /əˈwāt/ ▶ v. [trans.] (of a person) wait for (an event): *we await the proposals with impatience.* ■ (of an event or circumstance) be in store for (someone): *many dangers await them.* [ME: from Anglo-Norman Fr. *awaitier,* from *a-* 'to' + *waitier* 'to wait.']

a·wake /əˈwāk/ ▶ v. (past **a·woke** /əˈwōk/; past part. **a·wok·en** /əˈwōkən/) [intrans.] stop sleeping; wake from sleep. ■ [trans.] cause (someone) to wake from sleep: *my screams awoke my parents.* ■ regain consciousness: *I awoke six hours after the operation.* ■ (**awake to**) fig. become aware of; come to a realization of: *the authorities finally awoke to the extent of the problem.* ▶ adj. [predic.] not asleep: *the noise might keep you awake.* ■ (**awake to**) aware of: *too few are awake to the dangers.* [OE *āwæcnan, āwacian* 'come out of sleep' (see A-[2], WAKE[1]).]

a·wak·en /əˈwākən/ ▶ v. [trans.] rouse from sleep; cause to stop sleeping: *awakened by the telephone.* ■ [intrans.] stop sleeping: *he sighed but did not awaken.* ■ rouse (a feeling): *images can awaken emotions within us.* ■ (**awaken someone to**) make someone aware of (something): *the movie helped to awaken the public to the horrors of apartheid.* [OE *onwæcnan,* from *on* 'on' + *waken,* literary form of WAKE[1].]

a·wak·en·ing /əˈwāk(ə)niNG/ ▶ n. [in sing.] an act or moment of becoming suddenly aware of something. ■ formal an act of waking from sleep. ■ the beginning or rousing of something: *the awakening of democracy.* ▶ adj. [attrib.] coming into existence or awareness.

a·ward /əˈwôrd/ ▶ v. [with two objs.] give or order the giving of (something) as an official payment, compensation, or prize: *he was awarded the Purple Heart.* ■ grant or assign (a contract or commission) to (a person or organization). ▶ n. a prize or other mark of recognition given in honor of an achievement. ■ an amount of money paid to someone as an official payment, compensation, or grant: *a generous award given to promising young dancers.* ■ the action of giving a payment, compensation, or prize: *the award of an honorary doctorate | an award of damages.* —**a·ward·ee** /əˌwôrˈdē/ n. **a·ward·er** n. [ME: from OFr. *esguarder* 'consider,' from *es-* (from L. *ex* 'thoroughly') + *guarder* 'watch,' from Gmc., akin to WARD.]

a·ware /əˈwe(ə)r/ ▶ adj. [predic.] having knowledge or perception of a situation or fact: *most people are aware of the dangers of sunbathing.* ■ [with adverbial] concerned and well-informed about a particular situation or development: *a* **politically aware** *electorate.* —**a·ware·ness** n. [OE *gewær,* from West Gmc.; akin to Ger. *gewahr* and WARE[2].]

a·wash /əˈwôSH; əˈwäSH/ ▶ adj. [predic.] covered or flooded with water, esp. seawater or rain. ■ level with the surface of water, esp. the sea, so that it just washes over: *a rock awash outside the reef entrance.*

a·way /əˈwā/ ▶ adv. **1** to or at a distance from a particular place, person, or thing: *she landed badly, and crawled away | they walked* **away from** *the church in silence.* ■ at a specified distance: *when he was ten or twelve feet away, he stopped.* ■ at a specified future distance in time: *the wedding is only weeks away.* ■ toward a lower level; downward: *in front of them the land fell away to the river.* ■ conceptually to one side, so as no longer to be the focus of attention: *the museum has shifted its emphasis* **away from** *research toward exhibitions.* **2** into an appropriate place for storage or safekeeping: *he put away the lawn furniture.* ■ toward or into nonexistence: *the sound of hoofbeats died away.* **3** constantly, persistently, or continuously: *there was little Edgar crooning away.* ▶ adj. (of a sports competition) played at the opponents' grounds: *tomorrow night's away game at Yankee Stadium.*

– PHRASES **away with** said as an exhortation to overcome or be rid of something; let us be rid of: *away with poverty!* [OE *onweg, aweg* 'on one's way' (see A-[2], WAY).]

awe /ô/ ▶ n. a feeling of reverential respect mixed with fear or wonder: *they gazed in awe at the small mountain of diamonds.* ■ archaic capacity to inspire awe: *is it any wonder that Christmas Eve has lost its awe?* ▶ v. [trans.] (usu. **be awed**) inspire with awe: *they were both awed by the vastness of the forest.* [OE *ege* 'terror,' later from ON *agi.*]

a·weigh /əˈwā/ ▶ adj. Naut. (of an anchor) raised just clear of the sea or riverbed.

awe-in·spir·ing ▶ adj. arousing awe through being impressive, formidable, or magnificent.

awe·some /ˈôsəm/ ▶ adj. extremely impressive or daunting; inspiring great admiration, apprehension, or fear. ■ informal extremely good; excellent: —**awe·some·ly** adv. **awe·some·ness** n.

awe·struck /ˈôˌstrək/ (also **awe·strick·en** /ˈôˌstrikən/) ▶ adj. filled with or revealing awe.

aw·ful /ˈôfəl/ ▶ adj. **1** very bad or unpleasant: *the place smelled awful.* ■ extremely shocking; horrific: *awful, bloody images.* ■ [attrib.] used to emphasize the extent of something, esp. something unpleasant or negative: *I've made an awful fool of myself.* ■ (of a person) very unwell, troubled, or unhappy: *I felt awful for being so angry.* **2** archaic inspiring reverential wonder or fear. ▸ **adv.** [as submodifier] informal awfully; very: *we're an awful long way from the main road.* — **aw•ful•ness n.** [OE (see AWE, -FUL).]

aw•ful•ly /ˈôf(ə)lē/ ▸ **adv. 1** [as submodifier] (used esp. in spoken English) very: *an awfully nice man.* **2** very badly or unpleasantly: *we played awfully.*

a•while /əˈ(h)wīl/ ▸ **adv.** for a short time: *stand here awhile.*

a•whirl /əˈ(h)wərl/ ▸ **adj.** [predic.] in a whirl; whirling: *her mind was awhirl with images.*

awk•ward /ˈôkwərd/ ▸ **adj. 1** causing difficulty; hard to do or deal with: *one of the most awkward jobs is painting a ceiling | some awkward questions.* ■ esp. Brit. deliberately unreasonable or uncooperative: *you're being damned awkward!* **2** causing or feeling embarrassment or inconvenience: *put in a very awkward situation.* **3** not smooth or graceful; ungainly: *awkward movements.* ■ uncomfortable or abnormal: *sleeping in an awkward position.* — **awk•ward•ly adv. awk•ward•ness n.** [ME: from dial. *awk* 'backward,' (from ON *afugr* 'turned the wrong way').]

awk•ward age ▸ **n.** the period of adolescence marked by self-consciousness and moody behavior.

awl /ôl/ ▸ **n.** a small pointed tool used for piercing holes, esp. in leather. [OE *æl*, from Gmc.; akin to Ger. *Ahle*.]

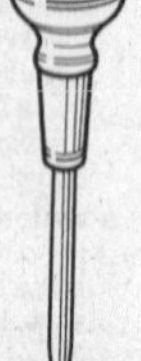

awl

awn /ôn/ ▸ **n.** Bot. a stiff bristle, esp. one of those growing from the ear or flower of barley, rye, and many grasses. — **awned adj.** [OE, from ON *ǫgn*.]

awn•ing /ˈôniNG/ ▸ **n.** a sheet of canvas or other material stretched on a frame and used to keep the sun or rain off a storefront, window, doorway, or deck. [17th C.: origin unknown.]

a•woke /əˈwōk/ past of AWAKE.

a•wo•ken /əˈwōkən/ past participle of AWAKE.

AWOL /ˈā,wôl/ ▸ **adj.** [predic.] Mil. absent from one's post but without intent to desert. [1920s: from *absent without (official) leave*.]

a•wry /əˈrī/ ▸ **adv. & adj.** away from the appropriate, planned, or expected course; amiss: [as adv.] *many youthful romances go awry.* ■ out of the normal or correct position; askew. [ME: from A-[2] + WRY.]

aw-shucks ▸ **adj.** [attrib.] informal (of a personal quality or manner) self-deprecating and shy: *his aw-shucks niceness disguised his conniving nature.* [20th C.: from AW + *shucks* (see SHUCK).]

ax /aks/ (also **axe**) ▸ **n. 1** a tool typically used for chopping wood, usually a steel blade attached at a right angle to a wooden handle. ■ fig. a measure intended to reduce costs drastically, esp. one that involves elimination of staff: *thirty workers are facing the ax.* **2** informal a musical instrument, esp. a jazz musician's saxophone or a bass guitar. ▸ **v.** [trans.] **1** end, cancel, or dismiss suddenly and ruthlessly: *the company is axing 125 jobs.* ■ reduce (costs or services) drastically: *the candidates all promised to ax spending.* **2** cut or strike with an ax, esp. violently or destructively: *the door had been axed by the firefighters.*
– PHRASES **have an ax to grind** have a self-serving reason for doing or being involved in something. [OE *æx*, from Gmc.; akin to Ger. *Axt*.]

ax•el /ˈaksəl/ (also **Ax•el**) ▸ **n.** a jump in figure skating with a forward takeoff from the forward outside edge of one skate to the backward outside edge of the other, with one and a half turns in the air. [1930s: named after *Axel* R. Paulsen (1885–1938), Norwegian skater.]

a•xen•ic /āˈzēnik; āˈzen-/ ▸ **adj.** esp. Bot. of, relating to, or denoting a culture that is free from living organisms other than the species required. — **a•xen•i•cal•ly** /-ik(ə)lē/ **adv.** [1940s: from A-[1] + Gk. *xenikos* 'alien.']

ax•es /ˈaksēz/ plural form of AXIS.

ax•i•al /ˈaksēəl/ ▸ **adj.** of, forming, or relating to an axis. ■ around an axis: *the axial rotation rate of the earth.* — **ax•i•al•ly adv.**

ax•il /ˈaksəl/ ▸ **n.** Bot. the upper angle between a leaf stalk or branch and the stem or trunk from which it is growing. [18th C.: from L. *axilla* (see AXILLA).]

axil

ax•il•la /akˈsilə/ ▸ **n.** (pl. **ax•il•lae** /akˈsilē/) Anat. the space below the shoulder through which vessels and nerves enter and leave the upper arm; armpit. ■ Bot. an axil. [17th C.: from L., dimin. of *ala* 'wing.']

ax•il•lar•y /ˈaksə,lerē/ ▸ **adj.** Anat. of or relating to the armpit: *enlargement of the axillary lymph nodes.* ■ Bot. in or growing from an axil: *axillary shoots.* Often contrasted with TERMINAL.

ax•il•lar•y bud ▸ **n.** a bud that grows from the axil of a leaf and may develop into a branch or flower cluster.

ax•i•om /ˈaksēəm/ ▸ **n.** a statement or proposition that is regarded as being established, accepted, or self-evidently true: *the axiom that supply equals demand.* ■ esp. Math. a statement or proposition on which an abstractly defined structure is based. [15th C.: ult. from Gk. *axiōma* 'what is thought fitting,' from *axios* 'worthy.']

ax•i•o•mat•ic /,aksēəˈmatik/ ▸ **adj.** self-evident or unquestionable. ■ [attrib.] esp. Math. relating to or containing axioms. — **ax•i•o•mat•i•cal•ly** /-ik(ə)lē/ **adv.**

ax•i•on /ˈaksē,än/ ▸ **n.** Physics a hypothetical subatomic particle postulated to account for the rarity of processes that break charge-parity symmetry. It is very light, electrically neutral, and pseudoscalar. [1970s: from AXIAL.]

ax•is /ˈaksis/ ▸ **n.** (pl. **ax•es** /ˈaksēz/) **1** an imaginary line about which a body rotates: *the earth revolves on its axis once every 24 hours.* ■ Geom. an imaginary straight line passing through the center of a symmetrical solid, and about which a plane figure can be conceived as rotating to generate the solid. ■ an imaginary line that divides something into equal or roughly equal halves. **2** Math. a fixed reference line for the measurement of coordinates. **3** a straight central part in a structure to which other parts are connected. ■ Bot. the central column of an inflorescence or other growth. ■ Zool. the skull and backbone of a vertebrate animal. **4** Anat. the second cervical vertebra. **5** an agreement or alliance between two or more countries that forms a center for an eventual larger grouping of nations: *the Anglo-American axis.* ■ **(the Axis)** the alliance of Germany and Italy formed before and during World War II, later extended to include Japan and other countries. [ME: from L., 'axle.']

ax•is deer (also **ax•is**) ▸ **n.** a deer (*Cervus axis*, family Cervidae) that has lyre-shaped antlers and a yellowish-brown coat with white spots, native to India and Sri Lanka. [17th C.: *axis* from L.]

ax•le /ˈaksəl/ ▸ **n.** a rod or spindle (either fixed or rotating) passing through the center of a wheel or group of wheels: [as adj.] *axle grease | axle loads.* [ME (*axle-tree*): from ON *ǫxultré*.]

Ax•min•ster /ˈaks,minstər/ (also **Axminster carpet**) ▸ **n.** a kind of machine-woven patterned carpet with a cut pile. [19th C.: named after *Axminster*, a town in southern England.]

ax•o•lotl /ˈaksə,lätl/ ▸ **n.** a salamander (*Ambystoma mexicanum*, family Ambystomatidae) of Mexico and the western US, which in natural conditions retains its aquatic newtlike larval form throughout life but is able to breed. [18th C.: from Nahuatl, from *atl* 'water' + *xolotl* 'servant.']

ax•on /ˈaksän/ ▸ **n.** the long threadlike part of a nerve cell along which impulses are conducted from the cell. — **ax•on•al** /ˈaksənl; akˈsänl/ **adj.** [19th C.: from Gk. *axōn* 'axis.']

ax•o•neme /ˈaksə,nēm/ ▸ **n.** Biol. the central strand of a cilium or flagellum. It is composed of an array of microtubules, typically in nine pairs around two single central ones. — **ax•o•ne•mal** /aksəˈnēməl/ **adj.** [20th C.: from Gk. *axōn* 'axis' + *nēma* 'thread.']

ax•o•no•met•ric /,aksənōˈmetrik/ ▸ **adj.** using or designating an orthographic projection of an object, such as a building, on a plane inclined to each of the three principal axes of the object; three-dimensional but without perspective.

ax•o•plasm /ˈaksə,plazəm/ ▸ **n.** Biol. the cytoplasm of a nerve axon. — **ax•o•plas•mic** /,aksəˈplazmik/ **adj.**

Ax•um var. of AKSUM.

ay /ī; ā/ ▸ **exclam. & n.** var. of AYE.

A•ya•cu•cho /,äyəˈkōōCHō/ a city in south central Peru; pop. 101,600.

a•yah /ˈäyə/ ▸ **n.** a native maid or nursemaid employed by Europeans in India. [Anglo-Ind., from Port. *aia* 'nurse,' fem. of *aio* 'tutor.']

a•ya•huas•ca /,äyəˈwäskə/ ▸ **n.** a tropical vine (genus *Banisteriopsis*, family Malpighiaceae) native to the Amazon region, noted for its hallucinogenic properties. ■ a hallucinogenic drink prepared from the bark of this. [1940s: from South Amer. Sp., from Quechua *ayawáskha*, from *aya* 'corpse' + *waskha* 'rope.']

a•ya•tol•lah /,äyəˈtōlə/ ▸ **n.** a Shiite religious leader in Iran. [1950s: from Pers., from Arab. *āyatu-llāh*, lit. 'token of God.']

A•ya•tol•lah Kho•mei•ni see KHOMEINI.

aye[1] /ī/ (also **ay**) ▸ **exclam.** archaic or dialect said to express assent; yes: *aye, you're right.* ■ **(aye, aye)** Naut. a response acknowledging an order: *aye, aye, captain.* ■ (in voting) I assent: *all in favor say, "aye."* ▸ **n.** an affirmative answer or assent, esp. in voting. [16th C.: prob. from I[2].]

aye[2] /ā,/ ▸ **adv.** archaic or Scot. always or still. [ME: from ON *ei, ey*; akin to L. *aevum* 'age,' Gk. *aie(i)* 'ever.']

aye-aye /ˈī ˈī/ ▸ **n.** a rare nocturnal Madagascan primate (*Daubentonia madagascariensis*) allied to the lemurs. The only member of the family Daubentoniidae, it has rodentlike incisor teeth and an elongated twiglike finger on each hand with which it pries insects from bark. [18th C.: from Fr., from Malagasy *aiay*.]

Ayer /e(ə)r/, Sir A. J. (1910–89), English philosopher; full name *Alfred Jules Ayer*. He was a proponent of logical positivism.

Ayers Rock /e(ə)rz/ a red rock mass in Northern Territory, Australia, southwest of Alice Springs, the largest monolith in the world. Aboriginal name ULURU.

A•ye•sha /äˈ(y)ēSHə/ the wife of Muhammad.

Ay•ma•ra /,īmäˈrä/ ▸ **n.** (pl. same or **-ras**) **1** a member of a South American Indian people inhabiting the high plateau region of Bolivia and Peru. **2** the language of this people, related to Quechua. ▸ **adj.** of or relating to this people or their language. [Sp.]

Ayr•shire /ˈersHər; -SHir/ ▸ **n.** an animal of a mainly white breed of dairy cattle. [19th C.: named after *Ayrshire*, a former Scottish county.]

A•yur•ve•da /,äyərˈvādə; -ˈvēdə/ ▸ **n.** the traditional Hindu system of medicine, which uses diet, herbal treatment, and yogic breathing. — **A•yur•ve•dic** /-ˈvedik/ **adj.** [from Sanskrit *āyus* 'life' + *veda* 'science.']

AZ ▸ **abbr.** Arizona (in official postal use).

A•zad Kash•mir /ˈäzäd käsHˈmi(ə)r; kasH-/ an autonomous state in northeastern Pakistan, formerly part of Kashmir; administrative center, Muzzafarabad.

a•zal•ea /əˈzālyə/ ▸ **n.** a deciduous flowering shrub (genus *Rhododendron*) of the heath family with clusters of brightly colored flowers. [18th C.: mod. L., from Gk., fem. of *azaleos* 'dry.']

Azerbaijan

Official name: Republic of Azerbaijan
Location: southwestern Asia, in the Caucasus, on the western shore of the Caspian Sea between Iran and Russia
Area: 33,300 square miles (86,100 sq km)
Population: 7,868,000
Capital: Baku
Languages: Azerbaijani (official), Russian, Armenian
Currency: Azerbaijani manat

a·zan /ä'zän/ ▶ **n.** the Muslim call to ritual prayer. [19th C.: from Arab. *aḏān* 'announcement.']

a·ze·o·trope /ā'zēə,trōp/ ▶ **n.** Chem. a mixture of two liquids that has a constant boiling point and composition throughout distillation. — **a·ze·o·trop·ic** /,āzēə'träpik; -'trōpik/ **adj.** [20th C.: from A-[1] + Gk. *zein* 'to boil' + *tropos* 'turning.']

Az·er·bai·jan /,azərbī'jän; ,äzər-/ a country in southwestern Asia. *See box.*

A·zer·bai·ja·ni /,azərbī'jänē; ,äzər-/ ▶ **adj.** of or relating to Azerbaijan or its people or their language. ▶ **n.** (pl. **-nis**) **1** a native or national of Azerbaijan or a person of Azerbaijani descent. **2** the Turkic language of Azerbaijan.

A·ze·ri /ə'zerē/ ▶ **n.** (pl. **-ris**) **1** a member of a Turkic people living in Azerbaijan, Armenia, and northern Iran. **2** the Azerbaijani language. ▶ **adj.** of, relating to, or denoting this people or their language. [from Turk. *azerî.*]

az·ide /'āzīd; 'azīd/ ▶ **n.** Chem. a compound containing the univalent group $-N_3-$. [20th C.: from AZO- + -IDE.]

a·zi·do·thy·mi·dine /,azidō'THīmə,dēn; ə,zī-; ə,zē-/ ▶ **n.** trademark for the drug ZIDOVUDINE.

az·i·muth /'azəməTH/ ▶ **n.** the direction of a celestial object from the observer, expressed as the angular distance from the north or south point of the horizon to the point at which a vertical circle passing through the object intersects the horizon. ■ the horizontal angle or direction of a compass bearing. — **az·i·muth·al** /,azə'məTHəl/ **adj.** [ME: from OFr. *azimut*, from Arab. *as-samt*, from *al* 'the' + *samt* 'way.']

az·i·muth·al pro·jec·tion /,azə'məTHəl/ ▶ **n.** a map projection in which a region of the earth is projected onto a plane tangential to the surface, typically at a pole or the equator.

az·ine /'azēn; 'āzēn/ ▶ **n.** Chem. a cyclic organic compound having a ring including one or (typically) more nitrogen atoms. [19th C.: from AZO- + -INE[4].]

azo- ▶ **prefix** Chem. containing two adjacent nitrogen atoms between carbon atoms: *azobenzene.* [from obs. *azote* 'nitrogen,' from Fr., from Gk. *azōos* 'without life.']

az·o·ben·zene /,azō'benzēn; -ben'zēn; ,āzō-/ ▶ **n.** Chem. a synthetic crystalline organic compound, $(C_6H_5)N{=}N(C_6H_5)$, used chiefly in dye manufacture.

az·o dye /'azō; 'āzō/ ▶ **n.** Chem. any of a large class of synthetic dyes whose molecules contain two adjacent nitrogen atoms between carbon atoms.

a·zo·ic /ā'zō-ik; ə'zō-/ ▶ **adj.** having no trace of life or organic remains. ■ (**Azoic**) Geol. another term for ARCHEAN. [19th C.: from Gk. *azōos* 'without life.']

a·zon·al /ā'zōnl/ ▶ **adj.** (esp. of soils) having no zonal organization or structure.

a·zo·o·sper·mi·a /,āzōə'spərmēə/ ▶ **n.** Med. absence of motile (and hence viable) sperm in the semen. — **a·zo·o·sper·mic** /-'spərmik/ **adj.**

A·zores /ə'zôrz; 'āzôrz/ a group of volcanic islands in the Atlantic Ocean, west of Portugal, a possession of Portugal but partially autonomous; pop. 241,590; capital, Ponta Delgada.

az·o·tu·ri·a /,azə't(y)o͝orēə/ ▶ **n.** Med. abnormal excess of nitrogen compounds in the urine. [19th C.: from obs. *azote* 'nitrogen.']

A·zov, Sea of /'az,ôf; 'ā,zôf/ an inland sea in southern Russia and Ukraine, separated from the Black Sea by the Crimea and linked to it by a narrow strait.

Az·ra·el /'azrē,el; ,äzrē'el/ Jewish Islamic Mythol. the angel who severs the soul from the body at death.

AZT ▶ **abbr.** trademark azidothymidine.

Az·tec /'aztek/ ▶ **n.** **1** a member of the American Indian people dominant in Mexico before the Spanish conquest of the 16th century. **2** the extinct language of this people, a Uto-Aztecan language from which modern Nahuatl is descended. ▶ **adj.** of, relating to, or denoting this people or their language. [from Fr. *Aztèque* or Sp. *Azteca*, from Nahuatl *aztecatl* 'person of Aztlan,' their legendary place of origin.]

az·ure /'azHər/ ▶ **adj.** bright blue in color, like a cloudless sky. ■ Heraldry blue. ▶ **n.** **1** a bright blue color. ■ literary the clear sky. **2** a small butterfly (*Celastrina* and other genera, family Lycaenidae) typically blue or purplish, with color differences between the sexes. [ME: from OFr. *asur, azur*, based on Arab. *al* 'the' + *lāzaward* (from Pers. *lāž ward* 'lapis lazuli').]

az·ur·ite /'azHə,rīt/ ▶ **n.** a blue mineral consisting of copper hydroxyl carbonate. It occurs as blue prisms or crystal masses, often with malachite. [19th C.: from AZURE.]

Azu·sa /ə'zo͞osə/ a city in southwestern California, northeast of Los Angeles; pop. 44,712.

az·y·gous /ā'zīgəs; 'azə-/ ▶ **adj.** Anat. & Biol. (of an organic structure) single; not existing in pairs. [19th C.: from Gk. *azugos* 'unyoked' (from A-[1] + *zugon* 'yoke.')]

Bb

B¹ /bē/ (also **b**) ▶ **n.** (pl. **Bs** or **B's**) **1** the second letter of the alphabet. ■ the second highest class of academic mark. ■ denoting the second-highest-earning socioeconomic category for marketing purposes, including intermediate management and professional personnel. ■ (usu. **b**) the second constant to appear in an algebraic equation. ■ Geol. denoting a soil horizon of intermediate depth, typically the subsoil. ■ the human blood type (in the ABO system) containing the B antigen and lacking the A. **2** (usu. **B**) Music the seventh note of the diatonic scale of C major. ■ a key based on a scale with B as its keynote.
– PHRASES **plan B** an alternative strategy.

B² ▶ **abbr.** ■ black (used in describing grades of pencil lead): *2HB pencils.* ■ (in personal ads) Black. ■ bomber (in designations of US aircraft types). ■ a dry cell battery size. ▶ **symb.** ■ the chemical element boron. ■ Physics magnetic flux density.

b ▶ **abbr.** ■ Physics barn(s). ■ (**b.**) born (used to indicate a date of birth): *George Lloyd (b. 1913).* ■ billion. ■ bass. ■ basso.

BA ▶ **abbr.** ■ Bachelor of Arts: *David Brown, BA.* ■ Baseball batting average. ■ Buenos Aires.

Ba ▶ **symb.** the chemical element barium.

baa /bä/ ▶ **v.** (**baas, baaed, baaing**) [intrans.] (of a sheep or lamb) bleat. ▶ **n.** the cry of a sheep or lamb. [16th C.: imitative.]

Ba·al /'bā(ə)l/ (also **Bel** /bel/) (pl. **Ba·a·lim** /'bāə,lim/ or **Ba·als**) a male fertility god whose cult was widespread in ancient Phoenician and Canaanite lands. [from Heb. *ba al* 'lord.']

Baal·bek /'bäl,bek; 'bāəl-/ a town in eastern Lebanon, site of the ancient city of Heliopolis.

Ba·ath Par·ty /bäTH; 'bä-äTH/ (also **Ba'ath**) a pan-Arab socialist party founded in Syria in 1943. Different factions of the Baath Party hold power in Syria and formerly held power in Iraq. — **Ba·ath·ism n. Ba·ath·ist adj. & n.** [*Baath*, from Arab. *ba ṯ* 'resurrection, renaissance.']

ba·ba¹ /'bä,bä/ (also **ba·ba au rhum** /ō 'rəm/) ▶ **n.** a small rich sponge cake, typically soaked in rum-flavored syrup. [19th C.: via Fr. from Pol., lit. 'married peasant woman.']

ba·ba² ▶ **n.** Indian, informal father (often as a proper name or as a familiar form of address). ■ a respectful form of address for an older man. ■ (often **Baba**) a holy man (often as a proper name or form of address). [from Hindi *bābā*.]

ba·ba gha·nouj /,bäbə gə'nōōZH/ (also **ba·ba ga·noush** /gə'nōōSH/) ▶ **n.** a thick sauce or spread made from ground eggplant and sesame seeds, olive oil, lemon, and garlic, typical of eastern Mediterranean cuisine. [from Egyptian Arabic, from Arab. *bābā*, lit. 'father' + *gannuug*, perh. a name.]

ba·bas·su /,bäbə'sōō/ (also **ba·ba·çú**) ▶ **n.** a Brazilian palm (genus *Orbignya*) that yields an edible oil sometimes used in cosmetics. [1920s: from Brazilian Port. *babaçú*, from Tupi *ybá* 'fruit' + *guasu* 'large.']

Bab·bage /'babij/, Charles (1791–1871), English mathematician and inventor. He designed a mechanical computer with Ada Lovelace (1815–52) that would perform calculations and print the results.

Bab·bitt¹ /'babit/, Milton Byron (1916–), US composer. His compositions developed from the twelve-note system of Arnold Schoenberg and Anton von Webern.

Bab·bitt² ▶ **n.** dated a materialistic, complacent, and conformist businessman. — **Bab·bitt·ry n.** [1922: George *Babbitt*, protagonist of the novel *Babbitt* by Sinclair Lewis.]

bab·ble /'babəl/ ▶ **v.** [intrans.] talk rapidly and continuously in a foolish, excited, or incomprehensible way: *he would* **babble on** *in Spanish.* ■ [reporting verb] utter something rapidly and incoherently: [with direct speech] *I gasped and babbled, "Look at this!"* | [trans.] *he began to babble an apology.* ■ reveal something secret or confidential by talking impulsively or carelessly: *he babbled to another convict* | [trans.] *my father* **babbled out** *the truth.* ■ [usu. as adj.] (**babbling**) (of a stream) make the continuous murmuring sound of water flowing over stones: *a babbling brook.* ▶ **n.** [in sing.] the sound of people talking quickly and in a way that is difficult or impossible to understand. ■ foolish, excited, or confused talk. ■ [usu. in comb. or with adj.] pretentious jargon from a specified field. ■ the continuous murmuring sound of water flowing over stones in a stream. ■ background disturbance caused by interference from conversations on other telephone lines. — **bab·bler n.** [ME: from Mid. Low Ger. *babbelen*, prob. of imitative origin.]

babe /bāb/ ▶ **n. 1** esp. literary a baby. ■ fig. an innocent or helpless person. **2** informal an affectionate form of address. ■ a form of address for a young woman or girl (often considered sexist). ■ a sexually attractive young woman or girl. [ME: prob. imitative of a child's speech.]

ba·bel /'babəl; 'bā-/ ▶ **n.** [in sing.] a confused noise, typically that made by a number of voices. ■ a scene of noisy confusion. [16th C.: *Babel* (see TOWER OF BABEL).]

Ba·bel, Tower of see TOWER OF BABEL.

ba·be·li·cious /,bābə'lisHəs; ,bab-/ ▶ **adj.** informal (esp. of a woman) sexually very attractive. [1992: coined in the film *Wayne's World*.]

ba·be·si·o·sis /bə,bēzē'ōsis/ (also **ba·be·si·a·sis** /,babi'zīəsis; -'sī-/) ▶ **n.** a disease of cattle and other livestock caused by protozoans of the genus *Babesia*, transmitted by the bite of ticks. Also called PIROPLASMOSIS. [20th C.: from mod. L. *Babesia*, Victor *Babès* (1854–1926), Romanian bacteriologist.]

Ba·bi /'bäbē/ ▶ **n.** an adherent of Babism.

ba·biche /bə'bēsH/ ▶ **n.** rawhide, typically formed into strips, as used by North American Indians for making fastenings, animal snares, snowshoes, etc. [19th C.: from Canad. Fr., from Micmac *a:papi:č*.]

babirusa

bab·i·ru·sa /,bäbə'rōōsə; ,bab-/ ▶ **n.** a forest-dwelling wild pig (*Babyrousa babyrussa*) with several upturned hornlike tusks, native to Malaysia. [17th C.: from Malay, from *babi* 'hog' + *rusa* 'deer.']

Bab·ism /'bäbizəm/ ▶ **n.** a religion founded in 1844 by the Persian Mirza Ali Muhammad of Shiraz (1819–50) (popularly known as "the Bab"), who taught that a new prophet would follow Muhammad. See also BAHA'I. [19th C.: via Pers. from Arab. *bāb* 'intermediary,' lit. 'gate.']

ba·boon /ba'bōōn/ ▶ **n.** a large Old World ground-dwelling monkey (*Papio, Mandrillus*, and other genera, family Cercopithecidae) with a long doglike snout and large teeth. Species include the drill and mandrill. ■ an ugly or uncouth person. [ME: from Old Fr. *babuin* or med. L. *babewynus*, perh. from OFr. *baboue* 'grimace.']

Ba·bo·qui·vi·ri Moun·tains /,bäbōkə'vi(ə)rē/ a range in southern Arizona that rises to 7,734 feet (2,357 m) at Baboquiviri Peak.

ba·bouche /bə'bōōsH/ ▶ **n.** a heelless slipper. [17th C.: from Fr., from Arab. *bābūj*, Pers. *pāpūš*, lit. 'foot covering.']

Ba·bruisk /bä'brōō-isk/ (also **Ba·bruysk, Bo·bruisk,** or **Bo·bruysk**) a river port in central Belarus, on the Berezina River; pop. 222,900.

ba·bu /'bäbōō/ ▶ **n.** (pl. **ba·bus**) Indian a respectful title or form of address for a man, esp. an educated one. ■ an office worker; a clerk. [from Hindi *bābū*, lit. 'father.']

ba·bul /bə'bōōl/ ▶ **n.** a tropical acacia of the pea family (*Acacia nilotica*) introduced from Africa, used as a source of fuel, gum arabic, and (formerly) tannin. [19th C.: from Hindi *babūl*.]

ba·bush·ka /bə'bōōSHkə/ ▶ **n.** (in Poland and Russia) an old woman or grandmother. ■ a headscarf tied under the chin. [20th C.: Pol., Russ., 'grandmother.']

Ba·bu·yan Is·lands /,bäbōō'yän/ a group of 24 volcanic islands lying to the north of the island of Luzon in the northern Philippines.

ba·by /'bābē/ ▶ **n.** (pl. **-bies**) **1** a very young child, esp. one newly or recently born. ■ a young or newly born animal. ■ the youngest member of a family or group. ■ a timid or childish person. ■ (**one's baby**) fig. one's particular responsibility, achievement, or concern: *"This is your baby," she said, handing him the brief.* **2** informal a young woman or a person with whom one is having a romantic relationship (often as a form of address). ■ a thing regarded with affection or familiarity. ▶ **adj.** [attrib.] comparatively small or immature of its kind: *a baby grand piano.* ■ (of vegetables) picked before reaching their usual size: *baby carrots.* ▶ **v.** (**-bies, -bied**) [trans.] treat (someone) as a baby; pamper or be overprotective toward: *her aunt babied her.*
– PHRASES **throw the baby out with the bathwater** discard something valuable along with other things that are inessential or undesirable. — **ba·by·hood n.** [ME: prob. imitative of a child's speech.]

ba·by blue ▶ **n.** a pale shade of blue. ■ (**baby blues**) informal blue eyes. ■ (**baby blues**) depression affecting a woman after giving birth; postnatal depression.

ba·by-blue-eyes ▶ **n.** a plant of western North America (genus *Nemophila*, family Hydrophyllaceae) with blue bowl-shaped flowers. Species include *N. menziesii* of California and southern Oregon.

ba·by boom ▶ **n.** informal a temporary marked increase in the birth rate, esp. the one following World War II. — **ba·by boom·er n.**

ba·by bug·gy ▶ **n.** a baby carriage.

ba·by bust ▶ **n.** informal a decrease in the birth rate. — **ba·by bust·er n.**

ba·by car·riage ▶ **n.** a four-wheeled carriage for a baby, typically with a retractable hood, pushed by a person on foot.

ba·by doll ▶ **n.** a doll designed to look like a baby. ■ a girl or woman with pretty, ingenuous, childlike looks. ▶ **adj.** [attrib.] denoting a style of women's clothing resembling that traditionally worn by a doll or young child, esp. short, high-waisted, short-sleeved dresses.

ba·by face ▶ **n.** a smooth round face like a baby's.

ba·by-faced ▶ **adj.** having a youthful or innocent face.

ba·by grand ▶ **n.** the smallest size of grand piano, about 4.5 feet (1.5 m) long.

ba·by·ish /ˈbābē-isʜ/ ▶ **adj.** derog. (of appearance or behavior) characteristic of a baby. ■ (of clothes or toys) suitable for a baby. — **ba·by·ish·ly adv. ba·by·ish·ness n.**

Bab·y·lon¹ /ˈbabəˌlän; -ˌlən/ **1** an ancient city in Mesopotamia, the capital of Babylonia in the 2nd millennium BC. The city was on the banks of the Euphrates River and was noted for its luxury, its fortifications, and, particularly, for the Hanging Gardens of Babylon. **2** a town on the southern shore of Long Island in New York that includes the villages of Babylon and Amityville; pop. 202,889.

Bab·y·lon² ▶ **n.** black English (chiefly among Rastafarians) a contemptuous or dismissive term for aspects of a society seen as degenerate or oppressive, esp. the police. [1940s: BABYLON¹.]

Bab·y·lo·ni·a /ˌbabəˈlōnēə/ an ancient region of Mesopotamia, formed when the kingdoms of Akkad in the north and Sumer in the south combined in the first half of the 2nd millennium BC.

Bab·y·lo·ni·an /ˌbabəˈlōnēən/ ▶ **n. 1** an inhabitant of Babylon or Babylonia. **2** the dialect of Akkadian spoken in ancient Babylon. ▶ **adj.** of or relating to Babylon or Babylonia.

Bab·y·lo·ni·an Cap·tiv·i·ty the captivity of the Israelites in Babylon, lasting from their deportation by Nebuchadnezzar in 586 BC until their release by Cyrus the Great in 539 BC.

ba·by oil ▶ **n.** a mineral oil used to soften the skin.

ba·by's breath ▶ **n.** a herbaceous plant (*Gypsophila paniculata*) of the pink family, with a delicate appearance. It bears tiny scented pink or white flowers.

ba·by·sit /ˈbābēˌsit/ ▶ **v.** (**-sit·ting;** past and past part. **-sat**) [intrans.] look after a child or children while the parents are out: *I babysit for my neighbor sometimes* | [trans.] *she was babysitting Sophie* | [as n.] (**babysitting**) *part-time jobs such as babysitting.* — **ba·by·sit·ter n.**

ba·by tooth ▶ **n.** another term for MILK TOOTH.

ba·ca·lao /ˌbäkəˈlou/ ▶ **n.** codfish, often dried or salted. [Sp.]

bac·ca·la /ˌbakəˈlä; ˈbakəˌlä/ ▶ **n.** Italian term for BACALAO.

bac·ca·lau·re·ate /ˌbakəˈlôrēit/ ▶ **n. 1** a college bachelor's degree. **2** an examination intended to qualify successful candidates for higher education. **3** a religious service held at some educational institutions before commencement, containing a farewell sermon to the graduating class. [17th C. (sense 1): from Fr. *baccalauréat* or med. L. *baccalaureatus*, from *baccalaureus* 'bachelor.']

bac·ca·rat /ˈbäkəˌrä; ˌbakəˈrä/ ▶ **n.** a gambling card game in which players hold two- or three-card hands, the winning hand being that giving the highest remainder when its face value is divided by ten. [19th C.: from Fr. *baccara*.]

bac·cate /ˈbakāt/ ▶ **adj.** bearing berries; berried. ■ of the nature of a berry; berrylike.

Bac·chae /ˈbakē; ˈbäkē/ the priestesses of Bacchus.

bac·cha·nal /ˌbäkəˈnäl; ˌbak-; ˈbakənl/ esp. literary ▶ **n. 1** an occasion of wild and drunken revelry. ■ a drunken reveler. **2** a priest, worshiper, or follower of Bacchus. ▶ **adj.** another term for BACCHANALIAN. [16th C.: from L. *bacchanalis*, after BACCHUS.]

Bac·cha·na·li·a /ˌbakəˈnālyə; ˌbäk-/ ▶ **plural n.** [also treated as sing.] the Roman festival of Bacchus. ■ (**bacchanalia**) drunken revelry.

bac·cha·na·li·an /ˌbäkəˈnālyən; -ˈnālēən; ˌbakə-/ ▶ **adj.** characterized by or given to drunken revelry; riotously drunken.

bac·chant /bəˈkänt; -ˈkant/ ▶ **n.** (pl. **-chants** or **-chan·tes** /-ˈkäntēz/; fem. **-chan·te** /-tē/) a priest, priestess, or follower of Bacchus. [16th C.: from Fr. *bacchante*, from L. *bacchari* 'celebrate the feast of Bacchus.']

Bac·chus /ˈbäkəs; ˈbak-/ Gk. Mythol. another name for DIONYSUS. — **Bac·chic** /ˈbakik/ **adj.** [L., from Gk. *Bakkhos*.]

Bach /bäkʜ; bäk/, Johann Sebastian (1685–1750), German composer. His large-scale choral works include *The Passion According to St. John* (1723), and the *Mass in B minor* (1733–38).

bach·e·lor /ˈbacʜ(ə)lər/ ▶ **n. 1** a man who is not and has never been married. ■ Zool. a male bird or mammal without a mate, esp. one prevented from breeding by a dominant male. **2** a person who holds an undergraduate degree from a university or college (only in titles or set expressions). — **bach·e·lor·hood n.** [ME: from OFr. *bacheler*.]

bach·e·lor a·part·ment ▶ **n.** an apartment occupied by a bachelor. ■ an apartment consisting of a single large room serving as bedroom and living room, with a separate bathroom.

bach·e·lor·ette /ˌbacʜ(ə)ləˈret/ ▶ **n. 1** a young unmarried woman. **2** a small bachelor apartment.

bach·e·lor·ette par·ty ▶ **n.** a party given for a woman who is about to get married.

bach·e·lor girl ▶ **n.** an independent, unmarried young woman.

bach·e·lor par·ty ▶ **n.** a party given for a man who is about to get married.

bach·e·lor's but·tons ▶ **plural n.** [treated as sing. or pl.] any of a number of ornamental plants that bear small, buttonlike, double flowers, in particular the vivid blue cornflower *Centaurea cyanus*.

Bach·man /ˈbäkmən/, Richard see KING⁴.

ba·cil·li·form /bəˈsiləˌfôrm/ ▶ **adj.** esp. Biol. rod-shaped.

ba·cil·lus /bəˈsiləs/ ▶ **n.** (pl. **-cil·li** /-ˈsilī/) a disease-causing bacterium. ■ a rod-shaped bacterium. — **bac·il·lar·y** /ˈbasəˌlerē/ **adj.** [19th C.: from late L., dimin. of L. *baculus* 'stick.']

bac·i·tra·cin /ˌbasiˈtrāsin/ ▶ **n.** an antibiotic obtained from the bacterium *Bacillus subtilis*, used topically for skin and eye infections.

back /bak/ ▶ **n. 1** the rear surface of the human body from the shoulders to the hips. ■ the corresponding upper surface of an animal's body. ■ the spine of a person or animal. ■ the part of a chair against which the sitter's back rests. ■ the part of a garment that covers a person's back. ■ a person's torso or body regarded in terms of wearing clothes. ■ a person's back regarded as carrying a load or bearing an imposition: *they wanted the government **off their backs**.* **2** the side or part of something that is away from the spectator or from the direction in which it moves or faces; the rear. ■ [in sing.] the position directly behind someone or something. ■ the side or part of an object opposed to the one that is normally seen or used; the less active, visible, or important part of something. ■ the part of a book where the pages are held together by a binding. **3** a player in a field game whose initial position is behind the front line. ■ the position taken by such a player. ▶ **adv. 1** toward the rear; in the opposite direction from the one that one is facing or traveling: *she moved back a pace.* ■ expressing movement of the body into a reclining position: *sit back and relax.* ■ at a distance away: *the officer pushed the crowd back.* ■ (**back of**) behind: *other people were back of him.* **2** expressing a return to an earlier or normal condition: *I went back to sleep.* ■ fashionable again: *sideburns are back.* **3** in or into the past: *he made his fortune back in 1955.* ■ at a place previously left or mentioned: *the folks back home are counting on him.* **4** in return: *they wrote back to me.* ▶ **v. 1** [trans.] give financial, material, or moral support to: *go up there and tell them—I'll back you up.* ■ bet money on (a person or animal) winning a race or contest: *he backed the horse at 33–1.* ■ be in favor of: *over 97 percent backed the changes.* ■ supplement in order to reinforce or strengthen: *US troops were **backed up** by forces from European countries.* **2** [trans.] (often **be backed**) cover the back of (an object) in order to support, protect, or decorate it: *a mirror backed with tortoiseshell.* ■ (esp. in popular music) provide musical accompaniment to (a singer or musician): *brisk guitar work backed by drums.* **3** [no obj., with adverbial of direction] walk or drive backward: *she tried to back away* | fig. *the administration **backed away from** the plan* | [trans.] *he backed the Mercedes into the yard.* ■ [intrans.] (of the wind) change direction counterclockwise around the points of the compass: *the wind had backed to the northwest.* The opposite of VEER¹. **4** [intrans.] (of a property) have its back adjacent to (a piece of land or body of water): *a row of cottages **backed on** the water.* ■ [trans.] (usu. **be backed**) lie behind or at the back of: *the promenade is backed by lots of cafes.* ▶ **adj.** [attrib.] **1** of or at the back of something: *the back pocket of his jeans.* ■ situated in a remote or subsidiary position: *back roads.* **2** (esp. of wages or something published or released) from or relating to the past: *she was owed back pay.* **3** directed toward the rear or in a reversed course: *back currents.* **4** Phonet. (of a sound) articulated at the back of the mouth.

– PHRASES **at someone's back** in pursuit or support of someone. **back and forth** to and fro. **someone's back is turned** someone's attention is elsewhere. **the back of beyond** a remote or inaccessible place. **the back of one's mind** used to express that something is in one's mind but is not consciously thought of or remembered. **back water** reverse the action of the oars while rowing, causing a boat to slow down or stop. **back the wrong horse** make a wrong or inappropriate choice. **behind someone's back** without a person's knowledge and in an unfair or dishonorable way. **get** (or **put**) **someone's back up** make someone annoyed or angry. **in back** at the back of something, esp. a building. **know something like the back of one's hand** be entirely familiar with a place or route. **on one's back** in bed recovering from an injury or illness. ■ full-length on the ground. **put one's back into** approach (a task) with vigor. **turn one's back on** ignore (someone) by turning away. ■ reject or abandon. **with one's back to** (or **up against**) **the wall** in a desperate situation; hard-pressed.

– PHRASAL VERBS **back down** withdraw a claim or assertion in the face of opposition. **back off** draw back from action or confrontation. ■ another way of saying *BACK DOWN*. **back out** withdraw from a commitment. **back up 1** (of vehicles) form a line due to congestion. **2** (of running water) accumulate behind an obstruction. **3** Comput. (of data) copy onto another file or medium. [OE *bæc*, from Gmc.; akin to ON *bak*.]

back·ache /ˈbakˌāk/ ▶ **n.** a prolonged pain in one's back.

back al·ley ▶ **n.** a narrow passage behind or between buildings. ▶ **adj.** [attrib.] secret or illegal, as might be found in a back alley: *a back-alley drug deal.*

back·bar /ˈbakˌbär/ ▶ **n.** a structure behind a bar counter, with shelves for holding bottles and supplies.

Back Bay a historic residential and commercial district in western Boston, Massachusetts, along the Charles River.

back·beat /ˈbak,bēt/ ▶**n.** Music a strong accent on one of the normally unaccented beats of the bar, used esp. in jazz and popular music.

back·bit·ing /ˈbak,bītiNG/ ▶**n.** malicious talk about someone who is not present. — **back·bite v. back·bit·er n.**

back·board /ˈbak,bôrd/ ▶**n.** a board placed at or forming the back of something, such as a collage or piece of electronic equipment. ■ Basketball an upright board behind the basket, off which the ball may rebound. ■ a board used to support a person's back, esp. after an accident.

back·bone /ˈbak,bōn/ ▶**n.** the series of vertebrae extending from the skull to the pelvis; the spine. ■ fig. the chief support of a system or organization; the mainstay. ■ fig. strength of character; firmness. ■ the spine of a book. ■ Biochem. the main chain of a polymeric molecule.

back·break·ing (also **back·break·ing**) ▶**adj.** [attrib.] (esp. of manual labor) physically demanding.

back burn·er ▶**n.** a state of inaction or suspension; a position of relatively little importance. ▶**v.** [trans.] (usu. **be back-burnered**) postpone consideration of or action on: *a test of the new ale has been back-burnered.*

back·cast /ˈbak,kast/ Fishing ▶**n.** a backward swing of a fishing line preparatory to casting. ▶**v.** (past and past part. **-cast**) [intrans.] make such a backward swing.

back·chan·nel /ˈbak,CHanl/ (also **back chan·nel**) ▶**n.** **1** a secondary or covert route for the passage of information. **2** Psychol. a sound or gesture made to give continuity to a conversation by a person who is listening to another.

back·chat /ˈbak,CHat/ ▶**n.** another term for **BACK TALK**.

back·coun·try /ˈbak,kəntrē/ ▶**n.** (**the backcountry**) sparsely inhabited rural areas; wilderness.

back·court /ˈbak,kôrt/ ▶**n.** (in tennis, basketball, and similar games) the part of each side of the court nearest the back wall or back boundary line. ■ the defensive players in a basketball team.

back·cross /ˈbak,krôs/ Genet. ▶**v.** [trans.] cross (a hybrid) with one of its parents or an organism with the same genetic characteristics as one of the parents: [as adj.] (**backcrossed**) *the backcrossed dogs were indistinguishable from purebred Dalmatians* | [intrans.] *they backcrossed with red-flowered parents.* ▶**n.** an instance of backcrossing. ■ the product of such a cross.

back·date /ˈbak,dāt/ ▶**v.** [trans.] put an earlier date to (a document or agreement) than the actual one.

back door ▶**n.** the door or entrance at the back of a building. ▶**adj.** (also **back·door**) [attrib.] (of an activity) clandestine; underhanded: *backdoor private deals.*

back·down /ˈbak,doun/ ▶**n.** an act of backing down.

back·draft /ˈbak,draft/ (Brit. **back·draught**) ▶**n.** **1** a current of air or water that flows backward down a chimney, pipe, etc. **2** a phenomenon in which a fire that has consumed all available oxygen suddenly explodes when more oxygen is made available. — **back·draft·ing n.**

back·drop /ˈbak,dräp/ ▶**n.** a painted cloth hung at the back of a theater stage as part of the scenery. ■ fig. the setting or background for a scene, event, or situation.

back end ▶**n.** the end of something that is farthest from the front or the working end. ▶**adj.** [attrib.] **1** relating to the end or outcome of a project, process, or investment: *many annuities have back-end surrender charges.* **2** Comput. denoting a subordinate processor or program, not directly accessed by the user, which performs a specialized function on behalf of a main processor or software system: *a back-end database server.*

back·er /ˈbakər/ ▶**n.** a person, institution, or country that supports something, esp. financially. ■ a person who bets on a horse.

back-fanged ▶**adj.** Zool. (of a snake such as a boomslang) having the rear one or two pairs of teeth modified as fangs, with grooves to conduct the venom. Compare with **FRONT-FANGED**.

back·field /ˈbak,fēld/ ▶**n.** Football the area of play behind either the offensive or defensive line. ■ the players positioned in this area.

back·fill /ˈbak,fil/ ▶**v.** [trans.] refill (an excavated hole) with the material dug out of it: *they backfill the hole.* ▶**n.** material used for backfilling.

back·fire ▶**v.** /ˈbak,fī(ə)r/ [intrans.] **1** (of an engine) undergo a mistimed explosion in the cylinder or exhaust. **2** (of a plan or action) rebound adversely on the originator; have the opposite effect to what was intended. ▶**n.** **1** a mistimed explosion in the cylinder or exhaust of a vehicle or engine. **2** a fire set intentionally to arrest the progress of an approaching fire by creating a burned area in its path.

back·flip /ˈbak,flip/ ▶**n.** a backward somersault done in the air with the arms and legs stretched out straight.

back-for·ma·tion ▶**n.** a word that is formed from an already existing word from which it appears to be a derivative, often by removal of a suffix (e.g., *laze* from *lazy* and *edit* from *editor*). ■ the process by which such words are formed.

back·gam·mon /ˈbak,gamən/ ▶**n.** a board game in which two players move their pieces around twenty-four triangular points according to the throw of dice, the winner being the first to remove all their pieces from the board. ■ the most complete form of win in this game. [17th C.: from **BACK** + **GAMMON**[2].]

back·ground /ˈbak,ground/ ▶**n.** **1** [in sing.] the area or scenery behind the main object of contemplation, esp. when perceived as a framework for it. ■ the part of a picture or design that serves as a setting to the main figures or objects, or that appears furthest from the viewer. ■ a position or function that is not prominent or conspicuous: *after that evening, Athens remained in the background.* **2** the general scene, surroundings, or circumstances. ■ the circumstances, facts, or events that influence, cause, or explain something: *the political and economic background* | [as adj.] *background information.* ■ a person's education, experience, and social circumstances. **3** a persistent level of some phenomenon or process, against which particular events or measurements are distinguished, in particular: ■ Physics low-intensity radiation from radioisotopes present in the natural environment. ■ unwanted signals, such as noise in the reception or recording of sound. **4** Comput. used to describe tasks or processes running on a computer that do not need input from the user. ▶**v.** [trans.] **1** form a background to. **2** put in the background; make inconspicuous: *such practices have been conveniently backgrounded in mainstream narratives.* **3** provide (someone) with background information.

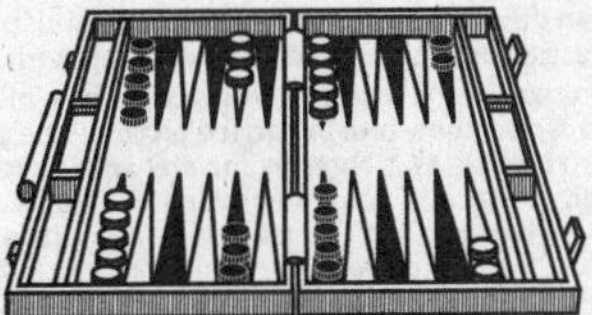
backgammon board and pieces

back·ground·er /ˈbak,groundər/ ▶**n.** an official briefing or handout giving background information.

back·ground mu·sic ▶**n.** music intended as an unobtrusive accompaniment to some activity or to provide atmosphere in a movie.

back·ground ra·di·a·tion ▶**n.** Astron. the uniform microwave radiation remaining from the big bang. See also **BIG BANG**.

back·hand /ˈbak,hand/ ▶**n.** **1** (in tennis and other racket sports) a stroke played with the back of the hand facing in the direction of the stroke, typically starting with the arm crossing the body. ■ a blow or stroke of any kind made in this way, or in a direction opposite to the usual. **2** handwriting that slopes to the left. ▶**v.** [trans.] strike with a backhanded blow or stroke: *in a flash, he backhanded Ace across the jaw.*

back·hand·ed /ˈbak,handid/ ▶**adj.** made with the back of the hand facing in the direction of movement. ■ fig. indirect; ambiguous or insincere: *coming from me, teasing is a backhanded compliment.* ▶**adv.** with the back of the hand or with the hand turned backward: *Frank hit him backhanded.*

back·hand·er /ˈbak,handər/ ▶**n.** a backhand stroke or shot in a game. ■ a blow made with the back of the hand.

back·hoe /ˈbak,hō/ (Brit. also **backhoe loader**) ▶**n.** a mechanical excavator that draws toward itself a bucket attached to a hinged boom.

backhoe

back·ing /ˈbakiNG/ ▶**n.** **1** support or help. ■ a layer of material that forms, protects, or strengthens the back of something. ■ (esp. in popular music) the music or singing that accompanies the main singer or soloist. **2** Phonet. the movement of the place of formation of a sound toward the back of the mouth.

back·ing track ▶**n.** a recorded musical accompaniment, esp. for a soloist to play or sing along with.

back is·sue ▶**n.** a past issue of a journal or magazine.

back·land /ˈbak,land/ ▶**n.** **1** (also **back·lands**) another term for **BACKCOUNTRY**. **2** land behind or beyond an area that is built on or otherwise developed.

back·lash /ˈbak,laSH/ ▶**n.** **1** [in sing.] a strong and adverse reaction by a large number of people, esp. to a social or political development. **2** recoil arising between parts of a mechanism. ■ degree of play between parts of a mechanism.

back·less /ˈbaklis/ ▶**adj.** (of a woman's garment) cut low at the back.

back·light /ˈbak,līt/ ▶**n.** illumination from behind. — **back·light·ing n.**

back·list /ˈbak,list/ ▶**n.** a publisher's list of older books still in print.

back·lit /ˈbak,lit/ ▶**adj.** (esp. in photography or of a graphic display) illuminated from behind.

back·load /ˈbak,lōd/ ▶**v.** [trans.] (usu. **be backloaded**) place more charges at the later stages of (a financial agreement) than at the earlier stages.

back·log /ˈbak,lôg; -,läg/ ▶**n.** an accumulation of something, esp. uncompleted work or matters that need to be dealt with. ■ a reserve; reserves.

back·lot /ˈbak,lät/ ▶**n.** an outdoor area in a movie studio where large exterior sets are made and some outside scenes are filmed.

back num·ber ▶**n.** an issue of a periodical earlier than the current one. ■ informal a person or thing seen as old-fashioned.

back off·ice an office or center in which the administrative work of a business is carried out, as opposed to its dealings with customers.

back·pack /ˈbak,pak/ ▶ n. a bag, often supported by a metal frame, with shoulder straps that allow it to be carried on someone's back. ■ a knapsack used by students as a bookbag, or any small bag carried on the back. ■ a load or piece of equipment carried on a person's back. ▶ v. [intrans.] [usu. as n.] (**backpacking**) travel or hike carrying one's belongings in a backpack: *a week's backpacking in the Pyrenees.* — **back·pack·er** n.

back·ped·al /ˈbak,pedl/ ▶ v. (**-ped·aled, -ped·al·ing** ; Brit. **-ped·alled, -ped·al·ling**) [intrans.] move the pedals of a bicycle backward in order to brake. ■ move hastily backward: *backpedaling furiously, he flipped a perfect pass.* ■ reverse one's previous action or opinion.

back·plane /ˈbak,plān/ ▶ n. a board to which the main circuit boards of a computer may be connected and that provides connections between them.

back·plate /ˈbak,plāt/ ▶ n. a plate placed at or forming the back of something.

back·rest /ˈbak,rest/ ▶ n. a support for a person's back when the person is seated.

back room ▶ n. a place where secret, administrative, or supporting work is done.

back·saw /ˈbak,sô/ ▶ n. a type of saw with a reinforced back edge that keeps the thin blade from being distorted.

back·scat·ter /ˈbak,skatər/ ▶ n. Physics deflection of radiation or particles through an angle of 180°. ■ radiation or particles that have been deflected in this way. ■ Photog. light from a flashgun or other light source that is deflected directly into a lens. ▶ v. [trans.] Physics deflect (radiation or particles) through an angle of 180°: [as adj.] (**backscattered**) *backscattered sound.*

back·scratch·er /ˈbak,skracHər/ ▶ n. a rod terminating in a clawed hand for scratching one's own back.

back·scratch·ing /ˈbak,skracHiNG/ ▶ n. the mutual providing of favors or services, esp. when the legitimacy of such dealings is doubtful.

back seat (also **back·seat**) ▶ n. a seat at the back of a vehicle.
– PHRASES **take a back seat** take or be given a less important position or role.

back·seat driv·er /ˈbakˈsēt/ ▶ n. a passenger in a car who gives the driver unwanted advice. — **back·seat driv·ing** n.

back·shift /ˈbak,sHift/ ▶ n. Gram. the changing of a present tense in direct speech to a past tense in reported speech (or a past tense to pluperfect).

back·side /ˈbak,sīd/ ▶ n. informal a person's buttocks. ■ the rear side or view of a thing.

back·slap·ping /ˈbak,slapiNG/ ▶ n. the action of effusively congratulating or encouraging someone, typically by slapping a person's back. ▶ adj. vigorously hearty. — **back·slap** v. & n. **back·slap·per** n.

back·slash /ˈbak,slasH/ ▶ n. a backward-sloping diagonal line (\), used to separate file and folder names in a path statement.

back·slide /ˈbak,slīd/ ▶ v. (past **-slid**; past part. **-slid** or **-slid·den** /-,slidn/) [intrans.] relapse into bad ways or error: *vegetarians backslide to T-bones* | [as n.] (**backsliding**) *there would be no backsliding.* — **back·slid·er** n.

back·space /ˈbak,spās/ ▶ n. **1** a key on a typewriter or computer keyboard that causes the carriage or cursor to move backward. **2** a device on a video recorder or camcorder that produces a slight backward run between shots to eliminate disturbance caused by the interruption of the scanning process. ▶ v. [intrans.] move a typewriter carriage or computer cursor back one or more spaces.

back·spin /ˈbak,spin/ ▶ n. a backward spin given to a moving ball, causing it to stop more quickly or rebound at a steeper angle on hitting a surface.

back·splash /ˈbak,splasH/ ▶ n. a panel behind a sink or stove that protects the wall from splashes.

back·stab·bing /ˈbak,stabiNG/ ▶ n. the action or practice of criticizing someone in a treacherous manner while feigning friendship. ▶ adj. (of a person) behaving in such a way. — **back·stab** v. **back·stab·ber** n.

back·stage /ˈbakˈstāj/ ▶ n. the area in a theater out of view of the audience. ▶ adj. of, relating to, or situated in the area behind the stage in a theater. ■ fig. secret: *backstage deals.* ▶ adv. in or to the backstage area in a theater: *I went backstage after the show.* ■ fig. not known to the public; in secret.

back·stairs /ˈbakˈste(ə)rz/ ▶ plural n. stairs at the back or side of a building. ▶ adj. [attrib.] underhanded or clandestine: *I won't make backstairs deals with politicians.*

back·stay /ˈbak,stā/ ▶ n. a stay on a sailing ship leading downward and aft from the upper part of a mast.

back·stitch /ˈbak,sticH/ ▶ n. sewing with overlapping stitches. ▶ v. sew using backstitches: [trans.] *you can simply backstitch the edges* | [intrans.] *having to backstitch through open loops.*

back·stop /ˈbak,stäp/ ▶ n. a person or thing placed at the rear of or behind something as a barrier, support, or reinforcement. ■ Baseball a high fence or similar structure behind the home plate area. ■ Baseball, informal a catcher. ■ fig. an emergency precaution or last resort. ▶ v. [trans.] support or reinforce: *the founding banks were backstopping the loans.* ■ Hockey act as goaltender for: *the man who backstopped the Edmonton Oilers.*

back·sto·ry /ˈbak,stôrē/ ▶ n. (pl. **-ries**) a history or background created for a fictional character in a motion picture or television program. ■ similar background information about a real person or thing that promotes fuller understanding of it.

back·street /ˈbak,strēt/ ▶ n. a minor street remote from a main road. ▶ adj. [attrib.] operating or performed secretly, and typically illegally.

back·stretch /ˈbakˈstrecH/ ▶ n. the part of a racecourse that is farthest from the grandstand and parallel to the homestretch.

back·stroke /ˈbak,strōk/ ▶ n. [in sing.] a swimming stroke performed on the back with the arms lifted alternately out of the water in a backward circular motion and the legs extended and kicking: *I concentrated on the backstroke* | [as adj.] *I won the backstroke event* | [as adv.] *they would swim freestyle and then backstroke.* ■ (**the backstroke**) a race, typically of a specified length or kind, in which such a style of swimming is used: *he was fifth in the 200-meter backstroke.* — **back·strok·er** n.

back·swept /ˈbak,swept/ ▶ adj. swept, slanted, or sloped backward: *his backswept hair.*

back·swim·mer /ˈbak,swimər/ ▶ n. a predatory aquatic bug (family Notonectidae, *Notonecta* and other genera) that swims on its back using its long back legs as oars. See also WATER BOATMAN.

backswimmer

back·swing /ˈbak,swiNG/ ▶ n. a backward swing, esp. of an arm or of a golf club when about to hit a ball.

back·sword /ˈbak,sôrd/ ▶ n. a sword with only one cutting edge.

back talk (also **back·talk**) ▶ n. informal rude or impertinent remarks made in reply to someone in authority.

back-to-back ▶ adj. consecutive: *back-to-back homers.* ▶ adv. (**back to back**) **1** (of two people) facing in opposite directions with backs touching: *they sat on the ground, leaning back to back.* **2** consecutively; in succession: *the games were played back to back.*

back-to-na·ture ▶ adj. [attrib.] advocating or relating to reversion to a simpler way of life: *a back-to-nature lifestyle.*

back·track /ˈbak,trak/ ▶ v. **1** [intrans.] retrace one's steps: *she had to bypass two farms and backtrack to them later* | fig. *to backtrack a little, the case is complex.* ■ fig. reverse one's previous action or opinion: *the unions have had to backtrack on their demands.* **2** [trans.] pursue, trace, or monitor: *he was able to backtrack the buck to a ridge nearby.*

back·up /ˈbak,əp/ ▶ n. **1** help or support. ■ a person or thing that can be called on if necessary. **2** Comput. the procedure for making extra copies of data in case the original is lost or damaged. ■ a copy of this type. **3** an overflow caused by a stoppage, as in water or automobile traffic.

back·ward /ˈbakwərd/ ▶ adj. **1** [attrib.] directed behind or to the rear. ■ looking toward the past, rather than being progressive; retrograde. **2** (of a person) having learning difficulties. ■ having made less than normal progress. ▶ adv. (also **back·wards**) **1** (of a movement) away from one's front; in the direction of one's back: *he took a step backward.* ■ in reverse of the usual direction or order: *counting backward.* ■ with the rear facing forward: *the canoe turned around backward.* **2** toward or into the past: *a look backward at his life.* ■ toward or into a worse state.
– PHRASES **backward and forward** in both directions alternately; to and fro. **bend** (or **lean**) **over backward to do something** informal make every effort, esp. to be fair or helpful. **know something backward** (**and forward**) be entirely familiar with something. — **back·ward·ly** adv. **back·ward·ness** n. [ME: from *abackward*, from ABACK.]

back·ward com·pat·i·ble (also **back·wards com·pat·i·ble**) ▶ adj. (of computer hardware or software) able to be used with an older piece of hardware or software without special adaptation or modification. — **back·ward com·pat·i·bil·i·ty** n.

back·wash /ˈbak,wôsH; -,wäsH/ ▶ n. the motion of receding waves. ■ a backward current of water or air created by the motion of an object through it. ■ fig. repercussions. ▶ v. [trans.] clean (a filter) by reversing the flow of fluid through it.

back·wa·ter ▶ n. /ˈbak,wôtər; -,wätər/ a part of a river not reached by the current, where the water is stagnant. ■ an isolated or peaceful place. ■ a place or condition in which no development or progress is taking place.

back·wind /ˈbak,wind/ Sailing ▶ v. [trans.] (of a sail or vessel) deflect a flow of air into the back of (another sail or vessel). ▶ n. a flow of air deflected into the back of a sail.

back·woods /ˈbakˈwo͝odz/ ▶ plural n. [often as adj.] remote uncleared forest land. ■ a remote or sparsely inhabited region, esp. one considered backward. — **back·woods·man** /-mən/ n.

back·yard /ˈbakˈyärd/ ▶ n. **1** a yard behind a house or other building. **2** the area close to where one lives regarded with proprietorial concern.

Ba·co·lod /bəˈkō,lôd/ a city in the central Philippines, on the northwestern coast of Negros; pop. 364,180.

Ba·con[1] /ˈbākən/, Francis, Baron Verulam and Viscount St. Albans (1561–1626), English philosopher. As a scientist he advocated the inductive method.

Ba·con[2], Francis (1909–92), Irish painter. His work chiefly depicts human figures in distorted postures.

Ba·con[3], Roger (*c.*1214–94), English philosopher, scientist, and monk. He emphasized the need for an empirical approach to scientific study.

ba·con /ˈbākən/ ▶ n. cured meat from the back or sides of a pig.
– PHRASES **bring home the bacon** informal **1** supply material provision or support; earn a living. **2** achieve success. [ME: from OFr., from Gmc., 'ham, flitch'; akin to BACK.]

Ba·co·ni·an /bā'kōnēən/ ▶ **adj.** of or relating to Sir Francis Bacon or his inductive method of reasoning. ■ relating to or denoting the theory that Bacon wrote the plays attributed to Shakespeare. ▶ **n.** an adherent of Bacon's philosophical system. ■ a supporter of the theory that Bacon wrote the plays attributed to Shakespeare.

bac·te·re·mi·a /,baktə'rēmēə/ (Brit. **bac·te·rae·m·ia**) ▶ **n.** Med. the presence of bacteria in the blood. — **bac·te·re·mic** /-mik/ **adj.** [19th C.: from BACTERIUM.]

bac·te·ri·a /bak'ti(ə)rēə/ plural form of BACTERIUM.

bac·te·ri·cide /bak'ti(ə)rə,sīd/ ▶ **n.** a substance that kills bacteria. — **bac·te·ri·cid·al** /-,ti(ə)rə'sīdl/ **adj.**

bacterio- (also **bacteri-**; also **bacter-** before a vowel) ▶ **comb. form** representing BACTERIUM.

bac·te·ri·o·log·i·cal /bak,ti(ə)rēə'läjikəl/ ▶ **adj.** [attrib.] of or relating to bacteriology or bacteria. ■ relating to or denoting germ warfare. — **bac·te·ri·o·log·ic** /-jik/ **adj.** **bac·te·ri·o·log·i·cal·ly** /-ik(ə)lē/ **adv.**

bac·te·ri·ol·o·gy /bak,ti(ə)rē'äləjē/ ▶ **n.** the study of bacteria. — **bac·te·ri·ol·o·gist** /-jist/ **n.**

bac·te·ri·ol·y·sis /bak,ti(ə)rē'äləsis/ ▶ **n.** Biol. the rupture of bacterial cells, esp. by an antibody. — **bac·te·ri·o·lyt·ic** /-,ti(ə)rēə'litik/ **adj.**

bac·te·ri·o·phage /bak'ti(ə)rēə,fāj/ ▶ **n.** Biol. a virus that parasitizes a bacterium by infecting it and reproducing inside it. [1920s: from BACTERIUM + Gk. *phagein* 'eat.']

bac·te·ri·o·stat /bak'ti(ə)rēə,stat/ ▶ **n.** a substance that prevents the multiplying of bacteria without destroying them. — **bac·te·ri·o·sta·sis** /-,ti(ə)rēə'stāsis/ **n.** **bac·te·ri·o·stat·ic** /-,ti(ə)rēə'statik/ **adj.** **bac·te·ri·o·stat·i·cal·ly** /-,ti(ə)rēə'statik(ə)lē/ **adv.** [20th C.: from BACTERIUM + Gk. *statos* 'standing.']

bac·te·ri·um /bak'ti(ə)rēəm/ ▶ **n.** (pl. **-te·ri·a** /-'ti(ə)rēə/) a member of a large group of unicellular microorganisms lacking organelles and an organized nucleus, including some that can cause disease. — **bac·te·ri·al** /-'ti(ə)rēəl/ **adj.** [19th C.: mod. L., from Gk. *baktērion*, dimin. of *baktēria* 'staff.']

bac·te·ri·u·ri·a /bak,ti(ə)rē'yo͝orēə/ ▶ **n.** Med. the presence of bacteria in the urine.

bac·te·rize /'baktə,rīz/ ▶ **v.** [trans.] (usu. **be bacterized**) treat with bacteria. — **bac·te·ri·za·tion** /,baktərə'zāsʜən/ **n.**

bac·te·roid /'baktə,roid/ ▶ **adj.** of the nature of or resembling a bacterium. ▶ **n.** a bacteroid organism or structure, esp. a modified cell formed by a symbiotic bacterium in a root nodule of a leguminous plant.

Bac·tri·a /'baktrēə/ an ancient country in central Asia, in the northern part of modern Afghanistan. — **Bac·tri·an** **adj. & n.**

Bac·tri·an cam·el /'baktrēən/ ▶ **n.** the two-humped camel (*Camelus bactrianus*) which has been domesticated but is still found wild (sometimes classified as *C. ferus*) in central Asia.

bad /bad/ ▶ **adj.** (**worse**; **worst**) **1** of poor quality; inferior or defective: *a bad diet.* ■ (of a person) not able to do something well; incompetent. **2** unpleasant or unwelcome. ■ unsatisfactory or unfortunate: *bad luck* | [as n.] (**the bad**) *taking the good with the bad.* ■ (of an unwelcome thing) serious; severe. ■ unfavorable; adverse. ■ harmful. ■ not suitable. **3** (of food) decayed; putrid. ■ (of the atmosphere) polluted; unhealthy. **4** (of parts of the body) injured, diseased, or causing pain. ■ [as complement] (of a person) unwell: *I feel bad.* **5** [as complement] regretful, guilty, or ashamed about something. **6** morally depraved; wicked. ■ naughty; badly behaved. **7** worthless; not valid. **8** (**bad·der, bad·dest**) informal good; excellent: *they want the baddest, best-looking Corvette there is.* ▶ **adv.** informal badly: *he beat her up real bad.*

– PHRASES **come to a bad end** see END. **from bad to worse** into an even worse state. **in a bad way** ill. ■ in trouble. **not (or not so) bad** informal fairly good: *he wasn't so bad after all.* **to the bad** to ruin. ■ in deficit. **too bad** informal used to indicate that something is regrettable but now beyond retrieval: *too bad, but that's the way it is.* — **bad·dish** **adj.** **bad·ness** **n.** [ME: perh. from OE *bǣddel* 'hermaphrodite.']

bad·ass /'bad,as/ informal ▶ **n.** a tough, aggressive, or uncooperative person. ▶ **adj.** **1** tough or aggressive: *a badass temper.* ■ particularly bad or severe. **2** formidable; excellent.

bad blood ▶ **n.** ill feeling.

bad break ▶ **n.** informal a piece of bad luck.

bad breath ▶ **n.** unpleasant-smelling breath; halitosis.

bad debt ▶ **n.** a debt that cannot be recovered.

bad·dy /'badē/ (also **bad·die**) informal ▶ **n.** (pl. **-dies**) a villain or criminal in a story, movie, etc.

bade /bad; bād/ past of BID[2].

bad egg ▶ **n.** see EGG[1] (sense 2).

Ba·den /'bädn/ a spa town in eastern Austria, south of Vienna; pop. 24,000.

Ba·den-Ba·den /,bädn 'bädn/ a spa town in the Black Forest in southwestern Germany; pop. 48,700.

Ba·den-Pow·ell /,bädn 'pōəl; 'pou-əl/, Robert Stephenson Smyth, 1st Baron Baden-Powell of Gilwell (1857–1941), English soldier. He founded the Boy Scout movement.

Ba·den-Würt·tem·berg /'wərtəm,bərg; 'vʏrtəm,berk/ a state of western Germany; capital, Stuttgart.

bad faith ▶ **n.** intent to deceive. ■ (in existentialist philosophy) refusal to confront facts or choices.

bad form ▶ **n.** an offense against current social convention.

badge /baj/ ▶ **n.** a distinctive emblem worn as a mark of office, membership, achievement, licensed employment, etc. ■ a distinguishing object or emblem. ■ fig. a feature or sign that reveals a particular condition or quality. ▶ **v.** [trans.] mark with a badge or other emblem. [ME: origin unknown.]

badger 1

badg·er /'bajər/ ▶ **n.** **1** a heavily built omnivorous nocturnal mammal of the weasel family, typically having a gray and black coat. Several genera and species include the North American *Taxidea taxus*, with a white stripe on the head. **2** (**Badger**) informal a native of Wisconsin. ▶ **v.** [trans.] ask (someone) repeatedly and annoyingly for something; pester: *they badgered him about the deals.* [16th C.: perh. from BADGE, from its distinctive head markings.]

bad hair day ▶ **n.** informal a day on which everything seems to go wrong, characterized as a day on which one's hair is particularly unmanageable.

bad·i·nage /,badn'äzʜ/ ▶ **n.** humorous conversation. [17th C.: from Fr., from *badiner* 'to joke,' from *badin* 'fool,' based on Provençal *badar* 'gape.']

bad·lands /'bad,landz/ ▶ **plural n.** extensive tracts of heavily eroded, uncultivable land with little vegetation. ■ (**the Badlands**) a barren plateau region of the western US, mainly in southwestern South Dakota and northwestern Nebraska, south of the Black Hills.

bad·ly /'badlē/ ▶ **adv.** (**worse, worst**) **1** in an unsatisfactory, inadequate, or unsuccessful way: *a badly managed company.* ■ in an unfavorable way: *try not to think badly of me.* ■ in an unacceptable or unpleasant way: *she was behaving badly.* **2** to a great or serious degree; severely: *I wanted a baby so badly.* ▶ **adj.** informal [as complement] guilty or regretful: *I felt badly about my unfriendliness.* See usage at BAD.

– PHRASES **badly off** in an unfavorable situation: *her belief that children are worse off when their parents divorce.* ■ having little money.

bad·min·ton /'badmintn/ ▶ **n.** a game with rackets in which a shuttlecock is volleyed across a net. See illustration at RACKET[1]. [*Badminton*, a country home in southwestern England.]

bad-mouth ▶ **v.** [trans.] informal criticize (someone or something); speak disloyally of: *no one wants to hire an individual who bad-mouths a prior employer.*

bad news ▶ **n.** informal an unpleasant or undesirable person or thing.

bad-tem·pered ▶ **adj.** easily annoyed or made angry. ■ characterized by anger or ungraciousness. — **bad-tem·pered·ly** **adv.**

Bae·de·ker /'bādikər; 'bed-/, Karl (1801–59), German publisher. He is known for the series of guidebooks to which he gave his name.

Baeke·land /'bakə,länt; 'bāk(ə)lənd/, Leo Hendrik (1863–1944), US chemist and inventor; born in Belgium. He developed Bakelite in 1907.

Bae·yer /'bāər/, Adolph Johann Friedrich Wilhelm von (1835–1917), German chemist. He synthesized indigo. Nobel Prize for Chemistry (1905).

Baf·fin /'bafən/, William (c.1584–1622), English explorer. He discovered the largest island of the Canadian Arctic in 1616; this and the bay between it and Greenland are named after him.

Baf·fin Bay an extension of the North Atlantic Ocean between Baffin Island and Greenland, linked to the Arctic Ocean by three passages.

Baf·fin Is·land an island in the Canadian Arctic Ocean, at the mouth of Hudson Bay.

baf·fle /'bafəl/ ▶ **v.** [trans.] **1** totally bewilder or perplex: *an unexplained occurrence that baffled everyone* | [as adj.] (**baffling**) *the baffling murder of her sister.* **2** restrain or regulate (a fluid, a sound, etc.): *to baffle the noise further, I pad the gunwales.* ▶ **n.** a device used to restrain the flow of a fluid, gas, or loose material or to prevent the spreading of sound or light in a particular direction. — **baf·fle·ment** **n.** (in sense 1 of the **verb**) **baf·fling·ly** **adv.** (in sense 1 of the **verb**). [16th C.: perh. akin to Fr. *bafouer* 'ridicule.']

bag /bag/ ▶ **n.** **1** a container of flexible material with an opening at the top, used for carrying things. ■ an amount held by such a container. ■ a thing resembling a bag in shape. ■ a woman's handbag or purse. ■ a piece of luggage. ■ Baseball a base. **2** the amount of game shot by a hunter. **3** (usu. **bags**) a loose fold of skin under a person's eye. **4** a sac in an animal, such as the udder of a cow. **5** derog. a woman, esp. an older one, perceived as unpleasant, bad-tempered, or unattractive. **6** (**one's bag**) informal one's particular interest or taste. ▶ **v.** (**bagged, bag·ging**) [trans.] **1** put (something) in a bag: *customers bagged their own groceries* | *we bagged up the apples.* **2** (of a hunter) succeed in killing or catching an animal: *in 1979, handgun hunters bagged 677 deer.* ■ fig. succeed in securing (something): *we've bagged three awards for excellence.* ■ informal take, occupy, or reserve (something) before someone else can do so: *get there early to bag a seat in the front row.* **3** [intrans.] (of clothes, esp. pants) hang loosely or lose shape: *these trousers never bag at the knee.* ■ swell or bulge. **4** quit; give up on: *it was a drag to be in the ninth grade at 17, so he bagged it.*

– PHRASES **bag and baggage** with all one's belongings: *he threw her out bag and baggage.* **a bag of bones** an emaciated person or animal. **a bag** (or **whole bag**) **of tricks** informal a set of ingenious plans, techniques, or resources. **be left holding the bag** see HOLD. **in the bag** informal **1** (of something desirable) as good as secured. **2** drunk: *I was half in the bag.* — **bag·ful** /-,fo͝ol/ n. (pl. **-fuls**). [ME: perh. from ON *baggi.*]

Ba·gan·da /bə'gändə/ (also **Gan·da**) ▶ **plural n.** (sing. **Mu·gan·da** /mo͞o'gändə/) a Bantu people of the kingdom of Buganda, now forming part of Uganda. Their language is Luganda. ▶ **adj.** of or relating to the Baganda. [a local name.]

ba·gasse /bə'gas/ ▶ **n.** the dry pulpy residue left after the extraction of juice from sugar cane, used as fuel for electricity generators, etc. [19th C.: from Fr., from Sp. *bagazo* 'pulp.']

bag·a·telle /,bagə'tel/ ▶ **n.** **1** a thing of little importance; a very easy task. **2** a game in which small balls are hit and then allowed to roll down a sloping board on which there are holes, each numbered with the score achieved if a ball goes into it, with pins acting as obstructions. **3** a short, light piece of music, esp. one for the piano. [17th C.: from Fr., from Ital. *bagatella*, perh. from *baga* 'baggage' or dimin. of L. *baca* 'berry.']

ba·gel /'bāgəl/ ▶ **n.** a dense bread roll in the shape of a ring, made by boiling dough and then baking it. [20th C.: from Yiddish *beygel.*]

bag·gage /'bagij/ ▶ **n.** personal belongings packed in suitcases for traveling; luggage. ■ the portable equipment of an army. ■ fig. past experiences or long-held ideas regarded as burdens and impediments. [ME: from OFr. *bagage* (from *baguer* 'tie up'), or *bagues* 'bundles.']

bag·gage claim ▶ **n.** [in sing.] the area in an airport where arriving passengers collect luggage that has been carried in the hold of the aircraft.

Bag·gie /'bagē/ ▶ **n.** (pl. **-gies**) trademark a plastic bag typically used for storing food. ■ (**baggie**) informal any small plastic bag.

bag·ging /'baging/ ▶ **n.** material out of which bags are made.

bag·gy /'bagē/ ▶ **adj.** (**-gi·er, -gi·est**) (of clothing) loose and hanging in folds. ■ (of eyes) with folds of puffy skin below them. ▶ **n.** (**baggies**) informal loose and wide-legged pants, shorts, or swim trunks. — **bag·gi·ly** /'bagəlē/ **adv.** **bag·gi·ness** **n.**

Bagh·dad /'bagdad; bag'dad/ the capital of Iraq, on the Tigris River; pop. 4,850,000.

bag la·dy ▶ **n.** informal a homeless woman who carries her possessions in shopping bags.

bag lunch ▶ **n.** a cold lunch prepared at home and carried in a bag to work, to school, or on an excursion.

bag·man /'bag,man; -mən/ ▶ **n.** (pl. **-men**) **1** informal an agent who collects or distributes the proceeds of illicit activities. **2** Canadian a political fund-raiser: *a Tory bagman.*

bagn·io /'banyō; 'bän-/ ▶ **n.** (pl. **-ios**) **1** archaic a brothel. **2** hist. an oriental prison. **3** hist. a bathhouse in Turkey or Italy. [16th C. (sense 2): from Ital. *bagno*, from L. *balneum* 'bath.']

bag of wa·ters ▶ **n.** the fluid-filled sac that contains and protects the fetus in the womb.

bag·pipe /'bag,pīp/ ▶ **n.** (usu. **bagpipes**) a musical instrument with reed pipes that are sounded by the pressure of wind emitted from a bag squeezed by the player's arm. — **bag·pip·er** /'bag,pīpər/ **n.**

bagpipes

ba·guette /ba'get/ ▶ **n.** **1** a long, narrow loaf of French bread. **2** [often as adj.] a gem, esp. a diamond, cut in a long rectangular shape: *a baguette diamond.* **3** Archit. a small molding, semicircular in section. [18th C. (sense 3): from Fr., from Ital. *bacchetto*, dimin. of *bacchio*, from L. *baculum* 'staff.']

bag·wig /'bag,wig/ ▶ **n.** a wig fashionable in the 18th century with the back hair enclosed in an ornamental bag.

bag·worm /'bag,wərm/ ▶ **n.** a moth of the family Psychidae, the caterpillar and flightless female of which live in a portable protective case constructed out of plant debris.

bah /bä/ ▶ **exclam.** an expression of contempt or disagreement: *You think it was an accident? Bah!* [19th C.: prob. from Fr.]

Ba·ha'i /bə'hī; -'hä-ē/ (also **Ba·ha·i**) ▶ **n.** (pl. **-ha'is**) a monotheistic religion founded in the 19th century as a development of Babism, emphasizing the essential oneness of humankind and of all religions and seeking world peace. The Baha'i faith was founded by the Persian Baha'ullah (1817–92) and his son Abdul Baha (1844–1921). ■ an adherent of the Baha'i faith. — **Ba·ha'·ism** **n.** [Pers., from Arab. *bahā'* 'splendor.']

Ba·ha·mas /bə'häməz/ a country in the West Indies. *See box.* — **Ba·ha·mi·an** /bə'hāmēən; -'hä-/ **adj.** & **n.**

Ba·ha·sa In·do·ne·sia /bə'häsə/ ▶ **n.** the official language of Indonesia. See INDONESIAN. [from Malay *bahasa* 'language.']

Ba·ha·sa Ma·lay·sia /bə'häsə/ ▶ **n.** the official language of Malaysia. See MALAY.

Ba·ha·wal·pur /bə'hä-wəl,po͝or/ a city in east central Pakistan, in Punjab province; pop. 250,000.

Ba·hi·a /bä'ēə; bə'hēə/ **1** a state of eastern Brazil, on the Atlantic coast; capital, Salvador. **2** former name for SALVADOR.

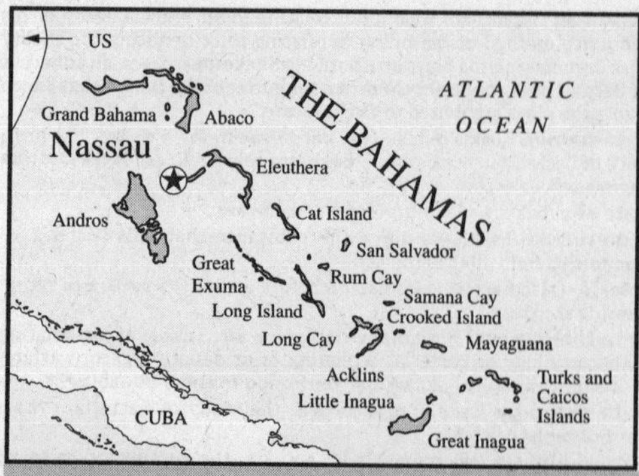

Bahamas, the

Official name: Commonwealth of the Bahamas
Location: northwestern West Indies, off the southeastern coast of Florida
Area: 3,900 square miles (10,100 sq km)
Population: 299,600
Capital: Nassau
Languages: English (official), Creole
Currency: Bahamian dollar

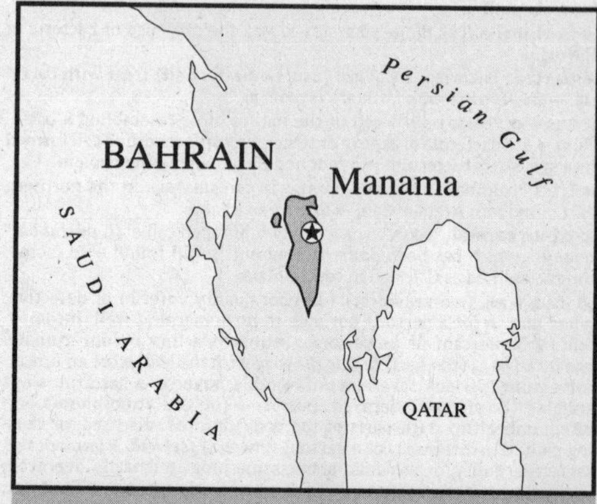

Bahrain

Official name: State of Bahrain
Location: western Asia, consisting of a group of islands in the Persian Gulf between Saudi Arabia and Qatar
Area: 240 square miles (670 sq km)
Population: 677,800
Capital: Manama
Languages: Arabic, English, Farsi, Urdu
Currency: Bahraini dinar

Ba·hí·a Blan·ca /bä'ēə 'blängkə/ a port in Argentina serving the southern part of the country; pop. 271,500.

Bah·rain /bä'rān/ a country in western Asia. *See box.* — **Bah·rain·i** /-'rānē/ **adj.** & **n.**

baht /bät/ ▶ **n.** (pl. same) the basic monetary unit of Thailand, equal to 100 satangs. [from Thai *bāt.*]

Ba·hu·tu /bä'ho͞oto͞o/ plural form of HUTU.

Bai·kal, Lake /bī'käl; -'kôl; -'kal/ (also **Baykal**) a large lake in southern Siberia; with a depth of 5,714 feet (1,743 m), the deepest lake in the world.

bail[1] /bāl/ ▶ **n.** the temporary release of an accused person awaiting trial, sometimes on condition that a sum of money be lodged to guarantee their appearance in court. ■ money paid by or for such a person as security. ▶ **v.** [trans.] (usu. **be bailed**) release or secure the release of (a prisoner) on payment of bail: *get bailed out of jail.* See also BAIL OUT at BAIL[3].

– PHRASES **jump bail** informal fail to appear for trial after being released on bail. **go bail** (or **stand bail**) act as surety for an accused person. **post bail** pay a sum of money as bail. — **bail·a·ble** **adj.** [ME: from OFr., lit. 'custody' from *bailler* 'take charge of,' from L. *bajulare* 'bear a burden.']

bail[2] ▶ **n.** **1** a bar that holds something in place, in particular: ■ Fishing a bar that guides fishing line on a reel. ■ a bar on a typewriter or computer printer that holds the paper steady. ■ Mountaineering a bar on a crampon that fits into a groove in the sole of a boot. ■ a bar separating horses in an open stable. **2** an arched handle, such as on a bucket or a teapot: [as adj.] *brass bail handles.* **3** (usu. **bails**) Cricket either of the two crosspieces bridging the stumps, which the bowler and fielders try to dislodge with the ball to get the batsman out. [ME: from OFr. *baile* 'palisade,' *baillier* 'enclose,' perh. from L. *baculum* 'rod.']

bail[3] ▶ **v.** [trans.] scoop water out of (a ship or boat): *the first priority is to **bail out** the boat with buckets.* ■ scoop (water) out of a ship or boat.
– PHRASAL VERBS **bail out** (of a member of an aircrew) make an emergency parachute descent from an aircraft; eject. ■ fig. become free of an obligation or commitment; discontinue an activity. **bail someone/something out** release someone or something from a difficulty; rescue. — **bail·er** **n.** [17th C.: from obs. *bail* 'bucket,' from Fr. *baille*, based on L. *bajulus* 'carrier.']

Bai·le Átha Cli·ath /blä 'klēə/ Irish name for **Dublin**.

bail·ee /bā'lē/ ▶ **n.** Law a person or party to whom goods are delivered for a purpose, such as custody or repair, without transfer of ownership.

bai·ley /'bālē/ ▶ **n.** (pl. **-leys**) the outer wall of a castle. ■ a court enclosed by this. [ME: prob. from OFr. *baile* 'palisade, enclosure' (see **bail**[2]).]

bail·ie /'bālē/ ▶ **n.** (pl. **-ies**) esp. hist. a municipal officer and magistrate in Scotland. [ME: from OFr. *bailli*.]

bail·iff /'bālif/ ▶ **n.** a person who performs certain actions under legal authority, in particular: ■ an official in a court of law who keeps order, looks after prisoners, etc. ■ esp. Brit. a sheriff's officer who executes writs and processes and carries out distraints and arrests. [ME: from OFr. *baillif*, form of *bailli*, based on L. *bajulus* 'manager.']

bail·i·wick /'bālə,wik/ ▶ **n.** Law the district or jurisdiction of a bailie or bailiff. ■ (**one's bailiwick**) informal one's sphere of operations or particular area of interest. [ME: from **bailie** + **wick**[2].]

bail·ment /'bālmənt/ ▶ **n.** Law an act of delivering goods to a bailee for a particular purpose, without transfer of ownership.

bail·or /'bālər/ ▶ **n.** Law a person or party that entrusts goods to a bailee.

bail·out /'bāl,out/ ▶ **n.** informal an act of giving financial assistance to a failing business or economy to save it from collapse.

bain-ma·rie /,ban mə'rē/ ▶ **n.** (pl. **bains-ma·rie** pronunc. same) a container holding hot water into which a pan is placed for slow cooking. [18th C.: Fr., translation of med. L. *balneum Mariae* 'bath of Maria.']

Baird /be(ə)rd/, John Logie (1888–1946), Scottish inventor. He made the first transatlantic transmission and demonstration of color television in 1928.

Bai·ri·ki /'bī,rēkē/ the capital of Kiribati, on South Tarawa Island; pop. 2,200.

bairn /be(ə)rn/ ▶ **n.** esp. Scot. & N. Engl. a child. [OE *bearn* from Gmc.; akin to **bear**[1], (v.).]

Bai·sak·hi /bī'säkē/ ▶ **n.** a Sikh festival held annually to commemorate the founding of the Khalsa by Gobind Singh in 1699. [from Sanskrit *Vaiśākha*, a month of the Hindu lunar year.]

bait /bāt/ ▶ **n.** **1** food used to entice fish or other animals as prey. ■ fig. an allurement; a thing intended to tempt or entice. **2** var. of **bate**. ▶ **v.** [trans.] **1** deliberately annoy or taunt (someone): *the boys reveled **in baiting him about** his love of literature.* ■ torment (a trapped or restrained animal), esp. by allowing dogs to attack it. **2** prepare (a hook, trap, net, or fishing area) with bait to entice fish or animals as prey: *she baited a trap with corn.* ■ fig. lure; entice. **3** [intrans.] archaic stop on a journey to take food or a rest: *they stopped to bait at an inn.* ■ [trans.] give food to (horses) on a journey: *while their horses were baited, they entered the public room.*
– PHRASES **fish or cut bait** informal stop vacillating and act on something or disengage from it. **rise to the bait** react to a provocation or temptation exactly as intended: *Jenny was being rude, but he never rose to the bait.* **with baited breath** misspelling of ***with bated breath***. See usage at **bated**. [ME: from ON *beit* 'pasture, food,' *beita* 'to hunt or chase.']

bait-and-switch ▶ **n.** the action (generally illegal) of advertising goods that are an apparent bargain, with the intention of substituting inferior or more expensive goods: [as adj.] *a bait-and-switch scheme.*

bait·fish /'bāt,fish/ ▶ **n.** a fish used as bait to catch a larger fish.

bai·za /'bīzə/ ▶ **n.** (pl. same or **bai·zas**) a monetary unit of Oman, equal to one thousandth of a rial.

baize /bāz/ ▶ **n.** a coarse, feltlike, woolen material that is typically green, used for covering billiard and card tables and for aprons. [16th C.: from Fr. *baies*, fem. pl. of *bai* 'chestnut-colored' (see **bay**[4]).]

Ba·ja Ca·li·for·nia /'bähä/ a mountainous peninsula in northwestern Mexico that extends southward from the border with California and separates the Gulf of California from the Pacific Ocean. Also called **Lower California**.

Ba·jan /'bājən/ ▶ **adj. & n.** informal term for ***Barbadian*** (see **Barbados**).

bake /bāk/ ▶ **v.** [trans.] **1** cook (food) by dry heat without direct exposure to a flame, typically in an oven or on a hot surface: [with two objs.] *I baked him a cake for his birthday* | [as adj.] (**baked**) *baked apples.* ■ [intrans.] (of food) be cooked in such a way: *the bread was baking on hot stones.* **2** (of the sun or other agency) subject (something) to dry heat, esp. so as to harden it: *the sun baked the earth.* ■ [intrans.] informal (of a person or place) be or become extremely hot in prolonged sun or hot weather: *the city was baking in a heat wave* | [as adj.] (**baking**) *the summer's baking heat.* ▶ **n.** [with adj.] a social gathering at which baked food is eaten: *lobster bakes.* [OE *bacan*, from Gmc.; akin to Ger. *backen*.]

baked A·las·ka ▶ **n.** sponge cake and ice cream in a meringue covering, cooked for a very short time. [named after the state of **Alaska**.]

baked beans ▶ **plural n.** short for **Boston baked beans**.

bake·house /'bāk,hous/ ▶ **n.** dated a building or area in which bread is made.

Ba·ke·lite /'bāk(ə),līt/ ▶ **n.** trademark an early form of brittle plastic made from formaldehyde and phenol, used chiefly for electrical equipment. [20th C.: Leo H. *Baekeland* (1863–1944), Belgian-born American chemist.]

Bak·er /'bākər/, Josephine (1906–75), US singer and dancer. She was a star of the Folies-Bergère in Paris.

bak·er /'bākər/ ▶ **n.** a person who makes bread and cakes, esp. commercially. ■ [often with adj.] an oven for a particular purpose: *a bread baker.*

Ba·ker Is·land an uninhabited island in the central Pacific Ocean. It was claimed by the US in 1857.

bak·er's doz·en ▶ **n.** a group or set of thirteen, from the former bakers' custom of adding an extra loaf to a dozen sold.

Ba·kers·field /'bākərz,fēld/ an industrial city in south central California; pop. 247,057.

bak·er's yeast ▶ **n.** a dried preparation of yeast used or suitable for use as leaven.

bak·er·y /'bāk(ə)rē/ ▶ **n.** (pl. **-er·ies**) a place where bread and cakes are made or sold. ■ baked goods such as bread and cakes.

bake·shop /'bāk,shäp/ ▶ **n.** a place where bread and cakes are made or sold.

bake·ware /'bāk,we(ə)r/ ▶ **n.** tins, trays, and other items placed in the oven during baking.

bak·ing pow·der ▶ **n.** a mixture of sodium bicarbonate and cream of tartar, used instead of yeast in baking.

bak·ing so·da ▶ **n.** sodium bicarbonate used in cooking, for cleaning, or in toothpaste.

ba·kla·va /,bäklə'vä/ ▶ **n.** a dessert originating in the Middle East made of phyllo pastry filled with chopped nuts and soaked in honey. [Turk.]

bak·sheesh /'bakshēsh; bak'shēsh/ ▶ **n.** (in parts of Asia) a sum of money given as alms, a tip, or a bribe. [based on Pers. *bakšiš*, from *bakšīdan* 'give.']

Bakst /bäkst/, Léon (1866–1924), Russian painter and designer; born *Lev Samuilovich Rozenberg*. He designed sets and costumes for the Ballets Russes.

Ba·ku /bä'ko͞o/ the capital of Azerbaijan, on the Caspian Sea; pop. 1,780,000.

bal·a·cla·va /,balə'klävə/ (also **balaclava helmet**) ▶ **n.** a close-fitting garment covering the whole head and neck except for parts of the face, typically made of wool. [19th C.: after the village of *Balaclava* (now Balaklava) in the Crimea.]

Bal·a·cla·va, Battle of /,balə'klävə/ a battle of the Crimean War, between Russia and an alliance of British, French, and Turkish forces in the port of Balaclava (now Balaklava) in the southern Crimea in 1854; noted as the scene of the Charge of the Light Brigade.

bal·a·lai·ka /,balə'līkə/ ▶ **n.** a guitarlike musical instrument with a triangular body and two, three, or four strings, popular in Russia and other Slavic countries. [18th C.: from Russ., of Tartar origin.]

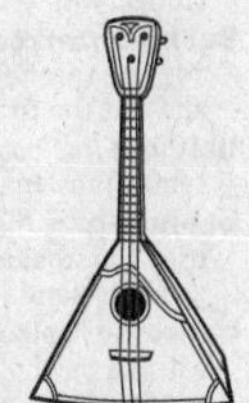
balalaika

bal·ance /'baləns/ ▶ **n.** **1** an even distribution of weight enabling someone or something to remain upright and steady: *she **lost her balance** before falling.* ■ stability of one's mind or feelings. ■ Sailing the ability of a boat to stay on course without adjustment of the rudder. **2** a condition in which different elements are equal or in the correct proportions. [in sing.] ***a balance between** work and relaxation.* ■ Art harmony of design and proportion. ■ [in sing.] the relative volume of various sources of sound: *the balance of the voices is good.* **3** an apparatus for weighing, esp. one with a central pivot, beam, and a pair of scales. ■ (**the Balance**) the zodiacal sign or constellation Libra. **4** a counteracting weight or force. ■ (also **balance wheel**) the regulating device in a clock or watch. **5** a predominating weight or amount; the majority. **6** a figure representing the difference between credits and debits in an account; the amount of money held in an account. ■ the difference between an amount due and an amount paid: *unpaid credit-card balances.* ■ [in sing.] an amount left over. ▶ **v.** [trans.] **1** keep or put (something) in a steady position so that it does not fall: *a mug that she **balanced on** her knee.* ■ [intrans.] remain in a steady position without falling. **2** offset or compare the value of (one thing) with another: *the cost needs to be **balanced against** the benefits.* ■ counteract, equal, or neutralize the weight or importance of: *he **balanced** his somber remarks **with** humor.* ■ establish equal or appropriate proportions of elements in: *balancing work and family life.* **3** compare debits and credits in (an account), typically to ensure that they are equal: *the council must **balance its books** each year.* ■ [intrans.] (of an account) have credits and debits equal.
– PHRASES **balance of payments** the difference in total value between payments into and out of a country over a period. **balance of power**

1 a situation in which nations of the world have roughly equal power. 2 the power held by a small group when larger groups are of equal strength. **balance of trade** the difference in value between a country's imports and exports. **in the balance** uncertain; at a critical stage: *his survival hung in the balance for days.* **on balance** with all things considered: *but on balance he was pleased.* **strike a balance** choose a moderate course or compromise. **throw** (or **catch**) **someone off balance** cause someone to become unsteady and in danger of falling. ■ fig. confuse or bewilder someone. — **bal·anc·er** n. [ME: from OFr. *balance* (n.), *balancer* (v.), based on late L. *(libra) bilanx* '(balance) having two scalepans,' from *bi-* + *lanx* 'scalepan.']

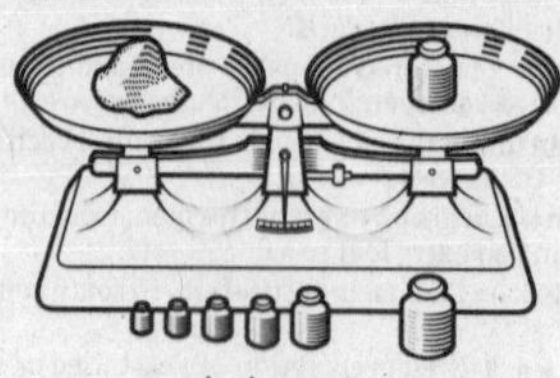
balance 3

bal·ance beam ▶n. a narrow horizontal bar raised off the floor, on which a gymnast balances while performing exercises. ■ [in sing.] the set of exercises performed on such a piece of equipment.

bal·anced /'balənst/ ▶adj. keeping or showing a balance; arranged in good proportions. ■ taking everything into account; fairly judged or presented. ■ (esp. of food) having different elements in the correct proportions: *a healthy, balanced diet.* ■ (of a person or state of mind) having no emotion lacking or too strong; stable. ■ (of an account or budget) having debits and credits equal. ■ (of an electrical circuit or signal) being symmetrical with respect to a reference point, typically ground.

bal·ance sheet ▶n. a statement of the assets, liabilities, and capital of a business or other organization at a particular point in time, detailing the balance of income and expenditure over the preceding period.

bal·ance wheel ▶n. the regulating device in a watch or clock.

Bal·an·chine /,balən'CHēn; 'balən,CHēn/, George (1904–83), US ballet dancer and choreographer; born in Russia; born *Georgi Melitonovich Balanchivadze.* In 1934, he cofounded the company that became the New York City Ballet.

bal·anc·ing act ▶n. an action or activity that requires a delicate balance between different situations or requirements.

bal·as ru·by /'baləs/ ▶n. a spinel of a delicate rose-red variety. [ME: from OFr. *balais*, from Arab. *balakš*, from Pers. *Badakšān*, district of Afghanistan.]

ba·la·ta /bə'lätə/ ▶n. a tropical American tree (esp. *Manilkara bidentata*) of the sapodilla family that bears edible fruit and produces latex. ■ the dried sap of this tree used as a substitute for rubber. [17th C.: from Carib *balatá.*]

Ba·la·ton, Lake /'bôlə,tōn; 'bälə,tän/ a large shallow lake in west central Hungary.

Bal·bo·a /bal'bōə/, Vasco Núñez de (1475–1519), Spanish explorer. In 1513 he reached the western coast of the isthmus of Darien (Panama) and was the first European to see the eastern Pacific Ocean.

bal·bo·a /bal'bōə/ ▶n. the basic monetary unit of Panama, equal to 100 centésimos. [named after Vasco Núñez de BALBOA.]

bal·brig·gan /bal'brigən/ ▶n. a fine, unbleached knitted cotton fabric, used for stockings and underwear. [19th C.: after the town of *Balbriggan* in Ireland.]

bal·co·ny /'balkənē/ ▶n. (pl. **-nies**) **1** a platform enclosed by a wall or balustrade on the outside of a building, with access from an upper-floor window or door. **2** (**the balcony**) the upstairs seats in a theater, concert hall, or auditorium. — **bal·co·nied** adj. [17th C.: from Ital. *balcone*, prob. ult. from Gmc.]

bald /bôld/ ▶adj. **1** having a scalp wholly or partly lacking hair: *starting to go bald.* ■ (of an animal) not covered by the usual fur, hair, or feathers. ■ (of a plant or an area of land) not covered by the usual leaves, bark, or vegetation. ■ (of a tire) having the tread worn away. **2** [attrib.] without any extra detail or explanation; plain or blunt: *the bald statement requires amplification.* — **bald·ish** adj. **bald·ly** adv. (in sense 2) *"I want to leave," Stephen said baldly.* **bald·ness** n. [ME: prob. from base meaning 'white patch.']

bal·da·chin /'bôldəkin/ (also **bal·da·quin**) ▶n. a ceremonial canopy of stone, metal, or fabric over an altar, throne, or doorway. [16th C.: from Ital. *baldacchino*, from *Baldacco* 'Baghdad.']

bald cy·press ▶n. a deciduous North American conifer (*Taxodium distichum*, family Taxodiaceae) with exposed buttress roots and ball-shaped cones, typically growing in swamps and on water margins.

bald ea·gle ▶n. a white-headed North American eagle (*Haliaeetus leucocephalus*) that includes fish among its prey. Now most common in Alaska, it is the national emblem of the US.

Bal·der /'bôldər/ Scand. Mythol. a son of Odin and god of the summer sun. He was invulnerable to all things except mistletoe, with which the god Loki, by a trick, induced the blind god Hödur to kill him.

bal·der·dash /'bôldər,dasH/ ▶n. senseless talk or writing; nonsense. [16th C.: origin unknown.]

bald-faced ▶adj. **1** (of an animal) having white markings on the face. **2** shameless and undisguised; bare-faced: *a bald-faced lie.*

bald eagle

bald·ing /'bôldiNG/ ▶adj. going bald.

bald·pate /'bôld,pāt/ ▶n. the American wigeon, in allusion to its white-crowned head.

bal·dric /'bôldrik/ ▶n. hist. a belt for a sword or other piece of equipment, worn over one shoulder and reaching down to the opposite hip. [ME *baudry*, from OFr. *baudre.*]

Bald·win[1] /'bôldwin/, Henry (1780–1844), US Supreme Court associate justice 1830–44.

Bald·win[2], James Arthur (1924–87), US writer and civil rights activist. His novels include *Go Tell It on the Mountain* (1953) and *Another Country* (1962).

Bald·win[3], Stanley, 1st Earl Baldwin of Bewdley (1867–1947), British prime minister 1923–24, 1924–29, 1935–37.

Bald·win Park a city in southwestern California, east of Los Angeles; pop. 69,330.

bald·y /'bôldē/ (also **bald·ie**) ▶n. (pl. **bald·ies**) derog. a baldheaded person.

Bâle /bäl/ French name for BASLE.

bale[1] /bāl/ ▶n. a bundle of paper, hay, cotton, etc., tightly wrapped and bound with cords or hoops. ■ the quantity in a bale as a measure, esp. 500 pounds of cotton. ▶v. [trans.] make (something) into bales: *they baled a lot of hay* | [as n.] (**baling**) *most baling has been finished.* [ME: prob. from MDu., from OFr.; ult. from Gmc., akin to BALL[1].]

bale[2] ▶n. archaic or literary evil considered as a destructive force. ■ evil suffered; physical torment or mental suffering. [OE *balu, bealu*, from Gmc.]

Bal·e·ar·ic Is·lands /,balē'arik/ (also **the Bal·e·ar·ics**) a group of Mediterranean islands off the eastern coast of Spain that form an autonomous region of Spain; capital, Palma (on the island of Majorca).

ba·leen /bə'lēn/ ▶n. whalebone. [ME: from OFr. *baleine*, from L. *balaena* 'whale.']

ba·leen whale ▶n. a whale (suborder Mysticeti) that has plates of whalebone in the mouth for straining plankton from the water. Baleen whales include the rorquals, humpback, right whales, and gray whale.

bale·fire /'bāl,fīr/ ▶n. a large open-air fire; a bonfire. [OE, from obs. *bale* 'great fire.']

bale·ful /'bālfəl/ ▶adj. threatening harm; menacing: *Bill shot a baleful glance in her direction.* ■ having a harmful or destructive effect. — **bale·ful·ly** adv. **bale·ful·ness** n.

bal·er /'bālər/ ▶n. a machine for making paper, hay, or cotton into bales.

Bal·four /'bal,fôr/, Arthur James, 1st Earl of Balfour (1848–1930), British prime minister 1902–05. In 1917, as foreign secretary, he issued the Balfour Declaration that favored a Jewish national home in Palestine.

Ba·li /'bälē; 'balē/ a mountainous island in Indonesia, to the east of Java; chief city, Denpasar; pop. 2,856,000.

Ba·li·nese /,bälə'nēz; -'nēs; ,bal-/ ▶adj. of or relating to Bali or its people or language. ▶n. (pl. same) **1** a native of Bali. **2** the Indonesian language of Bali. [from BALI.]

balk /bôk/ (Brit. also **baulk**) ▶v. [intrans.] **1** hesitate or be unwilling to accept an idea or undertaking: *any gardener will balk at enclosing the garden.* ■ [trans.] thwart or hinder (a plan or person): *his influence will be invoked to balk the law.* ■ [trans.] (**balk someone of**) prevent a person or animal from having (something): *the lions, fearing to be balked of their prey.* ■ (of a horse) refuse to go on. ■ [trans.] archaic miss or refuse (a chance or invitation). **2** Baseball (of a pitcher) make an illegal motion, penalized by an advance of the base runners. ▶n. **1** Baseball an illegal motion made by a pitcher that may deceive a base runner. **2** a roughly squared timber beam. **3** any area on a pool or billiard table in which play is restricted in some way. **4** a ridge left unplowed between furrows. [OE *balc*, from ON *bálkr* 'partition.']

Bal·kan·ize /'bôlkə,nīz/ ▶v. [trans.] divide (a region or body) into smaller mutually hostile states or groups. — **Bal·kan·i·za·tion** /,bôlkənə'zāSHən/ n. [1920s: from *Balkan* Peninsula.]

Bal·kans /'bôlkənz/ **1** (also **Bal·kan Moun·tains**) a range of mountains stretching east across Bulgaria. The highest peak is Botev Peak (7,793 feet; 2,375 m). **2** the countries in southeastern Europe that are south of the Danube and Sava rivers and are bounded by the Adriatic and Ionian seas (west), the Aegean and Black seas (east), and the Mediterranean Sea (south). — **Bal·kan** adj.

Bal·kan Wars /'bôlkən/ two wars of 1912–13 that were fought over the last European territories of the Ottoman Empire.

balk·line /'bôk,līn/ (also **balk line**) ▶n. a line on a billiard table marking off a restricted play area.

balk·y /'bôkē/ (Brit. also **baulk·y**) ▶adj. (**balk·i·er**, **balk·i·est**) reluctant; uncooperative.

Ball /bôl/, John (died 1381), English priest. He led the Peasants' Revolt and was hanged as a traitor.

ball[1] /bôl/ ▶n. **1** a solid or hollow sphere or ovoid, esp. one that is kicked, thrown, or hit in a game. ■ a ball-shaped object: *a ball of wool.* ■ hist. a solid nonexplosive missile for a firearm. ■ a game played with a ball, esp. baseball: *pro ball.* **2** Baseball a pitch delivered outside the strike zone that the batter does not attempt to hit. ■ Sports a pass of a ball from one player to another. **3** (in full **the ball of the foot**) the rounded protuberant part of the foot at the base of the big toe. ■ (in full **the ball of the thumb**) the rounded protuberant part of the hand at the base of the thumb. **4** (**balls**) vulgar slang testicles. ■ (**ball**) an act of sexual intercourse. ■ courage or nerve. ■ nonsense; rubbish (often said to express strong disagreement). ▶ **v.** [trans.] **1** (usu. **ball up**) squeeze or form (something) into a rounded shape: *Robert **balled up** his napkin.* ■ clench or screw up (one's fist) tightly. ■ [intrans.] form a round shape: *the fishing nets **ball up** and sink.* ■ wrap the rootball of (a tree or shrub) in burlap to protect it during transportation. **2** vulgar slang have sexual intercourse with.

– PHRASES **balled up 1** formed into a ball. **2** entangled; confused. **3** used as a euphemism for *constipated.* **the ball is in your court** it is up to you to make the next move. **a ball of fire** a person full of energy and enthusiasm. **keep the ball rolling** maintain the momentum of an activity. **keep one's eye on** (or **take one's eye off**) **the ball** keep (or fail to keep) one's attention focused on the matter in hand. **on the ball** alert to new ideas, methods, and trends. ■ indicating competence, alertness, or intelligence. **play ball** play a ball game such as baseball. ■ informal work willingly with others; cooperate: *if his lawyers won't play ball, there's nothing we can do.* ■ Baseball the umpire's command to begin or resume play. **start** (or **get** or **set**) **the ball rolling** set an activity in motion; make a start. **the whole ball of wax** informal everything. [ME: from ON *bǫllr*, from Gmc.]

ball² ▶ **n.** a formal social gathering for dancing.

– PHRASES **have a ball** informal enjoy oneself greatly; have a lot of fun. [17th C.: from Fr. *bal* 'a dance,' from late L. *ballare* 'to dance.']

bal·lad /'baləd/ ▶ **n.** a poem or song narrating a story in short stanzas. ■ a slow sentimental or romantic song. [15th C.: from OFr. *balade*, from Provençal *balada* 'dance, song to dance to.']

bal·lade /bə'läd/ ▶ **n. 1** a poem normally composed of three stanzas and an envoi. The last line of the opening stanza is used as a refrain, and the same rhymes, strictly limited in number, recur throughout. **2** a short, lyrical piece of music, esp. one for piano. [ME: earlier form of BALLAD.]

bal·lad·eer /ˌbalə'di(ə)r/ ▶ **n.** a singer or composer of ballads.

bal·lad·ry /'baladrē/ ▶ **n.** ballads collectively. ■ the art of writing or performing ballads.

bal·lad stan·za ▶ **n.** a four-line stanza in iambic meter in which the first and third unrhymed lines have four metrical feet and the second and fourth rhyming lines have three metrical feet.

ball and chain ▶ **n.** a heavy metal ball secured by a chain to the leg of a prisoner to prevent escape. ■ fig. a crippling encumbrance: *the ball and chain of debt.*

ball-and-sock·et joint ▶ **n.** a natural or manufactured joint or coupling, such as the hip joint, in which a partially spherical end lies in a socket, allowing multidirectional movement and rotation.

Bal·lard /'balərd/, J. G. (1930–), British writer; full name *James Graham Ballard*. He wrote the autobiograhical novel *Empire of the Sun* (1984).

bal·last /'baləst/ ▶ **n. 1** heavy material, such as gravel, placed low in a vessel to improve its stability. ■ a substance of this type carried in an airship or on a hot-air balloon to stabilize it, and jettisoned when greater altitude is required. ■ fig. something that gives stability or substance: *the film is an entertaining comedy with some serious ideas thrown in for ballast.* **2** gravel or coarse stone used to form the bed of a railroad track or road. ■ a mixture of coarse and fine aggregate for making concrete. **3** a passive component used in an electric circuit to moderate changes in current. ▶ **v.** [trans.] (usu. **be ballasted**) **1** give stability to (a ship) by putting a heavy substance in its bilge: *the vessel has been ballasted to give the necessary floating stability.* **2** form (the bed of a railroad line or road) with gravel or coarse stone.

– PHRASES **in ballast** (of a ship) laden only with ballast. [16th C.: prob. of Low Ger. or Scand. origin.]

ball bear·ing ▶ **n.** a bearing between a wheel and a fixed axle, in which the rotating part and the stationary part are separated by a ring of small solid metal balls that reduce friction. ■ a ball used in such a bearing.

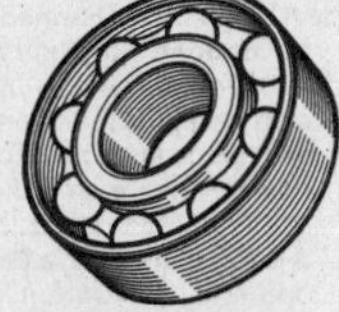
ball bearing

ball boy ▶ **n.** a boy who retrieves balls that go out of play during a game such as tennis or baseball, and who supplies players or umpires with new balls.

ball-break·er (also **ball-bust·er**) ▶ **n.** informal a person who is demanding of other people. ■ a demanding and punishing task or situation. — **ball-break·ing adj.**

ball·car·ri·er /'bôlˌkarēər/ ▶ **n.** Football a player in possession of the ball and attempting to advance it.

ball cock ▶ **n.** a valve that automatically fills a tank after liquid has been drawn from it.

bal·le·ri·na /ˌbalə'rēnə/ ▶ **n.** a female ballet dancer. [18th C.: from Ital., fem. of *ballerino* 'dancing master,' from *ballare* 'to dance.']

bal·let /ba'lā/ ▶ **n.** an artistic dance form performed to music using precise and highly formalized set steps and gestures. Classical ballet is characterized by light, graceful, fluid movements and the use of pointe shoes. ■ a creative work of this form or the music written for it. ■ a group of dancers who regularly perform such works. ■ [in sing.] fig. an elaborate or complicated interaction between people. [17th C.: from Fr., from Ital. *balletto*, dimin. of *ballo* 'a dance,' from late L. *ballare* 'to dance.']

bal·let·ic /ba'letik; bə-/ ▶ **adj.** of, relating to, or characteristic of ballet: *a graceful, balletic movement.* — **bal·let·i·cal·ly** /-ik(ə)lē/ **adv.**

bal·let·o·mane /bə'letəˌmān; ba-/ ▶ **n.** a ballet enthusiast. — **bal·let·o·ma·ni·a** /-ˌletə'mānēə/ **n.**

Ballets Russes /ˌbalā'ro͞os/ a ballet company formed in Paris in 1909 by Sergei Diaghilev.

ball float ▶ **n.** the spherical float attached to the pivoting arm of the ball cock in a toilet tank.

ball game ▶ **n. 1** a game played with a ball. ■ a baseball game. **2** [in sing.] informal a particular situation, esp. one that is completely different from the previous situation: *making the film was **a whole new ball game** for her.*

ball girl ▶ **n.** a girl who retrieves balls that go out of play during a game such as tennis or baseball, and who supplies players or umpires with new balls.

bal·lis·ta /bə'listə/ ▶ **n.** (pl. **-tae** /-tē/ or **-tas**) a catapult used in ancient warfare for hurling large stones. ■ a large crossbow for firing a spear. [16th C.: from L., based on Gk. *ballein* 'to throw.']

bal·lis·tic /bə'listik/ ▶ **adj.** [attrib.] **1** of or relating to projectiles or their flight. **2** moving under the force of gravity only.

– PHRASES **go ballistic** informal fly into a rage. — **bal·lis·ti·cal·ly** /-ik(ə)lē/ **adv.** [18th C.: from BALLISTA + -IC.]

bal·lis·tic mis·sile ▶ **n.** a missile with a high, arching trajectory that is initially powered and guided but falls under gravity onto its target.

bal·lis·tics /bə'listiks/ ▶ **plural n.** [treated as sing.] the science of projectiles and firearms. ■ the study of the effects (on a bullet, cartridge, or gun) of being fired.

ball light·ning ▶ **n.** a rare and little known kind of lightning having the form of a moving globe of light that persists for periods of up to a minute.

bal·locks ▶ **n.** var. of BOLLOCKS.

bal·lon /bə'lôn/ ▶ **n. 1** (in dancing) the ability to appear effortlessly suspended while performing movements during a jump. **2** var. of BALLOON (sense 3). [Fr., from Ital. *ballone*, from *balla* 'ball.']

bal·lo·net /ˌbalə'nā/ (also **bal·lon·net**) ▶ **n.** the compartment in a balloon or airship into which air or another gas can be forced in order to maintain the craft's shape as buoyant gas is released.

bal·loon /bə'lo͞on/ ▶ **n. 1** a brightly colored rubber sac inflated with air and then sealed at the neck, used as a children's toy or a decoration. ■ a round or pear-shaped outline in which the words or thoughts of characters in a comic strip or cartoon are written. **2** a large bag filled with hot air or gas to make it rise in the air, typically carrying a basket for passengers. **3** (also **balloon glass**) a large rounded drinking glass, used for brandy and other drinks. ▶ **v.** [intrans.] **1** swell out in a spherical shape; billow: *the trousers **ballooned out** below his waist* | [trans.] *the wind ballooned her sleeves.* ■ (of an amount of money) increase rapidly: *the company's debt has ballooned in the last five years* | [as adj.] (**ballooning**) *ballooning government spending.* ■ swell dramatically in size or number. ■ (of a person) increase rapidly and dramatically in weight: *I had ballooned on the school's starchy diet.* **2** travel by hot-air balloon: *he is famous for ballooning across oceans.* ▶ **adj.** resembling a balloon; puffed. [16th C.: from Fr. *ballon* or Ital. *ballone* 'large ball.']

bal·loon an·gi·o·plas·ty ▶ **n.** Med. surgical widening of a blocked or narrowed blood vessel, esp. a coronary artery, by means of a balloon catheter.

bal·loon cath·e·ter ▶ **n.** Med. a type of catheter with a small balloon that may be introduced into a canal, duct, or blood vessel and then inflated in order to clear an obstruction or dilate a narrowed region.

bal·loon·ing /bə'lo͞oniNG/ ▶ **n.** the sport or pastime of flying in a balloon. — **bal·loon·ist n.**

bal·loon mort·gage ▶ **n.** a mortgage in which a large portion of the borrowed principal is repaid in a single payment at the end of the loan period.

bal·loon pay·ment ▶ **n.** a repayment of the outstanding principal sum made at the end of a loan period, interest only having been paid hitherto.

bal·loon tire ▶ **n.** a large tire containing air at low pressure. — **bal·loon-tired adj.**

bal·loon vine ▶ **n.** a tropical American vine (*Cardiospermum halicacabum*, family Sapiondaceae) with inflated balloonlike pods.

bal·lot /'balət/ ▶ **n.** a process of voting, in writing and typically in secret. ■ (**the ballot**) the total number of votes cast in such a process. ■ the piece of paper used to record someone's vote in such a process. ■ a list of candidates or issues to be voted on. ■ the right to vote. ▶ **v.** (**-lot·ed, -lot·ing**) [trans.] (of an organization) elicit a secret vote from (members) on a particular issue: *the union is preparing to ballot its members.* ■ [intrans.] cast one's vote on a particular issue: *ambulance crews balloted unanimously to reject the deal.* ■ decide the allocation of (something) to applicants by drawing lots. [16th C.: from Ital. *ballotta*, dimin. of *balla* (see BALL¹).]

bal·lot box ▶ **n.** a sealed box into which voters put completed ballots.

■ (**the ballot box**) democratic principles and methods: *the remedy was the ballot box and not the court.*

ball·park /'bôl,pärk/ ▶ **n.** a baseball stadium or field. ■ informal a particular area or range: *this figure's in the ballpark.* ▶ **adj.** [attrib.] informal (of prices or costs) approximate; rough: *the **ballpark figure** is $400.*

ball-peen ham·mer ▶ **n.** a hammer with a rounded end opposite the face.

ball·point /'bôl,point/ (also **ballpoint pen**) ▶ **n.** a pen with a tiny ball as its writing point.

ball race ▶ **n.** Mech. either of the components of a ball bearing that have ring-shaped grooves in which the balls run.

ball·room /'bôl,ro͞om; -,ro͝om/ ▶ **n.** a large room used for dancing.

ball·room danc·ing ▶ **n.** formal social dancing in couples, popular as a recreation and also as a competitive activity, including the waltz, cha-cha, and foxtrot. — **ball·room dance n.**

balls·y /'bôlzē/ ▶ **adj.** (**balls·i·er, balls·i·est**) informal tough and courageous. — **balls·i·ness n.** [1950s: from BALL[1] (sense 4 of **n.**) + -Y[1].]

ball valve ▶ **n.** a one-way valve that is opened and closed by pressure on a ball that fits into a cup-shaped opening.

bal·ly·hoo /'balē,ho͞o/ informal ▶ **n.** extravagant publicity or fuss. ▶ **v.** (**-hoos, -hooed**) [trans.] praise or publicize extravagantly: [as adj.] (**ballyhooed**) *a much-ballyhooed musical extravaganza.* [19th C.: origin unknown.]

balm /bä(l)m/ ▶ **n.** **1** a fragrant ointment or preparation used to heal or soothe the skin. ■ fig. something that has a comforting, soothing, or restorative effect. **2** a tree with species in several families, in particular those of the genus *Commiphora* (family Burseraceae) that yields a fragrant resinous substance, typically one used in medicine. ■ such a substance. **3** (also **lemon balm** or **sweet balm**) a bushy herb of the mint family (*Melissa officinalis*) with leaves smelling and tasting of lemon. ■ used in names of other aromatic herbs of the mint family, e.g., **bee balm**. [ME: from OFr. *basme*, from L. *balsamum* (see BALSAM).]

bal·ma·caan /,balmə'kan; -'kän/ ▶ **n.** a loose overcoat with raglan sleeves.

balm of Gil·e·ad /'gilēəd/ ▶ **n.** **1** a fragrant medicinal resin obtained from certain kinds of tree. **2** a tree that yields such a resin, in particular: ■ an Arabian tree (*Commiphora gileadensis*, family Burseraceae). ■ the balsam poplar. ■ the balsam fir. [16th C.: *Gilead*, because this resin is assumed to be the substance mentioned in the Bible as coming from Gilead.]

bal·mor·al /bal'môrəl/ (also **Bal·mor·al**) ▶ **n.** **1** a type of brimless round cocked hat with a cockade attached. **2** a heavy laced leather walking boot. **3** hist. a stiff woolen or horsehair petticoat worn under a skirt. [19th C.: after BALMORAL CASTLE.]

Bal·mor·al Cas·tle a vacation residence of the British royal family, on the Dee River in Scotland.

balm·y /'bä(l)mē/ ▶ **adj.** (**balm·i·er, balm·i·est**) **1** (of the weather) pleasantly warm. **2** informal extremely foolish; eccentric: *he's gone balmy.* — **balm·i·ness n.**

bal·ne·ol·o·gy /,balnē'äləjē/ ▶ **n.** the study of therapeutic bathing and medicinal springs. ■ another term for BALNEOTHERAPY. — **bal·ne·o·log·i·cal** /-nēə'läjikəl/ **adj.** **bal·ne·ol·o·gist n.** [19th C.: from L. *balneum* 'bath.']

bal·ne·o·ther·a·py /,balnēō'THerəpē/ ▶ **n.** the treatment of disease by bathing in mineral springs. [19th C.: from L. *balneum* 'bath' + THERAPY.]

ba·lo·ney /bə'lōnē/ ▶ **n.** informal **1** foolish or deceptive talk; nonsense. [corruption of BOLOGNA.] **2** variant of BOLOGNA.

Bal·qash, Lake /bäl'käsh; bal'kash/ (also **Balkhash**) a shallow salt lake in Kazakhstan.

bal·sa /'bôlsə/ ▶ **n.** **1** (also **balsa wood**) a very lightweight wood used in particular for making models and rafts. **2** the fast-growing tropical American tree (*Ochroma lagopus* (or **pyramidale**), family Bombacaceae) from which this wood is obtained. [17th C.: from Sp., 'raft.']

bal·sam /'bôlsəm/ ▶ **n.** **1** an aromatic resinous substance, such as balm, exuded by various trees and shrubs and used as a base for certain fragrances and medical preparations. ■ an aromatic ointment or other resinous medicinal or cosmetic preparation. ■ a tree or shrub that yields balsam. **2** a herbaceous plant (genus *Impatiens*, family Balsaminaceae) cultivated for its flowers, which are typically pink or purple and carried high on the stem. — **bal·sam·ic** /bôl'samik/ **adj.** [OE, via L. from Gk. *balsamon.*]

bal·sam fir ▶ **n.** a North American fir tree (*Abies balsamea*) that yields Canada balsam.

bal·sam·ic vin·e·gar ▶ **n.** dark, sweet Italian vinegar that has been matured in wooden barrels.

bal·sam pop·lar ▶ **n.** a North American poplar tree (*Populus balsamifera*) that yields balsam.

Bal·sas, Rio /,rēō 'bôōlsəs/ a river that flows for 450 miles (725 km) through Mexico into the Pacific Ocean.

bal·sa wood ▶ **n.** see BALSA (sense 1).

Balt /bôlt/ ▶ **n.** **1** a speaker of a Baltic language; a Lithuanian or Latvian. **2** a native or inhabitant of one of the Baltic States of Lithuania, Latvia, and Estonia. ■ hist. a German-speaking inhabitant of any of these states. ▶ **adj.** of or relating to the Balts. [19th C.: from late L. *Balthae* 'dwellers near the Baltic Sea.']

Bal·tha·sar /bôl'THazər; bal-; 'bôlTHə,zär; 'bal-/ (also **Bal·tha·zar**) one of the three Magi.

Bal·tha·zar /bôl'THazər; bal-; 'bôlTHə,zär; 'bal-/ ▶ **n.** a very large wine bottle, with a capacity of 12 liters, equivalent to that of 16 ordinary wine bottles. [1930s: from *Balthazar*, king of Babylon (Dan. 5:1).]

Bal·tic /'bôltik/ ▶ **adj.** **1** of or relating to the Baltic Sea or the region surrounding it. **2** relating to a branch of the Indo-European family of languages consisting of Lithuanian, Latvian, and Old Prussian. ▶ **n.** **1** (**the Baltic**) the Baltic Sea or the Baltic States. **2** the Baltic languages collectively. [16th C.: from med. L. *Balticus*, from late L. *Balthae* (see BALT).]

Bal·tic Sea a sea in northern Europe that is linked with the North Sea.

Bal·tic States **1** the independent republics of Estonia, Latvia, and Lithuania. **2** the ten members of the Council of Baltic States established in 1992: Denmark, Estonia, Finland, Germany, Latvia, Lithuania, Norway, Poland, Russia, and Sweden.

Bal·ti·more /'bôltə,môr/ a city in northern Maryland on Chesapeake Bay; pop. 651,154.

Bal·ti·stan /,bôltə'stan; -'stän; ,bəl-/ a region of the Karakoram range of the Himalayas, to the south of K2 peak. Also called LITTLE TIBET.

Bal·to-Slav·ic /'bôltō 'slävik/ ▶ **n.** a branch of the Indo-European language family that includes the Baltic and Slavic languages. — **Bal·to-Slav·ic adj.**

Ba·lu·chi /bə'lo͞oCHē/ (also **Ba·luch** /-'lo͞oCH/) ▶ **n.** (pl. same or **-chis**) **1** a native or inhabitant of Baluchistan. **2** the Iranian language of Baluchistan. ▶ **adj.** of or relating to this people or their language. [from Pers. *Balūč(ī)*.]

Ba·lu·chi·stan /bə,lo͞oCHi'stan; -'stän/ **1** a mountainous region of western Asia that includes parts of Iran, Afghanistan, and Pakistan. **2** a province of western Pakistan; capital, Quetta.

Ba·lun·da /bə'lo͞ondə; -'lo͞on-/ ▶ **n.** plural form of LUNDA.

bal·us·ter /'baləstər/ ▶ **n.** a short pillar or column in a series supporting a rail or coping. ■ [as adj.] (of a furniture leg or other decorative item) having the form of a baluster. [17th C.: from Fr. *balustre*, from Ital. *balaustro*, from *balaust(r)a* 'wild pomegranate flower,' because of the resemblance to the curving calyx tube of the flower.]

bal·us·trade /'balə,strād/ ▶ **n.** a railing supported by balusters. — **bal·us·trad·ed adj.** [17th C.: from Fr., from *balustre*.]

Bal·zac /'bôlzak; 'bal-/, Honoré de (1799–1850), French writer. He wrote 91 interconnected novels and stories known collectively as *La Comédie humaine*. — **Bal·zac·i·an** /bôl'zakēən; bal-/ **adj.**

bam /bam/ ▶ **exclam.** used to imitate the sound of a hard blow or to convey the abruptness of an occurrence. [1920s: imitative.]

Ba·ma·ko /'bämə,kō; 'bam-/ the capital of Mali, in the south part of the country; pop. 646,000.

Bam·ba·ra /bäm'bärə/ ▶ **n.** (pl. same or **-ras**) a member of a native people living chiefly in Mali. ■ the Mande language of this people. ▶ **adj.** of or relating to this people or their language.

bam·bi·no /bam'bēnō/ ▶ **n.** (pl. **-ni** /-nē/) often humorous a baby or young child. ■ an image of the infant Jesus. [18th C.: Ital., dimin. of *bambo* 'silly.']

bam·boo /bam'bo͞o/ ▶ **n.** a giant woody grass (*Bambusa* and other genera), that grows chiefly in the tropics, where it is widely cultivated. ■ the hollow jointed stem of this plant, used as a cane or to make furniture and implements. [16th C.: from Du. *bamboes*, based on Malay *mambu*.]

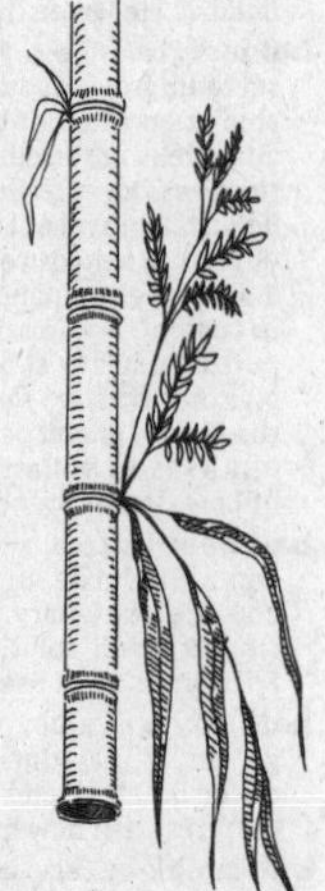

bamboo

bam·boo cur·tain ▶ **n.** (often **the Bamboo Curtain**) a political and economic barrier between China and noncommunist countries.

bam·boo shoot ▶ **n.** a young shoot of bamboo, eaten as a vegetable.

bam·boo·zle /bam'bo͞ozəl/ ▶ **v.** [trans.] informal fool or cheat (someone): *Tom Sawyer bamboozled the boys.* ■ (often **be bamboozled**) confound or perplex: *bamboozled by the number of savings plans being offered.* [18th C.: origin unknown.]

ban[1] /ban/ ▶ **v.** (**banned, ban·ning**) [trans.] (often **be banned**) officially or legally prohibit: *he was **banned from** driving for a year.* ■ officially exclude (someone) from a place. ▶ **n.** **1** an official or legal prohibition: *a **ban on** cigarette advertising.* ■ an official exclusion of a person from an organization, country, or activity. ■ archaic a curse. **2** a tacit prohibition by public opinion. [OE *bannan* 'summon by public proclamation,' from Gmc.; n. partly from OFr. *ban* 'proclamation.']

ban[2] /bän/ ▶ **n.** (pl. **ba·ni** /'bänē/) a monetary unit of Romania, equal to one hundredth of a leu. [Romanian.]

Ba·na·ba /bə'näbə; -'nabə/ an island in the western Pacific. It has been part of Kiribati since 1979. Also called OCEAN ISLAND.

ba·nal /'bānl; bə'nal; -'näl/ ▶ **adj.** so lacking in originality as to be obvious and boring. — **ba·nal·i·ty** /bə'nalitē/ **n.** (pl. **-ties**) **ba·nal·ly adv.** [18th C.: from Fr., from *ban* 'a call to arms'; ult. akin to BAN[1].]

ba·nan·a /bə'nanə/ ▶ **n.** **1** a long curved fruit that grows in clusters and has soft pulpy flesh and yellow skin when ripe. **2** (also **banana plant** or **banana tree**) the tropical and subtropical treelike plant (genus *Musa*, family Musaceae) that bears this fruit, with very large leaves. **3 adj.**

(**bananas**) informal insane or extremely silly: *he's beginning to think I'm bananas.*

– PHRASES **go bananas** informal go insane. ■ rave; cheer wildly. ■ become extremely angry or excited. **second banana** informal the second most important person in an organization or activity. **top banana** informal the most important person in an organization or activity. [16th C.: via Port. or Sp. from Mande.]

ba·nan·a belt ▶ n. informal a region with a comparatively warm climate.

ba·nan·a oil ▶ n. a colorless liquid, $CH_3CO_2C_5H_{11}$, with a bananalike odor used in flavorings and as a solvent.

ba·nan·a·quit /bə'nanə,kwit/ ▶ n. a small songbird (*Coereba flaveola*, family Coerebidae) with a curved bill, common in the West Indies and Central and South America. [see QUIT².]

ba·nan·a re·pub·lic ▶ n. usu. derog. a small nation, esp. in Central America, dependent on one crop or the influx of foreign capital.

ba·nan·a seat ▶ n. a narrow, elongated bicycle seat that curves up toward the rear.

ba·nan·a split ▶ n. a dessert made with a split banana, ice cream, sauce, whipped cream, nuts, and a cherry.

ba·nau·sic /bə'nôzik; -sik/ ▶ adj. formal not operating on a refined or elevated level; mundane. ■ relating to technical work. [19th C.: from Gk. *banausikos* 'of artisans.']

ban·co /'baNGkō/ ▶ exclam. used in baccarat, chemin de fer, and similar games to express a player's willingness to meet the banker's whole stake single-handed. [18th C.: via Fr. from Ital.]

band¹ /band/ ▶ n. **1** a flat, thin strip or loop of material put around something. ■ a strip of material forming part of a garment: *hatband.* ■ a plain ring for the finger, esp. a gold wedding ring. ■ Ornithol. a ring of metal placed around a bird's leg to identify it. ■ (**bands**) a collar with two hanging strips, worn by certain clerics and academics as part of their formal dress. ■ Mech. a belt connecting wheels or pulleys. **2** a stripe or elongated area of a different color, texture, or composition than its surroundings. **3** a range of frequencies or wavelengths in a spectrum (esp. of radio frequencies): *channels in the UHF band.* **4** (on a long-playing record) a set of grooves onto which sound has been recorded, separated from other sections of the record by grooves with no sound. **5** archaic a thing that restrains, binds, or unites. ▶ v. [trans.] (usu. **be banded**) **1** surround (an object) with something in the form of a strip or ring, typically for reinforcement or decoration: *doors are banded with iron.* ■ Ornithol. put a band on (a bird) for identification. **2** mark (something) with a stripe or stripes of a different color: *the bird's bill is banded across the middle with black* | [as adj.] (**banded**) *banded agate.* [OE (sense 5), from ON, reinforced by OFr. *bande*, from Gmc.; akin to BIND.]

band² ▶ n. **1** a group of people who have a common interest or purpose. ■ Anthropol. a subgroup of a tribe. **2** a group of musicians who play together, in particular: ■ a small group of musicians and vocalists who play pop, jazz, or rock music. ■ a group of musicians who play brass, wind, or percussion instruments. ■ informal an orchestra. **3** a herd or flock. ▶ v. [intrans.] (of people or organizations) form a group for a mutual purpose: *local people **banded together** to fight the company.* [ME: from OFr. *bande*, from Gmc.; akin to BANNER.]

Ban·da /'bandə/, Hastings Kamuzu (1906–97), dictator of Malawi 1964–94. Self-titled as the President for Life, he was defeated in Malawi's first truly democratic election in 1994.

band·age /'bandij/ ▶ n. a strip of material used to bind a wound or to protect an injured part of the body. ▶ v. [trans.] bind (a wound or a part of the body) with a protective strip of material: *bandage the foot so that the ankle is supported* | *the doctors **bandaged up** his wounds.* [16th C.: from Fr., from *bande* (see BAND²).]

band·ag·ing /'bandijiNG/ ▶ n. the action of binding a strip or strips of material around a wound or an injured part of the body. ■ the material used for this.

Band-Aid /'band ,ād/ ▶ n. trademark an adhesive bandage with a gauze pad in the center, used to cover minor wounds. ■ fig. (also **band-aid**) a temporary solution.

ban·dan·na /ban'danə/ (also **ban·dan·a**) ▶ n. a large handkerchief or neckerchief, often having a colorful pattern. [18th C.: prob. via Port. from Hindi.]

Ban·da·ra·nai·ke /,bəndərə'nīkə/, Sirimavo Ratwatte Dias (1916–2000), prime minister of Sri Lanka 1960–65, 1970–77, 1994–2000. She was the world's first woman prime minister.

Ban·dar Lam·pung /'bəndər 'läm,po͝oNG/ a city at the southern tip of Sumatra, in Indonesia; pop. 284,275. It was created in the 1980s by the amalgamation of Tanjungkarang and Telukbetung.

Ban·dar Se·ri Be·ga·wan /'bändär 'serē bə'gäwən/ the capital of Brunei, in the northern part of the country; pop. 52,300.

Ban·da Sea /'bandə; 'bändə/ a sea in eastern Indonesia, between the central and south Molucca Islands.

b. & b. (also **B&B**) ▶ abbr. bed and breakfast.

band·box /'band,bäks/ ▶ n. a cardboard box, typically circular, for carrying hats.

B&E ▶ abbr. breaking and entering.

ban·deau /ban'dō/ ▶ n. (pl. **-deaux** /-'dōz/) a narrow band worn around the head to hold the hair in position. ■ a woman's strapless top formed from a band of fabric fitting around the bust. [18th C.: from Fr., from OFr. *bandel*, dimin. of *bande* (see BAND²).]

ban·de·ril·la /,bandə'rēə/ ▶ n. a decorated dart thrust into a bull's neck or shoulders during a bullfight. [Sp., dimin. of *bandera* 'banner.']

ban·de·ril·le·ro /,bandərē'yerō/ ▶ n. (pl. **-ros**) a bullfighter who uses banderillas. [Sp.]

ban·de·role /'bandə,rōl/ (also **ban·de·rol**) ▶ n. a narrow flaglike object, in particular: ■ a long, narrow flag with a cleft end, flown at a masthead. ■ an ornamental streamer on a knight's lance. ■ a ribbonlike stone scroll bearing an inscription. [16th C.: from Fr., from Ital. *banderuola*, dimin. of *bandiera* 'banner.']

ban·di·coot /'bandi,ko͞ot/ ▶ n. a mainly insectivorous marsupial (family Peramelidae) native to Australia and New Guinea. Several genera and species, some of which are endangered or extinct, include the **short-nosed bandicoot** (*Isodon obesulus*). [18th C.: from Telugu *pandikokku*, lit. 'pig-rat.']

short-nosed bandicoot

ban·di·coot rat ▶ n. an Asian rat (genera *Bandicota* and *Nesokia*, family Muridae), esp. the large *B. indica*.

band·ing /'bandiNG/ ▶ n. **1** the presence or formation of visible stripes of contrasting color. ■ Biochem. the pattern of regions on a chromosome made visible by staining. ■ Biochem. the separation of molecules into bands of concentration in a gel. **2** the marking of individual birds or other animals with bands or rings.

ban·dit /'bandit/ ▶ n. (pl. **ban·dits** or **ban·dit·ti** /ban'ditē/) a robber or outlaw belonging to a gang and typically operating in an isolated or lawless area. ■ military slang an enemy aircraft.

– PHRASES **make out like a bandit** profit greatly from an activity.
—**ban·dit·ry** n. [16th C.: from Ital. *bandito*, lit. 'banned,' past part. of *bandire*.]

band·lead·er /'band,lēdər/ (also **band lead·er**) ▶ n. a player or conductor at the head of a musical band.

band·mas·ter /'band,mastər/ ▶ n. the conductor of a musical band, esp. a brass or military one.

ban·dog /'ban,dôg/ ▶ n. a dog bred for its strength and ferocity by crossing aggressive breeds. [ME (denoting a dog kept on a chain or "band").]

ban·do·lier /,bandə'li(ə)r/ (also **ban·do·leer**) ▶ n. a shoulder-belt with loops or pockets for cartridges. [16th C.: from Fr. *bandoulière*; perh. from Sp. *bandolera* (from *banda* 'sash'), or from Catalan *bandolera* (from *bandoler* 'bandit').]

bandolier

ban·do·ne·on /ban'dōnēən/ ▶ n. a type of concertina used esp. in South America. [via Sp. from German *Bandonion*, named after Heinrich *Band*, the 19th-cent. German musician who invented it, + *-on-* (as in *Harmonika* 'harmonica') + *-ion* (as in *Akkordion* 'accordion').]

ban·do·ra /ban'dôrə/ ▶ n. a bass stringed instrument of the cittern family, having a long neck and a scallop-shaped body. [16th C.: cf. Du. *bandoor*, Sp. *bandurria*.]

band·pass /'band,pas/ ▶ adj. (of a filter) transmitting only a set range of frequencies: *a 1–40 Hz bandpass filter.* ▶ n. the range of frequencies transmitted through such a filter.

band·saw /'band,sô/ (also **band saw**) ▶ n. an endless saw, consisting of a steel belt with a serrated edge running over wheels.

band·shell /'band,SHel/ (also **band shell**) ▶ n. a bandstand in the form of a large concave shell with special acoustic properties.

bands·man /'bandzmən/ ▶ n. (pl. **-men**) a player in a musical band, esp. a military or brass one.

band·stand /'band,stand/ ▶ n. a covered outdoor platform for a band to play on. ■ a raised platform for performing musicians in a restaurant or dance hall.

Ban·dung /'bän,do͝oNG/ a city in southern Indonesia; pop. 2,056,900.

band·wag·on /'band,wagən/ ▶ n. **1** a wagon used for carrying a band in a parade or procession. **2** [usu. in sing.] a particular activity or cause that has suddenly become fashionable or popular.

– PHRASES **jump** (or **climb**) **on the bandwagon** join others in doing or supporting something fashionable or likely to be successful.

band·width /'band,widTH/ ▶ n. Electron. a range of frequencies within a given band, in particular: ■ the range of frequencies used for transmitting a signal. ■ the range of frequencies over which a system or a device can operate effectively. ■ the transmission capacity of a computer network or other telecommunication system. ■ fig. the breadth of a person's interests or mental capacity.

ban·dy¹ /'bandē/ ▶ adj. (**-di·er**, **-di·est**) (of a person's legs) curved so as to be wide apart at the knees. ■ (often **bandy-legged**) (of a person) having legs that are curved in such a way; bowlegged. [17th C.: perh. from obs. *bandy* 'curved stick used in hockey.']

ban·dy² ▶ v. (**-dies**, **-died**) [trans.] (usu. **be bandied about/around**) pass

on or discuss an idea in a casual way: *$40,000 is the figure that has been bandied about.* ■ exchange; pass back and forth: *they bandied words.* ▶ n. a game similar to field hockey. ■ the stick used to play this game.
– PHRASES **bandy words with** argue pointlessly or rudely: *don't bandy words with me, Sir!* [16th C.: perh. from Fr. *bander* 'take sides,' from *bande* (see BAND[2]).]

bane /bān/ ▶ n. [usu. in sing.] a cause of great distress or annoyance. ■ archaic something, typically poison, that causes death. —**bane·ful** /-fəl/ adj. archaic. [OE *bana*, 'poison,' from Gmc.]

bane·ber·ry /'bān,berē/ ▶ n. (pl. **-ries**) a plant of the buttercup family (genus *Actaea*), native to north temperate regions, that bears spikes of white flowers followed by shiny berries. The many species include the North American **white baneberry** (*A. pachypoda*), with clusters of black-eyed white berries on red stalks. ■ the bitter, typically poisonous berry of this plant. [18th C.: from BANE in the sense 'poison.']

bang[1] /baNG/ ▶ n. **1** a sudden loud noise. ■ a sharp blow causing such a loud noise. ■ a sudden painful blow. **2** (**bangs**) a fringe of hair cut straight across the forehead. [from a use of the adv. *bang* to mean 'abruptly.'] **3** vulgar slang an act of sexual intercourse. **4** Comput. the character "!" ▶ v. **1** [trans.] strike or put down (something) forcefully and noisily, typically in anger or in order to attract attention: *he began to bang the table with his fist* | [intrans.] *someone was banging on the door.* ■ [with obj. and adverbial] come into contact with (something) suddenly and sharply, typically by accident: *I banged my head on the low beams* | [intrans.] *she banged into some shelves.* ■ [intrans.] make a sudden loud noise, typically repeatedly: *the shutter was banging in the wind.* ■ [with obj. and complement] (of a door) open or close violently and noisily: *he banged the kitchen door shut* | [no obj., with complement] *the door banged open and a man staggered out.* ■ [no obj., with adverbial of direction] (of a person) move around or do something noisily, esp. as an indication of anger or irritation. ■ [with obj. and adverbial of direction] (of a sports player) hit (a ball or a shot) forcefully and successfully: *in his second start he banged out two hits.* ■ vulgar slang (of a man) have sexual intercourse with (a woman). **2** cut (hair) in a fringe. ▶ adv. informal esp. Brit. exactly: *bang in the middle of town.* ■ completely: *bring your wardrobe bang up to date.* ▶ exclam. **1** used to express or imitate the sound of a sudden loud noise: *firecrackers went bang.* **2** used to convey the suddenness of an action or process: *the minute something becomes obsolete, bang, it's gone.*
– PHRASES **bang for one's** (or **the**) **buck** informal value for money; performance for cost. **get a bang out of** informal derive excitement or pleasure from. **go (off) with a bang** go successfully. **with a bang 1** abruptly. **2** impressively or spectacularly.
– PHRASAL VERBS **bang away at** informal do something in a persistent or dogged way. **bang something out** informal **1** play music noisily, enthusiastically, and typically unskillfully. **2** produce hurriedly or in great quantities. **bang someone/something up** informal damage or injure someone or something: *he banged up his knee.* [16th C.: imitative, perh. of Scand. origin; cf. ON *bang* 'hammering.']

bang[2] ▶ n. var. of BHANG.

Ban·ga·lore /,baNGgə'lôr/ a city in south central India, capital of the state of Karnataka; pop. 2,651,000.

ban·ga·lore tor·pe·do (also **Ban·ga·lore tor·pe·do**) ▶ n. a tube containing explosives used by infantry for blowing up barriers.

bang·er /'baNGər/ ▶ n. esp. Brit. **1** informal a sausage. **2** informal a car in poor condition. **3** a loud explosive firework.

Bang·kok /'baNGkäk; baNG'käk/ the capital and chief port of Thailand, on the Chao Phraya waterway; pop. 5,876,000.

Bang·la·desh /,bäNGglə'desH; ,baNGlə-/ a country in southern Asia. *See box.* —**Bang·la·desh·i** /-'desHē/ adj. & n.

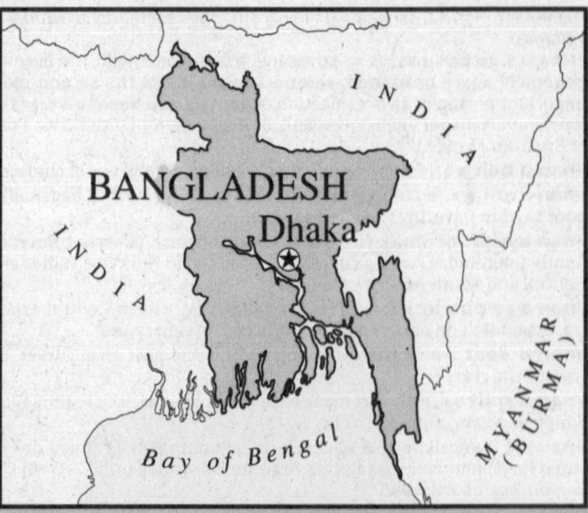

Bangladesh

Official name: People's Republic of Bangladesh
Location: southern Asia, in the Ganges River delta, northeast of India, on the Bay of Bengal
Area: 51,700 square miles (133,900 sq km)
Population: 141,340,000
Capital: Dhaka
Languages: Bengali (official), English
Currency: taka

ban·gle /'baNGgəl/ ▶ n. a rigid bracelet or anklet. [18th C.: from Hindi *bangli* 'glass bracelet.']

Ban·gor /'baNGgər/ a city in east central Maine, on the Penobscot River; pop. 31,473.

bang·tail /'baNG,tāl/ ▶ n. a horse's tail that has been cut straight across just below the level of the hocks.

Ban·gui /bäNG'gē; 'bäNG,gē/ the capital of the Central African Republic, in the southwestern part of the country, on the Ugandi River; pop. 596,800.

bang-up ▶ adj. informal excellent: *a bang-up job.*

ba·ni /'bänē/ plural form of BAN[2].

ban·ian ▶ n. var. of BANYAN.

ban·ish /'banisH/ ▶ v. [trans.] (often **be banished**) send (someone) away from a country or place as an official punishment: *they were banished to Siberia.* ■ forbid, abolish, or get rid of (something unwanted): *all thoughts of romance were banished from her head.* —**ban·ish·ment** n. [ME: from OFr. *baniss-*, stem of *banir*; ult. from Gmc., rel. to BAN[1].]

ban·is·ter /'banəstər/ (also **ban·nis·ter**) ▶ n. (also **banisters**) the structure formed by uprights and a handrail at the side of a staircase. ■ a single upright at the side of the staircase. [17th C.: from *barrister*, alt. of BALUSTER.]

Ban·ja Lu·ka /,bänyə 'lo͞okə/ a spa town in northern Bosnia and Herzegovina; pop. 143,000. It served as a base for Bosnian Serbs in the 1990s.

Ban·jar·ma·sin /,bänjər'mäsən; ,ban-/ a deep-water port in Indonesia, on southern Borneo; pop. 480,700.

ban·jo /'banjō/ ▶ n. (pl. **-jos** or **-joes**) a stringed musical instrument with a long neck and a round open-backed body consisting of parchment stretched over a metal hoop like a tambourine, played by plucking or with a plectrum. ■ an object resembling this in shape: [as adj.] *a banjo clock.* —**ban·jo·ist** n. [18th C.: black Amer. alt. of *bandore*; prob. based on Gk. *pandoura* 'three-stringed lute.']

banjo

Ban·jul /'bänjo͞ol/ the capital of Gambia; pop. 44,540. Until 1973 it was known as Bathurst.

bank[1] /baNGk/ ▶ n. **1** the land alongside or sloping down to a river or lake. **2** a slope, mass, or mound of a particular substance: *a bank of snow.* ■ an elevation in the seabed or a riverbed; a mudbank or sandbank. ■ a transverse slope given to a road, railroad, or sports track to enable vehicles or runners to maintain speed around a curve. ■ the sideways tilt of an aircraft when turning in flight. **3** a set or series of similar things, esp. electrical or electronic devices, grouped together in rows. ■ a tier of oars. **4** the cushion of a pool table: [as adj.] *a bank shot.* ▶ v. [trans.] **1** heap (a substance) into a mass or mound: *the rain banked the soil up behind the gate* | *snow was banked in humps at the roadside.* ■ [intrans.] rise or form into a mass or mound: *purple clouds banked up over the hills.* ■ heap a mass or mound of a substance against (something): *people were banking their houses with earth.* ■ heap (a fire) with tightly packed fuel so that it burns slowly: *she made a fire and banked it with dirt.* ■ edge or surround with a ridge or row of something: *steps banked with pots of chrysanthemums.* **2** (of an aircraft or vehicle) tilt or cause to tilt sideways in making a turn: [intrans.] *the plane banked* | [trans.] *I banked the aircraft steeply and turned.* ■ [intrans.] build (a road, railroad, or sports track) higher at the outer edge of a bend to facilitate fast cornering. **3** (in pool and other games) play (a ball) so that it rebounds off a surface such as a backboard or cushion. [ME: from ON *bakki*, from Gmc.; akin to BENCH. The senses 'set of similar things in sloping rows' and 'tier of oars' are from Fr. *banc*.]

bank[2] ▶ n. a financial establishment that invests money deposited by customers, pays it out when required, makes loans at interest, and exchanges currency. ■ a stock of something available for use when required: *a blood bank.* ■ a place where something may be safely kept: *the computer's memory bank.* ■ (**the bank**) the store of money or tokens held by the banker in some gambling or board games. ■ the person holding this store; the banker. ▶ v. [trans.] deposit (money or valuables) in a bank: *I banked the check.* ■ [intrans.] have an account at a particular bank: *he did not bank with the old family banks.* ■ informal (esp. of a competitor in a game or race) win or earn (a sum of money): *he banked $100,000 for a hole-in-one.* ■ store (something, esp. blood, tissue, or sperm) for future use: *the sperm is banked for the following spring.*
– PHRASES **break the bank** (in gambling) win more money than is held by the bank. ■ [usu. with negative] informal cost more than one can afford.
– PHRASAL VERBS **bank on** base one's hopes or confidence on. [15th C.: from Fr. *banque* or Ital. *banca*, from med. L. *banca, bancus*, from Gmc., akin to BANK[1].]

bank·a·ble /'baNGkəbəl/ ▶ adj. (esp. in the entertainment industry) certain to bring profit and success. ■ reliable: *a bankable assurance.* —**bank·a·bil·i·ty** /,baNGkə'bilitē/ n.

bank bal·ance ▶ n. the amount of money held in a bank account at a given moment.

bank barn ▶ n. a barn built on a slope.

bank·book /'baNGk,bo͝ok/ ▶ n. another term for PASSBOOK.

bank card ▶ n. a card issued by a bank for the purpose of identifying a customer, as at an automated teller machine.

bank dis·count ▶ n. interest computed on the face value of a loan and deducted in advance from the loan by the lending bank.

bank draft ▶ n. a check drawn by a bank on its own funds in another bank.

bank·er /'baNGkər/ ▶ n. an officer or owner of a bank or group of banks. ■ the person running the table, controlling play, or acting as dealer in some gambling or board games.

bank·er's hours ▶ plural n. short working hours (in reference to the typical opening hours of a bank in former times).

bank hol·i·day ▶ n. Brit. a day on which banks are officially closed, observed as a public holiday.

Ban Ki-moon /'bän gē 'mo͞on/ (1944–), South Korean diplomat; secretary general of the UN 2007– .

bank·ing /'baNGkiNG/ ▶ n. the business conducted or services offered by a bank. ■ the occupation of a banker: [as adj.] *to pursue a banking career.*

bank ma·chine ▶ n. another term for AUTOMATED TELLER MACHINE.

bank·note /'baNGk,nōt/ (also **bank note**) ▶ n. a piece of paper money, constituting a central bank's promissory note to pay a stated sum to the bearer on demand.

bank rate ▶ n. the rate of discount set by a central bank.

bank·roll /'baNGk,rōl/ ▶ n. a roll of paper money. ■ fig. financial resources. ▶ v. [trans.] informal support (a person, organization, or project) financially: *the project is bankrolled by wealthy expatriates.*

bank·rupt /'baNGk,rəpt; -rəpt/ ▶ adj. (of a person or organization) declared in law unable to pay outstanding debts: *the company was declared bankrupt* | *he committed suicide after going bankrupt.* ■ impoverished or depleted. ■ fig. completely lacking in a particular quality or value: *their cause is morally bankrupt.* ▶ n. a person judged by a court to be insolvent, whose property is taken and disposed of for the benefit of creditors. ▶ v. [trans.] reduce (a person or organization) to bankruptcy: *the strike nearly bankrupted the union.* [16th C.: from Ital. *banca rotta* 'broken bench,' from *banca* (see BANK[2]) and *rompere* 'to break.']

bank·rupt·cy /'baNGk,rəp(t)sē; -rəp(t)sē/ ▶ n. (pl. **-cies**) the state of being bankrupt: *many companies were facing bankruptcy* | [as adj.] *bankruptcy proceedings.* ■ fig. the state of being completely lacking in a particular quality or value: *the moral bankruptcy of terrorism.*

Banks /baNGks/, Sir Joseph (1743–1820), English botanist. He sailed around the world with James Cook 1768–71.

bank·si·a /'baNGksēə/ ▶ n. an evergreen Australian shrub (genus *Banksia*, family Proteaceae) that typically has narrow, leathery leaves and spikes of bottlebrushlike flowers. [mod. L., after Sir Joseph BANKS.]

bank state·ment ▶ n. a printed record of the balance in a bank account and the amounts that have been paid into it and withdrawn from it, issued periodically to the holder of the account.

Ban·ne·ker /'banikər/, Benjamin (1731–1806), US inventor, astronomer, and mathematician. The child of slaves, he helped to survey the District of Columbia 1790 and published an almanac 1791–1802.

ban·ner /'banər/ ▶ n. **1** (also **banner ad**) a long strip of cloth bearing a slogan or design, hung in a public place or carried in a demonstration or procession. ■ a flag on a pole used as the standard of a monarch, army, or knight. ■ fig. an idea or principle used to rally public opinion: *the administration is flying the free trade banner.* **2** (also **banner ad**) an advertisement on a Web site in the form of bar, column, or box at the edges of the main body of the page. ▶ adj. [attrib.] excellent; outstanding: *a banner year.*

– PHRASES **under the banner of** claiming to support a particular cause or set of ideas. ■ as part of a particular group or organization. — **ban·nered** adj. [ME: from OFr. *baniere*, ult. from Gmc. and rel. to BAND[2].]

ban·ner·et /'banərit; ,banə'ret/ ▶ n. hist. **1** a knight who commanded his own troops in battle under his own banner. **2** a knighthood given on the battlefield for courage. [ME: from OFr. *baneret*, lit. 'bannered,' from *baniere* 'banner.']

ban·ner head·line ▶ n. a newspaper headline running across a whole page, esp. one on the front page.

Ban·nis·ter /'banəstər/, Sir Roger Gilbert (1929–), British track and field athlete. In 1954, he became the first man to run a mile in under four minutes.

ban·nis·ter ▶ n. var. of BANISTER.

ban·nock /'banək/ ▶ n. a round, flat bread, typically unleavened, associated with Scotland and northern England. [OE *bannuc*, of Celtic origin; akin to Welsh *ban*.]

Ban·nock·burn, Battle of /'banək,bərn/ a battle that took place near Stirling in central Scotland in 1314, in which the English army of Edward II was defeated by the Scots under Robert the Bruce.

banns /banz/ ▶ plural n. a notice read out on three successive Sundays in a parish church, announcing an intended marriage and giving the opportunity for objections. [ME: pl. of BAN[1].]

ban·quet /'baNGkwit/ ▶ n. an elaborate and formal evening meal for many people, often followed by speeches. ■ an elaborate and extensive meal; a feast. ▶ v. (**-quet·ed, -quet·ing**) [trans.] entertain with a banquet: *there are halls for banqueting up to 3,000 people* | [as adj.] (**banqueting**) *a banqueting hall.* — **ban·quet·er** n. [15th C.: from Fr., dimin. of *banc* 'bench' (see BANK[1]).]

ban·quette /baNG'ket/ ▶ n. **1** an upholstered bench along a wall, esp. in a restaurant or bar. **2** a raised step behind a rampart. [17th C. (sense 2): from Fr., from Ital. *banchetta*, dimin. of *banca* 'bench' (see BANK[2]).]

ban·shee /'banshē/ ▶ n. (in Irish legend) a female spirit whose wailing warns of an impending death in a house. [17th C.: from Irish *bean sídhe*, from Old Irish *ben síde* 'woman of the fairies.']

ban·tam /'bantəm/ ▶ n. **1** a chicken of a small breed, of which the cock is noted for its aggressiveness. **2** short for BANTAMWEIGHT. [18th C.: prob. after *Bantam*, province in Java.]

ban·tam·weight /'bantəm,wāt/ ▶ n. a weight in boxing and other sports intermediate between flyweight and featherweight. In boxing it ranges from 112 to 118 pounds (51 to 54 kg). ■ a boxer or other competitor of this weight.

ban·ter /'bantər/ ▶ n. the playful and friendly exchange of teasing remarks. ▶ v. [intrans.] talk or exchange remarks in a good-humored teasing way: *the men bantered with the waitresses* | [as adj.] (**bantering**) *a bantering tone.* [17th C.: of unknown origin.]

Ban·ting /'bantiNG/, Sir Frederick Grant (1891–1941), Canadian physiologist. With the help of C. H. Best, he discovered insulin 1921–22 to treat diabetes. Nobel Prize for Physiology or Medicine (1923, shared with J. J. R. Macleod).

Ban·tu /'banto͞o/ ▶ n. (pl. same or **-tus**) **1** a member of an extensive group of native peoples of central and southern Africa. **2** the group of languages spoken by these peoples. ▶ adj. of or relating to these peoples or their languages. [pl. (in certain Bantu languages) of *-ntu* 'person.']

ban·yan /'banyən/ (also **ban·ian**) ▶ n. (also **banyan tree**) an Indian fig tree (*Ficus benghalensis*) whose branches produce aerial roots that later become accessory trunks. A mature tree may cover several acres in this manner. [16th C.: from Port., from Gujarati *vāṇiyo* 'man of the trading caste,' from Sanskrit (orig. applied by Europeans to a tree under which traders had built a pagoda.]

ban·zai /'ban'zī/ ▶ exclam. **1** a Japanese battle cry. **2** a form of greeting used to the Japanese emperor. ▶ adj. (esp. of Japanese troops) attacking fiercely and recklessly: *a banzai charge.* [Japanese, lit. 'ten thousand years (of life to you).']

ba·o·bab /'bāō,bab; 'bāō-/ ▶ n. a short tree (genus *Adansonia*, family Bombacaceae) with an enormously thick trunk and large edible fruit. [17th C.: prob. from an African language.]

Bao·tou /'bou'tō/ a city in Inner Mongolia, in northern China, on the Yellow River; pop. 1,180,000.

bap·tism /'baptizəm/ ▶ n. a person's initiation into a particular activity or role, typically one perceived as difficult: *his baptism as a politician.* ■ a ceremony or occasion at which this takes place. ■ fig. a religious experience likened to this.

– PHRASES **baptism of fire** a difficult or painful new undertaking or experience. — **bap·tis·mal** /bap'tizməl/ adj. [ME: from OFr. *baptesme*.]

bap·tist /'baptist/ ▶ n. **1** (**Baptist**) **2** a person who baptizes someone. [ME (sense 2): from OFr. *baptiste*, via ecclesiastical L. from eccles. Gk. *baptistēs*, from *baptizein* 'immerse, baptize.']

bap·tis·ter·y /'baptəstrē/ (also **bap·tis·try**) ▶ n. (pl. **-ter·ies**) the part of a church used for baptism. ■ hist. a building next to a church, used for baptism. ■ (in a Baptist chapel) a sunken receptacle used for baptism by total immersion. [ME: from OFr. *baptistere*, via ecclesiastical L. from eccles. Gk. *baptistērion*, from *baptizein* 'immerse, baptize.']

bap·tize /'baptīz; bap'tīz/ ▶ v. [with obj. and often with complement] administer baptism to (someone); christen: *he was baptized Joshua.* ■ admit (someone) into a specified church by baptism: *Mark had been baptized a Catholic.* ■ give a name or nickname to: *he baptized the science of narrative "narratology."* [ME: via OFr. from eccles. L. *baptizare*, from Gk. *baptizein* 'immerse, baptize.']

Bar. abbr. Bible Baruch.

bar[1] /bär/ ▶ n. **1** a long rod or rigid piece of wood, metal, or similar material, typically used as an obstruction, fastening, or weapon. ■ an amount of food or another substance formed into a regular narrow block. ■ a band of color or light, esp. on a flat surface. ■ see CROSSBAR. ■ a sandbank or shoal at the mouth of a harbor or an estuary. ■ Brit. a rail marking the end of each chamber in the Houses of Parliament. ■ Heraldry a charge in the form of a narrow horizontal stripe across the shield. **2** a counter across which alcoholic drinks or refreshments are served. ■ a room in a restaurant or hotel in which alcohol is served. ■ an establishment where alcohol and sometimes other refreshments are served. ■ [usu. with adj.] a small store or booth serving refreshments or providing a service: *a dairy bar.* **3** a barrier or restriction to an action or advance. **4** Music a measure of music or the time of a piece of music; bar. **5** (**the bar**) a partition in a courtroom, now usually notional, beyond which most persons may not pass and at which an accused person stands. ■ a similar partition in a legislative assembly. ■ a plea arresting an action or claim in a law case. ■ a particular court of law. ■ any kind of tribunal. **6** (**the Bar**) the legal profession. ■ lawyers collectively. ■ Brit. barristers collectively. ▶ v. (**barred, bar·ring**) [trans.] **1** fasten (something, esp. a door or window) with a bar or bars: *she bars the door.* ■ (usu. **be barred**) prevent or forbid the entrance or movement of: *boulders barred her passage* | *she was barred from a men-only dinner.* ■ prohibit

(someone) from doing something. ■ forbid (an activity) to someone: *the job she loved had been **barred** to her.* ■ exclude (something) from consideration: *nothing is **barred** in the crime novel.* ■ Law prevent or delay (an action) by objection. **2** (usu. **be barred**) mark (something) with bars or stripes: *his face was **barred** with light.* ▶ **prep.** esp. Brit. except for; apart from: *everyone, bar a few ascetics, thinks it desirable.*
– PHRASES **bar none** with no exceptions. **behind bars** in prison. — **barred** /bärd/ **adj.** *barred windows* | [in comb.] *a five-barred gate.* [ME: from OFr. *barre* (n.), *barrer* (v.), of unknown origin.]

bar² ▶ **n.** a unit of pressure equivalent to a hundred thousand newtons per square meter or approximately one atmosphere. [20th C.: from Gk. *baros* 'weight.']

Ba·ra·ta·ria Bay /ˌbärəˈtarēə; -ˈte(ə)rēə/ an inlet of the Gulf of Mexico in southeastern Louisiana.

bar·a·the·a /ˌbarəˈTHēə/ ▶ **n.** a fine woolen cloth, sometimes mixed with silk or cotton, used chiefly for coats and suits. [19th C.: of unknown origin.]

barb¹ /bärb/ ▶ **n. 1** a sharp projection near the end of an arrow, fishhook, or similar item, angled away from the main point so as to make extraction difficult. ■ a cluster of spikes on barbed wire. ■ fig. a deliberately hurtful remark: *his **barb** hurt more than she cared to admit.* ■ a beardlike filament at the mouth of some fish, such as barbel and catfish. ■ one of the fine hairlike filaments growing from the shaft of a feather, forming the vane. **2** a freshwater fish (*Barbus* and other genera) of the minnow family that typically has barbels around the mouth, popular in aquariums. [ME: from OFr. *barbe*, from L. *barba* 'beard.']

barb² ▶ **n.** a small horse of a hardy breed originally from North Africa. [17th C.: from Fr. *barbe*, from Ital. *barbero* 'of Barbary.']

Bar·ba·dos /bärˈbādəs; -dōs; -dōz/ a country in the West Indies, one of the Windward Islands; pop. 278,200; capital, Bridgetown. — **Bar·ba·di·an** /bärˈbādēən/ **adj. & n.**

bar·bar·i·an /bärˈbe(ə)rēən/ ▶ **n.** (in ancient times) a member of a community or tribe not belonging to one of the great civilizations (Greek, Roman, Christian). ■ an uncultured or brutish person. ▶ **adj.** of or relating to ancient barbarians. ■ uncultured; brutish. [ME: ult. from L. *barbarus* (see BARBAROUS).]

bar·bar·ic /bärˈbarik/ ▶ **adj. 1** savagely cruel; exceedingly brutal. **2** primitive; unsophisticated. ■ uncivilized and uncultured. — **bar·bar·i·cal·ly** /-ik(ə)lē/ **adv.**

bar·ba·rism /ˈbärbəˌrizəm/ ▶ **n. 1** absence of culture and civilization. ■ a word or expression that is badly formed according to traditional philological rules, such as formed from elements of different languages: *breathalyzer* (English and Greek) or *television* (Greek and Latin). **2** extreme cruelty or brutality.

bar·bar·i·ty /bärˈbaritē/ ▶ **n.** (pl. **-ties**) **1** extreme cruelty or brutality. **2** absence of culture and civilization.

bar·ba·rize /ˈbärbəˌrīz/ ▶ **v.** [trans.] [usu. as adj.] (**barbarizing**) cause to become savage or uncultured. — **bar·ba·ri·za·tion** /ˌbärbərəˈzāSHən/ **n.**

Bar·ba·ros·sa¹ /ˌbärbəˈräsə; -ˈrōsə/ see FREDERICK I.

Bar·ba·ros·sa², (c.1483–1546), Barbary pirate; born *Khair ad-Din.* He was notorious for his attacks on Christian vessels in the Mediterranean Sea.

bar·ba·rous /ˈbärbərəs/ ▶ **adj. 1** savagely cruel; exceedingly brutal. **2** primitive; uncivilized. ■ (esp. of language) coarse and unrefined. — **bar·ba·rous·ly adv.** [ME (sense 2): via L. from Gk. *barbaros* 'foreign.']

Bar·ba·ry /ˈbärbərē/ (also **Barbary States**) a former name for the Saracen countries of north and northwestern Africa, together with Moorish Spain. Compare with MAGHRIB.

Bar·ba·ry ape ▶ **n.** a tailless macaque monkey (*Macaca sylvana*) that is native to northwestern Africa and also found on the Rock of Gibraltar.

Bar·ba·ry Coast a former name for the Mediterranean coast of North Africa from Morocco to Egypt.

Bar·ba·ry sheep ▶ **n.** a short-coated sheep (*Ammotragus lervia*) with a long neck ruff, found in the high deserts of northern Africa. Also called AOUDAD.

Bar·ba·ry Wars two naval wars (1801–05, 1815) between the US and North Africa's Barbary States, which were supporting piracy throughout the trade routes of the Mediterranean. The second war was a conclusive US victory. Also called the TRIPOLITAN WARS.

bar·be·cue /ˈbärbiˌkyo͞o/ ▶ **n.** a meal or gathering at which meat, fish, or other food is cooked out of doors on a rack over an open fire or on a portable grill. ■ a portable grill used for the preparation of food at a barbecue, or a brick fireplace containing a grill. ■ food cooked in such a way. ▶ **v.** (**-cued, -cu·ing**) [trans.] cook (meat, fish, or other food) on a barbecue. [17th C.: from Sp. *barbacoa*, perh. from Arawak *barbacoa* 'wooden frame on posts.']

barbed /bärbd/ ▶ **adj.** having a barb or barbs. ■ fig. (of a remark or joke) deliberately hurtful.

barbed wire ▶ **n.** wire with clusters of short, sharp spikes set at intervals along it, used to make fences or in warfare as an obstruction.

bar·bel /ˈbärbəl/ ▶ **n. 1** a fleshy filament growing from the mouth or snout of a fish. **2** a large European freshwater fish (*Barbus barbus*) of the minnow family that has such filaments hanging from its mouth. **3** [with adj.] any of numerous marine or freshwater African fish with barbels around the mouth. [ME: via OFr. from late L. *barbellus*, dimin. of *barbus* 'barbel,' from *barba* 'beard.']

bar·bell /ˈbärˌbel/ ▶ **n.** a long metal bar to which disks of varying weights are attached at each end, used for weightlifting.

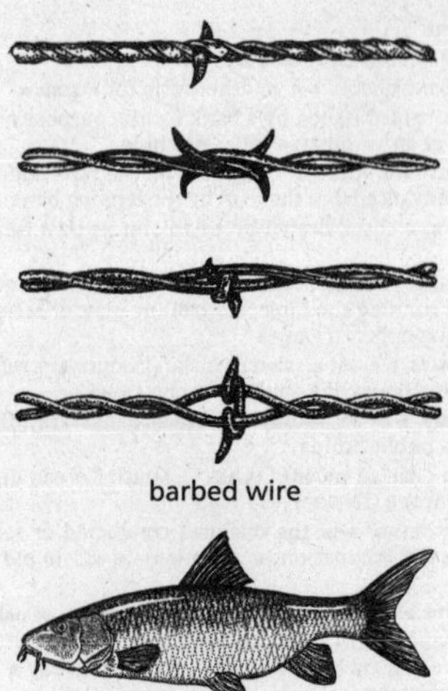

barbed wire

barbel 2

Bar·ber /ˈbärbər/, Samuel (1910–81), US composer. His works include *Adagio for Strings* (1936).

bar·ber /ˈbärbər/ ▶ **n.** a person who cuts hair, esp. men's, and shaves or trims beards as an occupation. ▶ **v.** [trans.] cut or trim (a man's hair). [ME: ult. from OFr. *barbe* (see BARB¹).]

bar·ber·ry /ˈbärˌberē; -bərē/ ▶ **n.** (pl. **-ries**) a thorny shrub (genus *Berberis*, family Berberidaceae) that bears yellow flowers and red or blue-black berries. [ME: from OFr. *berberis*.]

bar·ber·shop /ˈbärbərˌSHäp/ ▶ **n.** a shop where a barber works. ■ [often as adj.] a popular style of close harmony singing, typically for four male voices: *a barbershop quartet.*

bar·ber's itch ▶ **n.** ringworm of the face or neck communicated by unsterilized shaving apparatus.

bar·ber's pole (also **bar·ber pole**) ▶ **n.** a pole painted with spiraling red and white stripes and hung outside barbershops as a business sign.

bar·bet /ˈbärbit/ ▶ **n.** any of numerous large-headed, brightly colored, fruit-eating birds (family Capitonidae) that have stout bills with tufts of bristles at the base. [16th C.: from Fr., from *barbe* 'beard' (see BARB¹).]

bar·bette /bärˈbet/ ▶ **n.** a fixed armored housing at the base of a gun turret on a warship or armored vehicle. ■ hist. a platform on which a gun is placed to fire over a parapet. [18th C.: from Fr., dimin. of *barbe* 'beard' (see BARB¹).]

bar·bi·can /ˈbärbikən/ ▶ **n.** the outer defense of a city or castle, esp. a double tower above a gate or drawbridge. [ME: from OFr. *barbacane*; prob. based on Arab.]

bar·bi·cel /ˈbärbəˌsel/ ▶ **n.** any of the minute hooked filaments that interlock the barbules of a bird's feathers.

bar·bie /ˈbärbē/ ▶ **n.** (pl. **-bies**) informal, esp. Austral. a barbecue.

Bar·bie doll /ˈbärbē/ ▶ **n.** trademark a doll representing a conventionally attractive young woman. ■ informal a woman who is attractive in a glossily artificial way. [1950s: dimin. of the name *Barbara*.]

bar·bi·tal /ˈbärbiˌtäl; -ˌtôl/ ▶ **n.** a long-acting sedative and sleep-inducing drug, $C_6H_{12}O_3N_2$, of the barbiturate type. Alternative name: diethylbarbituric acid. [20th C.: from BARBITURIC ACID.]

bar·bi·tu·rate /bärˈbiCHərit; -əˌrāt/ ▶ **n.** any of a class of sedative and sleep-inducing drugs derived from barbituric acid. ■ Chem. a salt or ester of barbituric acid.

bar·bi·tu·ric ac·id /ˌbärbiˈCHo͝orik/ ▶ **n.** Chem. a synthetic organic acid, $C_4H_4O_3N_2$, from which the barbiturates are derived. [19th C.: from Fr. *barbiturique*, from Ger. *Barbitursäure*.]

Bar·bi·zon School /ˈbärbəˌzän/ a mid-19th-century school of French landscape painters who reacted against classical conventions and based their art on direct study of nature. Led by Théodore Rousseau, the group included Charles Daubigny and Jean-François Millet. [after *Barbizon*, a village near Paris.]

Bar·bour /ˈbärbər/, Philip Pendleton (1783–1841), US Supreme Court associate justice 1836–41.

Bar·bu·da /bärˈbo͞odə/ see ANTIGUA AND BARBUDA. — **Bar·bu·dan** /bärˈbo͞odn/ **adj. & n.**

bar·bule /ˈbärbyo͞ol/ ▶ **n.** a minute filament projecting from the barb of a feather. [19th C.: from L. *barbula*, dimin. of *barba* 'beard.']

barb·wire /ˈbärbˈwī(ə)r/ ▶ **n.** barbed wire.

bar·ca·role /ˈbärkəˌrōl/ (also **bar·ca·rolle**) ▶ **n.** a song traditionally sung by Venetian gondoliers. ■ a musical composition in the style of such a song. [18th C.: from Fr. *barcarolle*, from Venetian Ital. *barcarola* 'boatman's song,' from *barca* 'boat.']

Bar·ce·lo·na /ˌbärsəˈlōnə/ a city on the coast of northeastern Spain; pop. 1,653,175.

Bar·ce·lo·na chair ▶ **n.** trademark an armless chair with a curved stainless steel frame and leather cushions.

bar·chan /bär'kän/ ▶ n. a crescent-shaped shifting sand dune, concave on the leeward side. [19th C.: from Turkic *barkhan*.]

bar chart ▶ n. another term for BAR GRAPH.

bar code ▶ n. a machine-readable code in the form of numbers and a pattern of parallel lines of varying widths, printed on and identifying a product. Also called UNIVERSAL PRODUCT CODE.

bard[1] /bärd/ ▶ n. archaic or literary a poet, traditionally one reciting epics and associated with a particular oral tradition. ■ (**the Bard** or **the Bard of Avon**) Shakespeare. —**bard·ic** adj. [ME: from Scot. Gael. *bàrd*, Irish *bard*, Welsh *bardd*, of Celtic origin.]

bard[2] ▶ n. a slice of bacon placed on meat or game before roasting. ▶ v. [trans.] cover (meat or game) with slices of bacon. [18th C.: from Fr. *barde*, from *barde* 'armor for horse,' based on Arab. *barda'a* 'padded saddle.']

Bar·deen /bär'dēn/, John (1908–91), US physicist who co-invented the point-contact transistor in 1947 with Shockley and Brattain (shared Nobel Prize for Physics 1956). With Leon N. Cooper and John R. Schrieffer, he developed the microscopic theory of superconductivity in 1957 (shared Nobel Prize for Physics 1972).

bard·ol·a·try /bär'dälətrē/ ▶ n. humorous excessive admiration of Shakespeare. —**bard·ol·a·ter** (or **bard·o·la·tor**) /-'dälətər/ n.

Bar·do·li·no /,bärdl'ēnō/ ▶ n. a red wine from the Veneto region of Italy.

bare /be(ə)r/ ▶ adj. **1** (of a person or part of the body) not clothed or covered. ■ without the appropriate, usual, or natural covering: *bare floorboards.* ■ without the appropriate or usual contents. ■ unconcealed; without disguise: *an ordeal that lay* **bare** *a troubled past.* **2** without addition; basic and simple: *he outlined the bare essentials of the story.* ■ [attrib.] only just sufficient: *a bare majority.* ■ [attrib.] surprisingly small in number or amount. ▶ v. [trans.] uncover (a part of the body or other thing) and expose it to view: *he bared his chest.*
– PHRASES **bare all** take off all of one's clothes and display oneself to others. **the bare bones** the basic facts about something, without any detail. **bare one's soul** reveal one's innermost secrets and feelings to someone. **bare one's teeth** show one's teeth, typically when angry. **with one's bare hands** without using tools or weapons. —**bare·ness** n. [OE *bær* (n.), *barian* (v.), from Gmc.; akin to Du. *baar*.]

bare·back /'be(ə)r,bak/ ▶ adj. & adv. on an unsaddled horse or other animal: [as adj.] *a bareback circus rider* | [as adv.] *riding bareback.*

bare·boat /'be(ə)r,bōt/ ▶ adj. [attrib.] relating to or denoting a boat or ship hired without a crew. —**bare·boat·ing** n.

bare·faced /'be(ə)r,fāst/ ▶ adj. **1** [attrib.] shameless; undisguised: *a barefaced lie.* **2** having an uncovered face, so as to be exposed or vulnerable to something.

bare·foot /'be(ə)r,fo͝ot/ (also **bare·foot·ed** /-,fo͝otid/) ▶ adj. & adv. wearing nothing on the feet: [as adv.] *I won't walk barefoot.*

bare·foot doc·tor ▶ n. a paramedical worker with basic medical training working in a rural district in China.

ba·rège /bə'rezн/ (also **ba·rege**) ▶ n. a light, silky dress fabric resembling gauze, typically made from wool. [Fr., after *Barèges*, village in France.]

bare·hand /'be(ə)r,hand/ ▶ v. (in baseball) field with one's bare hand.

bare·hand·ed /'be(ə)r'handid/ ▶ adj. & adv. with nothing in or covering one's hands: *his barehanded catch.* ■ carrying no weapons.

bare·head·ed /'be(ə)r,hedid/ ▶ adj. & adv. without a covering for one's head.

Ba·reil·ly /bə'rālē/ a city in northern India, in Uttar Pradesh; pop. 583,000.

bare-knuck·le (also **bare-knuck·led** or **bare-knuck·les**) ▶ adj. [attrib.] (of a boxer or boxing match) without gloves. ■ informal with no scruples or reservations.

bare·leg·ged /'be(ə)r,legid/ ▶ adj. & adv. without a covering on the legs: *barelegged models.*

bare·ly /'be(ə)rlē/ ▶ adv. **1** only just; almost not: *she nodded, barely able to speak* | [as submodifier] *a barely perceptible pause.* ■ only a short time before: *they had barely sat down when forty policemen swarmed in.* **2** in a simple and sparse way: *their barely furnished house.* **3** archaic openly; explicitly.

Bar·en·boim /'barən,boim/, Daniel (1942–), Israeli pianist and conductor; born in Argentina. He was musical director of the Chicago Symphony Orchestra 1991–2006.

Bar·ents /'barənts; 'bär-/, Willem (died 1597), Dutch explorer. He discovered Spitsbergen and reached Novaya Zemlya.

Bar·ents Sea /'barəns; 'bärəns/ a part of the Arctic Ocean to the north of Norway and Russia.

barf /bärf/ informal ▶ v. [intrans.] vomit. ▶ n. vomited food. [1960s: of unknown origin.]

barf bag ▶ n. a bag provided for airplane passengers for use in case of vomiting associated with motion sickness.

bar·fly /'bär,flī/ ▶ n. (pl. **-flies**) informal a person who spends much time drinking in bars.

bar·gain /'bärgən/ ▶ n. **1** an agreement between two or more parties as to what each party will do for the other. **2** a thing bought or offered for sale more cheaply than is usual or expected. ▶ v. [intrans.] negotiate the terms and conditions of a transaction: *he* **bargained with** *the city council* | [as n.] (**bargaining**) *many statutes are passed by political bargaining.* ■ [trans.] (**bargain something away**) part with something after negotiation but get little or nothing in return. ■ (**bargain for/on**) be prepared for; expect: *I got more information than I'd bargained for.*
– PHRASES **drive a hard bargain** be uncompromising in making a deal. **into (in) the bargain** in addition to what was expected; moreover. **keep one's side of the bargain** carry out the promises one has made as part of an agreement. **strike a bargain** make a bargain; agree to a deal. —**bar·gain·er** n. [ME: from OFr. *bargaine* (n.), *bargaignier* (v.); prob. from Gmc. and akin to Ger. *borgen* 'borrow.']

bar·gain base·ment ▶ n. a part of a store where goods are sold cheaply, typically because they are old or imperfect: [as adj.] *bargain-basement prices.*

bar·gain·ing chip ▶ n. a potential concession or other factor that can be used to advantage in negotiations.

barge /bärj/ ▶ n. a long flat-bottomed boat for carrying freight, typically on canals and rivers, either under its own power or towed by another. ■ a long ornamental boat used for pleasure or ceremony. ■ a boat used by the chief officers of a warship. ▶ v. **1** [no obj., with adverbial of direction] move forcefully or roughly: *we can't just* **barge into** *a private garden.* ■ (**barge in**) intrude or interrupt rudely or awkwardly. ■ (chiefly in a sporting context) collide with: *deliberately* **barging into** *the umpire.* **2** [trans.] convey (freight) by barge. [ME (denoting a small seagoing vessel): from OFr., perh. based on Gk. *baris* 'Egyptian boat.']

barge·board /'bärj,bôrd/ ▶ n. a board, typically ornamental, fixed to the gable end of a roof to hide the ends of the roof timbers.

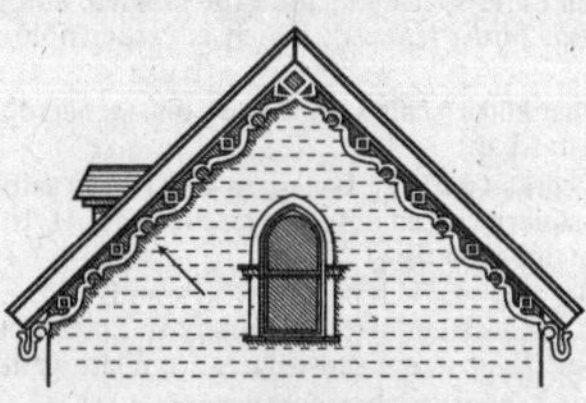
bargeboard

barg·ee /bär'jē/ ▶ n. esp. Brit. a bargeman.

Bar·gel·lo /bär'jelō; -'zнelō/ (also **bar·gel·lo**) ▶ n. a kind of embroidery in stitch patterns suggestive of flames. Also called FLAME STITCH. [1940s: after *Bargello* Palace in Florence, Italy.]

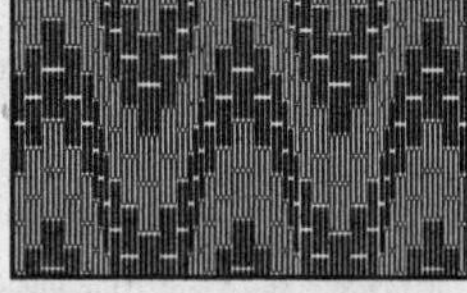
Bargello

barge·man /'bärjmən/ ▶ n. (pl. **-men**) a person who has charge of, or works on, a barge.

bar graph (also **bar chart**) ▶ n. a diagram in which the numerical values of variables are represented by the height or length of lines or rectangles of equal width.

Bar Harbor a town in south central Maine, on Mount Desert Island; pop. 4,443.

bar·hop /'bär,häp/ ▶ v. [intrans.] drink at a number of bars during a single day or evening.

Ba·ri /'bärē/ a seaport on the Adriatic coast of southeastern Italy; pop. 353,030.

bar·i·at·rics /,barē'atriks/ ▶ n. the branch of medicine that deals with the study and treatment of obesity. —**bar·i·at·ric** adj.

ba·ril·la /bə'rilə; -'rēə/ ▶ n. an impure alkali formerly made from the ashes of burned plants, esp. saltworts. [17th C.: from Sp. *barrilla*, dimin. of *barra* 'bar.']

Ba·ri·sal /'barə,sôl/ a port in southern Bangladesh, on the Ganges delta; pop. 180,010.

ba·ri·sta /bə'rēstə/ ▶ n. a person who serves in a coffee bar. [1980s: Italian, 'barman.']

bar·ite /'be(ə)rīt; 'bar-/ ▶ n. a mineral consisting of barium sulfate.

bar·i·tone /'bari,tōn/ ▶ n. **1** an adult male singing voice between tenor and bass. ■ a singer with such a voice. ■ a part written for such a voice. **2** an instrument that is second lowest in pitch in its family. ■ a large, valved brass instrument in coiled oval form. ▶ adj. second lowest in musical pitch. [17th C.: from Ital. *baritono*, from Gk. *barutonos*, from *barus* 'heavy' + *tonos* (see TONE).]

bar·i·um /'be(ə)rēəm; 'bar-/ ▶ n. the chemical element of atomic number 56, a soft white reactive metal of the alkaline earth group. (Symbol: **Ba**) ■ a mixture of barium sulfate and water, opaque to X-rays, that is swallowed to permit radiological examination of the stomach or intestines. [19th C.: from BARYTA + -IUM.]

bar·i·um sul·fate ▶ n. an odorless, insoluble white powder, $BaSO_4$, used in the making of pigments, paper, textiles, and plastics, and ingested as a contrasting agent in X-raying the digestive tract.

bark[1] /bärk/ ▶ n. the sharp explosive cry of certain animals, esp. a dog, fox, or seal. ■ a sound resembling this cry, typically one made by someone laughing or coughing. ▶ v. **1** [intrans.] (of a dog or other animal) emit a bark. ■ (of a person) make a sound, such as a cough or a laugh,

resembling a bark. **2** [trans.] utter (a command or question) abruptly or aggressively: *he began **barking out** his orders* | [with direct speech] *"Nobody is allowed up here," he barked* | [intrans.] *he was **barking at** me to make myself presentable.* ■ [intrans.] call out in order to sell or advertise something: *doormen bark at passersby.*
– PHRASES **someone's bark is worse than their bite** someone is not as ferocious as they appear or sound. **be barking up the wrong tree** informal be pursuing a mistaken or misguided line of thought or course of action. [OE *beorc* (n.), *beorcan* (v.), of Gmc. origin; possibly rel. to BREAK.]

bark[2] ▶ **n.** the tough, protective outer sheath of the trunk, branches, and twigs of a tree or woody shrub. ■ this material used for tanning leather, making dyestuffs, or as a mulch in gardening. ▶ **v.** [trans.] **1** strip the bark from (a tree or piece of wood). ■ scrape the skin off (one's shin) by accidentally hitting it against something hard. **2** tech. tan or dye (leather or other materials) using the tannins found in bark. — **barked adj.** [in comb.] *the red-barked dogwood.* [ME: from ON *bǫrkr*; perh. rel. to BIRCH.]

bark[3] ▶ **n.** (also **barque**) a sailing ship, typically with three masts, in which the foremast and mainmast are square-rigged and the mizzenmast is rigged fore-and-aft. ■ archaic or literary a ship or boat. [ME: var. of BARQUE.]

bark bee·tle ▶ **n.** a small wood-boring beetle of the family Scolytidae that tunnels under the bark of trees, which die if heavily infested. Its many genera and species include the **smaller European elm bark beetle** (*Scolytus multistriatus*), which is responsible for Dutch elm disease.

bar·keep·er /'bär,kēpər/ (also **bar·keep**) ▶ **n.** a person who owns or serves drinks in a bar.

bark·en·tine /'bärkən,tēn/ (Brit. **bar·quen·tine**) ▶ **n.** a sailing ship similar to a bark but square-rigged only on the foremast. [17th C.: from BARK[3], on the pattern of *brigantine*.]

bark·er /'bärkər/ ▶ **n.** informal a person who stands in front of a theater, sideshow, etc., and calls out to passersby to attract customers. [ME: from BARK[1] + -ER[1], the current sense dates from late 17th C.]

bark·ing deer ▶ **n.** another term for MUNTJAC.

Bark·ley /'bärklē/, Alben William (1877–1956), US vice president 1949–53. He also served in the US Senate 1927–49, 1955–56.

bar·ley /'bärlē/ ▶ **n.** a hardy cereal (genus *Hordeum*) that has coarse bristles extending from the ears, widely cultivated for use in brewing and stockfeed. ■ the grain of this plant. See also PEARL BARLEY. [OE *bærlic* (adj.), from *bære, bere* 'barley' + *-lic* (see -LY[1]).]

bar·ley·corn /'bärlē,kôrn/ ▶ **n.** a grain of barley. ■ a former unit of measurement (about a third of an inch) based on the length of a grain of barley.

bar·ley sug·ar ▶ **n.** an amber-colored candy made of boiled sugar, traditionally shaped as a twisted stick. ▶ **adj.** (**bar·ley-sug·ar**) [attrib.] shaped like twisted barley-sugar sticks.

bar·ley wa·ter ▶ **n.** a drink made from water and a boiled barley mixture, typically flavored with orange or lemon.

bar line ▶ **n.** Music a vertical line used in a musical score to mark a division between bars.

Bar·low knife /'bärlō/ ▶ **n.** a large single-bladed pocketknife. [named for Russell Barlow, 18th-cent. English inventor.]

barm /bärm/ ▶ **n.** the froth on fermenting malt liquor. [OE *beorma*, from West Gmc.]

bar·maid /'bär,mād/ ▶ **n.** **1** a waitress who serves drinks in a bar. **2** Brit. a woman bartender.

bar·man /'bärmən/ ▶ **n.** (pl. **-men**) esp. Brit. a male bartender.

Bar·me·cide /'bärmə,sīd/ (also **Bar·me·cid·al** /,bärmə'sīdl/) rare ▶ **adj.** [attrib.] illusory or imaginary and therefore disappointing. ▶ **n.** a person who offers benefits that are illusory or disappointing. [18th C.: from Arab. *Barmakī*, a prince in the *Arabian Nights' Entertainments*, who gave a beggar a feast with empty dishes.]

bar mitz·vah /,bär 'mitsvə/ ▶ **n.** the religious initiation ceremony of a Jewish boy who has reached the age of 13 and is regarded as ready to observe religious precepts and eligible to take part in public worship. ■ the boy undergoing this ceremony. ▶ **v.** [trans.] (usu. **be bar mitzvahed**) celebrate the bar mitzvah of (a boy). [19th C.: from Heb. *bar miṣwāh*, lit. 'son of the commandment.']

barn[1] /bärn/ ▶ **n.** a large farm building used for storing grain, hay, or straw or for housing livestock. ■ a large shed used for storing vehicles. ■ a large and unattractive building: *moved into that **barn of a house**.* [OE *bern, berern*, from *bere* 'barley' + *ern, ærn* 'house.']

barn[2] (abbr.: **b**) ▶ **n.** Physics a unit of area, 10–28 square meters, used esp. in particle physics. [1940s: appar. from phr. *as big as a barn door*.]

Bar·na·bas, St. /'bärnəbəs/ (died c.61), a leader of the early Christian Church. He founded the Cypriot Church.

bar·na·cle /'bärnəkəl/ ▶ **n.** a marine crustacean (class Cirripedia) with an external shell, which attaches itself permanently to a variety of surfaces. ■ used figuratively to describe a tenacious person or thing. — **bar·na·cled adj.** [16th C.: from med. L. *bernaca*, of unknown origin.]

bar·na·cle goose ▶ **n.** a goose (*Branta leucopsis*) with a white face and black neck, breeding in the arctic tundra of Greenland and northern Europe.

Bar·nard /'bärnərd/, Christiaan Neethling (1922–2001), South African physician. He performed the first human heart transplant in December 1967.

Bar·na·ul /,bərnə'ōōl/ a city in southern Russia, on the Ob River; pop. 603,000.

barn burn·er (also **barn·burn·er**) ▶ **n.** informal an event, typically a sports contest, that is very exciting or intense.

barn dance ▶ **n.** an informal social gathering for square dancing, originally held in a barn.

barn door ▶ **n.** the large door of a barn. ■ a target too large to be missed: *on the shooting range he **could not hit a barn door**.* ■ a hinged metal flap fitted to a spotlight to control the direction and intensity of its beam.

barn owl ▶ **n.** an owl (genus *Tyto*, family Tytonidae) with a heart-shaped face, dark eyes, and relatively long, slender legs. It typically nests in farm buildings or in holes in trees.

Barns·ley /'bärnzlē/ a town in northern England; pop. 217,300.

Barn·sta·ble /'bärnstəbəl/ a town in southeastern Massachusetts, on Cape Cod; pop. 40,949.

barn·storm /'bärn,stôrm/ ▶ **v.** [intrans.] tour rural districts giving theatrical performances, originally often in barns. ■ [trans.] make a rapid tour of (an area), typically as part of a political campaign. ■ travel around giving exhibitions of flying and performing aeronautical stunts. — **barn·storm·er n.**

barn swal·low ▶ **n.** see SWALLOW[2].

Bar·num /'bärnəm/, P. T. (1810–91), US showman; full name *Phineas Taylor Barnum*. In 1881, he founded the Barnum and Bailey Circus with Anthony Bailey (1847–1906).

Bar·num ef·fect ▶ **n.** Psychol. the tendency to accept certain information as true, such as character assessments or horoscopes, even when the information is so vague as to be worthless. [named after P. T. BARNUM; *Barnum* was formerly used to mean 'nonsense.']

barn·yard /'bärn,yärd/ ▶ **n.** the area of open ground around a barn. ▶ **adj.** (esp. of manners or language) typical of a barnyard; earthy.

baro- ▶ **comb. form** relating to pressure: *barotrauma* | *baroreceptor.* [from Gk. *baros* 'weight.']

bar·o·gram /'barə,gram/ ▶ **n.** a record traced by a barograph.

bar·o·graph /'barə,graf/ ▶ **n.** a barometer that records its readings on a moving chart. [19th C.: from Gk. *baros* 'weight.']

Ba·ro·lo /bə'rōlō/ ▶ **n.** a full-bodied red Italian wine from Barolo, a region of Piedmont.

ba·rom·e·ter /bə'rämitər/ ▶ **n.** an instrument measuring atmospheric pressure, used esp. in forecasting the weather and determining altitude. ■ something that reflects changes in circumstances or opinions: *furniture is **a barometer of** changing tastes.* — **bar·o·met·ric** /,barə'metrik/ **adj.** **bar·o·met·ri·cal** /,barə'metrikəl/ **adj.** **ba·rom·e·try n.** [17th C.: from Gk. *baros* 'weight.']

bar·o·met·ric pres·sure /,barə'metrik/ ▶ **n.** another term for ATMOSPHERIC PRESSURE.

bar·on /'barən/ ▶ **n.** a member of the lowest order of the British nobility. ■ a similar member of a foreign nobility. ■ hist. a person who held lands or property from the sovereign or a powerful overlord. ■ [with adj.] an important or powerful person in a specified business or industry: *a press baron.* [ME: from OFr., from med. L. *baro, baron-* 'man, warrior,' prob. of Gmc. origin.]

bar·on·age /'barənij/ ▶ **n.** **1** [treated as sing. or pl.] barons or nobles collectively. **2** an annotated list of barons or peers.

bar·on·ess /'barənis/ ▶ **n.** the wife or widow of a baron. ■ a woman holding the rank of baron either as a life peerage or as a hereditary rank.

bar·on·et /'barənit; ,barə'net/ ▶ **n.** a member of the lowest hereditary titled British order, with the status of a commoner but able to use the prefix "Sir." [ME: from Anglo-Latin *baronettus*, from L. *baro, baron-* 'man, warrior.']

bar·on·et·age /'barənitij; ,barə'netij/ ▶ **n.** **1** [treated as sing. or pl.] baronets collectively. **2** an annotated list of baronets.

bar·on·et·cy /'barənitsē/ ▶ **n.** (pl. **-cies**) the rank of a baronet.

ba·ro·ni·al /bə'rōnēəl/ ▶ **adj.** belonging or relating to a baron or barons. ■ suitable for a baron.

bar·o·ny /'barənē/ ▶ **n.** (pl. **-nies**) **1** the rank and estates of a baron. **2** hist. (in Ireland) a division of a county. **3** hist. (in Scotland) a large manor or estate.

ba·roque /bə'rōk/ ▶ **adj.** relating to or denoting a style of European architecture, music, and art of the 17th and 18th centuries that followed mannerism and is characterized by ornate detail. ■ highly ornate and extravagant in style. ▶ **n.** the baroque style. ■ the baroque period. [18th C.: from Fr. (orig. a pearl of irregular shape), from Port. *barroco*, Sp. *barrueco*, or Ital. *barocco*.]

bar·o·re·cep·tor /,barōri'septər/ ▶ **n.** Zool. a receptor sensitive to changes in pressure.

ba·rouche /bə'rōōsh/ ▶ **n.** hist. a four-wheeled horse-drawn carriage with a collapsible hood over the rear half, a seat in front for the driver, and seats facing each other for the passengers, used esp. in the 19th century. [19th C.: from Ger. dial. *Barutsche*, from Ital. *baroccio*, based on L. *birotus* 'two-wheeled,' from *bi-* 'having two' + *rota* 'wheel.'] *See illustration on next page.*

barque /bärk/ ▶ **n.** var. of BARK[3]. [ME: from OFr., prob. from Provençal *barca*, from late L. *barca* 'ship's boat.']

bar·quen·tine /'bärkən,tēn/ ▶ **n.** British spelling of BARKENTINE.

Bar·qui·si·me·to /,bärkēsē'mātō/ a city in northwestern Venezuela; pop. 602,620.

bar·rack[1] /'barək/ ▶ **v.** [trans.] (often **be barracked**) provide (soldiers) with accommodations in a building or set of buildings: *the granary in which the platoons were barracked.* [18th C.: from BARRACKS.]

barouche

bar·rack² ▶ **v.** [trans.] Brit. & Austral./NZ jeer loudly at (someone performing or speaking in public) in order to express disapproval or to create a distraction: *opponents barracked him when he addressed the opening parliamentary session* | [as n.] (**barracking**) *the disgraceful barracking which came from the mob.* ■ [intrans.] (**barrack for**) Austral./NZ give support and encouragement to: *I take it you'll be barracking for Labour tonight?* [19th C.: prob. from Northern Irish dial.]

bar·racks /'barəks/ ▶ **plural n.** [often treated as sing.] a building or group of buildings used to house soldiers. ■ a building or group of buildings used to house large numbers of people. [17th C.: *barrack* from Fr. *baraque*, from Ital. *baracca* or Sp. *barraca* 'soldier's tent.']

bar·racks bag ▶ **n.** a large cloth bag for carrying clothing, equipment, and personal items; a duffel bag.

bar·ra·coon /,barə'ko͞on/ ▶ **n.** hist. an enclosure in which black slaves were confined for a limited period. [19th C.: from Sp. *barracón*, from *barraca* 'soldier's tent.']

Pacific barracuda

bar·ra·cu·da /,barə'ko͞odə/ ▶ **n.** (pl. same or **-das**) a large, predatory tropical marine fish (genus *Sphyraena*, family Sphyraenidae) with a slender body and large jaws and teeth. Its several species include the inedible and poisonous **great barracuda** (*S. barracuda*) and the edible **Pacific barracuda** (*S. argentea*). [17th C.: of unknown origin.]

bar·rage /bə'räzʜ/ ▶ **n.** a concentrated artillery bombardment over a wide area. ■ fig. a concentrated outpouring, as of questions or blows. ▶ **v.** [trans.] (usu. **be barraged**) bombard (someone) with something: *his doctor was barraged with advice.* [19th C.: from Fr., from *barrer* 'to bar,' of unknown origin.]

bar·rage bal·loon ▶ **n.** a large balloon anchored to the ground by cables and often with netting suspended from it, serving as an obstacle to low-flying enemy aircraft.

bar·ran·ca /bə'räNGkə/ (also **bar·ran·co** /-kō/) ▶ **n.** (pl. **-cas** also **-cos**) a narrow, winding river gorge. [17th C.: from Sp.]

Bar·ran·quil·la /,bärən'kē(y)ə/ a city in northern Colombia, at the mouth of the Magdalena River; pop. 1,018,700.

bar·ra·try /'barətrē/ ▶ **n. 1** Law vexatious litigation or incitement to it. **2** hist. trade in the sale of church or state appointments. — **bar·ra·tor** /'barətər/ **n.** (hist.) (in sense 2). **bar·ra·trous** /-trəs/ **adj.** [ME: from OFr. *baraterie*, from *barater* 'deceive,' based on Gk. *prattein* 'do, perform, manage.']

Barr bod·y /bär/ ▶ **n.** Anat. Physiol. a small, densely staining structure in the cell nuclei of female mammals, consisting of a condensed, inactive X chromosome. It is regarded as diagnostic of genetic femaleness.

barre /bär/ ▶ **n.** a horizontal bar at waist level on which ballet dancers rest a hand for support during exercises. [20th C.: Fr., lit. 'bar.']

barred owl ▶ **n.** large gray-brown North American owl (*Strix varia*, family Strigidae) with brown eyes and a barred pattern across the chest.

bar·rel /'barəl/ ▶ **n. 1** a cylindrical container bulging out in the middle, traditionally made of wooden staves with metal hoops around them. ■ such a container together with its contents: *a barrel of beer.* ■ a measure of capacity used for beer and petroleum. In the US, it is usually equal to 31 gallons for beer and 42 gallons for petroleum. **2** a tube forming part of an object such as a gun or a pen. **3** the belly and loins of a four-legged animal such as a horse. ▶ **v.** (**-reled, -rel·ing** ; Brit. **-relled, -rel·ling**) **1** [no obj., with adverbial of direction] informal drive or move fast, often heedless of surroundings or conditions: *we barreled across the Everglades.* **2** [trans.] put into a barrel or barrels.
— PHRASES **a barrel of laughs** [often with negative] informal a source of fun or amusement. **on the barrel** (of payment) without delay. **over a barrel** informal in a helpless position; at someone's mercy. **with both barrels** informal with unrestrained force or emotion. [ME: from O Fr. *baril*, from med. L. *barriclus* 'small cask.']

bar·rel cac·tus ▶ **n.** a spiny, ribbed cylindrical cactus (*Ferocactus, Echinocereus* and other genera).

bar·rel-chest·ed ▶ **adj.** having a large rounded chest.

bar·rel dis·tor·tion ▶ **n.** a type of defect in optical or electronic images in which vertical or horizontal straight lines appear as convex curves.

bar·rel·head /'barəl,hed/ ▶ **n.** the flat top of a barrel.
— PHRASES **on the barrelhead** another way of saying ON THE BARREL (see BARREL).

bar·rel·house /'barəl,hous/ ▶ **n. 1** a cheap or disreputable bar. **2** [usu. as adj.] an unrestrained and unsophisticated style of jazz music. [19th C.: so named because of the rows of barrels along the walls of such a bar.]

bar·rel or·gan ▶ **n.** a mechanical musical instrument from which predetermined music is produced by turning a handle, played, esp. in former times, by street musicians.

bar·rel roll ▶ **n.** an aerobatic maneuver in which an aircraft follows a single turn of a spiral while rolling once about its longitudinal axis.

bar·rel vault ▶ **n.** Archit. a vault forming a half cylinder. — **bar·rel-vault·ed adj.**

bar·ren /'barən/ ▶ **adj. 1** (of land) too poor to produce much or any vegetation. ■ (of a tree or plant) not producing fruit or seed. ■ archaic (of a woman) unable to have children. ■ (of a female animal) not pregnant or unable to become so. ■ showing no results or achievements; unproductive. **2** (of a place or building) bleak and lifeless. ■ empty of meaning or value. ■ (**barren of**) devoid of. ▶ **n.** (usu. **barrens**) a barren tract or tracts of land. — **bar·ren·ness n.** [ME: from OFr. *barhaine*.]

Bar·rett /'barit/, Elizabeth, see BROWNING¹.

bar·rette /bə'ret/ ▶ **n.** a typically bar-shaped clip or ornament for the hair. [20th C.: from Fr., dimin. of *barre* 'bar.']

bar·ri·cade /'bari,kād/ ▶ **n.** an improvised barrier erected across a thoroughfare to prevent or delay the movement of opposing forces. ▶ **v.** [trans.] block or defend with such a barrier: *he barricaded the door with a bureau* | [as adj.] (**barricaded**) *barricaded streets.* ■ shut (oneself or someone) into a place by blocking all the entrances. [16th C.: from Fr., from *barrique* 'cask,' from Sp. *barrica*; rel. to BARREL (barrels being often used to build barricades).]

Bar·rie /'barē/, Sir J. M. (1860–1937), Scottish writer; full name *James Matthew Barrie*. His plays include *The Admirable Crichton* (1902) and *Peter Pan* (1904).

bar·ri·er /'barēər/ ▶ **n.** a fence or other obstacle that prevents movement or access. ■ a circumstance or obstacle that prevents communication or that keeps people or things apart: *a language barrier.* ■ something that prevents progress or success. ■ the starting gate of a racecourse. ■ (in full **barrier island**) a long narrow island lying parallel and close to the mainland, protecting the mainland from erosion and storms. [ME (denoting a fortification defending an entrance): from OFr. *barriere*; rel. to BARRE.]

bar·ri·er reef ▶ **n.** a coral reef running parallel to the shore but separated from it by a channel of deep water.

bar·ring /'bäriNG/ ▶ **prep.** except for; if not for: *barring a miracle, he's crippled for life.*

bar·ri·o /'bärē,ō/ ▶ **n.** (pl. **-os**) a district of a town in Spain and Spanish-speaking countries. ■ (in the US) the Spanish-speaking quarter of a town or city. ■ a poor neighborhood populated by Spanish-speaking people. [Sp., perh. from Arab.]

bar·ris·ter /'barəstər/ (also **bar·ris·ter-at-law**) ▶ **n.** esp. Brit. a lawyer entitled to practice as an advocate, particularly in the higher courts. Compare with ATTORNEY, SOLICITOR. [ME: from the n. BAR¹, perh. on the pattern of *minister*.]

bar·room /'bär,ro͞om; -,ro͝om/ ▶ **n.** a room where alcoholic drinks are served over a counter. ■ typical of a barroom: *a barroom brawl.*

Bar·row¹ /'barō/ a city in north central Alaska, the northernmost US city; pop. 4,581. Nearby Point Barrow is the northernmost point in the US.

Bar·row², Clyde Chestnut (1909–34), US robber and murderer. He and his partner, Bonnie Parker, shot and killed at least 13 people during a notorious two-year crime spree across the Southwest.

bar·row¹ /'barō/ ▶ **n.** a metal frame with two wheels used for transporting objects such as luggage. ■ a wheelbarrow. — **bar·row·load n.** [OE *bearwe* 'stretcher, bier,' of Gmc. origin; rel. to BEAR¹.]

bar·row² ▶ **n.** Archaeol. an ancient burial mound. [OE *beorg*, of Gmc. origin; rel. to Du. *berg*, Ger. *Berg* 'hill, mountain.']

bar·row³ ▶ **n.** a male pig castrated before maturity.

bar·ry /'barē/ ▶ **adj.** Heraldry divided into typically four, six, or eight equal horizontal bars of alternating tinctures. [15th C.: from Fr. *barré* 'barred, striped,' past part. of *barrer*.]

Bar·ry·more /'barə,môr/, a US family of actors, including Lionel (1878–1954), his sister Ethel (1879–1959), their brother John (1882–1942), and John's granddaughter Drew (1975–).

bar sin·is·ter ▶ **n.** popular and erroneous term for BEND SINISTER.

bar·stool /'bär,sto͞ol/ (also **bar stool**) ▶ **n.** a tall padded stool for customers at a bar to sit on.

Bar·stow /'bär,stō/ a city in south central California, in the Mojave Desert, northeast of Los Angeles; pop. 21,472.

Bart /bärt/, Lionel (1930–99), English composer and lyricist; born *Lionel Beglieter*. His musicals include *Oliver!* (1960).

Bart. ▶ **abbr.** Baronet.

bar tack ▶ **n.** a stitch made to strengthen a potential weak spot in a garment or other sewn item. — **bar-tacked adj. bar tack·ing n.**

bar·tend·er /'bär,tendər/ ▶ **n.** a person who mixes and serves drinks at a bar.

bar·ter /'bärtər/ ▶ **v.** [trans.] exchange (goods or services) for other goods or services without using money: *he often bartered a meal for drawings* | [intrans.] *the company is prepared to barter for Russian oil.* ▶ **n.** the action or system of exchanging goods or services without using money. ■ the goods or services used for such an exchange. — **bar·ter·er** n. [ME: prob. from OFr. *barater* 'deceive' (see BARRATRY).]

Barth[1] /bärTH/, John Simmons (1930–), US writer. His novels include *Giles Goat-Boy* (1966).

Barth[2] /bärt/, Karl (1886–1968), Swiss theologian. His *Epistle to the Romans* (1919) established a theocentric approach to contemporary religious thought.

Barthes /bärt/, Roland (1915–80), French writer and critic. He was a leading exponent of structuralism and semiology in literary criticism.

Bar·thol·di /bärˈtôldē/, (Frédéric) Auguste (1834–1904), French sculptor. He designed the Statue of Liberty.

Bar·tho·lin's gland /ˈbärtl-inz/ ▶ n. Anat. one of a pair of glands lying near the entrance of the vagina, which secrete a fluid that lubricates the vulva. [18th C.: named by Caspar *Bartholin* (1655–1738), Danish anatomist, as a tribute to his father.]

Bar·thol·o·mew, St. /bärˈTHäləˌmyo͞o/, one of the twelve Apostles; the patron saint of tanners. Feast day, August 24.

bar·ti·zan /ˈbärtəzən/ ▶ n. Archit. an overhanging corner turret at the top of a castle or church tower. [19th C.: from *bertisene*, var. of *bratticing* 'temporary breastwork,' from BRATTICE.]

Bart·lett[1] /ˈbärtlit/ a town in southwestern Tennessee, northeast of Memphis; pop. 40,543.

Bart·lett[2] (also **Bartlett pear**) ▶ n. a dessert pear of a juicy, early-ripening variety.

Bar·tók /ˈbärtäk; -tôk/, Béla (1881–1945), Hungarian composer, influenced by his native folk music.

Bar·to·lom·me·o /ˌbärtōləˈmāō/, Fra (*c*.1472–1517), Italian painter; born *Baccio della Porta*. A Dominican friar, he worked chiefly in Florence.

Bar·ton /ˈbärtn/, Clara (1821–1912), US nurse and social activist; full name *Clarissa Harlowe Barton*. In 1882, she founded the American Red Cross.

Ba·ruch[1] /bəˈro͞ok/, Bernard Mannes (1870–1965), US financier. He was chairman of the War Industries Board 1918–19 and US representative on the UN Atomic Energy Commission 1946.

Bar·uch[2] a book of the Apocrypha, attributed in the text to Baruch, the scribe of Jeremiah.

bar·ware /ˈbärˌwe(ə)r/ ▶ n. glassware used for preparing and serving alcoholic drinks.

bar·y·cen·tric /ˌbarəˈsentrik/ ▶ adj. [attrib.] of or relating to the center of gravity. — **bar·y·cen·ter** /ˈbarəˌsentər/ n. [19th C.: from Gk. *barus* 'heavy.']

bar·y·on /ˈbarēˌän/ ▶ n. Physics a subatomic particle, such as a nucleon or hyperon, that has a mass equal to or greater than that of a proton. — **bar·y·on·ic** /ˌbarēˈänik/ adj. [1950s: from Gk. *barus* 'heavy' + -ON.]

Ba·rysh·ni·kov /bəˈrisHnəˌkôf; -ˌkôv/, Mikhail Nikolaevich (1948–), US ballet dancer; born in Latvia. He was the American Ballet Theater's artistic director 1980–89.

ba·ry·ta /bəˈrītə/ ▶ n. Chem. barium hydroxide, $Ba(OH)_2$. [19th C.: from BARYTE, on the pattern of words such as *soda*.]

bar·yte /ˈbarīt/ (also **ba·ry·tes** /bəˈrītēz/) ▶ n. Brit. var. of BARITE.

bar·y·tone[1] /ˈbariˌtōn/ ▶ n. & adj. var. of BARITONE.

bar·y·tone[2] ▶ adj. Greek Gram. not having the acute accent on the last syllable. — **bar·y·tone** n.

ba·sal /ˈbāsəl; -zəl/ ▶ adj. [attrib.] esp. tech. forming or belonging to a bottom layer or base.

ba·sal bod·y (also **ba·sal gran·ule**) ▶ n. an organelle that forms the base of a flagellum or cilium. Also called KINETOSOME.

ba·sal cell ▶ n. a type of cell in the innermost layer of the epidermis.

ba·sal gan·gli·a ▶ plural n. Anat. a group of structures linked to the thalamus in the base of the brain and involved in coordination of movement.

ba·sal met·a·bol·ic rate ▶ n. the rate at which the body uses energy while at rest to keep vital functions going. — **ba·sal me·tab·o·lism** n.

ba·salt /bəˈsôlt/ ▶ n. a dark, fine-grained volcanic rock that sometimes displays a columnar structure. ■ a kind of black stoneware resembling such rock. — **ba·sal·tic** /-tik/ adj. [17th C.: from L. *basaltes*, from Gk. *basanitēs*, from *basanos* 'touchstone.']

bas·cule /ˈbaskyo͞ol/ (also **bascule bridge**) ▶ n. a type of bridge with a movable section that is raised and lowered using counterweights. ■ a movable section of road forming part of such a bridge. [19th C.: from Fr. (earlier *bacule*), 'seesaw,' from *battre* 'to bump' + *cul* 'buttocks.']

base[1] /bās/ ▶ n. **1** the lowest part or edge of something, esp. the part on which it rests or is supported. ■ Archit. the part of a column between the shaft and pedestal or pavement. ■ Bot. Zool. the end at which a part or organ is attached to the trunk or main part. ■ Geom. a line or surface on which a figure is regarded as standing. ■ Surveying a line of known length used in triangulation. ■ Heraldry the lowest part of a shield. ■ Heraldry the lower third of the field. **2** a conceptual structure or entity on which something draws or depends. ■ something used as a foundation or starting point for further work; a basis. ■ [with adj.] a group of people regarded as supporting an organization, for example by buying its products: *a client base*. **3** the main place where a person works or stays. ■ esp. Mil. a place used as a center of operations by the armed forces or others; a headquarters. ■ a place from which a particular activity can be carried out. **4** a main or important element or ingredient to which other things are added. ■ a substance used as a foundation for makeup. ■ a substance such as water or oil into which a pigment is mixed to form paint. **5** Chem. a substance capable of reacting with an acid to form a salt and water, or (more broadly) of accepting or neutralizing hydrogen ions. Compare with ALKALI. ■ Biochem. a purine or pyrimidine group in a nucleotide or nucleic acid. **6** Electron. the middle part of a bipolar transistor, separating the emitter from the collector. **7** Ling. the root or stem of a word or a derivative. ■ the uninflected form of a verb. **8** Math. a number used as the basis of a numeration scale. ■ a number in terms of which other numbers are expressed as logarithms. **9** Baseball one of the four stations that must be reached in turn to score a run. ▶ v. [trans.] **1** (often **be based**) have as the foundation for (something); use as a point from which (something) can develop: *the film is **based on** a novel*. **2** situate as the center of operations: *a research program based at the University of Arizona* | [as adj., in comb.] (**-based**) *a London-based band*.

– PHRASES **get to first base** [usu. with negative] informal achieve the first step toward one's objective. **first base, second base, third base** informal used to refer to progressive levels of sexual intimacy. **off-base** informal mistaken: *the boy is way off-base*. **touch base** informal briefly make or renew contact with (someone). [ME: from OFr., from L. *basis* 'base, pedestal,' from Gk.]

base[2] ▶ adj. (of a person or a person's actions or feelings) without moral principles; ignoble: *the electorate's baser instincts of greed and selfishness* | *we hope his motives are nothing so base as money*. ■ archaic denoting or befitting a person of low social class. ■ (of coins or other articles) not made of precious metal. — **base·ly** adv. **base·ness** n. [ME: from OFr. *bas*, from med. L. *bassus* 'short' (found in classical L. as a cognomen).]

base·ball /ˈbāsˌbôl/ ▶ n. a ball game played between two teams of nine on a field with a diamond-shaped circuit of four bases. It is played chiefly in the US, Canada, Latin America, and East Asia. ■ the hard ball used in this game.

base·board /ˈbāsˌbôrd/ ▶ n. a narrow wooden board running along the base of an interior wall.

base·born /ˈbāsˌbôrn/ ▶ adj. [attrib.] archaic of low birth or origin. ■ illegitimate.

base bur·ner ▶ n. a coal stove or furnace into which coal is fed automatically from a hopper as the lower layers are burned.

base dress·ing ▶ n. the application of manure or fertilizer to the earth, which is then plowed or dug in. Compare with TOP DRESSING. ■ manure or fertilizer applied in this way.

base ex·change (abbr.: **BX**) ▶ n. a nonprofit store for the purchase of personal items, clothing, refreshments, etc., at a naval or air force base.

base·head /ˈbāsˌhed/ ▶ n. informal a habitual abuser of freebase or crack cocaine. [1980s: from a shortened form of FREEBASE + -HEAD[2].]

base hit ▶ n. Baseball a fair ball hit such that the batter can advance safely to a base without aid of an error committed by the team in the field.

base hos·pi·tal ▶ n. a military hospital situated at some distance from the area of active operations during a war.

Ba·sel /ˈbäzəl/ German name for BASLE.

base·less /ˈbāslis/ ▶ adj. **1** without foundation in fact. **2** Archit. (of a column) not having a base between the shaft and pedestal. — **base·less·ly** adv. **base·less·ness** n.

base·line /ˈbāsˌlīn/ ▶ n. **1** a minimum or starting point used for comparisons. **2** (in tennis, volleyball, etc.) the line marking each end of the court. ■ Baseball the line between bases, which a runner must stay close to when running.

base·man /ˈbāsmən/ ▶ n. (pl. **-men**) Baseball a fielder designated to cover first, second, or third base.

base·ment /ˈbāsmənt/ ▶ n. the floor of a building partly or entirely below ground level. ■ Geol. the oldest formation of rocks underlying a particular area. [18th C.: prob. from archaic Du. *basement* 'foundation,' perh. from Ital. *basamento* 'column base.']

base met·al ▶ n. a common metal not considered precious, such as copper, tin, or zinc.

ba·sen·ji /bəˈsenjē/ ▶ n. (pl. **-jis**) a small hunting dog of a central African breed, which growls and yelps but does not bark. [1930s: a local word.]

base on balls (abbr.: **BB**) ▶ n. Baseball another term for WALK n. 3.

base pair ▶ n. Biochem. a pair of complementary bases in a double-stranded nucleic acid molecule, consisting of a purine in one strand linked by hydrogen bonds to a pyrimidine in the other. Cytosine always pairs with guanine, and adenine with thymine (in DNA) or uracil (in RNA). — **base pair·ing** n.

base path ▶ n. Baseball the straight-line path from one base to the next, defined by the position of the base runner while a play is being made.

base pay ▶ n. the base rate of pay for a job or activity, not including any additional payments such as overtime or bonuses.

base·plate /ˈbāsˌplāt/ ▶ n. a sheet of metal forming the bottom of an object.

base run·ner (also **base·run·ner**) ▶ n. Baseball a player on the team at bat who is on a base, or running between bases. — **base-run·ning** (or **base·run·ning**) n.

ba·ses /ˈbāsēz/ plural form of BASIS.

base u·nit ▶ n. a fundamental unit that is defined arbitrarily and not by combinations of other units. The base units of the SI system are the meter, kilogram, second, ampere, kelvin, mole, and candela.

bash /basH/ ▶ v. [trans.] informal strike hard and violently. ■ (**bash something in**) damage or break something by striking it violently. ■ [intrans.] (**bash into**) collide with: *the vehicle bashed into the back of them*. ■ fig.

criticize severely. ▶ **n.** informal **1** a heavy blow. **2** [usu. with adj.] informal a party or social event.

– PHRASAL VERBS **bash something out** produce something rapidly without preparation or attention to detail. [17th C. (as a v.): imitative, perh. a blend of BANG[1] and SMASH, DASH, etc.]

ba·shaw /bəˈSHô/ ▶ **n.** another term for PASHA.

bash·ful /ˈbaSHfəl/ ▶ **adj.** reluctant to draw attention to oneself; shy. —**bash·ful·ly adv. bash·ful·ness n.** [15th C.: from obs. *bash* 'make or become abashed' (from ABASH).]

bash·ing /ˈbaSHiNG/ ▶ **n.** [usu. with modifier] informal violent physical assault. ■ severe criticism.

Bash·kir /baSHˈki(ə)r/ ▶ **n. 1** a member of a Muslim people living in the southern Urals. **2** the Turkic language of this people. ▶ **adj.** of or relating to this people or their language. [via Russ. from Turkic *Baş¸kurt*.]

Bash·kir·i·a /baSHˈki(ə)rēə/ an autonomous republic in central Russia; pop. 3,964,000; capital, Ufa. Also called BASHKIR AUTONOMOUS REPUBLIC, BASHKORTOSTAN.

BASIC /ˈbāsik/ ▶ **n.** a simple high-level computer programming language that uses familiar English words, designed for beginners and formerly widely used on microcomputers. [1960s: acronym from *Beginners' All-purpose Symbolic Instruction Code*.]

ba·sic /ˈbāsik/ ▶ **adj. 1** forming an essential foundation or starting point; fundamental. ■ offering or consisting of the minimum required without elaboration or luxury; simplest or lowest in level. ■ common to or required by everyone; primary and ineradicable or inalienable. **2** Chem. having the properties of a base, or containing a base; having a pH above 7. Often contrasted with ACID or ACIDIC; compare with ALKALINE. ■ Geol. (of rock, esp. igneous rock) relatively poor in silica. ■ Metallurgy relating to or denoting steelmaking processes involving lime-rich refractories and slags. ▶ **n.** (**basics**) the essential facts or principles of a subject or skill. ■ essential food and other supplies. ■ Mil. basic training. [19th C.: from BASE[1] + -IC.]

ba·si·cal·ly /ˈbāsik(ə)lē/ ▶ **adv.** [often as submodifier] in the most essential respects; fundamentally: *a basically simple idea.* ■ [sentence adverb] used to indicate that a statement summarizes the most important aspects of a more complex situation: *I basically played the same tunes every night.*

Ba·sic Eng·lish ▶ **n.** a simplified form of English limited to 850 selected words, intended for international communication.

ba·sic·i·ty /bāˈsisitē/ ▶ **n.** Chem. the number of hydrogen atoms replaceable by a base in a particular acid.

ba·sic train·ing ▶ **n.** Mil. the initial period of training for new personnel, involving intense physical activity and behavioral discipline.

ba·sid·i·o·my·cete /bəˌsidēōˈmīsēt/ ▶ **n.** Bot. a fungus (phylum Basidiomycota; classes Basidiomycetes, Teliomycetes, and Ustomycetes) whose spores develop within basidia. Basidiomycetes include the majority of familiar mushrooms and toadstools. Compare with ASCOMYCETE. [19th C.: Anglicized sing. of mod. L. *Basidiomycetes*, from *basidium* (see BASIDIUM) + Gk. *mukētes* 'fungi.']

ba·sid·i·o·spore /bəˈsidēōˌspôr/ ▶ **n.** a spore produced by a basidium.

ba·sid·i·um /bəˈsidēəm/ ▶ **n.** (pl. **-sid·i·a** /-ˈsidēə/) a microscopic, club-shaped spore-bearing structure produced by certain fungi. [19th C.: mod. L., from Gk. *basidion*, dimin. of *basis* (see BASIS).]

Ba·sie /ˈbāsē/, Count (1904–84), US pianist and bandleader; born *William Basie*.

ba·si·fy /ˈbāsəˌfī/ ▶ **v.** [trans.] Chem. change into a base; alkalize.

bas·il /ˈbāzəl; ˈbazəl/ ▶ **n.** an aromatic annual herb (genus *Ocimum*) of the mint family, native to tropical Asia. ■ the leaves of this plant used as a culinary herb, esp. in Mediterranean dishes. [ME: from OFr. *basile*, via med. L. from Gk. *basilikon*, neut. of *basilikos* 'royal' (see BASILICA).]

Bas·il, St. /ˈbazəl; ˈbāzəl/ (*c.*330–379), bishop of Caesarea; known as **St. Basil the Great**. Brother of St. Gregory of Nyssa, he established a monastic rule.

bas·i·lar /ˈbasələr/ ▶ **adj.** [attrib.] of or situated at the base of something, esp. of the skull, or of the organ of Corti in the ear. [16th C.: from mod. L. *basilaris*, from L. *basis* (see BASIS).]

ba·si·lect /ˈbāzəˌlekt; ˈbaz-/ ▶ **n.** Ling. a less prestigious dialect or variety of a particular language (used esp. in the study of Creoles). —**ba·si·lec·tal** /ˌbāzəˈlektəl; ˌbaz-/ **adj.**

Ba·sil·i·an /bəˈzilyən; -ˈzilēən/ ▶ **adj.** of or relating to St. Basil the Great, or the order of monks and nuns following his monastic rule. ▶ **n.** a Basilian monk or nun.

ba·sil·i·ca /bəˈsilikə/ ▶ **n.** a large oblong hall or building with double colonnades and a semicircular apse, used in ancient Rome as a court of law or for public assemblies. ■ a similar building used as a Christian church. ■ the name given to certain churches granted special privileges by the pope. —**ba·sil·i·can adj.** [16th C.: from L., lit. 'royal palace,' from Gk. *basilikē*, fem. of *basilikos* 'royal,' from *basileus* 'king.']

bas·i·lisk /ˈbasəˌlisk; ˈbaz-/ ▶ **n. 1** a mythical reptile with a lethal gaze or breath, hatched by a serpent from a cock's egg. ■ Heraldry another term for COCKATRICE. **2** a long, slender, and mainly bright green lizard (*Basiliscus plumifrons*, family Iguanidae) found in Central America, the male of which has a crest running from the head to the tail. It can swim well and is able to run on its hind legs across the surface of water. [ME: via L. from Gk. *basiliskos* 'little king, serpent,' from *basileus* 'king.']

ba·sin /ˈbāsən/ ▶ **n. 1** a bowl for washing, typically attached to a wall and having faucets connected to a water supply; a washbasin. **2** a wide, round open container, esp. one used for holding liquid. **3** a natural depression on the earth's surface, typically containing water. ■ the

basilisk 2

tract of country that is drained by a river and its tributaries or drains into a lake or sea. ■ an enclosed area of water where vessels can be moored. ■ Geol. a circumscribed rock formation where the strata dip toward the center. —**ba·sin·ful** /-ˌfo͝ol/ **n.** [ME: from OFr. *bacin*, from med. L. *bacinus*, from *bacca* 'water container,' perh. of Gaulish origin.]

Ba·sin and Range Province a largely arid intermountain region of the southwestern US. The Great Basin and Death Valley are parts of the region.

bas·i·net /ˌbasəˈnet/ (also **bas·ci·net**) ▶ **n.** a medieval helmet of light steel, fitting close to the wearer's head and typically having a visor. [ME: from OFr. *bacinet* 'little basin.']

ba·sip·e·tal /bāˈsipitl/ ▶ **adj.** Bot. (of growth or development) downward toward the base or point of attachment. The opposite of ACROPETAL. ■ (of the movement of dissolved substances) inward from the shoot and root apexes. —**ba·sip·e·tal·ly adv.** [19th C.: from BASIS + L. *petere* 'seek.']

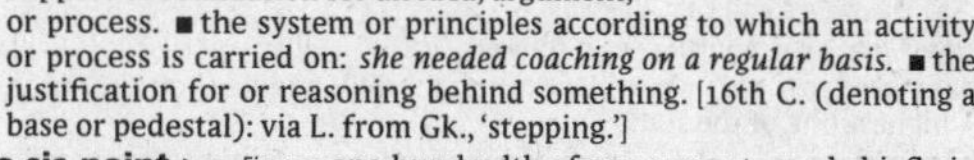

basinet

ba·sis /ˈbāsis/ ▶ **n.** (pl. **-ses** /-sēz/) the underlying support or foundation for an idea, argument, or process. ■ the system or principles according to which an activity or process is carried on: *she needed coaching on a regular basis.* ■ the justification for or reasoning behind something. [16th C. (denoting a base or pedestal): via L. from Gk., 'stepping.']

ba·sis point ▶ **n.** Finance one hundredth of one percent, used chiefly in expressing differences of interest rates.

bask /bask/ ▶ **v.** [intrans.] lie exposed to warmth and light, typically from the sun, for relaxation and pleasure: *sprawled figures basking in the afternoon sun.* ■ (**bask in**) fig. revel in and make the most of (something pleasing). [ME: perh. rel. to ON *batha* 'bathe.']

Bas·ker·ville /ˈbaskərˌvil/ ▶ **n.** a typeface much used in books. [19th C.: after John *Baskerville* (1706–75), English printer.]

bas·ket /ˈbaskit/ ▶ **n. 1** a container used to hold or carry things, typically made from interwoven strips of cane or wire. ■ a structure suspended from the envelope of a hot-air balloon for carrying the crew, equipment, and ballast. ■ Finance a group or range of currencies or investments. **2** Basketball a net fixed on a hoop used as the goal. ■ a goal scored. [ME: from OFr. *basket*.]

bas·ket·ball /ˈbaskitˌbôl/ ▶ **n.** a game played between two teams of five players in which goals are scored by throwing a ball through a netted hoop fixed above each end of the court. ■ the inflated ball used in this game.

bas·ket case ▶ **n.** informal a person or thing regarded as useless or unable to cope. [20th C.: orig. slang for a soldier who had lost all four limbs.]

bas·ket hilt ▶ **n.** a sword hilt with a guard resembling basketwork. —**bas·ket-hilt·ed adj.**

Bas·ket Mak·er ▶ **n.** a member of a culture of the southwestern US, forming the early stages of the Anasazi culture, from the 1st century BC until *c.*AD 700.

bas·ket-of-gold ▶ **n.** a cultivated evergreen alyssum of the cabbage family (*Alyssum saxatile*) with gray-green leaves and numerous small yellow flowers.

bas·ket·ry /ˈbaskitrē/ ▶ **n.** the craft of basket-making. ■ baskets collectively.

bas·ket star ▶ **n.** a brittlestar (genus *Gorgonocephalus*, family Gorgonocephalidae) having branched arms.

bas·ket weave ▶ **n.** a style of weave or a pattern resembling basketwork.

bas·ket-weav·ing /ˈbaskitˌwēviNG/ ▶ **n. 1** the art or activity of creating woven baskets. **2** humorous a college course that is thought to be very easy.

bas·ket·work /ˈbaskitˌwərk/ ▶ **n.** material woven in the style of a basket. ■ the craft of making such material.

bask·ing shark ▶ **n.** a large shark (*Cetorhinus maximus*, family Cetorhinidae) that feeds exclusively on plankton and often swims slowly close to the surface, found chiefly in the open ocean.

Basle /bäl/ a city in northwestern Switzerland; pop. 171,000. French name BÂLE, German name BASEL.

bas·ma·ti /bäsˈmätē/ (also **basmati rice**) ▶ **n.** a kind of long-grain Indian rice of a high quality. [from Hindi *bāsmatī*, lit. 'fragrant.']

bas mitz·vah /bäs 'mitsvə/ ▶ **n.** a variant of BAT MITZVAH.

ba·so·phil /'bāsəfil/ ▶ **n.** Physiol. a basophilic white blood cell.

ba·so·phil·ic /ˌbāsə'filik/ ▶ **adj.** Physiol. (of a cell or its contents) readily stained with basic dyes.

Ba·so·tho /bə'sōˌtō/ ▶ **n.** (pl. same or **-thos**) a member of the Sotho people of southern Africa, esp. Lesotho. [from Sesotho, from *ba-* (prefix denoting a pl.) + SOTHO.]

Basque /bask/ ▶ **n.** **1** a member of a people living in the Basque Country of France and Spain. **2** the language of this people, which has no known relation to any other language. ▶ **adj.** of or relating to the Basques or their language. [from Fr., from L. *Vasco.*]

basque /bask/ ▶ **n.** a close-fitting bodice extending from the shoulders to the waist and often with a short continuation below waist level. [19th C.: from BASQUE, referring to Basque dress.]

Basque Coun·try a region of the western Pyrenees in both France and Spain, the homeland of the Basque people. French name PAYS BASQUE.

Basque Prov·in·ces an autonomous region consisting of the provinces of Álava, Guipúzcoa, and Vizcaya in northern Spain; capital, Vitoria.

Bas·ra /'bäsrə; 'bäz-/ a port in Iraq, on the Shatt al-Arab waterway; pop. 616,700.

bas-re·lief /ˌbä rə'lēf/ ▶ **n.** Sculpture see RELIEF (sense 4). ■ a sculpture, carving, or molding in bas-relief. [17th C.: from Ital. *basso-rilievo* 'low relief.']

bass[1] /bās/ ▶ **n.** a voice, instrument, or sound of the lowest range, in particular: ■ the lowest adult male singing voice. ■ [as adj.] denoting the member of a family of instruments that is the lowest in pitch. See illustration at DRUM KIT. ■ informal a bass guitar or double bass. ■ the low-frequency output of a radio or audio system, corresponding to the bass in music. [ME: alt. of BASE[2].]

bass[2] /bas/ ▶ **n.** (pl. same or **bass·es**) **1** the common European freshwater perch. **2** any of a number of fish similar to or related to this, in particular: ■ a mainly marine fish found in temperate waters (family Percichthyidae or Moronidae). ■ an American fish (genera *Ambloplites* and *Micropterus*) of the freshwater sunfish family. See illustration at BLACK BASS, ROCK BASS. ■ a sea bass. [ME: alt. of dial. *barse*, of Gmc. origin; rel. to Du. *baars* and Ger. *Barsch.*]

bass[3] /bas/ ▶ **n.** another term for BAST. [17th C.: alt.]

bass clef /bās klef/ ▶ **n.** a clef placing F below middle C on the second-highest line of the staff.

bass drum /bās/ ▶ **n.** a large, two-headed drum that has a low booming sound.

Basse-Nor·man·die /'bäs ˌnôrmänˈdē/ a region of northwestern France that includes the Cherbourg peninsula and the city of Caen.

Basse·terre /bäs'ter/ the capital of St. Kitts and Nevis, on the island of St. Kitts; pop. 12,600.

Basse-Terre /bäs 'ter/ the main island of Guadeloupe.

bas·set horn /'basit/ ▶ **n.** an alto clarinet in F. [19th C.: from Ger., translation of Fr. *cor de bassette*, from Ital. *corno di bassetto*, from *corno* 'horn' + *di* 'of' + *bassetto* (dimin. of *basso* 'low').]

basset hound

bas·set hound ▶ **n.** a sturdy hunting dog of a breed with a long body, short legs, and big ears. [17th C.: from Fr., dimin. of *bas* 'low.']

bass fid·dle /bās/ ▶ **n.** another term for DOUBLE BASS.

bas·si·net /ˌbasə'net/ ▶ **n.** a baby's wicker cradle. [19th C.: from Fr., dimin. of *bassin* 'basin.']

bass·ist /'bāsist/ ▶ **n.** a person who plays a double bass or bass guitar.

bas·so /'basō; bä-/ ▶ **n.** (pl. **bas·sos** or **bas·si** /'bäsē/) a singer with a bass voice. [18th C.: Ital., 'low.']

bas·soon /bə'so͞on; ba-/ ▶ **n.** a bass instrument of the oboe family with a double reed. — **bas·soon·ist** /-nist/ **n.** [18th C.: from Fr. *basson*, from Ital. *bassone*, from *basso* 'low.']

bas·so pro·fun·do /prō'fəndō; -'fo͞on-/ ▶ **n.** (pl. **bas·so pro·fun·dos** or **bas·si pro·fun·di** /prō'fəndē/) a bass singer with an exceptionally low range. [19th C.: Ital., from *basso* 'low' + *profondo* 'deep.']

bas·so-re·lie·vo /ri'lēvō/ ▶ **n.** (pl. **-vos**) Sculpture another term for BAS-RELIEF (see RELIEF sense 4). [17th C.: from Ital. *basso-rilievo.*]

Bass Strait /'bas/ a channel that separates Tasmania from the mainland of Australia.

bassoon

bass vi·ol /'bās 'vīəl/ ▶ **n.** a viola da gamba. ■ a double bass.

bass·wood /'basˌwo͝od/ ▶ **n.** a North American linden tree (genus *Tilia*, family Tiliaceae), including the large-leaved *T. americana* (also called **American linden**) of the northern US and Canada. [17th C.: from BASS[3] + WOOD.]

bast /bast/ ▶ **n.** (also **bast fiber**) fibrous material from the phloem of a plant, used as fiber in matting, cord, etc. ■ Bot. the phloem or vascular tissue of a plant. [OE *bæst*; rel. to Du. *bast*, Ger. *Bast*; of unknown origin.]

bas·tard /'bastərd/ ▶ **n.** **1** archaic or derog. a person born of parents not married to each other. **2** informal an unpleasant or despicable person. ■ [with adj.] a person (used to suggest an emotion such as pity or envy). ■ a difficult or awkward thing, undertaking, or situation. ▶ **adj.** [attrib.] **1** archaic or derog. born of parents not married to each other; illegitimate. **2** (of a thing) no longer in its pure or original form; debased. ■ (of a handwriting script or typeface) showing a mixture of different styles. — **bas·tar·dy** **n.** (in sense 1 of the noun). [ME: via OFr. from med. L. *bastardus.*]

bas·tard·ize /'bastərˌdīz/ ▶ **v.** [trans.] **1** [often as adj.] (**bastardized**) corrupt or debase (something such as a language or art form). **2** archaic declare (someone) illegitimate: *to annul the marriage and bastardize the child.* — **bas·tard·i·za·tion** /ˌbastərdi'zāsʜən/ **n.**

bas·tard wing ▶ **n.** a group of small quill feathers on the first digit of a bird's wing.

baste[1] /bāst/ ▶ **v.** [trans.] pour juices or melted fat over (meat) during cooking in order to keep it moist. [15th C.: of unknown origin.]

baste[2] ▶ **v.** [trans.] Needlework tack with long, loose stitches in preparation for sewing. [ME: from OFr. *bastir* 'sew lightly,' ult. Gmc., akin to BAST.]

baste[3] ▶ **v.** [trans.] informal, dated beat (someone) soundly; thrash. [16th C.: perh. from BASTE[1].]

Ba·sti·a /'bästēə; bäst'yä/ the chief port of Corsica, on the northeastern coast; pop. 38,730.

Bas·tille /ba'stēl/ a fortress in Paris built in the 14th century and used in the 17th–18th centuries as a state prison. [via OFr. from Provençal *bastida*, from *bastir* 'build.']

Bas·tille Day ▶ **n.** July 14, the date of the storming of the Bastille in 1789, a national holiday in France.

bas·ti·na·do /ˌbastə'nādō; -'nädō/ esp. hist. ▶ **n.** a form of punishment or torture that involves caning the soles of someone's feet. ▶ **v.** (**-does, -doed**) [trans.] (usu. **be bastinadoed**) punish or torture (someone) in such a way. [16th C.: from Sp. *bastonada*, from *bastón* 'stick,' from late L. *bastum* 'stick.']

bas·tion /'basсʜən/ ▶ **n.** a projecting part of a fortification built at an angle to the line of a wall, so as to allow defensive fire in several directions. ■ a natural rock formation resembling such a fortification. ■ fig. an institution, place, or person strongly defending or upholding particular principles, attitudes, or activities. [16th C.: from Fr., from Ital. *bastione*, from *bastire* 'build.']

bast·naes·ite /'bast-nəˌsīt/ ▶ **n.** a yellow to brown mineral consisting of a fluoride and carbonate of cerium and other rare earth metals. [19th C.: from *Bastnäs*, a district in Sweden.]

Bas·togne /bä'stōn(yə)/ a town in southeastern Belgium; pop. 11,000. It was the scene of heavy fighting during the Battle of the Bulge in World War II.

Ba·su·to·land /bə'so͞otōˌland/ former name (until 1966) of LESOTHO.

bat[1] /bat/ ▶ **n.** an implement with a handle and a solid surface, usually of wood, used for hitting the ball in games such as baseball, cricket, and table tennis. ■ the person batting, esp. in cricket. ■ each of a pair of objects resembling table tennis bats, used by a person on the ground to guide a taxiing aircraft. ▶ **v.** (**bat·ted, bat·ting**) **1** [intrans.] (of a team or a player in sports such as baseball) take in turns the role of hitting rather than fielding. **2** [with obj. and adverbial of direction] hit at (someone or something) with the palm of one's hand: *he batted the flies away.*

– PHRASES **go to bat for** informal defend the interests of; support. **right off the bat** at the very beginning.

– PHRASAL VERBS **bat something around** informal discuss an idea or proposal casually or idly. [OE *batt* 'club,' perh. partly from OFr. *batte*, from *battre* 'to strike.']

bat[2] ▶ **n.** a mainly nocturnal mammal (order Chiroptera) capable of sustained flight, with membranous wings that extend between the fingers and connecting the forelimbs to the body and the hindlimbs to the tail.

– PHRASES **have bats in the** (usu. **old bat**) **belfry** informal be eccentric or crazy. **like a bat out of hell** informal very fast and wildly. [16th C.: alt. of ME *bakke*, of Scand. origin.]

bat[3] ▶ **v.** (**bat·ted, bat·ting**) [trans.] flutter one's eyelashes, typically in a flirtatious manner.

– PHRASES **not bat** (or **without batting**) **an eyelid** (or **eye**) informal show (or showing) no reaction. [19th C.: from dial. *bat* 'to wink, blink,' var. of obs. *bate* 'to flutter.']

Ba·taan /bə'tan; -'tän/ a peninsula and province in the Philippines, on the western part of the island of Luzon; pop. 426,000. It was the site of World War II battles and the "Death March."

Ba·tak /bə'täk/ ▶ **n.** **1** (pl. same or **-taks**) a member of a people of northern Sumatra. **2** the Indonesian language of this people. ▶ **adj.** of or relating to the Batak or their language. [the name in Batak.]

Ba·tan Is·lands /bä'tän/ the northernmost islands in the Philippines.

ba·ta·ta /bə'tätə/ ▶ **n.** (in the southern West Indies) sweet potato. [via Sp. from Taino.]

Ba·ta·vi·a /bə'tāvēə/ former name (until 1949) for JAKARTA.

Ba·ta·vi·an /bəˈtāvēən/ hist. archaic ▶ **adj.** of or relating to the ancient Germanic people who inhabited the island of Betuwe between the Rhine and the Waal (now part of the Netherlands). ■ of or relating to the people of the Netherlands. ■ of or relating to Jakarta in Indonesia (formerly the Dutch East Indies). ▶ **n.** a Batavian person. [from L. *Batavia* (from *Batavi* 'the people of Betuwe').]

bat·boy /ˈbat,boi/ ▶ **n.** a boy who is employed to look after and retrieve bats during a baseball game and as a general assistant at other times.

batch /baCH/ ▶ **n.** a quantity or consignment of goods produced at one time. ■ informal a number of things or people regarded as a group or set. ■ Comput. a group of records processed as a single unit, usually without input from a user. ▶ **v.** [trans.] arrange (things) in sets or groups. [15th C.: based on an OE word rel. to *bacan* (see BAKE).]

bate /bāt/ ▶ **v.** [intrans.] Falconry (of a hawk) beat the wings in an attempt to escape from the perch: *the hawks bated when the breeze got in their feathers.* [ME: from OFr. *batre* 'to beat.']

ba·teau /baˈtō/ ▶ **n.** (pl. **-teaux** /-ˈtōz/) a flat-bottomed riverboat used in eastern and central North America. [18th C.: Fr., lit. 'boat.']

bat·ed /ˈbātid/ ▶ **adj.** (in phrase **with bated breath**) in great suspense; very anxiously or excitedly. [16th C.: from the past part. of obs. *bate* 'restrain,' from ABATE.]

Bates·i·an mim·ic·ry /ˈbātsēən/ ▶ **n.** Zool. mimicry in which an edible animal is protected by its resemblance to a noxious one that is avoided by predators. Compare with MÜLLERIAN MIMICRY. [19th C.: after Henry W. *Bates* (1825–92), English naturalist.]

bat·fish /ˈbat,fiSH/ ▶ **n.** (pl. same or **-fish·es**) **1** a fish (family Ogcocephalidae) of tropical and temperate seas with a flattened body that is round or almost triangular when viewed from above. It typically has a hard or spiny covering. **2** a deep-bodied, laterally compressed marine fish (genus *Platax*, family Ephippidae) of the Indo-Pacific region that resembles an angelfish.

bat·fowl /ˈbat,foul/ ▶ **v.** [intrans.] catch birds at night by dazing them with a light and knocking them down or netting them.

bat·girl /ˈbat,gərl/ ▶ **n.** a girl who is employed to look after and retrieve bats during a baseball game and as a general assistant at other times.

Bath /baTH; bäTH/ a town in southwestern England; pop. 79,900.

bath[1] /baTH/ ▶ **n.** (pl. **baths** /baTHs; baTHz/) an act or process of immersing and washing one's body in a large container of water. ■ such a container and its contents; a bathtub. ■ [with adj.] any act of washing or cleansing oneself. ■ (usu. **baths**) a public establishment offering bathing facilities. ■ (**baths**) a resort with a mineral spring used for medical treatment. ■ a bathroom. ■ [with adj.] a container holding a liquid or other substance in which something is immersed, typically when undergoing a process such as film developing. ▶ **v.** [trans.] wash (someone) while immersing him or her in a container of water: *how to bath a baby.*
– PHRASES **take a bath** informal suffer a heavy financial loss. [OE *bæth*, of Gmc. origin; rel. to Du. *bad* and Ger. *Bad.*]

bath[2] ▶ **n.** an ancient Hebrew liquid measure equivalent to about 40 liters or 9 gallons. [from Heb. *bat.*]

bath chair ▶ **n.** dated a hooded wheelchair for invalids. [19th C.: after the city of BATH, from its hot springs.]

bathe /bāTH/ ▶ **v.** [intrans.] wash by immersing one's body in water. ■ spend time in the ocean or a lake, river, or swimming pool for pleasure. ■ [trans.] soak or wipe gently with liquid to clean or soothe: *she bathed and bandaged my knee.* ■ [trans.] wash (someone) in a bath. ■ [trans.] (usu. **be bathed**) fig. suffuse or envelop in something. — **bath·er** **n.** [OE *bathian*, of Gmc. origin; rel. to Du. and Ger. *baden.*]

bath·house /ˈbaTH,hous/ ▶ **n.** **1** a building with baths for communal use. **2** a building where swimmers change clothes.

Bath·i·nette /,baTHəˈnet/ ▶ **n.** trademark a portable folding bathtub for infants.

bath·ing cap ▶ **n.** a close-fitting elastic cap worn while swimming to keep the hair dry or to reduce friction.

bath·ing suit ▶ **n.** a garment worn for swimming; a swimsuit.

bath mat ▶ **n.** a mat for someone to stand on after getting out of a bathtub. ■ a rubber mat placed in the bottom of a bathtub to prevent someone from slipping.

bath·o·lith /ˈbaTHə,liTH/ ▶ **n.** Geol. a very large igneous intrusion extending deep in the earth's crust. [20th C.: coined in Ger. from Gk. *bathos* 'depth.']

ba·thos /ˈbāTHäs/ ▶ **n.** (esp. in a work of literature) an effect of anticlimax created by an unintentional lapse in mood from the sublime to the trivial or ridiculous. — **ba·thet·ic** /bəˈTHetik/ **adj.** [17th C.: from Gk., lit. 'depth.']

bath·robe /ˈbaTH,rōb/ ▶ **n.** a robe, typically made of terrycloth, worn esp. before and after taking a bath.

bath·room /ˈbaTH,ro͞om; -,ro͝om/ ▶ **n.** a room containing a bathtub or a shower and usually also a washbasin and a toilet. ■ a set of matching units to be fitted in such a room, esp. as sold together. ■ a room containing a toilet.
– PHRASES **go to** (or **use**) **the bathroom** urinate or defecate.

bath salts ▶ **plural n.** a crystalline substance that is dissolved in bathwater to soften or perfume the water.

Bath·she·ba /,baTHˈSHēbə/ (in the Bible) the mother of Solomon. She became David's wife after David sent her husband, Uriah the Hittite, to his death on the battlefield.

bath sponge ▶ **n.** a marine sponge (genera *Spongia* and *Hippospongia*; family Spongiidae) of warm waters, the fibrous skeleton of which is used as a sponge for washing.

bath·tub /ˈbaTH,təb/ ▶ **n.** a tub, usually installed in a bathroom, in which to bathe.

Bath·urst /ˈbaTHərst/ former name (until 1973) of BANJUL.

bathy- ▶ **comb. form** relating to depth: *bathymetry.* [from Gk. *bathus* 'deep.']

bath·y·al /ˈbaTHēəl/ ▶ **adj.** of or relating to the zone of the sea between the continental shelf and the abyssal zone.

ba·thym·e·ter /bəˈTHimitər/ ▶ **n.** an instrument used to measure the depth of water in oceans, seas, or lakes. [19th C.: from Gk. *bathos* 'depth.']

ba·thym·e·try /bəˈTHimitrē/ ▶ **n.** the measurement of depth of water in oceans, seas, or lakes. — **bath·y·met·ric** /,baTHəˈmetrik/ **adj.** [19th C.: from Gk. *bathus* 'deep.']

bath·y·pe·lag·ic /,baTHəpəˈlajik/ ▶ **adj.** Biol. (of fish and other organisms) inhabiting the deep sea where the environment is dark and cold, approximately 3,300–9,800 feet (1,000–3,000 m) below the surface.

bath·y·scaphe /ˈbaTHə,skaf/ ▶ **n.** esp. hist. a manned submersible vessel. [1940s: coined in Fr. from Gk. *bathus* 'deep' + *skaphos* 'ship.']

bath·y·sphere /ˈbaTHə,sfi(ə)r/ ▶ **n.** a manned spherical chamber for deep-sea observation, lowered by cable from a ship. [1930s: from Gk. *bathus* 'deep.']

ba·tik /bəˈtēk/ ▶ **n.** a method (originally used in Java) of producing colored designs on textiles by dyeing them, having first applied wax to the parts to be left undyed. ■ an item or piece of cloth treated in this way. [19th C.: from Javanese, lit. 'painted.']

Ba·tis·ta /bəˈtēstə/, Fulgencio (1901–73), president of Cuba 1940–44, 1952–59; full name *Fulgencio Batista y Zaldívar.* His second government was overthrown by Fidel Castro.

ba·tiste /bəˈtēst/ ▶ **n.** a fine, light linen or cotton fabric resembling cambric. [19th C.: from Fr. (earlier *batiche*); prob. rel. to *battre* 'to beat.']

bat·man /ˈbatmən/ ▶ **n.** (pl. **-men**) dated (in the British armed forces) an officer's personal servant. [18th C. (denoting an orderly in charge of the *bat horse* 'packhorse' that carried baggage): from OFr. *bat* (from med. L. *bastum* 'packsaddle').]

bat mitz·vah /bät ˈmitsvə/ ▶ **n.** a religious initiation ceremony for a Jewish girl aged twelve years and one day, regarded as the age of religious maturity. ■ the girl undergoing such a ceremony. [from Heb. *baṯ miṣwāh* 'daughter of the commandment.']

ba·ton /bəˈtän/ ▶ **n.** a short stick or staff or something resembling one, in particular: ■ a thin stick used by a conductor to direct an orchestra or choir. ■ Track & Field a short stick or tube passed from runner to runner in a relay race. ■ a long stick carried and twirled by a drum major. ■ a police officer's club. ■ Heraldry a narrow bend truncated at each end. ■ a short bar replacing some figures on the dial of a clock or watch. ■ (**batons**) one of the suits in some tarot packs, corresponding to wands in others. [16th C.: from Fr. *bâton*, earlier *baston*, from late L. *bastum* 'stick.']

Bat·on Rouge /,batn ˈro͞oZH/ the capital of Louisiana, in the southeast central part of the state, on the Mississippi River; pop. 227,818.

Ba·tra·chi·a /bəˈtrākēə/ Zool. another term, esp. formerly, for ANURA. — **ba·tra·chi·an** **n. & adj.** [mod. L. (pl.), from Gk. *batrakhos* 'frog.']

bats /bats/ ▶ **adj.** [predic.] informal, dated (of a person) crazy; insane. [20th C.: from the phr. *have bats in the belfry* (see BAT[2]).]

bats·man /ˈbatsmən/ ▶ **n.** (pl. **-men**) a player, esp. in baseball and cricket, who is batting or whose chief skill is in batting. — **bats·man·ship** **n.**

Bat·swa·na /bätˈswänə/ ▶ **n. & adj.** see TSWANA.

batt /bat/ ▶ **n.** a piece of felted material used for lining or insulating items such as quilts and sleeping bags. ■ a piece of fiberglass used to insulate buildings.

bat·tal·ion /bəˈtalyən/ ▶ **n.** a large body of troops ready for battle, esp. an infantry unit. ■ a large, organized group of people pursuing a common aim or sharing a major undertaking. [16th C.: from Fr. *bataillon*, from Ital. *battaglione*, from *battaglia* 'battle,' from L. (see BATTLE).]

batte·ment /ˈbatmənt/ ▶ **n.** [with adj.] Ballet a movement in which one leg is moved outward from the body and in again. [19th C.: Fr., lit. 'beating.']

Bat·ten /ˈbatn/, Jean (1909–82), New Zealand aviator. She was the first woman to fly from England to Australia and back 1934–35.

bat·ten[1] /ˈbatn/ ▶ **n.** a long, flat strip of wood or metal used to hold something in place. ■ a strip of wood or metal for securing the edges of a tarpaulin that covers a ship's hatch. ■ a strip of wood or plastic used to stiffen and extend the leech of a sail. ▶ **v.** [trans.] strengthen or fasten (something) with battens: *Stephen was **battening down the shutters.***
– PHRASES **batten down the hatches** Naut. secure a ship's hatch-tarpaulins, esp. when rough weather is expected. ■ fig. prepare for a difficulty or crisis. [15th C.: from OFr. *batant*, pres. part. of *batre* 'to beat,' from L. *battuere.*]

bat·ten[2] ▶ **v.** [intrans.] (**batten on**) thrive or prosper at the expense of (someone). [16th C.: from ON *batna* 'get better,' rel. to BETTER[1].]

bat·ten·ing /ˈbatn-iNG/ ▶ **n.** the application of battens. ■ a structure formed with battens.

bat·ter[1] /ˈbatər/ ▶ **v.** [trans.] strike repeatedly with hard blows; pound heavily and insistently: *a prisoner was **battered to death with a table leg.*** ■ [often as n.] (**battering**) subject (one's spouse, partner, or child) to repeated violence and assault. ■ [usu. as n.] (**battering**) fig. censure, criticize, or defeat severely. — **bat·ter·er** n. [ME: from OFr. *batre* 'to beat' (from L. *battuere*) + -ER[3].]

bat·ter[2] ▶ n. **1** a semiliquid mixture of flour, egg, and milk or water used in cooking, esp. for making cakes or for coating food before frying. **2** Print., esp. hist. a damaged area of metal type or a printing block. [ME: from OFr. *bateure* 'the action of beating,' from *batre* 'to beat.']

bat·ter[3] ▶ n. (in various sports, esp. baseball) a player who is batting.

bat·ter[4] ▶ n. a gradual backward slope in a wall or similar structure. ▶ v. [intrans.] (of a wall) have a receding slope.

bat·tered[1] /'batərd/ ▶ adj. injured by repeated blows or punishment. ■ having suffered repeated violence from a spouse, partner, or parent. ■ (of a thing) damaged by age and repeated use; shabby.

bat·tered[2] ▶ adj. (of food) coated in batter and deep-fried until crisp.

bat·tered child syn·drome ▶ n. the set of symptoms, injuries, and signs of mistreatment seen on a severely or repeatedly abused child.

bat·tered wom·an syn·drome ▶ n. the set of symptoms, injuries, and signs of mistreatment seen in a woman who has been repeatedly abused by a husband or other male figure.

bat·te·rie /'batərē/ ▶ n. Ballet the action of beating or crossing the legs together during a leap or jump. [18th C.: Fr., lit. 'beating.']

bat·ter·ing par·ent syn·drome ▶ n. the set of symptoms and signs indicating a psychological disorder in a parent or child-care provider resulting in a tendency toward repeated abuse of a child.

bat·ter·ing ram ▶ n. a heavy object swung or rammed against a door to break it down. ■ hist. a heavy beam, originally with an end in the form of a carved ram's head, used in breaching fortifications.

bat·ter·y /'batərē/ ▶ n. (pl. **-ies**) **1** a container consisting of one or more cells carrying an electric charge and used as a source of power. **2** a fortified emplacement for heavy guns. ■ an artillery subunit of guns, men, and vehicles. **3** a set of similar units of equipment, typically when connected together. ■ an extensive series, sequence, or range of things. **4** Law the crime or tort of unconsented physical contact with another person, even where the contact is not violent but merely menacing or offensive. See also ASSAULT AND BATTERY. **5** (**the battery**) Baseball the pitcher and the catcher in a game, considered as a unit. [ME: from Fr. *batterie*, from *battre* 'to strike,' from L. *battuere*.]

Bat·tery, the /'batərē/ a historic area at the southern end of Manhattan Island in New York City.

bat·ting ▶ n. cotton wadding prepared in sheets for use in quilts.

bat·ting av·er·age ▶ n. Baseball the average performance of a batter, expressed as a ratio of a batter's safe hits per official times at bat.

bat·ting cage ▶ n. Baseball an area for batting practice that is enclosed by fencing or netting.

bat·ting or·der ▶ n. Baseball the order in which batters take their turn at bat.

bat·tle /'batl/ ▶ n. a sustained fight between large, organized armed forces. ■ a lengthy and difficult conflict or struggle. ▶ v. [intrans.] fight or struggle tenaciously to achieve or resist something: *he has been battling against the illness.* ■ [trans.] engage in a fight or struggle against.
– PHRASES **battle it out** fight or compete to a definite conclusion. **do battle** fight; engage in conflict. **battle royal** (pl. **battles royal**) a fiercely contested fight or dispute. **battle stations** the positions taken by military personnel in preparation for battle (often used as a command or signal to prepare for battle). **half the battle** an important step toward achieving something. — **bat·tler** n. [ME: from OFr. *bataille* (n.), *batailler* (v.), based on late L. *battualia* 'military or gladiatorial exercises,' from L. *battuere* 'to beat.']

bat·tle-ax (also **bat·tle-axe**) ▶ n. **1** a large broad-bladed ax used in ancient warfare. **2** informal a formidably aggressive older woman.

Bat·tle Creek a city in southern Michigan, noted as a center of the cereal industry; pop. 53,540.

bat·tle·cruis·er /'batl,kro͞ozər/ ▶ n. hist. a large warship carrying similar armament to a battleship but faster and more lightly armored.

bat·tle cry ▶ n. a word or phrase shouted by soldiers going into battle to express solidarity and intimidate the enemy. ■ a slogan expressing the ideals of people promoting a cause.

bat·tle·dore /'batl,dôr/ ▶ n. hist. (also **battledore and shuttlecock**) a game played with a shuttlecock and rackets; a forerunner of badminton. ■ the small racket used in this. [ME: perh. from Provençal *batedor* 'paddle,' from *batre* 'to beat.']

bat·tle fa·tigue ▶ n. another term for SHELL SHOCK.

bat·tle·field /'batl,fēld/ (also **bat·tle·ground** /-,ground/) ▶ n. the piece of ground on which a battle is or was fought. ■ fig. a place or situation of strife or conflict.

bat·tle·front /'batl,frənt/ ▶ n. the region or line along which opposing armies engage in combat. ■ the area in which opponents or opposing ideas meet.

bat·tle group ▶ n. a military force created to fight together, typically consisting of several different types of troops.

bat·tle jack·et ▶ n. a style of waist-length jacket worn by army personnel. ■ any jacket of a similar cut.

bat·tle·ment /'batlmənt/ ▶ n. (usu. **battlements**) a parapet at the top of a wall, usually of a fort or castle, that has squared openings for shooting through. ■ a section of roof enclosed by this. — **bat·tle·ment·ed** adj. [ME: from OFr. *bataillier* 'fortify with turrets,' possibly rel. to BATTLE.]

bat·tle·ship /'batl,sHip/ ▶ n. a heavy warship with extensive armor protection and large-caliber guns. [18th C.: shortening of *line-of-battle ship*.]

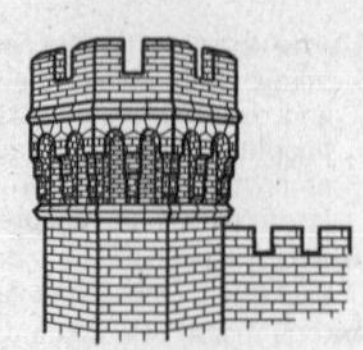
battlement

bat·tle·ship gray ▶ n. a bluish gray color, typically used for warships to reduce their visibility.

bat·tle·wag·on /'batl,wagən/ (also **bat·tle wag·on**) ▶ n. informal a battleship or an armored vehicle.

bat·tue /ba'to͞o/ ▶ n. the driving of game toward hunters by beaters. ■ a hunting party arranged in such a way. [19th C.: from Fr., fem. past part. of *battre* 'to beat,' from L. *battuere*.]

bat·ty /'batē/ ▶ adj. (**-ti·er, -ti·est**) informal crazy; insane. — **bat·ti·ly** adv. **bat·ti·ness** n. [20th C.: from BAT[2] + -Y[1].]

bat·wing /'bat,wiNG/ ▶ adj. [attrib.] (of a sleeve) having a deep armhole and a tight cuff. ■ (of a garment) having such sleeves.

bau·ble /'bôbəl/ ▶ n. **1** a small, showy trinket or decoration. ■ fig. something of no importance or worth. **2** hist. a baton formerly used as an emblem by jesters. [ME: from OFr. *baubel* 'child's toy,' of unknown origin.]

Bau·cis /'bôsis/ Gk. Mythol. the wife of Philemon.

baud /bôd/ ▶ n. (pl. same or **bauds**) esp. Comput. a unit used to express the speed of transmission of electronic signals, corresponding to one information unit or event per second. ■ a unit of data transmission speed for a modem of one bit per second. [1930s: coined in French after J. M. E. *Baudot* (1845–1903), French engineer.]

Bau·de·laire /,bōdə'le(ə)r; -dl'e(ə)r/, Charles Pierre (1821–67), French poet and critic, noted for *Les Fleurs du mal* (1857), a series of 101 lyrics.

Bau·dril·lard /,bōdrē'(y)är/, Jean (1929–2007), French sociologist and critic, associated with postmodernism.

Bau·haus /'bou,hous/ a school of design established by Walter Gropius in Weimar in 1919, known for its designs of objects based on functionalism and simplicity. [Ger., 'house of architecture,' from *Bau* 'building' + *Haus* 'house.']

baulk ▶ v. & n. Brit. var. of BALK.

baulk·y ▶ adj. British spelling of BALKY.

Baum /bôm; bäm/, Lyman Frank (1856–1919), US journalist and writer. His children's books include *The Wonderful Wizard of Oz* (1900).

Bau·mé scale /bō'mā; 'bōmā/ ▶ n. a scale with arbitrary markings, used with a hydrometer to measure the relative density of liquids. [named for Antoine Baumé (1728–1804), French chemist.]

Bausch /bousH/, John Jacob (1830–1926), US businessman; born in Germany. He cofounded the Bausch & Lomb Optical Company in 1853.

baux·ite /'bôksīt/ ▶ n. an amorphous clayey rock that is the chief commercial ore of aluminum. — **baux·it·ic** /bôk'sitik/ adj. [19th C.: from Fr., from *Les Baux* (a village in France, near where it was first found).]

Ba·var·i·a /bə've(ə)rēə/ a state in southern Germany, formerly an independent kingdom; capital, Munich. German name BAYERN.

Ba·var·i·an /bə've(ə)rēən/ ▶ adj. of or relating to Bavaria, its people, or their language. ▶ n. **1** a native or inhabitant of Bavaria. **2** the dialect of German used in Bavaria.

baw·bee /'bôbē/ ▶ n. Scot. & N. Irish a coin of low value. ■ hist. a former silver coin worth three (later six) Scottish pennies. [16th C.: after the laird of Sille*bawby*, mint master under James V.]

bawd /bôd/ ▶ n. archaic a woman in charge of a brothel. [ME: shortened from obs. *bawdstrot*, from OFr. *baudestroyt* 'procuress,' from *baude* 'shameless.']

bawd·ry /'bôdrē/ ▶ n. obscenity in speech or writing.

bawd·y /'bôdē/ ▶ adj. (**bawd·i·er, bawd·i·est**) (esp. humorously) indecent; raunchy. ▶ n. humorously indecent talk or writing. — **bawd·i·ly** adv. **bawd·i·ness** n.

bawd·y house ▶ n. archaic a brothel.

bawl /bôl/ ▶ v. **1** [reporting verb] shout or call out noisily and unrestrainedly: [with direct speech] *"Move!" bawled the drill sergeant* | [trans.] *lustily **bawling** out the hymns* | [intrans.] *Joe bawled with laughter.* **2** [intrans.] weep or cry noisily. ▶ n. a loud, unrestrained shout.
– PHRASAL VERBS **bawl someone out** reprimand someone angrily. [ME: imitative; possibly rel. to med. L. *baulare* 'to bark.']

bay[1] /bā/ ▶ n. a broad inlet of the sea where the land curves inward. ■ an indentation or recess in a range of hills or mountains. [ME: from OFr. *baie*, from Old Sp. *bahia*, of unknown origin.]

bay[2] ▶ n. **1** (also **bay tree, bay laurel**, or **sweet bay**) an evergreen Mediterranean shrub of the laurel family (*Laurus nobilis*), with deep green leaves and purple berries. Its aromatic leaves are used in cooking and were formerly used to make triumphal crowns for victors. **2** a similarly aromatic tree or shrub of North America, esp. the bayberry used in the preparation of bay rum. [ME (denoting the laurel berry): from OFr. *baie*, from L. *baca* 'berry.']

bay[3] ▶ n. a recessed or enclosed area, in particular: ■ a space created by a window-line projecting outward from a wall. ■ short for BAY WINDOW. ■ a section of wall between two buttresses or columns, esp. in the nave of a church. ■ [with adj.] a compartment with a particular function in a motor vehicle, aircraft, or ship. ■ an area allocated or marked off for a specified purpose. ■ short for SICKBAY. ■ Comput. a cabinet, or a space in the cabinet, into which an electronic device is installed. [ME: from OFr. *baie*, from *baer* 'to gape,' from med. L. *batare*.]

bay[4] ▶ adj. (of a horse) brown with black points. ▶ n. a bay horse. [ME: from OFr. *bai*, from L. *badius*.]

bay[5] ▶ v. [intrans.] (of a dog, esp. a large one) bark or howl loudly: *the dogs bayed.* ■ (of a group of people) shout loudly, typically to demand something. ■ [trans.] archaic bay at: *wolves baying at the moon.* ▶ n. the sound of baying, esp. that of hounds in close pursuit of their quarry.
– PHRASES **at bay** forced to confront one's attackers or pursuers; cornered. **bring someone/something to bay** trap or corner a person or animal being hunted or chased. **hold** (or **keep**) **someone/something at bay** prevent someone or something from approaching or having an effect. **stand at bay** turn to face one's pursuers. [ME (as a noun): from OFr. *(a)bai* (n.), *(a)baiier* (v.) 'to bark,' of imitative origin.]

ba·ya·dère /'bīə,de(ə)r/ ▶ n. a Hindu dancing girl, in particular one at a southern Indian temple. [from Fr., from Port. *bailadeira*, from *bailar* 'to dance.']

bay·ber·ry /'bā,berē; -bərē/ ▶ n. (pl. **-ries**) **1** a North American shrub (genus *Myrica*, family Myricaceae) with aromatic leathery leaves and waxy berries. See also **WAX MYRTLE**. **2** a tropical American shrub (*Pimenta racemosa*) of the myrtle family with aromatic leaves that are used in the preparation of bay rum. Also called **bay rum tree**. [17th C.: from **BAY**[2].]

Bay City industrial city in eastern Michigan, on the Saginaw River, near Lake Huron; pop. 38,936.

Bay·ern /'bīərn/ German name for **BAVARIA**.

Ba·yeux Tap·es·try /bä'yo͞o; bā'yo͞o/ a medieval English embroidery made between 1066 and 1077, telling the story of the Norman Conquest.

Bay·kal, Lake var. of **BAIKAL, LAKE**.

bay lau·rel ▶ n. another term for **BAY**[2].

bay leaf ▶ n. the aromatic, usually dried, leaf of the bay tree, used in cooking.

Bay of Pigs ▶ n. a bay in the Caribbean Sea in southwestern Cuba, site of a failed attempt in 1961 by US-trained Cuban exiles to invade Cuba and overthrow the government of Fidel Castro.

bay·o·net /'bāənit; ,bāə'net/ ▶ n. **1** a swordlike stabbing blade that may be fixed to the muzzle of a rifle for use in hand-to-hand fighting. **2** [as adj.] denoting an electrical or other fitting engaged by being pushed into a socket and twisted. ▶ v. (**-net·ed, -net·ing**) [trans.] stab (someone) with a bayonet. [17th C.: from Fr. *baïonnette*, from *Bayonne*, a town in France where they were first made.]

Bay·onne /bā'(y)ōn/ a city in northeastern New Jersey, on New York Bay; pop. 61,444.

bay·ou /'bīo͞o; 'bīō/ ▶ n. (pl. **-ous**) (in the southern US) a marshy outlet of a lake or river. [18th C.: from Louisiana Fr., from Choctaw *bayuk*.]

Bay·ou Teche /'bī,o͞o 'tesн/ a water route in south central Louisiana. Also called **the Teche**.

Bay·reuth /'bī,roit; bī'roit/ a town in Bavaria where festivals of Wagner's operas are held regularly.

bay rum ▶ n. an aromatic liquid, used esp. for the hair or as an aftershave, typically distilled from rum and the leaves of the bayberry.

bay·side /'bā,sīd/ ▶ adj. on or near the shore of a bay.

Bay·town /'bā,toun/ a city in southeastern Texas, east of Houston, a center of the oil industry; pop. 63,850.

bay tree ▶ n. see **BAY**[2].

bay win·dow ▶ n. a window built to project outward from an outside wall.

bay window

ba·zaar /bə'zär/ ▶ n. a market in a Middle-Eastern country. ■ a fund-raising sale of goods, typically for charity. ■ dated a large shop selling miscellaneous goods. [16th C.: from Ital. *bazarro*, from Turk., from Pers. *bāzār* 'market.']

ba·zoo /bə'zo͞o/ ▶ n. informal **1** a person's mouth. **2** a person's buttocks or anus. [19th C.: of unknown origin; cf. Du. *bazuin* 'trombone, trumpet.']

ba·zoo·ka /bə'zo͞okə/ ▶ n. **1** a short-range tubular rocket launcher used against tanks. **2** a trombonelike type of kazoo.

ba·zoom /bə'zo͞om/ ▶ n. (usu. **bazooms**) informal a woman's breast. [1950s: prob. an alt. of **BOSOM**.]

BB ▶ symb. a standard size of lead pellet used in air rifles. ▶ abbr. Baseball base on balls.

b-ball informal basketball.

BBC ▶ abbr. British Broadcasting Corporation.

BB gun ▶ n. an air rifle that fires BBs.

bbl. ▶ abbr. barrels (esp. of oil).

b-boy ▶ n. informal a young man involved with hip-hop culture. [1980s: *b*- prob. from **BEAT** (n.) or **BREAKDANCING**.]

BBQ ▶ abbr. informal barbecue.

BBS Comput. ▶ abbr. bulletin board system.

BC ▶ abbr. ■ before Christ (used to indicate that a date is before the Christian Era). ■ British Columbia (in official postal use).

bcc ▶ abbr. blind carbon copy, a copy of an e-mail sent to someone whose name and address is not visible to other recipients.

BCD ▶ abbr. ■ Mil. bad conduct discharge. ■ binary coded decimal.

BCE ▶ abbr. ■ Bachelor of Chemical Engineering. ■ Bachelor of Civil Engineering. ■ before the Common Era (used of dates before the Christian era, esp. by non-Christians).

B cell (also **B-cell**) ▶ n. Physiol. a lymphocyte not processed by the thymus gland, and responsible for producing antibodies. Also called **B LYMPHOCYTE**. Compare with **T CELL**. [*B* for **BURSA**, referring to the organ in birds where it was first identified.]

BCG ▶ abbr. Bacillus Calmette-Guérin, an antituberculosis vaccine.

B com·plex ▶ n. see **VITAMIN B**.

BD ▶ abbr. Bachelor of Divinity.

Bde ▶ abbr. Brigade.

bdel·li·um /'delēəm/ ▶ n. a fragrant resin produced by a number of trees related to myrrh, used in perfumes. [ME: via L. from Gk. *bdellion*, of Semitic origin.]

bdrm. ▶ abbr. bedroom.

BE ▶ abbr. ■ Bachelor of Education. ■ Bachelor of Engineering. ■ bill of exchange. ■ black English.

Be ▶ symb. the chemical element beryllium.

be /bē/ ▶ v. (sing. pres. **am** /am/; **are** /är/; **is** /iz/; pl. pres. **are**; 1st and 3rd sing. past **was** /wəz; wäz/; 2nd sing. past and pl. past **were** /wər/; pres. subjunctive **be**; past subjunctive **were**; pres. part. **be·ing** /'bēiNG/; past part. **been** /bin/) **1** (usu. **there is/are**) exist: *there are no easy answers | there once was a man.* ■ be present: *there is a boy sitting on the step | there were no curtains around the showers.* **2** [with adverbial] occur; take place: *the exhibition will be in November.* ■ occupy a position in space: *the Salvation Army store was on his left | she was not at the window.* ■ stay in the same place or condition: *she was here until about ten-thirty | he's a tough customer—**let him be**.* ■ attend: *the days when she was in school.* ■ come; go; visit: *he's from Missouri | I have just been to Thailand.* **3** [as copular verb] having the state, quality, identity, nature, role, etc., specified: *Amy was 91 | I want to be a teacher | father was not well | his hair's brown | "Be careful," Mr. Carter said.* ■ cost: *the tickets were $25.* ■ amount to: *one and one is two.* ■ represent: *let A be a square matrix of order* n. ■ signify: *we were everything to each other.* ■ consist of; constitute: *the monastery was several three-story buildings.* ▶ aux. v. **1** used with a present participle to form continuous tenses: *they are coming | he had been reading | she will be waiting.* **2** used with a past participle to form the passive mood: *it was done | it is said | his book will be published.* **3** [with infin.] used to indicate something due to happen: *construction is to begin next summer | I was to meet him at 6:30.* ■ used to express obligation or necessity: *you are to follow these orders.* ■ used to express possibility: *these snakes are to be found in North America.* ■ used to hypothesize about something that might happen: *if I were to lose | were she to cure me, what could I offer her?* **4** archaic used with the past participle of intransitive verbs to form perfect tenses: *I am returned | all humanity is fallen.*
– PHRASES **the be-all and end-all** informal a feature of an activity or a way of life that is of greater importance than any other. **be oneself** act naturally, according to one's character and instincts. **be that as it may** see **MAY**[1]. **be there for someone** be available to support or comfort someone while they are experiencing difficulties or adversities. **been there, done that** see **THERE**. **not be oneself** not feel well. **-to-be** [in comb.] of the future: *my bride-to-be.*
– PHRASAL VERBS **be about** see **ABOUT**. **be off** go away; leave: *he was anxious to be off.* [OE *bēon*, an irregular v. whose full conjugation derives from several orig. distinct verbs; the forms *am* and *is* are rel. to L. *sum* and *est*.]

be- ▶ prefix forming verbs. **1** all over; all around: *bespatter.* ■ thoroughly; excessively: *bewilder.* **2** (added to intransitive verbs) expressing transitive action: *bemoan.* **3** (added to adjectives and nouns) expressing transitive action: *befriend.* **4** (added to nouns) affect with: *befog.* ■ (added to adjectives) cause to be: *befoul.* **5** (forming adjectives ending in *-ed*) having; covered with: *bejeweled.* [OE, weak form of *bī* 'by.']

beach /bēcн/ ▶ n. a pebbly or sandy shore, esp. by the sea between high- and low-water marks. ▶ v. [trans.] run or haul up (a boat or ship) onto a beach: *a rowboat was beached* | [intrans.] *crews would not beach for fear of damaging craft.* ■ [often as adj.] (**beached**) cause (a whale or similar animal) to become stranded out of the water. ■ [intrans.] (of a whale or similar animal) become stranded out of the water. ■ (of an angler) land (a fish) on a beach. ■ fig. cause (someone) to suffer a loss. [16th C.: perh. akin to OE *bæce*, *bece* 'brook.']

beach ball ▶ n. a large inflatable ball used for playing games on the beach.

beach bug·gy ▶ n. another term for **DUNE BUGGY**.

beach bum ▶ n. informal a person who loafs on or around a beach.

beach·comb·er /'bēcн,kōmər/ ▶ n. **1** a vagrant who makes a living by searching beaches for articles of value and selling them. **2** a person who searches beaches for useful or interesting items. **3** a long wave rolling in from the sea; a comber.

beach flea ▶ n. a small crustacean (*Orchestia* and other genera, order Amphipoda) that typically lives among seaweed and leaps when disturbed. Also called **SAND FLEA, SAND HOPPER**.

beach·front /ˈbēcʜˌfrənt/ ▶ **n.** [usu. in sing.] the part of a coastal town next to and directly facing the sea.

beach·head /ˈbēcʜˌhed/ ▶ **n.** a defended position on a beach taken from the enemy by landing forces, from which an attack can be launched. [World War II: patterned after *bridgehead*.]

Beach-la-mar /ˌbēcʜ lə ˈmär/ ▶ **n.** another term for **BISLAMA**.

beach plum ▶ **n.** a maritime shrub of the rose family (*Prunus maritima*) related to the plum, native to northeastern North America. ■ the edible fruit of this tree.

beach·side /ˈbēcʜˌsīd/ ▶ **adj.** [attrib.] next to the beach.

beach·wear /ˈbēcʜˌwe(ə)r/ ▶ **n.** clothing suitable for wearing on the beach.

bea·con /ˈbēkən/ ▶ **n.** a fire or light set up in a high or prominent position as a warning, signal, or celebration. ■ a light or other visible object serving as a signal, warning, or guide, esp. at sea or on an airfield. ■ a radio transmitter whose signal helps to fix the position of a ship, aircraft, or spacecraft. ▶ **v.** shine like a beacon. [OE *bēacn* 'sign, portent, ensign,' of West Gmc. origin; rel. to **BECKON**.]

Bea·con Hill a historic neighborhood in downtown Boston, Massachusetts.

bead /bēd/ ▶ **n. 1** a small piece of glass, stone, or similar material, typically rounded and perforated for threading with others as a necklace or rosary or for sewing onto fabric. ■ (**beads**) a necklace made of a string of beads. ■ (**beads**) a rosary. **2** something resembling a bead or a string of beads, in particular: ■ a drop of a liquid on a surface. ■ a small knob forming the front sight of a gun. ■ the reinforced inner edge of a pneumatic tire that grips the rim of the wheel. ■ an ornamental molding resembling a string of beads or of a semicircular cross-section. ▶ **v.** [trans.] **1** [often as adj.] (**beaded**) decorate or cover with beads: *a beaded evening bag.* ■ string (beads) together. **2** (often **be beaded**) cover (a surface) with drops of moisture: *his face was **beaded with perspiration**.* [OE *gebed* 'prayer,' from Gmc.; akin to Ger. *Gebet*, also to **BID**[1].]

bead·ing /ˈbēdiɴɢ/ ▶ **n.** decoration or ornamental molding resembling a string of beads or of a semicircular cross section.

bea·dle /ˈbēdl/ ▶ **n.** Brit. a ceremonial officer of a church, college, or similar institution. ■ Scot. a church officer assisting the minister. ■ hist. a minor parish officer dealing with petty offenders. [OE *bydel* 'a person who makes a proclamation'; gradually superseded by OFr. *bedel*, ult. of Gmc. origin; rel. to Ger. *Büttel*, and **BID**[1].]

bead·work /ˈbēdˌwərk/ ▶ **n.** decorative work made of beads.

bead·y /ˈbēdē/ ▶ **adj.** (of a person's eyes) small, round, and gleaming. ■ (of a look) bright and penetrating. — **bead·i·ly** /ˈbēdəlē/ **adv.**

bead·y-eyed ▶ **adj.** having small, glinting eyes. ■ informal keenly observant, typically in a sinister or hostile way.

bea·gle /ˈbēgəl/ ▶ **n.** a small sturdy hound of a breed with a coat of medium length, bred esp. for hunting. — **bea·gler** /-g(ə)lər/ **n.** [15th C.: perh. from OFr. *beegueule* 'open-mouthed,' from *beer* 'open wide' + *gueule* 'throat.']

beagle

beak /bēk/ ▶ **n.** a bird's horny projecting jaws; a bill. ■ the similar horny projecting jaw of other animals, e.g., a turtle or squid. ■ informal a person's nose, esp. a hooked one. ■ a projection at the prow of an ancient warship, typically shaped to resemble the head of a bird or other animal, used to pierce the hulls of enemy ships. — **beaked adj.** [in comb.] *a yellow-beaked alpine chough.* [ME: from OFr. *bec*, from L. *beccus*, of Celtic origin.]

beaked whale ▶ **n.** a medium-sized whale (family Ziphiidae) with elongated jaws that form a beak.

beak·er /ˈbēkər/ ▶ **n.** a lipped cylindrical glass container for laboratory use. ■ archaic or literary a large drinking container with a wide mouth. [ME: from ON *bikarr*, perh. based on Gk. *bikos* 'drinking bowl.']

beak·y /ˈbēkē/ ▶ **adj.** informal (of a person's nose) resembling a bird's beak; hooked. ■ (of a person) having such a nose.

Beale Street /bēl/ a historic street in Memphis, Tennessee; associated with black music.

beam /bēm/ ▶ **n. 1** a long, sturdy piece of squared timber or metal spanning an opening or room, usually to support the roof or floor above. ■ another term for **BALANCE BEAM**. ■ a horizontal piece of squared timber or metal supporting the deck and joining the sides of a ship. ■ Naut. the direction of an object visible from the port or starboard side of a ship when it is perpendicular to the center line of the vessel. ■ a ship's breadth at its widest point. ■ [in sing.] informal the width of a person's hips. ■ the main stem of a stag's antler. ■ the crossbar of a balance. **2** a ray or shaft of light. ■ a directional flow of particles or radiation. ■ a series of radio or radar signals emitted to serve as a navigational guide for ships or aircraft. **3** [in sing.] a radiant or good-natured look or smile. ▶ **v. 1** [with obj. and adverbial of direction] transmit (a radio signal or broadcast) in a specified direction: *beaming a distress signal into space* | [intrans.] *the TV station begins beaming into homes in the new year.* ■ [trans.] (**beam someone up/down**) (in science fiction) transport someone instantaneously to another place, esp. to or from a spaceship: *Scotty, beam me up!* **2** [no obj., with adverbial of direction] (of a light or light source) shine brightly: *the sun's rays beamed down.* **3** [intrans.] smile radiantly: *she beamed with pleasure* ■ [trans.] express (an emotion) with a radiant smile: [with direct speech] *"Isn't that wonderful, Beatrice?" beamed the nun.* **4** (**beamed**) construct a ceiling with exposed beams.

– PHRASES **off** (or **way off**) **beam** informal on the wrong track; mistaken. **on the beam** informal on the right track. **on her** (or **its**) **beam-ends** (of a ship) heeled over on its side. [OE *bēam* 'tree, beam,' from West Gmc.; akin to Ger. *Baum*.]

beam com·pass (also **beam com·pass·es**) ▶ **n.** a drawing compass consisting of a horizontal rod or beam connected by sliding sockets to two vertical legs, used for drawing large circles.

beam·ish /ˈbēmisʜ/ ▶ **adj.** beaming with happiness, optimism, or anticipation.

beam split·ter ▶ **n.** a device for dividing a beam of light or other electromagnetic radiation into two or more separate beams.

beam·y /ˈbēmē/ ▶ **adj.** (of a ship) broad-beamed.

Bean /bēn/, Roy (*c.*1825–1903), US frontiersman; known as **Judge**.

bean /bēn/ ▶ **n. 1** an edible seed, typically kidney-shaped, growing in long pods on certain leguminous plants. ■ the hard seed of coffee, cocoa, and certain other plants. **2** a leguminous plant (*Phaseolus* and other genera) that bears such seeds in pods. **3** [with negative] (also **beans**) informal a very small amount or nothing at all of something (used emphatically): *I **didn't know beans about** being a step-parent.* **4** informal a person's head, typically when regarded as a source of common sense. ▶ **v.** [trans.] informal hit (someone) on the head.

– PHRASES **full of beans** informal lively; in high spirits. **a hill** (or **row**) **of beans** [with negative] anything of any importance or value: *three people **don't amount to a hill of beans**.* [OE *bēan*, from Gmc.; akin to Ger. *Bohne*.]

bean·bag /ˈbēnˌbag/ ▶ **n. 1** a small bag filled with dried beans and typically used in children's games. **2** a large cushion, typically filled with polystyrene beads, used as a seat.

bean·ball /ˈbēnˌbôl/ ▶ **n.** Baseball informal a ball pitched, esp. intentionally, at the batter's head.

bean count·er ▶ **n.** informal a person, typically an accountant or bureaucrat, perceived as placing excessive emphasis on controlling expenditure. — **bean count·ing n.**

bean curd ▶ **n.** another term for **TOFU**.

bean·er·y /ˈbēnərē/ ▶ **n.** (pl. **-er·ies**) a cheap restaurant.

bean·ie /ˈbēnē/ ▶ **n.** (pl. **-ies**) a small, close-fitting hat worn on the back of the head. [1940s: perh. from **BEAN** (in the sense 'head') + **-IE**.]

bean·pole /ˈbēnˌpōl/ ▶ **n.** a stick for supporting bean plants. ■ informal a tall, thin person.

bean sprouts ▶ **plural n.** the sprouting seeds of certain beans, esp. mung beans, used in Asian cooking.

bean·stalk /ˈbēnˌstôk/ ▶ **n.** the stem of a bean plant, proverbially fast growing and tall.

bear[1] /be(ə)r/ ▶ **v.** (past **bore**; past part. **borne**) [trans.] **1** (of a person) carry: *he was bearing a tray.* ■ (of a vehicle or boat) convey (passengers or cargo). ■ have or display as a visible mark or feature: *many of the papers bore his flamboyant signature.* ■ be called by (a name or title): *he bore the surname Tiller.* ■ (**bear oneself**) [with adverbial] carry or conduct oneself in a particular manner: *she bore herself with dignity.* **2** support: *walls that cannot bear a stone vault.* ■ take responsibility for: *no one likes to **bear the responsibility** for such decisions.* ■ be able to accept or stand up to: *it is doubtful whether either of these distinctions would **bear scrutiny**.* **3** endure (an ordeal or difficulty): *she bore the pain.* ■ [with modal and negative] manage to tolerate (a situation or experience): *she **could hardly bear** his sarcasm* | [with infin.] *I cannot bear to see you hurt* ■ (**cannot bear someone/something**) strongly dislike: *I can't bear caviar.* **4** give birth to (a child): *she bore six daughters* | [with two objs.] *his wife had borne him a son.* ■ (of a tree or plant) produce (fruit or flowers): *a squash that bears fruit shaped like cucumbers.* **5** [no obj., with adverbial of direction] turn and proceed in a specified direction: *bear left and follow the old road.*

– PHRASES **be borne in upon** come to be realized by: *the folly of her action was borne in on her with devastating precision.* **bear arms 1** carry firearms. **2** wear or display a coat of arms. **bear the brunt of** see **BRUNT**. **bear the burden of** suffer the consequences of. **bear fruit** fig. yield positive results: *plans for power-sharing may be about to bear fruit.* **bear someone a grudge** nurture a feeling of resentment against someone. **bear a hand** archaic help in a task or enterprise. **bear someone malice** (or **ill will**) [with negative] wish someone harm. **bear a resemblance** (or **similarity**) **to** resemble. **bear a relation** (or **relationship**) **to** [with negative] be logically consistent with: *the map didn't seem to bear any relation to the roads.* **bear the stamp of** be clearly identifiable with. **bear witness** (or **testimony**) **to** testify to. **bring pressure to bear on** attempt to coerce. **bring to bear 1** muster and use to effect: *she had reservations about how much influence she could bring to bear.* **2** aim (a weapon): *bringing his rifle to bear on a distant target.* **does not bear thinking about** is too terrible to contemplate. **grin and bear it** see **GRIN**. **have one's cross to bear** see **CROSS**.

– PHRASAL VERBS **bear away** another way of saying ***BEAR OFF***. **bear down** (of a woman in labor) exert downward pressure in order to push the baby out. ■ put pressure on someone or something. **bear down on** move quickly toward someone, in a purposeful or an intimidating manner. ■ take strict measures to deal with. **bear off** Sailing change course away from the wind. ■ Naut. steer away from something, typically the land. **bear on** be relevant to (something): *two kinds of theories that bear on literary studies.* ■ [with adverbial] be a burden on (someone): *a tax* *that will* **bear** *heavily on poorer households.* **bear something out** support or confirm something: *this assumption is not borne out by any evidence.* **bear up** remain cheerful in the face of adversity. **bear with** be patient or tolerant with. [OE *beran,* from an Indo-Eur. root shared by Gk. *pherein,* and L. *ferre.*]

bear[2] ▶ **n. 1** a large, heavy, mostly omnivorous mammal of the family Ursidae that walks on the soles of its feet, with thick fur and a very short tail. See illustration at BLACK BEAR. ■ a teddy bear. ■ informal a rough, unmannerly, or uncouth person. ■ a large, heavy, cumbersome man: *a lumbering bear of a man.* ■ (**the Bear**) informal a nickname for Russia. ■ (**the Bear**) the constellation Ursa Major or Ursa Minor. **2** Stock Market a person who forecasts that prices of stocks or commodities will fall, esp. a person who sells shares hoping to buy them back later at a lower price: [as adj.] *bear markets.* Often contrasted with BULL[1] (sense 2 of the **noun**).
– PHRASES **loaded for bear** informal fully prepared for any eventuality, typically a confrontation or challenge. [OE *bera,* from West Gmc.; akin to Ger. *Bär.*]

bear·a·ble /ˈbe(ə)rəbəl/ ▶ **adj.** able to be endured. — **bear·a·bly** /-blē/ **adv.**

bear·bait·ing /ˈbe(ə)rˌbātiNG/ ▶ **n.** hist. a form of entertainment that involved setting dogs to attack a captive bear.

bear·ber·ry /ˈbe(ə)rˌberē/ ▶ **n.** (pl. **-ries**) a creeping dwarf shrub of the heath family (genus *Arctostaphylos*) with pinkish flowers and bright red berries.

bear·cat /ˈbe(ə)rˌkat/ ▶ **n. 1** a bearlike climbing mammal, esp. the red panda. **2** a binturong. **3** Informal an aggressive or forceful person.

beard /bi(ə)rd/ ▶ **n. 1** a growth of hair on the chin and lower cheeks of a man's face. ■ a tuft of hair on the chin of certain mammals, for example a lion or goat. ■ an animal's growth or marking that is likened to a beard, e.g., the gills of an oyster, or the beak bristles of certain birds. ■ a tuft of hairs or bristles on certain plants, esp. the awn of a grass. **2** informal a person who carries out a transaction, typically a bet, for someone else in order to conceal the other's identity. ■ a person who pretends to have a romantic or sexual relationship with someone else in order to conceal the other's true sexual orientation. ▶ **v.** [trans.] boldly confront or challenge (someone formidable).
– PHRASES **beard the lion in his den** (or **lair**) confront or challenge someone on their own ground. — **beard·ed adj.** [in comb.] *a gray-bearded man.* **beard·less adj.** [OE, from West Gmc.; akin to Ger. *Bart.*]

beard·ed col·lie /ˈbi(ə)rdid/ ▶ **n.** a dog of a shaggy breed of collie with long hair on the face.

beard·ed vul·ture ▶ **n.** another term for LAMMERGEIER.

Beards·ley /ˈbi(ə)rdzlē/, Aubrey Vincent (1872–98), English illustrator, associated with art nouveau.

beard·tongue /ˈbi(ə)rdˌtəNG/ ▶ **n.** a North American plant of the figwort family (genus *Penstemon*), esp. the widespread **foxglove beardtongue** (*P. digitalis*) with showy, five-lobed flowers. Each blossom has a tuft of hair on one of its stamens.

bear·er /ˈbe(ə)rər/ ▶ **n. 1** a person or thing that carries or holds something: [in comb.] *a flag-bearer.* ■ a carrier of equipment on an expedition. ■ a person who carries the coffin at a funeral; pall-bearer. ■ a tree or plant that bears fruit or flowers. **2** a person who presents a check or other order to pay money. ■ [as adj.] payable to the possessor: *bearer bonds.*

bear·grass /ˈbe(ə)rˌgras/ (also **bear grass**) ▶ **n.** a North American plant with long, coarse, grasslike leaves, in particular: ■ a wild yucca. ■ a cultivated ornamental plant (*Xerophyllum tenax*) of the lily family, the leaves of which were formerly used by American Indians to make watertight baskets.

bear hug ▶ **n.** a rough, tight embrace.

bear·ing /ˈbe(ə)riNG/ ▶ **n. 1** [in sing.] a person's way of standing or moving. ■ the way one behaves or conducts oneself. **2** relation or relevance. **3** the level to which something bad can be tolerated. **4** a part of a machine that bears friction, esp. between a rotating part and its housing. ■ a ball bearing. **5** the direction or position of something, or the direction of movement, relative to a fixed point. It is typically measured in degrees, usually with magnetic north as zero: *the Point is on a bearing of 015°.* ■ (**one's bearings**) awareness of one's position relative to one's surroundings. **6** Heraldry a device or charge: *armorial bearings.* **7** the act, capability, or time of producing fruit or offspring.

bear·ing rein ▶ **n.** a fixed rein that causes the horse to raise its head and arch its neck.

bear·ish /ˈbe(ə)riSH/ ▶ **adj. 1** resembling or likened to a bear, typically in being rough, surly, or clumsy. **2** Stock Market characterized by falling share prices. ■ (of a dealer) inclined to sell because of an anticipated fall in prices. — **bear·ish·ly adv. bear·ish·ness n.**

bear mar·ket ▶ **n.** Stock Market a market in which prices are falling, encouraging selling.

Bé·ar·naise sauce /ˌberˈnāz/ ▶ **n.** a rich sauce thickened with egg yolks and flavored with tarragon. [*Béarnaise,* fem. of Fr. *Béarnais* 'of *Béarn,*' a region of southwestern France.]

bear·skin /ˈbe(ə)rˌskin/ ▶ **n.** the pelt of a bear, esp. when used as a rug or wrap. ■ a tall cap of black fur worn ceremonially by certain military troops.

Be·as /ˈbēäs/ a river in northern India that rises in the Himalayas and joins the Sutlej River in Punjab.

beast /bēst/ ▶ **n.** an animal, esp. a large or dangerous four-footed one. ■ (usu. **beasts**) a domestic animal, esp. a bovine farm animal. ■ archaic or humorous an animal as opposed to a human. ■ an inhumanly cruel, violent, or depraved person. ■ informal an objectionable or unpleasant person or thing. ■ (**the beast**) a person's brutish or untamed characteristics. ■ [with adj.] informal a thing or concept possessing a particular quality. [ME: from OFr. *beste,* based on L. *bestia.*]

beast·ie /ˈbēstē/ ▶ **n.** (pl. **-ies**) Scot. or humorous an animal, insect, or germ.

beast·ings ▶ **n.** var. of BEESTINGS.

beast·ly /ˈbēstlē/ ▶ **adj.** (**-li·er, -li·est**) **1** informal very unpleasant. ■ unkind; malicious. **2** archaic cruel and unrestrained. — **beast·li·ness n.**

beast of bur·den ▶ **n.** an animal such as a mule or donkey that is used for carrying loads.

beast of prey ▶ **n.** an animal, esp. a mammal, that kills and eats other animals.

beat /bēt/ ▶ **v.** (past **beat** ; past part. **beat·en**) [trans.] **1** strike (a person or an animal) repeatedly and violently so as to hurt or injure them, usually with an implement such as a club or whip. ■ strike (an object) repeatedly so as to make a noise. ■ [intrans.] (of an instrument) make a rhythmical sound through being struck: *drums were beating in the distance.* ■ strike (a carpet, blanket, etc.) repeatedly in order to remove dust. ■ remove (dust) from something by striking it repeatedly. ■ flatten or shape (metal) by striking it repeatedly with a hammer. ■ (**beat something against/on**) strike something against (something). ■ [intrans.] (**beat on/against**) strike repeatedly on: *Sidney beat on the door with the flat of his hand.* ■ [intrans.] (**beat at**) make striking movements toward: *Emmie began to beat at the flames.* ■ move across (an area of land) repeatedly striking at the ground cover in order to raise game birds for shooting. **2** defeat (someone) in a game, competition, election, or commercial venture. ■ informal baffle. ■ overcome (a problem, or disease). ■ do or be better than (a record or score). ■ informal be better than: *you can't beat the taste of fresh raspberries.* **3** succeed in getting somewhere ahead of (someone). ■ take action to avoid (difficult or inconvenient effects of an event or circumstance). **4** [intrans.] (of the heart) pulsate: *her heart beat faster with panic.* **5** (of a bird) move (the wings) up and down. ■ (of a bird or its wings) make rhythmic movements through (the air). ■ [intrans.] (of a bird) fly making rhythmic wing movements: *an owl beat low over the salt marsh.* **6** stir (cooking ingredients) vigorously with a fork, whisk, or beater to make a smooth or frothy mixture. **7** (**beat it**) informal leave: [in imper.] *now beat it, will you!* **8** [no obj., with adverbial of direction] Sailing sail into the wind, following a zigzag course with repeated tacking: *we beat southward.* ▶ **n. 1** a main accent or rhythmic unit in music or poetry. ■ a strong rhythm in popular music. ■ [in sing] a regular, rhythmic sound or movement. ■ the sound made when something, typically a musical instrument, is struck. ■ a pulsation of the heart. ■ a periodic variation of sound or amplitude due to the combination of two sounds, electrical signals, or other vibrations having similar but not identical frequencies. ■ the movement of a bird's wings. **2** an area allocated to a police officer to patrol. ■ a spell of duty allocated to a police officer. ■ an area regularly frequented by someone, typically a prostitute. ■ fig. a person's area of interest: *his beat is construction.* ■ an area regularly occupied by a shoal of freshwater fish. **3** a brief pause or moment of hesitation, typically one lasting a specified length. **4** informal short for BEATNIK. ▶ **adj. 1** [predic.] infomal completely exhausted: *I'm dead beat.* **2** [attrib.] of or relating to the beat generation or its philosophy: *beat poet Allen Ginsberg.*
– PHRASES **beat all** be amazing or impressive: *well, that beats all.* **beat around** (or **beat about**) **the bush** discuss a matter without coming to the point. **beat someone at their own game** see GAME[1]. **beat someone's brains out** see BRAIN. **beat one's breast** see BREAST. **beat the bushes** informal search thoroughly: *I was out beating the bushes for investors.* **beat the clock** perform a task quickly or within a fixed time limit. **beat a dead horse** waste energy on a lost cause or unalterable situation. **beat the drum for** see DRUM[1]. **beat the hell out of** informal **1** beat (someone) very severely. **2** surpass or defeat easily. **beat the living daylights out of** see DAYLIGHT (sense 2). **beat the pants off** informal prove to be vastly superior to. **beat a path to someone's door** (of a large number of people) hasten to make contact with someone regarded as interesting or inspiring. **beat a (hasty) retreat** withdraw, typically in order to avoid something unpleasant. **beat the shit out of** vulgar slang beat (someone) very severely. **beat the system** succeed in finding a means of getting around rules, regulations, or other means of control. **beat time** indicate or follow a musical tempo with a baton or other means. **beat someone to it** succeed in doing something or getting somewhere before someone else, to their annoyance. **miss a beat** see MISS[1]. **to beat all —s** that is infinitely better than all the things mentioned: *a PC screen saver to beat all screen savers.* **to beat the band** informal in such a way as to surpass all competition: *they were talking to beat the band.*
– PHRASAL VERBS **beat someone back** (usu. **be beaten back**) force (someone attempting to do something) to retreat. **beat down** (of the sun) radiate intense heat and brightness. ■ (of rain) fall hard and continuously. **beat someone down** force someone to reduce the price of something. **beat something down** quell defense or resistance. **beat one's meat** vulgar slang (of a man) masturbate. **beat off** vulgar slang (of a man) masturbate. **beat someone/something off** succeed in resisting an attacker or an attack. ■ win against a challenge or rival. **beat**

something out 1 produce a loud, rhythmic sound by striking something. **2** extinguish flames by striking at them with a suitable object. **beat someone up 1** assault and severely injure someone by hitting, kicking, or punching them repeatedly. **2** abuse someone verbally. **beat up on** another way of saying BEAT SOMEONE UP. — **beat·a·ble** adj. [OE *bēatan*, of Gmc. origin.]

beat·box /'bēt,bäks/ ▶ n. informal a drum machine. ■ a radio or radio cassette player used to play loud music, esp. rap. ▶ v. [intrans.] make rhythmical sounds with the voice in imitation of the rhythms of rap music.

beat·en /'bētn/ past participle of BEAT. ▶ adj. **1** having been defeated. ■ exhausted and dejected. **2** having been beaten or struck. ■ (of food) whipped to a uniform consistency. ■ (of metal) shaped by hammering, typically so as to give the surface a dimpled texture. ■ (of precious metal) hammered to form thin foil for ornamental use. **3** (of a path) well trodden; much used.
– PHRASES **off the beaten track** (or **path**) in or into an isolated place. ■ unusual: [as adj.] *off-the-beaten-track experiences.*

beat·er /'bētər/ ▶ n. **1** a person who hits someone or something, in particular: ■ a person employed to flush out or drive game birds for shooting by striking at the ground cover. ■ a person who beats metal in manufacturing. ■ [in comb.] a person who habitually hits someone: *a wife-beater.* **2** [often with adj.] an implement or machine used for beating something, in particular: ■ (in cooking) a device for whisking or blending ingredients. ■ an implement used to dislodge dirt from rugs and carpets by hitting them. ■ a stick for beating a drum. **3** [in comb.] informal a means of defeating or preventing something: *a recession-beater.*

beat gen·er·a·tion a movement of young people in the 1950s who rejected conventional society and favored Zen Buddhism, modern jazz, free sexuality, and recreational drugs.

be·a·tif·ic /,bēə'tifik/ ▶ adj. blissfully happy: *a beatific smile.* ■ Christian Theol. imparting holy bliss. — **be·a·tif·i·cal·ly** /-ik(ə)lē/ adv. [17th C.: from Fr. *béatifique* or L. *beatificus*, from *beatus* 'blessed.']

be·at·i·fi·ca·tion /bē,atəfi'kāsHən/ ▶ n. (in the Roman Catholic Church) declaration by the pope that a dead person is in a state of bliss, constituting a step toward canonization and permitting public veneration.

be·at·i·fy /bē'atə,fī/ ▶ v. (**-fies, -fied**) [trans.] (in the Roman Catholic Church) announce the beatification of. ■ make (someone) blissfully happy. [16th C.: from OFr. *beatifier* or eccles. Latin *beatificare*, from L. *beatus* 'blessed.']

beat·ing /'bētiNG/ ▶ n. **1** a punishment or assault in which the victim is hit repeatedly. **2** pulsation or throbbing, typically of the heart. **3** a defeat in a competitive situation.
– PHRASES **take a beating** informal suffer damage or hurt.

be·at·i·tude /bē'ati,t(y)o͞od/ ▶ n. supreme blessedness. ■ (**the Beatitudes**) the blessings listed by Jesus in the Sermon on the Mount (Matt. 5:3–11). ■ (**his/your Beatitude**) a title given to patriarchs in the Orthodox Church. [ME: from OFr. *beatitude* or L. *beatitudo*, from *beatus* 'blessed.']

beat·nik /'bētnik/ ▶ n. a young person in the 1950s and early 1960s belonging to a subculture associated with the beat generation. [1950s: from BEAT + *-nik* on the pattern of *sputnik*.]

Bea·ton /'bētn/, Sir Cecil Walter Hardy (1904–80), English photographer. He is noted for his fashion features and portraits of celebrities.

Be·a·trix /'bāə,triks; 'bē-/ (1938–), queen of the Netherlands (1980–); full name *Beatrix Wilhelmina Armgard.*

Beat·tie /'bētē/, Ann (1947–), US writer. Her novels include *Picturing Will* (1989), and *The Doctor's House* (2002).

beat-up ▶ adj. [attrib.] informal (of a thing) worn out by overuse; in a state of disrepair.

beau /bō/ ▶ n. (pl. **beaux** /bōz/ or **beaus**) dated **1** a boyfriend or male admirer. **2** a rich, fashionable young man; a dandy. [17th C.: from Fr., lit. 'handsome,' from L. *bellus.*]

beau·coup /bō'ko͞o; 'bo͞o,ko͞o/ ▶ n. informal an abundance; a large quantity. ▶ adj. many; much. ▶ adv. in abundance. [20th C.: Fr.]

Beau·fort scale /'bōfərt/ a scale of wind speed based on a visual estimation of the wind's effects, ranging from force 0 (less than 1 knot or 1 kph, "calm") to force 12 (64 knots or 118 kph and above, "hurricane"). [19th C.: named after Sir Francis *Beaufort* (1774–1857), the English admiral and naval hydrographer who devised it.]

Beau·fort Sea a part of the Arctic Ocean that lies to the north of Alaska and Canada.

beau geste /,bō 'zHest/ ▶ n. (pl. **beaux gestes** pronunc. same) a noble and generous act. [20th C.: Fr., lit. 'splendid gesture.']

beau i·dé·al /,bō ,ēdā'al; ī'dēəl/ ▶ n. a person or thing representing the highest possible standard of excellence in a particular respect. [19th C.: Fr., lit. 'ideal beauty.']

Beau·jo·lais /,bōzHə'lā/ ▶ n. a light red or (less commonly) white burgundy wine produced in the Beaujolais district of southeastern France.

Beau·mar·chais /,bōmär'sHā/, Pierre Augustin Caron de (1732–99), French playwright, noted for *The Barber of Seville* (1775).

beau monde /,bō 'mônd/ ▶ n. (**the beau monde**) fashionable society. [17th C.: Fr., lit. 'fine world.']

Beau·mont[1] /'bō,mänt/ a port in southeastern Texas, on the Neches River; pop. 114,323.

Beau·mont[2], Francis (1584–1616), English playwright. He worked with John Fletcher on many plays.

Beaune /bōn/ ▶ n. a red burgundy wine from the region around Beaune in eastern France.

Beau·re·gard /'bōri,gärd/, Pierre Gustave Toutant (1818–93), Confederate general in the American Civil War. Superintendent of the US Military Academy at West Point, he resigned in 1861 to join the cause of secession.

beaut /byo͞ot/ informal; ▶ n. a particularly fine example of something. ■ a beautiful person. [19th C.: abbrev. of BEAUTY or BEAUTIFUL.]

beau·te·ous /'byo͞otēəs/ ▶ adj. literary beautiful. [ME: from BEAUTY.]

beau·ti·cian /byo͞o'tisHən/ ▶ n. a person who does hair styling, manicures, and other beauty treatments.

beau·ti·ful /'byo͞otəfəl/ ▶ adj. pleasing the senses or mind aesthetically. ■ of a very high standard; excellent.
– PHRASES **the beautiful people 1** fashionable, glamorous, and privileged people. **2** (in the 1960s) hippies. **the body beautiful** an ideal of physical beauty. — **beau·ti·ful·ly** /-f(ə)lē/ adv. [as adj.] *the rules are beautifully simple.*

beau·ti·fy /'byo͞otə,fī/ ▶ v. (**-fies, -fied**) [trans.] improve the appearance of. — **beau·ti·fi·ca·tion** /,byo͞otəfi'kāsHən/ n. **beau·ti·fi·er** n.

beau·ty /'byo͞otē/ ▶ n. (pl. **-ties**) **1** a combination of qualities, such as shape, color, or form, that pleases the aesthetic senses, esp. the sight. ■ a combination of qualities that pleases the intellect or moral sense. ■ [as adj.] denoting something intended to make a woman more attractive. **2** a beautiful or pleasing thing or person, in particular: ■ a beautiful woman. ■ an excellent specimen or example of something. ■ (**the beauties of**) the pleasing or attractive features of something. ■ [in sing.] the best feature or advantage of something.
– PHRASES **beauty is in the eye of the beholder** proverb beauty cannot be judged objectively; for what one person finds beautiful or admirable may not appeal to another. **beauty is only skin-deep** proverb a pleasing appearance is not a guide to character. [ME: from OFr. *beaute*, based on L. *bellus* 'beautiful, fine.']

beau·ty bush (also **beau·ty·bush**) ▶ n. a deciduous Chinese shrub of the honeysuckle family (*Kolkwitzia amabilis*), with clusters of yellow-throated pink tubular flowers, widely cultivated as an ornamental.

beau·ty con·test ▶ n. a competition for a prize given to the woman judged the most beautiful. ■ a contest between rival institutions or political candidates that depends heavily on presentation.

beau·ty mark ▶ n. another term for BEAUTY SPOT (sense 2).

beau·ty par·lor (also **beauty salon** or **beauty shop**) ▶ n. an establishment in which hairdressing, makeup, and similar cosmetic treatments are carried out professionally.

beau·ty queen ▶ n. a woman judged most beautiful in a beauty contest.

beau·ty sleep ▶ n. humorous sleep considered to be sufficient to keep one looking young and beautiful.

beau·ty spot ▶ n. **1** a place known for its beautiful scenery. **2** a small natural or artificial mark such as a mole on a woman's face, considered to enhance another feature.

Beau·voir, Simone de, see DE BEAUVOIR.

beaux /bōz/ plural form of BEAU.

beaux arts /,bō 'zär/ ▶ plural n. **1** fine arts. **2** (usu. **Beaux Arts**) [as adj.] relating to the classical decorative style maintained by the École des Beaux-Arts in Paris, esp. in the 19th century. [from Fr. *beaux-arts.*]

bea·ver[1] /'bēvər/ ▶ n. (pl. same or **-vers**) a large semiaquatic broad-tailed rodent (genus *Castor*, family Castoridae), esp. *C. canadensis* of North America. It is noted for its habit of gnawing through tree trunks to fell the trees in order to feed on the bark and build dams. ■ the soft light brown fur of the beaver. ■ (also **beaver hat**) esp. hist. a hat made of felted beaver fur. ■ (also **beaver cloth**) a heavy woolen cloth resembling felted beaver fur. ■ fig. a very hardworking person. ▶ v. [intrans.] informal work hard: *Joe beavered away to keep things running.* [OE *beofor, befor*, from Gmc.; akin to Ger. *Biber*, from an Indo-Eur. root meaning 'brown.']

beaver[1]

bea·ver[2] ▶ n. the lower part of the face guard of a helmet in a suit of armor. [15th C.: from OFr. *baviere* 'bib,' from *baver* 'slaver.']

bea·ver·board /'bēvər,bôrd/ ▶ n. a kind of fiberboard used in building. [20th C.: from BEAVER[1] + BOARD.]

Bea·ver·ton /'bēvərtən/ a city in northwestern Oregon, west of Portland; pop. 76,129.

be·bop /'bē,bäp/ ▶ n. a type of jazz originating in the 1940s and characterized by complex harmony and rhythms. — **be·bop·per** n. [1940s: imitative.]

be·calm /bi'kä(l)m/ ▶ v. [trans.] (usu. **be becalmed**) leave (a sailing vessel) unable to move through lack of wind.

be·came /bi'kām/ past participle of BECOME.

be·cause /bi'kôz; -'kəz/ ▶ conj. for the reason that; since: *we did it because we felt it our duty.*
– PHRASES **because of** on account of; by reason of. [ME: from the phr. *by cause*, influenced by OFr. *par cause de* 'by reason of.']

bec·ca·fi·co /ˌbekəˈfēkō/ ▶ **n.** a European songbird, esp. a warbler, eaten as a delicacy. [Ital.]

bé·cha·mel /ˌbāsHəˈmel/ (also **béchamel sauce**) ▶ **n.** a rich white sauce made with milk infused with herbs and other flavorings. [named after the Marquis Louis de *Béchamel* (died 1703), steward to Louis XIV of France.]

be·chance /biˈcHans/ ▶ **v.** archaic happen; befall.

bêche-de-mer /ˌbesH də ˈmer/ ▶ **n.** (pl. same or **bêches-de-mer** pronunc. same) **1** a large sea cucumber that is eaten as a delicacy in China and Japan. Also called TREPANG. **2** var. of BEACH-LA-MAR. [18th C.: pseudo-Fr., alt. of Port. *bicho do mar*, lit. 'sea worm.']

beck[1] /bek/ ▶ **n.** esp. Brit. a mountain stream. [ME: from ON *bekkr*, from Gmc.; akin to Ger. *Bach*.]

beck[2] ▶ **n.** literary a gesture requesting attention, such as a nod or wave.
– PHRASES **at someone's beck and call** always having to be ready to obey someone's orders immediately. [ME: from archaic *beck*, abbreviated form of BECKON.]

Beck·er /ˈbekər/, Boris Franz (1967–), German tennis player. A six-time Grand Slam singles champion during 1985–96, he is also an Olympic gold medalist (1992).

beck·et /ˈbekit/ ▶ **n.** a loop of rope or similar device for securing loose items on a ship. [18th C.: of unknown origin.]

Beck·et, St. Tho·mas à /ə ˈbekit/ (*c.*1118–70), archbishop of Canterbury 1162–70. He was assassinated when he opposed Henry II.

Beck·ett /ˈbekit/, Samuel Barclay (1906–89), Irish playwright. He wrote *Waiting for Godot* (1952). Nobel Prize for Literature (1969).

Beck·mann[1] /ˈbekmən/, Ernst Otto (1853–1923), German chemist. He devised a method for determining a compound's molecular weight.

Beck·mann[2], Max (1884–1950), German painter. His paintings reflect events of World War I.

beck·on /ˈbekən/ ▶ **v.** [intrans.] make a gesture with the hand, arm, or head to encourage someone to come nearer or follow. ■ [with obj. and adverbial of direction] attract the attention of and summon (someone) in this way. [with obj. and infin.] *he beckoned Duncan to follow.* ■ fig. seem to be appealing or inviting. [OE *bīecnan*, *bēcnan*, of West Gmc. origin; rel. to BEACON.]

be·cloud /biˈkloud/ ▶ **v.** [trans.] cause to become obscure or muddled: *self-interest beclouds the issue.* ■ (usu. **be beclouded**) cover or surround with clouds.

be·come /biˈkəm/ ▶ **v.** (past **-came** ; past part. **-come**) **1** [no obj., with complement] begin to be: *they became angry.* ■ grow to be; turn into. ■ (of a person) qualify or be accepted as; acquire the status of. ■ (**become of**) (in questions) happen to: *what would become of her?* **2** [trans.] (of clothing) look good on or suit (someone). ■ be appropriate or suitable to (someone). [OE *becuman* 'come to a place, come (to be or do something)' (see BE-, COME), from Gmc. origin; akin to Ger. *bekommen* 'receive.']

be·com·ing /biˈkəmiNG/ ▶ **adj.** (esp. of clothing) flattering a person's appearance. ■ decorous. ▶ **n.** Philos. the process of coming to be something or of passing into a state. — **be·com·ing·ly adj.**

Bec·que·rel /ˌbek(ə)ˈrel/, Antoine-Henri (1852–1908), French physicist. He worked with Marie and Pierre Curie. Nobel Prize for Physics (1903, shared with the Curies).

bec·que·rel /ˈbekəˌrel/ (abbr.: **Bq**) ▶ **n.** Physics the SI unit of radioactivity, corresponding to one disintegration per second. [19th C.: named after A. H. BECQUEREL.]

BEd ▶ **abbr.** Bachelor of Education.

bed /bed/ ▶ **n.** **1** a piece of furniture for sleep or rest, typically a framework with a mattress and coverings. ■ a place or article used by a person or animal for sleep or rest: *a bed of straw.* ■ the time for sleeping: *it was time for bed.* ■ a bed and associated facilities making up a place for a patient in a hospital or for a guest at a hotel. ■ informal used with reference to a bed as the typical place for sexual activity. **2** an area of ground, typically in a garden, where flowers and plants are grown. **3** a flat base or foundation on which something rests or is supported, in particular: ■ the foundation of a road or railroad. ■ the open part of a truck, wagon, or railroad car, where goods are carried. ■ the flat surface beneath the baize of a billiard table. **4** a layer or pile of something, in particular: ■ a layer of food on which other foods are served. ■ a stratum or layer of rock or other geological material. ■ any mass or pile resembling a bed. **5** the bottom of the sea or a lake or river. ■ [with modifier] a place on the seabed where shellfish, esp. oysters or mussels, breed or are bred. ▶ **v.** (**bed·ded, bed·ding**) **1** [intrans.] settle down to sleep or rest for the night, typically in an improvised place: *he usually bedded down on newspapers in the church.* ■ (**bed someone/something down**) settle a person or animal down to sleep or rest for the night. ■ informal have sexual intercourse with. **2** transfer (a plant) from a pot or seed tray to a garden plot: *I bedded out these houseplants.* **3** (usu. **be bedded in/on**) fix firmly; embed. ■ lay or arrange (something, esp. stone) in a layer.
– PHRASES **bed of nails** a board with nails pointing out of it, as lain on by fakirs and ascetics. ■ fig. a problematic or uncomfortable situation. **bed of roses** [often with negative] used in reference to a situation or activity that is comfortable or easy: *farming is no bed of roses.* **be brought to bed** archaic (of a woman) give birth to a child. **get up on the wrong side of the bed** start the day in a bad temper. **in bed with** informal having sexual intercourse with. ■ fig. in undesirably close association with. **make a bed** fit a bed with sheets, blankets, and pillows. **put someone to bed** take or prepare someone, typically a child, for rest in bed. **put a newspaper to bed** informal prepare a newspaper for press. **take to one's bed** stay in bed because of illness. [OE *bed*, *bedd*, from Gmc.; akin to Ger. *Bett*.]

bed and break·fast (also **bed-and-break·fast**; abbr.: **b. & b.**) ▶ **n.** sleeping accommodations for a night and a meal in the morning, provided in guest houses and small hotels. ■ a guest house or small hotel offering such accommodations.

be·daub /biˈdôb/ ▶ **v.** [trans.] (usu. **be bedaubed**) literary smear or daub with a sticky substance.

be·daz·zle /biˈdazəl/ ▶ **v.** [trans.] (often **be bedazzled**) greatly impress (someone) with brilliance or skill. ■ cleverly outwit. — **be·daz·zle·ment n.**

bed·bug /ˈbedˌbəg/ ▶ **n.** a bloodsucking insect (family Cimicidae, *Cimex* and other genera) that is a parasite of birds and mammals, some species of which feed mainly on humans.

bedbug

bed·cham·ber /ˈbedˌcHāmbər/ ▶ **n.** archaic a bedroom.

bed·clothes /ˈbedˌklō(TH)z/ ▶ **plural n.** coverings for a bed, such as sheets and blankets.

bed·cov·er /ˈbedˌkəvər/ ▶ **n.** a bedspread.

bed·ded /ˈbedid/ ▶ **adj.** Geol. (of rock) deposited in layers or strata, esp. in a way specified.

bed·der /ˈbedər/ ▶ **n.** a plant suitable for use as a bedding plant.

bed·ding /ˈbediNG/ ▶ **n.** **1** coverings for a bed, such as sheets and blankets. ■ straw or similar material for animals to sleep on. **2** a base or bottom layer. **3** a display of bedding plants. **4** Geol. the stratification or layering of rocks.

bed·ding plant ▶ **n.** a plant set into a garden bed or container when it is about to bloom, usually an annual.

bed·dy-bye /ˈbedēˌbī/ ▶ **n.** a baby-talk word for bed or bedtime. [20th C.: from BED + -Y[2] and BYE-BYE.]

Bede, St. /bēd/ (*c.*673–735), English monk and historian; known as **the Venerable Bede**. He wrote *The Ecclesiastical History of the English People* (731).

be·deck /biˈdek/ ▶ **v.** [trans.] (often **be bedecked**) decorate: *he led us into a room bedecked with tinsel.*

be·dev·il /biˈdevəl/ ▶ **v.** (**-dev·iled, -dev·il·ing** ; also esp. Brit. **-dev·illed, -dev·il·ling**) [trans.] (of something bad) cause great and continual trouble to. ■ (of a person) torment or harass. — **be·dev·il·ment n.**

be·dew /biˈd(y)o͞o/ ▶ **v.** [trans.] literary cover or sprinkle with drops of water or other liquid.

bed·fel·low /ˈbedˌfelō/ ▶ **n.** a person who shares a bed with another. ■ fig. a person or thing allied or closely connected with another.

Bed·ford /ˈbedfərd/ a city in northeastern Texas, northeast of Fort Worth; pop. 43,762.

Bed·ford cord ▶ **n.** a tough woven fabric having prominent ridges, similar to corduroy. [19th C.: named after the town of Bedford, England.]

Bed·ford-Stuy·ve·sant /ˈstīvəsənt/ a section of Brooklyn in New York City.

be·dight /biˈdīt/ ▶ **adj.** archaic adorned: *a Christmas pudding bedight with holly.* [ME: past part. of archaic *bedight* 'equip, array' (see BE-, DIGHT).]

be·dim /biˈdim/ ▶ **v.** (**-dimmed, -dim·ming**) [trans.] literary cause to become dim.

be·di·zened /biˈdīzənd/ ▶ **adj.** literary dressed up or decorated gaudily. — **be·di·zen v.** [17th C.: from BE- (as an intensifier) + obs. *dizen* 'deck out,' prob. of Du. origin.]

bed·lam /ˈbedləm/ ▶ **n.** **1** a scene of uproar and confusion. **2** hist. (**Bedlam**) a former insane asylum in London. ■ archaic used allusively to refer to any insane asylum. [ME: early form of BETHLEHEM, referring to the hospital of St. Mary of Bethlehem in London, used as an asylum for the insane.]

bed lin·en ▶ **n.** sheets, pillowcases, and duvet covers.

Bed·ling·ton ter·ri·er /ˈbedliNGtən/ ▶ **n.** a terrier of a breed with a narrow head, long legs, and curly hair. [19th C.: after the village of *Bedlington* in northern England.]

Bedlington terrier

bed·mate /ˈbedˌmāt/ ▶ **n.** a person with whom a bed is shared, esp. a sexual partner.

Bed·ou·in /ˈbedo͞oin; ˈbedwin/ (also **Bed·u·in**) ▶ **n.** (pl. same) a nomadic Arab of the desert. ▶ **adj.** of or relating to the Bedouin. [from OFr.

beduin, based on Arab. *badawī*, (pl.) *badawīn* 'dwellers in the desert,' from *badw* 'desert.']

bed·pan /'bed,pan/ ▶ **n.** a receptacle used by a bedridden patient as a toilet.

bed·plate /'bed,plāt/ ▶ **n.** a metal plate forming the base of a machine.

bed·post /'bed,pōst/ ▶ **n.** any of the four upright supports of a bedstead. – PHRASES **between you and me and the bedpost** (or **the gatepost** or **the wall**) informal in strict confidence.

be·drag·gled /bi'dragəld/ ▶ **adj.** dirty and disheveled. — **be·drag·gle v.** [18th C.: from BE- 'thoroughly' + DRAGGLE + -ED[2].]

bed·rail /'bed,rāl/ ▶ **n.** a rail along the side of a bed connecting the headboard to the footboard.

bed rest ▶ **n.** confinement of an invalid to bed as part of treatment.

bed·rid·den /'bed,ridn/ ▶ **adj.** confined to bed by sickness or old age. [ME: from *bedrid* 'bedridden person,' from the v. RIDE.]

bed·rock /'bed,räk/ ▶ **n.** solid rock underlying loose deposits such as soil or alluvium. ■ fig. the fundamental principles on which something is based.

bed·roll /'bed,rōl/ ▶ **n.** a sleeping bag or other bedding rolled into a bundle.

bed·room /'bed,ro͞om; -,ro͝om/ (abbr.: **bdrm.**) ▶ **n.** a room for sleeping in: [in comb.] *a three-bedroom house.* ■ [as adj.] relating to sexual relations. ■ [as adj.] denoting a small town or suburb whose residents travel to work in a nearby city.

bed·side /'bed,sīd/ ▶ **n.** the space beside a bed, typically that of someone who is ill. – PHRASES **bedside manner** a doctor's approach or attitude toward a patient.

bed·sit /'bed,sit/ (also **bed·sit·ter** or **bed-sit·ting room**) ▶ **n.** Brit., informal a one-room apartment typically consisting of a combined bedroom and sitting room with cooking facilities.

bed·skirt /'bed,skərt/ ▶ **n.** a decorative drapery attached to the frame of a bed; a dust ruffle.

bed·sore /'bed,sôr/ ▶ **n.** a sore developed by an invalid because of pressure caused by lying in bed in one position. Also called DECUBITUS ULCER.

bed·spread /'bed,spred/ ▶ **n.** a decorative cloth used to cover a bed.

bed·stead /'bed,sted/ ▶ **n.** the framework of a bed on which the bedsprings and mattress are placed.

bed·straw /'bed,strô/ ▶ **n.** a herbaceous plant (genus *Galium*, family Rubiaceae) with small, lightly perfumed, white or yellow flowers and whorls of slender leaves, formerly used for stuffing mattresses.

bed·time /'bed,tīm/ ▶ **n.** [in sing.] the usual time when someone goes to bed.

Bed·u·in ▶ **n. & adj.** var. of BEDOUIN.

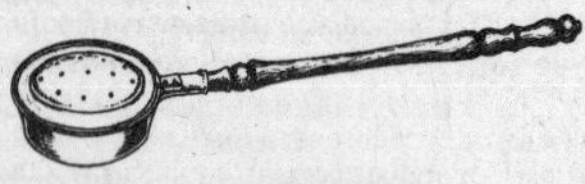

bed warmer

bed warm·er (also **bed·warm·er**) ▶ **n.** hist. a device for warming a bed, typically a metal pan filled with warm coals.

bed-wet·ting ▶ **n.** involuntary urination during sleep. — **bed-wet·ter n.**

bee /bē/ ▶ **n. 1** a honeybee. See illustration at HONEYBEE. **2** an insect of a large group (superfamily Apoidea, order Hymenoptera) to which the honeybee belongs, including many solitary as well as social kinds. See illustration at HONEYBEE. **3** [with adj.] a meeting for communal work or amusement: *a quilting bee.* – PHRASES **have a bee in one's bonnet** informal be preoccupied or obsessed about something, esp. a scheme or plan of action: **the bee's knees** informal an outstandingly good person or thing. [first used to denote something small and insignificant, transferred to the opposite sense in US slang.] [OE *bēo*, from Gmc.; akin to Ger. dial. *Beie*.]

bee balm ▶ **n.** another term for BERGAMOT (sense 3).

bee·bread /'bē,bred/ (also **bee bread**) ▶ **n.** honey or pollen used as food by bees.

beech /bēCH/ ▶ **n.** (also **beech tree**) a large tree (genera *Fagus* and *Nothofagus*) with smooth gray bark, glossy leaves, and hard, pale, fine-grained timber. Its fruit, a small triangular nut (**beechnut**), is an important food for numerous wild birds and mammals. The **beech family** (Fagaceae) also includes the oaks and chestnuts. [OE *bēce*, of Gmc. origin; rel. to L. *fagus* 'beech,' Gk. *phagos* 'edible oak.']

Bee·cham /'bēCHəm/, Sir Thomas (1879–1961), English conductor. He founded the London Philharmonic 1932 and the Royal Philharmonic 1947.

beech·drops /'bēCH,dräps/ ▶ **n.** a broomrape (*Epifagus virginiana*) that is parasitic on the roots of beech trees. Unlike most broomrapes, it has branching stems.

Bee·cher /'bēCHər/, Henry Ward (1813–87), US clergyman and orator who attacked political corruption and slavery.

beech·mast /'bēCH,mast/ ▶ **n.** (collectively, esp. when on the ground) the triangular brown nuts (**beechnuts**) of the beech tree, pairs of which are enclosed in a prickly case. [16th C.: from BEECH + MAST[2].]

beech·nut /'bēCH,nət/ ▶ **n.** see BEECH, BEECHMAST.

bee-eat·er ▶ **n.** a brightly colored insectivorous bird (*Merops* and other genera, family Meropidae) with a large head and a long down-curved bill, and typically with long central tail feathers.

beef /bēf/ ▶ **n. 1** the flesh of a cow, bull, or ox, used as food. ■ (pl. **beeves** /bēvz/) Farming a cow, bull, or ox fattened for its meat. ■ informal flesh or muscle, typically when well developed. ■ informal strength or power. **2** (pl. **beefs**) informal a complaint or grievance. **3** informal a criminal charge: *a drunk-driving beef.* ▶ **v.** [intrans.] informal complain. – PHRASAL VERBS **beef something up** informal give more substance or strength to something. [ME: from OFr. *boef*, from L. *bos*, *bov*- 'ox.']

beef·a·lo /'bēfə,lō/ ▶ **n.** (pl. same or **-loes**) a hybrid animal of a cross between cattle and buffalo. [1970s: blend of BEEF and BUFFALO.]

beef bour·gui·gnon ▶ **n.** var. of BOEUF BOURGUIGNON.

beef·cake /'bēf,kāk/ ▶ **n.** informal an attractive man with well-developed muscles.

beef·eat·er /'bēf,ētər/ ▶ **n.** a Yeoman Warder or Yeoman of the Guard in the Tower of London. [17th C.: (orig. a derogatory term for a well-fed servant).]

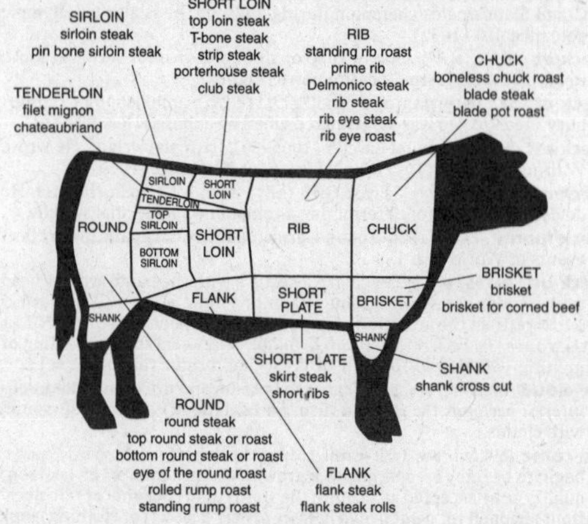

beef 1

bee fly ▶ **n.** a squat, hairy, beelike fly (family Bombyliidae) that hovers to feed from flowers using its long tongue. Its larvae usually parasitize other insects, esp. bees and wasps.

beef·steak /'bēf,stāk/ ▶ **n.** a thick slice of lean beef, typically from the rump and eaten grilled, broiled, or fried.

beef·steak fun·gus (also **beefsteak mushroom**) ▶ **n.** an edible reddish-brown bracket fungus (*Fistulina hepatica*, family Fistulinaceae) that resembles raw beef and is considered to be edible. Native to both Eurasia and North America, it usually grows on trees.

beef·steak to·ma·to ▶ **n.** a tomato of an exceptionally large and firm variety.

beef tea ▶ **n.** esp. Brit. a drink made from stewed extract of beef used as nourishment for invalids.

beef Wel·ling·ton ▶ **n.** a dish of beef, typically coated in pâté de foie gras, wrapped in puff pastry, and baked.

beef·wood /'bēf,wo͝od/ ▶ **n.** a tropical hardwood tree with close-grained red timber, esp. *Casuarina equisetifolia* (family Casuarinaceae), native to Australia and Southeast Asia.

beef·y /'bēfē/ ▶ **adj.** (**beef·i·er, beef·i·est**) **1** informal muscular or robust. ■ [attrib.] large and impressively powerful. **2** tasting like beef. — **beef·i·ly** /'bēfəlē/ **adv. beef·i·ness n.**

bee·hive /'bē,hīv/ ▶ **n. 1** a structure in which bees are kept, typically in the form of a dome or box. ■ [usu. as adj.] something having the domed shape of a traditional wicker beehive: *beehive ovens.* ■ a busy, crowded place. ■ (**the Beehive** or **the Beehive cluster**) another term for PRAESEPE. **2** a woman's domed and lacquered hairstyle, esp. popular in the 1960s. — **bee·hived adj.** (in sense 2).

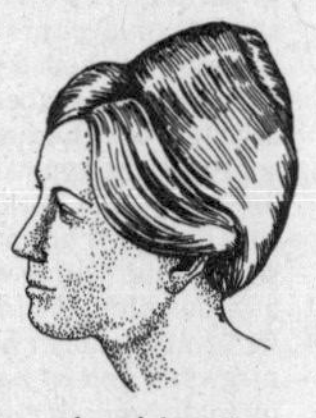

beehive 2

bee·keep·ing /'bē,kēpiNG/ ▶ **n.** the occupation of owning and breeding bees for their honey. — **bee·keep·er** /-,kēpər/ **n.**

bee·line /'bē,līn/ ▶ **n.** a straight line between two places. – PHRASES **make a beeline for** hurry directly to. [19th C.: from the straight line supposedly taken by a bee returning to the hive.]

Be·el·ze·bub /bē'elzə,bəb/ a name for the Devil. [from late L. *Beëlzebub*, translating Heb. *ba al zĕbûb* 'lord of flies,' a Philistine god (2 Kings 1:2), and Gk. *Beelzeboul* 'the Devil' (Matt. 12:24).]

been /bin/ past participle of BE.

Beene /bēn/, Geoffrey (1927–2004), US fashion designer.

beep /bēp/ ▶ **n.** a short, high-pitched sound emitted by electronic equipment or a vehicle horn. ▶ **v.** [intrans.] (of a horn or electronic device) produce such a sound. ■ [trans.] summon (someone) by means of a pager. [1920s: imitative.]

beep·er /ˈbēpər/ ▶ **n.** another term for PAGER.

beer /bi(ə)r/ ▶ **n.** an alcoholic drink made from yeast-fermented malt flavored with hops. ■ any of several other fermented drinks. [OE *bēor*, from West Gmc., based on monastic Latin *biber* 'a drink,' from L. *bibere* 'to drink.']

Beer·bohm /ˈbi(ə)r,bōm/, Max (1872–1956), English caricaturist and humorist; full name *Sir Henry Maximilian Beerbohm*.

Beer·en·aus·le·se /ˌberənˈous,lāzə/ ▶ **n.** a white wine of German origin or style made from selected individual grapes picked later than the general harvest. [Ger., from *Beeren* 'berries' + *aus* 'out' + *lese* 'picking.']

beer gar·den ▶ **n.** a garden, typically one attached to a bar or tavern, where beer is served.

beer hall ▶ **n.** a large room or building where beer is served.

beer mon·ey ▶ **n.** informal a small amount of money allowed or earned.

Beer·she·ba /bi(ə)rˈshēbə/ a town in southern Israel, on the northern edge of the Negev Desert; pop. 138,100.

beer-swill·ing ▶ **adj.** drinking a lot of beer. ■ disreputable, rowdy.

beer·y /ˈbi(ə)rē/ ▶ **adj.** informal relating to or characterized by the drinking of beer, typically in large amounts.

beest·ings /ˈbēstiNGz/ (also **beast·ings**) ▶ **n.** [treated as sing.] the first milk produced by a cow or goat after giving birth. [OE *bӯsting*, of West Gmc. origin; rel. to Ger. *Biest(milch)*.]

bee-stung ▶ **adj.** [attrib.] informal (of a woman's lips) full, red, and pouting.

bees·wax /ˈbēz,waks/ ▶ **n.** informal a person's concern or business.

beet /bēt/ ▶ **n.** a herbaceous plant (*Beta vulgaris*) of the goosefoot family, widely cultivated as a source of food for humans and livestock, and for processing into sugar. Some varieties are grown for their leaves and some for their large nutritious root. [OE *bēte*, of West Gmc. origin, from L. *beta*, perh. of Celtic origin.]

Bee·tho·ven /ˈbā,tōvən; ˈbāt,ō-/, Ludwig van (1770–1827), German composer. Despite increasing deafness, he was responsible for a prodigious output that includes 9 symphonies, 32 piano sonatas, 16 string quartets, and the Mass in D (1823).

bee·tle[1] /ˈbētl/ ▶ **n.** an insect of an order (Coleoptera) distinguished by having forewings typically modified into hard wing cases (elytra) that cover and protect the hind wings and abdomen. ■ (loosely) a similar insect, esp. a black one. ▶ **v.** [no obj., with adverbial of direction] informal make one's way hurriedly: *the tourist beetled off.* [OE *bitula, bitela* 'biter,' from the base of *bītan* 'to bite.']

bee·tle[2] ▶ **n.** a tool with a heavy head and a handle, used for tasks such as ramming, crushing, and driving wedges; a maul. ■ a machine used for heightening the luster of cloth by pressure from rollers. ▶ **v.** [trans.] ram, crush, or drive with a beetle. ■ finish (cloth) with a beetle. [OE *bētel*, of Gmc. origin; rel. to BEAT.]

bee·tle[3] ▶ **v.** [intrans.] [usu. as adj.] (**beetling**) (of a person's eyebrows) project or overhang threateningly: *piercing eyes beneath a beetling brow.* ▶ **adj.** [attrib.] (of a person's eyebrows) shaggy and projecting. — **bee·tle-browed adj.** [16th C.: back-form. from *beetle-browed*.]

beet leaf·hop·per ▶ **n.** a North American leafhopper (*Circulifer tenellus*) found west of the Mississippi River. A serious pest to beets and members of the gourd family, it is a principal carrier of the virus that causes curly top.

bee tree ▶ **n.** a hollow tree used by bees for a hive: *in the Appalachians, the tupelo is a prime bee tree.*

beet·root /ˈbēt,ro͞ot/ ▶ **n.** esp. Brit. the edible root of a beet, typically dark red and spherical and eaten as a vegetable.

beet sug·ar ▶ **n.** sugar obtained from sugar beet.

beeves /bēvz/ plural form of BEEF (sense 1).

be·fall /biˈfôl/ ▶ **v.** (past **-fell** ; past part. **-fall·en**) [trans.] literary (of something bad) happen to someone: *a tragedy befell his daughter* | [intrans.] *she was to blame for anything that befell.*

be·fit /biˈfit/ ▶ **v.** (**fit·ted, -fit·ting**) [trans.] be appropriate for; suit. — **be·fit·ting·ly adv.**

be·fog /biˈfäg/ ▶ **v.** (**-fogged, -fog·ging**) [trans.] cause to become confused.

be·fool /biˈfo͞ol/ ▶ **v.** [trans.] archaic make a fool of.

be·fore /biˈfôr/ ▶ **prep., conj., & adv. 1** during the period of time preceding (a particular event, date, or time): [as prep.] *she had to rest before dinner* | [as conj.] *they lived rough before they were arrested* | [as adv.] *his playing days had ended six years before.* **2** in front of: [as prep.] *the patterns swam before her eyes* | [as adv.] archaic *trotting through the city with guards running before and behind.* ■ [prep.] in front of and required to answer to (a court of law, tribunal, or other authority): *he could be taken before a magistrate for punishment.* **3** in preference to; with a higher priority than: [as prep.] *a woman who placed duty before all else* | [as conj.] *they would die before they would cooperate with each other.* [OE *beforan* (see BY, FORE), of Gmc. origin; rel. to Ger. *bevor*.]

be·fore·hand /biˈfôr,hand/ ▶ **adv.** before an action or event; in advance: *rooms must be booked beforehand.* [ME: from BEFORE + HAND.]

be·fore·time /biˈfôr,tīm/ ▶ **adv.** archaic previously; formerly.

be·foul /biˈfoul/ ▶ **v.** [trans.] make dirty; pollute.

be·friend /biˈfrend/ ▶ **v.** [trans.] act as a friend to (someone) by offering help or support.

be·fud·dle /biˈfədl/ ▶ **v.** [trans.] [usu. as adj.] (**befuddled**) make (someone) unable to think clearly. — **be·fud·dle·ment n.**

beg /beg/ ▶ **v.** (**begged, beg·ging**) **1** [reporting verb] ask (someone) earnestly or humbly for something: [trans.] *a leper **begged** Jesus **for help*** | [with obj. and infin.] *she begged me to say nothing to her father* | [intrans.] ***I must beg of you** not to act impulsively.* ■ ask for (something) earnestly or humbly: [with direct speech] *"Don't leave me," she begged.* ■ ask formally for (permission to do something): *I will now **beg leave*** | [no obj., with infin.] ***we beg to inform** you that we are instructed to wait.* **2** [intrans.] ask for something, typically food or money, as charity or a gift. ■ [trans.] acquire (something) from someone in this way. ■ live by acquiring food or money in this way. ■ (of a dog) sit up with the front paws raised expectantly.

– PHRASES **beg off** request to be excused from a question or obligation. **beg the question 1** (of a fact or action) raise a question or point that has not been dealt with; invite an obvious question. **2** assume the truth of an argument or proposition to be proved, without arguing it. **beg to differ** see DIFFER. **go begging** (of an article) be available for use because unwanted by others. ■ (of an opportunity) not be taken.

– PHRASAL VERBS **beg off** withdraw from a promise or undertaking. [ME: prob. from OE *bedecian*, of Gmc. origin; rel. to BID[1].]

be·gad /biˈgad/ ▶ **exclam.** archaic used to express surprise or for emphasis. [16th C.: alt. of *by God*.]

be·gan /biˈgan/ past of BEGIN.

be·gat /biˈgat/ archaic past of BEGET.

be·gem /biˈjem/ ▶ **v.** (**-gemmed, -gem·ming**) [trans.] [usu. as adj.] (**begemmed**) set or stud with gems: *a begemmed cross.*

be·get /biˈget/ ▶ **v.** (**-get·ting** ; past **-got** /-ˈgät/; past part. **-got·ten**) [trans.] literary **1** (typically of a man, sometimes of a man and a woman) bring (a child) into existence by the process of reproduction. **2** give rise to; bring about. — **be·get·ter n.** [OE *begietan* 'get,' (see BE-, GET).]

beg·gar /ˈbegər/ ▶ **n. 1** a person who lives by asking for money or food. **2** [with adj.] informal a person of a specified type, often one to be envied or pitied. ▶ **v.** [trans.] reduce (someone) to poverty.

– PHRASES **beggar belief** (or **description**) be too extraordinary to be believed or described. **beggars can't be choosers** proverb people with no other options must be content with what is offered. **set a beggar on horseback and he'll ride to the Devil** proverb someone unaccustomed to power or luxury will abuse or be corrupted by it. [ME: from BEG + -AR[3].]

beg·gar·ly /ˈbegərlē/ ▶ **adj.** poverty-stricken. ■ pitifully or deplorably bad. ■ very small and mean. — **beg·gar·li·ness n.**

beg·gar-my-neigh·bor ▶ **n.** a card game for two players in which the object is to acquire one's opponent's cards. Players alternately turn cards up and if an honor is revealed, the other player must find an honor within a specified number of turns or else forfeit the cards already played. ▶ **adj.** [attrib.] (also **beg·gar-thy-neigh·bor**) (esp. of national policy) self-aggrandizing at the expense of competitors.

beg·gar's purse ▶ **n.** an appetizer consisting of a crêpe stuffed with a savory filling.

beg·gar ticks (also **beg·gar's ticks**) ▶ **plural n.** [often treated as sing.] a plant (genus *Bidens*) of the daisy family with inconspicuous yellow flowers and small barbed fruit that cling to passing animals.

beg·gar·y /ˈbegərē/ ▶ **n.** a state of extreme poverty.

Be·gin /ˈbāgin; bəˈgēn/, Menachem (1913–92), prime minister of Israel 1977–83. His meetings with President Anwar al-Sadat of Egypt led to a peace treaty between the countries. Nobel Peace Prize (1978, shared with Sadat).

be·gin /biˈgin/ ▶ **v.** (**-gin·ning** ; past **-gan** /-ˈgan/; past part. **-gun** /-ˈgən/) **1** [trans.] start; perform or undergo the first part of (an action or activity): *the Communists have just begun to fight.* | (**begin to do/doing something**) *it was beginning to snow* | [intrans.] *she **began by** rewriting the syllabus.* ■ [intrans.] come into being or have its starting point at a certain time or place: *the ground campaign had begun.* ■ [intrans.] (of a person) hold a specific position or role before holding any other: *he **began as** a drummer.* ■ [intrans.] (of a thing) originate. ■ [intrans.] (**begin with**) have as a first element: *words beginning with a vowel.* ■ [intrans.] (**begin on/upon**) set to work at. ■ [with direct speech] start speaking by saying: *"I've got to go to the hotel," she began.* ■ [intrans.] (**begin at**) (of an article) cost at least (a specified amount): *rooms begin at $139.* **2** [no obj., with infin.] [with negative] informal not have any chance or likelihood of doing a specified thing: *circuitry that Karen could not begin to comprehend.*

– PHRASES **to begin with** at first. ■ in the first place. [OE *beginnan*, of Gmc. origin; rel. to Ger. *beginnen*.]

be·gin·ner /biˈginər/ ▶ **n.** a person just starting to learn a skill or take part in an activity.

– PHRASES **beginner's luck** good luck supposedly experienced by a beginner at a particular activity.

be·gin·ning /biˈginiNG/ ▶ **n.** [usu. in sing.] the point in time or space at which something starts. ■ the process of coming, or being brought into being. ■ the first part or earliest stage of something. ■ (usu. **beginnings**) the background or origins of anything. ▶ **adj.** new or inexperienced: *a beginning gardener.* ■ introductory or elementary.

– PHRASES **the beginning of the end** the event to which ending or failure can be traced.

be·gird /bi'gərd/ ▶ **v.** [trans.] esp. literary gird about or around; encompass. ■ besiege.

be·gone /bi'gôn; -'gän/ ▶ **exclam.** literary go away (as an expression of annoyance): *begone from my sight!*

be·go·nia /bi'gōnyə; -nēə/ ▶ **n.** a herbaceous plant (genus *Begonia*, family Begoniaceae) of warm climates, the bright flowers of which have brightly colored sepals but no petals. [mod. L., named after Michel *Bégon* (1638–1710), French amateur botanist who discovered the plant on the island of Santo Domingo and introduced it to Europe.]

be·got /bi'gät/ past of **BEGET**.

be·got·ten /bi'gätn/ past participle of **BEGET**.

be·grime /bi'grīm/ ▶ **v.** [trans.] [often as adj.] (**begrimed**) blacken with ingrained dirt: *paint flaking from begrimed walls.*

be·grudge /bi'grəj/ ▶ **v.** [trans.] **1** [with two objs.] envy (someone) the possession or enjoyment of (something): *she begrudged Martin his affluence.* **2** [trans.] give reluctantly or resentfully: *nobody begrudges a single penny spent on health.* — **be·grudg·ing·ly** **adv.**

be·guile /bi'gīl/ ▶ **v.** [trans.] **1** charm or enchant (someone), sometimes in a deceptive way: *every prominent American artist has been beguiled by Maine* | [as adj.] (**beguiling**) *a beguiling smile.* ■ trick (someone) into doing something. **2** dated help (time) pass pleasantly. — **be·guile·ment** **n.** **be·guil·er** **n.** **be·guil·ing·ly** **adv.** [ME: from **BE-** 'thoroughly' + obs. *guile* 'to deceive' (see **GUILE**).]

Beg·uine /'begēn; 'bā,gēn; bə'gēn/ ▶ **n.** (in the Roman Catholic Church) a member of a Dutch lay sisterhood, formed in the 12th century, and not bound by vows.

be·guine /bi'gēn/ ▶ **n.** a popular dance of West Indian origin, similar to the foxtrot. [1930s: from W. Ind. Fr., from Fr. *béguin* 'infatuation.']

be·gum /'bāgəm; 'bē-/ ▶ **n.** Indian a Muslim lady of high rank. ■ (**Begum**) the title of a married Muslim woman, equivalent to Mrs. [from Urdu *begam*, from eastern Turk. *bigim* 'princess,' fem. of *big* 'prince.']

be·gun /bi'gən/ past participle of **BEGIN**.

be·half /bi'haf/ ▶ **n.** (in phrase **on** (also **in**) **behalf of** (or **on someone's behalf**)) **1** in the interests of a person, group, or principle. **2** as a representative of: *he had to attend the funeral on Mama's behalf.* [ME: mixture of *on his halve* and *bihalve him*, 'on his side' (see **BY**, **HALF**).]

be·have /bi'hāv/ ▶ **v.** [intrans.] **1** [with adverbial] act or conduct oneself in a specified way, esp. toward others: *he always behaved like a gentleman.* ■ (of a machine or natural phenomenon) work or function in a specified way: *each car behaves differently.* **2** [often in imper.] conduct oneself in accordance with the accepted norms of a society or group: *you can go as long as you behave.* [ME: from **BE-** + **HAVE**, 'bear (oneself) in a particular way.']

be·haved /bi'hāvd/ ▶ **adj.** conducting oneself in a specified way: *some of the boys had been badly behaved* | [in comb.] *a well-behaved child.*

be·hav·ior /bi'hāvyər/ (Brit. **be·hav·iour**) ▶ **n.** the way in which one acts or conducts oneself, esp. toward others: *his insulting* ***behavior towards*** *me.* ■ the way in which an animal or person acts in response to a particular situation or stimulus: *the feeding behavior of predators.* ■ the way in which a natural phenomenon or a machine works or functions.
– PHRASES **be on one's best behavior** behave well when being observed: *warn them to be on their best behavior.* [ME: from **BEHAVE**.]

be·hav·ior·al /bi'hāvyərəl/ ▶ **adj.** involving, relating to, or emphasizing behavior.

be·hav·ior·al·ism /bi'hāvyərə,lizəm/ ▶ **n.** the methods and principles of the science of animal (and human) behavior. ■ advocacy of or adherence to a behavioral approach to social phenomena. — **be·hav·ior·al·ist** **n. & adj.**

be·hav·ior·al sci·ence ▶ **n.** the scientific study of human and animal behavior.

be·hav·ior·ism /bi'hāvyə,rizəm/ (Brit. **be·hav·iour·ism**) ▶ **n.** Psychol. the theory that human and animal behavior can be explained in terms of conditioning, without appeal to thoughts or feelings, and that psychological disorders are best treated by altering behavior patterns. ■ such study and treatment in practice. — **be·hav·ior·ist** **n. & adj.** **be·hav·ior·is·tic** /bi,hāvyə'ristik/ **adj.**

be·ha·vior mod·i·fi·ca·tion ▶ **n.** **1** the alteration of behavioral patterns through the use of such learning techniques as biofeedback and positive or negative reinforcement. **2** another term for **BEHAVIOR THERAPY**.

be·hav·ior ther·a·py ▶ **n.** the treatment of neurotic symptoms by training the patient's reactions to stimuli.

be·head /bi'hed/ ▶ **v.** cut off the head of (someone), typically as a form of execution: [as n.] (**beheading**) *Arabs have public beheadings.*

be·held /bi'held/ past and past participle of **BEHOLD**.

be·he·moth /bi'hēməTH; 'bēəməTH/ ▶ **n.** a huge or monstrous creature. ■ something enormous, esp. a big and powerful organization. [ME: from Heb. *bĕhēmōṯ*, intensive pl. of *bĕhēmāh* 'beast.']

be·hest /bi'hest/ ▶ **n.** literary a person's orders or command: *they had assembled* ***at his behest.*** [OE *behǣs* 'a vow,' from Gmc., meaning 'bid'; rel. to **HIGHT**.]

be·hind /bi'hīnd/ ▶ **prep.** **1** at or to the far side of (something), typically so as to be hidden by it: ■ expressing location: *the recording machinery was kept behind screens.* ■ fig. hidden from the observer: *the agony behind his decision to retire.* ■ expressing movement: *Jannie instinctively hid her cigarette behind her back.* ■ at the back of (someone), after they have passed through a door: *slamming the door behind her.* **2** in a line or procession, following or further back than (another member of the line or procession). **3** in support of or giving guidance to (someone else): *whatever you decide to do, I'll be behind you.* ■ guiding, controlling, or responsible for (an event or plan): *the reasoning behind their decisions.* **4** after the departure or death of (the person referred to): *he left behind him a manuscript.* **5** less advanced than (someone else) in achievement or development. **6** having a lower score than (another competitor). ▶ **adv.** **1** at or to the far side or the back side of something: *Campbell grabbed him from behind.* **2** in a place or time already past: *the adventure lay behind them.* **3** remaining after someone or something is gone: *don't leave me behind.* **4** further back than other members of a group. **5** (in a game or contest) having a score lower than that of the opposition. **6** slow or late in accomplishing a task: *getting* ***behind with*** *my work.* ■ in arrears. **7** underlying or motivating: *behind his winning facade lurks uncertainty.* ▶ **adj.** following; lagging. ▶ **n.** informal the buttocks: *sitting on her behind.*
– PHRASES **behind the curve** see **CURVE**. [OE *behindan*, *bihindan*, from *bi* 'by' + *hindan* 'from behind.']

be·hind·hand /bi'hīnd,hand/ ▶ **adj.** late or slow in doing something, esp. paying a debt. ■ archaic unaware of recent events. [16th C.: from **BEHIND** + **HAND**.]

be·hold /bi'hōld/ ▶ **v.** (past and past part. **-held**) [trans.] [often in imper.] archaic or literary see or observe (a thing or person, esp. a remarkable or impressive one): *behold your king!* | *the botanical gardens were a wonder to behold.*
– PHRASES **beauty is in the eye of the beholder** see **BEAUTY**. — **be·hold·er** **n.** [OE *bihaldan*, from *bi-* 'thoroughly' + *haldan* 'to hold.']

be·hold·en /bi'hōldən/ ▶ **adj.** [predic.] owing thanks or having a duty to someone in return for help or a service: *I don't like to be* ***beholden to*** *anybody.* [ME: former past part. of **BEHOLD**, in the otherwise unrecorded sense 'bound.']

be·hoof /bi'hōōf/ ▶ **n.** archaic benefit or advantage. [OE *behōf*, of West Gmc. origin; rel. to Ger. *Behuf* and **HEAVE**.]

be·hoove /bi'hōōv/ (Brit. **be·hove** /-'hōv/) ▶ **v.** [trans.] (**it behooves someone to do something**) formal it is a duty or responsibility for someone to do something; it is incumbent on: *it behooves any coach to study his predecessors.* ■ [with negative] it is appropriate or suitable; it befits: ***it ill behooves*** *the opposition constantly to decry the sale of arms to friendly countries.* [OE *behōfian*, from *behōf* (see **BEHOOF**).]

Beh·ring /'beriNG/, Emil Adolf von (1854–1917), German bacteriologist. He cofounded immunology. Nobel Prize for Physiology or Medicine (1901).

Bei·der·becke /'bīdər,bek/, Bix (1903–31), US jazz musician and composer; born *Leon Bismarck Beiderbecke.* He profoundly influenced the development of jazz.

beige /bāZH/ ▶ **adj.** of a pale sandy yellowish-brown color. ▶ **n.** a pale sandy yellowish-brown. [19th C.: from Fr., origin unknown.]

Beige Book ▶ **n.** a summary and analysis of economic activity and conditions, prepared with the aid of reports from the district Federal Reserve Banks and issued by the central bank of the Federal Reserve for its policy makers before a Federal Open Market Committee meeting.

bei·gnet /ben'yā/ ▶ **n.** **1** a fritter. **2** a square of fried dough eaten hot sprinkled with confectioners' sugar. [Fr., from archaic *buyne* 'hump, bump.']

Bei·jing /'bā'jiNG/ the capital of China, in the northeastern part of the country; pop. 6,920,000. It became the country's capital in 1421.

be·ing /'bēiNG/ present participle of **BE**. ▶ **n.** **1** existence: *the railroad* ***brought*** *many towns* ***into being.*** ■ living; being alive. **2** [in sing.] the nature or essence of a person. **3** a real or imaginary living creature, esp. an intelligent one. ■ a human being. ■ a supernatural entity.

Bei·ra /'bārə/ a port in eastern Mozambique; pop. 299,300.

Bei·rut /bā'rōōt/ the capital of Lebanon; pop. 1,500,000. It was damaged during civil war 1975–89.

Be·ja /'bājə/ ▶ **n.** (pl. same) **1** a member of a nomadic people living between the Nile and the Red Sea. **2** the Cushitic language of this people. ▶ **adj.** of or relating to this people or their language.

be·jab·bers /bi'jabərz/ (also **be·ja·bers** /-'jā-/) ▶ **exclam.** another way of saying **BEJESUS**. [19th C.: alt. of *by Jesus*.]

be·je·sus /bi'jēzəs/ (also **be·jee·zus**) ▶ **n.** informal an exclamation traditionally attributed to the Irish, used to express surprise or for emphasis.
– PHRASES **beat the bejesus out of someone** hit someone very hard or for a long time. **scare the bejesus out of someone** frighten someone very much.

be·jew·eled /bi'jōōəld/ (also **be·jew·elled**) ▶ **adj.** adorned with jewels.

Bel /bel/ another name for **BAAL**.

bel /bel/ ▶ **n.** a unit used in the comparison of power levels in electrical communication or of intensities of sound, corresponding to an intensity ratio of 10 to 1. See also **DECIBEL**. [1920s: from the name of Alexander Graham *Bell* (see **BELL**[2]).]

be·la·bor /bi'lābər/ ▶ **v.** [trans.] **1** argue or elaborate (a subject) in excessive detail: *they belabored the obvious.* **2** attack or assault (someone) physically or verbally.

Be·la·rus /,belə'rōōs; ,bā-/ a country in eastern Europe. Formerly called **WHITE RUSSIA**. *See box on next page.*

be·lat·ed /bi'lātid/ ▶ **adj.** coming or happening later than should have been the case. — **be·lat·ed·ly** **adv.** **be·lat·ed·ness** **n.** [17th C.: past part. of obs. *belate* 'delay' (see **BE-**, **LATE**).]

be·lay /bi'lā/ ▶ **v.** [trans.] **1** fix (a running rope) around a cleat, pin, rock, or other object, to secure it. ■ secure (a mountaineer) in this way: *he*

Belarus

Official name: Republic of Belarus
Location: eastern Europe, north of Ukraine
Area: 80,200 square miles (207,600 sq km)
Population: 10,328,000
Capital: Minsk
Languages: Belorusian, Russian
Currency: Belarusian ruble

Belgium

Official name: Kingdom of Belgium
Location: western Europe, on the southern shore of the North Sea and English Channel
Area: 11,700 square miles (30,200 sq km)
Population: 10,340,000
Capital: Brussels
Languages: Flemish and French (both official), German
Currency: euro

belayed his partner across the ice | [intrans.] *it is possible to belay here.* **2** [usu. in imper.] Nautical slang stop; enough!: *"Belay that, mister. Man your post."* ▶ **n. 1** an act of belaying. **2** a spike of rock or other hard material used for belaying. — **be·lay·er n.** [16th C.: from BE- + LAY[1].]

Be·la·ya Riv·er /ˈbyeləyə/ a river in eastern Russia that flows northwest for 700 miles (1,210 km) from the Ural Mountains to the Kama River.

be·lay·ing pin ▶ **n.** a pin or rod, typically of metal or wood, used on board ship and in mountaineering to secure a rope fastened around it.

bel can·to /bel ˈkäntō; ˈkan-/ ▶ **n.** a lyrical style of operatic singing using a full rich broad tone and smooth phrasing. [19th C.: Ital., lit. 'fine song.']

belch /belCH/ ▶ **v. 1** [intrans.] emit gas noisily from the stomach through the mouth. **2** [trans.] (often **belch out/forth/into**) (esp. of a chimney) send (smoke or flames) out or up: *a factory chimney belches out smoke.* ■ [intrans.] (often **belch from**) (of smoke or flames) pour out from a chimney or other opening: *flames belch from the wreckage.* ▶ **n.** an act of belching. [OE *belcettan*, prob. imitative.]

bel·dam /ˈbeldəm; -ˌdam/ (also **bel·dame**) ▶ **n.** archaic an old woman. ■ a malicious and ugly woman, esp. an old one; a witch. [ME: from OFr. *bel* 'beautiful' + DAM[2].]

be·lea·guer /biˈlēgər/ ▶ **v.** [trans.] [usu. as adj.] (**beleaguered**) lay siege to: *he is leading a relief force to the aid of the beleaguered city.* ■ beset with difficulties. [16th C.: from Du. *belegeren* 'camp around,' from *be-* '(all) around' + *leger* 'a camp.']

Be·lém /bāˈlem; bə-/ a city and port in northern Brazil, at the mouth of the Amazon River; pop. 1,244,640.

bel·em·nite /ˈbeləmˌnīt/ ▶ **n.** an extinct cephalopod (order Belemnoidea) with a bullet-shaped internal shell that is often found as a fossil in marine deposits of the Jurassic and Cretaceous periods. [17th C.: from mod. L. *belemnites*, based on Gk. *belemnon* 'dart.']

Bel·fast /ˈbelˌfast; belˈfast/ the capital of Northern Ireland; pop. 280,970. It suffered damage and population decline from the early 1970s because of sectarian violence.

bel·fry /ˈbelfrē/ ▶ **n.** (pl. **-fries**) a bell tower or steeple housing bells, esp. one that is part of a church. ■ a space for hanging bells in a church tower.
– PHRASES **bats in the** (or **one's**) **belfry** see BAT[2]. [ME *berfrey*, from OFr. *berfrei*, later *belfrei*, of West Gmc. origin.]

Bel·gae /ˈbeljē; ˈbelgī/ ▶ **plural n.** an ancient Celtic people inhabiting Gaul north of the Seine and Marne rivers. [from L.]

Bel·gaum /belˈgoum/ a city in western India, in the state of Karnataka; pop. 326,000.

Bel·gian /ˈbeljən/ ▶ **adj.** of or relating to Belgium. ▶ **n.** a native or national of Belgium or a person of Belgian descent.

Bel·gian en·dive ▶ **n.** another term for ENDIVE (sense 2).

Bel·gian hare ▶ **n.** a rabbit of a dark red long-eared domestic breed.

Bel·gian sheep·dog ▶ **n.** a dog of a medium-sized breed, similar in appearance to a German shepherd.

Bel·gian waf·fle ▶ **n.** a waffle made with a special tool to have large, deep indentations in it.

Bel·gic /ˈbeljik/ ▶ **adj.** of or relating to the Belgae.

Bel·gium /ˈbeljəm/ a country in western Europe. French name BELGIQUE, Flemish name BELGIË. *See box.*

Bel·go·rod /ˈbyelgərət; ˈbelgəˌräd/ a city in southern Russia; pop. 306,000.

Bel·grade /ˈbelˌgrād; -ˌgräd/ the capital of Serbia, on the Danube River; pop. 1,168,450.

Be·li·al /ˈbēlēəl/ a name for the Devil. [from Heb. *bĕliyya al* 'worthlessness.']

be·lie /biˈlī/ ▶ **v.** (**-ly·ing**) [trans.] **1** (of an appearance) fail to give a true notion or impression of (something); disguise or contradict: *his alert manner belied his years.* **2** fail to fulfill or justify (a claim or expectation); betray. [OE *belēogan* 'deceive by lying,' from BE- 'about' + *lēogan* 'to lie.']

be·lief /biˈlēf/ ▶ **n. 1** an acceptance that a statement is true or that something exists. ■ something one accepts as true or real; a firmly held opinion or conviction. ■ a religious conviction. **2** (**belief in**) trust, faith, or confidence in someone or something.
– PHRASES **be of the belief that** hold the opinion that; think. **beyond belief** astonishingly good or bad; incredible. **in the belief that** thinking or believing that. **to the best of my belief** in my genuine opinion; as far as I know. [ME: alt. of OE *gelēafa*; cf. BELIEVE.]

be·liev·a·ble /biˈlēvəbəl/ ▶ **adj.** (of an account or the person relating it) able to be believed; credible. ■ (of a fictional character or situation) convincing or realistic. —**be·liev·a·bil·i·ty** /biˌlēvəˈbilitē/ **n.**, **be·liev·a·bly adv.**

be·lieve /biˈlēv/ ▶ **v.** [trans.] **1** accept (something) as true; feel sure of the truth of: *the superintendent believed Lancaster's story.* ■ accept the statement of (someone) as true. ■ [intrans.] have faith, esp. religious faith: *there are those who do not really believe.* ■ (**believe something of someone**) feel sure that (someone) is capable of a particular action: *I wouldn't have believed it of Lois.* **2** [with clause] hold (something) as an opinion; think or suppose: *I believe we've already met.* | (**believe someone/something to be**) *four men were believed to be trapped.*
– PHRASES **be unable** (or **hardly able**) **to believe something** be amazed by something: *I couldn't believe what was happening.* **be unable** (or **hardly able**) **to believe one's eyes** (or **ears**) be amazed by what one sees or hears. **believe it or not** used to concede that a proposition or statement is surprising: *believe it or not, the speaker was Horace.* **believe me** (or **believe you me**) used to emphasize the truth of a statement or assertion: *believe me, she is a shrewd woman.* **don't you believe it!** used to express disbelief in the truth of a statement: *he says he is left of center, but don't you believe it!* **would you believe it?** used to express surprise at something one is relating: *they're still arguing, would you believe it?*
– PHRASAL VERBS **believe in 1** have faith in the truth or existence of. **2** be of the opinion that (something) is right, proper, or desirable. **3** have confidence in (a person or a course of action). [OE *belȳfan*, *belēfan*, alt. of *gelēfan*, of Gmc. origin; rel. to Ger. *glauben* and LIEF.]

be·liev·er /biˈlēvər/ ▶ **n. 1** a person who believes that a specified thing is effective, proper, or desirable. **2** an adherent of a particular religion; someone with religious faith.

Belize

Location: northeastern Central America, on the coast of the Caribbean Sea
Area: 8,800 square miles (22,800 sq km)
Population: 272,000
Capital: Belmopan
Languages: English (official), Creole, Spanish, Mayan, Carib
Currency: Belizean dollar

be·like /bi'līk/ ▶ **adv.** archaic probably; perhaps.

be·lit·tle /bi'litl/ ▶ **v.** [trans.] make (someone or something) seem unimportant: *this is not to belittle his role.* — **be·lit·tle·ment n. be·lit·tler n.**

Be·li·tung /bā'lētōōng/ (also **Bil·li·ton** /bi'lētōn/) an Indonesian island in the Java Sea.

Be·lize /bə'lēz/ a country in Central America. Former name (until 1973) **British Honduras**. *See box.* — **Be·li·zi·an** /-zēən/ **adj. & n.**

Be·lize Cit·y the principal seaport and former capital (until 1970) of Belize; pop. 46,000.

Bell[1], Alexander Graham (1847–1922), US inventor; born in Scotland. He invented a method for transmitting speech electrically and gave the first public demonstration of the telephone in 1876.

Bell[2], Currier, Ellis, and Acton, the pen names used by Charlotte, Emily, and Anne Brontë respectively.

Bell[3], Vanessa (1879–1961), English painter; born *Vanessa Stephen*; sister of Virginia Woolf. She was a member of the Bloomsbury Group.

bell[1] /bel/ ▶ **n.** **1** a hollow object, typically made of metal and having the shape of a deep inverted cup widening at the lip, that sounds a clear musical note when struck, typically by means of a clapper inside. ■ a device that includes or sounds like a bell, used to give a signal or warning. ■ the sound of a bell. ■ **(the bell)** (in boxing and other sports) a bell rung to mark the start or end of a round. **2** a bell-shaped object or part of one, such as the end of a trumpet. ■ the corolla of a bell-shaped flower. **3** **(bells)** a musical instrument consisting of a set of cylindrical metal tubes of different lengths, suspended in a frame and played by being struck with a hammer. Also called TUBULAR BELLS. **4** Naut. (preceded by a numeral) the time as indicated every half hour of a watch by the striking of the ship's bell one to eight times. ▶ **v.** **1** [trans.] provide with a bell or bells; attach a bell or bells to: *the young men were belling and hobbling the horses before releasing them* | [as adj.] **(belled)** *animals in gaudy belled harnesses.* **2** [intrans.] make a ringing sound likened to that of a bell: *the organ belling away.* **3** [intrans.] spread or flare outward like the lip of a bell: *her shirt* ***belled out*** *behind.*
– PHRASES **be saved by the bell** (in boxing and other sports) avoid being counted out by the ringing of the bell at the end of a round. ■ escape from danger narrowly or by an unexpected intervention. **bell the cat** take the danger of a shared enterprise upon oneself. **bells and whistles** informal attractive additional features or trimmings. **(as) clear** (or **sound) as a bell** perfectly clear or sound. **ring a bell** informal revive a distant recollection; sound familiar. **with bells on** informal enthusiastically. [OE *belle*, of Gmc. origin; rel. to Du. *bel*, and perh. to BELL[2].]

bell[2] ▶ **n.** the cry of a stag or buck at rutting time. ▶ **v.** [intrans.] (of a stag or buck) make this cry. [OE *bellan* 'to bellow,' from Gmc.; akin to Ger. *bellen* 'bark, bray,' and perh. to BELL[1].]

bel·la·don·na /,belə'dänə/ ▶ **n.** deadly nightshade. ■ a drug prepared from the leaves and root of this, containing atropine. [18th C.: from mod. L., from Ital. *bella donna* 'fair lady.']

bel·la·don·na lil·y ▶ **n.** the South African amaryllis.

bell·bird /'bel,bərd/ ▶ **n.** **1** a tropical American bird (genus *Procnias*) of the cotinga family, with loud explosive calls. There are wattles on the head of the male. **2** any of a number of Australasian songbirds with ringing bell-like calls.

bell-bot·toms ▶ **plural n.** trousers with a marked flare below the knee: [as adj.] **(bell-bottom)** *bell-bottom trousers.* — **bell-bot·tomed adj.**

bell·boy /'bel,boi/ ▶ **n.** another term for BELLHOP.

bell·bu·oy /'bel,bōōē; -,boi/ ▶ **n.** a buoy equipped with a bell rung by the motion of the sea.

bell cap·tain ▶ **n.** the supervisor of a group of bellboys.

bell curve ▶ **n.** Math. a graph of a normal (Gaussian) distribution, with a large rounded peak tapering away at each end.

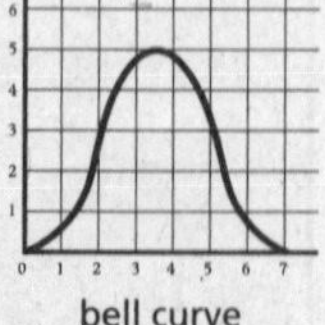

bell curve

belle /bel/ ▶ **n.** a beautiful girl or woman, esp. the most beautiful at a particular event or in a particular group.
– PHRASES **belle of the ball** the most beautiful and popular girl or woman at a dance. [17th C.: from Fr., feminine of *beau*, from L. *bella*, fem. of *bellus* 'beautiful.']

Bel·leau Wood /be'lō/ (French **Bois de Belleau**) a forest just east of Château-Thierry, the scene of a June 1918 US victory over the Germans.

belle é·poque /,bel ā'pôk/ ▶ **n.** the period of settled and comfortable life preceding World War I: [as adj.] *a romantic, belle-époque replica of a Paris bistro.* [20th C.: Fr., lit. 'fine period.']

Bel·ler·o·phon /bə'lerə,fän; -fən/ Gk. Mythol. a hero who slew the monster Chimera with the help of the winged horse Pegasus.

belles-let·tres /,bel 'letrə/ ▶ **plural n.** [also treated as sing.] **1** essays, particularly of literary and artistic criticism, written and read primarily for their aesthetic effect. **2** literature considered as a fine art. — **bel·let·rism** /bel'letrizəm/ **n.** **bel·let·rist** /bel'letrist/ **n.** **bel·let·ris·tic** /,belə'tristik/ **adj.** [17th C.: from Fr., lit. 'fine letters.']

Belle·ville /'bel,vil/ a city in southwestern Illinois; pop. 42,785.

Belle·vue /'bel,vyōō/ **1** a city in eastern Nebraska; pop. 44,382. **2** a city in northwestern Washington; pop. 109,569

Bell·flow·er /'bel,flou(-ə)r/ a city in southwestern California, southeast of Los Angeles; pop. 61,815.

bell·flow·er /'bel,flou(-ə)r/ ▶ **n.** a plant (genus *Campanula*, family Campanulaceae) with bell-shaped flowers that are usually blue, purple, pink, or white. Many kinds are cultivated as ornamentals.

bell·hop /'bel,häp/ an attendant in a hotel who performs services such as carrying guests' luggage.

bel·li·cose /'beli,kōs/ ▶ **adj.** demonstrating aggression and willingness to fight. — **bel·li·cos·i·ty** /,belə'käsitē/ **n.** [ME: from L. *bellicosus*, from *bellicus* 'warlike,' from *bellum* 'war.']

bel·lig·er·ence /bə'lijərəns/ (also **bel·lig·er·en·cy** /-ənsē/) ▶ **n.** aggressive or warlike behavior.

bel·lig·er·ent /bə'lijərənt/ ▶ **adj.** hostile and aggressive. ■ engaged in a war or conflict, as recognized by international law. ▶ **n.** a nation or person engaged in war or conflict, as recognized by international law. — **bel·lig·er·ent·ly adv.** [16th C.: from L. *belligerant-* 'waging war,' from the v. *belligerare*, from *bellum* 'war.']

Bel·ling·ham /'beliNG,ham/ a city in northwestern Washington; pop. 67,171.

Bel·lings·hau·sen Sea /'beliNGz,houzən/ the southeastern Pacific Ocean off the coast of Antarctica.

Bel·li·ni[1] /bə'lēnē/, an Italian family of painters in Venice that included Jacopo (*c.*1400–70) and his sons Gentile (*c.*1429–1507) and Giovanni (*c.*1430–1516).

Bel·li·ni[2], Vincenzo (1801–35), Italian composer. His operas include *La Sonnambula* (1831).

bell jar ▶ **n.** a bell-shaped glass cover used for covering delicate objects or used in a laboratory, typically for enclosing samples. ■ fig. an environment in which someone is protected or cut off from the outside world.

bell·man /'belmən/ ▶ **n.** (pl. **-men**) **1** another term for BELLHOP. **2** hist. a town crier.

Bel·loc /bə'lôk/ Hilaire (1870–1953), British writer; born in France. Full name *Joseph Hilaire Pierre René Belloc*. He wrote *Cautionary Tales* (1907).

Bel·low /'belō/, Saul (1915–2005), US writer; born in Canada. His novels include *The Adventures of Augie March* (1953) and *Humboldt's Gift* (1975). Nobel Prize for Literature (1976).

bel·low /'belō/ ▶ **v.** [intrans.] (of a person or animal) emit a deep loud roar, typically in pain or anger: ***he bellowed in agony*** | [as n.] **(bellowing)** *the bellowing of a bull.* ■ [reporting verb] shout something with a deep loud roar: [trans.] ***the watchers were bellowing encouragement*** | ***he bellowed out the order*** | [with direct speech] ***"God send the right!" he bellowed*** | [with infin.] ***his parents were bellowing at her to stop.*** ■ [trans.] sing (a song) loudly and tunelessly. ▶ **n.** a deep roaring shout or sound. [ME: perh. from late OE *bylgan*.]

bel·lows /'belōz; -əz/ ▶ **plural n.** [also treated as sing.] **1** a device with a bag that emits a stream of air when squeezed: ■ (also **pair of bellows**) a kind with two handles used for blowing air at a fire. ■ a kind used in a harmonium or small organ. **2** an object or device with concertinaed sides to allow it to expand and contract, such as a tube joining a lens to a camera body. [ME: prob. from OE *belga*, pl. of *belig* (see BELLY), a shortened form of *blæstbelig* 'blowing bag.']

pair of bellows

bell pep·per ▶ n. another term for SWEET PEPPER.

bell pull ▶ n. a cord or handle that rings a bell when pulled.

bell-ring·ing ▶ n. the activity or pastime of ringing church bells or handbells. — **bell-ring·er** n.

Bell's pal·sy ▶ n. paralysis of the facial nerve, causing muscular weakness in one side of the face. [19th C.: named after Sir Charles *Bell* (1774–1842), the Scottish anatomist who first described it.]

bell·weth·er /ˈbel,weTHər/ ▶ n. the leading sheep of a flock, with a bell on its neck. ■ an indicator or predictor of something.

bell·wort /ˈbel,wərt; -,wôrt/ ▶ n. a plant (genus *Uvularia*) of the lily family bearing slender yellow bell-like flowers and found chiefly in eastern North America.

bel·ly /ˈbelē/ ▶ n. (pl. **-lies**) the human trunk below the ribs, containing the stomach and bowels. ■ the front of this part of the body. ■ the stomach, esp. as representing the body's need for food. ■ the underside of a bird or other animal. ■ a cut of pork from the underside between the legs. ■ a pig's belly as food, esp. as a traded commodity. ■ the rounded underside of a ship or aircraft. ■ the top surface of an instrument of the violin family, across which the strings are placed. ▶ v. (**-lies, -lied**) **1** [intrans.] swell; bulge: *as she leaned forward her pullover **bellied out**.* ■ [trans.] cause to swell or bulge: *the wind **bellied** the sail **out**.* **2** [intrans.] (**belly up to**) informal move or sit close to (a bar or table): *regulars who bellied up to the bar.*

– PHRASES **go belly up** informal go bankrupt. — **bel·lied** adj. [usu. in comb.] *fat-bellied men.* [OE *belig* 'bag,' of Gmc. origin, from a base meaning 'swell, be inflated.']

bel·ly·ache /ˈbelē,āk/ informal ▶ n. an abdominal pain. ▶ v. [intrans.] complain noisily or persistently: *heads of departments **bellyaching about** lack of resources* | [as n.] (**bellyaching**) *there was plenty of bellyaching.* — **bel·ly·ach·er** n.

bel·ly·band /ˈbelē,band/ ▶ n. **1** a band placed round a horse's belly to harness it to the shafts of a cart. See illustration at HARNESS. **2** a cloth band placed around the belly of an infant to protect the navel. **3** a band wrapped around a product to prevent it from opening.

bel·ly but·ton ▶ n. informal a person's navel.

bel·ly dance ▶ n. a dance originating in the Middle East, typically performed by a woman and involving undulating movements of the belly and rapid gyration of the hips. — **bel·ly danc·er** n. **bel·ly danc·ing** n.

bel·ly·flop /ˈbelē,fläp/ informal ▶ n. a dive into water, landing flat on one's front. ■ fig. a commercial failure. ▶ v. (**-flopped, -flop·ping**) [intrans.] perform such a dive. ■ (of an aircraft) perform a belly landing.

bel·ly·ful /ˈbelē,fo͝ol/ ▶ n. (pl. **-fuls**) a quantity of food sufficient to fill one's stomach; a sustaining meal.

– PHRASES **have a** (or **one's**) **bellyful** informal become intolerant of someone or something after lengthy or repeated contact.

bel·ly land·ing ▶ n. a crash-landing of an aircraft on the underside of the fuselage, without lowering the undercarriage.

bel·ly laugh ▶ n. a loud, unrestrained laugh.

Bel·mo·pan /ˈbelmə,pan/ the capital of Belize since 1970, in the central part of the country. It is one of the smallest capital cities in the world; pop. 3,850.

Be·lo Ho·ri·zon·te /,bālō ,hôrəˈzôntā/ a city in eastern Brazil; pop. 2,020,160.

Be·loit /bəˈloit/ an industrial and academic city in southeastern Wisconsin; pop. 35,573.

be·long /biˈlôNG; -ˈläNG/ ▶ v. [intrans.] **1** [with adverbial of place] (of a thing) be rightly placed in a specified position: *learning to place the blame where it belongs.* ■ be rightly classified in or assigned to a specified category. **2** [usu. with adverbial of place] (of a person) fit in a specified place or environment: *she is a stranger, and doesn't belong here* | [as n.] (**belonging**) *we feel a real sense of belonging.* ■ have the right personal or social qualities to be a member of a particular group. ■ (**belong to**) be a member or part of (a particular group, organization, or class). **3** (**belong to**) be the property of. ■ be the rightful possession of; be due to. ■ (of a contest or period of time) be dominated by. — **be·long·ing·ness** n. [ME: from BE- (intensifier) + v. *long* 'belong,' based on OE *gelang* 'at hand.']

be·long·ings /biˈlôNGiNGz; -ˈläNG-/ ▶ plural n. one's movable possessions.

Be·lo·rus·sian /,belōˈrəSHən/ (also **Bye·lo·rus·sian** /,byelō-/) ▶ adj. of or relating to Belarus, its people, or its language. ▶ n. **1** a native or national of Belarus. ■ a person of Belorussian descent. **2** the East Slavic language of Belarus.

Be·lo·stok /,byeləˈstôk/ Russian name for BIAŁYSTOK.

be·lov·ed /biˈləv(i)d/ ▶ adj. dearly loved. ■ (**beloved by/of**) very popular with or much used by a specified set of people. ▶ n. a much loved person. [ME: past part. of obs. *belove* 'be pleasing,' later 'love.']

be·low /biˈlō/ ▶ prep. **1** extending underneath: *the tunnel below the crags.* **2** at a lower level or layer than. ■ lower in grade or rank than. **3** lower than (a specified amount, rate, or norm): *below freezing.* ▶ adv. at a lower level or layer: *he jumped from the window into the moat below.* ■ under the surface of the water. ■ on earth: *deflections of the stars from their proper orbits with fatal results here below.* ■ in hell: *traitors gnash their teeth below.* ■ lower than zero (esp. zero degrees Fahrenheit) in temperature: *it's 30 below.* ■ (in printed text) mentioned later or further down on the same page: *our nutritionist is pictured below right.* ■ Naut. below deck: *I'll go below and fix us a drink.*

– PHRASES **below (the) ground** beneath the surface of the ground. [ME: from BE- 'by' + LOW[1] (adj.).]

be·low decks (also **be·low deck**) ▶ adj. & adv. in or into the space below the main deck of a ship: [as adj.] *the sleeping quarters were below decks* | [as adv.] *nuclear weapons stored below decks.* ▶ plural n. (**belowdecks**) the space below the main deck of a ship.

Bel Pa·e·se /,bel päˈāzē/ ▶ n. trademark a rich, white, mild, creamy cheese of a kind originally made in Italy. [Ital., lit. 'fair country.']

Bel·sen /ˈbelsən/ a Nazi concentration camp in World War II, near the village of Belsen in northwestern Germany.

Bel·shaz·zar /ˈbelSHə,zär; belˈSHazər/ (6th century BC), last king of Babylon; son of Nebuchadnezzar.

belt /belt/ ▶ n. **1** a strip of leather or other material worn around the waist or across the chest, esp. in order to support clothes or carry weapons. ■ short for SEAT BELT. ■ a belt worn as a sign of rank or achievement. ■ a belt of a specified color, marking the attainment of a particular level in judo, karate, or similar sports: [as adj.] *brown-belt level.* ■ a person who has reached such a level. ■ (**the belt**) the punishment of being struck with a belt. **2** a strip of material used in various technical applications, in particular: ■ a continuous band of material used in machinery for transferring motion from one wheel to another. ■ a conveyor belt. ■ a flexible strip carrying machine-gun cartridges. **3** a strip or encircling band of something having a specified nature or composition that is different from its surroundings. **4** a heavy blow. **5** informal a gulp or shot of liquor. ▶ v. [trans.] **1** [with obj. and adverbial] fasten with a belt: *she belted her raincoat firmly.* ■ [no obj., with adverbial] be fastened with a belt. ■ attach or secure with a belt: *he was securely belted into the passenger seat.* **2** beat or strike (someone), esp. with a belt, as a punishment. ■ hit (something) hard. **3** gulp a drink quickly. **4** [no obj., with adverbial of direction] move quickly in a specified direction: *they belted along the empty road.* ■ (of rain) fall hard: *rain **belted down** on the roof.*

– PHRASES **below the belt** unfair or unfairly; disregarding the rules. **tighten one's belt** cut one's spending; live more frugally. **under one's belt 1** safely or satisfactorily achieved, experienced, or acquired: *I want to get more experience under my belt.* **2** (of food or drink) consumed.

– PHRASAL VERBS **belt something out** sing or play a song loudly and forcefully. — **belt·ed** adj. (usu. in sense 1 of the noun). [OE, of Gmc. origin, from L. *balteus* 'girdle.']

Bel·tane /ˈbeltān/ ▶ n. an ancient Celtic festival celebrated on May Day. [ME: from Scot. Gael. *bealltainn.*]

belt·ed gal·lo·way ▶ n. an animal belonging to a variety of the galloway breed of cattle.

belt·er /ˈbeltər/ ▶ n. informal a loud forceful singer. ■ a loud forceful song.

belt·ing /ˈbeltiNG/ ▶ n. **1** belts collectively, or material for belts. **2** a beating, esp. with a belt, as a punishment.

belt-tight·en·ing ▶ n. the introduction of rigorous reductions in spending.

belt·way /ˈbelt,wā/ ▶ n. a highway encircling an urban area. ■ (**Beltway**) [often as adj.] Washington, DC, esp. as representing the perceived insularity of the US government: *conventional beltway wisdom.* [transferred use by association with the beltway encircling Washington.]

Belt·way ban·dit ▶ n. informal a company that does a large percentage of its business as a federal government contractor. See BELTWAY.

be·lu·ga /bəˈlo͞ogə/ ▶ n. (pl. same or **-gas**) **1** a small, white-toothed whale (*Delphinapterus leucas*, family Monodontidae) related to the narwhal, living in herds mainly in Arctic coastal waters. Also called WHITE WHALE. **2** a very large sturgeon (*Huso huso*) occurring in the inland seas and associated rivers of central Eurasia. ■ (also **beluga caviar**) caviar obtained from this fish. [16th C. (sense 2): from Russ. *belukha* (sense 1), *beluga* (sense 2), both from *belyĭ* 'white.']

bel·ve·dere /ˈbelvi,di(ə)r/ ▶ n. a summerhouse or open-sided gallery, usually at rooftop level. [16th C.: from Ital., lit. 'fair sight.']

be·ly·ing /biˈlī-iNG/ present participle of BELIE.

be·ma /ˈbēmə/ ▶ n. (pl. **-mas** or **-ma·ta** /-mətə/) the altar part or sanctuary in ancient and Orthodox churches. ■ (**bi·ma, bi·mah**) Judaism the podium or platform in a synagogue from which the Torah and Prophets are read. ■ hist. the platform from which orators spoke in ancient Athens. [17th C.: from Gk. *bēma* 'step.']

Bem·ba /ˈbembə/ ▶ n. (pl. same) **1** a member of a native people of Zambia. **2** the Bantu language of this people. ▶ adj. of or relating to this people or their language. [of Bemba origin.]

be·mire /biˈmī(ə)r/ ▶ v. [trans.] archaic cover or stain with mud: *his shoes were bemired.* ■ (**be bemired**) be stuck in mud: *men and horses and wagons all bemired.*

be·moan /biˈmōn/ ▶ v. [trans.] often humorous express discontent or sorrow over (something): *single women bemoaning the absence of men.* [OE *bemǣnan* 'complain, lament,' from BE- + *mǣnan*, akin to MOAN.]

be·muse /biˈmyo͞oz/ ▶ v. [trans.] [usu. as adj.] (**bemused**) puzzle, confuse, or bewilder (someone): *her bemused expression.* — **be·mus·ed·ly** /-ˈmyo͞ozidlē/ adv. **be·muse·ment** n.

ben[1] /ben/ ▶ n. Scot. a high mountain or mountain peak (esp. in place names): *Ben Nevis.* [18th C.: from Scot. Gael. and Irish *beann.*]

ben[2] ▶ n. Scot. & N. Irish an inner room in a two-roomed cottage. [18th C.: dial. var. of ME *binne* 'within' (adv.), from OE *binnan* (rel. to Ger. *binnen*).]

Ben Bel·la /ben 'belə/, Muhammad Ahmed (1918–), president of Algeria 1963–65. He was overthrown in a military coup.

bench /bencH/ ▶n. **1** a long seat for several people, typically made of wood or stone. **2** a long, sturdy work table used by a carpenter, mechanic, scientist, or other worker. **3** (**the bench**) the office of judge or magistrate: *his appointment to the civil bench.* ■ a judge's seat in a court. ■ judges or magistrates collectively. **4** Brit. a seat in Parliament for politicians of a specified party or position: *the Conservative benches.* ■ the politicians occupying such a seat. **5** (**the bench**) a seat on which sports coaches and players sit during a game when they are not playing. **6** a flat ledge in masonry or on sloping ground. ▶v. [trans.] **1** exhibit (a dog) at a show: *Affenpinschers and Afghans were benched side by side.* **2** withdraw (a sports player) from play; substitute. **3** short for BENCH PRESS.
– PHRASES **on the bench 1** appointed as or in the capacity of a judge or magistrate: *he retired after twenty-five years on the bench.* **2** acting as one of the possible substitutes in a sports contest. [OE *benc*, of Gmc. origin; rel. to Ger. *Bank* and BANK[1].]

bench·er /'bencHər/ ▶n. Law (in the UK) a senior member of any of the Inns of Court.

Bench·ley /'bencHlē/ a family of US writers, including **Robert Charles** (1889–1945), a theater critic for *Life* magazine (1920–29) and the *New Yorker* (1929–40); his son **Nathaniel** (1915–81), a writer of humorous novels; and Nathaniel's son **Peter Bradford** (1940–2006), who wrote *Jaws* (1974).

bench·mark /'bencH,märk/ ▶n. **1** a standard or point of reference against which things may be compared or assessed. ■ a problem designed to evaluate the performance of a computer system: **2** a surveyor's mark cut in a wall, pillar, or building and used as a reference point in measuring altitudes. ▶v. [trans.] evaluate or check (something) by comparison with a standard: *we are **benchmarking** our performance against external criteria.* ■ [intrans.] evaluate or check something in this way: *we continue to benchmark against the competition.* ■ [intrans.] show particular results during a benchmark test: *the device should benchmark at between 100 and 150 MHz.*

bench·mark test ▶n. a test using a benchmark to evaluate a computer system's performance.

bench press ▶n. a bodybuilding and weightlifting exercise in which a lifter lies on a bench with feet on the floor and raises a weight with both arms. ▶v. (**bench-press**) [trans.] raise (a weight) in a bench press: *Josh can bench-press more than 400 pounds* | [intrans.] *my elbow hurts when I bench-press.*

bench run ▶n. & v. another term for BENCH TEST.

bench seat ▶n. a seat across the whole width of a car.

bench test esp. Comput. ▶n. a test carried out on a machine, a component, or software before it is released for use, to ensure that it works properly. ▶v. (**bench-test**) [trans.] run a bench test on (something): *they are offering you the chance to bench-test their applications.* ■ [intrans.] give particular results during a bench test: *it bench-tests two times faster than the previous version.*

bench·warm·er /'bencH,wôrmər/ ▶n. informal a sports player who does not get selected to play; a substitute.

bench war·rant ▶n. a written order issued by a judge authorizing the arrest of a person charged with some contempt, crime, or misdemeanor.

bench·work /'bencH,wərk/ ▶n. work carried out at a bench in a laboratory or workshop.

Bend /bend/ a city in central Oregon; pop. 52,029.

bend[1] /bend/ ▶v. (past **bent** /bent/) **1** [trans.] shape or force (something straight) into a curve or angle: *the wind bent the long grass.* ■ [intrans.] (of something straight) be shaped or forced into a curve or angle: *the oar bent as Lance heaved angrily at it.* ■ fig. force or be forced to submit: [trans.] *they want to **bend me to their will*** | [intrans.] *a refusal to **bend to mob rule.*** ■ [no obj., usu. with adverbial of direction] (of a road, river, or path) deviate from a straight line in a specified direction; have a sharply curved course: *the river slowly bends around Davenport.* **2** [intrans.] (of a person) incline the body downward from the vertical: *he **bent down** and picked her up* | [with infin.] *he bent to tie his shoelaces.* ■ [trans.] move (a jointed part of the body) to an angled position: *Irene bent her head over her work.* **3** [trans.] interpret or modify (a rule) to suit oneself or somebody else: *we cannot bend the rules, even for Darren.* **4** [trans.] direct or devote (one's attention or energies) to a task: *Eric **bent** all his efforts to persuading them to donate some blankets* | [intrans.] *she **bent** once more to the task of diverting the wedding guests.* **5** [trans.] Naut. attach (a sail or rope) by means of a knot: *sailors were **bending** sails to the spars.* ▶n. **1** a curve, esp. a sharp one, in a road, river, racecourse, or path. **2** a curved or angled part or form of something. **3** a kind of knot used to join two ropes, or to tie a rope to another object, e.g. a carrick bend. **4** (**the bends**) decompression sickness, esp. in divers.
– PHRASES **bend someone's ear** informal talk to someone, esp. with great eagerness or in order to ask a favor. **bend one's elbow** drink alcohol. **bend one's** (or **the**) **knee** fig. submit: *a country no longer willing to **bend its knee to foreign powers.*** **bend over backward** see BACKWARD. **around the bend** informal crazy; insane. — **bend·a·ble** adj. [OE *bendan* 'put in bonds,' from Gmc.; akin to BAND[1].]

bend[2] ▶n. Heraldry an ordinary in the form of a broad diagonal stripe from top left (dexter chief) to bottom right (sinister base) of a shield or part of one. [ME: from Anglo-Norman Fr. *bande*, OFr. *bende* 'flat strip.']

bend·er /'bendər/ informal ▶n. **1** [usu. in comb.] an object or person that bends something else: *a fender bender.* **2** a wild drinking spree.

bend sinister

bend sin·is·ter ▶n. Heraldry a broad diagonal stripe from top right to bottom left of a shield (a supposed sign of bastardy).

bend·y /'bendē/ ▶adj. (**bend·i·er, bend·i·est**) informal capable of bending; soft and flexible. — **bend·i·ness** n.

be·neath /bi'nēTH/ ▶prep. **1** extending or directly underneath, typically with close contact: *in the labyrinths beneath central Moscow.* ■ underneath so as to be hidden, covered, or protected. **2** at a lower level or layer than. ■ lower in grade or rank than. ■ considered of lower status or worth than. ■ behind (a physical surface). ■ behind or hidden behind (an appearance): *beneath the gloss of success.* ▶adv. **1** extending or directly underneath something: *allow air to circulate beneath.* **2** at a lower level or layer: *exposing the black earth beneath.* ■ behind or hidden behind an appearance: *the smile revealed the evil beneath.* [OE *binithan, bineothan*, from *bi* (see BY) + *nithan, neothan* 'below,' of Gmc. origin; rel. to NETHER.]

Ben·e·dict, St. /'beni,dikt/ (*c.*480–*c.*550), Italian monk. He established a monastery at Monte Cassino and his *Regula Monachorum* (the Rule of St. Benedict) formed the basis of Western monasticism.

Ben·e·dict XVI (1927–), pope 2005– ; born in Germany; born *Joseph Alois Ratzinger.* An extensively published theologian, he is noted for his defense of traditional Roman Catholic doctrine.

Ben·e·dic·tine ▶n. /,beni'dik,tēn; -tin/ **1** a monk or nun of an order following the rule of St. Benedict. **2** trademark a liqueur based on brandy, originally made by Benedictine monks in France. ▶adj. of St. Benedict or the Benedictines.

ben·e·dic·tion /,beni'diksHən/ ▶n. the utterance or bestowing of a blessing, esp. at the end of a religious service. ■ (**Benediction**) a service in which the congregation is blessed with the Blessed Sacrament, held mainly in the Roman Catholic Church. ■ devout or formal invocation of blessedness: *her arms outstretched in benediction.* ■ the state of being blessed. [ME: via OFr. from L. *benedictio(n-)*, from *benedicere* 'wish well, bless,' from *bene* 'well' + *dicere* 'say.']

Ben·e·dict's so·lu·tion /'beni,dikts/ (also **Benedict's reagent**) ▶n. a chemical solution of sodium or potassium citrate, sodium carbonate, and copper sulfate used in clinical urine tests for diabetes. [named after S. R. *Benedict* (1884–1936), Amer. chemist.]

Ben·e·dic·tus /,beni'diktəs/ ▶n. Christian Church **1** an invocation beginning *Benedictus qui venit in nomine Domini* (Blessed is he who comes in the name of the Lord) forming a set part of the Mass. **2** a canticle beginning *Benedictus Dominus Deus* (Blessed be the Lord God) from Luke 1:68–79. [16th C.: L., 'blessed,' past part. of *benedicere* 'wish well.']

ben·e·fac·tion /,benə'faksHən/ ▶n. a donation or gift. [17th C.: from late L. *benefactio(n-)*, from *bene facere* 'do good (to),' from *bene* 'well' + *facere* 'do.']

ben·e·fac·tive /,benə'faktiv/ Gram. ▶adj. denoting a semantic case or construction that expresses the person or thing that benefits from the action of the verb, for example *for you* in *I bought this for you.* ▶n. the benefactive case, or a word or expression in it.

ben·e·fac·tor /'benə,faktər; ,benə'faktər/ ▶n. a person who gives money or other help to a person or cause.

ben·e·fac·tress /'benə,faktris; ,benə'faktris/ ▶n. a female benefactor.

be·nef·ic /bə'nefik/ ▶adj. rare beneficent or kindly. ■ Astrol. relating to or denoting the planets Jupiter and Venus, traditionally considered to have a favorable influence. [17th C.: from L. *beneficus*, from *bene facere* 'do good (to).']

ben·e·fice /'benəfis/ ▶n. a permanent Church appointment, typically that of a rector or vicar, for which property and income are provided in respect of pastoral duties. — **ben·e·ficed** adj. [ME: via OFr. from L. *beneficium* 'favor, support,' from *bene* 'well' + *facere* 'do.']

be·nef·i·cent /bə'nefəsənt/ ▶adj. (of a person) generous or doing good. ■ resulting in good. — **be·nef·i·cence** n. **be·nef·i·cent·ly** adv. [17th C.: from L. *beneficent-* based on *bene facere* 'do good (to).']

ben·e·fi·cial /,benə'fisHəl/ ▶adj. favorable or advantageous; resulting in good. ■ Law of or relating to rights, other than legal title. — **ben·e·fi·cial·ly** adv. [ME: from late L. *beneficialis*, from *beneficium* 'support.']

ben·e·fi·ci·ar·y /,benə'fisHē,erē/ ▶n. (pl. **-ar·ies**) a person who derives advantage from something, esp. a trust, will, or life insurance policy.

ben·e·fit /'benəfit/ ▶n. **1** an advantage or profit gained from something. **2** a payment or gift made by an employer, the state, or an insurance company. **3** a public performance or other entertainment of which the proceeds go to a particular charitable cause. ▶v. (**-fit·ed, -fit·ing** or **-fit·ted, -fit·ting**) [intrans.] receive an advantage; profit; gain: *areas that would **benefit from** regeneration.* ■ [trans.] bring advantage to: *the bill will benefit the nation.*
– PHRASES **benefit of clergy 1** hist. exemption of the English clergy and nuns from the jurisdiction of the ordinary civil courts, granted in the Middle Ages but abolished in 1827. **2** ecclesiastical sanction or approval: *they lived together without benefit of clergy.* **the benefit of the doubt** a concession that a person or fact must be regarded as correct or justified, if the contrary has not been proven. **for the benefit of 1** in order to help, guide, or be of service to. **2** in order to interest or impress someone. **give someone the benefit of** often ironic explain or recount to someone at length. [ME: from OFr. *bienfet*, from L. *benefac-*

tum 'good deed,' from *bene facere*.]

Ben·e·lux /'benl,əks/ a collective name for Belgium, the Netherlands, and Luxembourg.

Be·neš /'benesн/, Edvard (1884–1948), president of Czechoslovakia 1935–38, 1945–48.

be·nev·o·lent /bə'nevələnt/ ▶ **adj.** well meaning and kindly. ■ (of an organization) serving a charitable rather than a profit-making purpose. — **be·nev·o·lence n. be·nev·o·lent·ly adv.** [ME: from OFr. *benivolent*, from L. *bene volent-* 'well wishing,' from *bene* 'well' + *velle* 'to wish.']

Ben·ford's Law /'benfərdz/ ▶ **n.** Math. the principle that in any large, randomly produced set of natural numbers, such as tables of logarithms or corporate sales statistics, around 30 percent will begin with the digit 1, 18 percent with 2, and so on, with the smallest percentage beginning with 9. [named for US physicist Frank Benford, who demonstrated the statistical validity of the phenomenon.]

BEng ▶ **abbr.** Bachelor of Engineering.

Ben·gal /ben'gôl; -'gäl; beNG-/ a region in the northeast of the Indian subcontinent that contains the Ganges and Brahmaputra river deltas. In 1947, it was divided into West Bengal, which remained a state of India, and East Bengal, which is now Bangladesh.

Ben·gal, Bay of a part of the Indian Ocean that lies between India and Myanmar (Burma) and Thailand.

Ben·ga·li /,beNG'gälē/ ▶ **n.** (pl. **-lis**) **1** a native of Bengal. **2** the Indic language of Bangladesh and West Bengal. ▶ **adj.** of or relating to Bengal, its people, or their language. [from Hindi *baṅgālī*.]

ben·ga·line /'beNGgə,lēn/ ▶ **n.** a strong ribbed fabric made of a mixture of silk and either cotton or wool. [19th C.: from Fr., from a similarity with archaic *Bengals* 'fabrics, usually silks, imported from Bengal.']

Ben·gal light /,beNG'gäl/ ▶ **n.** a kind of firework giving off a blue flame and used for lighting or signaling.

Ben·gha·zi /ben'gäzē; beNG-/ a port in northeastern Libya; pop. 485,400. It was the joint capital (with Tripoli) 1951–72.

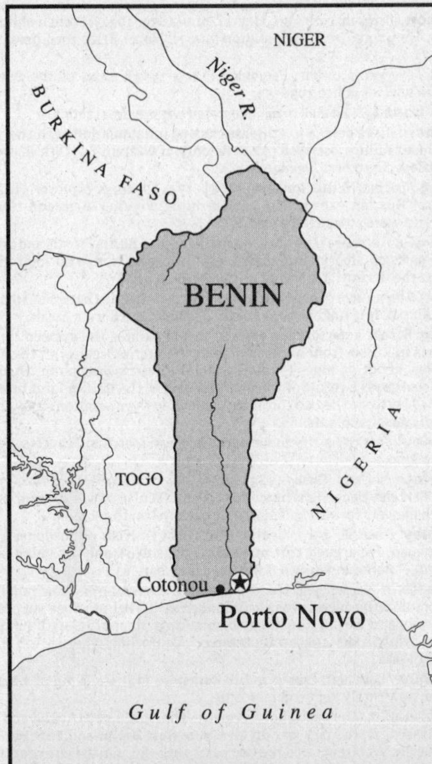

Benin

Official name: Republic of Benin
Location: West Africa, bordered by Nigeria to the east and Togo to the west
Area: 42,700 square miles (110,600 sq km)
Population: 7,250,000
Capital: Porto Novo
Languages: French (official), West African languages (including Fon and Yoruba)
Currency: CFA franc

Ben·guel·a /ben'gwelə; beNG-/ a city in Angola, on the Atlantic coast; pop. 155,000.

Ben·guel·a Cur·rent a cold ocean current that flows north from Antarctica along the west coast of southern Africa as far as Angola.

Ben-Gu·rion /ben 'go͝orēən/, David (1886–1973), prime minister of Israel 1948–53, 1955–63.

Be·ni Riv·er /'bānē/ a river that flows for 1,000 miles (1,600 km) through Bolivia.

Be·ni·cia /bə'nēsнə/ a city in north central California, north of San Francisco Bay; pop. 24,437.

be·night·ed /bi'nītid/ ▶ **adj. 1** in a state of pitiful or contemptible intellectual or moral ignorance, typically owing to a lack of opportunity. **2** overtaken by darkness. — **be·night·ed·ness n.** [16th C. (sense 2): past part. of archaic *benight* 'obscure' (see BE-, NIGHT).]

be·nign /bi'nīn/ ▶ **adj. 1** gentle; kindly. ■ (of a climate or environment) mild and favorable: ■ not harmful to the environment: [in comb.] *an ozone-benign refrigerant*. **2** Med. (of a disease) not harmful in effect: in particular, (of a tumor) not malignant. — **be·nign·ly adv.** [ME: from OFr. *benigne*, from L. *benignus*, prob. from *bene* 'well' + *-genus* '-born.']

be·nig·nant /bi'nignənt/ ▶ **adj. 1** kindly and benevolent. **2** Med. less common term for BENIGN (sense 2). ■ archaic having a good effect; beneficial. — **be·nig·nan·cy n. be·nig·nant·ly adv.**

be·nig·ni·ty /bi'nignitē/ ▶ **n.** (pl. **-ties**) kindness or tolerance toward others. ■ archaic an act of kindness.

be·nign ne·glect ▶ **n.** a noninterference that is intended to benefit someone or something more than continual attention would.

Be·nin /bə'nēn; -'nin/ a country in West Africa. Former name (until 1975) DAHOMEY. *See box.* — **Be·ni·nese** /,benə'nēz; -'nēs/ **adj. & n.**

Be·nin, Bight of a bay on the coast of Africa north of the Gulf of Guinea. Lagos is its chief port.

ben·i·son /'benəsən; -zən/ ▶ **n.** literary a blessing. [ME: from OFr. *beneiçun*, from L. *benedictio* (see BENEDICTION).]

Ben·ja·min /'benjəmən/ (in the Bible) a Hebrew patriarch; the youngest son of Jacob and Rachel. ■ the smallest tribe of Israel, traditionally descended from him.

ben·ne /'benē/ ▶ **n.** another term for SESAME. [18th C.: from Malay *bene*.]

Ben Ne·vis /ben 'nevəs/ a mountain in western Scotland that rises to 4,406 feet (1,343 m).

ben·ny[1] /'benē/ ▶ **n.** (pl. **-nies**) informal a tablet of Benzedrine.

ben·ny[2] ▶ **n.** (pl. **-nies**) informal a benefit attached to employment.

Be·no·ni /bə'nōnē/ a city in South Africa, east of Johannesburg; pop. 206,800.

Ben·sa·lem /ben'sāləm/ a township in southeastern Pennsylvania; pop. 58,434.

bent[1] /bent/ past and past participle of BEND[1]. ▶ **adj. 1** sharply curved or having an angle. **2** informal, esp. Brit. dishonest; corrupt: *a bent cop.* ■ stolen. ■ homosexual. **3** (**bent on**) determined to do or have something: *a mob bent on violence.* ▶ **n.** a natural talent or inclination: *a man of religious bent.*

– PHRASES **bent out of shape** informal angry or agitated.

bent[2] ▶ **n.** (also **bent grass**) a stiff grass (*Agrostis* and other genera) that is used for lawns and is a component of pasture and hay grasses. ■ the stiff flowering stalk of a grass. [ME: from OE *beonet* (in place names), from West Gmc.; akin to Ger. *Binse*.]

Ben·tham /'benтнəm/, Jeremy (1748–1832), English philosopher and jurist. He was a first major proponent of utilitarianism.

ben·thos /'benтнäs/ ▶ **n.** Ecol. the flora and fauna found on the bottom, or in the bottom sediments, of a sea, lake, or other body of water. — **ben·thic adj.** [19th C.: from Gk., 'depth of the sea.']

Ben·ton[1] /'bentn/, Thomas Hart (1782–1858), US politician. A Democrat from Missouri, he was a member of the US Senate 1821–51.

Ben·ton[2], Thomas Hart (1889–1975), US painter, a grandnephew of Senator Thomas Hart Benton. His paintings represent life in the Midwest.

ben·ton·ite /'bentn,īt/ ▶ **n.** a kind of absorbent clay formed by the breakdown of volcanic ash, used esp. as a filler. [19th C.: from Fort *Benton* in Montana, where it is found, + -ITE[1].]

bent·wood /'bent,wo͝od/ ▶ **n.** wood that is artificially shaped for use in making furniture.

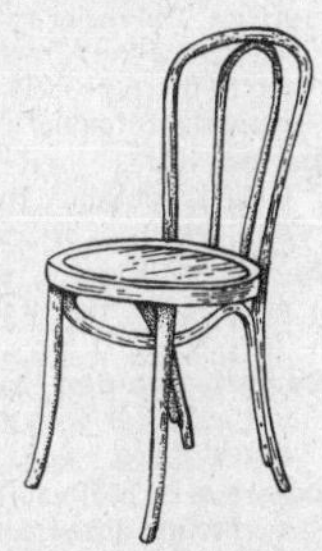
bentwood chair

Be·nue-Con·go /'bānwā/ ▶ **n.** a major branch of the Niger-Congo family of languages, spoken mainly in Nigeria and including Efik and Fula. ▶ **adj.** of, relating to, or denoting this group of languages. [from the names of rivers.]

Be·nue Riv·er /'bānwā/ a river that flows for 870 miles (1,400 km) from northern Cameroon into Nigeria, where it joins the Niger River.

be·numb /bi'nəm/ ▶ **v.** [trans.] [often as adj.] (**benumbed**) deprive of physical or emotional feeling: *a hoarse shout cut through* *his benumbed senses.* [15th C.: from obs. *benome*, past part. of *benim* 'deprive,' from BE- (expressing removal) + OE *niman* 'take.']

Ben·xi /'ben'CHē/ a city in northeastern China, in the province of Liaoning; pop. 920,000.

benz·al·de·hyde /ben'zaldə,hīd/ ▶ n. Chem. a colorless liquid aldehyde, C_6H_5CHO, with the odor of bitter almonds, used in the manufacture of dyes and perfumes.

Ben·ze·drine /'benzə,drēn/ ▶ n. trademark for AMPHETAMINE. [1930s: blend of BENZOIN and EPHEDRINE.]

ben·zene /'benzēn; ben'zēn/ ▶ n. a colorless volatile liquid hydrocarbon, C_6H_6, present in coal tar and petroleum, used in chemical synthesis. Its use as a solvent has been reduced because of its carcinogenic properties. [19th C.: from BENZOIN + -ENE.]

ben·zene hex·a·chlor·ide /,heksə'klôr,īd/ (abbr.: **BHC**) ▶ n. **1** a compound of benzene and chlorine, $C_6H_6Cl_6$, used as an insecticide. **2** used as a general term for LINDANE.

ben·zene ring ▶ n. Chem. the hexagonal unsaturated ring of six carbon atoms present in benzene and many other aromatic molecules.

ben·ze·noid /'benzə,noid/ ▶ adj. Chem. having the six-membered ring structure or aromatic properties of benzene.

ben·zi·dine /'benzi,dēn/ ▶ n. a crystalline base, $NH_2C_6H_4C_6H_4NH_2$, used in making dyes and in detecting blood stains.

ben·zine /'benzēn; ben'zēn/ (also **ben·zin** /'benzin/) ▶ n. a mixture of liquid hydrocarbons obtained from petroleum. [19th C. (denoting benzene): from BENZOIN + -INE[4].]

ben·zo·caine /'benzə,kān/ ▶ n. a white, odorless, crystalline powder, $NH_2C_6H_4C_6H_4NH_2$, used in ointments as a local anesthetic and to protect against sunburn.

ben·zo·di·az·e·pine /,benzō,dī'azə,pēn/ ▶ n. Med. any of a class of heterocyclic organic compounds used as tranquilizers, such as Librium and Valium. [1930s: from BENZENE + DI-[1] + AZO- + EPI- + -INE[4].]

ben·zo·ic ac·id /ben'zō-ik/ ▶ n. Chem. a white crystalline substance, C_6H_5COOH, present in benzoin and other plant resins, and used as a food preservative. — **ben·zo·ate** /'benzō,āt/ n.

ben·zo·in /'benzō-in; -zoin/ ▶ n. **1** (also **gum benzoin**) a fragrant gum resin obtained from a tropical eastern Asian tree (genus *Styrax*, family Styracaceae), used in medicines, perfumes, and incense. Also called GUM BENJAMIN. **2** Chem. a white crystalline aromatic ketone, $C_6H_5CHOHCOC_6H_5$, present in this resin. [16th C.: from Fr. *benjoin*, based on Arab. *lubānjāwī* 'incense of Java.']

ben·zo·phe·none /,benzōfi'nōn; -'fē,nōn/ ▶ n. a white, crystalline ketone, $C_6H_5COC_6H_5$, used in perfume, sunscreen, and as a flavoring agent.

ben·zo·py·rene /,benzō'pīrēn/ ▶ n. Chem. a compound, $C_{20}H_{12}$, that is the major carcinogen present in cigarette smoke. It also occurs in coal tar.

ben·zo·qui·none /,benzōkwi'nōn; -'kwinōn/ ▶ n. Chem. a yellow crystalline compound, $C_6H_4O_2$, related to benzene but having two hydrogen atoms replaced by oxygen.

ben·zo·yl /'benzō-il/ ▶ n. [as adj.] Chem. the acyl radical $-C(O)C_6H_5$, derived from benzoic acid: *benzoyl peroxide.*

ben·zo·yl per·ox·ide ▶ n. an antibacterial ingredient used in acne medications.

ben·zyl /'benzil/ ▶ n. [as adj.] Chem. the radical $-CH_2C_6H_5$, derived from toluene: *benzyl benzoate.*

Be·o·wulf /'bāə,wŏŏlf/ an Old English epic poem celebrating the legendary Scandinavian hero Beowulf.

be·queath /bi'kwēTH; -'kwēTH/ ▶ v. [trans.] leave (a personal estate or one's body) to a person or other beneficiary by a will: *an identical sum was bequeathed by Tomo.* ■ pass (something) on or leave (something) to someone else. — **be·queath·er** n. [OE *becwethan*, from BE- 'about' (expressing transitivity) + *cwethan* 'say' (see QUOTH).]

be·quest /bi'kwest/ ▶ n. a legacy. ■ the action of bequeathing something. [ME: from BE- 'about' + OE *cwis* 'speech,' influenced by BEQUEATH.]

be·rate /bi'rāt/ ▶ v. [trans.] scold or criticize (someone) angrily: *my son berated me for not giving him a Jewish upbringing.*

Ber·ber /'bərbər/ ▶ n. **1** a member of an indigenous people of North Africa. The majority of Berbers are settled farmers or (now) migrant workers. **2** the Afro-Asiatic language of these peoples. ▶ adj. of or relating to these peoples or their language. [from Arab. *barbar*, from Gk. *barbarus* 'foreigner' (see BARBARIAN).]

ber·be·rine /'bərbə,rēn/ ▶ n. Chem. a bitter yellow compound of the alkaloid class obtained from barberry and other plants. [19th C.: from *Berberis* (genus of barberry) + -INE[4].]

ber·ceuse /ber'sŏŏz; -'sœz/ ▶ n. (pl. **-ceuses** pronunc. same) a lullaby. ■ a piece of instrumental music in the style of a lullaby. [Fr., from *bercer* 'to rock.']

Berch·tes·ga·den /'berKHtəs,gädn/ a town in southern Germany, close to the border with Austria; pop. 8,186. Adolf Hitler had a fortified retreat there.

be·reave /bi'rēv/ ▶ v. (**be bereaved**) be deprived of a loved one through a profound absence, esp. due to the loved one's death: *the year after they had been bereaved* | [as adj.] (**bereaved**) *bereaved families* | [as pl. n.] (**the bereaved**) *those who counsel the bereaved.* — **be·reave·ment** n. [OE *berēafian* (see BE-, REAVE).]

be·reft /bi'reft/ archaic past participle of BEREAVE. ▶ adj. deprived of or lacking something, esp. a nonmaterial asset: *her room was stark and bereft of color.* ■ (of a person) lonely and abandoned, esp. through someone's death or departure.

Ber·e·ni·ce /,berə'nīsē; -'nēs/ (3rd century BC), Egyptian queen; wife of Ptolemy III. The constellation Coma Berenices (*Berenice's Hair*) is named after her.

be·ret /bə'rā/ ▶ n. a round flattish cap of felt or cloth. [19th C.: from Fr. *béret* 'Basque cap,' from Old Provençal *berret*, based on late L. *birrus* 'hooded cape.']

ber·et·ta ▶ n. var. of BIRETTA.

Berg /berKH/, Alban Maria Johannes (1885–1935), Austrian composer. He favored twelve-note composition.

berg /bərg/ ▶ n. short for ICEBERG.

ber·ga·mot /'bərgə,mät/ ▶ n. **1** an oily substance extracted from the rind of the fruit of a dwarf variety of the Seville orange tree, used in cosmetics and as flavoring in tea. **2** (also **bergamot orange**) the tree (*Citrus aurantium* subsp. *bergamia*) that bears this fruit. **3** an aromatic North American herb (*Monarda didyma*) of the mint family, grown for its bright flowers and used medicinally. Also called BEE BALM; OSWEGO TEA. [17th C. (sense 2): named after the city and province of *Bergamo* in northern Italy.]

Ber·gen /'bərgən; 'ber-/ a seaport in southwestern Norway; pop. 213,344.

Ber·ger /'bərgər/, Hans (1873–1941), German psychiatrist. He developed encephalography.

Ber·ge·rac see CYRANO DE BERGERAC.

ber·gère /ber'ZHer/ ▶ n. a long-seated upholstered armchair fashionable in the 18th century. ■ a later example of this, in which the upholstery is replaced with canework seat, back, and sides.

Ber·gi·us /'bergēŏŏs/, Friedrich Karl Rudolf (1884–1949), German chemist. Nobel Prize for Chemistry (1931, shared with Carl Bosch 1874–1940).

Berg·man /'bərgmən; 'ber(yə),män/, Ingmar (1918–), Swedish director; full name *Ernst Ingmar Bergman.* His movies include *The Seventh Seal* (1956), and *Saraband* (2003).

Berg·son /'bergsən; berk'sôn/, Henri Louis (1859–1941), French philosopher. He wrote *Creative Evolution* (1907). Nobel Prize for Literature (1927).

Be·ria /'byeryə/, Lavrenti Pavlovich (1899–1953), head of the Soviet Union's secret police 1938–53.

be·rib·boned /bi'ribənd/ ▶ adj. decorated with many ribbons.

ber·i·ber·i /'berē'berē/ ▶ n. a disease causing inflammation of the nerves and heart failure, ascribed to a deficiency of vitamin B_1. [18th C.: from Sinhalese, from *beri* 'weakness.']

Ber·ing /'beriNG/, Vitus Jonassen (1681–1741), Danish explorer. He led several Russian expeditions to determine whether Asia and North America were connected by land.

Be·rin·gi·a /bə'rinjēə/ the area consisting of the Bering Strait and adjacent parts of Siberia and Alaska, esp. in connection with migration across the Bering land bridge. — **Be·rin·gi·an** adj.

Ber·ing Sea an arm of the North Pacific Ocean that lies between Siberia and Alaska. It is linked to the Arctic Ocean by the Bering Strait.

Ber·ing Strait a narrow sea passage that separates the eastern tip of Siberia in Russia from Alaska and links the Arctic Ocean with the Bering Sea, about 53 miles (85 km) wide at its narrowest point. During the Ice Age, as a result of a drop in sea levels, the **Bering land bridge** formed between the two continents, allowing the migration of animals and dispersal of plants.

Berke·ley[1] /'bərklē/ a city in western California, on San Francisco Bay; pop. 102,724.

Berke·ley[2] /'bərklē/, Busby (1895–1976), US choreographer; born *William Berkeley Enos.* He is noted for his spectacular movie sequences in which dancers formed kaleidoscopic patterns on the screen.

Berke·ley[3] /'bärklē; 'bər-/, George (1685–1753), Irish philosopher and clergyman. He argued that material objects exist only by being perceived. — **Berke·le·ian·ism** /'bärklēə,nizəm; 'bər-/ n.

ber·ke·li·um /bər'kēlēəm/ ▶ n. the chemical element of atomic number 97, a radioactive metal of the actinide series. Berkelium does not occur naturally and was first made by bombarding americium with helium ions. (Symbol: **Bk**) [1949: from BERKELEY[1], California (where it was first made) + -IUM.]

Berk·shire /'bərksHər; -,sHir/ (in full **Berkshire Pig**) ▶ n. a pig of a black breed, now rarely kept commercially.

Ber·lin[1] /bər'lin/ the capital of Germany; pop. 3,102,500. At the end of World War II, the city was divided into **West Berlin** and **East Berlin**. The Berlin Wall separated the two parts 1961–89, which were reunited in 1990.

Ber·lin[2], Irving (1888–1989), US composer of popular music; born in Russia; born *Israel Baline.* He wrote more than 800 songs, including "God Bless America" (1939) and "White Christmas" (1942).

Ber·li·ner /bər'linər/ ▶ n. a native or citizen of Berlin. [19th C.: Ger.]

Ber·lin Wall a guarded wall built between East and West Berlin in 1961 by the communist authorities. It was opened in November 1989 after the collapse of the communist regime in East Germany and subsequently was dismantled.

Ber·lin work ▶ n. worsted embroidery on canvas.

Ber·li·oz /'berlē,ōz; ber'lyōz/, Hector (1803–69), French composer; full name *Louis-Hector Berlioz.* His works include the opera *Les Troyens* (1856–59).

berm /bərm/ ▶ n. a flat strip of land, raised bank, or terrace bordering a river or canal. ■ a path or grass strip beside a road. ■ an artificial ridge or embankment, e.g., as a defense against tanks. ■ a narrow space, esp. one between a ditch and the base of a parapet. [18th C.: from Fr. *berme*, from Du. *berm*.]

Ber·mu·da /bər'myo͞odə/ (also **the Ber·mu·das**) a British crown colony made up of about 150 small islands about 650 miles (1,046 km) east of the coast of North Carolina; pop. 58,000; capital, Hamilton. Inhabited since 1609, it now has internal self-government. — **Ber·mu·dan** /-'myo͞odn/ **adj. & n. Ber·mu·di·an** /-'myo͞odēən/ **adj. & n.**

Ber·mu·da grass ▶ **n.** a creeping grass (*Cynodon dactylon*) common in warmer parts of the world, used for lawns and pasture.

Ber·mu·da on·ion ▶ **n.** a variety of cultivated onion with a mild flavor and a flattened shape.

Ber·mu·da rig ▶ **n.** a tall yachting rig with a fore-and-aft tapering mainsail.

Ber·mu·da shorts (also **Ber·mu·das**) ▶ **plural n.** casual knee-length shorts.

Ber·mu·da Tri·an·gle an area of the western Atlantic Ocean between Florida, Bermuda, and Puerto Rico where a large number of ships and aircraft have disappeared mysteriously.

Ber·na·dette, St. /ˌbərnə'det/ (1844–79), French peasant girl; born *Marie Bernarde Soubirous*. Her visions of the Virgin Mary at Lourdes in 1858 led to the town's establishment as a center of pilgrimage.

Ber·na·dotte[1] /ˌbernə'dät; -'dôt/, Folke, Count (1895–1948), Swedish diplomat. As vice-president of the Swedish Red Cross he arranged the exchange of prisoners of war and in 1945 conveyed a German offer of capitulation to the Allies.

Ber·na·dotte[2], Jean Baptiste Jules (1763–1844), French soldier. He became king of Sweden (as Charles XIV) 1818–44.

Ber·nard, St. /bər'närd; ber'när/ (*c.*996–*c.*1081), French monk. He founded two hospices for travelers in the Alps.

Ber·nard of Clair·vaux, St. /bər'närd əv kler'vō; ber'när/ (1090–1153), French theologian. The first abbot of Clairvaux, his monastery was one of the chief centers of the Cistercian order.

Berne /bern; bərn/ (also **Bern**) the capital of Switzerland, in the west central part; pop. 134,620. ■ a canton of Switzerland. — **Ber·nese** /ber'nēz; -'nēs; bər-/ **adj. & n.**

Ber·nese moun·tain dog /'bərnēz; -nēs; bər'nēz; -'nēs/ ▶ **n.** a large muscular dog of a Swiss breed with a silky black coat, having white and russet markings.

Bern·hardt /'bərnˌhärt/, Sarah (1844–1923), French actress; born *Henriette Rosine Bernard*. She portrayed Cordelia in *King Lear*.

Ber·ni·ni /bər'nēnē/, Gian Lorenzo (1598–1680), Italian sculptor, painter, and architect. His work includes the altar canopy at St. Peter's in Rome.

Ber·noul·li /bər'no͞o(l)ē/ a Swiss family of mathematicians. Jakob (1654–1705), also known as *Jacques* or *James Bernoulli*, made discoveries in calculus, geometry, and the theory of probabilities. Johann (1667–1748), his brother, also known as *Jean* or *John Bernoulli*, contributed to differential and integral calculus. Daniel (1700–82), son of Johann, contributed to hydrodynamics and mathematical physics.

Ber·noul·li's prin·ci·ple ▶ **n.** the principle in hydrodynamics that an increase in the velocity of a stream of fluid results in a decrease in pressure. Also called **Bernoulli effect** or **Bernoulli theorem**. [Named for Daniel Bernoulli.]

Bern·stein[1] /'bərnˌstēn; -ˌstīn/, Carl (1944–), US journalist. A reporter for the *Washington Post*, he and Robert Woodward broke the story of the Watergate burglary.

Bern·stein[2], Leonard (1918–90), US composer, conductor, and pianist. He was a conductor with the New York Philharmonic Orchestra 1945–48, 1957–69. His works include *West Side Story* (1957).

ber·ried /'berēd/ ▶ **adj.** **1** bearing or covered with berries. **2** like a berry or berries, as in flavor or shape. **3** (of crustaceans or fish) bearing eggs.

ber·ry /'berē/ ▶ **n.** (pl. **-ries**) a small roundish juicy fruit without a stone. ■ Bot. any fruit that has its seeds enclosed in a fleshy pulp, for example, a banana or tomato. ■ any of various kernels or seeds, such as the coffee bean. ■ a fish egg or the roe of a lobster or similar creature. [OE *berie*, of Gmc. origin; rel. to Du. *bes* and Ger. *Beere*.]

ber·ry·ing /'bereiNG/ ▶ **n.** the activity of gathering berries: *let's go berrying.*

Ber·ry·man /'berēmən/, John (1914–72), US poet. His works include the award-winning *77 Dream Songs* (1964).

ber·seem clo·ver /bər'sēm/ ▶ **n.** a white-flowered clover (*Trifolium alexandrinum*), native to Egypt and Syria, and now an established forage plant in the southern US. Also called **EGYPTIAN CLOVER**.

ber·serk /bər'zərk; -'sərk/ ▶ **adj.** (of a person or animal) out of control with anger or excitement; wild or frenzied: *after she left him, he went berserk.* ■ (of a mechanical device or system) operating in a wild or erratic way; out of control. ■ (of a procedure, program, or activity) fluctuating wildly. [19th C. a wild Norse warrior): from ON *berserkr* (n.), prob. from *birn-*, *bjǫrn* (see **BEAR**[2]) + *serkr* 'coat.']

ber·serk·er /bər'zərkər; -'sər-/ ▶ **n.** an ancient Norse warrior who fought with a wild frenzy.

berth /bərTH/ ▶ **n.** **1** a ship's allotted place at a wharf or dock. **2** a fixed bed or bunk on a ship, train, or other means of transport. **3** informal (often in a sports context) a situation or position in an organization or event. ▶ **v.** [trans.] **1** moor (a ship) in its allotted place: *these modern ships can almost berth themselves.* ■ [intrans.] (of a ship) dock: *the Dutch freighter berthed at the Brooklyn docks.* **2** (of a passenger ship) provide a sleeping place for (someone).

– PHRASES **give a wide berth** steer (a ship) well clear of something while passing it. ■ stay away from someone or something. [17th C.: prob. from **BEAR**[1] + **-TH**[2].]

ber·tha /'bərTHə/ ▶ **n.** esp. hist. a deep collar, typically made of lace, attached to the top of a dress that has a low neckline. [19th C.: from the name *Bertha*.]

berth·ing /'bərTHiNG/ ▶ **n.** **1** the action of mooring a ship. **2** mooring position; accommodation in berths.

Ber·til·lon /'bərtl,än; ˌbertē'yôN/, Alphonse (1853–1914), French criminologist. He devised a system of body measurements (the **Bertillon system**) to identify criminals.

Ber·to·luc·ci /ˌbertl'o͞oCHē/, Bernardo (1940–), Italian director. He directed *Last Tango in Paris* (1972).

Ber·wyn /'bərwin/ a city in northeastern Illinois; pop. 45,426.

ber·yl /'berəl/ ▶ **n.** a transparent pale green, blue, or yellow mineral consisting of a silicate of beryllium and aluminum, sometimes used as a gemstone. [ME: from OFr. *beril*, via L. from Gk. *bērullos*.]

be·ryl·li·o·sis /bəˌrilē'ōsis/ ▶ **n.** Med. poisoning by beryllium or beryllium compounds, esp. by inhalation causing fibrosis of the lungs.

be·ryl·li·um /bə'rilēəm/ ▶ **n.** the chemical element of atomic number 4, a hard gray metal. (Symbol: **Be**)

Ber·ze·li·us /bər'zālēəs; -'zē-/, Jöns Jakob (1779–1848), Swedish chemist. He determined the atomic weights of many elements.

Bes /bes/ Egyptian Mythol. a grotesque god depicted as having short legs, an obese body, and an almost bestial face, who dispelled evil spirits.

Be·san·çon /bəˌzäN'sôN/ a city in northeastern France; pop. 119,200.

be·seech /bi'sēCH/ ▶ **v.** (past **-sought** or **-seeched**) [reporting verb] formal or literary ask (someone) urgently and fervently to do something; implore; entreat: [with obj. and infin.] *they beseeched him to stay* | [with obj. and direct speech] *"You have got to believe me," Gloria beseeched him* | [trans.] *they earnestly beseeched his forgiveness* | [as adj.] (**beseeching**) *a beseeching gaze.* — **be·seech·ing·ly adv.** [ME: from **BE-** (as an intensifier) + OE *sēcan* (see **SEEK**).]

be·seem /bi'sēm/ ▶ **v.** [trans.] archaic seem; befit.

be·set /bi'set/ ▶ **v.** (**-set·ting**; past and past part. **-set**) [trans.] **1** (of a problem or difficulty) trouble or threaten persistently: *the social problems that beset the inner city* | *she was beset with self-doubt* | [as adj.] *poverty is a besetting problem.* ■ surround and harass; assail on all sides: *I was beset by clouds of flies.* ■ hem in; enclose. **2** (**be beset with**) archaic be covered or studded with. [OE *besettan*, from **BE-** 'around' + *settan* (see **SET**[1]).]

be·shrew /bi'SHro͞o/ ▶ **v.** [trans.] archaic **1** make wicked; deprave. **2** invoke evil upon; curse; blame for a misfortune.

be·side /bi'sīd/ ▶ **prep.** **1** at the side of; next to: *on the table beside the bed.* ■ compared with. **2** in addition to; apart from.

– PHRASES **beside oneself** overcome with worry or anger; distraught: *she was* **beside herself** *with anguish.* **beside the point** see **POINT**. [OE *be sīdan* (adv.) 'by the side' (see **BY, SIDE**).]

be·sides /bi'sīdz/ ▶ **prep.** in addition to; apart from: *I have no other family besides my parents.* ▶ **adv.** in addition; as well: *I'm capable of doing the work, and a lot more besides.* ■ moreover; anyway: *I had no time to warn you. Besides, I wasn't sure.*

be·siege /bi'sēj/ ▶ **v.** [trans.] surround (a place) with armed forces in order to capture it or force its surrender; lay siege to: *the guerrillas continued to besiege other cities to the north* | [as adj.] (**besieged**) *the besieged city.* ■ crowd around oppressively; surround and harass: *she spent the whole day besieged by newsmen.* ■ (**be besieged**) be inundated by large numbers of requests or complaints: *the television station was* **besieged with** *calls.* — **be·sieg·er n.** [ME: alt. of *assiege*, from OFr. *asegier*.]

be·smear /bi'smi(ə)r/ ▶ **v.** [trans.] literary smear or cover with a greasy or sticky substance.

be·smirch /bi'smərCH/ ▶ **v.** [trans.] damage the reputation of (someone or something) in the opinion of others: *he had besmirched the good name of his family.* ■ literary make (something) dirty or discolored.

be·som /'bēzəm/ ▶ **n.** a broom made of twigs tied around a stick. [OE *besema*, from West Gmc.; akin to Ger. *Besen*.]

be·sot·ted /bi'sätid/ ▶ **adj.** **1** strongly infatuated: *he became* **besotted with** *his best friend's sister.* **2** archaic intoxicated; drunk. [16th C.: past part. of *besot* 'make foolishly affectionate,' from **BE-** 'cause to be' + **SOT**.]

be·sought /bi'sôt/ past and past participle of **BESEECH**.

be·spat·ter /bi'spatər/ ▶ **v.** [trans.] splash small drops of a liquid substance all over (an object or surface): *his shoes were* **bespattered with** *mud.*

be·speak /bi'spēk/ ▶ **v.** (past **-spoke**; past part. **-spok·en**) [trans.] **1** (of an appearance or action)

besom

PRONUNCIATION KEY ə *ago, up*; ər *over, fur*; a *hat*; ā *ate*; ä *car*; e *let*; ē *see*; i *fit*; ī *by*; NG *sing*; ō *go*; ô *law, for*; oi *toy*; o͝o *good*; o͞o *goo*; ou *out*; TH *thin*; T̲H̲ *then*; ZH *vision*

suggest; be evidence of: *the attractive tree-lined road bespoke money.* **2** order or reserve (something) in advance: *obtaining the affidavits that it has been necessary to bespeak.* **3** archaic speak to: *and in disgrace bespoke him thus.*

be·spec·ta·cled /bi'spektəkəld/ ▸ **adj.** (of a person) wearing eyeglasses.

be·spoke /bi'spōk/ past of BESPEAK. ▸ **adj.** [attrib.] esp. Brit. (of goods, esp. clothing) made to order: *a bespoke suit.* ▪ (of a trader) making such goods: *bespoke tailors.*

be·spo·ken /bi'spōkən/ past participle of BESPEAK.

be·sprent /bi'sprent/ ▸ **adj.** [archaic] sprinkled.

be·sprin·kle /bi'spriNGkəl/ ▸ **v.** [trans.] literary sprinkle all over with small drops or amounts of a substance: *their lips were **besprinkled with** flakes of pastry.*

Bes·sa·ra·bi·a /,besə'rābēə/ a region in eastern Europe. It now lies in Moldova and Ukraine. — **Bes·sa·ra·bi·an adj. & n.**

Bes·sel /'besəl/, Friedrich Wilhelm (1784–1846), German astronomer and mathematician. He determined the positions and distances of approximately 75,000 stars and predicted the existence of an eighth planet.

Bes·se·mer /'besəmər/, Sir Henry (1813–98), English inventor. By 1860 he had developed the Bessemer process, the first successful method of making steel in quantity at low cost.

Bes·se·mer proc·ess ▸ **n.** a steelmaking process, now largely superseded, in which carbon, silicon, and other impurities are removed from molten pig-iron by oxidation in a blast of air in a special tilting retort (a **Bessemer converter**).

Best /best/, Charles Herbert (1899–1978), Canadian physiologist; born in the US. He assisted F. G. Banting in research leading to the discovery of insulin in 1922.

best /best/ superlative of GOOD. ▸ **adj.** of the most excellent, effective, or desirable type or quality: *the best pitcher in the league | how to obtain the best results from your machine | her best black suit.* ▪ most enjoyable: *some of the best times of my life.* ▪ most appropriate, advantageous, or well advised: *do whatever you think best | it's best if we both go.* ▸ **adv.** superlative of WELL[1]. to the highest degree; most: *the one we liked best.* ▪ most excellently or effectively: *the best-dressed man in Hollywood.* ▪ most suitably, appropriately, or usefully: *this is best done at home.* ▸ **n.** (usu. **the best**) that which is the most excellent, outstanding, or desirable. ▪ the most meritorious aspect of a thing or person: *he **brought out the best in** people.* ▪ **(one's best)** the peak of condition; the highest standard or level that a person or thing can reach: *this is jazz **at its best**.* ▪ **(one's best)** one's finest or most formal clothes: *she dressed in her best.* ▪ (in sports) a record of a specified kind, esp. a personal one: *achieving a lifetime best of 12.0 seconds | **a personal best**.* ▸ **v.** [trans.] informal outwit or get the better of (someone): *she refused to allow herself to be bested.*

– PHRASES **all the best** said or written to wish a person well on ending a letter or parting. **as best one can** (or **may**) as effectively as possible under the circumstances. **at best** taking the most optimistic or favorable view: *signs of recovery are patchy at best.* **at** (or **in**) **the best of times** even in the most favorable circumstances. **be best friends** be mutually closest friends: *he's **best friends with** Eddie.* **be for** (or **all for**) **the best** be desirable in the end, although not at first seeming so. **one's best friend** one's closest or favorite friend. **the best of friends** very good friends. **the best of three** (or **five**, etc.) victory achieved by winning the majority of a specified (usually odd) number of games. **the best part of** most of: *it took them the best part of 10 years.* **best wishes** an expression of hope for someone's future happiness or welfare. ▪ written at the end of a letter. **one's best years** the most vigorous and productive period of one's life; one's prime. **do** (or **try**) **one's best** do all one can. **get the best of** overcome (someone). **had best do something** find it most sensible or well advised to do the thing mentioned: *I'd best be going.* **make the best of** derive what limited advantage one can from (something unsatisfactory or unwelcome). ▪ use (resources) as well as possible. **to the best of one's ability** (or **knowledge**) as far as one can do or know. **with the best of them** as well or as much as anyone. [OE *betest* (adj.), *betost, betst* (adv.), from Gmc.; akin to Ger. *best* and BETTER[1].]

best ball ▸ **n.** Golf the better score at a hole of two or more players competing as a team: [as adj.] *a best-ball match.*

best boy ▸ **n.** the assistant to the chief electrician of a movie crew.

bes·tial /'bēsCHəl; 'bes-/ ▸ **adj.** of or like an animal or animals. ▪ savagely cruel and depraved. — **bes·tial·ly adv.** [ME: via OFr. from late L. *bestialis*, from L. *bestia* 'beast.']

bes·ti·al·i·ty /,bēsCHē'alitē; ,bes-/ ▸ **n.** **1** savagely cruel or depraved behavior. **2** sexual intercourse between a person and an animal.

bes·ti·ar·y /'bēsCHē,erē; 'bes-/ ▸ **n.** (pl. **-ar·ies**) a descriptive or anecdotal treatise on various real or mythical kinds of animals, esp. a medieval work with a moralizing tone. [19th C.: from med. L. *bestiarium*, from L. *bestia* 'beast.']

be·stir /bi'stər/ ▸ **v.** (**-stirred, -stir·ring**) (**bestir oneself**) make a physical or mental effort; exert or rouse oneself: *they rarely bestir themselves.*

best man ▸ **n.** [in sing.] a male friend or relative chosen by a bridegroom to assist him at his wedding.

be·stow /bi'stō/ ▸ **v.** [trans.] confer or present (an honor, right, or gift): *the office was **bestowed on** him by the chief of state.* | fig. *she bestowed her nicest smile on Jim.* — **be·stow·al** /-əl/ **n.** [ME: from BE- (intensifier) + OE *stōw* 'place.']

be·strew /bi'strōō/ ▸ **v.** (past part. **-strewed** or **-strewn**) [trans.] literary cover or partly cover (a surface) with scattered objects: *the bride's train was **bestrewn with** rose petals.* ▪ (of objects) lie scattered over (a surface): *sweeping away the sand and rubbish that bestrewed it.*

be·stride /bi'strīd/ ▸ **v.** (past **-strode** ; past part. **-strid·den**) [trans.] stand astride over; span or straddle: fig. *creatures that bestride the dividing line between amphibians and reptiles.* ▪ sit astride on: *he bestrode his horse.*

best sell·er ▸ **n.** a book or other product that sells in very large numbers.

best-sell·ing ▸ **adj.** [attrib.] (of a book or other product) having very large sales; very popular: *a best-selling novel.*

bet /bet/ ▸ **v.** (**bet·ting** ; past **bet** or **bet·ted**) **1** [intrans.] risk something, usually a sum of money, against someone else's on the basis of the outcome of a future event, such as the result of a race or game: ***betting on** horses* | [with clause] *I would be prepared to bet that what he really wanted was to settle down* | [trans.] *most people would **bet** their life savings **on** this prospect.* ▪ [with obj. and clause] risk a sum of money against (someone) on the outcome or happening of a future event: [with two objs.] *I'll bet you $15 you won't find a single scratch.* **2** [with clause] informal feel sure: ***I bet** this place is really spooky late at night | he'll be surprised to see me, **I'll bet**.* ▸ **n.** an act of risking a sum of money in this way. ▪ a sum of money staked in this way. ▪ [with adj.] informal a candidate or course of action to choose; an option: ***your best bet** is to call a professional exterminator.* ▪ **(one's bet)** informal an opinion, typically one formed quickly or spontaneously.

– PHRASES **all bets are off** informal the outcome of a situation is unpredictable. **don't** (or **I wouldn't**) **bet on it** informal used to express doubt about an assertion or situation. **want to** (or **wanna**) **bet?** informal used to express vigorous disagreement with a confident assertion: *"You can't be with me every moment." "Want to bet?"* **you bet** informal you may be sure; certainly: *"Would you like this piece of pie?" "You bet!"* [16th C.: perh. a shortening of the obs. n. *abet* 'abetment.']

bet. ▸ **abbr.** between.

be·ta /'bātə/ ▸ **n.** the second letter of the Greek alphabet (Β, β), transliterated as 'b.' ▪ [as adj.] denoting the second of a series of items, categories, forms of a chemical compound, etc.: *beta carotene.* ▪ informal short for BETA TEST: *their database system is currently **in beta*** | [as adj.] *a beta version.* ▪ **(Beta)** [followed by Latin genitive] the second (usually second-brightest) star in a constellation: *Beta Virginis.* ▪ [as adj.] relating to beta decay or beta particles: *beta emitters.*

be·ta-ad·ren·er·gic ▸ **adj.** of, relating to, or affecting beta receptors.

be·ta block·er ▸ **n.** any of a class of drugs that prevent the stimulation of the adrenergic receptors responsible for increased cardiac action. Beta blockers are used to control heart rhythm, treat angina, and reduce high blood pressure.

Be·ta·cam /'bātə,kam/ ▸ **n.** trademark a high quality format for video cameras and recorders. ▪ a camera using this format.

be·ta·car·o·tene /,bātə'karə,tēn/ (also **be·ta-car·o·tene**) ▸ **n.** see CAROTENE.

be·ta cell ▸ **n.** any of the insulin-producing cells in the islets of Langerhans.

be·ta de·cay ▸ **n.** radioactive decay in which an electron is emitted.

be·ta en·dor·phin ▸ **n.** an endorphin produced in the pituitary gland that is a powerful pain suppressor.

be·ta glob·u·lin ▸ **n.** see GLOBULIN.

be·ta·ine /'bētə,ēn/ ▸ **n.** Chem. a crystalline compound, $(CH_3)_3N^+{-}CH_2CO_2^-$, with basic properties found in many plant juices. [19th C.: from L. *beta* 'beet' (because orig. isolated from beets) + -INE[4].]

be·take /bi'tāk/ ▸ **v.** (past **-took** ; past part. **-tak·en**) [trans.] (**betake oneself to**) literary go to: *I shall betake myself to my room.*

Be·ta·max /'bātə,maks/ ▸ **n.** trademark a format for video recorders, now largely obsolete.

be·ta par·ti·cle (also **beta ray**) ▸ **n.** Physics a fast-moving electron emitted by radioactive decay of substances. (The emission of beta particles was originally regarded as a ray.)

be·ta re·cep·tor ▸ **n.** an adrenergic receptor in the sympathetic nervous system, stimulation of which results esp. in increased cardiac activity.

be·ta rhythm ▸ **n.** Physiol. the normal electrical activity of the brain when conscious and alert, consisting of oscillations (**beta waves**) with a frequency of 18 to 25 hertz.

be·ta test ▸ **n.** a trial of machinery, software, or other products, in the final stages of its development, carried out by a party unconnected with its development. ▸ **v.** (**be·ta-test**) [trans.] subject (a product) to such a test.

be·ta·tron /'bātə,trän/ ▸ **n.** Physics an apparatus for accelerating electrons in a circular path by magnetic induction. [1940s: from BETA + -TRON.]

bet·cha /'beCHə/ ▸ **v.** a nonstandard contraction of "bet you," used in representing informal speech: *betcha can't find a better apartment.*

be·tel /'bētl/ ▸ **n.** **1** the leaf of an Asian evergreen climbing plant, used in the East as a mild stimulant. Parings of areca nut, lime, and cinnamon are wrapped in the leaf, which is then chewed, causing the saliva to go red and, with prolonged use, the teeth to go black. **2** the plant (*Piper betle*) of the pepper family from which these leaves are taken. [16th C.: via Port. from Malayalam *verrila*.]

Be·tel·geuse /'bētl,jōōs; -,jōōz; 'betl-/ (also **Be·tel·geux**) Astron. the tenth brightest star in the sky, in the constellation Orion. [Fr., alt. of Arab. *yad al-jauzā* 'hand of the giant' (Orion).]

be·tel nut ▸ **n.** another term for ARECA NUT. [Port. *betel.*]

be·tel palm ▸ **n.** another term for ARECA.

bête noire /ˌbāt ˈnwär; ˌbet/ ▶ **n.** (pl. **bêtes noires** pronunc. same or /ˈnwärz/) a person or thing that one particularly dislikes. [19th C.: Fr., lit. 'black beast.']

beth /bās; bāt; bet/ ▶ **n.** the second letter of the Hebrew alphabet.

Beth·el /ˈbeTHəl/ a town in the Catskill Mountains, in southeastern New York; pop. 3,693. It is the actual site of the 1969 Woodstock music festival.

beth·el /ˈbeTHəl/ ▶ **n.** **1** a holy place. **2** a chapel for seamen. **3** Brit. a Nonconformist chapel.

Be·thes·da /bəˈTHezdə/ an affluent unincorporated suburb in central Maryland. It is home to the National Institutes of Health; pop. 62,936.

be·think /biˈTHiNGk/ ▶ **v.** (past and past part. **-thought**) (**bethink oneself**) formal or archaic think on reflection; come to think: *he bethought himself of the verse from the Book of Proverbs* | [with clause] *the council bethought itself that this plan would leave room for future expansion.*

Beth·le·hem /ˈbeTHliˌhem; -lēəm/ **1** a small town 5 miles (8 km) south of Jerusalem, in the West Bank; pop. 14,000. It was the native city of King David and is said to be the birthplace of Jesus. **2** an industrial city in eastern Pennsylvania, on the Lehigh River; pop. 71,329.

Be·thune /bəˈTH(y)o͞on/, Mary McLeod (1875–1955), US educator. In 1904, she founded the Daytona Normal and Industrial Institute for Negro Girls, and was founder and first president 1935–49 of the National Council of Negro Women.

be·tide /biˈtīd/ ▶ **v.** [intrans.] literary happen: *I waited with beating heart, as yet not knowing what would betide.* ■ [trans.] happen to (someone): *she was trembling with fear lest worse might betide her.*
– PHRASES **woe betide** see WOE. [ME: from BE- (intensifier) + *tide* 'befall,' from OE *tīdan* 'happen,' from *tīd* (see TIDE).]

be·times /biˈtīmz/ ▶ **adv.** literary before the usual or expected time; early: *next morning I was up betimes.* [ME: from obs. *betime* (see BY, TIME).]

bê·tise /beˈtēz/ ▶ **n.** a foolish or ill-timed remark or action. [19th C.: Fr., lit. 'stupidity.']

be·to·ken /biˈtōkən/ ▶ **v.** [trans.] literary be a sign of; indicate: *she wondered if his cold, level gaze betokened indifference or anger.* ■ be a warning or indication of (a future event): *the falling comet betokened the true end of Merlin's powers.* [OE *betācnian*, from BE- (intensifier) + *tācnian* 'signify,' from Gmc.; akin to TOKEN.]

bet·o·ny /ˈbetn-ē/ ▶ **n.** (pl. **-nies**) a Eurasian plant (*Stachys officinalis*) of the mint family that bears spikes of showy purple flowers. ■ used in names of plants that resemble the betony, e.g., **wood betony**. [ME: from OFr. *betoine*, based on L. *betonica*.]

be·took /biˈto͝ok/ past of BETAKE.

be·tray /biˈtrā/ ▶ **v.** [trans.] be disloyal to: *he betrayed them.* ■ be disloyal to (one's country, organization, or ideology) by acting in the interests of an enemy. ■ treacherously inform an enemy of the existence or location of (a person or organization). ■ treacherously reveal (secrets or information). ■ fig. reveal the presence of; be evidence of: *she drew a deep breath that betrayed her indignation.* — **be·tray·al** /-əl/ **n.** **be·tray·er n.** [ME: from BE- 'thoroughly' + obs. *tray* 'betray,' from OFr. *trair*, based on L. *tradere* 'hand over.']

be·troth /bəˈtrōT͟H; -ˈtrôTH/ ▶ **v.** [trans.] (usu. **be betrothed**) dated enter into a formal agreement to marry: *soon I shall be betrothed to Isabel* | [as n.] (**betrothed**) *how long have you known your betrothed?* — **be·troth·al** /-əl/ **n.** [ME *betreuthe*: from BE- (expressing transitivity) + TRUTH]

Bet·tel·heim /ˈbetlˌhīm/, Bruno (1903–90), US psychologist; born in Austria. He developed revolutionary theories and therapies for autistic children.

Bet·ten·dorf /ˈbetnˌdôrf/ a city in southeastern Iowa, on the Mississippi River; pop. 31,275.

bet·ter[1] /ˈbetər/ ▶ **adj.** **1** comparative of GOOD and WELL. **2** of a more excellent or effective type or quality: *hoping for better weather* | *I'm better at algebra than Alice.* ■ more appropriate, advantageous, or well advised. **3** [predic.] partly or fully recovered from illness or injury: *she's much better today.* ■ fitter and healthier; less unwell: *we'll feel a lot better after a decent night's sleep.* ▶ **adv.** comparative of WELL[1]. more excellently or effectively: *Johnny could do better if he tried* | *instruments are generally better made these days.* ■ to a greater degree; more: *I liked it better when we lived in the country.* ■ more suitably, appropriately, or usefully: *the money could be better spent.* ▶ **n.** **1** the better one; that which is better: *the Natural History Museum book is by far the better of the two* | *a change* **for the better**. **2** (**one's betters**) esp. dated or humorous one's superiors in social class or ability: *amusing themselves by imitating their betters.* ▶ **v.** [trans.] improve on or surpass (an existing or previous level or achievement): *bettering his previous time by ten minutes.* ■ make (something) better; improve: *his ideas for bettering the working conditions.* ■ (**better oneself**) achieve a better social position or status: *the residents are mostly welfare mothers who have bettered themselves.* ■ overcome or defeat (someone): *she bettered him at archery.*
– PHRASES **be better off** be in a better position, esp. in financial terms: *the promotion would make her about $750 a year better off* | [as pl. n.] (**the better off**) *a paper read mainly by the better off.* **the —— the better** used to emphasize the importance or desirability of the quality or thing specified: *the sooner we're off, the better.* **the better part of** almost all of; most of. **better safe than sorry** proverb it's wiser to be cautious than to be hasty or rash and so do something you may later regret. **better than** more than. **the better to ——** so as to —— better: *he leaned closer the better to hear her.* **for better or (for) worse** whether the outcome is good or bad. **get the better of** (often of something immaterial) win an advantage over (someone); defeat or outwit. **go one better** narrowly surpass a previous effort or achievement. ■ narrowly outdo (another person). **had better do something** would find it wiser to do something; ought to do something: *you had better be careful.* **have the better of** be more successful in a contest. **no** (or **little**) **better than** just (or almost) the same as; merely. [OE *betera* (adj.), from Gmc.; akin to Ger. *besser* and BEST.]

bet·ter[2] ▶ **n.** var. of BETTOR.

bet·ter half ▶ **n.** informal a person's wife, husband, or partner.

bet·ter·ment /ˈbetərmənt/ ▶ **n.** the act or process of improving something. ■ the enhanced value of real property arising from local improvements.

bet·ting /ˈbetiNG/ ▶ **n.** the act of gambling money on the outcome of a race, game, or other unpredictable event.

bet·tor /ˈbetər/ (also **bet·ter**) ▶ **n.** a person who bets, typically regularly or habitually.

be·tween /biˈtwēn/ (abbr.: **bet.**) ▶ **prep.** **1** at, into, or across the space separating (two objects or regions): ■ expressing location: *traffic was at a standstill between exits 12 and 14* | *the border between Mexico and the United States.* ■ expressing movement to a point: *the dog crawled between us.* ■ expressing movement from one side or point to the other and back again: *traveling by train between London and Paris.* **2** in the period separating (two points in time): *they snack between meals.* **3** in the interval separating (two points on a scale): *a man aged between 18 and 30* | *the difference between income and expenditure.* **4** indicating a connection or relationship involving two or more parties: *the relationship between Pauline and Chris.* ■ with reference to a collision or conflict: *a collision in midair between two light aircraft above Geneva.* ■ with reference to a choice or differentiation involving two or more things being considered together. **5** by combining the resources or actions of (two or more people or other entities): *we have created something between us.* ■ shared by (two or more people or things): *they had drunk between them a bottle of Chianti.* ▶ **adv.** **1** in or along the space separating two objects or regions: *layers of paper with tar* **in between** | *from Leipzig to Dresden, with the gentle Elbe flowing between.* **2** in the period separating two points in time: *sets of exercises with no rest* **in between**.
– PHRASES **between ourselves** (or **you and me**) in confidence. **(in) between times** in the intervals between other actions. [OE *betwēonum*, from *be* 'by' + a Gmc. word rel. to TWO.]

be·twixt /biˈtwikst/ ▶ **prep. & adv.** archaic term for BETWEEN.
– PHRASES **betwixt and between** informal neither one thing nor the other. [OE *betwēox*, from *be* 'by' + a Gmc. word akin to TWO.]

beurre blanc /ˈbər ˈbläNGk/ ▶ **n.** a creamy sauce made with butter, onions or shallots, and vinegar or lemon juice, usually served with seafood dishes. [20th C.: Fr., lit. 'white butter.']

BEV ▶ **abbr.** Ling. Black English Vernacular.

BeV another term for GEV. [1940s: from *b*illion (10⁹) *e*lectron*v*olts.]

bev·a·tron /ˈbevəˌträn/ ▶ **n.** a synchrotron used to accelerate protons to energies in the billion electron-volt range. [1940s: from BEV + -TRON.]

bev·el /ˈbevəl/ ▶ **n.** a slope from the horizontal or vertical in carpentry and stonework; a sloping surface or edge. ■ (in full **bev·el square**) a tool for marking angles in carpentry and stonework. ▶ **v.** (**bev·eled, bev·el·ing** or **bev·elled, bev·el·ling**) [trans.] [often as adj.] (**beveled**) reduce (a square edge on an object) to a sloping edge: *a beveled mirror.* [16th C.: from OFr. *baif* 'open-mouthed,' from *baer* 'to gape' (see BAY[5]).]

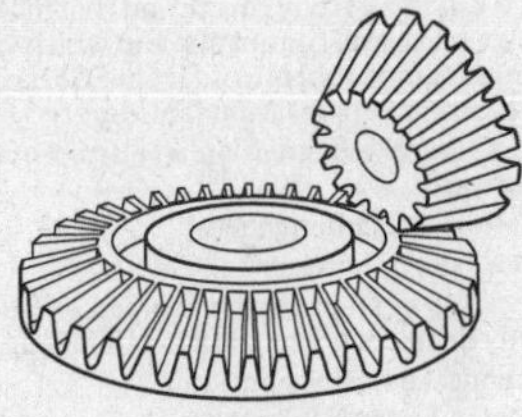

bevel gear

bev·el gear ▶ **n.** a gear working another gear at an angle to it by means of bevel wheels.

bev·el wheel ▶ **n.** a toothed wheel whose working face is oblique to the axis.

bev·er·age /ˈbev(ə)rij/ ▶ **n.** a drink, esp. one other than water. [ME: from OFr. *bevrage*, based on L. *bibere* 'to drink.']

Bev·er·ly /ˈbevərlē/ a city in northeastern Massachusetts; pop. 38,195.

Bev·er·ly Hills a city in California, northwest of Los Angeles; pop. 31,970. It is home to many movie stars.

Bev·in /ˈbevən/, Ernest (1881–1951), foreign secretary of Britain 1945–51. He helped to establish NATO in 1949.

bev·y /ˈbevē/ ▶ **n.** (pl. **bev·ies**) a large group of people or things of a particular kind. ■ a group of birds, particularly when closely gathered on the ground. [ME: of unknown origin.]

be·wail /bi'wāl/ ▶v. [trans.] express great regret, disappointment, or bitterness over (something) by complaining about it to others: *he bewailed the fact that heart trouble had slowed him down.* ■ cry or wail loudly about (something).

be·ware /bi'we(ə)r/ ▶v. [intrans.] [in imper. or infin.] be cautious and alert to the dangers of: *consumers were warned to **beware of** faulty packaging* | *Beware! Dangerous submerged rocks ahead* | [trans.] *we should beware the incompetence of legislators.* [ME: from *be ware* (see BE-, WARE[2]).]

be·whisk·ered /bi'(h)wiskərd/ ▶adj. having hair or whiskers growing on the face.

be·wigged /bi'wigd/ ▶adj. (of a person) wearing a wig.

be·wil·der /bi'wildər/ ▶v. [trans.] [often as adj.] (**bewildered**) cause (someone) to become perplexed and confused: *she seemed frightened and bewildered* | [as adj.] (**bewildering**) *a bewildering array of desserts.* —**be·wil·dered·ly** adv. **be·wil·der·ing·ly** adv. **be·wil·der·ment** n. [17th C.: from BE- 'thoroughly' + *wilder* 'go astray,' of unknown origin.]

be·witch /bi'wicн/ ▶v. [trans.] (often **be bewitched**) cast a spell on and gain a magical control over (someone): *he was bewitched.* ■ enchant and delight (someone): *they both were bewitched by the country and its culture* | [as adj.] (**bewitching**) *she was certainly a bewitching woman.* —**be·witch·ing·ly** adv. **be·witch·ment** n.

bey /bā/ ▶n. (pl. **beys**) hist. the governor of a district or province in the Ottoman Empire. ■ formerly used in Turkey and Egypt as a courtesy title. [Turk., mod. form of *beg* 'prince.']

be·yond /bē'änd; bi'yänd/ ▶prep. & adv. **1** at or to the further side of: [as prep.] *he pointed to a spot beyond the trees* | [as adv.] *there was the terminal and, beyond, an endless line of warehouses.* ■ [prep.] outside the physical limits or range of: *the land sloped away until far beyond sight it reached the Great Plains.* ■ fig. more extensive or extreme than: [as prep.] *what these children go through is **far beyond** what most adults endure in a lifetime.* | [as adv.] *pushing the laws to their limits **and beyond**.* **2** happening or continuing after (a specified time or event): [as prep.] *we can manage another two years, but beyond that the system is not viable.* **3** having progressed or achieved more than (a specified stage or level): [as prep.] *we need to get beyond square one.* ■ above or greater than (a specified amount): [as prep.] *the absenteeism had gone beyond 15%.* **4** [prep.] to a degree or condition where a specified action is impossible: *the landscape has changed beyond recognition.* ■ too much for (someone) to achieve or understand: *I did something that I thought was beyond me.* **5** [prep.] [with negative] apart from; except: *beyond telling us that she was well educated, he has nothing to say about her.* ▶n. (**the beyond**) the unknown after death: *messages from the beyond.*
– PHRASES **the back of beyond** see BACK. [OE *begeondan*, from *be* 'by' + *geondan*, from Gmc.; akin to YONDER.]

bez·ant /'bezənt/ ▶n. **1** hist. a gold or silver coin originally minted at Byzantium. **2** Heraldry a roundel or (i.e., a solid gold circle). [ME: from OFr. *besant*, from L. *Byzantius* 'Byzantine.']

bez·el /'bezəl/ ▶n. a grooved ring holding the glass or plastic cover of a watch face or other instrument in position. ■ a groove holding the crystal of a watch or the stone of a gem in its setting. [16th C.: from OFr.]

be·zique /bə'zēk/ ▶n. a trick-taking card game for two, played with a double pack of 64 cards, including the seven to ace only in each suit. ■ the holding of the queen of spades and the jack of diamonds in this game. [19th C.: from Fr. *bésigue*, perh. from Pers. *bāzīgar* 'juggler' or *bāzī* 'game.']

be·zoar /'bēzôr/ ▶n. a small stony concretion that may form in the stomachs of certain animals, esp. ruminants, and which was once used as an antidote for various ailments. [15th C.: from Fr. *bezoard*, based on Arab. *bāzahr, bādizahr*, from Pers. *pādzahr* 'antidote.']

b.f. ▶abbr. ■ Print. boldface. ■ board foot. ■ (also **b/f** or **B/F**) (in bookkeeping) brought forward.

BG (also **B Gen**) ▶abbr. brigadier general.

BGH ▶abbr. bovine growth hormone.

B-girl (also **bar girl**) ▶n. an attractive woman employed to encourage customers to buy drinks at a bar. [20th C.: alt. of *bar girl*.]

Bh ▶symb. the chemical element bohrium.

BHA ▶abbr. butylated hydroxyanisole, $C_{11}H_{16}O_2$, a synthetic antioxidant used to preserve fats and oils in food.

Bha·ga·vad·gi·ta /,bəgəvəd'gētə; ,bägəväd-/ (also **Gi·ta**) Hinduism a poem composed between the 2nd century BC and the 2nd century AD and incorporated into the Mahabharata. It stresses the importance of doing one's duty and of faith in God.

bhak·ti /'bəktē; 'bäk-/ ▶n. Hinduism devotional worship directed to one supreme deity, usually Vishnu (esp. in his incarnations as Rama and Krishna) or Shiva, by whose grace salvation may be attained by all regardless of sex, caste, or class. [Sanskrit.]

bhang /baNG/ (also **bang**) ▶n. the leaves and flowerheads of cannabis, used as a narcotic. [from Hindi *bhāṅg*.]

bhan·gra /'bäNGgrə/ ▶n. a type of popular music combining Punjabi folk traditions with Western pop music. [1960s: from Punjabi *bhāngrā*.]

Bha·rat /'bə-rət/ Hindi name for INDIA.

Bhav·na·gar /bou'nəgər/ a port in northwestern India, in Gujarat, on the Gulf of Cambay; pop. 401,000.

Bhn (also **BHN**) ▶abbr. Brinell hardness number.

Bhoj·pu·ri /,bōj'po͝orē/ ▶n. a Bihari language spoken in western Bihar and eastern Uttar Pradesh.

Bho·pal /bō'päl/ a city in central India, the capital of the state of Madhya Pradesh; pop. 1,604,000. In 1984, leakage of poisonous gas from a US-owned pesticide factory caused the deaths of about 2,500 people.

BHT ▶abbr. butylated hydroxytoluene, $C_{15}H_{24}O$, a synthetic antioxidant used to preserve fats and oils in foods, medicinal drugs, and cosmetics.

Bhu·ba·nes·war /,bo͞ovə'näsHwər/ a city in eastern India, capital of the state of Orissa; pop. 412,000.

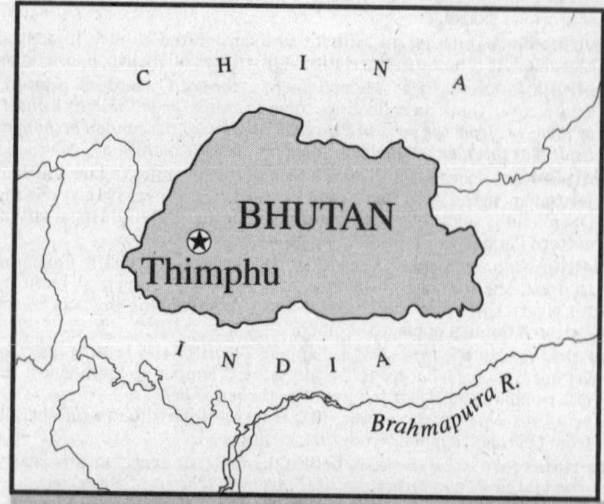

Bhutan

Official name: Kingdom of Bhutan
Location: southern Asia, on the southeastern slopes of the Himalayas
Area: 18,200 square miles (47,000 sq km)
Population: 810,000
Capital: Thimphu
Languages: Dzongkha (official), Nepali
Currency: ngultrum, Indian rupee

Bhu·tan /bo͞o'tän; -'tan/ a small independent kingdom in southern Asia. *See box.* —**Bhu·tan·ese** /,bo͞otn'ēz; -'ēs/ adj. & n.

Bhut·to[1] /'bo͞otō/, Benazir (1953–), prime minister of Pakistan 1988–90, 1993–96; daughter of Zulfikar Ali Bhutto. She was the first woman prime minister of a Muslim country.

Bhut·to[2], Zulfikar Ali (1928–79), president 1971–73 and prime minister 1973–77 of Pakistan. He was ousted by a military coup and executed.

BI ▶abbr. Block Island.

bi /bī/ ▶abbr. informal bisexual.

bi- (often **bin-** before a vowel) ▶comb. form two; having two: *bicolored* | *biathlon.* ■ occurring twice in every one: *biannual.* ■ occurring once in every two: *bicentennial* | *biennial.* ■ lasting for two: *biennial.* ■ doubly; in two ways: *biconcave.* ■ Chem. a substance having a double proportion of the radical, group, etc., indicated by the simple word: *bicarbonate.* ■ Bot. Zool. (of division and subdivision) twice over: *bipinnate.* [from L., earlier *dui-*, akin to Gk. *di-* 'two,' Sanskrit *dvi-* 'doubly.']

Bi ▶symb. the chemical element bismuth.

Bi·a·fra /bē'afrə; bī-/ a state proclaimed in 1967, when the Ibo people of Nigeria sought independence from the rest of the country. A civil war ensued, and by 1970 Biafra had ceased to exist. —**Bi·a·fran** adj. & n.

bi·a·ly /bē'älē/ ▶n. (pl. **-lys**) a flat bread roll topped with chopped onions. [20th C.: from *Bialystok*.]

Bia·ly·stok /'byäwi,stôk; -li-/ a city in northeastern Poland; pop. 270,568. Russian name BELOSTOK.

bi·an·nu·al /bī'anyo͞oəl/ ▶adj. occurring twice a year. Compare with BIENNIAL. —**bi·an·nu·al·ly** adv.

Biar·ritz /,bēə'rits; 'bēə,rits/ a city in southwestern France; pop. 28,890.

bi·as /'bīəs/ ▶n. **1** prejudice in favor of or against one thing, person, or group compared with another, usually in a way considered to be unfair: [in sing.] *a systematic **bias in favor of** the powerful.* ■ [in sing.] a concentration on or interest in one particular area or subject: *a discernible bias toward philosophy.* ■ Stat. a systematic distortion of a statistical result due to a factor not allowed for in its derivation. **2** an edge cut obliquely across the grain of a fabric. **3** in some sports, such as lawn bowling, the irregular shape given to a ball. ■ the oblique course that such a shape causes a ball to run. **4** Electron. a steady voltage, magnetic field, or other factor applied to an electronic system or device. ▶v. (**bi·ased, bi·as·ing** or **bi·assed, bi·as·sing**) **1** [trans.] (usu. **be biased**) show prejudice for or against (someone or something) unfairly: *the tests were **biased against** women* | [as adj.] (**biased**) *a biased view of the world.* ■ influence unfairly to invoke favoritism: *her story failed to bias the jury.* **2** give a bias to: *bias the ball.*
– PHRASES **cut on the bias** (of a fabric or garment) cut obliquely or diagonally across the grain. [16th C.: from Fr. *biais*, from Provençal, perh. based on Gk. *epikarsios* 'oblique.']

bi·as-cut ▶ adj. (of a garment or fabric) cut obliquely or diagonally across the grain.

bi·as-ply ▶ adj. (of a tire) having fabric layers with their threads running diagonally, crosswise to each other. Compare with RADIAL (sense 1).

bi·as tape (also **bias binding**) ▶ n. a narrow strip of fabric cut obliquely and used to bind edges.

bi·ath·lon /bīˈaTHlän/ ▶ n. an athletic contest combining two events, esp. cross-country skiing and rifle shooting. — **bi·ath·lete** /-lēt/ n. [1950s: from BI- + Gk. *athlon* 'contest.']

bi·ax·i·al /bīˈaksēəl/ ▶ adj. having or relating to two axes. ■ (of crystals) having two optic axes.

bib[1] /bib/ ▶ n. a piece of cloth or plastic fastened around the neck to keep clothes clean while eating. ■ the part above the waist of the front of an apron or overalls. ■ a loose-fitting, sleeveless garment. ■ a patch of color on the throat of a bird or other animal.
– PHRASES **one's best bib and tucker** informal one's finest clothes. [16th C.: prob. from BIB[2].]

bib[2] ▶ v. (**bibbed, bib·bing**) [with obj.] archaic drink (something alcoholic). [ME: prob. from L. *bibere* 'to drink.']

bibb let·tuce /bib/ (also **Bibb**) ▶ n. a butterhead lettuce that has crisp dark-green leaves. [19th C.: named after Jack *Bibb* (1789–1884), American horticulturalist.]

bib·cock /ˈbibˌkäk/ ▶ n. a faucet with a bent nozzle fixed at the end of a pipe. [18th C.: perh. from BIB[1] and COCK[1].]

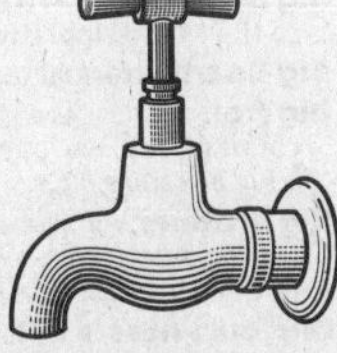
bibcock

bi·be·lot /ˈbib(ə)ˌlō/ ▶ n. a small, decorative ornament or trinket. [19th C.: from Fr., based on *bel* 'beautiful.']

bibl. (also **Bibl.**) ▶ abbr. biblical.

Bi·ble /ˈbībəl/ ▶ n. (**the Bible**) the Christian scriptures, consisting of the Old and New Testaments. ■ (**the Bible**) the Jewish scriptures, consisting of the Torah, the Prophets, and the Hagiographa. ■ (also **bible**) a copy of the Christian or Jewish scriptures. ■ a particular edition or translation of the Bible. ■ (**bible**) informal any authoritative book. ■ the scriptures of any religion. [ME: ult. from eccles. L. *biblia*, from Gk. *(ta) biblia* '(the) books,' from *biblion* 'book,' dimin. of *biblos* 'papyrus,' of Semitic origin.]

Bi·ble Belt ▶ n. (**the Bible Belt**) informal those areas of the southern and midwestern US and western Canada where Protestant fundamentalism is widely practiced.

Bi·ble-thump·ing ▶ adj. [attrib.] denoting a person who expounds or follows the teachings of the Bible in an aggressively evangelical way. — **Bi·ble-thump·er** n.

bib·li·cal /ˈbiblikəl/ (also **Bib·li·cal**) (abbr.: **bibl.** or **Bibl.**) ▶ adj. of, relating to, or contained in the Bible. ■ resembling the language or style of the Bible. ■ very great; on a large scale. — **bib·li·cal·ly** /-ik(ə)lē/ adv.

bib·li·cist /ˈbibləsist/ ▶ n. **1** one who is an expert in the Bible. **2** one who interprets the Bible literally. — **bib·li·cism** /-ˌsizəm/ n.

biblio- ▶ comb. form relating to a book or books: *bibliomania* | *bibliophile*. [from Gk. *biblion* 'book.']

bibliog. ▶ abbr. bibliography.

bib·li·og·ra·phy /ˌbiblēˈägrəfē/ (abbr.: **bibliog.**) ▶ n. (pl. **-phies**) a list of the books referred to in a scholarly work, usually printed as an appendix. ■ a list of the books of a specific author or publisher, or on a specific subject. ■ the history or systematic description of books, their authorship, printing, publication, editions, etc. ■ any book containing such information. — **bib·li·og·ra·pher** n. **bib·li·o·graph·ic** /-lēəˈgrafik/ adj. **bib·li·o·graph·i·cal** /-ˈgrafikəl/ adj. **bib·li·o·graph·i·cal·ly** /-lēəˈgrafik(ə)lē/ adv. [19th C.: from Fr. *bibliographie* or mod. L. *bibliographia*, from Gk. *biblion* 'book' + *-graphia* 'writing.']

bib·li·ol·a·try /ˌbiblēˈälətrē/ ▶ n. **1** an excessive adherence to the literal interpretation of the Bible. **2** an excessive love of books. — **bib·li·ol·at·er** /-ˈälətər/ n. **bib·li·ol·a·trous** /-ˈälətrəs/ adj.

bib·li·o·man·cy /ˈbiblēəˌmansē/ ▶ n. rare foretelling the future by interpreting a randomly chosen passage from a book, esp. the Bible.

bib·li·o·ma·ni·a /ˌbiblēəˈmānēə/ ▶ n. passionate enthusiasm for collecting and possessing books. — **bibli·o·ma·ni·ac** /-nēˌak/ n. & adj.

bib·li·o·phile /ˈbiblēəˌfīl/ ▶ n. a person who collects or has a great love of books. — **bib·li·o·phil·ic** /ˌbiblēəˈfilik/ adj. **bib·li·oph·i·ly** /ˌbiblēˈäfəlē/ n. [19th C.: from Fr., from Gk. *biblion* 'book' + *philos* 'loving.']

bib·li·o·pole /ˈbiblēəˌpōl/ ▶ n. archaic a person who buys and sells books, esp. rare ones. [18th C.: via L. from Gk. *bibliopōlēs*, from *biblion* 'book' + *pōlēs* 'seller.']

bib·li·o·the·ca /ˌbiblēəˈTHēkə/ ▶ n. (pl. **-cae** /-kē/ or **-cas**) a library. ■ a list of books in a catalog, esp. for use by a bookseller.

bib·li·ot·ics /ˌbiblēˈätiks/ ▶ plural n. [treated as sing.] the study of documents, handwriting, and writing materials to determine authenticity. — **bib·li·ot·ic** n. **bib·li·o·tist** /ˈbiblēətist/ n.

bib o·ver·alls ▶ plural n. another term for *OVERALLS* (see OVERALL).

bib·u·lous /ˈbibyələs/ ▶ adj. formal excessively fond of drinking alcohol. [17th C.: from L. *bibulus* 'freely drinking' (from *bibere* 'to drink.']

bi·cam·er·al /bīˈkamərəl/ ▶ adj. (of a legislative body) having two branches or chambers. — **bi·cam·er·al·ism** n. [19th C.: from BI- + L. *camera* 'chamber.']

bi·carb /bīˈkärb/ ▶ n. informal sodium bicarbonate.

bi·car·bo·nate /bīˈkärbəˌnāt; -nit/ ▶ n. Chem. a salt containing the anion HCO_3^-. ■ (also **bicarbonate of soda**) sodium bicarbonate.

bice /bīs/ (also **blue bice** or **bice blue**) ▶ n. a medium blue pigment made from basic copper carbonate. ■ the color of this. [ME: from OFr. *bis* 'dark gray.']

bi·cen·ten·ar·y /ˌbīsenˈtenərē/ ▶ n. & adj. another term for BICENTENNIAL.

bi·cen·ten·ni·al /ˌbīsenˈtenēəl/ ▶ n. (pl. **-ies**) the two-hundredth anniversary of a significant event. ▶ adj. [attrib.] of or relating to such an anniversary.

bi·ceph·a·lous /bīˈsefələs/ ▶ adj. having two heads. [19th C.: from BI- + Gk. *kephalē* 'head.']

bi·ceps /ˈbīseps/ ▶ n. (pl. same or **-ceps·es** /-sepsiz/) a muscle having two points of attachment at one end, in particular: ■ (also **bi·ceps bra·chi·i** /ˈbrākēˌī; -kēˌē; ˈbrak-/) the large muscle in the upper arm that turns the hand to face palm uppermost. ■ (also **bi·ceps fem·o·ris** /ˈfemərìs/) Anat. the muscle in the back of the thigh that helps to flex the leg. [17th C.: from L., lit. 'two-headed,' from *bi-* + *-ceps* (from *caput* 'head').]

Bi·chon Fri·sé /ˈbēsHän friˈzā; ˈfrēz; ˈbēsHôN frēˈzā/ (also **Bi·chon Fri·se**) ▶ n. (pl. **Bi·chons Fri·sés** pronunc. same) a small sturdy dog with a curly white coat and a tail that curves over its back.

Bichon Frisé

bi·chro·mate /bīˈkrōmāt/ ▶ adj. another term for DICHROMATE.

bi·cip·i·tal /bīˈsipitl/ ▶ adj. **1** two-headed. **2** of or relating to biceps.

bick·er /ˈbikər/ ▶ v. [intrans.] **1** argue about petty and trivial matters: *whenever the phone rings, they bicker over who must answer it* | [as n.] (**bickering**) *the constant bickering between Edgar and his mother.* **2** literary (of water) flow or fall with a gentle repetitive noise; patter: *the rain did beat and bicker.* ■ (of a flame or light) flash, gleam, or flicker. [ME: of unknown origin.]

bi·coast·al /bīˈkōstəl/ ▶ adj. of or relating to two coasts. ■ traveling frequently from one coast to the other. ■ located along both the east and west coasts.

bi·col·or /ˈbīˌkələr/ ▶ adj. having two colors. ▶ n. a bicolor blossom or animal. — **bi·col·ored** adj. & n.

bi·con·cave /bīˈkänˌkāv; ˌbīkänˈkāv/ ▶ adj. concave on both sides.

bi·con·vex /bīˈkänˌveks; ˌbīkänˈveks/ ▶ adj. convex on both sides.

bi·cul·tur·al /bīˈkəlCHərəl/ ▶ adj. having or combining the cultural attitudes and customs of two nations, peoples, or ethnic groups. — **bi·cul·tur·al·ism** n.

bi·cus·pid /bīˈkəspid/ ▶ adj. having two cusps or points. ▶ n. a tooth with two cusps. [19th C.: from BI- + L. *cuspis, cuspid-* 'point.']

bi·cus·pid valve ▶ n. Anat. another term for MITRAL VALVE.

bi·cy·cle /ˈbīsikəl/ ▶ n. a vehicle composed of two wheels held in a frame one behind the other, propelled by pedals and steered with handlebars attached to the front wheel. ▶ v. [intrans.] ride a bicycle in a particular direction: *bicycling around the island.* — **bi·cy·clist** /-siklist/ n. [19th C.: from BI- + Gk. *kuklos* 'wheel.']

bi·cy·clic /bīˈsīklik; -ˈsik-/ ▶ adj. Chem. having two rings of atoms in its molecule.

bid[1] /bid/ ▶ v. (**bid·ding**; past and past part. **bid**) [trans.] offer (a certain price) for something, esp. at an auction: *dealers bid a world record price for a snuff box* | [intrans.] *guests will **bid for** pieces of fine jewelry.* ■ [intrans.] (**bid for**) (of a contractor) offer to do (work) for a stated price; tender for: *nineteen companies have bid for the contract.* ■ [intrans.] (**bid for**) make an effort or attempt to achieve: *the two freshmen are bidding for places on the team.* ■ Bridge make a statement during the auction undertaking to make a certain number of tricks with a stated suit as trumps: *North bids four hearts* | [intrans.] *with this hand, South should not bid.* ▶ n. an offer of a price, esp. at an auction. ■ an offer to buy the shares of a company in order to gain control of it. ■ an offer to do work or supply goods at a stated price; a tender. ■ an attempt or effort to achieve something: [with infin.] *an investigation would be carried out **in a bid** to establish what had happened.* ■ Bridge an undertaking by a player in the auction to make a stated number of tricks with a stated suit as trumps. — **bid·der** n. [OE *bēodan* 'to offer,' of Gmc. origin; rel. to Ger. *bieten*.]

bid[2] ▶ v. (**bid·ding**; past **bid** or **bade** /bad; bād/; past part. **bid**) [trans.] **1** utter (a greeting or farewell) to: *a chance to bid farewell to their president.* **2** archaic or literary command or order (someone) to do something: *I did as he bade me.* ■ invite (someone) to do something.

– PHRASES **bid fair to** archaic or literary seem likely to: *the girl bade fair to be pretty.* [OE *biddan* 'ask,' of Gmc. origin; rel. to Ger. *bitten.*]

bid·da·ble /'bidəbəl/ ▶ **adj.** **1** meekly ready to accept and follow instructions; docile and obedient. **2** Bridge strong enough to justify a bid. — **bid·da·bil·i·ty** /ˌbidə'bilitē/ **n.**

bid·ding /'bidiNG/ ▶ **n.** **1** the offering of particular prices for something, esp. at an auction. ■ the offers made in such a situation. ■ (in bridge and whist) the action of stating before play how many tricks one intends to make. **2** the ordering or requesting of someone to do something.
– PHRASES **do someone's bidding** do what someone orders or requests, typically in a way considered overly slavish.

bid·ding pad·dle ▶ **n.** a paddle-shaped baton, usually marked with an identifying number, used to signal bids at auctions.

bid·dy /'bidē/ ▶ **n.** (pl. **-dies**) informal a woman, usually an elderly one, regarded as annoying or interfering. [17th C.: of unknown origin.]

bide /bīd/ ▶ **v.** [intrans.] archaic or dialect remain or stay somewhere: *how long must I bide here to wait?*
– PHRASES **bide one's time** wait quietly for a good opportunity to do something: *she bided her time, planning her escape.* [OE *bīdan*, of Gmc. origin.]

bi·det /bi'dā/ ▶ **n.** a low oval basin used for washing one's genital and anal area. [17th C.: from Fr., lit. 'pony,' from *bider* 'to trot.']

bi·don·ville /ˌbēdôN'vēl; bi'dôn,vēl/ ▶ **n.** a shanty town built of oil drums or other metal containers. [1950s: from Fr., from *bidon* 'container for liquids' + *ville* 'town.']

Bie·der·mei·er /'bēdər,mīər/ ▶ **adj.** denoting or relating to a style of furniture and interior decoration current in Germany 1815–48. [Gottlieb *Biedermeier*, German schoolmaster created by L. Eichrodt 1854.]

Bie·le·feld /'bēlə,feld/ a city in western Germany; pop. 322,130.

Bien Hoa /'byen 'hwä/ a city in southern Vietnam, north of Ho Chi Minh City; pop. 314,000.

biennale /ˌbē-en'älā/ ▶ **n.** a large art exhibition or music festival, usually one held biennially. [1930s: from Ital., lit. 'biennial.']

bi·en·ni·al /bī'enēəl/ ▶ **adj.** **1** taking place every other year. **2** (esp. of a plant) living or lasting for two years. ▶ **n.** **1** a plant that takes two years to grow from seed to fruition and die. Compare with ANNUAL, PERENNIAL. **2** an event taking place every two years. — **bi·en·ni·al·ly** **adv.** [17th C.: from L. *biennis* (from *bi-* 'twice' + *annus* 'year').]

bi·en·ni·um /bī'enēəm/ ▶ **n.** (pl. **-en·ni·ums** or **-en·ni·a** /-'enēə/) (usu. **the biennium**) a specified period of two years. [20th C.: from L., from *bi-* + *annus* 'year.']

bien pensant /ˌbyeN pän'säN/ ▶ **adj.** right-thinking; orthodox. ▶ **n.** (**bien-pensant**) a right-thinking or orthodox person. [Fr., from *bien* 'well' + *pensant*, pres. part. of *penser* 'think.']

bier /bi(ə)r/ ▶ **n.** a movable frame on which a coffin or a corpse is placed before burial or cremation or on which it is carried to the grave. [OE *bēr*, of Gmc. origin; rel. to Ger. *Bahre* and BEAR[1].]

bi·fa·cial /bī'fāsHəl/ ▶ **adj.** having two faces, in particular: ■ Bot. (of a leaf) having upper and lower surfaces that are structurally different. ■ Archaeol. (of a flint or other artifact) worked on both faces.

biff /bif/ informal ▶ **v.** [trans.] strike (someone) roughly or sharply, usually with the fist: *he biffed me on the nose.* ▶ **n.** a sharp blow with the fist. [19th C.: symbolic.]

bi·fid /'bīfid/ ▶ **adj.** Bot. Zool. (of a part of a plant or animal) divided by a deep cleft into two parts. [17th C.: from L. *bifidus*, from *bi-* 'doubly' + *fidus* (from *findere* 'to split').]

bi·fi·lar /bī'fīlər/ ▶ **adj.** consisting of or involving two threads or wires. [19th C.: from BI- + *filum* 'thread.']

bi·fla·gel·late /bī'flajəlit; -ˌlāt/ ▶ **adj.** having two flagella.

bi·fo·cal /'bī,fōkəl/ ▶ **adj.** (usually of a pair of eyeglasses) having lenses each with two focuses, one for distant vision and one for near vision. ▶ **n.** (**bifocals**) a pair of eyeglasses having two such parts.

bi·fold /'bī,fōld/ ▶ **adj.** double or twofold.

bi·func·tion·al /bī'fəNGksHənl/ ▶ **adj.** **1** having two functions. **2** Chem. having two highly reactive binding sites in each molecule.

bi·fur·cate ▶ **v.** /'bīfər,kāt/ divide into two branches or forks: [intrans.] *just below Cairo the river bifurcates* | [trans.] *the trail was bifurcated by a mountain stream.* ▶ **adj.** /bī'fərkāt; 'bīfərkit/ forked; branched. [17th C.: from med. L. *bifurcat-* 'divided into two forks,' from v. *bifurcare*, from L. *bifurcus* 'two-forked,' from *bi-* + *furca* 'fork.']

bi·fur·ca·tion /ˌbīfər'kāsHən/ ▶ **n.** the division of something into two branches or parts. ■ a thing divided in this way or either of the branches.

big /big/ ▶ **adj.** (**big·ger, big·gest**) **1** of considerable size, extent, or intensity. ■ [attrib.] of a large or the largest size. ■ grown up. ■ elder. ■ [attrib.] informal doing a specified action very often or on a very large scale. ■ informal on an ambitiously large scale. ■ informal popular or exciting interest among the public. ■ showing great enthusiasm. **2** of considerable importance or seriousness. ■ informal holding an important position or playing an influential role: *as a senior in college, he was a big man on campus.* **3** [predic.] informal, often ironic generous: *"I'm inclined to take pity on you." "That's big of you!"* ▶ **n.** (**the bigs**) informal the major league in a professional sport.
– PHRASES **big bucks** informal large amounts of money, esp. as pay or profit. **big idea** chiefly ironic a clever or important intention or scheme: *okay, what's the big idea?* **the big lie** a gross distortion or misrepresentation of the facts, esp. when used as a propaganda device by a politician or official body. **big screen** informal the movies. **big shot** informal an important or influential person. **big stick** informal the use or threat of force or power. **go over big** informal have a great effect; be a success. **in a big way** informal on a large scale; with great enthusiasm. **make it big** informal become very successful or famous. **talk big** informal talk confidently or boastfully. **think big** informal be ambitious. **too big for one's britches** (also **big noise**) informal conceited. — **big·gish** **adj.** **big·ness** **n.** [ME: of unknown origin.]

big·a·my /'bigəmē/ ▶ **n.** the act of marrying while already married to another person. — **big·a·mist** **n.** **big·a·mous** /-məs/ **adj.** [ME: from OFr. *bigamie*, from *bigame* 'bigamous,' from late L. *bigamus*, from *bi-* + Gk. *-gamos* 'married.']

Big Ap·ple nickname for New York City.

big band ▶ **n.** a large group of musicians playing jazz or dance music.

big bang (also **Big Bang**) ▶ **n.** Astron. the explosion of dense matter that, according to current cosmological theories, marked the origin of the universe.

Big Bear Lake a reservoir and recreational area in southern California, in the San Bernardino Mountains.

big beat ▶ **n.** popular music with a steady, prominent beat.

Big Ben the clock tower of the Houses of Parliament in London.

Big Bend Na·tion·al Park a US national park at a bend of the Rio Grande, in southern Texas, on the border with Mexico.

Big Black Riv·er a river in Mississippi that flows for 330 miles (530 km) to the Mississippi River.

Big Board informal term for the New York Stock Exchange.

big box ▶ **n.** [usu. as adj.] informal a very large store that sells goods at discount prices, esp. one specializing in a particular type of merchandise: *a big-box store.*

Big Broth·er ▶ **n.** informal a person or organization exercising total control over people's lives. — **Big Broth·er·ism** **n.** [1950s: after the head of state in Orwell's *Nineteen Eighty-four* (1949).]

big busi·ness ▶ **n.** large-scale or important financial or commercial activity.

big cat ▶ **n.** any of the large members of the cat family, including the lion, tiger, leopard, jaguar, snow leopard, clouded leopard, cheetah, and cougar.

Big Dip·per (also **big dipper**) ▶ **n.** a constellation of seven bright stars in Ursa Major (the Great Bear), containing the Pointers that indicate the direction to Polaris.

bi·gem·i·ny /bī'jemənē/ ▶ **n.** a cardiac rhythm in which each normal beat is followed by an abnormal one. — **bi·gem·i·nal** /-'jemənl/ **adj.**

bi·ge·ner·ic /ˌbījə'nerik/ ▶ **adj.** Bot. relating to or denoting a hybrid between two genera.

big·eye /'big,ī/ ▶ **n.** **1** (also **bigeye tuna**) a large migratory tuna (*Thunnus obesus*) that is very important to the commercial fishing industry. **2** a reddish, large-eyed fish (*Priacanthus arenatus*, family Priacanthidae) that lives in moderately deep waters of the tropical Atlantic and the western Indian Ocean.

Big·foot /'big,fo͝ot/ ▶ **n.** (pl. **-feet**) a large apelike creature resembling a yeti, supposedly found in northwestern America. Also called SASQUATCH. [from the size of its footprints.]

big game ▶ **n.** large animals hunted for sport: [as adj.] *a big-game hunter.*

big·gie /'bigē/ ▶ **n.** (pl. **-gies**) informal a big, important, or successful person or thing.

big·git·y /'bigitē/ (also **big·get·y**) ▶ **adj.** informal conceited, self-important, or boastful. ▶ **adv.** rudely; impudently.

big gun ▶ **n.** informal a powerful or influential person. ■ a significant or influential thing, esp. when presented as an ultimate means of persuasion.

big·head /'big,hed/ ▶ **n.** informal a conceited or arrogant person. — **big·head·ed** **adj.** **big·head·ed·ness** **n.**

big·heart·ed /'big,härtid/ ▶ **adj.** kind and generous.

big·horn /'big,hôrn/ (in full **American bighorn sheep**) ▶ **n.** a stocky brown North American wild sheep (*Ovis canadensis*) found esp. in the Rocky Mountains. Also called MOUNTAIN SHEEP.

bighorn (male)

Big·horn Moun·tains /'big,hôrn/ a range of the Rocky Mountains in Montana and Wyoming.

big house ▶ **n.** informal a prison.

bight /bīt/ ▶ **n.** a curve or recess in a coastline, river, or other geographical feature. ■ a loop of rope, as distinct from the rope's ends. [OE *byht* 'angle,' of Gmc. origin; rel. to BOW[2].]

Big Is·land a popular name for the island of HAWAII.

big league ▶ **n.** a group of teams in a professional sport, esp. baseball, competing for a championship at the highest level. ■ (**the big league**) informal a very successful or important group. — **big lea·guer** **n.**

big·mouth /'big,mouTH/ ▶ **n.** **1** informal an indiscreet or boastful person. **2** another term for LARGEMOUTH BASS (see BLACK BASS). — **big·mouthed** **adj.**

Big Mud·dy a popular name for the Missouri River.

big name ▸ **n.** informal a person who is famous in a certain sphere: *he's a big name in gymnastics.*

big·ot /ˈbigət/ ▸ **n.** a person who is bigoted. [16th C.: from Fr.]

big·ot·ed /ˈbigətid/ ▸ **adj.** obstinately convinced of the superiority or correctness of one's own opinions and prejudiced against those who hold different opinions. ■ expressing or characterized by prejudice and intolerance.

big·ot·ry /ˈbigətrē/ ▸ **n.** bigoted attitudes; intolerance toward those who hold different opinions from oneself.

big rig ▸ **n.** informal another term for TRACTOR-TRAILER.

big sci·ence ▸ **n.** informal scientific research that is expensive and involves large teams of scientists.

Big Sioux Riv·er a river in South Dakota and Iowa that flows to the Missouri River.

Big Spring a city in west Texas; pop. 23,093.

Big Sur /ˈsər/ a scenic locality in west central California, on the Pacific coast.

big tent ▸ **n.** used in reference to a political party's policy of permitting or encouraging a broad spectrum of views among its members.

big-tick·et ▸ **adj.** [attrib.] informal constituting a major expense.

big time informal ▸ **n.** (**the big time**) the highest or most successful level in a career, esp. in entertainment. ▸ **adv.** on a large scale; to a great extent: *they've messed up big time.* — **big-tim·er n.**

big top ▸ **n.** the main tent in a circus.

big tree ▸ **n.** another term for giant redwood (see REDWOOD).

big·wig /ˈbigˌwig/ ▸ **n.** informal an important person, usually in a particular sphere. Also called **big wheel**.

Bi·har /biˈhär/ a state in northeastern India; capital, Patna.

Bi·ha·ri /biˈhärē/ ▸ **n. 1** a native or inhabitant of Bihar. **2** a group of three related Indic languages, Bhojpuri, Maithili, and Magahi, spoken principally in Bihar. ▸ **adj.** of or relating to this people, their languages, or Bihar. [from Hindi *Bihārī*.]

bi·jou /ˈbēZHo͞o/ ▸ **adj.** (esp. of a residence or business establishment) small and elegant. ▸ **n.** (pl. **-joux** /-ZHo͞o(z)/) archaic a jewel or trinket. [Fr., from Breton *bizou* 'finger ring,' from *biz* 'finger.']

bi·jou·te·rie /bēˈZHo͞otərē/ ▸ **n.** jewelry or trinkets. [Fr., from BIJOU.]

bike /bīk/ informal ▸ **n.** a bicycle or motorcycle. ▸ **v.** [intrans.] ride a bicycle or motorcycle: *encourage people to bike to work.* [19th C.: abbrev.]

bik·er /ˈbīkər/ ▸ **n.** informal a motorcyclist. ■ a member of a motorcycle gang or club. ■ a cyclist.

bike·way /ˈbīkˌwā/ ▸ **n.** a path or lane for the use of bicycles.

Bi·ki·ni /biˈkēnē/ an atoll in the Marshall Islands, used by the US 1946–58 to test nuclear weapons.

bi·ki·ni /biˈkēnē/ ▸ **n.** (pl. **-nis**) a very brief two-piece swimsuit for women. ■ (also **bi·ki·nis**) scanty underpants. [1940s: named after BIKINI, where an atomic bomb was exploded in 1946 (because of the supposed 'explosive' effect created by the garment).]

bi·ki·ni line ▸ **n.** the area of skin around the edge of the bottom half of a bikini, used esp. with reference to the cosmetic removal of the pubic hair in this area.

bi·ki·ni wax ▸ **n.** an act of using hot wax to remove unwanted hair from around the bikini line.

Bi·kol /biˈkōl/ (also **Bi·col**) ▸ **n.** (pl. same or **-kols**) a member of an indigenous people of southeastern Luzon in the Philippines. ■ the Austronesian language of this people. ▸ **adj.** of or relating to this people or their language.

bi·la·bi·al /bīˈlābēəl/ ▸ **adj.** Phonet. (of a speech sound) formed by closure or near closure of the lips, as in *p, b, m, w*. ▸ **n.** a consonant sound made in such a way.

bi·lat·er·al /bīˈlatərəl/ ▸ **adj.** having or relating to two sides; affecting both sides. ■ involving two parties, usually countries. — **bi·lat·er·al·ly adv.**

bi·lat·er·al sym·me·try ▸ **n.** the property of being divisible into symmetrical halves on either side of a unique plane.

bi·lay·er /ˈbīˌlāər/ ▸ **n.** Biochem. a film two molecules thick (formed, e.g., by lipids).

Bil·ba·o /bilˈbou/ a city in northern Spain; pop. 372,200.

bil·ber·ry /ˈbilˌberē/ ▸ **n.** (pl. **-ries**) a hardy dwarf shrub (genus *Vaccinium*) of the heath family, closely related to the blueberry, with red drooping flowers and dark blue edible berries. ■ the small blue edible berry of this plant. [16th C.: prob. of Scand. origin; compare Dan. *bøllebær*.]

bil·bo /ˈbilbō/ ▸ **n.** (pl. **-bos** or **-boes**) a sword, noted for the temper and elasticity of its blade. [16th C.: from *Bilboa*, Engl. form of BILBAO.]

bil·boes /ˈbilbōz/ ▸ **plural n.** an iron bar with sliding shackles. [16th C.: of unknown origin.]

Bil·dungs·ro·man /ˈbildo͝oNGzrōˌmän; ˈbēldo͝oNGks-/ ▸ **n.** a novel dealing with a person's development or spiritual education. [Ger., from *Bildung* 'education' + *Roman* 'a novel.']

bile /bīl/ ▸ **n.** a bitter greenish-brown alkaline fluid that aids digestion and is secreted by the liver and stored in the gallbladder. ■ fig. anger; irritability. [16th C.: from Fr., from L. *bilis*.]

bile duct ▸ **n.** the duct that conveys bile from the liver and the gallbladder to the duodenum.

bi·lev·el /ˈbīˌlevəl/ (also **bi·lev·el**) ▸ **adj.** [attrib.] having or functioning on two levels; arranged on two planes. ■ denoting a style of two-story house in which the lower story is partially sunk below ground level, and the main entrance is between the two stories; split-level. ■ denoting a railroad passenger coach or a bus with seats on two levels. ▸ **n.** a bi-level house.

bilge /bilj/ ▸ **n.** the area on the outer surface of a ship's hull where the bottom curves to meet the vertical sides. ■ (**bilges**) the lowest internal portion of the hull. ■ fig., informal nonsense; rubbish. ▸ **v.** [trans.] archaic break a hole in the bilge of (a ship). [15th C.: prob. var. of BULGE.]

bilge keel ▸ **n.** each of a pair of plates or timbers fastened under the sides of the hull of a ship to provide lateral resistance to the water, prevent rolling, and support its weight in dry dock.

bil·har·zi·a /bilˈhärzēə/ ▸ **n.** a chronic disease, endemic in parts of Africa and South America, caused by infestation with blood flukes (schistosomes). Also called BILHARZIASIS or SCHISTOSOMIASIS. ■ the fluke (schistosome) itself. [19th C.: mod. L., after German physician T. *Bilharz* (1825–62).]

bil·har·zi·a·sis /ˌbilhärˈzīəsis/ ▸ **n.** Med. another term for BILHARZIA (the disease).

bil·i·ar·y /ˈbilēˌerē; ˈbilyərē/ ▸ **adj.** Med. of or relating to bile or the bile duct. [18th C.: from Fr. *biliaire*, from *bile* 'bile.']

bi·lin·e·ar /bīˈlinēər/ ▸ **adj.** Math. **1** rare of, relating to, or contained by two straight lines. **2** of, relating to, or denoting a function of two variables that is linear and homogeneous in both independently.

bi·lin·gual /bīˈliNGgwəl/ ▸ **adj.** (of a person) speaking two languages fluently. ■ (of a text or an activity) written or conducted in two languages. ■ (of a country, city, or other community) using two languages, esp. officially. ▸ **n.** a person fluent in two languages. — **bi·lin·gual·ism n.** [19th C.: from L. *bilinguis*, from *bi-* + *lingua* 'tongue.']

bil·ious /ˈbilyəs/ ▸ **adj.** affected by or associated with nausea or vomiting. ■ (of a color) lurid or sickly. ■ fig. spiteful; bad-tempered. ■ Physiol. of or relating to bile. — **bil·ious·ly adv. bil·ious·ness n.** [16th C.: from L. *biliosus*, from *bilis* 'bile.']

bil·i·ru·bin /ˈbiliˌro͞obin/ ▸ **n.** Biochem. an orange-yellow pigment formed in the liver. [19th C.: coined in Ger. from L. *bilis* 'bile' + *ruber* 'red.']

bil·i·ver·din /ˌbiləˈvərdn; ˈbiliˌvərdn/ ▸ **n.** Biochem. a green pigment excreted in bile.

bilk /bilk/ informal ▸ **v.** [trans.] **1** obtain or withhold money by deceit or without justification; cheat or defraud. ■ obtain (money) fraudulently. **2** archaic evade; elude. — **bilk·er n.** [17th C.: perh. a var. of BALK.]

bill[1] /bil/ ▸ **n. 1** an amount of money owed for goods supplied or services rendered, set out in a printed or written statement of charges: *the bill for their meal came to $17.* **2** a draft of a proposed law presented to a legislature for discussion. **3** a program of entertainment, esp. at a theater. **4** a banknote; a piece of paper money. **5** a poster or handbill. ▸ **v.** [trans.] **1** (usu. **be billed**) list (a person or event) in a program: *they were billed to appear but didn't show up.* ■ (**bill someone/something as**) describe someone or something in a particular, usually promotional, way, esp. as a means of advertisement: *he was billed as "the new Sean Connery."* **2** send a note of charges to (someone): [with two objs.] *he had been billed $3,000 for his license.* ■ charge (a sum of money): *we billed her $400,000.*

– PHRASES **fit** (or **fill**) **the bill** be suitable for a particular purpose. **foot** (or **pick up**) **the bill** see FOOT (sense 1 of the **verb**). — **bill·a·ble adj.** [ME: from Anglo-Norman Fr. *bille*, prob. based on med. L. *bulla* 'seal, sealed document.']

bill[2] ▸ **n.** the beak of a bird, esp. when it is slender, flattened, or weak, or belongs to a web-footed bird or a bird of the pigeon family. ■ the muzzle of a platypus. ■ the point of an anchor fluke. ■ a stiff brim at the front of a cap. ▸ **v.** [intrans.] (of birds, esp. doves) stroke bill with bill during courtship.

– PHRASES **bill and coo** informal exchange caresses or affectionate words; behave or talk in a loving way. — **billed adj.** [usu. in comb.] *the red-billed weaverbird.* [OE *bile*.]

bill[3] ▸ **n.** a medieval weapon like a halberd with a hook instead of a blade. [OE *bil*, of West Gmc. origin; rel. to Ger. *Bille* 'ax.']

bil·la·bong /ˈbiləˌbôNG/ ▸ **n.** Austral. a branch of a river forming a backwater or stagnant pool. [19th C.: from Wiradhuri *bilabang*, from *billa* 'water' + *bang* 'channel.']

bill·board /ˈbilˌbôrd/ ▸ **n.** a large outdoor board for displaying advertisements.

bill·bug /ˈbilˌbəg/ ▸ **n.** a typically large weevil (genus *Sphenophorus*, subfamily Rhynchophorinae, family Curculionidae) that feeds on various grasses and grains.

Bille·rica /bilˈrikə/ a town in northeastern Massachusetts; pop. 37,609.

bil·let[1] /ˈbilit/ ▸ **n.** a nonmilitary facility, where soldiers are lodged temporarily. ▸ **v.** (**-let·ed, -let·ing**) [with obj. and adverbial of place] (often **be billeted**) lodge (soldiers) in a particular place, esp. a civilian's house or other nonmilitary facility: *he didn't belong to the regiment billeted at the hotel.* [ME: from Anglo-Norman Fr. *billette*, dimin. of *bille* (see BILL[1]).]

bil·let[2] ▸ **n.** a thick piece of wood. ■ a small bar of metal for further processing. ■ Archit. each of a series of short cylindrical pieces inserted at intervals in decorative hollow moldings. ■ Heraldry a rectangle placed vertically as a charge. [ME: from OFr. *billette* and *billot*, diminutives of *bille* 'tree trunk,' from med. L. *billa, billus* 'branch.']

bil·let-doux /ˈbilā ˈdōō; ˈbēyā-/ ▶ **n.** (pl. **bil·lets-doux** pronunc. same or /-ˈdōōz/) dated or humorous a love letter. [17th C.: Fr., lit. 'sweet note.']

bill·fish /ˈbil,fisʜ/ ▶ **n.** (pl. same or **-fish·es**) a large, fast-swimming fish (family Istiophoridae) of open seas, with a streamlined body and a long, pointed spearlike snout. Its several species include the marlins, sailfish, and spearfishes.

bill·fold /ˈbil,fōld/ ▶ **n.** a thin wallet.

bill·hook /ˈbil,ho͝ok/ ▶ **n.** a tool with a sickle-shaped blade with a sharp inner edge, used for pruning or lopping branches or other vegetation.

bil·liard /ˈbilyərd/ ▶ **n. 1** (**billiards**) [usu. treated as sing.] a game usually for two people, played on a billiard table, in which three balls are struck with cues into pockets around the edge of the table. ■ (**billiard**) a game played on a billiard table with pockets, in which points are made by caroms, pocketing an object ball, or caroming the cue ball into a pocket. **2** a stroke in which the cue ball strikes two balls successively. [16th C.: from Fr. *billard*, dimin. of *bille* (see BILLET[2]).]

bill·ing /ˈbiliNG/ ▶ **n. 1** the action or fact of publicizing or being publicized in a particular way. ■ prominence in publicity, esp. as an indication of importance. **2** the process of making out or sending invoices. ■ the total amount of business conducted in a given time, esp. that of an advertising agency.

Bil·lings /ˈbiliNGz/ a city in south central Montana; pop. 89,847.

bil·lion /ˈbilyən/ ▶ **cardinal number** (pl. **-lions** or (with numeral or quantifying word) same) the number equivalent to the product of a thousand and a million; 1,000,000,000 or 109. ■ (**billions**) informal a very large number or amount of something. ■ a billion dollars (or pounds, etc.). — **bil·lionth** /-yənTH/ **ordinal number.** [17th C.: from Fr., from *bi-* + *(m)illion*.]

bil·lion·aire /ˈbilyə,ne(ə)r/ ▶ **n.** a person possessing assets worth at least a billion dollars (or pounds, etc.). [19th C.: from BILLION.]

bill of ex·change ▶ **n.** a written order to pay a sum of money on a given date to the drawer or to a named payee; a promissory note.

bill of fare ▶ **n.** dated a menu. ■ informal the selection of food available to or consumed by (a person or animal). ■ a program for a theatrical event.

bill of goods ▶ **n.** a consignment of merchandise.

– PHRASES **sell someone a bill of goods** deceive someone, usually by persuading them to accept something untrue or undesirable.

bill of health ▶ **n.** a certificate relating to the incidence of infectious disease on a ship or in the port from which it has sailed.

– PHRASES **a clean bill of health** a declaration or confirmation that someone is healthy or that something is in good condition.

bill of in·dict·ment ▶ **n.** a written accusation as presented to a grand jury.

bill of lad·ing ▶ **n.** a detailed list of a shipment of goods in the form of a receipt given by the carrier to the person consigning the goods.

Bill of Rights ▶ **n.** Law a statement of the rights of a class of people, in particular: ■ the first ten amendments to the US Constitution. ■ the English constitutional settlement of 1689.

bill of sale ▶ **n.** a certificate of transfer of personal property.

bil·lon /ˈbilən/ ▶ **n.** an alloy that contains gold or silver with copper or another base metal. [18th C.: from Fr., lit. 'bronze or copper money,' from *bille* (see BILLET[2]).]

bil·low /ˈbilō/ ▶ **n.** a large undulating mass of something, typically cloud, smoke, or steam. ■ archaic a large sea wave. ▶ **v.** [intrans.] (of fabric) fill with air and swell outward: *her dress* ***billowed out*** *around her.* ■ (of smoke, cloud, or steam) move or flow outward with an undulating motion. — **bil·low·y** /ˈbilō-ē/ **adj.** [16th C.: from ON *bylgja*.]

bil·ly /ˈbilē/ ▶ **n.** (pl. **-lies**) **1** short for BILLY GOAT. **2** (also **billy club**) a truncheon; a cudgel. [19th C.: from *Billy*, nickname for the name *William*.]

bil·ly goat ▶ **n.** a male goat.

Bil·ly the Kid see BONNEY.

bi·lobed /bīˈlōbd/ (also **bi·lo·bate** /-ˈlōbāt/) ▶ **adj.** having or consisting of two lobes.

bi·lo·ca·tion /,bīlōˈkāsʜən/ ▶ **n.** the supposed phenomenon of being in two places simultaneously.

Bi·loxi /biˈləksē; -ˈläksē/ a city in southeastern Mississippi, on the Gulf of Mexico; pop. 50,644.

bil·tong /ˈbil,tôNG/ ▶ **n.** esp. S. African lean meat that is salted and dried in strips. [Afrik., from Du. *bil* 'buttock' + *tong* 'tongue.']

bi·man·u·al /bīˈmanyo͞oəl/ ▶ **adj.** performed with both hands. — **bi·man·u·al·ly adv.**

bim·bo /ˈbimbō/ ▶ **n.** (pl. **-bos**) informal, derog. an attractive but empty-headed young woman, esp. one perceived as a willing sex object. — **bim·bette** /bimˈbet/ **n.** [20th C.: from Ital., lit. 'little child.']

bi·me·tal·lic /,bīməˈtalik/ ▶ **adj.** made or consisting of two metals. ■ hist. of or relating to bimetallism. [19th C.: from Fr. *bimétallique*, from *bi-* + *métallique* 'metallic.']

bi·met·al·lism /bīˈmetl,izəm/ ▶ **n.** hist. a system of allowing the unrestricted currency of two metals as legal tender at a fixed ratio to each other. — **bi·met·al·list n.**

bi·mil·le·nar·y /bīˈmilə,nerē ;/ ▶ **adj.** [attrib.] of or relating to a period of two thousand years or a two-thousandth anniversary. ▶ **n.** (pl. **-nar·ies**) a period of two thousand years or a two-thousandth anniversary.

Bim·i·ni /ˈbimənē/ (also **Biminis**) resort islands in the northwestern Bahamas. The legendary Fountain of Youth sought by Ponce de León was thought to be here.

bi·mod·al /bīˈmōdl/ ▶ **adj.** having or involving two modes, in particular (of a statistical distribution) having two maxima.

bi·mo·lec·u·lar /,bīməˈlekyələr/ ▶ **adj.** Chem. consisting of or involving two molecules.

bi·month·ly /bīˈmənTHlē/ ▶ **adj.** occurring or produced twice a month or every two months. ▶ **adv.** twice a month or every two months. ▶ **n.** (pl. **-lies**) a periodical produced twice a month or every two months.

bin /bin/ ▶ **n.** a receptacle for storing a specified substance. ■ a receptacle in which to deposit trash or recyclables. ■ Stat. each of a series of ranges of numerical value into which data are sorted in statistical analysis. ■ short for LOONY BIN. ▶ **v.** (**binned, bin·ning**) [trans.] place (something) in a bin. ■ Stat. group together (data) in bins. [OE *bin(n)*, *binne*, of Celtic origin; rel. to Welsh *ben* 'cart.']

bin- ▶ **prefix** var. of BI- before a vowel (as in *binaural*).

bi·na·ry /ˈbīnerē; -nərē/ ▶ **adj. 1** relating to, using, or expressed in a system of numerical notation that has 2 rather than 10 as a base. ■ in binary format. **2** relating to, composed of, or involving two things. ▶ **n.** (pl. **-ries**) **1** the binary system: binary notation. **2** something having two parts. ■ a binary star. [ME: from late L. *binarius*, from *bini* 'two together.']

bi·na·ry code ▶ **n.** Electron. a coding system using the binary digits 0 and 1 to represent a letter, digit, or other character in a computer or other electronic device.

bi·na·ry cod·ed dec·i·mal (abbr.: **BCD**) ▶ **n.** Electron. a system for coding a number in which each digit of a decimal number is represented individually by its binary equivalent. ■ a number represented in this way.

bi·na·ry dig·it ▶ **n.** one of two digits (0 or 1) in a binary system of notation.

bi·na·ry op·e·ra·tion ▶ **n.** a mathematical operation, such as addition or multiplication, performed on two elements of a set to derive a third element.

bi·na·ry star ▶ **n.** a system of two stars in which one star revolves around the other or both revolve around a common center.

bi·na·ry sys·tem ▶ **n. 1** a system in which information can be expressed by combinations of the digits 0 and 1. **2** a system consisting of two parts. ■ Astron. a star system containing two stars orbiting around each other.

bi·na·ry tree ▶ **n.** Comput. a data structure in which a record is linked to two successor records, usually referred to as the left branch when greater and the right when less than the previous record.

bi·nate /ˈbīnāt/ ▶ **adj.** Bot. growing in pairs. ■ composed of two equal parts. [19th C.: from mod. L. *binatus*, from L. *bini* 'two together.']

bi·na·tion·al /bīˈnasʜənl/ ▶ **adj.** concerning or consisting of two nations.

bin·au·ral /bīˈnôrəl; biˈnôr-/ ▶ **adj.** of, relating to, or used with both ears. ■ of or relating to sound recorded using two microphones and usually transmitted separately to the two ears of the listener.

bind /bīnd/ ▶ **v.** (past and past part. **bound**) [trans.] **1** tie or fasten (something) tightly. ■ restrain (someone) by the tying up of hands and feet. ■ wrap (something) tightly: *her hair was* ***bound up*** *in a towel.* ■ bandage (a wound). ■ (**be bound with**) (of an object) be encircled by something, typically metal bands, in order to strengthen it. ■ Ling. (of a rule or set of grammatical conditions) determine the relationship between (coreferential noun phrases). **2** cause (people) to feel that they belong together: *the comradeship that* ***bound*** *such a disparate bunch* ***together.*** ■ (**bind someone to**) cause someone to feel strongly attached to (a person or place). ■ cohere or cause to cohere in a single mass: [trans.] *with the protection of trees to* ***bind soil*** | | [intrans.] *clay is chiefly tiny soil particles that* ***bind together.*** ■ cause (ingredients) to cohere by adding another ingredient. ■ cause (painting pigments) to form a smooth medium by mixing them with oil. ■ hold by chemical bonding. ■ [intrans.] (**bind to**) combine with (a substance) through chemical bonding: *these proteins* ***bind to*** *calmodulin.* **3** formal impose a legal or contractual obligation on. ■ indenture (someone) as an apprentice: *he was* ***bound apprentice*** *at the age of sixteen.* ■ (**bind oneself**) formal make a contractual or enforceable undertaking. ■ secure (a contract), typically with a sum of money. ■ (**be bound by**) be hampered or constrained by. **4** fix together and enclose (the pages of a book) in a cover. **5** trim (the edge of a piece of material) with a decorative strip: *a ruffle with the edges* ***bound*** *in a contrasting color.* **6** Logic (of a quantifier) be applied to (a given variable) so that the variable falls within its scope. For example, in an expression of the form 'for every *x*, if *x* is a dog, *x* is an animal,' the universal quantifier is binding the variable *x*. ▶ **n. 1** a problematical situation. **2** formal a statutory constraint. **3** Brit. Music another term for TIE. **4** another term for BINE.

– PHRASES **bind someone hand and foot** see HAND.

– PHRASAL VERBS **bind off** cast off in knitting. **bind someone over** (usu. **be bound over**) (of a court of law) require someone to fulfill an obligation, typically by paying a sum of money as surety. [OE *bindan*, from Indo-Eur.; akin to Ger. *binden* and Sanskrit *bandh*.]

bind·er /ˈbīndər/ ▶ **n.** a thing or person that binds something, in particular: ■ a cover for holding loose sheets of paper, magazines, etc., together. ■ a substance that acts cohesively. ■ a reaping machine that binds grain into sheaves. ■ a bookbinder.

bind·er·y /ˈbīnd(ə)rē/ ▶ **n.** (pl. **-er·ies**) a workshop or factory in which books are bound.

bin·di /ˈbindē/ ▶ **n.** a decorative mark worn in the middle of the forehead by Indian women. [from Hindi *bindī*.]

bind·ing /ˈbīndiNG/ ▶ **n. 1** a strong covering holding the pages of a book together. ■ fabric used for binding material edges. **2** (also **ski binding**) Skiing a mechanical device fixed to a ski to grip a ski boot. **3** the action of fastening, holding together, or being linked by chemical bonds. ■ (in Chomskyan linguistics) the relationship between a referentially dependent form (such as a reflexive) and the independent noun phrase that determines its reference. ▶ **adj.** (of an agreement or promise) involving an obligation that cannot be broken.

bind·ing en·er·gy ▶ **n.** Physics the energy that holds a nucleus together.

bind·ing post ▶ **n.** Electron. a connector consisting of a threaded screw to which bare wires are attached and held in place by a nut.

bin·dle·stiff /ˈbindlˌstif/ ▶ **n.** informal a tramp or a hobo. [20th C.: prob. from an alt. of BUNDLE + STIFF.]

bind·weed /ˈbīndˌwēd/ ▶ **n.** a twining, often invasive plant (genera *Convolvulus* and *Calystegia*) of the morning glory family, with trumpet-shaped flowers.

bine /bīn/ ▶ **n.** a long flexible stem of a climbing plant, esp. the hop. [19th C.: dial. form of BIND.]

Bi·net /bəˈnā/, Alfred (1857–1911), French psychologist. With psychiatrist Théodore Simon (1873–1961), he was responsible for a pioneering system of intelligence tests.

Bi·net–Si·mon scale ▶ **n.** the measurement of intelligence by the application of a test (see BINET-SIMON TEST).

Bi·net–Si·mon test (also **Bi·net test**) ▶ **adj.** Psychol. a test used to measure intelligence, esp. that of children.

Bing /biNG/, Sir Rudolf (1902–97), British conductor; born in Austria. He was conductor and director of the Metropolitan Opera in New York City 1950–72.

bing /biNG/ ▶ **exclam.** indicating a sudden action or event: *Bing! They've hit you with something.* [19th C.: imitative.]

Bing cher·ry /biNG/ ▶ **n.** a heart-shaped, blackish-red cherry.

binge /binj/ informal ▶ **n.** a short period devoted to indulging in an activity, esp. drinking alcohol, to excess. ▶ **v.** (**bing·ing** or **binge·ing**) [intrans.] indulge in an activity, esp. eating, to excess: *some dieters say they cannot help binging on chocolate* | [as n.] (**binging**) *her secret binging and vomiting.* — **bing·er n.** [19th C.: of unknown origin.]

binge-eat·ing syn·drome ▶ **n.** see BULIMIA.

binge-purge syn·drome ▶ **n.** see BULIMIA.

Bing·ham /ˈbiNGəm/, George Caleb (1811–79), US painter. His paintings of the US frontier include *The Fur Traders Descending the Missouri* (1845).

Bing·ham·ton /ˈbiNGəmtən/ a city in south central New York, on the Susquehanna River; pop. 47,380.

bin·go /ˈbiNGgō/ ▶ **n.** a game in which players mark off numbers on cards as the numbers are drawn randomly by a caller, the winner being the first person to mark off five numbers in a row or another required pattern. ▶ **exclam.** used to express satisfaction or surprise. ■ a call by someone who wins a game of bingo. [1920s (interjection): of unknown origin.]

bin La·den /bin ˈlädn/, Osama (1957–), Saudi Arabian national and leader of the Islamist terrorist organization al Qaeda.

bin·na·cle /ˈbinəkəl/ ▶ **n.** housing for a ship's compass. [15th C.: from Sp. *bitácula, bitácora* or Port. *bitacola*, from L. ***habitaculum*** 'dwelling place,' from ***habitare*** 'inhabit.']

binnacle

bin·oc·u·lar /biˈnäkyələr/ ▶ **adj.** adapted for or using both eyes. [18th C.: from L. *bini* 'two together' + *oculus* 'eye.']

bin·oc·u·lars /biˈnäkyələrz/ ▶ **plural n.** an optical instrument with a lens for each eye, used for viewing distant objects.

bin·oc·u·lar vi·sion ▶ **n.** vision using two eyes with overlapping fields of view.

bi·no·mi·al /bīˈnōmēəl/ ▶ **n. 1** Math. an algebraic expression of the sum or the difference of two terms. **2** a two-part name, esp. the Latin name of a species of living organism (consisting of the genus followed by the specific epithet). **3** Gram. a noun phrase with two heads joined by a conjunction, in which the order is relatively fixed (as in *knife and fork*). ▶ **adj. 1** Math. consisting of two terms. ■ of or relating to a binomial or to the binomial theorem. **2** having or using two names, used esp. of the Latin name of a species of living organism. [16th C.: from Fr. *binôme* or mod. L. *binomium* (from *bi-* + Gk. *nomos* 'part, portion').]

bi·no·mi·al dis·tri·bu·tion ▶ **n.** Stat. a frequency distribution of the possible number of successful outcomes in a given number of trials in each of which there is the same probability of success.

bi·no·mi·al no·men·cla·ture ▶ **n.** Biol. the system of nomenclature using two terms, the first one indicating the genus and the second the species.

bi·no·mi·al the·o·rem ▶ **n.** a formula for finding any power of a binomial without multiplying at length.

bin·tu·rong /binˈto͝orôNG/ ▶ **n.** a tree-dwelling Asian civet (*Arctictis binturong*) with a coarse blackish coat and a muscular prehensile tail. [19th C.: from Malay.]

bi·nu·cle·ate /bīˈn(y)o͞oclēit; -ˌāt/ ▶ **adj.** having two nuclei.

bi·o /ˈbīō/ ▶ **n.** (pl. **-os**) informal **1** biology. **2** a biography. ▶ **adj.** informal **1** biological. **2** biographical.

bio- ▶ **comb. form** of or relating to life: *biosynthesis.* ■ biological; relating to biology: *biohazard.* ■ of living beings: *biogenesis.* [from Gk. *bios* 'human life.']

bi·o·ac·cu·mu·late /ˌbīōəˈkyo͞omyəˌlāt/ ▶ **v.** [intrans.] (of a substance) become concentrated inside the bodies of living things. — **bi·o·ac·cu·mu·la·tion** /-ˌkyo͞omyəˈlāSHən/ **n.**

bi·o·a·cou·stics /ˌbīōəˈko͞ostiks/ ▶ **plural n.** [treated as sing.] the branch of acoustics concerned with sounds produced by or affecting living organisms, esp. as relating to communication.

bi·o·ac·tive /ˌbīōˈaktiv/ ▶ **adj.** (of a substance) having a biological effect. — **bi·o·ac·tiv·i·ty** /-akˈtivitē/ **n.**

bi·o·as·say /ˌbīōəˈsā; -ˈasā/ ▶ **n.** measurement of the potency of a substance by its effect on living cells.

bi·o·as·tro·naut·ics /ˌbīōˌastrəˈnôtiks/ ▶ **n.** the study of the effects of space flight on living organisms.

bi·o·a·vail·a·bil·i·ty /ˌbīōəˌvāləˈbilitē/ ▶ **n.** Physiol. the proportion of a drug or other substance that enters the circulation when introduced into the body and so is able to have an active effect. — **bi·o·a·vail·a·ble** /-əˈvāləbəl/ **adj.**

bi·o·cat·a·lyst /ˌbīōˈkatl-ist/ ▶ **n.** a substance, such as an enzyme or hormone, that initiates or increases the rate of a chemical reaction. — **bi·o·cat·a·lyt·ic** /ˌbīōˌkatlˈitik/ **adj.**

bi·o·ce·no·sis /ˌbīōsiˈnōsis/ (also **bi·o·coe·no·sis**) ▶ **n.** (pl. **-ses** /-sēz/) Ecol. an association of different organisms forming an integrated community. [19th C.: mod. L., from BIO- + Gk. *koinōsis* 'sharing' (from *koinos* 'common').]

bi·o·cen·trism /ˌbīōˈsentrizəm/ ▶ **n.** the view or belief that the rights and needs of humans are not more important than those of other living things. — **bi·o·cen·tric adj. bi·o·cen·trist n.**

bi·o·chem·i·cal ox·y·gen de·mand /ˌbīōˈkemikəl/ (abbr.: **BOD**) ▶ **n.** the amount of oxygen dissolved in water necessary for microorganisms to decompose the organic matter in the water, used to measure pollution. Also called BIOLOGICAL OXYGEN DEMAND.

bi·o·chem·is·try /ˌbīōˈkeməstrē/ ▶ **n.** the branch of science concerned with the chemical and physicochemical processes that occur within living organisms. ■ processes of this kind. — **bi·o·chem·i·cal** /-ˈkemikəl/ **adj. bi·o·chem·i·cal·ly** /-ˈkemik(ə)lē/ **adv. bi·o·chem·ist** /-ˈkemist/ **n.**

bi·o·chip /ˈbīōˌCHip/ ▶ **n.** a microchip designed or intended to function in a biological environment, esp. inside a living organism. ■ a logical device analogous to the silicon chip, whose components are formed from biological molecules.

bi·o·cide /ˈbīəˌsīd/ ▶ **n. 1** a poisonous substance, esp. a pesticide. **2** the destruction of life. — **bi·o·cid·al** /ˌbīəˈsīdl/ **adj.**

bi·o·cli·ma·tol·o·gy /ˌbīōˌklīməˈtäləjē/ ▶ **n.** the study of climate in relation to living organisms. — **bi·o·cli·mat·o·log·i·cal** /-ˌklīmətlˈäjikəl/ **adj.**

bi·o·com·pat·i·ble /ˌbīōkəmˈpatəbəl/ ▶ **adj.** (esp. of materials used in surgical implants) not harmful to living tissue. — **bi·o·com·pat·i·bil·i·ty** /-ˌpatəˈbilitē/ **n.**

bi·o·com·put·ing /ˌbīōkəmˈpyo͞otiNG/ ▶ **n.** the design and construction of computers using biochemical components. ■ an approach to programming that seeks to emulate or model biological processes. ■ computing in a biological context or environment.

bi·o·con·trol /ˌbīōkənˈtrōl/ ▶ **n.** short for BIOLOGICAL CONTROL.

bi·o·con·ver·sion /ˌbīōkənˈvərZHən/ ▶ **n.** the conversion of organic matter into a source of energy through the action of microorganisms.

bi·o·de·grad·a·ble /ˌbīōdiˈgrādəbəl/ ▶ **adj.** (of a substance or object) capable of being decomposed by bacteria or other living organisms. — **bi·o·de·grad·a·bil·i·ty** /-ˌgrādəˈbilitē/ **n.**

bi·o·de·grade /ˌbīōdiˈgrād/ ▶ **v.** [intrans.] (of a substance or object) be decomposed by bacteria or other living organisms. — **bi·o·deg·ra·da·tion** /-ˌdegrəˈdāSHən/ **n.**

bi·o·di·ver·si·ty /ˌbīōdiˈvərsitē/ ▶ **n.** the variety of life in the world or in a particular habitat or ecosystem.

bi·o·dy·nam·ics /ˌbīōdīˈnamiks/ ▶ **plural n.** [treated as sing.] **1** the study of physical motion in living systems. **2** a method of organic farming involving such factors as the observation of lunar phases and planetary cycles and the use of incantations and ritual substances. — **bi·o·dy·nam·ic adj.**

bi·o·e·lec·tric /ˌbīō-iˈlektrik/ ▶ **adj.** of or relating to electrical phenomena produced within living organisms. — **bi·o·e·lec·tri·cal adj.**

bi·o·e·lec·tron·ics /ˌbīō-ilekˈträniks; -ˌēlek-/ ▶ **n.** the application of electronics in biological processes. — **bi·o·e·lec·tron·ic adj. bi·o·e·lec·tron·i·cal·ly** /-ik(ə)lē/ **adv.**

bi·o·en·er·get·ics /ˌbīōˌenərˈjetiks/ ▶ **plural n.** [treated as sing.] **1** the study of the transformation of energy in living organisms. **2** a system of alternative psychotherapy based on the belief that emotional healing can be aided through resolution of bodily tension. — **bi·o·en·er·get·ic adj.**

bi·o·en·gi·neer·ing /ˌbīōˌenjəˈni(ə)riNG/ ▶ **n. 1** another term for GENETIC ENGINEERING. **2** the use of artificial tissues, organs, or organ components to replace damaged or absent parts of the body. **3** the use in engineering or industry of biological organisms or processes. — **bi·o·en·gi·neer n. & v.**

bi·o·eth·ics /ˌbīōˈeTHiks/ ▶ **plural n.** [treated as sing.] the ethics of medical

PRONUNCIATION KEY ə *ago, up*; ər *over, fur*; a *hat*; ā *ate*; ä *car*; e *let*; ē *see*; i *fit*; ī *by*; NG *sing*; ō *go*; ô *law, for*; oi *toy*; o͝o *good*; o͞o *goo*; ou *out*; TH *thin*; T͟H *then*; ZH *vision*

and biological research. — **bi·o·eth·i·cal** /-'eTHikəl/ **adj.** **bi·o·eth·i·cist** /-'eTHəsist/ **n.**

bi·o·feed·back /ˌbīō'fēdˌbak/ ▶ **n.** the use of electronic monitoring of an automatic bodily function to train someone to acquire voluntary control of that function.

bi·o·film /'bīōˌfilm/ ▶ **n.** a thin, slimy film of bacteria that adheres to a surface.

bi·o·fla·vo·noid /ˌbīō'flāvəˌnoid/ ▶ **n.** any of a group of compounds occurring mainly in citrus fruits and black currants. Also called CITRIN. See also VITAMIN P.

bi·o·fu·el /'bīōˌfyo͞oəl/ ▶ **n.** a fuel derived directly from living matter.

bi·o·gas /'bīōˌgas/ ▶ **n.** gaseous fuel, esp. methane, produced by the fermentation of organic matter.

bi·o·gen·e·sis /ˌbīō'jenəsis/ ▶ **n.** the synthesis of substances by living organisms. ■ hist. the hypothesis that living matter arises only from other living matter. — **bi·o·ge·net·ic** /-jə'netik/ **adj.**

bi·o·ge·net·ic law /ˌbīōjə'netik/ ▶ **n.** the theory that evolutionary stages are repeated in the growth of a young animal.

bi·o·gen·ic /ˌbīō'jenik/ ▶ **adj.** [attrib.] produced or brought about by living organisms.

bi·o·ge·o·chem·i·cal /ˌbīōˌjēō'kemikəl/ ▶ **adj.** relating to or denoting the cycle in which chemical elements and simple substances are transferred between living systems and the environment. — **bi·o·ge·o·chem·ist** /-'kemist/ **n.** **bi·o·ge·o·chem·is·try** /-'kemәstrē/ **n.**

bi·o·ge·og·ra·phy /ˌbīōjē'ägrəfē/ ▶ **n.** the branch of biology that deals with the geographical distribution of plants and animals. — **bi·o·ge·og·ra·pher** **n.** **bi·o·ge·o·graph·ic** /-ˌjēə'grafik/ **adj.** **bi·o·ge·o·graph·i·cal** /-ˌjēə'grafikəl/ **adj.** **bi·o·ge·o·graph·i·cal·ly** /-ˌjēə'grafik(ə)lē/ **adv.**

bi·og·ra·phy /bī'ägrəfē/ ▶ **n.** (pl. **-phies**) an account of someone's life written by someone else. ■ writing of such a type as a branch of literature. ■ a human life in its course. — **bi·og·ra·pher** **n.** **bi·o·graph·ic** /ˌbīə'grafik/ **adj.** **bi·o·graph·i·cal** /ˌbīə'grafikəl/ **adj.** [17th C.: from Fr. *biographie* or mod. L. *biographia*, from med. Gk., from *bios* 'life' + *-graphia* 'writing.']

bi·o·haz·ard /'bīōˌhazərd/ ▶ **n.** a risk to human health or the environment arising from biological work.

Bi·o·ko /bē'ōkō/ an island in Equatorial Guinea, in the Gulf of Guinea. Malabo, the capital of Equatorial Guinea, is here. Formerly called Fernando Póo until 1973 and Macias Nguema 1973–79.

biol. ▶ **abbr.** ■ biological. ■ biologist. ■ biology.

bi·o·log·i·cal /ˌbīə'läjikəl/ (abbr.: **biol.**) ▶ **adj.** of or relating to biology or living organisms. ■ genetically related; related by blood. ■ containing enzymes to assist the process of cleaning. — **bi·o·log·i·cal·ly** /-ik(ə)lē/ **adv.**

bi·o·log·i·cal clock ▶ **n.** an innate mechanism that controls the physiological activities of an organism that change on a regular cycle.

bi·o·log·i·cal con·trol ▶ **n.** the control of a pest by the introduction of a natural enemy or predator.

bi·o·log·i·cal ox·y·gen de·mand (abbr.: **BOD**) ▶ **n.** another term for BIOCHEMICAL OXYGEN DEMAND.

bi·o·log·i·cal war·fare ▶ **n.** the use of toxins of biological origin or microorganisms as weapons of war.

bi·ol·o·gy /bī'äləjē/ (abbr.: **biol.**) ▶ **n.** the study of living organisms, divided into many specialized fields. ■ the plants and animals of a particular area. ■ the qualities of a particular organism or class of organisms. — **bi·ol·o·gist** /-jist/ **n.** [19th C.: coined in Ger., via Fr. from Gk. *bios* 'life.']

bi·o·lu·mi·nes·cence /ˌbīōˌlo͞omə'nesəns/ ▶ **n.** the biochemical emission of light by living organisms. ■ the light emitted in such a way. — **bi·o·lu·mi·nes·cent** /-'nesənt/ **adj.**

bi·o·mag·net·ism /ˌbīō'magniˌtizəm/ ▶ **n.** the interaction of living organisms with magnetic fields.

bi·o·mark·er /'bīōˌmärkər/ ▶ **n.** a naturally occurring molecule, gene, or characteristic by which a particular pathological or physiological process, disease, etc. can be identified.

bi·o·mass /'bīōˌmas/ ▶ **n.** the total quantity or weight of organisms in a given area or volume. ■ organic matter used as a fuel.

bi·o·ma·ter·i·al /ˌbīōmə'ti(ə)rēəl/ ▶ **n.** synthetic or natural material suitable for use in constructing artificial organs and prostheses or to replace bone or tissue.

bi·o·math·e·mat·ics /ˌbīōˌmaTHə'matiks/ ▶ **plural n.** [treated as sing.] the science of the application of mathematics to biology.

bi·ome /'bīˌōm/ ▶ **n.** Ecol. a large naturally occurring community of flora and fauna occupying a major habitat. [20th C.: from BIO- 'life' + -OME.]

bi·o·me·chan·ics /ˌbīōmə'kaniks/ ▶ **plural n.** [treated as sing.] the study of the mechanical laws relating to the movement or structure of living organisms.

bi·o·med·i·cal /ˌbīō'medikəl/ ▶ **adj.** of or relating to both biology and medicine. — **bi·o·med·i·cine** /-'medəsin/ **n.**

bi·o·me·te·or·ol·o·gy /ˌbīōˌmētēə'räləjē/ ▶ **n.** the study of the relationship between living organisms and weather. — **bi·o·me·te·o·ro·log·i·cal** /-ərə'läjikəl/ **adj.**

bi·o·met·rics /ˌbīō'metriks/ ▶ **n.** **1** another term for BIOMETRY. **2** another term for BIOSTATISTICS.

bi·o·met·ric sig·na·ture ▶ **n.** the unique pattern of a bodily feature such as the retina, fingerprint, or voice, encoded on an identity card and used for recognition and identification purposes.

bi·om·e·try /bī'ämitrē/ ▶ **n.** the application of statistical analysis to biological data. Also called BIOMETRICS. — **bi·o·met·ric** /ˌbīō'metrik/ **adj.** **bi·o·met·ri·cal** /ˌbīō'metrikəl/ **adj.** **bi·o·me·tri·cian** /ˌbīōmə'trisHən/ **n.**

bi·o·morph /'bīōˌmôrf/ ▶ **n.** a decorative form or object based on or resembling a living organism. ■ a graphical representation of an organism generated on a computer, used to model evolution. — **bi·o·mor·phic** /ˌbīō'môrfik/ **adj.**

bi·on·ic /bī'änik/ ▶ **adj.** having artificial body parts, esp. electromechanical ones. ■ informal having ordinary human powers increased by or as if by the aid of such devices (real or fictional). ■ of or relating to bionics. — **bi·on·i·cal·ly** /-ik(ə)lē/ **adv.** [1960s: from BIO-.]

bi·on·ics /bī'äniks/ ▶ **plural n.** [treated as sing.] the study of mechanical systems that function like living organisms or parts of living organisms.

bi·o·nom·ics /bīə'nämiks/ ▶ **plural n.** [treated as sing.] the study of the mode of life of organisms in their natural habitat and their adaptations to their surroundings; ecology. — **bi·o·nom·ic** **adj.** [19th C.: from BIO-.]

bi·o·phys·ics /ˌbīō'fiziks/ ▶ **plural n.** [treated as sing.] the science of the application of the laws of physics to biological phenomena. — **bi·o·phys·i·cal** /-'fizikəl/ **adj.** **bi·o·phys·i·cist** /-'fizəsist/ **n.**

biopic /'bīōˌpik/ ▶ **n.** informal a biographical movie. [1950s: blend of *biographical* and PIC.]

bi·o·pi·ra·cy /ˌbīō'pīrəsē/ ▶ **n.** bioprospecting that exploits plant and animal species by claiming patents to restrict their general use.

bi·o·pol·y·mer /ˌbīō'päləmər/ ▶ **n.** a polymeric substance occurring in living organisms, e.g., a protein, cellulose, or DNA.

bi·o·pros·pect·ing /ˌbīō'präspektiNG/ ▶ **n.** the search for plant and animal species from which medicinal drugs and other commercially valuable compounds can be obtained. — **bi·o·pros·pec·tor** /-'präspektər/ **n.** [1990s: from *bio(diversity) prospecting*.]

bi·op·sy /'bīäpsē/ ▶ **n.** (pl. **-sies**) an examination of tissue removed from a living body to discover the presence, cause, or extent of a disease. [19th C.: coined in Fr. from Gk. *bios* 'life' + *opsis* 'sight.']

bi·o·psy·chol·o·gy /ˌbīōsī'käləjē/ ▶ **n.** the branch of psychology concerned with its biological and physiological aspects.

bi·o·re·ac·tor /ˌbīōrē'aktər/ ▶ **n.** an apparatus in which a biological reaction or process is carried out.

bi·o·re·gion /'bīōˌrējən/ ▶ **n.** a region defined by characteristics of the natural environment rather than by man-made divisions. — **bi·o·re·gion·al** /ˌbīō'rējənl/ **adj.**

bi·o·rhythm /'bīōˌriT͟Həm/ ▶ **n.** a recurring cycle in the physiology or functioning of an organism, such as the daily cycle of sleeping and waking. ■ a cyclic pattern of physical, emotional, or mental activity said to occur in the life of a person. — **bi·o·rhyth·mic** /ˌbīō'riT͟Hmik/ **adj.**

BIOS /'bīōs/ ▶ **n.** Comput. a set of computer instructions in firmware that control input and output operations. [acronym from *Basic Input-Output System*.]

bi·o·sat·el·lite /ˌbīō'satlˌīt/ ▶ **n.** an artificial satellite that serves as an automated laboratory, conducting biological experiments on living organisms.

bi·o·sci·ence /'bīōˌsīəns/ ▶ **n.** any of the life sciences. — **bi·o·sci·en·tist** /ˌbīō'sīəntist/ **n.**

bi·o·se·cur·i·ty /ˌbīōsi'kyo͝oritē/ ▶ **n.** [often as adj.] procedures intended to protect humans or animals against disease or harmful biological agents: *biosecurity risks*.

bi·o·sen·sor /'bīōˌsensər/ ▶ **n.** a device that uses a living organism or biological molecules, esp. enzymes or antibodies, to detect the presence of chemicals.

bi·o·so·cial /ˌbīō'sōsHəl/ ▶ **adj.** of or relating to the interaction of biological and social factors.

bi·o·sphere /'bīəˌsfi(ə)r/ ▶ **n.** the regions of the surface and atmosphere of the earth or other planet occupied by living organisms. — **bi·o·spher·ic** /ˌbīə'sfi(ə)rik; -'sfer-/ **adj.** [19th C.: coined in Ger. from Gk. *bios* 'life' + *sphaira* (see SPHERE).]

bi·o·sta·tis·tics /ˌbīōstə'tistiks/ ▶ **plural n.** [treated as sing.] the branch of statistics that deals with data relating to living organisms. Also called BIOMETRICS. — **bi·o·sta·tis·ti·cal** /-tikəl/ **adj.** **bi·o·stat·is·ti·cian** /-ˌstatə'stisHən/ **n.**

bi·o·syn·the·sis /ˌbīō'sinTHəsis/ ▶ **n.** the production of complex molecules within living organisms or cells. — **bi·o·syn·thet·ic** /-sin'THetik/ **adj.**

bi·o·sys·tem·at·ics /ˌbīōˌsistə'matiks/ ▶ **plural n.** [treated as sing.] taxonomy based on the study of the genetic evolution of plant and animal populations. — **bi·o·sys·tem·a·tist** /-'sistəməˌtist/ **n.**

bi·o·ta /bī'ōtə/ ▶ **n.** Ecol. the animal and plant life of a particular region, habitat, or geological period. [20th C.: mod. L., from Gk. *biotē* 'life.']

bi·o·tech /ˌbīō'tek; 'bīōˌtek/ ▶ **n.** informal short for BIOTECHNOLOGY. ▶ **adj.** informal genetically modified: *biotech corn*.

bi·o·tech·nol·o·gy /ˌbīōtek'näləjē/ ▶ **n.** the exploitation of biological processes for industrial and other purposes.

bi·o·te·lem·e·try /ˌbīōtə'lemitrē/ ▶ **n.** the detection or measurement of human or animal physiological functions from a distance using a telemeter. — **bi·o·tel·e·me·tric** /-ˌtelə'metrik/ **adj.**

bi·o·ter·ror·ism /ˌbīō'terəˌrizəm/ ▶ **n.** terrorism involving the release of toxic biological agents.

bi·o·ther·a·py /ˌbīō'THerəpē/ ▶ **n.** (pl. **-pies**) the treatment of disease using substances obtained or derived from living organisms.

bi·ot·ic /bī'ätik/ ▶ **adj.** [attrib.] of, relating to, or resulting from living things, esp. in their ecological relations. [19th C.: from Fr. *biotique*, or via late L. from Gk. *biōtikos*, from *bios* 'life.']

bi·o·tin /'bīətin/ ▶ **n.** Biochem. a vitamin of the B complex, found in egg yolk, liver, and yeast. Also called VITAMIN H. [1930s: coined in Ger. from Gk. *bios* 'life.']

bi·o·tite /'bīə,tīt/ ▶ **n.** a black, dark brown, or greenish black micaceous mineral. [19th C.: named after J.-B. *Biot* (1774–1862), French mineralogist.]

bi·o·tope /'bīə,tōp/ ▶ **n.** Ecol. the region of a habitat associated with a particular ecological community. [1920s: from Ger. *Biotop*, based on Gk. *topos* 'place.']

bi·o·trans·for·ma·tion /,bīō,transfər'māshən/ ▶ **n.** the alteration of a substance within the body.

bi·o·type /'bīə,tīp/ ▶ **n.** a group of organisms having an identical genetic constitution.

bi·o·war·fare /,bīō'wôr,fe(ə)r/ ▶ **n.** biological warfare, including the use of toxins of biological origin or microorganisms as weapons of war.

bi·o·wea·pon /'bīō,wepən/ ▶ **n.** a harmful biological agent used as a weapon of war.

bi·par·ti·san /bī'pärtəzən/ ▶ **adj.** of or involving the agreement or cooperation of two political parties that usually oppose each other's policies. — **bi·par·ti·san·ship n.**

bi·par·tite /bī'pärtīt/ ▶ **adj.** involving or made by two separate parties. ■ tech. consisting of two parts: *a bipartite uterus.* [ME: from L. *bipartitus*, past part. of *bipartire*, from *bi-* + *partire* 'to part.']

bi·ped·al /bī'pedl/ ▶ **adj.** Zool. (of an animal) using only two legs for walking. — **bi·ped** /'bīped/ **n. & adj. bi·ped·al·ism** /bī'pedl,izəm/ **n. bi·pe·dal·i·ty** /,bīpi'dalitē/ **n.** [17th C.: from L. *bipes, biped-* (from *bi-* + *pes, ped-* 'foot').]

bi·phen·yl /bī'fenl/ ▶ **n.** Chem. an organic compound containing two phenyl groups bonded together.

bi·pin·nate /bī'pināt/ ▶ **adj.** Bot. (of a pinnate leaf) having leaflets that are further subdivided in a pinnate arrangement.

bi·plane /'bī,plān/ ▶ **n.** an early type of aircraft with two pairs of wings, one above the other.

biplane

bi·pod /'bī,päd/ ▶ **n.** a two-legged stand or support.

bi·po·lar /bī'pōlər/ ▶ **adj.** having or relating to two poles or extremities. ■ (of a plant or animal species) of or occurring in both polar regions. ■ (of a nerve cell) having two axons, one on either side of the cell body. ■ Electron. (of a transistor or other device) using both positive and negative charge carriers. — **bi·po·lar·i·ty** /,bīpō'laritē; -pə-/ **n.**

bi·po·lar dis·or·der ▶ **n.** a mental disorder marked by alternating periods of elation and depression. Also called (esp. formerly) MANIC DEPRESSION.

bi·ra·cial /bī'rāshəl/ ▶ **adj.** concerning or containing members of two racial groups.

bi·ra·mous /bī'rāməs/ ▶ **adj.** Zool. (esp. of crustacean limbs and antennae) dividing to form two branches. [19th C.: from BI- + RAMUS.]

birch /bərch/ ▶ **n.** **1** (also **birch tree**) a slender, fast-growing tree (genus *Betula*, family Betulaceae) that has thin bark (often peeling) and bears catkins. Birches grow chiefly in north temperate regions, some reaching the northern limit of tree growth. ■ (also **birch·wood**) the hard fine-grained pale wood of any of these trees. **2** (**the birch**) esp. hist. a punishment in which a person is flogged with a bundle of birch twigs. ▶ **v.** [trans.] esp. hist. beat (someone) with a bundle of birch twigs as a punishment. — **birch·en** /'bərchən/ **adj.** (archaic). [OE *bierce, birce*, of Gmc. origin; rel. to Ger. *Birke*.]

birch·bark /'bərch,bärk/ (also **birch bark**) ▶ **n.** the impervious bark of the North American paper birch, *Betula papyrifera*, used, esp. formerly by American Indians, to make canoes and containers. ■ a canoe of this material.

Birch·er /'bərchər/ ▶ **n.** a member or supporter of the John Birch Society, a conservative anticommunist American organization founded in 1958. [from the name of John *Birch*, a Baptist missionary and US Army Air Force officer, killed by Chinese communists in 1945.]

Bird /bərd/, Larry (1956–), US basketball player. He played forward for the Boston Celtics 1979–92.

bird /bərd/ ▶ **n.** **1** a warm-blooded egg-laying vertebrate (class Aves) distinguished by the possession of feathers, wings, and a beak and (typically) by being able to fly. ■ an animal of this type that is hunted for sport or used for food. ■ a clay pigeon. ■ informal an aircraft, spacecraft, satellite, or guided missile. **2** [usu. with adj.] informal a person of a specified kind or character: *I'm a pretty tough old bird.* ■ Brit., informal a young woman; a girlfriend.

– PHRASES **a bird in the hand is worth two in the bush** proverb it's better to be content with what you have than to risk losing everything by seeking to get more. **the birds and the bees** basic facts about sex and reproduction, as told to a child. **birds of a feather flock together** proverb people of the same sort or with the same tastes and interests will be found together. **eat like a bird** see EAT. **flip someone the bird** stick one's middle finger up at someone as a sign of contempt or anger. **(strictly) for the birds** informal not worth consideration; unimportant: *this piece of legislation is for the birds.* **give someone the bird** see FLIP SOMEONE THE BIRD. **have a bird** informal be very shocked or agitated. **a little bird told me** humorous used to say that the speaker knows something but prefers to keep the identity of the informant a secret. [OE *brid* 'chick.']

bird·bath /'bərd,bath/ ▶ **n.** a small basin filled with water for birds to bathe in.

bird·brain /'bərd,brān/ ▶ **n.** informal an annoyingly stupid and shallow person. — **bird·brained adj.**

bird·cage /'bərd,kāj/ ▶ **n.** a cage for pet birds. ■ an object resembling such a cage: *the elevator was an elegant and gilded birdcage.*

bird call ▶ **n.** a note uttered by a bird. ■ an instrument imitating such a sound.

bird cher·ry ▶ **n.** a small wild cherry tree or shrub with bitter black fruit, including the North American **pin cherry** (*Prunus pensylvanica*).

bird colo·nel ▶ **n.** informal a full colonel. [20th C.; from the silver eagle indicating the rank of full colonel.]

bird dog ▶ **n.** a gun dog trained to retrieve birds. ■ informal a person whose job involves searching. ▶ **v.** (**bird-dog**) [trans.] search out or pursue with dogged determination.

bird·er /'bərdər/ ▶ **n.** informal a bird-watcher.

bird flu ▶ **n.** an often fatal flu virus (family Orthomyxoviridae) of birds, esp. poultry, that is transmissible from them to humans, in whom it may also prove fatal.

bird·house /'bərd,hous/ ▶ **n.** a box, usually resembling a house, for a bird to make its nest in.

bird·ie /'bərdē/ ▶ **n.** (pl. **bird·ies**) **1** informal a little bird. **2** Golf a score of one stroke under par at a hole. ▶ **v.** (**bird·ie·ing**) Golf [trans.] play (a hole) with a score of one stroke under par: *she wound up birdieing the hole.*

bird·ing /'bərding/ ▶ **n.** the observation of birds in their natural habitats as a hobby.

bird·lime /'bərd,līm/ ▶ **n.** a sticky substance spread on twigs to trap small birds. ▶ **v.** spread with birdlime: *he birdlimed the branch.* ■ catch or trap with birdlime. ■ fig. entrap by clever deception; inveigle.

bird of par·a·dise ▶ **n.** **1** (pl. **birds of par·a·dise**) a tropical Australasian bird (family Paradisaeidae), the male of which is noted for the beauty and brilliance of its plumage and its spectacular courtship display. **2** (also **bird of paradise flower**) a southern African plant (genus *Strelitzia*, family Strelitziaceae), related to the banana. It bears a showy irregular flower with a long projecting tongue.

bird of pas·sage ▶ **n.** dated a migratory bird. ■ a person who does not stay anywhere for long.

bird of prey ▶ **n.** a predatory bird, distinguished by a hooked bill and sharp talons and belonging to the order Falconiformes (the diurnal birds of prey) or Strigiformes (the owls); a raptor.

bird pep·per ▶ **n.** a tropical American pepper (*Capsicum annuum* var. *glabriusculum*, or *C. frutescens* var. *typicum*), thought to be the ancestor of both sweet and chili peppers. ■ the small, red, very hot fruit of this plant. ■ a variety of small hot pepper grown in Asia or Africa.

bird·seed /'bərd,sēd/ ▶ **n.** any seed for feeding birds.

Birds·eye /'bərdz,ī/, Clarence (1886–1956), US inventor whose process of rapidly freezing foods in small packages revolutionized eating habits.

bird's-eye /'bərdz,ī/ ▶ **n.** **1** [usu. as adj.] any of a number of plants with small flowers that have contrasting petals and centers, in particular the **bird's-eye primrose** (*Primula farinosa*) and the **bird's-eye speedwell** (another term for GERMANDER SPEEDWELL). **2** (also **bird's-eye primrose**) a small, very hot chili pepper. **3** a small geometric pattern woven with a dot in the center, typically used in suiting and lining fabrics.

bird's-eye ma·ple ▶ **n.** the lumber from an American maple that contains eyelike markings.

bird's-eye view ▶ **n.** a general view from above. ■ a general view as if from above. ■ a broad, general, or superficial consideration (of something).

bird's-foot tre·foil (also **birds·foot tre·foil**) ▶ **n.** a small trifoliate plant (*Lotus corniculatus*) of the pea family with red-streaked yellow flowers and triple pods that resemble the feet of a bird.

bird·shot /'bərd,shät/ ▶ **n.** the smallest size of shot for sporting rifles or other guns.

bird's-nest ▶ **n.** **1** a North American brownish or yellowish flowering saprophytic plant (*Pterospora andromeda*) of the wintergreen family, with scalelike leaves and a lack of chlorophyll. **2** (also **bird's-nest fungus**) a fungus (family Nidulariaceae, class Basidiomycetes) of worldwide distribution that grows on dead wood and other plant debris. Its bowl-shaped fruiting body opens to reveal egg-shaped organs containing the spores.

bird·song /'bərd,sông/ ▶ **n.** the musical vocalizations of a bird, typically uttered by a male songbird in characteristic bursts or phrases for territorial purposes.

bird-watch·er (also **bird·watch·er**) ▶ **n.** a person who observes birds in their natural surroundings. — **bird-watch·ing n.**

Bird Wom·an see SACAJAWEA.

bi·re·frin·gent /,bīri'frinjənt/ ▶ **adj.** Physics having two different refractive indices. ■ Optics of or relating to optically anisotropic material. — **bi·re·frin·gence n.**

bi·reme /ˈbīˌrēm/ ▸ n. an ancient warship with two files of oarsmen on each side. [16th C.: from L. *biremis*, from *bi-* + *remus* 'oar.']

bi·ret·ta /bəˈretə/ (also **be·ret·ta**) ▸ n. a square cap with three flat projections on top, worn by Roman Catholic clergymen. [16th C.: from Ital. *berretta* or Sp. *birreta*, based on late L. *birrus* 'hooded cape.']

Bir·git·ta, St. /birˈgitə/ see BRIDGET, ST.[2]

Bir·ken·head /ˈbərkənˌhed/ a town in northwestern England, opposite Liverpool; pop. 116,000.

Bir·man /ˈbərmən/ ▸ n. a cat of a long-haired breed, typically with a cream body, a dark head, tail, and legs, and white paws.

Bir·ming·ham 1 /ˈbərmiNGəm/ a city in west central England; pop. 934,900. **2** /ˈbərmiNGˌham/ a city in north central Alabama; pop. 242,820.

birr /bər/ ▸ n. the basic monetary unit of Ethiopia, equal to 100 cents.

birth /bərTH/ ▸ n. the emergence of a baby or other young from the body of its mother; the start of life as a physically separate being. ■ a baby born. ■ the beginning or coming into existence of something. ■ origin, descent, or ancestry. ■ high or noble descent. ▸ v. [trans.] informal give birth to (a baby or other young): *she had carried him and birthed him* | [intrans.] *in spring the cows birthed.*
– PHRASES **give birth** bear a child or young. [ME: from ON *byrth*; rel. to BEAR[1].]

birth ca·nal ▸ n. the passageway from the womb through which a fetus passes during birth.

birth cer·tif·i·cate ▸ n. an official document issued to record a person's birth.

birth con·trol ▸ n. the practice of preventing unwanted pregnancies, typically by use of contraception.

birth con·trol pill ▸ n. a contraceptive pill.

birth·day /ˈbərTHˌdā/ ▸ n. the annual anniversary of the day on which a person was born. ■ the day of one's birth: *she shares a birthday with Paul McCartney.* ■ the anniversary of something starting or being founded.
– PHRASES **in one's birthday suit** humorous naked.

birth de·fect ▸ n. a physical, mental, or biochemical abnormality that is present at birth.

birth fam·i·ly ▸ n. one's biological parents and siblings, as opposed to adoptive relatives.

birth·ing /ˈbərTHiNG/ ▸ n. the action or process of giving birth.

birth·ing room ▸ n. a room in a hospital or other medical facility that is equipped for labor and childbirth and is designed to be comfortable and homelike.

birth·mark /ˈbərTHˌmärk/ ▸ n. a typically permanent brown or red mark on one's body from birth.

birth pang ▸ n. [usu. in pl.] another term for LABOR PAIN.

birth par·ent ▸ n. a biological as opposed to an adoptive parent.

birth·place /ˈbərTHˌplās/ ▸ n. the place where a person was born. ■ the place where something started or originated.

birth rate ▸ n. the number of live births per thousand of population per year.

birth·right /ˈbərTHˌrīt/ ▸ n. a particular right of possession or privilege one has from birth. ■ the possession or privilege itself. ■ a natural or moral right, possessed by everyone.

birth·stone /ˈbərTHˌstōn/ ▸ n. a gemstone popularly associated with the month or astrological sign of birth.

birth·weight /ˈbərTHˌwāt/ ▸ n. a baby's weight at birth.

birth·wort /ˈbərTHˌwərt; -ˌwôrt/ ▸ n. a climbing or herbaceous plant (genus *Aristolochia*, family Aristolochiaceae) that typically has heart-shaped leaves and deep-throated, often pipe-shaped, flowers. It was formerly used as an aid to childbirth and to induce abortion.

bis /bis/ ▸ adv. again, as a direction in a musical score indicating that a passage is to be repeated. [via Fr. and Ital. from L., lit. 'twice.']

bis- ▸ comb. form Chem. used to form the names of compounds containing two groups identically substituted or coordinated: *bis(2-aminoethyl) ether.*

Bis·cay, Bay of /ˈbisˌkā/ a part of the North Atlantic Ocean between the northern coast of Spain and the western coast of France.

Bis·cayne Bay /bisˈkān/ an inlet of the Atlantic Ocean in southeastern Florida.

bis·cot·ti /biˈskätē/ ▸ plural n. small, crisp rectangular twice-baked cookies made originally in Italy.

bis·cuit /ˈbiskit/ ▸ n. **1** a small, typically round cake of bread leavened with baking powder, baking soda, or sometimes yeast. ■ Brit. a cookie or cracker. **2** another term for BISQUE[3]. **3** a light brown color. **4** a small flat piece of wood used to join two mortised planks together. ▸ adj. light brown in color. — **bis·cuit·y** adj. [ME: from OFr. *bescuit*, based on L. *bis* 'twice' + *coctus*, past part. of *coquere* 'to cook' (because biscuits were orig. cooked in a twofold process: first baked and then dried out in a slow oven).]

bi·sect /bīˈsekt; ˈbīˌsekt/ ▸ v. [trans.] divide into two parts. ■ Geom. divide (a line, angle, shape, etc.) into two equal parts. — **bi·sec·tion** /bīˈsekSHən/ n. **bi·sec·tor** /bīˈsektər; ˈbīˌsek-/ n. [17th C.: from BI- + L. *sect-* (from *secare* 'to cut').]

bi·sex·u·al /bīˈsekSHo͞oəl/ ▸ adj. sexually attracted to both men and women. ■ Biol. having characteristics of both sexes. ▸ n. a person who is sexually attracted to both men and women. — **bi·sex·u·al·i·ty** /ˌbīsekSHo͞oˈalitē/ n.

Bish·kek /bisHˈkek/ the capital of Kyrgyzstan; pop. 625,000. Former name (until 1926) PISHPEK and (1926–91) FRUNZE.

Bish·op /ˈbisHəp/, Elizabeth (1911–79), US poet. Her poetry is collected in *North and South* (1946) and *A Cold Spring* (1955).

bish·op /ˈbisHəp/ ▸ n. **1** a senior member of the Christian clergy, typically in charge of a diocese and empowered to confer holy orders. **2** (also **bishop bird**) an African weaverbird (genus *Euplectes*), the male of which has red, orange, yellow, or black plumage. **3** a chess piece, typically with its top shaped like a miter, that can move in any direction along a diagonal on which it stands. **4** mulled and spiced wine. [OE *biscop, bisceop*, based on Gk. *episkopos* 'overseer,' from *epi* 'above' + *-skopos* '-looking.']

bish·op·ric /ˈbisHəprik/ ▸ n. the office or rank of a bishop. ■ a district under a bishop's control; a diocese. [OE *bisceoprīce*, from *bisceop* (see BISHOP) + *rīce* 'realm.']

Bis·la·ma /bisˈlämə/ ▸ n. an English-based pidgin language used as a lingua franca in Fiji and the Solomon Islands and as an official language in Vanuatu. Also called BEACH-LA-MAR. [alt. of Port. *bicho do mar* 'sea cucumber'(traded as a commodity, the word later being applied to the language of trade).]

Bis·marck[1] /ˈbizˌmärk/ the capital of North Dakota, in the south central part of the state; pop. 55,532.

Bis·marck[2] /ˈbizmärk; ˈbis-/, Otto Eduard Leopold von, Prince of Bismarck, Duke of Lauenburg (1815–98), Prussian chancellor of the German Empire 1871–90; also known as the **Iron Chancellor**. He was the driving force behind the unification of Germany.

Bis·marck Archipelago an island group in the western Pacific Ocean, part of Papua New Guinea. It includes New Britain, New Ireland, and several hundred other islands.

Bis·marck Sea an arm of the Pacific Ocean, northeast of New Guinea and north of New Britain. In 1943, the US destroyed a large Japanese naval force here.

bis·muth /ˈbizməTH/ ▸ n. the chemical element of atomic number 83, a brittle reddish-gray metal. (Symbol: **Bi**) ■ a compound of this element used medicinally. [17th C.: from mod. L. *bisemutum*, Latinization of Ger. *Wismut*.]

bi·son /ˈbīsən; -zən/ ▸ n. (pl. same) a humpbacked shaggy-haired wild ox (genus *Bison*) native to North America (*B. bison*) and Europe (*B. bonasus*). [ME: from L., ult. of Gmc. origin and rel. to WISENT.]

bisque[1] /bisk/ ▸ n. a rich, creamy soup typically made with shellfish, esp. lobster. [17th C.: Fr., lit. 'crayfish soup.']

bisque[2] ▸ n. an extra turn, point, or stroke allowed to a weaker player in croquet or court tennis. [17th C.: from Fr.]

bisque[3] ▸ n. **1** fired unglazed pottery. **2** a light brown color. ▸ adj. light brown in color.

Bis·sau /biˈsou/ the capital of Guinea-Bissau, in the western part of the country; pop. 125,000.

bi·sta·ble /bīˈstābəl/ ▸ n. an electronic circuit that has two stable states. ▸ adj. (of a system) having two stable states.

bis·ter /ˈbistər/ (also **bis·tre**) ▸ n. a brownish-yellowish pigment made from the soot of burned wood. ■ the color of this pigment. [18th C.: from Fr. *bistre*.]

bis·tort /ˈbistôrt/ ▸ n. a Eurasian herbaceous plant (genus *Polygonum*) of the dock family, with a spike of flesh-colored flowers and twisted root that is used medicinally. [16th C.: from Fr. *bistorte* or med. L. *bistorta*, from *bis* 'twice' + *torta* (fem. past part. of *torquere* 'to twist').]

bis·tou·ry /ˈbistərē/ ▸ n. (pl. **-ries**) a surgical knife with a long, narrow, straight or curved blade. [18th C.: from Fr. *bistouri*, orig. *bistorie* 'dagger.']

bis·tro /ˈbistrō; ˈbē-/ ▸ n. (pl. **-tros**) a small restaurant. [1920s: Fr.]

bi·sul·fate /bīˈsəlfāt/ (esp. Brit. also **bi·sul·phate**) ▸ n. Chem. a salt of the anion HSO_4^-.

bi·sul·fide /bīˈsəlfīd/ (esp. Brit. **bi·sul·phide**) ▸ n. another term for DISULFIDE.

bi·sul·fite /bīˈsəlfīt/ (esp. Brit. also **bi·sul·phite**) ▸ n. an acid sulfite containing the radical HSO_3.

bit[1] /bit/ ▸ n. **1** a small piece, part, or quantity of something. ■ (**a bit**) a fair amount. ■ (**a bit**) a short time or distance. ■ [with adj.] informal a set of actions or ideas associated with a specific group or activity: *she's gone off to do her theatrical bit.* **2** informal a unit of 12½ cents (used only in even multiples): *two bits was the going price for a softball.*
– PHRASES **a bit** somewhat; to some extent. **bit by bit** gradually. **a bit of a —** used to suggest that something is not severe or extreme, or is true only to a limited extent. ■ only a little —; a mere —: *we went on a bit of a walk.* **bits and pieces** an assortment of small items. **do one's bit** informal make a useful contribution to an effort or cause. **every bit as** see EVERY. **not a bit** not at all. **to bits 1** into pieces. **2** informal very much; to a great degree. [OE *bita* 'bite, mouthful,' of Gmc. origin; rel. to Ger. *Bissen* and BITE.]

bit[2] past of BITE.

bit[3] ▸ n. **1** a mouthpiece, typically made of metal, that is attached to a bridle and used to control a horse. **2** a tool or piece for boring or drilling. ■ the cutting or gripping part of a plane, pliers, or other tool. ■ the part of a key that engages with the lock lever. ■ the copper head of a soldering iron. ▸ v. [trans.] put a bit

bit[3] 2

into the mouth of (a horse). — **bit·ted** adj. [in comb.] *a double-bitted ax.* [OE *bite* 'biting, a bite,' of Gmc. origin; rel. to Ger. *Biss* and BITE.]

bit[4] ▶ n. Comput. a unit of information expressed as either a 0 or 1 in binary notation. [1940s: blend of BINARY and DIGIT.]

bi·tar·trate /bīˈtärtrāt/ ▶ n. an acid tartrate containing the radical $C_4H_5O_6$.

bitch /biCH/ ▶ n. **1** a female dog, wolf, fox, or otter. **2** informal, derog. a woman whom one dislikes or considers to be malicious or unpleasant. ■ [in sing.] informal a thing or situation that is unpleasant or difficult to deal with. ▶ v. [intrans.] informal express displeasure; grumble: *the guys were all bitching about commuting time.* [OE *bicce*, of Gmc. origin.]

bitch·er·y /ˈbiCHərē/ ▶ n. bitchy behavior.

bitch·ing /ˈbiCHiNG/ (also **bitch·en** or **bitch·in'** /ˈbiCHən/) ▶ adj. informal excellent. ▶ adv. [as submodifier] extremely: *it's bitchin' hot, ain't it?*

bitch-slap ▶ v. (**-slapped, -slap·ping**) vulgar slang [trans.] deliver a stinging blow to (someone), typically in order to humiliate them: *I'd bitch-slap her too if she mouthed off to me like that.* [1990s: originally black English, referring to a woman hitting or haranguing her male partner.]

bitch·y /ˈbiCHē/ informal ▶ adj. (**bitchier, bitchiest**) (of a person's comments or behavior) malicious or unpleasant. — **bitch·i·ly** /ˈbiCHəlē/ adv. **bitch·i·ness** n.

bite /bīt/ ▶ v. (past **bit** /bit/; past part. **bit·ten**) [intrans.] **1** (of a person or animal) use the teeth to cut into something in order to eat it: *Rosa **bit into** a cupcake* | [trans.] *he bit a mouthful from the sandwich.* ■ [trans.] (of an animal or a person) use the teeth in order to inflict injury on: *she had bitten her assailant.* ■ [trans.] (of a snake, insect, or arachnid) wound with a sting, pincers, or fangs: *getting bitten by mosquitoes.* ■ (**bite at**) (of an animal) snap at; attempt to bite: *it is not unusual for this dog to bite at its owner's hand.* ■ (of an acid) corrode a surface: *chemicals have **bitten** deep **into** the stone.* ■ (of a fish) take the bait or lure on the end of a fishing line into the mouth. ■ fig. (of a person) be persuaded to accept a deal or offer: *retailers should bite at this offer.* **2** (of a tool, tire, boot, etc.) grip a surface. ■ (of an object) press into a part of the body, causing pain: *the handcuffs **bit into** his wrists.* ■ fig. cause emotional pain: *Cheryl's betrayal had bitten deep.* ■ (of a policy or situation) take effect, with unpleasant consequences. ■ informal be very bad, unpleasant, or unfortunate. ▶ n. **1** an act of biting into something in order to eat it. ■ a piece cut off by biting. ■ informal a quick snack. ■ a small morsel of prepared food, intended to constitute one mouthful. ■ fig. a short piece of information. See also SOUND BITE. ■ a wound inflicted by an animal's or a person's teeth. ■ a wound inflicted by a snake, insect, or arachnid. ■ an act of bait being taken by a fish. ■ Dentistry the bringing together of the teeth in occlusion. ■ Dentistry the imprint of this in a plastic material. **2** a sharp or pungent flavor. ■ incisiveness or cogency of style. ■ a feeling of cold in the air or wind.

– PHRASES **one's bark is worse than one's bite** proverb said of someone whose fierce and intimidating manner is not felt by the speaker to reflect the person's nature. **be bitten by the —— bug** develop a passionate interest in a specified activity: *Joe was bitten by the showbiz bug.* **bite the big one** informal die. **bite the bullet** decide to do something difficult or unpleasant that one has been putting off or hesitating over. **bite the dust** informal be killed. ■ fig. fail; come to an end **bite the hand that feeds one** deliberately hurt or offend a benefactor. **bite someone's head off** see HEAD. **bite one's lip** dig one's front teeth into one's lip in embarrassment, grief, or annoyance, or to prevent oneself from saying something or to control oneself when experiencing physical pain. ■ fig. force oneself to remain silent even though annoyed, provoked, or in possession of information. **bite off more than one can chew** take on a commitment one cannot fulfill. **bite one's tongue** make a desperate effort to avoid saying something. **one could have bitten one's tongue off** used to show that someone profoundly and immediately regrets having said something. **once bitten, twice shy** proverb an unpleasant experience induces caution. **put the bite on** informal borrow or extort money from. **take a bite out of** informal reduce by a significant amount.

– PHRASAL VERBS **bite something back** refrain with difficulty from saying something, making a sound, or expressing an emotion: *Melissa bit back a scathing comment.* — **bit·er** n. [OE *bītan*, of Gmc. origin; rel. to Ger. *beissen*.]

bite-sized (also **bite-size**) ▶ adj. (of a piece of food) small enough to be eaten in one mouthful. ■ informal very small or short: *a series of bite-sized essays.*

bite·wing /ˈbītˌwiNG/ ▶ n. a dental film for X-raying the crowns of upper and lower teeth simultaneously and that is held in place by a tab between the teeth.

bit·ing /ˈbītiNG/ ▶ adj. (of insects and certain other animals) able to wound the skin with a sting or fangs. ■ (of wind or cold) so cold as to be painful. ■ (of wit or criticism) harsh or cruel. — **bit·ing·ly** adv.

bit·ing midge ▶ n. a very small fly (family Ceratopogonidae) that typically occurs in large swarms. The female has piercing mouthparts and feeds on the blood of a variety of animals including humans. Numerous genera and species includes the punkie (*Culicoides* and related genera).

bit·map /ˈbitˌmap/ Comput. ▶ n. a representation in which each item corresponds to one or more bits of information, esp. the information used to control the display of a computer screen. ▶ v. (**-mapped, -map·ping**) [trans.] represent (an item) as a bitmap.

BITNET /ˈbitˌnet/ (also **Bitnet**) trademark a data transmission network founded in 1981 to link North American academic institutions and to interconnect with other information networks.

bit part ▶ n. a small acting role in a play or a movie.

bit rate ▶ n. Electron. the number of bits per second that can be transmitted along a digital network.

bit·stream /ˈbitˌstrēm/ ▶ n. Electron. a stream of data in binary form. ■ (**Bitstream**) trademark a system of digital-to-analog signal conversion used in some audio CD players, in which the signal from the CD is digitally processed to give a signal at a higher frequency before being converted to an analog signal.

bitt /bit/ ▶ n. [usu. in pl.] any of the posts fixed in pairs on the deck of a ship, for fastening cables, belaying ropes, etc. ▶ v. [trans.] coil or fasten around the bitts.

bit·ten /ˈbitn/ past participle of BITE.

bit·ter /ˈbitər/ ▶ adj. **1** having a sharp, pungent taste or smell; not sweet. ■ (of chocolate) dark and unsweetened. **2** (of people or their feelings or behavior) angry, hurt, or resentful because of one's bad experiences or a sense of unjust treatment. **3** harsh or unpleasant, in particular: ■ (often used for emphasis) painful or unpleasant to accept or contemplate: *today's decision has come as **a bitter blow**.* ■ (of a conflict, argument, or opponent) full of anger and acrimony: *a bitter, five-year legal battle.* ■ (of wind, cold, or weather) intensely cold: *a bitter wind blowing from the east.* ▶ n. **1** [mass noun] Brit. beer that is strongly flavored with hops and has a bitter taste. **2** (**bitters**) [treated as sing] liquor that is flavored with the sharp pungent taste of plant extracts.

– PHRASES **to the bitter end** used to say that one will continue doing something until it is finished, no matter what. — **bit·ter·ly** adv. **bit·ter·ness** n. [OE *biter*, of Gmc. origin; rel. to Ger. *bitter*, and prob. to BITE.]

bit·ter al·mond ▶ n. see ALMOND (sense 2).

bit·ter al·oes ▶ n. see ALOE.

bit·ter·cress /ˈbitərˌkres/ ▶ n. a plant (genus *Cardamine*) of the cabbage family, with small white flowers. It grows widely as a weed of temperate areas.

bit·ter-end·er ▶ n. a person who holds out until the end no matter what.

bit·tern[1] /ˈbitərn/ ▶ n. a large marsh bird (genera *Botaurus* and *Ixobrychus*) of the heron family, with brown streaked plumage, including the **American bittern** (*B. lentiginosus*) and the **least bittern** (*I. exilis*). The males of certain species are noted for a deep booming call during the breeding season. [ME *bitore*, from OFr. *butor*, based on L. *butio* 'bittern' + *taurus* 'bull' (from its call).]

bit·tern[2] (also **bitterns**) ▶ n. a concentrated solution of various salts remaining after the crystallization of salt from seawater. [17th C.: prob. from the adj. BITTER.]

bit·ter or·ange ▶ n. another term for SEVILLE ORANGE.

bit·ter·root ▶ n. a plant (*Lewisia rediviva*) of the purslane family with showy pinkish-white flowers on short stems, found throughout the rocky areas of western North America.

Bit·ter·root Range part of the Rocky Mountains in western Montana and eastern Idaho.

bit·ter·sweet /ˈbitərˌswēt/ ▶ adj. (of food, drink, or flavor) sweet with a bitter aftertaste. ■ arousing pleasure tinged with sadness or pain: *bittersweet memories.* ▶ n. **1** another term for woody nightshade (see NIGHTSHADE). **2** (also **climbing bittersweet**) a vinelike climbing plant (genus *Celastrus*, family Celastraceae) that bears clusters of bright orange pods.

bit·ty /ˈbitē/ informal ▶ adj. (**bittier, bittiest**) tiny. — **bit·ti·ly** adv. **bit·ti·ness** n.

bi·tu·men /biˈt(y)o͞omən; bī-/ ▶ n. a black viscous mixture of hydrocarbons obtained naturally or as a residue from petroleum distillation. [ME: from L.]

bi·tu·mi·nize /biˈt(y)o͞oməˌnīz; bī-/ ▶ v. [trans.] convert into, impregnate with, or cover with bitumen. — **bi·tu·mi·ni·za·tion** /-ˌt(y)o͞oməniˈzāSHən/ n.

bi·tu·mi·nous /biˈt(y)o͞omənəs; bī-/ ▶ adj. [attrib.] of, containing, or of the nature of bitumen. [16th C.: ult. from L. *bituminosus*.]

bi·tu·mi·nous coal ▶ n. black coal having a relatively high volatile content.

bit·wise /ˈbitˌwīz/ ▶ adj. Comput. designating an operator in a programming language that manipulates the individual bits in a byte or word.

bi·va·lence /bīˈvāləns/ ▶ n. Logic the existence of only two states or truth values (e.g. true and false).

bi·va·lent /bīˈvālənt; ˈbivə-/ ▶ adj. **1** Biol. (of homologous chromosomes) associated in pairs. **2** Chem. another term for DIVALENT. ▶ n. Biol. a pair of homologous chromosomes.

bi·valve /ˈbīˌvalv/ ▶ n. an aquatic mollusk (class Bivalvia) that has a compressed body enclosed within two hinged shells, including oysters, clams, mussels, and scallops. Also called PELECYPOD or LAMELLIBRANCH.

biv·ou·ac /ˈbivo͞oˌak; ˈbivwak/ ▶ n. a temporary camp without tents or cover. ▶ v. [intrans.] (**bivouacked, bivouacking**) stay in such a camp: *the battalion was now bivouacked in a field.* [18th C.: from Fr., prob. from Swiss Ger. *Bîwacht* 'additional guard at night.']

bi·week·ly /bīˈwēklē/ ▶ adj. & adv. appearing or taking place every two weeks or twice a week: [as adj.] *a biweekly bulletin* | [as adv.] *undergo health checks biweekly.* ▶ n. (pl. **-lies**) a periodical that appears every two weeks or twice a week.

bi·year·ly /bī'yi(ə)rlē/ ▶ **adj. & adv.** appearing or taking place every two years or twice a year.

biz /biz/ ▶ **n.** [usu. in sing.] [usu. with adj.] informal a business, typically one connected with entertainment. [19th C.: abbrev.]

bi·zarre /bi'zär/ ▶ **adj.** very strange or unusual. — **bi·zarre·ness n.** [17th C.: from Fr., from Ital. *bizzarro* 'angry.']

bi·zarre·ly /bi'zärlē/ ▶ **adv.** in a very strange or unusual manner: *bizarrely attired musicians.* ■ [sentence adverb] used to express the opinion that something is very strange or unusual: ***bizarrely enough**, he began to trust his abductors.*

bi·zar·re·rie /bi'zärərē/ ▶ **n.** (pl. **-ries**) a thing considered extremely strange and unusual, typically in an amusing way. [18th C.: from Fr.]

Bi·zet /bi'zā/, Georges (1838–75), French composer; born *Alexandre César Léopold Bizet.* He is noted for the opera *Carmen* (1875).

BJ ▶ **abbr.** BLOW JOB.

Bjerk·nes /'byerknəs/, Vilhelm Frimann Koren (1862–1951), Norwegian geophysicist. He developed a theory of physical hydrodynamics for atmosphere and oceanic circulation.

Bk ▶ **symb.** the chemical element berkelium.

bk ▶ **abbr.** ■ bank. ■ book. ■ brick.

BL ▶ **abbr.** ■ Bachelor of Law. ■ Bachelor of Letters. ■ bill of lading.

bl ▶ **abbr.** ■ bale. ■ barrel. ■ black. ■ blue.

blab /blab/ informal ▶ **v.** (**blabbed, blab·bing**) [intrans.] reveal secrets by indiscreet talk: *she blabbed to the press* | [trans.] *there's no need to blab the whole story.* ▶ **n.** a person who blabs. [ME: prob. of Gmc. origin; ult. imitative.]

blab·ber /'blabər/ informal ▶ **v.** [intrans.] talk foolishly, mindlessly, or excessively: *she **blabbered on and on**.* ▶ **n.** a person who talks foolishly or indiscreetly. ■ foolish or mindless talk.

blab·ber·mouth /'blabər,mouTH/ ▶ **n.** informal a person who talks excessively or indiscreetly.

Black /blak/, Hugo Lafayette (1886–1971), US Supreme Court associate justice 1937–71.

black /blak/ ▶ **adj.** **1** of the very darkest color; the opposite of white; colored like coal, due to the absence of or complete absorption of light. ■ (of the sky or night) completely dark due to nonvisibility of the sun, moon, or stars, normally because of dense cloud cover. ■ deeply stained with dirt. ■ (of a plant or animal) dark in color as distinguished from a lighter variety. ■ (of coffee or tea) served without milk or cream. ■ of or denoting the suits spades and clubs in a deck of cards. **2** (also **Black**) of any human group having dark-colored skin, esp. of African or Australian Aboriginal ancestry. ■ of or relating to black people. **3** fig. (of a period of time or situation) characterized by tragic or disastrous events; causing despair or pessimism. ■ (of a person's state of mind) full of gloom or misery; very depressed. ■ (of humor) presenting tragic or harrowing situations in comic terms: *"Good place to bury the bodies," she joked with black humor.* ■ full of anger or hatred. ■ archaic very evil or wicked. ▶ **n.** **1** black color or pigment. ■ black clothes or material, often worn as a sign of mourning. ■ darkness, esp. of night or an overcast sky. **2** (also **Black**) a member of a dark-skinned people, esp. one of African or Australian Aboriginal ancestry. **3** (in a game or sport) a black piece or ball, in particular: ■ (often **Black**) the player of the black pieces in chess or checkers. ■ the black pieces in chess. ▶ **v.** [trans.] make black, esp. by the application of black polish: *blacking the prize bull's hooves.* ■ make visible parts of one's body black with polish or makeup, so as not to be seen at night or, esp. formerly, to play the role of a black person in a musical show, play, or movie: *white extras **blacking up** their faces to play Ethiopians.*

– PHRASES **black someone's eye** hit someone in the eye and cause bruising. **in the black** (of a person or organization) not owing any money; solvent. **look on the black side** informal view a situation from a pessimistic angle. **not as black as one is painted** informal not as bad as one is said to be.

– PHRASAL VERBS **black out** (of a person) undergo a sudden and temporary loss of consciousness. **black something out 1** (usu. **be blacked out**) extinguish all lights or completely cover windows, esp. for protection against an air attack or in order to provide darkness in which to show a movie. ■ subject a place to an electricity failure: *Chicago was blacked out yesterday.* **2** obscure something completely so that it cannot be read or seen. ■ (of a television company) suppress the broadcast of a program. — **black·ish adj. black·ly adv. black·ness n.** [OE *blæc*, of Gmc. origin.]

– USAGE **Black**, designating Americans of African heritage, became the most widely used and accepted term in the 1960s and 1970s, replacing **Negro**. It is not usually capitalized: *black Americans.* Through the 1980s, the more formal **African American** replaced **black** in much usage, but both are now generally acceptable. **Afro-American**, an earlier alternative to **black**, is heard mostly in anthropological and cultural contexts. **Colored people**, common early in the twentieth century, is now usually regarded as derogatory, although the phrase survives in the full name of the NAACP, the National Association for the Advancement of Colored People. An inversion, **people of color**, has gained some favor, but is also used in reference to other nonwhite ethnic groups: *a gathering spot for African Americans and other people of color interested in reading about their cultures.* See also usage at COLORED and PERSON OF COLOR.

black·a·moor /'blakə,mo͝or/ ▶ **n.** archaic a black African; a very dark-skinned person. [16th C.: from BLACK + MOOR.]

black and blue ▶ **adj.** discolored by bruising. ■ (of a person) covered in bruises.

black and tan ▶ **n.** **1** a terrier of a breed with a black back and tan markings on face, flanks, and legs. **2** a drink composed of stout (or porter) and ale. **3** informal an event or establishment that is attended or frequented by both blacks and whites.

Black and Tans an armed force recruited by the British government to fight Sinn Fein in Ireland in 1921. [from the colors of their uniform.]

black and white ▶ **adj.** **1** (of a photograph, movie, television program, or illustration) in black, white, shades of gray, and no other color. ■ (of a television) displaying images only in black, white, and shades of gray. **2** (of a situation or debate) involving clearly defined opposing principles or issues. ▶ **n.** informal a police car.

– PHRASES **in black and white 1** in writing or in print, and regarded as more reliable, credible, or formal than by word of mouth: *getting her contract down in black and white.* **2** in terms of clearly defined opposing principles or issues: *children think in black and white, good and bad.*

Black An·gus ▶ **n.** another term for ABERDEEN ANGUS.

black art ▶ **n.** (usu. **the black art**) another term for BLACK MAGIC. ■ often humorous a technique or practice considered mysterious and sinister.

black·ball /'blak,bôl/ ▶ **v.** [trans.] reject (someone), typically by means of a secret ballot: *her husband was blackballed.* [18th C.: from the practice of registering an adverse vote by placing a black ball in a ballot box.]

black bass

black bass /bas/ ▶ **n.** a popular North American sporting and food fish (genus *Micropterus*) of the freshwater sunfish family, in particular the **largemouth bass** (*M. salmoides*) and the **smallmouth bass** (*M. dolomieui*).

black bean ▶ **n.** a cultivated variety of bean plant having small black seeds, esp. a variety of soybean, used fermented in Asian cooking, and a Mexican variety of string bean. ■ the dried seed of such a plant used as a vegetable.

American black bear

black bear ▶ **n.** either of two species of medium-sized forest-dwelling bears: the **American black bear** (*Ursus americanus*), with a wide range of coat color, and the smaller **Asian black bear** (*Selenarctos thibetanus*).

Black·beard /'blak,bi(ə)rd/ (died 1718), English pirate; real name *Edward Teach.* He concentrated on the West Indies and the Virginia–North Carolina coast of America.

Black Belt /'blak 'belt/ an agricultural district in central Alabama and Mississippi, named for its rich soils.

black belt ▶ **n.** a black belt worn by an expert in judo, karate, and other martial arts. ■ a person qualified to wear this.

black·ber·ry /'blak,berē/ ▶ **n.** (pl. **-ies**) **1** an edible soft fruit, consisting of a cluster of soft purple-black drupelets. **2** the prickly climbing shrub (*Rubus fruticosus*) of the rose family that bears this fruit and that grows extensively in the wild.

black bile ▶ **n.** (in medieval science and medicine) one of the four bodily humors, believed to cause melancholy. Also called MELANCHOLY.

black birch ▶ **n.** another term for SWEET BIRCH.

black·bird /'blak,bərd/ ▶ **n.** **1** a European thrush (genus *Turdus*) with mainly black plumage. **2** an American bird (family Icteridae) with a strong pointed bill. The male has black plumage that is iridescent or has patches of red or yellow. Its several species include the **red-winged blackbird** (*Agelaius phoeniceus*).

black·board /'blak,bôrd/ ▶ **n.** a board with a smooth, dark, surface used for writing on with chalk.

black book ▶ **n.** (a book containing) a list of the names of people liable to censure or punishment.

black bot·tom pie ▶ **n.** pie with a bottom layer of chocolate cream or custard and a contrasting top layer, usually of whipped cream.

black box ▶ **n.** a flight recorder on an aircraft. ■ any complex piece of equipment, typically a unit in an electronic system, with contents that are mysterious to the user.

black bread ▶ **n.** a coarse, dark-colored rye bread.

black bry·o·ny ▶ **n.** see BRYONY (sense 2).

black·buck /'blak,bək/ ▶ **n.** a small Indian gazelle (*Antilope cervicapra*), the horned male of which has a black back and white underbelly, the female being hornless.

Black·burn /ˈblakˌbərn/ a town in northwestern England; pop. 132,800.

black·cap /ˈblakˌkap/ ▶ **n. 1** a mainly European warbler (*Sylvia atricapilla*, family Sylviidae) with a black cap in the male and a reddish-brown one in the female. **2** the black-capped chickadee. See CHICKADEE.

black cher·ry ▶ **n.** a large North American cherry tree (*Prunus serotina*) that yields valuable close-grained hard wood. ■ the bitter blackish fruit of this tree.

black·cock /ˈblakˌkäk/ ▶ **n.** (pl. same) the male of the black grouse.

black co·hosh /ˈkōhäsн/ ▶ **n.** see COHOSH.

black cur·rant ▶ **n. 1** a small round edible black berry that grows in loose hanging clusters. **2** the shrub (genus *Ribes*) of the gooseberry family that produces this fruit.

black·damp /ˈblakˌdamp/ ▶ **n.** choking or suffocating gas, typically underground carbon dioxide.

Black Death the great epidemic of bubonic plague that killed a large part of the population of Europe in the mid 14th century.

black dia·mond ▶ **n. 1** informal a lump of coal. **2** [usu. as adj.] a difficult ski slope. **3** another term for CARBONADO.

black dog ▶ **n.** informal used as a metaphor for melancholy or depression. [18th C.: orig. from a slang name for a base silver coin (usually a bad shilling).]

black duck ▶ **n.** a duck with black plumage, esp. the **American black duck** (*Anas rubripes*) of northeastern North America.

black·en /ˈblakən/ ▶ **v.** become or make black or dark, esp. as a result of burning, decay, or bruising: [intrans.] *watching the end blacken as it burned* | [trans.] *she blackened George's eye.* ■ [trans.] dye or color (the face or hair) black for camouflage or cosmetic effect: *with blackened faces.* ■ [intrans.] (of the sky) become dark as night or a storm approaches. ■ [trans.] fig. damage or destroy (someone's good reputation); defame.

black Eng·lish ▶ **n.** any of various nonstandard forms of English spoken by black people.

Black·ett /ˈblakit/, Patrick Maynard Stuart, Baron (1897–1974), English physicist. He modified the cloud chamber for the study of cosmic rays. Nobel Prize for Physics (1948).

black eye ▶ **n.** a bruised and discolored area around the eye resulting from a blow. ■ fig. a mark or source of dishonor or shame.

black-eyed pea ▶ **n.** another term for COWPEA.

black-eyed Su·san ▶ **n.** any of a number of flowers that have yellowish petals and a dark center, in particular *Rudbeckia hirta*, a North American flower of the daisy family with bristly leaves and stems.

black·face /ˈblakˌfās/ ▶ **n.** the makeup used by a nonblack performer playing a black role. ■ fig. used to imply patronization of blacks by whites or by institutions perceived to be insincerely or ineffectively nonracist.

black·fish /ˈblakˌfisн/ ▶ **n.** (pl. same or **-fish·es**) **1** any of a number of dark-colored fish, in particular: ■ an open-ocean fish (genera *Centrolophus* and *Schedophilus*, family Centrolophidae), related to the perches. ■ (**Alaska blackfish**) a small fish (*Dallia pectoralis*, family Umbridae) occurring along the Arctic coasts of Alaska and Siberia and noted for its ability to withstand freezing. **2** another term for PILOT WHALE.

black flag ▶ **n. 1** hist. a pirate's ensign, typically thought to feature a white skull and crossbones on a black background; Jolly Roger. **2** Auto Racing a black flag used to signal a driver to make an immediate pit stop as punishment for violating a rule or driving dangerously, or to force inspection of a hazardous condition.

black fly ▶ **n.** (pl. **-flies**) a small black, often swarming fly (*Simulium* and other genera, family Simuliidae), the female of which sucks blood and can transmit a number of serious human and animal diseases.

Black·foot /ˈblakˌfo͝ot/ ▶ **n.** (pl. same or **-feet**) **1** a member of a confederacy of North American Indian peoples of the northwestern plains. The confederacy consisted of three closely related tribes: the Blackfeet proper, the Bloods, and the Piegan. **2** the Algonquian language of this people. **3** a subdivision of the Teton Sioux. ▶ **adj.** of or relating to these peoples or the language of the Blackfeet proper.

Black For·est a hilly wooded region of southwestern Germany. German name SCHWARZWALD.

black frost ▶ **n.** a dry, invisible killing frost that turns vegetation black.

black gold ▶ **n.** informal petroleum.

black grouse ▶ **n.** (pl. same) a large Eurasian grouse (*Tetrao tetrix*), the male of which has glossy blue-black plumage and a lyre-shaped tail.

black·guard /ˈblagərd; ˈblakˌgärd/ ▶ **n.** dated a person who behaves in a dishonorable or contemptible way. ▶ **v.** [trans.] dated abuse or disparage (someone) scurrilously. — **black·guard·ly** **adj.** [16th C.: from BLACK + GUARD. The exact significance of the epithet 'black' is uncert. The sense 'scoundrel, villain' dates from the mid 18th C.]

black guil·le·mot ▶ **n.** a seabird (*Cepphus grylle*) of the auk family with black summer plumage and large white wing patches, breeding on the coasts of the Arctic and North Atlantic.

black gum ▶ **n.** another term for SOURGUM.

Black Hand ▶ **n.** a secret criminal and terrorist society in New York during the early 20th century. ■ any similar society.

Black Hawk (1767–1838), Indian chief; native name *Makataimeshekiakiak*. Leader of the Sauk and Fox, he fought to repossess Indian lands in the Black Hawk War 1832.

black·head /ˈblakˌhed/ ▶ **n. 1** a plug of sebum in a hair follicle, darkened by oxidation. **2** an infectious disease of turkeys producing discoloration of the head, caused by a protozoan.

Black Hills a mountain range in eastern Wyoming and western South Dakota. Mount Rushmore is here.

black hole ▶ **n.** Astron. a region of space having a gravitational field so intense that no matter or radiation can escape. ■ informal a figurative place of emptiness or aloneness. ■ informal, chiefly humorous a place where money, lost items, etc., are supposed to go, never to be seen again. ■ informal (of a system, practice, or institution) a state of inadequacy or excessive bureaucracy in which hopes, progress, etc., become futile.

black ice ▶ **n.** a transparent coating of ice.

Black Jack see PERSHING.

black·jack /ˈblakˌjak/ ▶ **n. 1** a gambling card game in which players try to acquire cards with a face value as close as possible to 21 without going over. Also called TWENTY-ONE, VINGT-ET-UN. **2** a short, leather-covered club used as a weapon. **3** hist. a pirate's black ensign. **4** hist. a tarred-leather container used for alcoholic drinks.

black·lead /ˈblakˌled/ ▶ **n.** another term for GRAPHITE.

black·leg /ˈblakˌleg/ ▶ **n. 1** any of a number of plant diseases in which part of the stem blackens and decays, in particular: ■ a fungal disease of cabbages and related plants (caused by *Leptosphaeria, Pleospora*, and other genera). ■ a bacterial disease of potatoes (caused by *Erwinia carotovora* subsp. *atroseptica*. **2** an acute infectious bacterial disease of cattle and sheep (caused by *Clostridium chauvoei*), resulting in necrosis in the legs.

black let·ter ▶ **n.** an early, ornate, bold style of type.

black light ▶ **n.** ultraviolet or infrared radiation, invisible to the eye.

black·list /ˈblakˌlist/ ▶ **n.** a list of people or products viewed with suspicion or disapproval. ▶ **v.** [trans.] (often **be blacklisted**) put (a person or product) on such a list: *workers were blacklisted.*

black lo·cust ▶ **n.** a North American tree (*Robinia pseudoacacia*) of the pea family, with compound leaves and dense hanging clusters of fragrant white flowers, widely grown as an ornamental.

black lung ▶ **n.** pneumoconiosis caused by inhalation of coal dust.

black mag·ic ▶ **n.** magic involving the supposed invocation of evil spirits for evil purposes.

black·mail /ˈblakˌmāl/ ▶ **n.** the action, treated as a criminal offense, of demanding money from a person in return for not revealing compromising or injurious information. ■ money demanded in this way. ■ the use of threats or the manipulation of someone's feelings to force them to do something. ▶ **v.** [trans.] demand money from (a person) in return for not revealing compromising or injurious information: *trying to blackmail him for $400,000.* ■ force (someone) to do something by using threats or manipulating their feelings: *he had* ***blackmailed*** *her into sailing with him.* — **black·mail·er** **n.** [16th C.: from BLACK + obs. *mail* 'tribute,' from ON *mál* 'agreement.']

black mam·ba ▶ **n.** a highly venomous, slender, olive-brown to dark gray snake (*Dendroaspis polylepis*, family Elapidae) that moves with great speed and agility. Native to eastern and southern Africa, it is the largest poisonous snake on the continent.

Black Ma·ri·a /məˈrīə/ ▶ **n.** informal a police vehicle for transporting prisoners.

black mark ▶ **n.** informal used to indicate that someone is remembered and regarded with disfavor.

black mar·ket ▶ **n.** (**the black market**) an illegal traffic or trade in officially controlled or scarce commodities. — **black mar·ke·teer** (also **black-mar·ke·teer**) **n.** **black-mar·ke·teer** **v.** **black mar·ket·er** **n.**

black mass (often **Black Mass**) ▶ **n.** a travesty of the Roman Catholic Mass in worship of Satan.

Black Me·sa an upland in northeastern Arizona, home to many of the Navajo.

black mon·ey ▶ **n.** income illegally obtained or not declared for tax purposes.

Black·more /ˈblakˌmôr/, R. D. (1825–1900), English writer and poet; full name *Richard Doddridge Blackmore*. He wrote the novel *Lorna Doone* (1869).

Black Moun·tains a range of the Appalachian Mountains in western North Carolina.

Black·mun /ˈblakmən/, Harry Andrew (1908–99), US Supreme Court associate justice 1970–94.

Black Mus·lim ▶ **n.** a member of the NATION OF ISLAM.

black na·tion·al·ism ▶ **n.** the advocacy of separate national status for black people, esp. in the US. — **black na·tion·al·ist** **n.**

black·out /ˈblakˌout/ ▶ **n. 1** a period when all lights must be turned out or covered to prevent them being seen by the enemy during an air raid. ■ (usu. **blackouts**) dark curtains put up in windows to cover lights during an air raid. ■ a failure of electrical power supply. ■ a moment in the theater when the lights on stage are suddenly turned off. **2** a suppression of information, esp. one imposed on the media by government. ■ a period during which a particular activity is prohibited. **3** a temporary loss of consciousness.

black oys·ter plant ▶ **n.** another term for SCORZONERA.

Black Pan·ther ▶ n. a member of a militant political organization set up in the US to fight for black rights.

black pan·ther ▶ n. a leopard that has black fur rather than the typical spotted coat.

black pep·per ▶ n. the dried black berries of the pepper (see PEPPER sense 2), widely used as a spice and a condiment either whole (peppercorns) or ground.

black·poll /ˈblak,pōl/ (also **blackpoll warbler**) ▶ n. a North American warbler (*Dendroica striata*), the male of which has a black cap, white cheeks, and white underparts streaked with black.

Black·pool /ˈblak,po͞ol/ a city in northwestern England; pop. 144,500.

black pow·der ▶ n. gunpowder.

Black Pow·er ▶ n. a movement in support of rights and political power for black people.

Black Prince (1330–76), eldest son of Edward III of England; name given to *Edward, Prince of Wales and Duke of Cornwall,* most likely because of the black armor he wore when fighting. He predeceased his father, and his son became King Richard II.

black pud·ding ▶ n. blood sausage.

black rasp·ber·ry ▶ n. **1** an edible soft fruit related to the blackberry, consisting of a cluster of black drupelets. **2** the prickly arching shrub (*Rubus occidentalis*) of the rose family that bears this fruit.

black rat ▶ n. a rat (*Rattus rattus*) with dark fur, large ears, and a long tail. Common in the tropics, it is found worldwide and is the chief host of the plague-transmitting flea. Also called ROOF RAT.

Black Riv·er a river that flows southeast for 300 miles (480 km) through Missouri and Arkansas.

black rot ▶ n. a disease of fruits and vegetables caused by bacteria or fungi.

black sal·si·fy ▶ n. another term for SCORZONERA.

Blacks·burg /ˈblaks,bərg/ a town in southwestern Virginia, in the Appalachian Mountains; pop. 39,573.

Black Sea an almost landlocked sea bounded by Ukraine, Russia, Georgia, Turkey, Bulgaria, and Romania and connected to the Mediterranean Sea through the Strait of Bosporus and the Sea of Marmara.

black sheep ▶ n. informal a member of a family or group who is regarded as a disgrace to them.

black·shirt /ˈblak,sʜərt/ ▶ n. a member of a fascist organization, in particular: ■ (in Italy) a member of a paramilitary group founded by Mussolini. ■ (in Nazi Germany) a member of the SS. [1920s: from the color of the Italian Fascist uniform.]

black·smith /ˈblak,smiᴛʜ/ ▶ n. a person who makes and repairs iron things by hand. ■ a farrier.

black·snake /ˈblak,snāk/ ▶ n. a long black American racer, esp. the common **Northern blacksnake** (*Coluber constrictor constrictor*), the adult of which is a patternless black, above and below.

black spot ▶ n. a disease of plants, esp. of roses, that produces black blotches on leaves.

Black·stone Riv·er /ˈblak,stōn/ a river that flows south through Massachusetts, to Pawtucket, Rhode Island, below which it is called the Seekonk River.

black·strap /ˈblak,strap/ ▶ n. a dark, viscous molasses, the byproduct of the final extraction phase of sugar refining.

black·tail deer /ˈblak,tāl/ (also **black-tailed deer**) ▶ n. a type of mule deer (*Odocoileus hemionus* subsp. *columbianus*) with black markings on the upper side of its tail, found in the western Cascade Mountains.

black tea ▶ n. **1** the most usual type of tea. Compare with GREEN TEA. **2** tea served without milk or cream.

black·thorn /ˈblak,ᴛʜôrn/ ▶ n. a thorny Eurasian shrub (*Prunus spinosa*) of the rose family that bears white flowers and astringent blue-black fruits. Also called SLOE.

black tie ▶ n. a black bow tie worn with a dinner jacket. ■ formal evening dress. ▶ adj. (**black-tie**) (of an event) requiring formal evening dress.

black·top /ˈblak,täp/ ▶ n. asphalt, tarmac, or other black material used for surfacing roads. ■ a road or area surfaced with such material. ▶ v. [trans.] surface (a road or area) with such material: *41 miles had been blacktopped to date.*

black tu·pe·lo ▶ n. another term for SOURGUM.

black vul·ture ▶ n. a large, aggressive American vulture (*Coragyps atratus*, family Cathartidae) with black plumage and a short square tail. Also called CARRION CROW.

black wal·nut ▶ n. see WALNUT.

Black War·ri·or Riv·er a river that flows across Alabama to join the Tombigbee River.

black wa·ter ▶ n. tech. waste water and sewage from toilets. Compare with GRAY WATER.

black·wa·ter fe·ver /ˈblak,wôtər; -,wätər/ ▶ n. a severe form of malaria in which blood cells are rapidly destroyed, resulting in dark urine.

black wid·ow ▶ n. a venomous American spider (*Latrodectus mactans*, family Theridiidae), the female of which has a black body with a red hourglass shape on its underside.

black widow

black·work /ˈblak,wərk/ ▶ n. a type of embroidery done in black thread on white cloth.

blad·der /ˈbladər/ ▶ n. **1** a membranous sac in humans and other animals, in which urine is collected for excretion. **2** anything inflated and hollow. ■ Bot. an inflated fruit or vesicle in various plants. [OE *blǣdre*, of Gmc. origin; rel. to Ger. *Blatter* and to BLOW[1].]

blad·der fern ▶ n. a small delicate fern (genus *Cystopteris*, family Dryopteridaceae) of Eurasia and North America, with rounded spore cases, growing on rocks and walls.

blad·der·nut /ˈbladər,nət/ (also **bladder nut**) ▶ n. a shrub or small tree (genus *Staphylea*, family Staphyleaceae) of north temperate regions that bears white flowers and inflated seed capsules. ■ the fruit of this shrub or tree.

blad·der worm ▶ n. an immature form of a tapeworm, which lives in the flesh of the secondary host.

blad·der·wort /ˈbladər,wərt; -,wôrt/ ▶ n. an aquatic plant (genus *Utricularia*, family Lentibulariaceae) of north temperate regions with small air-filled bladders that keep the plant afloat and trap tiny animals that provide additional nutrients.

blad·der·wrack /ˈbladər,rak/ (also **blad·der wrack**) ▶ n. a common brown shoreline seaweed (*Fucus vesiculosus*, class Phaeophyceae) that has tough straplike fronds containing air bladders that give buoyancy.

blade /blād/ ▶ n. **1** the flat cutting edge of a knife, saw, or other tool or weapon. ■ a razor blade. ■ literary a sword. ■ Archaeol. a long, narrow flake. **2** the flat, wide section of an implement or device such as an oar or a propeller. ■ a thin, flat metal runner on an ice skate. ■ a shoulder bone in a cut of meat, or the cut of meat itself. ■ the flat part of the tongue behind the tip. **3** a long, narrow leaf of grass or another similar plant. ■ Bot. the broad thin part of a leaf apart from the stalk. **4** informal, dated a dashing or energetic young man. — **blad·ed** adj. [in comb.] *double-bladed paddles.* [OE *blæd* 'leaf of a plant', of Gmc. origin.]

blague /bläg/ ▶ n. a joke or piece of nonsense. [19th C.: Fr., lit. 'nonsense.']

blah /blä/ informal ▶ exclam. used to substitute for actual words in contexts where they are felt to be too tedious or lengthy to give in full: *the typical kid, going out every night, blah, blah, blah.* ▶ n. **1** (also **blah-blah**) used to refer to something that is boring or without meaningful content. **2** (**the blahs**) depression. [20th C.: imitative.]

blain /blān/ ▶ n. rare an inflamed swelling or sore on the skin. See CHILBLAIN. [OE *blegen*, of West Gmc. origin; rel. to Du. *blein*.]

Blaine /blān/ a city in southeastern Minnesota; pop. 38,975.

Blair[1] /ble(ə)r/, John (1732–1800), US Supreme Court associate justice 1789–96, and a signer of the US Constitution.

Blair[2], Tony (1953–), prime minister of Britain 1997–2007; full name *Anthony Charles Lynton Blair.* He was elected leader of the Labour Party in 1994.

Blake[1] /blāk/, Eubie (1883–1983), US pianist and composer. A ragtime pianist, he wrote many of his songs with lyricist Noble Sissle (1889–1975).

Blake[2], William (1757–1827), English poet and painter. His poems mark the beginning of romanticism and are collected in *Songs of Innocence* (1789) and *Songs of Experience* (1794).

Bla·key /ˈblākē/, Art (1919–90), US drummer; full name *Arthur Blakey.* He was a pioneer of the bebop movement.

blame /blām/ ▶ v. [trans.] assign responsibility for a fault or wrong: *the inquiry **blamed** the engineer **for** the accident.* ■ (**blame something on**) assign the responsibility for something bad to (someone or something): *they blame youth crime on unemployment.* ▶ n. responsibility for a fault or wrong. ■ the action of assigning responsibility for a fault.
– PHRASES **be to blame** be responsible for a fault or wrong. **I don't** (or **can't**) **blame you** (or **her**, etc.) used to indicate that one agrees that the action or attitude taken was reasonable. **have only oneself to blame** be solely responsible for something bad that has happened. — **blam·a·ble** (also **blame·a·ble**) adj. **blame·ful** /-fəl/ adj. [ME: from OFr. *blamer, blasmer* (v.), ult. from Gk. *blasphēmein* (see BLASPHEME).]

blamed ▶ adj. & adv. informal used for emphasis, esp. to express disapprobation or annoyance: *a blamed old sodden-headed conservative.*

blame·less /ˈblāmlis/ ▶ adj. innocent of wrongdoing. — **blame·less·ly** adv. **blame·less·ness** n.

blame·wor·thy /ˈblām,wərᴛʜē/ ▶ adj. responsible for wrongdoing and deserving of censure or blame. — **blame·wor·thi·ness** n.

blanc fixe /ˈblaɴɢk ˈfiks; bläɴ ˈfēks/ ▶ n. barium sulfate in the form of a white powder used in making pigments and paper.

blanch /blanᴄʜ/ ▶ v. **1** [trans.] make white or pale by extracting color; bleach: *the cold light blanched her face.* ■ [trans.] whiten (a plant) by depriving it of light: *blanch endive by covering plants with large flowerpots.* ■ [intrans.] fig. (of a person) grow pale from shock, fear, or a similar emotion: *many people **blanch at** the suggestion.* **2** [trans.] prepare (vegetables) for freezing or further cooking by immersing briefly in boiling water. ■ peel (almonds) by scalding them. [ME: from OFr. *blanchir*, from *blanc* 'white,' ult. of Gmc. origin.]

Blan·chard /ˈblanᴄʜərd; bläɴˈsʜär/, Jean Pierre François (1753–1809), French balloonist. In 1785, with the American John Jeffries (1744–1819), he made the first crossing of the English Channel in a balloon.

blanc·mange /bləˈmänj; -ˈmäɴzʜ/ ▶ n. a sweet opaque gelatinous dessert made with cornstarch and milk. [ME *blancmanger*, from OFr. *blanc mangier*, from *blanc* 'white' + *mangier* 'eat' (used as a n. to mean 'food'). The shortened form without *-er* arose in the 18th C.]

bland /bland/ ▶ adj. lacking strong features or characteristics and therefore uninteresting. ■ (of food or drink) mild or insipid. ■ (of a person or behavior) showing no strong emotion; dull and unremarkable. — **bland·ly** adv. **bland·ness** n. [ME: from L. *blandus* 'soft, smooth.']

Blan·da /'blandə/, George Frederick (1927–), US football player, the first in the NFL to score more than 2,000 points.

bland·ish /'blandisн/ ▶ v. [trans.] archaic coax (someone) with kind words or flattery: *I was blandishing her with imprudences to get her off the subject.* [ME: from OFr. *blandiss-*, lengthened stem of *blandir*, from L. *blandiri*, from *blandus* 'soft, smooth.']

bland·ish·ment /'blandisнmənt/ ▶ n. a flattering or pleasing statement or action used to persuade someone gently to do something.

blank /blaNGk/ ▶ adj. **1** (of a surface or background) unrelieved by decorative or other features; bare, empty, or plain. ■ not written or printed on. ■ (of a document) with spaces left for a signature or details. ■ (of a tape) with nothing recorded on it. **2** showing incomprehension or no reaction. ■ having temporarily no knowledge or understanding. ■ lacking incident or result. **3** [attrib.] complete; absolute (used emphatically with negative force): *a blank refusal to negotiate.* ▶ n. **1** a space left to be filled in a document. ■ a document with blank spaces to be filled. **2** (also **blank cartridge**) a cartridge containing gunpowder but no bullet, used for training or as a signal. **3** an empty space or period of time, esp. in terms of a lack of knowledge or understanding. **4** an object that has no mark or design on it, in particular: ■ a roughly cut metal or wooden block intended for further shaping or finishing. ■ a domino with one or both halves blank. ■ a plain metal disk from which a coin is made by stamping a design on it. **5** a dash written instead of a word or letter, esp. instead of an obscenity or profanity. ■ used euphemistically in place of a noun regarded as obscene, profane, or abusive. ▶ v. [trans.] **1** cover up, obscure, or cause to appear blank or empty: *electronic countermeasures **blanked out** the radar signals.* ■ [intrans.] become blank or empty: *the picture **blanked out**.* ■ cut (a metal blank). **2** informal defeat (a sports opponent) without allowing the opposition to score: *Baltimore blanked Toronto in a 7–0 victory.*

– PHRASES **draw a blank** elicit no successful response; fail. **firing blanks** informal (of a man) infertile. — **blank·ly** adv. **blank·ness** n. [ME: from OFr. *blanc* 'white,' ult. of Gmc. origin.]

blank check ▶ n. a bank check with the amount left for the payee to fill in. ■ [in sing.] fig. unlimited freedom of action.

blan·ket /'blaNGkit/ ▶ n. **1** a large piece of woolen or similar material used as a bed covering or other covering for warmth. ■ fig. a thick mass or layer of a specified material that covers something completely. **2** Print. a rubber surface used for transferring the image in ink from the plate to the paper in offset printing. ▶ adj. covering all cases or instances; total and inclusive. ▶ v. (**-ket·ed, -ket·ing**) [trans.] cover completely with a thick layer of something: *the countryside **was blanketed** in snow.* ■ stifle or keep quiet (sound): *the double glazing blankets the noise.* ■ Sailing take wind from the sails of (another craft) by passing to windward. [ME (denoting undyed woolen cloth): from OFr. *blanc* 'white,' ult. of Gmc. origin.]

blan·ket·flow·er ▶ n. another term for GAILLARDIA.

blan·ket·ing /'blaNGkitiNG/ ▶ n. **1** material used for making blankets. **2** the action of covering something with or as if with a blanket.

blan·ket stitch ▶ n. a buttonhole stitch used on the edges of a blanket or other material too thick to be hemmed.

blank·e·ty /'blaNGkitē/ (also **blank·e·ty-blank**) ▶ adj. & n. informal used euphemistically to replace a word considered coarse or vulgar.

blank verse ▶ n. verse without rhyme, esp. that which uses iambic pentameter.

Blan·tyre /'blan,tī(ə)r/ a city in Malawi; pop. 331,600 (with Limbe, a town to the southeast).

blare /ble(ə)r/ ▶ v. [intrans.] sound loudly and harshly: *the ambulance arrived, siren blaring.* ■ [trans.] cause (something) to sound loudly and harshly. ▶ n. a loud harsh sound. [ME: from MDu. *blaren, bleren*, or Low Ger. *blaren*, of imitative origin.]

blar·ney /'blärnē/ ▶ n. talk that aims to charm, pleasantly flatter, or persuade. ■ amusing and harmless nonsense. ▶ v. (**-neys, -neyed**) [trans.] influence or persuade (someone) using charm and pleasant flattery. [18th C.: named after *Blarney*, a castle near Cork in Ireland, where there is a stone said to give the gift of persuasive speech to anyone who kisses it.]

bla·sé /blä'zā/ ▶ adj. unimpressed or indifferent to something because of over-familiarity. [19th C.: Fr., past part. of *blaser* 'cloy,' prob. ult. of Gmc. origin.]

blas·pheme /blas'fēm; 'blas,fēm/ ▶ v. speak irreverently about God or sacred things: *allegations that he had **blasphemed against** Islam.* — **blas·phem·er** /blas'fēmər; 'blasfəmər/ n. [ME: via OFr., ult. from Gk. *blasphēmein*, from *blasphēmos* 'evil-speaking.']

blas·phe·mous /'blasfəməs/ ▶ adj. sacrilegious against God or sacred things; profane. — **blas·phe·mous·ly** adv.

blas·phe·my /'blasfəmē/ ▶ n. (pl. **-mies**) the act or offense of speaking sacrilegiously about God or sacred things; profane talk.

blast /blast/ ▶ n. **1** a destructive wave of highly compressed air spreading outward from an explosion. ■ an explosion or explosive firing, esp. of a bomb. ■ fig. a forceful attack or assault. **2** a strong gust of wind or air. ■ a strong current of air used in smelting. **3** a single loud note of a horn, whistle, or other noisemaking device. **4** informal a severe reprimand. **5** informal an enjoyable experience or lively party. ▶ v. [trans.] **1** blow up or break apart (something solid) with explosives: *solid rock had to be **blasted away**.* ■ produce (damage or a hole) by means of an explosion: *the collision **blasted out** a tremendous crater.* ■ [trans.] force or throw (something) in a specified direction by impact or explosion: *the car was blasted thirty feet into the sky.* ■ shoot with a gun: *Fowler was blasted with an air rifle.* ■ [intrans.] move very quickly and loudly in a specified direction: *driving rain blasted through the smashed window.* ■ informal criticize fiercely. **2** make or cause to make a loud continuous musical or other noise: [intrans.] *music blasted out at full volume* | [trans.] *an impatient motorist blasted his horn.* **3** kick, strike, or throw (a ball) hard: *Ripken blasted the ball into right field.* **4** literary (of a wind or other natural force) wither, shrivel, or blight (a plant): *crops blasted on the eve of harvest.* ■ strike with divine anger: *damn and blast this awful place!* ■ destroy or ruin. ▶ exclam. esp. Brit., informal expressing annoyance: *"Blast! The car won't start!"*

– PHRASES **a blast from the past** informal something forcefully nostalgic. **(at) full blast** at maximum power or intensity.

– PHRASAL VERBS **blast off** (of a rocket or spacecraft) take off from a launching site. [OE *blǣst*, of Gmc. origin; rel. to BLAZE[3].]

-blast ▶ comb. form Biol. denoting an embryonic cell: *erythroblast.* Compare with -CYTE. [from Gk. *blastos* 'sprout.']

blast cell ▶ n. a primitive, undifferentiated blood cell, often found in the blood of those with acute leukemia.

blast·ed /'blastid/ ▶ adj. **1** [attrib.] informal used to express annoyance: *make your own blasted coffee!* **2** [attrib.] literary withered or blighted; laid waste. **3** [predic.] informal drunk.

blas·te·ma /bla'stēmə/ ▶ n. (pl. **-mas** or **-ma·ta** /-mətə/) the primary formative material of plants and animals, from which cells are developed. — **blas·te·mal** adj. **blas·te·mat·ic** /,blastə'matik/ adj.

blast·er /'blastər/ ▶ n. a person or thing that blasts. ■ (in science fiction) a weapon that emits a destructive blast. ■ a computer game in which the objective is to shoot as many enemies as possible.

blast fur·nace ▶ n. a smelting furnace in the form of a tower into which a blast of hot compressed air can be introduced from below.

blast·ing gel·a·tin ▶ n. another term for GELATIN.

blasto- ▶ comb. form relating to germination: *blastoderm.* [from Gk. *blastos* 'germ.']

blas·to·coel /'blastə,sēl/ (also **blas·to·coele**) ▶ n. the fluid-filled cavity of a blastula. Also called SEGMENTATION CAVITY. — **blas·to·coel·ic** /,blastə'sēlik/ adj.

blas·to·cyst /'blastə,sist/ ▶ n. Embryol. a mammalian blastula in which some differentiation of cells has occurred. Also called **blastodermic vesicle**.

blas·to·derm /'blastə,dərm/ ▶ n. Embryol. the layer of embryonic tissue that forms prior to the development of the embryonic axis. ■ the outer layer of cells that forms the wall of a blastula.

blas·to·disk /'blastə,disk/ (also **blas·to·disc**) ▶ n. Embryol. a blastula having the form of a disk of cells on top of the yolk in the eggs of reptiles and birds.

blast·off /'blast,ôf; -,äf/ ▶ n. the launching of a rocket or spacecraft.

blas·to·gen·e·sis /,blastə'jenəsis/ ▶ n. **1** the theory of the transmission of inherited characteristics by germ plasm. **2** asexual reproduction of an organism by budding. **3** the development of lymphocytes into larger undifferentiated cells that can undergo mitosis. — **blas·to·gen·ic** /-'jenik/ adj.

blas·to·ma /bla'stōmə/ ▶ n. (pl. **-mas** or **-ma·ta** /-mətə/) a neoplasm consisting of immature undifferentiated cells.

blas·to·mere /'blastə,mi(ə)r/ ▶ n. Embryol. a cell formed by cleavage of a fertilized ovum.

blas·to·my·co·sis /,blastəmī'kōsis/ ▶ n. Med. a disease caused by infection with parasitic fungi (**blastomycetes**, of the genus *Blastomyces*), affecting the skin or the internal organs.

blas·to·pore /'blastə,pôr/ ▶ n. the opening of an embryo's central cavity in the early stage of development.

blas·tu·la /'blascнələ/ ▶ n. (pl. **-las** or **-lae** /-,lē/) Embryol. an animal embryo at the early stage of development. Also called **blastosphere**. [19th C.: mod. L., from Gk. *blastos* 'sprout.']

blat /blat/ ▶ v. (**blat·ted, blat·ting**) [intrans.] make a bleating sound. ▶ n. a bleat or similar noise. [19th C.: imitative.]

bla·tant /'blātnt/ ▶ adj. (of bad behavior) done openly and unashamedly: *blatant lies.* ■ completely lacking in subtlety; very obvious. — **bla·tan·cy** /'blātnsē/ n. [16th C.: perh. alt. of Scots *blatand* 'bleating.']

bla·tant·ly /'blātntlē/ ▶ adv. in an unsubtle and unashamed manner. ■ [usu. as submodifier] used to emphasize the speaker's opinion that something disapproved of is clearly the case: *he found her remarks blatantly racist.*

Blatch·ford /blacнfərd/, Samuel (1820–93), US Supreme Court associate justice 1882–93.

blath·er /'bla<u>TH</u>ər/ (also **bleth·er** /'ble<u>TH</u>ər/ or **blith·er** /'bli<u>TH</u>ər/) ▶ v. [intrans.] talk long-windedly without making very much sense: *she began **blathering on about** spirituality* | [as n.] (**blathering**) *stop your blathering.* ▶ n. long-winded talk with no real substance. [ME: from ON *blathra* 'talk nonsense,' from *blathr* 'nonsense.']

blath·er·skite /'bla<u>TH</u>ər,skīt/ ▶ n. **1** a person who talks at great length without making much sense. ■ foolish talk; nonsense: *politicians get* *away all the time with their blatherskite.* **2** informal a scoundrel: *you lousy, thieving blatherskite!* [17th C.: from BLATHER + *skate* 'mean person.']

Bla·vat·sky /blə'vätskē; -'vätskē/, Helena Petrovna (1831–91), Russian spiritualist; born in Ukraine; born *Helena Petrovna Hahn*; known as **Madame Blavatsky**. In 1875, she cofounded the Theosophical Society.

blax·ploi·ta·tion /,blaksploi'tāsHən/ ▶ **n.** the exploitation of black people, esp. with regard to stereotyped roles in movies. [1970s: blend of *blacks* and EXPLOITATION.]

blaze[1] /blāz/ ▶ **n.** **1** a very large or fiercely burning fire. ■ a harsh bright light. ■ [in sing.] a very bright display of light or color: *the gardens are a blaze of color.* ■ [in sing.] fig. a conspicuous display or outburst of something: *their relationship broke up in a blaze of publicity.* **2** (**blazes**) informal used in various expressions of anger, bewilderment, or surprise as a euphemism for "hell": *"Go to blazes!" he shouted.* [with ref. to the flames associated with hell.] ▶ **v.** [intrans.] **1** burn fiercely or brightly: *the fire blazed merrily.* ■ shine brightly or powerfully: *the sun* **blazed down** | fig. *Barbara's eyes were* **blazing with** *anger* **2** (of a gun or a person firing a gun) fire repeatedly or indiscriminately. **3** informal achieve something in an impressive manner: *she blazed to a gold medal.* ■ [trans.] hit (a ball) with impressive strength: *he blazed a drive into the rough.*
– PHRASES **like blazes** informal very fast or forcefully. [see sense 2 of the n.] **with all guns blazing** informal with great determination and energy, typically without thought for the consequences.
– PHRASAL VERBS **blaze up** burst into flame. ■ fig. suddenly become angry. [OE *blæse* 'torch,' of Gmc. origin; akin to BLAZE[2].]

blaze[2] ▶ **n.** **1** a white spot or stripe on the face of a mammal or bird. ■ a broad white stripe running the length of a horse's face. **2** a mark made on a tree by cutting the bark so as to mark a route. ▶ **v.** (**blaze a trail**) mark out a path or route. ■ fig. set an example by being the first to do something; pioneer: *small firms would set the pace, blazing a trail for others to follow.* [17th C.: ult. of Gmc. origin; rel. to Ger. *Blässe* 'blaze' and BLAZE[1].]

blaze[3] ▶ **v.** [trans.] (of a newspaper) present or proclaim (news) in a prominent, typically sensational, manner. [ME: from Mid. Low Ger. or MDu. *blāzen* 'to blow'; rel. to BLOW[1].]

blaz·er /'blāzər/ ▶ **n.** a lightweight jacket. ■ a plain jacket, not forming part of a suit but considered appropriate for formal or semiformal wear. [19th C.: from BLAZE[1].]

blaz·ing star ▶ **n.** any of a number of North American plants, some of which are cultivated for their flowers, in particular: ■ a plant (genus *Liatris*) of the daisy family with tall spikes of purple or white flowers. ■ a plant (genus *Mentzelia*, family Loasaceae) of the western US, with toothed leaves and yellow flowers, esp. the **giant blazing star** (*M. laevicaulis*).

blazing star

bla·zon /'blāzən/ ▶ **v.** [trans.] **1** [with adverbial of place] display prominently or vividly. ■ report (news), esp. in a sensational manner: *their ordeal blazoned to the entire nation.* **2** Heraldry describe or depict (armorial bearings) in a correct heraldic manner. ■ inscribe or paint (an object) with arms or a name. ▶ **n.** Heraldry a correct description of armorial bearings. ■ archaic a coat of arms. [ME: from OFr. *blason* 'shield.']

bla·zon·ry /'blāzənrē/ ▶ **n.** Heraldry the art of describing or painting heraldic devices or armorial bearings. ■ [pl. n.] devices or bearings of this type.

bldg. ▶ **abbr.** building.

bleach /blēcH/ ▶ **v.** [trans.] whiten by exposure to sunlight or by a chemical process: [as adj.] (**bleached**) *permed and bleached hair.* ■ clean and sterilize: *a new formula to bleach and brighten clothing* ■ fig. deprive of vitality or substance: *his contributions to the album are bleached of personality.* ▶ **n.** a chemical (typically a solution of sodium hypochlorite or hydrogen peroxide) used to whiten or sterilize materials. [OE *blǣcan* (v.), *blǣce* (n.), from *blǣc* 'pale,' of Gmc. origin; rel. to BLEAK[1].]

bleach·er /'blēcHər/ ▶ **n.** **1** a person who bleaches textiles or other material. ■ a container or chemical used in bleaching. **2** (usu. **bleachers**) a cheap bench seat at a sports arena, typically in an outdoor uncovered stand. ■ (also **bleach·er·ite** /'blēcHə,rīt/) a person occupying such a seat: *the bleachers cheered.*

bleach·ing pow·der ▶ **n.** a powder containing calcium hypochlorite.

bleak[1] /blēk/ ▶ **adj.** (of an area of land) lacking vegetation and exposed to the elements. ■ (of a building or room) charmless and inhospitable; dreary. ■ (of the weather) cold and miserable. ■ (of a situation or future prospect) not hopeful or encouraging; unlikely to have a favorable outcome. ■ (of a person or a person's expression) cold and forbidding. — **bleak·ly** **adv.** **bleak·ness** **n.** [OE *blāc* 'shining, white;' from ON *bleikr*; from Gmc., akin to BLEACH.]

bleak[2] ▶ **n.** a small silvery shoaling fish (genera *Alburnus* and *Chalcalburnus*) of the minnow family, found in Eurasian rivers. [15th C.: from ON *bleikja*.]

blear /bli(ə)r/ archaic ▶ **v.** [trans.] make dim; blur: *you would blear your eyes with books.* ▶ **adj.** dim, dull, or filmy. ▶ **n.** a film over the eyes; a blur. [ME: prob. rel. to Mid. High Ger. *blerre* 'blurred vision.']

blear·y /'bli(ə)rē/ ▶ **adj.** (**blear·i·er**, **blear·i·est**) (of the eyes) unfocused or filmy from sleep or tiredness. — **blear·i·ly** /'bli(ə)rəlē/ **adv.** **blear·i·ness** **n.**

blear·y-eyed (also **blear-eyed**) ▶ **adj.** (of a person) having bleary eyes.

bleat /blēt/ ▶ **v.** [intrans.] (of a sheep, goat, or calf) make a characteristic wavering cry: *the lamb was bleating weakly.* ■ [reporting verb] speak or complain in a weak, querulous, or foolish way: *he bleated incoherently about the report.* ▶ **n.** [in sing.] the wavering cry made by a sheep, goat, or calf. ■ a person's plaintive cry. ■ informal a complaint. [OE *blǣtan*, of imitative origin.]

bleb /bleb/ ▶ **n.** a small blister on the skin. ■ a small bubble in glass or in a fluid. ■ Biol. a rounded outgrowth on the surface of a cell. [17th C.: var. of BLOB.]

bleed /blēd/ ▶ **v.** (past and past part. **bled** /bled/) **1** [intrans.] lose blood from the body as a result of injury or illness: *the cut was bleeding steadily* | *some casualties were left to* **bleed to death** | [as n.] (**bleeding**) *the bleeding has stopped now.* ■ (of a dye or color) seep into an adjacent color or area. ■ [intrans.] Print. (of an illustration or a design) be printed so as to run to the edge of the page: *the picture bleeds on three sides.* ■ [trans.] print and trim (an illustration or a design) in such a way. **2** [trans.] draw blood from (someone), esp. as a once-common method of treatment in medicine. ■ remove blood from (an animal carcass). ■ [trans.] informal drain (someone) of money or resources: *attempting to bleed unions of funds.* ■ [trans.] allow (fluid or gas) to escape from a closed system through a valve: *open the valves and bleed air from the pump chamber.* ■ [trans.] treat (a system) in this way: *bleeding the radiator at the air vent.* ▶ **n.** an instance of bleeding. ■ Print. an instance of printing to the edge of the page. ■ the escape of fluid or gas from a closed system through a valve. ■ the action or process of a dye, ink, or color seeping into an adjacent color or area.
– PHRASES **bleed someone dry** (or **white**) drain someone of all money or resources. **my heart bleeds** (**for you**) used ironically to express the speaker's belief that the person spoken to does not deserve the sympathetic response sought. [OE *blēdan*, of Gmc. origin; rel. to BLOOD.]

bleed·er /'blēdər/ ▶ **n.** informal a person who bleeds easily, esp. a hemophiliac. ■ a blood vessel that bleeds freely during surgery.

bleed·ing /'blēdiNG/ ▶ **adj.** [attrib.] Brit., vulgar slang used for emphasis or to express annoyance.

bleeding heart 2

bleed·ing heart ▶ **n.** **1** informal, derog. a person considered to be dangerously softhearted, typically someone considered too liberal in political beliefs. **2** any of a number of plants that have heart-shaped flowers, typically pink or red, in particular a popular garden plant (genus *Dicentra*, family Fumariaceae).

bleep /blēp/ ▶ **n.** a short high-pitched sound made by an electronic device as a signal or to attract attention. ■ a sound of this type used in broadcasting as a substitute for a censored word or phrase. ▶ **v.** [intrans.] (of an electronic device) make a short high-pitched sound or repeated sequence of sounds: *the screen flickered and bleeped.* ■ [trans.] substitute a bleep or bleeps for (a censored word or phrase): *cable operators have* **bleeped out** *the accuser's name.* ■ used in place of an expletive: *"what the bleep are we going to do?" he asked.* [1950s: imitative.]

bleep·ing /'blēpiNG/ ▶ **adj.** (of an electronic device) making a short high-pitched sound or sounds. ■ informal, often humorous used to express exasperation or annoyance, in place of an expletive: *we didn't do a bleeping thing.* [1950s: euphemistically for BLEEDING.]

blem·ish /'blemisH/ ▶ **n.** a small mark or flaw that spoils the appearance of something. ■ fig. a moral defect or fault. ▶ **v.** [trans.] [often as adj.] (**blemished**) spoil the appearance of (something) that is otherwise aesthetically perfect: *thousands of Web pages are blemished with embarrassing typos.* [ME: from OFr. *ble(s)miss-*, stem of *ble(s)mir* 'make pale'; prob. of Gmc. origin.]

blench[1] /blencH/ ▶ **v.** [intrans.] make a sudden flinching movement out of fear or pain: *he blenched and struggled to regain his composure.* [OE *blencan* 'deceive,' of Gmc. origin.]

blench[2] ▶ **v.** esp. dialect var. of BLANCH.

blend /blend/ ▶ **v.** [trans.] mix (a substance) with another substance so that they combine together as a mass: **blend** *the cornstarch* **with** *a tablespoon of water* | [intrans.] *add the grated cheese and blend well.* ■ [often as adj.] (**blended**) mix (different types of the same substance, such as tea, coffee, liquor, etc.) together so as to make a product of the desired quality: *a blended whiskey.* ■ put or combine (abstract things) together: *blend basic information for the novice with some scientific gardening for the more experienced* | [as n.] (**blending**) *a blending of romanticism.* ■ merge (a color) with another so that one is not clearly distinguishable from the other. ■ [intrans.] form a harmonious combination: *costumes, music, and lighting all **blend together** beautifully.* ■ (**blend in/into**) be unobtrusive or harmonious by being similar in appearance or behavior: *employ a bodyguard in the house, someone who would blend in.* ▶ **n.** a mixture of different things or people. ■ a mixture of different types or grades of a substance, such as tea, coffee, whiskey, etc. ■ a combination of different abstract things or qualities. ■ a word made up of the parts of others and combining their meanings, for example *motel* from *motor* and *hotel.* [ME: prob. of Scand. origin and rel. to ON *blanda* 'to mix.']

blende /blend/ ▶ **n.** another term for SPHALERITE. [17th C.: from Ger., from *blenden* 'deceive.']

blend·ed fam·i·ly ▶ **n.** a family consisting of a couple and their children from this and all previous relationships.

blend·er /'blendər/ ▶ **n.** a person or thing that mixes things together, in particular: ■ an electric mixing machine used in food preparation for liquefying, chopping, or puréeing.

Blen·heim¹ /'blenəm/ a battle in 1704 in Bavaria, in which the English defeated the French and the Bavarians. See MARLBOROUGH.

Blen·heim² ▶ **n.** a dog of a small red and white breed of spaniel. [19th C.: *Blenheim* palace, the Duke of Marlborough's seat in England.]

blen·ny /'blenē/ ▶ **n.** (pl. **-nies**) a small, spiny-finned, blunt-headed marine fish (*Blennius* and other genera, family Blennidae), typically living in shallow inshore or intertidal waters. Its scaleless skin is covered with a protective slime. ■ [with adj.] any of a number of other small fishes that resemble or are related to the true blennies, including the **hairy blenny** (*Labrisomus nuchipinnis*, family Clinidae), found esp. along the Atlantic coast from the Bahamas to Brazil. [18th C.: from L. *blennius*, from Gk. *blennos* 'mucus.']

hairy blenny

blent /blent/ literary past and past participle of BLEND.

bleph·a·ri·tis /ˌblefə'rītis/ ▶ **n.** Med. inflammation of the eyelid. [19th C.: from Gk. *blepharon* 'eyelid.']

bleph·a·ro·plas·ty /'blefərəˌplastē/ ▶ **n.** Med. surgical repair or reconstruction of an eyelid. [19th C.: from Gk. *blepharon* 'eyelid.']

bleph·a·ro·spasm /'blefərəˌspazəm/ ▶ **n.** involuntary tight closure of the eyelids. [19th C.: from Gk. *blepharon* 'eyelid.']

Blé·riot /'blārēˌō; ble(ə)r'yō/, Louis (1872–1936), French aviator. In 1909, he became the first person to cross the English Channel in a monoplane.

bles·bok /'blesˌbäk/ ▶ **n.** an antelope (*Damaliscus dorcas phillipsi*) with a mainly reddish-brown coat and white face, found in southwestern South Africa. It belongs to the same species as the bontebok. [19th C.: from Afrik., from Du. *bles* 'blaze' + *bok* 'buck.']

bless /bles/ ▶ **v.** [trans.] (of a priest) pronounce words in a religious rite, to confer or invoke divine favor upon. ■ consecrate (something) by a religious rite, action, or spoken formula. ■ (esp. in Christian Church services) call (God) holy; praise (God). ■ (**bless someone with**) (of God or some notional higher power) endow (someone) with a particular cherished thing or attribute. ■ express or feel gratitude to; thank. ■ (**bless oneself**) archaic make the Christian gesture of the sign of the cross. ■ used in expressions of surprise, endearment, gratitude, etc.: *bless my soul, Alan, what are you doing?*

– PHRASES **bless you!** said to a person who has just sneezed. [from *(may) God bless you.*] [OE *blēdsian, blētsian*, based on *blōd* 'blood' (i.e., orig. perh. 'mark or consecrate with blood').]

blessed /blest; 'blesid/ ▶ **adj.** **1** made holy; consecrated. ■ a title preceding the name of a dead person considered to have led a holy life, esp. a person formally beatified by the Roman Catholic Church. ■ used respectfully in reference to a dead person. ■ endowed with divine favor and protection. ■ bringing pleasure or relief as a welcome contrast to what one has previously experienced. ■ (**blessed with**) endowed with (a particular quality or attribute). **2** informal used in mild expressions of annoyance or exasperation. ▶ **plural n.** (**the Blessed** /'blesid/) those who live with God in heaven. — **bless·ed·ly** /'blesidlē/ **adv.**

bless·ed·ness /'blesidnis/ ▶ **n.** the state of being blessed with divine favor.

Bless·ed Vir·gin Mar·y /'blesid/ (also **Bles·sed Vir·gin**) (abbr.: **BVM**) a title given to Mary, the mother of Jesus. See MARY¹.

bless·ing /'blesiNG/ ▶ **n.** [in sing.] God's favor and protection. ■ a prayer asking for such favor and protection. ■ grace said before or after a meal. ■ a beneficial thing for which one is grateful; something that brings well-being. ■ a person's sanction or support.

– PHRASES **a blessing in disguise** an apparent misfortune that eventually has good results. **count one's blessings** see COUNT¹.

blest /blest/ ▶ **adj.** archaic or literary term for BLESSED.

bleth·er /'bleT͟Hər/ ▶ **n.** another term for BLATHER.

bleu cheese /blo͞o/ ▶ **n.** var. of BLUE CHEESE.

blew /blo͞o/ past of BLOW¹ and BLOW³.

blew·it /'blo͞oit/ (also **blew·its**) ▶ **n.** an edible wild mushroom (genus *Lepista*, family Tricholomataceae) of Europe and North America, with a pale buff or lilac cap and a lilac stem. [19th C.: prob. from BLUE.]

Bligh /blī/, William (1754–1817), British navy officer; captain of HMS *Bounty*. In 1789, part of his crew mutinied and set Bligh adrift. He landed safely at Timor a few weeks later.

blight /blīt/ ▶ **n.** a plant disease, esp. one caused by fungi such as mildews, rusts, and smuts. ■ informal anything that causes a plant disease or interferes with the healthy growth of a plant. ■ [in sing.] a thing that spoils or damages something. ■ an ugly or neglected urban area. ▶ **v.** [trans.] (usu. **be blighted**) infect (plants or a planted area) with blight: *a peach tree blighted by leaf curl.* ■ spoil, harm, or destroy: *the scandal blighted the careers of several politicians* | [as adj.] (**blighted**) *his father's blighted ambitions.* ■ [usu. as adj.] (**blighted**) subject (an urban area) to neglect: *blighted areas.* [16th C.: of unknown origin.]

blight·er /'blītər/ ▶ **n.** [with adj.] Brit., informal a person who is regarded with contempt, irritation, or pity: *you little blighter!* [19th C.: from BLIGHT.]

bli·mey /'blīmē/ ▶ **exclam.** Brit., informal used to express one's surprise, excitement, or alarm. [19th C.: alt. form of *(God) blind* (or *blame*) *me!*]

blimp /blimp/ ▶ **n.** **1** informal a small nonrigid airship. ■ an obese person. **2** a soundproof cover for a movie camera. — **blimp·ish adj.** [World War I (sense 1): of uncert. origin. Sense 2 from character invented by cartoonist David Low (1891–1963).]

blin /blin/ singular form of BLINI.

blind /blīnd/ ▶ **adj.** **1** unable to see; sightless. ■ [attrib.] (of an action, esp. a test or experiment) done without being able to see or without being in possession of certain information. ■ Aeron. (of flying) using instruments only. **2** [predic.] lacking perception or discernment: *he's absolutely blind where you're concerned.* ■ (**blind to**) unwilling or unable to appreciate or notice something apparent to others. ■ [attrib.] (of an action or state of mind) not controlled by reason or judgment: *they left in blind panic.* ■ [attrib.] not governed by purpose. **3** [attrib.] concealed or closed, in particular: ■ (of a corner or bend in a road) impossible to see around. ■ (of a door or window) walled up. ■ closed at one end. ■ (of a plant) without buds, eyes, or terminal flowers. **4** informal drunk. ▶ **v.** [trans.] **1** cause (someone) to be unable to see, permanently or temporarily: *eyes blinded with tears.* **2** (**be blinded**) deprive (someone) of understanding, judgment, or perception: *a clever tactician blinded by passion.* ■ (**blind someone with**) confuse or overawe someone with something difficult to understand. ▶ **n.** **1** [as pl. n.] (**the blind**) people who are unable to see. **2** an obstruction to sight or light, in particular: a screen for a window, esp. one on a roller or made of slats. **3** [in sing.] something designed to conceal one's real intentions. ■ a hiding place. ■ a camouflaged shelter used by hunters to get close to wildlife: *a duck blind.* ▶ **adv.** without being able to see clearly: *he was the first pilot to fly blind.* ■ without having all the relevant information; unprepared. ■ (of a stake in poker and other games) put up by a player before the cards dealt are seen.

– PHRASES **(as) blind as a bat** informal having very bad eyesight. **blind drunk** informal extremely drunk. **rob** (or **steal**) **someone blind** informal rob or cheat someone in a comprehensive or merciless way. **turn a blind eye** pretend not to notice. — **blind·ing adj. blind·ing·ly adv. blind·ly adv. blind·ness n.** [OE, of Gmc. origin; rel. to Ger. *blind.*]

blind al·ley ▶ **n.** an alley or road that is closed at one end. ■ fig. a course of action leading nowhere.

blind date ▶ **n.** a social engagement or date with a person one has not previously met. ■ either person of the couple on a blind date.

blind·er /'blīndər/ ▶ **n.** (**blinders**) a pair of small leather screens attached to a horse's bridle to prevent it seeing sideways and behind. Also called BLINKERS (see BLINKER). See illustration at HARNESS. ■ fig. something that prevents someone from gaining a full understanding of a situation.

blind·fish /'blīndˌfisH/ ▶ **n.** another term for CAVEFISH.

blind·fold /'blīndˌfōld/ ▶ **v.** [trans.] (often **be blindfolded**) deprive (someone) of sight by tying a piece of cloth around the head to cover the eyes. ▶ **n.** a piece of cloth tied around the head to cover someone's eyes. ▶ **adj.** literary wearing a blindfold. ■ (of a game of chess) conducted without sight of board and pieces. ▶ **adv.** with a blindfold covering the eyes. ■ done with great ease and confidence, as if it could have been done wearing a blindfold. [16th C.: alt. of *blindfeld*, past part. of obs. *blindfell* 'strike blind,' from OE *geblindfellan* (see BLIND, FELL²).]

blind gut ▶ **n.** the cecum.

blind·man's bluff /'blīndmənz/ (also **blind·man's buff**) ▶ **n.** a children's game in which a blindfolded player tries to catch others while being pushed about by them. [17th C.: *bluff*, alt. of *buff* 'a blow,' from OFr. *bufe* (see BUFFET²).]

blind pig ▶ **n.** another term for BLIND TIGER.

blind pool ▶ **n.** a company that sells stock without specifying how invested money will be spent.

blind side ▶ **n.** [in sing.] a direction in which a person has a poor view, typically of approaching danger. ■ the side opposite the one toward which a person is looking. ▶ **v.** (**blind·side**) [trans.] hit or attack (someone) on the blind side: *Jenkins blindsided Adams.* ■ (often **be blindsided**) catch (someone) unprepared; attack from an unexpected position.

blind·sight /'blīndˌsīt/ ▶ **n.** Med. the ability to respond to visual stimuli without consciously perceiving them.

blind snake ▶ **n.** a small burrowing insectivorous snake (esp. family Typhlopidae) that lacks a distinct head and has very small inefficient eyes. Also called WORM SNAKE.

blind spot ▶ n. **1** Anat. the point of entry of the optic nerve on the retina, insensitive to light. **2** an area where a person's view is obstructed. ■ an area in which a person lacks understanding or impartiality. **3** Telecom. a point within the normal range of a transmitter where there is unusually weak reception.

blind stitch ▶ n. a sewing stitch producing stitches visible on one side only. ▶ v. (**blind-stitch**) [trans.] sew (something) using such a stitch.

blind ti·ger ▶ n. informal an illegal bar.

blind trust ▶ n. a financial arrangement in which a person in public office gives the administration of private business interests to an independent trust in order to prevent conflict of interest.

blind·worm /ˈblīndˌwərm/ ▶ n. another term for SLOW-WORM.

bling /bliNG/ (also **bling-bling**) informal ▶ n. [often as adj.] expensive, ostentatious clothing and jewelery, or the wearing of them: *a backless bling bling orange top.* ▶ v. [intrans.] adopt a flamboyant or ostentatious lifestyle or appearance: *I'm blinging for the troops, so they can feel good.* [1990s: perh. imitative of light reflecting off jewelry, or of jewelry clashing together.]

blin·i /ˈblinē; ˈblē-/ (also **blin·y** or **blin·is**) ▶ plural n. (sing. **blin** /blin/) pancakes made from buckwheat flour and served with sour cream. [Russ. (pl.).]

blink /bliNGk/ ▶ v. [intrans.] **1** shut and open the eyes quickly: *she blinked, momentarily blinded* | [trans.] *he blinked his eyes nervously.* ■ [trans.] clear (dust or tears) from the eyes by this action: *she* **blinked away** *her tears.* ■ [trans.] (**blink back**) try to control or prevent (tears) by such an action: *Elizabeth blinked back tears.* ■ (**blink at**) look at (someone or something) with one's eyes opening and shutting, typically to register surprise or bewilderment. ■ (**blink at**) [usu. with negative] fig. react to (something) with surprise or disapproval: *he doesn't blink at the unsavory aspects of his subject.* ■ fig. back down from a confrontation. **2** (of a light or light source) shine intermittently or unsteadily. ▶ n. [in sing.] **1** an act of shutting and opening the eyes quickly. ■ fig. a moment's hesitation. **2** a momentary gleam of light.

– PHRASES **not blink an eye** show no reaction. **in the blink of an eye** (or **in a blink**) informal very quickly. **on the blink** informal (of a machine) not working properly; out of order. [ME: from *blenk*, Scots var. of BLENCH[1].]

blink·er /ˈbliNGkər/ ▶ n. **1** a device that blinks, esp. a vehicle's turn signal. **2** (**blinkers**) another term for *BLINDERS* (see BLINDER). ▶ v. [trans.] (often **be blinkered**) put blinders on (a horse). ■ fig. cause (someone) to have a narrow or limited outlook on a situation: *university education blinkers researchers so that they see poverty in terms of their own specialization.*

blink·ered /ˈbliNGkərd/ ▶ adj. (of a horse) wearing blinders. ■ fig. having or showing a limited outlook: *a small-minded, blinkered approach.*

blintz /blints/ (also **blint·ze** /ˈblintsə/) ▶ n. a thin rolled pancake filled with cheese or fruit and then fried or baked. [from Yiddish *blintse*, from Russ. *blinets* 'little pancakes.']

blin·y ▶ plural n. var. of BLINI.

blip /blip/ ▶ n. **1** a short high-pitched sound made by an electronic device. **2** a flashing point of light on a radar screen representing an object, typically accompanied by a high-pitched sound. **3** an unexpected, minor, and typically temporary deviation from a general trend. **4** a brief segment, esp. of a telecast. ▶ v. (**blipped, blip·ping**) **1** [intrans.] (of an electronic device) make a short high-pitched sound or succession of sounds. **2** [trans.] open (the throttle of a motor vehicle) momentarily. [19th C.: imitative.]

bliss /blis/ ▶ n. perfect happiness; great joy. ■ something providing such happiness. ■ a state of spiritual blessedness, typically that reached after death.

– PHRASAL VERBS **bliss out** [often as adj.] (**blissed out**) informal reach a state of perfect happiness, typically so as to be oblivious of everything else: *blissed-out hippies.* [OE *blīths, bliss*, of Gmc. origin; rel. to BLITHE.]

bliss·ful /ˈblisfəl/ ▶ adj. extremely happy; full of joy. ■ providing perfect happiness or great joy.

– PHRASES **blissful ignorance** fortunate unawareness of something unpleasant. — **bliss·ful·ly** adv. **bliss·ful·ness** n.

B-list /ˈbēˌlist/ ▶ n. see A-LIST.

blis·ter /ˈblistər/ ▶ n. a small bubble on the skin filled with serum and caused by friction, burning, or other damage. ■ a similar swelling, filled with air or fluid, on the surface of a plant, heated metal, painted wood, or other object. ■ Med., esp. hist. a preparation applied to the skin to form a blister. ▶ v. **1** [intrans.] form swellings filled with air or fluid on something: *the door began to blister* | [as adj.] (**blistered**) *he had blistered feet.* ■ [trans.] cause blisters to form on the surface of: *a caustic liquid that blisters the skin.* **2** criticize sharply. [ME: perh. from OFr. *blestre* 'swelling.']

blis·ter bee·tle ▶ n. a beetle (*Lytta* and other genera, family Meloidae) that, when alarmed or crushed, secretes a substance that causes blisters. The larvae are typically parasites of other insects.

blis·ter cop·per ▶ n. partly purified copper with a blistered surface formed during smelting.

blis·ter·ing /ˈblistəriNG/ ▶ adj. (of heat) intense. ■ fig. (of criticism) expressed with great vehemence. ■ extremely fast, forceful, or impressive.

blis·ter pack ▶ n. packaging in which a product is sealed in plastic, often with a cardboard backing.

blis·ter rust ▶ n. any of several destructive diseases of pine trees caused by fungi of the genus *Conartium*, resulting in orange blisters on the bark and branches.

blithe /blīTH; blīTH/ ▶ adj. showing a casual and cheerful indifference considered to be callous or improper. ■ happy or joyous. — **blithe·ly** adv. **blithe·ness** n. **blithe·some** /-səm/ adj. (literary). [OE *blīthe*, of Gmc. origin; rel. to Du. *blijde*, also to BLISS.]

blith·er /ˈbliTHər/ ▶ v. & n. another term for BLATHER.

blith·er·ing /ˈbliTHəriNG/ ▶ adj. [attrib.] informal senselessly talkative, babbling; used chiefly as an intensive to express annoyance or contempt.

BLitt (also **BLit**) ▶ abbr. ■ Bachelor of Letters. ■ Bachelor of Literature. [from L. *Baccalaureus Litterarum*.]

blitz /blits/ ▶ n. an intensive or sudden military attack. ■ informal a sudden, energetic, and concerted effort, typically on a specific task. ■ Football a charge of the passer by the defensive linebackers just after the ball is snapped. ■ (**the Blitz**) the German air raids on Britain in 1940. ■ a form of chess in which moves must be made at very short intervals. ▶ v. [trans.] (often **be blitzed**) attack or damage (a place or building) in a blitz: *Rotterdam had been blitzed.* ■ Football attack (the passer) in a blitz. [abbrev. of BLITZKRIEG.]

blitz·krieg /ˈblitsˌkrēg/ ▶ n. an intense military campaign intended to bring about a swift victory. [World War II: from Ger., lit. 'lightning war.']

Blix·en /ˈbliksən/, Karen Christentze, Baroness Blixen-Finecke (1885–1962), Danish writer; born *Karen Dinesen*; pen name *Isak Dinesen*. Her autobiography, *Out of Africa* (1937), was made into a movie in 1985.

bliz·zard /ˈblizərd/ ▶ n. a severe snowstorm with high winds and low visibility. ■ fig. an overabundance; a deluge. [19th C. ('violent blow'): of unknown origin.]

bloat[1] /blōt/ ▶ v. [trans.] cause to swell with fluid or gas. ■ [intrans.] become swollen with fluid or gas: [as n.] (**bloating**) *she suffered from abdominal bloating.* ▶ n. a disease of livestock characterized by an accumulation of gas in the stomach. [17th C.: from obs. *bloat* 'swollen,' perh. from ON *blautr* 'soft.']

bloat[2] ▶ v. [trans.] cure (a herring) by salting and smoking it lightly. [16th C.: rel. to *bloat* in *bloat herring* 'bloater.']

bloat·ed /ˈblōtid/ ▶ adj. (of part of the body) swollen with fluid or gas. ■ fig. excessive in size or amount. ■ fig. (of a person) excessively wealthy and pampered.

bloat·er[1] /ˈblōtər/ ▶ n. a herring cured by salting and light smoking.

bloat·er[2] ▶ n. another term for CISCO.

bloat·ware /ˈblōtˌwe(ə)r/ ▶ n. Comput., informal software whose usefulness is reduced because of the excessive disk-space and memory it requires.

BLOB ▶ n Comput. binary large objects.

blob /bläb/ ▶ n. a drop of a thick liquid or other viscous substance. ■ a spot of color. ■ an indeterminate mass or shape. ▶ v. [trans.] (often **be blobbed**) put small drops of thick liquid or spots of color on: *her nose was blobbed with paint.* — **blob·by** adj. [ME: perh. symbolic of a drop of liquid.]

bloc /bläk/ ▶ n. a combination of countries, parties, or groups sharing a common purpose. [20th C.: from Fr., lit. 'block.']

Bloch /bläk/, Ernest (1880–1959), US composer; born in Switzerland. His works include *Israel Symphony* (1912–16) and *Solomon* (1916).

block /bläk/ ▶ n. **1** a large solid piece of hard material, esp. rock, stone, or wood, typically with flat surfaces on each side. ■ a sturdy, flat-topped block used as a work surface, typically for chopping food. ■ (usu. **blocks**) any of a set of solid cubes used as a child's toy. ■ a block of stone or low wooden steps from which a rider mounts a horse. ■ Sports (usu. **blocks**) a starting block. ■ Print. a piece of wood or metal engraved for printing on paper or fabric. ■ (also **cylinder block** or **engine block**) the main body of an internal combustion engine, containing the pistons. ■ a head-shaped mold used for shaping hats or wigs. **2** the area bounded by four streets in a town or suburb. ■ the length of one side of such an area, typically as a measure of distance. **3** [with adj.] a building, esp. part of a complex, used for a particular purpose. ■ esp. Brit. a large single building subdivided into separate rooms, apartments, or offices. **4** a large quantity or allocation of things regarded as a unit. ■ Comput. a large piece of text processed as a unit. ■ an unseparated unit of at least four postage stamps in at least two rows, generally a group of four. **5** an obstacle to the normal progress or functioning of something. ■ Sports a hindering or stopping of an opponent's movement or action. ■ Tennis a shot in which the racket is held stationary rather than being swung back. ■ short for NERVE BLOCK. ■ a chock for stopping the motion of a wheel. **6** a flat area of something, typically a solid area of color. **7** a pulley or system of pulleys mounted in a case. **8** informal a person's head. ▶ v. [trans.] **1** make the movement or flow in (a passage, pipe, road, etc.) difficult or impossible: ***block up** the holes with sticky tape* | *a police cordon* **blocked off** *roads* | [as adj.] (**blocked**) *a blocked nose.* ■ put an obstacle in the way of (something proposed or attempted): *he stood up, blocking her escape.* ■ restrict the use or conversion of (currency or any other asset). ■ Sports hinder or stop the movement or action of (an opponent). ■ Sports stop (a blow or ball) from finding its mark. ■ Med. produce insensibility in (a part of the body) by injecting an anesthetic close to the nerves that supply it. ■ Bridge play in such a way that an opponent cannot establish (a long suit). **2** impress text or a design on (a book cover). **3** Theater design or plan the movements of actors on a stage or movie set. **4** shape or reshape (a hat) using a wooden mold.

– PHRASES **have been around the block (a few times)** informal (of a person) have a lot of experience. **the new kid on the block** informal a newcomer to a particular place or sphere of activity, typically someone who has yet to prove themselves. **on the (auction) block** for sale at auction. **put** (or **lay**) **one's head** (or **neck**) **on the block** informal put one's standing or reputation at risk by proceeding with a particular course of action.

– PHRASAL VERBS **block something in 1** mark something out roughly. ■ add something in a unit. ■ paint something with solid areas of color. **2** park one's car in such a way as to prevent another car from moving away. **block something out 1** stop something, typically light or noise, from reaching somewhere. ■ fig. exclude something unpleasant from one's thoughts or memory. **2** mark or sketch something out roughly. [ME ('log'): from OFr. *bloc* (n.), *bloquer* (v.), from MDu. *blok*.]

block·ade /bläˈkād/ ▶n. an act of sealing off a place to prevent goods or people from entering or leaving. ■ anything that prevents access or progress. ■ an obstruction of a physiological or mental function, esp. of a biochemical receptor. ▶v. [trans.] seal off (a place) to prevent goods or people from entering or leaving.

– PHRASES **run a blockade** (of a ship) manage to enter or leave a blockaded port. — **blockader** n. [17th C.: from BLOCK.]

block·ade-run·ner ▶n. **1** a vessel that runs or attempts to run into or out of a blockaded port. **2** the owner, master, or one of the crew of such a vessel.

block·age /ˈbläkij/ ▶n. an obstruction that makes movement or flow difficult or impossible.

block and tack·le ▶n. a mechanism consisting of ropes and one or more pulley-blocks, used for lifting or pulling heavy objects.

block·bust·er /ˈbläk,bəstər/ ▶n. informal a thing of great power or size, in particular: ■ a movie, book, or other product that is a great commercial success. ■ a huge aerial bomb capable of destroying targets within a wide area.

block·bust·ing /ˈbläk,bəstiNG/ ▶adj. very successful commercially. ▶n. the practice of persuading owners to sell property cheaply because of the fear of people of another race or class moving into the neighborhood, and thus profiting by reselling at a higher price.

block cap·i·tals ▶plural n. another term for BLOCK LETTERS.

block di·a·gram ▶n. a diagram showing in schematic form the general arrangement of parts or components of a complex system or process.

block·er /ˈbläkər/ ▶n. a person or thing that blocks, in particular: ■ Football a player whose task it is to block for the ballcarrier or kicker. ■ a substance that prevents or inhibits a given physiological function.

block and tackle

block grant ▶n. a grant from a central government that a local authority can allocate to a range of services.

block·head /ˈbläk,hed/ ▶n. informal a stupid person. — **block·head·ed** adj.

block heat·er ▶n. a device for heating the engine block of a vehicle.

block·house /ˈbläk,hous/ ▶n. a reinforced concrete shelter used as an observation point. ■ hist. a one-storied timber building with loopholes, used as a fort. ■ a house made of squared logs.

block·ing /ˈbläkiNG/ ▶n. **1** the action or process of obstructing movement, progress, or activity, in particular: ■ obstructing or impeding the actions of an opponent in a game, esp. (in ball sports) one who does not have control of the ball. ■ Psychiatry the sudden halting of the flow of thought or speech, as a symptom of schizophrenia or other mental disorder. ■ failure to recall an unpleasant memory or train of thought. **2** the grouping or treatment of things in blocks. ■ the physical arrangement of actors on a stage or movie set.

block·ish /ˈbläkisH/ ▶adj. **1** resembling a block. ■ big, bulky, or crude in form or appearance. **2** unintelligent and stupid.

Block Is·land (abbr.: **BI**) an island in southern Rhode Island, in the Atlantic Ocean at the eastern end of Long Island Sound.

block let·ters ▶plural n. plain capital letters.

block moun·tain ▶n. Geol. a mountain consisting of a block or blocks bounded by normal faults in the earth's crust.

block par·ty ▶n. a party for all the residents of a block or neighborhood.

block plane ▶n. a carpenter's plane with a blade set at an acute angle

block sys·tem ▶n. a system of railroad signaling that divides the track into sections and allows no train to enter a section that is not completely clear.

block·y /ˈbläkē/ ▶adj. of the nature of or resembling a block or blocks.

Bloem·fon·tein /ˈblo͞omfän,tān/ a city in central South Africa. It is the judicial capital of the country; pop. 300,150.

blog /blôg; bläg/ ▶n. a Web site on which an individual or group of users record opinions, information, etc. on a regular basis. ▶v. (**blogged, blog·ging**) [intrans.] add new material to or regularly update a blog. — **blog·ger** n.

blog·o·sphere /ˈblôgə,sfi(ə)r; ˈblä-/ ▶n. the world of weblogs.

bloke /blōk/ ▶n. Brit., informal a man; a fellow. [19th C.: from Shelta.]

blond /bländ/ ▶adj. (of hair) fair or pale yellow. ■ (of a person) having hair of a fair or pale yellow color. ■ (of a person) having fair hair and a light complexion, typically regarded as a racial characteristic. ■ (of wood and other substances) light in color or tone. ▶n. a person with fair hair and skin. — **blond·ish** adj. **blond·ness** n. [15th C.: via Fr. from med. L. *blundus* 'yellow.']

blonde /bländ/ ▶adj. (of a woman or a woman's hair) blond. ▶n. a blond-haired woman. [17th C.: from Fr., fem. of *blond*.]

Blood /bləd/ ▶n. (pl. same or **Bloods**) a member of a North American Indian people belonging to the Blackfoot Confederacy.

blood /bləd/ ▶n. **1** the red liquid that circulates in the arteries and veins of humans and other vertebrate animals, carrying oxygen to and carbon dioxide from the tissues of the body. ■ an internal bodily fluid, not necessarily red, that performs a similar function in invertebrates. ■ fig. violence involving bloodshed. ■ fig. a person's downfall or punishment, typically as retribution. **2** fig. temperament or disposition, esp. when passionate. **3** [with adj.] family background; descent or lineage. ■ [in comb.] a person of specified descent: *a mixed-blood.* ■ informal a fellow black person. **4** (usu. **Blood**) a member of a Los Angeles street gang.

– PHRASES **be like getting blood out of** (or **from**) **a stone** (or **turnip**) be extremely difficult (said in reference to obtaining something from someone). **blood and guts** informal violence and bloodshed, typically in fiction. **blood is thicker than water** proverb relationships and loyalties within a family are the strongest and most important ones. **blood, sweat, and tears** extremely hard work; unstinting effort. **blood will tell** proverb family characteristics cannot be concealed. **first blood 1** the first shedding of blood, esp. in a boxing match or formerly in dueling with swords. **2** the first point or advantage gained in a contest. **give blood** allow blood to be removed medically from one's body in order to be stored for use in transfusions. **have blood on one's hands** be responsible for someone's death. **have** (or **get**) **one's blood up** be in a fighting mood. **in one's blood** ingrained in or fundamental to one's character. **in cold blood** ruthlessly; without feeling. **make someone's blood boil** informal infuriate someone. **make someone's blood run cold** horrify someone. **new** (or **fresh**) **blood** new members admitted to a group. **out for (someone's) blood** set on getting revenge. **taste blood** achieve an early success that stimulates further efforts. **young blood** a younger member or members of a group. [OE *blōd*, of Gmc. origin; rel. to Ger. *Blut*.]

blood bank ▶n. a place where supplies of blood or plasma for transfusion are stored.

blood·bath /ˈbləd,baTH/ ▶n. an event or situation in which many people are killed in a violent manner.

blood-brain bar·ri·er ▶n. Physiology a filtering mechanism of the capillaries that blocks the passage of certain substances.

blood broth·er ▶n. a brother by birth. ■ a man who has sworn to treat another man as a brother.

blood cell ▶n. any of the kinds of cell normally found circulating in the blood.

blood clot ▶n. a gelatinous or semisolid mass of coagulated blood.

blood count ▶n. a determination of the number of corpuscles in a specific volume of blood. ■ the number found in such a procedure.

blood·cur·dling /ˈbləd,kərd(ə)liNG/ (also **blood-cur·dling**) ▶adj. causing terror or horror.

blood do·nor ▶n. a person who gives blood for transfusion.

blood·ed /ˈblədid/ ▶adj. [usu. in comb.] having blood or a temperament of a specified kind: *warm-blooded animals.* ■ (of horses or cattle) of good pedigree: *a blooded stallion.*

blood feud ▶n. a lengthy conflict between families.

blood·fin /ˈbləd,fin/ ▶n. a small South American freshwater fish (*Aphyocharax rubripinnis*, family Characidae) that is silvery-yellow with bright red fins, popular in aquariums.

blood fluke ▶n. another term for SCHISTOSOME.

blood group ▶n. any of the various types of human blood whose antigen characteristics determine compatibility in transfusion.

blood·guilt /ˈbləd,gilt/ ▶n. guilt resulting from murder or bloodshed. — **blood·guilt·y** adj.

blood·hound /ˈbləd,hound/ ▶n. a large hound of a breed with a very keen sense of smell, used in tracking.

bloodhound

blood·less /ˈblədlis/ ▶adj. **1** without blood. ■ (of a revolution or conflict) without violence or killing. ■ (of surgery or other medical procedures) spilling little or no blood. **2** (of the skin or a part of the body) drained of color. ■ (of a person) cold or unemotional. ■ lacking in vitality; feeble. — **blood·less·ly** adv. **blood·less·ness** n.

blood·let·ting /ˈbləd,letiNG/ ▶n. esp. hist. the surgical removal of some of a patient's blood for therapeutic purposes. ■ the violent killing and wounding of people during a war or conflict. ■ bitter division and quarreling within an organization.

blood·line /ˈbləd,līn/ ▶**n.** an animal's set of ancestors or pedigree. ■ a set of ancestors or line of descent of a person.

blood meal ▶**n.** dried blood used for feeding animals and as a fertilizer.

blood·mo·bile /ˈblədmə,bēl/ ▶**n.** a motor vehicle equipped for collecting blood from volunteer donors.

blood mon·ey ▶**n.** money paid in compensation to the family of someone who has been killed. ■ money paid to a hired killer. ■ money paid for information about a killer or killing.

blood or·ange ▶**n.** an orange of a variety with red or red-streaked flesh.

blood plate·let ▶**n.** see PLATELET.

blood poi·soning ▶**n.** the presence of microorganisms or their toxins in the blood, causing a diseased state; septicemia.

blood pres·sure ▶**n.** the pressure of the blood in the circulatory system, often measured for diagnosis since it is related to the force and rate of the heartbeat and the diameter and elasticity of the arterial walls.

blood pud·ding ▶**n.** another term for BLOOD SAUSAGE.

blood-red ▶**adj.** of the deep red color of blood. ▶**n.** a deep red.

blood re·la·tion (also **blood rel·a·tive**) ▶**n.** a person related to another by birth rather than by marriage.

blood·root /ˈbləd,ro͞ot; -,ro͝ot/ ▶**n.** a North American plant (*Sanguinaria canadensis*) of the poppy family that has white flowers and fleshy underground rhizomes that exude red sap when cut.

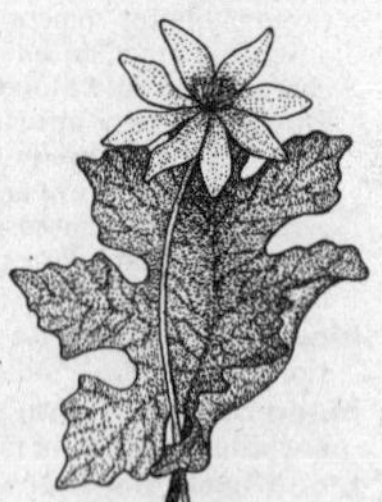

North American bloodroot

blood sau·sage (also **blood pudding**) ▶**n.** a dark sausage containing pork, dried pig's blood, and suet.

blood·shed /ˈbləd,sʜed/ ▶**n.** the killing or wounding of people.

blood·shot /ˈbləd,sʜät/ ▶**adj.** (of the eyes) inflamed or tinged with blood.

blood sport ▶**n.** (usu. **blood sports**) a sport involving the shedding of blood, esp. the hunting or killing of animals.

blood·stain /ˈbləd,stān/ ▶**n.** a stain caused by blood. —**blood·stained adj.**

blood·stock /ˈbləd,stäk/ ▶**n.** [treated as sing. or pl.] thoroughbred horses considered collectively.

blood·stone /ˈbləd,stōn/ ▶**n.** a type of green chalcedony spotted or streaked with red, used as a gemstone.

blood·stream /ˈbləd,strēm/ ▶**n.** [in sing.] the blood circulating through the body of a person or animal.

blood·suck·er /ˈbləd,səkər/ ▶**n.** **1** an animal or insect that sucks blood, esp. a leech or a mosquito. **2** a person who extorts money. ■ a person who lives off others; a parasite. — **blood·suck·ing adj.**

blood sug·ar ▶**n.** the amount of glucose in the blood.

blood test ▶**n.** a scientific examination of a sample of blood.

blood·thirst·y /ˈbləd,ᴛʜərstē/ ▶**adj.** (**-thirst·i·er, -thirst·i·est**) eager to shed blood. ■ (of a story or movie) containing or depicting much violence: *a bloodthirsty novel.* — **blood·thirst·i·ly** /-stəlē/ **adv. blood·thirst·i·ness n.**

blood type ▶**n.** another term for BLOOD GROUP.

blood typ·ing ▶**n.** the testing of a blood sample to determine an individual's blood group.

blood ves·sel ▶**n.** a tubular structure carrying blood through tissues and organs; a vein, artery, or capillary.

blood·worm /ˈbləd,wərm/ ▶**n.** **1** the bright red aquatic larva of a nonbiting midge (genus *Chironomus*), the blood of which contains hemoglobin that allows it to live in poorly oxygenated water. **2** another term for TUBIFEX.

blood·wort /ˈbləd,wərt; -,wôrt/ ▶**n.** any of various plants having red roots or leaves, esp. the red-veined dock.

blood·y[1] /ˈblədē/ ▶**adj.** (**blood·i·er, blood·i·est**) **1** covered, smeared, or running with blood. ■ composed of or resembling blood. **2** involving or characterized by bloodshed or cruelty. ▶**v.** (**blood·ies, blood·ied**) [trans.] (often **be bloodied**) cover or stain with blood.
– PHRASES **bloody** (or **bloodied**) **but unbowed** proud of what one has achieved despite having suffered great difficulties or losses. — **blood·i·ly adv. blood·i·ness n.**

blood·y[2] ▶**adj.** [attrib.] vulgar slang esp. Brit. used to express anger, annoyance, or shock, or simply for emphasis: *took your bloody time* | [as exclam.] *bloody Hell!—what was that?* | [as submodifier] *it's bloody cold outside.* [17th C.: from BLOODY[1].]

Blood·y Mar·y[1] the nickname of Mary I of England (see MARY[2]).

Blood·y Mar·y[2] ▶**n.** a drink consisting of vodka and seasoned tomato juice.

blood·y-mind·ed ▶**adj.** Brit., informal deliberately uncooperative. — **blood·y-mind·ed·ly adv. blood·y-mind·ed·ness n.**

bloo·ey /ˈblo͞oē/ (also **bloo·ie**) informal ▶**adv. & adj.** awry; amiss: [as adv.] *the ignition switch went blooey.* ▶**exclam.** used to convey that something has happened in an abrupt way: *and, blooey! He shot himself dead.* [1920s: of unknown origin.]

bloom[1] /blo͞om/ ▶**n.** **1** a flower, esp. one cultivated for its beauty. ■ the state or period of flowering. ■ the state or period of greatest beauty, freshness, or vigor. **2** [in sing.] a youthful or healthy glow in a person's complexion. **3** a delicate powdery surface deposit on certain fresh fruits, leaves, or stems. ■ (also **algal bloom**) a rapid growth of microscopic algae or cyanobacteria in water, often resulting in a colored scum on the surface. ■ a grayish-white appearance on chocolate caused by cocoa butter rising to the surface. ▶**v.** [intrans.] produce flowers; be in flower: *a rose tree bloomed on a ruined wall.* ■ come into or be in full beauty or health; flourish: *she bloomed as an actress.* ■ (of fire, color, or light) become radiant and glowing: *color bloomed in her cheeks.*
– PHRASES **the bloom is off the rose** something is no longer new, fresh, or exciting. [ME: from ON *blóm* 'flower,' *blómi* 'prosperity.']

bloom[2] ▶**n.** a mass of iron, steel, or other metal hammered or rolled into a thick bar for further working. ■ hist. an unworked mass of puddled iron. ▶**v.** [trans.] [usu. as n.] (**blooming**) make (metal) into such a mass. [OE *blōma.*]

Bloom·er /ˈblo͞omər/, Amelia Jenks (1818–94), US feminist. She founded the paper *Lily* 1849, and wore pants that came to be known as "bloomers."

bloom·er /ˈblo͞omər/ ▶**n.** [usu. in comb.] a plant that produces flowers at a specified time: *fragrant night-bloomers.* ■ [with adj.] a person who matures or flourishes at a specified time: *he was a late bloomer.*

bloo·mers /ˈblo͞omərz/ ▶**plural n.** women's loose-fitting knee-length underpants. ■ hist. women's and girls' loose-fitting trousers, gathered at the knee or the ankle. [19th C.: Amelia J. *Bloomer* (1818–94), American social reformer.]

Bloom·field[1] /ˈblo͞om,fēld/ a township in northeastern New Jersey; pop. 45,061.

Bloom·field[2], Leonard (1887–1949), US linguist. He was one of the founders of American structural linguistics.

bloom·ing /ˈblo͞omiɴɢ/ ▶**adj. & adv.** Brit., informal used for emphasis or to express annoyance: [as adj.] *I didn't learn a blooming thing* | [as submodifier] *a blooming good read.*

Bloom·ing·ton /ˈblo͞omiɴɢtən/ **1** a city in central Illinois; pop. 51,972. **2** a city in south central Indiana; pop. 69,291. **3** a city in southeastern Minnesota; pop. 85,172.

Blooms·bur·y /ˈblo͞omzbərē; -,berē/ an area of central London noted for its associations with the Bloomsbury Group. ■ [as adj.] associated with or similar to the Bloomsbury Group.

Blooms·bur·y Group a group of writers, artists, and philosophers living in or associated with Bloomsbury in the early 20th century. Members of the group, which included Virginia Woolf, Lytton Strachey, Vanessa Bell, and Roger Fry, were known for their unconventional lifestyles and attitudes.

bloop /blo͞op/ ▶**v.** [intrans.] informal make a mistake: *the company admitted it had blooped.* ■ [trans.] Baseball hit a ball weakly or make (a hit) from a poorly hit fly ball landing just beyond the reach of the infielders. ▶**n.** informal a mistake. ■ Baseball another term for BLOOPER (sense 2): [as adj.] *a bloop single.* — **bloop·y adj.** [1920s: imitative.]

bloop·er /ˈblo͞opər/ ▶**n.** informal **1** an embarrassing error. ■ a brief television or radio segment containing a humorous error, collected with others for broadcast as a group. **2** Baseball a weakly hit fly ball landing just beyond the reach of the infielders.

blos·som /ˈbläsəm/ ▶**n.** a flower or a mass of flowers on a tree or bush. ■ the state or period of flowering. ▶**v.** [intrans.] (of a tree or bush) produce flowers or masses of flowers: *the mango trees have blossomed again.* ■ mature or develop in a promising or healthy way: *their friendship blossomed into romance* | [as n.] (**blossoming**) *the blossoming of experimental theater.* ■ seem to grow or open like a flower. — **blos·som·y adj.** [OE *blōstm, blōstma* (n.), *blōstmian* (v.), of Gmc. origin; rel. to Du. *bloesem* and BLOOM[1].]

blot /blät/ ▶**n.** a dark mark or stain, typically one made by ink, paint, or dirt. ■ a shameful act or quality that tarnishes an otherwise good character or reputation. ■ Biochem. a procedure in which proteins or nucleic acids separated on a gel are transferred directly to an immobilizing medium for identification. ▶**v.** (**blot·ted, blot·ting**) [trans.] **1** dry (a wet surface or substance) using an absorbent material: *Guy blotted his face with a dust rag.* ■ Biochem. transfer by means of a blot. **2** mark or stain (something): [as adj.] (**blotted**) *the writing was messy and blotted.* ■ tarnish the good character or reputation of. **3** (**blot something out**) cover writing or pictures with ink or paint so that they cannot be seen. ■ obscure a view. ■ obliterate or disregard something painful in one's memory or existence. [ME: prob. of Scand. origin and akin to ON *blettr.*]

blotch /bläcʜ/ ▶**n.** an irregular patch or unsightly mark on a surface, typically the skin. ▶**v.** (usu. **be blotched**) cover with blotches: *her face was blotched and swollen with crying.* — **blotch·y adj.** [17th C.: partly an alt. of obs. *plotch*; partly a blend of BLOT and BOTCH.]

blot·ter /ˈblätər/ ▶**n.** **1** a sheet or pad of blotting paper inserted into a frame and kept on a desk. **2** a temporary recording book, esp. that used by police to record arrests and charges.

blot·ting pa·per ▶**n.** absorbent paper used for soaking up excess ink when writing.

blot·to /ˈblätō/ ▶**adj.** informal extremely drunk. [20th C.: from BLOT.]

blouse /blous; blouz/ ▶**n.** a woman's loose upper garment resembling a shirt. ■ a loose linen or cotton garment of a type worn by peasants and manual workers, typically belted at the waist. ■ a type of jacket worn as part of military uniform. ▶**v.** [with obj. and adverbial] make (a garment) hang in loose folds: *I bloused my trousers over my boots* | [intrans.] *my dress* *bloused out above my waist.* [19th C.: from Fr., of unknown origin.]

blous·on /ˈblouˌsän; -ˌzän/ ▶ n. a short loose-fitting jacket, typically bloused and finishing at the waist. [20th C.: from Fr., dimin. of BLOUSE.]

blow[1] /blō/ ▶ v. (past **blew**; past part. **blown**) **1** [intrans.] (of wind) move creating an air current: *a cold wind began to blow.* ■ [trans.] (of wind) cause to move; propel: *a gust of wind blew a cloud of smoke into his face.* ■ [intrans.] be carried, driven, or moved by the wind or an air current: *cotton curtains blowing in the breeze.* ■ [trans.] informal leave (a place): *I'm ready to blow town* | [intrans.] *I'd better blow.* **2** [intrans.] (of a person) expel air through pursed lips: *Willie took a deep breath, and blew.* ■ [trans.] use one's breath to propel: *he blew cigar smoke in her face.* ■ breathe hard; pant: *Uncle Albert was soon puffing and blowing.* ■ [trans.] cause to breathe hard; exhaust of breath: [as adj.] (**blown**) *an exhausted, blown horse.* ■ [trans.] (of a person) force air through the mouth into (an instrument) in order to make a sound. ■ (of such an instrument) make a noise through being blown into in such a way. ■ [trans.] sound (the horn of a vehicle). ■ informal play jazz or rock music in an unrestrained style. ■ [trans.] force air through a tube into (molten glass) in order to create an artifact. ■ [trans.] remove the contents of (an egg) by forcing air through it. ■ [with adverbial of place] (of flies) lay eggs in or on something: *to repel the flies that would otherwise blow on the buffalo hide.* ■ (of a whale) eject air and vapor through the blowhole. **3** [trans.] (of an explosion or explosive device) displace violently or send flying: *the back of his head had been blown away.* ■ [intrans.] (of a vehicle tire) burst suddenly while the vehicle is in motion. ■ burst or cause to burst due to pressure or overheating: [intrans.] *the engines sounded as if their exhausts had blown* | [trans.] *frost will have blown a compression joint.* ■ (of an electrical circuit) burn out or cause to burn out through overloading: [intrans.] *the fuse had blown* | [trans.] *the floodlights blew a fuse.* **4** [trans.] informal spend recklessly: *they blew $100,000.* **5** informal completely bungle (an opportunity): *politicians had blown it.* ■ (usu. **be blown**) expose (a stratagem): *a man whose cover was blown.* **6** (past part. **blowed**) [trans.] [usu. as imper.] Brit., informal damn: *"Well, blow me," he said, "I never knew that."* **7** [trans.] vulgar slang perform fellatio on. ▶ n. **1** [in sing.] a strong wind: *we're in for a blow.* **2** an act of blowing on an instrument. ■ [in sing.] an act of blowing one's nose. ■ [in sing.] informal a spell of playing jazz or rock music. ■ (in steelmaking) an act of sending an air or oxygen blast through molten metal in a converter. **3** informal cocaine.

– PHRASES **be blown off course** fig. (of a project) be disrupted by some circumstance. **be blown out of the water** fig. (of a person, idea, or project) be shown to lack all credibility. **blow** (or **clear**) **away the cobwebs** refresh oneself, typically by having some fresh air. **blow someone's brains out** informal kill someone with a shot in the head with a firearm. **blow the doors off** informal be considerably better or more successful than. **blow a fuse** see FUSE[1]. **blow a gasket** informal lose one's temper. **blow one's own horn** see HORN. **blow hot and cold** vacillate. **blow someone a kiss** kiss the tips of one's fingers then blow across them toward someone as a gesture of affection. **blow one's lid** (or **top** or **stack** or **cool**) informal lose one's temper. **blow the lid off** see LID. **blow me down** Brit. an exclamation of surprise. **blow someone's mind** informal affect someone very strongly. **blow one's nose** clear one's nose of mucus by blowing through it into a handkerchief. **blow off steam** see *LET OFF STEAM* at STEAM. **blow a raspberry** see RASPBERRY. **blow someone's socks off** see SOCK. **blow something to bits** (or **pieces** or **smithereens**) use explosives to destroy something, typically a building, completely. **blow something out of proportion** exaggerate the importance of something. **blow up in one's face** (of an action, project, or situation) go drastically wrong with damaging effects to oneself. **blow the whistle on** see WHISTLE. **blow with the wind** be incapable of maintaining a consistent course of action.

– PHRASAL VERBS **blow someone away** informal **1** kill someone using a firearm. **2** (**be blown away**) be extremely impressed. **blow in** informal (of a person) arrive unannounced. **blow off** lose one's temper and shout. **blow someone off** informal fail to keep an appointment with someone. ■ end a relationship with someone. **blow something off** informal ignore or make light of something. ■ fail to attend something: *Ivy blew off class.* **blow out 1** be extinguished by an air current. **2** (of a tire) puncture while the vehicle is in motion. **3** (of an oil or gas well) emit gas suddenly and forcefully. **4** (**blow itself out**) (of a storm) finally lose its force. **blow someone out** informal defeat someone convincingly. **blow something out 1** use one's breath to extinguish a flame. **2** informal render a part of the body useless. **blow over** (of trouble) fade away without serious consequences. **blow up 1** explode. ■ (of a person) lose one's temper. **2** (of a wind or storm) begin to develop. ■ (of a scandal or dispute) emerge or become public. **3** inflate. **blow something up 1** cause something to explode. **2** inflate something. ■ enlarge a photograph or text. [OE *blāwan*, from Indo-Eur.; akin to Ger. *blähen* 'blow up,' L. *flare* 'blow.']

blow[2] ▶ n. a powerful stroke with a hand, weapon, or hard object. ■ a sudden shock or disappointment.

– PHRASES **at one blow** by a single stroke; in one operation. **come to blows** start fighting after a disagreement. **soften** (or **cushion**) **the blow** make it easier to cope with a difficult change or upsetting news. **strike a blow for** (or **against**) act in support of (or opposition to). [ME: of unknown origin.]

blow[3] archaic literary ▶ v. (past **blew**; past part. **blown**) [intrans.] produce flowers or be in flower. ▶ n. the state or period of flowering. [OE *blōwan*, of Gmc. origin.]

blow·back /ˈblōˌbak/ ▶ n. **1** a process in which gases expand or travel in a direction opposite to the usual one. **2** the unintended adverse results of a political action or situation.

blow-by-blow ▶ adj. [attrib.] (of a description of an event) giving all the details in the order in which they occurred: *a blow-by-blow account of your rescue.*

blow·dart /ˈblōˌdärt/ ▶ n. a dart shot from a blowpipe.

blow·down /ˈblōˌdoun/ ▶ n. **1** a tree that has been blown down by the wind. ■ such trees collectively. ■ the blowing down of a tree or trees. **2** the removal of solids or liquids from a container or pipe, using pressure.

blow-dry ▶ v. [trans.] arrange (the hair) into a particular style while drying it with a hand-held dryer. ■ [as adj.] (**blow-dried**) fig. (of a person) well groomed, polished, and assured. ▶ n. [in sing.] an act of arranging the hair in such a way. — **blow-dryer** (also **blow·dri·er**) n.

blow·er /ˈblōər/ ▶ n. **1** a person or thing that blows, typically a mechanical device for creating a current of air. **2** informal, esp. Brit. a telephone.

blow·fish /ˈblōˌfisн/ ▶ n. (pl. same or **-fish·es**) any of a number of fishes that are able to inflate their bodies when alarmed.

blow·fly /ˈblōˌflī/ ▶ n. (pl. **-flies**) a large and typically metallic-colored fly (family Calliphoridae) that lays its eggs on meat and carcasses.

blow·gun /ˈblōˌgən/ ▶ n. a primitive weapon consisting of a long tube through which an arrow or dart is propelled by force of the breath.

blow·hard /ˈblōˌhärd/ informal ▶ n. a person who blusters and boasts in an unpleasant way.

blow·hole /ˈblōˌhōl/ ▶ n. a hole for blowing or breathing through, in particular: ■ the nostril of a whale on the top of its head. ■ a hole in ice through which seals, whales, and other aquatic animals breathe. ■ a vent for air or smoke in a tunnel or other structure. ■ a cavity in a metal casting, produced by the escape of air through the liquid metal.

blow job ▶ n. vulgar slang an act of fellatio.

blown /blōn/ past participle of BLOW[1]. ▶ adj. destroyed; spoiled. ■ informal (of a vehicle or its engine) provided with a turbocharger.

– PHRASES **blown away** extremely surprised; flabbergasted. **blown to bits** (or **smithereens**) completely destroyed.

blow·off /ˈblōˌôf/ ▶ n. the action of emitting a gas, typically to reduce pressure to a safe level.

blow·out /ˈblōˌout/ ▶ n. **1** a sudden rupture or malfunction of a part or apparatus due to pressure, in particular: ■ a bursting of an automobile tire. ■ fig. an outburst of anger; an argument. ■ an uprush of oil or gas from a well. ■ informal a melting of an electric fuse. **2** informal an easy victory in a sporting contest or an election. **3** informal a large or lavish meal or social gathering. **4** a hollow eroded by the wind. ▶ adj. huge; all-consuming.

blow·pipe /ˈblōˌpīp/ ▶ n. **1** another term for BLOWGUN. **2** a long tube by means of which molten glass is blown into the required shape. ■ a tube used to intensify the heat of a flame by blowing air or other gas through it at high pressure.

blows·y /ˈblouzē/ (also **blowz·y**) ▶ adj. (of a woman) coarse, untidy, and red-faced. — **blows·i·ly** /-zəlē/ adv. **blows·i·ness** n. [17th C.: from obs. *blowze* 'beggar's female companion.']

blow·torch /ˈblōˌtôrcн/ ▶ n. a portable device producing a hot flame that is directed onto a surface, typically to solder metal.

blow·up /ˈblōˌəp/ (also **blow-up**) ▶ n. **1** an enlargement of a photograph. **2** informal an outburst of anger. ▶ adj. [attrib.] inflatable.

blow·y /ˈblō-ē/ ▶ adj. (**blow·i·er, blow·i·est**) having or affected by strong winds; windy or windswept.

BLT ▶ n. informal a bacon, lettuce, and tomato sandwich.

blub·ber[1] /ˈbləbər/ ▶ n. the fat of sea mammals. ■ informal, derog. excessive human fat. — **blub·ber·y** adj. [ME: perh. symbolic.]

blub·ber[2] ▶ v. [intrans.] informal sob noisily and uncontrollably. [ME: prob. symbolic.]

blu·chers /ˈblo͝okərz; -cнərz/ ▶ plural n. hist. strong leather half-boots or high shoes. [19th C.: G. L. von *Blücher* (1742–1819), Prussian general.]

bludg·eon /ˈbləjən/ ▶ n. a thick stick with a heavy end, used as a weapon. ▶ v. [trans.] beat (someone) repeatedly with a bludgeon or other heavy object. ■ force or bully (someone) to do something. ■ (**bludgeon one's way**) make one's way by brute force. [18th C.: of unknown origin.]

blue /blo͞o/ ▶ adj. (**blu·er, blu·est**) **1** of a color intermediate between green and violet, as of the sky or sea on a sunny day. ■ (of a person's skin) having or turning such a color, esp. with cold or breathing difficulties. ■ (of a bird or other animal) having blue markings. ■ (of cats, foxes, or rabbits) having fur of a smoky gray color. ■ Physics denoting one of three colors of quark. **2** informal (of a person or mood) melancholy, sad, or depressed. **3** informal (of a movie, joke, or story) with sexual or pornographic content. ■ (of language) marked by cursing, swearing, and blasphemy. **4** informal rigidly religious or moralistic; puritanical. ▶ n. **1** blue color or pigment. ■ blue clothes or material. ■ a blue uniform, or a person wearing a blue uniform, such as a police officer or a baseball umpire. ■ (usu. **Blue**) the Union army in the Civil War, or a member of that army. **2** a blue thing, in particular: ■ a blue ball, piece, etc., in a game or sport. ■ (**the blue**) literary the sky or sea; the unknown. **3** [usu. with adj.] a small butterfly (family Lycaenidae), the male of which is predominantly blue while the female is typically brown. **4** another

term for **BLUING.** ▶ v. (**blues, blued, blu·ing** or **blue·ing**) **1** make or become blue: [trans.] *the light dims, bluing the retina* | [as adj.] (**blued**) *blued paper* | [intrans.] *the day would haze, the air bluing with afternoon.* ■ [trans.] heat (metal) so as to give it a grayish-blue finish: [as adj.] (**blued**) *blued hooks.* **2** [trans.] wash (white clothes) with bluing.
– PHRASES **do something until** (or **till**) **one is blue in the face** informal put all one's efforts into doing something to no avail. **once in a blue moon** informal very rarely. [because a "blue moon" is a phenomenon that never occurs.] **out of the blue** (or **out of a clear blue sky**) informal without warning; unexpectedly. [with ref. to a "blue" (i.e., clear) sky, from which nothing unusual is expected.] **talk a blue streak** informal speak continuously and at great length. — **blue·ness** n. [ME: from OFr. *bleu*, ult. of Gmc. origin and akin to OE *blǣwen* 'blue.']

blue ba·by ▶ n. a baby with a blue complexion from lack of oxygen in the blood due to a congenital defect of the heart or major blood vessels.

blue·back /'blo͞o,bak/ ▶ n. a bird or fish, esp. a trout or a sockeye salmon, having a bluish back.

Blue·beard /'blo͞o,bi(ə)rd/ a character in a tale by Charles Perrault, who killed several wives. ■ [as n.] (**a Bluebeard**) a man who murders his wives.

blue beat ▶ n. another term for **SKA.**

blue·bell /'blo͞o,bel/ ▶ n. **1** (also **English bluebell**) a widely cultivated European woodland plant (*Hyacinthoides nonscripta*) of the lily family that produces clusters of bell-shaped blue flowers in spring. **2** any of a number of other plants with blue bell-shaped flowers, in particular the bellflower and the Virginia bluebell.

blue·ber·ry /'blo͞o,berē/ ▶ n. (pl. **-ries**) **1** a hardy dwarf shrub (genus *Vaccinium*) of the heath family, with small, whitish drooping flowers and dark blue edible berries. **2** the small, sweet edible berry of this plant.

blue bice ▶ n. see **BICE.**

blue·bill /'blo͞o,bil/ ▶ n. any of a number of ducks with blue bills, esp. the scaup.

blue·bird /'blo͞o,bərd/ ▶ n. an American songbird (genus *Sialia*) of the thrush subfamily, the male of which has a blue head, back, and wings.

blue-black ▶ adj. black with a tinge of blue.

blue blood ▶ n. noble birth. ■ (also **blueblood**) a person of noble birth. — **blue-blood·ed** adj.

blue·bonnet /'blo͞o,bänit/ ▶ n. a blue-flowered lupine, esp. common in Texas.

blue book ▶ n. **1** a listing of socially prominent people. ■ (in full **Kelley Blue Book**) trademark a reference book listing the prices of used cars. ■ (**Blue Book**) a report issued by the government. **2** a blank book used for written examinations in high school and college.

blue·bot·tle /'blo͞o,bätl/ ▶ n. **1** a common blowfly (*Calliphora vomitoria*) with a metallic-blue body. **2** the wild cornflower.

blue box ▶ n. an electronic device used to access long-distance telephone lines illegally.

blue cheese ▶ n. cheese containing veins of blue mold, such as Gorgonzola and Danish Blue.

blue-chip ▶ adj. [attrib.] denoting companies or their shares considered to be a reliable investment. ■ of the highest quality.

blue chip·per ▶ n. a highly valued person.

blue coat ▶ n. a person who wears a blue coat, in particular: ■ a soldier in a blue uniform, esp. a Union soldier during the Civil War. ■ a police officer.

blue co·hosh ▶ n. see **COHOSH.**

blue-col·lar ▶ adj. [attrib.] of or relating to workers who wear work clothes or specialized protective clothing, as miners, mechanics, etc. Compare with **WHITE-COLLAR.**

blue crab ▶ n. a large edible swimming crab (*Callinectes sapidus*, family Portunidae) of the Atlantic coast of North America.

blue·curls /'blo͞o,kərlz/ ▶ n. a North American plant (genus *Trichostema*) of the mint family, with small blue flowers and blue-stalked, deeply curled stamens.

blue dev·il ▶ n. informal **1** a blue capsule containing a barbiturate. **2** (**blue devils**) a feeling of despondency or low spirits. **3** (**blue devils**) another term for **DELIRIUM TREMENS.**

blue crab

blue dog Dem·o·crat (also **Blue Dog Dem·o·crat**) ▶ n. in the US, a Democrat from a Southern state who has a conservative voting record.

blue-eyed grass ▶ n. a North American plant (genus *Sisyrinchium*) of the iris family, cultivated for its blue flowers.

blue·fin /'blo͞o,fin/ (also **bluefin tuna**) ▶ n. the most common large tuna (*Thunnus thynnus*), which occurs worldwide in warm seas. Probably the largest bony fish, it is an important food and game fish.

blue·fish /'blo͞o,fisʜ/ ▶ n. (pl. same or **-fish·es**) a predatory blue-colored marine fish (*Pomatomus saltatrix*, family Pomatomidae) of tropical and temperate waters, popular as a game fish.

blue flag ▶ n. a violet-flowered iris that grows in marshy places and wet meadows, in particular the **larger blue flag** (*Iris versicolor*) and the **slender blue flag** (*I. prismatica*).

blue flu ▶ n. a sick-out, esp. among police officers.

blue·gill /'blo͞o,gil/ ▶ n. an edible North American fish (*Lepomis macrochirus*) of the freshwater sunfish family, with a deep body and bluish cheeks and gill covers.

blue·grass /'blo͞o,gras/ ▶ n. **1** (also **Kentucky bluegrass**) a bluish-green grass that is widely grown for fodder, esp. in Kentucky and Virginia. **2** a kind of country music characterized by banjos, guitars, and high-pitched vocals.

blue-green al·gae ▶ plural n. another term for **CYANOBACTERIA** (see **CYANOBACTERIA**).

blue ground ▶ n. another term for **KIMBERLITE.**

blue gum ▶ n. a eucalyptus tree with blue-green aromatic leaves and smooth bark.

blue hel·met ▶ n. a member of a United Nations peacekeeping force.

blue·ish /'blo͞oisʜ/ ▶ adj. var. of **BLUISH.**

blue·jack·et /'blo͞o,jakit/ ▶ n. informal a sailor in the navy.

blue jay ▶ n. a common North American jay (*Cyanocitta cristata*) with a blue crest, back, wings, and tail.

blue jeans ▶ n. jeans made of blue denim.

blue law ▶ n. a law prohibiting certain activities, such as shopping, on a Sunday. ■ (in colonial New England) a strict religious law.

blue line ▶ n. Ice Hockey either of the two lines midway between the center of the rink and each goal.

blue mold ▶ n. a bluish fungus (*Penicillium* and other genera, phylum Ascomycota) that grows on food. Blue molds are deliberately introduced into some cheeses, and some kinds are used to produce antibiotics such as penicillin.

Blue Nile one of the two principal headwaters of the Nile River. It rises from Lake Tana in northwestern Ethiopia and flows about 1,000 miles (1,600 km) to meet the White Nile at Khartoum.

blue·nose /'blo͞o,nōz/ ▶ n. informal **1** a priggish or puritanical person. **2** (**Bluenose**) a person from Nova Scotia. — **blue·nosed** adj. (in sense 1).

blue note ▶ n. Music a minor interval where a major would be expected, used esp. in jazz.

blue-pen·cil ▶ v. [trans.] edit or make cuts in.

Blue Pe·ter ▶ n. a blue flag with a white square in the center, raised by a ship about to leave port.

blue plate (also **blue-plate**) ▶ adj. [attrib.] (of a restaurant meal) consisting of a full main course ordered as a single menu item.

blue·point /'blo͞o,point/ ▶ n. a small oyster, in particular one harvested at Blue Point, Long Island.

blue·print /'blo͞o,print/ ▶ n. a design plan or other technical drawing. ■ fig. something that acts as a plan, model, or template. ▶ v. [trans.] draw up (a plan or model): [as adj.] (**blueprinted**) *a neatly blueprinted scheme.* [19th C.: from the process in which prints were composed of white lines on a blue ground or of blue lines on a white ground.]

blue-rib·bon ▶ adj. [attrib.] of the highest quality; first-class. ■ (of a jury or committee) carefully or specially selected.

blue rib·bon ▶ n. (Brit. also **blue rib·and**) a badge made of blue ribbon and given as first prize to the winner of a competition. ■ (in the UK) a badge worn by members of the Order of the Garter.

Blue Ridge Moun·tains a range in the Appalachian Mountains in the eastern US that stretches from southern Pennsylvania to northern Georgia.

blue rinse ▶ n. a preparation used as a rinse on gray or white hair, intended to make it look more silver. ▶ adj. (**blue-rinse** or **blue-rinsed**) [attrib.] informal, derog. of or relating to elderly and conservative women.

blues /blo͞oz/ ▶ plural n. **1** [treated as sing. or pl.] (often **the blues**) melancholic music of black American folk origin, typically in a twelve-bar sequence. ■ [treated as sing.] a piece of such music. **2** (**the blues**) informal feelings of melancholy, sadness, or depression — **blues·y** adj. (in sense 1). [18th C.: from *blue devils* 'depression or delirium tremens.']

blue shark ▶ n. a long slender shark (*Prionace glauca*, family Carcharhinidae) with an indigo-blue back and white underparts, typically occurring in the open sea.

blue·shift /'blo͞o,sʜift/ (also **blue shift**) ▶ n. Astron. the displacement of the spectrum to shorter wavelengths in the light from distant celestial objects moving toward the observer. Compare with **REDSHIFT.**

blue-sky (also **blue-skies**) ▶ adj. [attrib.] informal not yet practical or profitable.

blue-sky law ▶ n. a law regulating the sale of securities, intended to protect the public from fraud.

Blue Springs a city in west central Missouri; pop. 48,080.

blue spruce ▶ n. a North American spruce (*Picea pungens*) with sharp, stiff blue-green needles, growing wild in the central Rocky Mountains.

blue state ▶ n. a US state that predominantly votes for or supports the Democratic Party. Compare with **RED STATE.** [from the typical color used to represent the Democratic Party on maps during elections.]

blue·stem /'blo͞o,stem/ ▶ n. a coarse North American prairie grass (genus *Andropogon*) with bluish leaf sheaths, often cultivated as forage.

blue·stock·ing /'blo͞o,stäkiɴɢ/ ▶ n. often derog. an intellectual or literary woman. [17th C.: referring to the less formal dress worn at London literary assemblies.]

blue·stone /'blo͞o,stōn/ ▶ n. any of various bluish or gray building stones.

■ any of the smaller stones made of dolerite found in the inner part of Stonehenge.

blu·et /ˈblo͞oit/ ▶ **n.** a low-growing North American plant (genus *Houstonia*, or *Hedyotis*) of the bedstraw family, with small four-petaled flowers and paired leaves. Bluets often grow in large groups. [18th C.: from Fr., dimin. of *bleu* 'blue.']

blue·throat /ˈblo͞oˌTHrōt/ ▶ **n.** a small, lively thrush (*Luscinia svecica*) found in northern Eurasia and Alaska. The male has a blue throat with a reddish spot in the center.

blue vit·ri·ol ▶ **n.** archaic crystalline copper sulfate.

blue·weed /ˈblo͞oˌwēd/ ▶ **n.** another term for **VIPER'S BUGLOSS.**

blue whale ▶ **n.** a migratory, mottled bluish-gray rorqual (*Balaenoptera musculus*), found in all oceans of the world. Known to grow as long as 110 feet (33 m) and weigh as much as 150 tons (136,000 kg), it is the largest animal ever to inhabit the earth.

bluff¹ /bləf/ ▶ **n.** an attempt to deceive someone into believing that one can or will do something. ▶ **v.** [intrans.] try to deceive someone as to one's abilities or intentions: *he's been bluffing all along* | [with direct speech] *"I am an accredited envoy," he bluffed.* ■ [trans.] mislead (someone) in this way: *the object is to **bluff** your opponent **into** submission.* ■ (in a card game) bet heavily on a weak hand in order to deceive opponents. ■ (**bluff one's way**) contrive a difficult escape or other achievement by maintaining a pretense.

– PHRASES **call someone's bluff** challenge someone thought to be bluffing. — **bluff·er n.** [17th C.: from Du. *bluffen* 'brag,' or *bluf* 'bragging.']

bluff² ▶ **adj.** direct in speech or behavior, but in a good-natured way. — **bluff·ly adv. bluff·ness n.** [18th C.: from **BLUFF³**.]

bluff³ ▶ **n. 1** a steep cliff, bank, or promontory. **2** Canadian a grove or clump of trees. ▶ **adj.** (of a cliff or a ship's bow) having a vertical or steep broad front. [17th C.: origin unknown.]

blu·ing /ˈblo͞oiNG/ (also **blue·ing**) ▶ **n. 1** esp. hist. blue powder used to preserve the whiteness of laundry. **2** a grayish-blue finish on metal produced by heating.

blu·ish /ˈblo͞oiSH/ (also **blue·ish**) ▶ **adj.** having a blue tinge; somewhat blue.

Blum /ˈblo͞om/, Léon (1872–1950), prime minister of France 1936–37, 1938, 1946–47. He introduced significant labor reforms.

Blume /blo͞om/, Judy Sussman (1938–), US writer. Her young adult's fiction includes *Are You There, God? It's Me, Margaret* (1970) and *Double Fudge* (2002).

Blu·men·bach /ˈblo͞omənˌbäKH/, Johann Friedrich (1752–1840), German physiologist and anatomist. He is regarded as the founder of physical anthropology.

blun·der /ˈbləndər/ ▶ **n.** a stupid or careless mistake. ▶ **v.** [intrans.] make such a mistake; act or speak clumsily: ***I blundered on** in my explanation* | [as adj.] (**blundering**) *blundering actors.* ■ [intrans.] move clumsily or as if unable to see: *we were blundering around in the darkness.* — **blun·der·er n. blun·der·ing·ly adv.** [ME: prob. of Scand. origin and rel. to **BLIND.**]

blunderbuss

blun·der·buss /ˈbləndərˌbəs/ ▶ **n.** hist. a short-barreled large-bored gun with a flared muzzle, used at short range. ■ fig. an action or way of doing something regarded as lacking in subtlety and precision. [17th C.: alt. of Du. *donderbus*, lit. 'thunder gun.']

blunge /blənj/ ▶ **v.** [trans.] mix (clay or other materials) with water in a revolving apparatus for use in ceramics. — **blung·er n.** [19th C.: blend of **BLEND** and **PLUNGE.**]

blunt /blənt/ ▶ **adj. 1** (of a knife, pencil, etc.) having a worn-down edge or point; not sharp. ■ having a flat or rounded end. **2** (of a person or remark) uncompromisingly forthright. ▶ **v.** make or become less sharp: [trans.] *wood can blunt your ax* | [intrans.] *the edge may blunt very rapidly.* ■ [trans.] fig. weaken or reduce (something): *their determination had been blunted.* — **blunt·ly adv. blunt·ness n.** [ME: perh. of Scand. origin and rel. to ON *blunda* 'shut the eyes.']

blur /blər/ ▶ **v.** (**blurred, blur·ring**) make or become unclear or less distinct: [trans.] *tears blurred her vision.* | [intrans.] *the pages blurred.* ▶ **n.** a thing that cannot be seen or heard clearly. ■ an indistinct memory or impression of events, typically because they happened very fast. — **blur·ry adj.** (**blurr·i·er, blurr·i·est**). [16th C. (in the sense 'smear that partially obscures something'): perh. rel. to **BLEAR.**]

blurb /blərb/ ▶ **n.** a short description of a book, movie, or other product written for promotional purposes and appearing on the cover of a book or in an advertisement. ▶ **v.** [trans.] informal write or contribute such a passage for (a book, movie, or other product). [20th C.: coined by Gelett Burgess (died 1951), American humorist.]

blurt /blərt/ ▶ **v.** [trans.] say (something) suddenly and without careful consideration: *she wouldn't **blurt out** words she did not mean* | [with direct speech] *"It wasn't my idea," Gordon blurted.* [16th C.: prob. imitative.]

blush /bləSH/ ▶ **v.** [intrans.] develop a pink tinge in the face from embarrassment or shame: *she blushed at the unexpected compliment* | [with complement] *Kate felt herself blushing scarlet.* ■ feel embarrassed or ashamed: [with infin.] *he blushed to think of how he'd paraded himself.* ■ [often as adj.] (**blushing**) (of a flower or other thing) be or become pink or pale red: *blushing blossoms.* ▶ **n. 1** a reddening of the face as a sign of embarrassment or shame. ■ a pink or pale red tinge. ■ another term for **BLUSHER. 2** (also **blush wine**) a wine with a slight pink tint made from red grape varieties.

– PHRASES **at first blush** at the first glimpse or impression. [OE *blyscan*; rel. to mod. Du. *blozen*.]

blush·er /ˈbləSHər/ ▶ **n.** a cosmetic of a powder or cream consistency used to give a warm color to the cheeks. Also called **BLUSH.**

blus·ter /ˈbləstər/ ▶ **v.** [intrans.] talk in a loud, aggressive, or indignant way with little effect: *you threaten and bluster* | [with direct speech] *"I don't care what he says," I blustered.* ■ (of a storm, wind, or rain) blow or beat fiercely and noisily: *a winter gale blustered.* ▶ **n.** loud, aggressive, or indignant talk with little effect. — **blus·ter·er n.** [ME: ult. imitative.]

blus·ter·y /ˈbləstərē/ ▶ **adj.** (of weather or a period of time) characterized by strong winds. ■ (of a wind) blowing in strong gusts.

blvd. ▶ **abbr.** boulevard.

B lym·pho·cyte (also **B-lymphocyte**) ▶ **n.** Physiol. another term for **B CELL.**

BM ▶ **abbr.** ■ Bachelor of Medicine. ■ Bachelor of Music. ■ basal metabolism. ■ black male. ■ board measure. ■ bowel movement. ■ British Museum.

BMI ▶ **abbr.** body mass index.

BMOC ▶ **abbr.** big man on campus.

B-mov·ie ▶ **n.** a low-budget movie.

BMR ▶ **abbr.** basal metabolic rate.

BMX ▶ **n.** organized bicycle racing on a dirt track, esp. for youngsters. ■ a kind of bicycle designed to be used for such racing. [1970s: from *bicycle motocross*, with *X* for *cross*.]

Bn. ▶ **abbr.** ■ Baron. ■ Battalion.

bn ▶ **abbr.** billion.

B'nai B'rith /bəˈnā ˈbriTH/ a Jewish organization founded in New York in 1843. It pursues educational, humanitarian, and cultural activities and attempts to safeguard the rights and interests of Jews. [Heb., lit. 'sons of the covenant.']

BO ▶ **abbr.** ■ informal body odor. ■ best offer. ■ box office. ■ back order. ■ (also **B/O** or **b/o**) (in bookkeeping) brought over.

bo ▶ **abbr.** best offer.

bo·a /ˈbōə/ ▶ **n. 1** a constrictor snake (family Boidae) that bears live young and may reach great size, native to America, Africa, Asia, and some Pacific islands. Its numerous species include the large **boa constrictor** (*Boa constrictor*) of tropical America. **2** a long thin stole of feathers or fur worn around a woman's neck, typically as part of evening dress. [ME: from L.]

boar /bôr/ ▶ **n.** (pl. same or **boars**) **1** (also **wild boar**) a tusked Eurasian wild pig (*Sus scrofa*) from which domestic pigs are descended. ■ the flesh of the wild boar as food. **2** an uncastrated domestic male pig. ■ the full-grown male of certain other animals, esp. a badger, guinea pig, or hedgehog. [OE *bār*, of West Gmc. origin; rel. to Ger. *Bär*.]

board /bôrd/ ▶ **n. 1** a long, thin, flat piece of wood or other hard material, used for floors or other building purposes. ■ (**the boards**) informal the stage of a theater. **2** a thin, flat, rectangular piece of wood or other stiff material used for various purposes, in particular: ■ a vertical surface on which to write or pin notices. ■ a horizontal surface on which to cut things, play games, or perform other activities. ■ a flat insulating sheet used as a mounting for an electronic circuit. ■ the piece of equipment on which a person stands in surfing, skateboarding, snowboarding, and certain other sports. ■ (**boards**) the wooden structure surrounding an ice-hockey rink. ■ (usu. **boards**) Basketball informal term for **BACKBOARD**, referring specifically to rebounding. ■ (**boards**) pieces of thick stiff cardboard or, originally, wood used for book covers. **3** [treated as sing. or pl.] a group of people constituted as the decision-making body of an organization. **4** the provision of regular meals when one stays somewhere, in return for payment or services. ■ archaic a table set for a meal. ▶ **v. 1** [trans.] get on or into (a ship, aircraft, or other vehicle): *we boarded the plane for Oslo* | [intrans.] they *can't board without a ticket.* ■ (**be boarding**) (of an aircraft) be ready for passengers to get on: *flight 172 to Istanbul is now boarding.* **2** [intrans.] live and receive regular meals in a house in return for payment or services: *the cousins boarded for a while with Ruby.* ■ (of a student) live at school during the semester in return for payment. ■ [trans.] (often **be boarded**) provide (a person or animal) with regular meals and somewhere to live in return for payment: *dogs may have to be **boarded** at kennels.* **3** [trans.] (**board something up**) cover or seal a window, storefront, or other structure with pieces of wood: *the shop was still boarded up* | [as adj.] (**boarded**) *boarded windows.*

– PHRASES **go by the board** (of something planned or previously upheld) be abandoned, rejected, or ignored. [earlier 'fall overboard.'] **on board** on or in a ship, aircraft, or other vehicle. ■ informal onto a team or group as a member. ■ informal (of a jockey) riding. ■ Baseball on base. **take something on board** informal fully consider or assimilate a new idea or situation. **tread the boards** informal appear on stage as an actor. [OE *bord*, of Gmc. origin.]

board cer·ti·fi·ca·tion /ˌsərtəfəˈkāSHən/ ▶ **n.** the process of examining and certifying the qualifications of a professional by a board of specialists in the field.

board-cer·ti·fied ▶ adj. having satisfied the requirements for board certification.

board·er /ˈbôrdər/ ▶ n. **1** a person who receives regular meals when staying somewhere, in return for payment or services. ■ a student who lives at school during the semester in return for payment. **2** a person who boards a ship during or after an attack. **3** a person who takes part in a sport using a board.

board foot ▶ n. (pl. **board feet**) a unit of volume for timber equal to 144 cubic inches.

board game ▶ n. any game played on a board, such as chess or checkers.

board·ing /ˈbôrdiNG/ ▶ n. **1** long, flat, thin pieces of wood used to build or cover something. **2** the procedure according to which students live at school during the semester in return for payment. **3** the action of getting on or into a ship, aircraft, or other vehicle.

board·ing·house /ˈbôrdiNG,hous/ (also **board·ing-house** or **board·ing house**) ▶ n. a house providing food and lodging for paying guests.

board·ing school ▶ n. a school where students reside during the semester.

board of ed·u·ca·tion ▶ n. a body of officials elected or appointed to oversee a local or statewide school system or systems. Compare with SCHOOL BOARD.

Board of Trade ▶ n. **1** another term for CHAMBER OF COMMERCE. ■ (also **Chicago Board of Trade**) the Chicago futures exchange. **2** (**Board of Trade**) a now nominal British government department within the Department of Trade and Industry concerned with commerce and industry.

board·room /ˈbôrd,ro͞om/ ▶ n. a room in which the members of a board meet regularly. ■ the directors of a company or organization considered collectively.

board·sail·ing /ˈbôrd,sāliNG/ ▶ n. another term for WINDSURFING. — **board·sail·or** /-,sālər/ n.

board·walk /ˈbôrd,wôk/ ▶ n. a wooden walkway across sand or marshy ground. ■ a promenade along a beach or waterfront.

Bo·as /ˈbōaz/, Franz (1858–1942), US anthropologist; born in Germany. He developed the linguistic and cultural components of ethnology. His works include *Race, Language, and Culture* (1940).

boast /bōst/ ▶ v. **1** [reporting verb] talk with excessive pride and self-satisfaction about one's achievements, possessions, or abilities: [with direct speech] *Ted used to boast, "I manage ten people"* | [with clause] *he boasted that he had taken part in the crime* | [intrans.] *she* ***boasted about*** *her exploits.* **2** [trans.] (of a person, place, or thing) possess (a feature that is a source of pride): *the hotel boasts high standards of comfort.* ▶ n. an act of talking with excessive pride and self-satisfaction. — **boast·er** n. **boast·ing·ly** adv. [ME: of unknown origin.]

boast·ful /ˈbōstfəl/ ▶ adj. showing excessive pride and self-satisfaction in one's achievements, possessions, or abilities. — **boast·ful·ly** adv. **boast·ful·ness** n.

boat /bōt/ ▶ n. **1** a small vessel propelled on water by oars, sails, or an engine. ■ (in general use) a ship of any size. **2** a serving dish in the shape of a boat. ▶ v. [intrans.] travel or go in a boat for pleasure: *they boated through fjords* | [as n.] (**boating**) *she likes to go boating.* ■ [trans.] transport (someone or something) in a boat in a specified direction: *they boated the timber down the lake.* ■ [trans.] to bring a caught fish into a boat.

– PHRASES **be in the same boat** informal be in the same unfortunate circumstances as others. **miss the boat** see MISS[1]. **off the boat** informal, often offens. recently arrived from a foreign country, and by implication naive or an outsider. **rock the boat** informal say or do something to disturb an existing situation. — **boat·ful** /-,fo͝ol/ n. (pl. **-fuls**). [OE *bāt*, of Gmc. origin.]

boat·bill /ˈbōt,bil/ ▶ n. (also **boat-billed her·on**) a small Central and South American heron (*Cochlearius cochlearius*) with a broad, flattened bill and a prominent black crest.

boat·build·ing /ˈbōt,bildiNG/ ▶ n. the occupation or industry of building boats. — **boat·build·er** n.

boat·el /bōˈtel/ ▶ n. **1** a waterside hotel with facilities for mooring boats. **2** a ship moored at a wharf and used as a hotel. [1950s: blend of BOAT and HOTEL.]

boat·er /ˈbōtər/ ▶ n. **1** a flat-topped hardened straw hat with a brim. **2** a person who uses or travels in a boat for pleasure.

boat·hook /ˈbōt,ho͝ok/ ▶ n. a long pole with a hook and a spike that is used for fending off or pulling a boat.

boat·house /ˈbōt,hous/ ▶ n. a shed at the edge of a river or lake used for housing boats.

boat·ing /ˈbōtiNG/ ▶ n. rowing or sailing in boats as a sport or form of recreation.

boat·load /ˈbōt,lōd/ ▶ n. a number of passengers or amount of cargo that will fill a ship or boat. ■ informal a large number of people.

boat·man /ˈbōtmən/ ▶ n. (pl. **-men**) a person who rents out or works on boats.

boat peo·ple ▶ plural n. refugees who have left a country by sea, in particular the Vietnamese who fled in small boats after the conquest of South Vietnam by North Vietnam in 1975.

boat shoe (also **deck shoe**) ▶ n. a type of loafer with a flexible rubber heel and sole to provide good traction on boat decks.

boat·swain /ˈbōsən/ (also **bo'sun** or **bo·sun**) ▶ n. a ship's officer in charge of equipment and the crew.

boat·swain's chair ▶ n. a seat suspended from ropes, used in rescues and for work on the body or masts of a ship or the face of a building.

boat train ▶ n. a train scheduled to connect with the arrival or departure of a boat.

boat·yard /ˈbōt,yärd/ ▶ n. a place where boats are built, repaired, or stored.

Bo·a Vis·ta /ˈbōə ˈvistə/ a town in northern Brazil; pop. 130,426.

bob[1] /bäb/ ▶ v. (**bobbed, bob·bing**) [intrans.] (of a thing) make a quick short movement up and down: *the boat bobbed up and down.* ■ [trans.] cause (something) to make such a movement: *she bobbed her head.* ■ [intrans.] make a sudden move in a particular direction so as to appear or disappear: *a lady* ***bobbed up*** *from beneath the counter.* ■ [intrans.] move up and down briefly in a curtsy. ▶ n. a movement up and down. ■ another term for BOBBER. ■ a curtsy.

– PHRASES **bob and weave** make rapid bodily movements up and down and from side to side, for example as an evasive tactic by a boxer. **bob for apples** try to catch floating or hanging apples with one's mouth alone, as a game. [ME: of unknown origin.]

bob[2] ▶ n. **1** a style in which the hair is cut short and evenly all around so that it hangs above the shoulders. **2** a weight on a pendulum, plumb line, or kite-tail. **3** a bobsled. **4** a short line at or toward the end of a stanza. **5** a horse's tail docked short. ▶ v. (**bobbed, bob·bing**) **1** [trans.] [usu. as adj.] (**bobbed**) cut (someone's hair) in a bob. **2** [intrans.] ride on a bobsled. [ME ('bunch'): of unknown origin.]

bob[3] Brit., informal ▶ n. (pl. same) a shilling. ■ used with reference to a moderately large but unspecified amount of money: *those vases are worth a few bob.* [18th C.: of unknown origin.]

bob[4] ▶ n. a change of order in bell-ringing. ■ used in names of change-ringing methods: *plain bob* | *bob minor.* [17th C.: perh. akin to BOB[1].]

bo·ba tea /ˈbōbə/ ▶ n. another term for BUBBLE TEA.

bob·ber /ˈbäbər/ ▶ n. a small float placed on a fishing line to hold the hook at the desired depth.

bob·bin /ˈbäbin/ ▶ n. a cylinder or cone holding thread, yarn, or wire. ■ a spool or reel. [16th C.: from Fr. *bobine.*]

bob·bi·net /,bäbəˈnet/ ▶ n. machine-made cotton net (imitating lace made with bobbins on a pillow). [19th C.: from BOBBIN + NET[1].]

bob·bin lace ▶ n. lace made by hand with thread wound on bobbins.

bob·ble[1] /ˈbäbəl/ ▶ n. a small ball made of strands of wool used as a decoration on a hat or on furnishings. — **bob·bly** adj. [1920s: dimin. of BOB[2].]

bob·ble[2] informal ▶ v. **1** [trans.] mishandle (a ball): *Andy bobbled the ball.* **2** [intrans.] move with an irregular bouncing motion. ▶ n. **1** a mishandling of a ball. **2** an irregular bouncing motion. [19th C.: frequentative of BOB[1].]

bob·by /ˈbäbē/ ▶ n. (pl. **-bies**) Brit., informal, dated a police officer. [19th C.: nickname for *Robert*, given name of Sir Robert PEEL.]

bob·by pin ▶ n. a kind of sprung hairpin or small clip. ▶ v. (**bob·by-pin**) [trans.] fix (hair) in place with such a pin or clip. [1930s: from BOB[2].]

bob·by socks (also **bob·by sox**) ▶ plural n. dated short socks reaching just above the ankle. [1940s: cf. BOB[2] in the sense 'cut short.']

bob·by-sox·er /ˈbäbē,säksər/ ▶ n. informal, dated an adolescent girl.

bob·cat /ˈbäb,kat/ ▶ n. a small North American cat (*Lynx rufus*) with a barred and spotted coat and a short tail. [19th C.: from BOB[2].]

Bo·bo-Diou·las·so /ˈbōbō dyo͞oˈlasō/ a city in southwestern Burkina Faso; pop. 269,000.

bob·o·link /ˈbäbə,liNGk/ ▶ n. a North American songbird (*Dolichonyx oryzivorus*) of the American blackbird family, with a finchlike bill. The male has black, buff, and white plumage. [18th C.: imitative of its call.]

bobolink

bob·sled /ˈbäb,sled/ ▶ n. a mechanically steered and braked sled, typically manned by crews of two or four, used for racing down a steep ice-covered run with banked curves. ▶ v. ride on a bobsled. — **bob·sled·ding** n.

bob·stay /ˈbäb,stā/ ▶ n. a rope used to hold down the bowsprit of a ship and keep it steady. [18th C.: prob. from BOB[1] + STAY[2].]

bob·tail /ˈbäb,tāl/ ▶ n. a docked tail of a horse or dog. ▶ adj. (also **bob·tailed**) fig. cut short; abbreviated. [16th C.: prob. from BOB[2] + TAIL[1].]

bob-weight ▶ n. a component used as a counterweight to a moving part in a machine.

bob·white /ˈbäbˈ(h)wīt/ (also **bobwhite quail**) ▶ n. a New World quail with mottled reddish-brown plumage, in particular the **northern** (or

bobsled

common) bobwhite (*Colinus virginianus*). [19th C.: imitative of its call.]

northern bobwhite

bo·cac·cio /bəˈkäCHō; -CHē-ō; bō-/ ▶ **n.** an edible rockfish (*Sebastes paucispinis*), of particular commercial importance in California.

Bo·ca Ra·ton /ˌbōkə rəˈtōn/ a city in southeastern Florida, north of Fort Lauderdale; pop. 61,492.

Boc·cac·ci·o /bəˈkäCHēˌō/, Giovanni (1313–75), Italian writer. He is noted for the *Decameron* (1348–58), a collection of 100 tales told by ten young people trying to escape the Black Death.

boc·ce /ˈbäCHē/ (also **boc·cie** or **boc·ci**) ▶ **n.** an Italian game similar to lawn bowling. [Ital., 'bowls,' pl. of *boccia* 'ball.']

Boche /bôSH; bäSH/ informal, dated ▶ **n.** a German, esp. a soldier. ■ (**the Boche**) Germans, esp. German soldiers, considered collectively. ▶ **adj.** German. [19th C.: Fr. soldiers' slang, orig. in the sense 'rascal,' later used in World War I meaning 'German.']

Bo·chum /ˈbōKHŏŏm; -kəm/ a city in the Ruhr valley in Germany; pop. 398,580.

bock /bäk/ (also **bock beer**) ▶ **n.** a strong dark beer brewed in the fall and drunk in the spring. [19th C.: ult. from Ger. *Eimbockbier* 'beer from *Einbeck*,' town in Hanover.]

BOD ▶ **abbr.** biochemical oxygen demand.

bod /bäd/ ▶ **n.** informal a body. ■ a physique. ■ esp. Brit. a person.

bo·da·cious /bōˈdāSHəs/ ▶ **adj.** informal excellent, admirable, or attractive. ■ audacious in a way considered admirable. [19th C.: perh. var. of dial. *boldacious*, blend of BOLD and AUDACIOUS.]

bode /bōd/ ▶ **v.** [intrans.] (**bode well/ill**) be an omen of a particular outcome: *their argument did not bode well for the future* | [trans.] *the 12 percent interest rate bodes dark days ahead for retailers.* [OE *bodian* 'proclaim,' from *boda* 'messenger,' of Gmc. origin; akin to Ger. *Bote*, and BID[1].]

bo·de·ga /bōˈdāgə/ ▶ **n.** a grocery store in a Spanish-speaking neighborhood. ■ a wineshop or wine cellar. [19th C.: from Sp., via L. from Gk. *apothēkē* 'storehouse.']

Bo·den·see /ˈbōdnˌzā/ German name for Lake Constance (see CONSTANCE, LAKE).

Bodh·ga·ya /ˈbōdˈgīə/ (also **Buddh Ga·ya** /ˈbŏŏdˈgīə/) a village in northeastern India, where Buddha attained enlightenment.

bo·dhi·satt·va /ˌbōdiˈsätvə; -ˈsət-/ (also **Bo·dhi·satt·va**) ▶ **n.** (in Mahayana Buddhism) a person who is able to reach nirvana but delays doing so out of compassion in order to save suffering beings. [19th C.: Sanskrit, 'person whose essence is perfect knowledge,' from *bodhi-* 'perfect knowledge' + *sattva* 'being.']

bo·dhi tree /ˈbōdē/ ▶ **n.** another term for BO TREE.

bod·hrán /ˈbôrän; -rən/ ▶ **n.** a shallow one-sided Irish drum played with a short two-headed drumstick. [Irish.]

bod·ice /ˈbädis/ ▶ **n.** the part of a woman's dress (excluding sleeves) that is above the waist. ■ a woman's vest, esp. a laced vest worn as an outer garment. ■ a woman's vest-like undergarment. [16th C.: pl. of BODY.]

bodice

bod·ice-rip·per ▶ **n.** informal, derog. humorous a sexually explicit romantic novel or movie with a historical setting. — **bod·ice-rip·ping adj.**

bod·i·less /ˈbädēlis/ ▶ **adj.** lacking a body. ■ having no material existence; insubstantial.

bod·i·ly /ˈbädl-ē/ ▶ **adj.** [attrib.] of or concerning the body. ■ material or actual as opposed to spiritual or incorporeal. ▶ **adv.** by taking hold of a person's body, esp. with force: *he hauled her bodily from the van.* ■ with one's whole body; with great force.

bod·kin /ˈbädkin/ ▶ **n.** a blunt thick needle with a large eye used esp. for drawing tape or cord through a hem. ■ a small pointed instrument used to pierce cloth or leather. ■ hist. a long pin used for fastening hair. ■ Print., esp. hist. a pointed tool used for removing pieces of metal type for correction. [ME: perh. of Celtic origin and rel. to Irish *bod*, 'dagger.']

Bod·lei·an Li·brar·y /ˈbädlēən/ the library of Oxford University, one of six copyright libraries in the UK.

Bod·ley /ˈbädlē/, Sir Thomas (1545–1613), English scholar. He enlarged the Oxford University library.

Bo·do·ni /bōˈdōnē/, Giambattista (1740–1813), Italian printer. He designed a typeface named for him.

bod·y /ˈbädē/ ▶ **n.** (pl. **bod·ies**) **1** the physical structure of a person or an animal, including the bones, flesh, and organs. ■ a corpse. ■ the physical and mortal aspect of a person as opposed to the soul or spirit. ■ informal a person's body regarded as an object of sexual desire. ■ informal, dated a person, often one of a specified type or character: *a motherly body at the bed and breakfast who always had aspirin in her apron pocket.* **2** the trunk apart from the head and the limbs. ■ [in sing.] (**the body of**) the main or central part of something, esp. a building or text. ■ the main section of a car or aircraft. ■ a large or substantial amount of something; a mass or collection of something. ■ (in pottery) a clay used for making the main part of ceramic ware, as distinct from a glaze. **3** a group of people with a common purpose or function, acting as an organized unit. **4** [often with adj.] tech. a distinct material object: *the falling body.* **5** a full or substantial quality of flavor in wine. ■ fullness or thickness of a person's hair. ▶ **v.** (**bod·ies, bod·ied**) [trans.] **1** (**body something forth**) give material form to something abstract. **2** build the bodywork of (a motor vehicle): *an era when automobiles were bodied over wooden frames.*
– PHRASES **body and soul** involving every aspect of a person; completely. **in a body** all together; as a group. **keep body and soul together** stay alive, esp. in difficult circumstances. **over my dead body** informal used to emphasize that one opposes something and would do anything to prevent it from happening. — **bod·ied adj.** [in comb.] *a wide-bodied jet.* [OE *bodig.*]

bod·y bag ▶ **n.** a bag used for carrying a corpse.

bod·y·board /ˈbädēˌbôrd/ ▶ **n.** a short light type of surfboard ridden in a prone position. — **bod·y·board·er n. bod·y·board·ing n.**

bod·y·build·ing /ˈbädēˌbildiNG/ ▶ **n.** the practice of strengthening and enlarging the muscles of the body through exercise. — **bod·y·build·er n.**

bod·y check ▶ **n.** a deliberate obstruction of a player (esp. in ice hockey) by placing one's body in the way. ▶ **v.** (**bod·y-check**) [trans.] obstruct (a player) in such a way.

bod·y cor·po·rate ▶ **n.** formal term for CORPORATION.

bod·y count ▶ **n.** a list or total of casualties.

bod·y dou·ble ▶ **n.** a stand-in for a movie actor used during stunt or nude scenes.

bod·y Eng·lish ▶ **n.** a bodily action after throwing, hitting, or kicking a ball, intended as an attempt to influence the ball's trajectory.

bod·y·guard /ˈbädēˌgärd/ ▶ **n.** a person or group of persons hired to escort and protect another person, esp. a dignitary.

bod·y lan·guage ▶ **n.** the process of communicating nonverbally through conscious or unconscious gestures and movements.

bod·y louse ▶ **n.** a louse (*Pediculus humanus humanus*) that infests the human body and is especially prevalent where hygiene is poor. Several diseases, including typhus, may be transmitted through its bite.

body louse

bod·y mass in·dex (abbr.: **BMI**) ▶ **n.** a weight-to-height ratio, calculated by dividing one's weight in kilograms by the square of one's height in meters and used as an indicator of obesity and underweight.

bod·y pierc·ing ▶ **n.** the piercing of holes in parts of the body other than the earlobes in order to insert rings or other decorative objects.

bod·y pol·i·tic ▶ **n.** (usu. **the body politic**) the people of a nation, state, or society considered collectively as an organized group of citizens.

bod·y shirt ▶ **n.** a close-fitting woman's garment for the upper body that is closed at the crotch. ■ a close-fitting blouse or shirt.

bod·y shop ▶ **n.** a garage where repairs to the bodies of vehicles are carried out.

bod·y·side /ˈbädeˌsīd/ ▶ **n.** the side of the body of a vehicle: [as adj.] *bodyside panels.*

bod·y·snatch·er /ˈbädēˌsnaCHər/ ▶ **n.** hist. a person who stole corpses from a graveyard for dissection. — **bod·y·snatch·ing n.**

bod·y stock·ing ▶ **n.** a woman's one-piece undergarment that covers the torso and legs.

bod·y·suit /ˈbädēˌsōōt/ ▶ **n.** a close-fitting one-piece stretch garment for women.

bod·y·surf /ˈbädēˌsərf/ ▶ **v.** [intrans.] [often as n.] (**bodysurfing**) float on the crest of incoming waves without using a board.

bod·y text ▶ **n.** (usu. **the body text**) the main part of a printed text.

bod·y wall ▶ **n.** the external surface of an animal body that encloses the body cavity and consists of ectoderm and mesoderm.

bod·y wave ▶ **n.** a soft, light permanent wave designed to give hair fullness.

bod·y·work /ˈbädēˌwərk/ ▶ **n.** **1** the metal outer shell of a vehicle. **2** therapies and techniques in complementary medicine that involve touching or manipulating the body. — **bod·y·work·er n.** (in sense 2).

bod·y wrap ▶ **n.** a type of beauty treatment involving the application of skin-cleansing ingredients to the body, which is then wrapped in hot towels.

boehm·ite /ˈbāmīt; ˈbō-/ ▶ **n.** a crystalline mineral compound, AlO(OH), composed of aluminum oxide and hydroxide and found in bauxite.

Boe·ing /ˈbō-iNG/, William Edward (1881–1956), US industrialist. In 1927, he founded what became Boeing Aircraft, United Aircraft, and United Airlines.

Boe·o·tia /bēˈōSHə/ a department in central Greece, north of the Gulf of Corinth, and a region of ancient Greece of which the chief city was Thebes. — **Boe·o·tian adj. & n.**

Boer /bôr; bo͝or/ esp. hist. ▶ **n.** a member of the Dutch and Huguenot population that settled in southern Africa in the late 17th century, whose descendants are the present-day Afrikaners. ▶ **adj.** of or relating to the Boers. [from Du. *boer* 'farmer.']

Boer Wars two wars fought by Great Britain in southern Africa between 1880 and 1902.

boeuf /bœf/ ▶ **n.** Cooking French word for BEEF, used in the names of various beef dishes.

boeuf bour·gui·gnon /ˈbœf ˌbo͝orgēˈnyôN/ ▶ **n.** a dish consisting of beef stewed in red wine. [20th C.: Fr., lit. 'Burgundy beef.']

boff /bäf/ informal ▶ **v.** [trans.] have sexual intercourse with (someone). ▶ **n.** an act of sexual intercourse. [1920s ('punch'): imitative.]

bof·fin /ˈbäfin/ ▶ **n.** informal, esp. Brit. a person engaged in scientific or technical research: *a computer boffin.* ■ a person with knowledge or a skill considered to be complex, arcane, and difficult: *he had a reputation as a tax boffin, a learned lawyer.* — **bof·fin·y** adj. [World War II: of unknown origin.]

bof·fo /ˈbäfō/ informal ▶ **adj.** **1** (of a review of a theatrical production, movie, etc.) wholeheartedly positive. ■ resoundingly successful or popular. **2** (of a laugh) deep and unrestrained. ■ boisterously funny. ▶ **n.** (pl. **-fos**) a success. [1940s: from *boff* 'roaring success.']

bof·fo·la /bäˈfōlə/ informal ▶ **n.** a joke or a line in a script meant to get a laugh. ▶ **adj.** (of a laugh) hearty and unrestrained. [1940s: extension of BOFF.]

Bo·fors gun /ˈbōfôrz/ ▶ **n.** a type of light antiaircraft gun. [1930s: *Bofors* in Sweden.]

bog /bäg; bôg/ ▶ **n.** wet muddy ground too soft to support a heavy body. ■ Ecol. wetland with acid, peaty soil, typically dominated by peat moss. Compare with FEN[1]. ▶ **v.** (**bogged, bog·ging**) [trans.] (usu. **be bogged down**) cause (a vehicle, person, or animal) to become stuck in mud or wet ground. ■ (**be bogged down**) fig. (of a person or process) be unable to make progress. — **bog·gy** adj. **bog·gi·ness** n. [ME: from Irish or Scot. Gael. *bogach,* from *bog* 'soft.']

bog as·pho·del ▶ **n.** a yellow-flowered marsh plant of the lily family, in particular *Narthecium americanum,* esp. abundant in New Jersey.

bog·bean /ˈbägˌbēn/ ▶ **n.** another term for BUCKBEAN.

bo·gey[1] /ˈbōgē/ Golf ▶ **n.** (pl. **-geys**) a score of one stroke over par at a hole. ■ archaic term for PAR[1] sense 1. ▶ **v.** (**-geys, -geyed**) [trans.] play (a hole) in one stroke over par. [19th C.: perh. from *Bogey,* 'the Devil' (see BOGEY[2]).]

bo·gey[2] /ˈbo͝ogē/ (also **bo·gy**) ▶ **n.** (pl. **-geys**) a person or thing that causes fear or alarm. ■ an evil or mischievous spirit. ■ military slang an enemy aircraft. [19th C.: prob. rel. to BOGLE.]

bo·gey·man /ˈbo͝ogēˌman; ˈbō-/ (also **boo·gey·man, bo·gy·man**) ▶ **n.** (pl. **-men**) (usu. **the bogeyman**) an imaginary evil spirit, referred to typically to frighten children. ■ a person or thing that is widely regarded as an object of fear.

bog·gle /ˈbägəl/ ▶ **v.** [intrans.] informal (of a person or a person's mind) be astonished or overwhelmed when trying to imagine something: *the mind boggles at the spectacle.* ■ [trans.] cause (a person or a person's mind) to be astonished in such a way: *the inflated salary of a CEO boggles the mind* | [as adj.] (**boggling**) *a boggling 1.5 trillion miles.* ■ (**boggle at**) (of a person) hesitate or be anxious at: *you never boggle at plain speaking.* [16th C.: prob. of dial. origin and akin to BOGLE.]

bo·gie /ˈbōgē/ ▶ **n.** (pl. **-gies**) esp. Brit. an undercarriage with four or six wheels pivoted beneath the end of a railroad car. [19th C.: of unknown origin.]

bog i·ron ▶ **n.** soft, spongy goethite deposited in bogs.

bo·gle /ˈbōgəl/ ▶ **n.** a phantom or goblin. ■ Scot. & N. Engl. a scarecrow. [16th C.: prob. rel. to BOGEY[2].]

bog moss ▶ **n.** another term for PEAT MOSS (sense 1).

bog myr·tle ▶ **n.** another term for SWEET GALE.

bog oak ▶ **n.** an ancient oak tree that has been preserved in a black state in peat.

Bog·o·mil /ˈbägəmil/ ▶ **n.** hist. a member of a heretical medieval Balkan sect professing a modified form of Manichaeism. — **Bog·o·mil·ism** n. [19th C.: from med. Gk. *Bogomilos,* from *Bogomil,* the person who first disseminated the heresy.]

Bo·go·tá /ˈbōgəˌtä; ˌbōgəˈtô/ the capital of Colombia, in the eastern Andes at about 8,560 feet (2,610 m); pop. 4,921,200. Official name SANTA FÉ DE BOGOTÁ.

bog rose·mar·y ▶ **n.** See ANDROMEDA.

bog spav·in ▶ **n.** a soft swelling of the joint capsule of the hock of horses.

bog·trot·ter /ˈbägˌträtər/ ▶ **n.** a person who lives or works among bogs. ■ informal, derog. an Irish person.

bo·gus /ˈbōgəs/ ▶ **adj.** not genuine or true; fake. — **bo·gus·ly** adv. **bo·gus·ness** n. [18th C.: of unknown origin.]

bo·gy /ˈbōgē; ˈbo͝ogē/ ▶ **n.** (pl. **-gies**) var. of BOGEY[2].

bo·gy·man ▶ **n.** var. of BOGEYMAN.

Bo Hai /ˈbō ˈhī/ (also **Po Hai**) an inlet of the Yellow Sea, on the coast of eastern China. Also called CHIHLI, GULF OF.

Bo·he·mi·a /bōˈhēmēə/ a region that forms the western part of the Czech Republic.

Bo·he·mi·an /bōˈhēmēən/ ▶ **n.** **1** a native or inhabitant of Bohemia. **2** (also **bo·he·mi·an**) a person who has informal and unconventional social habits, esp. an artist or writer. [19th C.: from Fr. *bohémien* 'gypsy.'] ▶ **adj.** **1** of or relating to Bohemia or its people. **2** (also **bo·he·mi·an**) having informal and unconventional social habits. — **Bo·he·mi·an·ism** n. (in sense 2 of the **adjective**).

bo·ho /ˈbōˌhō/ ▶ **n.** (pl. **-hos**) informal term for BOHEMIAN (sense 2). ▶ **adj.** informal term for BOHEMIAN (sense 2).

Bo·hol /bōˈhôl/ an island in the central Philippines.

Bohr /bôr/, Niels Hendrik David (1885–1962), Danish physicist. His theory of the structure of the atom incorporated quantum theory for the first time. He helped to develop the atom bomb. Nobel Prize for Physics (1922).

Bohr ef·fect ▶ **n.** a decrease in the amount of oxygen associated with hemoglobin and other respiratory compounds in response to a lowered blood pH resulting from increased carbon dioxide in the blood. [Danish physiologist Christian *Bohr* (1855–1911).]

bohr·i·um /ˈbôrēəm/ ▶ **n.** the chemical element of atomic number 107, a very unstable element made by high-energy atomic collisions. (Symbol: **Bh**)

Bohr the·o·ry ▶ **n.** Physics a theory of the structure of atoms stating that electrons revolve in discrete orbits around a positively charged nucleus and that radiation is given off or absorbed only when an electron moves from one orbit to another. [Danish physicist Niels Henrik David BOHR.]

bo·hunk /ˈbōˌhəNGk/ ▶ **n.** informal, offens. an immigrant from central or southeastern Europe, esp. a laborer. ■ a rough or uncivilized person. [20th C.: appar. from BOHEMIAN + *-hunk,* alt. of HUNGARIAN.]

boil[1] /boil/ ▶ **v.** **1** [trans.] heat (a liquid) to the temperature at which it bubbles and turns to vapor: *boil drinking water.* ■ (of a liquid) be at or reach this temperature: *he waited for the water to boil.* ■ heat (a container) until the liquid in it reaches such a temperature: [trans.] *she boiled the kettle.* ■ [intrans.] (of a container) be heated until the liquid in it reaches such a temperature: *the kettle boiled.* **2** [trans.] subject (something) to the heat of boiling liquid, in particular: ■ cook (food) by immersing in boiling water: *boil the potatoes until well done* | [as adj.] (**boiled**) *two boiled eggs.* ■ [intrans.] (of food) be cooked in boiling water: *the lobsters are boiling.* ■ wash or sterilize (clothes) in very hot water. ■ hist. execute (someone) by subjecting them to the heat of boiling liquid. **3** [intrans.] (of the sea or clouds) be turbulent and stormy: *a cliff with the black sea boiling below.* ■ (of a person or strong emotion) be stirred up or inflamed: *he was **boiling with rage.*** ▶ **n.** **1** [in sing.] the temperature at which a liquid bubbles and turns to vapor. ■ an act or process of heating a liquid to such a temperature. ■ fig. a state of vigorous activity or excitement. ■ an area of churning water. ■ Fishing a sudden rise of a fish at a fly. **2** an outdoor meal at which seafood is boiled. ■ a blend of seasonings added to water to enhance the flavor of boiled seafood.

– PHRASES **keep the pot boiling** maintain the momentum or interest value of something. **make one's blood boil** see BLOOD.

– PHRASAL VERBS **boil away** (of a liquid in a container) boil until the container is empty. **boil down to** be in essence a matter of: *everything boiled down to cash in the end.* **boil something down** reduce the volume of a liquid by boiling. **boil over** (of a liquid) flow over the sides of the container in boiling. ■ fig. (of a situation or strong emotion) become so excited or tense as to get out of control. [ME: from OFr. *boillir,* from L. *bullire* 'to bubble,' from *bulla* 'bubble.']

boil[2] ▶ **n.** an inflamed pus-filled swelling on the skin, typically caused by the infection of a hair follicle. [OE *bȳle, bȳl,* of West Gmc. origin; rel. to Ger. *Beule.*]

Boi·leau /bwäˈlō/, Nicholas (1636–1711), French critic; full name *Nicholas Boileau-Despréaux.* He was one of the founders of French literary criticism.

boil·er /ˈboilər/ ▶ **n.** a fuel-burning apparatus or container for heating water, in particular: ■ a household device providing a hot-water supply or serving a central heating system. ■ a tank for generating steam under pressure in a steam engine. See also STEAM BOILER. ■ dated a metal tub for washing or sterilizing clothes at a very high temperature.

boil·er·mak·er /ˈboilərˌmākər/ ▶ **n.** **1** a person who makes boilers. ■ a metalworker in heavy industry. **2** a shot of whiskey followed by a glass of beer as a chaser.

boil·er·plate /ˈboilərˌplāt/ ▶ **n.** **1** rolled steel for making boilers. **2** (**boilerplates**) smooth, overlapping, and undercut slabs of rock: *the ice-worn boilerplates.* **3** fig. writing that is clichéd or expresses a generally accepted opinion or belief: *he accepted Soviet boilerplate at face value.* ■ standardized pieces of text for use as clauses in contracts or as part of a computer program: *some sections have been written as boilerplate for use in all proposals.*

boil·er room ▶ **n.** a room in a building (typically in the basement) or a compartment in a ship containing a boiler and related heating equipment. ■ a room used for intensive telephone selling: [as adj.] *boiler-room stock salesmen.*

boil·er suit ▶ **n.** British term for COVERALLS (see COVERALL).

boil·ing point ▶ **n.** the temperature at which a liquid boils and turns to vapor. The boiling point for fresh water at sea level is 212°F (100°C). ■ fig. the point at which anger or excitement breaks out into violent expression: *racial tension surges to boiling point.*

boil·ing-wa·ter re·ac·tor (abbr.: **BWR**) ▶ **n.** a nuclear reactor in which the fuel is uranium oxide clad in zircaloy and the coolant and moderator is water, which is boiled to produce steam for driving turbines.

boing /boiNG/ ▶ **exclam.** representing the noise of a compressed spring suddenly released. ▶**n.** such a noise. ▶**v.** [intrans.] make such a noise. [1950s: imitative.]

Boi·se /'boisē; -zē/ the capital of Idaho, in in the southwestern part of the state; pop. 185,787.

boi·se·rie /bwäzə'rē/ ▶**n.** wooden paneling. [19th C.: Fr.]

bois·ter·ous /'boist(ə)rəs/ ▶**adj.** (of a person, event, or behavior) noisy, energetic, and cheerful; rowdy. ■ (of wind, weather, or water) wild or stormy. — **bois·ter·ous·ly adv. bois·ter·ous·ness n.** [ME: var. of *boistuous* 'rustic.']

boîte /bwät/ ▶**n.** (pl. same or **boîtes**) a small restaurant or nightclub.

Bo·kas·sa /bə'käsə/, Jean Bédel (1921–96), president of the Central African Republic 1972–76 and self-styled emperor 1976–79.

bok choy /'bäk 'CHoi/ ▶**n.** Chinese cabbage of a variety (*Brassica chinensis*) with smooth-edged tapering leaves. [from Chin. (Cantonese dial.) *paâk ts'oì* 'white vegetable.']

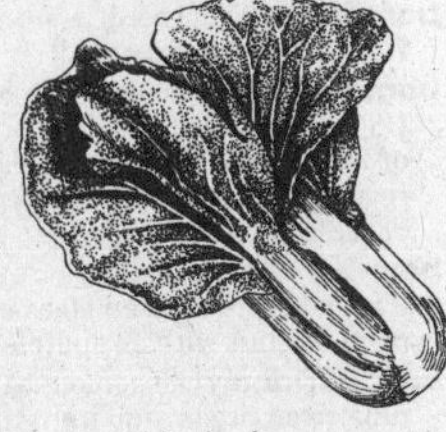

bok choy

bok·ken /'bäkən/ ▶**n.** a wooden sword used as a practice weapon in kendo.

Bok·mål /'bŏŏk,môl/ ▶**n.** one of two standard forms of the Norwegian language, a modified form of Danish. See **NORWEGIAN.** [from Norw. *bok* 'book' + *mål* 'language.']

bo·la /'bōlə/ (also **bo·las**) ▶**n.** (esp. in South America) a weapon consisting of balls connected by strong cord, which when thrown entangles the limbs of the quarry. [19th C.: from Sp. and Port. *bolas*, pl. of *bola* 'ball.']

bo·la tie /'bōlə/ ▶**n.** var. of **BOLO TIE.**

bold /bōld/ ▶**adj. 1** (of a person, action, or idea) showing an ability to take risks; confident and courageous. ■ dated (of a person or manner) so confident as to suggest a lack of shame or modesty. **2** (of a color or design) having a strong or vivid appearance. ■ (of a typeface) having thick strokes. **3** (of a cliff or coastline) steep or projecting. ▶**n.** a typeface with thick strokes.

– PHRASES **be** (or **make**) **so bold** (**as to do something**) formal dare to do something (often used when politely asking a question or making a suggestion). (**as**) **bold as brass** confident to the point of impudence. **a bold stroke** a daring action or initiative. **put a bold face on something** see **FACE.** — **bold·ly adv. bold·ness n.** [OE *bald*, of Gmc. origin; rel. to Ger. *bald* 'soon.']

bold·face /'bōld,fās/ ▶**n.** a typeface with thick strokes. See illustration at **TYPE.** ▶**adj.** printed or displayed in such a typeface. — **bold·faced adj.**

bole[1] /bōl/ ▶**n.** the trunk of a tree. [ME: from ON *bolr*; perh. rel. to **BALK.**]

bole[2] ▶**n.** fine, compact, earthy clay, typically of a reddish color, used as a pigment. [ME: from late L. *bolus* 'rounded mass' (see **BOLUS**).]

bo·lec·tion /bō'leksHən/ ▶**n.** [usu. as adj.] Archit. a decorative molding that separates two planes (or surfaces), esp. around a wooden panel, usually convex. [17th C.: of unknown origin.]

bo·le·ro /bə'le(ə)rō/ ▶**n.** (pl. **-ros**) **1** a Spanish dance in simple triple time. ■ a piece of music for this dance. **2** a woman's short open jacket. [18th C.: from Sp.]

bolero 2

bo·lete /bō'lēt/ (also **bo·le·tus** /-'lētəs/) ▶**n.** (pl. **-letes** or **-le·tus·es**) a mushroom or toadstool (genus *Boletus*, family Boletaceae) with pores rather than gills on the underside of the cap. Boletes often have a thick stem, and several kinds are edible. [from L., from Gk. *bōlitēs*, perh. from *bōlos* 'lump.']

Bol·eyn /bŏŏ'lin; 'bŏŏlin/, Anne (1507–36), second wife of Henry VIII; mother of Elizabeth I. She fell from favor when she failed to provide Henry with a male heir and was executed.

bo·lide /'bōlīd; 'bōlid/ ▶**n.** a large meteor that explodes in the atmosphere. [19th C.: from Fr., from L. *bolis, bolid-*, from Gk. *bolis* 'missile.']

Bol·ing·broke /'bōliNG,brŏŏk; 'bäl-; -,brōk/, the surname of Henry IV of England. (see **HENRY**[1]).

Bo·ling·brook /'bōliNG,brŏŏk/ a village in northeastern Illinois; pop. 40,843.

Bol·í·var /bə'lēvär; 'bäləvər/, Simón (1783–1830), Venezuelan patriot; known as **the Liberator**. He succeeded in driving the Spanish from Venezuela, Colombia, Peru, and Ecuador.

bol·i·var /bə'lēvär; 'bäləvər/ ▶**n.** the basic monetary unit of Venezuela, equal to 100 centimos. [named after S. **BOLÍVAR.**]

Bo·liv·i·a /bə'livēə/ a landlocked country in western South America. *See box.* — **Bo·liv·i·an adj. & n.**

bo·liv·i·a·no /bə,livē'änō/ ▶**n.** (pl. **-nos**) the basic monetary unit of Bolivia (1863–1962 and since 1987), equal to 100 centavos or cents. [19th C.: Sp., lit. 'Bolivian.']

Böll /bœl/, Heinrich Theodor (1917–85), German writer. His works include *Billiards at Half Past Nine* (1959). Nobel Prize for Literature (1972).

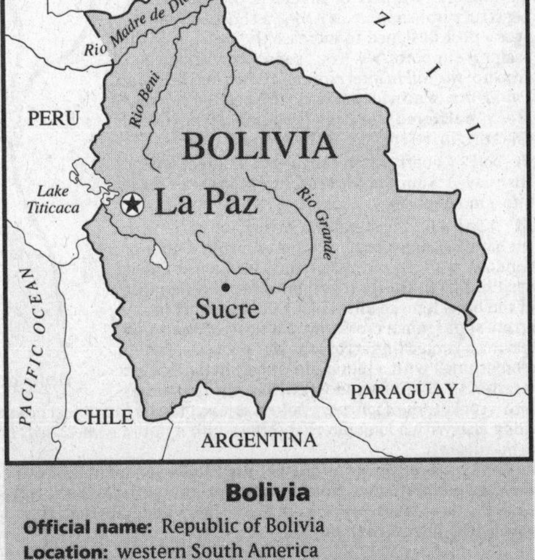

Bolivia

Official name: Republic of Bolivia
Location: western South America
Area: 418,800 square miles (1,084,400 sq km)
Population: 8,724,000
Capital: La Paz (seat of government); Sucre (legal capital and seat of judiciary)
Languages: Spanish, Aymara, Quechua (all official)
Currency: boliviano

boll /bōl/ ▶**n.** the rounded seed capsule of plants such as cotton or flax. [ME: from MDu. *bolle* 'rounded object'; rel. to **BOWL**[1].]

bol·lard /'bälərd/ ▶**n.** a short, thick post on the deck of a ship or on a wharf, to which a ship's rope may be secured. [ME (sense 1): perh. from ON *bolr* (see **BOLE**[1]) + **-ARD.**]

bol·lix /'bäliks/ vulgar slang ▶**v.** [trans.] (usu. **bollix something up**) bungle (a task). ▶**plural n.** var. of **BOLLOCKS.**

bol·locks /'bäləks/ (also **bal·locks** or **bol·lix**) vulgar slang, esp. Brit. ▶**n. 1** [in pl.] the testicles. **2** used to express contempt, annoyance, or defiance. [18th C.: pl. of *bollock*, var. of earlier *ballock*, of Gmc. origin; rel. to **BALL**[1].]

boll wee·vil ▶**n.** a small weevil (*Anthonomus grandis*, family Curculionidae) that feeds on the fibers of the cotton boll. It is a major pest of the American cotton crop. ■ informal in the US, a conservative Southern Democrat, esp. a member of Congress.

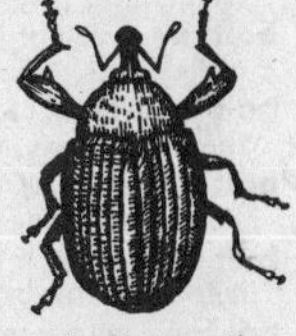

boll weevil

boll·worm /'bōl,wərm/ ▶**n.** a moth caterpillar that attacks the cotton boll, in particular: ■ (**pink bollworm**) a small moth (*Pectinophora gossypiella*, family Gelechiidae) that is a serious pest of the North American cotton crop. ■ (also **cotton bollworm**) another term for **CORN EARWORM.**

Bol·ly·wood /'bälē,wŏŏd/ ▶**n.** the Indian movie industry, based in Bombay. [1970s: blend of **BOMBAY** and **HOLLYWOOD.**]

bo·lo /'bōlō/ ▶**n. 1** (pl. **-los**) a large single-edged knife used in the Philippines. **2** variant of **BOLA. 3** short for **BOLO TIE.** [Sp.]

Bo·lo·gna /bə'lōnyə/ a city in northern Italy, northeast of Florence; pop. 411,800.

bo·lo·gna /bə'lōnē/ (also **bologna sausage**) ▶**n.** a sausage made of various meats, esp. beef and pork. [from **BOLOGNA.**]

bo·lom·e·ter /bō'lämitər/ ▶**n.** a sensitive electrical instrument for measuring radiant energy. — **bo·lo·met·ric** /,bōlə'metrik/ **adj.** [19th C.: from Gk. *bolē* 'ray of light.']

bo·lo·ney ▶**n.** var. of **BALONEY.**

bo·lo tie (also **bo·la tie** /'bōlə/) ▶**n.** a type of tie consisting of a cord worn around the neck with a large ornamental fastening at the throat. *See illustration on next page.*

Bol·she·vik /'bōlsHə,vik/ ▶**n.** hist. a member of the majority faction of the Russian Social Democratic Party, which was renamed the Communist Party after seizing power in the October Revolution of 1917. ■ esp. derog. (in general use) a person with politically subversive or radical views; a revolutionary. ▶**adj.** of, relating to, or characteristic of Bolsheviks

PRONUNCIATION KEY ə *ago, up*; ər *over, fur*; a *hat*; ā *ate*; ä *car*; e *let*; ē *see*; i *fit*; ī *by*; NG *sing*; ō *go*; ô *law, for*; oi *toy*; ŏŏ *good*; ōō *goo*; ou *out*; TH *thin*; T͟H *then*; ZH *vision*

or Bolshevism. — **Bol·she·vism** n. **Bol·she·vist** n. [Russ., from *bol'she* 'greater.']

bol·ster /'bōlstər/ ▶ n. (also **bolster pillow**) a long, thick pillow that is placed under other pillows for support. ■ a part of a vehicle or tool providing structural support. ■ Building a short timber cap over a post designed to increase the bearing of the beams it supports. ▶ v. [trans.] support or strengthen; prop up: *the fall in interest rates is starting to bolster confidence.* ■ provide (a seat) with padded support: [as adj.] (**bolstered**) *the heavily bolstered seat.* [OE, of Gmc. origin; rel. to Ger. *Polster*.]

bolo tie

Bolt /bōlt/, Robert Oxton (1924–95), English writer. His play *A Man for All Seasons* (1960) was made into a movie in 1967.

bolt[1] /bōlt/ ▶ n. **1** a metal pin or bar, in particular: ■ a bar that slides into a socket to fasten a door or window. ■ a long pin that screws into a nut and is used to fasten things together. ■ the sliding piece of the breech mechanism of a rifle. **2** a short heavy arrow shot from a crossbow. **3** a flash of lightning leaving a jagged line across the sky. ▶ v. [trans.] fasten (something) with a metal pin or bar, in particular: ■ fasten (a door or window) with a bar that slides into a socket: *the doors were bolted.* ■ [trans.] fasten (an object) to something else with a long pin that screws into a nut: *a camera was bolted to the aircraft.*
– PHRASES **a bolt from** (or **out of**) **the blue** a sudden and unexpected event or piece of news. **bolt upright** upright, with the back rigid and straight. **have shot one's bolt** informal have done all that is in one's power. [OE, 'arrow,' Ger. *Bolzen*.]

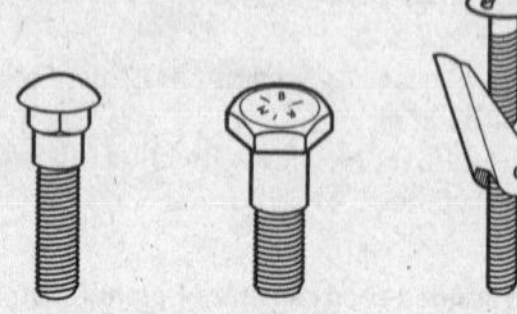

bolt[1] 1

bolt[2] ▶ v. **1** [intrans.] (of a horse or other animal) run away suddenly out of control: *the horses bolted.* ■ [intrans.] (of a person) move or run away suddenly. ■ [trans.] (in hunting) cause (a rabbit or fox) to run out of its burrow or hole. ■ (of a plant) grow quickly upward and stop flowering as seeds develop. **2** [trans.] (often **bolt something down**) eat or swallow (food) quickly: *puppies bolt down their food.*
– PHRASES **make a bolt for** try to escape by moving suddenly toward (something). [ME: from BOLT[1].]

bolt[3] ▶ n. a roll of fabric, originally as a measure. [ME: transferred use of BOLT[1].]

bolt[4] (also **boult**) ▶ v. [trans.] archaic pass (flour, powder, or other material) through a sieve. [ME: from OFr. *bulter*.]

bolt-ac·tion ▶ adj. (of a gun) having a breech that is opened by turning a bolt and sliding it back.

bolt-hole ▶ n. fig. a place where a person can escape and hide. ■ esp. Brit. a hole or burrow by which a rabbit or other wild animal can escape.

Bol·ton /'bōltn/ a town in northwestern England; pop. 253,300.

bolt-on ▶ adj. [attrib.] (of an extra part of a machine) able to be fastened on with a bolt or catch. ▶ n. an extra part that can be fastened onto a machine with a bolt or catch.

bolt rope ▶ n. a rope sewn around the edge of a vessel's sail to prevent tearing.

Boltz·mann /'bôltsmən/, Ludwig (1844–1906), Austrian physicist. He derived the Maxwell–Boltzmann equation for the distribution of energy among colliding atoms.

Boltz·mann's con·stant Chem. the ratio of the gas constant to Avogadro's number, equal to 1.381 × 10–23 joule per kelvin. (Symbol: **k**)

bo·lus /'bōləs/ ▶ n. (pl. **bo·luses**) a small rounded mass of a substance, esp. of chewed food at the moment of swallowing. ■ a type of large pill used in veterinary medicine. ■ Med. a single dose of a drug given all at once. [16th C.: via late L. from Gk. *bōlos* 'clod.']

Bol·za·no /bōlt'sänō; bōld'zänō/ a city in northeastern Italy; pop. 100,000.

bomb /bäm/ ▶ n. **1** a container filled with explosive, incendiary material, smoke, gas, or other destructive substance, designed to explode on impact or when detonated by a time mechanism, remote-control device, or lit fuse. ■ [with adj.] an explosive device fitted into a specified object. See also CAR BOMB, LETTER BOMB. ■ (**the bomb**) nuclear weapons considered collectively as agents of mass destruction. ■ a small pressurized container that sprays liquid, foam, or gas. **2** a thing resembling a bomb in impact, in particular: ■ (also **volcanic bomb**) a lump of lava thrown out by a volcano. ■ informal a movie, play, or other event that fails badly ■ a long forward pass or hit in a ball game. **3** informal an old car. ▶ v. **1** [trans.] attack (a place or vehicle) with a bomb or bombs: *London was bombed* | [as n.] (**bombing**) *a series of bombings.* **2** [intrans.] informal (of a movie, play, or other event) fail miserably: *a big-budget movie that bombed.* **3** [intrans.] Brit., informal move very quickly: *the bus came bombing along.* [17th C.: from Fr. *bombe*, from Ital. *bomba*, prob. from L. *bombus* 'booming, humming,' from Gk. *bombos*, of imitative origin.]

bom·bard /bäm'bärd/ ▶ v. [trans.] attack (a place or person) continuously with bombs, shells, or other missiles: *the city was bombarded by federal forces* | *supporters **bombarded** police **with** bottles.* ■ assail (someone) persistently, as with questions, criticisms, or information. ■ Physics direct a high-speed stream of particles at (a substance). ▶ n. /'bäm,bärd/ hist. a cannon of the earliest type, which fired a stone ball or large shot. — **bom·bard·ment** /bäm'bärdmənt/ n. [ME: from OFr. *bombarde*, prob. based on L. *bombus* (see BOMB).]

bom·barde /'bäm,bärd/ ▶ n. Music a medieval alto-pitched shawm. [ME: from OFr. (see BOMBARD).]

bom·bar·dier /,bämbə(r)'di(ə)r/ ▶ n. **1** a member of a bomber crew in the US Air Force responsible for sighting and releasing bombs. **2** a rank of noncommissioned officer in certain Canadian and British artillery regiments, equivalent to corporal. [16th C.: from Fr., from OFr. *bombarde* 'cannon.']

bom·bar·dier bee·tle ▶ n. a ground beetle (genus *Brachinus*, family Carabidae) that when alarmed discharges a puff of hot irritant vapor from its anus with an audible pop.

bom·bar·don /'bämbərdən; bäm'bärdn/ ▶ n. Music a type of valved bass tuba. ■ an organ stop imitating this. [19th C.: from Ital. *bombardone*, from *bombardo* 'cannon.']

bom·bast /'bämbast/ ▶ n. high-sounding language with little meaning. — **bom·bas·tic** /bäm'bastik/ adj. **bom·bas·ti·cal·ly** /bäm'bastik(ə)lē/ adv. [16th C. ('raw cotton'): from OFr. *bombace*, from med. L. *bombax*, *bombac-*, alt. of *bombyx* (see BOMBAZINE).]

Bom·bay /bäm'bā/ a city on the western coast of India; pop. 9,990,000. Official name (from 1995) **MUMBAI**.

bom·ba·zine /,bämbə'zēn; 'bämbə,zēn/ ▶ n. a twilled dress fabric of worsted and silk or cotton. [16th C.: from Fr. *bombasin*, from med. L. *bombacinum*, from *bombycinum*, neut. of *bombycinus* 'silken,' based on Gk. *bombux* 'silkworm.']

bomb bay ▶ n. a compartment in the fuselage of an aircraft in which bombs are held.

bombe /bäm(b)/ ▶ n. a frozen dome-shaped dessert. ■ a dome-shaped mold in which this dessert is made. [19th C.: Fr., lit. 'bomb.']

bom·bé /bäm'bā/ ▶ adj. (of furniture) rounded. [20th C.: Fr., lit. 'swollen out.']

bombed /bämd/ ▶ adj. **1** (of an area or building) subjected to bombing. **2** informal intoxicated by drink or drugs.

bombed-out ▶ adj. **1** [attrib.] (of a building or city) destroyed by bombing. **2** informal another term for BOMBED (sense 2).

bomb·er /'bämər/ ▶ n. **1** an aircraft designed to carry and drop bombs. **2** a person who plants, detonates, or throws bombs in a public place, esp. as a terrorist. **3** informal a cigarette containing marijuana. **4** short for BOMBER JACKET.

bomb·er jack·et ▶ n. a short jacket, usually leather, tightly gathered at the waist and cuffs by elasticized bands and typically having a zipper front.

bom·bi·nate /'bämbə,nāt/ ▶ v. [intrans.] literary buzz; hum: [as adj.] (**bombinating**) *her head had become a bombinating vacuum.* [19th C.: from med. L. *bombinat-* 'buzzed,' from the v. *bombinare*, from L. *bombus* 'humming' (see BOMBARD).]

bomb·let /'bämlit/ ▶ n. a small bomb.

bomb·proof /'bäm,prōōf/ ▶ adj. strong enough to resist the effects of a bomb blast.

bomb·shell /'bäm,shel/ ▶ n. **1** an overwhelming surprise or disappointment: *the news came as a bombshell.* **2** informal a very attractive woman: *a twenty-year-old **blonde bombshell**.* **3** dated an artillery shell.

bomb·sight /'bäm,sīt/ ▶ n. a mechanical or electronic device used in an aircraft for aiming bombs.

Bon, Cape /bôn/ a peninsula in northeastern Tunisia.

bo·na fide /'bōnə ,fīd; 'bänə/ ▶ adj. genuine; real. ▶ adv. esp. Law sincerely; without intention to deceive: *the court will assume that they have acted bona fide.* [16th C.: L., lit. 'with good faith,' ablative sing. of BONA FIDES.]

bo·na fi·des /'bōnə ,fīdz; 'fīdēz; 'bänə/ ▶ n. a person's honesty and sincerity of intention. ■ [treated as pl.] informal documentary evidence showing a person's legitimacy; credentials. [18th C.: L., lit. 'good faith.']

Bon·aire /bä'ne(ə)r; bə-/ a principal island of the Netherlands Antilles; chief town, Kralendijk; pop. 10,190.

bo·nan·za /bə'nanzə/ ▶ n. [often with adj.] a situation or event that creates a sudden increase in wealth, good fortune, or profits. ■ a large amount of something desirable: *the festive feature film bonanza.* [19th C.: from Sp., lit. 'prosperity,' from L. *bonus* 'good.']

Bo·na·parte /'bōnə,pärt/ (Italian **Buo·na·parte** /,bwōnä'pärtā/) a Corsican family, including the three French rulers named Napoleon.

bon ap·pé·tit /'bōn ,apə'tē/ ▶ exclam. used as a salutation to a person about to eat. [19th C.: Fr., lit. 'good appetite.']

Bon·a·ven·tu·ra, St. /,bōnə,ven'tōōrə/ (1221–74), Franciscan theologian; born *Giovanni di Fidanza*; known as **the Seraphic Doctor**. He wrote the official biography of St. Francis.

bon·bon /ˈbänˌbän/ ▶ n. a piece of candy, esp. one covered with chocolate. [18th C.: from Fr., reduplication of *bon* 'good.']

bond /bänd/ ▶ n. **1** (**bonds**) physical restraints used to hold someone or something prisoner, esp. ropes or chains. ■ a thing used to tie something or to fasten things together. ■ adhesiveness; ability of two objects to stick to each other. ■ fig. a force or feeling that unites people; a common emotion or interest. ■ (**bonds**) fig. restricting forces or circumstances; obligations. **2** an agreement or promise with legal force, in particular: ■ Law a deed by which a person is committed to make payment to another. ■ a certificate issued by a government or a public company promising to repay borrowed money at a fixed rate of interest at a specified time. ■ (of dutiable goods) a state of storage in a bonded warehouse until the importer pays the duty owing. ■ an insurance policy held by a company against losses resulting from circumstances such as bankruptcy or misconduct by employees. **3** (also **chemical bond**) a strong force of attraction holding atoms together in a molecule or crystal, resulting from the sharing or transfer of electrons. **4** [with adj.] Building any of the various patterns in which bricks are laid in order to ensure strength. **5** short for BOND PAPER. ▶ v. **1** join or be joined securely to something else, typically by means of an adhesive, heat, or pressure: [trans.] *press the material to **bond** the layers together* | [intrans.] *this material will **bond** well to stainless steel* | [as adj.] (**bonding**) *a bonding agent.* ■ [intrans.] fig. establish a relationship with someone based on shared feelings, interests, or experiences: *the failure to properly **bond** with their children* | [as n.] (**bonding**) *the film has some great male bonding scenes.* **2** join or be joined by a chemical bond. **3** [trans.] [usu. as adj.] (**bonding**) lay (bricks) in an overlapping pattern so as to form a strong structure. **4** [usu. as n.] (**bonding**) place (dutiable goods) in bond. [ME: var. of BAND[1].]

bond·age /ˈbändij/ ▶ n. **1** the state of being a slave. ■ fig. a state of being greatly constrained by circumstances or obligations. **2** sexual practice that involves the tying up or restraining of one partner. [ME: from Anglo-L. *bondagium*, from ME *bond* 'serf,' from ON *bóndi* 'tiller of the soil,' based on *búa* 'dwell.']

bond·ed /ˈbändid/ ▶ adj. [attrib.] **1** (of a thing) joined securely to another thing, esp. by an adhesive, a heat process, or pressure. ■ fig. emotionally or psychologically linked. ■ held by a chemical bond. **2** (of a person or company) bound by a legal agreement, in particular: ■ (of a debt) secured by bonds. ■ (of a worker or workforce) obliged to work for a particular employer, often in a condition close to slavery. **3** (of dutiable goods) placed in bond.

bond·ed ware·house ▶ n. a customs-controlled warehouse for holding imported goods until the duty is paid.

bond·maid /ˈbändˌmād/ ▶ n. archaic a slave girl.

bond·man /ˈbändmən/ ▶ n. archaic a serf; a slave.

bond pa·per ▶ n. high-quality writing paper.

bond·serv·ant /ˈbändˌsərvənt/ ▶ n. a person bound in service without wages. ■ a slave or serf.

bonds·man /ˈbändzmən/ ▶ n. (pl. **-men**) **1** a person who stands surety for a bond. **2** archaic a slave.

bond·wom·an /ˈbändˌwo͝omən/ ▶ n. (pl. **-wom·en**) a female bondservant or slave.

Bône /bōn/ former name for ANNABA.

bone /bōn/ ▶ n. **1** any of the pieces of hard, whitish tissue making up the skeleton in humans and other vertebrates. ■ (**bones**) a person's body. ■ (**bones**) a corpse or skeleton. ■ (**bones**) fig. the basic or essential framework of something. ■ a bone of an animal with meat on it, used as food for people or dogs. **2** the calcified material of which bones consist. ■ a substance similar to this such as ivory, dentin, or whalebone. ■ (often **bones**) a thing made of, or once made of, such a substance, for example a pair of dice. **3** the whitish color of bone. **4** vulgar slang a penis. ▶ v. **1** [trans.] remove the bones from (meat or fish). **2** [intrans.] (**bone up on**) informal study (a subject) intensively, often in preparation for something: *she boned up on languages.* **3** [trans.] vulgar slang (of a man) have sexual intercourse with (someone).

– PHRASES **a bag of bones** see BAG. **the bare bones** see BARE. **be skin and bones** see SKIN. **a bone of contention** a subject or issue over which there is continuing disagreement. **close to** (or **near**) **the bone** **1** (of a remark) penetrating and accurate to the point of causing hurt or discomfort. **2** destitute; hard up. **cut** (or **pare**) **something to the bone** reduce something to the bare minimum. (**as**) **dry as a bone** see DRY. **have a bone to pick with someone** informal have reason to disagree or be annoyed with someone. **have not a —— bone in one's body** (of a person) have not the slightest trace of the specified quality: *there's not a conservative bone in his body.* **in one's bones** felt, believed, or known deeply or instinctively. **make no bones about something** have no hesitation in stating or dealing with something, however awkward or distasteful it is. **to the bone** **1** (of a wound) so deep as to expose a person's bone. ■ (esp. of cold) affecting a person in a penetrating way. **2** (or **to one's bones**) used to emphasize that a person has a specified quality in an overwhelming or fundamental way. **throw a bone to** give someone a token concession without offering anything substantial. **what's bred in the bone will come out in the flesh** (or **blood**) proverb a person's behavior or characteristics are determined by heredity. **work one's fingers to the bone** work very hard. [OE *bān*, of Gmc. origin; rel. to Du. *been* and Ger. *Bein*.]

bone ash ▶ n. the mineral residue of calcined bones.

bone black ▶ n. fine charcoal made by burning animal bones in a closed container.

bone chi·na ▶ n. fine china made of clay mixed with bone ash.

boned /bōnd/ ▶ adj. [attrib.] **1** (of meat or fish) having had the bones removed before cooking or serving. **2** [in comb.] (of a person) having bones of the specified type: *she was fine-boned.* **3** (of a garment) stiffened with strips of plastic or whalebone to give shape to the figure or the garment.

bone-dry ▶ adj. completely or extremely dry.

bone·fish /ˈbōnˌfisн/ ▶ n. (pl. same or **-fish·es**) a silvery game fish (family Albulidae) of warm coastal waters, in particular *Albula vulpes*.

bone·head /ˈbōnˌhed/ ▶ n. informal a stupid person. — **bone·head·ed** adj.

bone·less /ˈbōnlis/ ▶ adj. (of a piece of meat or fish) having had the bones removed. ■ fig. (of a person) limp; with loose limbs. ■ fig. lacking physical or mental strength. — **bone·less·ly** adv.: *he collapsed bonelessly into an easy chair.*

bone mar·row ▶ n. see MARROW (sense 1).

bone·meal /ˈbōnˌmēl/ ▶ n. crushed or ground bones used as a fertilizer.

bon·er /ˈbōnər/ ▶ n. **1** informal a stupid mistake. **2** vulgar slang an erection of the penis. [20th C.: from BONE.]

bone·set /ˈbōnˌset/ ▶ n. a North American plant (genus *Eupatorium*) of the daisy family that bears clusters of small flowers and is used in herbal medicine. ■ the common comfrey (*Symphytum officinale*), used in herbal medicine. [its ground-up root was formerly used as a 'plaster' to set broken bones.]

bone·set·ter /ˈbōnˌsetər/ ▶ n. hist. a person, typically not formally qualified, who sets broken or dislocated bones.

bone spav·in ▶ n. osteoarthritis of the hock in horses.

bone-wea·ry (also **bone-tired**) ▶ adj. extremely tired.

bon·ey ▶ adj. var. of BONY.

bone·yard /ˈbōnˌyärd/ ▶ n. informal a cemetery. ■ a place where discarded cars are kept.

bon·fire /ˈbänˌfī(ə)r/ ▶ n. a large open-air fire used as part of a celebration, for burning trash, or as a signal. [ME: from BONE + FIRE.]

bong[1] /bäNG/ ▶ n. a low-pitched sound as of a bell. ▶ v. [intrans.] emit such a sound. [1920s (orig. US): imitative.]

bong[2] ▶ n. a water pipe used for smoking marijuana or other drugs. [1970s: from Thai *baung*, lit. 'wooden tube.']

bon·go[1] /ˈbäNGgō; ˈbôNG-/ (also **bongo drum**) ▶ n. (pl. **-gos** or **-goes**) either of a pair of small, long-bodied drums typically held between the knees and played with the fingers. [1920s: from L. Amer. Sp. *bongó*.]

bongo[1]

bon·go[2] ▶ n. (pl. same or **-gos**) a forest antelope (*Tragelaphus eurycerus*) that has a chestnut coat with narrow white vertical stripes, native to central Africa. [19th C.: from Kikongo.]

Bon·hoef·fer /ˈbänˌhôfər/, Dietrich (1906–45), German Lutheran theologian. He actively opposed Nazism and was involved in the German resistance movement.

bon·ho·mie /ˈbänəˌmē; ˌbänəˈmē/ ▶ n. cheerful friendliness; geniality. [18th C.: from Fr., from *bonhomme* 'good fellow.']

bon·ho·mous /ˈbänəməs/ ▶ adj. full of cheerful friendliness.

Bon·i·face, St. /ˈbänəfəs/ (680–754), Anglo-Saxon missionary; born *Wynfrith*; known as **the Apostle of Germany**. He was appointed primate of Germany in 732.

bo·ni·to /bəˈnētō/ ▶ n. (pl. **-tos**) a smaller relative of the tunas (*Sarda* and other genera), with dark oblique stripes on the back and important as a food and game fish. ■ (also **ocean bonito**) another term for SKIPJACK (sense 1). [16th C.: from Sp.]

bonk /bäNGk/ informal ▶ v. **1** [trans.] knock or hit (something) so as to cause a reverberating sound. **2** have sexual intercourse with (someone). ▶ n. **1** an act of knocking or hitting something that causes a reverberating sound. ■ a reverberating sound caused in such a way. **2** an act of sexual intercourse. [1930s: imitative.]

bon·kers /ˈbäNGkərz/ ▶ adj. [predic.] informal mad; crazy. [1940s: of unknown origin.]

bon mot /ˈbän ˈmō; ˌbôN ˈmō/ ▶ n. (pl. **bons mots** pronunc. same or /ˈmōz/) a witty remark. [18th C.: Fr., lit. 'good word.']

Bonn /bän/ a city in the state of North Rhine-Westphalia in Germany; pop. 296,240. It was the capital of the Federal Republic of Germany (West Germany) 1949–90.

Bon·nard /bôˈnär/, Pierre (1867–1947), French painter. His works continue and develop the Impressionist tradition.

bon·net /ˈbänit/ ▶ n. **1** a woman's or child's hat tied under the chin, typically with a brim framing the face. ■ (also **war bonnet**) the ceremonial feathered headdress of an American Indian. ■ a soft round brimless hat like a beret, esp. as worn by men and boys in Scotland. ■ Heraldry the velvet cap within a coronet. **2** a protective cover or cap over a machine or object, in particular: ■ a cowl on a chimney. ■ Brit. the hood of a car. **3** Sailing, hist. an additional canvas laced to the foot of a sail to catch more wind. — **bon·net·ed** adj. (in sense 1). [ME: from OFr. *bonet*, from med. L. *abonnis* 'headgear.']

Bon·ne·ville Dam /'bänə,vil/ a hydroelectric dam built in the 1930s on the Columbia River in Oregon.

Bon·ne·ville Salt Flats a desert in northwestern Utah, the site of automotive speed trials.

Bon·ney /'bänē/, William H. (1859–81), US outlaw; born *Henry McCarty*; known as **Billy the Kid**. A notorious robber and murderer, he was killed by Sheriff Pat Garrett (1850–1908).

Bon·nie Prince Char·lie /'bänē ,prins 'CHärlē/ see STUART[1].

bon·ny /'bänē/ (also **bon·nie**) esp. Scot. N. Engl. ▶ adj. (**-ni·er, -ni·est**) attractive; beautiful. ■ (of a baby) plump and healthy-looking. ■ sizable; considerable (usually expressing approval). ▶ n. (**my bonny**) literary used as a form of address for one's beloved or baby. — **bon·ni·ly** adv. **bon·ni·ness** n. [15th C.: perh. rel. to OFr. *bon* 'good.']

bon·ny clab·ber ▶ n. another term for CLABBER. [17th C.: from Irish *bainne clabair*, denoting thick milk for churning.]

bo·no·bo /bə'nōbō/ ▶ n. (pl. **-bos**) a chimpanzee (*Pan paniscus*) with a black face and black hair, found in the rain forests of the Democratic Republic of the Congo (formerly Zaire). Also called PYGMY CHIMPANZEE. [1950s: a local word.]

bon·sai /bän'sī; 'bänsī/ ▶ n. (pl. same) (also **bonsai tree**) an ornamental tree or shrub grown in a pot and artificially prevented from reaching its normal size. ■ the art of growing trees or shrubs in such a way. [1950s: from Japanese, from *bon* 'tray' + *sai* 'planting.']

bon·spiel /'bän,spēl/ ▶ n. esp. Scot. & Canadian a curling match. [16th C.: prob. of Low Ger. origin.]

bon·te·bok /'bäntē,bäk/ ▶ n. (pl. same or **-boks**) an antelope (*Damaliscus dorcas dorcas*) with a mainly reddish-brown coat and white face, found in eastern South Africa. It belongs to the same species as the blesbok. [18th C.: from Afrik., from Du. *bont* 'pied' + *bok* 'buck.']

bon ton /bän 'tän; bôN 'tôN/ ▶ n. the fashionable world.

bo·nus /'bōnəs/ ▶ n. a payment or gift added to what is usual or expected, in particular: ■ an amount of money added to wages on a seasonal basis, esp. as a reward for good performance. ■ something welcome and often unexpected that accompanies and enhances something that is itself good. ■ Basketball an extra free throw awarded to a fouled player when the opposing team has exceeded the number of team fouls allowed during a period. [18th C.: from L. *bonus* (masc.) 'good,' used for *bonum* (neut.) 'good thing.']

bon vi·vant /'bän vē'vänt; ,bôN vē'väN/ ▶ n. (pl. **bon vi·vants** or **bons vi·vants** pronunc. same or /-'vänts/) a person who enjoys a sociable and luxurious lifestyle. [17th C.: from Fr., lit. 'person living well,' from *bon* 'good' and *vivre* 'to live.']

bon vi·veur /'bän vē'vər; ,bôN vē'vœr/ ▶ n. (pl. **bon vi·veurs** or **bons vi·veurs** pronunc. same or /-'vərz/) another term for BON VIVANT. [19th C.: pseudo-French, from Fr. *bon* 'good' and *viveur* 'a living person.']

bon vo·yage /'bän voi'äZH; 'bōn; bôN/ ▶ exclam. used to express good wishes to someone about to go on a journey. [17th C.: Fr., lit. 'good journey.']

bon·y /'bōnē/ ▶ adj. (**bon·i·er, bon·i·est**) of or like bone. ■ (of a person or part of the body) so thin that the bones are prominent. ■ (of a fish eaten as food) having many bones. — **bon·i·ness** n.

bon·y fish ▶ n. a fish of a large class (Osteichthyes) distinguished by a skeleton of bone, and comprising the majority of modern fishes. Compare with CARTILAGINOUS FISH.

bon·y lab·y·rinth ▶ n. see LABYRINTH.

bonze /bänz/ ▶ n. a Japanese or Chinese Buddhist monk. [16th C.: prob. from Japanese *bonzō, bonsō* 'priest.']

boo /bōō/ ▶ exclam. **1** said suddenly to surprise someone: *"Boo!" she cried.* [prob. alt. of *bo*.] **2** said to show disapproval or contempt, esp. at a performance or athletic contest. ▶ n. an utterance of "boo" to show disapproval or contempt. ▶ v. (**boos, booed**) say "boo" to show disapproval or contempt: [intrans.] *they booed when he stepped on stage* | [trans.] *I was booed off the stage.*

– PHRASES **say boo** [with negative] say anything at all; utter a sound. [19th C. (sense 2): imitative of the lowing of oxen.]

boob[1] /bōōb/ informal ▶ n. **1** a foolish or stupid person. **2** Brit. an embarrassing mistake. [20th C.: abbrev. of BOOBY[1].]

boob[2] ▶ n. (usu. **boobs**) informal a woman's breast. [1950s: abbrev. of BOOBY[2], from dialect *bubby*, perh. rel. to Ger. dial. *Bübbi* 'teat.']

boob·oi·sie /,bōōbwä'zē/ ▶ n. informal stupid people as a class. [1920s: from BOOB[1].]

boo-boo ▶ n. informal a mistake. ■ informal a minor injury, such as a scratch. [1950s: reduplication of BOOB[1].]

boob tube informal ▶ n. (usu. **the boob tube**) television or a television set.

boo·by[1] /'bōōbē/ ▶ n. (pl. **-bies**) **1** a stupid or childish person. **2** a large tropical seabird (genus *Sula*) of the gannet family, with brown, black, or white plumage and often brightly colored feet. [17th C.: prob. from Sp. *bobo* (in both senses), from L. *balbus* 'stammering.']

boo·by[2] ▶ n. (pl. **-bies**) (usu. **boobies**) informal a woman's breast. [1930s: alt. of dial. *bubby* (see BOOB[2]).]

boo·by hatch ▶ n. informal, offens. a psychiatric hospital.

boo·by prize ▶ n. a prize given as a joke to the last-place finisher in a race or competition.

boo·by trap ▶ n. a thing designed to catch the unwary, in particular: ■ an apparently harmless object containing a concealed explosive device designed to kill or injure anyone who touches it. ■ a trap intended as a practical joke, such as an object placed on top of a door ajar, ready to fall on the next person to pass through. ▶ v. (**boo·by-trap**) [trans.] place a booby trap in or on (an object or area): [as adj.] (**booby-trapped**) *the area was booby-trapped.*

boo·dle /'bōōdl/ ▶ n. **1** informal money, esp. that gained or spent illegally or improperly. **2** (**boodles**) a great quantity, esp. of money. [17th C.: from Du. *boedel, boel* 'disorderly mass.']

boo·ga·loo /'bōōgə,lōō/ ▶ n. a dance to rock-and-roll music performed with swiveling and shuffling movements of the body, originally popular in the 1960s. ▶ v. (**-loos, -looed**) [intrans.] perform this dance. [1960s: perh. alt. of BOOGIE-WOOGIE.]

boog·er /'bŏŏgər/ ▶ n. **1** another term for BOGEYMAN. **2** informal a piece of dried nasal mucus.

boog·ey·man ▶ n. var. of BOGEYMAN.

boog·ie /'bŏŏgē/ ▶ n. (also **boog·ie-woog·ie** /'wŏŏgē/) (pl. **boog·ies**) a style of blues with a strong, fast beat. ■ informal a dance to fast pop or rock music. ▶ v. (**boog·ie·ing**) [intrans.] informal dance to fast pop or rock music: *ready to boogie down to the music.* ■ [intrans.] move or leave somewhere fast: *we'd better boogie on out of here.* [20th C.: of unknown origin.]

boog·ie board ▶ n. a short, light type of surfboard ridden in a prone position. — **boog·ie board·er** n.

boo·hoo /'bōō'hōō/ ▶ exclam. used to represent the sound of someone crying noisily. ▶ v. (**-hoos, -hooed**) [intrans.] cry noisily: *she broke down and boohooed.* [19th C.: imitative.]

book /bŏŏk/ ▶ n. **1** a written or printed work consisting of pages glued or sewn together along one side and bound in covers. ■ a literary composition that is published or intended for publication as such a work. ■ (**the books**) used to refer to studying. ■ a main division of a classic literary work, an epic, or the Bible. ■ the libretto of an opera or musical, or the script of a play. ■ (**the book**) the local telephone directory. ■ (**the Book**) the Bible. ■ informal a magazine. ■ fig. an imaginary record or list (often used to emphasize the thoroughness or comprehensiveness of someone's actions or experiences). **2** [with adj.] a bound set of blank sheets for writing or keeping records in. ■ (**books**) a set of records or accounts. ■ a bookmaker's record of bets accepted and money paid out. **3** a set of tickets, stamps, matches, checks, samples of cloth, etc., bound together. ▶ v. [trans.] **1** reserve (accommodations, a place, etc.); buy (a ticket) in advance: *I have booked a table at the Swan* | [intrans.] *book early to avoid disappointment.* ■ reserve accommodations for (someone): *his secretary had booked him into the Howard Hotel* | [with two objs.] *book me a single room at my usual hotel.* ■ engage (a performer or guest) for an occasion or event. ■ (**be booked (up)**) have all appointments or places reserved; be full: *I'm booked till 2008.* **2** make an official record of the name and other personal details of (a criminal suspect or offender): *the cop booked me.*

– PHRASES **bring someone to book** bring someone to justice; punish. **by the book** strictly according to the rules. **close the book on** lay aside; expend no further energy on. **in someone's bad** (or **good**) **books** esp. Brit. in disfavor (or favor) with a person. **in my book** in my opinion. **make book** take bets on the outcome of an event. **one for the books** an extraordinary feat or event. **on the books** contained in a book of laws or records. **People of the Book** Jews and Christians as regarded by Muslims. **take a leaf from** (or **out of**) **someone's book** imitate or emulate someone in a particular way. **throw the book at** informal charge or punish (someone) as severely as possible. **wrote the book** be the leader in the field. **you can't judge a book by its cover** proverb outward appearances are not a reliable indication of true character. — **book·a·ble** adj. [OE *bōc, bōcian* 'to grant by charter,' of Gmc. origin; rel. to Ger. *Buch* and prob. BEECH.]

book·bind·er /'bŏŏk,bīndər/ ▶ n. a person who binds books as a profession. — **book·bind·ing** n.

book·case /'bŏŏk,kās/ ▶ n. a set of shelves for books set in a surrounding frame or cabinet.

book club ▶ n. an organization that sells selected books to members or subscribers, often through the mail.

book·end /'bŏŏk,end/ ▶ n. a support for the end of a row of books to keep them upright, often one of a pair. ▶ v. [trans.] (usu. **be bookended**) informal occur or be positioned at the end or on either side of (something): *the narrative is bookended by a pair of incisive essays.*

book·er /'bŏŏkər/ ▶ n. short for BOOKING AGENT.

Book·er Prize /'bŏŏkər/ a literary prize awarded annually for a novel published by a British or Commonwealth citizen during the previous year.

book hand ▶ n. a formal style of handwriting as used by professional copiers of books before the invention of printing.

book·ie /'bŏŏkē/ ▶ n. (pl. **-ies**) informal term for BOOKMAKER.

book·ing /'bŏŏkiNG/ ▶ n. an act of reserving accommodations, travel, etc., or of buying a ticket in advance. ■ an engagement for a performance by an entertainer.

book·ing a·gent ▶ n. a person who makes engagements or reservations for others, in particular: ■ a person who arranges concert or club engagements for performers. ■ a person who makes travel arrangements for clients.

book·ish /'bŏŏkiSH/ ▶ adj. (of a person or way of life) devoted to reading and studying rather than worldly interests. ■ (of language or writing) literary in style or allusion. — **book·ish·ly** adv. **book·ish·ness** n.

book·keep·ing /ˈbo͝ok,kēpiNG/ ▶ **n.** the activity or occupation of keeping the financial records of a business. — **book·keep·er n.**

book learn·ing ▶ **n.** knowledge gained from books or study; mere theory.

book·let /ˈbo͝oklit/ ▶ **n.** a small book consisting of a few sheets, typically with paper covers.

book·louse /ˈbo͝ok,lous/ ▶ **n.** (pl. **-lice**) a minute insect (Liposcelidae and related families, order Psocoptera) that typically has reduced or absent wings and often lives in books or papers, where it feeds on mold.

book lung ▶ **n.** Zool. (in a spider or other arachnid) each of a pair of respiratory organs composed of many fine leaves.

book·mak·er /ˈbo͝ok,mākər/ ▶ **n.** a person who takes bets, calculates odds, and pays out winnings. — **book·mak·ing n.**

book·man /ˈbo͝okmən/ ▶ **n.** (pl. **-men**) a literary person, esp. one involved in the business of books.

book·mark /ˈbo͝ok,märk/ ▶ **n.** a strip of leather or other material used to mark one's place in a book. ■ Comput. a record of the address of a file, web page, or other data used to enable quick access by a user. ▶ **v.** Comput. record the address of (a file, web page, or other data) for quick access by a user: *be sure to bookmark eVote.*

book·mo·bile /ˈbo͝okmə,bēl/ ▶ **n.** a truck, van, or trailer serving as a mobile library. [1930s: from **BOOK**, on the pattern of *automobile.*]

Book of Chang·es ▶ **n.** another name for **I CHING.**

Book of Com·mon Prayer ▶ **n.** the official service book of the Church of England, compiled by Thomas Cranmer and others and first issued in 1549.

book page ▶ **n. 1** a page of a book. **2** a page of a newspaper or magazine devoted to book reviews.

book·plate /ˈbo͝ok,plāt/ ▶ **n.** a decorative label stuck in the front of a book, bearing the book owner's name.

book·rack /ˈbo͝ok,rak/ ▶ **n.** a rack or shelf for books. ■ a stand or rack for holding an open book. Also called **BOOKSTAND.**

book·sell·er /ˈbo͝ok,selər/ ▶ **n.** a person who sells books.

book·shelf /ˈbo͝ok,sHelf/ ▶ **n.** (pl. **-shelves**) a shelf on which books can be stored.

book·stall /ˈbo͝ok,stôl/ ▶ **n.** a stand where books are sold, typically secondhand. ■ esp. Brit. a newsstand.

book·stand /ˈbo͝ok,stand/ ▶ **n. 1** another term for **BOOKSTALL. 2** another term for **BOOKRACK.**

book·store /ˈbo͝ok,stôr/ (also esp. Brit. **book·shop** /-,sHäp/) ▶ **n.** a store where books are sold.

book val·ue ▶ **n.** the value of a security or asset as entered in a company's books. Often contrasted with **MARKET VALUE.**

book·work /ˈbo͝ok,wərk/ ▶ **n. 1** the activity of keeping records of accounts. **2** the studying of textbooks, as opposed to practical work.

book·worm /ˈbo͝ok,wərm/ ▶ **n. 1** informal a person devoted to reading. **2** the larva of a wood-boring beetle that feeds on the paper and glue in books.

Bool·e·an /ˈbo͞olēən/ ▶ **adj.** denoting a system of algebraic notation used to represent logical propositions, esp. in computing and electronics. ▶ **n.** Comput. a binary variable, having two possible values called "true" and "false." [19th C.: from the name of English mathematician George *Boole* (1815–64).]

boom¹ /bo͞om/ ▶ **n.** a loud, deep, resonant sound. ■ the characteristic resonant cry of the bittern. ▶ **v.** [intrans.] make a loud, deep, resonant sound: *thunder boomed in the sky.* ■ [with direct speech] say in a loud, deep, resonant voice: *"Silence!" boomed out by Ray himself.* ■ (of a bittern) utter its characteristic resonant cry. — **boom·y adj.** [ME: ult. imitative; perh. from Du. *bommen* 'to hum.']

boom² ▶ **n.** a period of great prosperity or rapid economic growth. ▶ **v.** [intrans.] enjoy a period of great prosperity or rapid economic growth: *business is booming.* — **boom·let** /ˈbo͞omlit/ **n. boom·y adj.** [19th C.: prob. from **BOOM¹**.]

boom³ ▶ **n.** a long pole or rod, in particular: ■ a pivoted spar to which the foot of a vessel's sail is attached ■ [often as adj.] a movable arm over a television or movie set, carrying a microphone or camera. ■ a long beam extending upward at an angle from the mast of a derrick, for guiding or supporting objects being moved or suspended. ■ a floating beam used to contain oil spills or to form a barrier across the mouth of a harbor or river. ■ a retractable tube for in-flight transferral of fuel between airplanes. [16th C.: from Du., 'beam'; rel. to **BEAM.**]

boom box ▶ **n.** informal a portable sound system, typically including radio and cassette or CD player, capable of powerful sound.

boom·er /ˈbo͞omər/ ▶ **n.** informal **1** short for ***BABY BOOMER*** (see **BABY BOOM**). **2** something large or notable of its kind, in particular: ■ a large wave. **3** informal a nuclear submarine with ballistic missiles. **4** a transient construction worker, esp. a bridge builder. [19th C.: prob. from v. **BOOM¹**.]

boo·mer·ang /ˈbo͞omə,raNG/ ▶ **n.** a curved flat piece of wood that can be thrown so as to return to the thrower, traditionally used by Australian Aboriginals as a hunting weapon. ▶ **v.** [intrans.] (of a plan or action) return to the originator, often with negative consequences: *misleading consumers will boomerang on a carmaker.* [19th C.: from Dharuk.]

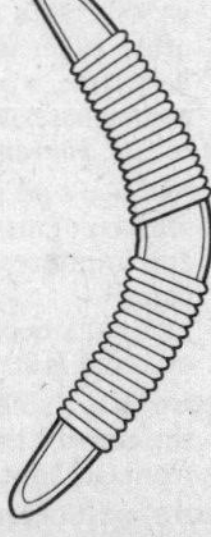

boomerang

boom·ing /ˈbo͞omiNG/ ▶ **adj. 1** having a period of great prosperity or rapid economic growth. **2** (of a sound or voice) loud, deep, and resonant.

boom·slang /ˈbo͞om,slaNG/ ▶ **n.** a large, highly venomous southern African tree snake (*Dispholidus typus*, family Colubridae), the male of which is bright green. [18th C.: from Afrik., from Du. *boom* 'tree' + *slang* 'snake.']

boom town (also **boom·town**) ▶ **n.** a town undergoing rapid growth due to sudden prosperity.

boon¹ /bo͞on/ ▶ **n. 1** [usu. in sing.] a thing that is helpful or beneficial. **2** archaic a favor or request. [ME: from ON *bón.*]

boon² ▶ **adj.** (of a companion or friend) close; intimate; favorite. [16th C.: from OFr. *bon*, from L. *bonus* 'good.']

boon·docks /ˈbo͞on,däks/ ▶ **plural n.** informal rough, remote, or isolated country. [1940s: *boondock* from Tagalog *bundok* 'mountain.']

boon·dog·gle /ˈbo͞on,dägəl; -,dôgəl/ informal ▶ **n.** work or activity that is wasteful or pointless but gives the appearance of having value. ■ a public project of questionable merit that typically involves political patronage and graft. ▶ **v.** [intrans.] waste money or time on such projects. [1930s: of unknown origin.]

Boone /bo͞on/, Daniel (*c.*1734–1820), American pioneer. He made trips west from Pennsylvania into the unexplored area that is now Kentucky. He later moved further west to what is now Missouri.

boon·ies /ˈbo͞onēz/ ▶ **plural n.** short for **BOONDOCKS.**

boor /bo͝or/ ▶ **n.** a rude, unmannerly person. ■ a clumsy person. ■ a peasant; a yokel. — **boor·ish adj. boor·ish·ly adv. boor·ish·ness n.** [16th C. ('peasant'): from Low Ger. *būr* or Du. *boer* 'farmer.']

boost /bo͞ost/ ▶ **v.** [trans.] help or encourage (something) to increase or improve: *measures to boost tourism.* ■ push from below; assist: *people they were trying to boost over a wall.* ■ amplify (an electrical signal). ■ informal steal, esp. by shoplifting or pickpocketing. ▶ **n.** a source of help or encouragement leading to increase or improvement. ■ an increase or improvement: *a boost in exports.* ■ a push from below. [19th C.: of unknown origin.]

boost·er /ˈbo͞ostər/ ▶ **n. 1** a person or thing that helps increase or promote something, in particular: ■ a keen promoter of a person, organization, or cause: [as adj.] *athletic booster clubs.* ■ [in comb.] a source of help or encouragement: *a great morale booster.* ■ Med. a dose of an immunizing agent increasing or renewing the effect of an earlier one. ■ the first stage of a rocket or spacecraft, used to give initial acceleration. ■ a device for increasing electrical voltage or signal strength. **2** informal a shoplifter.

boost·er ca·ble ▶ **n.** another term for **JUMPER CABLE.**

boost·er·ism /ˈbo͞ostə,rizəm/ ▶ **n.** the enthusiastic promotion of a person, organization, or cause.

boost·er seat ▶ **n.** an extra seat or cushion placed on an existing seat for a small child to sit on.

boot¹ /bo͞ot/ ▶ **n. 1** a sturdy item of footwear covering the foot, the ankle, and sometimes the leg below the knee. ■ a covering or sheath to protect a mechanical connection, as on a gearshift. ■ (also **Denver boot**) a clamp placed by the police on the wheel of an illegally parked vehicle to make it immobile. ■ a covering to protect the lower part of a horse's leg. ■ hist. an instrument of torture encasing and crushing the foot. **2** informal a hard kick. **3** Brit. the trunk of a car. **4** (also **boot up**) [usu. as adj.] the process of starting a computer and putting it into a state of readiness for operation. **5** Mil. a navy or marine recruit. ▶ **v.** [trans.] **1** [usu. as adj.] (**booted**) place boots on (oneself, another person, or an animal): *thin, booted legs.* **2** [trans.] kick (something) hard in a specified direction: *booting the ball into the stands.* ■ (in an athletic contest) misplay (a ball); mishandle (a play): *the infielder booted the ball.* ■ (**boot someone off**) force someone to leave a vehicle unceremoniously: *the driver booted two teenagers off the bus.* ■ (**boot someone out**) informal force someone to leave a place, institution, or job unceremoniously. **3** start (a computer) and put it into a state of readiness for operation: *the menu will be ready as soon as you **boot up** your computer* | [intrans.] *the system won't **boot** from the original drive.* **4** place a Denver boot on (an illegally parked car).
– PHRASES **die with one's boots on** die in battle or while actively occupied. **get the boot** informal be dismissed from one's job. **give someone the boot** informal dismiss someone from their job. **one's heart sank** (or **fell**) **into one's boots** used to refer to a sudden onset of depression or dismay. **you (can) bet your boots** informal used to express certainty about a situation or statement. [ME: from ON *bóti* or its source, OFr. *bote.*]

boot² ▶ **n.** (in phrase **to boot**) as well; in addition. [OE *bōt* 'advantage,' of Gmc. origin; rel. to Ger. *Busse* 'penance,' **BETTER¹**.]

boot·a·ble /ˈbo͞otəbəl/ ▶ **adj.** (of a disk) containing the software required to boot a computer.

boot·black /ˈbo͞ot,blak/ ▶ **n.** esp. hist. a person employed to polish boots and shoes.

boot camp ▶ **n.** a military training camp for new recruits. ■ a prison for youthful offenders, run on military lines.

boot·ee /ˈbo͞otē; bo͞oˈtē/ ▶ **n.** (pl. **-ees**) var. of **BOOTIE.**

Bo·ö·tes /bōˈōtēz/ Astron. a northern constellation (the Herdsman), said to represent a man holding the leash of two dogs (Canes Venatici) while driving a bear (Ursa Major). It contains the bright star Arcturus. [Gk.]

Booth[1] /bo͞oTH/, John Wilkes (1838–65), US actor. During a performance at Ford's Theater in Washington, DC, he assassinated President Abraham Lincoln.

Booth[2], William (1829–1912), English religious leader. He founded the Salvation Army in 1865.

booth /bo͞oTH/ ▶ **n.** **1** a small temporary tent or structure, used esp. for the sale or display of goods at a market or fair. ■ a small room where a vendor sits separated from customers by a window. **2** an enclosure or compartment for various purposes, such as telephoning, broadcasting, or voting. **3** a set of a table and benches in a restaurant or bar. [ME: from ON *buth*, based on *búa* 'dwell.']

Boo·thi·a, Gulf of /'bo͞oTHēə/ a gulf in the Canadian Arctic Ocean, in the Northwest Territories.

Boo·thi·a Pen·in·su·la a peninsula in northern Canada, in the Northwest Territories.

boot·ie /'bo͞otē/ (also **boot·ee**) ▶ **n.** (pl. **-ies**) **1** a soft shoe, typically knitted, worn by a baby. ■ any soft, socklike shoe. **2** a protective shoe or lining for a shoe. **3** a woman's short boot.

boot·jack /'bo͞ot,jak/ ▶ **n.** a device for holding a boot by the heel to ease withdrawal of one's foot.

boot·lace /'bo͞ot,lās/ ▶ **n.** a cord or leather strip for lacing boots.

boot·leg /'bo͞ot,leg/ ▶ **adj.** [attrib.] (esp. of liquor, computer software, or recordings) made, distributed, or sold illegally. ▶ **v.** (**-legged, -leg·ging**) [trans.] make, distribute, or sell (illicit goods, esp. liquor, computer software, or recordings) illegally: [as n.] (**bootlegging**) *domestic bootlegging was impossible to control* | [as adj.] (**bootlegged**) *bootlegged videos.* ▶ **n.** **1** an illegal musical recording, esp. one made at a concert. **2** Football a play in which the quarterback fakes a handoff and runs with the ball hidden next to his hip. — **boot·leg·ger n.** [19th C.: from the smugglers' practice of concealing bottles in their boots.]

boot·less /'bo͞otlis/ ▶ **adj.** archaic (of a task or undertaking) ineffectual; useless. [OE *bōtlēas* 'not able to be compensated for by payment' (see BOOT[2], -LESS).]

boot·lick·er /'bo͞ot,likər/ ▶ **n.** informal an obsequious or overly deferential person; a toady. — **boot·lick·ing n.**

boot·strap /'bo͞ot,strap/ ▶ **n.** **1** a loop at the back of a boot, used to pull it on. ■ [usu. as adj.] the technique of starting with existing resources to create something more complex and effective. **2** Comput. a technique of loading a program into a computer by means of a few initial instructions that enable the introduction of the rest of the program from an input device. ▶ **v.** [trans.] **1** get (oneself or something) into or out of a situation using existing resources: *the company is bootstrapping itself out of a marred financial past.* **2** start up (an enterprise), esp. one based on the Internet, with minimal resources. ▶ **adj.** (of a person or project) using one's own resources rather than external help.
– PHRASES **pull oneself up by one's (own) bootstraps** improve one's position by one's own efforts.

boot-up ▶ **n.** see BOOT[1] (sense 4).

boo·ty[1] /'bo͞otē/ ▶ **n.** valuable stolen goods, esp. those seized in war. ■ colloq. something gained or won. [ME: from Mid. Low Ger. *būte*, *buite* 'exchange.']

boo·ty[2] ▶ **n.** (pl. **-ties**) informal a person's buttocks.
– PHRASES **shake one's booty** dance energetically.

boo·ty·li·cious /,bo͞otē'lisHəs/ ▶ **adj.** informal sexually attractive. [1990s: from BOOTY[2], on the pattern of *delicious.*]

booze /bo͞oz/ informal ▶ **n.** alcohol, esp. hard liquor. ▶ **v.** [intrans.] drink alcohol, esp. in large quantities: *you used to booze a lot on expensive hard liquor* | [as n.] (**boozing**) *Michael is trying to quit boozing.* [ME *bouse*, from MDu. *būsen* 'drink to excess.']

booze·hound /'bo͞oz,hound/ ▶ **n.** informal a person who drinks alcohol regularly and heavily.

booz·er /'bo͞ozər/ ▶ **n.** informal a person who drinks large quantities of alcohol. ■ Brit. a pub or bar.

booz·y /'bo͞ozē/ ▶ **adj.** (**booz·i·er, booz·i·est**) informal intoxicated; addicted to drink. — **booz·i·ly** /-zəlē/ **adv.** **booz·i·ness n.**

bop[1] /bäp/ informal ▶ **n.** short for BEBOP. ▶ **v.** (**bopped, bop·ping**) [intrans.] dance to pop music: *bopping to the radio.* ■ move or travel energetically: *we had been bopping around the county all morning.* — **bop·per n.** [1940s: shortening of BEBOP.]

bop[2] informal ▶ **v.** (**bopped, bop·ping**) [trans.] hit; punch lightly: *I warned him I'd bop him on the nose.* ▶ **n.** a blow or light punch. [1930s: imitative.]

Bo·phu·that·swa·na /,bōpo͞o,tät'swänə/ a former homeland established in South Africa for the Tswana people.

bor. ▶ **abbr.** borough.

bo·ra /'bôrə/ ▶ **n.** a strong, cold, dry northeast wind blowing in the upper Adriatic. [19th C.: dial. var. of Ital. *borea*, from L. *boreas* 'north wind' (see BOREAL).]

Bo·ra-Bo·ra /,bôrə 'bôrə/ an island in the Society Islands group in French Polynesia.

bo·rac·ic /bə'rasik/ ▶ **adj.** another term for BORIC. [18th C.: from med. L. *borax*, *borac-* (see BORAX) + -IC.]

bor·age /'bôrij; 'bär-/ ▶ **n.** a herbaceous plant (*Borago officinalis*, family Boraginaceae) with bright blue flowers and hairy leaves, used medicinally and as a salad green. [ME: from OFr. *bourrache*, from med. L. *borrago*, perh. from Arab. *abū ḥurāš* 'father of roughness.']

bo·rane /'bôrān/ ▶ **n.** Chem. any of a series of unstable binary compounds of boron and hydrogen, analogous to the alkanes. [20th C.: from BORON + -ANE[2].]

Bo·rås /bo͞o'rôs/ a city in southwestern Sweden; pop. 101,770.

bo·rate /'bôrāt/ ▶ **n.** Chem. a salt in which the anion contains both boron and oxygen, as in borax.

bo·rax /'bôraks/ ▶ **n.** a white mineral, $Na_2B_4O_7(OH)_4.8H_2O$, in some alkaline salt deposits, used in making glass and ceramics, as a metallurgical flux, and as an antiseptic. [ME: from med. L., from Arab. *būraķ* from Pahlavi *būrak.*]

Bo·ra·zon /'bôrə,zän/ ▶ **n.** trademark an industrial abrasive consisting of boron nitride. [1950s: from BORON, with the insertion of AZO-.]

bor·bo·ryg·mus /,bôrbə'rigməs/ ▶ **n.** (pl. **-mi** /-mī/) tech. a rumbling or gurgling noise made by the movement of fluid and gas in the intestines. — **bor·bo·ryg·mic** /-mik/ **adj.** [18th C.: mod. L., from Gk. *borborugmos.*]

Bor·deaux[1] /bôr'dō/ a city in southwestern France; pop. 213,270.

Bor·deaux[2] ▶ **n.** (pl. same) a red, white, or rosé wine from the district of Bordeaux.

Bor·deaux mix·ture ▶ **n.** a fungicide for vines, fruit trees, and other plants composed of equal quantities of copper sulfate and calcium oxide in water. [19th C.: first used in the Bordeaux region.]

bor·de·laise /,bôrdl'āz/ ▶ **adj.** served with a sauce of red wine and onions: [postpositive] *lobster bordelaise.* [Fr., from *(à la) bordelaise* 'Bordeaux-style.']

bor·del·lo /bôr'delō/ ▶ **n.** (pl. **-los**) a brothel. [16th C.: from Ital., prob. from OFr. *bordel*, dimin. of *borde* 'cottage,' ult. from Gmc.]

Bor·den /'bôrdn/, Lizzie Andrew (1860–1927), US alleged murderess. She was accused of the ax murders of her father and stepmother in Fall River, Massachusetts, in 1892, but was acquitted.

bor·der /'bôrdər/ ▶ **n.** **1** a line separating two political or geographical areas, esp. countries. ■ a district near such a line. **2** the edge or boundary of something, or the part near it. **3** a band or strip, esp. a decorative one, around the edge of something. ■ a strip of ground along the edge of a lawn or path for planting flowers or shrubs. ▶ **v.** [trans.] form an edge along or beside (something): *a pool **bordered by** palm trees.* ■ (of a country or area) be adjacent to (another country or area): *regions bordering Azerbaijan* | [intrans.] *the mountains **bordering on** Afghanistan.* ■ [intrans.] (**border on**) fig. be close to an extreme condition: *a state of excitement bordering on hysteria.* ■ (usu. **be bordered with**) provide (something) with a decorative edge: *a curving driveway bordered with chrysanthemums.* [ME: from OFr. *bordeure*; ult. of Gmc. origin and rel. to BOARD.]

Bor·der col·lie ▶ **n.** (also **border collie**) a common working sheepdog, typically with a black and white coat, originating near the border between England and Scotland.

bord·er·er /'bôrdərər/ ▶ **n.** a person living near a border.

bord·er·land /'bôrdər,land/ ▶ **n.** (usu. **borderlands**) the district near a border. ■ fig. an area of overlap between two things.

bord·er·line /'bôrdər,līn/ ▶ **n.** a line marking a border. ■ fig. a division between two distinct (often extreme) conditions. ▶ **adj.** barely acceptable in quality or as belonging to a category; on the borderline.

bor·der state ▶ **n.** any of the Slave States that bordered the northern free states during the US Civil War. See also BORDER STATES. ■ a US state that borders Canada or Mexico. ■ a small country that borders a larger, more powerful country or that lies between two larger countries.

Bor·der States the US Slave States of Delaware, Maryland, Kentucky, Virginia, and Missouri that did not secede from the Union during the Civil War.

Bord·er ter·ri·er ▶ **n.** a small terrier with rough hair, originating near the border between England and Scotland.

Bor·det /bôr'dā/, Jules (1870–1961), Belgian bacteriologist and immunologist. He developed a vaccine for whooping cough. Nobel Prize for Physiology or Medicine (1919).

bor·dure /'bôrjər/ ▶ **n.** Heraldry a broad border used as a charge in a coat of arms, often as a mark of difference. [ME: var. of BORDER.]

bore[1] /bôr/ ▶ **v.** **1** [trans.] make (a hole) in something, esp. with a revolving tool: *they bored holes in the sides* | [intrans.] *the drill can bore through rock.* ■ [trans.] hollow out (a tube or tunnel). ■ [intrans.] (**bore into**) fig. (of a person's eyes) stare harshly at: *your blue eyes bore into me.* ■ [trans.] hollow out (a gun barrel or other tube). **2** [intrans.] make one's way through (a crowd). ▶ **n.** **1** the hollow part inside a gun barrel or other tube. ■ [often in comb.] the diameter of this; the caliber: *a small-bore rifle.* ■ [in comb.] a gun of a specified bore: *he shot a guard with a twelve-bore.* **2** short for BOREHOLE. [OE *borian* (v.), of Gmc. origin; rel. to Ger. *bohren.*]

bore[2] ▶ **n.** a person whose talk or behavior is dull and uninteresting. ■ [in sing.] a tedious situation or thing. ▶ **v.** [trans.] make (someone) feel weary and uninterested by tedious talk or dullness: *he'll bore you with all the details.*
– PHRASES **bore someone to death** (or **to tears**) weary (a person) in the extreme. [18th C.: origin unknown.]

bore[3] ▶ **n.** a steep-fronted wave caused by the meeting of two tides or by the constriction of a tide rushing up a narrow estuary. [17th C.: perh. from ON *bára* 'wave.']

bore[4] past of BEAR[1].

bo·re·al /'bôrēəl/ ▶ **adj.** of the North or northern regions. ■ Ecol. relating to or characteristic of the climatic zone south of the Arctic, esp. the cold temperate region dominated by taiga and forests of birch, poplar, and conifers. ■ (**Boreal**) Bot. relating to or denoting a phytogeographical kingdom comprising the arctic and temperate regions of Eurasia and North America. [ME: from late L. *borealis*, from L. *Boreas* 'god of the north wind,' from Gk.]

bored[1] /bôrd/ ▶ **adj.** feeling weary because one is unoccupied or lacks interest in one's current activity.

bored[2] ▶ **adj.** [in comb.] (of a gun) having a specified bore: *large-bored guns.*

bore·dom /'bôrdəm/ ▶ **n.** the state of feeling bored.

bo·reen /bô'rēn/ ▶ **n.** Irish a narrow country road. [19th C.: from Irish *bóithrín*, dimin. of *bóthar* 'road.']

bore·hole /'bôr,hōl/ ▶ **n.** a deep, narrow hole made in the ground, esp. to locate water or oil.

bor·er /'bôrər/ ▶ **n. 1** a worm, mollusk, insect, or insect larva that bores into wood and other plants, or rock. **2** a tool for boring.

bore·scope /'bôr,skōp/ ▶ **n.** an instrument used to inspect the inside of a structure through a small hole.

Borg /bôrg/, Björn Rune (1956–), Swedish tennis player. He won 11 Grand Slam singles titles during 1974–81.

Bor·ge /'bôrgə/, Victor (1909–2000), US pianist; born in Denmark. He was noted for his clowning while playing classical music.

Bor·ges /'bôr,hās/, Jorge Luis (1899–1986), Argentine writer. His short stories are collected in *A Universal History of Infamy* (1935).

Bor·gia /'bôrzhə/ an influential Spanish-Italian family of the Renaissance, including Cesare (*c.*1476–1507), a statesman, cardinal, and general noted for his corruption and ruthlessness. His sister, Lucrezia (1480–1519), is the subject of many legends of murderous complicity. Both were the illegitimate children of Cardinal Rodrigo Borgia (later Pope Alexander VI).

Bor·glum /'bôrgləm/, Gutzon (1867–1941) US sculptor; full name *John Gutzon de la Mothe Borglum.* He sculpted Mount Rushmore National Memorial in South Dakota, which features the heads of US presidents Washington, Jefferson, Lincoln, and T. Roosevelt. The work, begun in 1927, was completed in 1941 with the help of his son Lincoln (1912–86), full name *James Lincoln Borglum.*

bo·ric /'bôrik/ ▶ **adj.** Chem. of boron: *boric oxide.*

bo·ric ac·id ▶ **n.** Chem. a weakly acid crystalline compound, $B(OH)_3$, derived from borax and used as a mild antiseptic and in the manufacture of heat-resistant glass and enamels.

bor·ing /'bôriNG/ ▶ **adj.** not interesting; tedious. — **bor·ing·ly adv.**: [as submodifier] *the list is excoriated as boringly predictable.* **bor·ing·ness n.**

Bo·ris Go·du·nov /'bôrəs/ see **Godunov**.

bork /bôrk/ (also **Bork**) ▶ **v.** [trans.] informal obstruct (someone, esp. a candidate for public office) through systematic defamation or vilification: [as n.] (**borking**) *is fear of borking scaring people from public office?* [1980s: from the name of Robert *Bork* (born 1927), an American judge whose nomination to the Supreme Court (1987) was rejected following unfavorable publicity for his allegedly extreme views.]

Bor·laug /'bôr,lôg/, Norman Ernest (1914–), US agronomist, considered the father of the green revolution. He developed high-yielding cereals for cultivation in less developed countries. Nobel Peace Prize (1970).

Bor·mann /'bôrmən/, Martin (1900–*c.*1945), German politician. Considered to be Hitler's closest collaborator, he disappeared at the end of World War II.

Born /bôrn/, Max (1882–1970), German physicist. He helped to found quantum mechanics. Nobel Prize for Physics (1954, shared with Walther Bothe (1891–1957)).

born /bôrn/ past participle of **bear**[1] (sense 4). ▶ **adj.** existing as a result of birth: *he was born in Seattle* | [in comb.] *a German-born philosopher.* ■ [attrib.] having a natural ability to do a particular job or task. ■ [with infin.] perfectly suited or trained to do a particular job or task: *they are born to rule.* ■ (of a thing) brought into existence. ■ (**born of**) existing as a result of a particular situation or feeling.

– PHRASES **born and bred** by birth and upbringing, esp. when considered a typical product of a place. **born with a silver spoon in one's mouth** see **silver**. **I** (**she**, etc.) **wasn't born yesterday** used to remind someone that one isn't naive. **in all one's born days** used to express surprise or shock at something one has not encountered before. **there's one** (or **a sucker**) **born every minute** used to say that there are many gullible people. [OE *boren*, past part. of *beran* 'to bear' (see **bear**[1]).]

born-a·gain ▶ **adj.** converted to a personal faith in Christ (with reference to John 3:3). ■ fig. having the extreme enthusiasm of the newly converted or reconverted. ▶ **n.** a born-again Christian.

borne /bôrn/ past participle of **bear**[1] (senses 1, 2, 3, and 5). ▶ **adj.** [in comb.] carried or transported by: *waterborne bacteria* | *insect-borne pollen.*

Bor·ne·o /'bôrnē,ō/ a large island in the Malay Archipelago that consists of Kalimantan in Indonesia, Sabah and Sarawak (states of Malaysia), and Brunei. — **Bor·ne·an** /-nēən/ **adj.**

Born·holm /'bôrn,hō(l)m/ a Danish island in the Baltic Sea, southeast of Sweden.

Born·holm dis·ease ▶ **n.** a viral infection with fever and pain in the muscles of the ribs. [1930s: named after the island of **Bornholm**, where it was first described.]

born·ite /'bôrnīt/ ▶ **n.** a brittle reddish-brown crystalline mineral with an iridescent purple tarnish, consisting of a sulfide of copper and iron. [19th C.: from the name of Ignatius von *Born* (1742–91), Austrian mineralogist, + **-ite**[1].]

boro- ▶ **comb. form** Chem. representing **boron**.

Bo·ro·din /,bôrə'dēn/, Aleksandr Porfirevich (1833–87), Russian composer. His opera *Prince Igor* was completed after his death by Nikolai Rimsky-Korsakov and Aleksandr Glazunov (1865–1936).

Bo·ro·di·no, Bat·tle of /,bôrə'dēnō/ a battle in 1812 at Borodino, a village west of Moscow, at which Napoleon's forces defeated the Russian army.

bo·ron /'bôrän/ ▶ **n.** the chemical element of atomic number 5, a nonmetallic solid. It has some specialized uses, such as in alloy steels and nuclear control rods. (Symbol: **B**) — **bo·ride** /-rīd/ **n.** [19th C.: from **borax**.]

bo·ro·sil·i·cate /,bôrə'silikit; -,kāt/ ▶ **n.** [usu. as adj.] a low-melting-point glass made from a mixture of silica and boric oxide (B_2O_3).

bor·ough /'bərō; 'bə-rō/ (abbr.: **bor.**) ▶ **n.** a town or district that is an administrative unit, in particular: ■ an incorporated municipality in certain US states. ■ each of five divisions of New York City. ■ in Alaska, a district corresponding to a county elsewhere in the US. ■ Brit. a town (as distinct from a city) with a corporation and privileges granted by a royal charter. ■ Brit., hist. a town sending representatives to Parliament. [OE *burg, burh* 'fortress,' from Gmc.; akin to Ger. *Burg.*]

Bor·ro·mi·ni /,bôrə'mēnē/, Francesco (1599–1667), Italian architect. He was a leading figure of the Italian baroque style.

bor·row /'bärō; 'bôrō/ ▶ **v.** [trans.] take and use (something that belongs to someone else) with the intention of returning it: *he had **borrowed** a car **from** one of his colleagues* | [as adj.] (**borrowed**) *a borrowed jacket.* ■ take and use (money) from a person or bank under an agreement to pay it back later: *I borrowed money* | [intrans.] *lower interest rates will make it cheaper to borrow.* ■ take (a word, idea, or method) from another source and use it in one's own language or work: *the term is **borrowed from** Greek* | [intrans.] *designers consistently **borrow from** the styles of preceding generations.* ■ take and use (a book) from a library. ■ in subtraction, take a unit from the next larger denomination.

– PHRASES **be (living) on borrowed time** used to say that someone has continued to survive against expectations, with the implication that this will not be for much longer. **borrow trouble** take needless action that may have detrimental effects. — **bor·row·er n.** [OE *borgian* 'borrow against security,' from Gmc.; akin to Ger. *borgen.*]

bor·row·ing /'bärō-iNG; 'bôr-/ ▶ **n.** the action of borrowing something. ■ the action of taking and using money from a bank under an agreement to pay it back later. ■ a word, idea, or method taken from another source and used in one's own language or work.

Bor·sa·li·no /,bôrsə'lēnō/ ▶ **n.** (pl. **-nos**) trademark a man's wide-brimmed felt hat. [20th C.: from the name of the manufacturer.]

borscht /bôrsHt/ (also **borsch**) ▶ **n.** a Russian or Polish soup made with beets and usually served with sour cream. [from Russ. *borshch.*]

Borscht Belt /bôrsHt/ ▶ **n.** (**the Borscht Belt**) humorous a resort area in the Catskill Mountains frequented chiefly by Jewish guests.

bor·stal /'bôrstəl/ (also **Bor·stal**) ▶ **n.** Brit., hist. a custodial institution for youthful offenders. [20th C.: named after *Borstal*, England, where the first of these was established.]

bort /bôrt/ ▶ **n.** small, granular, opaque diamonds, used as an abrasive in cutting tools. Compare with **carbonado**. [17th C.: from Du. *boort.*]

borzoi

bor·zoi /'bôrzoi/ ▶ **n.** (pl. **-zois**) a large Russian wolfhound with a narrow head and silky coat. [19th C.: from Russ. *borzoĭ* (adj.), 'swift.']

Bosc /bäsk/ (also **Bosc pear**) ▶ **n.** a medium- to large-sized variety of pear, golden brown in color and often russeted. [named after L. *Bosc* d'Antic (1759–1828), French naturalist.]

bos·cage /'bäskij/ (also **bos·kage**) ▶ **n.** massed trees or shrubs. [ME: from OFr.; ult. of Gmc. origin and rel. to **bush**.]

Bosch /bäsH; bôsH/, Hieronymus (*c.*1450–1516), Dutch painter. He is noted for his works crowded with half-human, half-animal creatures and grotesque demons.

Bose /bōz/, Satyendra Nath (1894–1974), Indian physicist. With Albert Einstein, he described fundamental particles that later came to be known as *bosons.*

bosh /bäsh/ ▶ n. informal something regarded as absurd; nonsense. [19th C.: from Turk. *boş* 'empty.']

bosk /bäsk/ ▶ n. a thicket of bushes; a small wood.

bosk·y /'bäskē/ ▶ adj. wooded; covered by trees or bushes. [16th C.: from ME *bosk*, var. of BUSH.]

bo's'n ▶ n. var. of BOATSWAIN.

Bos·ni·a /'bäznēə/ short for BOSNIA–HERZEGOVINA. ■ a region in the Balkans that forms the larger, northern part of Bosnia–Herzegovina. — **Bos·ni·an** adj. & n.

Bos·ni·a–Her·ze·go·vi·na /,hertsəgō'vēnə ,hertsə'gōvənə/ (also **Bosnia and Herzegovina**) a country in southeastern Europe, in the Balkans, formerly a constituent republic of Yugoslavia. *See box.*

Bosnia and Herzegovina

Location: southeastern Europe in the Balkans
Area: 19,700 square miles (51,100 sq km)
Population: 4,007,000
Capital: Sarajevo
Language: Serbo-Croatian
Currency: marka

bos·om /'bo͝ozəm/ ▶ n. a woman's chest. ■ (usu. **bosoms**) a woman's breast. ■ a part of a woman's dress covering the chest. ■ the space between a person's clothing and chest used for carrying things. ■ (**the bosom of**) literary the loving care and protection of. ■ used to refer to the chest as the seat of emotions. ▶ adj. [attrib.] (of a friend) close or intimate. — **bos·omed** adj. [in comb.] *her small-bosomed physique.* [OE *bōsm*, from West Gmc.; akin to Ger. *Busen*.]

bos·om·y /'bo͝ozəmē/ ▶ adj. (of a woman) having large breasts.

bo·son /'bōsän/ ▶ n. Physics a subatomic particle, such as a photon, that has zero or integral spin and follows the statistical description given by S. N. Bose and Einstein. [1940s: named after S. N. BOSE + -ON.]

Bos·po·rus /'bäsp(ə)rəs/ (also **Bos·pho·rus** /'bäsf(ə)rəs/) a strait that connects the Black Sea with the Sea of Marmara.

boss[1] /bôs; bäs/ informal ▶ n. a person in charge of a worker or organization. ■ a person in control of a group or situation. ▶ v. [trans.] give (someone) orders in a domineering manner: ***bossing everyone around.*** ▶ adj. [attrib.] excellent; outstanding.
– PHRASES **be one's own boss** be self-employed. **show someone who's boss** make it clear that one is in charge. [19th C.: from Du. *baas* 'master.']

boss[2] ▶ n. a round knob, stud, or other protuberance, in particular: ■ a stud on the center of a shield. ■ Archit. a piece of ornamental carving covering the point where the ribs in a vault or ceiling cross. ■ Geol. a large mass of igneous rock protruding through other strata. ■ Mech. an enlarged part of a shaft. [ME: from OFr.]

boss[3] ▶ n. informal a cow. [19th C.: of unknown origin.]

bos·sa no·va /'bäsə 'nōvə; 'bô-/ ▶ n. a dance like the samba, originating in Brazil. ■ a piece of music for this dance or in its rhythm. [1960s: from Port., from *bossa* 'tendency' and *nova* (fem. of *novo*) 'new.']

Bos·sier Cit·y /'bōzhər/ a city in northwestern Louisiana; pop. 56,461.

boss·ism /'bôsizəm; 'bäs-/ ▶ n. a situation in which a political party is controlled by party managers.

boss·y[1] /'bôsē; 'bä-/ ▶ adj. (**boss·i·er**, **boss·i·est**) informal fond of giving people orders; domineering. — **boss·i·ly** /-səlē/ adv. **boss·i·ness** n.

boss·y[2] ▶ n. (pl. **boss·ies**) informal a cow or calf. [19th C.: of unknown origin.]

Bos·ton[1] /'bôstən/ the capital of Massachusetts, in the eastern part of the state; pop. 589,141. — **Bos·to·ni·an** /bô'stōnēən/ n. & adj.

Bos·ton[2] ▶ n. **1** a card game resembling solo whist. **2** a variation of the waltz or of the two-step.

Bos·ton baked beans ▶ plural n. a dish of baked beans with salt pork and molasses.

Bos·ton cream pie ▶ n. a two-layer cake filled with custard or cream and frosted, usually with chocolate.

Bos·ton fern ▶ n. a variety of sword fern (*Nephrolepis exaltata bostoniensis*), with long, arching bright green fronds, widely cultivated esp. as a hanging houseplant.

Bos·ton i·vy ▶ n. a Virginia creeper (*Parthenocissus tricuspidata*) with three-lobed leaves, cultivated for its foliage.

Bos·ton let·tuce ▶ n. a butterhead lettuce with medium or light green leaves.

Bos·ton rock·er ▶ n. a rocking chair with a decorative panel on a high spindled back and with arms and a seat that curves downward at the front.

Bos·ton Tea Par·ty a violent demonstration in 1773 by American colonists. Colonists boarded vessels in Boston harbor and threw the cargoes of tea into the water in protest at the imposition of a tax on tea by the British Parliament.

Bos·ton ter·ri·er ▶ n. a small smooth-coated terrier that originated in Massachusetts.

bo·sun (also **bo'sun**) ▶ n. var. of BOATSWAIN.

Bos·well /'bäzwəl; -,wel/, James (1740–95), Scottish writer. His works include *The Life of Samuel Johnson* (1791).

Bos·worth Field /'bäz,wərth/ (also **Battle of Bosworth**) a battle of the Wars of the Roses fought in 1485 near Market Bosworth in Leicestershire, England, during which Richard III was killed.

bot[1] /bät/ ▶ n. the larva of the botfly, which is an internal parasite of animals. [16th C.: prob. of Low Ger. origin.]

bot[2] ▶ n. (chiefly in science fiction) a robot. ■ Comput. an autonomous program on a network (esp. the Internet) that can interact with computer systems or users, esp. one designed to respond or behave like a player in an adventure game. [1980s: shortening of ROBOT.]

bot. ▶ abbr. ■ (with reference to journal titles) botanic; botanical; botany. ■ bottle. ■ bought.

bo·tan·i·cal /bə'tanikəl/ ▶ adj. of or relating to plants. ▶ n. (usu. **botanicals**) a substance obtained from a plant and used as an additive, esp. in gin or cosmetics. — **bo·tan·i·cal·ly** /-ik(ə)lē/ adv.

bo·tan·i·cal gar·den (also **bo·tan·ic gar·den**) ▶ n. an establishment where plants are grown for display to the public and often for scientific study.

bot·a·nize /'bätn,īz/ ▶ v. [intrans.] study plants, esp. in their natural habitat: *I'd always go off botanizing.* [18th C.: from mod. L. *botanizare*, from Gk. *botanizein* 'gather plants,' from *botanē* 'plant.']

Bot·a·ny /'bätn-ē/ (also **Botany wool**) ▶ n. [mass noun] merino wool, esp. from Australia. [19th C.: named after BOTANY BAY, from where the wool orig. came.]

bot·a·ny /'bätn-ē/ ▶ n. the scientific study of plants. ■ the plant life of a particular region, habitat, or geological period. — **bo·tan·ic** /bə'tanik/ adj. **bot·a·nist** n. [17th C.: from *botanic* (from Fr. *botanique*, based on Gk. *botanikos*, from *botanē* 'plant').]

Bot·a·ny Bay an inlet of the Tasman Sea just south of Sydney, Australia.

botch /bäch/ ▶ v. [trans.] informal carry out (a task) badly or carelessly: [as adj.] (**botched**) *a botched attempt to kill them.* ■ patch or repair (an object or damage) clumsily. ▶ n. (also **botch-up**) informal a bungled or badly carried out task or action. — **botch·er** n. [ME: origin unknown.]

bot·fly /'bät,flī/ ▶ n. (pl. **-flies**) a stout hairy-bodied fly with larvae that are internal parasites of mammals, in particular: ■ a fly (*Gasterophilus* and other genera, family Gasterophilidae) with larvae (bots) that develop within the guts of horses. ■ a fly of the warble fly family (Oestridae).

both /bōth/ ▶ adj. & pron. used to refer to two people or things, regarded and identified together: [as adj.] *both his parents indulged him* | [as pron.] *a picture of **both of** us together.* | ▶ adv. used before the first of two alternatives to emphasize that the statement being made applies to each (the other alternative being introduced by "and"): *they all loved to play, both the boys and the girls.*
– PHRASES **have it both ways** benefit from two incompatible ways of thinking or behaving. [ME: from ON *báthir*.]

Bo·tha[1] /'bōtə/, Louis (1862–1919), the first prime minister of the Union of South Africa 1910–19.

Bo·tha[2], P. W. (1916–2006), prime minister 1978–84 and president of South Africa 1984–89; full name *Pieter Willem Botha.* He introduced limited reforms to apartheid.

both·er /'bäthər/ ▶ v. **1** [with negative] take the trouble to do something: *nobody bothered locking the doors* | [with infin.] ***didn't bother to ask why.*** **2** (of a circumstance or event) worry, disturb, or upset (someone): *secrecy is an issue that bothers journalists.* ■ trouble or annoy (someone) by interrupting or causing inconvenience: *she didn't feel she could **bother** Mike **with** the problem.* ■ [intrans.] [usu. with negative] feel concern about or interest in: *don't **bother about** me* | [as adj.] (**bothered**) *I'm not particularly **bothered about** how I look.* ■ [with negative] (**bother oneself**) concern oneself: *he wasn't to **bother himself with** day-to-day things.* ▶ n. effort, worry, or difficulty. ■ (**a bother**) a person or thing that causes worry or difficulty. ■ [with negative] a nuisance or inconvenience: ***it's no bother**, it's on my way home.*
– PHRASES **can't be bothered (to do something)** be unwilling to make the effort to do something. **hot and bothered** in a state of anxiety or physical discomfort. [17th C. ('noise'): of Anglo-Irish origin; prob. rel. to Irish *bodhaire* 'noise.']

both·er·a·tion /ˌbäᴛʜəˈrāsʜən/ informal ▶n. effort, worry, or difficulty; bother. ▶exclam. dated used to express mild irritation or annoyance.

both·er·some /ˈbäᴛʜərsəm/ ▶adj. causing bother; troublesome: *most childhood stomachaches, though bothersome, aren't serious.*

Both·ni·a, Gulf of /ˈbäᴛʜnēə/ a northern arm of the Baltic Sea, between Sweden and Finland.

both·y /ˈbäᴛʜē/ (also **both·ie**) ▶n. (pl. **both·ies**) (in Scotland) a small hut or cottage. [18th C.: akin to Irish *both*, and perh. to BOOTH.]

Bo·tox /ˈbōˌtäks/ ▶n. trademark a drug prepared from botulin, used cosmetically to remove wrinkles by temporarily paralyzing facial muscles and medically to treat certain muscular conditions. — **Bo·toxed** adj. [1990s: from *bo(tulinum) tox(in).*]

bo tree /bō/ (also **bo·dhi tree** /ˈbōdē/) ▶n. a fig tree (*Ficus religiosa*) native to India and Southeast Asia, regarded as sacred by Buddhists. [19th C.: from Sinhalese *bōgaha* 'tree of knowledge.']

bot·ry·oi·dal /ˌbätrēˈoidl/ ▶adj. (chiefly of minerals) having a shape reminiscent of a cluster of grapes. [18th C.: from Gk. *botruoeidēs* (from *botrus* 'bunch of grapes') + -AL.]

bo·try·tis /bōˈtrītis/ ▶n. a fungus (genus *Botrytis*, phylum Ascomycota) that forms a grayish powdery mold on a variety of organic matter. It causes a number of fungal plant diseases and is deliberately cultivated (as noble rot) on the grapes used for certain wines. [mod. L., from Gk. *botrus* 'cluster of grapes.']

Bot·swa·na /bätˈswänə/ a landlocked country in southern Africa. *See box.* — **Bot·swa·nan** adj. & n.

Bot·ti·cel·li /ˌbätəˈcʜelē/, Sandro (1445–1510), Italian painter; born *Alessandro di Mariano Filipepi*. His works include *The Birth of Venus* (c.1480).

bottles

bot·tle /ˈbätl/ ▶n. a container, typically made of glass or plastic and with a narrow neck, used for storing drinks or other liquids. ■ the contents of such a container. ■ (**the bottle**) informal used in reference to heavy drinking. ■ a bottle fitted with a nipple for giving milk or other drinks to babies and very young children. ■ (**the bottle**) the milk given to a baby from such a bottle. ■ a large metal cylinder holding liquefied gas. ▶v. [trans.] (usu. **be bottled**) place (drinks or other liquid) in bottles or jars: *the wine is then bottled* | [as adj.] (**bottled**) *bottled beer.* ■ [usu. as adj.] (**bottled**) store (gas) in a container in liquefied form: *connecting the bottled gas to the stove.*
– PHRASES **hit the bottle** informal drink heavily.
– PHRASAL VERBS **bottle someone up** (usu. **be bottled up**) keep (someone) trapped or contained: *he had to stay bottled up in New York.* **bottle something up** repress or conceal feelings over a period of time: *learning how to express anger instead of bottling it up* | [as adj.] (**bottled up**) *Lily's bottled-up fury.* — **bot·tler** n. [ME: from OFr. *boteille*, from med. L. *butticula*, dimin. of late L. *buttis* 'cask' (see BUTT[4]).]

bot·tle bill ▶n. any of several US state laws that require deposits on beverages sold in recyclable bottles and cans.

bot·tle·brush /ˈbätlˌbrəsʜ/ ▶n. an Australian shrub or small tree (genus *Callistemon*) of the myrtle family, with spikes of scarlet or yellow flowers that resemble a cylindrical brush in shape. ■ any of a number of plants bearing similar flowers.

bot·tled gas ▶n. butane or propane gas stored under pressure in portable tanks.

bot·tle-feed ▶v. [trans.] feed (a baby) with milk from a bottle instead of from the mother's breast: [as adj.] (**bottle-fed**) *a bottle-fed baby.*

bot·tle green ▶n. a dark shade of green.

bot·tle jack ▶n. a large jack used for lifting heavy objects. See illustration at JACK[1].

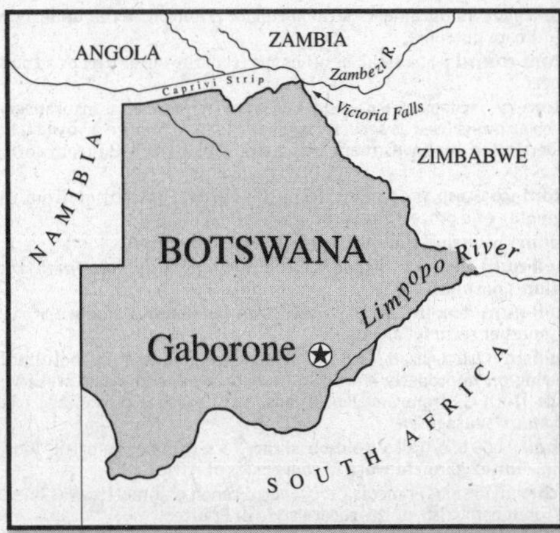

Botswana

Official name: Republic of Botswana
Location: southern Africa, bordered on the south by South Africa; the Kalahari Desert covers the western half
Area: 226,100 square miles (585,400 sq km)
Population: 1,560,000
Capital: Gaborone
Languages: English (official), Setswana
Currency: pula

bot·tle·neck /ˈbätlˌnek/ ▶n. **1** the neck or mouth of a bottle. **2** a point of congestion or blockage, in particular: ■ a narrow section of road or a junction that impedes traffic flow. ■ a situation that causes delay in a process or system. **3** a device shaped like the neck of a bottle, worn on a guitarist's finger to produce special sound effects. ■ (also **bottleneck guitar**) the style of guitar playing that uses such a device.

bot·tle·nose dol·phin /ˈbätlˌnōz/ (also **bot·tle-nosed dol·phin**) ▶n. a stout-bodied dolphin (*Tursiops truncatus*) with a distinct short beak, found in tropical and temperate coastal waters.

bot·tle tree ▶n. an Australian tree with swollen water-containing trunks, esp. *Adansonia gregorii* (a baobab) and *Brachychiton rupestre* (a relative of the flame tree).

bot·tom /ˈbätəm/ ▶n. (usu. **the bottom**) **1** the lowest point or part: *the bottom of the page.* ■ the lower surface of something. ■ the part on which a thing rests; the underside. ■ the ground under a sea, river, or lake. ■ (also **bottoms**) another term for BOTTOMLAND. ■ the seat of a chair. ■ the lowest position in a competition or ranking. ■ the basis or origin. ■ (also **bottoms**) the lower half of a two-piece garment. ■ the keel or hull of a ship, esp. the relatively flat portion on either side of the keel. **2** informal the buttocks. **3** Baseball the second half of an inning. **4** Physics one of six flavors of quark. ▶adj. in the lowest position. ▶v. [intrans.] (of a performance or situation) reach the lowest point before stabilizing or improving: *interest rates have bottomed out.*
– PHRASES **at bottom** basically; fundamentally: *at bottom, science is exploration.* **bet your bottom dollar** informal stake everything: *you can bet your bottom dollar it'll end in tears.* **the bottom falls** (or **drops**) **out** collapse or failure occurs. **bottoms up!** informal a call to finish one's drink. **from the bottom of one's heart** see HEART. **from the bottom up 1** completely and thoroughly. **2** by progressing from a lower or more fundamental starting point. **get to the bottom of** find an explanation for (a mystery). — **bot·tomed** adj. [in comb.] *a glass-bottomed boat* **bot·tom·most** adj. [OE *botm*, of Gmc. origin; rel. to Ger. *Boden* 'ground.']

bot·tom-dwell·ing ▶adj. (of an aquatic organism) dwelling on or near the bed of a body of water. ■ (of a person or organization) performing consistently poorly. ■ (of a person or organization) acting or performing questionably or unethically. — **bot·tom-dwell·er** n.

bot·tom feed·er ▶n. an aquatic creature that feeds at the bottom of a body of water. ■ fig. someone who profits from things cast off or left over by others.

bot·tom fer·men·ta·tion ▶n. a process in the brewing of certain beers in which the yeast falls to the bottom during fermentation.

bot·tom fish ▶n. a species of fish, such as flounder, that is a bottom feeder. ▶v. fish for species that are bottom fish. ■ make profits from investments that are of low value or out of favor.

bot·tom·land /ˈbätəmˌland/ ▶n. low-lying land, typically by a river.

bot·tom line ▶n. informal the final total of an account, balance sheet, or other financial document. ■ the ultimate criterion. ■ the underlying or ultimate outcome.

bot·tom round ▶ n. a steak or other cut from the outer part of a round of beef.

bot·tom·ry /ˈbätəmrē/ ▶ n. dated a system of merchant insurance in which a ship is used as security against a loan to finance a voyage, the lender losing the investment if the ship sinks. [16th C.: from BOTTOM ('ship').]

bot·tom-up ▶ adj. proceeding from the bottom upward or from the beginning of a process forward.

bot·u·lin /ˈbächəlin/ ▶ n. the bacterial toxin in botulism.

bot·u·li·num ▶ n. a rod-shaped bacterium (*Clostridium botulinum*) that produces botulin.

bot·u·li·num tox·in /ˌbächəˈlīnəm/ (also **bot·u·li·nus tox·in** /-ˈlīnəs/) ▶ n. another term for BOTULIN.

bot·u·lism /ˈbächəˌlizəm/ ▶ n. food poisoning caused by botulinum growing on improperly sterilized canned meats and other preserved foods. [19th C.: from Ger. *Botulismus*, orig. 'sausage poisoning,' from L. *botulus* 'sausage.']

bou·bou /ˈbo͞oˌbo͞o/ (also **boubou shrike**) ▶ n. a long, colorful, loose-fitting unisex garment worn in some parts of Africa.

Bou·cher /bo͞oˈshā/, François (1703–70), French painter. He was one of the foremost artists of the rococo style in France.

bou·clé /ˌbo͞oˈklā/ ▶ n. [often as adj.] yarn with a looped or curled ply, or fabric woven from this yarn. [19th C.: Fr., lit. 'buckled.']

Bou·dic·ca /bo͞oˈdikə/ (died AD 62), a queen of the Britons; also known as **Boadicea**. She revolted against the Romans but was eventually defeated.

bou·din /bo͞oˈdan; -ˈdaN/ ▶ n. a French type of blood sausage. ■ a spicy sausage used esp. in Louisiana cuisine. [19th C.: Fr., lit. 'blood sausage.']

bou·doir /ˈbo͞oˌdwär/ ▶ n. esp. hist. or humorous a woman's bedroom or private room. [18th C.: Fr., lit. 'sulking place'.]

bouf·fant /bo͞oˈfänt/ ▶ adj. [attrib.] (of a person's hair) styled so as to puff out in a rounded shape. ▶ n. a bouffant hairstyle. [19th C.: from Fr., lit. 'swelling,' pres. part. of *bouffer*.]

Bou·gain·ville¹ /ˈbo͞ogənˌvil; ˈbō-/ an island in the South Pacific Ocean, the largest of the Solomon Islands.

Bou·gain·ville² /ˌbo͞ogaNˈvēl/, Louis Antoine de (1729–1811), French explorer. He led the first French circumnavigation of the globe 1766–69.

bou·gain·vil·le·a /ˌbo͞ogənˈvilyə; -ˈvēə; ˌbō-/ (also **bou·gain·vil·lae·a**) ▶ n. an ornamental climbing plant (genus *Bougainvillea*, family Nyctaginaceae) that is widely cultivated in the tropics. The insignificant flowers are surrounded by brightly colored papery bracts. [named after Louis Antoine de *Bougainville* (see BOUGAINVILLE²).]

bough /bou/ ▶ n. a main branch of a tree. [OE *bōg*, *bōh* 'bough or shoulder,' of Gmc. origin; rel. to Ger. *Bug* 'ship's bow' and BOW³.]

bought /bôt/ past and past participle of BUY.

bought·en /ˈbôtn/ ▶ adj. dialect bought rather than homemade. [18th C.: dial. var. of BOUGHT.]

bou·gie /ˈbo͞ojē; -zhē/ ▶ n. (pl. **-gies**) Med. a thin, flexible surgical instrument for exploring or dilating a passage of the body. [18th C.: from Fr., lit. 'wax candle,' from Arab. *Bijāya*, the name of an Algerian town that traded in wax.]

bouil·la·baisse /ˌbo͞o(l)yəˈbās; ˈbo͞o(l)yəˌbās/ ▶ n. a stew or soup made with various kinds of fish. [Fr., from mod. Provençal *bouiabaisso* 'boil down.']

bouil·lon /ˈbo͞olyən; -yän/ ▶ n. a broth made by stewing meat, fish, or vegetables in water. [17th C.: Fr., lit. 'liquid in which something has boiled'.]

bouil·lon cube ▶ n. a cube of concentrated stock.

Boul·der /ˈbōldər/ a city in north central Colorado; pop. 94,673.

boul·der /ˈbōldər/ (also **bowl·der**) ▶ n. a large rock, typically one that has been worn smooth by erosion. — **boul·der·y** adj. [ME: shortened from earlier *boulderstone*, of Scand. origin.]

boul·der clay ▶ n. clay containing many large stones and boulders.

boule¹ /bo͞ol/ (also **boules** pronunc. same) ▶ n. **1** a French lawn game, played with metal balls. **2** a crystal, as of sapphire, synthetically manufactured by fusion and used as a gemstone. **3** a rounded loaf of bread. [20th C. (orig. denoting a form of roulette): Fr., lit. 'bowl.']

boule² /bo͞oˈlā; ˈbo͞olē/ ▶ n. a legislative body of ancient or modern Greece. [from Gk. *boulē* 'senate.']

boul·e·vard /ˈbo͝oləˌvärd/ (abbr.: **blvd.**) ▶ n. a wide street, typically lined with trees. [18th C.: Fr., lit. 'a rampart,' from Ger. *Bollwerk* (see BULWARK).]

bou·le·var·dier /ˌbo͝oləvärˈdi(ə)r/ ▶ n. a wealthy, fashionable socialite. [19th C.: from Fr.]

boul·e·vard strip ▶ n. a grassy strip between a road and a sidewalk.

bou·le·ver·se·ment /ˌbo͞oləˌversəˈmäN/ ▶ n. an inversion, esp. a violent one; an upset or upheaval.

Bou·lez /bo͞oˈlez/, Pierre (1925–), French composer conductor. He conducted the New York Philharmonic Orchestra 1971–78.

bounce /bouns/ ▶ v. [intrans.] (of an object, esp. a ball) move quickly away from a surface after hitting it; rebound: *the ball* ***bounced off*** *the rim* | [trans.] *he was bouncing the ball against the wall.* ■ [often with adv. or prep. phrase showing direction] rebound repeatedly: *the ball bounced away.* ■ (of light, sound, or an electronic signal) come into contact with an object or surface and be reflected back: *short sound waves* ***bounce off*** *even small objects.* ■ (of a thing) move up and down while remaining essentially in the same position. ■ (of a person) jump repeatedly up and down, typically on something springy. ■ [trans.] cause (a child) to move lightly up and down on one's knee as a game: *you used to bounce me on your knee.* ■ [often with adv. or prep. phrase showing direction] move in an energetic or happy manner: *Linda bounced in through the open front door.* ■ [often with adv. or prep. phrase showing direction] (of a vehicle) move jerkily along a bumpy surface. ■ (**bounce back**) fig. recover well after a setback: *admired for his ability to bounce back from injury.* ■ Baseball hit a ball that bounces before reaching a fielder: ***bouncing out*** *with the bases loaded* | [trans.] *bounced a grounder to third.* ■ informal (of a check) be returned by a bank when there are insufficient funds to meet it: *my rent check bounced.* ■ informal [trans.] write (a check) on insufficient funds: *I've never bounced a check.* ■ informal [trans.] dismiss (someone) from a job. ■ [trans.] informal eject (a troublemaker) forcibly from a nightclub or similar establishment. ▶ n. a rebound of a ball or other object. ■ an act of jumping or an instance of being moved up and down. ■ the power of rebounding. ■ a sudden rise in the level of something. ■ exuberant self-confidence. ■ health and body in the hair.

– PHRASES **bounce an idea off someone** informal share an idea with another person in order to get feedback on it. **be bouncing off the walls** informal be full of nervous excitement or agitation. [ME *bunsen* 'beat, thump,' perh. imitative, or from Low Ger. *bunsen* 'beat,' Du. *bons* 'a thump.']

bounc·er /ˈbounsər/ ▶ n. **1** a person employed by an establishment to prevent troublemakers from entering or to eject them from the premises. **2** Baseball a batted ball that bounces before being fielded.

bounc·ing /ˈbounsiNG/ ▶ adj. (of a ball) rebounding up and down. ■ (of a baby) vigorous and healthy. ■ lively and confident. ■ informal (of a check) returned by a bank because there are insufficient funds in an account to meet it.

bounc·ing Bet ▶ n. another term for SOAPWORT.

bounc·y /ˈbounsē/ ▶ adj. (**bounc·i·er**, **bounc·i·est**) bouncing well. ■ resilient; springy. ■ (of a person) confident and lively. ■ (of music) having a jaunty rhythm. ■ (of the hair) in good condition; having bounce. — **bounc·i·ly** /-səlē/ adv. **bounc·i·ness** n.

bound¹ /bound/ ▶ v. [intrans.] walk or run with leaping strides: *Louis came* ***bounding down*** *the stairs.* ■ (of an object, typically a round one) rebound from a surface: *bullets* ***bounded off*** *the veranda.* ▶ n. a leaping movement upward. [16th C.: from Fr., from late L. *bombitare*, from L. *bombus* 'humming.']

bound² ▶ n. (often **bounds**) a territorial limit; a boundary. ■ a limitation or restriction on feeling or action: *it is not* ***beyond the bounds of possibility*** *that the issue could arise again.* ■ tech. a limiting value. ▶ v. [trans.] (usu. **be bounded**) form the boundary of; enclose: *the ground was bounded by a main road on one side and a meadow on the other.* ■ place within certain limits; restrict.

– PHRASES **in bounds** Sports inside the regular playing area. **out of bounds** (of a place) outside the limits of where one is permitted to be. ■ Sports outside the regular playing area. ■ fig. beyond what is acceptable. [ME: from OFr. *bodne*, from med. L. *bodina*, earlier *butina*.]

bound³ ▶ adj. heading toward somewhere: *trains* ***bound for*** *Chicago* | [in comb.] *moon-bound astronauts.* ■ fig. destined or likely to have a specified experience: *they were* ***bound for*** *disaster.* [ME *boun*, from ON *búinn*, past part. of *búa* 'get ready.']

bound⁴ past and past participle of BIND. ▶ adj. **1** [in comb.] restricted or confined to a specified place: *his job kept him city-bound.* ■ prevented from operating normally by the specified conditions: *blizzard-bound Boston.* **2** [with infin.] certain to do or have something: *there is* ***bound to be*** *a change of plan.* ■ obliged by law, circumstances, or duty to do something. **3** [in comb.] (of a book) having a specified binding: *fine leather-bound books.* **4** Ling. (of a morpheme) unable to occur alone, e.g., *dis-* in *dismount.* **5** constipated.

– PHRASES **bound up in** focusing on, to the exclusion of all else. **bound up with** (or **in**) closely connected with or related to.

bound·a·ry /ˈbound(ə)rē/ ▶ n. (pl. **-ries**) a line that marks the limits of an area; a dividing line. ■ (often **boundaries**) fig. a limit of a subject or sphere of activity.

bound·a·ry con·di·tion ▶ n. Math. a condition that is required to be satisfied at all or part of the boundary of a region in which a set of differential equations is to be solved.

bound·a·ry lay·er ▶ n. a layer of more or less stationary fluid (such as water or air) immediately surrounding an immersed moving object.

bound·en /ˈboundən/ archaic past participle of BIND.

– PHRASES **one's bounden duty** a responsibility regarded as obligatory.

bound·er /ˈboundər/ ▶ n. informal, dated, chiefly Brit. a dishonorable man.

bound form ▶ n. a morpheme that occurs only as an element of a compound word and cannot stand on its own, such as *-ing* or *-er*.

bound·less /ˈboundlis/ ▶ adj. unlimited; immense. — **bound·less·ly** adv. [as submodifier] *the land was boundlessly fertile.* **bound·less·ness** n.

boun·te·ous /ˈbountēəs/ ▶ adj. archaic generously given or giving; bountiful. — **boun·te·ous·ly** adv. **boun·te·ous·ness** n. [ME: from OFr. *bontif*, *-ive* 'benevolent' (from *bonte* 'bounty').]

Boun·ti·ful /ˈbountəfəl/ a city in northern Utah; pop. 41,301.

boun·ti·ful /ˈbountəfəl/ ▶ adj. large in quantity; abundant. ■ giving generously. — **boun·ti·ful·ly** adv.

Boun·ty /ˈbountē/ a British ship on which in 1789 part of the crew, led by Fletcher Christian, mutinied against their commander, William Bligh, and set him adrift in an open boat.

boun·ty /ˈbountē/ ▶ **n.** (pl. **-ties**) **1** generosity; liberality. ■ abundance; plenty. **2** a monetary gift or reward, typically given by a government, in particular: ■ a sum paid for killing or capturing a person or animal: *there was a **bounty** on his head.* ■ hist. a sum paid to encourage trade. ■ a sum paid to army or navy recruits upon enlistment. ■ literary something given or occurring in generous amounts. [ME: from OFr. *bonte* 'goodness,' from L. *bonitas*, from *bonus* 'good.']

boun·ty hunt·er ▶ **n.** one who pursues a criminal or seeks an achievement for the sake of the reward.

bou·quet /bōˈkā; bo͞o-/ ▶ **n.** **1** an attractively arranged bunch of flowers, esp. one presented as a gift or carried at a ceremony. ■ fig. an expression of approval; a compliment. **2** a characteristic scent, esp. that of a wine or perfume. [18th C.: from Fr., from dial. var. of OFr. *bos* 'wood.']

bou·quet gar·ni /bōˈkā gärˈnē; bo͞o-/ ▶ **n.** (pl. **bou·quets gar·nis** pronunc. same) herbs, typically encased in a cheesecloth bag, used for flavoring a stew or soup. [19th C.: Fr., lit. 'garnished bouquet.']

Bour·bon[1] /ˈbo͝orbən/ the surname of a branch of the royal family of France.

Bour·bon[2] ▶ **n.** **1** a reactionary. **2** (also **Bourbon rose**) a rose (*Rosa* × *borboniana*) of a variety that flowers over a long period and has a rich scent. It is a natural hybrid of the China rose and the damask rose. [19th C.: from the name **BOURBON**[1].]

bour·bon /ˈbərbən/ ▶ **n.** a straight whiskey distilled from corn mash, malt, and rye. [19th C.: named after *Bourbon* County, Kentucky.]

Bour·bon·nais /ˌbo͝orbəˈnā/ a former duchy and province in central France; chief town, Moulins.

bour·don /ˈbo͝ordn/ ▶ **n.** the drone pipe of a bagpipe. [ME: from OFr., 'drone,' of imitative origin.]

bourg /bo͝org/ ▶ **n.** hist. a town or village under the shadow of a castle. ■ a French market town.

bour·geois /bo͝orˈZHwä; ˈbo͝orZHwä/ ▶ **adj.** of or characteristic of the middle class, typically with reference to its perceived materialistic values or conventional attitudes. ■ (in Marxist contexts) upholding the interests of capitalism; not communist. ▶ **n.** (pl. same) a bourgeois person. [16th C.: from Fr., from late L. *burgus* 'castle,' ult. of Gmc. origin and rel. to **BOROUGH**.]

bour·geoise /bo͝orˈZHwäz; ˈbo͝orZHwäz/ ▶ **adj.** of or characteristic of female members of the bourgeoisie. ▶ **n.** a female member of the bourgeoisie. [18th C.: Fr., fem. of *bourgeois*.]

bour·geoi·sie /ˌbo͝orZHwäˈzē/ ▶ **n.** (usu. **the bourgeoisie**) the middle class, typically referring to its perceived materialistic values or conventional attitudes. ■ (in Marxist contexts) the capitalist class who own most of society's wealth and means of production. [18th C.: Fr.]

Bour·gogne /bo͝orˈgôn(yə)/ French name for **BURGUNDY**.

Bour·gui·ba /bo͝orˈgēbə/, Habib ibn Ali (1903–2000), president of Tunisia 1957–87.

Bourke-White /ˈbərk ˌ(h)wīt/, Margaret (1906–71), US photojournalist. During World War II, she was the first female photographer to accompany US armed forces.

bourn[1] /bôrn; bo͝orn/ (also **bourne**) ▶ **n.** dialect a small stream, esp. one that flows intermittently or seasonally. [ME: var. of **BURN**[2].]

bourn[2] (also **bourne**) ▶ **n.** literary **1** a goal; a destination. **2** a limit; a boundary. [16th C.: from Fr. *borne*, from OFr. *bodne* (see **BOUND**[2]).]

Bourne·mouth /ˈbôrnməTH; ˈbo͝orn-/ a city in southern England; pop. 154,400.

bour·rée /bo͝oˈrā/ ▶ **n.** a lively French dance. ■ Ballet a series of fast little steps, with the feet close together, typically performed on pointe and giving the impression that the dancer is gliding over the floor. ▶ **v.** [intrans.] perform a bourrée. [17th C.: Fr., lit. 'faggot of twigs.']

bourse /bo͝ors/ ▶ **n.** a stock market in a non-English-speaking country, esp. France. ■ (**Bourse**) the Paris stock exchange. [16th C.: from Fr., lit. 'purse,' via med. L. from Gk. *bursa* 'leather.']

Bour·sin /bo͝orˈsaN/ ▶ **n.** trademark a kind of soft cheese from France.

bou·stro·phe·don /ˌbo͞ostrəˈfēdn/ ▶ **adj. & adv.** (of written words) from right to left and from left to right in alternate lines. [17th C.: from Gk., lit. 'as an ox turns in plowing,' from *bous* 'ox' + *-strophos* 'turning.']

bout /bout/ ▶ **n.** a short period of intense activity of a specified kind. ■ an attack of illness or strong emotion of a specified kind. ■ a wrestling or boxing match. [16th C.: from dial. *bought* 'bend, loop'; prob. of Low Ger. origin.]

bou·tade /bo͞oˈtäd/ ▶ **n.** formal a sudden outburst or outbreak. [17th C.: Fr., from *bouter* 'to thrust.']

bou·tique /bo͞oˈtēk/ ▶ **n.** **1** a small store selling fashionable clothes or accessories. **2** a business that serves a sophisticated or specialized clientele: *a small investment boutique* | [as adj.] *a boutique film.* — **bou·tique·y adj.** [18th C.: Fr., lit. 'small shop,' via L. from Gk. *apothēkē* 'storehouse.']

bou·ton /bo͞oˈtôn/ ▶ **n.** Anat. an enlarged part of a nerve fiber or cell, esp. an axon, where it forms a synapse with another nerve. [20th C.: from Fr., lit. 'button.']

bou·ton·nière /ˌbo͞otnˈi(ə)r/ ▶ **n.** a spray of flowers worn in a buttonhole. [19th C.: Fr., 'buttonhole,' from *bouton* 'button.']

Bou·tros-Gha·li /ˈbo͞otrôs ˈgälē/, Boutros (1922–), Egyptian diplomat. He was secretary-general of the UN 1992–96.

bou·vier /bo͞oˈvyā/ ▶ **n.** a large, rough-coated, powerful dog originating in Belgium.

bou·zou·ki /bo͞oˈzo͞okē/ ▶ **n.** (pl. **-kis** or **-kia** /-kyä/) a long-necked Greek instrument similar to the mandolin. [1950s: from mod. Gk. *mpouzouki*, possibly rel. to Turk. *bozuk* 'spoiled.']

bo·vid /ˈbōvid/ ▶ **n.** Zool. a mammal of the cattle family (Bovidae). [19th C.: from mod. L. *Bovidae*, from *bos*, *bov-* 'ox.']

bo·vine /ˈbōvīn; -vēn/ ▶ **adj.** of, relating to, or affecting cattle. ■ (of a person) slow-moving and dull-witted. ▶ **n.** an animal of the cattle group, which also includes buffaloes and bisons. — **bo·vine·ly adv.** [19th C.: from late L. *bovinus*, from L. *bos*, *bov-* 'ox.']

bo·vine growth hor·mone (abbr.: **BGH**) ▶ **n.** a natural hormone in cattle that helps regulate growth and milk production and that may be produced artificially and given to dairy cattle to increase the yield of milk. Also called **BOVINE SOMATROPIN**.

bo·vine spon·gi·form en·ceph·a·lop·a·thy ▶ **n.** see **BSE**.

bow[1] /bō/ ▶ **n.** **1** a knot tied with two loops and two loose ends, used esp. for tying shoelaces and decorative ribbons. ■ a decorative ribbon tied in such a knot. **2** a weapon for shooting arrows, made of a curved piece of wood joined at both ends by a taut string. ■ a bowman. **3** a long, partially curved rod with horsehair stretched along its length, used for playing the violin and other stringed instruments. ■ a single passage of such a rod over the strings. **4** a thing that is bent or curved in shape, in particular: ■ a curved stroke forming part of a letter (e.g., *b*, *p*). ■ a metal ring forming the handle of a key or pair of scissors. ■ a side piece or lens frame of a pair of glasses. ▶ **v.** **1** [trans.] play (a stringed instrument or music) using a bow: *the techniques by which the pieces were bowed.* **2** bend into the shape of a bow: *the sides are squeezed in or bowed out.* [OE *boga* 'bend, bow,' from Gmc.; akin to Ger. *Bogen* and **BOW**[2].]

bow[2] /bou/ ▶ **v.** [intrans.] bend the head or upper part of the body as a sign of respect, greeting, or shame: *he turned and **bowed to his father*** | [as adj.] (**bowed**) *councilors stood **with heads bowed*** | [trans.] *she knelt and bowed her head.* ■ [trans.] express (thanks, agreement, or other sentiments) by bending one's head respectfully. ■ [intrans.] bend the body in order to see or concentrate: [as adj.] *my mother sat bowed over a library book.* ■ [trans.] cause (something) to bend with age or under a heavy weight: *the vines **were bowed down with** flowers* | [intrans.] *the grass bowed down before the wind.* ■ submit to pressure or to someone's demands. ■ [trans.] usher (someone) in a specified direction while bowing respectfully: *a footman bowed her into the hallway.* ▶ **n.** an act of bending the head or upper body as a sign of respect or greeting.

– PHRASES **bow and scrape** behave in an obsequious way to someone in authority. **make one's bow** make one's first formal appearance in a particular role. **take a bow** (of an actor or entertainer) acknowledge applause after a performance by bowing.

– PHRASAL VERBS **bow out** withdraw or retire from an activity, role, or commitment. [OE *būgan* 'bend, stoop,' from Gmc.; akin to Ger. *biegen* and **BOW**[1].]

bow[3] /bou/ (also **bows**) ▶ **n.** the front end of a ship.

– PHRASES **on the bow** Naut. within 45° of the point directly ahead. **a (warning) shot across the bows** a statement or gesture intended to frighten someone into changing their course of action. [ME: from Low Ger. *boog*, Du. *boeg* 'shoulder or ship's bow'; rel. to **BOUGH**.]

bow com·pass /bō/ (also **bow com·pass·es**) ▶ **n.** a compass with jointed legs.

bowd·ler·ize /ˈbōdləˌrīz; ˈboud-/ ▶ **v.** [trans.] remove material that is considered improper or offensive from (a text or account), esp. with the result that it becomes weaker or less effective: [as adj.] (**bowdlerized**) *a bowdlerized version of the story.* — **bowd·ler·ism n.** **bowd·ler·i·za·tion** /ˌbōdləriˈzāSHən; ˌboud-/ **n.** [19th C.: from the name of Dr. Thomas *Bowdler* (1754–1825), who published an expurgated edition of Shakespeare in 1818, + **-IZE**.]

bow·el /ˈbou(ə)l/ (also **bow·els**) ▶ **n.** the part of the alimentary canal below the stomach; the intestine. ■ (**the bowels of ——**) used to refer to the parts deep inside something large: *the subterranean bowels of Manhattan.* [ME: from OFr. *bouel*, from L. *botellus*, dimin. of *botulus* 'sausage.']

bow·el move·ment ▶ **n.** an act of defecation. ■ the feces discharged in an act of defecation.

Bow·en /ˈbōən/, Elizabeth Dorothea Cole (1899–1973), British writer; born in Ireland. Her novels include *The Heat of the Day* (1949).

bow·er[1] /ˈbouər/ ▶ **n.** a pleasant shady place. ■ literary a summerhouse or country cottage. ■ literary a lady's private room or bedroom. ▶ **v.** [trans.] literary shade or enclose (a place or person): [as adj.] (**bowered**) *the bowered pathways.* [OE *būr* 'dwelling,' from Gmc.; akin to Ger. *Bauer* 'birdcage.']

bow·er[2] (also **bower anchor**) ▶ **n.** each of two anchors carried at a ship's bow. [15th C.: from **BOW**[3] + **-ER**[1].]

bow·er·bird /ˈbouərˌbərd/ ▶ **n.** a strong-billed Australasian bird (family Ptilonorhynchidae), noted for the male's habit of constructing an elaborate bower adorned with feathers, shells, and other objects to attract the female for courtship.

Bow·er·y /ˈbou(ə)rē/ a street and district of lower Manhattan in New York City.

bow·fin /ˈbō,fin/ ▶ n. a predatory American freshwater fish (*Amia calva*, family Amiidae) with a large blunt head and a long dorsal fin. It is able to survive for long periods out of water. [19th C.: from BOW[1] + FIN.]

bow-front·ed /bō/ ▶ adj. (of furniture) having a convexly curved front. — **bow front** n. & adj.

bow·head /ˈbō,hed/ (also **bowhead whale**) ▶ n. an Arctic right whale (*Balaena mysticetus*) with black skin, feeding by skimming the surface for plankton. [19th C.: from BOW[1] + HEAD.]

bow·hunt·ing /ˈbō,həntiNG/ ▶ n. the practice of hunting animals with a bow rather than a gun. — **bow·hunt·er** /-,həntər/ n.

Bow·ie[1] /ˈbo͞oē/ a town in west central Maryland; pop. 50,269.

Bow·ie[2] /ˈbōē; ˈbo͞oē/, Jim (1799–1836), US frontiersman; full name *James Bowie*. He shared command of the garrison that resisted the Mexican attack on the Alamo, where he was killed.

bow·ie knife /ˈbōē; ˈbo͞oē/ ▶ n. a long knife with a blade double-edged at the point. [19th C.: named after Jim BOWIE[2], or perh. his brother Rezin Pleasant *Bowie* (1793–1841).]

bow·knot /ˈbō,nät/ ▶ n. a double-looped knot in a ribbon, tie, or other fastening.

bowl[1] /bōl/ ▶ n. **1** a round, deep dish or basin used for food or liquid. ■ the contents of such a container. ■ [usu. in names] a decorative round dish awarded as a prize in a competition: *the McGeorge Rose Bowl.* ■ a rounded, concave part of an object. ■ Geog. a natural basin. **2** [in names] a stadium for sporting or musical events: *the Hollywood Bowl.* ■ a football game played after the regular season between leading or all-star teams. — **bowl·ful** /-,fo͞ol/ n. [OE *bolle, bolla*, of Gmc. origin; rel. to Du. *bol* 'round object,' also to BOLL.]

bowl[2] ▶ n. a ball usually made of a composition material and slightly asymmetrical so that it runs on a curved course, used in the game of lawn bowling. ■ a large ball with holes for gripping, used in tenpin bowling. ▶ v. **1** [trans.] roll (a ball or hoop) along the ground: *she snatched her hat off and bowled it ahead of her like a hoop.* **2** [trans.] Cricket deliver (a ball to a batsman): *Lillee bowled another bouncer* | [intrans.] *Sobers bowled to Willis.* **3** [intrans.] move rapidly and smoothly in a specified direction: *they bowled along the country roads.*
– PHRASAL VERBS **bowl someone over** knock someone down. ■ (usu. **be bowled over**) informal completely overwhelm or astonish someone, for example by one's good qualities or looks. [ME: from OFr. *boule*, from L. *bulla* 'bubble.']

bowl·der ▶ n. var. of BOULDER.

bow legs /bō/ ▶ plural n. legs that curve outward at the knee; bandy legs. — **bow-leg·ged** /ˈbō,legid/ adj.

bowl·er[1] /ˈbōlər/ ▶ n. **1** a player at tenpin bowling, lawn bowling, or skittles. **2** Cricket a member of the fielding side who bowls or is bowling.

bowl·er[2] (also **bowler hat**) ▶ n. a man's hard felt hat with a round dome-shaped crown. [19th C.: named after William *Bowler*, the English hatter who designed it in 1850.]

Bowles /bōlz/, Paul Frederick (1910–99), US writer and composer. His novels include *The Sheltering Sky* (1949). He set to music Tennessee Williams's *Blue Mountain Ballads* (1946).

bowl hair·cut ▶ n. a haircut done by or as if by inverting a bowl on the head and cutting off the exposed hair.

bow·line /ˈbōlin; ˈbō,līn/ ▶ n. **1** a rope attached to the weather leech of a square sail and leading forward, thus helping the ship sail nearer the wind. **2** a nonbinding knot for forming a nonslipping nonjamming loop at the end of a rope. See illustration at KNOT[1]. [ME: from Mid. Low Ger. *bōline*, MDu. *boechlijne*, from *boeg* 'ship's bow' + *lijne* 'line.']

bowl·ing /ˈbōliNG/ ▶ n. **1** the game of tenpin bowling. ■ the game of candlepin or duckpin bowling. ■ the game of lawn bowling. ■ the game of skittles. **2** Cricket the delivery of the ball.

bowl·ing al·ley ▶ n. a long narrow track along which balls are rolled in bowling or skittles. ■ a building containing such tracks.

Bowl·ing Green a city in west central Kentucky; pop. 49,296.

bowl·ing green ▶ n. an area of closely mown grass on which the game of lawn bowling is played.

bowls /bōlz/ ▶ plural n. [treated as sing.] British term for LAWN BOWLING. ■ Brit. tenpin bowling or skittles.

bow·man[1] /ˈbōmən/ ▶ n. (pl. **-men**) an archer.

bow·man[2] /ˈboumən/ ▶ n. (pl. **-men**) the rower who sits nearest the bow of a boat, esp. a racing boat.

Bow·man's cap·sule /ˈbōmənz/ ▶ n. a capsule-shaped membranous structure surrounding the glomerulus of each nephron in the kidneys of mammals that extracts wastes from the blood.

bow saw /bō/ ▶ n. a narrow saw stretched like a bowstring on a light frame.

bow·shot /ˈbō,SHät/ ▶ n. [in sing.] the distance to which a bow can send an arrow.

bow·sprit /ˈbou,sprit; ˈbō-/ ▶ n. a spar extending forward from a ship's bow, to which the forestays are fastened. [ME: from Mid. Low Ger. *bōgsprēt*, MDu. *boechspriet*, from *boech* 'bow' + *spriet* 'sprit.']

bow·string /ˈbō,striNG/ ▶ n. the string of an archer's bow. ▶ v. (past and past part. **-strung**) [trans.] hist. strangle with a bowstring (a former Turkish method of execution).

bow·string hemp ▶ n. another term for SANSEVIERIA.

bow tie /bō/ ▶ n. a necktie in the form of a bow or a knot with two loops. ■ a pattern used for patchwork quilts, resembling such a necktie.

bow win·dow /bō/ ▶ n. a curved bay window.

bow·wood /ˈbō,wo͝od/ ▶ n. another name for OSAGE ORANGE.

bow-wow /ˈbou ˈwou/ ▶ exclam. an imitation of a dog's bark.

bow·yer /ˈbōyər/ ▶ n. a person who makes or sells archers' bows.

box[1] /bäks/ ▶ n. **1** a container with a flat base and sides, typically square or rectangular and having a lid. ■ the contents of such a container. ■ short for BOOM BOX. ■ informal a casing containing a computer. ■ (**the box**) informal, chiefly Brit. television or a television set. ■ informal a coffin. **2** an area or space enclosed within straight lines, in particular: ■ an area on a printed page that is to be filled in or that is set off by a border. ■ an area on a computer screen for user input or displaying information. ■ an area marked out at an intersection that vehicles must not enter while waiting to proceed: *don't block the box.* ■ (**the box**) Baseball any of four rectangular areas designated for a specific purpose: the **batter's box** (occupied by the batter), the **catcher's box** (occupied by the catcher), and a **coach's box** near first base and third base (for each base coach). ■ (**the box**) Soccer the penalty area. **3** a small structure or building for a specific purpose, in particular: ■ a separate section or enclosed area within a larger building, esp. one reserved for a group of people in a theater or sports ground or for witnesses or the jury in a law court. **4** a protective casing for a piece of a mechanism. ■ informal short for GEARBOX. **5** a mailbox at a post office, newspaper office, or other facility where a person may arrange to receive correspondence. ▶ v. [trans.] [often as adj.] (**boxed**) put in or provide with a box. ■ enclose (a piece of text) within printed lines. ■ (**box someone in**) restrict the ability of (someone) to move freely.
– PHRASES **back through the box** Baseball (of a batted ball) hit in the direction of the pitcher and past second base. **in a box** restricted or limited. (also **the batter's box**) **out of the box** describing a newly purchased product that works immediately, without any special assembly or training. — **box·ful** /-,fo͞ol/ n. [OE, prob. from late L. *buxis*, from L. *pyxis* 'boxwood box,' from Gk. *puxos* (see BOX[3]).]

box[2] ▶ v. [intrans.] fight an opponent using one's fists; compete in the sport of boxing: *he boxed for England.* ▶ n. [in sing.] a slap with the hand on the side of a person's head given as a punishment or in anger. [ME: origin unknown.]

box[3] ▶ n. **1** (also **box tree**) a slow-growing European evergreen shrub or small tree (*Buxus sempervirens*, family Buxaceae) with glossy dark green leaves, often grown as a hedge and for topiary. ■ (also **box·wood**) the hard, heavy wood of this tree, formerly widely used for engraving and for musical instruments. **2** any of a number of trees that have similar wood or foliage, including several Australian eucalyptus trees. [OE, via L. from Gk. *puxos*.]

box[4] ▶ v. (in phrase **box the compass**) esp. Naut. **1** recite the compass points in correct (clockwise) order. **2** make a complete change of direction: *the breeze had boxed the compass.* [18th C.: perh. from Sp. *bojar* 'sail around,' from Mid. Low Ger. *bōgen* 'bend,' from the base of BOW[1].]

box·car /ˈbäks,kär/ ▶ n. an enclosed railroad freight car, typically with sliding doors on the sides.

box-cut·ter ▶ n. a thin, inexpensive razor-blade knife designed to open cardboard boxes.

box el·der ▶ n. an American maple (*Acer negundo*) of damp soils that has green or purplish twigs, and leaves similar to those of the ash.

Box·er /ˈbäksər/ ▶ n. a member of a fiercely nationalistic Chinese secret society that flourished in the 19th century. In 1899 the society led a Chinese uprising (**the Boxer Rebellion**) against Western domination that was eventually crushed by a combined European force, aided by Japan and the US. [from BOXER, translating Chin. *yì hé quán*, lit. 'righteous harmony fists.']

box·er /ˈbäksər/ ▶ n. **1** a person who takes part in boxing. **2** a medium-sized dog of a breed with a smooth brown coat and puglike face.

box·er shorts (also **boxers**) ▶ plural n. men's loose underpants similar in shape to the shorts worn by boxers.

box·fish /ˈbäks,fiSH/ ▶ n. (pl. same or **-fish·es**) a tropical marine fish (family Ostraciontidae) that has a shell of bony plates enclosing the body, from which spines project. Also called TRUNKFISH.

box·ing /ˈbäksiNG/ ▶ n. the sport or practice of fighting with the fists, esp. with padded gloves in a roped square ring according to prescribed rules.

Box·ing Day ▶ n. (in parts of the British Commonwealth) a public holiday celebrated on the first day (strictly, the first weekday) after Christmas Day. [19th C.: from the custom of giving tradespeople a Christmas box on this day.]

bowsprit

box·ing glove ▸ n. a heavily padded mitten worn in boxing.

box jel·ly·fish ▸ n. a jellyfish (class Cubozoa) with a box-shaped swimming bell, living in warm seas. See also SEA WASP.

box kite ▸ n. a tailless kite in the form of a long box open at each end.

box lunch ▸ n. an individual lunch carried in a box rather than a bag.

box of·fice ▸ n. a place at a theater or other arts establishment where tickets are bought or reserved. ■ [in sing.] used to refer to the commercial success of a movie, play, or actor in terms of the audience size or takings they command.

box pleat ▸ n. a pleat consisting of two parallel creases facing opposite directions and forming a raised section in between.

box score ▸ n. the tabulated results of a baseball game or other sporting event, with statistics given for each player's performance.

box seat ▸ n. **1** a seat in a box in a theater or stadium. **2** hist. a coachman's seat.

box kite

box so·cial ▸ n. a fund-raising event in which box lunches are auctioned off.

box spring ▸ n. each of a set of vertical springs housed in a frame in a mattress or upholstered chair base.

box stall ▸ n. an enclosed area in a barn in which a single animal can move around freely.

box step ▸ n. a dance step in which the feet describe the form of a square or rectangle.

box tur·tle ▸ n. a land-living North American turtle (genus *Terrapene*, family Emydidae) that has a lower shell with hinged lobes that can be drawn up tightly to enclose the animal. Its several species include the **eastern box turtle** (*T. carolina*) and the **western box turtle** (*T. ornata*).

eastern box turtle

box·wood /ˈbäks,wo͝od/ ▸ n. see BOX[3] (sense 1).

box wrench ▸ n. a cylindrical wrench with a hexagonal end fitting over the head of a nut, used esp. when the nut is difficult to reach.

box·y /ˈbäksē/ ▸ adj. (**box·i·er**, **box·i·est**) squarish in shape. ■ (of a room or space) cramped. ■ (of recorded sound) restricted in tone.

boy /boi/ ▸ n. **1** a male child or young man. ■ a son. ■ [with adj.] a male child or young man who does a specified job. **2** [usu. with adj.] used informally or lightheartedly to refer to a man: *the inspector was a **local boy**.* ■ dated used as a friendly form of address from one man to another, often from an older man to a young man: ***my dear boy**, don't say another word!* ■ dated, offens. (sometimes used as a form of address) a black male servant or worker. ■ used as a form of address to a male dog. ▸ **exclam.** informal used to express strong feelings, esp. of excitement or admiration: *oh boy, that's wonderful!*

– PHRASES **boys in blue** informal policemen; the police. **the big boys** men or organizations considered to be the most powerful and successful. **boys will be boys** used to express the view that mischievous or childish behavior is typical of boys or young men. **one of the boys** an accepted member of a group, esp. a group of men. — **boy·hood** n. [ME: origin unknown.]

bo·yar /bōˈyär/ ▸ n. hist. a member of the old aristocracy in Russia, next in rank to a prince. [16th C.: from Russ. *boyarin* 'grandee.']

boy·cott /ˈboi,kät/ ▸ v. [trans.] withdraw from commercial or social relations with (a country, organization, or person) as a punishment or protest. ■ refuse to buy or handle (goods) as a punishment or protest. ■ refuse to cooperate with or participate in (a policy or event). ▸ n. a punitive ban that forbids relations with other bodies, cooperation with a policy, or the handling of goods. [from the name of Captain C. C. *Boycott* (1832–97), an English land agent in Ireland.]

boy·friend /ˈboi,frend/ ▸ n. a regular male companion with whom one has a romantic or sexual relationship.

boy·ish /ˈboi-ISH/ ▸ adj. of, like, or characteristic of a male child or young man: *his famous boyish charm.* — **boy·ish·ly** adv. **boy·ish·ness** n.

Boyle /boil/, Robert (1627–91), Irish scientist. He was known for his experiments with the air pump that led to the law named after him.

Boyle's law Chem. a law stating that the pressure of a given mass of an ideal gas is inversely proportional to its volume at a constant temperature.

Boyne, Bat·tle of the /boin/ a battle fought near the Boyne River in Ireland in 1690, in which the Protestant army of William III defeated the Catholic army of James II.

Boyn·ton Beach /ˈbointən/ a city in southeastern Florida; pop. 46,194.

boy·o /ˈboiō/ ▸ n. (pl. **-os**) esp. Welsh & Irish, informal a boy or man (usually used as a form of address).

Boy Scout ▸ n. a member of an organization of boys, esp. the **Boy Scouts of America**. ■ an honest, friendly, and typically naive man: [as adj.] *his trademark Boy Scout smile.*

boy·sen·ber·ry /ˈboizən,berē/ ▸ n. (pl. **-ries**) **1** a large red edible blackberrylike fruit. **2** the shrubby plant (*Rubus loganobaccus*) that bears this fruit, which is a hybrid of several kinds of bramble. [1930s: named after Robert *Boysen* (died 1950), the American horticulturalist who developed it.]

Boys Town a village in east central Nebraska, noted as a home for troubled youth; pop. 794.

boy toy ▸ n. informal, derog. a young woman who offers herself as a sex object for young men. ■ a young man who offers himself as a sex object for women.

boy won·der ▸ n. an exceptionally talented young man or boy.

Boz /bäz/ a pen name of Charles Dickens.

bo·zo /ˈbōzō/ ▸ n. (pl. **-zos**) informal a stupid, rude, or insignificant person, esp. a man. [1920s: of unknown origin.]

BP ▸ abbr. ■ before the present (era): *18,000 years BP.* ■ blood pressure. ■ Baseball batting practice. ■ boiling point.

Bp. ▸ abbr. Bishop.

bp ▸ abbr. ■ baptized. ■ Biochem. base pair(s), as a unit of length in nucleic acid chains. ■ Finance basis point(s). ■ (**b.p.**) boiling point.

BPH Med. ▸ abbr. benign prostatic hyperplasia (or hypertrophy), an enlargement of the prostate gland common in elderly men.

BPh ▸ abbr. (also **BPhil**) Bachelor of Philosophy.

bpi Comput. ▸ abbr. bits per inch, used to indicate the density of data that can be stored on magnetic tape or similar media.

B-pic·ture ▸ n. another term for B-MOVIE.

bps Comput. ▸ abbr. bits per second.

Bq ▸ abbr. becquerel.

BR ▸ abbr. ■ bedroom(s). ■ bills receivable.

Br ▸ symb. the chemical element bromine.

Br. ▸ abbr. ■ British. ■ (with reference to religious orders) Brother.

bra /brä/ ▸ n. an undergarment worn by women to support the breasts. ■ (also **auto bra** or **car bra**) a carbon-based cover that fits over the front bumper of a car, absorbing the microwaves used in police radar equipment to minimize the risk of detection for the speeding motorist. [1930s: abbrev. of BRASSIERE.]

Bra·bant /brəˈbant/ a former duchy in western Europe, now divided into two provinces: North Brabant in the Netherlands, and Brabant in Belgium.

bra burn·er ▸ n. informal a feminist perceived as militant in the struggle for women's rights.

brace /brās/ ▸ n. **1** a device that clamps things tightly together or that gives support, in particular: ■ a device fitted to a weak neck, leg, or other part of the body for support. ■ a wire device fitted in the mouth to straighten the teeth. ■ a strengthening piece of iron or timber used in building and carpentry. ■ a tool in carpentry having a crank handle and a socket to hold a bit for boring. ■ a rope leading aft from each yardarm, used for trimming the sail. ■ (**braces**) British term for SUSPENDERS. **2** (pl. same) a pair of something, typically of birds or mammals killed in hunting: *thirty **brace of** grouse.* **3** either of the two marks { and }, used either to indicate that two or more items on one side have the same relationship as each other to the single item to which the other side points, or in pairs to show that words between them are connected. ■ Music a similar mark connecting staves to be performed at the same time. ▸ v. [trans.] make (a structure) stronger or firmer with wood, iron, or other forms of support: *the posts were braced by lengths of timber.* ■ press (one's body or part of one's body) firmly against something in order to stay balanced: *she **braced** her feet **against** a projecting shelf* | [as adj.] (**braced**) *he stood with legs braced.* ■ prepare (someone or oneself) for something difficult or unpleasant: *police **are braced for** a traffic nightmare.*

– PHRASAL VERBS **brace up** be strong or courageous. [ME: from OFr. *bracier* 'embrace,' based on L. *bracchia*, pl. of *bracchium* 'arm,' from Gk. *brakhiōn*.]

brace and bit ▸ n. a revolving tool with a D-shaped crank handle for boring.

brace·let /ˈbrāslit/ ▸ n. an ornamental band, hoop, or chain worn on the wrist or arm. ■ (**bracelets**) informal handcuffs. [ME: from OFr., from *bras* 'arm,' from L. *bracchium*.]

brac·er[1] /ˈbrāsər/ ▸ n. informal an alcoholic drink intended to prepare one for something difficult or unpleasant.

brac·er[2] ▸ n. a wristguard used in archery, fencing, and other sports. Also called ARMGUARD. ■ hist. a portion of a suit of armor covering the arm.

brace and bit

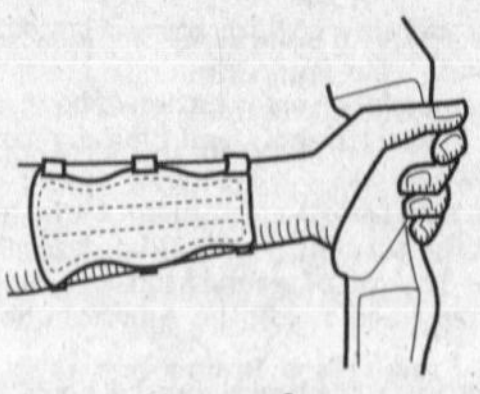
bracer[2]

[ME: from OFr. *braciere*, from *bras* 'arm' (see BRACELET).]

bra·cer·o /brə'se(ə)rō/ ▶ n. a Mexican laborer allowed into the United States for a limited time as a seasonal agricultural worker.

bra·chi·al /'brākēəl; 'brak-/ ▶ adj. Anat. of or relating to the arm, specifically the upper arm, or an armlike structure. ■ like an arm. ■ Zool. denoting the upper valve of a brachiopod's shell. [ME: from L. *brachialis*, from *brac(c)hium* 'arm.']

bra·chi·ate ▶ v. /'brākē,āt; 'brak-/ [no obj., usu. with adverbial of direction] (of certain apes) move by using the arms to swing from branch to branch: *the gibbons brachiate energetically.* ▶ adj. /'brākē,āt; 'brak-; -it/ Biol. branched, esp. having widely spread paired branches on alternate sides. ■ having arms. — **bra·chi·a·tion** /,brākē'āsнən; ,brak-/ n. **bra·chi·a·tor** /-,ātər/ n.

Brach·i·op·o·da /,brākēə'pōdə; ,brak-/ Zool. a phylum of marine invertebrates that comprises the lamp shells. — **bra·chi·o·pod** /'brākēə,päd; 'brak-/ n. [mod. L. (pl.), from Gk. *brakhiōn* 'arm' + *pous, pod-* 'foot.']

bra·chi·o·saur /'brākēə,sôr; 'brak-/ (also **bra·chi·o·sau·rus** /,brākēə'sôrəs; ,brak-/) ▶ n. a huge herbivorous dinosaur (genus *Brachiosaurus*, order Saurischia) of the late Jurassic to mid Cretaceous periods, with forelegs much longer than the hind legs. — **bra·chi·o·sau·ri·an** /,brākēə'sôr'ēən; ,brak-/ adj. [mod. L., from Gk. *brakhiōn* 'arm' + *sauros* 'lizard.']

bra·chis·to·chrone /brə'kistə,krōn/ ▶ n. a curve between two points along which a body can move under gravity in a shorter time than for any other curve. [18th C.: from Gk. *brakhistos* 'shortest' + *khronos* 'time.']

bra·chi·um /'brākēəm; 'brak-/ ▶ n. the arm, specifically the upper arm from shoulder to elbow.

brachy- ▶ comb. form short: *brachycephalic.* [from Gk. *brakhus* 'short.']

brach·y·ce·phal·ic /,brakēsə'falik/ ▶ adj. having a broad, short skull. Often contrasted with DOLICHOCEPHALIC. — **brach·y·ceph·a·ly** /-'sefəlē/ n.

brach·y·u·ra /,brakē'yŏŏrə/ a tribe or suborder of crustaceans that have short abdomens folded toward the ventral surface. It includes the true crabs. — **brach·y·u·ral** /-'yŏŏrəl/ adj. **brach·y·u·rous** /-'yŏŏrəs/ adj.

brach·y·u·ran /,brakē'yŏŏrən/ ▶ n. a crab belonging to the brachyura suborder of crustaceans.

brac·ing /'brāsiNG/ ▶ adj. 1 fresh and invigorating. 2 [attrib.] (of a support) serving to brace a structure. — **brac·ing·ly** adv. (in sense 1).

bra·ci·o·la /,brächē'ōlə; brä'chō-/ ▶ n. a thin slice of beef or other meat wrapped around a filling and cooked in wine.

brack·en /'brakən/ ▶ n. a tall fern (*Pteridium aquilinum*, family Dennstaedtiaceae) with coarse lobed fronds that occurs worldwide and can cover large areas. ■ (loosely) any large coarse fern resembling this. [ME: of Scand. origin; rel. to Dan. *bregne*.]

brack·et /'brakit/ ▶ n. 1 each of a pair of marks [ ] used to enclose words or figures so as to separate them from the context. 2 [with adj.] a category of people or things that are similar or fall between specified limits: *a high income bracket.* 3 a right-angled support attached to and projecting from a wall for holding a shelf, lamp, or other object. ■ a shelf fixed with such a support to a wall. 4 Mil. the distance between two artillery shots fired either side of the target to establish range. ▶ v. (**-et·ed, -et·ing**) [trans.] 1 (usu. **be bracketed**) place (one or more people or things) in the same category or group: *he is sometimes bracketed with the "new wave" of film directors.* 2 enclose (words or figures) in brackets: [as adj.] (**bracketed**) *the relevant data are included as bracketed points.* ■ Math. enclose (a complex expression) in brackets to denote that the whole of the expression rather than just a part of it has a particular relation, such as multiplication or division, to another expression. ■ fig. surround or enclose (someone or something) physically. ■ put (a belief or matter) aside temporarily: *he **bracketed off** the question of God.* 3 hold or attach (something) by means of a right-angled support. 4 Mil. establish the range of (a target) by firing two preliminary shots, one short of the target and the other beyond it. ■ Photog. establish (the correct exposure) by taking several pictures with slightly more or less exposure. [16th C.: from Fr. *braguette* or Sp. *bragueta* 'codpiece, bracket,' ult. from L. *braca*, (pl.) *bracae* 'breeches.']

brack·et creep ▶ n. movement into a higher tax bracket as taxable income increases.

brack·et fun·gus ▶ n. a fungus (class Basidiomycetes) that grows on living trees or dead wood, forming one or more shelflike projections that are the spore-producing bodies. Hyphae spread through the wood absorbing nutrients and can cause the death of the tree.

bract of a composite flower

brack·ish /'brakisн/ ▶ adj. (of water) slightly salty, as present in estuaries. ■ (of fish or other organisms) living in or requiring such water. ■ unpleasant or distasteful. — **brack·ish·ness** n. [16th C.: from obs. *brack* 'salty,' from Mid. Low Ger., MDu. *brac*.]

brac·o·nid /'brakənid/ ▶ n. Entomol. a small parasitic wasp that lays numerous eggs in a single host. [19th C.: from mod. L. *Braconidae*, from Gk. *brakhus* 'short.']

bract /brakt/ ▶ n. Bot. a modified leaf or scale, typically small, with a flower or flower cluster in its axil. Bracts are sometimes larger and more brightly colored than the true flower, as in a poinsettia. — **brac·te·ate** /-tēit; -tē,āt/ adj. [18th C.: from L. *bractea* 'thin plate of metal.']

brac·te·o·late /'braktēəlit; -,lāt/ ▶ adj. having bracteoles.

brac·te·ole /'braktē,ōl/ ▶ n. a small bract, esp. one on a floral stem.

brad /brad/ ▶ n. a small wire nail with a small, often asymmetrical head. See illustration at NAIL. [ME: from ON *broddr* 'spike.']

brad·awl /'brad,ôl/ ▶ n. a hand boring tool similar to a small, sharpened screwdriver.

Brad·bur·y /'brad,berē; -b(ə)rē/, Ray (1920–), US writer; full name *Raymond Douglas Bradbury*. His novels include *The Martian Chronicles* (1950) and *Farewell Summer* (2006).

Brad·dock /'bradək/, Edward (1695–1755), British commander of forces in America during the French and Indian War. He died while leading troops that were infamously routed at the Monongahela.

Bra·den·ton /'brādntən/ a city in southwestern Florida; pop. 43,779.

Brad·ford[1] /'bradfərd/ a city in northern England; pop. 449,100.

Brad·ford[2], William (1590–1657), American colonial leader. He signed the Mayflower Compact 1620 and governed Plymouth Colony sporadically 1621–56.

Brad·ley[1] /'bradlē/, Joseph (1813–92), US Supreme Court associate justice 1870–92.

Brad·ley[2], Milton (1836–1911), US entrepreneur. His board game "The Checkered Game of Life" led to the formation of Milton Bradley and Co. in 1864.

Brad·ley[3], Omar Nelson (1893–1981), US general. He commanded the land contingent during the Normandy campaign of 1944–45. After World War II, he served as chief of staff of the US Army 1948–49 and chairman of the US Joint Chiefs of Staff 1949–53.

Brad·street /'brad,strēt/, Anne Dudley (1612–72), American poet, the first published American female writer. Her poetry is collected in *The Tenth Muse Lately Sprung Up in America* (1650).

Bra·dy /'brādē/, Mathew W. (c.1823–96) US photographer, noted for his American Civil War photographs on and off the battlefield.

Bra·dy Bill (also **Brady Law**) ▶ n. a law that requires a waiting period for handgun purchases and background checks on those who wish to purchase them. [James S. Brady (1940–).]

Bra·dy bond ▶ n. a restructured commercial bank loan to poor countries, denominated in US dollars.

brad·y·car·di·a /,bradi'kärdēə/ ▶ n. Med. abnormally slow heart action. [19th C.: from Gk. *bradus* 'slow' + *kardia* 'heart.']

brad·y·kin·in /,bradi'kīnin; -'kinin/ ▶ n. Biochem. a compound released in the blood in some circumstances that causes contraction of smooth muscle and dilation of blood vessels. [1940s: from Gk. *bradus* 'slow' + *kinēsis* 'motion.']

brae /brā/ ▶ n. Scot. & N. Irish a steep bank or hillside. [ME: from ON *brá* 'eyelash.']

Brae·burn /'brābərn/ ▶ n. a dessert apple of a variety with crisp flesh, first grown in New Zealand.

brag /brag/ ▶ v. (**bragged, brag·ging**) [reporting verb] say in a boastful manner: [with direct speech] *"I found them," she bragged* | [with clause] *he brags that he wrote 300 pages in 10 days* | [intrans.] *they were **bragging about** how easy it had been.* ▶ n. 1 a gambling card game that is a simplified form of poker. 2 [in sing.] a boastful statement; an act of talking boastfully. ▶ adj. [attrib.] informal, excellent; first-rate. — **brag·ger** n. **brag·ging·ly** adv. [ME (adj., 'boastful'): of unknown origin.]

Bra·gan·za /brə'gänzə/ the dynasty that ruled Portugal from 1640 until the end of the monarchy in 1910 and Brazil (on its independence from Portugal) from 1822 until the formation of a republic in 1889.

Bragg /brag/, Sir William Henry (1862–1942), English physicist. He collaborated with his son, Sir (William) Lawrence Bragg (1890–1971), in developing the technique of X-ray diffraction. Nobel Prize for Physics (1915, shared with his son).

brag·ga·do·ci·o /,bragə'dōsнē,ō/ ▶ n. boastful or arrogant behavior. [16th C.: from *Braggadocchio*, a braggart in Spenser's Faerie Queene.]

brag·gart /'bragərt/ ▶ n. a person who boasts about achievements or possessions. [16th C.: from Fr. *bragard*, from *braguer* 'to brag.']

brag·ging rights ▶ n. (esp. of sports teams) the supposed right of a winning team and its fans to brag over the defeat of a close rival. ■ the supposed right to brag about an accomplishment.

Brahe /'brä,hē/, Tycho (1546–1601), Danish astronomer. He demonstrated that comets follow sun-centered paths.

Brah·ma /'brämə/ 1 the creator god in later Hinduism, who forms a triad with Vishnu the preserver and Shiva the destroyer. 2 another term for BRAHMAN (sense 2). [from Sanskrit *brahman*.]

Brah·ma bull n. another term for BRAHMAN sense 3.

Brah·man /'brämən/ (also **Brah·min** /-min/) ▶ n. (pl. **-mans** also **-mins**) 1 a member of the highest Hindu caste, that of the priesthood. [from Sanskrit *brāhmaṇa*.] 2 (in Hinduism) the ultimate reality underlying all phenomena. [from Sanskrit *brahman*.] 3 an ox (*Bos indicus*) of a humped breed originally domesticated in India that is tolerant of heat and drought. It is often included under the name *B. taurus* with other domestic cattle. Also called **Brahma bull**; **zebu**. — **Brah•man•ic** /brä'manik/ **adj.** **Brah•man•i•cal** /brä'manikəl/ **adj.**

Brah•ma•na /'brämənə/ ▶ **n.** (in Hinduism) any of the lengthy commentaries on the Vedas, composed in Sanskrit *c.*900–700 BC and containing expository material relating to Vedic sacrificial ritual.

Brah•man•ism /'brämə,nizəm/ (also **Brah•min•ism**) ▶ **n.** the complex sacrificial religion that emerged in post-Vedic India (*c.*900 BC) under the influence of the dominant priesthood (Brahmans), an early stage in the development of Hinduism.

Brah•ma•pu•tra /,brämə'pōōtrə/ a river in southern Asia that rises in the Himalayas and flows for 1,800 miles (2,900 km) to join the Ganges River on the Bay of Bengal.

Brah•min /'brämin/ ▶ **n. 1** var. of **Brahman**. **2** a socially or culturally superior person, esp. a member of the upper classes from New England. — **Brah•min•i•cal** /brä'minikəl/ **adj.** (in sense 1).

Brahms /brämz/, Johannes (1833–97), German composer and pianist. He wrote symphonies, concertos, chamber and piano music, and choral works.

braid /brād/ ▶ **n. 1** threads of silk, cotton, or other material woven into a decorative band for edging or trimming garments. **2** a length of hair made up of three or more interlaced strands: *women with long black braids.* ■ a length made up of three or more interlaced strands of any flexible material. ▶ **v.** [trans.] **1** interlace three or more strands of (hair or other flexible material) to form a length: *their long hair was tightly braided* | [as adj.] (**braided**) *braided manes.* **2** [often as adj.] (**braided**) edge or trim (a garment) with braid: *braided red trousers.* **3** [usu. as adj.] (**braided**) (of a river or stream) flow into shallow interconnected channels divided by deposited earth or alluvium. [OE *bregdan* 'make a sudden movement,' 'interweave,' of Gmc. origin; rel. to Du. *breien.*]

braid•ing /'brādiNG/ ▶ **n.** decorative braid or braided work.

brail /brāl/ Sailing ▶ **n.** (**brails**) small ropes that are led from the leech of a fore-and-aft sail to pulleys on the mast for temporarily furling it. ▶ **v.** [trans.] (**brail a sail up**) furl (a sail) by hauling on such ropes. [ME: from OFr. *braiel*, from med. L. *bracale* 'girdle,' from *braca* 'breeches.']

Bră•i•la /brə'ēlä/ a city in eastern Romania, on the Danube River; pop. 236,300.

Braille[1] /brāl/, Louis (1809–52), French educator. Blind from the age of three, he developed his own system of raised-point reading and writing.

Braille[2] ▶ **n.** a form of written language for the blind, in which characters are represented by patterns of raised dots that are felt with the fingertips. ▶ **v.** [trans.] print or transcribe in Braille.

braille•writ•er /'brāl,rītər/ ▶ **n.** a machine for writing braille.

brain /brān/ ▶ **n. 1** an organ of soft nervous tissue contained in the skull of vertebrates, functioning as the coordinating center of sensation and intellectual and nervous activity. ■ (**brains**) the substance of such an organ, typically that of an animal, used as food. ■ informal an electronic device with functions comparable to those of the human brain. **2** intellectual capacity. ■ (**the brains**) informal a clever person who supplies the ideas and plans for a group of people. ■ a person's mind. ■ an exceptionally intelligent person. ▶ **v.** [trans.] informal hit (someone) hard on the head with an object: *she brained me with a rolling pin.*
– PHRASES **beat** (or **blow**) **someone's brains out** informal injure or kill someone with a hard hit on the head. **have something on the brain** informal be obsessed with something: *John has cars on the brain.* [OE *brægen*, of West Gmc. origin; rel. to Du. *brein.*]

brain cell ▶ **n.** a cell in the tissue of the brain. ■ informal regarded as a unit of intellectual power.

brain•child /'brān,CHīld/ ▶ **n.** (pl. **-child•ren**) informal an idea or invention considered to be a particular person's creation.

brain cor•al ▶ **n.** a compact coral (*Diploria* and other genera, order Scleractinia) with a convoluted surface resembling that of the brain.

brain-dead ▶ **adj.** having suffered brain death. ■ informal extremely stupid.

brain death ▶ **n.** irreversible brain damage causing the end of independent respiration, regarded as indicative of death.

brain drain ▶ **n.** [in sing.] informal the emigration of highly trained or intelligent people from a particular country.

Braine /brān/, John Gerard (1922–86), English writer. He wrote the novel *Room at the Top* (1957).

brained /brānd/ ▶ **adj.** [in comb.] (of vertebrates) having an organ in the skull of a certain size or kind: *large-brained mammals.* ■ derog. (of a person) having an intellectual capacity of a certain quality or kind: *pea-brained Americans.*

brain fe•ver ▶ **n.** dated inflammation of the brain.

brain food ▶ **n.** food believed to be beneficial to the brain, esp. in increasing intellectual power.

brain•i•ac /'brānē,ak/ ▶ **n.** informal an exceptionally intelligent person. [1950s: blend of **brain** and **maniac**.]

brain•less /'brānlis/ ▶ **adj.** stupid; foolish. — **brain•less•ly adv. brain•less•ness n.**

brain•pan /'brān,pan/ ▶ **n.** informal a person's skull.

brain•pow•er /'brān,pouər/ ▶ **n.** mental ability; intelligence.

brain•sick /'brān,sik/ ▶ **adj.** diseased in the mind; mad or insane.

brain•stem /'brān,stem/ (also **brain stem**) ▶ **n.** Anat. the central trunk of the mammalian brain, consisting of the medulla oblongata, pons, and midbrain, and continuing downward to form the spinal cord.

brain•storm /'brān,stôrm/ ▶ **n. 1** a spontaneous group discussion to produce ideas and ways of solving problems. ■ informal a sudden clever idea. **2** informal a moment in which one is suddenly unable to think clearly or act sensibly. ▶ **v.** [intrans.] produce an idea or way of solving a problem by holding a spontaneous group discussion: [as n.] (**brainstorming**) *a brainstorming session.*

brain-teas•er (also **brain•teas•er, brain-twist•er**) ▶ **n.** informal a problem or puzzle, typically one designed to be solved for amusement. — **brain-teas•ing adj.**

brain trust ▶ **n.** a group of experts appointed to advise a government or politician.

brain•wash /'brān,wôSH; -,wäSH/ ▶ **v.** [trans.] make (someone) adopt radically different beliefs by using systematic and often forcible pressure: *the organization could brainwash young people.*

brain•wave /'brān,wāv/ ▶ **n.** (usu. **brainwaves**) an electrical impulse in the brain. ■ [usu. in sing.] informal a sudden clever idea.

brain•work /'brān,wərk/ ▶ **n.** mental activity or effort, esp. as opposed to physical labor.

brain•y /'brānē/ ▶ **adj.** (**brain•i•er, brain•i•est**) having or showing intelligence. — **brain•i•ly adv. brain•i•ness n.**

braise /brāz/ ▶ **v.** [trans.] fry (food) lightly and then stew it slowly in a closed container: [as adj.] (**braised**) *braised veal.* [18th C.: from Fr. *braiser*, from *braise* 'live coals.']

brake[1] /brāk/ ▶ **n.** a device for slowing or stopping a moving vehicle, typically by applying pressure to the wheels. ■ a thing that slows or hinders a process. ▶ **v.** [intrans.] make a moving vehicle slow down or stop by using a brake: *drivers who brake abruptly* | [as adj.] (**braking**) *an anti-lock braking system.* [18th C.: of unknown origin.]

brake[2] ▶ **n.** hist. an open horse-drawn carriage with four wheels.

brake[3] ▶ **n.** a toothed instrument used for crushing flax and hemp. ■ (also **brake harrow**) a heavy machine formerly used in agriculture for breaking up large lumps of earth. [ME: possibly rel. to Mid. Low Ger. *brake*, and perh. **break**.]

brake[4] (also **brake fern**) ▶ **n.** a coarse fern (genus *Pteris*, family Pteridaceae) of warm and tropical countries, frequently having the fronds divided into long linear segments. ■ archaic term for **bracken**. [ME: perh. abbrev. of **bracken**.]

brake drum ▶ **n.** a broad, very short cylinder attached to a wheel, against which the brake shoes press in a drum brake.

brake har•row ▶ **n.** see **brake**[3].

brake light ▶ **n.** a red light at the back of a vehicle that is automatically illuminated when the brakes are applied.

brake lin•ing ▶ **n.** a layer of asbestos or a similar material attached to a brake shoe to increase friction against the brake drum.

brake•man /'brākmən/ ▶ **n.** (pl. **-men**) **1** a railroad worker responsible for a train's brakes or for other duties such as those of a guard. **2** a person in charge of brakes, for instance in a bobsled.

brake pad ▶ **n.** either of the thin blocks that grip the disc in a disc brake.

brake shoe ▶ **n.** either of the long curved blocks that press on to the drum in a drum brake.

brak•ing dis•tance ▶ **n.** the approximate distance traveled before coming to a complete stop when the brakes are applied in a vehicle moving at a specified speed.

Bra•man•te /brä'mäntä/, Donato di Angelo (1444–1514), Italian architect. He established the concept of a huge central dome.

bram•ble /'brambəl/ ▶ **n.** a prickly scrambling wild shrub of the rose family, esp. a blackberry or (loosely) a dog rose. ■ any rough, prickly vine or shrub. — **bram•bly adj.** [OE *bræmbel, bræmel*, of Gmc. origin; rel. to **broom**.]

Bramp•ton /'bramtən/ a city in southeastern Ontario, west of Toronto; pop. 234,445.

bran /bran/ ▶ **n.** pieces of grain husk separated from flour after milling. [ME: from OFr.]

branch /branCH/ ▶ **n.** a part of a tree that grows out from the trunk or from a bough. ■ a lateral extension or subdivision extending from the main part of something, typically one extending from a river, road, or railroad. ■ a division or office of a large business or organization, operating locally or having a particular function. ■ a conceptual subdivision of something, esp. a family, group of languages, or a subject. ■ Comput. a control structure in which one of several alternative sets of program statements is selected for execution. ▶ **v.** [intrans.] (of a road or path) divide into one or more subdivisions. ■ (of a tree or plant) bear or send out branches: [as adj.] (**branched**) *identified by its branched stem.* ■ (**branch off**) diverge from the main route or part: *the road branched off at the town.* ■ (**branch out**) extend or expand one's activities or interests in a new direction: *the company is **branching out into** Europe.* — **branch•let** /-lit/ **n. branch•like adj. branch•y adj.** [ME: from OFr. *branche*, from late L. *branca* 'paw.']

bran•chi•a /'braNGkēə/ ▶ **n.** (pl. **-chi•ae** /-kē,ē/) the gills of fish and some invertebrate animals. — **bran•chi•al** /-kēəl/ **adj.** [17th C.: from L.

branchia, (plural) *branchiae*, from Gk. *brankhia* (pl.).]

Bran·chi·op·o·da /ˌbraNGkēˈəpōdə/ Zool. a class of small aquatic crustaceans that includes water fleas and fairy shrimps, which are distinguished by having gills upon the feet. — **bran·chi·o·pod** /ˈbraNGkēəˌpäd/ n. [mod. L. (pl.), from Gk. *brankhia* 'gills' + *pous, pod-* 'foot.']

branch·let /ˈbranCHlit/ ▶ n. a subdivision of a branch; a twig.

branch line ▶ n. a secondary railroad line branching off from a main line.

branch wa·ter (also **branch**) ▶ n. ordinary water, esp. when added to alcoholic drinks. ■ water from a stream or brook.

Bran·cu·si /branˈko͞osē; ˈbränˌko͞osH/, Constantin (1876–1957), Romanian sculptor. He reduced forms to their ultimate simplicity.

brand /brand/ ▶ n. **1** a type of product manufactured by a particular company under a particular name. ■ a brand name. ■ a particular type or kind of something. **2** an identifying mark burned on livestock or (esp. formerly) criminals or slaves with a branding iron. ■ archaic a branding iron. ■ fig. a habit, trait, or quality that causes someone public shame or disgrace. **3** a piece of burning or smoldering wood. ■ literary a torch. **4** literary a sword. ▶ v. [trans.] **1** mark (an animal, formerly a criminal or slave) with a branding iron. ■ mark indelibly: *an ointment that branded her with splotches.* ■ describe (someone or something) as something bad or shameful: *the media was* ***branding us as*** *communists* | [with obj. and complement] *she was branded a liar.* **2** assign a brand name to: [as adj.] (**branded**) *branded goods at low prices.* ■ [as n.] (**branding**) the promotion of a particular product or company by means of advertising and distinctive design. — **brand·er** n. [OE, of Gmc. origin; rel. to Ger. *Brand,* also to BURN[1].]

bran·dade /bränˈdäd/ ▶ n. a Provençal dish consisting of salt cod mixed into a purée with olive oil and milk. [Fr., from mod. Provençal *brandado*, lit. 'something that has been shaken.']

Bran·deis /ˈbrandīs/, Louis Dembitz (1856–1941), US Supreme Court associate justice 1916–39; born *Louis David Brandeis*. He was a leader of the American Zionist movement 1914–21.

Bran·den·burg /ˈbrandənˌbərg/ a state in northeastern Germany; capital, Potsdam.

Bran·den·burg Gate the only surviving city gate of Berlin, built 1788–91.

brand ex·ten·sion ▶ n. an instance of using an established brand name or trademark on new products, so as to increase sales.

brand im·age ▶ n. the impression of a product held by real or potential consumers.

brand·ing i·ron ▶ n. a metal implement that is heated and used to brand livestock or (esp. formerly) criminals or slaves.

bran·dish /ˈbrandisH/ ▶ v. [trans.] wave or flourish (something, esp. a weapon) as a threat or in anger or excitement. — **bran·dish·er** n. [ME: from OFr. *brandiss-*, stem of *brandir*; ult. of Gmc. origin and rel. to BRAND.]

brand·ling /ˈbrandliNG/ ▶ n. a red earthworm (*Eisenia fetida*) that has rings of a brighter color, often used as fishing bait.

brand name ▶ n. a name given by the maker to a product or range of products, esp. a trademark. ■ a familiar or widely known name: [as adj.] *brand-name status.*

brand new ▶ adj. completely new.

Brandt /bränt/, Willy (1913–92), chancellor of West Germany 1969–74; born *Herbert Ernst Karl Frahm*. He won international recognition for his policy of détente and for opening relations with the countries of the Eastern bloc. Nobel Peace Prize (1971).

bran·dy /ˈbrandē/ ▶ n. (pl. **-dies**) a strong alcoholic spirit distilled from wine or fermented fruit juice. [17th C.: from *brandwine*, from Du. *brandewijn*, from *branden* 'burn' + *wijn* 'wine.']

Bran·dy·wine Creek /ˈbrandēˌwīn/ a historic stream in southeastern Pennsylvania and northern Delaware, site of an American defeat by the British 1777.

branks /braNGks/ ▶ plural n. hist. an instrument of punishment for a scolding woman, consisting of an iron framework for the head and a sharp metal gag for restraining the tongue. [16th C.: cf. Ger. *Pranger* 'bit for a horse.']

bran·ni·gan /ˈbranigən/ ▶ n. informal a brawl or violent argument. [19th C.: perh. from the surname *Brannigan*.]

Bran·son /ˈbransən/ a city in southwestern Missouri, noted as a resort based on country music; pop. 3,706.

brant /brant/ ▶ n. (pl. same or **brants**) a small goose (*Branta bernicla*) with a mainly black head and neck, breeding in the arctic tundra of Eurasia and Canada.

Braque /bräk/, Georges (1882–1963), French painter. His collages were the first stage in the development of synthetic cubism.

brash[1] /brasH/ ▶ adj. self-assertive in a rude, noisy, or overbearing way. ■ strong, energetic, or irreverent. ■ (of a place or thing) having an ostentatious or tasteless appearance. — **brash·ly** adv. **brash·ness** n. [19th C. perh. from RASH[1].]

brash[2] ▶ n. a mass of fragments, esp. loose broken rock or ice. [18th C.: of unknown origin.]

Bra·sil /brəˈzil/ Portuguese name for BRAZIL[1].

Bra·sil·ia /brəˈzilyə/ the capital of Brazil since 1960, in the eastern central part; pop. 1,601,100.

Bra·şov /bräˈsHōv/ a city in central Romania; pop. 352,640. Hungarian name BRASSÓ. German name KRONSTADT.

brass /bras/ ▶ n. a yellow alloy of copper and zinc. ■ a decorative object made of such an alloy. ■ a memorial, typically medieval, consisting of a flat piece of inscribed brass, laid in the floor or set into the wall of a church. ■ a brass block or die used for stamping a design on a book binding. ■ Music brass wind instruments (including trumpet, horn, trombone) forming a band or a section of an orchestra. ■ (also **top brass**) informal people in authority or of high military rank. ■ informal in extended or metaphorical use referring to a person's hardness or effrontery: *he* ***had the brass to*** *show his face.*
– PHRASES **the brass ring** informal a prize or goal that someone strives for. [with ref. to the reward of a free ride given on a merry-go-round to the person hooking a brass ring suspended over the horses.]

bras·sard /brəˈsärd; ˈbrasärd/ ▶ n. a band worn on the sleeve, typically having an identifying mark and worn with a uniform. ■ hist. a piece of armor for the upper arm. [16th C.: from Fr., from *bras* 'arm.']

brass band ▶ n. a group of musicians playing brass instruments and sometimes also percussion.

brass-bound ▶ adj. trimmed or banded with brass fittings. ■ (of a person) adhering inflexibly to tradition or belief. ■ (of a person) brazen or impudent.

bras·se·rie /ˌbrasəˈrē/ ▶ n. (pl. **-ries**) an informal restaurant, esp. one in France or modeled on a French one and with a large selection of drinks. [19th C.: Fr., orig. 'brewery,' from *brasser* 'to brew.']

brass hat ▶ n. informal a high-ranking officer in the armed forces. [19th C.: from the gilt insignia on the caps of such officers.]

bras·si·ca /ˈbrasikə/ ▶ n. a plant of the genus *Brassica* (family Cruciferae) that includes cabbage, turnip, Brussels sprouts, and mustard. [19th C.: L., lit. 'cabbage.']

bras·siere /brəˈzi(ə)r/ ▶ n. full form of BRA. [20th C.: from Fr., lit. 'bodice.']

brass in·stru·ment ▶ n. a wind instrument, such as a trumpet or trombone, typically made of brass.

brass knuck·les ▶ n. a metal guard worn over the knuckles in fighting, esp. to increase the effect of the blows.

brass knuckles

Bras·só /ˈbräsH-sHō/ Hungarian name for BRAŞOV.

brass·ware /ˈbrasˌwe(ə)r/ ▶ n. utensils or other objects made of brass.

brass·y /ˈbrasē/ ▶ adj. (**brass·i·er, brass·i·est**) resembling brass, in particular: ■ bright or harsh yellow. ■ sounding like a brass musical instrument; harsh and loud. ■ (of a person, typically a woman) tastelessly showy or loud in appearance or manner. — **brass·i·ly** adv. **brass·i·ness** n.

brat /brat/ ▶ n. informal, derog. humorous a child, typically a badly behaved one. — **brat·tish** adj. **brat·tish·ness** n. **brat·ty** adj. [16th C.: perh. abbrev. of Scots *bratchet*, from OFr. *brachet* 'hound.']

Bra·ti·sla·va /ˌbrätəˈslävə/ the capital of Slovakia, a port on the Danube River; pop. 441,450. German name PRESSBURG; Hungarian name POZSONY.

brat pack ▶ n. informal a rowdy and ostentatious group of young celebrities, typically movie stars. — **brat pack·er** n.

Brat·tain /ˈbratn/, Walter Houser (1902–87), US physicist. He co-invented the point-contact transistor 1947. Nobel Prize for Physics (1956, shared with Bardeen and Shockley).

brat·tice /ˈbratis/ ▶ n. a partition or shaft lining in a coal mine, typically made of wood or heavy cloth. — **brat·ticed** adj. [ME: from OFr. *bretesche*, based on OE *brittisc* 'British.']

brat·tle /ˈbratl/ dialect ▶ n. a sharp rattling sound. ▶ v. [trans.] rattle (something). ■ [intrans.] produce a rattling sound. [16th C.: prob. imitative, from blend of BREAK and RATTLE.]

brat·wurst /ˈbrätˌwərst/ (also **brats**) ▶ n. a type of fine German pork sausage that is typically fried or grilled. [Ger., from *Brat* 'a spit' + *Wurst* 'sausage.']

Braun[1] /broun/, Eva (1910–45), German mistress of Adolf Hitler.

Braun[2] /broun/, Karl Ferdinand (1850–1918), German physicist. He invented the coupled system of radio transmission and the Braun tube (forerunner of the cathode-ray tube). Nobel Prize for Physics (1909, shared with Marconi).

Braun[3] /brôn; broun/, Wernher Magnus Maximilian von (1912–77), US engineer; born in Germany. He led the development of the V-2 rockets used by Germany during World War II. After the war he moved to the US, where he worked in the US space program.

Braun·schweig /ˈbrounˌsHwīg/ German name for BRUNSWICK.

braun·schwei·ger /ˈbrounˌsHwīgər/ ▶ n. a variety of smoked liver sausage.

bra·va /ˈbrävä; bräˈvä/ ▶ exclam. feminine of BRAVO[1].

bra·va·do /brəˈvädō/ ▶ n. a bold manner or a show of boldness intended to impress or intimidate. [16th C.: from Sp. *bravada*, from *bravo* 'bold' (see BRAVE).]

brave /brāv/ ▶ adj. ready to face and endure danger or pain; showing courage. ■ literary fine or splendid in appearance. ▶ n. **1** [as pl. n.] (**the brave**) people who are ready to face and endure danger or pain. **2** dated an American Indian warrior. ■ a young man who shows courage or a fighting spirit. ▶ v. [trans.] endure or face (unpleasant conditions or behavior) without showing fear: *we had to brave the heat.*

– PHRASES **brave new world** used to refer, often ironically, to a new and hopeful period in history resulting from major changes in society. **put a brave face on something** see FACE. — **brave·ly** adv. **brave·ness** n. [15th C.: from Fr., based on L. *barbarus* (see BARBAROUS).]

brav·er·y /ˈbrāv(ə)rē/ ▶ n. courageous behavior or character.

bra·vis·si·mo /bräˈvisəˌmō; -ˈvēsē-/ ▶ exclam. used to express great approval of a performance or performer.

bra·vo¹ /ˈbrävō/ ▶ exclam. used to express approval when a performer or other person has done something well. ▶ n. (pl. **-vos**) **1** a cry of bravo: *bravos rang out.* **2** a code word representing the letter B, used in radio communication. [18th C.: from Fr., from Ital., lit. 'bold.']

bra·vo² ▶ n. (pl. **-vos** or **-voes**) a thug or hired assassin. [16th C.: from Ital., from *bravo* 'bold (one).']

bra·vu·ra /brəˈv(y)o͝orə/ ▶ n. great technical skill and brilliance shown in a performance or activity. ■ the display of great daring. [18th C.: from Ital., from *bravo* 'bold.']

brawl /brôl/ ▶ n. a rough or noisy fight or quarrel. ▶ v. [intrans.] fight or quarrel in a rough or noisy way. ■ literary (of a stream) flow noisily. — **brawl·er** n. [ME: perh. rel. to BRAY¹.]

brawn /brôn/ ▶ n. **1** physical strength in contrast to intelligence. **2** Brit. meat from a pig's or calf's head that is cooked and pressed in a pot with jelly. [ME: from OFr. *braon* 'fleshy part of the leg,' of Gmc. origin; rel. to Ger. *Braten* 'roast meat.']

brawn·y /ˈbrônē/ ▶ adj. (**brawn·i·er**, **brawn·i·est**) physically strong; muscular. — **brawn·i·ness** n.

Brax·ton Hicks con·trac·tions /ˌbrakstən ˈhiks/ ▶ plural n. Med. intermittent weak contractions of the uterus occurring during pregnancy. [20th C.: John *Braxton Hicks* (1823–97), English gynecologist.]

brax·y /ˈbraksē/ ▶ n. a fatal bacterial infection of young sheep, caused by the bacterium *Clostridium septicum* and contracted by the ingestion of frozen grass or contaminated feed.

bray¹ /brā/ ▶ n. [usu. in sing.] the loud, harsh cry of a donkey or mule. ■ a sound, voice, or laugh resembling such a cry. ▶ v. [intrans.] make a loud, harsh cry or sound: *he brayed with laughter.* ■ [trans.] say (something) in a loud, harsh way: *vendors brayed the merits of spiced sausages.* [ME: from OFr. *brait* 'a shriek,' *braire* 'to cry,' perh. ult. of Celtic origin.]

bray² ▶ v. [trans.] archaic pound or crush (something) to small pieces, typically with a pestle and mortar. [ME: from OFr. *breier*, of Gmc. origin; rel. to BREAK.]

braze /brāz/ ▶ v. [trans.] [often as adj.] (**brazed**) form, fix, or join by soldering with an alloy of copper and zinc at high temperature. ▶ n. a brazed joint. [17th C.: from Fr. *braser* 'solder,' ult. of Gmc. origin.]

bra·zen /ˈbrāzən/ ▶ adj. **1** bold and without shame. **2** esp. literary made of brass. ■ harsh in sound.

– PHRASAL VERBS **brazen it** (or **something**) **out** endure an embarrassing or difficult situation by behaving with apparent confidence and lack of shame. — **bra·zen·ly** adv. **bra·zen·ness** n. [OE *bræsen* 'made of brass,' from *bræs* 'brass.']

bra·zier /ˈbrāzhər/ ▶ n. **1** a portable heater consisting of a pan or stand for holding lighted coals. **2** a barbecue. [17th C.: from Fr. *brasier*, from *braise* 'hot coals.']

Bra·zil¹ /brəˈzil/ the largest country in South America. Portuguese name BRASIL. *See box.*

Bra·zil² (also **bra·zil**) ▶ n. **1** (also **Brazil nut**) a large three-sided nut with an edible kernel, several of which grow inside a large woody capsule, borne on a South American forest tree (*Bertholletia excelsa*, family Lecythidaceae). **2** (also **Brazil wood**) a hard red wood obtained from a tropical tree (genus *Caesalpinia*) of the pea family, and from which dyes are obtained.

Bra·zil·ian /brəˈzilyən/ ▶ n. **1** a native or inhabitant of Brazil. **2** (**Brazilian wax**) a style of waxing a woman's pubic hair so that little or no hair remains. ▶ adj. relating to Brazil.

Braz·os Riv·er /ˈbrazəs/ a river that flows southeast for 840 miles (1,350 km) from northern Texas to the Gulf of Mexico.

Braz·za·ville /ˈbrazəˌvil; ˈbräzəˌvēl/ the capital of and a major port in the Republic of the Congo; pop. 2,936,000.

breach /brēch/ ▶ n. **1** an act of breaking or failing to observe a law, agreement, or code of conduct. ■ a break in relations. **2** a gap in a wall, barrier, or defense, esp. one made by an attacking army. ▶ v. [trans.] **1** make a gap in and break through (a wall, barrier, or defense): *the river breached its bank.* ■ break or fail to observe (a law, agreement, or code of conduct). **2** [intrans.] (of a whale) rise and break through the surface of the water.

– PHRASES **breach of the peace** an act of violent or noisy behavior that causes a public disturbance and is considered a criminal offense. **breach of promise** the action of breaking a sworn assurance to do something, formerly esp. to marry someone. [ME: from OFr. *breche*, ult. of Gmc. origin; rel. to BREAK.]

bread /bred/ ▶ n. food made of flour, water, and yeast or another leavening agent, mixed together and baked. ■ the bread or wafer used in the Eucharist. ■ informal the money or food that one needs in order to live.

– PHRASES **best** (or **greatest**) **thing since sliced bread** informal used to emphasize one's enthusiasm about a new idea, person, or thing. **bread and circuses** used to refer to a diet of entertainment or political policies on which the masses are fed to keep them happy and docile. **bread and water** a frugal diet that is eaten in poverty, chosen in abstinence, or given as a punishment. **bread and wine** the consecrated elements used in the celebration of the Eucharist; the sacrament of the Eucharist. **the bread of life** something regarded as a source of spiritual nourishment. **break bread** celebrate the Eucharist. ■ literary share a meal with someone. **cast one's bread upon the waters** do good without expecting gratitude or reward. **daily bread** the money or food that one needs in order to live. **know which side one's bread is buttered (on)** informal know where one's advantage lies. **one cannot live by bread alone** people have spiritual as well as physical needs. **take the bread out of** (or **from**) **people's mouths** deprive people of their livings by competition or unfair working practices. **want one's bread buttered on both sides** informal want more than is practicable or than is reasonable to expect. [OE *brēad*, of Gmc. origin; rel. to Ger. *Brot*.]

bread and but·ter ▶ n. a person's livelihood or main source of income, typically as earned by routine work: *their bread and butter is reporting local events* | [as adj.] *bread-and-butter occupations.* ■ an everyday or ordinary person or thing: *the bread and butter of non-League soccer* | [as adj.] *a good bread-and-butter player.*

bread-and-but·ter let·ter ▶ n. a letter expressing thanks for hospitality.

bread-and-but·ter pick·le ▶ n. a variety of sweet pickle made with thin-sliced cucumbers and various seasonings.

bread·bas·ket /ˈbredˌbaskit/ ▶ n. **1** a part of a region that produces cereals for the rest of it. **2** informal a person's stomach, considered as the target for a blow.

bread·board /ˈbredˌbôrd/ ▶ n. a board for making an experimental model of an electric circuit. ▶ v. [trans.] make (an experimental circuit).

bread·box /ˈbredˌbäks/ ▶ n. a box for storing bread and other baked goods.

bread·crumb /ˈbredˌkrəm/ ▶ n. (usu. **breadcrumbs**) a small fragment of bread. — **bread·crumbed** adj.

bread·ed /ˈbredid/ ▶ adj. (of food) coated with breadcrumbs and then fried: *lightly breaded chicken strips.*

bread·fruit /ˈbredˌfro͞ot/ ▶ n. **1** a large, round, starchy fruit, used as a vegetable and sometimes to make a substitute for flour. **2** (also **breadfruit tree**) the large evergreen tree (*Artocarpus altilis*) of the mulberry family that bears this fruit, widely cultivated on the islands of the Pacific and the Caribbean.

bread·line /ˈbredˌlīn/ ▶ n. a line of people waiting to receive free food.

bread mold ▶ n. any of various fungi, esp. of the genus *Rhizopus*, that grow on bread and other foods.

bread pud·ding ▶ n. a dessert consisting of slices of bread baked together with dried fruit, sugar, spices, eggs, and milk.

Brazil

Official name: Federative Republic of Brazil
Location: east central South America, on the South Atlantic, comprising nearly half the continent
Area: 3,265,900 square miles (8,456,500 sq km)
Population: 184,100,000
Capital: Brasilia
Languages: Portuguese (official), Spanish, English, French
Currency: real

bread·stick /ˈbredˌstik/ ▶ **n.** a long, thin, often crisp piece of bread.

bread·stuff /ˈbredˌstəf/ ▶ **n.** any bread product. ■ grain or flour used in the making of bread.

breadth /bredTH/ ▶ **n.** the distance or measurement from side to side of something; width. ■ wide range or extent. ■ the capacity to accept a wide range of ideas or beliefs. ■ dated a piece of cloth of standard or full width. ■ overall unity of artistic effect. [16th C.: from obs. *brede* 'breadth' (rel. to BROAD) + -TH[2].]

breadth·wise /ˈbredTHˌwīz/ (also **breadth·ways** /-ˌwāz/) ▶ **adv.** in a direction parallel with a thing's width.

bread·win·ner /ˈbredˌwinər/ ▶ **n.** a person who earns money to support a family. — **bread·win·ning n.**

break /brāk/ ▶ **v.** (past **broke**; past part. **brok·en**) **1** separate or cause to separate into pieces as a result of a blow, shock, or strain: [intrans.] *the rope broke with a loud snap* | [trans.] *windows in the street were broken by the blast.* ■ [trans.] (of a person or animal) sustain an injury involving the fracture of a bone or bones in (a part of the body). ■ [trans.] sustain such an injury to (a bone in the body). ■ [intrans.] (of a part of the body or a bone) sustain a fracture: *what if his leg had broken?* ■ [trans.] cause a cut or graze in (the skin): *the bite had broken the skin.* ■ make or become inoperative: [intrans.] *the machine has broken* | [trans.] *he's broken the video.* ■ (of the amniotic fluid surrounding a fetus) be or cause to be discharged when the sac is ruptured in the first stages of labor: [intrans.] *her water had broken.* ■ [trans.] open (a safe) forcibly. ■ [trans.] use (a piece of paper currency) to pay for something and receive change out of the transaction: *she had to break a ten.* ■ [trans.] exchange (a piece of paper currency of large denomination) for the same amount in smaller denominations. ■ [intrans.] (of two boxers or wrestlers) come out of a clinch, typically at the referee's command: *I was telling them to break.* ■ [trans.] unfurl (a flag or sail). ■ [trans.] succeed in deciphering (a code). ■ [trans.] open (a shotgun or rifle) at the breech. ■ [trans.] disprove (an alibi). ■ [trans.] invalidate (a will) through legal process. **2** [trans.] interrupt (a continuity, sequence, or course): *his concentration was broken by a sound.* ■ put an end to (a silence) by speaking or making contact. ■ make a pause in (a journey): *we will break our journey in Venice.* ■ [intrans.] stop proceedings in order to have a pause or vacation: *at mid-morning they* **broke for** *coffee.* ■ lessen the impact of (a fall). ■ stop oneself from being subject to (a habit). ■ put an end to (a tie in a game) by making a score. ■ [no obj., with adverbial] (chiefly of an attacking player or team, or of a military force) make a rush or dash in a particular direction: *the flight broke to the right and formed a defensive circle.* ■ surpass (a record). ■ disconnect or interrupt (an electrical circuit). ■ [intrans.] Sports (of a ball) swerve or dip in direction. **3** [trans.] fail to observe (a law, regulation, or agreement). ■ fail to continue with (a self-imposed discipline): *diets are broken all the time.* **4** [trans.] crush the emotional strength, spirit, or resistance of. ■ [intrans.] (of a person's emotional strength) give way: *her self-control finally broke.* ■ destroy the power of (a movement or organization). ■ destroy the effectiveness of (a strike), typically by moving in other people to replace the striking workers. ■ tame or train (a horse). **5** [intrans.] undergo a change or enter a new state, in particular: ■ (of the weather) change suddenly: *the weather broke, and thunder rumbled.* ■ (of a storm) begin violently. ■ (of dawn or day) begin with the sun rising: *dawn was just breaking.* ■ (of clouds) move apart and begin to disperse. ■ (of waves) curl over and dissolve into foam: *the sea breaking gently on the shore.* ■ (of a pitched baseball) curve or drop on its way toward the batter. ■ (of the voice) falter and change tone, due to emotion: *her voice broke as she relived the experience.* ■ (of a boy's voice) change in tone and register at puberty. ■ Phonology (of a vowel) develop into a diphthong, under the influence of an adjacent sound: [as n.] (**breaking**) *breaking due to a following r or h.* ■ (of prices on the stock exchange) fall sharply. ■ (of news or a scandal) suddenly become public. ■ [trans.] (**break something to someone**) make bad news known to someone. ■ make the first stroke at the beginning of a game of billiards, pool, or snooker. ▶ **n. 1** an interruption of continuity or uniformity. ■ an act of separating oneself from a state of affairs. ■ a change in the weather. ■ [with adj.] a change of line, paragraph, or page: *dotted lines show page breaks.* ■ a curve or drop in the path of a pitched baseball. ■ a change of tone in the voice due to emotion. ■ an interruption in an electrical circuit. ■ a rush or dash in a particular direction, esp. by an attacking player or team. ■ a breakout, esp. from prison. ■ a sudden decrease, typically in prices. ■ informal an opportunity or chance, esp. one leading to professional success. ■ (also **break of serve** or **service break**) Tennis the winning of a game against an opponent's serve. **2** a pause in work. ■ a short vacation. ■ a period of time taken out of one's professional activity in order to do something else. ■ a short solo or instrumental passage in jazz or popular music. **3** a gap or opening. **4** an instance of breaking; the point where something is broken. **5** Billiards & Snooker a player's turn to make the opening shot of a game or a rack.

– PHRASES **break the back of** do the hardest part of (a task). ■ overwhelm or defeat: *I thought we had broken the back of inflation.* **break the bank** see BANK[2]. **break bread** see BREAD. **break camp** see CAMP[1]. **break cover** (of game being hunted) emerge into the open. **break someone's heart** see HEART. **break the ice** see ICE. **break a leg!** informal good luck! **break the mold** see MOLD[1]. **break of day** dawn. **break ranks** see RANK[1]. **break (someone's) serve** (or **service**) win a game in a tennis match against an opponent's service. **break step** see STEP. **break wind** release gas from the anus. **give someone a break** [usu. in imper.] informal stop putting pressure on someone about something. ■ (**give me a break**) used to express contemptuous disagreement or disbelief about what has been said: *He's only 20 years old. Give me a break.* **make a break for** make a sudden dash in the direction of, typically in a bid to escape. **make a clean break** remove oneself completely and finally from a situation or relationship. **those are** (or **them's**) **the breaks** that is the way things turn out.

– PHRASAL VERBS **break away** (of a person) escape from someone's hold. ■ escape from the control of a person, group, or practice. ■ (of a competitor in a race) move into the lead. ■ (of a material or object) become detached from its base, typically through decay or under force. **break down 1** (of a machine or motor vehicle) suddenly cease to function. ■ (of a person) have the vehicle they are driving cease to function. ■ (of a relationship, agreement, or process) cease to continue; collapse. ■ lose control of one's emotions when in a state of distress: *the old woman broke down in tears.* ■ (of a person's health or emotional control) fail or collapse. **2** undergo chemical decomposition. **break something down 1** demolish a door or other barrier: *get the police to break the door down* | fig. *race barriers can be broken down by educational reform.* **2** separate something into a number of parts. ■ analyze information: *bar graphs show how the information can be broken down.* ■ convert a substance into simpler compounds by chemical action. **break even** reach a point in a business venture when the profits are equal to the costs. **break forth** burst out suddenly; emerge. **break free** another way of saying BREAK AWAY. **break in 1** force entry to a building: *someone trying to break in.* **2** [with direct speech] interject: *"I don't want to interfere," Mrs. Hendry broke in.* **break someone in** familiarize someone with a new job or situation: *there was no time to break in a new assistant.* ■ (**break a horse**) accustom a horse to a saddle and bridle, and to being ridden. **break something in** wear something, typically a pair of new shoes, until it becomes supple and comfortable. **break in on** interrupt. **break into 1** enter or open a (place, vehicle, or container) forcibly, typically for the purposes of theft. ■ succeed in winning a share of (a market or a position in a profession). ■ interrupt (a conversation). **2** (of a person) suddenly or unexpectedly burst forth into (laughter or song). ■ (of a person's face or mouth) relax into (a smile). **3** change one's pace to (a faster one): *Greg broke into a sprint.* **break off** become severed. ■ abruptly stop talking. **break something off** remove something from a larger unit or whole: *Tucker broke off a piece of bread.* ■ discontinue talks or relations. **break something open** open something forcibly. **break out** (of war, fighting, or similarly undesirable things) start suddenly. ■ (of a physical discomfort) suddenly manifest itself. **break out in** (of a person or a part of their body) be suddenly affected by an unpleasant sensation or condition: *something had caused him to break out in a rash.* **break out of** escape from. **break something out** informal open and start using something: *time to break out the champagne.* **break through** make or force a way through (a barrier): *demonstrators attempted to break through the police lines.* ■ fig. (of a person) achieve success in a particular area: *so many talented players are struggling to break through.* **break up** disintegrate; disperse. ■ (of a gathering) disband; end. ■ (of a couple in a relationship) part company. ■ start laughing uncontrollably: *the whole cast broke up.* ■ become emotionally upset. **break someone up** cause someone to become extremely upset. **break something up** cause something to separate into several pieces, parts, or sections. ■ bring a social event or meeting to an end by being the first person to leave. ■ disperse or put an end to a gathering. **break with** quarrel or cease relations with (someone). ■ act in a way that is not in accordance with (a custom or tradition). [OE *brecan* (v.), from Indo-Eur.; akin to Ger. *brechen*, L. *frangere* 'to break.']

break·a·ble /ˈbrākəbəl/ ▶ **adj.** capable of breaking or being broken easily. ▶ **n.** (**breakables**) things that are fragile and easily broken.

break·age /ˈbrākij/ ▶ **n.** the action of breaking something. ■ a thing that has been broken.

break·a·way /ˈbrākəˌwā/ ▶ **n. 1** a divergence or radical change from something established or long standing. ■ a secession of a number of people from an organization, typically following conflict or disagreement and resulting in the establishment of a new organization. **2** Sports a sudden attack or forward movement, esp. in a bicycle race or in hockey or football. **3** an object, such as a stage prop, designed to break apart easily.

break·beat /ˈbrākˌbēt/ ▶ **n.** Music a repeated sample of a drumbeat, usually forming a fast syncopated rhythm, used as a basis for dance music. ■ dance music featuring breakbeats.

break·bone fe·ver /ˈbrākˌbōn/ ▶ **n.** another term for DENGUE.

break·danc·ing /ˈbrākˌdansiNG/ ▶ **n.** an energetic and acrobatic style of street dancing, developed by American blacks. — **break·dance v. & n. break·danc·er n.**

break·down /ˈbrākˌdoun/ ▶ **n. 1** a failure of a relationship or of communication. ■ a collapse of a system of authority due to widespread transgression of the rules. ■ a sudden collapse in someone's mental health. ■ a mechanical failure. ■ [in sing.] the chemical or physical decomposition of something. **2** an explanatory analysis, esp. of statistics. **3** a lively, energetic American country dance.

break·er /ˈbrākər/ ▶ **n. 1** a heavy sea wave that breaks into white foam on the shore or a shoal. **2** a person or thing that breaks something: [in comb.] *a rule-breaker.* ■ a person who breaks horses. ■ short for CIRCUIT BREAKER. **3** a person who interrupts the conversation of others on a Citizens' Band radio channel, indicating a wish to transmit a message. ■ any CB radio user.

break·e·ven ▶ **n.** the point or state at which a person or company breaks even.

break·fast /ˈbrekfəst/ ▶ **n.** a meal eaten in the morning, the first of the day. ▶ **v.** [intrans.] have this meal: *she breakfasted on toast.*
– PHRASES **have** (or **eat**) **someone for breakfast** informal deal with or defeat someone with contemptuous ease. — **break·fast·er n. break·fast·less adj.** [ME: from the v. BREAK + FAST[2].]

break·front /ˈbrākˌfrənt/ ▶ **n.** a piece of furniture having the line of its front broken by a curve or angle.

break-in ▶ **n.** a forced or unconsented entry into a building, car, computer system, etc., typically to steal something.

break·ing and en·ter·ing ▶ **n.** the crime of entering a building by force so as to commit burglary.

break·ing point ▶ **n.** the moment of greatest strain at which someone or something gives way.

break·neck /ˈbrākˌnek/ ▶ **adj.** [attrib.] dangerously or extremely fast.

break·out /ˈbrākˌout/ ▶ **n. 1** a forcible escape, typically from prison. ■ [in sing.] (in soccer, hockey, and other sports) a sudden attack by a team that had been defending. **2** [in sing.] an outbreak. **3** an itemized list. **4** a sudden advance to a new level. **5** the deformation or splintering of wood, stone, or other material being drilled or planed. ▶ **adj.** informal **1** suddenly and extremely popular or successful. **2** denoting or relating to groups that break away from a conference or other larger gathering for discussion.

break point ▶ **n. 1** a place or time at which an interruption or change is made. ■ (usu. **break·point**) Comput. a place in a computer program where the sequence of instructions is interrupted, esp. by another program or by the operator. **2** Tennis the state of a game when the side receiving service needs only one more point to win the game. ■ a point of this nature. **3** another term for BREAKING POINT.

Break·spear /ˈbrākˌspi(ə)r/, Nicholas, see ADRIAN IV.

break·through /ˈbrākˌTHrōō/. ▶ **n.** a sudden, dramatic, and important discovery or development, esp. in science. ■ a significant and dramatic overcoming of a perceived obstacle, allowing the completion of a process.

break·up /ˈbrākˌəp/ ▶ **n.** an end to a relationship, typically a marriage. ■ a division of a country or organization into smaller autonomous units. ■ a physical disintegration of something.

break·wa·ter /ˈbrākˌwôtər; -ˌwätər/ ▶ **n.** a barrier built out into the sea to protect a coast or harbor from the force of waves.

bream[1] /brim; brēm/ ▶ **n.** (pl. same) a greenish-bronze deep-bodied freshwater fish (*Abramis brama*) of the minnow family, native to Europe and popular with anglers. ■ used in names of other fishes resembling or related to this, e.g., **sea bream.**

bream[2] /brēm/ ▶ **v.** [trans.] Naut., archaic clear (a ship or its bottom) of weeds, shells, or other accumulated matter by burning and scraping it. [15th C.: prob. of Low Ger. origin and rel. to BROOM.]

breast /brest/ ▶ **n.** either of the two soft, protruding organs on the upper front of a woman's body that secrete milk after pregnancy. ■ the corresponding but less-developed part of a man's body. ■ a person's chest. ■ the corresponding part of a bird or mammal. ■ a joint of meat or portion of poultry cut from such a part. ■ the part of a garment that covers the chest. ■ a person's chest regarded as the seat of the emotions. ▶ **v.** [trans.] face and move forward against or through (something): *I watched him breast the wave.* ■ reach the top of (a hill).
– PHRASES **beat one's breast** make an exaggerated show of sorrow, despair, or regret. **make a clean breast of something** see CLEAN. — **breast·ed adj.** [in comb.] *a bare-breasted woman* | *a crimson-breasted bird.* [OE *brēost*, of Gmc. origin; rel. to Ger. *Brust.*]

breast-beat·ing /ˈbrestˌbētiNG/ ▶ **n.** a loud, emotional expression of remorse.

breast·bone /ˈbrestˌbōn/ ▶ **n.** a thin, flat bone running down the center of the chest and connecting the ribs. Also called STERNUM.

breast-feed ▶ **v.** (past and past part. **-fed**) [trans.] (of a woman) feed (a baby) with milk from the breast: *she breast-fed her first child* | [intrans.] *sometimes it is not possible to breast-feed.* ■ [intrans.] (of a baby) feed from the breast: *the child began to breast-feed.*

breast-high ▶ **adj. & adv.** submerged to or as high as the breast: [as adj.] *we pushed through breast-high weeds* | [as adv.] *a cement patio fenced breast-high.*

breast im·plant ▶ **n.** Med. a prosthesis consisting of a gellike or fluid material in a flexible sac, implanted behind or in place of a female breast in reconstructive or cosmetic surgery.

breast·plate /ˈbrestˌplāt/ ▶ **n. 1** a piece of armor covering the chest. **2** Judaism in ancient times, a jeweled vestment covering the chest of the Jewish high priest. **3** a set of straps attached to the front of a saddle, which pass across the horse's chest and prevent the saddle from slipping backward. ■ the strap of a harness covering the chest of a horse.

breast·stroke /ˈbrestˌstrōk/ ▶ **n.** [in sing.] a style of swimming on one's front, in which the arms are pushed forward and then swept back in a circular movement, while the legs are tucked in toward the body and then kicked out in a corresponding movement. ■ (**the breaststroke**) a race, typically of a specified length or kind, in which such a style of swimming is used.

breast·work /ˈbrestˌwərk/ ▶ **n.** a low temporary defense or parapet.

breath /breTH/ ▶ **n.** an inhalation or exhalation of air from the lungs. ■ an exhalation of air by a person or animal that can be seen, smelled, or heard. ■ the physiological process of taking air into the lungs and expelling it again, esp. the ability to breathe easily. ■ the air taken into or expelled from the lungs. ■ archaic the power of breathing; life. ■ a brief moment; the time required for one act of respiration. ■ [in sing.] a slight movement of air. ■ [in sing.] a sign, hint, or suggestion: *he avoided the slightest breath of scandal.*
– PHRASES **a breath of fresh air** a small amount of or a brief time in the fresh air. ■ a refreshing change. **the breath of life** a thing that someone needs or depends on. **catch one's breath 1** cease breathing momentarily in surprise or fear. **2** rest after exercise to restore normal breathing. **don't hold your breath** informal used hyperbolically to indicate that something is likely to take a long time. **draw breath** breathe in. **get one's breath** (**back**) begin to breathe normally again after exercise or exertion. **hold one's breath** cease breathing temporarily. ■ fig. be in a state of suspense or anticipation. **in the same** (or **next**) **breath** at the same time. **last breath** the last moment of one's life (often used hyperbolically); death. **out of breath** gasping for air, typically after exercise. **save one's breath** stop wasting time in futile talk. **take someone's breath away** astonish or inspire someone with awed respect or delight. **under** (or **below**) **one's breath** in a very quiet voice; almost inaudibly. **waste one's breath** talk or give advice without effect. [OE *brǣth* 'smell, scent,' of Gmc. origin; rel. to BROOD.]

breath·a·ble /ˈbrēT͟Həbəl/ ▶ **adj.** (of the air) fit or pleasant to breathe. ■ (of clothes or material) admitting air to the skin and allowing sweat to evaporate.

breath·a·lyze /ˈbreTHəˌlīz/ ▶ **v.** [trans.] (usu. **be breathalyzed**) (of the police) use a breathalyzer to test the level of alcohol of (a driver).

breath·a·lyz·er /ˈbreTHəˌlīzər/ (also **Breath·a·lyz·er**) ▶ **n.** a device used by police for measuring the amount of alcohol in a driver's breath. [1960s: blend of BREATH and *(an)alyze.*]

breathe /brēT͟H/ ▶ **v.** [intrans.] take air into the lungs and then expel it, esp. as a regular physiological process: *she was wheezing as she breathed* | [trans.] *we are polluting the air we breathe.* ■ be or seem to be alive because of this: *at least I'm still breathing.* ■ literary (of wind) blow softly. ■ [with direct speech] say something with quiet intensity: *"We're together at last," she breathed.* ■ (of an animal or plant) respire or exchange gases: *plants breathe through their roots.* ■ [trans.] give an impression of (something): *the whole room breathed an air of hygienic efficiency.* ■ (of wine) be exposed to fresh air. ■ (of material or soil) admit or emit air or moisture.
– PHRASES **breathe** (**freely**) **again** relax after being frightened or tense about something. **breathe down someone's neck** follow closely behind someone. ■ constantly check up on someone. **breathe one's last** die. **breathe** (**new**) **life into** fill with enthusiasm and energy; reinvigorate. **breathe a sigh of relief** exhale noisily as a sign of relief (often used hyperbolically). **live and breathe** see LIVE[1]. **not breathe a word** remain silent about something; keep secret. [ME ('exhale'): from BREATH.]

breathed /breTHt/ ▶ **adj.** [usu. in comb.] having breath of a specified kind: *a foul-breathed poodle.* ■ (also /brēT͟Hd/) Phonet. unvoiced; voiceless.

breath·er /ˈbrēT͟Hər/ ▶ **n. 1** [in sing.] informal a brief pause for rest. **2** a vent or valve to release pressure or to allow air to move freely around something. **3** [with adj.] a person or animal that breathes in a particular way, or breathes a particular substance.

breath·ing /ˈbrēT͟HiNG/ ▶ **n. 1** the process of taking air into and expelling it from the lungs. **2** a sign in Greek (ʽ or ʼ) indicating the presence of an aspirate (**rough breathing**) or the absence of an aspirate (**smooth breathing**) at the beginning of a word.

breath·ing room n. sufficient room to move and breathe comfortably. ■ breathing space.

breath·ing space ▶ **n.** [in sing.] an opportunity to pause, relax, or decide what to do next.

breath·less /ˈbreTHlis/ ▶ **adj.** gasping for breath, typically due to exertion. ■ short of breath or appearing this way because of excitement or other strong feelings. ■ (of the air or weather) unstirred by a wind or breeze; stiflingly still. — **breath·less·ly adv. breath·less·ness n.**

breath·tak·ing /ˈbreTHˌtākiNG/ ▶ **adj.** astonishing or awe-inspiring in quality, so as to take one's breath away. — **breath·tak·ing·ly adv.**

breath test ▶ **n.** a test in which a driver is made to blow into a breathalyzer to check the amount of alcohol that has been drunk. ▶ **v.** (**breath-test**) [trans.] give (someone) such a test.

breath·y /ˈbreTHē/ ▶ **adj.** (**breath·i·er, breath·i·est**) producing or causing an audible sound of breathing, often related to physical exertion or strong feelings. — **breath·i·ly** /ˈbreTHəlē/ **adv. breath·i·ness n.**

brec·ci·a /ˈbrecHēə; ˈbresH-/ ▶ **n.** Geol. rock consisting of angular fragments of stones cemented together. — **brec·ci·ate** /-ēˌāt/ **v. brec·ci·a·tion** /ˌbrecHēˈāsHən; ˌbresH-/ **n.** [18th C.: from Ital., lit. 'gravel,' ult. of Gmc. origin and rel. to BREAK.]

Brecht /brekt; breKHt/, Bertolt (1898–1956), German playwright; full name *Eugen Berthold Friedrich Brecht.* He collaborated with Kurt Weill in *The Threepenny Opera* (1928) and also wrote *Mother Courage and Her Children* (1939).

Breck·in·ridge /ˈbrekənˌrij/, John Cabell (1821–75), vice president of the US 1857–61.

bred /bred/ past and participle of BREED. ▶ **adj.** [usu. in comb.] (of a person or animal) reared in a specified environment or way: *a city-bred man.*

Bre·da /brāˈdä; ˈbrādə/ a historic town in southwestern Netherlands; pop. 124,800.

bred-in-the-bone ▶ adj. firmly established; deep-rooted. ■ long established and unlikely to change; inveterate.

breech /brēCH/ ▶ n. **1** the part of a cannon behind the bore. ■ the back part of a rifle or gun barrel. **2** archaic a person's buttocks. ▶ v. [trans.] archaic put (a boy) into breeches after being in petticoats since birth. [OE *brēc* (pl. of *brōc*, of Gmc. origin; rel. to Du. *broek*), interpreted as sing.]

breech birth (also **breech delivery**) ▶ n. a delivery of a baby so positioned in the uterus that the buttocks or feet are delivered first.

breech·block /ˈbrēCH,bläk/ ▶ n. a metal block that closes the aperture at the back part of a rifle or gun barrel.

breech·clout /ˈbrēCH,klout/ ▶ n. (also **breech·cloth**) another term for LOINCLOTH.

breech·es /ˈbriCHiz; ˈbrē-/ ▶ plural n. short trousers fastened just below the knee, now chiefly worn for riding a horse or as part of ceremonial dress. ■ informal trousers.
– PHRASES **too big for one's breeches** see BIG. [ME: pl. of BREECH.]

breech·es bu·oy ▶ n. a lifebuoy with canvas breeches attached that, when suspended from a rope, can be used to transfer a passenger to safety from a ship.

breech·ing /ˈbrēCHiNG/ ▶ n. **1** a strong leather strap passing around the hindquarters of a horse harnessed to a vehicle. **2** hist. a thick rope used to secure the carriage of a cannon on a ship and to absorb the force of the recoil. **3** the hair or wool on the hindquarters of an animal.

breech-load·er ▶ n. a gun designed to have ammunition inserted at the breech rather than through the muzzle. — **breech-load·ing** adj.

breech pre·sen·ta·tion ▶ n. a position of a fetus in which the feet or buttocks appear first during birth.

breed /brēd/ ▶ v. (past and past part. **bred**) [trans.] cause (an animal) to produce offspring, typically in a controlled and organized way: *bitches may not be bred from more than once a year.* ■ [intrans.] (of animals) mate and then produce offspring: *toads are said to return to the pond of their birth to breed* | [as adj.] (**breeding**) *the breeding season.* ■ develop (a kind of animal or plant) for a particular purpose or quality: *these horses are bred for this sport.* ■ raise (livestock or animals). ■ rear and train (someone) to behave in a particular way or have certain qualities. ■ cause (something) to happen or occur, typically over a period of time: *success breeds confidence.* ■ Physics create (fissile material) by nuclear reaction. ▶ n. a stock of animals or plants within a species having a distinctive appearance and typically having been developed by deliberate selection. ■ a sort or kind of person or thing.
– PHRASES **a breed apart** a sort or kind or person that is very different from the norm. **a dying breed** a sort or kind of person that is slowly disappearing. **what's bred in the bone will come out in the flesh** (or **blood**) see BONE. [OE *brēdan* 'produce, bear,' of Gmc. origin; rel. to Ger. *brüten*, also to BROOD.]

breed·er /ˈbrēdər/ ▶ n. a person who breeds livestock, racehorses, other animals, or plants. ■ [with adj.] an animal that breeds at a particular time or in a particular way.

breed·er re·ac·tor ▶ n. a nuclear reactor that creates fissile material (typically plutonium-239 by irradiation of uranium-238) at a faster rate than it uses another fissile material (typically uranium-235) as fuel.

breed·ing /ˈbrēdiNG/ ▶ n. the mating and production of offspring by animals. ■ the activity of controlling the mating and production of offspring of animals. ■ training and education, esp. in proper social behavior. ■ the good manners regarded as characteristic of the aristocracy and conferred by heredity.

breed·ing ground ▶ n. an area where birds, fish, or other animals habitually breed. ■ [usu. in sing.] fig. a thing that favors the development or occurrence of something.

breeks /brēks/ ▶ plural n. Scottish term for BREECHES.

breeze[1] /brēz/ ▶ n. **1** a gentle wind. ■ [with adj.] a wind of force 2 to 6 on the Beaufort scale (4–27 knots or 4.5-31 mph). **2** informal a thing that is easy to do or accomplish. ▶ v. [no obj., with adverbial of direction] informal come or go in a casual or lighthearted manner: *I breezed in as if nothing were wrong.* ■ [intrans.] deal with something with apparently casual ease: *he breezed to victory.*
– PHRASES **shoot the breeze** see SHOOT. [16th C.: prob. from Old Sp. and Port. *briza* 'northeastern wind.']

breeze[2] ▶ n. small cinders mixed with sand and cement to make cinder blocks. [16th C.: from Fr. *braise*, (earlier) *brese* 'live coals.']

breeze·way /ˈbrēz,wā/ ▶ n. a roofed outdoor passage, as between a house and a garage.

breez·y /ˈbrēzē/ ▶ adj. (**breez·i·er, breez·i·est**) **1** pleasantly windy. **2** appearing relaxed, informal, and cheerily brisk. — **breez·i·ly** /-zəlē/ adv. **breez·i·ness** n.

breg·ma /ˈbregmə/ ▶ n. the point or area of the skull where the sagittal and coronal sutures joining the parietal and frontal bones come together.

Brem·en /ˈbrāmən; ˈbremən/ a state in northwestern Germany, comprising the city of Bremen and the port of Bremerhaven. ■ its capital, a port on the Weser River; pop. 537,600.

Brem·er·ha·ven /ˈbremər,hävən/ a seaport in northwestern Germany, on the North Sea coast; pop. 131,000.

Brem·er·ton /ˈbremərtən/ a city in west central Washington, on Puget Sound; pop. 38,142.

brems·strah·lung /ˈbrem,SHträləNG/ ▶ n. Physics electromagnetic radiation produced by the acceleration or esp. the deceleration of a charged particle after passing through the electric and magnetic fields of a nucleus. [1940s: from Ger., from *bremsen* 'to brake' + *Strahlung* 'radiation.']

Bren /bren/ (also **Bren gun**) ▶ n. a lightweight quick-firing machine gun. [blend of *Brno* (town in the Czech Republic where it was orig. made) and *Enfield* in England (where it was later made).]

Bren·nan /ˈbrenən/, William Joseph, Jr. (1906–97), US Supreme Court associate justice 1956–90.

Bren·ner Pass /ˈbrenər/ an Alpine pass at the border between Austria and Italy; altitude 4,450 feet (1,371 m).

Brent·wood /ˈbrent,wŏŏd/ a village in central Long Island in New York; pop. 45,218.

Bre·scia /ˈbrāSHə; ˈbreSHə/ a city in northern Italy, in Lombardy; pop. 196,770.

Bres·lau /ˈbres,lou/ German name for WROCŁAW.

Brest /brest/ **1** a port in northwestern France, on the Atlantic coast; pop. 153,100. **2** a city in Belarus; pop. 268,800. Former name (until 1921) BREST-LITOVSK. Polish name BRZEŚĆ NAD BUGIEM.

Bre·tagne /brəˈtänyə/ French name for BRITTANY.

breth·ren /ˈbreT͟Hrin/ archaic plural form of BROTHER. ▶ plural n. fellow Christians or members of a male religious order. See also BROTHER (sense 2). ■ used for humorous or rhetorical effect to refer to people belonging to a particular group.

Bret·on[1] /ˈbretn/ ▶ n. **1** a native of Brittany. **2** the Celtic language of Brittany, related to Cornish. ▶ adj. of or relating to Brittany or its people or language. [19th C.: from OFr., lit. 'Briton.']

Bret·on[2] /brəˈtôN/, André (1896–1966), French poet and critic. He outlined the philosophy of the surrealist movement 1924.

Bret·ton Woods /ˈbretn/ a resort in north central New Hampshire, site of 1944 UN conference at which the International Monetary Fund was formed.

Breu·er /ˈbroiər/, Marcel Lajos (1902–81), US architect; born in Hungary. He designed the Whitney Museum of American Art in New York City 1965–66. He is also known for his chair designs.

Bre·vard Coun·ty /brəˈvärd/ a county in east central Florida, the site of Cape Canaveral; pop. 398,978.

breve /brēv; brev/ ▶ n. **1** a musical note, rarely used in modern music, having the time value of two semibreves or whole notes. **2** a written or printed mark (˘) indicating a short or unstressed vowel. **3** hist. an authoritative letter from a pope or monarch. [ME: var. of BRIEF.]

bre·vet /brəˈvet; ˈbrevit/ ▶ n. [often as adj.] a former type of military commission conferred esp. for outstanding service by which an officer was promoted to a higher rank without the corresponding pay: *a brevet lieutenant.* ▶ v. (**-vet·ed** or **-vet·ted, -vet·ing** or **-vet·ting**) [trans.] confer a brevet rank on. [ME: from OFr. *brievet* 'little letter,' dimin. of *bref*.]

bre·vi·ar·y /ˈbrēvē,erē; ˈbrev-/ ▶ n. (pl. **-ar·ies**) a book containing the service for each day, to be recited by those in orders in the Roman Catholic Church. [ME: from L. *breviarium* 'summary,' from *breviare* 'abridge,' from *brevis* 'short.']

brev·i·ty /ˈbrevitē/ ▶ n. concise and exact use of words in writing or speech. ■ shortness of time.
– PHRASES **brevity is the soul of wit** proverb the essence of a witty statement lies in its concise wording and delivery. [15th C.: from OFr. *brievete*, from L. *brevitas*, from *brevis* 'brief.']

brew /bro͞o/ ▶ v. [trans.] **1** make (beer) by soaking, boiling, and fermentation. **2** make (tea or coffee) by mixing it with hot water: *I've just brewed some coffee* | [intrans.] *he did a crossword while the tea brewed.* **3** [intrans.] (of an unwelcome event or situation) begin to develop: *a storm was brewing.* ▶ n. **1** a kind of beer. ■ informal a serving of beer. **2** a cup or mug of tea or coffee. **3** a mixture of events, people, or things that interact to form a more potent whole.
– PHRASAL VERBS **brew up** Brit. make tea. — **brew·er** n. [OE *brēowan* (v.), of Gmc. origin; rel. to Ger. *brauen*.]

Brew·er /ˈbro͞oər/, David Josiah (1837–1910), US Supreme Court associate justice 1889–1910.

brew·er's yeast ▶ n. a yeast (*Saccharomyces cerevisiae*, phylum Ascomycota) used in breadmaking, winemaking, and the brewing of topfermenting beer, and as a source of vitamin B.

brew·er·y /ˈbro͞oərē/ ▶ n. (pl. **-er·ies**) a place where beer is made commercially. [17th C.: from BREW.]

brew·house /ˈbro͞o,hous/ ▶ n. a brewery.

brew·mas·ter /ˈbro͞o,mastər/ ▶ n. a person who supervises the brewing process in a brewery.

brew·pub /ˈbro͞o,pəb/ ▶ n. an establishment selling beer brewed on the premises and often including a restaurant.

brew·ski /ˈbro͞oskē/ ▶ n. informal a bottle, can, or glass of beer.

Brey·er /ˈbrīər/, Stephen Gerald (1938–), US Supreme Court associate justice 1994–.

Brezh·nev /ˈbreZH,nef; ˈbreZHnyif/, Leonid Ilich (1906–82), general secretary of the Soviet Communist Party 1964–82 and president of the Soviet Union 1977–82. His administration was marked by persecution of dissidents and an escalation of the Cold War.

bri·ar[1] /ˈbrī(ə)r/ ▶ n. var. of BRIER[1].

bri·ar[2] ▶ n. var. of BRIER[2].

bri·ar·root ▶ n. var. of BRIERROOT.

bri·ar·wood ▶ n. var. of BRIERWOOD.

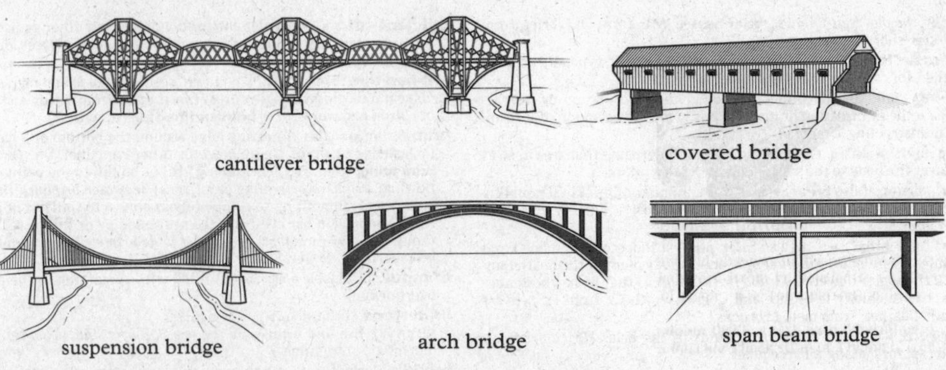

bridges

bribe /brīb/ ▶ **v.** [trans.] persuade (someone) to act in one's favor, typically illegally or dishonestly, by a gift of money or other inducement: *an undercover agent **bribed** the judge **into** giving a lenient sentence* | [intrans.] *he has no money to bribe with.* ▶ **n.** a sum of money or other inducement offered or given in this way. — **brib·a·ble adj. brib·er n.** [ME: from OFr. *briber, brimber* 'beg.']

brib·er·y /'brīb(ə)rē/ ▶ **n.** the giving or offering of a bribe.

bric-a-brac /'brik ə ˌbrak/ ▶ **n.** miscellaneous objects and ornaments of little value. [19th C.: from Fr., from obs. *à bric et à brac* 'at random.']

Brick /brik/ a township in southeastern New Jersey; pop. 76,119.

brick ▶ **n.** a small rectangular block typically made of fired or sun-dried clay, used in building. ■ bricks collectively as a building material. ■ a small, rectangular object. ▶ **v.** [with obj. and usu. with adverbial] (often **be bricked**) block or enclose with a wall of bricks.
– PHRASES **be built like a brick shithouse** see SHITHOUSE. **a brick short of a load** see SHORT. **hit** (or **run into**) **a brick wall** face an insuperable problem or obstacle while trying to do something. **like a ton of bricks** informal with crushing weight, force, or authority. **shit a brick** (or **bricks**) vulgar slang be extremely anxious or nervous. [ME: from Mid. Low Ger., MDu. *bricke, brike.*]

brick·bat /'brikˌbat/ ▶ **n.** a piece of brick, typically when used as a weapon. ■ a remark or comment that is highly critical and typically insulting.

brick·lay·er /'brikˌlāər/ ▶ **n.** a person whose job is to build walls, houses, and other structures with bricks. — **brick·lay·ing n.**

brick red ▶ **n.** a deep brownish red.

brick·work /'brikˌwərk/ ▶ **n.** the bricks in a wall, house, or other structure, typically in terms of their type or layout. ■ the craft or occupation of building walls, houses, or other structures with bricks.

brick·yard /'brikˌyärd/ ▶ **n.** a place where bricks are made.

bri·co·lage /ˌbrēkō'läzh; ˌbrikə-/ ▶ **n.** (pl. same or **-lag·es**) (in art or literature) construction or creation from a diverse range of available things. ■ something constructed or created in this way. [20th C.: Fr., from *bricoler* 'do odd jobs.']

bri·co·leur /ˌbrēkō'lər; ˌbrikə-/ ▶ **n.** a person who engages in bricolage. [20th C.: Fr., lit. 'handyman.']

brid·al /'brīdl/ ▶ **adj.** [attrib.] of or concerning a bride or a wedding. [ME: from OE *brȳd-ealu* 'wedding feast,' from *brȳd* 'bride' + *ealu* 'ale-drinking.']

brid·al wreath ▶ **n.** a spirea (*Spirea prunifolia*) with sprays of white flowers.

bride /brīd/ ▶ **n.** a woman on her wedding day or just before and after the event. [OE *brȳd*, of Gmc. origin; rel. to Ger. *Braut.*]

Bride, St. /brīd; brēd/ see BRIDGET, ST.[1]

bride·groom /'brīdˌgrōōm/ ▶ **n.** a man on his wedding day or just before and after the event. [OE *brȳdguma*, from *brȳd* 'bride' + *guma* 'man'; alt. by association with GROOM.]

bride price ▶ **n.** [in sing.] a sum of money or quantity of goods given to a bride's family by that of the groom, esp. in tribal societies.

brides·maid /'brīdzˌmād/ ▶ **n.** a girl or woman who accompanies a bride on her wedding day. [18th C.: alt. of *bridemaid.*]

bridge[1] /brij/ ▶ **n.** **1** a structure carrying a road, path, railroad, or canal across a river, ravine, road, railroad, or other obstacle. ■ something that makes a physical connection between two other things. ■ something that is intended to reconcile or form a connection between two things. ■ a partial denture supported by natural teeth on either side. See also BRIDGEWORK. ■ the support formed by the hand for the forward part of a billiard cue. ■ a long stick with a frame at the end that is used to support a cue for a shot that is otherwise hard to reach. ■ Music an upright piece of wood on a string instrument over which the strings are stretched. ■ Music a bridge passage or middle eight. ■ short for LAND BRIDGE. **2** the elevated, enclosed platform on a ship from which the captain and officers direct operations. **3** the upper bony part of a person's nose. ■ the central part of a pair of glasses, fitting over this. **4** an electric circuit with two branches across which a detector or load is connected, used to measure resistance or other property. ▶ **v.** [trans.] be a bridge over (something): *a walkway that bridged the gardens.* ■ build a bridge over (something): *earlier attempts to bridge the channel had failed.* ■ make (a difference between two groups) smaller or less significant.
– PHRASES **burn one's bridges** see BURN[1]. **cross that bridge when one comes to it** deal with a problem when and if it arises. — **bridge·a·ble adj.** [OE *brycg* (n.), of Gmc. origin; rel. to Ger. *Brücke.*]

bridge[2] ▶ **n.** a card game descended from whist, played by two partnerships of two players who at the beginning of each hand bid for the right to name the trump suit, the highest bid also representing a contract to make a specified number of tricks with a specified suit as trumps. [19th C.: of unknown origin.]

bridge·head /'brijˌhed/ ▶ **n.** a strong position secured by an army inside enemy territory from which to advance or attack.

bridge loan ▶ **n.** a sum of money lent by a bank to cover an interval between two transactions, typically the buying of one house and the selling of another.

bridge mix ▶ **n.** a mixture of various bite-size snack foods, such as nuts, raisins, and chocolates.

Bridge of Sighs a 16th-century enclosed bridge in Venice between the Doges' Palace and the state prison, crossed by prisoners to be tried or executed.

bridge pas·sage ▶ **n.** a transitional section in a musical composition leading to a new section or theme.

Bridge·port /'brijˌpôrt/ a city in southwestern Connecticut; pop. 139,529.

Bridg·es /'brijiz/, Robert Seymour (1844–1930), English poet. He was England's poet laureate 1913–30.

Bridg·et, St.[1] /'brijit/ (also **Bride** /brīd; brēd/ or **Brig·id** /'brijid/) (6th century), Irish abbess; also known as **St. Bridget of Ireland.**

Bridg·et, St.[2] (also **Bir·git·ta** /bir'gētə/) (*c.*1303–73), Swedish nun; also known as **St. Bridget of Sweden.**

Bridge·town /'brijˌtoun/ the capital of Barbados, a port on the southern coast; pop. 6,720.

bridge·work /'brijˌwərk/ ▶ **n.** **1** dental bridges collectively. ■ the construction or insertion of such bridges. **2** Building the component parts of a bridge. ■ the construction of bridges.

bridg·ing /'brijiNG/ ▶ **n.** the action of putting a bridge over something.

Bridg·man /'brijmən/, Percy Williams (1882–1961), US physicist. He worked with liquids and solids under very high pressures. Nobel Prize for Physics (1946).

bri·dle /'brīdl/ ▶ **n.** the headgear used to control a horse, consisting of buckled straps to which a bit and reins are attached. ■ a line, rope, or device that is used to restrain or control the action or movement of something. ▶ **v.** **1** [trans.] (usu. **be bridled**) put a bridle on (a horse). ■ bring (something) under control; curb: *the fact that he was their servant bridled his tongue.* **2** [intrans.] show one's resentment or anger, esp. by throwing up the head and drawing in the chin: *ranchers have **bridled at** excessive federal control.* [OE *brīdel* (noun), *brīdlian* (v.), of Gmc. origin; rel. to Du. *breidel* (n.).]

bri·dle path ▶ **n.** a path or track used for horseback riding.

Brie /brē/ ▶ **n.** a kind of soft, mild, creamy cheese with a firm, white skin. [*Brie* in France.]

brief /brēf/ ▶ **adj.** of short duration. ■ concise in expression; using few words. ■ (of a piece of clothing) not covering much of the body; scanty. ▶ **n.** a concise statement or summary. ■ a set of instructions given to a person about a job or task. ■ a written summary of the facts and legal points supporting one side of a case, for presentation to a court. ■ a letter from the pope to a person or community on a matter of discipline. ▶ **v.** [trans.] instruct or inform (someone) thoroughly, esp. in preparation for a task: *she briefed him on last week's decisions.*
– PHRASES **in brief** in a few words; in short. — **brief·ly adv.** [sentence adverb]

briefly, the plot is as follows... **brief·ness** n. [ME: from OFr. *brief*, from L. *brevis* 'short.']

brief·case /'brēf,kās/ ▶ n. a flat, rectangular container, typically made of leather, for carrying books and papers.

brief·ing /'brēfiNG/ ▶ n. a meeting for giving information or instructions. ■ the information or instructions given. ■ the action of informing or instructing someone.

briefs /brēfs/ ▶ plural n. close-fitting legless underpants that are cut so as to cover the body to the waist, in contrast to a bikini.

bri·er[1] /'brī(ə)r/ (also **bri·ar**) ▶ n. any of a number of prickly scrambling shrubs, esp. the sweetbrier and other wild roses. — **bri·er·y** adj. [OE *brǣr, brēr*.]

bri·er[2] (also **bri·ar**) ▶ n. **1** (also **brier pipe**) a tobacco pipe made from nodules borne at ground level by a large woody plant of the heath family. **2** the white-flowered shrub (*Erica arborea*) that bears these nodules, native chiefly to France and Corsica. [19th C.: from Fr. *bruyère* 'heath, heather,' from med. L. *brucus*.]

bri·er·root ▶ n. wood from the nodules of the brier (*Erica arborea*), used esp. for making tobacco pipes.

bri·er·wood ▶ n. another term for BRIERROOT.

Brig. ▶ abbr. ■ brigade. ■ brigadier.

brig /brig/ ▶ n. a two-masted, square-rigged ship with an additional gaff sail on the mainmast. ■ informal a prison, esp. on a warship. [18th C.: abbrev. of BRIGANTINE.]

bri·gade /bri'gād/ ▶ n. a subdivision of an army, typically consisting of a small number of infantry battalions and/or other units and often forming part of a division. ■ [usu. with adj.] an organization with a specific purpose, typically with a military or quasi-military structure: *the fire brigade.* ■ [in sing.] informal, often derog. a group of people with a common characteristic or dedicated to a common cause. ▶ v. [trans.] (often **be brigaded**) rare form into a brigade. ■ associate with (someone or something). [17th C.: from Fr., from Ital. *brigata* 'company,' from *brigare* 'contend,' from *briga* 'strife.']

brig·a·dier /,brigə'di(ə)r; 'brigə,di(ə)r/ ▶ n. a rank of officer in the British army, above colonel and below major general. [17th C.: from Fr.]

brig·a·dier gen·er·al ▶ n. (pl. **brig·a·dier gen·er·als**) an officer in the US Army, Air Force, or Marine Corps ranking above colonel and below major general.

brig·and /'brigənd/ ▶ n. literary a member of a gang that ambushes and robs people in forests and mountains. — **brig·and·age** /-əndij/ n. **brig·and·ry** /-əndrē/ n. [ME: from OFr., from Ital. *brigante*, lit. '(person) contending,' from *brigare* (see BRIGADE).]

brig·an·dine /'brigən,dēn/ ▶ n. hist. a coat of mail, typically one made of iron rings or plates attached to canvas or other fabric.

brig·an·tine /'brigən,tēn/ ▶ n. a two-masted sailing ship with a square-rigged foremast and a fore-and-aft-rigged mainmast. [16th C.: from OFr., from Ital. *brigantino*, from *brigante* (see BRIGAND).]

Briggs /brigz/, Henry (1561–1630), English mathematician. He is known for his work on logarithms.

bright /brīt/ ▶ adj. **1** giving out or reflecting a lot of light; shining. ■ full of light. ■ (of a period of time) having sunny, cloudless weather. ■ having a vivid color. ■ (of color) vivid and bold. **2** (of sound) clear, vibrant, and typically high-pitched. **3** (of a person, idea, or remark) intelligent and quick-witted. **4** giving an appearance of cheerful liveliness. ■ (of someone's future) likely to be successful and happy. ▶ adv. luminously. ▶ n. (**brights**) **1** bold and vivid colors: *gloves in neon brights.* **2** headlights switched to high beam.

– PHRASES **bright and early** very early in the morning. **the bright lights** the glamour and excitement of the city. **look on the bright side** be optimistic or cheerful in spite of difficulties. — **bright·ish** adj. **bright·ly** adv. **bright·ness** n. [OE *beorht*, of Gmc. origin.]

bright·en /'brītn/ ▶ v. make or become more light: [intrans.] *the day began to brighten* | [trans.] *the fire began to blaze fiercely, brightening the room.* ■ [trans.] make (something) more attractively and cheerfully colorful: *this colorful hanging ornament will brighten any room.* ■ make or become happier and more cheerful: [intrans.] *Sarah* **brightened up** *considerably* | [trans.] *she seems to brighten his life.*

bright-eyed ▶ adj. **1** having shining eyes. **2** alert and lively.

– PHRASES **bright-eyed and bushy-tailed** informal alert and lively; eager.

Bright·on /'brītn/ a resort city on the southern coast of England; pop. 133,400.

Brigh·ton Beach /'brītn/ a section of southern Brooklyn in New York City, east of Coney Island.

Bright's dis·ease ▶ n. a disease involving chronic inflammation of the kidneys. [19th C.: Richard *Bright* (1789–1858), English physician.]

bright·work /'brīt,wərk/ ▶ n. polished metalwork on ships or other vehicles.

Brig·id, St. /'brijəd; brēd/ see BRIDGET, ST.[1]

brill /bril/ ▶ n. a European flatfish (*Scophthalmus rhombus*, family Scophthalmidae) that resembles a turbot. [15th C.: of unknown origin.]

bril·liance /'brilyəns/ (also **bril·lian·cy**) ▶ n. intense brightness of light. ■ vividness of color. ■ exceptional talent or intelligence.

bril·liant /'brilyənt/ ▶ adj. **1** (of light) very bright and radiant. ■ (of a color) brightly and intensely vivid. **2** exceptionally clever or talented. ■ outstanding; impressive. ▶ n. a diamond of brilliant cut. — **bril·liant·ly** adv. [17th C.: from Fr. *brillant* 'shining,' pres. part. of *briller*, from Ital. *brillare*, prob. from L. *beryllus* (see BERYL).]

bril·liant cut ▶ n. a circular cut for diamonds and other gemstones in the form of two many-faceted pyramids joined at their bases, the upper one truncated near its apex.

bril·lian·tine /'brilyən,tēn/ ▶ n. **1** dated scented oil used on men's hair to make it look glossy. **2** shiny dress fabric made from cotton and mohair or cotton and worsted. — **bril·lian·tined** adj. (in sense 1).

brim /brim/ ▶ n. the projecting edge around the bottom of a hat. ■ the upper edge or lip of a cup, bowl, or other container. ▶ v. (**brimmed, brim·ming**) [often as adj.] (**brimming**) fill or be full to the point of overflowing: [intrans.] *a brimming cup* | [trans.] *seawater brimmed the riverbanks.* ■ fill something so completely as almost to spill out of it: *large tears brimmed in her eyes.* ■ fig. be possessed by or full of feelings or thoughts. — **brimmed** adj. [in comb.] *a wide-brimmed hat.* **brim·less** adj. [ME: perh. rel. to Ger. *Bräme* 'trimming.']

brim·ful /'brim,fo͝ol/ ▶ adj. [predic.] filled with something to the point of overflowing.

brim·stone /'brim,stōn/ ▶ n. archaic sulfur.

– PHRASES **fire and brimstone** see FIRE. [OE *brynstān*, prob. from *bryne* 'burning' + *stān* 'stone.']

brin·dle /'brindl/ ▶ n. a brownish or tawny color of animal fur, with streaks of other color. ■ an animal with such a coat. ▶ adj. (also **brin·dled**) (esp. of domestic animals) brownish or tawny with streaks of other color. [17th C.: back-form. from *brindled*, alt. of ME *brinded*, prob. of Scand. origin.]

brine /brīn/ ▶ n. water saturated or strongly impregnated with salt. ■ seawater. ■ tech. a strong solution of a salt or salts. ▶ v. [trans.] [often as adj.] (**brined**) soak in or saturate with salty water: *brined anchovies.* [OE *brīne*, of unknown origin.]

Bri·nell hard·ness test /bri'nel/ ▶ n. a test to determine the hardness of metals and alloys by hydraulically pressing a steel ball into the metal and measuring the resulting indentation. [Johan August Brinell (1849–1925), Swedish engineer.]

brine shrimp ▶ n. a small fairy shrimp (*Artemia salina*) that lives in brine pools and salt lakes, used as food for aquarium fish.

bring /briNG/ ▶ v. (past **brought** /brôt/) [with obj. and usu. with adverbial of direction] come to a place with (someone or something): *she brought Luke home* | [with two objs.] *Liz brought her a glass of water.* ■ cause (someone or something) to come to a place: *what brings you here?* | *a felony case brought before a jury.* ■ make (someone or something) move in a particular direction or way: *he brought his hands out of his pockets.* ■ cause (something): *the bad weather brought famine.* ■ cause (someone or something) to be in or change to a particular state or condition: *I'll give you some aspirin to* **bring down** *his temperature.* ■ (**bring someone in**) involve (someone) in a particular activity: *he has brought in a consultant.* ■ initiate (legal action) against someone: *riot and conspiracy charges should* **be brought against** *them.* ■ [usu. with negative] (**bring oneself to do something**) force oneself to do something unpleasant or distressing: *she could not bring herself to mention it.* ■ cause someone to receive (an amount of money) as income or profit: [with two objs.] *five more novels brought him $150,000.*

– PHRASES **bring home the bacon** see BACON. **bring something home to someone** see HOME. **bring the house down** make an audience respond with great enthusiasm, typically as shown by their laughter or applause. **bring something into play** cause something to begin operating or to have an effect; activate. **bring something to bear** exert influence or pressure so as to cause a particular result: *he was released after pressure had been brought to bear by the aid agencies.* **bring someone to book** see BOOK. **bring something to light** see LIGHT[1]. **bring someone/something to mind** cause one to remember or think of someone or something. **bring something to pass** esp. literary cause something to happen.

– PHRASAL VERBS **bring something about 1** cause something to happen. **2** cause a ship to head in a different direction. **bring something back** cause something to return. ■ reintroduce something. **bring someone down** cause someone to fall over, esp. by tackling them during a football game or rugby match. ■ cause someone to lose power: *the vote will not bring down the government.* ■ make someone unhappy. **bring someone/something down** cause an animal or person to fall over by shooting them. ■ cause an aircraft or bird to fall from the sky by shooting it. **bring something forth** archaic or literary give birth to. **bring something forward 1** move a meeting or event to an earlier date or time. **2** [often as adj.] (**brought forward**) in bookkeeping, transfer a total sum from the bottom of one page to the top of the next. **3** propose a plan, subject, or idea for consideration. **bring something in 1** introduce something, esp. a new law or product. **2** make or earn a particular amount of money. **3** (of a jury) give a decision in court. **bring someone off 1** be rescued from a ship in difficulties. **2** vulgar slang give someone or oneself an orgasm. **bring something off** achieve something successfully. **bring someone on** encourage someone who is learning something to develop or improve at a faster rate. **bring something on** cause something, typically something unpleasant, to occur or develop. ■ (**bring something on/upon**) be responsible for something, typically something unpleasant, that happens to oneself or someone else. **bring someone out 1** encourage one to feel more confident or sociable. **2** introduce (a young woman) formally into society. **3** introduce (a homosexual) into the homosexual subculture. **bring something out** produce and launch a new product or publication. ■ make something more evident; emphasize something. **bring someone around 1** restore someone to consciousness. **2** persuade someone to do something, esp. to adopt one's own point of view. **bring someone to** restore someone to consciousness. **bring something to** cause a boat to stop, esp. by turning into the wind. **bring up** (chiefly of a ship) come to a stop. **bring someone up** look after a child until it is an adult. ■ (**be brought up**) be taught as a child to adopt particular behavior or attitudes. **bring something up 1** vomit something. **2** raise a matter for discussion or consideration. — **bring·er** n. [OE *bringan*, of Gmc. origin; rel. to Ger. *bringen*.]

bring·down /'brinG,doun/ ▶n. a disappointment or letdown; comedown.

Brink /brinGk/, André Philippus (1935–), South African writer. His novel *Looking on Darkness* (1973) was the first novel in Afrikaans to be banned by the South African government.

brink /brinGk/ ▶n. an extreme edge of land before a steep or vertical slope. ■ a margin or bank of a body of water. ■ a point at which something, typically an unwelcome or disastrous event, is about to happen.
– PHRASES **on the brink of** about to experience something, typically a disastrous or unwelcome event. [ME: of Scand. origin.]

brink·man·ship /'brinGkmən,SHip/ (also **brinks·man·ship** /'brinGks mən-/) ▶n. the art or practice of pursuing a dangerous policy to the limits of safety before stopping, typically in politics.

brin·y /'brīnē/ ▶adj. of salty water or the sea; salty.

bri·o /'brēō/ ▶n. vigor or vivacity of style or performance. See also CON BRIO. [18th C.: from Ital.]

bri·oche /brē'ōSH; -'ôSH/ ▶n. a light, sweet yeast bread typically in the form of a small, round roll. [Fr.]

bri·quette /bri'ket/ (also **bri·quet**) ▶n. a block of compressed charcoal or coal dust used as fuel. [19th C.: from Fr., dimin. of *brique* 'brick.']

bris /bris/ ▶n. the Jewish ceremony of circumcision. Also called BRITH.

Bris·bane /'brizbən; -,bān/ the capital of Queensland, Australia, founded in 1824 as a penal colony; pop. 1,273,500.

brisk /brisk/ ▶adj. active, fast, and energetic. ■ (of the weather or wind) cold but fresh and enlivening. ■ sharp or abrupt. — **brisk·ly** adv. **brisk·ness** n. [16th C.: prob. from Fr. *brusque* (see BRUSQUE).]

bris·ket /'briskit/ ▶n. meat cut from the breast of an animal, typically a cow. [ME: perh. from ON *brjósk* 'cartilage.']

bris·ling /'brizliNG; 'bris-/ ▶n. (pl. same or **-lings**) a sprat, typically one seasoned and smoked in Norway and sold in a can. [20th C.: from Norw. and Dan.]

bris·tle /'brisəl/ ▶n. (usu. **bristles**) a short stiff hair, typically one of those on an animal's skin, a man's face, or a plant. ■ a stiff animal hair, or a man-made substitute, used to make a brush. ▶v. [intrans.] **1** (of hair or fur) stand upright away from the skin, esp. in anger or fear: *the hair on the back of his neck bristled.* ■ make one's hair or fur stand on end: *the cat bristled in annoyance.* ■ react angrily or defensively, typically by drawing oneself up. **2** (**bristle with**) be covered with or abundant in. [ME: from OE *byrst* (of Gmc. origin, rel. to Ger. *Borste*) + -LE[1].]

bris·tle·cone pine /'brisəl,kōn/ ▶n. a very long-lived shrubby pine (*Pinus longaeva*) of western North America. It has been used in dendrochronology to correct radiocarbon dating.

bris·tle·tail /'brisəl,tāl/ ▶n. a small wingless insect with bristles at the end of the abdomen, belonging to two orders: Thysanura (the three-bristled **true bristletails**, the silverfish) and Diplura (the **two-pronged bristletails**).

bris·tle worm ▶n. a marine annelid (class Polychaete) that has a segmented body with numerous bristles on the fleshy lobes of each segment.

bris·tling /'bris(ə)liNG/ ▶adj. **1** (esp. of hair) close-set, stiff, and spiky. **2** fig. aggressively brisk or tense.

bris·tly /'brislē/ ▶adj. (of hair or foliage) having a stiff and prickly texture. ■ covered with short stiff hairs.

Bris·tol /'bristl/ **1** a city in southwestern England, located on the Avon River; pop. 370,300. **2** a city in west central Connecticut; pop. 60,062. **3** a township in southeastern Pennsylvania, on the Delaware River; pop. 55,521.

Bris·tol board ▶n. fine, smooth pasteboard used for drawing or cutting. [19th C.: named after the city of BRISTOL in southwestern England.]

Bris·tol Chan·nel a wide inlet of the Atlantic Ocean between South Wales and the southwestern peninsula of England.

Brit /brit/ informal ▶n. a British person. ▶adj. British.

Brit·ain /'britn/ See GREAT BRITAIN.

Bri·tan·nia /bri'tanyə; -'tanēə/ the personification of Britain, usually depicted as a helmeted woman with shield and trident. [L. name for BRITAIN.]

Bri·tan·nia met·al ▶n. a silvery alloy consisting of tin with about 5–15 percent antimony and typically some copper, lead, or zinc.

Bri·tan·nic /bri'tanik/ ▶adj. dated (usually in names or titles) of Britain or the British Empire.

britch·es /'briCHiz/ ▶n. var. of BREECHES.
– PHRASES **too big for one's britches** see BIG.

brith /bris; brit/ ▶n. another term for BRIS. [For *brith milah*, from Heb. *berit mila* 'covenant of circumcision.']

Brit·i·cism /'briti,sizəm/ (also **Brit·ish·ism** /'briti,SHizəm/) ▶n. an idiom used in Britain but not in other English-speaking countries. [19th C.: from BRITISH.]

Brit·ish /'britiSH/ ▶adj. **1** of or relating to Great Britain or the United Kingdom, or to its people or language. **2** of the British Commonwealth or (formerly) the British Empire. ▶n. [as pl. n.] (**the British**) the British people. — **Brit·ish·ness** n. [OE *Brettisc* 'relating to the ancient Britons,' from *Bret* 'Briton,' from L. *Britto*, or its Celtic equivalent.]

Brit·ish Ant·arc·tic Ter·ri·to·ry that part of Antarctica claimed by Britain, including about 150,058 square miles (388,500 sq km) of the continent of Antarctica, the South Orkney and South Shetland islands.

Brit·ish Broad·cast·ing Cor·po·ra·tion (abbr.: **BBC**) a public corporation for radio and television broadcasting in Britain.

Brit·ish Co·lum·bi·a a province on the western coast of Canada; pop. 3,282,061; capital, Victoria.

Brit·ish Com·mon·wealth see COMMONWEALTH (sense 2).

Brit·ish Em·pire a former empire consisting of Great Britain and its possessions, dominions, and dependencies.

Brit·ish Eng·lish ▶n. English as used in Great Britain, as distinct from that used elsewhere.

Brit·ish·er /'britiSHər/ ▶n. informal (in North America and old-fashioned British English) a native or inhabitant of Britain.

Brit·ish In·di·a that part of the Indian subcontinent administered by the British from 1765 until 1947. See also INDIA.

Brit·ish In·di·an O·cean Ter·ri·to·ry a British dependency in the Indian Ocean consisting of the Chagos Archipelago and (until 1976) some other groups that now belong to the Seychelles.

Brit·ish Isles a group of islands off the coast of northwestern Europe, including Britain, Ireland, the Isle of Man, the Isle of Wight, the Hebrides, the Orkney Islands, the Shetland Islands, the Scilly Isles, and the Channel Islands.

Brit·ish·ism /'briti,SHizəm/ ▶n. var. of BRITICISM.

Brit·ish Mu·se·um a national museum of antiquities in Bloomsbury, London. Established with public funds in 1753, it includes among its holdings the Magna Carta, the Elgin Marbles, and the Rosetta Stone.

Brit·ish So·ma·li·land a former British protectorate on the coast of East Africa, part of Somalia since 1960.

Brit·ish ther·mal u·nit (abbr.: **Btu**, **BTU**) ▶n. the amount of heat needed to raise one pound of water at maximum density through one degree Fahrenheit, equivalent to 1.055 × 103 joules.

Brit·ish Vir·gin Is·lands see VIRGIN ISLANDS.

Brit·on /'britn/ ▶n. **1** a citizen or native of Great Britain. ■ a person of British descent. **2** one of the people of southern Britain before and during Roman times. [from OFr. *Breton*, from L. *Britto*, *Britton-*, or its Celtic equivalent.]

Brit·ta·ny /'britn-ē/ a region of northwestern France that forms a peninsula between the Bay of Biscay and the English Channel. French name BRETAGNE.

Brit·ten /'britn/, Benjamin, Lord Britten of Aldeburgh (1913–76), English composer; full name *Edward Benjamin Britten*. His operas include *Peter Grimes* (1945) and *A Midsummer Night's Dream* (1960).

brit·tle /'britl/ ▶adj. hard but liable to break or shatter easily. ■ (of a sound, esp. a person's voice) unpleasantly hard and sharp and showing signs of instability or nervousness. ■ (of a person or behavior) appearing aggressive or hard but unstable or nervous within. ▶n. a candy made from nuts and set melted sugar. — **brit·tle·ly** (or **brit·tly**) adv. **brit·tle·ness** n. [ME, ult. of Gmc. origin akin to OE *brēotan* 'break up.']

brit·tle bone dis·ease ▶n. Med. **1** another term for OSTEOGENESIS IMPERFECTA. **2** another term for OSTEOPOROSIS.

brit·tle frac·ture ▶n. fracture of a metal or other material occurring without appreciable prior plastic deformation.

brit·tle·star /'britl,stär/ ▶n. an echinoderm (*Ophiura* and other genera, class Ophiuroidea) with long, thin, flexible arms radiating from a small central disk.

Brit·ton·ic /bri'tänik/ ▶adj. & n. variant of BRYTHONIC. [from L. *Britto*, *Britton-* 'Briton.']

Brix scale /briks/ ▶n. a hydrometer scale for measuring the amount of sugar in a solution at a given temperature.

Br·no /'bərnō/ a city in the Czech Republic; pop. 388,000.

bro /brō/ ▶n. informal short for BROTHER. ■ [in sing.] a friendly greeting or form of address. ■ (**Bro.**) Brother (used before a first name when referring in writing to a member of a religious order of men).

broach[1] /brōCH/ ▶v. [trans.] **1** raise (a sensitive or difficult subject) for discussion: *he broached the subject.* **2** pierce (a cask) to draw liquor. ■ open and start using the contents of (a bottle or other container). **3** [intrans.] (of a fish or sea mammal) rise through the water and break the surface: *the salmon broach.* [ME: from OFr. *brochier*, based on L. *brocchus*, *broccus* 'projecting.']

broach[2] Naut. ▶v. [intrans.] (also **broach to**) (of a ship with the wind on the quarter) veer and pitch forward because of bad steering or a sea hitting the stern, causing it to present a side to the wind and sea, losing steerage, and possibly suffer serious damage: *we had broached badly, side on to the wind and sea.* ▶n. a sudden and hazardous veering of a ship having such consequences. [18th C.: of unknown origin.]

broad /brôd/ ▶adj. **1** having an ample distance from side to side; wide. ■ (after a measurement) giving the distance from side to side. ■ large

in area; spacious. **2** covering a large number and wide scope of subjects or areas. ■ having or incorporating a wide range of meanings, applications, or kinds of things; loosely defined. ■ including or coming from many people of many kinds. **3** general; without detail. ■ (of a hint) clear and unambiguous; not subtle. ■ somewhat coarse and indecent. ■ (of a phonetic transcription) showing only meaningful distinctions in sound and ignoring minor details. **4** (of a regional accent) very noticeable and strong. ▶**n.** informal a woman.
– PHRASES **broad in the beam** fat around the hips. **in broad daylight** during the day, when it is light, and surprising or unexpected for this reason. — **broad•ness n.** [OE *brād*, of Gmc. origin; rel. to Ger. *breit*.]

broad ar•row ▶**n.** a mark resembling a broad arrowhead, formerly used on British prison clothing and other government property.

broad•ax /ˈbrôd,aks/ (also **broad•axe**) ▶**n.** an ax with a wide head and a short handle.

broad•band /ˈbrôd,band/ ▶**adj.** of or using signals over a wide range of frequencies in high-capacity telecommunications, esp. as used for access to the Internet. ▶**n.** signals over such a range of frequencies.

broad bean ▶**n. 1** a large edible flat green bean that is typically eaten without the pod. Also called FAVA BEAN, HORSEBEAN. **2** the plant (*Vicia faba*) that yields these beans, often cultivated in gardens.

broad•bill /ˈbrôd,bil/ ▶**n. 1** a small, stocky bird (family Eurylaimidae) of the Old World tropics, with a flattened bill with a wide gape, and typically very colorful plumage. **2** a bird with a broad bill, esp. the shoveler or the scaup.

broad-brush ▶**adj.** lacking in detail and subtlety. ▶**n.** (**broad brush**) an approach characterized in this way.

broad•cast /ˈbrôd,kast/ ▶**v.** (past **-cast** or **-cast•ed** ; past part. **-cast** or **-cast•ed**) [trans.] **1** (often **be broadcast**) transmit (a program or some information) by radio or television: *the announcement was broadcast live* | [as n.] (**broadcasting**) *the 1920s was the dawn of broadcasting.* ■ [intrans.] take part in a radio or television transmission: *the station broadcasts 24 hours a day.* ■ tell (something) to many people; make widely known: *we don't want to broadcast our unhappiness.* **2** scatter (seeds) by hand or machine rather than placing in drills or rows. ▶**n.** a radio or television program or transmission. ▶**adj.** of or relating to such programs. ▶**adv.** by scattering: *green manure can be sown broadcast.* — **broad•cast•er n.** [18th C.: from BROAD + past part. of CAST[1].]

Broad Church ▶**n.** a tradition or group within the Anglican Church favoring a liberal interpretation of doctrine. ■ a group, organization, or doctrine that allows for and caters to a wide range of opinions and people.

broad•cloth /ˈbrôd,klôTH/ ▶**n.** clothing fabric of fine twilled wool or worsted, or plain-woven cotton.

broad•en /ˈbrôdn/ ▶**v.** [intrans.] become larger in distance from side to side; widen: *her smile broadened.* ■ expand to encompass more people, ideas, or things: *her interests broadened* | [trans.] *efforts to broaden classical music's appeal.*
– PHRASES **broaden one's horizons** expand one's range of interests, activities, and knowledge.

broad gauge ▶**n.** a railroad gauge that is wider than the standard gauge of 56.5 inches (1.435 m).

broad jump ▶**n.** another term for LONG JUMP.

broad•leaf /ˈbrôd,lēf/ ▶**adj.** another term for BROAD-LEAVED. ▶**n.** (pl. **-leaves** or **-leafs**) a tree or plant with wide flat leaves.

broad-leaved /ˈbrôd ,lēvd/ ▶**adj.** [attrib.] (of a tree or plant) having relatively wide, flat leaves rather than needles; nonconiferous. ■ (of a wood or woodland) consisting of trees with such leaves.

broad•loom /ˈbrôd,lo͞om/ ▶**n.** carpet woven in wide widths. — **broad•loomed adj.**

broad•ly /ˈbrôdlē/ ▶**adv. 1** in general and with the exception of minor details: *the climate is broadly similar in the two regions.* **2** widely and openly.

broad-mind•ed ▶**adj.** tolerant or liberal in one's views and reactions; not easily offended. — **broad-mind•ed•ness n. broad-mind•ed•ly adv.**

broad•sheet /ˈbrôd,SHēt/ ▶**n.** a large piece of paper printed on one side only with information; a broadside. ■ (also **broadsheet newspaper**) a newspaper with a large format regarded as more serious and less sensationalist than tabloids.

broad•side /ˈbrôd,sīd/ ▶**n. 1** a nearly simultaneous firing of all the guns from one side of a warship. ■ fig. a strongly worded critical attack. ■ the set of guns that can fire on each side of a warship. ■ the side of a ship above the water between the bow and quarter. **2** a sheet of paper printed on one side only, forming one large page; also called BROADSHEET. ▶**adv.** with the side turned to a particular thing: *the yacht was drifting broadside to the wind.* ■ on the side: *her car was hit broadside.* ▶**v.** [trans.] collide with the side of (a vehicle): *I had to skid my bike sideways to avoid broadsiding her.*

broad-spec•trum ▶**adj.** [attrib.] denoting antibiotics, pesticides, etc., effective against a large variety of organisms.

broad•sword /ˈbrôd,sôrd/ ▶**n.** a sword with a wide blade, used for cutting rather than thrusting.

broad•tail /ˈbrôd,tāl/ ▶**n.** a karakul sheep. ■ the fleece or wool from a karakul lamb.

Broad•way /ˈbrôd,wā/ a street that runs the length of Manhattan in New York City, famous for its theaters; its name has become synonymous with the commercial theater business.

broad•way /ˈbrôd,wā/ ▶**n.** (usually in names) a large open or main road.

broast /brōst/ ▶**v.** prepare food using a cooking process that combines broiling and roasting.

Brob•ding•nag•i•an /,bräbdiNGˈnagēən/ ▶**adj.** gigantic. ▶**n.** a giant. [18th C.: from *Brobdingnag*, a land (in Swift's *Gulliver's Travels*) where everything is of huge size.]

bro•cade /brōˈkād/ ▶**n.** a rich fabric, usually silk, woven with a raised pattern, typically with gold or silver thread. ▶**v.** [trans.] [usu. as adj.] (**brocaded**) weave (something) with this design: *a brocaded blanket.* [16th C.: from Sp. and Port. *brocado*, from Ital. *broccato*, from *brocco* 'twisted thread.']

Bro•ca's ar•e•a /ˈbrōkəz/ ▶**n.** Anat. a region of the brain concerned with the production of speech, located in the cortex of the dominant frontal lobe. [19th C.: P. Paul *Broca* (1824–80), French surgeon.]

broc•co•li /ˈbräk(ə)lē/ ▶**n.** a cabbage of a variety similar to the cauliflower, bearing heads of green or purplish flower buds. ■ the flower stalk and head eaten as a vegetable. [17th C.: from Ital., pl. of *broccolo* 'cabbage sprout,' dimin. of *brocco* 'shoot,' based on L. *brocchus, broccus* 'projecting.']

broc•co•li rabe /räb/ (also **broc•co•li raab**) ▶**n.** a leafy green vegetable with broccolilike buds and bitter-flavored greens.

bro•chette /brōˈSHet/ ▶**n.** a skewer or spit on which chunks of meat or fish are barbecued, grilled, or roasted: *beef and lamb en brochette.* ■ a dish of meat or fish chunks cooked in such a way. [Fr., dimin. of *broche* (see BROACH[1]).]

bro•chure /brōˈSHo͝or/ ▶**n.** a small book or magazine containing pictures and information about a product or service. [18th C.: from Fr., lit. 'something stitched,' from *brocher* (see BROACH[1]).]

Brock•en /ˈbräkən/ highest peak in the Harz Mountains, in central Germany; 3,747 feet (1,143 m).

brock•et /ˈbräkit/ (also **brocket deer**) ▶**n.** a small deer (genus *Mazama*) of Central and South America, with short, straight antlers. [ME: from Anglo-Norman Fr. *broquet*, dimin. of *broque*, var. of *broche* (see BROOCH).]

Brock•ton /ˈbräktən/ a city in southeastern Massachusetts; pop. 94,304.

Brod•sky /ˈbrädskē; ˈbrät-/, Joseph (1940–96), US poet; born in Russia; born *Iosif Aleksandrovich Brodsky*. He was the poet laureate of the US 1991. Nobel Prize for Literature (1987).

bro•gan /ˈbrōgən/ ▶**n.** a coarse, stout leather shoe reaching to the ankle. [19th C.: from Irish *brógán*, Scot. Gael. *brógan*, lit. 'small brogue.']

brogue[1] /brōg/ ▶**n.** a strong outdoor shoe with ornamental perforated patterns in the leather. ■ hist. a rough shoe of untanned leather, formerly worn in parts of Ireland and the Scottish Highlands. [16th C.: from Scot. Gael. and Irish *bróg*, from ON *brók* (rel. to BREECH).]

brogue[2] ▶**n.** [usu. in sing.] a marked accent, esp. Irish or Scottish, when speaking English. [18th C.: perh. from BROGUE[1].]

broi•der /ˈbroidər/ ▶**v.** [trans.] archaic ornament with embroidery.

broil[1] /broil/ ▶**v.** [trans.] cook (meat or fish) by exposure to direct, intense heat: *he broiled a wedge of sea bass* | [as adj.] (**broiled**) *a broiled sirloin steak.* ■ [intrans.] become very hot, esp. from the sun: *the countryside lay broiling in the sun.* [ME: from OFr. *bruler* 'to burn.']

broil[2] ▶**n.** archaic a quarrel or a commotion. [16th C.: from obs. *broil* 'to muddle.']

broil•er /ˈbroilər/ ▶**n. 1** (also **broil•er chick•en**) a young chicken suitable for roasting, grilling, or barbecuing. **2** a gridiron, grill, or special part of a stove for broiling meat or fish.

broke /brōk/ past (and archaic past participle) of BREAK. ▶**adj.** [predic.] informal having completely run out of money.
– PHRASES **go for broke** informal risk everything in an all-out effort.

bro•ken /ˈbrōkən/ past participle of BREAK. ▶**adj. 1** having been fractured or damaged and no longer in one piece or in working order. ■ rejected, defeated, or despairing. ■ sick or weakened. ■ (of a relationship) ended, typically by betrayal or faithlessness. ■ disrupted or divided. ■ (of an agreement or promise) not observed by one of the parties involved. **2** having gaps or intervals that break a continuity. ■ having an uneven and rough surface. ■ (of speech or a language) spoken falteringly and with many mistakes, as by a foreigner. ■ halting, as if overcome by emotion.
– PHRASES **broken record** a scratched record that repeats the same brief passage over and over. — **bro•ken•ly adv. bro•ken•ness n.**

Bro•ken Ar•row a city in northeastern Oklahoma, southeast of Tulsa; pop. 74,859.

bro•ken-down ▶**adj.** [attrib.] worn out and dilapidated by age, use, or ill-treatment. ■ (of a machine or vehicle) not functioning due to a mechanical failure. ■ (of a horse) with serious damage to the legs, in particular the tendons.

bro•ken-field Football ▶**adj.** relating to or occurring in the area beyond the line of scrimmage where defenders are relatively scattered. ■ informal (of a movement) with starts, stops, and changes of direction, in the manner of a broken-field ballcarrier.

bro•ken-heart•ed ▶**adj.** overwhelmed by grief or disappointment.

Bro•ken Hill 1 a town in New South Wales, Australia, a lead, silver, and zinc mining center; pop. 23,260. **2** former name (1904–65) for KABWE.

bro•ken home ▶**n.** a family in which the parents are divorced or separated.

bro•ken wind /wind/ ▶**n.** another term for COPD in horses. — **bro•ken-wind•ed adj.**

bro·ker /'brōkər/ ▶ **n.** a person who buys and sells goods or assets for others. ▶ **v.** [trans.] arrange or negotiate (a settlement, deal, or plan): *attempts to broker a cease-fire.* [ME: from Anglo-Norman Fr. *brocour.*]

bro·ker·age /'brōkərij/ ▶ **n.** the business or service of acting as a broker. ■ a fee or commission charged by a broker. ■ a company that buys or sells goods or assets for clients.

bro·ker-deal·er ▶ **n.** a brokerage firm that buys and sells securities on its own account as a principal before selling the securities to customers.

Brom·berg /'brämbərg/ German name for **Bydgoszcz**.

brome /brōm/ ▶ **n.** an oatlike grass (genus *Bromus*) sometimes grown for fodder or ornamental purposes. [18th C.: from mod. L. *Bromus*, from Gk. *bromos* 'oat.']

bro·me·li·ad /brō'mēlē,ad/ ▶ **n.** a plant (*Bromelia* and other genera, family Bromeliaceae) of tropical and subtropical America, typically having short stems with rosettes of stiff, usually spiny, leaves. Some kinds are epiphytic, and many are cultivated as houseplants. [19th C.: from mod. L. *Bromelia* (after Olaf *Bromel* (1639–1705), Swedish. botanist).]

bro·mic ac·id /'brōmik/ ▶ **n.** Chem. a strongly oxidizing acid, $HBrO_3$, known only in aqueous solutions. — **bro·mate** /'brōmāt/ **n.**

bro·mide /'brōmīd/ ▶ **n. 1** Chem. a compound of bromine with another element or group, esp. a salt containing the anion Br– or an organic compound with bromine bonded to an alkyl radical. ■ dated a sedative preparation containing potassium bromide. **2** a trite and unoriginal idea or remark, typically intended to soothe or placate. — **bro·mid·ic** /brō'midik/ **adj.** (in sense 2).

bro·min·ate /'brōmə,nāt/ ▶ **v.** [trans.] treat with bromine. ■ [usu. as adj.] (**brominated**) introduce one or more bromine atoms into a compound or molecule, usually in place of hydrogen. — **bro·mi·na·tion n.**

bro·mine /'brōmēn/ ▶ **n.** the chemical element of atomic number 35, a dark red fuming toxic liquid with a choking, irritating smell. It is a member of the halogen group and occurs chiefly as salts in seawater and brines. (Symbol: **Br**) [19th C.: from Fr. *brome*, from Gk. *brōmos* 'a stink.']

bro·mism /'brō,mizəm/ ▶ **n.** dated a condition of dullness and weakness due to excessive intake of bromide sedatives.

bromo- (usu. **brom-** before a vowel) ▶ **comb. form** Chem. representing **bromine**.

Bromp·ton cock·tail /'brämptən/ ▶ **n.** a powerful painkiller and sedative consisting of vodka or other liquor laced with morphine and sometimes also cocaine. [20th C.: said to be after *Brompton* Hospital, London.]

bronc /bräNGk/ ▶ **n.** informal short for **bronco**.

bron·chi /'bräNGkī; -kē/ plural form of **bronchus**.

bron·chi·a /'bräNGkēə/ ▶ **n.** rare the ramifications of the two main bronchi in the lungs.

bron·chi·al /'bräNGkēəl/ ▶ **adj.** of or relating to the bronchi or bronchioles.

bron·chi·al tube ▶ **n.** a bronchus or a primary branch off of one.

bron·chi·ec·ta·sis /,bräNGkē'ektəsis/ ▶ **n.** Med. abnormal widening of the bronchi or their branches, causing a risk of infection. [19th C.: from Gk. *bronkhia* (branches of the bronchi) + *ektasis* 'dilatation.']

bron·chi·ole /'bräNGkē,ōl/ ▶ **n.** Anat. any of the minute branches into which a bronchus divides. — **bron·chi·o·lar** /,bräNGkē'ōlər/ **adj.** [19th C.: from mod. L. *bronchiolus, bronchiolum*, diminutives of late L. *bronchia*, denoting the branches of the bronchi.]

bron·chi·tis /bräNG'kītis/ ▶ **n.** inflammation of the mucous membrane in the bronchial tubes. — **bron·chit·ic** /bräNG'kitik/ **adj. & n.**

bron·chi·um /'bräNGkēəm/ ▶ **n.** a bronchial tube smaller than a bronchus and larger than a bronchiole.

broncho- ▶ **comb. form** of or relating to the bronchi: *bronchopneumonia.* [from Gk. *bronkho-*, from *bronkhos* (see **bronchus**).]

bron·cho·di·la·tor /,bräNGkōdī'lātər; -di-; -'dīlātər/ ▶ **n.** Med. a drug that causes widening of the bronchi, e.g., any of those taken by inhalation for the alleviation of asthma.

bron·cho·pneu·mo·nia /,bräNGkōn(y)o͝o'mōnēə; -'mōnyə/ ▶ **n.** inflammation of the lungs, arising in the bronchi or bronchioles.

bron·cho·scope /'bräNGkə,skōp/ ▶ **n.** a fiber-optic cable that is passed into the windpipe in order to view the bronchi. — **bron·chos·co·py** /bräNG'käskəpē/ **n.**

bron·cho·spasm /'bräNGkə,spazəm/ ▶ **n.** Med. spasm of bronchial smooth muscle producing narrowing of the bronchi.

bron·chus /'bräNGkəs/ ▶ **n.** (pl. **-chi** /-kī; -kē/) any of the major air passages of the lungs that diverge from the windpipe. [17th C.: from late L., from Gk. *bronkhos* 'windpipe.']

bron·co /'bräNGkō/ ▶ **n.** (pl. **-cos**) a wild or half-tamed horse, esp. of the western US. [19th C.: from Sp., lit. 'rough, rude.']

bron·co·bust·er /'bräNGkō,bəstər/ ▶ **n.** informal a cowboy who breaks in wild or half-tamed horses.

Bron·të /'bräntē; -tā/ a family of English writers. Charlotte (1816–55) wrote *Jane Eyre* (1847). Her sister Emily (1818–48) wrote *Wuthering Heights* (1847). Their sister Anne (1820–49) authored *Agnes Grey* (1845). See also **Bell**[2].

bron·to·saur /'bräntə,sôr/ (also **bron·to·sau·rus** /,bräntə'sôrəs/) ▶ **n.** another, chiefly former, term for **apatosaur**. — **bron·to·sau·ri·an** /,bräntə'sôrēən/ **adj.** [mod. L., from Gk. *brontē* 'thunder' + *sauros* 'lizard.']

Bronx /bräNGks/ a borough in northeastern New York City, only borough on the mainland; pop. 1,332,650.

Bronx cheer ▶ **n.** a sound of derision or contempt made by blowing through closed lips with the tongue between them; a raspberry. [1920s: **Bronx**.]

bronze /bränz/ ▶ **n.** a yellowish-brown alloy of copper with up to one-third tin. ■ a yellowish-brown color. ■ a work of sculpture or other object made of bronze. ■ short for **bronze medal**. ▶ **adj.** made of or colored like bronze. ▶ **v.** [trans.] (usu. **be bronzed**) make (a person or part of the body) suntanned: *Alison was bronzed by outdoor life* | [as adj.] (**bronzed**) *bronzed arms.* ■ give a surface of bronze or something resembling bronze to. — **bronz·y adj.** [17th C.: from Fr. *bronze* (n.), *bronzer* (v.), from Ital. *bronzo*, prob. from Pers. *birinj* 'brass.']

Bronze Age a prehistoric period that followed the Stone Age and preceded the Iron Age, when certain weapons and tools came to be made of bronze rather than stone.

bronze med·al ▶ **n.** a medal made of bronze, customarily awarded for third place in a race or competition.

Bronze Star ▶ **n.** a US military decoration awarded for heroic or meritorious achievement not involving participation in aerial flight.

brooch /brōCH; bro͞oCH/ ▶ **n.** an ornament fastened to clothing with a hinged pin and catch. [ME: var. of *broach*, orig. 'skewer,' from OFr. *broche* 'spit,' based on L. *brocchus, broccus* 'projecting.']

brood /bro͞od/ ▶ **n.** a family of young animals, esp. of a bird, produced at one hatching or birth. ■ bee or wasp larvae. ■ informal all of the children in a family. ■ a group of things or people having a similar character. ▶ **v. 1** [intrans.] think deeply about something that makes one unhappy: *he brooded over his need to find a wife.* **2** [trans.] (of a bird) sit on (eggs) to hatch them. ■ (of a fish, frog, or invertebrate) hold (developing eggs) within the body. **3** [usu. foll. by over] (of silence, a storm, etc.) hang or hover closely: *a storm broods over the lake.* ▶ **adj.** [attrib.] (of an animal) kept to be used for breeding. [OE *brōd*, of Gmc. origin; rel. to Ger. *Brut*, also to **breed**.]

brood·er /'bro͞odər/ ▶ **n. 1** a heated house for chicks or piglets. **2** a person who broods about something.

brood·ing /'bro͞odiNG/ ▶ **adj.** showing deep unhappiness of thought. ■ appearing darkly menacing. — **brood·ing·ly adv.**

brood·y /'bro͞odē/ ▶ **adj.** (**brood·i·er, brood·i·est**) **1** (of a hen) wishing or inclined to incubate eggs. ■ informal (of a woman) having a strong desire to have a baby. **2** thoughtful and unhappy. — **brood·i·ly adv. brood·i·ness n.**

brook[1] /bro͝ok/ ▶ **n.** a small stream. — **brook·let** /-lit/ **n.** [OE *brōc*, rel. to Ger. *Bruch* 'marsh.']

brook[2] ▶ **v.** [trans.] [with negative] formal tolerate or allow (something, typically dissent or opposition): *Jenny would brook no criticism of Matthew.* [OE *brūcan* 'use, possess,' of Gmc. origin; rel. to Ger. *brauchen.*]

Brooke[1] /bro͝ok/, Edward William, III (1919–), US politician. A Republican from Massachusetts, he was the first African American to be elected to the US Senate (1966) by popular vote. He served until 1979.

Brooke[2], Rupert Chawner (1887–1915), English poet, noted for his World War I poetry, including *1914 and Other Poems* (1915).

Brook Farm an experimental commune in West Roxbury, Massachusetts set up by a group of US writers in the 1840s.

Brook·field /'bro͝ok,fēld/ a city in southeastern Wisconsin; pop. 35,184.

Brook·ha·ven /'bro͝ok,hāvən/ a town in New York, in eastern Long Island; pop. 407,779.

Brook·line /'bro͝ok,līn/ a town in eastern Massachusetts, on the west side of Boston; pop. 54,718.

Brook·lyn /'bro͝oklən/ a borough of New York City, at the southwestern corner of Long Island; pop. 2,465,326.

Brook·lyn Bridge a suspension bridge between southern Manhattan and northern Brooklyn in New York City, opened in 1883.

Brook·lyn·ese /,bro͝oklə'nēz; -'nēs/ ▶ **n.** a form of New York speech associated esp. with Brooklyn.

Brook·lyn Park a city in southeastern Minnesota; pop. 67,388.

Brook·ner /'bro͝oknər/, Anita (1928–), English writer. Her novels include *Hotel du Lac* (1984).

Brooks[1] /bro͝oks/, Cleanth (1906–94), US teacher and critic. A leading proponent of the New Criticism movement, he edited *The Southern Review* 1935–42 and taught at Yale University 1947–75.

Brooks[2], Gwendolyn (1917– 2000), US poet. She was the first African-American woman named as poetry consultant to the Library of Congress 1985–86.

Brooks Range /bro͝oks/ a mountain chain that extends across northern Alaska, the northwestern end of the Rocky Mountains.

brook trout ▶ **n.** see **char**[3].

broom /bro͞om; bro͝om/ ▶ **n. 1** a long-handled brush of bristles or twigs used for sweeping. **2** a shrub (genera *Cytisus* and *Genista*) of the pea family, with long, thin green stems and a profusion of flowers. [OE *brōm* (sense 2), of Gmc. origin; rel. to Du. *braam*, also to **bramble**.]

broom·corn /'bro͞om,kôrn; 'bro͝om-/ ▶ **n.** a variety of sorghum whose dried inflorescences are used to make brooms.

broom·rape /ˈbro͞omˌrāp; ˈbro͝om-/ ▶n. a parasitic plant (genus *Orobanche*, family Orobanchaceae) that bears tubular flowers on a leafless brown stem. It is attached by its tubers to the roots of a host plant. [16th C.: from BROOM + L. *rapum* 'tuber.']

broom·stick /ˈbro͞omˌstik; ˈbro͝om-/ ▶n. the long handle of a broom. ▪ a broom on which, in children's literature, witches are said to fly.

Bros. ▶plural n. brothers (in names of companies).

broth /bräTH; brôTH/ ▶n. **1** soup consisting of meat or vegetable chunks, and often rice, cooked in stock. ▪ meat or fish stock. **2** Microbiol. liquid medium containing proteins and other nutrients for the culture of bacteria. ▪ a liquid mixture for the preservation of tissue. [OE, of Gmc. origin; rel. to BREW.]

broth·el /ˈbräTHəl; ˈbrôTHəl/ ▶n. a house where men can visit prostitutes. [16th C.: from ME *brothel* 'prostitute,' rel. to OE *brēothan* 'deteriorate.']

broth·er /ˈbrəT͟Hər/ ▶n. **1** a man or boy in relation to other sons and daughters of his parents. ▪ a half-brother, stepbrother, or foster brother. ▪ a brother-in-law. ▪ a male associate or fellow member of an organization. ▪ informal a black man (chiefly used as a term of address among black people). ▪ a fellow human being. ▪ a thing that resembles or is connected to another thing. **2** (pl. also **breth·ren**) Christian Church a (male) fellow Christian. ▪ a member of a religious order or congregation of men: *a Benedictine brother.* ▶exclam. used to express annoyance or surprise. — **broth·er·li·ness** n. **broth·er·ly** adj. [OE *brōthor*, from Indo-Eur.; akin to Ger. *Bruder*, L. *frater*.]

broth·er·hood /ˈbrəT͟Hərˌho͝od/ ▶n. **1** the relationship between brothers. ▪ the feeling of kinship with and closeness to a group of people or all people. **2** an association, society, or community of people linked by a common interest, religion, or trade. ▪ a trade union. [ME: prob. from obs. *brotherred* (based on OE *-rǣden* 'condition'; compare KINDRED).]

broth·er-in-law ▶n. (pl. **broth·ers-in-law**) the brother of one's wife or husband. ▪ the husband of one's sister or sister-in-law.

brough·am /ˈbro͞oəm; ˈbrōəm/ ▶n. hist. a horse-drawn carriage with a roof, four wheels, and an open driver's seat in front. [19th C.: Lord *Brougham* (1778–1868).]

brought /brôt/ past and past participle of BRING.

brou·ha·ha /ˈbro͞ohäˌhä; bro͞oˈhähä/ ▶n. [usu. in sing.] a noisy and overexcited critical response, display of interest, or trail of publicity. [19th C.: from Fr., prob. imitative.]

Brou·wer /ˈbrou-ər/, Adriaen (*c.*1605–38), Flemish painter. He was an important link between Dutch and Flemish genre painting.

brow[1] /brou/ ▶n. **1** a person's forehead. ▪ (usu. **brows**) an eyebrow. **2** the summit of a hill or pass. — **-browed** adj. [in comb.] *furrow-browed.* [OE *brū* 'eyelash, eyebrow,' of Gmc. origin.]

brow[2] ▶n. a gangway from a ship to the shore. ▪ a hinged part of a ferry or landing craft forming a landing platform or ramp. [19th C.: prob. from Norw. *bru*, from ON *brú* 'bridge.']

brow·beat /ˈbrouˌbēt/ ▶v. (past **-beat**; past part. **-beat·en**) [trans.] intimidate (someone), typically into doing something, with stern or abusive words: *a witness is being browbeaten under cross-examination.*

Brown[1] /broun/, Ford Madox (1821–93), English painter. He also designed stained glass and furniture.

Brown[2], Helen Gurley (1922–), US editor and writer. She was editor in chief of *Cosmopolitan* magazine 1972–97 and author of *Sex and the Single Girl* (1962).

Brown[3], Henry Billings (1836–1913), US Supreme Court associate justice 1890–1906.

Brown[4], John (1800–59), US abolitionist. In 1859 he was executed after raiding an arsenal at Harpers Ferry, Virginia (later part of West Virginia), with the intention of arming slaves and starting a revolt.

Brown[5], Lancelot (1716–83), English landscape architect; known as **Capability Brown**. He evolved a style of natural-looking landscape parks.

brown /broun/ ▶adj. of a color produced by mixing red, yellow, and black, as of dark wood or rich soil. ▪ dark-skinned or suntanned. ▪ (of bread) made from a dark, unsifted, or unbleached flour. ▶n. brown color or pigment. ▪ brown clothes or material. ▶v. make or become brown, typically by cooking: [trans.] *food has been browned* | [intrans.] *bake until the cheese has browned.*

– PHRASES **(as) brown as a berry** (of a person) very suntanned. **do something up brown** do something thoroughly or completely. — **brown·ish** adj. **brown·ness** n. **brown·y** adj. [OE *brūn*, of Gmc. origin; rel. to Ger. *braun*.]

brown al·gae ▶plural n. algae (class Phaeophyceae, phylum Heterokonta) belonging to a large group that includes many seaweeds, typically olive brown or greenish in color. They contain xanthophyll in addition to chlorophyll.

brown bag ▶n. a bag made of opaque brown paper. ▪ a bag of such a kind in which a lunch is packed and carried to work, school, or informal functions. ▶v. [trans.] **(brown bag it)** take a packed lunch to work or school: *no school lunch, so I'm brown-bagging it.* — **brown bag·ger** n.

brown bag·ging ▶n. **1** the practice of bringing one's own packed lunch to work. **2** the practice of bringing one's own liquor to a restaurant or club that may supply setups but cannot sell alcoholic beverages.

brown bear ▶n. a large bear (*Ursus arctos*) with a coat color ranging from cream to black, occurring chiefly in forests in Eurasia and North America.

brown belt ▶n. a brown belt marking a high level of proficiency in judo, karate, or other martial arts, below that of a black belt. ▪ a person qualified to wear such a belt.

brown bet·ty ▶n. a baked pudding made with apples or other fruit and breadcrumbs.

brown coal ▶n. another term for LIGNITE.

brown dwarf ▶n. Astron. a celestial object intermediate in size between a giant planet and a small star, believed to emit mainly infrared radiation.

brown fat ▶n. a dark-colored adipose tissue with many blood vessels, involved in the rapid production of heat in hibernating animals and human babies.

brown·field /ˈbrounˌfēld/ ▶adj. [attrib.] (of an urban site for potential building development) having had previous development on it. Compare with GREENFIELD. ▶n. a former industrial or commercial site where future use is affected by real or perceived environmental contamination.

Brown·i·an mo·tion /ˈbrounēən/ ▶n. Physics the erratic random movement of microscopic particles in a fluid, as a result of continuous bombardment from molecules of the surrounding medium. [19th C.: Robert *Brown* (1773–1858), Scottish botanist.]

Brown·ie /ˈbrounē/ ▶n. (pl. **-ies**) **1** a member of the junior branch of the Girl Scouts, for girls aged between about 6 and 8. [named for the brownie elf emblem on the beanie hat that is part of the uniform.] **2** **(brownie)** a small square of rich cake, typically chocolate. **3** **(brownie)** a benevolent elf supposed to haunt houses and do housework secretly. [dimin. of BROWN; a "wee brown man" often appears in Scottish fairy tales.]

– PHRASES **brownie point** informal, humorous an imaginary award given to someone who does good deeds or tries to please.

Brown·ing[1] /ˈbrouniNG/ English poets. Elizabeth Barrett (1806–61) is noted for her *Sonnets of the Portuguese* (1850). Her husband, Robert (1812–89), established his name with *Dramatic Lyrics* (1842), which contained "The Pied Piper of Hamelin."

Brown·ing[2] ▶n. (also **Browning machine gun**) a type of water-cooled automatic machine gun. ▪ (also **Browning automatic**) a type of automatic pistol. ▪ (also **Browning automatic rifle**) a gas-operated automatic rifle, typically fired from a bipod. [20th C.: J. M. *Browning* (1855–1926), US designer of the weapons.]

brown-nose (also **brown·nose**) informal ▶n. (also **brown-nos·er**) a person who acts in a grossly obsequious way. ▶v. [trans.] curry favor with (someone) by acting in such a way: *academics were brown-nosing the senior faculty* | [intrans.] *I was not brown-nosing.*

brown·out /ˈbrounˌout/ ▶n. a partial blackout.

brown owl ▶n. another term for TAWNY OWL.

brown rat ▶n. a rat (*Rattus norvegicus*) found throughout the world, often regarded as a pest. Commonly kept as a laboratory animal, it is also bred in the albino form. Also called COMMON RAT, NORWAY RAT.

brown rec·luse (also **brown rec·luse spi·der**) ▶n. a brown venomous North American spider (*Loxosceles reclusa*, family Loxoscelidae), with a dark brown violin-shaped marking on the top of its orange-yellow head.

brown rice ▶n. unpolished rice with only the husk of the grain removed.

brown rot ▶n. a fungal disease causing the rotting and browning of parts of plants, in particular a disease of certain fruits (caused by fungi of the genus *Monilinia*, phylum Ascomycota).

brown sauce ▶n. a savory sauce made with fat and flour cooked to a brown color.

Brown·shirt /ˈbrounˌSHərt/ ▶n. esp. hist. a member of an early Nazi militia founded by Hitler in Munich in 1921, with brown uniforms resembling those of Mussolini's Blackshirts. Also called STORM TROOPS.

brown·stone /ˈbrounˌstōn/ ▶n. a kind of reddish-brown sandstone used for building. ▪ a building faced with such sandstone.

brown sug·ar ▶n. unrefined or partially refined sugar.

Browns·ville a city in southern Texas, on the Rio Grande and the Mexican border; pop. 98,962.

Brown Swiss ▶n. an animal of a brown breed of dairy cattle, originally bred in Switzerland.

brown-tail (also **brown-tail moth**) ▶n. a white moth (*Euproctis chrysorrhoea*, family Lymantriidae) with a brown tip on the abdomen. A pest of tree foliage, its caterpillars live communally in web tents and bear irritant hairs.

brown trout ▶n. (pl. same) the common trout (*Salmo trutta*) of Europe, a commonly stocked game fish in North America.

browse /brouz/ ▶v. [intrans.] **1** survey objects casually, esp. goods for sale: *he stopped to browse around a sporting goods store.* ▪ scan through a book or magazine superficially to gain an impression of the contents: *she browsed through the newspaper* | [trans.] *patrons can browse the shelves of the library.* ▪ [trans.] Comput. read or survey (data files), typically via a network. **2** (of an animal) feed on leaves, twigs, or other high-growing vegetation. ▶n. **1** [in sing.] an act of casual looking or reading. **2** vegetation, such as twigs and young shoots, eaten by animals. — **brows·a·ble** adj. [ME (sense 2 of the v.): from OFr. *broster*, from *brost* 'young shoot,' prob. of Gmc. origin.]

brows·er /ˈbrouzər/ ▶n. a person who looks casually through books or magazines or at things for sale. ▪ an animal that feeds mainly on high-growing vegetation. ▪ Comput. a program with a graphical user interface for displaying HTML files, used to navigate the World Wide Web.

brrr /bər/ ▶ **exclam.** used to express someone's reaction to feeling cold: *Brrr! It's a freezing cold day.*

Bruce[1] /brōōs/, Lenny (1925–66), US comedian; born *Leonard Alfred Schneider*. He flouted the bounds of respectability with his humor and was imprisoned for obscenity in 1961.

Bruce[2], Robert the, see **Robert** I.

bru·cel·lo·sis /ˌbrōōsəˈlōsis/ ▶ **n.** a bacterial disease typically affecting cattle and humans, caused esp. by the bacteria *Brucella abortus*. See also **undulant fever**. [1930s: from mod. L. *Brucella*: after Sir David *Bruce* (1855–1931), Scottish physician.]

bru·cine /ˈbrōōsēn; -sin/ ▶ **n.** a highly toxic alkaloid, $C_{23}H_{26}N_2O_4$, present in nux vomica.

Brue·gel /ˈbroigəl/ (also **Breu·ghel** or **Brue·ghel**) a family of Flemish painters. Pieter (*c.*1525–69), known as **Pieter Bruegel the Elder**, produced landscapes, religious allegories, and satires of peasant life. His son Pieter Bruegel the Younger, known as **Hell Bruegel**, is noted for his paintings of devils. Another son, Jan (1564–1638), known as **Velvet**, painted flower, landscape, and mythological pictures.

Bru·ges /brōōzh/ a city in northwestern Belgium, capital of the province of West Flanders; pop. 117,000. Flemish name **Brugge**.

Brug·ge /ˈbrʏgə/ Flemish name for **Bruges**.

bru·in /ˈbrōōin/ ▶ **n.** a bear, esp. in children's fables. [15th C.: from Du. *bruin* (see **brown**); name of the bear in 13th-cent. fable *Reynard the Fox.*]

bruise /brōōz/ ▶ **n.** an injury appearing as an area of discolored skin on the body, caused by a blow or impact rupturing underlying blood vessels. ■ a similar area of damage on a fruit, vegetable, or plant. ▶ **v.** [trans.] [often as adj.] (**bruised**) inflict such an injury on (someone or something): *a bruised knee.* ■ hurt (someone's feelings). ■ [intrans.] be susceptible to bruising: *potatoes bruise easily.* ■ crush or pound (something): *bruise the raisins before adding.* [OE *brȳsan* 'injure,' reinforced in ME by OFr. *bruisier* 'break.']

bruis·er /ˈbrōōzər/ ▶ **n.** informal, derog. a person who is tough and aggressive and enjoys a fight or argument. ■ a professional boxer.

bruis·ing /ˈbrōōziNG/ ▶ **adj.** causing a bruise or bruises. ■ fig. (of an antagonistic or competitive situation) conducted in an aggressive way and likely to have a stressful effect on those involved. ▶ **n.** bruises on the skin.

bruit /brōōt/ ▶ **v.** [with obj. and adverbial] spread (a report or rumor) widely: *I didn't want to have our relationship* ***bruited about*** *the office.* ▶ **n. 1** archaic a report or rumor. **2** a sound, typically an abnormal one, heard through a stethoscope; a murmur. [ME: from OFr. *bruit* 'noise,' from *bruire* 'to roar.']

bru·mal /ˈbrōōməl/ ▶ **adj.** literary of or relating to winter; wintry.

brume /brōōm/ ▶ **n.** literary mist or fog. [18th C.: from Fr., from L. *bruma* 'winter.']

Brum·ma·gem /ˈbrəməjəm/ (also **brum·ma·gem**) ▶ **adj.** [attrib.] cheap, showy, or counterfeit. [17th C.: dial. form of **Birmingham**, England.]

Brum·mell /ˈbrəməl/, George Bryan (1778–1840), English dandy; known as **Beau Brummell**. He was the arbiter of British fashion for the early 19th century.

brunch /brənCH/ ▶ **n.** a late morning meal eaten instead of breakfast and lunch. [19th C.: blend of **breakfast** and **lunch**.]

Brundt·land /ˈbrōōntˌländ/, Gro Harlem (1939–), prime minister of Norway 1981, 1986–89, and 1990–96. She chaired the World Commission on Environment and Development (the Brundtland Commission) in the 1980s and was director-general of the World Health Organization 1998–2003.

Bru·nei /brōōˈnī; ˈbrōōnī/ a constitutional sultanate on the northwestern coast of Borneo. *See box.* — **Bru·nei·an** /-ˈnīən/ **adj. & n.**

Bru·nel /brōōˈnel/, Isambard Kingdom (1806–59), English engineer. He designed the *Great Western* (1838), the first transatlantic steamship.

Bru·nel·les·chi /ˌbrōōnlˈeskē/, Filippo (1377–1446), Italian architect; born *Filippo di Ser Brunellesco*. He is noted for the dome of Florence Cathedral (1420–61).

bru·nette /brōōˈnet/ (also **bru·net**) ▶ **adj.** having dark brown hair. ■ (of hair) dark brown. [16th C.: from Fr., fem. of *brunet*, dimin. of *brun* 'brown.']

brung /brəNG/ dialect past and past participle of **bring**.

Brun·hild /ˈbrōōnˌhild; -ˌhilt/ Germanic Mythol. in the Nibelungenlied, the wife of Gunther, who instigated the murder of Siegfried.

Bru·no /ˈbrōōnō/, Giordano (1548–1600), Italian philosopher. As a supporter of the heliocentric Copernican view of the solar system, he was tried by the Inquisition for heresy and burned at the stake.

Bru·no, St. /ˈbrōōnō; brʏˈnō/ (*c.*1032–1101), French clergyman, born in Germany. He founded the Carthusian order in 1084.

Bruns·wick /ˈbrənzwik/ a former duchy in central Germany, incorporated into Lower Saxony. German name **Braunschweig**. ■ the capital of this former duchy, a city in Lower Saxony, Germany; pop. 259,130.

Bruns·wick stew ▶ **n.** a stew originally made with squirrel or rabbit, but now consisting of chicken and vegetables including onion and tomatoes.

brunt /brənt/ ▶ **n.** (**the brunt**) the worst part or chief impact of a specified thing: *education will* ***bear the brunt of*** *the cuts.* [ME ('a blow'): of unknown origin.]

bru·schet·ta /brōōˈsketə/ ▶ **n.** toasted Italian bread drenched in olive oil and served typically with garlic or tomatoes.

brush[1] /brəsH/ ▶ **n. 1** an implement with a handle, consisting of bristles, hair, or wire set into a block, used for cleaning or scrubbing, applying a liquid or powder to a surface, arranging the hair, or other purposes. ■ an act of sweeping, applying, or arranging with such an implement or with one's hand. ■ (usu. **brushes**) a thin stick set with long wire bristles, used to make a soft hissing sound on drums or cymbals. ■ the bushy tail of a fox. **2** a slight and fleeting touch. ■ a brief and typically unpleasant or unwelcome encounter with someone or something. **3** a piece of carbon or metal serving as an electrical contact with a moving part in a motor or alternator. ▶ **v. 1** [with obj. and adverbial] remove (dust or dirt) by sweeping or scrubbing: *he brushed himself down.* ■ [trans.] use a brush or one's hand to remove dust or dirt from (something). ■ [trans.] clean (one's teeth) by scrubbing with a brush. ■ [trans.] arrange (one's hair) by running a brush through it. ■ [trans.] apply a liquid to (a surface) with a brush. ■ apply (a liquid or substance) to a surface. **2** [intrans.] touch lightly and gently: *stems of grass* ***brush against*** *her legs.* ■ (**brush past**) touch fleetingly and in passing. ■ [trans.] push (something) away with a quick movement of the hand. ■ [trans.] (**brush something aside**) dismiss (something) curtly and confidently. ■ [trans.] (**brush someone/something off**) dismiss in an abrupt, contemptuous way.

– PHRASAL VERBS **brush someone back** Baseball, informal (of a pitcher) force a batter to step back to avoid being hit by a ball pitched close to the body. **brush up on** improve one's previously good knowledge of or skill at a particular thing. — **brush·less adj.** esp. tech. [ME: n. from Old Fr. *broisse*; v. partly from OFr. *brosser* 'to sweep.']

brush[2] ▶ **n.** undergrowth, small trees, and shrubs. ■ land covered with such growth. ■ cut brushwood. [ME: from OFr. *broce*, perh. based on L. *bruscum*, 'excrescence on the maple.']

brush·back /ˈbrəsHˌbak/ (also **brushback pitch**) ▶ **n.** Baseball a pitch aimed close to the body so that the batter must step back to avoid it.

brushed /brəsHt/ ▶ **adj.** having been treated with a brush, in particular: ■ (of fabric) having a soft raised nap. ■ (of metal) finished with a nonreflective surface.

brush fire (also **brush·fire**) ▶ **n. 1** a fire in brush or scrub. **2** a conflict that arises suddenly and is limited in scale. ■ a minor crisis.

brush-off ▶ **n.** [in sing.] informal a rejection or dismissal in which someone is treated as unimportant.

brush wolf ▶ **n.** another term for **coyote**.

brush·wood /ˈbrəsHˌwŏŏd/ ▶ **n.** undergrowth, twigs, and small branches, typically used for firewood or kindling.

brush·work /ˈbrəsHˌwərk/ ▶ **n.** the way in which painters use their brush, as evident in their paintings.

brush·y /ˈbrəsHē/ ▶ **adj. 1** covered in or consisting of brushwood. **2** Art relating to or displaying bold use of the brush in painting.

brusque /brəsk/ ▶ **adj.** abrupt or offhand in speech or manner. — **brusque·ly adv. brusque·ness n. brus·que·rie** /ˌbrəskəˈrē; ˌbrōō-/ **n.** (archaic). [17th C.: from Fr., 'lively, fierce,' from Ital. *brusco* 'sour.']

Brunei

Official name: Negara Brunei Darussalam
Location: southeast Asia on the northwest coast of Borneo, divided by parts of Malaysia
Area: 2,000 square miles (5300 sq km)
Population: 365,000
Capital: Bandar Seri Begawan
Languages: Malay (official), English, Chinese
Currency: Bruneian dollar

Brus·sels /ˈbrəsəlz/ the capital of Belgium, in the central part of the country; pop. 954,000. French name **Bruxelles**; Flemish name **Brussel**.

Brus·sels car·pet ▶ **n.** a carpet with a heavy woolen pile and a strong linen back. [18th C.: **Brussels** in Belgium.]

Brus·sels lace ▶ **n.** an elaborate kind of lace, typically with a raised design, made using a needle or lace pillow.

Brus·sels sprout (also **brus·sels sprout**) ▶ **n.** a vegetable consisting of the small compact bud of a variety of cabbage. ■ the plant that yields this vegetable, bearing many such buds along a tall single stem.

brut /bro͞ot/ ▶ **adj.** (of sparkling wine) unsweetened; very dry. [19th C.: Fr., lit. 'raw, rough.']

bru·tal /ˈbro͞otl/ ▶ **adj.** savagely violent. ■ punishingly hard or uncomfortable. ■ without any attempt to disguise unpleasantness. — **bru·tal·i·ty** /bro͞oˈtalitē/ **n.** **bru·tal·ly** **adv.** [15th C. (in the sense 'relating to the lower animals'): from OFr., or from med. L. *brutalis*, from *brutus* 'dull, stupid' (see **brute**).]

bru·tal·ism /ˈbro͞otl,izəm/ ▶ **n.** a style of architecture or art characterized by a deliberate plainness, crudity, or violence of imagery. — **bru·tal·ist** **n. & adj.**

bru·tal·ize /ˈbro͞otl,īz/ ▶ **v.** [trans.] attack (someone) in a savage and violent way. ■ (often **be brutalized**) desensitize (someone) to the pain or suffering of others by exposing them to violent behavior or situations: *he had been brutalized in prison* | [as adj.] (**brutalizing**) *the brutalizing effects of warfare.* — **bru·tal·i·za·tion** /ˈbro͞otliˈzāsHən/ **n.**

brute /bro͞ot/ ▶ **n.** a savagely violent person or animal: *he was a cold-blooded brute.* ■ informal a cruel, unpleasant, or insensitive person. ■ an animal as opposed to a human being. ■ something awkward, difficult, or unpleasant. ▶ **adj.** [attrib.] unreasoning and animallike. ■ merely physical. ■ harsh, fundamental, or inescapable. [ME: from OFr. *brut(e)*, from L. *brutus* 'dull, stupid.']

brut·ish /ˈbro͞otisH/ ▶ **adj.** resembling or characteristic of a brute. — **brut·ish·ly** **adv.** **brut·ish·ness** **n.**

Bru·tus[1] /ˈbro͞otəs/, Lucius Junius, (6th century BC), legendary founder of the Roman Republic.

Bru·tus[2], Marcus Junius (85–42 BC), Roman senator. With Cassius he led the conspirators who assassinated Julius Caesar in 44.

Brux·elles /bryˈsel/ French name for **Brussels**.

brux·ism /ˈbrəksizəm/ ▶ **n.** the involuntary or habitual grinding of the teeth, typically during sleep. [1930s: from Gk. *brukhein* 'gnash the teeth.']

Bry·an[1] /ˈbrīən/ a city in east central Texas; pop. 55,002.

Bry·an[2], William Jennings (1860–1925), US secretary of state 1913–15. A three-time Democratic nominee for US president, he is best known as a prosecuting attorney in the 1925 Scopes Trial.

Bry·ansk /brēˈänsk/ (also **Bri·ansk**) a city in western Russia, on the Desna River; pop. 456,000.

Bry·ant /ˈbrīənt/, William Cullen (1794–1878), US poet. He was co-owner and editor of the *New York Evening Post* 1829–78; his poems include "Thanatopsis" (1811) and "To a Waterfowl" (1821).

Bryce Can·yon /brīs/ a region in south central Utah, site of a national park noted for unusual rock formations.

Bryl·creem /ˈbril,krēm/ ▶ **n.** trademark a cream used on men's hair to give it a smooth, shiny appearance. — **Bryl·creemed** **adj.**

bry·ol·o·gy /brīˈäləjē/ ▶ **n.** the study of mosses and liverworts. — **bry·o·log·i·cal** /,brīəˈläjikəl/ **adj.** **bry·ol·o·gist** /-jist/ **n.** [19th C.: from Gk. *bruon* 'moss.']

bry·o·ny /ˈbrīənē/ ▶ **n.** (pl. **-nies**) **1** (also **white bryony**) a climbing Eurasian plant (*Bryonia dioica*) of the gourd family, with greenish-white flowers and red berries. **2** (**black bryony**) a climbing European plant (*Tamus communis*) of the yam family, with broad glossy leaves, poisonous red berries, and black tubers. [OE, via L. from Gk. *bruōnia*.]

Bry·oph·y·ta /brīˈäfitə/ Bot. a division of small, simple plants (division Bryophyta) that comprises the mosses and liverworts. They lack flowers and roots, reproduce by spores released from a stalked capsule, and are anchored to the soil by specialized hairs. — **bry·o·phyte** /ˈbrīə,fīt/ **n.** [mod. L. (pl.), from Gk. *bruon* 'moss' + *phuta* 'plants.']

Bry·o·zo·a /,brīəˈzōə/ Zool. a phylum of sedentary aquatic invertebrates that comprises the moss animals. — **bry·o·zo·an** **n. & adj.** [mod. L. (pl.), from Gk. *bruon* 'moss' + *zōia* 'animals.']

Bry·thon·ic /briˈTHänik/ (also **Brit·ton·ic** /briˈtänik/) ▶ **adj.** denoting, relating to, or belonging to the southern group of Celtic languages, consisting of Welsh, Cornish, and Breton. Compare with **Goidelic**. Also called **P-Celtic**. ▶ **n.** these languages collectively. [from Welsh *Brython* 'Britons.']

Brześć nad Bu·giem /bəˈZHESHCH näd ˈbo͝ogyem/ Polish name for **Brest** (sense 2.)

BS ▶ **abbr.** ■ Bachelor of Science. ■ balance sheet. ■ Blessed Sacrament. ■ vulgar slang used as a euphemism for "bullshit."

BSA ▶ **abbr.** Boy Scouts of America.

BSc ▶ **abbr.** Bachelor of Science.

B-school ▶ **abbr.** business school.

BSE ▶ **abbr.** bovine spongiform encephalopathy, a usually fatal disease of cattle affecting the central nervous system, causing agitation and staggering. Also (popularly) called **mad cow disease**.

B-side ▶ **n.** the less important side of a pop single record.

BST ▶ **abbr.** ■ bovine somatotropin, esp. as a hormone injected in cattle.

Bt. ▶ **abbr.** Baronet.

B2B ▶ **abbr.** business-to-business, denoting trade conducted via the Internet between businesses.

B-tree ▶ **n.** Comput. an organizational structure for information storage and retrieval in the form of a tree in which all terminal nodes are the same distance from the base, and all nonterminal nodes have between *n* and 2*n* subtrees or pointers (where *n* is an integer).

Btu (also **BTU**) ▶ **abbr.** British thermal unit(s).

btw ▶ **abbr.** by the way.

bu. ▶ **abbr.** ■ bureau. ■ bushel(s).

Bual /bwäl; bo͞oˈäl/ ▶ **n.** a variety of wine grape grown chiefly in Madeira. ■ a Madeira wine of a medium sweet type made from such grapes. [from Port. *boal*.]

bub /bəb/ ▶ **n.** informal an aggressive or rude way of addressing a boy or man. [19th C.: from *bubby* (perh. a child's form of **brother**), or Ger. *Bube* 'boy.']

bu·bal /ˈbyo͞obəl/ ▶ **n.** a hartebeest (*Alcelaphus buselaphus buselaphus*), esp. one of an extinct race that was formerly found in North Africa. [18th C.: from Fr. *bubale*, via L. from Gk. *boubalos* 'antelope.']

bub·ba /ˈbəbə/ ▶ **n.** informal **1** used as an informal or affectionate form of address to a brother. **2** derog. a working-class white male of the rural South. [20th C.: alt. of **brother**.]

bub·ble /ˈbəbəl/ ▶ **n.** **1** a thin sphere of liquid enclosing air or another gas. ■ an air- or gas-filled spherical cavity in a liquid or a solidified liquid such as glass or amber. ■ fig. a state or feeling that is unstable and unlikely to last. ■ a brief, sudden, upward change from a general trend. **2** a transparent domed cover or enclosure. ■ a place or position of isolated safety: *seeing foreign ports from a bubble.* ▶ **v.** [intrans.] (of a liquid) contain bubbles of air or gas rising to the surface. ■ [often as adj.] (**bubbling**) make a sound resembling this: *a bubbling fountain.* ■ (**bubble with or over with**) fig. (of a person) be exuberantly filled with an irrepressible positive feeling. ■ (**bubble up**) fig. (esp. of a negative feeling) become more intense and approach the point of being vehemently expressed.

– PHRASES **burst someone's bubble** see **burst**. [ME: partly imitative, partly alt. of **burble**.]

bub·ble and squeak ▶ **n.** Brit. cooked cabbage fried with cooked potatoes and often meat.

bub·ble bath ▶ **n.** liquid, crystals, or powder added to bathwater to make it foam and have a fragrant smell. ■ a bath of water with such a substance added.

bub·ble cham·ber ▶ **n.** Physics an apparatus designed to make the tracks of ionizing particles visible as a row of bubbles in a liquid.

bub·ble e·con·o·my ▶ **n.** an unstable expanding economy; in particular, a period of heightened prosperity and increased commercial activity in Japan in the late 1980s brought about by artificially adjusted interest rates.

bub·ble·gum /ˈbəbəl,gəm/ ▶ **n.** **1** chewing gum that can be blown into bubbles. ■ (also **bubblegum pink**) the bright pink color of such gum: [as adj.] *bubblegum capri pants.* **2** [usu. as adj.] a thing considered to be insipid, simplistic, or adolescent in taste or style: *rockers hate bubblegum pop.*

bub·ble·head /ˈbəbəl,hed/ ▶ **n.** informal a foolish or empty-headed person.

bub·ble mem·o·ry ▶ **n.** Comput. a type of memory in which data is stored as a pattern of magnetized regions in a thin layer of magnetic material.

bub·ble pack ▶ **n.** another term for **bubble wrap**.

bub·bler /ˈbəb(ə)lər/ ▶ **n.** a drinking fountain.

bub·ble tea ▶ **n.** a cold, frothy drink made with iced tea, sweetened milk or other flavorings, and usually with sweet black balls or "pearls" made from tapioca. Also called **boba tea**, **pearl tea**.

bub·ble wrap (trademark **Bub·ble Wrap**) ▶ **n.** plastic packaging material in sheets containing numerous small air cushions designed to protect fragile goods.

bub·bly /ˈbəb(ə)lē/ ▶ **adj.** (**-bli·er**, **-bli·est**) containing bubbles. ■ fig. (of a person) full of cheerful high spirits. ▶ **n.** informal champagne.

Bu·ber /ˈbo͞obər/, Martin (1878–1965), Israeli philosopher; born in Austria. An existentialist, he wrote *I and Thou* (1923).

bu·bo /ˈb(y)o͞obō/ ▶ **n.** (pl. **-boes**) a swollen, inflamed lymph node in the armpit or groin. — **bu·bon·ic** /b(y)o͞oˈbänik/ **adj.** [ME: from L., from Gk. *boubōn* 'groin.']

bu·bon·ic plague ▶ **n.** the commonest form of plague in humans, characterized by fever, delirium, and the formation of buboes, caused by the bacterium *Yersinia pestis*, and transmitted by rat fleas.

buc·cal /ˈbəkəl/ ▶ **adj.** tech. of or relating to the mouth. ■ of or relating to the cheek. [19th C.: from L. *bucca* 'cheek.']

buc·ca·neer /,bəkəˈni(ə)r/ ▶ **n.** hist. a pirate, originally off the Spanish-American coasts. ■ a daring, adventurous, and sometimes reckless person, esp. in business. — **buc·ca·neer·ing** **adj.** [17th C.: from Fr. *boucanier*, from *boucan* 'a frame on which to cook or cure meat,' from Tupi *mukem*.]

buc·ci·na·tor /ˈbəksə,nātər/ ▶ **n.** Anat. a flat, thin muscle in the wall of the cheek. [17th C.: from L., from *buccinare* 'blow a trumpet,' from *buccina*, a trumpet.]

Bu·ceph·a·lus /byo͞oˈsefələs/ the favorite horse of Alexander the Great, who tamed the horse as a boy and took it with him on his campaigns until its death, after a battle, in 326 BC.

Bu·chan·an /byo͞oˈkanən/, James (1791–1868), 15th president of the US 1857–61. A Pennsylvania Democrat, he served as US congressman 1821–31, minister to Russia 1832–34, US senator 1834–45, US secretary of state 1845–49, and minister to Great Britain 1853–56. A pro-slavery president, he failed to quell the tensions that led to civil war.

Bu·cha·rest /ˈbo͞okəˌrest/ the capital of Romania, in the southeastern part of the country; pop. 2,343,800. Romanian name **Bucureşti**.

Bu·chen·wald /ˈbo͞okənˌwôld/ a Nazi concentration camp in World War II, near Weimar in central Germany.

Büch·ner /ˈbo͞oknər; ˈbo͞ok-/, Eduard (1860–1917), German chemist. He identified several enzymes, notably zymase. Nobel Prize for Chemistry (1907).

Buck /bək/, Pearl S. (1892–1973), US writer; full name *Pearl Sydenstricker Buck*. Her life in China inspired her early novels, including *The Good Earth* (1931). Nobel Prize for Literature (1938).

buck[1] /bək/ ▶ **n.** **1** the male of some antlered animals, esp. the fallow deer, roe deer, reindeer, and antelopes. Compare with **doe**. ■ a male hare, rabbit, ferret, rat, or kangaroo. **2** a vaulting horse. **3** a vertical jump performed by a horse, with the head lowered, back arched, and back legs thrown out behind. **4** a fashionable and typically hell-raising young man. **5** (**bucks**) an oxford shoe made of buckskin. ▶ **v.** **1** [intrans.] (of a horse) to perform a buck: *he's got to get his head down to buck* | [trans.] *she bucked them off*. ■ (of a vehicle) make sudden jerky movements. **2** [trans.] oppose or resist (something that seems oppressive or inevitable). **3** [trans.] informal make (someone) more cheerful: *Bella and Jim need me to buck them up* | [intrans.] (**buck up**) *buck up, kid, it's not the end of the world*. ▶ **adj.** military slang lowest of a particular rank. [OE, partly from *buc* 'male deer' (of Gmc. origin, related to Ger. *Bock*); reinforced by rel. *bucca* 'male goat.']

buck[2] ▶ **n.** informal a dollar.
– PHRASES **big bucks** a lot of money. **a fast** (or **quick**) **buck** easily and quickly earned money. [19th C.: of unknown origin.]

buck[3] ▶ **n.** an article placed as a reminder before a player whose turn it is to deal at poker.
– PHRASES **the buck stops here** (or **with someone**) informal the responsibility for something cannot or should not be passed to someone else. **pass the buck** informal shift the responsibility for something to someone else. [19th C.: from the use of a buck-handled knife to indicate the dealer in poker.]

buck-and-wing ▶ **n.** esp. hist. a lively solo tap dance, typically done in wooden-soled shoes.

buck·a·roo /ˌbəkəˈro͞o/ ▶ **n.** a cowboy. [19th C.: alt. of **vaquero**.]

buck·bean /ˈbəkˌbēn/ ▶ **n.** a trifoliate plant (*Menyanthes trifoliata*, family Menyanthaceae) of bogs and shallow water, with creeping rhizomes and white or pinkish hairy flowers. Also called **bogbean**. [16th C.: from Flemish *bocks boonen* 'goat's beans.']

buck·board /ˈbəkˌbôrd/ ▶ **n.** a horse-drawn carriage with the body formed by a plank fixed to the axles. [19th C.: from *buck* 'body of a cart' (perh. var. of obs. *bouk* 'belly').]

buck·brush /ˈbəkˌbrəsʜ/ ▶ **n.** coarse vegetation on which wild deer browse.

buck·e·roo ▶ **n.** var. of **buckaroo**.

buck·et /ˈbəkit/ ▶ **n.** a roughly cylindrical open container, typically made of metal or plastic, with a handle, used to hold and carry liquids or other material. ■ the contents of such a container or the amount it can contain. ■ (**buckets**) informal large quantities of liquid, typically rain or tears. ■ Basketball a basket. ■ Comput. a unit of data that can be transferred from a secondary storage in a single operation. ■ a compartment on the outer edge of a waterwheel. ■ the scoop of a dredger or grain elevator. ■ a scoop attached by two movable forks to the front of a loader, digger, or tractor. ▶ **v.** (**buck·et·ed, buck·et·ing**) [intrans.] **1** (**it buckets, it is bucketing**, etc.) informal rain heavily: *it was still bucketing down*. **2** [with adverbial of direction] (of a vehicle) move quickly and jerkily: *the car came bucketing out of a side road*.
– PHRASES **a drop in the bucket** see **drop**. **kick the bucket** see **kick**.
— **buck·et·ful** /-ˌfo͝ol/ **n.** (pl. **-fuls**). [ME: from Anglo-Norman Fr. *buquet* 'tub,' perh. from OE *būc* 'pitcher.']

buck·et bri·gade ▶ **n.** a line of people who pass buckets of water from one to another to put out a fire.

buck·et seat ▶ **n.** a seat in a car or aircraft with a rounded back to fit one person.

buck·et shop ▶ **n.** informal, derog. an unauthorized office for speculating in stocks or currency using the funds of unwitting investors.

buck·eye /ˈbəkˌī/ ▶ **n.** **1** a North American tree or shrub (genus *Aesculus*, family Hippocastanaceae), related to the horse chestnut, with showy yellow, red, or white flowers. **2** (also **buckeye butterfly**) an orange and brown New World butterfly (*Junonia coenia*, family Nymphalidae) with conspicuous eyespots on the wings. **3** (**Buckeye**) informal a native of the state of Ohio (with reference to Ohio's abundance of buckeye trees).

buck fe·ver ▶ **n.** nervousness felt by novice hunters when they first sight game.

buck·hound ▶ **n.** a staghound of a small breed.

buck·le /ˈbəkəl/ ▶ **n.** a flat, typically rectangular frame with a hinged pin, used for joining the ends of a belt or strap. ■ a similarly shaped ornament, esp. on a shoe. ▶ **v.** **1** [trans.] fasten or decorate with a buckle: *he buckled his belt*. ■ [intrans.] (**buckle up**) fasten one's seat belt in a car

buckeye butterfly

or aircraft. **2** [intrans.] bend and give way under pressure or strain: *the earth buckled under the stress*. [from Fr. *boucler* 'to bulge.'] ■ [trans.] bend (something) out of shape. ■ fig. (of a person) yield or collapse under pressure.
– PHRASAL VERBS **buckle down** tackle a task with determination. [ME: from OFr. *bocle*, from L. *buccula* 'cheek strap of a helmet,' from *bucca* 'cheek.']

buck·ler /ˈbək(ə)lər/ ▶ **n.** hist. a small, round shield held by a handle or worn on the forearm. [ME: from OFr. *(escu) bocler*, lit. '(shield) with a boss,' from *bocle* 'boss' (see **buckle**).]

Buck·ley /ˈbəklē/, William Frank, Jr. (1925–), US journalist. Founder of the politically conservative *National Review* magazine 1955, he hosted the television discussion program "Firing Line" 1966–99.

buck·min·ster·ful·ler·ene /ˌbəkminstərˈfo͝oləˌrēn/ ▶ **n.** Chem. a form of carbon having molecules of 60 atoms arranged in a polyhedron resembling a geodesic sphere. See also **fullerene**. [1980s: Richard *Buckminster Fuller* (see **Fuller**[3]).]

buck na·ked (also **buck-nak·ed**) ▶ **adj.** informal completely naked.

buck·o /ˈbəkō/ ▶ **n.** (pl. **-oes** or **-os**) informal a young man (often as a form of address). [19th C.: from **buck**[1].]

buck-pass·ing ▶ **n.** the practice of shifting the responsibility for something to someone else.

buck·ra /ˈbəkrə/ ▶ **n.** (pl. same or **-ras**) informal, chiefly derog. a white person, typically a man. [18th C.: from Ibibio and Efik *(m)bakara* 'European, master.']

buck·ram /ˈbəkrəm/ ▶ **n.** coarse linen or other cloth stiffened with gum or paste and used typically as interfacing and in bookbinding. ■ fig., archaic stiffness of manner. ▶ **adj.** [attrib.] of or like such material. ■ fig., archaic (of a person) starchy or formal. [ME: from OFr. *boquerant*, perh. from **Bukhoro**.]

buck·saw /ˈbəkˌsô/ ▶ **n.** a type of saw typically set in an H-shaped frame and used with both hands.

buck·shee /bəkˈsʜē; ˈbəksʜē/ ▶ **adj.** informal, esp. Brit. free of charge: *a buckshee brandy*. [World War I: alt. of **baksheesh**.]

buck·shot /ˈbəkˌsʜät/ ▶ **n.** coarse lead shot used in shotgun shells.

buck·skin /ˈbəkˌskin/ ▶ **n.** **1** the skin of a male deer. ■ grayish leather with a suede finish, traditionally made from such skin but now more commonly made from sheepskin. ■ (**buckskins**) clothes or shoes made from such leather. ■ thick, smooth cotton or woolen fabric. **2** a horse of a grayish-yellow color. — **buck·skinned** **adj.**

buck·thorn /ˈbəkˌᴛʜôrn/ ▶ **n.** **1** a typically thorny North American shrub or small tree (genus *Rhamnus*, family Rhamnaceae). Some kinds yield dyes, and others have been used medicinally. **2** (also **buckthorn bumelia**) a thorny shrub or small tree (*Bumelia lycioides*) of the sapodilla family, with clusters of small white flowers, found esp. in the southern and central US. [16th C.: from **buck**[1] 'deer.']

buck·tooth ▶ **n.** an upper tooth that projects over the lower lip. — **buck·toothed** **adj.**

buck·wheat /ˈbəkˌ(h)wēt/ ▶ **n.** **1** an Asian plant (*Fagopyrum esculentum*) of the dock family. Cultivated in the US, it produces starchy seeds that are used for fodder and milled into flour. **2** (in full **buckwheat tree**) see **titi**[2]. [16th C.: from MDu. *boecweite* 'beech wheat.']

buck·y·balls /ˈbəkēˌbôlz/ ▶ **plural n.** Chem., informal spherical molecules of a fullerene, esp. buckminsterfullerene. Related cylindrical molecules are termed **buckytubes**.

bu·col·ic /byo͞oˈkälik/ ▶ **adj.** of or relating to the pleasant aspects of the countryside and country life. ▶ **n.** (usu. **bucolics**) a pastoral poem. [16th C.: via L. from Gk. *boukolikos*, from *boukolos* 'herdsman,' from *bous* 'ox.']

Bu·cu·reşti /ˌbo͞okəˈresʜt(y); -ˈresʜtē/ Romanian name for **Bucharest**.

bud[1] /bəd/ ▶ **n.** a compact knoblike growth on a plant that develops into a leaf, flower, or shoot. ■ Biol. an outgrowth from an organism (e.g., a yeast cell) that separates to form a new individual without sexual reproduction taking place. ■ [with adj.] Zool. (of an animal) a rudimentary leg or other appendage that has not yet grown, or never will grow, to full size. ▶ **v.** (**bud·ded, bud·ding**) [intrans.] Biol. (of a plant or animal) form a bud: *new blood vessels bud out from the vascular bed* | [trans.] *tapeworms bud off egg-bearing sections from their tail end*. ■ [trans.] graft a bud of (a plant) on to another plant.
– PHRASES **in bud** (of a plant) having newly formed buds. [ME: of unknown origin.]

PRONUNCIATION KEY ə *ago, up*; ər *over, fur*; a *hat*; ā *ate*; ä *car*; e *let*; ē *see*; i *fit*; ī *by*; ɴɢ *sing*; ō *go*; ô *law, for*; oi *toy*; o͝o *good*; o͞o *goo*; ou *out*; ᴛʜ *thin*; T͟H *then*; ᴢʜ *vision*

bud² ▶ **n.** informal a form of address, usually to a boy or man, used esp. when the name of the one being addressed is not known. [19th C.: abbrev. of BUDDY.]

Bu·da·pest /ˈbo͞odəˌpest; -ˌpesht/ the capital of Hungary, in the northern central part of the country; pop. 2,000,000.

Bud·dha /ˈbo͞odə; ˈbo͝odə/ (often **the Buddha**) a title given to the founder of Buddhism, Siddartha Gautama (*c.*563–*c.*483 BC). Born an Indian prince, he renounced wealth and family to become an ascetic, and after achieving enlightenment, a teacher. ■ [as n.] (**a buddha**) Buddhism a person who has attained full enlightenment. ■ a statue or picture of the Buddha. [Sanskrit, lit. 'enlightened,' past part. of *budh* 'know.']

Bud·dhism /ˈbo͞odizəm; ˈbo͝od-/ ▶ **n.** a widespread Asian religion or philosophy, founded by Siddartha Gautama in NE India in the 5th century BC, which teaches that enlightenment may be reached by elimination of earthly desires and of the idea of the self. — **Bud·dhist n. & adj. Bud·dhis·tic** /bo͞oˈdistik; bo͝o-/ **adj. Bud·dhis·ti·cal** /bo͞oˈdistikəl; bo͝o-/ **adj.**

bud·ding /ˈbədiNG/ ▶ **adj.** [attrib.] (of a plant) having or developing buds. ■ (of a part of the body) becoming larger as part of the process of normal growth. ■ (of a person) beginning and showing signs of promise in a particular career or field. ■ just beginning and showing promising signs of continuing.

bud·dle /ˈbədl/ ▶ **n.** a shallow inclined container in which ore is washed. [16th C.: of unknown origin.]

bud·dle·ia /ˈbədlēə; bədˈlēə/ ▶ **n.** a widely cultivated shrub (genus *Buddleia*, family Loganiaceae) with fragrant lilac, white, or yellow flowers. [mod. L.; Adam *Buddle* (died 1715), English botanist.]

bud·dy /ˈbədē/ informal ▶ **n.** (pl. **-dies**) a close friend. ■ a working companion with whom close cooperation is required. ▶ **v.** (**-dies, -died**) [intrans.] become friendly and spend time with: *I decided to **buddy up to** them.* [19th C.: perh. alt. of BROTHER.]

bud·dy-bud·dy ▶ **adj.** informal, chiefly derog. very friendly.

bud·dy sys·tem ▶ **n.** a cooperative arrangement whereby individuals are paired or teamed up and assume responsibility for one another's instruction, productivity, welfare, or safety.

Budge /bəj/, Don (1915–2000), US tennis player; born *John Donald Budge*. He was the first to win the four Grand Slam singles championships in one year, 1938.

budge /bəj/ ▶ **v.** [usu. with negative] make or cause to make the slightest movement: [intrans.] *the line in the bank hasn't budged* | [trans.] *I couldn't budge the door.* ■ [intrans.] (**budge over**) informal make room for another person by moving: *budge over, boys.* ■ [usu. with modal] change or make (someone) change an opinion: [intrans.] *he wouldn't budge* | [trans.] *neither bribe nor threat will budge him.* [16th C.: from Fr. *bouger* 'to stir,' based on L. *bullire* 'to boil.']

budg·er·i·gar /ˈbəjərēˌgär/ ▶ **n.** a small gregarious green Australian parakeet (*Melopsittacus undulatus*) with a yellow head. Popular as a pet bird, it has been bred in a variety of colors. [19th C.: of Aboriginal origin, perh. alt. of Kamilaroi *gijirrigaa*.]

budg·et /ˈbəjit/ ▶ **n.** **1** an estimate of income and expenditure for a set period of time. ■ an annual or other regular estimate of national revenue and expenditure put forward by the government, often including details of changes in taxation. ■ the amount of money needed or available for a purpose. **2** archaic a quantity of material, typically that which is written or printed. ▶ **v.** (**budg·et·ed, budg·et·ing**) [intrans.] allow or provide for in a budget: *the university is **budgeting for** a deficit* | [as adj.] (**budgeted**) *a budgeted figure of $31,000* | [as n.] (**budgeting**) *corporate planning and budgeting.* ■ [trans.] provide (a sum of money) for a particular purpose from a budget. ▶ **adj.** [attrib.] inexpensive: *a budget guitar.*
– PHRASES **on a budget** with a restricted amount of money: *we're traveling on a budget.* — **budg·et·ar·y** /-ˌterē/ **adj.** [ME: from OFr. *bougette*, dimin. of *bouge* 'leather bag,' from L. *bulga* 'bag, knapsack,' of Gaulish origin.]

budg·ie /ˈbəjē/ ▶ **n.** (pl. **-ies**) informal term for BUDGERIGAR.

Bud·weis /ˈbo͞otˌvīs/ German name for ČESKÉ BUDĚJOVICE.

bud·wood /ˈbədˌwo͝od/ ▶ **n.** short lengths of young branches with buds prepared for grafting on to the rootstock of another plant.

bud·worm /ˈbədˌwərm/ ▶ **n.** a moth caterpillar that is destructive to buds. See SPRUCE BUDWORM.

Bue·na Park /ˈbwānə; ˈbyo͞o-/ a city in southern California; pop. 68,784.

Bue·na·ven·tu·ra /ˌbwānəvenˈt(y)o͝orə; ˌbwenə-/ the chief Pacific Ocean port of Colombia; pop. 122,500.

Bue·na Vis·ta a village in northern Mexico, near Saltillo, site of US victory over Mexican forces in 1847.

Bue·nos Ai·res /ˌbwānəs ˈe(ə)rēz; ˈīriz/ the capital city and chief port of Argentina, in the eastern central part of the country, on the Plata River; pop. 2,961,000.

buff¹ /bəf/ ▶ **n.** **1** a yellowish-beige color. **2** a stout, dull yellow leather with a velvety surface. ■ a stick, wheel, or pad used for polishing or smoothing. ▶ **v.** [trans.] polish (something): *he buffed the glass.* ■ give (leather) a velvety finish by removing the surface of the grain. ▶ **adj.** **1** yellowish beige. **2** informal being in good physical shape with fine muscle tone.
– PHRASES **in the buff** informal naked. [16th C.: prob. from Fr. *buffle*, from Ital. *bufalo*, from late L. *bufalus* (see BUFFALO). The original sense in Engl. was 'buffalo,' later 'oxhide' or 'color of oxhide.']

buff² ▶ **n.** [with adj.] informal a person who is enthusiastically interested in and very knowledgeable about a particular subject. [20th C.: from BUFF¹, orig. applied to enthusiastic fire-watchers, from the buff uniforms formerly worn by New York volunteer firemen.]

Buf·fa·lo /ˈbəfəˌlō/ a city and port on Lake Erie in northwestern New York; pop. 292,648.

buf·fa·lo /ˈbəfəˌlō/ ▶ **n.** (pl. same, **-loes** or **-los**) **1** a heavily built wild ox with backswept horns, in particular: ■ four species native to South Asia (genus *Bubalus*), including the water buffalo and the anoa. ■ the Cape buffalo. ■ the North American bison. **2** (also **buf·fa·lo fish**) a large, thick-lipped, grayish-olive North American freshwater fish (genus *Ictiobus*, family Catostomidae). ▶ **v.** (**-loes, -loed**) [trans.] (often **be buffaloed**) informal overawe or intimidate (someone). ■ baffle (someone). [16th C.: prob. from Port. *bufalo*, from late L. *bufalus*, Gk. *boubalos* 'antelope.']

buf·fa·lo ber·ry ▶ **n.** a North American shrub (genus *Shepherdia*, family Elaeagnaceae) with silvery twigs and leaves and edible red or yellow berries. ■ the berry of this shrub.

Buf·fa·lo Bill (1846–1917), US showman; born *William Frederick Cody*. He gained his nickname for killing buffalo to feed the Union Pacific Railroad workers. He later traveled with his Wild West Show.

buf·fa·lo gnat ▶ **n.** another term for BLACK FLY.

buf·fa·lo grass ▶ **n.** any of a number of grasses, in particular a creeping grass (*Buchloe dactyloides*) of the North American plains, sometimes used for erosion control.

buf·fa·lo robe ▶ **n.** a rug, cloak, or blanket made from the dressed hide of a North American bison.

buf·fa·lo sol·dier ▶ **n.** (in US history) an African-American cavalry soldier.

Buf·fa·lo wings (also **buf·fa·lo wings** or **Buffalo chicken wings**) ▶ **plural n.** deep-fried chicken wings coated in a spicy sauce and usually served with blue cheese dressing.

buff·er /ˈbəfər/ ▶ **n.** **1** a person or thing that prevents incompatible or antagonistic people or things from coming into contact with or harming each other. **2** (also **buffer solution**) Chem. a solution that resists changes in pH when acid or alkali is added to it. **3** Comput. a temporary memory area or queue used when transferring data between devices or programs operating at different speeds. ▶ **v.** [trans.] **1** lessen or moderate the impact of (something): *the massage helped to buffer the strain.* **2** treat with a chemical buffer. [19th C.: prob. from obs. *buff* (v.), imitative of a blow.]

buff·er state ▶ **n.** a small neutral country, situated between two larger hostile countries, serving to prevent the outbreak of regional conflict.

buff·er zone ▶ **n.** a neutral area serving to separate hostile forces or nations. ■ an area of land designated for environmental protection.

buf·fet¹ /bəˈfā/ ▶ **n.** **1** a meal consisting of several dishes from which guests serve themselves. **2** a room or counter in a station, hotel, or other public building selling light meals or snacks. **3** a cabinet with shelves and drawers for keeping dinnerware and table linens. [18th C. (sense 3): from Fr., from OFr. *bufet* 'stool.']

buf·fet² /ˈbəfit/ ▶ **v.** (**-fet·ed, -fet·ing**) [trans.] (esp. of wind or waves) strike repeatedly and violently; batter: *the rough seas buffeted the coast* | [intrans.] *the wind was **buffeting at** their bodies.* ■ knock (someone) over or off course. ■ (often **be buffeted**) fig. (of misfortunes or difficulties) afflict or harm (someone) repeatedly or over a long period. ▶ **n.** **1** dated a blow, typically of the hand or fist. ■ fig. a shock or misfortune. **2** Aeron. another term for BUFFETING. [ME: from OFr. *buffeter* (v.), *buffet* (n.), dimin. of *bufe* 'a blow.']

buf·fet·ing /ˈbəfitiNG/ ▶ **n.** the action of striking someone or something repeatedly and violently. ■ fig. the action or result of afflicting or harming someone, typically repeatedly or over a long period. ■ Aeron. irregular oscillation of part of an aircraft, caused by turbulence.

buf·fle·head /ˈbəfəlˌhed/ ▶ **n.** a small North American diving duck (*Bucephala albeola*) with a large puffy head. The male has white plumage with a black back. [17th C. ('simpleton'): from obs. *buffle* 'buffalo.']

buf·fo /ˈbo͞ofō/ ▶ **n.** (pl. **-fos**) a comic actor in Italian opera or a person resembling such an actor. [18th C.: Ital., 'puff of wind,' from *buffare* 'to puff,' of imitative origin.]

Buf·fon /byˈfôN/, Georges-Louis Leclerc, Comte de (1707–88), French naturalist. A founder of paleontology, he emphasized the unity of all living species.

buf·foon /bəˈfo͞on/ ▶ **n.** a ridiculous but amusing person; a clown. — **buf·foon·ish adj.** [16th C.: from Fr. *bouffon*, from Ital. *buffone*, from med. L. *buffo* 'clown.']

buf·foon·er·y /bəˈfo͞onərē/ ▶ **n.** (pl. **-er·ies**) behavior that is ridiculous but amusing.

bug /bəg/ ▶ **n.** **1** a small insect. ■ informal a harmful microorganism, as a bacterium or virus. ■ an illness caused by such a microorganism. ■ [with adj.] fig., informal an enthusiastic, almost obsessive, interest in something: *they caught the sailing bug.* **2** (also **true bug**) Entomol. an insect of a large order (Hemiptera) distinguished by having mouthparts that are modified for piercing and sucking. **3** a concealed miniature microphone, used for surveillance. **4** an error in a computer program or system. ▶ **v.** (**bugged, bug·ging**) [trans.] **1** (often **be bugged**) conceal a miniature microphone in (a room, telephone, etc.) in order to monitor or record someone's conversations. ■ record or monitor (a conversation) in this way. **2** informal annoy or bother (someone).

– PHRASAL VERBS **bug off** informal go away. **bug out** informal **1** leave quickly. **2** chiefly fig. bulge outward. [17th C.: of unknown origin.]

bug·a·boo /'bəgə,bo͞o/ ▶ **n.** an object of fear or alarm; a bugbear. [18th C.: prob. of Celtic origin and rel. to Welsh *bwci bo* 'bogey.']

bug·bane /'bəg,bān/ ▶ **n.** a tall plant (genus *Cimicifuga*) of the buttercup family, with wandlike spikes of cream or yellow flowers. Its several species include the black cohosh.

bug·bear /'bəg,be(ə)r/ ▶ **n.** a cause of obsessive fear, irritation, or loathing. ■ archaic an imaginary being invoked to frighten children, typically a sort of hobgoblin supposed to devour them. [16th C.: prob. from obs. *bug* 'bogey' (of unknown origin) + BEAR[2].]

bug-eyed ▶ **adj. & adv.** with bulging eyes: [as adj.] *bug-eyed monsters* | [as adv.] *he stared bug-eyed at John.*

bug·ger /'bəgər; 'bo͝og-/ vulgar slang, esp. Brit. ▶ **n. 1** [with adj.] a contemptible or pitied person, typically a man. ■ a person with a particular negative quality or characteristic. ■ used as a term of affection or respect, typically grudgingly. **2** derog. a person who commits buggery. ▶ **v.** [trans.] penetrate the anus of (someone) during sexual intercourse; sodomize. ▶ **exclam.** used to express annoyance or anger.

– PHRASAL VERBS **bugger off** [usu. in imper.] go away. [ME (a heretic): from MDu., from OFr. *bougre*, orig. 'heretic,' from med. L. *Bulgarus* 'Bulgarian' (Bulgarians belonging to the Orthodox Church were regarded as heretical by Roman Catholics; heresy was associated with forbidden sexual practices).]

bug·ger·y /'bəgərē; 'bo͝og-/ ▶ **n.** anal intercourse.

bug·gy[1] /'bəgē/ ▶ **n.** (pl. **-gies**) a small or light vehicle, in particular: ■ a small motor vehicle, typically one with an open top. ■ short for BABY BUGGY. ■ hist. a light, horse-drawn vehicle for one or two people, with two or four wheels. [18th C.: of unknown origin.]

bug·gy[2] ▶ **adj.** (**-gi·er, -gi·est**) **1** infested with bugs. ■ (of a computer program or system) faulty in operation. **2** informal mad; insane.

bug·house /'bəg,hous/ informal ▶ **n.** offens. a mental hospital or asylum. ▶ **adj.** crazy; insane.

bug juice ▶ **n. 1** whisky or other liquor, esp. when of poor quality. **2** a sweet, artificially colored, non-carbonated soft drink.

bu·gle[1] /'byo͞ogəl/ ▶ **n.** a brass instrument like a small trumpet, typically without valves or keys and used for military signals. ■ a loud sound resembling that of a bugle, as the mating call of a bull elk. ▶ **v.** [intrans.] sound a bugle. ■ [trans.] sound (a note or call) on a bugle: *he bugled a warning.* ■ issue a loud sound resembling that of a bugle, particularly the mating call of a bull elk. — **bu·gler** /'byo͞og(ə)lər/ **n.** [ME: via OFr. from L. *buculus*, dimin. of *bos* 'ox.']

bu·gle[2] (also **bugleweed**) ▶ **n.** a creeping plant (esp. *Ajuga reptans*) of the mint family, with blue flowers held on upright stems. [ME: from late L. *bugula*.]

bu·gle[3] ▶ **n.** (also **bugle bead**) an ornamental tube-shaped glass or plastic bead sewn on to clothing. [16th C.: of unknown origin.]

bu·gloss /'byo͞oglôs; -gläs/ ▶ **n.** a bristly plant (*Anchusa, Lycopsis*, and other genera) of the borage family, with bright blue flowers. [ME: ult. from Gk. *bouglōssos* 'ox-tongued,' from *bous* 'ox' + *glōssa* 'tongue.']

buhl /bo͞ol/ ▶ **n.** brass, tortoiseshell, or other material cut to make a pattern and used for inlaying furniture. ■ work inlaid in such a way. [19th C.: from French *boule*, after André Charles *Boulle* (1642–1732), French cabinetmaker.]

buhr·stone /'bər,stōn/ (also **bur·stone** or **burr·stone**) a porous limestone formerly much used for millstones.

build /bild/ ▶ **v.** (past and past part. **built** /bilt/) [trans.] (often **be built**) construct (something, typically something large) by putting parts or material together over a period of time: *the factory was built in 1936.* ■ commission, finance, and oversee the building of (something). ■ (**build something in/into**) incorporate (something) and make it a permanent part of a structure, system, or situation: *engineers want to build in extra traction.* ■ Comput. compile (a program, database, index, etc.). ■ [intrans.] (of a program, database, index, etc.) be compiled. ■ establish and develop (a business, relationship, or situation) over a period of time. ■ [intrans.] (**build on**) use as a basis for further progress or development: *the nation should build on the talents of its workforce.* ■ increase the size, intensity, or extent of: *we built up confidence in our abilities* | [intrans.] *the air of excited anticipation builds.* ▶ **n. 1** the dimensions or proportions of a person's or animal's body. ■ the style or form of construction of something, typically a vehicle. **2** Comput. a compiled version of a program. ■ the process of compiling a program.

– PHRASES **build one's hopes up** become ever more hopeful or optimistic about something. **built upon/on sand** fig. without reliable foundations or any real substance. [OE *byldan*, from *bold, botl* 'dwelling,' of Gmc. origin; rel. to BOWER[1].]

build·down /'bild,doun/ ▶ **n.** a gradual, systematic reduction in numbers, esp. of nuclear weapons.

build·er /'bildər/ ▶ **n.** a person who constructs something by putting parts or material together over a period of time. ■ a person whose job is to construct or repair houses, or to contract for their construction and repair. ■ [usu. in comb.] a person or thing that creates or develops a particular thing: *breaking the record was a real confidence builder.*

build·ing /'bildiNG/ (abbr.: **bldg.**) ▶ **n. 1** a structure with a roof and walls, such as a house, school, store, or factory. **2** the process or business of constructing something. ■ the process of commissioning, financing, or overseeing the construction of something. ■ the process of creating or developing something over a period of time.

-building ▶ **comb. form** the process of constructing, shaping, developing, or forming a particular thing: *boat-building.* ■ the process of promoting something. ■ able to build: *reef-building coral.*

build·ing block ▶ **n.** a child's toy brick, typically made of wood or plastic. ■ fig. a basic unit from which something is built up.

build·up /'bild,əp/ ▶ **n.** [usu. in sing.] **1** a gradual accumulation or increase, typically of something negative and typically leading to a problem or crisis. **2** a period of excitement and preparation in advance of a significant event. ■ a favorable description in advance; publicity.

built /bilt/ past and past participle of BUILD. ▶ **adj.** (of a person) having a specified physical size or build: *a slightly built woman.*

built-in ▶ **adj.** [attrib.] forming an integral part of a structure or device. ■ (of a characteristic) inherent; innate.

built-up ▶ **adj. 1** (of an area) densely covered by houses or other buildings. **2** increased in height by the addition of parts. ■ (of a feeling) increasing in intensity over a period of time.

Bu·jum·bu·ra /,bo͞ojəm'bo͝orə/ the capital of Burundi, at the northeastern end of Lake Tanganyika; pop. 235,440.

Bu·kho·ro /bo͞o'KHôrō/ (also **Bu·kha·ra, Bo·kha·ra** /bo͞o'KHärə/) a city in southeastern Uzbekistan; pop. 246,200.

Bu·la·wa·yo /,bo͝olə'wā-ō; -'wī-ō/ a city in Zimbabwe; pop. 620,940.

bulb /bəlb/ ▶ **n. 1** a rounded underground storage organ present in some plants, notably those of the lily family, consisting of a short stem surrounded by fleshy scale leaves or leaf bases. Compare with CORM, RHIZOME. ■ a plant grown from an organ of this kind. ■ a similar underground organ such as a corm or a rhizome. **2** an object with a rounded or teardrop shape like a bulb, in particular: ■ a light bulb. ■ an expanded part of a glass tube such as that forming the reservoir of a thermometer. ■ a hollow flexible container with an opening through which the air can be expelled by squeezing, such as that used to fill a syringe. ■ a spheroidal dilated part at the end of an anatomical structure. — **bul·bar** /'bəlbər; -bär/ **adj.** [ME: via L. from Gk. *bolbos* 'onion, bulbous root.']

bul·bil /'bəlbil/ ▶ **n.** Bot. a small bulblike structure, esp. in the axil of a leaf or at the base of a stem, that may form a new plant. [19th C.: from mod. L. *bulbillus*, dimin. of *bulbus*.]

bul·bous /'bəlbəs/ ▶ **adj. 1** fat, round, or bulging. **2** (of a plant) growing from a bulb.

bul·bul /'bo͝ol,bo͝ol/ ▶ **n.** a tropical, often crested, African and Asian songbird (family Pycnonotidae) that typically has a melodious voice and drab plumage. [17th C.: from Pers., of imitative origin.]

Bul·ga·nin /bo͝ol'ganən/, Nikolai Aleksandrovich (1895–1975), premier of the Soviet Union 1955–58.

Bul·gar /'bəlgär; 'bo͝ol-/ ▶ **n.** a member of a Slavic people who settled in what is now Bulgaria in the 7th century. [from med. L. *Bulgarus*, from Old Church Slavic *Blŭgarinŭ*.]

bul·gar /'bəlgər/ (also **bul·gur, bulgar wheat**) ▶ **n.** a cereal food made from whole wheat partially boiled then dried. [1930s: from Turk. *bulgur* 'bruised grain.']

Bul·gar·i·a /,bəl'ge(ə)rēə; bo͝ol-/ a country in southeastern Europe. *See box on next page.*

Bul·gar·i·an /,bəl'ge(ə)rēən; bo͝ol-/ ▶ **n. 1** a native or national of Bulgaria. **2** the South Slavic language spoken in Bulgaria. ▶ **adj.** of or relating to Bulgaria, its people, or their language.

bulge /bəlj/ ▶ **n.** a rounded swelling or protuberance that distorts a flat surface. ■ (esp. in a military context) a piece of land that projects outward from an otherwise regular line. ■ [in sing.] informal a temporary unusual increase in number or size. ▶ **v.** [intrans.] swell or protrude to an unnatural or incongruous extent: *the veins in his neck bulged* | [as adj.] (**bulging**) *bulging eyes.* ■ be full of and distended with: *a briefcase bulging with documents.* — **bulg·y** **adj.** [ME: from OFr. *boulge*, from L. *bulga* (see BUDGET).]

bu·lim·a·rex·i·a /,bo͞olēmə'reksēə/ ▶ **n.** another term for BULIMIA NERVOSA (see BULIMIA). — **bu·lim·a·rex·ic** /-'reksik/ **adj. & n.** [1970s: blend of BULIMIA and ANOREXIA.]

bu·lim·i·a /bo͞o'limēə; 'lē-/ ▶ **n.** insatiable overeating as a medical condition, in particular: ■ (also **bu·lim·i·a ner·vo·sa** /nər'vōsə/) an emotional disorder in which bouts of extreme overeating are followed by depression and self-induced vomiting, purging, or fasting. Also called BINGE-PURGE SYNDROME. ■ an eating disorder in which a large quantity of food is consumed in a short period of time, often followed by feelings of guilt or shame. Also called BINGE-EATING SYNDROME. — **bu·lim·ic** /-'limik; 'lē-/ **adj. & n.** [ME: ult. from Gk. *boulimia* 'ravenous hunger,' from *bous* 'ox' + *limos* 'hunger.']

bulk /bəlk/ ▶ **n.** the mass or magnitude of something large. ■ a large mass or shape, for example of a building or a heavy body. ■ [as adj.] large in quantity or amount. ■ (**the bulk**) the majority or greater part of something. ■ roughage in food. ■ cargo that is an unpackaged mass such as grain, oil, or milk. ▶ **v. 1** [intrans.] be or seem to be of great size or importance: *territorial questions bulked large in diplomatic relations.* **2** [trans.] treat (a product) so that its quantity appears greater than it in fact is: *traders were bulking up their flour with chalk.* ■ [intrans.] (**bulk up**) build up body mass, typically in training for athletic events.

– PHRASES **in bulk 1** (esp. of goods) in large quantities, usually at a reduced price. **2** (of a cargo or commodity) loose; not packaged. [ME: 'cargo,' 'heap' prob. from ON *búlki* 'cargo.']

Bulgaria

Official name: Republic of Bulgaria
Location: southeastern Europe, on the western coast of the Black Sea
Area: 42,700 square miles (110,600 sq km)
Population: 7,517,000
Capital: Sofia
Language: Bulgarian
Currency: lev

bulk·head /ˈbəlk,hed/ ▶ **n.** a dividing wall or barrier between compartments in a ship, aircraft, or other vehicle. [15th C.: from ON *bálkr* 'partition.']

bulk mail ▶ **n.** a class of mail for sending out large numbers of identical items at a reduced rate.

bulk·y /ˈbəlkē/ ▶ **adj.** (**bulk·i·er, bulk·i·est**) taking up much space, typically inconveniently; large and unwieldy. ■ (of a person) heavily built. ■ (of clothing) made of a thick yarn or fabric. — **bulk·i·ly** /-kəlē/ **adv.** **bulk·i·ness n.**

bull[1] /bo͝ol/ ▶ **n.** **1** an uncastrated male bovine animal. ■ a large male animal, esp. a whale or elephant. ■ (**the Bull**) the zodiacal sign or constellation Taurus. **2** Stock Market a person who buys shares hoping to sell them at a higher price later. Often contrasted with BEAR[2]. ▶ **adj.** [attrib.] (of a part of the body, esp. the neck) resembling the corresponding part of a male bovine animal in build and strength. ▶ **v.** **1** [trans.] push or drive powerfully or violently: *he bulled the motorcycle clear of the tunnel.* **2** [intrans.] (**be bulling**) (of a cow) behave in a manner characteristic of being in heat.
– PHRASES **like a bull in a china shop** behaving recklessly and clumsily in a place or situation where one is likely to cause damage or injury. (**like**) **a red rag to a bull** see RED. **take the bull by the horns** deal bravely and decisively with a difficult, dangerous, or unpleasant situation. [OE *bula* (in names), from ON *boli*.]

bull[2] ▶ **n.** a papal edict. [ME: from OFr. *bulle*, from L. *bulla* 'bubble.']

bull[3] ▶ **n.** informal stupid or untrue talk or writing; nonsense. [17th C.: of unknown origin.]

bul·la /ˈbo͝olə/ ▶ **n.** (pl. **bul·lae** /ˈbo͝olē/) **1** Med. a bubblelike cavity filled with air or fluid, in particular: ■ a large blister containing serous fluid. ■ an abnormal air-filled cavity in the lung. **2** a round seal attached to a papal bull, typically made of lead. [L., lit. 'bubble.']

bul·lace /ˈbo͝olis/ ▶ **n.** a thorny shrub or small tree (*Prunus insititia*) of the rose family that bears purple-black fruits. See also DAMSON. [ME: from OFr. *buloce* 'sloe'.]

bul·late /ˈbo͝olāt/ ▶ **adj.** Bot. covered with rounded swellings like blisters. [18th C.: from L. *bullatus*, from *bulla* 'bubble.']

bull·bait·ing /ˈbo͝ol,bāting/ ▶ **n.** hist. the practice of setting dogs to harass and attack a tethered bull, popular as a sport in medieval Europe.

bull·bat /ˈbo͝ol,bat/ ▶ **n.** another term for NIGHTHAWK (sense 1).

bull·dog /ˈbo͝ol,dôg/ ▶ **n.** a dog of a sturdy smooth-haired breed with a large head and powerful protruding lower jaw, a flat wrinkled face, and a broad chest. ■ a person noted for courageous or stubborn tenacity. ■ informal (at Oxford and Cambridge Universities) an official who assists the proctors, esp. in disciplinary matters. ▶ **v.** (**-dogged, -dog·ging**) [trans.] wrestle (a steer) to the ground by holding its horns and twisting its neck: [as n.] (**bulldogging**) *cowboys compete in bulldogging.* — **bull·dog·ger n.**

bulldog

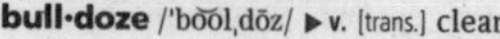

bull·doze /ˈbo͝ol,dōz/ ▶ **v.** [trans.] clear (ground) or destroy (buildings, trees, etc.) with a bulldozer. ■ fig., informal use insensitive force when dealing with (someone or something). [19th C.: from BULL[1] + *-doze*, alt. of the n. DOSE.]

bulldozer

bull·doz·er /ˈbo͝ol,dōzər/ ▶ **n.** a powerful tractor with a broad curved upright blade at the front for clearing ground. ■ fig. a person, army, or other body exercising irresistible power, esp. in disposing of obstacles or opposition.

bull·dyke /ˈbo͝ol,dīk/ (also **bull·dike** or **bull·dyk·er**) ▶ **n.** informal, offens. a particularly masculine lesbian.

bul·let /ˈbo͝olit/ ▶ **n.** **1** a projectile for firing from a rifle, revolver, or other small firearms, typically of metal, cylindrical and pointed, and sometimes containing an explosive. ■ used in similes and comparisons to refer to someone or something that moves very fast. ■ (in a sporting context) a very fast ball. **2** Print. a small solid circle printed just before a line of type, such as an item in a list, to emphasize it. [16th C.: from Fr. *boulet, boulette* 'small ball,' dimin. of *boule*, from L. *bulla* 'bubble.']

bul·le·tin /ˈbo͝olitn; -,tin/ ▶ **n.** a short official statement or broadcast summary of news. ■ a regular newsletter or printed report issued by an organization or society. [17th C.: from Fr., from Ital. *bullettino*, diminutive of *bulletta* 'passport,' dimin. of *bulla* 'seal, bull.']

bul·le·tin board ▶ **n.** a board for displaying notices. ■ Comput. (also **bulletin board system**) an information storage system designed to permit any authorized computer user to access and add to it from a remote terminal.

bul·let point ▶ **n.** each of several items in a list, typically the ideas or arguments in an article or presentation and typically printed with a bullet before each for emphasis.

bul·let·proof /ˈbo͝olit,pro͞of/ ▶ **adj.** designed to resist the penetration of bullets.

bul·let train ▶ **n.** informal a high-speed passenger train.

bull·fight /ˈbo͝ol,fīt/ ▶ **n.** a public spectacle, particularly in Spain and Latin America, at which a bull is goaded in a highly stylized manner and then killed. — **bull·fight·er n.**

bull·fight·ing /ˈbo͝ol,fīting/ ▶ **n.** the sport of goading and killing a bull as a public spectacle in an outdoor arena.

bull·finch /ˈbo͝ol,finch/ ▶ **n.** a stocky Eurasian finch (genus *Pyrrhula*) with a short, thick bill, and typically with gray or pinkish plumage, dark wings, and a white rump.

bull·frog /ˈbo͝ol,frôg; -,fräg/ ▶ **n.** a very large frog (genera *Rana* and *Pyxicephalus*, family Ranidae) that has a deep booming croak and is often a predator of smaller vertebrates.

bull·head /ˈbo͝ol,hed/ ▶ **n.** **1** (also **bullhead catfish**) an American freshwater catfish (family Ictaluridae) with four pairs of barbels around the mouth, including the **black bullhead** (*Ameiurus melas*). **2** a small, mainly freshwater Eurasian fish (genera *Cottus* and *Taurulus*) of the sculpin family, with a broad flattened head and spiny fins. **3** (also **bullhead lily**) a North American water lily (*Nuphar variegatum*) with globular yellow flowers.

bull·head·ed /ˈbo͝ol,hedid/ ▶ **adj.** determined in an obstinate or unthinking way. — **bull·head·ed·ly adv.** **bull·head·ed·ness n.**

bull·horn /ˈbo͝ol,hôrn/ ▶ **n.** an electronic device for amplifying the sound of the voice so it can be heard at a distance.

bul·lion /ˈbo͝olyən/ ▶ **n.** **1** gold or silver in bulk before coining, or valued by weight. **2** (also **bullion fringe**) ornamental braid or trimming made with twists of gold or silver thread. [ME: from Anglo-Norman Fr., 'a mint,' var. of OFr. *bouillon*, based on L. *bullire* 'to boil.']

bull·ish /ˈbo͝olish/ ▶ **adj.** **1** resembling a bull. ■ stupid or oafish; bullheaded. ■ assertively masculine; macho. **2** Stock Market characterized by rising share prices. ■ (of a dealer) inclined to buy because of an anticipated rise in prices. **3** feeling especially hopeful; optimistic. — **bull·ish·ly adv.** **bull·ish·ness n.**

bull kelp ▶ **n.** a very large brown seaweed (*Nereocystis* and other genera, class Phaeophyceae) found in Pacific and Antarctic waters, growing up to 165 feet (50 m) in length off the northwestern coasts of North America.

bull mar·ket ▶ **n.** Stock Market a market in which share prices are rising, encouraging buying.

bull·mas·tiff /ˈbo͝olˈmastif/ ▶ **n.** a dog of a crossbreed of bulldog and mastiff.

Bull Moose ▶ **n.** a supporter or member of the Progressive Party.

Bull Moose Par·ty ▶ **n.** another term for the PROGRESSIVE PARTY.

bull-necked ▶ **adj.** having a short, thick neck.

bull·nose /ˈbo͝ol,nōz/ tech. ▶ **adj.** (also **bull·nosed**) [attrib.] (of the edge of a surface) rounded. ■ (of a surface or object) having a rounded edge or edges. ▶ **n.** a rounded edge of this type.

bul·lock ▶ n. another term for STEER². [OE *bulluc*, dimin. of *bula* (see BULL¹).]

bull of the woods ▶ n. a sexually mature male of a large wild species, such as moose or elk. ■ fig. the supervisor of a logging camp.

bul·lous /ˈbo͝oləs/ ▶ adj. Med. characterized by blisters or bullae on the skin.

bull·pen /ˈbo͝olˌpen/ ▶ n. (also **bull pen**) an enclosure for bulls. ■ an exercise area for baseball pitchers. ■ the relief pitchers of a baseball team. ■ an open-plan office area. ■ a large cell in which prisoners are held before a court hearing.

bull·ring /ˈbo͝olˌriNG/ ▶ n. an arena where bullfights are held.

Bull Run a stream in eastern Virginia that was the scene of two Confederate victories in 1861 and 1862, during the Civil War.

bull·rush ▶ n. var. of BULRUSH.

bull ses·sion ▶ n. an informal, typically impromptu discussion, esp. among a small group. [1920s: from BULL³.]

bull's-eye ▶ n. (also **bulls·eye**) **1** the center of a target in sports such as archery, shooting, and darts. ■ a shot that hits such a target center. ■ fig. used to refer to something that achieves exactly the intended effect. **2** dated a hemisphere or thick disk of glass forming a small window in a ship or the glass of a lamp. ■ a thick knob or boss of glass at the center of a blown glass sheet.

bull shark

bull shark ▶ n. a large, stout-bodied aggressive shark (*Carcharhinus leucas*, family Carcharhinidae) of widespread distribution.

bull·shit /ˈbo͝olˌSHit/ vulgar slang ▶ n. stupid or untrue talk or writing; nonsense. ▶ v. (**-shit·ted, -shit·ting**) [trans.] talk nonsense to (someone), typically to be misleading or deceptive. — **bull·shit·ter** n. [20th C.: from BULL³.]

bull snake ▶ n. (also **bull·snake**) a constrictor (genus *Pituophis*, family Colubridae) found commonly on the plains and prairies of North America.

bull ter·ri·er ▶ n. a short-haired dog of a breed that is a cross between a bulldog and a terrier.

bull trout ▶ n. a North American trout (*Salvelinus confluentus*) that resembles the Dolly Varden, found in cold rivers and lakes.

bull·whip /ˈbo͝olˌ(h)wip/ ▶ n. a whip with a long heavy lash. ▶ v. (**-whipped, -whip·ping**) [trans.] strike or thrash with such a whip.

bul·ly¹ /ˈbo͝olē/ ▶ n. (pl. **-lies**) a person who uses strength or power to harm or intimidate those who are weaker. ▶ v. (**-lies, -lied**) [trans.] use superior strength or influence to intimidate (someone), typically to force him or her to do what one wants. [16th C.: prob. from MDu. *boele* 'lover.']

bul·ly² informal ▶ adj. very good; first-rate. ▶ exclam. (**bully for**) an expression of admiration or approval: *he got away—bully for him.* [16th C.: from BULLY¹.]

bul·ly³ (also **bully beef**) informal ▶ n. corned beef. [18th C.: alt. of Fr. *bouilli*, lit. 'boiled.']

bul·ly boy ▶ n. a tough or aggressive man.

bul·ly pul·pit ▶ n. [in sing.] a public office or position of authority that provides its occupant with an outstanding opportunity to speak out on any issue.

bul·ly·rag /ˈbo͝olēˌrag/ ▶ v. (**-ragged, -rag·ging**) [trans.] informal treat (someone) in a scolding or intimidating way: *he would* ***bullyrag*** *his staff* ***around.*** [18th C.: of unknown origin.]

bul·rush /ˈbo͝olˌrəSH/ (also **bull·rush**) ▶ n. **1** another term for CATTAIL. **2** a tall rushlike water plant (*Scirpus lacustris*) of the sedge family. Native to temperate regions of the northern hemisphere, it is used for weaving and is grown as an aid to water purification. **3** (in biblical use) a papyrus plant. [ME: prob. from BULL¹ 'large.']

bul·wark /ˈbo͝olˌwərk/ ▶ n. a defensive wall. ■ fig. a person, institution, or principle that acts as a defense. ■ (usu. **bulwarks**) an extension of a ship's sides above the level of the deck. [ME: from Mid. Low Ger. and MDu. *bolwerk*; rel. to BOLE¹ and WORK.]

Bul·wer-Lyt·ton /ˈbo͝olwər ˈlitn/ see LYTTON.

bum¹ /bəm/ informal ▶ n. **1** a vagrant. ■ a lazy or worthless person. **2** [in comb.] a person who devotes a great deal of time to a specified activity: *a ski bum.* ▶ v. (**bummed, bum·ming**) **1** [intrans.] travel, with no particular purpose or destination: *he* ***bummed around*** *Florida for a few months.* ■ pass one's time idly. **2** [trans.] get by asking or begging. ▶ adj. [attrib.] of poor quality; bad or wrong.

– PHRASES **give someone** (or **get**) **the bum's rush** forcibly eject someone (or be forcibly ejected) from a place or gathering. ■ abruptly dismiss someone (or be abruptly dismissed) for a poor idea or performance. **on the bum** traveling with rough provisions and with no fixed home; living as a vagrant. [19th C.: prob. from BUMMER.]

bum² ▶ n. Brit. informal buttocks. [ME: of unknown origin.]

bum·ber·shoot /ˈbəmbərˌSHo͞ot/ ▶ n. informal an umbrella. [19th C.: alt. of UMBRELLA and PARACHUTE.]

bum·ble /ˈbəmbəl/ ▶ v. **1** [no obj., with adverbial of direction] move or act in an awkward or confused manner: *they* ***bumbled around*** *the house.* **2** [intrans.] speak in a confused or indistinct way: *the succeeding speakers bumbled.* ■ [with adverbial] (of an insect) buzz or hum: *she watched a bee bumble among the flowers.* — **bum·bler** /-b(ə)lər/ n. [ME: from BOOM¹ + -LE⁴.]

bum·ble·bee /ˈbəmbəlˌbē/ ▶ n. a large hairy bee (genus *Bombus*, family Apidae) with a loud hum, living in small colonies in holes underground.

bum·boat /ˈbəmˌbōt/ ▶ n. a small vessel carrying provisions for sale to moored or anchored ships. [17th C.: from BUM¹ + BOAT.]

bum·mer /ˈbəmər/ ▶ n. informal **1** (**a bummer**) a thing that is annoying or disappointing. ■ an unpleasant reaction to a hallucinogenic drug. **2** a loafer or vagrant. ▶ exclam. informal used to express frustration or disappointment, typically sympathetically. [19th C.: perh. from Ger. *Bummler*, from *bummeln* 'to stroll.']

bump /bəmp/ ▶ n. **1** a light blow or a jolting collision. ■ the dull sound of such a blow or collision. ■ Aeron. a rising air current causing an irregularity in an aircraft's motion. **2** a protuberance on a level surface. ■ a swelling on the skin, esp. one caused by illness or injury. ■ dated or humorous a prominence on a person's skull, formerly thought to indicate a particular mental faculty; such a faculty. **3** a loosely woven fleeced cotton fabric used in upholstery and as lining material. ▶ v. **1** [intrans.] knock or run into someone or something, typically with a jolt: *I almost* ***bumped into him*** | [trans.] *she bumped the girl.* ■ (**bump into**) meet by chance. ■ [trans.] hurt or damage (something) by striking or knocking it against something else. ■ [trans.] cause to collide with something. **2** [no obj., with adverbial of direction] move or travel with much jolting and jarring: *the car* ***bumped along*** *the rutted track.* ■ [with obj. and adverbial of direction] push (something) jerkily in a specified direction. **3** [trans.] refuse (a passenger) a reserved place on an airline flight, typically because of deliberate overbooking. ■ cause to move from a job or position, typically in favor of someone else; displace.

– PHRASAL VERBS **bump someone off** informal murder someone. **bump someone up** informal move someone to a higher level or status; promote. **bump something up** informal **1** make larger, greater, or more numerous; increase. **2** make, complete, or release earlier than planned or expected. [16th C. (as a v.): imitative, perh. of Scand. origin.]

bump·er /ˈbəmpər/ ▶ n. **1** a horizontal bar fixed across the front or back of a motor vehicle to reduce damage in a collision or as a trim. **2** archaic a generous glassful of an alcoholic drink, typically one drunk as a toast. ▶ adj. exceptionally large, fine, or successful.

– PHRASES **bumper-to-bumper** very close together, as cars in a traffic jam.

bump·er stick·er ▶ n. a label carrying a slogan or advertisement fixed to a vehicle's bumper.

bump·kin /ˈbəmpkin/ ▶ n. an unsophisticated or socially awkward person from the countryside. — **bump·kin·ish** adj. [16th C.: perh. from Du. *boomken* 'little tree' or MDu. *bommekijn* 'little barrel.']

bump·tious /ˈbəmpSHəs/ ▶ adj. self-assertive or proud to an irritating degree. — **bump·tious·ly** adv. **bump·tious·ness** n. [19th C.: from BUMP.]

bump·y /ˈbəmpē/ ▶ adj. (**bump·i·er, bump·i·est**) (of a surface) uneven, with many patches raised above the rest. ■ (of a journey or other movement) involving sudden jolts and jerks, esp. caused by an uneven surface. ■ fig. fluctuating and unreliable; subject to unexpected difficulties. — **bump·i·ly** /-pəlē/ adv. **bump·i·ness** n.

bum rap ▶ n. [in sing.] informal a false charge, typically one leading to imprisonment. ■ fig. an unfair punishment or scolding.

bum-rush ▶ v. [trans.] suddenly force or barge one's way into.

bum steer ▶ n. informal a piece of false information or guidance. [1920s: from BUM² + STEER¹.]

bun /bən/ ▶ n. **1** a bread roll of various shapes and flavorings, typically sweetened and often containing dried fruit. **2** a hairstyle in which the hair is drawn back into a tight coil at the back of the head. **3** (**buns**) informal a person's buttocks.

– PHRASES **have a bun in the oven** informal be pregnant. [ME: of unknown origin.]

bunch /bənCH/ ▶ n. a number of things, typically of the same kind, growing or fastened together. ■ [in sing.] informal a group of people. ■ informal a large number or quantity; a lot. ▶ v. [trans.] collect or fasten into a compact group: *she bunched the carnations together.* ■ gather (cloth) into close folds. ■ [intrans.] (of cloth) gather into close folds: *his pants bunched around his ankles.* ■ [intrans.] form into a tight group or crowd. ■ [intrans.] (of muscles) flex or bulge.

– PHRASES **the best** (or **the pick**) **of the bunch** the best in a particular group. — **bunch·y** adj. [ME: of unknown origin.]

bunch·ber·ry /ˈbənCHˌberē/ ▶ n. (pl. **-ries**) a low-growing plant (*Cornus canadensis*) of the dogwood family that produces white flowers followed by red berries and bright red autumn foliage.

Bunche /bənCH/, Ralph Johnson (1904–71), US diplomat. Instrumental in the settlement of the Israeli-Arab conflict in 1948, he was the first African-American Nobelist. Nobel Peace Prize (1950).

bunch·flow·er /'bənCH,flouər/ ▶n. a North American plant (*Melanthium virginicum*) of the lily family, sometimes cultivated for its yellowish-green flowers.

bunch grass (also **bunch·grass**) ▶n. a grass (*Schizachyrium* and other genera) that grows in clumps, in particular *S. scoparium*, used for grazing and in erosion control, esp. on the Great Plains.

bun·co /'bəNGkō/ (also **bunko**) informal ▶n. (pl. **-cos**) [often as adj.] a swindle or confidence game. ▶v. (**-coes, -coed**) [trans.] dated swindle or cheat. [19th C.: perh. from Sp. *banca*, a card game.]

bun·combe ▶n. var. of BUNKUM.

bund[1] /bənd/ ▶n. an embankment or causeway, particularly in India and other Asian countries. [19th C.: from Urdu *band*, from Pers.]

bund[2] /bŏŏnd; bənd/ ▶n. an association, esp. a political one. ■ (**Bund**) a pro-Nazi German-American organization of the 1930s. ■ (**Bund**) an Ashkenazi Jewish socialist movement founded in Russia in 1897.

Bun·des·tag /'bŏŏndəs,täg/ the Lower House of Parliament in Germany. [Ger., from *Bund* 'federation' + *tagen* 'confer.']

bun·dle /'bəndl/ ▶n. a collection of things, or a quantity of material, tied or wrapped up together. ■ fig. a large quantity or collection, typically a disorganized one. ■ [in sing.] informal a person displaying a specified characteristic to a very high degree. ■ fig. a person, esp. a child, huddled or wrapped up. ■ a set of nerve, muscle, or other fibers running close together in parallel. ■ Comput. a set of software or hardware sold together. ■ (**a bundle**) informal a large amount of money. ▶v. **1** [trans.] tie or roll up (a number of things) together as though into a parcel: *she bundled up her clothes.* ■ [with obj. and adverbial] wrap or pack (something): *the figure was bundled in furs.* ■ (usu. **be bundled up**) dress (someone) in many clothes to keep warm: *they were bundled up in thick sweaters* | [intrans.] *I bundled up in my parka.* ■ Comput. sell (items of hardware and software) as a package. **2** [with obj. and adverbial of direction] (often **be bundled**) informal push or carry forcibly: *he was bundled into a van.* ■ send (someone) away hurriedly or unceremoniously: *the old man was bundled off into exile.* ■ [no obj., with adverbial of direction] (esp. of a group of people) move clumsily or in a disorganized way. **3** [intrans.] dated sleep fully clothed with another person, particularly during courtship, as a former local custom in New England and Wales.

– PHRASES **a bundle of fun** (or **laughs**) [often with negative] informal something extremely amusing or pleasant. **a bundle of nerves** informal a person who is extremely timid or tense. [ME: perh. from OE *byndelle* 'a binding,' reinforced by Low Ger. and Du. *bundel*.]

Bundt cake /bənt/ ▶n. trademarka ring-shaped cake made in a fluted tube pan, called a **Bundt pan**.

bung /bəNG/ ▶n. a stopper for closing a hole in a container. ▶v. [trans.] close with a stopper: *the casks are bunged before delivery.* ■ (**bung something up**) block (something), typically by overfilling it: *vegetable peelings bung up the sink.* [ME: from MDu. *bonghe* (n.).]

bun·ga·low /'bəNGgə,lō/ ▶n. a low house, with a broad front porch, having either no upper floor or upper rooms set in the roof, typically with dormer windows. [17th C.: from Hindi *baṅglā* 'belonging to Bengal.']

bun·gee /'bənjē/ ▶n. (also **bungee cord**) a long nylon-cased rubber band, used typically for securing luggage. [1930s ('elastic cord'): of unknown origin.]

bun·gee-jump·ing ▶n. the sport of leaping from a height while secured by a long nylon-cased rubber band from the ankles. — **bun·gee-jump** n., adj. **bun·gee-jump·er** n.

bung·hole /'bəNG,hōl/ ▶n. an aperture through which a cask can be filled or emptied.

bun·gle /'bəNGgəl/ ▶v. [trans.] carry out (a task) clumsily or incompetently, leading to failure or an unsatisfactory outcome: *she had bungled every attempt to help* | [as adj.] (**bungled**) *a bungled bank raid.* ■ [intrans.] [usu. as adj.] (**bungling**) make or be prone to making many mistakes: *a bungling amateur.* ▶n. a mistake or failure. —**bun·gler** /-g(ə)lər/ n. [16th C.: imitative.]

Bu·nin /'bŏŏnyin/, Ivan Alekseevich (1870–1953), Russian poet and writer, noted for themes of peasant life and love. Nobel Prize for Literature (1933).

bun·ion /'bənyən/ ▶n. a painful swelling on the first joint of the big toe. [18th C.: from OFr. *buignon*, from *buigne* 'bump on the head.']

bunk[1] /bəNGk/ ▶n. a narrow shelflike bed, typically one of two or more arranged one on top of the other. ▶v. [intrans.] sleep in a narrow berth or improvised bed, typically in shared quarters as a temporary arrangement: *they bunk together in the dormitory.* [18th C.: perh. rel. to BUNKER.]

bunk[2] ▶n. informal nonsense. [20th C.: abbrev. of BUNKUM.]

bunk bed ▶n. a piece of furniture consisting of two beds, one above the other, that form a unit.

bun·ker /'bəNGkər/ ▶n. **1** a large container or compartment for storing fuel. **2** a reinforced underground shelter, typically for use in wartime. **3** a hollow filled with sand, used as an obstacle on a golf course. ▶v. [trans.] **1** fill the fuel containers of (a ship); refuel. **2** (**be bunkered**) Golf (of a player) have one's ball lodged in a bunker: *he was bunkered at the fifth hole.* [16th C.: perh. rel. to BUNK[1].]

Bun·ker Hill /'bəNGkər/ a hill in northern Boston, Massachusetts. The first battle of the American Revolution was fought nearby on Breed's Hill in 1775.

bunk·house /'bəNGk,hous/ ▶n. a building offering basic sleeping accommodations for workers, visitors, or campers.

bunk·mate /'bəNGk,māt/ ▶n. a person who sleeps in an adjoining bunk or who shares one's sleeping quarters.

bun·ko ▶n. var. of BUNCO.

bun·kum /'bəNGkəm/ (also **bun·combe**) ▶n. informal nonsense. [19th C. *Buncombe* County in North Carolina, mentioned in inconsequential speech made by its congressman (*c.*1820).]

bun·ny /'bənē/ ▶n. (pl. **-nies**) informal (also **bunny rabbit**) a rabbit, esp. a young one. ■ [with adj.] informal a person of a specified type or in a specified mood. [17th C.: from dial. *bun* 'squirrel, rabbit.']

bun·ny-hop ▶v. [intrans.] jump forward in a crouched position. ■ [trans.] move (a vehicle) forward jerkily. ■ move a bicycle forward by jumping in the air while standing on the pedals. ■ [trans.] jump (an obstacle) on a bicycle in this way. ▶n. (usu. **bun·ny hop**) **1** a jump in a crouched position. ■ a short jump forward on a bicycle. ■ an obstacle on a cycling course. **2** a dance of hopping steps in which the participants face the same direction and form a line by placing their hands on the waist or shoulders of the person in front of them.

bun·ny slope ▶n. Skiing a gentle slope suitable for beginners.

Bun·sen /'bənsən/, Robert Wilhelm Eberhard (1811–99), German chemist. He designed the Bunsen burner in 1855.

Bun·sen burn·er ▶n. a small adjustable gas burner used in laboratories.

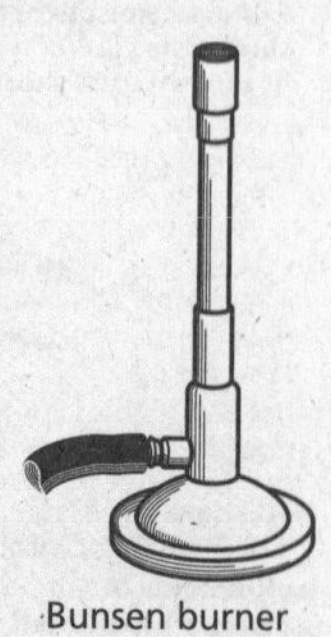
Bunsen burner

Bun·shaft /'bən,sHaft/, Gordon (1909–90), US architect, noted for his use of the International style in corporate architecture.

bunt[1] /bənt/ ▶v. [trans.] **1** Baseball (of a batter) gently tap (a pitched ball) without swinging in an attempt to make it more difficult to field: *the batter tried to bunt the ball* | [intrans.] *Phil bunted and got to first.* ■ (of a batter) help (a base runner) to progress to a further base by tapping a ball in such a way: *he bunted Davis to third.* **2** (of a person or animal) butt with the head or horns. ▶n. **1** Baseball an act or result of tapping a pitched ball in such a way. **2** an act of flying an aircraft in part of an outside loop. [18th C.: prob. rel. to the n. BUTT[1].]

bunt[2] ▶n. the baggy center of a fishing net or a sail. [16th C.: of unknown origin.]

bunt[3] ▶n. a disease of wheat caused by a smut fungus (*Tilletia caries*), the spores of which give off a smell of rotten fish. [17th C. (denoting the puffball fungus): of unknown origin.]

bunt·ing[1] /'bəntiNG/ ▶n. **1** an Old World seed-eating songbird (*Emberiza* and other genera, family Emberizidae) related to the finches, typically with brown streaked plumage and a boldly marked head. **2** a small New World songbird (genera *Passerina* and *Cyanocompsa*, family Emberizidae) of the cardinal subfamily (Cardinalinae), the male of which is brightly colored. [ME: of unknown origin.]

bunt·ing[2] ▶n. flags and other colorful festive decorations. ■ a loosely woven fabric used for such decoration. [18th C.: of unknown origin.]

bunt·line /'bənt,līn/ ▶n. a line for restraining the loose center of a sail while it is furled.

Bu·ñuel /bŏŏn'wel/, Luis (1900–83), Spanish director. His movies include *Belle de jour* (1967) and *The Discreet Charm of the Bourgeoisie* (1972).

bun·ya /'bənyə/ (also **bunya pine** or **bun·ya-bun·ya**) ▶n. a tall coniferous Australian tree (*Araucaria bidwillii*) of the monkey puzzle family that bears large cones containing edible seeds. [19th C.: from Wiradhuri.]

Bun·yan /'bənyən/, John (1628–88), English writer. His major work, *The Pilgrim's Progress* (1678–84), is an allegory recounting a spiritual journey. — **Bun·yan·esque** /,bənyə'nesk/ adj.

Buo·na·par·te /,bwōnä'pärtä/ see BONAPARTE.

Buo·nar·ro·ti /,bwänə'rôtē/, Michelangelo, see MICHELANGELO.

bu·oy /'bōō-ē; boi/ ▶n. an anchored float serving as a navigation mark, to show reefs or other hazards, or for mooring. ▶v. [trans.] **1** keep (someone or something) afloat: *I let the water* **buoy up** *my weight.* [via Sp. *boyar* 'to float,' from *boya* 'buoy.'] ■ (often **be buoyed**) cause to become cheerful or confident. ■ (often **be buoyed**) cause (a price) to rise to or remain at a high level. **2** mark with a buoy. [ME: prob. from MDu. *boye, boeie*, from Gmc., 'signal.']

buoy·an·cy /'boi-ənsē; 'bōōyənsē/ ▶n. the ability or tendency to float in water or other fluid. ■ the power of a liquid to keep something afloat. ■ fig. an optimistic and cheerful disposition. ■ fig. a high level of activity in an economy or stock market.

buoy·ant /'boi-ənt; 'bōōyənt/ ▶adj. able or apt to keep afloat or rise to the top of a liquid or gas. ■ (of a liquid or gas) able to keep something afloat. ■ fig. (of an economy, business, or market) involving or engaged in much activity. ■ fig. cheerful and optimistic. — **buoy·ant·ly** adv. [16th C.: from Fr. *bouyant* or Sp. *boyante*, pres. part. of *boyar* 'to float' (see BUOY).]

bup·kis /'bŏŏpkis; 'bəp-/ ▶n. informal nothing at all: *you know bupkis about fund-raising.* [from Yiddish.]

bup·pie /'bəpē/ ▶n. (pl. **-pies**) informal a young urban black professional; a black yuppie.

bur /bər/ (also **burr**) ▶n. **1** a prickly seed case or flowerhead that clings to animals and clothes. ■ [usu. as adj.] a plant that produces burs, e.g., bur reed. **2** [as adj.] denoting wood containing knots or other growths that show a pattern of dense swirls in the grain when sawn. **3** the coronet of a deer's antler. **4** var. of BURR (senses 2 and 3). [Senses 1, 2 are possibly of Scand. origin, akin to Dan. *burre* 'bur,'; sense 3 is possibly from Fr. (cf. *bourre* 'vine-bud').]

bur. ▶ abbr. bureau.

burb /bərb/ ▶ n. (usu. **the burbs**) informal short for SUBURB.

Bur·bank[1] /'bər,baNGk/ a city in southern California; pop. 93,640.

Bur·bank[2], Luther (1849–1926), US horticulturist. His experiments in cross-breeding led to new types and improved varieties of plants.

bur·ble /'bərbəl/ ▶ v. [intrans.] make a continuous murmuring noise: *the wind burbled at his ear.* ■ speak in an unintelligible or silly way, typically at unnecessary length: *he* **burbled on** *about annuities* | [trans.] *he was burbling inanities.* ■ Aeron. [often as n.] (**burbling**) (of an airflow) break up into turbulence. ▶ n. continuous murmuring noise. ■ rambling speech. [ME: imitative.]

bur·bot /'bərbət/ ▶ n. an elongated bottom-dwelling fish (*Lota lota*) of Eurasia and North America. It is the only freshwater fish of the cod family. [ME: from OFr. *borbete*, prob. from *borbe* 'mud.']

bur·den /'bərdn/ ▶ n. **1** a load, esp. a heavy one. ■ fig. a duty or misfortune that causes hardship, anxiety, or grief; a nuisance. ■ the main responsibility for achieving a specified aim or task. ■ a ship's carrying capacity; tonnage. **2** (**the burden**) the main theme or gist of a speech, book, or argument. ■ the refrain or chorus of a song. ▶ v. [trans.] (usu. **be burdened**) load heavily: *she walked forward* **burdened with** *a wooden box.* ■ fig. cause (someone) hardship or distress.
– PHRASES **burden of proof** the obligation to prove one's assertion. — **bur·den·some** /'-səm/ adj. [OE *byrthen*, of West Gmc. origin; rel. to BEAR[1].]

bur·dock /'bərdäk/ ▶ n. a large herbaceous plant (genus *Arctium*) of the daisy family. The hook-bearing flowers become woody burrs after fertilization and cling to animals' coats for seed dispersal. [16th C.: from BUR + DOCK[3].]

bu·reau /'byŏŏrō/ ▶ n. (pl. **bu·reaus** or **bu·reaux** /'byŏŏrōz/) **1** a chest of drawers. **2** (abbr.: **bur.**) an office or department for transacting particular business. ■ the office in a particular place of an organization based elsewhere. ■ a government department. [17th C.: from Fr., orig. 'baize,' from OFr. *burel*, prob. from *bure* 'dark brown,' based on Gk. *purros* 'red.']

bu·reauc·ra·cy /byŏŏ'räkrəsē/ ▶ n. (pl. **-cies**) a system of government in which most of the important decisions are made by state officials rather than by elected representatives. ■ a state or organization governed or managed according to such a system. ■ the officials in such a system, considered as a group or hierarchy. ■ excessively complicated administrative procedure, seen as characteristic of such a system. [19th C.: from Fr. *bureaucratie*, from *bureau* (see BUREAU).]

bu·reau·crat /'byŏŏrə,krat/ ▶ n. an official in a government department. ■ an administrator concerned with procedural correctness at the expense of people's needs. — **bu·reau·crat·ic** /,byŏŏrə'kratik/ adj. **bu·reau·crat·i·cal·ly** /,byŏŏrə'kratik(ə)lē/ adv.

bu·reau·crat·ese /byŏŏ,räkrə'tēz; -'tēs/ ▶ n. a style of speech or writing characterized by jargon, euphemism, and abstractions, held to be typical of bureaucrats.

bu·reauc·ra·tize /byŏŏ'räkrə,tīz/ ▶ v. [trans.] [usu. as adj.] (**bureaucratized**) govern (someone or something) by an excessively complicated administrative procedure: *bureaucratized welfare systems.* — **bu·reauc·ra·ti·za·tion** /-,räkrəti'zāSHən/ n.

bu·rette /byŏŏ'ret/ (also **bu·ret**) ▶ n. a graduated glass tube with a tap at one end, for delivering known volumes of a liquid, esp. in titrations. [19th C.: from Fr., from *buire* 'jug,' of Gmc. origin; rel. to Ger. *Bauch* 'stomach.']

burg /bərg/ ▶ n. an ancient or medieval fortress or walled town. ■ informal a town or city. [18th C.: from late L. *burgus* (see BURGESS); sense 2 from Ger. *Burg* 'castle'; rel. to BOROUGH.]

bur·gage /'bərgij/ ▶ n. hist. (in England and Scotland) tenure of land in a town held in return for service or annual rent. ■ a house or other property held by such tenure. [ME: from med. L. *burgagium*, from *burgus* 'fortified town,' of Gmc. origin, akin to BOROUGH.]

Bur·gas /'bərgəs/ a city in eastern Bulgaria, on the Black Sea; pop. 226,120.

bur·gee /bər'jē; 'bərjē/ ▶ n. a flag bearing the colors or emblem of a sailing club, typically triangular. [18th C.: perh. from Fr. *bourgeois* (see BURGESS) 'owner.']

bur·geon /'bərjən/ ▶ v. [intrans.] [often as adj.] (**burgeoning**) begin to grow or increase rapidly; flourish: *manufacturers are keen to cash in on the burgeoning demand.* ■ put forth young shoots; bud. [ME: from OFr. *bourgeonner* 'put out buds,' from *borjon* 'bud,' based on late L. *burra* 'wool.']

Bur·ger /'bərgər/, Warren Earl (1907–95), Chief Justice of the US 1969–86. He was a conservative, except in matters of civil rights.

burg·er /'bərgər/ ▶ n. short for HAMBURGER. ■ [with adj.] a particular variation of a hamburger with additional or substitute ingredients. [1930s (orig. US): abbrev.]

Bur·gess /'bərjəs/, Anthony (1917–93), English writer; pseudonym of *John Anthony Burgess Wilson.* He wrote *A Clockwork Orange* (1962).

bur·gess /'bərjis/ ▶ n. a person with municipal authority or privileges, in particular: ■ Brit., hist. a member of Parliament for a borough, corporate town, or university. ■ (in the US and also historically in the UK) a magistrate or member of the governing body of a town. ■ hist. a member of the assembly of colonial Maryland or Virginia. [ME: from Anglo-Norman Fr. *burgeis*, from late L. *burgus* 'castle'; rel. to BOROUGH.]

burgh /bərg; 'bərə/ ▶ n. archaic or Scot. a borough or chartered town. — **burgh·al** /'bərgəl/ adj. [ME: Scots form of BOROUGH.]

burgh·er /'bərgər/ ▶ n. archaic or humorous a citizen of a town or city, typically a member of the wealthy bourgeoisie.

bur·glar /'bərglər/ ▶ n. a person who commits burglary. — **bur·glar·i·ous** /bər'gle(ə)rēəs/ adj. (archaic). [16th C.: from legal Fr. *burgler* or Anglo-L. *burgulator, burglator*; rel. to OFr. *burgier* 'pillage.']

bur·glar·ize /'bərglə,rīz/ ▶ v. [trans.] (often **be burglarized**) enter (a building) illegally with intent to commit a crime, esp. theft.

bur·glar·proof /'bərglər,prōōf/ ▶ adj. protected against or providing protection against burglary.

bur·gla·ry /'bərglərē/ ▶ n. (pl. **-ries**) entry into a building illegally with intent to commit a crime, esp. theft.

bur·gle /'bərgəl/ ▶ v. another term for BURGLARIZE. [19th C.: back-form. from BURGLAR.]

bur·go·mas·ter /'bərgə,mastər/ ▶ n. the mayor of a Dutch, Flemish, German, Austrian, or Swiss town. [16th C.: from Du. *burgemeester*, from *burg* 'castle' + *meester* 'master.']

bur·go·net /'bərgə,net; ,bərgə'net/ ▶ n. hist. a kind of visored helmet. [16th C.: from Fr. *bourguignotte*, perh. fem. of *bourguignot* 'Burgundian.']

burgonet

bur·goo /bər'gōō/ ▶ n. a stew or thick soup, typically made for an outdoor meal. ■ an outdoor meal at which such food is served. ■ esp. Naut. a thick porridge. [from Arab. *burgul.*]

Bur·gos /'bŏŏrgōs/ a town in northern Spain; pop. 169,280.

Bur·goyne /'bər,goin; bər'goin/, John (1722–92), English general. He surrendered to the Americans at Saratoga (1777) during the American Revolution.

Bur·gun·di·an /bər'gəndēən/ ▶ n. a native or inhabitant of Burgundy. ■ hist. a member of a Germanic people that invaded Gaul from the east and established the kingdom of Burgundy in the 5th century AD. ▶ adj. of or relating to Burgundy or the Burgundians.

Bur·gun·dy /'bərgəndē/ a region and former duchy of eastern central France, the center of which is Dijon. French name BOURGOGNE.

bur·gun·dy /'bərgəndē/ (also **Bur·gun·dy**) ▶ n. (pl. **-dies**) a wine from Burgundy (usually taken to be red unless otherwise specified). ■ a deep red color like that of burgundy wine.

bur·i·al /'berēəl/ ▶ n. the action or practice of interring a dead body. ■ a ceremony at which someone's body is interred; a funeral. ■ Archaeol. a grave or the remains found in it. [OE *byrgels* 'grave' (interpreted as pl. in ME, hence the loss of *-s*), of Gmc. origin; rel. to BURY.]

bu·rin /'byŏŏrin/ ▶ n. a steel tool used for engraving in copper or wood. ■ Archaeol. a flint tool with a chisel point. [17th C.: from Fr.; perh. rel. to Old High Ger. *bora* 'boring tool.']

bur·ka /'bŏŏrkə/ (also **bur·kha, burqa**) ▶ n. a long, loose garment covering the whole body, worn in public by many Muslim women. [from Urdu and Pers. *burka'*, from Arab. *burku'*.]

Burke[1] /bərk/, Edmund (1729–97), British writer and politician. He wrote about political emancipation and moderation.

Burke[2], John (1787–1848), Irish writer. In 1826, he compiled the first edition of *Burke's Peerage*, still regarded as the authoritative guide to the British aristocracy.

Bur·ki·na Fa·so /bər'kēnə 'fäsō/ a landlocked country in western Africa. Former name (until 1984) UPPER VOLTA. *See box on next page.* — **Bur·ki·nan** /-'kēnən/ adj. & n.

Bur·kitt's lym·pho·ma /'bərkits/ ▶ n. Med. cancer of the lymphatic system, caused by the Epstein–Barr virus, chiefly affecting children in central Africa. [1960s: D. P. *Burkitt* (1911–93), British surgeon.]

burl /bərl/ ▶ n. a slub or lump in wool or cloth. ■ a rounded knotty growth on a tree, giving an attractive figure when polished and used esp. for handcrafted objects and veneers. [ME: from OFr. *bourle* 'tuft,' dimin. of *bourre* 'coarse wool,' from late L. *burra* 'wool.']

bur·lap /'bərlap/ ▶ n. coarse canvas woven from jute, hemp, or a similar fiber, used esp. for sacking. ■ lighter material of a similar kind used in dressmaking and furnishing. [17th C.: of unknown origin.]

bur·lesque /bər'lesk/ ▶ n. **1** a parody or comically exaggerated imitation of something, esp. in a literary or dramatic work. ■ humor that depends on comic imitation and exaggeration; absurdity. **2** a variety show, typically including striptease. ▶ v. (**-lesques, -lesqued, -lesqu·ing**) [trans.] cause to appear absurd by parodying or copying in an exaggerated form: *she struck a ridiculous pose that burlesqued her own vanity.* [17th C.: from Fr., from Ital. *burlesco*, from *burla* 'mockery.']

bur·ley /'bərlē/ ▶ n. (also **burley tobacco**) a tobacco of a light-colored variety grown mainly in Kentucky. [19th C.: of unknown origin.]

Bur·ling·ton /'bərliNGtən/ **1** a city in southern Ontario, Canada, on Lake Ontario; pop. 129,600. **2** a city in north central North Carolina, noted as a textile center; pop. 39,498. **3** a city in northwestern Vermont, the largest in the state, on Lake Champlain; pop. 38,889.

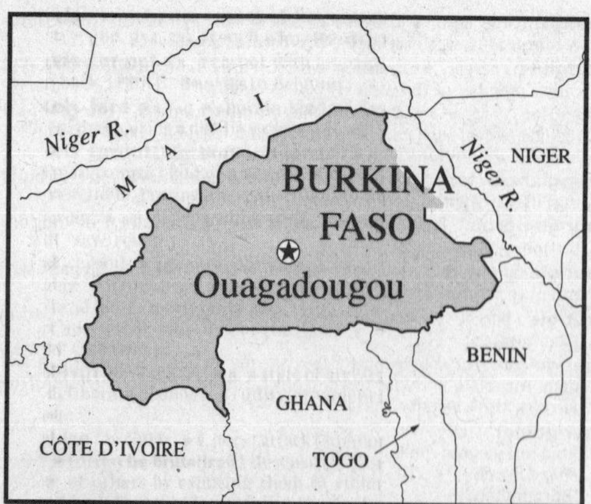

Burkina Faso

Location: western Africa, bordered on the west and north by Mali
Area: 105,700 square miles (273,800 sq km)
Population: 13,574,000
Capital: Ouagadougou
Languages: French (official), Sudanic African languages
Currency: CFA franc

bur·ly /'bərlē/ ▶ **adj.** (**-li·er, -li·est**) (of a person) large and strong; heavily built. — **bur·li·ness** n. [ME: prob. from an unrecorded OE word,'fit for the bower' (see BOWER[1], -LY[1]).]

Bur·ma /'bərmə/ see **MYANMAR.**

bur mar·i·gold ▶ **n.** another term for BEGGAR TICKS.

Bur·ma Road a route that links Lashio in Myanmar (Burma) to Kunming in China and covers 717 miles (1,154 km), used as a supply route by the Chinese during World War II.

Bur·mese /bər'mēz; -'mēs/ ▶ **n.** (pl. same) **1** a member of the largest ethnic group of Myanmar (Burma) in Southeast Asia. **2** a native or national of Myanmar. **3** the Tibeto-Burman language of the Burmese people, written in an alphabet derived from that of Pali and the official language of Myanmar. **4** (also **Burmese cat**) a cat of a short-haired breed originating in Asia. ▶ **adj.** of or relating to Myanmar, its people, or their language.

burn[1] /bərn/ ▶ **v.** (past and past part. **burned** or esp. Brit. **burnt** /bərnt/) **1** [intrans.] (of a fire) flame or glow while consuming a material such as coal or wood: *a fire burned and crackled.* ■ (of a candle or other source of light) be alight: *a light was burning in the hall.* ■ be or cause to be destroyed by fire. ■ [trans.] damage or injure by heat or fire. **2** [intrans.] (of a person, the skin, or a part of the body) become red and painful through exposure to the sun: *my skin sometimes burns.* ■ feel or cause to feel sore, hot, or inflamed, typically as a result of illness or injury. ■ (of a person's face) feel hot and flushed from an intense emotion such as shame or indignation. ■ (**be burning with**) be entirely possessed by (a desire or an emotion): *Martha was burning with curiosity.* **3** [trans.] use (a type of fuel) as a source of heat or energy. ■ [trans.] (of a person) convert (calories) to energy. **4** [trans.] produce (a compact disc) by copying from an original or master copy. **5** [no obj., with adverbial of direction] informal drive very fast: *he burned past us.* ▶ **n. 1** an injury caused by exposure to heat or flame. ■ a mark left on something as a result of being burned. ■ [with adj.] a feeling of heat and discomfort on the skin caused by friction, typically by a rope or razor. ■ a sensation of heat experienced on swallowing spicy food, hot liquid, or powerful alcohol. **2** consumption of a type of fuel as an energy source. ■ a firing of a rocket engine in flight. **3** an act of clearing vegetation by burning. ■ an area of land cleared in this way.
– PHRASES **be burned at the stake** hist. be executed by being burned alive in public, typically for heresy or witchcraft. **burn one's bridges** do something that makes it impossible to return to an earlier state. **burn the candle at both ends** go to bed late and get up early. **burn the midnight oil** read or work late into the night. **burn** (or **lay**) **rubber** informal drive very fast. **go for the burn** informal push one's body to the extremes when doing physical exercise. **money burns a hole in someone's pocket** someone has a strong urge to spend money as soon as they receive it. **slow burn** informal a state of slowly mounting anger or annoyance.
– PHRASAL VERBS **burn something down** (or **burn down**) (of a building or structure) destroy or be destroyed completely by fire. **burn something in/into** brand or imprint by burning: *designs are burned into the skin* | fig. *a childhood incident that was burned into her memory.* ■ Photog. expose one area of a print more than the rest. **burn something off** remove (a substance) using a flame. **burn out** be completely consumed and thus no longer aflame. ■ cease to function as a result of excessive heat or friction. **burn (oneself) out** ruin one's health or become completely exhausted through overwork. **burn someone out** make someone homeless by destroying their home by fire. **burn something out** completely destroy a building or vehicle by fire, so that only a shell remains. **burn up 1** (of a fire) produce brighter and stronger flames. **2** (of an object entering the earth's atmosphere) be destroyed by heat. **burn someone up** informal make someone angry. **burn something up** use up the calories or energy provided by food, rather than converting these to fat. [OE *birnan* 'be on fire', *bærnan* 'consume by fire,' from Gmc. base; rel. to Ger. *brennen*.]

burn[2] ▶ **n.** esp. Scot. & N. Engl. a small stream; a brook. [OE *burna, burn(e)*, of Gmc. origin; rel. to Ger. *Brunnen* 'well.']

burned /bərnd/ (also **burnt**) past and past participle of BURN[1]. ▶ **adj.** [attrib.] having been burned. ■ (of a taste) like that of food that has been charred in cooking. ■ (of sugar) cooked or heated until caramelized. ■ (usu. **burnt**) (of a warm color) dark or deep.

burned-out (also **burnt-out**) ▶ **adj.** (of a vehicle or building) destroyed or badly damaged by fire; gutted. ■ (of an electrical device or component) having failed through overheating. ■ (of a person) in a state of physical or mental collapse caused by overwork or stress. ■ informal (of a person) mentally or physically impaired from habitual drug use.

Burne-Jones /'bərn 'jōnz/, Sir Edward Coley (1833–98), English painter. His works include *The Mirror of Venus* (1875).

burn·er /'bərnər/ ▶ **n.** a thing that burns something or is burned, in particular: ■ a part of a stove, lamp, etc., that emits and shapes a flame. ■ an apparatus in which a fuel is used or an aromatic substance is heated. ■ [with adj.] an activity that uses something of a specified kind as energy. ■ informal a handgun.
– PHRASES **on the back** (or **front**) **burner** informal having low (or high) priority.

bur·net /bər'net; 'bərnit/ ▶ **n.** a herbaceous plant (genus *Sanguisorba*) of the rose family, with globular pinkish flowerheads and leaves composed of many small leaflets, in particular the edible **salad burnet** (*S. minor*). [ME: from OFr. *brunete, burnete*, diminutives of *brun* 'brown.']

Bur·nett /bər'net/, Frances Eliza Hodgson (1849–1924), US writer; born in England. Her children's novels include *Little Lord Fauntleroy* (1886) and *The Secret Garden* (1911).

burn-in ▶ **n.** damage to a computer or television screen, caused by being left on too long. ■ a reliability test in which a device is switched on for a long time.

burn·ing /'bərniNG/ ▶ **adj.** [attrib.] on fire. ■ very hot or bright. ■ fig. very keenly or deeply felt; intense. ■ fig. of urgent interest and importance; exciting or calling for debate. — **burn·ing·ly** adv.

burn·ing bush ▶ **n. 1** any of a number of shrubs noted for their bright red autumn foliage, in particular the kochia and the smoke tree. **2** any of a number of shrubs or trees with bright red leaves or fruits, in particular the purple-flowered North American *Euonymus atropurpurea* (family Celastraceae). **3** another term for GAS PLANT. [19th C.: Exod. 3:2.]

burn·ing glass ▶ **n.** a lens for concentrating the sun's rays on an object so as to set fire to it.

bur·nish /'bərnisH/ ▶ **v.** [trans.] [usu. as adj.] (**burnished**) polish (something, esp. metal) by rubbing: *burnished armor.* ■ fig. enhance or perfect (something such as a reputation or a skill). ▶ **n.** [in sing.] the shine on a highly polished surface. — **bur·nish·er** n. [ME: from OFr. *burniss-*, stem of *burnir*, var. of *brunir* 'make brown,' from *brun* 'brown.']

bur·noose /bər'nōōs/ (also **bur·nous**) ▶ **n.** a long, loose hooded cloak worn by Arabs. [16th C.: Fr., from Arab. *burnus*, from Gk. *birros* 'cloak.']

burn·out /'bərn,out/ ▶ **n. 1** the reduction of a fuel or substance to nothing through use or combustion. **2** physical or mental collapse caused by overwork or stress. ■ informal a habitual drug abuser. **3** failure of an electrical device or component through overheating.

Burns /bərnz/, Robert (1759–96), Scottish poet. He is also noted for his collection of old Scottish songs, including "Auld Lang Syne."

Burn·side /'bərn,sīd/, Ambrose Everett (1824–81), Union general in the American Civil War. His incompetence at the Battle of Fredericksburg in 1862 led to his transfer.

burn·side /'bərn,sīd/ ▶ **n.** (usu. **burnsides**) a mustache in combination with whiskers on the cheeks but no beard on the chin. [19th C.: General Ambrose *Burnside*.]

Burns·ville /'bərnz,vil/ a city in southeastern Minnesota; pop. 60,220.

burnt /bərnt/ ▶ **adj.** var. of BURNED.

burnt of·fer·ing ▶ **n. 1** an offering burned on an altar as a religious sacrifice. **2** (usu. **burnt offerings**) humorous overcooked or charred food.

burnt si·en·na ▶ **n.** see SIENNA.

burnt um·ber ▶ **n.** see UMBER (sense 1).

bur oak ▶ **n.** a North American oak (*Quercus macrocarpa*), with large fringed acorn cups. Also called MOSSYCUP OAK.

burp /bərp/ informal ▶ **v.** [intrans.] noisily release air from the stomach through the mouth; belch. ■ [trans.] make (a baby) belch after feeding, typically by patting its back. ▶ **n.** a noise made by air released from the stomach through the mouth; a belch. [1930s: imitative.]

burp gun ▶ **n.** informal a lightweight submachine gun.

bur·qa /'bŏŏrkə/ ▶ **n.** variant spelling of BURKA.

Burr /bər/, Aaron (1756–1836), vice president of the US 1801–05. In 1804, he killed Alexander Hamilton in a duel. Tried in 1806 for conspiracy to seize territory and create a North American nation independent of the US, he was acquitted but never overcame the label of traitor.

burr /bər/ ▶ **n.** **1** [in sing.] a rough sounding of the sound *r*, esp. with a uvular trill (a "French *r*") as in certain Northern England accents. ■ (loosely) a regional accent characterized by such a trill. ■ a whirring sound, such as a telephone ringing tone or the sound of cogs turning. **2** (also **bur**) a rough edge or ridge left on an object (esp. of metal) by the action of a tool or machine. **3** (also **bur**) a small rotary cutting tool with a shaped end, used chiefly in woodworking and dentistry. ■ a small surgical drill for making holes in bone, esp. in the skull. **4** a siliceous rock used for millstones. ■ a whetstone. **5** var. of **BUR.** ▶ **v. 1** [intrans.] speak with an accent in which the sound *r* is trilled: [with direct speech] *"I like to have a purrrpose," she burrs.* ■ make a whirring sound such as a telephone ringing tone or the sound of cogs turning. **2** [trans.] form a rough edge on (metal): *the handles were fixed by rivets burred over on the shield's front.*
– PHRASES **a burr under one's saddle** informal a persistent source of irritation. [var. of **BUR.** Sense 1 of n., v. prob. imitative.]

bur reed ▶ **n.** an aquatic reedlike plant (genus *Sparganium*, family Sparganiaceae) with rounded flowerheads and oily seeds.

burr·fish /'bər,fisH/ ▶ **n.** (pl. same or **-fish·es**) a porcupine fish (genus *Chilomycterus*) with spines that are permanently erected, occurring in tropical waters of the Atlantic and Pacific.

bur·ri·to /bə'rētō/ ▶ **n.** (pl. **-tos**) a Mexican dish consisting of a tortilla rolled around a filling, typically of beans or ground or shredded beef. [L. Amer. Sp., dimin. of Sp. *burro*, lit. 'donkey.']

bur·ro /'bərō; 'bo͝orō/ ▶ **n.** (pl. **-ros**) a small donkey used as a pack animal. [19th C.: from Sp.]

Bur·roughs[1] /'bərōz/, Edgar Rice (1875–1950), US writer. He wrote an adventure series that began with *Tarzan of the Apes* (1914).

Bur·roughs[2] /'bərōz/, William Seward (1914–97), US writer. His best-known writings, such as *Junkie* (1953) and *The Naked Lunch* (1959), deal with life as a drug addict.

bur·row /'bərō; 'bə-rō/ ▶ **n.** a hole or tunnel dug by a small animal, esp. a rabbit, as a dwelling. ▶ **v.** [intrans.] (of an animal) make a hole or tunnel, esp. to use as a dwelling: *moles burrowing away underground* | [as adj.] (**burrowing**) *burrowing earthworms* | [trans.] *the fish can burrow a hiding place.* ■ [with adverbial of direction] advance into or through something solid by digging or making a hole: *worms that burrow through dead wood.* ■ [with adverbial of direction] move underneath or press close to something in order to hide oneself or in search of comfort. ■ [trans.] move (something) in this way. ■ fig. make a thorough inquiry; investigate. — **bur·row·er n.** [ME: var. of **BOROUGH.**]

bur·ry /'bərē/ ▶ **adj. 1** having or containing burs; prickly. **2** (of speech) having a burr.

Bur·sa /'bərsə/ a city in northwestern Turkey; pop. 834,580. It was the capital of the Ottoman Empire 1326–1402.

bur·sa /'bərsə/ ▶ **n.** (pl. **-sae** /-sē/ or **-sas**) Anat. a fluid-filled sac or saclike cavity, esp. one countering friction at a joint. — **bur·sal adj.** [19th C.: from med. L., 'bag, purse,' from Gk. *bursa* 'leather.']

bur·sa of Fa·bri·cius /fa'brēsHəs/ ▶ **n.** Zool. a glandular sac opening into the cloaca of a bird, producing B cells. [19th C.: from **BURSA**, and a Latinized form of Girolama *Fabrici* (1533–1619), Italian anatomist.]

bur·sar /'bərsər/ ▶ **n. 1** a person who manages the financial affairs of a college or university. **2** esp. Scot. a student attending a college or university on a scholarship. [ME: from Fr. *boursier* or med. L. *bursarius*, from *bursa*.]

bur·sa·ry /'bərsərē/ ▶ **n.** (pl. **-ries**) **1** esp. Brit. a scholarship to attend a college or university. **2** the treasury of an institution, esp. a religious one.

burse /bərs/ ▶ **n.** a flat, square, fabric-covered case in which a folded corporal is carried to and from an altar in church.

bur·si·tis /bər'sītis/ ▶ **n.** Med. inflammation of a bursa, typically one in the knee, elbow, or shoulder.

burst /bərst/ ▶ **v.** (past and past part. **burst**) [intrans.] (of a container) break suddenly and violently apart, spilling the contents, typically as a result of an impact or internal pressure: *we inflated dozens of balloons and only one burst.* ■ [trans.] cause to break, esp. by puncturing: *he burst the balloon in my face.* ■ [trans.] (of contents) break open (a container) from the inside by growing too large to be held. ■ [trans.] suffer from the sudden breaking of (a bodily organ or vessel). ■ be so full as almost to break open. ■ feel a very strong or irrepressible emotion or impulse. ■ suddenly begin doing something as an expression of a strong feeling. ■ issue suddenly and uncontrollably, as though from a splitting container. ■ be opened suddenly and forcibly. ■ [with adverbial of direction] make one's way suddenly and typically violently: *he burst into the room without knocking.* ■ [trans.] separate (continuous stationery) into single sheets. ▶ **n.** an instance of breaking or splitting as a result of internal pressure or puncturing; an explosion. ■ a sudden issuing forth. ■ a sudden outbreak, typically short and often violent or noisy. ■ a short, sudden, and intense effort.
– PHRASES **burst someone's bubble** shatter someone's illusions about something or destroy someone's sense of well-being. [OE *berstan*, of Gmc. origin; rel. to Du. *bersten*.]

burst·er /'bərstər/ ▶ **n.** a thing that bursts, in particular: ■ Astron. a cosmic source of powerful short-lived bursts of X-rays or other radiation. ■ a violent gale. ■ a machine that separates continuous stationery into single sheets.

burst·y /'bərstē/ ▶ **adj.** informal or tech. occurring at intervals in short sudden episodes or groups. ■ relating to or denoting the transmission of data in short separate bursts of signals.

bur·then /'bər<u>TH</u>ən/ ▶ **n.** archaic form of **BURDEN.**

Bur·ton[1] /'bərtn/, Harold Hitz (1888–1964), US Supreme Court associate justice 1945–58.

Bur·ton[2], Sir Richard Francis (1821–90), English explorer and anthropologist. In 1858, he and John Hanning Speke were the first Europeans to see Lake Tanganyika.

bur·ton /'bərtn/ (also **bur·ton-tack·le**) ▶ **n.** esp. hist. a light two-block tackle for hoisting. [18th C.: alt. of ME *Breton tackle*.]

Bu·run·di /bə'ro͞ondē/ a central African country. *See box.* — **Bu·run·di·an** /-dēən/ **adj. & n.**

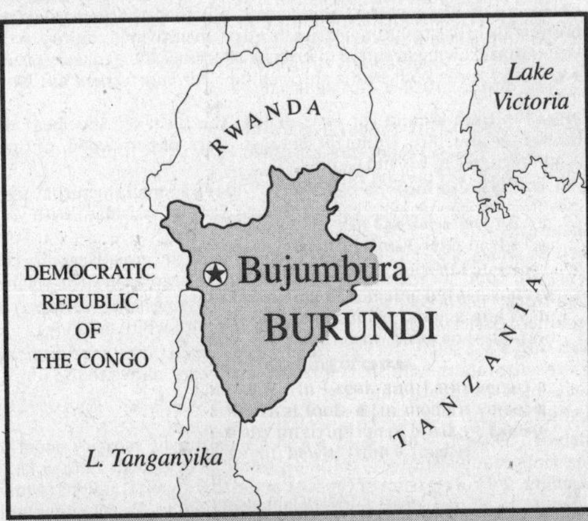

Burundi

Official name: Republic of Burundi
Location: east central Africa, on the northeastern side of Lake Tanganyika, south of Rwanda
Area: 9,900 square miles (25,700 sq km)
Population: 6,230,000
Capital: Bujumbura
Languages: French and Kirundi (both official), Swahili
Currency: Burundi franc

bur·y /'berē/ ▶ **v.** (**bur·ies, bur·ied**) [trans.] put or hide under ground: *he buried the box in the back garden* | [as adj.] (**buried**) *buried treasure.* ■ (usu. **be buried**) place (a dead body) in the earth, in a tomb, or in the sea, typically with funeral rites. ■ fig. lose (someone, typically a relative) through death. ■ completely cover; cause to disappear or become inconspicuous. ■ move or put out of sight. ■ fig. deliberately forget; conceal from oneself: *they had buried their feelings.* ■ overwhelm (an opponent) beyond hope of recovery. ■ (**bury oneself**) involve oneself deeply in something to the exclusion of other concerns.
– PHRASES **bury the hatchet** end a quarrel or conflict and become friendly. **bury one's head in the sand** ignore unpleasant realities. [OE *byrgan*, of West Gmc. origin; rel. to the v. **BORROW.**]

Bur·yat·i·a /bo͝or'yätēə/ (also **Bur·yat Re·pub·lic** /bo͝or'yät; 'bo͝oryät/) an autonomous republic in southeastern Russia, between Lake Baikal and the Mongolian border; pop. 1,049,000; capital, Ulan-Ude.

bus /bəs/ ▶ **n.** (pl. **bus·es** or **bus·ses**) **1** a large motor vehicle carrying passengers by road, esp. one serving the public on a fixed route and for a fare. **2** Comput. a distinct set of conductors carrying data and control signals within a computer system, to which pieces of equipment may be connected in parallel. ▶ **v.** (**bus·es, bused, bus·ing** or **bus·ses, bus·sed, bus·sing**) **1** [with obj. and adverbial of direction] (often **be bused**) transport in a communal road vehicle: *managerial staff was bused in and out of the factory.* ■ transport (a child of one race) to a school where another race is predominant, in an attempt to promote racial integration. **2** [trans.] remove (dirty tableware) from a table in a restaurant or cafeteria: *I'd never bused so many dishes in one night.* ■ remove dirty tableware from (a table): *Chad buses tables on weekends.* [19th C.: shortening of **OMNIBUS.**]

bus. ▶ **abbr.** business.

bus·boy /'bəs,boi/ ▶ **n.** a young man who clears tables in a restaurant or cafeteria. [19th C.: shortening of **OMNIBUS** + **BOY.**]

bus·by /'bəzbē/ ▶ **n.** (pl. **-ies**) a tall fur hat with a colored cloth flap hanging down on the right-hand side and often a plume on the top, worn by soldiers of certain regiments of hussars and artillerymen. ■ popular term for **BEARSKIN** (the cap). [18th C.: of unknown origin.]

Bush /bo͝osH/ a family of US politicians, prominent in the Republican Party. George Herbert Walker (1924–), 41st president of the US

1989–93, served in the House of Representatives 1967–71, as director of the CIA 1975–76, and as US vice president 1981–89. As president, he organized international action to expel the Iraqis from Kuwait following their invasion in 1990. His son George Walker (1946–), 43rd president of the US 2001–09, served as governor of Texas 1994–2001 before winning one of the closest and most controversial presidential contests in US history. The unpopularity of the war he launched in Iraq 2003 resulted in a general election in 2006 that gave both houses of Congress to the Democrats.

bush /bo͝osн/ ▶ **n.** a shrub or clump of shrubs with stems of moderate length. ■ a thing resembling such a shrub, esp. a clump of thick hair or fur. ■ vulgar slang a person's pubic hair, esp. that of a woman. ■ (**the bush**) (esp. in Australia and Africa) wild or uncultivated country. ■ the vegetation growing in such a district. ▶ **adj.** informal short for BUSH LEAGUE. ▶ **v.** [intrans.] spread out into a thick clump: *her hair bushed out like a halo.*

– PHRASES **beat around** (or **beat about**) **the bush** see BEAT. **beat the bushes** see BEAT. [ME: from OFr. *bos, bosc,* vars. of *bois* 'wood,' of Gmc. origin akin to Du. *bos* and Ger. *Busch.*]

bush ba·by (also **bush·ba·by**) ▶ **n.** (pl. **-bies**) a small nocturnal tree-dwelling African primate (genus *Galago,* family Lorisidae) with very large eyes.

bush bean ▶ **n.** a variety of bean plant whose bushy growth requires no support. Compare with POLE BEAN. ■ the edible bean from such a plant.

bush·buck /'bo͝osн,bək/ ▶ **n.** a small antelope (*Tragelaphus scriptus*) of southern Africa, with a reddish-brown coat with white markings.

bush dog ▶ **n.** a small, stocky carnivorous mammal (*Speothus venaticus*) of the dog family, with short legs and small ears, native to the forests of Central and South America.

bushed /bo͝osнt/ ▶ **adj.** informal tired out.

bush·el /'bo͝osнəl/ (abbr.: **bu.**) ▶ **n. 1** a measure of capacity equal to 64 pints (equivalent to 35.2 liters), used for dry goods. ■ fig. a large amount. **2** Brit. a measure of capacity equal to 8 imperial gallons (equivalent to 36.4 liters), used for dry goods and liquids. **3** a container with the capacity of a bushel.

– PHRASES **hide one's light under a bushel** see HIDE[1]. — **bush·el·ful** /-,fo͝ol/ **n.** (pl. **-fuls**). [ME: from OFr. *boissel,* perh. of Gaulish origin.]

bu·shi·do /'bo͝osнēdō/ ▶ **n.** the code of honor and morals developed by the Japanese samurai. [Japanese, from *bushi* 'samurai' + *dō* 'way.']

bush·ing /'bo͝osнiNG/ ▶ **n.** a metal lining for a round hole enclosing a revolving shaft. ■ more generally, a bearing for a revolving shaft. ■ a clamp that grips and protects an electric cable where it passes through a metal panel.

bush jack·et ▶ **n.** a belted cotton jacket with patch pockets.

bush league ▶ **n.** a minor league of a professional sport, esp. baseball. ▶ **adj.** (**bush-league**) informal not of the highest quality or sophistication; second-rate. — **bush lea·guer n.**

Bush·man /'bo͝osнmən/ ▶ **n.** (pl. **-men**) **1** a member of any of several aboriginal peoples of southern Africa, esp. of the Kalahari Desert. They are traditionally nomadic hunter-gatherers. Also called SAN. **2** the language of these peoples, now usually called SAN. **3** (**bushman**) a person who lives, works, or travels in the Australian bush.

bush·mas·ter /'bo͝osн,mastər/ ▶ **n.** a pit viper (*Lachesis muta*) of Central and South America, the largest venomous snake in the New World. [19th C.: perh. from obs. Du. *boschmeester,* from *bos* 'bush' + *meester* 'master.']

bush pig (also **African bush pig**) ▶ **n.** a wild pig (*Potamochoerus porcus* and *P. larvatus*) native to the forests and savannas of Africa and Madagascar.

bush pi·lot ▶ **n.** one who flies small aircraft into remote areas.

bush·rang·er /'bo͝osн,rānjər/ ▶ **n.** a person living far from civilization. ■ Austral., hist. an outlaw living in the bush.

bush·tit /'bo͝osн,tit/ (also **bush tit**) ▶ **n.** a small American long-tailed tit (*Psaltriparus minimus,* family Aegithalidae), with mainly pale gray plumage and sometimes a black mask.

bush·wa /'bo͝osнwä/ (also **bush·wah**) ▶ **n.** informal rubbish; nonsense. [20th C.: from Fr. *bourgeois.*]

bush·whack /'bo͝osн,(h)wak/ ▶ **v. 1** [intrans.] [often as n.] (**bushwhacking**) live or travel in wild or uncultivated country: *seven days of bushwhacking.* ■ [with adverbial of direction] cut or push one's way in a specified direction through dense vegetation: *he'd bushwhacked down the steep slopes.* **2** [intrans.] fight as a guerrilla in the bush. ■ [trans.] make a surprise attack on (someone) from a hidden place; ambush.

bush·whack·er /'bo͝osн,(h)wakər/ ▶ **n. 1** a person who clears woods and bush country. ■ a person who lives or travels in bush country. **2** a guerrilla fighter (originally in the American Civil War).

bush·y /'bo͝osнē/ ▶ **adj.** (**bush·i·er, bush·i·est**) **1** growing thickly into or so as to resemble a bush. **2** covered with bush or bushes. — **bush·i·ly** /'bo͝osнəlē/ **adv. bush·i·ness n.**

busi·ness /'biznis/ (**bus.**) ▶ **n. 1** a person's regular occupation, profession, or trade. ■ an activity that someone is engaged in. ■ a person's concern. ■ work that has to be done or matters that have to be attended to. **2** the practice of making one's living by engaging in commerce. ■ trade considered in terms of its volume or profitability. ■ a commercial house or firm. **3** [in sing.] informal an affair or series of events, typically a scandalous or discreditable one. ■ informal a group of related or previously mentioned things. **4** Theater actions other than dialogue performed by actors. **5** informal a scolding; harsh verbal criticism.

– PHRASES **business as usual** an ongoing and unchanging state of affairs despite difficulties or disturbances. **have no business** have no right to do something or be somewhere. **in business** operating, esp. in commerce. ■ informal able to begin operations. **in the business of** engaged in or prepared to engage in. **like nobody's business** informal to an extraordinarily high degree or standard. **mind one's own business** refrain from meddling in other people's affairs. [OE *bisignis* (see BUSY, -NESS).]

busi·ness card ▶ **n.** a small card printed with one's name, professional occupation, company position, business address, etc.

busi·ness cy·cle ▶ **n.** a cycle or series of cycles of economic expansion and contraction.

busi·ness day ▶ **n.** another term for WORKDAY.

busi·ness hours ▶ **plural n.** another term for OFFICE HOURS.

busi·ness·like /'biznis,līk/ ▶ **adj.** (of a person) carrying out tasks efficiently without wasting time or being distracted by personal or other concerns; systematic and practical. ■ (of clothing, furniture, etc.) designed or appearing to be practical rather than decorative. ■ excessively brisk or practical; severe or impersonal.

busi·ness·man /'biznis,man; -mən/ ▶ **n.** (pl. **-men**) a man who works in business or commerce, esp. at an executive level. ■ [with adj.] a person with a specified level of skill in financial matters.

busi·ness per·son (also **busi·ness·per·son**) ▶ **n.** a man or woman who works in business or commerce, esp. at an executive level.

busi·ness·wom·an /'biznis,wo͝omən/ ▶ **n.** a woman who works in business or commerce, esp. at an executive level. ■ [with adj.] a woman with a specified level of skill in financial affairs.

busk[1] /bəsk/ ▶ **v.** [intrans.] play music or otherwise perform for voluntary donations in the street or in subways: *busking on Philadelphia sidewalks* | [as n.] (**busking**) *busking was a real means of living.* ■ (**busk it**) informal improvise. — **busk·er n.** [17th C.: from obs. Fr. *busquer* 'seek,' from Ital. *buscare* or Sp. *buscar,* of Gmc. origin.]

busk[2] ▶ **n.** hist. a stay or stiffening strip for a corset. [16th C.: from Fr. *busc,* from Ital. *busco* 'splinter.']

bus·kin /'bəskin/ ▶ **n.** esp. hist. a calf-high or knee-high boot of cloth or leather. ■ a thick-soled laced boot worn by an ancient Athenian tragic actor to gain height. ■ (**the buskin**) the style or spirit of tragic drama. — **bus·kined adj.** [16th C.: prob. from OFr. *bouzequin,* from MDu. *broseken.*]

bus·man /'bəsmən/ ▶ **n.** (pl. **-men**) a driver of a bus.

– PHRASES **a busman's holiday** a vacation or form of recreation that involves doing the same thing that one does at work.

buss /bəs/ informal ▶ **n.** a kiss. ▶ **v.** [trans.] kiss. [16th C.: alt. of ME *bass* (n., v.), prob. from Fr. *baiser,* from L. *basiare.*]

bust[1] /bəst/ ▶ **n. 1** a woman's chest as measured around her breasts. ■ a woman's breasts, esp. considered in terms of their size. **2** a sculpture of a person's head, shoulders, and chest. [17th C.: from Fr. *buste,* from Ital. *busto,* from L. *bustum* 'tomb.']

bust[2] informal ▶ **v.** (past and past part. **bust·ed** or **bust**) [trans.] **1** break, split, or burst (something): *they bust the tunnel wide open.* ■ [intrans.] come apart or split open. ■ cause to collapse; defeat utterly: *he promised to bust the mafia.* ■ [intrans.] (**bust up**) (esp. of a married couple) separate, typically after a quarrel. ■ (**bust something up**) cause (something) to break up: *men hired to bust up union rallies.* ■ strike violently: *they wanted to bust me on the mouth.* ■ [intrans.] (**bust out**) break out; escape: *she busted out of prison.* ■ [intrans.] (in blackjack and similar card games) exceed the score of 21, losing one's stake. **2** raid or search (premises where illegal activity is suspected): *their house got busted.* ■ arrest: *he was busted for drugs.* ■ reduce (a soldier) to a lower rank; demote. ▶ **n. 1** a period of economic difficulty or depression. **2** a police raid. **3** a worthless thing. ▶ **adj.** bankrupt. [18th C.: var. of BURST.]

bus·tard /'bəstərd/ ▶ **n.** a large, heavily built Old World bird (family Otididae), in particular the **great bustard** (*Otis tarda*), which is the heaviest flying land bird. The males of most bustards have a spectacular courtship display. [15th C.: perh. Anglo-Norman Fr. blend of OFr. *bistarde* and *oustarde,* both from L. *avis tarda* 'slow bird.']

bus·tard quail ▶ **n.** the barred button quail (see BUTTON QUAIL).

bust·er /'bəstər/ ▶ **n.** esp. informal **1** a person or thing that breaks, destroys, or overpowers something: [in comb.] *a flu-buster.* ■ short for BRONCOBUSTER. **2** informal used as a mildly disrespectful or humorous form of address, esp. to a man or boy.

bus·tier /bo͞os'tyā/ ▶ **n.** a close-fitting strapless top worn by women. [1970s: Fr., from *buste.*]

bus·tle[1] /'bəsəl/ ▶ **v.** [no obj., with adverbial of direction] move in an energetic or noisy manner: *people bustled about.* ■ [with obj. and adverbial of direction] make (someone) move hurriedly in a particular direction: *she bustled us into the kitchen.* ■ [intrans.] (of a place) be full of activity: *the small harbor bustled with boats* | [as adj.] (**bustling**) *the bustling little town.* ▶ **n.** excited activity and movement. [ME: perh. var. of obs. *buskle,* frequentative of *busk* 'prepare,' from ON.]

bus·tle[2] ▶ **n.** hist. a pad or frame worn under a skirt and puffing it out behind. [18th C.: of unknown origin.]

bust·y /'bəstē/ ▶ **adj.** (**bust·i·er, bust·i·est**) informal (of a woman) having large breasts. — **bust·i·ness n.**

bus·y /'bizē/ ▶ **adj.** (**bus·i·er, bus·i·est**) having a great deal to do. ■ occupied with or concentrating on a particular activity or object of attention. ■ (of a place) full of activity. ■ excessively detailed or decorated; fussy. ■ (of a telephone line) engaged. ▶ **v.** (**bus·ies, bus·ied**) [trans.] (**busy oneself**) keep occupied: *she busied herself with her new home.*

— **bus·i·ly** /-lē/ adv. **bus·y·ness** n. [OE *bisgian* (v.), *bisig* (n.); rel. to Du. *bezig*.]

bus·y bee ▶ n. informal an industrious person.

bus·y·bod·y /ˈbizē,bädē/ ▶ n. (pl. **-bod·ies**) a meddling or prying person.

bus·y sig·nal ▶ n. a sound indicating that a telephone line is engaged, typically a repeated single bleep.

bus·y·work /ˈbizē,wərk/ ▶ n. work that keeps a person busy but has little value in itself.

but /bət/ ▶ conj. **1** used to introduce something contrasting with what has already been mentioned: ■ nevertheless; however: *he stumbled but didn't fall.* ■ on the contrary; in contrast: *I am clean but you are dirty.* **2** [with negative or in questions] used to indicate the impossibility of anything other than what is being stated: *they had no alternative but to follow.* **3** used to introduce a response expressing a feeling such as surprise or anger: *but why?* **4** used after an expression of apology for what one is about to say: *I'm sorry, but I can't pay you.* **5** [with negative] archaic without its being the case that: *it never rains but it pours.* ▶ prep. except; apart from; other than: *in Texas, we were never anything but poor* | *I trusted no one but him.* ■ used with repetition of certain words to give emphasis: *nobody, but nobody, was going to stop her.* ▶ adv. no more than; only: *he is but a shadow of his former self.* ▶ n. an argument against something; an objection: ***no buts**—just get out of here.*
– PHRASES **all but** see ALL. **anything but** see ANYTHING. **but for** except for. ■ if it were not for: *the game could be over but for you.* **but that** archaic other than that; except that: *who knows but that the pictures painted on air are eternal.* **but then** on the other hand; that being so: *it's a hard exam, but then they all are.* [OE *be-ūtan, būtan, būta* 'outside, without' (see BY, OUT).]

bu·ta·di·ene /,byo͞otəˈdīēn/ ▶ n. Chem. a colorless gaseous hydrocarbon, $CH_2{=}CHCH{=}CH_2$, made by catalytic dehydrogenation of butane and used in the manufacture of synthetic rubber. [20th C.: from BUTANE + DI-[1].]

bu·tane /ˈbyo͞otān; byo͞oˈtān/ ▶ n. Chem. a flammable hydrocarbon gas, $CH_3CH_2CH_2CH_3$, that is a constituent of petroleum and is used in bottled form as a fuel. It is a member of the alkane series. [19th C.: from BUTYL.]

bu·ta·no·ic ac·id /,byo͞otn'ō-ik/ ▶ n. systematic chemical name for BUTYRIC ACID. — **bu·ta·no·ate** /,byo͞otn'ōāt; byo͞oˈtanō,āt/ n.

bu·ta·nol /ˈbyo͞otn,ôl; -,äl/ ▶ n. Chem. either of two isomeric liquid alcohols, $CH_3CH_2CH_2CH_2OH$ and $CH_3CH_2CH(OH)CH_3$, used as solvents; butyl alcohol.

butch /bo͝och/ informal ▶ adj. manlike or masculine in appearance or behavior, typically aggressively or ostentatiously so. ▶ n. a mannish lesbian, often contrasted with a more feminine partner. [1940s: perh. abbrev. of BUTCHER.]

butch·er /ˈbo͝ochər/ ▶ n. **1** a person whose trade is cutting up and selling meat in a shop. ■ a person who slaughters and cuts up animals for food. ■ a person who kills or has people killed indiscriminately or brutally. **2** informal a person selling refreshments, newspapers, and other items on a train or in a stadium or theater. ▶ v. [trans.] (often **be butchered**) slaughter or cut up (an animal) for food: *the meat will be butchered.* ■ kill (someone) brutally. ■ fig. ruin (something) deliberately or through incompetence. [ME: ult. from OFr. *bochier*, from *boc* 'he-goat,' prob. akin to BUCK[1].]

butch·er·bird /ˈbo͝ochər,bərd/ ▶ n. a shrike, specifically one that impales its prey on thorns.

butch·er block ▶ n. a material used to make kitchen worktops and tables, consisting of strips of wood glued together.

butch·er knife ▶ n. a large, broad-bladed knife used for cutting meat.

butch·er's broom ▶ n. a low evergreen Eurasian shrub (*Ruscus aculeatus*) of the lily family, with flat shoots that give the appearance of stiff, spine-tipped leaves.

butch·er·y /ˈbo͝ochərē/ ▶ n. (pl. **-er·ies**) the savage killing of large numbers of people. ■ the work of slaughtering animals and preparing them for sale as meat.

butch hair·cut ▶ n. a haircut that is trimmed very close to the head; crewcut.

bute /byo͞ot/ ▶ n. informal term for PHENYLBUTAZONE.

bu·te·o /ˈbyo͞otē,ō/ ▶ n. a bird of prey of a group (*Buteo* and related genera, family Accipitridae) distinguished by broad wings that are used for soaring. [from L. *buteo* 'buzzard, hawk.']

Bu·the·le·zi /,bo͞otlˈāzē/, Chief Mangosuthu Gatsha (1928–), South African politician. He was leader of Zululand (later KwaZulu) 1970–94.

But·ler[1] /ˈbətlər/, Pierce (1866–1939), US Supreme Court associate justice 1922–39.

But·ler[2], Samuel (1612–80), English poet. He wrote the three-part satirical poem *Hudibras* (1663–78).

But·ler[3], Samuel (1835–1902), English writer. His novels include *The Way of All Flesh* (1903).

but·ler /ˈbətlər/ ▶ n. the chief manservant of a house. [ME: from OFr. *bouteillier* 'cupbearer,' from *bouteille* 'bottle.']

but·ler's pan·try ▶ n. a small service and storage room between a kitchen and a dining room.

butt[1] /bət/ ▶ v. [trans.] (of a person or animal) hit (someone or something) with the head or horns: *she **butted** him in the chest.* ■ strike (the head) against something. ▶ n. a push or blow, typically given with the head.
– PHRASAL VERBS **butt in** take part in a conversation or activity, or enter somewhere, without being invited or expected. **butt out** informal stop interfering. [ME: from OFr. *boter*, of Gmc. origin.]

butt[2] ▶ n. the person or thing at which criticism or humor, typically unkind, is directed. ■ (usu. **butts**) an archery or shooting target or range. ■ a mound on or in front of which a target is set up for archery or shooting. [ME (in the archery sense): from OFr. *but*, of unknown origin; perh. influenced by Fr. *butte* 'rising ground.']

butt[3] ▶ n. **1** (also **butt end**) the thicker end, esp. of a tool or a weapon. ■ the square end of a plank or plate meeting the end or side of another, as in the side of a ship. ■ the thicker or hinder end of a hide used for leather. **2** (also **butt end**) the stub of a cigar or a cigarette. **3** informal the buttocks. ■ the anus. **4** the trunk of a tree, esp. the part just above the ground. ▶ v. [intrans.] adjoin or meet end to end. ■ [trans.] join (pieces of stone, lumber, and other building materials) with the ends or sides flat against each other. [ME: n. appar. akin to Du. *bot* 'stumpy' and BUTTOCK; the v. partly from BUTT[2], reinforced by ABUT.]

butt[4] ▶ n. a cask, typically used for wine, ale, or water. ■ a liquid measure equal to 2 hogsheads (equivalent to 126 US gallons). [ME: from OFr. *bot*, from late L. *buttis*.]

Butte /byo͞ot/ a city in southwestern Montana, noted as a mining center; pop. 33,336.

butte /byo͞ot/ ▶ n. tech. an isolated hill with steep sides and a flat top (similar to but narrower than a mesa). [19th C.: from Fr., 'mound,' from OFr. *but*.]

but·ter /ˈbətər/ ▶ n. a pale yellow edible fatty substance made by churning cream and used as a spread or in cooking. ■ [with adj.] a substance of a similar consistency. ▶ v. [trans.] spread (something) with butter: *she buttered the toast* | [as adj.] (**buttered**) *buttered bread.*
– PHRASES **look as if butter wouldn't melt in one's mouth** informal appear gentle or innocent while typically being the opposite.
– PHRASAL VERBS **butter someone up** informal flatter or otherwise ingratiate oneself with someone. [OE *butere*, of West Gmc. origin; based on L. *butyrum*, from Gk. *bouturon* 'cow cheese'.]

but·ter-and-eggs ▶ n. see TOADFLAX.

but·ter·ball /ˈbətər,bôl/ ▶ n. informal a derogatory way of addressing or referring to a fat person. ■ a plump bird, esp. a turkey or bufflehead.

but·ter bean ▶ n. a lima bean, esp. one of a variety with large flat white seeds that are usually dried.

but·ter·bur /ˈbətər,bər/ ▶ n. a Eurasian waterside plant (genus *Petasites*) of the daisy family, the large soft leaves of which were formerly used to wrap butter. Extracts of the plant have been used medicinally as a powerful anticonvulsant.

but·ter·cup /ˈbətər,kəp/ ▶ n. a poisonous herbaceous plant (genus *Ranunculus*) with bright yellow cup-shaped flowers, common in grassland and as a garden weed. The **buttercup family** (Ranunculaceae) also includes anemones, celandines, aconites, clematises, and hellebores.

but·ter·cup squash ▶ n. a winter squash of a variety with dark green skin and orange flesh.

but·ter·fat /ˈbətər,fat/ ▶ n. the natural fat contained in milk and dairy products.

but·ter·fin·gers /ˈbətər,fiNGgərz/ ▶ n. (pl. same) informal a clumsy person, esp. one who fails to hold a catch. ■ clumsiness in handling something. — **but·ter·fin·gered** adj.

but·ter·fish /ˈbətər,fisH/ ▶ n. (pl. same or **-fish·es**) any of a number of fishes with oily flesh or slippery skin, in particular a deep-bodied edible fish (*Peprilus triacanthus*, family Stromateidae) of eastern North America.

but·ter·fly /ˈbətər,flī/ ▶ n. (pl. **-flies**) a nectar-feeding insect (superfamilies Papilionoidea and Hesperioidea, order Lepidoptera) with two pairs of large, typically colorful wings, distinguished from moths by having clubbed or dilated antennae, holding their wings erect when at rest, and being active by day. ■ a showy or frivolous person: *a social butterfly.* ■ (**butterflies**) informal a fluttering and nauseated sensation felt in the stomach when one is nervous. ■ (in full **butterfly stroke**) [in sing.] a stroke in swimming in which both arms are raised out of the water and lifted forward together. ■ [as adj.] having a two-lobed shape resembling the spread wings of a butterfly: *a butterfly clip.* ▶ v. (**-flies, -flied**) [trans.] split (a piece of meat) almost in two and spread it out flat.

but·ter·fly bush ▶ n. a Chinese buddleia (*Buddleia davidii*) cultivated for its large spikes of fragrant purplish-lilac or white flowers, which are highly attractive to butterflies.

but·ter·fly·fish ▶ n. any of a number of typically brightly colored or boldly marked fish of warm waters, in particular a reef-dwelling fish (*Chaetodon* and other genera, family Chaetodontidae) that is popular in marine aquariums.

but·ter·fly or·chid ▶ n. an epiphytic wild orchid (*Oncidium papilio*) of South America with large yellow and red flowers that somewhat resemble a butterfly in shape.

but·ter·fly stroke ▶ n. another term for BUTTERFLY (in swimming).

but·ter·fly valve ▶ n. **1** a valve consisting of a disk rotating on an axis across the diameter of a pipe to regulate the flow, as in the throttles of many engines. **2** a valve consisting of a pair of semicircular plates that are attached to a spindle across a pipe and hinged to allow flow only one way.

but·ter·fly weed ▶ n. a North American milkweed (*Asclepias tuberosa*) with bright orange flowers that are attractive to butterflies.

but·ter·head let·tuce /ˈbətərˌhed ˈletəs/ ▶ **n.** a class of lettuce varieties having soft leaves that grow in a loose head and are said to have the flavor of butter.

but·ter knife ▶ **n.** a blunt knife used for cutting or spreading butter or other similar spreads.

but·ter·milk /ˈbətərˌmilk/ ▶ **n.** the slightly sour liquid left after butter has been churned, used in baking or consumed as a drink. ■ a pale yellow color (used esp. to describe paint or wallpaper).

but·ter·nut /ˈbətərˌnət/ ▶ **n.** **1** a soft-timbered North American walnut tree (*Juglans cinerea*) that bears oblong sticky fruits. ■ the edible oily nut of this tree. **2** hist., informal a Confederate soldier or supporter. [from the fabric of the Confederate uniform, which was typically homespun and dyed with butternut extract.]

but·ter·nut squash ▶ **n.** a popular winter squash of a variety that has a bell-shaped fruit with sweet orange-yellow flesh.

but·ter·scotch /ˈbətərˌskäcʜ/ ▶ **n.** a flavor created by combining melted butter with brown sugar. ■ a candy with this flavor.

but·ter·weed /ˈbətərˌwēd/ ▶ **n.** a yellow-flowered plant (genus *Senecio*) of the daisy family, closely related to ragwort.

but·ter·wort /ˈbətərˌwərt; -ˌwôrt/ ▶ **n.** a carnivorous bog plant (genus *Pinguicula*, family Lentibulariaceae) of Eurasia and North America, with violet flowers borne above a rosette of yellowish-green greasy leaves that trap and digest small insects.

but·ter·y[1] /ˈbətərē/ ▶ **adj.** containing or tasting like butter. ■ covered with butter. — **but·ter·i·ness n.**

but·ter·y[2] ▶ **n.** (pl. **-ter·ies**) a pantry, or a room for storing wine and liquor. ■ Brit. a room, esp. in a college, where food is kept and sold to students. [ME: from Anglo-Norman Fr. *boterie* 'storeroom for casks,' from OFr. *bot* (see BUTT[4]).]

butt hinge ▶ **n.** a hinge attached to the abutting surfaces of a door and a door jamb.

butt·in·sky /bəˈtinskē/ ▶ **n.** (pl. **-skies**) a person who habitually butts in; an intruder or meddler.

butt joint ▶ **n.** (of wood, metal, etc.) a joint formed by two surfaces abutting at right angles.

but·tock /ˈbətək/ ▶ **n.** either of the two round fleshy parts that form the lower rear area of a human trunk. ■ (**buttocks**) the rump of an animal. [OE *buttuc*, prob. from base of BUTT[3] + -OCK.]

but·ton /ˈbətn/ ▶ **n.** a small disk or knob sewn on to a garment, either to fasten it by being pushed through a slit made for the purpose, or for decoration. ■ a knob on a piece of electrical or electronic equipment that is pressed to operate it. ■ a badge bearing a design or slogan and pinned to the clothing. ■ a small, round object resembling a button. ■ Fencing a knob fitted to the point of a foil to make it harmless. ▶ **v.** [trans.] fasten (clothing) with buttons. ■ (**button someone into**) fasten the buttons of a garment being worn by (someone). ■ [intrans.] (of a garment) be fastened with buttons: *a dress that buttons down the front.* ■ (**button it**) [often in imper.] informal stop talking.
– PHRASES **button one's lip** informal stop or refrain from talking. **on the button** informal punctually. ■ exactly right. **press the button** informal initiate an action or train of events, esp. nuclear war. **push** (or **press**) **someone's buttons** informal arouse or provoke a reaction in someone.
– PHRASAL VERBS **button something up 1** informal complete or conclude something satisfactorily. **2** [often as adj.] (**buttoned up**) repress or contain something: *keep public opinion buttoned up.* — **but·toned adj.** [in comb.] *a gold-buttoned blazer.* **but·ton·less adj.** [ME: from OFr. *bouton*, of Gmc. origin, akin to BUTT[1].]

but·ton·ball tree /ˈbətnˌbôl/ ▶ **n.** another term for SYCAMORE (sense 1).

but·ton·bush /ˈbətnˌbo͝osʜ/ ▶ **n.** a low-growing North American aquatic shrub (*Cephalanthus occidentalis*) of the bedstraw family, with small tubular flowers that form globular flowerheads.

but·ton-down ▶ **adj.** [attrib.] (of a collar) having points that are buttoned to the garment. ■ (of a shirt) having such a collar. ■ (of a person) conservative or unimaginative. ▶ **n.** a shirt with a button-down collar.

but·toned-up ▶ **adj.** reserved and not inclined to reveal information.

but·ton·hole /ˈbətnˌhōl/ ▶ **n.** a slit made in a garment to receive a button for fastening. ▶ **v.** [trans.] **1** informal attract the attention of and detain (someone) in conversation, typically against his or her will. **2** make slits for receiving buttons in (a garment).

but·ton·hol·er /ˈbətnˌhōlər/ ▶ **n.** an attachment for a sewing machine used to make buttonholes.

but·ton·hole stitch ▶ **n.** a looped stitch used for edging buttonholes or pieces of material. See illustration at EMBROIDERY.

but·ton·hook /ˈbətnˌho͝ok/ ▶ **n.** **1** a small hook with a long handle for fastening tight buttons (often formerly on buttoned boots or gloves). **2** Football a play in which a pass receiver runs straight downfield and then doubles back sharply toward the line of scrimmage.

but·ton quail ▶ **n.** a small, three-toed quaillike Old World bird (genus *Turnix*, family Turnicidae) related to the rails.

but·ton·wood /ˈbətnˌwo͝od/ ▶ **n.** **1** (also **buttonwood tree**) another term for SYCAMORE (sense 1). **2** either of two mangroves (*Conocarpus erectus* and *Laguncularia racemosa*, family Combretaceae) native mainly to tropical America, used in the production of tanbark and for charcoal.

but·tress /ˈbətris/ ▶ **n.** a projecting support of stone or brick built against a wall. ■ a projecting portion of a hill or mountain. ■ fig. a source of defense or support. ▶ **v.** [trans.] provide (a building or structure) with projecting supports built against its walls: [as adj.] (**buttressed**) *a buttressed wall.* ■ fig. increase the strength of or justification for; reinforce. [ME: from OFr. *(ars) bouterez* 'thrusting (arch),' from *boter* 'to strike' (see BUTT[1]).]

but·tress root ▶ **n.** a tree root whose upper, exposed parts project from the trunk like a buttress.

bu·tut /ˈbo͞oˌto͞ot/ ▶ **n.** (pl. same or **-tuts**) a monetary unit of the Gambia, equal to one hundredth of a dalasi.

bu·tyl /ˈbyo͞otl/ ▶ **n.** [as adj.] Chem. an alkyl radical $-C_4H_9$, derived from butane: *butyl acetate.* ■ short for BUTYL RUBBER. [19th C.: from BUTYRIC ACID.]

bu·tyl al·co·hol ▶ **n.** any of four isomeric alcohols used as solvents and in organic synthesis.

bu·tyl·ate /ˈbyo͞otlˌāt/ ▶ **v.** [trans.] Chem. to combine with a butyl group. — **bu·tyl·a·tion** /ˌbyo͞otlˈāsʜən/ **n.**

bu·tyl·ene /ˈbyo͞otlˌēn/ ▶ **n.** any of several isomeric hydrocarbons, C_4H_8, obtained from petroleum and used to make polymers and in organic synthesis.

bu·tyl rub·ber ▶ **n.** a synthetic rubber made by polymerizing isobutylene and isoprene.

bu·tyr·a·ceous /ˌbyo͞otəˈrāsʜəs/ ▶ **adj.** of or like butter.

bu·tyr·ic ac·id /byo͞oˈtirik/ ▶ **n.** Chem. a colorless, syrupy liquid organic acid, C_3H_7COOH, found in rancid butter and in arnica oil. [19th C.: *butyric* from L. *butyrum* (see BUTTER).]

bu·ty·rin /ˈbyo͞otərin/ ▶ **n.** any of three glyceryl esters of butyric acid, $C_3H_5(C_3H_4O_2)_3$, found naturally in butter.

bux·om /ˈbəksəm/ ▶ **adj.** (of a woman) plump, esp. with large breasts. — **bux·om·ness n.** [ME: from the stem of OE *būgan* 'to bend' (see BOW[2]) + -SOME[1].]

buy /bī/ ▶ **v.** (**buys, buy·ing** ; past and past part. **bought**) [trans.] **1** obtain in exchange for payment: *find some money to buy a house* | [with two objs.] *he bought me a new dress* | [intrans.] *no interest in buying into an entertainment company.* ■ (**buy someone out**) pay someone to give up an ownership, interest, or share. ■ procure the loyalty and support of (someone) by bribery. ■ [often with negative] be a means of obtaining (something) through exchange or payment: *money can't buy happiness.* ■ (often **be bought**) get by sacrifice or great effort: *greatness is dearly bought.* ■ [intrans.] make a profession of purchasing goods for a store or firm. **2** informal accept the truth of. **3** (**bought it**) informal used to say that someone has died. ▶ **n.** informal a purchase. ■ an act of purchasing something.
– PHRASES **buy the farm** informal die. **buy time** delay an event temporarily so as to have longer to improve one's own position. [OE *bycgan*, of Gmc. origin.]

buy-back ▶ **n.** the buying back of goods by the original seller. ■ the buying back by a company of its own shares. ■ a form of borrowing in which shares or bonds are sold with an agreement to repurchase them at a later date.

buy·er /ˈbīər/ ▶ **n.** a person who makes a purchase. ■ a person employed to select and purchase stock or materials for a large retail or manufacturing business, etc.
– PHRASES **a buyer's market** an economic situation in which goods or shares are plentiful and buyers can keep prices down.

buy-in ▶ **n.** **1** a purchase of shares by a broker after a seller has failed to deliver similar shares, the original seller being charged any difference in cost. **2** informal agreement to support a decision.

buy·out /ˈbīˌout/ ▶ **n.** the purchase of a controlling share in a company, esp. by its own managers.

buzz /bəz/ ▶ **n.** [in sing.] a low, continuous humming or murmuring sound, made by or similar to that made by an insect. ■ the sound of a buzzer or telephone. ■ informal a telephone call. ■ informal a rumor. ■ an atmosphere of excitement and activity. ■ informal a feeling of excitement or euphoria: *I got such a buzz out of seeing the kids' faces.* ▶ **v.** [intrans.] **1** make a humming sound: *mosquitoes were buzzing all around us.* ■ [often as n.] (**buzzing**) (of the ears) be filled with a humming sound: *a buzzing in my ears.* ■ signal with a buzzer: *the bell began to buzz for closing time* | [trans.] *he buzzed the stewardesses.* ■ [trans.] informal make a telephone call to (someone). **2** [with adverbial of direction] move quickly or busily: *she buzzed along the highway.* ■ [trans.] Aeron., informal fly very close to (another aircraft, the ground, etc.) at a high speed. **3** (of a place) have an air of excitement or purposeful activity: *the club is buzzing with excitement.* ■ (of a person's mind or head) be filled with excited or confused thoughts.
– PHRASAL VERBS **buzz off** [often in imper.] informal go away. [ME: imitative.]

buz·zard /ˈbəzərd/ ▶ **n.** a large hawklike bird of prey (family Accipitridae) with broad wings and a rounded tail, typically seen soaring in wide circles, in particular the common *Buteo buteo.* ■ a North American vulture, esp. a turkey vulture. [ME: from OFr. *busard*, based on L. *buteo* 'falcon.']

Buz·zards Bay /ˈbəzərdz/ an inlet of the Atlantic Ocean in southeastern Massachusetts, just southwest of Cape Cod.

buzz bomb ▶ **n.** informal a robot bomb, esp. the German V-1 used during World War II.

buzz cut ▶ **n.** a haircut in which all the hair is cut very close to the scalp.

buzz·er /ˈbəzər/ ▶ **n.** an electrical device, similar to a bell, that makes a buzzing noise and is used for signaling.
– PHRASES **at the buzzer** Sports at the end of a game or period of play.

buzz saw ▶ **n.** another term for CIRCULAR SAW.

buzz·word /ˈbəzˌwərd/ (also **buzz phrase**) ▶ **n.** informal a technical word or phrase that has become fashionable, typically as a slogan.

BVDs ▶ **plural n.** trademark a type of boxer shorts.

BVM ▶ **abbr.** Blessed Virgin Mary.

b/w ▶ **abbr.** black and white (used esp. to describe printing, movies, photographs, or television pictures).

bwa·na /ˈbwänə/ ▶ **n.** (in East Africa) a boss or master. ■ used as a form of address. [Kiswahili.]

BWI hist. ▶ **abbr.** British West Indies.

BWR ▶ **abbr.** boiling-water reactor.

by /bī/ ▶ **prep. 1** identifying the agent performing an action. ■ after a passive verb: *damage caused by fire.* ■ after a noun denoting an action: *further attacks by the mob.* ■ identifying the author of a text, idea, or work of art: *a book by Ernest Hemingway.* **2** [often with verbal n.] indicating the means of achieving something: *malaria can be controlled by attacking the parasite.* ■ indicating a term to which an interpretation is to be assigned: *what is meant by "fair?"* ■ indicating a name according to which a person is known: *she calls me by my last name.* ■ indicating the means of transport selected for a journey: *traveling by train.* ■ indicating the other parent of someone's child or children: *Richard is his son by his third wife.* ■ indicating the sire of a pedigree animal, esp. a horse. ■ in various phrases indicating how something happens: *I heard by chance that she has married again.* **3** indicating the amount or size of a margin. *the shot missed her by miles.* ■ indicating a quantity or amount: *billing is by the minute.* ■ in phrases indicating something happening repeatedly or progressively, typically with repetition of a unit of time: *colors changing minute by minute.* ■ identifying a parameter: *employment figures by age and occupation.* ■ expressing multiplication, often in dimensions: *a map measuring 24 by 36 inches.* **4** indicating a deadline or the end of a particular time period: *I've got to do this report by Monday.* **5** indicating location of a physical object beside a place or object: *the lamp was by the door.* ■ past; beyond: *I drove by our house.* **6** indicating the period in which something happens: *this animal hunts* **by night**. **7** concerning; according to. **8** used in mild oaths: *it was the least he could do, by God.* ▶ **adv.** so as to go past: *he let only a moment go by.* ▶ **n.** (pl. **byes**) var. of BYE[1].
– PHRASES **by and by** before long; eventually. **by the by** (or **bye**) incidentally; parenthetically: *where's Hector, by the by?* **by and large** on the whole; everything considered. **by oneself 1** alone. **2** unaided. **by way of** see WAY. [OE *bī, bi, be*, of Gmc. origin; rel. to Ger. *bei*.]

by- ▶ **prefix** subordinate; incidental; secondary: *by-form* | *by-product.*

Byb·los /ˈbibləs/ an ancient Mediterranean seaport, now Jebeil, north of Beirut in Lebanon.

by-blow ▶ **n.** Brit. **1** a side-blow not at the main target. **2** a man's illegitimate child.

by-catch ▶ **n.** the unwanted fish and other marine creatures trapped by commercial fishing nets during fishing for a different species.

Byd·goszcz /ˈbid,gôsн(cн)/ a city in north central Poland; pop. 381,530. German name BROMBERG.

bye[1] /bī/ ▶ **n. 1** the transfer of a competitor directly to the next round of a competition in the absence of an assigned opponent. **2** Golf one or more holes remaining unplayed after the match has been decided.
– PHRASES **by the bye** var. of BY THE BY (see BY). [16th C.: from the n. BY.]

bye[2] ▶ **exclam.** informal short for GOODBYE.

bye-bye ▶ **exclam.** informal way of saying GOODBYE. [18th C.: reduplication.]

by-e·lec·tion ▶ **n.** esp. Brit. an election to fill a vacancy arising during a term of office.

Bye·lo·rus·sian ▶ **adj. & n.** var. of BELORUSSIAN.

by-form ▶ **n.** a secondary form of a word: *"inquire" is a by-form of "enquire."*

by·gone /ˈbī,gôn/ ▶ **adj.** belonging to an earlier time. ▶ **n.** (usu. **bygones**) a thing dating from an earlier time.
– PHRASES **let bygones be bygones** forget past offenses or causes of conflict and be reconciled.

by·law /ˈbī,lô/ (also **by-law**) ▶ **n. 1** a rule made by a company or society to control the actions of its members. **2** a regulation made by a local authority; an ordinance. [ME: prob. from obs. *byrlaw* 'local law,' from ON *býjar*, genitive sing. of *býr* 'town.']

by·line /ˈbī,līn/ ▶ **n.** a line in a newspaper naming the writer of an article.

by·name /ˈbī,nām/ ▶ **n.** (also **by-name**) a sobriquet or nickname, esp. one given to distinguish people with the same given name.

BYOB ▶ **abbr.** bring your own bottle (or booze, or beer).

by·pass /ˈbī,pas/ ▶ **n.** a road passing around a town or its center to provide an alternative route for through traffic. ■ a secondary channel, pipe, or connection to allow a flow when the main one is closed or blocked. ■ an alternative passage made by surgery, typically to aid the circulation of blood. ■ a surgical operation to make such a passage. ▶ **v.** [trans.] go past or around: *bypass the farm.* ■ provide (a town) with a route diverting traffic from its center: *the town has been bypassed.* ■ avoid or circumvent (an obstacle or problem).

by·path /ˈbī,paтн/ ▶ **n.** (also **by-path**) an indirect route. ■ fig. a minor or obscure branch or detail of a subject.

by·play /ˈbī,plā/ ▶ **n.** (also **by-play**) secondary or subsidiary action or involvement in a play or movie.

by-prod·uct ▶ **n.** (also **by-prod·uct**) an incidental or secondary product made in the manufacture or synthesis of something else. ■ a secondary result, unintended but inevitably produced in doing or producing something else.

Byrd[1] /bərd/, Charlie (1925–99), US guitarist; full name *Charles Lee Byrd.* He introduced acoustic classical guitar techniques to jazz and popular music and was central to the samba and bossa nova movements of the 1960s.

Byrd[2], Richard Evelyn (1888–1957), US explorer. He was the first to fly over the South Pole 1929 and led further scientific expeditions to the Antarctic in 1933–34 and 1939–41.

Byrd[3], Robert Carlyle(1917–), US politician, the longest serving member of the US Congress. A Democrat from West Virginia, he has served in the US House of Representatives 1953–59 and the US Senate 1959–, and as president pro tem of the Senate 1989–95, 2001–03, 2007–.

byre /ˈbī(ə)r/ ▶ **n.** esp. Brit. a cowshed. [OE *býre*; perh. rel. to BOWER[1].]

Byrnes /bərnz/, James Francis (1879–1972), US Supreme Court associate justice 1941–42.

by·road /ˈbī,rōd/ ▶ **n.** (also **by-road**) a minor road.

By·ron /ˈbīrən/, George Gordon, 6th Baron (1788–1824), English poet, known as **Lord Byron**. His poetry includes the narrative *Childe Harold's Pilgrimage* (1812–18).

By·ron·ic /bīˈränik/ ▶ **adj.** characteristic of Lord Byron or his poetry. ■ (of a man) alluringly dark, mysterious, or moody.

bys·si·no·sis /,bisəˈnōsis/ ▶ **n.** a lung disease caused by prolonged inhalation of textile fiber dust. [19th C.: from L. *byssinus* 'made of byssus' (from Gk. *bussinos*).]

bys·sus /ˈbisəs/ ▶ **n.** (pl. **bys·sus·es** or **bys·si** /ˈbisī/) **1** hist. a fine textile fiber and fabric of flax. **2** Zool. a tuft of tough silky filaments by which mussels and some other bivalves adhere to rocks and other objects: [as adj.] *byssus threads.* — **bys·sal** /ˈbisəl/ **adj.** [ME: from L., from Gk. *bussos*, of Semitic origin.]

by·stand·er /ˈbī,standər/ ▶ **n.** a person who is present at an event or incident but does not take part.

by·street /ˈbī,strēt/ ▶ **n.** a side street off the main thoroughfare.

byte /bīt/ ▶ **n.** Comput. a group of binary digits or bits (usually eight) operated on as a unit. Compare with BIT[4]. ■ such a group as a unit of memory size. [1960s: an arbitrary formation based on BIT[4], BITE.]

by·town·ite /bīˈtounīt/ ▶ **n.** a mineral present in many basic igneous rocks, consisting of plagioclase feldspar with sodium and calcium. [19th C.: *Bytown*, former name of Ottawa, Canada, + -ITE[1].]

by·way /ˈbī,wā/ ▶ **n.** a road or track not following a main route; a minor road or path. ■ a little-known area or detail.

by·word /ˈbī,wərd/ ▶ **n.** a person or thing cited as a notorious and outstanding example or embodiment of something. ■ a word or expression summarizing a thing's characteristics or a person's principles.

by-your-leave ▶ **n.** request for permission. See also LEAVE[2].

Byz·an·tine /ˈbizən,tēn; -,tīn; bəˈzan-/ ▶ **adj.** of or relating to Byzantium, the Byzantine Empire, or the Eastern Orthodox Church. ■ of an ornate artistic and architectural style that developed in the Byzantine Empire and spread esp. to Italy and Russia. ■ (of a system or situation) excessively complicated, typically involving a great deal of administrative detail. ■ characterized by deviousness or underhanded procedure. ▶ **n.** a citizen of Byzantium or the Byzantine Empire. — **By·zan·tin·ism** /bəˈzantə,nizəm; bī-/ **n.**

Byz·an·tine Em·pire the empire in southeastern Europe and Asia Minor formed from the eastern part of the Roman Empire. It ended with the loss of Constantinople to the Ottoman Turks in 1453.

Byz·an·tin·ist /biˈzantənist; bī-/ ▶ **n.** a historian or other scholar specializing in the study of the Byzantine Empire.

Byz·an·ti·um /bəˈzantēəmw; -cнēəm/ an ancient Greek city, founded in the 7th century BC, site of the modern city of Istanbul. It was rebuilt by Constantine the Great in AD 324–330 as Constantinople.

Cc

C¹ /sē/ (also **c**) ▶ **n.** (pl. **Cs** or **C's**) **1** the third letter of the alphabet. ■ denoting the third in a set of items, categories, sizes, etc. ■ denoting the third of three or more hypothetical people or things. ■ the third highest class of academic grades. ■ (usu. **c**) the third fixed constant to appear in an algebraic expression, or a known constant. ■ denoting the lowest soil horizon, comprising parent materials. **2** a shape like that of a letter C: [in comb.] *C-springs.* **3** (usu. **C**) Music the first note of the diatonic scale of C major, the major scale having no sharps or flats. ■ a key based on a scale with C as its keynote. **4** the Roman numeral for 100. **5** (**C**) a high-level computer programming language originally developed for implementing the UNIX operating system. [formerly known as *B*, abbrev. of *BCPL.*]

C² ▶ **abbr.** ■ (**C.**) Cape (chiefly on maps): *C. Hatteras.* ■ Celsius or centigrade: *it was 29°C at noon.* ■ (©) copyright. ■ (in personal ads) Christian. ■ a 1.5 volt dry cell battery size. ■ Physics coulomb(s). ▶ **symb.** ■ Physics capacitance. ■ the chemical element carbon.

– PHRASES **the Big C** informal cancer.

c ▶ **abbr.** ■ cent(s). ■ [in comb.] (in units of measurement) centi-: *centistokes (cS).* ■ (**c.**) century or centuries. ■ (preceding a date or amount) circa; approximately. ■ (of water) cold. ■ colt. ▶ **symb.** Physics the speed of light in a vacuum: $E = mc^2$.

CA ▶ **abbr.** ■ California (in official postal use). ■ Central America. ■ chief accountant. ■ Canadian Scot. chartered accountant.

Ca ▶ **symb.** the chemical element calcium.

ca (also **ca.**) ▶ **abbr.** (preceding a date or amount) circa.

Caa·ba /'käəbə/ var. of KAABA.

CAB ▶ **abbr.** Civil Aeronautics Board.

cab /kab/ ▶ **n.** **1** short for TAXICAB. ■ hist. a horse-drawn vehicle for public hire. **2** the driver's compartment in a truck, bus, or train. ▶ **v.** (**cabbed, cab·bing**) [intrans.] travel in a taxi. [19th C.: abbrev. of CABRIOLET.]

ca·bal /kə'bäl; -'bal/ ▶ **n.** a secret political clique or faction: *a cabal of dissidents.* [16th C.: from Fr. *cabale,* from med. L. *cabala* (see CABBALA).]

Cab·a·la ▶ **n.** var. of KABBALAH.

ca·ba·let·ta /,kabə'letə; ,käbə-/ ▶ **n.** (pl. **-let·tas** or **-let·te** /-'letā/) a simple aria with a repetitive rhythm. ■ the uniformly quick final section of an aria. [19th C.: from Ital., var. of *coboletta* 'short stanza,' dimin. of *cobola,* from Old Provençal *cobla,* from L. *copula* 'connection.']

cab·a·lis·tic /,kabə'listik/ ▶ **adj.** relating to or associated with mystical interpretation or esoteric doctrine. See also KABBALAH. — **cab·a·lism** /'kabə,lizəm/ **n.** **cab·a·list** /'kabəlist/ **n.** [var. of *Kabbalistic:* see KABBALAH.]

ca·bal·le·ro /,kabə(l)'ye(ə)rō; -'le(ə)rō/ ▶ **n.** (pl. **-ros**) **1** a Spanish or Mexican gentleman. **2** (in the southwestern US) a horseman. [19th C.: Sp., 'gentleman,' based on L. *caballus* 'horse.']

ca·ban·a /kə'ban(y)ə/ ▶ **n.** a cabin, hut, or shelter, esp. one at a beach or swimming pool. [19th C.: from Sp. *cabaña,* from late L. *capana, cavana* 'cabin.']

cab·a·ret /,kabə'rā; 'kabə,rā/ ▶ **n.** entertainment held in a nightclub or restaurant while the audience eats or drinks at tables. ■ a nightclub or restaurant where such entertainment is performed. [17th C.: from OFr., lit. 'wooden structure,' via MDu. from Old Picard *camberet* 'little room.']

cab·bage /'kabij/ ▶ **n.** a cultivated plant (*Brassica oleracea*) eaten as a vegetable, having thick green or purple leaves surrounding a spherical heart or head of young leaves. ■ the leaves of this plant, eaten as a vegetable. ■ informal paper money. — **cab·bag·y adj.** [ME: from Old Fr. (Picard) *caboche* 'head,' var. of OFr. *caboce.*]

cab·bage palm ▶ **n.** any of a number of palms or palmlike plants that resemble a cabbage, in particular: ■ a Caribbean palm (*Roystonea oleraceae*) with edible buds that resemble a cabbage. ■ an evergreen plant (genus *Cordyline,* family Agavaceae) of warm regions, grown elsewhere as an indoor plant.

cab·bage pal·met·to ▶ **n.** see PALMETTO.

cab·bage rose ▶ **n.** a kind of rose with a large, round, compact double flower.

cab·bage·worm /'kabij,wərm/ ▶ **n.** any caterpillar that is a pest of cabbages, esp. that of the **cabbage white** butterfly (genus *Pieris,* family Pieridae).

Cab·ba·la /kə'bälə; 'kabələ/ ▶ **n.** var. of KABBALAH.

cab·bie /'kabē/ (also **cab·by**) ▶ **n.** (pl. **-bies**) informal a taxicab driver.

ca·ber /'kābər; 'käbər/ ▶ **n.** a roughly trimmed tree trunk used in the Scottish Highland sport of **tossing the caber**. This involves holding the caber upright and running forward to toss it so that it lands on the opposite end. [16th C.: from Scot. Gael. *cabar* 'pole.']

Ca·ber·net Sau·vi·gnon /,kabər'nā ,sōvin'yôN; -vē'nyôN/ ▶ **n.** a variety of black wine grape from the Bordeaux area of France, now grown throughout the world. ■ a red wine made from this grape.

Ca·be·za Pri·e·ta /kə'bāzə prē'ātə/ a national wildlife refuge in southwestern Arizona, in the Sonoran Desert.

cab·e·zon /'kabə,zän; -,zōn/ ▶ **n.** a heavy-bodied fish (*Scorpaenichthys marmoratus,* family Cottidae) with a broad tentacle above each eye and a green-brown body with white patches, found on the west coast of North America. [Sp.]

cab·in /'kabən/ ▶ **n.** **1** a private room or compartment on a ship. ■ the area for passengers in an aircraft. **2** a small shelter or house, made of wood and situated in a wild or remote area. [ME: from OFr. *cabane,* from Provençal *cabana,* from late L. *capanna, cavanna.*]

cab·in boy ▶ **n.** esp. hist. a boy employed to wait on a ship's officers or passengers.

cab·in class ▶ **n.** the intermediate class of accommodations on a passenger ship.

cab·in crew ▶ **n.** [treated as sing. or pl.] the members of an aircraft crew who attend to passengers or cargo.

cab·in cruis·er ▶ **n.** a recreational motorboat with sleeping accommodations.

Ca·bin·da /kə'bində/ an exclave of Angola at the mouth of the Congo River, separated from Angola by the Democratic Republic of the Congo. ■ the capital of this area; pop. 163,000.

cab·i·net /'kabənit/ ▶ **n.** **1** a cupboard with drawers or shelves for storing or displaying articles. ■ a wooden box, container, or piece of furniture housing a radio, television set, or speaker. **2** (in the US) a body of advisers to the President, composed of the heads of the executive departments of the government. ■ (also **Cabinet**) (in the UK, Canada, and other Commonwealth countries) the committee of senior ministers responsible for controlling government policy. **3** archaic a small private room. [16th C.: from CABIN.]

cab·i·net·mak·er /'kabənit,mākər/ ▶ **n.** a skilled carpenter who makes high-quality woodwork. — **cab·i·net·mak·ing n.**

cab·i·net min·is·ter ▶ **n.** (in the UK, Canada, and other Commonwealth countries) a member of a parliamentary cabinet.

cab·i·net·ry /'kabənitrē/ ▶ **n.** cabinets collectively.

cab·in fe·ver ▶ **n.** informal irritability, listlessness, and similar symptoms resulting from long confinement or isolation indoors during the winter.

ca·ble /'kābəl/ ▶ **n.** **1** a thick rope of wire or non-metallic fiber, typically used for construction, mooring ships, and towing vehicles. ■ the chain of a ship's anchor. ■ Naut. a length of 200 yards (182.9 m) or (in the US) 240 yards (219.4 m). ■ short for CABLE STITCH. ■ (also **cable molding**) Archit. a molding resembling twisted rope. **2** an insulated wire or wires having a protective casing and used for transmitting electricity or telecommunication signals: ■ a cablegram. ■ short for CABLE TELEVISION. ▶ **v.** [trans.] **1** contact or send a message to (someone) by cablegram. ■ transmit (a message) by cablegram. ■ [intrans.] send a cablegram. **2** (often **be cabled**) provide (an area or community) with power lines or with the equipment necessary for cable television. [ME: ult. from OFr. *chable,* from late L. *capulum* 'halter.']

ca·ble car ▶ **n.** **1** a transportation system, typically one traveling up and down a mountain, in which cars are suspended on a continuous moving cable driven by a motor at one end of the route. ■ a cabin on such a system. **2** a car on a cable railroad.

ca·ble·gram /'kābəl,gram/ ▶ **n.** hist. a telegraph message sent by cable: *Walter shot off a cablegram.*

ca·ble-laid ▶ **adj.** (of rope) made of three right-handed triple strands twisted together left-handed, used originally to make a large rope used for anchor cables.

ca·ble mo·dem ▶ **n.** a type of modem that connects a computer or local network to broadband Internet service through the same cable that supplies cable television service: [as adj.] *a cable-modem connection.*

ca·ble rail·way ▶ **n.** a railroad along which cars are drawn by a continuous cable, in particular: ■ a tramway on which the unpowered cars are attached, for as long as they are required to move, to a continuously moving cable running in a slot in the street. ■ a funicular.

ca·ble-read·y ▶ **adj.** [attrib.] adapted for cable television.

ca·ble re·lease ▸ **n.** Photog. a cable attached to the shutter release of a camera, allowing the photographer to open the shutter without touching or moving the camera.

ca·ble stitch ▸ **n.** a combination of knitted stitches done to resemble twisted rope.

ca·ble tel·e·vi·sion ▸ **n.** a system in which television programs are transmitted to the sets of subscribers by cable rather than by a broadcast signal.

ca·ble·way /ˈkābəlˌwā/ ▸ **n.** a transportation system in which goods are carried suspended from a continuous moving cable.

cab·man /ˈkabmən/ ▸ **n.** (pl. **-men**) a taxicab driver. ■ hist. the driver of a horse-drawn hackney carriage.

cab·o·chon /ˈkabəˌsHän/ ▸ **n.** a gem that is polished but not faceted.
– PHRASES **en cabochon** /än/ (of a gem) treated in this way. [16th C.: from Fr., dimin. of *caboche* 'head.']

ca·boo·dle /kəˈbo͞odl/ (also **ka·boo·dle**) ▸ **n.** (in phrase **the whole caboodle** or **the whole kit and caboodle**) informal the whole number or quantity of people or things in question. [19th C.: perh. from *kit and boodle.*]

ca·boose /kəˈbo͞os/ ▸ **n. 1** a railroad car with accommodations for the train crew, typically attached to the end of the train. ■ informal **(typically referring to a woman) buttocks. 2** archaic a kitchen on a ship's deck. [18th C.: from Du. *kabuis, kombuis.*]

Ca·bo·ra Bas·sa /kəˌbôrə ˈbäsə/ a lake on the Zambezi River in western Mozambique. Its waters are impounded by a dam and massive hydroelectric complex.

Cab·ot /ˈkabət/ a family of Italian explorers and navigators. John (*c.*1450–*c.*1498), Italian name *Giovanni Caboto*, sailed from Bristol, England, in 1497 in search of Asia, but in fact discovered the mainland of North America. His son, Sebastian (*c.*1475–1557), made a voyage in 1526 to explore the coast of Brazil and the Plate River.

cab·o·tage /ˈkabəˌtäzH; -bətij/ ▸ **n.** the right to operate sea, air, or other transportation services within a particular territory. ■ restriction of the operation of sea, air, or other transportation services within or into a particular country to that country's own transportation services. [19th C.: from Fr., from *caboter* 'sail along a coast,' perh. from Sp. *cabo* 'cape.']

Cab·ot Strait /ˈkabət/ an ocean passage between Newfoundland and Nova Scotia.

cab·o·ver /ˈkabˌōvər/ ▸ **n.** a truck where the driver's cab is mounted directly above the engine.

Ca·bri·ni /kəˈbrēnē/, St. Frances Xavier (1850–1917), US religious leader; born *Maria Francesca Cabrini* in Italy; known as **Mother Cabrini**. She founded the Missionary Sisters of the Sacred Heart in 1880 and became the first American saint in 1946.

cab·ri·ole /ˈkabrēˌōl/ ▸ **n.** Ballet a jump in which one leg is extended into the air forward or backward, the other is brought up to meet it, and the dancer lands on the second foot. [Fr., lit. 'light leap,' from *cabrioler* (earlier *caprioler*), from Ital. *capriolare* 'to leap in the air' (see CAPRIOLE).

cab·ri·ole leg ▸ **n.** a kind of curved leg characteristic of Chippendale and Queen Anne furniture.

cabriole leg

cab·ri·o·let /ˌkabrēəˈlā/ ▸ **n. 1** a car with a roof that folds down. **2** a light, two-wheeled carriage with a hood, drawn by one horse. [18th C.: Fr., from *cabrioler* 'to leap in the air' (see CABRIOLE).]

cabriolet 2

cab·stand /ˈkabˌstand/ ▸ **n.** a place for taxis to wait for passengers.

ca·ca·o /kəˈkou; kəˈkāō/ ▸ **n.** (pl. **-os**) **1** (also **cacao bean**) a beanlike seed from which cocoa, cocoa butter, and chocolate are made. **2** the small tropical American evergreen tree (*Theobroma cacao*, family Sterculiaceae) that bears these seeds in large, oval pods that grow on the trunk. [16th C.: via Sp. from Nahuatl *cacaua.*]

cac·cia·to·re /ˌkächəˈtôrē; ˌkacH-/ (also **cac·cia·to·ra** /-ˌtôrə/) ▸ **adj.** [postpositive] prepared in a spicy tomato sauce with mushrooms and herbs: *chicken cacciatore.* [Ital., lit. 'hunter.']

cach·a·lot /ˈkasHəˌlät; -ˌlō/ ▸ **n.** another term for SPERM WHALE. [18th C.: from Fr., from Sp. and Port. *cachalote*, from *cachola* 'big head.']

cache /kasH/ ▸ **n.** a collection of items of the same type stored in a hidden or inaccessible place. ■ a hidden or inaccessible storage place for valuables, provisions, or ammunition. ■ (also **cache memory**) Comput. an auxiliary memory from which high-speed retrieval is possible. ▸ **v.** [trans.] store away in hiding or for future use. ■ Comput. store (data) in a cache memory. ■ Comput. provide (hardware) with a cache memory. [18th C.: from Fr., from *cacher* 'to hide.']

ca·chec·tic /kəˈkektik/ ▸ **adj.** Med. relating to or having the symptoms of cachexia.

cache·pot /ˈkasHˌpät; ˈkasH(ə)ˌpō/ ▸ **n.** (pl. pronunc. same) an ornamental holder for a flowerpot. [19th C.: from Fr. *cache-pot*, from *cacher* 'to hide' + *pot* 'pot.']

cache-sexe /ˈkasHˌseks/ ▸ **n.** (pl. **cache-sexes** pronunc. same) a covering for a person's genitals, typically worn by erotic dancers or tribal peoples. [1920s: from Fr., from *cacher* 'to hide' and *sexe* 'genitals.']

ca·chet /kaˈsHā/ ▸ **n. 1** the state of being respected or admired; prestige. **2** a distinguishing mark or seal. ■ Philately a printed design added to an envelope to commemorate a special event. **3** a flat capsule enclosing a dose of unpleasant-tasting medicine. [17th C.: from Fr., from *cacher* 'to press,' based on L. *coactare* 'constrain.']

ca·chex·i·a /kəˈkeksēə/ ▸ **n.** Med. weakness and wasting of the body due to severe chronic illness. [16th C.: via late L. from Gk. *kakhexia*, from *kakos* 'bad' + *hexis* 'habit.']

cach·in·nate /ˈkakəˌnāt/ ▸ **v.** [intrans.] literary laugh loudly. — **cach·in·na·tion** /ˌkakəˈnāsHən/ **n.** [19th C.: from L. *cachinnat-* 'laughed loudly,' from v. *cachinnare*, of imitative origin.]

ca·chou /kaˈsHo͞o; ˈkasHo͞o/ ▸ **n.** (pl. **-chous**) **1** dated a pleasant-smelling lozenge sucked to mask bad breath. **2** var. of CATECHU. [16th C.: from Fr., from Port. *cachu*, from Malay *kacu.*]

ca·chu·cha /kəˈcHo͞ocHə/ ▸ **n.** a lively Spanish solo dance in 3/4 time, performed with castanet accompaniment.

ca·cique /kəˈsēk/ ▸ **n. 1** (in Latin America or the Spanish-speaking Caribbean) a native chief. **2** (in Spain or Latin America) a local political boss. [16th C.: from Sp. or Fr., from Taino.]

cack·le /ˈkakəl/ ▸ **v.** [intrans.] (of a bird, typically a hen or goose) give a raucous, clucking cry. ■ make a harsh sound resembling such a cry when laughing. ▸ **n.** the raucous clucking cry of a bird such as a hen or a goose. ■ a harsh laugh resembling such a cry. [ME: prob. from Mid. Low Ger. *kākelen*, partly imitative.]

cack·le·ber·ry /ˈkakəlˌberē/ ▸ **n.** humorous a hen's egg.

cac·o·de·mon /ˌkakəˈdēmən/ ▸ **n.** a malevolent spirit or person. [16th C.: from Gk. *kakodaimōn*, from *kakos* 'bad' + *daimōn* 'spirit.']

cac·o·dyl /ˈkakəˌdil/ ▸ **n.** Chem. a malodorous, toxic, spontaneously flammable liquid compound, $((CH_3)_2As)_2$, containing arsenic. ■ [as adj.] of or denoting the radical $-As(CH_3)_2$, derived from this. [19th C.: from Gk. *kakōdēs* 'stinking' (from *kakos* 'bad').]

cac·o·e·thes /ˌkakōˈēTHēz/ ▸ **n.** [in sing.] rare an irresistible urge to do something inadvisable. [16th C.: via L. from Gk. *kakoēthes* 'ill-disposed,' from *kakos* 'bad' + *ēthos* 'disposition.']

ca·cog·ra·phy /kəˈkägrəfē/ ▸ **n.** archaic bad handwriting or spelling. — **ca·cog·ra·pher n.** [16th C.: from Gk. *kakos* 'bad.']

cac·o·mis·tle /ˈkakəˌmisəl/ ▸ **n.** a nocturnal mammal (genus *Bassariscus*) of the raccoon family, with a dark-ringed tail, found in North and Central America. See also RING-TAILED CAT. [19th C.: from L. Amer. Sp. *cacomixtle*, from Nahuatl *tlacomiztli.*]

ca·coph·o·ny /kəˈkäfənē/ ▸ **n.** (pl. **-nies**) a harsh, discordant mixture of sounds: *a cacophony of deafening alarm bells* | fig. *a cacophony of architectural styles.* — **ca·coph·o·nous** /-nəs/ **adj.** [17th C.: from Fr. *cacophonie*, from Gk. *kakophōnia*, based on *kakos* 'bad' + *phōnē* 'sound.']

cac·tus /ˈkaktəs/ ▸ **n.** (pl. **-ti** /-tī; -tē/ or **-tus·es**) a succulent New World plant (family Cactaceae), chiefly of arid regions, with a thick, fleshy stem that typically bears spines, lacks leaves, and has brilliantly colored flowers. [17th C.: from L., from Gk. *kaktos* 'cardoon.']

ca·cu·mi·nal /kəˈkyo͞omənl/ ▸ **adj.** Phonet. another term for RETROFLEX. [19th C.: from L. *cacuminare* 'make pointed' (from *cacumen, cacumin-* 'top, summit').]

CAD /kad/ ▸ **abbr.** computer-aided design.

cad /kad/ ▸ **n.** dated humorous a man who behaves dishonorably, esp. toward a woman. — **cad·dish adj. cad·dish·ly adv. cad·dish·ness n.** [18th C.: abbrev. of CADDIE or CADET.]

ca·das·tre /kəˈdastər/ ▸ **n.** a register of property showing the extent, value, and ownership of land for taxation. — **ca·das·tral** /-ˌtrəl/ **adj.** [19th C.: from Fr., from *cadastre* 'register of property,' from Provençal *cadastro*, from Ital. *catastro* (earlier *catastico*), from late Gk. *katastikhon* 'list, register,' from *kata stikhon* 'line by line.']

ca·dav·er /kəˈdavər/ ▸ **n.** Med. or literary a corpse. — **ca·dav·er·ic adj.** [ME: from L., from *cadere* 'to fall.']

ca·dav·er·ine /kəˈdavəˌrēn/ ▸ **n.** a toxic liquid base, $H_2N(CH_2)_5NH_2$, formed by the putrefaction of proteins.

ca·dav·er·ous /kəˈdavərəs/ ▸ **adj.** resembling a corpse in being very pale, thin, or bony.

CADCAM (also **CAD/CAM**) ▸ **abbr.** computer-aided design, computer-aided manufacturing.

cad·die /ˈkadē/ (also **cad·dy**) ▸ **n.** (pl. **-dies**) a person who carries a golfer's clubs and provides other assistance during a match. ▸ **v.** (**cad·died, cad·dy·ing**) [intrans.] work as a caddie. [17th C. (orig. Scots, denoting a gentleman who joined the army without a commission, later coming to mean 'odd-job man'): from Fr. CADET.]

cad·dis·fly /ˈkadisˌflī/ (also **cad·dis fly**) ▸ **n.** (pl. **-flies**) a small, mothlike insect (order Trichoptera) with an aquatic larva (**caddisworm**) that typically builds a protective, portable case of sticks, stones, and other particles. [17th C.: of unknown origin.]

Cad·do·an /'kadō-ən/ ▶ **adj.** relating to or denoting a group of American Indian peoples formerly inhabiting the Midwest, or their languages. ▶ **n. 1** a member of any of these peoples. **2** the family of languages spoken by these peoples, possibly related to Siouan and Iroquoian. [from Caddo *kaduhdacu*, denoting a band belonging to this group.]

cad·dy[1] /'kadē/ ▶ **n.** (pl. **-dies**) [usu. with adj.] a small storage container, typically one with divisions: *a tool caddy.* See also TEA CADDY. [18th C.: from earlier *catty*, denoting a unit of weight of 113 lb. (0.61 kg.), from Malay *kati*.]

cad·dy[2] ▶ **n. & v.** var. of CADDIE.

Cade /kād/, Jack (died 1450), Irish rebel; full name *John Cade*. In 1450, he assumed the name of Mortimer and led the Kentish rebels against Henry VI.

ca·delle /kə'del/ ▶ **n.** a small, dark beetle (*Tenebroides mauritanicus*, family Cleridae) that is frequently found in food storage, where it scavenges and preys on other insects. [19th C.: from Fr., based on L. *catella, catellus* 'young (of an animal), little dog.']

ca·dence /'kādns/ ▶ **n. 1** a modulation or inflection of the voice. ■ such a modulation in reading aloud as implied by the structure and ordering of words and phrases in written text. ■ a fall in pitch of the voice at the end of a phrase or sentence. ■ rhythm: *the thumping cadence of the engines.* **2** Music a sequence of notes or chords comprising the close of a musical phrase. — **ca·denced adj.** [ME: via OFr. from Ital. *cadenza*, based on L. *cadere* 'to fall.']

ca·den·cy /'kādnsē/ ▶ **n.** esp. Heraldry the status of a younger branch of a family. [17th C.: based on L. *cadent-* 'falling,' from *cadere*.]

ca·den·tial /kā'dencHəl/ ▶ **adj.** of or relating to a cadenza or cadence. [19th C.: from CADENCE.]

ca·den·za /kə'denzə/ ▶ **n.** Music a virtuoso solo passage inserted into a movement in a concerto or other work, typically near the end. [18th C.: from Ital. (see CADENCE).]

ca·det /kə'det/ ▶ **n. 1** a young trainee in the armed services or police force. ■ a student in training at a military school. **2** formal archaic a younger son or daughter. ■ [usu. as adj.] a junior branch of a family: *a cadet branch of the family.* — **ca·det·ship n.** [17th C.: from Fr., ult. from a dimin. based on L. *caput* 'head.']

cadge /kaj/ ▶ **v.** [trans.] informal ask for or obtain (something to which one is not entitled): *he eats whenever he can cadge a meal.* | [intrans.] *they cadge, but timidly.* — **cadg·er n.** [17th C.: back-form. from *cadger* 'itinerant dealer.']

ca·di /'kädē; 'kā-/ (also **ka·di**) ▶ **n.** (pl. **ca·dis**) (in Islamic countries) a judge. [16th C.: from Arab. *ḳāḍī*, from *ḳaḍā* 'to judge.']

Ca·dil·lac /kädē'yäk; 'kadl,ak/, Antoine Laumet de La Mothe (1658–1730), French soldier and colonial administrator. He founded military posts at Mackinac in 1694 and Detroit in 1701.

Ca·diz /kə'diz; 'kādiz; 'kä-/ a city in southwestern Spain; pop. 156,560. Spanish name CÁDIZ.

Cad·me·an /kad'mēən; 'kadmēən/ ▶ **adj.** of or relating to Cadmus.

cad·mi·um /'kadmēəm/ ▶ **n.** the chemical element of atomic number 48, a silvery-white metal that occurs naturally in zinc ores and is obtained as a by-product of zinc smelting. It is used as a component in low melting point alloys and as a corrosion-resistant coating on other metals. (Symbol: **Cd**) [19th C.: from L. *cadmia* 'calamine.']

cad·mi·um yel·low ▶ **n.** a bright yellow pigment containing cadmium sulfide. Deeper versions are called **cadmium orange**; the addition of cadmium selenide gives **cadmium red.** ■ a bright yellow color.

Cad·mus /'kadməs/ Gk. Mythol. the traditional founder of Thebes in Boeotia. He killed a dragon, and when he sowed the dragon's teeth, there came up a harvest of armed men who began to fight one another. The survivors formed the ancestors of the Theban nobility.

ca·dre /'kadrē; -rā; 'käd-/ ▶ **n.** a small group of people specially trained for a particular purpose or profession. ■ a group of activists in a communist or other revolutionary organization. ■ a member of such a group. [19th C.: from Fr., from Ital. *quadro*, from L. *quadrus* 'square.']

ca·du·ce·us /kə'd(y)o͞osēəs; -sHəs/ ▶ **n.** (pl. **-ce·i** /-sē,ī; -sHē,ī/) an ancient Greek or Roman herald's wand, typically one with two serpents twined around it, carried by the messenger god Hermes or Mercury. ■ a representation of this, traditionally associated with the medical profession. [L., from Doric Greek *karukeion*, from Gk. *kērux* 'herald.']

caduceus

ca·du·ci·ty /kə'd(y)o͞ositē/ ▶ **n.** archaic the infirmity of old age; senility. ■ literary frailty or transitory nature. [18th C.: from Fr. *caducité*, from *caduc*, from L. *caducus* 'liable to fall,' from *cadere* 'to fall.']

ca·du·cous /kə'd(y)o͞okəs/ ▶ **adj.** esp. Bot. (of an organ or part) easily detached and shed at an early stage. [17th C.: from L. *caducus* 'liable to fall' (from *cadere*).]

CAE ▶ **abbr.** computer-aided engineering.

cae·cil·i·an /si'silyən/ (also **coe·cil·i·an**) ▶ **n.** Zool. a burrowing wormlike amphibian of a tropical order (Gymnophiona) distinguished by poorly developed eyes and lack of limbs. [from mod. L. *Caecilia*, from L. *caecilia* 'slow-worm.']

cae·cum ▶ **n.** (pl. **caeca**) British spelling of CECUM.

Caed·mon /'kadmən/ (7th century), Anglo-Saxon monk and poet. He is said to have been inspired in a vision to compose poetry on biblical themes.

Cae·lum /'sēləm/ Astron. a small and faint southern constellation (the Chisel), next to Eridanus. [L.]

Caen /käN/ a city in northern France, on the Orne River; pop. 115,620.

Caer·dydd /kär'dē<u>TH</u>/ Welsh name for CARDIFF.

Caer·phil·ly /kär'filē/ ▶ **n.** a kind of mild white cheese, originally made in Caerphilly in Wales.

Cae·sar[1] /'sēzər/, Gaius Julius (100–44 BC), Roman general and politician. He established the First Triumvirate with Pompey and Crassus in 60, fought the Gallic Wars 58–51, and invaded Britain 55–54. In 48, he became dictator of the Roman Empire. He was murdered on the Ides of March in a conspiracy led by Brutus and Cassius.

Cae·sar[2] ▶ **n.** a title used by Roman emperors, esp. those from Augustus to Hadrian. ■ an autocrat.
– PHRASES **Caesar's wife** a person who is required to be above suspicion. [ME: from L. *Caesar*, family name of Gaius JULIUS CAESAR.]

Caes·a·re·a /,sēzə'rēə; ,ses-; ,sez-/ an ancient port on the Mediterranean coast of Israel.

cae·sar·e·an /si'ze(ə)rēən/ ▶ **adj. & n. 1** (also **Cae·sar·e·an**) var. of CESAREAN. **2** (**Caesarean**) of or connected with Julius Caesar or the Caesars.

Caes·a·re·a Phi·lip·pi /'filə,pī; fə'lipī/ a city in ancient Palestine.

Cae·sar sal·ad ▶ **n.** a salad consisting of romaine lettuce and croutons served with a dressing of olive oil, lemon juice, raw egg, and Worcestershire sauce. [*Caesar* Cardini, early 20th-cent. Mexican restaurateur.]

cae·si·um /'sēzēəm/ ▶ **n.** British spelling of CESIUM.

cae·su·ra /si'zHo͝orə; -'zo͝orə/ ▶ **n.** (in Greek and Latin verse) a break between words within a metrical foot. ■ (in modern verse) a pause near the middle of a line. ■ any interruption or break. — **cae·su·ral adj.** [16th C.: from L., from *caes-* 'cut, hewn,' from v. *caedere*.]

CAF ▶ **abbr.** cost and freight.

ca·fard /ka'fär/ ▶ **n.** depression; melancholia. [from Fr.]

CAFE ▶ **abbr.** Corporate Average Fuel Economy.

ca·fé /ka'fā; kə-/ (also **ca·fe**) ▶ **n. 1** a small restaurant selling light meals and drinks. **2** a bar or nightclub. **3** a serving of coffee, esp. prepared European-style: [in comb.] *an assortment of cappuccinos and café mochas.* [19th C.: Fr., 'coffee or coffeehouse.']

ca·fé au lait /ka,fā ō 'lā/ ▶ **n.** coffee with milk. ■ the light brown color of this. [from Fr., lit. 'coffee with milk.']

ca·fé con le·che /'kafākän 'lecHā; ka'fā-; kə'fā-/ ▶ **n.** coffee with milk. [Sp., lit. 'coffee with milk.']

ca·fé fil·tre /,kafā 'fēlt(rə)/ ▶ **n.** coffee made with a filter over a cup or a pot.

ca·fé noir /,kafā 'nwär/ ▶ **n.** black coffee. [Fr.]

caf·e·te·ri·a /,kafi'ti(ə)rēə/ ▶ **n.** a restaurant or dining room in a school or a business in which customers serve themselves or are served from a counter and pay before eating. [19th C.: from L. Amer. Sp. *cafetería* 'coffee shop.']

caf·e·te·ri·a ben·e·fit ▶ **n.** an employee benefit selected from a variety of offerings under a fringe-benefit plan that can be tailored to fit individual needs.

caf·fein·at·ed /'kafə,nātid/ ▶ **adj.** (of coffee or tea) containing the natural amount of caffeine, or with caffeine added: *trying to avoid caffeinated beverages.*

caf·feine /ka'fēn; 'kafēn/ ▶ **n.** the alkaloid crystalline compound $C_8H_{10}N_4O_2$, found esp. in tea and coffee plants. It is a stimulant of the central nervous system. [19th C.: from Fr. *caféine*, from *café* 'coffee.']

caf·fè lat·te /,kafā 'lätā/ ▶ **n.** a drink made by adding a shot of espresso to a glass or cup of steamed milk. [Ital., lit. 'milk coffee.']

caf·tan ▶ **n.** var. of KAFTAN.

Ca·ga·yan Is·lands /,kägə'yän/ a group of small islands in the western Philippines, in the Sulu Sea.

Cage /kāj/, John Milton (1912–92), US composer. He was noted for his experimental approach, which included the use of aleatory music and periods of silence.

cage /kāj/ ▶ **n.** a structure of bars or wires in which birds or other animals are confined. ■ a prison cell or camp. ■ an open framework forming the compartment in an elevator. ■ a structure of crossing bars or wires designed to hold or support something. ■ Baseball a portable backstop situated behind the batter during batting practice. ■ (in hockey and other games) a goal made from a network frame. ■ an indoor athletic facility with areas fenced off for security. ▶ **v.** [trans.] (usu. **be caged**) confine in or as in a cage. ■ informal put in prison. [ME: via OFr. from L. *cavea*.]

cag·ey /'kājē/ (also **cag·y**) ▶ **adj.** informal reluctant to give information owing to caution or suspicion. — **cag·i·ly** /'kājilē/ **adv. cag·i·ness** (also **cag·ey·ness**) **n.** [20th C.: of unknown origin.]

Ca·glia·ri /'kälyərē; 'kal-/ the capital of the Italian island of Sardinia; pop. 211,720.

ca·hier /kä'yā/ ▶ **n.** (pl. same) an exercise book or notebook. [19th C.: from Fr.]

Ca·ho·kia /kə'hōkēə/ a village in southwestern Illinois; pop. 17,550.

PRONUNCIATION KEY ə *ago, up*; ər *over, fur*; a *hat*; ā *ate*; ä *car*; e *let*; ē *see*; i *fit*; ī *by*; NG *sing*; ō *go*; ô *law, for*; oi *toy*; o͝o *good*; o͞o *goo*; ou *out*; TH *thin*; <u>TH</u> *then*; ZH *vision*

The Cahokia Mounds, major pre-Columbian earthworks, are to the northeast.

ca·hoots /kə'ho͞ots/ ▶ **plural n.** (in phrase **in cahoots**) informal colluding or conspiring together secretly. [19th C.: of unknown origin.]

ca·how /kə'hou/ ▶ **n.** a large Atlantic petrel (*Pterodroma cahow*, family Procellariidae) that breeds in Bermuda. It is an endangered species. [17th C.: imitative of its call.]

CAI ▶ **abbr.** computer-assisted (or -aided) instruction.

cai·man /'kāmən/ (also **cay·man**) ▶ **n.** a semiaquatic reptile (*Caiman* and other genera, family Alligatoridae), similar to the alligator but with a heavily armored belly, native to tropical America. [16th C.: from Sp. *caimán*, Port. *caima-o*, from Carib *acayuman*.]

Cain /kān/ ▶ **n.** (in the Bible) the eldest son of Adam and Eve and murderer of his brother Abel.
– PHRASES **raise Cain** informal create trouble or a commotion.

ca·ique /kä'ēk; kīk/ ▶ **n. 1** a light rowboat used on the Bosporus. **2** a small eastern Mediterranean sailing ship. [17th C.: from Fr. *caïque*, from Ital. *caicco*, from Turk. *kayık*.]

cairn /ke(ə)rn/ ▶ **n. 1** a mound of rough stones built as a memorial or landmark, typically on a hilltop or skyline. ■ a prehistoric burial mound made of stones. **2** (also **cairn ter·ri·er**) a small terrier of a breed with short legs, a longish body, and a shaggy coat. [ME: from Scot. Gael. *carn*.]

Cairn·gorm Moun·tains /'ke(ə)rn,gôrm/ (also **the Cairn·gorms**) a mountain range in northern Scotland.

Cai·ro /'kīrō/ the capital of Egypt, a port on the Nile River; pop. 13,300,000. Arabic name **Al Qahira**. — **Cai·rene** /kī'rēn/ **adj. & n.**

cais·son /'kāsän; -sən/ ▶ **n. 1** a large watertight chamber, open at the bottom from which the water is kept out by air pressure and in which construction work may be carried out under water. ■ a floating vessel or watertight structure used as a gate across the entrance of a dry dock or basin. **2** hist. a chest or wagon for holding or conveying ammunition. [17th C.: from Fr., lit. 'large chest,' from Ital. *cassone*.]

cais·son dis·ease ▶ **n.** another term for **decompression sickness**.

cai·tiff /'kātif/ ▶ **n.** archaic a contemptible or cowardly person. [ME: from OFr. *caitif* 'captive,' based on L. *captivus* (see **captive**).]

ca·jole /kə'jōl/ ▶ **v.** [trans.] (often **cajole someone into doing something**) persuade someone to do something by sustained coaxing or flattery: *he cajoled her into selling the house* | [intrans.] *she cajoled to win his support.* — **ca·jole·ment n. ca·jol·er·y n.** [17th C.: from Fr. *cajoler*.]

Ca·jun /'kājən/ ▶ **n.** a member of any of the communities in southern Louisiana formed by descendants of French Canadians, speaking an archaic form of French. ▶ **adj.** of or relating to the Cajuns, esp. with reference to their folk music or spicy cuisine. [alt. of **Acadian**.]

Ca·jun Country a region of southern Louisiana that is inhabited largely by Cajuns.

cake /kāk/ ▶ **n.** an item of soft, sweet food made from a mixture of flour, shortening, eggs, sugar, and other ingredients, baked and often decorated. ■ an item of savory food formed into a flat, round shape, and typically baked or fried: *fish cakes.* ■ a flattish, compact mass of something, esp. soap. ▶ **v.** [trans.] (usu. **be caked**) (of a thick or sticky substance that hardens when dry) cover and become encrusted on (the surface of an object): *a pair of boots caked with mud.* ■ [intrans.] (of a thick or sticky substance) dry or harden into a solid mass: *the blood under his nose was beginning to cake.*
– PHRASES **a piece of cake** informal something easily achieved. **take the cake** surpass or exceed all others. **you can't have your cake and eat it (too)** proverb you can't enjoy both of two desirable but mutually exclusive alternatives. [ME: of Scand. origin; rel. to Swed. *kaka*.]

cake·box /'kāk,bäks/ ▶ **n.** a storage container for a round layer cake, with a surrounding cover that protects and preserves the cake. ■ a similarly shaped package for blank, recordable compact discs, with a central spindle on which discs are stacked.

cake·walk /'kāk,wôk/ ▶ **n. 1** informal an absurdly or surprisingly easy task. **2** a strutting dance popular at the end of the 19th century, developed from a black-American contest in graceful walking that had a cake as a prize. ▶ **v.** [intrans.] **1** informal achieve or win something easily: *he cakewalked to a 5-1 triumph.* **2** walk or dance in the manner of a cakewalk.

CAL ▶ **abbr.** computer-assisted (or -aided) learning.

Cal ▶ **abbr.** large calorie(s).

Cal. ▶ **abbr.** California.

cal. ▶ **abbr.** ■ calendar. ■ caliber. ■ calorie. ■ small calorie(s).

Cal·a·bar /'kalə,bär; ,kalə'bär/ a city in southeastern Nigeria; pop. 126,000.

Cal·a·bar bean ▶ **n.** the poisonous seed of a tropical West African climbing plant of the pea family (*Physostigma venosum*), containing physostigmine. [19th C.: named after **Calabar**.]

cal·a·bash /'kalə,basн/ ▶ **n.** (also **calabash tree**) an evergreen tropical American tree (*Crescentia cujete*, family Bignoniaceae) that bears fruit in the form of large woody gourds. ■ a gourd from this tree. ■ a water container, tobacco pipe, or other object made from the dried shell of this or a similar gourd. [17th C.: from Fr. *calebasse*, from Sp. *calabaza*, perh. from Pers. *karbuz* 'melon.']

cal·a·boose /'kalə,bo͞os/ ▶ **n.** informal a prison. [18th C.: from black Fr. *calabouse*, from Sp. *calabozo* 'dungeon.']

Ca·la·bri·a /kə'läbrēə; -'lā-/ a region of southwestern Italy; capital, Catanzaro. — **Ca·la·bri·an adj. & n.**

ca·la·di·um /kə'lādēəm/ ▶ **n.** (pl. **-ums**) a tropical South American plant (genus *Caladium*) of the arum family, cultivated for its brilliantly colored ornamental foliage. [mod. L., from Malay *keladi*.]

Cal·ais /ka'lā; 'kalā/ a city and ferry port in northern France; pop. 75,840.

cal·a·man·co /,kalə'maNGkō/ ▶ **n.** (pl. **-coes**) hist. a glossy woolen cloth checkered on one side only. [16th C.: of unknown origin.]

cal·a·man·der /'kalə,mandər/ ▶ **n.** another term for **coromandel**. [19th C.: from Sinhalese *kaḷu-madīriya*, perh. from **coromandel**.]

ca·la·ma·ri /,kälə'märē; ,kalə-/ ▶ **n.** squid served as food. [Ital., pl. of *calamaro*, from med. L. *calamarium* 'pen case,' from Gk. *kalamos* 'pen.']

cal·a·mi /'kalə,mī; -mē/ ▶ **n.** plural form of **calamus**.

cal·a·mine /'kalə,mīn/ ▶ **n.** a pink powder consisting of zinc carbonate and ferric oxide, used to make a soothing lotion or ointment. ■ dated smithsonite or a similar zinc ore. [ME: via OFr. from med. L. *calamina*, alt. of L. *cadmia*, from Gk. *kadmeia (gē)* 'Cadmean (earth),' from *Kadmos* 'Cadmus.']

cal·a·mint /'kalə,mint/ ▶ **n.** an aromatic Eurasian herbaceous plant or shrub (genus *Calamintha*) of the mint family, with blue or lilac flowers. [ME: from OFr. *calament*, based on Gk. *kalaminthē*.]

cal·a·mite /'kalə,mīt/ ▶ **n.** a jointed-stemmed swamp plant (*Calamites* and other genera, family Calamitaceae) of an extinct group related to the horsetails, growing to a height of 60 feet (18 m), a characteristic fossil of the Carboniferous coal measures. [mod. L., from **calamus**.]

ca·lam·i·ty /kə'lamitē/ ▶ **n.** (pl. **-ties**) an event causing great and often sudden damage or distress; a disaster. ■ disaster and distress. — **ca·lam·i·tous** /-itəs/ **adj. ca·lam·i·tous·ly** /-ətəslē/ **adv.** [ME: from OFr. *calamite*, from L. *calamitas*.]

Ca·lam·i·ty Jane /'jān/ (*c.*1852–1903), US frontierswoman; born *Martha Jane Canary* (or *Cannary*). She was noted for her skill at shooting and riding and was featured in Buffalo Bill's Wild West Show.

cal·a·mus /'kaləməs/ ▶ **n.** (pl. **-mi** /-,mī; -,mē/) **1** another term for **sweet flag**. ■ (also **calamus root**) a preparation of the aromatic root of the sweet flag. **2** Zool. the hollow lower part of the shaft of a feather; a quill. [ME: from L., from Gk. *kalamos*.]

ca·lan·do /kä'ländō/ ▶ **adv.** Music (esp. as a direction) gradually decreasing in tempo and volume of sound. [Ital., lit. 'slackening.']

ca·lash /kə'lasн/ ▶ **n.** another term for **calèche**.

Ca·la·ver·as Coun·ty /,kalə've(ə)rəs/ a rural county in east central California, associated with the 1840s gold rush and the writings of Mark Twain.

calc- ▶ **comb. form** (used chiefly in geological terms) of lime or calcium: *calcalkaline*. [from Ger. *Kalk* 'lime.']

cal·cal·ka·line /kal'kalkəlin; -,līn/ ▶ **adj.** Geol. (chiefly of rocks) relatively rich in both calcium and alkali metals.

cal·ca·ne·us /kal'kānēəs/ (also **cal·ca·ne·um** /-nēəm/) ▶ **n.** (pl. **-ne·i** /-nē,ī; -nē,ē/ or **-ne·a** /-nēə/) Anat. the large bone forming the heel. [18th C.: from L.]

cal·car·e·ous /kal'ke(ə)rēəs/ ▶ **adj.** containing calcium carbonate; chalky. [17th C.: from L. *calcarius* (from *calx, calc-* 'lime').]

cal·ce·o·lar·i·a /,kalsēə'le(ə)rēə/ ▶ **n.** a South American plant (genus *Calceolaria*) of the figwort family that is cultivated for its bright slipper-shaped flowers. Also called **pocketbook plant**. [18th C.: mod. L., from L. *calceolus*, dimin. of *calceus* 'shoe.']

cal·ces /'kalsēz/ plural form of **calx**.

calci- ▶ **comb. form** relating to calcium or its compounds: *calcifuge*. [from L. *calx, calc-* 'lime.']

cal·cic /'kalsik/ ▶ **adj.** (chiefly of minerals) containing or relatively rich in calcium.

cal·ci·cole /'kalsi,kōl/ ▶ **n.** Bot. a plant that grows best in calcareous soil. — **cal·cic·o·lous** /kal'sikələs/ **adj.** [19th C.: from **calci-** + L. *colere* 'inhabit.']

cal·cif·er·ol /kal'sifə,rôl; -,rōl/ ▶ **n.** Biochem. one of the D vitamins. Also called **vitamin D_2** (see **vitamin D**). [1930s: from **calciferous** + **-ol**.]

cal·cif·er·ous /kal'sifərəs/ ▶ **adj.** containing or producing calcium salts, esp. calcium carbonate.

cal·ci·fuge /'kalsə,fyo͞oj/ ▶ **n.** Bot. a plant that is not suited to calcareous soil.

cal·ci·fy /'kalsə,fī/ ▶ **v.** (**-fies, -fied**) [trans.] [usu. as adj.] (**calcified**) harden by deposition of or conversion into calcium carbonate or some other insoluble calcium compounds: *calcified cartilage.* — **cal·cif·ic** /kal'sifik/ **adj. cal·ci·fi·ca·tion** /,kalsəfi'kāsнən/ **n.**

cal·ci·mine /'kalsə,mīn/ (also **kal·so·mine**) ▶ **n.** a kind of white or pale blue wash for walls and ceilings. ▶ **v.** [trans.] whitewash with calcimine. [19th C.: of unknown origin.]

cal·cine /'kalsīn/ ▶ **v.** [trans.] [usu. as adj.] (**calcined**) reduce, oxidize, or desiccate by roasting or strong heat. — **cal·ci·na·tion** /kalsə'nāsнən/ **n.** [ME: from med. L. *calcinare*, from late L. *calcina* 'lime,' from L. *calx, calc-* 'lime' (see **calx**).]

cal·cite /'kalsīt/ ▶ **n.** a white or colorless mineral consisting of calcium carbonate. It is a major constituent of sedimentary rocks such as limestone, marble, and chalk. — **cal·cit·ic** /kal'sitik/ **adj.** [19th C.: coined in Ger. from L. *calx, calc-* 'lime' (see **calx**).]

cal·ci·to·nin /,kalsə'tōnən/ ▶ **n.** Biochem. a hormone secreted by the thyroid that has the effect of lowering blood calcium. [1960s: from **calci-** + **tonic**.]

cal·ci·um /'kalsēəm/ ▶n. the chemical element of atomic number 20, a soft gray alkaline earth metal. Its compounds occur naturally in limestone, fluorite, gypsum, and other minerals. Many physiological processes involve calcium ions, and calcium salts are an essential constituent of bone, teeth, and shells. (Symbol: **Ca**) [19th C.: from L. *calx, calc-* 'lime' (see CALX).]

cal·ci·um an·tag·o·nist ▶n. Med. a compound that reduces the influx of calcium into the cells of cardiac and smooth muscle, reducing the strength of contractions; used to treat angina and high blood pressure.

cal·ci·um car·bide ▶n. see CARBIDE.

cal·ci·um car·bon·ate ▶n. a white, insoluble solid, $CaCO_3$, occurring naturally as chalk, limestone, marble, and calcite, and forming mollusk shells and stony corals.

cal·ci·um chlo·ride ▶n. a white crystalline salt, $CaCl_2$, used to de-ice roads and as a drying agent.

cal·ci·um hy·drox·ide ▶n. a soluble white crystalline solid, $Ca(OH)_2$, commonly produced in the form of slaked lime.

cal·ci·um ox·ide ▶n. a white caustic alkaline solid, CaO, commonly produced in the form of quicklime.

cal·cu·la·ble /'kalkyələbəl/ ▶adj. able to be measured or assessed. — **cal·cu·la·bil·i·ty** /,kalkyələ'bilətē/ n. **cal·cu·la·bly** /-blē/ adv.

cal·cu·late /'kalkyə,lāt/ ▶v. [trans.] **1** determine (the amount or number of something) mathematically. ■ determine by reasoning, experience, or common sense; reckon or judge: *I calculated that she had been on vacation.* ■ [intrans.] (**calculate on**) include as an essential element in one's plans: *he calculated on maximizing pressure for policy revision.* **2** ■ (usu. **be calculated to do something**) intend (an action) to have a particular effect: *his last words were calculated to wound her.* ■ [with clause] suppose; believe. — **cal·cu·la·tive** /-,lātiv/ adj. [ME: from late L. *calculat-* 'counted,' from v. *calculare*, from *calculus* 'small pebble.']

cal·cu·lat·ed /'kalkyə,lātid/ ▶adj. (of an action) done with full awareness of the likely consequences. ■ carefully planned or intended: *vicious and calculated assaults.* ■ (of an amount or number) mathematically worked out or measured. — **cal·cu·lat·ed·ly** adv.

cal·cu·lat·ing /'kalkyə,lātiNG/ ▶adj. acting in a scheming and ruthlessly determined way. — **cal·cu·lat·ing·ly** adv.

cal·cu·la·tion /,kalkyə'lāSHən/ ▶n. a mathematical determination of the size or number of something. ■ (often **calculations**) an assessment of the risks, possibilities, or effects of a situation or course of action.

cal·cu·la·tor /'kalkyə,lātər/ ▶n. something used for making mathematical calculations, esp. a small electronic device with a keyboard and a visual display.

cal·cu·lus /'kalkyələs/ ▶n. **1** (pl. **-lus·es**) (also **infinitesimal calculus**) the branch of mathematics that deals with the finding and properties of derivatives and integrals of functions, by methods originally based on the summation of infinitesimal differences. The two main types are **differential calculus** and **integral calculus**. **2** (pl. **-lus·es**) Math. Logic a particular method or system of calculation or reasoning. **3** (pl. **-li** /-,lī; -lē/) Med. a concretion of minerals formed within the body, esp. in the kidney or gallbladder. ■ another term for TARTAR. [17th C.: from L., lit. 'small pebble.']

cal·cu·lus of var·i·a·tions ▶n. a form of calculus applied to expressions or functions in which the law relating the quantities is liable to variation, esp. to find what relation between the variables makes an integral a maximum or a minimum.

Cal·cut·ta /kal'kətə/ a city in eastern India, capital of the state of West Bengal; pop. 10,916,000. Official name (from 2000) **KOLKATA**. — **Cal·cut·tan** /-'kətn/ n. & adj.

Cal·de·cott /'kôldikət; -,kät/, Randolph (1846–86), English graphic artist. A medal awarded annually for the illustration of children's books is named for him.

Cal·der /'kôldər/, Alexander (1898–1976), US sculptor. He was one of the first artists to introduce movement into sculpture with his mobiles. His static sculptures are called "stabiles."

cal·de·ra /kal'derə; kôl-; -'di(ə)rə/ ▶n. a large volcanic crater, typically one formed by a major eruption leading to the collapse of the mouth of the volcano. [17th C.: from Sp., from late L. *caldaria* 'boiling pot.']

Cal·de·rón de la Bar·ca /,käldə'rōn dā lä 'bärkə/, Pedro (1600–81), Spanish playwright, noted for his numerous religious dramas.

cal·dron ▶n. var. of CAULDRON.

Cald·well /'kôld,wel/, Erskine Preston (1903–87), US writer. His novels include *Tobacco Road* (1932) and *God's Little Acre* (1933).

ca·lèche /kə'lesH/ (also **ca·leche** or **ca·lash** /-'lasH/) ▶n. hist. **1** a light low-wheeled carriage with a removable folding hood. **2** a woman's hooped silk hood. [17th C.: Fr., from Ger. *Kalesche*, from Pol. *kołasa*, from *koło* 'wheel.']

Cal·e·do·ni·an /,kalə'dōnēən/ ▶adj. (chiefly in names or geographical terms) of or relating to Scotland or the Scottish Highlands. [from *Caledonia*, L. name for northern Britain.]

Cal·e·do·ni·an Ca·nal a system of lochs and canals that cross Scotland.

cal·e·fa·cient /,kalə'fāSHənt/ ▶n. Med., archaic a drug or other agent causing a sensation of warmth. [17th C.: from L. *calefacient-* 'making warm,' from v. *calefacere*, from *calere* 'be warm' + *facere* 'make.']

cal·en·dar /'kaləndər/ (abbr.: **cal.** or **cal**) ▶n. a chart or series of pages showing the days, weeks, and months of a particular year. ■ a datebook. ■ a system by which the beginning, length, and subdivisions of the year are fixed. See also JEWISH CALENDAR, JULIAN CALENDAR, GREGORIAN CALENDAR. ■ a timetable of special days or events of a specified kind or involving a specified group: *the college calendar.* ■ a list of people or events connected with particular dates, esp. canonized saints and cases for trial. ▶v. [trans.] enter (something) in a calendar or timetable. — **ca·len·dric** /kə'lendrik/ adj. **ca·len·dri·cal** /kə'lendrikəl/ adj. [ME: from OFr. *calendier*, from L. *kalendarium* 'account book,' from *kalendae* (see CALENDS).]

cal·en·dar month ▶n. see MONTH.

cal·en·dar year ▶n. see YEAR (sense 2).

cal·en·der /'kaləndər/ ▶n. a machine in which cloth or paper is pressed by rollers to glaze or smooth it. ▶v. [trans.] press in such a machine. [15th C.: from Fr. *calendre* (n.), *calendrer* (v.).]

cal·ends /'kaləndz; 'kā-/ (also **kal·ends**) ▶plural n. the first day of the month in the ancient Roman calendar. [OE: from OFr. *calendes*, from L. *kalendae, calendae*; rel. to *calare* 'proclaim.']

ca·len·du·la /kə'lenjələ/ ▶n. a Mediterranean plant (genus *Calendula*) of the daisy family that includes the common (or pot) marigold. [mod. L., dimin. of *calendae* (see CALENDS).]

cal·en·ture /'kalən,CHŏŏr/ ▶n. feverish delirium supposedly caused by the heat in the tropics. [16th C.: from Fr., from Sp. *calentura* 'fever,' from *calentar* 'be hot,' based on L. *calere* 'be warm.']

calf[1] /kaf/ ▶n. (pl. **calves** /kavz/) **1** a young bovine animal, esp. a domestic cow or bull in its first year. ■ the young of some other large mammals, such as elephants, rhinoceroses, large deer and antelopes, and whales. ■ short for CALFSKIN. **2** a floating piece of ice detached from an iceberg.
– PHRASES **in** (or **with**) **calf** (of a cow) pregnant. **kill the fatted calf** see FAT. — **calf·like** adj. [OE *cælf*, of Gmc. origin; rel. to Ger. *Kalb*.]

calf[2] ▶n. (pl. **calves** /kavz/) the fleshy part at the back of a person's leg below the knee. [ME: from ON *kálfi*.]

calf·skin /'kaf,skin/ ▶n. leather made from the hide or skin of a calf, used chiefly in bookbinding and shoemaking.

Cal·ga·ry /'kalgərē/ a city in southern Alberta, in southwestern Canada; pop. 710,680.

Cal·houn /kal'hōōn/, John Caldwell (1782–1850), US politician. A South Carolina Democrat, he served as US vice president 1825–32 and in the US Senate 1832–43, 1845–50.

Ca·li /'kälē/ a city in western Colombia; pop. 1,624,400.

cal·i·ber /'kaləbər/ (Brit. **cal·i·bre**) (abbr.: **cal.** or **cal**) ▶n. **1** the quality of someone's character or the level of someone's ability. ■ the standard reached by something. **2** the internal diameter or bore of a gun barrel: [in comb.] *a .22 caliber repeater rifle.* ■ the diameter of a bullet, shell, or rocket. ■ the diameter of a body of circular section, such as a tube, blood vessel, or fiber. — **cal·i·bered** adj. [also in comb.]. [16th C.: from Fr. *calibre*, from Ital. *calibro*, perh. from Arab. *ḳālib* 'mold,' based on Gk. *kalapous* 'shoemaker's last.']

cal·i·brate /'kalə,brāt/ ▶v. [trans.] (often **be calibrated**) mark (a gauge or instrument) with a standard scale of readings. ■ correlate the readings of (an instrument) with those of a standard in order to check the instrument's accuracy. ■ adjust (experimental results) to take external factors into account or to allow comparison with other data. — **cal·i·bra·tor** /-,brātər/ n.

cal·i·bra·tion /kalə'brāSHən/ ▶n. the action or process of calibrating an instrument or experimental readings. ■ each of a set of graduations on an instrument.

ca·li·che /kə'lēsH/ ▶n. a mineral deposit of gravel, sand, and nitrates, found esp. in dry areas of South America. ■ an area of calcium carbonate formed in the soils of semiarid regions. [19th C.: from L. Amer. Sp.]

cal·i·co /'kali,kō/ ▶n. (pl. **-coes** or **-cos**) printed cotton fabric. ■ Brit. a type of cotton cloth, typically plain white or unbleached. ▶adj. (of an animal, typically a cat) multicolored or mottled. [16th C.: alt. of CALICUT.]

Cal·i·cut /'kalikət/ a city in southwestern India; pop. 420,000. Also called **KOZHIKODE**.

Calif. ▶abbr. California.

Cal·i·for·nia /,kalə'fôrnyə; -nēə/ a state in the western US, on the coast of the Pacific Ocean; pop. 33,871,648; capital, Sacramento; statehood, Sept. 9, 1850 (31). Formerly part of Mexico, it was ceded to the US in 1847, having briefly been independent. Large numbers of settlers were attracted to California in the 19th century, esp. during the gold rushes of the 1840s. — **Cal·i·for·nian** adj. & n.

Cal·i·for·nia, Gulf of an arm of the Pacific Ocean that separates Baja California from mainland Mexico.

Cal·i·for·nia Cur·rent a cold ocean current of the eastern Pacific Ocean.

Cal·i·for·nia pop·py ▶n. an annual poppy (*Eschscholzia californica*) native to western North America and cultivated for its brilliant yellow or orange flowers.

California poppy

Cal·i·for·nia sheeps·head ▶n. see SHEEPSHEAD.

PRONUNCIATION KEY ə *ago, up*; ər *over, fur*; a *hat*; ā *ate*; ä *car*; e *let*; ē *see*; i *fit*; ī *by*; NG *sing*; ō *go*; ô *law, for*; oi *toy*; ŏŏ *good*; ōō *goo*; ou *out*; TH *thin*; TH *then*; ZH *vision*

cal·i·for·ni·um /ˌkaləˈfôrnēəm/ ▶**n.** the chemical element of atomic number 98, a radioactive metal of the actinide series, first produced by bombarding curium with helium ions. (Symbol: **Cf**) [1950s: named after *University of California at Berkeley*.]

ca·lig·i·nous /kəˈlijənəs/ ▶**adj.** archaic misty, dim; obscure, dark. — **ca·lig·i·nos·i·ty** /kəˌlijəˈnäsitē/ **n.**

Ca·lig·u·la /kəˈligyələ/ (AD 12–41), Roman emperor 37–41; born *Gaius Julius Caesar Germanicus.* His reign was notorious for tyrannical excesses and depraved madness.

cal·i·per /ˈkaləpər/ (also **cal·li·per**) ▶**n.** (**calipers**) an instrument for measuring external or internal dimensions, having two hinged legs resembling a pair of compasses and in-turned or out-turned points. ■ (also **caliper rule**) an instrument performing a similar function but having one linear component sliding along another, with two parallel jaws and a vernier scale. ■ (also **brake caliper**) a motor-vehicle or bicycle brake consisting of two or more hinged components. [16th C.: appar. alt. of CALIBER.]

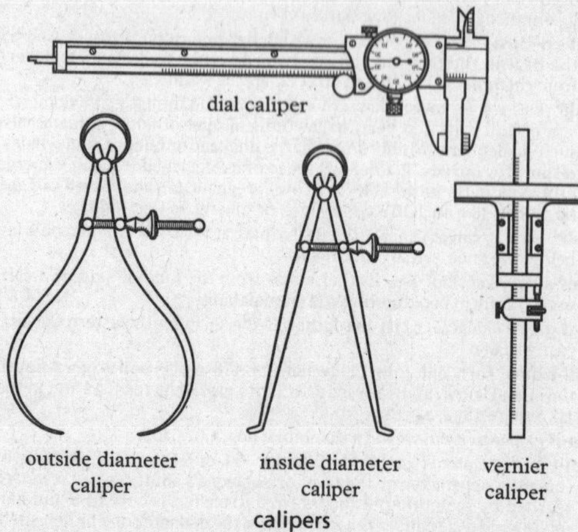

calipers

ca·liph /ˈkālif; ˈkal-/ ▶**n.** hist. the chief Muslim civil and religious ruler, regarded as the successor of Muhammad. — **cal·iph·ate** /ˈkāləˌfāt; -fit; ˈkal-/ **n.** [ME: from OFr. *caliphe*, from Arab. *ḵalīfa* meaning 'deputy' or 'successor,' from *ḵalafa* 'succeed.']

cal·is·then·ics /ˌkaləsˈᴛʜeniks/ (Brit. **cal·lis·then·ics**) ▶**plural n.** gymnastic exercises to achieve bodily fitness and grace of movement. — **cal·is·then·ic adj.** [19th C.: from Gk. *kallos* 'beauty' + *sthenos* 'strength' + -ICS.]

ca·lix /ˈkāliks; ˈkal-/ ▶**n. 1** var. of CALYX. **2** a chalice.

calk ▶**n. & v.** var. of CAULK.

call /kôl/ ▶**v. 1** [trans.] cry out to (someone) in order to summon them or attract their attention: *she heard Terry calling her* | [intrans.] *I heard you call.* ■ cry out (a word or words): *he heard a voice calling his name* ■ shout out or chant (the steps and figures) to people performing a square dance or country dance. ■ [intrans.] (of an animal, esp. a bird) make its characteristic cry. ■ telephone (a person or telephone number): *could I call you back?* ■ summon (something, esp. an emergency service or a taxicab) by telephone: *call the police!* ■ bring (a witness) into court to give evidence. ■ [with obj. and infin.] archaic inspire or urge (someone) to do something: *I am called to preach the Gospel.* ■ fix a date or time for (a meeting, strike, or election). ■ [intrans.] guess the outcome of tossing a coin: *"You call," he said. "Heads or tails?"* ■ predict the result of (a future event, esp. an election or a vote): *the race remains too close to call.* ■ Comput. cause the execution of (a subroutine). **2** Brit. [no obj., with adverbial of place] (of a person) pay a brief visit: *he called last night looking for you.* ■ (**call for**) stop to collect (someone) at the place where they are living or working: *I'll call for you around seven.* **3** [with obj. and complement] give (an infant or animal) a specified name: *they called their daughter Hannah.* ■ address or refer to (someone) by a specified name, title, endearment, or term of abuse: *please call me Lucy.* ■ refer to, consider, or describe (someone or something) as being: *he's the only person I call a friend.* ■ (of an umpire or other official in a game) pronounce (a ball, stroke, or other action) to be the thing specified: *the linesman called the ball wide.* ▶**n. 1** a cry made as a summons or to attract someone's attention. ■ the characteristic cry of a bird or other animal. ■ [with adj.] a series of notes sounded on a brass instrument as a signal to do something: *a bugle call to rise at 5:30.* ■ a telephone communication or conversation. ■ (**a call for**) an appeal or demand for: *the call for action was welcomed.* ■ a summons. ■ [in sing., with infin.] a vocation: *his call to be a disciple.* ■ [in sing.] a powerful force of attraction: *hikers can't resist the call of the Sierras.* ■ [usu. with negative] (**a call for**) a demand or need for (goods or services): *there was little call for Turkish food in Milltown.* ■ a shout by an official in a game indicating whether the ball has gone out of play, if a rule has been breached, etc.; the decision or ruling so made: *the umpire made a bad call.* ■ Bridge a bid, response, or double. ■ a direction in a square dance given by the caller. ■ a demand for payment of lent or unpaid capital. ■ Stock Market short for CALL OPTION. ■ a player's right or turn to make a bid in a card game. **2** a brief visit. ■ a visit or journey made in response to an emergency appeal for help.
– PHRASES **at call** another way of saying *ON CALL* (sense 2). **call someone's bluff** see BLUFF¹. **call collect** make a telephone call reversing the charges. **call something into question** cast doubt on something. **call it a day** see DAY. **call someone names** see NAME. **call of nature** see NATURE. **call the shots** (or **tune**) take the initiative in deciding how something should be done. **call a spade a spade** see SPADE¹. **call someone to account** see ACCOUNT. **call someone/something to mind** cause one to think of someone or something, esp. through similarity. ■ [with negative] remember someone or something: [with clause] *I cannot call to mind where I have seen you.* **on call 1** (of a person) able to be contacted in order to provide a professional service if necessary, but not formally on duty. **2** (of money lent) repayable on demand.
– PHRASAL VERBS **call for** make necessary. ■ draw attention to the need for. **call something forth** elicit a response. **call someone/something down** cause or provoke someone or something to appear or occur: *nothing called down the wrath of Nemesis quicker.* **call someone in** enlist someone's aid or services. **call something in** require payment of a loan or promise of money. **call someone/something off** order a person or dog to stop attacking someone. **call something off** cancel an event or agreement. **call on 1** pay a visit to (someone). **2** (also **call upon**) have recourse to. ■ [with infin.] demand that (someone) do something: *he called on the government to hold a plebiscite.* **call someone out 1** summon someone, esp. to deal with an emergency or to do repairs. **2** order or advise workers to strike. **3** challenge someone to a fight. **call someone up 1** informal telephone someone. **2** summon someone to serve in the army. ■ select someone to play in a team. **call something up** summon for use something that is stored or kept available: *icons that allow you to call up a graphic.* ■ fig. evoke something: *the special effects that called up the Mars landscape were impressive.* [OE *ceallian*, from ON *kalla* 'summon loudly.']

cal·la /ˈkalə/ ▶**n.** (usu. **calla lily**) a plant (genus *Zantedeschia*) of the arum family, with a large showy white spathe. ■ (also **wild calla**) another term for WATER ARUM. [19th C.: mod. L.]

call·a·ble /ˈkôləbəl/ ▶**adj.** Finance designating a bond that can be paid off earlier than the maturity date.

Cal·la·ghan /ˈkaləˌhan/, Leonard James, Baron Callaghan of Cardiff (1912–2005), prime minister of Britain 1976–79.

cal·la·loo /ˌkaləˈlo͞o; ˈkaləˌlo͞o/ (also **cal·la·lou**) ▶**n.** the spinachlike leaves of a tropical American plant (genus *Xanthosoma*) of the arum family, widely used in Caribbean cooking. ■ a soup or stew made with such leaves. [18th C.: from Amer. Sp. *calalú.*]

Ca·llao /kəˈyä-ō; kəˈyou/ a city in Peru, west of Lima; pop. 369,770.

Cal·las /ˈkaləs/, Maria (1923–77), Greek opera singer; born in the US; born *Cecilia Sofia Anna Maria Kalogeropoulou.* Noted for the dramatic effect of her voice, she was the preeminent soprano of her day.

call·back /ˈkôlˌbak/ ▶**n. 1** an invitation to return for a second audition or interview. **2** a telephone call made to return a call received. **3** a recall of a defective product. **4** an emergency call summoning an employee to work after hours. **5** Comput. a security feature used by systems accessed by telephone, in which a remote user must log on using a previously registered phone number, to which the system then places a return call.

call·board ▶**n.** a bulletin board in a theater on which announcements for the cast and crew are posted.

call box ▶**n. 1** a roadside telephone for use only in an emergency. **2** Brit. a public telephone booth.

call boy ▶**n. 1** a person in a theater who summons actors when they are due on stage. **2** a male prostitute who accepts appointments by telephone.

call cen·ter ▶**n.** an office set up to handle a large volume of telephone calls, esp. for taking orders and providing customer service.

call·er /ˈkôlər/ ▶**n. 1** a person who pays a brief visit or makes a telephone call. **2** a person who calls out numbers in a game of bingo or directions in a dance.

call·er ID ▶**n.** a facility that identifies and displays the telephone numbers of incoming calls made to a particular line.

call for·ward·ing ▶**n.** a telephone feature that allows calls made to one number to be forwarded to another specified number.

call girl ▶**n.** a female prostitute who accepts appointments by telephone.

Cal·lic·ra·tes /kəˈlikrəˌtēz/ (5th century BC), Greek architect. With Ictinus, he designed the Parthenon (447–438 BC).

cal·li·graph·ic /ˌkaliˈgrafik/ ▶**adj.** of or relating to calligraphy. ■ resembling lettering in shape.

cal·lig·ra·phy /kəˈligrəfē/ ▶**n.** decorative handwriting or handwritten lettering. ■ the art of producing decorative handwriting or lettering with a pen or brush. — **cal·li·graph** /ˈkaləˌgraf/ **v. cal·lig·ra·pher n. cal·lig·ra·phist n.** [17th C.: from Gk. *kalligraphia*, from *kalligraphos* 'person who writes beautifully.']

Cal·lim·a·chus /kəˈliməkəs/ (*c.*305–*c.*240 BC), Greek poet and scholar. He headed the library at Alexandria.

call-in ▶**n.** a radio or television program during which the listeners or viewers telephone the studio and participate. ■ a telephone conversation that is broadcast during such a program.

call·ing /ˈkôliNG/ ▶**n. 1** the loud cries or shouts of an animal or person. **2** [in sing.] a strong urge toward a particular way of life or career; a vocation. ■ a profession or occupation.

call·ing card ▶ n. **1** a card bearing a person's name and address, sent or left in lieu of a formal visit. ■ fig. an action or the result of an action by which someone or something can be identified: *a dog whose calling card is a nip at the ankles.* **2** a card that allows the user to make telephone calls from any phone and charge the cost to their home telephone number. ■ a prepaid card that allows the user to make telephone calls up to a specified value.

Cal·li·o·pe /kə'līəpē/ Greek Rom. Mythol. the Muse of epic poetry. [from Gk. *Kalliopē*, lit. 'having a beautiful voice.']

cal·li·o·pe /kə'līəpē/ ▶ n. esp. hist. a keyboard instrument resembling an organ but with the notes produced by steam whistles, used chiefly on showboats and in traveling fairs. [19th C.: from Gk. *Kalliopē* (see CALLIOPE).]

cal·li·per ▶ n. var. of CALIPER.

cal·li·pyg·i·an /ˌkalə'pijēən/ (also **cal·li·pyg·e·an**) ▶ adj. having well-shaped buttocks. —**cal·li·py·gous** /-'pīgəs/ **adj.** [18th C.: from Gk. *kallipūgos*, from *kallos* 'beauty' + *pūgē* 'buttocks.']

cal·lis·then·ics /ˌkaləs'THeniks/ ▶ plural n. British spelling of CALISTHENICS.

Cal·lis·to /kə'listō/ **1** Gk. Mythol. a nymph who was changed into a bear by Zeus. See also URSA MAJOR. **2** Astron. one of the Galilean moons of Jupiter, the eighth closest satellite to the planet.

call let·ters ▶ plural n. a sequence of letters used by a television or radio station as an identifying code.

call mon·ey ▶ n. money lent by a bank or other institution that is repayable on demand.

call num·ber ▶ n. a mark, esp. a number, on the spine of a library book, or listed in the library's catalog, indicating the book's location in the library.

call op·tion ▶ n. Stock Market an option to buy assets at an agreed price on or before a particular date.

cal·los·i·ty /kə'läsitē/ ▶ n. (pl. **-ties**) tech. a thickened and hardened part of the skin; a callus.

cal·lous /'kaləs/ ▶ adj. showing or having an insensitive and cruel disregard for others. ▶ n. var. of CALLUS. —**cal·lous·ly** adv. **cal·lous·ness** n. [ME (in the Latin sense): from L. *callosus* 'hard-skinned,' from *callum*, *callus* 'hardened skin.']

cal·loused /'kaləst/ (also **callused**) ▶ adj. (of a part of the body) having an area of hardened skin.

call-out ▶ n. **1** an instance of being summoned, esp. in order to deal with an emergency or to do repairs. **2** Print. a letter, word, number or other symbol identifying a specific part of an illustration.

cal·low /'kalō/ ▶ adj. (esp. of a young person) inexperienced and immature. —**cal·low·ly** adv. **cal·low·ness** n. [OE *calu* 'bald,' of West Gmc. origin, prob. from L. *calvus* 'bald.']

call sign (also **call signal**) ▶ n. a message, code, or tune that is broadcast by radio to identify the broadcaster or transmitter.

call to quar·ters ▶ n. a bugle call summoning soldiers to their barracks.

call-up ▶ n. [in sing.] an act of summoning someone or of being summoned to serve in the armed forces or on a sports team: [as adj.] *my call-up papers.*

cal·lus /'kaləs/ (also **cal·lous**) ▶ n. a thickened and hardened part of the skin. ■ Med. the bony healing tissue that forms around the ends of broken bone. ■ Bot. a hard formation of tissue, esp. new tissue formed over a wound. [16th C.: from L. *callus*, *callum* 'hardened skin.']

cal·lused /'kaləst/ ▶ adj. var. of CALLOUSED.

call wait·ing ▶ n. a service whereby someone on the telephone is notified of an incoming call and is able to place the first call on hold while answering the second.

calm /kä(l)m/ ▶ adj. **1** (of a person, action, or manner) not showing or feeling nervousness, anger, or other emotions. ■ (of a place) peaceful, esp. in contrast to recent violent activity: *the city was reported to be calm.* **2** (of the weather) pleasantly free from wind. ■ (of the sea) not disturbed by large waves. ▶ n. **1** the absence of violent or confrontational activity within a place or group. ■ the absence of nervousness, agitation, or excitement in a person: *his usual calm deserted him.* **2** the absence of wind. ■ still air represented by force 0 on the Beaufort scale (less than 1 knot). ■ (often **calms**) an area of the sea without wind. ▶ v. [trans.] make (someone) tranquil and quiet; soothe: *he lit a cigarette to calm his nerves.* ■ [intrans.] (**calm down**) (of a person) become tranquil and quiet: *I calmed down and lost my anxiety.* —**calm·ly** adv. **calm·ness** n. [ME: ult. from Gk. *kauma* 'heat.']

calm·a·tive /'kä(l)mətiv/ ▶ adj. (of a drug) having a sedative effect. ▶ n. a calmative drug.

cal·mod·u·lin /kal'mäjəlin/ ▶ n. Biochem. a protein that binds calcium and is involved in regulating a variety of activities in cells. [1970s: from *cal(cium)* + *modul(ate)* + -IN[1].]

cal·o·mel /'kaləməl; -ˌmel/ ▶ n. a white powder, Hg_2Cl_2, used as a purgative and a fungicide. Also called MERCURIC CHLORIDE. [17th C.: mod. L., perh. from Gk. *kalos* 'beautiful' + *melas* 'black.']

Ca·lo·o·can /ˌkalə'ōkän/ (also **Kaloocan**) a city in the Philippines, on southern Luzon; pop. 763,000.

ca·lor·ic /kə'lôrik; -'lär-/ ▶ adj. tech. of or relating to heat; calorific: *a caloric value of 7 calories per gram.* ▶ n. Physics, hist. a hypothetical fluid thought to be responsible for the phenomenon of heat. —**ca·lor·i·cal·ly** /-k(ə)lē/ adv. [18th C.: from Fr. *calorique*, from L. *calor* 'heat.']

cal·o·rie /'kal(ə)rē/ (abbr.: **cal.**) ▶ n. (pl. **-ries**) either of two units of heat energy: ■ (also **small calorie**) (abbr.: **cal**) the energy needed to raise the temperature of 1 gram of water through 1 °C (now usually defined as 4.1868 joules). ■ (also **large calorie**) (abbr.: **Cal**) the energy needed to raise the temperature of 1 kilogram of water through 1 °C, equal to one thousand small calories and often used to measure the energy value of foods. [19th C.: from French, from L. *calor* 'heat' + Fr. suffix *-ie* (see -Y[3]).]

cal·o·rif·ic /ˌkalə'rifik/ ▶ adj. relating to the amount of energy contained in food or fuel. ■ esp. Brit. (of food or drink) containing many calories and so likely to be fattening. —**cal·o·rif·i·cal·ly** /-ik(ə)lē/ adv.

cal·o·rim·e·ter /ˌkalə'rimitər/ ▶ n. an apparatus for measuring the amount of heat involved in a chemical reaction or other process. —**cal·o·ri·met·ric** /ˌkalərə'metrik/ **adj.** **cal·o·rim·e·try** /-'rimitrē/ **n.** [18th C.: from L. *calor*.]

cal·o·type /'kaləˌtīp/ (also **calotype process**) ▶ n. hist. an early photographic process in which negatives were made using paper coated with silver iodide. [19th C.: from Gk. *kalos* 'beautiful.']

calque /kalk/ Ling. ▶ n. another term for LOAN TRANSLATION. ▶ v. (**be calqued on**) originate or function as a loan translation of. [1930s: from Fr., lit. 'tracing,' from *calquer* 'to trace,' via Ital. from L. *calcare* 'to tread.']

cal·trop /'kaltrəp; 'kôl-/ (also **cal·trap**) ▶ n. **1** a spiked metal ball thrown on the ground to impede wheeled vehicles or (formerly) cavalry horses. **2** a creeping plant (genus *Tribulus*, family Zygophyllaceae) with woody carpels that typically have hard spines. **3** (also **water caltrop**) another term for WATER CHESTNUT (sense 3). [OE *calcatrippe*, 'a plant tending to catch the feet,' from med. L. *calcatrippa*, from *calx* 'heel' or *calcare* 'to tread' + word rel. to TRAP[1].]

cal·u·met /'kalyəˌmet; -mit; ˌkalyə'met/ ▶ n. a North American Indian peace pipe. [17th C.: from Fr., from late L. *calamellus* 'little reed,' dimin. of L. *calamus*.]

calumet

Cal·u·met Cit·y /'kalyəˌmet/ a city in northeastern Illinois, south of Chicago; pop. 37,840.

ca·lum·ni·ate /kə'ləmnēˌāt/ ▶ v. [trans.] formal make false and defamatory statements about: *Ezra Pound calumniated the Jews over the airwaves.* —**ca·lum·ni·a·tion** /kəˌləmnē'āSHən/ n. **ca·lum·ni·a·tor** /-ˌātər/ n.

cal·um·ny /'kaləmnē/ ▶ n. (pl. **-nies**) the making of false and defamatory statements in order to damage someone's reputation; slander. ■ a false and slanderous statement. —**ca·lum·ni·ous** /kə'ləmnēəs/ adj. [ME: from L. *calumnia*.]

cal·u·tron /'kalyəˌträn/ ▶ n. a device that uses large electromagnets to separate uranium isotopes from uranium ore. [from *Cal(ifornia) U(niversity) (cyclo)tron*.]

Cal·va·dos /ˌkalvə'dōs/ (also **cal·va·dos**) ▶ n. apple brandy made in the Calvados region of Normandy.

Cal·va·ry /'kalv(ə)rē/ the hill outside Jerusalem on which Jesus was crucified. ■ [as n.] (**a calvary**) a sculpture or picture representing the scene of the Crucifixion.

calve /kav/ ▶ v. **1** [intrans.] (of cows and certain other large animals) give birth to a calf. ■ [trans.] (of a person) help (a cow) give birth to a calf. **2** [trans.] (of an iceberg or glacier) split and shed (a smaller mass of ice). ■ [intrans.] (of a mass of ice) split off from an iceberg or glacier. [OE *calfian*, from *cælf* 'calf.']

calves /kavz/ plural form of CALF[1], CALF[2].

Cal·vin[1] /'kalvin/, John (1509–64), French theologian and reformer. On becoming a Protestant, he fled to Switzerland, where he attempted to reorder society on reformed Christian principles.

Cal·vin[2], Melvin (1911–97), US biochemist. He investigated photosynthesis and discovered the cycle of reactions (the **Calvin cycle**), that constitutes the dark reaction. Nobel Prize for Chemistry (1961).

Cal·vin·ism /'kalvəˌnizəm/ ▶ n. the Protestant theological system of John Calvin, which emphasizes the irresistibility of grace and the doctrine of predestination. —**Cal·vin·ist** n. **Cal·vin·is·tic** /ˌkalvə'nistik/ adj. **Cal·vin·is·ti·cal** /ˌkalvə'nistikəl/ adj.

Cal·vi·no /käl'vēnō; kal-/, Italo (1923–87), Italian writer; born in Cuba. His novels include *If on a Winter's Night a Traveler* (1979).

calx /kalks/ ▶ n. (pl. **cal·ces** /'kalsēz/) Chem., archaic a powdery metallic oxide formed when an ore or mineral has been heated. [ME: from L., 'lime,' prob. from Gk. *khalix* 'pebble, limestone.']

Ca·lyp·so /kə'lipsō/ Gk. Mythol. a nymph who kept Odysseus on her island, Ogygia, for seven years. [Gk., lit. 'she who conceals.']

ca·lyp·so /kə'lipsō/ ▶ n. (pl. **-sos**) a kind of West Indian music in syncopated African rhythm, typically with words improvised on a topical theme. —**ca·lyp·so·ni·an** /kəˌlip'sōnēən; ˌkalip-/ adj. & n. [1930s: of unknown origin.]

ca·lyx /ˈkāliks; ˈkal-/ (also **ca·lix**) ▶ **n.** (pl. **ca·ly·ces** /ˈkālə,sēz; ˈkal-/ or **ca·lyx·es**) **1** Bot. the sepals of a flower, typically forming a whorl that encloses the petals and forms a protective layer around a flower in bud. Compare with COROLLA. **2** Zool. a cuplike cavity or structure, in particular: ▪ a portion of the pelvis of a mammalian kidney. ▪ the cavity in a calcareous coral skeleton that surrounds the polyp. ▪ the plated body of a crinoid, excluding the stalk and arms. [17th C.: from L., from Gk. *kalux* 'case of a bud, husk,' rel. to *kaluptein* 'to hide.']

cal·zo·ne /kalˈzōn(ē),/ ▶ **n.** (pl. **-zo·ni** /-ˈzōnē/ or **-zo·nes** /-ˈzōn(ē)z/) a type of pizza that is folded in half before cooking to contain a filling. [Ital. dial., prob. from *calzone* 'trouser leg.']

CAM /kam/ ▶ **abbr.** computer-aided manufacturing.

cam /kam/ ▶ **n.** a projection on a rotating part in machinery, designed to make sliding contact with another part while rotating and to impart reciprocal or variable motion to it. ▪ short for CAMSHAFT. ▪ short for CAMERA[1]. [18th C.: from Du. *kam* 'comb.']

ca·ma·ra·de·rie /ˌkäm(ə)ˈrädərē; -ˈrad-; ˌkam-/ ▶ **n.** mutual trust and friendship among people who spend a lot of time together. [19th C.: from Fr., from *camarade* 'comrade.']

cam·a·ril·la /ˌkaməˈrilə; -ˈrēə/ ▶ **n.** a small group of people, esp. a group of advisers to a ruler or politician, with a shared, typically nefarious, purpose. [19th C.: from Sp., dimin. of *camara* 'chamber.']

Cam·a·ril·lo /ˌkaməˈrilō; -ˈrē(y)ō/ a city in southwestern California, west of Los Angeles; pop. 52,303.

cam·as /ˈkaməs/ (also **cam·ass** or **quam·ash**) ▶ **n.** a North American plant (genera *Camassia* and *Zigadenus*) of the lily family, cultivated for its starry blue or purple flowers. [19th C.: from Chinook Jargon *qamaš, qawaš*, perh. from Nootka.]

Cam·bay, Gulf of /kamˈbā/ an inlet of the Arabian Sea in western India. Also called **Gulf of Khambhat**.

cam·ber /ˈkambər/ ▶ **n.** a slightly convex or arched shape of a road or other horizontal surface. ▪ the slight sideways inclination of the front wheels of a motor vehicle. ▪ the extent of curvature of a section of an airfoil. — **cam·bered adj.** [ME: from OFr. *cambre*, dial. var. of *chambre* 'arched,' from L. *camurus* 'curved inward.']

cam·bi·um /ˈkambēəm/ ▶ **n.** (pl. **-bi·a** /-bēə/ or **-bi·ums**) Bot. a cellular plant tissue from which phloem, xylem, or cork grows by division, resulting (in woody plants) in secondary thickening. — **cam·bi·al** /-bēəl/ **adj.** [16th C.: from med. L., 'exchange.']

Cam·bo·di·a /kamˈbōdēə/ a country in Southeast Asia. Also officially called the KHMER REPUBLIC (1970–75) and KAMPUCHEA (1976–89). *See box.*

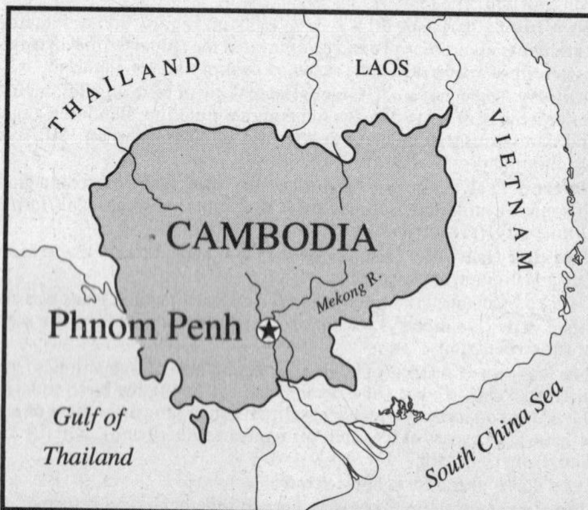

Cambodia

Official name: Kingdom of Cambodia
Location: Southeast Asia in Indochina, between Thailand and southern Vietnam
Area: 68,200 square miles (176,500 sq km)
Population: 13,363.000
Capital: Phnom Penh
Languages: Khmer (official), French, English
Currency: riel

Cam·bo·di·an /kamˈbōdēən/ ▶ **adj.** of or relating to Cambodia, its people, or their language. ▶ **n. 1** a native or national of Cambodia, or a person of Cambodian descent. **2** another term for KHMER (the language).

Cam·bri·an /ˈkambrēən; ˈkām-/ ▶ **adj. 1** (chiefly in names or geographical terms) Welsh: *the Cambrian Railway.* **2** Geol. of, relating to, or denoting the first period in the Paleozoic era (between the end of the Precambrian eon and the beginning of the Ordovician period, about 570 million to 510 million years ago), a time when there was extensive invertebrate life. ▪ [as n.] **(the Cambrian)** the Cambrian period or the system of rocks deposited during it. [17th C.: from L. *Cambria* 'Wales,' var. of *Cumbria*, from Welsh *Cymry* 'Welshman' or *Cymru* 'Wales.']

cam·bric /ˈkāmbrik/ ▶ **n.** a lightweight, closely woven white linen or cotton fabric. [ME: from *Kamerijk*, Flemish form of *Cambrai*, town in France.]

Cam·bridge /ˈkāmbrij/ **1** a city in eastern England; pop. 101,000. Cambridge University is located here. **2** a city in eastern Massachusetts, across from Boston; pop. 101,355. Harvard University and the Massachusetts Institute of Technology are here.

Cam·bridge·shire /ˈkāmbrijshər; -ˌshi(ə)r/ a county in eastern England; county seat, Cambridge.

Cam·by·ses /kamˈbīsēz/ (died 522 BC), king of Persia 529–522 BC; son of Cyrus. He is chiefly remembered for his conquest of Egypt in 525 BC.

cam·cord·er /ˈkamˌkôrdər/ ▶ **n.** a portable combined video camera and video recorder. [1980s: blend of CAMERA[1] and RECORDER.]

Cam·den /ˈkamdən/ a city in southwestern New Jersey; pop. 79,904.

came /kām/ past tense of COME.

cam·el /ˈkaməl/ ▶ **n. 1** a large, long-necked ungulate mammal (genus *Camelus*) of arid country, with long slender legs, broad cushioned feet, and either one or two fat-storing humps on the back. The **camel family** (Camelidae) also includes the llama and its relatives. See also ARABIAN CAMEL, BACTRIAN CAMEL. ▪ a fabric made from camel hair. ▪ a yellowish-brown color like that of camel hair. **2** an apparatus for raising a sunken ship, consisting of one or more watertight chests to provide buoyancy. ▪ a large floating fender used to keep a vessel off the dock. [OE, from L. *camelus*, from Gk. *kamēlos*, of Semitic origin.]

cam·el·back /ˈkaməlˌbak/ ▶ **n.** a back with a hump-shaped curve on a sofa.

cam·el·eer /ˌkaməˈli(ə)r/ ▶ **n.** a person who controls or rides a camel.

cam·el hair (also **cam·el's hair**) ▶ **n. 1** a fabric made from the hair of a camel. **2** [usu. as adj.] fine, soft hair from a squirrel's tail, used in artists' brushes.

cam·e·lid /kəˈmēlid; ˈkaməlid/ ▶ **n.** Zool. a mammal of the camel family (Camelidae).

ca·mel·lia /kəˈmēlyə/ ▶ **n.** an evergreen eastern Asian shrub (genus *Camellia*) of the tea family, grown for its showy flowers and shiny leaves. [mod. L., named after Joseph *Kamel* (Latinized as *Camellus*), Moravian botanist (1661–1706).]

Ca·mel·o·par·da·lis /kəˌmeləˈpärdl-is/ Astron. a large but inconspicuous northern constellation (the Giraffe), between Polaris and Perseus. [via L. from Gk. *kamēlopardalis*.]

Cam·e·lot /ˈkaməˌlät/ (in Arthurian legend) the place where King Arthur held his court. ▪ [as n.] **(a Camelot)** a place associated with glittering romance and optimism.

Cam·em·bert /ˈkaməmˌbe(ə)r/ ▶ **n.** a kind of rich, soft, creamy cheese with a whitish rind, originally made near Camembert in Normandy.

cam·e·o /ˈkamēˌō/ ▶ **n.** (pl. **-os**) **1** a piece of jewelry, typically oval in shape, consisting of a portrait in profile carved in relief on a background of a different color. **2** a short descriptive literary sketch that neatly encapsulates someone or something. ▪ a small part in a play or movie, played by a distinguished actor or a celebrity. [ME: from OFr. *camahieu, cama(h)u*.]

cam·er·a[1] /ˈkam(ə)rə/ ▶ **n.** a device for recording visual images in the form of photographs, movie film, or video signals.

– PHRASES **on** (or **off**) **camera** while being filmed or televised (or not being filmed or televised). [19th C.: from L. (see CAMERA[2]).]

cam·er·a[2] ▶ **n.** [in names] a chamber or round building: *the Radcliffe Camera.*

– PHRASES **in camera** esp. Law in private, in particular taking place in the private chambers of a judge. [17th C.: from L., 'vault,' from Gk. *kamara* 'object with an arched cover.']

cam·er·a lu·ci·da /ˈlo͞osidə/ ▶ **n.** an instrument in which rays of light are reflected by a prism to produce on a sheet of paper an image, from which a drawing can be made. [18th C.: from L., 'bright chamber.']

cam·er·a·man /ˈkam(ə)rəmən; -ˌman/ ▶ **n.** (pl. **-men**) a man whose profession involves operating a television or movie camera.

cam·er·a ob·scu·ra /əbˈskyo͝orə/ ▶ **n.** a darkened box with a convex lens or aperture for projecting the image of an external object onto a screen inside. It is important historically in the development of photography. [18th C.: from L., 'dark chamber.']

cam·er·a·per·son /ˈkam(ə)rəˌpərsən/ ▶ **n.** a cameraman or camerawoman (used as a neutral alternative).

cam·er·a-read·y ▶ **adj.** Print. (of matter to be printed) in the right form and of good enough quality to be reproduced photographically onto a printing plate.

cam·er·a·wom·an /ˈkam(ə)rəˌwo͝omən/ ▶ **n.** a woman whose profession involves operating a television or movie camera.

cam·er·a·work /ˈkam(ə)rəˌwərk/ ▶ **n.** the way in which cameras are used in a movie or television program: *discreet camerawork and underplayed acting.*

Cam·e·roon /ˌkaməˈro͞on/ a country on the western coast of Africa. French name CAMEROUN. *See box on next page.* — **Cam·e·roon·i·an adj. & n.**

cam·i·on /ˈkamēən/ ▶ **n.** a large truck or a bus. [Fr.]

cam·i·sole /ˈkaməˌsōl/ ▶ **n.** a woman's loose-fitting undergarment for the upper body, typically held up by shoulder straps and having decorative trimming. [19th C.: from Fr., based on late L. *camisia* 'shirt or nightgown.']

cam·o /ˈkamō/ ▶ **n.** informal short for CAMOUFLAGE.

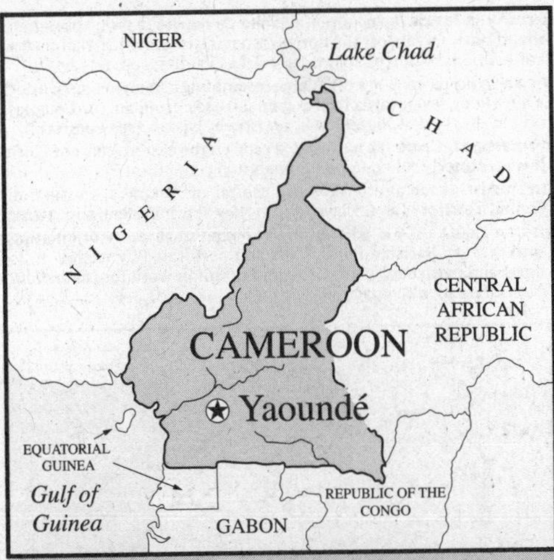

Cameroon

Official name: Republic of Cameroon
Location: west coast of Africa on the Bight of Biafra, east and southeast of Nigeria
Area: 181,300 square miles (469,400 sq km)
Population: 16,063,000
Capital: Yaoundé
Languages: English and French (both official), two dozen major African language groups
Currency: CFA franc

Ca·mõ·es /kə'moinsн/ (also **Ca·mo·ëns** /'kamō,ens/), Luis (Vaz) de (c.1524–80), Portuguese poet. His most noted work is *The Lusiads* (1572).

cam·o·mile ▶n. var. of CHAMOMILE.

Ca·mor·ra /kə'môrə/ (**the Camorra**) a secret criminal society originating in Naples and Neapolitan emigrant communities in the 19th century. [Ital., perh. from Sp. *camorra* 'quarrel.']

cam·ou·flage /'kamə,fläzн; -,fläj/ ▶n. the disguising of military personnel, equipment, and installations by painting or covering them to make them blend in with their surroundings. ■ the clothing or materials used for such a purpose. ■ an animal's natural coloring or form that enables it to blend in with its surroundings. ■ fig. actions or devices intended to disguise or mislead: *his apparent indifference was merely camouflage.* ▶v. [trans.] (often **be camouflaged**) hide or disguise the presence of (a person, animal, or object) by means of camouflage. [World War I: from Fr., from *camoufler* 'to disguise.']

Camp /kamp/, Walter Chauncey (1859–1925), US football coach. He coached at Yale University 1888–92 and was influential in shaping the rules of the sport.

camp[1] /kamp/ ▶n. **1** a place with temporary accommodations of huts, tents, or other structures, typically used by soldiers, refugees, prisoners, or travelers. ■ the people lodging in such a place: *the shot woke the whole camp.* ■ a recreational institution providing facilities for outdoor activities, sports, crafts, and other special interests and typically featuring rustic overnight accommodations. ■ temporary overnight lodging out of doors, typically in tents: *we pitched camp at a fine spot.* ■ a facility at which athletes train during the off-season: *football tryout camps.* **2** the supporters of a particular party or doctrine regarded collectively: *the conservative camp.* ▶v. [intrans.] live for a time in a camp, tent, or camper, as when on vacation. ■ lodge temporarily, esp. in an inappropriate or uncomfortable place: *we camped out for the night in a schoolroom.* ■ remain persistently in one place: *the press will be camping on your doorstep.*
– PHRASES **break camp** take down a tent or the tents of an encampment ready to leave. [16th C.: from Fr. *camp, champ,* from Ital. *campo,* from L. *campus* 'level ground.']

camp[2] informal ▶adj. deliberately exaggerated and theatrical in style, typically for humorous effect: *the movie seems more camp than shocking or gruesome.* ■ (of a man or his manner) ostentatiously and extravagantly effeminate: *a heavily made-up and highly camp actor.* ▶n. deliberately exaggerated and theatrical behavior or style: *Hollywood camp.* ▶v. [intrans.] (of a man) behave in an ostentatiously effeminate way: *he camped it up a bit for the cameras.* —**camp·i·ly** /'kampəlē/ adv. **camp·i·ness** n. **camp·y** adj. [20th C.: of unknown origin.]

cam·paign /kam'pān/ ▶n. a series of military operations intended to achieve a particular objective, confined to a particular area, or involving a specified type of fighting: *a desert campaign.* ■ an organized course of action to achieve a particular goal: *an advertising campaign.* ■ the organized actions that a political candidate undertakes to win an election. ▶v. [intrans.] work in an organized and active way toward a particular goal, typically a political or social one: *people who campaigned against child labor.* —**cam·paign·er** n. [17th C. (denoting a tract of open country): from Fr. *campagne* 'open country,' via Ital. from late L. *campania,* from *campus* 'level ground' (see CAMP[1]).]

cam·pa·ni·le /,kampə'nēlē; -'nēl/ ▶n. an Italian bell tower, esp. a freestanding one. [17th C.: from Ital., from *campana* 'bell.']

cam·pa·nol·o·gy /,kampə'näləjē/ ▶n. the art or practice of bell-ringing. —**cam·pa·no·log·i·cal** /,kampənl'äjikəl/ adj. **cam·pa·nol·o·gist** n. [19th C.: from mod. L. *campanologia,* from late L. *campana.*]

cam·pan·u·la /kam'panyələ/ ▶n. another term for BELLFLOWER. [mod. L., dimin. of late L. *campana.*]

cam·pan·u·late /kam'panyəlit; -,lāt/ ▶adj. Bot. (of a flower) bell-shaped, like a campanula.

Cam·pa·ri /käm'pärē/ ▶n. trademark a pinkish aperitif flavored with bitters. [named after the manufacturer.]

Camp·bell[1] /'kambəl/ a city in west central California, southwest of San Jose; pop. 36,048.

Camp·bell[2], John Archibald (1811–89), US Supreme Court associate justice 1853–61.

Camp·bell[3], Mrs. Patrick (1865–1940), English actress; born *Beatrice Stella Tanner.* She was noted for her portrayal of Eliza Doolittle in *Pygmalion* (1914).

Camp·bell-Ban·ner·man /'banərmən/, Sir Henry (1836–1908), British statesman; prime minister 1905–08.

Camp Da·vid the country retreat of the US president, in the Catoctin Mountains of Maryland.

Cam·pe·che /käm'pāснā; kam'pēснē/ a state in southeastern Mexico, on the Yucatán Peninsula. ■ its capital, on the Gulf of Mexico; pop. 172,200.

camp·er /'kampər/ ▶n. **1** a person who spends a vacation in a tent or camp. **2** a large motor vehicle with facilities for sleeping and cooking while camping.

cam·pe·si·no /,kampə'sēnō; ,käm-/ ▶n. (pl. **-nos**) (in Spanish-speaking regions) a peasant farmer.

camp·fire /'kamp,fī(ə)r/ ▶n. an open-air fire in a camp, used for cooking and as a focal point for social activity.

camp fol·low·er ▶n. a civilian who works in or is attached to a military camp. ■ a person who is nominally attached to a group but is not fully committed or does not make a substantial contribution to its activities.

camp·ground /'kamp,ground/ ▶n. a place used for camping, esp. one equipped with cooking grills, water, and bathrooms. ■ a place where a camp meeting is held.

cam·phor /'kamfər/ ▶n. a white, volatile, crystalline substance, a terpenoid ketone, $C_{10}H_{16}O$, with an aromatic smell and bitter taste, occurring in certain essential oils. [ME: from OFr. *camphore* or med. L. *camphora,* from Arab. *kāfūr,* via Malay from Sanskrit *karpūra.*]

cam·phor·ate /'kamfə,rāt/ ▶v. [trans.] [usu. as adj.] (**camphorated**) impregnate or treat with camphor.

cam·phor tree ▶n. an eastern Asian tree (*Cinnamomum camphora*) of the laurel family, that serves as the chief natural source of camphor.

Cam·pi·nas /käm'pēnəs; kän-/ a city in southeastern Brazil, northwest of São Paulo; pop. 835,000.

Cam·pi·on[1] /'kampēən/, Jane (1954–), New Zealand filmmaker. She wrote and directed *The Piano* (1993) and *In the Cut* (2003).

Cam·pi·on[2], St. Edmund (1540–81), English Jesuit priest and martyr.

cam·pi·on /'kampēən/ ▶n. a plant (genera *Silene* and *Lychnis*) of the pink family, typically having pink or white flowers with notched petals. [16th C.: perh. rel. to CHAMPION.]

camp meet·ing ▶n. a religious meeting held in the open air or in a tent, often lasting several days.

cam·po /'kampō; 'kämpō/ ▶n. (pl. **-pos**) (usu. **the campo**) (in South America, esp. Brazil) a grass plain with occasional stunted trees. [from Sp., Port., and Ital. *campo,* lit. 'field.']

Cam·po·bel·lo Is·land /,kampə'belō/ an island in southwestern New Brunswick, Canada, off Eastport in Maine, noted as the vacation home of President Franklin D. Roosevelt.

Cam·po Gran·de /'kän(m)poo 'grän(n)də/ a city in southwestern Brazil; pop. 489,000.

camp·o·ree /,kampə'rē/ ▶n. a local or regional camping event for Girl Scouts or Boy Scouts. [20th C.: blend of CAMP[1] and JAMBOREE.]

camp·site /'kamp,sīt/ ▶n. a place used for camping.

cam·pus /'kampəs/ ▶n. (pl. **-pus·es**) the grounds and buildings of a university or college. ■ the grounds of a school, hospital, or other institution. [18th C.: from L. *campus* 'field.']

Cam Ranh Bay /'kam 'rän/ an inlet of the South China Sea, in south central Vietnam. It was a major US military base during the Vietnam War.

cam·shaft /'kam,sнaft/ ▶n. a shaft with one or more cams attached to it, esp. one operating the valves in an internal combustion engine.

Ca·mus /ka'mo͞o/, Albert (1913–60), French writer; His works, closely aligned with existentialism, include *The Stranger* (1942) and *The Rebel* (1951). Nobel Prize for Literature (1957).

Can. ▶ abbr. Canada or Canadian.

can[1] /kan/ ▶ modal verb (3rd sing. pres. **can**; past **could** /ko͝od/) **1** be able to: *they can run fast | he can't afford it.* ■ be able to through acquired knowledge or skill: *I can speak Italian.* ■ have the opportunity or possibility to: *there are many ways vacationers can take money abroad.* ■ [with negative or in questions] used to express doubt or surprise about the possibility of something's being the case. *he can't have finished.* **2** be permitted to: *nobody could legally drink on the premises.* ■ used to request someone to do something: *can you open the window?* ■ used to make a suggestion or offer: *we can have another drink if you like.* **3** used to indicate that something is typically the case: *he could be very moody.* [OE *cunnan* 'know' from Indo-Eur.; akin to Ger. *können* 'to be able,' L. *gnoscere* 'know,' Gk. *gignōskein*.]

can[2] ▶ n. **1** a cylindrical metal container. ■ a small steel or aluminum container in which food or drink is hermetically sealed for storage over long periods. ■ the quantity of food or drink held by such a container. **2** (**the can**) informal prison. **3** (**the can**) informal the toilet. ▶ v. (**canned, can·ning**) [trans.] (often **be canned**) **1** preserve (food) in a can. **2** informal dismiss (someone) from their job. ■ reject (something) as inadequate.
– PHRASES **a can of worms** a complicated matter likely to prove awkward or embarrassing. **in the can** informal on tape or film and ready to be broadcast or released. — **can·ner** n. [OE *canne*, rel. to Ger. *Kanne*; either of Gmc. origin or from late L. *canna*.]

Ca·na /'kānə/ an ancient small town in Galilee where Christ is said to have performed his first miracle by changing water into wine (John 2:1–11).

Ca·naan /'kānən/ the biblical name for the area of ancient Palestine west of the Jordan River. — **Ca·naan·ite** /-nə,nīt/ n. & adj.

Can·a·da /'kanədə/ a country in northern North America. *See box.* — **Ca·na·di·an** /kə'nādēən/ n. & adj.

Can·a·da bal·sam ▶ n. a yellowish resin obtained from the balsam fir and used for mounting preparations on microscope slides.

Can·a·da goose ▶ n. a common North American goose (*Branta canadensis*) with a black head and neck, a white cheek patch, and a loud trumpeting call.

Can·a·da jay ▶ n. another term for GRAY JAY.

Ca·na·di·an foot·ball /kə'nādēən/ ▶ n. a form of football played in Canada, derived from rugby but now resembling American football.

Ca·na·di·an French ▶ n. the form of the French language written and spoken by French Canadians.

Ca·na·di·an goose ▶ n. another term for CANADA GOOSE.

Ca·na·di·an Riv·er a river that flows for 900 miles (1,450 km) from New Mexico to Oklahoma.

Ca·na·di·an Shield a plateau that occupies more than two fifths of the land area of Canada. Also called LAURENTIAN PLATEAU.

ca·naille /kə'nī; -'nāl/ ▶ n. (**the canaille**) derog. the common people; the masses. [Fr., from Ital. *canaglia* 'pack of dogs,' from *cane* 'dog.']

ca·nal /kə'nal/ ▶ n. an artificial waterway constructed to allow the passage of boats or ships inland or to convey water for irrigation. ■ a tubular duct in a plant or animal, serving to convey or contain food, liquid, or air: *the ear canal.* ■ Astron. any of a number of linear markings formerly reported as seen by telescope on the planet Mars. [ME: from OFr., alt. of *chanel* 'channel,' from L. *canalis* 'pipe,' from *canna* 'cane.']

ca·nal boat ▶ n. a long, narrow boat used on canals.

Ca·na·let·to /,kanl'etō/ (1697–1768), Italian painter; born *Giovanni Antonio Canal.* He painted the festivals and scenery of Venice.

can·a·lic·u·lus /,kanl'ikyələs/ ▶ n. (pl. **-li** /-,lī/) Anat. a small channel or duct. — **can·a·lic·u·lar** /-'ikyələr/ adj.

can·al·ize /'kanl,īz/ ▶ v. [trans.] convert (a river) into a navigable canal. ■ convey (something) through a duct or channel. ■ fig. give a direction or purpose to (something): *he canalized the enthusiasm of the diehards into party channels.* — **ca·nal·i·za·tion** /,kanl-ə'zāsʜən/ n.

Ca·nal Zone see PANAMA CANAL.

can·a·pé /'kanə,pā -pē/ ▶ n. **1** a small piece of bread or pastry with a savory topping. **2** a sofa, esp. a decorative French antique. [Fr.]

ca·nard /kə'när(d)/ ▶ n. **1** an unfounded rumor or story. **2** a small winglike projection attached to an aircraft forward of the main wing to provide extra stability or control. [19th C.: from Fr., lit. 'duck,' also 'hoax,' from OFr. *caner* 'to quack.']

Ca·nar·sie /kə'närsē/ a section of southeastern Brooklyn in New York City.

Ca·nar·y /kə'ne(ə)rē/, Martha Jane. See CALAMITY JANE.

ca·nar·y /kə'ne(ə)rē/ ▶ n. (pl. **-nar·ies**) **1** a mainly African finch (genus *Serinus*) with a melodious song, typically having yellowish-green plumage. ■ slang an informer. **2** (also **canary yellow**) a bright yellow color resembling the plumage of a canary. **3** (also **canary wine**) hist. a sweet wine from the Canary Islands, similar to Madeira. [16th C.: from Fr. *canari*, from Sp. *canario* 'canary' or 'person from the Canary Islands.']

ca·nar·y grass ▶ n. a tall grass (genus *Phalaris*, esp. *P. canariensis*) of northwestern Africa and the Canary Islands, used as food for caged birds.

Ca·nar·y Is·lands /kə'ne(ə)rē/ (also **the Ca·nar·ies**) a group of islands in the Atlantic Ocean, off the northwestern coast of Africa, that forms an autonomous region of Spain; capital, Las Palmas; pop. 1,557,530.

ca·nas·ta /kə'nastə/ ▶ n. a card game resembling rummy, using two decks. ■ a meld of seven cards in this game. [1940s: from Sp. (of Uruguayan origin), lit. 'basket,' based on L. *canistrum* 'basket' (see CANISTER).]

Ca·nav·er·al, Cape /kə'nav(ə)rəl/ a cape on the eastern coast of Florida. It was formerly called Cape Kennedy 1963–73.

Can·ber·ra /'kanb(ə)rə; -,berə/ the capital of Australia, in Australian Capital Territory (an enclave within New South Wales); pop. 310,000.

can·can /'kan,kan/ ▶ n. a lively, high-kicking stage dance originating in 19th-century Parisian music halls and performed by women in long skirts and petticoats: [19th C.: from Fr., child's word for *canard* 'duck,' from OFr. *caner* 'to quack.']

Canada

Location: extends across the northern part of the North American continent
Area: 3,561,200 square miles (9,221,000 sq km)
Population: 32,507,900
Capital: Ottawa
Languages: English and French (both official)
Currency: Canadian dollar

can·cel /'kansəl/ ▶ v. (**-celed, -cel·ing**; Brit. **-celled, -cel·ling**) [trans.] **1** decide or announce that (an arranged or planned event) will not take place. ■ annul or revoke (a formal arrangement that is in effect). ■ abolish or make void (a financial obligation). ■ mark, pierce, or tear (a ticket, check, or postage stamp) to show that it has been used or invalidated: [as adj.] *canceled checks.* **2** (of a factor or circumstance) neutralize or negate the force or effect of (another): *the electric fields may cancel each other out.* ■ Math. delete (an equal factor) from both sides of an equation or from the numerator and denominator of a fraction. ▶ n. **1** a mark made on a postage stamp to show that it has been used. **2** Print. a new page or section inserted in a book to replace the original text, typically to correct an error: [as adj.] *a cancel title page.* [ME: from OFr. *canceller*, from L. *cancellare*, from *cancelli* 'crossbars.']

can·cel·bot /'kansəl,bät/ ▶ n. Comput. a program that searches for and deletes specified postings from Internet newsgroups. [1990s: from CANCEL + BOT[2].]

can·cel·er /'kansələr/ (also **can·cel·ler**) ▶ n. a device used to cancel something, esp. one that makes a cancellation on a postage stamp.

can·cel·la·tion /,kansə'lāsʜən/ ▶ n. the action of canceling something that has been arranged or planned. ■ a crossing out of something written: *all cancellations on documents must be made indelibly.* ■ a mark placed on a postage stamp to show that it has been used. ■ Law the annulling of a legal document.

can·cel·lous /'kansələs/ ▶ adj. Anat. of or denoting bone tissue with a meshlike structure containing many pores, typical of the interior of mature bones. [19th C.: from L. *cancelli* 'crossbars.']

Can·cer /'kansər/ **1** Astron. a constellation (the Crab), said to represent a crab crushed under the foot of Hercules. It is most noted for the globular star cluster of Praesepe (the Beehive cluster). **2** Astrol. the fourth sign of the zodiac, which the sun enters at the northern summer solstice (about June 21). ■ (**a Cancer**) a person born when the sun is in this sign.
– PHRASES **tropic of Cancer** see TROPIC[1]. — **Can·cer·i·an** /kan'se(ə)rēən; -'si(ə)r-/ n. & adj. (in sense 2). [L.]

can·cer /'kansər/ ▶ n. the disease caused by an uncontrolled division of abnormal cells in a part of the body. ■ a malignant growth or tumor resulting from such a division of cells. ■ fig. a practice or phenomenon perceived to be evil or destructive and hard to contain or eradicate. — **can·cer·ous** /'kansərəs/ adj. [OE, from L., 'crab or creeping ulcer,' translating Gk. *karkinos*, said to have been applied to such tumors because the swollen veins around them resembled the limbs of a crab.]

can·cer clus·ter ▶ n. a geographic area with a statistically higher than average occurrence of cancer among its residents.

can·cer stick ▶ n. informal, humorous a cigarette.

can·croid /ˈkaNG,kroid/ ▶ adj. **1** Zool. like a crab, esp. in structure. **2** Med. (of a growth) resembling cancer.

Can·cún /kaNGˈkōōn; kan-/ a town in southeastern Mexico, on the Yucatán Peninsula; pop. 27,500.

can·de·la /kanˈdēlə; -ˈdelə/ (abbr.: **cd**) ▶ n. Physics the SI unit of luminous intensity. One candela is the luminous intensity, in a given direction, of a source that emits monochromatic radiation of frequency 540 × 1012Hz and has a radiant intensity in that direction of 1683 watt per steradian. [1950s: from L., 'candle.']

can·de·la·brum /,kandəˈläbrəm; -ˈlab-/ ▶ n. (pl. **-la·bra** /-ˈläbrə; -ˈlabrə/) a large branched candlestick or holder for several candles or lamps. [19th C.: from L., from *candela*.]

can·des·cent /kanˈdesənt/ ▶ adj. glowing with, or as with, heat. — **can·des·cence** n. **can·des·cent·ly** adv.

can·did /ˈkandid/ ▶ adj. **1** truthful and straightforward; frank. **2** (of a photograph of a person) taken informally, esp. without the subject's knowledge. — **can·did·ly** adv. **can·did·ness** n. [17th C.: from L. *candidus* 'white.']

can·di·da /ˈkandidə/ ▶ n. a yeastlike, parasitic fungus (genus *Candida*, phylum Ascomycota) that can cause an infection (**candidiasis**) such as athlete's foot and vaginitis. [mod. L., fem. of L. *candidus* 'white.']

can·di·date /ˈkandi,dāt; -dit/ ▶ n. a person who applies for a job or is nominated for election. ■ a person taking an examination: *doctoral candidates in literature.* ■ a person or thing regarded as suitable for or likely to receive a particular fate, treatment, or position: *she was the perfect* ***candidate for*** *a biography.* — **can·di·da·cy** /ˈkandidəsē/ n. **can·di·da·ture** /-,CHŏŏr; -CHər/ n. Brit. [17th C.: from L. *candidatus* 'white-robed,' also 'candidate for office,' from *candidus* 'white.']

can·dle /ˈkandl/ ▶ n. a cylinder or block of wax or tallow with a central wick that is lit to produce light as it burns. ■ (also **international candle**) Physics a unit of luminous intensity, superseded by the candela. ▶ v. [trans.] (often **be candled**) test (an egg) for freshness or fertility by holding it to the light.
– PHRASES **be unable to hold a candle to** informal be not nearly as good as. — **can·dler** /ˈkandlər; -dl-ər/ n. [OE *candel*, from L. *candela*, from *candere* 'be white.']

can·dle·ber·ry /ˈkandl,berē/ ▶ n. (pl. **-ries**) any of a number of trees or shrubs whose berries or seeds yield a wax or oil that can be used for making candles, esp. the bayberry or the candlenut.

can·dle·fish /ˈkandl,fisH/ ▶ n. (pl. same or **-fish·es**) a small, edible marine fish (*Thaleichthys pacificus*, family Osmeridae) with oily flesh, occurring on the west coast of North America. Also called EULACHON. [because the Chinook Indians formerly burned the bodies as candles.]

can·dle·hold·er /ˈkandl,hōldər/ ▶ n. a holder or support for a candle, typically one that is small or sturdy.

can·dle·light /ˈkandl,līt/ ▶ n. dim light provided by a candle or candles: *we dined* ***by candlelight.***

can·dle·lit /ˈkandl,lit/ ▶ adj. lit by a candle or candles: *a romantic candlelit dinner.*

Can·dle·mas /ˈkandlməs/ ▶ n. a Christian festival held on February 2 to commemorate the purification of the Virgin Mary and the Presentation of Christ in the Temple. Candles were blessed at this festival. [OE *Candelmæsse* (see CANDLE, MASS).]

can·dle·nut /ˈkandl,nət/ ▶ n. a southeast Asian evergreen tree (*Aleurites moluccana*) of the spurge family, with large seeds that yield an oil used for lighting and other purposes. Also called CANDLEBERRY.

can·dle·pow·er /ˈkandl,pou(ə)r/ ▶ n. illuminating power expressed in candelas or candles.

can·dle·snuff·er /ˈkandl,snəfər/ ▶ n. see SNUFFER.

can·dle·stick /ˈkandl,stik/ ▶ n. a support or holder for one or more candles, typically tall and thin.

can·dle·wick /ˈkandl,wik/ ▶ n. a thick, soft cotton fabric with a raised, tufted pattern. ■ the yarn used to make such a fabric. ■ tufted embroidery work made with heavy cotton yarn similar to that used to make wicks for candles.

can-do /ˈkan ˈdōō/ ▶ adj. [attrib.] informal characterized by or exhibiting a determination or willingness to take action and achieve results: *I like his can-do attitude.*

can·dor /ˈkandər; -dôr/ (Brit. **can·dour**) ▶ n. the quality of being open and honest in expression; frankness. [ME: from L. *candor* 'whiteness.']

C&W ▶ abbr. country and western (music).

can·dy /ˈkandē/ ▶ n. (pl. **-dies**) a sweet food made with sugar or syrup combined with fruit, chocolate, or nuts. ■ sugar crystallized by boiling and slow evaporation. ▶ v. (**-dies, -died**) [trans.] [often as adj.] (**candied**) preserve (fruit) by coating and impregnating it with a sugar syrup: *candied fruit.* [17th C. (v.): n. use from ME *sugar-candy*, from Fr. *sucre candi* 'crystallized sugar,' from Arab. *sukkar* 'sugar' + *ḳandī* 'candied,' based on Sanskrit *khaṇḍa* 'fragment.']

can·dy ap·ple ▶ n. an apple coated with a thin layer of cooked sugar or caramel and fixed on a stick. ■ (also **candy-apple red**) a bright red color.

can·dy-ass ▶ n. informal a timid, cowardly, or despicable person. — **can·dy-assed** adj.

can·dy cane ▶ n. a cylindrical stick of striped, sweet candy with a curved end, resembling a walking stick.

can·dy corn ▶ n. a form of chewy candy shaped like a large kernel of corn.

can·dy·man /ˈkandē,man/ ▶ n. (pl. **-men**) informal a person who sells illegal drugs.

can·dy-striped ▶ adj. (of material or a garment) patterned with alternating stripes of white and another color, typically pink. — **can·dy-stripe** adj. & n.

can·dy-strip·er /ˈstrīpər/ ▶ n. informal a teenage girl who does volunteer nursing in a hospital. [from the candy-striped uniforms.]

can·dy·tuft /ˈkandē,təft/ ▶ n. a European plant (genus *Iberis*) of the cabbage family, with small heads of white, pink, or purple flowers, often cultivated as a garden plant. [17th C.: from *Candy* (obs. form of *Candia*, former name of Crete).]

cane /kān/ ▶ n. **1** the hollow, jointed stem of a tall grass, esp. bamboo or sugar cane, or the stem of a slender palm such as rattan. ■ any plant that produces such stems. ■ stems of bamboo, rattan, or wicker used as a material for making furniture or baskets. ■ short for SUGAR CANE. ■ a flexible, woody stem of the raspberry plant or any of its relatives. **2** a length of cane or a slender stick, esp. one used as a support for plants, as a walking stick, or as an instrument of punishment. ■ (**the cane**) a form of corporal punishment used in certain schools, involving beating with a cane. ▶ v. [trans.] **1** (often **be caned**) beat with a cane as a punishment. **2** [usu. as adj.] (**caned**) make or repair (furniture) with cane. — **can·er** n. [ME: from OFr., via L. from Gk. *kanna, kannē*, of Semitic origin.]

cane·brake /ˈkān,brāk/ ▶ n. a piece of ground covered with a dense growth of canes.

cane chair ▶ n. a chair with a seat made of woven cane strips.

cane sug·ar ▶ n. sugar obtained from sugar cane.

Ca·nes Ve·nat·i·ci /ˈkānēz vəˈnatəsē; -,sī/ Astron. a small northern constellation (the Hunting Dogs), said to represent two dogs (Asterion and Chara) held on a leash by Boötes. [L.]

Ca·net·ti /kəˈnetē/, Elias (1905–94), British writer; born in Bulgaria. He wrote *Auto-da-Fé* (1936). Nobel Prize for Literature (1981).

Can·field /ˈkan,fēld/ ▶ n. a form of the card game patience or solitaire. [20th C.: named after Richard A. *Canfield* (1855–1914), Amer. gambler.]

ca·nic·u·lar /kəˈnikyələr/ ▶ adj. pertaining to a dog, in particular: ■ of or pertaining to the Dog Star, Sirius. ■ of or pertaining to the dog days.

can·id /ˈkanid; ˈkā-/ ▶ n. Zool. a mammal of the dog family (Canidae). [19th C.: from mod. L. *Canidae* (pl.), from L. *canis* 'dog.']

ca·nine /ˈkānīn/ ▶ adj. of, relating to, or resembling a dog or dogs. ■ Zool. of or relating to animals of the dog family. ▶ n. **1** a dog. ■ Zool. another term for CANID. **2** (also **canine tooth**) a pointed tooth between the incisors and premolars of a mammal, often greatly enlarged in carnivores. [ME (sense 2): from Fr., from L. *caninus*, from *canis* 'dog.']

ca·nine dis·tem·per ▶ n. see DISTEMPER[1] (sense 1).

Ca·nis Ma·jor /ˈkānis; ˈkan-/ Astron. a small constellation (the Great Dog), said to represent one of the dogs following Orion. It is just south of the celestial equator and contains the brightest star, Sirius. [L.]

Ca·nis Mi·nor /mīˈnôr/ Astron. a small constellation (the Little Dog), said to represent one of the dogs following Orion. It is close to the celestial equator and contains the bright star Procyon. [L.]

can·is·ter /ˈkanəstər/ ▶ n. a round or cylindrical container, typically of metal, used for storing such things as food, chemicals, or rolls of film. ■ a cylinder of pressurized gas, typically one that explodes when thrown or fired from a gun: *tear-gas canisters.* ■ hist. small bullets packed in cases that fit the bore of an artillery piece or gun: *a volley of canister.* [15th C.: from L. *canistrum*, from Gk. *kanastron* 'wicker basket,' from *kanna* 'reed' (see CANE).]

can·ker /ˈkaNGkər/ ▶ n. **1** a necrotic, fungal disease of apple and other trees causing damage to the bark. ■ an open lesion in plant tissue caused by infection or injury. ■ fungal rot in some fruits and vegetables, e.g., parsnips and tomatoes. **2** Med. an ulcerous condition or disease, in particular: ■ (also **canker sore**) a small ulcer of the mouth or lips. ■ another term for THRUSH[2] (sense 2). ■ ulceration of the throat and other orifices of birds, typically caused by a protozoal infection. ■ (also **ear can·ker**) inflammation of the ear of a dog, cat, or rabbit, typically caused by mites. ■ fig. a malign influence difficult to eradicate. ▶ v. **1** [intrans.] (of woody plant tissue) become infected with canker. **2** [trans.] [usu. as adj.] (**cankered**) infect with a corrupting bitterness: *he hated her with a cankered, shameful abhorrence.* — **can·ker·ous** /-kərəs/ adj. [ME: from OFr. *chancre*, from L. *cancer* 'crab' (see CANCER).]

can·ker·worm /ˈkaNGkər,wərm/ ▶ n. the caterpillar of a North American moth of the family Geometridae (esp. *Paleacrita vernata* and *Alsophila pometaria*) that can be a major pest of fruit and shade trees.

Can·more /ˈkan,môr/, the nickname of Malcolm III of Scotland (see MALCOLM).

can·na /ˈkanə/ (also **canna lily**) ▶ n. a lilylike, tropical American plant (genus *Canna*, family Cannaceae) widely cultivated for its bright flowers and ornamental straplike leaves. [from mod. L., from L. *canna* 'cane' (see CANE).]

can·na·bin /ˈkanəbin/ ▶ n. a poisonous resin extracted from cannabis.

can·nab·i·noid /ˈkanəbə,noid; kəˈnabə-/ ▶ n. Chem. any of a group of related compounds that include cannabinol and the active constituents of cannabis.

can·nab·i·nol /'kanəbə,nôl; -,nōl; kə'nabə-/ ▶ **n.** Chem. a crystalline compound, $C_{21}H_{26}O_2$, whose derivatives, esp. THC, are the active constituents of cannabis. [19th C.: from CANNABIS + -OL.]

can·na·bis /'kanəbis/ ▶ **n.** a plant (*Cannabis sativa*, family Cannabaceae) used to produce hemp fiber and as a mildly psychotropic drug. Also called HEMP, MARIJUANA. ■ a dried preparation of the flowering tops or other parts of this plant, or a resinous extract of it (**cannabis resin**). [from L., from Gk. *kannabis*.]

Can·nar·y /kə'ne(ə)rē/, Martha Jane. See CALAMITY JANE.

canned /kand/ ▶ **adj. 1** (of food or drink) preserved or supplied in a sealed can. **2** informal, often derog. (of music, laughter, or applause) prerecorded and therefore considered to be lacking in freshness and spontaneity.

can·nel coal /'kanl/ ▶ **n.** a hard, compact kind of bituminous coal. [16th C. (orig. a north. Engl. usage): of unknown origin.]

can·nel·li·ni bean /,kanl'ēnē/ ▶ **n.** a kidney-shaped bean of a medium-sized, creamy-white variety. [Ital. *cannellini*, lit. 'small tubes.']

can·nel·lo·ni /,kanl'ōnē/ ▶ **n.** rolls of pasta stuffed with a meat or vegetable mixture. [Ital., lit. 'large tubes,' from *cannello* 'tube.']

can·ne·lure /'kanl,(y)o͝or/ ▶ **n.** a groove around the cylindrical part of a bullet. [18th C.: from Fr., from *canneler* 'provide with a channel,' from *canne* 'reed, cane.']

can·ner·y /'kanərē/ ▶ **n.** (pl. **-ner·ies**) a factory where food is canned.

Cannes /kan; kän/ a city on the Mediterranean coast of France; pop. 69,360. An international film festival is held here annually.

can·ni·bal /'kanəbəl/ ▶ **n.** a person who eats the flesh of other human beings: [as adj.] *cannibal tribes.* ■ an animal that feeds on flesh of its own species. — **can·ni·bal·ism n. can·ni·bal·is·tic** /,kanəbə'listik/ **adj. can·ni·bal·is·ti·cal·ly** /,kanəbə'listik(ə)lē/ **adv.** [16th C.: from Sp. *Canibales* (pl.), var. of *Caribes*, a W. Ind. people reputed to eat humans (see CARIB).]

can·ni·bal·ize /'kanəbə,līz/ ▶ **v.** [trans.] **1** use (a machine) as a source of spare parts for another, similar machine. ■ use (the creative work of others) in one's own art: *high culture cannibalized mass culture.* ■ (of a company) reduce (the sales of one of its products) by introducing a similar, competing product. **2** (of an animal) eat (an animal of its own kind). — **can·ni·bal·i·za·tion** /,kanəbələ'zāsʜən/ **n.**

Can·niz·za·ro /,känēd'zärō/, Stanislao (1826–1910), Italian chemist. He introduced a unified system of atomic and molecular weights.

can·no·li /kə'nōlē/ ▶ **pl. n.** a dessert consisting of small deep-fried pastry tubes filled with sweetened ricotta cheese, nuts, chocolate bits, etc. [Ital., from *canna* 'reed.']

can·non /'kanən/ ▶ **n. 1** (pl. usu. same) a large, heavy piece of artillery, typically mounted on wheels, formerly used in warfare. ■ an automatic heavy gun that fires shells from an aircraft or tank. **2** Engin. a heavy cylinder or hollow drum that is able to rotate independently on a shaft. [ME: from Fr. *canon*, from Ital. *cannone* 'large tube,' from *canna* 'cane' (see CANE).]

can·non·ade /,kanə'nād/ ▶ **n.** a period of continuous, heavy gunfire. ▶ **v.** [intrans.] discharge heavy guns continuously.

can·non·ball /'kanən,bôl/ ▶ **n.** a round metal or stone projectile fired from a cannon in former times. ■ (also **cannonball dive**) a jump into water performed upright with the knees clasped to the chest.

can·non bone ▶ **n.** a long, tube-shaped bone in the lower leg of a horse or other large quadruped, between the fetlock and the knee or hock.

can·non·eer /,kanə'ni(ə)r/ ▶ **n.** hist. an artilleryman who positioned and fired a cannon.

can·non fod·der ▶ **n.** soldiers regarded merely as material to be expended in war.

can·non·ry /'kanənrē/ ▶ **n.** (pl. **-ries**) the use or discharge of cannon; artillery.

can·not /kə'nät; 'kan,(n)ät/ ▶ **contr.** can not.

can·nu·la /'kanyələ/ ▶ **n.** (pl. **-lae** /-lē; -,lī/ or **-las**) Surg. a thin tube inserted into a vein or body cavity to administer medicine, drain off fluid, or insert a surgical instrument. [17th C.: from L., 'small reed,' dimin. of *canna* (see CANE).]

can·nu·late /'kanyə,lāt/ ▶ **v.** [trans.] Surg. introduce a cannula or thin tube into (a vein or body cavity). — **can·nu·la·tion** /,kanyə'lāsʜən/ **n.**

can·ny /'kanē/ ▶ **adj.** (**-ni·er, -ni·est**) **1** having shrewdness, esp. in money or business matters. **2** N. English Scot. pleasant; nice: *she's a canny lass.* — **can·ni·ly** /'kanl-ē/ **adv. can·ni·ness n.** [16th C.: from CAN[1] ('know').]

ca·noe /kə'no͞o/ ▶ **n.** a narrow, keelless boat with pointed ends, propelled by a paddle or paddles. ▶ **v.** (**-noes, -noed, -noe·ing**) [no obj., with adverbial of direction] travel in or paddle a canoe: *he canoed down the Nile.* — **ca·noe·ing** /-'no͞oiɴɢ/ **ca·noe·ist** /-'no͞oist/ **n.** [16th C.: from Sp. *canoa*, from Arawak, from Carib *canaoua*.]

canoe

can·o·la /kə'nōlə/ ▶ **n.** an oilseed rape that yields a valuable cooking oil. [1970s: from CANADA + *-ola* (based on L. *oleum* 'oil').]

can·on[1] /'kanən/ ▶ **n. 1** a general law, rule, principle, or criterion by which something is judged. ■ a church decree or law. **2** a collection or list of sacred books accepted as genuine: *the biblical canon.* ■ the works of a particular author or artist that are recognized as genuine: *the Shakespeare canon.* ■ a list of literary or artistic works considered to be established as being of the highest quality: *Hopkins was established in the canon of English poetry.* **3** (also **canon of the Mass**) (in the Roman Catholic Church) the part of the Mass containing the words of consecration. **4** Music a piece in which the same melody is begun in different parts successively, so that the imitations overlap. [OE: from L., from Gk. *kanōn* 'rule.']

can·on[2] ▶ **n.** a member of the clergy on the staff of a cathedral, esp. a member of the chapter. ■ (also **canon regular** or **regular canon**) (in the Roman Catholic Church) a member of certain orders of clergy that live communally according to an ecclesiastical rule in the same way as monks. [ME: from OFr. *canonie*, from L. *canonicus* 'according to rule.']

ca·ñon /'kanyən/ ▶ **n.** var. of CANYON.

can·on·ess /'kanənis/ ▶ **n.** (in the Roman Catholic Church) a member of certain religious orders of women living communally according to an ecclesiastical rule in the same way as nuns.

ca·non·ic /kə'nänik/ ▶ **adj. 1** Music in canon form. **2** another term for CANONICAL. — **ca·non·i·cal·ly** /-ik(ə)lē/ **adv.**

ca·non·i·cal /kə'nänikəl/ ▶ **adj. 1** according to or ordered by canon law: *the canonical rites of the Roman Church.* **2** included in the list of sacred books officially accepted as genuine. ■ accepted as being accurate and authoritative. ■ (of an artist or work) belonging to the literary or artistic canon. ■ according to recognized rules or scientific laws: *canonical nucleotide sequences.* ■ Math. of or relating to a general rule or standard formula. **3** of or relating to a cathedral chapter or a member of it. ▶ **plural n.** (**canonicals**) the prescribed official dress of the clergy. — **ca·non·i·cal·ly** /-ik(ə)lē/ **adv.**

ca·non·i·cal hours ▶ **plural n.** the times of daily Christian prayer appointed in the breviary. ■ the offices set for these times, namely matins with lauds, prime, terce, sext, nones, vespers, and compline.

can·on·ic·i·ty /,kanə'nisitē/ ▶ **n.** the fact or status of being canonical: *established standards of canonicity.*

can·on·ist /'kanənist/ ▶ **n.** an expert in canon law. — **can·on·is·tic** /,kanə'nistik/ **adj.**

can·on·ize /'kanə,nīz/ ▶ **v.** [trans.] (often **be canonized**) (in the Roman Catholic Church) officially declare (a dead person) to be a saint. ■ fig. regard as being above reproach or of great significance: *we have canonized freedom of speech as an absolute value.* ■ accept into the literary or artistic canon: [as adj.] *a canonized writer.* ■ sanction by Church authority. — **can·on·i·za·tion** /,kanənə'zāsʜən/ **n.**

can·on law ▶ **n.** ecclesiastical law, esp. (in the Roman Catholic Church) that laid down by papal pronouncements.

can·on reg·u·lar ▶ **n.** see CANON[2].

can·on·ry /'kanənrē/ ▶ **n.** (pl. **-ries**) the office or benefice of a canon.

ca·noo·dle /kə'no͞odl/ ▶ **v.** [intrans.] informal kiss and cuddle amorously: *canoodling with her boyfriend.* [19th C.: of unknown origin.]

Ca·no·pic jar /kə'nōpik; -'näpik/ (also **Canopic vase**) ▶ **n.** a covered urn used in ancient Egyptian burials to hold the entrails from an embalmed body. [19th C.: from L. *Canopicus*, from *Canopus*, town in ancient Egypt.]

Ca·no·pus /kə'nōpəs/ Astron. the second brightest star in the sky, and the brightest in the constellation Carina. [L., from Gk. *Kanōpus*, pilot of the fleet of King Menelaus in the Trojan War.]

can·o·py /'kanəpē/ ▶ **n.** (pl. **-pies**) an ornamental cloth covering hung or held up over something, esp. a throne or bed. ■ fig. something hanging or perceived as hanging over a person or scene: *the canopy of twinkling stars.* ■ Archit. a rooflike projection or shelter. ■ the transparent plastic or glass cover of an aircraft's cockpit. ■ the expanding, umbrellalike part of a parachute, made of silk or nylon. ■ [in sing.] the uppermost trees or branches of the trees in a forest, forming a more or less continuous layer of foliage. ▶ **v.** (**-pies, -pied**) [trans.] [usu. as adj.] (**canopied**) cover or provide with a canopy: *a canopied bed.* [ME: from med. L. *canopeum*, alt. of L. *conopeum* 'mosquito net,' from Gk. *kōnōpeion* 'couch,' from *kōnōps* 'mosquito.']

ca·no·rous /kə'nôrəs; 'kanərəs/ ▶ **adj.** rare (of song or speech) melodious or resonant. [17th C.: from L. *canorus* (from *canere* 'sing').]

canst /kanst/ archaic second person singular present of CAN[1].

Cant. ▶ **abbr.** Bible Canticles.

cant[1] /kant/ ▶ **n. 1** hypocritical and sanctimonious talk, typically of a moral, religious, or political nature. **2** [as adj.] denoting a phrase or catchword temporarily current or in fashion: *they are misrepresented as, in the cant word of our day, uncaring.* ■ language peculiar to a specified group or profession and regarded with disparagement: *thieves' cant.* ▶ **v.** [intrans.] dated talk hypocritically and sanctimoniously about something. [16th C.: prob. from L. *cantare* 'to sing' (see CHANT).]

cant[2] ▶ **v.** [trans.] cause (something) to be in a slanting or oblique position; tilt: *he canted his head to look at the screen.* ■ [intrans.] take or have a slanting position: *mismatched slate roofs canted at all angles.* ▶ **n. 1** [in sing.] a slope or tilt. **2** a wedge-shaped block of wood, esp. one remaining after the better-quality pieces have been cut off. [ME: from Mid. Low Ger. *kant, kante*, MDu. *cant* 'side,' based on a Romance word rel. to med. L. *cantus* 'corner.']

can't /kant/ ▶ **contr.** cannot.

can·ta·bi·le /kän'täbə,lā/ Music ▶**adv. & adj.** in a smooth singing style. ▶**n.** a cantabile passage or movement. [Ital., lit. 'singable.']

Can·ta·brig·i·an /'kantə,brijēən/ ▶**adj.** of or relating to Cambridge, England, or Cambridge University. ▶**n.** a student or faculty member of Cambridge University. [16th C.: from L. *Cantabrigia* (see sense 1 of CAMBRIDGE).]

can·tal /'kan'täl; käN-/ ▶**n.** a hard, strong cheese made chiefly in the Auvergne. [named after *Cantal*, department of Auvergne.]

can·ta·loupe /'kantl,ōp/ ▶**n.** a small, round melon of a variety with orange flesh and ribbed skin. [18th C.: from Fr. *cantaloup*, from *Cantaluppi* near Rome.]

can·tan·ker·ous /kan'taNGkərəs/ ▶**adj.** bad-tempered, argumentative, and uncooperative. — **can·tan·ker·ous·ly adv. can·tan·ker·ous·ness n.** [18th C.: perh. blend of Anglo-Irish *cant* 'auction' and *rancorous*.]

can·ta·ta /kən'tätə/ ▶**n.** a medium-length narrative or descriptive piece of music with vocal solos and usually a chorus and orchestra. [18th C.: from Ital. *cantata (aria)* 'sung (air),' from *cantare* 'to sing.']

can·teen /kan'tēn/ ▶**n. 1** a restaurant provided by a military camp, college, factory, or company for its students or staff. **2** a small water bottle, as used by soldiers or campers. [18th C.: from Fr. *cantine*, from Ital. *cantina* 'cellar.']

can·ter /'kantər/ ▶**n.** [in sing.] a three-beat gait of a horse or other quadruped between a trot and a gallop. ■ a ride on a horse at such a speed. ▶**v.** [no obj., with adverbial of direction] (of a horse) move at a canter in a particular direction: *they cantered down into the village.* ■ [trans.] make (a horse) move at a canter. [18th C.: short for *Canterbury pace* or *Canterbury gallop*, from the supposed easy pace of medieval pilgrims to CANTERBURY.]

Can·ter·bur·y /'kantər,berē; -bərē/ a city in Kent, in southeastern England, the seat of the archbishop of Canterbury; pop. 39,700.

Can·ter·bur·y, Archbishop of ▶**n.** the archbishop of the southern province of the Church of England, who is Primate of All England and plays a leading role in the worldwide Anglican Church.

Can·ter·bur·y bell ▶**n.** a tall, sturdy cultivated bellflower (*Campanula medium*) with large blue, pink, or white flowers. [16th C.: named after the bells on Canterbury pilgrims' horses (see CANTER).]

can·thar·i·des /kan'THari,dēz/ ▶**plural n.** see SPANISH FLY. [ME: from L., pl. of *cantharis*, from Gk. *kantharis* 'Spanish fly.']

can·tha·rus /'kanTHərəs/ ▶**n.** (pl. **-ri** /-,rī; -rē/) (in ancient Greece and Rome) a large, two-handled drinking cup. [L., from Gk. *kantharos*.]

cant hook ▶**n.** a hinged metal hook at the end of a long handle, used for gripping and rolling logs.

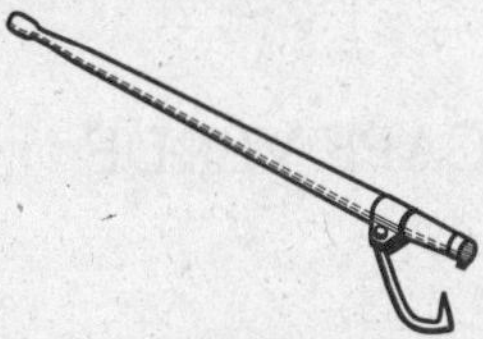

cant hook

can·thus /'kanTHəs/ ▶**n.** (pl. **-thi** /-THī; -THē/) the outer or inner corner of the eye, where the upper and lower lids meet. — **can·thic** /'kanTHik/ **adj.** [17th C.: from L., from Gk. *kanthos*.]

can·ti·cle /'kantikəl/ ▶**n. 1** a hymn or chant, typically with a biblical text, forming a regular part of a church service. **2** (**Can·ti·cles** or **Can·ti·cle of Can·ti·cles**) another name for SONG OF SONGS (esp. in the Vulgate Bible). [ME: from L. *canticulum* 'little song,' dimin. of *canticum*, from *canere* 'sing.']

can·ti·le·na /,kantl'ēnə/ ▶**n.** Music a lyrical vocal or instrumental melody in a composition. [18th C.: from Ital., from L., 'song.']

can·ti·le·ver /'kantl,ēvər; -,evər/ ▶**n.** a long projecting beam or girder fixed at only one end, used chiefly in bridge construction. ■ a long bracket or beam projecting from a wall to support a balcony, cornice, or similar structure. ▶**v.** [trans.] [usu. as adj.] (**cantilevered**) support by a cantilever or cantilevers: *a cantilevered deck.* ■ [no obj., with adverbial of direction] project as or like a cantilever: *a conveyor cantilevered out over the river.* [17th C.: of unknown origin.]

can·ti·le·ver bridge ▶**n.** a bridge in which each span is constructed from cantilevers built out sideways from piers. See illustration at BRIDGE[1].

can·til·late /'kantl,āt/ ▶**v.** [trans.] rare chant or intone (a passage of religious text). — **can·til·la·tion** /,kantl'āSHən/ **n.** [19th C.: from L. *cantillat-* 'hummed,' from v. *cantillare*, from *cantare* (see CHANT).]

can·ti·na /kan'tēnə/ ▶**n.** (esp. in a Spanish-speaking country or the southwestern US) a bar. [19th C.: from Sp. and Ital.]

can·tle /'kantl/ ▶**n.** the raised, curved part at the back of a horse's saddle. [ME: from Anglo-Norman Fr. *cantel*, ult. from med. L. *cantellus*, from *cantus* 'corner.']

can·to /'kantō/ ▶**n.** (pl. **-tos**) one of the sections into which certain long poems are divided. [16th C.: from Ital., lit. 'song,' from L. *cantus*.]

Can·ton[1] /kan'tän/ variant of GUANGZHOU.

Can·ton[2] /'kantn/ a city in northeastern Ohio; pop. 80,806. The Professional Football Hall of Fame is here.

can·ton /'kantn; 'kan,tän/ ▶**n. 1** a political or administrative subdivision of a country. ■ a state of the Swiss Confederation. **2** Heraldry a square charge smaller than a quarter and positioned in an upper corner of a shield. — **can·ton·al** /kan'tänl; 'kantnl/ **adj.** [16th C.: from OFr., lit. 'corner,' from Provençal, based on a Romance word rel. to med. L. *cantus* 'side.']

Can·ton·ese /,kantn'ēz; -'ēs/ ▶**adj.** of or relating to Canton (Guangzhou), its inhabitants, their dialect, or their cuisine. ▶**n.** (pl. same) **1** a native or inhabitant of Canton. **2** a form of Chinese spoken mainly in southeastern China (including Hong Kong). Also called YUE.

can·ton·ment /kan'tōnmənt; -'tän-/ ▶**n.** a military camp, esp. (hist.) a permanent military station in British India.

Can·tor /'kantər/, Georg (1845–1918), German mathematician; born in Russia. His work on numbers laid the foundations for the theory of sets.

can·tor /'kantər/ ▶**n. 1** an official who sings liturgical music in a synagogue. Also called HAZZAN. **2** (in formal Christian worship) a solo singer to whom the choir or congregation responds. — **can·to·ri·al** /kan'tôrēəl/ **adj.** [16th C.: from L., 'singer,' from *canere* 'sing' (see CHANT).]

can·trip /'kantrip/ ▶**n.** Scot., archaic a mischievous or playful act; a trick. [16th C.: of unknown origin.]

can·tus /'kantəs/ ▶**n.** the highest voice in polyphonic choral music. [16th C.: from L.]

can·tus fir·mus /'fərməs/ ▶**n.** (pl. **can·tus fir·mi** /'fərmī; -mē/) Music an existing melody used as the basis for a polyphonic composition. [19th C.: from L., lit. 'firm song.']

Ca·nuck /kə'nək/ ▶**n.** informal a Canadian, esp. a French Canadian (chiefly used by Canadians themselves and often derogatory in the US). [appar. from CANADA.]

Ca·nute /kə'n(y)ōōt/ (also **Cnut** or **Knut**) (died 1035), Danish king of England 1017–35, Denmark 1018–35, and Norway 1028–35; son of Sweyn I.

can·vas /'kanvəs/ ▶**n.** a strong, coarse unbleached cloth made from hemp, flax, or cotton, used to make sails and tents. ■ a piece of such cloth prepared for use as the surface for an oil painting. ■ an oil painting: *Turner's late canvases.* ■ a variety of canvas with an open weave, used as a basis for tapestry and embroidery. ■ (**the canvas**) the floor of a boxing or wrestling ring, having a canvas covering. ▶**v.** (**-vased, -vas·ing**) [trans.] (usu. **be canvased**) cover with canvas.
– PHRASES **under canvas** in a tent or tents. [ME: from Old North. Fr. *canevas*, based on L. *cannabis* 'hemp,' from Gk. *kannabis*.]

can·vas·back /'kanvəs,bak/ ▶**n.** a North American diving duck (*Aythya valisineria*) with a long, sloping black bill and a light grey back.

can·vas duck ▶**n.** a lightweight cotton or linen fabric.

can·vass /'kanvəs/ ▶**v. 1** [trans.] solicit votes from (electors in a district): *two workers canvassed some 2,000 voters* | [intrans.] *she canvassed for votes.* ■ question (someone) in order to ascertain their opinion on something: *they canvassed all members for their views.* ■ ascertain (someone's opinion) through questioning: *opinions were canvassed.* ■ try to obtain; request: *they're canvassing support among stockholders.* **2** [trans.] (often **be canvassed**) discuss thoroughly: *the issues were canvassed.* ▶**n.** [usu. in sing.] an act or process of attempting to secure votes or ascertain opinions. — **can·vass·er n.** [16th C.: from CANVAS.]

can·yon /'kanyən/ ▶**n.** a deep gorge, typically one with a river flowing through it, as found in North America. [19th C.: from Sp. *cañón* 'tube,' based on L. *canna* 'reed, cane.']

Can·yon de Chel·ly /də 'SHā(lē)/ a national monument in northeastern Arizona, on the Navajo Indian Reservation, noted for cliff dwellings and other ruins.

Can·yon·lands /'kanyən,landz/ a region in southeastern Utah, noted for its rock formations.

can·zo·ne /kan'zōnē; känt'sōnā/ ▶**n.** (pl. **-ni** /-nē/) an Italian or Provençal song or ballad. ■ a type of lyric resembling a madrigal. [16th C.: from Ital., 'song,' from L. *cantio(n-)* 'singing,' from *canere* 'sing.']

can·zo·net·ta /,kanzə'netə/ ▶**n.** (pl. **-net·tas** or **-net·te** /-'netē/) a short, light vocal piece, esp. in the Italian style of the 17th century. [16th C.: from Ital., 'little song,' dimin. of *canzone*, from L. *cantio(n-)* 'singing,' from *canere* 'sing.']

caou·tchouc /'kou,CHōōk; -,CHōō(k)/ ▶**n.** unvulcanized natural rubber. [18th C.: from Fr., from obs. Sp. *cauchuc*, from Quechua *kauchuk*.]

CAP ▶**abbr.** Civil Air Patrol.

cap /kap/ ▶**n. 1** a kind of soft, flat hat without a brim, and sometimes having a visor. ■ [with adj.] a kind of soft, close-fitting head covering worn for a particular purpose or as a mark of a particular profession or status. ■ an academic mortarboard. **2** a protective lid or cover for an object such as a bottle, the point of a pen, or a camera lens. ■ Dentistry an artificial protective covering for a tooth. ■ the top of a bird's head when distinctively colored. ■ the broad upper part of the fruiting body of most mushrooms and toadstools, at the top of a stem and bearing gills or pores. **3** ■ an upper limit imposed on spending or other activities. **4** short for PERCUSSION CAP. ▶**v.** (**capped, cap·ping**) [trans.] **1** put a lid or cover on. ■ (often **be capped**) form a covering layer or top part of: *several towers were capped by domes* | [as adj., in comb.] (**-capped**) *snow-capped mountains.* ■ put an artificial protective covering on (a tooth). ■ provide a fitting climax or conclusion to. ■ follow or reply to (a story, remark, or joke) by producing a better or more apposite one. **2** (often **be capped**) place a limit or restriction on (prices, expenditure, or other activity).

– PHRASES **cap** (or **hat**) **in hand** humbly asking for a favor. **set one's cap for** (or **at**) dated (of a woman) try to attract (a particular man) as a suitor. — **cap·ful** /-ˌfo͝ol/ n. (pl. **-fuls**). [OE *cæppe* 'hood,' from late L. *cappa*, perh. from L. *caput* 'head.']

cap. ▶ abbr. ■ capacity. ■ capital (city). ■ capital letter.

ca·pa·bil·i·ty /ˌkāpəˈbilitē/ ▶ n. (pl. **-ties**) (often **capability of doing** (or **to do**) **something**) power or ability. ■ (often **capabilities**) the extent of someone's or something's ability: ***beyond my capabilities.*** ■ [usu. with adj.] a facility on a computer for performing a specified task: *a graphics capability.* ■ [usu. with adj.] forces or resources giving a country or state the ability to undertake a particular kind of military action: *their nuclear weapons capability.*

Ca·pa·bil·i·ty Brown see BROWN[4].

ca·pa·ble /ˈkāpəbəl/ ▶ adj. [predic.] (**capable of doing something**) having the ability, fitness, or quality necessary to do or achieve a specified thing. ■ able to achieve efficiently whatever one has to do; competent. ■ open to or admitting of something: *events **capable of** rational explanation.* ■ ready or inclined to: *children **capable of** murder.* — **ca·pa·bly** adv. [16th C.: from Fr., from late L. *capabilis*, from L. *capere* 'take.']

ca·pa·cious /kəˈpāsнəs/ ▶ adj. having a lot of space inside; roomy: *a capacious van.* — **ca·pa·cious·ly** adv. **ca·pa·cious·ness** n. [17th C.: from L. *capax, capac-* 'capable.']

ca·pac·i·tance /kəˈpasitəns/ ▶ n. Physics the ability of a system to store an electric charge. ■ the ratio of the change in an electric charge in a system to the corresponding change in its electric potential. (Symbol: **C**)

ca·pac·i·tate /kəˈpasiˌtāt/ ▶ v. [trans.] formal archaic make (someone) capable of a particular action or legally competent to act in a particular way. — **ca·pac·i·ta·tion** /kəˌpasiˈtāsнən/ n.

ca·pac·i·tor /kəˈpasitər/ ▶ n. a device used to store an electric charge, consisting of one or more pairs of conductors separated by an insulator.

ca·pac·i·ty /kəˈpasitē/ ▶ n. (pl. **-ties**) **1** [in sing.] the maximum amount that something can contain: *seating capacity.* ■ [as adj.] fully occupying the available area or space: *a capacity crowd.* ■ the amount that something can produce: ***running at full capacity.*** ■ the total cylinder volume that is swept by the pistons in an internal combustion engine. ■ former term for CAPACITANCE. **2** the ability or power to do, experience, or understand something: ***her capacity for hard work.*** ■ [in sing.] a person's legal competence: *cases where a patient's testamentary capacity is in doubt.* **3** [in sing.] a specified role or position: ***in his capacity as** legal correspondent.* — **ca·pac·i·tive** /-tiv/ (also **ca·pac·i·ta·tive** /-ˌtātiv/) adj. (esp. Physics). [ME: from Fr. *capacité*, from L. *capacitas*, from *capax, capac-* 'that can contain,' from *capere* 'take.']

ca·par·i·son /kəˈparəsən/ ▶ n. an ornamental covering spread over a horse's saddle or harness. ▶ v. (**be caparisoned**) (of a horse) be decked out in rich decorative coverings. [16th C.: from obs. Fr. *caparasson*, from Sp. *caparazón* 'saddlecloth,' from *capa* 'hood.']

cape[1] /kāp/ ▶ n. a sleeveless cloak, typically a short one. ■ a part of a longer coat or cloak that falls loosely over the shoulders from the neckband. ▶ v. [trans.] skin the head and neck of (an animal) to prepare a hunting trophy. — **caped** adj. [16th C.: from Fr., from Provençal *capa*, from late L. *cappa* 'covering for the head.']

cape[2] ▶ n. **1** a headland or promontory. ■ (**the Cape**) the Cape of Good Hope. ■ (**the Cape**) Cape Cod, Massachusetts. ■ (**the Cape**) the former Cape Province of South Africa. **2** (**Cape**) short for CAPE COD (the style of house). [ME: from OFr. *cap*, from Provençal, based on L. *caput* 'head.']

Cape Bret·on Is·land /ˈbretn/ an island that forms northeastern Nova Scotia in eastern Canada.

Cape buf·fa·lo ▶ n. a large-horned buffalo (*Syncerus caffer*) with large horns, native to sub-Saharan Africa.

Cape Cod /ˈkäd/ (abbr.: **CC**) **1** a peninsula in southeastern Massachusetts. The Pilgrims landed on the northern tip of Cape Cod in November 1620. **2** (also **Cape**) a type of rectangular house with a deeply gabled roof.

Cape Col·o·ny early name (1814–1910) for the former CAPE PROVINCE.

Cape Cor·al a city in southwestern Florida, southwest of Fort Myers; pop. 102, 286.

Cape Fear Riv·er a river that flows for 200 miles (320 km) across eastern North Carolina to enter the Atlantic Ocean.

Cape Gi·rar·deau /jəˈrärdō/ a city in southeastern Missouri, on the Mississippi River; pop. 34,438.

cape goose·ber·ry ▶ n. a tropical South American plant (*Physalis peruviana*) of the nightshade family that bears soft, edible, yellow berries.

Cape jas·mine (also **Cape jessamine**) ▶ n. a fragrant Chinese gardenia (esp. *G. jasminoides*), some kinds of which have flowers that are used to perfume tea.

Ča·pek /ˈcнäpek/, Karel (1890–1938), Czech novelist and playwright. His plays include *R.U.R.* (*Rossum's Universal Robots*) (1920), from which the word *robot* originates, and *The Insect Play* (1921) a collaboration with his brother Josef (1887–1945).

cap·e·lin /ˈkap(ə)lin/ ▶ n. a small fish (*Mallotus villosus*) of the smelt family, found in North Atlantic coastal waters and used as food for humans and animals. [17th C.: from Fr., from Provençal *capelan*, from med. L. *cappellanus* 'custodian' (see CHAPLAIN).]

Ca·pel·la /kəˈpelə/ Astron. the sixth brightest star in the sky, and the brightest in the constellation Auriga. [L., 'she-goat,' dimin. of *caper* 'goat.']

Cape May a resort town in southern New Jersey; pop. 4,668.

Cape of Good Hope a mountainous promontory south of Cape Town, South Africa. It was sailed around for the first time by Vasco da Gama in 1497.

Cape Prov·ince a former province of South Africa, containing the Cape of Good Hope. In 1994 it was divided into the provinces of Northern Cape, Western Cape, and Eastern Cape.

ca·per[1] /ˈkāpər/ ▶ v. [no obj., with adverbial of direction] skip or dance about in a lively or playful way: *children capering about the room.* ▶ n. **1** a playful skipping movement: *she did a little caper.* **2** informal an activity or escapade, typically illicit or ridiculous. ■ an amusing or far-fetched story, esp. one presented on film or stage: *a cop caper about intergalactic drug dealers.*

– PHRASES **cut a caper** make a playful, skipping movement. — **ca·per·er** /ˈkāpərər/ n. [16th C.: abbrev. of CAPRIOLE.]

ca·per[2] ▶ n. **1** (usu. **capers**) the cooked and pickled flower buds of a spiny southern European shrub, used to flavor food. **2** the shrub (*Capparis spinosa*, family Capparidaceae) from which these buds are taken. [ME: from Fr. *câpres* or L. *capparis*, from Gk. *kapparis*.]

cap·er·cail·lie /ˌkapərˈkāl(y)ē/ (Scot. also **cap·er·cail·zie** /-ˈkālzē/) ▶ n. (pl. **-lies**) a large, turkeylike Eurasian grouse (genus *Tetrao*) of mature pine forests. [16th C.: from Scot. Gael. *capull coille*, lit. 'horse of the wood.']

cape·skin /ˈkāpˌskin/ ▶ n. a soft leather made from South African sheepskin.

Ca·pet /käˈpe; käˈpā; ˈkāpit/, Hugh (938–996), king of France 987–996; founder of the Capetian dynasty.

Ca·pe·tian /kəˈpēsнən/ ▶ adj. relating to or denoting the dynasty ruling France 987–1328. ▶ n. a member of this dynasty.

Cape Town a city in southwestern South Africa at the foot of Table Mountain, the legislative capital of the country; pop. 776,600.

Cape Verde /ˈvərd/ (also **Cape Verde Islands**) an island country in Africa. *See box.* — **Cape Ver·de·an** /ˈvərdēən/ adj. & n.

Cape Verde

Official name: Republic of Cape Verde
Location: Africa, consisting of a group of islands in the North Atlantic Ocean off the coast of Senegal
Area: 1,500 square miles (4,000 sq km)
Population: 415,300
Capital: Praia
Languages: Portuguese (official), Creole
Currency: Cape Verdean escudo

Cape York /ˈyôrk/ the northernmost point of Australia, on Torres Strait.

Cap-Ha·ï·tien /kăp ˈhāsнən; ä-ē'syaN/ a historic city in northern Haiti; pop. 133,000. It is the former capital of Haiti.

ca·pi·as /ˈkāpēəs/ ▶ n. (pl. **-as·es**) Law a writ ordering the arrest of a named person. [ME: from L. *capias*, lit. 'you are to seize,' from *capere* 'take.']

cap·il·lar·i·ty /ˌkapəˈlaritē/ ▶ n. the tendency of a liquid in a capillary tube or absorbent material to rise or fall as a result of surface tension. Also called CAPILLARY ACTION.

cap·il·lar·y /ˈkapəˌlerē/ ▶ n. **1** Anat. any of the branching blood vessels that form a network between the arterioles and venules. **2** (also **capillary tube**) a tube with an internal diameter of hairlike thinness. ▶ adj. [attrib.] of or relating to capillaries or capillarity. [17th C.: from L. *capillaris*, from *capillus* 'hair.']

cap·il·lar·y ac·tion ▶ n. another term for CAPILLARITY.

cap·il·lar·y at·trac·tion ▶ n. the tendency of a liquid in a capillary tube to rise as a result of surface forces.

cap·i·tal¹ /ˈkapitl/ ▶**n. 1** (also **capital city** or **town**) the most important city or town of a country or region, usually its seat of government. ■ [with adj.] a place associated more than any other with a specified activity or product: *the fashion capital of the world.* **2** wealth in the form of money or other assets owned by a person or organization or available or contributed for a particular purpose such as starting a company or investing. ■ the excess of a company's assets over its liabilities. ■ people who possess wealth and use it to control a society's economic activity, considered collectively. ■ [with adj.] fig. a valuable resource of a particular kind: *investment in human capital.* **3** (also **capital letter**) a letter of the size and form used to begin sentences and names. ▶**adj. 1** [attrib.] (of an offense or charge) punishable by the death penalty. **2** of or relating to wealth: *capital losses.* **3** of greatest political importance: *the capital city.* **4** [attrib.] (of a letter of the alphabet) large in size and of the form used to begin sentences and names. **5** informal, dated excellent: *he's a really capital fellow.* ▶**exclam.** Brit., informal, dated used to express approval, satisfaction, or delight: *That's splendid! Capital!*
– PHRASES **make capital out of** use to one's own advantage. — **cap·i·tal·ly adv.** (in sense 5). [ME: ult. from L. *caput* 'head.']

Ionic

Corinthian

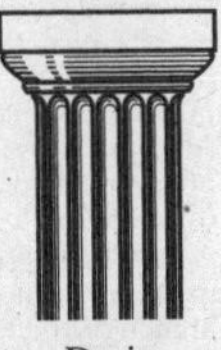
Doric

capitals

cap·i·tal² ▶**n.** Archit. the distinct, typically broader section at the head of a pillar or column. [ME: from OFr. *capitel*, from late L. *capitellum* 'little head,' dimin. of L. *caput.*]

cap·i·tal gain ▶**n.** (often **capital gains**) a profit from the sale of property or of an investment.

cap·i·tal gains tax ▶**n.** a tax levied on profit from the sale of property or of an investment.

cap·i·tal goods ▶**plural n.** goods that are used in producing other goods, rather than being bought by consumers. Often contrasted with CONSUMER GOODS.

cap·i·tal-in·ten·sive ▶**adj.** (of a business) requiring the investment of large sums of money.

cap·i·tal·ism /ˈkapətl,izəm/ ▶**n.** an economic and political system in which a country's trade and industry are controlled by private owners for profit.

cap·i·tal·ist /ˈkapətlist/ ▶**n.** a wealthy person who uses money to invest in trade and industry for profit in accordance with the principles of capitalism. ▶**adj.** practicing, supporting, or based on capitalism. — **cap·i·tal·is·tic** /,kapətlˈistik/ **adj.** **cap·i·tal·is·ti·cal·ly** /,kapətlˈistik(ə)lē/ **adv.**

cap·i·tal·ize /ˈkapətl,īz/ ▶**v. 1** [intrans.] (**capitalize on**) take the chance to gain advantage from. **2** [trans.] provide (a company or industry) with capital: [as adj.] (**capitalized**) *a highly capitalized industry.* **3** [trans.] realize (the present value of an income); convert into capital. ■ reckon (the value of an asset) by setting future benefits against the cost of maintenance: *a trader will want to capitalize repairs expenditure.* **4** [trans.] write or print (a word or letter) in capital letters. ■ begin (a word) with a capital letter. — **cap·i·tal·i·za·tion** /,kapətl-əˈzāsHən/ **n.**

cap·i·tal mar·ket ▶**n.** the part of a financial system concerned with raising capital by dealing in stocks, bonds, and other long-term investments.

cap·i·tal pun·ish·ment ▶**n.** the legally authorized killing of someone as punishment for a crime.

cap·i·tal ship ▶**n.** a large warship such as a battleship or aircraft carrier.

cap·i·tal sum ▶**n.** a lump sum of money payable to an insured person or paid as an initial fee or investment.

cap·i·tal ter·ri·to·ry ▶**n.** a territory containing the capital city of a country, e.g., in Australia or Nigeria.

cap·i·tate /ˈkapi,tāt/ ▶**adj.** Bot. Zool. ending in a distinct compact head. ▶**n.** (also **capitate bone**) Anat. the largest of the carpal bones, situated at the base of the palm of the hand. [17th C.: from L. *capitatus*, from *caput, capit-* 'head.']

cap·i·ta·tion /,kapiˈtāsHən/ ▶**n.** the payment of a fee or grant to a person or body providing services to a number of people, such that the amount paid is determined by the number of patients, pupils, or customers.

Cap·i·tol /ˈkapitl/ (usu. **the Capitol**) **1** the seat of the US Congress in Washington, DC. ■ (**cap·i·tol**) a building housing a legislative assembly. **2** the temple of Jupiter on the Capitoline Hill in ancient Rome. [from OFr. *capitolie, capitoile.*]

Cap·i·tol Hill the region around the Capitol building in Washington, DC.

Cap·i·tol Reef Na·tion·al Park a preserve in south central Utah, noted for its fossils and rock formations.

ca·pit·u·lar /kəˈpicHələr/ ▶**adj. 1** of or relating to a cathedral chapter. **2** Biol. of or relating to a capitulum. [16th C.: from late L. *capitularis*, from L. *capitulum.*]

ca·pit·u·lar·y /kəˈpicHə,lerē/ ▶**n.** (pl. **-lar·ies**) hist. a royal ordinance under the Merovingian dynasty.

ca·pit·u·late /kəˈpicHə,lāt/ ▶**v.** [intrans.] cease to resist an opponent or an unwelcome demand; surrender. — **ca·pit·u·la·tor** /-ˈlātər/ **n.** [16th C.: from Fr. *capituler*, from med. L. *capitulare* 'draw up under headings,' from L. *capitulum*, dimin. of *caput* 'head.']

ca·pit·u·la·tion /kə,picHəˈlāsHən/ ▶**n.** the action of surrendering or ceasing to resist an opponent or demand. ■ (**capitulations**) hist. an agreement or set of conditions.

ca·pit·u·lum /kəˈpicHələm/ ▶**n.** (pl. **-la** /-lə/) Biol. a compact head of a structure, in particular a dense, flat cluster of small flowers or florets, as in plants of the daisy family. [18th C.: from L., dimin. of *caput* 'head.']

cap·let /ˈkaplit/ (trademark **Cap·let**) ▶**n.** a coated oral medicinal tablet. [1930s: blend of CAPSULE and TABLET.]

cap'n /ˈkapm; ˈkapn/ ▶**n.** informal contraction of CAPTAIN, used in representing speech.

ca·po¹ /ˈkāpō; ˈkäpō/ (also **ca·potas·to**) ▶**n.** (pl. **-pos**) a clamp fastened across all the strings of a fretted musical instrument to raise their tuning. [19th C.: from Ital. *capo tasto*, lit. 'head stop.']

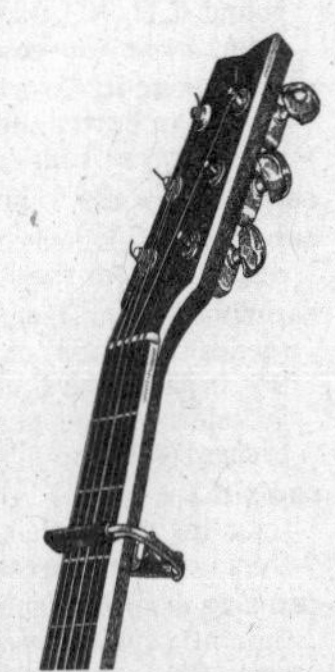
capo¹

ca·po² ▶**n.** (pl. **-pos**) the head of a crime syndicate, esp. the Mafia, or a branch of one. [1950s: from Ital., from L. *caput* 'head.']

cap of lib·er·ty ▶**n.** another term for LIBERTY CAP.

ca·pon /ˈkāpän; -pən/ ▶**n.** a castrated domestic cock fattened for eating. — **ca·pon·ize** /ˈkāpə,nīz/ **v.** [OE: from OFr., based on L. *capo, capon-.*]

ca·po·na·ta /,käpəˈnätə/ ▶**n.** a dish of eggplant, olives, and onions seasoned with herbs. [Ital.]

Ca·pone /kəˈpōn/, Al (1899–1947), US gangster; full name *Alphonse Gabriel Capone*; nicknamed **Scarface.** Notorious for his domination of organized crime in Chicago in the 1920s, he was imprisoned for federal income tax evasion in 1931.

ca·po tas·to /,käpōˈtästō/ ▶**n.** (pl. **-tos**) another term for CAPO¹.

Ca·pote /kəˈpōtē/, Truman (1924–84), US writer; born *Truman Streckfus Persons.* His works include *Breakfast at Tiffany's* (1958) and *In Cold Blood* (1966).

ca·pote /kəˈpōt/ ▶**n.** hist. a long cloak or coat with a hood, typically part of an army or company uniform. [19th C.: from Fr., dimin. of *cape* (see CAPE¹).]

Capp /kap/, Al (1909–79), US cartoonist; full name *Alfred Gerald Caplin.* His comic strip "Li'l Abner" 1934–77 used a setting of hillbilly culture to deliver political satire.

Cap·pa·do·cia /,kapəˈdōsHə/ an ancient region of central Asia Minor, between Lake Tuz and the Euphrates River. It was a center of early Christianity. — **Cap·pa·do·cian adj. & n.**

cap·pel·let·ti /,kapəˈletē/ ▶**n.** small pieces of pasta folded and stuffed with meat or cheese. [Ital., lit. 'little hats.']

cap·per /ˈkapər/ ▶**n.** informal a more surprising, upsetting, or entertaining event or situation than all others that have gone before.

cap·puc·ci·no /,käpəˈcHēnō; ,kap-/ ▶**n.** (pl. **-nos**) coffee made with milk that has been frothed up with pressurized steam. [1940s: from Ital., lit. 'Capuchin,' because its color resembles that of a Capuchin's habit.]

Ca·pra /ˈkaprə/, Frank (1897–1991), US director; born in Sicily; born *Francesco Rosario Capra.* His movies include *It Happened One Night* (1934) and *It's a Wonderful Life* (1945).

Ca·pri /kəˈprē; ˈkaprē; ˈkäprē/ an island off the western coast of Italy, south of Naples.

ca·pric·ci·o /kəˈprēcHē,ō; -cHō/ ▶**n.** (pl. **-os**) a lively piece of music, short and free in form. ■ a painting or other work of art representing a fantasy or a mixture of real and imaginary features. [17th C.: from Ital., lit. 'head with the hair standing on end,' from *capo* 'head' + *riccio* 'hedgehog.']

ca·price /kəˈprēs/ ▶**n. 1** a sudden and unaccountable change of mood or behavior. **2** Music another term for CAPRICCIO. [17th C.: from Fr., from Ital. (see CAPRICCIO).]

ca·pri·cious /kəˈprisHəs; -ˈprē-/ ▶**adj.** given to sudden and unaccountable changes of mood or behavior. — **ca·pri·cious·ly adv.** **ca·pri·cious·ness n.**

Cap·ri·corn /ˈkapri,kôrn/ Astrol. the tenth sign of the zodiac (the Goat), which the sun enters at the northern winter solstice (about December 21). Compare with CAPRICORNUS. ■ (**a Capricorn**) a person born when the sun is in this sign. — **Cap·ri·corn·i·an** /,kapriˈkôrnēən/ **n. & adj.** [OE, from L. *capricornus*, from *caper, capr-* 'goat' + *cornu* 'horn.']

Cap·ri·cor·nus /,kapriˈkôrnəs/ Astron. a constellation (the Goat), said to represent a goat with a fish's tail. It has few bright stars. Compare with CAPRICORN. [L. (see CAPRICORN).]

cap·rine /ˈkap,rīn/ ▶**adj.** of, relating to, or resembling goats. [ME: from L. *caprinus*, from *caper, capr-* 'goat.']

cap·ri·ole /ˈkaprē,ōl/ ▶**n.** a movement performed in classical riding, in which the horse leaps from the ground and kicks out with its hind legs.

■ a leap or caper in dancing, esp. a cabriole. [16th C.: from Fr., from Ital. *capriola* 'leap,' from *capriolo* 'roebuck,' from L. *capreolus*, dimin. of *caper*, *capr-* 'goat.']

ca·pri pants /kəˈprē/ (also **ca·pris**) ▶ **plural n.** close-fitting calf-length tapered pants, usually worn by women and girls. [1950s: named after CAPRI.]

Ca·pri·vi Strip /kəˈprēvē/ a narrow strip in northeastern Namibia that reaches the Zambezi River.

cap rock ▶ **n.** a layer of hard, impervious rock overlying and often sealing in a deposit of oil, gas, or coal.

ca·pro·ic ac·id /kəˈprō-ik/ ▶ **n.** Chem. a liquid fatty acid, $CH_3(CH_2)_4COOH$, present in milk fat and coconut and palm oils. Also called **hexanoic acid.** [19th C.: from L. *caper*, *capr-* 'goat.']

cap·ro·lac·tam /ˌkaprōˈlakˌtam/ ▶ **n.** Chem. a synthetic crystalline compound, $C_6H_{11}NO$, that is an intermediate in nylon manufacture. [1940s: from CAPROIC ACID + LACTAM.]

ca·pryl·ic ac·id /kəˈprilik/ ▶ **n.** Chem. a liquid fatty acid, $CH_3(CH_2)_6COOH$, present in butter and other fats. Also called ***n*-octanoic acid.** [19th C.: from L. *caper*, *capr-* 'goat.']

caps /kaps/ ▶ **abbr.** capital letters.

cap·sa·i·cin /kapˈsāəsin/ ▶ **n.** Chem. a compound, $C_{18}H_{27}NO_3$, that is responsible for the pungency of capsicums. [19th C.: alt. of *capsicine*.]

cap·si·cum /ˈkapsikəm/ ▶ **n.** (pl. **-cums**) a tropical American pepper plant (genus *Capsicum*) of the nightshade family; several species and varieties, in particular *C. annuum* var. *annuum*, the cultivated forms of which include sweet peppers and chili peppers. [16th C.: mod. L., perh. from L. *capsa* (see CASE[2]).]

cap·sid ▶ **n.** Microbiol. the protein coat or shell of a virus particle, surrounding the nucleic acid or nucleoprotein core. [1960s: coined in Fr. from L. *capsa* (see CASE[2]).]

cap·size /ˈkapˌsīz; kapˈsīz/ ▶ **v.** (of a boat) overturn in the water: [intrans.] *the craft capsized in heavy seas* | [trans.] *gale-force gusts capsized the dinghies.* ▶ **n.** [in sing.] an instance of capsizing. [18th C.: perh. based on Sp. *capuzar* 'sink by the head,' from *cabo* 'head' + *chapuzar* 'to dive.']

cap sleeve ▶ **n.** a sleeve extending only a short distance from the shoulder and tapering to nothing under the arm.

cap·stan /ˈkapstən/ ▶ **n.** a revolving cylinder with a vertical axis used for winding a rope or cable, powered by a motor or pushed around by levers. ■ the motor-driven spindle on a tape recorder that makes the tape travel past the head at constant speed. [ME: from Provençal *cabestan*, from *cabestre* 'halter,' from L. *capistrum*, from *capere* 'seize.']

capstan

cap·stone /ˈkapˌstōn/ ▶ **n.** a stone fixed on top of something, typically a wall.

cap·sule /ˈkapsəl; ˈkapˌso͞ol/ ▶ **n.** a small case or container, esp. a round or cylindrical one. ■ a small, soluble case of gelatin containing a dose of medicine, swallowed whole. ■ short for SPACE CAPSULE. ■ [as adj.] fig. (of a piece of writing) shortened but retaining the essence of the original; condensed: *a capsule review of the movie.* ■ Anat. a tough sheath or membrane that encloses something in the body, such as a kidney. ■ Biol. a gelatinous layer forming the outer surface of some bacterial cells. ■ Bot. a dry fruit that releases its seeds by bursting open when ripe, such as a pea pod. ■ Bot. the spore-producing structure of mosses and liverworts. — **cap·su·lar** /ˈkapsələr/ **adj.** **cap·su·late** /ˈkapsələt; -ˌlāt/ **adj.** [ME: via Fr. from L. *capsula*, dimin. of *capsa* (see CASE[2]).]

cap·sul·ize /ˈkapsəˌlīz/ ▶ **v.** [trans.] put (information) in compact form; summarize.

Capt. ▶ **abbr.** Captain.

cap·tain /ˈkaptən/ ▶ **n.** the person in command of a ship. ■ the pilot in command of a civil aircraft. ■ a naval officer of high rank, in particular (in the US Navy or Coast Guard) an officer ranking above commander and below commodore. ■ an army officer of high rank, in particular (in the US Army, Marine Corps, or Air Force) an officer ranking above first lieutenant and below major. ■ a police officer in charge of a precinct, ranking below a chief. ■ the head of a precinct's fire department. ■ the leader of a team, esp. in sports. ■ a powerful or influential person in a particular field. ■ a political party leader in a local district. ▶ **v.** [trans.] be the captain of (a ship, aircraft, or team). — **cap·tain·cy** /-tənsē/ **n.** [ME: from OFr. *capitain*, from late L. *capitaneus* 'chief,' from L. *caput*, *capit-* 'head.']

cap·tain's chair ▶ **n.** a wooden chair along whose side and back edges a row of vertical spindles supports a bar that forms the back and armrests.

cap·tain's mast ▶ **n.** see MAST[1].

cap·tan /ˈkapˌtan/ ▶ **n.** a synthetic fungicide derived from a mercaptan.

cap·tion /ˈkapsʜən/ ▶ **n.** a title or brief explanation appended to an article, illustration, or poster. ■ a piece of text appearing on a movie or television screen as part of a movie or broadcast. ■ Law the heading of a legal document. ▶ **v.** [trans.] (usu. **be captioned**) provide (an illustration) with a title or explanation: *the drawings were captioned with humorous texts.* [ME (in the sense 'seizing, capture'): from L. *caption-*, from *capere* 'take, seize.']

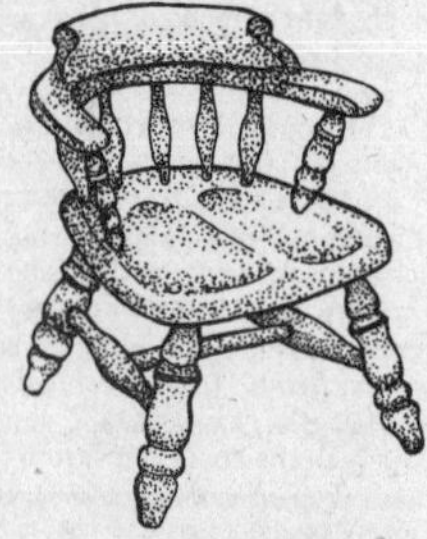
captain's chair

cap·tious /ˈkapsʜəs/ ▶ **adj.** formal (of a person) tending to find fault or raise petty objections. — **cap·tious·ly adv.** **cap·tious·ness n.** [ME: from OFr. *captieux* or L. *captiosus*, from *captio(n-)*.]

cap·ti·vate /ˈkaptəˌvāt/ ▶ **v.** [trans.] attract and hold the interest and attention of; charm. — **cap·ti·vat·ing·ly** /-ˌvātiɴGlē/ **adv.** **cap·ti·va·tion** /ˌkaptəˈvāsʜən/ **n.**

cap·tive /ˈkaptiv/ ▶ **n.** a person who has been taken prisoner or an animal that has been confined. ▶ **adj.** imprisoned or confined: *a captive animal.* ■ [attrib.] having no freedom to choose alternatives or to avoid something: *a captive audience.* ■ (of a facility or service) controlled by, and typically for the sole use of, an establishment or company: *a captive power plant.* [ME: from L. *captivus*, from *capere* 'seize, take.']

cap·tiv·i·ty /kapˈtivitē/ ▶ **n.** (pl. **-ties**) the condition of being imprisoned or confined.

cap·tor /ˈkaptər; -ˌtôr/ ▶ **n.** a person or animal that catches or confines another. [16th C.: from L., based on *capere*.]

cap·ture /ˈkapcʜər/ ▶ **v.** [trans.] take into one's possession or control by force: *the Russians captured 13,000 men* | fig. *the appeal captured the imagination of all.* ■ record or express accurately in words or pictures: *she did a series of sketches, trying to capture all his moods.* ■ Physics absorb (an atomic or subatomic particle). ■ (in chess and other board games) make a move that secures the removal of (an opposing piece) from the board. ■ Astron. (of a star, planet, or other celestial body) bring (a less massive body) permanently within its gravitational influence. ■ cause (data) to be stored in a computer or in a digital format. ▶ **n.** the action of capturing or of being captured. ■ a person or thing that has been captured. ■ Physics the absorption of an atomic or subatomic particle. — **cap·tur·er n.** [16th C.: from Fr., from L. *captura*, based on *capere*.]

Cap·u·chin /ˈkap(y)əsʜən; kəˈp(y)o͞o-/ ▶ **n.** **1** a friar belonging to a strict branch of the Franciscan order. **2** a cloak and hood formerly worn by women. **3** (**capuchin**) a South American monkey (genus *Cebus*) with a cap of hair on the head that has the appearance of a cowl. [16th C.: from obs. Fr., earlier form of *capucin*, from Ital. *cappuccino*, from *cappuccio* 'hood, cowl,' from *cappa* (see CAPE[1]), from the sharp-pointed hoods worn by the friars.]

cap·y·ba·ra /ˌkapəˈberə; -ˈbärə/ ▶ **n.** (pl. same or **-ras**) a South American mammal (*Hydrochoerus hydrochaeris*, family Hydrochaeridae) that resembles a large guinea pig. It lives in groups near water and is the largest living rodent. [17th C.: from Sp. *capibara* or Port. *capivara*, from Tupi *capiuára*, from *capí* 'grass' + *uára* 'eater.']

car /kär/ ▶ **n.** an automobile. ■ a vehicle that runs on rails, esp. a railroad car. ■ a railroad car of a specified kind: *the first-class cars.* ■ the passenger compartment of an elevator, cableway, airship, or balloon. ■ literary a chariot. — **car·ful** /-ˌfo͝ol/ **n.** (pl. **-fuls**). [ME: from Old North. Fr. *carre*, based on L. *carrum*, *carrus*, of Celtic origin.]

ca·ra·ba·o /ˌkarəˈbou; ˌkär-/ ▶ **n.** (pl. same or **-os**) another term for WATER BUFFALO. [20th C.: from Sp., from a local word in the Philippines.]

ca·ra·bid /ˈkarəbid; kəˈrabid/ ▶ **n.** Entomol. a fast-running beetle of a family (Carabidae) that comprises the predatory ground beetles. [19th C.: from mod. L. *Carabidae* (pl.), from L. *carabus*, a crab.]

car·a·bi·neer /ˌkarəbəˈni(ə)r/ (also **car·a·bi·nier**) ▶ **n.** hist. a cavalry soldier armed with a carbine. [17th C.: from Fr. *carabinier*, from *carabine* (see CARBINE).]

car·a·bi·ner /ˌkarəˈbēnər/ (also **kar·a·bi·ner**) ▶ **n.** a coupling link with a safety closure, used by rock climbers. [1930s: shortened from Ger. *Karabiner-haken* 'spring hook.']

ca·ra·bi·nie·re /ˌkarəbənˈye(ə)rē/ ▶ **n.** (pl. **-ri** pronunc. same) a member of the Italian paramilitary police. [Ital., lit. 'carabineer.']

car·a·cal /ˈkarəˌkal/ ▶ **n.** a long-legged lynxlike cat (*Felis caracal*) with black tufted ears and a uniform brown coat, native to Africa and western Asia. Also called **African lynx.** [19th C.: from Fr. or Sp., from Turk. *karakulak*, from *kara* 'black' + *kulak* 'ear.']

Car·a·cal·la /ˌkarəˈkalə/ (188–217), Roman emperor 211–217; born *Septimius Bassanius*; later called *Marcus Aurelius Severus Antoninus Augustus*. He granted citizenship to all free inhabitants of the Empire in 212.

ca·ra·ca·ra /ˌkarəˈkarə; ˌkärəˈkärə/ ▶ **n.** (pl. same or **-ras**) a large New World bird of prey of the falcon family, feeding largely on carrion. [19th C.: from Sp. or Port. *caracará*, from Tupi-Guarani, imitating its cry.]

Ca·ra·cas /kəˈräkəs; kəˈrakəs/ the capital of Venezuela, in the northern part of the country; pop. 1,824,890.

car·a·cole /ˈkarəˌkōl/ ▶ **n.** a half turn to the right or left by a horse. ▶ **v.** [intrans.] (of a horse) perform a caracole. [17th C.: from Fr. *caracole*, *caracol* 'snail's shell, spiral.']

car·a·cul ▶ **n.** var. of KARAKUL.

ca·rafe /kəˈraf; -ˈräf/ ▶ **n.** an open-topped glass flask typically used for serving wine or water. [18th C.: from Fr., from Ital. *caraffa*, prob. based on Arab. *garafa* 'draw water.']

car·a·ga·na /ˌkarəˈgänə; -ˈganə/ ▶ **n.** a leguminous shrub or small tree (genus *Caragana*) native to central Asia and Siberia, widely planted as an ornamental. [mod. L., of Turkic origin.]

Ca·ra·jás /ˌkärəˈzʜäs/ a mining region in northern Brazil, the site of rich deposits of iron ore.

ca·ram·ba /kəˈrämbə/ ▶ **exclam.** informal, often humorous an expression of surprise or dismay. [19th C.: from Sp.]

ca·ram·bo·la /ˌkarəmˈbōlə/ ▶ n. **1** a golden-yellow juicy fruit with a star-shaped cross section. Also called STAR FRUIT. **2** the small tropical tree (*Averrhoa carambola*, family Oxalidaceae) that bears this fruit. [16th C.: from Port., prob. from Marathi *karambal*.]

car·a·mel /ˈkarəməl; -ˌmel; ˈkärməl/ ▶ n. sugar or syrup heated until it turns brown, used as a flavoring or coloring for food or drink. ■ the light brown color of this substance: *a pale caramel.* ■ a soft candy made with sugar and butter that have been melted and further heated. [18th C.: from Fr., from Sp. *caramelo*.]

car·a·mel·ize /ˈkarəməˌlīz; ˈkärmə-/ ▶ v. [intrans.] (of sugar or syrup) be converted into caramel. ■ [trans.] cook (food) with sugar so that it becomes coated with caramel. — **car·a·mel·i·za·tion** /ˌkarəmələˈzāsʜən/ n.

ca·ran·gid /kəˈranjid; -ˈraɴɢgid/ ▶ n. Zool. a marine fish of the jack family (Carangidae), whose members typically have a sloping forehead and two dorsal fins.

car·a·pace /ˈkarəˌpās/ ▶ n. the hard upper shell of a turtle or crustacean. [19th C.: from Fr., from Sp. *carapacho*.]

car·at /ˈkarət/ ▶ n. **1** a unit of weight for precious stones and pearls, now equivalent to 200 milligrams. **2** chiefly British spelling of KARAT. [ME: from Fr., from Ital. *carato*, from Arab. *ḳīrāṭ*, from Gk. *keration* 'fruit of the carob.']

Ca·ra·vag·gio /ˌkarəˈväjō/, Michelangelo Merisi da (*c.*1571–1610), Italian painter. He was influential in the transition from late mannerism to baroque.

car·a·van /ˈkarəˌvan/ ▶ n. **1** hist. a group of people, esp. traders or pilgrims, traveling together across a desert in Asia or North Africa. ■ any large group of people, typically with vehicles or animals traveling together, in single file. **2** Brit. a vehicle equipped for living in, typically towed by a car and used for vacations. ■ a covered horse-drawn wagon. [15th C.: from Fr. *caravane*, from Pers. *kārwān*.]

car·a·van·sa·ry /ˌkarəˈvansərē/ (esp. Brit. also **car·a·van·se·rai** /-səˌrī/) ▶ n. (pl. **-sa·ries** or **-se·rais** /-səˌrīz/) **1** hist. an inn with a central courtyard for travelers in the deserts of Asia or North Africa. **2** a group of people traveling together; a caravan. [16th C.: from Pers. *kārwānsarāy*, from *kārwān* 'caravan' + *sarāy* 'palace.']

car·a·vel /ˈkarəˌvel; -vəl/ (also **car·vel** /ˈkärvel/) ▶ n. hist. a small, fast Spanish or Portuguese ship of the 15th–17th centuries. [16th C.: from Fr. *caravelle*, from Port. *caravela*, dimin. of *caravo*, via L. from Gk. *karabos* 'horned beetle' or 'light ship.']

car·a·way /ˈkarəˌwā/ ▶ n. (also **caraway seed**) the seeds of a Mediterranean plant (*Carum carvi*) of the parsley family, used for flavoring and as a source of oil. [ME: from med. L. *carui*, from Arab. *alkarāwiyā*, prob. from Gk. *karon* 'cumin.']

carb[1] /ˈkärb/ ▶ n. short for CARBURETOR.

carb[2] ▶ n. short for CARBOHYDRATE.

car·ba·mate /ˈkärbəˌmāt/ ▶ n. Chem. a salt or ester containing the anion NH_2COO- or the group $-OOCNH_2$, derived from the hypothetical compound **carbamic acid**. [19th C.: from *carbamic* (from CARBO- + AMIDE + -IC).]

car·ban·i·on /kärˈbanˌīən; -ˌīän/ ▶ n. Chem. an organic anion in which the negative charge is located on a carbon atom.

car·ba·ryl /ˈkärbəˌril/ ▶ n. a synthetic insecticide, $C_{12}H_{11}NO_2$, used to protect crops and in the treatment of fleas and lice. Alternative name: **1-naphthyl-N-methylcarbamate**. [20th C.: from CARBAMATE.]

car·ba·zole /ˈkärbəˌzōl/ ▶ n. Chem. a colorless crystalline substance, a tricyclic heteroaromatic compound, $C_{12}H_9N$, obtained from coal tar and used in dye production. [19th C.: from CARBO- + AZO-.]

car·bide /ˈkärbīd/ ▶ n. Chem. a binary compound of carbon with an element of lower or comparable electronegativity. ■ calcium carbide (CaC_2), used to generate acetylene by reaction with water.

car·bine /ˈkärbīn; -bēn/ ▶ n. a light automatic rifle. ■ hist. a short rifle or musket used by cavalry. [17th C.: from Fr. *carabine*, from *carabin* 'mounted musketeer.']

carbo- ▶ comb. form representing CARBON.

car·bo·hy·drate /ˌkärbəˈhīˌdrāt/ ▶ n. Biochem. any of a large group of organic compounds occurring in foods and living tissues and including sugars, starch, and cellulose. They contain hydrogen and oxygen in the same ratio as water (2:1) and typically can be broken down to release energy in the animal body.

car·bo·lat·ed /ˈkärbəˌlātid/ ▶ adj. impregnated with carbolic acid.

car·bol·ic ac·id /kärˈbälik/ ▶ n. phenol, esp. when used as a disinfectant.

car·bol·ic soap ▶ n. disinfectant soap containing phenol.

car·bo-load /ˈkärbōˌlōd/ ▶ v. [intrans.] eat large amounts of carbohydrates, in preparation for athletic endurance.

car bomb ▶ n. a bomb concealed in or under a parked car, used esp. by terrorists. ▶ v. (**car-bomb**) [trans.] attack with such a bomb. — **car bomb·er** n.

car·bon /ˈkärbən/ ▶ n. the chemical element of atomic number 6, a nonmetal that has two main forms (diamond and graphite), occurs in impure form in charcoal, soot, and coal, and is present in all organic compounds. (Symbol: **C**) ■ Chem. an atom of this element. ■ a rod of carbon in an arc light. ■ a piece of carbon paper or a carbon copy. [18th C.: from Fr. *carbone*, from L. *carbo, carbon-* 'coal, charcoal.']

car·bon-12 ▶ n. the commonest natural carbon isotope, of mass 12. It is the basis for the accepted scale of atomic mass units.

car·bon-14 ▶ n. a long-lived naturally occurring radioactive carbon isotope of mass 14, used in carbon dating and as a tracer in biochemistry.

car·bo·na·ceous /ˌkärbəˈnāsʜəs/ ▶ adj. (chiefly of rocks or sediments) consisting of or containing carbon or its compounds.

car·bo·na·do /ˌkärbəˈnādō; -ˈnädō/ ▶ n. (pl. **-dos**) a dark opaque diamond, used in abrasives and cutting tools. [19th C.: from Port.]

car·bo·na·ra /ˌkärbəˈnärə; -ˈnarə/ ▶ adj. denoting a pasta sauce made with bacon or ham, eggs, and cream. [Ital., lit. 'charcoal kiln.']

car·bo·nate /ˈkärbənit; -ˌnāt/ ▶ n. a salt of the anion $CO_3 2-$, typically formed by reaction of carbon dioxide with bases. ▶ v. /-ˌnāt/ [trans.] dissolve carbon dioxide in (a liquid) ■ Chem. convert into a carbonate, typically by reaction with carbon dioxide. — **car·bo·na·tion** /ˌkärbəˈnāsʜən/ n.

car·bon black ▶ n. a fine carbon powder used as a pigment, made by burning hydrocarbons in insufficient air.

car·bon cop·y ▶ n. a copy of written or typed material made with carbon paper. ■ fig. a person or thing identical or very similar to another.

car·bon cy·cle ▶ n. **1** the series of processes by which carbon compounds are interconverted in the environment, chiefly involving the incorporation of carbon dioxide into living tissue by photosynthesis and its return to the atmosphere through respiration, the decay of dead organisms, and the burning of fossil fuels. **2** Astron. the cycle of thermonuclear reactions believed to occur in stars, in which carbon nuclei are repeatedly formed and broken down in the conversion of hydrogen into helium.

car·bon dat·ing ▶ n. the determination of the age of an organic object from the relative proportions of the carbon isotopes carbon-12 and carbon-14 in it.

car·bon di·ox·ide ▶ n. a colorless, odorless gas, CO_2, produced by burning carbon and organic compounds and by respiration. It is naturally present in air (about 0.03 percent) and is absorbed by plants in photosynthesis.

car·bon di·sul·fide ▶ n. a colorless, toxic, flammable liquid, CS_2, used as a solvent, esp. for rubber and sulfur, and in the manufacture of viscose rayon, cellophane, and carbon tetrachloride.

car·bon fi·ber ▶ n. a material consisting of thin, strong crystalline filaments of carbon, used as a strengthening material.

car·bon foot·print ▶ adj. the amount of carbon dioxide emitted due to the the consumption of fossil fuels by a particular person, group, etc.

car·bon·ic /kärˈbänik/ ▶ adj. of or relating to carbon or its compounds, esp. carbon dioxide.

car·bon·ic ac·id ▶ n. a very weak acid, H_2CO_3, formed in solution when carbon dioxide dissolves in water.

car·bon·ic ac·id gas ▶ n. archaic term for CARBON DIOXIDE.

car·bon·ic an·hy·drase /anˈhīdrās; -drāz/ ▶ n. Biochem. an enzyme that catalyzes the conversion of dissolved bicarbonates into carbon dioxide.

Car·bon·if·er·ous /ˌkärbəˈnifərəs/ ▶ adj. Geol. of, relating to, or denoting the fifth period of the Paleozoic era (between the Devonian and Permian periods, about 360 to 286 million years ago), a time when extensive coal-bearing strata were formed. ■ (**the Carboniferous**) [as n.] the Carboniferous period or the system of rocks deposited during it.

car·bo·ni·um i·on /kärˈbōnēəm/ ▶ n. Chem. an organic cation in which the positive charge is located on a carbon atom. [20th C.: from CARBO- 'carbon.']

car·bon·ize /ˈkärbəˌnīz/ ▶ v. [trans.] convert into carbon, typically by heating or burning, or during fossilization. ■ [intrans.] coat with carbon. — **car·bon·i·za·tion** /ˌkärbənəˈzāsʜən/ n.

car·bon mon·ox·ide ▶ n. a colorless, odorless, toxic flammable gas, CO, formed by incomplete combustion of carbon.

car·bon·nade /ˌkärbəˈnäd/ ▶ n. a rich beef stew made with onions and beer. [17th C.: from Fr., from L. *carbo, carbon-* 'coal, charcoal.']

car·bon-neu·tral ▶ adj. making no net release of carbon dioxide to the atmosphere, esp. through offsetting emissions by planting trees.

car·bon pa·per ▶ n. thin paper coated with carbon or another pigmented substance, used for making copies of written or typed documents.

car·bon proc·ess ▶ n. a method of making photographic prints that uses a pigment, esp. carbon, contained in a sensitized tissue of gelatin.

car·bon sink ▶ n. Ecology a forest, ocean, or other natural environment viewed in terms of its ability to absorb carbon dioxide from the atmosphere.

car·bon steel ▶ n. steel in which the main alloying element is carbon, and whose properties are chiefly dependent on the percentage of carbon present.

car·bon tax ▶ n. a tax on fossil fuels, esp. those used by motor vehicles, intended to reduce the emission of carbon dioxide.

car·bon tet·ra·chlo·ride /ˌtetrəˈklôrīd/ ▶ n. a colorless, toxic, volatile liquid, CCl_4, used as a solvent, esp. for fats and oils.

car·bon·yl /ˈkärbəˌnil/ ▶ n. [as adj.] Chem. of or denoting the divalent radical $=C=O$, present in such organic compounds as aldehydes and esters, and in organic acids as part of the carboxyl group. ■ a coordination compound in which one or more carbon monoxide molecules are bonded as neutral ligands to a central metal atom.

car·bon·yl chlo·ride ▶ n. another term for PHOSGENE.

car·bo·run·dum /ˌkärbəˈrəndəm/ ▶ n. a very hard black solid consisting of silicon carbide, used as an abrasive. [19th C.: blend of CARBON and CORUNDUM.]

car·box·y·he·mo·glo·bin /kär,bäksē'hēmə,glōbin/ ▶ **n.** Biochem. a compound formed in the blood by the binding of carbon monoxide to hemoglobin. It is stable and therefore cannot absorb or transport oxygen.

car·box·yl /kär'bäksəl/ ▶ **n.** [as adj.] Chem. of or denoting the acid radical –COOH, present in most organic acids: *the carboxyl group.* [19th C.: from CARBO-.]

car·box·yl·ase /kär'bäksə,lās; -,lāz/ ▶ **n.** Biochem. an enzyme that catalyzes the addition of a carboxyl group to a specified substrate.

car·box·yl·ate /kär'bäksə,lāt; -lit/ Chem. ▶ **n.** a salt or ester of a carboxylic acid. ▶ **v.** [trans.] add a carboxyl group to (a compound). — **car·box·yl·a·tion** /kär,bäksə'lāsʜən/ **n.**

car·box·yl·ic ac·id /,kärbäk'silik/ ▶ **n.** Chem. an organic acid containing a carboxyl group, e.g., methanoic (or formic) acid and acetic acid.

car·boy /'kär,boi/ ▶ **n.** a large globular bottle with a narrow neck, typically protected by a frame and used for holding acids or other corrosive liquids. [18th C.: from Pers. *ḳarāba* 'large glass flagon.']

car bra ▶ **n.** see BRA.

carbs /kärbz/ ▶ **plural n.** informal dietary carbohydrates.

car·bun·cle /'kär,bəɴɢkəl/ ▶ **n.** **1** a multiple boil in the skin, typically infected with staphylococcus. **2** a bright red gem, esp. a garnet cut en cabochon. — **car·bun·cu·lar** /kär'bəɴɢkyələr/ **adj.** [ME: from OFr. *charbuncle*, from L. *carbunculus* 'small coal,' from *carbo* 'coal.']

car·bu·ret·ed /'kärb(y)ə,rātəd; -,retid/ (Brit. **car·bu·ret·ted**) ▶ **adj.** (of a vehicle or engine) having fuel supplied through a carburetor, rather than an injector. [19th C.: from archaic *carburet* 'carbide.']

car·bu·re·tor /'kärb(y)ə,rātər/ (also **car·bu·ra·tor**, Brit. **car·bu·ret·tor** or **car·bu·ret·ter**) ▶ **n.** a device in an internal combustion engine for mixing air with a fine spray of liquid fuel. [19th C.: from archaic *carburet* 'charge with a hydrocarbon.']

car·bu·rize /'kärb(y)ə,rīz/ ▶ **v.** [trans.] add carbon to (iron or steel), in particular by heating in the presence of carbon to harden the surface. — **car·bu·ri·za·tion** /,kärb(y)ərə'zāsʜən/ **n.** [19th C.: from Fr. *carbure* 'carbide.']

car·ca·jou /'kärkə,jo͞o; ,ᴢʜo͞o/ ▶ **n.** another term for the North American WOLVERINE. [18th C.: from Canad. Fr., from Montagnais *kwāhkwāčēw*.]

car·cass /'kärkəs/ (Brit. also **car·case**) ▶ **n.** the dead body of an animal. ■ the trunk of an animal such as a cow, sheep, or pig, for cutting up as meat. ■ the remains of a cooked bird after all the edible parts have been removed. ■ derog. humorous a person's body, living or dead. ■ the structural framework of a building, ship, or piece of furniture. ■ fig. the remains of something being discarded, dismembered, or worthless. [ME: from Anglo-Norman Fr. *carcois*, var. of OFr. *charcois*.]

car·cin·o·gen /kär'sinəjən; 'kärsənə,jen/ ▶ **n.** a substance capable of causing cancer in living tissue. [19th C.: from abbrev. of CARCINOMA.]

car·cin·o·gen·e·sis /,kärsənə'jenəsis/ ▶ **n.** the initiation of cancer formation.

car·cin·o·gen·ic /,kärsənə'jenik/ ▶ **adj.** having the potential to cause cancer. — **car·ci·no·ge·nic·i·ty** /-,nōjə'nisitē/ **n.**

car·ci·noid /'kärsə,noid/ ▶ **n.** Med. a tumor of a type occurring in the glands of the intestine or in the bronchi, and abnormally secreting hormones. [19th C.: from abbrev. of CARCINOMA.]

car·ci·no·ma /,kärsə'nōmə/ ▶ **n.** (pl. **-no·mas** or **-no·ma·ta** /-'nōmətə/) a cancer arising in the epithelial tissue of the skin or of the lining of the internal organs. — **car·ci·no·ma·tous** /-'nōmətəs/ **adj.** [18th C.: via L. from Gk. *karkinōma*, from *karkinos* 'crab.']

car coat ▶ **n.** a short, square-cut style of coat designed to be worn when driving a car.

Card. ▶ **abbr.** Cardinal.

card¹ /kärd/ ▶ **n.** **1** a piece of thick, stiff paper or thin pasteboard, in particular one used for writing or printing on. ■ such a piece of thick paper printed with a picture and used to send a message or greeting. ■ a small piece of such paper with a person's name and other details printed on it for purposes of identification, e.g., a business card. **2** a small rectangular piece of plastic issued by a bank, containing personal data in a machine-readable form and used chiefly to obtain cash or credit. ■ a similar piece of plastic used for other purposes such as paying for a telephone call or gaining entry to a room or building. **3** a playing card. ■ **(cards)** a game played with playing cards. **4** informal a person regarded as odd or amusing: *He laughed: "You're a card, you know."* **5** a program of events at a racetrack. ■ a record of scores in a sporting event; a scorecard. ■ a list of holes on a golf course, on which a player's scores are entered. ▶ **v.** [trans.] **1** write (something) on a card, esp. for indexing. **2** check the identity card of (someone), in particular as evidence of legal drinking age. **3** informal (in golf and other sports) score (a certain number of points on a scorecard).

– PHRASES **in the cards** informal very possible or likely. **play the —— card** exploit the specified issue or idea mentioned, esp. for political advantage: *he saw an opportunity to play the peace card.* **put** (or **lay**) **one's cards on the table** be completely open and honest in declaring one's resources, intentions, or attitude. [ME: from OFr. *carte*, from L. *carta*, *charta*, from Gk. *khartēs* 'papyrus leaf.']

card² ▶ **v.** [trans.] comb and clean (raw wool, hemp fibers, or similar material) with a sharp-toothed instrument in order to disentangle the fibers before spinning. ▶ **n.** a toothed implement or machine for this purpose. — **card·er n.** [ME: from OFr. *carde*, from Provençal *carda*, from *cardar* 'tease, comb,' based on L. *carere* 'to card.']

car·da·mom /'kärdəməm/ (also **car·da·mon** /-mən/) ▶ **n.** **1** the aromatic seeds of a plant of the ginger family, used as a spice and also medicinally. **2** the Southeast Asian plant (*Elettaria cardamomum*) that bears these seeds. [ME: ult. from Gk. *kardamōmon*, from *kardamon* 'cress' + *amōmon*, a spice plant.]

Car·da·mom Moun·tains /'kärdəməm/ a range of mountains in western Cambodia.

card·board /'kärd,bôrd/ ▶ **n.** pasteboard or stiff paper. ■ [as adj.] (of a character in a literary work) lacking depth and realism; artificial: *with its superficial, cardboard characters, the novel was typical of her work.*

card-car·ry·ing ▶ **adj.** [attrib.] registered as a member of a political party or labor union.

Cár·de·nas /'kärdā,näs; 'kärdn-əs/ a city in north central Cuba, east of Havana; pop. 63,000.

card·hold·er /'kärd,hōldər/ ▶ **n.** a person who has a credit card or debit card.

car·di·a /'kärdēə/ ▶ **n.** Anat. the upper opening of the stomach, where the esophagus enters. [18th C.: from Gk. *kardia*.]

car·di·ac /'kärdē,ak/ ▶ **adj.** [attrib.] **1** of or relating to the heart: *a cardiac arrest.* **2** of or relating to the part of the stomach nearest the esophagus. ▶ **n.** Med., informal a person with heart disease. [ME: ult. from Gk. *kardiakos*, from *kardia* 'heart.']

car·di·ac ar·rest ▶ **n.** a sudden, sometimes temporary, cessation of function of the heart.

car·di·ac mas·sage ▶ **n.** a procedure to resuscitate a patient suffering cardiac arrest or fibrillation by rhythmically compressing the chest and heart to restore circulation. Also called HEART MASSAGE.

car·di·ac mus·cle ▶ **n.** another term for MYOCARDIUM.

car·di·ac tam·pon·ade ▶ **n.** see TAMPONADE (sense 1).

car·di·al·gi·a /,kärdē'alj(ē)ə/ ▶ **n.** **1** heartburn. **2** another term for CARDIODYNIA.

Car·diff /'kärdif/ the capital of Wales, in the southern part of the country; pop. 272,600. Welsh name CAERDYDD.

car·di·gan /'kärdigən/ ▶ **n.** a knitted sweater fastening down the front, typically with long sleeves. [19th C. (Crimean War): named after the 7th Earl of *Cardigan*, whose troops first wore such garments.]

Car·din /kär'dᴀɴ; -'dan/, Pierre (1922–), French fashion designer.

car·di·nal /'kärdn-əl; 'kärd-nl/ ▶ **n.** **1** a leading dignitary of the Roman Catholic Church, nominated by the pope and collectively forming the Sacred College. ■ (also **cardinal red**) a deep scarlet color like that of a cardinal's cassock. **2** a New World songbird of the bunting family, with a stout bill and conspicuous crest, in particular the **northern** (or **common**) **cardinal** (*Cardinalis cardinalis*), the male of which is scarlet with a black face. ▶ **adj.** [attrib.] of the greatest importance; fundamental. — **car·di·nal·ate** /-it; -,āt/ **n.** (in sense 1 of the **noun**) **car·di·nal·ship n.** (in sense 1 of the **noun**). [OE, from L. *cardinalis*, from *cardo, cardin-* 'hinge.']

car·di·nal flow·er ▶ **n.** a tall scarlet-flowered lobelia of the bellflower family (*Lobelia cardinalis*), found in North America.

car·di·nal hu·mor ▶ **n.** see HUMOR (sense 3).

car·di·nal·i·ty /,kärdn'alitē/ ▶ **n.** (pl. **-ties**) Math. the number of elements in a set or other grouping.

car·di·nal num·ber ▶ **n.** a number denoting quantity (one, two, three, etc.).

car·di·nal point ▶ **n.** each of the four main points of the compass (north, south, east, and west).

car·di·nal sin ▶ **n.** **1** another name for DEADLY SIN. **2** chiefly humorous a serious error of judgment.

car·di·nal vir·tue ▶ **n.** each of the chief natural virtues of justice, prudence, temperance, and fortitude.

card in·dex ▶ **n.** a catalog or similar collection of information in which each item is entered on a separate card, and the cards are arranged in order, typically alphabetical.

card·ing wool ▶ **n.** short-stapled pieces of wool that result from the carding process, spun and woven to make standard-quality fabrics.

cardio- ▶ **comb. form** of or relating to the heart: *cardiograph* | *cardiopulmonary.* [from Gk. *kardia* 'heart.']

car·di·o ▶ **n.** informal cardiovascular exercise.

car·di·o·dyn·i·a /,kärdēō'dinēə/ ▶ **n.** pain in the region of the heart.

car·di·o·gram /'kärdēə,gram/ ▶ **n.** a record of muscle activity within the heart made by a cardiograph.

car·di·o·graph /'kärdēə,graf/ ▶ **n.** an instrument for recording heart muscle activity, such as an electrocardiograph. — **car·di·og·ra·pher** /,kärdē'ägrəfər/ **n.** **car·di·og·ra·phy** /,kärdē'ägrəfē/ **n.**

car·di·oid /'kärdē,oid/ ▶ **n.** Math. a heart-shaped curve traced by a point on the circumference of a circle as it rolls around another identical circle. [18th C.: from Gk. *kardioeidēs* 'heart-shaped,' from *kardia* 'heart' + *eidos* 'form.']

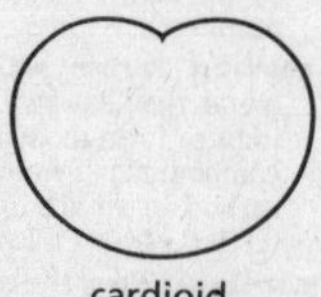
cardioid

car·di·ol·o·gy /,kärdē'äləjē/ ▶ **n.** the branch of medicine that deals with diseases and abnormalities of the heart. — **car·di·o·log·i·cal** /,kärdēə'läjikəl/ **adj.** **car·di·ol·o·gist** /-jist/ **n.**

car·di·o·meg·a·ly /,kärdēō'megəlē/ ▶ **n.** Med. abnormal enlargement of the heart. [1960s: from CARDIO- + Gk. *megas, megal-* 'great.']

car·di·o·my·op·a·thy /ˌkärdēˌōmīˈäpəᴛʜē/ ▶ n. Med. chronic disease of the heart muscle.

car·di·op·a·thy /ˌkärdēˈäpəᴛʜē/ ▶ n. heart disease.

car·di·o·pul·mo·nar·y /ˌkärdēōˈpo͝olməˌnerē; -ˈpəl-/ ▶ adj. Med. of or relating to the heart and the lungs.

car·di·o·pul·mo·nar·y re·sus·ci·ta·tion ▶ n. emergency medical procedures for restoring normal heartbeat and breathing to victims of heart failure, drowning, etc.

car·di·o·res·pi·ra·to·ry /ˌkärdēōˈresp(ə)rəˌtôrē; -rəˈspīrə-/ ▶ adj. Med. relating to the action of both heart and lungs.

car·di·o·vas·cu·lar /ˌkärdēōˈvaskyələr/ ▶ adj. Med. of or relating to the heart and blood vessels.

car·di·o·vas·cu·lar sys·tem ▶ n. another term for CIRCULATORY SYSTEM.

car·di·tis /kärˈdītəs/ ▶ n. Med. inflammation of the heart.

card key ▶ n. another term for KEY CARD.

card·mem·ber /ˈkärdˌmembər/ ▶ n. a holder of a particular credit or charge card.

car·doon /kärˈdo͞on/ ▶ n. a tall thistlelike southern European plant (*Cynara cardunculus*) of the daisy family, related to the globe artichoke, with edible leaves and roots. [17th C.: from Fr. *cardon*, from *carde* 'edible part of an artichoke,' based on L. *carduus, cardus* 'thistle, artichoke.']

Car·do·zo /kärˈdōzō/, Benjamin Nathan (1870–1938), US Supreme Court associate justice 1932–38.

card sharp (also **card sharper** or **card shark**) ▶ n. a person who cheats at cards in order to win money.

card ta·ble ▶ n. a square table for playing cards on, typically having legs that fold flat for storage.

CARE /ke(ə)r/ ▶ abbr. Cooperative for American Relief Everywhere, a large private organization that provides emergency and long-term assistance to people in need throughout the world.

care /ke(ə)r/ ▶ n. **1** the provision of what is necessary for the health, welfare, maintenance, and protection of someone or something. **2** serious attention or consideration applied to doing something correctly or to avoid damage or risk. ■ an object of concern or attention: *the cares of family life.* ■ a feeling of or occasion for anxiety: *without a care in the world.* ▶ v. [intrans.] **1** [often with negative] feel concern or interest; attach importance to something: *they don't* ***care about*** *human life.* ■ feel affection or liking: *you* ***care*** *very deeply* ***for*** *him.* ■ **(care for something/care to do something)** like or be willing to do or have something: *I don't care to listen to him.* **2 (care for)** look after and provide for the needs of: *he has animals to care for.*

– PHRASES **care of** at the address of: *write to me care of Anne.* **I** (or **he, she,** etc.) **couldn't** (or informal also **could**) **care less** informal used to express complete indifference. **for all you care** (or **he, she,** etc., **cares**) informal used to indicate that someone feels no interest or concern: *I could drown for all you care.* **take care 1** [often in imper.] be cautious; keep oneself safe. ■ said to someone on leaving them: *take care, see you soon.* **2** [with infin.] make sure of doing something: *he took care to provide himself with an escape clause.* **take care of 1** keep (someone or something) safe and provided for. **2** deal with (something). [OE *caru* (n.), *carian* (v.), of Gmc. origin; akin to Old High Ger. *chara* 'grief.']

ca·reen /kəˈrēn/ ▶ v. **1** [trans.] turn (a ship) on its side for cleaning, caulking, or repair. ■ [intrans.] (of a ship) tilt; lean over. **2** [no obj., with adverbial of direction] move swiftly and in an uncontrolled way in a specified direction. *an electric golf cart careened around the corner.* [16th C.: from Fr. *carène*, from Ital. *carena*, from L. *carina* 'a keel.']

ca·reer /kəˈri(ə)r/ ▶ n. an occupation undertaken for a significant period of a person's life and with opportunities for progress. ■ the time spent by a person in such an occupation or profession. ■ the progress through history of an institution or organization: *the court has had a checkered career.* ■ [as adj.] working permanently in or committed to a particular profession: *a career diplomat.* ■ [as adj.] (of a woman) interested in pursuing a profession rather than devoting all her time to child care and housekeeping. ▶ v. [no obj., with adverbial of direction] move swiftly and in an uncontrolled way in a specified direction: *the car careered across the road and went through a hedge.*

– PHRASES **in full career** archaic at full speed. [16th C.: from Fr. *carrière*, from Ital. *carriera*, based on L. *carrus* 'wheeled vehicle.']

ca·reer·ist /kəˈri(ə)rist/ ▶ n. a person whose main concern is for professional advancement, esp. one willing to achieve this by any means: [as adj.] *a careerist politician.* — **ca·reer·ism** n.

care·free /ˈke(ə)rˌfrē/ ▶ adj. free from anxiety or responsibility. — **care·free·ness** n.

care·ful /ˈke(ə)rfəl/ ▶ adj. **1** making sure of avoiding potential danger, mishap, or harm; cautious. ■ **(careful of/about)** anxious to protect (something) from harm or loss; solicitous: *careful of his reputation.* ■ prudent in the use of something, esp. money: ***careful with*** *money.* **2** done with or showing thought and attention: *a careful consideration of the facts.* — **care·ful·ly** adv. **care·ful·ness** n.

care·giv·er /ˈke(ə)rˌgivər/ ▶ n. a family member or paid helper who regularly takes care of a child or a sick, elderly, or disabled person. — **care·giv·ing** n. & adj.

care·less /ˈke(ə)rlis/ ▶ adj. not giving sufficient attention or thought to avoiding harm or errors. ■ (of an action or its result) showing or caused by a lack of attention: *a careless error.* ■ [predic.] **(careless of/about)** not concerned or worried about: *careless about his own safety.* ■ showing no interest or effort; casual: *a careless shrug.* — **care·less·ly** adv. **care·less·ness** n.

ca·ress /kəˈres/ ▶ v. [trans.] touch or stroke gently or lovingly: *she caressed the girl's forehead* | fig. [as adj.] **(caressing)** *the caressing warmth of the sun.* ▶ n. a gentle or loving touch. — **ca·ress·ing·ly** adv. [17th C.: from Fr. *caresser* (v.), *caresse* (n.), from Ital. *carezza*, based on L. *carus* 'dear.']

car·et /ˈkarit/ ▶ n. a mark (^, ʌ) placed below the line to indicate a proposed insertion in a printed or written text. [17th C.: from L., 'is lacking.']

care·tak·er /ˈke(ə)rˌtākər/ ▶ n. **1** a person employed to look after a public building or a house in the owner's absence. ■ [as adj.] holding power temporarily: *his was a caretaker regime.* **2** a person employed to look after people or animals. — **care·take** v.

care·worn /ˈke(ə)rˌwôrn/ ▶ adj. tired and unhappy because of prolonged worry: *a careworn expression.*

Car·ey /ˈke(ə)rē/, George Leonard, Baron Carey of Clifton (1935–), Archbishop of Canterbury 1991–2002. During his tenure, the Church of England allowed the ordination of women as priests.

car·fare /ˈkärˌfe(ə)r/ ▶ n. dated the fare for travel on a bus, subway, or similar mode of public transportation.

car·go /ˈkärgō/ ▶ n. (pl. **-goes** or **-gos**) freight carried on a ship, aircraft, or motor vehicle: *a cargo of oil.* [17th C.: from Sp. *cargo, carga*, from late L. *carricare, carcare* 'to load,' from L. *carrus* 'wheeled vehicle.']

car·go cult ▶ n. (in the Melanesian Islands) a system of belief based around the expected arrival of ancestral spirits in ships bringing cargoes of food and goods.

car·go pants ▶ n. loose-fitting casual slacks with large patch pockets on the thighs.

car·hop /ˈkärˌhäp/ ▶ n. informal, dated a waiter or waitress at a drive-in restaurant.

Car·i·a /ˈke(ə)rēə/ an ancient region of southwestern Asia Minor, northwest of Lycia. — **Car·i·an** adj. & n.

Car·ib /ˈkarib/ ▶ n. **1** a member of an indigenous South American people living mainly in coastal regions of French Guiana, Suriname, Guyana, and Venezuela. **2** the Cariban language of this people, now spoken in parts of northern South America. **Island Carib** is an extinct language of the Arawakan group, formerly used in the Lesser Antilles; **Black Carib**, spoken in parts of Central America, is derived from this. Also called GALIBI. ▶ adj. of or relating to the Caribs or their language. ■ of or relating to Island Carib or Black Carib. [from Sp. *caribe*, from Haitian Creole.]

Car·i·ban /ˈkarəbən; kəˈrē-/ ▶ adj. of, belonging to, or denoting a family of South American languages scattered widely throughout Brazil, Suriname, Guyana, Venezuela, and Colombia. ▶ n. this family of languages.

Car·ib·be·an /ˌkarəˈbēən; kəˈribēən/ ▶ n. **(the Caribbean)** the region consisting of the Caribbean Sea, its islands, and the surrounding coasts. ▶ adj. of or relating to this region.

Car·ib·be·an Sea the part of the Atlantic Ocean that lies between the Antilles and Central and South America.

ca·ri·be /kəˈrēbē/ ▶ n. another term for PIRANHA.

Car·i·boo Moun·tains /ˈkarəˌbo͞o/ a range of mountains in east central British Columbia, Canada.

barren ground caribou

car·i·bou /ˈkarəˌbo͞o/ ▶ n. (pl. same or **-bous**) a large North American reindeer (genus *Rangifer*), esp. the **woodland caribou** (*R. caribou*) and the **barren ground caribou** (*R. tarandus*). [17th C.: from Canad. Fr., from Micmac *alipu*, lit. 'snowshoveler.']

car·i·ca·ture /ˈkarikəᴄʜər; -ˌᴄʜo͝or/ ▶ n. a picture, description, or imitation of a person or thing in which certain characteristics are exaggerated to create a comic or grotesque effect. ■ the art or style of such exaggerated representation. ■ a ludicrous or grotesque version of someone or something: *he looked* ***a caricature of*** *his normal self.* ▶ v. [trans.] (usu. **be caricatured**) make or give a comically or grotesquely exaggerated representation of (someone or something): *a play that caricatures the legal profession.* — **car·i·ca·tur·al** /ˌkarikəˈᴄʜo͝orəl/ adj. **car·i·ca·tur·ist** n. [18th C.: from Fr., from Ital. *caricatura*, from *caricare* 'load, exaggerate,' from L. *carricare* (see CHARGE).]

car·ies /'ke(ə)rēz/ ▶ n. decay and crumbling of a tooth or bone. [16th C.: from L.]

car·il·lon /'karə,län; -lən/ ▶ n. a set of bells in a tower, played using a keyboard or by an automatic mechanism similar to a piano roll. ■ a tune played on such bells. — **car·il·lon·neur** /,karələ'nər/ n. [18th C.: from Fr., from OFr. *quarregnon* 'peal of four bells,' based on L. *quattuor* 'four.']

Ca·ri·na /kə'rīnə/ Astron. a southern constellation (the Keel) partly in the Milky Way, originally part of Argo. It contains the second brightest star in the sky, Canopus. [L.]

ca·ri·na /kə'rēnə; -'rī-/ ▶ n. (pl. **-nae** /-nē/ or **-nas**) esp. Biol. a keel-shaped structure, in particular: ■ Zool. the ridge of a bird's breastbone, to which the main flight muscles are attached. — **ca·ri·nal** adj. [18th C.: from L., 'keel.']

car·i·nate /'karə,nāt; -nit/ ▶ adj. having a keellike ridge. ■ (of a bird) having a deep ridge on the breastbone for the attachment of flight muscles. — **car·i·nat·ed** /-,nātid/ adj. **car·i·na·tion** /,karə'nāSHən/ n.

car·ing /'ke(ə)riNG/ ▶ adj. displaying kindness and concern for others. ▶ n. the work or practice of looking after those unable to care for themselves, esp. the sick and the elderly.

Car·i·o·ca /,karē'ōkə/ ▶ n. **1** a native of Rio de Janeiro. **2** (**carioca**) a Brazilian dance resembling the samba. [19th C.: from Port., from Tupi *kari'oka* 'house of the white man.']

car·i·o·gen·ic /,karēə'jenik/ ▶ adj. tech. causing tooth decay.

car·i·ole ▶ n. var. of CARRIOLE.

car·i·ous /'karēəs/ ▶ adj. (of bones or teeth) decayed. [16th C.: from L. *cariosus* (see CARIES).]

car·jack·ing /'kär,jakiNG/ ▶ n. the action of violently stealing an occupied car. — **car·jack** v. **car·jack·er** /-,jakər/ n. [1990s: blend of CAR and *hijacking*.]

cark·ing /'kärkiNG/ ▶ adj. [attrib.] archaic causing distress or worry: *her carking doubts*. [16th C.: pres. part. of ME *cark* 'worry,' from Old North. Fr. *carkier*, based on late L. *carcare* (see CHARGE).]

carl /kärl/ ▶ n. archaic a peasant or man of low birth. [OE: from ON *karl* 'man, freeman,' of Gmc. origin; rel. to CHURL.]

Car·lism /'kär,lizəm/ ▶ n. hist. a Spanish political movement in support of Don Carlos, brother of Fernando VII (died 1833), who claimed the throne in place of Fernando's daughter Isabella. — **Car·list** adj. & n.

car·load /'kär,lōd/ ▶ n. the number of people that can travel in an automobile. ■ the quantity of goods that can be carried in a railroad freight car.

Car·lo·vin·gi·an /,kärlə'vinj(ē)ən/ ▶ adj. & n. another term for CAROLINGIAN. [from Fr. *carlovingien*, from *Karl* 'Charles.']

Car·low /'kärlō/ a county in the Republic of Ireland, in the province of Leinster.

Carls·bad /'kärlz,bad/ **1** a city in southwestern California, north of San Diego; pop. 63,126. **2** a city in southeastern New Mexico, on the Pecos River; pop. 25,625. To the southwest is Carlsbad Caverns, a vast cave complex.

Car·lyle /kär'līl; 'kärlīl/, Thomas (1795–1881), Scottish historian and political philosopher. He wrote *The French Revolution: a History* (1837).

car·mak·er /'kär,mākər/ ▶ n. a manufacturer of automobiles.

car·man /'kärmən/ ▶ n. (pl. **-men** pronunc. same) dated a driver of a streetcar or horse-drawn carriage.

Car·mel /kär'mel/ a resort city in west central California, south of Monterey; pop. 4,239.

Car·mel, Mount /'kärməl/ a ridge of mountains near the Mediterranean coast in northwestern Israel. It is the biblical site of Elijah's defeat of the priests of Baal (I Kings 18).

Car·mel·ite /'kärmə,līt/ ▶ n. a friar or nun of a contemplative Catholic order founded at Mount Carmel during the Crusades. ▶ adj. of or relating to the Carmelites.

Car·mi·chael[1] /'kär,mīkəl/ a community in north central California; pop. 48,702.

Car·mi·chael[2], Hoagy (1899–1981), US pianist and composer; full name *Hoagland Howard Carmichael*. His songs include "Stardust" (1927–29) and "In the Cool, Cool, Cool of the Evening" (1951).

car·min·a·tive /kär'minətiv; 'kärmə,nātiv/ ▶ adj. Med. (chiefly of a drug) relieving flatulence. ▶ n. a drug of this kind. [ME: from OFr. *carminatif, -ive*, or med. L. *carminat-* 'healed,' from v. *carminare*, from L. *carmen* (see CHARM).]

car·mine /'kärmən; -,mīn/ ▶ n. a vivid crimson color. ■ a vivid crimson pigment made from cochineal. [18th C.: from Fr. *carmin*, based on Arab. *ķirmiz* (see KERMES).]

Car·nac /'kärnak/ the site in Brittany of nearly 3,000 megalithic stones dating from the Neolithic period.

car·nage /'kärnij/ ▶ n. the killing of a large number of people. [17th C.: from Fr., from Ital. *carnaggio*, ult. from L. *caro, carn-* 'flesh.']

car·nal /'kärnl/ ▶ adj. relating to physical, esp. sexual, needs and activities: *carnal desire*. — **car·nal·i·ty** /kär'nalitē/ n. **car·nal·ly** adv. [ME: from Christian L. *carnalis*, from *caro, carn-* 'flesh.']

car·nall·ite /'kärnl,īt/ ▶ n. a white or reddish mineral consisting of a hydrated chloride of potassium and magnesium. [19th C.: named after Rudolf von *Carnall* (1804–74), Ger. mining engineer.]

Car·nap /'kärnap/, Rudolf (1891–1970), US philosopher; born in Germany. He was a founding member of the logical positivist Vienna Circle.

car·nas·si·al /kär'nasēəl/ ▶ adj. Zool. denoting the large upper premolar and lower molar teeth of a carnivore, adapted for shearing flesh. ▶ n. a tooth of this type. [19th C.: from Fr. *carnassier* 'carnivorous,' based on L. *caro, carn-* 'flesh.']

car·na·tion /kär'nāSHən/ ▶ n. a double-flowered cultivated variety of clove pink (*Dianthus caryophyllus*) with gray-green leaves and showy pink, white, or red flowers. ■ a rosy pink color. [16th C.: perh. based on misreading of Arab. *ķaranful* 'clove or clove pink,' from Gk. *karyophullon*.]

car·nau·ba /kär'nôbə; -'noubə/ ▶ n. a northeastern Brazilian fan palm (*Copernicia cerifera*) whose leaves exude a yellowish wax. Also called WAX PALM. ■ (also **carnauba wax**) wax from this palm, formerly used as a polish and for making candles. [19th C.: from Port., from Tupi.]

Car·ne·gie /'kärnigē; kär'nāgē/, Andrew (1835–1919), US industrialist and philanthropist; born in Scotland. After building a fortune in the steel industry, he devoted his wealth to charitable purposes. He established the Carnegie Institute of Technology in 1900.

car·nel·ian /kär'nēlyən/ (also **cor·nel·ian** /kôr-/) ▶ n. a semiprecious stone consisting of an orange or orange-red variety of chalcedony. [ME: from OFr. *corneline*.]

car·net /kär'nā/ ▶ n. a permit, in particular: ■ a permit allowing use of certain campsites while traveling abroad. ■ a book of tickets for use on public transportation in some countries. [1920s: from Fr., 'notebook.']

Car·nic Alps /'kärnik/ (German name **Karnische Alpen**) a range of the Alps on the border of southern Austria and northeastern Italy.

car·ni·val /'kärnəvəl/ ▶ n. **1** a period of public revelry at a regular time each year, typically during the week before Lent. ■ fig. an exciting or riotous mixture of something. **2** a traveling amusement show or circus. — **car·ni·val·esque** /,kärnəvə'lesk/ adj. [16th C.: from Ital. *carnevale, carnovale*, based on L. *caro, carn-* 'flesh' + *levare* 'put away.']

Car·niv·o·ra /kär'nivərə/ Zool. an order of mammals that comprises the cats, dogs, bears, hyenas, weasels, civets, raccoons, and mongooses.

car·ni·vore /'kärnə,vôr/ ▶ n. an animal that feeds on flesh. ■ Zool. a mammal of the order Carnivora. [19th C.: from Fr., from L. *carnivorus*.]

car·niv·o·rous /kär'nivərəs/ ▶ adj. (of an animal) feeding on other animals. ■ (of a plant) able to trap and digest small animals, esp. insects. — **car·niv·o·rous·ly** adv. **car·niv·o·rous·ness** n. [16th C.: from L. *carnivorus*, from *caro, carn-* 'flesh' + *-vorus* (see -VOROUS).]

Car·not /kär'nō/, Nicolas Léonard Sadi (1796–1832), French physicist. He contributed to the theory of thermodynamics.

car·no·tite /'kärnə,tīt/ ▶ n. a lemon-yellow radioactive mineral consisting of hydrated vanadate of uranium and potassium, often found near petrified trees. [19th C.: named after Marie Adolphe *Carnot* (1839–1920), Fr. inspector of mines.]

car·ny /'kärnē/ (also **car·nie** or **car·ney**) ▶ n. [usu. as adj.] informal a carnival or amusement show. ■ a person who works in a carnival or amusement show.

car·ob /'karəb/ ▶ n. **1** a powder extracted from the carob bean, used as a substitute for chocolate. **2** (also **carob tree**) a leguminous Arabian evergreen tree (*Ceratonia siliqua*) that bears long brownish-purple edible pods. Also called **locust tree**. ■ (also **carob bean**) the edible pod of this tree. Also called **locust bean**. [ME: from OFr. *carobe*, from med. L. *carrubia*, from Arab. *ķarrūba*.]

car·ol /'karəl/ ▶ n. a religious folk song or popular hymn, particularly one associated with Christmas: *singing* ***Christmas carols*** *around the tree*. ▶ v. (**car·oled, car·ol·ing**; esp. Brit. **car·ol·led, car·ol·ling**) [intrans.] sing Christmas songs or hymns, esp. in a group: *we caroled from door to door.* ■ [trans.] sing or say (something) happily: *she was cheerfully caroling the words of the song*. — **car·ol·er** n. **car·ol·ing** n. [ME: from OFr. *carole* (n.), *caroler* (v.), of unknown origin.]

Car·ol Cit·y /'karəl/ a city in southeastern Florida; pop. 53,331.

Car·o·li·na /,karə'līnə/ a city in Puerto Rico, east of San Juan; pop. 162,404.

Car·o·li·na all·spice /,karə'līnə; ,ker-/ ▶ n. see ALLSPICE.

Car·o·li·na duck ▶ n. another term for WOOD DUCK.

Car·o·li·na par·a·keet ▶ n. a small, long-tailed, brightly colored North American parakeet (*Conuropsis carolinensis*), extinct since 1920.

Car·o·li·na rose ▶ n. another term for PASTURE ROSE.

Car·o·line /'karə,līn; -lin/ ▶ adj. **1** (also **Car·o·le·an** /,karə'lēən/) of or relating to the reigns of Charles I and II of England. **2** another term for CAROLINGIAN. [17th C.: from med. L. *Carolus* 'Charles.']

Car·o·line Is·lands /'karə,līn/ (also **the Car·o·lines**) islands in the western Pacific Ocean, north of the equator, that form the Federated States of Micronesia.

Car·o·lin·gi·an /,karə'linj(ē)ən/ (also **Car·lo·vin·gi·an**) ▶ adj. of or relating to the Frankish dynasty, founded by Charlemagne's father (Pepin III), that ruled in western Europe from 750 to 987. ▶ n. a member of the Carolingian dynasty. [alt. of earlier CARLOVINGIAN.]

Car·o·lin·gi·an Ren·ais·sance a period during the reign of Charlemagne and his successors, marked by achievements in art, learning, and music.

car·om /'karəm/ ▶ n. Billiards another term for BILLIARD (sense 2). ▶ v. [intrans.] make a carom; strike and rebound. [18th C.: abbrev. of *carambole*, from Sp. *carambola*, appar. from *bola* 'ball.']

car·o·tene /'karə,tēn/ ▶ n. Chem. an orange or red plant pigment found in carrots and many other plant structures. It is a terpenoid hydrocarbon with several isomers, of which one (**beta carotene**) is important in the diet as a precursor of vitamin A. [19th C.: coined in Ger. from L. *carota* (see CARROT).]

ca·rot·e·noid /kəˈrätn,oid/ ▶ n. Chem. any of a class of mainly yellow, orange, or red fat-soluble pigments, including carotene, which give color to plant parts such as ripe tomatoes and autumn leaves. They are terpenoids based on a structure having the formula $C_{40}H_{56}$.

Ca·roth·ers /kəˈrəTHərz/, Wallace Hume (1896–1937), US chemist. He developed nylon (1935).

ca·rot·id /kəˈrätid/ ▶ adj. of, relating to, or denoting the two main arteries that carry blood to the head and neck. ▶ n. each of these arteries. [17th C.: ult. from Gk. *karōtides*, pl. of *karōtis* 'drowsiness,' from *karoun* 'stupefy.']

ca·rot·id bod·y ▶ n. a small mass of receptors in the carotid artery sensitive to chemical change in the blood.

ca·rouse /kəˈrouz/ ▶ v. [intrans.] drink plentiful amounts of alcohol and enjoy oneself with others in a noisy, lively way. ▶ n. a noisy, lively drinking party. — **ca·rous·al** /-zəl/ n. **ca·rous·er** n. [16th C.: orig. as adv. meaning 'all out,' from Ger. *gar aus trinken*; hence 'drink heavily.']

car·ou·sel /ˌkarəˈsel; ˈkarə,sel/ (also **car·rou·sel**) ▶ n. a merry-go-round. ■ a rotating machine or device, in particular a conveyor system at an airport from which arriving passengers collect their luggage. [17th C.: from Fr. *carrousel*, from Ital. *carosello*.]

carp[1] /kärp/ ▶ n. (pl. same) a deep-bodied freshwater fish of the minnow family, typically with barbels around the mouth. Carp are farmed for food in some parts of the world. [ME: from OFr. *carpe*, from late L. *carpa*.]

carp[2] ▶ v. [intrans.] complain or find fault continually, typically about trivial matters. — **carp·er** n. [ME: from ON *karpa* 'brag.']

Car·pac·cio /kärˈpäCH(ē)ō/, Vittore (*c.*1455–1525), Italian painter, noted for his religious subjects.

car·pac·cio /kärˈpäCH(ē)ō/ ▶ n. an hors d'oeuvre of thin slices of raw beef or fish served with a sauce. [Ital., named after Vittore CARPACCIO (from his use of red pigments).]

car·pal /ˈkärpəl/ ▶ n. any of the eight small bones forming the wrist. See CARPUS. ■ any of the equivalent bones in an animal's forelimb. ▶ adj. of or relating to these bones. [18th C.: from CARPUS.]

car·pal tun·nel syn·drome ▶ n. a painful condition of the hand and fingers caused by compression of a major nerve where it passes over the carpal bones, caused by repetitive movements over a long period, or by fluid retention, and characterized by sensations of tingling, numbness, or burning.

Car·pa·thi·an Moun·tains /kärˈpāTHēən/ (also **the Car·p·ath·ians**) mountains that extend southeast from Poland and the Czech Republic into Romania.

car·pe di·em /ˌkärpāˈdē,em/ ▶ exclam. used to urge someone to make the most of the present time and give little thought to the future. [19th C.: L., 'seize the day!']

car·pel /ˈkärpəl/ ▶ n. Bot. the female reproductive organ of a flower, consisting of an ovary, a stigma, and usually a style. It may occur singly or as one of a group. — **car·pel·lar·y** /-pə,lerē/ adj. [19th C.: from Fr. *carpelle* or mod. L. *carpellum*, from Gk. *karpos* 'fruit.']

Car·pen·tar·i·a, Gulf of /ˌkärpənˈterēə/ a large bay on the northern coast of Australia.

car·pen·ter /ˈkärpəntər/ ▶ n. a person who makes and repairs wooden objects and structures. ▶ v. [trans.] (usu. **be carpentered**) make by shaping wood. ■ [intrans.] do the work of a carpenter. [ME: from Anglo-Norman Fr., from OFr. *carpentier, charpentier*, from late L. *carpentarius (artifex)* 'carriage (maker),' from *carpentum* 'wagon,' of Gaulish origin.]

car·pen·ter ant ▶ n. a large ant (genus *Camponotus*) that burrows into wood to nest.

car·pen·ter bee ▶ n. a large solitary bee (genus *Xylocopa*) that nests in tunnels bored in dead wood or plant stems.

car·pen·try /ˈkärpəntrē/ ▶ n. the activity or occupation of making or repairing things in wood. ■ the work made or done by a carpenter.

car·pet /ˈkärpit/ ▶ n. a floor or stair covering made from thick woven fabric. ■ a large rug, typically an oriental one: *priceless Persian carpets.* ■ fig. a thick or soft expanse or layer of something: ***carpets of*** *snowdrops and crocuses.* ▶ v. (**-pet·ed, -pet·ing**) [trans.] (usu. **be carpeted**) cover (a floor or stairs) with a carpet. ■ fig. cover with a thick or soft expanse or layer of something: *the meadows are carpeted with flowers.*
– PHRASES **call someone on the carpet** informal severely reprimand a subordinate. [ME: from OFr. *carpite* or med. L. *carpita*, based on L. *carpere* 'pull to pieces.']

car·pet·bag /ˈkärpit,bag/ ▶ n. a traveling bag of a kind originally made of carpeting or carpetlike material. ▶ v. [intrans.] act as a carpetbagger.

car·pet·bag·ger /ˈkärpit,bagər/ ▶ n. derog. a political candidate who seeks election in an area where they have no local connections. ■ hist. a person from the northern states who went to the South after the Civil War to profit from the Reconstruction.

car·pet bee·tle ▶ n. a small beetle (genus *Anthrenus*, family Dermestidae) whose larva is destructive to carpets, fabrics, and other materials.

car·pet-bomb ▶ v. [trans.] [often as n.] (**carpet-bombing**) bomb (an area) intensively.

car·pet·ing /ˈkärpitiNG/ ▶ n. carpets collectively. ■ the fabric from which carpets are made.

car·pet slip·per ▶ n. a soft slipper whose upper part is made of wool or thick cloth.

car·pet sweep·er ▶ n. a manual household implement used for sweeping carpets, having a revolving brush or brushes and a receptacle for dust and dirt.

car·pet·weed /ˈkärpit,wēd/ ▶ n. any of various dicotyledonous, usually succulent plants (family Aizoaceae) that typically grow in warm, sandy regions, esp. *Mollugo verticillata*, a North American weed that forms a dense mat on the ground.

car phone ▶ n. a cellular phone designed for use in a motor vehicle.

carpo- ▶ comb. form fruit: *carpophore.*

car·pool /ˈkär,po͞ol/ ▶ n. an arrangement among people to make a regular journey in a single vehicle, typically with each person taking turns to drive the others. ■ a group of people with such an arrangement. ▶ v. [intrans.] form or participate in a carpool. — **car·pool·er** n.

car·po·phore /ˈkärpə,fôr/ ▶ n. Bot. (in a flower) an elongated axis that raises the stem of the pistil above the stamens. ■ (in a fungus) the stem of the fruiting body. [19th C.: from Gk. *karpos* 'fruit.']

car·port /ˈkär,pôrt/ ▶ n. a shelter for a car consisting of a roof supported on posts, built beside a house.

car·pus /ˈkärpəs/ ▶ n. (pl. **-pi** /-pī; -pē/) the group of small bones between the main part of the forelimb and the metacarpus in terrestrial vertebrates. The eight bones of the human carpus form the wrist and part of the hand, and are arranged in two rows. [ME: from mod. L., from Gk. *karpos* 'wrist.']

Car·rac·ci /käˈräCHē/ a family of Italian painters. Annibale (1560–1609), his brother Agostino (1557–1602), and their cousin Ludovico (1555–1619) established a teaching academy at Bologna.

car·rack /ˈkarək/ ▶ n. a large merchant ship of a kind that operated in European waters from the 14th to the 17th century. [ME: from OFr. *caraque*; based on Arab. *ḳarāḳir*, pl. of *ḳurḳūra*, a merchant ship.]

car·ra·geen /ˈkarə,gēn/ (also **car·ra·gheen** or **car·ra·geen moss**) ▶ n. an edible red shoreline seaweed (*Chondrus crispus*) found in both Eurasia and North America and used to produce carrageenan. Also called IRISH MOSS. [19th C.: from Irish *carraigín*.]

car·ra·gee·nan /ˌkarəˈgēnən/ ▶ n. a substance extracted from red and purple seaweeds, consisting of a mixture of polysaccharides. It is used as a thickening or emulsifying agent in food products. [1960s: from CARRAGEEN.]

Car·ra·ra /kəˈrärə; -ˈre(ə)rə/ a town in northwestern Italy, known for its white marble.

car·re·four /ˈkarə,fo͝or; ˌkarəˈfo͝or/ ▶ n. a crossroads. ■ a public square, plaza, or marketplace where roads converge.

Car·rel /käˈrel/, Alexis (1873–1944), French surgeon. He carried out some of the first organ transplants. Nobel Prize for Physiology or Medicine (1912).

car·rel /ˈkarəl/ ▶ n. a small cubicle with a desk for the use of a reader or student in a library. [16th C.: appar. rel. to CAROL 'ring.']

car·riage /ˈkarij/ ▶ n. **1** a means of conveyance, in particular: ■ a four-wheeled passenger vehicle pulled by two or more horses. ■ a baby carriage. ■ a wheeled support for moving a heavy object such as a gun. ■ Brit. a passenger car of a train: *the first-class carriages.* **2** the transporting of items or merchandise from one place to another. ■ the cost of such a procedure. **3** a moving part of a machine that carries other parts into the required position: *a typewriter carriage.* **4** [in sing.] a person's bearing or deportment: *her carriage was graceful.* [ME: from Old North. Fr. *cariage*, from *carier* (see CARRY).]

car·riage house ▶ n. a building for housing a horse-drawn carriage, typically such a building that has been converted into a dwelling.

car·riage re·turn ▶ n. another term for RETURN (sense 5).

car·riage trade ▶ n. archaic those of sufficient wealth or social standing to travel by private carriage. ■ informal or humorous elite clientele.

car·riage·way /ˈkarij,wā/ ▶ n. Brit. each of the two sides of a divided highway or expressway.

car·rick bend /ˈkarik/ ▶ n. a kind of knot used to join ropes, esp. hawsers, end to end, esp. so that they can go around a capstan without jamming. [19th C.: from BEND[2]: *carrick* perh. alt. of CARRACK.]

car·ri·er /ˈkarēər/ ▶ n. **1** a person or thing that carries, holds, or conveys something. **2** a person or company that undertakes the professional conveyance of goods or people. ■ a vessel or vehicle for transporting people or things, esp. goods freight. ■ an aircraft carrier. ■ a company that provides facilities for conveying telecommunications messages. **3** a person or animal that transmits a disease-causing organism to others. Typically, the carrier suffers no symptoms of the disease. ■ a person or other organism that possesses a particular gene whose effect is masked by a dominant allele, so that the associated characteristic is not expressed but may be passed to offspring. **4** a substance used to support or convey another substance such as a pigment, catalyst, or radioactive material. ■ Physics short for CHARGE CARRIER. ■ Biochem. a molecule that transfers a specified molecule or ion within the body, esp. across a cell membrane.

car·ri·er pig·eon ▶ n. a homing pigeon trained to carry messages tied to its neck or leg.

car·ri·er wave ▶ n. a high-frequency electromagnetic wave modulated in amplitude or frequency to convey a signal.

car·ri·ole /ˈkarēˌōl/ (also **car·i·ole**) ▶ **n.** **1** hist. a small open horse-drawn carriage for one person. **2** (in Canada) a kind of sled pulled by a horse or dogs. [18th C.: from Fr., from Ital. *carriuola*, dimin. of *carro*, from L. *carrum* (see CAR).]

car·ri·on /ˈkarēən/ ▶ **n.** the decaying flesh of dead animals. [ME: from Anglo-Norman Fr. *caroine, caroigne*, based on L. *caro* 'flesh.']

car·ri·on crow ▶ **n.** **1** a medium-sized, typically all-black crow (*Corvus corone*), common throughout much of Eurasia. **2** another name for BLACK VULTURE (sense 1).

car·ri·on flow·er ▶ **n.** **1** a North American climbing plant (genus *Smilax*, esp. *S. herbacea*) with small white flowers that smell of decaying flesh. **2** another term for STAPELIA.

Car·roll /ˈkarəl/, Lewis (1832–98), English writer; pen name of *Charles Lutwidge Dodgson*. He wrote the children's classics *Alice's Adventures in Wonderland* (1865) and *Through the Looking Glass* (1871).

Car·roll·ton /ˈkarəltən/ a city in northeastern Texas, north of Dallas; pop. 82,169.

car·ron·ade /ˌkarəˈnād/ ▶ **n.** hist. a short large-caliber cannon, formerly in naval use. [18th C.: from *Carron*, Scotland.]

car·rot /ˈkarət/ ▶ **n.** **1** a tapering orange-colored root eaten as a vegetable. **2** a cultivated plant (*Daucus carota*) of the parsley family with feathery leaves, which yields this vegetable. **3** an offer of something enticing as a means of persuasion. [with allusion to the proverbial encouragement of a donkey to move by enticing it with a carrot.] [15th C.: from Fr. *carotte*, from L. *carota*, from Gk. *karōton*.]

car·rot·y /ˈkarətē/ ▶ **adj.** (of a person's hair or whiskers) orange-red in color.

car·rou·sel ▶ **n.** var. of CAROUSEL.

car·ry /ˈkarē/ ▶ **v.** (**-ries, -ried**) [trans.] **1** support and move (someone or something) from one place to another: *medics were carrying a wounded man on a stretcher.* ■ transport: *the train service carries 20,000 passengers daily.* ■ have on one's person and take with one wherever one goes: *the money he was carrying was enough to pay the fine.* ■ conduct; transmit: *nerves carry visual information from the eyes.* ■ be infected with (a disease) and liable to transmit it to others: *ticks carry Lyme disease.* ■ transfer (a figure) to an adjacent column during an arithmetical operation (e.g., when a column of digits adds up to more than ten). **2** support the weight of: *the bridge can carry even the heaviest loads.* ■ be pregnant with: *carrying twins.* ■ (**carry oneself**) stand and move in a specified way: *she carried herself with assurance.* ■ assume or accept (responsibility or blame): *they must carry the responsibility for the mess they have gotten us into.* ■ be responsible for the effectiveness or success of: *they relied on dialogue to carry the plot.* **3** have as a feature or consequence: *each bike carries a ten-year guarantee.* **4** take or develop (an idea or activity) to a specified point: *he carried the criticism much further.* ■ (of a gun or similar weapon) propel (a missile) to a specified distance. ■ (of a ball) move or be hit a specified distance: *the balls carry well in that ballpark.* ■ Golf hit the ball over and beyond (a particular point). **5** (often **be carried**) approve (a proposed measure) by a majority of votes: *the resolution was carried two-to-one.* ■ persuade (colleagues or followers) to support one's policy: *he could not carry the cabinet.* ■ gain (a state or district) in an election. **6** (of a newspaper or a television or radio station) publish or broadcast: *the paper carried an account of the crisis.* ■ (of a retail outlet) keep a regular stock of (particular goods for sale): *this store carries phonograph equipment.* ■ have visible on the surface: *the product carries the "UL" symbol.* ■ be known by (a name): *some products carry the same names as overseas beers.* **7** [intrans.] (of a sound or a person's voice) be audible at a distance: *his voice carried clearly across the room.* ▶ **n.** (pl. **-ries**) [usu. in sing.] **1** an act of lifting and transporting something from one place to another: *we did a carry of equipment from the camp.* ■ Football an act of running with the ball from scrimmage. ■ the action of keeping something, esp. a gun, on one's person: *this pistol is the right choice for off-duty carry.* ■ hist. a place or route between navigable waters over which boats or supplies had to be carried. ■ the transfer of a figure into an adjacent column (or the equivalent part of a computer memory) during an arithmetical operation. ■ Finance the maintenance of an investment position in a securities market, esp. with regard to the costs or profits accruing. **2** (in golf) the distance a ball travels before reaching the ground. ■ (in golf) the distance a ball must travel to reach a certain destination. ■ the range of a gun or similar weapon.

– PHRASES **carry conviction** be convincing. **carry the day** be victorious or successful. **carry weight** be influential or important: *the report is expected to carry considerable weight with the administration.*

– PHRASAL VERBS **be/get carried away** lose self-control. **carry something forward** transfer figures to a new page or account. ■ keep something to use or deal with at a later time. **carry someone/something off** take someone or something away by force. ■ (of a disease) kill someone. **carry something off** win a prize: *she failed to carry off the gold medal.* ■ succeed in doing something difficult: *he could not have carried it off without government help.* **carry on 1** continue an activity or task. ■ continue to move in the same direction. **2** informal behave in a specified way: *they carry on in a very adult fashion.* **3** informal be engaged in a love affair, typically one of which the speaker disapproves. **carry something on** engage in an activity. **carry something out** perform a task or planned operation. **carry over** extend beyond the normal or original area or time of application. **carry something over** retain something and apply or deal with it in a new context. ■ postpone an event. ■ another way of saying CARRY SOMETHING FORWARD. **carry something through** bring a project to completion. ■ bring something safely out of difficulties. [ME: from Anglo-Norman Fr. and Old North. Fr. *carier*, based on L. *carrus* 'wheeled vehicle.']

car·ry·all /ˈkarēˌôl/ ▶ **n.** **1** a large bag or case. **2** hist. a light carriage. ■ a large car or truck with seats facing each other along the sides.

car·ry·ing ca·pac·i·ty ▶ **n.** the number or quantity of people or things that can be conveyed or held by a vehicle or container. ■ Ecol. the number of people, other living organisms, or crops that a region can support without environmental degradation.

car·ry·ing charge ▶ **n.** **1** Finance an expense or effective cost arising from unproductive assets such as stored goods. **2** a sum payable for the conveying of goods.

car·ry·ing-on ▶ **n.** (pl. **car·ry·ings-on**) excited or overwrought behavior. ■ improper or immoral behavior: *the couple's public carrying-on embarrassed passersby.*

car·ry-on ▶ **n.** a bag or suitcase suitable for taking onto an aircraft as hand luggage.

car·ry-out ▶ **adj. & n.** another term for TAKEOUT (sense 1).

car·ry·o·ver (also **car·ry-o·ver**) ▶ **n.** [usu. in sing.] something transferred or resulting from a previous situation or context.

car·sick /ˈkärˌsik/ ▶ **adj.** affected with nausea caused by the motion of a car or other vehicle in which one is traveling. — **car·sick·ness n.**

Car·son[1] /ˈkärsən/ a city in southwestern California, south of Los Angeles; pop. 83,995.

Car·son[2], Kit (1809–68), US frontiersman; full name *Christopher Houston Carson*. Famed as an expedition guide for John C. Frémont, he later was a US Indian agent in the Southwest 1853–61.

Car·son[3], Rachel Louise (1907–64), US biologist and environmentalist. Her book *Silent Spring* (1962) is considered seminal in the development of environmentalism.

Car·son Cit·y /ˌkärsən/ the capital of Nevada, in the western part of the state; pop. 52,457.

cart /kärt/ ▶ **n.** a strong open vehicle with two or four wheels, typically used for carrying loads and pulled by a horse. ■ a light two-wheeled open vehicle pulled by a single horse and used as a means of transportation. ■ a shallow open container on wheels that can be pulled or pushed by hand. ■ a shopping cart. ▶ **v.** [trans.] **1** (often **be carted**) convey or put in a cart or similar vehicle. **2** [with obj. and adverbial of direction] informal carry (a heavy or cumbersome object) somewhere with difficulty: *they carted the piano down three flights of stairs.* ■ remove or convey (someone) somewhere unceremoniously: *they carted off the refugees in the middle of the night.* — **cart·er n. cart·ful** /-ˌfo͝ol/ **n.** (pl. **-fuls**). [ME: from ON *kartr*, akin to OE *cræt* 'chariot.']

cart·age /ˈkärtij/ ▶ **n.** the transporting of something in a cart or other vehicle. ■ the cost of such a procedure.

Car·ta·ge·na /ˌkärtəˈhānə; -ˈgānə/ **1** a city in southeastern Spain; pop. 172,150. **2** a port, resort, and oil-refining center in northwestern Colombia, on the Caribbean Sea; pop. 688,300.

carte blanche /ˈkärt ˈblänsh; ˈblänch/ ▶ **n.** complete freedom to act as one wishes or thinks best. [17th C.: Fr., lit. 'blank paper.']

carte de vi·site /ˌkärt də viˈzēt/ ▶ **n.** (pl. **cartes de vi·site** pronunc. same) hist. a small photographic portrait of someone, mounted on a piece of card. [19th C.: Fr., 'visiting card.']

car·tel /kärˈtel/ ▶ **n.** an association of manufacturers or suppliers that maintains prices at a high level and restricts competition. ■ esp. hist. a coalition or cooperative arrangement between political parties to promote a mutual interest. [19th C.: from Ger. *Kartell*, from Fr. *cartel*, from Ital. *cartello*, dimin. of *carta*, from L. *carta* (see CARD[1]).]

car·tel·ize /kärˈtelˌīz; ˈkärtl-/ ▶ **v.** [trans.] (of manufacturers or suppliers) form a cartel in (an industry or trade).

Car·ter[1] /ˈkärtər/, Angela (1940–92), English writer. Her novels include *The Magic Toyshop* (1967).

Car·ter[2], Elliott Cook (1908–), US composer, noted for his innovative approach to meter.

Car·ter[3], Howard (1874–1939), English archaeologist. In 1922 he discovered the tomb of Tutankhamen.

Car·ter[4], Jimmy (1924–), 39th president of the US 1977–81; full name *James Earl Carter, Jr.* A Georgia Democrat, he served as state senator 1962–66 and as governor 1971–74. As president, he hosted the talks that led to the Camp David agreements of 1978. His post-presidency life has been dedicated to the causes of peace and human rights. Nobel Peace Price 2002.

Car·te·sian /kärˈtēzhən/ ▶ **adj.** of or relating to Descartes and his ideas. ▶ **n.** a follower of Descartes. — **Car·te·sian·ism n.** [17th C.: from mod. L. *Cartesianus*, from *Cartesius*, Latinized form of *Descartes*.]

Car·te·sian co·or·di·nates ▶ **plural n.** Math. numbers that indicate the location of a point relative to a fixed reference point (the origin), being its shortest perpendicular distances from two fixed axes (or three planes defined by three fixed axes) that intersect at right angles at the origin.

Car·te·sian prod·uct ▶ **n.** Math. the product of two sets: the product of set X and set Y is the set that contains all ordered pairs (x, y) for which x belongs to X and y belongs to Y.

Car·thage /ˈkärthij/ an ancient city on the coast of North Africa near present-day Tunis. It fought with Rome during the Punic Wars and was finally destroyed by the Romans in 146 BC. — **Car·tha·gin·i·an** /ˌkärthəˈjinēən/ **n. & adj.**

cart horse ▶ **n.** Brit. a large, strong horse suitable for heavy work.

Car·thu·sian /kär'TH(y)o͞ozHən/ ▶ **n.** a monk or nun of a contemplative order founded by St. Bruno in 1084. ▶ **adj.** of or relating to this order. [from med. L. *Carthusianus*, from *Cart(h)usia*, L. name of *Chartreuse*, France.]

Car·tier /kär'tyā; 'kärtē,ā/, Jacques (1491–1557), French explorer. He was the first to establish France's claim to North America.

Car·tier-Bres·son /kär'tyā brā'sôN/, Henri (1908–2004), French photographer. *The Decisive Moment* (1952), a collection of his Western and Asian photographs, established him as an internationally recognized photojournalist.

Car·tier Is·lands /'kärtē,ā/ see **Ashmore and Cartier Islands**.

car·ti·lage /'kärtl-ij/ ▶ **n.** firm, whitish, flexible connective tissue found in various forms in the larynx, in the external ear, and in the articulating surfaces of joints. ■ a particular structure made of this tissue. — **car·ti·lag·i·noid** /,kärtl'ajə,noid/ **adj.** [ME: from Fr., from L. *cartilago, cartilagin-*.]

car·ti·lag·i·nous /,kärtl'ajənəs/ ▶ **adj.** Anat. (of a structure) made of cartilage. ■ Zool. (of a vertebrate animal) having a skeleton of cartilage.

car·ti·lag·i·nous fish ▶ **n.** a fish of a class (Chondrichthyes) distinguished by having a skeleton of cartilage rather than bone, including the sharks, rays, and chimeras. Compare with **bony fish**.

Cart·land /'kärtlənd/, Dame Barbara (1901–2000), English writer; full name *Dame Mary Barbara Hamilton Cartland McCorquodale*. She authored more than 700 books, mostly romantic fiction.

cart·load /'kärt,lōd/ ▶ **n.** the amount held by a cart.

car·to·gram /'kärtə,gram/ ▶ **n.** a map on which statistical information is shown in diagrammatic form. [19th C.: from Fr. *cartogramme*, from *carte* 'map' + *-gramme* (from Gk. *gramma* 'thing written').]

car·tog·ra·phy /kär'tägrəfē/ ▶ **n.** the science or practice of drawing maps. — **car·tog·ra·pher n. car·to·graph·ic** /,kärtə'grafik/ **adj. car·to·graph·i·cal** /,kärtə'grafikəl/ **adj. car·to·graph·i·cal·ly** /,kärtə'grafik(ə)lē/ **adv.** [19th C.: from Fr. *cartographie*, from *carte* 'map' (see **card**[1]) + *-graphie* (see **-graphy**).]

car·ton /'kärtn/ ▶ **n.** a light box or container, typically one made of waxed cardboard or plastic in which drinks or foodstuffs are packaged. [19th C.: from Fr., from Ital. *cartone* (see **cartoon**).]

car·toon /kär'to͞on/ ▶ **n. 1** a simple drawing showing the features of its subjects in an exaggerated way, esp. in a newspaper or magazine. ■ a comic strip. ■ fig. a simplified or exaggerated version or interpretation of something: *this movie is a cartoon of life in America.* **2** a motion picture using animation techniques to photograph a sequence of drawings rather than real people or objects. **3** a full-size drawing made by an artist as a preliminary design for a painting or other work of art. ▶ **v.** [trans.] (usu. **be cartooned**) make a drawing of (someone) in a simplified or exaggerated way. — **car·toon·ish adj. car·toon·ist n. car·toon·y adj.** [16th C.: from Ital. *cartone*, from *carta*, from L. *carta, charta* (see **card**[1]).]

car·toon·ing /kär'to͞oniNG/ ▶ **n.** the activity or occupation of drawing cartoons for newspapers or magazines.

car·touche /kär'to͞osH/ ▶ **n.** a carved tablet or drawing representing a scroll with rolled-up ends, used ornamentally or bearing an inscription. ■ Archaeol. an oval or oblong enclosing a group of Egyptian hieroglyphs, typically representing the name and title of a monarch. [17th C.: from Fr. *cartouche*, from Ital. *cartoccio*, from *carta*, from L. *carta, charta* (see **card**[1]).]

car·tridge /'kärtrij/ ▶ **n.** a container holding a spool of photographic film, a quantity of ink, or other item or substance, designed for insertion into a mechanism. ■ a casing containing a charge and a bullet or shot for small arms or an explosive charge for blasting. ■ a component carrying the stylus on the pickup head of a record player. [16th C.: from Fr. *cartouche*, from Ital. *cartoccio* (see **cartouche**).]

car·tridge belt ▶ **n.** a belt with pockets or loops for cartridges of ammunition.

car·tridge clip ▶ **n.** a metal frame or container that holds cartridges for loading into an automatic rifle or pistol.

cart·wheel /'kärt,(h)wēl/ ▶ **n. 1** the wheel of a cart. **2** a circular sideways handspring with the arms and legs extended. ▶ **v.** [intrans.] perform such a handspring or handsprings.

Cart·wright /'kärt,rīt/, Edmund (1743–1823), English engineer. He invented the power loom.

car·un·cle /kə'rəNGkəl; 'kar,əNG-/ ▶ **n.** a fleshy outgrowth, in particular: ■ a wattle of a bird such as a turkey. ■ the red prominence at the inner corner of the eye. ■ any outgrowth from a seed near the micropyle, attractive to ants that aid the seed's dispersal. — **ca·run·cu·lar** /kə'rəNGkyələr/ **adj.** [16th C.: obs. Fr., from L. *caruncula*, from *caro, carn-* 'flesh.']

Ca·ru·so /kə'ro͞osō; -zō/, Enrico (1873–1921), Italian opera singer. He was the first major tenor to be recorded on phonograph records.

carve /kärv/ ▶ **v.** [trans.] **1** (often **be carved**) cut (a hard material) in order to produce an aesthetically pleasing object or design. ■ produce (an object) by cutting and shaping a hard material: *the altar was carved from a block of solid jade.* ■ produce (an inscription or design) by cutting into hard material: *an inscription was carved over the doorway.* **2** cut (cooked meat) into slices for eating. ■ cut (a slice of meat) from a larger piece.
– PHRASAL VERBS **carve something out 1** take something from a larger whole, esp. with difficulty: *carving out a 5 percent share of the vote.* **2** establish or create something through painstaking effort: *he managed to carve out a successful photographic career for himself.* **carve something up** divide something ruthlessly into separate areas or domains: *West Africa was carved up by the Europeans.* [OE *ceorfan* 'cut, carve,' of West Gmc. origin; rel. to Du. *kerven*.]

car·vel ▶ **n.** var. of **caravel**.

car·vel-built ▶ **adj.** (of a boat or ship) having hull planks that do not overlap. Compare with **lapstrake**.

carv·en /'kärvən/ archaic past participle of **carve**.

Car·ver /'kärvər/, George Washington (c.1864–1943), US botanist and agricultural researcher. Born into slavery, he developed many products from peanuts, sweet potatoes, and soybeans.

car·ver /'kärvər/ ▶ **n. 1** a person who carves wood, stone, ivory, coral, etc., esp. professionally. **2** a knife designed for slicing meat. **3** a person who cuts and serves the meat at a meal.

carv·ing /'kärviNG/ ▶ **n.** an object or design cut from a hard material as an artistic work.

carv·ing knife ▶ **n.** a knife with a long blade used for carving cooked meat into slices.

car wash (also **car·wash**) ▶ **n.** a building containing equipment for washing motor vehicles automatically.

Cary /'karē; 'ke(ə)rē/ a town in east central North Carolina; pop. 94,536.

car·y·at·id /,karē'atid; 'karēə,tid/ ▶ **n.** (pl. **car·y·at·ids** or **car·y·at·i·des** /,karē'atə,dēz/) Archit. a stone carving of a draped female figure, used as a supporting column of a Greek or Greek-style building. [16th C.: ult. from Gk. *karuatides*, pl. of *karuatis* 'priestess of Artemis at Caryae,' from *Karuai* (Caryae) in Laconia.]

caryatid

car·y·op·sis /,karē'äpsis/ ▶ **n.** (pl. **-ses** /-,sēz/) Bot. a dry one-seeded fruit in which the ovary wall is united with the seed coat, typical of grasses and cereals. [19th C.: from mod. L., from Gk. *karuon* 'nut' + *opsis* 'appearance.']

ca·sa·ba /kə'säbə/ (also **cas·sa·ba**) ▶ **n.** a winter melon of a variety with a wrinkled yellow rind and sweet flesh. [20th C.: named after *Kasaba* (now Turgutlu) in Turkey.]

Ca·sa·blan·ca /,käsə'bläNGkə; ,kasə'blaNGkə/ a city in Morocco, on the Atlantic coast; pop. 2,943,000.

Ca·sals /kə'sälz/, Pablo (1876–1973), Spanish cellist.

Cas·a·no·va /,kazə'nōvə; ,kasə-/, Giovanni Jacopo (1725–98), Italian adventurer; full name *Giovanni Jacopo Casanova de Seingalt*. His memoirs describe his sexual encounters and other exploits.

cas·bah /'kasbä/ (also **kas·bah**) ▶ **n.** the citadel of a North African city. ■ (**the casbah**) the area surrounding such a citadel, typically the old part of a city. [18th C.: Fr., from Arab. *ḳaṣaba* 'citadel.']

cas·ca·bel /'kaskə,bel/ ▶ **n.** a small red chili pepper of a mild-flavored variety. [17th C.: from Sp., based on med. L. *cascabellus* 'little bell.']

cas·cade /kas'kād/ ▶ **n. 1** a small waterfall, typically one of several that fall in stages down a steep rocky slope. ■ a mass of something that falls or hangs in copious quantities: *a cascade of pink bougainvillea.* ■ a large number or amount of something occurring in rapid succession: *a cascade of antiwar literature.* **2** a process whereby something, typically information, is successively passed on: [as adj.] *the more people who are well briefed, the wider the cascade effect.* ■ a succession of devices or stages in a process, each of which initiates the next. ▶ **v. 1** [no obj., with adverbial of direction] (of water) pour downward rapidly and in large quantities: *water was cascading down the stairs.* ■ fall or hang in copious or luxuriant quantities. **2** [trans.] arrange (a number of devices or objects) in a series or sequence. [17th C.: from Fr., from Ital. *cascata*, from *cascare* 'to fall,' based on L. *casus* (see **case**[1]).]

Cas·cade Range a range of mountains in western North America that extends from southern British Columbia to northern California. Its highest peak is Mount Rainier. It also includes an active volcano, Mount St. Helens.

cas·car·a /kas'karə/ (also **cascara sa·gra·da** /sə'grädə/) ▶ **n. 1** a purgative made from the dried bark of an American buckthorn. **2** (also **cascara buckthorn**) the tree (*Rhamnus purshiana*) from which this bark is obtained, native to the Pacific Northwest. [19th C.: from Sp. *cáscara (sagrada)*, lit. '(sacred) bark.']

Cas·co Bay /'kaskō/ an inlet of the Atlantic Ocean in southern Maine.

case[1] /kās/ ▶ **n. 1** an instance of a particular situation; an example of something occurring: *a case of mistaken identity.* ■ [usu. in sing.] the situation affecting or relating to a particular person or thing: *I'll make an exception in your case.* ■ an incident or set of circumstances under police investigation. **2** an instance of a disease, injury, or problem. ■ a person suffering from a disease or injury. ■ the circumstances or particular problem of a person who requires or receives professional attention: *the welfare office discussed Gerald's case.* ■ [with adj.] informal a person whose situation is regarded as pitiable or as having no chance of

improvement: *a very sad case.* **3** a legal action, esp. one to be decided in a court of law. ■ a set of facts or arguments supporting one side in such a legal action. ■ a legal action that has been decided and may be cited as a precedent. ■ a set of facts or arguments supporting one side of a debate or controversy: *the case against tobacco advertising.* **4** Gram. any of the inflected forms of a noun, adjective, or pronoun that express the semantic relation of the word to other words in the sentence: *the accusative case.* ■ such a relation whether indicated by inflection or not.
– PHRASES **as the case may be** according to the circumstances (used when referring to two or more possible alternatives). **be the case** be so. **in any case** whatever happens or may have happened. ■ used to confirm or support a point or idea just mentioned: *he wasn't allowed out yet, and in any case he wasn't well enough.* **(just) in case 1** as a provision against something happening or being true. **2** if it is true that: *in case you haven't figured it out, let me explain.* **in case of** in the event of (a particular situation). **in that case** if that happens or has happened; if that is the situation. **on** (or **off**) **someone's case** informal continually (or no longer) criticizing or harassing someone. [ME: from OFr. *cas,* from L. *casus* 'fall,' rel. to *cadere* 'to fall.']

case² ▶ n. a container designed to hold or protect something. ■ the outer protective covering of a natural or manufactured object. ■ Brit. an item of luggage; a suitcase. ■ a box containing bottles or cans of a beverage, sold as a unit. ■ Print. a partitioned container for loose metal type. ■ each of the two forms, capital or minuscule, in which a letter of the alphabet may be written or printed. See also UPPERCASE, LOWERCASE. ▶ v. [trans.] (usu. **be cased**) **1** surround in a material or substance: *the towers are of steel cased in granite.* ■ enclose in a protective container. **2** informal reconnoiter (a place) before carrying out a robbery: *I was casing the joint.* [ME: from OFr. *casse, chasse,* from L. *capsa,* rel. to *capere* 'to hold.']

ca·se·a·tion /ˌkāsēˈāsʜən/ ▶ n. Med. a form of necrosis characteristic of tuberculosis, in which diseased tissue forms a firm, dry mass like cheese in appearance. — **ca·se·ate** /ˈkāsēˌāt/ v. [19th C.: from med. L. *caseatio(n-),* from L. *caseus* 'cheese.']

case·book /ˈkāsˌbo͝ok/ ▶ n. a book containing a selection of source materials on a particular subject.

case·bound /ˈkāsˌbound/ ▶ adj. tech. (of a book) in a hard cover.

case-hard·en ▶ v. [trans.] [often as adj.] (**case-hardened**) harden the surface of (a material). ■ give a hard surface to (iron or steel) by carburizing it. ■ fig. make (someone) callous or tough.

case his·to·ry ▶ n. a record of a person's background or medical history kept by a doctor or social worker.

ca·sein /kāˈsēn; ˈkāsēən/ ▶ n. the main protein present in milk and (in coagulated form) in cheese. It is used in processed foods and in adhesives and paints. [19th C.: from L. *caseus* 'cheese.']

case knife ▶ n. a type of dagger carried in a sheath.

case law ▶ n. (also **caselaw**) the law as established by the outcome of former cases.

case·load /ˈkāsˌlōd/ ▶ n. the amount of work (in terms of number of cases) with which a doctor, lawyer, or social worker is concerned at one time.

case·mate /ˈkāsˌmāt/ ▶ n. hist. a small room in the thickness of the wall of a fortress, with embrasures from which guns or missiles can be fired. ■ an armored enclosure for guns on a warship. [16th C.: from Fr., from Ital. *casamatta,* perh. from Gk. *khasma, khasmat-* (see CHASM).]

case·ment /ˈkāsmənt/ ▶ n. a window or part of a window set on a hinge so that it opens like a door. [ME: from Anglo-Latin *cassimentum,* from *cassa,* from L. *capsa* (see CASE²).]

ca·se·ous /ˈkāsēəs/ ▶ adj. Med. characterized by caseation. [17th C.: from L. *caseus* 'cheese.']

case-sen·si·tive ▶ adj. Comput. (of a program or function) differentiating between capital and lowercase letters. ■ (of input) treated differently depending on whether it is in capitals or lowercase text.

case shot ▶ n. hist. bullets or pieces of metal in an iron case fired from a cannon.

case stud·y ▶ n. **1** a process or record of research in which detailed consideration is given to the development of a particular matter over a period of time. **2** a particular instance of something used or analyzed to illustrate a principle.

case sys·tem ▶ n. a method of teaching law that emphasizes the analysis and discussion of selected cases.

case·work /ˈkāsˌwərk/ ▶ n. social work directly concerned with individuals, esp. that involving a study of a person's family history and personal circumstances. — **case·work·er** n.

cash¹ /kasʜ/ ▶ n. money in coins or notes, as distinct from checks, money orders, or credit. ■ money in any form, esp. when immediately available. ▶ v. [trans.] give or obtain notes or coins for (a check or money order). ■ Bridge lead (a high card) so as to take the opportunity to win a trick.
– PHRASES **cash in one's chips** informal die.
– PHRASAL VERBS **cash in** informal take advantage of or exploit (a situation). **cash something in** convert an insurance policy, savings account, or other investment into money. **cash something out** another way of saying *CASH SOMETHING IN.* — **cash·a·ble** adj. [16th C.: from OFr. *casse* or Ital. *cassa* 'box,' from L. *capsa* (see CASE²).]

cash² ▶ n. (pl. same) hist. a coin of low value from China, southern India, or Southeast Asia. [16th C.: from Port. *caixa,* from Tamil *kāsu.*]

cash and car·ry ▶ n. a system of trading whereby goods are paid for in full at the time of purchase and taken away by the purchaser. ■ a store operating this system.

cash-back ▶ adj. denoting a form of incentive offered to buyers of certain products whereby they receive a cash refund after making their purchase.

cash bar ▶ n. a bar at a social function at which guests buy drinks rather than having them provided free.

cash·box /ˈkasʜˌbäks/ ▶ n. a lockable metal box for keeping cash in.

cash cow ▶ n. informal a business, investment, or product that provides a steady income or profit. ■ a person or organization that is a source of easy profit.

cash crop ▶ n. a crop produced for its commercial value rather than for use by the grower. — **cash crop·ping** n.

cash·ew /ˈkasʜˌo͞o; kəˈsʜo͞o/ ▶ n. **1** (also **cashew nut**) an edible kidney-shaped nut, rich in oil and protein. **2** (also **cashew tree**) a bushy tropical American tree (*Anacardium occidentale*), bearing cashew nuts singly at the tip of each swollen fruit. The **cashew family** (Anacardiaceae) also includes the mangoes, pistachios, sumacs, and poison ivy. [16th C.: from Port., from Tupi *acajú, cajú.*]

cash·ew ap·ple ▶ n. the swollen edible fruit of the cashew tree, from which the cashew nut hangs, sometimes used to make wine.

cash flow ▶ n. the total amount of money being transferred into and out of a business, esp. as affecting liquidity.

cash·ier¹ /kaˈsʜi(ə)r/ ▶ n. a person handling payments and receipts in a store, bank, or other business. [16th C.: from Du. *cassier* or Fr. *caissier,* from *caisse* 'cash.']

cash·ier² ▶ v. [trans.] (usu. **be cashiered**) dismiss someone from the armed forces in disgrace because of a serious misdemeanor: *he was found guilty and cashiered.* ■ informal suspend or dismiss someone from an office, position, or membership. [16th C.: from Flemish *kasseren* 'disband, revoke,' from Fr. *casser,* from L. *quassare* (see QUASH).]

cash·less /ˈkasʜləs/ ▶ adj. characterized by the exchange of funds by check, debit or credit card, or various electronic methods rather than the use of cash.

cash ma·chine ▶ n. another term for **ATM**.

cash·mere /ˈkazʜˌmi(ə)r; ˈkasʜ-/ ▶ n. fine soft wool obtained from the Kashmir goat. ■ woolen material made from or resembling such wool. [17th C.: early spelling of KASHMIR.]

cash·mere goat ▶ n. var. of KASHMIR GOAT.

cash on de·liv·er·y (abbr.: **COD**) ▶ n. the system of paying for goods when they are delivered.

cash·point /ˈkasʜˌpoint/ ▶ n. Brit. another term for AUTOMATED TELLER MACHINE.

cash reg·is·ter ▶ n. a business machine for regulating money transactions with customers. It typically has a compartmental drawer for cash and it totals, displays, and records the amount of each sale.

cash-strapped ▶ adj. informal extremely short of money.

cas·ing /ˈkāsiɴɢ/ ▶ n. **1** a cover or shell that protects or encloses something: *a waterproof casing.* **2** the frame around a door or window.

ca·si·no /kəˈsēnō/ ▶ n. (pl. **-nos**) a public room or building where gambling games are played. [18th C.: from Ital., dimin. of *casa* 'house,' from L. *casa* 'cottage.']

cask /kask/ ▶ n. a large barrellike container, used for storing liquids, typically alcoholic drinks. ■ the quantity of liquid held in such a container. [16th C.: from Fr. *casque* or Sp. *casco* 'helmet.']

cas·ket /ˈkaskit/ ▶ n. a small ornamental box or chest for holding jewels, letters, or other valuable objects. ■ a coffin. [ME: perh. ult. from OFr. *cassette,* dimin. of *casse* (see CASE²).]

Cas·lon /ˈkazlän; -lən/ ▶ n. a kind of roman typeface first introduced in the 18th century. [19th C.: named after William *Caslon* (1692–1766), Engl. type founder.]

Cas·ne·wydd /käsˈne-wiᴛʜ/ Welsh name for NEWPORT.

Cas·par /ˈkaspər/ one of the three Magi.

Cas·per /ˈkaspər/ a city in east central Wyoming, on the North Platte River; pop. 49,644.

Cas·pi·an Sea /ˈkaspēən/ a large landlocked salt lake, bounded by Russia, Kazakhstan, Turkmenistan, Azerbaijan, and Iran. The world's largest body of inland water, it is 92 feet (28 m) below sea level.

casque /kask/ ▶ n. **1** hist. a helmet. **2** Zool. a helmetlike structure, such as that on the bill of a hornbill. [17th C.: from Fr., from Sp. *casco.*]

cas·sa·ba ▶ n. var. of CASABA.

Cas·san·dra /kəˈsandrə/ Gk. Mythol. a daughter of Priam, who was given the gift of prophecy by Apollo. He caused her prophecies, though true, to be disbelieved. ■ [as n.] (**a Cassandra**) a prophet of disaster, esp. one who is disregarded.

Cas·satt /kəˈsat/, Mary (1844–1926), US painter. Her paintings include *Lady at the Tea Table* (1885).

cas·sa·va /kəˈsävə/ ▶ n. **1** the starchy tuberous root of a tropical tree, used as food in tropical countries. Also called MANIOC. ■ a starch or flour obtained from such a root. **2** the shrubby tree (genus *Manihot*) of the spurge family from which this root is obtained, native to tropical America. [16th C.: from Taino *casávi, cazábbi.*]

Cas·se·grain tel·e·scope /ˈkasəˌgrān/ ▶ n. a reflecting telescope in which light reflected from a convex secondary mirror passes through a hole in the primary mirror. [19th C.: named after N. *Cassegrain* (1625–1712), Fr. astronomer.]

cas·se·role /ˈkasəˌrōl/ ▶ n. a kind of stew cooked slowly in an oven. ■ a large covered dish used for cooking such stews. ▶ v. [trans.] cook (food) slowly in such a dish. [18th C.: from Fr., diminutive of *casse* 'spoonlike container,' based on Gk. *kuathion*, dimin. of *kuathos* 'cup.']

cas·sette /kə'set/ ▸ **n.** a sealed plastic unit containing a length of audiotape wound on a pair of spools, for insertion into a recorder or playback device. ■ a similar unit containing videotape, film, or other material for insertion into a machine. [18th C.: from Fr., dimin. of *casse* (see CASE[2]).]

cas·sette deck ▸ **n.** a unit in hi-fi equipment for playing or recording audiocassettes.

cas·sette play·er ▸ **n.** a machine for playing audiocassettes. ■ another term for CASSETTE RECORDER.

cas·sette re·cord·er ▸ **n.** a tape recorder for recording and playing back audiocassettes.

cas·sette tape ▸ **n.** a cassette of audiotape or videotape.

cas·sia /'kasHə/ ▸ **n.** **1** a tree, shrub, or herbaceous plant (genus *Cassia*) of the pea family, native to warm climates and yielding a variety of products, including medicinal drugs. **2** (also **cassia bark**) the aromatic bark of an eastern Asian tree (*Cinnamomum aromaticum*) of the laurel family, yielding an inferior kind of cinnamon. [from L., via Gk. from Heb. *qěṣīāh*.]

cas·sin·gle /kə'siNGgəl/ ▸ **n.** an audiocassette with a single piece of music, esp. popular music, on each side. [1970s: blend of CASSETTE and SINGLE.]

Cas·si·ni /ka'sēnē/, Giovanni Domenico (1625–1712), French astronomer; born in Italy. He discovered the gap (Cassini's division) in Saturn's rings.

Cas·si·o·pe·ia /ˌkasēə'pēə/ **1** Gk. Mythol. the wife of Cepheus, king of Ethiopia, and mother of Andromeda. **2** Astron. a constellation near the north celestial pole, recognizable by the conspicuous "W" pattern of its brightest stars.

cas·sis /ka'sēs/ (also **crème de cas·sis** /ˌkrem də ka'sēs/) ▸ **n.** a syrupy liqueur flavored with black currants and produced mainly in Burgundy. [19th C.: Fr., lit. 'black currant,' appar. from L. *cassia* (see CASSIA).]

cas·sit·er·ite /kə'sitəˌrīt/ ▸ **n.** a reddish, brownish, or yellowish mineral consisting of tin dioxide. It is the main ore of tin. [19th C.: from Gk. *kassiteros* 'tin.']

Cas·sius /'kasHəs; 'kasēəs/, Gaius (died 42 BC), Roman general; full name *Gaius Cassius Longinus*. He took part in the assassination of Julius Caesar in 44 BC.

cas·sock /'kasək/ ▸ **n.** a full-length garment of a single color worn by certain Christian clergy, members of church choirs, and acolytes. — **cas·socked** **adj.** [16th C.: from Fr. *casaque* 'long coat,' from Ital. *casacca* 'riding coat,' prob. from Turkic *kazak* 'vagabond.']

cassock

cas·sou·let /ˌkasə'lā/ ▸ **n.** a stew made with meat and beans. [Fr., dimin. of dial. *cassolo* 'stewpan,' from Old Provençal *cassa* 'pan.']

cas·so·war·y /'kasəˌwerē/ ▸ **n.** (pl. **-war·ies**) a large flightless bird (genus *Casuarius*, family Casuariidae) native mainly to the forests of New Guinea. Its three species include the **double-wattled cassowary** (*C. casuarius*). [17th C.: from Malay *kesuari*.]

cassowary

cast[1] /kast/ ▸ **v.** (past **cast** /kast/) **1** [with obj., usu. with adverbial of direction] throw (something) forcefully in a specified direction: *lemmings cast themselves off the cliff* | fig. *some individuals are cast out from the group.* ■ throw (something) so as to cause it to spread over an area: *the fishermen cast a net around a school of tuna* | fig. *he cast his net far and wide for evidence.* ■ direct (one's eyes or a look) at something: *she cast down her eyes.* ■ [trans.] throw the hooked and baited end of (a fishing line) out into the water. ■ [trans.] register (a vote): *residents cast their votes.* ■ [trans.] Hunting let loose (hounds) on a scent. ■ [intrans.] Hunting (of a dog) search in different directions for a lost scent: *the dog cast for the vanished rabbit.* ■ [trans.] let down (an anchor or sounding line). **2** [with obj. and adverbial of place] cause (light or shadow) to appear on a surface: *the moon cast a pale light over the cottages* | fig. *costs were already casting a shadow over the program.* ■ cause (uncertainty or disparagement) to be associated with something: *I do not wish to cast aspersions on your honesty.* ■ cause (a magic spell) to take effect: *the witch cast a spell on her to turn her into a beast* | fig. *the city casts a spell on the visitor.* **3** [with obj. and adverbial of direction] discard: *the issue was cast from the list of concerns.* ■ shed (skin or horns) in the process of growth: *the antlers are cast each year.* ■ (of a horse) lose (a shoe). **4** [trans.] shape (metal or other material) by pouring it into a mold while molten. ■ make (a molded object) in this way: *a bell was cast for the church.* ■ arrange and present in a specified form or style: *he issued statements cast in tones of reason.* ■ calculate and record details of (a horoscope). ▸ **n.** **1** an object made by shaping molten metal or similar material in a mold. ■ (also **plaster cast**) a mold used to make such an object. ■ (also **plaster cast**) a bandage stiffened with plaster of Paris, molded to the shape of a limb that is broken and used to support and protect it. **2** an act of throwing something forcefully. ■ archaic at dice, a throw or a number thrown. ■ Fishing a throw of a fishing line. **3** [in sing.] [with adj.] the form or appearance of something, esp. someone's features: *she had a masculine cast of countenance.* ■ the character of something: *this question is for minds of a philosophical cast.* ■ the overall appearance of someone's skin or hair as determined by a tinge of a particular color: *the colors he wore emphasized the olive cast of his skin.* **4** a slight squint: *a cast in one eye.* **5** a convoluted mass of earth or sand ejected onto the surface by a burrowing worm. ■ a pellet regurgitated by a hawk or owl.

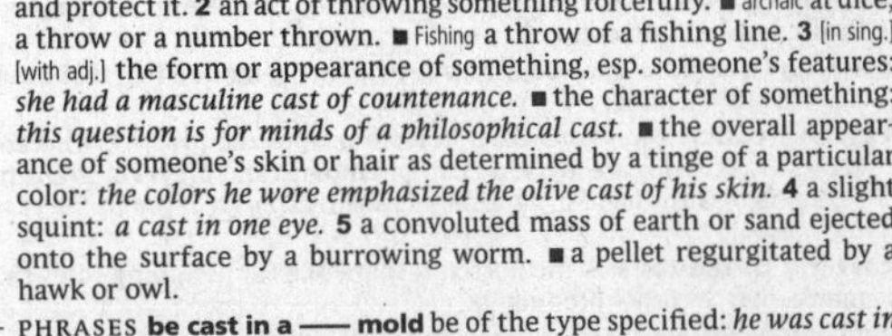

– PHRASES **be cast in a —— mold** be of the type specified: *he was cast in a cautious mold.* **cast one's eyes over** have a quick appraising look at. **cast one's mind back** think back to a particular event or time.

– PHRASAL VERBS **cast about** (or **around**) search far and wide (physically or mentally). **cast aside** discard or reject. **be cast away** be stranded after a shipwreck. **be cast down** feel depressed. **cast off** (or **cast something off**) **1** Knitting take the stitches off the needle by looping each over the next to finish the edge. **2** set a boat or ship free from its moorings. *Jack cast off our moorings.* ■ (**cast off**) (of a boat or ship) be set free from its moorings. **3** let loose a hunting hound or hawk. **4** Print. estimate the space that will be taken in print by manuscript copy. **cast someone off** exclude someone from a relationship. **cast on** (or **cast something on**) Knitting make the first row of a specified number of loops on the needle: *cast on and knit a few rows of stockinette stitch.* **cast something up 1** (of the sea) deposit something on the shore. **2** dated add up figures. [ME: from ON *kasta* 'to throw.']

cast[2] ▸ **n.** the actors taking part in a play, movie, or other production. ▸ **v.** (past and past part. **cast**) [trans.] assign a part in a play, movie, or other production to (an actor): *he was cast as the Spanish dancer* | fig. *a campaign for good nutrition, in which red meat is cast as the enemy.* ■ allocate parts in (a play, movie, or other production). [17th C.: from CAST[1].]

cas·ta·nets /ˌkastə'nets/ ▸ **plural n.** small concave pieces of wood, ivory, or plastic, joined in pairs by a cord and clicked together by the fingers as a rhythmic accompaniment to Spanish dancing. [17th C.: from Sp. *castañeta*, dimin. of *castaña*, from L. *castanea* 'chestnut.']

castanets

cast·a·way /'kastəˌwā/ ▸ **n.** a person who has been shipwrecked and stranded in an isolated place. ■ an outcast.

caste /kast/ ▸ **n.** each of the hereditary classes of Hindu society, distinguished by relative degrees of ritual purity or pollution and of social status. There are four basic classes: Brahman (priest), Kshatriya (warrior), Vaishya (merchant or farmer), and Shudra (laborer) | *a man of high caste.* ■ the system of dividing society into such classes. ■ any class or group of people who inherit exclusive privileges or are perceived as socially distinct. ■ Entomol. (in some social insects) a physically distinct individual with a particular function in the society. [16th C.: from Sp. and Port. *casta* 'race,' fem. of *casto* 'pure,' from L. *castus* 'chaste.']

Cas·tel Gan·dol·fo /'kästel gän'dôlfō; -'dälfō/ the summer residence of the pope, on Lake Albano.

cas·tel·lan /'kastələn/ ▸ **n.** hist. the governor of a castle. [ME: from Old North. Fr. *castelain*, from med. L. *castellanus*, from L. *castellum* (see CASTLE).]

cas·tel·lat·ed /'kastəˌlātid/ ▸ **adj.** **1** having battlements. ■ (of a nut or other mechanical part) having grooves or slots on its upper face. **2** having a castle or several castles. [17th C.: from med. L. *castellatus*, from L. *castellum* (see CASTLE).]

cas·tel·la·tions /ˌkastə'lāsHənz/ ▸ **plural n.** defensive or decorative parapets with regularly spaced notches; battlements. ■ (**castellation**) the use or building of such parapets.

cast·er /'kastər/ ▸ **n.** **1** a person who casts something or a machine for casting something. **2** Fishing a fly pupa used as bait. **3** each of a set of small wheels, free to swivel in any direction, fixed to the legs or base of a heavy piece of furniture so that it can be moved easily. **4** the angular inclination of a steering pivot or kingpin. **5** a small container with holes in the top, esp. one used for sprinkling sugar or pepper.

cas·ti·gate /'kastəˌgāt/ ▸ **v.** [trans.] formal reprimand (someone) severely. — **cas·ti·ga·tion** /ˌkastə'gāsHən/ **n.** **cas·ti·ga·tor** /-ˌgātər/ **n.** **cas·ti·ga·to·ry** /-gəˌtôrē/ **adj.** [17th C.: from L. *castigare* 'reprove,' from *castus* 'pure.']

Cas·tile /ka'stēl/ a region in central Spain, formerly an independent Spanish kingdom.

Cas·tile soap ▸ **n.** fine, hard white or mottled soap made with olive oil and sodium hydroxide. [ME: named after CASTILE.]

Cas·til·ian /kə'stilyən/ ▸ **n.** **1** a native of Castile. **2** the dialect of Spanish spoken in Castile, which is standard Spanish. ▸ **adj.** of or relating to Castile, Castilians, or the Castilian form of Spanish.

Cas·til·la-La Man·cha /kä'stē(l)yä lä 'mäncHə/ an autonomous region in central Spain; capital, Toledo.

PRONUNCIATION KEY ə *ago, up*; ər *over, fur*; a *hat*; ā *ate*; ä *car*; e *let*; ē *see*; i *fit*; ī *by*; NG *sing*; ō *go*; ô *law, for*; oi *toy*; o͝o *good*; o͞o *goo*; ou *out*; TH *thin*; T͟H *then*; ZH *vision*

Cas·til·la-Le·ón /kä'stē(l)yä lā'ōn/ an autonomous region in northern Spain; capital, Valladolid.

cast·ing /'kastiNG/ ▶n. an object made by pouring molten metal or other material into a mold.

cast·ing couch ▶n. informal used in reference to the practice whereby actors or actresses are awarded parts in movies and plays for granting sexual favors to the casting director: *she was no stranger to the casting couch.*

cast·ing di·rec·tor ▶n. the person responsible for assigning roles in a movie, play, or other production.

cast·ing vote ▶n. an extra vote given by a chairperson to decide an issue when the votes on each side are equal.

cast i·ron ▶n. a hard, brittle alloy of iron and carbon that can be readily cast in a mold and contains a higher proportion of carbon than steel does (typically 2.0–4.3 percent). ■ [as adj.] fig. firm and unchangeable.

cas·tle /'kasəl/ ▶n. a large building or group of buildings fortified against attack with thick walls, battlements and towers. ■ a magnificent mansion, esp. the home or former home of a member of the nobility. ■ Chess, informal old-fashioned term for ROOK[2]. ▶v. [intrans.] [often as n.] (**castling**) Chess make a special move in which the king is transferred from its original square two squares along the back rank toward the corner square of a rook, which is then transferred to the square passed over by the king. ■ [trans.] move (the king) in this way.
– PHRASES **castles in the air** (or **in Spain**) visionary unattainable schemes; daydreams. —**cas·tled** /'kasəld/ **adj.** (archaic). [OE: from Anglo-Norman Fr. and Old North. Fr. *castel*, from L. *castellum*, dimin. of *castrum* 'fort.']

cast·off /'kast,ôf/ ▶adj. no longer wanted; abandoned or discarded. ▶n. (usu. **castoffs**) something, esp. a garment, that is no longer wanted.

Cas·tor /'kastər/ **1** Gk. Mythol. the twin brother of Pollux. See DIOSCURI. **2** Astron. the second brightest star in the constellation Gemini, close to Pollux.

cas·tor /'kastər/ ▶n. a reddish-brown oily substance secreted by beavers, used in medicine and perfumes. [ME ('beaver'): ult. from Gk. *kastōr*.]

cas·tor bean ▶n. the seed of the castor-oil plant. It contains a number of poisonous compounds, esp. ricin, as well as castor oil. ■ the castor-oil plant.

cas·tor oil ▶n. a pale yellow oil obtained from castor beans, used as a purgative and a lubricant and in manufacturing oil-based products.

cas·tor-oil plant ▶n. an African shrub (*Ricinus communis*) of the spurge family with lobed serrated leaves, yielding the seeds from which castor oil is obtained.

cas·trate /'kasträt/ ▶v. [trans.] remove the testicles of (a male animal or man). ■ fig. deprive of power, vitality, or vigor. ▶n. a man or male animal whose testicles have been removed. —**cas·tra·tion** /ka'strāsHən/ **n.** **cas·tra·tor** /-trātər/ **n.** [16th C.: from L. *castrare*.]

cas·tra·to /kas'trätō/ ▶n. (pl. **-ti** /-tē/) hist. a male singer castrated in boyhood so as to retain a soprano or alto voice. [18th C.: from Ital., past part. of *castrare* (see CASTRATE).]

Cas·tries /kas'trē; 'kästrēs/ the capital of St. Lucia, a seaport on the northwestern coast; pop. 14,055.

Cas·tro /'kastrō/, Fidel (1927–), president of Cuba 1976– . After overthrowing President Batista, he set up a communist regime that survived the abortive Bay of Pigs invasion, the Cuban Missile Crisis, and the collapse of the Soviet bloc.

Cas·tro·ism /'kastrō,izəm/ ▶n. the political principles or actions of Fidel Castro or his adherents or imitators. —**Cas·tro·ist** **n. & adj.** **Cas·tro·ite** /-,īt/ **n. & adj.**

ca·su·al /'kazHōōəl/ ▶adj. **1** relaxed and unconcerned. ■ made or done without much thought or premeditation. ■ done or acting in a desultory way. ■ done or acting without sufficient care or thoroughness. **2** not regular or permanent: *casual jobs.* ■ (of a worker) employed on a temporary or irregular basis: *casual staff.* ■ (of a sexual relationship or encounter) occurring between people who are not regular or established sexual partners. **3** [attrib.] happening by chance; accidental. **4** without formality of style, manner, or procedure, in particular: ■ (of clothes or a style of dress) suitable for everyday wear rather than formal occasions. ■ (of a social event) not characterized by particular social conventions. ■ (of a place or environment) relaxed and friendly. ▶n. **1** a person who does something irregularly: *a number of casuals became regular customers.* ■ a worker employed on an irregular or temporary basis. **2** (**casuals**) clothes or shoes suitable for everyday wear rather than formal occasions. —**cas·u·al·ly** **adv.** **cas·u·al·ness** **n.** [ME: from OFr. *casuel* and L. *casualis*, from *casus* 'fall' (see CASE[1]).]

cas·u·al Fri·day ▶n. Friday as a day when office workers are allowed to dress more casually than usual.

cas·u·al·ty /'kazH(ōō)əltē/ ▶n. (pl. **-ties**) a person killed or injured in a war or accident. ■ fig. a person or thing badly affected by an event or situation: *the building industry has been one of the casualties of the recession.* ■ (chiefly in insurance) an accident, mishap, or disaster.

ca·su·a·ri·na /,kazHōōə'rēnə/ ▶n. a tree (genus *Casuarina*, family Casuarinaceae) with slender, jointed, drooping twigs that resemble horsetails and bear tiny scalelike leaves, native to Australia and Southeast Asia. [from mod. L. *casuarius* 'cassowary' (from the resemblance of the branches to the bird's feathers).]

cas·u·ist /'kazHōōist/ ▶n. a person who uses clever but unsound reasoning, esp. in relation to moral questions. ■ a person who resolves moral problems by the application of theoretical rules to particular instances. —**cas·u·is·tic** /,kazHōō'istik/ **adj.** **cas·u·is·ti·cal** /,kazHōō'istikəl/ **adj.** **cas·u·is·ti·cal·ly** /,kazHə'wistik(ə)lē/ **adv.** [17th C.: from Fr. *casuiste*, from Sp. *casuista*, from L. *casus* (see CASE[1]).]

cas·u·ist·ry /'kazHōōəstrē/ ▶n. the use of clever but unsound reasoning, esp. in relation to moral questions; sophistry. ■ the resolving of moral problems by the application of theoretical rules to particular instances.

ca·sus bel·li /'käsəs 'belē; 'kāsəs 'belī/ ▶n. (pl. same) an act or situation provoking or justifying war. [L., from *casus* (see CASE[1]) and *belli*, genitive of *bellum* 'war.']

CAT /'kat/ ▶abbr. ■ clear air turbulence. ■ computer-assisted (or -aided) testing. ■ Med. computerized axial tomography: [as adj.] *a CAT scan.*

cat[1] /kat/ ▶n. **1** a small domesticated carnivorous mammal (*Felis catus*), with soft fur, a short snout, and retractile claws. The **cat family** (Felidae) also includes the ocelot, serval, margay, lynx, and the big cats. ■ a wild animal of the cat family. See also BIG CAT. ■ used in names of catlike animals of other families, e.g., **ring-tailed cat**. ■ hist. short for CAT-O'-NINE-TAILS. ■ short for CATFISH. ■ short for CATHEAD. ■ short for CATBOAT. **2** informal (particularly among jazz enthusiasts) a person, esp. a man. ▶v. (**cat·ted**, **cat·ting**) [trans.] Naut. raise (an anchor) from the surface of the water to the cathead.
– PHRASES **a cat may look at a king** proverb even a person of low status or importance has rights. **has the cat got your tongue?** said to someone who, when expected to speak, remains silent. **let the cat out of the bag** informal reveal a secret carelessly or by mistake. **like a cat on a hot tin roof** informal very agitated or anxious. [OE *catt*, *catte*, of Gmc. origin; rel. to Ger. *Katze*.]

cat[2] ▶n. short for CATALYTIC CONVERTER.

cat[3] ▶n. short for CATAMARAN.

cata- (also **cat-**) ▶prefix **1** down; downward: *catadromous* | *cataract.* **2** wrongly; badly: *catachresis* | *catastrophe.* **3** completely; thoroughly: *catechize.* **4** against: *catapult.* [from Gk. *kata* 'down.']

ca·tab·o·lism /kə'tabə,lizəm/ ▶n. Biol. the breakdown of complex molecules in living organisms to form simpler ones, together with the release of energy; destructive metabolism. —**cat·a·bol·ic** /,katə'bälik/ **adj.** **ca·tab·o·lize** /-,līz/ **v.** [19th C.: from Gk. *katabolē* 'throwing down,' from *kata-* + *ballein* 'to throw.']

ca·tab·o·lite /kə'tabə,līt/ ▶n. Biochem. a product of catabolism.

cat·a·chre·sis /,katə'krēsis/ ▶n. (pl. **-ses** /-sēz/) the use of a word in a way that is not correct, for example, the use of *mitigate* for *militate*. —**cat·a·chres·tic** /-'krestik/ **adj.** [16th C.: from L., from Gk. *katakhrēsis*, from *katakhrēsthai* 'misuse,' from *kata-* 'down' + *khrēsthai* 'use.']

cat·a·clysm /'katə,klizəm/ ▶n. a large-scale and violent event in the natural world. ■ a sudden violent upheaval, esp. in a political or social context. —**cat·a·clys·mal** /,katə'klizməl/ **adj.** **cat·a·clys·mic** /,katə'klizmik/ **adj.** **cat·a·clys·mi·cal·ly** /-mik(ə)lē/ **adv.** [17th C.: from Fr. *cataclysme*, via L. from Gk. *kataklusmos* 'deluge,' from *kata-* 'down' + *kluzein* 'to wash.']

cat·a·comb /'katə,kōm/ ▶n. (usu. **catacombs**) an underground cemetery consisting of a subterranean gallery with recesses for tombs, as constructed by the ancient Romans. ■ an underground construction resembling or compared to such a cemetery. [OE, from late L. *catacumbas*.]

cat·a·di·op·tric /,katədī'äptrik/ ▶adj. Optics denoting an optical system that involves both the reflecting and refracting of light, in order to reduce aberration.

ca·tad·ro·mous /kə'tadrəməs/ ▶adj. Zool. (of a fish such as the eel) migrating down rivers to the sea to spawn. The opposite of ANADROMOUS. [19th C.: from CATA- + Gk. *dromos* 'running.']

cat·a·falque /'katə,fô(l)k; -,falk/ ▶n. a decorated wooden framework supporting the coffin of a distinguished person during a funeral or while lying in state. [17th C.: from Fr., from Ital. *catafalco*.]

Cat·a·lan /'katl,an; 'katl-ən/ ▶n. **1** a native of Catalonia. **2** a Romance language, widely spoken in Catalonia (where it has official status) and in Andorra, the Balearic Islands, and parts of southern France. ▶adj. of or relating to Catalonia, its people, or its language. [from Fr., from Sp. *catalán*, rel. to Catalan *català* 'Catalan,' *Catalunya* 'Catalonia.']

cat·a·lase /'katl,ās; -,āz/ ▶n. Biochem. an enzyme that catalyzes the reduction of hydrogen peroxide. [20th C.: from CATALYSIS + -ASE.]

cat·a·lec·tic /,katl'ektik/ Pros. ▶adj. (of a metrical line of verse) lacking one syllable in the last foot. ▶n. a line lacking a syllable in the last foot. [16th C.: from late L. *catalecticus*, from Gk. *katalēktikos*, from *katalēgein* 'leave off.']

cat·a·lep·sy /'katl,epsē/ ▶n. a medical condition characterized by a trance or seizure with a loss of sensation and consciousness and by rigidity of the body. —**cat·a·lep·tic** /,katl'eptik/ **adj. & n.** [ME: ult. from Gk. *katalēpsis*, from *katalambanein* 'seize upon.']

cat·a·lex·is /,katl'eksis/ ▶n. the absence of a syllable in the last foot of a line or verse.

cat·a·log /'katl,ôg; -,äg/ (also **cat·a·logue**) ▶n. a complete list of items, typically in alphabetical or other systematic order, in particular: ■ a list of all the books or resources in a library. ■ a publication containing details and often photographs of items for sale. ■ a descriptive list of works of art in an exhibition or collection giving detailed comments and explanations. ■ a list of courses offered by a university or college. ■ [in sing.] a series of unfortunate or bad things: *a catalog of dismal failures.* ▶v. (**-logs**, **-loged**, **-log·ing** ; also **-logues**, **-logued**, **-logu·ing**) [trans.] make a systematic list of (items of the same type). ■ enter (an item) in such a list. ■ list (similar situations, qualities, or events) in succession: *the report catalogs dangerous work practices in the company.* — **cat·a·log·er** (also **cat·a·logu·er**) **n.** [ME: via OFr. from late L. *catalogus*, from Gk. *katalogos*, from *katalegein* 'pick out.']

cat·a·logue rai·son·né /ˈkatl,ôg ,rāzəˈnā; -,äg/ ▶ **n.** (pl. **cat·a·logues rai·son·nés** /ˈkatl,ôg(z) ,rāzəˈnā; -,äg(z)/) a descriptive catalog of works of art with explanations and scholarly comments. [18th C.: Fr., lit. 'explained catalog.']

Cat·a·lo·ni·a /,katlˈōnēə/ an autonomous region in northeastern Spain; capital, Barcelona. The region has a strong separatist tradition. Catalan name CATALUNYA; Spanish name CATALUÑA.

ca·tal·pa /kəˈtalpə/ ▶ **n.** a tree (genus *Catalpa*, family Bignoniaceae) with large heart-shaped leaves, clusters of trumpet-shaped flowers, and long, slender beanlike seedpods, native to North America and eastern Asia. [from Gk.]

ca·tal·y·sis /kəˈtaləsis/ ▶ **n.** Chem. Biochem. the acceleration of a chemical reaction by a catalyst. [19th C.: from mod. L., from Gk. *katalusis*, from *kataluein* 'dissolve,' from *kata-* 'down' + *luein* 'loosen.']

cat·a·lyst /ˈkatl-ist/ ▶ **n.** a substance that increases the rate of a chemical reaction without itself undergoing any permanent chemical change. ■ fig. a person or thing that precipitates an event. — **cat·a·lyt·ic** /,katlˈitik/ **adj.** **cat·a·lyt·i·cal·ly** /-ik(ə)lē/ **adv.**

cat·a·lyt·ic con·vert·er ▶ **n.** a device in the exhaust system of a motor vehicle, containing a catalyst for converting pollutant gases into less harmful ones.

cat·a·lyze /ˈkatl,īz/ (Brit. **cat·a·lyse**) ▶ **v.** [trans.] cause or accelerate (a reaction) by acting as a catalyst. ■ fig. cause (an action or process) to begin.

cat·a·ma·ran /,katəməˈran; ˈkatəmə,ran/ ▶ **n.** a yacht or other boat with twin hulls in parallel. [17th C.: from Tamil *kaṭṭumaram*, lit. 'tied wood.']

catamaran

Cat·a·mar·ca /,kätəˈmärkə; ,katə-/ a city in northwestern Argentina; pop. 110,000.

cat·a·mite /ˈkatə,mīt/ ▶ **n.** archaic a boy kept for homosexual practices. [16th C.: from L. *catamitus*, via Etruscan from Gk. *Ganumēdēs* (see GANYMEDE).]

cat·a·mount /ˈkatə,mount/ (also **cat·a·moun·tain** /-,mountən/) ▶ **n.** a medium-sized or large wild cat, esp. a cougar. [ME: from *cat of the mountain*.]

Ca·ta·nia /kəˈtänyə; -ˈtān-; -ˈtānēə/ a city in southern Italy, at the foot of Mount Etna, in Sicily; pop. 364,180.

Ca·tan·za·ro /,kätän(d)ˈzärō/ a city in southern Italy, in the Calabria region; pop. 104,000.

ca·taph·o·ra /kəˈtafərə/ ▶ **n.** Gram. the use of a word or phrase that refers to or stands for a later word or phrase (e.g., the pronoun *he* in *he may be 37, but Jeff behaves like a teenager*). Compare with ANAPHORA. — **cat·a·phor·ic** /,katəˈfôrik/ **adj.** **cat·a·phor·i·cal·ly** /,katəˈfôrik(ə)lē/ **adv.** [1970s: from CATA- on the pattern of *anaphora*.]

cat·a·pho·re·sis /,katəfəˈrēsis/ ▶ **n.** another term for ELECTROPHORESIS.

cat·a·plasm /ˈkatə,plazəm/ ▶ **n.** another term for POULTICE.

cat·a·plex·y /ˈkatə,pleksē/ ▶ **n.** a medical condition in which strong emotion causes a person to suffer sudden physical collapse though remaining conscious. — **cat·a·plec·tic** /,katəˈplektik/ **adj.** [19th C.: from Gk. *kataplēxis* 'stupefaction,' from *kataplessein*, from *kata-* 'down' + *plēssein* 'strike.']

cat·a·pult /ˈkatə,pəlt; -,po͝olt/ ▶ **n.** a device in which accumulated tension is suddenly released to hurl an object some distance, in particular: ■ hist. a military machine worked by a lever and ropes for hurling large stones or other missiles. ■ a mechanical device for launching a glider or other aircraft, esp. from the deck of a ship. ■ esp. Brit. a slingshot. ▶ **v.** [with obj. and adverbial of direction] hurl or launch (something) in a specified direction with or as if with a catapult: *the explosion catapulted the car 30 yards along the road* | fig. *their music catapulted them to the top of the charts.* ■ [no obj., with adverbial of direction] move suddenly or at great speed as though hurled by a catapult: *the horse catapulted away from the fence.* [16th C.: from Fr. *catapulte* or L. *catapulta*, from Gk. *katapeltēs*, from *kata-* 'down' + *pallein* 'hurl.']

cat·a·ract /ˈkatə,rakt/ ▶ **n.** **1** a large waterfall. ■ a sudden rush of water; a downpour. **2** a medical condition in which the lens of the eye becomes progressively opaque, resulting in blurred vision. [ME: from L. *cataracta* 'floodgate,' from Gk. *kataraktēs* 'down-rushing,' from *katarassein*, from *kata-* + *arassein* 'strike.']

ca·tarrh /kəˈtär/ ▶ **n.** excessive discharge or buildup of mucus in the nose or throat, associated with inflammation of the mucous membrane. — **ca·tarrh·al** /kəˈtärəl/ **adj.** [16th C.: from Fr. *catarrhe*, ult. from Gk. *katarrhous*, from *katarrhein* 'flow down,' from *kata-* + *rhein* 'flow.']

cat·ar·rhine /ˈkatə,rīn/ Zool. ▶ **adj.** of or relating to primates of a group (infraorder Catarrhini, order Primates) that comprises the Old World monkeys, gibbons, great apes, and humans. They are distinguished by having nostrils that are close together and directed downward. Compare with PLATYRRHINE. ▶ **n.** a catarrhine primate. [19th C.: from CATA- + Gk. *rhis, rhin-* 'nose.']

ca·tas·ta·sis /kəˈtastəsis/ ▶ **n.** (pl. **-ses** /-,sēz/) the third part of the ancient drama, in which the action is heightened for the catastrophe.

ca·tas·tro·phe /kəˈtastrəfē/ ▶ **n.** an event causing great and often sudden damage or suffering. ■ the denouement of a drama, esp. a classical tragedy. — **cat·a·stroph·ic** /,katəˈsträfik/ **adj.** **cat·a·stroph·i·cal·ly** /-ik(ə)lē/ **adv.** [16th C.: from L. *catastropha*, from Gk. *katastrophē* 'overturning,' from *kata-* + *strophē* 'turning' (from *strephein* 'to turn').]

ca·tas·tro·phe the·o·ry ▶ **n.** a branch of mathematics concerned with systems displaying abrupt discontinuous change.

ca·tas·tro·phism /kəˈtastrə,fizəm/ **n.** ▶ **n.** Geol. the theory that changes in the earth's crust during geological history have resulted chiefly from sudden violent and unusual events. Often contrasted with UNIFORMITARIANISM. — **ca·tas·tro·phist** **n. & adj.**

cat·a·to·ni·a /,katəˈtōnēə/ ▶ **n.** Psychiatry abnormality of movement and behavior arising from a disturbed mental state. It may involve repetitive overactivity, catalepsy, or negativism. ■ informal a state of immobility and stupor. — **cat·a·ton·ic** /-ˈtänik/ **adj.** [19th C.: from CATA- + Gk. *tonos* 'tension.']

Ca·taw·ba /kəˈtôbə/ ▶ **n.** a North American variety of grape. ■ a white wine made from this grape. [named after the *Catawba* River.]

Ca·taw·ba Riv·er a river that flows for 300 miles (480 km) from North Carolina across much of South Carolina.

cat·bird /ˈkat,bərd/ ▶ **n.** a long-tailed North American songbird (*Dumetella carolinensis*) of the mockingbird family, with mainly dark gray or black plumage and catlike calls.

– PHRASES **in the catbird seat** informal in a superior or advantageous position. [said to be an allusion to a baseball player in the fortunate position of having no strikes and therefore three balls still to play (a ref. made in James Thurber's short story *The Catbird Seat*).]

cat·boat /ˈkat,bōt/ ▶ **n.** a sailboat with a single mast placed well forward and carrying only one sail. [19th C.: perh. from *cat* (a merchant ship).]

cat·bri·er /ˈkat,brī(ə)r/ (also **cat·bri·ar**) ▶ **n.** another term for GREENBRIER.

cat bur·glar ▶ **n.** a thief who enters a building by climbing to an upper story.

cat·call /ˈkat,kôl/ ▶ **n.** a shrill whistle or shout of disapproval, typically one made at a public meeting or performance. ■ a loud whistle or a comment of a sexual nature made by a man to a passing woman. ▶ **v.** [intrans.] make such a whistle, shout, or comment.

catch /kaCH; keCH/ ▶ **v.** (past **caught**) [trans.] **1** intercept and hold (something that has been thrown, propelled, or dropped). ■ intercept the fall of (someone). ■ seize or take hold of: *he caught hold of her arm.* ■ [intrans.] (**catch at**) grasp or try to grasp: *his hands caught at her arms as she turned away.* **2** capture (a person or animal that tries or would try to escape). ■ [no obj., with adverbial of place] (of an object) accidentally become entangled or trapped in something: *the bracelet always caught on her clothing.* ■ [with obj. and adverbial of place] (of a person) have (a part of one's body or clothing) become entangled or trapped in something: *she caught her foot in the bedspread* | fig. *companies were caught in a downward spiral.* ■ [with obj. and adverbial of place] (usu. **be caught**) fix or fasten in place: *her hair was caught back in a scrunchie.* **3** reach in time and board (a train, bus, or aircraft): *they caught the 12:15 from Chicago.* ■ reach or be in a place in time to see (a person, performance, program, etc.): *she ran downstairs to catch the news.* ■ come upon (someone) unexpectedly: *the snow caught us by surprise.* ■ (**be caught in**) (of a person) unexpectedly find oneself in (an unwelcome situation): *my sister was caught in a thunderstorm.* ■ (**catch it**) informal be punished or told off. ■ (often **be caught**) surprise (someone) in an incriminating situation or in the act of doing something wrong: *he was caught with bomb-making equipment in his home.* **4** engage (a person's interest or imagination). ■ perceive fleetingly: *she caught a glimpse of herself in the mirror.* ■ hear or understand (something said), esp. with effort: *he bellowed something Jess couldn't catch.* ■ succeed in evoking or representing: *the program caught something of the flavor of Minoan culture.* **5** [with obj. and adverbial of place] strike (someone) on a part of the body: *Ben caught him on the chin with an uppercut.* ■ accidentally strike (a part of one's body) against something: *she fell and caught her head on the corner of the hearth.* **6** contract (an illness) through infection or contagion. **7** [intrans.] become ignited, due to contact with flame, and start burning: *the rafters have caught.* ■ (of an engine) fire and start running. ▶ **n.** **1** an act of catching something, typically a ball. ■ an amount of fish caught: *a record catch of 6.9 billion pounds of fish.* ■ [in sing.] informal a person considered attractive, successful, or prestigious and so desirable as a partner or spouse. **2** a device for securing something such as a door, window, or box. **3** a hidden problem or disadvantage in an apparently ideal situation. **4** [in sing.] an unevenness in a person's voice caused by emotion. **5** Music a round, typically one with words arranged to produce a humorous effect.

– PHRASES **catch someone napping** see NAP[1]. **be caught short** see SHORT. **catch at straws** see STRAW. **catch one's breath** **1** draw one's breath in sharply as a reaction to an emotion. **2** recover one's breath after exertion. **catch one's death** (**of cold**) see DEATH. **catch someone's eye** **1** be noticed by someone: *a vase on a side table caught his eye.* **2** attract someone's attention by making eye contact. **catch fire** become ignited and burn. **catch someone in the act** see ACT. **catch the light** shine or glint in the light. **catch sight of** suddenly notice; glimpse.

– PHRASAL VERBS **catch on** informal **1** (of a practice or fashion) become popular. **2** understand what is meant or how to do something. **catch up** succeed in reaching a person who is ahead of one. ■ do work or other tasks that one should have done earlier. **catch up with 1** talk to (someone) one has not seen for some time in order to find out what they have been doing in the interim. **2** begin to have a damaging effect on: *the physical exertions began to catch up with Sue.* — **catch·a·ble** adj. [ME: ult. from OFr. *chacier*, based on L. *captare* 'try to catch,' from *capere* 'take.']

catch-all ▶ n. [usu. as adj.] a term or category that includes a variety of different possibilities.

catch-as-catch-can ▶ adj. [attrib.] using whatever methods or materials are available.

catch·er /ˈkacʜər; ˈkecʜ-/ ▶ n. a person or thing that catches something. ■ Baseball a fielder positioned behind home plate to catch pitches not hit by the batter and to execute defensive plays.

catch·fly /ˈkacʜ,flī; ˈkecʜ-/ ▶ n. (pl. **-flies**) a campion or similar plant (*Silene, Lychnis*, and other genera) of the pink family, with a sticky stem.

catch·ing /ˈkacʜiNG; ˈkecʜ-/ ▶ adj. [predic.] informal (of a disease) infectious: fig. *her enthusiasm is catching.*

catch·light /ˈkacʜ,līt; ˈkecʜ-/ ▶ n. a gleam of reflected light in the eye of a person or animal in a photograph.

catch·ment /ˈkacʜmənt; ˈkecʜ-/ ▶ n. the action of collecting water, esp. the collection of rainfall over a natural drainage area.

catch·ment ar·e·a ▶ n. **1** the area from which rainfall flows into a river, lake, or reservoir. **2** Brit. (also **catch·ment**) the area of a city, town, etc., from which a hospital's patients or school's students are drawn.

catch·pen·ny /ˈkacʜ,penē; ˈkecʜ-/ ▶ adj. [attrib.] having a cheap superficial attractiveness designed to encourage quick sales.

catch·phrase /ˈkacʜ,frāz; ˈkecʜ-/ ▶ n. a well-known sentence or phrase, typically one that is associated with a particular famous person.

catch-22 ▶ n. a dilemma from which there is no escape because of mutually conflicting or dependent conditions. [1970s: title of a novel by Joseph Heller (1961).]

catch-up (also **catchup**) ▶ n. informal an act of catching someone up in a particular activity.
– PHRASES **play catch-up** try to equal a competitor in a sport or game.

catch·weight /ˈkacʜ,wāt; ˈkecʜ-/ ▶ n. [usu. as adj.] esp. hist. unrestricted weight in a wrestling match or other sporting contest: *a catchweight contest.*

catch·word /ˈkacʜ,wərd; ˈkecʜ-/ ▶ n. **1** a briefly popular word or phrase encapsulating a concept: *"motivation" is a great catchword.* **2** a word printed or placed to attract attention. ■ Print., esp. hist. the first word of a page given at the foot of the previous one.

catch·y /ˈkacʜē; ˈkecʜē/ ▶ adj. (**catch·i·er, catch·i·est**) (of a tune or phrase) instantly appealing and memorable: *a catchy recruiting slogan.* — **catch·i·ly** /ˈkacʜəlē; ˈkecʜ-/ adv. **catch·i·ness** n.

cate /kāt/ ▶ n. (usu. **cates**) archaic a choice food; a delicacy. [ME: from obs. *acate* 'purchasing,' from OFr. *acat, achat*, based on L. *capere* 'take.']

cat·e·che·sis /,katəˈkēsis/ ▶ n. religious instruction given to a person in preparation for Christian baptism or confirmation, typically using a catechism. [18th C.: via eccles. L. from Gk. *katēkhēsis* 'oral instruction.']

cat·e·chet·i·cal /,katəˈketikəl/ ▶ adj. of or relating to religious instruction given to a person for Christian baptism or confirmation. ■ of or relating to religious teaching by questions and answers. — **cat·e·chet·ic** adj. **cat·e·chet·i·cal·ly** /-ik(ə)lē/ adv. [17th C.: from eccles. Gk. *katēkhētikos*, from *katēkhētēs* 'catechist,' from *katēkhein* 'instruct orally.']

cat·e·chin /ˈkatə,kin/ ▶ n. Chem. a crystalline compound, $C_{15}H_{14}O_6$, that is the major constituent of catechu. [19th C.: from CATECHU.]

cat·e·chism /ˈkatə,kizəm/ ▶ n. a summary of the principles of Christian religion in the form of questions and answers, used for the instruction of Christians. ■ a series of fixed questions, answers, or precepts used for instruction in other situations. — **cat·e·chis·mal** /,katəˈkizməl/ adj.

cat·e·chist /ˈkatəkist/ ▶ n. a teacher of the principles of Christian religion, esp. one using a catechism.

cat·e·chize /ˈkatə,kīz/ ▶ v. [trans.] instruct (someone) in the principles of Christian religion by means of question and answer, typically by using a catechism. ■ fig. put questions to or interrogate (someone). — **cat·e·chiz·er** n. [ME: via late L. from eccles. Gk. *katēkhizein*, from *katēkhein* 'instruct orally.']

cat·e·chol /ˈkatə,kôl; -,kōl/ ▶ n. Chem. a crystalline compound, $C_6H_4(OH)_2$, obtained by distilling catechu. [19th C.: from CATECHU.]

cat·e·chol·a·mine /katəˈkälə,mēn; -ˈkōlə-/ ▶ n. Biochem. any of a class of aromatic amines that includes a number of neurotransmitters such as epinephrine.

cat·e·chu /ˈkatə,cʜoo; -,sʜoo/ (also **ca·chou**) ▶ n. a vegetable extract containing tannin, esp. one (also called CUTCH) obtained from an Indian acacia tree (*Acacia catechu*), used chiefly for tanning and dyeing. [17th C.: mod. L., from Malay *kacu*.]

cat·e·chu·men /,katəˈkyoomən/ ▶ n. a Christian convert under instruction before baptism. ■ a young Christian preparing for confirmation. [ME: via eccles. L. from Gk. *katēkhoumenos* 'being instructed,' pres. part. of *katēkhein* 'instruct orally.']

cat·e·gor·i·cal /,katəˈgôrikəl/ ▶ adj. unambiguously explicit and direct: *a categorical assurance.* — **cat·e·gor·ic** adj. **cat·e·gor·i·cal·ly** /-ik(ə)lē/ adv. [16th C.: from late L. *categoricus* (from Gk. *katēgorikos*, from *katēgoria*: see CATEGORY).]

cat·e·gor·i·cal im·per·a·tive ▶ n. Philos. (in Kantian ethics) an unconditional moral obligation that is binding in all circumstances and is not dependent on a person's inclination or purpose.

cat·e·go·rize /ˈkatəgə,rīz/ ▶ v. [trans.] (often **be categorized**) place in a particular class or group. — **cat·e·go·ri·za·tion** /,katəgərəˈzāsʜən/ n.

cat·e·go·ry /ˈkatə,gôrē/ ▶ n. (pl. **-ries**) **1** a class or division of people or things regarded as having particular shared characteristics: *five categories of intelligence.* **2** Philos. one of a set of classes among which all things might be distributed. ■ one of the a priori conceptions applied by the mind to sense impressions. ■ a relatively fundamental philosophical concept. — **cat·e·go·ri·al** /,katəˈgôrēəl/ adj. [ME (sense 2): ult. from Gk. *katēgoria* 'statement,' from *katēgoros* 'accuser.']

ca·te·na /kəˈtēnə/ ▶ n. (pl. **-nae** /-nē; -nī/ or **-nas**) tech. a connected series or chain. ■ a connected series of texts written by early Christian theologians. [17th C.: from L., 'chain.']

cat·e·nar·y /ˈkatə,nerē; ˈkatn,erē/ ▶ n. (pl. **-nar·ies**) a curve formed by a wire, rope, or chain hanging freely from two points that are on the same horizontal level. ■ a wire, rope, or chain forming such a curve. ▶ adj. [attrib.] having the form of, involving, or denoting a curve of this type. [18th C.: from L. *catenarius* 'relating to a chain,' from *catena* 'chain.']

cat·e·nat·ed /ˈkatə,nātid; ˈkatn,ātid/ ▶ adj. tech. connected in a chain or series: *catenated molecules.* — **cat·e·na·tion** /,katəˈnāsʜən; ,katnˈāsʜən/ n. [19th C.: ult. from L. *catenat-* 'chained,' from v. *catenare*, from *catena*.]

ca·ter /ˈkātər/ ▶ v. [trans.] provide (food and drink), typically at social events and in a professional capacity: *he catered a lunch for 20 people.* ■ [intrans.] (**cater to**) provide with what is needed or required: *the school caters to children with learning difficulties.* ■ [intrans.] (**cater to**) try to satisfy (a particular need or demand): *he catered to her every whim.* — **ca·ter·er** n. [16th C.: from obs. *cater* 'caterer,' from OFr. *acateor* 'buyer,' from *acater* 'buy' (see CATE).]

cat·er·an /ˈkatərən/ ▶ n. hist. a warrior or raider from the Scottish Highlands. [ME: from Scot. Gael. *ceathairne* 'peasantry.']

cat·er-cor·nered /ˈkatē ,kôrnərd; ˈkatər/ (also **cat·er-cor·ner** or **cat·ty-cor·nered** or **kit·ty-cor·ner**) ▶ adj. & adv. situated diagonally opposite someone or something. [19th C.: from dial. *cater* 'diagonally,' from *cater* 'four on dice,' from Fr. *quatre* 'four,' from L. *quattuor*.]

cat·er·pil·lar /ˈkatə(r),pilər/ ▶ n. **1** the larva of a butterfly or moth, having a segmented wormlike body with three pairs of true legs and several pairs of leglike appendages. ■ (in general use) any similar larva of various insects, esp. sawflies. **2** (also **caterpillar track** or **tread**) trademark an articulated steel band passing around the wheels of a vehicle for travel on rough ground. ■ a vehicle with such tracks. [ME: perh. from a var. of OFr. *chatepelose*, lit. 'hairy cat,' influenced by obs. *piller* 'ravager.']

cat·er·waul /ˈkatər,wôl/ ▶ v. [intrans.] [often as n.] (**caterwauling**) (of a cat) make a shrill howling or wailing noise: *the caterwauling of a pair of bobcats* | [as adj.] (**caterwauling**) fig. *a caterwauling guitar.* ▶ n. a shrill howling or wailing noise. [ME: from CAT[1] + WAUL.]

cat·fish /ˈkat,fisʜ/ ▶ n. (pl. same or **-fish·es**) a freshwater or marine fish with whiskerlike barbels around the mouth, typically bottom-dwelling. Its many families include the Eurasian family Siluridae and the large North American family Ictaluridae.

cat·gut /ˈkat,gət/ ▶ n. a material used for the strings of musical instruments and for surgical sutures, made of the intestines of sheep or horses, but not cats.

Cath. ▶ abbr. ■ Cathedral. ■ Catholic.

Cath·ar /ˈkatʜär/ ▶ n. (pl. **Cath·ars** or **Cath·a·ri** /ˈkatʜə,rī; -rē/) a member of a heretical medieval Christian sect that professed a form of Manichaeism. — **Cath·a·rism** /ˈkatʜə,rizəm/ n. **Cath·a·rist** /ˈkatʜərist/ n. & adj. [17th C.: from med. L. *Cathari* (pl.), from Gk. *katharoi* 'the pure.']

ca·thar·sis /kəˈtʜärsis/ ▶ n. **1** the process of releasing, and thereby providing relief from, strong or repressed emotions. **2** Med., rare purgation. [19th C. (sense 2): from Gk. *katharsis*, from *kathairein* 'cleanse,' from *katharos* 'pure.']

ca·thar·tic /kəˈtʜärtik/ ▶ adj. **1** providing psychological relief through the expression of strong emotions; causing catharsis. **2** Med. (chiefly of a drug) purgative. ▶ n. Med. a purgative drug. — **ca·thar·ti·cal·ly** /-ik(ə)lē/ adv. [17th C.: via late L. from Gk. *kathartikos*, from *katharsis*.]

Ca·thay /kəˈtʜā; ka-/ the name by which China was known to medieval Europe. Also called KHITAI.

cat·head /ˈkat,hed/ ▶ n. a horizontal beam extending from each side of a ship's bow, used for raising and carrying an anchor.

ca·thec·tic /kəˈtʜektik/ ▶ adj. Psychoanal. of or relating to cathexis. [1920s: from Gk. *kathektikos* 'capable of holding.']

ca·the·dra /kəˈtʜēdrə/ ▶ n. (pl. **-drae** /-drē/) **1** a seat, specifically the chair of a bishop in his church. **2** a bishop's see. See also EX CATHEDRA.

ca·the·dral /kəˈtʜēdrəl/ ▶ n. the principal church of a diocese, with which the bishop is officially associated. [ME: from late L. *cathedralis*, from L. *cathedra* 'seat,' from Gk. *kathedra*.]

ca·the·dral ceil·ing ▶ n. a pointed or slanting ceiling of a room that rises through more than one floor.

Cath·er /ˈkat͟ʜər/, Willa Sibert (1876–1974), US writer; born *Wilella Sibert Cather*. Her novels include *O Pioneers!* (1913), *My Ántonia* (1918), and *Death Comes for the Archbishop* (1927).

Cath·er·ine, St. /ˈkatʜ(ə)rən/ (died c.307), early Christian martyr; known as **St. Catherine of Alexandria**. She opposed the persecution of Christians under the emperor Maxentius and refused to recant or to marry the emperor.

Cath·er·ine II (1729–96), empress of Russia; reigned 1762–96; known as **Catherine the Great**. She formed alliances with Prussia and Austria.

Cath·er·ine de' Me·di·ci /'kaTH(ə)rən də 'medəCHē/ (1519–89), queen of France; wife of Henry II. She ruled as regent 1560–74.

Cath·er·ine of Ar·a·gon (1485–1536), first wife of Henry VIII; youngest daughter of Ferdinand and Isabella of Castile; mother of Mary I. Henry's wish to annul his marriage to Catherine led eventually to England's break with the Roman Catholic Church.

Cath·er·ine wheel ▶ **n.** a firework in the form of a flat coil that spins when fixed to something solid. ■ Heraldry a wheel with curved spikes projecting around the circumference. [16th C.: named after St. *Catherine*.]

cath·e·ter /'kaTHitər/ ▶ **n.** Med. a flexible tube inserted through a narrow opening into a body cavity, particularly the bladder, for removing fluid. [17th C.: from late L., from Gk. *kathetēr*, from *kathienai* 'send down.']

cath·e·ter·ize /'kaTHitə,rīz/ ▶ **v.** [trans.] Med. insert a catheter into (a patient or body cavity). — **cath·e·ter·i·za·tion** /,kaTHitərə'zāSHən/ **n.**

ca·thex·is /kə'THeksis/ ▶ **n.** Psychoanal. the concentration of mental energy on one particular person, idea, or object (esp. to an unhealthy degree). [1920s: from Gk. *kathexis* 'retention,' translating Ger. *Libidobesetzung*.]

cath·ode /'kaTHōd/ ▶ **n.** the negatively charged electrode by which electrons enter an electrical device. The opposite of **ANODE**. ■ the positively charged electrode of an electrical device, such as a primary cell, that supplies current. — **cath·o·dal** /'kaTHōdl/ **adj.** **ca·thod·ic** /ka'THädik/ **adj.** [19th C.: from Gk. *kathodos* 'way down,' from *kata-* + *hodos* 'way.']

cath·ode ray ▶ **n.** a beam of electrons emitted from the cathode of a high-vacuum tube.

cath·ode-ray tube (abbr.: **CRT**) (also **cath·ode ray tube**) ▶ **n.** a high-vacuum tube in which cathode rays produce a luminous image on a fluorescent screen, used chiefly in televisions and computer terminals.

cath·o·lic /'kaTH(ə)lik/ ▶ **adj.** **1** (esp. of a person's tastes) including a wide variety of things; all-embracing. **2** (**Catholic**) of the Roman Catholic faith. ■ of or including all Christians. ■ of or relating to the historic doctrine and practice of the Western Church. ▶ **n.** (**Catholic**) a member of the Roman Catholic Church. — **cath·o·lic·i·ty** /,kaTH(ə)'lisətē/ **n.** **ca·thol·ic·ly** **adv.** [ME (sense 2): ult. from Gk. *katholikos* 'universal,' from *kata* 'with respect to' + *holos* 'whole.']

Cath·o·lic Church ▶ **n.** short for **ROMAN CATHOLIC CHURCH**.

Ca·thol·i·cism /kə'THälə,sizəm/ ▶ **n.** the faith, practice, and church order of the Roman Catholic Church. ■ adherence to the forms of Christian doctrine and practice that are generally regarded as Catholic rather than Protestant or Eastern Orthodox.

Ca·thol·i·cize /kə'THälə,sīz/ ▶ **v.** [trans.] make Roman Catholic; convert to Catholicism.

ca·thol·i·con /kə'THäli,kän; -kən/ ▶ **n.** **1** a comprehensive treatise. **2** a universal remedy; a panacea.

Ca·thol·i·cos /kə'THälikəs; -,käs/ ▶ **n.** (pl. **Ca·thol·i·cos·es** /kə,THäli'kō,sēz/ or **Ca·thol·i·coi** /kə'THäli,koi/) the Patriarch of the Armenian or the Nestorian Church. [17th C.: from med. Gk. *katholikos* (see **CATHOLIC**).]

cat·house /'kat,hous/ ▶ **n.** informal a brothel.

cat·i·on /'kat,īən; -,īän/ ▶ **n.** Chem. a positively charged ion, i.e., one that would be attracted to the cathode in electrolysis. The opposite of **ANION**. — **cat·i·on·ic** /,katī'änik/ **adj.** [19th C.: from **CATA-** or from **CATHODE**, + **ION**.]

cat·kin /'katkin/ ▶ **n.** a flowering spike of trees such as willow and hazel, typically downy, pendulous, and composed of flowers of a single sex. [16th C.: from obs. Du. *katteken* 'kitten.']

cat·like /'kat,līk/ ▶ **adj.** resembling a cat in appearance, action, or character, esp. by moving gracefully or stealthily.

cat·lin·ite /'katlə,nīt/ ▶ **n.** a red clay of the Upper Missouri region, the sacred pipestone of the American Indians. [19th C.: George *Catlin* (1796–1872), Amer. artist.]

cat lit·ter ▶ **n.** see **LITTER** (sense 3).

cat·mint /'kat,mint/ ▶ **n.** another term for **CATNIP**.

cat·nap /'kat,nap/ ▶ **n.** a short, light sleep; a doze. ▶ **v.** (**-napped, -nap·ping**) [intrans.] have such a sleep.

cat·nip /'kat,nip/ ▶ **n.** a plant (genus *Nepeta*) of the mint family, with downy leaves, purple-spotted white flowers, and a pungent smell attractive to cats. Also called **CATMINT**. [18th C.: from **CAT**[1] + *nip*, var. of dial. *nep*, *nept*, from med. L. *nepta*, from L. *nepeta* 'catmint.']

Ca·to /'kātō/, Marcus Porcius (234–149 BC), Roman statesman; known as **Cato the Elder** or **Cato the Censor**. As censor, he attempted to stem the growing influence of Greek culture.

cat-o'-nine-tails ▶ **n.** hist. a rope whip with nine knotted cords, formerly used (esp. at sea) to flog offenders.

Ca·tons·ville /'kātnz,vil/ a city in central Maryland, southwest of Baltimore; pop. 35,233.

ca·top·tric /kə'täptrik/ ▶ **adj.** Physics of or relating to a mirror, a reflector, or reflection. [18th C.: from Gk. *katoptrikos*, from *katoptron* 'mirror.']

ca·top·trics /kə'täptriks/ ▶ **plural n.** [treated as sing.] Physics the branch of optics that deals with reflection. [16th C.: from Gk. *katoptrikos* 'reflecting,' from *katoptron* 'mirror.']

cat rig ▶ **n.** the rig of a catboat with the single mast placed far forward.

Ca·tron /'kātrən/, John (c.1786–1865), US Supreme Court associate justice 1837–65.

CAT scan ▶ **n** an X-ray image made using computerized axial tomography. — **CAT scan·ner** **n.**

cat's cra·dle ▶ **n.** a child's game in which a loop of string is put around and between the fingers and complex patterns are formed.

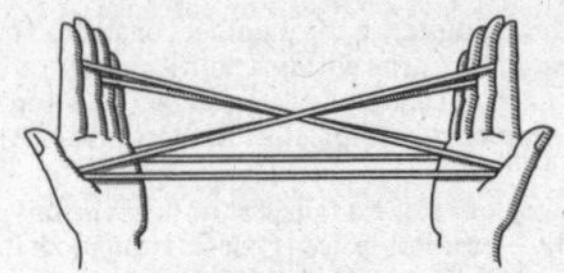

cat's cradle

cat scratch fe·ver (also **cat scratch disease**) ▶ **n.** an infectious disease occurring after a scratch by a cat's claw. Symptoms include mild fever and inflammation of the injury site and of the lymph glands.

cat's-eye ▶ **n.** a semiprecious stone, esp. chalcedony or chrysoberyl, with a chatoyant luster.

Cats·kill Moun·tains /'katskil/ (also **the Cats·kills**) a range of mountains in New York, part of the Appalachian system.

cat's me·ow ▶ **n.** (**the cat's meow**) another term for ***THE CAT'S PAJAMAS*** (see **CAT'S PAJAMAS**).

cat's pa·ja·mas ▶ **n.** (**the cat's pajamas**) informal, dated an excellent person or thing: *this car is the cat's pajamas.*

cat's-paw ▶ **n.** a person who is used by another, typically to carry out an unpleasant or dangerous task.

cat·suit /'kat,so͝ot/ ▶ **n.** a woman's jumpsuit, typically close-fitting.

cat·sup /'keCHəp; 'kaCHəp; 'katsəp/ ▶ **n.** var. of **KETCHUP**.

Catt /kat/, Carrie Clinton Lane Chapman (1859–1947), US civil rights activist who helped bring about the 19th Amendment to the US Constitution, granting women the right to vote, in 1920. That same year, she founded the League of Women Voters.

cat·tail /'kat,tāl/ ▶ **n.** a tall marsh plant (genus *Typha*, family Typhaceae) with long, reedlike leaves and brown, velvety cylindrical spikes of numerous tiny flowers. Also called **REED MACE, BULRUSH**.

cat·te·ry /'katərē/ ▶ **n.** (pl. **-ries**) a boarding or breeding establishment for cats.

cat·tish /'katiSH/ ▶ **adj.** another term for **CATTY**. — **cat·tish·ly** **adv.** **cat·tish·ness** **n.**

cat·tle /'katl/ ▶ **plural n.** **1** large ruminants (*Bos taurus*) with horns and cloven hoofs, domesticated for meat or milk, or as beasts of burden; cows. **2** similar animals of a group related to domestic cattle, including yak, bison, and buffalo. The **cattle family** (Bovidae) also includes the sheep, goats, goat-antelopes, and antelopes. [ME: from Anglo-Norman Fr. *catel*, var. of OFr. *chatel* (see **CHATTEL**).]

cat·tle call ▶ **n.** informal an open audition for parts in a play, movie, or other production.

cat·tle e·gret ▶ **n.** a small white heron (*Bubulcus ibis*) that feeds on insects around grazing cattle, native to southern Eurasia and Africa, and now found in North and South America.

cat·tle·man /'katlmən; -,man/ ▶ **n.** (pl. **-men**) a person who tends or rears cattle.

catt·ley·a /'katlēə; kat'lāə; kat'lēə/ ▶ **n.** a tropical American orchid (genus *Cattleya*) with brightly colored showy flowers and thick leaves, typically growing as an epiphyte. [19th C.: mod. L., named after William *Cattley* (died 1832), Engl. patron of botany.]

cat·ty /'katē/ ▶ **adj.** (**cat·ti·er, cat·ti·est**) **1** deliberately hurtful in one's remarks; spiteful. **2** of or relating to cats; catlike. — **cat·ti·ly** **adv.** **cat·ti·ness** **n.**

cat·ty-cor·nered ▶ **adj.** another term for **CATER-CORNERED**.

Ca·tul·lus /kə'tələs/, Gaius Valerius (*c.*84–*c.*54 BC), Roman poet. He is known for his love poems.

CATV ▶ **abbr.** community antenna television (i.e., cable television).

cat·walk /'kat,wôk/ ▶ **n.** a narrow walkway extending into an auditorium, esp. in an industrial installation, along which models walk to display clothes in fashion shows. ■ a narrow platform or stage.

Cau·ca Riv·er /'koukə/ a river in western Colombia that flows north from the Andes to the Magdalena River.

Cau·ca·sian /kô'kāZHən/ ▶ **adj.** **1** often offens. of or relating to one of the traditional divisions of humankind, covering a broad group of peoples from Europe, western Asia, and parts of India and North Africa. ■ white-skinned; of European origin. **2** of or relating to the Caucasus. **3** of or relating to a group of languages spoken in the region of the Caucasus. The most widely spoken is Georgian, of the small **South Caucasian** family, not related to the three **North Caucasian** families. ▶ **n.** often offens. a Caucasian person. ■ a white person; a person of European origin.

Cau·ca·soid /'kôkə,soid/ ▶ **adj.** of or relating to the Caucasian division of humankind.

Cau·ca·sus /'kôkəsəs/ (also **Cau·ca·sia** /kô'kāZHə/) a mountainous region in southeastern Europe that lies between the Black and Caspian seas.

Cau·chy /kô'SHē/, Augustin Louis, Baron (1789–1857), French mathematician. He contributed substantially to the founding of group theory and analysis.

cau·cus /'kôkəs/ ▶ **n.** (pl. **-cus·es**) **1** a meeting of the members of a legislative body who are members of a particular political party, to select candidates or decide policy. ■ the members of such a body. **2** a group of people with shared concerns within a political party or larger organization. ■ a meeting of such a group. ▶ **v.** (**-cused, -cus·ing**) [intrans.] hold or form such a group or meeting. [18th C.: perh. from Algonquian *cau'-cau'-as'u* 'adviser.']

cau·dal /'kôdl/ ▶ **adj.** of or like a tail. ■ at or near the tail or the posterior part of the body. — **cau·dal·ly adv.** [17th C.: from mod. L. *caudalis*, from L. *cauda* 'tail.']

cau·dal fin ▶ **n.** Zool. another term for TAIL FIN.

cau·date /'kôdāt/ ▶ **adj. 1** Anat. relating to or denoting the caudate nucleus. **2** Zool. (of an animal) having a tail. ▶ **n.** short for CAUDATE NUCLEUS.

cau·date nu·cle·us ▶ **n.** Anat. the upper of the two gray nuclei of the corpus striatum in the cerebrum of the brain.

cau·dex /'kôdeks/ ▶ **n.** (pl. **-di·ces** /-dəsēz/ or **-dex·es**) Bot. the axis of a woody plant, esp. a palm or tree fern, comprising the stem and root. [18th C.: from L., earlier form of CODEX.]

cau·dil·lo /kô'dēlyō; -'dēō; kou'dē(y)ō/ ▶ **n.** (pl. **-los**) (in Spanish-speaking regions) a military or political leader. [Sp., from late L. *capitellum*, dimin. of *caput* 'head.']

caught /kôt/ past and past participle of CATCH.

caul /kôl/ ▶ **n. 1** the amniotic membrane enclosing a fetus. ■ part of this membrane occasionally found on a child's head at birth, thought to bring good luck. **2** Anat. the omentum. [ME: perh. from OFr. *cale* 'head covering.']

caul·dron /'kôldrən/ (also **cal·dron**) ▶ **n.** a large metal pot with a lid and handle, used for cooking over an open fire. ■ fig. a situation characterized by instability and strong emotions. [ME: from Anglo-Norman Fr. *caudron*, based on L. *caldarium, calidarium* 'cooking pot,' from *calidus* 'hot.']

cau·li·flow·er /'kôli,flouər; 'käli-/ ▶ **n.** a cabbage of a variety that bears a large flowerhead of small creamy-white flower buds. ■ the immature flowerhead of this plant eaten as a vegetable. [16th C.: from obs. Fr. *chou fleuri* 'flowered cabbage,' prob. from Ital. *cavolfiore* or mod. L. *cauliflora*.]

cau·li·flow·er ear ▶ **n.** an ear that has become thickened or deformed as a result of repeated blows, typically in boxing.

caulk /kôk/ (also **calk**) ▶ **n.** (also **caulk·ing**) a waterproof filler and sealant, used in building work and repairs. ▶ **v.** [trans.] seal (a gap or seam) with such a substance. ■ stop up (the seams of a boat) with oakum and waterproofing material; make (a boat) watertight by this method. — **caulk·er n.** [ME: from Old North. Fr. *cauquer, caukier*, var. of *cauchier* 'tread,' from L. *calcare*, from *calx, calc-* 'heel.']

caus·al /'kôzəl/ ▶ **adj.** of, relating to, or acting as a cause. ■ Gram. Logic expressing or indicating a cause: *a causal conjunction.* — **caus·al·ly adv.**

cau·sal·gi·a /kô'zalj(ē)ə; -'sal-/ ▶ **n.** severe burning pain in a limb caused by injury to a peripheral nerve. [19th C.: from Gk. *kausos* 'fever.']

cau·sal·i·ty /kô'zalətē/ ▶ **n. 1** the relationship between cause and effect. **2** the principle that everything has a cause.

cau·sa·tion /kô'zāshən/ ▶ **n.** the action of causing something. ■ the relationship between cause and effect; causality.

caus·a·tive /'kôzətiv/ ▶ **adj.** acting as a cause. ■ Gram. expressing causation: *a causative verb.* ▶ **n.** a causative suffix.

cause /kôz/ ▶ **n. 1** a person or thing that gives rise to an action, phenomenon, or condition. ■ reasonable grounds for doing, thinking, or feeling something. **2** a principle, aim, or movement that, because of a deep commitment, one is prepared to defend or advocate: *she devoted her life to the cause of deaf people.* ■ [with adj.] something deserving of one's support, typically a charity: *money for a good cause.* **3** a matter to be resolved in a court of law. ■ an individual's case offered at law. ▶ **v.** [trans.] make (something) happen: *this disease can cause blindness.*
– PHRASES **cause of action** Law a fact or facts that enable a person to bring an action against another. **make common cause** unite in order to achieve a shared aim. **a rebel without a cause** a person who is dissatisfied with society but does not have a specific aim to fight for. — **cause·less adj. caus·er n.** [ME: from OFr., from L. *causa* (n.), *causare* (v.).]

'cause /kəz/ ▶ **conj.** informal short for BECAUSE.

cause cé·lè·bre /'kôz sə'leb(rə); 'kōz/ ▶ **n.** (pl. **causes cé·lè·bres** pronunc. same) a controversial issue that attracts a great deal of public attention. [18th C.: Fr., lit. 'famous case.']

cau·se·rie /,kōz(ə)'rē/ ▶ **n.** (pl. **-ries** pronunc. same) an informal article or talk, typically one on a literary subject. [Fr., from *causer* 'to talk.']

cause·way /'kôz,wā/ ▶ **n.** a raised road or track across low or wet ground. [ME: from *causey* (from Anglo-Norman Fr. *causee*, based on L. *calx* 'limestone') + WAY.]

caus·tic /'kôstik/ ▶ **adj. 1** able to burn or corrode organic tissue by chemical action. ■ fig. sarcastic in a scathing and bitter way: *the players were making caustic comments about the referee.* ■ fig. (of an expression or sound) expressive of such sarcasm. **2** Physics formed by the intersection of reflected or refracted parallel rays from a curved surface. ▶ **n. 1** a caustic substance. **2** Physics a caustic surface or curve. — **caus·ti·cal·ly** /-ik(ə)lē/ **adv. caus·tic·i·ty** /kô'stisitē/ **n.** [ME: via L. from Gk. *kaustikos*, from *kaustos* 'combustible,' from *kaiein* 'to burn.']

caus·tic pot·ash ▶ **n.** another term for POTASSIUM HYDROXIDE.

caus·tic so·da ▶ **n.** another term for SODIUM HYDROXIDE.

cau·ter·ize /'kôtə,rīz/ ▶ **v.** [trans.] Med. burn the skin or flesh of (a wound) with a heated instrument or caustic substance, typically to stop bleeding or prevent the wound from becoming infected. — **cau·ter·i·za·tion** /,kôtərə'zāshən/ **n.** [ME: from OFr. *cauteriser*, ult. from Gk. *kautēriazein*, from *kautērion* 'branding iron,' from *kaiein* 'to burn.']

cau·ter·y /'kôtərē/ ▶ **n.** (pl. **-ter·ies**) Med. an instrument or a caustic substance used for cauterizing. ■ the action of cauterizing something. [ME: via L. from Gk. *kautērion*.]

cau·tion /'kôshən/ ▶ **n. 1** care taken to avoid danger or mistakes. ■ a warning. **2** informal, dated an amusing or surprising person. ▶ **v.** [reporting verb] say something as a warning. ■ [intrans.] (**caution against**) warn or advise against (doing something): *advisers cautioned against tax increases.* [ME: from L. *caution-*, from *cavere* 'take heed.']

cau·tion·ar·y /'kôshə,nerē/ ▶ **adj.** serving as a warning.

cau·tious /'kôshəs/ ▶ **adj.** attentive to potential problems or dangers. ■ (of an action) characterized by such an attitude. — **cau·tious·ly adv. cau·tious·ness n.**

Cau·ver·y /'kôvərē/ (also **Ka·ver·i** pronunc. same or /'kä-/) a river in southern India that rises in northern Kerala and flows east for 475 miles (765 km) to the Bay of Bengal. It is held sacred by Hindus.

ca·va /'kävə/ ▶ **n.** a Spanish sparkling wine made in the same way as .

cav·al·cade /,kavəl'kād/ ▶ **n.** a formal procession of people walking, on horseback, or riding in vehicles. [16th C.: from Fr., from Ital. *cavalcata*, from *cavalcare* 'to ride,' based on L. *caballus* 'horse.']

cav·a·lier /,kavə'li(ə)r/ ▶ **n. 1** (**Cavalier**) hist. a supporter of King Charles I in the English Civil War. ■ archaic literary a courtly gentleman, esp. one acting as a lady's escort. ■ archaic a horseman, esp. a cavalryman. **2** (also **Cavalier King Charles**) a small spaniel of a breed with a moderately long, noncurly, silky coat. ▶ **adj.** showing a lack of proper concern; offhand. — **cav·a·lier·ly adv.** [16th C.: from Fr., ult. based on L. *caballus* 'horse.']

cav·al·ry /'kavəlrē/ ▶ **n.** (pl. **-ries**) [usu. treated as pl.] hist. soldiers who fought on horseback. ■ hist. a branch of an army made up of such soldiers. ■ modern soldiers who fight in armored vehicles. — **cav·al·ry·man** /-mən/ **n.** (pl. **-men**). [16th C.: from Fr. *cavallerie*, from Ital. *cavalleria*, from *cavallo* 'horse,' from L. *caballus*.]

cav·al·ry twill ▶ **n.** strong woolen twill used typically for making pants and sportswear.

Cav·an /'kavən/ a county in the Republic of Ireland.

cav·a·ti·na /,kavə'tēnə/ ▶ **n.** (pl. **-ne** /-nā/) Music a short operatic aria in simple style without repeated sections. ■ a similar piece of lyrical instrumental music. [19th C.: from Ital.]

cave /kāv/ ▶ **n.** a large underground chamber, typically of natural origin, in a hillside or cliff. ▶ **v.** [intrans.] **1** explore caves as a sport. **2** short for CAVE IN.
– PHRASAL VERBS **cave in** (or **cave something in**) (with reference to a roof or similar structure) subside or collapse or cause something to do this. ■ fig. yield or submit under pressure. — **cave·like adj. cav·er n.** [ME: from OFr., from L. *cava*, from *cavus* 'hollow.']

ca·ve·at /'kavē,ät; 'kä-; 'kā-/ ▶ **n.** a warning or proviso of specific stipulations, conditions, or limitations. ■ Law a notice, esp. in a probate, that certain actions may not be taken without informing the person who gave the notice. [16th C.: from L., lit. 'let a person beware.']

ca·ve·at emp·tor /'emp,tôr/ ▶ **n.** the principle that the buyer alone is responsible for checking the quality and suitability of goods before a purchase is made. [16th C.: L., lit. 'let the buyer beware.']

cave bear ▶ **n.** a large extinct bear (*Ursus spelaeus*) of the Pleistocene epoch, whose remains have been found in caves throughout Europe.

cave·fish /'kāv,fish/ ▶ **n.** (pl. same or **-fish·es**) a small colorless fish (*Amblyopsis, Typhlichthys*, and other genera, family Amblyopsidae) that lives only in limestone caves in North America. It has reduced or absent eyes, and the head and body are covered with papillae that are sensitive to vibration. Also called BLINDFISH.

cave-in ▶ **n.** a collapse of a roof or similar structure, typically underground. ■ [in sing.] fig. an instance of yielding or submitting under pressure: *the government's cave-in to industry pressure.*

cave·man /'kāv,man/ ▶ **n.** (pl. **-men**) a prehistoric man who lived in caves. ■ a man whose behavior is uncivilized or violent: [as adj.] *you can't change my mind by caveman tactics.*

Cav·en·dish /'kavəndish/, Henry (1731–1810), English chemist and physicist. He identified hydrogen.

cav·en·dish /'kavəndish/ ▶ **n.** tobacco softened, sweetened, and formed into cakes. [19th C.: prob. from the surname *Cavendish*.]

cave paint·ing ▶ **n.** a prehistoric picture on the interior of a cave, often depicting animals.

cav·ern /'kavərn/ ▶ **n.** a cave, or a chamber in a cave, typically a large one. ■ used in similes and comparisons to refer to a vast, dark space: *rouses me from the cavern of sleep.* [ME: from OFr. *caverne* or from L. *caverna*, from *cavus* 'hollow.']

cav·ern·ous /'kavərnəs/ ▶ **adj.** like a cavern in size, shape, or atmosphere. ■ fig. giving the impression of vast, dark depths: *his cavernous eyes.* — **cav·ern·ous·ly adv.**

cave·wom·an /'kāv,wo͝omən/ ▶ **n.** (pl. **-wom·en**) a prehistoric woman who lived in caves.

cav·i·ar /'kavē,är/ (also **cav·i·are**) ▶ **n.** the pickled roe of sturgeon or other large fish, eaten as a delicacy. [16th C.: from Ital. *caviale* or Fr. *caviar*, prob. from med. Gk. *khaviari*.]

cav·il /'kavəl/ ▶ **v.** [intrans.] make petty or unnecessary objections. ▶ **n.** an objection of this kind. — **cav·il·er n.** [16th C.: from Fr. *caviller*, from L. *cavillari*, from *cavilla* 'mockery.']

cav·ing /ˈkāviNG/ ▶ **n.** another term for SPELUNKING.

cav·i·ta·tion /ˌkavəˈtāSHən/ ▶ **n.** Physics the formation of an empty space within a solid object or body. ■ the formation of bubbles in a liquid, typically by the movement of a propeller through it.

cav·i·ty /ˈkavitē/ ▶ **n.** (pl. **-ties**) an empty space within a solid object, in particular the human body. ■ a decayed part of a tooth. — **cav·i·tar·y** /-iˌterē/ **adj.** [16th C.: from Fr. *cavité* or late L. *cavitas*, from L. *cavus* 'hollow.']

cav·i·ty wall ▶ **n.** a wall formed from two thicknesses of masonry with a space between them.

cav·ort /kəˈvôrt/ ▶ **v.** [intrans.] jump or dance around excitedly: *monkeys leap and cavort in the branches.* ■ informal apply oneself to sexual or disreputable pursuits: *he spent his nights cavorting with the glitterati.* [18th C.: perh. an alt. of CURVET.]

Ca·vour /kəˈvo͝or/, Camillo Benso, Conte di (1810–61), Italian statesman who promoted the cause of national unity.

ca·vy /ˈkāvē/ ▶ **n.** (pl. **-vies**) a South American rodent (family Caviidae) with a sturdy body and vestigial tail. Its several species include the guinea pig. [18th C.: from mod. L. *cavia*, from Galibi *cabiai*.]

caw /kô/ ▶ **n.** the harsh cry of a crow or similar bird. ▶ **v.** [intrans.] utter such a cry. [16th C.: imitative.]

Caw·ley /ˈkôlē/, Evonne Fay Goolagong (1951–), Australian tennis player. During 1971–80, she won 14 Grand Slam titles.

Cawn·pore /kônˈpôr/ var. of KANPUR.

Cax·ton /ˈkakstən/, William (*c.*1422–91), English printer. He printed the first book in English in 1474.

cay /kē; kā/ ▶ **n.** a low bank or reef of coral, rock, or sand. Compare with KEY². [17th C.: from Sp. *cayo* 'reef,' from Fr. *quai* 'quay.']

Cay·enne /kīˈen; kā-/ the capital and chief port of French Guiana; pop. 41,600.

cay·enne /kīˈen; kā-/ (also **cayenne pepper**) ▶ **n.** a pungent hot-tasting red powder prepared from ground dried chili peppers. [18th C.: from Tupi *kyynha*, *quiynha*, later associated with CAYENNE.]

Cay·ley /ˈkālē/, Arthur (1821–95), English mathematician. The **Cayley numbers**, a generalization of complex numbers, are named after him.

cay·man ▶ **n.** var. of CAIMAN.

Cay·man Is·lands /ˈkāmən/ (also **the Cay·mans**) a group of three islands in the Caribbean Sea, a British dependency; pop. 31,930; capital, George Town.

Ca·yu·ga /kāˈ(y)o͞ogə; kī-/ ▶ **n.** (pl. same or **-gas**) **1** a member of an American Indian people, one of the Five Nations, formerly inhabiting New York. **2** the Iroquoian language of this people. ▶ **adj.** of or relating to this people or their language. [from an Iroquoian place name.]

Cay·u·ga, Lake /kəˈyo͞ogə; kāˈ(y)o͞o-/ one of the Finger Lakes, in west central New York.

Cay·use /ˈkī(y)o͞os; kīˈ(y)o͞os/ ▶ **n.** (pl. same or **-us·es**) **1** a member of an American Indian people of Washington State and Oregon. **2** the language of this people, of unknown affinity. **3** (**cayuse**) an American Indian pony. ■ informal a horse. ▶ **adj.** of or relating to this people or their language. [prob. from Chinook Jargon, from Sp. *caballos*, 'horses.']

CB ▶ **abbr.** Citizens' Band (radio frequencies).

CBC ▶ **abbr.** Canadian Broadcasting Corporation.

CBS ▶ **abbr.** Columbia Broadcasting System.

CC ▶ **abbr.** ■ closed-captioned. ■ Cape Cod.

cc (also **c.c.**) ▶ **abbr.** ■ carbon copy (used as an indication that a duplicate has been or should be sent to another person). ■ cubic centimeter(s).

CCD ▶ **abbr.** Electron. ■ charge-coupled device, a high-speed semiconductor used chiefly in image detection. ■ Confraternity of Christian Doctrine.

C clef ▶ **n.** the soprano, alto, or tenor clef.

CCTV ▶ **abbr.** closed-circuit television.

CCU ▶ **abbr.** ■ cardiac care unit. ■ coronary care unit. ■ critical care unit.

CD ▶ **abbr.** ■ certificate of deposit. ■ civil defense. ■ compact disc. ■ corps diplomatique.

Cd ▶ **symb.** the chemical element cadmium.

cd ▶ **abbr.** ■ candela. ■ cord.

CDC ▶ **abbr.** Centers for Disease Control.

CD-I ▶ **abbr.** compact disc (interactive).

CDM ▶ **abbr.** cold dark matter.

CDMA ▶ **abbr.** Electron. Code Division Multiple Access, a generic term denoting a wireless interface based on advanced technology.

cDNA ▶ **abbr.** complementary DNA.

Cdr. (also **CDR**) ▶ **abbr.** Commander.

Cdre. ▶ **abbr.** Commodore.

CD-ROM /ˌsē ˌdē ˈräm/ ▶ **n.** a compact disc used as a read-only optical memory device for a computer. [1980s: from *compact disc read-only memory*.]

CDT ▶ **abbr.** Central Daylight Time (see CENTRAL TIME).

CD vid·e·o (abbr.: **CDV**) ▶ **n.** a video system in which both sound and picture are recorded on compact disc.

CE ▶ **abbr.** ■ Chemical Engineer. ■ Church of England. ■ civil engineer. ■ Common Era. ■ Corps of Engineers.

Ce ▶ **symb.** the chemical element cerium.

ce·a·no·thus /ˌsēəˈnōTHəs/ ▶ **n.** a North American shrub (genus *Ceanothus*) of the buckthorn family, cultivated for its dense clusters of small blue or white flowers. [mod. L., from Gk. *keanōthos*, a thistle.]

Ce·a·rá /ˌsāəˈrä/ a state in northeastern Brazil, on the Atlantic coast; capital, Fortaleza.

cease /sēs/ ▶ **v.** [intrans.] come to an end: *the hostilities had ceased and normal life was resumed* | [with infin.] *on his retirement the job will cease to exist.* ■ [trans.] bring (a specified action) to an end: *they were asked to cease all military activity.*

– PHRASES **never cease to** (in hyperbolic use) do something very frequently: *her exploits never cease to amaze me.* [ME: from OFr. *cesser*, from L. *cessare* 'stop,' from *cedere* 'to yield.']

cease-fire ▶ **n.** a temporary suspension of fighting, typically one during which peace talks take place; a truce. ■ an order or signal to stop fighting.

cease·less /ˈsēslis/ ▶ **adj.** constant and unending: *the fort was subjected to ceaseless bombardment.* — **cease·less·ly adv.**

Ceau·şes·cu /CHouˈSHeskoo/, Nicolae (1918–89), president of Romania and head of a Communist regime 1974–89. An uprising in December 1989 resulted in his downfall and execution.

Ce·bu /sāˈbo͞o/ an island in south central Philippines. ■ its chief city and port; pop. 610,000.

Ce·cil·ia, St. /səˈsilyə; -ˈsēlyə/ (2nd or 3rd century), Roman martyr. According to legend, she took a vow of celibacy but, when forced to marry, converted her husband to Christianity and both were martyred. She is the patron saint of church music.

ce·cro·pi·a /siˈkrōpēə/ ▶ **n.** **1** a fast-growing tropical American tree (genus *Cecropia*, family Cecropiaceae). Many cecropias have a symbiotic relationship with ants. **2** (also **cecropia moth**) a large North American silkworm moth (*Hyalophora cecropia*, family Saturniidae) with boldly marked red-dish-brown wings. [19th C.: mod. L., after *Cecrops*, king of Attica.]

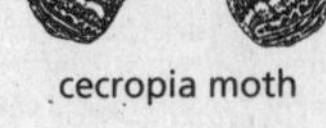

cecropia moth

ce·cum /ˈsēkəm/ (Brit. **cae·cum**) ▶ **n.** (pl. **-ca** /-kə/) Anat. a pouch connected to the junction of the small and large intestines. — **ce·cal** /-kəl/ **adj.** [ME: from L. *(intestinum) caecum* 'blind (gut).']

ce·dar /ˈsēdər/ ▶ **n.** any of a number of conifers that typically yield fragrant, durable timber, in particular: ■ a large tree (genus *Cedrus*) of the pine family, esp. the **cedar of Lebanon** (*C. libani*). ■ a tall slender North American or Asian tree (genus *Thuja*) of the cypress family, esp. the **western red cedar** (*T. plicata*) and the **northern white cedar** (*T. occidentalis*). [OE, from OFr. *cedre* or L. *cedrus*, from Gk. *kedros*.]

Ce·dar Falls a city in northeastern Iowa; pop. 36,145.

Ce·dar Ra·pids a city in east central Iowa; pop. 120,758.

ce·dar wax·wing ▶ **n.** a North American waxwing (*Bombycilla cedrorum*).

cede /sēd/ ▶ **v.** [trans.] give up (power or territory): *they ceded control of the schools to the government.* [16th C.: from Fr. *céder* or L. *cedere* 'to yield.']

ce·di /ˈsādē/ ▶ **n.** (pl. same or **-dis**) the basic monetary unit of Ghana, equal to 100 pesewas.

ce·dil·la /səˈdilə/ ▶ **n.** a mark (¸) written under the letter *c*, esp. in French, to show that it is pronounced like an *s* rather than a *k* (e.g., *façade*). [16th C.: from obs. Sp., earlier form of *zedilla*, dimin. of *zeda* (the letter Z), from Gk. *zēta*.]

cedar waxwing

cei·ba /ˈsābə/ ▶ **n.** a tall tropical American tree (*Ceiba pentandra*, family Bombacaceae) from which kapok is obtained. It is pollinated by bats. Also called KAPOK. [19th C.: via Sp. from Taino, lit. 'giant tree.']

ceil /sēl/ ▶ **v.** [trans.] (usu. **be ceiled**) archaic line or plaster the roof of (a building). [ME: perh. rel. to L. *celare* 'conceal.']

ceil·ing /ˈsēliNG/ ▶ **n.** **1** the upper interior surface of a room or other similar compartment. ■ fig. an upper limit, typically one set on prices, wages, or expenditure. See also GLASS CEILING. ■ the maximum altitude that a particular aircraft can reach. ■ the altitude of the base of a cloud layer. **2** the inside planking of a ship's bottom and sides. [ME: from CEIL.]

ceil·om·e·ter /sēˈlämitər/ ▶ **n.** a device for measuring and recording the height of clouds.

cel /sel/ ▶ **n.** a transparent sheet of celluloid or similar film material that can be drawn on, used in the production of cartoons. [20th C.: abbrev. of CELLULOID.]

cel·a·don /ˈseləˌdän/ ▶ **n.** a willow-green color: [as adj.] *paneling painted in celadon green.* ■ a gray-green glaze used on pottery, esp. that from China. ■ pottery made with this glaze. [18th C.: from Fr. *céladon* (color), named after the hero in d'Urfé's romance *L'Astrée* (1607–27).]

cel·an·dine /ˈselənˌdīn; -ˌdēn/ (also **lesser celandine**) ▶ **n.** a common plant (*Ranunculus ficaria*) of the buttercup family that produces

PRONUNCIATION KEY ə *ago, up*; ər *over, fur*; a *hat*; ā *ate*; ä *car*; e *let*; ē *see*; i *fit*; ī *by*; NG *sing*; ō *go*; ô *law, for*; oi *toy*; o͝o *good*; o͞o *goo*; ou *out*; TH *thin*; T͟H *then*; ZH *vision*

yellow flowers in the early spring. See also GREATER CELANDINE. [ME, from OFr. *celidoine*, based on Gk. *khelidōn* 'swallow.']

-cele ▶ **comb. form** var. of -COELE.

ce·leb /sə'leb/ ▶ **n.** informal a celebrity: *a TV celeb.*

Cel·e·bes /'selə,bēz; sə'lēbēz/ former name of SULAWESI.

Cel·e·bes Sea a part of the western Pacific Ocean south of the Philippines.

cel·e·brant /'seləbrənt/ ▶ **n. 1** a person who performs a rite, esp. a priest at the Eucharist. **2** a person who celebrates something: *birthday celebrants.*

cel·e·brate /'selə,brāt/ ▶ **v.** [trans.] **1** mark (a significant or happy day or event), typically with a social gathering: *his parents threw a party to celebrate his graduation.* ■ [intrans.] do something enjoyable to mark such an occasion: *she celebrated with a glass of champagne.* ■ reach (a birthday or anniversary): *the program celebrates its 40th birthday this year.* **2** perform (a religious ceremony) publicly and duly, in particular officiate at (the Eucharist). **3** honor or praise publicly: *a film celebrating the actor's career* | [as adj.] (**celebrated**) *a celebrated mathematician.* —**cel·e·bra·tor** /-,brātər/ **n. cel·e·bra·to·ry** /sə'lebrə,tôrē; 'seləbrə-/ **adj.** [ME: from L. *celebrat-* 'celebrated,' from the v. *celebrare*, from *celeber, celebr-* 'honored.']

cel·e·bra·tion /,selə'brāsHən/ ▶ **n.** the action of marking one's pleasure at an important event or occasion by engaging in enjoyable, typically social activity: *the birth of his son was a cause for celebration* | *a birthday celebration.* ■ a celebratory event or series of events.

ce·leb·ri·ty /sə'lebrətē/ ▶ **n.** (pl. **-ties**) a famous person. ■ the state of being well known: *his prestige and celebrity grew.*

ce·leb·u·tante /si'lebyŏŏ,tänt; -yə-/ ▶ **n.** a celebrity who is well known in fashionable society. [1930s: blend of CELEBRITY and DEBUTANTE.]

ce·ler·i·ac /sə'lerē,ak/ ▶ **n.** celery of a variety (*Apium graveolens rapaceum*) that forms a large swollen turniplike root. Also called CELERY ROOT. [18th C.: from CELERY.]

ce·ler·i·ty /sə'leritē/ ▶ **n.** archaic literary swiftness of movement. [15th C.: from L. *celeritas*, from *celer* 'swift.']

cel·er·y /'sel(ə)rē/ ▶ **n.** a cultivated plant (*Apium graveolens* var. *dulce*) of the parsley family, with closely packed succulent leafstalks that are eaten raw or cooked. [17th C.: from Fr. *céleri*, from Ital. dial. *selleri*, based on Gk. *selinon* 'parsley.']

cel·er·y root ▶ **n.** another term for CELERIAC.

cel·er·y salt ▶ **n.** a mixture of salt and ground celery seed used for seasoning.

ce·les·ta /sə'lestə/ ▶ **n.** (also **ce·leste**) a small keyboard instrument in which felted hammers strike a row of steel plates suspended over wooden resonators, giving an ethereal bell-like sound. [19th C.: pseudo-L., based on Fr. *céleste* 'heavenly.']

celesta

ce·les·tial /sə'lescHəl/ ▶ **adj.** [attrib.] positioned in or relating to the sky, or outer space as observed in astronomy. ■ belonging or relating to heaven. ■ supremely good: *the celestial beauty of music.* —**ce·les·tial·ly adv.** [ME: via OFr. from med. L. *caelestialis*, from L. *caelestis*, from *caelum* 'heaven.']

ce·les·tial e·qua·tor ▶ **n.** the projection into space of the earth's equator; an imaginary circle equidistant from the celestial poles.

ce·les·tial globe ▶ **n.** a spherical representation of the sky showing the constellations.

ce·les·tial ho·ri·zon ▶ **n.** see HORIZON (sense 1).

ce·les·tial lat·i·tude ▶ **n.** Astron. the angular distance of a point north or south of the ecliptic. Compare with DECLINATION (sense 1).

ce·les·tial lon·gi·tude ▶ **n.** Astron. the angular distance of a point east of the vernal equinox, measured along the ecliptic. Compare with RIGHT ASCENSION.

ce·les·tial me·chan·ics ▶ **plural n.** [treated as sing.] the branch of theoretical astronomy that deals with the calculation of the motions of celestial objects such as planets.

ce·les·tial nav·i·ga·tion ▶ **n.** the action of finding one's way by observing the sun, moon, and stars.

ce·les·tial pole ▶ **n.** Astron. the point on the celestial sphere directly above either of the earth's geographic poles, around which the stars and planets appear to rotate during the course of the night. The north celestial pole is currently within one degree of the star Polaris.

ce·les·tial sphere ▶ **n.** an imaginary sphere of which the observer is the center and on which all celestial objects are considered to lie.

ce·li·ac /'sēlē,ak/ (Brit. **coe·li·ac**) ▶ **adj. 1** Anat. of or relating to the abdomen. **2** Med. of, relating to, or affected by celiac disease. ▶ **n.** a person with celiac disease. [17th C.: from L. *coeliacus*, from Gk. *koiliakos*, from *koilia* 'belly.']

ce·li·ac dis·ease ▶ **n.** a disease in which chronic failure to digest food is triggered by hypersensitivity of the small intestine to gluten.

cel·i·bate /'seləbət/ ▶ **adj.** abstaining from marriage and sexual relations, typically for religious reasons. ■ having or involving no sexual relations. ▶ **n.** a person who abstains from marriage and sexual relations. —**cel·i·ba·cy** /-bəsē/ **n.** [19th C.: ult. from L. *caelibatus* 'celibacy,' from *caelebs, caelib-* 'unmarried.']

cell /sel/ ▶ **n. 1** a small room in which a prisoner is locked up or in which a monk or nun sleeps. ■ a small compartment in a larger structure such as a honeycomb. ■ hist. a small monastery or nunnery dependent on a larger one. **2** Biol. the smallest structural and functional unit of an organism, typically microscopic and consisting of cytoplasm and a nucleus enclosed in a membrane. Microscopic organisms typically consist of a single cell, which is either eukaryotic or prokaryotic. ■ an enclosed cavity in an organism. ■ fig. a small group forming a nucleus of political activity, typically a secret, subversive one: *the weapons may be used to arm terrorist cells.* ■ the local area covered by one of the short-range transmitters in a cellular telephone system. **3** a device containing electrodes immersed in an electrolyte, used for current-generation or electrolysis. ■ a unit in a device for converting chemical or solar energy into electricity. —**celled adj.** [in comb.] *a single-celled organism.* **cell-like adj.** [OE, from OFr. *celle* or L. *cella* 'storeroom.']

cel·la /'selə/ ▶ **n.** (pl. **cel·lae** /'selē/) the inner area of an ancient temple, esp. one housing the hidden cult image in a Greek or Roman temple. [17th C.: L., 'storeroom,' from *celare* 'hide.']

cel·lar /'selər/ ▶ **n.** a room below ground level in a house, typically one used for storing wine or coal: *the servants led us down into a cellar* | *a wine cellar.* ■ a stock of wine: *he spent years building up a remarkable cellar of aged Riojas.* ▶ **v.** [trans.] store (wine) in a cellar: *it is drinkable now but can be cellared for at least five years.* [ME: from OFr. *celier*, from late L. *cellarium* 'storehouse,' from *cella* 'storeroom.']

cel·lar·age /'selərij/ ▶ **n.** cellars collectively. ■ cellar space. ■ money charged for the use of a cellar or storehouse.

cel·lar·er /'selərər/ ▶ **n.** the person in a monastery who is responsible for food and drink.

cel·lar·et /,selə'ret/ (also **cel·lar·ette**) ▶ **n.** hist. a cabinet for keeping bottles of wine and liquor.

cell block ▶ **n.** a large single building or part of a complex subdivided into separate prison cells.

cell di·vi·sion ▶ **n.** Biol. the division of a cell into two daughter cells with the same genetic material.

Cel·li·ni /cHə'lēnē/, Benvenuto (1500–71), Italian goldsmith and sculptor. His autobiography is famous for its racy style and its vivid picture of contemporary Italian life. His sculptures include the bronze *Perseus* (1545–54).

cell line ▶ **n.** Biol. a cell culture developed from a single cell and therefore consisting of cells with a uniform genetic makeup.

cell-me·di·at·ed ▶ **adj.** Physiol. denoting the aspect of an immune response involving the action of white blood cells, rather than that of circulating antibodies. Often contrasted with HUMORAL.

cell mem·brane ▶ **n.** the semipermeable membrane surrounding the cytoplasm of a cell. Also called CYTOMEMBRANE.

cel·lo /'cHelō/ ▶ **n.** (pl. **-los**) a bass instrument of the violin family, held upright on the floor between the legs of the seated player. ■ a player of such an instrument. —**cel·list** /'cHelist/ **n.** [19th C.: shortening of VIOLONCELLO.]

cello

cel·lo·phane /'selə,fān/ ▶ **n.** a thin transparent wrapping material made from viscose: [as adj.] *a cellophane bag.* [20th C.: orig. a trademark.]

cell phone ▶ **n.** (also **cell·phone**) short for CELLULAR PHONE.

cel·lu·lar /'selyələr/ ▶ **adj. 1** of, relating to, or consisting of living cells. **2** denoting or relating to a telephone system that uses a number of short-range radio stations to cover the area that it serves, the signal being automatically switched from one station to another as the user travels. **3** (of a fabric item, such as a blanket or vest) knitted so as to form holes or hollows that trap air and provide extra insulation. **4** consisting of small compartments or rooms. —**cel·lu·lar·i·ty** /,selyə'laritē/ **n.** [18th C.: from Fr. *cellulaire*, from mod. L. *cellularis*, from *cellula* 'little chamber,' dimin. of *cella.*]

cel·lu·lar phone (also **cellular telephone**) ▶ **n.** a telephone with access to a cellular radio system so it can be used over a wide area, without a physical connection to a network.

cel·lu·lase /'selyə,lās; -,lāz/ ▶ **n.** Biochem. an enzyme that converts cellulose into glucose or a disaccharide. [20th C.: from CELLULOSE.]

cel·lu·lite /'selyə,līt/ ▶ **n.** persistent subcutaneous fat causing dimpling of the skin, esp. on women's hips and thighs. Not in technical use. [1960s: from Fr., from *cellule* 'small cell.']

cel·lu·li·tis /,selyə'lītis/ ▶ **n.** Med. inflammation of subcutaneous connective tissue.

cel·lu·loid /'selyə,loid/ ▶ **n.** a transparent flammable plastic made in sheets from camphor and nitrocellulose, formerly used for cinematographic film. ■ motion pictures as a genre. [19th C.: from CELLULOSE.]

cel·lu·lose /'selyə,lōs; -,lōz/ ▶ **n. 1** an insoluble substance that is the main constituent of plant cell walls and of vegetable fibers such as cotton. It is a polysaccharide consisting of chains of glucose monomers. **2** paint or lacquer consisting principally of cellulose acetate or nitrate in solution. — **cel·lu·lo·sic** /ˌselyəˈlōsik; -ˈlōzik/ **adj.** [19th C.: from Fr., from *cellule* 'small cell.']

cel·lu·lose ac·e·tate ▶ **n.** Chem. a nonflammable thermoplastic polymer made by acetylating cellulose, used as the basis of artificial fibers and plastic.

cel·lu·lose ni·trate ▶ **n.** another term for NITROCELLULOSE.

cel·lu·lose tri·ac·e·tate ▶ **n.** see TRIACETATE.

cell wall ▶ **n.** Biol. a rigid layer of polysaccharides lying outside the plasma membrane of the cells of plants, fungi, and bacteria. In the algae and higher plants, it consists mainly of cellulose.

ce·lom ▶ **n.** var. of COELOM.

ce·lo·sia /siˈlōzʜ(ē)ə/ ▶ **n.** a plant (genus *Celosia*) of the amaranth family with tiny red or yellow flowers in dense clusters. See also COCKSCOMB. [mod. L., from Gk. *kēlos* 'burned or dry' (from the burned appearance of the flowers in some species).]

Cel·si·us[1] /ˈselsēəs; ˈselsʜəs/, Anders (1701–44), Swedish astronomer. He is best known for his temperature scale.

Cel·si·us[2] (abbr.: **C**) ▶ **adj.** [postpositive when used with a numeral] of or denoting a scale of temperature on which water freezes at 0° and boils at 100° under standard conditions. ▶ **n.** (also **Celsius scale**) this scale of temperature.

Celt /kelt; selt/ ▶ **n.** a member of a group of peoples inhabiting much of Europe in pre-Roman times. Their culture developed in the late Bronze Age around the upper Danube, and reached its height in the La Tène culture (5th to 1st centuries BC) before being overrun by the Romans and Germanic peoples. ■ a native of any of the modern nations or regions in which Celtic languages are (or were) spoken; a person of Irish, Scottish, Manx, Welsh, or Cornish descent. [from L. *Celtae* (pl.), from Gk. *Keltoi*.]

celt /selt/ ▶ **n.** Archaeol. a prehistoric stone or metal implement with a beveled cutting edge, probably used as a tool or weapon. [18th C.: from med. L. *celtis* 'chisel.']

Celt·i·ber·i·an /ˌkeltīˈbi(ə)rēən; ˌselt-/ ▶ **n.** another term for IBERIAN (sense 3).

Celt·ic /ˈkeltik; ˈsel-/ ▶ **adj.** of or relating to the Celts or their languages, which constitute a branch of the Indo-European family and include Irish, Scottish Gaelic, Welsh, Breton, Manx, Cornish, and several extinct pre-Roman languages such as Gaulish. ▶ **n.** the Celtic language group. See also P-CELTIC, Q-CELTIC. — **Celt·i·cism** /ˈkeltəˌsizəm; ˈsel-/ **n.** **Celt·i·cist** /ˈkeltəˌsist; ˈsel-/ **n.** [16th C.: from L. *Celticus* (from *Celtae* 'Celts'), or from Fr. *Celtique* (from *Celte* 'Breton').]

Celt·ic cross ▶ **n.** a Latin cross with a circle around the center. See illustration at CROSS.

Celt·ic Sea a part of the Atlantic Ocean between southern Ireland and southwestern England.

cem·ba·lo /ˈcʜembəˌlō/ ▶ **n.** (pl. **-los**) another term for HARPSICHORD. — **cem·ba·list** /-bəlist/ **n.** [19th C.: from Ital., shortening of *clavicembalo*, from med. L. *clavicymbalum*, from L. *clavis* 'key' + *cymbalum* 'cymbal.']

ce·ment /siˈment/ ▶ **n.** a powdery substance made by calcining lime and clay, mixed with water to form mortar or mixed with sand, gravel, and water to make concrete. ■ a soft glue that hardens on setting: *rubber cement.* ■ fig. an element that unites a group of people: *traditional entertainment was a form of community cement.* ■ another term for CONCRETE. ■ a substance for filling cavities in teeth. ■ (also **cementum**) Anat. a thin layer of bony material that fixes teeth to the jaw. ■ Geol. the material that binds particles together in sedimentary rock. ▶ **v.** [trans.] attach with cement: *wooden posts were cemented into the ground.* ■ fig. settle or establish firmly: *the two companies are expected to cement an agreement soon.* ■ Geol. (of a material) bind (particles) together in sedimentary rock. — **ce·ment·er** **n.** [ME: from OFr. *ciment* (n.), *cimenter* (v.), from L. *caementum* 'quarry stone,' from *caedere* 'hew.']

ce·men·ta·tion /ˌsēmenˈtāsʜən/ ▶ **n.** **1** esp. Geol. the binding together of particles or other things by cement. **2** Metallurgy a process of altering a metal by heating it in contact with a powdered solid, esp. a former method of making steel by heating iron in contact with charcoal.

ce·ment·ite /siˈmentīt/ ▶ **n.** Metallurgy a hard, brittle iron carbide, Fe_3C, present in cast iron and most steels. [19th C.: from CEMENT + -ITE[1].]

ce·men·ti·tious /ˌsēmenˈtisʜəs/ ▶ **adj.** of the nature of cement: *a high-strength cementitious mortar that set within 1.5 hours.*

cem·e·ter·y /ˈseməˌterē/ ▶ **n.** (pl. **-ter·ies**) a burial ground; a graveyard. [ME: via late L. from Gk. *koimētērion* 'dormitory,' from *koiman* 'put to sleep.']

cen·a·cle /ˈsenikəl/ ▶ **n.** **1** a group of people, such as a discussion group or literary clique. **2** the room in which the Last Supper was held. [ME: from OFr. *cenacle*, from L. *cenaculum*, from *cena* 'dinner.']

ce·no·bite /ˈsenəˌbīt/ (also **coe·no·bite**) ▶ **n.** a member of a monastic community. — **ce·no·bit·ic** /ˌsenəˈbitik/ **adj.** **ce·no·bit·i·cal** /ˌsenəˈbitikəl/ **adj.** [ME: ult. from Gk. *koinobion* 'convent,' from *koinos* 'common' + *bios* 'life.']

ce·no·spe·cies /ˈsēnəˌspēsēz; -sʜēz/ ▶ **n.** a group of species whose members produce partially fertile hybrids when crossbred.

ce·no·taph /ˈsenəˌtaf/ ▶ **n.** a tomblike monument to someone buried elsewhere, esp. one commemorating people who died in a war. [17th C.: from Fr. *cénotaphe*, from late L. *cenotaphium*, from Gk. *kenos* 'empty' + *taphos* 'tomb.']

Ce·no·zo·ic /ˌsenəˈzōik/ ▶ **adj.** Geol. relating to or denoting the most recent era, beginning about 65 million years ago after the Mesozoic era and comprising the Tertiary and Quaternary periods. It has seen the rapid evolution and rise to dominance of mammals, birds, and flowering plants. ■ [as n.] (**the Cenozoic**) the Cenozoic era, or the system of rocks deposited during it. [19th C.: from Gk. *kainos* 'new' + *zōion* 'animal.']

cense /sens/ ▶ **v.** [trans.] perfume (something) ritually with the odor of burning incense. [ME: from OFr. *encenser*.]

cen·ser /ˈsensər/ ▶ **n.** a container in which incense is burned, typically during a religious ceremony. [ME: from OFr. *censier*, from *encensier*, from *encens* (see INCENSE[1]).]

cen·sor /ˈsensər/ ▶ **n.** **1** an official who examines material about to be released, such as books, movies, news, and art, and suppresses any parts considered obscene, politically unacceptable, or a threat to security. ■ Psychoanal. an aspect of the superego that is said to prevent certain ideas and memories from emerging into consciousness. **2** (in ancient Rome) either of two magistrates who held censuses and supervised public morals. ▶ **v.** [trans.] (often **be censored**) examine (a book, movie, etc.) officially and suppress unacceptable parts of it: *the movie was being censored because of its many violent scenes.* — **cen·so·ri·al** /senˈsôrēəl/ **adj.** [16th C.: from L., from *censere* 'assess.']

cen·so·ri·ous /senˈsôrēəs/ ▶ **adj.** severely critical of others. — **cen·so·ri·ous·ly** **adv.** **cen·so·ri·ous·ness** **n.**

cen·sor·ship /ˈsensərˌsʜip/ ▶ **n.** the practice of officially examining books, movies, etc., and suppressing unacceptable parts.

cen·sure /ˈsensʜər/ ▶ **v.** [trans.] (often **be censured**) express severe disapproval of (someone or something), typically in a formal statement. ▶ **n.** the expression of formal disapproval. — **cen·sur·a·ble** **adj.** [ME: ult. from L. *censura*, from *censere* 'assess.']

cen·sus /ˈsensəs/ ▶ **n.** (pl. **-sus·es**) an official count or survey of a population, typically recording various details of individuals. [17th C.: from L. 'registration of citizens and property,' from *censere* 'assess.']

cent /sent/ ▶ **n.** **1** a monetary unit of the U.S., Canada, and various other countries, equal to one hundredth of a dollar. ■ a coin of this value. ■ informal a small sum of money: *she saved every cent possible.* ■ [in sing.] [with negative] informal used for emphasis to denote any money at all: *he hadn't yet earned a cent.* **2** a monetary unit of some states of the European Union, equal to one hundredth of a euro. [ME: from Fr. *cent*, Ital. *cento*, or L. *centum* 'hundred.']

cent. ▶ **abbr.** ■ centigrade. ■ century.

cen·tas /ˈsentäs/ ▶ **n.** (pl. same) a monetary unit of Lithuania, equal to one hundredth of a litas.

cen·taur /ˈsentôr/ ▶ **n.** Gk. Mythol. a creature with the head, arms, and torso of a man and the body and legs of a horse. [via L. from Gk. *kentauros*, a Thessalonian tribe of expert horsemen.]

centaur

cen·tau·re·a /senˈtôrēə/ ▶ **n.** a composite plant of a genus (*Centaurea*) that includes the cornflower and knapweed. Several kinds are cultivated for their bright flowers. [mod. L., based on Gk. *kentauros*.]

Cen·tau·rus /senˈtôrəs/ Astron. a large southern constellation (the Centaur). It lies in the Milky Way and contains the stars Alpha and Proxima Centauri. [L.]

cen·tau·ry /ˈsentôrē/ ▶ **n.** (pl. **-ries**) a widely distributed herbaceous plant (*Centaurium* and related genera) of the gentian family, typically having pink petals atop long calyx tubes. Its many species include the wild *C. pulchellum* and the cultivated ornamental *C. scilloides*. [ME: from late L. *centaurea*, based on Gk. *kentauros*.]

cen·ta·vo /senˈtävō/ ▶ **n.** (pl. **-vos**) a monetary unit of Mexico, Brazil, Portugal, and certain other countries, equal to one hundredth of the basic unit. [Sp. and Port., from L. *centum* 'a hundred.']

cen·te·nar·i·an /ˌsentnˈe(ə)rēən/ ▶ **n.** a person who is one hundred or more years old. ▶ **adj.** [attrib.] one hundred or more years old.

cen·ten·ar·y /senˈtenərē; ˈsentnˌerē/ esp. Brit. ▶ **n.** (pl. **-ar·ies**) a centennial. ▶ **adj.** of or relating to a hundredth anniversary. [17th C.: from L. *centenarius* 'containing a hundred,' based on L. *centum* 'a hundred.']

cen·ten·ni·al /senˈtenēəl/ ▶ **adj.** of or relating to a hundredth anniversary. ▶ **n.** a hundredth anniversary. ■ a celebration of such an anniversary. [18th C.: from L. *centum* 'a hundred.']

cen·ter /ˈsentər/ (Brit. **cen·tre**) ▶ **n.** **1** the middle point of a circle or sphere, equidistant from every point on the circumference or surface. ■ a point or part that is equally distant from all sides, ends, or surfaces of something; the middle. ■ a pivot or axis of rotation: *the galactic rotation of the solar system around the galactic center.* ■ a political party or group holding moderate opinions. ■ Sports the middle player in a line or group in many games. ■ Football the offensive player who passes the ball to the quarterback. ■ Baseball short for CENTER FIELD. ■ a core, such as the filling in a piece of chocolate. ■ a conical adjustable support for a workpiece in a lathe or similar machine. **2** a place or group of buildings where a specified activity is concentrated: *a shopping center.* ■ a point at which an activity or quality is at its most intense and from which it spreads: *the city was **a center of** discontent.* ■ the point on which an

activity or process is focused: *two issues at the center of the healthcare debate.* ■ the most important place in the respect specified: *Geneva was then the center of the international world.* ▶ **v. 1** [intrans.] (**center around/on**) have (something) as a major concern or theme: *the plot centers on two young men.* ■ [trans.] (**center something around/on**) cause an argument or discussion to focus on (a specified issue): *he is centering his discussion on an analysis of patterns of mortality.* ■ (**be centered in**) (of an activity) occur mainly in or around (a specified place): *the mercantile association was centered in northern Germany.* **2** [trans.] place in the middle: *to center the needle, turn the knob.* ■ Football pass the ball back from the ground to another player to begin a down; snap.
– PHRASES **the center of attention** a person or thing that draws general attention. — **cen·ter·most adj.** [ME *centre*, based on Gk. *kentron* 'sharp point,' rel. to *kentein* 'to prick.']

cen·ter bit ▶ **n.** a drill bit with a sharp projecting point.

cen·ter·board /ˈsentər,bôrd/ ▶ **n.** a pivoted board that can be lowered through the keel of a sailboat to reduce sideways movement. Compare with DAGGERBOARD.

cen·tered /ˈsentərd/ (Brit. **cen·tred**) ▶ **adj. 1** in the center: *a centered oval window.* **2** [in comb.] having the specified subject as the focal element: *a computer-centered industry.* **3** (of a person) well balanced and confident or serene. **4** [in comb.] having a center or filling of a specified type: *a soft-centered chocolate.* — **cen·tered·ness n.**

cen·ter field (also **cen·ter·field**) ▶ **n.** Baseball the central part of the outfield, behind second base. ■ the position of an outfielder in this area: *Amaro played some center field when Dykstra went on the disabled list.* — **cen·ter field·er n.**

cen·ter·fire /ˈsentər,fī(ə)r/ ▶ **adj.** [attrib.] (of a gun cartridge) having the primer in the center of the base. ■ (of a gun) using such cartridges. ▶ **n.** a gun using such a cartridge.

cen·ter·fold /ˈsentər,fōld/ ▶ **n.** the two middle pages of a magazine, typically taken up by a single illustration or feature: *pull-out-and-keep centerfolds on superior quality paper* | [as adj.] *a centerfold poster of the person shown on the front cover.* ■ an illustration on such pages, typically a picture of a naked or scantily clad model: *the centerfold featured a nude woman* | [as adj.] *her centerfold body.*

cen·ter·ing /ˈsentəriNG/ ▶ **n.** Archit. framing used to support an arch or dome under construction.

cen·ter·line /ˈsentər,līn/ (also **center line**) ▶ **n.** a real or imaginary line through the center of something, esp. one following an axis of symmetry: *the road has a white center line* | *bore a series of holes along the center line.* ■ a painted line running down the middle of a road, dividing traffic traveling in opposite directions.

cen·ter of grav·i·ty ▶ **n.** a point from which the weight of a body or system may be considered to act. In uniform gravity it is the same as the center of mass.

cen·ter of mass ▶ **n.** a point representing the mean position of the matter in a body or system: *the center of mass of Venus.*

cen·ter·piece /ˈsentər,pēs/ ▶ **n.** a decorative piece or display placed in the middle of a dining or serving table. ■ an item or issue intended to be a focus of attention: *the tower is the centerpiece of the park.*

cen·ter punch ▶ **n.** a tool with a conical point for making an indentation in an object, to allow a drill to make a hole at the same spot without slipping.

cen·ter spread ▶ **n.** the two facing middle pages of a newspaper or magazine.

cen·ter stage ▶ **n.** [in sing.] the center of a stage. ■ the most prominent position: *oil remains at center stage, with demands for expanded drilling.* ▶ **adv.** at or toward the middle of a stage: *at the play's opening she stands center stage.* ■ in or toward a prominent position: *Asian countries have moved center stage for world business.*

cen·tes·i·mal /senˈtesəməl/ ▶ **adj.** of or relating to division into hundredths. — **cen·tes·i·mal·ly adv.** [19th C.: from L. *centesimus* 'hundredth,' from *centum* 'a hundred.']

cen·tes·i·mo /senˈtesə,mō; CHenˈtez-/ ▶ **n.** (pl. **-mos** or **-mi** /-mē/) a monetary unit of Italy until the introduction of the euro, worth one hundredth of a lira (used only in calculations).

cen·té·si·mo /senˈtesə,mō/ ▶ **n.** (pl. **-mos**) a monetary unit of Uruguay and Panama, equal to one hundredth of a peso in Uruguay and one hundredth of a balboa in Panama. [Sp.]

centi- ▶ **comb. form** used commonly in units of measurement: **1** one hundredth: *centiliter.* **2** hundred: *centigrade* | *centipede.* [from L. *centum* 'hundred.']

cen·ti·grade /ˈsentə,grād/ ▶ **adj.** [postpositive when used with a numeral] another term for CELSIUS². ■ having a scale of a hundred degrees. [19th C.: from Fr., from L. *centum* 'a hundred' + *gradus* 'step.']

cen·ti·gram /ˈsentə,gram/ (abbr.: **cg**) ▶ **n.** a metric unit of mass, equal to one hundredth of a gram.

cen·ti·li·ter /ˈsentə,lētər/ (Brit. **cen·ti·li·tre**) (abbr.: **cl**) ▶ **n.** a metric unit of capacity, equal to one hundredth of a liter.

cen·time /ˈsäntēm; ˈsen-/ ▶ **n.** a monetary unit of Switzerland and certain other countries (including France, Belgium, and Luxembourg until the introduction of the euro), equal to one hundredth of a franc or other decimal currency unit. ■ a coin of this value. [Fr., from L. *centesimus* 'hundredth,' from *centum* 'a hundred.']

cen·ti·me·ter /ˈsentə,mētər; ˈsän-/ (Brit. **cen·ti·me·tre**) (abbr.: **cm**) ▶ **n.** a metric unit of length, equal to one hundredth of a meter.

cen·ti·me·ter-gram-sec·ond sys·tem ▶ **n.** a system of measurement using the centimeter, the gram, and the second as basic units of length, mass, and time.

cen·ti·mo /ˈsentəmō/ ▶ **n.** (pl. **-mos**) a monetary unit of Spain (until the introduction of the euro) and a number of Latin American countries, equal to one hundredth of the peseta. [Sp.]

cen·ti·pede /ˈsentə,pēd/ ▶ **n.** a predatory myriapod invertebrate (class Chilopoda, several orders) with a flattened elongated body composed of many segments. Most segments bear a single pair of legs. [17th C.: from Fr. *centipède* or L. *centipeda*, from *centum* 'a hundred' + *pes, ped-* 'foot.']

cen·tra /ˈsentrə/ a plural form of CENTRUM.

cen·tral /ˈsentrəl/ ▶ **adj. 1** of, at, or forming the center: *the station has a central courtyard.* ■ accessible from a variety of places: *coaches met at a central location.* ■ Phonet. (of a vowel) articulated in the center of the mouth. **2** of the greatest importance; principal or essential: *his preoccupation with American history is* ***central to*** *his work* | *the rising crime rate remained the central campaign issue.* ■ [attrib.] (of a group or organization) having controlling power over a country or another organization: *central government.* ■ [attrib.] (of power or authority) in the hands of such a group: *local councils are increasingly subject to central control.* — **cen·tral·i·ty** /senˈtralitē/ **n. cen·tral·ly adv.** [17th C.: from Fr., or from L. *centralis*, from *centrum* (see CENTER).]

Cen·tral Af·ri·can Re·pub·lic a country in central Africa. *See box.*

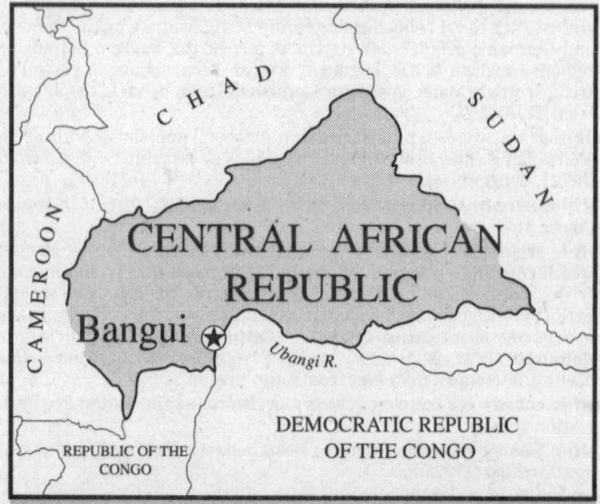

Central African Republic

Location: central Africa, north of the Democratic Republic of the Congo and south of Chad and Sudan
Area: 240,600 square miles (623,000 sq km)
Population: 3,742,000
Capital: Bangui
Languages: French (official), Arabic, Swahili
Currency: CFA franc

Cen·tral A·mer·i·ca the southernmost part of North America that links the continent to South America. — **Cen·tral A·mer·i·can adj. & n.**

cen·tral bank ▶ **n.** a national bank that provides financial and banking services for its country's government and commercial banking system, as well as implementing the government's monetary policy and issuing currency.

cen·tral cast·ing ▶ **n.** a department at a movie or television studio that hires actors for smaller parts.

cen·tral cit·y ▶ **n.** a heavily populated city at the center of a large metropolitan area.

Cen·tral Com·mand (abbr.: **Centcom**) a military strike force consisting of units from the US Army, Air Force, and Navy, established in 1979 (as the Rapid Deployment Force) to operate in the Middle East and North Africa.

cen·tral heat·ing ▶ **n.** a system for warming a building by heating water or air in one place and circulating it through pipes and radiators or vents.

Cen·tral In·tel·li·gence A·gen·cy (abbr.: **CIA**) a US federal agency responsible for coordinating government intelligence activities.

cen·tral·ism /ˈsentrə,lizəm/ ▶ **n.** a system that centralizes, esp. an administration. — **cen·tral·ist n. & adj.**

cen·tral·ize /ˈsentrə,līz/ ▶ **v.** [trans.] [often as adj.] (**centralized**) concentrate (control of an activity or organization) under a single authority: *a vast superstructure of centralized control.* ■ bring (activities) together in one place: *the ultimate goal is to centralize boxing under one umbrella.* — **cen·tral·i·za·tion** /,sentrələˈzāSHən/ **n.**

cen·tral lock·ing ▶ **n.** a locking system in a motor vehicle that enables the locks of all doors to be operated simultaneously by a single person.

cen·tral nerv·ous sys·tem ▶ **n.** Anat. the complex of nerve tissues that controls the activities of the body. In vertebrates it comprises the brain and spinal cord.

Cen·tral Park a large public park in the center of Manhattan in New York City.

Cen·tral Pow·ers the alliance of Germany, Austria–Hungary, Turkey, and Bulgaria during World War I. ■ the alliance of Germany, Austria–Hungary, and Italy between 1882 and 1914.

cen·tral proc·ess·ing u·nit (also **cen·tral proc·es·sor**) ▶ **n.** Comput. the part of a computer in which operations are controlled and executed.

Cen·tral time the standard time in a zone that includes the central states of the US and parts of central Canada, specifically: ■ (**Central Standard Time** abbrev.: **CST**) standard time based on the mean solar time at longitude 90° W., six hours behind Greenwich Mean Time. ■ (**Central Daylight Time** abbrev.: **CDT**) Central time during daylight saving time, seven hours behind Greenwich Mean Time.

Cen·tral Val·ley a lowland in central California that is drained in the north by the Sacramento River. It is also called the Sacramento Valley in the north; in the south, it is called the San Joaquin Valley.

cen·tre ▶ **n.** British spelling of CENTER.

cen·tric /ˈsentrik/ ▶ **adj.** **1** in or at the center; central: *centric and peripheral forces.* **2** Bot. (of a diatom) radially symmetrical. — **cen·tri·cal** /-trikəl/ **adj.** **cen·tric·i·ty** /senˈtrisitē/ **n.** [16th C.: from Gk. *kentrikos*, from *kentron* 'point.']

-centric ▶ **comb. form** having a specified center: *geocentric.* ■ forming an opinion or evaluation originating from a specified viewpoint: *Eurocentric* | *ethnocentric.* — **-centricity comb. form** in corresponding nouns. [from Gk. *kentrikos*.]

cen·trif·u·gal /senˈtrif(y)əgəl/ ▶ **adj.** Physics moving or tending to move away from a center. — **cen·trif·u·gal·ly adv.** [18th C.: from mod. L. *centrifugus*, from L. *centrum* (see CENTER) + *-fugus* 'fleeing' (from *fugere* 'flee').]

cen·trif·u·gal force ▶ **n.** Physics an apparent force that acts outward on a body moving around a center, arising from the body's inertia.

cen·tri·fuge /ˈsentrə,fyo͞oj/ ▶ **n.** a machine with a rapidly rotating container that applies centrifugal force to its contents, typically to separate fluids of different densities or liquids from solids. ▶ **v.** [trans.] (usu. **be centrifuged**) subject to the action of a centrifuge. ■ separate by centrifuge. — **cen·trif·u·ga·tion** /,sentrəfyo͞oˈgāsнən; sen,trif(y)ə-/ **n.**

cen·tri·ole /ˈsentrē,ōl/ ▶ **n.** Biol. a minute cylindrical organelle near the nucleus in animal cells, occurring in pairs and involved in the development of spindle fibers in cell division. [19th C.: from mod. L. *centriolum*, dimin. of *centrum* (see CENTER).]

cen·trip·e·tal /senˈtripətl/ ▶ **adj.** Physics moving or tending to move toward a center. — **cen·trip·e·tal·ly adv.** [18th C.: from mod. L. *centripetus*, from L. *centrum* (see CENTER) + *-petus* 'seeking' (from *petere* 'seek').]

cen·trip·e·tal force ▶ **n.** Physics a force that acts on a body moving in a circular path and is directed toward the center around which the body is moving.

cen·trist /ˈsentrist/ ▶ **adj.** having moderate political views or policies. ▶ **n.** a person who holds moderate political views. — **cen·trism** /-,trizəm/ **n.**

cen·troid /ˈsentroid/ ▶ **n.** Math. the center of mass of a geometric object of uniform density.

cen·tro·mere /ˈsentrə,mi(ə)r/ ▶ **n.** Biol. the point on a chromosome by which it is attached to a spindle fiber during cell division. — **cen·tro·mer·ic** /,sentrəˈmi(ə)rik; -ˈmerik/ **adj.** [1920s: from L. *centrum* (see CENTER) + Gk. *meros* 'part.']

cen·tro·some /ˈsentrə,sōm/ ▶ **n.** Biol. an organelle near the nucleus of a cell that contains the centrioles (in animal cells) and from which the spindle fibers develop in cell division. [19th C.: from L. *centrum* (see CENTER) + Gk. *sōma* 'body.']

cen·tro·sphere /ˈsentrə,sfi(ə)r/ ▶ **n.** **1** Biol. a region of clear, differentiated cytoplasm from which the asters extend during cell division and which contains the centriole(s) if present. **2** Geol. the central or inner part of the earth.

cen·trum /ˈsentrəm/ ▶ **n.** (pl. **-trums** or **-tra** /-trə/) Anat. the solid central part of a vertebra, to which the arches and processes are attached. [19th C.: from L.]

cen·tu·ple /senˈt(y)o͞opəl; ˈsent(y)o͞opəl/ ▶ **v.** [trans.] multiply by a hundred or by a large amount. [17th C.: ult. from L. *centuplex*, from *centum* 'hundred.']

cen·tu·ri·on /senˈt(y)o͝orēən/ ▶ **n.** the commander of a century in the ancient Roman army. [ME: from L. *centurion-*, from *centuria*.]

cen·tu·ry /ˈsenCH(ə)rē/ ▶ **n.** (pl. **-ries**) **1** a period of one hundred years: *a century ago most people walked to work.* ■ a period of one hundred years reckoned from the traditional date of the birth of Jesus Christ: *the fifteenth century.* **2** a group of one hundred things. **3** a company in the ancient Roman army, originally of one hundred men. ■ an ancient Roman political division for voting. **4** a bicycle race of one hundred miles: [as adj.] *the nation's largest single-day century ride.* — **cen·tu·ri·al** /senˈt(y)o͝orēəl/ **adj.** [ME (sense 3): from L. *centuria*, from *centum* 'hundred.']

cen·tu·ry plant ▶ **n.** a stemless agave (*Agave americana*) with long spiny leaves that produces a tall flowering stem after many years of growth and then dies. Also called AMERICAN ALOE.

CEO ▶ **abbr.** chief executive officer.

cep /sep/ (also **cèpe**) ▶ **n.** an edible European and North American bolete mushroom (*Boletus edulis*) with a smooth brown cap, a stout white stalk, and pores rather than gills, growing in dry woodland and much sought after as a delicacy. Also called KING BOLETE, PORCINI. [19th C.: from Fr. *cèpe*, from Gascon *cep* 'tree trunk,' from L. *cippus* 'stake.']

ce·phal·ic /səˈfalik/ ▶ **adj.** tech. of, in, or relating to the head. [ME: from OFr. *cephalique*, based on Gk. *kephalikos*, from *kephalē* 'head.']

-cephalic ▶ **comb. form** equivalent to -CEPHALOUS.

ce·phal·ic in·dex ▶ **n.** Anthropol. a number expressing the ratio of the maximum breadth of a skull to its maximum length.

ceph·a·lin /ˈsefəlin/ ▶ **n.** Biochem. any of a group of phospholipids present in cell membranes, esp. in the brain. [19th C.: from Gk. *kephalē* 'brain.']

ceph·a·li·za·tion /,sefələˈzāsнən/ ▶ **n.** Zool. the concentration of sense organs, nervous control, etc., at the anterior end of the body, forming a head and brain, both during evolution and in an embryo's development.

cephalo- ▶ **comb. form** relating to the head or skull: *cephalometry.* [from Gk. *kephalē* 'head.']

ceph·a·lom·e·ter /sefəˈlämitər/ ▶ **n.** a device for measuring the human head.

ceph·a·lom·e·try /,sefəˈlämitrē/ ▶ **n.** Med. measurement and study of the proportions of the head and face, esp. during development and growth. — **ceph·a·lo·met·ric** /-lōˈmetrik/ **adj.**

Ceph·a·lop·o·da /,sefəˈläpədə/ Zool. a class of predatory mollusks comprising octopuses, squids, and cuttlefish. They have a distinct head with large eyes and a ring of tentacles around a beaked mouth and are able to release a cloud of inky fluid to confuse predators. — **ceph·a·lo·pod** /ˈsefələ,päd/ **n.** [mod. L. (pl.), from Gk. *kephalē* 'head' + *pous, pod-* 'foot.']

ceph·a·lo·spo·rin /,sefəlōˈspôrən/ ▶ **n.** any of a group of semisynthetic broad-spectrum antibiotics resembling penicillin. [1950s: from mod. L. *Cephalosporium*, genus of fungi.]

ceph·a·lo·tho·rax /,sefəlōˈTHôraks/ ▶ **n.** (pl. **-tho·ra·ces** /-ˈTHôrə,sēz/ or **-tho·rax·es**) Zool. the fused head and thorax of spiders and other chelicerate arthropods.

-cephalous ▶ **comb. form** -headed (used commonly in medical, zoological, and botanical terms): *macrocephalous.* [based on Gk. *kephalē* 'head.']

ce·pheid /ˈsēfēəd; ˈsef-/ (also **cepheid variable**) ▶ **n.** Astron. a variable star having a regular cycle of brightness with a frequency related to its luminosity, so allowing estimation of its distance from the earth. [20th C.: from the name of the variable star *Delta Cephei*, which typifies this class of stars.]

Ce·phe·us /ˈsēfēəs; ˈsēfyo͞os/ Astron. a constellation near the north celestial pole. [after a king of Ethiopia, the husband of Cassiopeia.]

'cept /sep(t)/ ▶ **prep., conj., & v.** nonstandard contraction of EXCEPT used in representing speech.

ce·ram·ic /səˈramik/ ▶ **adj.** made of clay and hardened by heat. ■ of or relating to the manufacture of such articles. ▶ **n.** (**ceramics**) pots and other articles made from clay hardened by heat. ■ [usu. treated as sing.] the art of making such articles. ■ (**ceramic**) the material from which such articles are made. ■ (**ceramic**) any nonmetallic solid that remains hard when heated. — **ce·ram·i·cist** /səˈraməsist/ **n.** [19th C.: from Gk. *keramikos*, from *keramos* 'pottery.']

Ce·ram Sea /ˈsārām/ (also **Se·ram Sea**) the part of the western Pacific Ocean that is at the center of the Molucca Islands in Indonesia.

ce·ras·tes /səˈrastēz/ ▶ **n.** a North African viper (genus *Cerastes*) that has a hornlike spike over each eye. [ME: from L., from Gk. *kerastēs* 'horned,' from *keras* 'horn.']

ce·rat·ed /ˈsi(ə)rātid/ ▶ **adj.** **1** covered with wax or resin. **2** Ornithol. having a cere.

cer·a·top·si·an /,serəˈtäpsēən/ Paleontol. ▶ **n.** a gregarious quadrupedal herbivorous dinosaur (infraorder Ceratopsia, order Ornithischia) of a group found in the Cretaceous period, including the triceratops. It had a large beaked and horned head and a bony frill protecting the neck. ▶ **adj.** of or relating to the ceratopsians. [20th C.: from mod. L. *Ceratopsia* (pl.) (from Gk. *keras, kerat-* 'horn' + *ops* 'face').]

Cer·ber·us /ˈsərbərəs/ Gk. Mythol. a monstrous watchdog with three heads that guarded the entrance to Hades.

cer·car·i·a /sərˈke(ə)rēə/ ▶ **n.** (pl. **-car·i·ae** /-ˈke(ə)rē,ē/) Zool. a free-swimming larval stage in which a parasitic fluke passes from an intermediate host to another intermediate host or to the final vertebrate host. [19th C.: mod. L., from Gk. *kerkos* 'tail.']

cere /si(ə)r/ ▶ **n.** Ornithol. a waxy, fleshy covering at the base of the upper beak in some birds. [15th C.: from L. *cera* 'wax.']

ce·re·al /ˈsi(ə)rēəl/ ▶ **n.** a grain used for food, such as wheat, oats, or corn. ■ (usu. **cereals**) a grass producing such grain, grown as an agricultural crop. ■ a breakfast food made from roasted grain, typically eaten with milk. [19th C. (adj.): from L. *cerealis*, from *Ceres*, Roman goddess of agriculture.]

cer·e·bel·lum /,serəˈbeləm/ ▶ **n.** (pl. **-bel·lums** or **-bel·la** /-ˈbelə/) Anat. the part of the brain at the back of the skull in vertebrates. Its function is to coordinate and regulate muscular activity. — **cer·e·bel·lar** /-ˈbelər/ **adj.** [16th C.: from L., dimin. of CEREBRUM.]

ce·re·bral /səˈrēbrəl; ˈserəbrəl/ ▶ **adj.** **1** of the cerebrum of the brain: *a cerebral hemorrhage.* ■ intellectual rather than emotional or physical:

photography is a cerebral process. **2** Phonet. another term for RETROFLEX. — **ce·re·bral·ly** adv. [19th C.: from L. *cerebrum* 'brain.']

ce·re·bral aq·ue·duct ▶ n. Anat. a fluid-filled canal that runs through the midbrain connecting the third and fourth ventricles.

ce·re·bral pal·sy ▶ n. a condition marked by impaired muscle coordination (spastic paralysis) and/or other disabilities, typically caused by damage to the brain before or at birth. See also SPASTIC.

cer·e·bra·tion /ˌserəˈbrāsʜən/ ▶ n. tech. formal the working of the brain; thinking. — **cer·e·brate** /ˈserəˌbrāt/ v.

cerebro- ▶ comb. form of or relating to the brain: *cerebrospinal.* [from L. *cerebrum* 'brain.']

ce·re·bro·side /səˈrēbrəˌsīd; ˈserəbrə-/ ▶ n. Biochem. any of a group of complex lipids present in the sheaths of nerve fibers. [19th C.: from L. *cerebrum* 'brain' + -OSE².]

ce·re·bro·spi·nal /səˌrēbrōˈspīnl; ˌserəbrō-/ ▶ adj. Anat. of or relating to the brain and spine.

ce·re·bro·spi·nal flu·id ▶ n. Anat. clear watery fluid that fills the space between the arachnoid membrane and the pia mater.

ce·re·bro·vas·cu·lar /səˌrēbrōˈvaskyələr; ˌserəbrō-/ ▶ adj. Anat. relating to the brain and its blood vessels.

ce·re·brum /səˈrēbrəm; ˈserə-/ ▶ n. (pl. **-bra** /-brə/) Anat. the principal and most anterior part of the brain in vertebrates, located in the front area of the skull and consisting of two hemispheres. It is responsible for the integration of sensory and neural functions and the initiation and coordination of voluntary activity. See also TELENCEPHALON. [17th C.: from L., 'brain.']

cere·cloth /ˈsi(ə)rˌklôᴛʜ/ ▶ n. hist. waxed cloth typically used for wrapping a corpse. [ME: from *cered cloth,* from *cere* 'to wax,' from L. *cerare,* from *cera* 'wax.']

cere·ment /ˈserəmənt; ˈsi(ə)rmənt/ ▶ n. (usu. **cerements**) hist. waxed cloth for wrapping a corpse.

cer·e·mo·ni·al /ˌserəˈmōnēəl/ ▶ adj. **1** relating to or used for formal events of a religious or public nature. **2** (of a position or role) involving only nominal authority or power: *a ceremonial post.* ▶ n. the system of rules and procedures to be observed at a formal or religious occasion: *the procedure was conducted with all due ceremonial.* ■ a rite or ceremony: *a ceremonial called the ghost dance.* — **cer·e·mo·ni·al·ism** /-ˌlizəm/ n. **cer·e·mo·ni·al·ist** /-list/ n. **cer·e·mo·ni·al·ly** adv.

cer·e·mo·ni·ous /ˌserəˈmōnēəs/ ▶ adj. relating or appropriate to grand and formal occasions. ■ excessively polite; punctilious. — **cer·e·mo·ni·ous·ly** adv. **cer·e·mo·ni·ous·ness** n.

cer·e·mo·ny /ˈserəˌmōnē/ ▶ n. (pl. **-nies**) **1** a formal occasion, typically one celebrating a particular event or anniversary. ■ an act or series of acts performed according to a traditional form. **2** the ritual observances and procedures performed at formal occasions: *the new Queen was proclaimed with due ceremony.* ■ formal polite behavior: *he showed them to their table with great ceremony.*
– PHRASES **stand on ceremony** [usu. with negative] insist on the observance of formalities: *we don't stand on ceremony in this house.* [ME: from OFr. *ceremonie* or L. *caerimonia* 'religious worship.']

Ce·ren·kov /ᴄʜəˈrenɢkôv; -kôf; -kəf/, Pavel, see CHERENKOV.

Ce·ren·kov ra·di·a·tion (also **Che·ren·kov ra·di·a·tion**) ▶ n. Physics electromagnetic radiation emitted by particles moving through a medium at speeds greater than that of light in the same medium.

Ce·res /ˈsi(ə)rēz/ **1** Rom. Mythol. the goddess of grain and agriculture. Greek equivalent DEMETER. **2** Astron. the first asteroid to be discovered, and also the largest, with a diameter of 567 miles (913 km).

cer·e·sin /ˈserəsin/ ▶ n. a hard whitish paraffin wax used with or instead of beeswax. [19th C.: from mod. L. *ceres* (from L. *cera* 'wax').]

ce·re·us /ˈsi(ə)rēəs/ ▶ n. one of numerous neotropical cacti now or formerly included in the genus *Cereus.*

ce·ric /ˈsi(ə)rik/ ▶ adj. of cerium in its higher valency (4).

ce·rise /səˈrēs; -ˈrēz/ ▶ n. a bright or deep red color. ▶ adj. of a bright or deep red color. [19th C.: from Fr., lit. 'cherry.']

ce·ri·um /ˈsi(ə)rēəm/ ▶ n. the chemical element of atomic number 58, a silvery white metal. It is the most abundant of the lanthanide elements and is the main component of the alloy misch metal. (Symbol: **Ce**) [19th C.: named after the asteroid CERES.]

cer·met /ˈsərmet/ ▶ n. any of a class of heat-resistant materials made of ceramic and sintered metal. [1950s: blend of CERAMIC and METAL.]

CERN /sərn/ ▶ abbr. European Organization for Nuclear Research. [from Fr. *Conseil Européen pour la Recherche Nucléaire.*]

ce·ro /ˈsi(ə)rō/ ▶ n. (pl. same or **-ros**) a large fish (*Scomberomorus regalis*) of the mackerel family, valued as a food fish in the tropical western Atlantic. [19th C.: from Sp. *sierra* 'saw or sawfish.']

cero- ▶ comb. form of or relating to wax: *ceroplastic.* [from L. *cera* or Gk. *kēros* 'wax.']

ce·ro·plas·tic /ˌsi(ə)rōˈplastik; ˌserō-/ ▶ adj. of or relating to modeling in wax.

ce·rous /ˈsi(ə)rəs/ ▶ adj. of cerium in its lower valency (3).

Cer·ri·tos /səˈrētəs/ a city in southwestern California, southeast of Los Angeles; pop. 53,240.

Cer·ro Gor·do /ˈserōˈgôrdō/ a mountain pass in eastern Mexico, scene of an 1847 battle in the Mexican War.

cert. ▶ abbr. ■ certificate. ■ certified.

cer·tain /ˈsərtn/ ▶ adj. **1** known for sure; established beyond doubt. ■ having complete conviction about something; confident. **2** [attrib.] specific but not explicitly named or stated: *he raised certain personal problems with me.* ■ used when mentioning the name of someone not known to the reader or hearer: *a certain General Percy captured the town.* ▶ pron. (**certain of**) some but not all: *certain of his works have been edited.*
– PHRASES **for certain** without any doubt. [ME: from OFr., based on L. *certus* 'sure.']

cer·tain·ly /ˈsərtnlē/ ▶ adv. [sentence adverb] undoubtedly; definitely; surely: *it certainly isn't worth risking your life.* ■ (in answer to a question or command) yes; by all means: *"A good idea," she agreed. "Certainly!"*

cer·tain·ty /ˈsərtntē/ ▶ n. (pl. **-ties**) firm conviction that something is the case. ■ the quality of being reliably true: *a bewildering lack of certainty in the law.* ■ a fact that is definitely true or an event that is definitely going to take place: *an immediate transfer is a certainty.* ■ a person or thing that may be relied on: *he was a certainty for a gold medal.*
– PHRASES **for a certainty** beyond the possibility of doubt.

cer·tes /ˈsərtēz; sərts/ ▶ adv. archaic assuredly; I assure you. [ME: from OFr., based on L. *certus* 'sure.']

cer·ti·fi·a·ble /ˌsərtəˈfīəbəl/ ▶ adj. **1** able or needing to be certified. **2** officially recognized as needing treatment for a mental disorder. ■ informal crazy: *publishing has become insane and the people who work in it are certifiable.* — **cer·ti·fi·a·bly** /-blē/ adj.

cer·tif·i·cate ▶ n. /sərˈtifikit/ an official document attesting a certain fact, in particular: ■ a document recording a person's birth, marriage, or death. ■ a document describing a medical condition. ■ a document attesting a level of achievement in a course of study or training. ■ a document attesting ownership of a certain item. ▶ v. /-ˈtifəkāt/ [trans.] (usu. **be certificated**) provide with or attest in an official document. — **cer·ti·fi·ca·tion** /ˌsərtəfiˈkāsʜən/ n. [ME: from Fr. *certificat* or med. L. *certificatum,* from *certificare* (see CERTIFY).]

cer·tif·i·cate of de·pos·it (abbr.: **CD**) ▶ n. a certificate issued by a bank to a person depositing money for a specified length of time.

cer·ti·fied check ▶ n. a check guaranteed by a bank.

cer·ti·fied mail ▶ n. a postal service in which the sending and receipt of a letter or package are recorded.

cer·ti·fied pub·lic ac·count·ant (abbr.: **CPA**) ▶ n. a member of an officially accredited body of accountants.

cer·ti·fy /ˈsərtəˌfī/ ▶ v. (**-fies, -fied**) [trans.] (often **be certified**) attest or confirm in a formal statement. ■ [often as adj.] (**certified**) officially recognize (someone or something) as possessing certain qualifications or meeting certain standards. ■ officially declare insane. [ME: from OFr. *certifier,* from late L. *certificare,* from L. *certus* 'certain.']

cer·ti·o·ra·ri /ˌsərsʜ(ē)əˈrärē; -ˈre(ə)rī/ ▶ n. Law a writ or order by which a higher court reviews a decision of a lower court: *an order of certiorari.* [ME: from Law L., 'to be informed.']

cer·ti·tude /ˈsərtəˌt(y)o͞od/ ▶ n. absolute certainty or conviction that something is the case. ■ something that someone firmly believes is true. [ME: from late L. *certitudo,* from *certus* 'certain.']

ce·ru·le·an /səˈro͞olēən/ literary ▶ adj. deep blue in color like a clear sky. ▶ n. a deep sky-blue color. [17th C.: from L. *caeruleus* 'sky blue,' from *caelum* 'sky.']

ce·ru·men /səˈro͞omən/ ▶ n. technical term for EARWAX. [17th C.: mod. L., from L. *cera* 'wax.']

ce·ruse /səˈro͞os; ˈsi(ə)ro͞os/ ▶ n. archaic term for WHITE LEAD. [ME: via OFr. from L. *cerussa,* perh. from Gk. *kēros* 'wax.']

Cer·van·tes /sərˈvantēz; serˈväntās/, Miguel de (1547–1616), Spanish writer and playwright; full name *Miguel de Cervantes Saavedra.* He wrote *Don Quixote* (1605–15), a satire on chivalric romances.

cer·vi·cal /ˈsərvikəl/ ▶ adj. Anat. **1** of or relating to the narrow necklike passage forming the lower end of the uterus. **2** of or relating to the neck. [17th C.: from Fr., or from mod. L. *cervicalis,* from L. *cervix, cervic-* 'neck.']

cer·vi·ci·tis /ˌsərvəˈsītis/ ▶ n. Med. inflammation of the cervix.

cer·vid /ˈsərvid/ ▶ n. Zool. a mammal of the deer family (Cervidae). [19th C.: from mod. L. *Cervidae* (pl.), from L. *cervus* 'deer.']

cer·vine /ˈsərvīn; -vin/ ▶ adj. of or relating to deer; deerlike. [19th C.: from L. *cervinus,* from *cervus* 'deer.']

cer·vix /ˈsərviks/ ▶ n. (pl. **-vices** /-vəˌsēz/) the narrow necklike passage forming the lower end of the uterus. ■ tech. the neck. ■ a part of other bodily organs resembling a neck. [18th C.: L.]

ce·sar·e·an /siˈze(ə)rēən/ (also **cae·sar·e·an, Cae·sar·e·an,** or esp. Brit. **Cae·sar·i·an**) ▶ adj. of or effected by cesarean section. ▶ n. a cesarean section. [16th C.: from L. *Caesareus* 'of Caesar.']

ce·sar·e·an sec·tion ▶ n. a surgical operation for delivering a child by cutting through the wall of the mother's abdomen. [17th C.: from the story that Julius Caesar was delivered by this method.]

ce·si·um /ˈsēzēəm/ (Brit. **cae·si·um**) ▶ n. the chemical element of atomic number 55, a soft, silvery, extremely reactive metal. It belongs to the alkali metal group and occurs as a trace element in some rocks and minerals. (Symbol: **Cs**) [19th C.: from L. *caesius* 'grayish-blue.']

Čes·ké Bu·dě·jo·vi·ce /ˈᴄʜeske ˈbo͝odyəˌyôvitse/ a city in the southern Czech Republic; pop. 173,400. German name BUDWEIS.

ces·pi·tose /ˈsespiˌtōs/ ▶ adj. Bot. forming mats or growing in dense tufts or clumps.

cess ▶ n. (in phrase **bad cess to**) esp. Irish a curse on: *bad cess to the day I joined that band!* [19th C. (orig. Anglo-Irish).]

ces·sa·tion /se'sāsʜən/ ▶ n. a ceasing; an end. ■ a pause or interruption. [ME: from L. *cessatio(n-)*, from *cessare* 'cease.']

ces·sion /'sesʜən/ ▶ n. the formal giving up of rights, property, or territory, esp. by a state. [ME: from L. *cession-*, from *cedere* 'cede.']

cess·pit /'ses,pit/ ▶ n. a pit for the disposal of liquid waste and sewage. ■ fig. a disgusting or corrupt place or situation. [19th C.: from *cess* (supposed base of CESSPOOL.)]

cess·pool /'ses,po͞ol/ ▶ n. an underground container for the temporary storage of liquid waste and sewage. ■ fig. a disgusting or corrupt place. [17th C.: prob. alt. of *suspiral* 'vent,' from OFr. *souspirail* 'air hole,' based on L. *sub-* 'from below' + *spirare* 'breathe.']

ces·ta /'sestə/ a wicker basket used in jai alai to catch and throw the ball.

c'est la vie /,sā lä 'vē/ ▶ exclam. that's life; such is life. [20th C.:Fr.]

Ce·ta·cea /si'tāsʜ(ē)ə/ Zool. an order of marine mammals that comprises the whales, dolphins, and porpoises. These have a streamlined hairless body, no hind limbs, a horizontal tail fin, and a blowhole on top of the head for breathing. See also MYSTICETI, ODONTOCETI. — **ce·ta·cean** /si'tāsʜ(ē)ən/ n. & adj. [mod. L. (pl.), from L. *cetus*, from Gk. *kētos* 'whale.']

ce·tane /'sētān/ ▶ n. Chem. a colorless liquid hydrocarbon of the alkane series, $C_{16}H_{34}$, used as a solvent. [19th C.: from L. *cetus* 'whale,' from Gk. *kētos*.]

ce·tane num·ber ▶ n. a measure of the ignition properties of diesel fuel relative to cetane as a standard.

ce·te·ris pa·ri·bus /'kātəris 'parəbəs/ ▶ adv. formal with other conditions remaining the same. [17th C.: mod. L.]

ce·tol·o·gy /sē'täləjē/ ▶ n. the branch of zoology that deals with whales, dolphins, and porpoises.

cesta

Ce·tus /'sētəs/ Astron. a large northern constellation (the Whale), said to represent the sea monster that threatened Andromeda. It contains the variable star Mira. [L.]

ce·tyl al·co·hol /'sētl/ ▶ n. a waxy alcohol, $CH_3(CH_2)_{15}OH$, used in cosmetics and as an emulsifier.

Ce·u·ta /'ᴛʜāo͞otə; 'sā-/ a Spanish enclave, consisting of a port and a military post, on the coast of Morocco in northern Africa; pop. 67,615. With Melilla it forms a community of Spain.

Cé·vennes /sā'ven/ a mountain range in southern France.

ce·vi·che /sə'vēcʜā; -cʜē/ (also **se·vi·che**) ▶ n. a South American dish of marinated raw fish or seafood, typically garnished and served as an appetizer. [South Amer. Sp.]

Cey·lon /si'län; sā'län/ former name (until 1972) of SRI LANKA.

Cey·lon moss ▶ n. a red seaweed (*Gracilaria lichenoides*) of the Indian subcontinent, the main source of agar.

Cé·zanne /sā'zän/, Paul (1839–1906), French painter. Although his early work was identified with post-Impressionism, later paintings, such as the sequence *Bathers* (1890–1905), had an important influence on cubism.

CF ▶ abbr. ■ carried forward. ■ cost and freight. ■ cystic fibrosis.

Cf ▶ symb. the chemical element californium.

cf. ▶ abbr. compare with (used to refer a reader to another written work or another part of the same written work). [from L. *confer* 'compare.']

c.f. ▶ abbr. carried forward (used to refer to figures transferred to a new page or account).

CFA[1] (also **CFA franc**) ▶ n. **1** the basic monetary unit of Benin, Burkina Faso, Ivory Coast, Guinea-Bissau, Mali, Niger, Senegal, and Togo. [from Fr. *franc de la Communautè financiére de l'Afrique*.] **2** the basic monetary unit of Cameroon, Central African Republic, Chad, Republic of Congo, Equatorial Guinea, and Gabon. [from Fr. *franc de la Coopèration financiére africaine*.]

CFA[2] ▶ abbr. chartered financial analyst.

CFC Chem. ▶ abbr. chlorofluorocarbon.

cfm ▶ abbr. cubic feet per minute.

CFO ▶ abbr. chief financial officer.

CFS ▶ abbr. chronic fatigue syndrome.

cfs ▶ abbr. cubic feet per second.

CG ▶ abbr. ■ Coast Guard. ■ commanding general.

cg ▶ abbr. centigram(s).

CGI ▶ abbr. computer-generated imagery.

cGMP ▶ abbr. cyclic GMP.

cgs ▶ abbr. centimeter-gram-second.

CGT ▶ abbr. capital gains tax.

CH ▶ abbr. ■ courthouse. ■ custom house.

ch. ▶ abbr. ■ chaplain. ■ chapter. ■ church.

c.h. (also **C.H.**) ▶ abbr. clearinghouse.

Cha·blis /sʜa'blē; sʜə-; sʜä-/ ▶ n. a dry white burgundy wine from Chablis in eastern France.

cha-cha /'cʜä ,cʜä/ (also **cha-cha-cha** /-'cʜä/) ▶ n. a ballroom dance with small steps and swaying hip movements, performed to a Latin American rhythm. ■ music for or in the rhythm of such a dance. ▶ v. (**cha-chas, cha-chaed** or **cha-cha'd, cha-cha·ing**) [intrans.] dance the cha-cha. [1950s: L. Amer. Sp.]

cha·cha·la·ca /,cʜäcʜə'läkə/ ▶ n. a pheasantlike tree-dwelling bird (genus *Ortalis*) of the guan family, with a loud harsh call, found mainly in the forests of tropical America. [19th C.: via South Amer. Sp. from Nahuatl, of imitative origin.]

Cha·co /'cʜäkō/ another name for GRAN CHACO.

cha·conne /sʜä'kôn; -'kän; -'kən/ ▶ n. Music a composition in a series of varying sections in slow triple time, typically over a short repeated bass theme. Compare with PASSACAGLIA. ■ a stately dance performed to such music, popular in the 18th century. [17th C.: from Fr., from Sp. *chacona*.]

cha·cun à son goût /sʜä,kœɴ nä soɴ 'go͞o/ ▶ exclam. each to one's own taste. [19th C.: Fr.]

Chad /cʜad/ a landlocked country in north central Africa. *See box.* — **Chad·i·an** adj. & n.

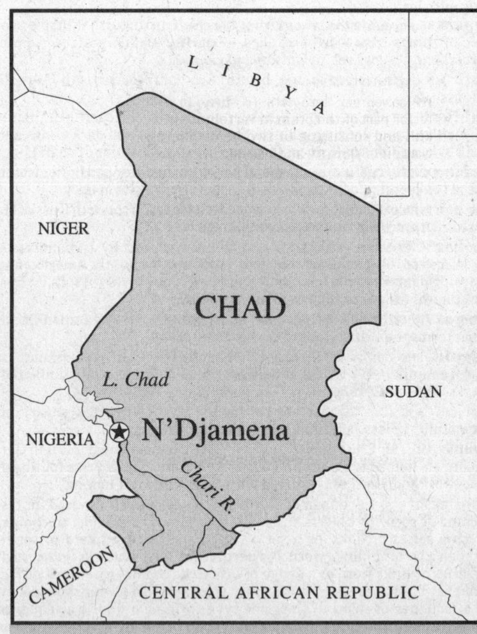

Chad

Official name: Republic of Chad
Location: north central Africa, south of Libya and north of the Central African Republic
Area: 486,300 square miles (1,259,200 sq km)
Population: 9,538,000
Capital: N'Djamena
Languages: French and Arabic (both official)
Currency: CFA franc

chad /cʜad/ ▶ n. a piece of waste material created by punching cards or tape. [1950s: of unknown origin.]

Chad·ic /'cʜadik/ ▶ n. a group of Afro-Asiatic languages spoken in the region of Lake Chad, of which the most important is Hausa. ▶ adj. of or relating to this group of languages.

Chad, Lake a shallow lake on the borders of Chad, Niger, and Nigeria in north central Africa.

chad·or /'cʜədər; 'cʜädôr/ (also **chad·ar** or **chud·dar**) ▶ n. a large piece of dark-colored cloth, typically worn by Muslim women, wrapped around the head and upper body to leave only the face exposed. [17th C.: from Urdu *chādar, chaddar*, from Pers. *čādar* 'sheet or veil.']

Chad·wick /'cʜadwik/, Sir James (1891–1974), English physicist. He discovered the neutron. Nobel Prize for Physics (1935).

chae·ta /'kētə/ ▶ n. (pl. **-tae** /-tē/) Zool. a stiff bristle made of chitin, esp. in an annelid. [19th C.: mod. L., from Gk. *khaitē* 'long hair.']

Chae·tog·na·tha /kē'tägnəᴛʜə/ Zool. a small phylum of marine invertebrates that comprises the arrow worms. — **chae·tog·nath** /'kētäg,naᴛʜ/ n. [mod. L. (pl.), from Gk. *khaitē* 'long hair' + *gnathos* 'jaw.']

chafe /cʜāf/ ▶ v. **1** [trans.] (of something restrictive or too tight) make (a part of the body) sore by rubbing against it: *the collar chafed his neck.* ■ [intrans.] (of a part of the body) be or become sore as a result of such rubbing. ■ [intrans.] (of an object) rub abrasively against another object. **2** [trans.] rub (a part of the body) to restore warmth or sensation. ■ restore (warmth or sensation) in this way. **3** become or make annoyed or impatient because of a restriction or inconvenience. ▶ **n.** wear or damage caused by rubbing.

– PHRASES **chafe at the bit** see CHOMP AT THE BIT at CHOMP. [ME: from OFr. *chaufer* 'make hot,' based on L. *calefacere*, from *calere* 'be hot' + *facere* 'make.']

chaf·er /'CHāfər/ ▶ **n.** a flying beetle (family Scarabaeidae), the adult and larva of which can be very destructive to foliage and plant roots, respectively. [OE *ceafor*, *cefer*, of Gmc. origin; rel. to Du. *kever*.]

chaff[1] /CHaf/ ▶ **n.** the husks of corn or other seed separated by winnowing or threshing. ■ chopped hay and straw used as fodder. ■ fig. worthless things; trash. ■ strips of metal foil or metal filings released in the atmosphere to obstruct radar detection or confuse radar-tracking missiles.

– PHRASES **separate the wheat from the chaff** distinguish valuable people or things from worthless ones. — **chaff·y** adj. [OE *cæf*, *ceaf*, prob. from Gmc., 'gnaw'; rel. to Du. *kaf* and CHAFER.]

chaff[2] ▶ **n.** lighthearted joking; banter. ▶ **v.** [trans.] tease. [19th C.: perh. from CHAFE.]

chaf·finch /'CHafinCH/ ▶ **n.** a Eurasian and North African finch (genus *Fringilla*), typically with a bluish top to the head and dark wings and tail. [OE *ceaffinc* 'chaff finch' (because it picks seeds out of chaff).]

chaf·ing dish /'CHāfiNG/ ▶ **n.** a metal pan with an outer pan of hot water, used for keeping food warm. [15th C.: from CHAFE 'warm up.']

Cha·gall /SHə'gäl/, Marc (1887–1985), French painter; born in Russia. He used rich emotive color and dream imagery.

Cha·gas' dis·ease /'SHägəs/ ▶ **n.** a disease caused by trypanosomes transmitted by bloodsucking bugs, endemic in South America and causing damage to the heart and central nervous system. [20th C.: Carlos *Chagas* (1879–1934), Brazilian physician.]

Cha·gos Ar·chi·pel·a·go /'CHägəs/ an island group in the Indian Ocean that forms the British Indian Ocean Territory.

cha·grin /SHə'grin/ ▶ **n.** distress or embarrassment at having failed or been humiliated. ▶ **v.** (**be chagrined**) feel distressed or humiliated. [17th C.: from Fr. *chagrin* (n.), lit. 'rough skin,' *chagriner* (v.).]

chai /CHī/ ▶ **n.** Indian tea made by boiling tea leaves with milk, sugar, and sometimes spices. [a term in various Indian languages.]

Chain /CHān/, Sir Ernst Boris (1906–79), British biochemist; born in Germany. He helped to isolate and purify penicillin. Nobel Prize for Physiology or Medicine (1945, shared with Florey and A. Fleming).

chain /CHān/ ▶ **n.** **1** a connected flexible series of metal links used for fastening or securing objects and pulling or supporting loads. ■ (**chains**) such a series of links, or a set of them, used to confine a prisoner. ■ such a series of links worn as a decoration; a necklace. ■ esp. Brit. such a series of links worn as a badge of office. ■ (**chains**) fig. a force or factor that binds or restricts someone. ■ (**chains**) short for SNOW CHAINS. **2** a sequence of items of the same type forming a line. ■ a sequence or series of connected elements. ■ a group of establishments, such as hotels, stores, or restaurants, owned by the same company. ■ a range of mountains. ■ a part of a molecule consisting of a number of atoms (typically carbon) bonded together in a linear sequence. ■ a figure in a quadrille or similar dance, in which dancers meet and pass each other in a continuous sequence. **3** a jointed measuring line consisting of linked metal rods. ■ the length of such a measuring line (66 ft.). ■ Football a measuring chain of ten yards, used in the determination of first downs. ▶ **v.** [trans.] fasten or secure with a chain. ■ confine with a chain.

– PHRASES **pull** (or **yank**) **someone's chain** informal tease someone, typically by leading them to believe something untrue. [ME: from OFr. *chaine*, *chaeine*, from L. *catena* 'a chain.']

chain gang ▶ **n.** a group of convicts chained together while working outside the prison.

chain let·ter ▶ **n.** one of a sequence of letters, each recipient in the sequence being requested to send copies to a specific number of other people.

chain-link ▶ **adj.** [attrib.] made of wire in a diamond-shaped mesh.

chain mail ▶ **n.** hist. armor made of small metal rings linked together.

chain·plate /'CHān,plāt/ ▶ **n.** a strong link or plate on a sailing ship's side, to which the shrouds are secured.

chain re·ac·tion ▶ **n.** a chemical reaction or other process in which the products themselves promote or spread the reaction. ■ the self-sustaining fission reaction spread by neutrons that occurs in nuclear reactors and bombs. ■ fig. a series of events, each caused by the previous one.

chain·saw /'CHān,sô/ ▶ **n.** a mechanical power-driven cutting tool with teeth set on a chain that moves around the edge of a blade.

chain-smoke ▶ **v.** [intrans.] smoke continually, esp. by lighting a new cigarette from the butt of the last one smoked. — **chain-smok·er** n.

chain stitch ▶ **n.** an ornamental stitch in which loops are crocheted or embroidered in a chain.

chain store ▶ **n.** one of a series of stores owned by one company and selling the same merchandise.

chain wheel ▶ **n.** a toothed wheel transmitting power by means of a chain fitted to its edges.

chair /CHe(ə)r/ ▶ **n.** **1** a separate seat for one person, typically with a back and four legs. ■ hist. a sedan chair. ■ short for CHAIRLIFT. **2** the person in charge of a meeting or organization (used as a neutral alternative to chairman or chairwoman). ■ an official position of authority, for example on a board of directors. **3** a professorship. **4** a particular seat in an orchestra: [as adj., in comb.] *fourth-chair trumpet.* **5** (**the chair**) short for ELECTRIC CHAIR. ▶ **v.** [trans.] act as chairperson of or preside over (an organization, meeting, or public event).

– PHRASES **take the chair** act as chairperson. [ME: from OFr. *chaiere*, from L. *cathedra* 'seat,' from Gk. *kathedra*.]

chair·la·dy /'CHe(ə)r,lādē/ ▶ **n.** (pl. **-dies**) another term for CHAIRWOMAN.

chair·lift /'CHe(ə)r,lift/ ▶ **n.** **1** a series of chairs hung from a moving cable, typically used for carrying passengers up and down a mountain. **2** a device for carrying people in wheelchairs from one floor of a building to another.

chair·man /'CHe(ə)rmən/ ▶ **n.** (pl. **-men**) a person, esp. a man, designated to preside over a meeting. ■ the permanent or long-term president of a committee, company, or other organization. ■ (**Chairman**) (since 1949) the leading figure in the Chinese Communist Party. — **chair·man·ship** n.

chair·per·son /'CHe(ə)r,pərsən/ ▶ **n.** a chairman or chairwoman (used as a neutral alternative).

chair·wom·an /'CHe(ə)r,wŏŏmən/ ▶ **n.** (pl. **-wom·en**) a woman designated to preside over committee or board meetings.

chaise /SHāz/ ▶ **n.** **1** esp. hist. a horse-drawn carriage for one or two people, typically one with an open top and two wheels. ■ another term for POST-CHAISE. **2** short for CHAISE LONGUE. [17th C.: from Fr., var. of *chaire* (see CHAIR).]

chaise longue /,SHāz 'lôNG/ ▶ **n.** (pl. **chaises longues** /'SHāz 'lôNG(z)/) a reclining chair with a lengthened seat forming a leg rest. [19th C.: Fr., lit. 'long chair.']

chaise lounge /'SHāz 'lounj; 'CHās/ ▶ **n.** variant of CHAISE LONGUE. [20th C.: alt.]

chak·ra /'CHäkrə/ ▶ **n.** (in Indian thought) each of the centers of spiritual power in the human body, usually considered to be seven in number. [from Sanskrit *cakra* 'wheel or circle,' from Indo-Eur., 'turn,' akin to WHEEL.]

Chal·ce·don /'kalsə,dän; kal'sēdn/ a former city on the Bosporus in Asia Minor, now part of Istanbul. Turkish name KADIKÖY.

Chal·ce·don, Coun·cil of /kal'sēdn; 'kalsə,dän/ the fourth ecumenical council of the Christian Church, held at Chalcedon in 451. — **Chal·ce·do·ni·an** /,kalsə'dōnēən/ n. & adj.

chal·ced·o·ny /kal'sedn-ē; CHal-; 'kalsə,dōnē; 'CHalsə-/ ▶ **n.** (pl. **-nies**) a type of quartz occurring in several different forms, including onyx and agate. — **chal·ce·don·ic** /,kalsə'dänik/ adj. [ME: from L. *calcedonius*, *chalcedonius*, from Gk. *khalkēdōn*.]

chal·cid /'kalsid/ (also **chalcid wasp**) ▶ **n.** a minute parasitic wasp of a large group (superfamily Chalcidoidea) whose members lay eggs inside the eggs of other insects. They typically have bright metallic coloration. [19th C.: from mod. L. *Chalcis*, from Gk. *khalkos* 'copper, brass.']

chal·co·cite /'kalkə,sīt/ ▶ **n.** cuprous sulfide, Cu_2S, an ore of copper, usu. occurring as black, fine-grained masses.

chal·co·py·rite /,kalkə'pīrīt/ ▶ **n.** a yellow mineral consisting of copper-iron sulfide, the principal ore of copper. [19th C.: from mod. L. *chalcopyrites*, from Gk. *khalkos* 'copper' + *purītes* (see PYRITE).]

Chal·de·a /kal'dēə/ an ancient country in what is now southern Iraq.

Chal·de·an /kal'dēən/ ▶ **n.** **1** a member of an ancient people who lived in Chaldea *c.*800 BC and ruled Babylonia 625–539 BC. They were renowned as astronomers and astrologers. **2** the Semitic language of the ancient Chaldeans. ■ a language related to Aramaic and spoken in parts of Iraq. ▶ **adj.** of or relating to ancient Chaldea or its people or language. ■ literary of or relating to astrology.

Chal·dee /'kaldē/ ▶ **n.** **1** the Semitic language of the ancient Chaldeans. **2** a native of ancient Chaldea. [from L. *Chaldaei* 'Chaldeans,' based on Gk. *Khaldaia*.]

chal·dron /'CHôldrən/ ▶ **n.** a chiefly British unit of dry measure, esp. a unit of approximately 36 bushels (of coal).

cha·let /SHa'lā; 'SHalā/ ▶ **n.** a wooden house or cottage with overhanging eaves, typically found in the Swiss Alps. ■ a similar building used as a ski lodge. [18th C.: from Swiss Fr., dimin. of OFr. *chasel* 'farmstead,' based on L. *casa* 'hut.']

chalet

chal·ice /'CHaləs/ ▶ **n.** hist. a large cup or goblet, typically used for drinking wine. ■ the wine cup used in the Christian Eucharist. [ME: via OFr. from L. *calix*, *calic-* 'cup.']

chalk /CHôk/ ▶ **n.** a soft white limestone (calcium carbonate) formed from the skeletal remains of sea creatures. ■ a similar substance (calcium sulfate), made into white or colored sticks used for drawing or writing. ■ Geol. a series of strata consisting mainly of chalk. ▶ **v.** [trans.] **1** draw or write with chalk. ■ draw or write on (a surface) with chalk. **2** rub (something, esp. a pool cue) with chalk.

– PHRASAL VERBS **chalk something out** sketch or plan something. **chalk**

something up 1 achieve something noteworthy. **2** ascribe something to a particular cause. [OE *cealc*, from L. *calx* (see CALX).]

chalk·board /ˈCHôk,bôrd/ ▶ n. another term for BLACKBOARD.

chalk talk ▶ n. a talk or lecture in which the speaker uses blackboard and chalk.

chalk·y /ˈCHôkē/ ▶ adj. (**chalk·i·er, chalk·i·est**) **1** consisting of or rich in chalk. **2** resembling chalk in texture or paleness of color. — **chalk·i·ness** n.

chal·lah /ˈhälə; ˈKHä-/ ▶ n. (pl. **chal·lahs** or **cha·lot(h)** /häˈlōt; -ˈlōs; KHä-/) a loaf of white leavened bread, typically braided, traditionally baked to celebrate the Jewish sabbath. [1920s: from Heb. *ḥallah*.]

chal·lenge /ˈCHalinj/ ▶ n. **1** a call to take part in a contest or competition, esp. a duel. ■ a task or situation that tests someone's abilities. ■ an attempt to win a contest or championship in a sport. **2** an objection or query as to the truth of something, often with an implicit demand for proof. ■ a sentry's call for a password or other proof of identity. ■ Law an objection regarding the eligibility or suitability of a jury member. **3** Med. exposure of the immune system to pathogenic organisms or antigens. ▶ v. [trans.] **1** invite (someone) to engage in a contest: *he challenged one of my men.* ■ enter into competition with or opposition against. ■ make a rival claim to or threaten someone's hold on (a position). ■ [with obj. and infin.] invite (someone) to do something that one thinks will be difficult or impossible; dare. ■ [usu. as adj.] (**challenging**) test the abilities of: *challenging and rewarding employment.* **2** dispute the truth or validity of. ■ Law object to (a jury member). ■ (of a sentry) call on (someone) for proof of identity. — **chal·lenge·a·ble** adj. **chal·leng·er** n. **chal·leng·ing·ly** adv. [ME: from OFr. *chalenge* (n.), *chalenger* (v.), from L. *calumnia* 'calumny,' *calumniari* 'calumniate.']

chal·lenged /ˈCHalinjd/ ▶ adj. [with submodifier or in comb.] (used euphemistically) impaired or disabled in a specified respect: *physically challenged.* ■ informal lacking or deficient in a specified respect.

Chal·leng·er /ˈCHalinjər/ ▶ n. a US space shuttle that exploded after launch on January 28, 1986.

chal·lis /ˈSHalē/ ▶ n. a soft lightweight clothing fabric made from silk and worsted. [19th C.: perh. from the surname *Challis*.]

chal·u·meau /,SHaləˈmō/ ▶ n. (pl. **-meaux** /-ˈmō(z)/) a reed instrument of the early 18th century from which the clarinet was developed. ■ (also **chalumeau register**) the lowest octave of the clarinet's range. [18th C.: from Fr., from L. *calamellus* 'little reed,' dimin. of *calamus*.]

cha·lu·pa /chəˈlo͝opə/ ▶ n. a fried tortilla in the shape of a boat, with a spicy filling. [19th C.: Spanish.]

cha·lyb·e·ate /kəˈlibēit/ ▶ adj. [attrib.] of or denoting natural mineral springs containing iron salts. [17th C.: from mod. L. *chalybeatus*, from L. *chalybs*, from Gk. *khalups*, *khalub-* 'steel.']

Cham /kam/ ▶ n. (pl. same or **Chams**) **1** a member of an indigenous people of Vietnam and Cambodia, who formed an independent kingdom from the 2nd to 17th centuries AD, and whose culture is strongly influenced by that of India. **2** either of two Austronesian languages of this people. ▶ adj. of or relating to this people, their culture, or their language.

Cha·mae·le·on /kəˈmēlyən; -lēən/ Astron. a small and faint southern constellation (the Chameleon), close to the south celestial pole. [from Gk.]

cha·mae·le·on ▶ n. esp. Brit. var. of CHAMELEON.

cham·ae·phyte /ˈkamə,fīt/ ▶ n. Bot. a woody plant whose resting buds are on or near the ground. [20th C.: from Gk. *khamai* 'on the ground.']

cham·ber /ˈCHāmbər/ ▶ n. **1** a hall used by a legislative or judicial body. ■ the body that meets in such a hall. ■ any of the houses of a legislature. **2** literary archaic a private room, typically a bedroom. ■ (**chambers**) Law a judge's room used for official proceedings not required to be held in open court. **3** an enclosed space or cavity. ■ a large underground cavern. ■ the part of a gun bore that contains the charge or bullet. ■ Biol. a cavity in a plant, animal body, or organ. **4** [as adj.] Music of or for a small group of instruments. ▶ v. [trans.] place (a bullet) into the chamber of a gun. — **cham·bered** adj. [ME: ult. from Gk. *kamara* 'object with an arched cover.']

cham·bered nau·ti·lus ▶ n. see NAUTILUS.

Cham·ber·lain[1] /ˈCHāmbərlən/, Arthur Neville (1869–1940), prime minister of Britain 1937–40. He pursued a policy of appeasement with Nazi Germany and signed the Munich Agreement in 1938.

Cham·ber·lain[2], Sir Austen (1863–1937), British statesman; full name *Joseph Austen Chamberlain*. As British foreign secretary 1924–29, he worked to secure peace in western Europe and bring Germany into the League of Nations. Nobel Peace Prize (1925, shared with Charles G. Dawes.).

Cham·ber·lain[3], Owen (1920–2006), US physicist. In 1955, he codiscovered the antiproton. Nobel Prize for Physics (1959, shared with E. G. Segrè 1905–89).

Cham·ber·lain[4], Wilt (1936–99), US basketball player; full name *Wilton Norman Chamberlain*; known as **Wilt the Stilt**. He played professionally 1959–73. Basketball Hall of Fame (1978).

cham·ber·maid /ˈCHāmbər,mād/ ▶ n. a maid who cleans bedrooms and bathrooms, esp. in a hotel.

cham·ber mu·sic ▶ n. instrumental music played by a small ensemble, with one player to a part, the most important form being the string quartet.

cham·ber of com·merce (abbr.: **C. of C.**) ▶ n. a local association to promote and protect the interests of the business community in a particular place.

cham·ber or·ches·tra ▶ n. a small orchestra.

cham·ber pot ▶ n. a bowl kept in a bedroom and used as a toilet, esp. at night.

Cham·ber·tin /,SHänberˈtaN/ ▶ n. a dry red burgundy wine of high quality from Gevrey Chambertin in eastern France.

cham·bray /ˈSHambrā; -brē/ ▶ n. a linen-finished gingham cloth with a white weft and a colored warp, producing a mottled appearance. [19th C.: *Cambrai*, France.]

cham·bré /ˈSHambrā; SHamˈbrā/ ▶ adj. [predic.] (of red wine) at room temperature. [1950s: Fr., past part. of *chambrer* 'bring to room temperature,' from *chambre* (see CHAMBER).]

common chameleon

cha·me·le·on /kəˈmēlyən; -lēən/ (esp. Brit. also **cha·mae·le·on**) ▶ n. a small Old World lizard (*Chamaeleo* and other genera, family Chamaeleonidae) with a prehensile tail, long extensible tongue, protruding eyes that rotate independently, and the ability to change color. Numerous species include the **common chameleon** (*C. chamaeleon*). ■ (also **American chameleon**) an anole. ■ fig. a changeable or inconstant person. — **cha·me·le·on·ic** /kə,mēlēˈänik/ adj. [ME: via L. *chamaeleon* from Gk. *khamaileōn*, from *khamai* 'on the ground' + *leōn* 'lion.']

cham·fer /ˈCHamfər/ ▶ v. [trans.] in carpentry, cut away (a right-angled edge or corner) to make a symmetrical sloping edge. ▶ n. a symmetrical sloping surface at an edge or corner. [16th C.: back-form. from *chamfering*, from Fr. *chamfrain*, from *chant* 'edge' (see CANT[2]) + *fraint* 'broken' (from OFr. *fraindre* 'break.']

cha·mise /SHəˈmēz/ ▶ n. an evergreen shrub (*Adenostoma fasciculatum*) of the rose family, with small narrow leaves, common in the chaparral of California. Also called GREASEWOOD. [19th C.: from Mex. Sp. *chamiso*.]

cham·ois /ˈSHamē/ ▶ n. **1** (pl. same /ˈSHamēz/) an agile goat-antelope (genus *Rupicapra*) with short hooked horns, found in mountainous areas of Europe from Spain to the Caucasus. **2** (pl. same) (also **chamois leather**) soft pliable leather made from the skin of sheep, goats, or deer. ■ a piece of such leather, used typically for washing windows or cars. [16th C.: from Fr.]

cham·o·mile /ˈkamə,mēl; -,mīl/ (also **cam·o·mile**) ▶ n. an aromatic European plant (*Anthemis* and other genera) of the daisy family, with white and yellow daisylike flowers. [ME: from OFr. *camomille*, from late L. *chamomilla*, from Gk. *khamaimēlon* 'earth apple.']

Cha·mor·ro /CHəˈmôrō/ ▶ n. **1** a member of the native people of the Mariana Islands (including Guam). **2** the Austronesian language of this people.

champ[1] /CHamp/ ▶ v. another term for CHOMP. [ME: imitative.]

champ[2] ▶ n. informal a champion.

Cham·pagne /SHänˈpänyə; SHamˈpān/ a region in northeastern France that now corresponds to the Champagne-Ardenne administrative region.

cham·pagne /SHamˈpān/ ▶ n. a white sparkling wine associated with celebration, typically that made in the Champagne region of France. ■ a pale cream or straw color.

Cham·pagne-Ar·denne /SHänˈpän yärˈden/ a region of northeastern France that consists of part of the Ardennes forest and Champagne.

Cham·paign /SHamˈpān/ a city in east central Illinois; pop. 67,518.

cham·paign /SHamˈpān/ ▶ n. literary open level countryside. [ME: from OFr. *champagne*, based on L. *campus* 'level ground.']

cham·pak /ˈCHəmpək; ˈCHam-/ ▶ n. an Asian evergreen tree (*Michelia champaca*) of the magnolia family, bearing fragrant orange flowers and sacred to Hindus and Buddhists. [from Sanskrit *campaka*.]

cham·per·ty /ˈCHampərtē/ ▶ n. Law an illegal agreement in which a person with no previous interest in a lawsuit finances it with a view to sharing the disputed property if the suit succeeds. — **cham·per·tous** /-təs/ adj. [ME: ult. from OFr. *champart* 'feudal lord's share of produce,' from L. *campus* 'field' + *pars* 'part.']

cham·pi·gnon /SHamˈpinyən; ,SHampēˈnyōn/ ▶ n. a small edible mushroom (*Agaricus campestris*, family Agaricaceae) with a light brown cap, growing in short grass in both Eurasia and North America and widely grown commercially. [16th C.: from Fr., dimin. of OFr. *champagne* 'open country' (see CHAMPAIGN).]

cham·pi·on /ˈCHampēən/ ▶ n. **1** a person who has defeated or surpassed all rivals in a competition, esp. in sports. **2** a person who fights or argues for a cause or on behalf of someone else. ■ hist. a knight who fought in single combat on behalf of the monarch. ▶ v. [trans.] support the cause of; defend. [ME: from OFr., from med. L. *campio(n-)* 'fighter,' from L. *campus* (see CAMP[1]).]

cham·pi·on·ship /ˈCHampēən,SHip/ ▶ n. **1** a contest for the position of champion in a sport, often involving a series of games or matches. ■ the position or title of the winner of such a contest. **2** the vigorous support or defense of someone or something.

Cham·plain /SHamˈplān/, Samuel de (1567–1635), French explorer. He established a settlement at Quebec in Canada in 1608.

Cham·plain, Lake /SHamˈplān/ a lake forming part of the border between the states of New York and Vermont, its northern tip extending into Quebec, Canada.

champ·le·vé /ˌshänlə'vā/ ▶ n. enamelwork in which hollows made in a metal surface are filled with colored enamel. [Fr., from *champ* 'field' + *levé* 'raised.']

Champs É·ly·sées /'shänz ˌālē'zā/ an avenue in Paris, France, that extends from the Place de la Concorde to the Arc de Triomphe.

chance /chans/ ▶ n. **1** a possibility of something happening. ■ (**chances**) the probability of something happening. ■ [in sing.] an opportunity to do or achieve something. ■ a ticket in a raffle or lottery. ■ Baseball an opportunity to make a defensive play, which if missed counts as an error. **2** the occurrence and development of events in the absence of any obvious design. ■ the unplanned and unpredictable course of events regarded as a power. ▶ adj. fortuitous; accidental. ▶ v. **1** [no obj., with infin.] do something by accident or without design: *if they chanced to meet.* ■ (**chance upon/on**) find or see by accident. **2** [trans.] informal do (something) despite its being dangerous or of uncertain outcome.
– PHRASES **by any chance** possibly (used in tentative inquiries or suggestions). **no chance** informal there is no possibility of that. **on the (off) chance** just in case. **stand a chance** [usu. with negative] have a prospect of success or survival. **take a chance** (or **chances**) behave in a way that leaves one vulnerable to danger or failure. ■ (**take a chance on**) put one's trust in (something or someone) knowing that it may not be safe or certain. **take one's chances** do something risky with the hope of success. [ME: from OFr. *cheance*, from *cheoir* 'fall, befall,' based on L. *cadere*.]

chan·cel /'chansəl/ ▶ n. the part of a church near the altar, reserved for the clergy and choir, and typically separated from the nave by steps or a screen. [ME: from OFr., from L. *cancelli* 'crossbars.']

chan·cel·ler·y /'chans(ə)lərē/ ▶ n. (pl. **-ler·ies**) **1** the position, office, or department of a chancellor. ■ the official residence of a chancellor. **2** an office attached to an embassy or consulate.

chan·cel·lor /'chans(ə)lər/ ▶ n. a senior state or legal official. ■ the head of the government in some European countries, such as Germany. ■ the presiding judge of a chancery court. ■ the president or chief administrative officer of a college or university. ■ esp. Brit. the nonresident honorary head of a college or university. ■ a bishop's law officer. ■ (**Chancellor**) short for CHANCELLOR OF THE EXCHEQUER. — **chan·cel·lor·ship** n. [OE, from OFr. *cancelier*, from late L. *cancellarius* 'porter, secretary.']

Chan·cel·lor of the Ex·cheq·uer ▶ n. the finance minister of the United Kingdom, responsible for preparing the nation's annual budgets.

Chan·cel·lors·ville /'chans(ə)lərzˌvil/ a historic locality in northeastern Virginia, site of a Civil War battle in May 1863.

chan·cer·y /'chans(ə)rē/ ▶ n. (pl. **-cer·ies**) **1** a court of equity. ■ equity. ■ hist. the court of a bishop's chancellor. **2** (in the Roman Catholic Church) the office of a diocese. **3** esp. Brit. an office attached to an embassy or consulate. **4** a public records office.
– PHRASES **in chancery** informal (of a boxer or wrestler) with their head held, contrary to the rules, between the opponent's arm and body and unable to avoid blows. [ME: contr. of CHANCELLERY.]

Chan·chi·ang /'jän jē'äng/ variant of ZHANJIANG.

chan·cre /'kangkər; 'shang-/ ▶ n. Med. a painless ulcer, particularly one developing on the genitals as a result of venereal disease. [16th C.: from Fr., from L. *cancer* 'creeping ulcer.']

chan·croid /'kangkroid; 'shang-/ ▶ n. a venereal infection causing ulceration of the lymph nodes in the groin. Also called SOFT CHANCRE.

chanc·y /'chansē/ ▶ adj. (**chanc·i·er, chanc·i·est**) informal subject to unpredictable changes and circumstances. — **chanc·i·ly** adv. **chanc·i·ness** n.

chan·de·lier /ˌshandl'i(ə)r/ ▶ n. a decorative hanging light with branches for several light bulbs or candles. [18th C.: from Fr., from *chandelle* 'candle,' from L. *candela*, from *candere* 'be white.']

chan·delle /shan'del; shän-/ ▶ n. a steep climbing turn executed in an aircraft to gain height while changing the direction of flight. [1970s: from Fr., lit. 'candle.']

Chan·di·garh /'chəndēgər/ **1** a Union Territory in northwestern India, created in 1966. **2** a city in this territory, capital of the states of Punjab and Haryana; pop. 503,000.

Chan·dler[1] /'chandlər/ a city in south central Arizona; pop. 176,581.

Chan·dler[2], Raymond Thornton (1888–1959), US writer. In his novels, he created private detective Philip Marlowe.

chan·dler /'chandlər/ ▶ n. **1** (also **ship chandler**) a dealer in supplies and equipment for ships and boats. **2** hist. a dealer in household items such as oil, soap, paint, and groceries. ■ a person who makes and sells candles. [ME: from OFr. *chandelier*, from *chandelle* (see CHANDELIER).]

chan·dler·y /'chandlərē/ ▶ n. (pl. **-dler·ies**) the warehouse or store of a chandler. ■ goods sold by a chandler.

Chan·dra·gup·ta Mau·ry·a /ˌchəndrə'go͝optə 'mourēə/ (c.325–297 BC), emperor of India. He founded the Mauryan empire.

Chan·dra·se·khar /ˌchəndrə'sākər/, Subrahmanyan (1910–95), US astronomer; born in India. He suggested that stars can collapse to form a dense white dwarf, provided that their mass does not exceed an upper limit (the **Chandrasekhar limit**).

Cha·nel /shə'nel/, Coco (1883–1971), French fashion designer; born *Gabrielle Bonheur Chanel.*

Chang·an /'chäng'än/ former name of XIAN.

Chang·chia·kow /'chäng 'jyä'kō/ variant of ZHANGJIAKOU.

Chang·chun /'chäng'cho͞on/ a city in northeastern China, capital of Jilin province; pop. 2,070,000.

change /chānj/ ▶ v. **1** make or become different: [trans.] *a proposal to change the law* | [intrans.] *beginning to change from green to gold.* ■ make or become a different substance entirely; transform. ■ [no obj., with complement] alter in terms of: *the ferns began to change shape.* ■ [intrans.] (of traffic lights) move from one color of signal to another. ■ (of a boy's voice) become deeper with the onset of puberty. ■ [intrans.] (of the moon) arrive at a fresh phase; become new. **2** [trans.] take or use another instead of. ■ move from one to another. ■ exchange; trade. ■ [intrans.] move to a different train, airplane, or subway line. ■ give up (something) in exchange for something else. ■ remove (something dirty or faulty) and replace it with another of the same kind. ■ put a clean diaper on (a baby or young child). ■ engage a different gear in a motor vehicle. ■ exchange (a sum of money) for the same amount in smaller denominations or in coins, or for different currency. ■ [intrans.] put different clothes on. ▶ n. **1** the act or instance of making or becoming different. ■ the substitution of one thing for another. ■ an alteration or modification. ■ a new or refreshingly different experience. ■ [in sing.] a clean garment or garments as a replacement for clothes one is wearing. ■ (**the change** or **the change of life**) informal menopause. ■ the moon's arrival at a fresh phase, typically at the new moon. **2** coins as opposed to paper currency. ■ money given in exchange for the same amount in larger denominations. ■ money returned to someone as the balance of the amount paid for something. **3** (usu. **changes**) an order in which a peal of bells can be rung.
– PHRASES **change color** blanch or flush. **change hands** (of a business or building) pass to a different owner. ■ (of money or a marketable commodity) pass to another person during a business transaction. **change one's mind** adopt a different opinion or plan. **change off** take turns. **a change of heart** a move to a different opinion or attitude. **change step** (in marching) alter one's step so that the opposite leg marks time. **change the subject** begin talking about something different, esp. to avoid embarrassment or the divulgence of confidences. **change one's tune 1** express a different opinion or behave in a different way. **2** change one's style of language or manner, esp. from an insolent to a respectful tone. **for a change** contrary to how things usually happen; for variety.
– PHRASAL VERBS **change over** move from one system or situation to another. — **change·ful** /'chānjfəl/ adj. [ME: from OFr. *change* (n.), *changer* (v.), from late L. *cambiare*, from L. *cambire* 'barter,' prob. of Celtic origin.]

change·a·ble /'chānjəbəl/ ▶ adj. **1** irregular; inconstant. **2** able to change or be changed. — **change·a·bil·i·ty** /ˌchānjə'bilətē/ n. **change·a·ble·ness** n. **change·a·bly** /-blē/ adv.

change·less /'chānjlis/ ▶ adj. remaining the same. — **change·less·ly** adv. **change·less·ness** n.

change·ling /'chānjling/ ▶ n. a child believed to have been secretly substituted by fairies for the parents' real child in infancy.

change·o·ver /'chānjˌōvər/ ▶ n. a change from one system or situation to another.

chang·er /'chānjər/ ▶ n. a person or thing that changes something. ■ a device that holds several computer disks or compact disks and is able to switch between them.

change-ring·ing ▶ n. the ringing of sets of church bells or handbells in a constantly varying order. — **change-ring·er** n.

change-up ▶ n. Baseball a deceptively slow pitch intended to throw off the batter's timing.

Chang Jiang /'chäng 'jyäng/ another name for YANGTZE.

Chang·sha /'chäng'shä/ the capital of Hunan province in eastern central China; pop. 1,300,000.

Chang·zhou /'chäng'jō/ a city in Jiangsu province in eastern China; pop. 670,000.

chan·nel /'chanl/ ▶ n. **1** a length of water wider than a strait, joining two larger areas of water, esp. two seas. ■ the navigable part of a waterway. ■ a hollow bed for a natural or artificial waterway. ■ (**the Channel**) the English Channel. ■ a narrow gap or passage. ■ a tubular passage or duct for liquid. ■ an electric circuit that acts as a path for a signal. ■ a groove or flute, esp. in a column. ■ Electron. the semiconductor region in a field-effect transistor that forms the main current path between the source and the drain. **2** a band of frequencies used in radio and television transmission, esp. as used by a particular station. ■ a service or station using such a band. **3** a medium for communication or the passage of information. ▶ v. (**-neled, -nel·ing** ; Brit. **-nelled, -nel·ling**) [trans.] **1** direct toward a particular end or object: *advertisers channel money into radio.* ■ guide along a particular route or through a specified medium. ■ (of a person) serve as a medium for (a spirit). **2** [usu. as adj.] (**channeled**) form channels or grooves in. [ME: from OFr. *chanel*, from L. *canalis* 'pipel,' from *canna* 'reed' (see CANE).]

chan·nel-hop ▶ v. [intrans.] informal **1** another term for CHANNEL-SURF. **2** travel across the English Channel and back frequently or for only a brief trip. — **chan·nel-hop·per** n.

Chan·nel Is·lands 1 a group of islands in the English Channel including Jersey, Guernsey, and Alderney; pop. 146,000. **2** another name for the SANTA BARBARA ISLANDS in California.

chan·nel·ize /'chanlˌīz/ ▶ v. [trans.] another term for CHANNEL (senses 1 and 2).

chan·nel-surf ▶ v. informal change frequently from one television channel to another, using a remote control device. — **chan·nel-surf·er** n. **chan·nel-surf·ing** n.

Chan·nel Tun·nel a rail tunnel under the English Channel, opened in

1994, that extends 31 miles (49 km) and links England and France; popularly called the Chunnel.

chan·son /SHän'sôn/ ▶ n. a French song. [Fr., from L. *cantio(n-)* 'singing,' from *canere* 'sing.']

chan·son de geste /SHän'sôn də 'ZHest/ ▶ n. (pl. **chan·sons de geste** /SHän'sôN(z)/) a medieval historical romance in French verse, typically one connected with Charlemagne. [19th C.: Fr., lit. 'song of heroic deeds.']

chant /CHant/ ▶ n. **1** a repeated rhythmic phrase, typically one shouted or sung in unison by a crowd. ■ a monotonous or repetitive song, typically an incantation or part of a ritual. **2** Music a short musical passage in two or more phrases used for singing unmetrical words; a psalm or canticle sung to such music. ■ the style of music consisting of such passages. ▶ v. [trans.] say or shout repeatedly in a sing-song tone. ■ sing or intone (a psalm, canticle, or sacred text). [ME: from OFr. *chanter* 'sing,' from L. *cantare*, frequentative of *canere*.]

chant·er /'CHantər/ ▶ n. **1** a person who chants something. **2** Music the pipe of a bagpipe with finger holes, on which the melody is played.

chan·te·relle /,SHantə'rel; ,SHänt-/ ▶ n. an edible woodland mushroom (*Cantharellus cibarius*, family Cantharellaceae) with a yellow funnel-shaped cap and a faint smell of apricots, found in both Eurasia and North America. [18th C.: from Fr., from mod. L. *cantharellus*, dimin. of *cantharus*, from Gk. *kantharos*, a container.]

chan·teuse /SHän'to͞oz; -'tœz/ ▶ n. a female singer of popular songs, esp. in a nightclub. [Fr., from *chanter* 'sing.']

chant·ey /'SHantē/ (also **chant·y**, **shant·y**, or **sea chant·ey**) ▶ n. a song with alternating solo and chorus, of a kind originally sung by sailors while performing physical labor together. [19th. C.: prob. from Fr. *chantez!* 'sing!,' imper. pl. of *chanter*.]

chan·ti·cleer /'CHantə,kli(ə)r; 'SHant-/ ▶ n. literary a name given to a rooster, esp. in fairy tales. [ME: from OFr. *Chantecler*, cock in the fable *Reynard the Fox*, from *chanter* 'sing,' + *cler* 'clear.']

Chan·til·ly lace ▶ n. a delicate kind of bobbin lace. [19th C.: *Chantilly*, town near Paris.]

chan·try /'CHantrē/ ▶ n. (pl. **-tries**) an endowment for a priest or priests to celebrate masses for the founder's soul. ■ a chapel, altar, or other part of a church endowed for such a purpose. [ME: from OFr. *chanterie*, from *chanter* 'to sing.']

chant·y ▶ n. (pl. **chant·ies**) var. of CHANTEY.

Cha·nu·kah ▶ n. var. of HANUKKAH.

Cha·nute /SHə'no͞ot/, Octave (1832–1910), US aviation pioneer; born in France. From 1898, he produced a number of gliders.

Chao Phra·ya /CHou 'prīə/ a major waterway in central Thailand, formed by the junction of the Ping and Nan rivers.

cha·os /'kāäs/ ▶ n. complete disorder and confusion. ■ Physics behavior so unpredictable as to appear random, owing to great sensitivity to small changes in conditions. ■ the formless matter supposed to have existed before the creation of the universe. ■ **(Chaos)** Gk. Mythol. the first created being. [15th C.: via Fr. and L. from Gk. *khaos* 'chasm, void.']

cha·os the·o·ry ▶ n. the branch of mathematics that deals with complex systems whose behavior is highly sensitive to slight changes in conditions, so that small alterations can give rise to strikingly great consequences.

cha·ot·ic /kā'ätik/ ▶ adj. in a state of complete confusion and disorder. ■ Physics of or relating to systems that exhibit chaos. — **cha·ot·i·cal·ly** /-ik(ə)lē/ adv. [18th C.: from CHAOS.]

chap[1] /CHap/ ▶ v. **(chapped, chap·ping)** [intrans.] (of the skin) become cracked, rough, or sore, typically through exposure to cold weather: ■ [trans.] [usu. as adj.] **(chapped)** (of the wind or cold) cause (skin) to crack in this way: *chapped lips*. ▶ n. a cracked or sore patch on the skin. [ME: of unknown origin.]

chap[2] ▶ n. informal, esp. Brit. a man or a boy. ■ dated a friendly form of address between men and boys. [16th C.: abbrev. of CHAPMAN.]

chap. ▶ abbr. chapter.

cha·pa·ra·jos /,SHapə'rā-ōs; -'rāəs/ (also **cha·pa·re·jos**) ▶ plural n. full form of CHAPS. [19th C.: from Mex. Sp. *chaparreras*, from *chaparra* (see CHAPARRAL).]

chap·ar·ral /,SHapə'ral/ ▶ n. vegetation consisting chiefly of tangled shrubs and thorny bushes. [19th C.: from Sp., from *chaparra* 'dwarf evergreen oak.']

cha·pa·ti /CHə'pätē/ (also **cha·pat·ti**) ▶ n. (pl. **-tis**) (in Indian cooking) a thin pancake of unleavened whole-grain bread cooked on a griddle. [from Hindi *capātī*, from *capānā* 'flatten.']

chap·book /'CHap,bo͝ok/ ▶ n. hist. a small pamphlet containing tales, ballads, or tracts, sold by peddlers. ■ a small paperback booklet, typically containing poems or fiction. [19th C.: from CHAPMAN.]

chape /CHāp/ ▶ n. **1** hist. the metal point of a scabbard. **2** the metal pin of a buckle. [ME: from OFr., lit. 'cape,' from late L. *cappa* 'cap.']

cha·peau /SHa'pō/ ▶ n. (pl. **-peaux** /-'pō(z)/) a hat. [15th C.: from Fr., from L. *cappellum*, dimin. of *cappa* 'cap.']

chap·el /'CHapəl/ ▶ n. a small building for Christian worship, typically one attached to an institution or private house. ■ regular services held in such a building. ■ a part of a large church or cathedral with its own altar and dedication. ■ a room or building in which funeral services are held. [ME: from OFr. *chapele*, from med. L. *cappella*, dimin. of *cappa*.]

Chap·el Hill a town in north central North Carolina; pop. 48,715.

chap·er·one /'SHapə,rōn/ (also **chap·er·on**) ▶ n. a person who accompanies and looks after another person or group of people, in particular: ■ dated an older woman responsible for the decorous behavior of a young unmarried girl at social occasions. ■ a person who takes charge of a child or group of children in public. ▶ v. [trans.] accompany and look after or supervise. — **chap·er·on·age** /-,rōnij; ,SHapə'rōnij/ n. [ME: from Fr., fem. of *chaperon* 'hood,' dimin. of *chape* (see CHAPE).]

chap·fall·en /'CHap,fôlən/ (also **chop·fall·en** /'CHäp-/) ▶ adj. archaic with one's lower jaw hanging due to extreme exhaustion or dejection. [16th C.: from *chap* 'jaw.']

chap·lain /'CHaplin/ ▶ n. a member of the clergy attached to a private chapel, institution, ship, branch of the armed forces, etc. — **chap·lain·cy** /'CHaplinsē/ n. [ME: from OFr. *chapelain*, from med. L. *cappellanus*, from *cappella* (see CHAPEL).]

chap·let /'CHaplit/ ▶ n. **1** a garland or wreath for a person's head. **2** a string of 55 beads (one third of the rosary number) for counting prayers, or as a necklace. **3** a metal support for the core of a hollow casting mold. — **chap·let·ed** adj. [ME: from OFr. *chapelet*, dimin. of *chapel* 'hat,' based on late L. *cappa* 'cap.']

Chap·lin /'CHaplin/, Charlie (1889–1977), English actor and director; full name *Sir Charles Spencer Chaplin*. He directed and starred in many short silent comedies, mostly playing a bowler-hatted tramp, a character that became his trademark.

Chap·man /'CHapmən/, John, see APPLESEED.

chap·man /'CHapmən/ ▶ n. (pl. **-men**) archaic a peddler. [OE *cēapman*, from *cēap* 'bargaining, trade' (see CHEAP) + MAN.]

Chap·pa·quid·dick Is·land /,CHapə'kwidik/ an island in southern Massachusetts, off the southeastern coast of Martha's Vineyard.

chaps /CHaps; SHaps/ ▶ plural n. leather pants without a seat, worn by a cowboy over ordinary pants to protect the legs. [19th C.: short for CHAPARAJOS.]

Chap Stick ▶ n. trademark a small stick of a cosmetic substance used to prevent chapping of the lips.

chap·tal·i·za·tion /,SHaptələ'zāSHən/ ▶ n. (in winemaking) the correction or improvement of must by the addition of calcium carbonate to neutralize acid, or of sugar to increase alcoholic strength. — **chap·tal·ize** /'SHaptə,līz/ v. [19th C.: Jean A. *Chaptal* (1756–1832), Fr. chemist.]

chap·ter /'CHaptər/ ▶ n. **1** a main division of a book, typically with a number or title. ■ fig. a period of time or an episode in a person's life, a nation's history, etc. **2** a local branch of a society. **3** the governing body of a religious community, esp. a cathedral or a knightly order. **4** a series or sequence.

– PHRASES **chapter and verse** an exact reference or authority. [ME: from OFr. *chapitre*, from L. *capitulum*, dimin. of *caput* 'head.']

Chap·ter 11 ▶ n. protection from creditors given to a company in financial difficulties for a limited period to allow it to reorganize.

Chap·ter 13 ▶ n. protection from creditors granted to individuals who legally file for bankruptcy, providing for repayment of debts by a court-approved plan.

Chap·ter 7 ▶ n. protection from creditors granted to individuals or companies who legally file for bankruptcy, providing for liquidation of certain assets to pay debts.

chap·ter house ▶ n. a building used for the meetings of the canons of a cathedral or other religious community. ■ a place where a college fraternity or sorority meets.

Cha·pul·te·pec /CHə'po͝oltə,pek/ a hill in Mexico City, Mexico, that was captured by the US in the Mexican War 1847.

char[1] /CHär/ ▶ v. **(charred, char·ring)** [trans.] (usu. **be charred**) partially burn (an object) so as to blacken its surface. ■ [intrans.] (of an object) become burned and discolored in such a way. ▶ n. material that has been charred. [17th C.: appar. back-form. from CHARCOAL.]

char[2] Brit., informal ▶ n. a charwoman. ▶ v. **(charred, char·ring)** [intrans.] work as a charwoman.

char[3] (also **charr**) ▶ n. (pl. same) a freshwater or marine fish (genus *Salvelinus*) of the salmon family, occurring in northern countries and widely valued as a food and game fish. Its several species include the North American **brook trout** (*S. fontinalis*) and the red-bellied **Arctic char** (*S. alpinus*). [17th C.: perh. of Celtic origin.]

char·a·cin /'karəsin/ ▶ n. a small and brightly colored freshwater fish (family Characidae) native to Africa and tropical America. Its numerous species include the piranhas and tetras. [19th C.: from mod. L. *Characinus*, from Gk. *kharax*, a fish, lit. 'stake.']

char·ac·ter /'kariktər/ ▶ n. **1** the mental and moral qualities distinctive to an individual. ■ the distinctive nature of something. ■ the quality of being individual, typically in an interesting or unusual way. ■ strength and originality in a person's nature. ■ a person's good reputation. **2** a person in a novel, play, or movie. ■ a part played by an actor. ■ [with adj.] a person seen in terms of a particular aspect of character. ■ informal an interesting or amusing individual. **3** a printed or written letter or symbol. ■ Comput. a symbol representing a letter or number. ■ Comput. the bit pattern used to store such a symbol. **4** esp. Biol. a characteristic, esp. one that assists in the identification of a species.

– PHRASES **in** (or **out of**) **character** in keeping (or not in keeping) with someone's usual pattern of behavior. — **char·ac·ter·ful** /-fəl/ adj.

char·ac·ter·ful·ly /-fəlē/ **adv. char·ac·ter·less adj.** [ME: from OFr. *caractere*, via L. from Gk. *kharaktēr* 'stamping tool.']

char·ac·ter ac·tor ▶ **n.** an actor who specializes in playing eccentric or unusual people rather than leading roles.

char·ac·ter as·sas·si·na·tion ▶ **n.** the malicious and unjustified harming of a person's good reputation.

char·ac·ter code ▶ **n.** Comput. the binary code used to represent a letter or number.

char·ac·ter·is·tic /ˌkariktəˈristik/ ▶ **adj.** typical of a particular person, place, or thing. ▶ **n. 1** a feature or quality belonging typically to a person, place, or thing and serving to identify it. **2** Math. the whole number or integral part of a logarithm, which gives the order of magnitude of the original number. — **char·ac·ter·is·ti·cal·ly** /-ik(ə)lē/ **adv.**

char·ac·ter·is·tic curve ▶ **n.** a graph showing the relationship between two variable but interdependent quantities.

char·ac·ter·ize /ˈkariktəˌrīz/ ▶ **v.** [trans.] **1** describe the distinctive nature or features of. **2** (often **be characterized**) (of a feature or quality) be typical or characteristic of: *the disease is **characterized by** weakening of the immune system.* — **char·ac·ter·i·za·tion** /ˌkariktərəˈzāsʜən/ **n.**

char·ac·ter rec·og·ni·tion ▶ **n.** the identification by electronic means of printed or written characters.

char·ac·ter·y /ˈkariktərē/ ▶ **n.** literary the expression of thought by symbols or characters; the symbols or characters collectively.

cha·rade /sʜəˈrād/ ▶ **n.** an absurd pretense intended to create a pleasant or respectable appearance. ■ (**charades**) a game in which players guess a word or phrase from pantomimed clues. [18th C.: from Fr., from Provençal *charrado* 'conversation,' from *charra* 'chatter,' perh. imitative.]

cha·ras /ˈcʜärəs/ ▶ **n.** a psychoactive resin from the flowerheads of hemp; cannabis resin. [from Hindi *caras*.]

char·broil /ˈcʜärˌbroil/ ▶ **v.** [trans.] [usu. as adj.] (**charbroiled**) grill (food, esp. meat) on a rack over charcoal: *charbroiled steak.* [1950s: blend of CHARCOAL and BROIL[1].]

char·coal /ˈcʜärˌkōl/ ▶ **n.** a porous black solid, consisting of an amorphous form of carbon, obtained as a residue when wood, bone, or other organic matter is heated in the absence of air. ■ briquettes of charcoal used for barbecuing. ■ a crayon made of charcoal and used for drawing. ■ a drawing made using charcoal. ■ a dark gray color. ▶ **v.** [usu. as adj.] (**charcoaled**) cook over charcoal: *charcoaled lobster.* ■ fig. darken or blacken as if with charcoal. [ME: prob. rel. to COAL.]

Char·cot /sʜärˈkō/, Jean-Martin (1825–93), French neurologist. He is a cofounder of modern neurology.

char·cu·te·rie /sʜärˌkōōtəˈrē; -ˈkōōtərē/ ▶ **n.** (pl. **-ries**) cold cooked meats collectively. ■ a store selling such meats. [Fr., from obs. *char* 'flesh' + *cuite* 'cooked.']

chard /cʜärd/ ▶ **n.** (also **Swiss chard**) a beet of a variety with broad white leaf stalks that may be prepared and eaten separately from the green parts of the leaf. ■ the blanched shoots of other plants, eaten as a vegetable, e.g., globe artichoke. [17th C.: from Fr. *carde*.]

Char·don·nay /ˌsʜärdnˈā/ ▶ **n.** a variety of white wine grape used for making champagne and other wines. ■ a wine made from this grape. [Fr.]

Cha·rente /sʜäˈränt/ a river in western France that flows west for 225 miles (360 km) to the Bay of Biscay.

charge /cʜärj/ ▶ **v.** [trans.] **1** demand (an amount) as a price from someone for a service rendered or goods supplied. ■ (**charge something to**) record the cost of something as an amount payable by (someone) or on (an account). **2** accuse (someone) of something, esp. an offense under law. ■ [with clause] make an accusation or assertion that. ■ Law accuse someone of (an offense). **3** entrust (someone) with a task as a duty or responsibility. **4** store electrical energy in (a battery or battery-operated device). ■ [intrans.] (of a battery or battery-operated device) receive and store electrical energy. ■ tech. formal load or fill (a container, gun, etc.) to the full or proper extent. ■ (usu. **be charged with**) fig. fill or pervade (something) with a quality or emotion: *the air was charged with menace.* **5** [intrans.] rush forward in attack. ■ [trans.] rush aggressively toward (someone or something) in attack. ■ [with adverbial of direction] move quickly and with impetus. **6** (usu. **be charged with**) Heraldry place a heraldic bearing on. ▶ **n. 1** a price asked for goods or services. ■ a financial liability or commitment. **2** an accusation, typically one formally made against a prisoner brought to trial. **3** the responsibility of taking care or control of someone or something. ■ a person or thing entrusted to the care of someone. ■ dated a responsibility or onerous duty assigned to someone. ■ an official instruction, esp. one given by a judge to a jury regarding points of law. **4** the property of matter that is responsible for electrical phenomena, existing in a positive or negative form. ■ the quantity of this carried by a body. ■ energy stored chemically for conversion into electricity. ■ the process of storing electrical energy in a battery. ■ [in sing.] informal a thrill. **5** a quantity of explosive to be detonated, typically in order to fire a gun or similar weapon. **6** a headlong rush forward, typically one made by attacking soldiers in battle. ■ the signal or call for such a rush. **7** Heraldry a device or bearing placed on a shield or crest.

– PHRASES **in charge** in control or with overall responsibility. **press** (or **prefer**) **charges** accuse someone formally of a crime so that they can be brought to trial. **take charge** assume control or responsibility. — **charge·a·ble adj.** [ME: ult. from late L. *carricare* 'to load,' from L. *carrus* 'wheeled vehicle.']

charge ac·count ▶ **n.** an account to which goods and services may be charged on credit.

charge card ▶ **n.** a credit card for use with an account that must be paid when a statement is issued.

charge car·ri·er ▶ **n.** Physics a particle that carries an electric charge. ■ a mobile electron or hole by which an electric charge passes through a semiconductor.

charge-cou·pled de·vice ▶ **n.** see **CCD**.

charged /cʜärjd/ ▶ **adj.** having an electric charge. ■ fig. filled with excitement, tension, or emotion.

char·gé d'af·faires /sʜärˌzʜä däˈfer/ (also **char·gé**) ▶ **n.** (pl. **char·gés d'af·faires** /sʜärˈzʜā(z)/) a diplomatic official who temporarily takes the place of an ambassador. ■ a state's diplomatic representative in a minor country. [18th C.: Fr., lit. 'in charge of affairs.']

Charge of the Light Bri·gade a British cavalry charge in 1854 during the Battle of Balaclava in the Crimean War.

charg·er[1] /ˈcʜärjər/ ▶ **n. 1** a horse trained for battle; a cavalry horse. **2** a device for charging a battery or battery-powered equipment. **3** a person who charges forward.

charg·er[2] (also **charger plate**) ▶ **n.** a large, flat dish; a platter. ■ a large plate placed under a dinner plate in some formal table settings. [ME: from Anglo-Norman Fr. *chargeour*, from *chargier* 'to load,' from late L. *carricare* (see CHARGE).]

char·grill /ˈcʜärˌgril/ ▶ **v.** [usu. as adj.] (**chargrilled**) grill (food, typically meat or fish) quickly at a high heat. [20th C.: on the pattern of *charbroil*.]

Cha·ri Riv·er /ˈsʜärē/ (also **Shari**) a river that flows for 660 miles (1,060 km) through the Central African Republic, Chad, and Cameroon.

char·i·ot /ˈcʜarēət/ ▶ **n.** hist. a two-wheeled horse-drawn vehicle used in ancient warfare and racing. ■ hist. a four-wheeled carriage with back seats and a coachman's seat. ■ literary a stately or triumphal carriage. ▶ **v.** [trans.] literary convey in or as in a chariot. [ME: from OFr., augmentative of *char* 'cart,' based on L. *carrus* 'wheeled vehicle.']

char·i·ot·eer /ˌcʜarēəˈti(ə)r/ ▶ **n.** a chariot driver. ■ (**the Charioteer**) the constellation Auriga.

char·ism /ˈkarizəm/ ▶ **n.** Theol. another term for CHARISMA (sense 2).

cha·ris·ma /kəˈrizmə/ ▶ **n. 1** compelling attractiveness or charm that can inspire devotion in others. **2** (pl. **-ma·ta** /-mətə/) (also **char·ism** /ˈkarizəm/) a divinely conferred power or talent. [17th C.: via eccles. L. from Gk. *kharisma*, from *kharis* 'favor.']

char·is·mat·ic /ˌkarizˈmatik/ ▶ **adj. 1** exercising a compelling charm that inspires devotion in others. **2** of or relating to the charismatic movement in the Christian Church that emphasizes gifts believed to be conferred by the Holy Spirit. ■ (of a power or talent) divinely conferred. ▶ **n.** an adherent of the charismatic movement. ■ a person who claims divine inspiration. — **char·is·mat·i·cal·ly** /-ik(ə)lē/ **adv.**

char·i·ta·ble /ˈcʜaritəbəl/ ▶ **adj. 1** of or relating to the assistance of those in need. ■ (of an organization or activity) officially recognized as devoted to the assistance of those in need. ■ generous in giving to those in need. **2** apt to judge others leniently or favorably. — **char·i·ta·ble·ness n. char·i·ta·bly** /-blē/ **adv.**

char·i·ty /ˈcʜaritē/ ▶ **n.** (pl. **-ties**) **1** the voluntary giving of help, typically money, to those in need. ■ help or money given in this way. **2** an organization set up to provide help and raise money for those in need. ■ such organizations viewed collectively as the object of fund-raising or donations. **3** kindness and tolerance in judging others.

– PHRASES **charity begins at home** proverb one's first responsibility is for the needs of one's own family and friends. [OE: from OFr. *charite*, from L. *caritas*, from *carus* 'dear.']

cha·ri·va·ri /ˌsʜivəˈrē; ˈsʜivəˌrē/ (also **shiv·a·ree**) ▶ **n.** (pl. **-va·ris**) esp. hist. a cacophonous mock serenade, typically performed by a group of people in derision of an unpopular person or in celebration of a marriage. ■ a series of discordant noises. [17th C.: from Fr.]

char·la·tan /ˈsʜärlətən; ˈsʜärlətn/ ▶ **n.** a person falsely claiming to have a special knowledge or skill; a fraud. — **char·la·tan·ism** /-ləṭəˌnizəm; -lətnˌizəm/ **n. char·la·tan·ry** /ˈsʜärlətənrē; -lətnrē/ **n.** [17th C.: from Fr., from Ital. *ciarlatano*, from *ciarlare* 'to babble.']

Char·le·magne /ˈsʜärləˌmān/ (742–814), king of the Franks 768–814 and Holy Roman Emperor (as Charles I) 800–814; Latin name *Carolus Magnus*; known as **Charles the Great**. As the first Holy Roman emperor, he promoted the arts and education.

Char·le·roi /ˌsʜärləˈrwä; -ˈroi/ a city in southwestern Belgium; pop. 206,200.

Charles[1] /cʜärlz/ the name of two kings of England, Scotland, and Ireland: ■ Charles I (1600–49), reigned 1625–49; son of James I. His reign was dominated by the events that led up to the English Civil War 1642–49. ■ Charles II (1630–85), reigned 1660–85; son of Charles I. He was restored to the throne after the collapse of Oliver Cromwell's regime.

Charles[2] the name of four kings of Spain: ■ Charles I (1500–58), reigned 1516–56; son of Philip I; Holy Roman Emperor (as Charles V) 1519–56. His reign dealt with the struggle against Protestantism in Germany, rebellion in Castile, and war with France 1521–44. ■ Charles II (1661–1700), reigned 1665–1700. He inherited a kingdom already in a decline that he was unable to halt. ■ Charles III (1716–88), reigned 1759–88. He improved Spain's position as an international power. ■ Charles IV (1748–1819), reigned 1788–1808. During the Napoleonic Wars he suffered the loss of the Spanish fleet.

Charles[3] the name of seven Holy Roman Emperors: ■ Charles I see CHARLEMAGNE. ■ Charles II (823–877), reigned 875–877. ■ Charles III (839–888), reigned 881–887. ■ Charles IV (1316–78), reigned 1355–78. ■ Charles V Charles I of Spain (see **Charles**[2]). ■ Charles VI (1685–1740), reigned 1711–40. His claim to the Spanish throne instigated the War of the Spanish Succession. ■ Charles VII (1697–1745), reigned 1742–45.

Charles VII (1403–61), king of France 1422–61. During his reign, after the intervention of Joan of Arc, the defeat of the English ended the Hundred Years War.

Charles XII (also **Karl XII** /kärl/) (1682–1718), king of Sweden 1697–1718.

Charles, Prince (1948–), son of Elizabeth II; full name *Charles Philip Arthur George, Prince of Wales*; heir apparent to Elizabeth II. He married Lady Diana Spencer in 1981; they had two children, Prince William Arthur Philip Louis (1982–) and Prince Henry Charles Albert David (1984–), and were divorced in 1996. In 2005 he married Mrs Camilla Parker Bowles (1947–); she became HRH the Duchess of Cornwall.

Charles' law (also **Charles's law**) Chem. a law stating that the volume of an ideal gas at constant pressure is directly proportional to the absolute temperature. [19th C.: named after Jacques A. C. *Charles* (1746–1823), the French physicist who first formulated it.]

Charles Mar·tel /'CHärlz mär'tel/ (*c.*688–741), Frankish ruler of the eastern part of the Frankish kingdom from 715 and the whole kingdom from 719; grandfather of Charlemagne.

Charles Riv·er /CHärlz/ a river that flows for 60 miles (100 km) through eastern Massachusetts to Boston Harbor.

Charles·ton[1] /'CHärlstən/ **1** the capital of West Virginia, in the southwestern part of the state; pop. 53,421. **2** a city and port in South Carolina; pop. 96,650.

Charles·ton[2] (also **charles·ton**) ▶ **n.** a lively dance of the 1920s that involved turning the knees inward and kicking out the lower legs. ▶ **v.** [intrans.] dance the Charleston. [1920s: named after **Charleston**[1] in South Carolina.]

Charles·town /'CHärlz,toun/ a neighborhood in northern Boston, Massachusetts, the site of Bunker Hill.

char·ley horse /'CHärlē/ ▶ **n.** [in sing.] informal a cramp or feeling of stiffness in an arm or leg. [19th C.: of unknown origin.]

Char·lie /'CHärlē/ ▶ **n.** **1** a code word representing the letter C, used in radio communication. **2** informal cocaine. **3** military slang, hist. a member of the Vietcong or the Vietcong collectively. [shortening of *Victor Charlie*, radio code for *VC*, representing *Vietcong*.] [19th C.: dimin. of the name *Charles*.]

char·lock /'CHär,läk; -lək/ ▶ **n.** a wild mustard (*Brassica kaber*, or *Sinapis arvensis*) with yellow flowers, commonly found in fields and along roadsides. [OE *cerlic, cyrlic*.]

Char·lotte /'SHärlət/ a city in southern North Carolina; pop. 540,828.

char·lotte /'SHärlət/ ▶ **n.** a dessert made of stewed fruit or mousse with a casing or covering of bread, sponge cake, ladyfingers, or breadcrumbs. [Fr., from the name *Charlotte*.]

Char·lotte A·ma·li·e /ə'mälyə/ the capital of the US Virgin Islands, a resort on the island of St. Thomas; pop. 52,660.

char·lotte russe /'rōōs/ ▶ **n.** a dessert consisting of custard enclosed in sponge cake or a casing of ladyfingers. [19th C.: Fr., lit. 'Russian charlotte.']

Char·lottes·ville /'SHärləts,vil/ a city in central Virginia; pop. 45,049.

Char·lotte·town /'SHärlət,toun/ the capital and chief port of Prince Edward Island, in eastern Canada; pop. 33,150.

charm /CHärm/ ▶ **n.** **1** the power or quality of giving delight or arousing admiration. ■ (usu. **charms**) an attractive or alluring characteristic. **2** a small ornament worn on a necklace or bracelet. **3** an object, act, or saying believed to have magic power. ■ an object kept or worn to ward off evil and bring good luck. **4** Physics one of six flavors of quark. ▶ **v.** [trans.] **1** delight greatly. ■ gain or influence by charm. **2** control or achieve by or as if by magic: [with adverbial] *she will charm your warts away.*
– PHRASES **turn on the charm** use one's ability to charm in order to influence someone. **work like a charm** be completely successful or effective. [ME: from OFr. *charme* (n.), *charmer* (v.), from L. *carmen* 'song.']

charmed /CHärmd/ ▶ **adj.** **1** (of a person's life) unusually lucky or happy as though protected by magic. **2** Physics (of a particle) possessing the property charm. ▶ **exclam.** dated expressing polite pleasure at an introduction: *charmed, I'm sure.*

charm·er /'CHärmər/ ▶ **n.** a person with an attractive, engaging personality. ■ a person who habitually seeks to impress or manipulate others by exploiting an ability to charm.

char·meuse /SHär'm(y)ōōz/ ▶ **n.** a soft, silky dress fabric. [20th C.: from Fr., fem. of *charmeur* 'charmer,' from *charmer* 'to charm.']

charm·ing /'CHärmiNG/ ▶ **adj.** pleasant or attractive. ■ (of a person or manner) polite, friendly, and likable. — **charm·ing·ly** adv.

char·mo·ni·um /CHär'mōnēəm/ ▶ **n.** (pl. **-ni·a** /-nēə/) Physics a combination of a charmed quark and an antiquark. [1970s: from **charm** (sense 4).]

char·nel /'CHärnl/ ▶ **n.** short for **charnel house**. ▶ **adj.** associated with death. [ME: from OFr., from med. L. *carnale*, neut. of *carnalis* (see **carnal**).]

char·nel house ▶ **n.** hist. a building or vault in which corpses or bones are piled. ■ fig. a place associated with violent death.

Cha·ro·lais /,SHarə'lā/ ▶ **n.** (pl. same) one of a breed of large white beef cattle. [19th C.: *Monts du Charollais*, hills in France.]

Char·on /'karən; 'ke(ə)r-/ **1** Gk. Mythol. an old man who ferried the souls of the dead across the Styx and Acheron rivers to Hades. **2** Astron. the only satellite of Pluto, discovered in 1978.

Cha·roph·y·ta /kə'räfitə/ Bot. a phylum that includes the stoneworts, which are frequently treated as a class (Charophyceae) of the green algae. — **char·o·phyte** /'karə,fīt/ **n.** [mod. L. (pl.), from *Chara* (genus) + Gk. *phuton* 'plant.']

charr /CHär/ (also **char**) ▶ **n.** var. of **char**[3]. [17th C.: perh. of Celtic origin.]

char·ro /'CHärō/ ▶ **n.** (pl. **-ros**) a Mexican horseman or cowboy, typically one in elaborate traditional dress. [20th C.: Mex. Sp., from Sp., lit. 'rustic.']

chart /CHärt/ ▶ **n.** a sheet of information in the form of a table, graph, or diagram. ■ (usu. **the charts**) a weekly listing of the current best-selling pop records. ■ a geographical map or plan, esp. one used for navigation by sea or air. ■ Med. a written record of information about a patient. ▶ **v.** **1** [trans.] make a map of (an area). ■ plot (a course) on a chart: *taking a route he had not charted.* ■ (usu. **be charted**) record on a chart. **2** [intrans.] (of a record) enter the weekly music charts at a particular position: *the record will probably chart at No. 74.* [16th C.: from Fr. *charte*, from L. *charta* 'paper' (see **card**[1]).]

chart·bust·er /'CHärt,bəstər/ ▶ **n.** informal a popular singer or group that makes a best-selling recording. ■ a best-selling recording.

char·ter /'CHärtər/ ▶ **n.** **1** a written grant by a country's legislative or sovereign power, by which an institution such as a company, university, or city is created and its rights and privileges defined. ■ a written constitution or description of an organization's functions. **2** the reservation of an aircraft, boat, or bus for private use. ■ an aircraft, boat, or bus that is reserved for private use. ■ a trip made by an aircraft, boat, or bus under charter. ▶ **v.** [trans.] **1** grant a charter to (a city, university, or other institution). **2** reserve (an aircraft, boat, or bus) for private use. [ME: from OFr. *chartre*, from L. *chartula*, dimin. of *charta* 'paper' (see **card**[1]).]

char·tered /'CHärtərd/ ▶ **adj.** [attrib.] Brit. (of an accountant, engineer, librarian, etc.) qualified as a member of a professional body that has a royal charter.

char·ter mem·ber ▶ **n.** an original or founding member of an organization.

char·ter school ▶ **n.** (in North America) a publicly funded independent school established by teachers, parents, or community groups under the terms of a charter with a local or national authority.

Chart·ism /'CHärtizəm/ ▶ **n.** a UK parliamentary reform movement of 1837–48, the principles of which were set out in a manifesto called *The People's Charter*. — **Chart·ist** **n. & adj.**

char·tist /'CHärtist/ ▶ **n.** a person who uses charts of financial data to predict future trends and to guide investment strategies. — **char·tism** /'CHärtizəm/ **n.**

Char·tres /'SHärt(rə)/ a city in northern France, noted for its Gothic cathedral; pop. 41,850.

char·treuse /SHär'trōōz; -'trōōs/ ▶ **n.** **1** a pale green or yellow liqueur made from brandy and aromatic herbs. ■ a pale yellow or green color resembling this liqueur. **2** a dish made in a mold using pieces of meat, vegetables, or (now most often) fruit in jelly. [*La Grande Chartreuse*, Carthusian monastery in France.]

char·wom·an /'CHär,wŏŏmən/ ▶ **n.** (pl. **-wom·en**) Brit., dated a woman employed to clean houses or offices. [16th C.: from obs. *char* or *chare* 'turn of work' (akin to **chore**).]

char·y /'CHe(ə)rē/ ▶ **adj.** (**char·i·er, char·i·est**) cautious; wary. ■ cautious about the amount one gives or reveals. — **char·i·ly** /'CHe(ə)rəlē/ **adv.** [OE *cearig* 'sorrowful, anxious,' of West Gmc. origin; rel. to **care**. The current sense arose in the mid 16th C.]

Cha·ryb·dis /kə'ribdis; CHə-/ Gk. Mythol. a dangerous whirlpool identified with Galofalo, in the strait of Messina, Sicily.

Chas. /CHaz/ ▶ **abbr.** Charles.

Chase[1] /CHās/, Salmon Portland (1808–73), Chief Justice of the US 1864–73.

Chase[2], Samuel (1741–1811), US Supreme Court associate justice 1796–1811.

chase[1] /CHās/ ▶ **v.** [trans.] **1** pursue in order to catch or catch up with: *police chased the stolen car* | [intrans.] *the dog **chased after** the stick.* ■ seek to attain. ■ seek the company of (a member of the opposite sex) in an obvious way. ■ [with obj. and adverbial of direction] drive or cause to go in a specified direction. **2** try to make contact with (someone) in order to get something owed or required. ■ make further investigation of (an unresolved matter). ▶ **n.** an act of pursuing someone or something.
– PHRASES **give chase** go in pursuit. [ME: from OFr. *chacier* (v.), *chace* (n.), based on L. *captare* 'continue to take,' from *capere* 'take.']

chase[2] ▶ **v.** [trans.] [usu. as adj.] (**chased**) engrave (metal, or a design on metal). [ME: appar. from *enchase*, from OFr. *enchasser*.]

chase[3] ▶ **n.** (in letterpress printing) a metal frame for holding the composed type and blocks being printed at one time. [16th C.: from Fr. *châsse*, from L. *capsa* 'box' (see **case**[2]).]

chase[4] ▶ **n.** **1** the part of a gun enclosing the bore. **2** a groove or furrow cut in the face of a wall or other surface to receive a pipe. [17th C.: from Fr. *chas* 'enclosed space,' from Provençal *cas, caus*, from med. L. *capsum* 'nave of a church.']

chas·er /'CHāsər/ ▶ **n.** **1** a person or thing that chases: [in comb.] *promotion-chasers.* **2** informal a drink taken after another of a different kind, typically a weak alcoholic drink after a stronger one. **3** a horse for steeplechasing.

Cha·sid ▶ n. var. of HASID.

Cha·sid·ism ▶ n. var. of HASIDISM.

chasm /ˈkazəm/ ▶ n. a deep fissure in the earth, rock, or another surface. ■ fig. a profound difference between people, viewpoints, feelings, etc. — **chas·mic** /ˈkazmik/ adj. (rare). [16th C.: from L. *chasma*, from Gk. *khasma* 'gaping hollow.']

chas·sé /SHaˈsā/ ▶ n. a gliding step in dancing in which one foot displaces the other. ▶ v. (**chas·séd, chas·sé·ing**) [intrans.] make such a step. [19th C.: Fr., lit. 'chased.']

chasse·pot /ˈSHas,pō/ ▶ n. a type of bolt-action breech-loading rifle used by the French army between 1866 and 1874. [Antoine A. Chassepot (1833–1905), its French designer.]

chas·seur /SHaˈsər/ ▶ n. (pl. same) hist. a soldier, usually in the light cavalry, equipped and trained for rapid movement, esp. in the French army. [18th C.: Fr., from *chasser*.]

Chas·sid ▶ n. var. of HASID.

Chas·sid·ism ▶ n. var. of HASIDISM.

chas·sis /ˈCHasē; ˈSHasē/ ▶ n. (pl. same) the base frame of a motor vehicle or other wheeled conveyance. ■ the outer structural framework of a piece of audio, radio, or computer equipment. [20th C.: from Fr. *châssis* 'frame,' based on L. *capsa* 'box' (see CASE[2]).]

chaste /CHāst/ ▶ adj. abstaining from extramarital, or from all, sexual intercourse. ■ not having any sexual nature or intention. ■ without unnecessary ornamentation; simple or restrained. — **chaste·ly** adv. **chaste·ness** n. [ME: from OFr., from L. *castus*.]

chas·ten /ˈCHāsən/ ▶ v. [trans.] (usu. **be chastened**) (of a reproof or misfortune) have a restraining or moderating effect on: *the director was chastened by his recent flops* | [as adj.] (**chastening**) *a chastening experience.* — **chas·ten·er** /ˈCHās(ə)nər/ n. [16th C.: from an obs. v. *chaste*, from OFr. *chastier*, from L. *castigare* 'castigate,' from *castus* 'chaste.']

chas·tise /CHasˈtīz/ ▶ v. [trans.] rebuke or reprimand severely. ■ dated punish, esp. by beating. — **chas·tise·ment** /CHasˈtīzmənt; ˈCHastəz-/ n. **chas·tis·er** n. [ME: appar. from v. *chaste* (see CHASTEN).]

chas·ti·ty /ˈCHastətē/ ▶ n. the state or practice of refraining from sexual intercourse.

chas·ti·ty belt ▶ n. hist. a garment or device designed to prevent a woman from having sexual intercourse.

chas·u·ble /ˈCHazəbəl; ˈCHazH-; ˈCHas-/ ▶ n. a sleeveless outer vestment worn by a Catholic or High Anglican priest when celebrating Mass, typically having a simple hole for the head. [ME: from OFr. *chesible*, from late L. *casubla*, alt. of L. *casula* 'hooded cloak,' dimin. of *casa* 'house.']

chasuble

chat[1] /CHat/ ▶ v. (**chat·ted, chat·ting**) [intrans.] talk in a friendly and informal way: *she chatted to her mother.* ▶ n. an informal conversation. [ME: shortening of CHATTER.]

chat[2] ▶ n. **1** [often in comb.] a small Old World songbird (*Saxicola* and other genera) of the thrush subfamily, with a harsh call and typically with bold black, white, and buff or chestnut coloration. **2** [with adj.] any of a number of small songbirds with harsh calls, esp. a New World warbler, (genera *Icteria* and *Granatellus*), that typically has a yellow or pink breast. [17th C.: prob. imitative.]

cha·teau /SHaˈtō/ (also **châ·teau**) ▶ n. (pl. **-teaux** /-ˈtō(z)/) a large French country house or castle. [18th C.: Fr., from OFr. *chastel* (see CASTLE).]

Cha·teau·bri·and /SHa,tōbrēˈäN/, François-René, Vicomte de (1768–1848), French writer and diplomat. His works include *Le Génie du Christianisme* (1802).

cha·teau·bri·and /SHa,tōbrēˈäN/ ▶ n. a thick tenderloin of beef, typically served with Béarnaise sauce. [19th C.: François-René, Vicomte de CHATEAUBRIAND.]

Cha·teau-Thierr·y /SHa,tō tyeˈrē/ a town in northern France, on the Marne River, site of a major World War I battle; pop. 15,000.

chat·e·lain /ˈSHatl,ān/ ▶ n. another term for CASTELLAN. [ME: from OFr. *chastelain*, from med. L. *castellanus*.]

chat·e·laine /ˈSHatl,ān/ ▶ n. dated a woman in charge of a large house. ■ hist. a set of short chains attached to a woman's belt, used for carrying keys or other items. [19th C.: from Fr. *châtelaine*, fem. of *châtelain* 'castellan.']

chat group ▶ n. a group of people who communicate regularly via the Internet, usually in real time but also by e-mail.

Chat·ham /ˈCHatəm/, 1st Earl of, see PITT.

Chat·ham Is·lands /ˈCHatəm/ two islands, Pitt and Chatham, in the southwestern Pacific Ocean, east of New Zealand.

chat line (also **chat·line**) ▶ n. a telephone service that allows conversation among a number of people who call into it separately. ■ the access to, or connection with, a chat room.

cha·toy·ant /SHəˈtoi-ənt/ ▶ adj. (of a gem, esp. when cut en cabochon) showing a band of bright reflected light caused by aligned inclusions in the stone. — **cha·toy·ance** n. **cha·toy·an·cy** /-ənsē/ n. [18th C.: Fr., pres. part. of *chatoyer* 'to shimmer.']

chat room ▶ n. an area on the Internet or other computer network where users can communicate.

Chat·ta·hoo·chee Riv·er /,CHatəˈhōōCHē/ a river that flows for 435 miles (700 km) through Georgia to the Apalachicola River.

Chat·ta·noo·ga /,CHatnˈōōgə/ a city in southeastern Tennessee; pop. 155,554.

chat·tel /ˈCHatl/ ▶ n. (in general use) a personal possession. ■ Law an item of property other than real estate. See also GOODS AND CHATTELS. [ME: from OFr. *chatel*, from med. L. *capitale*, from L. *capitalis*, from *caput* 'head.']

chat·ter /ˈCHatər/ ▶ v. [intrans.] talk rapidly or incessantly about trivial matters. ■ (of a bird, monkey, or machine) make a series of quick high-pitched sounds. ■ (of a person's teeth) click repeatedly together, typically from cold or fear. ▶ n. incessant trivial talk. ■ a series of quick high-pitched sounds. ■ undesirable vibration in a mechanism. — **chat·ter·y** adj. [ME: imitative.]

chat·ter·box /ˈCHatər,bäks/ ▶ n. informal a person who talks at length about trivial matters.

chat·ty /ˈCHatē/ ▶ adj. (**chat·ti·er, chat·ti·est**) (of a person) fond of talking in an easy, informal way. ■ (of a conversation, letter, etc.) informal and lively. — **chat·ti·ly** /ˈCHatl-ē/ adv. **chat·ti·ness** n.

Chau·bu·na·gun·ga·maug, Lake /CHô,bənəˈgəNGgə,môg/ a small lake in Webster, Massachusetts. The full form of its name, Chargoggagoggmanchaugagoggchaubunagungamaugg, is said to be the longest American place name.

Chau·cer /ˈCHôsər/, Geoffrey (c.1342–1400), English writer and poet. His *Canterbury Tales* (c.1387–1400) is a cycle of linked tales told by a group of pilgrims.

Chau·ce·ri·an /CHôˈsi(ə)rēən/ ▶ adj. of or relating to Chaucer or his style. ▶ n. an admirer, imitator, or student of Chaucer or his writing.

Chau·diere Riv·er /SHōˈdyer/ a river that flows north for 120 miles (190 km) from the Maine border to the St. Lawrence River.

chauf·feur /ˈSHōfər; SHōˈfər/ ▶ n. a person employed to drive a private or rented automobile. ▶ v. [trans.] drive (a car or a passenger in a car), typically as part of one's job. [19th C.: from Fr., lit. 'stoker,' from *chauffer* 'to heat.']

chaul·moo·gra /CHôlˈmōōgrə/ ▶ n. a tropical Asian evergreen tree (genus *Hydnocarpus*, family Flacourtiaceae) with narrow leathery leaves and oil-rich seeds. ■ (also **chaulmoogra oil**) the oil obtained from the seeds of this tree. It is used medically and as a preservative, and was formerly used in the treatment of leprosy. [19th C.: from Bengali *cāul-mugrā*.]

chausses /SHōs/ ▶ plural n. hist. pantaloons or close-fitting coverings for the legs and feet, in particular those forming part of a knight's armor. [15th C.: Fr., lit. 'clothing for the legs.']

Chau·tau·qua /SHəˈtôkwə/ ▶ n. a town in southwestern New York, on Chautauqua Lake, noted as the birthplace of a 19th-century popular education movement; pop. 4,666.

chau·vin·ism /ˈSHōvə,nizəm/ ▶ n. exaggerated or aggressive patriotism. ■ excessive or prejudiced loyalty or support for one's own cause, group, or gender. [19th C.: Nicolas *Chauvin*, Napoleonic veteran.]

chau·vin·ist /ˈSHōvənist/ ▶ n. a person displaying aggressive or exaggerated patriotism. ■ a person displaying excessive or prejudiced loyalty or support for a particular cause, group, or gender. ▶ adj. showing or relating to such excessive or prejudiced support or loyalty. — **chau·vin·is·tic** /,SHōvəˈnistik/ adj. **chau·vin·is·ti·cal·ly** /,SHōvəˈnistik(ə)lē/ adv.

Cha·vez /ˈCHävez; -ves; ˈSHä-/, Cesar Estrata (1927–93), US labor leader. In 1962, he founded the organization that became the United Farm Workers.

chaw /CHô/ informal ▶ n. an act of chewing something, esp. something not intended to be swallowed. ■ something chewed, esp. a wad of tobacco. ▶ v. [trans.] chew (something, esp. tobacco). [ME: var. of CHEW.]

Cha·yef·sky /CHīˈefskē; -ˈev-/, Paddy (1923–81), US playwright and screenwriter; born *Sidney Aaron Chayefsky*. His teleplay *Marty* (1953) was made into a movie in 1955. His other screenwriting credits include *Network* (1976).

cha·yo·te /CHäˈyōtē/ ▶ n. **1** a green pear-shaped tropical fruit that resembles cucumber in flavor. **2** the tropical American vine (*Sechium edule*) of the gourd family that yields this fruit, also producing an edible yam-like tuberous root. [19th C.: from Sp., from Nahuatl *chayotli*.]

CHD ▶ abbr. coronary heart disease.

Ch.E. ▶ abbr. Chemical Engineer.

cheap /CHēp/ ▶ adj. (of an item for sale) low in price; worth more than its cost. ■ charging low prices. ■ (of prices or other charges) low. ■ inexpensive because of inferior quality. ■ informal miserly; stingy. ■ of little worth because achieved in a discreditable way requiring little effort. ■ deserving of contempt. ▶ adv. at or for a low price: *a house that was going cheap.*

– PHRASES **dirt cheap** very cheap or cheaply. **on the cheap** informal at a low cost. — **cheap·ish** adj. **cheap·ly** adv. **cheap·ness** n. [15th C.: from obs. *good cheap* 'a good bargain,' from OE *cēap* 'trade,' based on L. *caupo* 'innkeeper.']

cheap·en /ˈCHēpən/ ▶ v. [trans.] reduce the price of. ■ degrade.

cheap·jack /ˈCHēp,jak/ ▶ n. a seller of cheap inferior goods, typically a hawker at a fair or market. ▶ adj. of inferior quality. [19th C.: from CHEAP + JACK[1].]

cheap·o /ˈCHēpō/ (also **cheap·ie**) ▶ adj. [attrib.] informal inexpensive and of poor quality. ▶ n. (pl. **-os**) an inexpensive thing of poor quality.

cheap·skate /ˈCHēp,skāt/ ▶ n. informal a stingy person. [19th C.: from CHEAP + *skate* 'mean person.']

cheat /CHēt/ ▸ **v. 1** [intrans.] act dishonestly or unfairly in order to gain an advantage, esp. in a game or examination: *she cheats at cards.* ■ [trans.] deceive or trick. ■ use inferior materials or methods unobtrusively in order to save time or money. ■ informal be sexually unfaithful. **2** [trans.] avoid (something undesirable) by luck or skill. ▸ **n.** a person who behaves dishonestly in order to gain an advantage. ■ an act of cheating; a fraud or deception. [ME: shortening of ESCHEAT.]

cheat·er /CHētər/ ▸ **n. 1** a person who acts dishonestly in order to gain an advantage. **2** (**cheaters**) informal a pair of glasses or sunglasses.

cheat sheet ▸ **n.** informal a piece of paper bearing written notes intended to aid one's memory, typically one used surreptitiously in an examination.

Che·bo·ksa·ry /ˌCHebäk'sär(y)ē/ a city in western central Russia, on the Volga River, capital of Chuvashia; pop. 429,000.

Che·chen /'CHeCHən/ ▸ **n.** (pl. same or **-chens**) **1** a member of the largely Muslim people inhabiting Chechnya. **2** the North Caucasian language of this people. ▸ **adj.** of or relating to this people or their language. [from obs. Russ. *chechen.*]

Chech·ny·a /'CHeCHnēə; CHeCH'nyä/ (also **Che·che·nia** /CHeCHə'nyə/) a republic in southwestern Russia; pop. 1,290,000; capital, Grozny. The republic declared itself independent of Russia in 1991 and was invaded by Russian troops in 1994. A peace treaty (1996) agreed the withdrawal of troops but Russian forces invaded again in 1999. Also called CHECHEN REPUBLIC.

check[1] /CHek/ ▸ **v.** [trans.] **1** examine (something) in order to determine its accuracy, quality, or condition, or to detect the presence of something: *the right to check all luggage* | [intrans.] *a blood test to check for anemia.* ■ verify or establish to one's satisfaction. ■ examine with a view to rectifying any fault or problem discovered. ■ (**check against**) verify the accuracy of something by comparing it with (something else). ■ another way of saying CHECK SOMETHING OFF. ■ another way of saying CHECK SOMETHING IN. ■ [intrans.] agree or correspond when compared. **2** stop or slow down the progress of (something undesirable). ■ curb or restrain (a feeling or emotion). ■ (**check oneself**) master an involuntary reaction. ■ Hockey hamper or neutralize (an opponent) with one's body or stick. ■ [intrans.] (**check against**) provide a means of preventing. ■ [intrans.] (of a hound) pause to make sure of or regain a scent. **3** [trans.] Chess move a piece or pawn so that (the opposing king) is under attack. ▸ **n. 1** an examination to test or ascertain accuracy, quality, or satisfactory condition. **2** a stopping or slowing of progress. ■ a means of control or restraint. ■ Hockey an act of hampering or neutralizing an opponent with one's body or stick. ■ a temporary loss of the scent in hunting. **3** Chess a move by which a piece or pawn directly attacks the opponent's king. If the defending player cannot counter the attack, the king is checkmated. **4** the bill in a restaurant. ■ (also **baggage/luggage check**) a token of identification for left luggage. ■ a counter used as a stake in a gambling game. **5** short for CHECK MARK. **6** a crack or flaw in timber. ▸ **exclam. 1** informal expressing assent or agreement. **2** used by a chess player to announce that the opponent's king has been placed in check.

– PHRASES **in check 1** under control. **2** Chess (of a king) directly attacked by an opponent's piece or pawn; (of a player) having the king in this position. **keep a check on** monitor.

– PHRASAL VERBS **check in** (or **check someone in**) arrive and register at a hotel or airport. **check something in** have one's baggage weighed and put aside for consignment to the hold of an aircraft on which one is booked to travel. ■ register and leave baggage for later pickup. **check into** register one's arrival at (a hotel). **check something off** tick or otherwise mark an item on a list to show that it has been dealt with. **check on 1** verify, ascertain, or monitor the state or condition of. **2** another way of saying CHECK UP ON. **check out** settle one's hotel bill before leaving. ■ informal die. **check someone/something out 1** establish the truth or inform oneself about someone or something. **2** (**check something out**) enter the price of goods in a supermarket into a cash register for addition and payment by a customer. ■ register something as having been borrowed. **check something over** inspect or examine something thoroughly. **check through** inspect or examine thoroughly. **check up on** investigate in order to establish the truth about or accuracy of. — **check·a·ble adj.** [ME (in chess): n. from OFr. *eschec*, from med. L. *scaccus*, via Arab. from Pers. *šāh* 'king.']

check[2] (Brit. **cheque**) ▸ **n.** a written order to a bank to pay a stated sum from the drawer's account. ■ the printed form on which such an order is written. [18th C.: var. of CHECK[1].]

check[3] ▸ **n.** a pattern of small squares. ■ a garment or fabric with such a pattern. ▸ **adj.** [attrib.] having such a pattern. [ME: prob. from CHECKER[2].]

check·book /'CHekˌbo͝ok/ ▸ **n.** a book of blank checks with a register for recording checks written.

check·box /'CHekˌbäks/ ▸ **n.** Comput. a small box on a computer screen that, when selected by the user, is filled with an X to show that the feature described alongside it has been enabled.

checked /CHekt/ ▸ **adj. 1** (of clothes or fabric) having a pattern of small squares. **2** Phonet. (of a vowel) followed by one or more consonants in the same syllable.

check·er[1] /'CHekər/ ▸ **n. 1** a person or thing that verifies or examines something. **2** a cashier in a supermarket.

check·er[2] (Brit. **cheq·uer**) ▸ **n. 1** (often **checkers**) a pattern of squares, typically alternately colored. **2** (**checkers**) [treated as sing.] a game for two players, with twelve pieces each, played on a checkerboard. ■ (**checker**) a round flat piece, usually red or black, used to play checkers. [ME: from EXCHEQUER.]

check·er·ber·ry /'CHekərˌberē/ ▸ **n.** (pl. **-ries**) a creeping evergreen North American shrub (*Gaultheria procumbens*) of the heath family, with spiny scented leaves and waxy white flowers. Also called WINTERGREEN. ■ the edible red fruit of this plant. [18th C.: from *checkers* 'berries of the service tree.']

check·er·board /'CHekərˌbôrd/ ▸ **n.** a board for playing checkers and certain other games, with a regular pattern of squares in alternating colors, typically black and white. ■ a pattern resembling such a board.

check·ered /'CHekərd/ ▸ **adj.** having a pattern of alternating squares of different colors. ■ fig. marked by periods of varied fortune or discreditable incidents: *his checkered past.*

check·ered flag ▸ **n. 1** Auto Racing a flag with a black and white checkered pattern, displayed to drivers as they finish a race. **2** victory in a race.

check·er·spot /'CHekərˌspät/ ▸ **n.** a North American butterfly (*Euphydryas* and other genera, family Nymphalidae) with pale markings on the wings that typically form a checkered pattern. Its several species include the **Baltimore checkerspot** (*E. phaeton*).

Baltimore checkerspot

check-in ▸ **n.** [often as adj.] the act of reporting one's presence and registering, typically at an airport or hotel. ■ the point at which such registration takes place.

check·ing ac·count (Canadian **cheq·uing ac·count**) ▸ **n.** an account at a bank against which checks can be drawn by the account depositor.

check·list /'CHekˌlist/ ▸ **n.** a list of items required, things to be done, or points to be considered, used as a reminder.

check mark ▸ **n.** a mark (✓) used to indicate that a textual item is correct or has been chosen or verified.

check·mate /'CHekˌmāt/ ▸ **n.** Chess a check from which a king cannot escape. ■ [as exclam.] (by a player) announcing that the opponent's king is in such a position. ■ fig. a final defeat or deadlock. ▸ **v.** [trans.] Chess put into checkmate. ■ fig. defeat or frustrate totally. [ME: from OFr. *eschec mat*, from Arab. *šāh māta*, from Pers. *šāh manad* 'the king is helpless.']

check·out /'CHekˌout/ ▸ **n. 1** a point at which goods are paid for in a supermarket or other store. **2** the administrative procedure followed when a guest leaves a hotel at the end of a stay.

check·point /'CHekˌpoint/ ▸ **n.** a barrier or manned entrance, typically at a border, where travelers are subject to security checks. ■ a place along the route of a long-distance race where the time for each competitor is recorded. ■ a location whose exact position can be verified visually or electronically, used by pilots to aid navigation.

check rein ▸ **n.** a bearing rein.

check·room /'CHekˌro͞om; -ˌro͝om/ ▸ **n.** a room in a public building where coats, hats, luggage, etc., may be left temporarily.

checks and bal·anc·es ▸ **plural n.** counterbalancing influences by which an organization or system is regulated, typically those ensuring that political power is not concentrated in the hands of individuals or groups.

check·sum /'CHekˌsəm/ ▸ **n.** a digit representing the sum of the correct digits in a piece of stored or transmitted digital data, against which later comparisons can be made to detect errors in the data.

check·up /'CHekˌəp/ ▸ **n.** a thorough examination, esp. a medical or dental one.

check valve ▸ **n.** a valve that closes to prevent backward flow of liquid.

ched·dar /'CHedər/ ▸ **n.** a kind of firm smooth cheese, originally made in Cheddar in southern England.

che·der /'KHedər; 'KHā-/ (also **he·der**) ▸ **n.** (pl. **che·da·rim** /KHe'därim/, **che·ders**) a school for Jewish children in which Hebrew and religious knowledge are taught. [19th C.: from Heb. *ḥeder* 'room.']

chee·cha·ko /CHi'CHäkō; -'CHôkō/ ▸ **n.** (pl. **-kos**) informal a person newly arrived in the mining districts of Alaska or northwestern Canada. [19th C.: Chinook Jargon.]

cheek /CHēk/ ▸ **n. 1** either side of the face below the eye. ■ either of the inner sides of the mouth. ■ informal either of the buttocks. ■ either of two side pieces or parts in a structure. **2** [in sing.] impertinent talk or behavior.

– PHRASES **cheek by jowl** close together; side by side. **cheek to cheek** (of two people dancing) with their heads close together in an intimate way. **turn the other cheek** refrain from retaliating when one has been attacked or insulted. — **cheeked adj.** [in comb.] *rosy-cheeked.* [OE *cē(a)ce*, *cēoce* 'cheek, jaw,' of West Gmc. origin; rel. to Du. *kaak.*]

cheek·bone /ˈCHēkˌbōn/ ▶ **n.** the bone below the eye.

cheek·piece /ˈCHēkˌpēs/ ▶ **n.** a part of an object that covers or rests on the cheek, in particular: ■ the portion of the stock of a rifle or shotgun that rests against the face when aiming from the shoulder. ■ either of the two straps of a horse's bridle joining the bit and the headpiece. ■ a bar on a horse's bit that lies outside the mouth.

cheek pouch ▶ **n.** a saclike fold of skin on either side of the mouth, esp. in squirrels, monkeys, and gophers, used for carrying food.

Cheek·to·wa·ga /ˌCHēktəˈwägə/ a town in western New York; pop. 94,019.

cheek·y /ˈCHēkē/ ▶ **adj.** (**cheek·i·er, cheek·i·est**) impudent or irreverent, typically in an endearing or amusing way. — **cheek·i·ly** /-kəlē/ **adv. cheek·i·ness n.**

cheep /CHēp/ ▶ **n.** a shrill squeaky cry made by a bird, typically a young one. ■ a sound resembling such a cry. ▶ **v.** [intrans.] make a shrill squeaky sound. [16th C.: imitative.]

cheer /CHi(ə)r/ ▶ **v. 1** [intrans.] shout for joy or in praise or encouragement: *she cheered from the sidelines.* ■ [trans.] praise or encourage with shouts. **2** [trans.] give comfort or support to. ■ (**cheer someone up** or **cheer up**) make or become less miserable. ▶ **n. 1** a shout of encouragement, praise, or joy. ■ a brief phrase shouted in unison by a crowd, typically led by cheerleaders, in support of an athletic team. **2** (also **good cheer**) cheerfulness, optimism, or confidence. ■ something that causes such feelings. ■ food and drink provided for a festive occasion.
– PHRASES **of good cheer** archaic cheerful; optimistic. **three cheers** three successive hurrahs shouted to express appreciation or congratulation. [ME: from OFr. *chiere* 'face,' from late L. *cara*, from Gk. *kara* 'head.']

cheer·ful /ˈCHi(ə)rfəl/ ▶ **adj.** noticeably happy and optimistic. ■ causing happiness by its nature or appearance. — **cheer·ful·ness n.**

cheer·ful·ly /ˈCHi(ə)rfəlē/ ▶ **adv.** in a way that displays happiness or optimism: *he was whistling cheerfully.* ■ in a way that inspires feelings of happiness. ■ readily and willingly.

cheer·i·o /ˌCHi(ə)rēˈō/ ▶ **exclam.** Brit., informal used as an expression of good wishes on parting; goodbye.

cheer·lead·er /ˈCHi(ə)rˌlēdər/ ▶ **n.** a person who leads cheers and applause, esp. at a sports event. ■ an enthusiastic and vocal supporter. — **cheer·lead v.** (past and past part. **-led**)

cheers /CHi(ə)rz/ ▶ **exclam.** informal expressing good wishes, in particular: ■ good wishes before drinking. ■ Brit. good wishes on parting or ending a conversation. ■ esp. Brit. gratitude or acknowledgment for something.

cheer·y /ˈCHi(ə)rē/ ▶ **adj.** (**cheer·i·er, cheer·i·est**) happy and optimistic. — **cheer·i·ly** /ˈCHi(ə)rəlē/ **adv. cheer·i·ness n.**

cheese[1] /CHēz/ ▶ **n. 1** a food made from the pressed curds of milk. ■ a molded mass of such food with its rind, often in a round flat shape. ■ a round flat object resembling a cheese. **2** informal the quality of being too obviously sentimental.
– PHRASES **say cheese** said by a photographer to encourage the subject to smile. [OE *cēse, cӯse*, from West Gmc., from L. *caseus*.]

cheese[2] (also **big cheese**) ▶ **n.** informal an important person. [19th C.: prob. from Urdu, from Pers. *čīz* 'thing.']

cheese·board /ˈCHēzˌbôrd/ ▶ **n.** a board on which cheese is served and cut. ■ a selection of cheeses.

cheese·burg·er /ˈCHēzˌbərgər/ ▶ **n.** a hamburger with a slice of cheese on it.

cheese·cake /ˈCHēzˌkāk/ ▶ **n. 1** a kind of rich dessert cake made with cream and soft cheese on a graham cracker, cookie, or pastry crust, typically topped with a fruit sauce. **2** informal photography, a movie, or art that portrays women in a manner emphasizing stereotypical sexual attractiveness.

cheese·cloth /ˈCHēzˌklôTH/ ▶ **n.** thin, loosely woven cloth of cotton, used originally for wrapping cheese.

cheese·cut·ter ▶ **n. 1** an implement for cutting cheese, esp. by means of a wire that can be pulled through the cheese. **2** (also **cheese-cutter cap**) informal a cap with a broad, square bill.

cheese·head /ˈCHēzˌhed/ ▶ **n. 1** informal a resident of Wisconsin, esp. a fan of the Green Bay Packers football team. **2** informal a blockhead; an idiot.

cheese·par·ing /ˈCHēzˌpe(ə)riNG/ ▶ **adj.** careful or stingy with money. ▶ **n.** stinginess.

cheese·steak /ˈCHēzˌstāk/ ▶ **n.** (also **Philly cheesesteak**) a sandwich containing thin-sliced sautéed beef, melted cheese, and typically sautéed onions, served in a long roll.

chees·y /ˈCHēzē/ ▶ **adj.** (**chees·i·er, chees·i·est**) **1** like cheese in taste, smell, or consistency. **2** informal cheap, unpleasant, or blatantly inauthentic. — **chees·i·ness n.**

chee·tah /ˈCHētə/ ▶ **n.** a large spotted cat (*Acinonyx jubatus*) found in Africa and parts of Asia. It is the fastest animal on land. [18th C.: from Hindi *cītā*, perh. from Sanskrit *citraka* 'leopard.']

Chee·ver /CHēvər/, John (1912–82), US writer. His novels include *The Wapshot Chronicle* (1957) and *Bullet Park* (1969).

chef /SHef/ ▶ **n.** a professional cook. [19th C.: Fr., lit. 'head.']

chef-d'œu·vre /SHā ˈdœv(rə); ˈdə(r)v/ ▶ **n.** (pl. **chefs-d'œu·vre** /SHāz ˈdœv(rə); ˈdə(r)v/) a masterpiece. [17th C.: Fr., lit. 'chief work.']

Che·foo /ˈjəˈfo͞o/ former name of **Yantai.**

cheiro- ▶ **comb. form** var. of **chiro-.**

Che·khov /ˈCHekôv; ˈCHekôf/, Anton Pavlovich (1860–1904), Russian playwright. His plays include *The Seagull* (1895) and *The Cherry Orchard* (1904).

Che·kiang /ˈjəˈkyäNG/ variant of **Zhejiang.**

che·la /ˈkēlə/ ▶ **n.** (pl. **-lae** /-lē; -lī/) Zool. a pincerlike claw, esp. of a crab or other crustacean. Compare with **chelicera.** [17th C.: mod. L., from L. *chele* or Gk. *khēlē* 'claw.']

che·late /ˈkēlāt/ ▶ **n.** Chem. a compound containing a ligand (typically organic) bonded to a central metal atom at two or more points. ▶ **adj.** Zool. (of an appendage) bearing chelae. ▶ **v.** [trans.] Chem. form a chelate with. — **che·la·tion** /kēˈlāsHən/ **n. che·la·tor** /-ˌlātər/ **n.**

che·lic·er·a /kəˈlisərə/ ▶ **n.** (pl. **-lic·er·ae** /-ˈlisərē/) Zool. either of a pair of appendages in front of the mouth in arachnids and some other arthropods, usually modified as pincerlike claws. Compare with **chela.** — **che·lic·er·al adj.** [19th C.: mod. L., from Gk. *khēlē* 'claw' + *keras* 'horn.']

Che·lic·er·at·a /kəˌlisəˈrätə/ Zool. a large group of arthropods (subphylum Chelicerata) that comprises the arachnids, sea spiders, and horseshoe crabs. They lack antennae, but possess a pair of chelicerae, a pair of pedipalps, and (typically) four pairs of legs. — **che·lic·er·ate** /kəˈlisəˌrāt; -rət/ **n. & adj.** [mod. L. (pl.), from Gk. *khēlē* 'claw' + *keras* 'horn.']

Chel·le·an /ˈSHelēən/ ▶ **adj. & n.** former term for **Abbevillian.** [19th C.: from Fr. *Chelléen*, from *Chelles*, near Paris.]

Chelms·ford /ˈCHelmsfərd/ a city in southeastern England, noted for its cathedral; pop. 152,418.

Che·lo·ni·a /kəˈlōnēə/ Zool. former term for **Testudines.** — **che·lo·ni·an n. & adj.** [mod. L. (pl.), from Gk. *khelōnē* 'tortoise.']

Chel·sea /ˈCHelsē/ **1** a residential district of London, on the northern bank of the Thames River. **2** a fashionable residential section of southern Manhattan in New York City, on the west side of the city.

Chel·sea boot ▶ **n.** an elastic-sided boot, typically with a high heel.

Chel·ya·binsk /CHelˈyäbinsk/ a city in southwestern Russia; pop. 1,148,000.

chem. ▶ **abbr.** ■ chemical. ■ chemist. ■ chemistry.

chemi- ▶ **comb. form** representing **chemical.** See also **chemo-.**

chem·i·cal /ˈkemikəl/ (abbr.: **chem.**) ▶ **adj.** of or relating to chemistry or the interactions of substances as studied in chemistry. ■ of or relating to chemicals. ■ relating to, involving, or denoting the use of poison gas or other chemicals as weapons of war. ▶ **n.** a compound or substance that has been purified or prepared, esp. artificially. — **chem·i·cal·ly** /-ik(ə)lē/ **adv.** [16th C.: from Fr. *chimique* or mod. L. *chimicus, chymicus*, from med. L. *alchymicus*, from *alchimia* (see **alchemy**).]

chem·i·cal a·buse ▶ **n.** another term for **substance abuse.**

chem·i·cal bond ▶ **n.** see **bond** (sense 3).

chem·i·cal com·pound ▶ **n.** see **compound**[1].

chem·i·cal de·pend·en·cy ▶ **n.** addiction to a mood- or mind-altering drug, such as alcohol or cocaine.

chem·i·cal en·gi·neer·ing ▶ **n.** the branch of engineering concerned with the design and operation of industrial chemical plants. — **chem·i·cal en·gi·neer n.**

chem·i·cal for·mu·la ▶ **n.** see **formula** (sense 1).

chem·i·cal re·ac·tion ▶ **n.** a process that involves rearrangement of the molecular or ionic structure of a substance, as opposed to a change in physical form or a nuclear reaction.

chemico- ▶ **comb. form** representing **chemical.**

chem·i·lum·i·nes·cence /ˌkemiˌlo͞oməˈnesəns/ ▶ **n.** the emission of light during a chemical reaction that does not produce significant quantities of heat. — **chem·i·lum·i·nes·cent adj.**

chem·in de fer /SHəˌman də ˈfe(ə)r/ ▶ **n.** a form of the card game baccarat. [19th C.: Fr., lit. 'railroad.']

che·mise /SHəˈmēz; -ˈmēs/ ▶ **n.** a dress hanging straight from the shoulders and giving the figure a uniform shape, popular in the 1920s. ■ a woman's loose-fitting undergarment or nightdress. ■ a priest's alb or surplice. ■ hist. a smock. [ME: from OFr., from late L. *camisia* 'shirt.']

chem·i·sette /ˌSHemiˈzet/ ▶ **n.** a woman's undergarment similar to a camisole, typically worn so as to be visible beneath an open-necked blouse or dress. [19th C.: Fr., dimin. of *chemise*.]

chem·i·sorp·tion /ˌkemiˈsôrpsHən; -ˈzôrp-/ ▶ **n.** Chem. adsorption in which the adsorbed substance is held by chemical bonds. — **chem·i·sorbed** /ˈkemiˌsôrbd/ **adj.** [1930s: from **chemi-** + shortened form of ***adsorption*** (see **adsorb**).]

chem·ist /ˈkemist/ (abbr.: **chem.**) ▶ **n.** an expert in chemistry; a person engaged in chemical research or experiments. [ME: from Fr. *chimiste*, from med. L. *alchimia* (see **alchemy**).]

chem·is·try /ˈkemistrē/ (abbr.: **chem.**) ▶ **n.** (pl. **-tries**) **1** the branch of science that deals with the identification of the substances of which matter is composed; the investigation of their properties and the ways in which they interact, combine, and change; and the use of these processes to form new substances. ■ the chemical composition and properties of a substance or body. ■ fig. a complex entity or process. **2** the emotional or psychological interaction between two people, esp. when experienced as a powerful mutual attraction.

Chem·nitz /ˈKHemnits/ a city in eastern Germany; pop. 310,000. Former name (from 1953) **Karl-Marx-Stadt.**

che·mo /ˈkēmō/ ▶ **n.** informal chemotherapy.

chemo- ▶ **comb. form** representing **chemical.** See also **chemi-.**

che·mo·au·to·troph /ˌkēmōˈôtəˌtrōf; ˌkemō-/ ▶ **n.** Biol. an organism, typically a bacterium, that derives energy from the oxidation of inorganic compounds. — **che·mo·au·to·tro·phic** /-ˌôtəˈtrōfik/ **adj. che·mo·au·tot·ro·phy** /-ˈôtəˌtrōfē/ **n.**

che·mo·pro·phy·lax·is /ˌkēmōˌprōfəˈlaksis; ˌkemō-/ ▶ n. the use of drugs to prevent disease. — **che·mo·pro·phy·lac·tic** adj.

che·mo·re·cep·tor /ˌkēmōriˈseptər; ˌkemō-/ ▶ n. Physiol. a sensory cell or organ responsive to chemical stimuli. — **che·mo·re·cep·tion** /-riˈsepsHən/ n.

che·mo·stat /ˈkēmōˌstat; ˈkemō-/ ▶ n. a system in which the chemical composition is kept at a controlled level, esp. for the culture of microorganisms.

che·mo·syn·the·sis /ˌkēmōˈsinTHəsəs; ˌkemō-/ ▶ n. Biol. the synthesis of organic compounds by energy derived from chemical reactions, typically in the absence of sunlight. Compare with PHOTOSYNTHESIS. — **che·mo·syn·thet·ic** /-sinˈTHetik/ adj.

che·mo·tax·is /ˌkēmōˈtaksis; ˌkemō-/ ▶ n. Biol. movement of a motile cell or organism, or part of one, in a direction corresponding to a gradient of increasing or decreasing concentration of a particular substance. — **che·mo·tac·tic** /-ˈtaktik/ adj.

che·mo·ther·a·py /ˌkēmōˈTHerəpē; ˌkemō-/ ▶ n. the treatment of disease, esp. cancer, by the use of chemical substances. — **che·mo·ther·a·pist** n.

che·mot·ro·pism /kiˈmätrəˌpizəm/ ▶ n. a tropism, esp. of a plant, in response to a particular substance. — **che·mo·trop·ic** /ˌkēmōˈträpik; -ˈtrō-; ˌkemō-/ adj. **che·mo·trop·i·cal·ly** /-ik(ə)lē/ adv.

chem·ur·gy /ˈkemərjē/ ▶ n. the chemical and industrial use of organic raw materials. — **chem·ur·gic** /kəˈmərjik; ke-/ adj. [1930s: from CHEMO-.]

Che·nab /CHəˈnäb/ a river in northern India and Pakistan that rises in the Himalayas and joins the Sutlej River in Punjab.

Che·nai /CHəˈnī/ official name (since 1995) for MADRAS.

Chen-chiang /ˈjən ˈjyäNG/ variant of ZHENJIANG.

Che·ney /ˈCHānē/, Dick (1941–), vice president of the US 2001– ; full name *Richard Bruce Cheney*. A conservative Republican from Wyoming, he was secretary of defense under President George Bush 1989–93.

Cheng·chow /ˈjəNGˈjō/ variant of ZHENGZHOU.

Cheng·du /ˈCHəNGˈdo͞o/ the capital of Sichuan province in western central China; pop. 2,780,000.

che·nille /SHəˈnēl/ ▶ n. a tufted velvety cord or yarn, used for trimming furniture and making carpets and clothing. ■ fabric made from such yarn. [18th C.: Fr.; lit. 'hairy caterpillar.']

Chen·nault /SHəˈnôlt/, Claire Lee (1890–1958), US general. During World War II, he formed the "Flying Tigers," a group of pilots, to aid China.

cheong·sam /ˈCHôNGˌsäm/ ▶ n. a straight, close-fitting silk dress with a high neck, short sleeves, and a slit skirt, worn traditionally by Chinese and Indonesian women. [Chin. (Cantonese dial.).]

cheongsam

Che·ops /ˈkēäps/ (*fl.* early 26th century BC), Egyptian pharaoh; Egyptian name **Khufu**. He commissioned the building of the Great Pyramid at Giza.

cheque ▶ n. British spelling of CHECK[3].

cheq·uer ▶ n. & v. British spelling of CHECKER[2].

Cher /SHe(ə)r/ a river in central France that rises in the Massif Central and flows north for 220 miles (350 km) to the Loire River near Tours.

Cher·bourg /ˈSHe(ə)rˌbo͝or(g); ˈSHər-/ a seaport and naval base in northwestern France; pop. 28,770.

Che·ren·kov /CHəˈreNGkôv; -kôf; -kəf/, Pavel Alekseevich (also **Ce·ren·kov**) (1904–90), Soviet physicist. He discovered the cause of blue light (now called CERENKOV RADIATION) emitted by radioactive substances underwater. Nobel Prize for Physics (1958, shared with Ilja Mikhailovich Frank 1908–90 and Igor Yevgenyevich Tamm 1895–1971).

Che·ren·kov ra·di·a·tion ▶ n. var. of CERENKOV RADIATION.

Che·re·po·vets /ˌCHerəpəˈv(y)ets/ a city in northwestern Russia; pop. 313,000.

cher·i·moy·a /ˌCHerəˈmoiə; ˌCHir-/ (also **chir·i·moy·a**) ▶ n. **1** a tropical American fruit with scaly green skin and a flavor like pineapple. **2** the small tree (*Annona cherimola*) of the custard apple family that bears this fruit, native to the Andes of Peru and Ecuador. [18th C.: from Sp., from Quechua, from *chiri* 'cold' + *muya* 'circle.']

cher·ish /ˈCHeriSH/ ▶ v. [trans.] protect and care for (someone) lovingly: *he cherished me in his heart.* ■ hold (something) dear. ■ (of a hope, idea, or memory) think of longingly or lovingly. [ME: from OFr. *cheriss-*, lengthened stem of *cherir*, from *cher* 'dear,' from L. *carus*.]

Cher·ka·sy /CHirˈkäsē/ a city in central Ukraine; pop. 297,000. Russian name CHERKASSY.

Cher·kessk /CHirˈk(y)esk/ a city in southern Russia, capital of Karachai-Cherkessia; pop 113,000.

Cher·nen·ko /CHirˈn(y)eNGkō/, Konstantin Ustinovich (1911–85), president of the Soviet Union 1984–85. He died after only thirteen months in office.

Cher·ni·hiv /CHirˈn(y)ēhəf/ a city in northern Ukraine; pop. 301,000. Russian name CHERNIGOV.

Cher·niv·tsi /ˌCHirniftˈsē/ a city in western Ukraine; pop. 257,000. Russian name CHERNOVTSY.

Cher·no·byl /CHirˈnōbil; CHərˈnōbəl/ a town near Kiev in Ukraine where an accident at a nuclear power station in 1986 resulted in radioactive contamination in Ukraine, Belarus, and other parts of Europe.

Cher·no·rech·ye /ˌCHərnəˈreCHə/ former name (until 1919) for DZERZHINSK.

cher·no·zem /ˈCHernəˌZHôm; -ˌzem/ ▶ n. Soil Science a fertile black soil rich in humus, found in temperate grasslands such as the Russian steppes and North American prairies. [19th C.: from Russ., from *chërnyĭ* 'black' + *zemlya* 'earth.']

Cher·o·kee /ˈCHerəkē/ ▶ n. (pl. same or **-kees**) **1** a member of an American Indian people of the southeastern US, now living on reservations in Oklahoma and North Carolina. **2** the Iroquoian language of this people, which has had its own script since 1820. ▶ adj. of or relating to this people or their language. [from Cherokee *tsaraki*.]

Cher·o·kee rose ▶ n. a climbing rose (*Rosa laevigata*) with fragrant white flowers, native to China and naturalized in the southern US.

che·root /SHəˈro͞ot/ ▶ n. a cigar with both ends open and untapered. [17th C.: from Fr. *cheroute*, from Tamil *curuṭṭu* 'roll of tobacco.']

cher·ry /ˈCHerē/ ▶ n. (pl. **-ries**) **1** a small, round stone fruit that is typically bright or dark red. **2** (also **cherry tree**) the tree (genus *Prunus*) of the rose family that bears such fruit. Cultivated, edible cherries are derived from the **mazzard** (or **sweet**) **cherry** (*P. avium*) and the **morello** (or **sour**) **cherry** (*P. cerasus*). ■ the wood of this tree. **3** a bright or deep red color. **4** [in sing.] vulgar slang the hymen, as representing a woman's virginity.

– PHRASES **a bowl of cherries** [usu. with negative] a pleasant or enjoyable situation or experience. [ME: from Old North. Fr. *cherise*, from med. L. *ceresia*, based on Gk. *kerasos*.]

Cher·ry Hill a township in southwestern New Jersey; pop. 69,965.

cher·ry lau·rel ▶ n. an evergreen shrub or small tree (*Prunus laurocerasus*) of the rose family, with leathery leaves, white flowers, and cherrylike fruits.

cher·ry-pick ▶ v. **1** [trans.] selectively choose (the most beneficial items) from what is available: *the company should not just cherry-pick its best assets.* **2** [intrans.] Sports in a game such as basketball, wait near the goal for a pass, which can be converted to an easy score. — **cher·ry-pick·ing** n.

cher·ry pick·er ▶ n. informal **1** a hydraulic crane with a railed platform at the end for raising and lowering people, for instance to work on overhead cables. **2** a person who cherry-picks.

cher·ry to·ma·to ▶ n. a spherical miniature tomato (esp. *Lycopersicon lycopersicum cerasiforme*), typically eaten in salad.

Cher·so·nese /ˈkərsəˌnēz; ˌkərsəˈnēz/ a name applied to several peninsulas, including the Gallipoli, the Crimea, the Jutland, and the Malay.

chert /CHərt; CHat/ ▶ n. a flintlike form of quartz composed of chalcedony. — **chert·y** adj. [17th C.: of unknown origin.]

Cher·toff /ˈCHərtôf/, Michael (1953–), US secretary of homeland security 2005– .

cher·ub /ˈCHerəb/ ▶ n. (pl. **cher·u·bim** /ˈCHerəˌbim/) a winged angelic being described in biblical tradition as attending on God, regarded in traditional Christian angelology as an angel of the second highest order of the ninefold celestial hierarchy. ■ (pl. **cher·u·bim** /ˈCHerəˌbim/ or **cher·ubs**) a representation of a cherub in art, depicted as a chubby, healthy-looking child with wings. ■ (pl. **cher·ubs**) a beautiful or innocent-looking child. [OE *cherubin*, ult. from Heb. *kĕrūḇ*, pl. *kĕrūḇîm*.]

che·ru·bic /CHəˈro͞obik/ ▶ adj. having the childlike innocence or plump prettiness of a cherub. — **che·ru·bi·cal·ly** /-bik(ə)lē/ adv.

Che·ru·bi·ni /ˌkerəˈbēnē/, Maria Luigi Carlo Zenobio Salvatore (1760–1842), Italian composer, principally known for his operas.

cher·vil /ˈCHərvəl/ ▶ n. a plant (*Anthriscus cerefolium*) of the parsley family, with small white flowers and delicate fernlike leaves that are used as a culinary herb. [OE, from L. *chaerephylla*, from Gk. *khairephullon*.]

Ches·a·peake /ˈCHesəˌpēk/ a port city in central Virginia; pop. 199,184.

Ches·a·peake Bay /ˈCHesəˌpēk/ a large inlet of the Atlantic Ocean that extends north for 200 miles (320 km) through Virginia and Maryland.

Chesh·ire[1] /ˈCHeSHər/ a county in western central England; county town, Chester.

Chesh·ire[2] (also **Cheshire cheese**) ▶ n. a kind of firm crumbly cheese, originally made in Cheshire, England.

Chesh·ire cat ▶ n. a cat depicted with a broad fixed grin, as popularized through Lewis Carroll's *Alice's Adventures in Wonderland* (1865). [18th C.: *Cheshire*, England.]

chess /CHes/ ▶ n. a board game of strategic skill for two players, the object of which is to put the opponent's king under a direct attack from which escape is impossible (*checkmate*). [ME: from OFr. *esches*, pl. of *eschec* 'a check' (see CHECK[1]).]

chess·board /ˈCHesˌbôrd/ ▶ n. a square board divided into sixty-four alternating dark and light squares, used for playing chess or checkers. *See illustration on next page.*

chess·man /ˈCHesˌman; -mən/ ▶ n. (pl. **-men**) a solid figure used as a chess piece.

chest /CHest/ ▶ n. **1** the front surface of a person's or animal's body between the neck and the abdomen. ■ the whole of a person's upper trunk, esp. with reference to physical size. ■ informal a woman's breasts. **2** a large strong box, typically made of wood and used for storage or

chessboard and pieces

shipping. ■ a small cabinet for medicines, toiletries, etc. ■ short for CHEST OF DRAWERS.
– PHRASES **get something off one's chest** informal say something that one has wanted to say for a long time, resulting in a feeling of relief. **play** (or **keep**) **one's cards close to one's chest** (or **vest**) informal be secretive and cautious about one's intentions. — **chest·ed** adj. [in comb.] *a bare-chested youth.* [OE *cest, cyst,* based on Gk. *kistē* 'box.']

Ches·ter /'CHestər/ **1** a city in western England, the county town of Cheshire; pop. 115,000. **2** a city in southeastern Pennsylvania; pop. 41,856.

Ches·ter·field /'CHestər,fēld/ a city in eastern Missouri; pop. 46,802.

ches·ter·field /'CHestər,fēld/ ▶ n. **1** a sofa with padded arms and back of the same height and curved outward at the top. ■ esp. Canadian any sofa or couch. **2** a man's plain straight overcoat, typically with a velvet collar. [19th C. (sense 2): after a 19th-cent. Earl of Chesterfield.]

Ches·ter·ton /'CHestərtən/, G. K. (1874–1936), English writer; full name *Gilbert Keith Chesterton.* His novels include *The Napoleon of Notting Hill* (1904) and a series of detective stories featuring Father Brown, a priest.

Ches·ter White ▶ n. a pig of a prolific white breed with drooping ears, developed in Pennsylvania.

chest·nut /'CHes(t),nət/ ▶ n. **1** (also **sweet chestnut**) a glossy brown nut that may be roasted and eaten. **2** (also **chestnut tree, sweet chestnut,** or **Spanish chestnut**) the large European tree (*Castanea sativa*) of the beech family that produces the edible chestnut, which develops within a bristly case, with serrated leaves and heavy timber. ■ (also **American chestnut**) a related tree (*C. dentata*), which succumbed to a fungal bark disease in the early 1900s. Once prolific in the eastern US, very few large specimens survived. ■ (also **Chinese chestnut**) a related tree (*C. mollissima*) native to China and Korea, cultivated elsewhere for its edible nut. ■ short for HORSE CHESTNUT. ■ used in names of trees and plants that are related to the sweet chestnut or that produce similar nuts, e.g., **water chestnut. 3** a deep reddish-brown color. ■ a horse of a reddish-brown color, with a brown mane and tail. **4** a small horny patch on the inside of each of a horse's legs. **5** colloq. a stale joke or anecdote. [16th C.: from OE *chesten* (from OFr. *chastaine,* via L. from Gk. *kastanea*) + NUT.]

chest·nut oak ▶ n. a North American oak (genus *Quercus*) that has leaves resembling those of the chestnut.

chest of drawers ▶ n. a piece of furniture consisting of a set of drawers in a frame, typically used for storing clothes.

chest·y /'CHestē/ ▶ adj. informal **1** (of a sound) produced deep in the chest. **2** (of a woman) having large or prominent breasts. **3** conceited and arrogant. — **chest·i·ly** adv. **chest·i·ness** n.

Ches·van var. of HESVAN.

che·trum /'CHētrəm; 'CHet-/ ▶ n. (pl. same or **-trums**) a monetary unit of Bhutan, equal to one hundredth of a ngultrum.

che·val-de-frise /SHə'val də 'frēz/ ▶ n. **1** a portable obstacle, consisting of a wooden frame covered with spikes or barbed wire, used by the military to close off a passage or block enemy advancement. **2** shards of glass or spikes set into masonry along the top of a wall.

che·val glass /SHə'val/ (also **cheval mirror**) ▶ n. a tall mirror fitted at its middle to an upright frame so that it can be tilted. [19th C.: *cheval* from Fr., 'frame.']

chev·a·lier /,SHevə'li(ə)r/ ▶ n. hist. a knight. ■ a chivalrous man. ■ a member of certain orders of knighthood or of modern French orders such as the Legion of Honor. ■ **(Chevalier)** Brit., hist. the title of James and Charles Stuart, pretenders to the British throne. [ME: from OFr., from med. L. *caballarius,* from L. *caballus* 'horse.']

Chev·i·ot /'SHevēət/ ▶ n. a sheep of a breed with short thick wool. ■ **(cheviot)** the wool or tweed cloth obtained from this breed.

chè·vre /'SHev(rə)/ ▶ n. cheese made with goat's milk. [1960s: Fr., lit. 'goat, she-goat,' from L. *capra.*]

chev·ron /'SHevrən/ ▶ n. a line or stripe in the shape of a V or an inverted V, esp. one on the sleeve of a uniform indicating rank or length of service. ■ Heraldry an ordinary in the form of a broad inverted V-shape. ■ Archit. a molding of continuous V-shaped patterns, common in Norman architecture. [ME: from OFr., based on L. *caper* 'goat.']

chevron

chev·ro·tain /'SHevrə,tān/ ▶ n. a small deerlike mammal (genera *Moschiola* and *Hyemoschus,* family Tragulidae) with short tusks, typically nocturnal and found in the tropical rain forests of Africa and South Asia. [18th C.: from Fr., diminutive of OFr. *chevrot,* dimin. of *chèvre* 'goat.']

Chev·y /'SHevē/ ▶ n. (pl. **chev·ys**) informal a Chevrolet car.

chev·y /'CHivē/ ▶ v. var. of CHIVVY.

Chevy Chase /'CHevē 'CHās/ a suburb in west central Maryland, north of Washington, DC; pop. 9,381.

chew /CHōō/ ▶ v. [trans.] bite and work (food) in the mouth with the teeth, esp. to make it easier to swallow: *he was chewing toast* | [intrans.] *he chewed for a moment, then swallowed.* ■ gnaw at (something) persistently, typically as a result of worry or anxiety. ▶ n. a repeated biting or gnawing of something. ■ something other than food that is meant for chewing.
– PHRASES **chew the cud** see CUD. **chew the fat** (or **rag**) informal chat in a leisurely way, esp. at length.
– PHRASAL VERBS **chew someone out** informal reprimand someone severely. **chew something over** discuss or consider something at length. **chew something up** chew food until it is soft or in small pieces. ■ damage or destroy something as if by chewing. — **chew·a·ble** adj. **chew·er** n. [usu. in comb.] *a tobacco-chewer.* [OE *cēowan,* of West Gmc. origin; rel. to Ger. *kauen.*]

chew·ing gum ▶ n. flavored gum for chewing.

chew·y /'CHōōē/ **1** adj. (**chew·i·er, chew·i·est**) (of food) needing to be chewed hard or for some time. **2** suitable for chewing. — **chew·i·ness** n.

Chey·enne[1] /SHī'an; -'en/ the capital of Wyoming, in the southeastern part of the state; pop. 53,011.

Chey·enne[2] ▶ n. (pl. same or **-ennes**) **1** a member of an American Indian people formerly living between the Missouri and Arkansas rivers but now on reservations in Montana and Oklahoma. **2** the Algonquian language of this people. ▶ adj. of or relating to the Cheyenne or their language. [Canad. Fr., from Dakota *šahíyena,* 'little Cree.']

Chey·enne Riv·er a river flowing 530 miles (850 km) from eastern Wyoming to the Missouri River in central South Dakota.

Cheyne-Stokes breath·ing /'CHān 'stōks; 'CHānē/ ▶ n. Med. a cyclical pattern of breathing in which movement gradually decreases to a complete stop and then returns to normal. It occurs in various medical conditions, and at high altitudes. [19th C.: John *Cheyne* (1777–1836), Scottish physician, and William *Stokes* (1804–78), Irish physician.]

chez /SHā/ ▶ prep. at the home of (used in imitation of French, often humorously): *I spent one summer chez Grandma.* [18th C.: Fr., from OFr. *chiese,* from L. *casa* 'cottage.']

chi[1] /kī/ ▶ n. the twenty-second letter of the Greek alphabet (Χ, χ), transliterated in the traditional Latin style as 'ch' (as in *Christ*) or in the modern style as 'kh' (as in *Khaniá* and in the etymologies of this dictionary).

chi[2] /CHē/ (also **qi** or **ki**) ▶ n. var. of QI.

chi·a /'CHēə/ ▶ n. a plant (*Salvia columbariae*) of the mint family with clusters of small two-lipped purple flowers.

Chiang Kai-shek /'CHANG 'kī'SHek; 'jyäNG/ (1887–1975), president of China 1928–31, 1943–49 and of Taiwan 1950–75. A general, he tried to unite China by military means in the 1930s but was defeated by the Communists. Forced to abandon mainland China in 1949, he set up a separate Nationalist Chinese State in Taiwan.

Chiang·mai /'jyäNG'mī/ a city in northwestern Thailand; pop. 164,900.

Chi·a·ni·na /,kēə'nēnə/ ▶ n. an animal of a large white breed of cattle, raised for its lean meat. [from Ital.]

Chi·an·ti /kē'äntē; -'antē/ (also **chi·an·ti**) ▶ n. (pl. **-tis**) a dry red wine, originally produced in Tuscany, Italy. [*Chianti* Mountains, Italy.]

Chi·a·pas /CHē'äpəs; 'CHäpəs/ a state in southern Mexico; capital, Tuxtla Gutiérrez.

chi·a·ro·scu·ro /kē,ärə'sk(y)ŏŏrō; kē,arə-/ ▶ n. the treatment of light and shade in drawing and painting. ■ an effect of contrasted light and shadow created by light falling unevenly or from a particular direction on something. [17th C.: from Ital., from *chiaro* 'clear' + *oscuro* 'dark.']

chi·as·ma /kī'azmə/ ▶ n. (pl. **-ma·ta** /-mətə/) Biol. the point at which paired chromosomes remain in contact after crossing over during meiosis. See also OPTIC CHIASMA. [19th C.: mod. L., from Gk. *chiasma* 'crosspiece,' from *khiazein* 'mark with the letter chi.']

chi·as·mus /kī'azməs/ ▶ n. a rhetorical or literary figure in which words, grammatical constructions, or concepts are repeated in reverse order, in the same or a modified form; e.g. 'Poetry is the record of the best and happiest moments of the happiest and best minds.' — **chi·as·tic** /kī'astik/ adj. [17th C.: mod. L., from Gk. *khiasmos* 'crosswise arrangement,' from *khiazein* 'mark with the letter chi,' from *khi* 'chi.']

Chi·ba /'CHēbə/ a city in Japan, on the island of Honshu; pop. 829,470.

Chib·cha /'CHibCHä/ ▶ n. (pl. same) **1** a member of a native people of Colombia whose well-developed political structure was destroyed by Europeans. **2** the Chibchan language of this people. ▶ adj. of or relating to the Chibcha or their language. [Amer. Sp., from Chibcha *zipa* 'chief.']

Chib·chan /'CHibCHən/ ▶ n. a language family of Colombia and Central America, most members of which are extinct or nearly so. ▶ adj. of or relating to this language family.

chi·bouk /CHə'bo͝ok; SHə-/ (also **chi·bouque**) ▶ **n.** a long Turkish tobacco pipe. [19th C.: Fr. *chibouque*, from Turk. *çubuk*, lit. 'tube.']

chic /SHēk/ ▶ **adj.** (**chic·er**, **chic·est**) elegantly and stylishly fashionable. ▶ **n.** stylishness and elegance, typically of a specified kind. — **chic·ly** **adv.** [19th C.: from Fr., prob. from Ger. *Schick* 'skill.']

Chi·ca·go /SHi'kôgō; -'kägō/ a city in northeastern Illinois, on Lake Michigan; pop. 2,896,016. — **Chi·ca·go·an** /-ən/ **n. & adj.**

Chi·ca·go Board of Trade ▶ **n.** see **BOARD OF TRADE** (sense 1).

Chi·ca·na /CHi'känə; SHi-/ ▶ **n.** (in North America) a girl or woman of Mexican origin or descent. [Mex. Sp., alt. of Sp. *mejicana* (fem.) 'Mexican.']

chi·cane /SHi'kān; CHi-/ ▶ **n.** **1** an artificial narrowing or turn on a road or auto-racing course. **2** dated (in card games) a hand without cards of one particular suit; a void. ▶ **v.** archaic [intrans.] employ trickery or chicanery. ■ [trans.] deceive or trick (someone). [17th C.: from Fr. *chicane* 'trickery,' *chicaner* 'quibble.']

chi·can·er·y /SHi'kānərē; CHi-/ ▶ **n.** the use of trickery to achieve a political, financial, or legal purpose.

Chi·ca·no /CHi'känō; SHi-/ ▶ **n.** (pl. **-nos**) (in North America) a person of Mexican origin or descent. See also **CHICANA**. [Mex. Sp., alt. of Sp. *mejicano* (masc.) 'Mexican.']

Chi·chén It·zá /CHi,CHen it'sä 'CHiCHən 'ētsə/ a site in northern Yucatán, Mexico, the center of the Mayan empire after AD 918 until about 1200.

Chi·ches·ter /'CHiCHəstər/, Sir Francis Charles (1901–72), English sailor. He was the first person to sail alone around the world 1966–67, stopping once.

Chi·che·wa /CHi'CHäwə/ ▶ **n.** another term for **NYANJA** (the language).

chi·chi /'SHēSHē; 'CHēCHē/ ▶ **adj.** attempting stylish elegance but achieving only an overelaborate affectedness. ▶ **n.** pretentious and overelaborate refinement. [20th C.: from Fr., of imitative origin.]

chick /CHik/ ▶ **n.** **1** a young bird, esp. one newly hatched. ■ a newly hatched domestic fowl. **2** informal a young woman. [ME: abbrev. of **CHICKEN**.]

chick·a·dee /'CHikədē/ ▶ **n.** a North American titmouse, in particular the **black-capped chickadee** (*Parus atricapillus*), with distinctive black cap and throat, and the similar but smaller **Carolina chickadee** (*P. carolinensis*). [19th C.: imitative.]

black-capped chickadee

Chick·a·mau·ga Creek /,CHikə'môgə/ a stream in northwestern Georgia; site of a Civil War battle 1863.

chick·a·ree /'CHikə,rē/ ▶ **n.** a squirrel (genus *Tamiasciurus*) with red fur, found in the coniferous forests of North America. [19th C.: imitative.]

Chick·a·saw /'CHikə,sô/ ▶ **n.** (pl. same or **-saws**) **1** a member of an American Indian people formerly resident in Mississippi and Alabama, and now in Oklahoma. **2** the Muskogean language of this people. ▶ **adj.** of or relating to this people or their language. [the name in Chickasaw.]

chick·en /'CHikən/ ▶ **n.** **1** a domestic fowl kept for its eggs or meat, esp. a young one. ■ meat from such a bird. **2** informal a game in which the first person to lose nerve and withdraw from a dangerous situation is the loser. ■ a coward. **3** informal (among homosexuals) an adolescent male. ▶ **adj.** [predic.] informal cowardly. ▶ **v.** [intrans.] (**chicken out**) informal withdraw from or fail in something through lack of nerve: *the referee chickened out of giving a penalty.*

– PHRASES **don't count your chickens before they're hatched** see **COUNT**[1]. [OE *cicen*, *cycen*, of Gmc. origin; rel. to Ger. *Küchlein* and prob. **COCK**[1].]

chick·en-and-egg ▶ **adj.** [attrib.] denoting a situation in which each of two things appears to be necessary to the other, making it impossible to say which came first.

chick·en breast ▶ **n.** Med. another term for **PIGEON BREAST**. — **chick·en-breast·ed** (also **chick·en-chest·ed**) **adj.**

chick·en feed ▶ **n.** food for poultry. ■ fig., informal an insignificant amount of money.

chick·en-fried steak ▶ **n.** a thin piece of beef that is lightly battered and fried until crisp.

chick·en hawk ▶ **n.** a hawk of a type that is reputed to prey on domestic fowl. ■ (also **chicken queen**) informal an older man who seeks young boys as sexual partners.

chick·en-heart·ed (also **chick·en-liv·ered**) ▶ **adj.** easily frightened; cowardly.

chick·en pox (also **chick·en·pox**) ▶ **n.** an infectious disease, esp. of children, causing a mild fever and a rash of itchy inflamed blisters. Also called **VARICELLA**. [18th C.: prob. of its mildness.]

chick·en·shit /'CHikən,SHit/ vulgar slang ▶ **adj.** worthless or contemptible (used as a general term of deprecation). ■ cowardly. ▶ **n.** a worthless or contemptible person. ■ something worthless or petty.

chick·en wire ▶ **n.** light wire netting with a hexagonal mesh.

chick·pea /'CHik,pē/ ▶ **n.** **1** a round yellowish seed, used widely as food. **2** the leguminous Old World plant (*Cicer arietinum*) that bears these seeds. [18th C.: from ME *chiche* (from OFr. *chiche*, *cice*, from L. *cicer* 'chickpea') + **PEA**.]

chick·weed /'CHik,wēd/ ▶ **n.** a small plant (*Stellaria*, *Cerastium*, and other genera) of the pink family with deeply cleft white petals, sometimes eaten by poultry.

chic·le /'CHikəl; 'CHiklē/ ▶ **n.** the milky latex of the sapodilla tree, used to make chewing gum. ■ another term for **SAPODILLA**. [via L. Amer. Sp. from Nahuatl *tzictli*.]

Chi·co /'CHēkō/ a city in northern California; pop. 59,954.

Chic·o·pee /'CHikə,pē/ a city in south central Massachusetts; pop. 54,653.

chic·o·ry /'CHikərē/ ▶ **n.** (pl. **-ries**) **1** a blue-flowered Mediterranean plant (*Cichorium intybus*) of the daisy family, cultivated for its edible salad leaves and carrot-shaped root. ■ the root of this plant, which is roasted and ground for use as an additive to or substitute for coffee. **2** another term for **ENDIVE**. [ME: from obs. Fr. *cicorée* 'endive,' via L. from Gk. *kikhorion*.]

chicory 1

chide /CHīd/ ▶ **v.** (past **chid·ed** or archaic **chid** /CHid/; past part. **chid·ed** or archaic **chid·den** /'CHidn/) [trans.] scold or rebuke: *she chided him for not replying.* — **chid·er** **n.** **chid·ing·ly** **adv.** [OE *cīdan*.]

chief /CHēf/ ▶ **n.** **1** a leader or ruler of a people or clan. ■ the person with the highest rank in an organization. ■ an informal form of address, esp. to someone of superior rank or status. **2** Heraldry an ordinary consisting of a broad horizontal band across the top of the shield. ■ the upper third of the field. ▶ **adj.** most important. ■ having or denoting the highest rank or authority.

– PHRASES **chief cook and bottle-washer** informal a person who performs a variety of important but routine tasks. **in chief** Heraldry at the top; in the upper part. **too many chiefs and not enough Indians** too many people giving orders and not enough people to carry them out. — **chief·dom** /-dəm/ **n.** **chief·ship** **n.** [ME: from OFr. *chief*, *chef*, based on L. *caput* 'head.']

chief jus·tice ▶ **n.** (the title of) the presiding judge in a supreme court. ■ (**Chief Justice of the United States**) (the formal title of) the chief justice of the US Supreme Court.

chief·ly /'CHēflē/ ▶ **adv.** above all; mainly. ■ for the most part; mostly.

chief mas·ter ser·geant ▶ **n.** a noncommissioned officer in the US Air Force ranking above senior master sergeant and below warrant officer.

chief of staff ▶ **n.** the senior staff officer of a service or command.

chief of state ▶ **n.** the titular head of a nation as distinct from the head of the government.

chief pet·ty of·fi·cer ▶ **n.** a senior noncommissioned officer in a navy, in particular an NCO in the US Navy or Coast Guard ranking above petty officer and below senior chief petty officer.

chief·tain /'CHēftən/ ▶ **n.** the leader of a people or clan. ■ informal a powerful member of an organization. — **chief·tain·cy** **n.** (pl. **-cies**) **chief·tain·ship** **n.** [ME and OFr. *chevetaine*, from late L. *capitaneus* (see **CAPTAIN**).]

chief war·rant of·fi·cer ▶ **n.** an member of the US armed forces ranking above warrant officer and below the lowest-ranking commissioned officer.

chiff·chaff /'CHif,CHaf/ ▶ **n.** a migratory Eurasian and North African warbler (genus *Phylloscopus*) with drab plumage. [late 18th C.: imitative.]

chif·fon /SHi'fän; 'SHifän/ ▶ **n.** a light, sheer fabric typically made of silk or nylon. ■ [as adj.] (of a cake or dessert) made with beaten egg whites to give a light consistency. [18th C.: from Fr., from *chiffe* 'rag.']

chif·fo·nade /,SHifə'nād; -'näd/ (also **chif·fon·nade**) ▶ **n.** (pl. same) a preparation of shredded or finely cut leaf vegetables, used as a garnish for soup. [Fr., from *chiffonner* 'to crumple.']

chif·fo·nier /,SHifə'ni(ə)r/ ▶ **n.** a tall chest of drawers, often with a mirror on top. [18th C.: from Fr. *chiffonnier*, *chiffonnière*, lit. 'ragpicker.']

chif·fo·robe /'SHifə,rōb/ ▶ **n.** a piece of furniture with drawers on one side and hanging space on the other. [20th C.: blend of **CHIFFONIER** and **WARDROBE**.]

chig·ger /'CHigər/ (also **jig·ger**) ▶ **n.** **1** a tiny mite (genus *Trombicula*, family Trombiculidae) whose parasitic larvae live on or under the skin of warm-blooded animals, where they cause irritation and dermatitis. **2** another term for **CHIGOE**. [18th C.: var. of **CHIGOE**.]

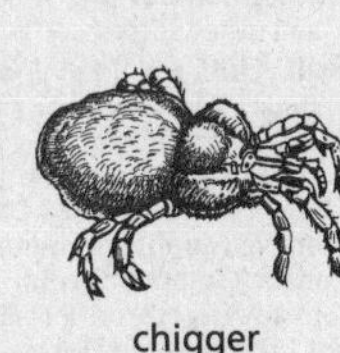
chigger

chi·gnon /'SHēnyän; SHēn'yän/ ▶ **n.** a knot or coil of hair arranged on the back of a woman's head. [18th C.: from Fr., orig. 'nape of the neck,' based on L. *catena* 'chain.']

chig·oe /'CHigō; 'CHē-/ ▶ **n.** a tropical flea (*Tunga penetrans*, family Tungidae), the female of which burrows and lays eggs beneath the host's

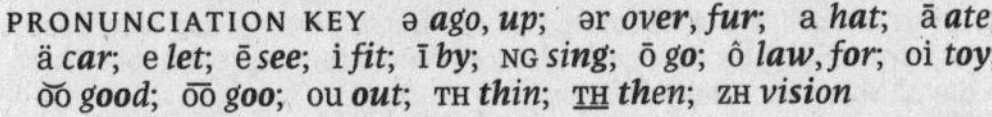
PRONUNCIATION KEY ə *ago, up*; ər *over, fur*; a *hat*; ā *ate*; ä *car*; e *let*; ē *see*; i *fit*; ī *by*; NG *sing*; ō *go*; ô *law, for*; oi *toy*; o͝o *good*; o͞o *goo*; ou *out*; TH *thin*; TH *then*; ZH *vision*

skin, causing painful sores. [17th C.: from Fr. *chique*, from a West Afr. language.]

Chih·li, Gulf of /'jir'lē; 'CHē'lē/ another name for **Bo Hai**.

Chi·hua·hua /CHə'wäwə; SHə-/ a state in northern Mexico. ■ its capital; pop. 530,490.

chi·hua·hua /CHə'wäwä; -wə; SHə-/ ▶ **n.** a small dog of a smooth-haired, large-eyed breed originating in Mexico.

chil·blain /'CHilblān/ ▶ **n.** a painful, itching swelling on the skin, typically on a hand or foot, caused by poor circulation in the skin when exposed to cold. — **chil·blained adj.** [16th C.: from **CHILL** + **BLAIN**.]

Child /CHīld/, Lydia Marie (1802–80), US abolitionist and writer; born *Lydia Marie Francis*. She was editor of the *National Anti-Slavery Standard* 1841–43.

child /CHīld/ ▶ **n.** (pl. **chil·dren**) a young human being below the age of full physical development or below the legal age of majority. ■ a son or daughter of any age. ■ an immature or irresponsible person. ■ a person who has little or no experience in a particular area. ■ (**children**) the descendants of a family or people. ■ (**child of**) a person or thing influenced by a specified environment.
– PHRASES **child's play** a task that is easily accomplished. **from a child** since childhood. **with child** formal pregnant. — **child·less adj. child·less·ness n.** [OE *cild*, of Gmc. origin.]

child·bear·ing /'CHīld,be(ə)riNG/ ▶ **n.** the process of giving birth to children.

child·bed fe·ver /'CHīld,bed/ ▶ **n.** another term for **PUERPERAL FEVER**.

child·birth /'CHīld,bərTH/ ▶ **n.** the action of giving birth to a child.

child care ▶ **n.** the action or skill of looking after children. ■ the care of children by a day-care center, babysitter, or other provider while parents are working.

child-cen·tered ▶ **adj.** giving priority to the interests and needs of children.

child·hood /'CHīld,hŏŏd/ ▶ **n.** the state of being a child. ■ the period during which a person is a child.

child·ish /'CHīldiSH/ ▶ **adj.** of, like, or appropriate to a child. ■ silly and immature. — **child·ish·ly adv. child·ish·ness n.**

child la·bor ▶ **n.** the use of children in industry or business, esp. when illegal or considered inhumane.

child·like /'CHīld,līk/ ▶ **adj.** (of an adult) having good qualities associated with a child.

child·proof /'CHīld,prōōf/ ▶ **adj.** designed to prevent children from injuring themselves or doing damage. ▶ **v.** [trans.] make inaccessible to children.

chil·dren /'CHildrən/ plural form of **CHILD**.

chil·dren of Is·ra·el see **ISRAEL**[1] (sense 1).

child re·straint ▶ **n.** a device used to control and protect a child in a motor vehicle.

child sup·port ▶ **n.** court-ordered payments, typically made by a noncustodial divorced parent, to support one's minor child or children.

Chil·e /'CHilē/ a country in southwestern South America. *See box.* — **Chil·e·an** /'CHilēən; CHə'lāən/ **adj. & n.**

chil·e[1] /'CHilē/ ▶ **n.** var. of **CHILI**.

chile[2] /CHīl/ ▶ **n.** nonstandard spelling of **CHILD**, used in representing chiefly southern US dialect.

chil·e re·lle·no /rə(l)'yānō/ ▶ **n.** (pl. **chil·es re·lle·nos**) (in Mexican cuisine) a stuffed chili pepper, typically battered and deep-fried. [20th C.: Sp., lit. 'stuffed chili.']

Chil·e salt·pe·ter ▶ **n.** another term for **SODIUM NITRATE**, esp. as a commercial product mined in Chile and other arid parts of the world.

chil·i /'CHilē/ (also **chil·i pep·per** or **chil·e** or Brit. **chil·li**) ▶ **n.** (pl. **chil·ies** or **chil·es** or Brit. **chil·lies**) a small hot-tasting pod of a variety of capsicum, used chopped (and often dried) in sauces, relishes, and spice powders. ■ short for **CHILI POWDER**. ■ (also **chile con carne** /kän 'kärnē; kən/) a spicy stew of beef and red chilies or chili powder, often with beans and tomatoes. [17th C.: from Sp. *chile*, from Nahuatl *chilli*.]

chil·i·ast /'kilē,ast/ ▶ **n.** another term for **MILLENARIAN**. — **chil·i·asm n. chil·i·as·tic** /,kilē'astik/ **adj.** [16th C.: via late L. from Gk. *khiliastēs*, from *khilias* 'a thousand years,' from *khilioi* 'thousand.']

chil·i dog ▶ **n.** a hot dog garnished with chili con carne.

chil·i pow·der ▶ **n.** a hot-tasting mixture of ground dried red chilies and other spices.

chill /CHil/ ▶ **n.** [in sing.] a moderate but unpleasant coldness. ■ (often **chills**) a lowered body temperature, often accompanied by shivering. ■ a feverish cold. ■ fig. a coldness of manner. ■ fig. a depressing influence. ■ a sudden and powerful unpleasant feeling, esp. of fear. ■ a metal mold or part of a mold, often cooled, designed to ensure rapid or even cooling of metal during casting. ▶ **v.** [trans.] **1** (often **be chilled**) make (someone) cold: *I'm chilled to the bone.* ■ cool (food or drink) in a refrigerator. **2** (often **be chilled**) horrify or frighten (someone). **3** (also **chill out**) [intrans.] informal calm down and relax: *I can lean back and chill* | *chill out, okay?* ■ pass time without a particular aim or purpose, esp. with other people. ▶ **adj.** chilly.
– PHRASES **chill someone's blood** horrify or terrify someone. **take the chill off** warm slightly. — **chill·ing·ly adv. chill·ness n. chill·some adj.** (literary). [OE *cele, ciele* 'cold,' of Gmc. origin; rel. to **COLD**.]

chill·er /'CHilər/ ▶ **n.** **1** a machine for cooling something, esp. a cold cabinet or refrigerator for keeping stored food a few degrees above freezing. **2** short for **SPINE-CHILLER**.

chill fac·tor ▶ **n.** another term for **WINDCHILL**.

chil·li ▶ **n.** (pl. **chil·lies**) British spelling of **CHILI**.

chil·lum /'CHiləm/ ▶ **n.** (pl. **-lums**) a hookah. ■ a pipe used for smoking marijuana. [from Hindi *cilam*.]

chill·y /'CHilē/ ▶ **adj.** (**chill·i·er, chill·i·est**) uncomfortably cool or cold. ■ (of a person) feeling cold. ■ unfriendly: *a chilly reception.* — **chill·i·ness n.**

Chi·lop·o·da /kī'läpədə/ Zool. a class of myriapod arthropods that comprises the centipedes. — **chi·lo·pod** /'kīlə,päd/ **n.** [mod. L. (pl.), from Gk. *kheilos* 'lip' + *pous, pod-* 'foot.']

Chil·pan·cin·go /,CHēlpän'siNGgō/ a city in southwestern Mexico, capital of the state of Guerrero; pop. 120,000.

Chi·lu·ba /CHə'lōōbə/ ▶ **n.** another term for **LUBA** (the language).

Chi·lung /'jē'lŏŏNG/ (also **Chi-lung, Kee·lung**) a chief port and naval base in Taiwan, at the northern tip of the island; pop. 357,000.

Chile

Official name: Republic of Chile
Location: southwestern South America, occupying a long Pacific coastal strip along the west borders of Bolivia and Argentina
Area: 289,200 square miles (748,800 sq km)
Population: 15,823,000
Capital: Santiago
Language: Spanish
Currency: Chilean peso

chi·mae·ra ▶ **n.** var. of **CHIMERA**.

chim·bley ▶ **n.** (pl. **-eys**) dialect form of **CHIMNEY**.

Chim·bo·ra·zo /,CHimbə'räzō; ,SHim-/ the highest peak in the Andes in Ecuador. It rises to 20,487 feet (6,310 m).

Chim·bo·te /CHēm'bōtā/ a port city in west central Peru, on the Pacific Ocean; pop. 297,000.

chime[1] /CHīm/ ▶ **n.** (often **chimes**) a bell or a metal bar or tube, typically one of a set tuned to produce a melodious series of ringing sounds when struck. ■ a sound made by such an instrument. ■ (**chimes**) a set of tuned metal rods used as an orchestral instrument. ■ (**chimes**) a

set of tuned bells used as a doorbell. ■ Bell-ringing a stroke of the clapper against one or both sides of a scarcely moving bell. ▶ **v.** [intrans.] **1** (of a bell or clock) make melodious ringing sounds, typically to indicate the time. ■ [trans.] (of a clock) make such sounds in order to indicate (the time). **2** be in agreement; harmonize.
– PHRASAL VERBS **chime in 1** interject a remark. **2** join in harmoniously. — **chim·er n.** [ME: prob. from OE *cimbal* (see CYMBAL).]

chime[2] (also **chimb**) ▶ **n.** the projecting rim at the end of a cask. [ME: prob. from OE word akin to Ger. *Kimme*.]

chi·me·ra /kī'mi(ə)rə; kə-/ (also **chi·mae·ra**) ▶ **n. 1** (**Chimera**) (in Greek mythology) a fire-breathing female monster with a lion's head, a goat's body, and a serpent's tail. ■ any mythical animal with parts taken from various animals. **2** a thing that is hoped or wished for but in fact is illusory or impossible to achieve. **3** Biol. an organism containing genetically different tissues, formed by processes such as fusion of early embryos, grafting, or mutation. ■ a DNA molecule with sequences derived from two or more different organisms, formed by laboratory manipulation. **4** (usu. **chimaera**) a cartilaginous marine fish (Chimaeridae and other families) with a long tail, an erect spine before the first dorsal fin, and typically a forward projection from the snout. — **chi·mer·ic** /-'mi(ə)rik; -'mer-/ **adj. chi·mer·i·cal** /kī'merikəl; kə-; -'mi(ə)r-/ **adj. chi·mer·i·cal·ly** /kī'merik(ə)lē; kə-; -'mi(ə)r-/ **adv.** [ME: via L. from Gk. *khimaira* 'she-goat or chimera.']

chi·mer·ism /kī'mi(ə)r,izəm; 'kīmə,rizəm/ ▶ **n.** Biol. the state of being a genetic chimera.

chi·mi·chan·ga /,CHimi'CHäNGgə; -'CHaNGgə/ ▶ **n.** a tortilla wrapped around a filling, typically of meat, and deep-fried. [Mex. Sp., lit. 'trinket.']

chi·mi·ne·a /CHimə'nēə/ (also **chi·me·ne·a**) ▶ **n.** an earthenware outdoor fireplace shaped like a lightbulb, with the bulbous end housing the fire and typically supported by a wrought-iron stand. [1990s: Sp., 'chimney.']

chiminea

chim·ney /'CHimnē/ ▶ **n.** (pl. **-neys**) a vertical channel or pipe that conducts smoke and combustion gases up from a fire or furnace and typically through the roof of a building. ■ the part of such a structure that extends above the roof. ■ a glass tube that protects the flame of a lamp. ■ a steep narrow cleft by which a rock face may be climbed. [ME: from OFr. *cheminee*, from late L. *caminata*, perh. based on Gk. *kaminos* 'oven.']

chim·ney cor·ner ▶ **n.** a warm seat at the side of an old-fashioned fireplace.

chim·ney pot ▶ **n.** an earthenware or metal pipe at the top of a chimney, narrowing the aperture and increasing the updraft.

chim·ney stack ▶ **n.** the part of a chimney that projects above a roof.

chim·ney sweep ▶ **n.** a person whose job is cleaning out the soot from chimneys.

chim·ney swift ▶ **n.** the common swift (*Chaetura pelagica*) found over the eastern part of North America, with mainly dark gray plumage.

chimney swift

chimp /CHimp/ ▶ **n.** informal term for CHIMPANZEE.

chim·pan·zee /,CHimpan'zē; -pən-; -'panzē/ ▶ **n.** a great ape (genus *Pan*) with large ears, mainly black coloration, and lighter skin on the face, native to the forests of western and central Africa. [18th C.: from Fr. *chimpanzé*, from Kikongo.]

Chin var. of JIN.

Ch'in var. of QIN.

chin /CHin/ ▶ **n.** the protruding part of the face below the mouth, formed by the apex of the lower jaw. ▶ **v.** [trans.] draw one's body up so as to bring one's chin level with or above (a horizontal bar) with one's feet off the ground, as an exercise.
– PHRASES **keep one's chin up** informal remain cheerful in difficult circumstances. **take it on the chin** endure or accept misfortune courageously or stoically. — **chinned adj.** [in comb.] *square-chinned.* [OE *cin, cinn*, from Indo-Eur.; akin to Du. *kin*, L. *gena* 'cheek,' Gk. *genus* 'jaw.']

Chi·na /'CHīnə/ a country in eastern Asia. *See box.*

chi·na /'CHīnə/ ▶ **n.** a fine white or translucent vitrified ceramic material. Also called PORCELAIN. ■ household tableware or other objects made from this or a similar material. [16th C.: from Pers. *chīnī* 'relating to China.']

Chi·na, Republic of official name for TAIWAN.

Chi·na as·ter ▶ **n.** a Chinese plant (*Callistephus chinensis*) of the daisy family, cultivated for its bright showy flowers.

chi·na·ber·ry /'CHīnə,berē/ (also **Chi·na·ber·ry**) ▶ **n.** (pl. **-ries**) (also **chinaberry tree**) a tall tree (*Melia azedarach*) of the mahogany family native to Asia and Australasia, bearing fragrant lilac flowers and yellow berries. ■ the fruit of this tree, used as beads and to make insecticides.

chi·na clay ▶ **n.** another term for KAOLIN.

Chi·na rose ▶ **n. 1** a Chinese rose (*Rosa chinensis*) that was introduced into Europe in the 19th century. ■ any of a number of garden rose varieties derived from crosses of this plant. **2** a tropical shrubby evergreen hibiscus (*Hibiscus rosa-sinensis*), cultivated for its large showy flowers.

Chi·na Sea a part of the Pacific Ocean off the coast of China, divided by the island of Taiwan into the **East China Sea** and the **South China Sea**.

chi·na stone ▶ **n.** partly kaolinized granite containing plagioclase feldspar, ground and mixed with kaolin to make porcelain.

Chi·na syn·drome ▶ **n.** a hypothetical sequence of events following the meltdown of a nuclear reactor, in which the core melts through its containment structure and deep into the earth. [1970s: CHINA (on the opposite side of the earth).]

Chi·na tea ▶ **n.** tea made from a small-leaved type of tea plant grown in China, typically flavored by smoke curing or the addition of flower petals.

Chi·na·town /'CHīnə,toun/ ▶ **n.** a district of any non-Chinese city, in which the population is predominantly of Chinese origin.

chi·na tree (also **Chi·na tree**) ▶ **n.** another term for CHINABERRY.

chi·na·ware /'CHīnə,we(ə)r/ ▶ **n.** dishes made of china.

chinch /CHinCH/ (also **chinch bug** /sinCH/) ▶ **n.** a plant-eating ground bug (family Lygaeidae) that forms large swarms on grasses and rushes. [17th C.: from Sp. *chinche*, from L. *cimex, cimic-*.]

chin·che·rin·chee /,CHinCHə'rinCHē; -rin'CHē/ ▶ **n.** a white-flowered South African lily (*Ornithogalum thyrsoides*). [20th C.: imitative of the sound made by rubbing its stalks together.]

chin·chil·la /CHin'CHilə/ ▶ **n.** a small South American rodent (genus *Chinchilla*, family Chinchillidae) with soft gray fur and a long bushy tail. ■ a cat or rabbit of a breed with silver-gray or gray fur. ■ the highly valued fur of the chinchilla, or of the chinchilla rabbit. [17th C.: from Sp., from Aymara or Quechua.]

chinchilla

Chin·co·teague Is·land /,SHiNGkə'tēg; ,CHiNG-/ an island off the coast of Virginia, west of Assateague Island.

Chin·co·teague po·ny ▶ **n.** a small, hardy horse found running wild on the islands of Chincoteague and Assateague off the Virginia and Maryland coasts.

Chin·dwin /'CHin'dwin/ a river that rises in northern Myanmar (Burma) and flows south for 550 miles (885 km) to meet the Irrawaddy River.

chine[1] /CHīn/ ▶ **n.** a backbone, esp. that of an animal as it appears in a

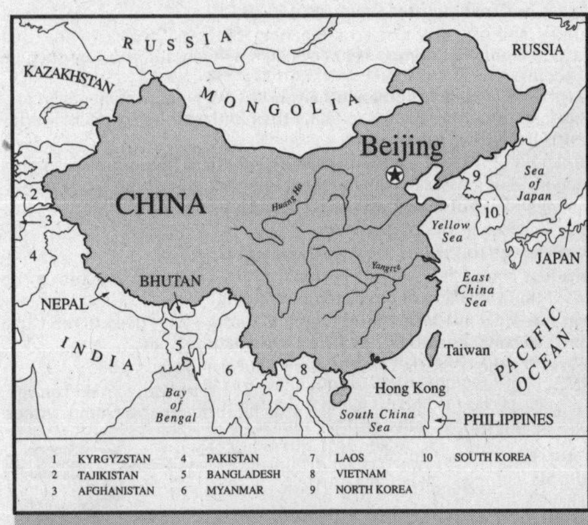

China

Official name: People's Republic of China
Location: eastern Asia
Area: 3,601,900 square miles (9,326,400 sq km)
Population: 1,298,847,000
Capital: Beijing
Language: Chinese (official form Mandarin)
Currency: yuan

cut of meat. ■ a cut of meat containing all or part of this. ■ a mountain ridge or arête. ▶**v.** [trans.] cut (meat) across or along the backbone. [ME: from OFr. *eschine*, based on blend of L. *spina* 'spine' and Gmc. word, 'narrow piece,' akin to SHIN.]

chine[2] ▶**n.** the angle where the bottom of a boat or ship meets the side. [ME: var. of CHIME[2].]

Chi·nese /CHĪ'nēz; -'nēs/ ▶**adj.** of or relating to China or its language, culture, or people. ■ belonging to or relating to the people forming the dominant ethnic group of China and widely dispersed elsewhere. Also called HAN. ▶**n.** (pl. same) **1** the Chinese language, a member of the Sino-Tibetan language family. It is the world's most commonly spoken first language. **2** a native or national of China, or a person of Chinese descent.

Chi·nese an·ise ▶**n.** another term for STAR ANISE.

Chi·nese black mush·room ▶**n.** another term for SHIITAKE MUSHROOM

Chi·nese box ▶**n.** each of a series of nested boxes.

Chi·nese cab·bage ▶**n.** an oriental cabbage (genus *Brassica*) that does not form a firm heart. See also BOK CHOY.

Chi·nese check·ers ▶**plural n.** [usu. treated as sing.] a board game for two to six players who attempt to move marbles or counters from one corner to the opposite one on a star-shaped board.

Chi·nese chest·nut ▶**n.** see CHESTNUT.

Chi·nese date ▶**n.** another term for JUJUBE.

Chi·nese fire drill ▶**n.** informal, often offens. a state of disorder or confusion. ■ a game in which the passengers of a motor vehicle that is stopped at an intersection get out of the vehicle, circle it, and return to their seats.

Chi·nese goose·ber·ry ▶**n.** another term for KIWI FRUIT.

Chi·nese lan·tern ▶**n.** **1** a collapsible paper lantern. **2** a plant (*Physalis alkekengi*) of the nightshade family with white flowers and globular orange fruits enclosed in an orange-red papery calyx.

Chinese lantern 2

Chi·nese pars·ley ▶**n.** another term for CORIANDER.

Chi·nese puz·zle ▶**n.** an intricate puzzle consisting of many interlocking pieces. ■ a very complicated or perplexing situation.

Chi·nese rad·ish ▶**n.** another term for DAIKON.

Chi·nese wall ▶**n.** an insurmountable barrier, esp. to the passage of information or communication. [20th C.: GREAT WALL OF CHINA.]

Chi·nese white ▶**n.** white pigment made from zinc oxide.

Chi·nese wind·lass ▶**n.** another term for DIFFERENTIAL WINDLASS.

Ch'ing var. of QING.

ching /CHING/ ▶**n.** an abrupt high-pitched ringing sound, typically one made by a cash register. [imitative.]

chink[1] /CHINGK/ ▶**n.** a narrow opening or crack, typically one that admits light. ■ a narrow beam or patch of light admitted by such an opening.

– PHRASES **a chink in someone's armor** a weak point in someone's character, arguments, or ideas, making them vulnerable to attack or criticism. [16th C.: rel. to CHINE[2].]

chink[2] ▶**v.** make or cause to make a light and high-pitched ringing sound, as of glasses or coins striking together. ▶**n.** a high-pitched ringing sound. [16th C.: imitative.]

chin·ka·pin ▶**n.** var. of CHINQUAPIN.

Chin·kiang /'jinjē'äNG/ variant of ZHENJIANG.

chin·less /'CHinlis/ ▶**adj.** (of a person) lacking a well-defined chin. ■ informal lacking strength of character; ineffectual.

chin mu·sic ▶**n.** informal **1** idle chatter. **2** Baseball, informal used to refer to a pitched ball that passes very close to the batter's chin.

Chi·no /'CHēnō/ a city in southwestern California; pop. 59,682.

chi·no /'CHēnō/ ▶**n.** (pl. **-os**) a cotton twill fabric, typically khaki-colored. ■ (**chinos**) casual pants made from such fabric. [1940s: from L. Amer. Sp., lit. 'toasted.']

Chino- ▶**comb. form** equivalent to SINO-.

chi·nois /SHin'wä; SHēn-/ ▶**n.** a cone-shaped sieve with a closely woven mesh for straining sauces.

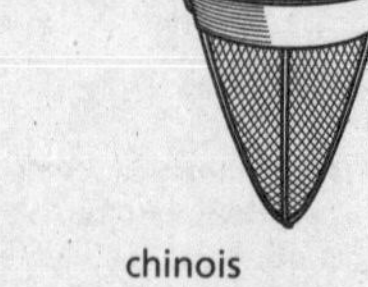

chinois

chi·noi·se·rie /SHēn,wäz(ə)'rē; -'wäzərē/ ▶**n.** (pl. **-ries**) the imitation or evocation of Chinese motifs and techniques in Western art, furniture, and architecture, esp. in the 18th century. ■ objects or decorations in this style. [19th C.: from Fr., from *chinois* 'Chinese.']

Chi·nook /SHə'no͝ok; CHə-/ ▶**n.** (pl. same or **-nooks**) **1** a member of an American Indian people originally inhabiting the region around the lower Columbia River in Oregon and Washington. **2** the Penutian language of this people. ▶**adj.** of or relating to the Chinook or their language. [from *c'inúk*, a Salishan word, name of a Chinook village.]

chi·nook /SHə'no͝ok; CHə-/ ▶**n.** **1** (also **chinook wind**) a warm dry wind that blows down the east side of the Rocky Mountains at the end of winter. **2** (also **chinook salmon**) a large North Pacific salmon (*Oncorhynchus tshawytscha*). An important commercial food fish, it is considered endangered. [19th C.: from CHINOOK.]

Chi·nook Jar·gon ▶**n.** an extinct pidgin composed of elements from Chinook, Nootka, English, French, and other languages, formerly used in the Pacific Northwest.

chin·qua·pin /'CHiNGkə,pin/ (also **chin·ka·pin**) ▶**n.** a North American chestnut tree, in particular the **Allegheny** (or **eastern**) **chinquapin** (*Castanea pumila*). ■ the edible nut of one of these trees. [17th C.: from Virginia Algonquian.]

chintz /CHints/ ▶**n.** printed multicolored cotton fabric with a glazed finish. [17th C. (as *chints*, pl. of *chint* 'cloth imported from India'): from Hindi *chīṃṭ* 'spattering, stain.']

chintz·y /'CHintsē/ ▶**adj.** (**chintz·i·er**, **chintz·i·est**) **1** of, like, or decorated with chintz. ■ brightly colorful but gaudy and tasteless. **2** informal miserly. — **chintz·i·ly adv.** **chintz·i·ness n.**

chin-up ▶**n.** another term for PULL-UP (sense 1).

chin·wag /'CHin,wag/ (also **chin wag**) informal ▶**n.** a chat. ▶**v.** (**-wagged**, **-wag·ging**) [intrans.] have a chat.

Chi·os /'kēäs; -ôs; 'kī-/ a Greek island in the Aegean Sea; pop. 52,690. Greek name KHIOS. — **Chi·an** /'kēən; 'kī-/ **n. & adj.**

chip /CHip/ ▶**n.** **1** a small piece of something removed in the course of chopping, cutting, or breaking something, esp. a hard material such as wood or stone. ■ a hole or flaw left by the removal of such a piece. **2** a thin slice of food made crisp by being fried, baked, or dried and typically eaten as a snack. ■ a small chunk of candy added to desserts or sweet snacks, esp. of chocolate. ■ (**chips**) esp. Brit. French fries. **3** short for MICROCHIP. **4** a counter used in certain gambling games to represent money. **5** (in golf, soccer, and other sports) a short lofted kick or shot with the ball. ■ Tennis a softly sliced return intended to land between the net and the opponent's service line. ▶**v.** (**chipped**, **chip·ping**) [trans.] **1** cut or break (a small piece) from the edge or surface of a hard material. ■ [intrans.] (of a material or object) break at the edge or on the surface: *the paint had chipped off the gate.* ■ cut pieces off (a hard material) to alter its shape or break it up. **2** (in golf, soccer, and other sports) kick or strike (a ball or shot) to produce a short lobbed shot or pass.

– PHRASES **a chip off the old block** informal someone who resembles his or her parent, esp. in character. **a chip on one's shoulder** informal a deeply ingrained grievance, typically about a particular thing. **when the chips are down** informal when a very serious and difficult situation arises: *Ivan can be a pain, but when the chips are down, he's always the first to help.*

– PHRASAL VERBS **chip away** gradually and relentlessly make something smaller or weaker. **chip in** (or **chip something in**) contribute something as one's share of a joint activity, cost, etc. [ME: rel. to OE *forcippian* 'cut off.']

chip·board /'CHip,bôrd/ ▶**n.** another term for PARTICLEBOARD.

Chip·e·wy·an /,CHipə'wīən/ ▶**n.** (pl. same or **-ans**) **1** a member of a Dene people of northwestern Canada. Do not confuse with CHIPPEWA. **2** the Athabaskan language of this people. ▶**adj.** of or relating to this people or their language. [from Cree *čīpwayān*, lit. '(wearing) pointed-skin (garments).']

chip·munk /'CHip,məNGk/ ▶**n.** a burrowing ground squirrel (genus *Tamias*) with cheek pouches and light and dark stripes running down the body. Its many species include the North American **eastern chipmunk** (*T. striatus*). [19th C.: from Ojibwa.]

eastern chipmunk

chi·pot·le /CHi'pōtlā/ ▶**n.** a smoked hot chili pepper used esp. in Mexican cooking. [Mex. Sp., from Nahuatl.]

Chip·pen·dale[1] /'CHipən,dāl/, Thomas (1718–79), English furniture maker. He produced furniture in a neoclassical vein.

Chip·pen·dale[2] ▶**adj.** (of furniture) designed, made by, or in the style of Thomas Chippendale.

chip·per[1] /'CHipər/ ▶**adj.** informal cheerful and lively. [19th C.: perh. from dial. *kipper* 'lively.']

chip·per[2] ▶**n.** a person or thing that turns something into chips. ■ a machine for chipping the trunks and limbs of trees.

Chip·pe·wa /'CHipə,wä; -,wä; -wə/ (also **Chip·pe·way** /-,wā/) ▶**n.** (pl. same) another term for OJIBWA. Do not confuse with CHIPEWYAN. [alt. of OJIBWA.]

chip·ping spar·row ▶**n.** a common American songbird (*Spizella passerina*) of the bunting family, with a chestnut crown and a white stripe over the eye. [19th C.: from *chip* 'chirp.']

chip·py /'CHipē/ informal ▶**n.** (also **chip·pie**) (pl. **-pies**) a promiscuous young woman, esp. a prostitute. ▶**adj.** touchy and irritable. ■ (of an ice-hockey game or player) rough and belligerent, with or incurring numerous penalties.

chip·set /'CHip,set/ ▶**n.** a collection of integrated circuits that form the set needed to make an electronic device such as a computer motherboard or portable telephone.

chip shot ▶**n.** Golf a stroke at which the ball is or must be chipped into the air.

Chi·rac /SHē'räk/, Jacques René (1932–), president of France (1995–2007). He previously served as prime minister 1974–76, 1986–88.

chi·ral /'kīrəl/ ▶ **adj.** Chem. asymmetric in such a way that the structure and its mirror image are not superimposable. — **chi·ral·i·ty** /kī'ralitē/ **n.** [19th C.: from Gk. *kheir* 'hand.']

chi-rho /'kī 'rō/ ▶ **n.** a monogram of chi (X) and rho (P) as the first two letters of Greek *Khristos* Christ, used as a Christian symbol.

Chir·i·ca·hua /,CHiri'käwə/ ▶ **n. 1** a member of an Apache people, formerly located in southern New Mexico, southeastern Arizona, and northern Mexico, now living primarily in Oklahoma and New Mexico. **2** the Athabaskan language of this people. ▶ **adj.** of or relating to this people or their language.

Chi·ri·ca·hua Moun·tains a range in southeastern Arizona, on the Mexican border.

chir·i·moy·a /,CHirə'moiə/ ▶ **n.** var. of CHERIMOYA.

chiro- (also **cheiro-**) ▶ **comb. form** of the hand or hands: *chiromancy.* [from Gk. *kheir* 'hand.']

chi·rog·ra·phy /kī'rägrəfē/ ▶ **n.** handwriting, esp. as distinct from typography. — **chi·ro·graph·ic** /,kīrə'grafik/ **adj.**

chi·ro·man·cy /'kīrə,mansē/ ▶ **n.** the prediction of a person's future from the lines on the palms of his or her hands; palmistry.

Chi·ron /'kīrən/ **1** Gk. Mythol. a learned centaur who acted as teacher to Jason, Achilles, and many other heroes. **2** Astron. asteroid 2060, discovered in 1977, which is unique in having an orbit lying mainly between the orbits of Saturn and Uranus.

chi·ron·o·mid /kī'ränəmid/ ▶ **n.** Entomol. an insect of a family (Chironomidae) that comprises the nonbiting midges. [19th C.: from mod. L. *Chironomidae* (pl.), based on Gk. *kheironomos* 'pantomime dancer.']

chi·rop·o·dy /kə'räpədē; SHə-/ ▶ **n.** another term for PODIATRY. — **chi·rop·o·dist n.** [19th C.: from CHIRO- + Gk. *pous, pod-* 'foot.']

chi·ro·prac·tic /,kīrə'praktik/ ▶ **n.** the diagnosis and manipulative treatment of misalignments of the joints, esp. those of the spinal column. — **chi·ro·prac·tor** /'kīrə,praktər/ **n.** [19th C.: from CHIRO- + Gk. *praktikos* 'practical,' from *prattein* 'do.']

Chi·rop·ter·a /kī'räptərə/ Zool. an order of mammals that comprises the bats. See also MEGACHIROPTERA, MICROCHIROPTERA. — **chi·rop·ter·an n. & adj.** [mod. L. (pl.), from CHIRO- + Gk. *pteron* 'wing.']

chirp /CHərp/ ▶ **v.** [intrans.] (typically of a small bird or an insect) utter a short, sharp, high-pitched sound. ■ [with direct speech] (of a person) say something in a lively and cheerful way: *"Good morning!" chirped Alex.* ▶ **n.** a short, sharp, high-pitched sound. — **chirp·er n.** [ME: imitative.]

chirp·y /'CHərpē/ ▶ **adj. (chirp·i·er, chirp·i·est)** informal cheerful and lively. — **chirp·i·ly** /'CHərpəlē/ **adv. chirp·i·ness n.**

chirr /CHər/ (also **churr**) ▶ **v.** [intrans.] (esp. of an insect) make a prolonged low trilling sound. ▶ **n.** a low trilling sound. [17th C.: imitative.]

chir·rup /'CHi(ə)rəp; 'CHər-/ ▶ **v. (-ruped, -ruping)** [intrans.] (esp. of a small bird) make repeated short high-pitched sounds; twitter. ■ [with direct speech] (of a person) say something in a high-pitched voice: *"Yes, Miss Honey," chirruped eighteen voices.* ▶ **n.** a short, high-pitched sound. — **chir·rup·y adj.** [16th C.: alt. of CHIRP.]

chis·el /'CHizəl/ ▶ **n.** a hand tool with a squared, beveled blade for shaping wood, stone, or metal. ▶ **v. (-eled, -el·ing;** Brit. **-elled, -el·ling)** [trans.] **1** cut or shape (something) with a chisel. **2** informal cheat or swindle (someone) out of something. — **chis·el·er n.** [ME: from Old North. Fr., based on L. *cis-*, var. of *caes-*, stem of *caedere* 'to cut.']

chis·eled /'CHizəld/ ▶ **adj.** (of wood or stone) shaped or cut with a chisel. ■ (of a facial feature, typically a man's) strongly and clearly defined.

Chis·holm /'CHizəm/, Shirley Anita St. Hill (1924–2005), US politician. A New York Democrat, she was the first African-American woman elected to Congress, where she served in the House of Representatives 1969–83.

Chis·holm Trail a 19th-century route primarily used for driving cattle from San Antonio, Texas to Abilene, Kansas.

Chi·şi·nă·u /,kēSHə'nou/ the capital of Moldova; pop. 665,000. Russian name KISHINYOV.

chi-square /kī/ ▶ **n.** [as adj.] relating to or denoting a statistical method assessing the goodness of fit between observed values and those expected theoretically. (Symbol: χ^2)

chit[1] /CHit/ ▶ **n.** a short official note, memorandum, or voucher, typically recording a sum owed. [18th C.: Anglo-Ind., from Hindi *ciṭṭhī* 'note.']

chit[2] ▶ **n.** an immature or disrespectful young woman. [ME: perh. akin to dial. *chit* 'sprout.']

Chi·ta /CHi'tä/ a city in southeastern Siberia, on the Trans-Siberian Railway; pop. 349,000.

chi·tal /'CHētl/ ▶ **n.** (pl. same) another term for AXIS DEER. [19th C.: from Hindi *cītal*, from Sanskrit *citrala* 'spotted,' from *citra* 'spot.']

chit·chat /'CHit,CHat/ (also **chit-chat**) informal ▶ **n.** inconsequential conversation. ▶ **v.** [intrans.] talk about trivial matters. [17th C.: reduplication of CHAT[1].]

chi·tin /'kītn/ ▶ **n.** Biochem. a fibrous substance consisting of polysaccharides and forming the major constituent in the exoskeleton of arthropods and the cell walls of fungi. — **chi·tin·ous** /'kītn-əs/ **adj.** [19th C.: from Fr. *chitine*, from Gk. *khitōn* (see CHITON).]

chi·ton /'kītn; -tän/ ▶ **n. 1** a long woolen tunic worn in ancient Greece. **2** a marine mollusk (class Polyplacophora) that has an oval flattened body with a shell of overlapping plates. [from Gk. *khitōn* 'tunic.']

Chit·ta·gong /'CHitə,gäNG; -,gôNG/ a seaport in southeastern Bangladesh; pop. 1,566,070.

chit·ter /'CHitər/ ▶ **v.** [intrans.] make a twittering or chattering sound. [ME: imitative.]

chit·ter·lings /'CHitlənz/ ▶ **plural n.** the smaller intestines of a pig, cooked for food. [ME: perh. rel. to Ger. *Kutteln.*]

Chi·tun·gwi·za /,CHētōōNG'gwēzə/ a city in northeastern Zimbabwe; pop. 274,000.

chiv·al·rous /'SHivəlrəs/ ▶ **adj.** (of a man or his behavior) courteous and gallant, esp. toward women. ■ of or relating to the historical notion of chivalry. — **chiv·al·rous·ly adv.**

chiv·al·ry /'SHivəlrē/ ▶ **n.** the medieval knightly system with its religious, moral, and social code. ■ hist. knights, noblemen, and horsemen collectively. ■ the combination of qualities expected of an ideal knight, esp. courage, honor, courtesy, justice, and a readiness to help the weak. ■ courteous behavior, esp. that of a man toward women. — **chi·val·ric** /SHə'valrik/ **adj.** [ME: from OFr. *chevalerie*, from med. L. *caballerius*, from late L. *caballarius* 'horseman' (see CHEVALIER).]

chives /CHīvz/ ▶ **plural n.** a small plant (*Allium schoenoprasum*) of the lily family, with purple-pink flowers and dense tufts of long tubular leaves that taste oniony and are used as a culinary herb. ■ the leaves from this plant. [ME: from OFr., dial. var. of *cive*, from L. *cepa* 'onion.']

chiv·vy /'CHivē/ (also **chiv·y** or **chev·y** /'CHevē/) ▶ **v. (-vies, -vied)** [trans.] tell (someone) repeatedly to do something: *an association that chivvies government into action.* [18th C.: probably from the ballad *Chevy Chase*, celebrating a skirmish (prob. the battle of Otterburn, 1388) on the Scot. border.]

Chka·lov /CHə'käləf/ former name (1938–57) for ORENBURG.

chlam·y·date /'klami,dāt/ ▶ **adj.** Zool. having a mantle or pallium like that of a mollusk.

chla·myd·e·ous /klə'midēəs/ ▶ **adj.** Bot. having or pertaining to a perianth or floral envelope.

chla·myd·i·a /klə'midēə/ ▶ **n.** (pl. same or **-myd·i·ae** /-'midē,ē/) a very small parasitic bacterium (genus *Chlamydia*, order Chlamydiales) that, like a virus, requires the biochemical mechanisms of another cell in order to reproduce. Bacteria of this type cause various diseases including trachoma, psittacosis, and nonspecific urethritis. — **chla·myd·i·al adj.** [1960s: mod. L. (pl.), from Gk. *khlamus, khlamud-* 'cloak.']

chla·myd·o·spore /klə'midə,spôr/ ▶ **n.** Bot. (in certain fungi) a thick-walled hyphal cell that functions as a spore. [19th C.: from Gk. *khlamus, khlamud-* 'mantle.']

chla·mys /'klaməs; 'klā-/ ▶ **n.** (pl. **chla·mys·es** or **chla·my·des** /'klaməidēz/) a short cloak worn by men in ancient Greece. [17th C.: from Gk. *khlamus* 'mantle.']

chlo·as·ma /klō'azmə/ ▶ **n.** a temporary condition, typically caused by hormonal changes, in which large brown patches form on the skin, mainly on the face. [19th C.: from Gk. *khloazein* 'become green.']

chlor- ▶ **comb. form** var. of CHLORO- before a vowel (as in *chloracne*).

chlor·ac·ne /klô'raknē/ ▶ **n.** Med. a skin disease resembling severe acne, caused by exposure to chlorinated chemicals.

chlo·ral /'klôrəl/ ▶ **n.** Chem. a colorless, viscous liquid, CCl_3CHO, made by chlorinating acetaldehyde. ■ short for CHLORAL HYDRATE. [19th C.: from Fr., blend of *chlore* 'chlorine' and *alcool* 'alcohol.']

chlo·ral hy·drate ▶ **n.** Chem. a colorless crystalline solid, $CCl_3CH(OH)_2$, made from chloral and used as a sedative.

chlo·ram·bu·cil /klô'rambyə,sil/ ▶ **n.** Med. a cytotoxic drug used in the treatment of cancer. [1950s: from *chlor(oethyl)am(inophenyl)bu(tyric acid)* + *-cil.*]

chlo·ra·mine /'klôrə,mēn/ ▶ **n.** Chem. an organic compound containing a chlorine atom bonded to nitrogen, esp. any of a group of sulfonamide derivatives used as antiseptics and disinfectants.

chlo·ram·phen·i·col /,klôram'fenə,kôl; -,kōl/ ▶ **n.** Med. an antibiotic obtained from the bacterium *Streptomyces venezuelae* or produced synthetically, used against serious infections such as typhoid fever. [1940s: from CHLORO- + *am(ide)* + PHENO- + *ni(tro-)* + *(gly)col.*]

chlor·dane /'klôrdān/ ▶ **n.** a synthetic viscous toxic compound, $C_{10}H_6Cl_8$, used as an insecticide. [1940s: from CHLOR- + *(in)dene* + -ANE[2].]

chlor·di·az·e·pox·ide /,klôrdī,azə'päksīd/ ▶ **n.** Med. a tranquilizer of the benzodiazepine group, used chiefly to treat anxiety and alcoholism. Also called LIBRIUM (trademark).

chlo·rel·la /klə'relə/ ▶ **n.** Biol. a common single-celled green alga (genus *Chlorella*) of both terrestrial and aquatic habitats, frequently turning stagnant water an opaque green. [mod. L., dimin. of Gk. *khlōros* 'green.']

chlo·ric /'klôrik/ ▶ **adj.** of, relating to, or containing chlorine in the pentavalent state.

chlo·ric ac·id ▶ **n.** Chem. a colorless liquid acid, $HClO_3$, with strong oxidizing properties. ■ any acid containing chlorine and oxygen.

chlo·ride /'klôrīd/ ▶ **n.** Chem. a compound of chlorine with another element or group. [19th C.: from CHLORINE + -IDE.]

chlo·ri·nate /'klôrə,nāt/ ▶ **v.** [trans.] [usu. as adj.] (**chlorinated**) impregnate or treat with chlorine. ■ Chem. introduce chlorine into (a compound). — **chlo·ri·na·tion** /,klôrə'nāSHən/ **n. chlo·ri·na·tor** /-,nātər/ **n.**

chlo·rine /ˈklôrēn/ ▶n. the chemical element of atomic number 17, a toxic, irritant, pale green gas. (Symbol: **Cl**) [19th C.: from Gk. *khlōros* 'green.']

chlo·rite[1] /ˈklôrīt/ ▶n. a dark green mineral consisting of a basic hydrated aluminosilicate of magnesium and iron. —**chlo·rit·ic** /klôˈritik/ adj. [18th C.: via L. from Gk. *khlōritis*, a stone.]

chlo·rite[2] ▶n. Chem. a salt of chlorous acid, containing the anion ClO_2^-. [19th C.: from CHLORINE.]

chlo·ri·toid /ˈklôrəˌtoid/ ▶n. a greenish-gray or black mineral resembling chlorite, found in metamorphosed clay sediments.

chloro- (usu. **chlor-** before a vowel) ▶comb. form **1** Biol. Mineral. green. **2** Chem. representing CHLORINE: *chloroquine*. [from Gk. *khlōros* 'green.']

chlo·ro·car·bon /ˈklôrōˌkärbən/ ▶n. a chemical compound that contains carbon and chlorine or carbon, chlorine, and hydrogen.

chlo·ro·fluor·o·car·bon /ˌklôrōˌflo͝orōˈkärbən/ (abbr.: **CFC**) ▶n. any of a class of compounds of carbon, hydrogen, chlorine, and fluorine, typically gases used chiefly in refrigerants and aerosol propellants.

chlo·ro·form /ˈklôrəˌfôrm/ ▶n. a colorless, volatile, sweet-smelling liquid, $CHCl_3$, used as a solvent and formerly as a general anesthetic. ▶v. [trans.] render (someone) unconscious with this substance. [19th C.: from CHLORO- + *form-* from FORMIC ACID.]

chlo·ro·my·ce·tin /ˌklôrōmīˈsētn/ ▶n. trademark for CHLORAMPHENICOL. [1940s: from CHLORO- + Gk. *mukēs, mukēt-* 'fungus.']

chlo·ro·phyll /ˈklôrəˌfil/ ▶n. a green pigment, present in all green plants and in cyanobacteria, responsible for the absorption of light to provide energy for photosynthesis. —**chlo·ro·phyl·lous** /ˌklôrəˈfiləs/ adj. [19th C.: coined in Fr. from Gk. *khlōros* 'green' + *phullon* 'leaf.']

Chlo·roph·y·ta /klôˈräfətə/ Bot. a phylum that comprises the green algae. They are more recently treated as a phylum of the kingdom Protista. —**chlo·ro·phyte** /ˈklôrəˌfīt/ n. [mod. L. (pl.), from Gk. *khlōros* 'green' + *phuton* 'plant.']

chlo·ro·plast /ˈklôrəˌplast/ ▶n. Bot. (in green plant cells) a plastid that contains chlorophyll and in which photosynthesis takes place. [19th C.: coined in Ger. from Gk. *khlōros* 'green' + *plastos* 'formed.']

chlo·ro·prene /ˈklôrəˌprēn/ ▶n. Chem. a colorless liquid, $CH_2{=}CClCH{=}CH_2$, made from acetylene and hydrochloric acid and polymerized to form neoprene. [1930s: from CHLORO- + shortened form of ISOPRENE.]

chlo·ro·quine /ˈklôrəˌkwēn/ ▶n. Med. a synthetic drug related to quinoline, chiefly used against malaria. [1940s: from CHLORO- + *quin(olin)e*.]

chlo·ro·sis /klôˈrōsəs/ ▶n. **1** Bot. abnormal reduction or loss of the normal green coloration of leaves of plants. **2** Med. anemia caused by iron deficiency, esp. in adolescent girls, causing a greenish complexion. —**chlo·rot·ic** /klôˈrätik/ adj.

chlo·ro·thi·a·zide /ˌklôrōˈTHīəˌzīd/ ▶n. Med. a synthetic drug used to treat fluid retention and high blood pressure.

chlo·rous ac·id /ˈklôrəs/ ▶n. Chem. a weak acid, $HClO_2$, with oxidizing properties, formed when chlorine dioxide dissolves in water.

chlor·prom·a·zine /klôrˈprämәˌzēn/ ▶n. Med. a synthetic drug used as a tranquilizer and sedative, and to prevent vomiting. [1950s: from CHLORO- + *prom(eth)azine*.]

chlor·tet·ra·cy·cline /ˌklôrtetrəˈsīklēn/ ▶n. Med. an antibiotic of the tetracycline group, obtained from the bacterium *Streptomyces aureofaciens* or produced synthetically, active against many bacterial and fungal infections.

cho·a·no·cyte /kōˈanəˌsīt/ ▶n. Zool. a flagellated cell with a collar of protoplasm at the base of the flagellum, numbers of which line the internal chambers of sponges. [19th C.: from Gk. *khoanē* 'funnel.']

choc·a·hol·ic ▶n. var. of CHOCOHOLIC.

chock /CHäk/ ▶n. **1** a wedge or block placed against a wheel or rounded object, to prevent it from moving. ■ a support on which a rounded structure, such as a cask or the hull of a boat, may be placed to keep it steady. **2** a fitting with a gap at the top, through which a rope or line is run. ▶v. [trans.] (often **be chocked**) prevent the forward movement of (a wheel or vehicle) with a chock. ■ support (a boat, cask, etc.) on chocks. [ME: prob. ult. from OFr. *çouche, çoche* 'block.']

chock·a·block /ˈCHäkəˌbläk/ (also **chock-a-block**) ▶adj. [predic.] informal crammed full of people or things. [19th C.: from *chock* (in CHOCK-FULL) and BLOCK.]

chock-full /ˈCHäk ˈfo͝ol; ˈCHək/ ▶adj. [predic.] informal filled to overflowing. [ME: of unknown origin.]

choc·o·hol·ic /ˌCHôkəˈhôlik; -ˈhälik; ˌCHä-/ (also **choc·a·hol·ic**) ▶n. informal a person who is addicted to or excessively fond of chocolate.

choc·o·late /ˈCHäk(ə)lit; ˈCHôk-/ ▶n. a food preparation in the form of a paste or solid block made from roasted and ground cacao seeds, typically sweetened. ■ a candy made of or covered with this. ■ a drink made by mixing milk with chocolate. ■ a deep brown color. —**choc·o·lat·y** (also **choc·o·lat·ey**) adj. [17th C.: from Fr. *chocolat* or Sp. *chocolate*, from Nahuatl *chocolatl* 'food made from cacao seeds,' influenced by unrelated *cacaua-atl* 'drink made from cacao.']

choc·o·late chip ▶n. [usu. as adj.] a small piece of chocolate used in making cookies and other sweet foods.

choc·o·late mousse ▶n. see MOUSSE.

cho·co·la·tier /ˌCHôk(ə)ləˈti(ə)r; ˌSHôkəläˈtyā/ ▶n. a maker or seller of chocolate. [19th C.: Fr.]

Choc·taw /ˈCHäktô/ ▶n. (pl. same or **-taws**) **1** a member of a native people now living mainly in Mississippi. **2** the Muskogean language of this people, closely related to Chickasaw. **3** Figure Skating a step from one edge of a skate to the other edge of the other skate in the opposite direction. ▶adj. of or relating to the Choctaw or their language. [from Choctaw *čahta*.]

choice /CHois/ ▶n. an act of selecting or making a decision when faced with two or more possibilities. ■ the right or ability to make, or possibility of making, such a selection. ■ a range of possibilities from which one or more may be selected. ■ a course of action, thing, or person that is selected or decided upon. ▶adj. **1** (esp. of food) of very good quality. **2** (of words, phrases, or language) rude and abusive.
– PHRASES **by choice** of one's own volition. **of choice** selected as one's favorite or the best. **of one's choice** that one chooses or has chosen. —**choice·ly** adv. **choice·ness** n. [ME: from OFr. *chois*, from *choisir* 'choose,' of Gmc. origin and rel. to CHOOSE.]

choil /CHoil/ ▶n. the end of a knife's cutting edge that is nearer to the handle. [19th C.: of unknown origin.]

choir /ˈkwī(ə)r/ ▶n. an organized group of singers, typically one that takes part in church services or performs regularly in public. ■ one of two or more subdivisions of such a group performing together. ■ the part of a cathedral or large church between the altar and the nave, used by the choir and clergy. ■ a group of instruments of one family playing together. [ME *quer, quere*, from OFr. *quer*, from L. *chorus* (see CHORUS).]

choir·boy /ˈkwī(ə)rˌboi/ ▶n. a boy who sings in a church or cathedral choir.

choir·girl /ˈkwī(ə)rˌgərl/ ▶n. a girl who sings in a church or cathedral choir.

choir·mas·ter /ˈkwī(ə)rˌmastər/ ▶n. the conductor of a choir.

choke[1] /CHōk/ ▶v. **1** [intrans.] (of a person or animal) have severe difficulty in breathing because of a constricted or obstructed throat or a lack of air. ■ [trans.] hinder or obstruct the breathing of (a person or animal) in such a way. ■ [trans.] retard the growth of or kill (a plant) by depriving it of light, air, or nourishment. ■ [trans.] (often **be choked with**) fill (a passage or space), esp. so as to make movement difficult or impossible. ■ [trans.] prevent or suppress (the occurrence of something). **2** [trans.] (often **be choked**) overwhelm and make (someone) speechless with a strong and typically negative feeling or emotion: *she was choked with angry emotion* | [intrans.] *I just choked up reading it.* ■ [intrans.] informal (in sports) fail to perform at a crucial point of a game or contest owing to a failure of nerve. **3** [trans.] enrich the fuel mixture in (a gasoline engine) by reducing the intake of air. ▶n. **1** a valve in the carburetor of a gasoline engine that is used to reduce the amount of air in the fuel mixture when the engine is started. ■ a knob that controls such a valve. ■ a narrowed part of a shotgun bore, typically near the muzzle and serving to restrict the spread of the shot. ■ informal an electrical inductor, esp. an inductance coil used to smooth the variations of an alternating current or to alter its phase. **2** an action or sound of a person or animal having or seeming to have difficulty in breathing.
– PHRASAL VERBS **choke something back** suppress a strong emotion or the expression of such an emotion. **choke something down** swallow something with difficulty. **choke up** (in sports) grip (a bat, racket, etc.) further from the narrow end than is usual. [ME: from OE *ācēocian* (v.), from *cēoce* (see CHEEK).]

choke[2] ▶n. the inedible mass of silky fibers at the center of a globe artichoke. [17th C.: prob. confusion of the ending of *artichoke* with CHOKE[1].]

choke·ber·ry /ˈCHōkˌberē/ ▶n. a North American shrub (genus *Aronia*) of the rose family, with white flowers and red autumn foliage, cultivated as an ornamental. ■ the berrylike fruit of this shrub, which is bitter and unpalatable.

choke chain ▶n. a chain formed into a loop by passing one end through a ring on the other, placed around a dog's neck to exert control by causing pressure on the windpipe when the dog pulls.

choke·cher·ry /ˈCHōkˌCHerē/ ▶n. a North American cherry (*Prunus virginiana*) with an edible astringent fruit that is more palatable when cooked.

choke·damp /ˈCHōkˌdamp/ ▶n. another term for BLACKDAMP.

choke·hold /ˈCHōkˌhōld/ ▶n. a tight grip around a person's neck, used to restrain him or her by restricting breathing.

choke point ▶n. a point of congestion or blockage.

chok·er /ˈCHōkər/ ▶n. **1** a close-fitting necklace or ornamental neckband. ■ a clerical or other high collar. **2** a cable looped around a log to drag it.

Chok·we /ˈCHäkwē/ ▶n. (pl. same) **1** a member of a people living in the Democratic Republic of the Congo (formerly Zaire) and northern Angola. **2** the Bantu language of this people. ▶adj. of or relating to this people or their language.

chok·y /ˈCHōkē/ ▶adj. (**chok·i·er, chok·i·est**) having or causing difficulty in breathing. ■ breathless and overwhelmed with emotion.

cho·la /ˈCHōlə/ ▶n. a Latin American woman or girl with Indian blood, or the girlfriend of a cholo; a mestiza. [19th C.: Amer. Sp. (see CHOLO).]

cho·lan·gi·og·ra·phy /kəˌlanjēˈägrəfē/ ▶n. Med. X-ray examination of the bile ducts, used to locate and identify an obstruction. —**cho·lan·gi·o·gram** /kəˈlanjēəˌgram/ n. [1930s: coined in Sp. from Gk. *kholē* 'bile' + *angeion* 'vessel' + *-graphia* (see -GRAPHY).]

chole- (also **chol-** before a vowel) ▶comb. form Med. Chem. relating to bile or the bile ducts: *cholesterol*. [from Gk. *kholē* 'bile.']

cho·le·cal·cif·er·ol /ˌkōləkalˈsifəˌrôl; -ˌrōl/ ▶n. Biochem. one of the D vitamins, formed by the action of sunlight on the skin. Also called VITAMIN D_3.

cholecyst- ▶**comb. form** relating to the gallbladder: *cholecystectomy.* [from mod. L. *cholecystis* 'gallbladder.']

cho·le·cys·tec·to·my /ˌkōləsisˈtektəmē/ ▶**n.** (pl. **-mies**) surgical removal of the gallbladder.

cho·le·cys·ti·tis /ˌkōləsisˈtītis/ ▶**n.** Med. inflammation of the gallbladder.

cho·le·cys·tog·ra·phy /ˌkōləsisˈtägrəfē/ ▶**n.** Med. X-ray examination of the gallbladder.

cho·le·cys·to·ki·nin /ˌkōləˌsistōˈkīnən/ ▶**n.** Biochem. a hormone that is secreted by cells in the duodenum and stimulates the release of bile into the intestine and the secretion of enzymes by the pancreas.

cho·le·li·thi·a·sis /ˌkōləliˈTHīəsəs/ ▶**n.** Med. the formation of gallstones.

cho·lent /ˈCHôlənt; ˈCHəl-/ ▶**n.** a Jewish Sabbath dish of slowly baked meat and vegetables, prepared on a Friday and cooked overnight. [from Yiddish *tsholnt.*]

chol·er /ˈkälər/ ▶**n.** (in medieval science and medicine) one of the four bodily humors, identified with bile, believed to be associated with a peevish or irascible temperament. Also called **YELLOW BILE.** [ME: from OFr. *colere* 'bile, anger,' from L. *cholera* 'diarrhea' (from Gk. *kholera*).]

chol·er·a /ˈkälərə/ ▶**n.** an infectious and often fatal bacterial disease of the small intestine, caused by the bacterium *Vibrio cholerae* and typically contracted from infected water supplies and causing severe vomiting and diarrhea. [ME: from L. (see **CHOLER**).]

chol·er·ic /ˈkälərik; kəˈlerik/ ▶**adj.** bad-tempered or irritable. ■ hist. influenced by or predominating in the humor called choler. — **chol·er·i·cal·ly** /-ik(ə)lē/ **adv.**

cho·les·ter·ol /kəˈlestəˌrôl; -ˌrōl/ ▶**n.** a compound of the sterol type, $C_{27}H_{45}OH$, found in most body tissues and important in metabolism; high concentrations in the blood are thought to promote atherosclerosis. [19th C.: from Gk. *kholē* 'bile' + *stereos* 'stiff.']

cho·lic ac·id /ˈkōlik/ ▶**n.** Biochem. a compound produced by oxidation of cholesterol. [19th C.: from Gk. *kholikos*, from *kholē* 'bile.']

cho·line /ˈkōlēn/ ▶**n.** Biochem. a strongly basic compound, $HON(CH_3)_3CH_2CH_2OH$, occurring widely in living tissues and important in the synthesis and transport of lipids. [19th C.: coined in Ger. from Gk. *kholē* 'bile.']

cho·lin·er·gic /ˌkōləˈnərjik/ ▶**adj.** Physiol. relating to or denoting nerve cells in which acetylcholine acts as a neurotransmitter. Contrasted with **ADRENERGIC.** [1930s: from **CHOLINE** + Gk. *ergon* 'work.']

cho·lin·es·ter·ase /ˌkōləˈnestəˌrās; -ˌrāz/ ▶**n.** Biochem. an enzyme, esp. acetylcholinesterase, that hydrolyzes esters of choline.

chol·la /ˈCHoi(y)ə/ ▶**n.** a cactus (genus *Opuntia*) with a cylindrical stem, native to Mexico and the southwestern US. [19th C.: ult. from Sp. *cholla* 'skull.']

cho·lo /ˈCHōlō/ ▶**n.** (pl. **-los**) a Latin American with Indian blood; a mestizo. ■ derog. a lower-class Mexican, esp. in an urban area. ■ a teenage boy, esp. in a Mexican-American community, who is a member of a street gang. [19th C.: Amer. Sp., from *Chololián* (now *Cholula*), in Mexico.]

chomp /CHämp; CHômp/ ▶**v.** [intrans.] **1** munch or chew vigorously and noisily. ■ (of a horse) make a noisy biting or chewing action. **2** fret impatiently. ▶**n.** [in sing.] a chewing noise or action.
– PHRASES **chomp** (or **champ** or **chafe**) **at the bit** be restless and impatient to start doing something. [mid 17th C.: prob. imitative.]

Chom·sky /ˈCHäm(p)skē/, Noam (1928–), US theoretical linguist; full name *Avram Noam Chomsky.* He is noted for expounding the theory of generative grammar.

Chon·drich·thy·es /känˈdrikTHēˌēz/ Zool. a class of fishes that includes those with a cartilaginous skeleton. Compare with **OSTEICHTHYES.** [mod. L., from Gk. *khondros* 'cartilage' + *ikhthus* 'fish.']

chon·drite /ˈkänˌdrīt/ ▶**n.** a stony meteorite containing small mineral granules (chondrules). — **chon·drit·ic** /känˈdritik/ **adj.** [19th C.: from Gk. *khondros* 'granule.']

chondro- ▶**comb. form** of or relating to cartilage: *chondrocyte.* [from Gk. *khondros* 'cartilage.']

chon·dro·cra·ni·um /ˌkändrōˈkrānēəm/ ▶**n.** Zool. Embryol. the primary skull of vertebrates, composed of cartilage, which in humans and most other vertebrates is replaced by bone during development.

chon·dro·cyte /ˈkändrəˌsīt/ ▶**n.** Biol. a cell that has secreted the matrix of cartilage and become embedded in it.

chon·dro·i·tin /känˈdroitn; -ˈdrō-itn/ ▶**n.** Biochem. a compound that is a major constituent of cartilage and other connective tissue. [19th C.: from **CHONDRO-** + **-ITE**[1].]

chon·drule /ˈkändrōōl/ ▶**n.** a spheroidal mineral grain present in large numbers in some stony meteorites.

Chong·jin /ˈCHəNGˈjēn/ a port on the northeastern coast of North Korea; pop. 754,100.

Chong·qing /ˈCHəNGˈkiNG/ (also **Chung·king**) a city in Sichuan province, in central China, on the Yangtze River; pop. 2,960,000.

choo-choo /ˈCHōō ˌCHōō/ (also **choo-choo train**) ▶**n.** a child's word for a railroad train or locomotive, esp. a steam engine. [20th C.: imitative.]

choose /CHōōz/ ▶**v.** (past **chose** ; past part. **cho·sen**) [trans.] pick out or select (someone or something) as being the best or most appropriate of two or more alternatives: *he chose a seat facing the door* | [intrans.] *many versions to choose from.* ■ [intrans.] decide on a course of action, typically after rejecting alternatives: [with infin.] *he chose to go.*
– PHRASES **cannot choose but do something** formal have no alternative to doing something. **there is little** (or **nothing**) **to choose between** there is little or no difference between. — **choos·er** **n.** [OE *cēosan*, of Gmc. origin; rel. to Du. *kiezen.*]

choos·y /ˈCHōōzē/ ▶**adj.** (**choos·i·er, choos·i·est**) informal overly fastidious in making a choice. — **choos·i·ly** /-zəlē/ **adv.** **choos·i·ness** **n.**

chop /CHäp/ ▶**v.** (**chopped, chop·ping**) [trans.] cut (something) into small pieces with repeated sharp blows using an ax or knife: *chop the celery into chunks.* ■ (**chop something off**) remove by cutting. ■ cut through the base of (something, esp. a tree) with blows from an ax or similar implement, in order to fell it. ■ strike (a ball) with a short heavy blow, as if cutting at something. ■ (usu. **be chopped**) abolish or reduce the size or extent of (something) in a way regarded as brutally sudden: *training courses are to be chopped.* ▶**n.** **1** a downward cutting blow or movement, typically with the hand. **2** a thick slice of meat, esp. pork or lamb, adjacent to, and typically including, a rib. **3** crushed or ground grain used as animal feed. **4** [in sing.] the broken motion of water, typically due to the action of the wind against the tide.
– PHRASES **chop logic** argue in a tiresomely pedantic way; quibble. [16th C.: from dial. use of *chop*, 'bandy words.'] [ME: var. of **CHAP**[1].]

chop-chop /ˈCHäp ˈCHäp/ ▶**adv. & exclam.** quickly; quick: *"Two beers, chop-chop," Jimmy called.* [19th C.: pidgin Engl., based on Chin. dial. *kuai-kuai.*]

chop·fall·en /ˈCHäpˌfôlən/ ▶**adj.** var. of **CHAPFALLEN.**

chop·house /ˈCHäpˌhous/ ▶**n.** a restaurant that specializes in steaks, chops, and similar fare.

Cho·pin[1] /ˈSHōpan; SHōˈpaN/, Frédéric François (1810–49), French composer and pianist; born in Poland; Polish name *Fryderyk Franciszek Szopen.*

Cho·pin[2] /ˈSHōpan/, Kate (1851–1904), US writer; born *Katherine O'Flaherty.* She wrote *Bayou Folk* (1894) and *The Awakening* (1899).

chop·per /ˈCHäpər/ ▶**n.** **1** a person, tool, or machine that chops. ■ a butcher's cleaver. ■ a device for regularly interrupting an electric current or a beam of light or particles. ■ (**choppers**) informal teeth. **2** informal a helicopter. **3** informal a motorcycle, esp. one with high handlebars and the front-wheel fork extended forward. **4** Baseball a batted ball that makes a high bounce after hitting the ground in fair territory.

chop·ping block /ˈCHäpiNG/ ▶**n.** a block for chopping something on, in particular: ■ a block for chopping wood. ■ a block for chopping food such as meat, vegetables, and herbs. ■ hist. an executioner's block.
– PHRASES **on the chopping block** likely to be abolished or drastically reduced.

chop·py /ˈCHäpē/ ▶**adj.** (**chop·pi·er, chop·pi·est**) (of a sea or river) having many small waves. — **chop·pi·ly** /ˈCHäpəlē/ **adv.** **chop·pi·ness** **n.** [17th C.: from **CHOP.**]

chops /CHäps/ ▶**plural n.** informal **1** a person's or animal's mouth or jaws. ■ a person's cheeks; jowls. **2** the technical skill of a musician, esp. one who plays jazz.
– PHRASES **bust one's chops** informal exert oneself. **bust someone's chops** informal nag or criticize someone. [ME: var. of archaic *chaps* 'jaws; sides of the face.']

chop shop ▶**n.** informal a place where stolen vehicles are dismantled so that the parts can be sold or used to repair other stolen vehicles.

chop·sock·y /ˈCHäpˌsäkē/ ▶**n.** [usu. as adj.] informal kung fu or a similar martial art, esp. as depicted in violent action movies. [1970s: perh. suggested by **CHOP SUEY.**]

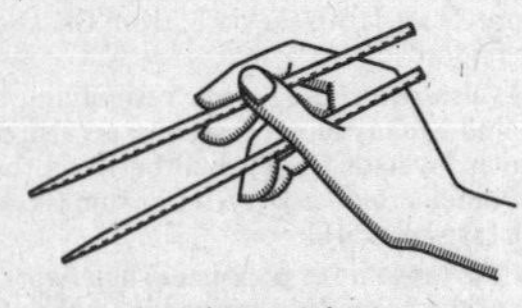

chopsticks

chop·stick /ˈCHäpˌstik/ ▶**n.** (usu. **chopsticks**) each of a pair of small, thin, tapered sticks of wood, ivory, or plastic, held together in one hand and used as eating utensils, esp. by the Chinese, the Japanese, and other people in eastern Asia. [17th C.: pidgin Engl., from *chop* 'quick.']

chop su·ey /ˌCHäp ˈsōōē/ ▶**n.** a Chinese-style dish of meat stewed and fried with bean sprouts, bamboo shoots, and onions, and often served with rice. [19th C.: from Chin. (Cantonese dial.) *tsaâp suì* 'mixed bits.']

cho·ral /ˈkôrəl/ ▶**adj.** composed for or sung by a choir or chorus. ■ engaged in or concerned with singing. — **cho·ral·ly** **adv.** [16th C.: from med. L. *choralis*, from L. *chorus* (see **CHORUS**).]

cho·rale /kəˈral; -ˈräl/ ▶**n.** **1** a musical composition (or part of one) consisting of or resembling a harmonized version of a simple, stately hymn tune. **2** a choir or choral society. [19th C.: from Ger. *Choral(gesang).*]

cho·ral speak·ing ▶**n.** the recitation of poetry or prose by a chorus or ensemble.

chord[1] /kôrd/ ▶**n.** a group of (typically three or more) notes sounded together, as a basis of harmony. ▶**v.** [intrans.] [usu. as n.] (**chording**) play, sing, or arrange notes in chords. — **chord·al** /ˈkôrdl/ **adj.** [ME *cord*, from **ACCORD.**]

chord² ▶**n.** **1** Math. a straight line joining the ends of an arc. ■ Aeron. the width of an airfoil from leading to trailing edge. ■ Engin. each of the two principal members of a truss. **2** Anat. var. of CORD. **3** literary a string on a harp or other instrument.
– PHRASES **strike** (or **touch**) **a chord** affect or stir someone's emotions. **strike** (or **touch**) **the right chord** skillfully appeal to or arouse a particular emotion in others. [16th C.: later spelling of CORD.]

Chor·da·ta /kôr'dätə; -'dātə/ Zool. a large phylum of animals that includes the vertebrates together with the sea squirts and lancelets. — **chor·date** /'kôrdət; -,dāt/ **n. & adj.** [mod. L. (pl.), from L. *chorda* (see CHORD²).]

chore /CHôr/ ▶**n.** a routine task, esp. a household one. ■ an unpleasant but necessary task. [18th C.: var. of obs. *char* or *chare* (see CHARWOMAN).]

cho·re·a /kə'rēə/ ▶**n.** Med. a neurological disorder characterized by jerky involuntary movements affecting esp. the shoulders, hips, and face. See also HUNTINGTON'S CHOREA, SYDENHAM'S CHOREA. [17th C.: via L. from Gk. *khoreia* 'dancing in unison,' from *khoros* 'chorus.']

cho·re·o·graph /'kôrēə,graf/ ▶**v.** [trans.] compose the sequence of steps and moves for (a performance of dance or ice skating). ■ fig. plan and control (an event or operation). — **cho·re·og·ra·pher** /,kôrē'ägrəfər/ **n.** [1940s: back-form. from CHOREOGRAPHY.]

cho·re·og·ra·phy /,kôrē'ägrəfē/ ▶**n.** the sequence of steps and movements in dance or figure skating, esp. in a ballet or other staged dance. ■ the art or practice of designing such sequences. ■ the written notation for such a sequence. — **cho·re·o·graph·ic** /,kôrēə'grafik/ **adj.** **cho·re·o·graph·i·cal·ly** /,kôrēə'grafik(ə)lē/ **adv.** [18th C.: from Gk. *khoreia* 'dancing in unison' (from *khoros* 'chorus').]

cho·ri·am·bus /,kôrē'ambəs/ (also **cho·ri·amb** /'kôrē,am(b)/) ▶**n.** (pl. **-bi** /-bī; -bē/) a metrical foot consisting of two short (or unstressed) syllables between two long (or stressed) ones. — **cho·ri·am·bic** /-'ambik/ **adj.** [18th C.: via late L. from Gk. *khoriambos*, from *khoreios* 'of the dance' + *iambos* (see IAMBUS).]

cho·ric /'kôrik/ ▶**adj.** belonging to, spoken by, or resembling a chorus in drama or recitation. [19th C.: via late L. from Gk. *khorikos*, from *khoros* 'chorus.']

cho·rine /'kôrēn/ ▶**n.** a chorus girl. [1920s: from CHORUS.]

chorio- ▶**comb. form** representing CHORION or CHOROID.

cho·ri·o·al·lan·to·ic /,kôrēō,alən'tō-ik/ ▶**adj.** Embryol. relating to or denoting fused chorionic and allantoic membranes around a fetus.

cho·ri·o·car·ci·no·ma /,kôrēō,kärsə'nōmə/ ▶**n.** (pl. **-no·mas** or **-no·ma·ta** /-'nōmətə/) Med. a malignant tumor of the uterus that originates in the cells of the chorion of a fetus.

cho·ri·oid /'kôrē,oid/ ▶**adj.** another term for CHOROID.

cho·ri·on /'kôrē,än/ ▶**n.** Embryol. the outermost membrane surrounding an embryo of a reptile, bird, or mammal. — **cho·ri·on·ic** /,kôrē'änik/ **adj.** [16th C.: from Gk. *khorion*.]

cho·ri·on·ic vil·lus sam·pling (abbr.: **CVS**) ▶**n.** Med. a test made in early pregnancy to detect congenital abnormalities in the fetus.

chor·is·ter /'kôrəstər; 'kär-/ ▶**n.** **1** a member of a choir, esp. a child or young person singing the treble part in a church choir. **2** a person who leads the singing of a church choir or congregation. [ME *queristre*, based on OFr. *cueriste*, from *quer* (see CHOIR).]

cho·ri·zo /CHə'rēzō; -sō/ ▶**n.** (pl. **-zos**) a spicy Spanish pork sausage.

cho·rog·ra·phy /kə'rägrəfē/ ▶**n.** esp. hist. the systematic description and mapping of regions or districts. — **cho·rog·ra·pher** /-fər/ **n.** **cho·ro·graph·ic** /,kôrə'grafik/ **adj.** [16th C.: via L. from Gk. *khōrographia*, from *khōra* or *khōros* 'region.']

cho·roid /'kôroid/ (also **cho·ri·oid**) ▶**adj.** resembling the chorion, particularly in containing many blood vessels. ▶**n.** (also **choroid coat**) the pigmented vascular layer of the eyeball between the retina and the sclera. — **cho·roi·dal** /kə'roidl/ **adj.** [17th C.: from Gk. *khoroeidēs* (adj.), based on *khorion* (see CHORION).]

cho·roid plex·us ▶**n.** (pl. same or **plex·uses**) a network of blood vessels in each ventricle of the brain. It is derived from the pia mater and produces the cerebrospinal fluid.

chor·o·pleth map /'kôrə,pleTH/ ▶**n.** a map that uses differences in shading, coloring, or the placing of symbols within predefined areas to indicate the average values of a property or quantity in those areas. Compare with ISOPLETH. [1930s: from Gk. *khōra* 'region' + *plēthos* 'multitude.']

Chor·ril·los /CHō'rēōs/ a town in west central Peru; pop. 213,000.

chor·tle /'CHôrtl/ ▶**v.** [intrans.] laugh in a breathy, gleeful way; chuckle. ▶**n.** a breathy, gleeful laugh. [1871: coined by Lewis Carroll; prob. blend of CHUCKLE and SNORT.]

cho·rus /'kôrəs/ ▶**n.** (pl. **-rus·es**) **1** a large organized group of singers, esp. one that performs together with an orchestra or opera company. ■ a group of singers or dancers performing together in a supporting role in a stage musical or opera. ■ a piece of choral music, esp. one forming part of a larger work such as an opera or oratorio. ■ a part of a song that is repeated after each verse, typically by more than one singer. ■ a simple song for group singing, esp. in informal Christian worship. **2** (in ancient Greek tragedy) a group of performers who comment on the main action, typically speaking and moving together. ■ a simultaneous utterance of something by many people. ■ a single character who speaks the prologue and other linking parts of the play, esp. in Elizabethan drama. ■ a section of text spoken by the chorus in drama. ■ a device used with an amplified musical instrument to give the impression that more than one instrument is being played. ▶**v.** (**-rused**, **-rus·ing**) [trans.] (of a group of people) say the same thing at the same time: *they chorused a noisy amen* | [with direct speech] *"Morning, Father," the children chorused.* [16th C.: from L., from Gk. *khoros*.]

cho·rus girl ▶**n.** a young woman who sings or dances in the chorus of a musical.

Cho·rzów /'hô,ZHōōf; 'kô-/ a city in southern Poland; pop. 133,000.

chose /CHōz/ past of CHOOSE.

cho·sen /'CHōzən/ past participle of CHOOSE. ▶**adj.** [attrib.] having been selected as the best or most appropriate.
– PHRASES **chosen few** a group of people who are special or different, typically in a way thought to be unfair. **chosen people** those selected by God for a special relationship with him, esp. the people of Israel; the Jews. ■ those destined to be saved by God; believing Christians.

chou·croute /SHōō'krōōt/ ▶**n.** pickled cabbage; sauerkraut. [Fr., from Ger. dial. *Surkrut* 'sauerkraut.']

Chou En-lai /'jō 'en 'lī/ variant of ZHOU ENLAI.

chough /CHəf/ ▶**n.** a black Eurasian and North African bird (genus *Pyrrhocorax*) of the crow family, with a down-curved bill and broad rounded wings, typically frequenting mountains and sea cliffs. [ME: prob. imitative.]

choux pastry /SHōō/ ▶**n.** very light pastry made with egg, typically used for eclairs and profiteroles. [19th C.: from *choux* or *chou* 'cake' (from Fr. *chou* 'cabbage, rosette.']

chow 2

chow /CHou/ ▶**n.** **1** informal food. **2** (also **chow chow**) a dog of a sturdy Chinese breed with a broad muzzle, a tail curled over the back, a bluish-black tongue, and typically a dense thick coat.
– PHRASAL VERBS **chow down** (or **chow something down**) informal eat. [19th C.: shortened from CHOW CHOW.]

chow chow /'CHou ,CHou/ ▶**n.** **1** another term for CHOW (sense 2). **2** (also **chow-chow**) a Chinese preserve of ginger, orange peel, and other ingredients, in syrup. **3** (also **chow-chow**) a mixed vegetable pickle. [18th C.: pidgin Engl.]

chow·der /'CHoudər/ ▶**n.** a rich soup typically containing fish, clams, or corn with potatoes and onions. [18th C.: perh. from Fr. *chaudière* 'stew pot,' rel. to Old North. Fr. *caudron* (see CAULDRON).]

chow·der·head /'CHoudər,hed/ ▶**n.** informal a stupid person. — **chow·der·head·ed** **adj.** [19th C.: prob. var. of *jolter-head* 'thick-headed person.']

chow mein /'CHou 'mān/ ▶**n.** a Chinese-style dish of fried noodles with shredded meat or seafood and vegetables. [19th C.: from Chin. *chǎo miàn* 'fried noodles.']

Chr. ▶**abbr.** Bible Chronicles.

chres·tom·a·thy /kre'stäməTHē/ ▶**n.** (pl. **-thies**) formal a selection of passages from an author or authors, designed to help in learning a language. [19th C.: from Gk. *khrēstomatheia*, from *khrēstos* 'useful' + *-matheia* 'learning.']

Chré·tien /krā'tyeN -'tyen/, Jean (1934–), prime minister of Canada 1993–2003; full name *Joseph Jacques Jean Chrétien*.

Chré·tien de Troyes /də 'trwä/ (12th century), French poet. His courtly romances on Arthurian themes include *Lancelot* (*c.*1177–81).

chrism /'krizəm/ ▶**n.** a mixture of oil and balsam, consecrated and used for anointing at baptism and in other rites of Catholic, Orthodox, and Anglican Churches. [OE, based on Gk. *khrisma* 'anointing,' from *khriein* 'anoint.']

chris·om /'krizəm/ ▶**n.** hist. a white robe put on a child at baptism. [ME: alt. of CHRISM.]

Chris·sake /krī(s)'sāk/ (also **chris·sake, Chris·sakes, chris·sakes**) ▶**n.** (in phrase **for Chrissake**) informal for Christ's sake (used as an exclamation, typically of annoyance or exasperation). [1920s.]

Christ /krīst/ ▶**n.** the title, also treated as a name, given to Jesus of Nazareth (see JESUS). ▶**exclam.** an oath used to express irritation, dismay, or surprise.
– PHRASES **before Christ** full form of **BC**. — **Christ·hood** **n.** **Christ·like** **adj.** **Christ·ly** **adj.** [OE *Crīst*, from L. *Christus*, from Gk. *Khristos*, lit. 'anointed,' from *khriein* 'anoint.']

Christ·church /'kris(t),CHərCH/ a city in New Zealand, on the eastern coast of South Island; pop. 303,400.

chris·ten /'krisən/ ▶**v.** [trans.] (often **be christened**) give (a baby) a Christian name at baptism as a sign of admission to a Christian Church: [with obj. and complement] *their daughter was christened Jeanette.* ■ give to (someone or something) a name that reflects a notable quality or characteristic: [with obj. and complement] *his colleagues christened him "Millipede."* ■ dedicate (a vessel, building, etc.) ceremonially. ■ informal use for the first time. — **chris·ten·er** /ˈkris(ə)nər/ n. [OE *crīstnian* 'make Christian,' from *crīsten* 'Christian,' from L. *Christianus*, from *Christus* 'Christ.']

Chris·ten·dom /ˈkrisəndəm/ ▸n. dated the worldwide body or society of Christians. ■ the Christian world. [OE *crīstendōm*, from *crīsten* (see CHRISTEN) + *-dōm* (see -DOM).]

Christ·er /ˈkrīstər/ ▸n. informal a sanctimonious or ostentatiously pious Christian.

Chris·tian[1] /ˌkrisCHən/, Fletcher (c.1764–93), English sailor. In April 1789, as first mate under Captain Bligh on the HMS *Bounty*, he seized the ship and cast Bligh and others adrift.

Chris·tian[2] ▸adj. of, relating to, or professing Christianity or its teachings. ■ informal having or showing qualities associated with Christians. ▸n. a person who has received Christian baptism or is a believer in Jesus Christ and his teachings. — **Chris·tian·i·za·tion** /ˌkrisCHənəˈzāSHən/ n. **Chris·tian·ize** /-ˌnīz/ v. **Chris·tian·ly** adv. [ME: from L. *Christianus*, from Gk. *Christianos* (see CHRIST).]

Chris·tian Broth·ers a Roman Catholic lay teaching order founded in France in 1684.

Chris·tian e·ra ▸n. (**the Christian era**) the period of time that begins with the traditional date of Christ's birth.

Chris·ti·an·i·a /ˌkristēˈanēə; ˌkrisCHē-/ (also **Kris·ti·an·i·a**) former name (1624–1924) of OSLO.

Chris·ti·an·i·ty /ˌkrisCHēˈanitē/ ▸n. the religion based on the person and teachings of Jesus of Nazareth, or its beliefs and practices. Christianity is today the world's most widespread religion, mainly divided between the Roman Catholic, Protestant, and Eastern Orthodox Churches. ■ Christian quality or character.

Chris·tian name ▸n. a name given to an individual that distinguishes him or her from other members of the same family and is used as an address of familiarity; a forename, esp. one given at baptism.

Chris·tian Sci·ence ▸n. the beliefs and practices of the Church of Christ Scientist, a Christian sect founded by Mary Baker Eddy in 1879. Members hold that only God and the mind have ultimate reality, and that sin and illness are illusions that can be overcome by prayer and faith. — **Chris·tian Sci·en·tist** n.

Chris·tian·sted /ˈkrisCHənˌsted/ a resort town on Saint Croix Island in the US Virgin Islands; pop. 2,555.

Chris·tie /ˈkristē/, Dame Agatha (1890–1976), English writer. Her works include the novel *Murder on the Orient Express* (1934) and the play *The Mousetrap* (1952).

Christ·mas /ˈkrisməs/ ▸n. (pl. **-mas·es**) the annual Christian festival celebrating Christ's birth, held on December 25. ■ the period immediately before and after December 25. ▸exclam. informal expressing surprise, dismay, or despair. — **Christ·mas·sy** /-məsē/ adj. [OE *Crīstes mæsse* (see CHRIST, MASS).]

Christ·mas cac·tus ▸n. a Brazilian cactus (*Schlumbergera bridgesii* or (*Schlumbergera x buckleyi*) with flattened segmented stems and red, pink, or white flowers, grown as a houseplant.

Christ·mas Day ▸n. the day on which the festival of Christmas is celebrated, December 25.

Christ·mas Eve the day or the evening before Christmas Day, December 24.

Christ·mas fern ▸n. an evergreen fern (*Polystichum acrostichoides*, family Polypodiaceae) with dark green leathery fronds that grow in circular clumps from a central rootstock.

Christ·mas Is·land 1 an island in the Indian Ocean, 200 miles (350 km) south of Java, an external territory of Australia since 1958; pop. 1,275. **2** former name (until 1981) of KIRITIMATI.

Christ·mas stock·ing ▸n. a real or ornamental stocking hung up by children on Christmas Eve for Santa Claus to fill with presents.

Christ·mas tree ▸n. a real or artificial evergreen tree set up and decorated with lights and ornaments as part of Christmas celebrations.

Christo- ▸comb. form of or relating to Christ: *Christology*. [from L. *Christus* or Gk. *Khristos* 'Christ.']

Chris·tol·o·gy /krisˈtäləjē/ ▸n. the branch of Christian theology relating to the person, nature, and role of Christ. — **Chris·to·log·i·cal** /ˌkristlˈäjikəl/ adj. **Chris·to·log·i·cal·ly** /ˌkristlˈäjik(ə)lē/ adv.

Chris·to·pher, St. /ˈkristəfər/ a legendary Christian martyr, adopted as the patron saint of travelers, since it is said that he once carried Christ in the form of a child across a river.

chris·to·phine /ˈkristəˌfēn/ (also **chris·to·phene**) ▸n. another term for CHAYOTE (sense 1). [prob. based on the Fr. given name *Christophe*.]

Christ's thorn ▸n. a thorny shrub popularly supposed to have formed Christ's crown of thorns, in particular either of two shrubs of the buckthorn family: ■ *Paliurus spina-christi* (also called JERUSALEM THORN). ■ *Ziziphus spina-christi* (also called CROWN OF THORNS).

chro·ma /ˈkrōmə/ ▸n. purity or intensity of color. [19th C.: from Gk. *khrōma* 'color.']

chro·maf·fin /krōˈmafin/ ▸adj. [attrib.] Physiol. denoting granules or vesicles containing epinephrine and norepinephrine, and the secretory cells of the adrenal medulla in which they are found. [20th C.: from CHROMO-[1] 'chromium' + L. *affinis* 'akin.']

chro·ma·key /ˈkrōməkē/ ▸n. a technique by which a block of a particular color in a video image can be replaced either by another color or by a separate image, enabling, for example, a weather forecaster to appear against a background of a computer-generated weather map. ▸v. (**-keys, -keyed**) [trans.] manipulate (an image) using this technique.

chro·mate /ˈkrōmāt/ ▸n. Chem. a salt in which the anion contains both chromium and oxygen, esp. one of the anion $CrO_4 2-$. [19th C.: from CHROMIC.]

chro·mat·ic /krōˈmatik/ ▸adj. **1** Music relating to or using notes not belonging to the diatonic scale of the key in which a passage is written. ■ (of a scale) ascending or descending by semitones. ■ (of an instrument) able to play all the notes of the chromatic scale. **2** of, relating to, or produced by color. — **chro·mat·i·cal·ly** /-ik(ə)lē/ adv. **chro·mat·i·cism** /-əˌsizəm/ n. [17th C.: ult. from Gk. *khrōmatikos*, from *khrōma, khrōmat-* 'color.']

chro·mat·ic ab·er·ra·tion ▸n. Optics the material effect produced by the refraction of different wavelengths of electromagnetic radiation through slightly different angles, resulting in a failure to focus.

chro·ma·tic·i·ty /ˌkrōməˈtisətē/ ▸n. the quality of color, independent of brightness.

chro·ma·tid /ˈkrōməˌtid/ ▸n. Biol. each of the two threadlike strands into which a chromosome divides longitudinally during cell division. Each contains a double helix of DNA.

chro·ma·tin /ˈkrōmətin/ ▸n. Biol. the material of which the chromosomes of organisms other than bacteria (i.e., eukaryotes) are composed.

chromato- (also **chromo-**) ▸comb. form color; of or in colors: *chromatopsia* | *chromosome*. [from Gk. *khrōma, khrōmat-* 'color.']

chro·mat·o·gram /krōˈmatəˌgram/ ▸n. a visible record (such as a series of colored bands, or a graph) showing the result of separation of the components of a mixture by chromatography.

chro·mat·o·graph /krōˈmatəˌgraf/ ▸n. an apparatus for performing chromatography. ■ another term for CHROMATOGRAM.

chro·ma·tog·ra·phy /ˌkrōməˈtägrəfē/ ▸n. Chem. the separation of a mixture by passing it in solution or suspension or as a vapor (as in gas chromatography) through a medium in which the components move at different rates. — **chro·mat·o·graph·ic** /krōˌmatəˈgrafik/ adj.

chro·mat·o·phore /krəˈmatəˌfôr; ˈkrōmətə-/ ▸n. a cell or plastid that contains pigment. — **chro·mat·o·phor·ic** /krəˌmatəˈfôrik; ˌkrōmətə-/ adj.

chrome /krōm/ ▸n. chromium plate as a decorative or protective finish on motor-vehicle fittings and other objects. ■ [as adj.] denoting compounds or alloys of chromium. [19th C.: from Fr., from Gk. *khrōma* 'color.']

chrome al·um ▸n. a reddish-purple crystalline compound, $K_2SO_4Cr_2(SO_4)_3.24H_2O$, used in solution in photographic processing and as a mordant in dyeing.

chromed /krōmd/ ▸adj. chromium-plated.

chrome leath·er ▸n. leather tanned with chromium salts.

chrome-mol·y /ˈkrōm ˈmōlē/ (also **chro·mol·y**) ▸n. a strong steel alloy made principally of chromium and molybdenum. [1980s: blend of CHROMIUM and MOLYBDENUM.]

chrome steel ▸n. a hard fine-grained steel containing chromium, used for making tools.

chro·mic /ˈkrōmik/ ▸adj. Chem. of chromium with a higher valence, usually three. Compare with CHROMOUS.

chro·mic ac·id ▸n. Chem. a corrosive and strongly oxidizing acid, H_2CrO_4, existing only in solutions of chromium trioxide.

chro·mi·nance /ˈkrōmənəns/ ▸n. the colorimetric difference between a given color in a television picture and a standard color of equal luminance. [1950s: from Gk. *khrōma* 'color.']

chro·mite /ˈkrōmīt/ ▸n. a brownish-black mineral that consists of a mixed oxide of chromium and iron and is the principal ore of chromium. [19th C.: from CHROME or CHROMIUM.]

chro·mi·um /ˈkrōmēəm/ ▸n. the chemical element of atomic number 24, a hard white metal used in stainless steel and other alloys. (Symbol: **Cr**) [19th C.: from CHROME + -IUM.]

chro·mi·um plate ▸n. a decorative or protective coating of metallic chromium. ■ metal with such a coating. ▸v. (**chro·mi·um-plate**) [trans.] coat with chromium, typically by electrolytic deposition.

chro·mi·um steel ▸n. another term for CHROME STEEL.

chro·mo /ˈkrōmō/ ▸n. (pl. **-mos**) **1** shortened form of CHROMOLITHOGRAPH. **2** informal chromoly.

chromo-[1] ▸comb. form Chem. representing CHROMIUM.

chromo-[2] ▸comb. form var. of CHROMATO-.

chro·mo·dy·nam·ics /ˌkrōmōdīˈnamiks/ ▸plural n. see QUANTUM CHROMODYNAMICS.

chro·mo·gen /ˈkrōməjən/ ▸n. a substance that can be readily converted into a dye or other colored compound.

chro·mo·gen·ic /ˌkrōməˈjenik/ ▸adj. involving the production of color or pigments, in particular: ■ Photog. denoting a modern process of film developing that uses couplers to produce black-and-white or color images of very high definition. ■ Photog. denoting any of a number of similar developing processes. ■ Microbiol. (of a bacterium) producing a pigment.

chro·mo·lith·o·graph /ˌkrōmōˈliTHəˌgraf/ hist. ▸n. a colored picture printed by lithography, esp. in the late 19th and early 20th centuries. ▸v. [trans.] print or produce (a picture) by this process. — **chro·mo·li·thog·ra·pher** /-liˈTHägrəfər/ n. **chro·mo·lith·o·graph·ic** /-ˌliTHəˈgrafik/ adj. **chro·mo·li·thog·ra·phy** /-liˈTHägrəfē/ n.

chro·mo·ly /krō'mälē/ var. of CHROME-MOLY.

chro·mo·phore /'krōmə,fôr/ ▶ n. Chem. an atom or group whose presence is responsible for the color of a compound. — **chro·mo·phor·ic** /,krōmə'fôrik/ adj.

chro·mo·plast /'krōmə,plast/ ▶ n. Bot. a colored plastid other than a chloroplast, typically containing a yellow or orange pigment. [19th C.: from CHROMO-[2] + Gk. *plastos* 'formed.']

chro·mo·some /'krōmə,sōm/ ▶ n. Biol. a threadlike structure of nucleic acids and protein found in the nucleus of most living cells, carrying genetic information in the form of genes. — **chro·mo·so·mal** /,krōmə'sōməl/ adj. [19th C.: coined in Ger. from Gk. *khrōma* 'color' + *sōma* 'body.']

chro·mo·some num·ber ▶ n. Genet. the characteristic number of chromosomes found in the cell nuclei of organisms of a particular species.

chro·mo·sphere /'krōmə,sfi(ə)r/ ▶ n. Astron. a reddish gaseous layer immediately above the photosphere of the sun or another star. — **chro·mo·spher·ic** /,krōmə'sfi(ə)rik; -'sferik/ adj.

chro·mous /'krōməs/ ▶ adj. Chem. of chromium with a valence of two; of chromium(II). Compare with CHROMIC.

Chron. ▶ abbr. Bible Chronicles.

chro·nax·ie /'krōnaksē; 'krä-/ ▶ n. Physiol. the minimum amount of time needed to stimulate a muscle or nerve fiber, using an electric current twice the strength required to elicit a threshold response.

chron·ic /'kränik/ ▶ adj. (of an illness) persisting for a long time or constantly recurring. Often contrasted with ACUTE. ■ (of a person) having such an illness. ■ (of a problem) long-lasting and difficult to eradicate. ■ (of a person) having a particular bad habit. — **chron·i·cal·ly** /-ik(ə)lē/ adv. **chro·nic·i·ty** /krä'nisətē/ n. [ME: from Fr. *chronique*, via L. from Gk. *khronikos* 'of time,' from *khronos* 'time.']

chron·ic fa·tigue syn·drome (abbr.: **CFS**) ▶ n. a medical condition of unknown cause, with fever, aching, and prolonged tiredness and depression, typically occurring after a viral infection.

chron·i·cle /'kränikəl/ ▶ n. a factual written account of important or historical events in the order of their occurrence. ■ a work of fiction or nonfiction that describes a particular series of events. ▶ v. [trans.] record (a related series of events) in a factual and detailed way. — **chron·i·cler** n. [ME: from Anglo-Norman Fr. *cronicle*, var. of OFr. *cronique*, via L. from Gk. *khronika* 'annals,' from *khronikos* (see CHRONIC).]

Chron·i·cles /'kränikəlz/ the name of two books of the Bible, recording the history of Israel and Judah until the return from Exile (536 BC).

chrono- ▶ comb. form relating to time: *chronometry.* [from Gk. *khronos* 'time.']

chron·o·bi·ol·o·gy /,kränōbī'äləjē; ,krō-/ ▶ n. the branch of biology concerned with natural physiological rhythms and other cyclical phenomena. — **chron·o·bi·ol·o·gist** n.

chron·o·graph /'kränə,graf; 'krō-/ ▶ n. an instrument for recording time with great accuracy. ■ a stopwatch. — **chron·o·graph·ic** /,kränə'grafik; ,krō-/ adj.

chron·o·log·i·cal /,kränl'äjikəl/ ▶ adj. relating to the establishment of dates and time sequences. ■ (of a record of several events) starting with the earliest and following the order in which they occurred. ■ calculated in terms of the passage of time rather than some other criterion. — **chron·o·log·i·cal·ly** adv.

chro·nol·o·gy /krə'näləjē/ ▶ n. (pl. **-gies**) the study of historical records to establish the dates of past events. ■ the arrangement of events or dates in the order of their occurrence. ■ a table or document displaying such an arrangement. — **chro·nol·o·gist** n.

chro·nom·e·ter /krə'nämətər/ ▶ n. an instrument for accurately measuring time.

chro·nom·e·try /krə'nämətrē/ ▶ n. the science of accurate time measurement. — **chron·o·met·ric** /,kränə'metrik; ,krō-/ adj. **chron·o·met·ri·cal** /,kränə'metrikəl; ,krō-/ adj. **chron·o·met·ri·cal·ly** /,kränə'metrik(ə)lē/ adv.

chron·o·scope /'kränə,skōp/ ▶ n. a device for measuring short time intervals, esp. in determining the velocity of projectiles, or a person's reaction time.

chron·o·stra·tig·ra·phy /,kränəstrə'tigrəfē; ,krō-/ ▶ n. the branch of geology concerned with establishing the absolute ages of strata. — **chron·o·strat·i·graph·ic** /-,stratə'grafik/ adj.

chrys·a·lis /'krisəlis/ (also **chrys·a·lid** /-,lid/) ▶ n. (pl. **-lis·es**) a quiescent insect pupa, esp. of a butterfly or moth. ■ the hard outer case of this, esp. after being discarded. ■ fig. a preparatory or transitional state. [17th C.: from L. *chrysal(l)is*, *chrysal(l)id-*, from Gk. *khrusallis*, from *khrusos* 'gold' color of the pupae of some species.]

chry·san·the·mum /kri'santHəməm/ ▶ n. (pl. **-mums**) a plant (genera *Chrysanthemum* and *Dendranthema*) of the daisy family, having brightly colored ornamental flowers and existing in many cultivated varieties. ■ a flower or flowering stem of this plant. [from L., from Gk. *khrusanthemon*, from *khrusos* 'gold' + *anthemon* 'flower.']

chrys·el·e·phan·tine /,kriselə'fantēn; -tīn/ ▶ adj. (of ancient Greek sculpture) overlaid with gold and ivory. [19th C.: from Gk. *khruselephantinos*, from *khrusos* 'gold' + *elephas*, *elephant-* 'elephant.']

Chrys·ler /'krīslər/, Walter Percy (1875–1940), US industrialist. He headed Buick Motor Co. 1916–21 and introduced the Chrysler automobile in 1924.

chrys·o·ber·yl /'krisə,berəl/ ▶ n. a greenish or yellowish-green mineral consisting of an oxide of beryllium and aluminum. [17th C.: from L. *chrysoberyllus*, from Gk. *khrusos* 'gold' + *bērullos* 'beryl.']

chrys·o·col·la /,krisə'kälə/ ▶ n. a greenish-blue mineral consisting of hydrated copper silicate. [16th C.: from L., from Gk. *khrusokolla*, a mineral.]

chrys·o·lite /'krisə,līt/ ▶ n. a yellowish-green or brownish variety of olivine. [ME: based on L. *chrysolithus*, based on Gk. *khrusos* 'gold' + *lithos* 'stone.']

chrys·o·mel·id /,krisə'melid; -'mēlid/ ▶ n. Entomol. a beetle of a family (Chrysomelidae) that comprises the leaf beetles and their relatives. [19th C.: from Gk. *khrusomēlon*, lit. 'golden apple.']

chrys·o·prase /'krisə,prāz/ ▶ n. an apple-green variety of chalcedony containing nickel. ■ (in the New Testament) a golden-green precious stone. [ME: from OFr. *crisopace*, via L. from Gk. *khrusoprasos*, from *khrusos* 'gold' + *prason* 'leek.']

Chrys·os·tom, St. John /'krisəstəm; kris'ästəm/ (*c.*347–407), bishop of Constantinople. His attempts to reform the corrupt state of the court, clergy, and people caused him to be banished in 403.

chrys·o·tile /'krisə,tīl/ ▶ n. a fibrous form of the mineral serpentine. Also called WHITE ASBESTOS. [19th C.: from Gk. *khrusos* 'gold' + *tilos* 'fiber.']

chthon·ic /'THänik/ (also **chtho·ni·an** /'THōnēən/) ▶ adj. concerning, belonging to, or inhabiting the underworld. [19th C.: from Gk. *khthōn* 'earth.']

chub /CHəb/ ▶ n. a thick-bodied European river fish (*Leuciscus cephalus*) of the minnow family, with a gray-green back and white underparts, popular with anglers. [ME: of unknown origin.]

chub·by /'CHəbē/ ▶ adj. (**-bi·er, -bi·est**) plump and rounded. — **chub·bi·ly** adv. **chub·bi·ness** n. [17th C.: from CHUB.]

chuck[1] /CHək/ informal ▶ v. [trans.] throw (something) carelessly or casually. ■ throw (something) away. ■ give up (a job or activity) suddenly. ■ break off a relationship with (a partner).
– PHRASES **chuck it all in** abandon a course of action or way of life, esp. for another that is radically different. — **chuck·er** n. [17th C.: from CHUCK[2].]

chuck[2] ▶ v. [trans.] touch (someone) playfully or gently under the chin. ▶ n. a playful touch under the chin. [17th C.: prob. from OFr. *chuquer*, 'to knock.']

chuck[3] ▶ n. **1** a device for holding a workpiece in a lathe or a tool in a drill, typically having three or four jaws that move radially in and out. **2** a cut of beef that extends from the neck to the ribs, typically used for stewing. [17th C., as var. of CHOCK.]

chuck[4] ▶ n. informal food or provisions. [19th C.: perh. same word as CHUCK[3].]

chuck[5] ▶ n. short for WOODCHUCK.

chuck-a-luck /'CHək ə ,lək/ ▶ n. a gambling game played with three dice.

chuck·hole /'CHək,hōl/ ▶ n. a hole or rut in a road or track.

chuck·le /'CHəkəl/ ▶ v. [intrans.] laugh quietly or inwardly. ▶ n. [in sing.] a quiet or suppressed laugh. — **chuck·ler** n. [16th C.: from *chuck* 'to cluck.']

chuck·le·head /'CHəkəl,hed/ ▶ n. informal a stupid person. — **chuck·le·head·ed** adj. [18th C.: from *chuckle* 'big and clumsy,' prob. rel. to CHUCK[3].]

chuck wag·on ▶ n. a wagon with cooking facilities providing food on a ranch, worksite, or campsite. [19th C.: *chuck.*]

chuck·wal·la /'CHək,wälə/ ▶ n. a large dark-bodied lizard (*Sauromalus obesus*, family Iguanidae), the male of which has a light yellow tail, native to the deserts of the southwestern US and Mexico. When threatened, it inflates itself with air to wedge itself into a crevice. [19th C.: from Mex. Sp. *chacahuala*, from Amer. Ind.]

chuck-will's-wid·ow /'CHək ,wilz/ ▶ n. a large nightjar (*Caprimulgus carolinensis*) native to eastern North America. [18th C.: imitative.]

chud·dar /'CHədər/ ▶ n. var. of CHADOR.

chuff /CHəf/ ▶ v. [intrans.] (of a steam engine) move with a regular sharp puffing sound. [20th C.: imitative.]

chug[1] /CHəg/ ▶ v. (**chugged, chug·ging**) [intrans.] emit a series of regular muffled explosive sounds, as of an engine running slowly. ■ [no obj., with adverbial of direction] (of a vehicle or boat) move slowly making such sounds. ▶ n. a muffled explosive sound or a series of such sounds. [19th C.: imitative.]

chug[2] (also **chug·a·lug** or **chug-a-lug** /'CHəgə,ləg/) ▶ v. (**chugged, chug·ging**) [trans.] informal consume (a drink) in large gulps without pausing. [1980s: imitative.]

Chu·gach Moun·tains /'CHōōgaCH; -gaSH/ a range of mountains, part of the Coast Ranges, in southern Alaska.

chu·kar /'CHōōkär; CHōō'kär/ (also **chukar partridge**) ▶ n. a Eurasian partridge (genus *Alectoris*) similar to the red-legged partridge, but with a call like a clucking domestic hen. [19th C.: from Sanskrit *cakora.*]

Chuk·chi /'CHōōkCHē/ (also **Chuk·chee**) ▶ n. (pl. same or **-chis**) **1** a member of an indigenous people of extreme northeastern Siberia. **2** the language of this people, which belongs to a small, isolated language family. ▶ adj. of or relating to this people or their language. [Russ. (pl.).]

Chuk·chi Sea part of the Arctic Ocean that lies between North America and Asia.

chuk·ker /'CHəkər/ (also **chuk·ka** /'CHəkə/) ▶ n. each of typically six periods into which play in a game of polo is divided, lasting 7 1/2 minutes. [19th C.: from Hindi *cakkar*, from Sanskrit *cakra* 'circle or wheel.']

Chu·la Vis·ta /,CHōōlə 'vistə/ a city in southwestern California, south of San Diego, near the Mexican border; pop. 173,556.

chum[1] /CHəm/ informal, dated ▶**n.** a close friend. ■a form of address expressing familiarity or friendliness. ▶**v.** (**chummed, chum·ming**) [intrans.] be friendly to or form a friendship with someone. —**chum·mi·ly adv. chum·mi·ness n. chum·my adj.** [17th C.: prob. short for *chamber-fellow*.]

chum[2] ▶**n.** chopped fish, fish fluids, and other material thrown overboard as angling bait. ■refuse from fish, esp. that remaining after expressing oil. ▶**v.** [intrans.] use chum as bait when fishing. [19th C.: of unknown origin.]

chum[3] (also **chum salmon**) ▶**n.** (pl. same or **chums**) a large North Pacific salmon (*Oncorhyncus keta*) that is commercially important as a food fish. [20th C.: from Chinook Jargon *tzum (samun)*, lit. 'spotted (salmon).']

Chu·mash /'CHōō,masH/ ▶**n.** (pl. same or **-mash·es**) **1** a member of an American Indian people inhabiting coastal parts of southern California. **2** the Hokan language of this people. ▶**adj.** of or relating to this people or their language. [Chumash, lit. 'islander.']

chump /CHəmp/ ▶**n.** informal a foolish person. ■an easily deceived person; a sucker. [18th C.: prob. a blend of CHUNK[1] and LUMP[1] or STUMP.]

Chun·chon /'CHōōn'CHən/ a city in northeastern South Korea, the capital of Kangwon province; pop. 179,000.

Chung·king /'CHŏŏNG'KING/ variant of **CHONGQING**.

Chung·shan /'CHŏŏNG 'SHän/ variant of **ZHONGSHAN**.

chunk[1] /CHəNGk/ ▶**n.** a thick, solid piece of something. ■[in sing.] an amount or part of something. ▶**v.** [trans.] divide (something) into chunks. [17th C.: appar. alt. of CHUCK[3].]

chunk[2] ▶**v.** [intrans.] move with or make a muffled, metallic sound: *the door chunked behind them.* [19th C.: imitative.]

chunk·y /'CHəNGkē/ ▶**adj.** (**chunk·i·er, chunk·i·est**) **1** (of a person) short and sturdy. ■bulky and solid. ■(of wool or a woolen garment) thick and bulky. **2** (of food) containing chunks. —**chunk·i·ly adv. chunk·i·ness n.**

Chun·nel /'CHənl/ ▶**n.** informal short for **CHANNEL TUNNEL**. [1920s: blend.]

chup·pah /'KHŏŏpə/ (also **chup·pa**) ▶**n.** (pl. **chup·pot** /'KHŏŏpōt; -ōs/) a canopy beneath which Jewish marriage ceremonies are performed. [19th C.: from Heb. *ḥuppāh* 'cover.']

Chu·qui·sa·ca /,CHŏŏkē'säkə/ former name (1539–1840) of **SUCRE**[1].

Church /CHərCH/, Frederick Edwin (1826–1900), US painter, known for his landscapes.

church /CHərCH/ ▶**n.** a building used for public Christian worship. ■(usu. **Church**) a particular Christian organization, typically one with its own clergy, buildings, and distinctive doctrines: *the Church of England.* ■(**the Church**) the hierarchy of clergy of such an organization, esp. the Roman Catholic Church or the Church of England. ■institutionalized religion as a political or social force. ■the body of all Christians. [OE *cir(i)ce, cyr(i)ce*, based on med. Greek *kurikon*, from Gk. *kuriakon (dōma)* 'Lord's (house),' from *kurios* 'master or lord.']

Church·es of Christ a number of Protestant denominations, chiefly in the US, originating in the Disciples of Christ but later separated over doctrinal issues.

Church Fa·thers ▶**n.** see **FATHER** (sense 3).

church·go·er /'CHərCH,gōər/ ▶**n.** a person who goes to church, esp. one who does so regularly. —**church·go·ing** /-,gō-iNG/ **n. & adj.**

Church·ill /'CHər,CHil; 'CHərCH,hil/, Sir Winston Leonard Spencer (1874–1965), prime minister of Britain 1940–45, 1951–55. He wrote *The Second World War* (1948–53). Nobel Prize for Literature (1953).

Church·ill Downs a racetrack in Louisville, Kentucky, site of the annual Kentucky Derby.

Church·ill Riv·er[1] a river that flows for 1,000 miles (1,600 km) from northern Saskatchewan across Manitoba to Hudson Bay.

Church·ill Riv·er[2] a river that flows for 600 miles (1,000 km) across eastern Labrador to the Labrador Sea. Its high falls generate hydroelectric power.

church·man /'CHərCHmən/ ▶**n.** (pl. **-men**) a male member of the Christian clergy or of a church.

Church of Christ, Sci·en·tist ▶**n.** the Christian Science Church.

Church of Eng·land the English branch of the Western Christian Church, which combines Catholic and Protestant traditions, rejects the pope's authority, and has the monarch as its titular head.

Church of Je·sus Christ of Lat·ter-Day Saints ▶**n.** the church of the Mormons.

Church of Rome ▶**n.** another term for **ROMAN CATHOLIC CHURCH**.

Church of Scot·land the national Christian Church in Scotland, established as Presbyterian in 1690.

Church Slav·ic (also **Church Sla·von·ic**) **n.** the liturgical language used in the Orthodox Church in Russia, Serbia, and some other countries. It is a modified form of Old Church Slavic.

church·ward·en /'CHərCH,wôrdn/ ▶**n.** **1** either of the two elected lay representatives in an Anglican parish, formally responsible for movable church property and for keeping order in church. ■a church administrator. **2** esp. Brit. a long-stemmed clay pipe.

church·wom·an /'CHərCH,wŏŏmən/ ▶**n.** (pl. **-wom·en**) a female member of the Christian clergy or of a church.

church·y /'CHərCHē/ ▶**adj.** **1** (of a person) excessively pious and consequently narrow-minded or intolerant. **2** resembling a church. —**church·i·ness n.**

church·yard /'CHərCH,yärd/ ▶**n.** an enclosed area surrounding a church, esp. as used for burials.

churl /CHərl/ ▶**n.** an impolite and mean-spirited person. [OE *ceorl*, of West Gmc. origin; rel. to Ger. *Kerl* 'fellow,' also to **CARL**.]

churl·ish /'CHərlisH/ ▶**adj.** rude in a mean-spirited and surly way. —**churl·ish·ly adv. churl·ish·ness n.**

churn /CHərn/ ▶**n.** a machine or container in which butter is made by agitating milk or cream. ▶**v.** **1** [trans.] (often **be churned**) agitate or turn (milk or cream) in a machine in order to produce butter. ■produce (butter) in such a way. **2** [intrans.] (of liquid) move about vigorously: *the seas churned.* ■[trans.] (often **be churned**) cause (liquid) to move in this way. ■[trans.] break up the surface of (an area of ground): *the earth had been churned up.* **3** [trans.] (of a broker) encourage frequent turnover of (investments) in order to generate commission.
– PHRASAL VERBS **churn something out** produce something routinely or mechanically, esp. in large quantities. [OE *cyrin*, of Gmc. origin; rel. to Mid. Low Ger. *kerne*.]

churr ▶**v. & n.** var. of **CHIRR**.

chur·ri·gue·resque /,CHŏŏrigə'resk/ (also **Chur·ri·gue·resque**) ▶**adj.** Archit. of or relating to the lavishly ornamented late Spanish baroque style. [19th C.: José Benito de *Churriguera* (1665–1725), Sp. architect.]

chur·ro /'CHŏŏrō/ ▶**n.** (pl. **-ros**)a Spanish sweet snack consisting of a strip of fried dough dusted with sugar or cinnamon. [Spanish.]

chute[1] /SHōōt/ (also **shoot**) ▶**n.** a sloping channel or slide for conveying things to a lower level. ■a water slide into a swimming pool. ■short for **CHUTE-THE-CHUTE**. [19th C.: from Fr., 'fall,' from OFr. *cheoite*, fem. past part. of *cheoir* 'to fall,' from L. *cadere*.]

chute[2] ▶**n.** informal a parachute. —**chut·ist** /'SHōōtist/ **n.** [1920s: shortened form.]

chute-the-chute (also **chute-the-chutes**) ▶**n.** a steep slide or roller coaster, esp. with water at the foot.

chut·ney /'CHətnē/ ▶**n.** (pl. **-neys**) a spicy condiment made of fruits or vegetables with vinegar, spices, and sugar, originating in India. [19th C.: from Hindi *caṭnī*.]

chutz·pah /'hŏŏtspə; 'KHŏŏtspä/ (also **chutz·pa** or **hutz·pah** or **hutz·pa**) ▶**n.** informal shameless audacity; impudence. [19th C.: Yiddish, from Aramaic *ḥuṣpā*.]

Chu·vash /'CHōōväsh; CHōō'väsH/ ▶**n.** (pl. same) **1** a member of a people living mainly in Chuvashia. **2** the language of this people, probably Turkic. ▶**adj.** of or relating to this people or their language.

Chu·vash·ia /CHōō'väsHēə/ a republic in central Russia, on the Volga; pop. 1,340,000; capital, Cheboksary.

chyle /kīl/ ▶**n.** Physiol. a milky fluid consisting of fat droplets and lymph. It drains from the lacteals of the small intestine into the lymphatic system during digestion. —**chy·lous** /'kīləs/ **adj.** [ME: from late L. *chylus*, from Gk. *khūlos* 'juice' (see **CHYME**).]

chy·lo·mi·cron /,kīlō'mīkrän/ ▶**n.** Physiol. a droplet of fat present in the blood or lymph after absorption from the small intestine. [1920s: from *chylo-* (from **CHYLE**).]

chyme /kīm/ ▶**n.** Physiol. the pulpy acidic fluid that passes from the stomach to the small intestine, consisting of gastric juices and partly digested food. —**chy·mous** /'kīməs/ **adj.** [ME: from late L. *chymus*, from Gk. *khūmos* 'juice.']

chy·mo·tryp·sin /,kīmō'tripsən/ ▶**n.** Biochem. a digestive enzyme that breaks down proteins in the small intestine. [1930s: from *chymo-* (from **CHYME**) + **TRYPSIN**.]

Ci ▶**abbr.** ■cirrus. ■curie.

CIA ▶**abbr.** Central Intelligence Agency.

cia·bat·ta /CHə'bätə/ (also **ciabatta bread**) ▶**n.** a type of flattish, open-textured Italian bread with a floury crust, made with olive oil. [Italian, literally 'slipper' (from its shape).]

ciao /CHou/ ▶**exclam.** informal used as a greeting at meeting or parting. [1920s: Ital., dial. alt. of *schiavo* '(I am your) slave,' from med. L. *sclavus* 'slave.']

ci·bo·ri·um /sə'bôrēəm/ ▶**n.** (pl. **-bo·ri·a** /-'bôrēə/) **1** a receptacle shaped like a cup with a cover, used for the reservation of the Eucharist. **2** a baldachin. [16th C.: via med. L. from Gk. *kibōrion* 'seed vessel of the water lily.']

ci·ca·da /sə'kādə; sə'kädə/ ▶**n.** a large homopterous insect (family Cicadidae, suborder Homoptera) with long transparent wings, occurring chiefly in warm countries. The male cicada makes a loud shrill droning noise after dark by vibrating two membranes on its abdomen. [ME: from L. *cicada, cicala*.]

cicada

cic·a·trix /'sikə,triks/ (also **cic·a·trice** /-,tris/) ▶**n.** (pl. **cic·a·tri·ces** /,sikə'trīsēz; sə'kātrə,sēz/) the scar of a healed wound. ■a scar on the bark of a tree. ■Bot. a mark on a stem left after a leaf or other part has become detached. —**cic·a·tri·cial** /,sikə'trisHəl/ **adj.** [ME: from L. *cicatrix* or OFr. *cicatrice*.]

cic·a·trize /ˈsikəˌtrīz/ ▶ **v.** (with reference to a wound) heal by scar formation: [trans.] *it was used to cicatrize certain types of wounds* | [intrans.] *his wound had cicatrized.* — **cic·a·tri·za·tion** /ˌsikətrəˈzāshən/ **n.** [ME: from OFr. *cicatriser*, from *cicatrice* (see CICATRIX).]

cic·e·ly /ˈsisilē/ (also **sweet cicely**) ▶ **n.** (pl. **-lies**) an aromatic white-flowered plant (genera *Myrrhis* and *Osmorhiza*) of the parsley family, with fernlike leaves. [16th C.: from L. *seselis*, from Gk.]

Cic·e·ro[1] /ˈsisəˌrō/ a town in northeastern Illinois; pop. 85,616.

Cic·e·ro[2], Marcus Tullius (106–43 BC), Roman orator and writer. A supporter of Pompey against Julius Caesar. In his speeches, he attacked Mark Antony, who had him put to death.

cic·e·ro·ne /ˌsisəˈrōnē; ˌchēchə-/ ▶ **n.** (pl. **-ro·ni** pronunc. same) a guide who gives information about antiquities and places of interest to sightseers. [18th C.: from Ital., from L. *Cicero, Ciceron-* (see CICERO[2]).]

Cic·e·ro·ni·an /ˌsisəˈrōnēən/ ▶ **adj.** characteristic of the work, thought, or style of Cicero.

cich·lid /ˈsiklid/ ▶ **n.** Zool. a perchlike freshwater fish of a family (Cichlidae) widely distributed in tropical countries. Cichlids provide a valuable source of food in some areas, and many are popular in aquariums. [19th C.: from mod. L. *Cichlidae* (pl.), from Gk. *kikhlē*, a fish.]

CID ▶ **abbr.** (in the UK) Criminal Investigation Department.

Cid, El /el ˈsid/ (also **the Cid**), Count of Bivar (*c.*1043–99), Spanish soldier; born *Rodrigo Díaz de Vivar*. A champion of Christianity against the Moors, he captured Valencia in 1094.

-cide ▶ **comb. form 1** denoting a person or substance that kills: *insecticide.* **2** denoting an act of killing: *homicide.* [via Fr.; sense 1 from L. *-cida*; sense 2 from L. *-cidium*, both from *caedere* 'kill.']

ci·der /ˈsīdər/ ▶ **n.** (also **sweet cider**) an unfermented drink made by crushing fruit, typically apples. ■ (also **hard cider**) an alcoholic drink made from fermented crushed fruit, typically apples. [ME: from OFr. *sidre*, based on eccles. Gk. *sikera*, from Heb. *šēkār* 'strong drink.']

ci-de·vant /ˌsē dəˈväɴ/ ▶ **adj.** [attrib.] former. [18th C.: Fr., lit. 'heretofore.']

Cien·fue·gos /syenˈfwāgōs/ a port city in south central Cuba, the capital of Cienfuegos province; pop. 124,000.

CIF (also **C.I.F.**) ▶ **abbr.** cost, insurance, freight (as included in a price).

cig /sig/ ▶ **n.** informal a cigarette.

ci·gar /siˈgär/ ▶ **n.** a cylinder of tobacco rolled in tobacco leaves for smoking.
– PHRASES **close, but no cigar** informal (of an attempt) almost, but not quite successful. [18th C.: from Fr. *cigare*, or from Sp. *cigarro*, prob. from Mayan *sik'ar* 'smoking.']

cig·a·rette /ˌsigəˈret; ˈsigəˌret/ (also **cig·a·ret**) ▶ **n.** a thin cylinder of finely cut tobacco rolled in paper for smoking. ■ a similar cylinder containing a narcotic, herbs, or a medicated substance. ■ (also **Cigarette**) trademark a long, sleek, narrow speedboat. [19th C.: from Fr., dimin. of *cigare*.]

cig·a·ril·lo /ˌsigəˈrilō; -ˈrē(y)ō/ ▶ **n.** (pl. **-los**) a small cigar. [19th C.: from Sp., dimin. of *cigarro* (see CIGAR).]

ci·gua·te·ra /ˌsēgwəˈterə/ ▶ **n.** poisoning by neurotoxins as a result of eating the flesh of a tropical marine fish that carries a toxic dinoflagellate. [19th C.: from Amer. Sp., from *cigua* 'sea snail.']

ci·lan·tro /siˈlantrō; -ˈlän-/ ▶ **n.** another term for CORIANDER (esp. the leaves). [1920s: from Sp., from L. *coliandrum* 'coriander.']

cil·i·a /ˈsilēə/ plural form of CILIUM.

cil·i·ar·y /ˈsilēˌerē/ ▶ **adj. 1** Biol. of, relating to, or involving cilia. **2** Anat. of or relating to the eyelashes or eyelids. ■ of or relating to the ciliary body of the eye.

cil·i·ar·y bod·y ▶ **n.** Anat. the part of the eye that connects the iris to the choroid.

cil·i·ate /ˈsilēˌāt; -ēit/ ▶ **n.** Zool. a single-celled animal of the phylum Ciliophora (kingdom Protista), distinguished by the possession of cilia or ciliary structures. The ciliates are a large and diverse group of advanced protozoans. ▶ **adj.** Zool. (of an organism, cell, or surface) bearing cilia. ■ Bot. (of a margin) having a fringe of hairs. — **cil·i·at·ed** /ˈsilēˌātid/ **adj.**

cil·ice /ˈsiləs/ ▶ **n.** haircloth. [16th C.: from Fr., from L. *cilicium*, from Greek *kilikion*, from *Kilikia*, the Gk. name for CILICIA.]

Ci·li·cia /səˈlishə/ an ancient region on the coast of southeastern Asia Minor. — **Ci·li·cian adj. & n.**

Ci·li·cian Gates /səˈlishən/ a mountain pass in the Taurus Mountains in southern Turkey.

cil·i·o·late /ˈsilēəlit; -ˌlāt/ ▶ **adj.** having cilia.

cil·i·um /ˈsilēəm/ ▶ **n.** (usu. in pl. **cil·i·a** /ˈsilēə/) Biol. Anat. a short, microscopic, hairlike vibrating structure. Cilia occur in large numbers on the surface of certain cells, either causing currents in the surrounding fluid, or, in some protozoans and other small organisms, providing propulsion. ■ an eyelash. — **cil·i·at·ed** /-ˌātid/ **adj.** **cil·i·a·tion** /ˌsilēˈāshən/ **n.** [18th C. (in the sense 'eyelash'): from L.]

Cim·ar·ron Riv·er /ˈsiməˌrän; -ˌrōn/ a river that flows for 600 miles (1,000 km) from New Mexico eastward to the Arkansas River near Tulsa.

ci·met·i·dine /sīˈmetəˌdēn/ ▶ **n.** Med. an antihistamine drug used to treat stomach acidity and peptic ulcers. It is a sulfur-containing derivative of imidazole. [1970s: from *ci-* (alt. of *cy-* in *cyano-*) + *met(hyl)* + -IDE.]

Cim·me·ri·an /səˈmi(ə)rēən; -ˈme(ə)r-/ ▶ **adj. 1** relating to or denoting members of an ancient nomadic people who overran Asia Minor in the 7th century BC. **2** Gk. Mythol. relating to or denoting members of a mythical people who lived in perpetual mist and darkness near the land of the dead. ▶ **n.** a member of the historical or mythological Cimmerian people. [via L. from Gk. *Kimmerios*.]

CINC ▶ **abbr.** Commander in Chief.

cinch /sinch/ ▶ **n. 1** informal an extremely easy task. ■ a sure thing; a certainty. **2** a girth for a Western saddle or pack. ▶ **v.** [trans.] **1** secure (a garment) with a belt. ■ fix (a saddle) securely by means of a girth; girth up (a horse). **2** informal make certain of. [19th C.: from Sp. *cincha* 'girth.']

cinch bug ▶ **n.** another term for CHINCH.

cin·cho·na /siNGˈkōnə; sinˈchōnə/ ▶ **n.** an evergreen South American tree or shrub (genus *Cinchona*) of the bedstraw family, with fragrant flowers and cultivated for its bark. ■ (also **cinchona bark**) the dried bark of this tree, a source of quinine. ■ a drug made from this bark. [18th C.: mod. L., after the Countess of *Chinchón* (died 1641).]

cin·cho·nine /ˈsiNGkəˌnēn; ˈsinchə-/ ▶ **n.** Chem. an alkaloid, $C_{19}H_{22}ON_2$, with antipyretic properties, derived from cinchona bark and used as a substitute for quinine.

cin·chon·ism /ˈsiNGkəˌnizəm; ˈsin-/ ▶ **n.** poisoning due to excessive ingestion of cinchona alkaloids.

Cin·cin·nat·i /ˌsinsəˈnatē/ a city in southwestern Ohio, on the Ohio River; pop. 331,285.

cinc·ture /ˈsiNGkchər/ ▶ **n. 1** literary a girdle or belt. **2** Archit. a ring at either end of a column shaft. [16th C.: from L. *cinctura*, from *cinct-* 'encircled,' from v. *cingere*.]

cin·der /ˈsindər/ ▶ **n.** a small piece of partly burned coal or wood that has stopped giving off flames but still has combustible matter in it. — **cin·der·y adj.** [OE *sinder* 'slag,' of Gmc. origin; rel. to Ger. *Sinter*.]

cin·der block ▶ **n.** a lightweight building brick made from small cinders mixed with sand and cement.

cin·der cone ▶ **n.** a cone formed around a volcanic vent by fragments of lava thrown out during eruptions.

Cin·der·el·la /ˌsindəˈrelə/ ▶ **n.** a person or thing of unrecognized or disregarded merit or beauty. ■ a drudge. ■ [as n.] a neglected aspect of something. [the heroine of a fairy tale, from CINDER + dimin. suffix *-ella*.]

cin·der track (also **cinder path**) ▶ **n.** a footpath or running track laid with fine cinders.

cin·e /ˈsinē/ ▶ **adj.** esp. Brit. cinematographic.

cine- ▶ **comb. form** representing CINEMATOGRAPHIC (see CINEMATOGRAPHY).

cin·e·ast /ˈsinēˌast/ (also **cin·é·aste** or **cin·e·aste**) ▶ **n.** a filmmaker. ■ an enthusiast for or devotee of movies or filmmaking. [1920s: from Fr. *cinéaste*, from *ciné* (from *cinéma*).]

cin·e·ma /ˈsinəmə/ ▶ **n.** esp. Brit. a movie theater. ■ the production of movies as an art or industry. [20th C.: from Fr. *cinéma*, abbrev. of *cinématographe*, from Gk. *kinēma* 'movement.']

cin·e·ma·theque /ˈsinəməˌtek/ ▶ **n. 1** a motion-picture library or archive. **2** a small movie theater, esp. one that shows avant-garde or classic movies. [1960s: from Fr. *cinémathèque*, from *cinéma* 'cinema.']

cin·e·mat·ic /ˌsinəˈmatik/ ▶ **adj.** of or relating to motion pictures. ■ having qualities characteristic of motion pictures. — **cin·e·mat·i·cal·ly** /-ik(ə)lē/ **adv.**

cin·e·ma·tize /ˈsinəməˌtīz/ ▶ **v.** [trans.] adapt (a play, story, etc.) to the cinema; make a movie of.

cin·e·ma·tog·ra·phy /ˌsinəməˈtägrəfē/ ▶ **n.** the art of making motion pictures.— **cin·e·ma·tog·ra·pher** /-fər/ **n.** **cin·e·mat·o·graph·ic** /-ˌmatəˈgrafik/ **adj.** **cin·e·mat·o·graph·i·cal·ly** /-ˌmatəˈgrafik(ə)lē/ **adv.**

ci·né·ma-vé·ri·té /ˈsinəmə ˌveriˈtā; ˈveriˌtā/ ▶ **n.** a style of filmmaking characterized by realistic, typically documentary motion pictures that avoid artificiality and artistic effect. ■ motion pictures of this style collectively. [20th C.: Fr., lit. 'cinema truth.']

cin·e·phile /ˈsiniˌfīl/ ▶ **n.** a person who is fond of motion pictures.

cin·e·plex /ˈsiniˌpleks/ (also **Cin·e·plex**) ▶ **n.** trademark a movie theater with several separate screens; a multiplex. [1970s: blend of CINEMA and COMPLEX.]

cin·e·rar·i·a /ˌsinəˈre(ə)rēə/ ▶ **n.** a plant (genus *Pericallis*) of the daisy family with compact masses of bright flowers, often cultivated as a houseplant. [mod. L., fem. of L. *cinerarius* 'of ashes,' from *cinis, ciner-* 'ashes.']

cin·e·rar·i·um /ˌsinəˈre(ə)rēəm/ ▶ **n.** (pl. **-ums**) a place where the ashes of the cremated dead are kept. — **cin·e·rar·y** /ˈsinəˌrerē/ **adj.** [19th C.: from late L., neut. of *cinerarius* 'of ashes.']

ci·ne·re·ous /səˈni(ə)rēəs/ ▶ **adj.** (esp. of hair or feathers) ash-gray. [ME: from L. *cinereus* 'similar to ashes.']

cin·gu·lum /ˈsiNGgyələm/ ▶ **n.** (pl. **-la** /-lə/) Anat. an encircling structure, in particular: ■ a curved bundle of nerve fibers in each hemisphere of the brain. ■ a ridge of enamel on the base or margin of the crown of a tooth. — **cin·gu·late** /-lit/ **adj.** [19th C.: from L., 'belt,' from *cingere* 'gird.']

cin·na·bar /ˈsinəˌbär/ ▶ **n.** a bright red mineral consisting of mercury sulfide, the only important ore of mercury and sometimes used as a pigment. ■ the bright red color of this; vermilion. [ME: from L. *cinnabaris*, from Gk. *kinnabari*.]

cin·nam·ic /səˈnamik/ ▶ **adj.** of cinnamon. ■ denoting an acidic crystalline powder (**cinnamic acid**), $C_9H_8O_2$, derived from cinnamon or produced synthetically and used in medicine and perfumery.

cin·na·mon /ˈsinəmən/ ▶ **n. 1** an aromatic spice made from the dried bark of a Southeast Asian tree. ■ flavored with cinnamon, or having a similar flavor. ■ a reddish- or yellowish-brown color resembling that of cinnamon. **2** (also **cinnamon tree**) the tree (genus *Cinnamomum*, family Lauraceae) that yields this spice. [ME: from OFr. *cinnamome* (from Greek *kinnamōmon*), and L. *cinnamon* (from Gk. *kinnamon*), both from a Semitic language.]

cin·na·mon bear ▶n. a North American black bear of a variety with reddish-brown hair.

cin·na·mon fern ▶n. a large North American fern (*Osmunda cinnamomea*, family Osmundaceae) whose fertile fronds are cinnamon-colored in spring.

cinque /sinGk; sanGk/ (also **cinq**) ▶n. the five on dice. [ME: from OFr. *cinc, cink*, from L. *quinque* 'five.']

cin·que·cen·to /ˌchinGkwiˈchentō/ ▶n. (**the cinquecento**) the 16th century as a period of Italian culture, with a reversion to classical forms. [Ital., lit. '500' (shortened from *milcinquecento* '1500').]

cinque·foil /ˈsinGkˌfoil; ˈsanGk-/ ▶n. **1** a widely distributed herbaceous plant (genus *Potentilla*) of the rose family, with compound leaves of five leaflets and five-petaled yellow flowers. **2** Art an ornamental design of five lobes arranged in a circle, e.g., in architectural tracery or heraldry. [ME: from L. *quinquefolium*, from *quinque* 'five' + *folium* 'leaf.']

rough-fruited cinquefoil

CIO ▶abbr. Congress of Industrial Organizations.

ci·on ▶n. var. of SCION (sense 1).

ci·pher /ˈsīfər/ (also **cy·pher**) ▶n. **1** a secret or disguised way of writing; a code. ■ a thing written in such a code. ■ a key to such a code. **2** dated a zero; a figure 0. ■ fig. a person or thing of no importance. **3** a monogram. ▶v. **1** [trans.] put (a message) into secret writing; encode. **2** [intrans.] archaic do arithmetic. [ME: from OFr. *cifre*, based on Arab. *ṣifr* 'zero.']

cir. (also **circ.**) ▶abbr. ■ circle. ■ circuit. ■ circular. ■ circulation. ■ circumference.

cir·ca /ˈsərkə/ ▶prep. (often preceding a date) approximately: *built circa 1935*. [19th C.: L.]

cir·ca·di·an /sərˈkādēən/ ▶adj. Physiol. (of biological processes) recurring naturally on a twenty-four-hour cycle. [1950s: from L. *circa* 'around' + *dies* 'day.']

Cir·cas·sian /sərˈkasHən/ ▶adj. relating to or denoting a group of peoples of the northwest Caucasus. ▶n. **1** a member of this people. **2** either of two North Caucasian languages of these peoples. [from *Circassia*, Latinized form of Russ. *Cherkes*, a district in the Caucasus.]

Cir·ce /ˈsərsē/ Gk. Mythol. an enchantress who lived with her wild animals on the island of Aeaea and who turned Odysseus's crew into swine. [via L. from Gk. *Kirkē*.]

cir·ci·nate /ˈsərsəˌnāt/ ▶adj. Bot. rolled up with the tip in the center, for example the young frond of a fern. [19th C.: from L. *circinatus*, past part. of *circinare* 'make round,' from *circinus* 'pair of compasses.']

Cir·ci·nus /ˈsərsənəs/ Astron. a small and faint southern constellation (the Compasses), in the Milky Way next to Centaurus. [L.]

cir·cle /ˈsərkəl/ (abbr.: **cir.** or **circ.**) ▶n. **1** a round plane figure whose boundary (the circumference) consists of points equidistant from a fixed center. See illustration at GEOMETRIC. ■ the line enclosing such a figure. ■ something in the shape of such a figure. ■ a group of people or things arranged to form such a figure. ■ a movement that follows the approximate circumference of such a figure. ■ a dark circular mark below each eye, typically caused by illness or tiredness. ■ a curved upper tier of seats in a theater. **2** a group of people with a shared profession, interests, or acquaintances. ▶v. [trans.] move all the way around (someone or something), esp. more than once: *the two dogs circle each other* | [intrans.] *we circled around the island.* ■ [trans.] (from the air) move in a ring-shaped path above (someone or something), esp. more than once. ■ [intrans.] (**circle back**) move in a wide loop back toward one's starting point. ■ (often **be circled**) form a ring around: *the monastery was circled by a huge wall.* ■ draw a line around.
– PHRASES **come** (or **turn**) **full circle** return to a past position or situation, esp. in a way considered to be inevitable. [OE, from OFr. *cercle*, from L. *circulus* 'small ring,' dimin. of *circus* 'ring.']

cir·cle dance ▶n. a country dance or folk dance, typically following a traditional set of steps, in which dancers form a circle.

cir·clet /ˈsərklit/ ▶n. a circular band, typically one made of precious metal, worn on the head as an ornament. [ME: from CIRCLE.]

cir·cuit /ˈsərkit/ (abbr.: **cir.** or **circ.**) ▶n. **1** a roughly circular line, route, or movement that starts and finishes at the same place. ■ a complete and closed path around which a circulating electric current can flow. ■ a system of electrical conductors and components forming such a path. **2** an established itinerary of events or venues used for a particular activity, typically involving public performance. ■ a series of sporting events in which the same players regularly take part. ■ a series of athletic exercises performed consecutively in one training session: [as adj.] *circuit training.* ■ a regular journey made by a judge around a particular district to hear cases in court. ■ a district of this type. ■ a judicial region formerly administered by traveling judges. ■ a chain of theaters or nightclubs under a single management. ▶v. [trans.] move all the way around (a place or thing): *the trains circuit the capital.* [ME: via OFr. from L. *circuitus*, from *circuire*, var. of *circumire* 'go around,' from *circum* 'around' + *ire* 'go.']

cir·cuit board ▶n. a thin rigid board containing an electric circuit; a printed circuit.

cir·cuit break·er ▶n. an automatic device for stopping the flow of current in an electric circuit as a safety measure.

cir·cu·i·tous /sərˈkyo͞oitəs/ ▶adj. (of a route or journey) longer than the most direct way. —**cir·cu·i·tous·ly** adv. **cir·cu·i·tous·ness** n.

cir·cuit rid·er ▶n. hist. a clergyman who traveled on horseback from church to church.

cir·cuit·ry /ˈsərkitrē/ ▶n. (pl. **-ries**) electric circuits collectively. ■ a circuit or system of circuits performing a particular function in an electronic device.

cir·cu·lar /ˈsərkyələr/ (abbr.: **cir.** or **circ.**) ▶adj. **1** having the form of a circle. ■ (of a movement or journey) starting and finishing at the same place and often following roughly the circumference of an imaginary circle. **2** Logic (of an argument) already containing an assumption of what is to be proved, and therefore fallacious. **3** [attrib.] (of a letter or advertisement) for distribution to a large number of people. ▶n. a letter or advertisement distributed to a large number of people. —**cir·cu·lar·i·ty** /ˌsərkyəˈlaritē/ n. **cir·cu·lar·ly** adv. [ME: from OFr. *circulier*, ult. from L. *circulus*.]

cir·cu·lar func·tion ▶n. Math. another term for TRIGONOMETRIC FUNCTION.

cir·cu·lar·ize /ˈsərkyələˌrīz/ ▶v. [trans.] **1** distribute a large number of letters, leaflets, or questionnaires to (a group of people) in order to advertise something or canvas opinion. **2** Biochem. make (a stretch of DNA) into a circular loop. —**cir·cu·lar·i·za·tion** /ˌsərkyələrəˈzāsHən/ n.

cir·cu·lar po·lar·i·za·tion ▶n. Physics polarization of an electromagnetic wave in which either the electric or the magnetic vector executes a circle perpendicular to the path of propagation with a frequency equal to that of the wave. It is frequently used in satellite communications.

cir·cu·lar saw ▶n. a power saw with a rapidly rotating toothed disk.

cir·cu·late /ˈsərkyəˌlāt/ ▶v. **1** move or cause to move continuously or freely through a closed system or area: [intrans.] *antibodies circulate in the bloodstream* | [trans.] *the fan circulates hot air.* ■ [intrans.] move around a social function in order to talk to many different people. **2** pass or cause to pass from place to place or person to person: [intrans.] *rumors of his arrest circulated* | [trans.] *they were circulating the list.* —**cir·cu·la·tive** /-ˌlātiv; -lətiv/ adj. **cir·cu·la·tor** /-ˌlātər/ n. [15th C.: from L. *circulat-*, from the v. *circulare*, from *circulus*.]

cir·cu·lat·ing dec·i·mal ▶n. another term for REPEATING DECIMAL.

cir·cu·lat·ing li·brar·y ▶n. hist. a small library with books lent for a small fee to subscribers.

cir·cu·la·tion /ˌsərkyəˈlāsHən/ (abbr.: **cir.** or **circ.**) ▶n. **1** movement to and fro or around something, esp. that of fluid in a closed system. ■ the continuous motion by which the blood travels through all parts of the body under the action of the heart. ■ the movement of sap through a plant. **2** the public availability or knowledge of something. ■ the movement, exchange, or availability of money in a country. ■ [in sing.] the number of copies sold of a newspaper or magazine: *the magazine had a large circulation.*
– PHRASES **in** (or **out of**) **circulation** available (or unavailable) to the public; in (or not in) general use. ■ used of a person who is seen (or not seen) in public.

cir·cu·la·to·ry /ˈsərkyələˌtôrē/ ▶adj. of or relating to the circulation of blood or sap.

cir·cu·la·to·ry sys·tem ▶n. Biol. the system that circulates blood and lymph through the body, consisting of the heart, blood vessels, blood, lymph, and the lymphatic vessels and glands. Also called CARDIOVASCULAR SYSTEM.

circum. ▶abbr. circumference.

circum- ▶prefix about; around: *circumambulate.* [from L. *circum* 'around.']

cir·cum·am·bi·ent /ˌsərkəmˈambēənt/ ▶adj. esp. literary surrounding. —**cir·cum·am·bi·ence** n. **cir·cum·am·bi·en·cy** n.

cir·cum·am·bu·late /ˌsərkəmˈambyəˌlāt/ ▶v. [trans.] formal walk all the way around. —**cir·cum·am·bu·la·tion** /-ˌambyəˈlāsHən/ n. **cir·cum·am·bu·la·to·ry** /-ˈambyələˌtôrē/ adj.

cir·cum·cise /ˈsərkəmˌsīz/ ▶v. [trans.] cut off the foreskin of (esp. a baby) esp. as a religious rite. ■ cut off the clitoris, and sometimes the labia, of (a girl or young woman) as a traditional practice among some peoples. [ME: ult. from L. *circumcis-* 'cut around,' from the v. *circumcidere*, from *circum* + *caedere* 'to cut.']

cir·cum·ci·sion /ˌsərkəmˈsizHən; ˈsərkəmˌsizHən/ ▶n. the action or practice of circumcising a young boy or man. See also FEMALE CIRCUMCISION. ■ (**Circumcision**) (in church use) the feast of the Circumcision of Jesus, January 1.

cir·cum·fer·ence /sərˈkəmf(ə)rəns/ (abbr.: **cir., circ.,** or **circum.**) ▶n. the enclosing boundary of a curved geometric figure, esp. a circle. See illustration at GEOMETRIC. ■ the distance around something. ■ the edge or region that entirely surrounds something. —**cir·cum·fer·en·tial** /sərˌkəmfəˈrencHəl/ adj. **cir·cum·fer·en·tial·ly** /sərˌkəmfəˈrencHəlē/ adv. [ME: from OFr. *circonference*, from L. *circumferentia*, from *circum* 'around' + *ferre* 'carry.']

cir·cum·flex /ˈsərkəmˌfleks/ ▶n. (also **circumflex accent**) a mark (^) placed over a vowel in some languages to indicate contraction, length, or pitch or tone. ▶ adj. Anat. bending around something else; curved: *circumflex coronary arteries.* [16th C.: from L. *circumflexus* (from *circum* 'around' + *flectere* 'to bend').]

cir·cum·flu·ent /sər'kəmflo͞oənt; ˌsərkəm'flo͞oənt/ ▶ adj. flowing around; surrounding. — **cir·cum·flu·ence** n. [16th C.: from L. *circumfluent-* 'flowing around,' from v. *circumfluere*, from *circum* + *fluere* 'to flow.']

cir·cum·lo·cu·tion /ˌsərkəmlō'kyo͞osʜən/ ▶ n. the use of many words where fewer would do, esp. in a deliberate attempt to be vague or evasive. — **cir·cum·loc·u·to·ry** /-'läkyəˌtôrē/ adj. [ME: from L. *circumlocutio(n-)*, from *circum* 'around' + *locutio(n-)* from *loqui* 'speak.']

cir·cum·lu·nar /ˌsərkəm'lo͞onər/ ▶ adj. moving or situated around the moon: *a circumlunar flight.*

cir·cum·nav·i·gate /ˌsərkəm'navəˌgāt/ ▶ v. [trans.] sail all the way around (something, esp. the world). ■ humorous go around or across (something): *he helped her to circumnavigate a frozen puddle.* — **cir·cum·nav·i·ga·tion** /-ˌnavə'gāsʜən/ n. **cir·cum·nav·i·ga·tor** /-ˌgātər/ n.

cir·cum·po·lar /ˌsərkəm'pōlər/ ▶ adj. situated around or inhabiting one of the earth's poles. ■ Astron. (of a star or motion) above the horizon at all times in a given latitude.

cir·cum·ro·tate /ˌsərkəm'rōtāt/ ▶ v. [intrans.] to revolve or turn like a wheel.

cir·cum·scribe /'sərkəmˌskrīb/ ▶ v. [trans.] (often **be circumscribed**) **1** restrict (something) within limits: *their movements were strictly monitored and circumscribed.* **2** Geom. draw (a figure) around another, touching it at points but not cutting it. Compare with INSCRIBE. — **cir·cum·scrib·er** n. **cir·cum·scrip·tion** /ˌsərkəm'skripsʜən/ n. [ME: from L. *circumscribere*, from *circum* 'around' + *scribere* 'write.']

cir·cum·so·lar /ˌsərkəm'sōlər/ ▶ adj. moving or situated around the sun.

cir·cum·spect /'sərkəmˌspekt/ ▶ adj. wary and unwilling to take risks. — **cir·cum·spec·tion** /ˌsərkəm'speksʜən/ n. **cir·cum·spect·ly** adv. [ME: from L. *circumspectus*, from *circumspicere* 'look around,' from *circum* + *specere* 'look.']

cir·cum·stance /'sərkəmˌstans; -stəns/ ▶ n. **1** (usu. **circumstances**) a fact or condition connected with or relevant to an event or action. ■ an event or fact that causes or helps to cause something to happen, typically something undesirable. **2** (**circumstances**) one's state of financial or material welfare.
– PHRASES **under no circumstances** never, whatever the situation is or might be. **under** (or **in**) **the circumstances** given the difficult nature of the situation. — **cir·cum·stanced** adj. [ME: from OFr. *circonstance* or L. *circumstantia*, from *circumstare* 'encircle,' from *circum* 'around' + *stare* 'stand.']

cir·cum·stan·tial /ˌsərkəm'stansʜəl/ ▶ adj. **1** (of evidence or a legal case) pointing indirectly toward someone's guilt but not proving it. **2** (of a description) containing full details. — **cir·cum·stan·ti·al·i·ty** /-ˌstansʜē'alitē/ n. **cir·cum·stan·tial·ly** adv.

cir·cum·stan·ti·ate /ˌsərkəm'stansʜēˌāt/ ▶ v. [trans.] rare set forth or support with circumstances or details. — **cir·cum·stan·ti·a·tion** /ˌsərkəm ˌstansʜē'āsʜən/ n.

cir·cum·ter·res·tri·al /ˌsərkəmtə'restrēəl; -tə'rescʜəl/ ▶ adj. moving or situated around the earth.

cir·cum·val·late /ˌsərkəm'valāt/ ▶ v. [trans.] literary surround with or as if with a rampart. ▶ adj. literary surrounded as if by a rampart. [17th C.: from L. *circumvallat-* from v. *circumvallare*, from *circum* 'around' + *vallare*, from *vallum* 'rampart.']

cir·cum·vent /ˌsərkəm'vent/ ▶ v. [trans.] find a way around (an obstacle). ■ overcome (a difficulty), typically in a clever and surreptitious way. — **cir·cum·ven·tion** /-'vencʜən/ n. [ME: from L. *circumvent-* 'skirted around,' from the v. *circumvenire*, from *circum* + *venire* 'come.']

cir·cum·vo·lu·tion /ˌsərkəmvə'lo͞osʜən/ ▶ n. a winding movement, esp. of one thing around another. [ME: from L. *circumvolut-* 'rolled around,' from the v. *circumvolvere*, from *circum* + *volvere* 'roll.']

cir·cum·volve /'sərkəmˌvälv/ ▶ v. rare rotate; revolve. ■ wind, fold, or twist around; enwrap.

cir·cus /'sərkəs/ ▶ n. (pl. **-cus·es**) **1** a traveling company of acrobats, trained animals, and clowns that gives performances, typically in a large tent, in a series of different places. ■ (in ancient Rome) a rounded or oblong arena lined with tiers of seats, used for equestrian and other sports and games. ■ informal a group of people involved in a particular sport who travel around to compete against one another in a series of different places. ■ informal a public scene of frenetic and noisily intrusive activity. **2** [in place names] Brit. a rounded open space in a city where several streets converge: *Piccadilly Circus.* [ME: from L., 'ring or circus.']

ci·ré /sə'rā/ (also **ci·re**) ▶ n. a fabric with a smooth shiny surface obtained by waxing and heating. [1920s: Fr., lit. 'waxed.']

cirque /sərk/ ▶ n. **1** Geol. a half-open steep-sided hollow at the head of a valley or on a mountainside, formed by glacial erosion. Also called CORRIE or CWM. **2** literary a ring, circlet, or circle. [17th C. (sense 2): from Fr., from L. *circus*.]

cir·rho·sis /sə'rōsis/ ▶ n. a chronic disease of the liver marked by degeneration of cells, inflammation, and fibrous thickening of tissue. It is typically a result of alcoholism or hepatitis. — **cir·rhot·ic** /sə'rätik/ adj. [19th C.: mod. L., from Gk. *kirrhos* 'tawny.']

Cir·ri·pe·di·a /ˌsirə'pēdēə; -'pedēə/ Zool. a class of crustaceans that comprises the barnacles. — **cir·ri·ped** /'sirəˌped/ n. **cir·ri·pede** /'sirəˌpēd/ n. [mod. L. (pl.), from L. *cirrus* 'a curl' + *pes, ped-* 'foot.']

cir·ro·cu·mu·lus /ˌsirō'kyo͞omyələs/ ▶ n. cloud forming a broken layer of small fleecy clouds at high altitude, usually 16,500–45,000 feet (5–13 km), typically with a rippled or granulated appearance.

cir·ro·stra·tus /ˌsirō'stratəs; -'strātəs/ ▶ n. cloud forming a thin, semitranslucent layer at high altitude, usually 16,500–45,000 feet (5–13 km).

cir·rus /'sirəs/ ▶ n. (pl. **cir·ri** /'sirī; 'sirē/) **1** cloud forming wispy filamentous tufted streaks at high altitude, usually 16,500–45,000 feet (5–13 km). **2** Zool. a slender tendril or hairlike filament, such as the appendage of a barnacle or the barbel of a fish. ■ Bot. a tendril. [18th C.: from L., lit. 'a curl.']

CIS ▶ abbr. Commonwealth of Independent States.

cis /sis/ ▶ adj. Chem. denoting or relating to a molecular structure in which two particular atoms or groups lie on the same side of a given plane in the molecule, in particular denoting an isomer in which substituents at opposite ends of a carbon–carbon double bond are on the same side of the bond: *the cis isomer of stilbene.* Compare with TRANS. [from CIS-.]

cis- ▶ prefix **1** on this side of; on the side nearer to the speaker: *cisatlantic.* ■ hist. on the side nearer to Rome: *cisalpine.* ■ (of time) closer to the present: *cis-Elizabethan.* Often contrasted with TRANS- or ULTRA-. **2** Chem. (usu. *cis-*) denoting molecules with cis arrangements of substituents: cis-*1,2-dichloroethylene.* [from L. *cis* 'on this side of.']

cis·al·pine /sis'alpīn/ ▶ adj. on the southern side of the Alps. [16th C.: from L. *cisalpinus*.]

Cis·al·pine Gaul /sis'alpīn/ see GAUL[1].

cis·at·lan·tic /ˌsisət'lantik/ ▶ adj. on the same side of the Atlantic as the speaker.

cis·co /'siskō/ ▶ n. (pl. **-coes**) a freshwater whitefish (genus *Coregonus*) of northern countries. Most species are migratory and are important food fishes. [19th C.: of unknown origin.]

cis·lu·nar /sis'lo͞onər/ ▶ adj. between the earth and the moon.

cis·mon·tane /sis'mäntān/ ▶ adj. on this side of the mountains, esp. the Alps. Compare with CISALPINE.

cis·plat·in /sis'platn/ ▶ n. Med. a cytotoxic drug, $Pt(NH_3)_2Cl_2$, containing platinum, used in cancer chemotherapy. [20th C.: from CIS- + PLATINUM.]

cist /sist; kist/ (also **kist**) ▶ n. Archaeol. a coffin or burial chamber made from stone or a hollowed tree. [19th C.: Welsh, lit. 'chest,' from L. *cista*, from Gk. *kistē* 'basket.']

Cis·ter·cian /sis'tərsʜən/ ▶ n. a monk or nun of an order founded in 1098 as a stricter branch of the Benedictines. ▶ adj. of or relating to this order: *a Cistercian abbey.* [from Fr. *cistercien*, from *Cistercium*, the L. name of *Cîteaux*, in France.]

cis·tern /'sistərn/ ▶ n. a tank for storing water, esp. one supplying taps or as part of a flushing toilet. ■ an underground reservoir for rainwater. [ME: from OFr. *cisterne*, from L. *cisterna*, from *cista* 'box.']

cis·tron /'sisträn/ ▶ n. Biochem. a section of a DNA or RNA molecule that codes for a specific polypeptide in protein synthesis. [1950s: from CIS- + TRANS-.]

cit. ▶ abbr. ■ citation. ■ cited. ■ citizen.

cit·a·del /'sitədl; -ˌdel/ ▶ n. a fortress, typically on high ground, protecting or dominating a city. [16th C.: from Fr. *citadelle*, or from Ital. *cittadella*, based on L. *civitas* 'city' (see CITY).]

ci·ta·tion /sī'tāsʜən/ (abbr.: **cit.**) ▶ n. **1** a quotation from or reference to a book, paper, or author, esp. in a scholarly work. ■ a mention of a praiseworthy act or achievement in an official report, esp. that of a member of the armed forces in wartime. ■ a note accompanying an award, describing the reasons for it. ■ Law a reference to a former tried case, used as guidance in the trying of comparable cases or in support of an argument. **2** Law a summons.

cite /sīt/ ▶ v. [trans.] (often **be cited**) **1** quote (a passage, book, or author) as evidence for or justification of an argument or statement, esp. in a scholarly work. ■ mention as an example. ■ praise (someone, typically a member of the armed forces) for a courageous act in an official dispatch. ■ Law induce a former tried case as a guide to deciding a comparable case or in support of an argument. **2** Law summon (someone) to appear in a court of law. ▶ n. a citation. — **cit·a·ble** adj. [ME: from OFr. *citer*, from L. *citare*, from *ciere, cire* 'to call.']

cith·a·ra /'sitʜərə; 'kitʜ-/ (also **kith·a·ra** /'kitʜ-/) ▶ n. an ancient Greek and Roman stringed musical instrument similar to the lyre. [L.]

cith·ern /'sitʜərn; 'sitʜ-/ ▶ n. var. of CITTERN.

cit·ied /'sitēd/ ▶ adj. made into or like a city; occupied by a city or cities.

cit·i·fied /'sitiˌfīd/ (also **cit·y·fied**) ▶ adj. often derog. characteristic of or adjusted to an urban environment. — **cit·i·fi·ca·tion** /ˌsitifi'kāsʜən/ n. **cit·i·fy** /-fī/ (**-fies, -fied**) v.

cit·i·zen /'sitizən; -sən/ (abbr.: **cit.**) ▶ n. a legally recognized subject or national of a state or commonwealth, either native or naturalized. ■ an inhabitant of a particular town or city.
– PHRASES **citizen of the world** a person who is at home in any country. — **cit·i·zen·ry** n. **cit·i·zen·ship** n. [ME: from Anglo-Norman Fr. *citezein*, alt. of OFr. *citeain*, based on L. *civitas* 'city' (see CITY).]

cit·i·zen's ar·rest ▶ n. an arrest by an ordinary person without a warrant, allowable in certain cases.

Cit·i·zens' Band (abbr.: **CB**) ▶ n. a range of radio frequencies that are allocated for local communication by private individuals, esp. by handheld or vehicle radio.

Ci·tlal·té·petl /sētˌläl'tāpetl/ the highest peak in Mexico, north of Orizaba; 18,503 feet (5,699 m). Spanish name PICO DE ORIZABA.

cit·ral /'sitrəl/ ▶ n. Chem. a fragrant liquid, $C_{10}H_{16}O$, occurring in citrus and lemongrass oils and used in flavorings and perfumes.

cit·rate /'sitrāt/ ▶ n. a salt or ester of citric acid.

cit·ric /ˈsitrik/ ▶ **adj.** derived from or related to citrus fruit. [18th C.: from L. *citrus* 'citron tree.']

cit·ric ac·id ▶ **n.** Chem. a sharp-tasting crystalline acid, $C_6H_8O_7$, present in the juice of lemons and other sour fruits. It is made commercially by the fermentation of sugar and used as a flavoring and setting agent.

cit·ric ac·id cy·cle ▶ **n.** another term for **KREBS CYCLE.**

cit·ri·cul·ture /ˈsitriˌkəlCHər/ ▶ **n.** the cultivation of citrus fruit trees.

cit·rin /ˈsitrin/ ▶ **n.** another term for **BIOFLAVONOID.**

cit·rine /siˈtrēn; ˈsitrēn/ ▶ **n.** (also **citrine quartz**) a glassy yellow variety of quartz. ■ a light greenish-yellow. [ME: from OFr. *citrin* 'lemon-colored,' from med. L. *citrinus*, from L. *citrus* 'citron tree.']

cit·ron /ˈsitrən/ ▶ **n.** a shrubby Asian citrus tree (*Citrus medica*) that bears large fruits similar to lemons, but with flesh that is less acid and peels that are thicker and more fragrant. ■ the fruit of this tree. [16th C.: from Fr., from L. *citrus* 'citron tree,' on the pattern of *limon* 'lemon.']

cit·ron·el·la /ˌsitrəˈnelə/ ▶ **n. 1** (also **citronella oil**) a fragrant natural oil used as an insect repellent and in perfume and soap manufacture. **2** the South Asian grass (*Cymbopogon nardus*) from which this oil is obtained. [19th C.: mod. L., from **CITRON** + dimin. suffix *-ella*.]

cit·ron·el·lal /ˌsitrəˈnelal/ ▶ **n.** a terpenoid aldehyde, $C_{10}H_{18}O$, found esp. in citronella, rose, and geranium oils.

cit·rus /ˈsitrəs/ ▶ **n.** (pl. **-rus·es**) a tree of the rue family belonging to the genus *Citrus*, which includes citron, lemon, lime, orange, and grapefruit. Native to Asia, citrus trees are widely cultivated in warm countries for their fruit, which has juicy flesh and pulpy rind. ■ (also **citrus fruit**) a fruit from such a tree. ▶ **adj.** (also **cit·rous**) of or relating to these trees or their fruits. — **cit·rus·y adj.** [19th C.: L., lit. 'citron tree, thuja.']

Cit·rus Heights /ˈsitrəs/ a community in north central California; pop. 107,439.

cit·tern /ˈsitərn/ (also **cith·ern** /ˈsiTHərn; ˈsiT͟H-/) ▶ **n.** a stringed instrument similar to a lute, with a flattened back and wire strings, used in Renaissance Europe. [16th C.: from L. *cithara*, from Gk. *kithara*, a harp.]

cit·y /ˈsitē/ ▶ **n.** (pl. **cit·ies**) **1** a large town. **2** (**the City**) the financial and commercial district of London, England. — **cit·y·ward** /-wərd/ **adj. & adv. cit·y·wards** /-wərdz/ **adv. cit·y·wide adj.** [ME (orig. denoting a town): from OFr. *cite*, from L. *civitas*, from *civis* 'citizen.']

cit·y desk ▶ **n.** the department of a newspaper dealing with local news.

cit·y ed·i·tor ▶ **n.** an editor dealing with local news in a newspaper or magazine.

cit·y fa·ther ▶ **n.** (usu. **city fathers**) a person concerned with or experienced in the administration of a city.

cit·y·fied /ˈsitiˌfīd/ ▶ **adj.** var. of **CITIFIED.**

cit·y hall (often **City Hall**) ▶ **n.** the administration building of a municipal government. ■ [treated as sing.] municipal offices or officers collectively.

cit·y man·ag·er ▶ **n.** an appointed official who directs the administration of a city.

Cit·y of Lon·don the part of London that is within the ancient boundaries, now part of the business and financial district.

cit·y plan·ning ▶ **n.** the planning and control of the construction, growth, and development of a city or town. — **cit·y plan·ner n.**

cit·y·scape /ˈsitēˌskāp/ ▶ **n.** the visual appearance of a city or urban area; a city landscape. ■ a picture of a city.

cit·y slick·er ▶ **n.** esp. derog. a person with the values generally associated with urban dwellers, typically regarded as unprincipled and untrustworthy.

cit·y-state ▶ **n.** esp. hist. a city that with its surrounding territory forms an independent state.

Ciu·dad Bo·lí·var /syo͞oˈdäd bōˈlēvär; syo͞oˈT͟HäT͟H/ a city in southeastern Venezuela, on the Orinoco River; pop. 225,850.

Ciu·dad del Es·te /del ˈestā/ a port city in southeastern Paraguay; pop. 134,000. Called (before 1989) **Puerto Presidente Stroessner.**

Ciu·dad Gua·ya·na /gīˈänə/ (also **Santo Tomé de Guayana**) a city in eastern Venezuela; pop. 543,000.

Ciu·dad Juá·rez /ˈhwäres/ (also **Juárez**) a city in northern Mexico; pop. 790,000.

Ciu·dad Re·al /rāˈäl/ a town in central Spain, capital of Ciudad Real province; pop. 475,000.

Ciu·dad Tru·jil·lo /tro͞oˈhē(l)yō/ former name (1936–61) for **SANTO DOMINGO.**

Ciu·dad Vic·to·ria /vēkˈtôryə/ a city in northeastern Mexico, capital of the state of Tamaulipas; pop. 207,830.

civ·et /ˈsivit/ ▶ **n.** (also **civet cat**) **1** a slender nocturnal carnivorous mammal (*Viverra* and other genera) with a barred and spotted coat and well-developed anal scent glands, native to Africa and Asia. The **civet family** (Viverridae) also includes the genets, linsang, and fossa, and formerly included the mongooses. ■ a strong musky perfume obtained from the secretions of the civet's scent glands. **2** another term for **CACOMISTLE.** ■ the fur of the cacomistle. [16th C.: from Fr. *civette*, from Ital. *zibetto*, from med. L. *zibethum*, from Arab. *zabād*, the perfume.]

civ·ic /ˈsivik/ ▶ **adj.** [attrib.] of or relating to a city or town, esp. its administration; municipal. ■ of or relating to the duties or activities of people in relation to their town, city, or local area. — **civ·i·cal·ly** /-ik(ə)lē/ **adv.** [16th C.: from Fr. *civique* or L. *civicus*, from *civis* 'citizen.']

civ·ic cen·ter ▶ **n.** a municipal building or building complex, often publicly financed, with space for conventions, sports events, and theatrical entertainment.

civ·ics /ˈsiviks/ ▶ **plural n.** [usu. treated as sing.] the study of the rights and duties of citizenship.

civ·ies ▶ **plural n.** var. of **CIVVIES.**

civ·il /ˈsivəl/ ▶ **adj. 1** [attrib.] of or relating to ordinary citizens and their concerns, as distinct from military or ecclesiastical matters. ■ (of disorder or conflict) occurring between citizens of the same country. ■ Law relating to private relations between members of a community; noncriminal. ■ Law of or relating to aspects of the civil (or code) law derived from European systems. **2** courteous and polite. **3** (of time measurement or a point in time) fixed by custom or law rather than being natural or astronomical: *civil twilight starts at sunset.* — **civ·il·ly adv.** [ME: via OFr. from L. *civilis*, from *civis*.]

civ·il court ▶ **n.** a court dealing with noncriminal cases.

civ·il death ▶ **n.** rare or esp. hist. the loss of a citizen's privileges through life imprisonment, banishment, etc.

civ·il de·fense ▶ **n.** the organization and training of civilians for the protection of lives and property during and after attacks in wartime.

civ·il dis·o·be·di·ence ▶ **n.** the refusal to comply with certain laws or to pay taxes and fines, as a peaceful form of political protest.

civ·il en·gi·neer ▶ **n.** an engineer who designs and maintains roads, bridges, dams, and similar structures. — **civ·il en·gi·neer·ing n.**

ci·vil·ian /səˈvilyən/ ▶ **n.** a person not in the armed services or the police force. ▶ **adj.** of, denoting, or relating to such a person.

ci·vil·ian·ize /səˈvilyəˌnīz/ ▶ **v.** [trans.] make (something) nonmilitary in character or function. — **ci·vil·ian·i·za·tion** /səˌvilyənəˈzāSHən/ **n.**

ci·vil·i·ty /səˈvilitē/ ▶ **n.** (pl. **-ties**) formal politeness and courtesy in behavior or speech. ■ (**civilities**) polite remarks used in formal conversation.

civ·i·li·za·tion /ˌsivələˈzāSHən/ ▶ **n.** the most advanced stage of human social development and organization. ■ the process by which a society or place reaches this stage. ■ the society, culture, and way of life of a particular area. ■ the comfort and convenience of modern life, regarded as available only in towns and cities.

civ·i·lize /ˈsivəˌlīz/ ▶ **v.** [trans.] [usu. as adj.] (**civilized**) bring (a place or people) to a stage of social, cultural, and moral development considered to be more advanced: *a civilized society.* ■ [as adj.] (**civilized**) polite and well-mannered. — **civ·i·liz·a·ble adj. civ·i·liz·er n.**

civ·il law ▶ **n.** the system of law concerned with private relations between members of a community rather than criminal, military, or religious affairs. Contrasted with **CRIMINAL LAW.** ■ the system of law predominant on the European continent and of which a form is in force in Louisiana, historically influenced by the codes of ancient Rome. Compare with **COMMON LAW.**

civ·il lib·er·ty ▶ **n.** the state of being subject only to laws established for the good of the community, esp. with regard to freedom of action and speech. ■ (**civil liberties**) a person's rights to be only so subject. — **civ·il lib·er·tar·i·an n.**

civ·il mar·riage ▶ **n.** a marriage solemnized as a civil contract without religious ceremony.

civ·il rights ▶ **plural n.** the rights of citizens to political and social freedom and equality.

civ·il serv·ant ▶ **n.** a member of the civil service.

civ·il serv·ice ▶ **n.** the permanent professional branches of a government's administration, excluding military and judicial branches and elected politicians.

civ·il un·ion ▶ **n.** a legally recognized union of a same-sex couple, with rights similar to those of marriage.

civ·il war ▶ **n.** a war between citizens of the same country.

civ·il year ▶ **n.** see **YEAR** (sense 2).

civ·vies /ˈsivēz/ informal ▶ **plural n.** civilian clothes, as opposed to a uniform. ▶ **adj.** [attrib.] (**civvy**) of or relating to civilians. [19th C.: abbrev.]

CJ ▶ **abbr.** chief justice.

CJD ▶ **abbr.** Creutzfeldt–Jakob disease.

Cl ▶ **symb.** the chemical element chlorine.

cl ▶ **abbr.** centiliter: *70 cl bottles.*

clab·ber /ˈklabər/ ▶ **n.** milk that has naturally clotted on souring. ▶ **v.** curdle or cause to curdle. [19th C.: shortening of **BONNY CLABBER.**]

cla·chan /ˈklaKHən/ ▶ **n.** (in Scotland or Northern Ireland) a small village or hamlet. [ME: from Scot. Gael. and Irish *clachán*.]

clack /klak/ ▶ **v.** make or cause to make a sharp sound or series of such sounds as a result of a hard object striking another: [intrans.] *the sound of her heels clacking* | [trans.] *he clacked the castanets.* ▶ **n.** a sharp sound or series of sounds made in such a way. — **clack·er n.** [ME: imitative.]

Clac·to·ni·an /klakˈtōnēən/ ▶ **adj.** Archaeol. of, relating to, or denoting a Lower Paleolithic culture represented by flint implements found at Clacton-on-Sea in southeastern England.

clad[1] /klad/ past participle of **CLOTHE.** ▶ **adj. 1** clothed: *clad in T-shirts and shorts* **2** provided with cladding: [in comb.] *copper-clad boards.*

clad² ▶v. (**clad·ding** ; past and past part. **clad·ded** or **clad**) [trans.] provide or encase with a covering or coating. [16th C. (in the sense 'clothe'): appar. from CLAD¹.]

clad·ding /ˈkladiNG/ ▶n. a covering or coating on a structure or material.

clade /klād/ ▶n. Biol. a group of organisms believed to have evolved from a common ancestor, according to the principles of cladistics. [1950s: from Gk. *klados* 'branch.']

cla·dis·tics /kləˈdistiks/ ▶plural n. [treated as sing.] Biol. a method of classification of animals and plants according to the proportion of measurable characteristics that they have in common. — **clad·ism** /ˈklād,izəm/ n. **cla·dis·tic** adj.

clado- ▶comb. form relating to a branch or branching: *cladogram.* [from Gk. *klados* 'branch or shoot.']

Cla·doc·er·a /kləˈdäsərə/ Zool. an order of minute branchiopod crustaceans that includes the water fleas. — **cla·doc·er·an** n. & adj. [mod. L. (pl.), from Gk. *klados* 'branch' + *keras* 'horn.']

clad·ode /ˈkladōd/ (also **clad·o·phyll** /ˈkladə,fil/) ▶n. Bot. a flattened leaflike stem. [19th C.: from Gk. *kladōdēs* 'with many shoots,' from *klados* 'shoot.']

clad·o·gen·e·sis /,kladəˈjenəsis/ ▶n. Biol. the formation of a new group of organisms or higher taxon by evolutionary divergence from an ancestral form. — **clad·o·ge·net·ic** /,kladōjəˈnetik/ adj.

clad·o·gram /ˈkladə,gram/ ▶n. Biol. a branching diagram showing the cladistic relationship between a number of species.

Clai·borne /ˈklābôrn/, Craig (1920–2000), US food critic. He was food editor for *The New York Times* 1957–70, 1974–88 and wrote *The New York Times Cookbook* (1961).

claim /klām/ ▶v. [trans.] state or assert that something is the case, typically without providing evidence or proof: *these sunblocks claim protection factors as high as 34.* ■ [trans.] assert that one has gained or achieved (something). ■ [trans.] formally request or demand; say that one owns or has earned (something). ■ [trans.] make a demand for (money) under the terms of an insurance policy. ■ call for (someone's notice and thought): *a most unwelcome event* ***claimed his attention.*** ■ cause the loss of (someone's life). ▶n. **1** an assertion of the truth of something, typically one that is disputed or in doubt. **2** a demand or request for something considered one's due. ■ an application for compensation under the terms of an insurance policy. ■ a right or title to something. ■ (also **mining claim**) a piece of land allotted to or taken by someone in order to be mined. — **claim·a·ble** adj. [ME: from OFr. *claime* (n.), *clamer* (v.), from L. *clamare* 'call out.']

claim·ant /ˈklāmənt/ ▶n. a person making a claim, esp. in a lawsuit or for a government-sponsored benefit.

clair·au·di·ence /kle(ə)rˈôdēəns/ ▶n. the supposed faculty of perceiving, as if by hearing, what is inaudible. — **clair·au·di·ent** adj. & n. [19th C.: from Fr. *clair* 'clear' + AUDIENCE.]

clair·voy·ance /kle(ə)rˈvoiəns/ ▶n. the supposed faculty of perceiving things or events in the future or beyond normal sensory contact. [19th C.: from Fr., from *clair* 'clear' + *voir* 'to see.']

clair·voy·ant /kle(ə)rˈvoiənt/ ▶n. a person who claims to have a supernatural ability to perceive events in the future or beyond normal sensory contact. ▶adj. having or exhibiting such an ability. — **clair·voy·ant·ly** adv. [17th C.: from Fr., from *clair* 'clear' + *voyant* 'seeing' (from *voir* 'to see').]

clam /klam/ ▶n. **1** a marine bivalve mollusk (subclass Heterodonta) with shells of equal size. ■ informal any of a number of edible bivalve mollusks, e.g., a scallop. **2** informal a dollar. **3** colloq. a shy or withdrawn person. ▶v. (**clammed, clamming**) [intrans.] **1** dig for or collect clams. **2** (**clam up**) informal abruptly stop talking, either for fear of revealing a secret or from shyness. [16th C.: appar. from earlier *clam* 'a clamp,' from OE *clam, clamm* 'a bond,' of Gmc. origin; rel. to Ger. *Klemme* and CLAMP.]

common Washington clam

cla·mant /ˈklāmənt; ˈklam-/ ▶adj. forcing itself urgently on the attention. — **cla·mant·ly** adv. [17th C.: from L. *clamant-* 'crying out,' from the v. *clamare.*]

clam·bake /ˈklam,bāk/ ▶n. an outdoor social gathering at which clams and other food are baked or steamed, traditionally in a pit, over heated stones and under a bed of seaweed.

clam·ber /ˈklambər; ˈklamər/ ▶v. [no obj., with adverbial of direction] climb, move, or get in or out of something in an awkward and laborious way: *I clambered out of the trench.* ▶n. [in sing.] a difficult climb or movement of this sort. [ME: prob. from *clamb*, obs. past tense of CLIMB.]

clam·dig·gers /ˈklam,digərz/ ▶n. close-fitting women's casual pants hemmed at mid-calf.

clam·my /ˈklamē/ ▶adj. (**clam·mi·er, clam·mi·est**) unpleasantly damp and sticky or slimy to touch. ■ (of air or atmosphere) damp and unpleasant. — **clam·mi·ly** adv. **clam·mi·ness** n. [ME: from dial. *clam* 'to be sticky,' of Gmc. origin; rel. to CLAY.]

clam·or /ˈklamər/ (Brit. **clam·our**) ▶n. [in sing.] a loud and confused noise, esp. that of people shouting vehemently. ■ a strongly expressed protest or demand, typically from a large number of people. ▶v. [intrans.] (of a group of people) shout loudly and insistently: *the crowds* ***clamored for*** *attention.* ■ make a vehement protest or demand: *scientists are* ***clamoring for*** *a ban on all chlorine substances.* — **clam·or·ous** /-ərəs/ adj. **clam·or·ous·ly** adv. **clam·or·ous·ness** n. [ME: via OFr. from L. *clamor*, from *clamare* 'cry out.']

clamp /klamp/ ▶n. a brace, band, or clasp used for strengthening or holding things together. ■ an electric circuit that serves to maintain the voltage limits of a signal at prescribed levels. ▶v. [with obj. and adverbial of place] (often **be clamped**) fasten (something) in place with a clamp: *the sander is clamped onto the workbench.* ■ fasten (two things) firmly together. ■ hold (something) tightly against or in another thing: *she clamped a hand over her mouth.*

– PHRASAL VERBS **clamp down** suppress or prevent something, typically in an oppressive or harsh manner. — **clamp·er** n. [ME: prob. of Du. or Low Ger. origin and rel. to CLAM.]

clamp·down /ˈklamp,doun/ ▶n. informal a severe or concerted attempt to suppress something.

clam·shell /ˈklam,SHel/ ▶n. the shell of a clam, formed of two roughly equal valves with a hinge. ■ a thing with hinged parts that open and shut in a manner resembling the parts of such a shell, such as a kind of mechanical digger, a portable computer, or a box for takeout food.

clan /klan/ ▶n. a group of close-knit and interrelated families (esp. associated with families in the Scottish Highlands). ■ often informal a family, esp. a large one: *the Kennedy clan.* ■ a group of people with a strong common interest. ■ informal a family or group of plants or animals. [ME: from Scot. Gael. *clann* 'family,' from Old Irish *cland*, from L. *planta* 'sprout.']

Clan·cy /ˈklansē/, Tom (1947–), US writer. His novels include *Hunt for Red October* (1985) and *The Teeth of the Tiger* (2003).

clan·des·tine /klanˈdestin; -tīn; -tēn; ˈklandəs-/ ▶adj. kept secret or done secretively, esp. because illicit. — **clan·des·tine·ly** adv. **clan·des·tin·i·ty** /,klandesˈtinitē/ n. [16th C.: from Fr. *clandestin* or L. *clandestinus*, from *clam* 'secretly.']

clang /klaNG/ ▶n. a loud, resonant metallic sound or series of sounds. ▶v. make or cause to make such a sound: [intrans.] *the plumbing clanged* | [trans.] *the belfry clangs its bell at 9 p.m.* [16th C.: imitative.]

clang·or /ˈklaNGər/ (Brit. **clang·our**) ▶n. [in sing.] a continuous loud banging or ringing sound. — **clang·or·ous** /ˈklaNGərəs/ adj. **clang·or·ous·ly** adv. [16th C.: from L. *clangor*, from *clangere* 'resound.']

clank /klaNGk/ ▶n. a loud, sharp sound or series of sounds, typically made by pieces of metal meeting or being struck together. ▶v. make or cause to make such a sound: [intrans.] *I heard the chain clanking* | [trans.] *Cassie bounced on the bed, clanking the springs.* — **clank·ing·ly** adv. [ME: imitative.]

clan·nish /ˈklanisн/ ▶adj. esp. derog. (of a group or their activities) tending to exclude others outside the group. — **clan·nish·ly** adv. **clan·nish·ness** n.

clans·man /ˈklanzmən/ ▶n. (pl. **-men**) a member of a clan, esp. a male member.

clans·wom·an /ˈklanz,wo͝omən/ ▶n. (pl. **-wom·en**) a female member of a clan.

clap¹ /klap/ ▶v. (**clapped, clap·ping**) [trans.] strike the palms of (one's hands) together repeatedly, typically in order to applaud: *Agnes clapped her hands* | [intrans.] *the crowd clapped.* ■ show approval of (a person or action) in this way. ■ strike the palms of (one's hands) together once, esp. as a signal. ■ slap (someone) encouragingly on the back or shoulder. ■ place (a hand) briefly against or over one's mouth or forehead as a gesture of dismay or regret. ■ (of a bird) flap (its wings) audibly. ▶n. **1** an act of striking together the palms of the hands, either once or repeatedly. ■ a friendly slap or pat on the back or shoulder. **2** an explosive sound, esp. of thunder.

– PHRASES **clap eyes on** see EYE. **clap (someone) in jail** (or **irons**) put (someone) in prison (or in chains).

– PHRASAL VERBS **clap (something) on** abruptly impose (a restrictive or punitive measure). [OE *clappan* 'throb, beat,' of imitative origin.]

clap² ▶n. (usu. **the clap**) informal a venereal disease, esp. gonorrhea. [16th C.: from OFr. *clapoir* 'venereal bubo.']

clap·board /ˈklabərd; ˈklap,bôrd/ ▶n. a long, thin, flat piece of wood with edges horizontally overlapping in series, used to cover the outer walls of buildings. ■ informal a house with outer walls covered in such pieces of wood. — **clap·board·ed** adj. [16th C.: partial translation of Low Ger. *klappholt* 'barrel stave,' from *klappen* 'to crack' + *holt* 'wood.']

clapped-out ▶adj. informal, esp. Brit. (of a vehicle, machine, or person) worn out from age or heavy use and unable to work or operate.

clap·per /ˈklapər/ ▶n. the free-swinging metal piece inside a bell that is made to strike the bell to produce the sound.

clap·per·board /ˈklapər,bôrd/ ▶n. a device of hinged boards that are struck together before filming as a signal to synchronize the starting of picture and sound machinery.

clap·per rail ▶n. a large grayish rail (*Rallus longirostris*) of American coastal marshes. It has a distinctive clattering rattlelike call. [from *clapper*, 'a device for making a loud sound.']

clap·trap /ˈklap,trap/ (also **clap-trap**) ▶n. absurd or nonsensical talk or ideas. [18th C.: from CLAP¹ + TRAP¹.]

claque /klak/ ▶n. a group of people hired to applaud (or heckle) a performer or public speaker. ■ a group of sycophantic followers. [19th C.: Fr., from *claquer* 'to clap.']

cla·queur /klaˈkər/ ▶n. a member of a claque. [19th C.: Fr., from *claquer* 'to clap.']

Clare /kle(ə)r/ a county in the Republic of Ireland, on the western coast in the province of Munster.

clar·ence /ˈklarəns/ (also **Clar·ence**) ▶ **n.** hist. a closed horse-drawn carriage with four wheels, seating four inside and two outside next to the coachman. [19th C.: the Duke of *Clarence*, later William IV.]

Clar·en·don /ˈklarəndən/, Edward Hyde, Earl of (1609–74), English chancellor of Oxford University 1660–67.

Clare of As·si·si, St. /kler/ (1194–1253), Italian abbess. She cofounded the order of Poor Ladies of San Damiano.

clar·et /ˈklarit/ ▶ **n.** a red wine from Bordeaux, or wine of a similar character made elsewhere. ■ a deep purplish-red color. [ME: from OFr. *(vin) claret* and med. L. *claratum (vinum)* 'clarified (wine),' from L. *clarus* 'clear.']

clar·i·fy /ˈklarəˌfī/ ▶ **v.** (**-fies, -fied**) [trans.] **1** make (a statement or situation) less confused and more clearly comprehensible. **2** [often as adj.] (**clarified**) melt (butter) in order to separate out the impurities. — **clar·i·fi·ca·tion** /ˌklarəfiˈkāsʜən/ **n.** **clar·i·fi·er n.** [ME: from OFr. *clarifier*, based on L. *clarus* 'clear.']

clar·i·net /ˌklarəˈnet/ ▶ **n.** a woodwind instrument with a single-reed mouthpiece, a cylindrical tube of dark wood with a flared end, and holes stopped by keys. — **clar·i·net·ist** /-ˈnetist/ (Brit. **clar·i·net·tist**) **n.** [18th C.: from Fr. *clarinette*, dimin. of *clarine*, a bell; rel. to CLARION.]

clarinet

clar·i·on /ˈklarēən/ ▶ **n.** esp. hist. a shrill, narrow-tubed war trumpet. ▶ **adj.** loud and clear. [ME: from med. L. *clario(n-)*, from L. *clarus* 'clear.']

clar·i·ty /ˈklaritē/ ▶ **n.** the quality of being clear, in particular: ■ the quality of coherence and intelligibility. ■ the quality of being easy to see or hear; sharpness of image or sound. ■ the quality of being certain or definite. ■ the quality of transparency or purity. [ME: from L. *claritas*, from *clarus* 'clear.']

Clark[1] /klärk/, George Rogers (1752–1818), American frontiersman. He defended the Illinois frontier against the British during the American Revolution.

Clark[2], Helen Elizabeth (1950–), prime minister of New Zealand 1999– .

Clark[3], Mark Wayne (1896–1984), US general. He served as chief of staff of the US Army ground forces in 1942 and as UN commander and commander in chief of the US Far East command 1952–53.

Clark[4], Tom Campbell (1899–1977), US Supreme Court associate justice 1949–67. He had been U.S. attorney general 1945–49.

Clark[5], William (1770–1838), US explorer. With Meriwether Lewis, he commanded an expedition 1804–06 across the North American continent.

Clarke[1] /klärk/, Sir Arthur Charles (1917–), English writer. He wrote, with Stanley Kubrick, the screenplay for the movie *2001: A Space Odyssey* (1968).

Clarke[2], John Hessin (1857–1945), US Supreme Court associate justice 1916–22.

Clark Fork Riv·er /ˈklärk/ a river that flows for 360 miles (580 km) from western Montana northwest to Pend Oreille Lake.

clark·i·a /ˈklärkēə/ ▶ **n.** a North American plant (genus *Clarkia*, family Onagraceae) with showy white, pink, or purple flowers, cultivated as a border plant in gardens. [mod. L., W. CLARK.]

Clarks·ville /ˈklärksˌvil; -vəl/ a city in north central Tennessee; pop. 103,445.

clar·y /ˈkle(ə)rē/ ▶ **n.** an aromatic herbaceous plant (genus *Salvia*) of the mint family, some kinds of which are used as culinary and medicinal herbs. [ME: from obs. Fr. *clarie*, from med. L. *sclarea*.]

clash /klasʜ/ ▶ **n.** **1** a violent confrontation. ■ an incompatibility leading to disagreement. **2** a mismatch of colors. ■ an inconvenient coincidence of the timing of events or activities. **3** a loud jarring sound made by or resembling that made by metal objects being struck together. ▶ **v.** **1** [intrans.] meet and come into violent conflict: *protestors clashed with police.* ■ have a forceful disagreement: *Clarke has frequently clashed with his colleagues.* ■ be incompatible or at odds: *his thriftiness clashed with Ross's largesse.* **2** [intrans.] (of colors) appear discordant or ugly when placed close to each other. ■ inconveniently occur at the same time. **3** [trans.] strike (cymbals) together, producing a loud discordant sound. — **clash·er n.** [16th C.: imitative.]

clasp /klasp/ ▶ **v.** [trans.] **1** grasp (something) tightly with one's hand: *he clasped her arm.* ■ place (one's arms) around something so as to hold it tightly: *Kate's arms were clasped around her knees.* ■ hold (someone) tightly. ■ (**clasp one's hands**) press one's hands together with the fingers interlaced: *he clasped his hands behind his head.* **2** archaic fasten (something) with a small device, typically a metal one: *one emerald clasped her robe.* ▶ **n.** **1** a device with interlocking parts used for fastening things together. ■ a silver bar on a medal ribbon, inscribed with the name of the battle at which the wearer was present. **2** [in sing.] an embrace. ■ a grasp or handshake. [ME: of unknown origin.]

clasp·ers /ˈklaspərz/ ▶ **plural n.** Zool. a pair of appendages under the abdomen of a male shark or ray, or at the end of the abdomen of a male insect, used to hold the female during copulation. [19th C.: from CLASP.]

clasp knife ▶ **n.** a pocketknife.

class /klas/ ▶ **n.** **1** a set or category of things having some property or attribute in common and differentiated from others by kind, type, or quality. ■ Biol. a principal taxonomic grouping that ranks above order and below phylum or division. **2** the system of ordering a society in which people are divided into sets based on perceived social or economic status. ■ a set in a society ordered in such a way. ■ informal impressive stylishness in appearance or behavior. **3** a group of students who are taught together. ■ an occasion when students meet with their teacher for instruction; a lesson. ■ a course of instruction. ■ all those graduating from a school or college in a particular year. ▶ **v.** [trans.] (often **be classed as**) assign or regard as belonging to a particular category: *conduct that is classed as criminal.* ▶ **adj.** [attrib.] informal showing stylish excellence.

– PHRASES **class act** a person or thing displaying impressive and stylish excellence. **in a class of** (or **on**) **its** (or **one's**) **own** unequaled, esp. in excellence or performance. [16th C.: from L. *classis* 'a division of the Roman people.']

class ac·tion ▶ **n.** Law a lawsuit filed or defended by an individual or small group acting on behalf of a large group.

class con·scious·ness ▶ **n.** awareness of one's place in a system of social classes, esp. (in Marxist terms) as it relates to the class struggle. — **class-con·scious adj.**

clas·sic /ˈklasik/ ▶ **adj.** judged over a period of time to be of the highest quality and outstanding of its kind. ■ (of a garment or design) of a simple elegant style not greatly subject to changes in fashion. ■ remarkably and instructively typical. ▶ **n.** **1** a work of art of recognized and established value. ■ a garment of a simple, elegant, and long-lasting style. ■ a thing that is memorable and a very good example of its kind. **2** (usu. **Classics**) a school subject that involves the study of ancient Greek and Latin literature, philosophy, and history. ■ (usu. **the classics**) the works of ancient Greek and Latin writers and philosophers. **3** a major sports tournament or competition, as in golf or tennis. [17th C.: from Fr. *classique* or L. *classicus* 'belonging to a division,' from *classis* (see CLASS).]

clas·si·cal /ˈklasikəl/ ▶ **adj.** **1** of or relating to ancient Greek or Latin literature, art, or culture. ■ (of art or architecture) influenced by ancient Greek or Roman forms or principles. ■ (of language) having the form used by the ancient standard authors. ■ based on the study of ancient Greek and Latin. **2** (typically of a form of art) regarded as representing an exemplary standard; traditional and long-established in form or style. **3** of or relating to the first significant period of an area of study. ■ Physics relating to or based upon concepts and theories that preceded the theories of relativity and quantum mechanics; Newtonian. — **clas·si·cal·ism n.** **clas·si·cal·i·ty** /ˌklasəˈkalətē/ **n.** **clas·si·cal·ly adv.**

clas·si·cal con·di·tion·ing ▶ **n.** Psychol. a learning process that occurs when two stimuli are repeatedly paired: a response at first elicited by the second stimulus is eventually elicited by the first stimulus alone.

clas·si·cal mu·sic ▶ **n.** serious or conventional music following long-established principles rather than a folk, jazz, or popular tradition. ■ (more specifically) music written in the European tradition during a period lasting approximately from 1750 to 1830, when forms such as the symphony, concerto, and sonata were standardized.

clas·si·cism /ˈklasəˌsizəm/ ▶ **n.** the following of ancient Greek or Roman principles and style in art and literature, associated with harmony, restraint, and adherence to standards of form and craftsmanship, esp. from the Renaissance to the 18th century. Often contrasted with ROMANTICISM. ■ the following of traditional and long-established theories or styles.

clas·si·cist /ˈklasəsist/ ▶ **n.** **1** a person who studies Classics (ancient Greek and Latin). **2** a follower of classicism in the arts.

clas·si·cize /ˈklasəˌsīz/ ▶ **v.** [intrans.] [usu. as adj.] (**classicizing**) imitate a classical style.

Clas·si·co /ˈklasikō/ ▶ **adj.** [postpositive] used in the classification of Italian wines produced in the region from which the type takes its name.

clas·si·fi·ca·tion /ˌklasəfəˈkāsʜən/ ▶ **n.** the action or process of classifying something according to shared qualities or characteristics. ■ Biol. the arrangement of animals and plants in taxonomic groups according to their observed similarities. ■ another term for TAXONOMY. ■ a category into which something is put.

clas·si·fied /ˈklasəˌfīd/ ▶ **adj.** arranged in classes or categories. ■ [attrib.] (of newspaper or magazine advertisements or the pages on which these appear) organized in categories according to what is being advertised. ■ (of information or documents) designated as officially secret and to which only authorized people may have access. ▶ **n.** (**classifieds**) small advertisements placed in a newspaper and organized in categories.

clas·si·fi·er /ˈklasəˌfīər/ ▶ **n.** a person or thing that classifies something. ■ Ling. an affix or word that indicates the semantic class to which a noun belongs, typically used in numerals or other expressions of counting, esp. in Chinese and Japanese, e.g. *head* in *two head of cattle.*

clas·si·fy /ˈklasəˌfī/ ▶ **v.** (**-fies, -fied**) [trans.] (often **be classified**) arrange (a group of people or things) in classes according to shared qualities: *mountain peaks are classified according to their shape.* ■ assign (someone or something) to a particular class or category: *elements are classified as metals or nonmetals.* ■ designate (documents or information) as officially secret or to which only authorized people may have access. — **clas·si·fi·a·ble** /ˌklasəˈfīəbəl/ **adj.** **clas·si·fi·ca·to·ry** /-fikəˌtôrē/ **adj.**

class in·ter·val ▶**n.** Stat. the size of each class into which a range of a variable is divided, as represented by the divisions of a histogram or bar chart.

class·ism /ˈklasˌizəm/ ▶**n.** prejudice against or in favor of people belonging to a particular social class. — **class·ist adj. & n.**

class·less /ˈklasləs/ ▶**adj.** (of a society) not divided into social classes. ■ not showing obvious signs of belonging to a particular social class. — **class·less·ness n.**

class·mate /ˈklasˌmāt/ ▶**n.** a fellow member of a class at school or college.

class·room /ˈklasˌro͞om; -ˌro͝om/ ▶**n.** a room, typically in a school, in which a class of students is taught.

class strug·gle ▶**n.** (in Marxist ideology) the conflict of interests between the workers and the ruling class in a capitalist society, regarded as inevitably violent.

class war (also **class war·fare**) ▶**n.** another term for CLASS STRUGGLE.

class·y /ˈklasē/ ▶**adj.** (**class·i·er**, **class·i·est**) informal stylish and sophisticated. — **class·i·ly adv.** **class·i·ness n.**

clast /klast/ ▶**n.** Geol. a constituent fragment of a clastic rock. [20th C.: back-form. from CLASTIC.]

clas·tic /ˈklastik/ ▶**adj.** Geol. denoting rocks composed of broken pieces of older rocks. [19th C.: from Fr. *clastique*, from Gk. *klastos* 'broken in pieces.']

clath·rate /ˈklaTHrāt/ ▶**n.** Chem. a compound in which molecules of one component are physically trapped within the crystal structure of another. [1940s: from L. *clathratus*, from *clathri* 'lattice bars,' from Gk. *klēthra*.]

clat·ter /ˈklatər/ ▶**n.** [in sing.] a continuous rattling sound as of hard objects falling or striking each other. ■ noisy rapid talk. ▶**v.** make or cause to make a continuous rattling sound: [intrans.] *her coffee cup clattered in the saucer* | [trans.] *she clattered cups and saucers onto a tray.* ■ [no obj., with adverbial of direction] fall or move with such a sound: *the knife clattered to the floor.* [OE of imitative origin.]

Claude Lor·raine /ˌklôd ləˈrān; ˌklōd ləˈren/ (also **Lor·rain**) (1600–82), French painter; born *Claude Gellée*. His works include *Ascanius and the Stag* (1682).

clau·di·ca·tion /ˌklôdəˈkāSHən/ ▶**n.** Med. limping. ■ (also **intermittent claudication**) a condition in which cramping pain in the leg is induced by exercise, typically caused by obstruction of the arteries. [ME: from L. *claudicatio(n-)*, from the v. *claudicare* 'to limp,' from *claudus* 'lame.']

Clau·di·us /ˈklôdēəs/ (10 BC–AD 54), Roman emperor 41–54; full name *Tiberius Claudius Drusus Nero Germanicus*. He restored order after Caligula's decadence and expanded the empire.

clause /klôz/ ▶**n.** **1** a unit of grammatical organization next below the sentence in rank and in traditional grammar said to consist of a subject and predicate. **2** a particular and separate article, stipulation, or proviso in a treaty, bill, or contract. — **claus·al** /ˈklôzəl/ **adj.** [ME: via OFr. *clause*, based on L. *claus-* 'closed,' from the v. *claudere*.]

Clau·se·witz /ˈklouzəˌvits/, Karl von (1780–1831), Prussian general. He wrote *On War* (1833).

Clau·si·us /ˈklouzēəs/, Rudolf (1822–88), German physicist, a founder of modern thermodynamics.

claus·tral /ˈklôstrəl/ ▶**adj.** of or relating to a cloister or religious house. ■ fig. enveloping; confining. [ME: from late L. *claustralis*, from L. *claustrum* 'lock' (see CLOISTER).]

claus·tra·tion /klôˈstrāSHən/ ▶**n.** confinement as if in a cloister.

claus·tro·pho·bi·a /ˌklôstrəˈfōbēə/ ▶**n.** extreme or irrational fear of confined places. — **claus·tro·phobe** /ˈklôstrəˌfōb/ **n.** [19th C.: mod. L., from L. *claustrum* 'lock, bolt.']

claus·tro·pho·bic /ˌklôstrəˈfōbik/ ▶**adj.** (of a person) suffering from claustrophobia: *crowds made him feel claustrophobic.* ■ (of a place or situation) inducing claustrophobia. ▶**n.** a person who suffers from claustrophobia. — **claus·tro·pho·bi·cal·ly adv.**

claus·trum /ˈklôstrəm; ˈklous-/ ▶**n.** (pl. **-tra** /-trə/) Anat. a thin layer of gray matter in each cerebral hemisphere between the lentiform nucleus and the insula. [19th C.: L.]

cla·vate /ˈklāvāt/ ▶**adj.** Bot. Zool. club-shaped; thicker at the apex than at the base. [17th C.: from mod. L. *clavatus*, from L. *clava* 'club.']

clave[1] /klāv/ ▶**n.** (usu. **claves**) Music one of a pair of hardwood sticks used to make a hollow sound when struck together. [1920s: from Latin Amer. Sp., from Sp. *clave* 'keystone,' from L. *clavis* 'key.']

clave[2] archaic past of CLEAVE[2].

clav·i·chord /ˈklavəˌkôrd/ ▶**n.** a small keyboard instrument producing a soft sound by metal blades attached to the ends of key levers that gently press the strings, popular from the early 15th to early 19th centuries. [ME: from med. L. *clavichordium*, from L. *clavis* 'key' + *chorda* 'string.']

clav·i·cle /ˈklavikəl/ ▶**n.** Anat. technical term for COLLARBONE. — **cla·vic·u·lar** /klaˈvikyələr; klə-/ **adj.** [17th C.: from L. *clavicula* 'small key,' dimin. of *clavis*.]

cla·vier /kləˈvi(ə)r; ˈklāvēər; ˈklav-/ ▶**n.** **1** the keyboard of a musical instrument. **2** a keyboard instrument, esp. one with strings, such as the harpsichord. [18th C.: from Ger. *Klavier*, from Fr. *clavier*, from med. L. *claviarius* 'key bearer,' from L. *clavis* 'key.']

clav·i·form /ˈklavəˌfôrm/ ▶**adj.** tech. another term for CLAVATE. [19th C.: from L. *clava* 'club.']

claw /klô/ ▶**n.** a curved pointed horny nail on each digit of the foot in birds, lizards, and some mammals. ■ either of a pair of small hooked appendages on an insect's leg. ■ the pincer of a crab, scorpion, or other arthropod. ■ a mechanical device resembling a claw, used for gripping or lifting. ▶**v.** **1** [intrans.] (of an animal or person) scratch or tear something with the claws or the fingernails: *the kitten clawed at my trousers* | [trans.] *her hands clawed his shoulders.* ■ clutch at something with the hands. ■ (**claw one's way**) make one's way with difficulty by hauling oneself forward with one's hands. ■ [trans.] (**claw something away**) try desperately to move or remove something with the hands: *rescuers clawed away rubble with their bare hands.* **2** [intrans.] (of a sailing ship) beat to windward: *the ability to claw off a lee shore.* — **clawed adj.** [often in comb.] *a short-clawed otter.* **claw·less adj.** [OE *clawu* (n.), *clawian* (v.), of West Gmc. origin; rel. to Ger. *Klaue*.]

claw ham·mer ▶**n.** **1** a hammer with one side of the head split and curved, used for extracting nails. See illustration at HAMMER. **2** (**claw-hammer**) a style of banjo playing in which the thumb and fingers strum or pluck the strings in a downward motion.

Clay[1] /klā/, Cassius, see ALI[2].

Clay[2], Henry (1777–1852), US secretary of state 1825–29; nicknamed **the Great Compromiser**. A renowned orator, he was Speaker of the House 1811–14, 1815–20.

clay /klā/ ▶**n.** a stiff, sticky fine-grained earth, typically yellow, red, or bluish-gray in color and often forming an impermeable layer in the soil. It can be molded when wet, and is dried and baked to make bricks, pottery, and ceramics. ■ tech. sediment with particles smaller than silt, typically less than 0.00016 inch (0.004 mm). ■ a hardened clay surface for a tennis court. ■ literary the substance of the human body.
– PHRASES **feet of clay** see FOOT. — **clay·ey** /ˈklā-ē/ **adj.** **clay·ish adj.** **clay·like adj.** [OE *clǣg*, of West Gmc. origin; rel. to Du. *klei*, also to CLEAVE[2].]

clay·ma·tion /klāˈmāSHən/ (also **Clay·ma·tion**) ▶**n.** a method of animation in which clay figures are filmed using stop-motion photography. [1980s: from CLAY + ANIMATION.]

clay min·er·al ▶**n.** any of a group of minerals that occur as minute sheetlike or fibrous crystals in clay. They are all hydrated aluminosilicates having layered crystal structures.

clay·more /ˈklāmôr/ ▶**n.** **1** hist. a two-edged broadsword used by Scottish Highlanders. ■ a single-edged broadsword having a hilt with a basket-work design. **2** a type of antipersonnel mine. [18th C.: from Scot. Gael. *claidheamh* 'sword' + *mór* 'great.']

clay pig·eon ▶**n.** a saucer-shaped piece of baked clay or other material thrown up in the air from a trap as a target for shooting.

-cle ▶**suffix** forming nouns such as *article*, *particle*, which were originally diminutives. [via Fr. from L. *-culus*, *-cula*, *-culum*.]

clean /klēn/ ▶**adj.** **1** free from dirt, marks, or stains. ■ having been washed since last worn or used. ■ [attrib.] (of paper) not yet marked by writing or drawing. ■ (of a person) attentive to personal hygiene. ■ free from pollutants or unpleasant substances. ■ free from or producing relatively little radioactive contamination. **2** morally uncontaminated; pure; innocent: *clean living.* ■ not sexually offensive or obscene: ***good clean fun.*** ■ showing or having no record of offenses or crimes: *a clean driving license.* ■ played or done according to the rules: *a clean fight.* ■ [predic.] informal not possessing or containing anything illegal, esp. drugs or stolen goods: *I searched him, and he was clean.* ■ [predic.] informal (of a person) not taking or having taken drugs or alcohol. ■ free from ceremonial defilement, according to Mosaic Law and similar religious codes. ■ (of an animal) not prohibited under such codes and fit to be used for food. **3** free from irregularities; having a smooth edge or surface: *a clean fracture.* ■ having a simple, well-defined, and pleasing shape. ■ (of an action) smoothly and skillfully done: *I made a clean takeoff.* ■ (of a taste, sound, or smell) giving a clear and distinctive impression to the senses; sharp and fresh. ■ (of timber) free from knots. ▶**adv.** **1** so as to be free from dirt, marks, or unwanted matter. **2** informal used to emphasize the completeness of a reported action, condition, or experience: *I clean forgot her birthday.* ▶**v.** [trans.] make (something or someone) free of dirt, marks, or mess, esp. by washing, wiping, or brushing: *chair covers should be easy to clean* | [intrans.] *he expected other people to **clean up after** him* | [as n.] (**cleaning**) *Anne will help with the cleaning.* ■ remove the innards of (fish or poultry) prior to cooking.
– PHRASES **(as) clean as a whistle** see WHISTLE. **clean bill of health** see BILL OF HEALTH. **clean someone's clock** informal give someone a beating. ■ defeat or surpass someone decisively. **clean house** do housework. ■ eliminate corruption or inefficiency. **a clean sweep 1** the removal of all unwanted people or things in order to start afresh. **2** the winning of all of a group of similar or related competitions, events, or matches. **clean up one's act** informal begin to behave in a better way, esp. by giving up alcohol, drugs, or illegal activities. **come clean** informal be completely honest; keep nothing hidden. **keep one's nose clean** see NOSE. **make a clean breast of something** (or **make a clean breast of it**) confess fully one's mistakes or wrongdoings. **wipe the slate clean** see WIPE.
– PHRASAL VERBS **clean someone out** informal use up or take all someone's money. **clean up** ■ make things or an area clean or neat. ■ informal make a substantial gain or profit. ■ win all the prizes available in a sporting competition or series of events. **clean something up** restore order or morality to. — **clean·a·ble adj.** **clean·ish adj.** **clean·ness n.** [OE *clǣne*, of West Gmc. origin; rel. to Ger. *klein* 'small.']

clean and jerk ▶ n. [in sing.] a two-movement weightlifting exercise in which a weight is raised above the head following an initial lift to shoulder level.

clean-cut ▶ adj. sharply outlined. ■ giving the appearance of neatness and respectability. ■ evoking or suggesting such respectability.

clean·er /ˈklēnər/ ▶ n. a person or thing that cleans something, in particular: ■ a person employed to clean the interior of a building. ■ (**the cleaners**) a place of business where clothes and fabrics are dry-cleaned. ■ a device for cleaning, such as a vacuum cleaner. ■ a chemical substance used for cleaning.
– PHRASES **take someone to the cleaners** informal take all someone's money or possessions in a dishonest or unfair way. ■ inflict a crushing defeat on someone.

clean·er fish ▶ n. a small fish (genus *Labroides*, family Labridae), esp. a striped wrasse, that is permitted to remove parasites from the skin, gills, and mouth of larger fishes, to their mutual benefit.

clean-limbed ▶ adj. (esp. of the human figure) slim; well formed and shapely.

clean·ly /ˈklēnlē/ ▶ adv. **1** in a way that produces no dirt, noxious gases, or other pollutants. **2** without difficulty or impediment; smoothly and efficiently. — **clean·li·ness** /ˈklenlēnis/ n.

clean room ▶ n. an environment free from dust and other contaminants, used chiefly for the manufacture of electronic components.

cleanse /klenz/ ▶ v. [trans.] make (something, esp. the skin) thoroughly clean: *this preparation will cleanse and tighten the skin* | [as adj.] (**cleansing**) *a cleansing cream.* ■ rid (a person, place, or thing) of something seen as unpleasant, unwanted, or defiling: *the mission to cleanse the nation of subversives.* ■ free (someone) from sin or guilt. ■ archaic (in biblical translations) cure (a leper). [OE *clǣnsian*, from *clǣne* (see CLEAN).]

cleans·er /ˈklenzər/ ▶ n. [often with adj.] a substance that cleanses, in particular: ■ a powder or liquid for scouring sinks, toilets, and bathtubs. ■ a cosmetic product for cleansing the skin.

clean-shav·en ▶ adj. (of a man) without a beard or mustache.

clean slate ▶ n. an absence of existing restraints or commitments.

clean·up /ˈklēn,əp/ (also **clean-up**) ▶ n. **1** an act of making a place clean or tidy. ■ an act of removing or putting an end to disorder, immorality, or crime. **2** [usu. as adj.] Baseball the fourth position in a team's batting order, typically for a power hitter likely to clear the bases by enabling runners to score: *LA's cleanup hitter* | [as adverb] *he batted cleanup.*

clear /ˈkli(ə)r/ ▶ adj. **1** easy to perceive, understand, or interpret. ■ leaving no doubt; obvious or unambiguous: *a clear case of poisoning.* ■ having or feeling no doubt or confusion. **2** free of anything that marks or darkens something, in particular: ■ (of a substance) transparent. ■ free of cloud, mist, or rain. ■ (of a person's skin) free from blemishes. ■ (of a person's eyes) unclouded; shining. ■ (of a color) pure and intense. **3** free of any obstructions or unwanted object: *his desktop was clear.* ■ (of a period of time) free of any appointments or commitments: *Saturday Mattie had a clear day.* ■ [predic.] (of a person) free of something undesirable or unpleasant: *he was **clear of** TB.* ■ (of a person's mind) free of something that impairs logical thought. ■ (of a person's conscience) free of guilt. **4** [predic.] (**clear of**) not touching; away from: *the truck was in the ditch, one wheel clear of the ground.* **5** [attrib.] (of a sum of money) net: *a clear profit of $1,100.* ▶ adv. **1** so as to be out of the way of or away from: *he leapt **clear of** the car.* ■ so as not to be obstructed or cluttered: *the floor was swept **clear of** litter.* **2** with clarity; distinctly: *she tossed her head to see the lake clear again.* **3** completely: *he got clear away.* ■ (**clear to**) all the way to: *you could see clear to the bottom.* ▶ v. **1** [intrans.] become free of something that marks, darkens, obstructs, or covers something, in particular: ■ (of the sky or weather) become free of cloud or rain: *we'll go out if the weather clears.* ■ (of a liquid) become transparent: *a wine that refuses to clear.* ■ become free of obstructions: *the boy's lungs cleared.* ■ gradually go away or disappear. ■ (of a person's face or expression) assume a happier aspect following previous confusion or distress. ■ (of a person's mind) regain the capacity for logical thought; become free of confusion. **2** [trans.] make (something) free of marks, obstructions, or unwanted items, in particular: ■ remove an obstruction or unwanted item or items from. ■ free (land) for cultivation or building by removing vegetation or existing structures. ■ free (one's mind) of unpleasantness or confusion. ■ cause people to leave (a building or place). **3** [trans.] remove (an obstruction or unwanted item) from somewhere. ■ esp. Soccer send (the ball) away from the area near one's goal. ■ discharge (a debt). **4** [trans.] get past or over (something) safely or without touching it. ■ jump (a specified height) in a competition. **5** [trans.] show or declare (someone) officially to be innocent: *the commission **cleared** the weightlifter **of** cheating.* **6** [trans.] give official approval or authorization to. ■ get official approval for (something): *press releases were **cleared with** the White House.* ■ (of a person or goods) satisfy the necessary requirements to pass through (customs): *I cleared customs quickly.* ■ pass (a check) through a clearinghouse so that the money goes into the payee's account. ■ [intrans.] (of a check) pass through a clearinghouse in such a way. **7** [trans.] earn or gain (an amount of money) as a net profit.
– PHRASES **as clear as mud** see MUD. **clear the air** make the air less sultry. ■ defuse or clarify an angry, tense, or confused situation by frank discussion. **(as) clear as a bell** see BELL[1]. **(as) clear as day** very easy to see or understand. **clear the decks** prepare for a particular event or goal by dealing with anything beforehand that might hinder progress. **clear the name of** show to be innocent. **clear the way** remove an obstacle or hindrance to allow progress. ■ [in imper.] stand aside: *Stand back, there! Clear the way!* **in clear** not encrypted; not in code. **in the clear** no longer in danger or suspected of something.
– PHRASAL VERBS **clear off** [usu. in imper.] informal go away. **clear out** informal leave quickly. **clear something out** remove the contents from something so as to tidy it or free it for alternative use. **clear up 1** (of an illness or other medical condition) become cured. **2** (of the weather) become brighter. ■ (of rain) stop. **clear something up 1** (also **clear up**) tidy something up by removing trash or other unwanted items. ■ remove trash or other unwanted items to leave something tidy. **2** solve or explain something. **3** cure an illness or other medical condition. — **clear·a·ble** adj. **clear·ness** n. [ME: from OFr. *cler*, from L. *clarus*.]

clear·ance /ˈkli(ə)rəns/ ▶ n. **1** the action or process of removing or getting rid of something or of something's dispersing. ■ [often with adj.] the removal of buildings, people, or trees from land so as to free it for alternative uses: *forest clearances.* ■ (in soccer and other games) a kick or hit that sends the ball out of a defensive zone. **2** official authorization for something to proceed or take place. ■ (also **security clearance**) official permission for someone to have access to classified information. ■ permission for an aircraft to take off or land at an airport. ■ the clearing of a person or ship by customs. ■ a certificate showing that such clearance has been granted. ■ the process of clearing checks through a clearinghouse. **3** clear space allowed for a thing to move past or under another.

clear·ance sale ▶ n. a sale of goods at reduced prices to get rid of superfluous stock or because the store is closing down.

clear-cut ▶ adj. **1** sharply defined; easy to perceive or understand. **2** (of an area) from which every tree has been cut down and removed. ▶ v. [trans.] cut down and remove every tree from (an area).

clear-eyed ▶ adj. having unclouded, bright eyes. ■ fig. having a shrewd understanding and no illusions.

clear·head·ed /ˈkli(ə)r,hedid/ (also **clear-head·ed**) ▶ adj. alert and thinking logically and coherently. — **clear·head·ed·ly** adv. **clear·head·ed·ness** n.

clear·ing /ˈkli(ə)riNG/ ▶ n. an open space in a forest, esp. one cleared for cultivation.

clear·ing·house /ˈkli(ə)riNG,hous/ (also **clear·ing house**) (abbr.: **c.h.** or **C.H.**) ▶ n. a bankers' establishment where checks and bills from member banks are exchanged, with only the balances to be paid in cash. ■ an agency or organization that collects and distributes something, esp. information.

clear·ly /ˈkli(ə)rlē/ ▶ adv. in such a way as to allow easy and accurate perception or interpretation. ■ [sentence adverb] without doubt; obviously: *clearly, there have been reversals here.*

clear-sight·ed ▶ adj. thinking clearly and sensibly; perspicacious and discerning. — **clear-sight·ed·ly** adv. **clear-sight·ed·ness** n.

clear·sto·ry ▶ n. (pl. **-ries**) var. of CLERESTORY.

Clear·wa·ter /ˈkli(ə)r,wôtər; -,wätər/ a city in west central Florida, on the Gulf of Mexico; pop. 108,787.

Clear·wa·ter Moun·tains a range in northern Idaho.

clear·wing /ˈkli(ə)r,wiNG/ (also **clearwing moth**) ▶ n. a day-flying moth (family Sesiidae) that has narrow mainly transparent wings and mimics a wasp or bee in appearance.

cleat

cleat /klēt/ ▶ n. a T-shaped piece of metal or wood, esp. on a boat or ship, to which ropes are attached. ■ one of a number of projecting pieces of metal, rubber, or other material on the sole of a shoe, designed to prevent the wearer from losing their footing. ■ (**cleats**) athletic shoes with a cleated sole, typically used when playing football. ■ a projection on a spar or other part of a ship, to prevent slipping. — **cleat·ed** /klētid/ adj. [ME: of West Gmc. origin; rel. to Ger. *Kloss* 'clod,' also to CLOT.]

cleav·age /ˈklēvij/ ▶ n. a sharp division; a split. ■ the hollow between a woman's breasts when supported, esp. as exposed by a low-cut garment. ■ Biol. cell division, esp. of a fertilized egg cell. ■ the splitting of rocks or crystals in a preferred plane or direction.

cleave[1] /klēv/ ▶ v. (past **clove** or **cleft** or **cleaved** /klēvd ;/ past part. **clo·ven** or **cleft** or **cleaved**) [trans.] split or sever (something), esp. along a natural line or grain. ■ split (a molecule) by breaking a particular chemical bond. ■ make a way through (something) forcefully, as if by splitting it apart: *Stan was **cleaving a path through** traffic* | [intrans.] *the warrior clove through their ranks.* ■ [intrans.] Biol. (of a cell) divide: *the egg cleaves to form a cluster of cells.* — **cleav·a·ble** adj. [OE *clēofan*, of Gmc. origin; rel. to Ger. *klieben*.]

cleave[2] ▶ v. [intrans.] (**cleave to**) literary stick fast to: *Rose's mouth was dry, her tongue cleaving to the roof of her mouth.* ■ adhere strongly to (a particular pursuit or belief). ■ become very strongly involved with or emotionally attached to (someone). [OE *cleofian, clifian, clīfan*, of West Gmc. origin; rel. to Ger. *kleben*, also to CLAY.]

Clea·ver /ˈklēvər/, Eldridge (1935–98), US civil rights activist. He wrote *Soul on Ice* (1968) about the black experience.

cleav·er /ˈklēvər/ ▶ n. a tool with a heavy broad blade, used by butchers for chopping meat.

cleav·ers /ˈklēvərz/ ▶ plural n. [treated as sing. or pl.] a widely distributed scrambling plant (*Galium aparine*) of the bedstraw family, with hooked bristles on the stem, leaves, and seeds that cling to fur and clothing. Also called GOOSEGRASS. [OE *clīfe*, rel. to CLEAVE[2].]

clef /klef/ ▶ n. Music any of several symbols placed at the left-hand end of a staff, indicating the pitch of the notes written on it. [16th C.: from Fr., from L. *clavis* 'key.']

cleft[1] /kleft/ past and past participle of CLEAVE[1]. ▶ adj. split, divided, or partially divided into two.

cleft[2] ▶ n. a fissure or split, esp. one in rock or the ground. ■ a vertical indentation in the middle of a person's forehead or chin. [ME *clift*: of Gmc. origin; rel. to Ger. *Kluft*, also to CLEAVE[1].]

cleft lip ▶ n. a congenital split in the upper lip on one or both sides of the center.

cleft pal·ate ▶ n. a congenital split in the roof of the mouth.

cleis·tog·a·my /klīˈstägəmē/ ▶ n. Bot. self-fertilization within a permanently closed flower. — **cleis·tog·a·mous** /-əməs/ adj. [19th C.: from Gk. *kleistos* 'closed' + *-gamy* (from *gamos* 'marriage').]

clem·a·tis /ˈklemətəs; kləˈmatəs/ ▶ n. a climbing plant (genus *Clematis*) of the buttercup family that bears white, pink, or purple flowers and feathery seeds. [L., from Gk. *klēmatis*, from *klēma* 'vine branch.']

Cle·men·ceau /ˌklemənˈsō; ˌklāmänˈsō/, Georges Eugène Benjamin (1841–1929), prime minister of France 1906–09, 1917–20. At the Versailles peace talks he pushed for a punitive settlement with Germany.

clem·en·cy /ˈklemənsē/ ▶ n. mercy; lenience. [ME: from L. *clementia*, from *clemens, clement-* 'clement.']

Clem·ens /ˈklemənz/, Samuel Langhorne, see TWAIN.

clem·ent /ˈklemənt/ ▶ adj. **1** (of weather) mild. **2** (of a person or a person's actions) merciful. [ME (sense 2): from L. *clemens, clement-*.]

Cle·men·te /kləˈmentā; -tē/, Roberto Walker (1934–72), US baseball player; born in Puerto Rico. An outfielder for the Pittsburgh Pirates 1955–72, he died in an airplane crash during a humanitarian mission.

clem·en·tine /ˈkleməntīn; -ˌtēn/ ▶ n. a tangerine of a deep orange-red North African variety. [1920s: from Fr. *clémentine*, from the name *Clément*.]

Clem·ent of Al·ex·an·dri·a, St. /ˈklemənt/ (*c.*150–*c.*215), Greek theologian; Latin name *Titus Flavius Clemens*. He related the ideas of Greek philosophy to the Christian faith.

Clem·ent, St. (1st century AD), pope (bishop of Rome) *c.*88–*c.*97; known as **St. Clement of Rome**.

clen·bu·te·rol /klenˈbyo͞otəˌrôl; -ˌrōl/ ▶ n. Med. a synthetic drug used to treat asthma. It also promotes the growth of muscle and has been used illegally by athletes to enhance performance. [1970s: from *c(h)l(oro-)* + *(ph)en(yl)* + *but(yl)* + *er* + -OL.]

clench /klench/ ▶ v. (with reference to the fingers or hand) close into a tight ball, esp. when feeling extreme anger: [trans.] *she clenched her fists* | [intrans.] *John's right hand clenched into a fist.* ■ (with reference to the teeth) press or be pressed tightly together, esp. with anger or determination or so as to suppress a strong emotion: [intrans.] *her teeth clenched in anger.* ■ [trans.] grasp (something) tightly, esp. with the hands or between the teeth: *he clenched the steering wheel.* ■ [intrans.] (of a muscular part of the body) tighten or contract sharply, esp. with strong emotion: *Mark felt his stomach clench in alarm.* ▶ n. [in sing.] a contraction or tightening of part of the body. ■ the state of being tightly closed or contracted. [OE ('fix securely'): of Gmc. origin; rel. to CLING.]

cle·o·me /klēˈōmē/ ▶ n. a chiefly tropical flowering plant (genus *Cleome*, family Capparidaceae) noted for its long stamens. [mod. L., from Gk., denoting a different plant.]

Cle·o·pa·tra /ˌklēəˈpatrə/ (69–30 BC), queen of Egypt 47–30; also known as **Cleopatra VII**. She formed a political and romantic alliance with Mark Antony, who was defeated at the Battle of Actium in 31. She is reputed to have committed suicide by being bitten by an asp.

Cle·o·pa·tra's Nee·dles a pair of ancient Egyptian granite obelisks, *c.*1475 BC, moved from Egypt in 1878, one to the Thames Embankment in London and the other to Central Park, New York.

clep·sy·dra /ˈklepsədrə/ ▶ n. (pl. **-dras** or **-drae** /-ˌdrē; -ˌdrī/) an ancient time-measuring device worked by a flow of water. [ME: via L. from Gk. *klepsudra*, based on *kleptein* 'steal' + *hudōr* 'water.']

clere·sto·ry /ˈkli(ə)rˌstôrē/ (also **clear·sto·ry**) ▶ n. (pl. **-ries**) the upper part of the nave, choir, and transepts of a large church, containing a series of windows. It is clear of the roofs of the aisles and admits light to the central parts of the building. [ME: from CLEAR + STORY[2].]

cler·gy /ˈklərjē/ ▶ n. (pl. **-gies**) [usu. treated as pl.] the body of all people ordained for religious duties, esp. in the Christian Church. [ME: from OFr., based on eccles. L. *clericus* 'clergyman' (see CLERIC).]

cler·gy·man /ˈklərjēmən/ ▶ n. (pl. **-men**) a male priest or minister of a Christian church.

cler·gy·wom·an /ˈklərjēˌwo͝omən/ ▶ n. (pl. **-wom·en**) a female priest or minister of a Christian church.

cler·ic /ˈklerik/ ▶ n. a priest or minister of a Christian church. ■ a priest or religious leader in any religion. [17th C.: from eccles. L. *clericus* 'clergyman,' from Gk. *klērikos* 'belonging to the Christian clergy,' from *klēros* 'lot, heritage.']

cler·i·cal /ˈklerikəl/ ▶ adj. **1** (of a job or person) concerned with or relating to work in an office, esp. routine tasks. **2** of or relating to the clergy. — **cler·i·cal·ism** /-ˌlizəm/ n. (in sense 2) **cler·i·cal·ist** /-ist/ n. (in sense 2) **cler·i·cal·ly** /-ik(ə)lē/ adv.

cler·i·cal col·lar ▶ n. a stiff upright white collar that fastens at the back, worn by the clergy in some churches.

cler·i·hew /ˈklerəˌhyo͞o/ ▶ n. a short comic or nonsensical verse, typically in two rhyming couplets with lines of unequal length and referring to a famous person. [1920s: Edmund *Clerihew* Bentley (1875–1956), Engl. writer.]

cler·i·sy /ˈklerəsē/ ▶ n. [usu. treated as pl.] a distinct class of learned or literary people. [19th C.: appar. influenced by Ger. *Klerisei*, based on Gk. *klēros* 'heritage.']

clerk /klərk/ ▶ n. **1** a person employed in an office or bank to keep records and to undertake other routine administrative duties. ■ an official in charge of the records of a local council or court. ■ a person employed by a judge, or being trained by a lawyer, who does legal research, etc. ■ a lay officer of a cathedral, parish church, college chapel, etc. **2** (also **desk clerk**) a receptionist in a hotel. ■ an assistant in a store; a salesclerk. **3** (also **clerk in holy orders**) formal a member of the clergy. ▶ v. [intrans.] work as a clerk: *eleven of us are clerking in auction houses.* — **clerk·ish** adj. [OE *cleric, clerc*, from eccles. L. *clericus* 'clergyman' (see CLERIC).]

clerk·ly /ˈklərklē/ ▶ adj. archaic of, relating to, or appropriate to a clerk. ■ scholarly; learned.

clerk·ship /ˈklərkˌship/ ▶ n. the position or status of a clerk, esp. in the legal profession.

Cler·mont-Fer·rand /klerˈmôn fəˈrän/ an industrial city in central France, capital of the Auvergne region; pop. 140,170.

Cleve·land[1] /ˈklēvlənd/ **1** a major port in northeastern Ohio, on Lake Erie; pop. 478,403. **2** a city in southeastern Tennessee; pop. 37,192.

Cleve·land[2], Grover (1837–1908), 22nd and 24th president of the US 1885–89, 1893–97; full name *Stephen Grover Cleveland*. A Democrat, he was governor of New York 1883–85. As president, he championed civil-service reform and revision of the tariff system.

Cleve·land Heights a city in northeastern Ohio; pop. 54,052.

clev·er /ˈklevər/ ▶ adj. (**clev·er·er, clev·er·est**) quick to understand, learn, and devise or apply ideas; intelligent. ■ skilled at doing or achieving something; talented: *she is clever with her hands.* ■ (of a thing, action, or idea) showing intelligence or skill; ingenious. ■ superficially ingenious or witty. ■ dated [usu. with negative] informal sensible; well-advised. — **clev·er·ly** adv. **clev·er·ness** n. [ME (in the sense 'quick to catch hold'): perh. of Du. or Low Ger. origin, and rel. to CLEAVE[2].]

clev·is /ˈklevis/ ▶ n. a U-shaped metal connector within which another part can be fastened by a bolt or pin passing through the ends of the connector. [16th C.: perh. rel. to CLEAVE[1].]

clew /klo͞o/ ▶ n. **1** the lower or after corner of a sail. **2** (**clews**) Naut. the cords by which a hammock is suspended. ■ (**clew**) a ball of thread (used esp. for the thread used by Theseus to mark his way out of the Cretan labyrinth). **3** archaic variant of CLUE. ▶ v. [trans.] (**clew a sail up**) Sailing haul up the clews of a sail to the yard or into the mast ready for furling. ■ (**clew a sail down**) lower an upper square sail by hauling down on the clew lines while slacking away on the halyard. [OE *cliwen, cleowen*, of Gmc. origin; rel. to Du. *kluwen*.]

CLI ▶ abbr. COST-OF-LIVING INDEX.

cli·ché /klēˈshā; kli-; ˈklēshā/ (also **cli·che**) ▶ n. **1** a phrase or opinion that is overused and betrays a lack of original thought. ■ a very predictable or unoriginal thing or person. **2** Print., esp. Brit. a stereotype or electrotype. [19th C.: Fr., past part. of *clicher* 'to stereotype.']

cli·chéd /klēˈshād; kli-; ˈklēshād/ (also **cli·ched**) ▶ adj. showing a lack of originality; based on frequently repeated phrases or opinions.

click /klik/ ▶ n. a short, sharp sound as of a switch being operated or of two hard objects coming quickly into contact. ■ Phonet. an ingressive consonantal stop produced by sudden withdrawal of the tongue from the soft palate, front teeth, or back teeth and hard palate, occurring in some southern African and other languages. ■ Comput. an act of pressing a mouse button. ▶ v. **1** make or cause to make a short, sharp sound: [intrans.] *the key clicked in the lock* ■ [no obj., with adverbial] move with such a sound: *Louise turned on her heels and clicked away.* ■ [trans.] Comput. press (a mouse button). ■ [intrans.] (**click on**) Comput. select (an item represented on the screen or a particular function) by pressing one of the buttons on the mouse when the cursor is over the appropriate symbol. **2** [intrans.] informal become suddenly clear or understandable: *finally it clicked what all the fuss had been about.* ■ become very comfortable with someone at the first meeting: *we just clicked.* ■ become successful or popular: *I don't think this issue has clicked with the voters.* [16th C.: imitative.]

click·a·ble /ˈklikəbəl/ ▶ adj. Comput. (of text or images on a computer screen) such that clicking on them with a mouse will produce a reaction.

click bee·tle ▶ n. a long, narrow beetle (family Elateridae) that can spring up with a click as a means of startling predators and escaping. Its larva is the wireworm.

click·er /ˈklikər/ ▶ n. a device that clicks. ■ a remote control keypad.

click lan·guage ▶ n. a language in which clicks are used.

click stop ▶ n. a control for the aperture of a camera lens that clicks into position at certain standard settings.

click·stream /ˈklikˌstrēm/ ▶ n. a series of mouse clicks made while using a Web site or in linking to multiple Web sites.

cli·ent /'klīənt/ ▶ n. **1** a person or organization using the services of a lawyer or other professional person or company. ▪ a person receiving social or medical services. ▪ (also **client state**) a nation dependent on another, more powerful nation. **2** Comput. (in a network) a desktop computer or workstation capable of obtaining information and applications from a server. ▪ (also **client application** or **program**) a program capable of obtaining a service provided by another program. **3** (in ancient Rome) a plebeian under the protection of a patrician. — **cli·ent·ship** n. [ME: from L. *cliens, client-*, var. of *cluens* 'heeding,' from *cluere* 'hear.']

cli·en·tele /ˌklīən'tel; ˌklē-/ ▶ n. [treated as sing. or pl.] clients collectively. ▪ the customers of a shop, bar, or place of entertainment. [16th C.: via Fr. from L. *clientela* 'clientship,' from *cliens, client-*.]

cli·en·tel·ism /ˌklīən'telizəm; ˌklē-/ (also **cli·ent·ism** /'klīənˌtizəm/) ▶ n. a social order that depends upon relations of patronage; in particular, a political approach that emphasizes or exploits such relations. — **cli·en·tel·is·tic** /-te'listik/ adj.

cli·ent-serv·er ▶ adj. Comput. denoting a computer system in which a central server provides data to a number of networked workstations.

cliff /klif/ ▶ n. a steep rock face, esp. at the edge of the sea: *a path along the top of rugged cliffs* | [as adj.] *the cliff face.* — **cliff·like** adj. **cliff·y** adj. [OE *clif*, of Gmc. origin; rel. to Du. *klif.*]

cliff·hang·er /'klifˌhaNGər/ ▶ n. an ending to an episode of a serial drama that leaves the audience in suspense. ▪ a story or event with a strong element of suspense. — **cliff·hang·ing** /-ˌhaNGiNG/ adj.

Clif·ford[1] /'klifərd/, Clark M. (1906–98), US statesman. He helped draft the legislation that established the Central Intelligence Agency (CIA).

Clif·ford[2], Nathan (1803–81), US Supreme Court associate justice 1858–81.

CliffsNotes /'klifsˌnōts/ ▶ n. Trademark a brand name for a series of prepared notes used as study guides for literary works and other school and college subjects.

Clif·ton /'kliftən/ a city in northeastern New Jersey; pop. 78,672.

cli·mac·ter·ic /klī'maktərik; ˌklīmak'terik/ ▶ n. a critical period or event. ▪ Med. the period of life when fertility and sexual activity are in decline; (in women) menopause. ▪ Bot. the ripening period of certain fruits such as apples, involving increased metabolism and only possible while still on the tree. ▶ adj. having extreme and far-reaching implications or results; critical. ▪ Med. occurring at, characteristic of, or undergoing the climacteric; (in women) menopausal. ▪ Bot. (of a fruit) undergoing a climacteric. [16th C.: ult. from Gk. *klimaktērikos*, from *klimaktēr* 'critical period,' from *klimax* 'ladder, climax.']

cli·mac·tic /klī'maktik; klə-/ ▶ adj. (of an action, event, or scene) exciting or thrilling and acting as a climax to a series of events. — **cli·mac·ti·cal·ly** /-ik(ə)lē/ adv. [19th C.: from CLIMAX.]

cli·mate /'klīmit/ ▶ n. the weather conditions prevailing in an area in general or over a long period. ▪ a region with particular prevailing weather conditions. ▪ the prevailing trend of public opinion or of another aspect of public life. — **cli·mat·ic** /klī'matik/ adj. **cli·mat·i·cal** /klī'matikəl/ adj. **cli·mat·i·cal·ly** /klī'matik(ə)lē/ adv. [ME: from OFr. *climat* or late L. *clima, climat-*, from Gk. *klima* 'slope, zone,' from *klinein* 'to slope.']

cli·ma·tol·o·gy /ˌklīmə'täləjē/ ▶ n. the scientific study of climate. — **cli·ma·to·log·i·cal** /ˌklīmətl'läjikəl/ adj. **cli·ma·tol·o·gist** /-jist/ n.

cli·max /'klīˌmaks/ ▶ n. the most intense, exciting, or important point of something; a culmination or apex. ▪ an orgasm. ▪ Ecol. the final stage in a succession in a given environment, at which a plant community reaches a state of equilibrium. ▪ Rhet. a sequence of ideas in increasing importance, force, or effectiveness. ▶ v. [intrans.] culminate in an exciting or impressive event; reach a climax: *the day climaxed with a gala concert.* ▪ [trans.] bring (something) to a climax: *the sentencing climaxed a seven-month trial.* ▪ have an orgasm. [16th C.: from late L., from Gk. *klimax* 'ladder, climax.']

climb /klīm/ ▶ v. **1** [trans.] go or come up (a slope, incline, or staircase), esp. by using the feet and sometimes the hands; ascend: *we began to climb the hill* | [intrans.] *the air became colder as they climbed higher.* ▪ [intrans.] (of an aircraft or the sun) go upward: *we climbed to 6,000 feet.* ▪ [intrans.] (of a road or track) slope upward or up: *the track climbed up a narrow valley.* ▪ (of a plant) grow up (a wall, tree, or trellis) by clinging with tendrils or by twining: *when ivy climbs a wall, it infiltrates any crack* | [intrans.] *there were roses climbing up the walls.* ▪ [intrans.] grow in scale, value, or power: *the stock market climbed 24 points.* ▪ move to a higher position in (a chart or table): *the song is climbing the charts.* **2** [intrans., with adverbial of direction] move with effort, esp. into or out of a confined space; clamber: *he climbed to a high bough.* ▪ (**climb into**) put on (clothes): *he climbed into his suit.* ▶ n. an ascent, esp. of a mountain or hill, by climbing. ▪ a mountain, hill, or slope that is climbed or is to be climbed. ▪ a recognized route up a mountain or cliff. ▪ an aircraft's flight upward. ▪ a rise or increase in value, rank, or power. — **climb·a·ble** adj. [OE *climban*, of West Gmc. origin; rel. to Ger. *klimmen*, also to CLAY.]

climb·er /'klīmər/ ▶ n. a person or animal that climbs. ▪ a mountaineer. ▪ a climbing plant. ▪ see SOCIAL CLIMBER.

climb·ing /'klīmiNG/ ▶ n. the sport or activity of ascending mountains or cliffs.

climb·ing perch ▶ n. a small, edible freshwater fish (family Anabantidae), native to Africa and Asia, that is able to breathe air and move over land.

climb·ing wall ▶ n. a wall at a sports center or in a gymnasium fitted with attachments to simulate a rock face for climbing practice.

clime /klīm/ ▶ n. (usu. **climes**) esp. literary a region considered with reference to its climate. [ME: from late L. *clima* (see CLIMATE).]

clin- ▶ comb. form var. of CLINO- shortened before a vowel.

clinch /klinCH/ ▶ v. [trans.] **1** confirm or settle (a contract or bargain). ▪ conclusively settle (an argument or debate). ▪ confirm the winning or achievement of (a game, competition, or victory): *his team clinched the title.* ▪ secure (a nail or rivet) by driving the point sideways when it has penetrated. ▪ fasten (a rope or fishing line) with a clinch knot. **2** [intrans.] grapple at close quarters, esp. (of boxers) so as to be too closely engaged for full-arm blows. ▪ (of two people) embrace. ▶ n. **1** a struggle or scuffle at close quarters, esp. (in boxing) one in which the fighters become too closely engaged for full-arm blows. ▪ an embrace, esp. an amorous one. **2** a knot used to fasten a rope to a ring, using a half hitch with the end seized back on its own part. [16th C.: var. of CLENCH.]

clinch·er /'klinCHər/ ▶ n. **1** a fact, argument, or event that settles a matter conclusively. **2** (in full **clincher tire**) a bicycle or automobile tire that has flange beads that fit into the wheel rim.

Clinch Riv·er /klinCH/ a river that flows for 300 miles (480 km) from southwestern Virginia to the Tennessee River.

cline /klīn/ ▶ n. a continuum with an infinite number of gradations from one extreme to the other. ▪ Biol. a gradation in one or more characteristics within a species or other taxon, esp. between different populations. — **clin·al** /'klīnl/ adj. [1930s: from Gk. *klinein* 'to slope.']

cling /kliNG/ ▶ v. (past and past part. **clung**) [intrans.] (**cling to/onto/on**) (of a person or animal) hold on tightly to: *she clung to Joe's arm* | fig. *she clung onto life.* ▪ (**cling to**) adhere or stick firmly or closely to; be hard to part or remove from: *the smell of smoke clung to their clothes.* ▪ (**cling to**) remain very close to: *the fish cling to the line of the weed.* ▪ remain persistently or stubbornly faithful to something: *she clung to her convictions.* ▪ be overly dependent on someone emotionally. ▶ n. (also **cling peach**) a clingstone peach. — **cling·er** n. [OE *clingan* 'stick together,' of Gmc. origin; rel. to MDu. *klingen* 'adhere,' also to CLENCH.]

cling·fish /'kliNGˌfiSH/ ▶ n. (pl. same or **-fish·es**) a small fish (family Gobiesocidae) occurring mainly in shallow or intertidal water, with a sucker for attachment to rocks and other surfaces.

cling·ing /'kliNGiNG/ ▶ adj. **1** (of a garment) fitting closely to the body and showing its shape. **2** overly dependent on someone emotionally.
– PHRASES **clinging vine** a person who is submissively dependent on another.

cling·stone /'kliNGˌstōn/ ▶ n. a peach or nectarine of a variety in which the flesh adheres to the stone. Contrasted with FREESTONE (sense 2).

cling·y /'kliNGē/ ▶ adj. (**cling·i·er, cling·i·est**) (of a person or garment) liable to cling; clinging. — **cling·i·ness** n.

clin·ic /'klinik/ ▶ n. **1** a place or hospital department where outpatients are given medical treatment or advice. ▪ an occasion or time when such treatment or advice is given. ▪ a gathering at a hospital bedside for the teaching of medicine. **2** a conference or short course on a particular subject. [19th C.: from Fr. *clinique*, from Gk. *klinikē (tekhnē)* 'bedside (art),' from *klinē* 'bed.']

clin·i·cal /'klinikəl/ ▶ adj. **1** of or relating to a clinic. ▪ of or relating to the observation and treatment of patients rather than laboratory studies. ▪ (of a disease or condition) causing observable symptoms. **2** efficient and unemotional; coldly detached. ▪ (of a room or building) bare, functional, and clean.

clin·i·cal·ly /'klinik(ə)lē/ ▶ adv. **1** as regards clinical medicine; in clinical terms. **2** efficiently and without emotion. ▪ [usu. as submodifier] in a very functional and clean manner: *a clinically clean kitchen.*

clin·i·cal psy·chol·o·gy ▶ n. the branch of psychology concerned with the assessment and treatment of mental illness and disability. — **clin·i·cal psy·chol·o·gist** n.

clin·i·cal ther·mom·e·ter ▶ n. a small medical thermometer with a short but finely calibrated range, for taking a person's temperature.

cli·ni·cian /klə'niSHən/ ▶ n. a doctor having direct contact with and responsibility for patients, rather than one involved with theoretical or laboratory studies.

clink[1] /kliNGk/ ▶ n. a sharp ringing sound, such as that made when metal or glass are struck. ▶ v. [intrans.] make such a sound: *his ring clinked against the crystal.* ▪ [trans.] cause (something) to make such a sound. ▪ [trans.] strike (a glass or glasses) with another to express friendly feelings toward one's companions before drinking. [ME (v.): prob. from MDu. *klinken.*]

clink[2] ▶ n. [in sing.] informal prison. [16th C. (orig. denoting a prison in London): of unknown origin.]

clink·er[1] /'kliNGkər/ ▶ n. the stony residue from burned coal or from a furnace. ▪ (also **clinker brick**) a brick with a vitrified surface. [17th C.: from obs. Du. *klinckaerd*, from *klinken* 'to clink.']

clink·er[2] ▶ n. informal something that is unsatisfactory, of poor quality, or a failure. ▪ a wrong musical note. [17th C.: from CLINK[1] + -ER[1].]

clink·er-built ▶ adj. (of a boat) having external planks secured with clinched nails such that the bottom edge of an upper plank overlaps the upper edge of a lower plank. Compare with CARVEL-BUILT. [18th C.: from *clink* (var. of CLINCH).]

clino- (usu. **clin-** before a vowel) ▶ comb. form slant; slope: *clinometer.*

cli·nom·e·ter /klī'nəmətər/ ▶ **n.** Surveying an instrument used for measuring the angle or elevation of slopes. [19th C.: from Gk. *klinein* 'to slope.']

cli·no·py·rox·ene /,klīnōpī'räksēn/ ▶ **n.** a mineral of the pyroxene group crystallizing in the monoclinic system. [20th C.: from *clino-* 'monoclinic.']

clin·quant /'kliNGkənt/ ▶ **adj.** glittering with gold and silver; tinseled. ▶ **n.** imitation gold leaf. ■ fig. literary or artistic tinsel; false glitter.

Clin·ton[1] /'klintən/ **1** a city in east central Iowa; pop. 27,772. **2** a city in southwest central Mississippi; pop. 23,347.

Clin·ton[2] a family of US politicians. Bill (1946–), full name *William Jefferson Clinton*, born *William Jefferson Blythe III*, was the 42nd president of the US 1993–2001. A Democrat, he was governor of Arkansas 1979–81, 1983–93. As president, he balanced the budget and brought economic prosperity. Impeached for impropriety, he was acquitted by the Senate in 1999. His wife, Hillary Rodham (1947–), born *Hillary Diane Rodham*, was the US first lady 1993–2001. A New York Democrat, she has served in the US Senate since 2001.

Clin·ton[3], DeWitt (1769–1828), US politician. As governor of New York 1817–23, 1825–28, he championed the Erie Canal.

Clin·ton[4], George (1739–1812), vice president of the US 1805–12.

Cli·o /'klīō; 'klēō/ **1** Greek Rom. Mythol. the Muse of history. **2** an award given annually for advertising achievement in television, radio, billboards, and other media. [from Gk. *kleiein* 'celebrate.']

cli·o·met·rics /,klīə'metriks/ ▶ **plural n.** [treated as sing.] a technique for the interpretation of economic history, based on the statistical analysis of population censuses, parish registers, and similar sources. — **cli·o·met·ric adj. cli·o·me·tri·cian** /-me'trisHən/ **n.** [1960s: from CLIO.]

clip[1] /klip/ ▶ **n.** a device, typically flexible or worked by a spring, for holding an object or objects together. ■ a device such as this used to hold paper currency. ■ a piece of jewelry fastened by a clip. ■ a metal holder containing cartridges for an automatic firearm. ▶ **v.** (**clipped, clip·ping**) [with adverbial of place] fasten or be fastened with a clip or clips: [trans.] *she clipped on a pair of earrings* | [intrans.] *the panels clip on to the framework.* [OE *clyppan* (v.), of West Gmc. origin.]

clip[2] ▶ **v.** (**clipped, clip·ping**) [trans.] **1** cut short or trim (hair, wool, nails, or vegetation) with shears or scissors: *clipping the hedge.* ■ trim or remove the hair or wool of (an animal). ■ (**clip something off**) cut off a thing or part of a thing with shears or scissors: *he clipped off a piece of wire* | fig. *she clipped two seconds off the old record.* ■ cut (a section) from a newspaper or magazine. ■ pare the edge of (a coin), esp. illicitly: *they clipped the edges of gold coins and melted the clippings down.* ■ speak (words) in a quick, precise, staccato manner: *"Yes?" The word was clipped short.* ■ Comput. process (an image) so as to remove the parts outside a certain area. ■ Electron. truncate the amplitude of (a signal) above or below predetermined levels. **2** strike briskly or with a glancing blow. ■ [with obj. and adverbial of direction] strike or kick (something, esp. a ball) briskly in a specified direction. **3** informal swindle or rob (someone). **4** [no obj., with adverbial of direction] informal move quickly in a specified direction: *we clip down the track.* ▶ **n. 1** an act of clipping or trimming something. ■ a short sequence taken from a movie or broadcast. ■ (also **wool clip**) the quantity of wool clipped from a sheep or flock. **2** informal a quick or glancing blow. **3** [in sing.] informal a specified speed or rate of movement, esp. when rapid.
– PHRASES **at a clip** informal at a time; all at once. [ME: from ON *klippa*, prob. imitative.]

clip art ▶ **n.** Comput. predrawn pictures and symbols that computer users can add to their documents, often provided with word-processing software and drawing packages.

clip·board /'klip,bôrd/ ▶ **n.** a small board with a spring clip at the top, used for holding papers and providing support for writing. ■ Comput. a temporary storage area where text or other data cut or copied from a file is kept until it is pasted into another file.

clip-clop /'klip ,kläp/ (also **clippety-clop**) ▶ **n.** [in sing.] the sound as of a horse's hoofs beating on a hard surface. ▶ **v.** [no obj., with adverbial of direction] move with such a sound: *the horses clip-clopped along the street.* [19th C.: imitative.]

clip joint ▶ **n.** informal a nightclub or bar that charges exorbitant prices.

clip-on ▶ **adj.** attached by a clip so as to be easy to fasten or remove. ▶ **n.** (usu. **clip-ons**) things, esp. sunglasses or earrings, that are attached by clips.

clip·per /'klipər/ ▶ **n. 1** (usu. **clippers**) an instrument for cutting or trimming small pieces off things. **2** a person who clips or cuts. **3** Electron. another term for LIMITER. **4** (also **clip·per ship**) a fast sailing ship, esp. one of 19th-century design with concave bow and raked masts.

clip·ping /'klipiNG/ ▶ **n.** (often **clippings**) a small piece trimmed from something. ■ an article cut from a newspaper or magazine.

clique /klēk; klik/ ▶ **n.** a small group of people with shared interests, who spend time together and exclude others. — **cli·quish adj. cli·quish·ness n.** [18th C.: from Fr., from OFr. *cliquer* 'make a noise.']

cli·quey /'klēkē; 'klikē/ ▶ **adj.** (**cli·qui·er, cli·qui·est**) (of a group or place) tending to form or hold exclusive groups. ■ (of music or art) appealing only to a small group or minority.

clit /klit/ ▶ **n.** vulgar slang short for CLITORIS.

cli·tel·lum /klī'teləm/ ▶ **n.** (pl. **-tel·la** /-'telə/) a raised band encircling the body of oligochaete worms and some leeches, made up of reproductive segments.

clit·ic /'klitik/ ▶ **n.** Gram. an enclitic or a proclitic. — **clit·i·ci·za·tion** /,klitəsə'zāsHən/ **n.** [1940s: from *(en)clitic* and *(pro)clitic.*]

clit·o·ri·dec·to·my /,klitərə'dektəmē/ ▶ **n.** (pl. **-mies**) excision of the clitoris; female circumcision.

clit·o·ris /'klitərəs/ ▶ **n.** a small sensitive and erectile part of the female genitals at the anterior end of the vulva. — **clit·o·ral** /'klitərəl/ **adj.** [17th C.: mod. L., from Gk. *kleitoris.*]

clit·ter /'klitər/ ▶ **v.** [intrans.] make a thin, vibratory, rattling sound: *a coded message clittered over the radio.* [16th C.: imitative.]

Clive /klīv/, Robert, 1st Baron Clive of Plassey (1725–74), British colonial administrator; known as **Clive of India**. He was governor of Bengal, India 1765–67.

cli·vi·a /'klīvēə; 'klivēə/ ▶ **n.** a southern African plant (genus *Clivia*) of the lily family, with dark green, straplike leaves and trumpet-shaped orange, red, or yellow flowers. [mod. L., from *Clive*, maiden name of Charlotte, Duchess of Northumberland (1787–1866).]

clo·a·ca /klō'ākə/ ▶ **n.** (pl. **-cae** /-,kē; -,sē/) Zool. a common cavity for the release of both excretory and genital products in birds, reptiles, amphibians, most fish, and monotremes, as well as certain invertebrates. — **clo·a·cal adj.** [16th C.: from L., rel. to *cluere* 'cleanse.']

cloak /klōk/ ▶ **n.** an outdoor overgarment, typically sleeveless, that hangs from the shoulders. ■ fig. something serving to hide or disguise something: *the cloak of secrecy on the arms trade.* ▶ **v.** [trans.] dress in a cloak. ■ fig. hide, cover, or disguise (something). [ME: from OFr. *cloke*, dial. var. of *cloche* 'bell, cloak,' from med. L. *clocca* 'bell.']

cloak-and-dag·ger ▶ **adj.** involving or characteristic of mystery, intrigue, or espionage.

cloak·room /'klōk,ro͞om; -,ro͝om/ ▶ **n.** a room in a public building where coats and other belongings may be left temporarily.

clob·ber[1] /'kläbər/ ▶ **v.** [trans.] informal hit (someone) hard. ■ treat or deal with harshly: *the recession clobbered the business.* ■ defeat heavily: [with obj. and complement] *the Braves clobbered the Cubs 23–10.* [World War II: of unknown origin.]

clob·ber[2] ▶ **v.** [trans.] add enameled decoration to (porcelain). [19th C.: of unknown origin.]

clo·chard /'klōsHərd; klō'sHär/ ▶ **n.** (pl. same) (in France) a beggar; a vagrant. [Fr., from *clocher* 'to limp.']

cloche /klōsH/ ▶ **n.** a small translucent cover for protecting or forcing outdoor plants. ■ (also **cloche hat**) a woman's close-fitting, bell-shaped hat. [19th C.: from Fr. (see CLOAK).]

clock[1] /kläk/ ▶ **n.** a mechanical or electrical device for measuring time, typically by hands on a round dial or by displayed figures. ■ (**the clock**) time taken as a factor in an activity, esp. in competitive sports: *they play against the clock* ■ informal a measuring device resembling a clock for recording things other than time, such as a speedometer, taximeter, or odometer. ■ see TIME CLOCK. ▶ **v.** [trans.] informal **1** attain or register (a specified time, distance, or speed): *Thomas clocked up forty years service* | [intrans.] *the book clocks in at 989 pages.* ■ achieve (a victory): *he clocked up his first win of the year.* ■ record as attaining a specified time or rate. **2** informal hit (someone), esp. on the head.
– PHRASES **around** (or **round**) **the clock** all day and all night. **run out the clock** Sports deliberately use as much time as possible in order to preserve one's own team's advantage.
– PHRASAL VERBS **clock in** (or **out**) (of an employee) punch in (or out). [ME: from Mid. Low Ger. and MDu. *klocke*, based on med. L. *clocca* 'bell.']

clock[2] ▶ **n.** dated an ornamental pattern on the side of a stocking or sock near the ankle. [16th C.: of unknown origin.]

clock·er /'kläkər/ ▶ **n.** informal a drug dealer, esp. one who sells cocaine or crack.

clock·mak·er /'kläk,mākər/ ▶ **n.** a person who makes and repairs clocks and watches. — **clock·mak·ing n.**

clock ra·di·o ▶ **n.** a combined radio and alarm clock that can be set so that the radio will come on at the desired time.

clock speed ▶ **n.** the operating speed of a computer or its microprocessor, defined as the rate at which it performs internal operations and expressed in cycles per second (megahertz).

clock-watch·er (also **clock watch·er**) ▶ **n.** an employee who is overly strict or zealous about not working more than the required hours. — **clock-watch v.**

clock·wise /'kläk,wīz/ ▶ **adv. & adj.** in a curve corresponding in direction to the movement of the hands of a clock.

clock·work /'kläk,wərk/ ▶ **n.** a mechanism with a spring and toothed gearwheels, used to drive a mechanical clock, toy, or other device. ▶ **adj.** [attrib.] driven by clockwork. ■ very smooth and regular. ■ repetitive and predictable: *it was a clockwork existence for the children.*
– PHRASES **like clockwork** very smoothly and easily. ■ with mechanical regularity.

clod /kläd/ ▶ **n. 1** a lump of earth or clay. **2** informal a stupid person (often used as a general term of abuse). [ME: var. of CLOT.]

clod·dish /'klädisH/ ▶ **adj.** foolish, awkward, or clumsy. — **clod·dish·ly adv. clod·dish·ness n.**

clod·hop·per /'kläd,häpər/ ▶ **n. 1** a large, heavy shoe. **2** informal a foolish, awkward, or clumsy person.

clod·hop·ping /'kläd,häpiNG/ ▶ **adj.** informal foolish, awkward, or clumsy.

clog /kläg; klôg/ ▶ **n. 1** a shoe with a thick wooden sole. **2** an encumbrance or impediment. ▶ **v.** (**clogged, clog·ging**) [trans.] fill or block with an accumulation of thick, wet matter: *gutters clogged up with leaves.* ■ [intrans.] become blocked in this way: *fat makes your arteries clog up.*

■ fill up or crowd (something) so as to obstruct passage: *tourists clog the roads.* [ME (in the sense 'block of wood'): of unknown origin.]

clog dance ▶ **n.** a dance performed in clogs with rhythmic beating of the feet. ■ a North American country tap dance of similar style. — **clog danc•er n. clog danc•ing n.**

clog•ger /ˈklägər; ˈklôgər/ ▶ **n. 1** a person who performs a clog dance. **2** someone or something that clogs.

clog•ging /kläging; ˈklôg-/ ▶ **n.** clog dancing.

cloi•son•né /ˌkloizəˈnā; ˌklwäz-/ (also **cloisonné enamel**) ▶ **n.** enamel work in which the different colors are separated by strips of flattened wire placed edgeways on a metal backing. [19th C.: Fr., lit. 'partitioned,' past part. of *cloisonner*.]

clois•ter /ˈkloistər/ ▶ **n.** a covered walk in a convent, monastery, college, or cathedral, with a wall on one side and a colonnade open to a quadrangle on the other. ■ (**the cloister**) monastic life. ■ a convent or monastery. ■ any place or position of seclusion. ▶ **v.** [trans.] seclude or shut up in or as if in a convent or monastery. — **clois•tral** /ˈkloistrəl/ **adj.** [ME: from OFr. *cloistre*, from L. *claustrum, clostrum* 'lock, enclosed place,' from *claudere* 'to close.']

cloister

clois•tered /ˈkloistərd/ ▶ **adj. 1** kept away from the outside world; sheltered: *a cloistered upbringing.* **2** having or enclosed by a cloister, as in a monastery.

clom•i•phene /ˈklämə,fēn; ˈklō-/ ▶ **n.** Med. a synthetic nonsteroidal drug used to treat infertility in women by stimulating ovulation.

clomp /klämp; klômp/ ▶ **v.** [no obj., with adverbial of direction] walk with a heavy tread: *she clomped down the steps.* [19th C.: imitative.]

clone /klōn/ ▶ **n.** Biol. a group of organisms or cells produced asexually from one ancestor or stock, to which they are genetically identical. ■ an individual organism or cell so produced. ■ a person or thing regarded as identical to another. ■ a microcomputer designed to simulate exactly the operation of another, typically more expensive, model. ▶ **v.** [trans.] propagate (an organism or cell) as a clone: *of the hundreds of new plants cloned, the best ones are selected.* ■ make an identical copy of. ■ Biochem. replicate (a fragment of DNA placed in an organism) so that there is enough to analyze or use in protein production. ■ illegally copy the security codes from (a mobile phone) to one or more others as a way of obtaining free calls. — **clon•al** /ˈklōnl/ **adj.** [20th C.: from Gk. *klōn* 'twig.']

clonk /klängk; klôngk/ another term for **CLUNK.** ▶ **v. 1** [intrans.] move with or make such a sound: *the horses clonked softly.* **2** [trans.] informal hit. — **clonk•y adj.** [19th C.: imitative.]

clo•nus /ˈklōnəs/ ▶ **n.** Med. muscular spasm involving repeated, often rhythmic, contractions. — **clon•ic** /ˈklänik/ **adj.** [19th C.: from Gk. *klonos* 'turmoil.']

clop /kläp/ ▶ **n.** [in sing.] a sound or series of sounds made by a horse's hooves on a hard surface. ▶ **v.** (**clopped, clop•ping**) [no obj., with adverbial of direction] (of a horse) move with such a sound: *the animal clopped on at a steady pace.* [19th C.: imitative.]

clo•qué /klōˈkā/ ▶ **n.** a fabric with an irregularly raised or embossed surface. [Fr., lit. 'blistered.']

close¹ /klōs/ ▶ **adj. 1** a short distance away or apart in space or time: *the hotel is close to the sea.* ■ with very little or no space in between; dense. ■ [predic.] (**close to**) very near to (being or doing something): *she was close to tears.* ■ (of a competitive situation) won or likely to be won by only a small amount or distance. ■ [attrib.] (of a final position in a competition) very near to the competitor immediately in front: *a close second.* ■ narrowly enclosed: *animals in close confinement.* ■ (of hair or grass) very short or near the surface. ■ Phonet. another term for **HIGH** (sense 7). **2** [attrib.] denoting a family member who is part of a person's immediate family, typically a parent or sibling. ■ (of a person or relationship) on very affectionate or intimate terms. ■ (of a connection or resemblance) strong. **3** (of observation, examination, etc.) done in a careful and thorough way: *we need to keep a close eye on this project.* ■ carefully guarded: *his whereabouts are a close secret.* ■ not willing to give away money or information; secretive: *he's very close about his work.* ■ following faithfully an original or model. **4** uncomfortably humid or airless. ▶ **adv.** in a position so as to be very near to someone or something; with very little space between: *he was holding her close.*

– PHRASES **close by** very near; nearby. **close to** (or **close on**) (of an amount) almost; very nearly. **close to the bone** see **BONE. close to one's heart** see **HEART. close to home** see **HOME. close up** very near: *close up she was no less pretty.* **close to the wind** Sailing (of a sailing vessel) pointed as near as possible to the direction from which the wind is blowing while still making headway. — **close•ly adv. close•ness n. clos•ish adj.** [ME: from OFr. *clos* (as n. and adj.), from L. *clausum* 'enclosure' and *clausus* 'closed,' past part. of *claudere*.]

close² /klōz/ ▶ **v. 1** move or cause to move so as to cover an opening: [intrans.] *she jumped into the train just as the doors were closing* | [trans.] *they closed the window.* ■ [trans.] block up (a hole or opening): *glass doors close off the living room from the hall.* ■ [trans.] bring two parts of (something) together so as to block its opening or bring it into a folded state. ■ [intrans.] gradually get nearer to someone or something: *they plotted a large group of aircraft closing fast.* ■ [intrans.] (**close around/over**) come into contact with (something) so as to encircle and hold it: *my fist closed around the weapon.* ■ [trans.] make (an electric circuit) continuous. **2** bring or come to an end: [trans.] *the meeting was closed* | [intrans.] *the concert closed with "Silent Night."* ■ [intrans.] (of a business, organization, or institution) cease to be in operation or accessible to the public, either permanently or at the end of a working day or other period of time: *the factory is to close with the loss of 150 jobs* | [trans.] *the country has been closed to outsiders.* ■ [intrans.] finish speaking or writing: *we close with a point about truth.* ■ [trans.] bring (a business transaction) to a satisfactory conclusion: *he closed the deal.* ■ [trans.] remove all the funds from (a bank account) and cease to use it. ■ [trans.] Comput. make (a data file) inaccessible after use, so that it is securely stored until required again. ▶ **n.** [in sing.] **1** the end of an event or of a period of time or activity: *the afternoon drew to a close.* ■ (**the close**) the end of a day's trading on a stock market: *at the close the Dow Jones average was down.* ■ Music the conclusion of a phrase; a cadence. **2** the shutting of something, esp. a door.

– PHRASES **close the door on** (or **to**) see **DOOR. close one's eyes to** see **EYE. close one's mind to** see **MIND. close ranks** see **RANK¹. close up shop** see **SHOP.**

– PHRASAL VERBS **close something down** (or **close down**) cause to cease or cease business or operation, esp. permanently. **close in** come nearer to someone being pursued: *the police were closing in on them.* ■ gradually surround, esp. with the effect of hindering movement or vision: *the weather has now closed in.* ■ (of days) get successively shorter with the approach of the winter solstice: *November was closing in.* **close something out** bring something to an end. **close up** (of a person's face) become blank and emotionless or hostile: *his face closed up angrily.* **close something up** (or **close up**) **1** cause to cease or cease operation or being used: *the broker advised me to close the house up.* **2** (**close up**) (of an opening) grow smaller or become blocked by something: *she felt her throat close up.* **close with** come near, esp. so as to engage with (an enemy force). — **clos•a•ble adj. clos•er n.** [ME: from OFr. *clos-*, stem of *clore*, from L. *claudere* 'to shut.']

close call /klōs/ ▶ **n.** a narrow escape from danger or disaster.

close-cropped /klōs/ (also **close•ly cropped**) ▶ **adj.** (typically of hair or grass) cut very short.

closed /klōzd/ ▶ **adj.** not open. ■ (of a business) having ceased trading, esp. for a short period: *he put the "Closed" sign up on the door.* ■ no longer under discussion or investigation; concluded. ■ (of a society or system) not communicating with or influenced by others; independent: *the perception of the Soviet Union as a closed society.* ■ limited to certain people; not open or available to all. ■ unwilling to accept new ideas. ■ Math. (of a set) having the property that the result of a specified operation on any element of the set is itself a member of the set. ■ Math. (of a set) containing all its limit points. ■ Geom. of or pertaining to a curve whose ends are joined.

closed cap•tion ▶ **n.** one of a series of subtitles to a television program, accessible through a decoder. ▶ **v.** (**closed-cap•tion**) [trans.] [usually as noun **closed-captioning**] provide (a program) with closed captions.

closed chain ▶ **n** Chem. a number of atoms bonded together to form a closed loop in a molecule.

closed-cir•cuit tel•e•vi•sion (abbr.: **CCTV**) ▶ **n.** a television system in which the video signals are transmitted from one or more cameras by cable to a restricted set of monitors.

closed cou•plet ▶ **n.** a rhyming couplet with end-stopped lines that is logically or grammatically complete: *Instruct the planets in what orbs to run,/Correct old Time, and regulate the Sun.*

closed-door ▶ **adj.** restricted; obstructive; secret.

closed-end ▶ **adj.** having a predetermined and fixed extent. ■ denoting an investment trust or company that issues a fixed number of shares.

closed sea•son ▶ **n.** a period between specified dates when fishing or the killing of game is forbidden.

closed shop ▶ **n.** a place of work where membership in a union is a condition for being hired and for continued employment. Compare with **UNION SHOP.**

closed u•ni•verse ▶ **n.** Astron. the condition in which there is sufficient matter in the universe to halt the expansion driven by the big bang and cause eventual recollapse.

close-fist•ed /klōs/ ▶ **adj.** unwilling to spend money; stingy.

close-fit•ting /klōs/ ▶ **adj.** (of a garment) fitting tightly and showing the contours of the body.

close-grained /klōs/ ▶ **adj.** (of wood, stone, or other material) having tightly packed fibers, crystals, or other structural elements.

close har·mo·ny /klōs/ ▶ **n.** Music harmony in which the notes of the chord are close together, typically in vocal music.

close-hauled /klōs/ ▶ **adj. & adv.** Sailing (of a ship) close to the wind.

close-in /klōs/ ▶ **adj.** only a short distance away. ■ near to the center of a town or city.

close-knit /klōs/ ▶ **adj.** (of a group of people) united or bound together by strong relationships and common interests.

close-mouthed /ˈklōs ˈmouTHd; ˈmouTHt/ ▶ **adj.** reticent; discreet.

close quar·ters /klōs/ ▶ **plural n.** a situation of being very or uncomfortably close to someone or something.

clos·er /ˈklōzər/ ▶ **n.** Baseball a relief pitcher who specializes in pitching to the final batters of a game if the pitcher's team has the lead.

close range /klōs/ ▶ **n.** a short distance between someone or something and a target.

close-ra·tio /klōs/ ▶ **adj.** (of a vehicle's gearbox) having gear ratios that are set at values not very different from each other.

close reach /klōs/ Sailing ▶ **n.** a point of sailing in which the wind blows from slightly forward of the beam: *we sailed **on a close reach** directly for Sharp's Island.*

close-set /klōs/ ▶ **adj.** (of two or more things) placed or occurring with little space in between.

close shave /klōs/ ▶ **n. 1** a shave in which the hair is cut very short. **2** informal another term for CLOSE CALL.

clos·et /ˈkläzit/ ▶ **n. 1** a small room or cupboard used for storing things. ■ archaic a small, private room used for prayer or study. **2** archaic a toilet. **3** (**the closet**) a state of secrecy or concealment, esp. about one's homosexuality. ▶ **adj.** [attrib.] secret; covert. ▶ **v.** (**clos·et·ed, clos·et·ing**) [trans.] (often **be closeted**) shut (someone) away, esp. in private conference or study: *he closeted himself in his room.* ■ in a state of concealment, esp. about one's homosexuality. [ME: from OFr., dimin. of *clos* 'closed' (see CLOSE[1]).]

clos·et dra·ma (also **closet play**) ▶ **n.** a play to be read rather than acted.

close-up /ˈklōs ˌəp/ ▶ **n.** a photograph, movie, or video taken at close range and showing the subject on a large scale. ■ an intimate and detailed description or study: [as adj.] *a close-up account of the violence.*

clos·ing date ▶ **n.** the last date by which something must be submitted for consideration, esp. a job application.

clos·ing price ▶ **n.** the price of a security at the end of the day's business in a financial market.

clos·ing time ▶ **n.** the regular time at which a restaurant, store, or other place closes to the public each day.

clos·trid·i·um /kläˈstridēəm/ ▶ **n.** (pl. **clos·trid·i·a** /kläˈstridēə/) Biol. an anaerobic bacterium of a large genus (*Clostridium*), typically rod-shaped and Gram-positive, that includes many pathogenic species, e.g., those causing tetanus, gas gangrene, botulism, and other forms of food poisoning. — **clos·trid·i·al** /-ˈstridēəl/ **adj.** [mod. L., based on Gk. *klōstēr* 'spindle.']

clo·sure /ˈklōZHər/ ▶ **n.** an act or process of closing something, esp. an institution, thoroughfare, or frontier, or of being closed. ■ a thing that closes or seals something, such as a cap or zipper. ■ a resolution or conclusion to a work or process. ■ a feeling that an emotional or traumatic experience has been resolved: *everyone needs closure after a divorce.* [ME: from OFr., from late L. *clausura*, from *claus-* 'closed,' from the v. *claudere*.]

clot /klät/ ▶ **n.** a thick mass of coagulated liquid, esp. blood, or of material stuck together. ▶ **v.** (**clot·ted, clot·ting**) form or cause to form into clots: [intrans.] *drugs that help blood to clot* | [trans.] *a blood protein known as factor VIII clots blood.* ■ [trans.] cover (something) with sticky matter. [OE *clott, clot*, of Gmc. origin; rel. to Ger. *Klotz*.]

cloth /klôTH/ ▶ **n.** (pl. **cloths** /klôTHz; klôTHs/) **1** woven or felted fabric made from wool, cotton, or other fiber. ■ a piece of cloth for a particular purpose, such as a dishcloth or a tablecloth. ■ a variety of cloth. **2** (**the cloth**) the clergy; the clerical profession. [OE *clāth*, rel. to Ger. *Kleid*.]

clothe /klōTH/ ▶ **v.** (past and past part. **clothed** or **clad**) [trans.] (often **be clothed in**) put clothes on (oneself or someone); dress: *she was clothed all in white.* ■ provide (someone) with clothes. ■ fig. cover (something) as if with clothes: *forests clothed the islands.* ■ fig. endow (someone) with a particular quality: *he is clothed with charisma.* [OE (in past part. *geclāded*), from *clāth* (see CLOTH).]

clothes /klō(TH)z/ ▶ **plural n. 1** items worn to cover the body. **2** bedclothes. [OE *clāthas*, pl. of *clāth* (see CLOTH).]

clothes horse ▶ **n.** a frame on which washed clothes are hung to air indoors. ■ informal, often derog. a determinedly fashionable person.

clothes·line /ˈklō(TH)zˌlīn/ ▶ **n.** a rope or wire on which washed clothes are hung to dry. ▶ **v.** [trans.] (chiefly in football and other games) knock down (a runner) by placing one's outstretched arm in the runner's path at neck level.

clothes moth ▶ **n.** a small, drab moth (family Tineidae) whose larvae feed on a range of animal fibers and can be destructive to clothing and other domestic textiles.

cloth·ier /ˈklōTHyər; -THēər/ ▶ **n.** a person or company that makes, sells, or deals in clothes or cloth. [ME *clother*, from CLOTH.]

cloth·ing /ˈklōTHiNG/ ▶ **n.** clothes collectively.

Clo·tho /ˈklōTHō/ Gk. Mythol. one of the three Fates. [Gk., lit. 'she who spins.']

cloth yard ▶ **n.** a unit for measuring cloth, formerly 37 inches but now a standard yard (36 inches).

clot·ted cream ▶ **n.** esp. Brit. thick cream obtained by heating milk slowly and then allowing it to cool while the cream content rises to the top in coagulated lumps.

clot·ting fac·tor ▶ **n.** Physiol. any of a number of substances in blood plasma that are involved in the clotting process, such as factor VIII.

clo·ture /ˈklōCHər/ ▶ **n.** (in a legislative assembly) a procedure for ending a debate and taking a vote. ▶ **v.** [trans.] apply the cloture to (a debate or speaker) in a legislative assembly. [19th C.: from Fr. *clôture*, from OFr. *closure* (see CLOSURE).]

cloud /kloud/ ▶ **n. 1** a visible mass of condensed water vapor floating in the atmosphere, typically high above the ground. ■ an indistinct or billowing mass, esp. of smoke or dust. ■ a large number of insects or birds moving together. ■ a vague patch of color in or on a liquid or transparent surface. **2** fig. a state or cause of gloom, suspicion, trouble, or worry. ■ a frowning or depressed look. ▶ **v. 1** [intrans.] (of the sky) become overcast with clouds. ■ [trans.] (usu. **be clouded**) darken (the sky) with clouds: *the western sky was still clouded.* ■ make or become less clear or transparent. **2** fig. make or become darkened or overshadowed, in particular: ■ [intrans.] (of someone's face or eyes) show worry, sorrow, or anger: *his expression **clouded over**.* ■ [trans.] (of such an emotion) show in (someone's face). ■ [trans.] make (a matter or mental process) unclear or uncertain; confuse. ■ [trans.] spoil or mar (something).

– PHRASES **every cloud has a silver lining** see SILVER. **have one's head in the clouds** (of a person) be out of touch with reality; be daydreaming. **in the clouds** out of touch with reality. **on cloud nine** extremely happy. [with ref. to a ten-part classification of clouds in which "nine" was next to the highest.] **under a cloud** under suspicion; discredited. — **cloud·let** /-lət/ **n.** [OE *clūd* 'mass of rock or earth'; prob. rel. to CLOT.]

cloud·ber·ry /ˈkloudˌberē/ ▶ **n.** (pl. **-ries**) a dwarf bramble (*Rubus chamaemorus*) with white flowers and edible orange fruit. [16th C.: appar. from CLOUD 'hill' + BERRY.]

cloud·burst /ˈkloudˌbərst/ ▶ **n.** a sudden, violent rainstorm.

cloud cham·ber ▶ **n.** Physics a device that contains air or gas supersaturated with water vapor and that is used to detect charged particles, X-rays, and gamma rays by the condensation trails that they produce.

cloud·ed leop·ard ▶ **n.** a large spotted cat (*Neofelis nebulosa*) that hunts in trees at twilight and is found in forests in Southeast Asia.

cloud·scape /ˈkloudˌskāp/ ▶ **n.** a large cloud formation considered in terms of its visual effect. [19th C.: from the n. CLOUD + *-scape* as in *landscape*.]

cloud seed·ing ▶ **n.** the dropping of crystals into clouds to cause rain.

cloud·y /ˈkloudē/ ▶ **adj.** (**cloud·i·er, cloud·i·est**) **1** (of the sky or weather) covered with or characterized by clouds; overcast. **2** (of a liquid) not transparent or clear. ■ (of a color) opaque; having white as a constituent: *cloudy reds.* ■ (of marble) variegated with cloudlike markings. ■ (of someone's eyes) misted with tears. ■ uncertain; unclear. — **cloud·i·ly** /ˈkloudl-ē/ **adv. cloud·i·ness n.**

clout /klout/ ▶ **n. 1** informal a heavy blow with the hand or a hard object. **2** informal influence or power, esp. in politics or business. ▶ **v.** [trans.] informal hit hard with the hand or a hard object. [OE *clūt* ('a patch or metal plate'); rel. to Du. *kluit* 'lump,' also to CLEAT.]

clove[1] /klōv/ ▶ **n. 1** the dried flower bud of a tropical tree, used as a pungent aromatic spice. ■ (**oil of cloves**) aromatic analgesic oil extracted from these buds and used medicinally, esp. for dental pain. **2** the Indonesian tree (*Syzygium aromaticum*, or *Eugenia caryophyllus*) of the myrtle family from which these buds are obtained. **3** (also **clove pink**) a clove-scented pink (*Dianthus caryophyllus*) that is the original type from which the carnation and other double pinks have been bred. [ME: from OFr. *clou de girofle*, lit. 'nail of gillyflower' (from its shape), GILLYFLOWER being orig. the name of the spice and later applied to the similarly scented pink.]

clove[2] ▶ **n.** any of the small bulbs making up a compound bulb of garlic, shallot, etc. [OE *clufu*, of Gmc. origin, akin to Ger. *Knoblauch* and CLEAVE[1].]

clove[3] past of CLEAVE[1].

clove hitch ▶ **n.** a knot by which a rope is secured by passing it twice around a spar or another rope that it crosses at right angles in such a way that both ends pass under the loop of rope at the front. See illustration at KNOT[1]. [18th C.: *clove*, past tense of CLEAVE[1].]

clo·ven /ˈklōvən/ past participle of CLEAVE[1]. ▶ **adj.** split or divided in two.

clo·ven hoof (also **cloven foot**) ▶ **n.** the divided hoof or foot of ruminants such as cattle, sheep, goats, antelopes, and deer. ■ a similar foot ascribed to a satyr, the god Pan, or to the Devil, sometimes used as a symbol or mark of the Devil. — **clo·ven-hoofed adj. clo·ven-foot·ed adj.**

clove pink ▶ **n.** see CLOVE[1] (sense 3).

clo·ver /ˈklōvər/ ▶ **n.** a herbaceous plant (genus *Trifolium*) of the pea family that has dense, globular flowerheads and leaves that are typically three-lobed. It is an important and widely grown fodder and rotational crop.

– PHRASES **in clover** in ease and luxury. [OE *clāfre*, of Gmc. origin; rel. to Ger. *Klee*.]

clo·ver·leaf /ˈklōvərˌlēf/ ▶ **n.** a junction of roads intersecting at different levels with connecting sections forming the pattern of a four-leaf clover. ▶ **adj.** having a shape or pattern resembling a leaf of clover, esp. a four-leaf clover.

Clo·vis[1] /ˈklōvis/ **1** a city in central California, in the San Joaquin Valley; pop. 68,468. **2** a city in eastern New Mexico; pop. 32,667.

Clo·vis[2] (465–511), king of the Franks 481–511. He extended Merovingian rule to Gaul and Germany and defeated the Visigoths at the battle of Poitiers 507.

Clo·vis[3] ▶ **n.** [usu. as adj.] Archaeol. a Paleo-Indian culture of Central and North America, dated to about 11,500–11,000 years ago and earlier. The culture is distinguished by heavy, leaf-shaped stone spearheads. Compare with FOLSOM. [CLOVIS[1], New Mexico.]

clown /kloun/ ▶ **n.** a comic entertainer, esp. one in a circus, wearing a traditional costume and exaggerated makeup. ■ a comical, silly, playful person. ■ a foolish or incompetent person. ▶ **v.** [intrans.] behave in a comical way; act playfully: *Harvey **clowned around** pretending to be a dog.* — **clown·ish adj. clown·ish·ly adv. clown·ish·ness n.** [16th C.: perh. of Low Ger. origin.]

clown·fish /ˈkloun,fisн/ ▶ **n.** (pl. same or **-fish·es**) a small, tropical marine fish (genera *Amphiprion* and *Premnas*, family Pomacentridae) with bold vertical stripes or other bright coloration.

cloy /kloi/ ▶ **v.** [trans.] [usu. as adj.] (**cloying**) disgust or sicken (someone) with an excess of sweetness, richness, or sentiment: *a romantic, rather cloying story* | [intrans.] *the first sip gives a malty taste that never cloys.* — **cloy·ing·ly adv.** [ME: shortening of obs. *accloy* 'stop up,' from OFr. *encloyer* 'drive a nail into,' based on L. *clavus* 'a nail.']

clo·za·pine /ˈklōzə,pēn/ ▶ **n.** Med. a sedative drug of the benzodiazepine group, used to treat schizophrenia. [20th C.: from *c(h)lo(ro)-* + elements of BENZODIAZEPINE.]

cloze test /klōz/ ▶ **n.** a test in which one is asked to supply words that have been removed from a passage in order to measure one's ability to comprehend text. [1950s: abbrev. of CLOSURE.]

CLU ▶ **abbr.** Civil Liberties Union.

club[1] /kləb/ ▶ **n.** an association or organization dedicated to a particular interest or activity. ■ the building or facilities used by such an association. ■ an organization or facility offering members social amenities, meals, and temporary residence. ■ a nightclub, esp. one playing fashionable dance music. ■ an organization constituted to play games in a particular sport. ■ [usu. with adj.] a commercial organization offering subscribers special benefits: *a shopping club.* ■ [usu. with adj.] a group of people, organizations, or nations having something in common. ▶ **v.** (**clubbed, club·bing**) [intrans.] informal go out to nightclubs. [17th C. (v.): from CLUB[2].]

club[2] ▶ **n. 1** a heavy stick with a thick end, esp. one used as a weapon. ■ short for GOLF CLUB. **2** (**clubs**) one of the four suits in a conventional pack of playing cards, denoted by a black trefoil. ■ a card of such a suit. ▶ **v.** (**clubbed, club·bing**) [trans.] beat (a person or animal) with a club or similar implement. [ME: from ON *clubba*, var. of *klumba*; rel. to CLUMP.]

club·ba·ble /ˈkləbəbəl/ ▶ **adj.** suitable for membership of a club because of one's sociability or popularity. — **club·ba·bil·i·ty** /,kləbəˈbilətē/ **n.**

club·by /ˈkləbē/ ▶ **adj.** (**-bi·er, -bi·est**) informal friendly and sociable with fellow members of a group or organization but not with outsiders.

club car ▶ **n.** a railroad car equipped with a lounge and other amenities.

club chair ▶ **n.** a thickly upholstered armchair of the type often found in clubs.

club face ▶ **n.** the side of the head of a golf club that strikes the ball.

club foot ▶ **n. 1** a deformed foot that is twisted so that the sole cannot be placed flat on the ground. It is typically congenital or a result of polio. **2** a woodland toadstool (*Clitocybe clavipes*, family Tricholomataceae) with a grayish-brown cap, primrose-yellow gills, and a stem with a swollen woolly base, found in Eurasia and North America. — **club-foot·ed adj.**

club·house /ˈkləb,hous/ ▶ **n. 1** a building or part of a building used by a sports team, esp. a baseball team, as a locker room. **2** a building or room used by a club. **3** a building in a sporting area, esp. a golf course, used for socializing and recreation.

club·land /ˈkləb,land/ ▶ **n.** the world of nightclubs and of people who frequent them.

club·man /ˈkləbmən; -,man/ ▶ **n.** (pl. **-men**) a man who is a member of a club, esp. of a gentleman's club.

club moss (also **club·moss**) ▶ **n.** a low-growing green plant (family Lycopodiaceae) that resembles a large moss, having branching stems with undivided leaves.

club·root /ˈkləb,rōōt; -,rōōt/ ▶ **n.** a disease of cabbages, turnips, and related plants, in which the root becomes swollen and distorted by a single large gall or groups of smaller galls, caused by the fungus *Plasmodiophora brassicae.*

club sand·wich ▶ **n.** a sandwich of meat, tomato, lettuce, and mayonnaise, with two layers of filling between three slices of toast or bread.

club so·da ▶ **n.** trademark another term for SODA (sense 1).

club steak ▶ **n.** another term for DELMONICO STEAK.

cluck /klək/ ▶ **n. 1** the characteristic short, guttural sound made by a hen. ■ a similar sound made by a person to express annoyance. **2** informal a stupid or foolish person. ▶ **v.** (also **cluck-cluck**) [intrans.] (of a hen) make a short, guttural sound. ■ [trans.] (of a person) make such a sound with (one's tongue) to express concern or disapproval. ■ [intrans.] (**cluck over/at/about**) express fussy concern about. [15th C.: imitative.]

clue /klōō/ ▶ **n. 1** a piece of evidence or information used in the detection of a crime or solving of a mystery. ■ a fact or idea that serves as a guide or aid in a task or problem. **2** a verbal formula giving an indication as to what is to be inserted in a particular space in a crossword or other puzzle. ▶ **v.** (**clues, clued, clue·ing**) [trans.] (**clue someone in**) informal inform someone about a particular matter: *Stella had clued her in about Peter.* [ME 'a ball of thread': var. of CLEW.]

clued-in ▶ **adj.** informal well-informed about a particular subject.

clue·less /ˈklōōləs/ ▶ **adj.** informal having no knowledge, understanding, or ability. — **clue·less·ly adv. clue·less·ness n.**

Clum·ber span·iel /ˈkləmbər/ ▶ **n.** a spaniel of a slow, heavily built breed. [19th C.: *Clumber* Park, estate in England.]

clump /kləmp/ ▶ **n. 1** a compacted mass or lump of something. ■ a small, compact group of people. ■ a small group of trees or plants growing closely together. ■ Physiol. an agglutinated mass of blood cells or bacteria, esp. as an indicator of the presence of an antibody to them. **2** the sound of heavy footsteps. ▶ **v.** [intrans.] **1** form into a clump or mass. **2** (also **clomp**) walk with a heavy tread. [ME: partly imitative, reinforced by Mid. Low Ger. *klumpe* and MDu. *klompe*; rel. to CLUB[2].]

clump·y /ˈkləmpē/ ▶ **adj.** (**clump·i·er, clump·i·est**) **1** (of shoes or boots) heavy and inelegant. **2** forming or showing a tendency to form clumps.

clum·sy /ˈkləmzē/ ▶ **adj.** (**-si·er, -si·est**) awkward in movement or in handling things. ■ done awkwardly or without skill or elegance. ■ difficult to handle or use; unwieldy. ■ lacking social skills and graces. — **clum·si·ly** /-zəlē/ **adv. clum·si·ness n.** [16th C.: from obs. *clumse* 'make numb,' prob. of Scand. origin and rel. to Swed. *klumsig.*]

clung /kləNG/ past and past participle of CLING.

Clu·ni·ac /ˈklōōnē,ak/ ▶ **adj.** of or relating to a reformed Benedictine monastic order founded at Cluny in eastern France in 910. ▶ **n.** a monk of this order.

clunk /kləNGk/ ▶ **n. 1** a heavy, dull sound such as that made by thick pieces of metal striking together. **2** informal a stupid or foolish person. ▶ **v.** [no obj., with adverbial] move with or make such a sound: *the machinery clunked into life.* [18th C.: imitative.]

clunk·er /ˈkləNGkər/ ▶ **n.** informal an old, run-down vehicle or machine. ■ a thing that is totally unsuccessful.

clunk·y /ˈkləNGkē/ ▶ **adj.** (**clunk·i·er, clunk·i·est**) informal **1** awkwardly solid, heavy, and outdated. **2** making a clunking sound.

clu·pe·oid /ˈklōōpē,oid/ Zool. ▶ **n.** a marine fish of a group (order Clupeiformes or suborder Clupeoidei) that includes the herring family together with the anchovies and related fish. ▶ **adj.** of or relating to fish of this group. [19th C.: from mod. L. *Clupeoidei* (pl.), from L. *clupea*, a river fish.]

clus·ter /ˈkləstər/ ▶ **n.** a group of similar objects growing closely together. ■ a group of people or similar objects positioned or occurring close together. ■ Astron. a group of stars or galaxies forming a relatively close association. ■ Ling. (also **consonant cluster**) a group of consonants pronounced in immediate succession, as *str* in *strong.* ■ a natural subgroup of a population, used for statistical sampling or analysis. ■ Chem. a group of atoms of the same element, typically a metal, bonded closely together in a molecule. ▶ **v.** [intrans.] be or come into a cluster or close group; congregate: *the children **clustered around** her skirts.* ■ Stat. (of data points) have similar numerical values: *students had scores clustering around 70 percent.* [OE *clyster*; prob. rel. to CLOT.]

clus·ter bomb ▶ **n.** a bomb that releases a number of projectiles on impact to injure or damage personnel and vehicles.

clus·tered /ˈkləstərd/ ▶ **adj.** [attrib.] growing or situated in a group.

clus·ter head·ache ▶ **n.** a type of severe headache that tends to recur over several weeks and in which the pain is usually limited to one side of the head.

clutch[1] /kləcн/ ▶ **v.** [trans.] grasp or seize (something) tightly or eagerly. ■ (also **clutch up**) become nervous and panicked. ▶ **n. 1** a tight grasp or an act of grasping something. ■ (**someone's clutches**) a person's power or control, esp. when perceived as cruel or inescapable. **2** a slim, flat handbag without handles or a strap. **3** (**the clutch**) an emergency or critical moment. **4** a mechanism for connecting and disconnecting a vehicle engine from its transmission system. ■ the pedal operating such a mechanism. ■ an arrangement for connecting and disconnecting the working parts of any machine.
– PHRASES **clutch at straws** see STRAW. [ME (in the sense 'bend, crook'): var. of obs. *clitch* 'close the hand,' from OE *clyccan* 'clench,' of Gmc. origin.]

clutch[2] ▶ **n.** a group of eggs fertilized at the same time, typically laid in a single session and (in birds) incubated together. ■ a brood of chicks. ■ a small group of people or things. [18th C.: prob. dial. *cletch*, rel. to ME *cleck* 'to hatch,' from ON *klekja.*]

Clu·tha /ˈklōōтнə/ a river at the southern end of the South Island, New Zealand, flowing for 213 miles (338 km) to the Pacific.

clut·ter /ˈklətər/ ▶ **n.** a collection of things lying about in an untidy mass. ■ an untidy state. ▶ **v.** [trans.] crowd (something) untidily; fill with clutter. [ME: var. of dial. *clotter* 'to clot.']

Clyde /klīd/ a river in western central Scotland that flows for 106 miles (170 km) northwest to the Firth of Clyde.

Clyde, Firth of the estuary of the Clyde River in western Scotland.

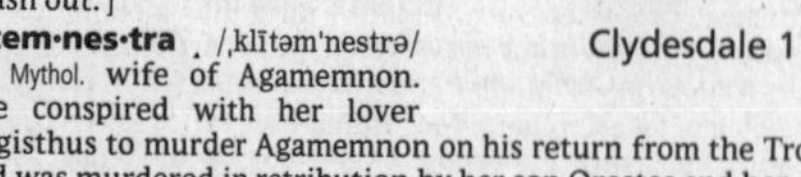
Clydesdale 1

Clydes·dale /ˈklīdzˌdāl/ ▶n. **1** a horse of a heavy, powerful breed, used for pulling heavy loads. **2** a dog of a small breed of terrier. [CLYDE.]

clyp·e·us /ˈklipēəs/ ▶n. (pl. **clyp·e·i** /ˈklipēˌī; -ēˌē/) Entomol. a broad plate at the front of an insect's head. —**clyp·e·al** /-pēəl/ adj. [19th C.: from L., lit. 'round shield.']

clys·ter /ˈklistər/ ▶n. archaic term for ENEMA. [ME: ult. from Gk. *klustēr* 'syringe,' from *kluzein* 'wash out.']

Cly·tem·nes·tra /ˌklītəmˈnestrə/ Gk. Mythol. wife of Agamemnon. She conspired with her lover Aegisthus to murder Agamemnon on his return from the Trojan War and was murdered in retribution by her son Orestes and her daughter Electra.

CM ▶abbr. ■ command module. ■ common meter or measure.

Cm ▶symb. the chemical element curium.

cm ▶abbr. centimeter(s).

Cmdr (also **Cmdr.**) ▶abbr. Commander.

Cmdre (also **Cmdre.**) ▶abbr. Commodore.

CMEA ▶abbr. Council for Mutual Economic Assistance.

CMOS ▶n. [often as adj.] Electron. a technology for making low-power integrated circuits. ■ a chip built using such technology. [1980s: from *Complementary Metal Oxide Semiconductor*.]

CMSgt ▶abbr. chief master sergeant.

CMV ▶abbr. cytomegalovirus.

cne·mi·al crest /ˈnēmēəl/ ▶n. Zool. (in the legs of many mammals, birds, and dinosaurs) a ridge at the front of the head of the tibia or tibiotarsus to which the main extensor muscle of the thigh is attached. [19th C.: *cnemial*, from Gk. *knēmē* 'tibia' + -AL.]

CNG ▶abbr. compressed natural gas.

Cni·dar·i·a /nīˈde(ə)rēə/ Zool. a phylum of aquatic invertebrate animals that comprises the coelenterates. —**cni·dar·i·an** n. & adj. [mod. L. (pl.), from Gk. *knidē* 'nettle.']

CNN ▶abbr. Cable News Network.

CNR hist. ▶abbr. Canadian National Railways.

CNS ▶abbr. central nervous system.

Cnut /kəˈno͞ot/ variant of CANUTE.

CO ▶abbr. ■ Colorado (in official postal use). ■ Commanding Officer. ■ conscientious objector.

Co ▶symb. the chemical element cobalt.

Co. ▶abbr. ■ company. ■ county.
– PHRASES **and Co.** used as part of the titles of commercial businesses to designate the partner or partners not named. ■ (also **and co.**) informal and the rest of them: *I waited for Mark and Co. to arrive.*

c/o ▶abbr. ■ care of. ■ carried over.

co- ▶prefix **1** (forming nouns) joint; mutual; common: *coeducation*. **2** (forming adjectives) jointly; mutually: *coequal*. **3** (forming verbs) together with another or others: *coproduce* | *co-own*. **4** Math. of the complement of an angle: *cosine*. ■ the complement of: *colatitude* | *coset*. [from L., orig. a form of COM-.]

CoA Biochem. ▶abbr. coenzyme A.

coach¹ /kōch/ ▶n. **1** a horse-drawn carriage, esp. a closed one. **2** a railroad car. ■ [as adj.] denoting economy class seating in an aircraft or train: *the cheapest coach-class fare*. **3** a bus, esp. one that is comfortably equipped and used for longer journeys. ▶v. [no obj., with adverbial of direction] travel by coach: *they coached to Claude's dwelling*. ▶adv. in economy class accommodations in an aircraft or train: *flying coach*. [16th C. (sense 1): from Fr. *coche*, from Hungarian *kocsi (szekér)* '(wagon) from *Kocs*,' a town in Hungary.]

coach² ▶n. an athletic instructor or trainer. ■ a tutor who gives private or specialized teaching. ▶v. [trans.] train or instruct (a team or player). ■ give (someone) extra or private teaching. ■ teach (a subject or sport) as a coach. ■ prompt or urge (someone) with instructions. [18th C.: from COACH¹.]

coach·man /ˈkōchmən/ ▶n. (pl. **-men**) a driver of a horse-drawn carriage.

coach·roof /ˈkōchˌro͞of; -ˌro͝of/ ▶n. a raised part of the cabin roof of a yacht.

coach screw ▶n. another term for LAG SCREW.

coach·whip /ˈkōchˌ(h)wip/ ▶n. a harmless, fast-moving North American snake (*Masticophis flagellum*, family Colubridae). The pattern of scales on its slender body is said to resemble a braided whip.

co·ac·tion /kōˈakshən/ ▶n. **1** compulsion; restraint; coercion. **2** concerted action; acting together.

co·a·dapt·ed /ˌkōəˈdaptid/ ▶adj. Biol. mutually adapted; mutually accommodating. —**co·a·dap·ta·tion** /ˌkōadəpˈtāshən/ n.

co·ad·ju·tant /kōˈajətənt/ ▶adj. helping another or others, or with another or others. ▶n. a person who thus helps.

co·ad·ju·tor /ˌkōəˈjo͞otər; kōˈajətər/ ▶n. a bishop appointed to assist a diocesan bishop, and often also designated as his successor. [ME: via OFr. from late L. *coadjutor*, from *co-* + *adjutor* 'assistant' (from *adjuvare* 'to help').]

co·ag·u·lant /kōˈagyələnt/ ▶n. a substance that causes blood or another liquid to coagulate.

co·ag·u·lase /kōˈagyəˌlās; -ˌlāz/ ▶n. Biochem. a bacterial enzyme that brings about the coagulation of blood or plasma and is produced by disease-causing forms of staphylococcus.

co·ag·u·late /kōˈagyəˌlāt/ ▶v. [intrans.] (of a fluid, esp. blood) change to a solid or semisolid state. ■ [trans.] cause (a fluid) to change to a solid or semisolid state: *epinephrine coagulates the blood*. —**co·ag·u·la·ble** /-ləbəl/ adj. **co·ag·u·la·tion** /kōˌagyəˈlāshən/ n. **co·ag·u·la·tive** /-ˌlātiv/ adj. **co·ag·u·la·tor** /-ˌlātər/ n. [ME: from L. *coagulat-* 'curdled,' from v. *coagulare*, from *coagulum* 'rennet.']

Co·a·hui·la /ˌkōəˈwēlə/ a state in northern Mexico, on the US border; capital, Saltillo.

coal /kōl/ ▶n. a combustible black or dark brown rock consisting mainly of carbonized plant matter, found mainly in underground deposits and widely used as fuel: [as adj.] *a coal fire*. ■ a red-hot piece of coal or other material in a fire. ▶v. [trans.] provide with a supply of coal.
– PHRASES **coals to Newcastle** something brought or sent to a place where it is already plentiful. **rake** (or **haul**) **someone over the coals** reprimand someone severely. —**coal·y** adj. [OE *col* ('ember'), from Gmc.; akin to Ger. *Kohle*.]

coal-black ▶adj. as black as coal; utterly black.

coal·er /ˈkōlər/ ▶n. **1** a ship that transports coal. **2** a large mechanized structure for loading coal on to a ship, railroad car, or steam locomotive.

co·a·lesce /ˌkōəˈles/ ▶v. [intrans.] come together and form one mass or whole. ■ [trans.] combine (elements) in a mass or whole. —**co·a·les·cence** /-ˈlesəns/ n. **co·a·les·cent** /-ˈlesənt/ adj. [16th C.: from L. *coalescere*, from *co-* + *alescere* 'grow up' (from *alere* 'nourish').]

coal·field /ˈkōlˌfēld/ ▶n. an extensive area containing underground coal deposits.

coal-fired ▶adj. heated, driven, or produced by the burning of coal: *a coal-fired power station*.

coal gas ▶n. a mixture of gases (chiefly hydrogen, methane, and carbon monoxide) obtained by the destructive distillation of coal and formerly used for lighting and heating.

co·a·li·tion /ˌkōəˈlishən/ ▶n. an alliance for combined action, especially a temporary alliance of political parties forming a government or of states. —**co·a·li·tion·ist** n. [17th C.: from med. L. *coalitio(n-)*, from *coalescere*.]

coal meas·ures ▶plural n. Geol. a series of strata of the Carboniferous period, including coal seams.

coal oil ▶n. another term for KEROSENE.

Coal·sack /ˈkōlˌsak/ (**the Coalsack**) Astron. a dark nebula of dust near the Southern Cross that gives the appearance of a gap in the stars of the Milky Way.

coal tar ▶n. a thick black liquid produced by the destructive distillation of bituminous coal. It contains benzene, naphthalene, phenols, aniline, and many other organic chemicals.

coam·ing /ˈkōming/ (also **coam·ings**) ▶n. a raised border around a ship's hatch serving to support the hatch covers and to keep out water. ■ a similar structure around the cockpit of a boat. [17th C.: of unknown origin.]

co·ap·ta·tion /ˌkōapˈtāshən/ ▶n. the adaptation or adjustment of things, parts, or people to each other. ■ Med. the drawing together of the separated tissue in a wound or fracture. [16th C.: from late L. *coaptatio(n-)*, from v. *coaptare*, from *co-* + *aptare* (from *aptus* 'apt').]

co·arc·tate /kōˈärktāt/ ▶adj. esp. Anat. Biol. pressed close together; contracted; confined. [ME: from L. *coarctatus*, past part. of *coarctare* 'press together.']

coarse /kôrs/ ▶adj. **1** rough or loose in texture or grain. ■ made of large grains or particles: *dry, coarse sand*. ■ (of grains or particles) large. ■ (of a person's features) not elegantly formed or proportioned. ■ (of food or drink) of inferior quality. **2** (of a person or a person's speech) rude, crude, or vulgar. —**coarse·ness** n. **coars·ish** adj. [ME ('ordinary or inferior'): possibly from COURSE.]

coarse-grained ▶adj. **1** coarse in texture or grain. ■ (of photographic film) having a noticeably grainy appearance. **2** coarse in manner or speech: *a coarse-grained man*.

coars·en /ˈkôrsən/ ▶v. make or become rough. ■ make or become crude, vulgar, or unpleasant.

co·ar·tic·u·la·tion /ˌkō-ärˌtikyəˈlāshən/ ▶n. Phonet. the articulation of two or more speech sounds together, so that one influences the other.

coast /kōst/ ▶n. **1** the part of the land near the sea; the edge of the land. ■ (**the Coast**) the Pacific coast of North America. **2** a run or movement in or on a vehicle without the use of power. ▶v. **1** [no obj., with adverbial of direction] (of a person or vehicle) move easily without using power. ■ [intrans.] act or make progress without making much effort. ■ slide down a snowy hill on a sled. **2** [no obj., with adverbial of direction] sail along the coast, esp. in order to carry cargo.
– PHRASES **the coast is clear** there is no danger of being observed or caught. [ME: from OFr. *coste* (n.), *costeier* (v.), from L. *costa* 'rib, side.']

coast·al /ˈkōstəl/ ▶adj. of, relating to, or near a coast.

coast·er /ˈkōstər/ ▶n. **1** a ship used to carry cargo along the coast. ■ [with adj.] a person who inhabits a specified coast. **2** a small tray or mat placed under a bottle or glass to protect the table underneath. **3** a toboggan. ■ short for ROLLER COASTER.

coast·guard /ˈkōstˌgärd/ (also **coast·guard**) ▶ n. (**Coast Guard**) a branch of the US armed forces responsible for the enforcement of maritime law and for the protection of life and property at sea. ■ (**the coastguard**) a civilian or volunteer organization keeping watch on the sea near a coast in order to assist people or ships in danger and to prevent smuggling.

coast·guards·man /ˈkōstˌgärdzmən/ ▶ n. a member of a coastguard, esp. the US Coast Guard.

coast·land /ˈkōstˌland/ ▶ n. (usu. **coastlands**) an expanse of land near the sea.

coast·line /ˈkōstˌlīn/ ▶ n. the outline of a coast, esp. with regard to its shape and appearance.

Coast Moun·tains a range that curves 1,000 miles (1,600 km) from British Columbia to Alaska, extending the line of the Cascade Mountains.

Coast Rang·es the name for various ranges that extend from southern California along the Pacific coast to Alaska.

coast to coast ▶ adj. & adv. all the way across an island or continent.

coast·ward /ˈkōstwərd/ (also **coast·wards**) ▶ adv. & adj. toward the coast.

coast·wise /ˈkōstˌwīz/ ▶ adj. & adv. along, following, or connected with the coast.

coat /kōt/ ▶ n. **1** an outer garment worn outdoors, having sleeves and typically extending below the hips. ■ a similar item worn indoors as a protective garment: *a laboratory coat.* ■ a man's jacket or tunic. ■ a woman's tailored jacket. **2** an animal's covering of fur or hair. ■ a structure, esp. a membrane, enclosing or lining an organ. ■ a skin, rind, or husk. ■ a layer of a plant bulb. ■ [with adj.] an outer layer or covering of a specified kind: *the protein coat of the virus.* **3** a covering of paint or similar material laid on a surface at one time: *a protective coat of varnish.* ▶ v. [trans.] (often **be coated**) provide with a layer or covering of something; apply a coat to. ■ (of a substance) form a covering to. — **coat·ed** adj. [in comb.] *shaggy-coated cattle.* [ME: from OFr. *cote.*]

coat check ▶ n. a cloakroom with an attendant.

coat dress ▶ n. a woman's tailored dress, typically fastening down the front and resembling a coat.

coat hang·er ▶ n. see HANGER (sense 2).

co·a·ti /kōˈätē/ (also **coatimundi** /kōˌätiˈməndē/) ▶ n. (pl. **-tis**) a mammal (genera *Nasua* and *Nasuella*) of the raccoon family found mainly in Central and South America, with a long, flexible snout and a ringed tail. [17th C.: from Sp. and Port., from Tupi *kua'ti*, from *cua* 'belt' + *tim* 'nose.']

coat·ing /ˈkōtiNG/ ▶ n. a thin layer or covering of something: *a coating of paint.* ■ material used for making coats.

coat of arms ▶ n. the distinctive heraldic bearings or shield of a person, family, corporation, or country.

coat of mail ▶ n. hist. a jacket covered with or composed of metal rings or plates, serving as armor.

coat·rack /ˈkōtˌrak/ ▶ n. a rack or stand with hooks on which to hang coats, hats, etc.

coat·room /ˈkōtˌro͞om; -ˌro͝om/ ▶ n. another term for CLOAKROOM.

Coats Land /ˈkōts/ a region of Antarctica, east of the Antarctic Peninsula.

coat stand ▶ n. another term for COATRACK.

coat·tail /ˈkōtˌtāl/ ▶ n. (usu. **coattails**) each of the flaps formed by the back of a tailcoat.
– PHRASES **on someone's coattails** undeservedly benefiting from another's success.

co·au·thor /kōˈôTHər/ ▶ n. a joint author. ▶ v. [trans.] be a joint author of (a book, paper, or report).

coax[1] /kōks/ ▶ v. [trans.] persuade (someone) gradually or by flattery to do something. ■ (**coax something from/out of**) use such persuasion to obtain something from: *we coaxed money out of my father.* ■ [with obj. and adverbial] manipulate (something) carefully into a particular shape or position. — **coax·er** n. **coax·ing·ly** adv. [16th C.: from obs. *cokes* 'simpleton.']

coax[2] /ˈkō-aks; kōˈaks/ informal ▶ n. coaxial cable. ▶ adj. coaxial: *coax connectors.*

co·ax·i·al /kōˈaksēəl/ ▶ adj. having a common axis. ■ (of a cable or line) consisting of two concentric conductors separated by an insulator. — **co·ax·i·al·ly** adv.

cob /käb/ ▶ n. **1** (also **corncob**) the central, cylindrical, woody part of the corn ear to which the grains, or kernels, are attached. **2** (also **cobnut**) a hazelnut or filbert, esp. one of a large variety. ■ a hazel or filbert bush. **3** a powerfully built, short-legged horse. **4** a male swan. [ME: origin unknown.]

co·bal·a·min /kōˈbaləmin/ ▶ n. Biochem. any of a group of cobalt-containing substances including cyanocobalamin (vitamin B_{12}). [1950s: blend of COBALT and VITAMIN.]

co·balt /ˈkōbôlt/ ▶ n. the chemical element of atomic number 27, a hard silvery-white magnetic metal. (Symbol: **Co**) ■ short for COBALT BLUE: [as adj.] *a cobalt sky.* — **co·bal·tic** /kōˈbôltik/ adj. **co·bal·tous** /kōˈbôltəs/ adj. [17th C.: from Ger. *Kobalt* 'demon' (from the belief that cobalt was harmful to the ores with which it occurred).]

co·balt blue ▶ n. a deep blue pigment containing cobalt and aluminum oxides. ■ the deep blue color of this.

Cobb /käb/, Ty (1886–1961), US baseball player; full name *Tyrus Raymond Cobb*; nicknamed **the Georgia Peach**. A Detroit Tiger 1905–26, his lifetime batting average (.367) is the highest in baseball history.

cob·ble[1] /ˈkäbəl/ ▶ n. (usu. **cobbles**) a cobblestone. [ME: from COB + -LE[2].]

cob·ble[2] ▶ v. [trans.] **1** dated repair (shoes). **2** (**cobble something together**) roughly assemble or put together something from available parts. [15th C.: back-form. from COBBLER.]

cob·bled /ˈkäbəld/ ▶ adj. (of an area or roadway) paved with cobbles: *a cobbled courtyard.*

cob·bler /ˈkäblər/ ▶ n. **1** a person who mends shoes as a job. **2** an iced drink made with wine or sherry, sugar, and lemon. **3** a fruit pie with a rich, thick, cakelike crust. [ME: of unknown origin.]

cob·ble·stone /ˈkäbəlˌstōn/ ▶ n. a small, round stone of a kind formerly used to cover road surfaces.

cob·by /ˈkäbē/ ▶ adj. (of horses, dogs, and other animals) shortish and thickset; stocky.

Cob·den /ˈkäbdən/, Richard (1804–65), English political activist who advocated free trade.

COBE /ˈkōbē/ a NASA satellite launched in 1989 to map the background microwave radiation from space in a search for evidence of the big bang. [acronym from *Cosmic Background Explorer.*]

co·bel·lig·er·ent /kōbəˈlijərənt/ ▶ n. any of two or more nations engaged in war as allies. — **co·bel·lig·er·ence** n.

co·bi·a /ˈkōbēə/ ▶ n. (pl. same) a large, edible game fish (*Rachycentron canadum*, family Rachycentridae) that lives in open waters of the Atlantic, Indian, and western Pacific oceans. Also called SERGEANT FISH. [19th C.: of unknown origin.]

cob·nut /ˈkäbˌnət/ ▶ n. see COB (sense 2).

COBOL /ˈkōbôl/ ▶ n. a computer programming language designed for use in commerce. [1960s: from *co(mmon) b(usiness) o(riented) l(anguage).*]

co·bra /ˈkōbrə/ ▶ n. a highly venomous snake (*Naja* and two other genera, family Elapidae) native to Africa and Asia that spreads the skin of its neck into a hood when disturbed. See illustration at SPECTACLED COBRA. [17th C.: from Port. *cobra de capello*, lit. 'snake with hood,' based on L. *colubra* 'snake.']

cob·web /ˈkäbˌweb/ ▶ n. (usu. **cobwebs**) a spider's web, esp. when old and covered with dust. ■ Zool. a tangled three-dimensional spider's web. ■ something resembling a cobweb in delicacy or intricacy: *white cobwebs of frost.* — **cob·webbed** adj. **cob·web·by** adj. [ME *coppeweb, copweb*, from obs. *coppe* 'spider' + WEB.]

co·ca /ˈkōkə/ ▶ n. a tropical American shrub (*Erythroxylum coca*, family Erythroxylaceae) that is widely grown for its leaves, which are a source of cocaine. ■ the dried leaves of this shrub, chewed as a stimulant by the native people of western South America. [16th C.: from Sp., from Aymara *kuka* or Quechua *koka.*]

co·caine /kōˈkān; ˈkōkān/ ▶ n. an addictive drug, $C_{17}H_{21}NO_4$, derived from coca or prepared synthetically, used as an illegal stimulant and sometimes medicinally as a local anesthetic. [19th C.: from COCA + -INE[4].]

coc·cid /ˈkäksid/ ▶ n. a homopteran insect of the family Coccidae; a scale insect.

coc·cid·i·a /käkˈsidēə/ ▶ plural n. (sing. **-cid·i·um** /-ˈsidēəm/) Biol. parasitic protozoa of a group (suborder Eimeriorina, phylum Sporozoa) that includes those that cause diseases such as coccidiosis and toxoplasmosis. — **coc·cid·i·an** adj. & n.

coc·cid·i·oi·do·my·co·sis /käkˌsidēˌoidōmīˈkōsəs/ ▶ n. a serious disease of the lungs and other tissues, caused by the fungus *Coccidioides immitis* and endemic in the warmer, arid regions of America. [1930s: from mod. L. *Coccidioides* + MYCOSIS.]

coc·cid·i·o·sis /käkˌsidēˈōsəs/ ▶ n. a disease of birds and mammals that chiefly affects the intestines, caused by coccidia (*Eimeria, Isopora*, and other genera).

coc·cid·i·um /käkˈsidēəm/ ▶ n. singular form of COCCIDIA.

coc·ci·nel·lid /ˌkäksəˈnelid/ ▶ n. Entomol. a beetle of a family (Coccinellidae) that includes the ladybugs. [19th C.: from mod. L. *Coccinellidae* (pl.), from *Coccinella*, from L. *coccineus* 'scarlet.']

coc·co·lith /ˈkäkəˌliTH/ ▶ n. Biol. a minute, rounded, calcareous platelet, numbers of which form the spherical shells of coccolithophores. [19th C.: from Gk. *kokkos* 'grain' + *lithos* 'stone.']

coc·cus /ˈkäkəs/ ▶ n. (pl. **coc·ci** /ˈkäkˌ(s)ī; ˈkäkˌ(s)ē/) Biol. any spherical or roughly spherical bacterium. — **coc·cal** /ˈkäkəl/ adj. **coc·coid** /ˈkäkoid/ adj. [18th C.: mod. L., from Gk. *kokkos* 'berry.']

coc·cyx /ˈkäksiks/ ▶ n. (pl. **-cy·ges** /-səˌjēz/ or **-cyx·es** /-siksiz/) a small, triangular bone at the base of the spinal column in humans and some apes, formed of fused vestigial vertebrae. — **coc·cyg·e·al** /käkˈsijēəl/ adj. [16th C.: via L. from Gk. *kokkux* 'cuckoo' (because its shape in humans resembles a cuckoo's bill).]

Co·cha·bam·ba /ˌkōCHəˈbämbə/ a city in western central Bolivia; pop. 404,100.

co·chair /ˈkōˌCHe(ə)r/ ▶ n. a person who is in charge of a meeting or organization jointly with another or others. ▶ v. [trans.] chair (a meeting) in this way.

Co·chin[1] /ˈkōˈCHin/ a city on the Malabar Coast of southwestern India; pop. 504,000.

Co·chin[2] /ˈkōCHin; ˈkäCHin/ (also **Cochin China**) ▶ **n.** a chicken of an Asian breed with feathery legs.

Co·chin-Chi·na /ˈkō,CHin/ the former name for the southern region of what is now Vietnam; formerly a French colony.

coch·i·neal /ˈkäCHə,nēəl; ˈkō-/ ▶ **n.** **1** a scarlet dye used chiefly for coloring food. ■ the dried bodies of a female scale insect, which are crushed to yield this dye. ■ a similar dye or preparation made from the oak kermes insect (see KERMES). **2** (**cochineal insect**) the scale insect (*Dactylopius coccus*, family Dactylopiidae) that is used for cochineal, native to Mexico and formerly widely cultivated on cacti. [16th C.: from Fr. *cochenille* or Sp. *cochinilla*, from L. *coccinus* 'scarlet,' from Gk. *kokkos* 'berry.']

Co·chise /kōˈCHēs/ (c.1812–74), American Indian chief. As leader of the Apaches, he resisted white encroachment on Indian lands.

coch·le·a /ˈkōklēə; ˈkäk-/ ▶ **n.** (pl. **-le·ae** /-lē,ē; -lē,ī/) the spiral cavity of the inner ear containing the organ of Corti, which produces nerve impulses in response to sound vibrations. — **coch·le·ar** **adj.** [16th C.: from L., 'snail shell or screw,' from Gk. *kokhlias*.]

coch·le·ate /ˈkäklēit; -,āt/ (also **coch·le·at·ed**) ▶ **adj.** esp. Bot. formed like a spiral shell; twisted.

Coch·ran /ˈkäkrən/, Jacqueline (c.1910–80), US aviator. In 1953, she became the first woman to break the sound barrier.

cock[1] /käk/ ▶ **n.** **1** a male bird, esp. a rooster. ■ [in comb.] used in names of birds, esp. game birds, e.g., **woodcock**. **2** vulgar slang a penis. **3** a firing lever in a gun which can be raised to be released by the trigger. **4** a stopcock. ▶ **v.** [trans.] **1** tilt (something) in a particular direction. ■ bend a (limb or joint) at an angle. ■ (of a male dog) lift (a back leg) in order to urinate. **2** raise the cock of (a gun) in order to make it ready for firing.

– PHRASES **at full cock** (of a gun) with the cock lifted to the position at which the trigger will act. **cock one's ear** (of a dog) raise its ears to an erect position. ■ (of a person) listen attentively to or for something. **cock of the walk** someone who dominates others within a group. [OE *cocc*, from med. L. *coccus*.]

cock[2] ▶ **n.** dated a small pile of hay, straw, or other material, with vertical sides and a rounded top. [ME: perh. of Scand. origin, akin to Norw. *kok* 'heap.']

cock·ade /käˈkād/ ▶ **n.** a rosette or knot of ribbons worn in a hat as a badge of office or party, or as part of a livery. — **cock·ad·ed** **adj.** [17th C.: from Fr. *cocarde*, from the fem. of obs. *coquard* 'saucy.']

cock-a-doo·dle-doo /,käk ə ,do͞odl ˈdo͞o/ ▶ **n.** used to represent the sound made by a cock when it crows.

cock-a-hoop /,käk ə ˈho͝op; ˈho͞op/ ▶ **adj.** [predic.] extremely and obviously pleased, esp. about a success. [17th C.: from *set cock a hoop*, appar. 'turn on the tap.']

cock-a-leek·ie /,käk ə ˈlēkē/ ▶ **n.** a Scottish soup traditionally made with chicken and leeks. [18th C.: from COCK[1] and LEEK.]

cock·a·ma·mie /ˈkäkə,māmē; ,käkəˈmāmē/ (also **cock·a·ma·my**) ▶ **adj.** informal ridiculous; implausible. [1940s: prob. an alt. of DECALCOMANIA.]

cock and bull sto·ry ▶ **n.** informal a ridiculous and implausible story.

cock·a·tiel /ˈkäkə,tēl/ ▶ **n.** a slender, long-crested Australian parrot (*Nymphicus hollandicus*) related to the cockatoos, with a mainly gray body, white shoulders, and a yellow and orange face. [19th C.: from Du. *kaketielje*, prob. dimin. of *kaketoe* 'cockatoo.']

cock·a·too /ˈkäkə,to͞o/ ▶ **n.** a large crested parrot, with typically white plumage tinged with pink or yellow. Numerous genera and species, esp. genus *Cacatua*, are found in Australia and eastern Indonesia. [17th C.: from Du. *kaketoe*, from Malay *kakatua*.]

cock·a·trice /ˈkäkətris; -,trīs/ ▶ **n.** another term for BASILISK (sense 1). ■ Heraldry a mythical animal depicted as a two-legged dragon (or wyvern) with a cock's head. [ME: from OFr. *cocatris*, from L. *calcatrix* 'tracker' (from *calcare* 'to tread').]

cock·chaf·er /ˈkäk,CHāfər/ ▶ **n.** a large brown European beetle (*Melolontha melolontha*, family Scarabaeidae). The adults damage foliage and flowers, and the larvae are a pest of cereal and grass roots. [18th C.: from COCK[1] + CHAFER.]

Cock·croft /ˈkäk,krôft/, Sir John Douglas (1897–1967), English physicist. In 1932, working with E. T. S. Walton, he succeeded in splitting the atom. Nobel Prize for Physics (1951, shared with Walton).

cock·crow /ˈkäk,krō/ (also **cock-crow** or **cock crow**) ▶ **n.** literary dawn: *the hour of cockcrow was still far off.*

cocked hat ▶ **n.** a brimless triangular hat pointed at the front, back, and top.

cock·er·el /ˈkäkərəl/ ▶ **n.** a young domestic cock. [ME: dimin. of COCK[1].]

cock·er span·iel /ˈkäkər/ (also **cock·er**) ▶ **n.** a small spaniel of a breed with a silky coat. [19th C.: from COCK[1].]

cock·eyed /ˈkäk,īd/ ▶ **adj.** informal crooked or askew; not level: *cockeyed camera angles.* ■ absurd; impractical. ■ drunk: *I got cockeyed.* ■ (of a person or a person's eyes) having a squint. [19th C.: appar. from the v. COCK[1] and EYE.]

cock·fight·ing /ˈkäk,fītiNG/ ▶ **n.** the practice of setting two cocks, their legs often fitted with sharp spurs, to fight each other. — **cock·fight** /ˈkäk,fīt/ **n.**

cock·le[1] /ˈkäkəl/ ▶ **n.** **1** an edible, burrowing bivalve mollusk (genus *Cardium*, family Cardiidae) with a strong ribbed shell. **2** (also **cock·le·shell**) literary a small shallow boat.

– PHRASES **warm the cockles of one's heart** give one a comforting feeling of pleasure or contentment. [ME: from OFr. *coquille* 'shell,' based on Gk. *konkhulion*, from *konkhē* 'conch.']

cock·le[2] ▶ **v.** [intrans.] (of paper) pucker in certain places so as to present a wrinkled or creased surface. [16th C.: from Fr. *coquiller* 'to blister,' from *coquille* (see COCKLE[1]).]

cock·le·bur /ˈkäkəl,bər/ ▶ **n.** a herbaceous plant (genus *Xanthium*) of the daisy family, with broad leaves and burred fruits. [19th C.: from COCKLE[2] + BURR.]

cock·loft /ˈkäk,lôft/ ▶ **n.** a small loft or attic.

cock·ney /ˈkäknē/ ▶ **n.** (pl. **-neys**) a native of East London. ■ the dialect or accent typical of such people. ▶ **adj.** of or characteristic of cockneys or their dialect or accent: *cockney humor.* — **cock·ney·ism** **n.** [17th C., orig. 'a town dweller regarded as puny.']

cock·pit /ˈkäk,pit/ ▶ **n.** **1** a compartment for the pilot and sometimes also the crew in an aircraft or spacecraft. ■ a similar compartment for the driver in a racecar. ■ a sunken area in the after deck of a boat providing space for members of the crew. **2** a place where a battle or other conflict takes place. ■ a place where cockfights are held. [16th C.: from COCK[1] + PIT[1].]

cock·roach /ˈkäk,rōCH/ ▶ **n.** a beetlelike insect (order Dictyoptera) with long antennae and legs, feeding by scavenging. Among the several species that have become established worldwide as pests in homes and food service establishments is the **American cockroach** (*Periplaneta americana*). [17th C.: from Sp. *cucaracha*, alt. by folk etymology.]

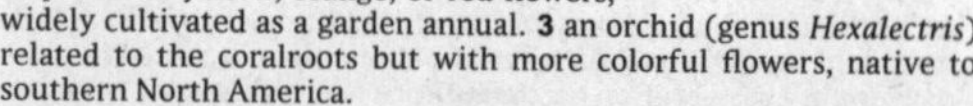
American cockroach

cocks·comb /ˈkäks,kōm/ ▶ **n.** **1** the crest or comb of a domestic cock. See illustration at WATTLE[2]. **2** a tropical plant (*Celosia cristata*) of the amaranth family, with a showy crest or plume of yellow, orange, or red flowers, widely cultivated as a garden annual. **3** an orchid (genus *Hexalectris*) related to the coralroots but with more colorful flowers, native to southern North America.

cocks·man /ˈkäksmən/ ▶ **n.** (pl. **-men**) vulgar slang a man reputed to be extremely virile or sexually accomplished. — **cocks·man·ship** **n.**

cock·spur thorn ▶ **n.** a North American hawthorn (*Crataegus crus-galli*) that is often cultivated for its rich orange autumn foliage.

cock·suck·er /ˈkäk,səkər/ ▶ **n.** vulgar slang a fellator. ■ a generalized term of abuse.

cock·sure /ˈkäk,SHo͝or/ ▶ **adj.** presumptuously or arrogantly confident. — **cock·sure·ly** **adv.** **cock·sure·ness** **n.** [16th C.: from archaic *cock* (euphemism for *God*) + SURE.]

cock·tail /ˈkäk,tāl/ ▶ **n.** **1** an alcoholic drink consisting of a spirit or several spirits mixed with other ingredients, such as fruit juice, lemonade, or cream. ■ a mixture of substances or factors, esp. when dangerous or unpleasant in its effects. **2** a dish consisting of small pieces of food, typically served cold at the beginning of a meal as an hors d'oeuvre: *a shrimp cocktail.* [17th C.: from COCK[1] + TAIL[1].]

cock·tail dress ▶ **n.** an elegant dress suitable for formal social occasions.

cock·tail lounge ▶ **n.** a bar, typically in a hotel, restaurant, or airport, where cocktails are served.

cock·tail ta·ble ▶ **n.** another term for COFFEE TABLE.

cock·teas·er /ˈkäk,tēzər/ (also **cock·tease**) ▶ **n.** vulgar slang a woman who leads a man to the mistaken belief that she is likely to have sexual intercourse with him.

cock·y /ˈkäkē/ ▶ **adj.** (**cock·i·er**, **cock·i·est**) conceited or arrogant, esp. in a bold or cheeky way. — **cock·i·ly** /ˈkäkəlē/ **adv.** **cock·i·ness** **n.** [16th C.: from COCK[1].]

co·co /ˈkōkō/ ▶ **n.** (pl. **-cos**) **1** [usu. as adj.] coconut. **2** W. Indian the root of the taro. [16th C.: from Sp. and Port., lit. 'grinning face.']

co·coa /ˈkōkō/ ▶ **n.** **1** a powder made from roasted and ground cacao seeds. ■ a hot drink made from such a powder. **2** var. of COCO, usu. regarded as a misspelling. [18th C.: alt. of CACAO.]

co·coa bean ▶ **n.** a cacao seed.

co·coa but·ter ▶ **n.** a fatty substance obtained from cocoa beans and used esp. in the manufacture of confectionery and cosmetics.

co·co·bo·lo /,kōkōˈbōlō/ ▶ **n.** (pl. **-los**) a tropical American tree (*Dalbergia retusa*) of the pea family, with hard, reddish timber used chiefly to make cutlery handles. [19th C.: via Sp. from Arawak *kakabali*.]

co·co de mer /ˈkōkō də ˈmer/ ▶ **n.** a tall palm tree (*Lodoicea maldivica*) native to the Seychelles. Its immense, seaborne nut, encased in a hard woody shell, is the largest known seed. ■ the large nut of this palm. [19th C.: from Fr. *coco-de-mer*, lit. 'coco from the sea.']

co·co·nut /ˈkōkə,nət/ (also **co·coa·nut**) ▶ **n.** **1** the large, oval, brown seed of a tropical palm, consisting of a hard shell lined with edible white flesh and containing a clear liquid. ■ the flesh of a coconut, esp. when used as food. **2** (also **coconut palm** or **tree**) the tall palm tree (*Cocos nucifera*) that yields this nut.

co·co·nut but·ter ▶ **n.** a solid fat obtained from the flesh of the coconut, and used in the manufacture of soap, candles, ointment, etc.

co·co·nut crab ▶ **n.** a large terrestrial crablike crustacean (*Birgus latro*, family Paguridae) that climbs coconut palms to feed on the nuts, found on islands in the Indo-Pacific area. Also called ROBBER CRAB.

co·co·nut milk ▶ **n.** the watery liquid found inside a coconut.

co·co·nut oil ▶ **n.** the fatty oil obtained from the coconut and used in cosmetics.

co·co·nut palm ▶ n. see COCONUT (sense 2).

co·coon /kəˈko͞on/ ▶ n. a silky case spun by the larvae of many insects for protection as pupae. ■ a similar structure made by other animals. ■ a covering that prevents the corrosion of metal equipment. ■ something that envelops or surrounds, esp. in a protective or comforting way. ▶ v. [trans.] (usu. **be cocooned**) envelop or surround in a protective or comforting way. ■ spray with a protective coating. ■ [intrans.] retreat from the stressful conditions of public life into the cozy private world of the family. — **co·coon·er** n. (in the last sense of the verb). [17th C.: from Fr. *cocon*, from med. Provençal *coucoun* 'eggshell, cocoon,' dimin. of *coca* 'shell.']

Co·cos Is·lands /ˈkōkəs/ a group of 27 small coral islands in the Indian Ocean, territory of Australia; pop. 603. Also called KEELING ISLANDS.

co·cotte /kôˈkôt; kəˈkät/ ▶ n. 1 (usu. **en cocotte**) a heatproof dish or small casserole in which individual portions of food can be both cooked and served. [20th C.: from Fr. *cocasse*, from L. *cucuma* 'cooking container.'] 2 dated a fashionable prostitute. [19th C.: Fr., from child's name for a hen.]

co·coun·sel·ing /ˈkōˌkounsəliNG; kōˈkoun-/ (also **co·coun·sel·ing**) ▶ n. a form of personal or psychological counseling in which two or more people alternate the roles of therapist and patient.

Coc·teau /käkˈtō/, Jean (1889–1963), French writer and director. His works include the novel *Les Enfants Terribles* (1929) and the play *Les Parents Terribles* (1948).

COD ▶ abbr. ■ cash on delivery. ■ collect on delivery.

cod /käd/ (also **cod·fish** /ˈkädˌfisH/) ▶ n. (pl. same) a large marine fish with a small barbel on the chin. The **cod family** (Gadidae) comprises many genera and species, in particular the North Atlantic *Gadus morhua*, of great commercial importance as a food fish and as a source of cod liver oil. [ME: perh. from OE *cod(d)* 'bag.']

cod

co·da /ˈkōdə/ ▶ n. Music the concluding passage of a piece or movement, typically forming an addition to the basic structure. ■ the concluding section of a dance, esp. of a pas de deux or the finale of a ballet in which the dancers parade before the audience. ■ a concluding event, remark, or section. [18th C.: Ital., from L. *cauda* 'tail.']

cod·dle /ˈkädl/ ▶ v. [trans.] 1 treat in an indulgent or overprotective way: *I was coddled and cosseted.* 2 cook (an egg) in water below the boiling point. — **cod·dler** n. [16th C.: sense 1 prob. dial. var. of obs. *caudle* 'administer invalids' gruel,' based on L.*calidus* 'warm.']

code /kōd/ ▶ n. 1 a system of words, letters, figures, or other symbols used to represent others, esp. for the purposes of secrecy. ■ a system of signals, such as sounds, light flashes, or flags, used to send messages: *Morse code.* ■ a series of letters, numbers, or symbols assigned to something for the purposes of classification or identification. 2 Comput. program instructions. 3 a systematic collection of laws or regulations, ■ a set of conventions governing behavior or activity in a particular sphere. ■ a set of rules and standards adhered to by a society, class, or individual. ▶ v. 1 [trans.] (usu. **be coded**) convert (the words of a message) into a particular code in order to convey a secret meaning. ■ express the meaning of (a statement or communication) in an indirect or euphemistic way. ■ assign a code to (something) for purposes of classification, analysis, or identification. 2 [intrans.] (**code for**) Biochem. specify the genetic sequence for (an amino acid or protein). ■ be the genetic determiner of (a characteristic).
– PHRASES **bring something up to code** renovate or update an old building in line with the latest building regulations. — **cod·er** n. [ME: via OFr. from L. *codex, codic-* (see CODEX).]

co·dec /ˈkōˌdek/ ▶ n. Electron. a microchip that compresses or decompresses data. [1960s: blend of *coder* and DECODER.]

co·de·fend·ant /ˌkōdiˈfendənt/ ▶ n. a joint defendant.

co·deine /ˈkōdēn/ ▶ n. Med. a sleep-inducing and analgesic drug, $C_{18}H_{21}No_3$, derived from morphine. [19th C.: from Gk. *kōdeia* 'poppy head.']

co·de·pend·en·cy /ˌkōdəˈpendənsē/ ▶ n. excessive emotional or psychological reliance on a partner, typically one with an illness or addiction. — **co·de·pend·ence** n. **co·de·pend·ent** adj. & n.

code-shar·ing ▶ n. agreement between two or more airlines to list certain flights in a reservation system under each other's names.

co·de·ter·mi·na·tion /ˌkōdiˌtərməˈnāsHən/ ▶ n. cooperation between management and workers in decision-making.

co·dex /ˈkōdeks/ ▶ n. (pl. **co·di·ces** /ˈkōdəˌsēz; ˈkä-/ or **co·dex·es**) an ancient manuscript text in book form. ■ an official list of medicines, chemicals, etc. [16th C.: from L., lit. 'block of wood.']

cod·fish /ˈkädˌfisH/ ▶ n. (pl. same or **-fish·es**) another term for COD.

codg·er /ˈkäjər/ ▶ n. informal an elderly man, esp. one who is old-fashioned or eccentric. [18th C.: perh. var. of *cadger*.]

co·di·ces /ˈkōdəˌsēz; ˈkä-/ plural form of CODEX.

cod·i·cil /ˈkädəsəl; -ˌsil/ ▶ n. an addition or supplement that explains, modifies, or revokes a will or part of one. — **cod·i·cil·la·ry** /ˌkädəˈsilərē/ adj. [ME: from L. *codicillus*, dimin. of *codex, codic-*.]

cod·i·fy /ˈkädəˌfī; ˈkō-/ ▶ v. (**-fies, -fied**) [trans.] arrange (laws or rules) into a systematic code. ■ arrange according to a plan or system. — **cod·i·fi·ca·tion** /ˌkädəfəˈkāsHən; ˌkō-/ n. **cod·i·fi·er** n.

cod·ing /ˈkōdiNG/ ▶ n. the process of assigning a code to something for the purposes of classification or identification. ■ a code assigned for such a purpose: *text type codings.* ■ Biochem. the process of coding genetically for an amino acid, protein, or characteristic.

cod·ling /ˈkädliNG/ ▶ n. an immature cod.

cod·ling moth (also **cod·lin moth**) ▶ n. a small, grayish moth (*Cydia pomonella*, family Tortricidae) whose larva feeds on apples. [ME: from Anglo-Norman Fr. *quer de lion* 'lionheart.']

cod liv·er oil ▶ n. oil pressed from the fresh liver of cod, which is rich in vitamins D and A.

co·do·main /ˈkōdōˌmān; ˌkōdōˈmān/ ▶ n. Math. a set that includes all the possible values of a given function.

co·don /ˈkōdän/ ▶ n. Biochem. a sequence of three nucleotides which together form a unit of genetic code in a DNA or RNA molecule. [1960s: from CODE + -ON.]

cod·piece /ˈkädˌpēs/ ▶ n. a pouch attached to a man's breeches or close-fitting hose to cover the genitals, worn in the 15th and 16th centuries. [from *cod* 'scrotum' (from OE *codd* 'bag').]

Co·dy /ˈkōdē/, William Frederick, see BUFFALO BILL.

coe·cil·i·an ▶ n. var. of CAECILIAN.

co·ed /ˈkōˌed/ informal ▶ n. dated a female student at a co-educational institution. ▶ adj. (of an institution or system) co-educational.

co·ed·u·ca·tion /ˌkōˌejəˈkāsHən/ ▶ n. the education of students of both sexes together. — **co·ed·u·ca·tion·al** /-sHənl/ adj.

co·ef·fi·cient /ˌkōəˈfisHənt/ ▶ n. 1 Math. a numerical or constant quantity placed before and multiplying the variable in an algebraic expression (e.g., 4 in $4xy$). 2 Physics a multiplier or factor that measures some property: *coefficients of elasticity* | *the drag coefficient.* [17th C.: from mod. L. *coefficient-*, from *com-* 'together' + *efficient-* 'accomplishing.']

co·ef·fi·cient of fric·tion ▶ n. the ratio between the force necessary to move one surface horizontally over another and the pressure between the two surfaces.

co·ef·fi·cient of vis·cos·i·ty ▶ n. Physics the degree to which a fluid resists flow under an applied force, expressed as the ratio of the shearing stress to the velocity gradient.

coe·la·canth /ˈsēləˌkanTH/ ▶ n. a large, bony marine fish (*Latimeria chalumnae*, family Latimeriidae) with a three-lobed tail fin and fleshy pectoral fins, found chiefly around the Comoro Islands. It was known only from fossils until one was found alive in 1938. [19th C.: from mod. L. *Coelacanthus*, from Gk. *koilos* 'hollow' + *akantha* 'spine.']

-coele (also **-cele**) ▶ comb. form Med. denoting a swelling or hernia in a specified part: *meningocele.* [from Gk. *kēlē* 'tumor.']

coe·len·ter·ate /siˈlentəˌrāt; -rit/ ▶ n. Zool. an aquatic invertebrate animal of the phylum Cnidaria (formerly Coelenterata), which includes jellyfishes, corals, and sea anemones. They are distinguished by having a tube- or cup-shaped body and a single opening ringed with tentacles. Also called CNIDARIAN. [19th C.: from mod. L. *Coelenterata*, from Gk. *koilos* 'hollow' + *enteron* 'intestine.']

coe·len·ter·on /siˈlentəˌrän/ ▶ n. (pl. **-ter·a** /-tərə/) the central gastric cavity of a coelenterate.

coe·li·ac ▶ n. British spelling of CELIAC.

coe·lom /ˈsēləm/ (also **ce·lom**) ▶ n. (pl. **coe·loms** or **coe·lom·a·ta** /siˈlōmətə/) Zool. the body cavity in metazoans, located between the intestinal canal and the body wall. — **coe·lo·mate** /ˈsēləˌmāt/ adj. & n. [19th C.: from Gk. *koilōma* 'cavity.']

coe·lo·stat /ˈsēləˌstat/ ▶ n. Astron. an advanced version of a heliostat, having a rotating mirror that continuously reflects the light from the same area of sky, allowing the path of a celestial object to be monitored. [19th C.: from L. *caelum* 'sky.']

coe·lur·o·saur /siˈlo͝orəˌsôr; sē-/ (also **coe·lur·o·sau·rus** /siˌlo͝orəˈsôrəs/) ▶ n. a small, slender, bipedal, carnivorous dinosaur with long forelimbs, from which birds are believed to have evolved. — **coe·lur·o·sau·ri·an** adj. [1950s: from Gk. *koilos* 'hollow' + *oura* 'tail' + *sauros* 'lizard.']

coe·no·cyte /ˈsēnəˌsīt/ ▶ n. Bot. a body of algal or fungal cytoplasm containing several nuclei enclosed in a single membrane. — **coe·no·cyt·ic** /ˌsēnəˈsitik/ adj. [20th C.: from Gk. *koinos* 'common.']

co·en·zyme /kōˈenzīm/ ▶ n. Biochem. a nonprotein compound necessary for the functioning of an enzyme.

co·en·zyme A ▶ n. Biochem. a coenzyme derived from pantothenic acid, important in respiration and many other biochemical reactions. [*A* from *acylation* (see ACYLATE).]

co·en·zyme Q ▶ n. another term for UBIQUINONE. [*Q* from QUINONE.]

co·e·qual /kōˈēkwəl/ ▶ adj. equal with one another; having the same rank or importance: *coequal partners.* ▶ n. a person or thing equal with another. — **co·e·qual·i·ty** /ˌkō-iˈkwälitē/ n.

co·erce /kōˈərs/ ▶ v. [trans.] persuade (an unwilling person) to do something by using force or threats. ■ obtain (something) by such means. — **co·er·ci·ble** adj. **co·er·cion** /kōˈərzHən; -sHən/ n. [ME: from L. *coercere* 'restrain,' from *co-* + *arcere* 'restrain.']

co·er·cive /kōˈərsiv/ ▶ adj. relating to or using force or threats: *coercive measures.* — **co·er·cive·ly** adv. **co·er·cive·ness** n.

PRONUNCIATION KEY ə *ago, up*; ər *over, fur*; a *hat*; ā *ate*; ä *car*; e *let*; ē *see*; i *fit*; ī *by*; NG *sing*; ō *go*; ô *law, for*; oi *toy*; o͝o *good*; o͞o *goo*; ou *out*; TH *thin*; TH *then*; ZH *vision*

co·er·cive force ▶ n. Physics another term for COERCIVITY.

co·er·civ·i·ty /ˌkōərˈsivitē/ ▶ n. Physics the resistance of a magnetic material to changes in magnetization. ■ the field intensity necessary to demagnetize it when fully magnetized.

co·es·sen·tial /ˌkō-iˈsenshəl/ ▶ adj. united or inseparable in essence or being. ■ having the same substance or essence. — **co·es·sen·ti·al·i·ty** /ˌkō-iˌsenshēˈalitē/ n. **co·es·sen·tial·ly** adv. **co·es·sen·tial·ness** n.

co·e·ta·ne·ous /ˌkō-iˈtānēəs/ ▶ adj. another term for COEVAL.

co·e·ter·nal /ˌkō-iˈtərnl/ ▶ adj. equally eternal; existing with something else eternally. — **co·e·ter·nal·ly** adv.

Coet·ze·e /kŏŏtˈsēə/, J. M. (1940–), South African writer; full name *John Maxwell Coetzee*. His novels include *Life and Times of Michael K* (1983) and *Slow Man* (2005). Nobel Prize for Literature (2003).

Coeur d'Alene /ˌkôr dlˈān/ a resort city in northwestern Idaho; pop. 34,514.

co·e·val /kōˈēvəl/ ▶ adj. having the same age or date of origin; contemporary. ▶ n. a person of roughly the same age as oneself; a contemporary. — **co·e·val·i·ty** /ˌkō-ēˈvalitē/ n. **co·e·val·ly** adv. [17th C. (as a n.): from late L. *coaevus*, from *co-* + L. *aevum* 'age.']

co·ev·o·lu·tion /ˌkō-evəˈlo͞oshən; -ēvə-/ ▶ n. Biol. the influence of closely associated species on each other in their evolution. — **co·ev·o·lu·tion·ar·y** /-shəˌnerē/ adj. **co·e·volve** /ˌkō-iˈvälv/ v.

co·ex·ist /ˌkō-igˈzist/ ▶ v. [intrans.] exist at the same time or in the same place. ■ (of nations or peoples) exist in mutual tolerance despite different ideologies or interests. — **co·ex·ist·ence** /-ˈzistəns/ n. **co·ex·ist·ent** /-ˈzistənt/ adj.

co·ex·ten·sive /ˌkō-ikˈstensiv/ ▶ adj. extending over the same space or time; corresponding exactly in extent. ■ (of a term) denoting the same referent as another.

co·fac·tor /ˈkōˌfaktər/ ▶ n. **1** a contributory cause of a disease. **2** Biochem. a substance (other than the substrate) essential for the activity of an enzyme. **3** Math. the quantity obtained from a determinant or a square matrix by removal of the row and column containing a specified element.

C. of C. ▶ abbr. Chamber of Commerce.

C. of E. ▶ abbr. Church of England.

cof·fee /ˈkôfē; ˈkäfē/ ▶ n. **1** a hot drink made from the roasted and ground beanlike seeds of a tropical shrub. ■ a cup of this drink. ■ these seeds raw, roasted and ground, or processed into a powder that dissolves in hot water. ■ a pale brown color like that of coffee mixed with milk. ■ a party or reception at which coffee is served. **2** the shrub (genus *Coffea*) of the bedstraw family that yields these seeds, two of which are contained in each red berry. Native to the Old World tropics, most coffee is grown in tropical America. [16th C.: from Turk. *kahveh*, from Arab. *ḳahwa*.]

cof·fee bar ▶ n. a bar or cafe serving coffee and light refreshments from a counter.

cof·fee bean ▶ n. a beanlike seed of the coffee shrub.

cof·fee cake ▶ n. **1** a cake or sweet bread, often flavored with cinnamon, eaten usually with coffee. **2** a coffee-flavored cake.

cof·fee·house /ˈkôfēˌhous; ˈkäfē-/ ▶ n. a place where coffee is served and people gather for music, poetry readings, and other informal entertainment.

cof·fee klatsch (also **cof·fee klatch**) ▶ n. var. of KAFFEEKLATSCH.

cof·fee shop ▶ n. a small, informal restaurant, as may be found in a hotel. ■ a shop serving coffee and light refreshments.

cof·fee ta·ble ▶ n. a small, low table, typically placed in front of a sofa.

cof·fee-ta·ble book ▶ n. a large, expensive, lavishly illustrated book, esp. one intended for casual reading.

cof·fer /ˈkôfər; ˈkäfər/ ▶ n. **1** a strongbox or small chest for holding valuables. ■ (**coffers**) the funds or financial reserves of a group or institution: *the federal government's empty coffers.* **2** a recessed panel in a ceiling. — **cof·fered** adj. (in sense 2). [ME: from OFr. *coffre* 'chest,' via L. from Gk. *kophinos* 'basket.']

cof·fer·dam /ˈkôfərˌdam; ˈkäfər-/ ▶ n. a watertight enclosure pumped dry to permit construction work below the waterline.

cof·fin /ˈkôfən; ˈkäfən/ ▶ n. a long, narrow box, typically of wood, in which a corpse is buried or cremated. ■ informal an old and unsafe aircraft or vessel. ▶ v. (**-fined, -fin·ing**) [trans.] put (a dead body) in a coffin. [ME: from OFr. *cofin* 'little basket,' from L. *cophinus* (see COFFER).]

cof·fin nail ▶ n. informal a cigarette.

cof·fle /ˈkôfəl; ˈkäfəl/ ▶ n. a line of animals or slaves fastened or driven along together. [18th C.: from Arab. *ḳāfila* 'caravan.']

co·found·er /ˈkōˈfoundər; ˈkōˌfoun-/ ▶ n. a joint founder. — **co·found** /kōˈfound/ v.

co·func·tion /ˈkōˌfəNGkshən/ ▶ n. Math. the trigonometric function of the complement of an angle or arc.

cog /käg/ ▶ n. a wheel or bar with a series of projections on its edge that transfers motion by engaging with projections on another wheel or bar. ■ each of such a series of projections. — **cogged** adj. [ME: prob. of Scand. origin, akin to Swed.]

co·gen·e·ra·tion /ˌkōˌjenəˈrāshən/ ▶ n. the generation of electricity and useful heat jointly.

co·gent /ˈkōjənt/ ▶ adj. (of an argument or case) clear, logical, and convincing. — **co·gen·cy** n. **co·gent·ly** adv. [17th C.: from L. *cogent-* 'compelling,' from the v. *cogere*, from *co-* + *agere* 'drive.']

cog·i·tate /ˈkäjəˌtāt/ ▶ v. [intrans.] formal or humorous think deeply about something; meditate or reflect. — **cog·i·ta·tion** /ˌkäjəˈtāshən/ n. **cog·i·ta·tive** /-ˌtātiv/ adj. **cog·i·ta·tor** /-ˌtātər/ n. [16th C.: from L. *cogitat-* 'considered,' from v. *cogitare*, from *co-* + *agitare* 'consider.']

co·gi·to /ˈkägiˌtō; ˈkäji-/ ▶ n. (usu. **the cogito**) Philos. the principle establishing the existence of a being from the fact of its thinking or awareness. [19th C.: L., lit. 'I think.']

co·gnac /ˈkōnyak; ˈkän-; ˈkôn-/ ▶ n. a high-quality brandy, properly that distilled in Cognac, France.

cog·nate /ˈkägnāt/ ▶ adj. **1** Ling. (of a word) having the same linguistic derivation as another; from the same original word or root (e.g., English *is*, German *ist*, Latin *est* from Indo-European *esti*). **2** formal related; connected. ■ related to or descended from a common ancestor. Compare with AGNATE. ▶ n. **1** Ling. a cognate word. **2** Law a blood relative. — **cog·nate·ly** adv. **cog·nate·ness** n. [17th C.: from L. *cognatus*, from *co-* + *natus* 'born.']

cog·ni·tion /kägˈnishən/ ▶ n. the mental action or process of acquiring knowledge and understanding through thought, experience, and the senses. ■ a result of this; a perception, sensation, or intuition. — **cog·ni·tion·al** /-shənl/ adj. **cog·ni·tive** /ˈkägnitiv/ adj. **cog·ni·tive·ly** adv. [ME: from L. *cognitio(n-)*, from *cognoscere* 'get to know.']

cog·ni·tive dis·so·nance /ˈkägnətiv/ ▶ n. Psychol. the state of having inconsistent thoughts, beliefs, or attitudes, esp. as relating to behavioral decisions and attitude change.

cog·ni·tive gram·mar ▶ n. a theory of language that seeks to characterize knowledge of grammar in terms of symbolic conceptual and semantic categories and general cognitive processes.

cog·ni·tive map ▶ n. a mental representation of one's physical environment.

cog·ni·tive sci·ence ▶ n. the study of thought, learning, and mental organization. — **cog·ni·tive sci·en·tist** n.

cog·ni·tive ther·a·py ▶ n. a type of psychotherapy in which negative patterns of thought about the self and the world are challenged in order to alter unwanted behavior patterns or treat mood disorders.

cog·ni·za·ble /ˈkägnəzəbəl; kägˈnī-/ ▶ adj. **1** formal perceptible; clearly identifiable. **2** Law within the jurisdiction of a court.

cog·ni·zance /ˈkägnəzəns/ (also **cog·ni·sance**) ▶ n. **1** formal knowledge, awareness, or notice. ■ Law the action of taking jurisdiction. ■ the action of taking judicial notice (of a fact beyond dispute). **2** Heraldry a distinctive device or mark, esp. an emblem or badge formerly worn by retainers of a noble house. [ME *conisance*, from OFr. *conoisance*, based on L. *cognoscere* 'get to know.']

cog·ni·zant /ˈkägnəzənt/ (also **cog·ni·sant**) ▶ adj. [predic.] formal having knowledge or being aware of.

cog·nize /kägˈnīz; ˈkägnīz/ ▶ v. [trans.] formal perceive, know, or become aware of. [19th C.: from COGNIZANCE.]

cog·no·men /kägˈnōmən; ˈkägnəmən/ ▶ n. an extra personal name given to an ancient Roman citizen, functioning rather like a nickname and typically passed down from father to son. ■ a name; a nickname. [L., from *co-* + *gnomen*, *nomen* 'name.']

co·gno·scen·te /ˌkänyəˈshentē; ˌkägnə-/ ▶ n. (pl. **-ti** /-tē/) a connoisseur; a discerning expert.

co·gno·scen·ti /ˌkänyōˈshentē; ˌkägnə-/ ▶ plural n. people who are considered to be especially well informed about a particular subject. [18th C.: from Ital. *conoscenti*, lit. 'people who know.']

cog rail·way ▶ n. a railroad with a toothed central rail between the bearing rails that engages with a cogwheel under the locomotive, providing traction for ascending and descending very steep slopes.

cog·wheel /ˈkägˌ(h)wēl/ ▶ n. another term for COG.

co·hab·it /kōˈhabit/ ▶ v. (**-hab·it·ed, -hab·it·ing**) [intrans.] live together and have a sexual relationship without being married. ■ coexist. — **co·hab·it·ant** n. **co·hab·i·ta·tion** /kōˌhabəˈtāshən/ n. **co·hab·it·er** n. [16th C.: from L. *cohabitare*, from *co-* + *habitare* 'dwell.']

Co·han /ˈkōhan/, George Michael (1878–1942), US composer. His songs include "Yankee Doodle Dandy" (1904) and "Give My Regards to Broadway" (1904).

co·heir /kōˈe(ə)r/ ▶ n. a joint heir.

co·heir·ess /kōˈe(ə)ris/ ▶ n. a joint heiress

co·here /kōˈhi(ə)r/ ▶ v. [intrans.] **1** be united; form a whole. **2** (of an argument or theory) be logically consistent. [16th C.: from L. *cohaerere*, from *co-* + *haerere* 'to stick.']

co·her·ent /kōˈhi(ə)rənt/ ▶ adj. **1** (of an argument, theory, or policy) logical and consistent. ■ (of a person) able to speak clearly and logically: *after one beer, he is not coherent.* **2** united as or forming a whole. **3** Physics (of waves) having a constant phase relationship. — **co·her·ence** n. **co·her·en·cy** n. (rare) **co·her·ent·ly** adv. [16th C.: from L. *cohaerent-* 'sticking together,' from *cohaerere*.]

co·he·sion /kōˈhēzhən/ ▶ n. the action or fact of forming a united whole: *the work at present lacks cohesion.* ■ Physics the sticking together of particles of the same substance. — **co·he·sive** /kōˈhēsiv; -ziv/ adj. **co·he·sive·ly** adv. **co·he·sive·ness** n. [17th C.: from L. *cohaes-* 'cleaved together,' from *cohaerere* (see COHERE).]

Cohn /kōn/, Ferdinand Julius (1828–98), German botanist. He was the first to devise a systematic classification of bacteria into genera and species.

co·ho /ˈkōhō/ (also **co·ho salmon** or **co·hoe**) ▶ n. (pl. same, **-hos**, or **-hoes**) a deep-bodied North Pacific salmon (*Oncorhynchus kisutch*) with small black spots. Also called SILVER SALMON. [19th C.: prob. from Salish.]

co·hort /'kōhôrt/ ▶ **n.** **1** [treated as sing. or pl.] an ancient Roman military unit, comprising six centuries, equal to one tenth of a legion. **2** [treated as sing. or pl.] a group of people banded together or treated as a group. ▪ a group of people with a common statistical characteristic: *the 1940–44 birth cohort of women.* **3** a supporter or companion. ▪ an accomplice or conspirator: *they arrested Cunningham and his cohorts.* [ME: from OFr. *cohorte*, or L. *cohors, cohort-* 'retinue.']

co·hosh /'kōhäsʜ/ ▶ **n.** either of two medicinal plants native to North America: ▪ (also **black cohosh**) a tall plant (*Cimicifuga racemosa*) of the buttercup family, with small white flowers. ▪ (also **blue cohosh**) a plant (*Caulophyllum thalictroides*) of the barberry family, with greenish flowers and deep blue berries. [18th C.: from Eastern Abnaki.]

co·host /'kō,hōst/ ▶ **n.** a joint host. ▶ **v.** [trans.] act as a joint host.

co·hune /kə'hōōn; kō-/ ▶ **n.** a Central American palm (*Orbignya cohune*) that is a valuable source of oil. ▪ (also **ca·houn**) the oil-rich nut of this palm. [18th C.: from Miskito.]

coif ▶ **n.** **1** /koif/ a woman's close-fitting cap, now only worn under a veil by nuns. **2** /kwäf; koif/ informal short for COIFFURE. ▶ **v.** /kwäf; koif/ (**coiffed, coif·fing;** also **coifed, coif·ing**) [trans.] style or arrange (someone's hair), typically in an elaborate way. ▪ style or arrange the hair of (someone). [ME: from OFr. *coife* 'headdress,' from late L. *cofia* 'helmet.']

coif·feur /kwä'fər/ ▶ **n.** a hairdresser. [19th C.: Fr., from *coiffer* (see COIF).]

coif·feuse /kwä'f(y)ōōz; -'fə(r)z/ ▶ **n.** a female hairdresser.

coif·fure /kwä'fyōōr/ ▶ **n.** a person's hairstyle, typically an elaborate one. — **coif·fured adj.** [17th C.: Fr., from *coiffer* 'arrange the hair,' in OFr. 'cover with a coif' (see COIF).]

coign /koin/ ▶ **n.** a projecting corner or angle of a wall or building. [ME: var. of COIN.]

coil[1] /koil/ ▶ **n.** a length of something wound or arranged in a spiral or sequence of rings: *a coil of rope.* ▪ a single ring or loop in such a sequence. ▪ a roll of postage stamps. ▪ a slow-burning spiral made with the dried paste of pyrethrum powder, which produces a smoke that inhibits mosquitoes from biting. ▪ (often **the coil**) an intrauterine contraceptive device in the form of a coil. ▪ an electrical device consisting of a length of wire arranged in a coil for converting the level of a voltage, producing a magnetic field, or adding inductance to a circuit: *a relay coil.* ▪ such a device used for transmitting high voltage to the spark plugs of an internal combustion engine. ▶ **v.** [trans.] arrange or wind (something long and flexible) in a joined sequence of concentric circles or rings. ▪ [no obj., with adverbial] move or twist into such an arrangement or shape. [16th C.: from OFr. *coillir*, from L. *colligere* 'gather together' (see COLLECT[1]).]

coil[2] ▶ **n.** archaic or dialect a confusion or turmoil.
– PHRASES **shuffle off this mortal coil** esp. humorous die. [16th C.: of unknown origin.]

coil spring ▶ **n.** a helical spring made from metal wire or a metal band.

Co·im·ba·tore /'koimbə,tôr/ a city in southern India, in the state of Tamil Nadu; pop. 853,000.

coin /koin/ ▶ **n.** a flat, typically round piece of metal with an official stamp, used as money. ▪ money in the form of coins. ▪ informal money. ▪ (**coins**) one of the suits in some tarot packs, corresponding to pentacles in others. ▶ **v.** [trans.] **1** make (coins) by stamping metal. ▪ make (metal) into coins. **2** invent or devise (a new word or phrase).
– PHRASES **the other side of the coin** the opposite or contrasting aspect of a matter. **pay someone back in his or her own coin** retaliate with similar behavior. **to coin a phrase** said ironically when introducing a banal remark or cliché. ▪ said when introducing a new expression or a variation on a familiar one. [ME: from OFr. *coin* 'wedge, die,' *coigner* 'to mint,' from L. *cuneus* 'wedge.']

coin·age /'koinij/ ▶ **n.** **1** coins collectively. ▪ the action or process of producing coins from metal. ▪ a system or type of coins in use: *decimal coinage.* **2** the invention of a new word or phrase. ▪ a newly invented word or phrase.

co·in·cide /,kōən'sīd; 'kōən,sīd/ ▶ **v.** [intrans.] occur at or during the same time. ▪ correspond in nature; tally. ▪ correspond in position; meet or intersect. ▪ be in agreement. [18th C.: from med. L. *coincidere*, from *co-* + *incidere* 'fall upon or into.']

co·in·ci·dence /kō'insədəns; -,dens/ ▶ **n.** **1** a remarkable concurrence of events or circumstances without apparent causal connection. **2** correspondence in nature or in time of occurrence. **3** Physics the presence of ionizing particles or other objects in two or more detectors simultaneously, or of two or more signals simultaneously in a circuit.

co·in·ci·dent /kō'insədənt; -,dent/ ▶ **adj.** occurring together in space or time. ▪ in agreement or harmony. — **co·in·ci·dent·ly adv.**

co·in·ci·den·tal /kō,insə'dentl/ ▶ **adj.** **1** resulting from a coincidence; done or happening by chance. **2** happening or existing at the same time. — **co·in·ci·den·tal·ly adv.**

coin·er /'koinər/ ▶ **n.** **1** hist. a person who coins money, in particular a maker of counterfeit coins. **2** a person who invents or devises a new word, sense, or phrase.

coin-op·er·at·ed (also **coin-op**) ▶ **adj.** operated by inserting coins in a slot: *coin-operated telephones.* ▶ **n.** a machine that is coin-operated.

co·in·sur·ance ▶ **n.** a type of insurance in which the insured pays a share of the payment made against a claim.

Coin·treau /kwän'trō/ ▶ **n.** trademark a colorless orange-flavored liqueur. [named after the *Cointreau* family, liqueur producers in France.]

coir /'koi(ə)r/ ▶ **n.** fiber from the outer husk of the coconut, used for making ropes and matting. [16th C.: from Malayalam *kayaṟu* 'cord, coir.']

co·i·tion /kō'isʜən/ ▶ **n.** another term for COITUS. [16th C.: from L. *coitio(n-)*, from the v. *coire*, from *co-* + *ire* 'go.']

co·i·tus /'kō-itəs; kō'ētəs/ ▶ **n.** formal sexual intercourse. — **co·i·tal** /'kō-itl; kō'ētl/ **adj.** [19th C.: from L., from *coire*.]

co·i·tus in·ter·rup·tus /intə'rəptəs/ ▶ **n.** sexual intercourse in which the penis is withdrawn before ejaculation. [from COITUS + L. *interruptus* 'interrupted.']

co·i·tus re·ser·va·tus /,rezər'vātəs; -'vätəs/ ▶ **n.** the postponement or avoidance of ejaculation, to prolong sexual intercourse. [from COITUS + L. *reservatus* 'reserved.']

co·jo·nes /kə'hōnāz; -nās/ ▶ **plural n.** informal a man's testicles. ▪ fig. courage; guts. [Sp.]

coke[1] /kōk/ ▶ **n.** a solid fuel made by heating coal in the absence of air so that the volatile components are driven off. ▪ carbon residue left after the incomplete combustion of gasoline or other fuels. ▶ **v.** [trans.] [usu. as n.] (**coking**) convert (coal) into coke. [ME: origin unknown.]

coke[2] ▶ **n.** informal term for COCAINE.

Coke-bot·tle ▶ **n.** [as adj.] informal denoting very thick lenses for glasses or glasses with such lenses.

Col. ▶ **abbr.** ▪ colonel. ▪ Bible Colossians.

col /käl/ ▶ **n.** the lowest point of a ridge or saddle between two peaks, typically affording a pass from one side of a mountain range to another. ▪ Meteorol. a region of slightly elevated pressure between two anticyclones. [19th C.: from Fr., lit. 'neck,' from L. *collum*.]

col. ▶ **abbr.** ▪ collected. ▪ college. ▪ colony. ▪ column.

col- ▶ **prefix** var. of COM- assimilated before *l* (as in *collocate, collude*).

COLA ▶ **abbr.** cost-of-living adjustment.

co·la /'kōlə/ ▶ **n.** **1** a brown carbonated drink that is flavored with an extract of cola nuts, or with a similar flavoring. [shortening of trademark *Coca-Cola*.] **2** (also **ko·la**) a small evergreen African tree (genus *Cola*, family Sterculiaceae) that is cultivated in the tropics for its seeds (cola nuts). [from Temne *k'ola* 'cola nut.']

col·an·der /'kələndər; 'kä-/ ▶ **n.** a perforated bowl used to strain off liquid from food, esp. after cooking. [ME: based on L. *colare* 'to strain.']

co·la nut (also **kola nut**) ▶ **n.** the seed of the cola tree, which contains caffeine and is chewed or made into a drink.

co·lat·i·tude /kō'lati,t(y)ōōd/ ▶ **n.** Astron. the complement of the latitude; the difference between latitude and 90°.

col·can·non /käl'kanən/ ▶ **n.** an Irish and Scottish dish of cabbage and potatoes boiled and pounded. [18th C.: from Irish *cál ceannan*, lit. 'white-headed cabbage.']

col·chi·cine /'kälcʜə,sēn; 'kälkə-/ ▶ **n.** Chem. a yellow alkaloid, $C_{22}H_{25}NO_6$, present in the corms of colchicums, used to relieve pain in cases of gout.

col·chi·cum /'kälcʜikəm; 'kälki-/ ▶ **n.** (pl. **-cums**) a plant of the genus *Colchicum*, which includes the autumn crocuses. ▪ the dried corm or seed of meadow saffron, which has analgesic properties and is used medicinally. [from L., from Gk. *kolkhikon* 'of Colchis.']

Col·chis /'kälkis/ an ancient region south of the Caucasus Mountains at the eastern end of the Black Sea. Greek name **Kolkhis**.

cold /kōld/ ▶ **adj.** **1** of or at a low or relatively low temperature, esp. when compared with the human body. ▪ (of food or drink) served or consumed without being heated or after cooling. ▪ (of an engine) not having been warmed up properly. ▪ (of a person) feeling uncomfortably cold. ▪ feeling or characterized by fear or horror. ▪ [as complement] informal unconscious: *she was out cold.* ▪ dead. **2** lacking affection or warmth of feeling; unemotional. ▪ not affected by emotion; objective: *cold statistics.* ▪ sexually unresponsive; frigid. ▪ depressing or dispiriting; not suggestive of warmth. ▪ (of a color) containing pale blue or gray. **3** (of the scent or trail of a hunted person or animal) no longer fresh and easy to follow: *the trail went cold.* ▪ [predic.] (in children's games) far from finding or guessing what is sought. **4** [as complement] without preparation or rehearsal; unawares: *going into the test cold.* ▶ **n.** **1** a low temperature, esp. in the atmosphere; cold weather; a cold environment. **2** a common viral infection in which the mucous membrane of the nose and throat becomes inflamed, typically causing running at the nose, sneezing, a sore throat, and other similar symptoms. ▶ **adv.** informal completely; entirely.
– PHRASES **as cold as ice** (or **stone** or **the grave**, etc.) very cold. **catch** (or **take**) **cold** become infected with a cold. **cold comfort** poor or inadequate consolation. **cold feet** loss of nerve or confidence. **the cold light of day** the objective realities of a situation. **the cold shoulder** a show of intentional unfriendliness; rejection. **cold-shoulder someone** reject or be deliberately unfriendly to someone. **down cold** see DOWN[1]. **in cold blood** without feeling or mercy; ruthlessly. **out in the cold** ignored; neglected. **throw** (or **pour**) **cold water on** be discouraging or negative about. — **cold·ish adj. cold·ness n.** [OE *cald*, from Gmc.; akin to Ger. *kalt* and L. *gelu* 'frost.']

cold-blood·ed ▶ **adj.** **1** (of a kind of animal) having a body temperature varying with that of the environment; poikilothermic. **2** without emotion or pity; deliberately cruel or callous. — **cold-blood·ed·ly adv. cold-blood·ed·ness n.**

cold-call ▶ v. [trans.] make an unsolicited call on (someone), by telephone or in person, in an attempt to sell goods or services. ▶ n. (**cold call**) an unsolicited call of this kind.

cold cash ▶ n. another term for HARD CASH.

cold cath·ode ▶ n. Electron. a cathode that emits electrons without being heated.

cold chis·el ▶ n. a chisel used for cutting metal.

cold-cock ▶ v. [trans.] informal knock (someone) out, esp. with a blow to the head.

cold cream ▶ n. a cosmetic preparation used for cleansing and softening the skin.

cold cuts ▶ plural n. slices of cold cooked meats.

cold dark mat·ter (abbr.: **CDM**) ▶ n. see DARK MATTER.

cold deck ▶ n. **1** informal a deck of cards that has been dishonestly arranged beforehand. **2** a pile of logs stored away from the immediate area where logging is taking place.

cold duck ▶ n. a type of sparkling wine made from burgundy and champagne.

cold frame ▶ n. a frame with a glass or plastic top in which small plants are grown and protected without artificial heat.

cold front ▶ n. Meteorol. the boundary of an advancing mass of cold air.

cold fu·sion ▶ n. nuclear fusion occurring at or close to room temperature.

cold-heart·ed ▶ adj. lacking affection or warmth. — **cold-heart·ed·ly** adv. **cold-heart·ed·ness** n.

cold light ▶ n. Physics light accompanied by little or no heat; luminescence.

cold·ly /ˈkōldlē/ ▶ adv. without affection or warmth of feeling; unemotionally.

cold-mold·ed ▶ adj. (of an object) molded from a resin that hardens without being heated. — **cold-mold·ing** n.

cold-rolled ▶ adj. Metallurgy (of metal) having been rolled into sheets while cold, resulting in a smooth hard finish. — **cold-roll·ing** n.

cold snap ▶ n. a sudden, brief spell of cold weather.

cold sore ▶ n. an inflamed blister in or near the mouth, caused by infection with the herpes simplex virus.

cold stor·age ▶ n. the keeping of something in a refrigerator or other cold place for preservation. ■ fig. the temporary postponement of something.

cold store ▶ n. a large refrigerated room for preserving food stocks at very low temperatures.

cold sweat ▶ n. a state of sweating induced by fear, nervousness, or illness.

cold tur·key informal ▶ n. the abrupt and complete cessation of taking a drug to which one is addicted. ▶ adv. in a sudden and abrupt manner.

cold war ▶ n. a state of political hostility existing between countries, characterized by threats, violent propaganda, subversive activities, and other measures short of open warfare, in particular: ■ (**the Cold War**) the state of political hostility that existed between the Soviet bloc countries and the US-led Western powers from 1945 to 1990.

cold wave ▶ n. **1** a spell of cold weather over a wide area. **2** a kind of permanent wave for the hair created by applying chemicals at room temperature.

cold-weld ▶ v. [trans.] join (a piece of metal) to another without the use of heat, by forcing them together so hard that the surface oxide films are disrupted and adhesion occurs.

cold-work ▶ v. [trans.] shape (metal) while it is cold. ▶ n. (**cold work**) the shaping of metal while it is cold.

Cole[1] /kōl/, Nat King (1919–65), US singer; born *Nathaniel Adams Coles*. He was the first African American to have his own radio 1948–49 and television 1956–57 series. His songs include "Mona Lisa" (1950).

Cole[2], Thomas (1801–48), US painter. He was a founder of the Hudson River School of painting.

cole /kōl/ ▶ n. esp. archaic a brassica, esp. cabbage, kale, or rape. [OE *cāwel, caul*, rel. to Du. *kool* and Ger. *Kohl*, from L. *caulis* 'stem, cabbage'; reinforced in ME by forms from ON *kál*. Cf. KALE.]

co·lec·to·my /kōˈlektəmē/ ▶ n. (pl. **-mies**) surgical removal of all or part of the colon.

Cole·man lan·tern /ˈkōlmən/ (also **Coleman lamp**) ▶ n. trademark a type of bright gasoline lamp used by campers.

Co·le·op·ter·a /ˌkōlēˈäptərə/ Entomol. an order of insects that comprises the beetles (including weevils), forming the largest order of animals on the earth. ■ [as pl. n.] (**coleoptera**) insects of this order; beetles. — **co·le·op·ter·an** /-tərən/ n. & adj. **co·le·op·ter·ist** n. **co·le·op·ter·ous** /-tərəs/ adj. [mod. L. (pl.), from Gk. *koleopteros*, from *koleos* 'sheath' + *pteron* 'wing.']

co·le·op·tile /ˌkōlēˈäpˌtīl/ ▶ n. Bot. a sheath protecting a young shoot tip in a grass or cereal. [19th C.: from Gk. *koleon* 'sheath' + *ptilon* 'feather.']

co·le·o·rhi·za /ˌkōlēəˈrīzə/ ▶ n. (pl. **-zae** /-zē/) Bot. a sheath protecting the root of a germinating grass or cereal grain. [19th C.: from Gk. *koleos* 'sheath' + *rhiza* 'root.']

Cole·ridge /ˈkōl(ə)rij/, Samuel Taylor (1772–1834), English poet. His *Lyrical Ballads* (1798), written with William Wordsworth, marked the start of English romanticism.

cole·seed /ˈkōlˌsēd/ ▶ n. old-fashioned term for RAPE[2]. [17th C.: from Du. *koolzaad* 'cabbage or rape seed.']

cole·slaw /ˈkōlˌslô/ ▶ n. sliced raw cabbage mixed with mayonnaise and other vegetables, eaten as a salad. [18th C.: from Du. *koolsla*, from *kool* 'cabbage' + *sla* (see SLAW).]

Co·lette /kəˈlet/ (1873–1954), French writer; born *Sidonie Gabrielle Claudine Colette*. Her novels include *Chéri* (1920).

co·le·us /ˈkōlēəs/ ▶ n. a tropical Southeast Asian plant (genus *Solenostemon*) of the mint family that has brightly colored variegated leaves and is popular as a houseplant. [mod. L., from Gk. *koleos* 'sheath.']

cole·wort /ˈkōlˌwərt; -ˌwôrt/ ▶ n. esp. archaic another term for COLE.

col·ic /ˈkälik/ ▶ n. severe, often fluctuating pain in the abdomen caused by intestinal gas or obstruction in the intestines and suffered esp. by babies. — **col·ick·y** adj. [ME: from OFr. *colique*, from late L. *colicus*, from *colon* (see COLON[2]).]

col·ic·root /ˈkälikˌro͞ot; -ˌro͝ot/ ▶ n. a North American plant (*Aletris farinosa*) of the lily family, with a rosette of leaves and a spike of small white or cream flowers. It was formerly used in the treatment of colic.

col·i·form bac·te·ri·um /ˈkōləˌfôrm; ˈkä-/ ▶ n. a rod-shaped bacterium, esp. *Escherichia coli* and members of the genus *Aerobacter*, found in the intestinal tract of humans and other animals. Also called COLON BACILLUS. [20th C.: from mod. L. *coli* 'of the colon.']

Co·li·ma /kəˈlēmə/ **1** a state in southwestern Mexico, on the Pacific coast. **2** the capital city of this state; pop. 58,000.

co·lin·e·ar /ˌkōˈlinēər/ (also **col·lin·e·ar**) ▶ adj. lying in the same straight line or linear sequence.

col·i·se·um /ˌkäləˈsēəm/ (also **col·os·se·um**) ▶ n. [in names] a large theater or stadium. [19th C.: from med. L., alt. of L. *colosseum* (see COLOSSEUM).]

co·li·tis /kəˈlītis; kō-/ ▶ n. Med. inflammation of the lining of the colon.

Coll. ▶ abbr. ■ Collateral. ■ Collected or Collection (used in written references to published works or sources). ■ College. ■ Colloquial.

col·lab·o·rate /kəˈlabəˌrāt/ ▶ v. [intrans.] work jointly on an activity, esp. to produce or create something. ■ cooperate traitorously with an enemy. — **col·lab·o·ra·tive** /kəˈlabərətiv/ adj. **col·lab·o·ra·tive·ly** adv. **col·lab·o·ra·tor** /-ˌrātər/ n. [19th C.: from L. *collaborat-* 'worked with,' from v. *collaborare*, from *col-* + *laborare* 'to work.']

col·lab·o·ra·tion /kəˌlabəˈrāSHən/ ▶ n. **1** the action of working with someone to produce or create something. ■ something produced or created in this way. **2** traitorous cooperation with an enemy. — **col·lab·o·ra·tion·ist** n. & adj. (sense 2).

col·lage /kəˈläZH; kô-; kō-/ ▶ n. a form of art in which various materials such as photographs and pieces of paper or fabric are arranged and stuck to a backing. ■ a composition made in this way. ■ a combination or collection of various things. — **col·lag·ist** n. [20th C.: from Fr., lit. 'gluing.']

col·la·gen /ˈkäləjən/ ▶ n. Biochem. the main structural protein found in animal connective tissue, yielding gelatin when boiled. [19th C.: from French *collagène*, from Gk. *kolla* 'glue' + Fr. *-gène* (see -GEN).]

col·lap·sar /kəˈlapsär/ ▶ n. Astron. an old star that has collapsed under its own gravity to form a white dwarf, neutron star, or black hole. [20th C.: from COLLAPSE.]

col·lapse /kəˈlaps/ ▶ v. [intrans.] **1** (of a structure) fall down or in; give way: *the roof collapsed on top of me.* ■ [trans.] cause (something) to fall in or give way. ■ (of a lung or blood vessel) fall inward and become flat and empty. ■ [trans.] cause (a lung or blood vessel) to do this. ■ fold or be foldable into a small space. **2** (of a person) fall down and become unconscious, typically through illness or injury. ■ informal sit or lie down as a result of tiredness or prolonged exertion: *exhausted, he collapsed on the bed.* **3** (of an institution or undertaking) fail suddenly and completely. ■ (of a price or currency) drop suddenly in value. ▶ n. an instance of a structure falling down or in. ■ a sudden failure of an institution or undertaking. ■ a physical or mental breakdown. [17th C.: from medical L. *collapsus*, past part. of *collabi*, from *col-* 'together' + *labi* 'to slip.']

col·laps·i·ble /kəˈlapsəbəl/ ▶ adj. (of an object) able to be folded into a small space: *a collapsible bed.* — **col·laps·i·bil·i·ty** /kəˌlapsəˈbilitē/ n.

col·lar /ˈkälər/ ▶ n. **1** a band of material around the neck of a shirt, dress, coat, or jacket, either upright or turned over and generally an integral part of the garment. ■ short for CLERICAL COLLAR. ■ a band of leather or other material put around the neck of a domestic animal, esp. a dog or cat. ■ a colored marking resembling a collar around the neck of a bird or other animal. ■ a heavy rounded part of the harness worn by a draft animal, which rests at the base of its neck on the shoulders. **2** a restraining or connecting band, ring, or pipe in machinery. **3** Bot. the part of a plant where the stem joins the roots. ▶ v. **1** put a collar on: *biologists who were collaring polar bears.* **2** [trans.] informal seize, grasp, or apprehend (someone): *police collared the culprit.* ■ approach aggressively and talk to (someone who wishes to leave). — **col·lared** adj. **col·lar·less** adj. [ME: from OFr. *colier*, from L. *collare*, from *collum* 'neck.']

col·lar beam ▶ n. a horizontal wooden joist or beam connecting two rafters and forming with them an A-shaped roof truss.

col·lar·bone /ˈkälərˌbōn/ ▶ n. either of the pair of bones joining the breastbone to the shoulder blades. Also called CLAVICLE.

col·lard /ˈkälərd/ (also **collards** or **collard greens**) ▶ n. esp. dialect a cabbage of a variety that does not develop a heart. [18th C.: from *colewort*, from COLE + WORT.]

col·lared dove /dəv/ ▶ n. an Old World dove (genus *Streptopelia*) related to the ringed turtle dove, with buff, gray, or brown plumage and a narrow black band around the back of the neck.

col·lared liz·ard ▶ n. a lizard (*Crotaphytus collaris*, family Iguanidae) that is typically marked with spots and bands and with a distinctive black-and-white collar. It is found in dry rocky areas in the southern US and Mexico.

col·lar stud ▶ n. a stud used to fasten a detachable collar to a shirt.

col·lar tie ▶ n. another term for COLLAR BEAM.

col·late /kə'lāt; 'kōlāt; 'kälāt/ ▶ v. [trans.] **1** collect and combine (texts, information, or sets of figures) in proper order. ■ compare and analyze (texts or other data). ■ Print. verify the order of (sheets of a book) by their signatures. **2** appoint (a priest) to a benefice. — **col·la·tor** /-tər/ n. [16th C.: from L. *collat-* 'brought together,' from *conferre* (see CONFER).]

col·lat·er·al /kə'lat(ə)rəl/ ▶ n. **1** something pledged as security for repayment of a loan. **2** a person having the same descent as another but by a different line. ▶ adj. **1** descended from the same stock but by a different line: *a collateral descendant of George Washington.* **2** additional but subordinate; secondary. ■ situated side by side; parallel: *collateral veins.* — **col·lat·er·al·i·ty** /kə,latə'ralitē/ n. **col·lat·er·al·ly** adv. [ME: from med. L. *collateralis*, from *col-* 'with' + *lateralis* (from *latus, later-* 'side').]

col·lat·er·al dam·age ▶ n. used euphemistically to refer to inadvertent casualties and destruction in civilian areas in the course of military operations.

col·lat·er·al·ize /kə'lat(ə)rə,līz/ ▶ v. [trans.] provide something as collateral for (a loan).

col·la·tion /kə'lāsHən; kō-; kä-/ ▶ n. **1** the action of collating something: *data management and collation.* **2** a light, informal meal. [ME: via OFr. from L. *collation-*, from *conferre* (see CONFER).]

col·league /'kälēg/ ▶ n. a person with whom one works, esp. in a profession or business. [16th C.: from Fr. *collègue*, from L. *collega* 'partner in office,' from *col-* 'with' + *legare* 'depute.']

col·lect[1] /kə'lekt/ ▶ v. [trans.] **1** bring or gather together (things, typically when scattered or widespread). ■ accumulate and store over a period of time. ■ systematically seek and acquire (items of a particular kind) as a hobby. ■ [intrans.] come together and form a group or mass. **2** call for and take away; fetch. ■ go somewhere and accept or receive (something), esp. as a right or due. ■ solicit and receive (donations), esp. for charity. ■ receive (money that is due); be paid. **3** (**collect oneself**) regain control of oneself, typically after a shock. ■ bring together and concentrate (one's thoughts). ▶ adv. & adj. (with reference to a telephone call) to be paid for by the person receiving it. [ME: ult. from L. *collect-* 'gathered together,' from v. *colligere*, from *col-* + *legere* 'choose.']

col·lect[2] /'kälekt; -likt/ ▶ n. (in church use) a short prayer, esp. one assigned to a particular day or season. [ME: from OFr. *collecte*, from L. *collecta* 'gathering,' fem. past part. of *colligere* (see COLLECT[1]).]

col·lec·ta·ne·a /,kälek'tānēə/ ▶ plural n. [also treated as sing.] passages, remarks, and other pieces of text collected from various sources. [17th C.: L., neut. pl. of *collectaneus* 'gathered together.']

col·lect·ed /kə'lektid/ ▶ adj. **1** (of a person) not perturbed or distracted. **2** [attrib.] (of individual works) brought together in one volume or edition: *Lenin's collected works.* ■ (of a volume or edition) containing all the works of a particular person or category. — **col·lect·ed·ly** adv. (in sense 1).

col·lect·i·ble /kə'lektəbəl/ (also esp. Brit. **col·lect·a·ble**) ▶ adj. **1** (of an item) worth collecting; of interest to a collector. **2** able to be collected. ▶ n. (usu. **collectibles**) an item valued and sought by collectors. — **col·lect·i·bil·i·ty** /kə,lektə'bilitē/ n.

col·lec·tion /kə'leksHən/ ▶ n. **1** the action or process of collecting someone or something. ■ a regular removal of mail for dispatch or of trash for disposal. ■ an instance of collecting money in a church service or for a charitable cause. ■ a sum collected in this way. **2** a group of things or people. ■ an assembly of items such as works of art, pieces of writing, or natural objects, esp. one systematically ordered. ■ (**collections**) an art museum's holdings organized by medium, such as sculpture, painting, or photography. ■ a book or recording containing various texts, poems, songs, etc. ■ a range of new clothes produced by a fashion house.

col·lec·tive /kə'lektiv/ ▶ adj. done by people acting as a group: *a collective protest.* ■ belonging or relating to all the members of a group. ■ (esp. of feelings or memories) common to the members of a group. ■ taken as a whole; aggregate. ▶ n. a cooperative enterprise. ■ a collective farm. — **col·lec·tive·ly** adv. **col·lec·tive·ness** n. **col·lec·tiv·i·ty** /kə,lek'tivitē; ,kälek-/ n.

col·lec·tive farm ▶ n. a jointly operated amalgamation of several farms, esp. one owned by the government.

col·lec·tive mem·o·ry ▶ n. the memory of a group of people, typically passed from one generation to the next.

col·lec·tive noun ▶ n. Gram. a count noun that denotes a group of individuals (e.g., *assembly, family*).

col·lec·tive un·con·scious ▶ n. (in Jungian psychology) the part of the unconscious mind that is derived from ancestral memory and experience and is common to all humankind, as distinct from the individual's unconscious.

col·lec·tiv·ism /kə'lektə,vizəm/ ▶ n. the practice or principle of giving a group priority over each individual in it. ■ the theory and practice of the ownership of land and the means of production by the people or the state. — **col·lec·tiv·ist** adj. & n. **col·lec·tiv·is·tic** /kə,lektə'vistik/ adj. **col·lec·ti·vize** /-tə,vīz/ v. **col·lec·ti·vi·za·tion** /kə,lektəvə'zāsHən/ n.

col·lec·tor /kə'lektər/ ▶ n. a person or thing that collects something, in particular: ■ a person who collects things of a specified type, professionally or as a hobby: *book collectors.* ■ an official who is responsible for collecting money owed to an organization or body. ■ Electron. the region in a bipolar transistor that absorbs charge carriers.

col·leen /kə'lēn; 'kälēn/ ▶ n. an Irish term for a girl or young woman. ■ an Irish girl or young woman. [19th C.: from Irish *cailín*, dimin. of *caile* 'countrywoman.']

col·lege /'kälij/ ▶ n. **1** an educational institution or establishment, in particular: ■ one providing higher education or specialized professional or vocational training. ■ (within a university) a school offering a general liberal arts curriculum leading only to a bachelor's degree. ■ the teaching staff and students of a college considered collectively: *the college was shocked by his death.* ■ the buildings and campus of a college. **2** an organized group of professional people with particular aims, duties, and privileges: [in names] *the electoral college.* [ME: from OFr., from L. *collegium* 'partnership,' from *collega* 'partner in office,' from *col-* 'with' + *legare* 'depute.']

Col·lege Board ▶ n. an organization that prepares and administers standardized tests that are used in college admission and placement.

Col·lege of Car·di·nals the body of cardinals of the Roman Catholic Church, founded in the 11th century and since 1179 responsible for the election of the pope. Also called SACRED COLLEGE.

Col·lege Sta·tion a city in east central Texas; pop. 52,456.

col·lege try ▶ n. a sincere effort or attempt at performing a difficult, or seemingly impossible, task.

col·le·gi·a /kə'legēə/ plural form of COLLEGIUM.

col·le·gi·al /kə'lēj(ē)əl/ ▶ adj. **1** relating to or involving shared responsibility, as among a group of colleagues. **2** another term for COLLEGIATE (sense 1). — **col·le·gi·al·i·ty** /kə,lējē'alitē/ n.

col·le·gian /kə'lējən/ ▶ n. a member of a college, esp. within a university.

col·le·giate /kə'lējit/ ▶ adj. **1** belonging or relating to a college or its students: *collegiate life.* **2** (of a university) composed of different colleges. [ME: from late L. *collegiatus*, from *collegium*.]

col·le·giate church ▶ n. a church endowed for a chapter of canons but without a bishop's see. ■ a church or group of churches established under two or more pastors.

col·le·gi·um /kə'lējēəm/ ▶ n. (pl. **-le·gi·a** /-'legēə/) **1** (in full **col·le·gi·um mu·si·cum** /'m(y)o͞ozikəm/) (pl. **col·le·gi·a mu·si·ca** /'m(y)o͞ozikə/) a society of amateur musicians, esp. one attached to a German or US college. **2** hist. an advisory or administrative board in Russia. [19th C.: from L.]

col le·gno /kō(l)'lānyō/ ▶ adv. (of a passage of music for a bowed instrument) played by hitting the strings with the back of the bow. [Ital., 'with the wood.']

Col·lem·bo·la /kə'lembələ/ Entomol. an order of insects that comprises the springtails. ■ [as pl. n.] (**collembola**) insects of this order; springtails. — **col·lem·bo·lan** /-bələn/ n. & adj. [mod. L. (pl.), from Gk. *kolla* 'glue' + *embolon* 'peg.']

Colles' frac·ture /kälz/ ▶ n. Med. a fracture of the lower end of the radius in the wrist with a characteristic backward displacement of the hand. [19th C.: named after Abraham *Colles* (1773–1843), Irish surgeon.]

col·let /'kälit/ ▶ n. a ring or lining that holds something, in particular: ■ a segmented band or sleeve put around a shaft or spindle and tightened so as to grip it. ■ a small collar in a clock to which the inner end of a balance spring is attached. ■ a flange or socket for setting a gem in jewelry. [ME: from OFr., dimin. of *col* 'neck,' from L. *collum*.]

col·lic·u·lus /kə'likyələs/ ▶ n. (pl. **-li** /-,lī; -,lē/) Anat. a small protuberance, esp. one of two pairs in the roof of the midbrain, involved respectively in vision and hearing. — **col·lic·u·lar** /-lər/ adj. [19th C.: from L., dimin. of *collis* 'hill.']

col·lide /kə'līd/ ▶ v. [intrans.] hit with force when moving: *she collided with someone.* ■ come into conflict or opposition. [17th C.: from L. *collidere*, from *col-* 'together' + *laedere* 'to strike.']

col·lid·er /kə'līdər/ ▶ n. Physics an accelerator in which two beams of particles are made to collide.

col·lie /'kälē/ ▶ n. (pl. **-lies**) a sheepdog of a breed originating in Scotland, having a long, pointed nose and thick, long hair. [17th C.: perh. from COAL.]

collie

PRONUNCIATION KEY ə *ago, up*; ər *over, fur*; a *hat*; ā *ate*; ä *car*; e *let*; ē *see*; i *fit*; ī *by*; NG *sing*; ō *go*; ô *law, for*; oi *toy*; o͝o *good*; o͞o *goo*; ou *out*; TH *thin*; T͟H *then*; ZH *vision*

col·lier /ˈkälyər/ ▶ **n.** esp. Brit. **1** a coal miner. **2** a ship carrying coal. [ME: from COAL + -IER.]

col·lier·y /ˈkälyərē/ ▶ **n.** (pl. **-ier·ies**) a coal mine and the buildings and equipment associated with it.

col·li·ga·tive /ˈkälə,gātiv/ ▶ **adj.** Chem. of or relating to the binding together of molecules.

col·li·mate /ˈkälə,māt/ ▶ **v.** [trans.] make (rays of light or particles) accurately parallel: [as adj.] (**collimated**) *a collimated electron beam.* ■ accurately align (an optical or other system). — **col·li·ma·tion** /,käləˈmāsʜən/ **n.** [19th C.: from L. *collimare,* erroneous reading of *collineare* 'align,' from *col-* 'with' + *linea* 'line.']

col·li·ma·tor /ˈkälə,mātər/ ▶ **n.** a device for producing a parallel beam of rays or radiation. ■ a small fixed telescope used for adjusting the line of sight of an astronomical telescope.

col·lin·e·ar /kəˈlinēər; kä-/ ▶ **adj.** Geom. (of points) lying in the same straight line. — **col·lin·e·ar·i·ty** /kə,linēˈaritē; kä-/ **n.**

Col·lins[1] /ˈkälinz/, Michael (1890–1922), Irish nationalist leader and politician. A member of Parliament for Sinn Fein, he commanded the Irish Free State forces in the civil war and became head of state but was assassinated ten days later.

Col·lins[2], William Wilkie (1824–89), English writer. His detective stories include *The Moonstone* (1868).

Col·lins[3] ▶ **n.** short for TOM COLLINS.

col·li·sion /kəˈlizʜən/ ▶ **n.** **1** an instance of one moving object or person striking violently against another. ■ an instance of conflict between opposing ideas, interests, or factions. **2** Comput. an event of two or more records being assigned the same location in memory. ■ an instance of simultaneous transmission by more than one node of a network.
– PHRASES **on (a) collision course** going in a direction that will lead to a collision with another moving object or person. ■ adopting an approach that is certain to lead to conflict with another person or group. — **col·li·sion·al** /-ˈlizʜənl/ **adj.** [ME: from late L. *collisio(n-),* from L. *collidere.*]

col·lo·cate ▶ **v.** /ˈkälə,kāt/ [intrans.] Ling. (of a word) be habitually juxtaposed with another with a frequency greater than chance: *"maiden" collocates with "voyage."* ▶ **n.** Ling. a word that is habitually juxtaposed with another with a frequency greater than chance. [16th C.: from L. *collocat-* 'placed together,' from v. *collocare,* from *col-* + *locare* 'to place.']

col·lo·ca·tion /,käləˈkāsʜən/ ▶ **n.** **1** Ling. the habitual juxtaposition of a particular word with another word or words with a frequency greater than chance. ■ a pair or group of words that are juxtaposed in such a way. **2** the action of placing things side by side or in position: *the collocation of the two pieces.*

col·lo·di·on /kəˈlōdēən/ ▶ **n.** a syrupy solution of nitrocellulose in a mixture of alcohol and ether, used for coating things, chiefly in surgery and in a former photographic process. [19th C.: from Gk. *kollōdēs* 'gluelike,' from *kolla* 'glue.']

col·loid /ˈkäloid/ ▶ **n.** a homogeneous, noncrystalline substance consisting of large molecules or ultramicroscopic particles of one substance dispersed through a second substance. ■ Anat. Med. a substance of gelatinous consistency. ▶ **adj.** [attrib.] of the nature of, relating to, or characterized by a colloid or colloids. — **col·loi·dal** /kəˈloidl/ **adj.** [19th C.: from Gk. *kolla* 'glue.']

col·lop /ˈkäləp/ ▶ **n.** a slice of meat. [ME: from Scand., akin to Swed. *kalops* 'meat stew.']

col·lo·qui·al /kəˈlōkwēəl/ ▶ **adj.** (of language) used in ordinary conversation; not formal or literary. — **col·lo·qui·al·ly** **adv.** [18th C.: from L. *colloquium.*]

col·lo·qui·al·ism /kəˈlōkwēə,lizəm/ ▶ **n.** a word or phrase that is not formal or literary, typically one used in ordinary or familiar conversation. ■ the use of such words or phrases.

col·lo·qui·um /kəˈlōkwēəm/ ▶ **n.** (pl. **-qui·ums** or **-qui·a** /-kwēə/) an academic conference or seminar. [16th C.: from L., from *colloqui* 'to converse,' from *col-* 'together' + *loqui* 'to talk.']

col·lo·quy /ˈkäləkwē/ ▶ **n.** (pl. **-quies**) **1** formal a conversation. **2** a gathering for discussion of theological questions. [ME: from L. *colloquium.*]

col·lo·type /ˈkälə,tīp/ ▶ **n.** Print. a process for making high-quality prints from a sheet of light-sensitive gelatin exposed photographically to the image without using a screen: [as adj.] *collotype printing.* ■ a print made by such a process. [19th C.: from Gk. *kolla.*]

col·lude /kəˈlo͞od/ ▶ **v.** [intrans.] come to a secret understanding for a harmful purpose; conspire. — **col·lud·er** **n.** [16th C.: from L. *colludere* from *col-* 'together' + *ludere* 'to play.']

col·lu·sion /kəˈlo͞ozʜən/ ▶ **n.** secret or illegal cooperation or conspiracy, esp. in order to cheat or deceive others. ■ Law such cooperation or conspiracy, esp. between ostensible opponents in a lawsuit. — **col·lu·sive** /-siv; -ziv/ **adj.** **col·lu·sive·ly** /-sivlē; -zivlē/ **adv.** [ME: from L. *collusion-,* from *colludere.*]

col·lu·vi·um /kəˈlo͞ovēəm/ ▶ **n.** Geol. material that accumulates at the foot of a steep slope. — **col·lu·vi·al** /-vēəl/ **adj.** [20th C.: from L. *colluvies* 'confluence,' from *colluere* 'to rinse,' from *col-* + *luere* 'to wash.']

col·ly·wob·bles /ˈkälē,wäbəlz/ ▶ **plural n.** informal, chiefly humorous stomach pain or queasiness. ■ intense anxiety or nervousness, esp. with such symptoms. [19th C.: from COLIC and WOBBLE.]

Colo. ▶ **abbr.** Colorado.

col·o·bo·ma /,käləˈbōmə/ ▶ **n.** Med. a congenital malformation of the eye causing defects in the lens, iris, or retina. [19th C.: mod. L., from Gk. *kolobōma* 'part removed in mutilation,' from *kolobos* 'cut short.']

col·o·bus /ˈkäləbəs/ (also **colobus monkey**) ▶ **n.** (pl. same) a slender, leaf-eating African monkey (genera *Colobus* and *Procolobus*) with silky fur, a long tail, and very small or absent thumbs. [mod. L., from Gk. *kolobos* 'curtailed.']

co·lo·cate /kōˈlōkāt; ˈkō,lō-/ ▶ **v.** (**be colocated**) share a location or facility with someone (or something) else: *a woman officer can often be colocated with her husband.*

col·o·cynth /ˈkälə,sinTH/ ▶ **n.** a tropical Old World climbing plant (*Citrullus colocynthis*) of the gourd family, which bears a pulpy fruit and has long been cultivated. Also called BITTER APPLE. ■ the pulpy fruit of this plant. ■ a bitter purgative drug obtained from this fruit. [16th C.: via L. from Gk. *kolokunthis.*]

Co·logne /kəˈlōn/ a city in western Germany, in North Rhine-Westphalia, on the Rhine River; pop. 956,690. German name **Köln**.

co·logne /kəˈlōn/ ▶ **n.** eau de cologne or similarly scented toilet water. [19th C.: named after COLOGNE.]

Co·lom·bi·a /kəˈləmbēə/ a country in northwestern South America. *See box.* — **Co·lom·bi·an** **adj.** & **n.**

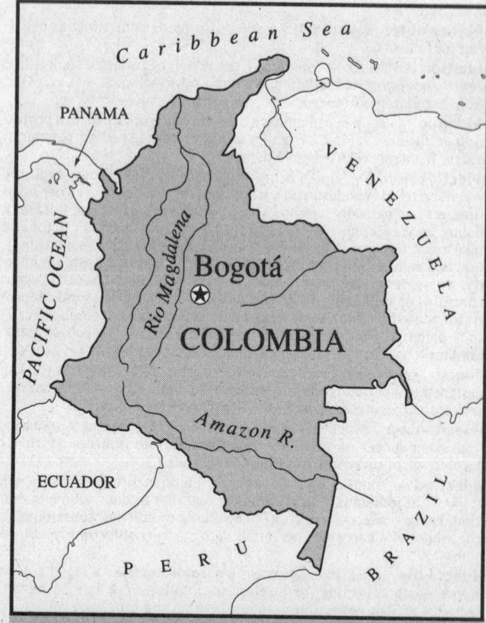

Colombia

Official name: Republic of Colombia
Location: extreme northwestern South America, bordering both the Pacific Ocean and the Caribbean Sea
Area: 401,100 square miles (1,038,700 sq km)
Population: 42,310,000
Capital: Bogotá
Language: Spanish
Currency: Colombian peso

Co·lom·bo /kəˈləmbō/ the capital of Sri Lanka, on the southwestern coast; pop. 615,000.

Co·lón /kəˈlōn/ the chief port of Panama, at the Caribbean Sea end of the Panama Canal; pop. 140,900.

co·lon[1] /ˈkōlən/ ▶ **n.** a punctuation mark (:) indicating: ■ that a writer is introducing a quotation or a list of items. ■ that a writer is separating two clauses of which the second expands or illustrates the first. ■ a statement of proportion between two numbers: *a ratio of 10:1.* ■ the separation of hours from minutes (and minutes from seconds) in a statement of time given in numbers: *4:30 p.m.* ■ the number of the chapter and verse respectively in biblical references: *Exodus 3:2.* [16th C.: via L. from Gk. *kōlon* 'limb, clause.']

co·lon[2] ▶ **n.** Anat. the main part of the large intestine, which passes from the cecum to the rectum and absorbs water and electrolytes from food that has remained undigested. [ME: via L. from Gk. *kolon.*]

co·lón /kəˈlōn/ ▶ **n.** (pl. **-lo·nes** /-ˈlōnās/) the basic monetary unit of Costa Rica and El Salvador, equal to 100 centimos in Costa Rica and 100 centavos in El Salvador. [from Cristóbal *Colón,* the Sp. name of Christopher Columbus (see COLUMBUS[2]).]

co•lon ba•cil•lus ▶ n. another term for COLIFORM BACTERIUM.

colo•nel /ˈkərnl/ ▶ n. an army officer of high rank, in particular (in the US Army, Air Force, and Marine Corps) an officer above a lieutenant colonel and below a brigadier general. ■ informal short for LIEUTENANT COLONEL. — **colo•nel•cy** /ˈkərnlsē/ n. (pl. **-cies**). [16th C.: from obs. Fr. *coronel*, from Ital. *colonnello* 'column of soldiers.']

co•lo•ni•al /kəˈlōnēəl; -nyəl/ ▶ adj. **1** of, relating to, or characteristic of a colony or colonies. ■ relating to the period of the British colonies in America before independence. ■ (esp. of architecture or furniture) made during or in the style of this period. **2** (of animals or plants) living in colonies. ▶ n. **1** a native or inhabitant of a colony. **2** a house built in colonial style. — **co•lo•ni•al•ly** adv.

co•lo•ni•al•ism /kəˈlōnēəˌlizəm; kəˈlōnyəˌlizəm/ ▶ n. the policy or practice of acquiring full or partial political control over another country, occupying it with settlers, and exploiting it economically. — **co•lo•ni•al•ist** n. & adj.

co•lon•ic /kōˈlänik; kə-/ ▶ adj. Anat. of, relating to, or affecting the colon. ▶ n. informal an act or instance of colonic irrigation, performed for its supposed therapeutic benefits.

co•lon•ic ir•ri•ga•tion ▶ n. a water enema given to flush out the colon.

col•o•nist /ˈkälənist/ ▶ n. a settler in or inhabitant of a colony.

col•o•nize /ˈkäləˌnīz/ ▶ v. [trans.] (of a country or its citizens) send settlers to (a place) and establish political control over it. ■ come to settle among and establish political control over (the indigenous people of an area). ■ appropriate (a place or domain) for one's own use. ■ Ecol. (of a plant or animal) establish itself in an area. — **col•o•ni•za•tion** /ˌkälənəˈzāsʜən/ n. **col•o•niz•er** n.

col•on•nade /ˌkäləˈnād/ ▶ n. a row of columns supporting a roof, an entablature, or arcade. ■ a row of trees or other tall objects. — **col•on•nad•ed** adj. [18th C.: from Fr., from *colonne* 'column,' from L. *columna*.]

co•lon•o•scope /kəˈlänəˌskōp/ ▶ n. Med. a flexible fiber-optic instrument inserted through the anus in order to examine the colon. — **co•lon•os•co•py** /ˌkōləˈnäskəpē/ n.

col•o•ny /ˈkälənē/ ▶ n. (pl. **-nies**) **1** a country or area under the full or partial political control of another country, typically a distant one, and occupied by settlers from that country. ■ a group of people living in such a country or area, consisting of the original settlers and their descendants and successors. **2** a group of people of one nationality or ethnic group living in a foreign city or country. ■ a place where a group of people with similar interests live together: *an artists' colony.* **3** Biol. a community of animals or plants of one kind living close together or forming a physically connected structure: *a colony of seals.* ■ a group of fungi or bacteria grown from a single spore or cell on a culture medium. [ME: from L. *colonia* 'settlement,' from *colonus* 'farmer,' from *colere* 'cultivate.']

col•o•phon /ˈkäləfən; -ˌfän/ ▶ n. a publisher's emblem or imprint, esp. one on the title page or spine of a book. ■ hist. a statement at the end of a book, typically with a printer's emblem, giving information about its authorship and printing. [17th C.: via late L. from Gk. *kolophōn* 'finishing touch.']

co•loph•o•ny /kəˈläfənē; ˈkäləˌfōnē/ ▶ n. another term for ROSIN. [ME: from L. *colophonia (resina)* '(resin) from *Colophon*,' in Lydia, Asia Minor.]

col•or /ˈkələr/ (Brit. **col•our**) ▶ n. **1** the property possessed by an object of producing different sensations on the eye as a result of the way it reflects or emits light. ■ one, or any mixture, of the constituents into which light can be separated in a spectrum or rainbow, sometimes including (loosely) black and white. ■ the use of all colors, not only black, white, and gray, in photography or television. ■ a substance used to give something a particular color: *lip color.* ■ fig. a shade of meaning. ■ fig. character or general nature. **2** the appearance of someone's skin; in particular: ■ pigmentation of the skin, esp. as an indication of someone's race. ■ a group of people considered as being distinguished by skin pigmentation. ■ rosiness of the complexion, esp. as an indication of someone's health. ■ redness of the face as a manifestation of an emotion, esp. embarrassment or anger. **3** vividness of visual appearance resulting from the presence of brightly colored things. ■ fig. picturesque or exciting features that lend a particularly interesting quality to something. ■ fig. variety of musical tone or expression: *orchestral color.* **4** (**colors**) an item or items of a particular color or combination of colors worn to identify an individual or a member of a school, group, or organization; in particular: ■ the clothes or accoutrements worn by a jockey or racehorse to indicate the horse's owner. ■ the flag of a regiment or ship. ■ a national flag. ■ the armed forces of a country, as symbolized by its flag. **5** Physics a quantized property of quarks that can take three values (designated blue, green, and red) for each flavor. **6** Mining a particle of gold remaining in a mining pan after most of the mud and gravel has been washed away. ▶ v. **1** [trans.] change the color of (something) by painting or dyeing it with crayons, paints, or dyes. ■ [intrans.] take on a different color. ■ use crayons to fill (a particular shape or outline) with color. ■ fig. make vivid or picturesque. **2** [intrans.] (of a person or their skin) show embarrassment or shame by becoming red; blush. ■ [trans.] cause (a person or their skin) to change in color. ■ [trans.] (of a particular color) imbue (a person's skin). ■ [trans.] fig. (of an emotion) imbue (a person's voice) with a particular tone. **3** [trans.] influence, esp. in a negative way; distort. ■ misrepresent by distortion or exaggeration.
– PHRASES **lend** (or **give**) **color to** make something seem true or probable. **person of color** see PERSON OF COLOR. **show one's true colors** reveal one's real character or intentions, esp. when these are disreputable or dishonorable. **under color of** under the pretext of. **with flying colors** see FLYING. [ME: ult. from L. *color*.]

col•or•a•ble /ˈkələrəbəl/ (Brit. **col•our•able**) ▶ adj. **1** apparently correct or justified: *a colorable legal claim.* ■ counterfeit. **2** capable of being colored: *colorable illustrations.*

Col•o•rad•o /ˌkäləˈrädō; -ˈradō/ **1** a river that rises in the Rocky Mountains of northern Colorado and flows southwest to the Gulf of California. **2** a river that flows east across Texas, from the Llano Estacado to the Gulf of Mexico. **3** a state in the central US; pop. 4,301,261; capital, Denver; statehood, Aug. 1, 1876 (38). Part of Colorado was acquired by the US with the Louisiana Purchase in 1803 and the rest was ceded by Mexico in 1848. — **Col•o•rad•an** /-ˈrädn; -ˈradn/ n. & adj.

Col•o•rad•o blue spruce ▶ n. another term for BLUE SPRUCE.

Col•o•ra•do Desert a region in southeastern California, west of the Colorado River.

Col•o•ra•do Pla•teau a region of arid uplands in the southwestern US; in Colorado, Utah, New Mexico, and Arizona.

Col•o•rad•o po•ta•to bee•tle ▶ n. a yellow- and black-striped leaf beetle (*Leptinotarsa decemlineata*, family Chrysomelidae) native to North America. The larvae are highly destructive to potato plants and have occurred in many countries. [19th C.: named after the state of COLORADO.]

Colorado potato beetle

Col•o•ra•do Springs a city in central Colorado, home to the US Air Force Academy; pop. 360,890.

Col•o•rad•o spruce ▶ n. another term for BLUE SPRUCE.

col•or•ant /ˈkələrənt/ (Brit. **col•our•ant**) ▶ n. a dye, pigment, or other substance that colors something.

col•or•a•tion /ˌkələˈrāsʜən/ ▶ n. **1** a visual appearance with regard to color. ■ the natural color or variegated markings of animals or plants. ■ a scheme or method of applying color. **2** a specified pervading character or tone of something. ■ a variety of musical or vocal expression. [17th C.: from late L. *coloratio(n-)*, from *colorare* 'to color.']

col•o•ra•tu•ra /ˌkələrəˈt(y)o͝orə; ˌkä-/ ▶ n. elaborate ornamentation of a vocal melody, esp. in operatic singing by a soprano. ■ (also **coloratura soprano**) a soprano skilled in such singing. [Ital., lit. 'coloring.']

col•or bar ▶ n. **1** a social system in which a group of people (typically nonwhite) are denied access to the same rights, opportunities, and facilities as other people (typically white) on the basis of skin color. **2** a strip on printed material or a screen display showing a range of colors, used to ensure that all colors are printed or displayed correctly.

col•or-blind (also **col•or•blind**) ▶ adj. **1** unable to distinguish certain colors, or (rarely in humans) any colors at all. See PROTANOPIA. **2** not influenced by racial prejudice. — **col•or-blind•ness** n.

col•or code ▶ n. a system of marking things with different colors as a means of identification. ▶ v. (**col•or-code**) [trans.] (usu. **be color-coded**) mark (things) with different colors as a means of identification. ■ mark different features of (something) with different colors: *the map is color-coded.*

co•lo•rec•tal /ˌkōlōˈrektəl/ ▶ adj. relating to or affecting the colon and the rectum.

col•ored /ˈkələrd/ (Brit. **col•oured**) ▶ adj. **1** having or having been given a color or colors, esp. as opposed to being black, white, or neutral. ■ fig. imbued with an emotive or exaggerated quality: ***highly colored** examples were used by both sides.* **2** (also **Colored**) wholly or partly of nonwhite descent (now usually offensive in the US). ■ (also **Coloured**) S. African used as an ethnic label for people of mixed ethnic origin. ■ relating to people who are wholly or partly of nonwhite descent. ▶ n. **1** (also **Colored**) dated offens. a person who is wholly or partly of nonwhite descent. ■ S. African a person of mixed ethnic origin speaking Afrikaans or English as their mother tongue. **2** (**coloreds**) clothes, sheets, etc., that are any color but white.
– USAGE **Colored** referring to skin color is first recorded in the early 17th century and was adopted in the US by emancipated slaves as a term of racial pride after the end of the Civil War. The word is still used in the National Association for the Advancement of Colored People (NAACP), but otherwise **colored** sounds old-fashioned at best, and possibly offensive.In South Africa, the term **colored** (normally written **Coloured**) has a different history. It is used to refer to people of mixed-race parentage rather than, as elsewhere, to refer to African peoples and their descendants, i.e., as a synonym for **black**. In modern use in this context, the term is not considered offensive or derogatory. See also usage at AFRICAN AMERICAN, BLACK, and PERSON OF COLOR.

col•or•fast /ˈkələrˌfast/ ▶ adj. dyed in colors that will not fade or be washed out. — **col•or•fast•ness** n.

col•or fil•ter ▶ n. a photographic filter that absorbs light of certain colors.

col•or•ful /ˈkələrfəl/ (Brit. **col•our•ful**) ▶ adj. **1** having much or varied color; bright: *a colorful array of fruit.* **2** full of interest; lively and exciting. ■ (of a person's life or background) involving variously disreputable activities. ■ (of language) vulgar or rude. — **col•or•ful•ly** /-f(ə)lē/ adv. **col•or•ful•ness** n.

col•or guard ▶ n. a uniformed group, esp. of soldiers, police officers, or school representatives, who parade or present their institution's flag (and sometimes their national flag) on ceremonial occasions.

col·or·im·e·ter /,kələ'rimitər/ ▶n. an instrument for measuring the intensity of color. — **col·or·i·met·ric** /,kələrə'metrik/ adj. **col·or·im·e·try** /,kələ'rimitrē/ n.

col·or·ing /'kələriNG/ (Brit. **col·our·ing**) ▶n. **1** the process or skill of applying a substance to something so as to change its original color. ■ the process of filling in a particular shape or outline with crayons. ■ a drawing produced in this way. **2** visual appearance with regard to color, in particular: ■ the arrangement of colors and markings on an animal. ■ the natural hues of a person's skin, hair, and eyes: *her fair coloring.* ■ fig. the pervading character or tone of something. **3** a substance used to give a particular color to something, esp. food.

col·or·ist /'kələrist/ (Brit. **col·our·ist**) ▶n. an artist or designer who uses color in a special or skillful way. ■ a person who tints black-and-white prints, photographs, or movies. ■ a hairdresser who specializes in dyeing people's hair.

col·or·is·tic /,kələ'ristik/ (Brit. **col·our·is·tic**) ▶adj. showing or relating to a special use of color. ■ having or showing a variety of musical or vocal expression: *the choir's coloristic resources.* — **col·or·is·ti·cal·ly** adv.

col·or·ize /'kələ,rīz/ (Brit. also **col·our·ize**) ▶v. [trans.] add color to (a black-and-white movie) by means of computer technology. — **col·or·i·za·tion** /,kələrə'zāSHən/ n. (trademark in the US) **col·or·iz·er** n. (trademark in the US).

col·or·less /'kələrləs/ (Brit.**col·our·less**) ▶adj. **1** (esp. of a gas or liquid) without color. ■ dull or pale in hue: *colorless cheeks.* **2** lacking distinctive character or interest; dull. — **col·or·less·ly** adv.

color line ▶n. another term for COLOR BAR (sense 1).

col·or phase ▶n. a genetic or seasonal variation in the color of the skin, pelt, or feathers of an animal.

col·or re·ver·sal ▶n. [usu. as adj.] Photog. the process of producing a positive image directly from another positive: *color reversal films.*

col·or sat·u·ra·tion ▶n. see SATURATION.

col·or scheme ▶n. an arrangement or combination of colors, esp. as used in interior decoration.

col·or sep·a·ra·tion ▶n. Photog. Print. any of three negative images of the same subject taken through green, red, and blue filters and combined to reproduce the full color of the original. ■ the production of such images.

col·or tem·per·a·ture ▶n. Astron. Physics the temperature at which a black body would emit radiation of the same color as a given object.

col·or ther·a·py ▶n. a system of alternative medicine based on the use of color, esp. projected colored light.

col·or wash ▶n. colored calcimine or tempera. ▶v. (**col·or-wash**) [trans.] paint (something) with colored calcimine or tempera.

col·or·way /'kələr,wā/ (Brit. **col·our·way**) ▶n. any of a range of combinations of colors in which a style or design is available.

col·or wheel ▶n. a circle with different colored sectors used to show the relationship between colors.

co·los·sal /kə'läsəl/ ▶adj. extremely large. ■ Archit. (of a giant order) having more than one story of columns. ■ Sculpture (of a statue) at least twice life size. — **co·los·sal·ly** adv.

Col·os·se·um /,kälə'sēəm/ ▶n. a vast amphitheater in Rome, begun by Vespasian c.AD 75. [from L., neut. of *colosseus* 'gigantic,' from *colossus.*]

Co·los·sians /kə'läSHənz/ a book of the New Testament, an epistle of St. Paul to the Church at Colossae in Phrygia.

co·los·sus /kə'läsəs/ ▶n. (pl. **-los·si** /-'läsī/ or **-los·sus·es**) a statue that is much bigger than life size. ■ fig. a person or thing of enormous size, importance, or ability. [ME: via L. from Gk. *kolossos.*]

Co·los·sus of Rhodes a huge bronze statue of the sun god Helios, one of the Seven Wonders of the World. Built *c.*280 BC, it was destroyed in an earthquake.

co·los·to·my /kə'lästəmē/ ▶n. (pl. **-mies**) a surgical operation in which a piece of the colon is diverted to an artificial opening in the abdominal wall so as to bypass a damaged part of the colon. ■ an opening so formed: [as adj.] *a colostomy bag.* [19th C.: from COLON² + Gk. *stoma* 'mouth.']

co·los·trum /kə'lästrəm/ ▶n. the first secretion from the mammary glands after giving birth, rich in antibodies. [16th C.: from L.]

col·our ▶n. & v. British spelling of COLOR.

col·po·scope /'kälpə,skōp/ ▶n. a surgical instrument used to examine the vagina and the cervix of the uterus. — **col·pos·co·py** /käl'päskəpē/ n. [20th C.: from Gk. *kolpos* 'womb.']

Colt¹ /kōlt/, Samuel (1814–62), US inventor, noted for advancing the manufacturing techniques of interchangeable parts and the production line. He invented a revolver in 1846 that is named after him.

Colt² ▶n. trademark a type of revolver.

colt /kōlt/ ▶n. a young, uncastrated male horse, in particular one less than four years old. [OE; perh. rel. to Swed. *kult* 'half-grown animal.']

col·ter /'kōltər/ ▶n. var. of COULTER.

colt·ish /'kōltiSH/ ▶adj. energetic but awkward in one's movements or behavior. — **colt·ish·ly** adv. **colt·ish·ness** n.

Col·ton /'kōltn/ a city in southwestern California; pop. 47,662.

Col·trane /'kōl,trān; kōl'trān/, John William (1926–67), US saxophonist who was a leading figure in avant-garde jazz.

colts·foot /'kōlts,fo͝ot/ ▶n. (pl. **-foots**) a Eurasian plant (*Tussilago farfara*) of the daisy family, with yellow flowers followed by large, heart-shaped leaves. It is used in herbal medicine, esp. for respiratory disorders.

col·u·brid /'käl(y)əbrid/ ▶n. Zool. a snake of a very large family (Colubridae) that includes the majority of harmless species, such as grass snakes and garter snakes. The few venomous species have grooved fangs in the rear of the upper jaw. [19th C.: from mod. L. *Colubridae* (pl.), from L. *coluber* 'snake.']

col·u·brine /'käl(y)ə,brīn/ ▶adj. rare, chiefly fig. of or belonging to a snake; snakelike. [16th C.: from L. *coluber* 'snake.']

co·lu·go /kə'lo͞ogō/ ▶n. (pl. **-gos**) another term for FLYING LEMUR. [18th C.: of unknown origin.]

Co·lum·ba /kə'ləmbə/ Astron. a small and faint southern constellation (the Dove), near Canis Major. [L.]

Co·lum·ba, St. (*c.*521–597), Irish abbot and missionary. He established a monastery at Iona *c.*563.

col·um·bar·i·um /,käləm'be(ə)rēəm/ ▶n. (pl. **-bar·i·a** /-'be(ə)rēə/) a room or building with niches for funeral urns to be stored. [18th C.: from L., lit. 'pigeon house'.]

Co·lum·bi·a /kə'ləmbēə/ **1** a river that rises in the Rocky Mountains of southeastern British Columbia and flows for 1,230 miles (1,953 km), first south and then west to the Pacific south of Seattle. **2** a community in central Maryland, planned and established in the 1960s; pop. 88,254. **3** a city in central Missouri; pop. 84,531. **4** the capital of South Carolina, in the central part of the state; pop. 116,278.

Co·lum·bi·a, District of see DISTRICT OF COLUMBIA.

col·um·bine /'käləm,bīn/ ▶n. an aquilegia with long-spurred flowers. Its several species include the white-flowered **Colorado blue columbine** (*A. coerulea*) with blue sepals, and the red-flowered *A. canadensis.* [ME: from OFr. *colombine,* from med. L. *colombina* 'dovelike,' from L. *columba* 'dove.']

Colorado blue columbine

co·lum·bite /'käləm,bīt/ ▶n. a black mineral, typically occurring as dense, tabular crystals, consisting of an oxide of iron, manganese, niobium, and tantalum. It is the chief ore of niobium. [19th C.: from COLUMBIUM + -ITE¹.]

co·lum·bi·um /kə'ləmbēəm/ ▶n. old-fashioned term for NIOBIUM. [19th C.: mod. L., from *Columbia* 'America.']

Co·lum·bus¹ /kə'ləmbəs/ **1** a city in western Georgia, on the Chattahoochee River; pop. 185,781. **2** the capital of Ohio, in the central part of the state; pop. 711,470.

Co·lum·bus², Christopher (1451–1506), Spanish explorer; born in Italy; Italian name *Cristoforo Colombo*; Spanish name *Cristóbal Colón.* Spanish monarchs Ferdinand and Isabella sponsored his 1492 expedition to the New World.

Co·lum·bus Day ▶n. a legal holiday commemorating the discovery of the New World by Christopher Columbus in 1492. It is observed by most states on the second Monday of October.

col·u·mel·la /,käl(y)ə'melə/ ▶n. (pl. **-mel·lae** /-'melī; -'melē/) Biol. a structure resembling a small column and typically forming a central axis. — **col·u·mel·lar** /-'melər/ adj. [16th C.: from L., 'small column.']

col·umn /'käləm/ ▶n. **1** an upright pillar, typically cylindrical and made of stone or concrete, supporting an entablature, arch, or other structure or standing alone as a monument. ■ a similar vertical, roughly cylindrical thing. ■ an upright shaft forming part of a machine and typically used for controlling it. **2** a vertical division of a page or text. ■ a vertical arrangement of figures or other information. ■ a section of a newspaper or magazine regularly devoted to a particular subject or written by a particular person. **3** one or more lines of people or vehicles moving in the same direction. ■ Mil. a narrow-fronted deep formation of troops in successive lines. ■ a military force deployed in such a formation. ■ a similar formation of ships in a fleet or convoy. — **co·lum·nar** /kə'ləmnər/ adj. **col·umned** /'käləmd/ adj. [ME: from OFr. *columpne,* L. *columna* 'pillar.']

col·um·nat·ed /'käləm,nātid/ ▶adj. Archit. supported on or having columns.

co·lum·ni·a·tion /kə,ləmnē'āSHən/ ▶n. Archit. the use or arrangement of columns.

col·umn inch ▶n. a one-inch length of a column in a newspaper or magazine.

col·um·nist /'käləmnist/ ▶n. a journalist contributing regularly to a newspaper or magazine.

co·lure /kə'lo͝or/ ▶n. Astron. either of two great circles intersecting at right angles at the celestial poles and passing through the ecliptic at either the equinoxes or the solstices. [ME: from late L. *coluri* (pl.), from Gk. *kolourai (grammai)* 'truncated (lines),' from *kolouros* 'truncated.']

co·ly /'kōlē/ ▶n. (pl. **-lies**) another term for MOUSEBIRD. [19th C.: from mod. L. *Colius,* from Gk. *kolios,* denoting a type of woodpecker.]

col·za /'kälzə; 'kōlzə/ ▶n. another term for RAPE². [18th C.: ult. from Du. *koolzaad,* from *kool* 'cole' + *zaad* 'seed.']

COM /käm/ ▶abbr. ■ computer output on microfilm or microfiche. ■ (also **Com.**) Commodore.

com- (also **co-**, **col-**, **con-**, or **cor-**) ▶ **prefix** with; together; jointly; altogether: *combine* | *command* | *collude.* [from L. *cum* 'with.']

co·ma[1] /'kōmə/ ▶ **n.** a state of deep unconsciousness that lasts for a prolonged or indefinite period, caused esp. by severe injury or illness. [17th C.: mod. L., from Gk. *kōma* 'deep sleep'; rel. to *koitē* 'bed.']

co·ma[2] ▶ **n.** (pl. **co·mae** /'kōmē/) Astron. a diffuse cloud of gas and dust surrounding the nucleus of a comet. [17th C.: via L. from Gk. *komē* 'hair of the head.']

Co·ma Ber·e·ni·ces /'kōmə ˌberə'nīsēz/ Astron. an inconspicuous northern constellation (Berenice's Hair), said to represent the tresses of Queen Berenice. It contains a large number of galaxies. [L.]

Co·man·che /kə'manchē/ ▶ **n.** (pl. same or **-ches**) **1** a member of an American Indian people of the southwestern US. **2** the Uto-Aztecan language of this people. ▶ **adj.** of or relating to this people or their language. [Sp., from Ute *kɨmmanči* 'strangers'.]

Co·ma·neci /ˌkōmə'nēch; -'nāch/, Nadia Elena (1961–), Romanian gymnast. In 1976, she became the first Olympic gymnast to earn a perfect score.

com·a·tose /'kōməˌtōs; 'kämə-/ ▶ **adj.** of or in a state of deep unconsciousness for a prolonged or indefinite period, esp. as a result of severe injury or illness. ■ humorous (of a person or thing) extremely exhausted, lethargic, or sleepy. [17th C.: from Gk. *kōma, kōmat-* 'sleep.']

comb /kōm/ ▶ **n.** **1** a strip of plastic, metal, or wood with a row of narrow teeth, used for untangling or arranging the hair. ■ [in sing.] an instance of untangling or arranging the hair with such a device: *she gave her hair a comb.* ■ a short curved device of this type, worn by women to hold hair in place or as an ornament. **2** something resembling a comb in function or structure, in particular: ■ a device for separating and dressing textile fibers. ■ a row of brass points for collecting the electricity in an electrostatic generator. **3** the red fleshy crest on the head of a domestic fowl, esp. a rooster. **4** short for HONEYCOMB (sense 1). ▶ **v.** [trans.] **1** untangle or arrange (the hair) by drawing a comb through it. ■ (**comb something out**) remove something from the hair by drawing a comb through it. ■ curry (a horse). **2** prepare (wool, flax, or cotton) for manufacture with a comb. ■ [usu. as adj.] (**combed**) treat (a fabric) in such a way. **3** search carefully and systematically. — **comb·like adj.** [OE *camb*, from Gmc.; akin to Ger. *Kamm*.]

com·bat /'kämˌbat/ ▶ **n.** fighting between armed forces. ■ nonviolent conflict or opposition. ▶ **v.** /kəm'bat; 'kämˌbat/ (**-bat·ed** or **-bat·ted**, **-bat·ing** or **-bat·ting**) [trans.] take action to reduce, destroy, or prevent (something undesirable). [16th C.: from Fr. *combattre* (v.), from late L. *combattere*, from *com-* + *battere*, var. of L. *batuere* 'to fight.']

com·bat·ant /kəm'batnt; 'kämbətənt/ ▶ **n.** a person engaged in fighting during a war. ■ a nation at war with another. ■ a person engaged in conflict or competition with another. ▶ **adj.** engaged in fighting during a war.

com·bat fa·tigue ▶ **n.** **1** more recent term for SHELL SHOCK. **2** (**combat fatigues**) a uniform of a type to be worn into combat.

com·bat·ive /kəm'bativ/ ▶ **adj.** ready or eager to fight; pugnacious. — **com·bat·ive·ly adv. com·bat·ive·ness n.**

comb-back ▶ **n.** a high-backed Windsor chair with a straight top rail: [as adj.] *a comb-back rocker.*

comb·er /'kōmər/ ▶ **n.** **1** a long curling sea wave. **2** a person or machine that separates and straightens the fibers of cotton or wool.

com·bi·na·tion /ˌkämbə'nāshən/ ▶ **n.** **1** the act or an instance of combining; the process of being combined. ■ [as adj.] uniting different uses, functions, or ingredients. ■ the state of being joined or united in such a way. ■ Chem. the joining of substances in a compound with new properties. ■ Chem. the state of being in a compound. **2** a set of people or things that have been combined. ■ an arrangement of elements. ■ a sequence of numbers or letters used to open a combination lock: [as adj.] *a combination briefcase.* ■ (in various sports and games) a coordinated and effective sequence of moves. ■ (in equestrian sports) a jump consisting of two or more elements. **3** Math. a selection of a given number of elements from a larger number without regard to their arrangement. — **com·bi·na·tion·al** /-shənl/ **adj. com·bi·na·tive** /'kämbəˌnātiv; kəm'bīnətiv/ **adj. com·bi·na·to·ri·al** /ˌkämbənə'tôrēəl; kəmˌbīnə-/ **adj.** (Math.) **com·bi·na·to·ri·al·ly** /ˌkämbənə'tôrēəlē; kəmˌbīnə-/ **adv.** (Math.) **com·bi·na·to·ry** /kəm'bīnəˌtôre; 'kämbənə-/ **adj.**

com·bi·na·tion lock ▶ **n.** a lock that is opened by rotating a dial or set of dials, marked with letters or numbers, through a specific sequence.

com·bi·na·tion ov·en ▶ **n.** an oven operating by both conventional heating and microwaves.

com·bi·na·tion ther·a·py ▶ **n.** treatment in which a patient is given two or more drugs (or other therapeutic agents) for a single disease.

com·bi·na·tor·ics /ˌkämbənə'tôriks; kəmˌbīnə-/ ▶ **plural n.** [treated as sing.] the branch of mathematics dealing with combinations of objects belonging to a finite set in accordance with certain constraints, such as those of graph theory. [1940s: from *combinatorial*.]

com·bine[1] ▶ **v.** /kəm'bīn/ [trans.] unite; merge. ■ [intrans.] Chem. unite to form a compound. ■ [intrans.] unite for a common purpose. ■ engage in simultaneously. ▶ **n.** /'kämbīn/ a group of people or companies acting together for a commercial purpose. — **com·bin·a·ble adj.** [ME: from late L. *combinare* 'join two by two,' from *com-* + L. *bini* 'two together.']

com·bine[2] /'kämbīn/ ▶ **n.** (in full **combine harvester**) an agricultural machine that cuts, threshes, and cleans a grain crop in one operation. ▶ **v.** [trans.] harvest (a crop) by means of a combine.

comb·ings /'kōmingz/ ▶ **plural n.** hairs removed with a comb.

comb·ing wool ▶ **n.** long-stapled wool with straight, parallel fibers, suitable for combing and making into high-quality fabrics, in particular worsted. Compare with CARDING WOOL.

com·bin·ing form /kəm'bīning/ ▶ **n.** Gram. a linguistic element used in combination with another element to form a word.

comb jel·ly ▶ **n.** a small, luminescent marine animal (phylum Ctenophora) with a jellyfishlike body bearing rows of fused cilia for propulsion.

com·bo /'kämbō/ ▶ **n.** (pl. **-bos**) informal **1** a small jazz, rock, or pop band. **2** a combination, typically of different foods: [as adj.] *the combo platter.* [1920s: abbrev. of COMBINATION + **-o**.]

com·bo box ▶ **n.** Comput., informal a type of dialog box containing a combination of controls, such as sliders, text boxes, and drop-down lists.

comb·over /'kōmˌōvər/ (also **comb-o·ver**) ▶ **n.** hair that is combed over a bald spot in an attempt to cover it.

com·bust /kəm'bəst/ ▶ **v.** [trans.] consume by fire. ■ [intrans.] be consumed by fire. [15th C.: ult. from L. *combustus*, past part. of *comburere* 'burn up.']

com·bus·ti·ble /kəm'bəstəbəl/ ▶ **adj.** able to catch fire and burn easily: *highly combustible paint thinner.* ■ fig. excitable; easily annoyed. ▶ **n.** a combustible substance. — **com·bus·ti·bil·i·ty** /kəmˌbəstə'bilitē/ **n.**

com·bus·tion /kəm'bəschən/ ▶ **n.** the process of burning something: *the combustion of fossil fuels.* ■ Chem. rapid chemical combination of a substance with oxygen, producing heat and light. — **com·bus·tive** /-'bəstiv/ **adj.**

com·bus·tion cham·ber ▶ **n.** an enclosed space in which combustion takes place, esp. in an engine or furnace.

Comdr. ▶ **abbr.** commander.

come /kəm/ ▶ **v.** (past **came** /kām/; past part. **come**) **1** [no obj., usu. with adverbial of direction] move or travel toward or into a place thought of as near or familiar to the speaker. ■ arrive at a specified place. ■ (of a thing) reach or extend to a specified point. ■ (**be coming**) approach: *someone was coming* | *she heard the train coming.* ■ travel in order to be with a specified person, to do a specified thing, or to be present at an event. ■ [with pres. part.] join someone in participating in a specified activity or course of action: *do you want to come fishing tomorrow?* ■ (**come along/on**) make progress; develop. ■ [in imper.] (also **come, come!**) said to someone when correcting, reassuring, or urging them on: *"Come, come, child, no need to thank me."* **2** [intrans.] occur; happen; take place. ■ be heard, perceived, or experienced. ■ [with adverbial] (of a quality) become apparent or noticeable through actions or performance: *your style and personality must come through.* ■ (**come across** or **off** or Brit. **over**) (of a person) appear or sound in a specified way; give a specified impression: *he'd always come across as a decent guy.* ■ (of a thought or memory) enter one's mind. **3** [no obj., with complement] take or occupy a specified position in space, order, or priority. ■ achieve a specified place in a race or contest. **4** [no obj., with complement] pass into a specified state, esp. one of separation or disunion. ■ (**come to/into**) reach or be brought to a specified situation or result. ■ [with infin.] reach eventually a certain condition or state of mind. **5** [no obj., with adverbial] be sold, available, or found in a specified form: *the cars come with a variety of extras.* **6** [intrans.] informal have an orgasm. ▶ **prep.** informal when a specified time is reached or event happens. ▶ **n.** informal semen ejaculated at orgasm.

– PHRASES **as —— as they come** used to describe someone or something that is a supreme example of the quality specified: *Smith is as tough as they come.* **come again?** informal used to ask someone to repeat or explain something they have said. **come and go** arrive and then depart again; move around freely. ■ exist or be present for a limited time; be transitory: *health fads come and go.* **come from behind** win after lagging. **come off it** [in imper.] informal said when vigorously expressing disbelief. **come to nothing** have no significant or successful result in the end. **come to pass** esp. literary happen; occur. **come to rest** eventually cease moving. **come to that** (or **if it comes to that**) informal in fact (said to introduce an additional point). **come to think of it** on reflection (said when an idea or point occurs to one while one is speaking). **come what may** no matter what happens. **have it coming** (**to one**) informal be due for retribution on account of something bad that one has done: *his uppity sister-in-law had it coming to her.* **how come?** informal said when asking how or why something happened or is the case. **to come** (following a noun) in the future. **where someone is coming from** informal someone's meaning, motivation, or personality.

– PHRASAL VERBS **come about 1** happen; take place. **2** (of a ship) change direction. **come across 1** meet or find by chance. **2** informal hand over or provide what is wanted: *she has come across with some details.* ■ (of a woman) agree to have sexual intercourse with a man. **come along** [in imper.] said when encouraging someone or telling them to hurry up. **come around** (esp. Brit. also **round**) **1** recover consciousness: *I'd just come around from a drunken stupor.* **2** be converted to another person's opinion: *I came around to her point of view.* **3** (of a date or regular occurrence) recur; be imminent again. **come at** launch oneself at (someone); attack. **come away** be left with a specified feeling, impression, or result after doing something. **come back 1** (in sports) recover from a deficit. **2** reply or respond to someone, esp. vigorously. **come before** be dealt with by (a judge or court). **come between** interfere with or disturb the relationship of (two people): *I let my stupid pride come between us.* **come by 1** call casually and briefly as a visitor. **2** manage to acquire or obtain (something). **come down 1** (of a building or other structure) collapse or be demolished. ■ (of an aircraft) crash or crash-land. **2** be handed down by tradition or inheritance. **3** reach a decision or recommendation in favor of one side or another. **4** informal experience the lessening of an excited or euphoric feeling, esp. one produced by a narcotic drug. **come down on** criticize or punish (someone) harshly. **come down to** (of a situation or outcome) be dependent on (a specified factor). **come down with** begin to suffer from (a specified illness): *I came down with influenza.* **come for** (of police or other officials) arrive to arrest or detain (someone). **come forward** volunteer oneself for a task or post or to give evidence about a crime. **come from** originate in; have as its source. ■ be the result of. ■ have as one's place of birth or residence. ■ be descended from. **come in 1** join or become involved in an enterprise. ■ have a useful role or function. ■ [with complement] prove to have a specified good quality: *the money came in handy.* **2** [with complement] finish a race in a specified position: *the favorite came in first.* **3** (of money) be earned or received regularly. **4** [in imper.] begin speaking or make contact, esp. in radio communication. **5** (of a tide) rise; flow. **come in for** receive or be the object of (a reaction), typically a negative one: *he has come in for a lot of criticism.* **come into** suddenly receive (money or property), esp. by inheriting it. **come of** result from: *no good will come of it.* ■ be descended from: *she came of Neapolitan stock.* **come off 1** (of an action) succeed; be accomplished. ■ fare in a specified way in a contest. **2** become detached or be detachable from something. **come on 1** (of a state or condition) start to arrive or happen. **2** (also **come upon**) meet or find by chance. **3** [in imper.] said when encouraging someone to do something or to hurry up or when one feels that someone is wrong or foolish. ■ said or shouted to express support, for example for a sports team. **come on to** informal make sexual advances toward. **come out 1** (of a fact) emerge; become known. ■ happen as a result. ■ (of a photograph) be produced satisfactorily or in a specified way: *I hope my photographs come out all right.* ■ (of the result of a calculation or measurement) emerge at a specified figure. **2** (of a book or other work) appear; be released or published. **3** declare oneself as being for or against something: *residents have come out against the proposals.* **4** [with complement] achieve a specified placing in an examination or contest. ■ acquit oneself in a specified way: *surprisingly, it's Penn who comes out best.* **5** (of a stain) be removed or able to be removed. **6** informal openly declare that one is homosexual. **7** dated (of a young upper-class woman) make one's debut in society. **come out with** say (something) in a sudden, rude, or incautious way. **come over 1** (of a feeling or manner) begin to affect (someone). **2** change to another side or point of view. **come through 1** succeed in surviving or dealing with (an illness or ordeal): *she's come through the operation very well.* **2** (of a message) be sent and received. ■ (of an official decree) be processed and notified. **come to 1** (also **come to oneself**) recover consciousness. **2** (of an expense) reach in total; amount to. **3** (of a ship) come to a stop. **come under 1** be classified as or among. **2** be subject to (an influence or authority). ■ be subjected to (pressure or aggression): *his vehicle came under mortar fire.* **come up** (of an issue, situation, or problem) occur or present itself, esp. unexpectedly. ■ (of a specified time or event) approach or draw near. ■ (of a legal case) reach the time when it is scheduled to be dealt with. **come up against** be faced with or opposed by (something such as an enemy or problem). **come up with** produce (something), esp. when pressured or challenged. **come upon 1** attack by surprise. **2** see COME ON (sense 2). [OE *cuman*, from Gmc.; akin to Ger. *kommen*.]

come·a·long ▶ n. informal a hand-operated winch.

come·back /ˈkəmˌbak/ ▶ n. **1** a return by a well-known person, esp. an entertainer or sports player, to the activity in which they have formerly been successful. ■ a return to fashion of an item, activity, or style. **2** informal a quick reply to a critical remark. ■ [usu. with negative] the opportunity to seek redress: *there's no comeback if he messes up your case.*

co·me·di·an /kəˈmēdēən/ ▶ n. an entertainer whose act is designed to make an audience laugh. ■ often ironic an amusing or entertaining person. ■ a comic actor.

Co·mé·die Fran·çaise /ˌkômādē fräNˈsez/ the French national theater (used for both comedy and tragedy), in Paris, founded in 1680 by Louis XIV.

co·me·di·enne /kəˌmēdēˈen/ ▶ n. a female comedian.

com·e·do·gen·ic /ˌkämədōˈjenik/ ▶ adj. tending to cause blackheads by blocking the pores of the skin.

come·down /ˈkəmˌdoun/ ▶ n. informal **1** a loss of status or importance. **2** a feeling of disappointment or depression. ■ [in sing.] a lessening of the sensations generated by a narcotic drug as its effects wear off.

com·e·dy /ˈkämədē/ ▶ n. (pl. **-dies**) professional entertainment consisting of jokes and satirical sketches, intended to make an audience laugh. ■ a movie, play, or broadcast program intended to make an audience laugh. ■ the style or genre of such types of entertainment. ■ the humorous or amusing aspects of something. ■ a play characterized by its humorous or satirical tone and its depiction of amusing people or incidents, in which the characters ultimately triumph over adversity: *Shakespeare's comedies.* ■ the dramatic genre represented by such plays: *satiric comedy.* Compare with TRAGEDY (sense 2).
– PHRASES **comedy of errors** a situation made amusing by bungling and incompetence. — **co·me·dic** /kəˈmēdik/ adj. [ME: from OFr. *comedie*, via L. from Gk. *kōmōidia*, from *kōmōidos* 'comic poet,' from *kōmos* 'revel' + *aoidos* 'singer.']

com·e·dy of man·ners ▶ n. a comedy that satirizes behavior in a particular social group, esp. the upper classes.

come-hith·er informal, dated ▶ adj. flirtatious; sexually inviting: *nymphs with come-hither looks.* ▶ n. [in sing.] a flirtatious or enticing manner.

come·ly /ˈkəmlē/ ▶ adj. (**-li·er, -li·est**) (typically of a woman) pleasant to look at; attractive. ■ archaic agreeable; suitable. — **come·li·ness** n. [ME: prob. from *becomely* 'fitting,' from BECOME.]

come-on ▶ n. informal a thing that is intended to lure or entice. ■ a gesture or remark that is intended to attract someone sexually: *she was giving me the come-on.* ■ a marketing ploy, such as a free or cheap offer.

com·er /ˈkəmər/ ▶ n. **1** [with adj.] a person who arrives somewhere: *feeding every comer is still a sacred duty.* See also ALL COMERS at ALL; LATECOMER; NEWCOMER. **2** [in sing.] informal a person or thing likely to succeed.

co·mes·ti·ble /kəˈmestəbəl/ formal humorous ▶ n. (usu. **comestibles**) an item of food. ▶ adj. edible. [15th C.: ult. from med. L. *comestibilis*, from L. *comest-* 'eaten up,' from *comedere*, from *com-* 'altogether' + *edere* 'eat.']

com·et /ˈkämit/ ▶ n. a celestial object consisting of a nucleus of ice and dust and, when near the sun, a "tail" of gas and dust particles pointing away from the sun. — **com·et·ar·y** /ˈkämiˌterē/ adj. [late OE, from L. *cometa*, from Gk. *komētēs* 'long-haired (star),' from *komē* 'hair.']

come·up·pance /kəˈməpəns/ ▶ n. [usu. in sing.] informal a punishment or fate that someone deserves.

com·fit /ˈkəmfit; ˈkäm-/ ▶ n. dated a candy consisting of a nut, seed, or other center coated in sugar. [ME: from OFr. *confit*, from L. *confectum*, neut. past part. of *conficere* 'put together.']

com·fort /ˈkəmfərt/ ▶ n. **1** a state of physical ease and freedom from pain or constraint. ■ (**comforts**) things that contribute to physical ease and well-being. ■ prosperity and the pleasant lifestyle secured by it. **2** consolation for grief or anxiety: *a few words of comfort.* ■ [in sing.] a person or thing that gives consolation. ■ a person or thing that gives satisfaction. **3** dialect a warm quilt. ▶ v. [trans.] soothe in grief; console. ■ help (someone) feel at ease; reassure.
– PHRASES **too — for comfort** causing physical or mental unease by an excess of the specified quality: *it can be too hot for comfort in July and August.* — **com·fort·ing·ly** adv. [ME: from OFr. *conforter* (v.), from late L. *confortare* 'strengthen,' from *com-* (intensifier) + L. *fortis* 'strong.']

com·fort·a·ble /ˈkəmfərtəbəl; ˈkəmftərbəl/ ▶ adj. **1** (esp. of clothes or furnishings) providing physical ease and relaxation: *invitingly comfortable beds.* ■ (of a person) physically relaxed and free from constraint. ■ not in pain (used esp. of a hospital patient). ■ free from stress or fear. ■ free from financial worry; having an adequate standard of living. **2** as large as is needed or wanted: *a comfortable income.* ■ with a wide margin: *a comfortable victory.* ▶ n. dialect a warm quilt. — **com·fort·a·ble·ness** n. **com·fort·a·bly** adv.

com·fort·er /ˈkəmfərtər/ ▶ n. **1** a warm quilt. **2** a person or thing that provides consolation. ■ (**Comforter**) the Holy Spirit. **3** dated a woolen scarf.

com·fort sta·tion ▶ n. a public restroom for travelers.

com·fort zone ▶ n. a place or situation where one feels safe or at ease and without stress.

com·frey /ˈkəmfrē/ ▶ n. (pl. **-freys**) a Eurasian plant (genus *Symphytum*) of the borage family, with large hairy leaves and clusters of purplish or white bell-shaped flowers. See also BONESET. [ME: from Anglo-Norman Fr. *cumfirie*, based on L. *conferva*, from *confervere* 'heal, boil together.']

com·fy /ˈkəmfē/ ▶ adj. (**-fi·er, -fi·est**) informal comfortable. — **com·fi·ly** /-fəlē/ adv. **com·fi·ness** n. [19th C.; abbrev.]

com·ic /ˈkämik/ ▶ adj. causing or meant to cause laughter: *comic and fantastic exaggeration.* ■ [attrib.] relating to or in the style of comedy. ▶ n. **1** a comedian, esp. a professional one. **2** (**comics**) comic strips. [16th C.: via L. from Gk. *kōmikos*, from *kōmos* 'revel.']

com·i·cal /ˈkämikəl/ ▶ adj. amusing. — **com·i·cal·i·ty** /ˌkäməˈkalitē/ n. **com·i·cal·ly** /-ik(ə)lē/ adv.

Co·mice /kōˈmēs; ˈkämis/ (in full **Doyenne du Comice**) ▶ n. a large yellow dessert pear. [19th C.: from Fr., lit. 'association,' referring to the *Comice Horticole* of Angers, France, where this variety was developed.]

com·ic re·lief ▶ n. comic episodes in a dramatic or literary work that offset more serious sections. ■ a character or characters providing this. ■ comical episodes that serve to release tension in real life.

com·ic strip ▶ n. a sequence of drawings in boxes that tell an amusing story, typically printed in a newspaper or comic book.

com·ing /ˈkəmiNG/ ▶ adj. [attrib.] **1** due to happen or just beginning: *work is due to start in the coming year.* **2** likely to be important or successful in the future. ▶ n. [in sing.] an arrival or an approach.
– PHRASES **comings and goings** the busy movements of a person or group of people, esp. in and out of a place. **not know if one is coming or going** informal be confused, esp. as a result of being very busy.

Co·mi·no /kəˈmēnō/ the smallest of the three main islands of Malta.

COMINT /ˈkämint/ ▶ abbr. communications intelligence.

Com·in·tern /ˈkäminˌtərn/ the Third International, a communist organization (1919–43). See INTERNATIONAL. [from Russ. *Komintern*, blend of *kom(munisticheskiĭ)* 'communist' and *intern(atsional)* 'international.']

com·i·ty /ˈkämitē/ ▶ n. (pl. **-ties**) **1** courtesy and considerate behavior toward others. **2** an association of nations for their mutual benefit. ■ (also **comity of nations**) the mutual recognition by nations of the laws and customs of others. [16th C.: from L. *comitas*, from *comis* 'courteous.']

comm /käm/ ▶ n. short for COMMUNICATION.

comm. ▶ abbr. ■ commerce. ■ commercial. ■ commission. ■ commissioner. ■ committee. ■ common.

com·ma /'kämə/ ▶n. **1** a punctuation mark (,) indicating a pause between parts of a sentence. It is also used to separate items in a list and to mark the place of thousands in a large numeral. **2** Music a minute interval or difference of pitch. **3** (also **comma butterfly**) a butterfly (genus *Polygonia*, family Nymphalidae) that has wings with irregular, ragged edges and typically a white or silver comma-shaped mark on the underside of each hind wing. Its numerous species include the common **eastern comma** (*P. comma*) of eastern North America. [16th C.: via L. from Gk. *komma* 'short clause,' from *koptein* 'cut.']

comma 3

Com·ma·ger /'kämәjәr/, Henry Steele (1902–98), US educator and writer. His works include *The American Mind* (1951) and *The Empire of Reason* (1977).

com·mand /kә'mand/ ▶v. **1** [reporting verb] give an authoritative order. ■ [trans.] Mil. have authority over; be in charge of (a unit). ■ [trans.] dominate (a strategic position) from a superior height. **2** [trans.] be in a strong enough position to secure. ■ deserve and receive. ▶n. an authoritative order. ■ Comput. an instruction or signal that causes a computer to perform one of its basic functions. ■ authority, esp. over armed forces. ■ [in sing.] the ability to use or control something: *he had a brilliant command of English.* ■ [treated as sing. or pl.] Mil. a group of officers exercising control over a particular group or operation. ■ Mil. a body of troops or a district under the control of a particular officer.
– PHRASES **at someone's command** at someone's disposal; available. [ME: from OFr. *comander* (v.) from late L. *commandare*, from *com-* (intensifier) + *mandare* 'commit.']

com·mand and con·trol ▶n. [usu. as adj.] esp. Mil. the running of an armed force or other organization: *a command-and-control bunker.*

com·man·dant /'kämәn,dant; -,dänt/ ▶n. an officer in charge of a particular force or institution: *the West Point commandant of cadets.*

com·mand-driv·en ▶adj. Comput. (of a program or computer) operated by means of commands keyed in by the user or issued by another program or computer.

com·mand e·con·o·my ▶n. an economy in which production, investment, prices, and incomes are determined centrally by a government.

com·man·deer /,kämәn'di(ә)r/ ▶v. [trans.] officially take possession or control of (something), esp. for military purposes. ■ take possession of (something) without authority. ■ [with obj. and infin.] enlist (someone) to help in a task, typically against the person's will. [19th C.: from Afrik. *kommandeer*, ult. from Fr. *commander* (see COMMAND).]

com·mand·er /kә'mandәr/ (abbr.: **Comdr.**) ▶n. **1** a person in authority, esp. over a body of troops or a military operation: *the commander of a paratroop regiment.* ■ a naval officer of high rank, in particular (in the US Navy or Coast Guard) an officer ranking above lieutenant commander and below captain. ■ (in certain metropolitan police departments) the officer in charge of a division, district, precinct, or squad. **2** a member of a higher class in some orders of knighthood. — **com·mand·er·ship** n.

com·mand·er in chief (also **Com·mand·er in Chief**) ▶n. (pl. **com·mand·ers in chief**) a head of state or officer in supreme command of a country's armed forces. ■ an officer in charge of a major subdivision of a country's armed forces, or of its forces in a particular area.

com·mand·ing /kә'mandiNG/ ▶adj. [attrib.] (in military contexts) having a position of authority. ■ (of an advantage or position) controlling; superior: *a commanding 13-6 lead.* ■ indicating or expressing authority; imposing. ■ (of a place or position) dominating physically; giving a wide view. — **com·mand·ing·ly** adv.

com·mand lan·guage ▶n. Comput. a computer programming language composed chiefly of a set of commands or operators, used esp. for communicating with the operating system of a computer.

com·mand·ment /kә'mandmәnt/ ▶n. a divine rule, esp. one of the Ten Commandments. ■ a rule to be observed as strictly as one of the Ten Commandments.

com·mand mod·ule (abbr.: **CM**) ▶n. the detachable control portion of a manned spacecraft.

com·man·do /kә'mandō/ ▶n. (pl. **-dos**) a soldier specially trained to carry out raids. [18th C.: from Port., from *commandar* 'to command,' (see COMMAND).]

com·mand per·for·mance ▶n. a presentation of a play, opera, or other show at the request of royalty.

com·mand post ▶n. the place from which a military unit is commanded.

com·mand ser·geant ma·jor ▶n. a noncommissioned officer in the US Army ranking above first sergeant.

comme ci, comme ça /kôm 'sē kôm 'sä/ ▶adv. (in answer to a question) neither very good nor very bad; so-so. [20th C.: Fr., lit. 'like this, like that.']

com·me·dia dell'ar·te /kә'mādēә dәl 'ärtē/ ▶n. an improvised kind of popular comedy in Italian theaters in the 16th–18th centuries, based on stock characters. [Ital., 'comedy of art.']

comme il faut /,kôm ēl 'fō/ ▶adj. [predic.] correct in behavior or etiquette. [18th C.: Fr., lit. 'as is necessary.']

com·mem·o·ra·to·ry /kә'memәrә,tôrē/ ▶adj. serving to commemorate; commemorative.

com·mem·o·rate /kә'memә,rāt/ ▶v. [trans.] recall and show respect for (someone or something) in a ceremony. ■ serve as a memorial to. ■ mark (a significant event). ■ (often **be commemorated**) celebrate (an event, a person, or a situation) by doing or building something. — **com·mem·o·ra·tor** /-,rātәr/ n. [16th C.: from L. *commemorare*, from *com-* 'altogether' + *memorare* 'relate' (from *memor* 'mindful').]

com·mem·o·ra·tion /kә,memә'rāsHәn/ ▶n. remembrance, typically expressed in a ceremony. ■ a ceremony or celebration in which a person or event is remembered: *VJ-Day commemorations in August.*
– PHRASES **in commemoration** as a reminder, esp. a ritual or official one.

com·mem·o·ra·tive /kә'mem(ә)rәtiv; -ә,rātiv/ ▶adj. acting as a memorial or mark of an event or person: *a commemorative plaque.* ▶n. an object such as a stamp or coin made to mark an event or honor a person. Compare with DEFINITIVE.

com·mence /kә'mens/ ▶v. begin; start. [ME: from OFr. *commencier*, based on L. *com-* (intensifier) + *initiare* 'begin.']

com·mence·ment /kә'mensmәnt/ ▶n. **1** [usu. in sing.] a beginning or start: *at the commencement of training.* **2** a ceremony in which degrees or diplomas are conferred on graduating students.

com·mend /kә'mend/ ▶v. [trans.] **1** (often **be commended**) praise formally or officially. ■ present as suitable for approval or acceptance; recommend: *I commend her to you without reservation.* ■ cause to be acceptable or pleasing. **2** (**commend someone/something to**) entrust someone or something to: *I commend them to your care.* [ME: from L. *commendare*, from *com-* (intensifier) + *mandare* 'commit.' Cf. COMMAND.]

com·mend·a·ble /kә'mendәbәl/ ▶adj. deserving praise: *commendable restraint.* — **com·mend·a·bly** adv.

com·men·da·tion /,kämәn'dāsHәn; -,men-/ ▶n. praise. ■ an award involving special praise.

com·men·sal /kә'mensәl/ ▶adj. Biol. of, relating to, or exhibiting commensalism. ▶n. Biol. a commensal organism, such as many bacteria. — **com·men·sal·i·ty** /,kämen'salitē/ n. [19th C.: from med. L. *commensalis*, from *com-* 'sharing' + *mensa* 'a table.']

com·men·sal·ism /kә'mensә,lizәm/ ▶n. Biol. an association between two organisms in which one benefits and the other derives neither benefit nor harm.

com·men·su·ra·ble /kә'mensәrәbәl; -sHәr-/ ▶adj. **1** measurable by the same standard: *the finite is not commensurable with the infinite.* **2** [predic.] (**commensurable to**) rare proportionate to. **3** Math. (of numbers) in a ratio equal to a ratio of integers. — **com·men·su·ra·bil·i·ty** /kә,mensәrә'bilәtē; -sHәr-/ n. **com·men·su·ra·bly** /-blē/ adv.

com·men·su·rate /kә'mensәrit; -sHә-/ ▶adj. corresponding in size or degree; in proportion. — **com·men·su·rate·ly** adv. [17th C.: from late L. *commensuratus*, from *com-* 'together' + *mensuratus*, past part. of *mensurare* 'to measure.']

com·ment /'käment/ ▶n. a remark expressing an opinion or reaction. ■ discussion, esp. of a critical nature, of an issue or event. ■ an indirect expression of the views of the creator of an artistic work. ■ an explanatory note in a book or other written text. ■ Comput. a piece of text placed within a program to help other users to understand it, which the computer ignores when running the program. ▶v. [reporting verb] express an opinion or reaction. ■ [trans.] Comput. place a piece of explanatory text within (a program) to assist other users. ■ [trans.] Comput. turn (part of a program) into a comment so that the computer ignores it when running the program.
– PHRASES **no comment** used in refusing to answer a question, esp. in a sensitive situation. — **com·ment·er** n. [ME: from L. *commentum* 'contrivance,' neut. past part. of *comminisci* 'devise.']

com·men·tar·y /'kämәn,terē/ ▶n. (pl. **-tar·ies**) the expression of opinions or explanations about an event or situation: *an editorial commentary.* ■ a descriptive spoken account (esp. on radio or television) of an event or a performance as it happens. ■ a set of explanatory or critical notes on a text.

com·men·tate /'kämәn,tāt/ ▶v. [intrans.] report on an event as it occurs, esp. for a news or sports broadcast; provide a commentary. [19th C.: back-form. from COMMENTATOR.]

com·men·ta·tor /'kämәn,tātәr/ ▶n. a person who comments on events, esp. on television or radio. ■ a person who writes a commentary on a text.

com·merce /'kämәrs/ (abbr.: **comm.**) ▶n. **1** the activity of buying and selling, esp. on a large scale. **2** dated social dealings between people. [16th C.: from Fr., or from L. *commercium* 'trade,' from *com-* 'together' + *mercium* (from *merx, merc-* 'merchandise').]

com·mer·cial /kә'mәrsHәl/ (abbr.: **comm.**) ▶adj. **1** concerned with or engaged in commerce. **2** making or intended to make a profit.

PRONUNCIATION KEY ә *ago, up*; әr *over, fur*; a *hat*; ā *ate*; ä *car*; e *let*; ē *see*; i *fit*; ī *by*; NG *sing*; ō *go*; ô *law, for*; oi *toy*; o͝o *good*; o͞o *goo*; ou *out*; TH *thin*; T͟H *then*; ZH *vision*

■ having profit, rather than artistic or other value, as a primary aim: *their work is too commercial.* **3** [attrib.] (of television or radio) funded by the revenue from broadcast advertisements. **4** (of chemicals) supplied in bulk and not of the highest purity. ▶ **n.** a television or radio advertisement. — **com·mer·ci·al·i·ty** /kə,mərshē'alitē/ **n.** **com·mer·cial·ly adv.**

com·mer·cial art ▶ **n.** art used in advertising and selling.

com·mer·cial bank ▶ **n.** a bank that offers services to the general public and to companies.

com·mer·cial break ▶ **n.** an interruption in the transmission of broadcast programming during which advertisements are broadcast.

com·mer·cial·ism /kə'mərshə,lizəm/ ▶ **n.** emphasis on the maximizing of profit. ■ derog. practices and attitudes that are concerned with the making of profit at the expense of quality.

com·mer·cial·ize /kə'mərshə,līz/ ▶ **v.** [trans.] (usu. **be commercialized**) make (an organization or activity) commercial: *the museum has been commercialized.* ■ exploit or spoil for the purpose of gaining profit. — **com·mer·cial·i·za·tion** /kə,mərshələ'zāshən/ **n.**

com·mer·cial pa·per ▶ **n.** short-term unsecured promissory notes issued by companies.

com·mer·cial space ▶ **n.** see **SPACE** (sense 1).

com·mer·cial ve·hi·cle ▶ **n.** a vehicle used for carrying goods or fare-paying passengers.

com·mie /'kämē/ (also **Com·mie**) informal, derog. ▶ **n.** (pl. **-mies**) a communist. ▶ **adj.** communist.

com·mi·na·tion /,kämə'nāshən/ ▶ **n.** the action of threatening divine vengeance. ■ the recital of divine threats against sinners in the Anglican Liturgy for Ash Wednesday. — **com·min·a·to·ry** /'kämənə,tôrē; kə'minə-/ **adj.** [ME: from L. *comminatio(n-)*, from *comminari*, from *com-* (intensifier) + *minari* 'threaten.']

com·min·gle /kə'miNGgəl; kä-/ ▶ **v.** mix; blend.

com·mi·nut·ed /'kämə,n(y)o͞otəd/ ▶ **adj.** tech. reduced to minute particles or fragments. ■ Med. (of a fracture) producing multiple bone splinters. [17th C.: ult. from L. *comminuere*, from *com-* 'together' + *minuere* 'lessen.']

com·mi·nu·tion /,kämə'n(y)o͞oshən/ ▶ **n.** tech. the action of reducing a material, esp. an ore, to minute particles or fragments.

com·mis /kə'mē; kô-/ (also **commis chef**) ▶ **n.** (pl. same) a junior chef. [1930s: from Fr., 'deputy,' past part. of *commettre* 'entrust,' from L. *committere* (see **COMMIT**).]

com·mis·er·ate /kə'mizə,rāt/ ▶ **v.** [intrans.] express or feel sympathy or pity; sympathize. — **com·mis·er·a·tion** /kə,mizə'rāshən/ **n.** **com·mis·er·a·tive** /-rətiv/ **adj.** [16th C.: from L. *commiserat-* 'commiserated,' from the v. *commiserari*, from *com-* 'with' + *miserari* 'to lament' (from *miser* 'wretched').]

com·mish /kə'misH/ ▶ **n.** informal **1** short for **COMMISSIONER.** **2** short for **COMMISSION:** *out of commish.*

com·mis·sar /'kämə,sär; ,kämə'sär/ ▶ **n.** an official of the Communist Party, esp. in the former Soviet Union or present-day China, responsible for political education and organization. ■ a head of a government department in the former Soviet Union before 1946. ■ fig. a strict or prescriptive figure of authority: *our academic commissars.* [20th C.: from Russ. *komissar*, from Fr. *commissaire*, from med. L. *commissarius.*]

com·mis·sar·i·at /,kämə'se(ə)rēit/ ▶ **n.** **1** esp. Mil. a department for the supply of food and equipment. **2** a government department of the USSR before 1946. [16th C.: from Fr. *commissariat*, from med. L. *commissarius.*]

com·mis·sar·y /'kämə,serē/ ▶ **n.** (pl. **-sar·ies**) **1** a restaurant in a movie studio, military base, prison, or other institution. ■ a store that sells food and drink to members of an organization, esp. a grocery store on a military base. **2** a deputy or delegate. — **com·mis·sar·i·al** /,kämə'se(ə)rēəl/ **adj.** [ME: from med. L. *commissarius* 'person in charge,' from *committere* (see **COMMIT**).]

com·mis·sion /kə'misHən/ (abbr.: **comm.**) ▶ **n.** **1** the authority to perform a task or certain duties. ■ an instruction, command, or duty given to a person or group of people. ■ an order for something, esp. a work of art, to be produced. ■ a work produced in response to such an order. **2** a group of people officially charged with a particular function. **3** an amount of money, typically a set percentage of the value involved, paid to an agent in a commercial transaction. **4** a warrant conferring the rank of officer in an army, navy, or air force: *he has resigned his commission.* **5** the action of committing a crime or offense. ▶ **v.** [trans.] **1** give an order for or authorize the production of (something such as a building, piece of equipment, or work of art). ■ [with obj. and infin.] order or authorize (a person or organization) to do or produce something. ■ [with obj. and infin.] give (an artist) an order for a piece of work. **2** bring (something newly produced, such as a factory or machine) into working condition. ■ bring (a warship) into readiness for active service. **3** (usu. **be commissioned**) appoint (someone) to the rank of officer in the armed services.

– PHRASES **in commission** (of a ship, vehicle, machine, etc.) in use or in service. **out of commission** not in service; not in working order. ■ (of a person) unable to work or function normally, esp. through illness or injury. — **com·mis·sion·a·ble adj.** [ME: via OFr. from L. *commissio(n-)*, from *committere* 'entrust' (see **COMMIT**).]

com·mis·sion·er /kə'misH(ə)nər/ (abbr.: **comm.**) ▶ **n.** a person appointed by a commission to perform a specific task: *the traffic commissioner.* ■ a person appointed as a member of a government commission: *the New York State Health Commissioner.* ■ a person appointed to regulate a particular sport: *the baseball commissioner.* ■ a representative of the supreme authority in an area. — **com·mis·sion·er·ship n.**

com·mis·sure /'kämə,sho͝or/ ▶ **n.** tech. a junction, joint, or seam, in particular: ■ Anat. the joint between two bones. ■ Anat. a band of nerve tissue connecting the hemispheres of the brain, the two sides of the spinal cord, etc. ■ Anat. the line where the upper and lower lips or eyelids meet. — **com·mis·su·ral** /,kämə'sho͝orəl/ **adj.** [ME: from L. *commissura* 'junction,' from *committere* 'join' (see **COMMIT**).]

com·mit /kə'mit/ ▶ **v.** (**-mit·ted, -mit·ting**) [trans.] **1** carry out or perpetrate (a mistake, crime, or immoral act): *he committed an uncharacteristic error.* **2** pledge or bind (a person or an organization) to a certain course or policy. ■ pledge or set aside (resources) for future use. ■ (**be committed to**) be in a long-term emotional relationship with (someone). ■ (**be committed to**) be dedicated to (something). **3** send, entrust, or consign, in particular: ■ consign (someone) officially to prison, esp. on remand. ■ send (a person or case) for trial. ■ send (someone) to be confined in a psychiatric hospital: *he had been committed for treatment.* ■ (**commit something to**) transfer something to (a state or place). ■ refer (a legislative bill) to a committee. — **com·mit·ta·ble adj.** **com·mit·ter n.** [ME: from L. *committere* 'join, entrust', from *com-* 'with' + *mittere* 'send.']

com·mit·ment /kə'mitmənt/ ▶ **n.** **1** the act of committing or the state of being committed. ■ dedication; application. ■ a pledge or undertaking. ■ an act of pledging or setting aside something. **2** (usu. **commitments**) an engagement or obligation that restricts freedom of action.

com·mit·ment or·der ▶ **n.** an order authorizing the admission and detention of a patient in a psychiatric hospital.

com·mit·tal /kə'mitl/ ▶ **n.** **1** the action of sending a person to an institution, esp. prison or a psychiatric hospital. **2** the burial of a corpse.

com·mit·ted /kə'mitid/ ▶ **adj.** feeling dedication and loyalty to a cause, activity, or job; wholeheartedly dedicated: *a committed Christian.*

com·mit·tee /kə'mitē/ ▶ **n.** **1** [treated as sing. or pl.] a group of people appointed for a specific function, typically consisting of members of a larger group. ■ such a body appointed by a legislature to consider the details of proposed legislation. **2** Law a person who has been judicially committed to the charge of another because of insanity or mental retardation.

com·mit·tee·man /kə'mitēmən; -,man/ ▶ **n.** (pl. **-men**) (in the US) a male local political party leader.

com·mit·tee·wom·an /kə'mitē,wo͝omən/ ▶ **n.** (pl. **-wom·en**) (in the US) a female local political party leader.

com·mix /kə'miks/ ▶ **v.** [trans.] archaic mix; mingle. — **com·mix·ture** /kə'mikscHər/ **n.** [ME: from L. *commixtus*, from *com-* 'with' + *mixtus* 'mixed.']

com·mo /'kämō/ ▶ **n.** informal communication, esp. as a departmental function in an organization.

com·mode /kə'mōd/ ▶ **n.** **1** a piece of furniture containing a concealed chamber pot. ■ a toilet. ■ hist. a movable washstand. **2** a chest of drawers or chiffonier of a decorative type popular in the 18th century. [18th C.: from Fr., lit. 'convenient,' from L. *commodus.*]

com·mod·i·fy /kə'mädə,fī/ ▶ **v.** (**-fies, -fied**) [trans.] turn into or treat as a commodity. — **com·mod·i·fi·ca·tion** /kə,mädəfi'kāshən/ **n.**

com·mo·di·ous /kə'mōdēəs/ ▶ **adj.** formal (esp. of furniture or a building) roomy and comfortable. — **com·mo·di·ous·ly adv.** **com·mo·di·ous·ness n.** [ME: from Fr. *commodieux* or med. L. *commodiosus*, based on L. *commodus* 'convenient.']

com·mod·i·tize /kə'mädi,tīz/ ▶ **v.** another term for **COMMODIFY.** — **com·mod·i·ti·za·tion** /kə,mäditə'zāshən/ **n.**

com·mod·i·ty /kə'mäditē/ ▶ **n.** (pl. **-ties**) a raw material or primary agricultural product that can be bought and sold, such as copper or coffee. ■ a useful or valuable thing, such as water or time. [ME: from OFr. *commodite* or L. *commoditas*, from *commodus.*]

com·mo·dore /'kämə,dôr/ ▶ **n.** a naval officer of high rank, in particular an officer in the US Navy or Coast Guard ranking above captain and below rear admiral. ■ the president of a yacht club. ■ the senior captain of a shipping line. [17th C.: prob. from Du. *komandeur*, from Fr. *commandeur* 'commander.']

com·mon /'kämən/ ▶ **adj.** (**-mon·er, -mon·est**) **1** occurring, found, or done often; prevalent. ■ (of an animal or plant) found or living in relatively large numbers; not rare. ■ ordinary; of ordinary qualities; without special rank or position. ■ (of a quality) of a sort or level to be generally expected: *common decency.* ■ of the most familiar type: *the common or vernacular name.* ■ denoting the most widespread or typical species of an animal or plant. **2** showing a lack of taste and refinement; vulgar. **3** shared by, coming from, or done by more than one. ■ belonging to, open to, or affecting the whole of a community or the public: *common land.* ■ Math. belonging to two or more quantities. **4** Gram. (in Latin and certain other languages) of or denoting a gender of nouns that are conventionally regarded as masculine or feminine, contrasting with neuter. ■ (in English) denoting a noun that refers to individuals of either sex (e.g., *teacher*). **5** Pros. (of a syllable) able to be either short or long. **6** Law (of a crime) of relatively minor importance. ▶ **n.** **1** a piece of open land for public use, esp. in a village or town. **2** (in the Christian Church) a form of service used for each of a group of occasions.

– PHRASES **the common good** the benefit or interests of all. **common ground** a point or argument accepted by both sides in a dispute. ■ ideas or interests shared by different people. **common knowledge** something known by most people. **common property** a thing or things held jointly. ■ something known by most people. **the common touch** the ability to get along with or appeal to ordinary people. **in common 1** in joint use or possession; shared. **2** of joint interest: *the two men had little in common.* See also TENANCY IN COMMON. **in common with** in the same way as: *in common with other officers, I had to undertake guard duties.* — **com·mon·ness** n. [ME: from OFr. *comun* (adj.), from L. *communis.*]

com·mon·al·i·ty /ˈkämə͵nalitē/ ▶ n. (pl. **-ties**) **1** [in sing.] the state of sharing features or attributes. ■ a shared feature or attribute. **2** (**the commonality**) another term for COMMONALTY. [ME (sense 2): var. of COMMONALTY.]

com·mon·al·ty /ˈkämənl-tē/ ▶ n. [treated as pl.] (**the commonalty**) esp. hist. people without special rank or position; common people: *a petition by the earls, barons, and commonalty of the realm.* ■ the general body of a group. [ME: from OFr. *comunalte*, from med. L. *communalitas*, from L. *communis* 'common.']

com·mon car·ri·er ▶ n. a person or company that transports goods or passengers on regular routes at set rates. ■ a company providing public telecommunications facilities.

com·mon chord ▶ n. Music a triad containing a root, a major or minor third, and a perfect fifth.

com·mon cold ▶ n. (**the common cold**) another term for COLD (sense 2).

com·mon coun·cil ▶ n. a town or city council in some parts of the US and Canada, and in London.

com·mon de·nom·i·na·tor ▶ n. Math. a shared multiple of the denominators of several fractions. See also LOWEST COMMON DENOMINATOR. ■ fig. a feature shared by all members of a group.

com·mon di·vi·sor ▶ n. Math. a number that can be divided into all of the other numbers of a given set without any remainder. Also called **common factor**.

com·mon·er /ˈkämənər/ ▶ n. an ordinary person, without rank or title.

Com·mon E·ra ▶ n. (**the Common Era**) another term for CHRISTIAN ERA.

com·mon frac·tion ▶ n. a fraction expressed by a numerator and a denominator, not decimally.

com·mon gen·der ▶ n. **1** the gender of those nouns in English that are not limited to either sex, such as cousin or spouse. **2** in some languages, such as Latin, the gender of those nouns that may be either masculine or feminine but not neuter. **3** in some languages, such as modern Danish, the gender of those nouns derived from the earlier masculine and feminine genders that do not belong to the neuter gender.

com·mon law ▶ n. the part of English law that is derived from custom and judicial precedent rather than statutes. Often contrasted with STATUTORY LAW. ■ the body of English law as adopted and modified separately by the different states of the US and by the federal government. Compare with CIVIL LAW. ■ [as adj.] denoting a partner in a marriage by common law (which recognized unions created by mutual agreement and public behavior), not by a civil or ecclesiastical ceremony: *a common-law husband.* ■ [as adj.] denoting a partner in a long-term relationship of cohabitation.

com·mon log·a·rithm ▶ n. a logarithm to the base 10.

com·mon·ly /ˈkämənlē/ ▶ adv. very often; frequently.

com·mon mar·ket ▶ n. a group of countries imposing few or no duties on trade with one another and a common tariff on trade with other countries. ■ (**the Common Market**) a name for the European Economic Community or European Union, used esp. in the 1960s and 1970s.

com·mon me·ter (also **common measure**) (abbr.: **CM**) ▶ n. a metrical pattern for hymns in which the stanzas have four lines containing eight and six syllables alternately rhyming *abcb* or *abab*.

com·mon mul·ti·ple ▶ n. Math. a number into which each number in a given set may be evenly divided.

com·mon noun ▶ n. Gram. a noun denoting a class of objects or a concept as opposed to a particular individual. Often contrasted with PROPER NOUN.

com·mon·place /ˈkämən͵plās/ ▶ adj. not unusual; ordinary. ■ not interesting or original; trite. ▶ n. **1** a usual or ordinary thing. ■ a trite saying or topic; a platitude. **2** a notable quotation copied into a commonplace book. — **com·mon·place·ness** n. [16th C.: translation of L. *locus communis*, rendering Gk. *koinos topos* 'general theme.']

com·mon·place book ▶ n. a book into which notable extracts from other works are copied for personal use.

Com·mon Prayer the liturgy of the Anglican Communion, originally set forth in the *Book of Common Prayer* of Edward VI (1549).

com·mon rat ▶ n. another term for BROWN RAT.

com·mon room ▶ n. a room in a school, college, or other educational institution for use of students or staff outside teaching hours. ■ a room in a residential facility for the recreational use of all residents.

com·mons /ˈkämənz/ ▶ plural n. **1** a dining hall in a residential school or college. **2** [treated as sing.] land or resources belonging to or affecting the whole of a community. ■ a public park of a town or city. **3** (**the Commons**) short for HOUSE OF COMMONS. [ME: pl. of COMMON.]

com·mon salt ▶ n. see SALT (sense 1).

com·mon sense ▶ n. good sense and sound judgment in practical matters. — **com·mon·sen·si·cal** /͵kämənˈsensikəl/ adj.

com·mon sol·dier ▶ n. see SOLDIER (sense 1).

com·mon stock ▶ plural n. (also **com·mon stocks**) shares entitling their holder to dividends that vary in amount and may even be missed, depending on the fortunes of the company. Compare with PREFERRED STOCK.

com·mon time ▶ n. Music a rhythmic pattern in which there are four beats, esp. four quarter notes, in a measure.

com·mon·weal /ˈkämən͵wēl/ ▶ n. (**the commonweal**) the welfare of the public.

com·mon·wealth /ˈkämən͵welTH/ ▶ n. **1** an independent country or community, esp. a democratic republic. ■ an aggregate or grouping of countries or other bodies. ■ a community or organization of shared interests in a nonpolitical field. ■ a self-governing unit voluntarily grouped with the US, such as Puerto Rico. ■ a formal title of some of the states of the US, esp. Kentucky, Massachusetts, Pennsylvania, and Virginia. ■ the title of the federated Australian states. ■ (**the Commonwealth**) the republican period of government in Britain between the execution of Charles I in 1649 and the Restoration of Charles II in 1660. **2** (**the Commonwealth**) (in full **the Commonwealth of Nations**) an association of the UK with states that were previously part of the British Empire, and dependencies.

Com·mon·wealth of In·de·pend·ent States (abbr.: **CIS**) a confederation of independent states that were formerly part of the Soviet Union, established in 1991; including Armenia, Belarus, Kazakhstan, Kyrgyzstan, Moldova, Russia, Tajikistan, Turkmenistan, Ukraine, and Uzbekistan.

com·mo·tion /kəˈmōSHən/ ▶ n. a state of confused and noisy disturbance. ■ civil insurrection: *damage caused by civil commotion.* [ME: from L. *commotio(n-)*, from *com-* 'altogether' + *motio* (see MOTION).]

com·move /kəˈmo͞ov/ ▶ v. [trans.] move violently; agitate or excite.

com·mu·nal /kəˈmyo͞onl/ ▶ adj. **1** shared by all members of a community; for common use. ■ of, relating to, or done by a community: *communal achievement.* ■ involving the sharing of work and property: *communal living.* **2** (of conflict) between different communities, esp. those having different religions or ethnic origins. — **com·mu·nal·i·ty** /͵kämyəˈnalitē/ n. **com·mu·nal·ly** adv. [19th C.: from Fr., from late L. *communalis*, from *communis* (see COMMON).]

com·mu·nal·ism /kəˈmyo͞onl͵izəm/ ▶ n. **1** a principle of political organization based on federated communes. ■ the principle or practice of living together and sharing possessions and responsibilities. **2** allegiance to one's own ethnic group rather than to the wider society. — **com·mu·nal·ist** adj. & n. **com·mu·nal·is·tic** /kə͵myo͞onlˈistik/ adj. **com·mu·nal·i·za·tion** /kə͵myo͞onl-əˈzāSHən/ n. **com·mu·nal·ize** /-͵īz/ v.

com·mu·nard /͵kämyəˈnär(d)/ ▶ n. a member of a commune. [19th C.: from Fr.]

com·mune[1] /ˈkämyo͞on/ ▶ n. **1** a group of people living together and sharing possessions and responsibilities. ■ a communal settlement in a communist country. **2** the smallest French territorial division for administrative purposes. ■ a similar division elsewhere. **3** (**the Commune**) the group that seized the municipal government of Paris in the French Revolution and played a leading part in the Reign of Terror until suppressed in 1794. [17th C. (sense 2): from Fr., from med. L. *communia*, neut. pl. of L. *communis* 'common.']

com·mune[2] /kəˈmyo͞on/ ▶ v. [intrans.] **1** (**commune with**) share one's intimate thoughts or feelings with (someone or something), esp. when the exchange is on a spiritual level. ■ feel in close spiritual contact with. **2** Christian Church receive Holy Communion. [ME: from OFr. *comuner* 'to share,' from *comun* (see COMMON).]

com·mu·ni·ca·ble /kəˈmyo͞onikəbəl/ ▶ adj. able to be communicated to others. ■ (of a disease) able to be transmitted from one sufferer to another; contagious or infectious. — **com·mu·ni·ca·bil·i·ty** /kə͵myo͞onikəˈbilitē/ n. **com·mu·ni·ca·bly** /-blē/ adv.

com·mu·ni·cant /kəˈmyo͞onikənt/ ▶ n. Christian Church a person who receives Holy Communion.

com·mu·ni·cate /kəˈmyo͞oni͵kāt/ ▶ v. **1** [intrans.] share or exchange information, news, or ideas. ■ [trans.] impart or pass on (information, news, or ideas): *he communicated his findings to the inspector.* ■ [trans.] convey or transmit (an emotion or feeling) in a nonverbal way. ■ succeed in conveying one's ideas or in evoking understanding in others. ■ (of two people) be able to share and understand each other's thoughts and feelings. ■ [trans.] (usu. **be communicated**) pass on (an infectious disease) to another person or animal. ■ [trans.] transmit (heat or motion): *the heat is communicated through a small brass grating.* ■ [often as adj.] (**communicating**) (of two rooms) have a common connecting door. **2** [intrans.] Christian Church receive Holy Communion. — **com·mu·ni·ca·tor** /-͵kātər/ n. **com·mu·ni·ca·to·ry** /-kə͵tôrē/ adj. [16th C.: from L. *communicat-* 'shared,' from the v. *communicare*, from *communis* 'common.']

com·mu·ni·ca·tion /kə͵myo͞oniˈkāSHən/ ▶ n. **1** the imparting or exchanging of information or news. ■ a letter or message containing such information or news. ■ the successful conveying or sharing of ideas and feelings. ■ social contact. **2** (**communications**) means of connection between people or places, in particular: ■ the means of sending or receiving information, such as telephone lines or computers. ■ the means of traveling or of transporting goods, such as roads or railroads. ■ [treated as sing.] the field of study concerned with the transmission of information by various means.

– PHRASES **lines of communication** the connections between an army in the field and its bases. ■ any system for communicating information or ideas. — **com·mu·ni·ca·tion·al** /-ˈkāSHənl/ adj.

com·mu·ni·ca·tions sat·el·lite (also **com·mu·ni·ca·tion sat·el·lite**)

▶ n. a satellite placed in orbit around the earth in order to relay television, radio, and telephone signals.

com·mu·ni·ca·tion the·o·ry (also **com·mu·ni·ca·tions the·o·ry**) ▶ n. the branch of knowledge dealing with the principles and methods by which information is conveyed.

com·mu·ni·ca·tive /kə'myo͞oni,kātiv; -nikətiv/ ▶ adj. ready to talk or impart information. ■ relating to the conveyance or exchange of information: *the communicative process in literary texts.* — **com·mu·ni·ca·tive·ly** adv.

com·mun·ion /kə'myo͞onyən/ ▶ n. **1** the sharing or exchanging of intimate thoughts and feelings, esp. when the exchange is on a mental or spiritual level. ■ common participation in a mental or emotional experience. **2** (often **Communion** or **Holy Communion**) the service of Christian worship at which bread and wine are consecrated and shared. See EUCHARIST. ■ the consecrated bread and wine so administered and received: *the priests gave him Holy Communion.* ■ reception of the consecrated bread and wine at such a service. **3** a relationship of recognition and acceptance between Christian churches or denominations, or between individual Christians or Christian communities and a church (signified by a willingness to give or receive the Eucharist). ■ a group of Christian communities or churches that recognize one another's ministries or that of a central authority: *the Anglican communion.*
– PHRASES **make one's communion** receive bread and wine that has been consecrated at a Eucharist, as a sacramental, spiritual, or symbolic act of receiving the presence of Christ. [ME: from L. *communio(n-)*, from *communis* 'common.']

com·mun·ion of saints ▶ n. [in sing.] a fellowship between Christians living and dead.

com·mu·ni·qué /kə,myo͞oni'kā; kə'myo͞oni,kā/ (also **com·mu·ni·que**) ▶ n. an official announcement or statement, esp. one made to the media. [19th C.: from Fr., past part. of *communiquer* 'communicate.']

com·mu·nism /'kämyə,nizəm/ (often **Communism**) ▶ n. a political theory derived from Karl Marx, advocating class war and leading to a society in which all property is publicly owned and each person works and is paid according to their abilities and needs. See also MARXISM. — **com·mu·nist** n. & adj. **com·mu·nis·tic** /,kämyə'nistik/ adj. [19th C.: from Fr. *communisme*, from *commun* (see COMMON).]

Com·mu·nism Peak a peak in the Pamir Mountains of Tajikistan, rising to 24,590 feet (7,495 m); the highest mountain in the former Soviet Union. Former names MOUNT GARMO and STALIN PEAK.

com·mu·ni·tar·i·an·ism /kə,myo͞oni'te(ə)rēə,nizəm/ ▶ n. a theory or system of social organization based on small self-governing communities. ■ an ideology that emphasizes the responsibility of the individual to the community and the social importance of the family unit. — **com·mu·ni·tar·i·an** adj. & n. [19th C.]

com·mu·ni·ty /kə'myo͞onitē/ ▶ n. (pl. **-ties**) **1** a group of people living together in one place, esp. one practicing common ownership: *a community of nuns.* ■ all the people living in a particular area or place: *local communities.* ■ a particular area or place considered together with its inhabitants: *a rural community.* ■ (**the community**) the people of a district or country considered collectively, esp. in the context of social values and responsibilities; society. ■ [as adj.] denoting a worker or resource designed to serve the people of a particular area: *community health services.* **2** [usu. with adj.] a group of people having a religion, race, profession, or other particular characteristic in common: *Rhode Island's Japanese community.* ■ a body of nations or states unified by common interests: [in names] *the European Community.* **3** a feeling of fellowship with others, as a result of sharing common attitudes, interests, and goals. ■ [in sing.] a similarity or identity: *writers who shared a community of interests.* ■ joint ownership or liability. **4** Ecol. a group of interdependent organisms of different species growing or living together in a specified habitat: *communities of insectivorous birds.* ■ a set of species found in the same habitat or ecosystem at the same time.
– PHRASES **the international community** the countries of the world considered collectively. [ME: from OFr. *comunete*, L. *communitas*, from *communis* 'common.']

com·mu·ni·ty an·ten·na tel·e·vi·sion (abbr.: **CATV**) ▶ n. another term for CABLE TELEVISION.

com·mu·ni·ty cen·ter ▶ n. a place where people from a particular community can meet for social, educational, or recreational activities.

com·mu·ni·ty chest ▶ n. a fund for charitable activities among the people in a particular area.

com·mu·ni·ty col·lege ▶ n. a nonresidential junior college offering courses to people living in a particular area.

com·mu·ni·ty po·lic·ing ▶ n. the system of allocating police officers to particular areas so that they become familiar with the local inhabitants.

com·mu·ni·ty pro·per·ty ▶ n. property owned jointly by a husband and wife.

com·mu·ni·ty serv·ice ▶ n. voluntary work intended to help people in a particular area. ■ Law unpaid work, intended to be of social use, that an offender is required to do instead of going to prison.

com·mu·nize /'kämyə,nīz/ ▶ v. [trans.] cause (a country, people, or economic activity) to be organized on the principles of communism. — **com·mu·ni·za·tion** /,kämyənə'zāsʜən/ n. [19th C.: from L. *communis* (see COMMON) + -IZE.]

com·mu·tate /'kämyə,tāt/ ▶ v. [trans.] regulate or reverse the direction of (an alternating electric current), esp. to make it a direct current. [19th C.: from L. *commutat-* 'exchanged,' from *commutare* (see COMMUTE).]

com·mu·ta·tion /,kämyə'tāsʜən/ ▶ n. **1** action or the process of commuting a judicial sentence. ■ the conversion of a legal obligation or entitlement into another form, e.g., the replacement of an annuity or series of payments by a single payment. **2** the process of commutating an electric current. **3** Math. the property of having a commutative relation.

com·mu·ta·tion tick·et ▶ n. a ticket issued at a reduced rate by a railroad or bus company, entitling the holder to travel a given route a fixed number of times or during a specified period.

com·mu·ta·tive /'kämyə,tātiv; kə'myo͞otətiv/ ▶ adj. Math. involving the condition that a group of quantities connected by operators gives the same result whatever the order of the quantities involved, e.g., $a \times b = b \times a$.

com·mu·ta·tor /'kämyə,tātər/ ▶ n. an attachment, connected to the armature of a motor or generator, through which electrical connection is made and which ensures that the current flows as direct current. ■ a device for reversing the direction of flow of electric current.

com·mute /kə'myo͞ot/ ▶ v. **1** [intrans.] travel some distance between one's home and place of work on a regular basis. **2** [trans.] reduce (a judicial sentence, esp. a sentence of death) to one less severe. ■ (**commute something for/into**) change one kind of payment or obligation for (another). ■ replace (an annuity or other series of payments) with a single payment. **3** [intrans.] Math. (of two operations or quantities) have a commutative relationship. ▶ n. a regular journey of some distance to and from one's place of work. — **com·mut·a·ble** adj. **com·mut·a·bil·i·ty** /kə,myo͞otə'bilitē/ n. **com·mut·er** n. [ME: from L. *commutare*, from *com-* 'altogether' + *mutare* 'to change.']

Co·mo, Lake /'kōmō/ a lake in the foothills of the Alps in northern Italy.

Co·mo·do·ro Ri·va·da·vi·a /,kōmō'dôrō ,rēvä'dävēə/ a port in southeastern Argentina, on the Atlantic coast; pop. 124,000.

co·mon·o·mer /kō'mänəmər/ ▶ n. Chem. one of the monomers that constitutes a copolymer.

Com·o·ros /'kämə,rōz; kə'môrōz; -ōs/ a country in Africa that consists of a group of islands in the Indian Ocean, north of Madagascar; pop. 651,000; capital, Moroni. — **Com·o·ran** /'kämərən; kə'môrən/ adj. & n.

comp /kämp/ informal ▶ n. short for: ■ a composition. ■ a complimentary ticket or voucher. ■ compensation. ■ a musical accompaniment. ■ a comprehensive examination. ▶ v. [trans.] **1** play (music) as an accompaniment, esp. in jazz or blues. **2** give (something) away free, esp. as part of a promotion. **3** short for COMPOSITE. ▶ adj. [attrib.] complimentary; free.

comp. ▶ abbr. ■ companion. ■ comparative. ■ compensation. ■ compilation. ■ compiled. ■ compiler. ■ complete. ■ composite. ■ composition. ■ compositor. ■ comprehensive.

com·pact[1] ▶ adj. /kəm'pakt; käm-; 'käm,pakt/ closely and neatly packed together; dense. ■ having all the necessary components or features neatly fitted into a small space: *a compact car.* ■ (of a person or animal) small, solid, and well-proportioned. ■ (of speech or writing) concise in expression: *a compact summary of the play.* ▶ v. /kəm'pakt; käm-/ [trans.] (often **be compacted**) exert force on (something) to make it more dense; compress. ■ [intrans.] (of a substance) become compressed in this way: *the snow hardened and compacted.* ■ express in fewer words; condense. ▶ n. /'käm,pakt/ **1** a small flat case containing face powder, a mirror, and a powder puff. **2** something that is a small and conveniently shaped example of its kind, in particular: ■ short for COMPACT CAR. **3** Metallurgy a mass of powdered metal compacted together in preparation for sintering. — **com·pac·tion** /kəm'paksʜən/ n. **com·pact·ly** adv. **com·pact·ness** n. **com·pac·tor** /kəm'paktər; käm-; 'käm,paktər/ (also **com·pact·er**) n. [ME: from L. *compact-* 'put together,' from *compingere*, from *com-* 'together' + *pangere* 'fasten.']

com·pact[2] /'käm,pakt/ ▶ n. a formal agreement or contract between two or more parties. ▶ v. /kəm'pakt; käm-; 'käm,pakt/ [trans.] make or enter into (a formal agreement) with another party or parties. [16th C.: from L. *compactum*, past part. of *compacisci*, from *com-* 'with' + *pacisci* 'make a covenant.' Cf. PACT.]

com·pact car ▶ n. a medium-sized car.

com·pact disc (also **com·pact disk**) (abbr.: **CD**) ▶ n. a small plastic disc on which music or other digital information is stored, and from which the information can be read using reflected laser light. See also CD-ROM.

com·pa·dre /kəm'pädrā/ ▶ n. (pl. **-pa·dres**) informal a way of addressing or referring to a friend or companion. [19th C.: Sp., lit. 'godfather.']

com·pan·ion[1] /kəm'panyən/ ▶ n. **1** a person or animal with whom one spends a lot of time or with whom one travels. ■ a person who shares the experiences of another, esp. when these are unpleasant or unwelcome. ■ a person with similar tastes and interests to one's own and with whom one has a friendly relationship: *drinking companions.* ■ a person's long-term sexual partner outside marriage. ■ a person, esp. an unmarried or widowed woman, employed to live with and assist another. ■ Astron. a star, galaxy, or other celestial object that is close to or associated with another. **2** one of a pair of things intended to complement or match each other: [as adj.] *a companion volume.* ■ [usu. in names] a book that provides information about a particular subject: *the Oxford Companion to English Literature.* ▶ v. [trans.] formal accompany: *he is companioned by a pageboy.* [ME: from OFr. *compaignon*, lit. 'one who breaks bread with another,' based on L. *com-* 'together with' + *panis* 'bread.']

com·pan·ion[2] ▶ n. Naut. a covering over the hatchway leading below decks. [18th C.: from obs. Du. *kompanje* 'quarterdeck,' based on Ital. *(camera della) compagna* '(storeroom for) provisions.']

com·pan·ion·a·ble /kəm'panyənəbəl/ ▶ **adj.** (of a person) friendly and sociable: *a companionable young man.* ■ (of a shared situation) relaxed and pleasant. — **com·pan·ion·a·ble·ness n. com·pan·ion·a·bly adv.**

com·pan·ion an·i·mal ▶ **n.** a pet or other domestic animal.

com·pan·ion·ate /kəm'panyənit/ ▶ **adj.** formal (of a marriage or relationship) between partners or spouses as equal companions. ■ (of a person) acting as a companion.

com·pan·ion plant·ing ▶ **n.** the close planting of different plants that enhance each other's growth or protect each other from pests. — **com·pan·ion plant n. com·pan·ion-plant v.**

com·pan·ion·ship /kəm'panyən,SHip/ ▶ **n.** a feeling of fellowship or friendship.

com·pan·ion·way /kəm'panyən,wā/ ▶ **n.** a set of steps leading from a ship's deck down to a cabin or lower deck.

com·pa·ny /'kəmpənē/ ▶ **n.** (pl. **-nies**) **1** a commercial business. **2** the fact or condition of being with another or others, esp. in a way that provides friendship and enjoyment. ■ a person or people seen as a source of such friendship and enjoyment. ■ the person or group of people whose society someone is currently sharing. ■ a visiting person or group of people. **3** a number of individuals gathered together, esp. for a particular purpose. ■ a body of soldiers, esp. the smallest subdivision of an infantry battalion, typically commanded by a major or captain: *the troops of C Company.* ■ a group of actors, singers, or dancers who perform together. **4** (**the Company**) informal the Central Intelligence Agency. ▶ **v.** (**-nies, -nied**) [intrans.] (**company with**) literary associate with; keep company with.

– PHRASES **and company** used after a person's name to denote those people usually associated with them: *the psycholinguistics of Jacques Lacan and company.* ■ used in the name of a business to denote other unspecified partners: *Little, Brown and Company.* **be in good company** be in the same situation as someone important or respected. **in company** with another person or a group of people. **in company with** together with. **keep someone company** accompany or spend time with someone in order to prevent them from feeling lonely or bored. ■ engage in the same activity as someone else in order to be sociable. **keep company with** associate with habitually. **part company** see PART. [ME (in senses 2 and 3): from OFr. *compainie*; rel. to *compaignon* (see COMPANION[1]).]

com·pa·ny car ▶ **n.** a car provided by a company for the business and sometimes private use of an employee.

com·pa·ny of·fi·cer ▶ **n.** an army officer serving within an infantry company.

com·pa·ra·ble /'kämp(ə)rəbəl/ ▶ **adj.** (of a person or thing) able to be likened to another; similar. ■ of equivalent quality; worthy of comparison. — **com·pa·ra·bil·i·ty** /,kämp(ə)rə'bilitē/ **n.**

com·pa·ra·bly /'kämp(ə)rəblē; kəm'parəblē/ ▶ **adv.** in a similar way or to a similar degree.

com·par·a·tist /kəm'parətist/ ▶ **n.** a person who carries out comparative study, esp. of language or literature.

com·par·a·tive /kəm'parə,tiv/ ▶ **adj.** **1** perceptible by comparison; relative. **2** of or involving comparison between two or more branches of science or subjects of study. **3** Gram. (of an adjective or adverb) expressing a higher degree of a quality, but not the highest possible (e.g., *braver*; *more fiercely*). Contrasted with POSITIVE, SUPERLATIVE. ■ (of a clause) involving comparison (e.g., *their memory is not as good as it used to be*). ▶ **n.** Gram. a comparative adjective or adverb. ■ (**the comparative**) the middle degree of comparison.

com·par·a·tive ad·van·tage ▶ **n.** the ability of an individual or group to carry out a particular economic activity (such as making a specific product) more efficiently than another activity.

com·par·a·tive lin·guis·tics ▶ **plural n.** [treated as sing.] the study of similarities and differences between languages, in particular the comparison of related languages with a view to reconstructing forms in their lost parent languages.

com·par·a·tive·ly /kəm'parə,tivlē/ ▶ **adv.** [as submodifier] to a moderate degree as compared to something else; relatively: *inflation was comparatively low.*

com·par·a·tor /kəm'parətər/ ▶ **n.** a device for comparing a measurable property or thing with a reference or standard. ■ an electronic circuit for comparing two electrical signals. ■ something used as a standard for comparison.

com·pare /kəm'pe(ə)r/ ▶ **v.** [trans.] **1** estimate, measure, or note the similarity or dissimilarity between. ■ (**compare something to**) point out the resemblances to; liken to. ■ (**compare something to**) draw an analogy between one thing and (another) for the purposes of explanation or clarification. ■ [no obj., with adverbial] have a specified relationship with another thing or person in terms of nature or quality. ■ [no obj., usu. with negative] be of an equal or similar nature or quality. **2** (usu. **be compared**) Gram. form the comparative and superlative degrees of (an adjective or an adverb): *words of one syllable are usually compared by "-er" and "-est."*

– PHRASES **beyond** (or **without**) **compare** of a quality or nature surpassing all others of the same kind. **compare notes** (of two or more people) exchange ideas, opinions, or information about a particular subject. [ME: from OFr. *comparer*, from L. *comparare*, from *compar* 'like, equal,' from *com-* 'with' + *par* 'equal.']

com·par·i·son /kəm'parəsən/ ▶ **n.** **1** the act or instance of comparing. ■ an analogy. ■ the quality of being similar or equivalent. **2** Gram. the formation of the comparative and superlative forms of adjectives and adverbs.

– PHRASES **bear** (or **stand**) **comparison** be of sufficient quality to be likened favorably to someone or something of the same kind. **beyond comparison** another way of saying BEYOND COMPARE (see COMPARE). **by/in comparison** when compared. [ME: from OFr. *comparesoun*, from L. *comparatio(n-)*, from *comparare*.]

com·part·ment /kəm'pärtmənt/ ▶ **n.** **1** a separate section or part of something, in particular: ■ a division of a railroad car marked by partitions: *a first-class compartment.* ■ a section of a container in which certain items can be kept separate from others. ■ a watertight division of a ship: *the aft cargo compartment.* ■ fig. an area in which something can be considered in isolation from other things. **2** Heraldry a grassy mound or other support depicted below a shield. ▶ **v.** [trans.] (usu. **be compartmented**) divide (something) into separate parts or sections. — **com·part·men·ta·tion** /kəm,pärtmen'tāSHən; -mən-/ **n.** [16th C.: from Fr. *compartiment*, based on late L. *compartiri* 'divide.']

com·part·men·tal /kəm,pärt'mentl/ ▶ **adj.** characterized by division into separate sections. — **com·art·men·tal·ly** /-'mentl-ē/ **adv.**

com·part·men·tal·ize /kəm,pärt'mentl,īz/ ▶ **v.** [trans.] divide into sections or categories. — **com·part·men·tal·ism n. com·part·men·tal·i·za·tion** /kəm,pärtmentl-ə'zāSHən/ **n.**

com·pass /'kəmpəs/ ▶ **n.** **1** (also **magnetic compass**) an instrument containing a magnetized pointer that shows the direction of magnetic north and bearings from it. **2** (also **pair of compasses**) an instrument for drawing circles and arcs and measuring distances between points, consisting of two arms linked by a movable joint, one arm ending in a point and the other usually carrying a pencil or pen. **3** [in sing.] the range or scope of something: *the political repercussions that are beyond the compass of this book.* ■ the enclosing limits of an area. ■ the range of notes that can be produced by a voice or a musical instrument. [ME: from OFr. *compas* (n.), based on L. *com-* 'together' + *passus* 'a step or pace.']

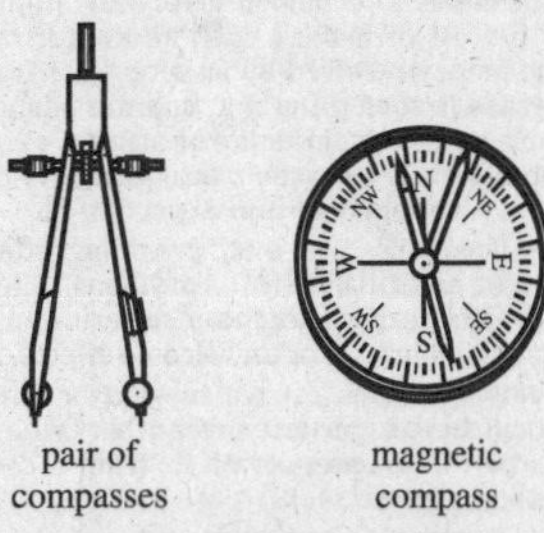

compasses

com·pass card ▶ **n.** a circular rotating card showing the 32 principal bearings, forming the indicator of a magnetic compass.

com·pas·sion /kəm'paSHən/ ▶ **n.** sympathetic pity and concern for the sufferings or misfortunes of others: *the victims should be treated with compassion.* [ME: via OFr. from eccles. L. *compassio(n-)*, from *compati* 'suffer with.']

com·pas·sion·ate /kəm'paSHənit/ ▶ **adj.** feeling or showing sympathy and concern for others. — **com·pas·sion·ate·ly adv.**

com·pas·sion·ate leave ▶ **n.** an absence from work granted to someone as the result of particular personal circumstances, esp. the death of a close relative.

com·pass rose ▶ **n.** a circle showing the principal directions printed on a map or chart.

com·pass saw ▶ **n.** a handsaw with a narrow blade for cutting curves.

com·pat·i·ble /kəm'patəbəl/ ▶ **adj.** (of two things) able to exist or occur together without conflict. ■ (of two people) able to have a harmonious relationship: well-suited: *it's a pity we're not compatible.* ■ (of one thing) consistent with another. ■ (of a computer, a piece of software, or other device) able to be used with a specified piece of equipment or software without special adaptation or modification. ▶ **n.** a computer that can use software designed for another make or type. — **com·pat·i·bil·i·ty** /kəm,patə'bilitē/ **n. com·pat·i·bly** /-blē/ **adv.** [ME: from Fr., from med. L. *compatibilis*, from *compati* 'suffer with.']

com·pa·tri·ot /kəm'pātrēət/ ▶ **n.** a fellow citizen or national of a country. [16th C.: from Fr. *compatriote*, from late L. *compatriota* (translating Gk. *sumpatriōtēs*), from *com-* 'together with' + *patriota* (see PATRIOT).]

com·peer /'käm,pi(ə)r; käm'pi(ə)r/ ▶ **n.** formal a person of equal rank, status, or ability. [ME: from OFr. *comper*, from *com-* 'with' + *per*, from L. *par* 'equal' (cf. PEER[2]).]

com·pel /kəm'pel/ ▶ **v.** (**-pelled, -pel·ling**) [with obj. and infin.] force or oblige (someone) to do something. ■ [trans.] bring about (something) by the use of force or pressure. ■ [with obj. and adverbial of direction] literary drive forcibly: *by heav'n's high will compell'd from shore to shore.* [ME: from L. *compellere*, from *com-* 'together' + *pellere* 'drive.']

com·pel·la·ble /kəm'peləbəl/ ▶ **adj.** Law (of a witness) able to be made to attend court or testify.

com·pel·ling /kəm'peliNG/ ▶ **adj.** evoking interest, attention, or admiration in a powerfully irresistible way. ■ not able to be refuted; inspiring conviction. ■ not able to be resisted; overwhelming. — **com·pel·ling·ly** adv.

com·pen·di·ous /kəm'pendēəs/ ▶ **adj.** formal containing or presenting the essential facts of something in a comprehensive but concise way: *a compendious study.* — **com·pen·di·ous·ly** adv. **com·pen·di·ous·ness** n. [ME: from OFr. *compendieux*, from L. *compendiosus* 'advantageous, brief,' from *compendium* 'profit, saving, abbreviation.']

com·pen·di·um /kəm'pendēəm/ ▶ **n.** (pl. **-di·ums** or **-di·a** /-dēə/) a collection of concise but detailed information about a particular subject. ■ a collection of things, esp. one systematically gathered. [16th C.: from L., 'profit, saving' (lit. 'what is weighed together'), from *compendere*, from *com-* 'together' + *pendere* 'weigh.']

com·pen·sa·ble /kəm'pensəbəl/ ▶ **adj.** (of a loss or hardship) for which compensation can be obtained. [17th C.: Fr., from *compenser*, from L. *compensare* 'weigh (something) against (another).']

com·pen·sate /'kämpən,sāt/ ▶ **v. 1** [trans.] recompense (someone) for loss, suffering, or injury, typically by the award of a sum of money. ■ pay (someone) for work performed. **2** [intrans.] **(compensate for)** make up for (something unwelcome or unpleasant) by exerting an opposite force or effect. ■ act to neutralize or correct (a deficiency or abnormality in a physical property or effect). ■ Psychol. attempt to conceal or offset (a disability or frustration) by development in another direction. **3** [trans.] Mech. provide (a pendulum) with extra or less weight to neutralize the effects of temperature, etc. — **com·pen·sa·tive** /kəm'pensətiv; 'kämpən,sātiv/ adj. **com·pen·sa·tor** /-,sātər/ n. [17th C. (in the sense 'counterbalance'): from L. *compensat-* 'weighed against,' from the v. *compensare*, from *com-* 'together' + *pensare* (frequentative of *pendere* 'weigh').]

com·pen·sa·tion /,kämpən'sāsHən/ ▶ **n.** something, typically money, awarded to someone as a recompense for loss, injury, or suffering. ■ the action or process of making such an award: *the compensation of victims.* ■ the money received by an employee from an employer as a salary or wages. ■ something that counterbalances or makes up for an undesirable or unwelcome state of affairs. ■ Psychol. the process of concealing or offsetting a psychological difficulty by developing in another direction. — **com·pen·sa·tion·al** /-sHənl/ adj.

com·pen·sa·to·ry /kəm'pensə,tôrē/ ▶ **adj.** providing, effecting, or aiming at compensation, in particular: ■ (of a payment) intended to recompense someone who has experienced loss, suffering, or injury. ■ reducing or offsetting the unpleasant or unwelcome effects of something.

com·pete /kəm'pēt/ ▶ **v.** [intrans.] strive to gain or win something by defeating or establishing superiority over others who are trying to do the same. ■ take part in a contest. [17th C.: from L. *competere*, 'strive,' from *com-* 'together' + *petere* 'seek.']

com·pe·tence /'kämpətəns/ (also **com·pe·ten·cy**) ▶ **n. 1** the ability to do something successfully or efficiently. ■ the scope of a person's or group's knowledge or ability. ■ a skill or ability. ■ the legal authority of a court or other body to deal with a particular matter. ■ the ability of a criminal defendant to stand trial, as gauged by their mental ability to understand the proceedings and to assist defense lawyers. ■ (also **linguistic** or **language competence**) Ling. a speaker's subconscious, intuitive knowledge of the rules of their language. Often contrasted with PERFORMANCE. ■ Biol. Med. effective performance of the normal function. **2** dated an income large enough to live on, typically unearned.

com·pe·tent /'kämpətənt/ ▶ **adj.** having the necessary ability, knowledge, or skill to do something successfully. ■ (of a person) efficient and capable. ■ acceptable and satisfactory, though not outstanding. ■ (chiefly of a court or other body) accepted as having legal authority to deal with a particular matter. ■ (of a criminal defendant) able to understand the charges and to aid in defending themselves. ■ Biol. Med. capable of performing the normal function effectively. — **com·pe·tent·ly** adv. [ME: from L. *competent-*, from *competere* 'be fit' (see COMPETE).]

com·pe·ti·tion /,kämpə'tisHən/ ▶ **n.** the activity or condition of competing: *there is fierce competition between banks | at this conservatory, competition for admissions is stiff.* ■ an event or contest in which people compete. ■ the action of participating in such an event or contest: *in the heat of competition.* ■ [in sing.] the person or people with whom one is competing, esp. in a commercial or sporting arena; the opposition. ■ Ecol. interaction between organisms, populations, or species, in which birth, growth and death depend on gaining a share of a limited environmental resource.

com·pet·i·tive /kəm'petətiv/ ▶ **adj. 1** of, relating to, or characterized by competition. ■ having or displaying a strong desire to be more successful than others: *she had a competitive streak.* **2** as good as or better than others of a comparable nature: *a car industry competitive with any in the world.* ■ (of prices) low enough to compare well with those of rival merchants. — **com·pet·i·tive·ly** adv. **com·pet·i·tive·ness** n.

com·pet·i·tive ex·clu·sion ▶ **n.** Ecol. the inevitable elimination from a habitat of one of two different species with identical needs for resources.

com·pet·i·tor /kəm'petitər/ ▶ **n.** an organization or country that is engaged in commercial or economic competition with others: *our main industrial competitors.* ■ a person who takes part in a contest.

com·pi·la·tion /,kämpə'lāsHən/ ▶ **n. 1** the action or process of producing something, esp. a list, book, or report, by assembling information from other sources. **2** a thing, esp. a book, record, or broadcast program, that is put together by assembling previously separate items: *there are thirty-three stories in this compilation.*

com·pile /kəm'pīl/ ▶ **v.** [trans.] **1** produce (something, esp. a list, report, or book) by assembling information collected from other sources. ■ collect (information) in order to produce something. ■ accumulate (a specified score). **2** Comput. (of a computer) convert (a program) into a machine-code or lower-level form in which the program can be executed. — **com·pil·er** n. [ME: from OFr. *compiler* or L. *compilare* 'plunder.']

comp·ing /'kämpiNG/ ▶ **n. 1** the process of making composite images, esp. electronically. **2** the action of playing a musical accompaniment, esp. in jazz or blues.

com·pla·cent /kəm'plāsənt/ ▶ **adj.** showing smug or uncritical satisfaction with oneself or one's achievements. — **com·pla·cen·cy** /-sənsē/ (or **complacence**) n. **com·pla·cent·ly** adv. [17th C.: from L. *complacere* 'please.']

com·plain /kəm'plān/ ▶ **v.** [reporting verb] express dissatisfaction or annoyance about a state of affairs or an event: [with clause] *local authorities complained that they lacked sufficient resources.* ■ [intrans.] **(complain of)** state that one is suffering from (a pain or other symptom of illness): *he began to complain of headaches.* ■ [intrans.] state a grievance. ■ [intrans.] literary make a mournful sound: *let the warbling flute complain.* ■ [intrans.] (of a structure or mechanism) groan or creak under strain. — **com·plain·er** n. **com·plain·ing·ly** adv. [ME: from OFr. *complaindre*, from med. L. *complangere* 'bewail,' from *com-* (intensifier) + *plangere* 'to lament.']

com·plain·ant /kəm'plānənt/ ▶ **n.** Law a plaintiff in certain lawsuits.

com·plaint /kəm'plānt/ ▶ **n. 1** a statement that a situation is unsatisfactory or unacceptable. ■ a reason for dissatisfaction: *I have no complaints about the hotel.* ■ the expression of dissatisfaction. ■ Law the plaintiff's reasons for proceeding in a civil action. **2** [often with adj.] an illness or medical condition, esp. a relatively minor one. [ME: from OFr. *complainte*, fem. past part. of *complaindre*.]

com·plai·sant /kəm'plāsənt/ ▶ **adj.** willing to please others; obliging; agreeable. — **com·plai·sance** n. **com·plai·sant·ly** adv. [17th C.: Fr., from *complaire* 'acquiesce,' from L. *complacere* 'please.']

com·pleat /kəm'plēt/ ▶ **adj. & v.** archaic spelling of COMPLETE.

com·plect·ed /kəm'plektid/ ▶ **adj.** [in comb.] having a specified complexion. [19th C.: appar. from COMPLEXION.]

com·ple·ment ▶ **n.** /'kämpləmənt/ **1** a thing that completes or brings to perfection. **2** [in sing.] a number or quantity of something required to make a group complete. ■ the number of people required to crew a ship. ■ Geom. the amount in degrees by which a given angle is less than 90°. ■ Math. the members of a set that are not members of a given subset. **3** Gram. one or more words, phrases, or clauses governed by a verb (or by a nominalization or a predicative adjective) that complete the meaning of the predicate. **4** Physiol. a group of proteins present in blood plasma and tissue fluid that combine with an antigen–antibody complex to bring about the lysis of foreign cells. ▶ **v.** /-,ment; -mənt/ [trans.] add to (something) in a way that enhances or improves it; make perfect. ■ add to or make complete. — **com·ple·men·tal** /,kämplə'mentl/ adj. [ME: from L. *complere* 'fill up' (see COMPLETE).]

com·ple·men·tar·i·ty /,kämpləmen'taritē/ ▶ **n.** (pl. **-ties**) a complementary relationship or situation. ■ Physics the concept that two contrasted theories, such as the wave and particle theories of light, may be able to explain a set of phenomena, although each separately only accounts for some aspects.

com·ple·men·ta·ry /,kämplə'ment(ə)rē/ ▶ **adj. 1** completing; forming a complement. ■ (of two or more different things) combining in such a way as to enhance or emphasize each other's qualities. ■ Biochem. (of gene sequences, nucleotides, etc.) related by the rules of base pairing. **2** [attrib.] of or relating to complementary medicine. — **com·ple·men·ta·ri·ly** /,kämplə'mentrəlē; -men'terəlē/ adv. **com·ple·men·ta·ri·ness** n.

com·ple·men·ta·ry an·gle ▶ **n.** either of two angles whose sum is 90°.

com·ple·men·ta·ry col·ors ▶ **plural n.** colors directly opposite each other in the color spectrum, such as red and green or blue and orange, that when combined in the right proportions, produce white light.

com·ple·men·ta·ry dis·tri·bu·tion ▶ **n.** Ling. the occurrence of speech sounds in mutually exclusive contexts.

com·ple·men·ta·ry DNA ▶ **n.** Biochem. synthetic DNA in which the sequence of bases is complementary to that of a given example of DNA.

com·ple·men·ta·ry func·tion ▶ **n.** Math. the part of the general solution of a linear differential equation that is the general solution of the associated homogeneous equation obtained by substituting zero for the terms not containing the dependent variable.

com·ple·men·ta·ry med·i·cine ▶ **n.** any of a range of medical therapies that fall beyond the scope of scientific medicine but may be used alongside it in the treatment of disease and ill health. Examples include acupuncture and osteopathy. See also ALTERNATIVE MEDICINE.

com·ple·men·ta·tion /,kämpləmen'tāsHən/ ▶ **n.** the action of complementing something.

com·ple·men·tiz·er /'kämpləmen,tīzər; -mən-/ ▶ **n.** Gram. a word or morpheme that marks an embedded clause as functioning as a complement, typically a subordinating conjunction or infinitival *to.*

com·plete /kəm'plēt/ ▶ **adj. 1** having all the necessary or appropriate parts. ■ (of all the works of a particular author) collected together in one volume or edition: *the complete works of Shakespeare.* ■ entire;

full. ■ [predic.] having run its full course; finished. **2** [attrib.] (often used for emphasis) to the greatest extent or degree; total. ■ (also **com•pleat**) esp. humorous skilled at every aspect of a particular activity; consummate: *these articles are for the compleat mathematician.* ▶**v.** [trans.] **1** finish making or doing. ■ Football (esp. of a quarterback) successfully throw (a forward pass) to a receiver: *he completed 12 of 16 passes for 128 yards.* **2** make (something) whole or perfect. ■ write the required information on (a form or questionnaire).
– PHRASES **complete with** having something as an additional part or feature: *the detachable keyboard comes complete with numeric keypad.* — **com•plete•ness n. com•plet•er n.** [ME: from OFr. *complet* or L. *completus*, from *complere* 'fill up,' from *com-* (intensifier) + *plere* 'fill.']

com•plete game ▶**n.** Baseball a game in which one pitcher pitches all innings without relief.

com•plete•ly /kəm'plētlē/ ▶**adv.** totally; utterly.

com•ple•tion /kəm'plēsʜən/ ▶**n.** the action or process of finishing something. ■ the state of being finished. ■ Football a successful forward pass. ■ Law the final stage in the sale of a property, at which point it legally changes ownership: *the risk stays with the seller until completion.* ■ the action of writing the required information on a form.

com•ple•tist /kəm'plētist/ ▶**n.** an obsessive, typically indiscriminate, collector or fan of something.

com•ple•tive /kəm'plētiv/ ▶**n.** Gram. a word or morpheme that adds a sense of completeness to a word or phrase (e.g., *up* in the phrase *break up*).

com•plex ▶**adj.** /käm'pleks; kəm-; 'kämpleks/ **1** consisting of many different and connected parts. ■ not easy to analyze or understand; complicated or intricate. **2** Math. denoting or involving numbers or quantities containing both a real and an imaginary part. **3** Chem. denoting an ion or molecule in which one or more groups are linked to a metal atom by coordinate bonds. ▶**n.** /'kämpleks/ **1** a group of similar buildings or facilities on the same site: *a new apartment complex.* ■ a group or system of different things that are linked in a close or complicated way; a network. **2** Psychoanal. a related group of emotionally significant ideas that are completely or partly repressed and that cause psychic conflict leading to abnormal mental states or behavior. ■ informal a disproportionate concern or anxiety about something. **3** Chem. an ion or molecule in which one or more groups are linked to a metal atom by coordinate bonds. ■ any loosely bonded species formed by the association of two molecules. ▶**v.** /käm'pleks; kəm-; 'kämpleks/ [trans.] (usu. **be complexed**) Chem. make (an atom or compound) form a complex with another. ■ [intrans.] form a complex. — **com•plex•a•tion** /käm,plek'sāsʜən; kəm-/ **n.** (Chem.) **com•plex•ly adv.** [17th C.: from L. *complexus*, from *complectere* 'embrace,' later associated with *complexus* 'plaited.']

com•plex plane ▶**n.** an infinite two-dimensional space representing the set of complex numbers, esp. one in which Cartesian coordinates represent the real and imaginary parts of the complex numbers.

com•plex con•ju•gate ▶**n.** Math. each of two complex numbers having their real parts identical and their imaginary parts of equal magnitude but opposite sign.

com•plex•ion /kəm'pleksʜən/ ▶**n.** **1** the natural color, texture, and appearance of a person's skin, esp. of the face: *an attractive girl with a pale complexion.* **2** the general aspect or character of something. — **com•plex•ioned adj.** [often in comb.] *they were both fair-complexioned.* [ME: via OFr. from L. *complexio(n-)* 'combination,' from *complectere* 'comprise.']

com•plex•i•ty /kəm'pleksitē/ ▶**n.** (pl. **-ties**) the state or quality of being intricate or complicated. ■ (usu. **complexities**) a factor involved in a complicated process or situation.

com•plex sen•tence ▶**n.** Gram. a sentence containing a subordinate clause or clauses.

com•pli•ance /kəm'plīəns/ (also **com•pli•an•cy** /-'plīənsē/) ▶**n.** **1** the action or fact of complying with a wish or command. ■ (**compliance with**) the state or fact of according with or meeting rules or standards. ■ unworthy or excessive acquiescence. **2** Physics the property of a material of undergoing elastic deformation or (of a gas) change in volume when subjected to an applied force. It is equal to the reciprocal of stiffness. ■ Med. the ability of an organ to distend in response to applied pressure.

com•pli•ant /kəm'plīənt/ ▶**adj.** **1** inclined to agree with others or obey rules, esp. to an excessive degree; acquiescent: *good-humored, eagerly compliant girls.* ■ meeting or in accordance with rules or standards. **2** Physics & Med. having the property of compliance. — **com•pli•ant•ly adv.**

com•pli•cate /'kämpli,kāt/ ▶**v.** [trans.] make (something) more difficult or confusing by causing it to be more complex. ■ Med. introduce complications in (an existing condition): *smoking may complicate pregnancy.* — **com•pli•cat•ed adj. com•pli•cat•ed•ly adv.** [17th C.: from L. *complicare*, from *com-* 'together' + *plicare* 'to fold.']

com•pli•ca•tion /,kämplə'kāsʜən/ ▶**n.** **1** a circumstance that complicates something; a difficulty. ■ an involved or confused condition or state. **2** Med. a secondary disease or condition aggravating an already existing one.

com•plic•it /kəm'plisit/ ▶**n.** involved with others in an illegal activity or wrongdoing.

com•plic•i•ty /kəm'plisitē/ ▶**n.** the state of being involved with others in an illegal activity or wrongdoing.

com•pli•ment ▶**n.** /'kämpləmənt/ a polite expression of praise or admiration. ■ an act or circumstance that implies praise or respect. ■ (**compliments**) congratulations or praise expressed to someone: *my compliments on your cooking.* ■ (**compliments**) greetings or regards, esp. when sent as a message. ▶**v.** /-,ment/ [trans.] politely congratulate or praise (someone) for something. ■ praise (something) politely.
– PHRASES **compliments of the season** used as a seasonal greeting at Christmas or the New Year. **pay one's compliments** send or express formal greetings. **return the compliment** give a compliment in return for another. ■ retaliate or respond in kind. **with someone's compliments** (or **the compliments of**) used to express the fact that what one is giving is free. [17th C.: from Fr. *compliment*, based on L. *complementum* 'fulfillment.']

com•pli•men•ta•ry /,kämplə'mentərē; -'mentrē/ ▶**adj.** **1** expressing a compliment; praising or approving. **2** given or supplied free of charge.

com•pli•men•tary close (also **complimentary closing**) ▶**n.** the part of a letter that immediately precedes the writer's signature, consisting of words such as *Sincerely, Cordially, Very truly yours*, etc.

com•pline /'kämplin; -plīn/ ▶**n.** a service of evening prayers forming part of the Divine Office of the Western Christian Church, traditionally said (or chanted) before retiring for the night. [ME: from OFr. *complie*, fem. past part. of obs. *complir* 'to complete,' from L. *complere* 'fill up.']

com•ply /kəm'plī/ ▶**v.** (**-plies, -plied**) [intrans.] (of a person or group) act in accordance with a wish or command. ■ (of an article) meet specified standards. [16th C. (in sense 'fulfill, accomplish,' later 'fulfill the requirements of courtesy'): from Ital. *complire*, Catalan *complir*, Sp. *cumplir*, from L. *complere* 'fill up, fulfill' (see COMPLETE); cf. COMPLIMENT.]

com•po•nent /kəm'pōnənt/ ▶**n.** a part or element of a larger whole, esp. a part of a machine or vehicle. ■ Physics each of two or more forces, velocities, or other vectors acting in different directions that are together equivalent to a given vector. ▶**adj.** [attrib.] constituting part of a larger whole; constituent. [17th C.: from L. *component-* 'putting together,' from the v. *componere*, from *com-* 'together' + *ponere* 'put.' Cf. COMPOUND[1].]

com•port[1] /kəm'pôrt/ ▶**v.** **1** (**comport oneself**) formal conduct oneself; behave. **2** [intrans.] (**comport with**) accord with; agree with. [ME: from L. *comportare*, from *com-* 'together' + *portare* 'carry.']

com•port[2] /'kämpôrt/ ▶**n.** another term for COMPOTE (sense 2). [19th C.: appar. an abbrev. of Fr. *comportier*, var. of *compotier* 'dessert dish.']

com•port•ment /kəm'pôrtmənt/ ▶**n.** behavior; bearing.

com•pose /kəm'pōz/ ▶**v.** [trans.] **1** write or create (a work of art, esp. music or poetry). ■ write or phrase (a letter or piece of writing) with care and thought: *the first sentence is so hard to compose.* ■ order or arrange (parts) to form a whole, esp. in an artistic way: *make an attempt to compose your images.* **2** (usu. **be composed**) (of elements) constitute or make up (a whole). ■ be (a specified number or amount) of a whole. **3** calm or settle (oneself or one's features or thoughts). **4** prepare (a text) for printing by manually, mechanically, or electronically setting up the letters and other characters in the order to be printed. ■ set up (letters and characters) in this way. [ME: from OFr. *composer*, from L. *componere* (see COMPONENT).]

com•posed /kəm'pōzd/ ▶**adj.** having one's feelings and expression under control; calm. — **com•pos•ed•ly** /-'pōzidlē/ **adv.**

com•pos•er /kəm'pōzər/ ▶**n.** a person who writes music, esp. as a professional occupation.

com•pos•ite /kəm'päzit; käm-/ ▶**adj.** **1** made up of various parts or elements. ■ (esp. of a constructional material) made up of recognizable constituents. ■ (of a railroad car) having compartments of more than one class or function. ■ Math. (of an integer) being the product of two or more factors greater than one; not prime. **2** (**Composite**) relating to or denoting a classical order of architecture consisting of elements of the Ionic and Corinthian orders. **3** Bot. relating to or denoting plants of the daisy family (Compositae). ▶**n.** **1** a thing made up of several parts or elements. ■ a composite constructional material. **2** Bot. a plant of the daisy family (Compositae). **3** (**Composite**) the Composite order of architecture. ▶**v.** [trans.] [usu. as n.] (**compositing**) combine (two or more images) to make a single picture, esp. electronically. ■ amalgamate (two or more similar resolutions). — **com•pos•ite•ly adv. com•pos•ite•ness n.** [ME: via Fr. from L. *compositus*, past part. of *componere* 'put together.']

com•pos•ite pho•to•graph ▶**n.** a photograph made by overlapping or juxtaposing two or more separate images.

com•po•si•tion /,kämpə'zisʜən/ ▶**n.** **1** the nature of something's ingredients or constituents; the way in which a whole or mixture is made up. ■ the action of putting things together; formation or construction. ■ a thing composed of various elements. ■ [often as adj.] a compound artificial substance, esp. one serving the purpose of a natural one: *composition flooring.* ■ Ling. the formation of words into a compound word. ■ Math. the successive application of functions to a variable, the value of the first function being the argument of the second, and so on. ■ Physics the process of finding the resultant of a number of forces. **2** a work of music, literature, or art. ■ the action or art of producing such a work. ■ an essay, esp. one written by a student. ■ the artistic arrangement of the parts of a picture. **3** the preparing of text for printing by setting up the characters in order. See COMPOSE (sense 4). **4** a legal agreement to pay an amount of money in lieu of a larger debt or other obligation.

■ an amount of money paid in this way. —**com·po·si·tion·al** /-SHənl/ **adj.** **com·po·si·tion·al·ly** /-SHənl-ē/ **adv.** [ME: via OFr. from L. *composition-*, from *componere* 'put together.']

com·pos·i·tor /kəm'päzitər/ ▶**n.** Print. a person who arranges type for printing or keys text into a composing machine.

com·pos men·tis /ˌkämpəs 'mentəs/ ▶**adj.** [predic.] having full control of one's mind; sane. [17th C.: L.]

com·post /'kämpōst/ ▶**n.** decayed organic material used as a plant fertilizer. ■ a mixture of this with loam soil and/or other ingredients, used as a growing medium. ▶**v.** [trans.] make (vegetable matter or manure) into compost: *don't compost heavily infested plants.* ■ treat (soil) with compost. [ME: from OFr. *composte*, from L. *composita, compositum*, past part. of *componere* 'put together.']

com·post heap (also **compost pile**) ▶**n.** a pile of garden and organic kitchen refuse that decomposes to produce compost.

com·po·sure /kəm'pōZHər/ ▶**n.** the state or feeling of being calm and in control of oneself.

com·pote /'kämpōt/ ▶**n.** **1** fruit preserved or cooked in syrup. ■ a dish consisting of fruit salad or stewed fruit. **2** a bowl-shaped dessert dish with a stem. [17th C.: from Fr., from OFr. *composte* 'mixture' (see COMPOST).]

com·pound¹ ▶**n.** /'kämpound/ a thing that is composed of two or more separate elements; a mixture. ■ (also **chemical compound**) a substance formed from two or more elements chemically united in fixed proportions. ■ a word made up of two or more existing words, such as *steamship.* ▶**adj.** /'kämpound; käm'pound; kəm'pound/ [attrib.] made up or consisting of several parts or elements, in particular: ■ (of a word) made up of two or more existing words or elements: *a compound noun.* ■ (of interest) payable on both capital and the accumulated interest: *compound interest.* Compare with SIMPLE. ■ Biol. (esp. of a leaf, flower, or eye) consisting of two or more simple parts or individuals in combination. ▶**v.** /kəm'pound; käm'pound; 'kämpound/ [trans.] **1** (often **be compounded**) make up (a composite whole); constitute. ■ mix or combine (ingredients or constituents): *yellow pastas compounded with lemon zest or saffron.* ■ calculate (interest) on previously accumulated interest. ■ (of a sum of money invested) increase by compound interest. **2** make (something bad) worse; intensify the negative aspects of. **3** Law forbear from prosecuting (a felony) in exchange for money or other consideration. ■ settle (a debt or other matter) in this way. —**com·pound·a·ble** /kəm'poundəbəl; käm-/ **adj.** [ME *compoune* (v.), from OFr. *compoun-*, stem of *compondre*, from L. *componere* 'put together.']

com·pound² /'kämpound/ ▶**n.** an area enclosed by a fence, in particular: ■ an open area in which a factory or large house stands. ■ an open area in a prison, prison camp, or work camp. [17th C.: from Port. *campon* or Du. *kampoeng*, from Malay *kampong* 'enclosure.']

com·pound-com·plex sen·tence ▶**n.** a sentence having two or more coordinate independent clauses and one or more dependent clauses.

com·pound·er /käm'poundər; kəm-; 'kämpoundər/ ▶**n.** a person who mixes or combines ingredients in order to produce an animal feed, medicine, or other substance.

com·pound eye ▶**n.** an eye consisting of an array of numerous small visual units, as found in insects and crustaceans. Contrasted with SIMPLE EYE.

com·pound frac·tion ▶**n.** a fraction in which either the numerator or the denominator, or both, contain one or more fractions.

com·pound frac·ture ▶**n.** an injury in which a broken bone pierces the skin, causing a risk of infection.

com·pound in·ter·val ▶**n.** Music an interval greater than an octave.

com·pound leaf ▶**n.** a leaf of a plant consisting of several or many distinct parts (leaflets) joined to a single stem.

com·pound sen·tence ▶**n.** a sentence with more than one subject or predicate.

com·pound time ▶**n.** Music musical rhythm or meter in which each beat in a bar is subdivided into three smaller units, so having the value of a dotted note. Compare with SIMPLE TIME.

com·pre·hend /ˌkämpri'hend/ ▶**v.** [trans.] **1** [often with negative] grasp mentally; understand. **2** formal include, comprise, or encompass. —**com·pre·hend·er** **n.** [ME: from OFr. *comprehender*, or L. *comprehendere*, from *com-* 'together' + *prehendere* 'grasp.']

com·pre·hen·si·ble /ˌkämpri'hensəbəl/ ▶**adj.** able to be understood; intelligible. —**com·pre·hen·si·bil·i·ty** /-ˌhensə'bilitē/ **n.** **com·pre·hen·si·bly** **adv.**

com·pre·hen·sion /ˌkämpri'henCHən/ ▶**n.** the action or capability of understanding something. [ME: from Fr. *compréhension* or L. *comprehensio(n-)*, from *comprehendere* 'seize, comprise.']

com·pre·hen·sive /ˌkämpri'hensiv/ ▶**adj.** complete; including all or nearly all elements or aspects of something: *a comprehensive list of sources.* ■ of large content or scope; wide-ranging. ■ (of automobile insurance) providing coverage for most risks, including damage to the policyholder's own vehicle. ■ (also **comprehensive examination** or **comp**) an examination testing a student's command of a special field of knowledge. —**com·pre·hen·sive·ly** **adv.** **com·pre·hen·sive·ness** **n.**

com·press ▶**v.** /kəm'pres/ [trans.] (often **be compressed**) flatten by pressure; squeeze; press. ■ [intrans.] be squeezed or pressed together or into a smaller space: *the land is sinking as the soil compresses.* ■ squeeze or press (two things) together: *Violet compressed her lips together grimly.* ■ express in a shorter form; abridge. ■ Comput. alter the form of (data) to reduce the amount of storage necessary. ■ [as adj.] (**compressed**) esp. Biol. having a narrow shape as if flattened, esp. sideways. ▶**n.** /'kämpres/ a pad of absorbent material pressed onto part of the body to relieve inflammation or stop bleeding: *a cold compress.* —**com·press·i·bil·i·ty** /kəmˌpresə'bilitē/ **n.** **com·press·i·ble** **adj.** **com·pres·sive** /-'presiv/ **adj.** [ME: ult. from late L. *compressare*, frequentative of L. *comprimere*, from *com-* 'together' + *premere* 'to press'; or from *compress-* 'pressed together,' from *comprimere.*]

com·pressed air ▶**n.** air that has been compressed to a pressure higher than atmospheric pressure.

com·pres·sion /kəm'preSHən/ ▶**n.** the action of compressing or being compressed. ■ the reduction in volume (causing an increase in pressure) of the fuel mixture in an internal combustion engine before ignition. —**com·pres·sion·al** /-SHənl/ **adj.**

com·pres·sive strength ▶**n.** the resistance of a material to breaking under compression. Compare with TENSILE STRENGTH.

com·pres·sor /kəm'presər/ ▶**n.** an instrument or device for compressing something. ■ a machine used to supply air or other gas at increased pressure, e.g., to power a gas turbine. ■ an electrical amplifier that reduces the dynamic range of a signal.

com·prise /kəm'prīz/ ▶**v.** [trans.] consist of; be made up of: *the country comprises twenty states.* ■ make up; constitute. [ME: from Fr., 'comprised,' fem. past part. of *comprendre*, from OFr. *comprehender* (see COMPREHEND).]

com·pro·mise /'kämprəˌmīz/ ▶**n.** an agreement or a settlement of a dispute that is reached by each side making concessions. ■ a middle state between conflicting opinions or actions reached by mutual concession or modification. ■ the acceptance of standards that are lower than is desirable. ▶**v.** **1** [intrans.] settle a dispute by mutual concession. **2** [trans.] weaken (a reputation or principle) by accepting standards that are lower than is desirable. ■ [intrans.] accept standards that are lower than is desirable: *we were not prepared to* ***compromise on safety.*** ■ bring into disrepute or danger by indiscreet, foolish, or reckless behavior. —**com·pro·mis·er** **n.** [ME: from OFr. *compromis*, from late L. *compromissum* 'a consent to arbitration,' neut. past part. of *compromittere*, from *com-* 'together' + *promittere* (see PROMISE).]

com·pro·mis·ing /'kämprəˌmīziNG/ ▶**adj.** (of information or a situation) revealing an embarrassing or incriminating secret about someone.

compte ren·du /'kônt räN'dY; räN'd(y)o͞o/ ▶**n.** (pl. **comptes ren·dus** pronunc. same) a formal report or review. [19th C.: Fr., lit. 'account rendered.']

Comp·ton¹ /'kämptən/ a city in southwestern California; pop. 93,493.

Comp·ton², Arthur Holly (1892–1962), US physicist. Nobel Prize for Physics (1927, shared with C. Wilson).

Comp·ton ef·fect ▶**n.** Physics an increase in wavelength of X-rays or gamma rays that occurs when they are scattered. [20th C.: named after A. H. *Compton* (see COMPTON²).]

comp·trol·ler /kən'trōlər; käm(p)'trōlər/ ▶**n.** a controller (used in the title of some financial officers). [15th C.: var. of CONTROLLER.]

com·pul·sion /kəm'pəlSHən/ ▶**n.** **1** the action or state of forcing or being forced to do something; constraint. **2** an irresistible urge to behave in a certain way, esp. against one's conscious wishes. [ME: via OFr. from late L. *compulsio(n-)*, from *compellere* 'drive.']

com·pul·sive /kəm'pəlsiv/ ▶**adj.** **1** resulting from or relating to an irresistible urge, esp. one that is against one's conscious wishes: *compulsive eating.* ■ (of a person) acting as a result of such an urge. **2** irresistibly interesting or exciting; compelling. —**com·pul·sive·ly** **adv.** **com·pul·sive·ness** **n.**

com·pul·so·ry /kəm'pəlsərē/ ▶**adj.** required by law or a rule; obligatory. | ■ involving or exercising compulsion; coercive. —**com·pul·so·ri·ly** /-sərəlē/ **adv.** **com·pul·so·ri·ness** **n.**

com·punc·tion /kəm'pəNG(k)SHən/ ▶**n.** [usu. with negative] a feeling of guilt or moral scruple that follows the doing of something bad: *spend the money* ***without compunction.*** ■ a pricking of the conscience. —**com·punc·tion·less** **adj.** **com·punc·tious** /-SHəs/ **adj.** **com·punc·tious·ly** /-SHəslē/ **adv.** [ME: from OFr. *componction*, based on L. *compungere* 'prick sharply,' from *com-* (intensifier) + *pungere* 'to prick.']

com·pu·ta·tion /ˌkämpyo͝o'tāSHən/ ▶**n.** the action of mathematical calculation. ■ the use of computers, esp. as a subject of research or study.

com·pu·ta·tion·al /ˌkämpyo͝o'tāSHənl/ ▶**adj.** using computers: *the computational analysis of English.* ■ of or relating to computers. ■ of or relating to the process of mathematical calculation. —**com·pu·ta·tion·al·ly** **adv.**

com·pu·ta·tion·al lin·guis·tics ▶**plural n.** [treated as sing.] the branch of linguistics in which the techniques of computer science are applied to the analysis and synthesis of language and speech.

com·pute /kəm'pyo͞ot/ ▶**v.** [trans.] (often **be computed**) calculate or reckon (a figure or amount). ■ [intrans.] make a calculation, esp. using a computer. ■ [no obj., with negative] informal seem reasonable; make sense. [from the phr. *does not compute*, once used as an error message in computing.] —**com·put·a·bil·i·ty** /kəmˌpyo͞otə'bilitē/ **n.** **com·put·a·ble** **adj.** **com·put·a·bly** **adv.** **com·put·ist** **n.** [17th C.: from Fr. *computer* or L. *computare*, from *com-* 'together' + *putare* 'to settle (an account).']

com·put·er /kəm'pyo͞otər/ ▶**n.** an electronic device for storing and processing data, typically in binary form, according to instructions given to it in a variable program. ■ a person who makes calculations, esp. with a calculating machine.

com·put·er an·i·ma·tion ▶**n.** see ANIMATION.

com·put·er con·fer·enc·ing ▶ n. the use of computer and telecommunications technology to hold discussions between three or more people operating computers in separate locations.

com·put·er dat·ing ▶ n. the use of computer databases to identify potentially compatible partners for people.

com·put·er·ese /kəm,pyōōtə'rēz; -'rēs/ ▶ n. the jargon associated with computers. ■ the symbols and rules of a computer programming language.

com·put·er-friend·ly ▶ adj. 1 suitable for use with computers; compatible with computers. 2 (of a person) well disposed toward computers.

com·put·er game ▶ n. a game played using a computer, typically a video game.

com·put·er graph·ics ▶ plural n. another term for GRAPHICS (sense 3).

com·put·er·ist /kəm'pyōōtərist/ ▶ n. a (frequent) user of computers.

com·put·er·ize /kəm'pyōōtə,rīz/ ▶ v. [trans.] [often as adj.] (**computerized**) convert to a system that is operated or controlled by computer. ■ convert (information) to a form that is stored or processed by computer. — **com·put·er·i·za·tion** /kəm,pyōōtərə'zāsHən/ n.

com·put·er-lit·er·ate ▶ adj. (of a person) having sufficient knowledge and skill to be able to use computers; familiar with the operation of computers. — **com·put·er lit·er·a·cy** n.

com·put·er pro·gram·mer ▶ n. a person who writes programs for the operation of computers, esp. as an occupation.

com·put·er sci·ence ▶ n. the study of the principles and use of computers.

com·put·er vi·rus ▶ n. see VIRUS.

com·put·ing /kəm'pyōōtiNG/ ▶ n. the use or operation of computers.

com·rade /'käm,rad; 'kämrəd/ ▶ n. a companion who shares one's activities or is a fellow member of an organization. ■ (also **comrade-in-arms**) a fellow soldier or serviceman. — **com·rade·ly** adj. **com·rade·ship** n. [16th C.: from Fr. *camerade*, from Sp. *camarada* 'roommate,' from L. *camera* 'chamber.']

Com·sat /'kämsat/ n. trademark the Communications Satellite Corporation, a private corporation authorized by Congress to develop commercial communications satellite systems. ■ (**comsat**) informal a communications satellite. [1960s: blend.]

Com·stock·er·y /'käm,stäkərē; 'kəm-/ ▶ n. excessive opposition to supposed immorality in the arts. [named for Anthony Comstock (1844–1915), US author and reformer.]

Com·stock Lode /'käm,stäk/ a historic gold and silver source in the Virginia Mountains of western Nevada.

Comte /kôNt/, Auguste (1798–1857), French philosopher. He was a cofounder of sociology. — **Comt·ism** /'kôNtizəm/ n.

con[1] /kän/ informal ▶ v. (**conned, con·ning**) [trans.] persuade (someone) to do or believe something, typically by use of a deception. ▶ n. an instance of deceiving or tricking someone. [abbrev. of CONFIDENCE, as in *confidence game*.]

con[2] ▶ n. a disadvantage. [from L. *contra* 'against.']

con[3] ▶ n. informal a convict.

con[4] var. of CONN.

con[5] ▶ n. informal a convention, esp. one for science-fiction enthusiasts. [1970s: abbrev.]

con- ▶ prefix var. of COM- assimilated before *c, d, f, g, j, n, q, s, t, v*, and sometimes before vowels (as in *concord, condescend, confide*, etc.). [L. var. of *com-*.]

Co·na·kry /'känəkrē/ the capital and chief port of Guinea, on the Atlantic coast; pop. 950,000.

con a·mo·re /,kän ə'môrā/ ▶ adv. Music (esp. as a direction) with tenderness. [Ital., 'with love.']

Co·nan Doyle /'kōnən 'doil/ see DOYLE.

co·na·tion /kō'nāsHən/ ▶ n. Philos. Psychol. the mental faculty of purpose, desire, or will to perform an action; volition. [17th C.: from L. *conatio(n-)*, from *conari* 'to try.']

con bri·o /kän 'brēō; kōn/ ▶ adv. Music (esp. as a direction) with vigor. [Ital.]

con·cat·e·nate /kən'katn,āt/ ▶ v. [trans.] formal tech. link (things) together in a chain or series. — **con·cat·e·na·tion** /kən,katn'āsHən/ [15th C.: from late L. *concatenat-* 'linked together,' from v. *concatenare*, from *con-* 'together' + *catenare*, from *catena* 'chain.']

con·cave /kän'kāv; 'kän,kāv/ ▶ adj. having an outline or surface that curves inward like the interior of a circle or sphere. Compare with CONVEX (sense 1). See illustration at CONVEX. — **con·cave·ly** adv. [ME: from L. *concavus*, from *con-* 'together' + *cavus* 'hollow.']

con·cav·i·ty /kän'kavitē/ ▶ n. (pl. **-ties**) the state or quality of being concave. ■ a concave surface or thing.

con·ca·vo-con·cave /kän'kāvō kän'kāv/ ▶ adj. another term for BICONCAVE.

con·ca·vo-con·vex /kän'kāvō kän'veks/ ▶ adj. (of a lens) concave on one side and convex on the other and thickest at the periphery.

con·ceal /kən'sēl/ ▶ v. [trans.] keep from sight; hide. ■ keep (something) secret; prevent from being known or noticed: *love that they had to conceal from others*. — **con·ceal·a·ble** adj. **con·ceal·ment** n. [ME: from OFr. *conceler*, from L. *concelare*, from *con-* 'completely' + *celare* 'hide.']

con·ceal·er /kən'sēlər/ ▶ n. a flesh-toned cosmetic stick used to cover facial blemishes and dark circles under the eyes.

con·cede /kən'sēd/ ▶ v. 1 [reporting verb] admit that something is true or valid after first denying or resisting it. ■ [trans.] admit (defeat) in a contest: *he conceded defeat*. ■ [trans.] admit defeat in (a contest). 2 [trans.] surrender or yield (something that one possesses): *to concede all the territory he'd won*. ■ grant (a right, privilege, or demand). ■ (in sports) fail to prevent the scoring of (a goal or point) by an opponent. ■ allow (a lead or advantage) to slip: *he took an early lead that he never conceded*. — **con·ced·er** n. [15th C.: from Fr. *concéder* or L. *concedere*, from *con-* 'completely' + *cedere* 'yield.']

con·ceit /kən'sēt/ ▶ n. 1 excessive pride in oneself. 2 a fanciful expression in writing or speech; an elaborate metaphor. ■ an artistic effect or device. ■ a fanciful notion. [ME: from CONCEIVE.]

con·ceit·ed /kən'sētid/ ▶ adj. excessively proud of oneself; vain. — **con·ceit·ed·ly** adv. **con·ceit·ed·ness** n.

con·ceiv·a·ble /kən'sēvəbəl/ ▶ adj. capable of being imagined or grasped mentally. — **con·ceiv·a·bil·i·ty** /kən,sēvə'bilitē/ n.

con·ceiv·a·bly /kən'sēvəblē/ ▶ adv. [sentence adverb] it is conceivable or imaginable that.

con·ceive /kən'sēv/ ▶ v. [trans.] (often **be conceived**) 1 become pregnant with (a child). ■ [intrans.] (of a woman) become pregnant. 2 form or devise (a plan or idea) in the mind. ■ form a mental representation of; imagine. ■ become affected by (a feeling): *he conceived a passion for football*. [ME: from OFr. *concevoir*, from L. *concipere*, from *com-* 'together' + *capere* 'take.']

con·cel·e·brate /kän'selə,brāt/ ▶ v. [trans.] Christian Church officiate jointly at (a Mass): *to concelebrate a Mass with other priests*. — **con·cel·e·brant** /-brənt/ n. **con·cel·e·bra·tion** /kän,selə'brāsHən/ n. [19th C.: from L. *concelebrat-* 'celebrated together,' from the v. *concelebrare*, from *con-* 'together' + *celebrare* (see CELEBRATE).]

con·cen·ter /kən'sentər; kän-/ ▶ v. [trans.] concentrate (something) in a small space or area. ■ [intrans.] come together or collect at a common center: *his thoughts concenter there monotonously*. [16th C.: from Fr. *concentrer*, from L. *con-* 'together' + *centrum* 'center.']

con·cen·trate /'känsən,trāt/ ▶ v. 1 [intrans.] focus one's attention or mental effort on a particular object or activity: *she couldn't concentrate on the movie*. ■ (**concentrate on/upon**) do or deal with (one particular thing) above all others. 2 [trans.] (often **be concentrated**) gather (people or things) together in numbers or in a mass to one point. ■ [intrans.] come together in this way: *troops were concentrating at the western front*. ■ increase the strength or proportion of (a substance or solution) by removing or reducing the water or other diluting agent or by selective accumulation of atoms or molecules. ▶ n. a substance made by removing water or other diluting agent; a concentrated form of something, esp. food. — **con·cen·tra·tive** /-,trātiv/ adj. **con·cen·tra·tor** /-,trātər/ n. [17th C.: Latinized form of CONCENTER, or from Fr. *concentrer* 'to concentrate.']

con·cen·trat·ed /'känsən,trātid/ ▶ adj. 1 wholly directed to one thing; intense: *a concentrated campaign*. 2 gathered in one place. ■ (of a substance or solution) present in a high proportion relative to other substances; having had water or other diluting agent removed or reduced. — **con·cen·trat·ed·ly** adv.

con·cen·tra·tion /,känsən'trāsHən/ ▶ n. 1 the action or power of focusing one's attention or mental effort. ■ (**concentration on/upon**) dealing with one particular thing above all others. 2 a close gathering of people or things. ■ the action of gathering together closely. 3 the relative amount of a given substance contained within a solution or in a particular volume of space; the amount of solute per unit volume of solution. ■ the action of strengthening a solution by the removal of water or other diluting agent or by the selective accumulation of atoms or molecules.

con·cen·tra·tion camp ▶ n. a place where large numbers of political prisoners or members of persecuted minorities are imprisoned, esp. in Nazi Germany and occupied Europe in 1933–45.

con·cen·tric /kən'sentrik; kän-/ ▶ adj. of or denoting circles, arcs, or other shapes that share the same center, the larger often completely surrounding the smaller. — **con·cen·tri·cal·ly** adv. **con·cen·tric·i·ty** /,känsen'trisitē/ n. [ME: from OFr. *concentrique* or med. L. *concentricus*, from *con-* 'together' + *centrum* 'center.']

Con·cep·ción /kän,sepsē'ōn/ a city in southern central Chile; pop. 294,000.

con·cept /'känsept/ ▶ n. an abstract idea; a general notion. ■ a plan or intention; a conception. ■ an idea or invention to help sell or publicize a commodity. ■ Philos. an idea or mental picture of a group or class of objects formed by combining all their aspects. ■ [as adj.] (of a car or other vehicle) produced as an experimental model to test the viability of new design features. [16th C.: from L. *conceptum* 'something conceived,' from *concipere* (see CONCEIVE).]

con·cept al·bum ▶ n. a rock album featuring a cycle of songs expressing a particular theme or idea.

con·cep·tion /kən'sepsHən/ ▶ n. 1 the action of conceiving a child or of a child being conceived. ■ the forming or devising of a plan or idea. 2 the way in which something is perceived or regarded. ■ a general notion; an abstract idea. ■ a plan or intention. ■ understanding; ability to imagine: *he had no conception of politics*. — **con·cep·tion·al** /-sHənl/ adj. [ME: via OFr. from L. *conceptio(n-)*, from the v. *concipere* (see CONCEIVE).]

con·cep·tu·al /kən'sepCHo͞oəl/ ▶**adj.** of, relating to, or based on mental concepts. —**con·cep·tu·al·ly** /kəm'sepCHo͞oəlē/ **adv.** [17th C.: from med. L. *conceptualis*, from L. *concept-* 'conceived,' from the v. *concipere* (see CONCEPT).]

con·cep·tu·al art (also **con·cept art**) ▶**n.** art in which the idea presented by the artist is considered more important than the finished product, if any exists.

con·cep·tu·al·ism /kən'sepCHo͞oə,lizəm/ ▶**n.** Philos. the theory that universals can be said to exist, but only as concepts in the mind. —**con·cep·tu·al·ist n.**

con·cep·tu·al·ize /kən'sepCHo͞oə,līz/ ▶**v.** [trans.] form a concept or idea of (something): *we can more easily conceptualize speed in miles per hour.* —**con·cep·tu·al·i·za·tion** /kən,sepCHo͞oələ'zāSHən/ **n. con·cep·tu·al·iz·er n.**

con·cep·tus /kən'septəs/ ▶**n.** (pl. **-tus·es**) tech. the embryo in the uterus, esp. during the early stages of pregnancy. [18th C.: from L., lit. 'conception, embryo.']

con·cern /kən'sərn/ ▶**v.** [trans.] **1** relate to; be about. ■ be relevant or important to; affect or involve. ■ (**be concerned with**) regard it as important or interesting to do something. ■ (**be concerned in**) formal have a specific connection with or responsibility for. ■ (**concern oneself with**) interest or involve oneself in. **2** worry (someone); make anxious. ▶**n. 1** anxiety; worry. ■ a cause of anxiety or worry. **2** a matter of interest or importance to someone. ■ (**concerns**) affairs; issues. **3** a business; a firm: *a small, debt-ridden concern.*

– PHRASES **as** (or **so**) **far as —— is concerned** as regards the interests or case of ——: *the measures are irrelevant as far as inflation is concerned.* **have no concern with** formal have nothing to do with. **to whom it may concern** a formula placed at the beginning of a letter or document when the identity of the reader or readers is unknown. [ME: from Fr. *concerner* or late L. *concernere*, from *con-* (intensifier) + *cernere* 'sift.']

con·cerned /kən'sərnd/ ▶**adj.** worried, troubled, or anxious: *the villagers are concerned about burglaries.* —**con·cern·ed·ly** /-'sərnidlē/ **adv.**

con·cern·ing /kən'sərniNG/ ▶**prep.** on the subject of or in connection with; about: *dreadful stories concerning a horrible beast.*

con·cert ▶**n.** /'känsərt/ **1** a musical performance given in public, typically by several performers or of several separate compositions. ■ [as adj.] of, relating to, or denoting the performance of music written for opera, ballet, or theater on its own without the accompanying dramatic action: *the concert version of the fourth interlude from the opera.* See also CONCERT PERFORMANCE. **2** formal agreement, accordance, or harmony. ▶**v.** /kən'sərt/ [trans.] formal arrange (something) by mutual agreement or coordination.

– PHRASES **in concert 1** acting jointly. **2** (of music or a performer) giving a public performance; live. [16th C.: from Fr. *concerter*, from Ital. *concertare* 'harmonize.']

con·cer·tan·te /,käsər'täntē; ,känCHər-; -tā/ ▶**adj. 1** denoting a piece of music containing one or more solo parts, typically of less prominence or weight than in a concerto. See also SINFONIA CONCERTANTE. **2** esp. hist. denoting prominent instrumental parts present throughout a piece of music, esp. in baroque and early classical compositions. [Ital., 'harmonizing,' from *concertare.*]

con·cert band ▶**n.** a relatively large group of brass, woodwind, and percussion players that performs in a concert hall, as distinguished from a marching band.

con·cert·ed /kən'sərtəd/ ▶**adj. 1** [attrib.] jointly arranged, planned, or carried out; coordinated. ■ strenuously carried out; done with great effort. **2** (of music) arranged in several parts of equal importance: *concerted secular music for voices.*

con·cert·go·er /'känsərt,gōər/ ▶**n.** a person who attends a concert, esp. one who does so regularly.

con·cert grand ▶**n.** the largest size of grand piano, up to 2.75 m long, used for concerts.

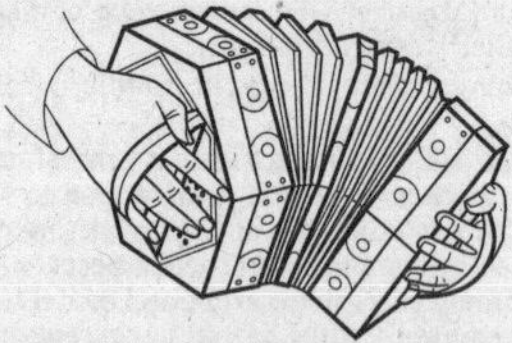

concertina

con·cer·ti·na /,känsər'tēnə/ ▶**n.** a small musical instrument, typically polygonal in form, played by stretching and squeezing between the hands, to work a central bellows that blows air over reeds, each note being sounded by a button. Compare with ACCORDION. ■ [as adj.] opening or closing in multiple folds: *concertina doors.* ▶**v.** (**-ti·naed** /-'tēnəd/) [trans.] extend, compress, or collapse in folds like those of a concertina. [19th C.: from CONCERT + -INA.]

con·cer·ti·no /,känCHər'tēnō/ ▶**n.** (pl. **-nos**) **1** a simple or short concerto. **2** a solo instrument or solo instruments playing with an orchestra. [18th C.: Ital., dimin. of *concerto* (see CONCERTO).]

con·cert·ize /'känsər,tīz/ ▶**v.** [intrans.] give a concert or concerts.

con·cert·mas·ter /'känsərt,mastər/ ▶**n.** (fem. **con·cert·mis·tress**) the leading first-violin player in some orchestras.

con·cer·to /kən'CHertō/ ▶**n.** (pl. **-tos** or **-ti** /-tē/) a musical composition for a solo instrument or instruments accompanied by an orchestra, esp. one conceived on a relatively large scale. [18th C.: Ital., from *concertare* 'harmonize.']

con·cer·to gros·so /'grōsō; 'grô-/ ▶**n.** (pl. **con·cer·ti gros·si** /'grōsē; 'grô-/) a musical composition for a group of solo instruments accompanied by an orchestra. The term is used mainly of baroque works. [18th C.: Ital., lit. 'big concerto.']

con·cert o·ver·ture ▶**n.** a piece of music in the style of an overture but intended for independent performance.

con·cert per·for·mance ▶**n. 1** a performance of a piece of music written for an opera, ballet, religious service, etc., at a concert without the accompanying dramatic action, dance, or liturgy. **2** a performance of a piece of music at a live concert.

con·cert pitch ▶**n.** Music a standard for the tuning of musical instruments, in which the note A above middle C has a frequency of 440 Hz. ■ fig. a state of readiness, efficiency, and keenness.

con·ces·sion /kən'seSHən/ ▶**n. 1** a thing that is granted, esp. in response to demands; a thing conceded. ■ the action of conceding, granting, or yielding something. ■ (**a concession to**) a gesture, esp. a token one, made in recognition of a demand or prevailing standard. **2** a preferential allowance or rate given by an organization: *tax concessions.* **3** the right to use land or other property for a specified purpose, granted by a government, company, or other controlling body: *new logging concessions.* ■ a commercial operation within the premises of a larger concern, typically selling refreshments. [ME: from L. *concessio(n-)*, from the v. *concedere* (see CONCEDE).]

con·ces·sion·aire /kən,seSHə'ne(ə)r/ (also **con·ces·sion·er**) ▶**n.** the holder of a concession or grant, esp. for the use of land or commercial premises. [19th C.: from Fr. *concessionnaire*, from L. *concessio(n)-*.]

con·ces·sion·al /kən'seSHənl/ ▶**adj.** [attrib.] (of a rate or allowance) constituting a concession.

con·ces·sive /kən'sesiv/ ▶**adj. 1** characterized by, or tending to concession. **2** Gram. (of a preposition or conjunction) introducing a phrase or clause denoting a circumstance that might be expected to preclude the action of the main clause, but does not (e.g., *in spite of, although*).

conch /käNGk; känCH;/ ▶**n.** (pl. **conchs** /käNGks;/ or **conch·es** /'känCHiz/) **1** (also **conch shell**) a tropical marine mollusk (*Strombus* and other genera, family Strombidae) with a spiral shell that may bear long projections and have a flared lip. ■ a shell of this kind blown like a trumpet to produce a musical note, often depicted as played by Tritons and other mythological figures. **2** Archit. the roof of a semicircular apse, shaped like half a dome. **3** another term for CONCHA. [ME: from L. *concha* 'shell,' from Gk. *konkhē* 'mussel, cockle.']

con·cha /'käNGkə/ ▶**n.** (pl. **-chae** /-kē; -kī/) Anat. Zool. a body part that resembles a spiral shell, in particular: ■ the depression in the external ear leading to its central opening. ■ any of several thin, scroll-like (turbinate) bones in the sides of the nasal cavity. [16th C.: from L. (see CONCH).]

con·chif·er·ous /käNG'kifərəs/ ▶**adj.** producing, bearing, or characterized by the presence of shells.

con·chi·o·lin /käNG'kīəlin/ ▶**n.** Zool. a tough, insoluble protein secreted by mollusks, forming the organic matrix of the shell within which calcium carbonate is deposited. [19th C.: from L. *concha* 'shell' + the dimin. suffix *-iola* + -IN[1].]

con·choi·dal /käNG'koidl/ ▶**adj.** esp. Mineral. denoting a type of fracture in a solid (such as flint or quartz) that results in a smooth rounded surface resembling the shape of a scallop shell.

con·chol·o·gy /käNG'käləjē/ ▶**n.** the scientific study or collection of mollusk shells. Compare with MALACOLOGY. —**con·cho·log·i·cal** /,käNGkə'läjikəl/ **adj. con·chol·o·gist n.** [18th C.: from Gk. *konkhē* 'shell.']

con·cierge /kôN'syerZH; ,känsē'erZH/ ▶**n. 1** (esp. in France) a caretaker of an apartment complex or a small hotel, typically one living on the premises. **2** a hotel employee whose job is to assist guests by making theater and restaurant reservations, etc. [16th C.: Fr., prob. based on L. *conservus* 'fellow slave.']

con·cil·i·ar /kən'silēər/ ▶**adj.** of, relating to, or proceeding from a council, esp. an ecclesiastical one. [17th C.: from med. L. *consiliarius* 'counselor,' from L. *concilium* (see COUNCIL).]

con·cil·i·ate /kən'silē,āt/ ▶**v.** [trans.] stop (someone) from being angry or discontented; placate; pacify. ■ [intrans.] act as a mediator. ■ formal reconcile; make compatible: *all complaints about charges will be conciliated if possible.* —**con·cil·i·a·tion** /kən,silē'āSHən/ **n. con·cil·i·a·tive** /-'silēətiv; -ē,ātiv/ **adj. con·cil·i·a·tor** /-,ātər/ **n.** [16th C.: from L. *conciliat-* 'combined,' from *concilium* (see COUNCIL).]

con·cil·i·a·to·ry /kən'silēə,tôrē/ ▶**adj.** intended or likely to placate or pacify: *a conciliatory approach.* —**con·cil·i·a·to·ri·ness n.**

con·cise /kən'sīs/ ▶**adj.** giving a lot of information clearly and in a few words; brief but comprehensive. —**con·cise·ly adv. con·cise·ness n. con·ci·sion** /-'sizHən/ **n.** [16th C.: from Fr. *concis* or L. *concisus*, past part. of *concidere* 'cut up, cut down,' from *con-* 'completely' + *caedere* 'to cut.']

con·clave /'känklāv/ ▶**n.** a private meeting. ■ (in the Roman Catholic Church) the assembly of cardinals for the election of a pope. ■ the meeting place for such an assembly. [ME: via Fr. from L. *conclave* 'lockable room,' from *con-* 'with' + *clavis* 'key.']

con·clude /kən'klo͞od/ ▶**v. 1** [trans.] bring (something) to an end. ■ [intrans.]

come to an end: *the talk concluded with slides.* ■ formally and finally settle or arrange (a treaty or agreement). **2** arrive at a judgment or opinion by reasoning. ■ [with direct speech] say in conclusion: *"It's a wicked old world," she concluded.* [ME: from L. *concludere*, from *con-* 'completely' + *claudere* 'shut.']

con·clu·sion /kən'klo͞oZHən/ ▸ **n.** **1** the end or finish of an event or process. ■ the summing-up of an argument or text. ■ the settling or arrangement of a treaty or agreement. **2** a judgment or decision reached by reasoning: *each research group came to a similar conclusion.* ■ Logic a proposition that is reached from given premises.
– PHRASES **in conclusion** lastly; to sum up. **jump** (or **leap**) **to conclusions** make a hasty judgment before learning or considering all the facts. [ME: from L. *conclusio(n-)*, from the v. *concludere* (see CONCLUDE).]

con·clu·sive /kən'klo͞osiv; -ziv/ ▸ **adj.** (of evidence or argument) serving to prove a case; convincing. ■ (of a victory) achieved easily or by a large margin. — **con·clu·sive·ly adv. con·clu·sive·ness n.**

con·coct /kən'käkt/ ▸ **v.** [trans.] make (a dish or meal) by combining various ingredients. ■ create or devise (said esp. of a story or plan). — **con·coct·er n. con·coc·tion** /kən'käksHən/ **n.** [16th C.: from L. *concoct-*, 'cooked together,' from *concoquere*.]

con·com·i·tance /kən'kämitəns/ ▸ **n.** (also **con·com·i·tan·cy**) the fact of existing or occurring together with something else. ■ Theol. the doctrine that the body and blood of Christ are each present in both the bread and the wine of the Eucharist.

con·com·i·tant /kən'kämitənt/ formal ▸ **adj.** naturally accompanying or associated. ▸ **n.** a phenomenon that naturally accompanies or follows something. — **con·com·i·tant·ly adv.** [17th C.: from late L. *concomitant-* 'accompanying,' from *concomitari*, from *con-* 'together with' + *comitari*, from L. *comes* 'companion.']

Con·cord[1] /'käNGkərd; -kôrd/ **1** a city in north central California; pop. 121,780. **2** a town in northeastern Massachusetts; pop. 16,993. Battles here and at Lexington in April 1775 marked the start of the American Revolution. **3** the capital of New Hampshire, in the southern part of the state; pop. 40,687. **4** a city in south central North Carolina; pop. 55,977.

Con·cord[2] ▸ **n.** a variety of dessert grape developed at Concord, Massachusetts.

con·cord /'käNGkôrd; 'kän-/ ▸ **n.** **1** formal agreement or harmony between people or groups. ■ a treaty. **2** Gram. agreement between words in gender, number, case, person, etc. **3** Music a chord that is pleasing or satisfactory in itself. [ME: from OFr. *concorde*, from L. *concordia*, from *concors* 'of one mind,' from *con-* 'together' + *cor, cord-* 'heart.']

con·cord·ance /kən'kôrdns/ ▸ **n.** **1** an alphabetical list of words present in a text, usually with citations of the passages concerned: *a concordance to the Bible.* **2** formal agreement. ■ Med. the inheritance by two related individuals (esp. twins) of the same genetic characteristic, such as susceptibility to a disease. ▸ **v.** [trans.] [often as adj.] (**concordanced**) make a concordance of: *the value of concordanced information.* [ME: from OFr., from med. L. *concordantia*, from *concordant-* 'being of one mind' (see CONCORDANT).]

con·cord·ant /kən'kôrdnt/ ▸ **adj.** in agreement; consistent: *the answers were roughly concordant.* ■ Geol. corresponding in direction with the planes of adjacent or underlying strata. ■ Med. (of twins) inheriting the same genetic characteristic, such as susceptibility to a disease. ■ Music in harmony. — **con·cord·ant·ly adv.**

con·cor·dat /kən'kôrdat/ ▸ **n.** an agreement or treaty, esp. one between the Vatican and a secular government relating to matters of mutual interest. [17th C.: from Fr., or from L. *concordatum*, neut. past part. of *concordare* 'be of one mind.']

Con·corde /'käNGkôrd; 'kän-/ a supersonic airliner able to cruise at twice the speed of sound.

Con·cord grape ▸ **n.** a cultivated variety of fox grape, used to make wine, juice, and jellies.

Con·cor·dia /kän'kôrdēə/ a port city in northeastern Argentina; pop. 139,000.

con·course /'känkôrs; 'käNG-/ ▸ **n.** **1** a large open area inside or in front of a public building, as in an airport or train station: *the domestic arrivals concourse.* **2** formal a crowd or assembly of people. ■ the action of coming together or meeting. [ME: from OFr. *concours*, from L. *concursus*, from *concurs-* 'run together,' from *concurrere* (see CONCUR).]

con·cres·cence /kən'kresəns/ ▸ **n.** Biol. the coalescence or growing together of parts originally separate. — **con·cres·cent** /-'kresənt/ **adj.** [17th C.: from CON- 'together' + *-crescence*.]

con·crete ▸ **adj.** /kän'krēt; 'känkrēt; kən'krēt/ existing in a material or physical form; real or solid; not abstract. ■ specific; definite. ■ (of a noun) denoting a material object as opposed to an abstract quality, state, or action. ▸ **n.** /'känkrēt; kän'krēt/ a heavy, rough building material made from a mixture of broken stone or gravel, sand, cement, and water, that can be spread or poured into molds and that forms a stonelike mass on hardening. ▸ **v.** /'känkrēt; kän'krēt/ [trans.] (often **be concreted**) cover (an area) with concrete: ■ [trans.] fix in position with concrete: *the post is concreted into the ground.*
– PHRASES **be set in concrete** (of a policy or idea) be fixed and unalterable. — **con·crete·ly adv. con·crete·ness n.** [ME: from Fr. *concret* or L. *concretus*, past part. of *concrescere* 'grow together.']

con·crete jun·gle ▸ **n.** a city or area of a city that has a high density of large, unattractive, modern buildings and that is perceived as an unpleasant living environment.

con·crete mu·sic ▸ **n.** another term for MUSIQUE CONCRÈTE.

con·crete po·et·ry ▸ **n.** poetry in which the meaning or effect is conveyed partly or wholly by visual means, using patterns of words or letters and other typographical devices.

con·cre·tion /kən'krēsHən; kän-/ ▸ **n.** a hard solid mass formed by the local accumulation of matter, esp. within the body or within a mass of sediment. ■ the formation of such a mass. — **con·cre·tion·ar·y** /-SHə,nerē/ **adj.**

con·cret·ism /kän'krētizəm; 'känkrē,tiz-/ ▸ **n.** the theory or practice of concrete poetry, in which the visual arrangement of words in patterns or forms on the page takes precedence over the semantic or phonetic elements involved.

con·cre·tize /'känkrə,tīz; kän'krētīz/ ▸ **v.** [trans.] make (an idea or concept) real; give specific or definite form to: *the theme park is an attempt to concretize our fantasies.* — **con·cret·i·za·tion** /,känkrētə'zāsHən; ,käNGkrətə-/ **n.**

con·cu·bine /'käNGkyə͝o,bīn/ ▸ **n.** esp. hist. (in polygamous societies) a woman who lives with a man but has lower status than his wife or wives. ■ archaic a mistress. — **con·cu·bi·nage** /kən'kyo͞obənij; kän-/ **n. con·cu·bi·nar·y** /kən'kyo͞obə,nerē; kän-/ **adj.** [ME: from OFr., from L. *concubina*, from *con-* 'with' + *cubare* 'to lie.']

con·cu·pis·cence /kän'kyo͞opisəns; kən-/ ▸ **n.** formal strong sexual desire; lust. [ME: ult. from L. *concupiscere*, from *con-* (intensifier) + *cupere* 'to desire.']

con·cu·pis·cent /kän'kyo͞opisənt; kən-/ ▸ **adj.** formal filled with sexual desire; lustful: *concupiscent dreams.*

con·cur /kən'kər/ ▸ **v.** (**-curred, -cur·ring**) [intrans.] **1** be of the same opinion; agree. ■ (**concur with**) agree with (a decision, opinion, or finding): *we strongly concur with this recommendation.* **2** happen or occur at the same time; coincide. — **con·cur·rence** /-'kərəns/ **n. con·cur·ren·cy** /-'kərənsē/ **n.** [ME: from L. *concurrere* 'run together,' from *con-* 'together' + *currere* 'to run.']

con·cur·rent /kən'kərənt; -'kə-rənt/ ▸ **adj.** existing, happening, or done at the same time. ■ (of two or more prison sentences) to be served at the same time. ■ Math. (of three or more lines) meeting at or tending toward one point. — **con·cur·rent·ly adv.**

con·cur·rent res·o·lu·tion ▸ **n.** a resolution adopted by both houses of a legislative assembly that does not require the signature of the chief executive and that does not have the force of law.

con·cuss /kən'kəs/ ▸ **v.** [trans.] [usu. as adj.] (**concussed**) hit the head of (a person or animal), causing temporary unconsciousness or confusion. — **con·cus·sive** /-'kəsiv/ **adj.** [16th C.: from L. *concuss-* 'dashed together,' from v. *concutere*, from *con-* 'together' + *quatere* 'shake.']

con·cus·sion /kən'kəsHən/ ▸ **n.** **1** temporary unconsciousness caused by a blow to the head. Also, loosely, aftereffects such as confusion or temporary incapacity. **2** a violent shock as from a heavy blow.

con·demn /kən'dem/ ▸ **v.** [trans.] **1** express complete disapproval of, typically in public; censure. **2** sentence (someone) to a particular punishment, esp. death: *the rebels had been condemned to death.* ■ (usu. **be condemned**) officially declare (something, esp. a building) to be unfit for use. ■ prove or show the guilt of. ■ (of circumstances) force (someone) to endure something unpleasant or undesirable. — **con·dem·na·ble** /-'dem(n)əbəl/ **adj. con·dem·na·tion** /,kändem'nāsHən; -dəm-/ **n. con·dem·na·to·ry** /-'demnə,tôrē/ **adj.** [ME: from OFr. *condemner*, from L. *condemnare*, from *con-* (intensifier) + *damnare* 'inflict loss on' (see DAMN).]

con·den·sate /'kändən,sāt; -den-; kən'densāt/ ▸ **n.** liquid formed by condensation. ■ Chem. a compound produced by a condensation reaction.

con·den·sa·tion /,känden'sāsHən; -dən-/ ▸ **n.** **1** water that collects as droplets on a cold surface when humid air is in contact with it. **2** the process of becoming more dense, in particular: ■ the conversion of a vapor or gas to a liquid. ■ (also **condensation reaction**) Chem. a reaction in which two molecules combine to form a larger molecule, producing a small molecule such as H_2O as a byproduct. ■ Psychol. the fusion of two or more images, ideas, or symbolic meanings into a single composite or new image, as a primary process in unconscious thought exemplified in dreams. **3** a concise version of something, esp. a text.

con·dense /kən'dens/ ▸ **v.** **1** [trans.] make (something) denser or more concentrated. ■ [usu. as adj.] (**condensed**) thicken (a liquid) by reducing the water content, typically by heating: *condensed soup.* ■ express (a piece of writing or speech) in fewer words; make concise. ■ (**condensed**) (in word processing) (of character spacing) reduced. **2** [intrans.] be changed from a gas or vapor to a liquid. ■ [trans.] cause (a gas or vapor) to be changed to a liquid: *the cold air was condensing his breath.* — **con·den·sa·ble adj.** [ME: from OFr. *condenser* or L. *condensare*, from *condensus* 'very thick,' from *con-* 'completely' + *densus* 'dense.']

con·densed milk ▸ **n.** canned milk that has been thickened by evaporation and sweetened.

con·dens·er /kən'densər/ ▸ **n.** a person or thing that condenses something, in particular: ■ an apparatus or container for condensing vapor. ■ a lens or system of lenses for collecting and directing light. ■ another term for CAPACITOR.

con·de·scend /,kändə'send/ ▸ **v.** [intrans.] show feelings of superiority; patronize. ■ [with infin.] do something in a haughty way, as though it is below one's dignity or level of importance. — **con·de·scend·ence** /-'sendəns/ **n.** (rare). **con·de·scen·sion** /-'sencHən/ **n.** [ME: from OFr.

condescendre, from eccles. L. *condescendere*, from *con-* + *descendere* 'descend.']

con·de·scend·ing /ˌkändəˈsendiNG/ ▶ **adj.** acting in a way that betrays a feeling of patronizing superiority. ■ (of an action) demonstrating such an attitude. — **con·de·scend·ing·ly adv.**

con·dign /kənˈdīn/ ▶ **adj.** formal (of punishment or retribution) appropriate to the crime or wrongdoing; fitting and deserved. — **con·dign·ly adv.** [ME: from OFr. *condigne*, from L. *condignus*, from *con-* 'altogether' + *dignus* 'worthy.']

con·di·ment /ˈkändəmənt/ ▶ **n.** a substance such as salt or ketchup that is used to add flavor to food. [ME: from L. *condimentum*, from *condire* 'to pickle.']

con·di·tion /kənˈdisHən/ ▶ **n.** **1** [usu. with adj.] the state of something, esp. with regard to its appearance, quality, or working order. ■ a person's or animal's state of health or physical fitness. ■ [often with adj.] an illness or other medical problem: *a heart condition.* ■ [in sing.] a particular state of existence: *a condition of misery.* **2** (**conditions**) [often with adj.] the circumstances affecting the way in which people live or work, esp. with regard to their safety or well-being. ■ the factors or prevailing situation influencing the performance or the outcome of a process: *present market conditions.* ■ the prevailing state of the weather, ground, sea, or atmosphere at a particular time, esp. as it affects a sporting event. **3** a state of affairs that must exist or be brought about before something else is possible or permitted. ▶ **v.** [trans.] **1** (often **be conditioned**) have a significant influence on or determine (the manner or outcome of something). ■ train or accustom (someone or something) to behave in a certain way or to accept certain circumstances. **2** bring (something) into the desired state for use: *a product for conditioning leather.* ■ [often as adj.] (**conditioned**) make (a person or animal) fit and healthy. ■ apply something to (the skin or hair) to give it a healthy or attractive look or feel: *I condition my hair regularly.* ■ [often as adj.] (**conditioned**) bring (beer or stout) to maturation after fermentation while the yeast is still present: [in comb.] *cask-conditioned real ales.* ■ [intrans.] (of a beer or stout) undergo such a process. **3** set prior requirements on (something) before it can occur or be done.

– PHRASES **in** (or **out of**) **condition** in a fit (or unfit) physical state. **in no condition to do something** certainly not fit or well enough to do something: *you're in no condition to tackle the stairs.* **on condition that** with the stipulation that. [ME: from OFr. *condicion* (n.), from L. *condicio(n-)* 'agreement,' from *condicere* 'agree,' from *con-* 'with' + *dicere* 'say.']

con·di·tion·al /kənˈdisHənl/ ▶ **adj.** **1** subject to one or more conditions or requirements being met; made or granted on certain terms. **2** Gram. (of a clause, phrase, conjunction, or verb form) expressing a condition. ▶ **n.** **1** Gram. Philos. a conditional clause or conjunction. ■ a statement or sentence containing a conditional clause. **2** Gram. the conditional mood of a verb, for example *should die* in *if I should die.* — **con·di·tion·al·i·ty** /kənˌdisHəˈnalitē/ **n.** **con·di·tion·al·ly adv.**

con·di·tion·al prob·a·bil·i·ty ▶ **n.** Stat. the probability of an event (*A*), given that another (*B*) has already occurred.

con·di·tioned re·sponse (also **conditioned reflex**) ▶ **n.** Psychol. an automatic response established by training to an ordinarily neutral stimulus. See also CLASSICAL CONDITIONING.

con·di·tion·er /kənˈdisH(ə)nər/ ▶ **n.** a substance or appliance used to improve or maintain something's condition: *add a water conditioner to neutralize chlorine.*

con·do /ˈkändō/ ▶ **n.** (pl. **-dos**) informal short for CONDOMINIUM: *a high-rise condo.*

con·dole /kənˈdōl/ ▶ **v.** [intrans.] (**condole with**) express sympathy for (someone); grieve with. [16th C.: from Christian L. *condolere*, from *con-* 'with' + *dolere* 'grieve, suffer.']

con·do·lence /kənˈdōləns/ ▶ **n.** (usu. **condolences**) an expression of sympathy, esp. on the occasion of a death.

con·dom /ˈkändəm; ˈkən-/ ▶ **n.** a thin rubber sheath worn on a man's penis during sexual intercourse as a contraceptive and/or as a protection against infection. [18th C.: origin unknown.]

con·do·min·i·um /ˌkändəˈminēəm/ ▶ **n.** (pl. **-ums**) a building or complex of buildings containing a number of individually owned apartments or houses. ■ each of the individual apartments or houses in such a building or complex. ■ the system of ownership by which these operate, in which owners have full title to the individual apartment or house and an undivided interest in the shared parts of the property. [18th C.: mod. L., from *con-* + *dominium* 'right of ownership' (see DOMINION).]

con·done /kənˈdōn/ ▶ **v.** [trans.] [often with negative] accept and allow (behavior that is considered morally wrong or offensive) to continue. ■ approve or sanction (something), esp. with reluctance. — **con·don·a·ble adj.** **con·do·na·tion** /ˌkändəˈnāsHən; -dō-/ **n.** **con·don·er n.** [19th C.: from L. *condonare* 'refrain from punishing,' from *con-* 'altogether' + *donare* 'give.']

con·dor /ˈkändôr; -dər/ ▶ **n.** a large New World vulture with a bare head and mainly black plumage, living in mountainous country and spending much time soaring. Two species: the **Andean condor** (*Vultur gryphus*) of South America and the **California condor** (*Gymnogyps californianus*), which is close to extinction in the wild. [17th C.: from Sp. *cóndor*, from Quechua *kuntur*.]

California condor

con·dot·tie·re /ˌkändätēˈerē; ˌkändəˈtyerē/ ▶ **n.** (pl. **-tie·ri** pronunc. same) hist. a leader or a member of a troop of mercenaries, esp. in Italy. [Ital., from *condotto* 'troop under contract,' based on *condurre* 'conduct.']

con·duce /kənˈd(y)o͞os/ ▶ **v.** [intrans.] (**conduce to**) formal help to bring about (a particular situation or outcome). [ME: from L. *conducere* 'bring together.']

con·du·cive /kənˈd(y)o͞osiv/ ▶ **adj.** making a certain situation or outcome likely or possible.

con·duct ▶ **n.** /ˈkänˌdəkt/ **1** the manner in which a person behaves, esp. on a particular occasion or in a particular context. **2** the action or manner of managing an activity or organization: *his conduct of the campaign.* ▶ **v.** /kənˈdəkt/ **1** [trans.] organize and carry out. ■ direct the performance of (a piece of music or a musical ensemble). ■ [with obj. and adverbial of direction] lead or guide (someone) to or around a particular place. ■ Physics transmit (a form of energy such as heat or electricity) by conduction. **2** (**conduct oneself**) behave in a specified way. — **con·duct·i·ble** /kənˈdəktəbəl/ **adj.** **con·duct·i·bil·i·ty** /kənˌdəktəˈbilitē/ **n.** [ME: from OFr., from L. *conduct-* 'brought together,' from the v. *conducere*.]

con·duct·ance /kənˈdəktəns/ ▶ **n.** the degree to which an object conducts electricity, calculated as the ratio of the current that flows to the potential difference present. This is the reciprocal of the resistance, and is measured in siemens or mhos. (Symbol: **G**)

con·duct dis·or·der ▶ **n.** a range of antisocial types of behavior displayed in childhood or adolescence.

con·duc·tion /kənˈdəksHən/ ▶ **n.** the process by which heat or electricity is directly transmitted through a substance when there is a difference of temperature or of electrical potential between adjoining regions, without movement of the material. ■ the process by which sound waves travel through a medium. ■ the transmission of impulses along nerves. ■ the conveying of fluid through a pipe or other channel.

con·duc·tive /kənˈdəktiv/ ▶ **adj.** having the property of conducting something (esp. heat or electricity). ■ of or relating to conduction. — **con·duc·tive·ly adv.**

con·duc·tiv·i·ty /ˌkändəkˈtivitē; kənˌdək-/ ▶ **n.** (pl. **-ties**) (also **electrical conductivity**) the degree to which a specified material conducts electricity, calculated as the ratio of the current density in the material to the electric field that causes the flow of current. It is the reciprocal of the resistivity. ■ (also **thermal conductivity**) the rate at which heat passes through a specified material, expressed as the amount of heat that flows per unit time through a unit area with a temperature gradient of one degree per unit distance.

con·duc·tor /kənˈdəktər/ ▶ **n.** **1** a person who directs the performance of an orchestra or choir. **2** a person in charge of a train, streetcar, or other public conveyance, who collects fares and sells tickets. **3** Physics a material or device that conducts or transmits heat, electricity, or sound, esp. when regarded in terms of its capacity to do this. ■ another term for LIGHTNING ROD. — **con·duc·to·ri·al** /ˌkändəkˈtôrēəl; kənˌdək-/ **adj.** **con·duc·tor·ship n.** (in sense 1).

con·duc·tress /kənˈdəktrəs/ ▶ **n.** a female conductor, esp. in a bus or other passenger vehicle.

con·duit /ˈkänd(y)o͞oit; -d(w)it/ ▶ **n.** a channel for conveying water or other fluid: *a conduit for conveying water to the power plant* | fig. *the office acts as a conduit for ideas to flow throughout the organization.* ■ a tube or trough for protecting electric wiring: *the gas pipe should not be close to any electrical conduit.* [ME: from OFr., from med. L. *conductus*.]

con·dyle /ˈkändīl/ ▶ **n.** Anat. a rounded protuberance at the end of some bones, forming an articulation with another bone. — **con·dy·lar** /ˈkändələr/ **adj.** **con·dy·loid** /ˈkändəˌloid/ **adj.** [17th C.: from Fr., from L. *condylus*, from Gk. *kondulos* 'knuckle.']

con·dy·lo·ma /ˌkändəˈlōmə/ ▶ **n.** (pl. **-mas** or **-ma·ta** /-mətə/) Med. a raised growth on the skin resembling a wart, typically in the genital region, caused by viral infection or syphilis and transmissible by contact. — **con·dy·lom·a·tous** /-mətəs/ **adj.** [ME: via L. from Gk. *kondulōma* 'callous lump,' from *kondulos* 'knuckle.']

cone /kōn/ ▶ **n.** **1** a solid or hollow object that tapers from a circular or roughly circular base to a point. ■ Math. a surface or solid figure generated by the straight lines that pass from a circle or other closed curve to a single point (the vertex) not in the same plane as the curve. A cone with the vertex perpendicularly over the center of a circular base is a **right circular cone.** ■ (also **traffic cone**) a plastic cone-shaped object that is used to separate off or close sections of a road. ■ an edible wafer container shaped like a cone in which ice cream is served. ■ a conical mountain or peak, esp. one of volcanic origin. ■ (also **pyrometric cone**) a ceramic pyramid that melts at a known temperature and is used to indicate the temperature of a kiln. ■ short for CONE SHELL. **2** the dry fruit of a conifer, typically tapering to a rounded end and formed of a tight array of overlapping scales on a central axis that separate to release the seeds. ■ a flower resembling a pine cone, esp. that of the hop plant. **3** Anat. a light-sensitive cell of one of the two types present in the retina of the eye, responding mainly to bright light and responsible for sharpness of vision and color perception. Compare with ROD (sense 5). [ME: from Fr. *cône*, via L. from Gk. *kōnos*.]

coned /kōnd/ ▶ **adj.** conical. ■ having cones.

cone·flow·er /'kōn,flouər/ ▶ **n.** a North American plant (*Rudbeckia*, *Echinacea*, and other genera) of the daisy family that has flowers with conelike disks that appear to consist of soft spines.

purple coneflower

cone shell ▶ **n.** a predatory mollusk (genus *Conus*, family Conidae) of warm seas, with a conical shell that typically displays intricate patterns. It captures prey by injecting venom, which can be lethal to humans.

Con·es·to·ga wag·on /,känə'stōgə/ ▶ **n.** hist. a large covered wagon used for long-distance travel, typically carrying pioneers in the westward migration. [18th C.: named after *Conestoga*, a town in Pennsylvania.]

co·ney /'kōnē/ (also **co·ny**) ▶ **n.** (pl. **-neys**) **1** Brit. & Heraldry a pika. ■ a rabbit. ■ rabbit fur. ■ (in biblical use) a hyrax. **2** a small fish, esp. a grouper (*Epinephelus fulvus*), found on the coasts of the tropical western Atlantic, with variable coloration. [ME: from OFr. *conin*, from L. *cuniculus*.]

Co·ney Is·land[1] /'kōnē/ a resort and amusement park in Brooklyn, New York City, in southern Long Island.

Co·ney Is·land[2] ▶ **n.** informal a hot dog. [named after **Coney Island**, where the hot dog was created and introduced.]

con·fab /'kän,fab; kən'fab/ informal ▶ **n.** an informal private conversation or discussion. ■ a meeting or conference of members of a particular group. ▶ **v.** /kən'fab; 'kän,fab/ (**-fabbed, -fab·bing**) [intrans.] engage in informal private conversation. [abbrev. of *confabulation*.]

con·fab·u·late /kən'fabyə,lāt/ ▶ **v.** [intrans.] **1** formal engage in conversation; talk. **2** Psychiatry fabricate imaginary experiences as compensation for loss of memory. — **con·fab·u·la·tion** /-,fabyə'lāsHən/ **n.** **con·fab·u·la·to·ry** /-lə,tôrē/ **adj.** [17th C.: from L. *confabulat-* 'chatted together,' from v. *confabulari*, from *con-* + *fabulari* (from *fabula* 'fable').]

con·fec·tion /kən'feksHən/ ▶ **n.** **1** a dish or delicacy made with sweet ingredients. ■ an elaborately constructed thing, esp. a frivolous one: *the city is a classical confection of shimmering gold.* ■ a fashionable or elaborate article of women's dress. **2** the action of mixing or compounding something. — **con·fec·tion·ar·y** /-SHə,nerē/ **adj.**

con·fec·tion·er /kən'feksHənər/ ▶ **n.** a person whose occupation is making or selling candy and other sweets.

con·fec·tion·ers' sug·ar (also **con·fec·tion·er's sug·ar**) ▶ **n.** finely powdered sugar with cornstarch added, used for making icings and candy.

con·fec·tion·er·y /kən'feksHə,nerē/ ▶ **n.** (pl. **-er·ies**) candy and other sweets considered collectively. ■ a shop that sells such items.

con·fed·er·a·cy /kən'fedərəsē/ ▶ **n.** (pl. **-cies**) a league or alliance, esp. of confederate states. ■ (**the Confederacy**) another term for **Confederate States of America**. ■ an alliance formed for an unlawful purpose; a conspiracy. [ME: from OFr. *confederacie*, based on L. *confoederare* 'join together in league' (see **confederation**).]

con·fed·er·ate ▶ **adj.** /kən'fedərit/ [attrib.] joined by an agreement or treaty. ■ (**Confederate**) of or relating to the Confederate States of America: *the Confederate flag.* ▶ **n.** /kən'fedərit/ **1** a person one works with, esp. in something secret or illegal; an accomplice. **2** (**Confederate**) a supporter of the Confederate States of America. ▶ **v.** /-,rāt/ [trans.] [usu. as adj.] (**confederated**) bring (states or groups of people) into an alliance: *Switzerland is a model for the new confederated Europe.* [ME: from late L. *confoederatus* (see **federate**).]

Con·fed·er·ate States of A·mer·i·ca (also **the Con·fed·er·a·cy**) the 11 Southern states (Alabama, Arkansas, Florida, Georgia, Louisiana, Mississippi, North Carolina, South Carolina, Tennessee, Texas, and Virginia) that seceded from the United States in 1860–61, thus precipitating the Civil War.

con·fed·er·a·tion /kən,fedə'rāsHən/ ▶ **n.** an organization that consists of a number of parties or groups united in an alliance or league. ■ a more or less permanent union of countries with some or most political power vested in a central authority. ■ the action of confederating or the state of being confederated: *a referendum on confederation.* — **con·fed·er·al** /kən'fedərəl/ **adj.** [ME: ult. from late L. *confederatio(n-)*, from L. *confoederare*, from *con-* 'together' + *foederare* 'join in league with' (from *foedus* 'league').]

con·fer /kən'fər/ ▶ **v.** (**-ferred, -fer·ring**) **1** [trans.] grant or bestow (a title, degree, benefit, or right). **2** [intrans.] have discussions; exchange opinions. — **con·fer·ment** **n.** (in sense 1). **con·fer·ra·ble** **adj.** **con·fer·ral** /-'fərəl/ **n.** (in sense 1). [ME: from L. *conferre*, from *con-* 'together' + *ferre* 'bring.']

con·fer·ee /,känfə'rē/ ▶ **n.** **1** a person who attends a conference. **2** a person on whom something is conferred.

con·fer·ence /'känf(ə)rəns/ ▶ **n.** **1** a formal meeting for discussion. ■ a formal meeting that typically takes place over a number of days and involves people with a shared interest, esp. one held regularly by an association or organization. ■ [usu. as adj.] a linking of several telephones or computers, so that each user may communicate with the others simultaneously. **2** an association of sports teams that play each other. **3** the governing body of some Christian churches, esp. the Methodist Church. ▶ **v.** [intrans.] [usu. as n.] (**conferencing**) take part in a conference or conference call: *video conferencing.*
– PHRASES **in conference** in a meeting.

Con·fer·ence on Dis·ar·ma·ment a committee with forty nations as members that seeks to negotiate multilateral disarmament.

con·fess /kən'fes/ ▶ **v.** [reporting verb] admit or state that one has committed a crime or is at fault in some way. ■ admit or acknowledge something reluctantly, typically because one feels slightly ashamed or embarrassed. ■ [trans.] declare (one's religious faith): *150 people confessed faith in Christ.* ■ declare one's sins formally to a priest. ■ [trans.] (of a priest) hear the confession of (someone) in such a way: *St. Ambrose would weep bitter tears when confessing a sinner.* [ME: from OFr. *confesser*, from L. *confessus*, past part. of *confiteri* 'acknowledge,' from *con-* + *fateri* 'declare.']

con·fes·sant /kən'fesənt/ ▶ **n.** a person who confesses to a priest; a penitent.

con·fess·ed·ly /kən'fesədlē/ ▶ **adv.** by one's own admission.

con·fes·sion /kən'fesHən/ ▶ **n.** **1** a formal statement admitting that one is guilty of a crime. ■ an admission or acknowledgment that one has done something that one is ashamed or embarrassed about. ■ a formal admission of one's sins with repentance and desire of absolution, esp. privately to a priest as a religious duty: *she still had not been to confession.* ■ (**confessions**) often humorous intimate revelations about a person's private life or occupation, esp. as presented in a sensationalized form in a book, newspaper, or movie: *confessions of a driving instructor.* **2** (also **confession of faith**) a statement setting out essential religious doctrine. ■ (also **Confession**) the religious body or church sharing a confession of faith. ■ a statement of one's principles: *his words are a political confession of faith.*

con·fes·sion·al /kən'fesHənl/ ▶ **n.** **1** an enclosed stall in a church divided by a screen or curtain in which a priest sits to hear people confess their sins. **2** an admission or acknowledgment that one has done something that one is ashamed or embarrassed about. ▶ **adj.** **1** (esp. of speech or writing) in which a person reveals or admits to private thoughts or past incidents, esp. ones that cause shame or embarrassment. ■ of or relating to religious confession. **2** of or relating to confessions of faith or doctrinal systems: *the confessional approach to religious education.*

con·fes·sor /kən'fesər/ ▶ **n.** **1** a priest who hears confessions and gives absolution and spiritual counsel. ■ a person to whom another confides personal problems. **2** a person who avows religious faith in the face of opposition, but does not suffer martyrdom. **3** a person who makes a confession.

con·fet·ti /kən'fetē/ ▶ **n.** small pieces of colored paper thrown during a celebration such as a wedding. [19th C.: from Ital., lit. 'sweets,' from L. *confectum*, neut. past part. of *conficere* 'put together.']

con·fi·dant /'känfə,dant; -,dänt/ ▶ **n.** (fem. **con·fi·dante** pronunc. same) a person with whom one shares a secret or private matter, trusting them not to repeat it. [17th C.: alt. of **confident**.]

con·fide /kən'fīd/ ▶ **v.** [reporting verb] tell someone about a secret or private matter while trusting them not to repeat it to others. ■ [intrans.] (**confide in**) trust (someone) enough to tell them of such a secret or private matter. ■ [trans.] (**confide something to**) dated entrust something to (someone) for safekeeping. — **con·fid·ing·ly** **adv.** [ME: from L. *confidere* 'have full trust.']

con·fi·dence /'känfidəns; -,dens/ ▶ **n.** the feeling or belief that one can rely on someone or something; firm trust: *we had every confidence in the staff.* ■ the state of feeling certain about the truth of something. ■ a feeling of self-assurance arising from one's appreciation of one's own abilities or qualities. ■ the telling of private matters or secrets with mutual trust. ■ (often **confidences**) a secret or private matter told to someone under such a condition of trust.
– PHRASES **in someone's confidence** in a position of trust with someone. **take someone into one's confidence** tell someone one's secrets.

con·fi·dence game ▶ **n.** a swindle in which the victim is persuaded to trust the swindler in some way.

con·fi·dence in·ter·val ▶ **n.** Stat. a range of values so defined that there is a specified probability that the value of a parameter lies within it.

con·fi·dence lev·el ▶ **n.** Stat. the probability that the value of a parameter falls within a specified range of values.

con·fi·dence lim·it ▶ **n.** Stat. either of the extreme values of a confidence interval.

con·fi·dence man ▶ **n.** old-fashioned term for **con man**.

con·fi·dent /'känfidənt; -,dent/ ▶ **adj.** feeling or showing confidence in oneself; self-assured. ■ feeling or showing certainty about something. — **con·fi·dent·ly** **adv.** [16th C.: ult. from L. *confident-* 'having full trust,' from the v. *confidere*, from *con-* + *fidere* 'trust.']

con·fi·den·tial /,känfi'dencHəl/ ▶ **adj.** intended to be kept secret: *confidential information.* ■ (of a person's tone of voice) indicating that what one says is private or secret. ■ [attrib.] entrusted with private or restricted information: *a confidential secretary.* — **con·fi·den·ti·al·i·ty** /-,dencHē'alitē/ **n.** **con·fi·den·tial·ly** **adv.**

con·fig·u·ra·tion /kən,fig(y)ə'rāsHən/ ▶ **n.** an arrangement of elements in a particular form, figure, or combination. ■ Chem. the fixed three-dimensional relationship of the atoms in a molecule, defined by the bonds between them. Compare with **conformation**. ■ Comput. the arrangement in which items of computer hardware or software are interconnected: *standard configuration.* ■ Psychol. another term for **gestalt**. — **con·fig·u·ra·tion·al** /-sHənl/ **adj.**

con·fig·ure /kən'figyər/ ▶v. [trans.] (often **be configured**) shape or put together in a particular form or configuration. ■ Comput. arrange or order (a computer system or an element of it) so as to fit it for a designated task. — **con·fig·ur·a·ble** adj. [ME: from L. *configurare* 'shape after a pattern,' from *con-* + *figurare* 'to shape' (from *figura* 'shape').]

con·fine ▶v. /kən'fīn/ [trans.] (**confine someone/something to**) keep or restrict someone or something within certain limits of (space, scope, quantity, or time). ■ (**confine someone to/in**) restrain or forbid someone from leaving (a place): *the troops were confined to their barracks.* ■ (**be confined to**) (of a person) be unable to leave (one's bed, home, or a wheelchair) because of illness or disability. ■ (**be confined**) dated (of a woman) remain in bed for a period before, during, and after the birth of a child. ▶n. (**confines** /'känfīn/) the borders or boundaries of a place, esp. with regard to their restricting freedom of movement. ■ fig. the limits or restrictions of something abstract, esp. a subject or sphere of activity. — **con·fine·ment** n. [ME: from Fr. *confins* (pl. n.), from L. *confinia*, from *confinis* 'bordering,' from *con-* 'with' + *finis* 'end.']

con·fined /kən'fīnd/ ▶adj. (of a space) restricted in area or volume; cramped.

con·firm /kən'fərm/ ▶v. [trans.] **1** establish the truth or correctness of (something previously believed, suspected, or feared to be the case). ■ [reporting verb] state with assurance that a report or fact is true. ■ (**confirm someone in**) reinforce someone in (an opinion, belief, or feeling): *he fueled his misogyny by cultivating women who confirmed him in this view.* ■ make (a provisional arrangement or appointment) definite. ■ make (something, esp. a person's appointment to a position or an agreement) formally valid; ratify. ■ formally declare (someone) to be appointed to a particular position: *he was **confirmed as** the new peace envoy.* **2** administer the religious rite of confirmation to. — **con·firm·a·tive** /-mətiv/ adj. **con·firm·a·to·ry** /-mə,tôrē/ adj. [ME: from OFr. *confermer*, from L. *confirmare*, from *con-* 'together' + *firmare* 'strengthen' (from *firmus* 'firm').]

con·fir·ma·tion /,känfər'māshən/ ▶n. **1** the action of confirming something or the state of being confirmed. **2** (in the Christian Church) the rite at which a baptized person affirms Christian belief and is admitted as a full member of the church. ■ the Jewish ceremony of bar mitzvah or bat mitzvah.

con·firmed /kən'fərmd/ ▶adj. (of a person) firmly established in a particular habit, belief, or way of life and unlikely to change: *a confirmed bachelor.*

con·fis·cate /'känfə,skāt/ ▶v. [trans.] take or seize (someone's property) with authority. ■ take (a possession, esp. land) as a penalty and give it to the public treasury. — **con·fis·ca·tion** /,känfə'skāshən/ n. **con·fis·ca·tor** /-,skātər/ n. **con·fis·ca·to·ry** /kən'fiskə,tôrē/ adj. [16th C.: from L. *confiscat-* 'put away in a chest,' from v. *confiscare*, based on *con-* 'together' + *fiscus* 'chest.']

con·fit /kôn'fē/ ▶n. duck or other meat cooked slowly in its own fat. [Fr., 'conserved,' from *confire* 'prepare.']

con·fi·ture /'känfi,choor/ ▶n. a preparation of preserved fruit. ■ a confection.

con·fla·grant /kən'flāgrənt/ ▶adj. on fire; blazing.

con·fla·gra·tion /,känflə'grāshən/ ▶n. an extensive fire that destroys a great deal of land or property. [15th C.: from L. *conflagratio(n-)*, from v. *conflagrare*, from *con-* + *flagrare* 'to blaze.']

con·flate /kən'flāt/ ▶v. [trans.] combine (two or more texts, ideas, etc.) into one: *the urban crisis conflates a number of different economic and social issues.* — **con·fla·tion** /-'flāshən/ n. [ME: from L. *conflat-* 'kindled,' from v. *conflare*, from *con-* + *flare* 'to blow.']

con·flict ▶n. /'känflikt/ a serious disagreement or argument, typically a protracted one: *the eternal **conflict between** the sexes.* ■ a prolonged armed struggle. ■ an incompatibility between two or more opinions, principles, or interests. ■ Psychol. a condition in which a person experiences a clash of opposing wishes or needs. ▶v. /kən'flikt; 'kän,flikt/ [intrans.] be incompatible or at variance; clash. ■ [as adj.] (**conflicted**) having or showing confused and mutually inconsistent feelings. — **con·flic·tive** /kən'fliktiv; 'känflik-/ adj. **con·flic·tu·al** /kən'flikchooəl/ adj. [ME: from L. *conflict-* 'struck together,' from v. *confligere*, from *con-* 'together' + *fligere* 'to strike.']

con·flu·ence /'känflooəns; kən'flooəns/ ▶n. the junction of two rivers, esp. rivers of approximately equal width. ■ an act or process of merging.

con·flu·ent /'känflooənt; kən'flooənt/ ▶adj. flowing together or merging: *warm confluent smells.* [15th C.: from L. *confluere*, from *con-* 'together' + *fluere* 'to flow.']

con·flux /'kän,fləks/ ▶n. another term for CONFLUENCE. [17th C.: from late L. *confluxus*, from *con-* 'together' + *fluxus* (see FLUX).]

con·fo·cal /kän'fōkəl/ ▶adj. having a common focus or foci: *confocal ellipses.*

con·form /kən'fôrm/ ▶v. [intrans.] comply with rules, standards, or laws. ■ (of a person) behave according to socially acceptable conventions or standards: *the pressure to conform.* ■ be similar in form or type; agree: [ME: from L. *conformare*, from *con-* + *formare* 'to form.']

con·form·a·ble /kən'fôrməbəl/ ▶adj. (usu. **conformable to**) (of a person) disposed or accustomed to conform to what is acceptable or expected. ■ similar in form or nature; consistent. ■ Geol. (of strata in contact) deposited in a continuous sequence, and typically having the same direction of stratification. — **con·form·a·bil·i·ty** /-,fôrmə'bilitē/ n. **con·form·a·bly** adv.

con·for·mal /kən'fôrməl/ ▶adj. (of a map projection or a mathematical mapping) preserving the correct angles between directions within small areas, though distorting distances. — **con·for·mal·ly** adv.

con·form·ance /kən'fôrməns/ ▶n. another term for CONFORMITY.

con·for·ma·tion /,känfôr'māshən; -fər-/ ▶n. the shape or structure of something, esp. an animal. ■ Chem. any of the spatial arrangements that the atoms in a molecule may adopt and freely convert between, esp. by rotation about individual single bonds. Compare with CONFIGURATION. — **con·for·ma·tion·al** /-shənl/ adj.

con·form·er /kən'fôrmər/ ▶n. Chem. a form of a compound having a particular molecular conformation. [1960s: blend of *conformational* and ISOMER.]

con·form·ist /kən'fôrmist/ ▶n. a person who conforms to accepted behavior or established practices. ▶adj. (of a person or activity) conforming to accepted behavior or established practices; conventional. — **con·form·ism** n.

con·form·i·ty /kən'fôrmitē/ ▶n. compliance with standards, rules, or laws. ■ behavior in accordance with socially accepted conventions or standards. ■ similarity in form or type; agreement in character. ■ Geol. (of strata in contact) a continuous sequence of deposits, typically in parallel strata.

con·found /kən'found/ ▶v. [trans.] **1** cause surprise or confusion in (someone), esp. by acting against their expectations. ■ prove (a theory, expectation, or prediction) wrong. ■ defeat (a plan, aim, or hope). **2** (often **be confounded with**) mix up (something) with something else so that the individual elements become difficult to distinguish. ▶exclam. dated used to express anger or annoyance: *oh, confound it, where is the thing?* [ME: from OFr. *confondre*, from L. *confundere* 'pour together.']

con·found·ed /kən'foundəd; kän-/ ▶adj. [attrib.] informal, dated used for emphasis, esp. to express anger or annoyance: *he was a confounded nuisance.* — **con·found·ed·ly** adv.

con·fra·ter·ni·ty /,känfrə'tərnitē/ ▶n. (pl. **-ties**) a brotherhood, esp. with a charitable or religious purpose. [ME: ult. from med. L. *confraternitas* (see CONFRÈRE).]

con·frère /'känfrer; kän'frer; kôn'frer/ (also **con·frere**) ▶n. a fellow member of a profession; a colleague. [mid 18th C.: Fr., from med. L. *confrater*, from *con-* + *frater* 'brother.']

con·front /kən'frənt/ ▶v. [trans.] meet (someone) face to face with hostile or argumentative intent. ■ face up to and deal with (a problem or difficult situation). ■ compel (someone) to face or consider something, esp. by way of accusation. ■ (often **be confronted**) (of a problem, difficulty, etc.) present itself to (someone) so that dealing with it cannot be avoided. ■ (usu. **be confronted**) appear or be placed in front of (someone) so as to unsettle or threaten. [16th C.: from Fr. *confronter*, from med. L. *confrontare*, from L. *con-* 'with' + *frons, front-* 'face.']

con·fron·ta·tion /,känfrən'tāshən/ ▶n. a hostile or argumentative meeting or situation between opposing parties. — **con·fron·ta·tion·al** /-shənl/ adj.

Con·fu·cian /kən'fyooshən/ ▶adj. of or relating to Confucius or Confucianism. ▶n. an adherent of Confucianism.

Con·fu·cian·ism /kən'fyooshə,nizəm/ ▶n. a system of philosophical and ethical teachings founded by Confucius and developed by Mencius. — **Con·fu·cian·ist** n. & adj.

Con·fu·cius /kən'fyooshəs/ (551–479 BC), Chinese philosopher; Latinized name of *Kongfuze* (*K'ung Fu-tzu*) "Kong the master." His ideas about the importance of practical moral values, collected by his disciples in the *Analects*, formed the basis of the philosophy known as Confucianism.

con·fus·a·ble /kən'fyoozəbəl/ ▶adj. able or liable to be confused with something else. ▶n. a word or phrase that is easily confused with another in meaning or usage, such as *mitigate*, which is often confused with *militate*. — **con·fus·a·bil·i·ty** /kən,fyoozə'bilitē/ n.

con·fuse /kən'fyooz/ ▶v. [trans.] cause (someone) to become bewildered or perplexed. ■ make (something) more complex or less easy to understand. ■ identify wrongly; mistake. — **con·fus·ing·ly** adv. [ME: from OFr. *confus*, from L. *confusus*, past part. of *confundere* 'mingle together.']

con·fused /kən'fyoozd/ ▶adj. (of a person) unable to think clearly; bewildered. ■ showing bewilderment: *a confused expression crossed her face.* ■ not in possession of all one's mental faculties, esp. because of old age. ■ lacking order and thus difficult to understand. ■ lacking clear distinction of elements; jumbled. — **con·fus·ed·ly** /-'fyoozidlē/ adv.

con·fu·sion /kən'fyoozhən/ ▶n. **1** lack of understanding; uncertainty. ■ a situation of panic; a breakdown of order: *the shaken survivors retreated in confusion.* ■ a disorderly jumble. **2** the state of being bewildered or unclear in one's mind about something: *she looked about her in confusion.* ■ the mistaking of one person or thing for another.

con·fute /kən'fyoot/ ▶v. [trans.] formal prove (a person or an assertion) to be wrong. — **con·fu·ta·tion** /,känfyoo'tāshən/ n. [16th C.: from L. *confutare* 'answer conclusively,' from *con-* + base of *refutare* 'refute.']

Cong. ▶abbr. ■ Congress. ■ Congressional. ■ Congregational.

con·ga /'käNGgə/ ▶n. **1** a Latin American dance of African origin, usually with several people in a

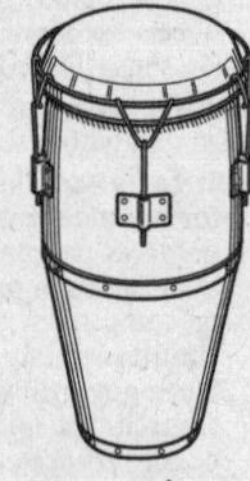

conga drum

single line, one behind the other. **2** (also **conga drum**) a tall, narrow, low-toned drum beaten with the hands. ▶ **v.** (**-gas, -gaed** /-gəd/ or **-ga'd, -ga·ing** /-gə-iNG/) [intrans.] dance the conga. [1930s: from L. Amer. Sp., from Sp., fem. of *congo* 'Congolese.']

con game ▶ **n.** informal term for CONFIDENCE GAME.

con·gé /kôN'zHā; 'känjā/ ▶ **n.** [in sing.] an unceremonious dismissal of someone; a leavetaking. [ME: from OFr. *congie*, from L. *commeatus* 'leave of absence,' from *commeare* 'go and come.']

con·geal /kən'jēl/ ▶ **v.** [intrans.] solidify or coagulate, esp. by cooling: *the blood had congealed into blobs.* ■ fig. take shape or coalesce, esp. to form a satisfying whole: *the ballet failed to congeal as a single oeuvre.* — **con·geal·a·ble adj.** [ME: ult. from L. *congelare*, from *con-* + *gelare* 'freeze' (from *gelu* 'frost').]

con·gee /'känjē; kôN'zHā/ ▶ **n.** (in Chinese cooking) broth or porridge made from rice. [from Tamil *kañci*.]

con·ge·la·tion /ˌkänjə'lāsHən/ ▶ **n.** the process of congealing or the state of being congealed. [ME: from L. *congelatio(n-)*, from *congelare* (see CONGEAL).]

con·ge·ner /kən'jēnər/ ▶ **n.** **1** a thing or person of the same kind or category as another. ■ an animal or plant of the same genus as another. **2** a minor chemical constituent, esp. one that gives a distinctive character to a wine or liquor or is responsible for some of its physiological effects. — **con·gen·er·ous** /kən'jenərəs; kän-; -'jēnərəs/ **adj.** [18th C.: from L., from *con-* 'together with' + *genus, gener-* 'race, stock.']

con·gen·ial /kən'jēnyəl/ ▶ **adj.** (of a person) pleasant because of a personality, qualities, or interests that are similar to one's own. | ■ (of a thing) pleasant or agreeable because suited to one's taste or inclination. — **con·ge·ni·al·i·ty** /-jēnē'alitē/ **n.** **con·gen·ial·ly adv.**

con·gen·i·tal /kən'jenətl/ ▶ **adj.** (esp. of a disease or physical abnormality) present from birth. ■ (of a person) having a particular trait from birth or by firmly established habit: *a congenital liar.* — **con·gen·i·tal·ly adv.** [18th C.: from L. *congenitus*, from *con-* 'with' + *genitus* (past part. of *gignere* 'beget').]

con·ger /'käNGgər/ (also **conger eel**) ▶ **n.** a large edible predatory eel (*Conger* and other genera, family Congridae) of shallow coastal waters. [ME: from OFr. *congre*, via L. from Gk. *gongros*.]

con·ge·ries /'känjərēz/ ▶ **n.** (pl. same) a disorderly collection; a jumble. [16th C.: from L. *congeries* 'heap, pile,' from *congerere* 'heap up.']

con·gest·ed /kən'jestid/ ▶ **adj.** blocked up with or too full of something, in particular: ■ (of a road or place) so crowded with traffic or people as to hinder freedom of movement. ■ (of the respiratory tract) blocked with mucus so as to hinder breathing. ■ (of a part of the body) abnormally full of blood: *congested arteries.* [19th C.: past part. of *congest*, from L. *congest-* 'heaped up,' from the v. *congerere*, from *con-* 'together' + *gerere* 'bring.']

con·ges·tion /kən'jescHən/ ▶ **n.** the state of being congested: *the new bridge should ease congestion in the area.*

con·ges·tive /kən'jestiv/ ▶ **adj.** Med. involving or produced by congestion of a part of the body.

con·ges·tive heart fail·ure ▶ **n.** a weakness of the heart that leads to a buildup of fluid in the lungs and surrounding body tissues.

con·glob·u·late /kən'gläbyəlit/ ▶ **v.** [intrans.] rare join closely together. [18th C.: from L. *globulus* 'globule.']

con·glom·er·ate ▶ **n.** /kən'glämərit/ **1** a number of different things or parts that are put or grouped together to form a whole but remain distinct entities. ■ [often with adj.] a large corporation formed by the merging of separate and diverse firms. **2** Geol. a coarse-grained sedimentary rock composed of rounded fragments (> 2 mm) within a matrix of finer grained material: *the sediments vary from coarse conglomerate to fine silt and clay.* ▶ **adj.** /-rit/ of or relating to a conglomerate, esp. a large corporation: *conglomerate businesses.* ▶ **v.** /-ˌrāt/ [intrans.] gather together into a compact mass. ■ form a conglomerate by merging diverse businesses. — **con·glom·er·a·tion** /kənˌglämə'rāsHən/ **n.** [ME: from L. *conglomeratus*, past part. of *conglomerare*, from *con-* + *glomus, glomer-* 'ball.']

Con·go /'käNGgō/ **1** a river in central Africa that rises in northern Democratic Republic of the Congo (formerly Zaire) and flows for 2,880 miles (4,630 km) to the west and then southwest to the Atlantic Ocean. Also called ZAIRE RIVER. **2** (often **the Congo**) (official name **Republic of the Congo**) a country in west central Africa. *See box.*

Con·go, Democratic Republic of the a country in central Africa. Formerly called (until 1997) ZAIRE. *See box.*

Con·go·lese /ˌkäNGgə'lēz; -'lēs/ ▶ **adj.** of or relating to the Congo or the Democratic Republic of the Congo (formerly Zaire). ▶ **n.** (pl. same) **1** a native or inhabitant of the Congo or the Democratic Republic of the Congo. **2** any of the Bantu languages spoken in the Congo region, in particular Kikongo. [from Fr. *Congolais*.]

con·grats /kən'grats/ ▶ **plural n.** informal congratulations: [as exclam.] *"Congrats on your exams, Cal!"*

con·grat·u·late /kən'gracHəˌlāt; -'grajə-/ ▶ **v.** [trans.] give (someone) one's good wishes when something special or pleasant has happened to them. ■ praise (someone) for a particular achievement. ■ (**congratulate oneself**) feel pride or satisfaction: *she congratulated herself on her powers of deduction.* — **con·grat·u·la·tor** /-ˌlātər/ **n.** **con·grat·u·la·to·ry** /-lətôrē/ **adj.** [16th C.: from L. *congratulat-* 'congratulated,' from the v. *congratulari*, from *con-* 'with' + *gratulari* 'show joy' (from *gratus* 'pleasing').]

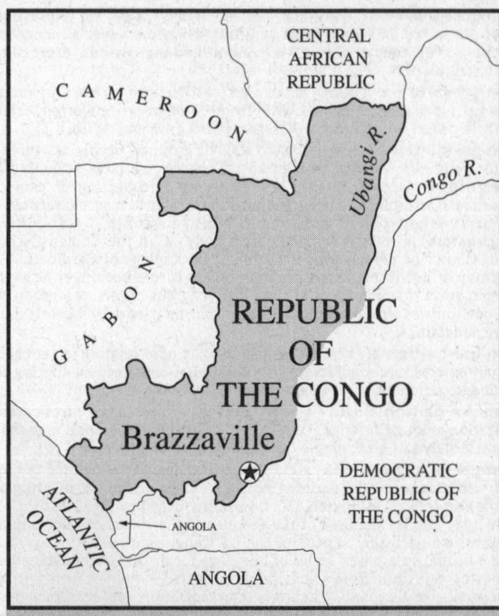

Congo, Republic of the

Location: west central Africa, west of the Democratic Republic of the Congo, with a short coastline on the Atlantic Ocean
Area: 131,900 square miles (341,500 sq km)
Population: 2,998,000
Capital: Brazzaville
Languages: French (official), Lingala, Kikongo, other Bantu languages
Currency: CFA franc

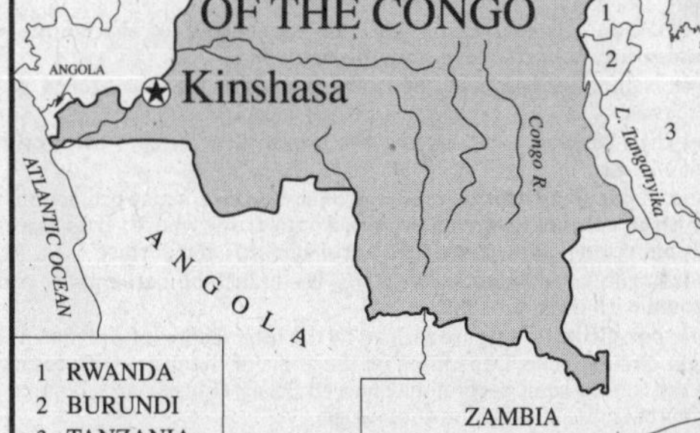

Congo, Democratic Republic of the

Location: central Africa, north of Angola and Zambia, with a very short coastline on South Atlantic Ocean
Area: 875,700 square miles (2,267,600 sq km)
Population: 58,317,700
Capital: Kinshasa
Languages: French (official), Lingala, Swahili, and others
Currency: Congolese franc

PRONUNCIATION KEY ə *ago, up*; ər *over, fur*; a *hat*; ā *ate*; ä *car*; e *let*; ē *see*; i *fit*; ī *by*; NG *sing*; ō *go*; ô *law, for*; oi *toy*; o͝o *good*; o͞o *goo*; ou *out*; TH *thin*; T͟H *then*; ZH *vision*

con·grat·u·la·tion /kən,graCHə'lāSHən; -,grajə-/ ▶**n.** an expression of praise for an achievement or good wishes on a special occasion; the act of congratulating. ■ **(congratulations)** words expressing congratulation.

con·gre·gate ▶**v.** [intrans.] /'käNGgri,gāt/ gather into a crowd or mass. ▶**adj.** /-git; -,gāt/ communal. [ME: from L. *congregat-* 'collected,' from the v. *congregare*, from *con-* + *gregare* (from *grex*, *greg-* 'a flock').]

con·gre·ga·tion /,käNGgri'gāSHən/ ▶**n. 1** a group of people assembled for religious worship. ■ a group of people regularly attending a particular place of worship. **2** a gathering or collection of people, animals, or things: *large congregations of birds may cause public harm.* ■ the action of gathering together in a crowd. **3** (often **Congregation**) a council or deliberative body. ■ (in the Roman Catholic Church) a permanent committee of the College of Cardinals. **4** a group of people obeying a common religious rule but under less solemn vows than members of the older religious orders. ■ a group of communities within a religious order sharing particular historical or regional links.

con·gre·ga·tion·al /,käNGgri'gāSHənl/ ▶**adj. 1** of or relating to a congregation: *congregational singing.* **2** (**Congregational**) of or adhering to Congregationalism: *the Congregational Church.*

Con·gre·ga·tion·al·ism /,käNGgri'gāSHənl,izəm/ ▶**n.** a system of organization among Christian churches whereby individual local churches are largely self-governing. — **Con·gre·ga·tion·al·ist n. & adj.**

con·gress /'käNGgrəs; 'kän-/ ▶**n. 1** the national legislative body of a country. ■ (**Congress**) the national legislative body of the US, meeting at the Capitol in Washington, DC. It was established by the Constitution of 1787 and is composed of the Senate and the House of Representatives. ■ a particular session of the US Congress: *the 104th Congress.* **2** a formal meeting or series of meetings for discussion between delegates, esp. those from a political party or trade union or from within a particular discipline. **3** a society or organization, esp. a political one. **4** the action of coming together: *sexual congress.* — **con·gres·sion·al** /kən'greSHənl/ **adj.** [ME: from L. *congressus*, from *congredi* 'meet,' from *con-* + *gradi* 'walk.']

Con·gres·sion·al Med·al of Hon·or ▶**n.** see MEDAL OF HONOR.

con·gress·man /'käNGgrəsmən; 'kän-/ ▶**n.** (pl. **-men**) a member of the US Congress (also used as a form of address), usually specifically a member of the US House of Representatives.

Con·gress of In·dus·tri·al Or·gan·i·za·tions (abbr.: **CIO**) a federation of North American trade unions, organized largely by industry rather than craft. In 1955 it merged with the American Federation of Labor to form the AFL-CIO.

con·gress·per·son /'käNGgrəs,pərsən; 'kän-/ (pl. **congresspeople** or **congresspersons**) ▶**n.** a member of a legislative congress, esp. the US House of Representatives.

con·gress·wom·an /'käNGgrəs,wo͝omən; 'kän-/ ▶**n.** (pl. **-wom·en**) a female member of the US Congress (also used as a form of address).

Con·greve /'käNGgrēv; 'kängrēv/, William (1670–1729), English playwright. His plays include *Love for Love* (1695) and *The Way of the World* (1700).

con·gru·ent /kən'gro͞oənt; 'käNGgro͞oənt/ ▶**adj. 1** in agreement or harmony. **2** Geom. (of figures) identical in form; coinciding exactly when superimposed. — **con·gru·ence n. con·gru·en·cy n. con·gru·ent·ly adv.** [ME: from L. *congruent-* 'agreeing,' from the v. *congruere*, from *con-* + *ruere* 'fall.']

con·gru·ous /'käNGgro͞oəs/ ▶**adj.** in agreement or harmony. — **con·gru·i·ty** /kən'gro͞oitē/ **n. con·gru·ous·ly adv.**

con·ic /'känik/ esp. Math. ▶**adj.** of a cone. ▶**n.** short for CONIC SECTION. See also CONICS.

con·i·cal /'känikəl/ ▶**adj.** having the shape of a cone. — **con·i·cal·ly** /-ik(ə)lē/ **adv.**

con·i·cal pro·jec·tion (also **con·ic pro·jec·tion**) ▶**n.** a map projection in which an area of the earth is projected onto a cone whose vertex is usually above one of the poles, then unrolled onto a flat surface.

con·ics /'käniks/ ▶**plural n.** [treated as sing.] the branch of mathematics concerned with conic sections.

con·ic sec·tion ▶**n.** a figure formed by the intersection of a plane and a right circular cone. Depending on the angle of the plane with respect to the cone, a conic section may be a circle, an ellipse, a parabola, or a hyperbola. See illustration at GEOMETRIC.

co·nid·i·um /kə'nidēəm/ ▶**n.** (pl. **-nid·i·a** /-'nidēə/) Bot. a spore produced asexually by various fungi at the tip of a specialized hypha. [19th C.: mod. L., from Gk. *konis* 'dust' + the dimin. suffix *-idium*.]

co·ni·fer /'känəfər; kō-/ ▶**n.** a tree that bears cones and evergreen needlelike or scalelike leaves. Its several families include the pines and firs (Pinaceae) and the cypresses (Cupressaceae). Conifers are of major importance as the source of softwood, and also supply resins and turpentine. — **co·nif·er·ous** /kə'nifərəs/ **adj.** [19th C.: from L., lit. 'cone-bearing,' from *conus* (see CONE).]

co·ni·ine /'kōnē,ēn; kō'nē-in/ ▶**n.** Chem. a volatile poisonous alkaloid, $C_8H_{17}N$, found in hemlock and other plants. It affects the motor nerves, causing paralysis and asphyxia. [19th C.: from L. *conium* (from Gk. *kōneion* 'hemlock') + -INE[4].]

conj. ▶**abbr.** conjunction.

con·jec·tur·al /kən'jekCHərəl/ ▶**adj.** based on or involving conjecture. — **con·jec·tur·al·ly adv.**

con·jec·ture /kən'jekCHər/ ▶**n.** an opinion or conclusion formed on the basis of incomplete information. ■ an unproven mathematical or scientific theorem. ■ (in textual criticism) the suggestion or reconstruction of a reading of a text not present in the original source. ▶**v.** [trans.] form an opinion or supposition about (something) on the basis of incomplete information. ■ (in textual criticism) propose (a reading). — **con·jec·tur·a·ble adj.** [ME: ult. from L. *conjectura*, from *conicere* 'put together in thought,' from *con-* + *jacere* 'throw.']

con·join /kən'join/ ▶**v.** [trans.] formal join; combine. — **con·joint** /kən'joint/ **adj. con·joint·ly adv.** [ME: from OFr. *conjoindre*, from L. *conjungere*, from *con-* + *jungere* 'to join.']

con·joined twin /kən'joind/ ▶**n.** either of a pair of twins who are physically joined at birth, sometimes sharing organs, and sometimes separable by surgery (depending on the degree of fusion).

con·ju·gal /'känjəgəl/ ▶**adj.** of or relating to marriage or the relationship between husband and wife: *conjugal loyalty.* — **con·ju·gal·i·ty** /,känjə'galitē/ **n. con·ju·gal·ly adv.** [16th C.: from L. *conjugalis*, from *conjux*, *conjug-* 'spouse,' from *con-* + *jugum* 'a yoke.']

con·ju·gal rights ▶**plural n.** the rights, esp. to sexual relations, regarded as exercisable in law by each partner in a marriage.

con·ju·gal vis·it ▶**n.** Law a visit to a prisoner, by the spouse of the prisoner, especially for sexual relations.

con·ju·gate ▶**v.** /'känjə,gāt/ **1** [trans.] Gram. give the different forms of (a verb in an inflected language) as they vary according to voice, mood, tense, number, and person. **2** [intrans.] Biol. (of bacteria or unicellular organisms) become temporarily united in order to exchange genetic material. ■ (of gametes) become fused. **3** [trans.] Chem. be combined with or joined to reversibly. ▶**adj.** /'känjəgit; -,gāt/ coupled, connected, or related, in particular: ■ Chem. (of an acid or base) related to the corresponding base or acid by loss or gain of a proton. ■ Math. joined in a reciprocal relation, esp. having the same real parts and equal magnitudes but opposite signs of imaginary parts. Short for COMPLEX CONJUGATE. ■ Geom. (of angles) adding up to 360°; (of arcs) combining to form a complete circle. ■ Biol. (esp. of gametes) fused. ▶**n.** /'känjəgit; -,gāt/ a thing that is conjugate or conjugated, in particular: ■ esp. Biochem. a substance formed by the reversible combination of two or more others. ■ a mathematical value or entity having a reciprocal relation with another. See also COMPLEX CONJUGATE. — **con·ju·ga·tive** /'känjə,gātiv/ **adj.** [15th C.: from L. *conjugare*, from *con-* 'together' + *jugum* 'yoke.']

con·ju·gat·ed /'känjə,gātid/ ▶**adj.** [attrib.] another term for CONJUGATE, in particular: ■ Chem. relating to or denoting double or triple bonds in a molecule that are separated by a single bond, across which some sharing of electrons occurs. ■ (of a substance) reversibly combined with another.

con·ju·ga·ted pro·tein ▶**n.** a complex protein, such as hemoglobin, consisting of amino acids combined with other substances.

con·ju·ga·tion /,känjə'gāSHən/ ▶**n. 1** the formation or existence of a link or connection between things, in particular: ■ Biol. the temporary union of two bacteria or unicellular organisms for the exchange of genetic material. ■ Biol. the fusion of two gametes, esp. when they are of a similar size. ■ esp. Biochem. the combination of two substances. ■ Chem. the sharing of electron density between nearby multiple bonds in a molecule. ■ Math. the solution of a problem by transforming it into an equivalent problem of a different form, solving this, and then reversing the transformation. **2** Gram. the variation of the form of a verb in an inflected language such as Latin, by which are identified the voice, mood, tense, number, and person. ■ the class in which a verb is put according to the manner of this variation. — **con·ju·ga·tion·al** /-SHənl/ **adj.**

con·junct ▶**adj.** /kən'jəNGkt; kän-/ joined together, combined, or associated. ■ Music of or relating to the movement of a melody between adjacent notes of the scale. ■ Astrol. in conjunction with: *Moon conjunct Jupiter.* ▶**n.** /'kän,jəNGkt/ each of two or more things that are joined or associated. ■ Logic each of the terms of a conjunctive proposition. ■ Gram. an adverbial whose function is to join two sentences or other discourse units (e.g., *however*, *anyway*, *in the first place*). [ME: from L. *conjunctus*, past part. of *conjungere* (see CONJOIN).]

con·junc·tion /kən'jəNGkSHən/ ▶**n. 1** the act of joining or the condition of being joined. ■ an instance of two or more events or things occurring at the same point in time or space ■ Astron. & Astrol. an alignment of two planets or other celestial objects so that they appear to be in the same, or nearly the same, place in the sky. **2** Gram. a word used to connect clauses or sentences or to coordinate words in the same clause (e.g., *and*, *but*, *if*).
– PHRASES **in conjunction** together. — **con·junc·tion·al** /-SHənl/ **adj.**

con·junc·ti·va /,känjəNGk'tīvə; kən,jəNGk-/ ▶**n.** Anat. the mucous membrane that covers the front of the eye and lines the inside of the eyelids. — **con·junc·ti·val adj.** [ME: from med. L. *(membrana) conjunctiva* 'conjunctive (membrane),' based on L. *conjungere* (see CONJOIN).]

con·junc·tive /kən'jəNGktiv/ ▶**adj.** serving to join; connective: *the conjunctive tissue.* ■ involving the combination or co-occurrence of two or more conditions or properties. ■ Gram. of the nature of or relating to a conjunction. ▶**n.** Gram. a word or expression acting as a conjunction. — **con·junc·tive·ly adv.**

con·junc·ti·vi·tis /kən,jəNG(k)tə'vītis/ ▶**n.** Med. inflammation of the conjunctiva of the eye.

con·junc·ture /kən'jəNGkCHər/ ▶**n.** a combination of events: *the peculiar political conjunctures that led to war.* ■ a state of affairs: *the wider political conjuncture.*

con·jur·a·tion /ˌkänjo͝oˈrāsHən/ ▶ n. a magic incantation or spell. ■ the performance of something supernatural by means of a magic incantation or spell.

con·jure /ˈkänjər; ˈkən-/ ▶ v. [trans.] make (something) appear unexpectedly or seemingly from nowhere as if by magic. ■ call (an image) to mind. ■ (of a word, sound, smell, etc.) cause someone to feel or think of (something). ■ call upon (a spirit or ghost) to appear, by means of a magic ritual.
– PHRASES **a name to conjure with** the name of an important person within a particular sphere of activity: *on the merger scene his is a name to conjure with.* [ME: from OFr. *conjurer* 'to plot,' from L. *conjurare* 'conspire,' from *con-* + *jurare* 'swear.']

con·jure wom·an ▶ n. (masc. **con·jure man**) a sorceress, esp. one who practices voodoo.

con·jur·ing /ˈkänjəriNG; ˈkən-/ ▶ n. [often as adj.] the performance of tricks that are seemingly magical, typically involving sleight of hand: *a conjuring trick.*

con·ju·ror /ˈkänjərər; ˈkən-/ (also **con·jur·er**) ▶ n. a person who conjures.

conk[1] /käNGk; kôNGk/ ▶ v. [intrans.] (**conk out**) informal (of a machine) break down: *my car conked out.* ■ (of a person) faint or go to sleep. ■ die. [World War I: of unknown origin.]

conk[2] informal ▶ v. [trans.] hit (someone) on the head. [19th C.: perh. an alt. of CONCH.]

conk[3] ▶ n. a hairstyle in which curly or kinky hair is straightened. v. [trans.] straighten curly or kinky hair.

con man (also **con artist**) ▶ n. informal a person who cheats or tricks someone by means of a confidence game.

con mo·to /kän ˈmōtō/ ▶ adv. Music (esp. as a direction) with movement: *andante con moto.* [Ital.]

Conn. ▶ abbr. Connecticut.

conn /kän/ (also **con**) Naut. ▶ v. [trans.] direct the steering of (a ship): *he conned a Boston whaler.* ▶ n. (**the conn**) the action or post of conning a ship. [17th C.: appar. weakened form of obs. *cond* 'guide,' based on L. *conducere* (see CONDUCE).]

Con·nacht /ˈkänôt; kəˈnôt/ (also **Con·naught**) a province in southwestern Republic of Ireland.

con·nate /ˈkänāt; käˈnāt/ ▶ adj. **1** (esp. of ideas or principles) existing in a person or thing from birth; innate. ■ of the same or similar nature; allied; congenial. **2** Biol. (of parts) united so as to form a single part. **3** Geol. (of water) trapped in sedimentary rock during its deposition. [17th C.: from late L. *connatus*, past part. of *connasci*, from *con-* + *nasci* 'be born.']

con·nat·u·ral /kəˈnacH(ə)rəl; kä-/ ▶ adj. belonging naturally; innate: *religion is connatural with man.* — **con·nat·u·ral·ly** adv. [16th C.: from late L. *connaturalis*, from *con-* 'together'+ L. *naturalis* 'natural.']

Con·naught var. of CONNACHT.

con·nect /kəˈnekt/ ▶ v. [trans.] (often **be connected**) bring together or into contact so that a real or notional link is established. ■ join together so as to provide access and communication. ■ link to a power or water supply. ■ put (someone) into contact by telephone. ■ [intrans.] (of a train, bus, aircraft, etc.) be timed to arrive at its destination before another train, aircraft, etc., departs so that passengers can transfer from one to the other: *the bus **connects with** trains from Union Station.* ■ associate or relate in some respect. ■ think of as being linked or related: *I didn't connect the two incidents at the time.* ■ (of a thing) provide or have a link or relationship with (someone or something): *there was no evidence to **connect** Jeff **with** the theft.* ■ [intrans.] form a relationship or feel an affinity. ■ [intrans.] informal (of a blow) hit the intended target. — **con·nect·a·ble** adj. **con·nect·ed·ly** adv. **con·nect·ed·ness** n. [ME: from L. *connectere*, from *con-* 'with' + *nectere* 'bind.']

Con·nect·i·cut /kəˈnetikət/ a state in the northeastern US, on the coast of the Atlantic Ocean's Long Island Sound, one of the six New England states; pop. 3,405,565; capital, Hartford; statehood, Jan. 9, 1788 (5). One of the original thirteen states. The Fundamental Orders, adopted by the Connecticut Colony in 1639, is often considered the first democratic constitution in America.

Con·nect·i·cut Riv·er the longest river in New England, flows south for 407 miles (655 km), from northern New Hampshire on the Quebec border, between New Hampshire and Vermont, through western Massachusetts and central Connecticut to Long Island Sound.

con·nect·ing rod ▶ n. a rod connecting two moving parts in a mechanism, esp. in an engine or pump.

con·nec·tion /kəˈneksHən/ (Brit. also **con·nex·ion**) ▶ n. **1** a relationship in which a person, thing, or idea is linked or associated with something else: *the **connections between** social attitudes and productivity | sufferers deny that their problems have any **connection with** drugs.* ■ the action of linking one thing with another: *connection to the Internet.* ■ the placing of parts of an electric circuit in contact so that a current may flow. ■ a link between pipes or electrical components: *it is important to ensure that all connections between the wires are properly made.* ■ a link between two telephones: *she replaced the receiver before the connection was made.* ■ an arrangement or opportunity for catching a connecting train, bus, aircraft, etc.: *ferry connections are sporadic in the off season.* ■ such a train, bus, etc.: *we had to wait for our connection to Frankfurt.* ■ (**connections**) people with whom one has social or professional contact or to whom one is related, esp. those with influence and able to offer one help: *he had connections with the music industry.* **2** informal a supplier of narcotics: *she introduced Jean to a number of her male drug connections.* ■ a narcotics sale or purchase. **3** esp. hist. an association of Methodist churches.
– PHRASES **in connection with** with reference to; concerning: *detectives are questioning two men in connection with alleged criminal damage.* **in this** (or **that**) **connection** with reference to this (or that): *of value in this connection was the work done by the state police.* — **con·nec·tion·al** /-sHənl/ adj. [ME: from L. *connexio(n-)*, from *connectere.*]

con·nec·tive /kəˈnektiv/ ▶ adj. connecting: *connective words and phrases.* ▶ n. something that connects, in particular: ■ Gram. a word or phrase whose function is to link linguistic units together. ■ Zool. a bundle of nerve fibers connecting two nerve centers or ganglia, esp. in invertebrate animals.

con·nec·tive tis·sue ▶ n. Anat. tissue that connects, supports, binds, or separates other tissues or organs, typically having relatively few cells embedded in an amorphous matrix, often with collagen or other fibers, and including cartilaginous, fatty, and elastic tissues.

con·nec·tiv·i·ty /kəˌnekˈtivitē/ ▶ n. the state or extent of being connected or interconnected. ■ Comput. capacity for the interconnection of platforms, systems, and applications: *connectivity between Sun and Mac platforms.*

con·nect·or /kəˈnektər/ ▶ n. [often with adj.] a thing that links two or more things together: *a pipe connector.* ■ a device for keeping two parts of an electric circuit in contact. ■ a short road or highway that connects two longer roads or highways.

Con·ne·ma·ra /ˌkänəˈmärə; -ˈmarə/ a mountainous coastal region in Galway, in western Republic of Ireland.

Con·ne·ma·ra po·ny (also **Con·ne·ma·ra**) ▶ n. a pony of a hardy breed originally from Ireland, typically gray.

con·nex·ion /kəˈneksHən/ ▶ n. British spelling of CONNECTION.

conn·ing tow·er ▶ n. the superstructure of a submarine, from which it can be commanded when on the surface, and containing the periscope.

con·nip·tion /kəˈnipsHən/ ▶ n. informal a fit of rage or hysterics: *the casting choice gave the writers a conniption.* [19th C.: prob. an invented word.]

con·niv·ance /kəˈnīvəns/ ▶ n. willingness to secretly allow or be involved in an immoral or illegal act.

con·nive /kəˈnīv/ ▶ v. [intrans.] (**connive at/in**) secretly allow (something considered immoral, illegal, or harmful) to occur. ■ conspire to do something considered immoral, illegal, or harmful. — **con·niv·er** n. [17th C.: from Fr. *conniver* or L. *connivere* 'shut the eyes (to),' from *con-* + a word akin to *nictare* 'to wink.']

con·niv·ent /kəˈnīvənt/ ▶ adj. Bot. coming into contact; converging and touching but not fused together.

con·nois·seur /ˌkänəˈsər; -ˈso͝or/ ▶ n. an expert judge in matters of taste: *a connoisseur of music.* — **con·nois·seur·ship** n. [18th C.: from obs. Fr., from *conoistre* 'know.']

Con·nol·ly /ˈkänəlē/, Maureen Catherine (1934–69), US tennis player; known as **Little Mo**. In 1953, she became the first woman to win the tennis Grand Slam.

Con·nor /ˈkänər/, Dennis Walter (1942–), US sailor. Winner of the America's Cup 1974, 1980, 1987, 1988.

Con·nors /ˈkänərz/, Jimmy (1952–), US tennis player; full name *James Scott Connors.* He won eight Grand Slam singles titles and two Grand Slam doubles titles during 1974–83.

con·no·ta·tion /ˌkänəˈtāsHən/ ▶ n. an idea or feeling that a word invokes for a person in addition to its literal or primary meaning. ■ the implication of such ideas or feelings. ■ Philos. the abstract meaning or intension of a term, which forms a principle determining which objects or concepts it applies to. Often contrasted with DENOTATION.

con·note /kəˈnōt/ ▶ v. [trans.] (of a word) imply or suggest (an idea or feeling) in addition to the literal or primary meaning. ■ (of a fact) imply as a consequence or condition. — **con·no·ta·tive** /ˈkänəˌtātiv/ adj. [17th C.: from med. L. *connotare* 'mark in addition,' from *con-* + *notare* 'to note' (from *nota* 'a mark').]

con·nu·bi·al /kəˈn(y)o͞obēəl/ ▶ adj. literary of or relating to marriage or the relationship of husband and wife; conjugal: *their connubial bed.* — **con·nu·bi·al·i·ty** /kəˌn(y)o͞obēˈalitē/ n. **con·nu·bi·al·ly** adv. [17th C.: from L. *connubialis*, from *connubium* 'marriage,' from *con-* 'with' + *nubere* 'marry.']

co·no·dont /ˈkōnəˌdänt/ ▶ n. (also **conodont animal**) an extinct marine animal (class Conodonta, phylum Chordata) of the Cambrian to Triassic periods, having a long wormlike body and numerous small teeth. It is now believed to be the earliest vertebrate. ■ (also **conodont element**) a tooth of this animal. [19th C.: from mod. L. *Conodonta* (pl.), from Gk. *kōnos* 'cone' + *odous, odont-* 'tooth.']

co·noid /ˈkōnoid/ ▶ adj. (also **co·noi·dal** /kōˈnoidl/) esp. Zool. approximately conical in shape. ▶ n. a conoid object.

con·quer /ˈkäNGkər/ ▶ v. [trans.] overcome and take control of (a place or people) by use of military force. ■ successfully overcome (a problem or weakness). ■ climb (a mountain) successfully. ■ gain the love, admiration, or respect of (a person or group of people). — **con·quer·a·ble** /-kərəbəl/ adj. **con·quer·or** /-kərər/ n. [ME: from OFr. *conquerre*, based on L. *conquirere* 'win,' from *con-* + *quaerere* 'seek.']

con·quest /ˈkänkwest; ˈkäNG-/ ▶ n. the subjugation and assumption of control of a place or people by use of military force. ■ a territory that has been gained in such a way: *colonial conquests.* ■ (**the Conquest**) the invasion and assumption of control of England by William of Normandy in 1066. See also **Norman Conquest.** ■ the overcoming of a problem or weakness: *the conquest of inflation.* ■ a person whose affection or favor has been won. [ME: from OFr. *conquest(e)*, based on L. *conquirere* (see **conquer**).]

con·quis·ta·dor /kôNG'kēstə,dôr; kän'k(w)istə-; kən-/ ▶ **n.** (pl. **-quis·ta·do·res** /-,kēstə'dôrēz; -ās; -,k(w)istə-/ or **-quis·ta·dors**) a conqueror, esp. one of the Spanish conquerors of Mexico and Peru in the 16th century. [19th C.: Sp.]

Con·rad[1] /'känrad/, Charles, Jr. (1930–99), US astronaut 1962–73; nicknamed **Pete.** As *Apollo 12* commander in 1969, he became the third man to set foot on the moon.

Con·rad[2], Joseph (1857–1924), British writer; born in Poland; born *Józef Teodor Konrad Korzeniowski.* His novels include *Lord Jim* (1900) and *Chance* (1913).

con·san·guine /kän'saNGgwin/ ▶ **adj.** another term for **consanguineous.** — **con·san·guin·e·al** /,känsaNG'gwinēəl/ **adj.**

con·san·guin·e·ous /,känsaNG'gwinēəs/ ▶ **adj.** relating to or denoting people descended from the same ancestor. — **con·san·guin·i·ty** /-'gwinitē/ **n.** [17th C.: from L. *consanguineus* 'of the same blood' (from *con-* + *sanguis* 'blood.')]

con·science /'känCHəns/ ▶ **n.** an inner feeling or voice viewed as acting as a guide to the rightness or wrongness of one's behavior.
– PHRASES **in (good) conscience** by any reasonable standard; by all that is fair. **on one's conscience** weighing heavily and guiltily on one's mind. — **con·science·less adj.** [ME: via OFr. from L. *conscientia*, from *conscient-* 'being privy to,' from the v. *conscire*, from *con-* + *scire* 'know.']

con·science clause ▶ **n.** a clause that makes concessions to the consciences of those affected by a law, e.g., one allowing doctors opposed to abortions to refuse to perform them.

con·science mon·ey ▶ **n.** money paid because of feelings of guilt, esp. about a payment that one has evaded.

con·science-strick·en ▶ **adj.** made uneasy by a guilty conscience.

con·sci·en·tious /,känCHē'enCHəs/ ▶ **adj.** (of a person) wishing to do what is right, esp. to do one's work or duty well and thoroughly. ■ (of work or a person's manner) showing such an attitude. ■ relating to a person's conscience. — **con·sci·en·tious·ly adv. con·sci·en·tious·ness n.** [17th C.: from Fr. *consciencieux*, from med. L. *conscientiosus*, from L. *conscientia* (see **conscience**).]

con·sci·en·tious ob·jec·tor ▶ **n.** a person who for reasons of conscience objects to serving in the military. — **con·sci·en·tious ob·jec·tion n.**

con·scious /'känCHəs/ ▶ **adj.** aware of and responding to one's surroundings; awake. ■ having knowledge of something; aware. ■ [predic.] (**conscious of**) painfully aware of; sensitive to. ■ [in comb.] concerned with or worried about a particular matter. ■ (of an action or feeling) deliberate and intentional. ■ (of the mind or a thought) directly perceptible to and under the control of the person concerned. — **con·scious·ly adv.** [16th C.: from L. *conscius* 'knowing with others' (from *conscire* 'be privy to.')]

con·scious·ness /'känCHəsnəs/ ▶ **n.** the state of being awake and aware of one's surroundings. ■ the awareness or perception of something by a person. ■ the fact of awareness by the mind of itself and the world.

con·scious·ness-rais·ing ▶ **n.** the activity of seeking to make people more aware of personal, social, or political issues: [as adj.] *a consciousness-raising group.*

con·script ▶ **v.** /kən'skript/ [trans.] (often **be conscripted**) enlist (someone) compulsorily, typically into the armed services. ▶ **n.** /'känskript/ a person enlisted compulsorily. [18th C.: from Fr. *conscrit*, from L. *conscriptus*, past part. of *conscribere* 'enroll.']

con·scrip·tion /kən'skripSHən/ ▶ **n.** compulsory enlistment for state service, typically into the military.

con·se·crate /'känsi,krāt/ ▶ **v.** [trans.] (usu **be consecrated**) make or declare (something, typically a church) sacred; dedicate formally to a religious or divine purpose. ■ (in Christian belief) make (bread or wine) into the body or blood of Christ. ■ ordain (someone) to a sacred office, typically that of bishop: [with obj. and complement] *he was consecrated bishop.* ■ informal devote (something) exclusively to a particular purpose. — **con·se·cra·tion** /,känsi'krāSHən/ **n. con·se·cra·tor** /-,krātər/ **n. con·se·cra·to·ry** /-krə,tôrē/ **adj.** [ME: from L. *consecrat-* 'dedicated,' from v. *consecrare*, from *con-* + *sacrare* 'dedicate,' from *sacer* 'sacred.']

con·sec·u·tive /kən'sekyətiv/ ▶ **adj.** following continuously. ■ in unbroken or logical sequence. ■ Gram. expressing consequence or result. ■ Music denoting intervals of the same kind (esp. fifths or octaves) occurring in succession between two parts or voices. — **con·sec·u·tive·ly adv. con·sec·u·tive·ness n.** [17th C.: from Fr. *consécutif*, from med. L. *consecutivus*, from L. *consecut-* 'followed closely,' from v. *consequi.*]

con·sen·su·al /kən'senCHōōəl/ ▶ **adj.** relating to or involving consent, esp. mutual consent. ■ relating to or involving consensus. — **con·sen·su·al·ly adv.** [18th C.: from L. *consensus.*]

con·sen·sus /kən'sensəs/ ▶ **n.** [usu. in sing.] general agreement. [17th C.: from L., 'agreement,' from *consens-* 'agreed,' from the v. *consentire.*]

con·sent /kən'sent/ ▶ **n.** permission for something to happen or agreement to do something. ▶ **v.** [intrans.] give permission for something to happen: *he consented to a search by a detective.* ■ [with infin.] agree to do something.
– PHRASES **by common consent** with the agreement of all. **informed consent** permission granted in the knowledge of the possible consequences, typically that which is given by a patient to a doctor for treatment with full knowledge of the possible risks and benefits. [ME: from OFr. *consente* (n.), *consentir* (v.), from L. *consentire*, from *con-* 'with' + *sentire* 'feel.']

con·se·quence /'känsikwəns; -,kwens/ ▶ **n. 1** a result or effect of an action or condition. **2** [often with negative] importance or relevance. *the past is of no consequence.* ■ dated social distinction: *a woman of consequence.*
– PHRASES **in consequence** as a result. **take the consequences** accept responsibility for the negative results of one's action.

con·se·quent /'känsikwənt; -,kwent/ ▶ **adj.** following as a result or effect. ■ Geol. (of a stream or valley) having a direction or character determined by the original slope of the land before erosion. ▶ **n.** a thing that follows another. ■ Logic the second part of a conditional proposition, whose truth is stated to be conditional upon that of the antecedent. ■ Math. the second term of a ratio. [ME: via OFr. from L. *consequent-* 'overtaking,' from the v. *consequi.*]

con·se·quen·tial /,känsə'kwenCHəl/ ▶ **adj. 1** following as a result or effect. ■ Law resulting from an act, but not immediately and directly. **2** important; significant. — **con·se·quen·ti·al·i·ty** /,känsə,kwenCHē'alitē/ **n. con·se·quen·tial·ly adv.**

con·se·quent·ly /'känsikwəntlē; -,kwentlē/ ▶ **adv.** as a result.

con·serv·an·cy /kən'sərvənsē/ ▶ **n.** (pl. **-cies**) **1** [in names] a body concerned with the preservation of nature, specific species, or natural resources. **2** the conservation of something, esp. wildlife and the environment. [18th C.: alt. of obs. *conservacy*, based on L. *conservatio(n-).*]

con·ser·va·tion /,känsər'vāSHən/ ▶ **n.** the action of conserving something, in particular: ■ preservation, protection, or restoration of the natural environment, natural ecosystems, vegetation, and wildlife. ■ preservation, repair, and prevention of deterioration of archaeological, historical, and cultural sites and artifacts. ■ prevention of excessive or wasteful use of a resource. ■ Physics the principle by which the total value of a physical quantity (such as energy, mass, or linear or angular momentum) remains constant in a system. — **con·ser·va·tion·al** /-SHənl/ **adj.** [ME: from L. *conservatio(n-)*, from *conservare.*]

con·ser·va·tion·ist /,känsər'vāSHənist/ ▶ **n.** a person who advocates or acts for the protection and preservation of the environment and wildlife.

con·ser·va·tion of charge ▶ **n.** a principle stating that the total electric charge of an isolated system is fixed.

con·ser·va·tion of en·er·gy ▶ **n.** a principle stating that energy cannot be created or destroyed, but can be altered from one form to another.

con·ser·va·tion of mass ▶ **n.** a principle stating that mass cannot be created or destroyed.

con·serv·a·tive /kən'sərvətiv/ ▶ **adj.** holding to traditional attitudes and values and cautious about change or innovation, typically in politics or religion. ■ (of dress or taste) sober and conventional. ■ (of an estimate) purposely low for the sake of caution. ■ (of surgery or medical treatment) intended to control rather than eliminate a condition, with existing tissue preserved as far as possible. ■ (**Conservative**) of or relating to the Conservative Party of Great Britain or a similar party in another country. ▶ **n.** a person who is averse to change and holds to traditional values and attitudes, typically in politics. ■ (**Conservative**) a supporter or member of the Conservative Party of Great Britain or a similar party in another country. — **con·serv·a·tism** /kən'sərvə,tizəm/ **n. con·serv·a·tive·ly adv. con·serv·a·tive·ness n.**

Con·serv·a·tive Ju·da·ism ▶ **n.** a form of Judaism, particularly prevalent in North America, that seeks to preserve Jewish tradition and ritual but has a more flexible approach to the interpretation of the law than Orthodox Judaism.

Con·serv·a·tive Par·ty ▶ **n.** a political party promoting free enterprise and private ownership, in particular a major British party that emerged from the old Tory Party in the 1830s and 1840s.

con·ser·va·toire /kən'sərvə,twär/ ▶ **n.** another term for **conservatory** (sense 1). [18th C.: Fr., based on L. *conservare.*]

con·ser·va·tor /kən'sərvətər; -,tôr; 'känsər,vātər/ ▶ **n.** a person responsible for the repair and preservation of works of art, buildings, or other things of cultural or environmental interest. ■ a guardian or protector.

con·serv·a·to·ry /kən'sərvə,tôrē/ ▶ **n.** (pl. **-ries**) **1** a college for the study of classical music or other arts. **2** a room with a glass roof and walls, attached to a house and used as a greenhouse or a sunroom.

con·serve /kən'sərv/ ▶ **v.** [trans.] protect (something, esp. an environmentally or culturally important place or thing) from harm or destruction. ■ prevent the wasteful or harmful overuse of (a resource). ■ Physics maintain (a quantity such as energy or mass) at a constant overall total. ■ (usu. **be conserved**) Biochem. retain (a particular amino acid, nucleotide, or sequence of these) unchanged in different protein or DNA molecules. ■ preserve (food, typically fruit) with sugar. ▶ **n.** /'kän,sərv/ a sweet food made by preserving fruit with sugar; jam. [ME: from OFr. *conserver* (v.), *conserve* (n.), from L. *conservare* 'to preserve,' from *con-* 'with' + *servare* 'to keep.']

con·sid·er /kən'sidər/ ▶ **v.** [trans.] (often **be considered**) think carefully about (something), typically before making a decision: *each application is considered* | [as adj.] (**considered**) *it is my considered opinion that we should wait.* ■ think about and be drawn toward (a course of action). ■ [trans.] regard (someone or something) as having a specified quality. ■ believe; think. ■ take (something) into account when making an assessment or judgment. ■ look attentively at.
– PHRASES **all things considered** taking everything into account. [ME:

from OFr. *considerer*, from L. *considerare* 'examine,' perh. based on *sidus, sider-* 'star.']

con·sid·er·a·ble /kən'sid(ə)rəbəl/ ▶ **adj.** notably large in size, amount, or extent. ■ (of a person) having merit or distinction. — **con·sid·er·a·bly** /-blē/ **adv.**

con·sid·er·ate /kən'sidərət/ ▶ **adj.** careful not to cause inconvenience or hurt to others. — **con·sid·er·ate·ly adv. con·sid·er·ate·ness n.**

con·sid·er·a·tion /kən,sidə'rāsʜən/ ▶ **n. 1** careful thought, typically over a period of time. ■ a fact or a motive taken into account in deciding or judging something. ■ thoughtfulness and sensitivity toward others. **2** a payment or reward. ■ Law (in a contractual agreement) anything given or promised or forborne by one party in exchange for the promise or undertaking of another.
– PHRASES **in consideration of** on account of. ■ in return for. **take into consideration** take into account. **under consideration** being thought about.

con·sid·er·ing /kən'sidəriɴɢ/ ▶ **prep. & conj.** taking into consideration: [as prep.] *considering the conditions, it's very good* | [as conj.] *considering that he was the youngest on the field, he played well.* ▶ **adv.** informal taking everything into account.

con·si·glie·re /,kônsē'lye-re/ ▶ **n.** (pl. **-ri** /-rē/) an adviser, esp. to a crime boss.

con·sign /kən'sīn/ ▶ **v.** [trans.] deliver (something) to a person's custody, typically in order for it to be sold. ■ send (goods) by a public carrier. ■ (**consign someone/something to**) assign; commit decisively or permanently. — **con·sign·ee** /,kănsə'nē; ,kănsī-; kən,sī'nē/ **n. con·sign·or** /kən'sīnər/ **n.** [ME: from Fr. *consigner* or L. *consignare* 'mark with a seal.']

con·sign·ment /kən'sīnmənt/ ▶ **n.** a batch of goods destined for or delivered to someone. ■ the action of consigning or delivering something. ■ agreement to pay a supplier of goods after the goods are sold. *clothing on consignment.*

con·sist ▶ **v.** /kən'sist/ [intrans.] (**consist of**) be composed or made up of. ■ (**consist in**) have as an essential feature. ▶ **n.** Railroad the set of vehicles forming a complete train. [ME: from L. *consistere* 'stand firm,' from *con-* + *sistere* 'stand.']

con·sist·ence /kən'sistəns/ ▶ **n.** another term for CONSISTENCY.

con·sist·en·cy /kən'sistənsē/ (also **con·sist·ence** /-təns/) ▶ **n.** (pl. **-cies**) **1** conformity in the application of something, typically that which is necessary for the sake of logic, accuracy, or fairness. ■ the achievement of a level of performance that does not vary greatly in quality over time. **2** the way in which a substance, typically a liquid, holds together; thickness or viscosity.

con·sist·ent /kən'sistənt/ ▶ **adj.** (of a person, behavior, or process) unchanging in achievement or effect over a period of time. ■ [predic.] compatible or in agreement with something: *injuries consistent with falling.* ■ (of an argument or set of ideas) not containing any logical contradictions. — **con·sist·ent·ly adv.** [16th C.: from L. *consistent-*, from *consistere.*]

con·sis·to·ry /kən'sistərē/ ▶ **n.** (pl. **-ries**) a church council or court, in particular: ■ (in the Roman Catholic Church) the council of cardinals, with or without the pope. ■ (also **consistory court**) (in the Church of England) a diocesan court presided over by a bishop. ■ (in other churches) a local administrative body. — **con·sis·to·ri·al** /,kănsis'tôrēəl; kən-/ **adj.** [ME: from Anglo-Norman Fr. *consistorie*, from late L. *consistorium*, from *consistere.*]

con·so·ci·a·tion /kăn,sōsʜē'āsʜən; -,sōsē-/ ▶ **n. 1** a group or association of a distinctive type, in particular: ■ a political system formed by the cooperation of different, esp. antagonistic, social groups on the basis of shared power. ■ Zool. a group of animals of the same species that interact more or less equally with each other. ■ dated an association of Congregational Churches. **2** dated close association or fellowship. — **con·so·ci·a·tion·al** /-sʜənl/ **adj. con·so·ci·a·tion·al·ism** /-sʜənl,izəm/ **n.** [16th C.: from L. *consociatio(n-)*, from v. *consociare*, from *con-* + *sociare* 'to associate' (from *socius* 'fellow').]

con·so·la·tion /,kănsə'lāsʜən/ ▶ **n.** comfort received by a person after a loss or disappointment. ■ a person or thing providing such comfort. ■ Sports a round or contest for tournament entrants who have been eliminated before the finals, often to determine third and fourth place. — **con·sol·a·to·ry** /kən'sōlə,tôrē/ **adj.**

con·so·la·tion prize ▶ **n.** a prize given to a competitor who narrowly fails to win or who finishes last.

con·sole[1] /kən'sōl/ ▶ **v.** [trans.] comfort (someone) at a time of grief or disappointment. — **con·sol·a·ble adj. con·sol·er n. con·sol·ing·ly adv.** [17th C.: from Fr. *consoler*, from L. *consolari*, from *con-* 'with' + *solari* 'soothe.']

con·sole[2] /'kănsōl/ ▶ **n. 1** a panel or unit accommodating controls for electronic or mechanical equipment. ■ a cabinet for television or radio equipment. ■ the cabinet or enclosure containing the keyboards, stops, pedals, etc., of an organ. ■ a monitor and keyboard in a multiuser computer system. **2** an ornamented bracket with scrolls or corbel supporting a cornice, shelf, or tabletop. **3** a support between the seats of an automobile that has indentations for holding small items. [17th C.: from Fr., perh. from *consolider*, from L. *consolidare* (see CONSOLIDATE).]

con·sole ta·ble /'kăn,sōl/ ▶ **n.** a table supported by ornamented brackets, either movable or fixed against a wall.

con·sol·i·date /kən'sălə,dāt/ ▶ **v. 1** [trans.] make (something) physically stronger or more solid. ■ reinforce or strengthen (one's position or power). ■ combine (a number of things) into a single more effective or coherent whole. ■ combine (a number of financial accounts or funds) into a single overall account or set of accounts. ■ combine (two or more legal actions involving similar questions) into one for action by a court. **2** [intrans.] become stronger or more solid. — **con·sol·i·da·tion** /-,sălə'dāsʜən/ **n. con·sol·i·da·tor** /-,dātər/ **n.** [16th C.: from L. *consolidare*, from *con-* 'with' + *solidare* 'make firm' (from *solidus* 'solid').]

con·som·mé /,kănsə'mā/ ▶ **n.** a clear soup made with concentrated stock. [Fr., past part. of *consommer* 'consume,' from L. *consummare* (see CONSUMMATE).]

con·so·nance /'kănsənəns/ ▶ **n.** agreement or compatibility between opinions or actions. ■ the recurrence of similar sounds, esp. consonants, in close proximity (chiefly as used in prosody). ■ Music the combination of notes that are in harmony with each other due to the relationship between their frequencies.

con·so·nant /'kănsənənt/ ▶ **n.** a basic speech sound in which the breath is at least partly obstructed and which can be combined with a vowel to form a syllable. Contrasted with VOWEL. ■ a letter representing such a sound. ▶ **adj. 1** [attrib.] denoting or relating to such a sound or letter. **2** [predic.] (**consonant with**) in agreement or harmony with: *the findings are consonant with other research.* ■ Music making a harmonious interval or chord. — **con·so·nan·tal** /,kănsə'nantl/ **adj. con·so·nant·ly adv.** [ME: via OFr. from L. *consonare* 'sound together,' from *con-* + *sonare* 'to sound' (from *sonus* 'sound').]

con·sort[1] ▶ **n.** /'kănsôrt/ a wife, husband, or companion, in particular the spouse of a reigning monarch. ■ a ship sailing in company with another. ▶ **v.** /kən'sôrt; 'kănsôrt/ [intrans.] (**consort with**) habitually associate with (someone), typically with the disapproval of others. ■ (**consort with/to**) archaic agree or be in harmony with. [ME: via Fr. from L. *consors* 'partner,' from *con-* 'with' + *sors, sort-* 'destiny.']

con·sort[2] /'kănsôrt/ ▶ **n.** a small group of musicians performing together, typically playing instrumental music of the Renaissance period. [16th C.: earlier form of CONCERT.]

con·sor·ti·um /kən'sôrsʜ(ē)əm; -'sôrtēəm/ ▶ **n.** (pl. **-ti·a** /-tēə; -sʜ(ē)ə/ or **-ti·ums**) **1** an association, typically of business companies. **2** Law the right of association and companionship with one's husband or wife. [19th C.: from L., from *consors* (see CONSORT[1]).]

con·spe·cif·ic /,kănspə'sifik/ Biol. ▶ **adj.** (of animals or plants) belonging to the same species. ▶ **n.** (usu. **conspecifics**) a member of the same species. — **con·spec·i·fic·i·ty** /kăn,spesə'fisitē/ **n.**

con·spec·tus /kən'spektəs/ ▶ **n.** a summary or overview of a subject. [19th C.: from L., past part. of *conspicere.*]

con·spic·u·ous /kən'spikyōōəs/ ▶ **adj.** standing out so as to be clearly visible. ■ attracting notice or attention.
– PHRASES **conspicuous by one's absence** obviously not present in a place where one should be. — **con·spi·cu·i·ty** /,kănspi'kyōōitē/ **n. con·spic·u·ous·ly adv. con·spic·u·ous·ness n.** [16th C.: from L. *conspicuus* (from *conspicere* 'look at attentively,' from *con-* + *specere* 'look at.')]

con·spir·a·cist /kən'spirəsist/ ▶ **n.** a person who supports a conspiracy theory.

con·spir·a·cy /kən'spirəsē/ ▶ **n.** (pl. **-cies**) a secret plan by a group to do something unlawful or harmful. ■ the action of plotting or conspiring.
– PHRASES **a conspiracy of silence** an agreement to say nothing about an issue that should be generally known. [ME: from Anglo-Norman Fr. *conspiracie*, alt. of OFr. *conspiration*, based on L. *conspirare* (see CONSPIRE).]

con·spir·a·cy the·o·ry ▶ **n.** a belief that some covert but influential organization is responsible for an unexplained event.

con·spir·a·tor /kən'spirətər/ ▶ **n.** a person who takes part in a conspiracy. — **con·spir·a·to·ri·al** /kən,spirə'tôrēəl/ **adj. con·spir·a·to·ri·al·ly** /kən,spirə'tôrēəlē/ **adv.**

con·spire /kən'spī(ə)r/ ▶ **v.** [intrans.] make secret plans jointly to commit an unlawful or harmful act. ■ [with infin.] (of events or circumstances) seem to be working together to bring about a particular result, typically to someone's detriment. [ME: from OFr. *conspirer*, from L. *conspirare* 'agree,' from *con-* 'with' + *spirare* 'breathe.']

con spi·ri·to /kăn 'spiri,tō; 'kōn-/ ▶ **adv.** Music (as a direction) vigorously; in a spirited manner.

Con·sta·ble /'kănstəbəl/, John (1776–1837), English painter, noted for his landscapes.

con·sta·ble /'kănstəbəl/ ▶ **n. 1** a peace officer with limited policing authority, typically in a small town. **2** the governor of a royal castle. ■ hist. the highest-ranking official in a royal household. [ME: from OFr. *conestable*, from late L. *comes stabuli* 'count of the stable.']

con·stab·u·lar·y /kən'stabyə,lerē/ ▶ **n.** (pl. **-lar·ies**) the constables of a district, collectively. ■ an armed police force organized as a military unit. ▶ **adj.** [attrib.] of or relating to a constabulary.

Con·stance, Lake /'kănstəns/ a lake in southeastern Germany, on the borders of Germany, Switzerland, and Austria. German name **BODENSEE.**

con·stan·cy /'kănstənsē/ ▶ **n.** the quality of being faithful and dependable. ■ the quality of being enduring and unchanging.

con·stant /'kănstənt/ ▶ **adj.** occurring continuously over a period of time. ■ remaining the same over a period of time. ■ (of a person) unchangingly faithful and dependable. ▶ **n.** a situation or state of

PRONUNCIATION KEY ə *ago, up*; ər *over, fur*; a *hat*; ā *ate*; ä *car*; e *let*; ē *see*; i *fit*; ī *by*; ɴɢ *sing*; ō *go*; ô *law, for*; oi *toy*; ŏŏ *good*; ōō *goo*; ou *out*; ᴛʜ *thin*; ᴛʜ *then*; ᴢʜ *vision* affairs that does not change. ■ Math. a quantity or parameter that does not change its value whatever the value of the variables, under a given set of conditions. ■ Physics a number expressing a relation or property that remains the same in all circumstances, or for the same substance under the same conditions. — **con·stant·ly** adv. [ME: from OFr., from L. *constant-* 'standing firm,' from v. *constare*, from *con-* + *stare* 'stand.']

Con·stan·ţa /kōn'stäntsə; kôn-/ (also **Con·stan·za**) a port in southeastern Romania, on the Black Sea; pop. 349,000.

con·stant·an /'känstən,tan/ ▶ n. a copper–nickel alloy used in electrical work for its high resistance. [20th C.: from CONSTANT.]

Con·stan·tine[1] /'känstən,tēn/ a city in northeastern Algeria; pop. 449,000.

Con·stan·tine[2] /'känstən,tēn; -,tīn/ (c.274–337), Roman emperor; known as **Constantine the Great**. He was the first Roman emperor to be converted to Christianity. In 330, he moved the capital to Byzantium, renaming it Constantinopolis (Constantinople).

Con·stan·ti·no·ple /,känstantn'ōpəl/ the former name of Istanbul, from AD 330 until the capture of the city by the Turks in 1453.

con·sta·tive /'känstətiv; kən'stātiv/ Ling. ▶ adj. denoting a speech act or sentence that is a statement declaring something to be the case. Often contrasted with PERFORMATIVE. ▶ n. a constative speech act or sentence. [20th C.: from L. *constat-* 'established' (from the v. *constare*).]

con·stel·late /'känstə,lāt/ ▶ v. literary form or cause to form into a cluster or group; gather together.

con·stel·la·tion /,känstə'lāshən/ ▶ n. a group of stars forming a pattern that is traditionally named after its apparent form or identified with a mythological figure. Modern astronomers divide the sky into eighty-eight constellations with defined boundaries. ■ a group or cluster of related things. [ME: via OFr. from late L. *constellatio(n-)*, based on L. *stella* 'star.']

con·ster·nate /'känstər,nāt/ ▶ v. [trans.] fill (someone) with anxiety.

con·ster·na·tion /,känstər'nāshən/ ▶ n. feelings of anxiety or dismay, typically at something unexpected. [17th C.: from L. *consternatio(n-)*, from v. *consternare* 'lay prostrate.']

con·sti·pat·ed /'känstə,pātid/ ▶ adj. (of a person or animal) affected with constipation. ■ fig. slow-moving; restricted or inhibited in some way. — **con·sti·pate** /-,pāt/ v. [16th C.: from L. *constipat-* 'pressed together,' from v. *constipare*, from *con-* + *stipare* 'press.']

con·sti·pa·tion /,känstə'pāshən/ ▶ n. a condition in which there is difficulty in emptying the bowels, usually associated with hardened feces. ■ fig. a high level of constraint or restriction; a pronounced lack of ease.

con·stit·u·en·cy /kən'stichōōənsē/ ▶ n. (pl. **-cies**) a body of voters in a specified area who elect a representative to a legislative body. ■ esp. Brit. the area represented in this way. ■ a body of customers or supporters.

con·stit·u·ent /kən'stichōōənt/ ▶ adj. [attrib.] **1** being a part of a whole. **2** being a voting member of a community or organization and having the power to appoint or elect. ■ able to make or change a political constitution. ▶ n. **1** a member of a constituency. **2** a component part of something. ■ Ling. the common part of two or several more complex forms, e.g., *gentle* in *gentleman, gentlemanly, ungentlemanly*. ■ Ling. a word or construction that is part of a larger construction. [15th C.: from L. *constituent-* 'establishing,' from *constituere* (see CONSTITUTE).]

con·sti·tute /'känstə,t(y)ōōt/ ▶ v. [trans.] **1** be (a part) of a whole. ■ (of people or things) combine to form (a whole). ■ be or be equivalent to (something). **2** (usu. **be constituted**) give legal or constitutional form to (an institution); establish by law. [ME: from L. *constitut-* 'established,' from v. *constituere*, from *con-* + *statuere* 'set up.']

con·sti·tu·tion /,känstə't(y)ōōshən/ ▶ n. **1** a body of fundamental principles or established precedents according to which a state or other organization is acknowledged to be governed. ■ a written record of this. ■ (**the Constitution**) the basic written set of principles and precedents of federal government in the US, which came into operation in 1789 and has since been modified by twenty-seven amendments. **2** the composition of something. ■ the forming or establishing of something. **3** a person's physical state with regard to vitality, health, and strength. ■ a person's mental or psychological makeup.

con·sti·tu·tion·al /,känstə't(y)ōōshənl/ ▶ adj. **1** of or relating to an established set of principles governing a state. ■ in accordance with or allowed by such principles. **2** of or relating to someone's physical or mental condition. ▶ n. dated a walk, typically one taken regularly to maintain or restore good health. — **con·sti·tu·tion·al·i·ty** /-,t(y)ōōshə'nalitē/ n. **con·sti·tu·tion·al·ly** adv.

con·sti·tu·tion·al·ism /,känstə't(y)ōōshənl,izəm/ ▶ n. constitutional government. ■ adherence to such a system of government. — **con·sti·tu·tion·al·ist** n.

con·sti·tu·tion·al·ize /,känstə't(y)ōōshənl,īz/ ▶ v. [trans.] make subject to explicit provisions of a country's constitution.

con·sti·tu·tive /'känstə,t(y)ōōtiv; kən'stichətiv/ ▶ adj. **1** having the power to establish or give organized existence to something. **2** forming a part or constituent of something; component. ■ forming an essential element of something. **3** Biochem. relating to an enzyme or enzyme system that is continuously produced in an organism, regardless of the needs of cells. — **con·sti·tu·tive·ly** adv.

con·strain /kən'strān/ ▶ v. [trans.] (often **be constrained**) severely restrict the scope, extent, or activity of. ■ compel or force (someone) toward a particular course of action. ■ [usu. as adj.] (**constrained**) cause to appear unnaturally forced, typically because of embarrassment. ■ literary confine forcibly; imprison. — **con·strain·ed·ly** /-nidlē/ adv. [ME: from OFr. *constraindre*, from L. *constringere* 'bind tightly together.']

con·straint /kən'strānt/ ▶ n. a limitation or restriction. ■ stiffness of manner and inhibition in relations between people. [ME: from OFr. *constreinte*, fem. past part. of *constraindre*.]

con·strict /kən'strikt/ ▶ v. [trans.] make narrower, esp. by encircling pressure: *chemicals that constrict the blood vessels* | [as adj.] (**constricted**) *constricted air passages*. ■ [intrans.] become narrower. ■ (of a snake) coil around (prey) in order to asphyxiate it. ■ fig. restrict. — **con·stric·tion** /-'strikshən/ n. **con·stric·tive** adj. [18th C.: from L. *constrict-* 'bound tightly together,' from *constringere* (see CONSTRAIN).]

con·stric·tor /kən'striktər/ ▶ n. **1** a snake (families Boidae and Pythonidae, and some members of other families, esp. Colubridae) that kills by coiling around its prey and asphyxiating it. **2** (also **constrictor muscle**) Anat. a muscle whose contraction narrows a vessel or passage. ■ each of the muscles that constrict the pharynx.

con·struct ▶ v. /kən'strəkt/ [trans.] build or erect (something, typically a building, road, or machine). ■ form (an idea or theory) by bringing together various conceptual elements, typically over a period of time. ■ Gram. form (a sentence) according to grammatical rules. ■ Geom. draw or delineate (a geometric figure) accurately to given conditions. ▶ n. /'kän,strəkt/ an idea or theory containing various conceptual elements, typically one considered to be subjective and not based on empirical evidence. ■ Ling. a group of words forming a phrase. ■ a physical thing that is deliberately built or formed. — **con·struct·i·ble** adj. **con·struc·tor** /-tər/ n. [ME: from L. *construct-* 'heaped together,' from v. *construere*, from *con-* + *struere* 'to pile.']

con·struc·tion /kən'strəkshən/ ▶ n. the building of something, typically a large structure. ■ such activity considered as an industry. ■ the style or method used in the building of something. ■ a building or other structure. ■ the creation or formation of an abstract entity. ■ an interpretation or explanation. ■ Gram. the arrangement of words according to syntactical rules. — **con·struc·tion·al** /-shənl/ adj. **con·struc·tion·al·ly** /-shənl-ē/ adv.

con·struc·tion·ism /kən'strəkshə,nizəm/ ▶ n. another term for CONSTRUCTIVISM.

con·struc·tion·ist /kən'strəkshənist/ ▶ n. **1** another term for CONSTRUCTIVIST (see CONSTRUCTIVISM). **2** a person who puts a particular construction upon a legal document, esp. the US Constitution. — **con·struc·tion·ism** n.

con·struc·tive /kən'strəktiv/ ▶ adj. **1** serving a useful purpose; tending to build up. **2** Law derived by inference; implied by operation of law; not obvious or explicit. **3** Math. relating to, based on, or denoting proofs that show how an entity may in principle be constructed or arrived at in a finite number of steps. — **con·struc·tive·ly** adv. **con·struc·tive·ness** n.

con·struc·tiv·ism /kən'strəkti,vizəm/ ▶ n. **1** Art a style or movement in which assorted mechanical objects are combined into abstract mobile structural forms. The movement originated in Russia in the 1920s and has influenced many aspects of modern architecture and design. [transliterating Russ. *konstruktivizm*.] **2** Math. a view which admits as valid only constructive proofs and entities demonstrable by them, implying that the latter have no independent existence. — **con·struc·tiv·ist** n.

con·strue /kən'strōō/ ▶ v. (**-strues, -strued, -stru·ing**) [trans.] (often **be construed**) interpret (a word or action) in a particular way. ■ dated analyze the syntax of (a text, sentence, or word). ■ dated translate (a passage or author) word for word, typically aloud. — **con·stru·a·ble** adj. **con·stru·al** /-'strōōəl/ n. [ME: from L. *construere* (see CONSTRUCT).]

con·sub·stan·tial /,känsəb'stanchəl/ ▶ adj. of the same substance or essence (used esp. of the three persons of the Trinity in Christian theology). — **con·sub·stan·ti·al·i·ty** /-,stanchē'alitē/ n. [ME: from eccles. L. *consubstantialis*, from *con-* 'with' + *substantialis* (see SUBSTANTIAL).]

con·sub·stan·ti·a·tion /,känsəb,stanchē'āshən/ ▶ n. Christian Theol. the doctrine, esp. in Lutheran belief, that the substance of the bread and wine coexists with the body and blood of Christ in the Eucharist. Compare with TRANSUBSTANTIATION.

con·sue·tude /'känswi,t(y)ōōd/ ▶ n. an established custom, esp. one having legal force. — **con·sue·tu·di·nar·y** /,känswi't(y)ōōdn,erē/ adj. [ME: from OFr., or from L. *consuetudo* (see CUSTOM).]

con·sul /'känsəl/ ▶ n. **1** an official appointed by a government to live in a foreign city and protect and promote the government's citizens and interests there. **2** (in ancient Rome) one of the two annually elected chief magistrates who jointly ruled the republic. ■ any of the three chief magistrates of the first French republic (1799–1804). — **con·su·lar** /'käns(y)ələr/ adj. **con·sul·ship** n. [ME: from L., rel. to *consulere* 'take counsel.']

con·su·late /'känsəlit/ ▶ n. **1** the place or building in which a consul's duties are carried out. ■ the office, position, or period of office of a consul. **2** hist. the period of office of a Roman consul. ■ (**the consulate**) the system of government by consuls in ancient Rome. **3** (**the Consulate**) the government of the first French republic (1799–1804) by three consuls.

con·sul gen·er·al ▶ n. (pl. **con·suls gen·er·al**) a consul of the highest status, stationed in a major city and supervising other consuls in the district.

con·sult /kən'səlt/ ▶ v. [trans.] seek information or advice from (someone with expertise). ■ have discussions or confer with (someone), typically before undertaking a course of action. ■ refer for information to (a book, watch, etc.) in order to ascertain something. — **con·sul·ta·tive**

/-'səltətiv/ adj. [16th C.: from Fr. *consulter*, from L. *consultare*, frequentative of *consulere* 'take counsel.']

con·sult·an·cy /kən'səltnsē/ ▶ n. (pl. **-cies**) a professional practice that gives expert advice within a particular field, esp. business. ■ the work of giving such advice.

con·sult·ant /kən'səltnt/ ▶ n. a person who provides expert advice professionally.

con·sul·ta·tion /,känsəl'tāsнən/ ▶ n. the action or process of formally consulting or discussing. ■ a meeting with an expert or professional, such as a medical doctor, in order to seek advice.

con·sult·ing /kən'səltiNG/ ▶ adj. [attrib.] (of a senior person in a professional or technical field) engaged in the business of giving advice to others in the same field. ■ (of a business or company) giving specialist advice. ▶ n. the business of giving specialist advice to other professionals, typically in financial and business matters.

con·sult·ing room ▶ n. a room in which a doctor or other therapeutic practitioner examines patients.

con·sum·a·ble /kən'sōōməbəl/ ▶ adj. (of an item for sale) intended to be used up and then replaced. ▶ n. (usu. **consumables**) a commodity that is intended to be used up relatively quickly.

con·sume /kən'sōōm/ ▶ v. [trans.] eat, drink, or ingest (food or drink). ■ buy (goods or services). ■ use up (a resource). ■ (esp. of a fire) completely destroy. ■ (usu. **be consumed**) (of a feeling) absorb all of the attention and energy of (someone): *Carolyn was consumed with guilt* | [as adj.] (**consuming**) *a consuming passion.* — **con·sum·ing·ly** adv. [ME: from L. *consumere*, from *con-* 'altogether' + *sumere* 'take up.']

con·sum·er /kən'sōōmər/ ▶ n. a person who purchases goods and services for personal use. ■ a person or thing that eats or uses something.

con·sum·er goods ▶ plural n. goods bought and used by consumers, rather than by manufacturers for producing other goods. Often contrasted with CAPITAL GOODS.

con·sum·er·ism /kən'sōōmə,rizəm/ ▶ n. 1 the protection or promotion of the interests of consumers. 2 often derog. the preoccupation of society with the acquisition of consumer goods. — **con·sum·er·ist** adj. & n. **con·sum·er·is·tic** /kən,sōōmə'ristik/ adj.

con·sum·er price in·dex (abbr.: **CPI**) ▶ n. an index of the variation in prices paid by typical consumers for retail goods and other items.

con·sum·er re·search ▶ n. the investigation of the needs and opinions of consumers, esp. with regard to a particular product or service.

con·sum·mate ▶ v. /'kānsə,māt/ [trans.] make (a marriage or relationship) complete by having sexual intercourse. ■ complete (a transaction or attempt); make perfect. ▶ adj. /'känsəmit; kən'səmit/ showing a high degree of skill and flair; complete or perfect. — **con·sum·mate·ly** /'känsəmətlē; kən'səmətlē/ adv. **con·sum·ma·tor** /'känsə,mātər/ n. [ME: from L. *consummat-* 'brought to completion,' from the v. *consummare*, from *con-* + *summa* 'sum.']

con·sum·ma·tion /,känsə'māsнən/ ▶ n. the point at which something is complete or finalized. ■ the action of making a marriage or relationship complete by having sexual intercourse.

con·sump·tion /kən'səm(p)sнən/ ▶ n. 1 the using up of a resource. ■ the eating, drinking, or ingesting of something. ■ an amount of something that is used up or ingested. ■ the purchase and use of goods and services by the public. ■ the reception of information or entertainment, esp. by a mass audience. 2 dated a wasting disease, esp. pulmonary tuberculosis. [ME: from L. *consumptio(n-)*, from *consumere* (see CONSUME).]

con·sump·tive /kən'səm(p)tiv/ ▶ adj. 1 dated affected with a wasting disease, esp. pulmonary tuberculosis. 2 esp. derog. of or relating to the using up of resources. ▶ n. dated a person with a wasting disease, esp. pulmonary tuberculosis. — **con·sump·tive·ly** adv.

cont. ▶ abbr. ■ contents. ■ continued.

con·tact ▶ n. /'käntakt/ 1 the state or condition of physical touching. ■ the state or condition of communicating or meeting. ■ [as adj.] activated by or operating through physical touch: *contact dermatitis.* ■ a connection for the passage of an electric current from one thing to another, or a part or device by which such a connection is made. ■ (**contacts**) contact lenses. 2 a meeting, communication, or relationship with someone. ■ a person who may be communicated with for information or assistance, esp. with regard to one's job. ■ a person who has associated with a patient with a contagious disease (and so may carry the infection). ▶ v. /'käntakt; kən'takt/ [trans.] communicate with (someone), typically in order to give or receive specific information. — **con·tact·a·ble** /'käntaktəbəl; kən'tak-/ adj. [17th C.: from L. *contactus*, from *contact-* 'touched,' from v. *contingere*, from *con-* 'with' + *tangere* 'to touch.']

con·tact flight (also **contact flying**) ▶ n. navigation of an aircraft by the observation of landmarks.

con·tact lens ▶ n. a thin plastic lens placed directly on the surface of the eye to correct visual defects.

con·tac·tor /'kän,taktər; kən'tak-/ ▶ n. a device for making and breaking an electric circuit.

con·tact per·son ▶ n. a person who provides a link for information or representation between two parties.

con·tact print ▶ n. a photographic print made by placing a negative directly onto sensitized paper, glass, or film and illuminating it. ▶ v. (**con·tact-print**) [trans.] make a photograph from (a negative) in this way.

con·tact sheet ▶ n. a piece of photographic paper onto which several or all of the negatives on a roll of film have been contact printed.

con·tact sport ▶ n. a sport in which the participants necessarily come into bodily contact with one another.

Con·ta·gem /,kōntə'zнām/ a city in Minas Gerais state in southeastern Brazil; pop. 491,000.

con·ta·gion /kən'tājən/ ▶ n. the communication of disease from one person to another by close contact. ■ a disease spread in such a way. ■ fig. the spreading of a harmful idea or practice. ■ a contagium. [ME: from L. *contagio(n-)*, from *con-* 'with' + base of *tangere* 'to touch.']

con·ta·gious /kən'tājəs/ ▶ adj. (of a disease) spread from one person or organism to another by direct or indirect contact. ■ (of a person or animal) likely to transmit a disease by contact with other people or animals. ■ fig. (of an emotion, feeling, or attitude) likely to spread to and affect others. — **con·ta·gious·ly** adv. **con·ta·gious·ness** n.

con·ta·gium /kən'tājəm; -jēəm/ ▶ n. (pl. **-gi·a** /-jə; -jēə/) a substance or agent, such as a virus, by which a contagious disease is transmitted.

con·tain /kən'tān/ ▶ v. [trans.] 1 have or hold (someone or something) within. ■ be made up of (a number of things); consist of. ■ (of a number) be divisible by (a factor) without a remainder. 2 control or restrain (oneself or a feeling). ■ prevent (a severe problem) from increasing in extent or intensity. — **con·tain·a·ble** adj. [ME: from OFr. *contenir*, from L. *continere*, from *con-* + *tenere* 'to hold.']

con·tain·er /kən'tānər/ ▶ n. an object that can be used to hold or transport something. ■ a large metal box of a standard design and size used for the transportation of goods by road, rail, sea, or air.

con·tain·er·ize /kən'tānə,rīz/ ▶ v. [trans.] [usu. as adj.] (**containerized**) pack into or transport by container: *containerized cargo.* — **con·tain·er·i·za·tion** /-,tānərə'zāsнən/ n.

con·tain·er port ▶ n. a port that specializes in handling goods transported in containers.

con·tain·er ship ▶ n. a ship that is designed to carry goods stowed in containers.

con·tain·ment /kən'tānmənt/ ▶ n. the action of keeping something harmful under control or within limits. ■ the action or policy of preventing the expansion of a hostile country or influence.

con·tam·i·nate /kən'tamə,nāt/ ▶ v. [trans.] (often **be contaminated**) make (something) impure by exposure to or addition of a poisonous or polluting substance. — **con·tam·i·nant** /-'tamənənt/ n. **con·tam·i·na·tion** /-,tamə'nāsнən/ n. **con·tam·i·na·tor** /-,nātər/ n. [ME: from L. *contaminat-* 'made impure,' from v. *contaminare*, from *contamen* 'contact,' from *con-* + base of *tangere* 'to touch.']

con·te /kônt/ ▶ n. a short story as a form of literary composition. ■ a medieval narrative tale. [Fr., based on L. *computare* 'reckon.']

con·té /kôn'tā/ (also trademark **Con·té**) ▶ n. a kind of hard, grease-free crayon used as a medium for artwork. [19th C.: named after Nicolas J. *Conté* (1755–1805), Fr. inventor.]

con·temn /kən'tem/ ▶ v. [trans.] archaic treat or regard with contempt. — **con·temn·er** /-'tem(n)ər/ n. [ME: from L. *contemnere*, from *con-* + *temnere* 'despise.']

con·tem·plate /'käntəm,plāt/ ▶ v. [trans.] look thoughtfully for a long time at. ■ think about. ■ [intrans.] think profoundly and at length; meditate. ■ have in mind as a probable though not certain intention. — **con·tem·pla·tor** /-,plātər/ n. [16th C.: from L. *contemplat-* 'surveyed,' from v. *contemplari*, based on *templum* 'place for observation.']

con·tem·pla·tion /,käntəm'plāsнən/ ▶ n. the action of looking thoughtfully at something for a long time. ■ deep reflective thought. ■ the state of being thought about or planned. ■ religious meditation. ■ (in Christian spirituality) a form of prayer or meditation in which a person seeks to pass beyond mental images and concepts to a direct experience of the divine.

con·tem·pla·tive /kən'templətiv; 'käntəm,plātiv/ ▶ adj. expressing or involving prolonged thought. ■ involving or given to deep silent prayer or religious meditation. ▶ n. a person whose life is devoted primarily to prayer, esp. in a monastery or convent. — **con·tem·pla·tive·ly** adv.

con·tem·po·ra·ne·ous /kən,tempə'rānēəs/ ▶ adj. existing or occurring in the same period of time. — **con·tem·po·ra·ne·i·ty** /-rə'nē-itē; -rə'nā-itē/ n. **con·tem·po·ra·ne·ous·ly** adv. **con·tem·po·ra·ne·ous·ness** n. [17th C.: from L., from *con-* 'with' + *temporaneus* (from *tempus*, *tempor-* 'time').]

con·tem·po·rar·y /kən'tempə,rerē/ ▶ adj. 1 living or occurring at the same time. ■ dating from the same time. 2 belonging to or occurring in the present. ■ following modern ideas or fashion in style or design. ▶ n. (pl. **-rar·ies**) a person or thing living or existing at the same time as another. ■ a person of roughly the same age as another. — **con·tem·po·rar·i·ly** /kən,tempə're(ə)rəlē/ adv. **con·tem·po·rar·i·ness** n. [17th C.: from med. L. *contemporarius*, from *con-* 'with' + *tempus*, *tempor-* 'time.']

con·tempt /kən'tem(p)t/ ▶ n. the feeling that a person or a thing is beneath consideration, worthless, or deserving scorn. ■ disregard for something that should be taken into account. ■ (also **contempt of court**) the offense of being disobedient to or disrespectful of a court of law and its officers. ■ the offense of being similarly disobedient to or disrespectful of the lawful operation of a legislative body (e.g., its investigations).

– PHRASES **beneath contempt** utterly worthless or despicable. **hold someone/something in contempt** consider someone or something to be unworthy of respect or attention. [ME: from L. *contemptus*, from *contemnere* (see CONTEMN).]

con·tempt·i·ble /kən'tem(p)təbəl/ ▶ **adj.** deserving contempt; despicable. — **con·tempt·i·bly** /-blē/ **adv.**

con·temp·tu·ous /kən'tem(p)CHōōəs/ ▶ **adj.** showing contempt; scornful. — **con·temp·tu·ous·ly adv. con·temp·tu·ous·ness n.** [16th C.: from med. L. *contemptuosus*, from L. *contemptus*.]

con·tend /kən'tend/ ▶ **v. 1** [intrans.] (**contend with/against**) struggle to surmount (a difficulty or danger). ■ (**contend for**) engage in a competition or campaign in order to win or achieve (something). **2** [with clause] assert something as a position in an argument. — **con·tend·er n.** [ME: from OFr. *contendre* or L. *contendere*, from *con-* 'with' + *tendere* 'strive.']

con·tent[1] /kən'tent/ ▶ **adj.** [attrib.] in a state of peaceful happiness. ■ satisfied with a certain level of achievement, good fortune, etc., and not wishing for more. ▶ **v.** [trans.] satisfy (someone). ■ (**content oneself with**) accept as adequate despite wanting more or better. ▶ **n.** a state of satisfaction: *the greater part of the century was a time of content.*

– PHRASES **to one's heart's content** to the full extent of one's desires. [ME: via OFr. from L. *contentus* 'satisfied,' past part. of *continere* (see CONTAIN).]

con·tent[2] /'käntent/ ▶ **n. 1** (usu. **contents**) the things that are held or included in something. ■ [usu. in sing.] [with adj.] the amount of a particular constituent occurring in a substance: *a low fat content.* ■ (**contents** or **table of contents**) a list of the titles of chapters or sections contained in a book or periodical. **2** the substance or material dealt with in a speech, literary work, etc., as distinct from its form or style. [ME: from med. L. *contentum*, neut. past part. of *continere* (see CONTAIN).]

con·tent·ed /kən'tentəd/ ▶ **adj.** happy and at ease. ■ expressing happiness and satisfaction. ■ willing to accept something; satisfied. — **con·tent·ed·ly adv. con·tent·ed·ness n.**

con·ten·tion /kən'tenCHən/ ▶ **n. 1** heated disagreement. **2** an assertion, esp. one maintained in argument.

– PHRASES **in contention** having a good chance of success in a contest. [ME: from L. *contentio(n-)*, from *contendere*.]

con·ten·tious /kən'tenCHəs/ ▶ **adj.** causing or likely to cause an argument; controversial. ■ involving heated argument. ■ (of a person) given to arguing or provoking argument. ■ Law relating to or involving differences between contending parties. — **con·ten·tious·ly adv. con·ten·tious·ness n.**

con·tent·ment /kən'tentmənt/ ▶ **n.** a state of happiness and satisfaction.

con·ter·mi·nous /kän'tərmənəs; kən-/ ▶ **adj.** sharing a common boundary. ■ having the same area, context, or meaning. — **con·ter·mi·nous·ly adv.** [17th C.: from L. *conterminus* (from *con-* 'with' + *terminus* 'boundary').]

con·tes·sa /kən'tesə/ ▶ **n.** an Italian countess. [Ital., from late L. *comitissa* (see COUNTESS).]

con·test ▶ **n.** /'käntest/ an event in which people compete for supremacy in a sport, activity, or particular quality. ■ a competition for a political position. ■ a dispute or conflict. ▶ **v.** /kən'test; 'käntest/ [trans.] **1** engage in competition to attain (a position of power). ■ take part in (a competition or election). **2** oppose (an action, decision, or theory) as mistaken or wrong. ■ engage in dispute about.

– PHRASES **no contest 1** another term for NOLO CONTENDERE. **2** a competition, comparison, or choice of which the outcome is a foregone conclusion. ■ a decision by the referee to declare a boxing match invalid on the grounds that one or both of the boxers are not making serious efforts. — **con·test·a·ble** /kən'testəbəl/ **adj. con·test·er** /kən'testər; 'kän,tes-/ **n.** [16th C.: from L. *contestari* 'call upon to witness,' from *con-* 'with' + *testare* 'to witness.']

con·test·ant /kən'testənt/ ▶ **n.** a person who takes part in a contest or competition.

con·tes·ta·tion /,käntəs'tāSHən/ ▶ **n.** formal the action or process of disputing or arguing.

con·text /'käntekst/ ▶ **n.** the circumstances that form the setting for an event, statement, or idea, and in terms of which it can be fully understood and assessed. ■ the parts of something written or spoken that immediately precede and follow a word or passage and clarify its meaning.

– PHRASES **in context** considered together with the surrounding words or circumstances. **out of context** without the surrounding words or circumstances and so not fully understandable. — **con·text·less adj. con·tex·tu·al** /kən'teksCHōōəl/ **adj. con·tex·tu·al·ly** /kən'teksCHəwəlē/ **adv.** [ME: from L. *contextus*, from *con-* 'with' + *texere* 'to weave.']

con·tex·tu·al·ism /kən'teksCHōōə,lizəm/ ▶ **n.** Philos. a doctrine that emphasizes the importance of the context of inquiry in a particular question. — **con·tex·tu·al·ist n.**

con·tex·tu·al·ize /kən'teksCHōōə,līz/ ▶ **v.** [trans.] place or study in context. — **con·tex·tu·al·i·za·tion** /kən,teksCHōōələ'zāSHən/ **n.**

con·tex·ture /kən'teksCHər/ ▶ **n.** the fact or manner of being woven or linked together to form a connected whole. ■ a mass of things interwoven together; a fabric. ■ the putting together of words and sentences in connected composition; the construction of a text. ■ a connected literary structure; a continuous text.

con·ti·gu·i·ty /,käntə'gyōōitē/ ▶ **n.** the state of bordering or being in direct contact with something.

con·tig·u·ous /kən'tigyōōəs/ ▶ **adj.** sharing a common border; touching. ■ next or together in sequence. — **con·tig·u·ous·ly adv.** [16th C.: from L. *contiguus* 'touching,' from *contingere* (see CONTINGENT).]

con·ti·nent[1] /'käntn-ənt/ ▶ **n.** any of the world's main continuous expanses of land (Africa, Antarctica, Asia, Australia, Europe, North America, South America). ■ (also **the Continent**) the mainland of Europe as distinct from the British Isles. ■ a mainland contrasted with islands. [16th C.: from L. *terra continens* 'continuous land.']

con·ti·nent[2] ▶ **adj. 1** able to control movements of the bowels and bladder. **2** exercising self-restraint, esp. sexually. — **con·ti·nence n. con·ti·nent·ly adv.** [ME: from L. *continent-* 'holding together,' from *continere* (see CONTAIN).]

con·ti·nen·tal /,käntn'entl/ ▶ **adj. 1** [attrib.] forming or belonging to a continent. **2** coming from or characteristic of mainland Europe. **3** (also **Continental**) pertaining to the 13 original colonies of the US. ▶ **n. 1** an inhabitant of mainland Europe. **2** (**Continental**) a member of the colonial army in the American Revolution. **3** (also **Continental**) a piece of paper currency used at the time of the American Revolution. — **con·ti·nen·tal·ly adv.**

Con·ti·nen·tal Ar·my the army raised by the Continental Congress of 1775, with George Washington as commander.

con·ti·nen·tal break·fast ▶ **n.** a light breakfast, typically consisting of coffee and rolls with butter and jam.

con·ti·nen·tal cli·mate ▶ **n.** a relatively dry climate with very hot summers and very cold winters, characteristic of the central parts of Asia and North America.

Con·ti·nen·tal Con·gress each of the three congresses held by the American colonies (in 1774, 1775, and 1776, respectively) in revolt against British rule. The second, convened in the wake of the battles at Lexington and Concord, created a Continental Army, which eventually won the American Revolution.

con·ti·nen·tal crust ▶ **n.** Geol. the relatively thick part of the earth's crust that forms the large landmasses. It is generally older and more complex than the oceanic crust.

Con·ti·nen·tal Di·vide the series of ridges in the Rocky Mountains in North America that form a watershed that separates the rivers flowing east from those flowing west. Also called GREAT DIVIDE.

con·ti·nen·tal drift ▶ **n.** the gradual movement of the continents across the earth's surface through geological time. See PLATE TECTONICS

con·ti·nen·tal shelf ▶ **n.** the area of seabed around a large landmass where the sea is relatively shallow compared with the open ocean.

con·ti·nen·tal slope ▶ **n.** the slope between the outer edge of the continental shelf and the deep ocean floor.

con·tin·gence /kən'tinjəns/ ▶ **n.** touching; contact. ■ connection; affinity.

con·tin·gen·cy /kən'tinjənsē/ ▶ **n.** (pl. **-cies**) a future event or circumstance that is possible but cannot be predicted with certainty. ■ a provision for such an event or circumstance. ■ an incidental expense. ■ the absence of certainty in events. ■ Philos. the absence of necessity; the fact of being so without having to be so.

con·tin·gen·cy plan ▶ **n.** a plan designed to take a possible future event or circumstance into account.

con·tin·gen·cy ta·ble ▶ **n.** Stat. a table showing the distribution of one variable in rows and another in columns, used to study the association between the two variables.

con·tin·gent /kən'tinjənt/ ▶ **adj. 1** subject to chance. ■ (of losses, liabilities, etc.) that can be anticipated to arise if a particular event occurs. ■ Philos. true by virtue of the way things in fact are and not by logical necessity. **2** [predic.] (**contingent on/upon**) occurring or existing only if (certain other circumstances) are the case; dependent on. ▶ **n.** a group of people united by some common feature, forming part of a larger group. ■ a body of troops or police sent to join a larger force in an operation. — **con·tin·gent·ly adv.** [ME: from L. *contingere* 'befall,' from *con-* 'with' + *tangere* 'to touch.']

con·tin·u·al /kən'tinyōōəl/ ▶ **adj.** frequently recurring; always happening. ■ having no interruptions. — **con·tin·u·al·ly adv.** [ME: from OFr. *continuel*, based on L. *continuus* (see CONTINUOUS).]

con·tin·u·ance /kən'tinyōōəns/ ▶ **n. 1** formal the state of remaining in existence or operation. ■ the time for which a situation or action lasts. ■ the state of remaining in a particular position or condition. **2** Law a postponement or adjournment.

con·tin·u·ant /kən'tinyōōənt/ ▶ **n.** Phonet. a consonant that is sounded with the vocal tract only partly closed, allowing the breath to pass through and the sound to be prolonged (as with *f, l, m, n, r, s, v*). ▶ **adj.** of, relating to, or denoting a continuant.

con·tin·u·a·tion /kən,tinyōō'āSHən/ ▶ **n.** the action of carrying something on over a period of time or the process of being carried on. ■ the state of remaining in a particular position or condition. ■ [usu. in sing.] a part that is attached to and an extension of something else.

con·tin·u·a·tive /kən'tinyōōətiv; -,ātiv/ Ling. ▶ **adj.** (of a word or phrase) having the function of moving a discourse or conversation forward. ▶ **n.** a word or phrase of this type (e.g., *yes, well, as I was saying*).

con·tin·u·a·tor /kən'tinyōō,ātər/ ▶ **n.** a person or thing that continues something or maintains continuity.

con·tin·ue /kən'tinyōō/ ▶ **v.** (**-ues, -ued, -u·ing**) **1** [intrans.] persist in an activity or process. ■ remain in existence or operation. ■ [trans.] carry on with (something that one has begun). ■ remain in a specified position or state. ■ [with adverbial of direction] carry on traveling in the same direction: *they continued northward.* ■ [intrans.] (of a road, river, etc.) extend farther in the same direction. **2** recommence or resume after interruption. ■ [intrans.] carry on speaking after a pause or interruption. ■ [trans.] Law postpone or adjourn (a legal proceeding). — **con·tin·u·er** n. [ME: from OFr. *continuer*, from L. *continuare*, from *continuus* (see CONTINUOUS).]

con·tin·ued frac·tion ▶ n. Math. a fraction of infinite length whose denominator is a quantity plus a fraction, which latter fraction has a similar denominator, and so on.

con·tin·u·ing ed·u·ca·tion ▶ n. education provided for adults after they have left the formal education system, consisting typically of short or part-time courses.

con·ti·nu·i·ty /ˌkäntn'(y)o͞oitē/ ▶ n. (pl. **-ties**) **1** the unbroken and consistent existence or operation of something over a period of time. ■ a state of stability and the absence of disruption. ■ (often **continuity between/with**) a connection or line of development with no sharp breaks. **2** the maintenance of continuous action and self-consistent detail in the various scenes of a movie or broadcast. ■ the linking of broadcast items, esp. by a spoken commentary.

con·tin·u·o /kən'tinyo͞oˌō/ (also **bas·so con·tin·u·o**) ▶ n. (pl. **-os**) (in baroque music) an accompanying part that includes a bass line and harmonies, typically played on a keyboard instrument and with other instruments such as cello or bass viol. [18th C.: Ital. *basso continuo* 'continuous bass.']

con·tin·u·ous /kən'tinyo͞oəs/ ▶ adj. **1** forming an unbroken whole; without interruption. ■ forming a series with no exceptions or reversals. ■ Math. (of a function) of which the graph is a smooth unbroken curve, i.e., one such that as the value of *x* approaches any given value *a*, the value of *f(x)* approaches that of *f(a)* as a limit. **2** Gram. another term for PROGRESSIVE (sense 3). — **con·tin·u·ous·ly** adv. **con·tin·u·ous·ness** n. [17th C.: from L. *continuus* 'uninterrupted,' from *continere* 'hang together' (from *con-* 'with' + *tenere* 'hold').]

con·tin·u·ous wave ▶ n. an electromagnetic wave, esp. a radio wave, having a constant amplitude.

con·tin·u·um /kən'tinyo͞oəm/ ▶ n. (pl. **-u·a** /-yo͞oə/) [usu. in sing.] a continuous sequence in which adjacent elements are not perceptibly different from each other, although the extremes are quite distinct. ■ Math. the set of real numbers. [17th C.: from L., neut. of *continuus*.]

con·tort /kən'tôrt/ ▶ v. twist or bend out of its normal shape. — **con·tor·tion** /kən'tôrsHən/ n. [ME: from L. *contort-* 'twisted around,' from v. *contorquere*, from *con-* + *torquere* 'twist.']

con·tor·tion·ist /kən'tôrsHənist/ ▶ n. an entertainer who twists and bends their body into strange and unnatural positions.

con·tour /'käntŏŏr/ ▶ n. (usu. **contours**) an outline, esp. one representing or bounding the shape or form of something. ■ an outline of a natural feature such as a hill or valley. ■ short for CONTOUR LINE. ■ a line joining points on a diagram at which some property has the same value. ■ a way in which something varies, esp. the pitch of music or the pattern of tones in an utterance. ▶ v. [trans.] **1** (usu. **be contoured**) mold into a specific shape, typically one designed to fit into something else. **2** mark (a map or diagram) with contour lines. **3** (of a road or railroad) follow the outline of (a topographical feature), esp. along a contour line. [17th C.: from Fr., from Ital. *contorno*, from *contornare* 'draw in outline,' from *con-* + *tornare* 'to turn.']

con·tour feath·er ▶ n. any of the mainly small feathers that form the outline of an adult bird's plumage.

con·tour line ▶ n. a line on a map joining points of equal height above or below sea level.

con·tour map ▶ n. a map marked with contour lines.

con·tra /'käntrə/ (also **Con·tra**) ▶ n. a member of a guerrilla force in Nicaragua that opposed the left-wing Sandinista government 1979–90, and was supported by the US for much of that time. It was officially disbanded in 1990, after the Sandinistas' electoral defeat. [abbrev. of Sp. *contrarevolucionario* 'counterrevolutionary.']

contra- ▶ prefix **1** against; opposite; contrasting: *contradict*. **2** Music (of instruments or organ stops) pitched an octave below: *contralto*. [from L. *contra* 'against.']

con·tra·band /'käntrəˌband/ ▶ n. goods that have been imported or exported illegally. ■ trade in smuggled goods. ■ (also **contraband of war**) goods forbidden to be supplied by neutrals to those engaged in war. ■ during the US Civil War, a slave who escaped or was transported across Union lines. ▶ adj. imported or exported illegally, either in defiance of a total ban or without payment of duty. ■ relating to traffic in illegal goods. — **con·tra·band·ist** n. [16th C.: from Sp. *contrabanda*, from Ital. *contrabando*, from *contra-* 'against' + *bando* 'ban.']

con·tra·bass /'käntrəˌbās/ ▶ n. another term for DOUBLE BASS. ▶ adj. [attrib.] denoting a musical instrument with a range an octave lower than the normal bass range. [18th C.: from Ital. *contrabasso*, from *contra-* 'pitched an octave below' + *basso* (see BASS[1]).]

con·tra·bas·soon /ˌkäntrəbə'so͞on; -ba-/ ▶ n. a bassoon that is larger and longer than the normal type and sounds an octave lower in pitch.

con·tra·cep·tion /ˌkäntrə'sepsHən/ ▶ n. the deliberate use of artificial methods or other techniques to prevent pregnancy as a consequence of sexual intercourse. [19th C.: from CONTRA- + shortened form of CONCEPTION.]

con·tra·cep·tive /ˌkäntrə'septiv/ ▶ adj. (of a method or device) serving to prevent pregnancy. ■ of or relating to contraception. ▶ n. a device or drug serving to prevent pregnancy.

con·tract ▶ n. /'käntrakt/ a written or spoken agreement, esp. one concerning employment, sales, or tenancy, that is intended to be enforceable by law. ■ the branch of law concerned with the making and observation of such agreements. ■ informal an arrangement for someone to be killed by a hired assassin. ■ Bridge the declarer's undertaking to win the number of tricks bid with a stated suit as trump. ■ dated a formal agreement to marry. ▶ v. **1** /kən'trakt/ [intrans.] decrease in size, number, or range. ■ (of a muscle) become shorter or tighter in order to effect movement of part of the body. ■ [trans.] shorten (a word or phrase) by combination or elision. **2** /'käntrakt; kən'trakt/ [intrans.] enter into a formal and legally binding agreement. ■ secure specified rights or undertake specified obligations in a formal and legally binding agreement. ■ [with obj. and infin.] impose an obligation on (someone) to do something by means of a formal agreement. ■ [trans.] (**contract something out**) arrange for work to be done by another organization. ■ [trans.] dated formally enter into (a marriage). ■ [trans.] enter into (a friendship or other relationship). **3** /kən'trakt/ [trans.] catch or develop (a disease or infectious agent). **4** /kən'trakt/ [trans.] become liable to pay (a debt). — **con·tract·ee** /ˌkäntrak'tē/ n. **con·trac·tive** /kən'traktiv; 'käntraktiv/ adj. [ME: via OFr. from L. *contractus*, from *contract-* 'drawn together,' from v. *contrahere*, from *con-* 'together' + *trahere* 'draw.']

con·tract·a·ble /kən'traktəbəl/ ▶ adj. (of a disease) able to be caught.

con·tract bridge /'käntrakt/ ▶ n. the standard form of the card game bridge, in which only tricks bid and won count toward the game, as opposed to auction bridge.

con·tract·i·ble /kən'traktəbəl/ ▶ adj. able to be shrunk or capable of contracting.

con·trac·tile /kən'traktl; -tīl/ ▶ adj. Biol. & Physiol. capable of or producing contraction. — **con·trac·til·i·ty** /ˌkäntrak'tilitē/ n.

con·trac·tion /kən'traksHən/ ▶ n. the process of becoming smaller. ■ the process in which a muscle becomes or is made shorter and tighter. ■ (usu. **contractions**) a shortening of the uterine muscles occurring at intervals before and during childbirth. ■ a word or group of words resulting from shortening an original form. ■ the process of shortening a word by combination or elision.

con·trac·tor /'käntraktər/ ▶ n. a person or company that undertakes a contract to provide materials or labor to perform a service or do a job.

con·trac·tu·al /kən'trakcHo͞oəl/ ▶ adj. agreed in a contract. ■ having similar characteristics to a contract. — **con·trac·tu·al·ly** adv.

con·trac·ture /kən'trakcHər/ ▶ n. Med. a condition of shortening and hardening of muscles, tendons, or other tissue, often leading to deformity and rigidity of joints. — **con·trac·tur·al** /-cHərəl/ adj.

con·tra·dance /'käntrəˌdans/ ▶ n. a country dance in which the couples form lines facing each other. [19th C.: var. of CONTREDANSE.]

con·tra·dict /ˌkäntrə'dikt/ ▶ v. [trans.] deny the truth of (a statement), esp. by asserting the opposite. ■ assert the opposite of a statement made by (someone). ■ be in conflict with. — **con·tra·dic·tor** /-'diktər/ n. [16th C.: from L. *contradict-* 'spoken against,' from v. *contradicere*, orig. *contra dicere* 'speak against.']

con·tra·dic·tion /ˌkäntrə'diksHən/ ▶ n. a combination of statements, ideas, or features of a situation that are opposed to one another. ■ a person, thing, or situation in which inconsistent elements are present. ■ the statement of a position opposite to one already made.

– PHRASES **contradiction in terms** a statement or group of words associating objects or ideas that are incompatible.

con·tra·dic·to·ry /ˌkäntrə'dikt(ə)rē/ ▶ adj. mutually opposed or inconsistent. ■ containing elements that are inconsistent or in conflict. ■ Logic (of two propositions) so related that one and only one must be true. Compare with CONTRARY. ▶ n. (pl. **-ries**) Logic a contradictory proposition. — **con·tra·dic·to·ri·ly** /-'dikt(ə)rəlē/ adv. **con·tra·dic·to·ri·ness** n.

con·tra·dis·tinc·tion /ˌkäntrədə'stiNGksHən/ ▶ n. distinction made by contrasting the different qualities of two things.

con·tra·fac·tu·al /ˌkäntrə'fakcHo͞oəl/ ▶ adj. another term for COUNTERFACTUAL.

con·trail /'känˌtrāl/ ▶ n. a trail of condensed water from an aircraft or rocket at high altitude, seen as a white streak against the sky. [1940s: abbrev. of *condensation trail*.]

con·tra·in·di·cate /ˌkäntrə'indəˌkāt/ ▶ v. [trans.] (usu. **be contraindicated**) Med. (of a condition or circumstance) suggest or indicate that (a particular technique or drug) should not be used in the case in question. — **con·tra·in·di·ca·tion** /-ˌində'kāsHən/ n.

con·tra·lat·er·al /ˌkäntrə'latərəl; -'latrəl/ ▶ adj. Med. relating to or denoting the side of the body opposite to that on which a particular structure or condition occurs.

con·tral·to /kən'traltō/ ▶ n. (pl. **-tos**) the lowest female singing voice. ■ a singer with such a voice. ■ a part written for such a voice. [18th C.: Ital., from *contra-* + ALTO.]

con·tra·po·si·tion /ˌkäntrəpə'zisHən/ ▶ n. Logic conversion of a proposition from *all A is B* to *all not-B is not-A*. — **con·tra·pos·i·tive** /-'päzitiv/ adj. & n. [16th C.: from late L. *contrapositio(n-)*, from v. *contraponere*, from *contra-* + *ponere* 'to place.']

con·trap·tion /kən'trapsHən/ ▶ n. a machine or device that appears strange or unnecessarily complicated, and often badly made or unsafe. [19th C.: perh. from blend of CONTRIVE and TRAP[1].]

con·tra·pun·tal /ˌkäntrəˈpəntl/ ▶**adj.** Music of or in counterpoint. ■ (of a piece of music) with two or more independent melodic lines. — **con·tra·pun·tal·ly** **adv.** **con·tra·pun·tist** **n.** [19th C.: from Ital. *contrapunto* (see COUNTERPOINT).]

con·trar·i·an /kənˈtre(ə)rēən; kän-/ ▶**n.** a person who opposes or rejects popular opinion, esp. in stock exchange dealing. ▶**adj.** opposing or rejecting popular opinion; going against current practice. — **con·trar·i·an·ism** **n.**

con·tra·ri·e·ty /ˌkäntrəˈrīitē/ ▶**n.** 1 opposition or inconsistency between two or more things. 2 Logic contrary opposition. [ME: from OFr. *contrariete*, from late L. *contrarietas*, from *contrarius* (see CONTRARY).]

con·trar·i·wise /ˈkän,tre(ə)rē,wīz; kənˈtre(ə)rē-/ ▶**adv.** in the opposite way or order. ■ [sentence adverb] in contrast to something that has just been stated or mentioned.

con·trar·y /ˈkän,tre(ə)rē/ ▶**adj.** 1 opposite in nature, direction, or meaning. ■ (of two or more statements, beliefs, etc.) opposed to one another. ■ (of a wind) blowing in the direction opposite to one's course; unfavorable. ■ Logic (of two propositions) so related that one or neither but not both must be true. Compare with CONTRADICTORY. 2 perversely inclined to disagree or to do the opposite of what is expected or desired. ▶**n.** (pl. **-trar·ies**) 1 (**the contrary**) the opposite. 2 Logic a contrary proposition.
– PHRASES **contrary to** conflicting with; counter to. **on** (or **quite**) **the contrary** used to intensify a denial of what has just been implied or stated. **to the contrary** with the opposite meaning or implication. — **con·trar·i·ly** /-əlē/ **adv.** **con·trar·i·ness** **n.** [ME: from Anglo-Norman Fr. *contrarie*, from L. *contrarius*, from *contra* 'against.']

con·trast ▶**n.** /ˈkäntrast/ the state of being strikingly different from something else, typically something in juxtaposition or close association. ■ the degree of difference between tones in a television picture, photograph, or other image. ■ enhancement of the apparent brightness or clarity of a design provided by the juxtaposition of different colors or textures. ■ the action of calling attention to notable differences. ■ [in sing.] a thing or person having qualities noticeably different from another. ▶**v.** /ˈkän,trast; kənˈtrast/ [intrans.] differ strikingly. ■ [trans.] compare in such a way as to emphasize differences. — **con·trast·ing·ly** /ˈkän,trastiNGlē; kənˈtras-/ **adv.** **con·tras·tive** /kənˈtrastiv; ˈkän,tras-/ **adj.** [17th C.: from Fr. *contraste* (n.), *contraster* (v.), based on L. *contra-* 'against' + *stare* 'stand.']

con·trast me·di·um /ˈkän,trast/ ▶**n.** Med. a substance introduced into a part of the body in order to improve the visibility of internal structure during radiography.

con·trast·y /ˈkäntrastē/ ▶**adj.** informal (of a photograph, movie, or television picture) showing a high degree of contrast.

con·tra·vene /ˌkäntrəˈvēn/ ▶**v.** [trans.] violate the prohibition or order of (a law, treaty, or code of conduct). ■ conflict with (a right, principle, etc.), esp. to its detriment. — **con·tra·ven·er** **n.** [16th C.: from late L. *contravenire*, from L. *contra-* 'against' + *venire* 'come.']

con·tra·ven·tion /ˌkäntrəˈvenCHən/ ▶**n.** an action that violates a law, treaty, or other ruling.
– PHRASES **in contravention of** in a manner contrary and disobedient to (a law or other ruling). [16th C.: via Fr. from med. L. *contraventio(n-)*, from late L. *contravenire*.]

con·tre·danse /ˈkäntrə,dans; ˌkôNtrəˈdäNs/ ▶**n.** (pl. same) a French form of country dance, originating in the 18th century and related to the quadrille. ■ a piece of music for such a dance. ■ another term for CONTRADANCE. [Fr., alt. of Engl. COUNTRY DANCE, by association with *contre* 'against.']

con·tre·temps /ˈkäntrə,täN; ˌkôNtrəˈtäN/ ▶**n.** (pl. same /-ˌtäN(z); -ˈtäN(z)/) an unexpected and unfortunate occurrence. ■ a minor dispute or disagreement. [17th C.: Fr., orig. 'motion out of time,' from *contre-* + *temps* 'time.']

con·trib·ute /kənˈtribyo͞ot; -byət/ ▶**v.** [trans.] give (something, esp. money) in order to help achieve or provide something. ■ [intrans.] (**contribute to**) help to cause or bring about. ■ supply (an article) for publication. ■ [intrans.] give one's views in a discussion. — **con·trib·u·tive** /-yətiv/ **adj.** [16th C.: from L. *contribut-* 'brought together,' from v. *contribuere*, from *con-* 'with' + *tribuere* 'bestow.']

con·tri·bu·tion /ˌkäntrəˈbyo͞oSHən/ ▶**n.** a gift or payment to a common fund or collection. ■ the part played by a person or thing in bringing about a result or helping something to advance. ■ an article or other piece of writing submitted for publication in a collection.

con·trib·u·tor /kənˈtribyətər/ ▶**n.** a person or thing that contributes something, in particular: ■ a person who writes articles for a magazine or newspaper. ■ a person who donates money to a cause. ■ a causal factor in the existence or occurrence of something.

con·trib·u·to·ry /kənˈtribyə,tôrē/ ▶**adj.** 1 playing a part in bringing something about. 2 (of or relating to a pension or insurance plan) operated by means of a fund into which people pay.

con·trite /kənˈtrīt/ ▶**adj.** feeling or expressing remorse or penitence; affected by guilt. — **con·trite·ly** **adv.** **con·trite·ness** **n.** [ME: from OFr. *contrit*, from L. *contritus*, past part. of *conterere* 'grind down,' from *con-* + *terere* 'rub.']

con·tri·tion /kənˈtriSHən/ ▶**n.** the state of feeling remorseful and penitent. ■ (in the Roman Catholic Church) the repentance of past sins during or after confession.

con·triv·ance /kənˈtrīvəns/ ▶**n.** a thing that is created skillfully and inventively to serve a particular purpose. ■ the use of skill to bring something about or create something. ■ a device, esp. in literary or artistic composition, that gives a sense of artificiality.

con·trive /kənˈtrīv/ ▶**v.** [trans.] create or bring about (an object or a situation) by deliberate use of skill and artifice. ■ [with infin.] manage to do something foolish or create an undesirable situation. — **con·triv·a·ble** **adj.** **con·triv·er** **n.** [ME: from OFr. *contreuve-*, stem of *controver* 'imagine,' from med. L. *contropare* 'compare.']

con·trived /kənˈtrīvd/ ▶**adj.** deliberately created rather than arising naturally or spontaneously. ■ giving a sense of artificiality.

con·trol /kənˈtrōl/ ▶**n.** 1 the power to influence or direct people's behavior or the course of events. ■ the ability to manage a machine or other moving object. ■ the restriction of an activity, tendency, or phenomenon. ■ the power to restrain something, esp. one's own emotions or actions. ■ (often **controls**) a means of limiting or regulating something. ■ a switch or other device by which a machine is regulated. ■ [with adj.] the place where a particular item is verified. ■ the base from which a system or activity is directed. ■ Bridge a high card that will prevent opponents from establishing a particular suit. ■ Comput. short for CONTROL KEY. 2 Stat. a group or individual used as a standard of comparison for checking the results of a survey or experiment. 3 a member of an intelligence organization who personally directs the activities of a spy. ▶**v.** (**-trolled, -trol·ling**) 1 [trans.] determine the behavior or supervise the running of. ■ maintain influence or authority over. ■ limit the level, intensity, or numbers of. ■ (**control oneself**) remain calm and reasonable despite provocation. ■ regulate (a mechanical or scientific process). ■ [as adj.] (**controlled**) (of a drug) restricted by law with respect to use and possession. 2 Stat. [intrans.] (**control for**) take into account (an extraneous factor that might affect results) when performing an experiment. ■ check; verify.
– PHRASES **in control** able to direct a situation, person, or activity. **out of control** no longer possible to manage. **under control** (of a danger or emergency) being dealt with successfully and competently. — **con·trol·la·bil·i·ty** /kən,trōləˈbilitē/ **n.** **con·trol·la·ble** **adj.** **con·trol·la·bly** /-əblē/ **adv.** [ME: from Anglo-Norman Fr. *contreroller* 'keep a copy of a roll,' from med. L. *contrarotulare*, from *contrarotulus* 'copy of a roll,' from *contra-* 'against' + *rotulus* 'a roll.']

con·trol freak ▶**n.** informal a person who feels an obsessive need to exercise control and to take command of any situation.

con·trol key ▶**n.** Comput. a key that alters the function of another key if both are pressed at the same time.

con·trol·ler /kənˈtrōlər/ ▶**n.** a person or thing that directs or regulates something. ■ a person in charge of an organization's finances. — **con·trol·ler·ship** **n.** [ME: from Anglo-Norman *contrerollour*, from *contreroller*.]

con·trol·ling in·ter·est ▶**n.** the holding by one person or group of the stock of a business, enough to give the holder a means of exercising control.

con·trol rod ▶**n.** a rod of a neutron-absorbing substance used to vary the output power of a nuclear reactor.

con·trol tow·er ▶**n.** a building at an airport from which movements of air and runway traffic are controlled.

con·tro·ver·sial /ˌkäntrəˈvərSHəl; -ˈvərsēəl/ ▶**adj.** giving rise or likely to give rise to public disagreement. — **con·tro·ver·sial·ist** **n.** **con·tro·ver·sial·ly** **adv.**

con·tro·ver·sy /ˈkäntrə,vərsē/ ▶**n.** (pl. **-sies**) disagreement, typically when prolonged, public, and heated. [ME: from L. *controversia*, from *controversus* 'turned against,' from *contro-* (var. of *contra-* 'against') + *versus*, past part. of *vertere* 'turn.']

con·tro·vert /ˈkäntrə,vərt; ˌkäntrəˈvərt/ ▶**v.** [trans.] deny the truth of (something). ■ argue about (something). — **con·tro·vert·i·ble** **adj.** [16th C.: from L. *controversus* (see CONTROVERSY).]

con·tu·ma·cious /ˌkänt(y)əˈmāSHəs/ ▶**adj.** archaic or Law (esp. of a defendant's behavior) stubbornly or willfully disobedient to authority. — **con·tu·ma·cious·ly** **adv.** [16th C.: from L. *contumax*, *contumac-* (perh. from *con-* 'with' + *tumere* 'to swell') + -IOUS.]

con·tu·ma·cy /kənˈt(y)o͞oməsē; ˈkänt(y)əməsē/ ▶**n.** archaic or Law stubborn refusal to obey or comply with authority, esp. a court order or summons. [ME: from L. *contumacia* 'inflexibility,' from *contumax* (see CONTUMACIOUS).]

con·tu·me·li·ous /ˌkänt(y)əˈmēlēəs/ ▶**adj.** archaic (of behavior) scornful and insulting; insolent. — **con·tu·me·li·ous·ly** **adv.**

con·tu·me·ly /kənˈt(y)o͞oməlē; ˈkänt(y)ə,mēlē; ˈkänt(y)o͞omlē/ ▶**n.** (pl. **-lies**) insolent or insulting language or treatment. [ME: ult. from L. *contumelia*, perh. from *con-* 'with' + *tumere* 'to swell.']

con·tuse /kənˈt(y)o͞oz/ ▶**v.** [trans.] (usu. **be contused**) injure (a part of the body) without breaking the skin, forming a bruise. [ME: from L. *contus-* 'bruised,' from v. *contundere*, from *con-* 'together' + *tundere* 'beat.']

con·tu·sion /kənˈto͞oZHən/ ▶**n.** a region of injured tissue or skin in which blood capillaries have been ruptured; a bruise.

co·nun·drum /kəˈnəndrəm/ ▶**n.** (pl. **-drums**) a confusing and difficult problem or question. ■ a question asked for amusement, typically one with a pun in its answer; a riddle. [16th C.: of unknown origin.]

con·ur·ba·tion /ˌkänərˈbāSHən/ ▶**n.** an extended urban area, typically consisting of several towns merging with the suburbs of one or more cities. [20th C.: from CON- + L. *urbs*, *urb-* 'city.']

con·ure /ˈkänyər; -ˌyo͝or/ ▶**n.** a Central and South American parakeet (*Aratinga*, *Pyrrhura*, and other genera) typically with green plumage and patches of other colors. [19th C.: from mod. L. *conurus*, from Gk. *kōnos* 'cone' + *oura* 'tail.']

con·va·lesce /ˌkänvəˈles/ ▶ **v.** [intrans.] recover one's health and strength over a period of time after an illness or operation. [15th C.: from L. *convalescere*, from *con-* + *valescere* 'grow strong' (from *valere* 'be well').]

con·va·les·cent /ˌkänvəˈlesənt/ ▶ **adj.** (of a person) recovering from an illness or operation. ■ [attrib.] relating to convalescence. ▶ **n.** a person recovering from an illness or operation. — **con·va·les·cence n.**

con·vect /kənˈvekt/ ▶ **v.** [trans.] transport (heat or material) by convection. ■ [intrans.] (of a fluid or fluid body) undergo convection. [19th C.: back-form. from CONVECTION.]

con·vec·tion /kənˈveksHən/ ▶ **n.** the movement caused within a fluid by the tendency of hotter and therefore less dense material to rise, and colder, denser material to sink under the influence of gravity, which consequently results in transfer of heat. — **con·vec·tion·al** /-sHənl/ **adj.** **con·vec·tive adj.** [19th C.: from late L. *convectio(n-)*, from L. *convehere*, from *con-* 'with' + *vehere* 'carry.']

con·vec·tion cell ▶ **n.** a self-contained convective zone in a fluid in which upward motion of warmer fluid in the center is balanced by downward motion of cooler fluid at the periphery.

con·vec·tion ov·en ▶ **n.** a cooking device that heats food by the circulation of hot air.

con·vec·tor /kənˈvektər/ ▶ **n.** a heating appliance that circulates warm air by convection.

con·vene /kənˈvēn/ ▶ **v.** [trans.] call people together for (a meeting). ■ assemble or cause to assemble for a common purpose. — **con·ven·a·ble adj. con·ven·er n. con·ve·nor** /-ˈvēnər/ **n.** [ME: from L. *convenire* 'assemble,' from *con-* 'with' + *venire* 'come.']

con·ven·ience /kənˈvēnyəns/ ▶ **n.** the state of being able to proceed with something with little effort or difficulty. ■ the quality of contributing to such a state. ■ a thing that contributes to an easy and effortless way of life.

– PHRASES **at one's convenience** at a time or place that suits one. **at one's earliest convenience** as soon as one can without difficulty.

con·ven·ience food ▶ **n.** a food, typically a complete meal, that has been preprepared commercially and so requires little preparation by the consumer.

con·ven·ience store ▶ **n.** a store with extended opening hours and in a convenient location, stocking a limited range of household goods and groceries.

con·ven·ient /kənˈvēnyənt/ ▶ **adj.** fitting in well with a person's needs, activities, and plans. ■ involving little trouble or effort. ■ [predic.] (**convenient to**) situated so as to allow easy access to. ■ occurring in a place or at a time that is useful. — **con·ven·ient·ly adv.** [sentence adverb] *he lived, conveniently, in Paris.* [ME: from L. *convenient-* 'assembling,' from *convenire*.]

con·vent /ˈkänvent/ ▶ **n.** a Christian community under monastic vows, esp. one of nuns. ■ (also **convent school**) a school, esp. one for girls, run by such a community. ■ the building or buildings occupied by such a community. [ME: from OFr., from L. *conventus* 'assembly,' from *convenire* (see CONVENE).]

con·ven·ti·cle /kənˈventikəl/ ▶ **n.** hist. a secret or unlawful religious meeting, typically of people with nonconformist views. [ME: from L. *conventiculum* 'assembly,' dimin. of *conventus* 'assembly.']

con·ven·tion /kənˈvencHən/ ▶ **n.** **1** a way in which something is usually done, esp. within a particular area or activity. ■ behavior that is considered acceptable or polite to most members of a society. ■ Bridge an artificial bid by which a bidder tries to convey specific information about the hand to their partner. **2** an agreement between countries covering particular matters, esp. one less formal than a treaty. **3** a large meeting or conference, esp. of members of a political party or a particular profession. ■ an assembly of the delegates of a political party to select candidates for office. ■ an organized meeting of enthusiasts for a television program, movie, or literary genre. ■ a body set up by agreement to deal with a particular issue. [ME: via OFr. from L. *conventio(n-)* 'meeting,' from *convenire*.]

con·ven·tion·al /kənˈvencHənl/ ▶ **adj.** based on or in accordance with what is generally done or believed. ■ (of a person) concerned with what is generally held to be acceptable at the expense of individuality and sincerity. ■ (of a work of art or literature) following traditional forms and genres. ■ (of weapons or power) nonnuclear. ■ Bridge (of a bid) intended to convey a particular meaning according to an agreed upon convention. Often contrasted with NATURAL. — **con·ven·tion·al·ism n. con·ven·tion·al·ist** /-ist/ **n. con·ven·tion·al·i·ty** /-ˌvencHəˈnalitē/ **n. con·ven·tion·al·ize** /-ˌīz/ **v. con·ven·tion·al·ly adv.**

con·ven·tion·al mem·o·ry ▶ **n.** Comput. (in a personal computer running DOS) the first 640k of memory where programs to be run must be loaded.

con·ven·tion·eer /kənˌvencHəˈni(ə)r/ ▶ **n.** a person attending a convention.

con·ven·tu·al /kənˈvencHo͞oəl/ ▶ **adj.** relating or belonging to a convent. ■ relating to the less strict order of the Franciscans, living in large convents. ▶ **n.** a person who lives in or is a member of a convent. [ME: from med. L. *conventualis*, from L. *conventus* 'assembly.']

con·verge /kənˈvərj/ ▶ **v.** [intrans.] (of several people or things) come together from different directions so as eventually to meet. ■ (**converge on/upon**) come from different directions and meet at (a place). ■ (of a number of things) gradually change so as to become similar or develop something in common. ■ (of lines) tend to meet at a point. ■ Math. (of a series) approximate in the sum of its terms toward a definite limit. [17th C.: from late L. *convergere*, from *con-* 'with' + L. *vergere* 'incline.']

con·ver·gence /kənˈvərjəns/ (also **con·ver·gen·cy** /-jənsē/) ▶ **n.** the process or state of converging. ■ Biol. the tendency of unrelated animals and plants to evolve superficially similar characteristics under similar environmental conditions. ■ (also **convergence zone**) a location where airflows or ocean currents meet, characteristically marked by upwelling (of air) or downwelling (of water).

con·ver·gent /kənˈvərjənt/ ▶ **adj.** coming closer together, esp. in characteristics or ideas. ■ relating to convergence. ■ Math. (of a series) approaching a definite limit as more of its terms are added. ■ Biol. relating to or denoting evolutionary convergence. ■ (of thought) tending to follow well-established patterns.

con·ver·sant /kənˈvərsənt/ ▶ **adj.** [predic.] familiar with or knowledgeable about something. — **con·ver·sance n. con·ver·san·cy** /-sənsē/ **n.**

con·ver·sa·tion /ˌkänvərˈsāsHən/ ▶ **n.** the informal exchange of ideas by spoken words. ■ an instance of this.

– PHRASES **make conversation** talk for the sake of politeness without having anything to say. [ME: via OFr. from L. *conversatio(n-)*, from *conversari* (see CONVERSE[1]).]

con·ver·sa·tion·al /ˌkänvərˈsāsHənl/ ▶ **adj.** appropriate to an informal conversation. ■ consisting of or relating to conversation. — **con·ver·sa·tion·al·ly adv.**

con·ver·sa·tion·al·ist /ˌkänvərˈsāsHənl-ist/ ▶ **n.** a person who is good at or fond of engaging in conversation.

con·ver·sa·tion piece ▶ **n.** **1** a type of genre painting in which a group of figures are posed in a landscape or domestic setting, popular esp. in the 18th century. **2** an object whose unusual quality makes it a topic of conversation.

con·ver·sa·tion-stop·per ▶ **n.** informal an unexpected or outrageous remark that cannot easily be answered.

con·ver·sa·zi·o·ne /ˌkänvərˌsätsēˈōnē; -ˈōnā/ ▶ **n.** (pl. **-nes** or **-ni** /-nē/) a scholarly social gathering held for discussion of literature and the arts. [Ital., from L. *conversatio* (see CONVERSATION).]

con·verse[1] /kənˈvərs/ ▶ **v.** [intrans.] engage in conversation. — **con·vers·er n.** [ME: from OFr. *converser*, from L. *conversari* 'keep company (with),' from *con-* + *versare*, frequentative of *vertere* 'to turn.']

con·verse[2] ▶ **n.** /ˈkänvərs/ a situation, object, or statement that is the reverse of another, or that corresponds to it but with certain terms transposed. ■ Math. a theorem whose hypothesis and conclusion are the conclusion and hypothesis of another. ▶ **adj.** /ˈkänvərs; kənˈvərs/ having characteristics that are the reverse of something else already mentioned. [ME: from L. *conversus* 'turned around,' past part. of *convertere*.]

con·verse·ly /ˈkänvərslē; kənˈvərslē/ ▶ **adv.** introducing a statement or idea that reverses one that has just been made or referred to.

con·ver·sion /kənˈvərzHən/ ▶ **n.** **1** the act or an instance of converting or the process of being converted. ■ the fact of changing one's religion or beliefs or the action of persuading someone else to change theirs. ■ Christian Theol. repentance and change to a godly life. ■ the adaptation of a building for a new purpose. ■ Law the changing of real into personal property, or of joint into separate property, or vice versa. ■ Psychiatry the manifestation of a mental disturbance as a physical disorder or disease. ■ Logic the transposition of the subject and predicate of a proposition according to certain rules to form a new proposition by inference. **2** Football the act of scoring an extra point or points after having scored a touchdown. ■ the act of gaining a first down. **3** Law the action of wrongfully dealing with goods in a manner inconsistent with the owner's rights. ■ Physics the change in a quantity's numerical value as a result of using a different unit of measurement. [ME: via OFr. from L. *conversio(n-)*, from *convers-* 'turned around,' from *convertere*.]

con·ver·sion fac·tor ▶ **n.** **1** an arithmetical multiplier for converting a quantity expressed in one set of units into an equivalent expressed in another. **2** Econ. the manufacturing cost of a product relative to the cost of raw materials.

con·vert ▶ **v.** /kənˈvərt/ **1** [trans.] cause to change in form, character, or function. ■ [intrans.] change or be able to change from one form to another. ■ [intrans.] change one's religious faith or other beliefs. ■ persuade (someone) to do this. ■ change (money, stocks, or units in which a quantity is expressed) into others of a different kind. ■ adapt (a building) to make it suitable for a new purpose. ■ Logic transpose the subject and predicate of (a proposition) according to certain rules to form a new proposition by inference. **2** [trans.] score from (a penalty kick, pass, or other opportunity) in a sport or game. ■ [intrans.] Football score an extra point or points after having scored a touchdown by kicking a goal (one point) or running another play into the end zone (two points). ■ [intrans.] Football advance the ball far enough during a down to earn a first down. ▶ **n.** /ˈkänvərt/ a person who has been persuaded to change their religious faith or other beliefs. [ME: from OFr. *convertir*, based on L. *convertere* 'turn around,' from *con-* + *vertere* 'turn.']

con·vert·er /kənˈvərtər/ (also **con·ver·tor**) ▶ **n.** a person or thing that converts something. ■ a device for altering the nature of an electric current or signal, esp. from AC to DC or vice versa, or from analog to digital or vice versa. ■ a retort used in steelmaking. ■ short for CATALYTIC CONVERTER. ■ Comput. a program that converts data from one format to another. ■ a camera lens that changes the focal length of another lens by a set amount.

con·vert·i·ble /kən'vərtəbəl/ ▶ **adj.** able to be changed in form, function, or character. ■ (of a car) having a folding or detachable roof. ■ (of currency) able to be converted into other forms, esp. into gold or US dollars. ■ (of a bond or stock) able to be converted into common or preferred stock. ■ Logic (of terms) synonymous. ▶ **n. 1** a car with a folding or detachable roof. **2** (usu. **convertibles**) a convertible security. — **con·vert·i·bil·i·ty** /-,vərtə'bilitē/ **n.**

con·vex /kän'veks; 'känveks; kən'veks/ ▶ **adj. 1** having an outline or surface curved like the exterior of a circle or sphere. Compare with CONCAVE. **2** (of a polygon) having only interior angles measuring less than 180°. — **con·vex·i·ty** /kän'veksitē; kən-/ **n. con·vex·ly adv.** [16th C.: from L. *convexus* 'vaulted.']

convex and concave

con·vex·o-con·cave /kən,veksō'känkāv; -kän'kāv/ ▶ **adj.** (of a lens) convex on one side and concave on the other and thickest in the center.

con·vex·o-con·vex /kən,veksō'kän,veks; -kän'veks/ ▶ **adj.** another term for BICONVEX.

con·vey /kən'vā/ ▶ **v.** [trans.] transport or carry to a place. ■ make (an idea, impression, or feeling) known or understandable to someone. ■ communicate (a message or information). ■ Law transfer the title to (property). — **con·vey·a·ble adj.** [ME: from OFr. *conveier*, from med. L. *conviare*, from *con-* 'with' + L. *via* 'way.']

con·vey·ance /kən'vāəns/ ▶ **n. 1** the action or process of transporting someone or something from one place to another. ■ a means of transportation; a vehicle. ■ the action of making an idea, feeling, or impression known or understandable to someone. **2** Law the legal process of transferring property from one owner to another. ■ a legal document effecting such a process.

con·vey·anc·ing /kən'vāənsiNG/ ▶ **n.** the branch of law concerned with the preparation of documents for the transferring of property. ■ the action of preparing documents for the transfer of property. — **con·vey·anc·er n.**

con·vey·or /kən'vāər/ (also **con·vey·er**) ▶ **n.** a person or thing that transports or communicates something. ■ a conveyor belt.

con·vey·or belt ▶ **n.** a continuous moving band of fabric, rubber, or metal used for transporting objects from one place to another.

con·vict ▶ **v.** /kən'vikt/ [trans.] (often **be convicted**) declare (someone) to be guilty of a criminal offense by the verdict of a jury or the decision of a judge in a court of law. ▶ **n.** /'känvikt/ a person found guilty of a criminal offense and serving a sentence of imprisonment. [ME: from L. *convict-* 'demonstrated,' from *convincere* (see CONVINCE).]

con·vic·tion /kən'vikSHən/ ▶ **n. 1** a formal declaration that someone is guilty of a criminal offense, made by the verdict of a jury or the decision of a judge in a court of law. **2** a firmly held belief or opinion. ■ the quality of showing that one is firmly convinced of what one believes or says.

con·vince /kən'vins/ ▶ **v.** [trans.] cause (someone) to believe firmly in the truth of something. ■ [with obj. and infin.] persuade (someone) to do something. — **con·vinc·er n. con·vin·ci·ble adj.** [16th C.: from L. *convincere*, from *con-* 'with' + *vincere* 'conquer.']

con·vinced /kən'vinst/ ▶ **adj.** completely certain about something. ■ [attrib.] firm in one's belief, esp. with regard to a particular cause or issue.

con·vinc·ing /kən'vinsiNG/ ▶ **adj.** capable of causing someone to believe that something is true or real. ■ (of a victory or a winner) leaving no margin of doubt; clear. — **con·vinc·ing·ly adv.**

con·viv·i·al /kən'vivēəl; -'vivyəl/ ▶ **adj.** (of an atmosphere or event) friendly, lively, and enjoyable. ■ (of a person) cheerful and friendly; jovial. — **con·viv·i·al·i·ty** /kən,vivē'alitē/ **n. con·viv·i·al·ly adv.** [17th C.: from L. *convivialis*, from *convivium* 'a feast,' from *con-* 'with' + *vivere* 'live.']

con·vo·ca·tion /,känvə'kāSHən/ ▶ **n. 1** a large formal assembly of people. ■ a formal ceremony at a college or university, as for the conferring of awards. **2** the action of calling people together for a large formal assembly. — **con·vo·ca·tion·al** /-SHənl/ **adj.** [ME: from L. *convocatio(n-)*, from *convocare* (see CONVOKE).]

con·voke /kən'vōk/ ▶ **v.** [trans.] formal call together or summon (an assembly or meeting). [16th C.: from L. *convocare*, from *con-* + *vocare* 'call.']

con·vo·lute /'känvə,lo͞ot/ ▶ **adj** Biol. rolled longitudinally upon itself, as a leaf in the bud.

con·vo·lut·ed /'känvə,lo͞otid/ ▶ **adj.** (esp. of an argument, story, or sentence) extremely complex and difficult to follow. ■ esp. tech. intricately folded, twisted, or coiled. — **con·vo·lut·ed·ly adv.** [18th C.: past part. of *convolute*, from L. *convolutus*, past part. of *convolvere*.]

con·vo·lu·tion /,känvə'lo͞oSHən/ ▶ **n.** (often **convolutions**) a coil or twist, esp. one of many. ■ a thing that is complex and difficult to follow. ■ a sinuous fold in the surface of the brain. ■ the state of being coiled or twisted, or the process of becoming so. — **con·vo·lu·tion·al** /-SHənl/ **adj.**

con·volve /kən'välv; -'vôlv/ ▶ **v.** [trans.] rare roll or coil together; entwine. [16th C.: from L. *convolvere* 'roll together,' from *con-* + *volvere* 'roll.']

con·vol·vu·lus /kən'välvyələs; -'vôl-/ ▶ **n.** (pl. **-lus·es**) a twining plant (genus *Convolvulus*) of the morning glory family with trumpet-shaped flowers, some kinds of which are invasive, while others are cultivated for their bright flowers. [16th C.: L., lit. 'bindweed,' from *convolvere* (see CONVOLVE).]

con·voy /'kän,voi/ ▶ **n.** a group of ships or vehicles traveling together, typically accompanied by armed troops, warships, or other vehicles for protection. ▶ **v.** /'kän,voi; kən'voi/ [trans.] (of a warship or armed troops) accompany (a group of ships or vehicles) for protection.
– PHRASES **in convoy** (of traveling vehicles) as a group; together. [ME: from Fr. *convoyer*, from med. L. *conviare* (see CONVEY).]

con·vul·sant /kən'vəlsənt/ ▶ **adj.** (chiefly of drugs) producing sudden, involuntary muscle contractions. ▶ **n.** a convulsant drug.

con·vulse /kən'vəls/ ▶ **v.** [intrans.] (of a person) suffer violent involuntary contraction of the muscles, producing contortion of the body or limbs. ■ [trans.] (usu. **be convulsed**) (of an emotion, laughter, or physical stimulus) cause (someone) to make sudden, violent, uncontrollable movements. ■ [trans.] fig. throw (a country) into violent social or political upheaval. [17th C.: from L. *convuls-* 'pulled violently,' from *convellere*, from *con-* + *vellere* 'to pull.']

con·vul·sion /kən'vəlSHən/ ▶ **n.** (often **convulsions**) a sudden, violent, irregular movement of a limb or of the body, caused by involuntary contraction of muscles and associated esp. with brain disorders such as epilepsy, the presence of certain toxins or other agents in the blood, or fever in children. ■ (**convulsions**) uncontrollable laughter. ■ an earthquake or other violent or major movement of the earth's crust. ■ fig. a violent social or political upheaval.

con·vul·sive /kən'vəlsiv/ ▶ **adj.** producing or consisting of convulsions. — **con·vul·sive·ly adv.**

Con·way /'känwā/ a city in central Arkansas; pop. 43,167.

co·ny ▶ **n.** (pl. **-nies**) var. of CONEY.

coo /ko͞o/ ▶ **v.** (**coos, cooed**) [intrans.] (of a pigeon or dove) make a soft murmuring sound. ■ (of a baby) make a soft murmuring sound similar to this, expressing contentment. ■ (of a person) speak in a soft gentle voice, typically to express affection. ▶ **n.** [in sing.] a soft murmuring sound made by a dove or pigeon.
– PHRASES **bill and coo** see BILL². [17th C.: imitative.]

co-oc·cur /,kō ə'kər/ ▶ **v.** [intrans.] occur together or simultaneously. — **co-oc·cur·rence** /ə'kərəns/ **n.**

Cook¹ /ko͝ok/, Captain James (1728–79), English explorer. On his first expedition to the Pacific 1768–71, he explored the coasts of New Zealand, New Guinea, and the east coast of Australia. He was killed in a skirmish with the Hawaiians.

Cook², Thomas (1808–92), English entrepreneur. In 1841, with the first publicly advertised excursion train in England, he laid the foundations for the tourist and travel-agent industry.

cook /ko͝ok/ ▶ **v. 1** [trans.] prepare (food, a dish, or a meal) by combining and heating the ingredients in various ways. ■ [intrans.] (of food) be heated so that the condition required for eating is reached. ■ (**cook something down**) heat food and cause it to thicken and reduce in volume. ■ [intrans.] (**cook down**) (of food being cooked) be reduced in volume in this way. ■ (**be cooking**) informal be happening or planned: *what's cooking on the alternative fuels front?* **2** [trans.] informal alter dishonestly; falsify. ■ (**be cooked**) be in an inescapably bad situation: *if I can't talk to him, I'm cooked.* **3** [intrans.] informal perform or proceed vigorously or well. ▶ **n.** [often with adj.] a person who prepares and cooks food, esp. as a job or in a specified way.
– PHRASES **cook the books** informal alter facts or figures dishonestly or illegally. **cook someone's goose** informal cause someone's downfall.
– PHRASAL VERBS **cook something up** concoct a story, excuse, or plan, esp. an ingenious or devious one. — **cook·a·ble adj.** [OE *cōc* (n.), from pop. L. *cocus*, from L. *coquus*.]

Cook, Mount the highest peak in New Zealand, in the Southern Alps; 12,349 feet (3,764 m).

cook·book /'ko͝ok,bo͝ok/ ▶ **n.** a book containing recipes and other information about the preparation and cooking of food.

Cooke /ko͝ok/, Jay (1821–1905), US financier. The founder of a Philadelphia bank 1861, he helped to finance the American Civil War and western railroads.

cook·er /'ko͝okər/ ▶ **n.** esp. Brit. an appliance used for cooking food.

cook·er·y /'ko͝okərē/ ▶ **n.** (pl. **-er·ies**) **1** the practice or skill of preparing and cooking food. **2** a place in which food is cooked; a kitchen.

cook·house /'ko͝ok,hous/ ▶ **n. 1** a kitchen or dining hall in a military camp. **2** an outdoor kitchen in a warm country.

cook·ie /'ko͝okē/ ▶ **n.** (pl. **-ies**) **1** a small sweet cake, typically round, flat, and crisp. **2** [with adj.] informal a person of a specified kind: *a tough cookie with one eye on her bank account.* **3** Comput. a packet of data sent by an Internet server to a browser, which is returned by the browser each time it subsequently accesses the same server, used to identify the user or track their access to the server.
– PHRASES **that's the way the cookie crumbles** informal that's how things turn out (often used of an undesirable but unalterable situation). [18th C.: from Du. *koekje* 'little cake,' dimin. of *koek*.]

cook·ie cut·ter ▶ **n.** a device with sharp edges for cutting cookie dough into a particular shape. ■ [as adj.] denoting something mass-produced or lacking any distinguishing characteristics.

cook·ie jar ▶ **n.** a jar to hold cookies.

– PHRASES **with one's hand in the cookie jar** engaged in surreptitious theft from one's employer.

cook·ie sheet ▶n. a flat metal tray on which cookies are baked.

cook·ing /ˈko͝okiNG/ ▶n. the process of preparing food by heating it. ■ the practice or skill of preparing food. ■ food that has been prepared in a particular way. ■ [as adj.] suitable for or used in cooking.

Cook In·let an inlet of the Gulf of Alaska, west of the Kenai Peninsula.

Cook Is·lands a group of 15 islands in the southwestern Pacific between Tonga and French Polynesia, a self-governing territory of New Zealand; pop. 18,000; capital, Avarua.

cook·out /ˈko͝okˌout/ ▶n. a party or gathering where a meal is cooked and eaten outdoors.

Cook·son /ˈko͝oksən/, Dame Catherine Anne (1906–98), English writer. She wrote light romantic fiction such as the Mary Ann series (1956–67).

Cook's tour ▶n. informal a rapid tour of many places. [20th C.: from the name of the travel agent Thomas *Cook* (see COOK[2]).]

Cook Strait the strait that separates the North and the South island of New Zealand.

cook·top /ˈko͝okˌtäp/ ▶n. a cooking unit, usually with hot plates or burners, built into or fixed on the top of a cabinet or other surface.

cook·ware /ˈko͝okˌwe(ə)r/ ▶n. pots, pans, or dishes in which food can be cooked.

cool /ko͞ol/ ▶adj. **1** of or at a fairly low temperature. ■ soothing or refreshing because of its low temperature. ■ (esp. of clothing) keeping one from becoming too hot. ■ showing no friendliness toward a person or enthusiasm for an idea or project. ■ free from excitement or anxiety. ■ calmly audacious. ■ (of jazz, esp. modern jazz) restrained and relaxed. **2** informal fashionably attractive or impressive. ■ excellent. ■ used to express acceptance or agreement: *if people want to freak out at our clubs, that's cool.* **3** (**a cool ——**) informal used to emphasize a specified quantity or amount, esp. of money: *a cool $15,000.* ▶n. **1** (**the cool**) a fairly low temperature. ■ a time or place at which the temperature is pleasantly low. ■ calmness; composure. **2** the quality of being fashionably attractive or impressive. ▶v. become or cause to become less hot. ■ become or cause to become calm or less excited. ■ [usu. in imper.] (**cool it**) informal behave in a less excitable manner.

– PHRASES **cool down** recover from strenuous physical exertion by doing gentle stretches and exercises; warm down. **cool one's heels** be kept waiting. **keep** (or **lose**) **one's cool** informal maintain (or fail to maintain) a calm and controlled attitude. **play it cool** see PLAY. — **cooled** adj. [in comb.] *a water-cooled engine.* **cool·ish** adj. **cool·ly** adv. **cool·ness** n. [OE *cōl* (n.), *cōlian* (v.), of Gmc. origin; rel. to Du. *koel*, also to COLD.]

cool·ant /ˈko͞olənt/ ▶n. a liquid or gas that is used to remove heat from something.

cool·er /ˈko͞olər/ ▶n. **1** a device or container for keeping things cool, in particular: ■ an insulated container for keeping food and drink cool. ■ a refrigerated room. **2** a tall drink, esp. a mixture of wine, fruit juice, and soda water. **3** (**the cooler**) informal prison or a prison cell.

Coo·ley's a·ne·mi·a /ˈko͞olēz/ ▶n. another term for THALASSEMIA. [1930s: Thomas B. *Cooley* (1871–1945), Amer. pediatrician.]

cool·head·ed /ˈko͞olˌhedəd/ ▶adj. not easily worried or excited.

Cool·idge /ˈko͞olij/, Calvin (1872–1933), 30th president of the US 1923–29; full name *John Calvin Coolidge.* A Republican, he was governor of Massachusetts 1919–20 and US vice president 1921–23, succeeding to the presidency when President Harding died. Elected to a full term in 1924, he was noted for noninterference in foreign affairs.

coo·lie /ˈko͞olē/ ▶n. (pl. **-lies**) offens. an unskilled native laborer in India, China, and some other Asian countries. [17th C.: from Hindi and Telugu *kūlī* 'day-laborer.']

coo·lie hat ▶n. a broad conical straw hat as worn by laborers in some Asian countries.

cool·ing-off pe·ri·od ▶n. an interval during which two people or groups who are in disagreement can try to settle their differences before taking further action. ■ an interval after a sales contract is agreed upon during which the purchaser can decide to cancel without loss.

cool·ing tow·er ▶n. a tall, open-topped, cylindrical concrete tower, used for cooling water or condensing steam from an industrial process.

coolth /ko͞olTH/ ▶n. esp. humorous **1** pleasantly low temperature. **2** articles, activities, or people perceived as fashionable. [16th C.: from COOL.]

coon /ko͞on/ ▶n. **1** short for RACCOON. **2** informal, derog. a black person.

– PHRASES **a coon's age** informal a long time.

coon·can /ˈko͞onˌkan/ ▶n. a card game for two players, originally from Mexico, similar to rummy. [19th C.: probably from Sp. *con quién* 'with whom?']

coon·hound /ˈko͞onˌhound/ ▶n. a dog of an American breed, used to hunt raccoons.

Coon Rapids a city in southeastern Minnesota, on the Mississippi River; pop. 61,607.

coon·skin /ˈko͞onˌskin/ ▶n. the pelt of a raccoon.

coop /ko͞op; ko͝op/ ▶n. a cage or pen for poultry. ▶v. [trans.] (usu. **be cooped up**) confine in a small space. ■ put or keep (a fowl) in a cage or pen.

– PHRASES **fly the coop** see FLY[1]. [ME *cowpe*, based on L. *cupa*.]

co-op /ˈkōˌäp; kōˈäp/ ▶n. informal a cooperative society, business, or enterprise.

Coop·er[1] /ˈko͞opər/, James Fenimore (1789–1851), US writer, noted for the Leatherstocking Tales, a series of novels about the American frontier.

Coo·per[2], Leon Neil (1930–). See BARDEEN.

coop·er /ˈko͞opər; ˈko͝opər/ ▶n. a maker or repairer of casks and barrels. ▶v. [trans.] make or repair (a cask or barrel). [ME *cowper*, from MDu., Mid. Low Ger. *kūper*, from *kūpe* 'tub, vat,' based on L. *cupa*.]

coop·er·age /ˈko͞opərij; ˈko͝op-/ ▶n. a cooper's business or premises. ■ the making of barrels and casks.

co·op·er·ate /kōˈäpəˌrāt/ (also **co-op·er·ate**) ▶v. [intrans.] act jointly; work toward the same end. ■ assist someone or comply with their requests. — **co·op·er·ant** /-ərənt/ n. **co·op·er·a·tor** /-əˌrātər/ n. [16th C.: from eccles. L. *cooperat-* 'worked together,' from the v. *cooperari*, from *co-* 'together' + *operari* 'to work.']

co·op·er·a·tion /kōˌäpəˈrāSHən/ (also **co-op·er·a·tion**) ▶n. the process of working together to the same end. ■ assistance, esp. by ready compliance with requests. ■ Econ. the formation and operation of cooperatives.

co·op·er·a·tive /kōˈäp(ə)rətiv/ (also **co-op·er·a·tive**) ▶adj. involving mutual assistance in working toward a common goal. ■ willing to be of assistance. ■ (of a farm, business, etc.) owned and run jointly by its members, with profits or benefits shared among them. ▶n. a farm, business, or other organization that is owned and run jointly by its members, who share the profits or benefits. — **co·op·er·a·tive·ly** adv. **co·op·er·a·tive·ness** n.

Co·op·er·a·tive Re·pub·lic of Guy·a·na official name for GUYANA.

Coo·per's hawk ▶n. a North American hawk (*Accipiter cooperii*) resembling but smaller than the goshawk. [19th C.: named after William *Cooper* (1798–1864), Amer. naturalist.]

Coo·pers·town /ˈko͞opərzˌtoun; ˈko͝op-/ a resort village in central New York, site of the Baseball Hall of Fame; pop. 2,180.

coop·er·y /ˈko͞opərē; ˈko͝op-/ ▶n. (pl. **-ries**) another term for COOPERAGE.

co-opt /kōˈäpt; ˈkōˌäpt/ ▶v. [trans.] (often **be co-opted**) appoint to membership of a committee or other body by invitation of the existing members. ■ divert to or use in a role different from the usual or original one. ■ adopt (an idea or policy) for one's own use. — **co-op·ta·tion** /ˌkōäpˈtāSHən/ n. **co-op·tion** /kōˈäpSHən/ n. **co-op·tive** /-ˈäptiv/ adj. [17th C.: from L. *cooptare*, from *co-* 'together' + *optare* 'choose.']

co·or·di·nate (also **co-or·di·nate**) ▶v. /kōˈôrdnˌāt/ **1** [trans.] bring the different elements of (a complex activity or organization) into a relationship that will ensure efficiency or harmony. ■ [intrans.] negotiate with others in order to work together effectively. ■ [intrans.] match or harmonize attractively. **2** Chem. form a coordinate bond to (an atom or molecule). ▶adj. /kōˈôrdn-it/ **1** equal in rank or importance. ■ Gram. (of parts of a compound sentence) equal in rank and fulfilling identical functions. **2** Chem. denoting a type of covalent bond in which one atom provides both the shared electrons. ▶n. /kōˈôrdn-it/ **1** Math. each of a group of numbers used to indicate the position of a point, line, or plane. **2** (**coordinates**) matching items of clothing. — **co·or·di·na·tive** /kōˈôrdn-ətiv; ˈôrdnˌātiv/ adj. **co·or·di·na·tor** /-dnˌātər/ n. [17th C.: from co- + L. *ordinare* (from *ordo* 'order').]

Co·or·di·nat·ed U·ni·ver·sal Time (abbr.: **UTC**) another term for GREENWICH MEAN TIME.

co·or·di·nat·ing con·junc·tion ▶n. a conjunction placed between words, phrases, clauses, or sentences of equal rank, e.g., *and, but, or.* Contrasted with SUBORDINATING CONJUNCTION.

co·or·di·na·tion /kōˌôrdnˈāSHən/ ▶n. **1** the process or state of coordinating or being coordinated. ■ the organization of the different elements of a complex body or activity so as to enable them to work together effectively. ■ cooperative effort resulting in an effective relationship. ■ the ability to use different parts of the body together smoothly and efficiently. **2** Chem. the linking of atoms by coordinate bonds.

co·or·di·na·tion num·ber ▶n. Chem. the number of atoms or ions immediately surrounding a central atom in a complex or crystal.

coot /ko͞ot/ ▶n. **1** (pl. same) an aquatic bird (genus *Fulica*) of the rail family, with blackish plumage, lobed feet, and a bill that extends back onto the forehead as a horny shield. **2** informal a foolish or eccentric person, typically an old man. [ME: prob. of Du. or Low Ger. origin and rel. to Du. *koet*.]

coot·er /ˈko͞otər/ ▶n. a North American river turtle (genus *Pseudemys*, family Emydidae) with a dull brown shell and typically having yellow stripes on the head. [19th C.: of unknown origin.]

coot·ie /ˈko͞otē/ ▶n. informal a body louse. ■ a children's term for an imaginary germ quality transmitted by obnoxious or slovenly people. [World War I: perh. from Malay *kutu* 'biting insect.']

cop[1] /käp/ informal ▶n. a police officer. ▶v. (**copped, cop·ping**) [trans.] **1** catch or arrest (an offender). ■ incur (something unwelcome). ■ obtain (an illegal drug). ■ steal. ■ receive or attain (something welcome). **2** strike (an attitude or pose).

– PHRASES **cop a feel** informal fondle someone sexually, esp. in a surreptitious way or without their permission. **cop a plea** engage in plea bargaining.

– PHRASAL VERBS **cop out** avoid doing something that one ought to do. **cop to** accept or admit to. [18th C. (as a v.): perh. from obs. *cap* 'arrest,' from OFr. *caper* 'seize,' from L. *capere*. The n. is from COPPER[2].]

cop[2] ▶n. a conical or cylindrical roll of thread wound onto a spindle. [18th C.: possibly from OE *cop* 'summit, top.']

Co·pa·ca·ba·na Beach /ˌkōpəkəˈbanə/ a resort on the Atlantic coast of Brazil near Rio de Janeiro.

co·pa·cet·ic /ˌkōpəˈsetik/ (also **co·pa·set·ic**) ▶ **adj.** informal in excellent order. [20th C.: of unknown origin.]

co·pal /ˈkōpəl/ ▶ **n.** resin from any of a number of tropical trees of the pea and monkey puzzle families, used to make varnish. [16th C.: via Sp. from Nahuatl *copalli* 'incense.']

Co·pán /kōˈpän/ the ruins of an ancient Mayan city in western Honduras.

co·part·ner /ˈkōˌpärtnər/ ▶ **n.** a partner or associate, esp. an equal partner in a business. — **co·part·ner·ship n.**

co·pay /ˈkōˌpā/ ▶ **n.** short for COPAYMENT.

co·pay·ment /kōˈpāmənt/ ▶ **n.** (also **co·pay**) (of insurance policies) a payment owed by the person insured at the time a covered service is rendered, covering part of the cost of the service.

COPD Med. ▶ **abbr.** chronic obstructive pulmonary disease, involving constriction of the airways and difficulty or discomfort in breathing.

cope[1] /kōp/ ▶ **v.** [intrans.] (of a person) deal effectively with something difficult. ■ (of a machine or system) have the capacity to deal successfully with. — **cop·er n.** [ME ('come to blows'): from OFr. *coper, colper,* from *cop, colp* 'a blow,' via L. from Gk. *kolaphos* 'blow with the fist.']

cope[2] ▶ **n.** a long, loose cloak worn by a priest or bishop on ceremonial occasions. ■ tech. literary a thing resembling or likened to a cloak. ▶ **v.** [trans.] [usu. as adj.] (**coped**) (in building) cover (a joint or structure) with a coping. [ME: from med. L. *capa,* var. of late L. *cappa* (see CAP).]

cope[2]

co·peck /ˈkōpek/ ▶ **n.** chiefly British var. of KOPEK.

Co·pen·ha·gen /ˈkōpənˌhägən; -ˌhāgən/ the capital and chief port of Denmark, on the eastern part of Zealand; pop. 466,700. Danish name KØBENHAVN.

Co·pep·o·da /kōˈpepədə/ Zool. a large class of small aquatic crustaceans, many of which occur in plankton and some of which are parasitic on larger aquatic animals. — **co·pe·pod** /ˈkōpəˌpäd/ **n.** [mod. L., from Gk. *kōpē* 'handle, oar' + *pous, pod-* 'foot.']

Co·per·ni·can sys·tem /kəˈpərnikən/ (also **Copernican theory**) ▶ **n.** Astron. the theory that the sun is the center of the solar system, with the planets (including the earth) orbiting around it. Compare with PTOLEMAIC SYSTEM. [17th C.: named after COPERNICUS.]

Co·per·ni·cus /kəˈpərnikəs/, Nicolaus (1473–1543), Polish astronomer; Latinized name of *Mikołaj Kopernik.* He proposed a model of the solar system in which the planets orbit in perfect circles around the sun; his work ultimately led to rejection of the established geocentric cosmology.

cope·stone /ˈkōpˌstōn/ ▶ **n.** a flat stone forming part of a coping. ■ fig. a finishing touch or crowning achievement. [16th C.: from COPE[2].]

cop·i·er /ˈkäpēər/ ▶ **n.** a machine that makes exact copies of something, esp. documents, video or audio recordings, or software.

co·pi·lot /ˈkōˌpīlət/ ▶ **n.** a second pilot in an aircraft. ▶ **v.** [trans.] act as the copilot of (an aircraft).

cop·ing /ˈkōpiNG/ ▶ **n.** the top, typically sloping, course of a brick or stone wall. [16th C.: from v. COPE[2].]

cop·ing saw ▶ **n.** a saw with a very narrow blade stretched across a U-shaped frame, used for cutting curves in wood. [1920s: from COPE[2].]

cop·ing stone ▶ **n.** chiefly British term for COPESTONE.

co·pi·ous /ˈkōpēəs/ ▶ **adj.** abundant in supply or quantity. — **co·pi·ous·ly adv. co·pi·ous·ness n.** [ME: from OFr. *copieux* or L. *copiosus,* from *copia* 'plenty.']

co·pla·nar /kōˈplānər; -ˈnär/ ▶ **adj.** Geom. in the same plane. — **co·pla·nar·i·ty** /ˌkōˌplāˈne(ə)ritē/ **n.**

Cop·land /ˈkōplənd/, Aaron (1900–90), US composer. He established a distinctive American style in his compositions, which include *Appalachian Spring* (1944).

Cop·ley /ˈkäplē/, John Singleton (1738–1815), US painter, noted for portraits of well-known people.

co·pol·y·mer /kōˈpäləmər/ ▶ **n.** Chem. a polymer made by reaction of two different monomers, with units of more than one kind.

co·po·lym·er·ize /kōˈpäləməˌrīz/ ▶ **v.** [trans.] Chem. polymerize together to form a copolymer. — **co·po·lym·er·i·za·tion** /ˌkōˌpäləmərəˈzāSHən/ **n.**

cop-out ▶ **n.** informal an instance of avoiding a commitment or responsibility.

cop·per[1] /ˈkäpər/ ▶ **n.** **1** a red-brown metal, the chemical element of atomic number 29. A ductile metal, it is a very good conductor of heat and electricity and is used esp. for electrical wiring. (Symbol: **Cu**) **2** dated a copper coin, esp. a penny. **3** a reddish-brown color like that of copper. **4** [with adj.] a small, typically orange or purple butterfly (genus *Lycaena,* family Lycaenidae) of North America and Eurasia. Its numerous species include the **American copper** (*L. phlaeas*) of the eastern US and arctic North America. ▶ **v.** [trans.] cover or coat (something) with copper. [OE *copor, coper,* based on late L. *cuprum,* from L. *cyprium aes* 'Cyprus metal.']

copper[1] 4

cop·per[2] ▶ **n.** informal a police officer. [19th C.: from COP[1].]

cop·per·as /ˈkäpərəs/ ▶ **n.** green crystals of hydrated ferrous sulfate, esp. as an industrial product. [ME *coperose,* ult. from med. L. *cuperosa,* lit. 'flower of copper,' from late L. *cuprum* (see COPPER[1]) + *rosa* 'rose.']

cop·per beech ▶ **n.** a variety of European beech tree with purplish-brown leaves.

cop·per·head /ˈkäpərˌhed/ ▶ **n.** any of a number of stout-bodied venomous snakes with coppery-pink or reddish-brown coloration, in particular a North American pit viper (*Agkistrodon contortrix*).

cop·per·plate /ˈkäpərˌplāt/ ▶ **n.** **1** a polished copper plate with a design engraved or etched into it. ■ a print made from such a plate. **2** a style of neat, round handwriting, usually slanted and looped, the thick and thin strokes being made by pressure with a flexible metal nib. ▶ **adj.** of or in copperplate writing.

cop·per·smith /ˈkäpərˌsmiTH/ ▶ **n.** a person who makes things out of copper.

cop·per sul·fate ▶ **n.** a blue crystalline solid, $CuSO_4.5H_2O$, used in electroplating and as a fungicide.

cop·per·y /ˈkäpərē/ ▶ **adj.** like copper, esp. in color.

cop·pice /ˈkäpəs/ chiefly Brit. ▶ **n.** an area of woodland in which the trees or shrubs are, or formerly were, periodically cut back to ground level to stimulate growth and provide firewood or timber. ▶ **v.** [trans.] cut back (a tree or shrub) to ground level periodically to stimulate growth. [ME: from OFr. *copeiz,* based on med. L. *colpus* 'a blow' (see COPE[1]). Cf. COPSE.]

Cop·po·la /ˈkäpələ/, Francis Ford (1939–), US filmmaker, noted for his directing of *The Godfather* (1972) and its two sequels (1974, 1990).

cop·ra /ˈkäprə/ ▶ **n.** dried coconut kernels, from which oil is obtained. [16th C.: via Port. and Sp. from Malayalam *koppara* 'coconut.']

copro- ▶ **comb. form** of or relating to dung or feces: *coprophilia.* [from Gk. *kopros* 'dung.']

co·proc·es·sor /kōˈpräsesər; -səsər/ ▶ **n.** Comput. a microprocessor designed to supplement the capabilities of the primary processor.

cop·ro·la·li·a /ˌkäprəˈlālēə/ ▶ **n.** Psychiatry the involuntary and repetitive use of obscene language, as a symptom of mental illness or organic brain disease. [19th C.: from Gk. *kopros* 'dung' + *lalia* 'speech, chatter.']

cop·ro·lite /ˈkäprəˌlīt/ ▶ **n.** Paleontol. a piece of fossilized dung.

cop·rol·o·gy /kəˈpräləjē/ ▶ **n.** another term for SCATOLOGY.

co·proph·a·gy /kəˈpräfəjē/ (also **cop·ro·pha·gia** /ˌkäprəˈfāj(ē)ə/) ▶ **n.** Zool. the eating of feces or dung. — **cop·ro·phag·ic** /ˌkäprəˈfajik/ **adj. co·proph·a·gous** /-ˈpräfəgəs/ **adj.** (esp. Zool.).

cop·ro·phil·i·a /ˌkäprəˈfilēə/ ▶ **n.** abnormal interest and pleasure in feces and defecation.

cops and rob·bers ▶ **plural n.** a children's game of hiding and chasing, in which the participants pretend to be police and criminals. ■ fig. a simplistic polarization of the conflict between criminals and police, seen virtually as a game; a lifestyle centered around this.

copse /käps/ ▶ **n.** a small group of trees. [16th C.: shortened from COPPICE.]

Copt /käpt/ ▶ **n.** **1** a native Egyptian in the Hellenistic and Roman periods. **2** a member of the Coptic Church. [from Fr. *Copte* or mod. L. *Coptus,* from Arab. *al-ḳibṭ, al-ḳubṭ* 'Copts,' based on Gk. *Aiguptios* 'Egyptian.']

cop·ter /ˈkäptər/ ▶ **n.** informal term for HELICOPTER.

Cop·tic /ˈkäptik/ ▶ **n.** the language of the Copts, which represents the final stage of ancient Egyptian. It now survives only as the liturgical language of the Coptic Church. ▶ **adj.** of or relating to the Copts or their language.

Cop·tic Church the native Christian Church in Egypt, traditionally founded by St. Mark, and adhering to the Monophysite doctrine. The Coptic community now makes up about 5 percent of Egypt's population.

cop·u·la /ˈkäpyələ/ ▶ **n.** Logic Gram. a connecting word, in particular a form of the verb *be* connecting a subject and complement. Also called LINKING VERB. — **cop·u·lar** /ˈkäpyələr/ **adj.** [17th C.: from L., 'connection,' from *co-* 'with' + *apere* 'fasten.']

cop·u·late /ˈkäpyəˌlāt/ ▶ **v.** [intrans.] have sexual intercourse. — **cop·u·la·tion** /ˌkäpyəˈlāSHən/ **n. cop·u·la·to·ry** /-lə,tôrē/ **adj.** [ME: from L. *copulat-* 'fastened together,' from v. *copulare,* from *copula.*]

cop·u·la·tive /ˈkäpyəˌlātiv; -ˌlətiv/ ▶ **adj.** **1** Gram. (of a word) connecting words or clauses linked in sense. Compare with DISJUNCTIVE. ■ connecting a subject and predicate. **2** of or relating to sexual intercourse. — **cop·u·la·tive·ly adv.**

cop·y /ˈkäpē/ ▶**n.** (pl. **cop·ies**) **1** a thing made to be similar or identical to another. **2** a single specimen of a particular book, record, or other publication or issue. **3** matter to be printed. ■ material for a newspaper or magazine article. ■ the text of an advertisement. ▶**v.** (**cop·ies, cop·ied**) [trans.] make a similar or identical version of; reproduce. ■ Comput. reproduce (data stored in one location) in another location. ■ write out information that one has read or heard. ■ behave in a similar way to; do the same as. ■ imitate or reproduce (an idea or style) rather than creating something original. ■ (**copy something to**) send a copy of a letter to (a third party). — **cop·y·a·ble** (or **cop·i·a·ble**) **adj.** [ME: from OFr. *copie* (n.), *copier* (v.), from L. *copia* 'abundance.']

cop·y·book /ˈkäpēˌbo͝ok/ ▶**n.** a book containing models of handwriting for learners to imitate. ▶**adj.** [attrib.] exactly in accordance with established criteria; perfect. ■ tritely conventional.

cop·y·cat /ˈkäpēˌkat/ ▶**n.** informal, derog. (esp. in children's use) a person who copies another's behavior, dress, or ideas. ■ [as adj.] denoting an action, typically a crime, carried out in imitation of another.

cop·y·desk /ˈkäpēˌdesk/ ▶**n.** a desk in a newspaper office at which copy is edited for printing.

cop·y·ed·it /ˈkäpēˌedit/ (also **cop·y·ed·it**) ▶**v.** [trans.] edit (text to be printed) by checking its consistency and accuracy. — **cop·y·ed·i·tor** /-ˌeditər/ (also **cop·y ed·i·tor**) **n.**

cop·y·hold /ˈkäpēˌhōld/ ▶**n.** Brit., hist. tenure of land based on manorial records.

cop·y·hold·er /ˈkäpēˌhōldər/ ▶**n.** **1** (also **cop·y hold·er**) a clasp or stand for holding sheets of text while it is keyed or typed. **2** Brit., hist. a person who holds land in copyhold.

cop·y·ist /ˈkäpē-ist/ ▶**n.** a person who makes copies, esp. of handwritten documents or music. ■ a person who imitates the styles of others, esp. in art.

cop·y·read /ˈkäpēˌrēd/ ▶**v.** [trans.] read and edit (text) for a newspaper, magazine, or book; copyedit. — **cop·y·read·er n.**

cop·y·right /ˈkäpēˌrīt/ ▶**n.** the exclusive legal right, given to an originator or an assignee to print, publish, perform, film, or record literary, artistic, or musical material, and to authorize others to do the same. ▶**v.** [trans.] secure copyright for (such material).

cop·y·writ·er /ˈkäpēˌrītər/ ▶**n.** a person who writes the text of advertisements or publicity material. — **cop·y·writ·ing n.**

coq au vin /ˌkōk ō ˈvaN; ˌkäk/ ▶**n.** a casserole of chicken pieces cooked in red wine. [20th C.: Fr., lit. 'cock in wine.']

co·quet /kōˈket/ ▶**v.** flirt, or flirt with. ▶**n.** dated a man who flirts.

co·quet·ry /ˈkōkitrē; kōˈketrē/ ▶**n.** flirtatious behavior or a flirtatious manner. [17th C.: from Fr. *coquetterie*, from *coqueter* 'to flirt,' from *coquet* 'wanton' (see COQUETTE).]

co·quette /kōˈket/ ▶**n.** a woman who flirts. — **co·quet·tish adj. co·quet·tish·ly adv. co·quet·tish·ness n.** [17th C.: Fr., fem. of *coquet* 'wanton,' dimin. of *coq* 'cock.']

co·qui·na /kōˈkēnə/ ▶**n.** **1** a soft limestone of broken shells, used in road-making in the Caribbean and Florida. **2** (also **coquina clam**) a small bivalve mollusk (genus *Donax*, family Donacidae) with a wedge-shaped shell that has a wide variety of colors and patterns. [19th C.: from Sp., lit. 'cockle,' based on L. *concha* (see CONCH).]

co·qui·to /kōˈkētō/ ▶**n.** (pl. **-tos**) a thick-trunked Chilean palm tree (*Jubaea chilensis*) that yields large amounts of sweet sap (palm honey) and fiber. [19th C.: from Sp., dimin. of *coco* 'coconut.']

Cor. ▶**abbr.** ■ coroner. ■ Bible Corinthians.

cor /kôr/ ▶**exclam.** Brit., informal expressing surprise, excitement, admiration, or alarm.

– PHRASES **cor blimey** /ˌkôr ˈblīmē/ see BLIMEY. [1930s: alt. of GOD.]

cor- ▶**prefix** var. of COM- assimilated before *r* (as in *corrode, corrugate*).

cor·a·cle /ˈkôrəkəl; ˈkär-/ ▶**n.** (esp. in Wales and Ireland) a small, round boat made of wickerwork covered with a watertight material, propelled with a paddle. [16th C.: from Welsh *corwgl, cwrwgl*, rel. to Irish *curach* 'small boat.']

cor·a·coid /ˈkôrəˌkoid/ ▶**n.** (also **coracoid process**) Anat. a short projection from the shoulder blade in mammals, to which part of the biceps is attached. [18th C.: from mod. L. *coracoides*, from Gk. *korakoeidēs* 'ravenlike,' from *korax* 'raven.']

cor·al /ˈkôrəl; ˈkär-/ ▶**n.** **1** a hard stony substance secreted by certain marine coelenterates as an external skeleton, typically forming large reefs in warm seas. ■ precious red coral, used in jewelry. ■ the pinkish-red color of red coral. **2** a sedentary, typically colonial coelenterate (class Anthozoa) of warm and tropical seas, with a calcareous, horny, or soft skeleton. **3** the unfertilized roe of a lobster or scallop, which is used as food and becomes reddish when cooked. — **cor·al·loid** /-ˌloid/ **adj.** (esp. Biol. & Zool.). [ME: via OFr. from L. *corallum*, from Gk. *korallion, kouralion*.]

cor·al bells ▶**n.** a red-flowered heuchera (*Heuchera sanguinea*) native to the southwestern US, but established elsewhere with many ornamental cultivars.

cor·al·ber·ry /ˈkôrəlˌberē; ˈkär-/ ▶**n.** (pl. **-ries**) an evergreen North American shrub (*Symphoricarpos orbiculatus*) of the honeysuckle family, with fragrant white flowers followed by deep red berries.

cor·al fun·gus ▶**n.** a widely distributed fungus (*Clavulina, Ramaria*, and other genera) that produces a fruiting body composed of upright branching fingerlike projections that resemble coral, found in Eurasia and North America.

Cor·al Ga·bles a city in southeastern Florida, on Biscayne Bay; pop. 42,249.

cor·al·line /ˈkôrəˌlīn/ ▶**n.** (also **coralline alga** or **coralline seaweed**) a branching reddish seaweed (family Corallinaceae) with a calcareous jointed stem, in particular *Corallina officinalis*, common on the coasts of the North Atlantic. ■ a sedentary colonial marine animal, esp. a bryozoan. ▶**adj.** esp. Geol. derived or formed from coral. ■ of the pinkish-red color of precious red coral. ■ resembling coral: *coralline sponges*. [16th C.: the n. from Ital. *corallina*, dimin. of *corallo* 'coral,' based on L. *corallum*.]

cor·al·root /ˈkôrəlˌro͞ot; ˈkärəl-; -ˌro͝ot/ ▶**n.** (also **coralroot orchid**) a leafless orchid (genus *Corallorhiza*) that has inconspicuous flowers and lacks chlorophyll. It has a pale knobbly rhizome that obtains nourishment from decaying organic matter.

Cor·al Sea part of the western Pacific Ocean surrounded by Australia, New Guinea, and Vanuatu.

cor·al snake ▶**n.** a brightly colored venomous snake (*Micrurus* and other genera) of the cobra family, typically having conspicuous bands of red, yellow, white, and black.

Cor·al Springs a city in southeastern Florida; pop. 117,549.

cor·beil /ˈkôrbəl; kôrˈbā/ ▶**n.** Archit. a representation in stone of a basket of flowers. [18th C.: from Fr. *corbeille* 'basket,' from late L. *corbicula* 'small basket,' dimin. of *corbis*.]

cor·beille /ˈkôrbəl; kôrˈbā/ ▶**n.** an elegant basket of flowers or fruit. [19th C.: Fr., 'basket.']

cor·bel /ˈkôrbəl/ ▶**n.** a projection jutting out from a wall to support a structure above it. ▶**v.** (**-beled, -bel·ing**; esp. Brit. **-belled, -bel·ling**) [trans.] (often **be corbeled out**) support (a structure such as an arch or balcony) on corbels. [ME: from OFr., dimin. of *corp* 'crow,' from L. *corvus* 'raven.']

cor·bel ta·ble ▶**n.** a projecting course of bricks or stones resting on corbels.

Cor·bett /ˈkôrbit/, James John (1866–1933), US boxer; nicknamed **Gentleman Jim**. He won two world heavyweight championships 1892, 1897.

cor·bie /ˈkôrbē/ ▶**n.** (pl. **-bies**) Scot. a raven, crow, or rook. [ME: from OFr. *corb*, var. of *corp* 'crow' (see CORBEL).]

cor·bie·steps /ˈkôrbēˌsteps/ (also **cor·bie steps**) ▶**n.** the steplike projections on the sloping part of a gable, common in Flemish architecture and 16th- and 17th-century Scottish buildings. Also called CROW STEPS.

Cor·bin /ˈkôrbin/, Margaret (1751–1800), American heroine; born *Margaret Cochran*. After her husband's death in the attack on Fort Washington in 1776 during the American Revolution, she took his place at his cannon.

Cor·co·va·do /ˌkôrkōˈvädō/ a peak that rises to 2,310 feet (711 m) on the south side of Rio de Janeiro. A statue of Christ, 131 feet (40 m) high, stands on its summit.

Cor·cy·ra /kôrˈsīrə/ ancient Greek name for CORFU.

cord /kôrd/ ▶**n.** **1** long thin flexible string or rope made from several twisted strands. ■ a length of such material, typically one used to fasten or move a specified object. ■ an anatomical structure resembling a length of cord (e.g., the spinal cord, the umbilical cord). ■ a flexible insulated cable used for carrying electric current to an appliance. **2** ribbed fabric, esp. corduroy. ■ (**cords**) informal corduroy pants. ■ a cordlike rib on fabric. **3** a measure of cut wood, usually 128 cubic feet (3.62 cu m). ▶**v.** [trans.] attach a cord to.

– PHRASES **cut the (umbilical) cord** fig. cease to rely on someone or something protective or supportive and begin to act independently. — **cord·like adj.** [ME: from OFr. *corde*, from L. *chorda*, from Gk. *khordē* 'string.']

cord·age /ˈkôrdij/ ▶**n.** cords or ropes, esp. in a ship's rigging.

cor·date /ˈkôrdāt/ ▶**adj.** Bot. Zool. heart-shaped. [17th C.: from L. *cordatus* 'wise,' from *cor, cord-* 'heart.']

Cor·day /kôrˈdā/, Charlotte (1768–93), French assassin; full name *Marie Anne Charlotte Corday d'Armont*. In 1793, she killed revolutionary leader Jean Paul Marat.

cord·ed /ˈkôrdid/ ▶**adj.** **1** (of cloth) ribbed. ■ (of a tensed muscle) standing out so as to resemble a piece of cord. **2** equipped with a cord.

cord·grass /ˈkôrdˌgras/ ▶**n.** a coarse wiry coastal grass (genus *Spartina*) that is sometimes used to stabilize mudflats.

cor·dial /ˈkôrjəl/ ▶**adj.** warm and friendly. ■ strongly felt. ▶**n.** **1** another term for LIQUEUR. **2** a comforting or pleasant-tasting medicine. — **cor·dial·i·ty** /ˌkôrjēˈalitē/ **n.** **cor·dial·ly adv.** [ME: from med. L. *cordialis*, from L. *cor, cord-* 'heart.']

cor·di·er·ite /ˈkôrdēəˌrīt/ ▶**n.** a dark blue mineral occurring chiefly in metamorphic rocks. It consists of an aluminosilicate of magnesium, and also occurs as a dichroic gem variety. [19th C.: Pierre L. A. *Cordier* (1777–1861), French geologist.]

cor·di·form /ˈkôrdəˌfôrm/ ▶**adj.** heart-shaped.

cor·dil·le·ra /ˌkôrdlˈ(y)erə/ ▶**n.** a system or group of parallel mountain ranges together with the intervening plateaus and other features, esp. in the Andes or the Rockies. [18th C.: from Sp., from *cordilla*, dimin. of *cuerda* 'cord.']

cord•ing /ˈkôrdiNG/ ▶n. cord or braid, esp. that used as a decorative fabric trimming.

cord•ite /ˈkôrdīt/ ▶n. a smokeless explosive made from nitrocellulose, nitroglycerine, and petroleum jelly, used in ammunition. [19th C.: from CORD.]

cord•less /ˈkôrdlis/ ▶adj. (of an electrical appliance or telephone) working without connection to a main supply or central unit. ▶n. (usu. **the cordless**) a cordless telephone.

Cor•do•ba /ˈkôrdəbə; -dəvə/ (also **Cor•do•va**) **1** a city in Andalusia, in southern Spain; pop. 309,200. Spanish name CÓRDOBA. **2** a city in central Argentina; pop. 1,198,000.

cor•do•ba /ˈkôrdəbə; -dəvə/ ▶n. the basic monetary unit of Nicaragua, equal to 100 centavos. [F. Fernández de *Córdoba*, 16th-cent. Spanish governor of Nicaragua.]

cor•don /ˈkôrdn/ ▶n. **1** a line or circle of police, soldiers, or guards preventing access to or from an area or building. **2** an ornamental cord or braid. **3** Archit. another term for STRINGCOURSE. ▶v. [trans.] (**cordon off**) prevent access to or from (an area or building) by surrounding it with police or other guards. [ME: from Ital. *cordone*, augmentative of *corda*, and Fr. *cordon*, dimin. of *corde*, from L. *chorda* 'string.']

cor•don bleu /ˌkôrdôN ˈblœ/ ▶adj. Cooking of the highest class. ■ [postpositive] denoting a dish consisting of an escalope of veal or chicken rolled, filled with cheese and ham, and then fried in breadcrumbs. ▶n. a cook of the highest class. [18th C.: Fr., lit. 'blue ribbon.']

cor•don sa•ni•taire /ˌkôrdôN ˌsänēˈter/ ▶n. (pl. **cor•dons sa•ni•taires** pronunc. same) a guarded line preventing anyone from leaving an area infected by a disease and thus spreading it. ■ a measure designed to prevent communication or the spread of undesirable influences. ■ a series or chain of small neutral buffer states around a larger, potentially dangerous or hostile state. [19th C.: Fr., from *cordon* 'line, border' (see CORDON) + *sanitaire* 'sanitary.']

Cor•do•va /ˈkôrdəvə/ English name for CORDOBA.

cor•do•van /ˈkôrdəvən/ ▶n. a kind of soft leather made originally from goatskin and now from horsehide. [16th C.: from Sp. *cordován*, former spelling of *cordobán* 'of Cordoba.']

cor•du•roy /ˈkôrdəˌroi/ ▶n. a thick cotton fabric with velvety ribs. ■ (**corduroys**) pants or overalls made of corduroy. [18th C.: prob. from CORD + *duroy*, a kind of worsted.]

cor•du•roy road ▶n. hist. a road made of tree trunks laid across a swamp.

cord•wood /ˈkôrdˌwo͝od/ ▶n. wood that has been cut into uniform lengths, used esp. as firewood.

CORE /kôr/ ▶abbr. Congress of Racial Equality.

core /kôr/ ▶n. **1** the tough central part of various fruits, containing the seeds. **2** the central or most important part of something, in particular: ■ [often as adj.] the part of something that is central to its existence or character. ■ an important or unchanging group of people forming the central part of a larger body. ■ the dense central region of a planet, esp. the nickel–iron inner part of the earth. ■ the central part of a nuclear reactor, which contains the fissile material. ■ a tiny ring of magnetic material used in a computer memory to store one bit of data, now superseded by semiconductor memories. ■ the inner strand of an electrical cable or rope. ■ a piece of soft iron forming the center of an electromagnet or an induction coil. ■ an internal mold filling a space to be left hollow in a casting. ■ a cylindrical sample of rock, ice, or other material obtained by boring with a hollow drill. ■ Archaeol. a piece of flint from which flakes or blades have been removed. ▶v. [trans.] remove the tough central part and seeds from (a fruit).
– PHRASES **to the core** to the depths of one's being. ■ used to indicate that someone possesses a characteristic to a very high degree.
— **cor•er** n. [ME: of unknown origin.]

core dump ▶n. Comput. a dump of the contents of main memory, carried out typically as an aid to debugging.

co•ref•er•en•tial /ˌkōˌrefəˈrenCHəl/ ▶adj. Ling. (of two elements or units) having the same reference. — **co•ref•er•ence** /kōˈref(ə)rəns; ˈkō-/ n.

co•re•li•gion•ist /ˌkōriˈlijənist/ ▶n. an adherent of the same religion as another person.

Co•rel•li /kəˈrelē/, Arcangelo (1653–1713), Italian violinist and composer.

co•re•op•sis /ˌkôrēˈäpsis/ ▶n. a plant (genus *Coreopsis*) of the daisy family, cultivated for its rayed, typically yellow, flowers. [mod. L., from Gk. *koris* 'bug' + *opsis* 'appearance.']

co•re•spond•ent (also **co-re•spond•ent**) ▶n. **1** a joint defendant in a lawsuit, esp. one on appeal. **2** a person cited in a divorce case as having committed adultery with the respondent.

Cor•fu /kôrˈfo͞o; ˈkôrf(y)o͞o/ one of the largest of the Ionian Islands, off the west coast of mainland Greece, known in ancient times as Corcyra; pop. 105,350. Greek name KÉRKIRA.

cor•gi /ˈkôrgē/ ▶n. (pl. **cor•gis**) short for WELSH CORGI.

co•ri•a•ceous /ˌkôrēˈāSHəs/ ▶adj. tech. resembling or having the texture of leather. [17th C.: from late L. *coriaceus* (from L. *corium* 'leather') + -OUS.]

co•ri•an•der /ˈkôrēˌandər; ˌkôrēˈandər/ ▶n. an aromatic Mediterranean plant (*Coriandrum sativum*) of the parsley family, the leaves and seeds of which are used as culinary herbs. [ME: from OFr. *coriandre*, from L. *coriandrum*, from Gk. *koriannon*.]

Cor•inth /ˈkôrinTH; ˈkär-/ a city on the northeastern coast of the Peloponnese, in Greece; pop. 27,400, slightly northeast of the site of an ancient city of the same name. Greek name KÓRINTHOS.

Cor•inth, Gulf of an inlet of the Ionian Sea that extends between the Peloponnese and central Greece. Also called LEPANTO, GULF OF.

Cor•inth, Isthmus of a narrow neck of land that links the Peloponnese with central Greece.

Cor•inth Ca•nal a shipping channel that crosses the Isthmus of Corinth, linking the Gulf of Corinth and the Saronic Gulf.

Co•rin•thi•an /kəˈrinTHēən/ ▶adj. **1** belonging or relating to Corinth, esp. the ancient city. ■ relating to or denoting the lightest and most ornate of the classical orders of architecture (used esp. by the Romans), characterized by flared capitals with rows of acanthus leaves. See illustration at CAPITAL². **2** involving or displaying the highest standards of sportsmanship. ▶n. **1** a native of Corinth. **2** the Corinthian order of architecture.

Co•rin•thi•ans /kəˈrinTHēənz/ either of two books of the New Testament, epistles of St. Paul to the Church at Corinth.

Cor•i•o•la•nus /ˌkôrēəˈlānəs/, Gaius (or Gnaeus) Marcius (5th century BC), Roman general. He captured the Volscian town of Corioli.

Co•ri•o•lis ef•fect /ˌkôrēˈōləs/ ▶n. Physics an effect whereby a mass moving in a rotating system experiences a force perpendicular to the direction of motion and to the axis of rotation (influencing, for example, the formation of cyclonic weather systems). [20th C.: Gaspard *Coriolis* (1792–1843), French engineer.]

co•ri•um /ˈkôrēəm/ ▶n. esp. Zool. another term for DERMIS. [19th C.: from L., 'skin.']

Cork /kôrk/ a county in the Republic of Ireland, in the province of Munster, on the Celtic Sea. ■ its county town; pop. 127,000.

cork /kôrk/ ▶n. the buoyant, light brown substance obtained from the outer bark layer of the cork oak. ■ a bottle stopper, esp. one made of cork. ■ a piece of cork used as a float for a fishing line or net. ■ Bot. a protective layer of dead cells immediately below the bark of woody plants. ▶v. [trans.] (often **be corked**) **1** close or seal (a bottle) with a cork. ■ [as adj.] (**corked**) (of wine) spoiled by tannin from the cork. **2** draw with burnt cork. — **cork•like** adj. [ME: based on Arab. *al-* 'the' and (prob.) L. *quercus* 'oak.']

cork•age /ˈkôrkij/ ▶n. a charge made by a restaurant or hotel for serving wine that has been brought in by a customer.

cork cam•bi•um ▶n. Bot. tissue in the stem of a plant that gives rise to cork on its outer surface and a layer of cells containing chlorophyll on its inner surface.

cork•er /ˈkôrkər/ ▶n. dated an excellent or astonishing person or thing.

cork oak (also **cork tree**) ▶n. an evergreen Mediterranean oak (*Quercus suber*), the outer layer of the bark of which is the source of cork.

cork•screw /ˈkôrkˌskro͞o/ ▶n. a device for pulling corks from bottles, consisting of a spiral metal rod that is inserted into the cork and a handle that extracts it. ■ [usu. as adj.] a thing with a spiral shape or movement. ▶v. [intrans.] move or twist in a spiral motion.

cork•wood /ˈkôrkˌwo͝od/ ▶n. a shrub or tree that yields light porous timber, in particular the American *Leitneria floridana* (family Leitneriaceae).

cork•y /ˈkôrkē/ ▶adj. (**cork•i•er**, **cork•i•est**) **1** corklike. **2** (of wine) corked.

corm /kôrm/ ▶n. a rounded underground storage organ in plants such as crocuses, gladioli, and cyclamens, consisting of a swollen stem base covered with scale leaves. Compare with BULB (sense 1), RHIZOME. [19th C.: from mod. L. *cormus*, from Gk. *kormos* 'trunk.']

cor•mel /ˈkôrməl; kôrˈmel/ ▶n. a small corm growing at the side of a mature corm.

corm•let /ˈkôrmlit/ ▶n. a small corm growing at the base of a mature corm.

cor•mo•rant /ˈkôrmərənt/ ▶n. a large voracious diving bird (genera *Phalacrocorax* and *Nannopterum*, family Phalacrocoracidae) with a long neck, long hooked bill, short legs, and mainly dark plumage. Its species include the North American **double-crested cormorant** (*P. auritus*). [ME: from OFr. *cormaran*, from med. L. *corvus marinus* 'sea raven.']

double-crested cormorant

corn¹ /kôrn/ ▶n. **1** a North American cereal plant (*Zea mays*) that yields large grains, or kernels, set in rows on a cob. ■ the grains of this. ■ Brit. the chief cereal crop of a district, esp. (in England) wheat or (in Scotland) oats. **2** informal something banal or sentimental: *the movie is pure corn.* [OE, of Gmc. origin; rel. to Ger. *Korn*.]

corn² ▶n. a small, painful area of thickened skin on the foot, esp. on the toes, caused by pressure. [ME: via Anglo-Norman Fr. from L. *cornu* 'horn.']

corn•ball /ˈkôrnˌbôl/ informal ▶adj. trite and sentimental. ▶n. a person with trite or sentimental ideas.

corn beef ▶n. corned beef.

Corn Belt name for parts of the US Midwest, esp. Illinois and Iowa, where corn is a major crop.

corn bor•er ▶n. a moth (family Pyralidae) whose larvae feed upon and bore into corn, in particular *Ostrinia nubilalis*, introduced from Europe into North America, and *Diatraea* (or *Zeadiatraea*) *grandiosella* of the southern US.

corn·bread /ˈkôrn,bred/ (also **corn bread**) ▶ n. a type of bread made from cornmeal and typically leavened without yeast.

corn cake (also **corn·cake**) ▶ n. cornbread made in the form of flat cakes.

corn·cob /ˈkôrn,käb/ (also **corn cob**) ▶ n. see COB (sense 1).

corn·cob pipe ▶ n. a tobacco pipe with a bowl made from a dried corncob.

corn cock·le (also **corn·cock·le**) ▶ n. a Mediterranean plant (*Agrostemma githago*) of the pink family, with bright pink or purple flowers and poisonous seeds, introduced into Britain and North America and often a prolific weed in fields of grain. [18th C.: from CORN[1] + *cockle* (from OE *coccul* 'corn cockle,' perh. via L. from Gk. *kokkos* 'berry').]

corn crake (also **corn·crake**) ▶ n. a secretive Eurasian crake (*Crex crex*) inhabiting coarse grasslands, with mainly brown streaked plumage and a distinctive double rasping call.

corn crib (also **corn·crib**) ▶ n. a bin or ventilated building for storing unhusked ears of corn.

corn dodg·er ▶ n. a small, hard fried or baked cornmeal cake. ▪ a boiled cornmeal dumpling.

corn dog ▶ n. a hot dog covered in cornmeal batter, fried, and served on a stick.

cor·ne·a /ˈkôrnēə/ ▶ n. the transparent layer forming the front of the eye. — **cor·ne·al** adj. [ME: from med. L. *cornea tela* 'horny tissue,' from L. *cornu* 'horn.']

corn ear·worm ▶ n. an American moth (*Heliothis zea*, family Noctuidae) whose larva is a pest of corn, cotton, and tomatoes.

corned /kôrnd/ ▶ adj. [attrib.] (of food) preserved in salt water: *corned beef.*

Cor·neille /kôrˈnā(l)/, Pierre (1606–84), French playwright. His plays include *Le Cid* (1637).

cor·ne·i·tis /,kôrnēˈītis/ ▶ n. Med. inflammation of the cornea.

cor·nel /ˈkôrnl; -nel/ ▶ n. a dogwood, esp. of a dwarf variety.

cor·nel·ian /kôrˈnēlyən/ ▶ n. var. of CARNELIAN.

cor·ne·ous /ˈkôrnēəs/ ▶ adj. formal hornlike; horny. [17th C.: from L. *corneus* (from *cornu* 'horn').]

cor·ner /ˈkôrnər/ ▶ n. **1** a place or angle where two or more sides or edges meet. ▪ an area inside a room, box, or square-shaped space, near the place where two or more edges or surfaces meet. ▪ a place where two streets meet. ▪ fig. a difficult or awkward situation. ▪ first or third base on a baseball diamond. ▪ a sharp bend in a road. **2** a part, region, or area, esp. one regarded as secluded or remote. ▪ a position in which one dominates the supply of a particular commodity. **3** short for CORNER KICK. **4** Boxing & Wrestling each of the diagonally opposite ends of the ring, where a contestant rests between rounds. ▪ a contestant's supporters or seconds. **5** Baseball each of the two parallel sides of home plate, which are perceived as defining the vertical edges of the strike zone. ▶ v. [trans.] **1** (often **be cornered**) force (a person or animal) into a place or situation from which it is hard to escape. ▪ detain (someone) in conversation, typically against their will. **2** control (a market) by dominating the supply of a particular commodity. ▪ establish a corner in (a commodity). **3** [intrans.] (of a vehicle or driver) go around a bend in a road.

– PHRASES **(just) around** (or **round**) **the corner** very near. **cut corners** see CUT. **in someone's corner** acting as a second, to a boxer. ▪ on someone's side; giving someone support and encouragement. **on** (or **at** or **in**) **every corner** everywhere. **see someone/something out of** (or **from**) **the corner of one's eye** see someone or something at the edge of one's field of vision. **turn the corner** see TURN. [ME: from Anglo-Norman Fr., based on L. *cornu* 'horn, tip, corner.']

cor·ner·back /ˈkôrnər,bak/ ▶ n. Football a defensive back positioned to the outside of the linebackers.

cor·nered /ˈkôrnərd/ ▶ adj. [in comb.] having a specified number of places or angles where the edges or sides meet: *six-cornered hats.* ▪ having a specified number of parties involved.

cor·ner kick (also **cor·ner**) ▶ n. Soccer a free kick taken by the attacking side from a corner of the field after the ball has been sent over the end line outside the goal by a defender.

cor·ner·stone /ˈkôrnər,stōn/ ▶ n. a stone that forms the base of a corner of a building, joining two walls. ▪ an important quality or feature on which a particular thing depends or is based.

cor·ner·wise /ˈkôrnər,wīz/ ▶ adv. at an angle of approximately 45°; diagonally.

cor·net /kôrˈnet/ ▶ n. Music a brass instrument resembling a trumpet but shorter and wider. ▪ a compound organ stop with a powerful treble sound. — **cor·net·ist** /-ˈnetist/ (also **cor·net·tist**) n. [ME: from OFr., dimin. of var. of L. *cornu* 'horn.']

cor·net·to /kôrˈnetō/ (also **cor·nett** /-ˈnet/) ▶ n. (pl. **-net·ti** /-ˈnetē/ or **-netts**) a woodwind instrument of the 16th and 17th centuries, typically curved, with finger holes and a cup-shaped mouthpiece. [19th C.: from Ital., dimin. of *corno* 'horn,' from L. *cornu*.]

corn-fed (also **corn·fed**) ▶ adj. fed on corn. ▪ informal plump; well fed. ▪ informal provincial; unsophisticated.

corn·field /ˈkôrn,fēld/ ▶ n. a field in which corn is grown.

corn·flakes /ˈkôrn,flāks/ ▶ plural n. a breakfast cereal consisting of toasted flakes made from corn.

corn flour ▶ n. flour made from corn. ▪ (usu. **corn·flour**) British term for CORNSTARCH.

corn·flow·er /ˈkôrn,flouər/ ▶ n. a slender Eurasian plant (genus *Centaurea*) of the daisy family, with flowers that are typically a deep, vivid blue. ▪ (also **cornflower blue**) a deep, vivid blue color.

corn·husk·ing /ˈkôrn,həskiNG/ ▶ n. the removal of husks from ears of corn. ▪ the husking of corn by several people as a social event. Also called HUSKING BEE. — **corn·husk·er** n.

cor·nice /ˈkôrnis/ ▶ n. **1** an ornamental molding around the wall of a room just below the ceiling. ▪ a horizontal molded projection crowning a building or structure, esp. the uppermost member of the entablature of an order, surmounting the frieze. **2** an overhanging mass of hardened snow at the edge of a mountain precipice. — **cor·niced** adj. **cor·nic·ing** n. [16th C.: from Fr. *corniche*, from Ital. *cornice*, perh. from L. *cornix* 'crow.']

cor·niche /ˈkôrnisH; kôrˈnēsH/ ▶ n. a road cut into the edge of a cliff, esp. one running along a coast. [19th C.: from Fr. (see CORNICE).]

Cor·nish /ˈkôrnisH/ ▶ adj. of or relating to Cornwall, or its people or language. ▶ n. **1** [as pl. n.] (**the Cornish**) the people of Cornwall collectively. **2** the extinct Brythonic language of Cornwall — **Cor·nish·man** /-mən/ n. (pl. **-men**) **Cor·nish·wom·an** /-,wo͝omən/ n. (pl. **-wom·en**). [ME: from the first element of CORNWALL + -ISH[1].]

corn·meal /ˈkôrn,mēl/ ▶ n. meal made from ground, dried corn.

corn oil ▶ n. an oil obtained from the germ of corn, used in cooking and salad dressings.

corn pone ▶ n. see PONE. ▶ adj. (**corn-pone**) often derog. rustic; unsophisticated.

corn·rows /ˈkôrn,rōz/ ▶ plural n. a style of braiding and plaiting the hair in narrow strips to form geometric patterns on the scalp.

corn sal·ad ▶ n. a small blue-flowered plant (*Valerianella locusta*, family Valerianaceae) widely cultivated for its edible narrow leaves. Also called LAMB'S LETTUCE, MACHE.

corn·silk /ˈkôrn,silk/ ▶ n. each of the long silklike filiform styles of the female flower of corn.

corn snake ▶ n. a long North American rat snake (*Elaphe guttata*) with a spear-shaped mark between the eyes. [17th C.: so named because often found in cornfields.]

corn snow ▶ n. snow with a rough granular surface resulting from alternate thawing and freezing. [from *corn* in the dial. sense 'granule.']

corn·stalk /ˈkôrn,stôk/ ▶ n. the stem of a corn plant.

corn·starch /ˈkôrn,stärCH/ ▶ n. finely ground corn flour, used as a thickener in cooking.

corn sug·ar ▶ n. dextrose, esp. when made from cornstarch.

corn syr·up ▶ n. syrup made from cornstarch, consisting of dextrose, maltose, and dextrins.

cor·nu /ˈkôrn(y)o͞o/ ▶ n. (pl. **-nu·a** /-n(y)o͞oə/) Anat. a structure with a shape likened to a horn, in particular: ▪ a horn-shaped projection of the thyroid cartilage or of certain bones (such as the hyoid and the coccyx). ▪ either of the two lateral cavities of the uterus, into which the Fallopian tubes pass. ▪ each of three elongated parts of the lateral ventricles of the brain. — **cor·nu·al** /-n(y)o͞oəl/ adj. [17th C.: from L., 'horn.']

cor·nu·co·pi·a /,kôrn(y)əˈkōpēə/ ▶ n. a symbol of plenty consisting of a goat's horn overflowing with flowers, fruit, and corn. ▪ an ornamental container shaped like such a horn. ▪ an abundant supply of good things of a specified kind. — **cor·nu·co·pi·an** adj. [16th C.: from late L., from L. *cornu copiae* 'horn of plenty.']

Corn·wall /ˈkôrn,wôl; -wəl/ **1** a county occupying the extreme southwestern peninsula of England; county town, Truro. **2** a port city in eastern Ontario, on the St. Lawrence River; pop. 47,137.

Corn·wal·lis /kôrnˈwälis/, Charles, 1st Marquis (1738–1805), English general who surrendered the British forces at Yorktown in 1781, ending the fighting in the American Revolution.

corn·y /ˈkôrnē/ ▶ adj. (**corn·i·er**, **corn·i·est**) informal trite, banal, or mawkishly sentimental. — **corn·i·ly** /ˈkôrnl-ē/ adv. **corn·i·ness** n. [1930s: from 'rustic.']

co·rol·la /kəˈrälə; -ˈrōlə/ ▶ n. Bot. the petals of a flower, typically forming a whorl within the sepals and enclosing the reproductive organs. Compare with CALYX. [17th C.: from L., dimin. of *corona* 'crown.']

cor·ol·lar·y /ˈkôrə,lerē; ˈkär-/ ▶ n. (pl. **-lar·ies**) a proposition that follows from (and is often appended to) one already proved. ▪ a direct or natural consequence or result. ▶ adj. forming a proposition that follows from one already proved. ▪ associated; supplementary. [ME: from L. *corollarium* 'gratuity,' from *corolla*.]

cor·o·man·del /,kôrəˈmandəl; ,kär-/ ▶ n. **1** a fine-grained, grayish-brown wood streaked with black, used in furniture. Also called CALAMANDER. **2** the Sri Lankan tree (*Diospyros quaesita*, family Ebenaceae) that yields this wood. ▶ adj. denoting a form of Asian lacquerware with intaglio designs. [COROMANDEL COAST.]

Cor·o·man·del Coast /,kôrəˈmandəl/ the southeastern coast of India, from Point Calimere to the mouth of the Krishna River.

Co·ro·na /kəˈrōnə/ a city in southwestern California, southwest of Riverside; pop. 76,095.

co·ro·na¹ /kə'rōnə/ ▶ **n.** (pl. **-nae** /-nē; -nī/) **1** Astron. the rarefied gaseous envelope of the sun and other stars. The sun's corona is normally visible only during a total solar eclipse when it is seen as an irregularly shaped pearly glow surrounding the darkened disk of the moon. ■ (also **corona discharge**) Physics the glow around a conductor at high potential. ■ a small circle of light seen around the sun or moon, due to diffraction by water droplets. **2** Anat. a crown or crownlike structure. ■ Bot. the cup-shaped or trumpet-shaped outgrowth at the center of a daffodil or narcissus flower. **3** a circular chandelier in a church. **4** Archit. a part of a cornice having a broad vertical face. [16th C. (sense 4): from L., 'wreath, crown.']

co·ro·na² ▶ **n.** a long, straight-sided cigar. [19th C.: from Sp. *La Corona*, lit. 'the crown.']

Co·ro·na Aus·tra·lis /kə'rōnə ô'strālis; ä'strā-/ Astron. a small southern constellation (the Southern Crown), with no bright stars. [L.]

Co·ro·na Bo·re·al·is /bôrē'alis/ Astron. a northern constellation (the Northern Crown), in which the main stars form a small but prominent arc. [L.]

cor·o·nach /'kôrənəкн; 'kär-/ ▶ **n.** (in Scotland or Ireland) a funeral song. [16th C.: from Scot. Gael. *corranach* (Irish *coranach*), from *comh-* 'together' + *rànach* 'outcry.']

Co·ro·na·do /,kôrə'nädō; ,kär-/, Francisco Vásquez de (*c.*1510–54), Spanish explorer whose expeditions opened the American Southwest to Spanish colonization.

co·ro·na·graph /kə'rōnə,graf/ ▶ **n.** an instrument that blocks out light emitted by the sun's actual surface so that the corona can be observed.

cor·o·nal¹ /'kôrənl; 'kär-/ ▶ **adj. 1** of or relating to the crown or corona of something, in particular: ■ Astron. of or relating to the corona of the sun or another star. ■ Anat. of or relating to the crown of the head. **2** Anat. of or in the coronal plane: *coronal imaging.* **3** Phonet. (of a consonant) formed by raising the tip or blade of the tongue toward the hard palate. ▶ **n.** Phonet. a coronal consonant. [ME (in the sense 'relating to the crown of the head'): from L. *coronalis*, from *corona* 'crown.']

cor·o·nal² /'kôrənl; 'kär-; kə'rōnl/ ▶ **n.** a garland or wreath for the head. ■ literary a small crown; a coronet. [ME: appar. from Anglo-Norman Fr., from *corune* 'crown, wreath' (see **crown**).]

cor·o·nal plane ▶ **n.** Anat. an imaginary plane dividing the body into dorsal and ventral parts.

cor·o·nal su·ture ▶ **n.** Anat. the transverse suture in the skull separating the frontal bone from the parietal bones.

cor·o·nar·y /'kôrə,nerē; 'kär-/ ▶ **adj.** Anat. relating to or denoting the arteries that surround and supply the heart. ■ relating to or denoting a structure that encircles a part of the body. ▶ **n.** (pl. **-nar·ies**) short for **coronary thrombosis**. [17th C.: from L. *coronarius*, from *corona* 'crown.']

cor·o·nar·y ar·ter·y ▶ **n.** an artery supplying blood to the heart.

cor·o·nar·y oc·clu·sion ▶ **n.** partial or total obstruction of a coronary artery, usually resulting in a myocardial infarction (heart attack).

cor·o·nar·y si·nus ▶ **n.** a wide venous channel about 2.25 centimeters in length that receives blood from the coronary veins and empties into the right atrium of the heart.

cor·o·nar·y throm·bo·sis ▶ **n.** a blockage of the flow of blood to the heart, caused by a blood clot in a coronary artery.

cor·o·nar·y vein ▶ **n.** any of several veins that drain blood from the heart wall and empty into the coronary sinus.

cor·o·na·tion /,kôrə'nāsнən; ,kär-/ ▶ **n.** the ceremony of crowning a sovereign or a sovereign's consort. [ME: via OFr. from med. L. *coronatio(n-)*, from *coronare* 'to crown,' from *corona* (see **crown**).]

co·ro·na·vi·rus /kə'rōnə,vīrəs/ ▶ **n.** Med. any of a group of RNA viruses that cause a variety of diseases in humans and other animals.

cor·o·ner /'kôrənər; 'kär-/ ▶ **n.** an official who holds inquests into violent, sudden, or suspicious deaths. ■ hist. in England, an official responsible for safeguarding the private property of the Crown. — **cor·o·ner·ship n.** [ME: from Anglo-Norman Fr. *coruner*, from *corune* 'a crown' (see **crown**).]

cor·o·net /,kôrə'net; ,kär-/ ▶ **n. 1** a small or relatively simple crown, esp. as worn by lesser royalty and peers. ■ a circular decoration for the head, esp. one made of flowers. **2** a ring of bone at the base of a deer's antler. ■ the band of tissue on the lowest part of a horse's pastern, containing the horn-producing cells from which the hoof grows. — **cor·o·net·ed adj.** [ME: from OFr. *coronete* 'small crown or garland,' dimin. of *corone* (see **crown**).]

Corp. ▶ **abbr.** ■ **(Corp)** informal corporal. ■ corporation.

cor·po·ra /'kôrpərə/ plural form of **corpus**.

cor·po·ral¹ /'kôrp(ə)rəl/ ▶ **n.** a low-ranking noncommissioned officer in the armed forces, in particular (in the US Army) an NCO ranking above private first class and below sergeant or (in the US Marine Corps) an NCO ranking above lance corporal and below sergeant. [16th C.: from Fr., from Ital. *caporale*, prob. based on L. *corpus, corpor-* 'body (of troops).']

cor·po·ral² ▶ **adj.** of or relating to the human body. — **cor·po·ral·ly adv.** [ME: via OFr. from L. *corporalis*, from *corpus, corpor-* 'body.']

cor·po·ral³ ▶ **n.** a cloth on which the chalice and paten are placed during the celebration of the Eucharist. [ME: from med. L. *corporale (pallium)* 'body (cloth),' from L. *corpus, corpor-* 'body.']

cor·po·ral·i·ty /,kôrpə'ralitē/ ▶ **n.** rare material or corporeal existence. [ME: from late L. *corporalitas*, from L. *corporalis* 'relating to the body' (see **corporal²**).]

cor·po·ral pun·ish·ment ▶ **n.** physical punishment, such as caning or flogging.

cor·po·rate /'kôrp(ə)rit/ ▶ **adj.** of or relating to a corporation, esp. a large company or group. ■ Law (of a company or group of people) authorized to act as a single entity and recognized as such in law. ■ of or shared by all the members of a group. ▶ **n.** a corporate company or group. — **cor·po·rate·ly adv.** [15th C.: from L. *corporatus*, past part. of *corporare* 'form into a body,' from *corpus, corpor-* 'body.']

cor·po·rate raid·er ▶ **n.** a financier who makes a practice of making hostile takeover bids for companies, to control their policies or to resell them for a profit.

cor·po·rate wel·fare ▶ **n.** government support or subsidy of private business, such as by tax incentives.

cor·po·ra·tion /,kôrpə'rāsнən/ ▶ **n.** a company or group of people authorized to act as a single entity (legally a person) and recognized as such in law. ■ (also **municipal corporation**) a group of people elected to govern a city, town, or borough. [ME: from late L. *corporatio(n-)*, from L. *corporare* 'combine in one body.']

cor·po·rat·ism /'kôrp(ə)rə,tizəm/ ▶ **n.** the control of a state or organization by large interest groups. — **cor·po·rat·ist adj. & n.**

cor·po·ra·tize /'kôrp(ə)rə,tīz/ ▶ **v.** [trans.] convert (a state organization) into an independent commercial company.

cor·po·re·al /kôr'pôrēəl/ ▶ **adj.** of or relating to a person's body, esp. as opposed to their spirit. ■ having a body. ■ Law consisting of material objects; tangible. — **cor·po·re·al·i·ty** /kôr,pôrē'alitē/ **n. cor·po·re·al·ly adv.** [ME: from late L. *corporealis*, from L. *corporeus* 'bodily,' from *corpus, corpor-* 'body.']

cor·po·re·i·ty /,kôrpə'rē-itē; -'rā-itē/ ▶ **n.** rare the quality of having a physical body or existence. [17th C.: from Fr. *corporéité* or med. L. *corporeitas*, from L. *corporeus* 'composed of flesh,' from *corpus, corpor-* 'body.']

cor·po·sant /'kôrpə,sant; -zant/ ▶ **n.** archaic an appearance of St. Elmo's fire on a mast, rigging, or other structure. [16th C.: from Old Sp., Port., and Ital. *corpo santo* 'holy body.']

corps /kôr/ ▶ **n.** (pl. **corps** /kôrz/) [often in names] a main subdivision of an armed force in the field, consisting of two or more divisions: *the 5th Army Corps.* ■ a branch of a military organization assigned to a particular kind of work. ■ [with adj.] a body of people engaged in a particular activity: *the press corps.* ■ short for **corps de ballet**. [16th C.: from Fr., from L. *corpus* 'body.']

corps de bal·let /,kôr də ba'lā/ ▶ **n.** [treated as sing. or pl.] the members of a ballet company who dance together as a group. ■ the members of the lowest rank of dancers in a ballet company. [19th C.: Fr.]

corpse /kôrps/ ▶ **n.** a dead body, esp. of a human being rather than an animal. [ME: alt. of **corse** by association with L. *corpus*.]

corps·man /'kôrmən/ ▶ **n.** an enlisted member of a military medical unit. ■ a member of a civilian, esp. a paramedical, corps.

cor·pu·lent /'kôrpyələnt/ ▶ **adj.** (of a person) fat. — **cor·pu·lence n. cor·pu·len·cy n.** [ME: from L. *corpulentus*, from *corpus* 'body.']

cor·pus /'kôrpəs/ ▶ **n.** (pl. **-po·ra** /-pərə/ or **-pus·es**) **1** a collection of written texts, esp. the entire works of a particular author or a body of writing on a particular subject. ■ a collection of written or spoken material in machine-readable form, assembled for the purpose of studying linguistic structures, frequencies, etc. **2** Anat. the main body or mass of a structure. ■ the central part of the stomach, between the fundus and the antrum. [ME: from L., 'body.']

cor·pus cal·lo·sum /ka'lōsəm/ ▶ **n.** (pl. **cor·po·ra cal·lo·sa** /'kôrpərə ka'lōsə/) Anat. a broad band of nerve fibers joining the two hemispheres of the brain. [18th C.: from **corpus** and L. *callosum*, neut. of *callosus* 'tough.']

Cor·pus Chris·ti¹ /,kôrpəs 'kristē/ a city and port in southern Texas; pop. 277,454.

Cor·pus Chris·ti² a feast of the Western Christian Church commemorating the institution of the Eucharist, observed on the Thursday after Trinity Sunday. [L., lit. 'body of Christ.']

cor·pus·cle /'kôr,pəsəl/ ▶ **n.** Biol. a minute body or cell in an organism, esp. a red or white cell in the blood of vertebrates. ■ hist. a minute particle regarded as the basic constituent of matter or light. — **cor·pus·cu·lar** /kôr'pəskyələr/ **adj.** [17th C.: from L. *corpusculum* 'small body,' dimin. of *corpus*.]

cor·pus de·lic·ti /də'liktī; -tē/ ▶ **n.** Law the facts and circumstances constituting a breach of a law. ■ concrete evidence of a crime, such as a corpse. [L., lit. 'body of offense.']

cor·pus lu·te·um /'lōōtēəm/ ▶ **n.** (pl. **cor·po·ra lu·te·a** /'lōōtēə/) Anat. a hormone-secreting structure that develops in an ovary after an ovum has been discharged but degenerates after a few days unless pregnancy has begun. [18th C.: from **corpus** and L. *luteum*, neut. of *luteus* 'yellow.']

cor·pus stri·a·tum /strī'ātəm/ ▶ **n.** (pl. **cor·po·ra stri·a·ta** /strī'ātə/) Anat. part of the basal ganglia of the brain, comprising the caudate and lentiform nuclei. [from **corpus** and L. *striatum*, neut. of *striatus* 'grooved.']

corr. ▶ **abbr.** ■ correction. ■ correspondence.

cor·ral /kə'ral/ ▶ **n.** a pen for livestock, esp. cattle or horses, on a farm or ranch. ■ hist. a defensive enclosure of encamped wagons. ▶ **v.** (**-ralled, -ral·ling**) [trans.] put or keep (livestock) in a corral. ■ fig. gather (a group of people or things) together. ■ hist. form (wagons) into a corral. [16th C.: from Sp. and Old Port., perh. based on L. *currere* 'to run.']

cor·rect /kə'rekt/ ▶ **adj.** free from error; in accordance with fact or truth. ■ [predic.] not mistaken in one's opinion or judgment; right. ■ (of a thing or course of action) meeting the requirements of or most appropriate for a particular situation or activity. ▪ (of a person or their appearance or behavior) conforming to accepted social standards; proper. ▪ conforming to a particular political or ideological orthodoxy. See also POLITICALLY CORRECT. ▶ v. [trans.] put right (an error or fault). ▪ mark the errors in (a written or printed text). ▪ tell (someone) that they are mistaken: *I wish he had corrected me when I gave the wrong answer.* ▪ counteract or rectify. ▪ adjust (an instrument) to function accurately or in accord with a standard. ▪ adjust (a numerical result or reading) to allow for departure from standard conditions. — **cor·rect·a·ble** adj. **cor·rect·ly** adv. **cor·rect·ness** n. [ME (as a verb): from L. *correct-* 'made straight,' from the v. *corrigere*, from *cor-* 'together' + *regere* 'guide.']

cor·rec·tion /kəˈrekSHən/ ▶ n. the action or process of correcting something. ▪ a change that rectifies an error or inaccuracy. ▪ used to introduce an amended version of something one has just said. ▪ a quantity adjusting a numerical result to allow for a departure from standard conditions. ▪ a temporary reversal in an overall trend of stock market prices, esp. a brief fall during an overall increase. ▪ punishment, esp. that of criminals in prison intended to rectify their behavior. [ME: via OFr. from L. *correctio(n-)*, from *corrigere* 'make straight, bring into order' (see CORRECT).]

cor·rec·tion·al /kəˈreksHənl/ ▶ adj. of or relating to the punishment of criminals in a way intended to rectify their behavior.

cor·rec·ti·tude /kəˈrektə,t(y)o͞od/ ▶ n. correctness, esp. conscious correctness in one's behavior. [19th C.: blend of CORRECT and RECTITUDE.]

cor·rec·tive /kəˈrektiv/ ▶ adj. designed to correct or counteract something harmful or undesirable. ▶ n. a thing intended to correct or counteract something else. — **cor·rec·tive·ly** adv. [16th C.: from Fr. *correctif, -ive* or late L. *correctivus*, from L. *correct-* 'brought into order,' from the v. *corrigere* (see CORRECT).]

cor·rec·tor /kəˈrektər/ ▶ n. a person or thing that corrects something, esp. a computer program or electronic device with a specified function.

Cor·reg·gio /kəˈrej(ē)ō/, Antonio Allegri da (*c.*1494–1534), Italian painter; born *Antonio Allegri*. His work influenced the rococo style of the 18th century.

Cor·reg·i·dor /kəˈregə,dôr/ an island in the Philippines at the entrance to Manila Bay, scene of World War II battles and now a national shrine.

cor·re·late ▶ v. /ˈkôrə,lāt; ˈkär-/ [intrans.] have a mutual relationship or connection, in which one thing affects or depends on another. ▪ [trans.] establish such a relationship or connection between. ▶ n. /-lit/ each of two or more related or complementary things. [17th C. (as a n.): back-form. from CORRELATION and CORRELATIVE.]

cor·re·la·tion /,kôrəˈlāSHən/ ▶ n. a mutual relationship or connection between two or more things. ▪ Stat. interdependence of variable quantities. ▪ Stat. a quantity measuring the extent of such interdependence. ▪ the process of establishing a relationship or connection between two or more measures. — **cor·re·la·tion·al** /-SHənl/ adj. [16th C.: from med. L. *correlatio(n-)*, from *cor-* 'together' + *relatio* (see RELATION).]

cor·re·la·tion co·ef·fi·cient ▶ n. Stat. a number between −1 and +1 calculated so as to represent the linear dependence of two variables or sets of data. (Symbol: **r**.)

cor·rel·a·tive /kəˈrelətiv/ ▶ adj. having a mutual relationship; corresponding. ▪ Gram. (of words such as *neither* and *nor*) corresponding to each other and regularly used together. ▶ n. a word or concept that has a mutual relationship with another word or concept. — **cor·rel·a·tive·ly** adv. **cor·rel·a·tiv·i·ty** /kə,reləˈtivitē/ n. [16th C.: from med. L. *correlativus*, from *cor-* 'together' + late L. *relativus* (see RELATIVE).]

cor·re·spond /,kôrəˈspänd; ,kär-/ ▶ v. [intrans.] **1** have a close similarity; match or agree almost exactly. ▪ be analogous or equivalent in character, form, or function. ▪ represent. **2** communicate by exchanging letters. [ME: from OFr. *correspondre*, from med. L. *correspondere*, from *cor-* 'together' + L. *respondere* (see RESPOND).]

cor·re·spond·ence /,kôrəˈspändəns; ,kär-/ ▶ n. **1** a close similarity, connection, or equivalence. **2** communication by exchanging letters with someone. ▪ letters sent or received. — **cor·re·spond·en·cy** n. (rare). [ME: via OFr. from med. L. *correspondentia*, from *correspondent-* 'corresponding' (see CORRESPONDENT).]

cor·re·spond·ence course ▶ n. a course of study in which student and teachers communicate by mail.

cor·re·spond·ence school ▶ n. a college offering correspondence courses.

cor·re·spond·ent /,kôrəˈspändənt; ,kär-/ ▶ n. a person who writes letters to a person or a newspaper, esp. on a regular basis. ▪ [often with adj.] a person employed to report for a newspaper or broadcasting organization, typically on a particular subject or from a particular country. ▶ adj. corresponding.

cor·re·spond·ing /,kôrəˈspändiNG; ,kär-/ ▶ adj. **1** similar in character, form, or function. ▪ able to be matched, joined, or interlocked. **2** dealing with written communication; having this responsibility. ▪ having an honorary association with a group, esp. at a distance (from the group's headquarters). — **cor·re·spond·ing·ly** adv.

cor·re·spond·ing an·gles ▶ plural n. Math. the angles that occupy the same relative position at each intersection where a straight line crosses two others. If the two lines are parallel, the corresponding angles are equal.

cor·ri·da /kôˈrēdə/ ▶ n. a bullfight. [19th C.: from Sp. *corrida de toros* 'running of bulls.']

cor·ri·dor /ˈkôrədər; ˈkär-; -,dôr/ ▶ n. a long passage in a building from which doors lead into rooms. ▪ [often with adj.] a belt of land between two other areas, typically having a particular feature or giving access to a particular area. ▪ [with adj.] a belt of land following a road, river, or other route of passage.
– PHRASES **the corridors of power** the senior levels of government or administration, where covert influence is regarded as being exerted and significant decisions are made. [16th C.: from Fr., from Ital. *corridore*, alt. of *corridoio* 'running place,' from *correre* 'to run,' from L. *currere*.]

cor·rie /ˈkôrē; ˈkärē/ ▶ n. (pl. **-ries**) a cirque, esp. one in the mountains of Scotland. [16th C.: from Scot. Gael. and Irish *coire* 'cauldron, hollow.']

cor·ri·gen·dum /,kôriˈjendəm; ,kär-/ ▶ n. (pl. **-gen·da** /-ˈjendə/) a thing to be corrected, typically an error in a printed book. [19th C.: L., neut. gerundive of *corrigere* (see CORRECT).]

cor·ri·gi·ble /ˈkôrijəbəl; ˈkär-/ ▶ adj. capable of being corrected, rectified, or reformed. — **cor·ri·gi·bil·i·ty** /,kôrijəˈbilitē; ,kär-/ n. [ME: via Fr. from med. L. *corrigibilis*, from L. *corrigere* 'to correct.']

cor·rob·o·rate /kəˈräbə,rāt/ ▶ v. [trans.] confirm or give support to (a statement, theory, or finding). — **cor·rob·o·ra·tion** /kə,räbəˈrāSHən/ n. **cor·rob·o·ra·tive** /-ˈräb(ə)rətiv/ adj. **cor·rob·o·ra·tor** /-,rātər/ n. **cor·rob·o·ra·to·ry** /-ˈräb(ə)rə,tôrē/ adj. [16th C.: from L. *corroborat-* 'strengthened,' from v. *corroborare*, from *cor-* 'together' + *roborare*, from *robur* 'strength.']

cor·rob·o·ree /kəˈräbə,rē/ ▶ n. an Australian Aboriginal dance ceremony that may take the form of a sacred ritual or an informal gathering. ▪ esp. Austral. a party or other social gathering, esp. a lively one. [from Dharuk *garaabara*, denoting a style of dancing.]

cor·rode /kəˈrōd/ ▶ v. [trans.] destroy or damage (metal, stone, or other materials) slowly by chemical action. ▪ [intrans.] (of metal or other materials) be destroyed or damaged in this way. ▪ fig. destroy or weaken (something) gradually. — **cor·rod·i·ble** adj. [ME: from L. *corrodere*, from *cor-* (expressing intensive force) + *rodere* 'gnaw.']

cor·ro·sion /kəˈrōZHən/ ▶ n. the process of corroding metal, stone, or other materials. ▪ damage caused by such a process. [ME: ult. from late L. *corrosio(n-)*, from L. *corrodere*.]

cor·ro·sive /kəˈrōsiv; -ziv/ ▶ adj. tending to cause corrosion. ▶ n. a corrosive substance. — **cor·ro·sive·ly** adv. **cor·ro·sive·ness** n. [ME: from OFr. *corosif, -ive*, from med. L. *corrosivus*, from L. *corros-* 'gnawed through,' from the v. *corrodere* (see CORRODE).]

cor·ro·sive sub·li·mate ▶ n. rare another term for MERCURIC CHLORIDE.

cor·ru·gate /ˈkôrə,gāt; ˈkär-/ ▶ v. contract or cause to contract into wrinkles or folds. [ME: from L. *corrugat-* 'wrinkled,' from v. *corrugare*, from *cor-* (intensive) + *rugare* (from *ruga* 'wrinkle').]

cor·ru·gat·ed /ˈkôrə,gātid; ˈkär-/ ▶ adj. (of a material, surface, or structure) shaped into alternate ridges and grooves. — **cor·ru·ga·tion** /,kôrəˈgāSHən; ,kär-/ n.

cor·rupt /kəˈrəpt/ ▶ adj. **1** having or showing a willingness to act dishonestly in return for money or personal gain. ▪ evil or morally depraved. ▪ archaic (of organic or inorganic matter) in a state of decay; rotten or putrid: *a corrupt and rotting corpse.* **2** (of a text or manuscript) debased or made unreliable by errors or alterations. ▪ (of a computer database or program) having errors introduced. ▶ v. [trans.] **1** cause to act dishonestly in return for money or personal gain. ▪ cause to become morally depraved. ▪ archaic infect; contaminate. **2** (often **be corrupted**) change or debase by making errors or unintentional alterations. ▪ cause errors to appear in (a computer program or database). — **cor·rupt·er** n. **cor·rupt·i·bil·i·ty** /kə,rəptəˈbilitē/ n. **cor·rupt·i·ble** adj. **cor·rup·tive** adj. **cor·rupt·ly** adv. [ME: from L. *corruptus*, past part. of *corrumpere* 'mar,' from *cor-* 'altogether' + *rumpere* 'to break.']

cor·rup·tion /kəˈrəpSHən/ ▶ n. **1** dishonest or fraudulent conduct by those in power, typically involving bribery. ▪ the action of making someone or something morally depraved or the state of being so. ▪ archaic decay; putrefaction. **2** the process by which something, typically a word or expression, is changed from its original state to one that is regarded as erroneous or debased. ▪ the process of causing errors to appear in a computer program or database. [ME: via OFr. from L. *corruptio(n-)*, from *corrumpere* 'mar, bribe, destroy' (see CORRUPT).]

cor·rup·tion·ist /kəˈrəpSHə,nist/ ▶ n. one who practices or endorses corruption, esp. in politics.

cor·sage /kôrˈsäZH; -ˈsäj/ ▶ n. **1** a spray of flowers worn pinned to a woman's clothes. **2** the upper part of a woman's dress. [19th C. (sense 2): Fr., from OFr. *cors* 'body,' from L. *corpus*.]

cor·sair /ˈkôrse(ə)r/ ▶ n. archaic **1** a pirate. ▪ a privateer, esp. one operating along the southern coast of the Mediterranean in the 17th century. **2** a pirate ship. [16th C.: from Fr. *corsaire*, from med. L. *cursarius*, from *cursus* 'a raid,' from L. *cursus* 'course,' from *currere* 'to run.']

Corse /kôrs/ French name for CORSICA.

corse /kôrs/ ▶ n. archaic a corpse. [ME: from OFr. *cors* 'body,' from L. *corpus*.]

cor·se·let /ˈkôrs(ə)lit/ ▶ n. **1** hist. a piece of armor covering the trunk. **2** var. of CORSELETTE. [15th C.: from OFr. *corslet*, dimin. of *cors* 'body.']

cor·se·lette /ˈkôrs(ə)lit/ (also **cor·se·let**) ▶ n. a woman's foundation garment combining corset and brassière. [1920s: from *corselet* (see CORSELET).]

cor·set /ˈkôrsit/ ▶ **n.** a woman's tightly fitting undergarment extending from below the chest to the hips, worn to shape the figure. ■ a similar garment worn by men or women to support a weak or injured back. ■ hist. a tightly fitting laced or stiffened outer bodice or dress. — **cor·set·ed** adj. **cor·set·ry** n. [ME: from OFr., dimin. of *cors* 'body,' from L. *corpus*.]

cor·se·tière /ˌkôrsiˈti(ə)r; -ˈtyer/ ▶ **n.** a woman who makes or fits corsets. [19th C.: Fr., fem. of *corsetier*, from *corset*.]

Cor·si·ca /ˈkôrsikə/ an island off the western coast of Italy, an administrative region of France; pop. 249,740; chief towns, Ajaccio and Bastia. French name **Corse**.

Cor·si·can /ˈkôrsikən/ ▶ **adj.** of or relating to Corsica, its people, or their language. ▶ **n. 1** a native of Corsica. **2** the language of Corsica, which originated as a dialect of Italian.

cor·tège /kôrˈtezʜ; ˈkôrtezʜ/ ▶ **n.** a solemn procession, esp. for a funeral. ■ a person's entourage or retinue. [17th C.: from Fr., from Ital. *corteggio*, from *corteggiare* 'attend court,' from *corte* 'court,' from L. *cohors, cohort-* 'retinue.']

Cor·tes /ˈkôrtes/ the legislative assembly of Spain and formerly of Portugal. [Sp. and Port., pl. of *corte* 'court,' from L. *cohors, cohort-* 'yard, retinue.']

Cor·tés /kôrˈtes; -ˈtez/ (also **Cor·tez**), Hernando (1485–1547), Spanish conquistador. He overthrew the Aztec empire by conquering its capital, Tenochtitlán, in 1519 and by deposing its emperor, Montezuma.

cor·tex /ˈkôrteks/ ▶ **n.** (pl. **-ti·ces** /-təˌsēz/) Anat. the outer layer of the cerebrum (the **cerebral cortex**), composed of folded gray matter and playing an important role in consciousness. ■ an outer layer of another organ or body part such as a kidney (the **renal cortex**), the cerebellum, or a hair. ■ Bot. an outer layer of tissue immediately below the epidermis of a stem or root. — **cor·ti·cal** /ˈkôrtikəl/ adj. [ME: from L., 'bark.']

cor·ti·cate /ˈkôrtiˌkāt; -ikit/ ▶ **adj.** Bot. having a cortex, bark, or rind. — **cor·ti·ca·tion** /ˌkôrtəˈkāsʜən/ n. [19th C.: from L. *corticatus*, from *cortex, cortic-* 'bark.']

cortico- ▶ **comb. form** representing **cortex**, used esp. with reference to the adrenal and cerebral cortices. [from L. *cortex, cortic-* 'bark.']

cor·ti·coid /ˈkôrtiˌkoid/ ▶ **n.** another term for **corticosteroid**.

cor·ti·co·ster·oid /ˌkôrtikōˈsteroid; -ˈsti(ə)roid/ ▶ **n.** Biochem. any of a group of steroid hormones produced in the adrenal cortex or made synthetically. There are two kinds: glucocorticoids and mineralocorticoids. They have various metabolic functions and some are used to treat inflammation.

cor·ti·cos·ter·one /kôrtiˈkästəˌrōn/ ▶ **n.** Biochem. a hormone secreted by the adrenal cortex, one of the glucocorticoids.

cor·ti·co·tro·pin /ˌkôrtikōˈtrōpin/ (also **cor·ti·co·troph·in** /-ˈtrāfin/) ▶ **n.** Biochem. another term for **adrenocorticotropic hormone**.

cor·ti·sol /ˈkôrtəˌsôl; -ˌsōl/ ▶ **n.** Biochem. another term for **hydrocortisone**.

cor·ti·sone /ˈkôrtəˌsōn/ ▶ **n.** Biochem. a hormone produced by the adrenal cortex. One of the glucocorticoids, it is also made synthetically for use as an anti-inflammatory and anti-allergy agent. [1940s: from *17-hydroxy-11-dehydrocorticosterone*.]

co·run·dum /kəˈrəndəm/ ▶ **n.** extremely hard aluminum oxide, used as an abrasive. Ruby and sapphire are varieties of corundum. [18th C.: from Tamil *kuruntam*, Telugu *kuruvindam*.]

Co·run·na /kəˈrənə/ a port in northwestern Spain; pop. 251,300. Spanish name **La Coruña**.

co·rus·cant /kəˈrəskənt/ ▶ **adj.** literary glittering; sparkling. [15th C.: from L. *coruscant-* 'vibrating, glittering,' from the v. *coruscare*.]

cor·us·cate /ˈkôrəˌskāt; ˈkär-/ ▶ **v.** [intrans.] literary (of light) flash or sparkle. — **cor·us·ca·tion** /ˌkôrəˈskāsʜən/ n. [18th C.: from L. *coruscat-* 'glittered,' from the v. *coruscare*.]

cor·us·cat·ing /ˈkôrəˌskātiɴɢ/ ▶ **adj.** flashing; sparkling. ■ brilliant or striking in content or style.

cor·vée /ˈkôrvā; kôrˈvā/ ▶ **n.** hist. a day's unpaid labor owed by a vassal to his feudal lord. ■ forced labor exacted in lieu of taxes, in particular that on public roads. [ME: from OFr., based on L. *corrogare* 'ask for.']

cor·vette /kôrˈvet/ ▶ **n.** a small warship designed for convoy escort duty. ■ hist. a sailing warship with one tier of guns. [17th C.: from Fr., from Du. *korf*, a ship, + dimin. suffix *-ette*.]

cor·vid /ˈkôrvid/ ▶ **n.** Ornithol. a bird of the crow family (Corvidae); a crow. [20th C.: from mod. L. *Corvidae* (pl.), from L. *corvus* 'raven.']

cor·vi·na /kôrˈvēnə/ ▶ **n.** a marine food and game fish (genus *Cynoscion*) of the drum family, found on the Pacific coasts of California and Mexico and sometimes living in fresh water. [18th C.: from Sp. and Port.]

cor·vine /ˈkôrvīn/ ▶ **adj.** of or like a raven or crow, esp. in color. [17th C.: from L. *corvinus*, from *corvus* 'raven.']

Cor·vus /ˈkôrvəs/ Astron. a small southern constellation (the Crow or Raven), south of Virgo. [L.]

cor·y·ban·tic /ˌkôrəˈbantik/ ▶ **adj.** wild; frenzied. [17th C.: from *Corybantes*, Latin name of the priests of Cybele, a Phrygian goddess, from Gk. *Korubantes*.]

co·ryd·a·lis /kəˈridl-əs/ ▶ **n.** a plant (genus *Corydalis*) of the poppy family with spurred tubular flowers, found in north temperate regions. [mod. L., from Gk. *korudallis* 'crested lark.']

cor·ymb /ˈkôrim(b); ˈkär-/ ▶ **n.** Bot. a flower cluster whose lower stalks are proportionally longer so that the flowers form a flat or slightly convex head. — **co·rym·bose** /ˈkôrəmˌbōs; ˈkär-; -ˌbōz/ adj. [18th C.: from Fr. *corymbe* or L. *corymbus*, from Gk. *korumbos* 'cluster.']

cor·y·phée /ˌkôrəˈfā/ ▶ **n.** a leading dancer in a corps de ballet. [Fr., via L. from Gk. *koruphaios* 'leader of a chorus,' from *koruphē* 'head.']

co·ry·za /kəˈrīzə/ ▶ **n.** Med. catarrhal inflammation of the mucous membrane in the nose, caused esp. by a cold or by hay fever. [16th C.: from L., from Gk. *koruza* 'nasal mucus.']

cos[1] /käs; kôs/ (also **cos lettuce**) ▶ **n.** another term for **romaine**. [17th C.: *Cos*, an Aegean island.]

cos[2] ▶ **abbr.** cosine.

Co·sa Nos·tra /ˌkōsə ˈnōstrə; ˌkōzə/ a US criminal organization resembling and related to the Mafia. [Ital., lit. 'our affair.']

co·sec /ˈkōsek/ ▶ **abbr.** cosecant.

co·se·cant /kōˈsēkant; -kənt/ ▶ **n.** Math. the ratio of the hypotenuse (in a right-angled triangle) to the side opposite an acute angle; the reciprocal of sine. [18th C.: from mod. L. *cosecant-*, from **co-** + L. *secant-* 'cutting' (from v. *secare*).]

co·seis·mal /kōˈsīzməl; -ˈsīs-/ ▶ **adj.** relating to points on the earth's surface affected by an earthquake simultaneously. ▶ **n.** a line on a map connecting such points. [19th C.: from **co-** 'jointly' + *seismal* (from Gk. *seismos* 'earthquake,' from *seien* 'to shake').]

co·set /ˈkōˌset/ ▶ **n.** Math. a set composed of all the products obtained by multiplying each element of a subgroup in turn by one particular element of the group containing the subgroup.

cosh[1] /käsʜ/ esp. Brit., informal ▶ **n.** a thick heavy stick or bar used as a weapon; a bludgeon. ▶ **v.** [trans.] hit (someone) on the head with a cosh. [19th C.: of unknown origin.]

cosh[2] Math. ▶ **abbr.** hyperbolic cosine. [from **cos**[2] + *-h* for *hyperbolic*.]

co·sig·na·tory /kōˈsignəˌtôrē/ (also **co-sig·na·to·ry**) ▶ **n.** a person or state signing a treaty or other document jointly with others.

Cos·i·mo de' Me·di·ci /ˈkôzēˌmō də ˈmedəcʜē/ (1389–1464), Italian banker; known as **Cosimo the Elder**. He laid the foundations for the Medici family's power in Florence, becoming the city's ruler in 1434.

co·sine /ˈkōˌsīn/ ▶ **n.** Math. the trigonometric function that is equal to the ratio of the side adjacent to an acute angle (in a right-angled triangle) to the hypotenuse.

cos·met·ic /käzˈmetik/ ▶ **adj.** involving or relating to treatment intended to restore or improve a person's appearance. ■ designed or serving to improve the appearance of the body, esp. the face. ■ affecting only the appearance of something rather than its substance. ▶ **n.** (usu. **cosmetics**) a product applied to the body, esp. the face, to improve its appearance. — **cos·met·i·cal·ly** adv. [17th C.: from Fr. *cosmétique*, from Gk. *kosmētikos*, from *kosmein* 'adorn,' from *kosmos* 'adornment.']

cos·me·ti·cian /ˌkäzmiˈtisʜən/ ▶ **n.** a person who sells or applies cosmetics as an occupation.

cos·me·tol·o·gy /ˌkäzmiˈtäləjē/ ▶ **n.** the professional skill or practice of beautifying the face, hair, and skin. — **cos·me·to·log·i·cal** /-təˈläjikəl/ adj. **cos·me·tol·o·gist** n.

cos·mic /ˈkäzmik/ ▶ **adj.** of or relating to the universe or cosmos, esp. as distinct from the earth. ■ inconceivably vast. — **cos·mi·cal** adj. **cos·mi·cal·ly** adv.

cos·mic dust ▶ **n.** small particles of matter distributed throughout space.

cos·mic ray ▶ **n.** a highly energetic atomic nucleus or other particle traveling through space at a speed approaching that of light.

cos·mic string ▶ **n.** another term for **string** (sense 5).

cosmo- ▶ **comb. form** of or relating to the world or the universe: *cosmography*. [from Gk. *kosmos* 'world.']

cos·mo·gen·e·sis /ˌkäzməˈjenəsis/ ▶ **n.** the origin or evolution of the universe. — **cos·mo·ge·net·ic** /-jəˈnetik/ adj. **cos·mo·gen·ic** /-ˈjenik/ adj.

cos·mog·o·ny /käzˈmägənē/ ▶ **n.** (pl. **-nies**) the branch of science that deals with the origin of the universe, esp. the solar system. ■ a theory regarding this. — **cos·mo·gon·ic** /ˌkäzməˈgänik/ adj. **cos·mo·gon·i·cal** /ˌkäzməˈgänikəl/ adj. **cos·mog·o·nist** n. [17th C.: from Gk. *kosmogonia*, from *kosmos* 'order or world' + *-gonia* '-begetting.']

cos·mog·ra·phy /käzˈmägrəfē/ ▶ **n.** (pl. **-phies**) the science that deals with the general features of the universe, including the earth. The branches of cosmography include astronomy, geography, and geology. ■ a description or representation of the universe or the earth. — **cos·mog·ra·pher** /-fər/ n. **cos·mo·graph·ic** /ˌkäzməˈgrafik/ adj. **cos·mo·graph·i·cal** /ˌkäzməˈgrafikəl/ adj. [ME: ult. from Gk. *kosmographia*, from *kosmos* (see **cosmos**[1]) + *-graphia* 'writing.']

cos·mo·log·i·cal ar·gu·ment /ˌkäzməˈläjikəl/ ▶ **n.** Philos. an argument for the existence of God that claims that all things in nature depend on something else for their existence (i.e., are contingent), and that the whole cosmos must therefore itself depend on a being that exists independently or necessarily. Compare with **ontological argument** and **teleological argument**.

cos·mol·o·gy /käzˈmäləjē/ ▶ **n.** (pl. **-gies**) the science of the origin and development of the universe. Modern astronomy is dominated by the big bang theory, which brings together observational astronomy and particle physics. ■ an account or theory of the origin of the universe. — **cos·mo·log·i·cal** /ˌkäzməˈläjikəl/ adj. **cos·mol·o·gist** n. [17th C.: from Fr. *cosmologie* or mod. L. *cosmologia*, from Gk. *kosmos* 'world' + *-logia* 'discourse.']

cos·mo·naut /ˈkäzməˌnôt; -ˌnät/ ▶ **n.** a Russian astronaut. [1950s: from **cosmos**[1].]

cos·mop·o·lis /käzˈmäpəlis/ ▶ **n.** a city inhabited by people from many different countries. [19th C.: from Gk. *kosmos* 'world' + *polis* 'city.']

cos·mo·pol·i·tan /ˌkäzmə'pälitn/ ▶**adj.** familiar with and at ease in many different countries and cultures. ■ including people from many different countries. ■ having an exciting and glamorous character associated with travel and a mixture of cultures. ■ (of a plant or animal) found all over the world. ▶**n. 1** a cosmopolitan person. ■ a cosmopolitan organism or species. **2** a cocktail made with Cointreau, lemon vodka, cranberry juice, and lime juice. —**cos·mo·pol·i·tan·ism n. cos·mo·pol·i·tan·ize** /-ˌīz/ **v.** [17th C. (as a n.): from COSMOPOLITE + -AN.]

cos·mop·o·lite /käz'mäpəˌlīt/ ▶**n.** a cosmopolitan person. [17th C.: from Fr., from Gk. *kosmopolitēs*, from *kosmos* 'world' + *politēs* 'citizen.']

cos·mos[1] /'käzməs; -ˌmōs; -ˌmäs/ ▶**n.** (**the cosmos**) the universe seen as a well-ordered whole. ■ a system of thought. [ME: from Gk. *kosmos* 'order or world.']

cos·mos[2] ▶**n.** an ornamental plant (genus *Cosmos*) of the daisy family with single or double dahlialike flowers. [from Gk. *kosmos*.]

Cos·sack /'käsak; -ək/ ▶**n.** a member of a people of southern Russia, Ukraine, and Siberia, noted for their horsemanship and military skill. ■ a member of a Cossack military unit. ▶**adj.** of, relating to, or characteristic of the Cossacks. [16th C.: from Russ. *kazak* from Turkic, 'nomad.']

cos·set /'käsit/ ▶**v.** (**-set·ed, -set·ing**) [trans.] care for and protect in an overindulgent way. [16th C.: prob. from Anglo-Norman Fr. *coscet* 'cottager,' from OE *cotsǣta* 'cottar.']

cost /kôst/ ▶**v.** (past and past part. **cost**) [trans.] **1** (of an object or an action) require the payment of (a specified sum of money) before it can be acquired or done. ■ cause the loss of. ■ [with two objs.] involve (someone) in (an effort or unpleasant action). ■ informal be expensive for (someone). **2** (past and past part. **cost·ed**) estimate the price of. ▶**n.** an amount that has to be paid or spent to buy or obtain something. ■ the effort, loss, or sacrifice necessary to achieve or obtain something. ■ (**costs**) legal expenses, esp. those allowed in favor of the winning party or against the losing party in a suit.

– PHRASES **at all costs** (or **at any cost**) regardless of the price to be paid or the effort needed. **at cost** at cost price; without profit to the seller. **cost an arm and a leg** see ARM[1]. **cost someone dearly** (or **dear**) involve someone in a serious loss or a heavy penalty. [ME: from OFr. *coust* (n.), *couster* (v.), based on L. *constare* 'stand firm.']

cos·ta /'kästə/ ▶**n.** (pl. **-tae** /-tē; -tī/) Bot. Zool. a rib, midrib, or riblike structure. ■ Entomol. the main vein running along the leading edge of an insect's wing. [19th C.: from L.]

Cos·ta Bra·va /ˌkôstə 'brävə/ a resort region on the Mediterranean coast of northeastern Spain.

cost ac·count·ing ▶**n.** the recording of all the costs incurred in a business in a way that can be used to improve its management. —**cost ac·count·ant n.**

Cos·ta del Sol /ˌkōstə del 'sōl/ a resort region on the Mediterranean coast of southern Spain.

cos·tal /'kästəl/ ▶**adj.** of or relating to the ribs. ■ Anat. Zool. of or relating to a costa. [17th C.: from Fr., from mod. L. *costalis*, from L. *costa* 'rib.']

Cos·ta Me·sa /ˌkōstə 'māsə; ˌkästə/ a city in southwestern California, on the Pacific Ocean; pop. 96,357.

co·star /'kōˌstär; kō'stär/ (also **co-star**) ▶**n.** a leading actor or actress appearing in a movie, on stage, etc., with another or others of equal importance. ▶**v.** [intrans.] appear in a production as a costar. ■ [trans.] (of a production) include as a costar.

Cos·ta Ri·ca /ˌkōstə 'rēkə; ˌkôstə; ˌkästə/ a republic in Central America. *See box.* —**Cos·ta Ri·can** /'rēkən/ **adj. & n.**

cos·tate /'kästāt; 'kästit/ ▶**adj.** Bot. Zool. ribbed; possessing a costa. [19th C.: from L. *costatus*, from *costa* 'rib.']

cost-ben·e·fit ▶**adj.** [attrib.] relating to or denoting a process that assesses the relation between the cost of an undertaking and the value of the resulting benefits.

cost-ef·fec·tive ▶**adj.** effective or productive in relation to its cost. —**cost-ef·fec·tive·ly adv. cost-ef·fec·tive·ness n.**

cost-ef·fi·cient ▶**adj.** another term for COST-EFFECTIVE. —**cost-ef·fi·cien·cy n.**

cos·tive /'kästiv; 'kôstiv/ ▶**adj.** constipated. ■ slow or reluctant in speech or action; unforthcoming. —**cos·tive·ly adv. cos·tive·ness n.** [ME: via OFr. from L. *constipatus* 'pressed together' (see CONSTIPATED).]

cost·ly /'kôstlē/ ▶**adj.** (**-li·er, -li·est**) costing a lot; expensive. ■ causing suffering, loss, or disadvantage. —**cost·li·ness n.**

cost·mar·y /'kôstˌme(ə)rē; 'käst-/ ▶**n.** (pl. **-mar·ies**) an aromatic plant (*Balsamita major*) of the daisy family, formerly used in medicine and for flavoring ale. [ME: from obs. *cost* (via Gk. *kostos*, from Sanskrit *kuṣṭha*, a plant) + *Mary*, mother of Christ.]

cost of liv·ing ▶**n.** the level of prices relating to a range of everyday items.

cost-of-liv·ing in·dex (abbr.: **CLI**) ▶**n.** former term for CONSUMER PRICE INDEX.

cost-plus ▶**adj.** [attrib.] relating to or denoting a method of pricing a service or product in which a fixed profit factor is added to the costs.

cos·tume /'käst(y)o͞om/ ▶**n.** a set of clothes in a style typical of a particular country or historical period. ■ a set of clothes worn by an actor or other performer for a particular role or by someone attending a masquerade. ■ a set of clothes, esp. a woman's ensemble, for a particular occasion or purpose; an outfit. ▶**v.** /'käs't(y)o͞om; 'käst(y)o͞om/ [trans.] dress (someone) in a particular set of clothes. [18th C.: from Fr., from

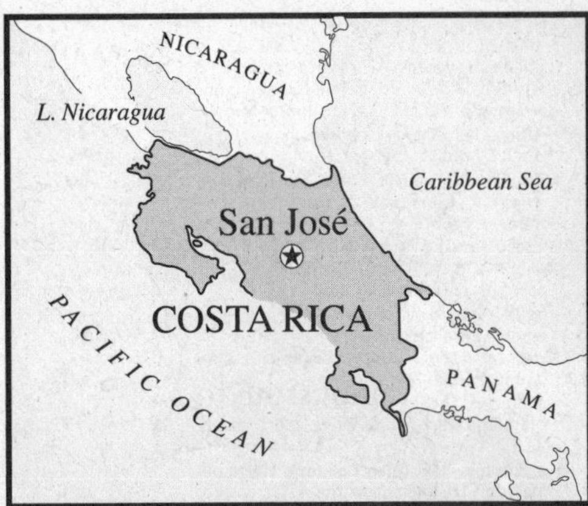

Costa Rica

Official name: Republic of Costa Rica
Location: southern Central America, with coastlines on the Caribbean Sea to the east and the Pacific Ocean to the west
Area: 19,600 square miles (50,700 sq km)
Population: 3,956,000
Capital: San José
Language: Spanish (official)
Currency: Costa Rican colon

Ital. *custume* 'custom,' from L. *consuetudo* (see CUSTOM).]

cos·tume jew·el·ry ▶**n.** jewelry made with inexpensive materials or imitation gems.

cos·tum·er /'käst(y)o͞omər; kä'st(y)o͞o-/ (also esp. Brit. **cos·tu·mi·er**) /kä'st(y)o͞omēər/ ▶**n.** a person or company that makes or supplies theatrical or fancy-dress costumes. [19th C.: from Fr. *costumier*, from *costumer* 'dress in a costume' (see COSTUME).]

co·sy ▶**adj.** British spelling of COZY.

cot[1] /kät/ ▶**n.** a type of bed, in particular: ■ a camp bed, particularly a portable, collapsible one. ■ a plain narrow bed. [17th C.: from Hindi *khāṭ* 'bedstead.']

cot[2] ▶**n.** a small shelter for livestock. [OE, of Gmc. origin; cf. ON *kytja* 'hovel'; rel. to COTE.]

cot[3] Math. ▶**abbr.** cotangent.

co·tan·gent /kō'tanjənt/ ▶**n.** Math. (in a right-angled triangle) the ratio of the side (other than the hypotenuse) adjacent to a particular acute angle to the side opposite the angle.

cote /kōt; kät/ ▶**n.** a shelter for mammals or birds, esp. pigeons. [OE ('cottage'), of Gmc. origin; rel. to COT[2].]

Côte d'Azur /ˌkōt dä'zʏr; -də'zo͝or/ a coastal area of southeastern France, along the Mediterranean Sea, roughly coterminous with the French Riviera.

Côte d'I·voire /ˌkōt dēv'wär/ a country in West Africa. *See box on next page.*

co·te·rie /'kōtərē; ˌkōtə'rē/ ▶**n.** (pl. **-ries**) a small group of people with shared interests or tastes, esp. one that is exclusive of other people. [18th C.: from Fr., based on Mid. Low Ger. *kote* 'cote.']

co·ter·mi·nous /kō'tərmənəs/ ▶**adj.** having the same boundaries or extent in space, time, or meaning. —**co·ter·mi·nous·ly adv.** [18th C.: alt. of CONTERMINOUS.]

coth /käTH/ ▶**abbr.** hyperbolic cotangent. [from COT[3] + *-h* for *hyperbolic*.]

co·thur·nus /kō'THərnəs/ ▶**n. 1** a thick-soled boot or buskin worn by actors in Greek tragedy. **2** an elevated style of acting in classical tragic drama.

co·tid·al line /kō'tīdl/ ▶**n.** a line on a map connecting points at which a tidal level, esp. high tide, occurs simultaneously.

co·til·lion /kə'tilyən/ ▶**n. 1** a dance with elaborate steps and figures, in particular: ■ an 18th-century French dance based on the contredanse. ■ a quadrille. **2** a formal ball, esp. one at which debutantes are presented. [18th C.: from Fr. *cotillon*, lit. 'petticoat dance,' dimin. of *cotte*, from OFr. *cote*.]

co·to·ne·as·ter /kə'tōnēˌastər; 'kätnˌēstər/ ▶**n.** a small-leaved shrub (genus *Cotoneaster*) of the rose family, cultivated as a hedging plant or for its bright red berries. [18th C.: mod. L., from L. *cotoneum* (see QUINCE).]

Co·to·nou /ˌkōtn'o͞o/ the largest city, chief port, and commercial and political center of Benin; pop. 536,830.

Co·to·pax·i /ˌkōtə'päksē; -'paksē/ the highest active volcano in the world, in the Andes in central Ecuador. It rises to 19,142 feet (5,896 m).

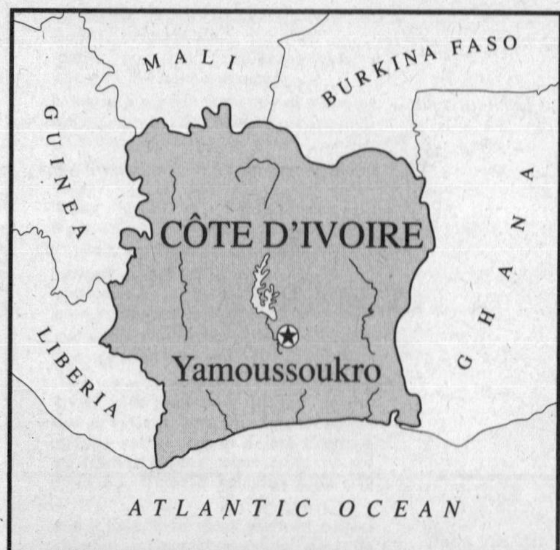

Côte d'Ivoire

Official name: Republic of Côte d'Ivoire
Location: West Africa, bordered on the west by Liberia and Guinea, and on the east by Ghana
Area: 122,800 square miles (318,000 sq km)
Population: 16,393,200
Capital: Yamoussoukro
Languages: French (official), West African languages
Currency: CFA franc

Cots·wold /'kätswōld; -wəld/ ▶ **n.** a sheep of a breed with fine wool, often used to produce crossbred lambs. ▶ **adj.** of or relating to the Cotswolds.

Cots·wold Hills (also **the Cots·wolds**) a range of limestone hills in southwestern England.

cot·ta /'kätə/ ▶ **n.** a short garment resembling a surplice, worn typically by Catholic priests and servers. [19th C.: from Ital.; ult. rel. to COAT.]

cot·tage /'kätij/ ▶ **n.** a small simple house, typically one near a lake or beach. ■ a dwelling forming part of a farm establishment, used by a worker. [ME: from Anglo-Norman Fr. *cotage* and Anglo-L. *cotagium*, from COT² or COTE.]

cot·tage cheese ▶ **n.** soft, lumpy white cheese made from the curds of slightly soured milk.

cot·tage in·dus·try ▶ **n.** a business or manufacturing activity carried on in a person's home.

Cott·bus /'kätbōōs/ a city in southeastern Germany, in the state of Brandenburg; pop. 123,320.

cot·ter pin /'kätər/ (also **cot·ter**) ▶ **n.** a metal pin used to fasten two parts of a mechanism together. ■ a split pin that is opened out after being passed through a hole. [17th C.: of unknown origin.]

cot·ton /'kätn/ ▶ **n. 1** a soft white fibrous substance that surrounds the seeds of a tropical and subtropical plant and is used as textile fiber and thread for sewing. ■ absorbent cotton. **2** (also **cot·ton plant**) the plant (genus *Gossypium*) of the mallow family that is commercially grown for this product. Oil and a protein-rich flour are also obtained from the seeds. ▶ **v.** [intrans.] informal **1** (**cotton on**) begin to understand: *he cottoned on to what I was trying to say.* **2** (**cotton to**) have a liking for. —**cot·ton·y adj.** [ME: from OFr. *coton*, from Arab. *ḳuṭn*.]

cot·ton bat·ting ▶ **n.** light, soft cotton fibers formed into layers, used esp. for filling quilts, cushions, etc.

Cot·ton Belt ▶ **n.** (**the Cotton Belt**) informal a region of the US South where cotton is the historic main crop.

cot·ton can·dy ▶ **n.** a mass of fluffy spun sugar, usually pink or white, wrapped around a stick or a paper cone.

cot·ton gin ▶ **n.** a machine for separating cotton from its seeds.

cot·ton grass ▶ **n.** a sedge (genus *Eriophorum*) that typically grows on swampy land in the northern hemisphere, producing tufts of long white silky hairs.

cot·ton·mouth /'kätn,mouTH/ ▶ **n.** a large, dangerous semiaquatic pit viper (*Agkistrodon piscivorus*) that inhabits lowland swamps and waterways of the southeastern US. When threatening, it opens its mouth wide to display the white interior. Also called WATER MOCCASIN.

cot·ton-pick·ing (also **cot·ton-pick·in'**) ▶ **adj.** [attrib.] informal used for emphasis, esp. with disapproval or reproach: *just a cotton-picking minute!*

cot·ton·seed /'kätn,sēd/ ▶ **n.** the seed of the cotton plant, yielding cottonseed oil.

cot·ton stain·er ▶ **n.** a North American bug (genus *Dysdercus*, family Pyrrhocoridae) that feeds on cotton bolls, causing reddish staining of the fibers.

cot·ton·tail /'kätn,tāl/ ▶ **n.** an American rabbit (genus *Sylvilagus*) that has a speckled brownish coat and a white underside to the tail.

cot·ton·wood /'kätn,wŏŏd/ ▶ **n.** a North American poplar with seeds covered in white cottony hairs.

cot·ton wool ▶ **n.** raw cotton.

cot·y·le·don /,kätl'ēdn/ ▶ **n.** Bot. an embryonic leaf in seed-bearing plants, one or more of which are the first leaves to appear from a germinating seed. —**cot·y·le·don·ar·y** /-'ēdn,erē/ **adj.** [16th C.: from L., from Gk. *kotulēdōn* 'cup-shaped cavity,' from *kotulē* 'cup.']

couch /kouCH/ ▶ **n.** a long upholstered piece of furniture for several people to sit on. ■ a reclining seat with a headrest at one end on which a psychoanalyst's subject or doctor's patient lies while undergoing treatment. ▶ **v.** [trans.] **1** (usu. **be couched in**) express (something) in language of a specified style. **2** [intrans.] literary lie down. ■ [trans.] lay down; spread out. **3** archaic lower (a spear) to the position for attack. **4** [usu. as n.] (**couching**) esp. hist. treat (a cataract) by pushing the lens of the eye downward and backward, out of line with the pupil. **5** (in embroidery) fix (a thread) to a fabric by stitching it down flat with another thread.
– PHRASES **on the couch** undergoing psychoanalysis or psychiatric treatment. [ME: from OFr. *couche* (n.), *coucher* (v.), from L. *collocare* 'place together' (see COLLOCATE).]

couch·ant /'kouCHənt/ ▶ **adj.** [usu. postpositive] Heraldry (of an animal) lying with the body resting on the legs and the head raised: *two lions couchant.* [ME: Fr., 'lying,' pres. part. of *coucher* (see COUCH).]

cou·chette /kōō'SHet/ ▶ **n.** a railroad car with seats convertible into sleeping berths. ■ a berth in such a car. [1920s: Fr., dimin. of *couche* 'a couch.']

couch grass /kouCH; kōōCH/ ▶ **n.** a coarse, often troublesome grass (genera *Elymus* and *Agropyron*) with long creeping roots. [16th C.: var. of QUITCH.]

couch po·ta·to /'kouCH/ ▶ **n.** informal a person who spends little or no time exercising and a great deal of time watching television.

cou·dé /kōō'dā/ ▶ **adj.** relating to or denoting a telescope in which the rays are bent to a focus at a fixed point off the axis. ▶ **n.** a telescope constructed in this way. [19th C.: Fr., lit. 'bent at right angles,' past part. of *couder*, from *coude* 'elbow,' from L. *cubitum*.]

cou·gar /'kōōgər/ ▶ **n.** a large American wild cat (*Felis concolor*) with a plain tawny to grayish coat, found from Canada to Patagonia. Also called MOUNTAIN LION, PUMA, PANTHER, and CATAMOUNT. [18th C.: from Fr. *couguar*, abbrev. of mod. L. *cuguarcarana*, from Guarani *guaçuarana*.]

cough /kôf/ ▶ **v.** [intrans.] expel air from the lungs with a sudden sharp sound. ■ (of an engine) make a sudden harsh noise, esp. as a sign of malfunction. ■ [trans.] force (something, esp. blood) out of the lungs or throat by coughing. ■ [trans.] (**cough something out**) say something in a harsh, abrupt way. ▶ **n.** an act or sound of coughing. ■ a condition of the respiratory organs causing coughing.
– PHRASAL VERBS **cough something up** (or **cough up**) give something reluctantly, esp. money or information that is due or required. [ME: of imitative origin; rel. to Ger. *keuchen* 'to pant.']

cough drop ▶ **n.** a medicated lozenge sucked to relieve a cough or sore throat.

cough syr·up ▶ **n.** liquid medicine taken either to suppress or expectorate a cough.

could /kŏŏd/ ▶ **modal verb** past of CAN¹. ■ used to indicate possibility: *they could be right.* ■ used in making polite requests: *could I use the phone?* ■ used in making suggestions: *you could always phone him.* ■ used to indicate annoyance because of something that has not been done: *they could have told me!* ■ used to indicate a strong inclination to do something.

could·n't /'kŏŏdnt/ ▶ **contr.** could not.

couldst /kŏŏdst/ (also **could·est** /'kŏŏdist/) ▶ **aux. v.** archaic second person singular of COULD.

cou·lee /'kōōlē/ ▶ **n.** a deep ravine. [19th C.: from Fr. *coulée* '(lava) flow,' from *couler* 'to flow,' from L. *colare* 'to strain or flow,' from *colum* 'strainer.']

cou·lis /'kōōlē/ ▶ **n.** (pl. same) a thin fruit or vegetable purée, used as a sauce. [Fr., from *couler* 'to flow.']

cou·lisse /kōō'lēs/ ▶ **n. 1** a flat piece of scenery at the side of the stage in a theater. ■ (**the coulisses**) the spaces between these pieces of scenery; the wings. **2** a groove, or a grooved timber, in which a movable partition slides up and down. [19th C.: Fr., fem. of *coulis* 'sliding,' based on L. *colare* 'to flow.']

cou·loir /kōōl'wär/ ▶ **n.** a steep, narrow gully on a mountainside. [19th C.: Fr., 'gully,' from *couler* 'to flow.']

cou·lomb /'kōō,läm; -,lōm/ (abbr.: **C**) ▶ **n.** Physics the SI unit of electric charge, equal to the quantity of electricity conveyed in one second by a current of one ampere. [19th C.: Charles-Augustin de *Coulomb* (1736–1806), French engineer.]

Cou·lomb's law Physics a law stating that like charges repel and opposite charges attract, with a force proportional to the product of the charges and inversely proportional to the square of the distance between them. [18th C.: C.-A. de *Coulomb* (see COULOMB).]

coul·ter /'kōltər/ (also **col·ter**) ▶ **n.** a vertical cutting blade fixed in front of a plowshare. ■ the part of a seed drill that makes the furrow for the seed.

cou·ma·rin /'ko͞omərin/ ▶**n.** Chem. a vanilla-scented bicyclic ketone, $C_9H_6O_2$, found in many plants, formerly used for flavoring food. ■ any derivative of this. [19th C.: from Fr. *coumarine*, from *coumarou*, via Port. and Sp. from Tupi *cumarú* 'tonka bean.']

cou·ma·rone /'ko͞omə,rōn/ ▶**n.** Chem. an organic bicyclic compound, C_8H_6O, present in coal tar, used to make thermoplastic resins chiefly for paints and varnishes. [19th C.: from COUMARIN + -ONE.]

coun·cil /'kounsəl/ ▶**n.** an advisory, deliberative, or legislative body of people formally constituted and meeting regularly. ■ a body of people elected to manage the affairs of a city, county, or other municipal district. ■ an ecclesiastical assembly. ■ an assembly or meeting for consultation or advice. [OE: from Anglo-Norman Fr. *cuncile*, from L. *concilium* 'assembly,' from *con-* 'with' + *calare* 'summon.']

Coun·cil Bluffs a city in southwestern Iowa, on the Missouri River, opposite Omaha in Nebraska; pop. 58,268.

coun·cil·man /'kounsəlmən/ ▶**n.** (pl. **-men**) a person, esp. a man, who is a member of a council, esp. a municipal one.

coun·ci·lor /'kouns(ə)lər/ (also esp. Brit. **coun·cil·lor**) ▶**n.** a member of a council. — **coun·ci·lor·ship n.** [ME: alt. of COUNSELOR, by association with COUNCIL.]

coun·cil·wom·an /'kounsəl,wo͝omən/ ▶**n.** (pl. **-wom·en**) a woman who is a member of a council, esp. a municipal one.

coun·sel /'kounsəl/ ▶**n.** **1** advice, esp. that given formally. ■ consultation, esp. to seek or give advice. **2** (pl. same) the lawyer or lawyers conducting a case. ▶**v.** (**-seled, -sel·ing**; esp. Brit. **-selled, -sel·ling**) [trans.] give advice to (someone). ■ give professional psychological help and advice to (someone). ■ recommend (a course of action).
– PHRASES **keep one's own counsel** say nothing about what one believes, knows, or plans. **take counsel** discuss a problem. [ME: via OFr. *counseil* (n.), *conseiller* (v.), from L. *consilium* 'advice,' rel. to *consulere* (see CONSULT).]

coun·sel·ing /'kouns(ə)liNG/ (also esp. Brit. **coun·sel·ling**) ▶**n.** the provision of assistance and guidance in resolving personal, social, or psychological problems and difficulties, esp. by a trained person on a professional basis.

coun·se·lor /'kouns(ə)lər/ (also esp. Brit. **coun·sel·lor**) ▶**n.** **1** a person trained to give guidance on personal, social, or psychological problems. ■ [often with adj.] a person who gives advice on a specified subject. **2** a person who supervises children at a camp. **3** a trial lawyer. **4** a senior officer in the diplomatic service.

count¹ /kount/ ▶**v.** **1** [trans.] determine the total number of (a collection of items). ■ [intrans.] recite numbers in ascending order, usually starting at the number one. ■ [intrans.] (**count down**) recite or display numbers backward to zero to indicate the time remaining before the launch of a rocket or the start of an operation. ■ [intrans.] (**count down**) prepare for a significant event in the short time remaining before it. **2** [trans.] take into account; include. ■ (**count someone in**) include someone in an activity or the plans for it. ■ consider (someone or something) to possess a specified quality or fulfill a specified role. ■ [intrans.] be regarded as possessing a specified quality or fulfilling a specified role. **3** [intrans.] be significant. ■ (of a factor) play a part in influencing opinion for or against someone or something. ■ (**count for**) be worth (a specified amount). ■ (**count toward**) be included in an assessment of (a final result or amount). ■ (**count on/upon**) rely on. ▶**n.** **1** an act of determining the total number of something. ■ the total determined by such an action. **2** an act of reciting numbers in ascending order, up to the specified number. ■ Boxing an act of reciting numbers up to ten by the referee when a boxer is knocked down, the boxer being considered knocked out if still down when ten is reached. ■ Baseball the number of balls and strikes that have been charged to the batter, as recalculated with each ball or strike. **3** a point for discussion or consideration. ■ Law a separate charge in an indictment. **4** the measure of the fineness of a yarn expressed as the weight of a given length or the length of a given weight. ■ a measure of the fineness of a woven fabric expressed as the number of warp or weft threads in a given length.
– PHRASES **count one's blessings** be grateful for what one has. **count the cost** calculate the consequences of something, typically a careless or foolish action. **count the days** (or **hours**) be impatient for time to pass. **down** (or Brit. **out**) **for the count** Boxing defeated by being knocked to the canvas and unable to rise within ten seconds. ■ unconscious or soundly asleep. ■ defeated.
– PHRASAL VERBS **count someone out 1** complete a count of ten seconds over a fallen boxer to indicate defeat. **2** informal exclude someone from an activity or the plans for it. **3** (in children's games) select a player for dismissal or a special role by using a counting rhyme. **count something out** take items one by one from a stock of something, esp. money, keeping a note of how many one takes. [ME (as n.): from OFr. *counte* (n.), *counter* (v.), from the verb *computare* 'calculate' (see COMPUTE).]

count² ▶**n.** a European nobleman whose rank corresponds to that of an English earl. — **count·ship n.** [ME: from OFr. *conte*, from L. *comes*, *comit-* 'companion,' from *com-* 'with' + *it-* 'gone' (from *ire* 'go').]

count·down /'kount,doun/ ▶**n.** [usu. in sing.] an act of counting numerals in reverse order to zero, esp. to time the last seconds before the launching of a rocket or missile. ■ (often **countdown to**) the final moments before a significant event and the procedures carried out during this time. ■ a digital display that counts down.

coun·te·nance /'kountn-əns/ ▶**n.** **1** a person's face or facial expression. **2** support. ▶**v.** [trans.] admit as acceptable or possible.
– PHRASES **keep one's countenance** maintain one's composure, esp. by refraining from laughter. **keep someone in countenance** help someone to remain calm and confident. **out of countenance** disconcerted or unpleasantly surprised. [ME: from OFr. *contenance* 'bearing,' from *contenir* (see CONTAIN).]

coun·ter¹ /'kountər/ ▶**n.** **1** a long flat-topped fixture in a store or bank across which business is conducted with customers. ■ a similar structure used for serving food and drinks in a cafeteria or bar. ■ a countertop. **2** an apparatus used for counting. ■ a person who counts something, for example votes in an election. ■ Physics an apparatus used for counting individual ionizing particles or events. **3** a small disk used as a place marker or for keeping the score in board games. ■ a token representing a coin.
– PHRASES **behind the counter** serving in a store or bank. **over the counter** by ordinary retail purchase, with no need for a prescription or license: [as adj.] *over-the-counter medicines.* ■ (of share transactions) taking place outside the stock exchange system. **under the counter** (or **table**) (with reference to goods bought or sold) surreptitiously and typically illegally. [ME (sense 3): from OFr. *conteor*, from med. L. *computatorium*, from L. *computare* (see COMPUTE).]

coun·ter² ▶**v.** [trans.] speak or act in opposition to. ■ [intrans.] respond to hostile speech or action. ■ [intrans.] Boxing give a return blow while parrying. ▶**adv.** (**counter to**) in the opposite direction to or in conflict with: *some actions ran counter to the call for leniency.* ▶**adj.** responding to something of the same kind, esp. in opposition. See also COUNTER-. ▶**n.** **1** [usu. in sing.] a thing that opposes or prevents something else. ■ an answer to an argument or criticism. ■ Boxing a blow given while parrying; a counterpunch. **2** the curved part of the stern of a ship projecting aft above the waterline. [ME: from OFr. *contre*, from L. *contra* 'against'; or from COUNTER-.]

coun·ter- ▶**prefix** denoting opposition, retaliation, or rivalry: *counterattack.* ■ denoting movement or effect in the opposite direction: *counterbalance.* ■ denoting correspondence, duplication, or substitution: *counterpart.* [from Anglo-Norman Fr. *countre-*, OFr. *contre*, from L. *contra* 'against.']

coun·ter·act /'kountər,akt/ ▶**v.** [trans.] act against (something) in order to reduce its force or neutralize it. — **coun·ter·ac·tion** /,kountər'akSHən/ **n.** **coun·ter·ac·tive** /kountər'aktiv/ **adj.**

coun·ter·at·tack /'kountərə,tak/ ▶**n.** an attack made in response to one by an enemy or opponent. ▶**v.** [intrans.] attack in response. — **coun·ter·at·tack·er n.**

coun·ter·bal·ance ▶**n.** /'kountər,baləns/ a weight that balances another weight. ■ a factor having the opposite effect to that of another and so preventing it from exercising a disproportionate influence. ▶**v.** /,kountər'baləns/ [trans.] (of a weight) balance (another weight). ■ neutralize or cancel by exerting an opposite influence.

coun·ter·blow /'kountər,blō/ ▶**n.** a blow given in return.

coun·ter·bore /'kountər,bôr/ ▶**n.** a drilled hole that has a flat-bottomed enlargement at its mouth. ■ a drill whose bit has a uniform smaller diameter near the tip, for drilling counterbores in one operation. ▶**v.** [trans.] drill a counterbore in (an object).

coun·ter·change /'kountər,CHānj/ ▶**v.** [trans.] change (places or parts); interchange. ▶**n.** change that is equivalent in degree but opposite in effect to a previous change.

coun·ter·charge /'kountər,CHärj/ ▶**n.** an accusation made in turn by someone against their accuser. ■ a charge by police or an armed force in response to one made against them.

count·er·check /'kountər,CHek/ ▶**n.** **1** a second check for security or accuracy. **2** a restraint. ▶**v.** [trans.] archaic stop (something) by acting to cancel or counteract it.

coun·ter·claim /'kountər,klām/ ▶**n.** a claim made to rebut a previous claim. ■ Law a claim made by a defendant against the plaintiff. ▶**v.** [intrans.] esp. Law make a counterclaim for something.

coun·ter·clock·wise /,kountər'kläkwīz/ ▶**adv. & adj.** in the opposite direction to the way in which the hands of a clock move around.

coun·ter·con·di·tion·ing /,kountərkən'disH(ə)niNG/ ▶**n.** a technique employed in animal training, and in the treatment of phobias and similar conditions in humans, in which behavior incompatible with a habitual undesirable pattern is induced. Compare with DECONDITION (sense 2).

coun·ter·cul·ture /'kountər,kəlCHər/ ▶**n.** a way of life and set of attitudes opposed to or at variance with the prevailing social norm.

coun·ter·cur·rent ▶**n.** /'kountər,kərənt; -,kə-rənt/ a current flowing in an opposite direction to another. ▶**adv.** /,kountər'kərənt/ in or with opposite directions of flow.

coun·ter·es·pi·o·nage /,kountər'espēə,näzH; -,näj/ ▶**n.** activities designed to prevent or thwart spying by an enemy.

coun·ter·fac·tu·al /,kountər'fakCHo͞oəl/ Philos. ▶**adj.** relating to or expressing what has not happened or is not the case. ▶**n.** a counterfactual conditional statement (e.g., *If kangaroos had no tails, they would topple over*).

coun·ter·feit /'kountər,fit/ ▶**adj.** made in exact imitation of something valuable or important with the intention to deceive or defraud. ■ pretended; sham. ▶**n.** a fraudulent imitation of something else; a forgery.

▶ v. [trans.] imitate fraudulently. ■ pretend to feel or possess (an emotion or quality). ■ literary resemble closely. — **coun·ter·feit·er** n. [ME: ult. from OFr. *contrefait*, past part. of *contrefaire*, from L. *contra-* 'against' + *facere* 'make.']

coun·ter·foil /'kountər,foil/ ▶ n. esp. Brit. the part of a check, receipt, ticket, or other document that is torn off and kept as a record by the person issuing it.

coun·ter·in·sur·gen·cy /,kountər-in'sərjənsē/ ▶ n. [usu. as adj.] military or political action taken against the activities of guerrillas or revolutionaries.

coun·ter·in·tel·li·gence /,kountər-in'teləjəns/ ▶ n. activities designed to prevent or thwart spying, intelligence gathering, and sabotage by an enemy or other foreign entity.

coun·ter·in·tu·i·tive /,kountər-in't(y)o͞oitiv/ ▶ adj. contrary to intuition or to common-sense expectation. — **coun·ter·in·tu·i·tive·ly** adv.

coun·ter·ir·ri·tant /,kountər'iritənt/ ▶ n. esp. hist. something such as heat or an ointment that is used to produce surface irritation of the skin, thereby counteracting underlying pain or discomfort. — **coun·ter·ir·ri·ta·tion** /-,iri'tāshən/ n.

coun·ter·mand /,kountər'mand; 'kountər,mand/ ▶ v. [trans.] revoke (an order). ■ cancel an order for (goods). ■ revoke an order issued by (another person). ■ declare (voting) invalid. [ME: from OFr. *contremander* (v.), *contremand* (n.), from med. L. *contramandare*, from *contra-* 'against' + *mandare* 'to order.']

coun·ter·march /'kountər,märch/ ▶ v. [intrans.] march in the opposite direction or back along the same route. ▶ n. an act or instance of marching in this way.

coun·ter·meas·ure /'kountər,mezhər/ ▶ n. an action taken to counteract a danger or threat.

coun·ter·mine /'kountər,mīn/ Mil. ▶ n. an excavation dug to intercept another dug by an enemy. ▶ v. [trans.] dig a countermine against.

coun·ter·of·fen·sive /'kountər-ə,fensiv/ ▶ n. an attack made in response to one from an enemy, typically on a large scale or for a prolonged period.

coun·ter·of·fer /'kountər,ôfər; -,äfər/ ▶ n. an offer made in response to another.

coun·ter·pane /'kountər,pān/ ▶ n. dated a bedspread. [17th C.: alt. of obs. COUNTERPOINT, from OFr. *contrepointe*, based on med. L. *culcitra puncta* 'quilted mattress.']

coun·ter·part /'kountər,pärt/ ▶ n. **1** a person or thing holding a position or performing a function that corresponds to that of another person or thing in a different area. **2** Law one of two or more copies of a legal document.

coun·ter·plot /'kountər,plät/ ▶ n. a plot intended to thwart another plot. ▶ v. (**-plot·ted, -plot·ting**) [intrans.] devise a counterplot.

coun·ter·point /'kountər,point/ ▶ n. **1** Music the art or technique of setting, writing, or playing a melody or melodies in conjunction with another, according to fixed rules. ■ a melody played in conjunction with another. **2** an argument, idea, or theme used to create a contrast with the main element. ▶ v. [trans.] **1** Music add counterpoint to (a melody). **2** (often **be counterpointed**) emphasize by contrast. ■ compensate for. [ME: from OFr. *contrepoint*, from med. L. *contrapunctum* '(song) marked against,' from *contra-* + *punctum*, from *pungere* 'to prick.']

coun·ter·poise /'kountər,poiz/ ▶ n. a factor, force, or influence that balances or neutralizes another. ■ a counterbalancing weight. ▶ v. [trans.] have an opposing and balancing effect on. ■ bring into contrast. [ME: from OFr. *contrepois*, from *contre* 'against' + *pois* from L. *pensum* 'weight.']

coun·ter·pose /,kountər'pōz/ ▶ v. [trans.] set against or in opposition to. — **coun·ter·po·si·tion** /-pə'zishən/ n.

coun·ter·pro·duc·tive /,kountərprə'dəktiv/ ▶ adj. having the opposite of the desired effect.

coun·ter·punch /'kountər,pənch/ Boxing ▶ n. a punch thrown in return for one received. ▶ v. [intrans.] throw a counterpunch. — **coun·ter·punch·er** n.

Coun·ter-Ref·or·ma·tion the reform of the Church of Rome in the 16th and 17th centuries that was stimulated by the Protestant Reformation.

coun·ter·rev·o·lu·tion /'kountər,revə'lo͞oshən/ ▶ n. a revolution opposing a former one or reversing its results. — **coun·ter·rev·o·lu·tion·ar·y** /-,nerē/ adj. & n.

coun·ter·scarp /'kountər,skärp/ ▶ n. the outer wall of a ditch in a fortification. Compare with SCARP. [16th C.: from Fr. *contrescarpe*, from Ital. *controscarpa*.]

coun·ter·shad·ing /'kountər,shāding/ ▶ n. Zool. protective coloration of some animals in which parts normally in shadow are light and those exposed to the sky are dark. — **coun·ter·shad·ed** adj.

coun·ter·shaft /'kountər,shaft/ ▶ n. a machine driveshaft that transmits motion from the main shaft to where it is required, such as the drive axle in a vehicle.

coun·ter·sign /'kountər,sīn/ ▶ v. [trans.] add a signature to (a document already signed by another person). ▶ n. archaic a signal or password given in reply to a soldier on guard. — **coun·ter·sig·na·ture** /,kountər'signəchər; -,cho͝or/ n.

coun·ter·sink /'kountər,singk/ ▶ v. (past and past part. **-sunk**) [trans.] enlarge and bevel the rim of (a drilled hole) so that a screw, nail, or bolt can be inserted flush with the surface. ■ drive (a screw, nail, or bolt) into such a hole.

coun·ter·spy /'kountər,spī/ ▶ n. (pl. **-spies**) a spy engaged in counterespionage.

coun·ter·stain /'kountər,stān/ Biol. ▶ n. an additional dye used in a microscopy specimen to produce a contrasting background or to make clearer the distinction between different kinds of tissue. ▶ v. [trans.] treat (a specimen) with a counterstain.

coun·ter·ten·or /'kountər,tenər/ ▶ n. Music the highest male adult singing voice (sometimes distinguished from the male alto voice by its strong, pure tone). ■ a singer with such a voice. [ME: from Fr. *contre-teneur*, from obs. Ital. *contratenore*, based on L. *tenor* (see TENOR[1]).]

coun·ter·ter·ror·ism /,kountər'terə,rizəm/ ▶ n. political or military activities designed to thwart terrorism. — **coun·ter·ter·ror·ist** n. & adj.

coun·ter·top /'kountər,täp/ ▶ n. a flat surface for working on, esp. in a kitchen.

coun·ter·trade /'kountər,trād/ ▶ n. international trade by exchange of goods rather than by currency purchase.

coun·ter·trans·fer·ence /,kountər,trans'fərəns; -,tranz-/ ▶ n. Psychoanal. the emotional reaction of the analyst to the subject's contribution. Compare with TRANSFERENCE.

coun·ter·vail /,kountər'vāl/ ▶ v. [trans.] [usu. as adj.] (**countervailing**) offset the effect of (something) by countering it with something of equal force. [ME: from Anglo-Norman Fr. *contrevaloir*, from L. *contra valere* 'be of worth against.']

coun·ter·weight /'kountər,wāt/ ▶ n. another term for COUNTERBALANCE.

count·ess /'kountis/ ▶ n. the wife or widow of a count or earl. ■ a woman holding the rank of count or earl in her own right.

coun·ti·an /'kountēən/ ▶ n. [with adj.] an inhabitant of a particular county: *a Sussex Countian.*

count·ing /'kounting/ ▶ prep. taking account of when reaching a total; including.

count·ing·house /'kounting,hous/ ▶ n. hist. an office or building in which the accounts and money of a person or company were kept.

count·less /'kountlis/ ▶ adj. too many to be counted; very many.

count noun ▶ n. Gram. a noun that can form a plural and, in the singular, can be used with the indefinite article (e.g., *books, a book*). Contrasted with MASS NOUN.

count pal·a·tine ▶ n. (pl. **counts pal·a·tine**) hist. a feudal lord having royal authority within a region of a kingdom. ■ a high official of the Holy Roman Empire with royal authority within his domain. [see PALATINE[1].]

coun·tri·fied /'kəntri,fīd/ (also **coun·try·fied**) ▶ adj. reminiscent or characteristic of the country, esp. in being unsophisticated. [17th C.: past part. of *countrify* 'make rural.']

coun·try /'kəntrē/ ▶ n. (pl. **-tries**) **1** a nation with its own government, occupying a particular territory. ■ (**the country**) the people of a nation. ■ the land of a person's birth or citizenship. **2** (often **the country**) districts and small settlements outside large towns, cities, or the capital. **3** an area or region with regard to its physical features. ■ a region associated with a particular person, esp. a writer, or with a particular work. **4** short for COUNTRY MUSIC.
– PHRASES **across country** not keeping to roads. [ME: from OFr. *cuntree*, from med. L. *contrata (terra)* '(land) lying opposite,' from L. *contra* 'against, opposite.']

coun·try and west·ern ▶ n. another term for COUNTRY MUSIC. ▶ adj. (usu. **country-and-western**) (also **country-western**) of or relating to this music: *country-and-western singers.*

coun·try club ▶ n. a club with sporting and social facilities, set in a suburban area.

coun·try cous·in ▶ n. a person with an unsophisticated and provincial appearance or manners.

coun·try dance ▶ n. a traditional type of social English dance, in particular one performed by couples facing each other in long lines.

coun·try·fied ▶ adj. var. of COUNTRIFIED.

coun·try gen·tle·man ▶ n. a rich man of social standing who owns and lives on an estate in a rural area.

coun·try house ▶ n. a large house in the country, typically the home of a wealthy or aristocratic family.

coun·try·man /'kəntrēmən/ ▶ n. (pl. **-men**) **1** a person living or born in a rural area, esp. one engaged in a typically rural occupation. **2** a person from the same country or region as someone else.

coun·try mile ▶ n. informal a very long way.

coun·try mu·sic ▶ n. a form of popular music originating in the rural southern US. It is traditionally a mixture of ballads and dance tunes played characteristically on fiddle, guitar, steel guitar, drums, and keyboard. Also called COUNTRY AND WESTERN.

coun·try rock[1] ▶ n. Geol. the rock that encloses a mineral deposit, igneous intrusion, or other feature.

coun·try rock[2] ▶ n. a type of popular music that is a blend of rock and country music.

coun·try·side /'kəntrē,sīd/ ▶ n. the land and scenery of a rural area. ■ the inhabitants of such an area.

coun·try·wide /'kəntrē'wīd/ ▶ adj. & adv. extending throughout a nation.

coun·try·wom·an /'kəntrē,wo͝omən/ ▶ n. (pl. **-wom·en**) **1** a woman living or born in a rural area, esp. one engaged in a typically rural occupation. **2** a woman from the same country or district as someone else.

coun·ty /'kountē/ ▶ n. (pl. **-ties**) a territorial division of some countries, forming the chief unit of local administration. ■ [treated as sing. or pl.] the people of such a territorial division collectively. ■ (in the US) a political and administrative division of a state. — **coun·ty·wide** adj. & adv. [ME: from OFr. *conte*, from L. *comitatus*, from *comes, comit-* (see COUNT[2]).]

coun·ty court ▶ n. a court in some states with civil and criminal jurisdiction for a given county.

coun·ty seat ▶ n. the town that is the governmental center of a county.

coup /ko͞o/ ▶ n. (pl. **coups** /ko͞oz/) **1** (also **coup d'é·tat**) a sudden, violent, and illegal seizure of power from a government. **2** a notable or successful stroke or move. **3** hist. (among North American Indians) an act of touching an armed enemy in battle as a deed of bravery, or an act of first touching an item of the enemy's in order to claim it. [18th C.: from Fr., from med. L. *colpus* 'blow' (see COPE[1]).]

coup de fou·dre /ˌko͞o də 'fo͞od(rə)/ ▶ n. (pl. **coups de fou·dre** pronunc. same) a sudden unforeseen event, in particular an instance of love at first sight. [18th C.: Fr., lit. 'stroke of lightning.']

coup de grâce /ˌko͞o də 'gräs/ ▶ n. (pl. **coups de grâce** pronunc. same) a final blow or shot given to kill a wounded person or animal. [17th C.: Fr., lit. 'stroke of grace.']

coup de main /ˌko͞o də 'maN/ ▶ n. (pl. **coups de main** pronunc. same) a sudden surprise attack, esp. one made by an army during war. [18th C.: Fr., lit. 'stroke of hand.']

coup de maî·tre /ˌko͞o də 'met(rə)/ ▶ n. (pl. **coups de maî·tre** pronunc. same) a master stroke. [Fr.]

coup d'é·tat /ˌko͞o dā'tä/ ▶ n. (pl. **coups d'é·tat** /ˌko͞o dā 'tä(z)/) another term for COUP (sense 1). [17th C.: Fr., lit. 'blow of state.']

coup de thé·â·tre /ˌko͞o də tā'ät(rə)/ ▶ n. (pl. **coups de thé·â·tre** pronunc. same) a sensational or dramatically sudden action or turn of events, esp. in a play. [18th C.: Fr., lit. 'blow of theater.']

coup d'œil /ˌko͞o 'dœē/ ▶ n. (pl. **coups d'œil** pronunc. same) a glance that takes in a comprehensive view. [18th C.: Fr., lit. 'stroke of eye.']

coupe[1] /ko͞op/ (also **cou·pé** /ko͞o'pā/) ▶ n. **1** a car with a fixed roof, two doors, and a sloping rear. **2** hist. a four-wheeled enclosed carriage for two passengers and a driver. **3** hist. an end compartment in a railroad car, with seats on only one side. [19th C. (sense 2): from Fr. *carrosse coupé*, lit. 'cut carriage.']

coupe[2] ▶ n. a shallow glass or glass dish, typically with a stem, in which desserts or champagne are served. ■ a dessert served in such a dish. [19th C.: Fr., lit. 'goblet.']

cou·ple /'kəpəl/ ▶ n. **1** two individuals of the same sort considered together. ■ informal an indefinite small number. **2** [treated as sing. or pl.] two people who are married, engaged, or otherwise closely associated romantically or sexually. ■ a pair of partners in a dance or game. ■ Mech. a pair of equal and parallel forces acting in opposite directions, and tending to cause rotation about an axis perpendicular to the plane containing them. ▶ v. [trans.] (often **be coupled to/with**) combine. ■ connect (a railroad vehicle or a piece of equipment) to another. ■ [intrans.] (**couple up**) join to form a pair. ■ [intrans.] dated have sexual intercourse. ■ connect (two electrical components) using electromagnetic induction, electrostatic charge, or an optical link. — **cou·ple·dom** /-dəm/ n. [ME: from OFr. *cople* (n.), *copler* (v.), from L. *copula* (n.), *copulare* (v.), from *co-* 'together' + *apere* 'fasten.']

cou·pler /'kəp(ə)lər/ ▶ n. something that connects two things, esp. mechanical components or systems. ■ Music a device in an organ for connecting two manuals, or a manual with pedals, so that they both sound when only one is played. ■ Music (also **octave coupler**) a similar device for connecting notes with their octaves above or below. ■ (also **acoustic coupler**) a modem that converts digital signals from a computer into audible sound signals and vice versa, so that the former can be transmitted and received over telephone lines.

cou·plet /'kəplit/ ▶ n. two lines of verse, usually in the same meter and joined by rhyme, forming a unit. [16th C.: from Fr., dimin. of *couple*.]

cou·pling /'kəp(ə)liNG/ ▶ n. **1** a device for connecting parts of machinery. ■ a fitting on the end of a railroad vehicle for connecting it to another. **2** the pairing of two items. ■ sexual intercourse. ■ an interaction between two electrical components by electromagnetic induction, electrostatic charge, or optical link.

coupling 1

cou·pon /'k(y)o͞oˌpän/ ▶ n. **1** a voucher entitling the holder to a discount off a particular product. ■ a detachable portion of a bond that is given up in return for a payment of interest. **2** a form in a newspaper or magazine that may be filled in and sent for a purchase or information. [19th C.: from Fr., lit. 'piece cut off,' from *couper* 'cut,' from OFr. *colper* (see COPE[1]).]

cou·pon bond ▶ n. an investment bond on which interest is paid by coupons.

cou·pon clip·per ▶ n. informal a person with a large number of coupon bonds.

coup stick /ko͞o/ ▶ n. (among North American Indians) a decorated stick recording coups attained by the warrior.

cour·age /'kərij; 'kə-rij/ ▶ n. the ability to do something that frightens one. ■ strength in the face of pain or grief.
– PHRASES **have the courage of one's convictions** act on one's beliefs despite danger or disapproval. **pluck up** (or **screw up** or **take**) **courage** make an effort to do something that frightens one. **take one's courage in both hands** nerve oneself to do something that frightens one. [ME: from OFr. *corage*, from L. *cor* 'heart.']

cou·ra·geous /kə'rājəs/ ▶ adj. not deterred by danger or pain; brave. — **cou·ra·geous·ly** adv. **cou·ra·geous·ness** n.

cou·rante /ko͝o'ränt; -'rant/ ▶ n. a 16th-century court dance consisting of short advances and retreats. ■ a piece of music written for or in the style of such a dance, typically one forming a movement of a suite. [16th C.: Fr., lit. 'running,' fem. pres. part. of *courir*.]

Cour·bet /ko͝or'bā/, Gustave (1819–77), French painter. His works include *Burial at Ornans* (1850).

cou·reur de bois /ko͞oˌrər də 'bwä/ ▶ n. (pl. **cou·reurs de bois** pronunc. same) hist. (in Canada and the northern US) a woodsman or trader of French origin. [18th C.: Fr., lit. 'wood runner.']

cour·i·er /'ko͝orēər; 'kərēər/ ▶ n. **1** a messenger who transports goods or documents, in particular: ■ a company or employee of a company that transports commercial packages and documents. ■ a messenger for an underground or espionage organization. **2** a person employed to guide and assist a group of tourists. ▶ v. [trans.] (often **be couriered**) send or transport (goods or documents) by courier. [ME: from OFr. *coreor*; later from Fr. *courier*; based on L. *currere* 'to run.']

Cour·règes /ko͝o'rezH/, André (1923–), French fashion designer, noted for futuristic and youth-oriented styles.

course /kôrs/ ▶ n. **1** [in sing.] the route or direction followed by a ship, aircraft, road, or river. ■ the way in which something progresses or develops. ■ a procedure adopted to deal with a situation. ■ the route of a race or similar sporting event. ■ an area of land set aside and prepared for racing, golf, or another sport. **2** a dish, or a set of dishes served together, forming one of the successive parts of a meal. **3** a series, in particular: ■ a series of lectures or lessons in a particular subject, typically leading to a qualification. ■ Med. a series of repeated treatments or doses of medication. **4** Archit. a continuous horizontal layer of brick, stone, or other material in a building. ▶ v. [intrans.] (of liquid) move without obstruction; flow.
– PHRASES **a matter of course** see MATTER. **the course of nature** events or processes that are normal and to be expected. **in the course of** — **1** undergoing the specified process. **2** during the specified period. ■ during and as a part of the specified activity. **in the course of time** as time goes by. **in due course** see DUE. **of course** used to introduce an idea or turn of events as being obvious or to be expected. ■ used to give or emphasize agreement or permission. ■ introducing a qualification or admission. **off course** not following the intended route. **on course** following the intended route. **run** (or **take**) **its course** complete its natural development without interference. [ME: from OFr. *cours*, from L. *cursus*, from *curs-* 'run,' from v. *currere*.]

cours·er[1] /'kôrsər/ ▶ n. literary a swift horse. [ME: from OFr. *corsier*, based on L. *cursus* (see COURSE).]

cours·er[2] ▶ n. a fast-running ploverlike bird (genera *Cursorius* and *Rhinoptilus*, family Glareolidae) typically found in open country in Africa and Asia. [18th C.: from mod. L. *Cursorius* 'adapted for running,' from *cursor* 'runner,' from *currere*, 'to run.']

cours·er[3] ▶ n. a person who hunts animals such as hares with greyhounds using sight rather than scent. [17th C.: from COURSER[1].]

course·ware /'kôrsˌwe(ə)r/ ▶ n. computer programs or other material designed for use in an educational or training course.

course·work /'kôrsˌwərk/ (also **course work**) ▶ n. written or practical work done by a student during a course of study, usually assessed in order to count toward a final mark or grade.

cours·ing /'kôrsiNG/ ▶ n. the sport of hunting game animals such as hares with greyhounds using sight rather than scent.

Court /kôrt/, Margaret Smith (1942–), Australian tennis player. She won a record 62 Grand Slam events.

court /kôrt/ ▶ n. **1** (also **court of law**) a tribunal presided over by a judge, judges, or a magistrate in civil and criminal cases. ■ any of various other tribunals, such as military courts. ■ the place where such a tribunal meets. ■ (**the court**) the judge or judges presiding at such a tribunal. **2** a quadrangular area, either open or covered, marked out for ball games such as tennis or basketball. ■ a quadrangular area surrounded by a building or group of buildings. ■ a subdivision of a building, usually a large hall extending to the ceiling with galleries and staircases. **3** the establishment, retinue, and courtiers of a sovereign. ■ a sovereign and his or her councilors, constituting a ruling power. ■ a sovereign's residence. ▶ v. [trans.] dated be involved with romantically, typically with the intention of marrying. ■ (of a male bird or other animal) try to attract (a mate). ■ pay special attention to (someone) in an attempt to win their support or favor. ■ go to great lengths to win (favorable attention). ■ risk incurring (misfortune) because of the way one behaves.
– PHRASES **go to court** take legal action. **hold court** see HOLD[1]. **in court** appearing as a party or an attorney in a court of law. **out of court** **1** before a legal hearing can take place. **2** treated as impossible or not worthy of consideration. **pay court to** pay flattering attention to someone in order to win favor. [ME: from OFr. *cort*, from L. *cohors, cohort-* 'yard or retinue.']

court bouil·lon /ko͝or 'bo͞o(l)yän; ˌko͝or bo͞o'yôn/ ▶ n. a stock made from

PRONUNCIATION KEY ə *ago, up*; ər *over, fur*; a *hat*; ā *ate*; ä *car*; e *let*; ē *see*; i *fit*; ī *by*; NG *sing*; ō *go*; ô *law, for*; oi *toy*; o͝o *good*; o͞o *goo*; ou *out*; TH *thin*; T͟H *then*; ZH *vision*

wine and vegetables, typically used in fish dishes. [Fr., from *court* 'short' and BOUILLON.]

cour·te·ous /'kərtēəs/ ▶ **adj.** polite, respectful, or considerate in manner. — **cour·te·ous·ly adv. cour·te·ous·ness n.** [ME: from OFr. *corteis*, based on L. *cohors* 'yard, retinue.']

cour·te·san /'kôrtəzən; 'kər-/ ▶ **n.** a prostitute, esp. one with wealthy or upper-class clients. [16th C.: from Fr. *courtisane*, from obs. Ital. *cortigiana*, fem. of *cortigiano* 'courtier,' from *corte* (see COURT).]

cour·te·sy /'kərtəsē/ ▶ **n.** (pl. **-sies**) the showing of politeness in one's attitude and behavior toward others. ■ (often **courtesies**) a polite speech or action, esp. one required by convention. ■ [as adj.] (esp. of transport) supplied free of charge to people who are already paying for another service.

– PHRASES **by courtesy** as a favor rather than by right. **(by) courtesy of** given or allowed by. ■ informal as a result of; thanks to. [ME: from OFr. *cortesie*, from *corteis* (see COURTEOUS).]

cour·te·sy ti·tle ▶ **n.** a title given to someone, esp. the son or daughter of a peer, that has no legal validity.

court·house /'kôrt,hous/ ▶ **n.** **1** a building in which a judicial court is held. **2** a building containing the administrative offices of a county.

cour·ti·er /'kôrtēər; 'kôrCHər/ ▶ **n.** a person who attends a royal court as a companion or adviser to the king or queen. ■ a person who fawns and flatters in order to gain favor or advantage.

court·ly /'kôrtlē/ ▶ **adj.** (**-li·er, -li·est**) **1** polished or refined, as befitting a royal court. **2** given to flattery; obsequious. — **court·li·ness n.**

court·ly love ▶ **n.** a highly conventionalized medieval tradition of love between a knight and a married noblewoman.

court-mar·tial ▶ **n.** (pl. **courts-mar·tial** or **court-mar·tials**) a judicial court for trying members of the armed services accused of offenses against military law. ▶ **v.** (**-mar·tialed, -mar·tial·ing**; Brit. **-mar·tialled, -mar·tial·ling**) [trans.] try (someone) by such a court.

court of ap·peals ▶ **n.** a court to which appeals are taken in a federal circuit or a state.

court of claims ▶ **n.** a court in which claims against the government are adjudicated.

court of in·quir·y ▶ **n.** a tribunal appointed in the armed forces to investigate a matter and decide whether a court-martial is called for.

court of law ▶ **n.** see COURT (sense 1).

court of rec·ord ▶ **n.** a court whose proceedings are recorded and available as evidence of fact.

Court of St. James's the British sovereign's court.

court or·der ▶ **n.** a direction issued by a court or a judge requiring a person to do or not do something.

court plas·ter ▶ **n.** hist. sticking plaster made of silk or other cloth with an adhesive such as isinglass. [18th C.: so named because it was formerly used by ladies at court for beauty spots.]

court rec·ord ▶ **n.** see RECORD (sense 1).

court·room /'kôrt,ro͞om; -,ro͝om/ ▶ **n.** the place or room in which a court of law meets.

court·ship /'kôrt,SHip/ ▶ **n.** a period during which a couple develop a romantic relationship, esp. with a view to marriage. ■ behavior designed to persuade someone to marry one. ■ the behavior of male birds and other animals aimed at attracting a mate. ■ the process of attempting to win a person's favor or support: *the country's courtship of foreign investors.*

court ten·nis ▶ **n.** the original form of tennis, played with a solid ball on an enclosed court divided into equal but dissimilar halves.

court·yard /'kôrt,yärd/ ▶ **n.** an unroofed area that is completely or partially enclosed by walls or buildings, typically one forming part of a castle or large house.

cous·cous /'ko͞os,sko͞os/ ▶ **n.** a type of North African semolina made from crushed durum wheat. ■ a spicy dish made by steaming or soaking such granules and adding meat, vegetables, or fruit. [17th C.: from Fr., from Arab. *kuskus*, from *kaskasa* 'to pound,' prob. of Berber origin.]

cous·in /'kəzən/ ▶ **n.** (also **first cousin**) a child of one's uncle or aunt. ■ a person belonging to the same extended family. ■ a thing related or analogous to another. ■ (usu. **cousins**) a person of a kindred culture, race, or nation. ■ hist. a title formerly used by a sovereign in addressing another sovereign or a noble of their own country.

– PHRASES **first cousin once removed 1** a child of one's first cousin. **2** one's parent's first cousin. **first cousin twice removed 1** a grandchild of one's first cousin. **2** one's grandparent's first cousin. **second cousin** a child of one's parent's first cousin. **second cousin once removed 1** a child of one's second cousin. **2** one's parent's second cousin. **third cousin** a child of one's parent's second cousin. — **cous·in·hood n. cous·in·ly adj. cous·in·ship n.** [ME: from OFr. *cosin*, from L. *consobrinus* 'mother's sister's child,' from *con-* 'with' + *sobrinus* 'second cousin' (from *soror* 'sister').]

cous·in-ger·man ▶ **n.** (pl. **cous·ins-ger·man**) old-fashioned term for COUSIN. [ME: from Fr. *cousin germain* (see COUSIN, GERMAN).]

Cous·teau /ko͞o'stō/, Jacques-Yves (1910–97), French oceanographer. He is known primarily for his documentaries and popular television series on marine life.

couth /ko͞oTH/ humorous ▶ **adj.** [predic.] cultured, refined, and well mannered. ▶ **n.** good manners; refinement. [19th C.: back-form. from UNCOUTH.]

cou·ture /ko͞o'to͝or; -'tyr/ ▶ **n.** the design and manufacture of fashionable clothes to a client's specific requirements and measurements. See also HAUTE COUTURE. ■ such clothes. [1920s: Fr., 'sewing.']

cou·tu·ri·er /ko͞o'to͝orēər; -'to͝orē,ā/ ▶ **n.** a fashion designer who manufactures and sells clothes that have been tailored to a client's specific requirements and measurements.

cou·tu·ri·ère /ko͞o'to͝orēər; -,to͝orē'e(ə)r/ ▶ **n.** a female couturier.

cou·vade /ko͞o'väd/ ▶ **n.** the custom in some cultures in which a man takes to his bed and goes through certain rituals when his child is being born, as though he were physically affected by the birth. [19th C.: Fr., from *couver* 'to hatch,' from L. *cubare* 'lie down.']

co·va·lent /kō'välənt/ ▶ **adj.** Chem. of, relating to, or denoting chemical bonds formed by the sharing of electrons between atoms. Often contrasted with IONIC. — **co·va·lence n. co·va·lent·ly adv.**

co·var·i·ance /kō've(ə)rēəns/ ▶ **n.** **1** Math. the property of a function of retaining its form when the variables are linearly transformed. **2** Stat. the mean value of the product of the deviations of two variates from their respective means.

co·var·i·ant /kō've(ə)rēənt/ Math. ▶ **n.** a function of the coefficients and variables of a given function that is invariant under a linear transformation except for a factor equal to a power of the determinant of the transformation. ▶ **adj.** changing in such a way that mathematical interrelations with another simultaneously changing quantity or set of quantities remain unchanged. ■ of, having the properties of, or relating to a covariant.

cove /kōv/ ▶ **n.** **1** a small sheltered bay. **2** a sheltered recess, esp. one in a mountain. **3** Archit. a concave arched molding, esp. one formed at the junction of a wall with a ceiling. ▶ **v.** [trans.] [usu. as adj.] (**coved**) Archit. provide (a room, ceiling, etc.) with a cove. [OE *cofa* 'chamber,' of Gmc. origin; rel. to Ger. *Koben* 'pen.']

co·vel·lite /kō'velīt; 'kōvə,līt/ ▶ **n.** a blue mineral consisting of copper sulfide, typically occurring as a coating on other copper minerals. [19th C.: named after Nicolò *Covelli* (1790–1829), Italian chemist, + -ITE[1].]

cov·en /'kəvən/ ▶ **n.** a group or gathering of witches who meet regularly. ■ fig., often derog. a secret or close-knit group of associates. [17th C.: var. of COVIN.]

cov·e·nant /'kəvənənt/ ▶ **n.** an agreement. ■ Law a contract drawn up by deed. ■ Law a clause in a contract. ■ Theol. an agreement that brings about a relationship of commitment between God and his people. The Jewish faith is based on the biblical covenants made with Abraham, Moses, and David. See also ARK OF THE COVENANT. ▶ **v.** [intrans.] agree, esp. by lease, deed, or other legal contract.

– PHRASES **Old Covenant** Christian Theol. the covenant between God and Israel in the Old Testament. **New Covenant** Christian Theol. the covenant between God and the followers of Jesus Christ. — **cov·e·nan·tal** /,kəvə'nantl/ **adj. cov·e·nant·er** (also esp. Law **cov·e·nan·tor**) **n.** [ME: from OFr., pres. part. of *covenir* 'agree,' from L. *convenire* (see CONVENE).]

cov·e·nan·tee /,kəvənən'tē; -nan-/ ▶ **n.** Law the person to whom a promise by covenant is made.

cov·e·nant of grace ▶ **n.** (in Calvinist theology) the covenant between God and humanity that was established by Jesus Christ at the Atonement.

cov·e·nant of works ▶ **n.** (in Calvinist theology) the covenant between God and humanity that was broken by Adam's sin at the Fall.

Cov·ent Gar·den /'kəvənt/ a district in central London.

Cov·en·try /'kəvəntrē; 'käv-/ an industrial city in central England; pop. 292,600.

cov·er /'kəvər/ ▶ **v.** [trans.] **1** (often **be covered**) put something such as a cloth or lid on top of or in front of (something) in order to protect or conceal it. ■ envelop in a layer of something, esp. dirt. ■ scatter a layer of loose material over (a surface, esp. a floor), leaving it completely obscured. ■ lie over or adhere to (a surface), as decoration or to conceal something. ■ protect (someone) with a garment or hat. ■ extend over (an area). ■ travel (a specified distance). **2** deal with (a subject) by describing or analyzing its most important aspects or events. ■ investigate, report on, or publish or broadcast pictures of (an event). ■ work in, have responsibility for, or provide services to (a particular area). ■ (of a rule or law) apply to (a person or situation). **3** (of a sum of money) be enough to pay (a bill or cost). ■ (of insurance) protect against a liability, loss, or accident involving financial consequences. ■ (**cover oneself**) take precautionary measures so as to protect oneself against future blame or liability. **4** disguise the sound or fact of (something) with another sound or action. ■ [intrans.] (**cover for**) disguise the illicit absence or wrongdoing of (someone) in order to spare them punishment. ■ [intrans.] (**cover for**) temporarily take over the job of (a colleague) in their absence. **5** aim a gun at (someone) in order to prevent them from moving or escaping. ■ protect (an exposed person) by shooting at an enemy. ■ (of a fortress, gun, or cannon) have (an area) within range. ■ (in team games) take up a position ready to defend against (an opposing player). ■ Baseball be in position at (a base) ready to catch a thrown ball. **6** Bridge play a higher card on (a high card) in a trick. **7** record or perform a new version of (a song) originally performed by someone else. ▶ **n.** **1** a thing that lies on, over, or around something, esp. in order to protect or conceal it. ■ a thin solid object that seals a container or hole; a lid. ■ a thick protective outer part or page of a book or magazine. ■ Philately a card or envelope that has traveled through the mail or that contains postal markings. ■ (**the covers**) bedclothes. **2** physical shelter or protection sought by people in danger. ■ undergrowth, trees, or other vegetation used as a shelter by hunted animals. See also COVERT (sense 1). ■ an activity or organization used as a means of concealing an illegal or secret activity. ■ [in sing.] an identity or activity adopted by a person, typically a spy, to conceal their true activities. ■ military support given when someone is in danger from or being attacked by an enemy. ■ Ecol. the amount of ground covered by a vertical projection of the vegetation, usually expressed as a percentage. **3** short for COVER CHARGE. **4** a place setting at a table in a restaurant. [rendering Fr. *couvert*.] **5** (also **cover version**) a recording or performance of a previously recorded song made esp. to take advantage of the original's success.

– PHRASES **break cover** suddenly leave a place of shelter, esp. vegetation, when being hunted or pursued. **cover one's ass** (or **back**) informal foresee and avoid the possibility of attack or criticism. **cover all bases** (or **cover all the bases**) include all relevant subject matter. ■ prepare for all likely circumstances. **cover a multitude of sins** conceal or gloss over many problems or defects. **cover one's position** purchase securities in order to be able to fulfill a commitment to sell. **cover one's tracks** conceal evidence of what one has done. **from cover to cover** from beginning to end of a book or magazine. **take cover** protect oneself from attack by ducking down into or under a shelter. **under cover of** concealed by. ■ while pretending to do something. **under plain cover** in an envelope or parcel without any marks to identify the sender. **under separate cover** in a separate envelope.

– PHRASAL VERBS **cover something up** put something on, over, or around something, esp. in order to conceal or disguise it. ■ try to hide or deny the fact of an illegal or illicit action or activity. — **cov·er·a·ble** adj. [ME: from OFr. *covrir*, from L. *cooperire*, from *co-* + *operire* 'to cover.']

cov·er·age /'kəv(ə)rij/ ▶ n. the extent to which something deals with or applies to something else. ■ the treatment of an issue by the media. ■ the amount of protection given by an insurance policy. ■ the area reached by a particular broadcasting station or advertising medium. ■ Football the manner in which a defender or a defensive team covers a player, an area, or a play.

cov·er·all /'kəvərˌôl/ ▶ n. (usu. **coveralls**) a full-length protective outer garment often zipped up the front. ■ [as adj.] inclusive.

cov·er charge ▶ n. a flat fee paid for admission to a restaurant, bar, club, etc.

cov·er crop ▶ n. a crop grown for the protection and enrichment of the soil.

Cov·er·dale /'kəvərˌdāl/, Miles (1488–1568), English scholar. He translated the first complete printed English Bible in 1535.

cov·ered wag·on ▶ n. a horse- or mule-drawn wagon topped with a canvas-covered framework, the common transport for the western-moving North American pioneers of the 19th century. See also CONESTOGA WAGON, PRAIRIE SCHOONER.

cov·er girl ▶ n. a female model whose picture appears on magazine covers.

cov·er glass ▶ n. another term for COVERSLIP.

cov·er·ing /'kəv(ə)riNG/ ▶ n. a thing used to cover something else, typically to protect or conceal it. ■ [usu. in sing.] a layer of something that covers something else.

cov·er·let /'kəvərlit/ ▶ n. a bedspread. [ME: from Anglo-Norman Fr. *covrelet*, from OFr. *covrir* 'to cover' + *lit* 'bed.']

cov·er let·ter ▶ n. a letter sent with, and explaining the contents of, another document or a parcel of goods.

cov·er sheet ▶ n. **1** a page sent as the first page of a fax transmission, identifying the sender, number of pages, etc. **2** a page placed before a manuscript or report, typically with the name of the author, title of the book or report, and date.

cov·er·slip /'kəvərˌslip/ (also **cov·er slip**) ▶ n. a small, thin piece of glass used to cover and protect a specimen on a microscope slide.

cov·er sto·ry ▶ n. **1** a magazine article that is illustrated or advertised on the front cover. **2** a fictitious account invented to conceal a person's identity or reasons for doing something.

co·vert ▶ adj. /'kōvərt; kō'vərt; 'kəvərt/ not openly acknowledged or displayed. ▶ n. /'kəvərt; 'kōvərt/ **1** a shelter or hiding place. ■ a thicket in which game can hide. **2** Ornithol. any of the feathers covering the bases of the main flight or tail feathers of a bird. **3** Law (of a woman) married and under the authority and protection of her husband. — **co·vert·ly** /'kōvərtlē; kō'vərtlē; 'kəvərtlē/ adv. **co·vert·ness** n. [ME: from OFr., 'covered,' past part. of *covrir* (see COVER).]

cov·er·ture /'kəvərˌCHŏŏr; -CHər/ ▶ n. **1** literary protective or concealing covering. **2** Law, hist. the legal status of a married woman, considered to be under her husband's protection and authority. [ME: from OFr., from *covrir* 'to cover.']

cov·er-up (also **cov·er·up**) ▶ n. **1** an attempt to prevent discovery of the truth about a serious mistake or crime. **2** a loose outer garment, typically worn over a swimsuit or exercise outfit.

cov·er ver·sion ▶ n. see COVER (sense 5).

cov·et /'kəvit/ ▶ v. (**cov·et·ed, cov·et·ing**) [trans.] yearn to possess or have (something). — **cov·et·a·ble** adj. [ME: from OFr. *cuveitier*, based on L. *cupiditas* (see CUPIDITY).]

cov·et·ous /'kəvitəs/ ▶ adj. having or showing a great desire to possess something, typically something belonging to someone else. — **cov·et·ous·ly** adv. **cov·et·ous·ness** n.

cov·ey /'kəvē/ ▶ n. (pl. **-eys**) a small party or flock of birds, esp. partridge. ■ fig. a small group of people or things. [ME: from OFr. *covee*, fem. past part. of *cover*, from L. *cubare* 'lie down.']

cov·in /'kəvin; 'kō-/ (also **cov·ine**) ▶ n. archaic fraud; deception. [ME: from OFr., from med. L. *convenium*, from L. *convenire* (see CONVENE).]

Co·vi·na /kō'vēnə/ a city in southwestern California; pop. 46,837.

Cov·ing·ton /'kəviNGtən/ a city in northern Kentucky; pop. 43,370.

cow[1] /kou/ ▶ n. a fully grown female animal of a domesticated breed of ox, used as a source of milk or beef. See CATTLE. ■ (loosely) a domestic bovine animal, regardless of sex or age. ■ (in farming) a female domestic bovine animal that has borne more than one calf. Compare with HEIFER. ■ the female of certain other large animals, for example elephant, whale, seal, or reindeer.

– PHRASES **have a cow** informal become angry, excited, or agitated. **till the cows come home** informal for an indefinitely long time. [OE *cū*, of Gmc. origin; rel. to Du. *koe* and Ger. *Kuh*, from an Indo-Eur. root shared by L. *bos* and Gk. *bous*.]

cow[2] ▶ v. [trans.] (usu. **be cowed**) cause (someone) to submit to one's wishes by intimidation. [16th C.: prob. from ON *kúga* 'oppress.']

cow·a·bun·ga /ˌkou-ə'bəNGgə/ ▶ exclam. informal used to express delight or satisfaction. [1940s: prob. fanciful.]

cow·age /'kouij/ (also **cow·hage**) ▶ n. a leguminous climbing plant, *Mucuna pruriens*, with hairy pods that cause stinging and itching. [17th C.: from Hindi *kaunc*.]

Cow·ard /'kouərd/, Sir Noel Pierce (1899–1973), English playwright and composer. His witty, satirical plays include *Private Lives* (1930).

cow·ard /'kouərd/ ▶ n. a person who lacks the courage to do or endure dangerous or unpleasant things. ▶ adj. literary excessively afraid of danger or pain. [ME: from OFr. *couard*, based on L. *cauda* 'tail.']

cow·ard·ice /'kouərdis/ ▶ n. lack of bravery. [ME: from OFr. *couardise*, from *couard* (see COWARD).]

cow·ard·ly /'kouərdlē/ ▶ adj. lacking courage. ■ (of an action) carried out against a person who is unable to retaliate: *a cowardly attack on a helpless victim*. ▶ adv. archaic in a way that shows a lack of courage. — **cow·ard·li·ness** n.

cow·bane /'kouˌbān/ ▶ n. any of a number of tall poisonous plants of the parsley family, growing in swampy or wet habitats, including water hemlock. [18th C.: from COW[1] + BANE.]

cow·bell /'kouˌbel/ ▶ n. a bell hung around a cow's neck in order to help locate the animal by the noise it makes. ■ a similar bell used as a percussion instrument, typically without a clapper and struck with a stick.

cow·ber·ry /'kouˌberē/ ▶ n. (pl. **-ries**) another term for MOUNTAIN CRANBERRY.

cow·bird /'kouˌbərd/ ▶ n. a New World songbird (genera *Molothrus* and *Scaphidura*, family Icteridae) with dark plumage and a relatively short bill, typically laying its eggs in other birds' nests.

cow·boy /'kouˌboi/ ▶ n. **1** a man, typically one on horseback, who herds and tends cattle, esp. in the western US and as represented in westerns and novels. **2** informal a person who is reckless or careless, esp. when driving an automobile.

cow·boy boot ▶ n. a style of boot with a pointed toe and a moderately high heel, extending to mid-calf.

cow·catch·er /'kouˌkaCHər; -ˌkeCHər/ ▶ n. a metal frame at the front of a locomotive for pushing aside cattle or other obstacles on the line.

cow chip ▶ n. informal a dried cowpat.

cow·er /'kouər/ ▶ v. [intrans.] crouch down in fear. [ME: from Mid. Low Ger. *kūren* 'lie in wait.']

cow·fish /'kouˌfiSH/ ▶ n. (pl. same or **-fish·es**) a boxfish (esp. *Lactoria diaphana*) with spines that resemble horns on the head, and typically with other spines on the back and sides.

cow flop (also **cow·flop** or esp. Canadian **cow flap** or **cow·flap**) ▶ n. informal a cowpat.

cow·girl /'kouˌgərl/ ▶ n. a female equivalent of a cowboy, esp. as represented in westerns and novels.

cow·hage ▶ n. var. of COWAGE.

cow·hand /'kouˌhand/ ▶ n. a person employed to tend or ranch cattle; a cowboy or cowgirl.

cow·herd /'kouˌhərd/ ▶ n. a person who tends grazing cattle. [OE, from COW[1] + obs. *herd* 'herdsman.']

cow·hide /'kouˌhīd/ ▶ n. a cow's hide. ■ leather made from such a hide. ■ a whip made from such leather.

cowl /koul/ ▶ n. a large loose hood, esp. one forming part of a monk's habit. ■ a monk's hooded, sleeveless habit. ■ a cloak with wide sleeves worn by members of Benedictine orders. ■ the hood-shaped covering of a chimney or ventilation shaft. ■ the part of a motor vehicle that supports the windshield and houses the dashboard. ■ another term for COWLING. — **cowled** adj. [OE *cugele*, *cūle*, from eccles. Latin *cuculla*, from L. *cucullus* 'hood of a cloak.']

cow·lick /'kouˌlik/ ▶ n. a lock of hair that grows in a direction different from the rest and that resists being combed flat.

cowl·ing /'kouliNG/ ▶ n. the removable cover of a vehicle or aircraft engine.

cowl neck ▶ n. a neckline on a woman's garment that hangs in draped folds: [as adj.] *a cowl-neck sweater*.

cow·man /'koumən; -ˌman/ ▶ n. (pl. **-men**) a person who owns or is in charge of a cattle ranch. ■ a cowboy.

co·work·er /'kō,wərkər; kō'wərkər/ ▶ n. a fellow worker.

cow pars·nip ▶ n. a bad-smelling plant (*Heracleum maximum*) of the parsley family that can reach a height of 10 feet (3 m).

cow·pat /'kou,pat/ ▶ n. a flat, round piece of cow dung.

cow·pea /'kou,pē/ ▶ n. a plant (*Vigna unguiculata*) of the pea family, native to the Old World tropics and cultivated in the southern US for animal feed and human consumption. ■ the seed of this plant as food.

Cow·per /'ko͞opər; 'ko͝opər; 'koupər/, William (1731–1800), English poet, noted for the poem *The Task* (1785) and for the comic ballad *John Gilpin* (1782).

Cow·per's gland /'koupərz; 'ko͞opərz; 'ko͝opərz/ ▶ n. Anat. either of a pair of small glands that open into the urethra at the base of the penis and secrete a constituent of seminal fluid. [18th C.: William *Cowper* (1666–1709), English anatomist.]

cow·poke /'kou,pōk/ ▶ n. informal a cowboy.

cow po·ny ▶ n. a small horse trained for use in cattle ranching.

cow·pox /'kou,päks/ ▶ n. a viral disease of cows' udders which, when contracted by humans through contact, resembles mild smallpox, and was the basis of the first smallpox vaccines.

cow·punch·er /'kou,pənCHər/ ▶ n. informal a cowboy.

cow·punk /'kou,pəNGk/ ▶ n. a type of popular music combining elements of country and western with those of punk rock. ■ a singer or musician who performs this type of music.

cow·rie /'kourē/ (also **cow·ry**) ▶ n. (pl. **-ries**) a marine mollusk (genus *Cypraea*, family Cypraeidae) that has a smooth, glossy, domed shell with a long narrow opening, typically brightly patterned and popular with collectors. ■ the flattened yellowish shell of the **money cowrie** (*C. moneta*), formerly used as money in parts of Africa and the Indo-Pacific area. [17th C.: from Hindi *kauṛī*.]

co·write /kō'rīt; 'kō,rīt/ ▶ v. [trans.] write (something) together with another person. — **co·writ·er** n.

cow shark ▶ n. a dull gray or brown shark (*Hexanchus griseus*, family Hexanchidae) that lives mainly in deep water, esp. in the North Atlantic and Mediterranean.

cow·shed /'kou,SHed/ ▶ n. a farm building in which cattle are kept when not in a pasture, or in which they are milked.

cow·slip /'kou,slip/ ▶ n. **1** a European primula (*Primula veris*) with clusters of drooping fragrant yellow flowers in spring. **2** any of a number of herbaceous plants, in particular the marsh marigold and the Virginia bluebell. [OE *cūslyppe*, from *cū* 'cow' + *slipa*, *slyppe* 'slime,' i.e., cow slobber or dung.]

cow·town /'kou,toun/ (also **cow town**) ▶ n. a town or city in a cattle-raising area of western North America. ■ fig. a small, isolated, or unsophisticated town.

cox /käks/ ▶ n. a coxswain, esp. of a racing boat. ▶ v. [trans.] act as a coxswain for (a racing boat or crew).

cox·a /'käksə/ ▶ n. (pl. **cox·ae** /'käksē; -sī/) Anat. the hipbone or hip joint. ■ Entomol. the first or basal segment of the leg of an insect. — **cox·al** adj. [17th C.: from L., 'hip.']

cox·al·gi·a /käk'salj(ē)ə/ ▶ n. pain in the hip joint.

cox·comb /'käks,kōm/ ▶ n. **1** dated a vain and conceited man; a dandy. **2** var. of **COCKSCOMB** (sense 2). — **cox·comb·ry** n. (pl. **-ries**) (in sense 1). **cox·comb·er·y** /-,kōmərē/ n. [16th C.: var. of **COCKSCOMB**, 'jester's cap.']

Cox·sack·ie vi·rus /käk'sakē; ko͝ok-/ (also **cox·sack·ie virus** or **cox·sack·ie·vi·rus**) ▶ n. Med. any of a group of enteroviruses that cause various respiratory, neurological, and muscular diseases in humans. [1940s: *Coxsackie*, New York.]

cox·swain /'käksən/ ▶ n. the steersman of a ship's boat, lifeboat, racing boat, or other boat. — **cox·swain·ship** n. [ME: from obs. *cock* + **SWAIN**. Cf. **BOATSWAIN**.]

coy /koi/ ▶ adj. (**coyer**, **coyest**) (esp. of a woman) making a pretense of shyness or modesty that is intended to be alluring but is often regarded as irritating. ■ reluctant to give details, esp. about something regarded as sensitive. ■ dated quiet and reserved; shy. — **coy·ly** adv. **coy·ness** n. [ME ('quiet'): from OFr. *coi*, *quei*, from L. *quietus* (see **QUIET**).]

coy·dog /'koi,dôg/ ▶ n. the hybrid offspring of a coyote and a dog.

Co·yo·a·cán /,koi-ōə'kän/ a municipality within the Federal District of Mexico, a suburb of Mexico City; pop. 640,000.

coy·o·te /kī'ōtē; 'kīōt/ ▶ n. **1** (pl. same or **-tes**) a wolflike wild dog (*Canis latrans*) native to North America. **2** informal a person who smuggles Latin Americans across the US border, typically for a high fee. [18th C.: from Mex. Sp., from Nahuatl *coyotl*.]

coy·pu /'koipo͞o/ ▶ n. (pl. **-pus**) another term for **NUTRIA**. [18th C.: from Araucanian.]

coz /kəz/ ▶ n. an informal word for cousin, used esp. as a term of address. [16th C.: abbrev.]

coz·en /'kəzən/ ▶ v. [trans.] trick or deceive. ■ obtain by deception. — **coz·en·age** /-ənij/ n. **coz·en·er** n. [16th C.: perh. from obs. Ital. *cozzonare* 'to cheat,' from *cozzone* 'middleman, broker,' from L. *cocio* 'dealer.']

Co·zu·mel /,kōzo͞o'mel/ a resort island off the northeastern coast of the Yucatán Peninsula in Mexico.

co·zy /'kōzē/ (Brit. **co·sy**) ▶ adj. (**-zi·er**, **-zi·est**) giving a feeling of comfort, warmth, and relaxation. ■ (of a relationship or conversation) intimate and relaxed. ■ avoiding or not offering challenge or difficulty; complacent. ■ (of a transaction or arrangement) working to the mutual advantage of those involved (used to convey a suspicion of corruption). ▶ n. (pl. **-zies**) a cover to keep a teapot hot. ▶ v. (**-zies**, **-zied**) [trans.] informal impart a feeling or quality of comfort to (something). ■ [trans.] informal give (someone) a feeling of comfort or complacency. ■ [intrans.] (**cozy up to**) snuggle up to. ■ [intrans.] (**cozy up to**) ingratiate oneself with. — **co·zi·ly** /-zəlē/ adv. **co·zi·ness** n. [18th C. (orig. Scots): of unknown origin.]

CP ▶ abbr. ■ cerebral palsy. ■ Command Post. ■ Finance commercial paper. ■ Communist Party. ■ (also **cp**) candlepower.

cp. ▶ abbr. compare.

CPA ▶ abbr. certified public accountant.

cpd. ▶ abbr. compound.

CPI ▶ abbr. consumer price index.

Cpl. ▶ abbr. corporal.

CPO ▶ abbr. Chief Petty Officer.

CPR ▶ abbr. cardiopulmonary resuscitation.

cps (also **c.p.s.**) ▶ abbr. ■ Comput. characters per second. ■ cycles per second.

Cpt. ▶ abbr. Captain.

CPU ▶ abbr. Comput. central processing unit.

CPUSA ▶ abbr. Communist Party USA.

CR ▶ abbr. ■ Conditioned reflex. ■ Conditioned response. ■ Costa Rica.

Cr ▶ symb. the chemical element chromium.

cr ▶ abbr. ■ credit. ■ creditor.

crab[1] /krab/ ▶ n. **1** a crustacean (order Decapoda, class Malacostraca) with a broad carapace, stalked eyes, and five pairs of legs, the first pair of which are modified as pincers. See illustration at **BLUE CRAB**. ■ the flesh of a crab as food. ■ (**the Crab**) the zodiacal sign or constellation Cancer. **2** (also **crab louse**) a louse (*Phthirus pubis*, family Pediculidae) that infests human body hair, esp. in the genital region, causing extreme irritation. ■ (**crabs**) informal an infestation of crab lice. **3** a machine for lifting heavy weights. ▶ v. **1** [trans.] move sideways or obliquely. **2** [intrans.] fish for crabs.
– PHRASES **catch a crab** Rowing make a faulty stroke in which the oar is under water too long or misses the water altogether. — **crab·ber** n. **crab·like** adj. & adv. [OE *crabba*, of Gmc. origin; rel. to Ger. *Krebs*; also to **CRAB**[3].]

crab[2] ▶ n. short for **CRAB APPLE**.

crab[3] ▶ n. informal an irritable person. ▶ v. (**crabbed**, **crab·bing**) informal **1** [intrans.] grumble, typically about something petty: *on picnics, I would crab about sand in my food.* **2** [trans.] act so as to spoil: *you're trying to crab my act.* [16th C.: from Low Ger. *krabben*; rel. to **CRAB**[1].]

crab ap·ple (also **crab·ap·ple**) ▶ n. **1** a small, sour apple. **2** the small tree (genus *Malus*) of the rose family that bears this fruit. [ME: *crab* perh. an alt. of Scots and north. Engl. *scrab*.]

crab·bed /'krabid/ ▶ adj. **1** (of handwriting) ill-formed and hard to decipher. ■ (of style) contorted and difficult to understand: *crabbed legal language.* **2** ill-humored: *a crabbed, unhappy middle age.* — **crab·bed·ly** adv. **crab·bed·ness** n. [ME: from **CRAB**[1].]

crab·by /'krabē/ ▶ adj. (**crab·bi·er**, **crab·bi·est**) irritable. — **crab·bi·ly** /'krabəlē/ adv. **crab·bi·ness** n.

crab·grass /'krab,gras/ ▶ n. a creeping grass (*Digitaria* and other genera) that can become a serious weed.

crab louse ▶ n. see **CRAB**[1] (sense 2).

crab·meat /'krab,mēt/ ▶ n. the flesh of a crab as food.

Crab Neb·u·la Astron. an irregular patch of luminous gas in the constellation Taurus, perhaps the remnant of a supernova seen by Chinese astronomers in 1054. At its center is the first pulsar to be observed visually, and it is a strong source of high-energy radiation.

crab pot ▶ n. a trap for crabs.

crab spi·der ▶ n. a spider (family Thomisidae) with long front legs, moving with a crablike sideways motion.

crab tree ▶ n. see **CRAB APPLE** (sense 2).

crab·wise /'krab,wīz/ ▶ adv. & adj. (of movement) sideways, typically in an awkward way.

crack /krak/ ▶ n. **1** a line along which something has split without breaking into separate parts. ■ a narrow space between two surfaces, esp. ones that have broken or been moved apart. ■ fig. a vulnerable point; a flaw. **2** a sharp or explosive noise. ■ a sharp blow, esp. one that makes a noise. ■ a sudden harshness or change in pitch in a person's voice. **3** informal a joke, typically a critical or unkind one. **4** [in sing.] informal an attempt to gain or achieve something: *I thought I **had a crack at** winning.* ■ a chance to attack or compete with someone. **5** (also **crack cocaine**) a hard, crystalline form of cocaine broken into small pieces and smoked. ▶ v. **1** break or cause to break without a complete separation of the parts: [intrans.] *the ice had cracked* | [trans.] *a stone cracked the glass on his car.* ■ break or cause to break open or apart: [intrans.] *the landmasses have cracked up and moved around* | [trans.] *she cracked an egg into the pan.* ■ [trans.] break (grain) into coarse pieces. ■ [trans.] open slightly: *he cracks open his door.* ■ fig. give way or cause to give way under torture or strain: [intrans.] *the witnesses cracked and the truth came out* | [trans.] *no one can crack them.* ■ [intrans.] (**crack up**) informal suffer an emotional breakdown under pressure. ■ (**crack up**) informal burst or cause to burst into laughter. **2** make or cause to make a sharp or explosive sound: [trans.] *he cracked his whip.* ■ [intrans.] knock against something, making a noise on impact: *her knees cracked against metal.* ■ [trans.] hit (someone or something) hard, making a sharp noise. ■ [intrans.] (of a voice, esp. of an adolescent boy or a person under strain) suddenly change in pitch.

3 [trans.] informal find a solution to; decipher or interpret. ■ break into (a safe). **4** [trans.] tell (a joke). **5** [trans.] decompose (hydrocarbons) by heat and pressure to produce lighter hydrocarbons, esp. in oil refining: [as n.] (**cracking**) *catalytic cracking.* ▶ **adj.** [attrib.] very good, esp. at a specific activity: *he is a crack shot.*

– PHRASES **crack a book** informal open a book and read it; study. **crack of dawn** very early in the morning; daybreak. **cracked up to be** [with negative] informal asserted to be (of someone or something described too favorably): *life on tour is not as glamorous as it's cracked up to be.* **fall** (or **slip**) **through the cracks** escape from or be missed by something organized to catch or deal with one. **get cracking** informal act quickly and energetically.

– PHRASAL VERBS **crack down on** informal take severe measures against. [OE *cracian* 'make an explosive noise'; of Gmc. origin; rel. to Du. *kraken* and Ger. *krachen.*]

crack·a·jack /ˈkrakəˌjak/ ▶ **adj.** var. of CRACKERJACK.

crack·brained /ˈkrakˌbrānd/ ▶ **adj.** informal extremely foolish; crazy.

crack·down /ˈkrakˌdoun/ ▶ **n.** severe measures against undesirable or illegal people or behavior: *a crackdown on crime.*

cracked /krakt/ ▶ **adj. 1** showing lines of breakage without coming apart. ■ (of a person's voice) having an unusual harshness or pitch, often due to distress. **2** [predic.] informal insane.

crack·er /ˈkrakər/ ▶ **n. 1** a thin, crisp wafer often eaten with cheese or other savory toppings. **2** a person or thing that cracks. ■ an installation for cracking hydrocarbons: *a catalytic cracker.* **3** often offens. another term for POOR WHITE. **4** esp. Brit. a paper cylinder that makes a sharp noise when pulled apart, releasing a small toy or other novelty. ■ a firework exploding with a sharp noise.

crack·er·bar·rel ▶ **adj.** [attrib.] (esp. of a philosophy) simple and unsophisticated. [19th C.: with ref. to the barrels of soda crackers once found in country stores.]

crack·er·jack /ˈkrakərˌjak/ informal ▶ **adj.** exceptionally good. ▶ **n.** an exceptionally good person or thing.

crack·head /ˈkrakˌhed/ ▶ **n.** informal a person who habitually takes crack cocaine.

crack house ▶ **n.** a place where crack cocaine is traded.

crack·le /ˈkrakəl/ ▶ **v.** [intrans.] make a rapid succession of slight cracking noises: *the fire crackled.* ■ fig. give a sense of great tension or animation. ▶ **n. 1** the sound of a rapid succession of slight cracking sounds. **2** a pattern of minute surface cracks on painted or varnished surfaces, glazed ceramics, or glass. — **crack·ly** /ˈkrak(ə)lē/ **adj.** [ME: from CRACK + -LE[4].]

crack·ling /ˈkraklin; -liNG/ ▶ **n.** the crisp, fatty skin of roast pork.

crack·pot /ˈkrakˌpät/ informal ▶ **n.** an eccentric or foolish person. ▶ **adj.** [attrib.] impractical.

crack-up (also **crackup**) ▶ **n.** [usu. in sing.] informal **1** a collapse under strain. **2** an act of breaking up or splitting apart. **3** an automobile accident.

crack·y /ˈkrakē/ ▶ **n.** (in phrase **by cracky**) dated, informal an exclamation used for emphasis.

Crac·ow /ˈkräkou; ˈkräko͞of/ a city in southern Poland, on the Vistula River; pop 750,540. Polish name KRAKÓW.

-cracy ▶ **comb. form** denoting a particular form of government, rule, or influence: *democracy.* [from Fr. *-cratie,* via med. L. from Gk. *-kratia* 'power, rule.']

cra·dle /ˈkrādl/ ▶ **n. 1** an infant's bed or crib, typically one mounted on rockers. ■ fig. a place, process, or event in which something originates or flourishes. ■ fig. infancy. **2** a framework resembling a cradle, in particular: ■ a framework for a vessel during construction or repairs. ■ the part of a telephone on which the handset rests when not in use. ■ a frame over a hospital bed to prevent the bedclothes from touching a patient. ▶ **v.** [trans.] **1** hold gently and protectively. ■ fig. be the place of origin of. **2** place (a telephone handset) in its cradle. [OE *cradol,* of uncert. origin; perh. rel. to Ger. *Kratte* 'basket.']

cra·dle cap ▶ **n.** a skin condition sometimes seen in babies, characterized by scales on the top of the head.

cra·dling /ˈkrādliNG; ˈkrādl-iNG/ ▶ **n.** Archit. a framework used as a structural support in a ceiling.

craft /kraft/ ▶ **n. 1** an activity involving skill in making things by hand. ■ (**crafts**) work or objects made by hand. ■ a skilled activity or profession. ■ skill in carrying out one's work. ■ skill used in deceiving others. ■ the members of a skilled profession. ■ (**the Craft**) Freemasons. **2** (pl. same) a boat or ship. ■ an airplane or spaceship. ▶ **v.** [trans.] use skill in making (something): *he crafted the chair* | [as adj.] (**crafted**) *a beautifully crafted object.* — **craft·er n.** [OE *cræft* 'strength, skill,' of Gmc. origin; rel. to Du. *kracht,* Ger. *Kraft,* and Swed. *kraft* 'strength.']

crafts·man /ˈkraf(t)smən/ ▶ **n.** (pl. **-men**) a person who is skilled in a particular craft or art. — **crafts·man·ship n.**

crafts·per·son /ˈkraf(t)sˌpərsən/ ▶ **n.** (pl. **-peo·ple** /-ˌpēpəl/) a person skilled in a particular craft or art.

crafts·wom·an /ˈkraf(t)sˌwo͝omən/ ▶ **n.** (pl. **-wom·en**) a woman who is skilled in a particular craft or art.

craft un·ion ▶ **n.** a labor union of people of the same skilled craft.

craft·y /ˈkraftē/ ▶ **adj.** (**craft·i·er, craft·i·est**) clever at achieving one's aims by indirect or deceitful methods. ■ of, involving, or relating to indirect or deceitful methods. — **craft·i·ly adv. craft·i·ness n.**

crag /krag/ ▶ **n.** a steep or rugged cliff or rock face. [ME: of Celtic origin.]

crag·gy /ˈkragē/ ▶ **adj.** (**-gi·er, -gi·est**) (of a landscape) having many crags. ■ (of a cliff or rock face) rough and uneven. ■ (of a man's face) rough-textured. — **crag·gi·ly** /ˈkragəlē/ **adv. crag·gi·ness n.**

Cra·io·va /krīˈōvə/ a city in southwestern Romania; pop. 300,030.

crake /krāk/ ▶ **n.** a bird (*Porzana* and other genera) of the rail family, esp. one with a short bill like the corn crake. ■ the rasping cry of the corn crake. [ME (orig. denoting a crow or raven): from ON *kráka, krákr,* of imitative origin.]

cram /kram/ ▶ **v.** (**crammed, cram·ming**) [trans.] (often **be crammed**) completely fill (a place or container) to the point of overflowing: *the ashtray was crammed with cigarette butts* | *how you've managed to cram everyone in.* ■ [intrans.] enter a place or space that is or seems to be too small: *they all crammed into the car.* ■ put (something) into something that seems to be too small to contain it: *he crammed the sandwiches into his mouth.* ■ [intrans.] study intensively just before an examination. [OE *crammian,* of Gmc. origin; rel. to Du. *krammen* 'to cramp or clamp.']

cram·ming /ˈkramiNG/ ▶ **n.** the fraudulent adding of unauthorized charges to a customer's phone bill.

cramp /kramp/ ▶ **n.** a painful, involuntary muscle contraction, typically caused by fatigue or strain. ■ (**cramps**) abdominal pain caused by menstruation. ▶ **v. 1** [trans.] restrict or inhibit the development of. **2** [intrans.] suffer from sudden and painful contractions of a muscle or muscles.

– PHRASES **cramp someone's style** informal prevent a person from acting freely or naturally. [ME: from Mid. Low Ger. and MDu. *krampe.*]

cramped /kram(p)t/ ▶ **adj. 1** feeling or causing to feel confined or hemmed in. ■ restricting or inhibiting the development of someone or something. ■ (of handwriting) small and difficult to read. **2** suffering from a cramp.

cram·pon /ˈkrampän/ ▶ **n.** (usu. **crampons**) a spiked plate fixed to a boot for walking on ice or in rock climbing. [ME: from OFr., of Gmc. origin.]

Cra·nach /ˈkränəKH/ two German painters of religious subjects, Lucas (1472–1553), known as **Cranach the Elder**, and his son Lucas (1515–86), known as **Cranach the Younger**.

cran·ber·ry /ˈkranˌberē; -bərē/ ▶ **n.** (pl. **-ries**) **1** a small, red, acid berry used in cooking. **2** the evergreen dwarf shrub (genus *Vaccinium*) of the heath family that yields this fruit, esp. the North American *V. macrocarpon,* which thrives in boggy places. [17th C.: from Ger. *Kranbeere* or Low Ger. *kranebeere* 'crane-berry.']

Crane[1] /krān/, Hart (1899–1932), US poet; full name *Harold Hart Crane.* He published only two books—*White Buildings* (1926), a collection, and *The Bridge* (1930), a mystical epic poem.

Crane[2], Stephen (1871–1900), US writer, noted for his American Civil War novel *The Red Badge of Courage* (1895).

crane[1] /krān/ ▶ **n.** a machine used for moving heavy objects, typically by suspending them from a projecting arm or beam. ■ a moving platform for a television or movie camera. ▶ **v. 1** [intrans.] stretch out one's neck in order to see something: *she craned forward.* ■ [trans.] stretch out (one's neck) in this way. **2** [trans.] move (a heavy object) with a crane: *the wheelhouse is craned into position on the hull.* [ME: from CRANE[2].]

crane[1]

crane[2] ▶ **n.** a tall, long-legged, long-necked bird (*Grus* and other genera, family Gruidae), typically with white or gray plumage. [OE, of Gmc. origin; rel. to Du. *kraan* and Ger. *Kran,* from an Indo-Eur. root shared by L. *grus* and Gk. *geranos.*]

crane fly ▶ **n.** a slender, two-winged fly (family Tipulidae) with very long legs, in particular the large and common *Tipula maxima.*

cranes·bill /ˈkrānzˌbil/ ▶ **n.** a wild geranium, typically with lobed leaves and purple or pink five-petaled flowers.

cra·ni·al /ˈkrānēəl/ ▶ **adj.** Anat. of or relating to the skull or cranium.

cra·ni·al in·dex ▶ **n.** another term for CEPHALIC INDEX.

cra·ni·al nerve ▶ **n.** Anat. each of twelve pairs of nerves that arise from the brain, not from the spinal cord, and pass through separate apertures in the skull.

cra·ni·ate /ˈkrānēˌāt; -nē-it/ Zool. ▶ **n.** an animal that possesses a skull. ▶ **adj.** of or relating to the craniates. [19th C.: from mod. L. *craniatus,* from med. L. *cranium* (see CRANIUM).]

cranio- ▶ **comb. form** relating to the skull: *craniotomy.* [from Gk. *kranion* 'skull.']

cra·ni·o·ce·re·bral /ˌkrānēōsəˈrēbrəl; -ˈserəbrəl/ ▶ **adj.** relating to or involving the cranium and the cerebrum.

cra·ni·ol·o·gy /ˌkrānēˈäləjē/ ▶ **n.** hist. the study of the shape and size of skulls of different human races. ■ another term for PHRENOLOGY. — **cra·ni·o·log·i·cal** /-nēəˈläjikəl/ **adj. cra·ni·ol·o·gist n.**

cra·ni·om·e·ter /ˌkrānēˈämitər/ ▶ **n.** a device for measuring the external dimensions of the skull.

cra·ni·om·e·try /ˌkrānēˈämətrē/ ▶ **n.** hist. the measurement of skulls, esp. in relation to craniology. — **cra·ni·o·met·ric** /ˌkrānēəˈmetrik/ **adj.**

PRONUNCIATION KEY ə *ago, up;* ər *over, fur;* a *hat;* ā *ate;* ä *car;* e *let;* ē *see;* i *fit;* ī *by;* NG *sing;* ō *go;* ô *law, for;* oi *toy;* o͝o *good;* o͞o *goo;* ou *out;* TH *thin;* T͟H *then;* ZH *vision*

cra·ni·o·sa·cral ther·a·py /ˌkrānēōˈsakrəl; -ˈsākrəl/ ▶**n.** a system of alternative medicine intended to relieve pain and tension by gentle manipulations of the skull.

cra·ni·ot·o·my /ˌkrānēˈätəmē/ ▶**n.** surgical opening into the skull.

cra·ni·um /ˈkrānēəm/ ▶**n.** (pl. **-ni·ums** or **-ni·a** /-nēə/) Anat. the skull, esp. the part enclosing the brain. [ME: via med. L. from Gk. *kranion* 'skull.']

crank[1] /kraNGk/ ▶**v.** [trans.] turn the crankshaft of (an internal combustion engine), typically to start the engine. ■ turn (a handle), typically to start an engine. ■ (**crank something up**) informal increase the intensity of something: *he cranked up the foghorn to full volume.* ■ (**crank something out**) informal produce something regularly and routinely: *researchers cranked out worthy studies.* ▶**n.** **1** a part of an axle or shaft bent out at right angles, for converting reciprocal to circular motion or vice versa. **2** informal methamphetamine. [OE *cranc* (recorded in *crancstæf*, denoting a weaver's implement), rel. to *crincan* (see CRINGE).]

crank[2] ▶**n.** an eccentric person, esp. one obsessed by a particular subject or theory. ■ a bad-tempered person. [19th C.: back-form. from CRANKY.] ▶**adj.** from or denoting a malicious or mischievous person: *she was the target of crank calls.*

crank·case /ˈkraNGkˌkās/ ▶**n.** a case or covering enclosing a crankshaft.

crank·shaft /ˈkraNGkˌSHaft/ ▶**n.** a shaft driven by a crank.

crank·y /ˈkraNGkē/ ▶**adj.** (**crank·i·er, crank·i·est**) informal ill-tempered; irritable. —**crank·i·ly** /-kəlē/ **adv.** **crank·i·ness n.** [18th C.: perh. from obs. *(counterfeit) crank* 'a rogue feigning sickness,' from Du. or Ger. *krank* 'sick.']

Cran·mer /ˈkranmər/, Thomas (1489–1556), archbishop of Canterbury 1532–56. He was responsible for the compilation of the Book of Common Prayer (1549).

cran·ny /ˈkranē/ ▶**n.** (pl. **-nies**) a narrow space or opening. [ME: from OFr. *crane* 'notched,' from *cran*, from pop. L. *crena* 'notch.']

Cran·ston /ˈkranstən/ a city in central Rhode Island; pop. 79,269.

crap[1] /krap/ vulgar slang ▶**n.** **1** something that is of extremely poor quality. ■ nonsense. ■ rubbish; junk. **2** excrement. ■ [in sing.] an act of defecation. ▶**v.** (**crapped, crap·ping**) [intrans.] defecate. [ME: rel. to Du. *krappe*, from *krappen* 'pluck or cut off.']

crap[2] ▶**n.** a losing throw of 2, 3, or 12 in craps. ▶**v.** [intrans.] (**crap out**) informal make a losing throw at craps. ■ withdraw from or give up on because of fear or fatigue: *entrepreneurs crap out and turn their companies over to others.* ■ fail. ■ (of a machine) break down. [20th C.: from CRAPS.]

crape /krāp/ ▶**n.** archaic spelling of CREPE.

crape myr·tle (also **crepe myr·tle**) ▶**n.** an ornamental Asian shrub or small tree (genus *Lagerstroemia*, family Lythraceae) with pink, white, or purplish crinkled petals.

crap·per /ˈkrapər/ ▶**n.** vulgar slang a toilet.

crap·pie /ˈkrapē/ ▶**n.** (pl. **-pies**) a North American fish (genus *Pomoxis*) of the freshwater sunfish family. [19th C.: of unknown origin.]

crap·py /ˈkrapē/ ▶**adj.** (**-pi·er, -pi·est**) vulgar slang of extremely poor quality. ■ disgusting or unpleasant. ■ [predic.] ill.

craps /kraps/ ▶**plural n.** [treated as sing.] a gambling game played with two dice. See also CRAP[2]. [19th C.: perh. from CRAB[1] or *crab's eyes*, denoting the lowest throw (two ones) at dice.]

crap·shoot /ˈkrapˌSHo͞ot/ ▶**n.** a game of craps. ■ informal a risky or uncertain matter. —**crap·shoot·er n.**

crap·u·lent /ˈkrapyələnt/ ▶**adj.** literary of or relating to the drinking of alcohol or drunkenness. —**crap·u·lence n.** **crap·u·lous** /-yələs/ **adj.** [17th C.: from late L. *crapulentus* 'very drunk,' from L. *crapula* 'inebriation,' from Gk. *kraipalē* 'drunken headache.']

cra·que·lure /ˌkrak(ə)ˈlo͝or; ˈkrak(ə)ˌlo͝or/ ▶**n.** a network of fine cracks in the paint or varnish of a painting. [20th C.: Fr., from *craqueler* 'to crackle.']

crash /kraSH/ ▶**v.** **1** [intrans.] (of a moving object) collide violently with another object: *the coffin slid down the hill and crashed.* ■ [trans.] cause (a moving object) to collide in this way. ■ (of an aircraft) fall from the sky and violently hit the land or sea. ■ [trans.] cause (an aircraft) to fall from the sky in this way. ■ informal (of a business, a market, or a price) fall suddenly and disastrously in value. ■ Comput. (of a machine, system, or software) fail suddenly. ■ informal go to sleep, esp. suddenly or in an improvised setting. **2** [intrans.] move with force and sudden loud noise: [with adverbial of direction] *huge waves crashed down on us.* ■ [trans.] move (something) in this way: *she crashed down the telephone.* ■ make a sudden loud noise: *the thunder crashed.* **3** [trans.] informal enter (a party) without an invitation. ▶**n.** **1** a violent collision, typically of one moving object with another or with an obstacle. ■ an instance of an aircraft falling to the land or sea. ■ a sudden loud noise as of something breaking or hitting another object. **2** a sudden large drop in the value or price of something, esp. shares of stock. ■ the sudden collapse of a business. ■ Comput. a sudden failure which puts a system out of action. ▶**adj.** [attrib.] done rapidly or urgently and involving a concentrated effort: *a crash diet.* ▶**adv.** with a sudden loud sound: *crash went the bolt.*
– PHRASES **crash and burn** informal come to grief or fail spectacularly. [ME: imitative.]

crash-dive ▶**v.** [intrans.] (of a submarine) dive rapidly and steeply in an emergency. ■ (of an aircraft) plunge steeply into a crash. ▶**n.** (**crash dive**) a steep dive of this kind by a submarine or aircraft.

crash hel·met ▶**n.** a helmet worn by a motorcyclist or a race car driver to protect the head in case of a crash.

crash·ing /ˈkraSHiNG/ ▶**adj.** informal complete; total (used for emphasis): *a crashing bore.* —**crash·ing·ly adv.**

crash-land ▶**v.** [intrans.] (of an aircraft) land in an emergency, typically without lowering the landing gear: [as n.] (**crash landing**) *a plane made a crash landing.*

crash-test ▶**v.** [trans.] crash (a vehicle) under controlled conditions to evaluate its ability to withstand impact. ▶**n.** (**crash test**) a test of this kind.

crash·wor·thy /ˈkraSHˌwərT͟Hē/ ▶**adj.** (of a vehicle or an aircraft) relatively able to withstand a crash. —**crash·wor·thi·ness n.**

crass /kras/ ▶**adj.** lacking sensitivity or due consideration: *crass assumptions that men make about women.* —**cras·si·tude** /ˈkrasiˌt(y)o͞od/ **n.** **crass·ly adv.** **crass·ness n.** [15th C. (in the sense 'dense or coarse (in constitution or texture)'): from L. *crassus* 'solid, thick.']

Cras·sus /ˈkrasəs/, Marcus Licinius (*c.*115–53 BC), Roman politician. He was part of the First Triumvirate 60 BC, along with Caesar and Pompey.

-crat ▶**comb. form** denoting a member or supporter of a particular form of government: *plutocrat* | *technocrat.* [from Fr. *-crate*, from adjectives ending in *-cratique* (see -CRATIC).]

crate /krāt/ ▶**n.** **1** a slatted wooden case used for transporting or storing goods. ■ a container divided into small individual units, used for transporting or storing bottles. **2** informal, dated an old and dilapidated vehicle. ▶**v.** [trans.] (often **be crated**) pack (something) in a crate. —**crate·ful** /ˈkrātˌfo͝ol/ **n.** (pl. **-fuls**). [ME: perh. rel. to Du. *krat* 'tailgate of a wagon,' earlier 'box of a coach,' of unknown origin.]

Cra·ter /ˈkrātər/ Astron. a faint southern constellation (the Cup), said to represent the goblet of Apollo.

cra·ter /ˈkrātər/ ▶**n.** **1** a large, bowl-shaped cavity in the ground or on the surface of a planet or the moon caused by an explosion, the impact of a meteorite, etc. ■ a large pit or hollow forming the mouth of a volcano. ■ a cavity or hole in any surface. **2** a large bowl used in ancient Greece for mixing wine. ▶**v.** [trans.] form a crater in (a surface): *the offensive power to crater the enemy's runways* | [as adj.] (**cratered**) *the heavily cratered moon.* [17th C.: via L. from Gk. *kratēr* 'mixing bowl,' from *krasis* 'mixture.']

Cra·ter Lake a lake that fills a volcanic crater in the Cascade Mountains in southwestern Oregon; 1,968 feet (600 m) deep.

-cratic ▶**comb. form** relating to a particular kind of government or rule: *democratic.* —**-cratically comb. form** in corresponding adverbs. [from Fr. *-cratique*, from *-cratie* (see -CRACY).]

C rations ▶**plural n.** a type of canned food formerly used by US soldiers. [C for *combat.*]

cra·vat /krəˈvat/ ▶**n.** a strip of fabric worn around the neck and tucked inside an open-necked shirt. —**cra·vat·ted adj.** [17th C.: from Fr. *cravate*, from *Cravate* 'Croat', because of the scarf worn by Croatian mercenaries in France.]

crave /krāv/ ▶**v.** [trans.] feel a powerful desire for (something): *give the infants the human touch they crave.* ■ dated ask for (something). —**crav·er n.** [OE *crafian* (in the sense 'demand, claim as a right'), of Gmc. origin; rel. to Swed. *kräva*, Dan. *kræve* 'demand.']

cra·ven /ˈkrāvən/ ▶**adj.** contemptibly lacking in courage; cowardly. —**cra·ven·ly adv.** **cra·ven·ness n.** [ME *cravant* 'defeated,' perh. via Anglo-Norman Fr. from OFr. *cravante*, past part. of *cravanter* 'crush, overwhelm,' based on L. *crepare* 'burst.']

crav·ing /ˈkrāviNG/ ▶**n.** a powerful desire for something.

craw /krô/ ▶**n.** dated the crop of a bird or insect. ■ esp. humorous the stomach of a person or animal.
– PHRASES **stick in one's craw** see STICK[2]. [ME: from or rel. to MDu. *crāghe* or Mid. Low Ger. *krage* 'neck, throat.']

craw·dad /ˈkrôˌdad/ ▶**n.** a freshwater crayfish. [20th C.: fanciful alt. of CRAWFISH.]

craw·fish /ˈkrôˌfiSH/ ▶**n.** (pl. same or **-fish·es**) a freshwater crayfish. ▶**v.** [intrans.] informal retreat from a position: *the networks, intimidated by the public outcry, had begun to crawfish.* [17th C.: var. of CRAYFISH.]

crawl /krôl/ ▶**v.** **1** [intrans.] (of a person) move on the hands and knees or by dragging the body close to the ground: *they crawled out from under the table.* ■ (of an insect or small animal) move slowly along a surface: *the spider was crawling up Nicky's arm.* ■ (of a vehicle) move at a very slow pace: *traffic was crawling along.* ■ swim using the crawl. ■ [intrans.] informal behave obsequiously or ingratiatingly in the hope of gaining favor: *don't come crawling back to me later.* **2** (**be crawling with**) be covered or crowded with insects or people, to an extent that is disgusting or objectionable: *the place was crawling with soldiers.* ▶**n.** [in sing.] **1** an act of moving on one's hands and knees or dragging one's body along the ground. ■ a slow rate of movement, typically that of a vehicle. **2** a swimming stroke involving alternate overarm movements and rapid kicks of the legs.
– PHRASES **make someone's skin crawl** see SKIN. —**crawl·y adj.** [ME: of unknown origin; possibly rel. to Swed. *kravla* and Dan. *kravle.*]

crawl·er /ˈkrôlər/ ▶**n.** a thing that crawls or moves at a slow pace, esp. an insect. ■ Comput. a program that searches the World Wide Web, typically in order to create an index of data.

crawl space ▶**n.** an area of limited height under a floor or roof, giving access to wiring and plumbing.

cray·fish /ˈkrāˌfiSH/ ▶**n.** (pl. same or **-fish·es**) a nocturnal freshwater crustacean (*Astacus*, *Cambarus*, and other genera) that resembles a small lobster and inhabits streams and rivers. ■ another term for SPINY

LOBSTER. [ME: from OFr. *crevice*, of Gmc. origin and rel. to Ger. *Krebs* (see CRAB[1]). In the 16th C. or earlier the second syllable was alt. by association with FISH[1].]

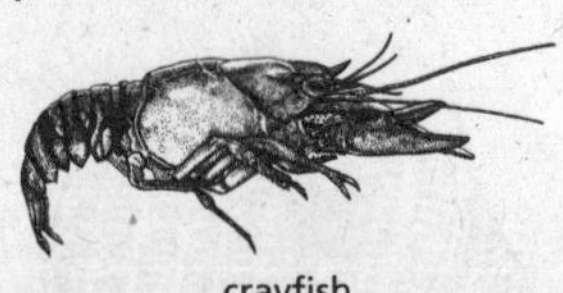

crayfish

cray·on /ˈkrāän; ˈkrāən/ ▶n. a pencil or stick of colored chalk or wax, used for drawing. ▶v. draw with a crayon or crayons. [17th C.: from Fr., from *craie* 'chalk,' from L. *creta*.]

craze /krāz/ ▶n. an enthusiasm for a particular activity or object that typically achieves widespread but short-lived popularity: *the craze for bungee jumping.* ▶v. [trans.] **1** [usu. as adj.] (**crazed**) wildly insane or excited: *a crazed killer* | [in comb.] *power-crazed dictators.* **2** (often **be crazed**) produce a network of fine cracks on (a surface): *frozen over but crazed with cracks.* ■ [intrans.] develop such cracks. [ME: perh. of Scand. origin and rel. to Swed. *krasa* 'crunch.']

cra·zy /ˈkrāzē/ informal ▶adj. (**-zi·er, -zi·est**) **1** mentally deranged, esp. as manifested in a wild or aggressive way: *Stella went crazy and assaulted a visitor.* ■ extremely annoyed or angry: *the noise was **driving me crazy.*** ■ foolish. **2** extremely enthusiastic: [in comb.] *a football-crazy bunch of boys.* **3** appearing absurdly out of place or in an unlikely position. ▶n. (pl. **-zies**) a mentally deranged person.
– PHRASES **like crazy** to a great degree. — **cra·zi·ly** /-zilē/ adv. **cra·zi·ness** n.

cra·zy bone ▶n. another term for FUNNY BONE.

Cra·zy Horse (*c.* 1849–77), Sioux Indian chief; Sioux name *Ta-Sunko-Witko*. He led the confederation that defeated General Custer at Little Bighorn in 1876.

cra·zy quilt ▶n. a patchwork quilt made with patches of varying sizes, shapes, colors, and fabrics.

CRC ▶abbr. ■ Print. camera-ready copy. ■ Civil Rights Commission. ■ Comput. cyclic redundancy check (or code).

creak /krēk/ ▶v. [intrans.] (of an object) make a harsh, high-pitched sound when moved or when pressure or weight is applied: *the stairs creaked* | [with complement] *the garden gate creaked open.* ■ fig. show weakness: *stock prices creaked to a mixed finish.* ▶n. a harsh scraping or squeaking sound. — **creak·ing·ly** adv. [ME (as a v. in the sense 'croak'): imitative.]

creak·y /ˈkrēkē/ ▶adj. (**creak·i·er, creak·i·est**) (of an object) making or liable to make a high-pitched sound when moved or weight is applied: *creaky stairs.* ■ (of a voice) making such a sound. ■ fig. appearing old-fashioned; decrepit: *a creaky legal system.* — **creak·i·ly** /-kəlē/ adv. **creak·i·ness** n.

cream /krēm/ ▶n. **1** the thick white or pale yellow fatty liquid that rises to the top on raw milk, used in cooking. ■ the part of a liquid that gathers at the top. ■ fig. the very best of a group: *the paper's readership is **the cream of** American society.* ■ a semisolid food containing cream or milk or having the consistency of cream. **2** a thick liquid or semisolid preparation applied to the skin: *shaving cream.* **3** a very pale yellow or off-white color. ▶v. [trans.] **1** work (butter) to form a smooth soft paste. ■ [usu. as adj.] (**creamed**) mix with milk or cream: *creamed turnips.* ■ add cream to (coffee). **2** informal defeat soundly, esp. in a sports contest. ■ (often **be creamed**) collide violently with (someone), esp. in a car: *she got creamed by a speeding car.* **3** [intrans.] vulgar slang (of a person) be sexually aroused, esp. to the point of producing sexual secretions. ■ [trans.] wet (one's underpants) from such arousal. [ME: from OFr. *cresme*, from a blend of late L. *cramum* (prob. of Gaulish origin) and eccles. L. *chrisma* (see CHRISM).]

cream cheese ▶n. soft, rich cheese made from unskimmed milk and cream.

cream·er /ˈkrēmər/ ▶n. **1** a cream or milk substitute for adding to coffee or tea. **2** a small container for cream. **3** hist. a dish used for skimming cream off milk. ■ a machine used for separating cream from milk.

cream·er·y /ˈkrēmərē/ ▶n. (pl. **-er·ies**) a place where butter and cheese are produced. ■ dated a shop where dairy products are sold.

cream of tar·tar ▶n. a white, crystalline, acidic compound, $HOOC(CHOH)_2COOK$, obtained as a by-product of wine fermentation and used chiefly in baking powder.

cream puff ▶n. **1** a light pastry filled with cream. **2** informal a weak or ineffectual person. ■ [as adj.] denoting something of little consequence or difficulty: *a cream-puff assignment.* **3** informal a used car or other item in excellent condition.

cream so·da ▶n. a carbonated, vanilla-flavored soft drink.

cream·y /ˈkrēmē/ ▶adj. (**cream·i·er, cream·i·est**) resembling cream in consistency or color: *beat eggs until creamy* | *creamy white flowers.* ■ containing a lot of cream: *a creamy dressing.* — **cream·i·ly** /-məlē/ adv. **cream·i·ness** n.

crease /krēs/ ▶n. **1** a line or ridge produced by folding, pressing, or crushing: *trousers with creases.* ■ a wrinkle or furrow in the skin, typically of the face, caused by age or a particular facial expression. **2** (usu. **the crease**) an area around the goal in ice hockey or lacrosse. ▶v. [trans.] **1** make a crease in (cloth or paper): *he was careful not to crease his dinner jacket* | [as adj.] (**creased**) *a creased piece of paper.* ■ cause a crease to appear temporarily in (the face or its features), typically as a result of the expression of an emotion: *a frown creased her forehead.* **2** (of a bullet) graze (someone or something), causing little damage. [16th C.: prob. a var. of CREST.]

cre·ate /krēˈāt/ ▶v. [trans.] bring (something) into existence: *he created a lake* | *170 jobs were created.* ■ cause (something) to happen as a result of one's actions: *divorce only created problems for children.* ■ [trans.] invest (someone) with a new rank or title: *he was created a baronet.* [ME: from L. *creat-* 'produced,' from the v. *creare*.]

cre·a·tine /ˈkrēəˌtēn; ˈkrēətn/ ▶n. Biochem. a compound, $C_4H_9N_3O_2$, formed in protein metabolism and present in much living tissue. It is involved in the supply of energy for muscular contraction. [19th C.: formed irregularly from Gk. *kreas* 'meat' + -INE[4].]

cre·a·tine phos·phate ▶n. another term for PHOSPHOCREATINE.

cre·at·i·nine /krēˈatnˌēn; -in/ ▶n. Biochem. a compound, $C_4H_7N_3O$, the anhydride of creatine, that is excreted in the urine.

cre·a·tion /krēˈāsʜən/ ▶n. **1** the action or process of bringing something into existence: *job creation.* ■ a thing made or invented, esp. something showing artistic talent. **2** (**the Creation**) the bringing into existence the universe, esp. when regarded as an act of God. ■ everything so created; the universe. **3** the action or process of investing someone with a new rank or title.

cre·a·tion·ism /krēˈāsʜəˌnizəm/ ▶n. the belief that the universe and living organisms originate from divine creation, as in the biblical account, rather than by processes such as evolution. ■ another term for CREATION SCIENCE. — **cre·a·tion·ist** n. & adj.

cre·a·tion sci·ence ▶n. the interpretation of scientific knowledge in accord with belief in the Bible, esp. the creation of matter, life, and humankind in six days.

cre·a·tive /krēˈātiv/ ▶adj. relating to or involving the imagination or original ideas, esp. in the production of an artistic work: *creative writing.* ■ (of a person) having good imagination or original ideas: *Homer, the creative genius of Greek epic.* ▶n. a person who is creative, esp. in a professional context. — **cre·a·tive·ly** adv. **cre·a·tive·ness** n.

cre·a·tive ac·count·ing ▶n. informal the use of loopholes in financial regulation in order to gain advantage or present figures in a misleadingly favorable light.

cre·a·tiv·i·ty /ˌkrēāˈtivitē/ ▶n. the use of the imagination or original ideas, esp. in the production of an artistic work.

cre·a·tor /krēˈātər/ ▶n. a person or thing that brings something into existence. ■ (**the Creator**) used as a name for God.

crea·ture /ˈkrēcʜər/ ▶n. an animal, as distinct from a human being. ■ an animal or person. ■ a fictional or imaginary being, typically a frightening one. ■ [with adj.] a person of a specified kind, typically one viewed with pity, contempt, or desire: *you heartless creature!* ■ a person or organization under the control of another: *the teacher was the creature of his employer.*
– PHRASES **creature of habit** a person who follows an unvarying routine. [ME (in the sense 'something created'): via OFr. from late L. *creatura*, from the v. *creare* (see CREATE).]

crea·ture com·forts ▶plural n. material comforts that contribute to physical ease and well-being, such as good food and accommodations.

crèche /kresʜ/ ▶n. a model or tableau representing the scene of Jesus Christ's birth. [18th C.: Fr.]

Cré·cy, Battle of /krāˈsē/ a battle between the English and the French in 1346 near the village of Crécy-en-Ponthieu in Picardy, the first major English victory of the Hundred Years War.

cred /kred/ ▶n. informal term for STREET CREDIBILITY.

cre·dal /ˈkrēdl/ (also **creed·al**) ▶adj. of or relating to a statement of Christian or other religious belief.

cre·dence /ˈkrēdns/ ▶n. **1** acceptance of something as true: *psychoanalysis finds little credence among laymen.* ■ the likelihood of being true; plausibility: *being called upon as an expert **lends credence** to one's opinions.* **2** [usu. as adj.] a small side table, shelf, or niche in a church for holding the elements of the Eucharist before they are consecrated: *a credence table.*
– PHRASES **give credence to** accept as true. [ME: via OFr. from med. L. *credentia*, from L. *credent-* 'believing,' from the v. *credere*.]

cre·den·tial /krəˈdencʜəl/ ▶n. (usu. **credentials**) a qualification, achievement, personal quality, etc., used to indicate suitability for something: *academic credentials.* ■ a document or certificate proving a person's identity or qualifications. ■ a letter of introduction given by a government to an ambassador before a new posting. [ME: from med. L. *credentialis*, from *credentia* (see CREDENCE).]

cre·den·za /krəˈdenzə/ ▶n. a sideboard or cupboard. [19th C.: Ital., from med. L. *credentia* (see CREDENCE).]

cred·i·bil·i·ty /ˌkredəˈbilitē/ ▶n. the quality of being trusted: *the government's loss of credibility.* ■ the quality of being convincing or believable: *the book's anecdotes have scant regard for credibility.* ■ another term for STREET CREDIBILITY.

cred·i·bil·i·ty gap ▶n. an apparent difference between what is said or promised and what happens or is true. ■ a lack of trust in a person's or institution's statements and motives: *the enemy is a continuing credibility gap.*

cred·i·ble /'kredəbəl/ ▶**adj.** able to be believed; convincing. ■ capable of persuading people that something will happen or be successful: *a credible threat.* —**cred·i·bly** /-blē/ **adv.** [ME: from L. *credibilis*, from *credere* 'believe.']

cred·it /'kredit/ ▶**n.** **1** the ability to obtain goods or services before payment, based on the trust that payment will be made in the future: *unlimited credit.* ■ the money made available in such an arrangement: *the bank refused to extend credit* | [as adj.] *exceeding his credit limit.* **2** an entry recording a sum received, listed on the right-hand column of an account. The opposite of DEBIT. ■ a payment received. **3** public acknowledgment or praise given or received when responsibility for an action or idea is apparent: *the president claims credit for each accomplishment.* ■ [in sing.] a source of pride, typically someone or something that reflects well on another person or organization: *he's a credit to his mother.* ■ (usu. **credits**) an acknowledgment of a contributor's services to a creative work, typically a list that is scrolled down the screen at the beginning or end of a movie or program. **4** the acknowledgment of a student's completion of a course that counts toward a degree or diploma. ■ a unit of study counting toward a degree or diploma: *he earned 17 credits.* ■ acknowledgment of merit in an examination which is reflected in the grades awarded: *students receive credit for accuracy.* **5** good reputation: *a citizen of credit and renown.* ▶**v.** (**cred·it·ed, cred·it·ing**) [trans.] (often **be credited**) **1** publicly acknowledge someone as a participant in the production of (something published or broadcast): *the screenplay is credited to two Japanese writers.* ■ (**credit someone with**) ascribe (an achievement or quality) to someone: *credited with painting one hundred canvases.* **2** add (an amount of money) to an account: *this deferred tax can be credited to the profit and loss account.* **3** believe (something surprising or unlikely): *you would hardly credit it—but it was true.*

– PHRASES **credit where credit is due** praise given when it is deserved. **do someone credit** (or **do credit to someone**) make someone worthy of praise or respect: *your concern does you credit.* **give someone credit for** commend someone for (a quality or achievement), esp. with reluctance or surprise. **have something to one's credit** have achieved something notable: *65 tournament wins to his credit.* **on credit** with an arrangement to pay later. **on the credit side** as a good aspect of the situation: *on the credit side, the text is highly readable.* **to one's credit** used to indicate that something praiseworthy has been achieved, esp. despite difficulties: *to her credit, she never betrayed a confidence.* [16th C.: from Fr. *crédit*, prob. via Ital. *credito* from L. *creditum*, neut. past part. of *credere* 'believe, trust.']

cred·it·a·ble /'kreditəbəl/ ▶**adj.** (of an effort or action) deserving acknowledgment and praise but not necessarily successful: *a creditable 2–4 defeat.* —**cred·it·a·bil·i·ty** /ˌkreditə'bilitē/ **n.** **cred·it·a·bly adv.**

cred·it an·a·lyst ▶**n.** a person employed to assess the credit rating of people or companies.

cred·it bu·reau ▶**n.** a company that collects the credit ratings of individuals and makes them available to credit card companies, financial institutions, etc.

cred·it card ▶**n.** a plastic card issued by a bank, business, etc., for the purchase of goods or services on credit.

cred·it line ▶**n.** another term for LINE OF CREDIT (see LINE[1]).

cred·i·tor /'kreditər/ ▶**n.** a person or company to whom money is owed.

cred·it rat·ing ▶**n.** an estimate of the ability to fulfill financial commitments, based on previous dealings. ■ the process of assessing this.

cred·it un·ion ▶**n.** a nonprofit financial cooperative offering deposit accounts, low-interest loans, etc.

cred·it·worth·y /'kreditˌwərT͟Hē/ ▶**adj.** considered suitable to receive credit, esp. because of being reliable in paying money back in the past. —**cred·it·wor·thi·ness n.**

cre·do /'krēdō; 'krādō/ ▶**n.** (pl. **-dos**) a statement of the beliefs or aims that guide someone's actions: *he announced his credo in his first editorial.* ■ (**Credo**) a Christian creed in Latin. ■ (**Credo**) a musical setting of the Nicene Creed. [ME: L., 'I believe.' Cf. CREED.]

cre·du·li·ty /krə'd(y)o͞olitē/ ▶**n.** a tendency to be too ready to believe that something is real or true.

cred·u·lous /'krejələs/ ▶**adj.** having or showing too great a readiness to believe things. —**cred·u·lous·ly adv.** **cred·u·lous·ness n.** [16th C.: from L. *credulus* (from *credere* 'believe') + -OUS.]

Cree /krē/ ▶**n.** (pl. same or **Crees**) **1** a member of an American Indian people living in central Canada. **2** the Algonquian language of this people. ▶**adj.** of or relating to the Cree or their language. [from Canad. Fr. *Cris*, abbrev. of *Cristinaux*, from Algonquian *kiriš̆tinō*.]

creed /krēd/ ▶**n.** a system of Christian or other religious belief; a faith. ■ (often **the Creed**) a formal statement of Christian beliefs, esp. the Apostles' Creed or the Nicene Creed. ■ a set of beliefs or aims that guide someone's actions: *a political creed.* [OE, from L. CREDO.]

creed·al /'krēdl/ ▶**adj.** var. of CREDAL.

Creek /krēk/ ▶**n.** (pl. same) **1** a member of a confederacy of native peoples of the southeastern US in the 16th to 19th centuries whose descendants now live mainly in Oklahoma. **2** the Muskogean language of this confederacy. ▶**adj.** of, relating to, or denoting this confederacy. [from CREEK.]

creek /krēk; krik/ ▶**n.** a stream, brook, or minor tributary of a river. ■ an inlet, a channel, or other narrow waterway.

– PHRASES **be up the creek** informal (also **be up the creek without a paddle**) be in severe trouble, esp. with no clear solution. **be up shit creek** see SHIT. [ME: from OFr. *crique* or from ON *kriki* 'nook.']

creel /krēl/ ▶**n.** **1** a wicker basket for carrying fish. **2** a rack holding bobbins or spools for spinning. [ME: of unknown origin. Sense 2 (perh. the same word) dates from the mid 19th C.]

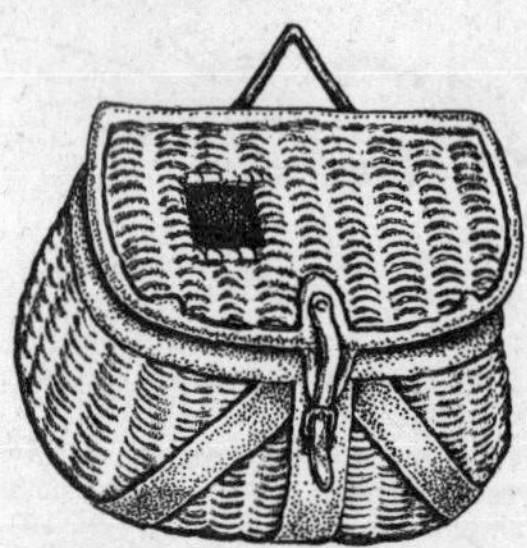

creel 1

creep /krēp/ ▶**v.** (past and past part. **crept** /krept/) [intrans.] **1** [usu. with adverbial of direction] move slowly and carefully, esp. in order to avoid being heard or noticed: *they were taught how to creep up on an enemy.* ■ (of a thing) move very slowly at a steady pace: *the fog was creeping up from the marsh.* ■ (of a plant) grow along the ground or other surface by means of extending stems or branches: [as adj.] (**creeping**) *creeping rhizomes.* ■ (of a plastic solid) undergo gradual deformation under stress. **2** (**creep in/into**) (of an unwanted characteristic or fact) occur gradually and almost imperceptibly: *errors crept into his game* | [as adj.] (**creeping**) *creeping centralization of power.* ■ (**creep up**) increase slowly but steadily: *interest rates have been creeping up.* ▶**n.** **1** informal a detestable person. **2** slow movement at a steady pace: *this slow creep of costs.* ■ the tendency of a car with automatic transmission to move when in gear without the accelerator being pressed. ■ the gradual downward movement of disintegrated rock or soil due to gravity: *stones slip down the slopes by soil creep.* ■ the gradual deformation of a plastic solid under stress.

– PHRASES **give someone the creeps** informal induce a feeling of revulsion or fear in someone. [OE *crēopan* 'move with the body close to the ground,' of Gmc. origin; rel. to Du. *kruipen*.]

creep·er /'krēpər/ ▶**n.** **1** Bot. any plant that grows along the ground, around another plant, or up a wall by means of extending stems or branches. **2** [with adj.] any of a number of small birds that creep around in trees, vegetation, etc., including the North American **brown creeper** (*Certhia americana*, family Certhiidae). **3** a low, wheeled platform on which a mechanic lies while working on the underside of a motor vehicle.

creep·ing Char·lie /'krēpiNG/ ▶**n.** a creeping or trailing plant, in particular: ■ another term for MONEYWORT. ■ another term for GROUND IVY.

creep·ing Jen·ny ▶**n.** another term for MONEYWORT.

creep·y /'krēpē/ ▶**adj.** (**creep·i·er, creep·i·est**) informal causing fear or unease: *creepy feelings in a strange house.* —**creep·i·ly** /-pəlē/ **adv.** **creep·i·ness n.**

creese ▶**n.** archaic spelling of KRIS.

cre·mate /'krēmāt; kri'māt/ ▶**v.** [trans.] (usu. **be cremated**) dispose of (a dead body) by burning it to ashes. —**cre·ma·tion** /kri'māSHən/ **n.** [19th C. (as *cremation*): from L. *cremare* 'burn.']

cre·ma·to·ry /'krēməˌtôrē; 'krem-/ (also **crematorium** /ˌkrēmə'tôrēəm; ˌkrem-/) ▶**n.** (pl. **-ries**) a place where a dead person's body is cremated. ▶**adj.** of or relating to cremation. [19th C.: mod. L., from *cremare* 'burn.']

crème an·glaise /ˌkrem äNG'glez; -'glāz/ ▶**n.** a rich egg custard. [Fr., lit. 'English cream.']

crème brû·lée /ˌkrem bro͞o'lā/ ▶**n.** (pl. **crèmes brû·lées** pronunc. same, or **crème brû·lées** /bro͞o'lāz/) a dessert of custard topped with caramelized sugar. [19th C.: Fr., lit. 'burned cream.']

crème car·a·mel /ˌkrem karə'mel; 'karəˌmel/ ▶**n.** (pl. **crèmes car·a·mel** pronunc. same, or **crème car·a·mels** /-'melz; -ˌmelz/) a custard dessert made with whipped cream and eggs, topped with caramel. [20th C.: Fr., lit. 'caramel custard.']

crème de ca·ca·o /ˌkrem də kə'kou; 'kōkō/ ▶**n.** a chocolate-flavored liqueur. [20th C.: Fr., lit. 'cream of cacao.']

crème de cas·sis /ˌkrem də ka'sēs/ ▶**n.** see CASSIS. [Fr., lit. 'cream of black currant.']

crème de la crème /ˌkrem də lə 'krem/ ▶**n.** the best of a particular kind: *the crème de la crème of the dancers.* [19th C.: Fr., lit. 'cream of the cream.']

crème de menthe /ˌkrēm də 'menTH; 'mint; ˌkrēm/ ▶**n.** a peppermint-flavored liqueur. [20th C.: Fr., lit. 'cream of mint.']

crème fraiche /ˌkrem 'fresH/ ▶**n.** a thick cream made from heavy cream with the addition of buttermilk, sour cream, or yogurt. [from Fr. *crème fraîche*, lit. 'fresh cream.']

Cre·mo·na /krə'mōnə/ a city in northern Italy, in Lombardy; pop. 75,160; famous for violins made between the 16th and 18th centuries.

cre·nate /'krēnāt/ ▶**adj.** Bot. & Zool. (esp. of a leaf or shell) having a round-toothed or scalloped edge. Compare with CRENULATE. —**cre·nat·ed adj.** **cre·na·tion** /kri'nāSHən/ **n.** [18th C. (earlier as *crenated*): from mod. L.

crenatus, from pop. L. *crena* 'notch.']

cren·el /'krenl/ (also **cre·nelle** /krə'nel/) ▶ **n.** an indentation in the battlements of a fort or castle, used for shooting or firing missiles through. [15th C.: from OFr., based on pop. L. *crena* 'notch.']

cren·el·late /'krenl,āt/ (also **cren·e·late**) ▶ **v.** [trans.] [as adj.] **(crenellated)** esp. hist. provide (a wall) with battlements.

cren·el·la·tions /,krenl'āsнən z/ ▶ **plural n.** the battlements of a castle or other building.

cren·u·late /'krenyəlit; -yə,lāt/ ▶ **adj.** tech. (esp. of a leaf, shell, or shoreline) having a finely scalloped or notched outline or edge. Compare with **CRENATE**. —**cren·u·lat·ed adj. cren·u·la·tion** /,krenyə'lāsнən/ **n.** [18th C.: from mod. L. *crenulatus*, from *crenula*, dimin. of *crena* 'notch.']

cre·o·dont /'krēə,dänt/ ▶ **n.** a carnivorous mammal (order Creodonta) of the early Tertiary period, ancestral to modern carnivores. [19th C.: from mod. L. *Creodonta* (pl.), from Gk. *kreas* 'flesh' + *odous, odont-* 'tooth.']

Cre·ole /'krēōl/ (also **cre·ole**) ▶ **n. 1** a person of mixed European and black descent, esp. in the Caribbean. ■ a descendant of European settlers in the Caribbean or Central or South America. ■ a white descendant of French settlers in Louisiana and other parts of the southern US. **2** a tongue formed from the contact of two unrelated languages: *a Portuguese-based Creole.* ▶ **adj.** of or relating to a Creole or Creoles. —**cre·o·li·za·tion** /,krēələ'zāsнən/ **n. cre·o·lize** /'krēə,līz/ **v.** [from Fr. *créole, criole*, from Sp. *criollo*, prob. from Port. *crioulo* 'black person born in Brazil, home-born slave,' from *criar* 'to breed,' from L. *creare* 'produce, create.']

cre·o·sol /'krēə,sôl; -,sōl/ ▶ **n.** Chem. a colorless liquid, $C_8H_{10}O_2$, that is the chief constituent of wood-tar creosote.

cre·o·sote /'krēə,sōt/ ▶ **n.** a dark brown oil distilled from coal tar and used as a wood preservative. ■ a colorless, pungent, oily liquid, containing creosol and other compounds, distilled from wood tar and used as an antiseptic. ▶ **v.** [trans.] treat (wood) with creosote. [19th C.: coined in Ger. from Gk. *kreas* 'flesh' + *sōtēr* 'preserver,' with ref. to its antiseptic properties.]

cre·o·sote bush ▶ **n.** a shrub (*Larrea tridentata*, family Zygophyllaceae) native to arid parts of Mexico and the western US with leaves that smell of creosote.

crepe (also **crêpe**) ▶ **n. 1** /krāp/ a light, thin fabric with a wrinkled surface: [as adj.] *a crepe bandage.* ■ (also **crepe rubber**) hard-wearing wrinkled rubber, used esp. for the soles of shoes. **2** /krāp/ black silk, formerly used for mourning clothes. **3** /krāp; krep/ a thin pancake. —**crep·ey adj.** [18th C.: Fr., from OFr. *crespe* 'curled, frizzed,' from L. *crispus*.]

crepe de chine /,krāp də 'sнēn/ (also **crepe de Chine**) ▶ **n.** a fine crepe of silk or similar fabric. [19th C.: Fr., lit. 'crêpe of China.']

crepe myr·tle ▶ **n.** var. of **CRAPE MYRTLE**.

crepe pa·per ▶ **n.** thin, crinkled paper resembling crepe, used esp. for making decorations.

crêpe su·zette /,krāp so͝o'zet/ ▶ **n.** (pl. **crêpes su·zette** pronunc. same) a dessert of crepes flamed and served in alcohol.

crep·i·tate /'krepə,tāt/ ▶ **v.** [intrans.] make a crackling sound: *the night crepitates with a whistling cacophony* | [as adj.] **(crepitating)** *crepitating electricity.* [17th C. (in the sense 'break wind'): from L. *crepitat-* 'crackled, rustled,' from the v. *crepitare*, from *crepare* 'to rattle.']

crep·i·ta·tion /,krepə'tāsнən/ ▶ **n.** a crackling or rattling sound. ■ Med. a crackling sound made in breathing by a person with an inflamed lung.

crep·i·tus /'krepətəs/ ▶ **n.** Med. a grating sound or sensation produced by friction between bone and cartilage or the fractured parts of a bone. ■ the production of crepitations in the lungs; rale. [19th C.: from L., from *crepare* 'rattle.']

cré·pon /'krāpän/ ▶ **n.** a fabric resembling crepe, but heavier and with a more pronounced crinkled effect. [19th C.: Fr.]

crept /krept/ past and past participle of **CREEP**.

cre·pus·cu·lar /krə'pəskyələr/ ▶ **adj.** of, resembling, or relating to twilight. ■ Zool. (of an animal) appearing or active in twilight. [17th C.: from L. *crepusculum* 'twilight' + **-AR**[1].]

cre·pus·cule /kri'pəskyo͞ol/ ▶ **n.** the period of partial darkness at the beginning or end of the day; twilight.

cresc. (also **cres.**) Music ▶ **abbr.** crescendo.

cre·scen·do /krə'sнendō/ ▶ **n.** (pl. **-dos** or **-di** /-dē/) Music a gradual increase in loudness. ■ Music a passage of music performed in this way. ■ the loudest point reached in a gradually increasing sound: *her voice was rising to a crescendo.* ■ a progressive increase in force or intensity: *a crescendo of misery.* ■ the most intense point reached in this; a climax. ▶ **adv. & adj.** Music with a gradual increase in loudness: [as adj.] *a crescendo kettledrum roll.* ▶ **v.** **(-does, -doed)** [intrans.] increase in loudness or intensity: *the cheers began to crescendo.* [18th C.: Ital., pres. part. of *crescere* 'to increase,' from L. *crescere* 'grow.']

cres·cent /'kresənt/ ▶ **n. 1** the curved sickle shape of the waxing or waning moon. ■ a representation of such a shape used as an emblem of Islam or Turkey. ■ **(the Crescent)** esp. hist. the political power of Islam or the Ottoman Empire. **2** a thing that has the shape of a single curve, esp. one that is broad in the center and tapers to a point at each end: *a three-mile crescent of golden sand.* ▶ **adj. 1** [attrib.] in the shape of a crescent: *a crescent moon.* **2** literary growing, increasing, or developing. —**cres·cen·tic** /krə'sentik/ **adj.** [ME *cressant*, from OFr. *creissant*, from L. *crescere* 'grow.']

cres·cent wrench ▶ **n.** an adjustable wrench with a crescent-shaped head.

cre·sol /'krēsôl; -sōl/ ▶ **n.** Chem. each of three isomeric crystalline compounds, $CH_3C_6H_4OH$, present in coal-tar creosote, used as disinfectants. [19th C.: from **CREOSOTE** + **-OL**.]

cress /kres/ ▶ **n.** a plant (*Barbarea* and other genera) of the cabbage family, typically having small white flowers and pungent, often edible leaves. [OE *cresse, cærse*, of West Gmc. origin; rel. to Du. *kers* and Ger. *Kresse*.]

Cres·si·da /'kresədə/ (in medieval legends of the Trojan War) the daughter of Calchas, a priest.

crest /krest/ ▶ **n. 1** a comb or tuft of feathers, fur, or skin on the head of a bird or other animal. ■ a thing resembling this, esp. a plume on a helmet. **2** the top of something, esp. a mountain or hill. ■ the curling top of a wave. ■ Anat. a ridge on the surface of a bone. ■ the ridge on the neck of a horse or other mammal. **3** Heraldry a distinctive device borne above the shield of a coat of arms, or reproduced on writing paper or silverware, to represent a family or corporate body. ▶ **v.** [trans.] reach the top of (something such as a hill or wave): *she crested a hill.* ■ [intrans.] (of a river) rise to its highest level: *the river was expected to crest at eight feet above flood stage.* ■ [intrans.] (of a wave) form a curling top. ■ **(be crested)** have attached at the top: *his helmet was* ***crested with*** *spikes.* [ME: from OFr. *creste*, from L. *crista* 'tuft, plume.']

crest·ed /'krestid/ ▶ **adj. 1** (of a bird or other animal) having a comb or tuft of feathers, fur, or skin on the head: [in comb.] *a plush-crested jay.* **2** emblazoned with a coat of arms or other emblem.

crest·fal·len /'krest,fôlən/ ▶ **adj.** sad and disappointed. [16th C.: lit. having a fallen crest.]

cres·yl /'kresəl; -sil/ ▶ **n.** [as adj.] Chem. of or denoting a radical $-OC_6H_4CH_3$, derived from a cresol.

Cre·ta·ceous /krə'tāsнəs/ ▶ **adj.** Geol. of, relating to, or denoting the last period of the Mesozoic era, between the Jurassic and Tertiary periods. ■ [as n.] **(the Cretaceous)** the Cretaceous period, from about 146 million to 65 million years ago, or the system of rocks deposited during it. The first flowering plants emerged, and the dinosaurs died out abruptly toward the end of it. [17th C.: from L. *cretaceus* (from *creta* 'chalk') + **-OUS**.]

Cre·ta·ceous–Ter·ti·ar·y bound·a·ry (also **K/T boundary**) Geol. the division between the Cretaceous and Tertiary periods, about 65 million years ago.

Crete /krēt/ a Greek island in the eastern Mediterranean Sea. Greek name **KRÍTI**. —**Cre·tan** /'krētn/ **adj. & n.**

cre·tic /'krētik/ ▶ **n.** Pros. a metrical foot containing one short or unstressed syllable between two long or stressed ones. [16th C.: from L. *Creticus*, from Gk. *Krētikos*, from *Krētē* 'Crete.']

cre·tin /'krētn/ ▶ **n.** a stupid person (used as a general term of abuse). ■ Med., dated a person deformed and mentally handicapped due to a congenital thyroid deficiency. —**cre·tin·ism n. cre·tin·ous** /-tn-əs/ **adj.** [18th C.: from French *crétin*, from Swiss Fr. *crestin* 'Christian' (from L. *Christianus*).]

cre·tonne /'krētän; kri'tän/ ▶ **n.** a heavy cotton fabric, typically with a floral pattern, used for upholstery. [19th C.: from Fr., of unknown origin.]

Creutz·feldt–Ja·kob dis·ease /'kroitsfelt 'yäkôb/ ▶ **n.** a fatal degenerative disease affecting nerve cells in the brain, causing sensory disturbances, dementia, and seizures. [1930s: named after H. G. *Creutzfeldt* (1885–1964) and A. *Jakob* (1882–1927), German neurologists.]

cre·vasse /krə'vas/ ▶ **n.** a deep open crack, esp. one in a glacier. ■ a breach in the embankment of a river or canal. [19th C.: from Fr., from OFr. *crevace* (see **CREVICE**).]

crev·ice /'krevis/ ▶ **n.** a narrow opening or fissure, esp. in a rock or wall. [ME: from OFr. *crevace*, from *crever* 'to burst,' from L. *crepare* 'to rattle, crack.']

crew /kro͞o/ ▶ **n.** [treated as sing. or pl.] a group of people who operate a vessel, aircraft, spacecraft, or train. ■ such a group other than the officers. ■ the group that rows a racing shell. ■ the sport of rowing a racing shell. ■ a group of people who work closely together, in a job that is technically difficult: *an ambulance crew.* ■ informal, a group of people associated in some way: *a crew of computer geeks.* ▶ **v.** [trans.] (often **be crewed**) provide (a craft or vehicle) with people to operate it: *the boat is crewed by 5 people.* ■ [intrans.] act as a member of a crew: *I've never crewed for a world-famous yachtsman before.* —**crew·man** /'kro͞omən/ **n.** (pl. **-men**). [ME: from OFr. *creue* 'augmentation, increase,' fem. past part. of *croistre* 'grow,' from L. *crescere*.]

crew cut ▶ **n.** a very short haircut for men and boys.

crew·el /'kro͞oəl/ ▶ **n.** a thin, loosely twisted, worsted yarn used for tapestry and embroidery. [15th C.: of unknown origin.]

crew·el work ▶ **n.** embroidery or tapestry done with crewel yarn on linen cloth.

crew neck ▶ **n.** a close-fitting, round neckline, esp. on a sweater or T-shirt: [as adj.] *a crew-neck sweater.* ■ a sweater with such a neckline.

crib /krib/ ▶ **n. 1** a young child's bed with barred or latticed sides. ■ a barred container for animal fodder; a manger. **2** informal a translation of a text for use by students. ■ a thing that has been plagiarized: *is the* *song a crib from Mozart's "Don Giovanni?"* **3** short for CRIBBAGE. ■ the cards discarded by the players at cribbage, counting to the dealer. **4** (also **crib·work**) a heavy timber framework used in foundations for a building or to line a mine shaft. ▶ v. (**cribbed, crib·bing**) [trans.] informal copy (another work) illicitly or without acknowledgment: *he didn't want anybody to crib the answers from him* | [intrans.] *he **cribbed** from other researchers.* ■ archaic steal. — **crib·ber** /'kribər/ n. [OE (in the sense 'manger'), of Gmc. origin; rel. to Du. *krib, kribbe* and Ger. *Krippe*.]

crib·bage /'kribij/ ▶ n. a card game for two to four players, in which the objective is to play so that the value of one's cards played reaches exactly 15 or 31. [17th C.: rel. to CRIB.]

crib·bage board ▶ n. a board with pegs and holes, used for scoring at cribbage.

crib death ▶ n. informal term for SUDDEN INFANT DEATH SYNDROME.

crib·ri·form /'kribrə,fôrm/ ▶ adj. Anat. a perforated anatomical structure, in particular the plate of the ethmoid bone through which the olfactory nerves pass. [18th C.: from L. *cribrum* 'sieve' + -IFORM.]

crib·work /'krib,wərk/ ▶ n. see CRIB (sense 5).

Crick /krik/, Francis Harry Compton (1916–2004), English biophysicist. With J. D. Watson, he proposed the double helix structure of the DNA molecule. Nobel Prize for Physiology or Medicine (1962, shared with Watson and M. H. F. Wilkins).

crick[1] /krik/ ▶ n. a pain or stiffness in the neck or back. ▶ v. [trans.] strain (one's neck or back), causing painful stiffness: [as adj.] (**cricked**) *a cricked neck.* [ME: of unknown origin.]

crick[2] ▶ n. dialect creek.

crick·et[1] /'krikit/ ▶ n. an insect (family Gryllidae) related to the grasshoppers. The male produces a characteristic rhythmical chirping sound. See illustration at FIELD CRICKET. [ME: from OFr. *criquet*, from *criquer* 'to crackle,' of imitative origin.]

crick·et[2] ▶ n. an outdoor game played on a large grass field with ball, bats, and two wickets, between teams of eleven players, the object of the game being to score more runs than the opposition.
– PHRASES **not cricket** Brit., informal a thing contrary to traditional standards of fairness or rectitude. — **crick·et·er** n. **crick·et·ing** adj. [16th C.: of unknown origin.]

crick·et[3] ▶ n. a low stool, typically with a rectangular or oval seat and four legs splayed out.

cri·coid /'krīkoid/ ▶ n. (also **cricoid cartilage**) Anat. the ring-shaped cartilage of the larynx. [18th C.: from mod. L. *cricoides* 'ring-shaped,' from Gk. *krikoeidēs*, from *krikos* 'ring.']

cri de cœur /,krē də 'kər/ ▶ n. (pl. **cris de cœur** /,krē(z)/) a passionate appeal, complaint, or protest. [20th C.: Fr., lit. 'cry from the heart.']

cried /krīd/ past and past participle of CRY.

cri·er /'krīər/ ▶ n. an officer who makes public announcements in a court of justice. ■ short for TOWN CRIER. ■ a person who shouts out announcements about their wares; a hawker. [ME: from OFr. *criere*, from *crier* 'to shout.']

cri·key /'krīkē/ ▶ exclam. Brit., informal an expression of surprise: *Crikey! I never thought I'd see you again.* [19th C.: euphemism for CHRIST.]

crime /krīm/ ▶ n. an action or omission that constitutes an offense that may be prosecuted by the state and is punishable by law: *shoplifting was a serious crime.* ■ illegal activities: *the victims of crime.* ■ an action or activity that, although not illegal, is considered to be evil, shameful, or wrong: *a crime against humanity* | [with infin.] *it's a crime to keep a creature in a tank.* [ME (in the sense 'wickedness, sin'): via OFr. from L. *crimen* 'judgment, offense,' based on *cernere* 'to judge.']

Cri·me·a /krī'mēə/ (usu. **the Crimea**) a peninsula in Ukraine between the Sea of Azov and the Black Sea. — **Cri·me·an** adj.

Cri·me·an War /krī'mēən/ a war (1853–56) in which an alliance of Great Britain, France, Sardinia, and Turkey defeated Russia.

crime-fight·ing ▶ n. the action of working to reduce the incidence of crime. — **crime-fight·er** n.

crime pas·si·on·nel /,krēm ,pasyə'nel/ ▶ n. (pl. **crimes pas·si·on·nels** pronunc. same) a crime, typically a murder, committed in a fit of sexual jealousy. [20th C.: Fr., lit. 'crime of passion.']

crime wave ▶ n. a sudden increase in the number of crimes committed in a country or area.

crime writ·er ▶ n. a writer of detective stories or thrillers.

crim·i·nal /'krimənl/ ▶ n. a person who has committed a crime. ▶ adj. of or relating to a crime: *criminal damage.* ■ Law of or relating to crime as opposed to civil matters: *a criminal court.* ■ informal (of an action or situation) deplorable and shocking. — **crim·i·nal·i·ty** /,krimə'nalitē/ n. **crim·i·nal·ly** adv. [ME (as an adj.): from late L. *criminalis*, from L. *crimen, crimin-* (see CRIME).]

crim·i·nal·ize /'krimənl,īz/ ▶ v. [trans.] make (an activity) illegal: *the law that criminalizes assisted suicide.* ■ make (someone) a criminal by making their activities illegal: *these punitive measures would criminalize travelers.* — **crim·i·nal·i·za·tion** /,krimənl-ə'zāshən/ n.

crim·i·nal jus·tice sys·tem ▶ n. the system of law enforcement that is involved in apprehending, prosecuting, defending, sentencing, and incarcerating those suspected of or charged with criminal offenses.

crim·i·nal law ▶ n. a system of law concerned with those who commit crimes. Contrasted with CIVIL LAW. ■ a law belonging to this system.

crim·i·nal re·cord ▶ n. a history of being convicted for crime. ■ a list of a person's previous criminal convictions.

crim·i·nol·o·gy /,krimə'näləjē/ ▶ n. the scientific study of crime and criminals. — **crim·i·no·log·i·cal** /,krimənl'äjikəl/ adj. **crim·i·nol·o·gist** /-jist/ n. [19th C.: from L. *crimen, crimin-* 'crime' + -LOGY.]

crimp /krimp/ ▶ v. [trans.] compress (something) into small folds or ridges: *she crimped the edge of the pie.* ■ squeeze (metal) so as to bend or corrugate it. ■ connect (a wire or cable) in this way. ■ [often as adj.] (**crimped**) make waves in (hair) with a curling iron. ■ informal have a limiting or adverse effect on (something): *the drought could crimp their income potential.* ▶ n. a curl, wave, or folded or compressed edge. ■ a small connecting piece for crimping wires or lines together. ■ informal a restriction or limitation: *the crimp on take-home pay.*
– PHRASES **put a crimp in** informal have an adverse effect on. — **crimp·er** n. **crimp·y** adj. [OE *gecrympan*, of Gmc. origin; rel. to Du. *krimpen* 'shrink, wrinkle.']

crim·son /'krimzən/ ▶ adj. of a rich deep red color inclining to purple. ▶ n. a rich deep red color inclining to purple. [ME: from obs. Fr. *cramoisin* or Old Sp. *cremesin*, based on Arab. *ḳirmizī*, from *ḳirmiz* (see KERMES). Cf. CARMINE.]

cringe /krinj/ ▶ v. (**cring·ing**) [intrans.] bend one's head and body in fear or in a servile manner: *he **cringed** away from the blow* | [as adj.] (**cringing**) *surrounded by cringing yes-men.* ■ experience an inward shiver of embarrassment or disgust: *I **cringed** at the fellow's stupidity.* ▶ n. an act of cringing in fear. ■ a feeling of embarrassment or disgust. — **cring·er** n. [ME *crenge, crenche*, rel. to OE *cringan, crincan* 'bend, yield, fall in battle,' Ger. *krank* 'sick.']

cringe·wor·thy /'krinj,wər<u>TH</u>ē/ ▶ adj. informal causing feelings of embarrassment or awkwardness: *the play's cast was excellent, but the dialogue was unforgivably cringeworthy.*

crin·kle /'kriNGkəl/ ▶ v. [intrans.] form small creases or wrinkles in the surface of something, esp. the skin of the face as the result of a facial expression: *his face **crinkled** up in a smile* | [as adj.] (**crinkled**) *crinkled foliage.* ■ [trans.] cause to form such creases or wrinkles: *he crinkled his eyes in a smile.* ■ [trans.] cause (something) to make a crackling or rustling sound: *we tried not to crinkle the plastic as we unwrapped the pies.* ▶ n. a wrinkle or crease found on the surface of something: *there was a crinkle of suspicion on her forehead.* ■ the sound of crinkling: *I heard the crinkle of clothing.* — **crin·kly** /-k(ə)lē/ adj. [ME: rel. to OE *crincan* (see CRINGE).]

crin·kle-cut ▶ adj. (esp. of French fries) cut with wavy edges.

Cri·noid·e·a /krī'noidēə/ Zool. a class of echinoderms that comprises the sea lilies and feather stars. They have slender, feathery arms and (in some kinds) a stalk for attachment. — **cri·noid** /'krīnoid/ n. & adj. **cri·noi·dal** /'krīnoidl/ adj. [mod. L. (pl.), from Gk. *krinoeidēs* 'lilylike,' from *krinon* 'lily.']

crin·o·line /'krinl-in/ ▶ n. **1** hist. a stiffened or hooped petticoat worn to make a long skirt stand out. **2** a stiff fabric of horsehair and cotton or linen thread, typically used to stiffen petticoats or as a lining. [19th C.: from Fr., formed irregularly from L. *crinis* 'hair' + *linum* 'thread.']

crip /krip/ ▶ n. informal **1** derog. a disabled person. [20th C.: abbrev. of CRIPPLE.] **2** (usu. **Crip**) a member of a Los Angeles street gang.

cripes /krīps/ ▶ exclam. informal a euphemism for Christ. [20th C.: alt. of CHRIST.]

crip·ple /'kripəl/ ▶ n. **1** dated, offens. a person who is unable to walk or move properly because of disability or injury to their back or legs. **2** a person who is disabled in a specified way: *an emotional cripple.* ▶ v. [trans.] (often **be crippled**) cause (someone) to become unable to move or walk properly. ■ cause severe and disabling damage to (a machine). ■ cause a severe and almost insuperable problem for: *countries are crippled by their debts.* — **crip·pler** /'krip(ə)lər/ n. [OE: from two words, *crypel* and *crēopel*, both of Gmc. origin and rel. to CREEP.]

cri·sis /'krīsis/ ▶ n. (pl. **-ses** /-,sēz/) a time of intense difficulty, trouble, or danger. ■ a time when a difficult or important decision must be made: [as adj.] *a crisis point of history.* ■ the turning point of a disease after which the outcome is either recovery or death. ■ the point in a play or story when a crucial conflict takes place, determining the outcome. [ME: medical L., from Gk. *krisis* 'decision,' from *krinein* 'decide.']

cri·sis cen·ter ▶ n. a facility where individuals with personal crises can obtain help or advice. ■ an office or agency that routes information and coordinates action during an emergency or disaster.

cri·sis man·age·ment ▶ n. the use of expert managers by a business or government to limit damage or danger from a crisis. ■ the tendency to take action only after a crisis has developed.

crisp /krisp/ ▶ adj. **1** firm, dry, and brittle, esp. in a way considered pleasing or attractive: *crisp bacon.* ■ (of a fruit or vegetable) firm, indicating freshness: *crisp lettuce.* ■ (of the weather) cool, fresh, and invigorating: *a crisp autumn day.* ■ (of paper or cloth) smooth, stiff, and uncreased: *a crisp $5 bill.* ■ (of hair) having tight, stiff curls. **2** (of speaking or writing) decisive and matter-of-fact, without hesitation or detail: *they were cut off with a crisp "Thank you."* ▶ n. a baked fruit dessert with a crunchy topping of brown sugar, butter, and flour: *rhubarb crisp.* ▶ v. [trans.] give (something, esp. food) a crisp surface by heating it: *crisp the pita rounds in the oven.* ■ [intrans.] (of food) acquire a crisp surface in this way: *open the foil so that the bread browns and crisps.*
– PHRASES **burn something to a crisp** burn something completely, leaving only a charred remnant. — **crisp·ly** adv. **crisp·ness** n. [OE: from L. *crispus* 'curled.']

cris·pate /'krispāt; -pit/ ▶ adj. Bot. (esp. of a leaf) having a wavy or curly edge. [19th C.: from L. *crispatus*, past part. of *crispare* 'to curl.']

crisp·er /ˈkrispər/ ▶ **n.** a compartment at the bottom of a refrigerator for storing fruit and vegetables.

crisp·y /ˈkrispē/ ▶ **adj.** (**crisp·i·er, crisp·i·est**) (of food, typically cooked) having a pleasingly firm, dry, and brittle surface or texture: *crispy fried bacon.* — **crisp·i·ness n.**

criss·cross /ˈkrisˌkrôs/ ▶ **n.** a pattern of intersecting straight lines or paths. ▶ **adj.** (of a pattern) containing a number of straight lines or paths that intersect each other: *a crisscross pattern.* ▶ **adv.** in a pattern of intersecting straight lines: *the swords were strung crisscross on his back.* ▶ **v.** [trans.] (usu. **be crisscrossed**) form a pattern of intersecting lines or paths on (a place): *the hill was crisscrossed with sheep tracks.* ■ [intrans.] intersect repeatedly: *the streets crisscrossed in a grid pattern.* ■ move or travel, going back and forth repeatedly: *the President crisscrossed America.* [17th C.: from *Christ-cross*, from *Christ's cross*.]

cris·ta /ˈkristə/ ▶ **n.** (pl. **-tae** /-tē; -tī/) **1** Anat. Zool. a ridge or crest. **2** Biol. each of the partitions in a mitochondrion. — **cris·tate** /ˈkristāt/ **adj.** [19th C.: from L., 'tuft, plume, crest.']

cris·to·bal·ite /kriˈstōbəˌlīt/ ▶ **n.** a form of silica that is the main component of opal and also occurs as small octahedral crystals. [19th C.: named after *Cerro San Cristóbal* in Mexico, where it was discovered, + **-ITE**[1].]

cri·te·ri·on /krīˈti(ə)rēən/ ▶ **n.** (pl. **-te·ri·a** /-ˈti(ə)rēə/) a principle or standard by which something may be judged or decided: *violating safety criteria.* — **cri·te·ri·al** /-ˈti(ə)rēəl/ **adj.** [17th C.: from Gk. *kritērion* 'means of judging,' from *kritēs* (see **CRITIC**).]

cri·te·ri·um /krīˈti(ə)rēəm/ ▶ **n.** a one-day bicycle race on a circuit road course.

crit·ic /ˈkritik/ ▶ **n.** **1** a person who expresses an unfavorable opinion of something. **2** a person who judges the merits of literary, artistic, or musical works, esp. one who does so professionally. [16th C.: from L. *criticus*, from Gk. *kritikos*, from *kritēs* 'a judge,' from *krinein* 'judge, decide.']

crit·i·cal /ˈkritikəl/ ▶ **adj.** **1** expressing adverse or disapproving judgments: ***critical of** many US programs.* **2** expressing or involving an analysis of a creative work or performance: *she never won the critical acclaim she sought.* ■ (of a published literary or musical text) incorporating a scholarly analysis and commentary: *a critical edition of a Bach sonata.* **3** having the potential to become disastrous; at a point of crisis: *the situation was still critical.* ■ (of a person) extremely ill and at risk of death: *he had been **in critical condition** since undergoing surgery.* ■ having decisive importance in the success or failure of something: *temperature is a critical factor.* **4** [attrib.] Math. Physics relating to or denoting a point of transition from one state to another. ■ (of a nuclear reactor or fuel) maintaining a self-sustaining chain reaction: *the reactor is due to **go critical** in October.* — **crit·i·cal·i·ty** /ˌkritəˈkalitē/ **n.** (in senses 3 and 4) **crit·i·cal·ly** /ˈkritik(ə)lē/ **adv.** [as submodifier] *he's critically ill.* **crit·i·cal·ness n.**

crit·i·cal ap·pa·rat·us ▶ **n.** see **APPARATUS** (sense 3).

crit·i·cal list ▶ **n.** [in sing.] a list of those who are critically ill in the hospital.

crit·i·cal mass ▶ **n.** Physics the minimum amount of fissile material needed to maintain a nuclear chain reaction. ■ fig. the minimum required to start or maintain a venture: *a critical mass of users.*

crit·i·cal path ▶ **n.** the sequence of stages determining the minimum time needed for an operation.

crit·i·cal path a·nal·y·sis ▶ **n.** the mathematical analysis of working procedures to determine the critical path.

crit·i·cal pe·ri·od ▶ **n.** Psychol. a period during someone's development in which a particular skill or characteristic is believed to be most readily acquired.

crit·i·cal point ▶ **n.** **1** Chem. a point on a phase diagram at which the liquid and gas phases of a substance have the same density, and so are indistinguishable. **2** Math. a point on a curve with a gradient of zero.

crit·i·cal pres·sure ▶ **n.** Chem. the pressure of a gas or vapor in its critical state.

crit·i·cal state ▶ **n.** Chem. the state of a substance when it is at the critical point, i.e., at critical temperature and pressure.

crit·i·cal tem·per·a·ture ▶ **n.** Chem. the temperature of a gas or vapor in its critical state. Above this temperature, a gas cannot be liquefied by pressure alone.

crit·i·cal the·o·ry ▶ **n.** a philosophical approach to culture, and esp. to literature, that seeks to confront the social, historical, and ideological forces and structures that produce and constrain it.

crit·i·cal vol·ume ▶ **n.** Chem. the volume occupied by a unit mass of a gas or vapor in its critical state.

crit·i·cism /ˈkritəˌsizəm/ ▶ **n.** **1** the expression of disapproval of someone or something based on perceived faults or mistakes: *he ignored the criticisms of his friends.* **2** the analysis and judgment of a literary or artistic work: *methods of criticism supported by literary theories.* ■ an article, book, or comment containing such analysis: *I only read poetry and criticism.* ■ the scholarly investigation of literary or historical texts to determine their origin or intended form.

crit·i·cize /ˈkritəˌsīz/ ▶ **v.** [trans.] **1** indicate the faults of (someone or something) in a disapproving way: *they criticized the failure of Western nations | technicians were **criticized for** defective workmanship.* **2** form and express a judgment of (a literary or artistic work): *a literary text may be criticized on two grounds: the semantic and the expressive.* — **crit·i·ciz·a·ble adj. crit·i·ciz·er n.**

cri·tique /kriˈtēk/ ▶ **n.** a detailed analysis and assessment of something, esp. a literary, philosophical, or political theory. ▶ **v.** (**-tiques, -tiqued, -tiqu·ing**) [trans.] evaluate (a theory or practice) in a detailed and analytical way: *the authors critique the methods used in research.* [17th C. (as a n.): from Fr., based on Gk. *kritikē tekhnē* 'critical art.']

crit·ter /ˈkritər/ ▶ **n.** informal dialect a living creature; an animal. [19th C.: var. of **CREATURE**.]

croak /krōk/ ▶ **n.** a deep hoarse sound made by a frog. ■ a sound resembling this, esp. one made by a person. ▶ **v.** [intrans.] **1** (of a frog) make a characteristic deep hoarse sound. ■ (of a person) make a similar sound when speaking or laughing: *"Thank you," I croaked.* **2** informal die. ■ [trans.] kill (someone). [ME (as a v.): imitative.]

croak·er /ˈkrōkər/ ▶ **n.** an animal or fish that makes a deep, hoarse sound. ■ another term for **DRUM**[2].

croak·y /ˈkrōkē/ ▶ **adj.** (**croak·i·er, croak·i·est**) (of a person's voice) deep and hoarse. — **croak·i·ly** /-kəlē/ **adv.**

Cro·at /ˈkrōat; ˈkrōät; krōt/ ▶ **n.** **1** a native or national of Croatia, or a person of Croatian descent. **2** the South Slavic language of the Croats, almost identical to Serbian but written in the Roman alphabet. See **SERBO-CROAT**. ▶ **adj.** of or relating to the Croats or their language. — **Cro·a·tian** /krōˈāshən/ **n. & adj.** [from mod. L. *Croatae* (pl.), from Serbo-Croat *Hrvat*.]

Cro·a·tia /krōˈāshə/ a country in southeastern Europe. Croatian name **HRVATSKA**. *See box.*

Croatia

Official name: Republic of Croatia
Location: southeastern Europe, on the Adriatic Sea
Area: 21,800 square miles (56,400 sq km)
Population: 4,760,000
Capital: Zagreb
Languages: Croatian, Serbian (small minorities speak Czech, German, Hungarian, Italian, and Slovak)
Currency: kuna

croc /kräk/ ▶ **n.** informal a crocodile.

Cro·ce /ˈkrōchā/, Benedetto (1866–1952), Italian philosopher. He wrote *Philosophy of Spirit* (1902–17).

cro·chet /krōˈshā/ ▶ **n.** a handicraft in which yarn is looped into a patterned fabric with a hooked needle. ■ fabric or items made in such a way. ▶ **v.** (**-cheted** /-ˈshād/, **-chet·ing** /-ˈshā-iNG/) [trans.] make (a garment or piece of fabric) in such a way: *she crocheted the shawl herself.* — **cro·chet·er** /-ˈshā-ər/ **n.** [19th C.: from Fr., dimin. of *croc* 'hook,' from ON *krókr*.]

cro·ci /ˈkrōkī; -sī/ plural form of **CROCUS**.

cro·cid·o·lite /krōˈsidlˌīt/ ▶ **n.** a fibrous blue or green mineral consisting of a silicate of iron and sodium. Also called ***BLUE ASBESTOS***. [19th C.: from Gk. *krokis, krokid-* 'nap of cloth' + **-LITE**.]

crock[1] /kräk/ ▶ **n.** **1** an earthenware pot or jar. **2** (also vulgar slang **crock of shit**) a thing that is considered to be complete nonsense. [OE *croc, crocca*, of Gmc. origin; rel. to ON *krukka*.]

crock[2] informal ▶ **n.** an old, feeble person. [ME: perh. from Flemish, and prob. rel. to **CRACK**.]

crock·er·y /ˈkräkərē/ ▶ **n.** dishes, cups, and similar items, esp. ones made of earthenware or china. [18th C.: from obs. *crocker* 'potter,' from **CROCK**[2].]

Crock·ett /ˈkräkit/, Davy (1786–1836), US frontiersman and politician; full name *David Crockett*. From Tennessee, he served in the US House of Representatives 1827–35 and fought for the cause of Texas independence. He was killed at the siege of the Alamo.

Crock·pot /ˈkräk,pät/ ▶ **n.** trademark a large electric cooking pot used to cook stews and other dishes slowly.

croc·o·dile /ˈkräkə,dīl/ ▶ **n.** a large predatory semiaquatic reptile (*Crocodylus* and two other genera, family Crocodylidae) with long jaws, long tail, short legs, and a horny textured skin, using submersion and stealth to approach prey unseen. See illustration at AMERICAN CROCODILE. ■ leather made from crocodile skin, used esp. to make bags and shoes. [ME *cocodrille, cokadrill*, from OFr. *cocodrille*, via med. L. from Gk. *krokodilos* 'worm of the stones,' from *krokē* 'pebble' + *drilos* 'worm.']

croc·o·dile bird ▶ **n.** the Egyptian plover, which is said to feed on insects parasitic on crocodiles.

croc·o·dile tears ▶ **plural n.** tears that are insincere.

croc·o·dil·i·an /,kräkəˈdilēən/ ▶ **n.** Zool. a large, predatory, semiaquatic reptile of the order Crocodylia, which comprises the crocodiles, alligators, caimans, and gharial. ▶ **adj.** of or relating to such reptiles.

cro·cus /ˈkrōkəs/ ▶ **n.** (pl. **-cus·es** or **-ci** /-kī; -sī/) a small, spring-flowering plant (genus *Crocus*) of the iris family that grows from a corm and bears bright yellow, purple, or white flowers. See also AUTUMN CROCUS. [ME: via L. from Gk. *krokos*, of Semitic origin and rel. to Heb. *karkōm*.]

Croe·sus /ˈkrēsəs/ (6th century BC), last king of Lydia *c.*560–546 BC. He was renowned for his great wealth.

croft /krôft/ Brit. ▶ **n.** a small rented farm, esp. one in Scotland, comprising a plot of arable land attached to a house, sharing pasturage with other such farms. ■ an enclosed field used for tillage or pasture, typically attached to a house and worked by the occupier. ▶ **v.** [trans.] farm (land) as a croft or crofts. — **croft·er n.** [OE: of unknown origin.]

Crohn's dis·ease /ˈkrōnz/ ▶ **n.** a chronic inflammatory disease of the intestines, esp. the colon and ileum. [1930s: named after Burrill B. *Crohn* (1884–1983), American pathologist, who was among the first to describe it.]

crois·sant /k(r)wäˈsänt; -ˈsäN/ ▶ **n.** a crescent-shaped roll made of flaky pastry, often eaten for breakfast. [19th C.: Fr. (see CRESCENT).]

Cro-Mag·non man /krō ˈmagnən; ˈmanyən/ ▶ **n.** the earliest form of modern human in Europe. Their appearance *c.*35,000 years ago marked the beginning of the Upper Paleolithic and the apparent decline and disappearance of Neanderthal man; the group persisted at least into the Neolithic period. [*Cro-Magnon*, the name of a hill in the Dordogne, France, where remains were found in 1868.]

crom·lech /ˈkrämlek; -leKH/ ▶ **n.** (in Wales) a megalithic tomb consisting of a large flat stone laid on upright ones. Also called DOLMEN. ■ (in Brittany) a circle of standing stones. [Welsh, from *crom*, fem. of *crwm* 'arched' + *llech* 'flat stone,' sense 2 via Fr. from Breton *krommlec'h*.]

Crom·well[1] /ˈkrämwəl; -,wel/, Oliver (1599–1658), English general and politician. He was the leader of the victorious Parliamentary forces (or Roundheads) in the English Civil War and became Lord Protector of the Commonwealth 1653–58.

Crom·well[2], Thomas (*c.*1485–1540), English statesman. He presided over Henry VIII's divorce from Catherine of Aragon (1533) and his break with the Roman Catholic Church.

crone /krōn/ ▶ **n.** an old woman who is thin and ugly. [ME: via MDu. *croonje, caroonje* 'carcass, old ewe,' from Old North. Fr. *caroigne* 'carrion, cantankerous woman' (see CARRION).]

Cro·nin /ˈkrōnin/, A. J. (1896–1981), Scottish writer; full name *Archibald Joseph Cronin*. His novels include *The Citadel* (1937).

Cron·kite /ˈkräNGkīt; ˈkrän-/, Walter Leland, Jr. (1916–), US television journalist, noted for anchoring the *CBS Evening News* 1962–81.

Cro·nus /ˈkrōnəs/ (also **Kro·nos**) Gk. Mythol. the supreme god until dethroned by Zeus. The youngest son of Uranus (Heaven) and Gaia (Earth), Cronus overthrew and castrated his father and then married his sister Rhea. Fated to be overcome by one of his male children, Cronus swallowed all of them as soon as they were born, but when Zeus was born, Rhea deceived him and hid the baby away. Roman equivalent SATURN.

cro·ny /ˈkrōnē/ ▶ **n.** (pl. **-nies**) informal, often derog. a close friend or companion. [17th C.: from Gk. *khronios* 'long-lasting,' from *khronos* 'time.']

cro·ny·ism /ˈkrōnē,izəm/ ▶ **n.** derog. the appointment of friends and associates to positions of authority, without proper regard to their qualifications.

crook /kro͝ok/ ▶ **n. 1** the hooked staff of a shepherd. ■ a bishop's crozier. ■ a bend in something, esp. at the elbow in a person's arm. ■ a piece of extra tubing that can be fitted to a brass instrument to lower the pitch by a set interval. ■ a metal tube on which the reed of some wind instruments is set. **2** informal a person who is dishonest or a criminal. ▶ **v.** [trans.] bend (something, esp. a finger as a signal): *he crooked a finger for the waitress.* [ME (in the sense 'hooked tool or weapon'): from ON *krókr* 'hook.']

crook·ed /ˈkro͝okid/ ▶ **adj.** (**crook·ed·er, crook·ed·est**) bent or twisted out of shape or out of place. ■ (of a smile or grin) with the mouth sloping down on one side; lopsided. ■ informal dishonest; illegal. — **crook·ed·ly adv. crook·ed·ness n.**

crook·neck /ˈkro͝ok,nek/ (also **crookneck squash**) ▶ **n.** a squash of a club-shaped variety with a curved neck and warty skin.

croon /kro͞on/ ▶ **v.** [intrans.] hum or sing in a soft, low voice, esp. in a sentimental manner: *she was crooning to the child* | [trans.] *the vocalist crooned smoky blues.* ■ say in a soft, low voice: *"Goodbye, you lovely darling," she crooned.* ▶ **n.** [in sing.] a soft, low voice or tone. — **croon·er n.** [15th C.: from Mid. Low Ger. and MDu. *krōnen* 'groan, lament.']

crop /kräp/ ▶ **n. 1** a cultivated plant that is grown as food: *the main crops were oats and barley.* ■ an amount of such plants or their produce harvested at one time. ■ an abundance of something, esp. a person's hair: *a thick crop of wiry hair.* ■ the number of farm animals born in a particular year on one farm. ■ a group of related people or things appearing or occurring at one time: *the current crop of politicians.* **2** a hairstyle in which the hair is cut very short. **3** short for RIDING CROP. **4** a pouch in a bird's gullet where food is stored or prepared for digestion. ■ a similar organ in an insect or earthworm. ▶ **v.** (**cropped, crop·ping**) [trans.] **1** cut (something, esp. hair) very short: [as adj.] (**cropped**) *cropped blond hair.* ■ (of an animal) eat the tops of (plants): *the horse was cropping the grass.* ■ trim parts of (a photograph) to improve a picture or to fit a given space. **2** (often **be cropped**) harvest (plants or their produce): *hay is cropped several times through the summer.* ■ sow or plant (land) with plants to produce food or fodder, esp. on a commercial scale: *cropped in cotton.*

– PHRASAL VERBS **crop out** (of rock) appear or be exposed at the surface of the earth. **crop up** appear, occur, or come to one's notice unexpectedly: *some urgent business had cropped up.* [OE, of Gmc. origin; rel. to Ger. *Kropf*.]

crop cir·cle ▶ **n.** an area of standing crops that has been flattened in the form of a circle or other pattern.

crop dust·ing ▶ **n.** the spraying of powdered or liquid pesticide or fertilizer on crops, esp. from the air.

crop·per /ˈkräpər/ ▶ **n. 1** [usu. with adj.] a plant that yields a crop of a specified kind or in a specified way. **2** a machine or person that cuts or trims something, such as carpet pile during manufacture. **3** a person who raises a crop, esp. as a sharecropper.

– PHRASES **come a cropper** informal fall heavily. ■ suffer a defeat or disaster: *the club's challenge for the championship has come a cropper.*

crop ro·ta·tion ▶ **n.** see ROTATION.

crop top ▶ **n.** a woman's garment or undergarment for the upper body, cut so that it reveals the midriff.

cro·quet /krōˈkā/ ▶ **n.** a game played on a lawn, in which colored wooden balls are driven through a series of wickets by means of mallets. ▶ **v.** (**-queted** /-ˈkād/, **-quet·ing** /-ˈkā-iNG/) [trans.] drive away (an opponent's ball) by holding one's own ball against it and striking this with the mallet. [19th C.: perh. a dial. form of Fr. *crochet* 'hook.']

cro·quette /krōˈket/ ▶ **n.** a small roll of chopped vegetables, meat, or fish, fried in breadcrumbs: *a potato croquette.* [Fr., from *croquer* 'to crunch.']

crore /krôr/ ▶ **n.** Indian ten million; one hundred lakhs, esp. of rupees, units of measurement, or people. [from Hindi *karoṛ*, based on Sanskrit *koṭi* 'ten million.']

cro·sier ▶ **n.** var. of CROZIER.

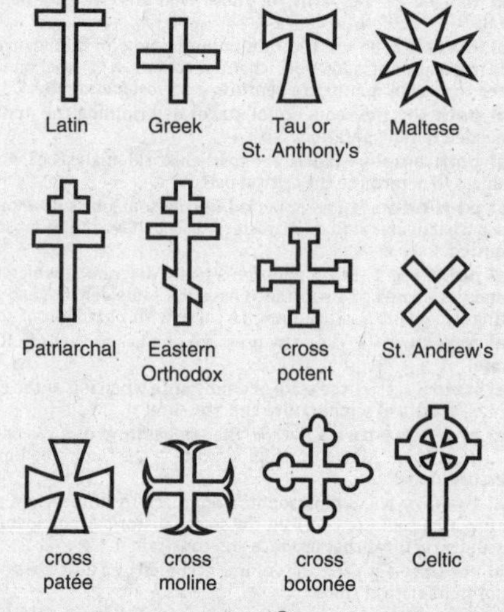

cross 2

cross /krôs/ ▶ **n. 1** a mark, object, or figure formed by two short intersecting lines or pieces (+ or ×). ■ a mark of this type (×) made to represent a signature by a person who cannot write. ■ Brit. a mark of this type (×) used to show that something is incorrect or unsatisfactory. **2** an upright post with a transverse bar, as used in antiquity for crucifixion. ■ (**the Cross**) the cross on which Jesus was crucified. ■ this, or a representation of it, as an emblem of Christianity. ■ fig. a thing that is unavoidable and has to be endured: *a cross we have to bear.* ■ a cross-shaped decoration awarded for valor or in some orders of knighthood. ■ (**the Cross**) the constellation Southern Cross. Also called CRUX. **3** an animal or plant resulting from crossbreeding; a hybrid: *a Devon* *and Holstein cross.* ■ **(a cross between)** a mixture or compromise of two things: *a cross between a hamburger and a burrito.* **4** a sideways or transverse movement, in particular: ■ Soccer a pass across the field toward the center close to one's opponents' goal. ■ Boxing a blow delivered across and over the opponent's lead: *a right cross.* ▶ **v.** [trans.] **1** go or extend across or to the other side of (a path, road, stretch of water, or area): *he has crossed the Atlantic twice* | [intrans.] *we* ***crossed over*** *the bridge.* ■ go across or climb over (an obstacle or boundary): *he attempted to cross the border* | [intrans.] *we* ***crossed over*** *a fence.* ■ [intrans.] **(cross over)** (esp. of an artist or artistic style) begin to appeal to a different audience, esp. a wider one: *an animator who crossed over to live action.* **2** [intrans.] intersect: *the two lines cross at 90°.* ■ [trans.] cause (two things) to intersect: *cross the cables in opposing directions.* ■ [trans.] place (something) crosswise: *Michele crossed her arms.* ■ [intrans.] (of a letter) be sent before receipt of another from the person being written to: *our letters crossed.* **3** draw a line or lines across: *cross the t's.* ■ **(cross someone/something off)** delete a name or item on a list as being no longer required or involved. ■ **(cross something out)** delete an incorrect or inapplicable word or phrase by drawing a line through it. **4** **(cross oneself)** make the sign of the cross in front of one's chest as a sign of Christian reverence or to invoke divine protection. **5** Soccer pass (the ball) toward the center when attacking. **6** cause (an animal of one species, breed, or variety) to interbreed with one of another species, breed, or variety: *hounds were* ***crossed with*** *wolves.* ■ cross-fertilize (a plant). **7** oppose (someone): *no one dared cross him.* ▶ **adj.** annoyed: *he seemed to be very cross.*

– PHRASES **at cross purposes** having different aims from one another: *talking at cross purposes.* **cross one's fingers** (or **keep one's fingers crossed**) put one finger across another for good luck. ■ hope that someone or something will be successful. **cross my heart** (**and hope to die**) used to emphasize the truthfulness of what one is saying, sometimes reinforced by making a sign of the cross over one's chest. **cross one's mind** (of a thought) occur to one, esp. transiently: *the idea never crossed my mind.* **cross someone's path** meet or encounter someone. **get one's wires** (or **lines**) **crossed** become wrongly connected by telephone. ■ have a misunderstanding. **the way of the Cross** see WAY. — **cross·ly adv. cross·ness n.** [OE (in the sense 'monument in the form of a cross'): from ON *kross*, from Old Irish *cros*, from L. *crux*.]

cross- ▶ **comb. form 1** denoting movement or position across something: *cross-channel.* ■ denoting interaction: *cross-pollinate.* ■ passing from side to side; transverse: *crosspiece.* **2** describing the form or figure of a cross: *crossbones.* [from CROSS.]

cross·bar /'krôs,bär/ ▶ **n.** a horizontal bar fixed across another bar or between two upright bars, in particular: ■ (in sports) the bar between the two upright posts of a goal. ■ the horizontal bar on the frame of a bicycle.

cross·beam /'krôs,bēm/ ▶ **n.** a transverse beam.

cross-bed·ding ▶ **n.** Geol. layering within a stratum and at an angle to the main bedding plane.

cross·bill /'krôs,bil/ ▶ **n.** a thickset finch (genus *Loxia*) with a crossed bill adapted for extracting seeds from the cones of conifers. The plumage is typically red in the male and olive green in the female.

cross·bones /'krôs,bōnz/ ▶ **n.** see *SKULL AND CROSSBONES* at SKULL.

cross-bor·der ▶ **adj.** [attrib.] passing or occurring across a border between two countries: *cross-border trade.*

cross·bow /'krôs,bō/ ▶ **n.** a bow of a kind that is fixed across a wooden support and has a groove for the bolt and a mechanism for drawing and releasing the string.

cross·breed /'krôs,brēd/ ▶ **n.** an animal or plant produced by mating or hybridizing two different species, breeds, or varieties: [as adj.] *a crossbreed Labrador.* ▶ **v.** [trans.] produce (an animal or plant) in this way. ■ hybridize (a breed, species, or variety) with another. ■ [intrans.] (of an animal or plant) breed with a different breed, species, or variety.

cross-check ▶ **v.** [trans.] **1** verify (figures or information) by using an alternative source or method: *always try to cross-check your bearings.* **2** Ice Hockey obstruct (an opponent) illegally with the stick held horizontally in both hands. ▶ **n. 1** an instance of verifying something by using an alternative source or method: *as a cross-check, they were also asked to give their date of birth.* **2** Ice Hockey an illegal obstruction using the stick held horizontally in both hands.

cross-col·or ▶ **n.** colored interference in a color television receiver caused by the misinterpretation of high-frequency luminance detail as color information.

cross-con·nec·tion ▶ **n.** a connection made between two or more distinct things, typically parts of different networks or circuits.

cross-coun·try ▶ **adj. 1** across fields or countryside, as opposed to on roads or tracks: *cross-country walking.* ■ [attrib.] of, relating to, or denoting the sport of running, riding, or driving along a course in the countryside, as opposed to around a track. ■ [attrib.] of, relating to, or denoting skiing over relatively flat or hilly terrain. **2** across a region or country, in particular: ■ not keeping to main or direct roads, routes, or railroad lines: [as adv.] *if you are traveling cross-country, choose where you walk with care.* ■ traveling to many different parts of a country. ▶ **n.** a cross-country race or competition. ■ the sport of cross-country running, riding, skiing, or driving.

cross·court /'krôs,kôrt/ ▶ **adv. & adj.** (of a stroke in tennis and other racket sports) hit diagonally across the court: [as adj.] *a crosscourt volley.*

cross cous·in ▶ **n.** each of two cousins who are children of a brother and sister.

cross-cul·tur·al ▶ **adj.** [attrib.] of, relating to, or comparing different cultures: *cross-cultural understanding.*

cross·cur·rent /'krôs,kərənt; -,kə-rənt/ ▶ **n.** a current in a river or sea that flows across another. ■ fig. a process or tendency that is in conflict with another: *strong crosscurrents of debate.*

cross·cut /'krôs,kət/ ▶ **v.** [trans.] **1** cut (wood or stone) across its main grain or axis. **2** [trans.] alternate (one sequence) with another when editing a movie. ▶ **n. 1** a diagonal cut, esp. one across the main grain or axis of wood or stone. ■ Mining a cutting made across the course of a vein or the general direction of the workings. **2** an instance of alternating between two or more sequences when editing a movie.

cross·cut saw ▶ **n.** a saw with a handle at each end, used by two people for cutting trees across the grain.

cross-dress ▶ **v.** [intrans.] wear clothing typical of the opposite sex. — **cross-dress·er n.**

crosse /krôs/ ▶ **n.** the stick used in lacrosse. [19th C.: from Fr., from OFr. *croce* 'bishop's crook,' ult. of Gmc. origin and rel. to CRUTCH.]

cross-ex·am·ine ▶ **v.** [trans.] question (a witness called by the other party) in a court of law to undercut testimony already given. Compare with DIRECT EXAMINATION. ■ question (someone) aggressively or in great detail. — **cross-ex·am·i·na·tion n. cross-ex·am·in·er n.**

cross-eyed ▶ **adj.** having one or both eyes turned inward toward the nose, either from focusing on something very close, through temporary loss of control of focus, or as a permanent condition.

cross-fade ▶ **v.** [intrans.] (in sound or movie editing) make a picture or sound appear or be heard gradually as another disappears or becomes silent. ▶ **n.** an act or instance of cross-fading.

cross-fer·ti·lize ▶ **v.** [trans.] fertilize (a plant) using pollen from another plant of the same species. ■ [intrans.] (of two plants) fertilize each other. ■ fig. stimulate development of (something) with an exchange of information: *sessions between the two groups cross-fertilize ideas.* — **cross-fer·ti·li·za·tion n.**

cross·fire /'krôs,fī(ə)r/ ▶ **n.** gunfire from two or more directions crossing the same area: *a photographer was killed in the crossfire.* ■ fig. used to refer to a situation in which two or more groups are arguing with each other: *grape growers* ***caught in the crossfire*** *of the boycott.*

cross·flow /'krôs,flō/ ▶ **n.** a type of engine cylinder head in which the intake ports are on the opposite side of the engine from the exhaust ports.

cross-grain ▶ **adj.** [attrib.] running across the regular grain in timber: *cross-grain swelling.*

cross-grained ▶ **adj.** (of timber) having a grain that runs across the regular grain. ■ stubbornly contrary or bad-tempered.

cross·hairs /'krôs,he(ə)rz/ ▶ **plural n.** a pair of fine wires or lines crossing at right angles at the focus of an optical instrument or gun sight, for use in positioning, aiming, or measuring. ■ a representation of this used as a cursor on a computer screen.

cross·hatch /'krôs,haCH/ ▶ **v.** [trans.] [often as n.] **(crosshatching)** (in drawing or graphics) shade (an area) with intersecting sets of parallel lines.

cross·head /'krôs,hed/ ▶ **n.** a bar or block between the piston rod and connecting rod in a steam engine.

cross in·dex ▶ **n.** a note or cross reference in a book or list that refers the reader to other material. ▶ **v.** **(cross-in·dex)** [trans.] index (something) under another heading as a cross reference.

cross in·fec·tion ▶ **n.** the transfer of infection, esp. to a hospital patient with a different infection or between different species of animal or plant.

cross·ing /'krôsiNG/ ▶ **n. 1** a place where two roads, two railroad lines, or a road and a railroad line cross. ■ the action of moving across or over something: *the crossing of the Pyrenees.* ■ a journey across water in a ship. ■ a place at which one may safely cross something, esp. a street. ■ a place at which one can cross a border between countries. **2** crossbreeding.

cross·ing o·ver ▶ **n.** Genet. the exchange of genes between homologous chromosomes, resulting in a mixture of parental characteristics in offspring.

cross-leg·ged /'leg(i)d/ ▶ **adj. & adv.** (of a seated person) with the legs crossed at the ankles and the knees bent outward: [as adv.] *John sat cross-legged on the floor.*

cross-link ▶ **n.** a chemical bond between chains of atoms in a polymer or other complex molecule. ▶ **v.** make or become linked with such a bond. ■ [trans.] connect (something) by a series of transverse links. — **cross-link·age n.**

cross·match /'krôs,maCH/ Med. ▶ **v.** [trans.] [often as n.] **(crossmatching)** test the compatibility of (a donor's and a recipient's blood or tissue). ▶ **n.** an instance of such testing.

cross·mem·ber /'krôs,membər/ ▶ **n.** a transverse structural piece that adds support to a motor-vehicle chassis or other construction.

cross of Lor·raine ▶ **n.** another term for LORRAINE CROSS.

cros·sop·te·ryg·i·an /krô,säptə'rijēən/ Zool. ▶ **n.** a lobe-finned fish, such as the coelacanth. ▶ **adj.** of or relating to such fishes. [19th C.: from mod. L. *Crossopterygii*, from Gk. *krossos* 'tassel' + *pterux, pterug-* 'fin.']

cross·o·ver /ˈkrôsˌōvər/ ▶ **n.** **1** a point or place of crossing from one side to the other. ■ a short track joining two adjacent railroad lines. **2** the process of achieving success in a different field or style, esp. in popular music. **3** a person who votes for a candidate in a different political party than the one they usually support. **4** [as adj.] relating to or denoting trials of medical treatment in which experimental subjects and control groups are exchanged after a set period.

cross·o·ver dis·tor·tion ▶ **n.** Electron. distortion occurring when a signal changes from positive to negative or vice versa.

cross·patch /ˈkrôsˌpacʜ/ ▶ **n.** informal a bad-tempered person. [18th C.: from the adj. CROSS + obs. *patch* 'fool, clown,' perh. from Ital. *pazzo* 'madman.']

cross peen ▶ **n.** a hammer having a peen that lies crossways to the length of the shaft.

cross·piece /ˈkrôsˌpēs/ ▶ **n.** a beam or bar fixed or placed across something else.

cross-plat·form ▶ **adj.** Comput. able to be used on different types of computers or with different software packages: *a cross-platform game*.

cross-pol·li·nate ▶ **v.** [trans.] pollinate (a flower or plant) with pollen from another flower or plant. — **cross-pol·li·na·tion** **n.**

cross-post·ing ▶ **n.** the simultaneous sending of a message to more than one newsgroup or other distribution system on the Internet in such a way that the receiving software at individual sites can detect and ignore duplicates.

cross-pres·sure ▶ **v.** [trans.] expose (someone) to different, incompatible opinions.

cross prod·uct ▶ **n.** another term for VECTOR PRODUCT.

cross-ques·tion ▶ **v.** [trans.] question (someone) in great detail; cross-examine. *it seemed ungrateful to cross-question him* | [as n.] (**cross-questioning**) *the cross-questioning of Lopez*.

cross-re·ac·tion ▶ **n.** Biochem. the reaction of an antibody with an antigen other than the one that gave rise to it. — **cross-re·act** **v.** **cross-re·ac·tive** **adj.** **cross-re·ac·tiv·i·ty** **n.**

cross-re·fer ▶ **v.** [intrans.] (of a text) refer to another text or part of a text, typically in order to elaborate on a point: *the database cross-refers to the printed book*. ■ [trans.] refer (someone) to another text. ■ (of a person) follow a cross reference from one part of a text to another, or one text to another.

cross ref·er·ence ▶ **n.** a reference to another text or part of a text, typically given in order to elaborate on a point. ▶ **v.** [trans.] (usu. **be cross-referenced**) provide with cross references to another text or part of a text.

cross·roads /ˈkrôsˌrōdz/ ▶ **n.** an intersection of two or more roads. ■ a point at which a crucial decision must be made that will have far-reaching consequences: *we stand again at a historic crossroads*. ■ (**crossroad**) a road that crosses a main road or joins two main roads.

cross sec·tion ▶ **n.** a surface or shape that is or would be exposed by making a straight cut through something, esp. at right angles to an axis. ■ a thin strip of organic tissue or other material removed by making two such cuts. ■ a diagram representing what such a cut would reveal. ■ a typical or representative sample of a larger group, esp. of people. ■ Physics a quantity having the dimensions of an area which expresses the probability of a given interaction between particles. ▶ **v.** (**cross-sec·tion**) [trans.] make a cross section of (something). — **cross-sec·tion·al** **adj.**

cross-sell ▶ **v.** [trans.] sell (a different product or service) to an existing customer.

cross-slide ▶ **n.** a sliding part on a lathe or planing machine that is supported by the saddle and carries the tool in a direction at right angles to the bed of the machine.

cross-stitch Needlework ▶ **n.** a stitch formed of two stitches crossing each other. See illustration at EMBROIDERY. ■ needlework done using such stitches. ▶ **v.** [trans.] sew or embroider using such stitches.

cross street ▶ **n.** a street crossing another or connecting two streets.

cross-sub·si·dize ▶ **v.** [trans.] subsidize (a business or activity) out of the profits of another business or activity. — **cross-sub·si·di·za·tion** **n.** **cross-sub·si·dy** **n.**

cross·talk /ˈkrôsˌtôk/ ▶ **n.** **1** unwanted transfer of signals between communication channels. **2** casual conversation.

cross·tie /ˈkrôsˌtī/ ▶ **n.** a wooden or concrete beam laid transversely under the rails of a railroad track to support it.

cross-tol·er·ance ▶ **n.** resistance to the effects of a substance because of exposure to a pharmacologically similar substance: *cross-tolerance of barbiturates with alcohol was observed*.

cross·town /ˈkrôsˌtoun/ ▶ **adj. & adv.** running or leading across a town.

cross-train ▶ **v.** [intrans.] learn another skill, esp. one related to one's current job.

cross-train·ing ▶ **n.** training in two or more sports in order to improve fitness and performance, esp. in a main sport.

cross·walk /ˈkrôsˌwôk/ ▶ **n.** a marked part of a road where pedestrians have the right of way to cross.

cross·ways /ˈkrôsˌwāz/ ▶ **adv.** another term for CROSSWISE.

cross·wind /ˈkrôsˌwind/ ▶ **n.** a wind blowing across one's direction of travel.

cross·wise /ˈkrôsˌwīz/ ▶ **adv.** in the form of a cross. ■ diagonally; transversely.

cross·word /ˈkrôsˌwərd/ (also **crossword puzzle**) ▶ **n.** a puzzle consisting of a grid of squares and blanks into which words crossing vertically and horizontally are written according to clues. [said to have been invented by the journalist Arthur Wynne, whose puzzle (called a "word-cross") appeared in the *New York World* on December 21, 1913.]

cros·ti·ni /krôˈstēnē/ ▶ **plural n.** small pieces of toasted or fried bread served with a topping as an appetizer. [Ital., pl. of *crostino* 'little crust.']

cro·tale /ˈkrōtäl; ˈkrōtl/ ▶ **n.** (usu. **crotales**) a small tuned cymbal. [1930s: Fr., from L. *crotalum* 'a type of castanet,' from Gk. *krotalon*.]

crotch /kräcʜ/ ▶ **n.** the part of the human body between the legs where they join the torso. ■ the part of a garment that passes between the legs. ■ a fork in a tree, road, or river. [16th C.: perh. akin to OFr. *croche* 'crozier,' based on ON *krókr* 'hook.']

crotch·et /ˈkräcʜit/ ▶ **n.** a perverse or unfounded belief or notion. [ME: from OFr. *crochet*, dimin. of *croc* 'hook,' from ON *krókr*.]

crotch·et·y /ˈkräcʜitē/ ▶ **adj.** irritable. — **crotch·et·i·ness** **n.** [19th C.: from CROTCHET + -Y[1].]

crotch·less /ˈkräcʜlis/ ▶ **adj.** (of a garment) having a hole cut so as to leave the genitals uncovered.

cro·ton /ˈkrōtn/ ▶ **n.** **1** a strong-scented tree, shrub, or herbaceous plant (genus *Croton*) of the spurge family, native to tropical and warm regions. Its numerous species include *C. laccifer*, the host plant for the lac insect. **2** a small Indo-Pacific evergreen tree or shrub (genus *Codiaeum*) of the spurge family, grown for its colorful ornamental foliage. [mod. L., from Gk. *krotōn* 'sheep tick.']

cro·ton oil ▶ **n.** a foul-smelling oil, formerly used as a purgative, obtained from the seeds of a tropical Asian croton tree (*Croton tiglium*).

Cro·ton Riv·er /ˈkrōtn/ a river in eastern New York that flows into the Hudson. It is the source of New York City's water.

crouch /kroucʜ/ ▶ **v.** [intrans.] adopt a position in which the knees are bent and the upper body is brought forward and down, typically in order to avoid detection or to defend oneself: *we crouched down in the trench*. ■ (**crouch over**) bend over so as to be close to (someone or something): *she was crouching over a flower*. ▶ **n.** [in sing.] a crouching stance or posture. [ME: perh. from OFr. *crochir* 'be bent,' from *croche* (see CROTCH).]

croup[1] /kro͞op/ ▶ **n.** inflammation of the larynx and trachea in children, associated with infection and causing breathing difficulties. — **croup·y** **adj.** [18th C.: from dial. *croup* 'to croak,' of imitative origin.]

croup[2] ▶ **n.** the rump or hindquarters, esp. of a horse. [ME: from OFr. *croupe*, ult. of Gmc. origin and rel. to CROP.]

croup·i·er /ˈkro͞opēˌā; -pēər/ ▶ **n.** the person in charge of a gaming table, gathering in and paying out money or tokens. [18th C.: Fr., from OFr. *cropier* 'pillion rider, rider on the croup,' rel. to OFr. *croupe* (see CROUP[2]).]

crous·tade /kro͞oˈstäd/ ▶ **n.** a crisp piece of bread or pastry hollowed to receive a savory filling. [Fr., from OFr. *crouste* or Ital. *crostata* 'tart' (from *crosta* 'crust').]

croute /kro͞ot/ ▶ **n.** a piece of toasted bread on which savory snacks can be served. See also EN CROUTE. [Fr. *croûte* (see CRUST).]

crou·ton /ˈkro͞otän; kro͞oˈtän/ ▶ **n.** a small piece of fried or toasted bread served with soup or used as a garnish. [from Fr. *croûton*, from *croûte* (see CRUST).]

Crow /krō/ ▶ **n.** (pl. same or **Crows**) **1** a member of an American Indian people inhabiting eastern Montana. **2** the Siouan language of this people. ▶ **adj.** of or relating to this people or their language.

crow[1] /krō/ ▶ **n.** **1** a large perching bird (genus *Corvus*) with mostly glossy black plumage, a heavy bill, and a raucous voice. The **crow family** (Corvidae) also includes the ravens, jays, magpies, choughs, and nutcrackers. **2** (**the Crow**) the constellation Corvus.
– PHRASES **as the crow flies** in a straight line: *it's 22 miles away, as the crow flies*. **eat crow** informal be humiliated by having to admit one's defeats or mistakes. [OE *crāwe*, of West Gmc. origin; rel. to Du. *kraai* and Ger. *Krähe*, also to CROW[2].]

crow[2] ▶ **v.** (past **crowed** or Brit. **crew** /kro͞o/) [intrans.] (of a cock) utter its characteristic loud cry. ■ (of a person) make a sound expressing a feeling of happiness or triumph: *Ruby crowed with delight*. ■ say something in a tone of gloating satisfaction. ▶ **n.** [usu. in sing.] the cry of a cock. ■ a sound made by a person expressing triumph or happiness: *she gave a little crow of triumph*. [OE *crāwan*, of West Gmc. origin; rel. to Ger. *krähen*, also to CROW[1]; ult. imitative.]

crow·bait /ˈkrōˌbāt/ ▶ **n.** informal, derog. an old horse.

crow·bar /ˈkrōˌbär/ ▶ **n.** an iron bar with a flattened end, used as a lever. ▶ **v.** (**-barred**, **-bar·ring**) [with obj. and complement] use a crowbar to open (something).

crow·ber·ry /ˈkrōˌberē/ ▶ **n.** (pl. **-ries**) a creeping heatherlike dwarf shrub (genus *Empetrum*, family Empetraceae) with small, needle-shaped leaves and black or reddish berries. ■ the edible but flavorless berry of this plant.

crowd /kroud/ ▶ **n.** a large number of people gathered together, typically in a disorganized or unruly way. ■ an audience. ■ informal, often derog. a group of people who are linked by a common interest or activity: *I've broken away from that whole junkie crowd*. ■ (**the crowd**) the mass or multitude of people, esp. those considered to be drearily ordinary or anonymous. ■ a large number of things regarded collectively. ▶ **v.** [trans.] (often **be crowded**) (of a number of people) fill (a space) almost completely, leaving little or no room for movement. ■ [intrans.] (**crowd into**) (of a number of people) move into (a space, esp. one that seems too small): *they crowded into the cockpit.* ■ [intrans.] **(crowd around)** (of a group of people) form a tightly packed mass around (someone or something). ■ move too close to (someone), either aggressively or in a way that causes discomfort or harm: *don't crowd her, she needs air.* ■ **(crowd someone/something out)** exclude someone or something by taking their place. ■ [intrans.] **(crowd in on)** fig. overwhelm and preoccupy (someone). ■ Baseball (of a batter) stand very close to (the plate) when batting. — **crowd·ed·ness** n. [OE *crūdan* 'press, hasten,' of Gmc. origin.]

crowd-pull·er ▶ n. informal an event, person, or thing that attracts a large audience.

crow·foot /'krō,fo͝ot/ ▶ n. a plant (genus *Ranunculus*) of the buttercup family, typically having lobed or divided leaves and white or yellow flowers. Many kinds are aquatic with flowers held above the water.

crown /kroun/ ▶ n. **1** a circular ornamental headdress worn by a monarch as a symbol of authority, usually made of or decorated with precious metals and jewels. ■ **(the Crown)** the reigning monarch, representing a country's government. ■ (usu. **the Crown**) the power or authority residing in the monarchy. ■ an ornament, emblem, or badge shaped like a crown. ■ a wreath of leaves or flowers, esp. that worn as an emblem of victory in ancient Greece or Rome. ■ an award or distinction gained by a victory or achievement, esp. in sports. **2** the top or highest part of something. ■ the top part of a person's head or a hat. ■ the part of a plant just above and below the ground from which the roots and shoots branch out. ■ the upper branching or spreading part of a tree or other plant. ■ the upper part of a cut gem, above the girdle. ■ the part of a tooth projecting from the gum. ■ an artificial replacement or covering for the upper part of a tooth. ■ the point of an anchor at which the arms reach the shaft. **3** (also **crown piece**) a British coin with a face value of five shillings or 25 pence, now minted only for commemorative purposes. **4** (in full **metric crown**) a paper size, now standardized at 384 × 504 mm. ■ (in full **crown octavo**) a book size, now standardized at 186 × 123 mm. ■ (in full **crown quarto**) a book size, now standardized at 246 × 189 mm. ▶ v. [trans.] **1** (usu. **be crowned**) ceremonially place a crown on the head of (someone) in order to invest them as a monarch. ■ [with obj. and complement] declare or acknowledge (someone) as the best, esp. at a sport: *he was crowned world champion last September.* ■ (in checkers) promote (a piece) to king by placing another on top of it. ■ rest on or form the top of. ■ fit a crown to (a tooth). ■ informal hit on the head. **2** be the triumphant culmination of (an effort or endeavor, esp. a prolonged one): *years of struggle were crowned by a state visit to Paris.* **3** [intrans.] (of a baby's head during labor) fully appear in the vaginal opening prior to emerging.

– PHRASES **crowning glory** the best and most notable aspect of something. ■ esp. humorous a person's hair. **to crown it all** as the final event in a series of particularly fortunate or unfortunate events. [ME: from Anglo-Norman Fr. *corune* (n.), *coruner* (v.), OFr. *corone* (n.), *coroner* (v.), from L. *corona* 'wreath, chaplet.']

crown col·o·ny a British colony whose legislature and administration is controlled by the Crown, represented by a governor.

crowned head ▶ n. (usu. **crowned heads**) a king or queen.

crown e·ther ▶ n. Chem. any of a class of organic compounds whose molecules are large rings containing a number of ether linkages.

crown fire ▶ n. a forest fire that spreads from treetop to treetop.

crown glass ▶ n. glass made without lead or iron, originally in a circular sheet. Formerly used in windows, it is now used as optical glass of low refractive index.

crown jew·els ▶ plural n. the crown and other ornaments and jewelry worn or carried by the sovereign on certain state occasions. ■ **(crown jewel)** a prized asset, achievement, or person: *the stadium will be the crown jewel of sporting arenas.*

Crown land ▶ n. (also **Crown lands**) land belonging to the British Crown. ■ land belonging to the state in some parts of the Commonwealth.

crown lens ▶ n. a lens made of crown glass and usu. forming one component of an achromatic lens.

crown mold·ing ▶ n. another term for CORNICE (sense 1).

crown of thorns ▶ n. **1** (also **crown-of-thorns-star·fish**) a large spiky starfish (*Acanthaster planci*) of the tropical Indo-Pacific, feeding on coral and sometimes causing great damage to reefs. **2** an ornamental Madagascan shrub (*Euphorbia milii*) of the spurge family, with bright red flowers and many slender thorns. ■ any of a number of other thorny plants, esp. Christ's thorn.

crown piece ▶ n. see CROWN (sense 3).

Crown Point a town in northeastern New York, on Lake Champlain, scene of much military action during the 18th century.

crown prince ▶ n. (in some countries) a male heir to a throne.

crown prin·cess ▶ n. the wife of a crown prince. ■ (in some countries) a female heir to a throne.

crown roast ▶ n. a roast of rib pieces of pork or lamb arranged like a crown in a circle with the bones pointing upward.

crown saw ▶ n. another term for HOLE SAW.

crown wheel ▶ n. a gearwheel or cogwheel with teeth that project from the face of the wheel at right angles, used esp. in the gears of motor vehicles.

crow's-foot ▶ n. (pl. **-feet**) **1** (usu. **crow's-feet**) a branching wrinkle at the outer corner of a person's eye. **2** a mark, symbol, or design formed of lines diverging from a point, resembling a bird's footprint.

crow's-nest ▶ n. a shelter or platform fixed near the top of the mast of a vessel as a place for a lookout to stand.

crow steps ▶ plural n. another term for CORBIESTEPS. — **crow-stepped** adj.

croze /krōz/ ▶ n. a groove at the end of a cask or barrel to receive the edge of the head. ■ a cooper's tool for making such grooves. [17th C.: perh. from Fr. *creux, creuse* 'hollow.']

cro·zier /'krōzhər/ (also **cro·sier**) ▶ n. a hooked staff carried by a bishop as a symbol of pastoral office. ■ the curled top of a young fern. [ME: partly from Old Fr. *croisier* 'cross bearer,' from *crois* 'cross,' based on L. *crux*; reinforced by OFr. *crocier* 'bearer of a bishop's crook,' from *croce* (see CROSSE).]

CRT ▶ abbr. cathode-ray tube.

cru /kro͞o; krʏ/ ▶ n. (pl. **crus** pronunc. same) (in France) a vineyard or group of vineyards, esp. one of recognized superior quality. See also GRAND CRU, PREMIER CRU. [Fr., from *crû*, lit. 'growth,' past part. of *croître*.]

cru·ces /'kro͞osēz/ plural form of CRUX.

cru·cial /'kro͞oshəl/ ▶ adj. decisive or critical, esp. in the success or failure of something. ■ of great importance. — **cru·ci·al·i·ty** /,kro͞oshē'alitē/ n. **cru·cial·ly** adv. [18th C. (in the sense 'cross-shaped'): from Fr., from L. *crux, cruc-* 'cross.']

cru·ci·ate /'kro͞osh(ē)it; -shē,āt/ ▶ adj. Anat. Bot. cross-shaped. [19th C.: from L. *cruciatus*, from *crux, cruc-* 'cross.']

cru·ci·ate lig·a·ment ▶ n. Anat. either of a pair of ligaments in the knee that cross each other and connect the femur to the tibia.

cru·ci·ble /'kro͞osəbəl/ ▶ n. a ceramic or metal container in which metals or other substances may be melted or subjected to very high temperatures. ■ a place or occasion of severe test or trial: *the crucible of combat.* ■ a place or situation in which different elements interact to produce something new. [ME: from med. L. *crucibulum* 'night lamp, crucible,' from L. *crux, cruc-* 'cross.']

cru·ci·fer /'kro͞osəfər/ ▶ n. **1** Bot. a plant of the cabbage family (Cruciferae), whose flowers have four petals arranged in a cross. **2** a person carrying a cross or crucifix in a procession. — **cru·cif·er·ous** /kro͞o'sifərəs/ adj. [16th C.: from Christian Latin, from L. *crux, cruc-* 'cross.']

cru·ci·fix /'kro͞osə,fiks/ ▶ n. a representation of a cross with a figure of Jesus Christ on it. [ME: via OFr. from eccles. Latin *crucifixus*, from L. *cruci fixus* 'fixed to a cross.']

cru·ci·fix·ion /,kro͞osə'fikshən/ ▶ n. esp. hist. the execution of a person by nailing or binding them to a cross. ■ **(the Crucifixion)** the killing of Jesus Christ in such a way. ■ **(Crucifixion)** [in sing.] an artistic representation or musical composition based on this event.

cru·ci·form /'kro͞osə,fôrm/ ▶ adj. having the shape of a cross: *a cruciform sword.* ■ of or denoting a church having a cross-shaped plan with a nave and transepts. ▶ n. a thing shaped like a cross. [17th C.: from L. *crux, cruc-* 'cross' + -IFORM.]

cru·ci·fy /'kro͞osə,fī/ ▶ v. (**-fies, -fied**) [trans.] (often **be crucified**) esp. hist. put (someone) to death by nailing or binding them to a cross. ■ criticize (someone) severely and unrelentingly: *our fans would crucify us if we lost.* ■ cause anguish to (someone): *she'd been crucified by his departure.* — **cru·ci·fi·er** n. [ME: from OFr. *crucifier*, from late L. *crucifigere*, from L. *crux, cruc-* 'cross' + *figere* 'fix.' Cf. CRUCIFIX.]

crud /krəd/ ▶ n. informal a substance that is disgusting or unpleasant, typically because of its dirtiness. ■ nonsense. — **crud·dy** /'krədē/ adj. [ME: var. of CURD.]

crude /kro͞od/ ▶ adj. **1** in a natural or raw state; not yet processed or refined: *crude oil.* ■ Stat. (of figures) not adjusted or corrected: *the crude mortality rate.* ■ (of an estimate or guess) likely to be only approximately accurate. **2** constructed in a rudimentary or makeshift way. ■ (of an action) showing little finesse or subtlety and as a result unlikely to succeed. **3** (of language, behavior, or a person) offensively coarse or rude, esp. in relation to sexual matters. ▶ n. natural petroleum. — **crude·ly** adv. **crude·ness** n. **cru·di·ty** /'kro͞oditē/ n. [ME: from L. *crudus* 'raw, rough.']

crude tur·pen·tine ▶ n. see TURPENTINE (sense 1).

cru·di·tés /,kro͞odi'tā/ ▶ plural n. assorted raw vegetables served as an hors d'oeuvre, typically with a sauce into which they may be dipped. [pl. of Fr. *crudité* 'rawness, crudity,' from L. *crudus* 'raw, rough.']

cru·el /'kro͞oəl/ ▶ adj. (**-el·er, -el·est**; Brit. **-el·ler, -el·lest**) causing pain or suffering: *I can't stand people who are cruel to animals.* ■ having or showing a sadistic disregard for the pain or suffering of others. — **cru·el·ly** adv. [ME: via OFr. from L. *crudelis*, rel. to *crudus* (see CRUDE).]

cru·el·ty /'kro͞oəltē/ ▶ n. (pl. **-ties**) callous indifference to or pleasure in causing pain and suffering. ■ behavior that causes pain or suffering to a person or animal. ■ Law behavior that causes physical or mental harm to another, esp. a spouse, whether intentionally or not. [ME: from OFr. *crualte*, based on L. *crudelitas*, from *crudelis* (see CRUEL).]

cru·el·ty-free ▶ adj. (of cosmetics or other commercial products) manufactured or developed by methods that do not involve experimentation on animals.

cru·et /'kro͞oit/ ▶ n. **1** a small container for salt, pepper, oil, or vinegar for use at a dining table. **2** (in church use) a small container for the wine or water to be used in the celebration of the Eucharist. [ME (sense 2): from Anglo-Norman Fr., dimin. of OFr. *crue* 'pot,' from Old Saxon *krūka*; rel. to CROCK[2].]

Cruik·shank /ˈkrŏŏk,shangk/, George (1792–1878), English painter, illustrator, and caricaturist.

cruise /krōōz/ ▶ **v.** [no obj., with adverbial] sail about in an area without a precise destination, esp. for pleasure. ■ take a vacation on a ship or boat following a predetermined course, usually calling at several ports. ■ (of a vehicle or person) travel or move slowly around without a specific destination in mind. ■ (of a motor vehicle or aircraft) travel smoothly at a moderate or economical speed. ■ achieve an objective with ease, esp. in sports. ■ [trans.] informal wander about (a place) in search of a sexual partner. ■ [trans.] informal attempt to pick up (a sexual partner): *he was cruising a pair of sailors.* ▶ **n.** a voyage on a ship or boat taken for pleasure or as a holiday and usually calling in at several places.
– PHRASES **cruising for a bruising** informal heading or looking for trouble. [17th C. (as a v.): prob. from Du. *kruisen* 'to cross,' from *kruis* 'cross,' from L. *crux*.]

cruise mis·sile ▶ **n.** a low-flying missile that is guided to its target by an on-board computer.

cruis·er /ˈkrōōzər/ ▶ **n.** **1** a relatively fast warship larger than a destroyer and less heavily armed than a battleship. **2** a yacht or motorboat with passenger accommodations, designed for leisure use. ■ a person who goes on a pleasure cruise. **3** an automobile that can be driven smoothly at high speed. ■ a police patrol car.

cruis·er·weight /ˈkrōōzər,wāt/ ▶ **n.** in professional boxing, a weight between light heavyweight and heavyweight, ranging from 175 to 190 pounds (79 to 85 kg). ■ a boxer of this weight.

cruis·ing speed ▶ **n.** a speed for a particular vehicle, ship, or aircraft, usually below maximum, that is comfortable and economical.

crul·ler /ˈkrələr/ ▶ **n.** a small cake made of rich dough twisted or curled and fried in deep fat. [19th C.: from Du. *kruller*, from *krullen* 'to curl.']

crumb /krəm/ ▶ **n.** **1** a small fragment of bread, cake, or cracker. ■ a very small amount of something: *the budget provided few crumbs of comfort.* ■ the soft inner part of a loaf of bread. ■ a dessert topping made of brown sugar, butter, flour, and spices: [as adj.] *apple crumb pie.* ■ (usu. **crumb rubber**) granulated rubber, usually made from recycled car tires. **2** informal an objectionable or contemptible person. ▶ **v.** [trans.] cover (food) with breadcrumbs. [OE *cruma*, of Gmc. origin; rel. to Du. *kruim* and Ger. *Krume*.]

crum·ble /ˈkrəmbəl/ ▶ **v.** [intrans.] break or fall apart into small fragments, esp. over a period of time as part of a process of deterioration. ■ [trans.] cause (something) to break apart into small fragments: *the easiest way to crumble blue cheese.* ■ (of an organization, relationship, or structure) disintegrate gradually over a period of time. [ME: prob. from an OE word rel. to CRUMB.]

crum·bly /ˈkrəmblē/ ▶ **adj.** (**-blier, -bli·est**) consisting of or easily breaking into small fragments. — **crum·bli·ness** **n.**

crumb struc·ture ▶ **n.** the porous structure or condition of soil when its particles are moderately aggregated.

crumb·y /ˈkrəmē/ ▶ **adj.** (**crumb·i·er, crumb·i·est**) **1** like or covered in crumbs. **2** var. of CRUMMY.

crum·horn /ˈkrəm,hôrn/ ▶ **n.** var. of KRUMMHORN.

crum·my /ˈkrəmē/ (also **crumb·y**) informal ▶ **adj.** (**-mi·er, -mi·est**) dirty, unpleasant, or of poor quality: *a crummy little room.* ■ [predic.] unwell; ill: *I'm crummy and want to get better.* — **crum·mi·ly** /ˈkrəməlē/ **adv.** **crum·mi·ness** **n.** [19th C.: var. of CRUMBY.]

crump /krəmp/ ▶ **n.** a loud thudding sound, esp. one made by an exploding bomb or shell. ▶ **v.** [intrans.] make such a sound. [17th C.: imitative.]

crum·pet /ˈkrəmpit/ ▶ **n.** a thick, flat, savory cake with a soft, porous texture, made from a yeast mixture cooked on a griddle and eaten toasted and buttered. [17th C.: of unknown origin.]

crum·ple /ˈkrəmpəl/ ▶ **v.** [trans.] crush (something, typically paper or cloth) so that it becomes creased and wrinkled. ■ [intrans.] become bent, crooked, or creased. ■ [intrans.] (of a person) suddenly flop down to the ground so that their body appears bent or broken. ■ [intrans.] (of a person's face) suddenly sag and show an expression of desolation. ■ [intrans.] suddenly lose force or effectiveness. ▶ **n.** a crushed fold, crease, or wrinkle. — **crum·ply** **adj.** [ME: from obs. *crump* 'make or become curved,' from OE *crump* 'bent, crooked,' of West Gmc. origin.]

crum·ple zone ▶ **n.** a part of a motor vehicle, esp. the extreme front and rear, designed to crumple easily in a crash and absorb the main force of an impact.

crunch /krənch/ ▶ **v.** **1** [trans.] crush (a hard or brittle foodstuff) with the teeth, making a loud but muffled grinding sound: *she paused to crunch a gingersnap.* ■ [intrans.] make such a sound, esp. when walking or driving over gravel or an icy surface. ■ strike or crush noisily: *two cab drivers who had just crunched fenders.* **2** process large amounts of information or perform operations of great complexity, esp. by computer. ▶ **n.** **1** [usu. in sing.] a loud muffled grinding sound made when crushing, moving over, or hitting something. **2** (**the crunch**) informal a crucial point or situation, typically one at which a decision with important consequences must be made. ■ a severe shortage of money or credit. **3** a physical exercise designed to strengthen the abdominal muscles; a sit-up. [19th C. (as a v.): var. of 17th-cent. *cranch* (prob. imitative).]

crunch·er /ˈkrənchər/ ▶ **n.** informal **1** a critical or vital point; a crucial or difficult question. **2** a computer, system, or person able to perform operations of great complexity or to process large amounts of information. See also NUMBER CRUNCHER.

crunch·y /ˈkrənchē/ ▶ **adj.** (**crunch·i·er, crunch·i·est**) **1** making a sharp noise when bitten or crushed and (of food) pleasantly crisp: *bake until the topping is crunchy.* **2** informal politically and environmentally liberal: *a song that incorporates whale-singing seems pretty crunchy.* — **crunch·i·ly** **adv.** **crunch·i·ness** **n.**

crunk /krəngk/ ▶ **n.** a type of hip-hop or rap music characterized by repeated shouted catchphrases and elements typical of electronic dance music, such as prominent bass. ▶ **adj.** chiefly black slang (of a person) very excited or full of energy: *get crunk with some raw hip hop.* [1990s: perh. an alt. past part. of CRANK[1] or a blend of CRAZY and DRUNK.]

crup·per /ˈkrəpər/ ▶ **n.** a strap buckled to the back of a saddle and looped under the horse's tail to prevent the saddle or harness from slipping forward. See illustration at HARNESS. [ME: from OFr. *cropiere*, rel. to *croupe* (see CROUP[2]).]

cru·ra /ˈkrŏŏrə/ plural form of CRUS.

cru·ra ce·re·bri /ˈkrŏŏrə ˈserə,brī; ˈkerə,brē/ plural form of CRUS CEREBRI.

cru·ral /ˈkrŏŏ(ə)rəl/ ▶ **adj.** Anat. Zool. of or relating to the leg or the thigh. ■ of or relating to any part called "crus," for example, the crura cerebri. [16th C.: from L. *cruralis*, from *crus, crur-* 'leg.']

crus /krōōs; krəs/ ▶ **n.** (pl. **cru·ra** /ˈkrŏŏrə/) Anat. an elongated part of an anatomical structure, esp. one that occurs in the body as a pair. See CRUS CEREBRI. [18th C.: L., lit. 'leg.']

cru·sade /krōōˈsād/ ▶ **n.** (often **Cru·sade**) a medieval military expedition, one of a series made by Europeans to recover the Holy Land from the Muslims in the 11th, 12th, and 13th centuries. ■ an organized campaign concerning a political, social, or religious issue, typically motivated by a fervent desire for change. ▶ **v.** [intrans.] lead or take part in a campaign concerning a social, political, or religious issue. — **cru·sad·er** **n.** [16th C.: from Fr. *croisade*, an alt. of earlier *croisée*, lit. 'the state of being marked with the cross,' based on L. *crux, cruc-* 'cross'.]

crus ce·re·bri /ˈserə,brī; ˈkerə,brē/ ▶ **n.** (pl. **cru·ra ce·re·bri** /ˈkrŏŏrə/) Anat. either of two symmetrical tracts of nerve fibers at the base of the midbrain, linking the pons and the cerebral hemispheres. [18th C.: from L., lit. 'leg of the brain.']

crush /krəsh/ ▶ **v.** [trans.] press or squeeze (someone or something) with force or violence, typically causing serious damage or injury. ■ reduce (something) to a powder or pulp by exerting strong pressure on it: *you can crush a pill between two spoons.* ■ crease or crumple (cloth or paper). ■ (of a government or state) violently subdue (opposition or a rebellion). ■ bring about a feeling of overwhelming disappointment or embarrassment in (someone). ▶ **n.** **1** [usu. in sing.] a crowd of people pressed closely together, esp. in an enclosed space. **2** informal a brief but intense infatuation for someone, esp. someone unattainable or inappropriate. **3** a drink made from the juice of pressed fruit. — **crush·a·ble** **adj.** **crush·er** **n.** **crush·ing·ly** **adv.** [ME: from OFr. *cruissir* 'gnash (teeth) or crack,' of unknown origin.]

crust /krəst/ ▶ **n.** the tough outer part of a loaf of bread. ■ a hard, dry scrap of bread. ■ a slice of bread from the end of the loaf. ■ a layer of pastry covering a pie. ■ a hardened layer, coating, or deposit on the surface of something, esp. something soft: *a crust of snow.* ■ the outermost layer of rock of which a planet consists, esp. the part of the earth above the mantle: *the earth's crust.* ■ a deposit of tartrates and other substances formed in wine aged in the bottle, esp. port. ▶ **v.** [intrans.] form into a hard outer layer. ■ [trans.] cover with a hard outer layer. — **crus·tal** /ˈkrəstəl/ **adj.** (Geol.). [ME: from OFr. *crouste*, from L. *crusta* 'rind, shell, crust.']

Crus·ta·cea /krəˈstāshə/ Zool. a large group (Subphylum or phylum Crustacea) of mainly aquatic arthropods that include crabs, lobsters, shrimps, wood lice, barnacles, and many minute forms. They are very diverse, but most have four or more pairs of limbs and several other appendages. ■ [as pl. n.] (**crustacea**) arthropods of this group. — **crus·ta·cean** **n.** & **adj.** **crus·ta·ceous** /-shəs/ **adj.** [mod. L. (pl.), from *crusta* (see CRUST).]

crust·ed /ˈkrəstəd/ ▶ **adj.** **1** having or forming a hard top layer or covering: *she washed away the crusted blood.* ■ denoting a style of unfiltered, blended port that deposits a sediment in the bottle. **2** old-fashioned; venerable.

crus·tose /ˈkrəs,tōs/ ▶ **adj.** Bot. (of a lichen or alga) forming or resembling a crust.

crust·y /ˈkrəstē/ ▶ **adj.** (**crust·i·er, crust·i·est**) **1** having a crisp or hard outer layer. *crusty bread.* ■ (of a substance) acting as a hard outer layer. **2** (esp. of an old person) outspoken and irritable. — **crust·i·ly** /ˈkrəstəlē/ **adv.** **crust·i·ness** **n.**

crutch /krəch/ ▶ **n.** a long stick with a crosspiece at the top, used as a support under the armpit by a lame person. ■ [in sing.] fig. a thing used for support or reassurance: *they use the Internet as a crutch for their loneliness.* ▶ **v.** [intrans.] move by means of or as if by means of crutches: *I was crutching down a long corridor.* [OE *crycc, cryc*, of Gmc. origin.]

Crux /krəks; krŏŏks/ Astron. another term for the SOUTHERN CROSS.

crux /krəks; krŏŏks/ ▶ **n.** (pl. **crux·es** or **cru·ces** /ˈkrōōsēz/) (**the crux**) the decisive or most important point at issue. ■ a particular point of difficulty. [17th C.: from L., lit. 'cross.']

cru·za·do /krōōˈzädō/ ▶ **n.** (pl. **-dos**) the basic monetary unit of Brazil from 1988 to 1990, equal to 100 centavos. [from Port. *cruzado, crusado* 'marked with the cross.']

cru·zei·ro /krōōˈze(ə)rō/ ▶ **n.** (pl. **-ros**) the basic monetary unit of Brazil from 1990 to 1993, equal to 100 centavos. [Port., lit. 'large cross.']

cry /krī/ ▶ **v.** (**cries, cried**) [intrans.] shed tears, esp. as an expression of distress or pain. ■ shout or scream, esp. to express one's fear, pain, or grief. ■ [with direct speech] say something in an excited or anguished tone of voice. ■ (**cry out for**) fig. demand as a self-evident requirement or solution. ■ (of a bird or other animal) make a loud characteristic

call. ■ [trans.] (of a hawker) proclaim (wares) for sale in the street. ▶ **n.** (pl. **cries**) a spell of weeping. ■ a loud inarticulate shout or scream expressing a powerful feeling or emotion: *a cry of despair.* ■ a distinctive call of a bird or other animal. ■ a loud excited utterance of a word or words. ■ the call of a hawker selling wares on the street. ■ an urgent appeal or entreaty. ■ a demand or opinion expressed by many people.
– PHRASES **cry one's eyes** (or **heart**) **out** weep bitterly and at length. **cry for the moon** ask for what is unattainable or impossible. **cry foul** protest strongly about a real or imagined wrong or injustice. **cry from the heart** a passionate and honest appeal or protest. **cry wolf** see WOLF. **for crying out loud** informal used to express one's irritation or impatience. **in full cry** used to describe hounds baying in keen pursuit. **it's no use crying over spilt** (or **spilled**) **milk** see MILK.
– PHRASAL VERBS **cry off** informal go back on a promise or fail to keep to an arrangement. [ME: from OFr. *crier* (v.), *cri* (n.), from L. *quiritare* 'raise a public outcry.']

cry·ba·by /'krī,bābē/ ▶ **n.** (pl. **-bies**) a person, esp. a child, who sheds tears frequently or readily.

cry·er /'krīər/ ▶ **n.** archaic spelling of CRIER.

cry·ing /'krī-iNG/ ▶ **adj.** [attrib.] very great: *it would be **a crying shame** to let some other woman have it.*

cryo- ▶ **comb. form** involving or producing cold, esp. extreme cold: *cryostat* | *cryosurgery.* [from Gk. *kruos* 'frost.']

cry·o·bi·ol·o·gy /,krīōbī'äləjē/ ▶ **n.** the branch of biology that deals with the properties of organisms and tissues at low temperatures. — **cry·o·bi·o·log·i·cal** /-,bīə'läjəkəl/ **adj.** **cry·o·bi·ol·o·gist** /-jist/ **n.**

cry·o·gen /'krīəjən/ ▶ **n.** a substance used to produce very low temperatures.

cry·o·gen·ics /,krīə'jeniks/ ▶ **plural n.** [treated as sing.] the branch of physics dealing with the production and effects of very low temperatures. ■ another term for CRYONICS. — **cry·o·gen·ic adj.** **cry·o·gen·i·cal·ly** /-ik(ə)lē/ **adv.**

cry·o·glob·u·lin /,krīə'gläbyəlin/ ▶ **n.** Biochem. a protein that occurs in the blood in certain disorders. It can be precipitated out of solution below 10°C, causing obstruction in the fingers and toes.

cry·o·lite /'krīə,līt/ ▶ **n.** a white or colorless mineral consisting of a fluoride of sodium and aluminum. It is added to bauxite as a flux in aluminum smelting.

cry·om·e·ter /krī'ämitər/ ▶ **n.** a thermometer for measuring very low temperatures.

cry·on·ics /krī'äniks/ ▶ **plural n.** [treated as sing.] the practice or technique of deep-freezing the bodies of those who have died of an incurable disease, in the hope of a future cure. — **cry·on·ic adj.** [1960s: contr. of CRYOGENICS.]

cry·o·pre·cip·i·tate /,krīōpri'sipətit; -'sipə,tāt/ ▶ **n.** esp. Biochem. a substance precipitated from a solution, esp. from the blood, at low temperatures.

cry·o·pre·serve /,krīōpri'zərv/ ▶ **v.** [trans.] Biol. Med. preserve (cells or tissues) by cooling them below the freezing point of water. — **cry·o·pres·er·va·tion** /-,prezər'vāSHən/ **n.**

cry·o·scope /'krīə,skōp/ ▶ **n.** an instrument used to determine the freezing point of a liquid or a solution.

cry·o·stat /'krīə,stat/ ▶ **n.** an apparatus for maintaining a very low temperature. ■ an apparatus for taking very fine slices of tissue while it is kept very cold.

cry·o·sur·ger·y /,krīō'sərjərē/ ▶ **n.** surgery using the local application of intense cold to destroy unwanted tissue.

crypt /kript/ ▶ **n. 1** an underground room or vault beneath a church, used as a chapel or burial place. **2** Anat. a small tubular gland, pit, or recess. [ME: from L. *crypta*, from Gk. *kruptē* 'a vault,' from *kruptos* 'hidden.']

crypt·a·nal·y·sis /,kriptə'naləsis/ ▶ **n.** the art or process of deciphering coded messages without the key. — **crypt·an·a·lyst** /,krip'tanl-ist/ **n.** **crypt·an·a·lyt·ic** /-tanl'itik/ **adj.** **crypt·an·a·lyt·i·cal** /-tanl'itikəl/ **adj.**

cryp·tic /'kriptik/ ▶ **adj. 1** having a meaning that is mysterious or obscure. ■ (of a crossword) having difficult clues that indicate the solutions indirectly. **2** Zool. (of coloration or markings) serving to camouflage an animal in its natural environment. — **cryp·ti·cal·ly** /-tik(ə)lē/ **adv.** [17th C.: from late L. *crypticus*, from Gk. *kruptikos*, from *kruptos* 'hidden.']

cryp·to /'kriptō/ ▶ **n. 1** short for CRYPTOGRAPHY. **2** (pl. **-tos**) informal a person having a secret allegiance to a political creed, esp. communism.

crypto- ▶ **comb. form** concealed; secret: *cryptogram.* [from Gk. *kruptos* 'hidden.']

cryp·to·bi·o·sis /,kriptəbī'ōsis/ ▶ **n.** Biol. a physiological state in which metabolic activity is reduced to an undetectable level without disappearing altogether. It is known in certain plant and animal groups adapted to survive periods of extremely dry conditions. — **cryp·to·bi·ot·ic** /,kriptə,bī'ätik/ **adj.**

cryp·to·clas·tic /,kriptō'klastik/ ▶ **adj.** Geol. composed of microscopic fragments.

cryp·to·crys·tal·line /,kriptō'kristə,lin; -,līn; -,lēn/ ▶ **adj.** having a crystalline structure visible only when magnified.

cryp·to·gam /'kriptə,gam/ ▶ **n.** Bot., dated a plant that has no true flowers or seeds, including ferns, mosses, liverworts, lichens, algae, and fungi. — **cryptogamous** /krip'tägəməs/ **adj.** [19th C.: ult. from Gk. *kruptos* 'hidden' + *gamos* 'marriage.']

cryp·to·gam·ic /,kriptə'gamik/ ▶ **adj.** Bot. of, relating to, or denoting cryptogams. ■ Ecol. (of a desert soil or surface crust) covered with or consisting of a fragile black layer of cyanobacteria, mosses, and lichens.

cryp·to·gen·ic /,kriptə'jenik/ ▶ **adj.** (of a disease) of obscure or uncertain origin.

cryp·to·gram /'kriptə,gram/ ▶ **n. 1** a text written in code. **2** a symbol or figure with secret or occult significance.

cryp·tog·ra·phy /krip'tägrəfē/ ▶ **n.** the art of writing or solving codes. — **cryp·tog·ra·pher n.** **cryp·to·graph·ic** /,kriptə'grafik/ **adj.** **cryp·to·graph·i·cal·ly** /,kriptə'grafik(ə)lē/ **adv.**

cryp·tol·o·gy /krip'täləjē/ ▶ **n.** the study of codes, or the art of writing and solving them. — **cryp·to·log·i·cal** /,kriptə'läjikəl/ **adj.** **cryp·tol·o·gist** /-jist/ **n.**

cryp·to·me·ri·a /,kriptə'mi(ə)rēə/ ▶ **n.** a tall, conical, coniferous tree (*Cryptomeria japonica*, family Taxodiaceae), native to China and Japan, with long, curved, spirally arranged leaves and short cones. Also called JAPANESE CEDAR. [mod. L., from CRYPTO- 'hidden' + Gk. *meros* 'part.']

cryp·to·nym /'kriptə,nim/ ▶ **n.** a code name. — **cryp·ton·y·mous** /krip'tänəməs/ **adj.**

cryp·to·spor·i·di·um /,kriptəspə'ridēəm/ ▶ **n.** a parasitic coccidian protozoan found in the intestinal tract of many vertebrates, where it can cause disease. [20th C.: from CRYPTO- 'concealed' + mod. L. *sporidium* 'small spore.']

Cryp·to·zo·ic /,kriptə'zō-ik/ ▶ **adj.** Geol. of, relating to, or denoting the period (the Precambrian) in which rocks contain no, or only slight, traces of living organisms. Compare with PHANEROZOIC. [20th C.: from Gk. *kruptos* 'hidden' + *zōē* 'life' + -IC.]

cryp·to·zo·ic /,kriptə'zō-ik/ ▶ **adj.** Ecol. (of small invertebrates) living on the ground but hidden in the leaf litter, or under stones or pieces of wood. — **cryp·to·zo·a** /-'zōə/ **plural n.** [19th C.: from Gk. *kruptos* 'hidden' + *zōē* 'life' + -IC.]

crys·tal /'kristl/ ▶ **n. 1** a piece of a homogeneous solid substance having a naturally geometrically regular form with symmetrically arranged plane faces. ■ Chem. any solid consisting of a symmetrical, ordered, three-dimensional aggregation of atoms or molecules. ■ Electron. a crystalline piece of semiconductor used as an oscillator or transducer. ■ a clear transparent mineral, esp. quartz. ■ a piece of crystalline substance believed to have healing powers. ■ informal short for CRYSTAL METH (methamphetamine). **2** (also **crystal glass**) highly transparent glass with a high refractive index: [as adj.] *a crystal chandelier.* ■ articles made of such glass. ■ the glass over a watch face. ▶ **adj.** clear and transparent like crystal.
– PHRASES **crystal clear** completely transparent and unclouded. ■ unambiguous; easily understood. [OE from OFr. *cristal*, from L. *crystallum*, from Gk. *krustallos* 'ice, crystal.']

crys·tal ball ▶ **n.** a solid globe of glass or rock crystal, used by fortunetellers and clairvoyants for crystal-gazing.

crys·tal form ▶ **n.** a set of crystal faces defined according to their relationship to the crystal axes.

crys·tal-gaz·ing ▶ **n.** looking intently into a crystal ball with the aim of seeing images relating to future or distant events. ■ fig. attempting to forecast the future.

crys·tal heal·ing (also **crystal therapy**) ▶ **n.** the use of the healing powers of crystals in alternative medicine.

crys·tal lat·tice ▶ **n.** the symmetrical three-dimensional arrangement of atoms inside a crystal.

crys·tal·lif·er·ous /,kristl'ifərəs/ (also **crys·tal·lig·er·ous** /-tl'ijərəs/) ▶ **adj.** bearing, containing, or producing crystals.

crys·tal·lin /'kristl-in/ ▶ **n.** Biochem. a protein of the globulin class present in the lens of the eye. [19th C.: from L. *crystallum* 'crystal' + -IN¹.]

crys·tal·line /'kristl-in; -,īn; -,ēn/ ▶ **adj.** having the structure and form of a crystal; composed of crystals. ■ literary very clear: *he writes a crystalline prose.* — **crys·tal·lin·i·ty** /,kristl'initē/ **n.**

crys·tal·line lens ▶ **n.** the transparent elastic structure behind the iris by which light is focused onto the retina of the eye.

crys·tal·lite /'kristl,īt/ ▶ **n.** an individual perfect crystal or region of regular crystalline structure in a material, typically of a metal or a partly crystalline polymer. ■ a very small crystal.

crys·tal·lize /'kristl,īz/ ▶ **v.** form or cause to form crystals: [intrans.] *when most liquids freeze they crystallize.* ■ fig. make or become definite and clear. ■ [usu. as adj.] (**crystallized**) coat and impregnate (fruit or petals) with sugar as a means of preserving them. — **crys·tal·liz·a·ble** /'kristl,īzəbəl; ,kristl'īzəbəl/ **adj.** **crys·tal·li·za·tion** /,kristlə'zāSHən/ **n.**

crys·tal·log·ra·phy /,kristl'ägrəfē/ ▶ **n.** the branch of science concerned with the structure and properties of crystals. — **crys·tal·log·ra·pher** /-fər/ **n.** **crys·tal·lo·graph·ic** /-ə'grafik/ **adj.** **crys·tal·lo·graph·i·cal·ly** /-ə'grafik(ə)lē/ **adv.**

crys·tal·loid /'kristl,oid/ ▶ **adj.** resembling a crystal in shape or structure. ▶ **n. 1** Bot. a small, crystallike mass of protein in a plant cell. **2** Chem. a substance that, when dissolved, forms a true solution rather than a colloid and is able to pass through a semipermeable membrane.

crys·tal meth ▶ **n.** see METH (sense 1).

crys·tal set (also **crystal radio**) ▶ **n.** a simple early form of radio receiver with a crystal touching a metal wire as the rectifier (instead of a tube or transistor), and no amplifier or loudspeaker.

crys·tal sys·tem ▶ n. each of seven categories of crystals (cubic, tetragonal, orthorhombic, trigonal, hexagonal, monoclinic, and triclinic) classified according to the possible relations of the crystal axes.
crys·tal ther·a·py ▶ n. another term for CRYSTAL HEALING.
Cs ▶ symb. the chemical element cesium.
c/s ▶ abbr. cycles per second.
CSA ▶ abbr. Confederate States of America.
csar·das /'CHärdäSH; -däs/ (also **czar·das**) ▶ n. var. of CZARDAS.
CSC ▶ abbr. Civil Service Commission.
CSF ▶ abbr. cerebrospinal fluid.
CSM ▶ abbr. ■ command and service modules (see COMMAND MODULE). ■ command sergeant major.
CST ▶ abbr. Central Standard Time (see CENTRAL TIME).
CT ▶ abbr. ■ computerized (or computed) tomography. ■ Connecticut (in official postal use).
ct. ▶ abbr. ■ carat: *18 ct. gold.* ■ cent. ■ county. ■ court.
cte·nid·i·um /tə'nidēəm/ ▶ n. (pl. **-nid·i·a** /-'nidēə/) Zool. a comblike structure, esp. a respiratory organ or gill in a mollusk, consisting of an axis with a row of projecting filaments. [19th C.; mod. L., from Gk. *ktenidion*, dimin. of *kteis, kten-* 'comb.']
cte·noid /'tēnoid; 'ten,oid/ ▶ adj. Zool. (of fish scales) having many tiny projections on the edge like the teeth of a comb, as in many bony fishes. Compare with GANOID and PLACOID. [19th C.: from Gk. *kteis, kten-* 'comb' + -OID.]
Cte·noph·o·ra /ti'näfərə/ Zool. a small phylum of aquatic invertebrates that comprises the comb jellies. — **cten·o·phore** /'tenə,fôr/ n. [mod. L. (pl.), from Gk. *kteis, kten-* 'comb' + *pherein* 'to bear.']
ctn. ▶ abbr. ■ carton. ■ Math. cotangent.
CTS ▶ abbr. carpal tunnel syndrome.
CT scan ▶ n another term for CAT SCAN. — **CT scan·ner** n.
Cu ▶ symb. the chemical element copper. [from late L. *cuprum*.]
cu. ▶ abbr. cubic (in units of measurement: for example, cu. ft. = cubic feet).
cua·dril·la /kwä'drē(l)yə/ ▶ n. a matador's team of assistants, including picadors and banderilleros. [19th C.: Sp.]
cub /kəb/ ▶ n. the young of a fox, bear, lion, or other carnivorous mammal. ▶ v. (**cubbed, cub·bing**) [intrans.] give birth to cubs: *both share the same earth during the first ten days after cubbing.* [16th C.: of unknown origin.]
Cu·ba /'kyo͞obə/ a country in the western West Indies. *See box.* — **Cu·ban** adj. & n.

Cuba

Official name: Republic of Cuba
Location: one large island and many smaller surrounding islands in the western West Indies, in the Caribbean Sea at the mouth of the Gulf of Mexico, about 90 miles (144 km) south of Florida
Area: 42,800 square miles (110,900 sq km)
Population: 11,308,000
Capital: Havana
Language: Spanish
Currency: Cuban peso

Cu·ba li·bre /,k(y)o͞obə 'lēbrā/ ▶ n. (pl. **Cu·ba li·bres**) a cocktail typically containing cola, lime juice, rum, and a garnish of lime. [19th C.: Amer. Sp., lit. 'free Cuba.']
Cu·ban·go /ko͞o'bäNGgō/ another name for OKAVANGO.
Cu·ban heel /'kyo͞obən/ ▶ n. a moderately high, straight-sided heel on a shoe or boot.
Cu·ban Mis·sile Cri·sis a crisis in October 1962, following the discovery by the US of Soviet nuclear missiles in Cuba. President John F. Kennedy demanded their removal and announced a naval blockade of the island; the Soviet leader Khrushchev acceded to the US demands a week later.
cu·ba·ture /'kyo͞obə,CHər/ ▶ n. the determination of the volume of a solid. [17th C.: from the v. CUBE.]
cub·by /'kəbē/ ▶ n. (pl. **-bies**) a cubbyhole. [17th C. (orig. Scots, denoting a straw basket): rel. to dial. *cub* 'stall, pen, hutch,' of Low Ger. origin.]
cub·by·hole /'kəbē,hōl/ ▶ n. a small, enclosed compartment or room.
cube /kyo͞ob/ ▶ n. a symmetrical three-dimensional shape, either solid or hollow, contained by six equal squares. ■ a block of something with six sides: *a sugar cube.* ■ Math. the product of a number multiplied by its square, represented by a superscript figure 3. ▶ v. [trans.] **1** Math. raise (a number or value) to its cube. **2** cut (food) into small cubes. **3** tenderize (meat) by scoring a pattern of small squares into its surface: [as adj.] (**cubed**) *cubed steaks.* [16th C.: from OFr., or via L. from Gk. *kubos.*]
cu·beb /'kyo͞obeb/ ▶ n. a tropical shrub (genus *Piper*) of the pepper family that bears pungent berries. [ME: from OFr. *cubebe*, from Sp. Arabic *kubēba*, from Arab. *kubāba*.]
cube root ▶ n. the number that produces a given number when cubed.
cu·bic /'kyo͞obik/ ▶ adj. having the shape of a cube. ■ [attrib.] denoting a unit of measurement equal to the volume of a cube whose side is one of the linear unit specified: *15 billion cubic meters of water.* ■ measured or expressed in such units. ■ involving the cube (and no higher power) of a quantity or variable: *a cubic equation.* ■ of or denoting a crystal system or three-dimensional geometric arrangement having three equal axes at right angles. ▶ n. Math. a cubic equation, or a curve described by one. — **cu·bi·cal** adj. **cu·bi·cal·ly** /-bik(ə)lē/ adv.
cu·bi·cle /'kyo͞obikəl/ ▶ n. a small partitioned-off area of a room. [ME (in the sense 'bedroom'): from L. *cubiculum*, from *cubare* 'lie down.']
cu·bic zir·co·ni·a ▶ n. a colorless form of zirconia that is similar to diamond in refractivity and appearance.
cu·bi·form /'kyo͞obi,fôrm/ ▶ adj. tech. cube-shaped.
cub·ism /'kyo͞obizəm/ ▶ n. an early 20th-century style and movement in art, esp. painting, in which perspective with a single viewpoint was abandoned and use was made of simple geometric shapes, interlocking planes, and, later, collage. It was created by Picasso and Braque. — **cub·ist** n. & adj. **cub·is·tic** /kyo͞o'bistik/ adj.
cu·bit /'kyo͞obit/ ▶ n. an ancient measure of length, approximately equal to the length of a forearm. It was typically about 18 inches or 44 cm, though there was a **long cubit** of about 21 inches or 52 cm. [ME: from L. *cubitum* 'elbow, forearm, cubit.']
cu·bi·tal /'kyo͞obitl/ ▶ adj. **1** Anat. of the forearm or the elbow: *the cubital vein.* **2** Entomol. of the cubitus.
cu·bi·tus /'kyo͞obitəs/ ▶ n. Entomol. the fifth longitudinal vein from the anterior edge of an insect's wing. [19th C.: from L.]
cu·boid /'kyo͞oboid/ ▶ adj. more or less cubic in shape. ▶ n. **1** Geom. a solid that has six rectangular faces at right angles to each other. **2** (also **cuboid bone**) Anat. a squat tarsal bone on the outer side of the foot, articulating with the heel bone and the fourth and fifth metatarsals. — **cu·boi·dal** /-boidl/ adj.
cub re·port·er ▶ n. informal a young or inexperienced newspaper reporter.
Cub Scout ▶ n. a member of the junior branch of the Boy Scouts, for boys aged about 8 to 10.
cuck·old /'kəkəld; -ōld/ ▶ n. archaic the husband of an adulteress, often regarded as an object of derision. ▶ v. [trans.] (of a man) make (another man) a cuckold by having a sexual relationship with his wife. ■ (of a man's wife) make (her husband) a cuckold. — **cuck·old·ry** /-əldrē/ n. [OE, from OFr. *cucuault*, from *cucu* 'cuckoo' (from the cuckoo's habit of laying its egg in another bird's nest).]
cuck·oo /'ko͞oko͞o; 'ko͝oko͞o/ ▶ n. **1** a medium-sized long-tailed bird, typically with a gray or brown back and barred or pale underparts. Many cuckoos lay their eggs in the nests of small songbirds. The **cuckoo family** (Cuculidae) also includes roadrunners and anis. **2** informal a crazy person. ▶ adj. informal crazy. [ME: from OFr. *cucu*, imitative of its call.]
cuck·oo clock ▶ n. a clock that strikes the hour with a sound like a cuckoo's call and typically has a mechanical cuckoo that emerges with each note.
cuck·oo·flow·er /'ko͞oko͞o,flouər; 'ko͝oko͞o-/ ▶ n. a spring-flowering plant (*Cardamine pratensis*) of the cabbage family, with pale lilac flowers, growing in damp meadows and by streams.
cuck·oo·pint /'ko͞oko͞o,pīnt; 'ko͝oko͞o-/ ▶ n. the common European wild arum (*Arum maculatum*), similar to jack-in-the-pulpit, with a pale spathe and a purple or green spadix followed by bright red berries. [ME: from earlier *cuckoo-pintle*, from PINTLE 'penis.']
cuck·oo spit ▶ n. whitish froth found in compact masses on leaves and plant stems, exuded by the nymphs of froghoppers.
cu·cum·ber /'kyo͞o,kəmbər/ ▶ n. **1** a long, green-skinned fruit with watery flesh, usually eaten raw in salads or pickled. **2** the widely cultivated climbing plant (*Cucumis sativus*) of the gourd family that yields this fruit, native to the Chinese Himalayan region.
– PHRASES **(as) cool as a cucumber** untroubled by heat, stress, or exertion. ■ calm and relaxed. [ME: from OFr. *cocombre, coucombre*, from L. *cucumis, cucumer-*.]
cu·cum·ber mo·sa·ic ▶ n. a viral disease affecting plants of the gourd family, spread by beetles and aphids and causing mottling and stunting.
cu·cur·bit /kyo͞o'kərbit/ ▶ n. a plant of the gourd family (Cucurbitaceae), which includes melon, pumpkin, squash, and cucumber. ■ a gourd-shaped vessel forming the lower part of an alembic. — **cu·cur·bi·ta·ceous** /kyo͞o,kərbə'tāSHəs/ adj. [ME: from OFr. *cucurbite*, from L. *cucurbita*.]
Cú·cu·ta /'ko͞oko͞o,tä/ a city in northern Colombia; pop. 450,000.
cud /kəd/ ▶ n. partly digested food returned from the first stomach of ruminants to the mouth for further chewing.

– PHRASES **chew the cud** 1 (of a ruminant) further chew partly digested food. 2 think or talk reflectively. [OE *cwidu, cudu*, of Gmc. origin.]

cud·dle /ˈkədl/ ▶ v. [trans.] hold close in one's arms as a way of showing love or affection. ■ [no obj., with adverbial] lie or sit close and snug. ▶ n. a prolonged and affectionate hug. — **cud·dle·some** /-səm/ adj. [16th C.: of unknown origin.]

cud·dly /ˈkədlē; ˈkədl-ē/ ▶ adj. (**-dli·er, -dli·est**) attractive, endearing, and pleasant to cuddle.

cudg·el /ˈkəjəl/ ▶ n. a short thick stick used as a weapon. ▶ v. (**cudg·eled, cudg·el·ing** ; Brit. **cudg·el·led, cudg·el·ling**) [trans.] beat with a cudgel.
– PHRASES **cudgel one's brain** (or **brains**) think hard about a problem. **take up the cudgels** start to defend or support someone or something strongly. [OE *cycgel*, of unknown origin.]

cue[1] /kyo͞o/ ▶ n. a thing said or done that serves as a signal to an actor or other performer to enter or to begin their speech or performance. ■ a signal for action. ■ a piece of information or circumstance that aids the memory in retrieving details not recalled spontaneously. ■ Psychol. a feature of something perceived that is used in the brain's interpretation of the perception. ■ a hint or indication about how to behave in particular circumstances. ■ a facility for playing through an audio or video recording very rapidly until a desired starting point is reached. ▶ v. (**cues, cued, cue·ing** or **cu·ing**) [trans.] give a cue to or for. ■ act as a prompt or reminder. ■ set a piece of audio or video equipment in readiness to play (a particular part of the recorded material).
– PHRASES **on cue** at the correct moment: *right on cue the door opened.* **take one's cue from** follow the example or advice of. [16th C.: of unknown origin.]

cue[2] ▶ n. a long, straight, tapering wooden rod for striking the ball in pool, billiards, snooker, etc. ▶ v. (**cues, cued, cue·ing** or **cu·ing**) [intrans.] use such a rod to strike the ball. [18th C.: var. of QUEUE.]

cue ball ▶ n. the ball, usually a white one, that is to be struck with the cue in pool, billiards, snooker, etc.

cue card ▶ n. a card held beside a camera for a television broadcaster to read from while appearing to look into the camera.

cued speech /kyo͞od/ ▶ n. a type of sign language that uses hand movements combined with mouth shapes to communicate to the hearing impaired.

Cuen·ca /ˈkwenGkə/ a city in the Andes in southern Ecuador; pop. 239,900.

Cuer·na·va·ca /ˌkwernəˈväkə/ a town in central Mexico, capital of the state of Morelos; pop. 400,000.

cues·ta /ˈkwestə/ ▶ n. Geol. a ridge with a gentle slope on one side and a steep slope on the other. [19th C.: from Sp., 'slope,' from L. *costa* 'rib, flank.']

cuff[1] /kəf/ ▶ n. 1 the end part of a sleeve, where the material of the sleeve is turned back or a separate band is sewn on. ■ the part of a glove covering the wrist. ■ the turned-up end of a trouser leg. ■ the top part of a boot, typically padded or turned down. ■ an inflatable bag wrapped around the arm when blood pressure is measured. 2 (**cuffs**) informal handcuffs. ▶ v. [trans.] informal secure with handcuffs.
– PHRASES **off the cuff** informal without preparation. — **cuffed** adj. [in comb.] *a double-cuffed striped shirt.* [ME (denoting a glove or mitten): of unknown origin.]

cuff[2] ▶ v. [trans.] strike (someone) with an open hand, esp. on the head. ▶ n. [usu. in sing.] a blow given with an open hand. [16th C.: origin unknown.]

cuff link ▶ n. (usu. **cuff links**) a device for fastening together the sides of a shirt cuff, typically a pair of linked studs or a single plate connected to a short swiveling rod, passed through a hole in each side of the cuff.

Cu·fic /ˈk(y)o͞ofik/ ▶ n. & adj. var. of KUFIC.

Cu·ia·bá /ˌko͞oyəˈbä/ a river port in west central Brazil, on the Cuiabá River, capital of Mato Grosso state; pop. 389,070.

cui bo·no? /kwē ˈbōnō/ ▶ exclam. who stands, or stood, to gain (from a crime, and so might have been responsible for it)? [17th C.: L., lit. 'to whom (is it) a benefit?']

cui·rass /kwiˈras; kyo͝oˈras/ ▶ n. 1 hist. a piece of armor consisting of breastplate and backplate fastened together. ■ a hard protective cover on an animal. 2 Med. an artificial ventilator that encloses the body, leaving the limbs free, and forces air in and out of the lungs by changes in pressure. [ME: from OFr. *cuirace*, based on late L. *coriaceus* (adj.), from *corium* 'leather.']

cuirass 1

cui·ras·sier /ˌkwi(ə)rəˈsi(ə)r; ˌkyo͝or-/ ▶ n. hist. a cavalry soldier wearing a cuirass. [16th C.: Fr., from *cuirasse*, from OFr. *cuirace* (see CUIRASS).]

cui·sine /kwiˈzēn/ ▶ n. a style or method of cooking, esp. as characteristic of a particular country, region, or establishment. ■ food cooked in a certain way: *sampling the local cuisine.* [18th C.: Fr., lit. 'kitchen'.]

cuisse /kwis/ (also **cuish** /kwisH/) ▶ n. (usu. **cuisses** or **cuishes**) hist. a piece of armor for the thigh. [ME (orig. in the plural): from OFr. *cuisseaux*, pl. of *cuissel*, from late L. *coxale*, from *coxa* 'hip.']

cuke /kyo͞ok/ ▶ n. informal term for CUCUMBER.

Cul·bert·son /ˈkəlbərtsən/, Ely (1891–1955), US contract bridge player; born in Romania. He formalized a system of bidding.

culch ▶ n. var. of CULTCH.

Cul·dee /ˈkəldē/ ▶ n. an Irish or Scottish monk of the 8th to 12th centuries, living as a recluse. [ME: from med. L. *culdeus*, from med. L. *culdeus* ult. from Old Irish *céle dé*, lit. 'companion of God.']

cul-de-sac /ˈkəl di ˌsak/ ▶ n. (pl. **cul-de-sacs** or **culs-de-sac** /ˈkəl(z)-/) a street or passage closed at one end. ■ fig. a route or course leading nowhere. ■ Anat. a vessel, tube, or sac open at only one end. [18th C. (orig. in anatomy): Fr., lit. 'bottom of a sack.']

-cule ▶ suffix forming nouns such as *molecule, reticule*, which were originally diminutives. [from Fr. *-cule* or L. *-culus, -cula, -culum*.]

cu·lex /ˈkyo͞oleks/ (also **culex mosquito**) ▶ n. (pl. **-li·ces** /-ləˌsēz/) a mosquito (genus *Culex*, family Culicidae) common in cool climates. They do not transmit malaria, but can pass on a variety of other parasites including those causing filariasis. — **cu·li·cine** /ˈkyo͞oləˌsīn/ adj. & n. [19th C.: L., lit. 'gnat.']

Cu·lia·cán Ro·sa·les /ˌko͞olyəˈkän rōˈsäləs; rōˈzäləs/ a city in northwestern Mexico, capital of the state of Sinaloa; pop. 662,110.

cu·li·nar·y /ˈkələˌnerē; ˈkyo͞olə-/ ▶ adj. of or for cooking: *culinary skills.* — **cu·li·nar·i·ly** /-ˌnerəlē/ adv. [17th C.: from L. *culinarius*, from *culina* 'kitchen.']

cull /kəl/ ▶ v. [trans.] (usu. **be culled**) select from a large quantity; obtain from a variety of sources. ■ reduce the population of (a wild animal) by selective slaughter. ■ send (an inferior or surplus animal on a farm) to be slaughtered. ■ literary pick (flowers or fruit). ▶ n. a selective slaughter of wild animals. ■ [usu. as adj.] an inferior or surplus livestock animal selected for killing: *a cull cow.* — **cull·er** n. [ME: from OFr. *coillier*, based on L. *colligere* (see COLLECT[1]).]

Cul·len /ˈkələn/, Countee (1903–46), US poet. Leader of the Harlem Renaissance, his works are collected in volumes such as *The Black Christ* (1929).

cul·let /ˈkəlit/ ▶ n. recycled broken or waste glass used in glassmaking. [19th C.: var. of COLLET.]

Cul·lo·den, Battle of /kəˈlädn/ the last battle of the Jacobite uprising of 1745–6, in which British forces under the Duke of Cumberland crushed the Jacobite army of Charles Edward Stuart.

cul·ly /ˈkəlē/ ▶ n. (pl. **-lies**) Brit., informal (often as a form of address) a man; a friend. [17th C.: origin unknown.]

Culm /kəlm/ ▶ n. Geol. a series of Carboniferous strata in southwestern England, mainly shale and limestone with some thin coal seams. ■ (**culm**) archaic coal dust or slack. [ME: prob. rel. to COAL.]

culm /kəlm/ ▶ n. the hollow stem of a grass or cereal plant, esp. that bearing the flower. [17th C.: from L. *culmus* 'stalk.']

cul·men /ˈkəlmən/ ▶ n. (pl. **-mi·na** /-mənə/) 1 Ornithol. the upper ridge of a bird's bill. 2 Anat. a small region in the brain on the anterior surface of the cerebellum. [17th C.: from L., contr. of *columen* 'top.']

cul·mi·nant /ˈkəlmənənt/ ▶ adj. at or forming the top or highest point.

cul·mi·nate /ˈkəlməˌnāt/ ▶ v. [intrans.] reach a climax or point of highest development: *the tensions culminated in World War II.* ■ [trans.] be the climax or point of highest development of: *her book culminated a research project on Escher.* ■ archaic or Astrol. (of a celestial body) reach or be at the meridian. [17th C.: from L. *culmen* 'summit.']

cul·mi·na·tion /ˌkəlməˈnāsHən/ ▶ n. [in sing.] the highest or climactic point of something, esp. as attained after a long time. ■ chiefly Astrol. the reaching of the meridian by a celestial body.

cu·lottes /ˈk(y)o͞oläts; k(y)o͞oˈläts/ ▶ plural n. women's knee-length trousers, cut with very full legs to resemble a skirt. [19th C.: Fr., 'breeches,' dimin. of *cul* 'rump,' from L. *culus*.]

cul·pa·ble /ˈkəlpəbəl/ ▶ adj. deserving blame. — **cul·pa·bil·i·ty** /ˌkəlpəˈbilitē/ n. **cul·pa·bly** adv. [ME: from OFr. *culpable*, ult. from L. *culpa* 'fault, blame.']

cul·prit /ˈkəlprit/ ▶ n. a person responsible for a crime or other misdeed. ■ the cause of a problem or defect. [17th C.: perh. from the abbrev. *cul. prist*, for *Culpable: prest d'averrer notre bille* '(You are) guilty: (We are) ready to prove our indictment.']

cult /kəlt/ ▶ n. a system of religious veneration and devotion directed toward a particular figure or object. ■ a relatively small group of people having religious beliefs or practices regarded by others as strange or sinister. ■ a misplaced or excessive admiration for a particular person or thing: *a cult of personality.* ■ [usu. as adj.] a person or thing that is popular or fashionable, esp. among a particular section of society. — **cul·tic** adj. **cult·ish** adj. **cult·ish·ness** n. **cult·ism** n. **cult·ist** n. [17th C.: from Fr. *culte* or L. *cultus* 'worship,' from *cult-* 'inhabited,' from the v. *colere*.]

cultch /kəlcH/ (also **culch**) ▶ n. the mass of stones, broken shells, and grit of which an oyster bed is formed. [17th C.: origin unknown.]

cul·ti·gen /ˈkəltəjən/ ▶ n. Bot. a plant species or variety known only in cultivation, esp. one with no known wild ancestor. [20th C.: from *cultivated* + -GEN.]

cul·ti·var /ˈkəltəˌvär/ ▶ n. Bot. a plant variety produced in cultivation by selective breeding and usually designated in the style *Taxus baccata* "Variegata." See also VARIETY (sense 2). [1920s: blend of CULTIVATE and VARIETY.]

cul·ti·vate /ˈkəltəˌvāt/ ▶ v. [trans.] 1 prepare and use (land) for crops or gardening. ■ break up (soil) in preparation for sowing or planting. ■ raise or grow (plants), esp. on a large scale for commercial purposes.

■ Biol. grow or maintain (living cells or tissue) in culture. **2** try to acquire or develop (a quality, sentiment, or skill). ■ try to win the friendship or favor of (someone). ■ [usu. as adj.] (**cultivated**) apply oneself to improving or developing (one's mind or manners): *a cultivated and educated man.* — **cul·ti·va·ble** /-vəbəl/ **adj. cul·ti·vat·a·ble** /-ˌvātəbəl/ **adj. cul·ti·va·tion** /ˌkəltəˈvāsHən/ **n.** [17th C.: from med. L. *cultivat-* 'prepared for crops,' from the v. *cultivare,* from *colere.*]

cul·ti·va·tor /ˈkəltəˌvātər/ ▶ **n.** a person or thing that cultivates something. ■ a mechanical implement for breaking up the ground and uprooting weeds.

cul·tur·al /ˈkəlCHərəl/ ▶ **adj.** of or relating to the ideas, customs, and social behavior of a society. ■ of or relating to the arts and to intellectual achievements. — **cul·tur·al·ly adv.**

cul·tur·al an·thro·pol·o·gy ▶ **n.** see ANTHROPOLOGY.

Cul·tur·al Rev·o·lu·tion a political upheaval in China 1966–68 intended to bring about a return to revolutionary Maoist beliefs.

cul·ture /ˈkəlCHər/ ▶ **n. 1** the arts and other manifestations of human intellectual achievement regarded collectively. ■ a refined understanding or appreciation of this. ■ the customs, arts, social institutions, and achievements of a particular nation, people, or other social group. ■ [with adj.] the attitudes and behavior characteristic of a particular social group: *the drug culture.* **2** Biol. the cultivation of bacteria, tissue cells, etc., in an artificial medium containing nutrients: *the cells proliferate readily in culture.* ■ a preparation of cells obtained in such a way: *the bacterium was isolated in two blood cultures.* ■ the cultivation of plants: *this variety of lettuce is popular for its ease of culture.* ▶ **v.** [trans.] Biol. maintain (tissue cells, bacteria, etc.) in conditions suitable for growth. [ME (denoting a cultivated piece of land): the n. from Fr. *culture* or directly from L. *cultura* 'growing, cultivation'; the v. from obs. Fr. *culturer* or med. L. *culturare,* both based on L. *colere* (see CULTIVATE).]

cul·ture-bound ▶ **adj.** restricted in character or outlook by belonging or referring to a particular culture.

cul·tured /ˈkəlCHərd/ ▶ **adj. 1** characterized by refined taste and manners and good education. **2** Biol. (of tissue cells, bacteria, etc.) grown or propagated in an artificial medium. ■ (of a pearl) formed around a foreign body inserted into an oyster.

cul·ture shock ▶ **n.** the feeling of disorientation experienced by someone who is suddenly subjected to an unfamiliar culture, way of life, or set of attitudes.

cul·ture vul·ture ▶ **n.** informal a person who is very interested in the arts, esp. to an obsessive degree.

cul·tus /ˈkəltəs/ ▶ **n.** tech. a system or variety of religious worship. [19th C.: L. (see CULT).]

Cul·ver Cit·y /ˈkəlvər/ a city in southwestern California, an industrial and filmmaking center; pop. 38,793.

cul·ver·in /ˈkəlvərin/ ▶ **n. 1** a 16th- or 17th- century cannon with a relatively long barrel for its bore, typically about 10 to 13 feet long. **2** a kind of handgun of the 15th and 16th centuries. [15th C. (sense 2): from OFr. *coulevrine,* from *couleuvre* 'snake,' based on L. *colubra.*]

cul·vert /ˈkəlvərt/ ▶ **n.** a tunnel carrying a stream or open drain under a road or railroad. ▶ **v.** [trans.] (usu. **be culverted**) channel (a stream or drain) through a culvert. [18th C.: origin unknown.]

cum[1] /ko͝om; kəm/ ▶ **prep.** [usu. in comb.] combined with; also used as (used to describe things with a dual nature or function): *a study-cum-bedroom.* [19th C.: L.]

cum[2] /kəm/ ▶ **n.** informal var. of COME.

cum. ▶ **abbr.** cumulative.

Cu·ma·ná /ˌko͞omäˈnä/ a historic port city in northeastern Venezuela, capital of Sucre state, on the Caribbean coast; pop. 212,000.

cum·ber /ˈkəmbər/ ▶ **v.** [trans.] dated hamper or hinder (someone or something). ■ obstruct (a path or space). ▶ **n.** archaic a hindrance, obstruction, or burden. [ME: prob. from ENCUMBER.]

Cum·ber·land Gap /ˈkəmbərlənd/ a historic pass through the Appalachian Mountains, at the Virginia, Kentucky, and Tennessee borders.

Cum·ber·land Riv·er a river that flows from southeastern Kentucky to the Ohio River.

cum·ber·some /ˈkəmbərsəm/ ▶ **adj.** large or heavy and therefore difficult to carry or use; unwieldy. ■ slow or complicated and therefore inefficient. — **cum·ber·some·ly adv. cum·ber·some·ness n.**

Cum·bri·a /ˈkəmbrēə/ a county in northwestern England, formed in 1974; county town, Carlisle. An ancient British kingdom, it includes the Lake District and much of the northern Pennines. — **Cum·bri·an adj. & n.**

cum·brous /ˈkəmbrəs/ ▶ **adj.** poetic or literary term for CUMBERSOME. — **cum·brous·ly adv. cum·brous·ness n.**

cum gra·no sal·is /ko͝om ˌgränō ˈsälis/ ▶ **adv.** (in phrase **take something cum grano salis**) another way of saying *TAKE SOMETHING WITH A GRAIN OF SALT* (see SALT). [L., lit. 'with a grain of salt.']

cum·in /ˈkəmən; ˈk(y)o͞o-/ (also **cum·min**) ▶ **n. 1** the aromatic seeds of a plant of the parsley family, used as a spice, esp. ground and used in curry powder. **2** the small, slender plant (*Cuminum cyminum*) that bears this fruit and grows from the Mediterranean to central Asia. [OE *cymen,* from L. *cuminum,* from Gk. *kuminon,* prob. of Semitic origin.]

cum·mer·bund /ˈkəmərˌbənd/ ▶ **n.** a sash worn around the waist, esp. as part of a man's evening clothes. [17th C.: from Urdu and Pers. *kamar-band.*]

cum·mings /ˈkəmiNGz/, e. e. (1894–1962), US poet and novelist; full name *Edward Estlin Cummings.* His poems use experimental typography (most notably the absence of capital letters) and sharp satire.

cum·quat /ˈkəmkwät/ ▶ **n.** var. of KUMQUAT.

cu·mu·late /ˈkyo͞omyəˌlāt/ ▶ **v.** [trans.] gather together and combine: *the systems cumulate data over a period of years.* ■ [intrans.] be gathered together and combined: *all unpaid dividend payments cumulate and are paid when earnings are sufficient.* — **cu·mu·la·tion** /ˌkyo͞omyəˈlāsHən/ **n.** [16th C.: from L. *cumulus* 'a heap.']

cu·mu·la·tive /ˈkyo͞omyələtiv; -ˌlātiv/ ▶ **adj.** increasing or increased in quantity, degree, or force by successive additions. — **cu·mu·la·tive·ly adv. cu·mu·la·tive·ness n.**

cu·mu·la·tive vot·ing ▶ **n.** a system of voting in an election in which each voter is allowed as many votes as there are candidates and may give all to one candidate or varying numbers to several.

cu·mu·li·form /ˈkyo͞omyələˌfôrm/ ▶ **adj.** (of a cloud) developed in a predominantly vertical direction.

cu·mu·lo·nim·bus /ˌkyo͞omyəlōˈnimbəs/ ▶ **n.** (pl. **-nim·bi** /-ˈnimbī; -bē/) Meteorol. a cloud forming a towering mass with a flat base at fairly low altitude and often a flat top, as in thunderstorms.

cu·mu·lus /ˈkyo͞omyələs/ ▶ **n.** (pl. **-li** /-ˌlī; -lē/) Meteorol. a cloud forming rounded masses heaped on each other above a flat base at fairly low altitude. — **cu·mu·lous** /-ləs/ **adj.** [17th C.: from L., 'heap.']

cunc·ta·tion /kəNGkˈtāsHən/ ▶ **n.** the action or an instance of delaying; tardy action.

cu·ne·ate /ˈkyo͞onēˌāt; -nē-it/ ▶ **adj.** esp. Anat. Bot. wedge-shaped. [19th C.: from L. *cuneus* 'wedge' + -ATE[2].]

cu·ne·i·form /kyo͞oˈnēəˌfôrm; ˈkyo͞on(ē)ə-/ ▶ **adj.** denoting or relating to the wedge-shaped characters used in the ancient writing systems of Mesopotamia, Persia, and Ugarit, surviving mainly impressed on clay tablets. ■ Anat. denoting three bones of the tarsus (ankle) between the navicular bone and the metatarsals. ■ esp. Biol. wedge-shaped: *the eggs are cuneiform.* ▶ **n.** cuneiform writing. [17th C.: from Fr. *cunéiforme* or mod. L. *cuneiformis,* from L. *cuneus* 'wedge.']

Cu·ne·ne /ko͞oˈnānə/ a river that rises in southwest Angola and flows south and then west for 156 miles (250 km) to the Atlantic.

cun·ner /ˈkənər/ ▶ **n.** an edible greenish-gray wrasse (*Tautogolabrus adspersus*) that lives along the Atlantic coast of North America. [17th C.: perh. associated with archaic *conder,* a lookout who alerts fishing boats to shoals of herring.]

cun·ni·lin·gus /ˌkənlˈiNGgəs/ ▶ **n.** stimulation of the female genitals using the tongue or lips. [19th C.: from L., from *cunnus* 'vulva' + *lingere* 'lick.']

cun·ning /ˈkəniNG/ ▶ **adj. 1** having or showing skill in achieving one's ends by deceit or evasion. ■ ingenious: *cunning defenses.* **2** attractive; quaint: *the baby will look cunning in pink.* ▶ **n.** skill in achieving one's ends by deceit. ■ ingenuity: *what cunning it took just to survive.* — **cun·ning·ly adv. cun·ning·ness n.** [ME: perh. from ON *kunnandi* 'knowledge' or perh. from ME *cunne,* an obs. var. of CAN[1].]

Cun·ning·ham /ˈkəniNGˌham/, Merce (1919–), US dancer and choreographer. He danced with the Martha Graham dance company 1939–45 and formed his own company in 1953.

Cu·no·be·li·nus /ˌk(y)o͞onōbəˈlīnəs; -ˈlē-/ variant of CYMBELINE.

cunt /kənt/ ▶ **n.** vulgar slang a woman's genitals. ■ derog. a woman. [ME: of Gmc. origin; rel. to Swed. dial. *kunta.*]

cup /kəp/ ▶ **n. 1** a small, bowl-shaped container for drinking from, typically having a handle and used with a matching saucer for hot drinks. ■ the contents of such a container. ■ a measure of capacity used in cooking, equal to half a pint (0.237 liter). ■ (in church use) a chalice used at the Eucharist. ■ the wine of the Eucharist. ■ one's portion or share, as of sorrow or joy: *I submit to God's will and drink this cup for his satisfaction.* ■ an ornamental trophy in the form of a cup. ■ (**Cup**) such a contest. ■ (**cups**) one of the suits in a tarot pack. **2** a cup-shaped thing, in particular: ■ either of the two parts of a bra shaped to contain or support one breast. ■ this as a measure of breast size. ■ a jockstrap having a protective reinforcement of rigid plastic or metal. ■ Golf the hole on a putting green or the container in it. **3** a mixed drink served at parties, typically flavored with fruit juices and containing wine or cider. ▶ **v.** (**cupped, cupping**) [trans.] **1** form (one's hand or hands) into the curved shape of a cup. ■ place the curved hand or hands around. **2** Med., hist. bleed (someone) by using a heated glass in which a partial vacuum is formed by cooling: *Dr. Ross ordered me to be cupped.*
— PHRASES **in one's cups** informal drunk. **not one's cup of tea** informal not what one likes or is interested in. [OE: from pop. L. *cuppa,* prob. from L. *cupa* 'tub.']

cup·bear·er ▶ **n.** chiefly hist. literary a person who serves wine, esp. in a royal or noble household.

cup·board /ˈkəbərd/ ▶ **n.** a cabinet or closet, usually with a door and shelves, used for storage. *a kitchen cupboard.*

cup·cake /ˈkəpˌkāk/ ▶ **n. 1** a small cake baked in a cup-shaped container and typically iced. **2** an attractive woman (often as a term of address). ■ a weak or effeminate man.

cu·pel /kyo͞oˈpel; ˈkyo͞opəl/ ▶ **n.** a shallow, porous container in which gold or silver can be refined or assayed by melting with a blast of hot air, which oxidizes lead or other base metals. ▶ **v.** (**-peled, -pel·ing**; Brit. **-pel·led, -pel·ling**) [trans.] assay or refine (a metal) in such a container. — **cu·pel·la·tion** /ˌkyo͞opəˈlāsHən/ **n.** [17th C. (as a n.): from Fr. *coupelle,* dimin. of *coupe* 'goblet.']

Cu·per·ti·no /ˌkōōpər'tēnō/ a city in north central California; pop. 40,263.

cup·ful /'kəpˌfōōl/ ▶ n. (pl. **-fuls**) the amount held by a cup. ■ another term for CUP as a measure in cooking.

Cu·pid /'kyōōpəd/ Rom. Mythol. the god of love. He is represented as a naked, winged boy with a bow and arrows, with which he wounds his victims. Greek equivalent EROS. ■ [as n.] (also **cupid**) a representation of a naked winged child, typically carrying a bow. [a personification of L. *cupido* 'desire,' from *cupere* 'to desire.']

cu·pid·i·ty /kyōō'piditē/ ▶ n. greed for money or possessions. [ME: from OFr. *cupidite* or L. *cupiditas*, ult. from *cupere* 'to desire.']

Cu·pid's bow ▶ n. a shape like that of the double-curved bow often shown carried by Cupid, esp. at the top edge of a person's upper lip.

cu·po·la /'kyōōpələ/ ▶ n. a small dome, esp. a small dome on a drum on top of a larger dome, adorning a roof or ceiling. ■ a gun turret; a small domed hatch above a gun turret on some tanks. ■ (also **cupola furnace**) a cylindrical furnace for refining metals, with openings at the bottom for blowing in air and originally with a dome leading to a chimney above. — **cu·po·laed** adj. [16th C.: Ital., from late L. *cupula* 'small cask,' dimin. of *cupa* 'cask.']

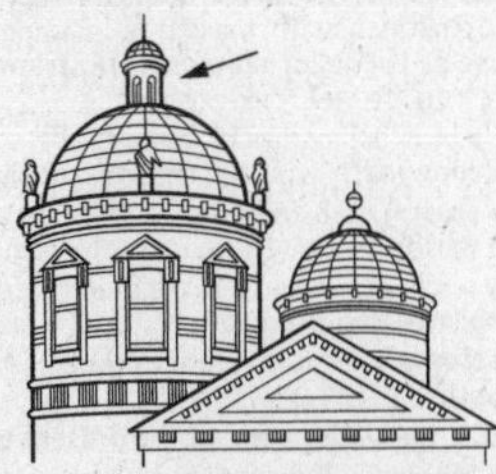

cupola

cup·pa /'kəpə/ Brit., informal ▶ n. a cup of tea: *a good strong cuppa.* ▶ contr. cup of.

cup·py /'kəpē/ ▶ adj. (**-pi·er**, **-pi·est**) (of ground) full of shallow depressions.

cupr- ▶ comb. form var. of CUPRO- shortened before a vowel (as in *cuprammonium*).

cu·pram·mo·ni·um /ˌk(y)ōōprə'mōnēəm/ ▶ n. [as adj.] Chem. a complex ion, $Cu(NH_3)_4 2+$, formed in solution when ammonia is added to copper salts.

cu·pre·ous /'k(y)ōōprēəs/ ▶ adj. dated or literary of or like copper. [17th C.: from late L. *cuprum* 'copper.']

cu·pric /'k(y)ōōprik/ ▶ adj. Chem. of copper with a valence of two; of copper(II). Compare with CUPROUS. [18th C.: from late L. *cuprum* 'copper.']

cu·prite /'k(y)ōōprīt/ ▶ n. a dark red or brownish black mineral consisting of cuprous oxide.

cupro- (also **cupr-**) ▶ comb. form of or relating to copper: *cupronickel.* [from late L. *cuprum.*]

cu·pro·nick·el /ˌk(y)ōōprō'nikəl/ ▶ n. an alloy of copper and nickel, esp. in the proportions 3:1 as used in "silver" coins.

cu·prous /'k(y)ōōprəs/ ▶ adj. Chem. of copper with a valence of one; of copper(I). [17th C.: partly directly from late L. *cuprum* 'copper' (reinforced by CUPRIC) + -OUS.]

cu·pule /'kyōōpyōōl/ ▶ n. Bot. & Zool. a cup-shaped organ, structure, or receptacle in a plant or animal. [ME: from late L. *cupula* (see CUPOLA).]

cur /kər/ ▶ n. an aggressive dog or one that is in poor condition, esp. a mongrel. ■ informal a contemptible man. [ME: prob. orig. in *cur-dog*, perh. from ON *kurr* 'grumbling.']

cur. ▶ abbr. ■ currency. ■ current.

cur·a·ble /'kyōōrəbəl/ ▶ adj. (of a disease or condition) able to be cured. ■ (of plastic, varnish, etc.) able to be hardened by some additive or other agent. — **cur·a·bil·i·ty** /ˌkyōōrə'bilitē/ n.

Cu·ra·çao /ˌk(y)ōōrə'sō; -'sou/ the largest island in the Netherlands Antilles, north of the Venezuelan coast; pop. 144,100; chief town, Willemstad.

cu·ra·çao /'kyōōrəˌsō; -ˌsou/ ▶ n. (pl. **-çaos**) a liqueur flavored with the peel of bitter oranges. [19th C.: CURAÇAO.]

cu·ra·cy /'kyōōrəsē/ ▶ n. (pl. **-cies**) the office, position, or work of a curate: *I was in England serving my curacy.*

cu·ran·de·ro /ˌkyōōrən'derō/ ▶ n. (pl. **-de·ros**) (fem. **cu·ran·de·ra** /-'derə/) (in Spain and Latin America) a healer who uses folk remedies. [Sp., from *curar* 'to cure,' from L. *curare.*]

cu·ra·re /k(y)ōō'rärē/ ▶ n. a bitter, resinous substance obtained from the bark and stems of certain South American plants (families Menispermaceae and Loganiaceae). It paralyzes the motor nerves and is traditionally used by some Indian peoples to poison their arrows and blowpipe darts. [18th C.: from a Carib word, partly via Sp. and Port.]

cu·ras·sow /'k(y)ōōrəˌsou; -ˌsō/ ▶ n. a large, crested, pheasantlike bird (genera *Crax* and *Nothocrax*) of the guan family, found in tropical American forests. The male is typically black. [17th C.: Anglicized form of CURAÇAO.]

cu·rate¹ /'kyōōrit; -rāt/ ▶ n. (also **assistant curate**) a member of the clergy engaged as assistant to a vicar, rector, or parish priest. ■ archaic a minister with pastoral responsibility. [ME: from med. L. *curatus*, from L. *cura* 'care.']

cu·rate² /'kyōōrāt/ ▶ v. [trans.] (usu. **be curated**) select, organize, and look after the items in (a collection or exhibition). — **cu·ra·tion** /kyə'rāshən/ n. [19th C.: back-form. from CURATOR.]

cu·rate's egg ▶ n. Brit. a thing that is partly good and partly bad: *this book is a bit of a curate's egg.* [20th C.: from a cartoon in *Punch* (1895) depicting a meek curate who, given a stale egg at the bishop's table, assures his host that "parts of it are excellent."]

cur·a·tive /'kyōōrətiv/ ▶ adj. able to cure something, typically disease. ▶ n. a medicine or remedy. — **cur·a·tive·ly** adv.

cu·ra·tor /'kyōōrātər; -ətər; kyōō'rātər;/ ▶ n. a keeper or custodian of a museum or other collection. — **cu·ra·to·ri·al** /ˌkyōōrə'tôrēəl/ adj. **cu·ra·tor·ship** n. [ME: from OFr. *curateur*, from L. *curator*, from *curare* (see CURE).]

curb /kərb/ ▶ n. **1** a stone or concrete edging to a street or path. **2** a check or restraint on something. **3** (also **curb bit**) a type of bit that is widely used in western riding. **4** a swelling on the back of a horse's hock, caused by spraining a ligament. ▶ v. [trans.] **1** restrain or keep in check. ■ restrain (a horse) by means of a curb. **2** lead (a dog being walked) near the curb to urinate or defecate. [15th C.: from OFr. *courber* 'bend,' from L. *curvare* (see CURVE).]

curb·ing /'kərbiNG/ ▶ n. the concrete or stones collectively forming a curb.

curb mar·ket ▶ n. a market for selling shares not dealt with on the normal stock exchange.

curb roof ▶ n. another term for GAMBREL.

curb serv·ice ▶ n. service, esp. at a restaurant, extended to customers remaining in their parked vehicles.

curb·side /'kərbˌsīd/ ▶ n. [usu. as adj.] the side of a road or sidewalk that is nearer to the curb.

curb·stone /'kərbˌstōn/ ▶ n. a long, narrow stone or concrete block, laid end to end with others to form a curb.

curb weight ▶ n. the weight of an automobile without occupants or baggage.

cur·cu·li·o /kər'kyōōlēˌō/ ▶ n. (pl. **-os**) a beetle of the weevil family, esp. one that is a pest of fruit trees. [mod. L., genus.]

cur·cu·ma /'kərkyəmə/ ▶ n. a tropical Asian plant (genus *Curcuma*, family Zingiberaceae) that includes turmeric, zedoary, and other species that yield spices, dyes, and medicinal products. [mod. L., from Arab. *kurkum* 'saffron,' from Sanskrit *kuṅkuma.*]

curd /kərd/ ▶ n. (also **curds**) a soft, white substance formed when milk sours, used as the basis for cheese. ■ a fatty substance found between the flakes of poached salmon. — **curd·y** adj. [ME: of unknown origin.]

curd cheese ▶ n. esp. Brit. a mild, soft, smooth cheese made from skimmed milk curd.

cur·dle /'kərdl/ ▶ v. separate or cause to separate into curds or lumps: [intrans.] *take care not to let the milk curdle* | [trans.] *making cheese by curdling milk.*
– PHRASES **make one's blood curdle** fill one with horror. — **cur·dler** n. [16th C.: frequentative of obs. *curd* 'congeal.']

cure /kyōōr/ ▶ v. [trans.] **1** relieve (a person or animal) of the symptoms of a disease or condition: *he was cured of the disease* | fig. *science has not cured us of our superstitions.* ■ eliminate (a disease, condition, or injury) with medical treatment. ■ solve (a problem): *stopping foreign investment is no way to cure the fundamental problem.* **2** preserve (meat, fish, tobacco, or an animal skin) by various methods such as salting, drying, or smoking: *some farmers cured their own bacon.* ■ harden (rubber, plastic, concrete, etc.) after manufacture by a chemical process such as vulcanization. ■ [intrans.] undergo this process. ▶ n. **1** a substance or treatment that cures a disease or condition ■ restoration to health: *beyond cure.* ■ a solution to a problem: *the cure is to improve the clutch operation.* **2** the process of curing rubber, plastic, or other material. **3** a Christian minister's pastoral charge or area of responsibility for spiritual ministry: *the cure of souls.* ■ a parish. — **cur·er** n. [ME: from OFr. *cure*, both from L. *cura* 'care.']

cu·ré /kyōō'rā; 'kyōōrā/ ▶ n. a parish priest in a French-speaking country or region. [Fr., from med. L. *curatus* (see CURATE¹).]

cure-all ▶ n. a medicine or other remedy that will supposedly cure any ailment. ■ a solution to any problem.

cu·ret·tage /ˌkyōōrə'täzh/ ▶ n. Surg. the use of a curette, esp. on the lining of the uterus. See DILATATION AND CURETTAGE.

cu·rette /kyōō'ret/ ▶ n. a surgical instrument used to remove material by a scraping action, esp. from the uterus. ▶ v. [trans.] clean or scrape with a curette. [18th C. (as a n.): from Fr., from *curer* 'cleanse,' from L. *curare* (see CURE).]

cur·few /'kərfyōō/ ▶ n. a regulation requiring people to remain indoors between specified hours, typically at night. ■ the hour designated as the beginning of such a restriction. ■ the daily signal indicating this. [ME: from OFr. *cuevrefeu*, from *cuvrir* 'to cover' + *feu* 'fire.']

Cu·ri·a /'kyōōrēə/ the papal court at the Vatican, by which the Roman

Catholic Church is governed —**Cu·ri·al** adj. [19th C.: from L. *curia*, denoting the senate of cities other than Rome.]

Cu·rie /kyo͝o'rē; 'kyo͝orē/, Marie (1867–1934), born in Poland, and Pierre (1859–1906), French physicists. Working together on the mineral pitchblende, they discovered the elements polonium and radium. After her husband's accidental death, Marie isolated radium. Nobel Prize for Physics (1903, both shared with Becquerel); Nobel Prize for Chemistry (1911, Marie).

cu·rie /'kyo͝orē; kyo͝o'rē/ (abbr.: **Ci**) ▶n. (pl. **-ries**) a unit of radioactivity, corresponding to 3.7×10^{10} disintegrations per second. ■ the quantity of radioactive substance that has this amount of activity. [20th C.: named after Pierre and Marie CURIE.]

cu·ri·o /'kyo͝orē,ō/ ▶n. (pl. **-os**) a rare, unusual, or intriguing object. [abbrev. of CURIOSITY.]

cu·ri·o·sa /,kyo͝orē'ōsə; -'ōzə/ ▶plural n. curiosities, esp. erotic or pornographic books or articles. [19th C.: from L., neut. pl. of *curiosus* (see CURIOUS).]

cu·ri·os·i·ty /,kyo͝orē'äsitē/ ▶n. (pl. **-ties**) **1** a strong desire to know or learn something. **2** a strange or unusual object or fact.
– PHRASES **curiosity killed the cat** proverb being inquisitive about other people's affairs may get you into trouble.

cu·ri·ous /'kyo͝orēəs/ ▶adj. **1** eager to know or learn something. ■ expressing curiosity. **2** strange; unusual. —**cu·ri·ous·ly** adv. **cu·ri·ous·ness** n. [ME: from OFr. *curios*, from L. *curiosus* 'careful,' from *cura* 'care.']

Cu·ri·ti·ba /,ko͝orə'tēbə/ a city in southern Brazil, capital of the state of Paraná; pop. 1,315,035.

cu·ri·um /'kyo͝orēəm/ ▶n. the chemical element of atomic number 96, a radioactive metal of the actinide series. Curium does not occur naturally and was first made by bombarding plutonium with helium ions. (Symbol: **Cm**) [1940s: mod. L., from the name of Marie and Pierre CURIE.]

curl /kərl/ ▶v. form or cause to form into a curved or spiral shape: [intrans.] *her fingers curled around the microphone* | [trans.] *she used to curl her hair with rags.* ■ [intrans.] **(curl up)** sit or lie with the knees drawn up. ■ move or cause to move in a spiral or curved course: [no obj., with adverbial of direction] *smoke curling across the sky.* ■ (with reference to one's mouth or upper lip) raise or cause to raise slightly on one side as an expression of contempt or disapproval. ■ (in weight training) lift (a weight) using only the hands, wrists, and forearms. ▶n. **1** a lock of hair having a spiral or coiled form. ■ a thing having a spiral or inwardly curved form: *a curl of smoke.* ■ a curling movement: *the sneering curl of his lip.* ■ (with reference to a person's hair) a state or condition of being curled: *your hair has a natural curl.* ■ see LEAF CURL. ■ a weightlifting exercise involving movement of only the hands, wrists, and forearms. **2** Math. the vector product of the operator del and a given vector.
– PHRASES **make someone's hair curl** informal shock or horrify someone. [ME: from obs. *crulle* 'curly,' from MDu. *krul*.]

curl·er /'kərlər/ ▶n. (usu. **curlers**) a roller or clasp around which a lock of hair is wrapped to curl it.

cur·lew /'kərlo͞o; 'kərlyo͞o/ ▶n. (pl. same or **-lews**) a large wading bird (genus *Numenius*) of the sandpiper family, with a long down-curved bill and brown streaked plumage. Its several species include the North American **long-billed curlew** (*N. americanus*). [ME: from OFr. *courlieu*, alt. of imitative *courlis*.]

long-billed curlew

Cur·ley /'kərlē/, James Michael (1874–1958), US politician. An urban political boss, he was mayor of Boston for four terms between 1914 and 1950, and governor of Massachusetts 1935–37.

curl·i·cue /'kərli,kyo͞o/ (also **curl·y·cue**) ▶n. a decorative curl or twist in calligraphy or in the design of an object. [19th C.: from CURLY + CUE² (in the sense 'pigtail'), or *-cue* representing the letter *q*.]

curl·ing /'kərliNG/ ▶n. a game played on ice, esp. in Scotland and Canada, in which large, round, flat stones are slid across the surface toward a mark.

curl·ing i·ron ▶n. a heated rod used for rolling a person's hair into curls.

curl·ing stone ▶n. a large, polished, circular stone with an iron handle on top, used in the game of curling.

curl·y /'kərlē/ ▶adj. (**curl·i·er**, **curl·i·est**) made, grown, or arranged in curls or curves. —**curl·i·ness** n.

curl·y·cue ▶n. var. of CURLICUE.

curl·y en·dive ▶n. see ENDIVE.

curl·y kale ▶n. kale of a variety with dark green, tightly curled leaves.

cur·ly top (also **curly top disease**) ▶n. a viral disease affecting plants, esp. beets and gourds, spread by beetles, esp. the beet leafhopper. Infected plants become dwarfed and have puckered, distorted foliage.

curl·y-wurl·y /-'wərlē/ ▶adj. informal twisting and curling. [18th C.: reduplication of CURLY.]

cur·mudg·eon /kər'məjən/ ▶n. a bad-tempered or surly person. —**cur·mudg·eon·li·ness** n. **cur·mudg·eon·ly** adj. [16th C.: of unknown origin.]

cur·rach /'kərə(KH); 'kə-rə(KH)/ (also **cur·ragh**) ▶n. Irish and Scottish term for CORACLE. [ME: from Irish and Scot. Gael. *curach* 'small boat.' Cf. CORACLE.]

cur·ragh ▶n. var. of CURRACH.

cur·ra·jong ▶n. var. of KURRAJONG.

cur·rant /'kərənt; 'kə-rənt/ ▶n. **1** a small dried fruit, from a seedless variety of grape native to the eastern Mediterranean region, now widely produced in California. **2** a Eurasian shrub (genus *Ribes*) of the gooseberry family that produces small edible black, red, or white berries. ■ a berry from such a shrub. [ME *raisons of Corauntz*, translating Anglo-Norman Fr. *raisins de Corauntz* 'grapes of Corinth.']

cur·ren·cy /'kərənsē; 'kə-rənsē/ ▶n. (pl. **-cies**) **1** a system of money in general use in a particular country. **2** the fact or quality of being generally accepted or in use. ■ the time during which something is in use or operation.

cur·rent /'kərənt; 'kə-rənt/ ▶adj. belonging to the present time; happening or being used or done now. ■ in common or general use. ▶n. a body of water or air moving in a definite direction, esp. through a surrounding body of water or air in which there is less movement. ■ a flow of electricity which results from the ordered directional movement of electrically charged particles. ■ a quantity representing the rate of flow of electric charge, usually measured in amperes. ■ the general tendency or course of events or opinion. [ME: from OFr. *corant* 'running,' from *courre* 'run,' from L. *currere* 'run.']

cur·rent af·fairs ▶plural n. events of political or social interest and importance happening in the world at the present time.

cur·rent as·sets ▶plural n. cash and other assets that are expected to be converted to cash within a year. Compare with FIXED ASSETS.

cur·rent den·si·ty ▶n. Physics the amount of electric current flowing per unit cross-sectional area of a material.

cur·rent li·a·bil·i·ties ▶plural n. amounts due to be paid to creditors within twelve months.

cur·rent·ly /'kərəntlē; 'kə-rəntlē/ ▶adv. at the present time.

cur·ri·cle /'kərikəl/ ▶n. hist. a light, open, two-wheeled carriage pulled by two horses side by side. [18th C.: from L. *curriculum* 'chariot,' from *currere* 'to run.']

cur·ric·u·lum /kə'rikyələm/ ▶n. (pl. **-la** /-lə/ or **-lums**) the subjects comprising a course of study in a school or college. —**cur·ric·u·lar** /-lər/ adj. [19th C.: from L. (see CURRICLE).]

cur·ric·u·lum vi·tae /kə'rik(y)ələm 'vītē; 'vētī/ (abbr.: **CV**) ▶n. (pl. **cur·ric·u·la vi·tae** /kə'rik(y)ələ/) a brief account of a person's education, qualifications, and experience, typically sent with a job application. [20th C.: L., lit. 'course of life.']

Cur·ri·er /'kərēər; 'kə-rēər/, Nathaniel (1813–88), US lithographer. With James Ives in 1857 he established Currier & Ives, which produced prints of American scenes.

cur·ri·er /'kərēər; 'kə-rēər/ ▶n. a person who curries leather. [ME: from OFr. *corier*, from L. *coriarius*, from *corium* 'leather.']

cur·rish /'kərisH/ ▶adj. **1** like a cur; snappish. **2** ignoble. —**cur·rish·ly** adv. **cur·rish·ness** n.

cur·ry¹ /'kərē; 'kə-rē/ ▶n. **1** (pl. **-ries**) a dish of meat, vegetables, etc., cooked in an Indian-style spicy sauce and served with rice. **2** curry powder. ▶v. (**-ries, -ried**) [trans.] [usu. as adj.] (**curried**) prepare or flavor with a sauce of hot-tasting spices. [16th C.: from Tamil *kari*.]

cur·ry² ▶v. (**-ries, -ried**) [trans.] **1** groom (a horse) with a rubber or plastic curry-comb. **2** hist. treat (tanned leather) to improve its properties. ■ archaic thrash; beat.
– PHRASES **curry favor** ingratiate oneself with someone through obsequious behavior. [ME: from OFr. *correier*, ult. of Gmc. origin.]

cur·ry-comb ▶n. a hand-held device with serrated ridges, used for removing dirt out of a horse's coat or for cleaning brushes with which a horse is being groomed.

cur·ry pow·der ▶n. a mixture of finely ground spices, such as turmeric, ginger, and coriander, used for making curry.

curse /kərs/ ▶n. **1** a solemn utterance to invoke a supernatural power to inflict harm or punishment on someone or something. ■ [usu. in sing.] a cause of harm or misery. ■ (**the curse**) informal menstruation. **2** an offensive word or phrase used to express anger or annoyance. ▶v. **1** [trans.] invoke or use a curse against: *the family had been cursed.* ■ (**be cursed with**) be afflicted with: *owners have been cursed with bankruptcies.* **2** [intrans.] utter offensive words in anger or annoyance. ■ [trans.] address with such words. —**curs·er** n. [OE, of unknown origin.]

curs·ed /'kərsid; kərst/ ▶adj. [attrib.] informal, dated used to express annoyance or irritation. —**curs·ed·ly** /'kərsidlē/ adv. **curs·ed·ness** /'kərsidnəs/ n.

cur·sil·lo /kər'sē(l)yō/ ▶n. (pl. **-los**) a spiritual retreat by a group of Roman Catholics, organized by lay people and originating in Spain. [1950s: Sp., lit. 'little course.']

cur·sive /'kərsiv/ ▶adj. written with the characters joined. ▶n. writing with such a style. —**cur·sive·ly** adv. [18th C.: from med. L. *cursivus*, from L. *curs-* 'run,' from the v. *currere*.]

cur·sor /'kərsər/ ▶n. a movable indicator on a computer screen identifying the point that will be affected by input from the user. ■ esp. hist. the transparent slide engraved with a hairline that is part of a slide rule. [ME: from L., 'runner' (see CURSIVE).]

cur·so·ri·al /kər,sôrēəl/ ▶adj. Zool. having limbs adapted for running.

cur·so·ry /'kərsərē/ ▶adj. hasty and therefore not thorough or detailed. —**cur·so·ri·ly** /'kərsərəlē/ adv. **cur·so·ri·ness** n. [17th C.: from L. *cursorius* 'of a runner,' from *cursor* (see CURSOR).]

curst /kərst/ ▶ adj. archaic spelling of CURSED.

curt /kərt/ ▶ adj. rudely brief. *his reply was curt.* — **curt·ly** adv. **curt·ness** n. [ME: from L. *curtus* 'cut short.']

cur·tail /kər'tāl/ ▶ v. [trans.] (often **be curtailed**) reduce in extent or quantity; restrict. ■ (**curtail someone of**) archaic deprive someone of (something): *I that am curtailed of this fair proportion.* — **cur·tail·ment** /kər'tālmənt/ n. [15th C.: from obs. *curtal* 'horse with a docked tail,' from Fr. *courtault*, from *court* 'short,' from L. *curtus*.]

cur·tain /'kərtn/ ▶ n. a piece of material suspended at the top to form a screen, typically movable sideways along a rail, found as one of a pair at a window. ■ (**the curtain**) a screen of heavy cloth or other material that can be raised or lowered at the front of a stage. ■ a raising or lowering of such a screen at the beginning or end of an act or scene. ■ (**curtains**) informal a disastrous outcome: *it looked like curtains for me.* ▶ v. [trans.] [often as adj.] (**curtained**) provide with a curtain or curtains.
– PHRASES **bring down the curtain on** bring to an end. [ME: from OFr. *cortine*, from late L. *cortina*, translation of Gk. *aulaia*, from *aulē* 'court.']

cur·tain call ▶ n. the appearance of one or more performers on stage after a performance to acknowledge the audience's applause.

cur·tain lec·ture ▶ n. dated an instance of a wife reprimanding her husband in private. [17th C.: orig. a reprimand given behind bed curtains.]

cur·tain rais·er ▶ n. an entertainment or other arts event happening just before a longer or more important one: *Bach's Sinfonia in B flat was an ideal curtain-raiser to Mozart's last piano concerto.*

cur·tain speech ▶ n. a speech of thanks or appreciation to an audience, made after a performance by an actor playing a leading role, typically from the front of the stage with the curtains closed.

cur·tain wall ▶ n. a fortified wall around a medieval castle, typically one linking towers together. ■ a wall that encloses the space within a building but does not support the roof, typically on a modern high-rise.

cur·tal /'kərtl/ ▶ adj. archaic shortened, abridged, or curtailed. ▶ n. hist. a dulcian or bassoon of the late 16th to early 18th century. [15th C.: from Fr. *courtault*, from *court* 'short' + the pejorative suffix *-ault*.]

cur·ta·na /kər'tänə; -'tānə/ ▶ n. Brit. the unpointed sword carried in front of English sovereigns at their coronation to represent mercy. [ME: from Anglo-L. *curtana (spatha)* 'shortened (sword),' from OFr. *cortain*, the name of the sword belonging to ROLAND.]

curtesy /'kərtəsē/ ▶ n. (pl. **-sies**) Law, hist. a tenure by which a husband, after his wife's death, held certain kinds of property that she had inherited.

cur·ti·lage /'kərtl-ij/ ▶ n. an area of land attached to a house and forming one enclosure with it: *the roads within the curtilage of the development site.* [ME: from Anglo-Norman Fr., var. of OFr. *courtillage*, from *courtil* 'small court,' from *cort* 'court.']

Cur·tis /'kərtis/, Benjamin Robbins (1809–74), US Supreme Court associate justice 1851–57.

Cur·tiss /'kərtəs/, Glenn Hammond (1878–1930), US aviation pioneer. He invented the aileron and in 1911 demonstrated the first practical seaplane.

curt·sy /'kərtsē/ (also **curt·sey**) ▶ n. (pl. **-sies** or **-seys**) a woman's or girl's formal greeting made by bending the knees with one foot in front of the other. ▶ v. (**-sies, -sied** or **-seys, -seyed**) [intrans.] perform such an action: *she curtsied onto the stage.* [16th C.: var. of COURTESY.]

cur·va·ceous /kər'vāsHəs/ ▶ adj. (esp. of a woman or a woman's figure) having an attractively curved shape. — **cur·va·ceous·ness** n.

cur·va·ture /'kərvəCHər; -,CHŏŏr/ ▶ n. the fact of being curved or the degree to which something is curved: *spinal curvature | the curvature of the earth.* ■ Geom. the degree to which a curve deviates from a straight line, or a curved surface deviates from a plane. ■ a numerical quantity expressing this.

curve /kərv/ ▶ n. a line or outline that gradually deviates from being straight for some or all of its length. ■ a place where a road deviates from a straight path: *the vehicle rounded a curve.* ■ (**curves**) a curving contour of a woman's figure. ■ a line on a graph (whether straight or curved) showing how one quantity varies with respect to another: *the population curve.* ■ a system in which grades are assigned to students based on their performance relative to other students, regardless of their actual knowledge of the subject. ■ Baseball another term for CURVEBALL. ▶ v. form or cause to form a curve.
– PHRASES **ahead of** (or **behind**) **the curve** (esp. of a business or politician) ahead of (or lagging behind) current thinking or trends. [ME: from L. *curvare* 'to bend,' from *curvus* 'bent.']

curve·ball /'kərv,bôl/ ▶ n. Baseball a ball that is pitched with a snap of the wrist and a strong downward spin, which causes the ball to drop suddenly and deceptively veer away from home plate.

cur·vet /kər'vet/ ▶ n. (of a horse) a graceful or energetic leap. ▶ v. (**-vet·ted, -vet·ting** or **-vet·ed, -vet·ing**) [intrans.] rare (of a horse) leap gracefully or energetically. [16th C.: from Ital. *corvetta*, dimin. of *corva*, earlier form of *curva* 'a curve,' from L. *curvus* 'bent.']

cur·vi·lin·e·ar /,kərvə'linēər/ ▶ adj. contained by or consisting of a curved line or lines. — **cur·vi·lin·e·ar·ly** adv. [18th C.: from *curvi-* 'curved,' from L. *curvus*.]

cur·vi·ros·tral /,kərvə'rästrəl/ ▶ adj. with a curved beak.

curv·y /'kərvē/ ▶ adj. (**curv·i·er, curv·i·est**) having many curves: *a curvy stretch of road.* ■ informal (esp. of a woman's figure) shapely and voluptuous. — **curv·i·ness** n.

cus·cus /'kəskəs; 'kŏŏskŏŏs/ ▶ n. a phalanger with a rounded head and prehensile tail, native to New Guinea and northern Australia, in particular the **spotted cuscus** (*Spilocuscus maculatus*) and the **gray cuscus** (*Phalanger orientalis*). [17th C.: via Fr. and Du. from a local name in the Molucca Islands.]

cu·sec /'kyōōsek/ ▶ n. a unit of flow (esp. of water) equal to one cubic foot per second. [20th C.: abbrev. of *cubic foot per second*.]

Cush /kŏŏsH/ **1** (in the Bible) the eldest son of Ham and grandson of Noah (Gen. 10:6). **2** the southern part of ancient Nubia, first mentioned in Egyptian records of the Middle Kingdom. In the Bible it is the country of the descendants of Cush.

cu·shaw /kŏŏ'sHô; 'kōōsHô/ (also **cushaw squash**) ▶ n. a large winter squash of a variety with a curved neck. [16th C.: of unknown origin.]

cush-cush /'kŏŏsH ,kŏŏsH/ ▶ n. a tropical American yam (*Dioscorea trifida*). [19th C.: perh. ult. of Afr. origin.]

Cush·ing /'kŏŏsHiNG/, William (1732–1810), US Supreme Court associate justice 1789–1810.

Cush·ing's dis·ease /'kŏŏsHiNGz/ ▶ n. Cushing's syndrome as caused by a tumor of the pituitary gland.

Cush·ing's syn·drome ▶ n. Med. a metabolic disorder caused by overproduction of corticosteroid hormones by the adrenal cortex and often involving obesity and high blood pressure. [1930s: named after Harvey W. *Cushing* (1869–1939), American surgeon.]

cush·ion /'kŏŏsHən/ ▶ n. a pillow or pad stuffed with a mass of soft material, used as a comfortable support for sitting or leaning on. ■ something providing support or protection against impact. ■ the elastic lining of the sides of a billiard table, from which the ball rebounds. ■ the layer of air supporting a hovercraft or similar vehicle. ▶ v. [trans.] soften the effect of an impact on. ■ fig. mitigate the adverse effects of. — **cush·ioned** adj. **cush·ion·y** adj. [ME: from OFr. *cuissin*, based on a L. word meaning 'cushion for the hip,' from *coxa* 'hip, thigh'.]

Cush·it·ic /kŏŏ'sHitik; ,kə-/ ▶ n. a group of East African languages of the Afro-Asiatic family spoken mainly in Ethiopia and Somalia, including Somali and Oromo. ▶ adj. of or relating to this group of languages.

cush·y /'kŏŏsHē/ ▶ adj. (**cush·i·er, cush·i·est**) informal **1** (of a job, task, or situation) undemanding, easy, or secure: *cushy jobs that pay you to ski.* **2** (of furniture) comfortable. — **cush·i·ness** n. [World War I (orig. Anglo-Ind.): from Urdu *ḳushī* 'pleasure,' from Pers. *ḳuš*.]

cusp /kəsp/ ▶ n. **1** a pointed end where two curves meet, in particular: ■ Archit. a projecting point between small arcs in Gothic tracery. ■ a cone-shaped prominence on the surface of a tooth, esp. of a molar or premolar. ■ Anat. a pocket or fold in the wall of the heart or a major blood vessel that fills and distends if the blood flows backward, so forming part of a valve. ■ Math. a point at which the direction of a curve is abruptly reversed. ■ each of the pointed ends of a crescent, esp. of the moon. **2** Astrol. the initial point of an astrological sign or house: *he was Aries on the cusp with Taurus.* ■ fig. a point between two different situations or states, when a person or thing is poised between the two or just about to move from one to the other. — **cus·pate** /'kəspət; -,pāt/ adj. **cusped** adj. **cus·pi·date** /'kəspə,dāt/ adj. [16th C. (sense 2): from L. *cuspis* 'point or apex.']

cus·pid /'kəspid/ ▶ n. a tooth with a single cusp or point; a canine tooth.

cus·pi·dor /'kəspi,dôr/ ▶ n. a spittoon. [18th C.: from Port., lit. 'spitter.']

cuss /kəs/ informal ▶ n. **1** an annoying or stubborn person or animal: *he was certainly an unsociable cuss.* **2** another term for CURSE (sense 2). ▶ v. another term for CURSE (sense 2).

cuss·ed /'kəsid/ ▶ adj. informal awkward; stubborn; annoying. — **cuss·ed·ly** adv. **cuss·ed·ness** n. [19th C. (orig. US): var. of CURSED.]

cuss word ▶ n. informal a swear word.

cus·tard /'kəstərd/ ▶ n. a dessert or sweet sauce made with milk, eggs, and sugar. [ME *crustarde, custarde* from OFr. *crouste* (see CRUST).]

cus·tard ap·ple ▶ n. **1** a large, fleshy, tropical fruit with a sweet yellow pulp. **2** the tree (genus *Annona*, family Annonaceae) that bears this fruit, native to Central and South America.

Cus·ter /'kəstər/, George Armstrong (1839–76), US general. He was killed, along with all 266 of his men, in a clash (known as Custer's Last Stand) with a Sioux-Cheyenne force at Little Bighorn in Montana.

cus·to·di·an /kəs'tōdēən/ ▶ n. a person who has responsibility for or looks after something, such as a museum, financial assets, or a culture or tradition. ■ a person employed to clean and maintain a building. — **cus·to·di·an·ship** n.

cus·to·dy /'kəstədē/ ▶ n. the protective care or guardianship of someone or something. ■ imprisonment. ■ Law parental responsibility and usually physical guardianship, esp. as allocated to one of two divorcing parents. — **cus·to·di·al** /kə'stōdēəl/ adj. [ME: from L. *custodia*, from *custos* 'guardian.']

cus·tom /'kəstəm/ ▶ n. a traditional and widely accepted way of behaving or doing something that is specific to a particular society, place, or time. ■ [in sing.] a thing that one does habitually: *it was my custom to nap for an hour every day.* ■ Law established practice or usage having the force of law or right. ▶ adj. [attrib.] made or done to order for a particular customer: *a custom guitar.* [ME: from OFr. *coustume*, based on L. *consuetudo*, from *consuetus*, past part. of *consuescere* 'accustom,' from *con-* + *suescere* 'become accustomed.']

cus·tom·ar·y /ˈkəstəˌmerē/ ▶**adj.** according to the customs or usual practices associated with a particular society, place, or set of circumstances. ■ [attrib.] according to a person's habitual practice. ■ Law established by or based on custom rather than common law or statute. — **cus·tom·ar·i·ly** /ˌkəstəˈme(ə)rəlē/ **adv. cus·tom·ar·i·ness n.**

cus·tom-built ▶**adj.** another term for CUSTOM-MADE.

cus·tom·er /ˈkəstəmər/ ▶**n. 1** a person or organization that buys goods or services from a store or other business. **2** [with adj.] a person or thing of a specified kind that one has to deal with: *a tough customer.*

cus·tom·ize /ˈkəstəˌmīz/ ▶**v.** [trans.] (often **be customized**) modify (something) to suit a particular individual or task.

cus·tom-made ▶**adj.** made to a particular customer's order.

cus·toms /ˈkəstəmz/ ▶**plural n.** the official department that administers and collects the duties levied by a government on imported goods. ■ the place at a port, airport, or frontier where officials check incoming goods, travelers, or luggage. ■ (usu. **customs duties**) the duties levied by a government on imported goods.

cus·toms un·ion ▶**n.** a group of countries that have agreed to charge the same import duties as each other and usually to allow free trade between themselves.

cut /kət/ ▶**v.** (**cut·ting** ; past and past part. **cut**) [trans.] **1** make an opening, incision, or wound in (something) with a sharp-edged tool or object. **2** remove (something) from something larger by using a sharp implement. ■ informal castrate (an animal, esp. a horse). ■ remove the foreskin of a penis; circumcise. ■ (**cut something out**) make something by cutting. ■ (**cut something out**) remove, exclude, or stop eating or doing something undesirable. ■ (**cut something out**) separate an animal from the main herd. **3** divide into pieces with a knife or other sharp implement: *cut the beef into thin slices.* ■ make divisions in (something). ■ separate (something) into two; sever. ■ (**cut something down**) make something, esp. a tree, fall by cutting it through at the base. ■ (**cut someone down**) (of a weapon, bullet, or disease) kill or injure someone. **4** make or form (something) by using a sharp tool to remove material: *workmen cut a hole in the pipe.* ■ make or design (a garment) in a particular way. ■ make (a path, tunnel, or other route) by excavation, digging, or chopping. **5** trim or reduce the length of (something, esp. grass or a person's hair or fingernails) by using a sharp implement. **6** reduce the amount or quantity of: *I should cut down my sugar intake.* ■ abridge (a text, movie, or performance) by removing material. ■ Comput. delete (part of a text or other display) completely or so as to insert a copy of it elsewhere. See also CUT AND PASTE. ■ (in sports) remove (a player) from a team's roster. ■ end or interrupt the provision of (something, esp. power or food supplies). ■ (**cut something off**) block the usual means of access to a place. ■ absent oneself deliberately from (something one should normally attend, esp. school). ■ switch off (an engine or a light). **7** (of a line) cross or intersect (another line). ■ [intrans.] (**cut across**) pass or traverse, esp. so as to shorten one's route. ■ [intrans.] (**cut across**) have an effect regardless of (divisions or boundaries between groups). ■ [intrans.] (**cut along**) informal, dated leave or move hurriedly: *you can cut along now.* **8** dated ignore or refuse to recognize (someone). **9** [no obj., often in imper.] stop filming or recording. ■ [with adverbial] move to another shot in a movie: *cut to a dentist's office.* ■ [trans.] make (a movie) into a coherent whole by removing parts or placing them in a different order. **10** make (a sound recording). **11** [intrans.] divide a pack of playing cards by lifting a portion from the top, either to reveal a card at random or to place the top portion under the bottom portion. **12** Golf slice (the ball). **13** adulterate (a drug) or dilute (alcohol) by mixing it with another substance: *speed cut with rat poison.* **14** (**cut it**) informal come up to expectations; meet requirements: *this CD player doesn't quite cut it.* ▶**n. 1** an act of cutting, in particular: ■ [in sing.] a haircut. ■ a stroke or blow given by a sharp-edged implement or by a whip or cane. ■ fig. a wounding remark or act. ■ [often with adj.] a reduction in amount or size: *she took a 20% pay cut.* ■ (in sports) a removal of a player from a team's roster. ■ an act of removing part of a play, movie, or book. ■ an immediate transition from one scene to another in a movie. ■ Golf the halfway point of a golf tournament where half of the players are eliminated. **2** a result of cutting something, in particular: ■ a long narrow incision in the skin made by something sharp. ■ a long narrow opening or incision made in a surface or piece of material. ■ a piece of meat cut from a carcass: *a good lean cut of beef.* ■ [in sing.] informal a share of the profits from something. ■ a recording of a piece of music: *a cut from his forthcoming album.* ■ a version of a movie after editing: *the director's cut.* ■ a passage cut or dug out, as a railroad cutting or a new channel made for a river or other waterway. ■ a woodcut. **3** [in sing.] the way or style in which something, esp. a garment or someone's hair, is cut.

– PHRASES **be cut out for** (or **to be**) [usu. with negative] informal have exactly the right qualities for a particular role, task, or job: *I'm just not cut out to be a policeman.* **a cut above** informal noticeably superior to. **cut and dried** [often with negative] (of a situation) completely settled or decided. [18th C.: orig. used to distinguish the herbs of herbalists' shops from growing herbs.] **cut and run** informal make a speedy or sudden departure from an awkward or hazardous situation. **cut and thrust** Fencing the use of both the edge and the point of one's sword while fighting. ■ a spirited and rapid interchange of views. ■ a situation or sphere of activity regarded as carried out under adversarial conditions. **cut both ways** (of a point or statement) serve both sides of an argument. ■ (of an action or process) have both good and bad effects. **cut the corner** take the shortest course by going across and not around a corner. **cut corners** undertake something in what appears to be the easiest, quickest, or cheapest way, esp. by omitting to do something important or ignoring rules. **cut the crap** [often in imper.] vulgar slang get to the point; state the real situation. **cut someone dead** completely ignore someone. **cut a deal** informal come to an arrangement, esp. in business; make a deal. **cut someone down to size** informal deflate someone's exaggerated sense of self-worth. **cut something down to size** reduce the size or power of something, e.g., an organization, regarded as too large or powerful. **cut a —— figure** present oneself or appear in a particular way. **cut from the same cloth** of the same nature; similar. **cut in line** push into a line of people in order to be served or dealt with before one's turn. **cut it fine** see FINE[1]. **cut it out** [usu. in imper.] informal used to ask someone to stop doing or saying something that is annoying or offensive: *I'm sick of that joke; cut it out, can't you?* **cut loose** distance oneself from a person, group, or system by which one is unduly influenced or on which one is overdependent. ■ begin to act without restraint. **cut one's losses** abandon an enterprise or course of action that is clearly going to be unprofitable or unsuccessful before one suffers too much loss or harm. **cut the mustard** informal come up to expectations; reach the required standard. **cut no ice** informal have no influence or effect. **cut someone off** (or **down**) **in their prime** bring someone's life or career to an abrupt end while they are at the peak of their abilities. **cut someone/something short** interrupt someone or something; bring an abrupt or premature end to something said or done. **cut someone to pieces** kill or severely injure someone. ■ fig. totally defeat someone. **cut a** (or **the**) **rug** informal dance, typically in an energetic or accomplished way: *you can cut a rug when dance bands take to the stage.* **cut one's teeth** acquire initial practice or experience in a particular sphere of activity or with a particular organization. **cut a tooth** (of a baby) have a tooth appear through the gum. **cut to the chase** informal come to the point: *cut to the chase—what is it you want us to do?* **have one's work cut out** see WORK. **make the cut** [usu. with negative] Golf equal or better a required score, thus avoiding elimination from the last two rounds of a four-round tournament. **miss the cut** Golf fail to equal or better a required score, thus being eliminated from the last two rounds of a four-round tournament.

– PHRASAL VERBS **cut in 1** interrupt someone while they are speaking. **2** pull in too closely in front of another vehicle after having overtaken it. **3** (of a motor or other mechanical device) begin operating, esp. when triggered automatically by an electrical signal. **4** dated interrupt a dancing couple to take over from one partner. **cut someone in** informal include someone in a deal and give them a share of the profits. **cut into** interrupt the course of: *Victoria's words cut into her thoughts.* **cut someone off** interrupt someone while they are speaking. ■ interrupt someone during a telephone call by breaking the connection. ■ prevent someone from receiving or being provided with something, esp. power or water. ■ reject someone as one's heir; disinherit someone. ■ prevent someone from having access to somewhere or someone; isolate someone from something they previously had connections with: *we were cut off from reality.* ■ informal (of a driver) overtake someone and pull in too closely in front of them. **cut out 1** (of a motor or engine) suddenly stop operating. **2** informal (of a person) leave quickly, esp. so as to avoid a boring or awkward situation. **cut someone out** exclude someone. **cut up** informal behave in a mischievous or unruly manner. **cut someone up** informal criticize someone severely: *my kids cut him up about his appetite all the time.* [ME: prob. from Gmc. origin and akin to Icelandic *kuti* 'small blunt knife.']

cut and paste ▶**n.** a process used in assembling text on a word processor or computer, in which items are removed from one part and inserted elsewhere. ▶**v.** [trans.] move (an item of text) using this technique.

cu·ta·ne·ous /kyo͞oˈtānēəs/ ▶**adj.** of, relating to, or affecting the skin: *cutaneous pigmentation.* [16th C.: from mod. L. *cutaneus* (from L. *cutis* 'skin') + -OUS.]

cut·a·way /ˈkətəˌwā/ ▶**n.** [often as adj.] **1** a thing made or designed with a part cut out or absent, in particular: ■ a coat or jacket with the front cut away below the waist so as to curve back to the tails. ■ a diagram or drawing with some external parts left out to reveal the interior. **2** a shot in a movie that is of a different subject from those to which it is joined in editing.

cutaway jacket

cut·back /ˈkətˌbak/ ▶**n.** an act or instance of reducing something, typically expenditures.

cutch /kəCH/ ▶**n.** see CATECHU.

cut·down /ˈkətˌdoun/ ▶**n. 1** a decrease or reduction. [as adj.] **2** Surg. a procedure of cutting into a vein in order to insert a needle or cannula.

cute /kyo͞ot/ ▶**adj. 1** attractive in a pretty or endearing way. ■ informal sexually attractive. **2** informal affectedly or superficially clever. — **cute·ly adv. cute·ness n.** [18th C.: shortening of ACUTE.]

cute·sy /ˈkyo͞otsē/ ▶**adj.** informal cute to a sentimental or mawkish extent: *hair pulled back in cutesy little bows.*

cut·ey ▶**n.** var. of CUTIE.

cut glass ▶**n.** glass that has been ornamented by having patterns cut into it by grinding and polishing: [as adj.] *a cut-glass vase.*

Cuth·bert, St. /ˈkəTHbərt/ (c. 635–687), English monk.

cu·ti·cle /ˈkyo͞otikəl/ ▶**n. 1** the outer layer of living tissue, in particular: ■ Bot. & Zool. a protective and waxy or hard layer covering the epidermis of a plant, invertebrate, or shell. ■ the outer cellular layer of a hair. ■ Zool. another term for EPIDERMIS. **2** the dead skin at the base of a fingernail or toenail. —**cu·tic·u·lar** /kyo͞oˈtikyələr/ **adj.** [15th C.: from L. *cuticula*, dimin. of *cutis* 'skin.']

cut·ie /ˈkyo͞otē/ (also **cutie pie**) ▶**n.** informal an attractive or endearing person.

cut·in /ˈkyo͞otn/ ▶**n.** Biochem. a waxy, water-repellent substance occurring in the cuticle of plants and consisting of highly polymerized esters of fatty acids. [19th C.: from CUTIS + -IN[1].]

cut-in ▶**n.** a shot in a movie that is edited into another shot or scene.

cu·tis /ˈkyo͞otis/ ▶**n.** Anat. the true skin or dermis. [17th C.: from L., 'skin.']

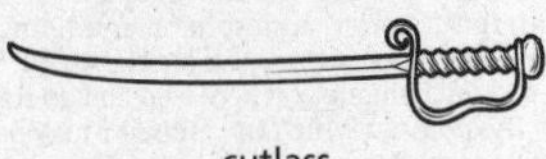
cutlass

cut·lass /ˈkətləs/ ▶**n.** a short sword with a slightly curved blade, formerly used by sailors. [16th C.: from Fr. *coutelas*, based on L. *cultellus* 'small knife' (see CUTLER).]

cut·lass·fish /ˈkətləs,fisн/ ▶**n.** (pl. same or **-fish·es**) a long, slender marine fish (*Trichiurus* and other genera, family Trichiuridae) with sharp teeth and a dorsal fin running the length of the back.

cut·ler /ˈkətlər/ ▶**n.** a person who makes or sells cutlery. [ME: from OFr. *coutelier*, from *coutel* 'knife,' from L. *cultellus*, dimin. of *culter* 'knife, plowshare.']

cut·ler·y /ˈkətlərē/ ▶**n.** **1** cutting utensils, esp. knives for cutting food. **2** knives, forks, and spoons used for eating or serving food.

cut·let /ˈkətlit/ ▶**n.** a portion of sliced meat breaded and served either grilled or fried. ■ a flat croquette of minced meat, nuts, or pulses, typically covered in breadcrumbs and fried. [18th C.: from Fr. *côtelette*, earlier *costelette*, dimin. of *coste* 'rib,' from L. *costa*.]

cut·off /ˈkət,ôf/ (also **cut-off**) ▶**adj.** [attrib.] **1** of or constituting a limit. **2** (of a device) producing an interruption or cessation of a power or fuel supply. **3** (of an item of clothing) having been cut short. **4** (of a person) isolated from or no longer having access to someone or something. ▶**n.** **1** a point or level that is a designated limit of something. **2** an act of stopping or interrupting the supply or provision of something. ■ a device for producing an interruption or cessation of a power or fuel supply. ■ a sudden drop in amplification or responsiveness of an electric device at a certain frequency: [as adj.] *a cutoff frequency of 8 Hz.* ■ the stopping of the supply of steam to the cylinders of a steam engine when the piston has traveled a set percentage of its stroke. **3** (**cutoffs**) shorts made by cutting off the legs of a pair of jeans or other trousers above or at the knee and leaving the edges unhemmed. **4** a shortcut. **5** Geol. a pattern of a meandering stream in which a channel cuts a new course to bypass a meander bend.

cut·out /ˈkət,out/ (also **cut-out**) ▶**n.** **1** a shape of a person or thing cut out of cardboard or another material. ■ fig. a person perceived as characterless or as lacking in individuality. *this film's protagonists are cardboard cutouts.* **2** a hole cut in something for decoration or to allow the insertion of something else. **3** a device that automatically breaks an electric circuit for safety and either resets itself or can be reset.

cut·o·ver /ˈkət,ōvər/ ▶**n.** a rapid transition from one phase of a business enterprise or project to another. ▶**adj.** [attrib.] (of land) having had its saleable timber felled and removed.

cut·purse /ˈkət,pərs/ ▶**n.** archaic term for PICKPOCKET.

cut-rate (also **cut-price**) ▶**adj.** [attrib.] for sale at a reduced or unusually low price: *cut-rate tickets.* ■ offering goods at such prices: *a cut-rate furniture store.*

cut·scene /ˈkət,sēn/ ▶**n.** (in computer games) a scene that develops the story line and is often shown on completion of a certain level, or when the player's character dies.

cut·ter /ˈkətər/ ▶**n.** **1** a person or thing that cuts something, in particular: ■ [often with adj.] a tool for cutting something, esp. one intended for cutting a particular thing or for producing a particular shape: *a glass cutter.* ■ a person who cuts or edits movies. ■ a person in a tailoring establishment who takes measurements and cuts the cloth. ■ a person who reduces or cuts down on something, esp. expenditures. **2** a light, fast coastal patrol boat. ■ a ship's boat used for carrying light stores or passengers. ■ hist. a small fore-and-aft-rigged sailing ship with one mast, more than one headsail, and a running bowsprit, used as a fast auxiliary. ■ a yacht with a gaff-rigged mainsail and two foresails.

cut·throat /ˈkət,тнrōt/ ▶**n.** **1** a murderer or other violent criminal. **2** (also **cutthroat trout**) a trout (*Salmo clarki*) of western North America, with red or orange markings under the jaw. ▶**adj.** (of a competitive situation or activity) fierce and intense; involving the use of ruthless measures: *the cutthroat world of fashion.* ■ (of a person) using ruthless methods in a competitive situation: *cutthroat manufacturers.* ■ relating to a game or contest in which individuals score against the other players. ■ denoting a form of whist (or other card game normally for four) played by three players.

cut·ting /ˈkətiNG/ ▶**n.** **1** (often **cuttings**) a piece cut off from something, esp. what remains when something is being trimmed or prepared. ■ a piece cut from a plant for propagation. ■ Brit. a clipping from a newspaper or periodical. **2** the action of someone or something that cuts. **3** an open passage excavated through higher ground for a railroad, road, or canal. ▶**adj.** capable of cutting something. ■ fig. (esp. of a comment) causing emotional pain; hurtful. ■ fig. (of the wind) bitterly cold. —**cut·ting·ly** **adv.**

cut·ting edge ▶**n.** edge of a tool's blade. ■ [in sing.] the latest stage in the development of something. ■ [in sing.] a person or factor that contributes a dynamic quality to a situation and thereby puts one at an advantage over one's rivals. ■ fig. incisiveness and directness of expression. ▶**adj.** (**cut·ting-edge**) at the latest or most advanced stage of development; innovative or pioneering.

cut·ting·ly /ˈkətiNGlē/ ▶**adv.** in an unkind or hurtful way: *he can be cuttingly rude.*

cut·ting room ▶**n.** a room in a production studio where film or videotape is cut and edited.

cut·tle /ˈkətl/ ▶**n.** a cuttlefish. [OE *cudele* 'cuttlefish,' from Gmc.; akin to *codd* 'bag,' referring to its ink bag.]

cut·tle·bone /ˈkətl,bōn/ ▶**n.** the flattened oval internal skeleton of the cuttlefish,made of white, lightweight, chalky material.

cut·tle·fish /ˈkətl,fisн/ ▶**n.** (pl. same or **-fish·es**) a marine mollusk (*Sepia* and other genera, class Cephalopoda) with eight arms and two long tentacles that are used for grabbing prey. [16th C.: from CUTTLE + FISH[1].]

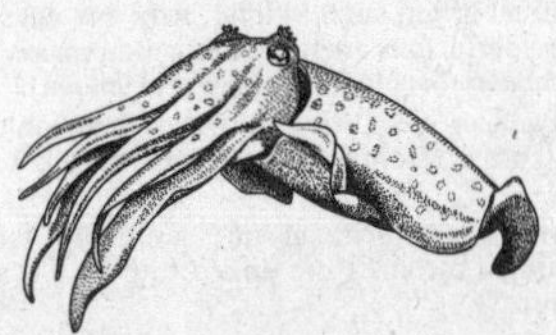
cuttlefish

cut-up (also **cut up**) ▶**adj.** **1** divided into pieces by cutting. ■ (of a soft piece of ground) having an uneven surface after the passage of heavy vehicles or animals: *the ground was deeply cut up where the cattle had strayed.* **2** [predic.] informal (of a person) very distressed. ▶**n.** **1** a film or sound recording made by cutting and editing material from preexisting recordings. **2** (**cutup**) informal a person fond of making jokes or playing pranks.

cut·wa·ter /ˈkət,wôtər; -,wätər/ ▶**n.** **1** the forward edge of a ship's prow. **2** a wedge-shaped projection on the pier of a bridge, which divides the flow of water and prevents debris from becoming trapped against the pier.

cut·work /ˈkət,wərk/ ▶**n.** embroidery or lace with parts cut out and the edges oversewn or filled with needlework designs. ■ appliqué work in which the pattern is cut out and sewn on.

cut·worm /ˈkət,wərm/ ▶**n.** a moth caterpillar (family Noctuidae) that lives in the upper layers of the soil and eats through the stems of young plants at ground level.

cu·vée /k(y)o͞oˈvā/ ▶**n.** a type, blend, or batch of wine, esp. champagne. [19th C.: Fr., 'vatful,' from *cuve* 'cask,' from L. *cupa*.]

cu·vette /kyo͞oˈvet/ ▶**n.** Biochem. a straight-sided, optically clear container for holding liquid samples in a spectrophotometer or other instrument. [18th C.: from Fr., dimin. of *cuve* 'cask,' from L. *cupa*.]

Cu·vi·er /ko͞oˈvyā/, Georges Léopold Chrétien Frédéric Dagobert, Baron (1769–1832), French naturalist. He founded the science of paleontology.

cuz /kəz/ (also **'cuz** or **coz**) ▶**conj.** informal short for BECAUSE.

Cuz·co /ˈko͞oskō/ a city in the Andes in southern Peru; pop. 275,000; ancient capital of the Inca empire.

CV ▶**abbr.** ■ cardiovascular. ■ curriculum vitae.

cv ▶**abbr.** cultivated variety.

CVS ▶**abbr.** ■ cardiovascular system. ■ chorionic villus sampling.

CVT ▶**abbr.** continuously variable transmission.

cwm /ko͝om; ko͞om/ ▶**n.** a cirque, esp. one in the mountains of Wales. [19th C.: Welsh.]

CWO ▶**abbr.** Chief Warrant Officer.

c.w.o. ▶**abbr.** cash with order.

cwt. ▶**abbr.** hundredweight.

CY ▶**abbr.** calendar year.

-cy ▶**suffix** **1** denoting state or condition: *bankruptcy.* **2** denoting rank or status: *baronetcy.* [from L. *-cia, -tia* and Gk. *-k(e)ia, -t(e)ia*.]

cy·an /ˈsīan; ˈsīən/ ▶**n.** a greenish-blue color, one of the primary subtractive colors, complementary to red. [19th C.: from Gk. *kuaneos* 'dark blue.']

cy·an·a·mide /sīˈanəmid; -,mīd/ ▶**n.** Chem. an acidic crystalline compound, CH_2N_2, made as an intermediate in the industrial production of ammonia. ■ a salt of this containing the anion CN_22-, esp. the calcium salt (**calcium cyanamide**) used as a fertilizer. [19th C.: blend of CYANOGEN and AMIDE.]

cy·an·ic /sīˈanik/ ▶**adj.** rare blue; azure.

cy·an·ic ac·id /ˈsīə,nāt; -nət/ ▶**n.** Chem. a colorless, poisonous, volatile, strongly acidic liquid, HOCN. [19th C.: from CYANOGEN.]

cy·a·nide /ˈsīə,nīd/ ▶**n.** Chem. a salt or ester of hydrocyanic acid, containing the anion CN− or the group −CN. The salts are generally extremely toxic. Compare with NITRILE. ■ sodium or potassium cyanide used as a poison or in the extraction of gold and silver. [19th C.: from CYANOGEN + -IDE.]

cy·a·nine /ˈsīəˌnēn; -nin/ ▶ **n.** a blue pigment that is a mixture of cobalt blue and Prussian blue.

cy·a·nite /ˈsīəˌnīt/ ▶ **n.** variant of KYANITE.

cyano- ▶ **comb. form** **1** relating to the color blue, esp. dark blue: *cyanosis*. **2** representing CYANIDE. [from Gk. *kuan(e)os* 'dark blue.']

cy·a·no·ac·ry·late /ˌsīənōˈakrəˌlāt; sīˈanō-/ ▶ **n.** Chem. any of a class of compounds that are cyanide derivatives of acrylates.

Cy·a·no·bac·te·ri·a /ˌsīəˌnō-bakˈti(ə)rēə; sīˌanō-/ Biol. a division of microorganisms (class Cyanophyceae, kingdom Eubacteria) that are related to the bacteria but are capable of photosynthesis. They are prokaryotic and represent the earliest known form of life on the earth. ■ [as pl. n.] (**cyanobacteria**) microorganisms of this division. Also called BLUE-GREEN ALGAE. [mod. L. (plural), from Gk. *kuaneos* 'dark blue' + pl. of BACTERIUM.]

cy·a·no·co·bal·a·min /ˌsīəˌnō-kōˈbaləmin; sīˌanō-/ ▶ **n.** a vitamin found in foods of animal origin such as liver, fish, and eggs, a deficiency of which can cause pernicious anemia. Also called VITAMIN B_{12}. [1950s: from CYANOGEN and *cobalamin* (blend of COBALT and VITAMIN).]

cy·a·no·gen /sīˈanəjən/ ▶ **n.** Chem. a colorless, flammable, highly poisonous gas, C_2N_2. [19th C.: from Fr. *cyanogène*, from Gk. *kuanos* 'dark blue mineral' + *-gène*.]

cy·a·no·hy·drin /ˌsīənōˈhīdrin; sīˌanō-/ ▶ **n.** Chem. an organic compound containing a carbon atom linked to both a cyanide group and a hydroxyl group.

cy·a·no·phyte /ˈsīənəˌfīt; sīˈanə-/ ▶ **n.** Biol. a microorganism of the division Cyanobacteria.

cy·a·no·sis /ˌsīəˈnōsis/ ▶ **n.** Med. a bluish discoloration of the skin. — **cy·a·not·ic** /ˌsīəˈnätik/ **adj.**

cy·an·o·type /ˈsīənəˌtīp; sīˈanə-/ ▶ **n.** a photographic blueprint.

cy·ath·i·um /sīˈaTHēəm/ ▶ **n.** (pl. **-ath·i·a** /-ˈaTHēə/) Bot. the characteristic inflorescence of the spurges, resembling a single flower. It consists of a cup-shaped involucre of fused bracts enclosing several greatly reduced male flowers and a single female flower. [19th C.: mod. L., from Gk. *kuathion*, dimin. of *kuathos* 'cup.']

Cyb·e·le /ˈsibəlē/ Mythol. a mother goddess worshiped esp. in Phrygia and later in Greece and the Roman Empire, with her consort Attis.

cy·ber /ˈsībər/ ▶ **adj.** of the culture of computers, information technology, and virtual reality: *the cyber age*. [abbrev. of CYBERNETICS.]

cyber- ▶ **comb. form** relating to electronic communication networks and virtual reality: *cyberpunk | cyberspace*. [back-form. from CYBERNETICS.]

cy·ber·naut /ˈsībərˌnôt; -ˌnät/ ▶ **n.** Comput. a person who wears sensory devices in order to experience virtual reality. ■ a person who uses the Internet. [1990s: from CYBER-, on the pattern of *astronaut* and *aeronaut*.]

cy·ber·net·ics /ˌsībərˈnetiks/ ▶ **plural n.** [treated as sing.] the science of communications and automatic control systems in both machines and living things. — **cy·ber·net·ic adj. cy·ber·ne·ti·cian** /-nəˈtisHən/ **n. cy·ber·net·i·cist** /-ˈnetəsist/ **n.** [1940s: from Gk. *kubernētēs* 'steersman,' from *kubernan* 'to steer.']

cy·ber·pho·bi·a /ˌsībərˈfōbēə/ ▶ **n.** extreme or irrational fear of computers or technology. — **cy·ber·phobe** /ˈsībərˌfōb/ **n. cy·ber·pho·bic** /-ˈfōbik/ **adj. & n.**

cy·ber·punk /ˈsībərˌpəNGk/ ▶ **n.** a genre of science fiction set in a lawless subculture of an oppressive society dominated by computer technology. ■ a writer of such science fiction. ■ a person who accesses computer networks illegally.

cy·ber·sex /ˈsībərˌseks/ ▶ **n.** sexual arousal using computer technology, esp. by wearing virtual reality equipment or by exchanging messages via the Internet.

cy·ber·space /ˈsībərˌspās/ ▶ **n.** the notional environment in which communication over computer networks occurs.

cy·ber·ter·ror·ism /ˌsībərˈterəˌrizəm/ ▶ **n.** the politically motivated use of computers and information technology to cause severe disruption or widespread fear in society: *a bill that would make it easier for law enforcement to wiretap computers and combat cyberterrorism*. — **cy·ber·ter·ror·ist n.**

cy·borg /ˈsībôrg/ ▶ **n.** a fictional or hypothetical person whose physical abilities become superhuman by mechanical elements built into the body. [1960s: blend of CYBER- and ORGANISM.]

cy·cad /ˈsīkəd; ˈsīkad/ ▶ **n.** a palmlike plant (genus *Cycas* and other genera, family Cycadaceae) of tropical and subtropical regions, bearing large male or female cones. [19th C.: from mod. L. *Cycas*, *Cycad-* (order name), from supposed Gk. *kukas*, scribal error for *koikas*, pl. of *koix* 'Egyptian palm.']

Cyc·la·des /ˈsikləˌdēz/ a group of Greek islands in the southern Aegean Sea. Greek name **KIKLÁDHES**.

Cy·clad·ic /sīˈkladik; si-/ ▶ **adj.** of or relating to the Cyclades. ■ Archaeol. of a Bronze Age civilization that flourished in the Cyclades, dated to c. 3000–1050 BC. ■ [as n.] (**the Cycladic**) the Cycladic culture or period.

cy·cla·mate /ˈsīkləˌmāt; -mət/ ▶ **n.** Chem. a salt of a synthetic acid, a cyclohexyl derivative of sulfamic acid. [1950s: contr. of *cyclohexylsulphamate*.]

cy·cla·men /ˈsīkləmən; ˈsik-/ ▶ **n.** (pl. same or **-mens**) a European plant (genus *Cyclamen*) of the primrose family, having pink, red, or white flowers with backward-curving petals and widely grown as a houseplant. [mod. L., based on Gk. *kuklaminos*, perh. from *kuklos* 'circle.']

cy·cle /ˈsīkəl/ ▶ **n.** **1** [often with adj.] a series of events that are regularly repeated in the same order. ■ the period of time taken to complete a single sequence of such events. ■ tech. a recurring series of successive operations or states, as in the working of an internal combustion engine, or in the alternation of an electric current or a wave: *four cycles of intake, combustion, ignition, and exhaust*. ■ Biol. a recurring series of events or metabolic processes in the lifetime of a plant or animal. ■ Biochem. a series of successive metabolic reactions in which a product is regenerated and reused. ■ Ecol. the movement of a simple substance through the soil, rocks, water, atmosphere, and living organisms. See CARBON CYCLE, NITROGEN CYCLE. ■ Comput. a single set of hardware operations, esp. that by which memory is accessed and an item is transferred to or from it, to the point at which the memory may be accessed again. ■ Physics a cycle per second; one hertz. **2** a complete set or series: *one of a cycle of seven*. ■ a series of songs, stories, plays, or poems composed around a particular theme: *Wagner's Ring Cycle*. **3** a bicycle or tricycle. ■ [in sing.] a ride on a bicycle. ▶ **v.** **1** [no obj., with adverbial of direction] ride a bicycle. **2** [intrans.] move in or follow a regularly repeated sequence of events: *cycle between boom and slump*. [ME: from OFr., from late L. *cyclus*, from Gk. *kuklos* 'circle.']

cy·cle of e·ro·sion ▶ **n.** Geol., dated an idealized course of landscape evolution, passing from youthful stages to old age.

cy·clic /ˈsīklik; ˈsik-/ ▶ **adj.** **1** occurring in cycles; regularly repeated: *nature is replete with cyclic processes*. ■ Math. (of a group) having the property that each element of the group can be expressed as a power of one particular element. ■ relating to or denoting a musical or literary composition with a recurrent theme or structural device. **2** Math. of or relating to a closed curve. ■ Geom. (of a polygon) having all its vertices lying on a circle. ■ Chem. (of a compound) having a molecular structure containing one or more closed rings of atoms. ■ Bot. (of a flower) having its parts arranged in whorls. — **cy·cli·cal adj.** (in sense 1) **cy·cli·cal·ly** /-k(ə)lē/ **adv.**

cy·clic AMP ▶ **n.** Biochem. a cyclic form of adenosine monophosphate (adenylic acid) that helps control many enzyme-catalyzed processes in living cells.

cy·clic GMP (abbr. **cGMP**) ▶ **n.** a cyclic version of the nucleotide guanosine monophosphate. In cellular metabolism, it aids in cell growth and division.

cy·clic re·dun·dan·cy check (also **cyclic redundancy code**) (abbr.: **CRC**) ▶ **n.** Comput. a data code that detects errors during transmission, storage, or retrieval.

cy·clin /ˈsīklin/ ▶ **n.** Biochem. any of a number of proteins associated with the cycle of cell division that are thought to initiate certain processes of mitosis. [1980s: from CYCLE + -IN[1].]

cy·cling /ˈsīk(ə)liNG/ ▶ **n.** the sport or activity of riding a bicycle.

Cy·cli·oph·o·ra /ˌsiklēˈäfərə; ˌsī-/ Zool. a new phylum proposed for a minute marine invertebrate (*Symbion pandora*) discovered in 1996 attached to the mouthparts of lobsters. [mod. L. (pl.), from Gk. *kuklios* 'circular' + *pherein* 'to bear.']

cy·clist /ˈsīk(ə)list/ ▶ **n.** a person who rides a bicycle.

cy·clize /ˈsīk(ə)ˌlīz/ ▶ **v.** Chem. undergo or cause to undergo a reaction in which one part of a molecule becomes linked to another to form a closed ring. — **cy·cli·za·tion** /ˌsīk(ə)ləˈzāsHən/ **n.**

cyclo- ▶ **comb. form** **1** circular: *cyclorama*. **2** relating to a cycle or cycling: *cyclocross*. **3** cyclic: *cycloparaffin*. [from Gk. *kuklos* 'circle,' or directly from CYCLE or CYCLIC.]

cy·clo·ad·di·tion /ˌsīklōəˈdisHən/ ▶ **n.** Chem. an addition reaction in which a cyclic molecule is formed.

cy·clo·al·kane /ˌsīklōˈalkān/ ▶ **n.** Chem. another term for CYCLOPARAFFIN.

cy·clo·cross /ˈsīkləˌkrôs/ (also **cy·clo-cross**) ▶ **n.** cross-country racing on bicycles.

cy·clo·hex·ane /ˌsīklōˈheksān/ ▶ **n.** Chem. a colorless, flammable liquid cycloparaffin, C_6H_{12}, obtained from petroleum and used as a solvent and paint remover.

cy·clo·hex·yl /ˌsīkləˈheksəl/ ▶ **n.** [as adj.] Chem. of or denoting the cyclic hydrocarbon radical $-C_6H_{11}$, derived from cyclohexane.

cy·cloid /ˈsīkloid/ ▶ **n.** Math. a curve (resembling a series of arches) traced by a point on a circle being rolled along a straight line. — **cy·cloi·dal** /sīˈkloidl/ **adj.** [17th C.: from Gk. *kukloeidēs* 'circular,' from *kuklos* 'circle.']

cy·clom·e·ter /sīˈklämətər/ ▶ **n.** **1** an instrument for measuring circular arcs. **2** an instrument on a bicycle for measuring the distance.

cy·clone /ˈsīklōn/ ▶ **n.** Meteorol. winds rotating inward to an area of low atmospheric pressure, with a counterclockwise (northern hemisphere) or clockwise (southern hemisphere) circulation; a depression. ■ another term for TROPICAL STORM. — **cy·clon·ic** /sīˈklänik/ **adj. cy·clon·i·cal·ly** /sīˈklänik(ə)lē/ **adv.** [19th C.: prob. from Gk. *kuklōma* 'wheel, coil of a snake,' from *kuklos* 'circle.']

cy·clo·par·af·fin /ˌsīklōˈparəfin/ ▶ **n.** Chem. a hydrocarbon with a molecule containing a ring of carbon atoms joined by single bonds.

cy·clo·pe·an /ˌsīkləˈpēən; sīˈklōpēən/ (also **cy·clo·pi·an**) ▶ **adj.** **1** denoting ancient masonry made with massive irregular blocks: *cyclopean stone walls*. [by association with the great size of the Cyclops.] **2** of or resembling a Cyclops: *a cyclopean eye*.

cy·clo·pe·di·a /ˌsīkləˈpēdēə/ (also **cy·clo·pae·di·a**) ▶ **n.** archaic (except in book titles) an encyclopedia. — **cy·clo·pe·dic adj.**

cy·clo·pen·ta·di·ene /ˌsīkləˌpentə'dīēn; ˌsiklə-/ ▶n. a colorless toxic liquid derived from the distillation of coal tar, insoluble in water and soluble in alcohol.

cy·clo·phos·pha·mide /ˌsīklō'fäsfəˌmīd/ ▶n. Med. a synthetic cytotoxic drug used in treating leukemia and lymphoma and as an immunosuppressive agent.

cy·clo·ple·gia /ˌsīklə'plēj(ē)ə/ ▶n. paralysis of the ciliary muscle of the eye.

cy·clo·pro·pane /ˌsīklō'prōpān/ ▶n. Chem. a flammable, gaseous synthetic compound, C_3H_6, which has some use as a general anesthetic.

Cy·clops /'sīkläps/ ▶n. (pl. **Cy·clops** or **Cy·clops·es** or **Cy·clo·pes** /sī'klōpēz/) Gk. Mythol. a member of a race of savage one-eyed giants. [via L. from Gk. *Kuklōps*, lit. 'round-eyed,' from *kuklos* 'circle' + *ōps* 'eye.']

cy·clo·ram·a /ˌsīklə'ramə; -'rämə/ ▶n. a circular picture of a 360° scene, viewed from inside. ■ a cloth stretched tight in an arc around the back of a stage set, often used to depict the sky. — **cy·clo·ram·ic** /-'ramik/ adj. [19th C.: from CYCLO-.]

cy·clo·spo·rine /ˌsīklə'spôrin; -ēn/ (also **cy·clo·spo·rin A**, **cy·clo·spo·rin**) ▶n. Med. a drug with immunosuppressive properties used to prevent the rejection of grafts and transplants. It is obtained from the fungus *Trichoderma polysporum*. [1970s: from CYCLO- + *-sporin* (from L. *spora* 'spore') + -IN¹.]

cy·clo·stome /'sīkləˌstōm/ ▶n. Zool. an eellike, jawless vertebrate (subclass Cyclostomata, superclass Agnatha) with a round sucking mouth. [19th C.: from CYCLO- + Gk. *stoma* 'mouth.']

cy·clo·style /'sīkləˌstīl/ ▶n. an early device for duplicating handwriting, in which a pen with a small toothed wheel pricks holes in a sheet of waxed paper, which is then used as a stencil. ▶v. [trans.] [usu. as adj.] (**cyclostyled**) duplicate with such a device: *a cyclostyled leaflet*. [19th C.: from CYCLO- 'circular.']

cy·clo·thy·mi·a /ˌsīklə'THīmēə/ ▶n. Psychiatry, dated a mental state of marked swings of mood between depression and elation; manic-depressive tendency. — **cy·clo·thy·mic** /-'THīmik/ adj. [1920s: from CYCLO- + Gk. *thumos* 'temper.']

cy·clo·tron /'sīkləˌträn/ ▶n. Physics a device in which charged atomic and subatomic particles are accelerated by an alternating electric field while following an outward spiral or circular path in a magnetic field.

cy·der ▶n. archaic spelling of CIDER.

cyg·net /'signət/ ▶n. a young swan. [ME: from Anglo-Norman Fr. *cignet*, dimin. of OFr. *cigne* 'swan,' based on Gk. *kuknos*.]

Cyg·nus /'signəs/ Astron. a prominent northern constellation (the Swan), said to represent a flying swan that was the form adopted by Zeus on one occasion.

cyl. ▶abbr. cylinder.

cyl·in·der /'siləndər/ ▶n. a solid geometric figure with straight parallel sides and a circular or oval section. ■ a solid or hollow body, object, or part with such a shape. ■ a piston chamber in a steam or internal combustion engine. ■ a cylindrical container for liquefied gas under pressure. ■ a rotating metal roller in a printing press. ■ Archaeol. a cylinder seal. — **cy·lin·dric** /sə'lindrik/ adj. **cy·lin·dri·cal** /sə'lindrikəl/ adj. **cy·lin·dri·cal·ly** /sə'lindrik(ə)lē/ adv. [16th C.: from L. *cylindrus*, from Gk. *kulindros* 'roller,' from *kulindein* 'to roll.']

cyl·in·der block ▶n. see BLOCK (sense 1).

cyl·in·der head ▶n. the end cover of a cylinder in an internal combustion engine.

cyl·in·der lock ▶n. a lock with the keyhole and tumbler mechanism contained in a cylinder.

cyl·in·der seal ▶n. Archaeol. a small, barrel-shaped stone object with a hole down the center and an incised design or cuneiform inscription. It was originally rolled on soft clay to indicate ownership or to authenticate a document and was used chiefly in Mesopotamia.

cyl·in·droid /'silənˌdroid/ ▶n. a figure or body resembling a cylinder. ▶adj. resembling a cylinder in shape.

cy·ma /'sīmə/ ▶n. (pl. **-mas** or **-mae** /-mē; -mī/) **1** Archit. a cornice molding with an S-shaped cross section. Compare with OGEE. **2** Bot. var. of CYME. [16th C.: mod. L., from Gk. *kuma* 'wave or wavy molding.']

cym·bal /'simbəl/ ▶n. a musical instrument consisting of a slightly concave round brass plate that is either struck against another one or struck with a stick to make a ringing or clashing sound. See also illustration at DRUM KIT. — **cym·bal·ist** n. [OE, from L. *cymbalum*, from Gk. *kumbalon*, from *kumbē* 'cup.']

cymbals

cym·ba·lom /'simbələm/ (also **cim·ba·lom**) ▶n. a large Hungarian dulcimer. [19th C.: from Hungarian, from Ital. *cembalo*, *cimbalo*, from L. *cymbalum* (see CYMBAL).]

Cym·be·line /'simbəˌlēn/ (also **Cu·no·be·li·nus** /ˌk(y)o͞onōbə'līnəs/) (died c.AD 42), English chieftain. He made the town of Camulodunum (Colchester) his capital and established a mint.

cym·bid·i·um /ˌsim'bidēəm/ ▶n. (pl. **-ums**) a widely cultivated tropical Asiatic orchid (genus *Cymbidium*, family Orchidaceae) with arching stems bearing several flowers. [mod. L., from Gk. *kumbē* 'cup.']

cyme /sīm/ ▶n. Bot. a flower cluster with a central stem bearing a single terminal flower that develops first, the other flowers in the cluster developing as terminal buds of lateral stems. Compare with RACEME. — **cy·mose** /'sīmōs/ adj. [18th C.: from Fr., lit. 'summit' based on L. *cyma*.]

cy·moid /'sīmoid/ ▶adj. resembling a cyma or a cyme.

Cym·ric /'kəmrik; 'kim-/ ▶adj. Welsh in language or culture. ▶n. the Welsh language. [19th C.: from Welsh *Cymru* 'Wales,' *Cymry* 'the Welsh,' + -IC.]

Cym·ru /'kəmrē; 'kim-/ Welsh name for WALES.

Cyn·e·wulf /'kinəˌwo͝olf; 'ko͞on-/ (late 8th–9th centuries), Anglo-Saxon poet. His poems include *Juliana* and *Elene*.

cyn·ic /'sinik/ ▶n. **1** a person who believes that people are motivated purely by self-interest rather than acting for honorable or unselfish reasons. ■ a person who questions whether something will happen or is worthwhile. **2** (**Cynic**) a member of a school of ancient Greek philosophers founded by Antisthenes, marked by an ostentatious contempt for ease and pleasure. — **cyn·i·cism** /'sinəˌsizəm/ n. [16th C. (sense 2): from L. *cynicus*, from Gk. *kunikos*; prob. orig. from *Kunosarges*, the name of a gymnasium where Antisthenes taught.]

cyn·i·cal /'sinikəl/ ▶adj. **1** believing that people are motivated by self-interest; distrustful of human sincerity or integrity. ■ doubtful as to whether something will happen or is worthwhile. ■ contemptuous; mocking: *he gave a cynical laugh*. **2** concerned only with one's own interests and disregarding accepted standards to achieve them: *Stalin's cynical deal with Hitler*. — **cyn·i·cal·ly** adv.

cyno- ▶comb. form of or relating to dogs: *cynodont*. [from Gk. *kuōn*, *kun-* 'dog.']

cyn·o·dont /'sīnəˌdänt/ ▶n. a carnivorous, mammallike fossil reptile (suborder Cynodontia, order Therapsida) of the late Permian and Triassic periods, with well-developed, specialized teeth. [19th C.: from Gk. *kuōn*, *kun-* 'dog' + *odous*, *odont-* 'tooth.']

cy·no·sure /'sīnəˌSHo͝or; 'sin-/ ▶n. [in sing.] a person or thing that is the center of attention or admiration. [16th C.: based on Gk. *kunosoura* 'dog's tail' (also 'Ursa Minor'), from *kuōn*, *kun-* 'dog' + *oura* 'tail.']

cy·pher ▶n. var. of CIPHER.

cy·pher·punk /'sīfərˌpəNGk/ ▶n. a person who uses encryption when accessing a computer network to ensure privacy, esp. from government authorities. [1990s: on the pattern of *cyberpunk*.]

cy·pres /sē'prā/ ▶adv. & adj. Law as near as possible to the testator's or donor's intentions when these cannot be precisely followed. [19th C.: from a late Anglo-Norman French var. of Fr. *si près* 'so near.']

Cy·press /'sīprəs/ a city in south central California; pop. 42,655.

cy·press /'sīprəs/ (also **cypress tree**) ▶n. an evergreen coniferous tree (*Cupressus* and other genera, family Cupressaceae) with small, rounded, woody cones and flattened shoots bearing small, scalelike leaves. ■ a tree of this type, or branches from it, as a symbol of mourning. ■ used in names of similar coniferous trees of other families, e.g., **bald cypress**. [ME: from OFr. *cipres*, from late L. *cypressus*, from Gk. *kuparissos*.]

cy·press knees ▶plural n. the cone-shaped exposed growths on the buttress roots of a bald cypress.

Cyp·ri·an, St. /'siprēən/ (died 258), Carthaginian bishop and martyr.

cy·pri·nid /'siprənid/ ▶n. Zool. a fish of the minnow (or carp) family (Cyprinidae). [19th C.: from mod. L. *Cyprinidae* (pl.), based on Gk. *kuprinos* 'carp.']

cyp·ri·noid /'siprəˌnoid/ Zool. ▶n. a fish of a large group (order Cypriniformes) that includes the carps, suckers, and loaches, and (in some classification schemes) the characins. ▶adj. of or relating to fish of this group. [19th C.: from mod. L. *Cyprinoidea*, based on L. *cyprinus* 'carp' (from Gk. *kuprinos*).]

Cyp·ri·ot /'siprēət; -ˌät/ ▶n. **1** a native or national of Cyprus. **2** the dialect of Greek used in Cyprus. ▶adj. of or relating to Cyprus or its people or the Greek dialect used there. [from Gk. *Kupriōtes*, from *Kupros* 'Cyprus.']

cyp·ri·pe·di·um /ˌsiprə'pēdēəm/ ▶n. (pl. **-ums**) an orchid of a genus (*Cypripedium*) that comprises the lady's slippers. [mod. L., from Gk. *Kupris* 'Aphrodite' + *pedilon* 'slipper.']

Cy·prus /'sīprəs/ an island country in southeastern Europe, in the eastern Mediterranean Sea, south of the Turkish coast; pop. 775,000; capital, Nicosia.

cyp·se·la /'sipsələ/ ▶n. (pl. **-lae** /-lē/) Bot. a dry, single-seeded fruit formed from a double ovary, of which only one develops into a seed, as in the daisy family. [19th C.: mod. L., from Gk. *kupselē* 'hollow vessel.']

Cyr·a·no de Ber·ge·rac /'sirənō də 'bərZH(ə)ˌrak/, Savinien (1619–55), French soldier and writer. His large nose, presumably an object of ridicule that led to many duels, was exaggerated and immortalized in Rostand's play *Cyrano de Bergerac* (1897).

Cyr·e·na·ic /ˌsirəˈnāik/ ▶**adj.** of or denoting the hedonistic school of philosophy, which was founded *c.*400 BC by Aristippus the Elder of Cyrene. ▶**n.** a follower of this school of philosophy. — **Cyr·e·na·i·cism** /-ˈnāəˌsizəm/ **n.**

Cyr·e·na·i·ca /ˌsirəˈnāikə/ a region in northeastern Libya that borders the Mediterranean Sea, settled by Greeks *c.*640 BC.

Cy·re·ne /sīˈrēnē/ an ancient Greek city in North Africa, near the coast in Cyrenaica.

Cyr·il, St. /ˈsirəl/ (826–869), Greek missionary who is said to have invented the Cyrillic alphabet.

Cy·ril·lic /səˈrilik/ ▶**adj.** denoting the alphabet used by many Slavic peoples, chiefly those with a historical allegiance to the Orthodox Church, and used for Russian, Bulgarian, Serbian, and Ukrainian. ▶**n.** the Cyrillic alphabet. [19th C.: named after St. *Cyril* (see CYRIL, ST.).]

Cyr·il of Al·ex·an·dri·a, St. (died 444), leader of the early Christian Church. The patriarch of Alexandria, he opposed Nestorius, the patriarch of Constantinople.

Cy·rus[1] /ˈsīrəs/ (died *c.*530 BC), king of Persia 559–530 BC; father of Cambyses; known as **Cyrus the Great**. He founded the Achaemenid dynasty.

Cy·rus[2] (died 401 BC), Persian prince; known as **Cyrus the Younger**. On the death of his father, Darius II, in 405 BC, he revolted against his brother, who had succeeded to the throne as Artaxerxes II.

cyst /sist/ ▶**n.** Biol. in an animal or plant, a thin-walled, hollow organ or cavity containing a liquid secretion; a sac, vesicle, or bladder. ■ Med. in the body, a membranous sac or cavity of abnormal character containing fluid. ■ a tough protective capsule enclosing the larva of a parasitic worm or the resting stage of an organism. [18th C.: from late L. *cystis*, from Gk. *kustis* 'bladder.']

cys·tec·to·my /sisˈtektəmē/ ▶**n. 1** (pl. **-mies**) a surgical operation to remove the urinary bladder. **2** a surgical operation to remove an abnormal cyst.

cys·te·ine /ˈsistiˌēn; ˈsistēn/ ▶**n.** Biochem. a sulfur-containing amino acid, $HSCH_2CH(NH_2)COOH$, that occurs in keratins and other proteins, often in the form of cystine, and is a constituent of many enzymes. [19th C.: from CYSTINE + *-eine* (var. of -INE[4]).]

cys·tic /ˈsistik/ ▶**adj. 1** esp. Med. of, relating to, or characterized by cysts. ■ Zool. (of a parasite or other organism) enclosed in a cyst: *the cystic stage.* **2** of or relating to the urinary bladder or the gallbladder: *the cystic artery.*

cys·ti·cer·cus /ˌsistəˈsərkəs; -ˈkərkəs/ ▶**n.** (pl. **-cer·ci** /-ˈsərsī; -ˈsərkī/) Zool. a larval tapeworm that is at a stage in which the anterior end is inverted in a sac, and that is typically found encysted in the muscle tissue of the host. — **cys·ti·cer·coid** /-ˈsərkoid/ **adj. & n.** [19th C.: mod. L., from Gk. *kustis* 'bladder' + *kerkos* 'tail.']

cys·tic fi·bro·sis ▶**n.** a hereditary disorder affecting the exocrine glands. It causes the production of abnormally thick mucus, leading to the blockage of the pancreatic ducts, intestines, and bronchi and often resulting in respiratory infection.

cys·tine /ˈsistēn/ ▶**n.** Biochem. a compound, $C_6H_{12}N_2O_4S_2$, that is an oxidized dimer of cysteine and is the form in which cysteine often occurs in organic tissue. [19th C.: from Gk. *kustis* 'bladder.']

cys·ti·tis /sisˈtītis/ ▶**n.** Med. inflammation of the urinary bladder.

cysto- ▶**comb. form** of or relating to the urinary bladder: *cystotomy.* [from Gk. *kustis* 'bladder.']

cyst·oid /ˈsistoid/ ▶**adj.** of the nature of a cyst. ▶**n.** a cystoid formation.

cys·to·scope /ˈsistəˌskōp/ ▶**n.** Med. an instrument inserted into the urethra for examining the urinary bladder. — **cys·to·scop·ic** /ˌsistəˈskäpik/ **adj. cys·tos·co·py** /siˈstäskəpē/ **n.**

cys·tot·o·my /siˈstätəmē/ ▶**n.** (pl. **-mies**) a surgical incision into the urinary bladder.

-cyte ▶**comb. form** Biol. denoting a mature cell: *lymphocyte.* Compare with -BLAST. [from Gk. *kutos* 'vessel.']

Cyth·er·e·a /ˌsiᴛʜəˈrēə/ ▶**n.** another name for APHRODITE. [from L. *Cythera* 'Kithira,' the name of an Ionian island.]

Cyth·er·ean /ˌsiᴛʜəˈrēən/ ▶**adj.** Astron. of or relating to the planet Venus. ■ of or relating to the goddess Cytherea.

cyt·i·dine /ˈsitiˌdēn; ˈsī-/ ▶**n.** Biochem. a nucleoside composed of cytosine linked to ribose, obtained from RNA by hydrolysis. [20th C.: from CYTO- + -IDE + -INE[4].]

cyto- ▶**comb. form** Biol. of a cell or cells: *cytology* | *cytoplasm.* [from Gk. *kutos* 'vessel.']

cy·to·ar·chi·tec·ton·ics /ˌsītōˌärkitekˈtäniks/ ▶**plural n.** [treated as sing. or pl.] another term for CYTOARCHITECTURE. — **cy·to·ar·chi·tec·ton·ic adj.**

cy·to·ar·chi·tec·ture /ˌsītōˈärkiˌtekᴄʜər/ ▶**n.** Anat. the arrangement of cells in a tissue, esp. in specific areas of the cerebral cortex characterized by the arrangement of their cells and each associated with particular functions. Also called CYTOARCHITECTONICS. — **cy·to·ar·chi·tec·tur·al** /-ˌärkiˈtekᴄʜərəl/ **adj. cy·to·ar·chi·tec·tur·al·ly** /-ˌärkiˈtekᴄʜərəlē/ **adv.**

cy·to·cen·tri·fuge /ˌsītəˈsentrəˌfyo͞oj/ Biol. ▶**n.** a centrifuge used for depositing cells suspended in a liquid onto a slide for microscopic examination. ▶**v.** [trans.] deposit (cells) on a slide using such a centrifuge.

cy·to·cha·la·sin /ˌsītōkəˈlāsin/ ▶**n.** Biochem. any of a group of polycyclic compounds produced by fungi and used in research for their property of interfering with cell processes. [1960s: from CYTO- + Gk. *khalasis* 'dislocation.']

cy·to·chem·is·try /ˌsītəˈkeməstrē/ ▶**n.** the chemistry of living cells, esp. as studied microscopically. — **cy·to·chem·i·cal** /-ˈkemikəl/ **adj.**

cy·to·chrome /ˈsītəˌkrōm/ ▶**n.** Biochem. any of a number of compounds consisting of heme bonded to a protein.

cy·to·gen·e·sis /ˌsītəˈjenəsis/ (also **cy·tog·e·ny** /sīˈtäjənē/) ▶**n.** the formation and development of cells.

cy·to·ge·net·ics /ˌsītōjəˈnetiks/ ▶**plural n.** [treated as sing.] Biol. the study of inheritance in relation to the structure and function of chromosomes. — **cy·to·ge·net·ic adj. cy·to·ge·net·i·cal** /-ikəl/ **adj. cy·to·ge·net·i·cal·ly** /-ik(ə)lē/ **adv. cy·to·ge·net·i·cist** /-jəˈnetəsist/ **n.**

cy·to·kine /ˈsītəˌkīn/ ▶**n.** Physiol. any of a number of substances, such as interferon, secreted by certain cells of the immune system and having an effect on other cells.

cy·to·ki·ne·sis /ˌsītōkəˈnēsis; -kī-/ ▶**n.** Biol. the cytoplasmic division of a cell at the end of mitosis or meiosis, bringing about the separation into two daughter cells.

cy·to·ki·nin /ˌsītəˈkīnin/ ▶**n.** another term for KININ (sense 2).

cy·tol·o·gy /sīˈtäləjē/ ▶**n.** the branch of biology concerned with the structure and function of plant and animal cells. — **cy·to·log·i·cal** /ˌsītlˈäjikəl/ **adj. cy·to·log·i·cal·ly** /ˌsītlˈäjik(ə)lē/ **adv. cy·tol·o·gist** /-jist/ **n.**

cy·tol·y·sis /sīˈtäləsis/ ▶**n.** Biol. the dissolution or disruption of cells, esp. by an external agent. — **cy·to·lyt·ic** /ˌsītlˈitik/ **adj.**

cy·to·me·gal·ic /ˌsītōmiˈgalik/ ▶**adj.** Med. characterized by enlarged cells, esp. with reference to a disease caused by a cytomegalovirus.

cy·to·meg·a·lo·vi·rus /ˌsītəˌmegəlōˈvīrəs/ (abbr.: **CMV**) ▶**n.** Med. a kind of herpesvirus that usually produces very mild symptoms in an infected person but may cause severe neurological damage in people with weakened immune systems and in the newborn.

cy·to·mem·brane /ˌsītəˈmembrān/ ▶**n.** another term for CELL MEMBRANE.

cy·to·path·ic /ˌsītəˈpaᴛʜik/ (also **cy·to·path·o·gen·ic** /ˌsītəˌpaᴛʜəˈjenik/) ▶**adj.** of, pertaining to, or producing damage to living cells.

cy·to·phil·ic /ˌsītəˈfilik/ ▶**adj.** having an affinity for living cells.

cy·to·pho·tom·e·try /ˌsītəfōˈtämətrē/ ▶**n.** Biol. the investigation of the contents of cells by measuring the light they allow through after staining. — **cy·to·pho·tom·e·ter** /-ˈtämətər/ **n. cy·to·pho·to·met·ric** /-ˌfōtəˈmetrik/ **adj.**

cy·to·plasm /ˈsītəˌplazəm/ ▶**n.** Biol. the material or protoplasm within a living cell, excluding the nucleus. — **cy·to·plas·mic** /ˌsītəˈplazmik/ **adj.**

cy·to·plast /ˈsītəˌplast/ ▶**n.** the intact cytoplasmic content of a single cell.

cy·to·sine /ˈsītəˌsēn/ ▶**n.** Biochem. a compound, $C_4H_5N_3O$, found in living tissue as a constituent base of nucleic acids.

cy·to·skel·e·ton /ˌsītəˈskelitn/ ▶**n.** Biol. a microscopic network of protein filaments and tubules in the cytoplasm of many living cells, giving them shape and coherence. — **cy·to·skel·e·tal** /-ˈskelitl/ **adj.**

cy·to·sol /ˈsītəˌsäl; -ˌsôl/ ▶**n.** Biol. the aqueous component of the cytoplasm of a cell, within which various organelles and particles are suspended. — **cy·to·sol·ic** /ˌsītəˈsälik; -ˈsôlik/ **adj.**

cy·to·stat·ic /ˌsītəˈstatik/ ▶**adj.** inhibiting cell growth and division. ▶**n.** any substance that inhibits cell growth and division.

cy·to·tax·on·o·my /ˌsītətakˈsänəmē/ ▶**n.** taxonomy based on cytological (and esp. cytogenetic) study.

cy·to·tox·ic /ˌsītəˈtäksik/ ▶**adj.** toxic to living cells. — **cy·to·tox·ic·i·ty** /-täkˈsisitē/ **n.**

cy·to·tox·ic T cell ▶**n.** another term for KILLER CELL.

cy·to·tox·in /ˌsītəˈtäksin/ ▶**n.** a substance toxic to cells.

Cy Young A·ward ▶**n.** Baseball an annual award to the outstanding pitcher in each of the major leagues. [named in honor of pitching great Cy Young.]

czar /zär; (t)sär/ (also **tsar** or **tzar**) ▶**n.** an emperor of Russia before 1917: [as title] *Czar Nicholas II.* ■ a South Slav ruler in former times, esp. one reigning over Serbia in the 14th century. ■ [usu. with adj.] a person with great authority or power in a particular area: *America's new drug czar.* — **czar·dom** /-dəm/ **n. czar·ism n. czar·ist n. & adj.** [from Russ. *tsar'*, representing L. *Caesar*.]

czar·das /ˈᴄʜärdäsʜ/ (also **csar·das**) ▶**n.** (pl. same) a Hungarian dance with a slow introduction and a fast, wild finish. [19th C.: from Hungarian *csárdás*, from *csárda* 'inn.']

czar·e·vich /ˈzärəˌviᴄʜ; ˈ(t)sär-/ (also **tsarevich** or **czarevitch**) ▶**n.** hist. the eldest son of an emperor of Russia. [18th C.: Russ., lit. 'son of a czar.']

cza·rev·na /zäˈrevnə; (t)sä-/ ▶**n. 1** a daughter of a czar. **2** the wife of a czarevich.

cza·ri·na /zäˈrēnə; (t)sä-/ (also **tsarina** or **tzarina**) ▶**n.** hist. an empress of Russia before 1917. [via Ital. and Sp. from Ger. *Czarin, Zarin*, fem. of *Czar, Zar*.]

Czech /ᴄʜek/ ▶**n. 1** a native or national of the Czech Republic or (formerly) Czechoslovakia, or a person of Czech descent. **2** the West Slavic language spoken in the Czech Republic, closely related to Slovak. ▶**adj.** of or relating to the Czechs or their language. [Polish spelling of Czech *Čech*.]

Czech·o·slo·va·ki·a /ˌᴄʜekəsləˈväkēə; -ˈvakēə/ a former country in central Europe; capital, Prague. Created out of the northern part of the Austro-Hungarian empire in 1918, it became a Communist state in 1948; with the collapse of Communism in the early 1990s, the country was divided into two independent nations, the Czech Republic and

Czech Republic

Location: central Europe, south of Poland and southeast of Germany
Area: 29,900 square miles (77,300 sq km)
Population: 10,298,700
Capital: Prague
Language: Czech
Currency: Czech koruna

Slovakia (1993). — **Czech·o·slo·vak** /-ˈslōväk; -vak/ **n. & adj. Czech·o·slo·va·ki·an adj. & n.**

Czech Re·pub·lic a country in central Europe. *See box.*

Czę·sto·cho·wa /ˌCHENstəˈhōvə/ a city in south central Poland; pop. 258,000.

Dd

D[1] /dē/ (also **d**) ▶ **n.** (pl. **Ds** or **D's**) **1** the fourth letter of the alphabet. ■ denoting the fourth in a set of items, categories, sizes, etc. ■ the fourth highest category of academic mark. **2** (**D**) a shape like that of a capital D: [in comb.] *the D-shaped handle.* ■ a loop or ring of this shape. **3** (usu. **D**) Music the second note of the diatonic scale of C major. ■ a key based on a scale with D as its keynote. **4** the Roman numeral for 500.

D[2] ▶ **abbr.** ■ Democrat or Democratic. ■ depth (in the sense of the dimension of an object from front to back). ■ Chem. dextrorotatory: *D-glucose.* ■ (with a numeral) dimension(s) or dimensional: *a 3-D model.* ■ (in tables of sports results) drawn. ■ (on an automatic gearshift) drive. ■ (in personal ads) divorced. ▶ **symb.** ■ Physics electric flux density. ■ Chem. the hydrogen isotope deuterium.

d ▶ **abbr.** ■ date. ■ (in genealogies) daughter. ■ day(s): *orbital period (Mars): 687.0d.* ■ deceased. ■ deep. ■ [in comb.] (in units of measurement) deci-. ■ (in travel timetables) departs. ■ (**d.**) died (used to indicate a date of death): *Barents, Willem (d.1597).* ■ divorced. ■ Brit. penny or pence (of predecimal currency): *£20 10s 6d.* [from L. *denarius* 'penny.'] ■ Chem. denoting electrons and orbitals possessing two units of angular momentum: *d-electrons.* [*d* from *diffuse.*] ▶ **symb.** ■ Math. diameter. ■ Math. denoting a small increment in a given variable: *dy/dx.*

'd ▶ **contr.** ■ had. ■ would.

DA ▶ **abbr.** ■ district attorney. ■ Doctor of Arts. ■ informal duck's ass.

D/A Electron. ▶ **abbr.** digital to analog.

da ▶ **abbr.** [in comb.] (in units of measurement) deca-.

DAB ▶ **abbr.** digital audio broadcasting.

dab[1] /dab/ ▶ **v.** (**dabbed, dabbing**) [trans.] **1** press against (something) lightly with a piece of absorbent material in order to clean or dry it: ***he dabbed his mouth with his napkin*** | [intrans.] ***she dabbed at her eyes with a handkerchief.*** ■ apply (a substance) with light quick strokes: ***she dabbed disinfectant on the cut.*** **2** aim at or strike with a light blow. ▶ **n.** a small amount of something: ***a dab of chocolate.*** [ME: symbolic.]

dab[2] ▶ **n.** a small flatfish (*Limanda* and other genera, family Pleuronectidae, and genus *Citharichthys*, family Bothidae), found chiefly in the North Atlantic. [ME: of unknown origin.]

dab·ber /'dabər/ ▶ **n.** a rounded pad used to apply ink to a surface.

dab·ble /'dabəl/ ▶ **v.** [trans.] immerse (one's hands or feet) partially in water and move them around gently. ■ [intrans.] (of a duck or other waterbird) move the bill around in shallow water while feeding: ***teal dabble in the shallows.*** ■ [intrans.] fig. take part in an activity in a casual or superficial way: ***he dabbled in writing.*** — **dab·bler** /'dab(ə)lər/ **n.** [16th C.: from obs. Du. **dabbelen**, or a frequentative of the v. DAB[1].]

dab·bling duck /'dab(ə)liNG/ ▶ **n.** a freshwater duck that typically feeds in shallow water by dabbling and upending. Compare with DIVING DUCK.

dab·chick /'dab,CHik/ ▶ **n.** a small grebe (genera *Tachybaptus* and *Podilymbus*), esp. the little grebe. [16th C.: the first element is perh. rel. to DIP and DEEP.]

DAC Electron. ▶ **abbr.** digital to analog converter.

da ca·po /dä 'käpō/ Music ▶ **adv.** (esp. as a direction) repeat from the beginning. Compare with DAL SEGNO. ▶ **adj.** [attrib.] including the repetition of a passage at the beginning: *da capo arias.* [Ital., lit. 'from the head.']

Dac·ca /'däkä/ var. of DHAKA.

dace /dās/ ▶ **n.** (pl. same) a small freshwater fish (*Leuciscus, Agosia,* and other genera) of the minnow family, typically living in running water. [ME: from OFr. **dars** (see DART).]

da·cha /'däCHə/ ▶ **n.** a country house or cottage in Russia, typically used as a second or vacation home. [19th C.: Russ., orig. 'grant (of land).']

Da·chau /'däKHou/ a city in Bavaria in southwestern Germany, near Munich, site of a Nazi concentration camp from 1933 until 1945; pop. 33,000.

dachs·hund /'däksənd; 'däks,ho͝ont/ ▶ **n.** a dog of a short-legged, long-bodied breed. [19th C.: from Ger., lit. 'badger dog.']

Da·ci·a /'däSH(ē)ə/ an ancient country in southeastern Europe in what is now northwestern Romania. — **Da·ci·an** /-ən/ **adj.** & **n.**

da·cite /'dā,sīt/ ▶ **n.** Geol. a volcanic rock resembling andesite but containing free quartz. — **da·cit·ic** /dā'sitik/ **adj.** [18th C.: DACIA.]

da·coit /də'koit/ ▶ **n.** a member of a band of armed robbers in India or Myanmar (Burma). — **da·coit·y** /-'koitē/ **n.** [from Hindi *ḍakait*, from *ḍakaitī* 'robbery by a gang.']

Da·cron /'dākrän; 'dakrän/ ▶ **n.** trademark a synthetic polyester (polyethylene terephthalate) with tough, elastic properties, used as a textile fabric. [1950s: an invented name.]

dac·tyl /'daktl/ ▶ **n.** Pros. a metrical foot consisting of one stressed syllable followed by two unstressed syllables or (in Greek and Latin) one long syllable followed by two short syllables. — **dac·tyl·ic** /dak'tilik/ **adj.** [ME: via L. from Gk. **daktulos**, lit. 'finger' (the three bones of the finger corresponding to the three syllables).]

dad /dad/ ▶ **n.** informal one's father. [16th C.: perh. imitative of a young child's first syllables *da, da.*]

Da·da /'dädä/ ▶ **n.** an early 20th-century international movement in art, literature, music, and film, repudiating and mocking artistic and social conventions and emphasizing the illogical and absurd. — **Da·da·ism n. Da·da·ist n.** & **adj. Da·da·is·tic** /,dädä'istik/ **adj.** [Fr., lit. 'hobbyhorse.']

da·da /'dada; -də/ ▶ **n.** informal one's father. [17th C.: see DAD.]

dad·dy /'dadē/ ▶ **n.** (pl. **-dies**) informal one's father.

daddy longlegs

dad·dy long·legs ▶ **n.** any of numerous arachnids with a globular body and long thin legs, including the common *Phalangium opilio*. Also called HARVESTMAN.

da·do /'dādō/ ▶ **n.** (pl. **-dos**) the lower part of the wall of a room, below about waist height, if it is a different color or has a different covering than the upper part. ■ a groove cut in the face of a board, into which the edge of another board is fixed. ■ Archit. the part of a pedestal between the base and the cornice. [17th C.: from Ital., lit. 'dice or cube,' from L. *datum* 'something given, starting point' (see DATUM).]

Da·dra and Na·gar Ha·ve·li /də'drä and ,nəgər ə'velē/ a Union Territory in western India, on the Arabian Sea; pop. 138,500; capital, Silvassa.

Daed·a·lus /'dedl-əs/ Gk. Mythol. the inventor of carpentry, who is said to have built the labyrinth for Minos, king of Crete. Minos imprisoned him and his son Icarus, but they escaped using wings that Daedalus made and fastened with wax.

dae·mon[1] /'dēmən/ (also **dai·mon**) ▶ **n.** **1** (in ancient Greek belief) a divinity or supernatural being of a nature between gods and humans. **2** archaic spelling of DEMON[1]. — **dae·mon·ic** /di'mänik/ **adj.** [16th C.: common spelling of DEMON[1] until the 19th cent.]

dae·mon[2] (also **de·mon**) ▶ **n.** Comput. a background process that handles requests for services such as print spooling and is dormant when not required. [1980s: perh. from *d(isk) a(nd) e(xecution) mon(itor)* or from *de(vice) mon(itor)*, or merely a transferred use of DEMON[1].]

daf·fo·dil /'dafə,dil/ ▶ **n.** a bulbous plant (genus *Narcissus*) of the lily family that typically bears bright yellow flowers with a long trumpet-shaped center (corona). [16th C.: from ME *affodill*, from med. L. *affodilus*, var. of L. *asphodilus* (see ASPHODEL). The initial *d-* is unexplained.]

daf·fy /'dafē/ ▶ **adj.** (**-fi·er, -fi·est**) informal silly; mildly eccentric: *daffy anecdotes.* ■ crazy: *you must both be daffy.* — **daf·fi·ness n.** [19th C.: from north. Engl. dial. *daff* 'simpleton' + -Y[1]; perh. rel. to DAFT.]

daft /daft/ ▶ **adj.** informal, silly; foolish. ■ crazy: *have you gone daft?* ■ [predic.] (**daft about**) infatuated with: *we were all daft about him.* [OE *gedæfte* 'mild, meek,' of Gmc. origin; rel. to Gothic *gadaban* 'become or be fitting.']

da Ga·ma /də 'gämə/, Vasco (*c.*1469–1524), Portuguese explorer. He led the first European expedition around the Cape of Good Hope in 1497, crossed the Indian Ocean, and arrived in Calicut, India, in 1498.

Da·ge·stan /,dägə'stän; ,dagə'stan/ an autonomous republic in southwestern Russia, on the Caspian Sea; pop. 1,823,000; capital, Makhachkala.

dag·ger /'dagər/ ▶ **n.** a short knife with a pointed and edged blade, used as a weapon. ■ Print. another term for OBELUS.

– PHRASES **at daggers drawn** in bitter enmity. **look daggers at** glare angrily or venomously at. [ME: perh. from obs. *dag* 'pierce, stab.']

dag·ger·board /'dagər,bôrd/ ▶ **n.** a board that slides vertically through the keel of a sailboat to reduce sideways movement. Compare with CENTERBOARD.

da·go /'dāgō/ ▶ n. (pl. -gos or -goes) informal, offens. an Italian, Spanish, or Portuguese-speaking person. [19th C.: from the Spanish given name *Diego* (equivalent to *James*).]

Da·gon /'dāgän/ (in the Bible) a national deity of the ancient Philistines, represented as a fish-tailed man. [via L. and Gk. from Heb. *dāgôn*, perh. from *dāgān* 'corn,' but said (according to folk etymology) to be from *dāg* 'fish.']

da·guerre·o·type /də'ge(ə)rə,tīp/ (also **da·guer·ro·type**) ▶ n. a photograph taken by an early process employing an iodine-sensitized silvered plate and mercury vapor. [19th C.: from Fr. *daguerréotype*, named after Louis-Jacques-Mandé *Daguerre* (1789–1851), its French inventor.]

Dag·wood sand·wich /'dag,wŏŏd/ (also **Dag·wood**) ▶ n. a thick sandwich with a variety of different fillings. [1970s: *Dagwood* Bumstead, a comic-strip character.]

dah /dä/ ▶ n. (in Morse code) another term for DASH. [World War II: imitative.]

da·ha·be·ah /,dähə'bēə/ (also **da·ha·bee·yah**) ▶ n. a passenger boat used on the Nile. [19th C.: from Arab., lit. 'golden.']

Dahl /däl/, Roald (1916–90), British writer. His works for children include *James and the Giant Peach* (1961) and *Charlie and the Chocolate Factory* (1964).

dahl ▶ n. var. of DHAL.

dahl·ia /'dalyə; 'däl-/ ▶ n. a tuberous-rooted Mexican plant (genus *Dahlia*) of the daisy family, cultivated for its brightly colored single or double flowers. [mod. L., named in honor of Andreas *Dahl* (1751–89), Swedish botanist.]

Da·ho·mey /də'hōmē/ former name (until 1975) of BENIN.

dai·kon /'dīkän; -kən/ ▶ n. a radish of a variety with a large slender white root that is typically eaten cooked, esp. in Eastern cuisine, and is also used for fodder. [Japanese, from *dai* 'large' + *kon* 'root.']

dai·ly /'dālē/ ▶ adj. [attrib.] done, produced, or occurring every day or every weekday: *a daily newspaper.* ■ relating to the period of a single day: *boats can be rented for a daily rate.* ▶ adv. every day: *the museum is open daily.* ▶ n. (pl. **-lies**) informal **1** a newspaper published every day except Sunday. **2** (**dailies**) the first prints from cinematographic takes, made rapidly for producers or editors; the rushes.
– PHRASES **daily life** the activities and experiences that constitute a person's normal existence. [ME: from DAY + -LY[1], -LY[2].]

dai·ly dou·ble ▶ n. Horse Racing a single bet on the winners of two named races in a day.

dai·ly doz·en ▶ n. [in sing.] informal, dated regular exercises, esp. those done first thing in the morning.

dai·mon /'dīmōn/ ▶ n. (pl. **-mons** or **-mo·nes** /-mə,nēz/) var. of DAEMON[1]. — **dai·mon·ic** /dī'mänik/ adj.

dai·myo /'dīmyō/ (also **dai·mio**) ▶ n. (pl. **-myos**) hist. (in feudal Japan) one of the great lords who were vassals of the shogun. [Japanese, from *dai* 'great' + *myō* 'name.']

dain·ty /'dāntē/ ▶ adj. (**-ti·er, -ti·est**) **1** delicately small and pretty: *a dainty lace handkerchief.* ■ (of a person) delicate and graceful in build or movement. ■ (of food) particularly good to eat: *a dainty morsel.* **2** fastidious or difficult to please, typically concerning food: *a dainty appetite.* ▶ n. (pl. **-ties**) (usu. **dainties**) something good to eat; a delicacy. — **dain·ti·ly** adv. **dain·ti·ness** n. [ME: from OFr. *daintie, deintie* 'choice morsel, pleasure,' from L. *dignitas* 'worthiness or beauty,' from *dignus* 'worthy.']

dai·qui·ri /'dakərē; 'dīkə-/ ▶ n. (pl. **-ris**) a cocktail containing rum and lime juice. [*Daiquiri* district in Cuba.]

Dai·ren /'dī'rən; -'ren/ former name of DALIAN.

dair·y /'de(ə)rē/ ▶ n. (pl. **dair·ies**) a building, room, or establishment for the storage, processing, and distribution of milk and milk products. ■ a store where milk and milk products are sold. ■ food made from or containing milk. ▶ adj. [attrib.] containing or made from milk. ■ concerned with or involved in the production of milk: *a dairy farmer.* [ME *deierie*, from *deie* 'dairymaid' (in OE *dǣge* 'female servant'), of Gmc. origin; rel. to DOUGH.]

dair·y·ing /'de(ə)rē-iNG/ ▶ n. the business of producing, storing, and distributing milk and its products.

dair·y·maid /'de(ə)rē,mād/ ▶ n. archaic a woman employed in a dairy.

dair·y·man /'de(ə)rēmən; -,man/ ▶ n. (pl. **-men**) a man who is employed in a dairy or sells dairy products.

da·is /'dāis; 'dī-/ ▶ n. a low platform for a lectern, seats of honor, or a throne. [ME: from OFr. *deis*, from L. *discus* 'disk or dish' (later 'table').]

dai·sy /'dāzē/ ▶ n. (pl. **-sies**) a small grassland plant (family Compositae) that has flowers with a yellow disk and white rays. It has given rise to many ornamental garden varieties. The most familiar North American daisy is *Chrysanthemum leucanthemum*.
– PHRASES **(as) fresh as a daisy** healthy and full of energy. **pushing up (the) daisies** informal dead and buried. [OE *dæges ēage* 'day's eye.']

dai·sy chain ▶ n. a string of daisies threaded together by their stems. ■ fig. a string of associated people or things. ■ informal a sexual activity in which participants serve as partners to different people simultaneously. ▶ v. (**dai·sy-chain**) [trans.] Comput. connect (several devices) together in a linear series. — **dai·sy-chain·a·ble** adj.

dai·sy cut·ter ▶ n. a 15,000-pound bomb that is dropped from a transport plane. It explodes just above the ground with a shock wave that forms a shallow impact crater several hundred feet in diameter and is used for clearing dense vegetation in creating landing zones and as a weapon of intimidation.

Dak. ▶ abbr. Dakota.

Da·kar /dä'kär; 'dakär/ the capital of Senegal, a port on the Atlantic coast of West Africa; pop. 1,641,350.

Da·ko·ta[1] /də'kōtə/ a former territory of the US that became the states of North Dakota and South Dakota. — **Da·ko·tan** /də'kōtn/ n. & adj.

Da·ko·ta[2] ▶ n. (pl. same or **-tas**) **1** a member of a North American Indian people of the upper Mississippi valley and the surrounding plains. **2** the Siouan language of this people. Also called SIOUX. ▶ adj. of or relating to this people or their language. [19th C.: the name in Dakota, lit. 'allies.']

Da·ko·ta Riv·er another name for JAMES RIVER (sense 1).

dal[1] ▶ abbr. decaliter(s).

dal[2] ▶ n. var. of DHAL.

Da·lai La·ma /'dälī 'lämə/ ▶ n. the spiritual head of Tibetan Buddhism and, until the establishment of Chinese communist rule, the spiritual and temporal ruler of Tibet. The present Dalai Lama escaped to India in 1959 when Tibet was invaded by the Chinese and was awarded the Nobel Peace Prize in 1989. [17th C.: from Tibetan, lit. 'ocean guru.']

da·la·si /də'läsē/ ▶ n. (pl. same or **-sis** /-sēz/) the basic monetary unit of Gambia, equal to 100 butut. [a local word.]

Dal·croze /dal'krōz/ see JAQUES-DALCROZE.

Dale /dāl/, Sir Henry Hallett (1875–1968), English physiologist. He investigated the role of histamine in anaphylactic shock and allergy and the role of acetylcholine as a natural neurotransmitter. Nobel Prize for Physiology or Medicine (1936, shared with Loewi).

dale /dāl/ ▶ n. a valley, esp. a broad one. [OE *dæl*, of Gmc. origin; rel. to Ger. *Tal*, also to DELL.]

Da·li /'dälē; dä'lē/, Salvador (1904–89), Spanish painter. A surrealist, his works include *The Persistence of Memory* (1931) and *Christ of St. John of the Cross* (1951).

Da·lian /'dä'lyan/ a port on the Liaodong Peninsula in northeastern China. It is now part of the urban complex of Luda. Former name DAIREN.

Da·lit /'dälit/ ▶ n. (in the traditional Indian caste system) a member of the lowest caste. See also UNTOUCHABLE, SCHEDULED CASTE. [via Hindi from Sanskrit *dalita* 'oppressed.']

Dal·las /'daləs/ a city in northeastern Texas; pop. 1,188,580.

dal·li·ance /'dalēəns; 'dalyəns/ ▶ n. a casual romantic or sexual relationship. ■ brief or casual involvement with something: *Berkeley was my last* ***dalliance with*** *the education system.*

Dall sheep /dôl/ (also **Dall's sheep**) ▶ n. a wild North American sheep (*Ovis dalli*) found in mountainous country from Alaska to British Columbia. [20th C.: named after William H. *Dall* (1845–1927), US naturalist.]

dal·ly /'dalē/ ▶ v. (**-lies, -lied**) [intrans.] **1** act or move slowly: *workers were loafing, dallying, or goofing off.* **2** have a casual romantic or sexual liaison with someone: *he should stop* ***dallying with*** *movie stars.* ■ show a casual interest in something, without committing oneself seriously: *the company has been* ***dallying with*** *the idea of opening a new office.* [ME: from OFr. *dalier* 'to chat.']

Dal·ma·tia /dal'māsH(ē)ə/ an ancient region in what is now southwestern Croatia. It once formed part of the Roman province of Illyricum.

Dal·ma·tian /dal'māsHən/ ▶ n. **1** a dog of a white, short-haired breed with dark spots. **2** a native or inhabitant of Dalmatia.

dal se·gno /däl 'sānyō/ ▶ adv. Music (esp. as a direction) repeat from the point marked by a sign. Compare with DA CAPO. [Ital., 'from the sign.']

Dal·ton /'dôltn/, John (1766–1844), English chemist. He produced the first table of comparative atomic weights.

dal·ton /'dôltn/ ▶ n. Chem. a unit used in expressing the molecular weight of proteins, equivalent to atomic mass unit. [1930s: named after John DALTON.]

dal·ton·ism /'dôltn,izəm/ ▶ n. another term for PROTANOPIA, a form of color-blindness. [19th C.: J. DALTON + -ISM.]

Da·ly Cit·y /'dālē/ a city in north central California, southwest of San Francisco; pop. 92,311.

dam[1] ▶ abbr. decameter(s).

dam[2] /dam/ ▶ n. a barrier constructed to hold back water and raise its level, the resulting reservoir being used in the generation of electricity or as a water supply. ■ a barrier of branches in a stream, constructed by a beaver to provide a deep pool and a lodge. ■ any barrier resembling a dam. ■ a rubber sheet used to keep saliva from the teeth during dental operations. ▶ v. (**dammed, dam·ming**) [trans.] build a dam across (a river or lake). ■ hold back or obstruct (something): *the closed lock gates* ***dammed up*** *the canal.* [ME: from Mid. Low Ger. or MDu.; rel. to OE *fordemman* 'close up.']

dam[3] ▶ n. the female parent of an animal, esp. a domestic mammal. [ME (denoting a human mother): alt. of DAME.]

dam·age /'damij/ ▶ n. **1** physical harm caused to something in such a way as to impair its value, usefulness, or normal function. ■ unwel-

come and detrimental effects: *the **damage to** his reputation was considerable.* **2** (**damages**) a sum of money claimed or awarded in compensation for a loss or an injury. ▶**v.** [trans.] inflict physical harm on (something) so as to impair its value, usefulness, or normal function: [as adj.] (**damaged**) *damaged ligaments* | [as adj.] (**damaging**) *extreme heat can be very **damaging to** color film.* ■ have a detrimental effect on: *the scandal could damage his career.*
– PHRASES **what's the damage?** informal, humorous used to ask the cost of something. —**dam·ag·ing·ly adv.** [ME: from OFr., from *dam, damne* 'loss or damage,' from L. *damnum* 'loss or hurt'; cf. **DAMN**.]

dam·aged goods ▶**plural n.** merchandise that has deteriorated in quality. ■ fig., derog. a person regarded as inadequate or impaired in some way: *I was just damaged goods, another misfit.*

Dam·an and Di·u /də'män and 'dē-o͞o/ a Union Territory in India; pop. 101,400; capital, Daman.

dam·ar ▶**n. & adj.** var. of **DAMMAR**.

Dam·a·scene /'damə,sēn; ,damə'sēn/ ▶**adj.** of or relating to the city of Damascus. ■ of, relating to, or resembling the conversion of St. Paul on the road to Damascus. ■ (often **damascene**) relating to or denoting a process of inlaying a metal object with gold or silver decoration. ▶**n.** a native or inhabitant of Damascus.

dam·a·scened /'damə,sēnd; ,damə'sēnd/ ▶**adj.** (of iron or steel) given a wavy pattern by hammer-welding and repeated heating and forging. ■ (of a metal object) inlaid with gold or silver decoration.

Da·mas·cus /də'maskəs/ the capital of Syria; pop. 1,497,000. It has existed as a city for over 4,000 years.

dam·ask /'daməsk/ ▶**n.** **1** a figured woven fabric with a pattern visible on both sides, typically used for table linen and upholstery. ■ a tablecloth made of this material. **2** short for **DAMASK ROSE**. ▶**adj.** made of or resembling damask. ■ literary having the velvety pink or light red color of a damask rose. ▶**v.** [trans.] weave with figured designs. [ME: from *Damaske*, early form of *Damascus*.]

dam·ask rose ▶**n.** a sweet-scented rose (*Rosa damascena*) of an old variety (or hybrid) that is typically pink or light red in color. The velvety petals are used to make attar.

dame /dām/ ▶**n.** **1** (**Dame**) (in the UK) the title given to a woman equivalent to the rank of knight. ■ a woman holding this title. **2** informal a woman. ■ archaic or humorous an elderly or mature woman. [ME (denoting a female ruler): via OFr. from L. *domina* 'mistress.']

dame's rock·et ▶**n.** a herbaceous plant (*Hesperis matronalis*) of the cabbage family, cultivated for its long spikes of mauve or white flowers that are fragrant in the evening.

dam·fool /'dam'fo͞ol/ informal, dated ▶**adj.** (also **dam·fool·ish**) [attrib.] (of a person) thoroughly foolish and stupid. ▶**n.** a stupid or foolish person.

Dam·i·et·ta /,damē'etə/ the eastern branch of the Nile delta. Arabic name **DUMYAT**. ■ a port at the mouth of this delta; pop. 113,000.

da·min·o·zide /də'minə,zīd/ ▶**n.** a growth retardant, $C_6H_{12}N_2O_3$, sprayed on vegetables and fruit, esp. apples, to enhance the quality of the crop. In the US, the use of daminozide is restricted due to potential health risks.

dam·mar /'damər/ (also **dam·ar**) ▶**n.** resin used to make varnish. It is obtained from mainly Indo-Malaysian trees of the families Araucariaceae (genus *Agathis*), Dipterocarpaceae (genera *Hopea, Shorea*, and *Vatica*), and Burseraceae (genus *Canarium*). [17th C.: from Malay *damar* 'resin.']

dam·mit /'damit/ ▶**exclam.** used to express anger and frustration. [19th C.: alt. of *damn it*.]

damn /dam/ ▶**v.** [trans.] (in Christian belief) (of God) condemn (a person) to suffer eternal punishment in hell: *be forever damned with Lucifer.* ■ (**be damned**) be doomed to misfortune or failure: *the enterprise was damned.* ■ condemn, esp. by the public expression of disapproval. ■ curse (someone or something): *damn him for making this sound trivial.* ▶**exclam.** informal expressing anger, surprise, or frustration. ▶**adj.** [attrib.] informal used for emphasis, esp. to express anger or frustration: *turn that damn thing off!* | [as submodifier] *don't be so damn silly!*
– PHRASES —— **be damned** used to express rejection of someone or something previously mentioned: *"Glory be damned!"* **damn well** informal used to emphasize a statement, esp. when the speaker is angry: *this is your mess and you can damn well clear it up!* **damn someone/something with faint praise** praise someone or something so unenthusiastically as to imply condemnation. **I'll be** (or **I'm**) **damned if** informal used to express a strong negative: *I'll be damned if I'll call her.* **not be worth a damn** informal have no value or validity at all. **not give a damn** see **GIVE**. **well I'll be** (or **I'm**) **damned** informal used as an expression of surprise.

dam·na·ble /'damnəbəl/ ▶**adj.** **1** extremely bad or unpleasant: *leave this damnable place behind.* **2** subject to or worthy of divine condemnation. —**dam·na·bly adv.** [ME (in the sense 'worthy of condemnation'): from OFr. *dam(p)nable*, from L. *dam(p)nabilis*, from *dam(p)nare* 'inflict loss on' (see **DAMN**).]

dam·na·tion /dam'nāsʜən/ ▶**n.** (in Christian belief) condemnation to eternal punishment in hell. ▶**exclam.** expressing anger or frustration.

dam·na·to·ry /'damnə,tôrē/ ▶**adj.** conveying or causing censure or damnation.

damned /damd/ ▶**adj.** **1** (in Christian belief) condemned by God to suffer eternal punishment in hell: [as pl. n.] (**the damned**) *the spirits of the damned.* **2** [attrib.] informal used for emphasis, esp. to express anger or frustration: *it's none of your damned business* | [as submodifier] *she's too damned arrogant.* ■ (**damnedest**) used to emphasize the surprising nature of something: *the damnedest thing I ever saw.* ▶**adv.** extremely; exceedingly.
– PHRASES **damned well** informal used for emphasis when the speaker is angry or irritated: *you can damned well tell him yourself!* **do** (or **try**) **one's damnedest** do or try one's utmost.

damn·ing /'damiɴɢ/ ▶**adj.** (of a circumstance or piece of evidence) strongly suggesting guilt or error: *presented with damning affidavits.* ■ extremely critical: *last year's damning report on the industry.* —**damn·ing·ly adv.**

Dam·o·cles /'damə,klēz/ a legendary courtier who praised the happiness of Dionysius I. To show him how precarious this happiness was, Dionysius seated him with a sword hung by a single hair over his head.
– PHRASES **sword of Damocles** used to refer to a precarious situation.

Da·mon /'dāmən/ a legendary Syracusan of the 4th century BC whose friend Pythias was sentenced to death by Dionysius I. Damon stood bail for Pythias, who returned to save him, and was himself reprieved.

damp /damp/ ▶**adj.** slightly wet: *her hair was still damp from the shower.* ▶**n.** moisture diffused through the air or a solid substance or condensed on a surface, typically with detrimental or unpleasant effects. ▶**v.** [trans.] **1** make (something) slightly wet: *damp a small area with water.* **2** control or restrain (a feeling or a state of affairs): *she tried to **damp down** her feelings of despair.* ■ make (a fire) burn less strongly by reducing the flow of air to it. **3** restrict the amplitude of vibrations on (a piano or other musical instrument) so as to reduce the volume of sound: *rapidly damping the cymbals.* ■ Physics progressively reduce the amplitude of (an oscillation or vibration): *concrete structures **damp out** any vibrations.* ■ reduce the level of (a noise or sound): *the ground mist clung to the hedgerows, **damping down** all sound.* —**damp·ish adj. damp·ly adv. damp·ness n.** [ME: of West Gmc. origin; rel. to a Mid. Low Ger. word meaning 'vapor, steam, smoke.']

damp·en /'dampən/ ▶**v.** [trans.] **1** make slightly wet: *the fine rain dampened her face.* **2** make less strong or intense: *nothing could dampen her enthusiasm.* ■ reduce the amplitude of (a sound source): *slider switches on the mixers can dampen the drums.* —**damp·en·er n.**

damp·er /'dampər/ ▶**n.** a person or thing that has a depressing, subduing, or inhibiting effect: *another damper on reactor development was the problem of safeguards.* ■ Music a pad that silences a piano string except when removed by means of a pedal or by the note being struck. ■ a device for reducing mechanical vibration, in particular a shock absorber on a motor vehicle. ■ a conductor used to reduce hunting in an electric motor or generator. ■ a movable metal plate in a flue or chimney, used to regulate the draft and so control the rate of combustion.
– PHRASES **put a damper on** have a depressing, subduing, or inhibiting effect on.

damp·ing /'dampiɴɢ/ ▶**n.** **1** tech. a decrease in the amplitude of an oscillation as a result of energy being drained from the system to overcome frictional or other resistive forces. ■ a mechanism or system for bringing about such a decrease. ■ a method of bringing about a decrease in oscillatory peaks in an electric current or voltage using an energy-absorbing or resistance circuit. **2** short for **DAMPING-OFF**.

damp·ing-off ▶**n.** a plant disease occurring in excessively damp conditions, in particular the collapse and death of seedlings as a result of a fungal infection.

dam·sel /'damzəl/ ▶**n.** archaic or literary a young unmarried woman.
– PHRASES **damsel in distress** often humorous a young woman in trouble (with the implication that she needs to be rescued, as by a prince in a fairy tale). [ME: from OFr. *dameisele, damisele*, based on L. *domina* 'mistress.']

dam·sel·fish /'damzəl,fisʜ/ ▶**n.** (pl. same or **-fish·es**) a small brightly colored tropical fish (*Chromis* and other genera, family Pomacentridae) that lives in or near coral reefs.

dam·sel·fly /'damzəl,flī/ ▶**n.** (pl. **-flies**) a slender insect related to the dragonflies, typically resting with the wings folded back along the body.

dam·son /'damzən; -sən/ ▶**n.** **1** a small purple-black plumlike fruit. ■ a dark purple color. **2** (also **damson tree**) the small deciduous tree (*Prunus domestica* subsp. *insititia*) of the rose family that bears this fruit, probably derived from the bullace. [ME *damascene*, from L. *damascenum (prunum)* '(plum) of Damascus.']

Dan /dan/ (in the Bible) a Hebrew patriarch, son of Jacob and Bilhah. ■ the tribe of Israel traditionally descended from him. ■ an ancient town in the north of Canaan.

Dan. ▶**abbr.** Bible Daniel.

dan[1] /dän; dan/ ▶**n.** any of ten degrees of advanced proficiency in judo or karate. ■ a person who has achieved such a degree. [1940s: from Japanese.]

dan[2] /dan/ (also **dan buoy**) ▶**n.** a small marker buoy with a lightweight flagpole. [17th C.: of unknown origin.]

Da·na[1] /'dānə/, Charles Anderson (1819–97), US journalist. He was the owner and editor of the *New York Sun* 1868–97.

Da·na[2], James Dwight (1813–95), US naturalist, geologist, and mineralogist. He founded a classification of minerals based on chemistry and physics.

Da·na[3], Richard Henry (1815–82), US adventurer and writer. He wrote an account of his voyage around Cape Horn in *Two Years Before the Mast* (1840).

Dan·a·e /'danə,ē/ Gk. Mythol. the daughter of Acrisius, king of Argos. An oracle foretold that her son would kill her father. To evade this, Acrisius imprisoned her, but Zeus visited her as a shower of gold and she conceived Perseus, who killed Acrisius by accident.

Da·na·ids /də'nā-idz; 'danē-idz/ Gk. Mythol. the daughters of Danaus, king of Argos, who were compelled to marry the sons of his brother Aegyptus. All but one, Hypermnestra, murdered their husbands on the wedding night, and were punished in Hades by being sent to fill a leaky jar with water.

Da Nang /'dä 'näNG; də 'naNG/ a city in central Vietnam; pop. 382,670. It was a US military base during the Vietnam War. Former name **TOURANE**.

Dan·bury /'dan,berē; -b(ə)rē/ a city in west central Connecticut; pop. 74,848.

dance /dans/ ▶ **v.** [intrans.] **1** move rhythmically to music, typically following a set sequence of steps: *their cheeks were pressed together as they danced.* ■ [trans.] perform (a particular dance or a role in a ballet): *they danced a tango.* ■ [with obj. and adverbial of direction] lead (someone) in a particular direction while dancing: *I danced her out of the room.* **2** [with adverbial of direction] (of a person) move in a quick and lively way: *Sheila danced in gaily.* ■ [with adverbial of place] move up and down lightly and quickly: *midges danced over the stream.* ■ (of someone's eyes) sparkle with pleasure or excitement. ▶ **n.** a series of movements that match the speed and rhythm of a piece of music. ■ a particular sequence of steps and movements constituting a particular form of dancing. ■ steps and movements of this type considered as an activity or art form: *she has studied dance with Martha Graham.* ■ a social gathering at which people dance. ■ a set of lively movements resembling a dance: *he gesticulated comically and did a little dance.* ■ a piece of music for dancing to. ■ (also **dance music**) music for dancing to, esp. in a nightclub. ■ a set of stylized movements performed by certain animals.
– PHRASES **dance attendance on** do one's utmost to please someone by attending to all possible needs or requests. **dance to someone's tune** comply completely with someone's demands and wishes. —**dance·a·bil·i·ty n. dance·a·ble adj.** [ME: from OFr. *dancer* (v.), *dance* (n.), of unknown origin.]

dance band ▶ **n.** a band that plays music suitable for dancing, esp. swing.

dance card ▶ **n.** dated a card bearing the names of a woman's prospective partners at a formal dance.

dance floor ▶ **n.** an area of uncarpeted floor, typically in a nightclub or restaurant, reserved for dancing.

dance hall ▶ **n. 1** a large public hall or building where people pay to enter and dance. **2** (**dance·hall**) an uptempo style of dance music originating in Jamaica and derived from reggae, in which a DJ improvises lyrics over a recorded instrumental backing track or to the accompaniment of live musicians.

dance of death ▶ **n.** a medieval allegorical representation in which a personified Death leads people to the grave, designed to emphasize the equality of all before death. Also called **DANSE MACABRE**.

danc·er /'dansər/ ▶ **n.** a person who dances or whose profession is dancing.

dan·cer·cise /'dansər,sīz/ (also **dan·cer·cize**) ▶ **n.** a system of aerobic exercise using dance movements. [1960s: blend of **DANCE** and **EXERCISE**.]

danc·ing girl ▶ **n.** a female professional dancer, esp. an erotic dancer or a member of the chorus in a musical.

D and C ▶ **abbr.** dilatation and curettage.

dan·de·li·on /'dandl,īən/ ▶ **n.** a widely distributed weed (genus *Taraxacum*) of the daisy family, with a rosette of leaves, bright yellow flowers followed by globular heads of seeds with downy tufts, and stems containing a milky latex. [ME: from Fr. *dent-de-lion*, translation of med. L. *dens leonis* 'lion's tooth.']

dan·de·li·on greens ▶ **plural n.** fresh dandelion leaves used as a salad vegetable or herb.

dan·der[1] /'dandər/ ▶ **n.** (in phrase **get/have one's dander up**) informal lose one's temper. [19th C.: of unknown origin.]

dan·der[2] ▶ **n.** skin flakes in an animal's fur or hair. [18th C.: rel. to **DANDRUFF**.]

Dan·die Din·mont /'dandē'dinmänt/ ▶ **n.** a terrier of a breed with short legs, a long body, and a rough coat. [19th C.: named after a farmer in Sir Walter Scott's *Guy Mannering*.]

dan·di·fied /'dandi,fīd/ ▶ **adj.** (of a man) showing excessive concern about his clothes or appearance. ■ self-consciously sophisticated or elaborate.

dan·dle /'dandl/ ▶ **v.** [trans.] move (a baby or young child) up and down in a playful or affectionate way. ■ move (something) lightly up and down: *dandling the halter rope, he gently urged the pony's head up.* [16th C.: of unknown origin.]

Dan·dong /'dän'dōōNG/ a port in northeastern China, near the mouth of the Yalu River; pop. 660,500.

dan·druff /'dandrəf/ ▶ **n.** small pieces of dead skin in a person's hair. —**dan·druff·y adj.** [16th C.: *-ruff*, perh. rel. to ME *rove* 'scurfiness.']

dan·dy /'dandē/ ▶ **n.** (pl. **-dies**) **1** a man unduly devoted to style, neatness, and fashion in dress and appearance. **2** informal, dated an excellent thing of its kind. ▶ **adj.** (**-di·er, -di·est**) **1** informal excellent: *upgrading seemed a dandy idea* | *things are all fine and dandy.* **2** relating to or characteristic of a dandy. —**dan·dy·ish adj. dan·dy·ism n.** [18th C.: perh. a shortened form of *Jack-a-dandy* 'conceited fellow,' from *Dandy*, a nickname for *Andrew*.]

dan·dy roll (also **dandy roll·er**) ▶ **n.** a roller that is used to solidify partly formed paper during its manufacture, and to impress the water mark.

Dane /dān/ ▶ **n.** a native or national of Denmark, or a person of Danish descent. ■ hist. one of the Viking invaders of the British Isles in the 9th–11th centuries. [OE *Dene*; influenced by ON *Danir* and late L. *Dani* (both pl.).]

Dan·forth an·chor /'dan,fôrTH/ ▶ **n.** a type of stockless lightweight anchor with flat flukes.

dang /daNG/ ▶ **adj., exclam. & v.** informal euphemism for **DAMN**.

dan·ger /'dānjər/ ▶ **n.** the possibility of suffering harm or injury: *his life was in danger.* ■ a person or thing that is likely to cause harm or injury: *drought is a danger.* ■ the possibility of something unwelcome or unpleasant: *there was no danger of the champagne running out.*
– PHRASES **in danger of** likely to incur or to suffer from: *the animal is in danger of extinction.* **out of danger** (of an injured or ill person) not expected to die. [ME: from OFr. *dangier*, based on L. *dominus* 'lord.']

dan·ger·ous /'dānjərəs/ ▶ **adj.** able or likely to cause harm or injury. —**dan·ger·ous·ness n.**

dan·gle /'daNGgəl/ ▶ **v.** [no obj., with adverbial of place] hang or swing loosely: *saucepans dangled from a rail* | [trans.] *they were dangling their legs over the water.* ■ [trans.] fig. offer (an enticing incentive) to someone.
– PHRASES **keep someone dangling** keep someone in an uncertain position. —**dan·gler n. dan·gly adj.** [16th C.: symbolic.]

dan·gling par·ti·ci·ple /'daNGg(ə)liNG/ ▶ **n.** Gram. a participle intended to modify a noun that is not actually present in the text.

Dan·iel[1] /'danyəl/ a Hebrew prophet (6th century BC), who spent his life as a captive at the court of Babylon. In the Bible he was delivered by God from the lions' den. ■ a book of the Bible containing his prophecies.

Dan·iel[2], Peter Vivian (1784–1860), US Supreme Court associate justice 1841–60. He was appointed to the Court by President Van Buren.

dan·i·o /'danē,ō/ ▶ **n.** (pl. **-os**) a small, typically brightly colored freshwater fish (genera *Danio* and *Brachydanio*) of the minnow family, native to India and Southeast Asia. [mod. L. (genus name).]

Dan·ish /'dānisH/ ▶ **adj.** of or relating to Denmark or its people or language. ▶ **n. 1** the North Germanic language of Denmark, which is also the official language of Greenland and the Faeroes. **2** [as pl. n.] (**the Danish**) the people of Denmark. **3** informal short for **DANISH PASTRY**.

Dan·ish blue ▶ **n.** a soft, salty, strong-flavored white cheese with blue veins.

Dan·ish pas·try ▶ **n.** a pastry made of sweetened yeast dough with toppings or fillings such as fruit, nuts, or cheese.

dank /daNGk/ ▶ **adj.** disagreeably damp, musty, and typically cold. —**dank·ly adv. dank·ness n.** [ME: prob. of Scand. origin and rel. to Swed. *dank* 'marshy spot.']

Dan·mark /'dän,märk/ Danish name for **DENMARK**.

Dan·ne·brog /'danə,bräg/ ▶ **n.** the Danish national flag. [18th C.: Danish, lit. 'Dan. cloth.']

Da·no-Nor·we·gian /'dānō nôr'wējən/ ▶ **n.** another term for **BOKMÅL**.

Dan Riv·er /dan/ a river that flows for 180 miles (290 km) from southwestern Virginia into North Carolina to the Roanoke River.

danse ma·ca·bre /'däns mə'käbrə/ ▶ **n.** another term for **DANCE OF DEATH**. [Fr. (see also **MACABRE**).]

dan·seur /dän'sər/ ▶ **n.** a male ballet dancer. [Fr., from *danser* 'to dance.']

dan·seuse /dän'sōōz; -'sœz/ ▶ **n.** a female ballet dancer. [19th C.: Fr., lit. 'female dancer.']

Dan·te /'däntā; 'dan-/ (1265–1321), Italian poet; full name *Dante Alighieri*. He wrote *The Divine Comedy* (c.1309–20), an epic poem that describes his spiritual journey through Hell and Purgatory and finally to Paradise. —**Dan·te·an** /'däntēən; 'dan-/ **adj. Dan·tesque** /dän'tesk/ (also **Dante-esque** /,däntā'esk/) **adj.**

Dan·ton /dän'tôN/, Georges Jacques (1759–94), French revolutionary. He revolted against the severity of the Revolutionary Tribunal and was executed on Robespierre's orders.

Dan·ube /'danyōōb/ a river that rises in southwestern Germany and flows for about 1,770 miles (2,850 km) into the Black Sea. It is the second longest river in Europe (after the Volga). German name **DONAU**. —**Dan·u·bi·an** /dan'yōōbēən/ **adj.**

Dan·ville /'dan,vil/ a city in southern Virginia; pop. 48,411.

Dan·zig /'däntsig; 'dant-/ German name for **GDAŃSK**.

dap /dap/ ▶ **v.** (**dapped, dap·ping**) [intrans.] fish by letting the fly bob lightly on the water without letting the line touch the water. [17th C.: symbolic.]

Daph·ne /'dafnē/ Gk. Mythol. a nymph who was turned into a laurel bush to save her from Apollo.

daph·ne /'dafnē/ **n.** a small Eurasian shrub (genus *Daphne*, family Thymelaeaceae) with sweet-scented flowers and, typically, evergreen leaves. [ME (denoting the laurel or bay tree): from Gk. *daphnē*, **Daphne**.]

daph·ni·a /ˈdafnēə/ ▸ **n.** (pl. same) a tiny and semitransparent freshwater crustacean (genus *Daphnia*, order Cladocera) with long antennae and prominent eyes, often used as food for aquarium fish. Also called **water flea**. [mod. L., from Gk. *Daphnē*, **Daphne**.]

Daph·nis /ˈdafnis/ Gk. Mythol. a Sicilian shepherd who, according to one version of the legend, was struck with blindness for his infidelity to the nymph Echenaïs.

dap·per /ˈdapər/ ▸ **adj.** (typically of a man) neat and trim in dress, appearance, or bearing. — **dap·per·ly adv. dap·per·ness n.** [ME: prob. from a Mid. Low Ger. or MDu. word meaning 'strong, stout.']

dap·ple /ˈdapəl/ ▸ **v.** [trans.] (usu. **be dappled**) mark with spots or rounded patches: *the floor was dappled with pale moonlight* | [as adj.] (**dappled**) *dappled sunlight lay upon her straight brown hair.* ▸ **n.** a patch or spot of color or light. ■ an animal whose coat is marked with patches or spots. [16th C.: perh. rel. to ON *depill* 'spot.']

Dap·sang /däpˈsäNG/ another name for **K2**.

dap·sone /ˈdapsōn/ ▸ **n.** Med. a sulfur compound, $(H_2NC_6H_4)_2SO_2$, with bacteriostatic action, used chiefly in the treatment of leprosy. [1950s: *dipara-aminophenyl sulfone*.]

Da·qing /ˈdäˈCHING/ (also **Ta·ching**) a city in northeastern China, in Heilongjiang province; pop. 996,800.

DAR ▸ **abbr.** Daughters of the American Revolution.

Dard /därd/ ▸ **n.** **1** a member of a group of peoples inhabiting eastern Afghanistan, northern Pakistan, and Kashmir. **2** a group of languages, including Kashmiri, usually classified as Indic but showing strong Iranian influence. ▸ **adj.** of or relating to the Dards or their languages. — **Dard·ic n. & adj.** [the name in Dard.]

Dar·da·nelles /ˌdärdnˈelz/ a narrow strait between Europe and Asiatic Turkey (called the Hellespont in classical times) that links the Sea of Marmara with the Aegean Sea. It is 38 miles (60 km) long.

Dare /de(ə)r/, Virginia (1587–?), first English child born in North America. Born on Roanoke Island, Virginia, she disappeared with the other 117 Roanoke colonists, as was discovered in 1591.

dare /de(ə)r/ ▸ **v.** (3rd sing. pres. usu. **dare** before an expressed or implied infinitive without **to**) **1** [usu. with infin. with or without **to**] [often with negative] have the courage to do something: *a story he dare not write down.* **2** [with obj. and infin.] defy or challenge (someone) to do something: *she was daring him to disagree* | [trans.] *swap with me, I dare you.* **3** [trans.] literary take the risk of; brave. ▸ **n.** a challenge, esp. to prove courage: *athletes who eat ground glass on a dare.*

– PHRASES **don't you dare** used to order someone threateningly not to do something. **how dare you** used to express indignation. **I dare say** (or **dare·say**) used to indicate that one believes something is probable. — **dar·er n.** [OE *durran*, rel. to Gothic *gadaursan*, from an Indo-Eur. root shared by Gk. *tharsein* 'be bold.']

dare·dev·il /ˈde(ə)rˌdevəl/ ▸ **n.** a reckless person who enjoys doing dangerous things. ▸ **adj.** [attrib.] reckless and daring. — **dare·dev·il·ry n.**

Dar es Sa·laam /ˌdär es səˈläm/ the capital of Tanzania; pop. 1,360,850.

Da·ri /ˈdärē/ ▸ **n.** the form of Persian spoken in Afghanistan.

Dar·i·en /därˈyen; ˌde(ə)rēˈen/ a sparsely populated province in eastern Panama. The name was formerly applied to the whole of the Isthmus of Panama.

Dar·i·en, Gulf of part of the Caribbean Sea between Panama and Colombia.

dar·ing /ˈde(ə)riNG/ ▸ **adj.** (of a person or action) adventurous or audaciously bold: *a daring crime.* ■ boldly unconventional: *a pretty girl in daring clothes.* ▸ **n.** adventurous courage: *the daring of climbers.* — **dar·ing·ly adv.**

dar·i·ole /ˈdarēˌōl/ (also **dariole mold**) ▸ **n.** (in French cooking) a small, round metal mold.

Da·ri·us I /ˈderēəs/ (c.550–486 BC), king of Persia 521–486 BC; known as **Darius the Great**. He invaded Greece but was defeated at Marathon (490 BC).

Dar·jee·ling /därˈjēliNG/ ▸ **n.** a high-quality tea grown in the mountainous regions of northern India.

dark /därk/ ▸ **adj.** **1** with little or no light. ■ hidden from knowledge; mysterious: *a dark secret.* ■ (of a theater) closed; not in use: *on Tuesdays he'd wait tables because the theater was dark.* **2** (of a color or object) not reflecting much light; approaching black in shade: *dark green.* ■ (of someone's skin, hair, or eyes) brown or black in color. ■ (of a person) having such skin, hair, or eyes: *both my father and I are very dark.* ■ fig. (of a sound or taste) having richness or depth: *a distinctive dark, sweet flavor.* ■ served or drunk with only a little or no milk or cream. **3** (of a period of time or situation) characterized by tragedy, unhappiness, or unpleasantness: *dark days.* ■ gloomily pessimistic. ■ (of an expression) angry; threatening. ■ suggestive of or arising from evil characteristics or forces; sinister: *so many dark deeds.* **4** Phonet. denoting a velarized form of the sound of the letter *l* (as in *pull*). ▸ **n.** **1** (**the dark**) the absence of light in a place: *Carolyn was sitting in the dark.* ■ nightfall: *I'll be home before dark.* **2** a dark color or shade, esp. in a painting.

– PHRASES **in the dark** in a state of ignorance about something: *we're clearly being **kept in the dark** about what's happening.* **a shot** (or **stab**) **in the dark** an act whose outcome cannot be foreseen; a mere guess. — **dark·ish adj. dark·some adj.** (literary). [OE *deorc*, of Gmc. origin, prob. distantly rel. to Ger. *tarnen* 'conceal.']

dark ad·ap·ta·tion ▸ **n.** the eye's adjustment to low light intensities, involving reflex dilation of the pupil and activation of the rod cells in preference to the cone cells. — **dark-a·dapt·ed adj.**

Dark Ag·es **1** the period in western Europe between the fall of the Roman Empire and the high Middle Ages, c.AD 500–1100, during which Germanic tribes swept through Europe and North Africa, often attacking and destroying towns and settlements. ■ a period of supposed unenlightenment: ***the dark ages of racism.*** ■ (**the dark ages**) humorous or derog. an obscure or little-regarded period in the past, esp. as characterizing an outdated attitude or practice. **2** Archaeol. a period in Greece and the Aegean from the end of the Bronze Age until the beginning of the archaic period.

dark choc·o·late ▸ **n.** slightly bitter chocolate, of a deep brown color, without added milk.

Dark Con·ti·nent hist. a name given to Africa at a time when it was little known to Europeans.

dark cur·rent ▸ **n.** the residual electric current flowing in a photoelectric device when there is no incident illumination.

dark·en /ˈdärkən/ ▸ **v.** **1** make or become dark or darker: [as adj.] (**darkened**) *a darkened room.* ■ [trans.] fig. (of an unpleasant event or state of affairs) cast a shadow over something; spoil: *the abuse darkened the rest of their lives.* **2** make or become gloomy, angry, or unhappy. ■ [intrans.] (of someone's eyes or expression) show anger or another strong negative emotion. ■ [trans.] (of such an emotion) show in (someone's eyes or expression).

– PHRASES **darken someone's door** visit someone's home: *never darken my door again!* — **dark·en·er n.**

dark horse ▸ **n.** **1** a person about whom little is known, esp. someone whose abilities and potential for success are concealed: [as adj.] *a dark-horse candidate.* **2** a competitor or candidate who has little chance of winning, or who wins against expectations: *a preseason dark horse as the nation's top collegiate football team.*

dark·ie /ˈdärkē/ ▸ **n.** var. of **darky**.

dark line ▸ **n.** Physics a line in an absorption spectrum, appearing as a black line at visible wavelengths.

dark·ling /ˈdärkliNG/ ▸ **adj.** literary of or relating to growing darkness: *the darkling sky.*

dark·ling bee·tle ▸ **n.** a dark-colored nocturnal beetle (family Tenebrionidae), typically with reduced or absent wings.

dark·ly /ˈdärklē/ ▸ **adv.** **1** in a threatening, mysterious, or ominous way: *"You can't trust him," said Jacob darkly.* ■ in a depressing or pessimistic way: *I wondered darkly if I was wasting my time.* **2** with a dark color.

dark mat·ter ▸ **n.** Astron. (in some cosmological theories) nonluminous material that is postulated to exist in space and that could take any of several forms including weakly interacting particles (**cold dark matter**) or high-energy randomly moving particles created soon after the big bang (**hot dark matter**).

dark neb·u·la ▸ **n.** Astron. a nonluminous nebula of dust and gas that is observable because it obscures light from other sources.

dark·ness /ˈdärknis/ ▸ **n.** **1** the partial or total absence of light: *the office was in darkness.* ■ night: *make camp before darkness.* ■ the quality of being dark in color. **2** wickedness or evil. ■ unhappiness, distress, or gloom. ■ secrecy or mystery. ■ lack of spiritual or intellectual enlightenment; ignorance.

dark re·ac·tion ▸ **n.** Biochem. the cycle of reactions (the Calvin cycle) that occurs in the second phase of photosynthesis and does not require the presence of light. It involves the fixation of carbon dioxide and its reduction to carbohydrate and the dissociation of water, using chemical energy stored in ATP.

dark·room /ˈdärkˌro͞om; -ˌro͝om/ ▸ **n.** a room from which normal light is excluded, used for developing photographs.

dark star ▸ **n.** Astron. a starlike object that emits little or no visible light. Its existence is inferred from other evidence, such as the eclipsing of other stars.

dark·y /ˈdärkē/ (also **dark·ie**) ▸ **n.** (pl. **dark·ies**) informal, offens. a person with black or dark skin.

dar·ling /ˈdärliNG/ ▸ **n.** used as an affectionate form of address to a beloved person. ■ a lovable or endearing person: *he's a darling.* ■ a person who is particularly popular with a certain group: *she is the darling of the media.* ▸ **adj.** [attrib.] beloved. ■ (esp. in affected use) pretty; charming.

– PHRASES **be a darling** used as a friendly or encouraging preface to a request: *be a darling and don't mention I'm here.* — **dar·ling·ness n.** [OE *dēorling* (see **dear**, **-ling**).]

Dar·ling Riv·er /ˈdärliNG/ a river in southeastern Australia that flows southwest for 1,712 miles (2,757 km).

Darm·stadt /ˈdärmˌstat; -ˌSHtät/ a town in western Germany, in the state of Hesse; pop. 140,040.

darm·stadt·i·um /därmˈstatēəm; -ˈSHtä-/ ▸ **n.** the synthetic chemical element of atomic number 110. It is a superheavy metal that decays in thousandths of a second. (Symbol: **Ds**) [21st C.: after a laboratory in *Darmstadt*, Germany, where the element was first created.]

darn[1] /därn/ ▸ **v.** [trans.] mend (knitted material or a hole in this) by weaving

PRONUNCIATION KEY ə *ago, up*; ər *over, fur*; a *hat*; ā *ate*; ä *car*; e *let*; ē *see*; i *fit*; ī *by*; NG *sing*; ō *go*; ô *law, for*; oi *toy*; o͝o *good*; o͞o *goo*; ou *out*; TH *thin*; TH *then*; ZH *vision*

yarn across the hole with a needle: *I darn my socks.* ■ embroider (material) with a large running stitch. ▶ n. a place in a garment that has been mended in such a way. [17th C.: perh. from dial. *dern* 'to hide,' from OE *diernan*, of West Gmc. origin.]

darn[2] (also **durn**) ▶ v., adj. & exclam. informal euphemism for DAMN.

darned /därnd/ (also **durned** /dərnd/) ▶ adj. informal euphemism for DAMNED. — **darned·est** adj.

dar·nel /'därnl/ ▶ n. a Eurasian ryegrass (genus *Lolium*), esp. the widespread *L. temulentum* with poisonous seeds. [ME: appar. rel. to Fr. (Walloon dial.) *darnelle*.]

darn·er /'därnər/ ▶ n. **1** a darning needle. **2** a large slender-bodied dragonfly (family Aeshnidae). Also called DARNING NEEDLE. [said to be so named because of the popular belief that the dragonfly sews up the lips and eyelids of people sleeping.]

darn·ing /'därniNG/ ▶ n. the skill or activity of one who darns. ■ articles being darned or needing to be darned.

darn·ing egg ▶ n. an egg-shaped piece of wood or other smooth hard material used to stretch and support material being darned.

darn·ing nee·dle ▶ n. a long sewing needle with a large eye, used in darning. ■ another term for DARNER (sense 2).

Darn·ley /'därnlē/, Henry Stewart (or Stuart), Lord (1545–67), Scottish nobleman; second husband of Mary, Queen of Scots; father of James I of England.

Dar·row /'darō/, Clarence Seward (1857–1938), US lawyer, noted for his role as defense counsel in the 1925 Scopes Trial.

dart /därt/ ▶ n. **1** a small pointed missile that can be thrown or fired. ■ a small pointed missile with a feather or plastic tail, used in the game of darts. ■ an act of running somewhere suddenly and rapidly: *the cat made a dart for the door.* ■ fig. a sudden, intense pang of a particular emotion: *a dart of panic.* ■ Zool. a dartlike calcareous organ of a snail forming part of the reproductive system, exchanged during copulation. **2** a tapered tuck stitched into a garment in order to shape it. ▶ v. [no obj., with adverbial of direction] move or run somewhere suddenly or rapidly: *she darted across the street.* ■ [with obj. and adverbial of direction] cast (a look or one's eyes) suddenly and rapidly in a particular direction. ■ [trans.] shoot (an animal) with a dart, typically in order to administer a drug. [ME: from OFr., accusative of *darz*, *dars*, from a West Gmc. word meaning 'spear, lance.']

dart·board /'därt,bôrd/ ▶ n. a circular board marked with numbered segments, used as a target in the game of darts.

dart·er /'därtər/ ▶ n. **1** another term for ANHINGA. **2** a small North American freshwater fish (genera *Etheostoma* and *Percina*, family Percidae), the male of which may develop bright coloration during the breeding season.

darts /därts/ ▶ plural n. [usu. treated as sing.] an indoor game in which small pointed missiles with feather or plastic flights are thrown at a circular target marked with numbers in order to score points.

Dar·win /'därwən/, Charles Robert (1809–82), English historian and geologist; a proponent of the theory of evolution by natural selection. His works include *On the Origin of Species* (1859) and *The Descent of Man* (1871). — **Dar·win·i·an** /där'winēən/ adj. **Dar·win·ism** /-,nizəm/ n. **Dar·win·ist** /-nist/ n. & adj.

dash /dasH/ ▶ v. **1** [no obj., with adverbial of direction] run or travel somewhere in a great hurry: *I dashed into the garden* | *I must dash, I'm late.* ■ (often **dash about/around**) move about in a great hurry, esp. in the attempt to do several things in a short period of time. **2** [with obj. and adverbial of direction] strike or fling (something) somewhere with great force, esp. so as to have a destructive effect; hurl: *the ship was dashed upon the rocks.* ■ [no obj., with adverbial of direction] strike forcefully against something. ■ [trans.] destroy or frustrate (a person's hopes or expectations). ■ [trans.] cause (someone) to lose confidence; dispirit. ▶ n. **1** [in sing.] an act of running somewhere suddenly and hastily: *she made a dash for the door.* ■ a journey or period of time characterized by urgency or eager haste: *a 20-mile dash to the airport.* ■ a short fast race run in one heat; a sprint: *the 100-yard dash.* **2** a small quantity of a substance, esp. a liquid, added to something else: *whiskey with a dash of soda.* ■ fig. a small amount of a particular quality adding piquancy or distinctiveness to something else: *a casual atmosphere with a dash of sophistication.* **3** a horizontal stroke in writing or printing to mark a pause or break in sense, or to represent omitted letters or words. ■ the longer signal of the two used in Morse code. Compare with DOT. ■ Music a short vertical mark placed above or beneath a note to indicate that it is to be performed in a very staccato manner. **4** impetuous or flamboyant vigor and confidence; panache. **5** short for DASHBOARD.

– PHRASAL VERBS **dash something off** write something hurriedly and without much premeditation. [ME: prob. symbolic.]

dash·board /'dasH,bôrd/ ▶ n. the panel facing the driver of a vehicle or the pilot of an aircraft, containing instruments and controls. ■ hist. a board of wood or leather in front of a carriage, to keep out mud.

da·sheen /da'sHēn/ ▶ n. another term for TARO. [19th C. (orig. W. Ind.): of unknown origin.]

dash·er /'dasHər/ ▶ n. **1** informal a person who dresses or acts flamboyantly or stylishly. **2** a plunger for agitating cream in a churn. **3** Hockey the ledge along the top of the boards of a rink.

da·shi·ki /də'sHēkē/ ▶ n. (pl. **-kis**) a loose, brightly colored shirt or tunic, originally from West Africa. [from Yoruba or Hausa.]

dash·ing /'dasHiNG/ ▶ adj. (of a man) attractive in a romantic, adventurous way. ■ stylish or fashionable. — **dash·ing·ly** adv.

das·sie /'dasē/ ▶ n. (pl. **-sies**) a hyrax, esp. the rock hyrax of southern Africa. [18th C.: from Afrik., from South Afr. Dutch *dasje*, dimin. of Du. *das* 'badger.']

das·tard /'dastərd/ ▶ n. dated or humorous a dishonorable or despicable person. — **das·tard·li·ness** n. **das·tard·ly** adj. [ME: prob. from *dazed*.]

das·y·ure /'dasē,yŏŏr/ ▶ n. another term for QUOLL. [19th C.: from Fr., from mod. L. *dasyurus*, from Gk. *dasus* 'rough, hairy' + *oura* 'tail.']

DAT /dat/ ▶ abbr. digital audiotape.

da·ta /'datə; 'dātə/ ▶ n. facts and statistics collected together for reference or analysis. See also DATUM. ■ Comput. the quantities, characters, or symbols on which operations are performed by a computer, being stored and transmitted in the form of electrical signals and recorded on magnetic, optical, or mechanical recording media. ■ Philos. things known or assumed as facts, making the basis of reasoning or calculation. [17th C.: from L., pl. of DATUM.]

da·ta bank (also **da·ta·bank**) ▶ n. Comput. a large repository of data on a particular topic, sometimes formed from more than one database, and accessible by many users.

da·ta·base /'datə,bās; 'dā-/ ▶ n. a structured set of data held in a computer, esp. one that is accessible in various ways.

da·ta·base man·age·ment sys·tem (abbr.: **DBMS**) ▶ n. Comput. software that handles the storage, retrieval, and updating of data in a computer system.

dat·a·ble /'dātəbəl/ (also **date·a·ble**) ▶ adj. able to be dated to a particular time.

da·ta com·mun·i·ca·tions ▶ n. the electronic transmission of encoded information to, from, or between computers.

da·ta·glove /'datə,gləv; 'dā-/ ▶ n. Comput. a device, worn like a glove, that allows the manual manipulation of images in virtual reality.

da·ta proc·ess·ing ▶ n. a series of operations on data, esp. by a computer, to retrieve, transform, or classify information. — **da·ta proc·es·sor** n.

da·ta set ▶ n. Comput. a collection of related sets of information that is composed of separate elements but can be manipulated as a unit by a computer.

da·ta ter·mi·nal ▶ n. Comput. a terminal at which a person can enter data into a computer-based system or receive data from one.

da·ta ware·house ▶ n. Comput. a large store of data accumulated from a wide range of sources within a company and used to guide management decisions. — **da·ta ware·hous·ing** n.

date[1] /dāt/ ▶ n. **1** the day of the month or year as specified by a number. ■ a particular day or year when a given event occurred or will occur: *significant dates like 1776 and 1789* | *they've set a date for the wedding.* ■ (**dates**) the years of a person's birth and death or of the beginning and end of a period or event. ■ the period of time to which an artifact or structure belongs. ■ a written, printed, or stamped statement on an item giving the day, month, and year of writing, publication, or manufacture. **2** informal a social or romantic appointment or engagement: *a student on a date with someone he met in class.* ■ a person with whom one has such an engagement. ■ an appointment. ■ a musical or theatrical engagement or performance, esp. as part of a tour: *possible live dates in the near future.* ▶ v. [trans.] **1** establish or ascertain the date of (an object or event): *they date the paintings to 1460.* ■ mark with a date: *sign and date the document* | [as adj.] (**dated**) *a signed and dated painting.* ■ [intrans.] have its origin at a particular time; have existed since: *the controversy dates back to 1986.* **2** indicate or expose as being old-fashioned: *disco—that word alone dates me.* ■ [intrans.] seem old-fashioned: [as adj.] (**dated**) *his style would sound dated nowadays.* **3** informal go out with (someone in whom one is romantically or sexually interested).

– PHRASES **to date** until now: *their finest work to date.* — **dat·er** n. [ME: via OFr. from med. L. *data*, fem. past part. of *dare* 'give'; from the L. formula used in dating letters, *data (epistola)* '(letter) given or delivered,' to record a particular time or place.]

date[2] ▶ n. **1** a sweet, dark brown, oval fruit containing a hard stone, often eaten dried. **2** (also **date palm**) the tall palm tree (*Phoenix dactylifera*) that bears clusters of this fruit, native to western Asia and North Africa. [ME: from OFr., via L. from Gk. *daktulos* 'finger.']

date·a·ble ▶ adj. var. of DATABLE.

date·book /'dāt,bŏŏk/ ▶ n. a book with spaces for each day of the year in which one notes appointments or important information for each day.

date·less /'dātlis/ ▶ adj. **1** not clearly belonging to any particular period, therefore not likely to go out of date. ■ (of a document or stamp) having no date mark. **2** not having, or incapable of having, social or romantic appointments or engagements.

Date Line (also **International Date Line**) an imaginary north–south line along the 180th meridian, adopted in 1884, to the east of which the date is a day earlier than it is to the west.

date·line /'dāt,līn/ ▶ n. a line at the head of a dispatch or special article in a newspaper showing the date and place of writing.

date palm ▶ n. see DATE[2].

date rape ▶ n. rape committed by the victim's escort.

date-rape drug ▶ n. a drug that causes temporary loss of memory or inhibition, surreptitiously given to a girl or a woman so that her date may sexually abuse or rape her.

date stamp ▶ n. a stamped mark indicating a date, typically used on food packaging or mailed envelopes. ■ an adjustable stamp used to make such a mark. ▶ v. (**date-stamp**) [trans.] mark (something) with a date stamp.

dat·ing serv·ice ▶ n. an agency that arranges introductions for people seeking romantic partners.

da·tive /ˈdātiv/ Gram. ▶ adj. (in Latin, Greek, German, and other languages) denoting a case of nouns and pronouns, and words in grammatical agreement with them, indicating an indirect object or recipient. ▶ n. a noun or other word of this type. ■ (**the dative**) the dative case. [ME: from L. *(casus) dativus* '(case) of giving,' from *dat-* 'given,' from the v. *dare.*]

Da·tong /ˈdäˈto͝oNG/ a city in northern China, in Shanxi province; pop. 1,090,000.

da·tum /ˈdātəm; ˈdatəm/ ▶ n. (pl. **da·ta** /ˈdātə; ˈdatə/) **1** a piece of information. See usage note at DATA. ■ an assumption or premise from which inferences may be drawn. See SENSE DATUM. **2** a fixed starting point of a scale or operation. [18th C.: from L., neut. past part. of *dare* 'give.']

da·tum line (also **datum level**) ▶ n. a standard of comparison or point of reference. ■ Surveying an assumed surface used as a reference for the measurement of heights and depths. ■ a line to which dimensions are referred on engineering drawings, and from which measurements are calculated.

da·tu·ra /dəˈt(y)o͝orə/ ▶ n. a shrubby annual plant (genus *Datura*) of the nightshade family, with large trumpet-shaped flowers. Native to southern North America, daturas contain toxic or narcotic alkaloids with hallucinogenic properties. [mod. L., from Hindi *dhatūrā.*]

daub /dôb/ ▶ v. [trans.] coat or smear (a surface) with a thick or sticky substance in a carelessly rough or liberal way: *she **daubed** her face with night cream.* ■ spread (a thick or sticky substance) on a surface in such a way: *a canvas with paint **daubed** on it.* ■ paint (words or drawings) on a surface in such a way. ▶ n. **1** plaster, clay, or another substance used for coating a surface, esp. when mixed with straw and applied to laths or wattles to form a wall. ■ a patch or smear of a thick or sticky substance. **2** a painting executed without much skill. [ME: from OFr. *dauber,* from L. *dealbare* 'whiten, whitewash,' based on *albus* 'white.']

daub·er /ˈdôbər/ ▶ n. a crude or inartistic painter. ■ an implement used for daubing.

Dau·bi·gny /ˌdôbēˈnyē/, Charles François (1817–78), French painter. He was a member of the Barbizon School.

daugh·ter /ˈdôtər; ˈdä-/ ▶ n. a girl or woman in relation to her parents. ■ a female offspring of an animal. ■ a female descendant: *the sons and daughters of Adam.* ■ a woman considered as the product of a particular person, influence, or environment. ■ literary a thing personified as a daughter in relation to its origin or source: *Italian, the eldest daughter of ancient Latin.* ■ Physics a nuclide formed by the radioactive decay of another. ▶ adj. Biol. originating through division or replication: *daughter cells.* — **daugh·ter·hood** n. **daugh·ter·ly** adj. [OE *dohtor,* of Gmc. origin; rel. to Du. *dochter* and Ger. *Tochter,* from an Indo-Eur. root shared by Gk. *thugatēr.*]

daugh·ter-in-law ▶ n. (pl. **daugh·ters-in-law**) the wife of one's son.

Daugh·ters of the A·mer·i·can Rev·o·lu·tion (abbr.: **DAR**) a patriotic society whose membership is limited to female descendants of those who aided the cause of independence.

Dau·mier /dōˈmyā/, Honoré (1808–78), French painter and lithographer. His lithographs satirized French society and politics.

daunt /dônt; dänt/ ▶ v. [trans.] (usu. **be daunted**) make (someone) feel intimidated or apprehensive.
– PHRASES **nothing daunted** without having been made fearful or apprehensive: *nothing daunted, the committee set to work.* [ME: from OFr. *danter,* from L. *domitare,* frequentative of *domare* 'to tame.']

daunt·ing /ˈdôntiNG; ˈdän-/ ▶ adj. seeming difficult to deal with in anticipation; intimidating: *a daunting task.* — **daunt·ing·ly** adv.

daunt·less /ˈdôntlis; ˈdänt-/ ▶ adj. showing fearlessness and determination: *dauntless bravery.* — **daunt·less·ly** adv. **daunt·less·ness** n.

dau·phin /ˈdôfin/ ▶ n. hist. the eldest son of the king of France. [Fr., from the family name of the lords of the Dauphiné.]

dau·phi·nois /ˌdôfinˈwä/ (also **dau·phi·noise** /-ˈwäz/) ▶ adj. (of potatoes or other vegetables) sliced and cooked in milk, typically with a topping of cheese. [Fr., 'from the province of Dauphiné.']

Da·vao /ˈdävou; däˈvou/ a seaport in the southern Philippines, on the island of Mindanao; pop. 850,000.

da·ven /ˈdävən/ ▶ v. (**da·vened, da·ven·ing**) [intrans.] (in Judaism) recite the prescribed liturgical prayers. [Yiddish.]

Dav·en·port /ˈdavənˌpôrt/ a city in southeastern Iowa, on the Mississippi River; pop. 98,359.

dav·en·port /ˈdavənˌpôrt/ ▶ n. a large upholstered sofa, typically able to be converted into a bed.

Da·vid[1] /ˈdāvid/ (died *c.*962 BC), king of Judah and Israel *c.*1000–*c.*962 BC, traditionally regarded as the author of the Psalms. In the biblical account, he killed the Philistine Goliath and, on Saul's death, became king, making Jerusalem his capital.

Da·vid[2] the name of two kings of Scotland: ■ David I (*c.*1084–1153), reigned 1124–53; sixth son of Malcolm III. In 1136, he invaded England but was defeated in 1138. ■ David II (1324–71), reigned 1329–71; son of Robert the Bruce.

Da·vid[3] /däˈvēd/, Jacques-Louis (1748–1825), French artist, noted for neoclassical paintings.

Da·vid, St. /ˈdāvəd/ (6th century), Welsh monk regarded as the patron saint of Wales; Welsh name **Dewi** /ˈde-wē/.

da Vin·ci /də ˈvinCHē/, Leonardo. See LEONARDO DA VINCI.

Da·vis /ˈdāvis/ an academic and agricultural city in north central California; pop. 46,209.

Da·vis[1] /ˈdāvis/, Angela Yvonne (1944–), US civil rights activist. She wrote *Women, Race and Class* (1980).

Da·vis[2] a family of US military officers. In 1940, Benjamin Oliver (1877–1970) became the first African-American general in the US Army. His son, **Benjamin Oliver Davis, Jr.** (1912–2002), commanded the Tuskegee Airmen in World War II and became the first African-American air force general in 1954.

Da·vis[3], David (1815–86), US Supreme Court associate justice 1862–77.

Da·vis[4], Jefferson (1808–89), president of the Confederate States of America 1862–65, during the American Civil War. A US senator from Mississippi (1847–51, 1857–61), he withdrew from the Senate when Mississippi seceded from the Union.

Da·vis Cup an annual tennis championship for men, first held in 1900, between teams from different countries. [Dwight F. *Davis* (1879–1945), US doubles champion.]

Da·vis Moun·tains a range in southwestern Texas, site of the Mount Locke observatory and several resorts.

Da·vis·son /ˈdāvəsən/, Clinton Joseph (1881–1958), US physicist. With L. H. Germer (1896–1971), he discovered electron diffraction. Nobel Prize for Physics (1937, shared with George P. Thomson 1892–1975).

Da·vis Strait a sea passage 400 miles (645 km) long that separates Greenland from Baffin Island and connects Baffin Bay with the Atlantic Ocean.

da·vit /ˈdavit; ˈdā-/ ▶ n. a small crane on board a ship, esp. one of a pair for suspending or lowering a lifeboat. [15th C.: from OFr. *daviot,* dimin. of *david,* a tool.]

Da·vy /ˈdāvē/, Sir Humphry (1778–1829), English chemist. He discovered nitrous oxide (laughing gas) and the elements sodium, potassium, magnesium, calcium, strontium, and barium.

Da·vy Jones's lock·er /ˌdāvē ˈjōnz(əz)/ ▶ n. informal the bottom of the sea, esp. regarded as the grave of those drowned at sea. [from *Davy Jones,* denoting the evil spirit of the sea.]

daw /dô/ ▶ n. another term for JACKDAW. [ME: of Gmc. origin; rel. to Ger. *Dohle.*]

daw·dle /ˈdôdl/ ▶ v. [intrans.] waste time; be slow. ■ [with adverbial of direction] move slowly and idly: *Ruth dawdled back through the woods.* — **daw·dler** /ˈdôd(ə)lər/ n. [17th C.: rel. to dial. *daddle, doddle* 'dally.']

Dawes /dôz/, Charles Gates (1865–1951), US vice president 1925–29. Following World War I, he helped to formulate the 1923 plan for restructuring Germany's economy. Nobel Peace Prize (1925, shared with Sir Austen Chamberlain).

dawn /dôn; dän/ ▶ n. the first appearance of light in the sky before sunrise: *the rose-pink light of dawn.* ■ fig. the beginning of a phenomenon or period of time, esp. one considered favorable. ▶ v. [intrans.] **1** (of a day) begin: [with complement] *Thursday dawned bright and sunny.* ■ fig. come into existence: *a new era of land-use policy was dawning.* **2** become evident to the mind; be perceived or understood: *the awful truth was beginning to **dawn on** him* | [as adj.] (**dawning**) *he smiled with dawning recognition.*
– PHRASES **from dawn to dusk** all day; ceaselessly. [15th C. (as a v.): back-form. from ME DAWNING.]

dawn cho·rus ▶ n. [in sing.] the singing of a large number of birds before dawn each day, particularly during the breeding season.

dawn·ing /ˈdôniNG; ˈdä-/ ▶ n. literary dawn. ■ the beginning or first appearance of something. [ME: alt. of earlier *dawing,* from OE *dagian* 'to dawn,' of Gmc. origin; rel. to Du. *dagen* and Ger. *tagen,* also to DAY.]

dawn red·wood ▶ n. a coniferous tree (*Metasequoia glyptostroboides,* family Taxodiaceae) with deciduous needles, known only as a fossil until it was found growing in southwestern China in 1941. Also called METASEQUOIA.

Daw·son /ˈdôsən/ a town in the west central Yukon Territory, on the Klondike and Yukon rivers, center of a gold rush after 1896; pop. 1,287.

DAX ▶ abbr. Deutsche Aktienindex, the German stock exchange.

Day[1] /dā/, Dorothy (1897–1980), US journalist and social activist. She founded the *Catholic Worker* newspaper with Peter Maurin (1877–1949) in 1933.

Day[2], William Rufus (1849–1923), US Supreme Court associate justice 1903–22.

day /dā/ ▶ n. **1** a period of twenty-four hours as a unit of time, reckoned from one midnight to the next, corresponding to a rotation of the earth on its axis. ■ the part of this period when it is light; the time between sunrise and sunset: *she sleeps all day* | *the animals hunt **by day.*** ■ the time spent working during such a period. ■ Astron. a single rotation of a planet in relation to its primary. ■ Astron. the period on a planet when its primary star is above the horizon. **2** (usu. **days**) a particular period of the past; an era: *the laws were strict in those days.* ■ (**the day**) the present time: *the political issues of the day.* ■ [with adj.] a day associated with a particular event or purpose: *graduation day* | *Christmas Day.*

■ a day's endeavor, or the period of an endeavor, esp. as bringing success: *speed and surprise would win the day.* ■ [usu. with adj.] (**days**) a particular period in a person's life or career: *my student days.* ■ (**one's day**) the successful, fortunate, or influential period of a person's life or career: *a matinée idol in his day.* ■ (**one's days**) the span of someone's life. ▶ **adj.** [attrib.] carried out during the day as opposed to at night: *my day job.* ■ (of a person) working during the day as opposed to at night: *a day nurse.*

– PHRASES **all in a** (or **the**) **day's work** (of something unusual or difficult) accepted as part of someone's normal routine or as a matter of course. **any day** informal at any time: *you can take me dancing any day of the week.* ■ (used to express one's strong preference for something) under any circumstances. ■ very soon: *expected to give birth any day.* **at the end of the day** see END. **by the day** gradually and steadily: *the campaign is growing by the day.* **call it a day** end a period of activity, esp. resting content that enough has been done. **day after day** on each successive day, esp. over a long period. **day and night** all the time. **day by day** gradually and steadily. **day in, day out** continuously or repeatedly over a long period of time. **day of reckoning** the time when past mistakes or misdeeds must be punished or paid for. **from day one** from the very beginning. **have had one's** (or **its**) **day** be no longer popular, successful, or influential: *power dressing has had its day.* **if someone is a day** at least (added to a statement about a person's age): *he must be seventy if he's a day.* **in this day and age** at the present time; in the modern era. **not someone's day** used to convey that someone has had a bad day. —— **of the day** a thing currently considered to be particularly interesting or important: *the story of the day.* **one day** (or **one of these days**) at some time in the future. **one of those days** a day when several things go wrong. **that will** (or **that'll**) **be the day** informal that will never happen. **these days** at present. **those were the days** used to assert that a particular past time was better than the present. **to the day** exactly: *it's four years to the day since we won the lottery.* **to this day** up to the present time; still. [OE *dæg*, of Gmc. origin; rel. to Du. *dag* and Ger. *Tag*.]

Day·ak /'dīak/ (also **Dy·ak**) ▶ **n.** (pl. same or **-aks**) **1** a member of a group of indigenous peoples inhabiting parts of Borneo. **2** the group of Austronesian languages spoken by these peoples. ▶ **adj.** of or relating to these peoples or their languages. [19th C.: Malay, lit. 'up-country.']

Da·yan /dä'yän/, Moshe (1915–81), Israeli general. He was minister of defense during the Six Day War (June 5–10, 1967), in which Israel defeated an Egyptian, Jordanian, and Syrian alliance.

day·bed /'dā,bed/ ▶ **n.** a couch that can be made up into a bed.

day·book /'dā,bo͝ok/ ▶ **n.** an account book in which a day's transactions are entered for later transfer to a ledger. ■ a diary.

day·break /'dā,brāk/ ▶ **n.** the time in the morning when daylight first appears; dawn: *she set off at daybreak.*

day care ▶ **n.** daytime care for the needs of people who cannot be fully independent, such as children or the elderly.

day·dream /'dā,drēm/ ▶ **n.** a series of pleasant thoughts that distract one's attention from the present. ▶ **v.** [intrans.] indulge in such a series of thoughts. — **day·dream·er n. day·dream·y adj.**

day·flow·er /'dā,flouər/ ▶ **n.** a plant (genus *Commelina*, family Commelinaceae) related to the spiderwort, with short-lived, typically blue flowers.

Day-Glo /'dā,glō/ (also **day-glo**) ▶ **n.** trademark a fluorescent paint or other coloring. [1950s: blend of DAY and GLOW.]

day job ▶ **n.** a person's regular job and main source of income, usually performed during the normal business day.

day la·bor ▶ **n.** unskilled labor paid by the day. — **day la·bor·er n.**

Day Lew·is /'dā 'lo͞oəs/, C. (1904–72), English poet and critic; full name *Cecil Day Lewis.* He was Britain's poet laureate 1968–72.

day·light /'dā,līt/ ▶ **n. 1** the natural light of the day. ■ the first appearance of light in the morning; dawn. ■ fig. visible distance between one person or thing and another. **2** (**daylights**) used to emphasize the severity or thoroughness of an action: *my father beat the living daylights out of them.* [from *daylights* 'eyes.']

– PHRASES **see daylight** begin to understand what was previously puzzling or unclear.

day·light sav·ing time (also **day·light sav·ings time**) ▶ **n.** time as adjusted to achieve longer evening daylight, esp. in summer, by setting the clocks an hour ahead of the standard time.

day·lil·y /'dā,lilē/ (also **day lil·y**) ▶ **n.** a lily (genus *Hemerocallis*) that bears large yellow, red, or orange flowers, each flower lasting only one day.

day·long /'dā'lôNG/ ▶ **adj.** of a day's duration; lasting all day.

day·mare /'dā,me(ə)r/ ▶ **n.** a frightening or oppressive trance or hallucination experienced while awake. [17th C.: from DAY, on the pattern of *nightmare*.]

day nurs·er·y ▶ **n.** a place where young children are cared for during the working day.

Day of A·tone·ment another term for YOM KIPPUR.

Day of Judg·ment another term for JUDGMENT DAY.

day room (also **day·room**) ▶ **n.** a room used for daytime recreation, esp. a communal room in an institution.

day·sail /'dā,sāl/ ▶ **v.** [intrans.] sail a yacht for a single day.

day·sail·er /'dā,sālər/ ▶ **n.** a sailboat without a cabin, designed for day trips.

day school ▶ **n.** a nonresidential school, typically a private one.

day shift ▶ **n.** a period of time worked during the daylight hours in a hospital, factory, etc., as opposed to the night shift. ■ [treated as sing. or pl.] the employees who work during this period.

day·side /'dā,sīd/ ▶ **n.** Astron. the side of a planet that is facing its primary star.

Days of Awe ▶ **plural n.** another term for HIGH HOLIDAYS.

day stu·dent ▶ **n.** a student who attends classes at a boarding school or college but who does not live at the school.

day·time /'dā,tīm/ ▶ **n.** the time of the day between sunrise and sunset.

day-to-day ▶ **adj.** [attrib.] happening regularly every day: *the day-to-day management of the classroom.* ■ ordinary; everyday: *our day-to-day life.* ■ short-term; without consideration for the future: *for day-to-day survival.* ■ Sports (of an injured player) not playing owing to a minor injury that is being treated and evaluated on a daily basis. ▶ **n.** [in sing.] an ordinary, everyday routine. ▶ **adv.** on a daily basis: *the information to be traded is determined day-to-day.*

Day·ton /'dātn/ a city in western Ohio; pop. 166,179.

Day·to·na Beach /dā'tōnə/ a city in northeastern Florida, on the Atlantic coast; pop. 61,921.

day trad·ing ▶ **n.** the buying and selling of securities on the same day, often online, on the basis of small, short-term price fluctuations. — **day-trade v. day trad·er n.**

day trip ▶ **n.** an excursion completed in one day. — **day-trip·per** (or **day trip·per**) **n.**

day·wear /'dā,we(ə)r/ ▶ **n.** articles of casual clothing suitable for informal or everyday occasions.

day·work /'dā,wərk/ ▶ **n.** casual work paid for on a daily basis. — **day·work·er n.**

daze /dāz/ ▶ **v.** [trans.] (usu. **be dazed**) make (someone) unable to think or react properly; stupefy; bewilder. ▶ **n.** [in sing.] a state of stunned confusion or bewilderment: *he was walking around in a daze.* — **daz·ed·ly** /'dāzidlē/ **adv.** [ME: back-form. from *dazed* (adj.), from ON *dasathr* 'weary'; cf. Swed. *dasa* 'lie idle.']

daz·zle /'dazəl/ ▶ **v.** [trans.] (of a bright light) blind (a person) temporarily: *she was dazzled by the headlights.* ■ fig. amaze or overwhelm (someone) with a particular impressive quality. ▶ **n.** brightness that confuses someone's vision temporarily: [in sing.] *a dazzle of red spotlights.* — **daz·zle·ment n.** [15th C. (in the sense 'be dazzled'): frequentative of the V. DAZE.]

daz·zler /'daz(ə)lər/ ▶ **n.** a person or thing that dazzles.

daz·zling /'daz(ə)liNG/ ▶ **adj.** extremely bright, esp. so as to blind the eyes temporarily. ■ fig. extremely impressive, beautiful, or skillful. — **daz·zling·ly adv.**

Db ▶ **symb.** the chemical element dubnium.

dB ▶ **abbr.** decibel(s).

dba (also **d/b/a**) ▶ **abbr.** ■ doing business as.

DBMS ▶ **abbr.** database management system.

DBS ▶ **abbr.** ■ direct broadcasting by satellite. ■ direct-broadcast satellite.

dbx ▶ **n.** trademark electronic circuitry designed to increase the dynamic range of reproduced sound and reduce noise in the system. [1970s: from DB 'decibel' + *x* (representing *expander*).]

DC ▶ **abbr.** ■ Music da capo. ■ direct current. ■ District of Columbia: *Washington, DC.* ■ Doctor of Chiropractic.

DCC ▶ **abbr.** ■ digital compact cassette.

DCL ▶ **abbr.** Doctor of Civil Law.

DCM ▶ **abbr.** (in the UK) Distinguished Conduct Medal, awarded for bravery.

DD ▶ **abbr.** ■ Mil. dishonorable discharge. ■ Doctor of Divinity.

D-Day ▶ **n.** the day (June 6, 1944) in World War II on which Allied forces invaded northern France by means of beach landings in Normandy. ■ the day on which an important operation is to begin or a change to take effect. [from *D* for *day* + DAY. Cf. H-HOUR.]

DDE ▶ **n.** Comput. a standard allowing data to be shared between different programs. [1980s: abbrev. of *Dynamic Data Exchange*.]

DDR ▶ **abbr.** German Democratic Republic. [abbrev. of Ger. *Deutsche Demokratische Republik*.]

D.D.S. ▶ **abbr.** ■ Doctor of Dental Science. ■ Doctor of Dental Surgery.

DDT ▶ **abbr.** dichlorodiphenyltrichloroethane, $CCl_3CH(C_6H_4Cl)_2$, a synthetic organic compound introduced in the 1940s and used as an insecticide. DDT tends to persist in the environment and become concentrated in animals at the head of the food chain. Its use is now widely banned.

DE ▶ **abbr.** ■ Football defensive end. ■ Delaware (in official postal use).

de- ▶ **prefix 1** (forming verbs and their derivatives) down; away: *descend* | *deduct.* ■ completely: *denude* | *derelict.* **2** (added to verbs and their derivatives) denoting removal or reversal: *deaerate* | *de-ice.* **3** denoting formation from: *deverbal.* [from L. *de* 'off, from'; sense 2 via OFr. *des-* from L. *dis-*.]

dea·con /'dēkən/ ▶ **n.** (in Catholic, Anglican, and Orthodox churches) an ordained minister of an order ranking below that of priest. ■ (in some Protestant churches) a lay officer appointed to assist a minister, esp. in secular affairs. ▶ **v.** [trans.] appoint or ordain as a deacon. — **dea·con·ship n.** [OE *diacon*, via eccles. L. from Gk. *diakonos* 'servant.']

dea·con·ess /'dēkənis/ ▶ **n.** (in the early church and some modern churches) a woman with duties similar to those of a deacon.

de·ac·ti·vate /dē'aktə,vāt/ ▶ **v.** **1** [trans.] make (something, typically technical equipment or a virus) inactive by disconnecting or destroying it. **2** [trans.] Mil. remove from active duty. — **de·ac·ti·va·tion** /dē,aktə'vāSHən/ **n.** **de·ac·ti·va·tor** /-vātər/ **n.**

dead /ded/ ▶ **adj.** **1** no longer alive. ■ (of a part of the body) having lost sensation; numb. ■ having or displaying no emotion, sympathy, or sensitivity: *a cold, dead voice.* ■ no longer current, relevant, or important: *pollution had become a dead issue.* ■ devoid of living things. ■ resembling death: *a dead faint.* ■ (of a place or time) characterized by a lack of activity or excitement. ■ (of money) not financially productive. ■ (of sound) without resonance; dull. ■ (of a color) not glossy or bright. ■ (of a piece of equipment) no longer functioning, esp. because of a fault: *the phone had gone dead.* ■ (of an electric circuit or conductor) carrying or transmitting no current. ■ no longer burning. ■ (of air or water) not circulating; stagnant. ■ (of a glass or bottle) empty or no longer being used. ■ (of the ball in a game) out of play. ■ (of a playing field, ball, or other surface) lacking springiness or bounce. **2** [attrib.] complete; absolute: *we sat in dead silence.* ▶ **adv.** [often as submodifier] absolutely; completely. ■ exactly: *they arrived dead on time.* ■ straight; directly: *flares were seen dead ahead.* ▶ **n.** [as pl. n.] (**the dead**) those who have died.

– PHRASES **dead and buried** over; finished: *the incident is dead and buried.* **(as) dead as a** (or **the**) **dodo** see DODO. **(as) dead as a doornail** see DOORNAIL. **dead from the neck up** informal stupid. **dead in the water** (of a ship) unable to move. ■ fig. unable to function effectively: *the economy is dead in the water.* **dead meat** informal in serious trouble: *if anyone finds out, you're dead meat.* **the dead of night** the quietest, darkest part of the night. **the dead of winter** the coldest part of winter. **dead on** exactly right: *her judgment was dead on.* **dead on arrival** used to describe a person who is declared dead immediately upon arrival at a hospital. ■ fig. (of an idea, etc.) declared ineffective without ever having been put into effect. **dead on one's feet** informal extremely tired. **dead set against** informal strongly opposed to. **dead to the world** informal fast asleep. **make a dead set at** see SET[2]. **over my dead body** see BODY. **wouldn't be seen** (or **caught**) **dead** informal used to express strong dislike for a particular thing. — **dead·ness** **n.** [OE *dēad*, of Gmc. origin: rel. to Du. *dood* and Ger. *tot*, also to DIE[1].]

dead air ▶ **n.** an unintended interruption of the video or audio signal during a television or radio broadcast.

dead·beat /'ded,bēt/ ▶ **n.** informal a person who tries to evade paying debts. ■ (also **deadbeat dad**) a man who avoids paying child support. ■ an idle, feckless, or disreputable person. ▶ **adj.** (of a clock escapement or other mechanism) without recoil.

dead·bolt /'ded,bōlt/ ▶ **n.** a bolt engaged by turning a knob or key, rather than by spring action.

dead cen·ter ▶ **n.** the position of a crank when it is in line with the connecting rod and not exerting torque.

dead duck ▶ **n.** informal **1** an unsuccessful or useless person or thing: *totalitarianism is a dead duck.* **2** a person who is beyond help; one who is doomed.

dead·en /'dedn/ ▶ **v.** [trans.] make (a noise or sensation) less intense: *ether was used to deaden the pain.* ■ deprive of the power of sensation: *diabetes can deaden the nerve endings.* ■ deprive of force or vitality; stultify: *the syllabus has deadened the teaching process* | [as adj.] (**deadening**) *a deadening routine.* ■ make (someone) insensitive to something: *laughter might deaden us to the moral issue.* — **dead·en·er** **n.**

dead end ▶ **n.** an end of a road or passage from which no exit is possible; a cul-de-sac. ■ a road or passage having such an end. ■ a situation offering no prospects of progress or development. ▶ **v.** [intrans.] (**dead-end**) (of a road or passage) come to a dead end.

dead·eye /'ded,ī/ ▶ **n.** **1** Sailing a circular wooden block with a groove around the circumference to take a lanyard, used singly or in pairs to tighten a shroud. **2** informal an expert marksman.

dead·fall /'ded,fôl/ ▶ **n.** **1** a trap consisting of a heavy weight positioned to fall on an animal. **2** a tangled mass of fallen trees and brush. ■ a fallen tree.

dead hand ▶ **n.** an undesirable persisting influence. ■ Law see MORTMAIN.

dead·head /'ded,hed/ (also **dead-head**) ▶ **n.** **1** (**Deadhead**) a fan and follower of the rock group The Grateful Dead. **2** informal a commercial carrier with no paying passengers or freight on a trip. ■ a passenger or member of an audience with a free ticket. ■ informal a boring or unenterprising person. **3** a sunken or partially submerged log. ▶ **v.** **1** [intrans.] informal (of a commercial driver, etc.) complete a trip without paying passengers or freight: *trucks deadheading into California.* ■ ride (in a plane or other vehicle) without paying for a ticket. **2** [trans.] remove dead flowerheads from (a plant) to encourage further blooming.

dead heat ▶ **n.** a situation in or result of a race in which two or more competitors are exactly even. ▶ **v.** [intrans.] (**dead-heat**) run or finish a race exactly even.

dead lan·guage ▶ **n.** a language no longer in everyday spoken use, such as Latin.

dead let·ter ▶ **n.** **1** a law or treaty that has not been repealed but is ineffectual or defunct in practice. ■ fig. a thing that is impractical or obsolete. **2** a letter that is undeliverable and unreturnable.

dead lift ▶ **n.** Weightlifting a lift made from a standing position, without the use of a bench or other equipment.

dead·light /'ded,līt/ ▶ **n.** **1** a protective cover or shutter fitted over a porthole or window on a ship. **2** a skylight designed not to be opened.

dead·line /'ded,līn/ ▶ **n.** the latest time or date by which something should be completed: *the deadline for submissions is February 5th.*

dead load ▶ **n.** the intrinsic weight of a structure or vehicle, excluding the weight of passengers or goods. Often contrasted with LIVE LOAD.

dead·lock /'ded,läk/ ▶ **n.** [in sing.] a situation, typically one involving opposing parties, in which no progress can be made: *an attempt to break the deadlock.* ▶ **v.** [trans.] [intrans.] (usu. **be deadlocked**) cause (a situation or opposing parties) to come to a point where no progress can be made because of fundamental disagreement: *the jurors were deadlocked on six charges.* ■ **cause (a contest or game) to be in a tie.**

dead loss ▶ **n.** a venture or situation that produces no profit whatsoever.

dead·ly /'dedlē/ ▶ **adj.** (**-li·er**, **-li·est**) causing or able to cause death: *a deadly weapon.* ■ filled with hate: *his voice was cold and deadly.* ■ (typically in the context of shooting or sports) extremely accurate, effective, or skillful: *his aim is deadly.* ■ informal extremely boring. ■ [attrib.] complete; total: *she was in deadly earnest.* ▶ **adv.** [as submodifier] in a way resembling or suggesting death; as if dead: *her skin was deadly pale.* ■ extremely: *a deadly serious remark.* — **dead·li·ness** **n.**

dead·ly night·shade ▶ **n.** a poisonous Eurasian plant (*Atropa belladonna*) of the nightshade family, with drooping purple flowers and black cherrylike fruit. Also called BELLADONNA.

dead·ly sin ▶ **n.** (in Christian tradition) a sin regarded as leading to damnation, esp. one of a traditional list of seven. See SEVEN DEADLY SINS.

dead·man /'ded,man/ ▶ **n.** an object buried in or secured to the ground for the purpose of providing anchorage or leverage.

dead-man's float ▶ **n.** a floating position, often used by beginning swimmers, in which a person lies face down in the water with arms outstretched or extended forward and legs extended backward.

dead man's han·dle (also **dead man's pedal**) ▶ **n.** (esp. in a diesel or electric train) a lever that acts as a safety device by shutting off power when not held in place by the driver.

dead march ▶ **n.** a slow, solemn piece of music suitable to accompany a funeral procession.

dead-net·tle ▶ **n.** an Old World plant (*Lamium* and related genera) of the mint family, with leaves that resemble those of a nettle but lack stinging hairs.

dead·pan /'ded,pan/ ▶ **adj.** deliberately impassive or expressionless: *a deadpan tone.* ▶ **adv.** in a deadpan manner. ▶ **v.** (**-panned**, **-pan·ning**) [with direct speech] say something amusing while affecting a serious manner.

dead reck·on·ing ▶ **n.** the process of calculating one's position, esp. at sea, by estimating the direction and distance traveled rather than by using landmarks, astronomical observations, or electronic navigation methods.

dead ring·er ▶ **n.** a person or thing that seems exactly like someone or something else.

Dead Sea a salt lake or inland sea in the Jordan valley. Its surface is 1,300 feet (400 m) below sea level.

Dead Sea scrolls a collection of Hebrew and Aramaic manuscripts discovered near Qumran between 1947 and 1956. Dating from shortly before AD 66, the scrolls include texts of many books of the Bible; they are some 1,000 years older than previously known versions.

dead set ▶ **n.** see SET[2] (sense 2).

dead time ▶ **n.** time in which someone or something is inactive or unable to act productively. ■ Physics the period after the recording of a particle or pulse when a detector is unable to record another.

dead weight (also **dead·weight**) ▶ **n.** the weight of an inert person or thing. ■ a heavy or oppressive burden. ■ the total weight of cargo, stores, etc., that a ship carries or can carry at a particular draft. ■ another term for DEAD LOAD. ■ Farming animals sold by the estimated weight of salable meat that they will yield.

dead white Eu·ro·pe·an male (also **dead white male**) ▶ **n.** informal a writer, philosopher, or other significant figure whose importance and talents may have been exaggerated by virtue of his belonging to a historically dominant gender and ethnic group.

Dead·wood /'ded,wo͝od/ a city in western South Dakota, in the Black Hills, known for its 1870s gold rush and Boot Hill cemetery; pop. 1,830.

dead·wood /'ded,wo͝od/ ▶ **n.** a branch or part of a tree that is dead. ■ fig. people or things that are no longer useful or productive.

dead zone ▶ **n.** an area of the ocean that is depleted of oxygen, frequently due to pollution.

de·aer·ate /dē'e(ə)rāt/ ▶ **v.** [trans.] (usu. **be deaerated**) partially or completely remove dissolved air from (something). — **de·aer·a·tion** /,dē-e(ə)'rāSHən/ **n.**

deaf /def/ ▶ **adj.** lacking the power of hearing or having impaired hearing: [as pl. n.] (**the deaf**) *subtitles for the deaf.* ■ unwilling or unable to hear or pay attention to something: *she is deaf to all advice.*

– PHRASES **(as) deaf as a post** completely or extremely deaf. **fall on deaf ears** (of a statement or request) be ignored. **turn a deaf ear** refuse to listen or respond to a statement or request. — **deaf·ness** **n.** [OE *dēaf*, of Gmc. origin; rel. to Du. *doof* and Ger. *taub*, from an Indo-Eur. root shared by Gk. *tuphlos* 'blind.']

deaf-blind ▶ **adj.** having a severe impairment of both hearing and vision.

deaf·en /'defən/ ▶ **v.** [trans.] (usu. **be deafened**) cause (someone) to lose the power of hearing permanently or temporarily: *we were deafened by the explosion.* ■ (of a loud noise) overwhelm (someone) with sound. ■ (**deafen someone to**) (of a sound) cause someone to be unaware of (other sounds): *the noise deafened him to Ron's approach.*

deaf·en·ing /'defəniNG/ ▶ **adj.** (of a noise) so loud as to make it impossible to hear anything else. — **deaf·en·ing·ly adv.**

de·af·fer·en·ta·tion /dē,afəren'tāSHən/ ▶ **n.** Biol. the interruption or destruction of the afferent connections of nerve cells, performed esp. in animal experiments to demonstrate the spontaneity of locomotor movement. — **de·af·fer·ent·ed** /dē'afə,rentid/ **adj.**

deaf-mute ▶ **n.** a person who is both deaf and unable to speak. ▶ **adj.** (of a person) both deaf and unable to speak. ■ of or relating to such people.

deal[1] /dēl/ ▶ **v.** (past and past part. **dealt** /delt/) **1** [trans.] distribute (cards) in an orderly rotation to the players for a game or round: *the cards were dealt for the last hand* | [with two objs.] | fig. *fate dealt her a different hand.* ■ (**deal someone in**) include a new player in a card game by giving them cards. ■ distribute or mete out (something) to a person or group. **2** [intrans.] take part in commercial trading of a particular commodity: *directors were prohibited from **dealing in** the company's shares.* ■ fig. be concerned with: *a movie that **deals in** ideas and issues.* ■ informal buy and sell illegal drugs. **3** [intrans.] (**deal with**) take measures concerning (someone or something), esp. with the intention of putting something right: *unable to deal with the crisis.* ■ cope with (a difficult person or situation). ■ [with adverbial] treat (someone) in a particular way: *life had dealt harshly with her.* ■ have relations with (a person or organization), esp. in a commercial context: *the bank deals directly with the private sector.* ■ take or have as a subject; discuss. **4** [with two objs.] inflict (a blow) on (someone or something). ▶ **n. 1** an agreement entered into by two or more parties for their mutual benefit, esp. in a business or political context. ■ an attractive price on a commodity for a purchaser; a bargain. ■ [with adj.] a particular form of treatment given or received: *working mothers get a bad deal.* **2** a significant but unspecified amount of something: *he lost **a great deal of** blood.* **3** [in sing.] the process of distributing the cards to players in a card game. ■ a player's turn to distribute cards. ■ the round of play following this. ■ the set of hands dealt to the players.

– PHRASES **a big deal** informal [usu. with negative] a thing considered important: *they don't make a big deal out of minor irritations.* ■ an important person. ■ (**big deal**) used to express one's contempt for something regarded as impressive or important by another person. **a raw** (or **rough**) **deal** informal a situation in which someone receives unfair or harsh treatment. **cut a deal** informal make an agreement. **it's a deal** informal used to express one's assent to an agreement. [OE *dǣlan* 'divide,' 'participate,' of Gmc. origin; rel. to Du. *deel* and Ger. *Teil* 'part' (n.), also to DOLE.]

deal[2] ▶ **n.** fir or pine wood, esp. when sawn into planks of a standard size. ■ a plank of such wood. [ME: from Mid. Low Ger. and MDu. *dele* 'plank.']

deal·er /'dēlər/ ▶ **n. 1** a person or business that buys and sells goods: *a car dealer.* ■ a person who buys and sells shares, securities, or other financial assets as a principal (rather than as a broker or agent). See also BROKER-DEALER. ■ informal a person who buys and sells drugs. **2** the player who distributes the cards at the start of a game or hand. — **deal·er·ship n.** (in sense 1).

deal·fish /'dēl,fiSH/ ▶ **n.** (pl. same or **-fish·es**) a slender silvery fish (*Trachipterus arcticus*, family Trachipteridae) with a dorsal fin running the length of the body, living in the northeastern Atlantic. [19th C.: from DEAL[2].]

de·a·lign /,dēə'līn/ ▶ **v.** [intrans.] (of a voter) withdraw allegiance to a political party. — **de·a·lign·ment n.**

deal·ing /'dēliNG/ ▶ **n. 1** (usu. **dealings**) a business relation or transaction. ■ a personal connection or association with someone. ■ the activity of buying and selling a particular commodity: *car dealing.* **2** the particular way in which someone behaves toward others: *fair dealing came naturally to him.*

dealt /delt/ past participle of DEAL[1].

Dean /dēn/, John Wesley III (1938–), US political adviser. He was the chief witness in the Watergate hearings 1973–74 and was convicted of conspiracy. He wrote *Blind Ambition* (1976).

dean /dēn/ ▶ **n. 1** the head of a university faculty or department. ■ a college or university official, esp. one with disciplinary and advisory functions. ■ the leader or senior member of a group. **2** the head of the chapter of a cathedral or collegiate church. [ME: from OFr. *deien*, from late L. *decanus* 'chief of a group of ten,' from *decem* 'ten.' Cf. DOYEN.]

dean's list ▶ **n.** a list of students recognized for academic achievement during a semester by the dean of the college they attend.

dear /di(ə)r/ ▶ **adj. 1** regarded with deep affection; cherished by someone: *a dear friend* | *he is very dear to me.* ■ used in speech as a way of addressing a person in a polite way: *Martin, my dear fellow.* ■ used as part of the polite introduction to a letter. ■ endearing; sweet: *a dear little puppy.* **2** expensive. ■ (of money) available as a loan only at a high rate of interest. ▶ **n.** used as an affectionate or friendly form of address. ■ a sweet or endearing person. ▶ **adv.** at a high cost: *they buy property cheaply and sell dear.* ▶ **exclam.** used in expressions of surprise, dismay, or sympathy: *oh dear, I've upset you.*

– PHRASES **for dear life** see LIFE. — **dear·ness n.** [OE *dēore*, of Gmc. origin; rel. to Ger. *teuer* 'expensive.']

Dear·born /'di(ə)r,bôrn; -bərn/ a city in southeastern Michigan, southwest of Detroit; pop. 97,775.

dear·est /'di(ə)rist/ ▶ **adj. 1** most loved or cherished. **2** most expensive: *beer is dearest in Germany.* ▶ **n.** used as an affectionate form of address to a much-loved person. ■ a much-loved person.

Dear John let·ter (also **Dear John**) ▶ **n.** informal a letter from a woman to a man, esp. a serviceman, terminating a personal relationship.

dear·ly /'di(ə)rlē/ ▶ **adv. 1** very much. **2** with much loss or suffering; at great cost.

dearth /dərTH/ ▶ **n.** [in sing.] a scarcity or lack of something: *there is a dearth of evidence.* [ME *derthe* (see DEAR, -TH[2]).]

death /deTH/ ▶ **n.** the action or fact of dying or being killed; the end of the life of a person or organism. ■ an instance of a person or an animal dying. ■ the state of being dead: *even in death, she was beautiful.* ■ the permanent ending of vital processes in a cell or tissue. ■ (**Death**) [in sing.] the personification of the power that destroys life, often represented in art and literature as a skeleton or an old man holding a scythe. ■ [in sing.] fig. the destruction or permanent end of something: *the death of her hopes.* ■ fig., informal a damaging or destructive state of affairs.

– PHRASES **at death's door** (esp. in hyperbolic use) so ill that one might die. **be the death of** (often used hyperbolically or humorously) cause someone's death: *you'll be the death of me with all your questions.* **be in at the death** be present when a hunted animal is caught and killed. ■ be present when something fails or comes to an end. **catch one's death (of cold)** informal catch a severe cold or chill. **do someone to death** kill someone. **do something to death** perform or repeat something so frequently that it becomes tediously familiar. **a fate worse than death** a terrible experience, esp. that of seduction or rape. **like death warmed over** (or **up**) informal extremely tired or ill. **a matter of life and death** see LIFE. **put someone to death** kill someone, esp. with official sanction. **till** (or **until**) **death us do part** for as long as both persons in a couple live. **to death** used of a particular action or process that results in someone's death: *he was stabbed to death.* ■ used to emphasize the extreme nature of a specific action, feeling, or state of mind: *I'm sick to death of you.* **to the death** until dead: *a fight to the death.* — **death·like adj.** [OE *dēath*, of Gmc. origin; rel. to Du. *dood* and Ger. *Tod*, also to DIE[1].]

death·bed /'deTH,bed/ ▶ **n.** the bed where someone is dying or has died. ■ used in reference to the time when someone is dying: [as adj.] *a deathbed confession.*

death ben·e·fit ▶ **n.** the amount paid to a beneficiary upon the death of an insured person.

death blow ▶ **n.** an impact or stroke that causes death. ■ fig. an event, circumstance, or action that ends something abruptly: *it was Galileo Galilei who dealt the death blow to the geocentric theory.*

death camp ▶ **n.** a prison camp, esp. one for political prisoners or prisoners of war, in which many die from poor conditions or from mass execution.

death cer·tif·i·cate ▶ **n.** an official statement, signed by a physician, of the cause, date, and place of a person's death.

death-deal·ing ▶ **adj.** capable of causing death.

death in·stinct ▶ **n.** Psychoanal. an innate desire for self-annihilation, thought to be manifest in the conservative and regressive tendency of the psyche to reduce tension. Compare with LIFE INSTINCT.

death knell ▶ **n.** [in sing.] the tolling of a bell to mark someone's death. ■ fig. an event that heralds the end or destruction of something: *the death knell for the peace plan.*

death·less /'deTHlis/ ▶ **adj.** esp. literary or humorous immortal: *deathless beauty.* — **death·less·ness n.**

death·ly /'deTHlē/ ▶ **adj.** (**-li·er**, **-li·est**) resembling or suggestive of death.

death mask ▶ **n.** a plaster cast taken of a dead person's face, used to make a mask or model.

death pen·al·ty ▶ **n.** the punishment of execution, administered to someone convicted of a capital crime.

death rate ▶ **n.** the ratio of deaths to the population of a particular area during a particular period of time, usually calculated as the number of deaths per one thousand people per year.

death rat·tle ▶ **n.** a gurgling sound heard in a dying person's throat.

death row /'rō/ ▶ **n.** a prison block or section for prisoners sentenced to death.

death sen·tence ▶ **n.** Law a sentence to be put to death for a capital crime. ■ fig. a disastrous result or outcome.

death's head ▶ **n.** a human skull as a symbol of mortality.

death's-head hawk moth ▶ **n.** a large European hawk moth (*Acherontia atropos*, family Sphingidae) with a skull-like marking on the thorax and a very large caterpillar.

death squad ▶ **n.** an armed paramilitary group formed to kill particular people, esp. political opponents.

death tax ▶ **n.** another term for ESTATE TAX, INHERITANCE TAX.

death toll ▶ **n.** the number of deaths resulting from a particular cause, esp. an accident, battle, or natural disaster.

death trap ▶ **n.** a place, structure, or vehicle that is potentially dangerous: *the theaters were often death traps.*

Death Val·ley a deep arid desert basin below sea level in southeastern California and southwestern Nevada. It contains the lowest point in the US at Badwater, which is 282 feet (86 m) below sea level.

death war·rant ▶ n. an official order for the execution of a condemned person: fig. *in making his announcement he has signed his political death warrant.*

death·watch /'deTH,wäCH/ ▶ n. **1** a vigil kept beside a dead or dying individual. ■ a guard set over a person due for execution. **2** (also **deathwatch beetle**) a small beetle (*Xestobium rufovillosum*, family Anobiidae) with damaging, wood-burrowing larvae. The adult makes a ticking sound that was formerly believed to portend death.

death wish ▶ n. a desire for someone's death, esp. an unconscious desire for one's own death. Compare with DEATH INSTINCT.

deb /deb/ ▶ n. informal short for DEBUTANTE.

de·ba·cle /di'bakəl; -'bäkəl/ ▶ n. a sudden and ignominious failure; a fiasco. [19th C.: from Fr. *débâcle*, from *débâcler* 'unleash,' from *dé-* 'un-' + *bâcler* 'to bar' (from L. *baculum* 'staff').]

de·bal·last /dē'baləst/ ▶ v. [trans.] remove ballast from (a ship) in order to increase its buoyancy.

de·bar /dē'bär; di-/ ▶ v. (**-barred, -bar·ring**) [trans.] (usu. **be debarred**) exclude or prohibit (someone) officially from doing something. — **de·bar·ment** n. [ME: from Fr. *débarrer*, from OFr. *desbarrer* 'unbar,' from *des-* (expressing reversal) + *barrer* 'to bar.']

de·bark[1] /dē'bärk; di-/ ▶ v. [intrans.] leave a ship or aircraft. ■ [trans.] unload (cargo or troops) from a ship or aircraft. — **de·bar·ka·tion** /,dēbär'kāSHən/ n. [17th C.: from Fr. *débarquer*.]

de·bark[2] ▶ v. [trans.] remove (the bark) from a tree.

de·base /di'bās/ ▶ v. [trans.] reduce (something) in quality or value; degrade. ■ lower the moral character of (someone): *war debases people.* ■ hist. lower the value of (coinage) by reducing the content of precious metal. — **de·base·ment** n. **de·bas·er** n. [16th C.: from DE- 'down' + the obs. v. *base* (cf. ABASE) 'to lower.']

de·bat·a·ble /di'bātəbəl/ ▶ adj. open to discussion or argument. ■ hist. (of land) on the border between two countries and claimed by each. — **de·bat·a·bly** /-blē/ adv.

de·bate /di'bāt/ ▶ n. a formal discussion on a particular topic in a public meeting or legislative assembly, in which opposing arguments are put forward. ■ an argument about a particular subject, esp. one in which many people are involved: *the national debate on abortion | there has been much debate about prices.* ▶ v. [trans.] argue about (a subject), esp. in a formal manner. ■ [with clause] consider a possible course of action in one's mind before reaching a decision.
– PHRASES **be open to debate** be unproven; require further discussion. **under debate** being discussed or disputed. — **de·bat·er** n. [ME: via OFr. from L. *dis-* (expressing reversal) + *battere* 'to fight.']

de·bauch /di'bôCH/ ▶ v. [trans.] destroy or debase the moral purity of; corrupt. ■ dated seduce (a woman): *he debauched schoolgirls.* ▶ n. a bout of excessive indulgence in sensual pleasures, esp. eating and drinking. ■ the habit or practice of such indulgence; debauchery: *his life had been spent in debauch.* — **de·bauched** adj. **de·bauch·er** n. [16th C.: from Fr. *débaucher* (v.) 'turn away from one's duty,' from OFr. *desbaucher*.]

deb·au·chee /di,bô'CHē/ ▶ n. a person given to excessive indulgence in sensual pleasures.

de·bauch·er·y /di'bôCHərē/ ▶ n. excessive indulgence in sensual pleasures.

de Beau·voir /də bō'vwär; də 'bōvwär/, Simone (1908–86), French philosopher, writer, and feminist. She wrote *The Second Sex* (1949).

de·ben·ture /di'benCHər/ ▶ n. (also **debenture bond**) an unsecured loan certificate issued by a company, backed by general credit rather than by specified assets. [ME: from L. *debentur* 'are owing' (from *debere* 'owe').]

de·bil·i·tate /di'bili,tāt; dē-/ ▶ v. [trans.] [often as adj.] (**debilitating**) make (someone) weak and infirm: *a debilitating disease* | [as adj.] (**debilitated**) *a woman who felt chronically debilitated for years.* ■ hinder, delay, or weaken. — **de·bil·i·tat·ing·ly** adv. **de·bil·i·ta·tion** /di,bili'tāSHən/ n. **de·bil·i·ta·tive** /di'bili,tātiv/ adj. [16th C.: from L. *debilitat-* 'weakened,' from the v. *debilitare*, from *debilitas* (see DEBILITY).]

de·bil·i·ty /di'bilitē/ ▶ n. physical weakness, esp. as a result of illness. [ME: from OFr. *debilite*, from L. *debilitas*, from *debilis* 'weak.']

deb·it /'debit/ ▶ n. an entry recording an amount owed, listed on the left-hand side or column of an account. The opposite of CREDIT. ■ a payment made or owed. ▶ v. (**deb·it·ed, deb·it·ing**) [trans.] (usu. **be debited**) (of a bank or other financial organization) remove (an amount of money) from a customer's account, typically as payment for services or goods. ■ remove an amount of money from (a bank account).
– PHRASES **on the debit side** as an unsatisfactory aspect of the situation. [ME (in the sense 'debt'): from Fr. *débit*, from L. *debitum* 'something owed' (see DEBT).]

deb·it card ▶ n. a card issued by a bank allowing the holder to transfer money electronically to another bank account when making a purchase.

deb·o·nair /,debə'ne(ə)r/ ▶ adj. (of a man) confident, stylish, and charming. — **deb·o·nair·ly** adv. [ME: from OFr. *debonaire*, from *de bon aire* 'of good disposition.']

de·bone /dē'bōn/ ▶ v. remove the bones from (meat, poultry, or fish), esp. before cooking.

Deb·o·rah /'deb(ə)rə/ a biblical prophet. She inspired the Israelite army to defeat the Canaanites.

de·bouch /di'bouCH; -'bo͞oSH/ ▶ v. [no obj., with adverbial of direction] emerge from a narrow or confined space into a wide, open area: *the stream debouches into a silent pool.* — **de·bouch·ment** n. [18th C.: from Fr. *déboucher*, from *dé-* (expressing removal) + *bouche* 'mouth' (from L. *bucca* 'cheek').]

De·bre·cen /'debrət,sen/ an industrial and commercial city in eastern Hungary; pop. 217,290.

de·bride·ment /di'brēdmənt/ ▶ n. Med. the removal of damaged tissue or foreign objects from a wound. [19th C.: from Fr., from *débrider*, lit. 'unbridle,' based on *bride* 'bridle' (of Gmc. origin).]

de·brief /dē'brēf/ ▶ v. [trans.] question (someone, typically a soldier or spy) about a completed mission or undertaking. ▶ n. a series of questions about a completed mission or undertaking. — **de·brief·er** n.

de·bris /də'brē; dā-/ ▶ n. scattered fragments, typically of something wrecked or destroyed. ■ loose natural material consisting esp. of broken pieces of rock. ■ dirt or refuse. [18th C.: from Fr. *débris*, from obs. *débriser* 'break down.']

de Bro·glie /də 'brôyə; də 'brōi/, Louis-Victor, Prince (1892–1987), French physicist. He was the first to suggest that subatomic particles can also have the properties of waves. Nobel Prize for Physics (1929).

debt /det/ ▶ n. something, typically money, that is owed or due: *I paid off my debts.* ■ the state of owing money: *the firm is heavily in debt.* ■ [usu. in sing.] a feeling of gratitude for a service or favor: *a debt of thanks.*
– PHRASES **be in someone's debt** owe gratitude to someone for a service or favor. [ME *dette*: from OFr., based on L. *debitum* 'something owed,' past part. of *debere* 'owe.']

debt of hon·or ▶ n. a debt that is not legally recoverable, esp. one lost in gambling.

debt·or /'detər/ ▶ n. a person or institution that owes a sum of money.

debt se·cu·ri·ty ▶ n. a negotiable or tradable liability or loan.

de·bug /dē'bəg/ ▶ v. (**-bugged, -bug·ging**) [trans.] **1** identify and remove errors from (computer hardware or software). **2** detect and remove concealed microphones from (an area). **3** remove insects from (something), esp. with a pesticide. ▶ n. the process of identifying and removing errors from computer hardware or software.

de·bug·ger /dē'bəgər/ ▶ n. a computer program that assists in the detection and correction of errors in computer programs.

de·bunk /di'bəNGk/ ▶ v. [trans.] expose the falseness or hollowness of (a myth, idea, or belief). ■ reduce the inflated reputation of (someone), esp. by ridicule: *comedy takes delight in debunking heroes.* — **de·bunk·er** n. **de·bunk·er·y** n.

de·burr /dē'bər/ (also **de·bur**) ▶ v. (**-burred, -bur·ring**) [trans.] neaten and smooth the rough edges or ridges of (an object, typically one made of metal): *hand tools for deburring holes in metal.*

De·bus·sy /,debyo͞o'sē; ,dā-/, Claude (1862–1918), French composer; full name *Achille Claude Debussy.* His music characterizes the transition from romantic to modernist.

de·but /dā'byo͞o/ ▶ n. a person's first appearance or performance in a particular capacity or role. ■ the first public appearance of a new product or presentation of a theatrical show: *the car makes its world debut.* ■ [as adj.] denoting the first recording or publication of a group, singer, or writer: *a debut album.* ■ dated the first appearance of a debutante in society. ▶ v. [no obj., with adverbial] perform in public for the first time: *the Rolling Stones debuted at the Marquee.* ■ (of a new product) be launched. ■ [trans.] (of a company) launch (a new product). [18th C.: from Fr. *début*, from *débuter* 'lead off.']

deb·u·tante /'debyo͝o,tänt; 'debyə-/ ▶ n. an upper-class young woman making her first appearance in fashionable society. [19th C.: from Fr. *débutante* (fem.) 'leading off,' from the v. *débuter*.]

De·bye /də'bī/, Peter Joseph William (1884–1966), US physicist; born in the Netherlands. Nobel Prize for Chemistry (1936).

de·bye /di'bī/ (also **debye unit**) ▶ n. Chem. a unit used to express electric dipole moments of molecules. One debye is equal to 3.336 × 10–30 coulomb meter. [20th C.: named after P. J. DEBYE.]

Dec. ▶ abbr. December.

dec. ▶ abbr. deceased.

deca- (also **dec-** before a vowel) ▶ comb. form (used commonly in units of measurement) ten; having ten: *decahedron | decane.* [from Gk. *deka* 'ten.']

dec·ade /'dekād/ ▶ n. **1** a period of ten years. ■ a period of ten years beginning with a year ending in 0: *the fourth decade of the nineteenth century.* **2** a set, series, or group of ten, in particular: ■ /'dekid/ each of the five divisions of each chapter of the rosary. — **dec·a·dal** /'dekədl/ adj. [ME: via OFr. and late L. from Gk. *deka* 'ten.']

dec·a·dence /'dekədəns/ ▶ n. moral or cultural decline, esp. after a peak of achievement. ■ behavior reflecting such a decline. ■ luxurious self-indulgence. [16th C.: from Fr. *décadence*, from med. L. *decadentia*; rel. to DECAY.]

dec·a·dent /'dekədənt/ ▶ adj. characterized by or reflecting a state of moral or cultural decline. ■ luxuriously self-indulgent. ▶ n. a person who is luxuriously self-indulgent. ■ (often **Decadent**) a member of a

PRONUNCIATION KEY ə *ago, up*; ər *over, fur*; a *hat*; ā *ate*; ä *car*; e *let*; ē *see*; i *fit*; ī *by*; NG *sing*; ō *go*; ô *law, for*; oi *toy*; o͝o *good*; o͞o *goo*; ou *out*; TH *thin*; T͟H *then*; ZH *vision*

group of late 19th-cent. French and English poets associated with the Aesthetic Movement. — **dec·a·dent·ly** adv.

de·caf /ˈdēˌkaf/ ▶ n. informal decaffeinated coffee.

de·caf·fein·ate /dēˈkafəˌnāt/ ▶ v. [trans.] [usu. as adj.] (**decaffeinated**) remove most or all of the caffeine from (coffee or tea): *decaffeinated coffee.* — **de·caf·fein·a·tion** /dēˌkafəˈnāsʜən/ n.

dec·a·gon /ˈdekəˌgän/ ▶ n. a plane figure with ten straight sides and angles. — **de·cag·o·nal** /dəˈkagənl/ adj. [17th C.: via med. L. from Gk. *dekagōnon*, neut. (used as a n.) of *dekagōnos* 'ten-angled.']

dec·a·gram /ˈdekəˌgram/ (also **dek·a·gram**) ▶ n. a metric unit of mass or weight, equal to 10 grams.

dec·a·he·dron /ˌdekəˈhēdrən/ ▶ n. (pl. **-drons** or **-dra** /-drə/) a solid figure with ten plane faces. — **dec·a·he·dral** /-drəl/ adj.

de·cal /ˈdēˌkal/ ▶ n. a design prepared on special paper for transfer onto another surface. [1950s: abbrev. of DECALCOMANIA.]

de·cal·ci·fied /dēˈkalsəˌfīd/ ▶ adj. (of rock or bone) containing a reduced quantity of calcium salts. — **de·cal·ci·fi·ca·tion** /dēˌkalsəfiˈkāsʜən/ n. **de·cal·ci·fi·er** n.

de·cal·co·ma·ni·a /dēˌkalkəˈmānēə/ ▶ n. the process of transferring designs from prepared paper onto glass or porcelain. ■ a technique used by some surrealist artists that involves pressing paint between sheets of paper. [19th C.: from Fr. *décalcomanie*, from *décalquer* 'transfer a tracing' + *-manie* '-mania' (with ref. to the enthusiasm for the process in the 1860s).]

dec·a·li·ter /ˈdekəˌlētər/ (also **dek·a·li·ter**) (abbr.: **dal** or **dkl**) ▶ n. a metric unit of capacity, equal to 10 liters.

Dec·a·logue /ˈdekəˌlôg; -ˌläg/ ▶ n. (usu. **the Decalogue**) the Ten Commandments. [ME: via Fr. from Gk. *dekalogos*, from *hoi deka logoi*, lit. 'the ten sayings.']

De·cam·er·on /diˈkamərən; -ˌrän/ a work by Boccaccio, written between 1348 and 1358, containing a hundred tales supposedly told in ten days by ten people who had fled from the Black Death.

dec·a·me·ter /ˈdekəˌmētər/ (also **dek·a·me·ter**) (abbr.: **dam** or **dkm**) ▶ n. a metric unit of length, equal to 10 meters. — **dec·a·met·ric** /ˌdekəˈmetrik/ adj.

de·camp /diˈkamp/ ▶ v. [intrans.] depart suddenly, esp. to relocate one's business or household in another area: *now he has decamped to Hollywood.* ■ abscond hurriedly to avoid prosecution or detection. ■ archaic break up or leave a military camp. — **de·camp·ment** n. [17th C.: from Fr. *décamper*, from *dé-* (expressing removal) + *camp* 'camp.']

dec·an /ˈdekən/ ▶ n. Astrol. each of three equal ten-degree divisions of a sign of the zodiac. [16th C.: from late L. *decanus* 'chief of a group of ten' (see DEAN).]

dec·ane /ˈdekān/ ▶ n. Chem. a colorless liquid hydrocarbon, $C_{10}H_{22}$, of the alkane series, present in petroleum products such as kerosene.

de·cant /diˈkant/ ▶ v. [trans.] gradually pour (liquid, typically wine or a solution) from one container into another, esp. without disturbing the sediment. ■ fig. empty out; move as if by pouring. [17th C.: from med. L. *decanthare*, from L. *de-* 'away from' + *canthus* 'edge, rim,' from Gk. *kanthos* 'corner of the eye.']

de·cant·er /diˈkantər/ ▶ n. a stoppered glass container into which wine is decanted.

de·cap·i·tate /diˈkapiˌtāt/ ▶ v. [trans.] cut off the head of (a person or animal). ■ cut the end or top from (something). ■ fig. attempt to undermine (a group or organization) by removing its leaders. — **de·cap·i·ta·tion** /diˌkapiˈtāsʜən/ n. **de·cap·i·ta·tor** /-ˌtātər/ n. [17th C.: from late L. *decapitat-* 'decapitated,' from the v. *decapitare*, from *de-* + *caput, capit-* 'head.']

De·cap·o·da /diˈkapədə/ Zool. **1** an order of crustaceans that includes shrimps, crabs, and lobsters. They have five pairs of walking legs and are typically marine. **2** a former order of cephalopods that includes squids and cuttlefishes, having eight arms and two long tentacles. Compare with OCTOPODA. — **dec·a·pod** /ˈdekəˌpäd/ n. & adj. [mod. L. (pl.), from DECA- 'ten' + Gk. *pous, pod-* 'foot.']

de·cap·su·late /dēˈkapsŏŏˌlāt/ ▶ v. [trans.] Surg. remove the capsule or covering from (a kidney or other encapsulated organ). — **de·cap·su·la·tion** /dēˌkapsŏŏˈlāsʜən/ n.

de·car·bon·ize /dēˈkärbəˌnīz/ ▶ v. [trans.] remove carbon or carbonaceous deposits from (an engine or other metal object). — **de·car·bon·i·za·tion** /dēˌkärbənəˈzāsʜən/ n. **de·car·bon·iz·er** n.

de·car·bu·rize /dēˈkärb(y)əˌrīz/ ▶ v. [trans.] Metallurgy remove carbon from (iron or steel); decarbonize. — **de·car·bu·ri·za·tion** /dēˌkärb(y)ərəˈzāsʜən/ n.

dec·a·syl·lab·ic /ˌdekəsiˈlabik/ Pros. ▶ adj. (of a metrical line) consisting of ten syllables. ▶ n. a metrical line of ten syllables.

de·cath·lon /diˈkaтʜlän/ ▶ n. an athletic event in which each competitor takes part in the same prescribed ten events (100-meter dash, long jump, shot put, high jump, 400-meter dash, 110-meter hurdles, discus, pole vault, javelin, and 1,500-meter run). — **de·cath·lete** /-ˈkaтʜlēt/ n. [20th C.: from DECA- 'ten' + Gk. *athlon* 'contest.']

De·ca·tur[1] /diˈkātər/ **1** a city in northern Alabama, on the Tennessee River; pop. 53,929. **2** a city in central Illinois; pop. 81,860.

De·ca·tur[2], Stephen (1779–1820), US naval commander, noted for his heroism in the Barbary Wars and the War of 1812.

de·cay /diˈkā/ ▶ v. [intrans.] (of organic matter) rot or decompose through the action of bacteria and fungi. ■ [trans.] cause to rot or decompose: *the fungus will decay soft timber.* ■ (of a building or area) fall into disrepair; deteriorate. ■ decline in quality, power, or vigor. ■ Physics (of a radioactive substance, particle, etc.) undergo change to a different form by emitting radiation. ■ tech. (of a physical quantity) undergo a gradual decrease: *the time taken for the current to decay to zero.* ▶ n. the state or process of rotting or decomposition. ■ structural or physical deterioration: *the old barn fell into decay.* ■ rotten matter or tissue. ■ the process of declining in quality, power, or vigor. ■ Physics the change of a radioactive substance, particle, etc., into another by the emission of radiation. ■ tech. gradual decrease in the magnitude of a physical quantity. [ME: from OFr. *decair*, based on L. *decidere* 'fall down or off,' from *de-* 'from' + *cadere* 'fall.']

Dec·can /ˈdekən; -an/ a plateau in southern India, bounded by the Malabar Coast, the Coromandel Coast, and the Vindhaya mountains.

de·cease /diˈsēs/ ▶ n. [in sing.] formal or Law death. [ME: from OFr. *deces*, from L. *decessus* 'death,' past part. (used as a n.) of *decedere* 'to die.']

de·ceased /diˈsēst/ formal Law ▶ n. (**the deceased**) a person who has died: *in memory of the deceased.* ▶ adj. dead; no longer living.

de·ce·dent /diˈsēdnt/ ▶ n. Law a person who has died. [16th C.: from L. *decedent-* 'dying,' from the v. *decedere* (see DECEASE).]

de·ceit /diˈsēt/ ▶ n. the action or practice of deceiving someone by concealing or misrepresenting the truth. ■ a dishonest act or statement. ■ deceitful disposition or character. [ME: from OFr., past part. (used as a n.) of *deceveir* 'deceive.']

de·ceit·ful /diˈsētfəl/ ▶ adj. (of a person) deceiving or misleading others, typically on a habitual basis. ■ intended to deceive or mislead. — **de·ceit·ful·ly** adv. **de·ceit·ful·ness** n.

de·ceive /diˈsēv/ ▶ v. [trans.] (of a person) cause (someone) to believe something that is not true, typically in order to gain some personal advantage. ■ (often **be deceived**) (of a thing) give a mistaken impression: *the area may seem to offer nothing of interest, but don't be deceived* | [intrans.] *everything about him was intended to deceive.* ■ (**deceive oneself**) fail to admit to oneself that something is true. ■ be sexually unfaithful to (one's regular partner). — **de·ceiv·a·ble** adj. **de·ceiv·er** n. [ME: from OFr. *deceivre*, from L. *decipere* 'catch, ensnare, cheat.']

de·cel·er·ate /dēˈseləˌrāt/ ▶ v. [intrans.] (of a vehicle, machine, or process) reduce speed; slow down. ■ [trans.] cause to move more slowly. — **de·cel·er·a·tion** /-ˌseləˈrāsʜən/ n. **de·cel·er·a·tor** /-ˌrātər/ n. **de·cel·er·om·e·ter** /-ˌseləˈrämitər/ n. [19th C.: from DE- (expressing removal) + a shortened form of ACCELERATE.]

De·cem·ber /diˈsembər/ ▶ n. the twelfth month of the year. [ME: from L., from *decem* 'ten' (being orig. the tenth month of the Roman year).]

De·cem·brist /diˈsembrist/ ▶ n. a member of a group of Russian revolutionaries who in December 1825 led an unsuccessful revolt against Czar Nicholas I.

de·cen·cy /ˈdēsənsē/ ▶ n. (pl. **-cies**) behavior that conforms to accepted standards of morality or respectability: *she had the decency to come and confess.* ■ modesty and propriety: *too low-cut for decency.* ■ (**decencies**) the requirements of accepted or respectable behavior. ■ (**decencies**) things required for a reasonable standard of life.

de·cen·ni·al /diˈsenēəl/ ▶ adj. recurring every ten years. ■ lasting for or relating to a period of ten years. — **de·cen·ni·al·ly** adv. [17th C.: from L. *decennium* 'a decade,' from *decennis* 'of ten years' (from *decem* 'ten' + *annus* 'year'), + -AL.]

de·cen·ni·um /diˈsenēəm/ ▶ n. (pl. **-cen·ni·a** /-ˈsenēə/ or **-cen·ni·ums**) a decade. [17th C.: from L., from *decem* 'ten' + *annus* 'year.']

de·cent /ˈdēsənt/ ▶ adj. **1** conforming with generally accepted standards of respectable or moral behavior. ■ appropriate; fitting: *they would meet again after a decent interval.* ■ not likely to shock or embarrass others: *a decent high-necked dress.* ■ informal sufficiently clothed to see visitors: *make yourself decent.* **2** [attrib.] of an acceptable standard; satisfactory: *a decent cup of coffee.* ■ good. ■ kind, obliging, or generous.

– PHRASES **do the decent thing** take the most honorable or appropriate course of action, even if is not necessarily in one's own interests. — **de·cent·ly** adv. [16th C.: from L. *decent-* 'being fitting,' from the v. *decere.*]

de·cen·ter /dēˈsentər/ (Brit. **de·cen·tre**) ▶ v. [trans.] displace from the center or from a central position. ■ remove or displace (the individual human subject, such as the author of a text) from a primary place or central role: [as n.] (**decentering**) *the egocentric infant develops by a progressive decentering.*

de·cen·tral·ize /dēˈsentrəˌlīz/ ▶ v. [trans.] [often as adj.] (**decentralized**) transfer (authority) from central to local government. ■ move departments of (a large organization) away from a single administrative center to other locations, usually granting them some degree of autonomy. — **de·cen·tral·ist** n. & adj. **de·cen·tral·i·za·tion** /dēˌsentrəliˈzāsʜən/ n.

de·cep·tion /diˈsepsʜən/ ▶ n. the action of deceiving someone. ■ a thing that deceives. [ME: from late L. *deceptio(n-)*, from *decipere* 'deceive.']

de·cep·tive /diˈseptiv/ ▶ adj. giving an appearance or impression different from the true one; misleading. — **de·cep·tive·ness** n.

de·cep·tive·ly /diˈseptivlē/ ▶ adv. [usu. as submodifier] in a way or to an extent that gives a misleading impression. ■ to a lesser extent than appears the case: *the idea was deceptively simple.* ■ to a greater extent than appears the case: *the deceptively spacious lounge.*

de·cer·ti·fy /dēˈsərtəˌfī/ ▶ v. (**-fies, -fied**) [trans.] remove a certificate or certification from (someone or something), typically for failure to comply with a regulating authority's rules or standards. — **de·cer·ti·fi·ca·tion** /-ˌsərtəfiˈkāsʜən/ n.

de·chris·tian·i·za·tion /dēˌkrisCʜənəˈzāsʜən/ ▶ n. the action or process or removing Christian influences or characteristics from something. —**de·chris·tian·ize** /-ˈkrischəˌnīz/ v.

deci- ▶ comb. form (used commonly in units of measurement) one tenth: *deciliter.* [from L. *decimus* 'tenth.']

dec·i·bel /ˈdesəˌbel; -bəl/ (abbr.: **dB**) ▶ n. a unit used to measure the intensity of a sound or the power level of an electrical signal by comparing it with a given level on a logarithmic scale. ■ (in general use) a degree of loudness: *his voice went up several decibels.* [20th C.: from DECI- 'ten' + BEL.]

de·cide /diˈsīd/ ▶ v. [intrans.] come to a resolution in the mind as a result of consideration. ■ [trans.] cause to come to such a resolution: *this business about the letter decided me.* ■ make a choice from a number of alternatives: *she had decided on her plan of action* | *I've decided against having children.* ■ give a judgment concerning a matter or legal case. ■ [trans.] come to a decision about (something). ■ [trans.] resolve or settle (a question or contest). —**de·cid·a·ble** adj. **de·cid·er** n. [ME: from Fr. *décider,* from L. *decidere* 'determine,' from *de-* 'off' + *caedere* 'cut.']

de·cid·ed /diˈsīdid/ ▶ adj. [attrib.] (of a quality) definite; unquestionable: *a decided improvement.* ■ (of a person) having clear opinions; resolute. ■ [attrib.] (of a legal case) that has been resolved. —**de·cid·ed·ness** n.

de·cid·ed·ly /diˈsīdidlē/ ▶ adv. **1** [usu. as submodifier] undoubtedly; undeniably: *he looked decidedly sad.* **2** in a decisive and confident way. —**de·cid·ed·ness** /-didnis/ n.

de·cid·u·ous /diˈsijo͞oəs/ ▶ adj. (of a tree or shrub) shedding its leaves annually. Often contrasted with EVERGREEN. ■ denoting the milk teeth of a mammal, which are shed after a time. —**de·cid·u·ous·ly** adv. **de·cid·u·ous·ness** n. [17th C.: from L. *deciduus* (from *decidere* 'fall down or off') + -OUS.]

dec·ile /ˈdesīl; -əl/ ▶ n. Stat. each of ten equal groups into which a population can be divided according to the distribution of values of a particular variable: *the lowest income decile of the population.* ■ each of the nine values of the random variable that divide a population into ten such groups. [17th C.: from Fr. *décile,* from a med. L. deriv. of L. *decem* 'ten.']

dec·i·li·ter /ˈdesəˌlētər/ (Brit. **dec·i·li·tre**) (abbr.: **dl**) ▶ n. a metric unit of capacity, equal to one tenth of a liter.

dec·i·mal /ˈdesəməl/ ▶ adj. relating to or denoting a system of numbers and arithmetic based on the number ten, tenth parts, and powers of ten. ▶ n. (also **decimal fraction**) a fraction whose denominator is a power of ten and whose numerator is expressed by figures placed to the right of a decimal point. ■ the system of decimal numerical notation. —**dec·i·mal·ly** adv. [17th C.: from mod. L. *decimalis* (adj.), from L. *decimus* 'tenth.']

dec·i·mal·ize /ˈdesəməˌlīz/ ▶ v. [trans.] convert (a system of coinage or weights and measures) to a decimal system. —**dec·i·mal·i·za·tion** /ˌdesəmələˈzāshən/ n.

dec·i·mal place ▶ n. the position of a digit to the right of a decimal point.

dec·i·mal point ▶ n. a dot placed after the figure representing units in a decimal fraction.

dec·i·mate /ˈdesəˌmāt/ ▶ v. [trans.] (often **be decimated**) **1** kill, destroy, or remove a large percentage of. ■ drastically reduce the strength or effectiveness of (something): *plant viruses that can decimate yields.* **2** hist. kill one in every ten of (a group of soldiers or others) as a punishment for the whole group. —**dec·i·ma·tion** /ˌdesəˈmāshən/ n. **dec·i·ma·tor** /-ˌmātər/ n. [ME: from L. *decimat-* 'taken as a tenth,' from the v. *decimare,* from *decimus* 'tenth.']

dec·i·me·ter /ˈdesəˌmētər/ (Brit. **dec·i·me·tre**) (abbr.: **dm**) ▶ n. a metric unit of length, equal to one tenth of a meter. —**dec·i·met·ric** /ˌdesəˈmetrik/ adj.

de·ci·pher /diˈsīfər/ ▶ v. [trans.] convert (a text written in code, or a coded signal) into normal language. ■ succeed in understanding, interpreting, or identifying (something). —**de·ci·pher·a·ble** adj. **de·ci·pher·ment** n.

de·ci·sion /diˈsizhən/ ▶ n. a conclusion or resolution reached after consideration. ■ the action or process of deciding something or of resolving a question. ■ a formal judgment. ■ the ability or tendency to make decisions quickly; decisiveness. ■ Boxing the awarding of a fight, in the absence of a knockout, to the boxer with the most points. ■ Baseball a win or a loss assigned to a pitcher. [ME: from L. *decisio(n-),* from *decidere* 'determine' (see DECIDE).]

de·ci·sion sup·port sys·tem (abbr.: **DSS**) ▶ n. Comput. a set of related computer programs and the data required to assist with analysis and decision-making within an organization.

de·ci·sion the·o·ry ▶ n. the mathematical study of strategies for optimal decision-making between options involving different risks or expectations of gain or loss depending on the outcome. Compare with GAME THEORY.

de·ci·sive /diˈsīsiv/ ▶ adj. settling an issue; producing a definite result. ■ (of a person) having or showing the ability to make decisions quickly and effectively. —**de·ci·sive·ly** adv. **de·ci·sive·ness** n.

De·cius /ˈdēsh(ē)əs/, Gaius Messius Quintus Trajanus (*c.*201–251), Roman emperor 249–251. He promoted systematic persecution of the Christians.

deck /dek/ ▶ n. **1** a structure of planks or plates, approximately horizontal, extending across a ship or boat at any of various levels, esp. one of those at the highest level and open to the weather. ■ the accommodations on a particular deck of a ship: *the first-class deck.* ■ a floor or platform resembling or compared to a ship's deck, esp. the floor of a pier or a platform for sunbathing. ■ a platformlike structure, typically made of lumber and unroofed, attached to a house or other building. ■ a level of a large, open building, esp. a sports stadium. ■ (**the deck**) informal the ground or floor: *there was a thud when I hit the deck.* ■ the flat part of a skateboard or snowboard. **2** a component or unit in sound-reproduction equipment that incorporates a playing or recording mechanism for discs or tapes. **3** a pack of cards. ▶ v. [trans.] **1** (usu. **be decked**) decorate or adorn brightly or festively: *Ingrid was decked out in her Sunday best.* **2** informal knock (someone) to the ground with a punch.
– PHRASES **below decks** see BELOW DECKS. **clear the decks** see DECK. **not playing with a full deck** informal mentally deficient. **on deck** on or onto a ship's main deck. ■ fig. ready for action or work. ■ Baseball next to hit in the batting order. —**decked** adj. [in comb.] *a three-decked vessel.* [ME: from MDu. *dec* 'covering, roof, cloak,' *dekken* 'to cover.']

deck chair ▶ n. a folding chair of wood and canvas, typically used on the deck of passenger ships.

-decker ▶ comb. form having a specified number of decks or layers: *double-decker.*

deck·hand /ˈdekˌhand/ ▶ n. a member of a ship's crew whose duties include maintenance of hull, decks, and superstructure, mooring, and cargo handling.

deck·ing /ˈdeking/ ▶ n. **1** the material of the deck of a ship, a floor, or a platform. **2** the action of ornamenting something.

deck·le /ˈdekəl/ ▶ n. (also **deckle strap**) a device in a papermaking machine for limiting the size of the sheet, consisting of a continuous belt on either side of the wire. [18th C.: from Ger. *Deckel,* dimin. of *Decke* 'covering.']

deck·le edge ▶ n. the rough uncut edge of a sheet of paper, formed by a deckle. —**deck·le-edged** adj.

deck of·fi·cer ▶ n. an officer in charge of the above-deck workings and maneuvers at sea of a ship or boat.

deck shoe another term for BOAT SHOE.

de·claim /diˈklām/ ▶ v. [reporting verb] utter or deliver words or a speech in a rhetorical or impassioned way, as if to an audience. ■ [intrans.] (**declaim against**) forcefully protest against or criticize (something). —**de·claim·er** n. **de·clam·a·to·ry** /-ˈklaməˌtôrē/ adj. [ME: from Fr. *déclamer* or L. *declamare,* from *de-* (expressing thoroughness) + *clamare* 'to shout.']

dec·la·ma·tion /ˌdekləˈmāshən/ ▶ n. the action or art of declaiming. [ME: from L. *declamatio(n-),* from *declamare.*]

de·clar·ant /diˈkle(ə)rənt/ esp. Law ▶ n. **1** a person or party who makes a formal declaration. ■ an alien who has signed a declaration of intent to become a US citizen. **2** a person who makes a statement, even an informal one. ▶ adj. making or having made a formal declaration.

dec·la·ra·tion /ˌdekləˈrāshən/ ▶ n. a formal or explicit statement or announcement. ■ the formal announcement of the beginning of a state or condition. ■ a listing of goods, property, income, etc., subject to duty or tax. ■ a statement asserting or protecting a legal right. ■ a written public announcement of intentions or of the terms of an agreement. ■ Law a plaintiff's statement of claims in proceedings. ■ Law an affirmation made instead of taking an oath. ■ the naming of trump in a card game.

Dec·la·ra·tion of In·de·pen·dence a document declaring the US to be independent of the British Crown, signed on July 4, 1776, by the congressional representatives of the Thirteen Colonies.

de·clar·a·tive /diˈkle(ə)rətiv; -ˈklar-/ ▶ adj. **1** of the nature of or making a declaration: *declarative statements.* ■ Gram. (of a sentence or phrase) taking the form of a simple statement. **2** Comput. denoting high-level programming languages that can be used to solve problems without an exact procedure being specified. ▶ n. a statement in the form of a declaration. ■ Gram. a declarative sentence or phrase. —**de·clar·a·tive·ly** adv.

de·clare /diˈkle(ə)r/ ▶ v. **1** [reporting verb] say something in a solemn and emphatic manner. ■ [trans.] formally announce the beginning of (a state or condition): *Spain declared war on Britain in 1796.* ■ [with obj. and complement] pronounce or assert (a person or thing) to be something specified: *the mansion was declared a fire hazard.* ■ [intrans.] (**declare for/against**) openly align oneself for or against (a party or position) in a dispute. ■ [intrans.] announce oneself as a candidate for an election: *he declared last April.* ■ (**declare oneself**) reveal one's intentions or identity. **2** [trans.] acknowledge possession of (taxable income or dutiable goods). **3** [trans.] announce that one holds (certain combinations of cards) in a card game.
– PHRASES **well, I declare** (or **I do declare**) an exclamation of incredulity, surprise, or vexation. —**de·clar·a·ble** adj. **de·clar·a·to·ry** /-ˈkle(ə)rəˌtôrē/ adj. **de·clar·ed·ly** /-ˈkle(ə)ridlē/ adv. [ME: from L. *declarare,* from *de-* 'thoroughly' + *clarare* 'make clear' (from *clarus* 'clear').]

de·clar·er /diˈkle(ə)rər/ ▶ n. Bridge the player whose bid establishes the suit of the contract and who must therefore play both their own hand and the exposed hand of the dummy.

dé·clas·sé /ˌdākläˈsā/ (also **dé·clas·sée**) ▶ adj. having fallen in social status: *his parents were poor and déclassé.* [19th C.: Fr., 'removed from one's class, degraded,' past participle of *déclasser*.]

de·clas·si·fy /dē'klasə,fī/ ▶ **v.** (**-fies, -fied**) [trans.] (often **be declassified**) officially declare (information or documents) to be no longer secret. — **de·clas·si·fi·ca·tion** /dē,klasəfi'kāshən/ **n.**

de·claw /dē'klô/ ▶ **v.** [trans.] remove the claws from.

de·clen·sion /di'klenshən/ ▶ **n.** (in the grammar of Latin, Greek, and other languages) the variation of the form of a noun, pronoun, or adjective, by which its grammatical case, number, and gender are identified. ■ the class to which a noun or adjective is assigned according to the manner of this variation. — **de·clen·sion·al** /-shənl/ **adj.** [ME *declinson*, from OFr. *declinaison*, from *decliner* 'to decline.']

dec·li·na·tion /,deklə'nāshən/ ▶ **n. 1** Astron. the angular distance of a point north or south of the celestial equator. Compare with RIGHT ASCENSION and CELESTIAL LATITUDE. ■ the angular deviation of a compass needle from true north (because the magnetic north pole and the geographic north pole do not coincide). **2** formal refusal. — **dec·li·na·tion·al** /-shənl/ **adj.** [ME: from L. *declinatio(n-)*, from the v. *declinare* (see DECLINE).]

dec·li·na·tion ax·is ▶ **n.** Astron. the axis of an equatorially mounted telescope that is at right angles to the polar axis, about which the telescope is turned in order to view points at different declinations but at a constant right ascension.

de·cline /di'klīn/ ▶ **v. 1** [intrans.] become smaller, fewer, or less; decrease: *the birth rate continued to decline.* ■ diminish in strength or quality; deteriorate. **2** [trans.] politely refuse (an invitation or offer). ■ [with infin.] politely refuse to do something. **3** [intrans.] (esp. of the sun) move downward. **4** [trans.] (in the grammar of Latin, Greek, and certain other languages) state the forms of (a noun, pronoun, or adjective) corresponding to cases, number, and gender. ▶ **n.** [in sing.] a gradual and continuous loss of strength, numbers, or quality. ■ a fall in value or price: *able to halt the stock's decline.* — **de·clin·a·ble adj. de·clin·er n.** [ME: from OFr. *decliner*, from L. *declinare* 'bend down, turn aside,' from *de-* 'down' + *clinare* 'to bend.']

de·clin·ing years ▶ **plural n.** a person's old age, esp. when regarded as the time when health, vigor, and mental faculties deteriorate. ■ fig. the period leading up to the demise of something, often characterized by a loss of effectiveness.

de·cliv·i·ty /di'klivitē/ ▶ **n.** (pl. **-ties**) a downward slope. — **de·cliv·i·tous** /-təs/ **adj.** [17th C.: from L. *declivitas*, from *declivis* 'sloping down,' from *de-* 'down' + *clivus* 'a slope.']

dec·o /'dekō/ ▶ **n. 1** short for ART DECO. **2** (in scuba diving) short for DECOMPRESSION.

de·coc·tion /di'käkshən/ ▶ **n.** the liquor resulting from concentrating the essence of a substance by heating or boiling, esp. a medicinal preparation made from a plant: *a decoction of a root.* ■ the action or process of extracting the essence of something. [ME: from late L. *decoctio(n-)*, from *decoquere* 'boil down,' from *de-* + *coquere* 'cook.']

de·code /di'kōd/ ▶ **v.** [trans.] convert (a coded message) into intelligible language. ■ analyze and interpret (a verbal or nonverbal communication or image): *a handbook to help parents decode street language.* ■ convert (audio or video signals) into another form, e.g., to analog from digital in sound reproduction. ▶ **n.** informal a translation of a coded message. — **de·cod·a·ble adj.**

de·cod·er /di'kōdər/ ▶ **n.** a person or thing that analyzes and interprets something.

de·col·late /'dekə,lāt; 'dēkə-/ ▶ **v.** [intrans.] separate sheets of paper, such as multi-ply computer paper, into different piles. — **de·col·la·tion** /,dekə'lāshən; ,dēkə-/ **n. de·col·la·tor** /-,lātər/ **n.**

dé·colle·tage /dā,käl(ə)'täzh ,dekələ-/ ▶ **n.** a low neckline on a woman's dress or top. [19th C.: Fr., from *décolleter* 'expose the neck,' from *dé-* (expressing removal) + *collet* 'collar of a dress.']

dé·colle·té /dā,käl(ə)'tā ,dekələ-/ ▶ **adj.** (also **dé·colle·tée**) (of a woman's dress or top) having a low neckline. ▶ **n.** a low neckline on a woman's dress or top. [19th C.: Fr., past part. of *décolleter* 'expose the neck.']

de·col·o·nize /dē'kälə,nīz/ ▶ **v.** [trans.] (of a country) withdraw from (a colony), leaving it independent. — **de·col·o·ni·za·tion** /-,kälənə'zāshən/ **n.**

de·col·or·ize /dē'kələ,rīz/ ▶ **v.** [trans.] remove the color from: *ethane decolorizes bromine water.* — **de·col·or·i·za·tion** /-,kələrə'zāshən/ **n.**

de·com·mis·sion /,dēkə'mishən/ ▶ **v.** [trans.] withdraw (someone or something) from service, in particular: ■ make (a nuclear reactor or weapon) inoperative, and dismantle and decontaminate it to make it safe. ■ take (a ship) out of service.

de·com·pen·sa·tion /dē,kämpən'sāshən/ ▶ **n.** Med. the failure of an organ (esp. the liver or heart) to compensate for the functional overload resulting from disease. ■ Psychiatry the failure to generate effective psychological coping mechanisms in response to stress. — **de·com·pen·sat·ed** /-'kämpən,sātid/ **adj.**

de·com·pose /,dēkəm'pōz/ ▶ **v.** [intrans.] (of a dead body or other organic matter) decay; become rotten. ■ [trans.] cause (something) to decay or rot. ■ (of a chemical compound) break down into component elements or simpler constituents. ■ [trans.] break down (a chemical compound) into its component elements or simpler constituents. — **de·com·pos·a·ble adj. de·com·po·si·tion** /dē,kämpə'zishən/ **n.** [18th C.: from Fr. *décomposer*, from *de-* (expressing reversal) + *composer*.]

de·com·pos·er /,dēkəm'pōzər/ ▶ **n.** an organism, esp. a soil bacterium, fungus, or invertebrate, that decomposes organic material. ■ a device or installation that is used to break down a chemical substance.

de·com·press /,dēkəm'pres/ ▶ **v.** [trans.] relieve of compressing forces, in particular: ■ expand (compressed computer data) to its normal size so that it can be read and processed by a computer. ■ subject (a diver) to decompression. ■ [intrans.] informal calm down and relax.

de·com·pres·sion /,dēkəm'preshən/ ▶ **n.** a release of compressing forces, in particular: ■ reduction in air pressure: *decompression of the aircraft cabin.* ■ a gradual reduction of air pressure on a person who has been experiencing high pressure while diving in order to prevent decompression sickness. ■ the process of expanding computer data to its normal size so that it can be read by a computer. ■ a surgical procedure that relieves excessive pressure on an internal part of the body such as the cranium or spinal cord.

de·com·pres·sion sick·ness ▶ **n.** a condition that results when sudden decompression causes nitrogen bubbles to form in the tissues of the body. It is suffered particularly by divers (who often call it **the bends**). Also called CAISSON DISEASE.

de·com·pres·sor /,dēkəm'presər/ ▶ **n.** an instrument or device for decompressing something. ■ a computer program that decompresses data by digitally expanding it to its original size and form.

de·con·di·tion /,dēkən'dishən/ ▶ **v.** [trans.] **1** [usu. as adj.] (**deconditioned**) cause to lose fitness or muscle tone, esp. through lack of exercise. **2** [usu. as n.] (**deconditioning**) Psychiatry reform or reverse (previously conditioned behavior), esp. in the treatment of phobia and other anxiety disorders in which the fear response to certain stimuli is brought under control. Compare with COUNTERCONDITIONING. ■ informal persuade (someone) to abandon a habitual mode of thinking.

de·con·gest /,dēkən'jest/ ▶ **v.** [trans.] relieve the congestion of (something). — **de·con·ges·tion** /-'jeschən/ **n.**

de·con·ges·tant /,dēkən'jestənt/ ▶ **adj.** (chiefly of a medicine) used to relieve nasal congestion. ▶ **n.** a decongestant medicine.

de·con·se·crate /dē'känsi,krāt/ ▶ **v.** [trans.] (usu. **be deconsecrated**) transfer (a building) from sacred to secular use. — **de·con·se·cra·tion** /-,känsi'krāshən/ **n.**

de·con·struct /,dēkən'strəkt/ ▶ **v.** [trans.] analyze (a text or a linguistic or conceptual system) by deconstruction, typically in order to expose its hidden internal assumptions and contradictions and subvert its apparent significance or unity. ■ (in general use) dismantle. — **de·con·struc·tive adj.** [19th C.: back-form. from DECONSTRUCTION.]

de·con·struc·tion /,dēkən'strəkshən/ ▶ **n.** a method of critical analysis of philosophical and literary language that emphasizes the internal workings of language and conceptual systems, the relational quality of meaning, and the assumptions implicit in forms of expression. — **de·con·struc·tion·ism n. de·con·struc·tion·ist adj. & n.** [19th C. (orig. in the general sense 'taking to pieces'): from DE- (expressing reversal) + CONSTRUCTION.]

de·con·tam·i·nate /,dēkən'tamə,nāt/ ▶ **v.** [trans.] neutralize or remove dangerous substances, radioactivity, or germs from (an area, object, or person). — **de·con·tam·i·na·tion** /-,tamə'nāshən/ **n.**

de·con·tex·tu·al·ized /,dēkən'tekschōōə,līzd/ ▶ **adj.** considered in isolation from its context. — **de·con·tex·tu·al·i·za·tion** /-,tekschōōələ'zāshən/ **n. de·con·tex·tu·al·ize v.**

de·con·trol /,dēkən'trōl/ ▶ **v.** (**-trolled, -trol·ling**) [trans.] release (a commodity, market, etc.) from controls or restrictions. ▶ **n.** the action of decontrolling something.

de·con·vo·lu·tion /dē,känvə'lōōshən/ ▶ **n.** a process of resolving something into its constituent elements or removing complication in order to clarify it.

de·cor /dā'kôr; di-/ ▶ **n.** the furnishing and decoration of a room. ■ the decoration and scenery of a stage. [19th C.: from Fr. *décor*, from the v. *décorer*, from L. *decorare* 'embellish' (see DECORATE).]

dec·o·rate /'dekə,rāt/ ▶ **v.** [trans.] **1** make (something) look more attractive by adding ornament to it. ■ provide (a room or building) with a color scheme, paint, wallpaper, etc. **2** confer an award or medal on (a member of the armed forces): *he was decorated for outstanding bravery.* [16th C. (in the sense 'to grace or honor'): from L. *decoratus* 'embellished' (past part. of *decorare*), from *decus, decor-* 'beauty, honor, or embellishment.']

dec·o·ra·tion /,dekə'rāshən/ ▶ **n. 1** the process or art of decorating or adorning something. ■ ornamentation. ■ a thing that serves as an ornament. ■ the application of paint or wallpaper in a room or building. ■ the paint or wallpaper applied. **2** a medal or award conferred as an honor.

Dec·o·ra·tion Day ▶ **n.** another term for MEMORIAL DAY.

dec·o·ra·tive /'dek(ə)rətiv; 'dekə,rātiv/ ▶ **adj.** serving to make something look more attractive; ornamental. ■ relating to decoration: *a decorative artist.* — **dec·o·ra·tive·ly adv. dec·o·ra·tive·ness n.**

dec·o·ra·tive arts ▶ **plural n.** the arts concerned with the production of high-quality objects that are both useful and beautiful.

dec·o·ra·tor /'dekə,rātər/ ▶ **n.** a person who decorates, in particular: ■ a person whose job is to design the interior of someone's home, by choosing colors, carpets, materials, and furnishings.

dec·o·rous /'dekərəs; di'kôrəs/ ▶ **adj.** in keeping with good taste and propriety; polite and restrained. — **dec·o·rous·ly adv. dec·o·rous·ness n.** [17th C. (in the sense 'appropriate, seemly'): from L. *decorus* 'seemly' + -OUS.]

de·cor·ti·cate /dē'kôrti,kāt/ ▶ **v.** [trans.] **1** [often as adj.] (**decorticated**) tech. remove the bark, rind, or husk from: *decorticated peanuts.* **2** subject to surgical decortication. ▶ **adj.** Biol. & Psychol. of or relating to an animal that has had the cortex of the brain removed or separated. [17th C.:

from L. *decorticat-* 'stripped of its bark,' from the v. *decorticare*, from *de-* (expressing removal) + *cortex, cortic-* 'bark.']

de·cor·ti·ca·tion /dē,kôrti'kāsHən/ ▶ n. the removal of the outer layer or cortex from a structure, esp. the lung, brain, or other organ. ■ Med. the operation of removing fibrous scar tissue that prevents expansion of the lung.

de·co·rum /di'kôrəm/ ▶ n. behavior in keeping with good taste and propriety. ■ etiquette. [16th C.: from L., neut. of *decorus* 'seemly.']

de·cou·page /,dākōō'päzH/ ▶ n. the decoration of the surface of an object with paper cut-outs. [1960s: Fr., from *découper* 'cut out.']

de·cou·ple /dē'kəpəl/ ▶ v. [trans.] separate, disengage, or dissociate (something) from something else: *the mountings effectively* ***decouple*** *movements of the engine* ***from*** *those of the wheels.* ■ make the interaction between (electrical components) so weak that there is little transfer of energy between them, esp. to remove unwanted AC distortion or oscillations in circuits with a common power supply. ■ muffle the sound or shock of (a nuclear explosion) by causing it to take place in an underground cavity.

de·coy ▶ n. /'dē,koi/ **1** a bird or mammal, or an imitation of one, used by hunters to attract other birds or mammals: [as adj.] *a decoy duck.* ■ a person or thing used to lure an animal or person into a trap. ■ a fake or nonworking article, esp. a weapon, used to mislead or misdirect. **2** a pond from which narrow netted channels lead, into which wild ducks may be enticed for capture. ▶ v. /di'koi/ [with obj. and adverbial of direction] lure or entice (a person or animal) away from an intended course, typically into a trap. [16th C. (earlier as *coy*): from Du. *de kooi* 'the decoy,' from MDu. *de kouw* 'the cage,' from L. *cavea* 'cage.']

de·crease ▶ v. /di'krēs/ [intrans.] become smaller or less in size, amount, intensity, or degree. ■ [trans.] make smaller or less in size, amount, intensity, or degree. ▶ n. /'dēkrēs; di'krēs/ an instance or example of becoming smaller or less: *a decrease in births.* ■ the action or process of becoming smaller or fewer.

– PHRASES **on the decrease** becoming less common or widespread; decreasing. — **de·creas·ing·ly** /di'krēsiNGlē/ adv. [ME: from OFr. *decreis* (n.), *decreistre* (v.), based on L. *decrescere*, from *de-* 'down' + *crescere* 'grow.']

de·cree /di'krē/ ▶ n. an official order issued by a legal authority. ■ the issuing of such an order: *the king* ***ruled by decree.*** ■ a judgment or decision of certain law courts. ▶ v. (**-crees, -creed, -cree·ing**) [trans.] order (something) by decree. [ME: from OFr. *decre, decret*, from L. *decretum* 'something decided,' from *decernere* 'decide.']

dec·re·ment /'dekrəmənt/ ▶ n. a reduction or diminution. ■ an amount by which something is reduced or diminished. ■ Physics the ratio of the amplitudes in successive cycles of a damped oscillation. ▶ v. [trans.] esp. Comput. cause a discrete reduction in (a numerical quantity). [17th C. (as a n.): from L. *decrementum* 'diminution,' from the stem of *decrescere* 'to decrease.']

de·crep·it /di'krepit/ ▶ adj. (of a person) elderly and infirm. ■ worn out or ruined because of age or neglect. — **de·crep·i·tude** /-,t(y)ōōd/ n. [ME: from L. *decrepitus*, from *de-* 'down' + *crepitus*, past part. of *crepare* 'rattle, creak.']

de·crep·i·tate /di'krepi,tāt/ ▶ v. [intrans.] tech. (of a crystal or an inclusion of something within a crystal) disintegrate audibly when heated. — **de·crep·i·ta·tion** /-,krepi'tāsHən/ n. [17th C.: from DE- 'away' + L. *crepitat-* 'crackled,' from the v. *crepitare*, frequentative of *crepare* 'rattle' (see DECREPIT).]

de·cre·scen·do /,dēkrə'sHendō/ ▶ n. (pl. **-dos**), **adv., adj., & v.** (**-dos, -doed**) another term for DIMINUENDO. [19th C.: Ital., lit. 'decreasing.']

de·cres·cent /di'kresənt/ ▶ adj. [attrib.] (of the moon) waning. [17th C.: from L. *decrescent-* 'growing less,' from the v. *decrescere* (see DECREASE).]

de·cre·tal /di'krētl/ ▶ n. a papal decree concerning a point of canon law. ▶ adj. of the nature of a decree. [ME: from late L. *decretale*, neut. of *decretalis* (adj.), from L. *decret-* 'decided,' from the v. *decernere*.]

de·crim·i·nal·ize /dē'kriminl,īz/ ▶ v. [trans.] cease by legislation to treat (something) as illegal. — **de·crim·i·nal·i·za·tion** /-,kriminl-i'zāsHən/ n.

de·cry /di'krī/ ▶ v. (**-cries, -cried**) [trans.] publicly denounce: *they decried human rights abuses.* — **de·cri·er** n. [17th C.: from DE- 'down' + CRY, on the pattern of Fr. *décrier* 'cry down.']

de·crypt /di'kript/ ▶ v. [trans.] make (a coded or unclear message) intelligible. ▶ n. a text that has been decoded. — **de·cryp·tion** /-'kripsHən/ n. [1930s: from DE- (expressing reversal) + *crypt* as in *encrypt*.]

de·cub·i·tus ul·cer ▶ n. technical term for BEDSORE.

de·cum·bent /di'kəmbənt/ ▶ adj. Bot. (of a plant or part of a plant) lying along the ground or along a surface, with the extremity curving upward. [18th C.: from L. *decumbent-* 'lying down,' from the verb *decumbere*, based on *de-* 'down' + a v. rel. to *cubare* 'to lie.']

de·cur·rent /di'kərənt; -'kə-rənt/ ▶ adj. Bot. (of a fungus gill, leaf, etc.) extending down the stem below the point of attachment. ■ (of a shrub or the crown of a tree) having several roughly equal branches. [18th C.: from L. *decurrent-* 'running down,' from the v. *decurrere*.]

de·curved /dē'kərvd/ ▶ adj. Biol. (esp. of a bird's bill) curved downward.

de·cus·sate /'dekə,sāt; di'kəsāt/ tech. ▶ v. [reciprocal] (of two or more things) cross or intersect each other to form an X: *the fibers decussate in the collar.* ▶ adj. shaped like an X. ■ Bot. (of leaves) arranged in opposite pairs, each pair being at right angles to the pair below. — **de·cus·sa·tion** /,dekə'sāsHən/ n. [17th C.: from L. *decussatus*, past part. of *decussare* 'divide crosswise,' from *decussis* (describing the figure X, i.e., the Roman numeral for the number 10), from *decem* 'ten.']

de·den·dum /di'dendəm/ ▶ n. Engin. the radial distance from the pitch circle of a cogwheel or worm wheel to the bottom of the tooth space or groove. Compare with ADDENDUM. [20th C.: from L., 'to be given up, surrendered.']

ded·i·cate /'dedi,kāt/ ▶ v. [trans.] devote (time, effort, or oneself) to a particular task or purpose: *Joan has* ***dedicated*** *her life* ***to*** *animals.* ■ devote (something) to a particular subject or purpose. ■ (usu. **be dedicated**) cite (a book or other artistic work) as being issued or performed in someone's honor: *the novel is* ***dedicated to*** *the memory of my mother.* ■ open (a building or other facility) formally for public use. ■ (usu. **be dedicated**) ceremonially assign (a church or other building) to a deity or saint. — **ded·i·ca·tee** /,dedikā'tē/ n. **ded·i·ca·tor** /-,kātər/ n. **ded·i·ca·to·ry** /-kə,tôrē/ adj. [ME: from L. *dedicat-* 'devoted, consecrated,' from the v. *dedicare*.]

ded·i·cat·ed /'dedi,kātid/ ▶ adj. (of a person) devoted to a task or purpose; having single-minded loyalty or integrity: *dedicated doctors.* ■ (of a thing) exclusively allocated to or intended for a particular service or purpose. — **ded·i·cat·ed·ly** adv.

ded·i·ca·tion /,dedi'kāsHən/ ▶ n. **1** the quality of being dedicated or committed to a task or purpose. **2** the words with which a book or other artistic work is dedicated. ■ the action of formally opening a building or other facility for public use. ■ the action of dedicating a church or other building to a deity or saint. ■ an inscription dedicating a church or other building in this way.

de dicto /dā 'diktō/ ▶ adj. Philos. relating to the form of an assertion or expression itself, rather than any property of a thing it refers to. Compare with DE RE. [Latin, 'from what is said.']

de·duce /di'd(y)ōōs/ ▶ v. [trans.] arrive at (a fact or a conclusion) by reasoning; draw as a logical conclusion. — **de·duc·i·ble** /-səbəl/ adj. [ME (in the sense 'lead or convey'): from L. *deducere*, from *de-* 'down' + *ducere* 'lead.']

de·duct /di'dəkt/ ▶ v. [trans.] subtract or take away (an amount or part) from a total. [ME: from L. *deduct-* 'taken or led away,' from the v. *deducere*.]

de·duct·i·ble /di'dəktəbəl/ ▶ adj. able to be deducted, esp. from taxable income or tax to be paid. See also TAX-DEDUCTIBLE. ▶ n. (in an insurance policy) a specified amount of money that the insured must pay before an insurance company will pay a claim. — **de·duct·i·bil·i·ty** /-,dəktə'bilitē/ n.

de·duc·tion /di'dəksHən/ ▶ n. **1** the action of deducting or subtracting something. ■ an amount that is or may be deducted from something, esp. from taxable income or tax to be paid. **2** the inference of particular instances by reference to a general law or principle. Often contrasted with INDUCTION. ■ a conclusion that has been deduced.

de·duc·tive /di'dəktiv/ ▶ adj. characterized by the inference of particular instances from a general law. ■ based on reason and logical analysis of available facts: *I used my deductive powers.* — **de·duc·tive·ly** adv.

de Du·ve /də 'dōōv; də 'dyv/, Christian René (1917–), Belgian biochemist; born in Britain. He was a pioneer in the study of cell biology. Nobel Prize for Physiology or Medicine (1974, shared with Albert Claude 1899–1983 and George Palade 1912–).

Dee /dē/ **1** a river in northeastern Scotland that flows east to the North Sea at Aberdeen. **2** a river that rises in North Wales and flows past Chester and on into the Irish Sea.

deed /dēd/ ▶ n. **1** an action that is performed intentionally or consciously: *doing good deeds.* ■ a brave or noble act. ■ action or performance. **2** a legal document that is signed and delivered, esp. one regarding the ownership of property or legal rights. See also TITLE DEED. ▶ v. [trans.] convey or transfer (property or rights) by legal deed: *they deeded their property to their children.* [OE *dēd, dǣd*, of Gmc. origin; rel. to Du. *daad* and Ger. *Tat*, from an Indo-Eur. root shared by DO[1].]

dee·jay /'dē,jā/ informal ▶ n. a disc jockey. ▶ v. (**-jays, -jayed, -jay·ing**) [intrans.] act as, or hold a job as, a disc jockey. [1950s: from *DJ*.]

deem /dēm/ ▶ v. [with obj. and complement] regard or consider in a specified way. [OE *dēman*, of Gmc. origin; rel. to Du. *doeman*, also to DOOM.]

de-em·pha·size /dē'emfə,sīz/ ▶ v. [trans.] reduce the importance or prominence given to (something). — **de-em·pha·sis** /-fə,sis/ n.

de-en·er·gize /dē'enər,jīz/ ▶ v. [trans.] disconnect (an electric circuit) from a power supply. ■ [intrans.] undergo loss of electrical power.

deep /dēp/ ▶ adj. **1** extending far down from the top or surface: *a deep gorge.* ■ extending or situated far in or down from the outer edge or surface: *deep in the woods.* ■ [predic.] (after a measurement and in questions) extending a specified distance from the top, surface, or outer edge: *200 feet deep.* ■ [in comb.] as far up or down as a specified point: *standing waist-deep in the river.* ■ [predic.] in a specified number of ranks one behind another: [in comb.] *standing three-deep at the bar.* ■ taking in or giving out a lot of air: *she took a deep breath.* ■ Baseball far back in the outfield: *a hit into deep left field.* **2** very intense or extreme: *she was in deep trouble.* ■ (of an emotion or feeling) intensely felt: *deep disappointment.* ■ profound or penetrating in awareness or understanding: *a deep analysis.* ■ difficult to understand. ■ [predic.] (**deep in**) fully absorbed or involved in (a state or activity). ■ (of a person) unpredictable and secretive. **3** (of sound) low in pitch and full in tone; not shrill. **4** (of color) dark and intense: *a deep pink.* ▶ n. (**the deep**) literary the sea:

denizens of the deep. ■ (usu. **deeps**) a deep part of the sea: *the dark and menacing deeps.* ■ (usu. **deeps**) fig. a remote and mysterious region. ▶ **adv.** far down or in; deeply: *traveling deep into the countryside* | fig. *his passion runs deep.* ■ (in sports) distant from the start of a play or the forward line of one's team: *the defense played deep.*
– PHRASES **the deep end** the end of a swimming pool where the water is deepest. **go off** (or **go in off**) **the deep end** informal give way immediately to an emotional outburst, esp. of anger. ■ go mad; behave extremely strangely. **in deep** informal inextricably involved in or committed to a situation. **in deep water** (or **waters**) informal in trouble or difficulty. **jump** (or **be thrown**) **in at the deep end** informal face a difficult problem or undertaking with little experience of it. — **deep·ness** **n.** [OE *dēop* (adj.), *dīope, dēope* (adv.), of Gmc. origin; rel. to Du. *diep* and Ger. *tief*, also to DIP.]

deep breath·ing ▶ **n.** breathing with long breaths, esp. as exercise or a method of relaxation.

deep-dis·count ▶ **adj.** denoting financial securities carrying a low rate of interest relative to prevailing market rates and issued at a discount to their redemption value, thus mainly providing capital gain rather than income. ■ heavily discounted; greatly reduced in price.

deep-dish ▶ **adj. 1** (of a pie) baked in a deep dish to allow for a large filling: *deep-dish apple pie.* ■ (of a pizza) baked in a deep dish and having a thick dough base. **2** informal extreme or thoroughgoing: *a deep-dish Catholic.*

deep-dyed ▶ **adj.** informal thoroughgoing; complete.

deep·en /ˈdēpən/ ▶ **v.** make or become deep or deeper.

deep freeze ▶ **n.** (also **deep freez·er**) a refrigerated cabinet or room in which food can be quickly frozen and kept for long periods at a low temperature. ■ fig. a place or situation in which progress or activity is suspended. ▶ **v.** (**deep-freeze**) [trans.] [often as adj.] (**deep-frozen**) store (something) in a deep freeze.

deep-fry ▶ **v.** [trans.] [as adj.] (**deep-fried**) fry (food) in an amount of fat or oil sufficient to cover it completely.

deep-laid ▶ **adj.** (of a scheme) secret and elaborate.

deep·ly /ˈdēplē/ ▶ **adv.** far down or in: *he breathed deeply* | *fragments of rock were deeply embedded within the wood.* ■ intensely: [as submodifier] *she was deeply hurt.*

deep mourn·ing ▶ **n.** a state of mourning, conventionally expressed by wearing only black clothing. ■ the black clothing worn by someone in deep mourning.

deep pock·ets ▶ **n.** abundant financial resources.

deep-root·ed ▶ **adj.** (of a plant) deeply implanted. ■ firmly embedded in thought, behavior, or culture, and so having a persistent influence. — **deep-root·ed·ness** **n.**

deep sea ▶ **n.** [usu. as adj.] the deeper parts of the ocean, esp. those beyond the edge of the continental shelf.

deep-seat·ed ▶ **adj.** firmly established at a deep or profound level: *deep-seated anxiety.*

deep-set ▶ **adj.** (of a person's eyes) positioned deeply in the head. ■ embedded firmly: *the bees found only a few deep-set plants.* ■ long-established, ingrained, or profound: *a deep-set enmity.*

deep-six ▶ **v.** [trans.] informal destroy or dispose of (something) irretrievably. [1920s: perh. from the custom of burial at sea at a depth of six fathoms.]

Deep South (**the Deep South**) the southeastern region of the US that is regarded as embodying traditional Southern culture and traditions.

deep space ▶ **n.** another term for OUTER SPACE.

deep struc·ture ▶ **n.** (in generative grammar) the abstract representation of the syntactic structure of a sentence.

deep throat ▶ **n.** informal a concealed informant, esp. one who is hated by those persons informed upon. [1970s: from the pseudonym used by a Watergate informant, from the title of a pornographic movie (1972).]

deer /di(ə)r/ ▶ **n.** (pl. same) a hoofed grazing or browsing animal (family Cervidae), with branched bony antlers that are shed annually and typically borne only by the male. See illustration at WHITETAIL DEER. See also MOUSE DEER, MUSK DEER. [OE *dēor*, also orig. denoting any quadruped, used in the (now archaic) phr. *small deer* meaning 'small creatures collectively'; of Gmc. origin; rel. to Du. *dier*, Ger. *Tier*.]

Deere /di(ə)r/, John (1804–86), US industrialist. He founded John Deere & Co. in 1868 to manufacture steel plows.

Deer·field Beach /ˈdi(ə)rˌfēld/ a resort city in southeastern Florida, north of Fort Lauderdale; pop. 46,325.

deer·fly /ˈdi(ə)rˌflī/ ▶ **n. 1** a bloodsucking horsefly (genus *Chrysops*, family Tabanidae) that can transmit various diseases, including tularemia. **2** a bloodsucking louse fly (*Lipoptena cervi*, family Hippoboscidae) that is a parasite of deer.

deerfly 1

deer·hound /ˈdi(ə)rˌhound/ ▶ **n.** a large dog of a rough-haired breed resembling the greyhound.

deer lick ▶ **n.** a place where deer come to lick salt, either from a block of salt placed there or from a natural source.

deer mouse ▶ **n.** a mainly nocturnal mouse (genus *Peromyscus*, family Muridae) found in a wide range of habitats in North and Central America.

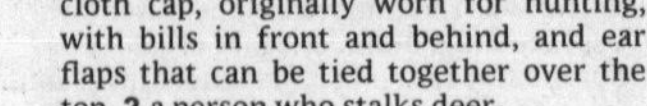

deer·skin /ˈdi(ə)rˌskin/ ▶ **n.** leather made from a deer's skin.

deer·stalk·er /ˈdi(ə)rˌstôkər/ ▶ **n. 1** a soft cloth cap, originally worn for hunting, with bills in front and behind, and ear flaps that can be tied together over the top. **2** a person who stalks deer.

deerstalker 1

de-es·ca·late /dēˈeskəˌlāt/ ▶ **v.** [trans.] reduce the intensity of (a conflict or potentially violent situation). — **de-es·ca·la·tion** /-ˌeskəˈlāshən/ **n.**

Deet /dēt/ ▶ **trademark** a brand of diethyltoluamide, a colorless oily liquid with a mild odor, used as an insect repellent.

def /def/ ▶ **adj.** esp. black slang excellent: *a truly def tattoo.* [1980s: prob. an alt. of DEATH.]

de·face /diˈfās/ ▶ **v.** [trans.] spoil the surface or appearance of (something), e.g., by drawing or writing on it. ■ mar; disfigure. — **de·face·ment** **n.** **de·fac·er** **n.** [ME: from OFr. *desfacier*, from *des-* (expressing removal) + *face* 'face.']

de fac·to /di ˈfaktō; dā/ ▶ **adv.** in fact, whether by right or not. Often contrasted with DE JURE. ▶ **adj.** [attrib.] denoting someone or something that is such in fact: *a de facto one-party system.* [17th C.: L., literally 'of fact.']

de·fal·cate /diˈfalkāt; -ˈfôl-/ ▶ **v.** [trans.] formal embezzle (funds with which one has been entrusted). — **de·fal·ca·tion** /ˌdēfalˈkāshən; -fôl-/ **n.** **de·fal·ca·tor** /-kātər/ **n.** [16th C.: from med. L. *defalcat-* 'lopped,' from the v. *defalcare*, from *de-* 'away from, off' + L. *falx, falc-* 'sickle.']

de·fame /diˈfām/ ▶ **v.** [trans.] damage the good reputation of (someone); slander or libel. — **def·a·ma·tion** /ˌdefəˈmāshən/ **n.** **de·fam·a·to·ry** /-ˈfaməˌtôrē/ **adj.** **de·fam·er** **n.** [ME: from OFr. *diffamer*, from L. *diffamare* 'spread evil report,' from *dis-* (expressing removal) + *fama* 'report.']

de·fang /dēˈfaNG/ ▶ **v.** [trans.] remove the fangs from (an animal, esp. a reptile): *defang the wolves.* ■ render harmless or ineffectual.

de·fat /dēˈfat/ ▶ **v.** (**-fat·ted, -fat·ting**) [trans.] [usu. as adj.] (**defatted**) remove fat from (food): *soup made with defatted chicken stock.*

de·fault /diˈfôlt/ ▶ **n. 1** failure to fulfill an obligation, esp. to repay a loan or appear in a court of law. **2** a preselected option adopted by a computer program or other mechanism when no alternative is specified by the user or programmer. ▶ **v.** [intrans.] **1** fail to fulfill an obligation, esp. to repay a loan or to appear in a court of law: *some had defaulted on student loans.* ■ [trans.] declare (a party) in default and give judgment against that party. **2** (**default to**) (of a computer program or other mechanism) revert automatically to (a preselected option).
– PHRASES **by default** because of a lack of opposition: *they won the election by default.* ■ through lack of positive action rather than conscious choice. **in default** guilty of failing to repay a loan or appear in a court of law: *the company is in default on its loans.* **in default of** in the absence of. [ME: from OFr. *defaut*, from *defaillir* 'to fail,' based on L. *fallere* 'disappoint, deceive.']

de·fault·er /diˈfôltər/ ▶ **n.** a person who fails to fulfill a duty, obligation, or undertaking, esp. to pay a debt. ■ a person who fails to complete a course of medical treatment.

de·fea·sance /diˈfēzəns/ ▶ **n.** Law the action or process of rendering something null and void. ■ a clause or condition which, if fulfilled, renders a deed or contract null and void. [ME (as a legal term): from OFr. *defesance*, from *defaire, desfaire* 'undo' (see DEFEAT).]

de·feat /diˈfēt/ ▶ **v.** [trans.] win a victory over (someone) in a battle or other contest; overcome or beat. ■ prevent (someone) from achieving an aim. ■ prevent (an aim) from being achieved. ■ reject or block (a motion or proposal). ■ be impossible for (someone) to understand: *this line of reasoning defeats me.* ■ Law render null and void; annul. ▶ **n.** an instance of defeating or being defeated. [ME: from OFr. *desfait* 'undone,' past part. of *desfaire*, from med. L. *disfacere* 'undo.']

de·feat·ed /diˈfētid/ ▶ **adj.** having been beaten in a battle or other contest: *the defeated army.* ■ demoralized and overcome by adversity. — **de·feat·ed·ly** **adv.**

de·feat·ist /diˈfētist/ ▶ **n.** a person who expects or is excessively ready to accept failure. ▶ **adj.** demonstrating expectation or acceptance of failure. — **de·feat·ism** **n.**

def·e·cate /ˈdefiˌkāt/ ▶ **v.** [intrans.] discharge feces from the body. — **def·e·ca·tion** /ˌdefiˈkāshən/ **n.** **def·e·ca·tor** /-ˌkātər/ **n.** **def·e·ca·to·ry** /-kəˌtôrē/ **adj.** [ME: from L. *defaecat-* 'cleared of dregs,' from the v. *defaecare*, from *de-* (expressing removal) + *faex, faec-* 'dregs.']

de·fect[1] ▶ **n.** /ˈdēfekt/ a shortcoming, imperfection, or lack: *genetic defects* | *the property is free from defect.* [ME: from L. *defectus*, past part. of *deficere* 'desert or fail,' from *de-* (expressing reversal) + *facere* 'do.']

de·fect[2] /diˈfekt/ ▶ **v.** [intrans.] abandon one's country or cause in favor of an opposing one: *he defected to the Soviet Union after the war.* — **de·fec·tion** /diˈfekshən/ **n.** **de·fec·tor** /-tər/ **n.** [16th C.: from L. *defect-* 'failed,' from the v. *deficere* (see DEFECT[1]).]

de·fec·tive /diˈfektiv/ ▶ **adj.** imperfect or faulty. ■ lacking or deficient: *dystrophin is commonly defective in muscle tissue.* ■ Gram. (of a word) not having all the inflections normal for the part of speech. — **de·fec·tive·ly** **adv.** **de·fec·tive·ness** **n.**

de·fem·i·nize /dēˈfeməˌnīz/ ▶ **v.** [trans.] deprive of feminine characteristics.

de·fend /diˈfend/ ▶ **v.** [trans.] resist an attack made on (someone or something); protect from harm or danger: *we shall defend our country.* ■ speak or write in favor of (an action or person); attempt to justify: *he* *defended his policy of imposing high taxes.* ■ conduct the case for (the party being accused or sued) in a lawsuit. ■ compete to retain (a title or seat) in a contest or election. ■ [intrans.] (in sports) protect one's goal rather than attempt to score against one's opponents. — **de·fend·a·ble** adj. [ME: from OFr. *defendre*, from L. *defendere*, from *de-* 'off' + *-fendere* 'to strike.']

de·fend·ant /di'fendənt/ ▶ n. an individual, company, or institution sued or accused in a court of law. Compare with PLAINTIFF.

de·fend·er /di'fendər/ ▶ n. a person who defends someone or something: *a defender of family values.*

de·fen·es·tra·tion /dē,fenə'strāsʜən/ ▶ n. formal or humorous the action of throwing someone or something out of a window. — **de·fen·es·trate** /-'fenə,strāt/ v. [17th C.: from mod. L. *defenestratio(n-)*, from *de-* 'down from' + L. *fenestra* 'window.']

de·fense /di'fens; 'dēfens/ (Brit. **de·fence**) ▶ n. **1** the action of defending from or resisting attack. ■ attempted justification or vindication of something: *he spoke in defense of a disciplined approach.* ■ an instance of defending a title or seat in a contest or election. ■ military measures or resources for protecting a country. ■ a means of protecting something from attack. ■ (**defenses**) fortifications or barriers against attack. ■ (in sports) the action or role of defending one's goal against the opposition. ■ (**the defense**) the players in a team who perform this role. **2** the case presented by or on behalf of the party being accused or sued in a lawsuit. **3** one or more defendants in a trial. ■ (usu. **the defense**) [treated as sing. or pl.] the counsel for the defendant in a lawsuit. [ME: from OFr. *defens*, from late L. *defensum* (neut.), *defensa* (fem.), past participles of *defendere* 'defend.']

de·fense·less /di'fenslis/ ▶ adj. without defense or protection; totally vulnerable. — **de·fense·less·ness** n.

de·fense·man /di'fensmən/ ▶ n. (pl. **-men**) (in ice hockey and lacrosse) a player in a defensive position.

de·fense mech·an·ism ▶ n. an automatic reaction of the body against disease-causing organisms. ■ a mental process (e.g., repression or projection) initiated, typically unconsciously, to avoid conscious conflict or anxiety.

de·fen·si·ble /di'fensəbəl/ ▶ adj. **1** justifiable by argument: *a morally defensible penal system.* **2** able to be protected. — **de·fen·si·bil·i·ty** /di,fensə'bilitē/ n. **de·fen·si·bly** adv.

de·fen·sive /di'fensiv/ ▶ adj. **1** used or intended to defend or protect: *troops in defensive positions.* ■ [attrib.] (in sports) relating to or intended as defense. **2** very anxious to challenge or avoid criticism.
– PHRASES **on the defensive** expecting or resisting criticism or attack. — **de·fen·sive·ness** n.

de·fen·sive end ▶ n. Football either of the two defensive players positioned at either end of the linemen.

de·fen·sive·ly /di'fensivlē/ ▶ adv. in a defensive manner: *"No, I didn't," he replied defensively.* ■ (in sports) in terms of defense.

de·fer[1] /di'fər/ ▶ v. (**-ferred, -fer·ring**) [trans.] put off (an action or event) to a later time; postpone. — **de·fer·ment** n. **de·fer·ra·ble** adj. **de·fer·ral** /-'fərəl/ n. [ME: from OFr. *differer* 'defer or differ,' from L. *differre*, from *dis-* 'apart' + *ferre* 'bring, carry.']

de·fer[2] ▶ v. (**-ferred, -fer·ring**) [intrans.] (**defer to**) submit humbly to (a person or a person's wishes or qualities): *he deferred to Tim's superior knowledge.* — **de·fer·rer** n. [ME: from OFr. *deferer*, from L. *deferre* 'carry away, refer (a matter),' from *de-* + *ferre* 'bring, carry.']

def·er·ence /'defərəns/ ▶ n. humble submission and respect.

def·er·en·tial /,defə'rencʜəl/ ▶ adj. showing deference; respectful: *people were always deferential to him.* — **def·er·en·tial·ly** adv.

de·ferred an·nu·i·ty ▶ n. an annuity that commences only after a lapse of some specified time after the final purchase premium has been paid.

de·fer·ves·cence /,dēfər'vesəns; ,defər-/ ▶ n. Med. the abatement of a fever as indicated by a decrease in bodily temperature. — **de·fer·vesce** /-'ves/ v. [18th C.: from L. *defervescent-* 'ceasing to boil,' from the v. *defervescere*.]

de·fi·ance /di'fīəns/ ▶ n. open resistance; bold disobedience. [ME: from OFr., from *defier* 'defy.']

de·fi·ant /di'fīənt/ ▶ adj. showing defiance. — **de·fi·ant·ly** adv.

de·fib·ril·la·tion /dē,fibrə'lāsʜən/ ▶ n. Med. the stopping of fibrillation of the heart by administering a controlled electric shock in order to allow restoration of the normal rhythm. — **de·fib·ril·late** /dē'fibrə,lāt/ v.

de·fib·ril·la·tor /dē'fibrə,lātər/ ▶ n. Med. an apparatus used to control heart fibrillation by application of an electric current to the chest wall or heart.

de·fi·cien·cy /di'fisʜənsē/ ▶ n. (pl. **-cies**) a lack or shortage: *vitamin A deficiency in children.* ■ a failing or shortcoming.

de·fi·cien·cy dis·ease ▶ n. a disease caused by the lack of some essential or important element in the diet, usually a particular vitamin or mineral. See also IMMUNODEFICIENCY.

de·fi·cient /di'fisʜənt/ ▶ adj. [predic.] not having enough of a specified quality or ingredient. ■ insufficient or inadequate. ■ (also **mentally deficient**) offens. having a mental handicap. [16th C.: from L. *deficient-* 'failing,' from the v. *deficere* (see DEFECT[1]).]

def·i·cit /'defəsit/ ▶ n. the amount by which something, esp. a sum of money, is too small. ■ an excess of expenditure or liabilities over income or assets in a given period. ■ (in sports) the amount or score by which a team or individual is losing: *came back from a 3–0 deficit.* ■ tech. a deficiency or failing, esp. in a neurological or psychological function: *deficits in speech comprehension.* [18th C.: via Fr. from L. *deficit* 'it is lacking,' from the v. *deficere* (see DEFECT[1]).]

def·i·cit fi·nanc·ing ▶ n. government funding of spending by borrowing.

def·i·cit spend·ing ▶ n. government spending, in excess of revenue, of funds raised by borrowing rather than from taxation.

def·i·lade /'defə,lād; ,defə'lād/ Mil. ▶ n. the protection of a position, vehicle, or troops against enemy observation or gunfire. ▶ v. [trans.] protect (a position, vehicle, or troops) against enemy observation or gunfire. [19th C.: from Fr. *défiler* 'protect.']

de·file[1] /di'fīl/ ▶ v. [trans.] sully, mar, or spoil. ■ desecrate or profane (something sacred). — **de·file·ment** n. **de·fil·er** n. [ME: alt. of obsolete *defoul*, from OFr. *defouler* 'trample down,' influenced by obs. *befile* 'befoul, defile.']

de·file[2] /di'fīl; 'dē,fīl -/ ▶ n. a steep-sided, narrow gorge or passage (originally one requiring troops to march in single file). [17th C.: from Fr. *défilé* (n.), *défiler* (v.), from *dé* 'away from' + *file* 'column, file.']

de·fine /di'fīn/ ▶ v. [trans.] **1** state or describe exactly the nature, scope, or meaning of. ■ give the meaning of (a word or phrase), esp. in a dictionary. ■ make up or establish the character of: *the football team defines their identity.* **2** mark out the boundary or limits of. ■ make clear the outline of; delineate. — **de·fin·a·ble** adj. **de·fin·er** n. [ME: from OFr. *definer*, from a var. of L. *definire*, from *de-* (expressing completion) + *finire* 'finish' (from *finis* 'end').]

de·fin·ing mo·ment ▶ n. an event that typifies or determines all subsequent related occurrences.

def·i·nite /'defənit/ ▶ adj. clearly stated or decided; not vague or doubtful: *we had no definite plans.* ■ clearly true or real; unambiguous. ■ [predic.] (of a person) certain or sure about something: *you're very definite about that!* ■ clear or undeniable (used for emphasis). ■ having exact and discernible physical limits or form. — **def·i·nite·ness** n. [16th C.: from L. *definitus*, past part. of *definire* (see DEFINE).]

def·i·nite ar·ti·cle ▶ n. Gram. a determiner (*the* in English) that introduces a noun phrase and implies that the thing mentioned has already been mentioned, or is common knowledge, or is about to be defined (as in *the book on the table*; *the famous poet and short story writer*). Compare with INDEFINITE ARTICLE.

def·i·nite in·te·gral ▶ n. Math. an integral expressed as the difference between the values of the integral at specified upper and lower limits of the independent variable.

def·i·nite·ly /'defənitlē/ ▶ adv. without doubt (used for emphasis): *I will definitely be at the airport to meet you.* ■ in a definite manner; clearly.

def·i·ni·tion /,defə'nisʜən/ ▶ n. **1** a statement of the exact meaning of a word, esp. in a dictionary. ■ an exact statement or description of the nature, scope, or meaning of something. ■ the action or process of defining something. **2** the degree of distinctness in outline of an object, image, or sound, esp. of an image in a photograph or on a screen. ■ the capacity of an instrument or device for making images distinct in outline: [in comb.] *high-definition television.*
– PHRASES **by definition** by its very nature; intrinsically. — **def·i·ni·tion·al** /-sʜənl/ adj. **def·i·ni·tion·al·ly** adv. [ME: from L. *definitio(n-)*, from *definire*.]

de·fin·i·tive /di'finitiv/ ▶ adj. **1** (of a conclusion or agreement) done or reached decisively and with authority: *a definitive diagnosis.* ■ (of a book or other text) the most authoritative of its kind: *the definitive biography of Harry Truman.* **2** (of a postage stamp) for general use and typically of standard design, not special or commemorative. ▶ n. a definitive postage stamp. — **de·fin·i·tive·ly** adv.

de·fin·i·tive host ▶ n. Biol. an organism that supports the adult or sexually reproductive form of a parasite. Compare with INTERMEDIATE HOST.

def·la·grate /'deflə,grāt/ ▶ v. Chem., dated burn away or cause (a substance) to burn away with a sudden flame and rapid, sharp combustion. — **def·la·gra·tor** /-'grātər/ n. [18th C.: from L. *deflagrat-* 'burned up,' from the v. *deflagrare*, from *de-* 'away, thoroughly' + *flagrare* 'to burn.']

def·la·gra·tion /,deflə'grāsʜən/ ▶ n. the action of heating a substance until it burns away rapidly. ■ tech. combustion that propagates through a gas or across the surface of an explosive at subsonic speeds, driven by the transfer of heat. Compare with DETONATION.

de·flate /di'flāt/ ▶ v. **1** [trans.] let air or gas out of (a tire, balloon, or similar object): *he deflated one of the tires.* ■ [intrans.] be emptied of air or gas: *the balloon deflated.* **2** cause (someone) to suddenly lose confidence or feel less important. ■ reduce the level of (an emotion or feeling). **3** Econ. bring about a general reduction of price levels in (an economy). — **de·fla·tor** /-'flātər/ n. [19th C.: from DE- (expressing reversal) + *-flate* (as in *inflate*).]

de·fla·tion /di'flāsʜən/ ▶ n. **1** the action or process of deflating or being deflated. **2** Econ. reduction of the general level of prices in an economy. **3** Geol. the removal of particles of rock, sand, etc., by the wind. — **de·fla·tion·ist** n. & adj.

de·fla·tion·ar·y /di'flāsʜə,nerē/ ▶ adj. of, characterized by, or tending to cause economic deflation.

de·flect /di'flekt/ ▶ v. [with obj. and usu. with adverbial of direction] cause (something) to change direction by interposing something; turn aside from a straight course. ■ [no obj., with adverbial of direction] (of an object) change direction after hitting something: *the ball deflected off his body.* ■ cause (someone) to deviate from an intended purpose. ■ cause (something) to change orientation. [16th C.: from L. *deflectere*, from *de-* 'away from' + *flectere* 'to bend.']

de·flec·tion /di'fleksʜən/ (also **de·flex·ion**) ▶ **n.** the action or process of deflecting or being deflected. ■ the amount by which something is deflected.

de·flec·tor /di'flektər/ ▶ **n.** a device that deflects something.

de·flexed /di'flekst/ ▶ **adj.** tech. (typically of plant or animal structures) bent or curving downward or backward: *a deflexed beak.* [19th C. (earlier as *deflex*): from L. *deflexus* 'bent away' (past part. of *deflectere*) + -ED[1].]

de·flow·er /dē'flouər/ ▶ **v.** [trans.] **1** dated or literary deprive (a woman) of her virginity. **2** [usu. as adj.] (**deflowered**) strip (a plant or garden) of flowers: *deflowered rose bushes.* [ME: from OFr. *desflourer*, from a var. of late L. *deflorare*, from *de-* (expressing removal) + L. *flos, flor-* 'a flower.']

de·fo·cus /dē'fōkəs/ ▶ **v.** (**-fo·cused**, **-fo·cus·ing** or **-fo·cussed**, **-fo·cus·sing**) [trans.] cause (an image, lens, or beam) to go out of focus. ■ [intrans.] go out of focus: *the view defocused.* ■ take the focus of interest or activity away from (something).

De·foe /də'fō/, Daniel (1660–1731), English writer. He wrote *Robinson Crusoe* (1719), considered the first British novel.

de·fog·ger /dē'fôgər; -'fä-/ ▶ **n.** a device on a vehicle that removes condensation from the windshield. — **de·fog v.**

de·fo·li·ant /dē'fōlēənt/ ▶ **n.** a chemical that removes the leaves from trees and plants.

de·fo·li·ate /dē'fōlē,āt/ ▶ **v.** [trans.] remove leaves from (a tree, plant, or area of land), for agricultural purposes or as a military tactic. — **de·fo·li·a·tion** /dē,fōlē'āsʜən/ **n.** [18th C.: from late L. *defoliat-* 'stripped of leaves,' from the v. *defoliare*, from *de-* (expressing removal) + *folium* 'leaf.']

de·fo·li·a·tor /dē'fōlē,ātər/ ▶ **n.** an adult or larval insect that strips all the leaves from a tree or shrub. ■ a machine that removes the leaves from a root crop.

de·force /di'fôrs/ ▶ **v.** [trans.] Law withhold (land or other property) wrongfully or forcibly from the rightful owner. [ME: from Anglo-Norman Fr. *deforcer*, from *de-* (expressing removal) + *forcer* 'to force.']

De For·est /də 'fôrəst; 'fär-/, Lee (1873–1961), US physicist. He designed a triode valve that was crucial to the development of radio communication, television, and computers.

de·for·est /dē'fôrist; -'fär-/ ▶ **v.** [trans.] (often **be deforested**) clear (an area) of forests or trees. — **de·for·est·a·tion** /dē,fôrə'stāsʜən; -,fär-/ **n.**

de·form /di'fôrm/ ▶ **v.** [trans.] distort the shape or form of; make misshapen. ■ [intrans.] become distorted or misshapen; undergo deformation: *the suspension deforms slightly on corners.* — **de·form·a·ble adj.** [ME: from OFr. *desformer*, via med. L. from L. *deformare*, from *de-* (expressing reversal) + *forma* 'a shape.']

de·for·ma·tion /,dēfôr'māsʜən; ,defər-/ ▶ **n.** the action or process of changing in shape or distorting, esp. through the application of pressure. ■ the result of such a process: *the deformation will be temporary.* ■ an altered form of a word, esp. one used to avoid overt profanity (e.g., *dang* for *damn*). — **de·for·ma·tion·al** /-sʜənl/ **adj.**

de·form·i·ty /di'fôrmitē/ ▶ **n.** (pl. **-ties**) a deformed part, esp. of the body; a malformation. ■ the state of being deformed or misshapen. [ME: from OFr. *desformite*, from L. *deformitas*, from *deformis* 'misshapen.']

de·frag /dē'frag/ ▶ **v.** (**-fragged**, **-frag·ging**) [trans.] Comput. short for DEFRAGMENT. ▶ **n.** an instance of defragging a disk, or the utility that does this.

de·frag·ment /,dēfrag'ment/ ▶ **v.** [trans.] Comput. (of software) reduce the fragmentation of (a file) by concatenating parts stored in separate locations on a disk. — **de·frag·men·ta·tion** /dē,fragmən'tāsʜən; -men-/ **n.** **de·frag·ment·er n.**

de·fraud /di'frôd/ ▶ **v.** [trans.] illegally obtain money from (someone) by deception. — **de·fraud·er n.** [ME: from OFr. *defrauder* or L. *defraudare*, from *de-* 'from' + *fraudare* 'to cheat' (from *fraus, fraud-* 'fraud').]

de·fray /di'frā/ ▶ **v.** [trans.] provide money to pay (a cost or expense). — **de·fray·a·ble adj.** **de·fray·al** /-'frāəl/ **n.** **de·fray·ment n.** [ME: from Fr. *défrayer*, from *dé-* (expressing removal) + obs. *frai* 'cost, expenses' (from med. L. *fredum* 'a fine').]

de·frock /dē'fräk/ ▶ **v.** [trans.] deprive (a person in holy orders) of ecclesiastical status. ■ [usu. as adj.] (**defrocked**) deprive (someone) of professional status or membership in a prestigious group: *a defrocked psychiatrist.*

de·frost /di'frôst/ ▶ **v.** [trans.] remove frost or ice from (the windshield of a motor vehicle). ■ thaw (frozen food) before cooking it. ■ [intrans.] (of frozen food) thaw before being cooked. ■ free (the interior of a refrigerator) of accumulated ice, usually by turning it off for a period. ■ [intrans.] (of a refrigerator) become free of accumulated ice in this way: *let the fridge defrost.* — **de·frost·er n.**

deft /deft/ ▶ **adj.** neatly skillful and quick in one's movements: *a deft piece of footwork.* ■ demonstrating skill and cleverness. — **deft·ly adv.** **deft·ness n.** [ME: var. of DAFT.]

de·funct /di'fəNGkt/ ▶ **adj.** no longer existing or functioning: *the defunct communist common market.* [16th C.: from L. *defunctus* 'dead,' past part. of *defungi* 'carry out, finish,' from *de-* (expressing reversal) + *fungi* 'perform.']

de·fuse /dē'fyo͞oz/ ▶ **v.** [trans.] remove the fuse from (an explosive device) in order to prevent it from exploding. ■ fig. reduce the danger or tension in (a difficult situation).

de·fy /di'fī/ ▶ **v.** (**-fies**, **-fied**) [trans.] openly resist or refuse to obey: *a woman who defies convention.* ■ (of a thing) make (an action or quality) almost impossible: *his actions defy belief.* ■ [with obj. and infin.] appear to be challenging (someone) to do or prove something: *he glowered at her, defying her to mock him.* — **de·fi·er n.** [ME: from OFr. *desfier*, based on L. *dis-* (expressing reversal) + *fidus* 'faithful.']

deg. ▶ **abbr.** degree(s).

dé·ga·gé /,dāgä'zʜā/ ▶ **adj.** unconcerned or unconstrained; relaxed. ▶ **n.** (pl. same) Ballet pointing of the foot to an open position with an arched instep slightly off the floor. [17th C.: Fr., past part. of *dégager* 'set free.']

De·gas /dā'gä/, Edgar (1834–1917), French painter and sculptor; full name *Hilaire Germain Edgar Degas.* He is known for his paintings of ballet dancers.

de·gas /dē'gas/ ▶ **v.** (**-gassed**, **-gas·sing**) make or become free of unwanted or excess gas: [trans.] *the column has not been degassed* | [intrans.] *the summit craters were degassing freely.*

de Gaulle /də 'gôl/, Charles André Joseph Marie (1890–1970), French general and president 1959–69. He is remembered for his assertive advocacy of France's independence from foreign power.

de·gauss /dē'gous/ ▶ **v.** [trans.] [often as n.] (**degaussing**) Electron. remove unwanted magnetism from (a television or monitor) in order to correct color disturbance. — **de·gauss·er n.**

de·gen·er·a·cy /di'jenərəsē/ ▶ **n.** the state or property of being degenerate.

de·gen·er·ate ▶ **adj.** /di'jenərit/ **1** having lost the physical, mental, or moral qualities considered normal and desirable; showing evidence of decline. **2** tech. lacking some property, order, or distinctness of structure previously or usually present, in particular: ■ Math. relating to or denoting an example of a particular type of equation, curve, or other entity that is equivalent to a simpler type, often occurring when a variable or parameter is set to zero. ■ Physics relating to or denoting an energy level that corresponds to more than one quantum state. ■ Physics relating to or denoting matter at densities so high that gravitational contraction is counteracted either by the Pauli exclusion principle or by an analogous quantum effect between closely packed neutrons. ■ Biol. having reverted to a simpler form as a result of losing a complex or adaptive structure present in the ancestral form. ▶ **n.** an immoral or corrupt person. ▶ **v.** /di'jenərāt/ [intrans.] decline or deteriorate physically, mentally, or morally. — **de·gen·er·a·cy** /di'jenə,rāt/ **n.** **de·gen·er·ate·ly** /-rəsē/ **adv.** **de·gen·er·a·tive** /-ritlē/ **adj.** [15th C.: from L. *degeneratus*, from the v. *degenerare*, from *degener* 'debased,' from *de-* 'away from' + *genus, gener-* 'race, kind.']

de·gen·er·a·tion /di,jenə'rāsʜən/ ▶ **n.** the state or process of being or becoming degenerate; decline or deterioration. ■ Med. deterioration and loss of function in the cells of a tissue or organ.

de·gen·er·a·tive joint dis·ease ▶ **n.** another term for OSTEOARTHRITIS.

de·gla·ci·a·tion /dē,glāsʜē'āsʜən; -,glāsē-/ ▶ **n.** Geol. the disappearance of ice from a previously glaciated region. ■ a period of geological time during which this takes place: *the last deglaciation.*

de·glaze /dē'glāz/ ▶ **v.** [trans.] dilute meat sediments in (a pan) in order to make a gravy or sauce, typically using wine: *deglaze the pan with the white wine.* [19th C.: from Fr. *déglacer*.]

de·glu·ti·tion /,dēglo͞o'tisʜən/ ▶ **n.** tech. the action or process of swallowing. — **de·glu·ti·tive** /dē'glo͞otətiv/ **adj.** [17th C.: from Fr. *déglutition* or mod. L. *deglutitio(n-)*, from *deglutire* 'swallow down.']

deg·ra·da·tion /,degrə'dāsʜən/ ▶ **n.** the condition or process of degrading or being degraded. ■ Geol. the wearing down of rock by disintegration.

de·grade /di'grād/ ▶ **v.** **1** [trans.] treat or regard (someone) with contempt or disrespect. ■ lower the character or quality of. **2** break down or deteriorate chemically. ■ [trans.] Physics reduce (energy) to a less readily convertible form. ■ [trans.] Geol. wear down (rock) and cause it to disintegrate. — **de·grad·a·bil·i·ty** /di,grādə'bilitē/ **n.** **de·grad·a·ble adj.** **deg·ra·da·tive** /'degrə,dātiv/ **adj.** **de·grad·er n.** [ME: from OFr. *degrader*, from eccles. Latin *degradare*, from *de-* 'down, away from' + L. *gradus* 'step or grade.']

de·grad·ing /di'grādiNG/ ▶ **adj.** causing a loss of self-respect; humiliating. — **de·grad·ing·ly adv.**

de·gran·u·late /dē'granyə,lāt/ ▶ **v.** [intrans.] Physiol. (of a cell) lose or release granules of a substance, typically as part of an immune reaction. — **de·gran·u·la·tion** /dē,granyə'lāsʜən/ **n.**

de·grease /dē'grēs/ ▶ **v.** [trans.] [often as n.] (**degreasing**) remove excess grease or fat from (something). — **de·greas·ant** /-'grēsənt/ **n.** **de·greas·er n.**

de·gree /di'grē/ ▶ **n.** **1** [in sing.] the amount, level, or extent to which something happens or is present. **2** a unit of measurement of angles, one three-hundred-and-sixtieth of the circumference of a circle: *set at an angle of 45 degrees.* (Symbol: °) **3** a stage in a scale or series, in particular: ■ a unit in any of various scales of temperature, intensity, or hardness: *water boils at 100 degrees Celsius.* (Symbol: °) ■ [in comb.] each of a set of grades (usually three) used to classify burns according to their severity. See FIRST-DEGREE, SECOND-DEGREE, THIRD-DEGREE. ■ [in comb.] a legal grade of crime or offense, esp. murder: *second-degree murder.* ■ [often in comb.] a step in direct genealogical descent: *second-*

degree relatives. ■ Music a position in a musical scale, counting upward from the tonic or fundamental note: *the lowered third degree of the scale.* ■ Math. the class into which an equation falls according to the highest power of unknowns or variables present: *an equation of the second degree.* **4** an academic rank conferred by a college or university after examination or after completion of a course of study, or as an honor on a distinguished person: *a degree in zoology.* ■ a rank in an order of Freemasonry.
– PHRASES **by degrees** a little at a time; gradually. **to a degree** to some extent. [ME: from OFr., based on L. *de-* 'down' + *gradus* 'step or grade.']

de·gree of free·dom ▶ n. each of a number of independently variable factors affecting the range of states in which a system may exist, in particular: ■ Physics a direction in which independent motion can occur. ■ Chem. each of a number of independent factors required to specify a system at equilibrium. ■ Stat. the number of independent values or quantities which can be assigned to a statistical distribution.

de·gres·sive /di'gresiv/ ▶ adj. reducing by gradual amounts. ■ (of taxation) at successively lower rates on lower amounts. [20th C.: from L. *degress-* 'descended' (from the v. *degredi*, from *de-* 'down' + *gradi* 'walk') + -IVE.]

de·gust /di'gəst/ ▶ v. [trans.] rare taste (something) carefully, so as to appreciate it fully. — **de·gus·ta·tion** /ˌdēgə'stāsʜən/ n. [17th C.: from L. *degustare*, from *de-* 'completely' + *gustare* 'to taste.']

de Hav·il·land, Olivia (1916–), US actress; born in Japan; sister of Joan Fontaine. She is noted for her role as Melanie Hamilton in *Gone with the Wind* (1939). She also starred in *To Each His Own* (Academy Award, 1946) and *The Heiress* (Academy Award, 1949).

de·hisce /di'his/ ▶ v. [intrans.] tech. (of a pod or seed vessel, or of a cut or wound) gape or burst open. — **de·his·cence** /-'hisəns/ n. **de·his·cent** /-'hisənt/ adj. [17th C.: from L. *dehiscere*, from *de-* 'away' + *hiscere* 'begin to gape' (from *hiare* 'gape').]

de·horn /dē'hôrn/ ▶ v. [trans.] remove the horns from (an animal).

de·hors /də'(h)ôr/ ▶ prep. Law other than, not including, or outside the scope of: *the plea shows that no request, dehors the letter, existed.* [18th C.: OFr. (mod. Fr., adv. and n.).]

de·hu·man·ize /dē'(h)yo͞oməˌnīz/ ▶ v. [trans.] deprive of positive human qualities: [as adj.] (**dehumanizing**) *the dehumanizing effects of war.* — **de·hu·man·i·za·tion** /dēˌ(h)yo͞oməni'zāsʜən/ n.

de·hu·mid·i·fi·er /ˌdē(h)yo͞o'midəˌfīər/ ▶ n. a device that removes excess moisture from the air.

de·hu·mid·i·fy /ˌdē(h)yo͞o'midəˌfī/ ▶ v. (**-fies, -fied**) [trans.] remove moisture from (the air or a gas). — **de·hu·mid·i·fi·ca·tion** /-midəfi'kāsʜən/ n.

de·hy·drate /dē'hīdrāt/ ▶ v. [trans.] [often as adj.] (**dehydrated**) cause (a person or a person's body) to lose a large amount of water. ■ [intrans.] lose a large amount of water from the body. ■ remove water from (food) in order to preserve and store it: *dehydrated mashed potatoes.* — **de·hy·dra·tion** /ˌdēhī'drāsʜən/ n. **de·hy·dra·tor** /-tər/ n. [19th C.: from DE- (expressing removal) + Gk. *hudōr, hudr-* 'water.']

de·hy·dro·gen·ase /dē'hīdrəjəˌnās; -ˌnāz/ ▶ n. Biochem. an enzyme that catalyzes the removal of hydrogen atoms from a particular molecule, particularly in the electron transport chain reactions of cell respiration in conjunction with the coenzymes NAD and FAD: [with adj.] *glucose-6-phosphate dehydrogenase.*

de·hy·dro·gen·ate /dē'hīdrəjəˌnāt/ ▶ v. [trans.] Chem. remove a hydrogen atom or atoms from (a compound). — **de·hy·dro·gen·a·tion** /dēˌhīdrəjə'nāsʜən/ n.

de-ice /dē'īs/ ▶ v. [trans.] remove ice from. — **de-ic·er** n.

de·i·cide /'dēəˌsīd/ ▶ n. the killer of a god. ■ the killing of a god. — **de·i·cid·al** /ˌdēə'sīdl/ adj. [17th C.: from eccles. L. *deicida* 'killer of a god,' or directly from L. *deus* 'god' + -CIDE.]

deic·tic /'dīktik/ Ling. ▶ adj. of, relating to, or denoting a word or expression whose meaning is dependent on the context in which it is used, e.g., *here, you, me, that one there*, or *next Tuesday*. Also called **indexical**. ▶ n. a deictic word or expression. — **deic·ti·cal·ly** /-tik(ə)lē/ adv. [19th C.: from Gk. *deiktikos, deiktos* 'demonstrative.']

de·i·fy /'dēəˌfī/ ▶ v. (**-fies, -fied**) [trans.] (usu. **be deified**) worship, regard, or treat (someone or something) as a god. — **de·i·fi·ca·tion** /ˌdēəfi'kāsʜən/ n. [ME: from OFr. *deifier*, from eccles. L. *deificare*, from *deus* 'god.']

Deigh·ton /'dātn/, Len (1929–), English writer; full name *Leonard Cyril Deighton*. His spy thrillers include *The Ipcress File* (1962).

deign /dān/ ▶ v. [no obj., with infin.] do something that one considers to be beneath one's dignity. [ME: from OFr. *degnier*, from L. *dignare, dignari* 'deem worthy,' from *dignus* 'worthy.']

De·i gra·ti·a /'de-ē 'grätsēə/ ▶ adv. by the grace of God. [17th C.: L.]

deil /dēl/ ▶ n. Scottish form of DEVIL.

Dei·mos /'dīmäs/ Astron. the outer, and smaller, of the two satellites of Mars, discovered in 1877. Heavily cratered, it has a diameter of 8 miles (12 km). Compare with PHOBOS.

de·in·dus·tri·al·i·za·tion /ˌdē-inˌdəstrēəli'zāsʜən/ ▶ n. a change from industry to other forms of activity. ■ decline in industrial activity in a region or economy: *severe deindustrialization with substantial job losses.* — **de·in·dus·tri·al·ize** /-'dəstrēəˌlīz/ v.

dei·non·y·chus /dī'nänikəs/ ▶ n. a dromaeosaurid dinosaur (genus *Deinonychus*, family Dromaeosauridae) of the mid Cretaceous period, growing up to 11 feet (3.3 m) in length. [mod. L., from Gk. *deinos* 'terrible' + *onux, onukh-* 'claw.']

de·in·sti·tu·tion·al·ize /dēˌinstə't(y)o͞osʜənlˌīz/ ▶ v. [trans.] discharge (a long-term inmate) from an institution such as a mental hospital or prison. — **de·in·sti·tu·tion·al·i·za·tion** /-ˌt(y)o͞osʜənl-ə'zāsʜən/ n.

de·i·on·ize /dē'īəˌnīz/ ▶ v. [trans.] [usu. as adj.] (**deionized**) remove the ions or ionic constituents from (a substance, esp. water). — **de·i·on·i·za·tion** /dēˌīənə'zāsʜən/ n. **de·i·on·iz·er** n.

de·ism /'dē-izəm/ ▶ n. belief in the existence of a supreme being, specifically of a creator who does not intervene in the universe. Compare with THEISM. — **de·ist** n. **de·is·tic** /dē'istik/ adj. **de·is·ti·cal** /dē'istikəl/ adj. [17th C.: from L. *deus* 'god' + -ISM.]

de·i·ty /'dē-itē/ ▶ n. (pl. **-ties**) a god or goddess (in a polytheistic religion): *a deity of ancient Greece.* ■ divine status, quality, or nature: *a ruler driven by delusions of deity.* ■ (usu. **the Deity**) the creator and Supreme Being (in a monotheistic religion such as Christianity). ■ a representation of a god or goddess, such as a statue or carving. [ME: from OFr. *deite*, from eccles. L. *deitas*, from *deus* 'god.']

dé·jà vu /ˌdāzʜä 'vo͞o/ ▶ n. a feeling of having already experienced the present situation. ■ tedious familiarity. [20th C.: Fr., lit. 'already seen.']

de·ject·ed /di'jektid/ ▶ adj. sad and depressed; dispirited: *he stood in the street looking dejected.* — **de·ject·ed·ly** adv.

de·jec·tion /di'jeksʜən/ ▶ n. a sad and depressed state; low spirits: *he was slumped in deep dejection.* [ME: from L. *dejectio(n-)*, from *deicere* 'throw down,' from *de-* + *jacere* 'to throw.'']

de ju·re /di 'jo͝orē; dā 'jo͝orā/ ▶ adv. according to rightful entitlement or claim; by right. Often contrasted with DE FACTO. ▶ adj. denoting something or someone that is rightfully such: *he had been de jure king since his father's death.* [16th C.: L., lit. 'of law.']

dek·a·gram ▶ n. var. of DECAGRAM.

dek·a·li·ter ▶ n. var. of DECALITER.

dek·a·me·ter ▶ n. var. of DECAMETER.

deke /dēk/ Ice Hockey ▶ n. a deceptive movement or feint that induces an opponent to move out of position. ▶ v. [with obj. and adverbial] draw (a player) out of position by such a movement. [1960s: shortened form of DECOY.]

de Klerk /də 'klerk/, F. W. (1936–), South African president 1989–94; full name *Frederik Willem de Klerk*. He freed Nelson Mandela in 1990, lifted the ban on membership in the African National Congress, and opened the negotiations that led to the first democratic elections in 1994. Nobel Peace Prize (1993, shared with Nelson Mandela).

de Koo·ning /də 'ko͞onɪɴɢ/, Willem (1904–97), US painter; born in the Netherlands. He was a leading exponent of abstract expressionism.

Del. ▶ abbr. Delaware.

De·la·croix /ˌdelə'krwä/, Eugène (1798–1863), French painter; full name *Ferdinand Victor Eugène Delacroix*. He was the leading figure of the French romantic school.

de la Mare /ˌdel ə 'me(ə)r/, Walter John (1873–1956), English poet known for his children's poetry.

de·lam·i·nate /dē'laməˌnāt/ ▶ v. divide or become divided into layers: [trans.] *delaminating the horn into thin sheets* | [intrans.] *the plywood was starting to delaminate.* [19th C.: from DE- 'away' + L. *lamina* 'thin plate' + -ATE[3].]

De·lau·nay /dəlô'nā/, Robert (1885–1941), French painter. With his wife, Sonia Delaunay-Terk (1885–1979), he was one of the founding members of Orphism.

Del·a·ware[1] /'deləˌwe(ə)r/ **1** a river in the northeastern US. It rises in the Catskill Mountains and flows south for about 280 miles (450 km) to Delaware Bay. It forms the eastern border of Pennsylvania. **2** a state in the eastern US, on the Atlantic coast; pop. 683,600; capital, Dover; statehood, Dec. 7, 1787 (1). One of the original thirteen states, it was the first to ratify the US Constitution.

Del·a·ware[2] ▶ n. (pl. same or **-wares**) **1** a member of an American Indian people formerly inhabiting the Delaware River valley of New Jersey and eastern Pennsylvania. **2** either of two Algonquian languages (Munsi and Unami) spoken by this people. ▶ adj. of or relating to the Delaware or their languages.

de·lay /di'lā/ ▶ v. [trans.] make (someone or something) late or slow: *the train was delayed.* ■ [intrans.] be late or slow; loiter. ■ postpone or defer (an action). ▶ n. a period of time by which something is late or postponed. ■ the action of delaying or being delayed: *I set off without delay.* ■ Electron. the time interval between the propagation of an electrical signal and its reception. ■ an electronic device that introduces such an interval, esp. in an audio signal. — **de·lay·er** n. [ME: from OFr. *delayer* (v.).]

de·layed-ac·tion ▶ adj. [attrib.] operating or effective after a predetermined length of time. ▶ n. (**de·layed ac·tion**) the operation of something after a predetermined length of time.

de·lay·ing ac·tion ▶ n. action taken to gain time, esp. a military engagement that delays the advance of an enemy.

de·lay·ing tac·tics ▶ plural n. tactics designed to defer or postpone something in order to gain an advantage for oneself.

de·lay line ▶ n. a device producing a specific desired delay in the transmission of a signal. ■ a set of mirrors controlling the path lengths between outlying telescopes and a central receiver.

de·le /'dēlē/ ▶ v. (**de·led, de·le·ing**) [trans.] delete or mark (a part of a text) for deletion. ▶ n. a proofreader's sign indicating matter to be deleted. [18th C.: L., 'blot out! efface!,' imperative of *delere*.]

de·lec·ta·ble /di'lektəbəl/ ▶ adj. (of food or drink) delicious. ■ esp. humorous extremely beautiful. — **de·lec·ta·bil·i·ty** /-,lektə'bilitē/ n. **de·lec·ta·bly** adv. [ME: via OFr. from L. *delectabilis*, from *delectare* 'to charm' (see DELIGHT).]

de·lec·ta·tion /,dēlek'tāsHən/ ▶ n. formal, esp. humorous pleasure and delight: *a box of chocolates for their delectation.*

del·e·gate ▶ n. /'deligit/ a person sent or authorized to represent others, in particular, an elected representative sent to a conference. ■ a member of a committee. ▶ v. /'deli,gāt/ [trans.] entrust (a task or responsibility) to another person, typically one who is less senior than oneself: *he delegates routine tasks.* ■ [with obj. and infin.] send or authorize (someone) to do something as a representative. — **del·e·ga·ble** /-gəbəl/ adj. **del·e·ga·cy** /-gəsē/ n. **del·e·ga·tor** /-,gātər/ n. [ME: from L. *delegatus* 'sent on a commission,' from the v. *delegare*, from *de-* 'down' + *legare* 'depute.']

del·e·ga·tion /,deli'gāsHən/ ▶ n. [treated as sing. or pl.] a body of delegates or representatives; a deputation. ■ the act or process of delegating or being delegated.

de·le·git·i·mize /,dēli'jitə,mīz/ ▶ v. [trans.] withdraw legitimate status or authority from (someone or something): *efforts to delegitimize nuclear weapons.* — **de·le·git·i·mi·za·tion** /-,jitəmə'zāsHən/ n.

de·lete /di'lēt/ ▶ v. [trans.] remove or obliterate (written or printed matter), esp. by drawing a line through it or marking it with a delete sign: *the passage was deleted.* ■ (usu. **be deleted**) remove (data) from a computer's memory. ■ (**be deleted**) Genet. (of a section of genetic code, or its product) be lost or excised from a nucleic acid or protein sequence. ■ remove (a product, esp. a recording) from the catalog of those available for purchase. ▶ n. a command or key on a computer that erases text. [ME (in the sense 'destroy'): from L. *delet-* 'blotted out, effaced,' from the v. *delere*.]

del·e·te·ri·ous /,deli'ti(ə)rēəs/ ▶ adj. causing harm or damage. — **del·e·te·ri·ous·ly** adv. [17th C.: via med. L. from Gk. *dēlētērios* 'noxious' + -OUS.]

de·le·tion /di'lēsHən/ ▶ n. **1** the action or process of deleting something: *deletion of a file.* **2** Genet. the loss or absence of a section from a nucleic acid molecule or chromosome.

de·lex·i·cal /dē'leksikəl/ ▶ adj. Ling. (of a verb) having little or no meaning in its own right, for example *take* in *take a photograph.*

Delft /delft/ a town in the Netherlands; pop. 89,400. It is noted for its pottery.

delft /delft/ ▶ n. English or Dutch tin-glazed earthenware, typically decorated by hand in blue on a white background. — **delft·ware** /-,we(ə)r/ n. [17th C.: DELFT.]

Del·hi /'delē/ a Union Territory in north central India that contains the cities of Old and New Delhi; pop. 7,175,000. **Old Delhi**, a walled city on the Jumna River, was made the capital of the Mogul empire in 1638 by Shah Jahan (1592–1666). **New Delhi**, the capital of India, was built 1912–29.

del·i /'delē/ ▶ n. (pl. **del·is**) informal short for DELICATESSEN.

De·li·an /'dēlēən/ ▶ adj. of or relating to Delos. ▶ n. a native or inhabitant of Delos.

De·li·an League an alliance of ancient Greek city-states, dominated by Athens, that joined first against the Persians and then against the Spartans in the fifth and fourth centuries BC. Also called the **Athenian empire**.

de·lib·er·ate ▶ adj. /di'libərit/ done consciously and intentionally: *a deliberate attempt to provoke conflict.* ■ fully considered; not impulsive: *a deliberate decision.* ■ done or acting in a careful and unhurried way. ▶ v. /-,rāt/ [intrans.] engage in long and careful consideration: *she deliberated over the menu.* ■ [trans.] consider (a question) carefully. — **de·lib·er·ate·ly** /-əritlē/ adv. **de·lib·er·ate·ness** /-əritnis/ n. **de·lib·er·a·tor** /-ə,rātər/ n. [ME (as an adj.): from L. *deliberatus*, 'considered carefully,' past part. of *deliberare*, from *de-* 'down' + *librare* 'weigh' (from *libra* 'scales').]

de·lib·er·a·tion /di,libə'rāsHən/ ▶ n. **1** long and careful consideration or discussion. **2** slow and careful movement or thought.

de·lib·er·a·tive /di'libərətiv; -ə,rātiv/ ▶ adj. relating to or intended for consideration or discussion. — **de·lib·er·a·tive·ly** adv.

del·i·ca·cy /'delikəsē/ ▶ n. (pl. **-cies**) **1** the quality of being delicate, in particular: ■ fineness or intricacy of texture or structure. ■ susceptibility to illness or adverse conditions; fragility. ■ the quality of requiring discretion or sensitivity: *the delicacy of the situation.* ■ tact and consideration. ■ accuracy of perception; sensitiveness. **2** a choice or expensive food: *a Chinese delicacy.*

del·i·cate /'delikit/ ▶ adj. **1** very fine in texture or structure; of intricate workmanship or quality. ■ (of a color or a scent) subtle and subdued. ■ (of food or drink) subtly and pleasantly flavored. **2** easily broken or damaged; fragile: *delicate china.* ■ (of a person, animal, or plant) susceptible to illness or adverse conditions: *his delicate health.* ■ (of a state or condition) easily upset or damaged. **3** requiring sensitive or careful handling. ■ (of a person or an action) tactful and considerate. ■ skillful and finely judged; deft: *his delicate ball-playing skills.* ■ (of an instrument) highly sensitive. ▶ n. informal a delicate fabric or garment made of such fabric. — **del·i·cate·ly** adv. **del·i·cate·ness** n. [ME: from Fr. *délicat* or L. *delicatus*.]

del·i·ca·tes·sen /,delikə'tesən/ ▶ n. a store selling cold cuts, cheeses, a variety of salads, etc. ■ a counter or section within a supermarket or grocery store at which a range of such foods is available. ■ foods of this type collectively. [19th C.: from Ger. *Delikatessen* or Du. *delicatessen*, from Fr. *délicatesse* 'delicateness,' from *délicat* (see DELICATE).]

De·li·cious /di'lisHəs/ ▶ n. a red or yellow variety of eating apple.

de·li·cious /di'lisHəs/ ▶ adj. highly pleasant to the taste. ■ delightful: *a delicious irony.* — **de·li·cious·ly** adv. **de·li·cious·ness** n. [ME: via OFr. from late L. *deliciosus*, from L. *deliciae* (pl.) 'delight, pleasure.']

de·lict /di'likt/ ▶ n. Law a violation of the law; a tort. [ME: from L. *delictum* 'something showing fault,' neut. past part. of *delinquere* (see DELINQUENT).]

de·light /di'līt/ ▶ v. [trans.] please (someone) greatly. ■ [intrans.] (**delight in**) take great pleasure in. ▶ n. great pleasure. ■ a cause or source of great pleasure. [ME: from OFr. *delitier* (v.), *delit* (n.), from L. *delectare* 'to charm,' frequentative of *delicere*.]

de·light·ed /di'lītid/ ▶ adj. feeling or showing great pleasure: *a delighted smile.* — **de·light·ed·ly** adv.

de·light·ful /di'lītfəl/ ▶ adj. causing delight; charming. — **de·light·ful·ly** adv. **de·light·ful·ness** n.

De·li·lah /di'līlə/ (in the Bible) a woman who betrayed Samson to the Philistines. ■ [as n.] (**a Delilah**) a seductive and wily temptress.

de·lim·it /di'limit/ ▶ v. (**-lim·it·ed, -lim·it·ing**) [trans.] determine the limits or boundaries of. — **de·lim·i·ta·tion** /-,limi'tāsHən/ n. **de·lim·it·er** n. [19th C.: from Fr. *délimiter*, from L. *delimitare*, from *de-* 'down, completely' + *limitare* (from *limes, limit-* 'boundary, limit').]

de·lin·e·ate /di'linē,āt/ ▶ v. [trans.] describe or portray (something) precisely. ■ indicate the exact position of (a border or boundary). — **de·lin·e·a·tion** /-,linē'āsHən/ n. **de·lin·e·a·tor** /-,ātər/ n. [16th C.: from L. *delineat-* 'outlined,' from the v. *delineare*, from *de-* 'out, completely' + *lineare* (from *linea* 'line').]

de·lin·quen·cy /di'liNGkwənsē/ ▶ n. (pl. **-cies**) minor crime, esp. that committed by young people. ■ formal neglect of one's duty. ■ a failure to pay an outstanding debt.

de·lin·quent /di'liNGkwənt/ ▶ adj. (typically of a young person or that person's behavior) showing or characterized by a tendency to commit crime, particularly minor crime: *delinquent children.* ■ in arrears. ■ formal failing in one's duty. ▶ n. a delinquent person: *young delinquents.* — **de·lin·quent·ly** adv. [15th C.: from L. *delinquent-* 'offending,' from the v. *delinquere*, from *de-* 'away' + *linquere* 'to leave.']

del·i·quesce /,deli'kwes/ ▶ v. [intrans.] (of organic matter) become liquid, typically during decomposition. ■ Chem. (of a solid) become liquid by absorbing moisture from the air. — **del·i·ques·cence** /-'kwesəns/ n. **del·i·ques·cent** /-'kwesənt/ adj.

de·lir·i·ous /di'li(ə)rēəs/ ▶ adj. in an acutely disturbed state of mind resulting from illness or intoxication and characterized by restlessness, illusions, and incoherence of thought and speech. ■ in a state of wild excitement or ecstasy. — **de·lir·i·ant** /-ənt/ adj. **de·lir·i·ous·ly** adv.

de·lir·i·um /di'li(ə)rēəm/ ▶ n. an acutely disturbed state of mind that occurs in fever, intoxication, and other disorders. ■ wild excitement or ecstasy. [16th C.: from L., from *delirare* 'deviate, be deranged' (lit. 'deviate from the furrow'), from *de-* 'away' + *lira* 'ridge between furrows.']

de·lir·i·um tre·mens /di'li(ə)rēəm 'trēmənz/ ▶ n. a psychotic condition typical of withdrawal in chronic alcoholics, involving tremors, hallucinations, anxiety, and disorientation. [19th C.: from L., 'trembling delirium.']

de·lish /di'lisH/ ▶ adj. informal delicious.

de·list /dē'list/ ▶ v. [trans.] remove (something) from a list, in particular: ■ remove (a security) from the official register of a stock exchange. ■ remove (a product) from the list of those sold by a particular retailer.

de·liv·er /di'livər/ ▶ v. [trans.] **1** bring and hand over (a letter, parcel, or ordered goods) to the proper recipient or address. ■ formally hand over (someone). ■ obtain (a vote) in favor of a candidate or cause. ■ launch or aim (a blow, a ball, or an attack): *the pitcher winds up to deliver the ball.* ■ provide (something promised or expected). ■ (**deliver someone/something from**) save, rescue, or set free from. ■ (**deliver someone/something up**) surrender someone or something: *to deliver up to justice a member of his own family.* ■ Law acknowledge that one intends to be bound by (a deed), either explicitly by declaration or implicitly by formal handover. **2** state in a formal manner. ■ (of a judge or court) give (a judgment or verdict). **3** assist in the birth of. ■ give birth to: *she will deliver a child.* ■ (**be delivered of**) give birth to. ■ assist (a woman) in giving birth.

– PHRASES **deliver the goods** informal provide what is promised or expected. — **de·liv·er·er** n. [ME: from OFr. *delivrer*, based on L. *de-* 'away' + *liberare* 'set free.']

de·liv·er·a·ble /di'livərəbəl/ ▶ adj. able to be delivered. ▶ n. (usu. **deliverables**) a thing able to be provided, esp. as a product of a development process.

de·liv·er·ance /di'livərəns/ ▶ n. **1** the action of being rescued or set free: *prayers for deliverance.* **2** a formal or authoritative utterance.

de·liv·er·y /di'livərē/ ▶ n. (pl. **-er·ies**) **1** the action of delivering letters, packages, or ordered goods. ■ a regular or scheduled occasion for this: *there will be 15 deliveries a week.* ■ an item or items delivered on a particular occasion. ■ Law the formal or symbolic handing over of property, esp. a sealed deed, to a grantee or third party. **2** the process of giving birth. **3** an act of throwing or bowling a ball or striking a blow: *a quick delivery that sent the ball zinging.* ■ the style or manner of such an action. **4** the manner or style of giving a speech. **5** the supply or provision of something.

– PHRASES **take delivery of** receive (something purchased): *we took delivery of the software in February.*

dell /del/ ▶ **n.** literary a small valley, usually among trees. [OE, of Gmc. origin; rel. to Du. *del* and DALE.]

del·la Quer·cia /ˌdelə ˈkwerchə/, Jacopo (*c.*1374–1438), Italian sculptor. He sculpted the biblical reliefs on the portal of San Petronio in Bologna (1425–35).

del·la Rob·bia /ˌdelə ˈrōbēə; ˈräb-/, Luca (1400–82), Italian sculptor. He sculpted the relief panels in Florence Cathedral.

Del·mar·va Peninsula /delˈmärvə/ a region that includes parts of *Delaware, Maryland,* and *Virginia.* Chesapeake Bay lies to the west.

Del·mon·i·co steak /delˈmäniˈkō/ ▶ **n.** a small steak cut from the front section of the short loin of beef. Also called CLUB STEAK. [named for Lorenzo Delmonico (1813–81), Swiss-born US restaurateur.]

de·lo·cal·ize /dēˈlōkəˌlīz/ ▶ **v.** [trans.] detach or remove (something) from a particular place or location. ■ not limit to a particular location: [as n.] (**delocalizing**) *delocalizing of finance capital.* ■ (**be delocalized**) Chem. (of electrons) be shared among more than two atoms in a molecule. — **de·lo·cal·i·za·tion** /-ˌlōkələˈzāshən/ **n.**

De·los /ˈdēläs; ˈdelōs/ a small Greek island in the Aegean Sea, regarded as the center of the Cyclades. It was considered to be sacred to Apollo in classical times and, according to legend, was the birthplace of Apollo and Artemis. Greek name DHÍLOS.

de·louse /dēˈlous/ ▶ **v.** [trans.] rid (a person or animal) of lice and other parasitic insects.

Del·phi /ˈdelfī/ one of the most important religious sanctuaries of the ancient Greek world, dedicated to Apollo, situated on the lower southern slopes of Mount Parnassus. Greek name DHELFOÍ.

Del·phic /ˈdelfik/ (also **Del·phi·an** /-fēən/) ▶ **adj.** of or relating to the ancient Greek oracle at Delphi. ■ (typically of a pronouncement) deliberately obscure or ambiguous.

del·phin·i·um /delˈfinēəm/ ▶ **n.** (pl. **-ums**) a plant (genus *Delphinium*) of the buttercup family that bears tall spikes of typically blue flowers. [mod. L., from Gk. *delphinion* 'larkspur,' from *delphin* 'dolphin.']

Del·phi·nus /delˈfīnəs/ Astron. a small constellation (the Dolphin), just north of the celestial equator near Cygnus.

del Sar·to /del ˈsärtō/, Andrea, see SARTO.

del·ta[1] /ˈdeltə/ ▶ **n. 1** the fourth letter of the Greek alphabet (Δ, δ), transliterated as "d." ■ [as adj.] the fourth in a series of items, categories, etc.: *delta hepatitis.* **2** a code word representing the letter D, used in radio communication. ▶ **symb.** ■ (δ) Math. variation of a variable or function. ■ (Δ) Math. a finite increment. ■ (δ) Astron. declination.

del·ta[2] ▶ **n.** a triangular tract of sediment deposited at the mouth of a river. — **del·ta·ic** /delˈtāik/ **adj.** [16th C.: from the Gk. letter (see DELTA[1]).]

Del·ta Force an elite US Army unit that performs rescue operations and special forces work.

del·ta rays ▶ **plural n.** Physics rays of low penetrative power consisting of slow electrons or other particles ejected from atoms by the impact of ionizing radiation.

del·ta rhythm ▶ **n.** electrical activity of the brain at a frequency of around 1–8 Hz, typical of sleep. The resulting oscillations, detected using an electroencephalograph, are called **delta waves.**

Del·ta, the a region in northern Mississippi that lies between the Yazoo and Mississippi rivers. Also called the **Yazoo Delta** or **Mississippi Delta.**

del·ta-v (also **del·ta-vee**) ▶ **n.** informal acceleration. [20th C.: *v* for *velocity.*]

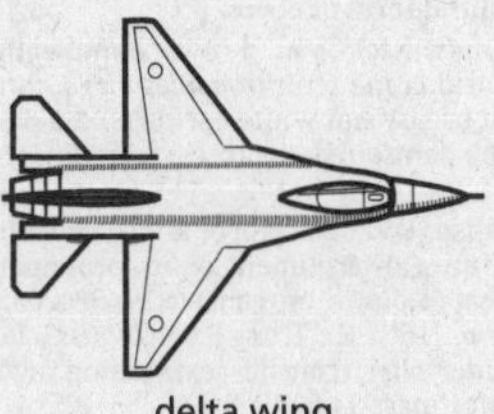

delta wing

del·ta wing ▶ **n.** the single triangular swept-back wing on some aircraft, typically on military aircraft. — **del·ta-winged adj.**

del·toid /ˈdeltoid/ ▶ **adj.** tech. triangular. ■ denoting a thick triangular muscle covering the shoulder joint and used for raising the arm away from the body. ▶ **n.** a deltoid muscle. ■ each of the three parts of a deltoid muscle, attached at the front, side, and rear of the shoulder. [18th C.: from Fr. *deltoïde,* or via mod. L. from Gk. *deltoeidēs.*]

de·lude /diˈlo͞od/ ▶ **v.** [trans.] impose a misleading belief upon (someone); deceive; fool. — **de·lud·ed·ly adv. de·lud·er n.** [ME: from L. *deludere* 'to mock,' from *de-* (with pejorative force) + *ludere* 'to play.']

del·uge /ˈdel(y)o͞oj/ ▶ **n.** a severe flood. ■ (**the Deluge**) the biblical Flood (recorded in Genesis 6–8). ■ a heavy fall of rain. ■ fig. a great quantity of something arriving at the same time. ▶ **v.** [trans.] (usu. **be deluged**) inundate with a great quantity of something. ■ flood: *the country was deluged with rain.* [ME: from OFr., var. of *diluve,* from L. *diluvium,* from *diluere* 'wash away.']

de·lu·sion /diˈlo͞ozhən/ ▶ **n.** an idiosyncratic belief or impression that is firmly maintained despite being contradicted by what is generally accepted as reality, typically a symptom of mental disorder. ■ the action of deluding someone or the state of being deluded: *what a capacity television has for delusion.*

– PHRASES **delusions of grandeur** a false impression of one's own importance. — **de·lu·sion·al** /-zhənl/ **adj.** [ME: from late L. *delusio(n-),* from the v. *deludere.*]

de·lu·sive /diˈlo͞osiv/ ▶ **adj.** giving a false or misleading impression: *the delusive light of Venice.* — **de·lu·sive·ly adv. de·lu·sive·ness n.**

de·lu·so·ry /diˈlo͞osərē; -zərē/ ▶ **adj.** another term for DELUSIVE.

de·lust·er /dēˈləstər/ ▶ **v.** [trans.] remove the luster from (a textile), typically by chemical treatment.

de·luxe /diˈləks/ ▶ **adj.** luxurious or sumptuous; of a superior kind: *a deluxe hotel.* [19th C.: from Fr. *de luxe,* literally 'of luxury.']

delve /delv/ ▶ **v.** [intrans.] reach inside a receptacle and search for something: *she delved in her pocket.* ■ research or make painstaking inquiries into something. ■ [trans.] literary dig; excavate. — **delv·er n.** [OE *delfan* 'dig,' of West Gmc. origin; rel. to Du. *delven.*]

Dem. ▶ **abbr.** Democrat.

de·mag·net·ize /dēˈmagniˌtīz/ ▶ **v.** [trans.] remove magnetic properties from. — **de·mag·net·i·za·tion** /-ˌmagnitəˈzāshən/ **n. de·mag·net·iz·er n.**

dem·a·gogue /ˈdeməˌgäg/ ▶ **n.** a political leader who seeks support by appealing to popular desires and prejudices rather than by using rational argument. ■ (in ancient Greece and Rome) a leader or orator who espoused the cause of the common people. — **dem·a·gog·ic** /ˌdeməˈgäjik; -ˈgägik; -ˈgōjik/ **adj. dem·a·gogu·er·y** /ˈdeməˌgägərē/ **n. dem·a·go·gy** /ˈdeməˌgäjē; -ˌgōjē/ **n.** [17th C.: from Gk. *dēmagōgos,* from *dēmos* 'the people' + *agōgos* 'leading' (from *agein* 'to lead').]

de Mainte·non /də maNtˈnôN/ see MAINTENON.

de·mand /diˈmand/ ▶ **n.** an insistent and peremptory request, made as if by right. ■ (**demands**) pressing requirements: *he's got enough **demands** on his time already.* ■ Econ. the desire of purchasers, consumers, clients, employers, etc., for a particular commodity, service, or other item. ▶ **v.** [reporting verb] ask authoritatively or brusquely. ■ [trans.] insist on having: *an outraged public demanded retribution.* ■ require; need: *an activity demanding detailed knowledge.* ■ Law call into court; summon.

– PHRASES **in demand** sought after. **on demand** as soon as or whenever required. — **de·mand·er n.** [ME (as a noun): from OFr. *demande* (n.), *demander* (v.), from L. *demandare* 'hand over, entrust,' from *de-* 'formally' + *mandare* 'to order.']

de·mand de·pos·it ▶ **n.** a deposit of money that can be withdrawn without prior notice.

de·mand draft ▶ **n.** a financial draft payable on demand.

de·mand feed·ing ▶ **n.** the practice of feeding a baby when it cries to be fed rather than at set times.

de·mand·ing /diˈmandiNG/ ▶ **adj.** (of a task) requiring much skill or effort: *she has a busy and demanding job.* ■ (of a person) making others work hard or meet high standards. — **de·mand·ing·ly adv.**

de·mand-led (also **de·mand-driv·en**) ▶ **adj.** Econ. caused or determined by demand from consumers or clients.

de·mand note ▶ **n.** a formal request for payment. ■ another term for DEMAND DRAFT.

de·mar·cate /diˈmärkāt; ˈdēmärˌkāt/ (also **de·mar·kate**) ▶ **v.** [trans.] set the boundaries or limits of. ■ separate or distinguish from. [19th C.: backform. from DEMARCATION.]

de·mar·ca·tion /ˌdēmärˈkāshən/ ▶ **n.** the action of fixing the boundary or limits of something. ■ a dividing line. — **de·mar·ca·tor** /diˈmärkātər/ **n.** [18th C.: from Sp. *demarcación,* from *demarcar* 'mark the bounds of,' ult. of Gmc. origin and rel. to MARK[1].]

dé·marche /dāˈmärsh/ ▶ **n.** a political step or initiative. [17th C.: Fr., from *démarcher* 'take steps.']

de·mas·si·fy /dēˈmasiˌfī/ ▶ **v.** (**-fies, -fied**) [trans.] divide or break up (a social or political unit) into its component parts. — **de·mas·si·fi·ca·tion** /-ˌmasifiˈkāshən/ **n.**

de·ma·te·ri·al·ize /ˌdēməˈti(ə)rēəˌlīz/ ▶ **v.** [intrans.] become free of physical substance, in particular: ■ (in science fiction) disappear through some imagined technological process. ■ become spiritual rather than physical. ■ [trans.] [usu. as adj.] (**dematerialized**) replace (physical records or certificates) with a paperless computerized system. — **de·ma·te·ri·al·i·za·tion** /-ˌti(ə)rēələˈzāshən/ **n.**

de Mau·pas·sant /də ˌmōpəˈsänt; də mōpaˈsäN/, Guy, see MAUPASSANT.

deme /dēm/ ▶ **n. 1** a political division of Attica in ancient Greece. ■ an administrative division in modern Greece. **2** Biol. a subdivision of a population consisting of closely related plants, animals, or people, typically breeding mainly within the group. [from Gk. *dēmos* 'people.']

PRONUNCIATION KEY ə *ago, up;* ər *over, fur;* a *hat;* ā *ate;* ä *car;* e *let;* ē *see;* i *fit;* ī *by;* NG *sing;* ō *go;* ô *law, for;* oi *toy;* o͝o *good;* o͞o *goo;* ou *out;* TH *thin;* T͟H *then;* ZH *vision*

de·mean /di'mēn/ ▶ **v.** [trans.] [often as adj.] (**demeaning**) cause a severe loss in the dignity of and respect for (someone or something). ■ (**demean oneself**) do something that is beneath one's dignity. [17th C.: from DE- 'away, down' + the adj. MEAN[2], on the pattern of *debase*.]

de·mean·or /di'mēnər/ (Brit. **de·mean·our**) ▶ **n.** outward behavior or bearing: *a quiet, somber demeanor.* [15th C.: from DEMEAN 'to conduct,' from OFr. *demener*, based on L. *de-* 'away' + *minare* 'to drive,' from *minari* 'threaten.']

de' Med·i·ci[1], Catherine, see CATHERINE DE' MEDICI.

de' Med·i·ci[2], Cosimo, see COSIMO DE' MEDICI.

de' Med·i·ci[3], Giovanni, the name of Pope Leo X (see LEO[1]).

de' Med·i·ci[4], Lorenzo, see LORENZO DE' MEDICI.

de Méd·i·cis, Marie, see MARIE DE MÉDICIS.

de·ment·ed /di'mentid/ ▶ **adj.** suffering from dementia. ■ informal driven to behave irrationally due to anger, distress, or excitement. — **de·ment·ed·ly** adv. **de·ment·ed·ness** n. [17th C.: past part. of earlier *dement* 'drive mad,' from OFr. *dementer* or late L. *dementare*, from *demens* 'out of one's mind.']

dé·men·ti /,dāmän'tē/ ▶ **n.** an official denial of a published statement. [Fr., from *démentir* 'contradict or accuse of lying.']

de·men·tia /di'mensHə/ ▶ **n.** Med. a chronic or persistent disorder of the mental processes caused by brain disease or injury and marked by memory disorders, personality changes, and impaired reasoning. [18th C.: from L., from *demens, dement-* 'out of one's mind.']

Dem·e·ra·ra /,demə're(ə)rə; -'rärə/ a river in northern Guyana. It flows north for about 200 miles (320 km) to the Atlantic Ocean.

dem·e·ra·ra /,demə're(ə)rə; -'rärə/ ▶ **n.** **1** (also **demerara sugar**) light brown cane sugar coming originally and chiefly from Guyana. **2** (also **demerara rum**) a dark rum fermented from molasses, made in Guyana. [19th C.: DEMERARA.]

de·mer·it /di'merit/ ▶ **n.** **1** a feature or fact deserving censure: *the merits and demerits of these proposals.* **2** a mark awarded against someone for a fault or offense. [ME: from OFr. *desmerite* or L. *demeritum* 'something deserved,' neut. past part. of *demereri*, from *de-* 'thoroughly' + *mereri* 'to merit.']

Dem·e·rol /'demə,rôl; -,räl/ ▶ **n.** trademark for MEPERIDINE.

de·mer·sal /di'mərsəl/ ▶ **adj.** (typically of fish) living close to the floor of the sea or a lake. Often contrasted with PELAGIC. [19th C.: from L. *demersus* (past part. of *demergere* 'submerge, sink,' from *de-* 'down' + *mergere* 'plunge') + -AL.]

de·mesne /di'mān/ ▶ **n.** hist. **1** land attached to a manor and retained for the owner's own use. **2** Law, hist. possession of real property in one's own right. [ME: from OFr. *demeine* 'belonging to a lord,' from L. *dominicus*, from *dominus* 'lord, master.']

De·me·ter /di'mētər/ Gk. Mythol. the goddess of cereal grains, mother of Persephone. She is associated with Cybele; her symbol is typically an ear of wheat. Roman equivalent CERES. See also PERSEPHONE.

demi- ▶ **prefix** **1** half; half-size: *demitasse.* **2** partially; in an inferior degree: *demigod.* [via Fr. from med. L. *dimedius* 'half,' from earlier *dimidius*.]

dem·i-glace /'demē ,glas/ (also **de·mi-glaze** /,glāz/) ▶ **n.** a rich, glossy brown sauce from which the liquid has been partly evaporated, typically flavored with wine and served with meat. [20th C.: Fr., lit. 'half glaze.']

dem·i·god /'demē,gäd/ ▶ **n.** (fem. **dem·i·god·dess** /'demē,gädis/) a being with partial or lesser divine status, such as a minor deity, the offspring of a god and a mortal, or a mortal raised to divine rank. ■ fig. a person who is greatly admired or feared.

dem·i·john /'demē,jän/ ▶ **n.** a bulbous, narrow-necked bottle holding from 3 to 10 gallons of liquid. [18th C.: prob. an alt. of Fr. *dame-jeanne* 'Lady Jane.']

de·mil·i·ta·rize /dē'militə,rīz/ ▶ **v.** [trans.] [usu. as adj.] (**demilitarized**) remove all military forces from (an area): *a demilitarized zone.* — **de·mil·i·ta·ri·za·tion** /-,militərə'zāsHən/ **n.**

de Mille /də 'mil/, Agnes George (1905–93), US dancer and choreographer; the niece of director Cecil B. De Mille. She choreographed the ballet *Rodeo* (1942) and the Broadway musical *Paint Your Wagon* (1951).

De Mille /də 'mil/, Cecil B. (1881–1959), US producer and director; full name *Cecil Blount De Mille*. His epic movies include *The Ten Commandments* (1923, 1956).

dem·i·monde /'demē,mänd/ (also **dem·i-monde**) ▶ **n.** (in 19th-century France) the class of women considered to be of doubtful morality and social standing. ■ a group of people considered to be on the fringes of respectable society: *the demimonde of arms deals.* — **dem·i·mon·daine** /,demēmän'dān/ (also **demi-mondaine**) **n.** [19th C.: from Fr. *demi-monde*, lit. 'half-world.']

de·min·er·al·ize /dē'minərə,līz/ ▶ **v.** [trans.] [often as adj.] (**demineralized**) remove salts from (water). ■ deprive (teeth or bones) of minerals, causing loss of tooth enamel or softening of the skeleton. — **de·min·er·al·i·za·tion** /-,minərələ'zāsHən/ **n.**

de·mise /di'mīz/ ▶ **n.** [in sing.] **1** a person's death. ■ the end or failure of an enterprise or institution. **2** Law conveyance or transfer of property or a title by demising. ▶ **v.** [trans.] Law convey or grant (an estate) by will or lease. ■ transmit (a sovereign's title) by death or abdication. [ME: from Anglo-Norman Fr., past part. of OFr. *desmettre* 'dismiss,' based on L. *dimittere* (see DISMISS).]

dem·i-sec /'demē,sek/ ▶ **adj.** (of wine) medium dry. [20th C.: Fr., literally 'half-dry.']

dem·i·tasse /'demē,täs; -,tas/ ▶ **n.** a small coffee cup. [19th C.: from Fr., literally 'half-cup.']

dem·i·urge /'demē,ərj/ ▶ **n.** a being responsible for the creation of the universe, in particular: ■ (in Platonic philosophy) the Maker or Creator of the world. ■ (in Gnosticism and other theological systems) a heavenly being, subordinate to the Supreme Being, that is considered to be the controller of the material world and antagonistic to all that is purely spiritual. — **dem·i·ur·gic** /,demē'ərjik/ **adj.** **dem·i·ur·gi·cal** /,demē'ərjikəl/ **adj.** [17th C.: via eccles. L. from Gk. *dēmiourgos* 'craftsman,' from *dēmios* 'public' (from *dēmos* 'people') + *-ergos* 'working.']

dem·o /'demō/ informal ▶ **n.** (pl. **-os**) a demonstration of the capabilities of something, typically computer software or a musical group: [as adj.] *we hired them to produce a demo tape.* ▶ **v.** (**-os, -oed**) [trans.] demonstrate the capabilities of (software or equipment). ■ record (a song) for demonstration purposes: *they've already demoed twelve new songs.*

de·mo·bi·lize /dē'mōbə,līz/ ▶ **v.** [trans.] (usu. **be demobilized**) take (troops) out of active service, typically at the end of a war: *he was demobilized in February 1946.* ■ [intrans.] cease military operations. — **de·mo·bi·li·za·tion** /-,mōbələ'zāsHən/ **n.**

de·moc·ra·cy /di'mäkrəsē/ ▶ **n.** (pl. **-cies**) a system of government by the whole population or all the eligible members of a state, typically through elected representatives. ■ a state governed in such a way. ■ control of an organization or group by the majority of its members. ■ the practice or principles of social equality. [16th C.: from Fr. *démocratie*, via late L. from Gk. *dēmokratia*, from *dēmos* 'the people' + *-kratia* 'power, rule.']

dem·o·crat /'demə,krat/ ▶ **n.** **1** an advocate or supporter of democracy. **2** (**Democrat**) a member of the Democratic Party.

dem·o·crat·ic /,demə'kratik/ ▶ **adj.** **1** of, relating to, or supporting democracy or its principles. ■ favoring or characterized by social equality; egalitarian. **2** (**Democratic**) of or relating to the Democratic Party. — **dem·o·crat·i·cal·ly** /-ik(ə)lē/ **adv.**

Dem·o·crat·ic Par·ty one of the two main US political parties (the other being the Republican Party); it follows a liberal program and tends to promote a strong central government and expansive social programs.

Dem·o·crat·ic Re·pub·li·can Par·ty a US political party that was founded in 1792 by Thomas Jefferson and was a forerunner of the modern Democratic Party.

de·moc·ra·tize /di'mäkrə,tīz/ ▶ **v.** [trans.] (often **be democratized**) introduce a democratic system or democratic principles to: *public institutions need to be democratized.* ■ make (something) accessible to everyone: *mass production has not democratized fashion.* — **de·moc·ra·ti·za·tion** /-,mäkrətə'zāsHən/ **n.**

De·moc·ri·tus /də'mäkritəs; dē-/ (*c.*460–*c.*370 BC), Greek philosopher. He developed the atomic theory originated by his teacher Leucippus.

de·mod·u·late /dē'mäjə,lāt/ ▶ **v.** [trans.] Electron. extract (a modulating signal) from its carrier. ■ separate a modulating signal from (its carrier). — **de·mod·u·la·tion** /-,mäjə'lāsHən/ **n.** **de·mod·u·la·tor** /-,lātər/ **n.**

dem·o·graph·ic /,demə'grafik/ ▶ **adj.** relating to the structure of populations. ▶ **n.** a particular sector of a population: *the drink is popular with a young demographic.* — **dem·o·graph·i·cal** **adj.** **dem·o·graph·i·cal·ly** /-ik(ə)lē/ **adv.**

dem·o·graph·ics /,demə'grafiks/ ▶ **plural n.** statistical data relating to the population and particular groups within it: *the demographics of book buyers.*

de·mog·ra·phy /di'mägrəfē/ ▶ **n.** the study of statistics such as births, deaths, income, or the incidence of disease, which illustrate the changing structure of human populations. ■ the composition of a particular human population: *Europe's demography is changing.* — **de·mog·ra·pher** /-fər/ **n.** [19th C.: from Gk. *dēmos* 'the people' + -GRAPHY.]

de·moi /'dēmoi/ plural form of DEMOS.

dem·oi·selle /,dem(w)ə'zel/ ▶ **n.** **1** (also **demoiselle crane**) a small, graceful Old World crane (*Anthropoides virgo*, family Gruidae) with a black head and breast and white ear tufts. **2** a damselfly, esp. of the genus *Agrion*. **3** a damselfish. [16th C.: from Fr., from OFr. *dameisele* 'damsel.']

de·mol·ish /di'mälisH/ ▶ **v.** [trans.] pull or knock down (a building). ■ comprehensively refute (an argument or its proponent). ■ informal overwhelmingly defeat (a player or team). ■ humorous eat up (food) quickly. — **de·mol·ish·er** **n.** [16th C.: from Fr. *démoliss-*, lengthened stem of *démolir*, from L. *demoliri*, from *de-* (expressing reversal) + *moliri* 'construct' (from *moles* 'mass').]

dem·o·li·tion /,demə'lisHən/ ▶ **n.** the action or process of demolishing or being demolished. ■ informal an overwhelming defeat. [16th C.: via Fr. from L. *demolitio(n-)*, from the v. *demoliri* (see DEMOLISH).]

dem·o·li·tion der·by ▶ **n.** a competition in which typically older cars are driven into each other until only one is left running.

de·mon[1] /'dēmən/ ▶ **n.** **1** an evil spirit or devil, esp. one thought to possess a person or act as a tormentor in hell. ■ a cruel, evil, or destructive person or thing. ■ [often as adj.] a forceful, fierce, or skillful performer of a specified activity. ■ reckless mischief; devilry. **2** another term for DAEMON[1] (sense 1).

– PHRASES **like a demon** in a very forceful, fierce, or skillful way: *he worked like a demon.* [ME: from med. L., from L. *daemon*, from Gk.

daimōn 'deity, genius'; in sense 1 also from L. *daemonium* 'lesser or evil spirit.']

de·mon² ▶ n. var. of DAEMON².

de·mon·e·tize /dē'mäni,tīz/ ▶ v. [trans.] (usu. **be demonetized**) deprive (a coin or precious metal) of its status as money. — **de·mon·e·ti·za·tion** /-,mänitə'zāsHən/ n. [19th C.: from Fr. *démonétiser*, from *dé-* (expressing reversal) + L. *moneta* 'money.']

de·mo·ni·ac /di'mōnē,ak/ ▶ adj. of, like, or characteristic of a demon or demons. ▶ n. a person believed to be possessed by an evil spirit. — **de·mo·ni·a·cal** /,dēmə'nīəkəl/ adj. **de·mo·ni·a·cal·ly** /,dēmə'nīək(ə)lē/ adv. [ME: from OFr. *demoniaque*, from eccles. L. *daemoniacus*, from *daemonium* 'lesser or evil spirit.']

de·mon·ic /di'mänik/ ▶ adj. of, resembling, or characteristic of demons or evil spirits. ■ fiercely energetic or frenzied: *in a demonic hurry.* — **de·mon·i·cal·ly** adv.

de·mon·ize /'dēmə,nīz/ ▶ v. [trans.] portray as wicked and threatening. — **de·mon·i·za·tion** /,dēməni'zāsHən/ n.

demono- ▶ comb. form of or relating to demons. [from Gk. *daimōn* 'demon.']

de·mon·ol·a·try /,dēmə'nälətrē/ ▶ n. the worship of demons.

de·mon·ol·o·gy /,dēmə'näləjē/ ▶ n. the study of demons or of demonic belief. — **de·mon·o·log·i·cal** /-nə'läjikəl/ adj. **de·mon·ol·o·gist** /-jist/ n.

de·mo·nop·o·lize /,dēmə'näpə,līz/ ▶ v. [trans.] introduce competition into (a market or economy) by privatizing previously nationalized assets. — **de·mo·nop·o·li·za·tion** /-,näpələ'zāsHən/ n.

de·mon·stra·ble /di'mänstrəbəl/ ▶ adj. clearly apparent or capable of being logically proved. — **de·mon·stra·bil·i·ty** /-,mänstrə'bilitē/ n.

de·mon·stra·bly /di'mänstrəblē/ ▶ adv. clearly and undeniably: *the situation is demonstrably unfair.*

dem·on·strate /'demən,strāt/ ▶ v. **1** [trans.] clearly show the existence or truth of (something) by giving proof or evidence. ■ give a practical exhibition and explanation of (how a machine, skill, or craft works or is performed). ■ show or express (a feeling or quality) by one's actions. **2** [intrans.] take part in a public demonstration. [16th C.: from L. *demonstrat-* 'pointed out,' from the v. *demonstrare.*]

dem·on·stra·tion /,demən'strāsHən/ ▶ n. **1** the action or process of showing the existence or truth of something by giving proof or evidence. ■ something that proves or makes evident: *the letter was a demonstration of good faith.* ■ the outward showing of feeling. ■ a practical exhibition and explanation of how something works or is performed. ■ a show of military force. **2** a public meeting or march protesting against something or expressing views on a political issue.

de·mon·stra·tive /di'mänstrətiv/ ▶ adj. **1** (of a person) tending to show feelings, esp. of affection, openly. **2** serving as conclusive evidence of something; giving proof: *demonstrative evidence.* ■ involving demonstration, esp. by scientific means. **3** Gram. (of a determiner or pronoun) indicating the person or thing referred to (e.g., *this, that, those*). ▶ n. Gram. a demonstrative determiner or pronoun. — **de·mon·stra·tive·ly** adv. **de·mon·stra·tive·ness** n.

dem·on·stra·tor /'demən,strātər/ ▶ n. **1** a person who takes part in a public protest meeting or march. **2** a person who shows how a particular piece of equipment works or how a skill or craft is performed.

de Mont·fort /də 'mäntfərt; -fôrt/, Simon, see MONTFORT.

de·mor·al·ize /di'môrə,līz/ ▶ v. [trans.] [usu. as adj.] (**demoralized**) cause (someone) to lose confidence or hope; dispirit: *by the end of the month, the army was demoralized and scattered.* — **de·mor·al·i·za·tion** /-,môrələ'zāsHən/ n. **de·mor·al·iz·ing** adj. **de·mor·al·iz·ing·ly** adv. [18th C.: from Fr. *démoraliser*, from *dé-* (expressing reversal) + *moral* 'moral,' from L. *moralis.*]

de·mos /'dēmäs/ ▶ n. (pl. **-moi** /-moi/) the common people of an ancient Greek state. ■ the populace as a political unit, esp. in a democracy. [from Gk. *dēmos.*]

De·mos·the·nes /də'mäsTHə,nēz/ (384–322 BC), Athenian orator. His political speeches urged resistance against Philip II of Macedon.

de·mote /di'mōt/ ▶ v. [trans.] (often **be demoted**) give (someone) a lower rank or less senior position, usually as a punishment. [19th C.: from DE- 'down' + a shortened form of PROMOTE.]

de·mot·ic /di'mätik/ ▶ adj. denoting or relating to the kind of language used by ordinary people; popular or colloquial: *a demotic idiom.* ■ relating to or denoting the form of modern Greek used in everyday speech and writing. Compare with KATHAREVOUSA. ■ relating to or denoting a simplified, cursive form of ancient Egyptian script, dating from *c.*650 BC and replaced by Greek in the Ptolemaic period. Compare with HIERATIC. ▶ n. ordinary colloquial speech. ■ demotic Greek. ■ demotic Egyptian script. [19th C.: from Gk. *dēmotikos* 'popular,' from *dēmotēs* 'one of the people,' from *dēmos* 'the people.']

de·mo·tion /di'mōsHən/ ▶ n. reduction in rank or status: *too many demotions would weaken morale.*

de·mount·a·ble /dē'mountəbəl/ ▶ adj. able to be dismantled or removed from its setting and readily reassembled or repositioned. — **de·mount** v.

Demp·sey /'dem(p)sē/, Jack (1895–1983), US boxer; full name *William Harrison Dempsey.* He was world heavyweight champion 1919–26.

de·mul·cent /di'məlsənt/ Med. ▶ adj. (of a substance) relieving inflammation or irritation. ▶ n. a substance that relieves irritation of the mucous membranes in the mouth by forming a protective film. [18th C.: from L. *demulcent-* 'stroking caressingly,' from the v. *demulcere*, from *de-* 'away' + *mulcere* 'soothe.']

de·mur /di'mər/ ▶ v. (**-murred, -mur·ring**) [intrans.] raise doubts or objections or show reluctance. ■ Law, dated put forward a demurrer. ▶ n. [usu. with negative] the action or process of objecting to or hesitating over something. [ME: from OFr. *demourer* (v.), *demeure* (n.), based on L. *de-* 'away, completely' + *morari* 'delay.']

de·mure /di'myŏŏr/ ▶ adj. (**-mur·er, -mur·est**) (of a woman or her behavior) reserved, modest, and shy. ■ (of clothing) lending such an appearance. — **de·mure·ly** adv. **de·mure·ness** n. [ME: perh. from OFr. *demoure*, past part. of *demourer* 'remain, stay' (see DEMUR).]

de·mur·rage /di'mərij; -'mə-rij/ ▶ n. Law a charge payable to the owner of a chartered ship in respect of failure to load or discharge the ship within the time agreed.

de·mur·ral /di'mərəl; -'mə-rəl/ ▶ n. the action of demurring.

de·mur·rer /di'mərər; -'mə-rər/ ▶ n. an objection. ■ Law, dated an objection that an opponent's point is irrelevant or invalid, while granting the factual basis of the point.

de·my /di'mī/ (in full **metric demy**) ▶ n. a paper size, now standardized at 564 × 444 mm. ■ (in full **demy octavo**) a book size, now standardized at 216 × 138 mm. ■ (in full **demy quarto**) a book size, now standardized at 276 × 219 mm. [ME: from DEMI-, or from its source, Fr. *demi* 'half.']

de·my·e·li·nate /dē'mīələ,nāt/ ▶ v. [trans.] [usu. as adj.] (**demyelinating**) Med. cause the loss or destruction of myelin in (nerve tissue). — **de·my·e·li·na·tion** /-,mīələ'nāsHən/ n.

de·mys·ti·fy /dē'mistə,fī/ ▶ v. (**-fies, -fied**) [trans.] make (a difficult or esoteric subject) clearer and easier to understand: *this book attempts to demystify technology.* — **de·mys·ti·fi·ca·tion** /-,mistəfi'kāsHən/ n.

de·my·thol·o·gize /,dēmi'THälə,jīz/ ▶ v. [trans.] reinterpret (a subject or text) so that it is free of mythical or heroic elements.

den /den/ ▶ n. a wild animal's lair or habitation. ■ informal a small, comfortable room in a house where a person can pursue an activity in private. ■ a place where people meet in secret, typically to engage in some illicit activity: *an opium den.* ■ a small subdivision of a Cub Scout pack. ▶ v. (**denned, den·ning**) [intrans.] (of a wild animal) live in or retreat to a den: *the cubs denned in late autumn.* [OE *denn*, of Gmc. origin; rel. to Ger. *Tenne* 'threshing floor.']

De·na·li /də'nälē/ another name for Mount McKinley (see MCKINLEY, MOUNT).

de·nar /di'när/ ▶ n. the basic monetary unit of the former Yugoslav Republic of Macedonia. [based on L. *denarius*; cf. DINAR.]

de·nar·i·us /di'ne(ə)rēəs/ ▶ n. (pl. **-nar·i·i** /-'ne(ə)rē,ī/) an ancient Roman silver coin, originally worth ten asses. [ME: L., literally 'containing ten,' from *deni* 'in tens,' from *decem* 'ten.']

de·na·tion·al·ize /dē'nasHənl,īz/ ▶ v. [trans.] **1** transfer (a nationalized industry or institution) from public to private ownership. **2** deprive (a country or person) of nationality or national characteristics. — **de·na·tion·al·i·za·tion** /-,nasHənl-ə'zāsHən/ n.

de·nat·u·ral·ize /dē'nacHərə,līz/ ▶ v. [trans.] **1** make (something) unnatural. **2** deprive (someone) of citizenship of a country. — **de·nat·u·ral·i·za·tion** /-,nacHərələ'zāsHən/ n.

de·na·tur·ant /dē'nācHərənt/ ▶ n. a substance added to alcohol to make it unfit for drinking. ■ Biochem. a substance that causes denaturation of proteins or other biological compounds.

de·na·ture /dē'nācHər/ ▶ v. [trans.] [often as adj.] (**denatured**) take away or alter the natural qualities of. ■ make (alcohol) unfit for drinking by the addition of toxic or foul-tasting substances. ■ Biochem. destroy the characteristic properties of (a protein or other biological macromolecule) by heat, acidity, or other effects that disrupt its molecular conformation. ■ [intrans.] (of a substance) undergo this process. — **de·na·tur·a·tion** /dē,nācHə'rāsHən/ n.

de·na·zi·fi·ca·tion /dē,nätsəfi'kāsHən/ ▶ n. the process of bringing the leaders of the National Socialist regime in Germany to justice and of purging Nazism from public life, carried out esp. between 1945 and 1948.

den·dri·form /'dendrə,fôrm/ ▶ adj. having the shape or form of a tree.

den·drite /'dendrīt/ ▶ n. **1** Physiol. a short branched extension of a nerve cell, along which impulses received from other cells at synapses are transmitted to the cell body. Compare with AXON. **2** a crystal or crystalline mass with a branching, treelike structure. ■ a natural treelike or mosslike marking on a piece of rock or mineral. [18th C.: from Fr., from Gk. *dendritēs* 'treelike,' from *dendron* 'tree.']

den·drit·ic /den'dritik/ ▶ adj. tech. having a branched form resembling a tree. ■ Physiol. of or relating to a dendrite or dendrites. ■ (of a solid) consisting of crystalline dendrites: *dendritic salt.* — **den·drit·i·cal·ly** adv.

dendro- ▶ comb. form of or relating to a tree or trees. [from Gk. *dendron* 'tree.']

den·dro·chro·nol·o·gy /,dendrōkrə'näləjē/ ▶ n. the science or technique of dating events, environmental change, and archaeological artifacts by using the characteristic patterns of annual growth rings in trees. — **den·dro·chron·o·log·i·cal** /-,kränl'äjikəl/ adj. **den·dro·chro·nol·o·gist** /-jist/ n.

den·dro·gram /'dendrə,gram/ ▶ n. a tree diagram, esp. one showing taxonomic relationships.

den·droid /'dendroid/ ▶**adj.** Biol. (of an organism or structure) tree-shaped; branching. ■ Paleontol. denoting graptolites of a type that formed many-branched colonies, found chiefly in the Ordovician and Silurian periods. ▶**n.** Paleontol. a graptolite of this type. [19th C.: from DENDRO- 'tree' + -OID.]

den·drol·o·gy /den'dräləjē/ ▶**n.** the scientific study of trees. —**den·dro·log·i·cal** /ˌdendrə'läjikəl/ **adj. den·drol·o·gist** /-jist/ **n.**

den·dron /'dendrän/ ▶**n.** another term for DENDRITE (sense 1).

De·ne /di'nā/ ▶**n.** (pl. same) **1** a member of a group of American Indian peoples of the Canadian Northwest and Alaska, traditionally speaking Athabaskan languages. **2** any of the languages of these peoples. ▶**adj.** of or relating to these peoples or their languages. [from Fr. *Déné*, from an Athabaskan word meaning 'people.']

Den·eb /'deneb/ Astron. the brightest star in the constellation Cygnus, a yellow supergiant.

De·neb·o·la /də'nebələ/ Astron. the second brightest star in the constellation Leo.

de·ner·vate /dē'nərvāt/ ▶**v.** [trans.] Med. remove or cut off the nerve supply from (an organ or other body part). —**de·ner·va·tion** /ˌdēnər'vāsHən/ **n.**

den·gue /'deNGgē; -gā/ (also **dengue fever**) ▶**n.** a debilitating viral disease of the tropics, transmitted by mosquitoes, and causing sudden fever and acute pains in the joints. [19th C.: from W. Ind. Sp., from Kiswahili *dinga* (in full *kidingapopo*).]

Deng Xiao·ping /'dəNG 'SHOU'piNG/ (also **Teng Hsiao-p'ing**) (1904–97), Chinese communist leader. He led China from 1977. In 1989, his orders led to the massacre of some 2,000 pro-democracy demonstrators in Beijing's Tiananmen Square.

Den Haag /ˌden 'häg/ Dutch name for The Hague (see HAGUE).

de·ni·a·ble /di'nīəbəl/ ▶**adj.** able to be denied. —**de·ni·a·bil·i·ty** /-ˌnīə'bilitē/ **n. de·ni·a·bly adv.**

de·ni·al /di'nīəl/ ▶**n.** the action of declaring something to be untrue: *she shook her head in denial.* ■ the refusal of something requested or desired. ■ a statement that something is not true. ■ Psychol. failure to acknowledge an unacceptable truth or emotion or to admit it into consciousness, used as a defense mechanism. ■ short for SELF-DENIAL. ■ disavowal of a person as one's leader.

de·ni·er /də'ni(ə)r; 'denyər/ ▶**n.** a unit of weight by which the fineness of silk, rayon, or nylon yarn is measured, equal to the weight in grams of 9000 meters of the yarn and often used to describe the thickness of hosiery: *840 denier nylon.* [ME: via OFr. from L. *denarius* (see DENARIUS).]

den·i·grate /'deniˌgrāt/ ▶**v.** [trans.] criticize unfairly; disparage: *there is a tendency to denigrate the poor.* —**den·i·gra·tion** /ˌdeni'grāsHən/ **n. den·i·gra·tor** /-ˌgrātər/ **n. den·i·gra·to·ry** /-grəˌtôrē/ **adj.** [ME: from L. *denigrat-* 'blackened,' from the v. *denigrare*, from *de-* 'away, completely' + *nigrare* (from *niger* 'black').]

den·im /'denəm/ ▶**n.** a sturdy cotton twill fabric, typically blue, used for jeans, overalls, and other clothing. ■ (**denims**) clothing made of such fabric. [17th C. (as *serge denim*): from Fr. *serge de Nimes*.]

Den·is, St. /'denis; də'nē/ (also **Den·ys**) (died *c.*250), French bishop; born in Italy; Roman name *Dionysius*. He is the patron saint of France.

de·ni·tri·fy /dē'nītrəˌfī/ ▶**v.** (**-fies, -fied**) [trans.] (chiefly of bacteria) remove the nitrates or nitrites from (soil, air, or water) by chemical reduction. —**de·ni·tri·fi·ca·tion** /-ˌnītrəfi'kāsHən/ **n.**

den·i·zen /'denəzən/ ▶**n.** formal or humorous an inhabitant or occupant of a particular place. —**den·i·zen·ship n.** [ME *deynseyn*, via Anglo-Norman Fr. from OFr. *deinz* 'within' (from L. *de* 'from' + *intus* 'within') + *-ein* (from L. *-aneus* '-aneous').]

De·niz·li /ˌdeniz'lē/ a city in southwestern Turkey, the site of ancient ruins; pop. 203,000.

Den·mark /'denmärk/ a country in northwestern Europe. Danish name DANMARK. *See box.*

den moth·er ▶**n.** the female leader of a den of Cub Scouts.

de·nom·i·nal /dē'nämənl/ ▶**adj.** [attrib.] (of a word) derived from a noun. ▶**n.** a verb or other word that is derived from a noun.

de·nom·i·nate /di'näməˌnāt/ ▶**v.** **1** (**be denominated**) (of sums of money) be expressed in a specified monetary unit. **2** [with obj. and complement] formal call; name. [ME: from L. *denominat-* 'named,' from the v. *denominare*, from *de-* 'away, formally' + *nominare* 'to name' (from *nomen, nomin-* 'name').]

de·nom·i·na·tion /diˌnämə'nāsHən/ ▶**n.** **1** a recognized autonomous branch of the Christian Church. ■ a group or branch of any religion. **2** the face value of a banknote, a coin, or a postage stamp. ■ the rank of a playing card within a suit, or of a suit relative to others. **3** formal a name or designation, esp. one serving to classify a set of things. ■ the action of naming or classifying something.

de·nom·i·na·tion·al /diˌnämə'nāsHənl/ ▶**adj.** relating to or according to the principles of a particular religious denomination: *denominational relief agencies.* —**de·nom·i·na·tion·al·ism** /-ˌizəm/ **n.**

de·nom·i·na·tor /di'näməˌnātər/ ▶**n.** Math. the number below the line in a common fraction; a divisor. ■ a figure representing the total population in terms of which statistical values are expressed.

de·no·ta·tion /ˌdēnō'tāsHən/ ▶**n.** the literal or primary meaning of a word, in contrast to the feelings or ideas that the word suggests. ■ the action or process of indicating or referring to something by means of a word, symbol, etc. ■ Philos. the object or concept to which a term refers, or the set of objects of which a predicate is true. Often contrasted with CONNOTATION. —**de·no·ta·tion·al** /-sHənl/ **adj.**

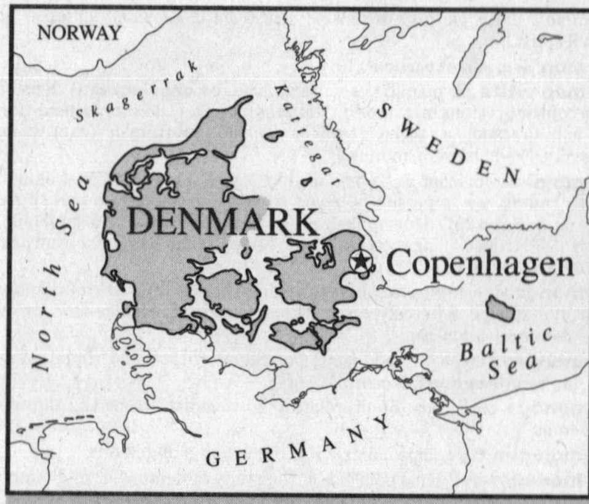

Denmark

Official name: Kingdom of Denmark
Location: northwestern Europe, on the Jutland peninsula, between the North and Baltic seas
Area: 16,400 square miles (42,400 sq km)
Population: 5,400,000
Capital: Copenhagen
Languages: Danish (official), Faroese, German
Currency: Danish krone

de·note /di'nōt/ ▶**v.** [trans.] be a sign of; indicate: *this mark denotes quality.* ■ (often **be denoted**) stand as a name or symbol for. —**de·no·ta·tive** /'dēnōˌtātiv; di'nōtətiv/ **adj.** [16th C.: from Fr. *dénoter* or L. *denotare*, from *de-* 'away, thoroughly' + *notare* 'observe, note' (from *nota* 'a mark').]

de·noue·ment /ˌdānōō'mäN/ ▶**n.** the final part of a play, movie, or narrative in which the strands of the plot are drawn together and matters are resolved. ■ the climax of a chain of events, usually when something is decided or made clear. [18th C.: Fr. *dénouement*, from *dénouer* 'unknot.']

de·nounce /di'nouns/ ▶**v.** [trans.] publicly declare to be wrong or evil. ■ inform against. —**de·nounce·ment n. de·nounc·er n.** [ME: from OFr. *denoncier*, from L. *denuntiare* 'give official information,' based on *nuntius* 'messenger.']

de no·vo /dā 'nōvō; di/ ▶**adv. & adj.** starting from the beginning; anew. [17th C.: L., literally 'from new.']

Den·pa·sar /den'päsär/ a city in Indonesia, on the southern coast of Bali; pop. 261,200.

dense /dens/ ▶**adj.** closely compacted in substance. ■ having the constituent parts crowded closely together: *an estuary dense with marine life.* ■ fig. (of a text) hard to understand because of complexity of ideas. ■ informal (of a person) stupid. —**dense·ly adv. dense·ness n.** [ME: from L. *densus*.]

den·si·fy /'densəˌfī/ ▶**v.** (**-fies, -fied**) [trans.] [often as adj.] (**densified**) make (something) more dense. —**den·si·fi·ca·tion** /ˌdensəfi'kāsHən/ **n.**

den·sim·e·ter /den'simitər/ ▶**n.** an instrument for measuring density, esp. of liquids. [19th C.: from L. *densus* 'dense' + -METER.]

den·si·tom·e·ter /ˌdensi'tämitər/ ▶**n.** **1** an instrument for measuring the photographic density of an image on a film or photographic print. **2** a device for measuring the optical density of a material by measuring the amount of light it reflects or transmits. —**den·si·to·met·ric** /-sitə'metrik/ **adj. den·si·to·met·ri·cal·ly** /-sitə'metrik(ə)lē/ **adv. den·si·tom·e·try n.**

den·si·ty /'densitē/ ▶**n.** (pl. **-ties**) the degree of compactness of a substance: *bone density.* ■ Comput. a measure of the amount of information on a storage medium (tape or disk). ■ Physics degree of consistency measured by the quantity of mass per unit volume. ■ the opacity of a photographic image. ■ the quantity of people or things in a given area or space.

den·si·ty func·tion ▶**n.** short for PROBABILITY DENSITY FUNCTION.

dent /dent/ ▶**n.** a slight hollow in a hard, even surface made by a blow or by the exertion of pressure. ■ a diminishing effect; a reduction. ▶**v.** [trans.] mark with a dent. ■ have an adverse effect on; diminish. [ME: var. of DINT.]

dent. ▶**abbr.** ■ dental. ■ dentist. ■ dentistry.

den·tal /'dentl/ ▶**adj.** **1** [attrib.] of or relating to the teeth. ■ (abbr.: **dent.**) of or relating to dentistry. **2** Phonet. (of a consonant) pronounced with the tip of the tongue against the upper front teeth (as *th*) or the alveolar ridge (as *n, d, t*). ▶**n.** Phonet. a dental consonant. —**den·tal·ize** /'dentlˌīz/ **v.** (Phonet.) **den·tal·ly adv.** [16th C.: from late L. *dentalis*, from L. *dens, dent-* 'tooth.']

den·tal dam ▶ n. a thin sheet of latex used by dentists to isolate a tooth being worked on. ■ a thin sheet of latex used as a prophylactic device during cunnilingus and anilingus.

den·tal floss ▶ n. a soft thread of floss silk or similar material used to clean between the teeth.

den·tal for·mu·la ▶ n. Zool. a formula expressing the number and kinds of teeth possessed by a mammal.

den·tal hy·gien·ist ▶ n. an ancillary dental worker specializing in scaling and polishing teeth and in giving advice on cleaning the teeth. — **den·tal hy·giene** n.

den·ta·li·um /den'tālēəm/ ▶ n. tooth shells used as ornaments or as a form of currency. [mod. L., from late L. *dentalis* (see DENTAL).]

den·tal tech·ni·cian ▶ n. a person who makes and repairs artificial teeth.

den·ta·ry /'dentərē/ ▶ n. (pl. **-ries**) Zool. the anterior bone of the lower jaw, which bears the teeth. In mammals it forms the whole of the lower jaw (or mandible). [19th C.: from late L. *dentarius*, from L. *dens, dent-* 'tooth.']

den·tate /'dentāt/ ▶ adj. Bot. & Zool. having a toothlike or serrated edge.

den·telle /den'tel/ ▶ n. (pl. pronunc. same) ornamental tooling used in bookbinding, resembling lace edging. [19th C.: from Fr., 'lace,' from *dent* 'tooth' + the diminutive suffix *-elle*.]

den·ti·cle /'dentikəl/ ▶ n. Zool. a small tooth or toothlike projection. [ME: from L. *denticulus*, dimin. of *dens, dent-* 'tooth.']

den·tic·u·late /den'tikyəlit/ ▶ adj. having small teeth or toothlike projections; finely toothed. — **den·tic·u·lat·ed** /-,lātid/ adj.

den·ti·frice /'dentəfris/ ▶ n. a paste or powder for cleaning the teeth. [ME: from Fr., from L. *dentifricium*, from *dens, dent-* 'tooth' + *fricare* 'to rub.']

den·til /'dentl; -til/ ▶ n. [often as adj.] (in classical architecture) one of a number of small, rectangular blocks resembling teeth and used as a decoration under the soffit of a cornice: *a dentil frieze.* [16th C.: from Ital. *dentello* or obs. Fr. *dentille*, dimin. of *dent* 'tooth,' from L. *dens, dent-*.]

den·tin /'dentn; -tin/ (also **den·tine** /'dentēn/) ▶ n. hard, dense, bony tissue forming the bulk of a tooth beneath the enamel. — **den·tin·al** /'dentn-əl/ adj. [19th C.: from L. *dens, dent-* 'tooth' + -IN[1].]

den·tist /'dentist/ (abbr.: **dent.**) ▶ n. a person qualified to treat the diseases and conditions that affect the teeth and gums, esp. the repair and extraction of teeth and the insertion of artificial ones. — **den·tist·ry** n. [18th C.: from Fr. *dentiste*, from *dent* 'tooth,' from L. *dens, dent-*.]

den·ti·tion /den'tisʜən/ ▶ n. the arrangement or condition of the teeth in a particular species or individual. [16th C.: from L. *dentitio(n-)*, from *dentire* 'teethe,' from *dens, dent-* 'tooth.']

den·ture /'dencʜər/ ▶ n. (usu. **dentures**) a removable plate or frame holding one or more artificial teeth. [19th C.: from Fr., from *dent* 'tooth,' from L. *dens, dent-*.]

de·nude /di'n(y)o͞od/ ▶ v. [trans.] (often **be denuded**) strip (something) of its covering, possessions, or assets; make bare. — **den·u·da·tion** /,den(y)o͞o'dāsʜən/ n. [ME: from L. *denudare*, from *de-* 'completely' + *nudare* 'to bare' (from *nudus* 'naked').]

de·nu·mer·a·ble /dē'n(y)o͞omərəbəl/ ▶ adj. Math. able to be counted by a one-to-one correspondence with the infinite set of integers. — **de·nu·mer·a·bil·i·ty** /-,n(y)o͞omərə'bilitē/ n. **de·nu·mer·a·bly** adv. [20th C.: from late L. *denumerare* 'count out' + -ABLE.]

de·nun·ci·a·tion /di,nənsē'āsʜən/ ▶ n. public condemnation of someone or something. ■ the action of informing against someone. — **de·nun·ci·a·tor** /-'nənsē,ātər/ n. **de·nun·ci·a·to·ry** /-'nənsēə,tôrē/ adj. [ME: from L. *denuntiatio(n-)*, from the v. *denuntiare* (see DENOUNCE).]

Den·ver[1] /'denvər/ the capital of Colorado, in the central part of the state; pop. 554,636. It is situated at an altitude of 5,280 feet (1,608 m).

Den·ver boot ▶ n. see BOOT[1] (sense 1). [20th C.: *Denver*, Colorado, where the boot was introduced in 1949.]

de·ny /di'nī/ ▶ v. (**-nies, -nied**) [trans.] refuse to admit the truth or existence of (something). ■ [with two objs.] refuse to give (something requested or desired) to (someone). ■ refuse to accept or agree to. ■ refuse to acknowledge or recognize; disown. ■ (**deny oneself**) refrain from satisfying oneself. [ME: from OFr. *deni-*, stressed stem of *deneier*, from L. *denegare*, from *de-* 'formally' + *negare* 'say no.']

Den·ys, St. see DENIS, ST.

de·o·dar /'dēə,där/ ▶ n. a tall, conical Himalayan cedar (*Cedrus deodara*, family Pinaceae) that is native to the Himalayas and has drooping branches and large barrel-shaped cones. [19th C.: from Hindi *deodār*, from Sanskrit *devadāru* 'divine tree.']

de·o·dor·ant /dē'ōdərənt/ ▶ n. a substance that removes or conceals unpleasant smells, esp. bodily odors. [19th C.: from DE- (expressing removal) + L. *odor* 'smell' + -ANT.]

de·o·dor·ize /dē'ōdə,rīz/ ▶ v. [trans.] remove or conceal an unpleasant smell in. — **de·o·dor·i·za·tion** /-,ōdərə'zāsʜən/ n. **de·o·dor·iz·er** n.

De·o gra·ti·as /'dāō 'grätsēəs/ ▶ exclam. thanks be to God. [16th C.: L.]

De·o vo·len·te /'dāō və'lentē/ ▶ adv. God willing; if nothing prevents it. [18th C.: L.]

de·ox·i·dize /dē'äksi,dīz/ ▶ v. [trans.] remove combined oxygen from (a substance, usually a metal). — **de·ox·i·da·tion** /-,äksi'dāsʜən/ n. **de·ox·i·diz·er** n.

de·ox·y·cor·ti·cos·ter·one /dē,äksē,kôrti'kästə,rōn/ ▶ n. Biochem. a corticosteroid hormone involved in regulating the salt and water balance in the human body.

de·ox·y·gen·ate /dē'äksijə,nāt/ ▶ v. [trans.] [usu. as adj.] (**deoxygenated**) remove oxygen from: *deoxygenated air.* — **de·ox·y·gen·a·tion** /-,äksijə'nāsʜən/ n.

de·ox·y·ri·bo·nu·cle·ic ac·id /dē,äksē,rībōn(y)o͞o'klēik/ ▶ n. see **DNA**. [1930s: *deoxyribonucleic* from a blend of DEOXYRIBOSE and NUCLEIC ACID.]

de·ox·y·ri·bose /dē,äksē'rībōs; -bōz/ ▶ n. Biochem. a sugar, $C_5H_{10}O_4$, derived from ribose by replacing a hydroxyl group with hydrogen. The isomer **2-deoxyribose** is a constituent of DNA.

dep. ▶ abbr. ■ departs. ■ deputy.

de·part /di'pärt/ ▶ v. [intrans.] leave, typically in order to start a journey. ■ (**depart from**) deviate from (an accepted, prescribed, or traditional course of action). [ME: from OFr. *departir*, based on L. *dispertire* 'to divide.']

de·part·ed /di'pärtid/ ▶ adj. deceased. ▶ n. (**the departed**) a particular dead person or dead people.

de·part·ment /di'pärtmənt/ ▶ n. a division of a large organization such as a government, university, business, or shop, dealing with a specific subject, commodity, or area of activity: *the English department.* ■ an administrative district in France and other countries. ■ (**one's department**) informal an area of special expertise or responsibility. ■ [with adj.] informal the specified subject under discussion. [ME: from OFr. *departement*, from *departir* (see DEPART).]

de·part·men·tal /di,pärt'mentl; ,dēpärt-/ ▶ adj. concerned with or belonging to a department of an organization. — **de·part·men·tal·ly** adv.

de·part·men·tal·ize /di,pärt'mentl,īz; ,dēpärt-/ ▶ v. [trans.] (usu. **be departmentalized**) divide (an organization or its work) into departments. — **de·part·men·tal·i·za·tion** /-,mentl-ə'zāsʜən/ n.

De·part·ment of Ag·ri·cul·ture ▶ n. the department of the US government that administers federal programs related to food production and rural life.

de·part·ment store ▶ n. a large store stocking many varieties of goods in different departments.

de·par·ture /di'pärcʜər/ ▶ n. the action of leaving, typically to start a journey. ■ a deviation from an accepted, prescribed, or traditional course of action or thought. ■ Naut. the east–west distance between two points, esp. as traveled by a ship or aircraft and expressed in miles.

de·paup·er·ate /di'pôpərit/ ▶ adj. Biol. (of a flora, fauna, or ecosystem) lacking in numbers or variety of species. ■ (of a plant or animal) imperfectly developed. [ME (in the sense 'impoverished'): from med. L. *depauperatus*, past part. of *depauperare*, from *de-* 'completely' + *pauperare* 'make poor' (from *pauper* 'poor').]

de·pend /di'pend/ ▶ v. [intrans.] **1** (**depend on/upon**) be controlled or determined by. **2** (**depend on/upon**) rely on. ■ need or require for financial or other support: *a town that depended heavily upon the wool industry.* ■ be grammatically dependent on.

– PHRASES **depending on** being conditioned by; contingent on. **it** (or **that**) (**all**) **depends** used to express uncertainty or qualification in answering a question. [ME: from OFr. *dependre*, from L. *dependere*, from *de-* 'down' + *pendere* 'hang.']

de·pend·a·ble /di'pendəbəl/ ▶ adj. trustworthy and reliable. — **de·pend·a·bil·i·ty** /-,pendə'bilitē/ n. **de·pend·a·bly** adv.

de·pend·ence /di'pendəns/ ▶ n. the state of relying on or being controlled by someone or something else. ■ reliance on someone or something for financial support. ■ addiction to drink or drugs: *she struggled to fight her dependence.*

de·pend·en·cy /di'pendənsē/ ▶ n. (pl. **-cies**) **1** a dependent or subordinate thing, esp. a country or province controlled by another. **2** dependence.

de·pend·ent /di'pendənt/ ▶ adj. **1** [predic.] (**dependent on/upon**) contingent on or determined by. **2** requiring someone or something for financial, emotional, or other support. ■ unable to do without. ■ Gram. (of a clause, phrase, or word) subordinate to another clause, phrase, or word. ▶ n. (Brit. also **de·pend·ant**) a person who relies on another, esp. a family member, for financial support. — **de·pend·ent·ly** adv.

de·pend·ent var·i·a·ble ▶ n. Math. a variable (often denoted by *y*) whose value depends on that of another.

de·per·son·al·i·za·tion /dē,pərsənələ'zāsʜən/ ▶ n. the action of divesting someone or something of human characteristics or individuality. ■ Psychiatry a state in which one's thoughts and feelings seem unreal or not to belong to oneself, or in which one loses all sense of identity.

de·per·son·al·ize /dē'pərsənə,līz/ ▶ v. [trans.] divest of human characteristics or individuality: *medical technology depersonalizes treatment.*

de·pict /di'pikt/ ▶ v. [trans.] show or represent by a drawing, painting, or other art form. ■ portray in words; describe. — **de·pict·er** n. **de·pic·tion** /-'piksʜən/ n. [ME: from L. *depict-* 'portrayed,' from the v. *depingere*, from *de-* 'completely' + *pingere* 'to paint.']

de·pig·ment /dē'pigmənt/ ▶ v. [trans.] [usu. as adj.] (**depigmented**) reduce or remove the pigmentation of (the skin). — **de·pig·men·ta·tion** /-,pigmən'tāsʜən/ n.

dep·i·late /ˈdepəˌlāt/ ▶**v.** [trans.] remove the hair from. —**dep·i·la·tion** /ˌdepəˈlāsʜən/ **n. dep·i·la·tor** /-ˌlātər/ **n.** [16th C.: from L. *depilat-* 'stripped of hair,' from the v. *depilare*, from *de-* (expressing removal) + *pilare* (from *pilus* 'hair').]

de·pil·a·to·ry /diˈpiləˌtôrē/ ▶**adj.** used to remove unwanted hair. ▶**n.** (pl. **-ries**) a cream or lotion for removing unwanted hair.

de·plane /dēˈplān/ ▶**v.** [intrans.] disembark from an aircraft: *we landed and deplaned.*

de·plete /diˈplēt/ ▶**v.** [often as adj.] (**depleted**) use up the supply of; exhaust the abundance of. ■ [intrans.] diminish in number or quantity. ■ exhaust. —**de·ple·tion** /-ˈplēsʜən/ **n.** [19th C.: from L. *deplet-* 'emptied out,' from the v. *deplere*, from *de-* (expressing reversal) + *plere* 'fill' (from *plenus* 'full').]

de·ple·tion al·low·ance /diˈplēsʜən/ ▶**n.** a tax concession allowable to a company whose normal business activities (in particular oil extraction) reduce the value of its own assets.

de·plor·a·ble /diˈplôrəbəl/ ▶**adj.** deserving strong condemnation. ■ shockingly bad in quality. —**de·plor·a·bly adv.**

de·plore /diˈplôr/ ▶**v.** [trans.] feel or express strong disapproval of (something): *we deplore this act of violence.* —**de·plor·ing·ly adv.** [16th C.: from Fr. *déplorer* or Ital. *deplorare*, from L. *deplorare*, from *de-* 'away, thoroughly' + *plorare* 'bewail.']

de·ploy /diˈploi/ ▶**v.** [trans.] move (troops) into position for military action. ■ [intrans.] (of troops) move into position for such action. ■ bring into effective action; utilize. —**de·ploy·ment n.** [18th C.: from Fr. *déployer*, from L. *displicare* and late L. *deplicare* 'unfold or explain,' from *dis-*, *de-* 'un-' + *plicare* 'to fold.']

de·plume /dēˈplo͞om/ ▶**v.** [trans.] deprive (a bird) of feathers. [ME: from OFr. *desplumer* or med. L. *deplumare*, from *des-*, *de-* (expressing reversal) + L. *pluma* 'feather.']

de·po·lar·ize /dēˈpōləˌrīz/ ▶**v.** [trans.] Physics reduce or remove the polarization of: *the threshold necessary to depolarize the membrane.* —**de·po·lar·i·za·tion** /-ˌpōlərəˈzāsʜən/ **n.**

de·po·lit·i·cize /ˌdēpəˈlitiˌsīz/ ▶**v.** [trans.] remove from political activity or influence. —**de·po·lit·i·ci·za·tion** /-ˌlitisəˈzāsʜən/ **n.**

de·po·lym·er·ize /dēˈpäləməˌrīz/ ▶**v.** [trans.] Chem. break (a polymer) down into monomers or other smaller units. ■ [intrans.] undergo this process. —**de·po·lym·er·i·za·tion** /-ˌpäləmərəˈzāsʜən/ **n.**

de·po·nent /diˈpōnənt/ ▶**adj.** Gram. (of a verb, esp. in Latin or Greek) passive or middle in form but active in meaning. ▶**n. 1** Gram. a deponent verb. **2** Law a person who makes a deposition or affidavit under oath. [ME: from L. *deponent-* 'laying aside, putting down,' from the v. *deponere*, from *de-* 'down' + *ponere* 'place.']

de·pop·u·late /dēˈpäpyəˌlāt/ ▶**v.** [trans.] substantially reduce the population of (an area). —**de·pop·u·la·tion** /-ˌpäpyəˈlāsʜən/ **n.**

de·port /diˈpôrt/ ▶**v.** [trans.] expel (a foreigner) from a country, typically on the grounds of illegal status or for having committed a crime. ■ exile (a native) to another country. —**de·port·a·ble adj. de·por·ta·tion** /ˌdēpôrˈtāsʜən/ **n.** [16th C.: from Fr. *déporter*, from L. *deportare*, from *de-* 'away' + *portare* 'carry.']

de·port·ment /diˈpôrtmənt/ ▶**n.** a person's behavior or manners.

de·pose /diˈpōz/ ▶**v.** [trans.] **1** remove from office suddenly and forcefully. **2** Law testify to or give (evidence) on oath, typically in a written statement. **3** Law to question (a witness) in deposition. [ME: from OFr. *deposer*, from L. *deponere* (see DEPONENT), but influenced by L. *depositus*.]

de·pos·it /diˈpäzit/ ▶**n. 1** a sum of money placed or kept in a bank account, usually to gain interest. ■ an act of placing money in a bank account. **2** a sum payable as a first installment on the purchase of something or as a pledge for a contract, the balance being payable later. ■ a returnable sum payable on the rental of something, to cover any possible loss or damage. **3** a layer or body of accumulated matter. ■ a natural layer of sand, rock, coal, or other material. ▶**v.** (**-it·ed**, **-it·ing**) **1** [with obj. and usu. with adverbial of place] put or set down (something or someone) in a specific place, typically unceremoniously: *just deposit your books on the table.* ■ (usu. **be deposited**) (of water, the wind, or other natural agency) lay down (matter) gradually as a layer or covering. ■ lay (an egg). **2** [trans.] store or entrust with someone for safekeeping. ■ pay (a sum of money) into a bank account. ■ pay (a sum) as a first installment or as a pledge for a contract. [16th C.: from L. *depositum* (n.), med. L. *depositare* (v.), both from L. *deposit-* 'laid aside,' from the v. *deponere*.]

de·pos·i·tar·y /diˈpäziˌterē/ (also **de·pos·i·to·ry**) ▶**n.** (pl. **-tar·ies**) a person to whom something is lodged in trust. ▶**adj.** (of a share or receipt) representing a share in a foreign company.

dep·o·si·tion /ˌdepəˈzisʜən/ ▶**n. 1** the action of deposing someone, esp. a monarch. **2** Law the process of giving sworn evidence. **3** Law the written record of a witness's out-of-court testimony. ■ a formal, usually written, statement to be used as evidence outside court. **4** the action of depositing something. **5** (**the Deposition**) the taking down of the body of Christ from the Cross.

de·pos·i·tor /diˈpäzitər/ ▶**n.** a person who keeps money in a bank account.

de·pos·i·to·ry /diˈpäziˌtôrē/ ▶**n.** (pl. **-ries**) **1** a place where things are stored. **2** var. of DEPOSITARY.

de·pot /ˈdēpō; ˈdepō/ ▶**n.** a place for the storage of large quantities of equipment, food, or some other commodity. ■ a railroad or bus station. ■ a place where buses, trains, or other vehicles are housed and maintained. ■ the headquarters of a regiment. [18th C.: from Fr. *dépôt*, from L. *depositum*.]

de·prave /diˈprāv/ ▶**v.** [trans.] make (someone) immoral or wicked. —**dep·ra·va·tion** /ˌdeprəˈvāsʜən/ **n.** [ME: from OFr. *depraver* or L. *depravare*, from *de-* 'down, thoroughly' + *pravus* 'crooked, perverse.']

de·praved /diˈprāvd/ ▶**adj.** morally corrupt.

de·prav·i·ty /diˈpravitē/ ▶**n.** (pl. **-ties**) moral corruption. ■ a wicked or morally corrupt act. [17th C.: alt. of obs. *pravity*, from L. *pravitas*, from *pravus* 'crooked, perverse.']

dep·re·cate /ˈdepriˌkāt/ ▶**v.** [trans.] **1** express disapproval of. **2** another term for DEPRECIATE (sense 2). —**dep·re·cat·ing·ly adv. dep·re·ca·tion** /ˌdepriˈkāsʜən/ **n. dep·re·ca·tive** /-ˌkātiv/ **adj. dep·re·ca·tor** /-ˌkātər/ **n. dep·re·ca·to·ry** /-kəˌtôrē/ **adj.** [17th C.: from L. *deprecat-* 'prayed against,' from the v. *deprecari*, from *de-* + *precari* 'pray.']

de·pre·ci·ate /diˈprēsʜēˌāt/ ▶**v. 1** [intrans.] diminish in value over a period of time. ■ reduce the recorded value in a company's books of (an asset) each year over a predetermined period. **2** [trans.] disparage or belittle (something). —**de·pre·ci·a·to·ry** /-sʜēəˌtôrē/ **adj.** [ME (sense 2): from late L. *depreciat-* 'lowered in price, undervalued,' from the v. *depreciare*, from L. *de-* 'down' + *pretium* 'price.']

de·pre·ci·a·tion /diˌprēsʜēˈāsʜən/ ▶**n.** a reduction in the value of an asset with the passage of time, due in particular to wear and tear. ■ decrease in the value of a currency relative to other currencies.

dep·re·da·tion /ˌdeprəˈdāsʜən/ ▶**n.** (usu. **depredations**) an act of attacking or plundering. [15th C.: from Fr. *déprédation*, from late L. *depraedatio(n-)*, from *depraedari* 'plunder.']

de·press /diˈpres/ ▶**v.** [trans.] **1** make (someone) feel utterly dispirited or dejected. ■ reduce the level or strength of activity in (something, esp. an economic or biological system). **2** push or pull (something) down into a lower position. —**de·press·i·ble adj.** [ME: from OFr. *depresser*, from late L. *depressare*, frequentative of *deprimere* 'press down.']

de·pres·sant /diˈpresənt/ ▶**adj.** (chiefly of a drug) reducing functional or nervous activity. ▶**n.** a depressant drug. ■ an influence that depresses economic or other activity: *higher taxation is a depressant.*

de·pressed /diˈprest/ ▶**adj.** (of a person) in a state of general unhappiness or despondency. ■ (of a person) suffering from clinical depression. ■ (of a place or economic activity) suffering the damaging effects of a lack of demand or employment. ■ (of an object or part of an object) in a physically lower position, having been pushed or forced down.

de·press·ing /diˈpresiɴɢ/ ▶**adj.** causing or resulting in a feeling of miserable dejection. ■ causing a damaging reduction in economic activity. —**de·press·ing·ly adv.**

de·pres·sion /diˈpresʜən/ ▶**n. 1** severe despondency and dejection, accompanied by feelings of hopelessness and inadequacy. ■ Med. a condition of mental disturbance, typically with lack of energy and difficulty in maintaining concentration or interest in life. ■ a long and severe recession in an economy or market. ■ (**the Depression** or **the Great Depression**) the financial and industrial slump of 1929 and subsequent years. **2** the lowering or reducing of something. ■ the action of pressing down on something. ■ a sunken place or hollow on a surface. ■ Astron. & Geog. the angular distance of an object below the horizon or a horizontal plane. ■ Meteorol. a region of lower atmospheric pressure, esp. a cyclonic weather system.

De·pres·sion glass ▶**n.** machine-pressed, tinted glassware that was mass-produced in the US from the late 1920s to the 1940s and often used as giveaways to persuade customers to purchase goods.

de·pres·sive /diˈpresiv/ ▶**adj.** causing feelings of hopelessness, despondency, and dejection. ■ Med. relating to or tending to suffer from clinical depression: *a depressive illness.* ■ causing a reduction in strength, effectiveness, or value. ▶**n.** Med. a person suffering from or with a tendency to suffer from depression.

de·pres·sor /diˈpresər/ ▶**n. 1** Anat. (also **depressor muscle**) a muscle whose contraction pulls down the part of the body to which it is attached. ■ any of several specific muscles in the face: [followed by Latin genitive] *depressor anguli oris.* **2** Physiol. a nerve whose stimulation results in a lowering of blood pressure. **3** an instrument for pressing something down.

de·pres·sur·ize /dēˈpresʜəˌrīz/ ▶**v.** [trans.] release the pressure of the gas inside (a pressurized vehicle or container). ■ [intrans.] (of a pressurized vehicle or container) lose pressure. —**de·pres·sur·i·za·tion** /-ˌpresʜərəˈzāsʜən/ **n.**

dep·ri·va·tion /ˌdeprəˈvāsʜən/ ▶**n.** the damaging lack of material benefits considered to be basic necessities in a society. ■ the lack or denial of something considered to be a necessity.

de·prive /diˈprīv/ ▶**v.** [trans.] deny (a person or place) the possession or use of something. —**de·priv·al** /-ˈprīvəl/ **n.** [ME: from OFr. *depriver*, from med. L. *deprivare*, from *de-* 'away, completely' + *privare* (see PRIVATE).]

de·prived /diˈprīvd/ ▶**adj.** suffering a severe and damaging lack of basic material and cultural benefits. ■ (of a person) suffering a lack of a specified benefit that is considered important.

de pro·fun·dis /ˌdā prəˈfo͝ondis/ ▶**n.** a cry of appeal expressing one's deepest feelings of sorrow or anguish. [ME: L., lit. 'from the depths.']

de·pro·gram /dēˈprōgram; -grəm/ ▶**v.** (**-grammed**, **-gram·ming** or **-gramed**, **-gram·ing**) [trans.] release (someone) from apparent brainwashing, typically that of a religious cult, by the systematic reindoctrination of conventional values.

de·pro·tein·ize /dē'prōtē(ə),nīz/ ▶ v. [trans.] remove the protein from (a substance), usually as a stage in chemical purification. — **de·pro·tein·i·za·tion** /-,prōtē(ə)nə'zāsHən/ n.

Dept. ▶ abbr. Department.

depth /depTH/ ▶ n. **1** the distance from the top or surface of something to its bottom. ■ distance from the nearest to the farthest point of something or from the front to the back. ■ used to specify the distance below the top or surface of something to which someone or something percolates or at which something happens: [in sing.] *loosen the soil to a depth of 8 inches.* ■ the apparent existence of three dimensions in a picture, photograph, or other two-dimensional representation; perspective. ■ lowness of pitch. **2** complexity and profundity of thought. ■ extensive and detailed study or knowledge. ■ intensity of emotion, usually considered as a laudable quality. ■ intensity of color. **3** (**the depths**) a point far below the surface. ■ (also **the depth**) the worst or lowest part or state. ■ a time when one's negative feelings are at their most intense. ■ a place that is remote and inaccessible. **4** Sports the strength of a team in its reserve players.
– PHRASES **hidden depths** usually admirable but previously unnoticed qualities of a person. ■ obscure or secretive aspects of a situation. **in depth** in great detail; comprehensively and thoroughly. See also IN-DEPTH. **out of one's depth** in water too deep to stand in. ■ fig. beyond one's knowledge or ability to cope. [ME: from DEEP + -TH².]

depth charge ▶ n. an explosive charge designed to be dropped from a ship or aircraft and to explode under water at a preset depth, used for attacking submarines.

depth find·er ▶ n. an echo sounder or other device for measuring water depth, esp. for navigation and fishing.

depth gauge ▶ n. a device fitted to a drill bit to ensure that the hole drilled does not exceed the required depth.

depth·less /'depTHlis/ ▶ adj. unfathomably deep. ■ fig. shallow and superficial. — **depth·less·ly** adv.

depth of field ▶ n. the distance between the nearest and the furthest objects that give an image judged to be in focus in a camera.

depth of fo·cus ▶ n. the distance between the two extreme axial points behind a lens at which an image is judged to be in focus.

depth per·cep·tion ▶ n. the ability to perceive the relative distance of objects in one's visual field.

depth sound·er ▶ n. another term for ECHO SOUNDER.

dep·u·ta·tion /,depyə'tāsHən/ ▶ n. a group of people appointed to undertake a mission or take part in a formal process on behalf of a larger group.

de·pute /di'pyo͞ot/ ▶ v. [with obj. and infin.] appoint or instruct (someone) to perform a task for which one is responsible. ■ delegate (authority or a task). [ME: via OFr. from L. *deputare* 'consider to be, assign,' from *de-* 'away'+ *putare* 'think over, consider.']

dep·u·tize /'depyə,tīz/ ▶ v. [trans.] make (someone) a deputy: *some officers will be deputized as marshals.* ■ [intrans.] temporarily act or speak as a deputy.

dep·u·ty /'depyətē/ ▶ n. (pl. **-ties**) a person whose immediate superior is a senior figure within an organization and who is empowered to act as a substitute for this superior. ■ a parliamentary representative in certain countries. — **dep·u·ty·ship** n. [ME: from OFr. *depute,* from late L. *deputatus,* past part. of *deputare* (see DEPUTE).]

De Quin·cey /də 'kwinsē/, Thomas (1785–1859), English writer. He wrote *Confessions of an English Opium Eater* (1822).

de·rac·in·ate /di'rasə,nāt/ ▶ v. [trans.] literary tear (something) up by the roots. — **de·rac·i·na·tion** /-,rasə'nāsHən/ n. [16th C.: from Fr. *déraciner,* from *dé-* (expressing removal) + *racine* 'root' (based on L. *radix*).]

de·rac·i·nat·ed /di'rasə,nātid/ ▶ adj. another term for DÉRACINÉ.

dé·ra·ci·né /dā,räsi'nā/ ▶ adj. uprooted or displaced from one's geographical or social environment. ▶ n. a person who has been or feels displaced. [20th C.: Fr., lit. 'uprooted.']

de·rail /dē'rāl/ ▶ v. [trans.] (usu. **be derailed**) cause (a train or trolley car) to leave its tracks accidentally. ■ [intrans.] (of a train or trolley car) accidentally leave the tracks. ■ [trans.] fig. obstruct (a process) by diverting it from its intended course. — **de·rail·ment** n. [19th C.: from Fr. *dérailler,* from *dé-* (expressing removal) + *rail* 'rail.']

de·rail·leur /di'rālər/ ▶ n. a bicycle mechanism that moves the chain out and up, allowing it to shift to different cogs. [1930s: from Fr., from *dérailler* 'derail.']

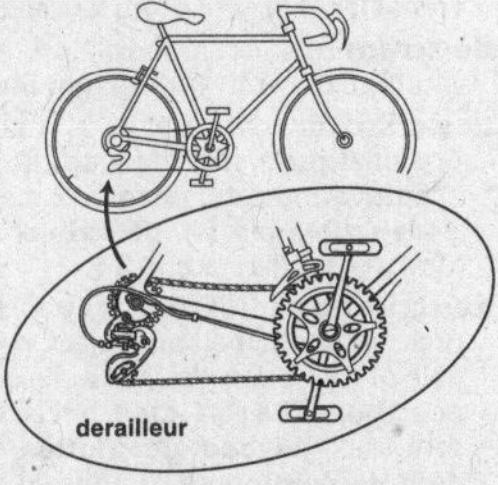

derailleur

De·rain /də'raN/, André (1880–1954), French painter. He was an exponent of fauvism.

de·range /di'rānj/ ▶ v. [trans.] [usu. as adj.] (**deranged**) cause (someone) to become insane: *a deranged man.* ■ throw (something) into confusion; cause to act irregularly: *stress deranges the immune system.* — **de·range·ment** n. [18th C.: from Fr. *déranger,* from OFr. *desrengier,* lit. 'move from orderly rows.']

de·rate /dē'rāt/ ▶ v. [trans.] reduce the power rating of (a component or device): *the engines were derated to 90 horse power.*

Der·by¹ /'därbē/ a city in north central England, on the Derwent River; pop. 214,000.

Der·by² /'därbē/ Edward George Geoffrey Smith Stanley, 14th Earl of (1799–1869), British prime minister 1852, 1858–59, 1866–68.

Der·by³ /'dərbē/ ▶ n. (pl. **-bies**) **1** an annual horse race for three-year-olds, founded in 1780 by the 12th Earl of Derby. The race is run on Epsom Downs in England in late May or early June. ■ a similar race elsewhere: *the Kentucky Derby.* ■ (**derby**) a sporting contest open to the general public: *sign up for the fishing derby.* **2** (**derby**, also **derby hat**) a bowler hat.

Derby³ 2

Der·by·shire /'därbēsHər; -,sHi(ə)r/ a county in north central England.

de re /dā 'rā/ ▶ adj. Philos. relating to the properties of things mentioned in an assertion or expression, rather than to the assertion or expression itself. Compare with DE DICTO. [Latin, literally 'about the thing.']

de·re·cho /dā'rācHō/ ▶ n. a line of intense, widespread, and fast-moving windstorms and sometimes thunderstorms that moves across a great distance and is characterized by damaging straight-line winds. [Sp., lit. 'straight.']

de·ref·er·ence /dē'ref(ə)rəns/ ▶ v. [trans.] Comput. obtain the address of a data item held in another location from (a pointer).

de·reg·u·late /dē'regyə,lāt/ ▶ v. [trans.] remove regulations or restrictions from. — **de·reg·u·la·tion** /-,regyə'lāsHən/ n. **de·reg·u·la·to·ry** /-lə,tôrē/ adj.

der·e·lict /'derə,likt/ ▶ adj. in a very poor condition as a result of disuse and neglect. ■ (of a person) shamefully negligent in not having done what one should have done. ▶ n. a person without a home, job, or property. ■ a piece of property, esp. a ship, abandoned by the owner and in poor condition. [17th C.: from L. *derelictus* 'abandoned,' past part. of *derelinquere,* from *de-* 'completely' + *relinquere* 'forsake.']

der·e·lic·tion /,derə'liksHən/ ▶ n. the state of having been abandoned and become dilapidated. ■ (usu. **dereliction of duty**) the shameful failure to fulfill one's obligations.

de·re·press /,dēri'pres/ ▶ v. [trans.] Biochem. & Genet. activate (enzymes, genes, etc.) from an inoperative or latent state. — **de·re·pres·sion** /-'presHən/ n.

de·re·strict /,dēri'strikt/ ▶ v. [trans.] remove restrictions from. — **de·re·stric·tion** /-'striksHən/ n.

de·ride /di'rīd/ ▶ v. [trans.] express contempt for; ridicule. — **de·rid·er** n. [16th C.: from L. *deridere* 'scoff at.']

de ri·gueur /də ri'gər; rē'gœr/ ▶ adj. required by etiquette or current fashion. [19th C.: Fr., lit. 'in strictness.']

de·ri·sion /di'rizHən/ ▶ n. contemptuous ridicule or mockery. — **de·ris·i·ble** /-'rizəbəl/ adj. [ME: via OFr. from late L. *derisio(n-),* from *deridere* 'scoff at.']

de·ri·sive /di'rīsiv/ ▶ adj. expressing contempt or ridicule: *a harsh, derisive laugh.* — **de·ri·sive·ly** adv. **de·ri·sive·ness** n.

de·ri·so·ry /di'rīsərē; -zərē/ ▶ adj. **1** ridiculously small or inadequate: *a derisory pay rise.* **2** another term for DERISIVE.

der·i·va·tion /,derə'vāsHən/ ▶ n. **1** the obtaining or developing of something from a source or origin. ■ the formation of a word from another word or from a root in the same or another language. ■ Ling. (in generative grammar) the set of stages that link the abstract underlying structure of an expression to its surface form. ■ Math. a sequence of statements showing that a formula, theorem, etc., is a consequence of previously accepted statements. ■ Math. the process of deducing a new formula, theorem, etc., from previously accepted statements. **2** origin; extraction. ■ something derived; a derivative. — **der·i·va·tion·al** /-sHənl/ adj.

de·riv·a·tive /di'rivətiv/ ▶ adj. (typically of an artist or work of art) imitative of the work of another person, and usually disapproved of for that reason. ■ originating from, based on, or influenced by. ■ [attrib.] (of a financial product) having a value deriving from an underlying variable asset. ▶ n. something that is based on another source. ■ (often **derivatives**) an arrangement or instrument (such as a future, option, or warrant) whose value derives from and is dependent on the value of an underlying asset: [as adj.] *the derivatives market.* ■ a word derived from another or from a root in the same or another language. ■ a substance that is derived chemically from a specified compound: *crack is a highly addictive cocaine derivative.* ■ Math. an expression representing the rate of change of a function with respect to an independent variable. — **de·riv·a·tive·ly** adv.

de·rive /di'rīv/ ▶ v. [trans.] (**derive something from**) obtain something from (a specified source). ■ (**derive something from**) base a concept on a logical extension or modification of (another concept). ■ [intrans.] (**derive from**) (of a word) have (a specified word, usually of another language) as a root or origin: *the word "punch" derives from the Hindustani "pancha."* ■ [intrans.] (**derive from**) arise from or originate in (a specified source). ■ (**be derived from**) Ling. (of an expression in a natural language) be linked by a set of stages to (its underlying abstract form). ■ (**be derived from**) (of a substance) be formed or prepared by (a chemical or physical process affecting another substance). ■ Math. obtain (a function or equation) from another by a sequence of logical steps, for example by differentiation. — **de·riv·a·ble** adj. [ME: from OFr. *deriver* or L. *derivare*, from *de-* 'down, away' + *rivus* 'brook, stream.']

derm /dərm/ ▶ n. another term for DERMIS.

der·ma[1] /'dərmə/ ▶ n. another term for DERMIS. [18th C.: mod. L., from Gk. 'skin.']

der·ma[2] ▶ n. beef or chicken intestine, stuffed and cooked in dishes such as kishke. [from Yiddish *derme*, pl. of *darm* 'intestine'; rel. to OE *tharm* 'intestine.']

der·ma- (also **dermo-**) ▶ comb. form skin: *dermabrasion.* [from Gk., *derma.*]

derm·a·bra·sion /,dərmə'brāzhən/ ▶ n. the removal of superficial layers of skin with a rapidly revolving abrasive tool, as a technique in cosmetic surgery. [1950s: from Gk. *derma* 'skin' + ABRASION.]

Der·map·te·ra /dər'maptərə/ Entomol. an order of insects that comprises the earwigs. — **der·map·ter·an** n. & adj. **der·map·ter·ous** /-tərəs/ adj. [mod. L. (pl.), from Gk. *derma* 'skin' + *pteron* 'wing.']

der·ma·ti·tis /,dərmə'tītis/ ▶ n. inflammation of the skin resulting from direct irritation by an external agent or an allergic reaction to it. Compare with ECZEMA. [19th C.: from Gk. *derma, dermat-* 'skin' + -ITIS.]

dermato- ▶ comb. form of or relating to the skin. [from Gk. *derma, dermat-* 'skin, hide.']

der·ma·tol·o·gy /,dərmə'täləjē/ ▶ n. the branch of medicine concerned with the diagnosis and treatment of skin disorders. — **der·ma·to·log·i·cal** /-mətl'äjikəl/ adj. **der·ma·to·log·i·cal·ly** /-mətl'äjik(ə)lē/ adv. **der·ma·tol·o·gist** /-jist/ n.

der·ma·tome /'dərmə,tōm/ ▶ n. Embryol. the lateral wall of each somite in a vertebrate embryo, giving rise to the connective tissue of the skin. Compare with MYOTOME, SCLEROTOME. ■ Physiol. an area of the skin supplied by nerves from a single spinal root.

der·mat·o·my·co·sis /dər,matəmī'kōsis; 'dərmə,tō-/ ▶ n. (pl. **-ses** /-,sēz/) a fungal infection of the skin, esp. by a dermatophyte.

der·mat·o·my·o·si·tis /dər,matə,mīə'sītis; 'dərmə,tō-/ ▶ n. Med. inflammation of the skin and underlying muscle tissue, typically occurring as an autoimmune condition or associated with internal cancer.

der·mat·o·phyte /dər'matə,fīt; 'dərmətə-/ ▶ n. a pathogenic fungus (*Trichophyton* and other genera) that grows on skin and other body surfaces, causing ringworm and related diseases. — **der·mat·o·phyt·ic** /dər,matə'fitik; ,dərmətə-/ adj.

der·mat·o·phy·to·sis /dər,matəfī'tōsis/ ▶ n. (pl. **-ses** /-sēz/) another term for DERMATOMYCOSIS.

der·ma·to·sis /,dərmə'tōsis/ ▶ n. (pl. **-ses** /-sēz/) a disease of the skin, esp. one that does not cause inflammation.

der·mis /'dərmis/ ▶ n. tech. the skin. ■ Anat. the thick layer of living tissue below the epidermis that forms the true skin. — **der·mal** /-məl/ adj. **der·mic** adj. (rare). [19th C.: mod. L., suggested by *epidermis.*]

der·moid /'dərmoid/ ▶ n. short for DERMOID CYST.

der·moid cyst ▶ n. Med. an abnormal growth (teratoma) containing epidermis, hair follicles, and sebaceous glands, derived from residual embryonic cells.

Der·mop·ter·a /dər'mäptərə/ Zool. a small order of mammals that comprises the flying lemurs or colugos. [mod. L. (pl.), from Gk. *derma* 'skin' + *pteron* 'wing.']

der·nier cri /'dernyā'krē/ ▶ n. (**the/le dernier cri**) the very latest fashion. [19th C.: Fr., lit. 'last cry.']

der·o·gate /'derə,gāt/ ▶ v. formal **1** [trans.] disparage (someone or something). **2** [intrans.] (**derogate from**) detract from. **3** [intrans.] (**derogate from**) deviate from (a set of rules or agreed form of behavior). — **de·rog·a·tive** /di'rägətiv/ adj. [ME: from L. *derogat-* 'abrogated,' from the v. *derogare*, from *de-* 'aside, away' + *rogare* 'ask.']

der·o·ga·tion /,derə'gāshən/ ▶ n. **1** an exemption from or relaxation of a rule or law. **2** the perception or treatment of someone as being of little worth.

de·rog·a·to·ry /di'rägə,tôrē/ ▶ adj. showing a critical or disrespectful attitude. — **de·rog·a·to·ri·ly** /-,tôrəlē/ adv.

der·rick /'derik/ ▶ n. **1** a kind of crane with a movable pivoted arm for moving or lifting heavy weights, esp. on a ship. **2** the framework over an oil well or similar boring that holds the drilling machinery. [17th C.: from *Derrick*, the surname of a hangman in London, England.]

Der·ri·da /,deri'dä/, Jacques (1930–2004), French philosopher who developed the theory of deconstruction.

der·ri·ère /,derē'e(ə)r/ ▶ n. informal euphemistic term for a person's buttocks. [18th C.: Fr., lit. 'behind.']

der·ring-do /'deriNG 'doo/ ▶ n. dated or humorous action displaying heroic courage: *tales of derring-do.* [16th C.: from late ME *dorryng do* 'daring to do,' misprinted as *derrynge do.*]

der·rin·ger /'derinjər/ ▶ n. a small pistol that has a large bore and is very effective at close range. [19th C.: Henry Deringer (1786–1868), American gunsmith.]

derringer

der·ris /'deris/ ▶ n. **1** an insecticide made from the powdered roots of certain tropical plants containing rotenone. **2** a woody, climbing plant (genus *Derris*) of the pea family that bears leathery pods and has tuberous roots from which this insecticide is obtained. [19th C.: mod. L., from Gk., 'leather covering.']

Der·ry /'derē/ see LONDONDERRY.

der·vish /'dərvisH/ ▶ n. a Muslim (specifically Sufi) religious man who has taken vows of poverty and austerity. Dervishes first appeared in the 12th century; they were noted for their wild or ecstatic rituals and were known as **dancing**, **whirling**, or **howling dervishes** according to the practice of their order. [from Turk. *dervis*, from Pers. *darvīš* 'poor,' (as a n.) 'religious mendicant.']

DES ▶ abbr. diethylstilbestrol.

de·sa·cral·ize /dē'sākrə,līz/ ▶ v. [trans.] remove the religious or sacred status from. — **de·sa·cral·i·za·tion** /-,sākrələ'zāshən/ n.

de Sade /də 'säd/, Marquis, see SADE.

de·sal·i·nate /dē'salə,nāt/ ▶ v. [trans.] [usu. as adj.] (**desalinated**) remove salt from (seawater). — **de·sal·i·na·tion** /-,salə'nāshən/ n. **de·sal·i·na·tor** /-,nātər/ n.

de·sal·in·ize /dē'salə,nīz/ ▶ v. another term for DESALINATE. — **de·sal·in·i·za·tion** /-,salənə'zāshən/ n.

de·salt /dē'sôlt/ ▶ v. another term for DESALINATE.

de·sa·pa·re·ci·do /,desə,pärə'sēdō/ ▶ n. (pl. **-dos**) (esp. in South America), a person who has disappeared, presumed killed by the military or police. [20th C.: Sp., lit. 'disappeared.']

de·sat·u·rate /dē'sacHə,rāt/ ▶ v. [trans.] make less saturated; cause to become unsaturated. — **de·sat·u·ra·tion** /-,sacHə'rāshən/ n.

des·ca·mi·sa·do /,deskamə'sädō/ ▶ n. (pl. **-dos**) (in Latin America) a very poor person. [19th C.: Sp., lit. 'shirtless.']

des·cant ▶ n. /'deskant/ Music an independent treble melody usually sung or played above a basic melody. ■ archaic or literary a melodious song. ■ a discourse on a theme or subject. ▶ v. /des'kant/ [intrans.] talk tediously or at length. [ME: from OFr. *deschant*, from med. L. *discantus* 'refrain.']

Des·cartes /dā'kärt/, René (1596–1650), French philosopher and mathematician. He concluded that everything was open to doubt except conscious experience.

de·scend /di'send/ ▶ v. [intrans.] **1** move or fall downward. ■ [trans.] move down (a slope or stairs): *the vehicle descended a ramp.* ■ (of a piece of land) be on a slope or incline and extend downward. ■ come or go down a scale, esp. from superior to inferior: [as adj.] (**descending**) *descending order of usefulness.* ■ Music (of sound) become lower in pitch. ■ (**descend to**) act in a specified way far below one's usual standards: *she descended to self-pity.* ■ (**descend into**) (of a situation or group of people) reach (a state considered undesirable): *descended into chaos.* **2** (**descend on/upon**) make a sudden attack on. ■ make an unexpected and typically unwelcome visit to. ■ (of a feeling or atmosphere) develop suddenly and be felt throughout a place or by a person or group: *gloom descended on the Democratic Party headquarters.* ■ (of night or darkness) begin to occur. **3** (**be descended from**) be a blood relative of (a specified ancestor). ■ (of an asset) pass by inheritance, typically from parent to child: *his lands descended to his eldest son.* — **de·scend·ent** /-'sendənt/ adj. [ME: from OFr. *descendre*, from L. *descendere*, from *de-* 'down' + *scandere* 'to climb.']

de·scend·ant /di'sendənt/ ▶ n. a person, plant, or animal that is descended from a particular ancestor. ■ a machine, artifact, system, etc., that has developed from an earlier version.

de·scend·er /di'sendər/ ▶ n. a part of a letter that extends below the level of its base of a letter (as in *g* and *p*). See illustration at ASCENDER. ■ a letter having such a part.

de·scend·i·ble /di'sendəbəl/ ▶ adj. Law (of property) able to be inherited by a descendant.

de·scend·ing co·lon ▶ n. Anat. the part of the large intestine that passes downward on the left side of the abdomen toward the rectum.

de·scent /di'sent/ ▶ n. **1** [usu. in sing.] an action of moving downward, dropping, or falling. ■ a downward slope, esp. a path or track. ■ a moral, social, or psychological decline into a specified undesirable state. **2** the origin or background of a person in terms of family or nationality: *of Hungarian descent.* ■ the transmission of qualities, property, or privileges by inheritance. **3** (**descent on**) a sudden, violent attack. [ME: from OFr. *descente*, from *descendre* (see DESCEND).]

de·scram·ble /dē'skrambəl/ ▶ v. [trans.] convert or restore (a signal) to intelligible form. — **de·scram·bler** n.

de·scribe /di'skrīb/ ▶ v. [trans.] **1** give an account in words of (someone or something), including all the relevant characteristics, qualities, or events. ■ indicate; denote. **2** mark out or draw (a geometric figure). — **de·scrib·a·ble** adj. **de·scrib·er** n. [ME: from L. *describere*, from *de-* 'down' + *scribere* 'write.']

de·scrip·tion /di'skripshən/ ▶ n. **1** a spoken or written representation or account of a person, object, or event: *people who had seen him were able to give a description.* ■ the action of giving such a representation or account. **2** a sort, kind, or class of people or things.
– PHRASES **beyond description** to a great and astonishing extent. **defy description** be so unusual or remarkable as to be impossible to describe. **answers** (or **fits**) **the description** has the qualities specified. [ME: via OFr. from L. *descriptio(n-)*, from *describere* 'write down.']

de·scrip·tive /di'skriptiv/ ▶ adj. **1** serving or seeking to describe. ■ Gram. (of an adjective) assigning a quality rather than restricting the application of the expression modified, e.g., *blue* as distinct from *few.*

2 describing or classifying without expressing feelings or judging. ■ Ling. denoting or relating to an approach to language analysis that describes accents, forms, structures, and usage without making value judgments. Often contrasted with PRESCRIPTIVE. — **de·scrip·tive·ly** adv. **de·scrip·tive·ness** n.

de·scrip·tor /di'skriptər/ ▶ n. an element or term that has the function of describing, identifying, or indexing, in particular: ■ Ling. a word or expression used to describe or identify something. ■ Comput. a piece of stored data that indicates how other data is stored.

de·scry /di'skrī/ ▶ v. (**-scries, -scried**) [trans.] literary catch sight of. [ME: apparently from Old Fr. *descrier* 'to cry,' lit. 'cry apart,' perhaps confused with obsolete *descry* 'describe.']

des·e·crate /'desi,krāt/ ▶ v. [trans.] (often **be desecrated**) treat (a sacred place or thing) with violent disrespect; violate. — **des·e·cra·tion** /,desi'krāsʜən/ n. **des·e·cra·tor** /-,krātər/ n. [17th C.: from DE- (expressing reversal) + a shortened form of CONSECRATE.]

de·seed /dē'sēd/ ▶ v. [trans.] [usu. as adj.] (**deseeded**) remove the seeds from (a plant, vegetable, or fruit). — **de·seed·er** n.

de·seg·re·gate /dē'segri,gāt/ ▶ v. [trans.] end a policy of racial segregation in. — **de·seg·re·ga·tion** /dē,segri'gāsʜən/ n.

de·sen·si·tize /dē'sensi,tīz/ ▶ v. [trans.] make less sensitive. ■ make (someone) less likely to feel shock or distress at scenes of cruelty, violence, or suffering by overexposure to such images. ■ free (someone) from a phobia or neurosis by gradually exposing the person to the thing that is feared. — **de·sen·si·ti·za·tion** /dē,sensitə'zāsʜən/ n. **de·sen·si·tiz·er** n.

Des·er·et /,dezə'ret/ the name proposed in the 1840s by Mormon settlers for what became Utah.

de·sert[1] /də'zərt/ ▶ v. [trans.] abandon (a person, cause, or organization) in a way considered disloyal or treacherous. ■ [usu. as adj.] (**deserted**) (of a number of people) leave (a place), causing it to appear empty. ■ (of a quality or ability) fail (someone), esp. at a crucial moment when most needed. ■ [intrans.] Mil. (of a soldier) illegally run away from military service. — **de·ser·tion** /-'zərsʜən/ n. [ME: from OFr. *deserter*, from late L. *desertare*, from L. *desertus* 'left waste' (see DESERT[2]).]

des·ert[2] /'dezərt/ ▶ n. a dry, barren area of land, esp. one covered with sand. ■ a lifeless and unpleasant place, esp. one consisting of or covered with a specified substance. ■ a situation or area considered uninteresting: *a cultural desert.* ▶ adj. [attrib.] barren or dull: *overgrazing has created desert conditions.* ■ uninhabited and desolate. — **de·ser·tic** adj. [ME: via OFr. from late L. *desertum* 'something left waste,' neut. past part. of *deserere* 'leave, forsake.']

de·sert[3] /di'zərt/ ▶ n. (usu. **deserts**) a person's worthiness or entitlement to reward or punishment.
– PHRASES **get** (or **receive**) **one's just deserts** receive the appropriate reward or (more usually) punishment for one's actions. [ME: via OFr. from *deservir* 'serve well' (see DESERVE).]

de·sert·er /də'zərtər/ ▶ n. a member of the armed forces who deserts. [17th C.: from DESERT[1].]

de·sert·i·fi·ca·tion /di,zərtəfi'kāsʜən/ ▶ n. the process by which fertile land becomes desert, typically as a result of drought, deforestation, or inappropriate agriculture.

des·ert var·nish /'dezərt/ ▶ n. Geol. a dark, hard film of oxides formed on exposed rock surfaces in arid regions.

de·serve /də'zərv/ ▶ v. [trans.] do something or have or show qualities worthy of (reward or punishment). — **de·serv·ed·ly** /-'zərvidlē/ adv. [ME: from OFr. *deservir*, from L. *deservire* 'serve well or zealously.']

de·serv·ing /də'zərviɴɢ/ ▶ adj. worthy of being treated in a particular way, typically of being given assistance. — **de·serv·ing·ly** adv. **de·serv·ing·ness** n.

de·sex /dē'seks/ ▶ v. [trans.] [usu. as adj.] (**desexed**) 1 deprive (someone) of sexual qualities or attraction. *Lawrence portrays feminists as shrill, humorless, and desexed.* 2 castrate or spay (an animal).

de·sex·u·al·ize /dē'seksʜo͞oə,līz/ ▶ v. [trans.] deprive of sexual character or the distinctive qualities of a sex. — **de·sex·u·al·i·za·tion** /-,seksʜo͞oələ'zāsʜən/ n.

des·ha·bille /,dezə'bēl; -'bē/ ▶ n. var. of DISHABILLE.

de·si /'dāsē/ (also **de·shi**) Indian ▶ adj. 1 local; indigenous. ■ derog. rustic; unsophisticated. 2 unadulterated or pure. ▶ n. a person of Indian, Pakistani, or Bangladeshi birth or descent who lives abroad. [via Hindi from Sanskrit *deśa* 'country, land.']

De Si·ca /də 'sēkə/, Vittorio (1901–74), Italian filmmaker. His movies include *Bicycle Thief* (1948) and *Two Women* (1960).

des·ic·cant /'desikənt/ ▶ n. a hygroscopic substance used as a drying agent.

des·ic·cate /'desi,kāt/ ▶ v. [trans.] [usu. as adj.] (**desiccated**) remove the moisture from (something, esp. food), typically in order to preserve it. ■ [as adj.] (**desiccated**) fig. lacking interest, passion, or energy. — **des·ic·ca·tion** /-,desi'kāsʜən/ n. **des·ic·ca·tive** /-,kātiv/ adj. [16th C.: from L. *desiccat-* 'made thoroughly dry,' from the v. *desiccare*.]

des·ic·ca·tor /'desi,kātər/ ▶ n. a glass container or other apparatus holding a drying agent for removing moisture from specimens and protecting them from water vapor in the air.

de·sid·er·ate /di'sidə,rāt/ ▶ v. [trans.] archaic feel a keen desire for (something lacking or absent). [17th C.: from L. *desiderat-* 'desired,' from the v. *desiderare*.]

de·sid·er·a·tive /di'sidərətiv; -,rātiv/ ▶ adj. Gram. (in Latin and other inflected languages) denoting a verb formed from another and expressing a desire to do the act denoted by the root verb (such as Latin *esurire* 'want to eat,' from *edere* 'eat'). ■ having, expressing, or relating to desire. ▶ n. Gram. a desiderative verb. [16th C.: from late L. *desiderativus*, from L. *desiderat-* 'desired,' from the v. *desiderare* (see DESIDERATE).]

de·sid·er·a·tum /di,sidə'rätəm; -'rātəm; -,zidə-/ ▶ n. (pl. **-ta** /-tə/) something that is needed or wanted: *integrity was a desideratum.*

de·sign /də'zīn/ ▶ n. 1 a plan or drawing produced to show the look and function or workings of a building, garment, or other object before it is built or made. ■ the art or action of conceiving of and producing such a plan or drawing. ■ an arrangement of lines or shapes created to form a pattern or decoration. 2 purpose, planning, or intention that exists or is thought to exist behind an action, fact, or material object. ▶ v. [trans.] decide upon the look and functioning of (a building, garment, or other object), typically by making a detailed drawing of it. ■ (often **be designed**) do or plan (something) with a specific purpose or intention in mind.
– PHRASES **by design** as a result of a plan; intentionally. **have designs on** aim to obtain (something desired), typically in a secret and dishonest way. [ME: from L. *designare* 'to designate.']

des·ig·nate ▶ v. /'dezig,nāt/ [trans.] (often **be designated**) appoint (someone) to a specified position. ■ officially assign a specified status or ascribe a specified name or quality to. ■ signify; indicate. ▶ adj. /-nit; -,nāt/ [postpositive] appointed to an office or position but not yet installed: *the Director designate.* — **des·ig·na·tor** /-,nātər/ n. [17th C.: from L. *designatus* 'designated,' past part. of *designare*, based on *signum* 'a mark.']

des·ig·nat·ed driv·er ▶ n. a member of a group who abstains from alcohol in order to drive the others safely.

des·ig·nat·ed hit·ter ▶ n. Baseball a nonfielding player named before the start of a game to be in the batting order, typically in place of the pitcher.

des·ig·na·tion /,dezig'nāsʜən/ ▶ n. the choosing and naming of someone to be the holder of a position. ■ the action of choosing a place for a special purpose or giving it a special status. ■ a name, description, or title, typically officially bestowed.

de·sign·ed·ly /də'zīnidlē/ ▶ adv. deliberately in order to produce a specific effect.

des·ig·nee /,dezig'nē/ ▶ n. a person who has been designated.

de·sign·er /də'zīnər/ ▶ n. a person who plans the form, look, or workings of something before its being made or built, typically by drawing it in detail. ■ [as adj.] made by or having the expensive sophistication of a prestigious fashion designer. ■ [as adj.] upscale and fashionable.

de·sign·er drug ▶ n. a synthetic analog of an illegal drug, esp. one devised to circumvent drug laws. ■ a fashionable artificial drug.

de·sign·ing /də'zīniɴɢ/ ▶ adj. [attrib.] acting in a calculating, deceitful way.

de·sir·a·ble /də'zī(ə)rəbəl/ ▶ adj. wanted or wished for as being an attractive, useful, or necessary course of action. ■ (of a person) arousing sexual desire. ▶ n. a desirable person, thing, or quality. — **de·sir·a·bil·i·ty** n. **de·sir·a·ble·ness** n. **de·sir·a·bly** adv.

de·sire /də'zī(ə)r/ ▶ n. a strong feeling of wanting to have something or wishing for something to happen. ■ strong sexual feeling or appetite. ▶ v. [trans.] strongly wish for or want (something). ■ want (someone) sexually. ■ archaic express a wish to (someone); request or entreat. [ME: from OFr. *desirer*, from L. *desiderare* (see DESIDERATE).]

de·sir·ous /di'zīrəs/ ▶ adj. [predic.] having or characterized by desire: *peoples desirous of peace.*

de·sist /di'sist/ ▶ v. [intrans.] cease; abstain. [ME: from OFr. *desister*, from L. *desistere*, from *de-* 'down from' + *sistere* 'to stop' (reduplication of *stare* 'to stand').]

desk /desk/ ▶ n. a piece of furniture with a flat or sloped surface and typically with drawers, at which one can read, write, or do other work. ■ Music a position in an orchestra at which two players share a music stand. ■ a counter in a hotel, bank, or airport at which a customer may check in or obtain information. ■ [with adj.] a specified section of a news organization, esp. a newspaper. [ME: from med. L. *desca*, based on L. *discus* (see DISCUS).]

desk-bound ▶ adj. restricted to working in an office, rather than in an active, physical capacity.

de·skill /dē'skil/ ▶ v. [trans.] reduce the level of skill required to carry out (a job). ■ make the skills of (a worker) obsolete.

desk job ▶ n. a job based at a desk, esp. as opposed to one in active military or police service.

desk·top /'desk,täp/ ▶ n. the working surface of a desk. ■ [as adj.] denoting a piece of equipment, such as a microcomputer, suitable for use at an ordinary desk. ■ a desktop computer. ■ the working area of a computer screen regarded as a representation of a notional desktop and containing icons representing items such as files and a wastebasket.

desk·top pub·lish·ing (abbr.: **DTP**) ▶ n. the production of printed matter by means of a printer linked to a desktop computer, with special software.

des·man /'desmən/ ▶ n. a small, semiaquatic European mammal (family

Talpidae) related to the mole, with a long, tubular muzzle and webbed toes. [18th C.: via Fr. and Ger. from Swed. *desman-råtta* 'muskrat,' from *desman* 'musk.']

des·mid /'dezmid/ ▸ **n.** Biol. a single-celled, freshwater alga (family Desmidiaceae) that appears to be composed of two rigid cells with a shared nucleus. The presence of desmids is usually an indicator of unpolluted water. [19th C.: from mod. L. *Desmidium* (genus name), from Gk. *desmos* 'band, chain.']

des·moid /'dezmoid/ ▸ **adj.** Med. denoting a type of fibrous tumor of muscle and connective tissue, typically in the abdomen. [19th C.: from Gk. *desmos* 'bond' or *desmē* 'bundle' + -OID.]

Des Moines /di 'moin/ the capital of Iowa, in the south central part of the state; pop. 198,682.

des·mo·some /'dezmə,sōm/ ▸ **n.** Biol. a structure by which two adjacent cells are attached, formed from protein plaques in the cell membranes linked by filaments. — **des·mo·so·mal** /,dezmə'sōməl/ **adj.** [1930s: from Gk. *desmos* 'bond, chain.']

Des·na Riv·er /dyis'nä; də'snä/ a river that rises in western Russia and flows for 550 miles (885 km) to enter the Dnieper River near Kiev.

des·o·late ▸ **adj.** /'desəlit/ (of a place) deserted of people and in a state of bleak and dismal emptiness. ■ feeling or showing misery, unhappiness, or loneliness: *I suddenly felt desolate and bereft.* ▸ **v.** /'desə,lāt/ [trans.] make (a place) bleakly and depressingly empty or bare. ■ (usu. **be desolated**) make (someone) feel utterly wretched and unhappy. — **des·o·late·ly** **adv.** **des·o·late·ness** /-litnis/ **n.** **des·o·la·tor** /-,lātər/ **n.** [ME: from L. *desolatus* 'abandoned,' past part. of *desolare*, from *de-* 'thoroughly' + *solus* 'alone.']

des·o·la·tion /,desə'lāsʜən/ ▸ **n.** a state of complete emptiness or destruction. ■ anguished misery or loneliness.

de·sorb /dē'sôrb; -'zôrb/ ▸ **v.** [trans.] Chem. cause the release of (an adsorbed substance) from a surface. ■ [intrans.] (of an adsorbed substance) become released. — **de·sorb·ent** **adj.** & **n.** **de·sorb·er** **n.** **de·sorp·tion** /-'zôrpsʜən; -'sôrp-/ **n.** [1920s: orig. as *desorption* (from *de-* 'away' + *adsorption*), from which *desorb* is a back-form.]

de So·to /də 'sōtō/, Hernando (c.1496–1542), Spanish explorer. He explored much of what is now the southeastern US, as far west as Oklahoma.

de·spair /di'spe(ə)r/ ▸ **n.** the complete loss or absence of hope. ▸ **v.** [intrans.] lose or be without hope: *to despair of ever knowing.*

– PHRASES **be the despair of** be the cause of a feeling of hopelessness in (someone else). — **des·pair·ing·ly** **adv.** [ME: from OFr. *desperer*, from L. *desperare*, from *de-* 'down from' + *sperare* 'to hope.']

des·patch ▸ **v.** & **n.** var. of DISPATCH.

des·per·a·do /,despə'rädō/ ▸ **n.** (pl. **-does** or **-dos**) a desperate or reckless person, esp. a criminal. — **des·per·a·do·ism** **n.** [17th C.: pseudo-Sp. alt. of the obs. n. *desperate*.]

des·per·ate /'despərit/ ▸ **adj.** feeling, showing, or involving a hopeless sense that a situation is so bad as to be impossible to deal with. ■ (of an act or attempt) tried in despair or when everything else has failed; having little hope of success. ■ (of a situation) extremely bad, serious, or dangerous. ■ [predic.] (of a person) having a great need or desire for something. ■ (of a person or fight) violent or dangerous. — **des·per·ate·ness** **n.** [ME: from L. *desperatus* 'deprived of hope,' past part. of *desperare* (see DESPAIR).]

des·per·ate·ly /'despəritlē/ ▸ **adv.** in a way that shows despair. ■ used to emphasize the extreme degree of something.

des·per·a·tion /,despə'rāsʜən/ ▸ **n.** a state of despair, typically one that results in rash or extreme behavior.

des·pi·ca·ble /di'spikəbəl/ ▸ **adj.** deserving hatred and contempt. — **des·pi·ca·bly** **adv.** [16th C.: from late L. *despicabilis*, from *despicari* 'look down on.']

de Spi·no·za /də spi'nōzə/, Baruch, see SPINOZA.

de·spise /di'spīz/ ▸ **v.** [trans.] feel contempt or a deep repugnance for. — **de·spis·er** **n.** [ME: from OFr. *despire*, from L. *despicere*, from *de-* 'down' + *specere* 'look at.']

de·spite /di'spīt/ ▸ **prep.** without being affected by; in spite of. ▸ **n.** archaic or literary **1** outrage; injury. **2** contempt; disdain.

– PHRASES **despite** (or **in despite**) **of** archaic in spite of. **despite oneself** used to indicate that one did not intend or expect to do the thing mentioned. — **de·spite·ful** /-fəl/ **adj.** (archaic or literary). [ME: from OFr. *despit*, from L. *despectus* 'looking down on,' past part. of *despicere* (see DESPISE).]

Des Plaines /des 'plānz/ a city in northeastern Illinois; pop. 58,720.

de·spoil /di'spoil/ ▸ **v.** [trans.] (often **be despoiled**) steal or violently remove valuable or attractive possessions from; plunder: *a church despoiled of its icons.* — **de·spoil·er** **n.** **de·spoil·ment** **n.** **de·spo·li·a·tion** /-,spōlē'āsʜən/ **n.** [ME: from OFr. *despoillier*, from L. *despoliare* 'rob, plunder' (from *spolia* 'spoil').]

de·spond /di'spänd/ ▸ **v.** [intrans.] archaic become dejected and lose confidence. ▸ **n.** a state of unhappiness and low spirits. [17th C.: from L. *despondere* 'give up,' from *de-* 'away' + *spondere* 'to promise.']

de·spond·en·cy /di'spändənsē/ ▸ **n.** a state of low spirits caused by loss of hope or courage. — **de·spond·ence** /-dəns/ **n.**

de·spond·ent /di'spändənt/ ▸ **adj.** in low spirits from loss of hope or courage. — **de·spond·ent·ly** **adv.**

des·pot /'despət/ ▸ **n.** a ruler or other person who holds absolute power, typically exercising it cruelly. — **des·pot·ic** /di'spätik/ **adj.** **des·pot·i·cal·ly** /di'spätik(ə)lē/ **adv.** [16th C.: from French *despote*, via med. L. from Gk. *despotēs* 'master.']

des·pot·ism /'despə,tizəm/ ▸ **n.** the exercise of absolute power, esp. in a cruel and oppressive way. ■ a country or political system where the ruler holds absolute power.

des·qua·mate /'deskwə,māt/ ▸ **v.** [intrans.] (of a layer of cells, e.g., of the skin) come off in scales or flakes. — **des·qua·ma·tion** /,deskwə'māsʜən/ **n.** **des·qua·ma·tive** /-,mātiv/ **adj.** [18th C.: from L. *desquamat-* 'scaled,' from the v. *desquamare*, from *de-* 'away from' + *squama* 'a scale.']

des·sert /di'zərt/ ▸ **n.** the sweet course eaten at the end of a meal. [16th C.: from Fr., past part. of *desservir* 'clear the table,' from *des-* + *servir* 'to serve.']

des·sert·spoon /di'zərt,spo͞on/ ▸ **n.** a spoon used for dessert, smaller than a tablespoon and larger than a teaspoon. — **des·sert·spoon·ful** /-fo͝ol/ **n.** (pl. **-fuls**).

des·sert wine ▸ **n.** a sweet wine drunk with or following dessert.

de·sta·bi·lize /dē'stābə,līz/ ▸ **v.** [trans.] upset the stability of; cause unrest in. — **de·sta·bi·li·za·tion** /-,stābələ'zāsʜən/ **n.**

de Staël /də 'stäl/, Madame (1766–1817), French writer; born *Anne Louise Germaine Necker*.

de·stain /dē'stān/ ▸ **v.** [trans.] Biol. selectively remove stain from (a specimen for microscopy, a chromatography gel, etc.) after it has previously been stained.

de-Sta·lin·i·za·tion /dē ,stälənə'zāsʜən/ ▸ **n.** (in communist countries) the policy of eradicating the memory or influence of Joseph Stalin and Stalinism.

De Stijl /də 'stīl/ a Dutch art movement founded in 1917 by Theo van Doesburg (1883–1931) and Piet Mondrian. The movement favored an abstract, economical style. It was influential on the Bauhaus and constructivist movements. [Du., lit. 'the style.']

des·ti·na·tion /,destə'nāsʜən/ ▸ **n.** the place to which someone or something is going or being sent.

des·tine /'destin/ ▸ **v.** [trans.] intend or choose (someone or something) for a particular purpose or end. [ME: from OFr. *destiner*, from L. *destinare* 'make firm, establish.']

des·tined /'destind/ ▸ **adj.** [predic.] (of a person's future) developing as though according to a plan. ■ (**destined to**) certain to meet (a particular fate). ■ (**destined for**) intended for or traveling toward (a particular place). ■ [attrib.] preordained.

des·ti·ny /'destinē/ ▸ **n.** (pl. **-nies**) the events that will necessarily happen to a particular person or thing in the future. ■ the hidden power believed to control what will happen in the future; fate. [ME: from OFr. *destinee*, from L. *destinata*, fem. past part. of *destinare* 'make firm, establish.']

des·ti·tute /'desti,t(y)o͞ot/ ▸ **adj.** without the basic necessities of life. ■ [predic.] (**destitute of**) not having. — **des·ti·tu·tion** /,desti't(y)o͞osʜən/ **n.** [ME (in the sense 'deserted, abandoned, empty'): from L. *destitutus*, past part. of *destituere* 'forsake,' from *de-* 'away from' + *statuere* 'to place.']

des·tri·er /'destrēər/ ▸ **n.** a medieval knight's warhorse. [ME: from OFr., based on L. *dextera* 'the right hand,' from *dexter* 'on the right.']

de·stroy /di'stroi/ ▸ **v.** [trans.] put an end to the existence of (something) by damaging or attacking it. ■ completely ruin or spoil (something). ■ ruin (someone) emotionally or spiritually. ■ defeat (someone) utterly. ■ (usu. **be destroyed**) kill (a sick, savage, or unwanted animal) by humane means. [ME: from OFr. *destruire*, based on L. *destruere*, from *de-* (expressing reversal) + *struere* 'build.']

de·stroy·er /di'stroiər/ ▸ **n.** a small, fast warship, esp. one equipped to attack submarines and defend fleets. ■ someone or something that destroys.

de·stroy·ing an·gel ▸ **n.** a deadly poisonous white woodland toadstool (*Amanita virosa*, family Amanitaceae) of Eurasia and North America.

de·struct /di'strəkt/ ▸ **v.** [trans.] destroy (something, typically a guided missile). ▸ **n.** [in sing.] [usu. as adj.] the deliberate causing of terminal damage. [1950s: back-form. from DESTRUCTION.]

de·struct·i·ble /di'strəktəbəl/ ▸ **adj.** able to be destroyed. — **de·struct·i·bil·i·ty** /-,strəktə'bilitē/ **n.**

de·struc·tion /di'strəksʜən/ ▸ **n.** the action or process of causing so much damage to something that it no longer exists or cannot be repaired. ■ the action or process of killing or being killed. ■ the ruination or ending of a system or state of affairs. ■ [in sing.] a cause of someone's ruin. [ME: from L. *destructio(n-)*, from the v. *destruere* (see DESTROY).]

de·struc·tive /di'strəktiv/ ▸ **adj.** causing great and irreparable harm or damage. ■ tending to negate or disparage; negative and unhelpful. — **de·struc·tive·ly** **adv.** **de·struc·tive·ness** **n.**

de·struc·tive dis·til·la·tion ▸ **n.** Chem. decomposition of a solid by heating it in a closed container and collecting the volatile constituents given off.

des·ue·tude /'deswi,t(y)o͞od/ ▸ **n.** formal a state of disuse: *the docks fell into desuetude.* [17th C.: from Fr., based on L. *desuescere*, from *de-* (expressing reversal) + *suescere* 'be accustomed.']

de·sul·fur·ize /dē'səlf(y)ə,rīz/ (also **de·sul·phu·rize**) ▸ **v.** [trans.] remove sulfur or sulfur compounds from (a substance). — **de·sul·fu·ri·za·tion** /-,səlfəri'zāsʜən/ **n.** **de·sul·fu·riz·er** **n.**

des·ul·to·ry /'desəl,tôrē/ ▸ **adj.** lacking a plan, purpose, or enthusiasm. ■ (of conversation or speech) going from one subject to another in a halfhearted way; unfocused: *desultory conversation.* ▪ occurring randomly or occasionally. —**des·ul·to·ri·ly** /-,tôrəlē/ adv. **des·ul·to·ri·ness** n. [16th C.: from L. *desultorius* 'superficial,' lit. ('relating to a vaulter'), from *desultor* 'vaulter,' from *desilire* 'leap down.']

de·syn·chro·nize /dē'siNGkrə,nīz/ ▶v. [trans.] disturb the synchronization of; put out of step or phase. —**de·syn·chro·ni·za·tion** /-,siNGkrənə'zāsHən/ n.

de·tach /di'tacH/ ▶v. [trans.] **1** disengage (something or part of something) and remove it. ▪ [intrans.] be easily removable. ▪ (**detach oneself from**) leave or separate oneself from (a group or place). ▪ (**detach oneself from**) avoid or put an end to any connection or association with. **2** (usu. **be detached**) Mil. send (a group of soldiers or ships) on a separate mission. —**de·tach·a·bil·i·ty** /-,tacHə'bilitē/ n. **de·tach·a·ble** adj. [16th C.: from Fr. *détacher*, from *des-* (expressing reversal) + *attacher* 'attach.']

de·tached /di'tacHt/ ▶adj. separate or disconnected, in particular: ▪ (of a house or other building) not joined to another on either side. ▪ aloof and objective. —**de·tach·ed·ly** /-'tacHidlē/ adv.

de·tached ret·i·na ▶n. a retina that has become separated from the underlying choroid tissue at the back of the eye, causing loss of vision in the affected area.

de·tach·ment /di'tacHmənt/ ▶n. **1** the state of being objective or aloof. **2** Mil. a group of troops, aircraft, or ships sent away on a separate mission. ▪ a party of people separated from a larger group. **3** the action or process of detaching; separation.

de·tail /di'tāl; 'dētāl/ ▶n. **1** an individual feature, fact, or item. ▪ a minor or less significant item or feature. ▪ a minor decorative feature of a building or work of art. ▪ the style or treatment of such features. ▪ a small part of a picture or other work of art reproduced separately for close study. ▪ (**details**) itemized facts or information about someone; personal particulars. **2** a small detachment of troops or police officers given a special duty: *the candidate's security detail.* ▪ [often with adj.] a special duty assigned to such a detachment. ▶v. [trans.] **1** describe item by item; give the full particulars of. **2** [with obj. and infin.] assign (someone) to undertake a particular task. **3** clean (a motor vehicle) intensively and minutely.

– PHRASES **go into detail** give a full account of something. **in detail** as regards every feature or aspect; fully. —**de·tail·er** n. (in sense 3 of the verb). [17th C.: from Fr. *détail*, from *dé-* (expressing separation) + *tailler* 'to cut' (based on L. *talea* 'cutting').]

de·tailed /di'tāld; 'dētāld/ ▶adj. having many details or facts; showing attention to detail. ▪ (of a work of art) executed with many minor decorative features.

de·tail·ing /'dētāliNG/ ▶n. small, decorative features on a building, garment, or work of art.

de·tain /di'tān/ ▶v. [trans.] keep (someone) in official custody, typically for questioning about a crime or in politically sensitive situations. ▪ keep (someone) from proceeding; hold back. —**de·tain·ment** n. [ME: from OFr. *detenir*, from L. *detinere*, from *de-* 'aside' + *tenere* 'to hold.']

de·tain·ee /,di,tā'nē; ,dētā'nē/ ▶n. a person held in custody, esp. for political reasons.

de·tain·er /di'tānər; dē-/ ▶n. **1** Law the action of detaining or withholding property. ▪ the detention of a person in custody. ▪ an order authorizing the continued detention of a person in custody. **2** esp. Law a person who detains someone or something.

de·tect /di'tekt/ ▶v. [trans.] discover or identify the presence or existence of. ▪ discover or investigate (a crime or its perpetrators). ▪ discern (something intangible or barely perceptible). —**de·tect·a·ble** adj. **de·tect·a·bly** adv. [ME: from L. *detect-* 'uncovered,' from the v. *detegere*, from *de-* (expressing reversal) + *tegere* 'to cover.']

de·tec·tion /di'teksHən/ ▶n. the action or process of identifying the presence of something concealed. ▪ the work of a detective in investigating a crime. ▪ another term for ***DEMODULATION*** (see **DEMODULATE**).

de·tec·tive /di'tektiv/ ▶n. a person, esp. a police officer, whose occupation is to investigate and solve crimes. ▪ [as adj.] denoting a particular rank of police officer. ▪ [as adj.] concerning crime and its investigation: *detective work.*

de·tec·tive sto·ry (also **detective novel**) ▶n. a story whose plot revolves around the investigation and solving of a crime.

de·tec·tor /di'tektər/ ▶n. [often with adj.] a device or instrument designed to detect the presence of a particular object or substance. ▪ another term for ***DEMODULATOR*** (see **DEMODULATE**).

de·tent /di'tent/ ▶n. a catch in a machine that prevents motion until released. ▪ (in a clock) a catch that regulates striking. [17th C.: from Fr. *détente*, from OFr. *destente*, from *destendre* 'slacken,' from *des-* (expressing reversal) + L. *tendere* 'to stretch.']

dé·tente /dā'tänt/ (also **de·tente**) ▶n. the easing of hostility or strained relations, esp. between countries. [20th C.: Fr., lit. 'loosening, relaxation.']

de·ten·tion /di'tensHən/ ▶n. the action of detaining someone or the state of being detained in official custody, esp. as a political prisoner. ▪ the punishment of being kept in school after hours. [ME: from late L. *detentio(n-)*, from L. *detinere* 'hold back' (see **DETAIN**).]

de·ten·tion cen·ter ▶n. an institution where people are held in detention for short periods, in particular illegal immigrants, refugees, people awaiting trial or sentence, or youthful offenders.

de·ter /di'tər/ ▶v. (**-terred, -ter·ring**) [trans.] discourage (someone) from doing something, typically by instilling doubt or fear of the consequences. ▪ prevent the occurrence of. [16th C.: from L. *deterrere*, from *de-* 'away from' + *terrere* 'frighten.']

de·terge /di'tərj/ ▶v. [trans.] rare cleanse thoroughly. [17th C.: from Fr. *déterger* or L. *detergere* 'wipe away.']

de·ter·gent /di'tərjənt/ ▶n. a water-soluble cleansing agent that combines with impurities and dirt to make them more soluble and differs from soap in not forming a scum with the salts in hard water. ▪ any additive with a similar action, e.g., an oil-soluble substance that holds dirt in suspension in lubricating oil. ▶adj. of or relating to such compounds or their action. —**de·ter·gence** n. **de·ter·gen·cy** n.

de·te·ri·o·rate /di'ti(ə)rēə,rāt/ ▶v. [intrans.] become progressively worse. —**de·te·ri·o·ra·tion** /-,ti(ə)rēə'rāsHən/ n. **de·te·ri·o·ra·tive** /-,rātiv/ adj. [16th C.: from late L. *deteriorat-* 'worsened,' from the v. *deteriorare*, from L. *deterior* 'worse.']

de·ter·mi·na·ble /di'tərminəbəl/ ▶adj. **1** able to be firmly decided or definitely ascertained. **2** Law capable of being brought to an end under given conditions; terminable.

de·ter·mi·nant /di'tərminənt/ ▶n. **1** a factor that decisively affects the nature or outcome of something. ▪ Biol. a gene or other factor that determines the character and development of a cell or group of cells in an organism, a set of which forms an individual's idiotype. **2** Math. a quantity obtained by the addition of products of the elements of a square matrix according to a given rule. ▶adj. serving to determine or decide something.

de·ter·mi·nate /də'tərmənit/ ▶adj. having exact and discernible limits or form. ▪ Bot. (of a flowering shoot) having the main axis ending in a flower bud and therefore no longer extending in length, as in a cyme. —**de·ter·mi·na·cy** /-minəsē/ n. **de·ter·mi·nate·ly** adv. **de·ter·mi·nate·ness** n.

de·ter·mi·na·tion /di,tərmə'nāsHən/ ▶n. **1** firmness of purpose; resoluteness. **2** the process of establishing something exactly, typically by calculation or research. ▪ Law the settlement of a dispute by the authoritative decision of a judge or arbitrator. ▪ Law a judicial decision or sentence. **3** the controlling or deciding of something's nature or outcome. **4** Law the cessation of an estate or interest. **5** archaic a tendency to move in a fixed direction.

de·ter·mi·na·tive /də'tərmə,nātiv; -nətiv/ ▶adj. [predic.] esp. Law serving to define. ▶n. Gram.another term for **DETERMINER**.

de·ter·mine /di'tərmin/ ▶v. [trans.] **1** cause (something) to occur in a particular way. ▪ firmly decide: [with infin.] *she determined to tackle him the next day* | [intrans.] *he determined on a plan.* **2** ascertain or establish exactly, typically as a result of research or calculation. ▪ Math. specify the value, position, or form of (a mathematical or geometric object) uniquely. **3** Law, archaic bring or come to an end. [ME: from OFr. *determiner*, from L. *determinare* 'limit, fix,' from *de-* 'completely' + *terminare* 'terminate.']

de·ter·mined /di'tərmind/ ▶adj. having made a firm decision and being resolved not to change it. ▪ processing or displaying resolve. —**de·ter·mined·ly** adv. **de·ter·mined·ness** n.

de·ter·min·er /di'tərminər/ ▶n. **1** a person or thing that determines or decides something. **2** Gram. a modifying word that determines the kind of reference a noun or noun group has, e.g., *a, the, every.* See also **DEFINITE ARTICLE, INDEFINITE ARTICLE.**

de·ter·min·ism /di'tərmə,nizəm/ ▶n. Philos. the doctrine that all events, including human action, are ultimately determined by causes external to the will. —**de·ter·min·ist** n. & adj. **de·ter·min·is·tic** /-,tərmə'nistik/ adj. **de·ter·min·is·ti·cal·ly** /-,tərmə'nistik(ə)lē/ adv.

de·ter·rent /di'tərənt/ ▶n. a thing that discourages or is intended to discourage someone from some act. ▪ a nuclear weapon or weapons system regarded as deterring an enemy from attack. ▶adj. able or intended to deter. —**de·ter·rence** n.

de·test /di'test/ ▶v. [trans.] dislike intensely. —**de·test·er** n. [15th C.: from L. *detestari*, from *de-* 'down' + *testari* 'witness.']

de·test·a·ble /di'testəbəl/ ▶adj. deserving intense dislike. —**de·test·a·bly** adv.

de·tes·ta·tion /,dēte'stāsHən/ ▶n. intense dislike. ▪ archaic a detested person or thing.

de·throne /dē'THrōn/ ▶v. [trans.] remove (a ruler, esp. a monarch) from power. ▪ fig. remove from a position of authority or dominance. —**de·throne·ment** n.

det·i·nue /'detn,(y)o͞o/ ▶n. Law an action to recover wrongfully detained goods or possessions. ▪ such wrongful detention. [ME: from OFr. *detenue*, past part. of *detenir* 'detain.']

det·o·nate /'detn,āt/ ▶v. explode or cause to explode. —**det·o·na·tive** /-,ātiv/ adj. [18th C.: from L. *detonat-* 'thundered down or forth,' from the v. *detonare*, from *de-* 'down' + *tonare* 'to thunder.']

det·o·na·tion /,detn'āsHən/ ▶n. the action of causing a bomb or explosive device to explode. ▪ a loud explosion. ▪ tech. combustion of a substance that is initiated suddenly and propagates extremely rapidly, giving rise to a shock wave. Compare with **DEFLAGRATION**. ▪ premature combustion of fuel in an internal combustion engine, causing knocking.

det·o·na·tor /'detn,ātər/ ▶n. a device or a small, sensitive charge used to detonate an explosive.

de·tour /'dē,to͝or/ ▶ **n.** a long or roundabout route taken to avoid something or to make a visit along the way. ■ an alternative route for use by traffic when the usual road is temporarily closed. ▶ **v.** [no obj., with adverbial of direction] take a long or roundabout route: *he detoured around the walls.* ■ [trans.] avoid or bypass (something) by taking such a route. [18th C.: from Fr. *détour* 'change of direction,' from *détourner* 'turn away.']

de·tox /'dē,täks/ informal ▶ **n.** short for DETOXIFICATION: *he ended up in detox for three months.* ▶ **v.** short for DETOXIFY.

de·tox·i·cate /dē'täksi,kāt/ ▶ **v.** another term for DETOXIFY. — **de·tox·i·ca·tion** /-,täksi'kāshən/ **n.**

de·tox·i·fi·ca·tion /dē,täksəfi'kāshən/ ▶ **n.** the process of removing toxic substances or qualities. ■ medical treatment of an alcoholic or drug addict involving abstention from drink or drugs until the bloodstream is free of toxins.

de·tox·i·fy /dē'täksə,fī/ ▶ **v.** (**-fies, -fied**) [trans.] remove toxic substances or qualities from. ■ (usu. **be detoxified**) treat (an alcoholic or drug addict) to remove the effects of drink or drugs in order to help overcome addiction. ■ [intrans.] abstain from drink and drugs until the bloodstream is free of toxins. ■ [intrans.] become free of poisonous substances or qualities. — **de·tox·i·fi·er n.** [20th C.: from DE- (expressing removal) + L. *toxicum* 'poison' + -FY.]

de·tract /di'trakt/ ▶ **v. 1** [intrans.] (**detract from**) reduce or take away the worth or value of. ■ [trans.] deny or take away (a quality or achievement) so as to make its subject seem less impressive. **2** [trans.] (**detract someone/something from**) divert or distract (someone or something) away from. — **de·trac·tion** /-'trakshən/ **n.** **de·trac·tive** /-'traktiv/ **adj.** [ME: from L. *detract-* 'drawn away,' from the v. *detrahere*, from *de-* 'away from' + *trahere* 'draw.']

de·trac·tor /di'traktər/ ▶ **n.** a person who disparages someone or something.

de·train /dē'trān/ ▶ **v.** [intrans.] leave a train. ■ [trans.] cause or assist to leave a train. — **de·train·ment n.**

de·trib·al·ize /dē'trībə,līz/ ▶ **v.** [trans.] [usu. as adj.] (**detribalized**) remove (someone) from a traditional tribal social structure. ■ remove a traditional tribal social structure from (a culture). — **de·trib·al·i·za·tion** /-,trībələ'zāshən/ **n.**

det·ri·ment /'detrəmənt/ ▶ **n.** the state of being harmed or damaged. ■ a cause of harm or damage. [ME: from OFr., from L. *detrimentum*, from *deterere* 'wear away.']

det·ri·men·tal /,detrə'mentl/ ▶ **adj.** tending to cause harm. — **det·ri·men·tal·ly adv.**

de·tri·tion /di'trishən/ ▶ **n.** rare the action of wearing away by friction. [17th C.: from med. L. *detritio(n-)*, from *detri-*, stem of *deterere* 'wear away.']

de·tri·tus /di'trītəs/ ▶ **n.** waste or debris of any kind. ■ gravel, sand, silt, or other material produced by erosion. ■ organic matter produced by the decomposition of organisms. — **de·tri·tal** /-tl/ **adj.** [18th C.: from Fr. *détritus*, from L. *detritus*, from *deterere* 'wear away.']

De·troit /di'troit/ a city and shipping center in northeastern Michigan; pop. 951,270.

de trop /də 'trō/ ▶ **adj.** not wanted; unwelcome: *she had no grasp of the conversation and felt herself de trop.* [18th C.: Fr., lit. 'excessive.']

de Troyes /də 'trwä/, Chrétien, see CHRÉTIEN DE TROYES.

de·tu·mes·cence /,dēt(y)o͞o'mesəns/ ▶ **n.** the process of subsiding from a state of tension, swelling, or (esp.) sexual arousal. — **de·tu·mesce** /-'mes/ **v.** **de·tu·mes·cent adj.** [17th C.: from L. *detumescere*, from *de-* 'down, away' + *tumescere* 'to swell.']

Deu·ca·li·on /d(y)o͞o'kālēən/ Gk. Mythol. the son of Prometheus. With his wife Pyrrha he survived a flood sent by Zeus to punish human wickedness.

deuce[1] /d(y)o͞os/ ▶ **n. 1** a thing representing, or represented by, the number two, in particular: ■ the two on dice or playing cards. ■ a throw of two at dice. ■ informal, dated a two-dollar bill. **2** Tennis the tie score of 40-all in a game, at which a player needs two consecutive points to win the game. [15th C.: from OFr. *deus* 'two,' from L. *duos*.]

deuce[2] ▶ **n.** (**the deuce**) informal used as a euphemism for "devil" in expressions of annoyance, impatience, or surprise or for emphasis.
– PHRASES **a** (or **the**) **deuce of a ——** used to emphasize how bad, difficult, or serious something is. [17th C.: from Low Ger. *duus*, prob. of the same origin as DEUCE[1].]

deuc·ed /'d(y)o͞osid/ informal, dated ▶ **adj.** [attrib.] used for emphasis, esp. to express disapproval or frustration. — **deuc·ed·ly adv.** [as submodifier] *they're deucedly hard to find.*

de·us ex ma·chi·na /'dāəs eks 'mäkənə; -'mak-/ ▶ **n.** an unexpected power or event saving a hopeless situation, esp. as a plot device in a play or novel. [17th C.: mod. L., translation of Gk. *theos ek mēkhanēs* 'god from the machinery.']

Deut. ▶ **abbr.** Bible Deuteronomy.

deu·ter·ag·o·nist /,d(y)o͞otə'ragənist/ ▶ **n.** the person second in importance to the protagonist in a drama. [19th C.: from Gk. *deuteragōnistēs*, from *deuteros* 'second' + *agōnistēs* 'actor.']

deu·ter·a·nope /'d(y)o͞otərə,nōp/ ▶ **n.** a person suffering from deuteranopia.

deu·ter·a·no·pi·a /,d(y)o͞otərə'nōpēə/ ▶ **n.** color-blindness resulting from insensitivity to green light, causing confusion of greens, reds, and yellows. Compare with PROTANOPIA. [20th C.: from DEUTERO- 'second.']

deu·ter·at·ed /'d(y)o͞otə,rātid/ (also **deu·te·ri·at·ed** /d(y)o͞o'ti(ə)rē,ātid/) ▶ **adj.** Chem. (of a compound) in which the ordinary isotope of hydrogen has been replaced with deuterium. — **deu·ter·a·tion** /,d(y)o͞otə'rāshən/ **n.**

deu·te·ri·um /d(y)o͞o'ti(ə)rēəm/ ▶ **n.** Chem. a stable isotope of hydrogen with a mass approximately twice that of the usual isotope, used as a fuel in thermonuclear bombs. Heavy water (D_2O) is used as a moderator in nuclear reactors. (Symbol: **D**) [1930s: mod. L., from Gk. *deuteros* 'second.']

deutero- ▶ **comb. form** second: *Deutero-Isaiah.* ■ secondary: *deuterocanonical.* [from Gk. *deuteros* 'second.']

deu·ter·o·ca·non·ical /,d(y)o͞otə,rōkə'nänikəl/ ▶ **adj.** (of sacred books or literary works) forming a secondary canon.

Deu·ter·o-I·sa·iah /,d(y)o͞otə,rō ī'zāə/ the supposed later author of Isaiah 40–55.

deu·ter·on /'d(y)o͞otə,rän/ ▶ **n.** the nucleus of a deuterium atom, consisting of a proton and a neutron. [1930s: from Gk. *deuteros* 'second,' on the pattern of *proton*.]

Deu·ter·on·o·my /,d(y)o͞otə'ränəmē/ the fifth book of the Bible, containing a recapitulation of the Ten Commandments and much of the Mosaic law.

Deutsch·land /'doich,länt/ German name for GERMANY.

Deutsch·mark /'doich,märk/ (also **Deutsch·e Mark** /'doichə/) ▶ **n.** the basic monetary unit of Germany (until the introduction of the euro), equal to 100 pfennigs. [20th C.: from Ger. *deutsche Mark* 'German mark.']

deut·zi·a /'d(y)o͞otsēə/ ▶ **n.** an ornamental shrub (genus *Deutzia*) of the hydrangea family, with white or pinkish flowers, native to Asia and Central America. [mod. L., named after Johann van der *Deutz*, 18th-cent. Dutch patron of botany.]

de·va /'dāvə/ Hinduism ▶ **n.** a member of a class of benevolent divine beings in the Vedic period. Compare with ASURA. ■ Indian (in general use) a god. [19th C.: Sanskrit, literally 'shining one,' later 'god.']

de Va·le·ra /,devə'lerə; ,dā-/, Eamon (1882–1975), president of the Republic of Ireland 1959–73; born in the US. Founder of the Fianna Fáil Party in 1926, and president of the Irish Free State from 1932, he was largely responsible for the new constitution of 1937 that created the state of Eire.

de·val·ue /dē'valyo͞o/ ▶ **v.** (**-val·ues, -val·ued, -val·u·ing**) [trans.] reduce or underestimate the worth or importance of. ■ (often **be devalued**) Econ. reduce the official value of (a currency) in relation to other currencies. — **de·val·u·a·tion** /,dēvalyo͞o'āshən/ **n.**

De·va·na·ga·ri /,dävə'nägərē/ ▶ **n.** the alphabet used for Sanskrit, Hindi, and other Indian languages. [18th C.: Sanskrit, from *deva* 'god' + *nāgarī* (from *nagara* 'town'), an earlier name of the script.]

dev·as·tate /'devə,stāt/ ▶ **v.** [trans.] destroy or ruin (something). ■ cause (someone) severe and overwhelming shock or grief. — **dev·as·ta·tion** /,devə'stāshən/ **n.** **dev·as·ta·tor** /-,stātər/ **n.** [17th C.: from L. *devastat-* 'laid waste,' from the v. *devastare*, from *de-* 'thoroughly' + *vastare* 'lay waste.']

dev·as·tat·ing /'devə,stātiNG/ ▶ **adj.** highly destructive or damaging. ■ causing severe shock, distress, or grief. ■ informal extremely impressive, effective, or attractive. — **dev·as·tat·ing·ly adv.**

de·vein /dē'vān/ ▶ **v.** [trans.] remove the main central vein from (a shrimp or prawn).

de·vel·op /di'veləp/ ▶ **v.** (**-vel·oped, -vel·op·ing**) **1** grow or cause to grow and become more mature, advanced, or elaborate: [intrans.] *motion pictures developed into mass entertainment* | [trans.] *entrepreneurs develop their skills through trial and error.* ■ [intrans.] [often as adj.] (**developing**) (of a poor agricultural country) become more economically and socially advanced. ■ [trans.] convert (land) to a new purpose by constructing buildings or making other use of its resources. ■ construct or convert (a building) so as to improve existing resources. ■ [trans.] elaborate (a musical theme) by modification of the melody, harmony, or rhythm. ■ [trans.] Chess bring (a piece) into play from its initial position on a player's back rank. ■ Geom. [trans.] convert (a curved surface) conceptually into a plane figure as if by unrolling. ■ [trans.] Math. expand (a function, etc.) in the form of a series. **2** start to exist, experience, or possess: [intrans.] *a strange closeness developed* | [trans.] *I developed an interest in law.* **3** [trans.] treat (a photographic film) with chemicals to make a visible image. — **de·vel·op·a·ble adj.** [17th C.: from Fr. *développer*, based on L. *dis-* 'un-' + a second element of unknown origin.]

de·vel·oped /di'veləpt/ ▶ **adj.** advanced or elaborated to a specified degree. ■ (of a person or part of the body) having specified physical proportions. ■ (of a country or region) advanced economically and socially.

de·vel·op·er /di'veləpər/ ▶ **n.** a person or organization that develops something. ■ [with adj.] a person who grows or matures at a specified time or rate. ■ a chemical agent used for treating photographic film to make a visible image.

de·vel·op·ment /di'veləpmənt/ ▶ **n. 1** the process of developing or being developed. ■ a specified state of growth or advancement. ■ a new and refined product or idea. ■ an event constituting a new stage in a changing situation. ■ the process of converting land to a new purpose by constructing buildings or making use of its resources. ■ an area of land with new buildings on it. **2** the process of starting to experience or suffer from an ailment or feeling. **3** the process of treating photographic film with chemicals to make a visible image.

de·vel·op·men·tal /di,veləp'mentl/ ▶ **adj.** concerned with the development of someone or something. ■ concerned with the evolution of animals and plants: *developmental biology.* — **de·vel·op·men·tal·ly adv.**

dé·vel·op·pé /də,velə'pā/ ▶ **n.** (pl. **-pés** pronunc. same) Ballet a movement in which one leg is raised to the knee of the supporting leg, then unfolded and kept in a fully extended position. [20th C.: Fr., past part. of *développer* 'develop.']

de·verb·al /dē'vərbəl/ ▶ **adj.** (of a noun or adjective) derived from a verb. ▶ **n.** a deverbal noun or adjective.

De·vi /'dāvē/ Hinduism the supreme goddess, often identified with Parvati and Shakti. ■ (**devi**) Indian (in general use) a goddess.

de·vi·ance /'dēvēəns/ ▶ **n.** the fact or state of departing from usual or accepted standards, esp. in social or sexual behavior. — **de·vi·an·cy** /-ənsē/ **n.**

de·vi·ant /'dēvēənt/ ▶ **adj.** departing from usual or accepted standards, esp. in social or sexual behavior. ■ usu. offens. homosexual. ▶ **n.** a deviant person or thing.

de·vi·ate ▶ **v.** /'dēvē,āt/ [intrans.] depart from an established course. ■ depart from usual or accepted standards. ▶ **n. & adj.** /'dēvēit/ old-fashioned term for DEVIANT. — **de·vi·a·tor** /-,ātər/ **n.** [16th C.: from late L. *deviat-* 'turned out of the way,' from the v. *deviare*, from *de-* 'away from' + *via* 'way.']

de·vi·a·tion /,dēvē'āsHən/ ▶ **n.** **1** the action of departing from an established course or accepted standard. **2** Stat. the amount by which a single measurement differs from a fixed value such as the mean. **3** the deflection of a vessel's compass needle caused by iron in the vessel, varying with the vessel's heading. — **de·vi·a·tion·ism n. de·vi·a·tion·ist n.**

de·vice /di'vīs/ ▶ **n.** **1** a thing made or adapted for a particular task, esp. a mechanism or electronic instrument. ■ an explosive contrivance; a bomb. ■ archaic the design or look of something: *works of strange device.* **2** a plan, scheme, or trick with a particular aim. ■ a turn of phrase intended to produce a particular effect in speech or a literary work: *a rhetorical device.* **3** a drawing or design. ■ an emblematic or heraldic design.
– PHRASES **leave someone to their own devices** leave someone to do as they wish without supervision. [ME: from OFr. *devis*, based on L. *divis-* 'divided,' from the v. *dividere.*]

dev·il /'devəl/ ▶ **n.** **1** (usu. **the Devil**) (in Christian and Jewish belief) the chief evil spirit; Satan. ■ an evil spirit; a demon. ■ a very wicked or cruel person. ■ a mischievously clever or self-willed person. ■ [with adj.] informal a person with specified characteristics: *the poor devil | a lucky devil.* ■ (**the devil**) fighting spirit; wildness. ■ (**the devil**) a thing that is very difficult or awkward to do or deal with. **2** (**the devil**) expressing surprise or annoyance in various questions or exclamations: *"Where the devil is he?"* **3** an instrument or machine, esp. one with sharp teeth or spikes, used for tearing or other destructive work. **4** informal, dated a junior assistant of a lawyer or other professional. See also PRINTER'S DEVIL. ▶ **v.** (**dev·iled, dev·il·ing**; Brit. **dev·illed, dev·il·ling**) **1** [intrans.] informal, dated act as a junior assistant for a lawyer or other professional. **2** [trans.] harass or worry (someone); bedevil.
– PHRASES **between the devil and the deep (blue) sea** caught in a dilemma. **devil a ——** archaic not even one or any: *the devil a man of you stirred himself over it.* **devil-may-care** cheerful and reckless. **a devil of a ——** informal used to emphasize great size or degree. **the devil is in the details** the details of a matter are its most problematic aspect. **the devil to pay** serious trouble to be dealt with. **the devil's own ——** informal used to emphasize the difficulty or seriousness of something: *he was in the devil's own hurry.* **go to the devil 1** said in angry rejection or condemnation of someone. **2** fall into moral depravity. **like the devil** with great speed or energy. **play the devil with** have a damaging or disruptive effect on. **speak** (or **talk**) **of the devil** said when a person appears just after being mentioned. [OE *dēofol*, via late L. from Gk. *diabolos* 'accuser, slanderer' (used in the Septuagint to translate Heb. *śāṭān* 'Satan'), from *diaballein* 'to slander.']

dev·iled /'devəld/ ▶ **adj.** (of food) cooked with hot seasoning: *deviled eggs.*

dev·il·fish /'devəl,fisH/ ▶ **n.** (pl. same or **-fish·es**) any of a number of marine creatures that are perceived as having a sinister appearance, in particular a devil ray, a stonefish, or an octopus or squid.

dev·il·ish /'devəlisH/ ▶ **adj.** of, like, or appropriate to a devil in evil and cruelty. ■ mischievous and rakish. ■ very difficult to deal with or use. ▶ **adv.** [as submodifier] informal, dated very; extremely. — **dev·il·ish·ness n.**

dev·il·ish·ly /'devəlisHlē/ ▶ **adv.** in a devilish manner. ■ [as submodifier] informal very; extremely.

dev·il·ment /'devəlmənt/ ▶ **n.** reckless mischief; wild spirits.

dev·il ray ▶ **n.** a large, long-tailed ray (family Mobulidae) that has a fleshy, hornlike projection on each side of the mouth. It occurs on or near the surface of warm seas and feeds on plankton.

dev·il·ry /'devəlrē/ ▶ **n.** wicked activity. ■ reckless mischief. ■ black magic; dealings with the devil.

dev·il's ad·vo·cate ▶ **n.** a person who expresses a contentious opinion in order to provoke debate or test the strength of the opposing arguments. ■ hist. the popular title of the person appointed by the Roman Catholic Church to challenge a proposed beatification or canonization, or the verification of a miracle.

dev·il's food cake ▶ **n.** a rich chocolate cake.

Dev·il's Is·land a rocky island off the coast of French Guiana, a penal settlement 1852–1953.

dev·il's paint·brush ▶ **n.** a deep orange European hawkweed (*Hieracium aurantiacum*), naturalized in North America.

dev·il's walk·ing stick ▶ **n.** See HERCULES-CLUB.

dev·il·try /'devəltrē/ ▶ **n.** archaic variant of DEVILRY.

de·vi·ous /'dēvēəs/ ▶ **adj.** **1** showing a skillful use of underhanded tactics to achieve goals. **2** (of a route or journey) longer and less direct than the most straightforward way. — **de·vi·ous·ly adv. de·vi·ous·ness n.** [16th C.: from L. *devius* (from *de-* 'away from' + *via* 'way') + -OUS.]

de·vise /di'vīz/ ▶ **v.** [trans.] **1** plan or invent (a complex procedure, system, or mechanism) by careful thought. **2** Law leave (real estate) to someone by the terms of a will. ▶ **n.** Law a clause in a will leaving real estate to someone. — **de·vis·a·ble adj. de·vi·see** /di,vī'zē/ **n.** (in sense 2). **de·vis·er n. de·vi·sor** /-'vīzər/ **n.** (in sense 2). [ME: from OFr. *deviser*, from L. *divis-* 'divided,' from the v. *dividere.*]

de·vi·tal·ize /dē'vītl,īz/ ▶ **v.** [trans.] [usu. as adj.] (**devitalized**) deprive of strength and vigor. — **de·vi·tal·i·za·tion** /dē,vītl-ə'zāsHən/ **n.**

de·vit·ri·fy /dē'vitrə,fī/ ▶ **v.** (**-fies, -fied**) [intrans.] (of glass or vitreous rock) become hard, opaque, and crystalline. ■ [trans.] make hard, opaque, and crystalline. — **de·vit·ri·fi·ca·tion** /-,vitrəfi'kāsHən/ **n.**

de·voice /dē'vois/ ▶ **v.** [trans.] Phonet. make (a vowel or voiced consonant) voiceless.

de·void /di'void/ ▶ **adj.** [predic.] (**devoid of**) entirely lacking or free from: *a voice devoid of emotion.* [ME: past part. of obs. *devoid* 'cast out,' from OFr. *devoidier.*]

de·voir /dəv'wär/ ▶ **n.** archaic a person's duty: *you have done your devoir right well.* ■ (**pay one's devoirs**) pay one's respects formally. [ME: from OFr. *deveir*, from L. *debere* 'owe.']

dev·o·lu·tion /,devə'lo͞osHən/ ▶ **n.** the transfer or delegation of power to a lower level, esp. by central government to local or regional administration. ■ formal descent or degeneration to a lower or worse state. ■ Law the legal transfer of property from one owner to another. ■ Biol. evolutionary degeneration. — **dev·o·lu·tion·ar·y** /-,nerē/ **adj. dev·o·lu·tion·ist n.** [15th C.: from late L. *devolutio(n-)*, from L. *devolvere.*]

de·volve /di'välv/ ▶ **v.** [trans.] transfer or delegate (power) to a lower level, esp. from central government to local or regional administration. ■ [intrans.] (**devolve on/upon/to**) (of duties or responsibility) pass to (a body or person at a lower level). ■ [intrans.] (**devolve into**) formal degenerate or be split into. — **de·volve·ment n.** [ME: from L. *devolvere*, from *de-* 'down' + *volvere* 'to roll.']

Dev·on[1] /'devən/ (also **Dev·on·shire** /-sHər; -,sHi(ə)r/) a county in southwestern England; county town, Exeter.

Dev·on[2] ▶ **n.** an animal of a breed of red beef cattle. [19th C.: named after the county of *Devon* (see DEVON[1]).]

De·vo·ni·an /di'vōnēən/ ▶ **adj.** **1** of or relating to Devon. **2** Geol. of, relating to, or denoting the fourth period of the Paleozoic era, between the Silurian and Carboniferous periods. During this period, which lasted from about 409 million to 363 million years ago, fish became abundant; the first amphibians evolved, and the first forests appeared. ▶ **n.** **1** a native or inhabitant of Devon. **2** (**the Devonian**) Geol. the Devonian period or the system of rocks deposited during it.

Dev·on·shire cream /'devənsHər; -,sHi(ə)r/ ▶ **n.** clotted cream.

de·vote /di'vōt/ ▶ **v.** [trans.] **1** (**devote something to**) give all or a large part of one's time or resources to (a person, activity, or cause). **2** archaic invoke or pronounce a curse upon. [16th C.: from L. *devot-* 'consecrated,' from the v. *devovere*, from *de-* 'formally' + *vovere* 'to vow.']

de·vot·ed /di'vōtid/ ▶ **adj.** **1** very loving or loyal. **2** [predic.] (**devoted to**) given over to the display, study, or discussion of. — **de·vot·ed·ly adv.** (sense 1) **de·vot·ed·ness n.** (sense 1).

dev·o·tee /,devə'tē; -'tā/ ▶ **n.** a person who is very interested in and enthusiastic about someone or something: *a devotee of Chinese calligraphy.* ■ a strong believer in a particular religion or god: *devotees thronged the temple.*

de·vo·tion /di'vōsHən/ ▶ **n.** love, loyalty, or enthusiasm for a person, activity, or cause. ■ religious worship or observance. ■ (**devotions**) prayers or religious observances.

de·vo·tion·al /di'vōsHənl/ ▶ **adj.** of or used in religious worship.

de·vour /di'vou(ə)r/ ▶ **v.** [trans.] eat (food or prey) hungrily or quickly. ■ (of fire, disease, or other forces) consume (someone or something) destructively. ■ read (something) quickly and eagerly. ■ (**be devoured**) (of a person) be totally absorbed by an unpleasant feeling. — **de·vour·er n. de·vour·ing·ly adv.** [ME: from OFr. *devorer*, from L. *devorare*, from *de-* 'down' + *vorare* 'to swallow.']

de·vout /di'vout/ ▶ **adj.** having or showing deep religious feeling or commitment. ■ totally committed to a cause or belief. — **de·vout·ly adv. de·vout·ness n.** [ME: from OFr. *devot*, from L. *devotus* 'devoted.']

de Vries /də 'vrēz/, Hugo (1848–1935), Dutch plant physiologist and geneticist. He worked on osmosis and water relations in plants.

DEW ▶ **abbr.** ■ distant early warning.

dew /d(y)o͞o/ ▶ **n.** tiny drops of water that form on cool surfaces at night, when atmospheric vapor condenses. ■ [in sing.] a beaded or glistening liquid resembling such drops. ▶ **v.** [trans.] wet (a part of someone's body) with a beaded or glistening liquid. [OE *dēaw*, from Gmc.; akin to Ger. *Tau.*]

de·wan ▶ **n.** var. of DIWAN.

Dew·ar /ˈd(y)o͞oər/, Sir James (1842–1923), Scottish chemist and physicist. He devised the vacuum flask.

dew·ar /ˈd(y)o͞oər/ ▶ **n.** a double-walled flask of metal or silvered glass with a vacuum between the walls, used to hold liquids at well below ambient temperature. [19th C.: named after Sir James DEWAR.]

de·wa·ter /dēˈwôtər; -ˈwät-/ ▶ **v.** [trans.] drain (a waterlogged or flooded area). ■ remove water from (sediment or waste materials).

dew·ber·ry /ˈd(y)o͞oˌberē/ ▶ **n.** (pl. **-ries**) a trailing European bramble (*Rubus caesius*) with soft prickles and edible, blackberrylike fruit, which has a dewy white bloom on the skin. ■ the blue-black fruit of this plant.

dew·claw /ˈd(y)o͞oˌklô/ ▶ **n.** a rudimentary inner toe present in some dogs. ■ a false hoof on an animal such as a deer, which is formed by its rudimentary side toes. [16th C.: appar. from the nouns DEW and CLAW.]

dewclaw

dew·drop /ˈd(y)o͞oˌdräp/ ▶ **n.** a drop of dew.

Dew·ey /ˈd(y)o͞o-ē/, George (1837–1917), US admiral, noted as the hero of the Battle of Manila Bay in 1898.

Dew·ey[2] /ˈd(y)o͞o-ē/, John (1859–1952), US philosopher. He espoused the educational theory that children learn best by doing.

Dew·ey[3], Melvil (1851–1931), US librarian. He devised a decimal system of classifying books.

Dew·ey[4], Thomas Edmund (1902–71), US politician. He was governor of New York 1943–55 and the Republican presidential candidate in 1944 and 1948.

Dew·ey dec·i·mal clas·si·fi·ca·tion (also **Dewey system**) ▶ **n.** a decimal system of library classification that uses a three-figure code to represent the major branches of knowledge, and allows finer classification by the addition of further figures after a decimal point. [19th C.: named after M. *Dewey*.]

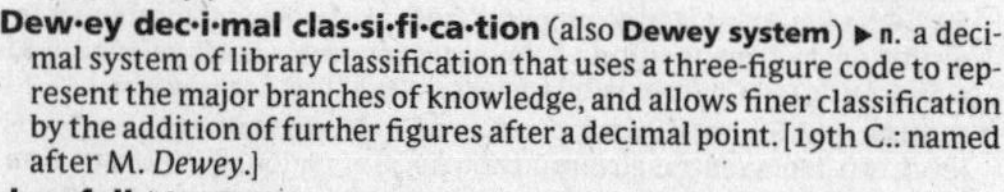

dew·fall /ˈd(y)o͞oˌfôl/ ▶ **n.** literary the formation of dew, or the time of the evening when dew begins to form. ■ the film of dew covering an area.

De·wi /ˈdāwē/ Welsh name for St. David (see DAVID, ST.).

dew·lap /ˈd(y)o͞oˌlap/ ▶ **n.** a fold of loose skin hanging from the neck or throat of an animal or bird, esp. that present in many cattle. [ME: from DEW and LAP[1].]

dewlap

de·worm /dēˈwərm/ ▶ **v.** [trans.] treat (an animal) to free it of worms. — **de·worm·er** **n.**

dew point ▶ **n.** the atmospheric temperature (varying according to pressure and humidity) below which water droplets begin to condense and dew can form.

dew worm ▶ **n.** an earthworm, in particular one used as fishing bait.

dew·y /ˈd(y)o͞o-ē/ ▶ **adj.** (**dew·i·er**, **dew·i·est**) wet with dew. ■ (of a person's skin) appearing soft and lustrous. ■ youthful and fresh. — **dew·i·ly** /ˈd(y)o͞oəlē/ **adv.** **dew·i·ness** **n.**

dew·y-eyed ▶ **adj.** having eyes that are moist with tears (used typically to indicate that a person is nostalgic, naive, or sentimental).

dex /deks/ ▶ **n.** informal short for DEXEDRINE.

Dex·e·drine /ˈdeksəˌdrēn; -ˌdrin/ ▶ **n.** trademark for *AMPHETAMINE SULFATE*.

dex·ter[1] /ˈdekstər/ ▶ **adj.** [attrib.] archaic & Heraldry of, on, or toward the right-hand side (in a coat of arms, from the bearer's point of view, i.e., the left as it is depicted). The opposite of SINISTER. [16th C.: from L., 'on the right.']

dex·ter[2] ▶ **n.** an animal of a small, hardy breed of Irish cattle. [19th C.: said to have been named after the breeder.]

dex·ter·i·ty /dekˈsteritē/ ▶ **n.** skill in performing tasks, esp. with the hands. [16th C.: from Fr. *dextérité*, from L. *dexteritas*, from *dexter* 'on the right.']

dex·ter·ous /ˈdekst(ə)rəs/ (also **dex·trous**) ▶ **adj.** demonstrating neat skill, esp. with the hands. ■ mentally adroit; clever. — **dex·ter·ous·ly** **adv.** **dex·ter·ous·ness** **n.** [17th C. (in the sense 'mentally adroit, clever'): from L. *dexter* 'on the right' + **-OUS**.]

dex·tral /ˈdekstrəl/ ▶ **adj.** of or on the right side or the right hand (the opposite of SINISTRAL), in particular: ■ right-handed. ■ Zool. (of a spiral mollusk shell) with whorls rising to the right and coiling in a counterclockwise direction. ▶ **n.** a right-handed person. — **dex·tral·i·ty** /dekˈstralitē/ **n.** **dex·tral·ly** **adv.**

dex·tran /ˈdekstran; -strən/ ▶ **n.** Chem. a carbohydrate gum formed by the fermentation of sugars and consisting of polymers of glucose. ■ Med. a solution containing a hydrolyzed form of this, used as a substitute for blood plasma. [19th C.: from DEXTRO- + -AN.]

dex·trin /ˈdekstrin/ ▶ **n.** a soluble gummy substance obtained by hydrolysis of starch, used as a thickening agent and in adhesives and dietary supplements. [19th C.: from DEXTRO- + -IN[1].]

dextro- ▶ **comb. form** on or to the right: *dextrorotatory*. [from L. *dexter*, *dextr-* 'right.']

dex·tro·ro·ta·to·ry /ˌdekstrəˈrōtəˌtôrē/ ▶ **adj.** Chem. (of a compound) having the property of rotating the plane of a polarized light ray to the right, i.e., clockwise facing the oncoming radiation. The opposite of LEVOROTATORY. — **dex·tro·ro·ta·tion** /-ˌrōˈtāsʜən/ **n.**

dex·trose /ˈdekstrōs/ ▶ **n.** Chem. the dextrorotatory form of glucose (and the predominant naturally occurring form). [19th C.: from L. *dexter*, *dextr-* 'on the right' + -OSE[2].]

dex·trous ▶ **adj.** var. of DEXTEROUS.

DF ▶ **abbr.** ■ direction finder.

DFC ▶ **abbr.** Distinguished Flying Cross.

DG ▶ **abbr.** ■ Dei gratia, by the grace of God. ■ Deo gratias, thanks be to God.

DH ▶ **abbr.** ■ Doctor of Humanities. ■ Baseball designated hitter.

Dhah·ran /däˈrän; ˌdähəˈrän/ a town in eastern Saudi Arabia near the Persian Gulf; pop. 74,000.

Dha·ka /ˈdäkə; ˈdakə/ (also **Dac·ca**) the capital of Bangladesh, in the central part of the country; pop. 3,637,890. — **Dha·kai** /ˈdäkī; ˈdakī/ **adj.**

dhal /däl/ (also **dal** or **dahl**) ▶ **n.** lentils, a common foodstuff in India. ■ a dish made with these. [from Hindi *dāl*.]

Dhan·bad /ˈdänˌbäd/ a city in northeastern India, in Bihar; pop. 818,000.

dhar·ma /ˈdärmə/ ▶ **n.** **1** Hinduism the principle of cosmic order. ■ virtue, righteousness, and duty, esp. social and caste duty in accord with the cosmic order. **2** Buddhism the teaching or religion of the Buddha. ■ one of the fundamental elements of which the world is composed. [18th C.: Sanskrit, literally 'decree or custom.']

dhar·na /ˈdärnə/ ▶ **n.** Indian a mode of compelling payment or compliance, by sitting at the debtor's or offender's door without eating until the demand is complied with. ■ a peaceful demonstration. [from Hindi *dharnā* 'sitting in restraint, placing.']

Dha·ruk /ˈdəro͝ok/ ▶ **n.** an Aboriginal language of the area around Sydney, Australia, now extinct.

Dhar·war /därˈwär/ a city in southern India, twinned with Hubli, in Karnataka state; pop. 648,000.

Dhau·la·gi·ri /ˌdouləˈgi(ə)rē/ a mountain in Nepal, in the Himalayas, that rises to 26,810 feet (8,172 m).

Dhel·foí /t͟hel'fē/ Greek name for DELPHI.

dhikr /ˈt͟hikər/ ▶ **n.** Islam a form of devotion, associated with Sufism, in which the worshiper is absorbed in the rhythmic repetition of the name of God. ■ a Sufi ceremony in which this is practiced.

Dhí·los /ˈt͟hēlôs/ Greek name for DELOS.

dhole /dōl/ ▶ **n.** a wild Asian dog (*Cuon alpinus*) with a sandy coat and a black, bushy tail. [19th C.: of unknown origin.]

dho·ti /ˈdōtē/ ▶ **n.** (pl. **dho·tis**) a loincloth worn by male Hindus. [from Hindi *dhotī*.]

dhow

dhow /dou/ ▶ **n.** a lateen-rigged ship with one or two masts, used in the Indian Ocean. [18th C.: from Arab. *dāwa*.]

dhur·rie /ˈdo͝orē/ (also **dur·rie**) ▶ **n.** (pl. **-ries**) a heavy cotton rug of Indian origin. [from Hindi *darī*.]

dhya·na /dīˈyänə/ ▶ **n.** (in Hindu and Buddhist practice) profound meditation that is the penultimate stage of yoga. [from Sanskrit *dhyāna*.]

DI ▶ **abbr.** drill instructor.

di-[1] ▶ **comb. form** twice; two-; double: *dichromatic*. ■ Chem. containing two atoms, molecules, or groups of a specified kind: *dioxide*. [from Gk. *dis* 'twice.']

di-[2] ▶ **prefix** var. of DIS- before *l, m, n, r, s* (followed by a consonant), and *v*; also often before *g*, and sometimes before *j*. [from L.]

di-[3] ▶ **prefix** var. of DIA- before a vowel (as in *dielectric*).

dia. ▶ **abbr.** diameter.

dia- (also **di-** before a vowel) ▶ **prefix** **1** through; across: *diameter* | *diaphanous* | *diuretic*. **2** apart: *diakinesis*. [from Gk. *dia* 'through.']

di·a·base /ˈdīəˌbās/ ▶ **n.** Geol. another term for DOLERITE. [19th C.: from Fr., from *di-* 'two' + *base* 'base,' thus 'rock with two bases.']

di·a·be·tes /ˌdīəˈbētēz; -tis/ ▶ **n.** a disorder of the metabolism causing excessive thirst and the production of large amounts of urine. [16th C.: via L. from Gk., literally 'siphon,' from *diabainein* 'go through.']

di·a·be·tes in·sip·i·dus /inˈsipidəs/ ▶ **n.** a rare form of diabetes caused by a deficiency of the pituitary hormone vasopressin, which regulates kidney function. [19th C.: from DIABETES + L. *insipidus* 'insipid.']

di·a·be·tes mel·li·tus /mə'lītəs; 'meli-/ ▶ n. the commonest form of diabetes, caused by a deficiency of the pancreatic hormone insulin, which results in a failure to metabolize sugars and starch. Sugars accumulate in the blood and urine, and the byproducts of alternative fat metabolism disturb the acid–base balance of the blood, causing a risk of convulsions and coma. [19th C.: from DIABETES + L. *mellitus* 'sweet.']

di·a·be·tic /ˌdīə'betik/ ▶ adj. having diabetes. ■ relating to or designed to relieve diabetes. ▶ n. a person suffering from diabetes.

di·a·ble·rie /dē'äblərē/ ▶ n. reckless mischief; charismatic wildness. ■ archaic sorcery supposedly assisted by the devil. [18th C.: from Fr., from *diable*, from eccles. L. *diabolus* 'devil.']

di·a·bol·i·cal /ˌdīə'bälikəl/ (also **di·a·bol·ic**) ▶ adj. belonging to or so evil as to recall the Devil. — **di·a·bol·i·cal·ly** adv.

di·ab·o·lism /dī'abəˌlizəm/ ▶ n. worship of the Devil. ■ devilish or atrociously wicked conduct. — **di·ab·o·list** n. [17th C.: from eccles. L. *diabolus* or Gk. *diabolos* 'devil' + -ISM.]

di·ab·o·lize /dī'abəˌlīz/ ▶ v. [trans.] archaic represent as diabolical.

di·a·chron·ic /ˌdīə'kränik/ ▶ adj. concerned with the way in which something, esp. language, has developed and evolved through time. Often contrasted with SYNCHRONIC. — **di·a·chro·ne·i·ty** /-krə'nā-itē/ n. **di·a·chron·i·cal·ly** adv. **di·a·chron·is·tic** /-ˌkrə'nistik/ adj. **di·ach·ro·ny** /dī'akrənē/ n. [19th C.: from DIA- 'through' + Gk. *khronos* 'time' + -IC.]

di·ac·o·nal /dī'akənl/ ▶ adj. relating to a deacon, or to the role of a deacon. [17th C.: from eccles. L. *diaconalis*, from *diaconus* (see DEACON).]

di·ac·o·nate /dī'akənit; -ˌnāt/ ▶ n. the office of deacon, or a person's tenure of it. ■ a body of deacons collectively.

di·a·crit·ic /ˌdīə'kritik/ ▶ n. a sign, such as an accent or cedilla, which when written above or below a letter indicates a difference in pronunciation from the same letter when unmarked or differently marked. ▶ adj. (of a mark or sign) indicating a difference in pronunciation.

di·a·crit·i·cal /ˌdīə'kritikəl/ ▶ adj. (of a mark or sign) serving to indicate different pronunciations of a letter above or below which it is written. — **di·a·crit·i·cal·ly** adv.

di·a·del·phous /ˌdīə'delfəs/ ▶ adj. Bot. (of stamens) united by their filaments so as to form two groups. [19th C.: from DI-[1] 'two' + Gk. *adelphos* 'brother' + -OUS.]

di·a·dem /'dīəˌdem/ ▶ n. a jeweled crown or headband worn as a symbol of sovereignty. ■ (**the diadem**) archaic the authority or dignity symbolized by a diadem. — **di·a·demed** adj. [ME: from OFr. *diademe*, via L. from Gk. *diadēma* 'the regal headband of the Persian kings,' from *diadein* 'bind around.']

di·aer·e·sis ▶ n. var. of DIERESIS.

diag. ▶ abbr. ■ diagonal. ■ diagram.

di·a·gen·e·sis /ˌdīə'jenəsis/ ▶ n. Geol. the physical and chemical changes occurring during the conversion of sediment to sedimentary rock. — **di·a·ge·net·ic** /-jə'netik/ adj. **di·a·ge·net·i·cal·ly** /-jə'netik(ə)lē/ adv.

Di·a·ghi·lev /dē'ägəˌlef/, Sergei (Pavlovich) (1872–1929), Russian ballet impresario. In 1909, in Paris, he formed the Ballets Russes.

di·ag·nose /ˌdīəg'nōs/ ▶ v. [trans.] identify the nature of (an illness or other problem) by examination of the symptoms. ■ (usu. **be diagnosed**) identify the nature of the medical condition of (someone). — **di·ag·nos·a·ble** adj. [19th C.: back-form. from DIAGNOSIS.]

di·ag·no·sis /ˌdīəg'nōsis/ ▶ n. (pl. **-ses** /-ˌsēz/) **1** the identification of the nature of an illness or other problem by examination of the symptoms. **2** the distinctive characterization in precise terms of a genus, species, or phenomenon. [17th C.: mod. L., from Gk., from *diagignōskein* 'distinguish, discern,' from *dia* 'apart' + *gignōskein* 'recognize, know.']

di·ag·nos·tic /ˌdīəg'nästik/ ▶ adj. **1** concerned with the diagnosis of illness or other problems. ■ (of a symptom) distinctive, and so indicating the nature of an illness. **2** characteristic of a particular species, genus, or phenomenon. ▶ n. **1** a distinctive symptom or characteristic. ■ Comput. a program or routine that helps a user to identify errors. **2** (**diagnostics**) the practice or techniques of diagnosis. — **di·ag·nos·ti·cal·ly** adv. **di·ag·nos·ti·cian** /-näs'tisнən/ n.

di·ag·o·nal /dī'agənl/ (abbr.: **diag.**) ▶ adj. (of a straight line) joining two opposite corners of a square, rectangle, or other straight-sided shape. ■ (of a line) straight and at an angle; slanting. ▶ n. a straight line joining two opposite corners of a square, rectangle, or other straight-sided shape. ■ Math. the set of elements of a matrix that lie on a line joining two opposite corners. ■ a slanting straight pattern or line. ■ Chess a slanting row of squares whose color is the same. — **di·ag·o·nal·ly** adv. [16th C.: from L. *diagonalis*, from Gk. *diagōnios* 'from angle to angle,' from *dia* 'through' + *gōnia* 'angle.']

di·a·gram /'dīəˌgram/ ▶ n. (abbr.: **diag.**) a simplified drawing showing the appearance, structure, or workings of something; a schematic representation. ■ Geom. a figure composed of lines that is used to illustrate a definition or statement or to aid in the proof of a proposition. ▶ v. (**-gramed, -gram·ing**; also **-grammed, -gram·ming**) [trans.] represent (something) in graphic form. — **di·a·gram·mat·ic** /ˌdīəgrə'matik/ adj. **di·a·gram·mat·i·cal·ly** /ˌdīəgrə'matik(ə)lē/ adv. [17th C.: from L. *diagramma*, from Gk., from *diagraphein* 'mark out by lines,' from *dia* 'through' + *graphein* 'write.']

di·a·ki·ne·sis /ˌdīəkə'nēsis/ ▶ n. (pl. **-ses** /-sēz/) Biol. the fifth and last stage of the prophase of meiosis, following diplotene, when the separation of homologous chromosomes is complete and crossing over has occurred. [20th C.: from DIA- 'through, across' + Gk. *kinēsis* 'motion.']

di·al /'dī(ə)l/ ▶ n. a face of a clock, watch, or sundial marked to show units of time. ■ a similar face or flat plate with a scale and pointer for showing measurements of weight, volume, pressure, compass direction, etc. ■ a disk with numbered holes on a telephone, used to make a call by inserting a finger in each of the holes corresponding to the number to be called and turning the disk. ■ a plate or disk on a radio, stove, washing machine, etc., tuned to select a wavelength or setting. ▶ v. (**di·aled, di·al·ing**; Brit. **di·alled, di·al·ling**) [trans.] call (a telephone number) by turning a dial. ■ (**dial something up**) gain access to a service using a telephone line. ■ indicate or regulate by means of a dial: *you dial in tone settings*. [ME: from med. L. *diale* 'clock dial,' based on L. *dies* 'day.']

di·al-a- ▶ comb. form denoting a service available for booking by telephone: *dial-a-ride*.

di·a·lect /'dīəˌlekt/ ▶ n. a particular form of a language that is peculiar to a specific region or social group. — **di·a·lec·tal** /ˌdīə'lektəl/ adj. [16th C.: from Fr. *dialecte*, or via L. from Gk. *dialektos* 'way of speaking,' from *dialegesthai* 'converse with' (see DIALOGUE).]

di·a·lec·tic /ˌdīə'lektik/ Philos. ▶ n. (also **di·a·lec·tics**) [usu. treated as sing.] **1** the art of investigating or discussing the truth of opinions. **2** inquiry into metaphysical contradictions and their solutions. ■ the existence or action of opposing social forces, concepts, etc. **3** (in Kant) the criticism of the contradictions that arise from supposing knowledge of objects beyond the limits of experience, e.g., the soul. **4** (in Hegel) the process of thought by which apparent contradictions (which he termed thesis and antithesis) are seen to be part of a higher truth (synthesis). ▶ adj. of or relating to dialectic or dialectics; dialectical.

di·a·lec·ti·cal /ˌdīə'lektikəl/ ▶ adj. **1** relating to the logical discussion of ideas and opinions. **2** concerned with or acting through opposing forces. — **di·a·lec·ti·cal·ly** adv.

di·a·lec·ti·cal ma·te·ri·al·ism ▶ n. the Marxist theory (adopted as the official philosophy of the Soviet communists) that political and historical events result from the conflict of social forces and are interpretable as a series of contradictions and their solutions. The conflict is believed to be caused by material needs. — **di·a·lec·ti·cal ma·te·ri·al·ist** n. & adj.

di·a·lec·ti·cian /ˌdīəlek'tisнən/ ▶ n. a person skilled in philosophical debate.

di·a·lec·tics /ˌdīə'lektiks/ ▶ plural n. & adj. see DIALECTIC.

di·a·lec·tol·o·gy /ˌdīəlek'täləjē/ ▶ n. the branch of linguistics concerned with the study of dialects. — **di·a·lec·to·log·i·cal** /-ˌlektə'läjikəl/ adj. **di·a·lec·tol·o·gist** /-jist/ n.

di·al·er /'dī(ə)lər/ ▶ n. a device or piece of software for calling telephone numbers automatically.

di·a·log box /'dīəˌlôg; -ˌläg/ ▶ n. Comput. a small area on screen, in which the user is prompted to provide information or select commands.

di·a·log·ic /ˌdīə'läjik/ ▶ adj. relating to or in the form of dialogue. — **di·a·log·i·cal** adj.

di·al·o·gism /dī'aləˌjizəm/ ▶ n. the use in a text of different tones or viewpoints, whose interaction or contradiction is important to the text's interpretation.

di·a·logue /'dīəˌlôg; -ˌläg/ (also **di·a·log**) ▶ n. conversation between two or more people as a feature of a book, play, or movie. ■ a discussion between two or more people or groups, esp. one directed toward exploration of a particular subject or resolution of a problem. ▶ v. [intrans.] take part in a conversation or discussion to resolve a problem. ■ [trans.] provide (a movie or play) with a dialogue. [ME: from OFr. *dialoge*, via L. from Gk. *dialogos*, from *dialegesthai* 'converse with,' from *dia* 'through' + *legein* 'speak.']

di·al tone ▶ n. a sound that a telephone produces indicating that a caller may start to dial.

di·al·y·sis /dī'aləsis/ ▶ n. (pl. **-ses** /-sēz/) Chem. the separation of particles in a liquid on the basis of differences in their ability to pass through a membrane. ■ Med. the clinical purification of blood thus, as a substitute for the normal function of the kidney. — **di·a·lyt·ic** /ˌdīə'litik/ adj. [19th C.: via L. from Gk. *dialusis*, from *dialuein* 'split, separate,' from *dia* 'apart' + *luein* 'set free.']

di·a·lyze /'dīəˌlīz/ (Brit. **di·a·lyse**) ▶ v. [trans.] purify (a mixture) by means of dialysis. ■ treat (a patient) by means of dialysis. [19th C.: from DIALYSIS, on the pattern of *analyze*.]

diam. ▶ abbr. ■ diameter.

di·a·mag·net·ic /ˌdīəmag'netik/ ▶ adj. Physics (of a substance or body) tending to become magnetized in a direction at 180° to the applied magnetic field. — **di·a·mag·net** /'dīəˌmagnit/ n. **di·a·mag·net·i·cal·ly** adv. **di·a·mag·net·ism** /-'magnəˌtizəm/ n.

di·a·man·té /ˌdēəmän'tā/ ▶ adj. decorated with artificial jewels. ▶ n. artificial jewels. ■ fabric or costume jewelry decorated with artificial jewels. [20th C.: Fr., lit. 'set with diamonds,' past part. of *diamanter*, from *diamant* 'diamond.']

di·a·man·tine /ˌdīə'mantīn; 'dīəˌman-; -tēn/ ▶ adj. made from or reminiscent of diamonds. [16th C.: from Fr. *diamantin*, from *diamant* 'diamond.']

di·am·e·ter /dī'amitər/ (abbr.: **diam.**) ▶ n. **1** a straight line passing from side to side through the center of a body or figure, esp. a circle or sphere. See illustration at GEOMETRIC. ■ the length of this line. ■ a transverse measurement of something; width or thickness. **2** a unit of linear measurement of magnifying power. — **di·am·e·tral** /-trəl/ **adj.** [ME: from OFr. *diametre*, via L. from Gk. *diametros (grammē)* '(line) measuring across,' from *dia* 'across' + *metron* 'measure.']

di·a·met·ri·cal /ˌdīəˈmetrikəl/ ▶ **adj.** **1** used to emphasize how completely different two or more things are: *he's the diametrical opposite of Gabriel.* **2** of or along a diameter. — **di·a·met·ric adj. di·a·met·ri·cal·ly adv.**

di·am·ine /ˈdīəˌmēn; dīˈamin/ ▶ **n.** Chem. a compound whose molecule contains two amino groups, esp. when not part of amide groups.

dia·mond /ˈdī(ə)mənd/ ▶ **n.** **1** a precious stone consisting of a clear and typically colorless crystalline form of pure carbon, the hardest naturally occurring substance. ■ a tool with a small stone of such a kind for cutting glass. ■ in extended and metaphorical use with reference to the brilliance, form, or hardness of diamonds. **2** [often as adj.] a figure with four straight sides of equal length forming two opposite acute angles and two opposite obtuse angles; a rhombus. ■ **(diamonds)** one of the four suits in a conventional pack of playing cards, denoted by a red figure of such a shape. ■ a card of this suit: *she led a losing diamond.* ■ the area delimited by the four bases of a baseball field, forming a square shape. ■ a baseball field.
– PHRASES **diamond in the rough** a person who is generally of good character but lacks manners, education, or style. [ME: from OFr. *diamant*, from med. L. *diamas, diamant-*, var. of L. *adamans* (see ADAMANT).]

dia·mond·back /ˈdī(ə)məndˌbak/ ▶ **n.** **1** (also **diamondback rattlesnake**) a large, common North American rattlesnake (genus *Crotalus*) with diamond-shaped markings. **2** another term for TERRAPIN (sense 1).

dia·mond·back moth ▶ **n.** a small, grayish moth (*Plutella xylostella*, family Yponomeutidae) that displays a pattern of diamonds along its back when the wings are folded.

dia·mond-cut ▶ **adj.** **1** cut with facets like a diamond. **2** cut into the shape of a diamond.

Dia·mond Head a volcanic crater in Hawaii, on Oahu.

dia·mond wed·ding (also **diamond wedding anniversary**) ▶ **n.** the sixtieth (or seventy-fifth) anniversary of a wedding.

Di·an·a /dīˈanə/ Rom. Mythol. an early Italian goddess associated with hunting, virginity, and, in later literature, with the moon. Greek equivalent ARTEMIS.

Di·an·a, Prin·cess of Wales (1961–97), British princess; wife of Prince Charles 1981–96; born *Lady Diana Frances Spencer.* Known for her humanitarian outreach, she died in an automobile accident in Paris.

Di·a·net·ics /ˌdīəˈnetiks/ ▶ **plural n.** [treated as sing.] a system developed by the founder of the Church of Scientology, L. Ron Hubbard, that aims to relieve psychosomatic disorder by cleansing the mind of harmful mental images. [1950s: from Gk. *dianoētikos* 'relating to thought' + -ICS.]

di·an·thus /dīˈanTHəs/ ▶ **n.** (pl. **-thus·es**) a flowering plant of the pink family that belongs to the genus *Dianthus*, including the carnations and sweet william. [from Gk. *Dios* 'of Zeus' + *anthos* 'a flower.']

di·a·pa·son /ˌdīəˈpāzən; -sən/ ▶ **n.** (also **open diapason** or **stopped diapason**) an organ stop sounding a main register of flue pipes, typically of eight-foot pitch. ■ literary the entire compass, range, or scope of something. ■ fig. a swelling burst of harmony. [ME: via L. from Gk. *dia pasōn (khordōn)* 'through all (notes).']

di·a·pause /ˈdīəˌpôz/ Zool. ▶ **n.** a period of suspended development in an insect, other invertebrate, or mammal embryo, esp. during unfavorable environmental conditions. ▶ **v.** [intrans.] [usu. as adj.] **(diapausing)** (of an insect or other animal) undergo such a period of suspended development.

di·a·pe·de·sis /ˌdīəpəˈdēsis/ ▶ **n.** Med. the passage of blood cells through the intact walls of the capillaries, typically accompanying inflammation. [17th C.: mod. L., based on Gk. *dia* 'through' + *pēdan* 'throb or leap.']

dia·per /ˈdī(ə)pər/ ▶ **n.** **1** a piece of absorbent material wrapped around a baby's bottom and between its legs to absorb and retain urine and feces. **2** a linen or cotton fabric woven in a repeating pattern of small diamonds. ■ a repeating geometric or floral pattern used to decorate a surface. ▶ **v.** [trans.] **1** put a diaper on (a baby). **2** decorate (a surface) with a repeating geometric or floral pattern. [ME (denoting a costly fabric): from OFr. *diapre*, from med. L. *diasprum*, from med. Gk. *diaspros* (adj.), from *dia* 'across' + *aspros* 'white.']

dia·per rash ▶ **n.** inflammation of a baby's skin caused by prolonged contact with a damp diaper.

di·aph·a·nous /dīˈafənəs/ ▶ **adj.** (esp. of fabric) light, delicate, and translucent. [17th C.: from med. L. *diaphanus*, from Gk. *diaphanēs*, from *dia* 'through' + *phainein* 'to show.']

di·a·phone /ˈdīəˌfōn/ ▶ **n.** a low-pitched fog signal operated by compressed air, characterized by the "grunt" that ends each note.

di·a·pho·re·sis /ˌdīəfəˈrēsis/ ▶ **n.** tech. sweating, esp. to an unusual degree as a symptom of disease or a side effect of a drug. [17th C.: via late L. from Gk., from *diaphorein* 'carry off, sweat out,' from *dia* 'through' + *phorein* 'carry.']

di·a·pho·ret·ic /ˌdīəfəˈretik/ ▶ **adj.** Med. (chiefly of a drug) inducing perspiration. ■ (of a person) sweating heavily.

di·a·phragm /ˈdīəˌfram/ ▶ **n.** **1** a dome-shaped, muscular partition separating the thorax from the abdomen in mammals. It plays a major role in breathing, as its contraction increases the volume of the thorax and so inflates the lungs. **2** a thin sheet of material forming a partition. ■ a taut, flexible membrane in mechanical or acoustic systems. ■ a thin contraceptive cap fitting over the cervix. **3** a device for varying the effective aperture of the lens in a camera or other optical system. — **di·a·phrag·mat·ic** /ˌdīəfragˈmatik/ **adj.** [ME: from late L. *diaphragma*, from Gk., from *dia* 'through, apart' + *phragma* 'a fence.']

di·aph·y·sis /dīˈafəsis/ ▶ **n.** (pl. **-ses** /-ˌsēz/) Anat. the shaft or central part of a long bone. Compare with EPIPHYSIS. [19th C.: from Gk. *diaphusis* 'growing through,' from *dia* 'through' + *phusis* 'growth.']

di·a·pir /ˈdīəˌpir/ ▶ **n.** Geol. a domed rock formation in which a core of rock has moved upward to pierce the overlying strata. — **di·a·pir·ic** /ˌdīəˈpirik/ **adj. di·a·pir·ism n.** [20th C.: from Gk. *diapeirainein* 'pierce through,' from *dia* 'through' + *peirainein* (from *peran* 'pierce').]

di·a·pos·i·tive /ˌdīəˈpäzitiv/ ▶ **n.** a positive photographic slide or transparency.

di·ar·chy /ˈdīˌärkē/ (also **dy·ar·chy**) ▶ **n.** (pl. **-chies**) government by two independent authorities. — **di·ar·chal** /dīˈärkəl/ **adj. di·ar·chic** /dīˈärkik/ **adj.** [19th C.: from DI-[1] 'two' + Gk. *arkhia* 'rule.']

di·a·rist /ˈdīərist/ ▶ **n.** a person who writes a diary. — **di·a·ris·tic** /ˌdīəˈristik/ **adj.**

di·ar·rhe·a /ˌdīəˈrēə/ (Brit. **di·ar·rhoe·a**) ▶ **n.** a condition in which feces are discharged from the bowels frequently and in a liquid form. — **di·ar·rhe·al adj. di·ar·rhe·ic** /-ˈrēik/ **adj.** [ME: via late L. *diarrhoea* from Gk. *diarrhoia*, from *diarrhein* 'flow through,' from *dia* 'through' + *rhein* 'to flow.']

di·a·ry /ˈdīərē/ ▶ **n.** (pl. **-ries**) a book in which one keeps a daily record of events and experiences. ■ a datebook. [16th C.: from L. *diarium*, from *dies* 'day.']

Di·as /ˈdēəs; ˈdēäsH/ (also **Di·az** /ˈdēəsH/), Bartolomeu (*c.*1450–1500), Portuguese explorer. In 1488, he became the first European to sail around the Cape of Good Hope.

di·as·po·ra /dīˈaspərə/ ▶ **n.** (often **the Diaspora**) Jews living outside Israel. ■ the dispersion of the Jews beyond Israel. The main diaspora began in the 8th–6th centuries BC, and even before the sack of Jerusalem in AD 70, the number of Jews dispersed by the diaspora was greater than that living in Israel. ■ the dispersion of any people from their original homeland. ■ the people so dispersed. [Gk., from *diaspeirein* 'disperse,' from *dia* 'across'+ *speirein* 'scatter.']

di·a·spore /ˈdīəˌspôr/ ▶ **n.** Bot. a spore, seed, or other structure that functions in plant dispersal; a propagule.

di·a·stase /ˈdīəˌstās; -ˌstāz/ ▶ **n.** Biochem.another term for AMYLASE. [19th C.: from Gk. *diastasis* 'separation,' from *dia* 'apart' + *stasis* 'placing.']

di·a·ste·ma /ˌdīəˈstēmə/ ▶ **n.** (pl. **-ma·ta** /-mətə/) a gap between the teeth. [19th C.: via late L. from Gk. *diastēma* 'space between.']

di·as·to·le /dīˈastl-ē/ ▶ **n.** Physiol. the phase of the heartbeat when the heart muscle relaxes and allows the chambers to fill with blood. Often contrasted with SYSTOLE. — **di·as·tol·ic** /ˌdīəˈstälik/ **adj.** [16th C.: via late L. from Gk., 'separation, expansion,' from *diastellein*, from *dia* 'apart' + *stellein* 'to place.']

di·a·tes·sa·ron /ˌdīəˈtesərən/ ▶ **n.** the four Gospels combined into a single narrative.

di·a·ther·my /ˈdīəˌTHərmē/ ▶ **n.** a medical and surgical technique involving the production of heat in a part of the body by high-frequency electric currents, to stimulate the circulation, relieve pain, destroy unhealthy tissue, or cause bleeding vessels to clot. [20th C.: from DIA- 'through' + *thermon* 'heat.']

di·ath·e·sis /dīˈaTHəsis/ ▶ **n.** **1** [usu. with adj.] Med. a tendency to suffer from a particular medical condition: *a bleeding diathesis.* **2** Ling. another term for VOICE (sense 4). [17th C.: mod. L., from Gk., 'disposition,' from *diatithenai* 'arrange.']

di·a·tom /ˈdīəˌtäm/ ▶ **n.** Biol. a single-celled alga (class Bacillariophyceae) that has a cell wall of silica. Many kinds are planktonic. — **di·a·to·ma·ceous** /ˌdīətəˈmāsHəs/ **adj.** [19th C.: from mod. L. *Diatoma* (genus name), from Gk. *diatomos* 'cut in two,' from *diatemnein* 'to cut through.']

di·a·to·ma·ceous earth ▶ **n.** a soft, crumbly, porous sedimentary deposit formed from the fossil remains of diatoms.

di·a·tom·ic /ˌdīəˈtämik/ ▶ **adj.** Chem. consisting of two atoms.

di·at·o·mite /dīˈatəˌmīt/ ▶ **n.** Geol. a fine-grained sedimentary rock formed from consolidated diatomaceous earth.

di·a·ton·ic /ˌdīəˈtänik/ ▶ **adj.** Music (of a scale, interval, etc.) involving only notes proper to the prevailing key without chromatic alteration. ■ (of a melody or harmony) constructed from such a scale. [17th C.: from Fr. *diatonique*, or via late L. from Gk. *diatonikos* 'at intervals of a tone,' from *dia* 'through' + *tonos* 'tone.']

di·a·treme /ˈdīəˌtrēm/ ▶ **n.** Geol. a long, vertical pipe or plug formed when gas-filled magma forced its way up through overlying strata. [20th C.: from DIA- 'through' + Gk. *trēma* 'perforation.']

di·a·tribe /ˈdīəˌtrīb/ ▶ **n.** a forceful and bitter verbal attack against someone or something. [16th C.: from Fr., via L. from Gk. *diatribē* 'spending of time, discourse,' from *dia* 'through' + *tribein* 'rub.']

Di·az /ˈdēəsH/ var. of DIAS.

Dí·az /ˈdē-äs/, Porfirio (1830–1915), president of Mexico 1877–80, 1884–1911.

di·az·e·pam /dīˈazəˌpam/ ▶ **n.** a tranquilizing muscle-relaxant drug, $C_{16}H_{13}N_2OCl$, used chiefly to relieve anxiety. Also called VALIUM. [1960s: blend of BENZODIAZEPINE and AMIDE.]

di·az·i·non /dīˈazəˌnän/ ▶ **n.** an organophosphorus insecticide derived from pyrimidine. [20th C.: from *diazine* (see DI-[1], AZINE) + *-on.*]

di·az·o /dī'azō/ (also **di·az·o·type** /-ˌtīp/) ▶**n.** a copying or coloring process using a diazo compound decomposed by ultraviolet light: [as adj.] *diazo printers.*

di·az·o com·pound ▶**n.** Chem. an organic compound containing two nitrogen atoms bonded together, esp. a diazonium compound. [19th C.: *diazo* from DIAZONIUM.]

di·a·zo·ni·um /dīə'zōnēəm/ ▶**n.** [as adj.] Chem. an organic cation containing the group $-N_2+$ bonded to an organic group. Aromatic diazonium compounds are typically intensely colored and include many synthetic dyes. [19th C.: coined in Ger. from *diazo-* + *-onium* (from AMMONIUM).]

di·ba·sic /dī'bāsik/ ▶**adj.** Chem. (of an acid) having two replaceable hydrogen atoms.

dib·ble /'dibəl/ ▶**n.** a pointed hand tool for making holes in the ground for seeds or young plants. ▶**v.** [trans.] make (a hole) in soil with a dibble. ■ sow (a seed or plant) with a dibble. [ME.]

dibs /dibz/ ▶**plural n.** informal money.
– PHRASES **have first dibs on** have the first right to or choice of: *they never got first dibs on great prospects.* [18th C.: from earlier *dib-stones.*]

dice /dīs/ ▶**n.** (pl. same) a small cube with each side having a different number of spots on it, ranging from one to six, thrown and used in gambling and other games involving chance. See also DIE[2]. ■ a game played with dice. ■ small cubes of food. ▶**v. 1** [intrans.] play or gamble with dice. **2** [trans.] cut (food or other matter) into small cubes.
– PHRASES **no dice** informal used to refuse a request or indicate no chance of success. **roll** (or **throw**) **of the dice** a risky attempt to do or achieve something. — **dic·er n.** [ME: from OFr. *des,* pl. of *de* (see DIE[2]).]

di·cen·tra /dī'sentrə/ ▶**n.** a plant of the genus *Dicentra* (family Fumariaceae), esp. (in gardening) a bleeding heart. [mod. L., from Gk. *dikentros,* from *di-* 'two' + *kentron* 'spur, sharp point.']

di·cen·tric /dī'sentrik/ Genet. ▶**adj.** (of a chromosome) having two centromeres. ▶**n.** a chromosome of this type.

dic·ey /'dīsē/ ▶**adj.** (**dic·i·er, dic·i·est**) informal unpredictable and potentially dangerous.

di·cha·si·um /dī'kāzн(ē)əm; -zēəm/ ▶**n.** (pl. **-si·a** /-zнēə; -zēə/) Bot. a cyme in which each flowering branch gives rise to two or more branches symmetrically placed. [19th C.: mod. L., from DI-[1] 'two' + Gk. *khasis* 'separation.']

di·chog·a·my /dī'kägəmē/ ▶**n.** Bot. the ripening of the stamens and pistils of a flower at different times, so that self-fertilization is prevented. Compare with HOMOGAMY (sense 3). — **di·chog·a·mous** /-məs/ **adj.** [19th C.: from Gk. *dikho-* 'apart, in two' + *gamos* 'marriage.']

di·chot·ic /dī'kätik/ ▶**adj.** involving or relating to the simultaneous stimulation of the right and left ear by different sounds. [20th C.: from Gk. *dikho-* 'apart' + *ous, ōt-* 'ear' + -IC.]

di·chot·o·mize /dī'kätəˌmīz/ ▶**v.** [trans.] regard or represent as divided or opposed.

di·chot·o·mous /dī'kätəməs/ ▶**adj.** exhibiting or characterized by dichotomy. ■ Bot. (of branching) in which the axis is divided into two branches. — **di·chot·o·mous·ly adv.** [17th C.: via late L. from Gk. *dikhotomos* (from *dikho-* 'in two' + *temnein* 'to cut') + -OUS.]

di·chot·o·my /dī'kätəmē/ ▶**n.** (pl. **-mies**) [usu. in sing.] a division or contrast between two things that are or are represented as being opposed or entirely different. ■ Bot. repeated branching into two equal parts.

di·chro·ic /dī'krō-ik/ ▶**adj.** (of a crystal) showing different colors when viewed from different directions, or (more generally) having different absorption coefficients for light polarized in different directions. — **di·chro·ism** /'dīkrōˌizəm/ **n.** [19th C.: from Gk. *dikhroos* (from *di-* 'twice' + *khrōs* 'color') + -IC.]

di·chro·mate /dī'krōmāt/ ▶**n.** Chem. a salt, typically red or orange, containing the anion Cr_2O_72-.

di·chro·ma·tism /dī'krōməˌtizəm/ ▶**n. 1** (typically in an animal species) the occurrence of two different kinds of coloring. **2** color-blindness in which only two of the three primary colors can be discerned. — **di·chro·mat·ic** /ˌdīkrō'matik/ **adj.**

dick[1] /dik/ ▶**n.** vulgar slang a penis. ▶**v. 1** [intrans.] vulgar slang handle something inexpertly; meddle: *he started **dicking around** with the controls.* **2** [trans.] vulgar slang (of a man) have sexual intercourse with (someone). [16th C. (in the general sense 'fellow'): nickname for the given name *Richard.*]

dick[2] ▶**n.** dated, informal a detective. [20th C.: perh. an arbitrary shortening of DETECTIVE, or from obs. slang *dick* 'look,' from Romany.]

dick·cis·sel /dik'sisəl; 'dikˌsisəl/ ▶**n.** a sparrowlike North American songbird (*Spiza americana*) of the bunting family, with a black-and-white throat and bright yellow breast. [19th C.: imitative of its call.]

Dick·ens /'dikinz/, Charles John Huffam (1812–70), English writer. His works include *Oliver Twist* (1837–38) and *David Copperfield* (1850).

dick·ens /'dikinz/ ▶**n.** [in sing.] informal, dated used for emphasis, euphemistically invoking the Devil: *they work like the dickens* | *in a dickens of a rush.* ■ (**the dickens**) used when asking questions to express annoyance or surprise: *what the dickens is it?* [16th C.: prob. a use of the surname *Dickens.*]

Dick·en·si·an /di'kenzēən/ ▶**adj.** of or reminiscent of the novels of Charles Dickens, esp. in suggesting the poor social conditions or comically repulsive characters that they portray: *the garrets of Dickensian London.*

dick·er /'dikər/ ▶**v.** [intrans.] **1** engage in petty argument or bargaining. **2** treat something casually or irresponsibly; toy with something. — **dick·er·er n.** [19th C.: perh. from obs. *dicker* 'set of ten (hides),' used as a unit of trade, based on L. *decem* 'ten.']

Dick·ey /'dikē/, James Lafayette (1923–97), US writer. His works include poetry in *Buckdancer's Choice* (1965) and the novel *Deliverance* (1970).

dick·ey /'dikē/ (also **dick·y**) ▶**n.** (pl. **dick·eys** or **dick·ies**) informal **1** a false shirtfront. **2** dated, esp. Brit. a folding outside seat at the back of a vehicle; a rumble seat. ■ hist., esp. Brit. a driver's seat in a carriage. [18th C.: perh. partly from *Dicky,* nickname for *Richard.*]

dick·ey bird ▶**n.** informal used by children to refer to a little bird.

dick·head /'dikˌhed/ ▶**n.** vulgar slang a stupid, irritating, or ridiculous person, particularly a man.

Dick·in·son /'dikinsən/, Emily Elizabeth (1830–86), US poet. Her poems use an elliptical language and reflect a reclusive life.

dick·y /'dikē/ ▶**adj.** (**dick·i·er, dick·i·est**) Brit., informal (of a part of the body, a structure, or a device) not strong, healthy, or functioning reliably. [18th C.: perh. from the given name *Dick.*]

di·cot /'dīkät/ ▶**n.** short for DICOTYLEDON.

di·cot·y·le·don /dīˌkätl'ēdn/ ▶**n.** Bot. a flowering plant (class Dicotyledoneae or Magnoliopsida) with an embryo that bears two cotyledons (seed leaves). Dicotyledons constitute the larger of the two great divisions of flowering plants, and typically have broad, stalked leaves with netlike veins (e.g., daisies, hawthorns, oaks). Compare with MONOCOTYLEDON. — **di·cot·y·le·don·ous** /-əs/ **adj.**

di·crot·ic /dī'krätik/ ▶**adj.** Med. denoting a pulse in which a double beat is detectable for each beat of the heart. [19th C.: from Gk. *dikrotos* 'beating twice' + -IC.]

dict. ▶**abbr.** ■ dictation. ■ dictionary.

dic·ta /'diktə/ plural form of DICTUM.

Dic·ta·phone /'diktəˌfōn/ (also **dic·ta·phone**) ▶**n.** trademark a small cassette recorder used to record speech for transcription at a later time.

dic·tate ▶**v.** /'diktāt/ [trans.] **1** lay down authoritatively; prescribe: *attempts to dictate policy* | [intrans.] *the right to **dictate to** me.* ■ control or decisively affect; determine: *choice is often dictated by availability* | [intrans.] *a review process can be changed **as circumstances dictate.*** **2** say or read aloud (words to be typed, written down, or recorded on tape). ▶**n.** (usu. **dictates**) an order or principle that must be obeyed. [16th C.: from L. *dictat-* 'dictated,' from the v. *dictare.*]

dic·ta·tion /dik'tāsнən/ ▶**n. 1** (abbr.: **dict.**) the action of saying words aloud to be typed, written down, or recorded on tape. ■ the activity of taking down a passage that is read aloud by a teacher as a test of spelling, writing, or language skills. ■ an utterance that is typed, written down, or recorded. **2** the action of giving orders authoritatively or categorically.

dic·ta·tor /'diktātər/ ▶**n. 1** a ruler with total power over a country, typically one who has obtained power by force. ■ a person who tells people what to do in an autocratic way or who determines behavior in a particular sphere. ■ (in ancient Rome) a chief magistrate with absolute power, appointed in an emergency. **2** a machine that records words spoken into it, used for personal or administrative purposes.

dic·ta·to·ri·al /ˌdiktə'tôrēəl/ ▶**adj.** of or typical of a ruler with total power. ■ having or showing a tendency to tell people what to do in an autocratic way. — **dic·ta·to·ri·al·ly adv.**

dic·ta·tor·ship /dik'tātərˌsнip; 'diktātər-/ ▶**n.** government by a dictator. ■ a country governed by a dictator. ■ absolute authority in any sphere.

dic·tion /'diksнən/ ▶**n. 1** the choice and use of words and phrases in speech or writing. **2** the style of enunciation in speaking or singing. [16th C.: from L. *dictio(n-),* from *dicere* 'to say.']

dic·tion·ar·y /'diksнəˌnerē/ (abbr.: **dict.**) ▶**n.** (pl. **-ar·ies**) a book that lists the words of a language in alphabetical order and gives their meaning, or that gives the equivalent words in a different language. ■ a reference book on any subject, the items of which are arranged in alphabetical order. [16th C.: from med. L. *dictionarium (manuale)* or *dictionarius (liber)* 'manual or book of words,' from L. *dictio* (see DICTION).]

dic·tum /'diktəm/ ▶**n.** (pl. **-ta** /-tə/ or **-tums**) a formal pronouncement from an authoritative source. ■ a short statement that expresses a general truth or principle. ■ Law short for OBITER DICTUM. [16th C.: from L., lit. 'something said,' neuter past part. of *dicere.*]

dic·ty /'diktē/ ▶**adj.** black slang ostentatiously stylish; pretentious. [20th C.: of unknown origin.]

did /did/ past of DO[1].

di·dac·tic /dī'daktik/ ▶**adj.** intended to teach, particularly in having moral instruction as an ulterior motive. ■ in the manner of a teacher, particularly so as to treat someone in a patronizing way. — **di·dac·ti·cal·ly adv. di·dac·ti·cism** /-təˌsizəm/ **n.** [17th C.: from Gk. *didaktikos,* from *didaskein* 'teach.']

did·dle /'didl/ ▶**v.** informal **1** [trans.] (usu. **be diddled**) cheat or swindle (someone) so as to deprive them of something: *he'd been **diddled out of** his change.* ■ deliberately falsify (something). **2** [intrans.] informal pass time aimlessly or unproductively: *why **diddle around** with slow costly* *tests?* ■ **(diddle with)** play or mess with. **3** [trans.] vulgar slang have sexual intercourse with (someone). — **did·dler** n. [19th C.: probably from the name of Jeremy *Diddler*, a character in the farce *Raising the Wind* (1803) by the Irish dramatist James Kenney (1780–1849).]

did·dly-squat /ˈdidlē ˌskwät/ (also **did·dly**, **did·dley**, or **dood·ly-squat**) ▶ **pron.** [usu. with negative] informal anything: *she didn't care diddly-squat what Darryl thought.* [20th C.: prob. from slang *doodle* 'excrement' + SQUAT in the sense 'defecate.']

Di·de·rot /ˈdēdəˌrō/, Denis (1713–84), French philosopher. He was editor of the *Encyclopédie* (1751–76).

didg·er·i·doo /ˌdijərēˈdo͞o/ (also **didj·er·i·doo** or **didj·er·i·du**) ▶ **n.** an Australian Aboriginal wind instrument in the form of a long wooden tube, traditionally made from a hollow branch, which is blown to produce a deep, resonant sound, varied by rhythmic accents of timbre and volume. [1920s: imitative; from an Aboriginal language.]

did·n't /ˈdidnt/ ▶ **contr.** did not.

Di·do /ˈdīdō/ (in the *Aeneid*) the queen and founder of Carthage, who fell in love with the shipwrecked Aeneas and killed herself when he deserted her.

di·do /ˈdīdō/ ▶ **n.** (pl. **-does** or **-dos**) (in phrase **cut/cut up didoes**) informal perform mischievous tricks or deeds. [19th C.: of unknown origin.]

Did·rik·son /ˈdidriksən/, Babe, see ZAHARIAS.

didst /didst/ archaic second person singular past of DO[1].

di·dym·i·um /dīˈdimēəm/ ▶ **n.** Chem. a mixture containing the rare earth elements praseodymium and neodymium, used to color glass for optical filters. It was originally regarded as a single element. [19th C.: from Gk. *didumos* 'twin' + *-ium*.]

die[1] /dī/ ▶ **v.** (**dy·ing** /ˈdī-iNG/) [intrans.] **1** (of a person, animal, or plant) stop living. ■ **(die for)** be killed for (a cause). ■ [with complement] have a specified status at the time of one's death. ■ **(die out)** become extinct. ■ be forgotten: *her name will never die.* ■ [with adverbial] become less loud or strong. ■ **(die back)** (of a plant) decay from the tip toward the root. ■ **(die off)** die one after another until few or none are left. ■ be no longer under the influence of something: *we died to such sentiments.* ■ (of a fire or light) stop burning or gleaming. ■ informal (of a machine) stop functioning. ■ literary have an orgasm. **2** informal used to emphasize that one wants to do or have something very much: *they must be dying for a drink.* ■ informal used to emphasize how keenly one feels something: *I'm simply dying of thirst.* **3** informal used to emphasize feelings of shock, embarrassment, amusement, or misery: *I nearly died when I saw them.*

– PHRASES **die hard** disappear or change very slowly. **die on the vine** be unsuccessful at an early stage. **never say die** used to encourage someone in a difficult situation. **to die for** informal extremely good or desirable. [ME: from ON *deyja*, of Gmc. origin; rel. to DEAD.]

die[2] ▶ **n.** **1** singular form of DICE. ■ Archit. the cubical part of a pedestal between the base and the cornice; a dado or plinth. **2** (pl. **dies**) a device for cutting or molding metal into a particular shape. ■ an engraved device for stamping a design on coins or medals.

– PHRASES **the die is cast** an event has happened or a decision has been made that cannot be changed. [ME: from OFr. *de*, from L. *datum* 'something given or played,' neut. past part. of *dare*.]

die·back /ˈdīˌbak/ ▶ **n.** a condition in which a tree or shrub begins to die from the tip of its leaves or roots backward, owing to disease or an unfavorable environment.

die-cast ▶ **adj.** (of a metal object) formed by pouring molten metal into a reusable mold. ▶ **v.** [trans.] [usu. as n.] **(die-casting)** make (a metal object) in this way.

dief·fen·bach·i·a /ˌdēfənˈbäkēə/ ▶ **n.** a plant (genus *Dieffenbachia*) of the arum family that includes dumb cane and its relatives. [mod. L., named after Ernst *Dieffenbach* (1811–55), German horticulturalist.]

die·hard /ˈdīˌhärd/ ▶ **n.** [often as adj.] a person who strongly opposes change or who continues to support something in spite of opposition.

die-in ▶ **n.** informal a demonstration in which people lie down as if dead.

di·el /ˈdī(ə)l; ˈdē(ə)l/ ▶ **adj.** Biol. denoting or involving a period of 24 hours: *tidal and diel cycles.* [1930s: from L. *dies* 'day' + *-(a)l* (see -AL).]

diel·drin /ˈdēldrin/ ▶ **n.** a toxic insecticide, $C_{12}H_8Cl_6O$, now largely banned because of its persistence in the environment. [1940s: from Otto *Diels* (1876–1954), German chemist, + ALDRIN.]

di·e·lec·tric /ˌdīəˈlektrik/ Physics ▶ **adj.** having the property of transmitting electric force without conduction; insulating. ▶ **n.** a medium or substance with such a property; an insulator. — **di·e·lec·tri·cal·ly** adv.

Dien Bien Phu /ˌdyen ˌbyen ˈfo͞o/ a village in northwestern Vietnam, site of a French military post captured by the Vietminh in 1954, ending French rule in Indo-China.

di·en·ceph·a·lon /ˌdīenˈsefəˌlän/ ▶ **n.** Anat. the caudal (posterior) part of the forebrain, containing the epithalamus, thalamus, hypothalamus, and ventral thalamus and the third ventricle. Compare with TELENCEPHALON. — **di·en·ce·phal·ic** /-səˈfalik/ adj. [19th C.: from DI-[3] 'across' + Gk. *enkephalos* 'brain.']

di·ene /ˈdīēn/ ▶ **n.** Chem. an unsaturated hydrocarbon containing two double bonds between carbon atoms.

di·er·e·sis /dīˈerəsis/ (also **di·aer·e·sis**) ▶ **n.** (pl. **-ses** /-ˌsēz/) **1** a mark (¨) placed over a vowel to indicate that it is sounded in a separate syllable, as in *naïve, Brontë.* ■ the division of a sound into two syllables, esp. by sounding a diphthong as two vowels. **2** Pros. a natural rhythmic break in a line of verse where the end of a metrical foot coincides with the end of a word. [16th C.: via L. from Gk. *diairesis* 'separation,' from *diairein* 'take apart,' from *dia* 'apart' + *hairein* 'take.']

die·sel /ˈdēzəl; -səl/ ▶ **n.** (also **diesel engine**) an internal combustion engine in which heat produced by the compression of air in the cylinder is used to ignite the fuel. ■ a heavy petroleum fraction used as fuel in diesel engines. — **die·sel·ize** /-ˌlīz/ v. [19th C.: Rudolph *Diesel* (1858–1913), German engineer.]

die·sel-e·lec·tric ▶ **adj.** denoting or relating to a locomotive driven by the electric current produced by a diesel-engined generator. ▶ **n.** a locomotive of this type.

die-sink·er ▶ **n.** a person who engraves dies used to stamp designs on coins or medals.

Di·es I·rae /ˈdēās ˈi(ə)rā/ ▶ **n.** a Latin hymn formerly sung in a Mass for the dead. [L., literally 'day of wrath.']

di·es non /ˌdēāz ˈnän/ ▶ **n.** (pl. same) a day on which no legal business can be done, or which does not count for legal or other purposes. [L., short for *dies non juridicus* 'nonjudicial day.']

die·stock /ˈdīˌstäk/ ▶ **n.** a hand tool used in the cutting of external screw threads, consisting of a holder for the die that is turned using long handles.

di·es·trus /dīˈestrəs/ ▶ **n.** Zool. (in most female mammals) a period of sexual inactivity between recurrent periods of estrus.

di·et[1] /ˈdī-it/ ▶ **n.** the kinds of food that a person, animal, or community habitually eats. ■ a special course of food to which one restricts oneself, either to lose weight or for medical reasons. ■ [as adj.] (of food or drink) with reduced fat or sugar content. ■ fig. a regular occupation or series of activities in which one participates. ▶ **v.** (**di·et·ed**, **di·et·ing**) [intrans.] restrict oneself to small amounts or special kinds of food in order to lose weight: *it is difficult to diet in a house full of cupcakes.* — **di·et·er** n. [ME: from OFr. *diete*, via L. from Gk. *diaita* 'a way of life.']

di·et[2] ▶ **n.** a legislative assembly in certain countries. ■ hist. a regular meeting of the states of a confederation. ■ Scots Law a meeting or session of a court. [ME: from med. L. *dieta* 'day's work' also 'meeting of councilors.']

die·tar·y /ˈdī-iˌterē/ ▶ **adj.** of or relating to diets or dieting. ■ provided by one's diet. ▶ **n.** (pl. **-tar·ies**) dated a regulated or restricted diet.

di·e·tet·ic /ˌdī-iˈtetik/ ▶ **adj.** concerned with diet and nutrition. — **di·e·tet·i·cal·ly** adv.

di·e·tet·ics /ˌdī-iˈtetiks/ ▶ **plural n.** [treated as sing.] the branch of knowledge concerned with the diet and its effects on health, esp. with the practical application of a scientific understanding of nutrition.

di·eth·yl e·ther /dīˈeTHəl ˈēTHər/ ▶ **n.** see ETHER (sense 1).

di·eth·yl·stil·bes·trol /dīˌeTHəlstilˈbestrôl/ ▶ **n.** another term for STILBESTROL.

di·e·ti·tian /ˌdī-iˈtiSHən/ (also **di·e·ti·cian**) ▶ **n.** an expert on diet and nutrition.

Dieu et mon droit /ˈdyo͝o āmôN ˈdwä/ ▶ **n.** God and my right (the motto of the British monarch). [Fr.]

dif- ▶ **prefix** var. of DIS-assimilated before *f* (as in *diffraction, diffuse.*). [from L., var. of DIS-.]

dif·fer /ˈdifər/ ▶ **v.** [intrans.] be unlike or dissimilar. ■ disagree.

– PHRASES **agree to differ** cease to argue about something because neither party will compromise or be persuaded. **beg to differ** politely disagree. [ME: from OFr. *differer* 'differ, defer,' from L. *differre*, from *dis-* 'from, away' + *ferre* 'bring, carry.']

dif·fer·ence /ˈdif(ə)rəns/ ▶ **n.** a point or way in which people or things are not the same. ■ the state or condition of being dissimilar or unlike. ■ a disagreement, quarrel, or dispute. ■ a quantity by which amounts differ; the remainder left after subtraction of one value from another.

– PHRASES **make a** (or **no**) **difference** have an effect (or no effect) on a person or situation. **with a difference** having a new or unusual feature or treatment.

dif·fer·ent /ˈdif(ə)rənt/ ▶ **adj.** **1** not the same as another or each other; unlike in nature, form, or quality. ■ informal novel and unusual. **2** distinct; separate. — **dif·fer·ent·ly** adv. **dif·fer·ent·ness** n. [ME: via OFr. from L. *different-* 'carrying away, differing,' from the v. *differre* (see DIFFER).]

dif·fer·en·ti·a /ˌdifəˈrenSH(ē)ə/ ▶ **n.** (pl. **-ti·ae** /-SHēˌē/) a distinguishing mark or characteristic. ■ esp. Philos. an attribute that distinguishes a species of thing from other species of the same genus. [17th C.: from L., lit. 'difference,' from *different-* 'carrying away' (see DIFFERENT).]

dif·fer·en·ti·a·ble /ˌdifəˈrenSHəbəl/ ▶ **adj.** able to be differentiated. — **dif·fer·en·ti·a·bil·i·ty** /-ˌrenSHəˈbilitē/ n.

dif·fer·en·tial /ˌdifəˈrenSHəl/ esp. tech. ▶ **adj.** [attrib.] of, showing, or depending on a difference; differing or varying according to circumstances or relevant factors. ■ constituting a specific difference; distinctive. ■ Math. relating to infinitesimal differences or to the derivatives of functions. ■ of or relating to a difference in a physical quantity. ▶ **n.** a difference between amounts of things. ■ Math. an infinitesimal difference between successive values of a variable. ■ (also **differential gear**) a set of gears allowing a vehicle's driven wheels to revolve at different speeds when going around corners. — **dif·fer·en·tial·ly** adv.

dif·fer·en·tial cal·cu·lus ▶ **n.** a branch of mathematics concerned with the determination, properties, and application of derivatives and differentials. Compare with INTEGRAL CALCULUS.

dif·fer·en·tial co·ef·fi·cient ▶ n. Math. another term for DERIVATIVE.

dif·fer·en·tial e·qua·tion ▶ n. an equation involving derivatives of a function or functions.

dif·fer·en·tial wind·lass ▶ n. a hoisting device consisting of two drums of different diameters on the same axis and turning at the same rate, so that a line wound on the larger drum and unwound from the smaller drum provides a mechanical advantage in lifting. Also called **Chinese windlass**.

dif·fer·en·ti·ate /ˌdifəˈrensHēˌāt/ ▶ v. [trans.] **1** recognize or ascertain what makes (someone or something) different. ■ [intrans.] (**differentiate between**) identify differences between (two or more things or people). ■ make (someone or something) appear different or distinct. **2** tech. make or become different in the process of growth or development. **3** Math. transform (a function) into its derivative. — **dif·fer·en·ti·a·tion** /-ˌrensHēˈāsHən/ n. **dif·fer·en·ti·a·tor** /-ˌātər/ n.

dif·fer·ent·ly a·bled ▶ adj. disabled.

dif·fi·cult /ˈdifiˌkəlt; -kəlt/ ▶ adj. needing much effort or skill to accomplish, deal with, or understand. ■ characterized by or causing hardships or problems. ■ (of a person) not easy to please or satisfy. — **dif·fi·cult·ly** adv. (rare) **dif·fi·cult·ness** n. [ME: back-form. from DIFFICULTY.]

dif·fi·cul·ty /ˈdifiˌkəltē/ ▶ n. (pl. **-ties**) the state or condition of being difficult. ■ a thing that is hard to accomplish, deal with, or understand. ■ (often **difficulties**) a situation that is difficult or dangerous. [ME: from L. *difficultas*, from *dis-* (expressing reversal) + *facultas* 'ability, opportunity.']

dif·fi·dent /ˈdifidənt/ ▶ adj. modest or shy because of a lack of self-confidence. — **dif·fi·dence** n. **dif·fi·dent·ly** adv. [ME: from L. *diffident-* 'failing in trust,' from the v. *diffidere*, from *dis-* (expressing reversal) + *fidere* 'to trust.']

dif·fract /diˈfrakt/ ▶ v. [trans.] Physics cause to undergo diffraction. — **dif·frac·tive** adj. **dif·frac·tive·ly** adv. [19th C.: from L. *diffract-* 'broken in pieces,' from the v. *diffringere*, from *dis-* 'away, from' + *frangere* 'to break.']

dif·frac·tion /diˈfraksHən/ ▶ n. the process by which a beam of light or other system of waves is spread out as a result of passing through a narrow aperture or across an edge, typically accompanied by interference between the wave forms produced.

dif·frac·tion grat·ing ▶ n. a plate of glass or metal ruled with very close parallel lines, producing a spectrum by diffraction and interference of light.

dif·frac·tom·e·ter /ˌdifrakˈtämitər/ ▶ n. an instrument for measuring diffraction, chiefly used to determine the structure of a crystal by analysis of the diffraction of X-rays.

dif·fuse ▶ v. /diˈfyo͞oz/ spread or cause to spread over a wide area or among a large number of people. ■ become or cause (a fluid, gas, individual atom, etc.) to become intermingled with a substance by movement, typically in a specified direction or at specified speed. ■ [trans.] cause (light) to glow faintly by dispersing it in many directions. ▶ adj. /diˈfyo͞os/ spread out over a large area; not concentrated. ■ (of disease) not localized in the body. ■ lacking clarity or conciseness. — **dif·fuse·ly** /-ˈfyo͞oslē/ adv. **dif·fuse·ness** /-ˈfyo͞osnis/ n. [ME: from L. *diffus-* 'poured out,' from the v. *diffundere*, from *dis-* 'away' + *fundere* 'pour.']

dif·fus·er /diˈfyo͞ozər/ (also **dif·fu·sor**) ▶ n. a thing that diffuses something, in particular: ■ an attachment or duct for broadening an airflow and reducing its speed. ■ Photog. a device that spreads the light from a source evenly, reducing harsh shadows.

dif·fus·i·ble /diˈfyo͞ozəbəl/ ▶ adj. able to intermingle by diffusion.

dif·fu·sion /diˈfyo͞ozHən/ ▶ n. the spreading of something more widely. ■ the action of spreading the light from a light source evenly so as to reduce glare and harsh shadows. ■ Chem. the intermingling of substances by the natural movement of their particles. ■ Anthropol. the dissemination of elements of culture to another region or people. — **dif·fu·sive** /-siv/ adj. (Chem.).

dif·fu·sion·ist /diˈfyo͞ozHənist/ Anthropol. ▶ adj. advocating the theory of the dissemination of elements of culture to another region or people. ▶ n. an advocate of such a theory. — **dif·fu·sion·ism** /-ˌnizəm/ n.

dif·fu·siv·i·ty /ˌdifyo͞oˈsivitē/ ▶ n. (pl. **-ties**) Physics a measure of the capability of a substance or energy to be diffused or to allow something to pass by diffusion.

dig /dig/ ▶ v. (**dig·ging** ; past **dug** /dəg/) **1** [intrans.] break up and move earth with a tool or machine, or with hands, paws, snout, etc.: *the boar had been digging for roots* | [trans.] *she had to dig the garden.* ■ [trans.] make (a hole, grave, etc.) by breaking up and moving earth in such a way. ■ [with obj. and adverbial] extract from the ground by breaking up and moving earth: *they dug up fossils.* ■ (**dig in**) (of a soldier) protect oneself by making a trench or similar ground defense. ■ [in imper.] (**dig in**) informal used to encourage someone to start eating with gusto and have as much as they want. ■ [trans.] (**dig something in/into**) push or poke something in or into. ■ [trans.] excavate (an archaeological site). ■ [trans.] (**dig something out**) bring out something that is hidden or has been stored for a long time. ■ (**dig into**) informal find money from (somewhere): *members have to dig deep into their pockets.* ■ [no obj., with adverbial] search or rummage in a specified place: *Catherine dug into her handbag.* ■ engage in research; conduct an investigation. ■ [trans.] (**dig something up/out**) discover information after a search or investigation. **2** [trans.] informal, dated like, appreciate, or understand. ▶ n. **1** [in sing.] an act or spell of digging. ■ an archaeological excavation. **2** a push or poke with one's elbow, finger, etc. ■ informal a remark intended to mock or criticize.
– PHRASES **dig up dirt** informal discover and reveal damaging information about someone. **dig oneself into a hole** (or **dig a hole for oneself**) get oneself into an awkward or restrictive situation. **dig in one's heels** resist stubbornly; refuse to give in. **dig's one's own grave** see GRAVE[1]. [ME: perh. from OE *dīc* 'ditch.']

di·gam·ma /dīˈgamə/ ▶ n. the sixth letter of the early Greek alphabet (ϝ, ϝ), pronounced as "w." It became obsolete in many dialects before the Classical period. [17th C.: via L. from Gk., from *di-* 'twice' + GAMMA.]

di·gas·tric /dīˈgastrik/ (also **digastric muscle**) ▶ n. Anat. each of a pair of muscles that run under the jaw and act to open it. [17th C.: from mod. L. *digastricus*, from *di-* 'twice' + Gk. *gastēr* 'belly.']

di·ge·ra·ti /dijəˈrätē/ ▶ plural n. people with expertise or professional involvement in information technology. [1990s: blend of DIGITAL and LITERATI.]

di·gest ▶ v. /diˈjest; dī-/ [trans.] break down (food) in the stomach and intestines into substances that can be used by the body. ■ understand or assimilate (new information or the significance of something) by a period of reflection. ■ arrange (something) in a systematic or convenient order, esp. by reduction. ■ Chem. treat (a substance) with heat, enzymes, or a solvent in order to decompose it or extract essential components. ▶ n. /ˈdījest/ **1** a compilation or summary of material or information. ■ a periodical consisting of condensed versions of pieces of writing or news published elsewhere. ■ a methodical summary of a body of laws. ■ (**the Digest**) the compendium of Roman law compiled in the reign of Justinian. **2** Chem. a substance or mixture obtained by digestion. [ME: from L. *digest-* 'distributed, dissolved, digested,' from the v. *digerere*, from *di-* 'apart' + *gerere* 'carry.']

di·gest·er /diˈjestər; dī-/ ▶ n. Chem. a container in which substances are treated with heat, enzymes, or a solvent in order to promote decomposition or extract essential components.

di·gest·i·ble /diˈjestəbəl; dī-/ ▶ adj. (of food) able to be digested. ■ (of information) easy to understand or follow. — **di·gest·i·bil·i·ty** /-ˌjestəˈbilitē/ n.

di·ges·tif /ˌdējesˈtēf/ ▶ n. a drink or portion of food drunk or eaten in order to aid the digestion. [20th C.: Fr., lit. 'digestive.']

di·ges·tion /diˈjescHən; dī-/ ▶ n. the process of breaking down food by mechanical and enzymatic action in the stomach and intestines into substances that can be used by the body. ■ a person's capacity to break down food in such a way. ■ Chem. the process of treating a substance by means of heat, enzymes, or a solvent to promote decomposition or extract essential components.

di·ges·tive /diˈjestiv; dī-/ ▶ adj. of or relating to the process of digesting food. ■ (of food or medicine) aiding or promoting the process of digestion. ▶ n. a food or medicine that aids or promotes the digestion of food. — **di·ges·tive·ly** adv.

di·ges·tive gland ▶ n. Zool. a glandular organ of digestion present in crustaceans, mollusks, and certain other invertebrates.

dig·ger /ˈdigər/ ▶ n. a person, animal, or large machine that digs earth: [in comb.] *a grave-digger.* ■ (**Digger**, in full **Digger Indian**) offens. a North American Indian of any of several tribes that subsisted on roots dug from the ground.

dig·ger wasp ▶ n. a solitary wasp (families Sphecidae and Pompilidae) that typically excavates a burrow in sandy soil, filling it with paralyzed insects or spiders for its larvae to feed on.

dig·gings /ˈdiginGz/ ▶ plural n. **1** a site such as a mine or goldfield that has been excavated. ■ material that has been dug from the ground. **2** Brit., informal, dated lodgings.

dight /dīt/ ▶ adj. archaic clothed or equipped. ▶ v. [trans.] literary make ready for a use or purpose; prepare: *let the meal be dighted.* [ME: past part. of archaic *dight* 'order, deal with,' based on L. *dictare* 'compose.']

dig·it /ˈdijit/ ▶ n. **1** any of the numerals from 0 to 9, esp. when forming part of a number. **2** a finger (including the thumb) or toe. ■ Zool. an equivalent structure at the end of the limbs of many higher vertebrates. [ME: from L. *digitus* 'finger, toe.']

dig·it·al /ˈdijitl/ ▶ adj. **1** relating to or using signals or information represented by discrete values (digits) of a physical quantity, such as voltage or magnetic polarization, to represent arithmetic numbers or approximations to numbers from a continuum of logical expressions and variables: *digital TV.* Often contrasted with ANALOG. ■ involving or relating to the use of computer technology: *the digital revolution.* ■ (of a clock or watch) showing the time by means of displayed digits rather than hands or a pointer. **2** of or relating to a finger or fingers. — **dig·it·al·ly** adv.

dig·it·al cam·er·a ▶ n. a camera that records and stores digital images.

dig·it·al cash (also **digital money**) ▶ n. money that may be transferred electronically from one party to another during a transaction.

dig·it·al com·pact cas·sette (abbr.: **DCC**) ▶ n. a format for tape cassettes similar to ordinary audiocassettes but with digital rather than analog recording.

dig·it·al com·press·ion ▶ n. a method of reducing the number of bits (zeros and ones) in a digital signal by using mathematical algorithms to eliminate redundant information.

dig·i·tal·in /,diji'talin/ ▶ **n.** a drug containing the active constituents of digitalis. [19th C.: from DIGITALIS + -IN[1].]

dig·i·tal·is /,diji'talis/ ▶ **n.** a drug prepared from the dried leaves of foxglove and containing substances (notably digoxin and digitoxin) that stimulate the heart muscle. [18th C.: from mod. L., from *digitalis (herba)* '(plant) relating to the finger,' from *digitus* 'finger, toe.']

dig·i·tal·ize[1] /'dijitl,īz/ ▶ **v.** another term for DIGITIZE. — **dig·i·tal·i·za·tion** /,dijitl-ə'zāsHən/ **n.**

dig·i·tal·ize[2] ▶ **v.** [trans.] Med. administer digitalis or digoxin to (a patient with a heart complaint). — **dig·i·tal·i·za·tion** /,dijitl-ə'zāsHən/ **n.**

dig·it·al lock·er ▶ **n.** Comput. an Internet service that allows registered users to access music, movies, videos, photographs, videogames, and other multimedia files.

dig·i·tal-to-an·a·log con·vert·er ▶ **n.** an electronic device for converting digital signals to analog form.

dig·i·tate /'diji,tāt/ ▶ **adj.** tech. shaped like a spread hand.

dig·i·ta·tion /,diji'tāsHən/ ▶ **n.** **1** Zool. & Bot. a fingerlike protuberance or division. **2** Comput. the process of converting data to digital form.

dig·i·ti·grade /'dijiti,grād/ ▶ **adj.** Zool. (of a mammal) walking on its toes and not touching the ground with its heels, as a dog, cat, or rodent. Compare with PLANTIGRADE. [19th C.: from L. *digitus* 'finger, toe' + *-gradus* '-walking.']

dig·i·tize /'diji,tīz/ ▶ **v.** [trans.] [usu. as adj.] (**digitized**) convert (pictures or sound) into a digital form that can be processed by a computer. — **dig·i·ti·za·tion** /,dijitə'zāsHən/ **n.** **dig·i·tiz·er n.**

dig·i·tox·in /,diji'täksin/ ▶ **n.** Chem. a compound with similar properties to digoxin and found with it in the foxglove and similar plants.

di·glos·si·a /dī'glôsēə; -'glä-/ ▶ **n.** Ling. a situation in which two languages (or two varieties of the same language) are used under different conditions within a community, often by the same speakers. The term is usually applied to languages with distinct "high" and "low" (colloquial) varieties, such as Arabic. — **di·glos·sic** /-sik/ **adj.** [1950s: from Gk. *diglōssos* 'bilingual.']

dig·ni·fied /'digni,fīd/ ▶ **adj.** having or showing a composed or serious manner that is worthy of respect. — **dig·ni·fied·ly adv.**

dig·ni·fy /'dignə,fī/ ▶ **v.** (**-fies, -fied**) [trans.] make (something) seem worthy and impressive. ■ (often **be dignified**) give an impressive name to (someone or something that one considers worthless). *dumps are increasingly* ***dignified as*** *landfills.* [ME: from OFr. *dignefier*, from late L. *dignificare*, from L. *dignus* 'worthy.']

dig·ni·tar·y /'digni,terē/ ▶ **n.** (pl. **-tar·ies**) a person considered to be important because of high rank or office.

dig·ni·ty /'dignitē/ ▶ **n.** (pl. **-ties**) the state or quality of being worthy of honor or respect. ■ a composed or serious manner or style. ■ a sense of pride in oneself; self-respect. ■ a high or honorable rank or position.
– PHRASES **stand on one's dignity** insist on being treated with due respect. [ME: from OFr. *dignete*, from L. *dignitas*, from *dignus* 'worthy.']

dig·ox·in /dij'äksin/ ▶ **n.** Chem. a poisonous compound present in the foxglove and other plants. It is a steroid glycoside and is used in small doses as a cardiac stimulant. [1930s: contr. of DIGITOXIN.]

di·graph /'dī,graf/ ▶ **n.** a combination of two letters representing one sound, as in *ph* and *ey*. ■ Print. a character consisting of two joined letters; a ligature. — **di·graph·ic** /dī'grafik/ **adj.**

di·gress /dī'gres/ ▶ **v.** [intrans.] leave the main subject temporarily in speech or writing. — **di·gress·er n.** **di·gres·sion** /-'gresHən/ **n.** **di·gres·sive** /-'gresiv/ **adj.** **di·gres·sive·ly** /-'gresivlē/ **adv.** **di·gres·sive·ness** /-'gresivnis/ **n.** [16th C.: from L. *digress-* 'stepped away,' from the v. *digredi*, from *di-* 'aside' + *gradi* 'to walk.']

digs /digz/ ▶ **plural n.** informal living quarters. [19th C.: short for *diggings*.]

di·he·dral /dī'hēdrəl/ ▶ **adj.** having or contained by two plane faces. ▶ **n.** an angle formed by two plane faces. ■ Aeron. inclination of an aircraft's wing from the horizontal, esp. upward away from the fuselage. Compare with ANHEDRAL. [18th C.: from DI-[1] 'two' + *-hedral* (see -HEDRON).]

di·hy·brid /dī'hībrid/ ▶ **n.** Genet. a hybrid that is heterozygous for alleles of two different genes.

di·hy·dric /dī'hīdrik/ ▶ **adj.** Chem. (of an alcohol) containing two hydroxyl groups. [19th C.: from DI-[1] 'two' + HYDROGEN + -IC.]

Di·jon /dē'zHôN; dē'zHän/ a city in east central France; pop. 151,640.

Di·jon mus·tard ▶ **n.** a medium-hot mustard, typically prepared with white wine and originally made in Dijon, France.

dik-dik /'dik ,dik/ ▶ **n.** a dwarf antelope (genus *Madoqua*) found on the dry savanna of Africa. [19th C.: a local word in East Africa, imitative of its call.]

dike[1] /dīk/ (also **dyke**) ▶ **n.** **1** a long wall or embankment built to prevent flooding from the sea. ■ [often in place names] a low wall or earthwork serving as a boundary or defense: *Offa's Dike.* ■ a causeway. ■ Geol. an intrusion of igneous rock cutting across existing strata. Compare with SILL. **2** a ditch or watercourse. ▶ **v.** [trans.] [often as adj.] (**diked**) provide (land) with a wall or embankment to prevent flooding.
– PHRASES **put one's finger in the dike** attempt to stem the advance of something undesirable. [ME: from ON *dík*, rel. to DITCH.]

dike[2] ▶ **n.** var. of DYKE[2].

dik·tat /dik'tät/ ▶ **n.** an order or decree imposed by someone in power without popular consent. [1930s: from Ger., from L. *dictatum* 'something dictated,' neut. past part. of *dictare*.]

di·lap·i·date /di'lapi,dāt/ ▶ **v.** [trans.] archaic cause (something) to fall into disrepair or ruin. — **di·lap·i·da·tion** /di,lapi'dāsHən/ **n.** [16th C.: from L. *dilapidat-* 'demolished,' from the v. *dilapidare*, from *di-* 'apart, abroad' + *lapis, lapid-* 'stone.']

di·lap·i·dat·ed /di'lapi,dātid/ ▶ **adj.** (of a building or object) in a state of disrepair or ruin as a result of age or neglect.

di·lat·an·cy /dī'lātnsē/ ▶ **n.** Chem. the phenomenon exhibited by some fluids, sols, and gels in which they become more viscous or solid under pressure.

dil·a·ta·tion /,dilə'tāsHən; ,dī-/ ▶ **n.** esp. Med. & Physiol. the process of becoming dilated. ■ the action of dilating a vessel or opening. ■ a dilated part of a hollow organ or vessel.

di·la·ta·tion and cu·ret·tage (also **di·la·tion and cu·ret·tage**) (abbr.: **D and C**) ▶ **n.** Med. a surgical procedure involving dilatation of the cervix and curettage of the uterus, performed after a miscarriage or for the removal of cysts or tumors.

di·late /'dīlāt; dī'lāt/ ▶ **v.** **1** make or become wider, larger, or more open. **2** [intrans.] (**dilate on**) speak or write at length on (a subject). — **di·lat·a·ble adj.** **di·la·tion** /dī'lāsHən/ **n.** [ME: from OFr. *dilater*, from L. *dilatare* 'spread out,' from *di-* 'apart' + *latus* 'wide.']

di·la·tor /'dīlātər; dī'lātər/ ▶ **n.** a thing that dilates something, in particular: ■ (also **dilator muscle**) Anat. a muscle whose contraction dilates an organ or aperture, such as the pupil of the eye. ■ a surgical instrument for dilating a tube or cavity in the body. ■ a vasodilatory drug.

dil·a·to·ry /'dilə,tôrē/ ▶ **adj.** slow to act. ■ intended to cause delay: *dilatory tactics.* — **dil·a·to·ri·ly** /,dilə'tôrəlē/ **adv.** **dil·a·to·ri·ness n.** [ME: from late L. *dilatorius* 'delaying,' from L. *dilator* 'delayer,' from *dilat-* 'deferred,' from the v. *differre*.]

dil·do /'dildō/ ▶ **n.** (pl. **-dos**) an object shaped like an erect penis used for sexual stimulation. ■ vulgar slang a stupid or ridiculous person. [16th C.: of unknown origin.]

di·lem·ma /di'lemə/ ▶ **n.** a situation in which a difficult choice has to be made between two or more alternatives, esp. equally undesirable ones. ■ informal a difficult situation or problem. ■ Logic an argument forcing an opponent to choose either of two unfavorable alternatives. [16th C.: via L. from Gk. *dilēmma*, from *di-* 'twice' + *lēmma* 'premise.']

dil·et·tante /,dili'tänt/ ▶ **n.** (pl. **-tan·ti** /-'täntē/ or **-tantes**) a person who claims an area of interest, such as the arts, without real commitment or knowledge. ■ archaic a person with an amateur interest in the arts. — **dil·et·tan·tish adj.** **dil·et·tant·ism n.** [18th C.: from Ital., 'person loving the arts,' from *dilettare* 'to delight,' from L. *delectare*.]

dil·i·gence[1] /'dilijəns/ ▶ **n.** careful and persistent work or effort.

dil·i·gence[2] ▶ **n.** hist. a public stagecoach. [17th C.: from Fr., shortened from *carrosse de diligence* 'coach of speed.']

dil·i·gent /'dilijənt/ ▶ **adj.** having or showing care and conscientiousness in one's work or duties. — **dil·i·gent·ly adv.** [ME: via OFr. from L. *diligens, diligent-* 'assiduous,' from *diligere* 'love, take delight in.']

dill /dil/ ▶ **n.** an aromatic herb (*Anethum graveolens*) of the parsley family, with fine blue-green leaves and yellow flowers. The leaves and seeds are used esp. for flavoring and for medicinal purposes. ■ (also **dill·weed** or **dill weed**) the fresh or dried leaves of this plant used to flavor food. [OE *dile, dyle*; rel. to Ger. *Dill*.]

Dil·lin·ger /'dilinjər/, John (1903–34), US bank robber. Noted for his high-profile outlawry, he was named "Public Enemy Number 1."

dill pick·le ▶ **n.** pickled cucumber flavored with dill.

dil·ly /'dilē/ ▶ **n.** (pl. **-lies**) [usu. in sing.] informal an excellent example of a particular type of person or thing. [19th C.: alt. of DELIGHTFUL or DELICIOUS.]

dil·ly-dal·ly ▶ **v.** (**-lies, -lied**) [intrans.] informal waste time through aimless wandering or indecision. [17th C.: reduplication of DALLY.]

dil·u·ent /'dilyo͞oənt/ tech. ▶ **n.** a substance used to dilute something. ▶ **adj.** acting to cause dilution. [18th C.: from L. *diluent-* 'dissolving,' from the v. *diluere*.]

di·lute /di'lo͞ot; dī-/ ▶ **v.** [trans.] (often **be diluted**) make (a liquid) thinner or weaker by adding water or another solvent to it. ■ make (something) weaker in force, content, or value by modifying it or adding other elements to it. ■ reduce the value of (a shareholding) by issuing more shares without increasing the values of assets. ▶ **adj.** (of a liquid) made thinner or weaker by having had water or another solvent added to it. ■ Chem. (of a solution) having a relatively low concentration of solute. ■ (of color or light) weak or low in concentration. — **di·lut·er n.** [16th C.: from L. *dilut-* 'washed away, dissolved,' from the v. *diluere*.]

di·lu·tion /di'lo͞osHən; dī-/ ▶ **n.** the action of making a liquid more dilute. ■ the action of making something weaker in force, content, or value. ■ a liquid that has been diluted. ■ the degree to which a solution has been diluted. ■ a reduction in the value of a shareholding due to the issue of additional shares in a company without an increase in assets. — **di·lu·tive** /-'lo͞otiv/ **adj.** (esp. Finance).

di·lu·vi·al /di'lo͞ovēəl/ ▶ **adj.** of or relating to a flood or floods, esp. the biblical Flood. [17th C.: from late L. *diluvialis*, from *diluvium* 'deluge,' from *diluere* 'wash away.']

di·lu·vi·an /di'lo͞ovēən/ ▶ **adj.** another term for DILUVIAL.

dim /dim/ ▶ **adj.** (**dim·mer, dim·mest**) **1** (of a light, color, or illuminated object) not shining brightly or clearly. ■ (of an object or shape) made difficult to see by darkness, shade, or distance. ■ (of a room or space) made difficult to see in by darkness. ■ (of the eyes) not able to see clearly. ■ (of a sound) indistinct or muffled. ■ (of prospects) not giving cause for hope or optimism. **2** not clearly recalled or formulated

in the mind. ■ informal stupid or slow to understand. ▶ v. (**dimmed, dim·ming**) make or become less bright. ■ [trans.] lower (a vehicle's headlights) from high to low beam. ■ make or become less intense or favorable. ■ make or become less able to see clearly. ■ make or become less clear in the mind.
– PHRASES **take a dim view of** regard with disapproval. — **dim·ly** adv. **dim·mish** adj. **dim·ness** n. [OE *dim, dimm*, of Gmc. origin; rel. to Ger. dial. *timmer*.]

dim. ▶ abbr. ■ dimension. ■ diminuendo. ■ diminutive.

Di·Mag·gi·o /də'majē,ō/, Joe (1914–99), US baseball player; full name *Joseph Paul DiMaggio*; called *Joltin' Joe* and the *Yankee Clipper*. He was center fielder for the New York Yankees 1936–42, 1946–51.

dime /dīm/ ▶ n. a ten-cent coin. ■ informal a small amount of money. ■ informal used to refer to something small in size, area, or degree.
– PHRASES **a dime a dozen** informal very common and of no particular value. **get off the dime** informal be decisive and show initiative. **on a dime** informal used to refer to a maneuver that can be performed by a moving vehicle or person within a small area or short distance: ***turn on a dime***. [ME: from OFr. *disme*, from L. *decima pars* 'tenth part.']

dime nov·el ▶ n. hist. a cheap, popular novel, typically a melodramatic romance or adventure story.

di·men·sion /di'menCHən/ ▶ n. **1** an aspect or feature of a situation, problem, or thing: *sun-dried tomatoes add a new dimension to this sauce.* **2** (usu. **dimensions**) a measurable extent of some kind, such as length, breadth, depth, or height. ■ a mode of linear extension of which there are three in space and two on a flat surface, which corresponds to one of a set of coordinates specifying the position of a point. ■ Physics an expression for a derived physical quantity in terms of fundamental quantities such as mass, length, or time, raised to the appropriate power (acceleration, for example, having the dimension of *length* × *time*−2). ▶ v. [trans.] (often **be dimensioned**) cut or shape (something) to particular measurements. ■ mark (a diagram) with measurements. — **di·men·sion·al** /-CHənl/ adj. [in comb.] *multidimensional scaling;* **di·men·sion·al·i·ty** /di,menCHə'nalitē/ n. **di·men·sion·al·ly** /-CHənl-ē/ adj. **di·men·sion·less** adj. [ME: via OFr. from L. *dimensio(n-)*, from *dimetiri* 'measure out.']

di·mer /'dīmər/ ▶ n. Chem. a molecule or molecular complex consisting of two identical molecules linked together. — **di·mer·ic** /dī'merik/ adj. [1930s: from DI-[1] 'two,' on the pattern of *polymer*.]

di·mer·ize /'dīmə,rīz/ ▶ v. [intrans.] Chem. combine with a similar molecule to form a dimer. — **di·mer·i·za·tion** /,dīmərə'zāSHən/ n.

dim·er·ous /'dimərəs/ ▶ adj. Bot. & Zool. having parts arranged in groups of two. ■ consisting of two joints or parts. [19th C.: from mod. L. *dimerus* (from Gk. *dimerēs* 'bipartite') + -OUS.]

dime store ▶ n. a shop selling cheap merchandise (originally one where the maximum price was a dime). ■ [as adj.] cheap and inferior: *plastic dime-store toys.*

dim·e·ter /'dimitər/ ▶ n. Pros. a line of verse consisting of two metrical feet. [16th C.: via late L. from Gk. *dimetros* 'of two measures,' from *di-* 'twice' + *metron* 'a measure.']

di·meth·yl sulf·ox·ide /dī'meTHəl səl'fäksīd/ (esp. Brit. **di·meth·yl sulph·ox·ide**) (abbr.: **DMSO**) ▶ n. Chem. a colorless liquid, $(CH_3)_2SO$, used as a solvent and synthetic reagent. Used in medicinal preparations, it readily penetrates the skin.

di·min·ish /di'miniSH/ ▶ v. make or become less. ■ [trans.] make (someone or something) seem less impressive or valuable.
– PHRASES **(the law of) diminishing returns** used to refer to a point at which the level of profits or benefits gained is less than the amount of money or energy invested. — **di·min·ish·a·ble** adj. [ME: blend of archaic *minish* 'diminish' (based on L. *minutia* 'smallness') and obs. *diminue* 'speak disparagingly' (based on L. *deminuere* 'lessen').]

di·min·ished /di'miniSHt/ ▶ adj. **1** made smaller or less. ■ [predic.] made to seem less impressive or valuable. **2** [attrib.] Music denoting or containing an interval that is one semitone less than the corresponding minor or perfect interval.

di·min·ished ca·pac·i·ty ▶ n. Law an unbalanced mental state that is considered to make a person less answerable for a crime and is recognized as grounds to reduce the charge.

di·min·u·en·do /di,minyōō'endō/ Music ▶ n. (pl. **-dos** or **-di** /-dē/) a decrease in loudness. ■ a passage to be performed with such a decrease. ▶ adv. & adj. (esp. as a direction) with a decrease in loudness. ▶ v. (**-dos, -doed**) [intrans.] decrease in loudness or intensity. [Ital., lit. 'diminishing,' from *diminuire*, from L. *deminuere* 'lessen'.]

dim·i·nu·tion /,dimə'n(y)ōōSHən/ ▶ n. a reduction in the size, extent, or importance of something. ■ Music the shortening of the time values of notes in a melodic part. [ME: via OFr. from L. *deminutio(n-)*, from the v. *deminuere* (see DIMINISH).]

di·min·u·tive /di'minyətiv/ ▶ adj. extremely or unusually small. ■ (of a word, name, or suffix) implying smallness, either actual or imputed in token of affection, scorn, etc., (e.g., *teeny, -let, -kins*). ▶ n. a smaller or shorter thing, in particular: ■ a diminutive word or suffix. ■ a shortened form of a name, typically used informally. — **di·min·u·tive·ly** adv. **di·min·u·tive·ness** n.

dim·i·ty /'dimitē/ ▶ n. a hard-wearing, sheer cotton fabric woven with raised stripes or checks. [ME: from Ital. *dimito* or med. L. *dimitum*, from Gk. *dimitos*, from *di-* 'twice' + *mitos* 'warp thread.']

dim·mer /'dimər/ ▶ n. **1** (also **dimmer switch**) a device for varying the brightness of an electric light. **2** a headlight with a low beam.

di·mor·phic /dī'môrfik/ ▶ adj. esp. Biol. occurring in or representing two distinct forms. — **di·mor·phism** n. [19th C.: from Gk. *dimorphos* (from *di-* 'twice' + *morphē* 'form') + -IC.]

dim·ple /'dimpəl/ ▶ n. a small depression in the flesh, either one that exists permanently or one that forms in the cheeks when one smiles. ■ [often as adj.] a slight depression in the surface of something: *a sheet of dimple foam.* ▶ v. [trans.] produce a dimple or dimples in the surface of (something). ■ [intrans.] form or show a dimple or dimples. — **dim·ply** adj. [ME: of Gmc. origin; rel. to Ger. *Tümpel* 'pond.']

dim sum /'dim 'səm/ ▶ n. a Chinese dish of small steamed or fried savory dumplings containing various fillings, served as a snack or main course. [from Chin. (Cantonese dial.) *tim sam*, from *tim* 'dot' and *sam* 'heart.']

dim·wit /'dim,wit/ ▶ n. informal a stupid or silly person. — **dim·wit·ted** adj. **dim·wit·ted·ly** adv. **dim·wit·ted·ness** n.

DIN /din/ ▶ n. any of a series of technical standards originating in Germany and used internationally, esp. to designate electrical connections, film speeds, and paper sizes: [as adj.] *a DIN socket.* [20th C.: from *Deutsche Industrie-Norm* 'Ger. Industrial Standard.']

din /din/ ▶ n. [in sing.] a loud, unpleasant, and prolonged noise. ▶ v. (**dinned, din·ning**) **1** [trans.] (**be dinned into**) (of a fact) be instilled in (someone) by constant repetition. **2** [intrans.] make a loud, unpleasant, and prolonged noise. [OE *dyne, dynn* (noun), *dynian* (v.), of Gmc. origin; rel. to ON *dynr* (n.).]

di·nar /di'när/ ▶ n. **1** the basic monetary unit of the states of Yugoslavia, equal to 100 paras. **2** the basic monetary unit of certain countries of the Middle East and North Africa, equal to 1000 fils in Jordan, Bahrain, and Iraq, 1000 dirhams in Libya, 100 centimes in Algeria, and 10 pounds in the Sudan. **3** a monetary unit of Iran, equal to one hundredth of a rial. [from Arab. and Pers. *dīnār*, Turk. and Serbo-Croat *dinar*, via late Gk. from L. *denarius* (see DENARIUS).]

Di·nar·ic Alps /di'narik/ a mountain range in the Balkans that runs from Slovenia, through Croatia, Bosnia, and Montenegro, to Albania.

din-din /'din ,din/ ▶ n. a child's word for dinner.

dine /dīn/ ▶ v. [intrans.] eat dinner. ■ (**dine out**) eat dinner in a restaurant or the home of friends. ■ (**dine on**) eat (something) for dinner. ■ (**dine out on**) regularly entertain friends with (a humorous story or interesting piece of information). ■ [trans.] take (someone) to dinner.
– PHRASES **wine and dine** see WINE. [ME: from OFr. *disner*, prob. from *desjëuner* 'to break fast,' from *des-* (expressing reversal) + *jëun* 'fasting' (from L. *jejunus*).]

din·er /'dīnər/ ▶ n. **1** a person who is eating, typically a customer in a restaurant. **2** a dining car on a train. ■ a restaurant with a long counter and booths, originally one designed to resemble a dining car on a train.

di·ne·ro /di'ne(ə)rō/ ▶ n. informal money. [19th C.: Sp., 'coin, money.']

Din·e·sen /'dinəsən/, Isak, see BLIXEN.

di·nette /dī'net/ ▶ n. a small room or part of a room used for eating meals. ■ a set of table and chairs for such an area.

ding[1] /diNG/ ▶ v. [intrans.] make a ringing sound. ▶ exclam. used to imitate a metallic ringing sound resembling a bell. [17th C.: imitative.]

ding[2] ▶ n. informal a blow, esp. a mark or dent on the bodywork of a car, boat, or other vehicle. ▶ v. [trans.] informal dent (something). ■ hit (someone), esp. on the head. [ME: prob. of Scand. origin.]

ding-a-ling /'diNG ə ,liNG/ ▶ n. **1** [in sing.] the ringing sound of a bell. **2** informal an eccentric or stupid person. [19th C.: imitative.]

Ding an sich /,diNG än 'siSH/ ▶ n. (in Kant's philosophy) a thing as it is in itself, not mediated through perception by the senses or conceptualization, and therefore unknowable. [19th C.: Ger., lit. 'thing in itself.']

ding·bat /'diNG,bat/ informal ▶ n. **1** a stupid or eccentric person. **2** a typographical device other than a letter or numeral (such as an asterisk), used to signal divisions in text or to replace letters. [19th C.: perh. based on obs. *ding* 'to beat.']

ding-dong /'diNG ,dôNG; ,däNG/ ▶ n. informal a silly or foolish person. ▶ adv. & adj. **1** with the simple alternate chimes of or as of a bell. **2** [as adj.] informal (of a contest) evenly matched and intensely waged: *the game was a ding-dong battle.* [16th C.: imitative.]

ding·er /'diNGər/ ▶ n. informal a thing outstanding of its kind. [19th C.: shortening of HUMDINGER.]

din·ghy /'diNGē/ ▶ n. (pl. **-ghies**) a small boat for recreation or racing, esp. an open boat with a mast and sails. ■ a small, inflatable rubber boat. ■ the smallest of a ship's boats. [19th C.: from Hindi *ḍiṅgī*.]

din·gle /'diNGgəl/ ▶ n. literary or dialect a deep wooded valley or dell. [ME: of unknown origin.]

din·gle·ber·ry /'diNGəl,berē/ ▶ n. (pl. **-ries**) **1** vulgar slang a particle of fecal matter attached to the anal hair. **2** vulgar slang a foolish or inept person. [20th C.: from *dingle* of unknown origin + BERRY.]

din·go /'diNGgō/ ▶ n. (pl. **-goes** or **-gos**) a wild or half-domesticated dog (*Canis dingo*) with a sandy-colored coat, found in Australia. [18th C.: from Dharuk *din-gu* 'domesticated dingo.']

ding·us /'diNGgəs/ ▶ n. (pl. **ding·us·es**) informal used to refer to something whose name the speaker cannot remember, is unsure of, or is humorously or euphemistically omitting: *here's a doohickey—and there's the dingus.* [19th C.: via Afrik. from Du. *ding* 'thing.']

dinosaurs 1

din·gy /ˈdinjē/ ▶ **adj.** (**-gi·er**, **-gi·est**) gloomy and drab. — **din·gi·ly** /-əlē/ **adv.** **din·gi·ness** **n.** [18th C.: perh. based on OE *dynge* 'dung.']

din·ing car ▶ **n.** a railroad car equipped as a restaurant.

din·ing hall ▶ **n.** a large room, typically in a school or other institution, in which people eat meals together.

din·ing room ▶ **n.** a room in a house or hotel in which meals are eaten.

din·ing ta·ble ▶ **n.** a table on which meals are served in a dining room.

dink[1] /diNGk/ ▶ **n.** (pl. **-ies**) informal a partner in a well-off working couple with no children. [1980s: acronym from *double income, no kids.*]

dink[2] esp. Tennis ▶ **n.** a drop shot. ▶ **v.** [trans.] hit (the ball) with a drop shot. [1930s: symbolic.]

Din·ka /ˈdiNGkə/ ▶ **n.** (pl. same or **-kas**) **1** a member of a Sudanese people of the Nile basin. **2** the Nilotic language of this people, with about 1.4 million speakers. ▶ **adj.** of or relating to this people or their language. [from the local word *Jieng* 'people.']

din·kum /ˈdiNGkəm/ ▶ **adj.** Austral./NZ, informal (of an article or person) genuine.
– PHRASES **fair dinkum** used to emphasize that or query whether something is genuine or true. ■ used to emphasize that behavior complies with accepted standards. [19th C.: of unknown origin.]

dink·y /ˈdiNGkē/ ▶ **adj.** (**dink·i·er**, **dink·i·est**) informal small; insignificant. [18th C.: from Scots and north. Engl. dial. *dink* 'neat, trim,' of unknown origin.]

din·ner /ˈdinər/ ▶ **n.** the main meal of the day, taken either around midday or in the evening. ■ a formal evening meal, typically one in honor of a person or event. [ME: from OFr. *disner*: see **DINE**).]

din·ner jack·et ▶ **n.** a man's short jacket without tails, typically a black one, worn with a bow tie for formal occasions in the evening.

din·ner ring ▶ **n.** a woman's dress ring, usually with a large stone or an ornate setting, often worn on special occasions.

din·ner serv·ice (also **dinner set**) ▶ **n.** a set of matching dishes for serving a meal.

din·ner the·a·ter ▶ **n.** a theater in which a meal is included in the price of a ticket.

din·ner·ware /ˈdinər,we(ə)r/ ▶ **n.** tableware, including plates, glassware, and cutlery.

din·o·flag·el·late /,dīnōˈflajəlit; -,lāt/ ▶ **n.** Biol. a single-celled organism (division Dinophyta, or class Dinophyceae, division Chromophycota) with two flagella, occurring in large numbers in marine plankton and also found in fresh water. Some produce toxins that can accumulate in shellfish. [19th C.: from mod. L. *Dinoflagellata* (pl.), from Gk. *dinos* 'whirling' + L. *flagellum* 'small whip' (see **FLAGELLUM**).]

di·no·saur /ˈdīnə,sôr/ ▶ **n.** **1** a fossil reptile of the Mesozoic era, often reaching an enormous size. The dinosaurs are placed, according to their hip structure, in two distantly related orders (see **ORNITHISCHIAN** and **SAURISCHIAN**). **2** a person or thing that is outdated or has become obsolete because of failure to adapt to changing circumstances. — **di·no·sau·ri·an** /,dīnəˈsôrēən/ **adj.** & **n.** [19th C.: from mod. L. *dinosaurus*, from Gk. *deinos* 'terrible' + *sauros* 'lizard.']

dint /dint/ ▶ **n.** **1** an impression or hollow in a surface. **2** archaic a blow or stroke, typically one made with a weapon in fighting. ■ force of attack; impact. ▶ **v.** [trans.] mark (a surface) with impressions or hollows.
– PHRASES **by dint of** by means of. [OE *dynt* 'stroke with a weapon.']

di·oc·e·san /dīˈäsisən/ ▶ **adj.** of or concerning a diocese. ▶ **n.** the bishop of a diocese.

di·o·cese /ˈdīəsis; -,sēz; -,sēs/ ▶ **n.** (pl. **-ces·es**) a district under the pastoral care of a Christian bishop. [ME: from OFr. *diocise*, based on Gk. *dioikēsis* 'administration, diocese,' from *dioikein* 'keep house, administer.']

Di·o·cle·tian /,dīəˈklēSHən/ (245–313), Roman emperor 284–305; full name *Gaius Aurelius Valerius Diocletianus*. In 286 he divided the empire between himself in the east and Maximian in the west.

di·ode /ˈdī,ōd/ ▶ **n.** Electron. a semiconductor device with two terminals, typically allowing the flow of current in one direction only. ■ a thermionic tube having two electrodes (an anode and a cathode). [20th C.: from **DI-**[1] 'two' + a shortened form of **ELECTRODE**.]

di·oe·cious /dīˈēSHəs/ ▶ **adj.** Biol. (of a plant or invertebrate animal) having the male and female reproductive organs in separate individuals. Compare with **MONOECIOUS**. — **di·oe·cy** /ˈdīēsē/ **n.** [18th C.: from mod. L. *Dioecia*, from **DI-**[1] 'two' + Gk. *-oikos* 'house.']

Di·og·e·nes /dīˈäjə,nēz/ (*c.*400–*c.*325 BC), Greek philosopher. A Cynic, he emphasized self-sufficiency.

di·ol /ˈdīôl/ ▶ **n.** Chem. an alcohol containing two hydroxyl groups in its molecule.

Di·o·mede Is·lands /ˈdīə,mēd/ two islands in the Bering Strait; Big Diomede belongs to Russia, and Little Diomede belongs to the US.

Di·o·ne /dīˈōnē/ Astron. a satellite of Saturn, the twelfth closest to the planet, discovered by Cassini in 1684.

Di·o·ny·sian /,dīəˈnisHən; -ˈnisēən; -ˈnīsē-/ (also **Di·o·ny·si·ac** /-ˈnisē,ak; -ˈnīsē-/) ▶ **adj.** **1** Gk. Mythol. of or relating to the god Dionysus. **2** of or relating to the sensual, spontaneous, and emotional aspects of human nature: *dark, grand Dionysian music.* Compare with **APOLLONIAN**.

Di·o·ny·si·us /,dīəˈnisēəs; -ˈnisHəs/ the name of two rulers of Syracuse: ■ Dionysius I (*c.*430–367 BC), reigned 405–367; known as **Dionysius the Elder**. He waged three wars against the Carthaginians. ■ Dionysius II (*c.*397–*c.*344 BC), son of Dionysius I; ruled 367–357 and 346–344; known as **Dionysius the Younger**. He lacked his father's military ambitions and signed a peace treaty with Carthage in 367.

Di·o·ny·si·us Ex·ig·u·us /egˈzigyōōəs/ (died *c.*556), Scythian monk. He is noted for developing in 505 the system of dates BC and AD.

Di·o·ny·si·us of Hal·i·car·nas·sus /,halikärˈnasəs/ (1st century BC), Greek historian. He wrote a history of Rome.

Di·o·ny·si·us the Ar·e·op·a·gite /,arēˈäpə,gīt; -jīt/ (1st century AD), Greek churchman. His conversion by St. Paul is recorded in Acts, and according to tradition he went on to become the first bishop of Athens.

Di·o·ny·sus /,dīəˈnisəs/ Gk. Mythol. a Greek god, son of Zeus and Semele. In later traditions he is a god of wine who inspires music and poetry. Also called **BACCHUS**.

di·op·side /dīˈäpsīd/ ▶ **n.** a mineral occurring as white to pale green crystals in metamorphic and basic igneous rocks. It consists of a calcium and magnesium silicate of the pyroxene group, often also containing iron and chromium. [19th C.: from Fr., from **DI-**[3] 'through' + Gk. *opsis* 'aspect.']

di·op·tase /dīˈäptās; -tāz/ ▶ **n.** a rare mineral occurring as emerald green or blue-green crystals. It consists of a hydrated silicate of copper. [19th C.: from Fr., formed irregularly from Gk. *dioptos* 'transparent.']

di·op·ter /dīˈäptər/ ▶ **n.** a unit of refractive power that is equal to the reciprocal of the focal length (in meters) of a given lens. [16th C.: from Fr., from L. *dioptra*, from Gk., from *di-* 'through' + *optos* 'visible.']

di·op·tric /dīˈäptrik/ ▶ **adj.** of or relating to the refraction of light, esp. in the organs of sight or in devices that aid or improve the vision.

di·op·trics /dīˈäptriks/ ▶ **plural n.** [treated as sing.] the branch of optics that deals with refraction.

Di·or /dēˈôr/, Christian (1905–57), French fashion designer. His collection featured 1947's New Look.

di·o·ram·a /ˌdīəˈramə; -ˈrä-/ ▶ **n.** a model representing a scene with three-dimensional figures, either in miniature or as a large-scale museum exhibit. ■ esp. hist. a scenic painting, viewed through a peephole, in which changes in color and direction of illumination simulate changes in the weather, time of day, etc. ■ a miniature movie set used for special effects or animation. [19th C.: coined in Fr. from **DIA-** 'through,' on the pattern of *panorama*.]

di·o·rite /ˈdīəˌrīt/ ▶ **n.** Geol. a speckled, coarse-grained igneous rock consisting essentially of plagioclase and hornblende or other mafic minerals. — **di·o·rit·ic** /ˌdīəˈritik/ **adj.** [19th C.: coined in Fr., formed irregularly from Gk. *diorizein* 'distinguish' + **-ITE**[1].]

Di·os·cu·ri /ˌdīəˈskyŏŏrē/ Greek & Rom. Mythol. the twins Castor and Pollux, born to Leda after her seduction by Zeus.

di·os·gen·in /ˌdī-äzˈjenin; dīˈäzjənin/ ▶ **n.** Chem. a steroid compound obtained from Mexican yams and used in the synthesis of steroid hormones. [1930s: from *dios-* + *genin*, steroids.]

di·ox·ane /dīˈäksān/ (also **di·ox·an** /-ˈäksän; -sən/) ▶ **n.** Chem. a colorless, toxic liquid, $C_4H_8O_2$, used as an organic solvent. [20th C.: from **DI-**[1] 'two' + **OX-** 'oxygen' + **-AN** (or **-ANE**[2]).]

di·ox·ide /dīˈäksīd/ ▶ **n.** Chem. an oxide containing two atoms of oxygen in its molecule or empirical formula.

di·ox·in /dīˈäksin/ ▶ **n.** a highly toxic and environmentally persistent compound, $C_{12}H_4O_2Cl_4$, produced as a byproduct in some manufacturing processes, notably herbicide production and paper bleaching.

Dip. ▶ **abbr.** diploma.

dip /dip/ ▶ **v.** (**dipped, dip·ping**) **1** [trans.] (**dip something in/into**) put or let something down quickly or briefly in or into (liquid). ■ [intrans.] (**dip into**) put a hand or tool into (a bag or container) in order to take something out. ■ [intrans.] (**dip into**) spend from or make use of (one's financial resources). ■ [intrans.] (**dip into**) read only parts of (a book) in a desultory manner. ■ take (snuff). ■ immerse (sheep) in a chemical solution that kills parasites. ■ make (a candle) by immersing a wick repeatedly in hot wax. ■ informal, dated baptize (someone) by immersion in water. **2** [intrans.] sink or drop downward. ■ (of a level or amount) become lower or smaller, typically temporarily. ■ (of a road, path, or area of land) slope downward. ■ [trans.] lower or move (something) downward. ▶ **n. 1** a brief swim. ■ a brief immersion in liquid. ■ short for **SHEEP DIP**. ■ a cursory read of part of a book. **2** a thick sauce in which pieces of food are dunked before eating. ■ a quantity that has been scooped up from a mass. **3** a brief downward slope followed by an upward one. ■ an act of sinking or dropping briefly before rising again. **4** tech. the extent to which something is angled downward from the horizontal, in particular: ■ (also **magnetic dip**) the angle made with the horizontal at any point by the earth's magnetic field, or by a magnetic needle in response to this. ■ Geol. the angle a stratum makes with the horizontal. ■ Astron. & Surveying the apparent depression of the horizon from the line of observation, due to the curvature of the earth. **5** informal, dated a pickpocket. **6** informal a stupid or foolish person. **7** archaic a candle made by immersing a wick repeatedly in hot wax.
– PHRASES **dip one's toe into** (or **in**) put one's toe briefly in (water), typically to check the temperature. ■ begin to do or test (something) cautiously. [OE *dyppan*, of Gmc. origin; rel. to **DEEP**.]

di·pep·tide /dīˈpeptīd/ ▶ **n.** Biochem. a peptide composed of two amino-acid residues.

di·phen·hy·dra·mine /ˌdīfenˈhīdrəˌmēn/ ▶ **n.** Med. an antihistamine compound, $C_{17}H_{21}NO$, used for the symptomatic relief of allergies. [1940s: from *diphen-* (denoting the presence of two phenyl groups) + **HYDR-** + **AMINE**.]

di·phen·yl·a·mine /dīˈfenl-əˌmēn; -ˈfē-/ ▶ **n.** Chem. a synthetic crystalline compound, $(C_6H_5)_2NH$, with basic properties, used in making dyes and as an insecticide and larvicide.

diph·the·ri·a /difˈTHi(ə)rēə; dip-/ ▶ **n.** a highly contagious disease caused by the bacterium *Corynebacterium diphtheriae* and characterized by the formation of a breath-obstructing membrane in the throat and by a potentially fatal toxin in the blood. — **diph·the·ri·al adj. diph·the·rit·ic** /ˌdifTHəˈritik; ˌdip-/ **adj.** [19th C.: mod. L., from Fr. *diphthérie* (earlier *diphthérite*), from Gk. *diphthera* 'skin, hide.']

diph·the·roid /ˈdifTHəˌroid; ˈdip-/ ▶ **n.** Microbiol. any bacterium of the genus *Corynebacterium* (which includes the diphtheria bacillus), esp. one that does not cause disease. ▶ **adj.** [attrib.] Med. similar to diphtheria.

diph·thong /ˈdifTHäNG; ˈdip-; -THôNG/ ▶ **n.** a sound formed by the combination of two vowels in a single syllable, in which the sound begins as one vowel and moves toward another (as in *coin, loud,* and *side*). Often contrasted with **MONOPHTHONG, TRIPHTHONG**. ■ a digraph representing the sound of a diphthong or single vowel (as in *feat*). ■ a compound vowel character; a ligature (such as *æ*). — **diph·thon·gal** /difˈTHäNGgəl; dip-; -ˈTHôNG-/ **adj.** [ME: from Fr. *diphtongue*, via late L. from Gk. *diphthongos*, from *di-* 'twice' + *phthongos* 'voice, sound.']

diph·thong·ize /ˈdifTHäNGˌ(g)īz; dip-; -THôNG-/ ▶ **v.** [trans.] change (a vowel) into a diphthong. — **diph·thong·i·za·tion** /ˌdifTHäNG(g)əˈzāSHən; ˌdip-; -THôNG-/ **n.**

di·ple·gia /dīˈplēj(ē)ə/ ▶ **n.** [mass noun] Med. paralysis of corresponding parts on both sides of the body, typically affecting the legs more severely than the arms. [19th C.: from **DI-**[1] 'two,' on the pattern of *hemiplegia* and *paraplegia*.]

diplo- ▶ **comb. form** double: *diplococcus*. [from Gk. *diplous* 'double.']

dip·lo·blas·tic /ˌdiplōˈblastik/ ▶ **adj.** Zool. having a body derived from only two embryonic cell layers (ectoderm and endoderm, but no mesoderm), as in sponges and coelenterates.

dip·lo·coc·cus /ˌdiplōˈkäkəs/ ▶ **n.** (pl. **-coc·ci** /-ˈkäk(s)ī; -(s)ē/) a bacterium that occurs as pairs of cocci, e.g., pneumococcus.

di·plod·o·cus /diˈplädəkəs/ ▶ **n.** a huge, herbivorous dinosaur (genus *Diplodocus*) of the late Jurassic period, with a long, slender neck and tail. [mod. L., from **DIPLO-** 'double' + Gk. *dokos* 'wooden beam.']

dip·loid /ˈdiploid/ Genet. ▶ **adj.** (of a cell or nucleus) containing two complete sets of chromosomes, one from each parent. Compare with **HAPLOID**. ■ (of an organism or part) composed of diploid cells. ▶ **n.** a diploid cell, organism, or species. — **dip·loi·dy** /-loidē/ **n.** [19th C.: from Gk. *diplous* 'double' + **-OID**.]

di·plo·ma /diˈplōmə/ ▶ **n.** a certificate awarded by an educational establishment to show that someone has successfully completed a course of study. ■ an official document or charter. [17th C.: via L. from Gk. *diplōma* 'folded paper,' from *diploun* 'to fold,' from *diplous* 'double.']

di·plo·ma·cy /diˈplōməsē/ ▶ **n.** the profession, activity, or skill of managing international relations, typically by a country's representatives abroad. ■ the art of dealing with people in a sensitive and effective way.

dip·lo·mat /ˈdipləˌmat/ ▶ **n.** an official representing a country abroad. ■ a person who can deal with people in a sensitive and effective way. [19th C.: from Fr. *diplomate*, back-form. from *diplomatique* 'diplomatic,' from L. *diploma* (see **DIPLOMA**).]

dip·lo·mate /ˈdipləˌmāt/ ▶ **n.** a person who holds a diploma, esp. a doctor certified as a specialist by a board of examiners.

dip·lo·mat·ic /ˌdipləˈmatik/ ▶ **adj. 1** of or concerning the profession, activity, or skill of managing international relations. ■ having or showing an ability to deal with people in a sensitive and effective way. **2** (of an edition or copy) exactly reproducing an original version. — **dip·lo·mat·i·cal·ly adv.**

dip·lo·mat·ic corps ▶ **n.** the body of diplomats residing in a particular country.

dip·lo·mat·ic im·mu·ni·ty ▶ **n.** the privilege of exemption from certain laws and taxes granted to diplomats by the country in which they are working.

di·plo·ma·tist /diˈplōmətist/ ▶ **n.** old-fashioned term for **DIPLOMAT**.

dip·lont·ic /dipˈläntik/ ▶ **n.** Genet. (of an alga or other lower plant) having a life cycle in which the main form, except for the gametes, is diploid. Compare with **HAPLONTIC**. — **dip·lont** /ˈdiplänt/ **n.** [1920s: from **DIPLO-** 'double' + Gk. *ōn, ont-* 'being' (from *einai* 'be, exist') + **-IC**.]

di·plo·pi·a /diˈplōpēə/ ▶ **n.** technical term for **DOUBLE VISION**.

Di·plo·po·da /ˌdipləˈpōdə/ Zool. a class of myriapod arthropods that comprises the millipedes. — **dip·lo·pod** /ˈdipləˌpäd/ **n.** [mod. L. (pl.), from Gk. *diploos* 'double' + *pous, pod-* 'foot.']

dip·lo·tene /ˈdipləˌtēn/ ▶ **n.** Biol. the fourth stage of the prophase of meiosis, following pachytene, during which the paired chromosomes begin to separate into two pairs of chromatids. [1920s: from **DIPLO-** 'double' + Gk. *tainia* 'band.']

di·pole /ˈdīˌpōl/ ▶ **n.** Physics a pair of equal and oppositely charged or magnetized poles separated by a distance. ■ an antenna consisting of a horizontal metal rod with a connecting wire at its center. ■ Chem. a molecule in which a concentration of positive electric charge is separated from a concentration of negative charge. — **di·po·lar** /dīˈpōlər/ **adj.**

di·pole mo·ment ▶ **n.** Physics & Chem. the mathematical product of the separation of the ends of a dipole and the magnitude of the charges.

dip·per /ˈdipər/ ▶ **n. 1** a short-tailed songbird (genus *Cinclus*, family Cinclidae), frequenting fast-flowing streams and able to swim, dive, and walk under water to feed. **2** a ladle or scoop. **3** a person who immerses something in liquid.

dip·py /ˈdipē/ ▶ **adj.** (**dip·pi·er, dip·pi·est**) informal stupid; foolish. [20th C.: of unknown origin.]

dip·so /ˈdipsō/ ▶ **n.** (pl. **-sos**) informal a person suffering from dipsomania; an alcoholic.

dip·so·ma·ni·a /ˌdipsəˈmānēə/ ▶ **n.** alcoholism, specifically in a form characterized by intermittent bouts of craving for alcohol. — **dip·so·ma·ni·ac** /-nēˌak/ **n. dip·so·ma·ni·a·cal** /-məˈnīəkəl/ **adj.** [19th C.: from Gk. *dipso-* (from *dipsa* 'thirst') + **-MANIA**.]

dip·stick /ˈdipˌstik/ ▶ **n. 1** a graduated rod for measuring the depth of a liquid, esp. oil in a vehicle's engine. **2** informal a stupid or inept person.

Dip·ter·a /ˈdiptərə/ Entomol. a large order of insects that comprises the two-winged or true flies, which have the hind wings reduced to form balancing organs (halteres). It includes many biting forms, such as mosquitoes and tsetse flies, that are vectors of disease. ■ [as pl. n.] (**diptera**) insects of this order; flies. — **dip·ter·an n. & adj.** [mod. L. (plural), from Gk. *diptera*, neut. pl. of *dipteros* 'two-winged,' from *di-* 'two' + *pteron* 'wing.']

dip·ter·al /ˈdiptərəl/ ▶ **adj.** Archit. having a double peristyle. [19th C.: from L. *dipteros* (from Gk., from *di-* 'twice' + *pteron* 'wing') + **-AL**.]

dip·ter·ous /ˈdiptərəs/ ▶ **adj. 1** Entomol. of or relating to flies of the order Diptera. **2** Bot. having two winglike appendages.

dip·tych /ˈdiptik/ ▶ **n. 1** a painting, esp. an altarpiece, on two hinged wooden panels that may be closed like a book. **2** an ancient writing tablet consisting of two hinged leaves with waxed inner sides. [17th C.: via late L. from late Gk. *diptukha* 'pair of writing tablets,' based on *di-* 'twice' + *ptukhē* 'a fold.']

dir. ▶ **abbr.** director.

Di·rac /də'räk/, Paul Adrian Maurice (1902–84), English physicist. He described the behavior of the electron. Nobel Prize for Physics (1933, shared with Schrödinger).

dire /dī(ə)r/ ▶ **adj.** (of a situation or event) extremely serious or urgent. ■ (of a warning or threat) presaging disaster. — **dire·ly adv. dire·ness n.** [16th C.: from L. *dirus* 'fearful, threatening.']

di·rect /di'rekt; dī-/ ▶ **adj.** extending or moving from one place to another by the shortest way without changing direction or stopping. ■ without intervening factors or intermediaries. ■ (of a person or their behavior) going straight to the point; frank. ■ (of evidence or proof) bearing immediately and unambiguously upon the facts at issue. ■ (of light or heat) proceeding from a source without being reflected or blocked. ■ (of genealogy) proceeding in continuous succession from parent to child. ■ [attrib.] (of a quotation) taken from someone's words without being changed. ■ complete (used for emphasis). ■ perpendicular to a surface; not oblique. ■ Astron. & Astrol. (of apparent planetary motion) proceeding from west to east in accord with actual motion. ▶ **adv.** with no one or nothing in between. ■ by a straight route or without breaking a journey. ▶ **v.** [trans.] **1** control the operations of; manage or govern. ■ supervise and control (a movie, play, or other production, or the actors in it). ■ (usu. **be directed**) train and conduct (a group of musicians). **2** [with obj. and adverbial of direction] aim (something) in a particular direction or at a particular person. ■ tell or show (someone) how to get somewhere. ■ address or give instructions for the delivery of (a letter or parcel). ■ focus or concentrate (one's attention, efforts, or feelings) on. ■ (**direct something at/to**) address a comment to or aim a criticism at. ■ (**direct something at**) target a product specifically at (someone). ■ archaic guide or advise (someone or their judgment) in a course or decision. **3** [with obj. and infin.] give (someone) an official order or authoritative instruction. — **di·rect·ness n.** [ME: from L. *directus*, past part. of *dirigere*, from *di-* 'distinctly' or *de-* 'down' + *regere* 'put straight.']

di·rect ac·cess ▶ **n.** the facility of retrieving data immediately from any part of a computer file, without having to read the file from the beginning. Compare with RANDOM ACCESS and SEQUENTIAL ACCESS.

di·rect ac·tion ▶ **n.** the use of strikes, demonstrations, or other public forms of protest rather than negotiation to achieve one's demands.

di·rect cur·rent (abbr.: **DC**) ▶ **n.** an electric current flowing in one direction only. Compare with ALTERNATING CURRENT.

di·rect de·pos·it ▶ **n.** the electronic transfer of a payment directly from the account of the payer to the recipient's account.

di·rect di·al·ing ▶ **n.** the facility of making a telephone call without connection by the operator. — **di·rect di·al adj.**

di·rect dis·course ▶ **n.** another term for DIRECT SPEECH.

di·rect-drive ▶ **adj.** [attrib.] denoting or relating to mechanical parts driven directly by a motor, without a belt or other device to transmit power.

di·rect ex·am·i·na·tion ▶ **n.** Law the questioning of a witness by the party that has called that witness to give evidence, in order to support the case that is being made. Also called EXAMINATION-IN-CHIEF. Compare with CROSS-EXAMINE.

di·rec·tion /di'reksHən; dī-/ ▶ **n. 1** a course along which someone or something moves. ■ the course that must be taken in order to reach a destination. ■ a point to or from which a person or thing moves or faces. ■ a general way in which someone or something is developing. ■ general aim or purpose. **2** the management or guidance of someone or something. ■ the work of supervising and controlling the actors and other staff in a movie, play, or other production. ■ (**directions**) instructions on how to reach a destination or about how to do something. ■ an authoritative order or command. [ME (sense 2): from L. *directio(n-)*, from the v. *dirigere* (see DIRECT).]

di·rec·tion·al /di'reksHənl; dī-/ ▶ **adj. 1** relating to or indicating the direction in which someone or something is situated, moving, or developing. **2** having a particular direction of motion, progression, or orientation. ■ relating to, denoting, or designed for the projection, transmission, or reception of light, radio, or sound waves in or from a particular direction or directions. — **di·rec·tion·al·i·ty** /di,reksHə'nalitē; dī-/ **n. di·rec·tion·al·ly adv.**

di·rec·tion find·er ▶ **n.** a special radio receiver with a system of antennas for locating the source of radio signals, used as an aid to navigation.

di·rec·tion·less /di'reksHənlis/ ▶ **adj.** lacking in general aim or purpose: *I feel directionless and miserable.*

di·rec·tive /di'rektiv/ ▶ **n.** an official or authoritative instruction. ▶ **adj.** involving the management or guidance of operations.

di·rect·ly /di'rektlē/ ▶ **adv. 1** without changing direction or stopping. ■ at once; immediately. ■ dated in a little while; soon. **2** with nothing or no one in between. ■ exactly in a specified position. **3** in a frank way. ▶ **conj.** Brit. as soon as: *she fell asleep directly she got into bed.*

di·rect mail ▶ **n.** unsolicited advertising sent to prospective customers through the mail. — **di·rect mail·ing n.**

di·rect mar·ket·ing ▶ **n.** the business of selling products or services directly to the public, e.g., by mail order or telephone selling, rather than through retailers.

di·rect ob·ject ▶ **n.** a noun phrase denoting a person or thing that is the recipient of the action of a transitive verb, for example *the dog* in *Jimmy fed the dog.* Compare with INDIRECT OBJECT.

Di·rec·toire /,direk'twär/ ▶ **adj.** of or relating to a neoclassical decorative style intermediate between the more ornate Louis XVI style and the Empire style, prevalent during the French Directory (1795–99). [18th C.: Fr., from Late L. *directorius*, from *director* 'one who directs, director.']

di·rec·tor /di'rektər/ (abbr.: **dir.**) ▶ **n.** a person who is in charge of an activity, department, or organization. ■ a member of the board of people that manages or oversees the affairs of a business. ■ a person who supervises the actors, camera crew, and other staff for a movie, play, television program, or similar production. — **di·rec·to·ri·al** /di,rek'tôrēəl; ,dīrek-/ **adj. di·rec·tor·ship n.**

di·rec·to·rate /di'rektərit/ ▶ **n.** [treated as sing. or pl.] the board of directors of a company. ■ a section of a government department in charge of a particular activity: *the Directorate of Intelligence.*

di·rec·tor gen·er·al ▶ **n.** (also **di·rec·tor-gen·er·al**) (pl. **di·rec·tors gen·er·al**) esp. Brit. the chief executive of a large organization.

di·rec·tor's chair ▶ **n.** a folding armchair with crossed legs and a canvas seat and back piece.

director s chair

di·rec·to·ry /di'rektərē/ ▶ **n.** (pl. **-ries**) **1** a book listing individuals or organizations alphabetically or thematically with details such as names, addresses, and telephone numbers. ■ Comput. a file that consists solely of a set of other files (which may themselves be directories). **2** esp. hist. a book of directions for the conduct of Christian worship, esp. in Presbyterian and Roman Catholic Churches. **3** (**the Directory**) the French revolutionary government in France 1795–99, comprising two councils and a five-member executive. It maintained an aggressive foreign policy but could not control events at home and was overthrown by Napoleon Bonaparte.

di·rec·to·ry as·sis·tance ▶ **plural n.** a telephone service used to find out someone's telephone number.

di·rec·tress /di'rektris/ (also **di·rec·trice**) ▶ **n.** a female director. [17th C.: from DIRECTOR + -ESS[1]; the var. *directrice* is an adopted Fr. form.]

di·rec·trix /di'rektriks/ ▶ **n.** (pl. **-tri·ces** /-trə,sēz/) Geom. a fixed line used in describing a curve or surface. [18th C.: from med. L., lit. 'directress.']

di·rect speech ▶ **n.** the reporting of speech by repeating the actual words of a speaker, for example *"I'm going," she said.* Contrasted with REPORTED SPEECH.

di·rect tax ▶ **n.** a tax, such as income tax, that is levied on the income or profits of the person who pays it, rather than on goods or services.

dire·ful /'dī(ə)rfəl/ ▶ **adj.** archaic or literary extremely bad; dreadful. — **dire·ful·ly adv.**

dire wolf ▶ **n.** a large wolf (*Canis dirus*) of the Pleistocene epoch that preyed on large mammals.

dirge /dərj/ ▶ **n.** a lament for the dead, esp. one forming part of a funeral rite. ■ a mournful song, piece of music, or poem. — **dirge·ful** /-fəl/ **adj.** [ME: from L. *dirige!* 'direct!']

dir·ham /də'ram/ ▶ **n. 1** the basic monetary unit of Morocco and the United Arab Emirates, equal to 100 centimes in Morocco and 100 fils in the United Arab Emirates. **2** a monetary unit of Libya and Qatar, equal to one thousandth of a dinar in Libya and one hundredth of a riyal in Qatar. [from Arab., from Gk. *drakhmē*, denoting an Attic weight or coin.]

dir·i·gi·ble /'dirijəbəl; də'rijə-/ ▶ **adj.** capable of being steered, guided, or directed. ▶ **n.** a dirigible airship, esp. one with a rigid structure. See illustration at AIRSHIP. [16th C.: from L. *dirigere* 'to direct' + -IBLE.]

di·ri·gisme /'diri,zHizəm; ,diri'zHizəm; ,dērē'zHēsm(ə)/ ▶ **n.** state control of economic and social matters. — **di·ri·giste** /,diri'zHēst; ,dirē-/ **adj.** [1950s: from Fr., from the v. *diriger*, from L. *dirigere* 'to direct.']

dir·i·ment im·ped·i·ment /'dirəmənt/ ▶ **n.** (in ecclesiastical law) a factor that invalidates a marriage, such as the existence of a prior marriage. [19th C.: *diriment* from L. *diriment-* 'interrupting,' from the v. *dirimere.*]

dirk /dərk/ ▶ **n.** a short dagger of a kind formerly carried by Scottish Highlanders. [16th C.: of unknown origin.]

dirn·dl /'dərndl/ ▶ **n. 1** (also **dirndl skirt**) a full, wide skirt with a tight waistband. **2** a woman's dress in the style of Alpine peasant costume, with such a skirt and a close-fitting bodice. [1930s: from south Ger. dial., dimin. of *Dirne* 'girl.']

dirt /dərt/ ▶ **n.** a substance, such as mud or dust, that soils someone or something. ■ loose soil or earth; the ground. ■ [usu. as adj.] earth used to make a surface for a road, floor, or other area of ground. ■ short for DIRT TRACK. ■ informal excrement. ■ a state or quality of uncleanliness. ■ informal gossip, esp. information about someone's activities or private life that could prove damaging if revealed. ■ obscene or sordid material. ■ informal a worthless or contemptible person or thing.

– PHRASES **do someone dirt** informal harm someone's reputation maliciously. **drag the name of someone** (or **something**) **through the dirt** informal give someone or something a bad reputation through bad behavior or damaging revelations. **eat dirt** informal suffer insults or humiliation. [ME: from ON *drit* 'excrement,' an early sense in Engl.]

dirndl 2

dirt bike ▶ n. a motorcycle designed for use on rough terrain, such as unsurfaced roads or tracks, and used esp. in scrambling.

dirt cheap ▶ adv. & adj. informal extremely cheap.

dirt farm·er ▶ n. a farmer who makes a living from a farm, typically without the help of hired labor. — **dirt farm** n.

dirt poor ▶ adv. & adj. extremely poor.

dirt track ▶ n. a course made of rolled cinders or earth for motor or flat racing. — **dirt track·er** n.

dirt·y /ˈdərtē/ ▶ adj. (**dirt·i·er, dirt·i·est**) covered or marked with an unclean substance. ■ causing a person or environment to become unclean. ■ (of a nuclear weapon) producing considerable radioactive fallout. ■ (of a color) not bright, clear, or pure. ■ concerned with sex in an unpleasant or obscene way. ■ [attrib.] informal used to emphasize one's disgust for someone or something. ■ (of an activity) dishonest; dishonorable. ■ (of weather) rough, stormy, and unpleasant. ■ (of popular music) having a distorted or rasping tone. ▶ v. (**dirt·ies, dirt·ied**) [trans.] cover or mark with an unclean substance. ■ cause to feel or appear morally tainted.
– PHRASES **get one's hands dirty** do manual, menial, or other hard work. ■ informal become involved in dishonest or dishonorable activity. **play dirty** informal act in a dishonest or unfair way. **talk dirty** informal speak about sex in a coarse or obscene way. **wash one's dirty laundry in public** see WASH. — **dirt·i·ly** adv. **dirt·i·ness** n.

dirt·y mon·ey ▶ n. money obtained unlawfully or immorally.

dirt·y old man ▶ n. informal an older man who is sexually interested in younger women or girls.

dirt·y pool ▶ n. informal dishonest, unfair, or unsportsmanlike conduct.

dirt·y trick ▶ n. a dishonest or unkind act. ■ (**dirty tricks**) underhanded political or commercial activity designed to discredit an opponent.

dirt·y word ▶ n. an offensive or indecent word. ■ fig. a thing regarded with dislike or disapproval.

dirt·y work ▶ n. activities or tasks that are unpleasant or dishonest and given to someone else to undertake.

dis /dis/ informal ▶ v. (also **diss**) (**dissed, diss·ing**) [trans.] act or speak in a disrespectful way toward. ▶ n. disrespectful talk. [1980s: abbrev. of DISRESPECT.]

dis- ▶ prefix **1** expressing negation: *dislike* | *disquiet.* **2** denoting reversal or absence of an action or state: *dishonor* | *disintegrate.* ■ denoting separation: *discharge* | *disengage.* ■ denoting expulsion: *disbar* | *disinherit.* **3** denoting removal of the thing specified: *disbud* | *dismember.* **4** expressing completeness or intensification of an unpleasant or unattractive action: *discombobulate* | *disgruntled.* [from L., sometimes via OFr. *des-*.]

dis·a·bil·i·ty /ˌdisəˈbilitē/ ▶ n. (pl. **-ties**) a physical or mental condition that limits a person's movements, senses, or activities. ■ a disadvantage or handicap, esp. one imposed or recognized by the law.

dis·a·ble /disˈābəl/ ▶ v. [trans.] (of a disease, injury, or accident) limit (someone) in their movements, senses, or activities. *it's an injury that could disable somebody for life* | [intrans.] *anxiety can disrupt and disable.* ■ put out of action. — **dis·a·ble·ment** n.

dis·a·bled /disˈābəld/ ▶ adj. (of a person) having a physical or mental condition that limits movements, senses, or activities. ■ (of an activity, organization, or facility) specifically designed for or relating to people with such a physical or mental condition.
– USAGE See usage at HANDICAPPED and LEARNING DISABILITY.

dis·a·bled list (abbr.: **DL**) Sports a list of players who are not available for play, owing to injury.

dis·a·buse /ˌdisəˈbyo͞oz/ ▶ v. [trans.] persuade (someone) that an idea or belief is mistaken: *he quickly disabused me of my belief.*

di·sac·cha·ride /dīˈsakəˌrīd/ ▶ n. Chem. any of a class of sugars whose molecules contain two monosaccharide residues.

dis·ac·cord /ˌdisəˈkôrd/ ▶ n. rare lack of agreement or harmony. ▶ v. [intrans.] archaic disagree; be at variance.

dis·ad·van·tage /ˌdisədˈvantij/ ▶ n. an unfavorable circumstance or condition that reduces the chances of success or effectiveness. ▶ v. [trans.] place in an unfavorable position in relation to someone or something else.
– PHRASES **at a disadvantage** in an unfavorable position relative to someone or something else. **to one's disadvantage** so as to cause harm to one's interests or standing.

dis·ad·van·taged /ˌdisədˈvantijd/ ▶ adj. (of a person or area) in unfavorable circumstances, esp. with regard to financial or social opportunities.

dis·ad·van·ta·geous /disˌadvənˈtājəs/ ▶ adj. involving or creating unfavorable circumstances that reduce the chances of success or effectiveness. — **dis·ad·van·ta·geous·ly** adv.

dis·af·fect·ed /ˌdisəˈfektid/ ▶ adj. dissatisfied with the people in authority and no longer willing to support them. — **dis·af·fect·ed·ly** adv.

dis·af·fec·tion /ˌdisəˈfeksʜən/ ▶ n. a state or feeling of being dissatisfied with the people in authority and no longer willing to support them.

dis·af·fil·i·ate /ˌdisəˈfilēˌāt/ ▶ v. [trans.] (of a group or organization) end its official connection with (a subsidiary group). ■ [intrans.] (of a subsidiary group) end such a connection. — **dis·af·fil·i·a·tion** /ˌdisəˌfilēˈāsʜən/ n.

dis·af·firm /ˌdisəˈfərm/ ▶ v. [trans.] Law repudiate; declare void. — **dis·af·fir·ma·tion** /disˌafərˈmāsʜən/ n.

dis·ag·gre·gate /disˈagriˌgāt/ ▶ v. [trans.] separate (something) into its component parts. — **dis·ag·gre·ga·tion** /-ˌagriˈgāsʜən/ n.

dis·a·gree /ˌdisəˈgrē/ ▶ v. (**-a·grees, -a·greed, -a·gree·ing**) [intrans.] **1** have or express a different opinion. ■ (**disagree with**) disapprove of. **2** (of statements or accounts) be inconsistent or fail to correspond. ■ (**disagree with**) (of food, climate, or an experience) have an adverse effect on (someone).

dis·a·gree·a·ble /ˌdisəˈgrēəbəl/ ▶ adj. unpleasant or unenjoyable. ■ unfriendly and bad-tempered. — **dis·a·gree·a·ble·ness** n. **dis·a·gree·a·bly** /-blē/ adv.

dis·a·gree·ment /ˌdisəˈgrēmənt/ ▶ n. lack of consensus or approval. ■ lack of consistency or correspondence.

dis·al·low /ˌdisəˈlou/ ▶ v. [trans.]. (usu. **be disallowed**) refuse to declare valid. — **dis·al·low·ance** /ˌdisəˈlouəns/ n.

dis·am·big·u·ate /ˌdisamˈbigyo͞oˌāt/ ▶ v. [trans.] remove uncertainty of meaning from (an ambiguous sentence, phrase, or other linguistic unit). — **dis·am·big·u·a·tion** /-ˌbigyo͞oˈāsʜən/ n.

dis·ap·pear /ˌdisəˈpi(ə)r/ ▶ v. [intrans.] cease to be visible. ■ cease to exist or be in use. ■ (of a thing) be lost or impossible to find. ■ (of a person) go missing or (in coded political language) be killed.

dis·ap·pear·ance /ˌdisəˈpi(ə)rəns/ ▶ n. [usu. in sing.] an instance or fact of someone or something ceasing to be visible. ■ an instance or fact of someone going missing or (in coded political language) being killed. ■ an instance or fact of something being lost or stolen. ■ the process or fact of something ceasing to exist or be in use.

dis·ap·point /ˌdisəˈpoint/ ▶ v. [trans.] fail to fulfill the hopes or expectations of (someone). ■ prevent (hopes or expectations) from being realized. [ME: from OFr. *desappointer.*]

dis·ap·point·ed /ˌdisəˈpointid/ ▶ adj. (of a person) sad or displeased because someone or something has failed to fulfill one's hopes or expectations. ■ (of hopes or expectations) prevented from being realized. — **dis·ap·point·ed·ly** adv.

dis·ap·point·ing /ˌdisəˈpointiɴɢ/ ▶ adj. failing to fulfill someone's hopes or expectations. — **dis·ap·point·ing·ly** adv.

dis·ap·point·ment /ˌdisəˈpointmənt/ ▶ n. the feeling of sadness or displeasure caused by the nonfulfillment of one's hopes or expectations.

dis·ap·pro·ba·tion /disˌaprəˈbāsʜən/ ▶ n. strong disapproval, typically on moral grounds.

dis·ap·prov·al /ˌdisəˈpro͞ovəl/ ▶ n. possession or expression of an unfavorable opinion.

dis·ap·prove /ˌdisəˈpro͞ov/ ▶ v. [intrans.] have or express an unfavorable opinion about something. ■ [trans.] officially refuse to agree to. — **dis·ap·prov·er** n. **dis·ap·prov·ing·ly** adv.

dis·arm /disˈärm/ ▶ v. [trans.] **1** take a weapon or weapons away from (a person, force, or country). ■ [intrans.] (of a country or force) give up or reduce its armed forces or weapons. ■ remove the fuse from (a bomb), making it safe. ■ deprive (a ship, etc.) of its means of defense. **2** allay the hostility or suspicions of. ■ deprive of the power to injure or hurt. [ME: from OFr. *desarmer.*]

dis·ar·ma·ment /disˈärməmənt/ ▶ n. the reduction or withdrawal of military forces and weapons.

dis·arm·ing /disˈärmiɴɢ/ ▶ adj. (of manner or behavior) having the effect of allaying suspicion or hostility, esp. through charm. — **dis·arm·ing·ly** adv.

dis·ar·range /ˌdisəˈrānj/ ▶ v. [trans.] (often **be disarranged**) make (something) untidy or disordered. — **dis·ar·range·ment** n.

dis·ar·ray /ˌdisəˈrā/ ▶ n. a state of disorganization or untidiness. ▶ v. [trans.] **1** throw (someone or something) into a state of disorganization or untidiness. **2** literary strip (someone) of clothing. [ME: from Anglo-Norman Fr. *dissairay.*]

dis·ar·tic·u·late /ˌdisärˈtikyəˌlāt/ ▶ v. [trans.] separate (bones) at the joints. ■ break up and disrupt the logic of (an argument or opinion). — **dis·ar·tic·u·la·tion** /-ˌtikyəˈlāsʜən/ n.

dis·as·sem·ble /ˌdisəˈsembəl/ ▶ v. [trans.] (often **be disassembled**) take (something) to pieces. ■ Comput. translate (a program) from machine code into a symbolic language. — **dis·as·sem·bly** /-blē/ n.

dis·as·sem·bler /ˌdisəˈsemb(ə)lər/ ▶ n. Comput. a program for converting machine code into a low-level symbolic language.

dis·as·so·ci·ate /ˌdisəˈsōsʜēˌāt; -ˈsōsē-/ ▶ v. another term for DISSOCIATE. — **dis·as·so·ci·a·tion** /ˌdisəˌsōsʜēˈāsʜən; -ˌsōsē-/ n.

dis·as·ter /diˈzastər/ ▶ n. a sudden event, such as an accident or a natural catastrophe, that causes great damage or loss of life. ■ [as adj.] denoting a genre of films that use natural or accidental catastrophe as the mainspring of plot and setting. ■ an event or fact that has unfortunate consequences. ■ informal a person, act, or thing that is a failure.
– PHRASES **be a recipe for disaster** be extremely likely to have unfortunate consequences. [16th C.: from Ital. *disastro* 'ill-starred event,' from *dis-* (expressing negation) + *astro* 'star' (from L. *astrum*).]

dis·as·ter ar·e·a ▶ n. an area in which a major disaster has recently occurred. ■ [in sing.] informal a place, situation, person, or activity regarded as chaotic, ineffectual, or failing in some fundamental respect.

dis·as·trous /diˈzastrəs/ ▶ adj. causing great damage. ■ informal highly unsuccessful. — **dis·as·trous·ly** adv.

dis·a·vow /ˌdisəˈvou/ ▶ v. [trans.] deny any responsibility or support for. — **dis·a·vow·al** /-ˈvouəl/ n. [ME: from OFr. *desavouer.*]

dis·band /dis'band/ ▶v. [trans.] (usu. **be disbanded**) cause (an organized group) to break up. ■ [intrans.] (of an organized group) break up and stop functioning as an organization. — **dis·band·ment** n. [16th C.: from obs. Fr. *desbander*.]

dis·bar /dis'bär/ ▶v. (**-barred, -bar·ring**) [trans.] **1** (usu. **be disbarred**) expel (a lawyer) from the Bar, so that they no longer have the right to practice law. **2** exclude (someone) from something. — **dis·bar·ment** n.

dis·be·lief /ˌdisbə'lēf/ ▶n. inability or refusal to accept that something is true or real. ■ lack of faith in something.

dis·be·lieve /ˌdisbə'lēv/ ▶v. [trans.] be unable to believe (someone or something). ■ [intrans.] have no faith in God, spiritual beings, or a religious system. — **dis·be·liev·er** n. **dis·be·liev·ing·ly** adv.

dis·bud /dis'bəd/ ▶v. (**-bud·ded, -bud·ding**) [trans.] remove superfluous or unwanted buds from (a plant). ■ Farming remove the horn buds from (a young animal).

dis·bur·den /dis'bərdn/ ▶v. [trans.] relieve (someone or something) of a burden or responsibility. ■ archaic relieve (someone's mind) of worries and anxieties.

dis·burse /dis'bərs/ ▶v. [trans.] (often **be disbursed**) pay out (money from a fund). — **dis·burs·al** /-səl/ n. **dis·burse·ment** n. **dis·burs·er** n. [16th C.: from OFr. *desbourser*, from *des-* (expressing removal) + *bourse* 'purse.']

disc ▶n. var. of DISK.

dis·calced /dis'kalst/ ▶adj. denoting or belonging to one of several strict orders of Catholic friars or nuns who go barefoot or wear only sandals. [17th C.: based on L. *discalceatus*, from *dis-* (expressing removal) + *calceatus* (from *calceus* 'shoe').]

dis·card ▶v. /dis'kärd/ [trans.] get rid of (someone or something) as no longer useful or desirable. ■ (in bridge, whist, and similar card games) play (a card that is neither of the suit led nor a trump), when one is unable to follow suit. ▶n. /'diskärd/ a person or thing rejected as no longer useful or desirable. ■ (in bridge, whist, and similar card games) a card played which is neither of the suit led nor a trump, when one is unable to follow suit. — **dis·card·a·ble** /dis'kärdəbəl/ adj. [16th C. (orig. in the sense 'reject (a playing card)'): from DIS- (expressing removal) + the n. CARD[1].]

dis·car·nate /dis'kärnit; -nāt/ ▶adj. (of a person or being) not having a physical body. [19th C.: from DIS- 'without' + L. *caro, carn-* 'flesh' or late L. *carnatus* 'fleshy.']

disc brake ▶n. a type of vehicle brake employing the friction of pads against a disc that is attached to the wheel.

disc cam·er·a ▶n. a camera in which the frames of film are formed on a disc, rather than on a long strip.

dis·cern /di'sərn/ ▶v. [trans.] perceive or recognize (something). ■ distinguish (someone or something) with difficulty by sight or with the other senses. — **dis·cern·er** n. **dis·cern·i·ble** adj. **dis·cern·i·bly** /-əblē/ adv. [ME: via OFr. from L. *discernere*, from *dis-* 'apart' + *cernere* 'to separate.']

dis·cern·ing /di'sərniNG/ ▶adj. having or showing good judgment. — **dis·cern·ing·ly** adv.

dis·cern·ment /di'sərnmənt/ ▶n. the ability to judge well.

dis·charge ▶v. /dis'CHärj/ [trans.] **1** (often **be discharged**) tell (someone) officially that they can or must leave, in particular: ■ send (a patient) out of the hospital because they are judged fit to go home. ■ dismiss or release (someone) from a job, esp. from service in the armed forces or police. ■ release (someone) from the custody or restraint of the law. ■ relieve (a juror or jury) from serving in a case. ■ Law relieve (a bankrupt) of liability. ■ release (a party) from a contract or obligation. **2** allow (a liquid, gas, or other substance) to flow out from where it has been confined: *industrial plants discharge highly toxic materials into rivers* | [intrans.] *the overflow should discharge in an obvious place.* ■ (of an orifice or diseased tissue) emit (pus, mucus, or other liquid): *the swelling will discharge pus* | [intrans.] *the eyes began to discharge.* ■ (often **be discharged**) Physics release or neutralize the electric charge of (an electric field, battery, or other object): *the electrostatic field that builds up can be discharged* | [intrans.] *batteries discharge slowly.* ■ (of a person) fire (a gun or missile): *discharge as many barrels as you wish.* ■ [intrans.] (of a firearm) be fired: *the gun discharged.* ■ (of a person) allow (an emotion) to be released. ■ unload (cargo or passengers) from a ship: *the ferry was discharging passengers* | [intrans.] *ships were waiting to discharge.* **3** do all that is required to fulfill (a responsibility) or perform (a duty). ■ pay off (a debt or other financial claim). **4** Law (of a judge or court) cancel (an order of a court). ■ cancel (a contract) because of completion or breach. ▶n. /'disˌCHärj/ **1** the action of discharging someone from a hospital or from a job. ■ an act of releasing someone from the custody or restraint of the law. ■ Law the action of relieving a bankrupt from residual liability. **2** the action of allowing a liquid, gas, or other substance to flow out from where it is confined. ■ the quantity of material allowed to flow out in such a way. ■ the emission of pus, mucus, or other liquid from an orifice or from diseased tissue. ■ Physics the release of electricity from a charged object. ■ a flow of electricity through air or other gas, esp. when accompanied by emission of light. ■ the action of firing a gun or missile. ■ the action of unloading a ship of its cargo or passengers. **3** the action of doing all that is required to fulfill a responsibility or perform a duty. ■ the payment of a debt or other financial claim. **4** Law the action of canceling an order of a court. — **dis·charge·a·ble** /dis'CHärjəbəl/ adj. **dis·charg·er** /dis'CHärjər/ n. [ME: from OFr. *descharger*, from late L. *discarricare* 'unload,' from *dis-* (expressing reversal) + *carricare* 'to load' (see CHARGE).]

dis·charge lamp /'disˌCHärj/ ▶n. a lamp in which the light is produced by a discharge tube.

dis·charge tube /'disˌCHärj/ ▶n. a tube containing charged electrodes and filled with a gas in which ionization is induced by an electric field. The gas molecules emit light as they return to the ground state.

dis·ci·ple /di'sīpəl/ ▶n. a personal follower of Jesus during his life, esp. one of the twelve Apostles. ■ a follower or student of a teacher, leader, or philosophy. ▶v. [trans.] guide (someone) in becoming a follower of Jesus or another leader. — **dis·ci·ple·ship** n. **dis·cip·u·lar** /-'sipyələr/ adj. [OE, from L. *discipulus* 'learner,' from *discere* 'learn.']

Dis·ci·ples of Christ a Protestant denomination, originating among American Presbyterians in the early 19th century and found chiefly in the US, which rejects creeds and regards the Bible as the only basis of faith.

dis·ci·pli·nar·i·an /ˌdisəplə'ne(ə)rēən/ ▶n. a person who believes in or practices firm discipline.

dis·ci·pli·nar·y /'disəpləˌnerē/ ▶adj. concerning or enforcing discipline.

dis·ci·pline /'disəplin/ ▶n. **1** the practice of training people to obey rules or a code of behavior, using punishment to correct disobedience. ■ the controlled behavior resulting from such training. ■ activity or experience that provides mental or physical training. ■ a system of rules of conduct. **2** a branch of knowledge, typically one studied in higher education. ▶v. [trans.] train (someone) to obey rules or a code of behavior, using punishment to correct disobedience. ■ (often **be disciplined**) punish or rebuke (someone) formally for an offense. ■ (**discipline oneself to do something**) train oneself to do something in a controlled and habitual way. — **dis·ci·plin·a·ble** adj. **dis·ci·pli·nal** /-nəl/ adj. [ME: via OFr. from L. *disciplina* 'instruction, knowledge,' from *discipulus* (see DISCIPLE).]

dis·ci·plined /'disəplind/ ▶adj. showing a controlled form of behavior or way of working.

disc jock·ey (also **disk jock·ey**) ▶n. a person who introduces and plays recorded popular music, esp. on radio or at a disco.

dis·claim /dis'klām/ ▶v. [trans.] refuse to acknowledge; deny. ■ Law renounce a legal claim to (a property or title). [ME: from Anglo-Norman Fr. *desclamer*, from *des-* (expressing reversal) + *clamer* 'to claim' (see CLAIM).]

dis·claim·er /dis'klāmər/ ▶n. a statement that denies something, esp. responsibility. ■ Law an act of repudiating another's claim or renouncing one's own.

dis·close /dis'klōz/ ▶v. [trans.] make (secret or new information) known. ■ allow (something) to be seen, esp. by uncovering it. — **dis·clos·er** n. [ME: from OFr. *desclos-*, stem of *desclore*, based on L. *claudere* 'to close.']

dis·clo·sure /dis'klōZHər/ ▶n. the action of making new or secret information known. ■ a fact, esp. a secret, that is made known.

dis·co /'diskō/ informal ▶n. (pl. **-cos**) **1** (also **di·sco·theque** /'diskəˌtek/) a club or party at which people dance to pop music. **2** pop music intended mainly for dancing to at discos, typically soul-influenced and melodic with a regular bass beat and popular particularly in the late 1970s. ▶v. (**-coes, -coed**) [intrans.] attend or dance at such a club or party. [1960s (orig. US): abbrev.]

dis·cog·ra·phy /dis'kägrəfē/ ▶n. (pl. **-phies**) a descriptive catalog of musical recordings, particularly those of a particular performer or composer. ■ all of a performer's or composer's recordings considered as a body of work. ■ the study of musical recordings and compilation of descriptive catalogs. — **dis·cog·ra·pher** n. [1930s: from DISC + -GRAPHY, on the pattern of *biography*.]

dis·coid /'diskoid/ ▶adj. tech. shaped like a disc. ▶n. a thing that is shaped like a disc, particularly a type of ancient stone tool. — **dis·coi·dal** /dis'koidl/ adj.

dis·col·or /dis'kələr/ ▶v. [intrans.] become a different, less attractive color. ■ [trans.] change or spoil the color of. — **dis·col·or·a·tion** /-ˌkələ'rāSHən/ n. [ME: from OFr. *descolorer* or med. L. *discolorare*, from *des-*, *dis-* (expressing reversal) + L. *colorare* 'to color.']

dis·com·bob·u·late /ˌdiskəm'bäbyəˌlāt/ ▶v. [trans.] humorous disconcert or confuse (someone). [19th C.: prob. based on DISCOMPOSE or DISCOMFIT.]

dis·com·fit /dis'kəmfit/ ▶v. (**-fit·ed, -fit·ing**) [trans.] (usu. **be discomfited**) make (someone) feel uneasy or embarrassed. — **dis·com·fi·ture** /dis'kəmfiˌCHər/ n. [ME: from OFr. *desconfit*, past part. of *desconfire*, based on L. *dis-* (expressing reversal) + *conficere* 'put together' (see CONFECTION).]

dis·com·fort /dis'kəmfərt/ ▶n. lack of physical comfort. ■ slight pain. ■ a state of mental unease. ▶v. [trans.] make (someone) feel uneasy. ■ [often as adj.] (**discomforting**) cause (someone) slight pain. [ME: from OFr. *desconforter* (v.), *desconfort* (n.), from *des-* (expressing reversal) + *conforter* 'to comfort' (see COMFORT).]

dis·com·mode /ˌdiskə'mōd/ ▶v. [trans.] formal cause (someone) trouble or inconvenience. — **dis·com·mo·di·ous** /-'mōdēəs/ adj. **dis·com·mod·i·ty** /-'mäditē/ n. [18th C.: from obs. Fr. *discommoder*, var. of *incommoder* (see INCOMMODE).]

dis·com·pose /ˌdiskəm'pōz/ ▶v. [trans.] [often as adj.] (**discomposed**) disturb or agitate (someone). — **dis·com·po·sure** /-'pōZHər/ n.

dis·con·cert /ˌdiskən'sərt/ ▶v. [trans.] disturb the composure of; unsettle. — **dis·con·cert·ed·ly** adv. **dis·con·cer·tion** /-'sərSHən/ n. **dis·con·cert·ment** n. (rare). [17th C.: from obs. Fr. *desconcerter*, from *des-* (expressing reversal) + *concerter* 'bring together.']

dis·con·cert·ing /ˌdiskən'sərtiNG/ ▶adj. causing one to feel unsettled. — **dis·con·cert·ing·ly** adv.

dis·con·firm /ˌdiskənˈfərm/ ▶**v.** [trans.] show that (a belief or hypothesis) is not or may not be true. — **dis·con·fir·ma·tion** /disˌkänfərˈmāsʜən/ **n.** **dis·con·fir·ma·to·ry** /-məˌtôrē/ **adj.**

dis·con·form·i·ty /ˌdiskənˈfôrmitē/ ▶**n.** (pl. **-ties**) **1** lack of conformity. **2** Geol. a break in a sedimentary sequence that does not involve a difference of inclination between the strata on each side of the break. Compare with UNCONFORMITY.

dis·con·nect /ˌdiskəˈnekt/ ▶**v.** [trans.] break the connection of or between. ■ take (an electrical device) out of action by detaching it from a power supply. ■ interrupt or terminate (a telephone conversation) by breaking the connection. ■ (usu. **be disconnected**) terminate the connection of (a household) to water, electricity, gas, or telephone, typically because of nonpayment of bills. — **dis·con·nec·tion** /-ˈneksʜən/ **n.**

dis·con·nect·ed /ˌdiskəˈnektid/ ▶**adj.** having a connection broken. ■ [predic.] (of a person) lacking contact with reality. ■ (of speech, writing, or thought) lacking a logical sequence; incoherent. — **dis·con·nect·ed·ly adv. dis·con·nect·ed·ness n.**

dis·con·so·late /disˈkänsəlit/ ▶**adj.** without consolation or comfort; unhappy. ■ (of a place or thing) causing or showing a complete lack of comfort; cheerless. — **dis·con·so·late·ly adv. dis·con·so·late·ness n. dis·con·so·la·tion** /-ˌkänsəˈlāsʜən/ **n.** [ME: from med. L. *disconsolatus*, from *dis-* (expressing reversal) + L. *consolatus* (past part. of *consolari* 'to console').]

dis·con·tent /ˌdiskənˈtent/ ▶**n.** lack of contentment; dissatisfaction with one's circumstances. ■ a person who is dissatisfied, typically with the prevailing social or political situation. — **dis·con·tent·ment n.**

dis·con·tent·ed /ˌdiskənˈtentid/ ▶**adj.** dissatisfied, esp. with one's circumstances. — **dis·con·tent·ed·ly adv. dis·con·tent·ed·ness n.**

dis·con·tin·ue /ˌdiskənˈtinyo͞o/ ▶**v.** (**-tin·ues, -tin·ued, -tin·u·ing**) [trans.] cease doing or providing (something), typically something provided on a regular basis. ■ (usu. **be discontinued**) stop making (a particular product). ■ cease taking (medication or a medical treatment). ■ cease taking (a newspaper or periodical) or paying (a subscription). — **dis·con·tin·u·ance** /-yo͞oəns/ **n. dis·con·tin·u·a·tion** /-ˌtinyo͞oˈāsʜən/ **n.**

dis·con·ti·nu·i·ty /ˌdiskäntn'(y)o͞oitē/ ▶**n.** (pl. **-ties**) a distinct break in physical continuity or sequence in time. ■ a sharp difference of characteristics between parts of something. ■ Math. a point at which a function is discontinuous or undefined.

dis·con·tin·u·ous /ˌdiskənˈtinyo͞oəs/ ▶**adj.** having intervals or gaps. ■ Math. (of a function) having at least one discontinuity, and whose differential coefficient may become infinite. — **dis·con·tin·u·ous·ly adv.**

dis·cord /ˈdiskôrd/ ▶**n. 1** disagreement between people. ■ lack of agreement or harmony between things. **2** Music lack of harmony between notes sounding together. ■ a chord that (in conventional harmonic terms) is regarded as unpleasing or requiring resolution by another. ■ any interval except a unison, an octave, a perfect fifth or fourth, a major or minor third and sixth, or their octaves. ■ a single note dissonant with another. ▶**v.** [intrans.] archaic (of people) disagree. ■ (of things) be different or in disharmony: ***views apt to discord with those of the administration.*** [ME: from OFr. *descord* (n.), *descorder* (v.), from L. *discordare*, from *discors* 'discordant,' from *dis-* (expressing negation, reversal) + *cor, cord-* 'heart.']

dis·cord·ant /disˈkôrdnt/ ▶**adj. 1** disagreeing or incongruous. ■ characterized by quarreling and conflict. **2** (of sounds) harsh and jarring because of a lack of harmony.
– PHRASES **strike a discordant note** appear strange and out of place.
— **dis·cord·ance n. dis·cor·dan·cy** /-dnsē/ **n. dis·cord·ant·ly adv.**

dis·co·theque /ˈdiskəˌtek/ ▶**n.** another term for DISCO (sense 1). [1950s: from Fr. *discothèque*, orig. 'record library,' on the pattern of *bibliothèque* 'library.']

dis·count ▶**n.** /ˈdisˌkount/ a deduction from the usual cost of something, typically given for prompt or advance payment or to a special category of buyers. ■ Finance a percentage deducted from the face value of a bill of exchange or promissory note when it changes hands before the due date. ▶**v.** /ˈdisˌkount; disˈkount/ [trans.] **1** deduct an amount from (the usual price of something). ■ reduce (a product or service) in price. ■ buy or sell (a bill of exchange) before its due date at less than its maturity value. **2** regard (a possibility, fact, or person) as being unworthy of consideration because it lacks credibility. ▶**adj.** /ˈdisˌkount/ (of a store or business) offering goods for sale at discounted prices. ■ at a price lower than the usual one.
– PHRASES **at a discount** below the nominal or usual price. Compare with *AT A PREMIUM* (see PREMIUM). — **dis·count·a·ble** /disˈkountəbəl/ **adj. dis·count·er n.** [17th C.: from obs. Fr. *descompte* (n.), *descompter* (v.), or from Ital. *(di)scontare*, both from med. L. *discomputare*, from L. *dis-* (expressing reversal) + *computare* (see COMPUTE).]

dis·coun·te·nance /disˈkountn-əns/ ▶**v.** [trans.] (usu. **be discountenanced**) **1** refuse to approve of (something). **2** disturb the composure of.

dis·count house ▶**n. 1** another term for DISCOUNT STORE. **2** Brit. a company that buys and sells bills of exchange.

dis·count rate ▶**n.** Finance **1** the minimum interest rate set by the Federal Reserve for lending to other banks. **2** a rate used for discounting bills of exchange.

dis·count store ▶**n.** a store that sells goods at less than the normal retail price.

dis·cour·age /disˈkərij; -ˈkə-rij/ ▶**v.** [trans.] cause (someone) to lose confidence or enthusiasm. ■ prevent or seek to prevent (something) by showing disapproval or creating difficulties. ■ persuade (someone) against an action. — **dis·cour·age·ment n. dis·cour·ag·er n. dis·cour·ag·ing·ly adv.** [ME: from OFr. *descouragier*, from *des-* (expressing reversal) + *corage* 'courage.']

dis·course ▶**n.** /ˈdisˌkôrs/ written or spoken communication or debate. ■ a formal discussion of a topic in speech or writing. ■ Ling. a connected series of utterances; a text or conversation. ▶**v.** /disˈkôrs/ [intrans.] speak or write authoritatively about a topic: ***she discoursed on the history of Europe.*** ■ engage in conversation: ***he spent an hour discoursing with his supporters in the courtroom.*** [ME: from OFr. *discours*, from L. *discursus* 'running to and fro,' from the v. *discurrere*, from *dis-* 'away' + *currere* 'to run.']

dis·cour·te·ous /disˈkərtēəs/ ▶**adj.** showing rudeness and a lack of consideration for other people. — **dis·cour·te·ous·ly adv. dis·cour·te·ous·ness n.**

dis·cour·te·sy /disˈkərtəsē/ ▶**n.** (pl. **-sies**) rude and inconsiderate behavior. ■ an impolite act or remark.

dis·cov·er /disˈkəvər/ ▶**v.** [trans.] **1** find (something or someone) unexpectedly or in the course of a search. ■ become aware of (a fact or situation). ■ be the first to find or observe (a place, substance, or scientific phenomenon). ■ perceive the attractions of (an activity or subject) for the first time. ■ be the first to recognize the potential of (an actor, singer, or musician). **2** archaic divulge (a secret). ■ disclose the identity of (someone). ■ display (a quality or feeling). — **dis·cov·er·a·ble adj. dis·cov·er·er n.** [ME: from OFr. *descovrir*, from late L. *discooperire*, from L. *dis-* (expressing reversal) + *cooperire* 'cover completely' (see COVER).]

dis·cov·er·y /disˈkəvərē/ ▶**n.** (pl. **-ies**) **1** the action or process of discovering or being discovered. ■ a person or thing discovered. **2** Law the compulsory disclosure, by a party to an action, of relevant documents referred to by the other party.

dis·cred·it /disˈkredit/ ▶**v.** (**-cred·it·ed, -cred·it·ing**) [trans.] harm the good reputation of (someone or something). ■ cause (an idea or piece of evidence) to seem false or unreliable. ▶**n.** loss or lack of reputation or respect. ■ a person or thing that is a source of disgrace.

dis·cred·it·a·ble /disˈkreditəbəl/ ▶**adj.** tending to bring harm to a reputation. — **dis·cred·it·a·bly adv.**

dis·creet /disˈkrēt/ ▶**adj.** (**-creet·er, -creet·est**) careful and circumspect in one's speech or actions, esp. to avoid causing offense or to gain an advantage. ■ intentionally unobtrusive. — **dis·creet·ly adv. dis·creet·ness n.** [ME: from OFr. *discret*, from L. *discretus* 'separate,' past part. of *discernere* 'discern.']

dis·crep·an·cy /disˈkrepənsē/ ▶**n.** (pl. **-cies**) a lack of compatibility or similarity between two or more facts. — **dis·crep·ant** /-pənt/ **adj.** [17th C.: from L. *discrepantia*, from *discrepare* 'be discordant,' from *dis-* 'apart, away' + *crepare* 'to creak.']

dis·crete /disˈkrēt/ ▶**adj.** individually separate and distinct. — **dis·crete·ly adv. dis·crete·ness n.** [ME: from L. *discretus* 'separate.']

dis·cre·tion /disˈkresʜən/ ▶**n. 1** the quality of behaving or speaking in such a way as to avoid causing offense or revealing private information. **2** the freedom to decide what should be done in a particular situation. [ME: via OFr. from L. *discretio(n-)* 'separation,' from *discernere* (see DISCERN).]

dis·cre·tion·ar·y /disˈkresʜəˌnerē/ ▶**adj.** available for use at the discretion of the user. ■ denoting or relating to investment funds placed with a broker or manager who has discretion to invest them on the client's behalf.

dis·cre·tion·ar·y in·come ▶**n.** income remaining after deduction of taxes, other mandatory charges, and expenditure on necessary items. Compare with DISPOSABLE INCOME.

dis·crim·i·na·ble /disˈkrimənəbəl/ ▶**adj.** able to be discriminated; distinguishable. — **dis·crim·i·na·bil·i·ty** /disˌkrimənəˈbilitē/ **n. dis·crim·i·na·bly adv.**

dis·crim·i·nant /disˈkrimənənt/ ▶**n.** an agent or characteristic that enables things, people, or classes to be distinguished from one another. ■ Math. a function of the coefficients of a polynomial equation whose value gives information about the roots of the polynomial. See also DISCRIMINANT FUNCTION.

dis·crim·i·nant func·tion ▶**n.** Stat. a function of several variates used to assign items into one of two or more groups. The function for a particular set of items is obtained from measurements of the variates of items that belong to a known group.

dis·crim·i·nate /disˈkriməˌnāt/ ▶**v.** [intrans.] **1** recognize a distinction; differentiate. ■ [trans.] perceive or constitute the difference in or between. **2** make an unjust or prejudicial distinction in the treatment of different categories of people or things, esp. on the grounds of race, sex, or age. — **dis·crim·i·nate·ly** /-nitlē/ **adv. dis·crim·i·na·tive** /-ˌnātiv; -nətiv/ **adj.** [17th C.: from L. *discriminat-* 'distinguished between,' from the verb *discriminare*, from *discrimen* 'distinction,' from the v. *discernere* (see DISCERN).]

dis·crim·i·nat·ing /disˈkriməˌnātiɴɢ/ ▶**adj.** (of a person) having or showing refined taste or good judgment. — **dis·crim·i·nat·ing·ly adv.**

dis·crim·i·na·tion /disˌkriməˈnāsʜən/ ▶**n. 1** the unjust or prejudicial treatment of different categories of people or things, esp. on the grounds of race, age, or sex. **2** recognition and understanding of the difference between one thing and another. ■ the ability to discern what is of high quality; good judgment or taste. ■ Psychol. the ability to distinguish between different stimuli. **3** Electron. the selection of a signal having a required characteristic, such as frequency or amplitude, by means of a discriminator that rejects all unwanted signals.

dis·crim·i·na·tor /dis'krimə,nātər/ ▶ **n.** **1** a characteristic that enables things, people, or classes to be distinguished from one another. **2** Electron. a circuit or device that only produces an output when the input exceeds a fixed value. ■ a circuit that converts a frequency-modulated signal into an amplitude-modulated one.

dis·crim·i·na·to·ry /dis'krimənə,tôrē/ ▶ **adj.** making or showing an unfair or prejudicial distinction between different categories of people or things, esp. on the grounds of race, age, or sex.

dis·cur·sive /dis'kərsiv/ ▶ **adj.** **1** digressing from subject to subject. ■ (of a style of speech or writing) fluent and expansive rather than formulaic or abbreviated. **2** of or relating to discourse or modes of discourse. **3** Philos., archaic proceeding by argument or reasoning rather than by intuition. — **dis·cur·sive·ly adv. dis·cur·sive·ness n.** [16th C.: from med. L. *discursivus*, from L. *discurs-*, lit. 'gone hastily to and fro,' from the v. *discurrere* (see **DISCOURSE**).]

dis·cus /'diskəs/ ▶ **n.** (pl. **-cus·es**) a heavy thick-centered disk thrown by an athlete, in ancient Greek games or in modern field events. ■ the athletic event or sport of throwing the discus. [via L. from Gk. *diskos*.]

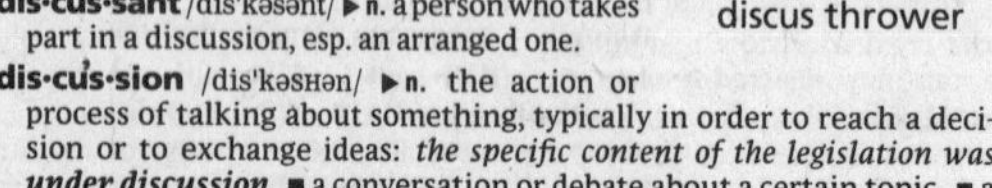

discus thrower

dis·cuss /dis'kəs/ ▶ **v.** [trans.] talk about (something) with another person or group of people. ■ talk or write about (a topic) in detail, taking into account different ideas and opinions. — **dis·cuss·a·ble adj. dis·cuss·er n.** [ME: from L. *discuss-* 'dashed to pieces,' later 'investigated,' from the v. *discutere*, from *dis-* 'apart' + *quatere* 'shake.']

dis·cus·sant /dis'kəsənt/ ▶ **n.** a person who takes part in a discussion, esp. an arranged one.

dis·cus·sion /dis'kəsHən/ ▶ **n.** the action or process of talking about something, typically in order to reach a decision or to exchange ideas: *the specific content of the legislation was under discussion.* ■ a conversation or debate about a certain topic. ■ a detailed treatment of a particular topic in speech or writing.

dis·dain /dis'dān/ ▶ **n.** the feeling that someone or something is unworthy of one's consideration or respect; contempt. ▶ **v.** [trans.] consider to be unworthy of one's consideration. ■ refuse or reject (something) out of feelings of pride or superiority. [ME: from OFr. *desdeignier*, based on L. *dedignari*, from *de-* (expressing reversal) + *dignari* 'consider worthy' (from *dignus* 'worthy').]

dis·dain·ful /dis'dānfəl/ ▶ **adj.** showing or feeling contempt or lack of respect. — **dis·dain·ful·ly adv. dis·dain·ful·ness n.**

dis·ease /di'zēz/ ▶ **n.** a disorder of structure or function in a human, animal, or plant, esp. one that produces specific signs or symptoms or that affects a specific location and is not simply a direct result of physical injury. ■ fig. a particular quality, habit, or disposition regarded as adversely affecting a person or group of people. [ME: from OFr. *desaise* 'lack of ease,' from *des-* (expressing reversal) + *aise* 'ease.']

dis·eased /di'zēzd/ ▶ **adj.** suffering from disease. ■ fig. abnormal and corrupt.

dis·e·con·o·my /,disi'känəmē/ ▶ **n.** (pl. **-mies**) an economic disadvantage such as an increase in cost arising from an increase in the size of an organization.

dis·em·bark /,disem'bärk/ ▶ **v.** [intrans.] leave a ship, aircraft, or other vehicle. — **dis·em·bar·ka·tion** /dis,embär'kāsHən/ **n.** [16th C.: from Fr. *désembarquer*, Sp. *desembarcar*, or Ital. *disimbarcare*, based on L. *barca* 'ship's boat.']

dis·em·bar·rass /,disem'barəs/ ▶ **v.** (**disembarrass oneself of/from**) free oneself of (a burden or nuisance). ■ [trans.] rare make (someone or something) free from embarrassment. — **dis·em·bar·rass·ment n.**

dis·em·bod·ied /,disem'bädēd/ ▶ **adj.** separated from or existing without the body. ■ (of a sound) lacking any obvious physical source.

dis·em·bod·y /,disem'bädē/ ▶ **v.** (**-bod·ies, -bod·ied**) [trans.] separate or free (something) from its concrete form. — **dis·em·bod·i·ment n.**

dis·em·bogue /,disem'bōg/ ▶ **v.** (**-bogues, -bogued, -bogu·ing**) [intrans.] literary (of a river or stream) emerge or be discharged in quantity; pour out. [16th C.: from Sp. *desembocar*, from *des-* (expressing reversal) + *embocar* 'run into a creek or strait' (based on *boca* 'mouth').]

dis·em·bow·el /,disem'bouəl/ ▶ **v.** (**-bow·eled, -bow·el·ing**; Brit. **-bow·elled, -bow·el·ling**) [trans.] cut open and remove the internal organs of. — **dis·em·bow·el·ment n.**

dis·em·pow·er /,disem'pouər/ ▶ **v.** [trans.] make (a person or group) less powerful or confident. — **dis·em·pow·er·ment n.**

dis·en·chant /,disen'cHant/ ▶ **v.** [trans.] (usu. **be disenchanted**) free (someone) from illusion; disappoint. — **dis·en·chant·ing·ly adv. dis·en·chant·ment n.** [16th C.: from Fr. *désenchanter*, from *dés-* (expressing reversal) + *enchanter* (see **ENCHANT**).]

dis·en·cum·ber /,disen'kəmbər/ ▶ **v.** [trans.] free from or relieve of an encumbrance.

dis·en·dow /,disen'dou/ ▶ **v.** [trans.] deprive (someone or something) of an endowment. — **dis·en·dow·ment n.**

dis·en·fran·chise /,disen'franCHīz/ (also **dis·fran·chise** /dis'franCHīz/) ▶ **v.** [trans.] deprive (someone) of the right to vote. ■ [as adj.] (**disenfranchised**) deprived of power; marginalized. ■ deprive (someone) of a right or privilege. ■ archaic deprive (someone) of the rights and privileges of a free inhabitant of a borough, city, or country. — **dis·en·fran·chise·ment n.**

dis·en·gage /,disen'gāj/ ▶ **v.** [trans.] detach, free, loosen, or separate (something). ■ detach oneself; get loose. ■ [intrans.] become released. ■ remove (troops) from an area of conflict.

dis·en·gaged /,disen'gājd/ ▶ **adj.** emotionally detached.

dis·en·gage·ment /,disen'gājmənt/ ▶ **n.** **1** the action or process of withdrawing from involvement in a particular activity, situation, or group. ■ the withdrawal of military forces or the renunciation of military or political influence in a particular area. ■ the process of separating or releasing something or of becoming separated or released. ■ archaic the breaking off of an engagement to be married. **2** emotional detachment; objectivity.

dis·en·tail·ment /,disen'tālmənt/ ▶ **n.** Law the action of freeing property from entail. — **dis·en·tail v.**

dis·en·tan·gle /,disen'taNGgəl/ ▶ **v.** [trans.] free (something or someone) from an entanglement; extricate. ■ remove knots or tangles from (wool, rope, or hair). — **dis·en·tan·gle·ment n.**

dis·en·thrall /,disen'THrôl/ (Brit. **dis·en·thral**) ▶ **v.** [trans.] literary set free. — **dis·en·thrall·ment n.**

dis·e·qui·lib·ri·um /dis,ēkwə'librēəm/ ▶ **n.** a loss or lack of balance or stability. ■ a loss or lack of equilibrium in relation to supply, demand, and prices.

dis·es·tab·lish /,disi'stablisH/ ▶ **v.** [trans.] (usu. **be disestablished**) deprive (an organization, esp. a country's national church) of its official status. — **dis·es·tab·lish·ment n.**

dis·es·teem /,disi'stēm/ dated ▶ **n.** low esteem or regard. ▶ **v.** [trans.] have a low opinion of.

di·seuse /dē'zo͞oz/ ▶ **n.** a female entertainer who performs monologues. [19th C.: Fr., lit. 'talker,' fem. of *diseur*, from *dire* 'to say.']

dis·fa·vor /dis'fāvər/ (Brit. **dis·fa·vour**) ▶ **n.** disapproval or dislike. ■ the state of being disliked. ▶ **v.** [trans.] regard or treat (someone or something) with disfavor.

dis·fig·ure /dis'figyər/ ▶ **v.** [trans.] spoil the attractiveness of. — **dis·fig·u·ra·tion** /-,figyə'rāsHən/ **n. dis·fig·ure·ment n.** [ME: from OFr. *desfigurer*, based on L. *figura* 'figure.']

dis·fran·chise /dis'franCHīz/ ▶ **v.** another term for **DISENFRANCHISE**.

dis·gorge /dis'gôrj/ ▶ **v.** [trans.] cause to pour out. ■ (of a building or vehicle) discharge (the occupants). ■ yield or give up (funds, esp. funds that have been dishonestly acquired). ■ eject (food) from the throat or mouth. ■ [intrans.] (of a river) empty into a sea. — **dis·gorge·ment n.** [15th C.: from OFr. *desgorger*, from *des-* (expressing removal) + *gorge* 'throat.']

dis·grace /dis'grās/ ▶ **n.** loss of reputation or respect, esp. as the result of a dishonorable action. ■ [in sing.] a person or thing regarded as shameful and unacceptable: *he's a disgrace to the legal profession.* ▶ **v.** [trans.] bring shame or discredit on (someone or something). ■ (**be disgraced**) fall from favor or lose a position of power or honor. [16th C.: via Fr. from Ital. *disgrazia*, from *dis-* (expressing reversal) + L. *gratia* 'grace.']

dis·grace·ful /dis'grāsfəl/ ▶ **adj.** shockingly unacceptable. — **dis·grace·ful·ly adv.**

dis·grun·tled /dis'grəntld/ ▶ **adj.** angry or dissatisfied. — **dis·grun·tle·ment n.** [17th C.: from **DIS-** (as an intensifier) + dial. *gruntle* 'utter little grunts,' from **GRUNT**.]

dis·guise /dis'gīz/ ▶ **v.** [trans.] give (someone or oneself) a different appearance in order to conceal one's identity. ■ make (something) unrecognizable by altering its appearance, sound, taste, or smell. ■ conceal the nature or existence of (a feeling or situation). ▶ **n.** a means of altering one's appearance or concealing one's identity. ■ the state of having altered one's appearance in order to conceal one's identity. ■ the concealing of one's true intentions or feelings. — **dis·guise·ment n.** (archaic). [ME: from OFr. *desguisier*.]

dis·gust /dis'gəst/ ▶ **n.** a feeling of revulsion or profound disapproval aroused by something unpleasant or offensive. ▶ **v.** [trans.] (often **be disgusted**) cause (someone) to feel revulsion or profound disapproval. — **dis·gust·ed·ly adv.** [16th C.: from early mod. Fr. *desgoust* or Ital. *disgusto*, from L. *dis-* (expressing reversal) + *gustus* 'taste.']

dis·gust·ful /dis'gəstfəl/ ▶ **adj.** old-fashioned term for **DISGUSTING**.

dis·gust·ing /dis'gəstiNG/ ▶ **adj.** arousing revulsion or strong indignation. — **dis·gust·ing·ly adv. dis·gust·ing·ness n.**

dish /disH/ ▶ **n.** **1** a shallow, typically flat-bottomed container for cooking or serving food: *an ovenproof dish.* ■ the food contained or served in such a container. ■ a particular variety or preparation of food served as part of a meal. ■ (**the dishes**) all the items that have been used in the preparation, serving, and eating of a meal. ■ [usu. with adj.] a shallow, concave receptacle, esp. one intended to hold a particular substance. ■ (also **dish aerial**) a bowl-shaped radio antenna. See also **SATELLITE DISH**. **2** informal a sexually attractive person. ■ (**one's dish**) dated a thing that one particularly enjoys or does well. ▶ **v.** [trans.] (**dish something out/up**) put (food) onto a plate or plates before a meal. ■ (**dish something out**) dispense something in a casual or indiscriminate way. ■ (**dish it out**) informal subject others to criticism or punishment. ■ [intrans.] informal gossip or share information, esp. information of an intimate or scandalous nature.

– PHRASES **dish the dirt** informal reveal or spread scandalous information or gossip.
– PHRASAL VERBS **dish off** pass to a teammate, esp. in basketball. — **dish·ful** /-ˌfo͝ol/ n. (pl. **-fuls**). [OE *disc* 'plate, bowl,' based on L. *discus* (see DISCUS).]

dis·ha·bille /ˌdisəˈbēl/ (also **des·ha·bille**) ▶ n. the state of being only partly or scantily clothed. [17th C.: from Fr. *déshabillé* 'undressed.']

dish an·ten·na ▶ n. a receiver or transmitter of electromagnetic energy, esp. microwaves or radiowaves, that consists of a reflector shaped like a shallow dish.

dis·har·mo·ny /disˈhärmənē/ ▶ n. lack of harmony or agreement. — **dis·har·mo·ni·ous** /ˌdis-härˈmōnēəs/ adj. **dis·har·mo·ni·ous·ly** /ˌdis-härˈmōnēəslē/ adv.

dish·cloth /ˈdisHˌklôTH/ ▶ n. a cloth for washing or drying dishes.

dish·cloth gourd ▶ n. another term for LOOFAH.

dis·heart·en /disˈhärtn/ ▶ v. [trans.] (often **be disheartened**) cause (someone) to lose determination or confidence. — **dis·heart·en·ing·ly** adv. **dis·heart·en·ment** n.

dished /disHt/ ▶ adj. having the shape of a dish; concave.

di·shev·eled /diˈsHevəld/ (Brit. **di·shev·elled**) ▶ adj. (of a person's hair, clothes, or appearance) untidy; disordered. — **di·shev·el** /-ˈsHevəl/ v. **di·shev·el·ment** n. [ME: from obs. *dishevely*, from OFr. *deschevele*, past part. of *descheveler* (based on *chevel* 'hair,' from L. *capillus*).]

dis·hon·est /disˈänist/ ▶ adj. behaving or prone to behave in an untrustworthy or fraudulent way. ■ intended to mislead or cheat. — **dis·hon·est·ly** adv.

dis·hon·es·ty /disˈänəstē/ ▶ n. (pl. **-ties**) deceitfulness shown in someone's character or behavior. ■ a fraudulent or deceitful act.

dis·hon·or /disˈänər/ (Brit. **dis·hon·our**) ▶ n. a state of shame or disgrace. ▶ v. [trans.] **1** bring shame or disgrace on. ■ archaic violate the chastity of (a woman); rape. **2** fail to observe or respect (an agreement or principle). ■ refuse to accept or pay (a check or a promissory note).

dis·hon·or·a·ble /disˈänərəbəl/ (Brit. **dis·hon·our·a·ble**) ▶ adj. bringing shame or disgrace on someone or something. — **dis·hon·or·a·ble·ness** n. **dis·hon·or·a·bly** adv.

dis·hon·or·a·ble dis·charge ▶ n. the dismissal of someone from the armed forces as a result of criminal or morally unacceptable actions.

dish·pan /ˈdisHˌpan/ ▶ n. a large basin in which dishes are washed.

dish·pan hands ▶ plural n. red, rough, or chapped hands caused by sensitivity to or excessive use of household detergents or other cleaning agents.

dish·rag /ˈdisHˌrag/ ▶ n. a dishcloth.

dish tow·el ▶ n. a cloth for drying washed dishes, utensils, and glasses.

dish·wash·er /ˈdisHˌwôsHər; -ˌwäsHər/ ▶ n. **1** a machine for washing dishes automatically. **2** a person employed to wash dishes.

dish·wa·ter /ˈdisHˌwôtər; -ˌwätər/ ▶ n. dirty water in which dishes have been washed.
– PHRASES **dull as dishwater** see DULL.

dish·y /ˈdisHē/ ▶ adj. (**dish·i·er**, **dish·i·est**) informal sexually attractive. ■ scandalous or gossipy.

dis·il·lu·sion /ˌdisəˈlo͞ozHən/ ▶ n. disappointment resulting from the discovery that something is not as good as one believed it to be. ▶ v. [trans.] cause (someone) to realize that a belief or an ideal is false. — **dis·il·lu·sion·ment** n.

dis·il·lu·sioned /ˌdisəˈlo͞ozHənd/ ▶ adj. disappointed in someone or something that one discovers to be less good than one had believed.

dis·in·cen·tive /ˌdisinˈsentiv/ ▶ n. a factor, esp. a financial disadvantage, that tends to discourage people from doing something.

dis·in·cli·na·tion /disˌinkləˈnāsHən; -ˌiNGklə-/ ▶ n. [in sing.] a reluctance or lack of enthusiasm.

dis·in·clined /ˌdisinˈklīnd/ ▶ adj. [predic., with infin.] unwilling; reluctant.

dis·in·cor·po·rate /ˌdisinˈkôrpəˌrāt/ ▶ v. [trans.] dissolve (a corporate body).

dis·in·fect /ˌdisinˈfekt/ ▶ v. [trans.] clean (something) with a disinfectant in order to destroy bacteria. — **dis·in·fec·tion** /-ˈfeksHən/ n. [16th C.: from Fr. *désinfecter*, from *dés-* (expressing reversal) + *infecter* 'to infect.']

dis·in·fect·ant /ˌdisinˈfektənt/ ▶ n. a chemical liquid that destroys bacteria. ▶ adj. causing the destruction of bacteria.

dis·in·fest /ˌdisinˈfest/ ▶ v. [trans.] rid (someone or something) of infesting vermin. — **dis·in·fes·ta·tion** /-ˌinfeˈstāsHən/ n.

dis·in·fla·tion /ˌdisinˈflāsHən/ ▶ n. reduction in the rate of inflation. — **dis·in·fla·tion·ar·y** /-ˌnerē/ adj.

dis·in·for·ma·tion /disˌinfərˈmāsHən/ ▶ n. false information that is intended to mislead, esp. that released by a government to a rival power or the media.

dis·in·gen·u·ous /ˌdisinˈjenyo͞oəs/ ▶ adj. not candid or sincere, typically by pretending that one knows less about something than one really does. — **dis·in·gen·u·ous·ly** adv. **dis·in·gen·u·ous·ness** n.

dis·in·her·it /ˌdisinˈherit/ ▶ v. (**-her·it·ed**, **-her·it·ing**) [trans.] change one's will or take other steps to prevent (someone) from inheriting one's property. — **dis·in·her·i·tance** /-ˈheritəns/ n. [ME: from DIS- (expressing removal) + *inherit* in the obs. sense 'make someone an heir.']

dis·in·hib·it /ˌdisinˈhibit/ ▶ v. (**-hib·it·ed**, **-hib·it·ing**) [trans.] make (someone or something) less inhibited. — **dis·in·hi·bi·tion** /disˌinhiˈbisHən/ n.

dis·in·te·grate /disˈintəˌgrāt/ ▶ v. [intrans.] break up into parts, typically as the result of impact or decay. ■ (of a society, family, or other social group) weaken or break apart. ■ informal deteriorate mentally or physically. ■ Physics undergo or cause to undergo disintegration at a subatomic level. — **dis·in·te·gra·tive** /-ˌgrātiv/ adj. **dis·in·te·gra·tor** /-ˌgrātər/ n.

dis·in·te·gra·tion /disˌintəˈgrāsHən/ ▶ n. the process of losing cohesion. ■ the process of coming to pieces. ■ breakdown of the personality. ■ Physics a process in which a nucleus or other subatomic particle emits a smaller particle or divides into smaller particles.

dis·in·ter /ˌdisinˈtər/ ▶ v. (**-terred**, **-ter·ring**) [trans.] dig up (something that has been buried, esp. a corpse). ■ discover (something that is well hidden). — **dis·in·ter·ment** n.

dis·in·ter·est /disˈint(ə)rist/ ▶ n. **1** the state of not being influenced by personal involvement in something; impartiality. **2** lack of interest in something.

dis·in·ter·est·ed /disˈintəˌrestid; -tristid/ ▶ adj. **1** not influenced by considerations of personal advantage. **2** having or feeling no interest in something. — **dis·in·ter·est·ed·ly** adv. **dis·in·ter·est·ed·ness** n. [17th C.: past part. of the rare verb *disinterest* 'rid of interest or concern,' from DIS- (expressing removal) + the v. INTEREST.]

dis·in·ter·me·di·a·tion /ˌdisintərˌmēdēˈāsHən/ ▶ n. reduction in the use of banks and savings institutions as intermediaries in the borrowing and investment of money, in favor of direct involvement in the securities market.

dis·in·vest /ˌdisinˈvest/ ▶ v. [intrans.] withdraw or reduce an investment: *the industry began to disinvest, and share prices have fallen* | [trans.] *a move to disinvest shares.* — **dis·in·vest·ment** n.

dis·in·vite /ˌdisinˈvīt/ ▶ v. [trans.] withdraw or cancel an invitation to (someone).

dis·jec·ta mem·bra /disˈjektə ˈmembrə/ ▶ plural n. scattered fragments, esp. of written work. [L., alt. of *disjecti membra poetae* (used by Horace) 'limbs of a dismembered poet.']

dis·join /disˈjoin/ ▶ v. separate; take or come apart. [ME: from OFr. *desjoindre*, from L. *disjungere*, from *dis-* (expressing reversal) + *jungere* 'to join.']

dis·joint /disˈjoint/ ▶ v. [trans.] disturb the cohesion or organization of. ■ dated take apart at the joints. ▶ adj. Math. (of two or more sets) having no elements in common. [ME: from OFr. *desjoint* 'separated,' from the v. *desjoindre* (see DISJOIN).]

dis·joint·ed /disˈjointid/ ▶ adj. lacking a coherent sequence or connection. — **dis·joint·ed·ly** adv. **dis·joint·ed·ness** n.

dis·junct /disˈjəNGkt/ ▶ adj. disjoined and distinct from one another. ■ of or relating to the movement of a melody from one note to another by a leap. ▶ n. /ˈdisˌjəNGkt/ **1** Logic each of the terms of a disjunctive proposition. **2** Gram. another term for SENTENCE ADVERB.

dis·junc·tion /disˈjəNGksHən/ ▶ n. **1** the process or an act of disjoining; separation. ■ a lack of correspondence or consistency. **2** Logic the relationship between two distinct alternatives. ■ a statement expressing this relationship (esp. one using the word "or"). [ME: from L. *disjunctio(n-)*, from *disjungere* 'disjoin' (see DISJUNCT).]

dis·junc·tive /disˈjəNGktiv/ ▶ adj. **1** lacking connection. **2** Gram. (of a conjunction) expressing a choice between two mutually exclusive possibilities, for example *or* in *she asked if he was going or staying.* Compare with COPULATIVE. ■ Logic (of a proposition) expressing alternatives. ▶ n. Gram. a disjunctive conjunction or other word. ■ Logic a disjunctive proposition. — **dis·junc·tive·ly** adv.

dis·junc·ture /disˈjəNGkCHər/ ▶ n. a separation or disconnection.

disk /disk/ (also **disc**) ▶ n. **1** a flat, thin, round object: *heavy metal disks the size of hockey pucks* | *onion soup ladled over a disk of cheese.* ■ an information storage device for a computer in the shape of a round flat plate that can be rotated to give access to all parts of the surface. The data may be stored either magnetically (in a **magnetic disk**) or optically (in an **optical disk** such as a CD-ROM). ■ (**disc**) short for COMPACT DISC. ■ (**disc**) dated a phonograph record. ■ (**discs**) one of the suits in some tarot packs, corresponding to coins in others. **2** a shape or surface that is round and flat in appearance. **3** a roundish, flattened part in an animal or plant, in particular: ■ (**disc** or **in·ter·ver·te·bral disc**) a layer of cartilage separating adjacent vertebrae in the spine. ■ Bot. (in a composite flowerhead of the daisy family) a close-packed cluster of disk florets in the center, forming the yellow part of the flowerhead. — **disk·less** adj. [17th C.: from Fr. *disque* or L. *discus* (see DISCUS).]

disk drive ▶ n. a device that allows a computer to read from and write to computer disks.

disk·ette /disˈket/ ▶ n. another term for FLOPPY DISK.

disk flo·ret ▶ n. Bot. (in a composite flowerhead of the daisy family) any of a number of small, tubular, and usually fertile florets that form the disk. In rayless plants such as the tansy, the flowerhead is composed entirely of disk florets. Compare with RAY FLORET.

disk har·row ▶ n. a harrow with cutting edges consisting of a row of concave disks set at an oblique angle.

disk jock·ey ▶ n. var. of DISC JOCKEY.

disk op·er·at·ing sys·tem ▶ n. see DOS.

dis·like /dis'līk/ ▶ v. [trans.] feel distaste for or hostility toward. ▶ n. a feeling of distaste or hostility. ■ a thing to which one feels aversion. — **dis·lik·a·ble** (also **dis·like·a·ble**) adj.

dis·lo·cate /dis'lōkāt; 'dislō,kāt/ ▶ v. [trans.] disturb the normal arrangement or position of (something, typically a joint in the body). ■ (often **be dislocated**) disturb the organization of; disrupt. ■ (often **be dislocated**) move from its proper place or position. [16th C.: prob. a back-form. from DISLOCATION.]

dis·lo·ca·tion /,dislō'kāshən/ ▶ n. disturbance from a proper, original, or usual place or state. ■ injury or disability caused when the normal position of a joint or other part of the body is disturbed. ■ Crystallog. a displacement of part of a crystal lattice structure. [ME: from OFr., or from med. L. *dislocatio(n-)*, from the v. *dislocare* 'put out of place,' based on L. *locare* 'to place.']

dis·lodge /dis'läj/ ▶ v. [trans.] remove from an established or fixed position. — **dis·lodge·a·ble** adj. **dis·lodg·ment** (also **dis·lodge·ment**) n. [ME: from OFr. *deslogier*, from *des-* (expressing reversal) + *logier* 'encamp,' from *loge* (see LODGE).]

dis·loy·al /dis'loiəl/ ▶ adj. failing to be loyal to a person, country, or body to which one has obligations. ■ (of an action, speech, or thought) demonstrating a lack of loyalty. — **dis·loy·al·ly** adv. **dis·loy·al·ty** /-tē/ n.

dis·mal /'dizməl/ ▶ adj. depressing; dreary. ■ (of a person or a mood) gloomy. ■ informal pitifully or disgracefully bad. — **dis·mal·ly** adv. **dis·mal·ness** n. [ME: from earlier *dismal* (n.), denoting the two days in each month that in med. times were believed to be unlucky, from Anglo-Norman Fr. *dis mal*, from med. L. *dies mali* 'evil days.']

dis·mal sci·ence ▶ n. [in sing.] (usu. **the dismal science**) humorous economics.

Dis·mal Swamp another name for GREAT DISMAL SWAMP.

dis·man·tle /dis'mantl/ ▶ v. [trans.] (often **be dismantled**) take to pieces. — **dis·man·tle·ment** n. **dis·man·tler** n. [16th C.: from OFr. *desmanteler*, from *des-* (expressing reversal) + *manteler* 'fortify' (from L. *mantellum* 'cloak').]

dis·mast /dis'mast/ ▶ v. [trans.] break or topple the mast or masts of (a ship).

dis·may /dis'mā/ ▶ v. [trans.] (usu. **be dismayed**) cause (someone) to feel consternation and distress. ▶ n. consternation and distress, typically that caused by something unexpected. [ME: from OFr., based on L. *dis-* (expressing negation) + the Gmc. base of MAY[1].]

dis·mem·ber /dis'membər/ ▶ v. [trans.] cut off the limbs of (a person or animal). ■ partition or divide up (a territory or organization). — **dis·mem·ber·ment** n. [ME: from OFr. *desmembrer*, based on L. *dis-* 'apart' + *membrum* 'limb.']

dis·miss /dis'mis/ ▶ v. [trans.] order or allow to leave; send away. ■ discharge from employment or office. ■ treat as unworthy of serious consideration. ■ deliberately cease to think about. ■ [intrans.] (of a group assembled under someone's authority) disperse. ■ Law refuse further hearing to (a case). ■ (in sports) defeat or end an opponent's turn. — **dis·miss·al** /-əl/ n. **dis·miss·i·ble** adj. [ME: from med. L. *dismiss-*, var. of L. *dimiss-* 'sent away,' from the v. *dimittere*.]

dis·mis·sive /dis'misiv/ ▶ adj. feeling or showing that something is unworthy of consideration. — **dis·mis·sive·ly** adv. **dis·mis·sive·ness** n.

dis·mount /dis'mount/ ▶ v. **1** [intrans.] alight from a horse, bicycle, or other thing that one is riding. ■ [trans.] cause to fall or alight. **2** [trans.] remove (something) from its support. ▶ n. Gymnastics a move in which a gymnast jumps off an apparatus or completes a floor exercise.

Dis·ney /'diznē/, Walt (1901–66), US cartoonist and producer; full name *Walter Elias Disney*. He debuted his most famous character, Mickey Mouse, in 1928 and produced hundreds of animated shorts and feature-length movies, live-action movies, wildlife documentaries, and television shows. His theme park Disneyland (1955) spawned Disney-trademarked theme parks around the world.

Dis·ney·land ▶ n. a theme park in Anaheim, California, that opened in 1955. ■ a large, bustling place filled with colorful attractions. ■ a place of fantasy or make-believe.

Dis·ney World an amusement park in Lake Buena Vista, Florida. Formally **Walt Disney World**.

dis·o·be·di·ence /,disə'bēdēəns/ ▶ n. failure or refusal to obey rules or someone in authority.

dis·o·be·di·ent /,disə'bēdēənt/ ▶ adj. refusing to obey rules or someone in authority. — **dis·o·be·di·ent·ly** adv.

dis·o·bey /,disə'bā/ ▶ v. [trans.] fail to obey (rules, a command, or someone in authority). — **dis·o·bey·er** n.

dis·o·blige /,disə'blīj/ ▶ v. [trans.] offend (someone) by not acting in accordance with their wishes. [16th C.: from Fr. *désobliger*, based on L. *obligare* 'oblige.']

dis·o·blig·ing /,disə'blījiNG/ ▶ adj. deliberately unhelpful; uncooperative.

di·so·my /dī'sōmē/ ▶ n. Genet. the condition of having a chromosome represented twice in a chromosomal complement. — **di·so·mic** adj. [20th C.: from DI-[1] 'two' + -SOME[3] + -Y[3].]

dis·or·der /dis'ôrdər/ ▶ n. a state of confusion. ■ the disruption of peaceful and law-abiding behavior. ■ Med. a disruption of normal physical or mental functions; a disease or abnormal condition. ▶ v. [trans.] [usu. as adj.] (**disordered**) disrupt the systematic functioning or neat arrangement of. ■ Med. disrupt the healthy or normal functioning of. [15th C.: alt. of earlier *disordain*, from OFr. *desordener*, based on L. *ordinare* 'ordain.']

dis·or·der·ly /dis'ôrdərlē/ ▶ adj. lacking organization; untidy. ■ involving or contributing to a breakdown of peaceful and law-abiding behavior. — **dis·or·der·li·ness** n.

dis·or·der·ly con·duct ▶ n. Law unruly behavior constituting a minor offense.

dis·or·der·ly house ▶ n. Law, archaic a brothel.

dis·or·gan·ize /dis'ôrgə,nīz/ ▶ v. [trans.] disrupt the systematic order or functioning of. — **dis·or·gan·i·za·tion** /-,ôrgənə'zāshən/ n.

dis·or·gan·ized /dis'ôrgə,nīzd/ ▶ adj. not properly planned and controlled. ■ (of a person) unable to plan one's activities efficiently.

dis·o·ri·ent /dis'ôrē,ent/ ▶ v. [trans.] [often as adj.] (**disoriented**) make (someone) lose their sense of direction. ■ make (someone) feel confused. [17th C.: from Fr. *désorienter* 'turn from the east.']

dis·o·ri·en·tate /dis'ôrēən,tāt/ ▶ v. esp. Brit. another term for DISORIENT. — **dis·o·ri·en·ta·tion** /-,ôrēən'tāshən/ n.

dis·own /dis'ōn/ ▶ v. [trans.] refuse to acknowledge or maintain any connection with. — **dis·own·er** n. **dis·own·ment** n.

dis·par·age /di'sparij/ ▶ v. [trans.] regard or represent as being of little worth. — **dis·par·age·ment** n. **dis·par·ag·ing·ly** adv. [ME: from OFr. *desparagier* 'marry someone of unequal rank,' based on L. *par* 'equal.']

dis·pa·rate /'dispərit; di'sparit/ ▶ adj. essentially different in kind; not allowing comparison. ■ containing elements very different from one another. ▶ n. (**disparates**) archaic things so unlike that there is no basis for comparison. — **dis·pa·rate·ly** adv. **dis·pa·rate·ness** n. [ME: from L. *disparatus* 'separated,' from the v. *disparare*, from *dis-* 'apart' + *parare* 'to prepare.']

dis·par·i·ty /di'sparitē/ ▶ n. (pl. **-ties**) a great difference. [16th C.: from Fr. *disparité*, from late L. *disparitas*, based on L. *paritas* 'parity.']

dis·pas·sion·ate /dis'pashənit/ ▶ adj. not influenced by strong emotion, and so able to be rational and impartial. — **dis·pas·sion** /-shən/ n. **dis·pas·sion·ate·ly** adv. **dis·pas·sion·ate·ness** n.

dis·patch /dis'pach/ (also **des·patch**) ▶ v. [trans.] **1** send off to a destination or for a purpose. **2** deal with (a task, problem, or opponent) quickly and efficiently. ■ kill. ▶ n. **1** the sending of someone or something to a destination or for a purpose. ■ speed in action. **2** an official report on state or military affairs. ■ a report sent in by a newspaper's correspondent from a faraway place. **3** the killing of someone or something. — **dis·patch·er** n. [16th C.: from Italian *dispacciare* or Spanish *despachar* 'expedite,' from *dis-*, *des-* (expressing reversal) + the base of Ital. *impacciare*, Sp. *empachar* 'hinder.']

dis·patch box ▶ n. (also **dispatch case**) a container for dispatches, esp. official state or military documents.

dis·pel /dis'pel/ ▶ v. (**-pelled**, **-pel·ling**) [trans.] make (a doubt, feeling, or belief) disappear. ■ drive (something) away; scatter. — **dis·pel·ler** n. [ME: from L. *dispellere*, from *dis-* 'apart' + *pellere* 'to drive.']

dis·pen·sa·ble /dis'pensəbəl/ ▶ adj. able to be replaced or done without; superfluous. — **dis·pen·sa·bil·i·ty** /-,pensə'bilitē/ n.

dis·pen·sa·ry /dis'pensərē/ ▶ n. (pl. **-ries**) **1** a room where medicines are prepared and provided. **2** a clinic provided by public or charitable funds.

dis·pen·sa·tion /,dispən'sāshən; -pen-/ ▶ n. **1** exemption from a rule or usual requirement. ■ permission to be exempted from the laws or observances of a church. **2** a system of order, government, or organization of a nation, community, etc., esp. as existing at a particular time. ■ (in Christian theology) a divinely ordained order prevailing at a particular period of history. ■ archaic an act of divine providence. **3** the action of distributing or supplying something. — **dis·pen·sa·tion·al** /-shənl/ adj.

dis·pense /dis'pens/ ▶ v. **1** [trans.] distribute or provide (a service or information) to a number of people. ■ (of a machine) supply (a product or cash). ■ (of a pharmacist) make up and give out (medicine) according to a doctor's prescription. **2** [intrans.] (**dispense with**) manage without; get rid of. ■ give special exemption from (a law or rule). ■ [trans.] grant (someone) an exemption from a religious obligation.

– PHRASES **dispense with someone's services** dismiss someone from a job. [ME: via OFr. from L. *dispensare* 'continue to weigh out or disburse,' from the v. *dispendere*, based on *pendere* 'weigh.']

dis·pens·er /dis'pensər/ ▶ n. a person or thing that dispenses something. ■ [often with adj.] an automatic machine or container that is designed to release a specific amount of something.

dis·per·sal /dis'pərsəl/ ▶ n. the action or process of distributing things or people over a wide area. ■ the splitting up of a group or gathering of people, causing them to leave in different directions. ■ the splitting up and selling off of a collection of artifacts or books.

dis·per·sant /dis'pərsənt/ ▶ n. a liquid or gas used to disperse small particles in a medium.

dis·perse /dis'pərs/ ▶ v. [trans.] distribute or spread over a wide area. ■ go or cause to go in different directions or to different destinations. ■ cause (gas, smoke, mist, or cloud) to thin out and eventually disappear. ■ [intrans.] thin out and disappear. ■ Physics divide (light) into constituents of different wavelengths. ■ Chem. distribute (small particles) uniformly in a medium. ▶ adj. [attrib.] Chem. denoting a phase dispersed in another phase, as in a colloid. — **dis·pers·er** n. **dis·pers·i·ble** adj. **dis·per·sive** /-siv/ adj. [ME: from L. *dispers-* 'scattered,' from the v. *dispergere*, from *dis-* 'widely' + *spargere* 'scatter, strew.']

dis·per·sion /dis'pərzhən; -shən/ ▶ n. the action or process of distributing things or people over a wide area. ■ the state of being dispersed over a wide area. ■ Ecol. the pattern of distribution of individuals within a habitat. ■ (also **the Dispersion**) another term for DIASPORA. ■ a mixture of one substance dispersed in another medium. ■ Physics the separation of white light into colors, or the separation of any radiation according to wavelength. ■ Stat. the extent to which values of a variable differ from a fixed value such as the mean.

dis·pir·it /di'spirit/ ▶v. [trans.] (often **be dispirited**) cause (someone) to lose enthusiasm or hope. — **dis·pir·it·ed·ly** adv. **dis·pir·it·ed·ness** n. **dis·pir·it·ing·ly** adv.

dis·place /dis'plās/ ▶v. [trans.] take over the place, position, or role of (someone or something). ■ cause (something) to move from its proper or usual place. ■ (usu. **be displaced**) force (someone) to leave their home, typically because of war, persecution, or natural disaster. ■ remove (someone) from a job or position of authority against their will. [16th C.: from OFr. *desplacer*.]

dis·placed per·son ▶n. a person who is forced to leave their home country because of war, persecution, or natural disaster; a refugee.

dis·place·ment /dis'plāsmənt/ ▶n. **1** the moving of something from its place or position. ■ the removal of someone or something by someone or something else that takes their place. ■ the enforced departure of people from their homes, typically because of war, persecution, or natural disaster. ■ the amount by which a thing is moved from its normal position. **2** the occupation by a submerged body or part of a body of a volume that would otherwise be occupied by a fluid. ■ the amount or weight of fluid that would fill such a volume in the case of a floating ship, used as a measure of the ship's size. ■ tech. the volume swept by a reciprocating system, as in a pump or engine. **3** Psychoanal. the unconscious transfer of an intense emotion from its original object to another one. **4** Physics the component of an electric field due to free separated charges, regardless of any polarizing effects. ■ the vector representing such a component. ■ the flux density of such an electric field.

dis·place·ment ton ▶n. see TON[1] (sense 1).

dis·play /dis'plā/ ▶v. [trans.] make a prominent exhibition of (something) in a place where it can be easily seen. ■ (of a computer or other device) show (information) on a screen. ■ give a conspicuous demonstration of (a quality, emotion, or skill). ■ [intrans.] (of a male bird, reptile, or fish) engage in a specialized pattern of behavior that is intended to attract a mate. ▶n. **1** a performance, show, or event intended for public entertainment. ■ a collection of objects arranged for public viewing. ■ a notable or conspicuous demonstration of a particular type of behavior, emotion, or skill. ■ conspicuous or flashy exhibition; ostentation. ■ a specialized pattern of behavior by the males of some species of birds, reptiles, and fish that is intended to attract a mate. ■ Print. the arrangement and choice of type in a style intended to attract attention. **2** an electronic device for the visual presentation of data. ■ the process or facility of presenting data on a computer screen or other device. ■ the data shown on a computer screen or other device. — **dis·play·er** n. [ME: from OFr. *despleier*, from L. *displicare* 'scatter, disperse.']

dis·play ad ▶n. a large advertisement, esp. in a newspaper or magazine, that features eye-catching type or illustrations.

dis·play type ▶n. large or eye-catching type used for headings or advertisements.

dis·please /dis'plēz/ ▶v. [trans.] make (someone) feel annoyed or dissatisfied. — **dis·pleas·ing·ly** adv. [ME: from OFr. *desplaisir*, from *des-* (expressing reversal) + *plaisir* 'to please,' from L. *placere*.]

dis·pleas·ure /dis'plezнər/ ▶n. a feeling of annoyance or disapproval. ▶v. [trans.] archaic annoy; displease. [ME: from OFr. *desplaisir* (see DISPLEASE).]

dis·port /dis'pôrt/ ▶v. [intrans.] archaic humorous enjoy oneself unrestrainedly; frolic: *a painting of lords and ladies **disporting themselves** by a lake.* ▶n. diversion from work or serious matters; recreation or amusement. ■ archaic a pastime, game, or sport. [ME: from OFr. *desporter*, from *des-* 'away' + *porter* 'carry' (from L. *portare*).]

dis·pos·a·ble /dis'pōzəbəl/ ▶adj. **1** (of an article) intended to be used once and then thrown away. ■ (of a person or idea) able to be dispensed with; easily dismissed. **2** (chiefly of financial assets) readily available for the owner's use as required. ▶n. an article designed to be thrown away after use. — **dis·pos·a·bil·i·ty** /-ˌpōzə'bilitē/ n.

dis·pos·a·ble in·come ▶n. income remaining after deduction of taxes and other mandatory charges, available to be spent or saved as one wishes. Compare with DISCRETIONARY INCOME.

dis·pos·al /dis'pōzəl/ ▶n. **1** the action or process of throwing away or getting rid of something. ■ (also **dis·pos·er**) informal an electrically operated device fitted to the waste pipe of a kitchen sink for grinding up food waste. **2** the sale of shares, property, or other assets. **3** the arrangement or positioning of something.
– PHRASES **at one's disposal** available for one to use whenever or however one wishes.

dis·pose /dis'pōz/ ▶v. **1** [intrans.] (**dispose of**) get rid of by throwing away or giving or selling to someone else. ■ informal kill; destroy. ■ overcome (a rival or threat). ■ informal consume (food or drink) quickly or enthusiastically. **2** [with obj. and adverbial] arrange in a particular position: *the chief disposed his attendants in a circle.* ■ bring (someone) into a particular frame of mind. ■ [intrans.] literary determine the course of events. *the city proposed, but the unions disposed.* — **dis·pos·er** n. [ME: from OFr. *disposer*, from L. *disponere* 'arrange,' influenced by *dispositus* 'arranged.']

dis·posed /dis'pōzd/ ▶adj. [predic., usu. with infin.] inclined or willing. ■ [with submodifier] having a specified attitude to or toward: *favorably **disposed** toward the proposals.*

dis·po·si·tion /ˌdispə'zisнən/ ▶n. **1** a person's inherent qualities of mind and character. ■ [often with infin.] an inclination or tendency. **2** the way in which something is placed or arranged, esp. in relation to other things. ■ the action of arranging or ordering people or things in a particular way. ■ (**dispositions**) military preparations, in particular the stationing of troops ready for attack or defense. **3** Law the action of distributing or transferring property or money to someone, in particular by bequest. **4** the power to deal with something as one pleases: *with railroads at his disposition, he would have triumphed.* ■ archaic the determination of events, esp. by divine power. [ME: via OFr. from L. *dispositio(n-)*, from *disponere* 'arrange' (see DISPOSE).]

dis·pos·i·tive /dis'päzitiv/ ▶adj. relating to or bringing about the settlement of an issue or the disposition of property. ■ Law dealing with the disposition of property by deed or will. ■ dealing with the settling of international conflicts by an agreed disposition of disputed territories.

dis·pos·sess /ˌdispə'zes/ ▶v. [trans.] (often **be dispossessed**) deprive (someone) of something that they own, typically land or property: *they were **dispossessed of** lands and properties.* ■ oust (a person) from a dwelling or position. — **dis·pos·ses·sion** /-'zesнən/ n. [15th C.: from OFr. *despossesser*, from *des-* (expressing reversal) + *possesser* 'possess.']

dis·praise /dis'prāz/ ▶n. rare censure; criticism. ▶v. [trans.] archaic express censure or criticism of (someone). [ME: from OFr. *despreisier*, based on late L. *depreciare* (see DEPRECIATE).]

dis·proof /dis'pro͞of/ ▶n. a set of facts that prove that something is untrue. ■ the action of proving that something is untrue.

dis·pro·por·tion /ˌdisprə'pôrsнən/ ▶n. an instance of being out of proportion with something else. — **dis·pro·por·tion·al** /-sнənl/ adj. **dis·pro·por·tion·al·i·ty** /-ˌpôrsнə'nalitē/ n. **dis·pro·por·tion·al·ly** /-sнənl-ē/ adv. [16th C.: from DIS- (expressing absence) + PROPORTION, on the pattern of Fr. *disproportion*.]

dis·pro·por·tion·ate[1] /ˌdisprə'pôrsнənit/ ▶adj. too large or too small in comparison with something else. — **dis·pro·por·tion·ate·ly** adv. **dis·pro·por·tion·ate·ness** n.

dis·pro·por·tion·ate[2] /ˌdisprə'pôrsнəˌnāt/ ▶v. [intrans.] Chem. undergo disproportionation: *water disproportionates to oxygen and hydrogen.*

dis·pro·por·tion·a·tion /ˌdisprəˌpôrsнə'nāsнən/ ▶n. Chem. a reaction in which a substance is simultaneously oxidized and reduced, giving two different products.

dis·prove /dis'pro͞ov/ ▶v. [trans.] prove that (something) is false. — **dis·prov·a·ble** adj. [ME: from OFr. *desprover*.]

dis·put·a·ble /dis'pyo͞otəbəl/ ▶adj. not established as fact, and so open to question or debate. — **dis·put·a·bly** adv.

dis·pu·ta·tion /ˌdispyo͝o'tāsнən/ ▶n. debate or argument. ■ formal academic debate. — **dis·put·a·tive** /-'pyo͞otətiv/ adj.

dis·pu·ta·tious /ˌdispyo͝o'tāsнəs/ ▶adj. (of a person) fond of having heated arguments. ■ (of an argument or situation) motivated by or causing strong opinions. — **dis·pu·ta·tious·ly** adv. **dis·pu·ta·tious·ness** n.

dis·pute ▶n. /dis'pyo͞ot/ a disagreement, argument, or debate. ▶v. [trans.] argue about (something); discuss heatedly: *I disputed the charge on the bill* | [intrans.] *he taught and disputed with local poets.* ■ question whether (a statement or alleged fact) is true or valid. ■ compete for; strive to win. ■ archaic resist (a landing or advance).
– PHRASES **beyond dispute** certain or certainly; without doubt. **open to dispute** not definitely decided. — **dis·pu·tant** /-'pyo͞otnt/ n. **dis·put·er** n. [ME: via OFr. from L. *disputare* 'to estimate' (in late L. 'to dispute'), from *dis-* 'apart' + *putare* 'reckon.']

dis·qual·i·fi·ca·tion /disˌkwäləfi'kāsнən/ ▶n. the action of disqualifying or the state of being disqualified. ■ a fact or condition that disqualifies someone from a position or activity.

dis·qual·i·fy /dis'kwäləˌfī/ ▶v. (**-fies, -fied**) [trans.] (often **be disqualified**) pronounce (someone) ineligible for an office or activity because of an offense or infringement: *he was **disqualified from** driving.* ■ eliminate (someone) from a competition because of an infringement of the rules. ■ (of a feature or characteristic) make (someone) unsuitable for an office or activity.

dis·qui·et /dis'kwī-it/ ▶n. a feeling of anxiety or worry. ▶v. [trans.] [usu. as adj.] (**disquieted**) make (someone) worried or anxious.

dis·qui·et·ing /dis'kwī-itiNG/ ▶adj. inducing feelings of anxiety or worry. — **dis·qui·et·ing·ly** adv.

dis·qui·e·tude /dis'kwī-iˌt(y)o͞od/ ▶n. a state of uneasiness or anxiety.

dis·qui·si·tion /ˌdiskwə'zisнən/ ▶n. a long or elaborate essay or discussion on a particular subject. — **dis·qui·si·tion·al** /-sнənl/ adj. (archaic). [15th C.: via Fr. from L. *disquisitio(n-)* 'investigation,' based on *quaerere* 'seek.']

Dis·rae·li /diz'rālē/, Benjamin, 1st Earl of Beaconsfield (1804–81), prime minister of Britain 1868, 1874–80. He ensured that Britain bought a controlling interest in the Suez Canal (1875).

dis·rate /dis'rāt/ ▶v. [trans.] (usu. **be disrated**) reduce (a sailor) to a lower rank.

dis·re·gard /ˌdisri'gärd/ ▶v. [trans.] pay no attention to; ignore. ▶n. the action or state of disregarding or ignoring something.

dis·rel·ish /dis'relisн/ archaic ▶n. a feeling of dislike or distaste. ▶v. [trans.] regard (something) with dislike or distaste.

dis·re·mem·ber /ˌdisri'membər/ ▶v. [trans.] dialect fail to remember.

dis·re·pair /ˌdisri'pe(ə)r/ ▶n. poor condition of a building or structure due to neglect.

dis·rep·u·ta·ble /dis'repyətəbəl/ ▶adj. not considered to be respectable in character or appearance. —**dis·rep·u·ta·ble·ness** n. **dis·rep·u·ta·bly** adv.

dis·re·pute /ˌdisrə'pyōōt/ ▶n. the state of being held in low esteem by the public.

dis·re·spect /ˌdisri'spekt/ ▶n. lack of respect or courtesy. ▶v. [trans.] informal show a lack of respect for; insult. —**dis·re·spect·ful** /-fəl/ adj. **dis·re·spect·ful·ly** /-fəlē/ adv.

dis·robe /dis'rōb/ ▶v. [intrans.] take off one's clothes. ■ take off the clothes worn for an official ceremony. ■ [trans.] undress (someone). [ME: from DIS- (expressing reversal) + ROBE, perh. on the pattern of Fr. *desrober*.]

dis·rupt /dis'rəpt/ ▶v. [trans.] interrupt (an event, activity, or process) by causing a disturbance or problem. ■ drastically alter or destroy the structure of (something). —**dis·rupt·er** (also **dis·rup·tor** /-tər/) n. **dis·rup·tion** /-'rəpsHən/ n. [ME: from L. *disrupt-* 'broken apart,' from the v. *disrumpere*.]

dis·rup·tive /dis'rəptiv/ ▶adj. causing or tending to cause disruption. —**dis·rup·tive·ly** adv. **dis·rup·tive·ness** n.

diss ▶v. var. of DIS.

dis·sat·is·fac·tion /disˌsatis'faksHən/ ▶n. lack of satisfaction.

dis·sat·is·fied /dis'satisˌfīd/ —**dis·sat·is·fied·ly** adv.

dis·sat·is·fy /dis'satisˌfī/ ▶v. (-fies, -fied) [trans.] fail to satisfy (someone).

dis·sav·ing /dis'sāviNG/ ▶n. the action of spending more than one has earned in a given period. ■ (**dissavings**) the excess amount spent. —**dis·sav·er** n.

dis·sect /di'sekt; dī-/ ▶v. [trans.] (often **be dissected**) methodically cut up (a body, part, or plant) in order to study its internal parts. ■ analyze (something) in minute detail. —**dis·sec·tion** /-'seksHən/ n. **dis·sec·tor** /-tər/ n. [16th C.: from L. *dissect-* 'cut up,' from the v. *dissecare*, from *dis-* 'apart' + *secare* 'to cut.']

dis·sect·ed /di'sektid; dī-/ ▶adj. **1** having been cut up for anatomical study. **2** having a divided form or structure, in particular: ■ Bot. (of a leaf) divided into many deep lobes. ■ Geol. (of a plateau or upland) divided by a number of deep valleys.

dis·sem·ble /di'sembəl/ ▶v. [intrans.] conceal one's true motives, feelings, or beliefs. ■ [trans.] disguise or conceal (a feeling or intention). —**dis·sem·blance** /-bləns/ n. **dis·sem·bler** n. [ME: alt. of obs. *dissimule*, via OFr. from L. *dissimulare* 'disguise, conceal.']

dis·sem·i·nate /di'semaˌnāt/ ▶v. [trans.] spread or disperse (something, esp. information) widely. ■ [usu. as adj.] (**disseminated**) spread throughout an organ or the body. —**dis·sem·i·na·tion** /-ˌsemə'nāsHən/ n. **dis·sem·i·na·tor** /-ˌnātər/ n. [ME: from L. *disseminat-* 'scattered,' from the v. *disseminare*, from *dis-* 'abroad' + *semen, semin-* 'seed.']

dis·sem·i·nule /di'semaˌnyōōl/ ▶n. Bot. a part of a plant that serves to propagate it, such as a seed or a fruit. [20th C.: from *dissemination*.]

dis·sen·sion /di'sensHən/ ▶n. disagreement that leads to discord. [ME: via OFr. from L. *dissensio(n-)*, from the v. *dissentire* (see DISSENT).]

dis·sen·sus /di'sensəs/ ▶n. widespread dissent. [1960s: from DIS- (expressing reversal) + a shortened form of CONSENSUS, or from L. *dissensus* 'disagreement.']

dis·sent /di'sent/ ▶v. [intrans.] hold or express opinions that are at variance with those previously, commonly, or officially expressed. ■ separate from an established or orthodox church because of doctrinal disagreement. ▶n. the expression or holding of opinions at variance with those previously, commonly, or officially held. ■ (also **Dissent**) refusal to accept the doctrines of an established or orthodox church; nonconformity. [ME: from L. *dissentire* 'differ in sentiment.']

dis·sent·er /di'sentər/ ▶n. a person who dissents. ■ (**Dissenter**) Brit., hist. a member of a nonestablished church; a Nonconformist.

dis·sen·tient /di'sensHənt/ ▶adj. in opposition to a majority or official opinion. ▶n. a person who opposes a majority or official opinion. [17th C.: from L. *dissentient-* 'differing in opinion,' from the v. *dissentire*.]

dis·sep·i·ment /di'sepəmənt/ ▶n. Bot. Zool. a partition in a part or organ; a septum. [18th C.: from L. *dissaepimentum*, from *dissaepire* 'make separate,' from *dis-* (expressing separation) + *saepire* 'divide by a hedge.']

dis·ser·ta·tion /ˌdisər'tāsHən/ ▶n. a long essay on a particular subject, esp. one written as a requirement for the Doctor of Philosophy degree. —**dis·ser·ta·tion·al** /-sHənl/ adj. [17th C.: from L. *dissertatio(n-)*, from *dissertare* 'continue to discuss,' from *disserere* 'examine, discuss.']

dis·serv·ice /dis'sərvis/ ▶n. [usu. in sing.] a harmful action: *you have done a disservice to the African people.*

dis·sev·er /di'sevər/ ▶v. [trans.] rare divide or sever (something). —**dis·sev·er·ance** /-'sev(ə)rəns/ n. **dis·sev·er·ment** n. [ME: from OFr. *dessevrer*, from late L. *disseparare*, from *dis-* (expressing intensive force) + L. *separare* 'to separate.']

dis·si·dence /'disidəns/ ▶n. protest against official policy; dissent.

dis·si·dent /'disidənt/ ▶n. a person who opposes official policy, esp. that of an authoritarian state. ▶adj. in opposition to official policy. [16th C.: from L. *dissident-* 'sitting apart, disagreeing,' from *dis-* 'apart' + *sedere* 'sit.']

dis·sim·i·lar /di'similər/ ▶adj. not alike; different. —**dis·sim·i·lar·i·ty** /-ˌsimə'laritē/ n. **dis·sim·i·lar·ly** adv.

dis·sim·i·late /di'simaˌlāt/ ▶v. [trans.] Ling. change (a sound in a word) in order to be unlike the sounds near it: *in "pilgrim," from Latin "peregrinus," the first "r" is dissimilated to "l."* ■ [intrans.] (of a sound) undergo such a change. —**dis·sim·i·la·tion** /-ˌsimə'lāsHən/ n. **dis·sim·i·la·to·ry** /-ləˌtôrē/ adj. [19th C.: from DIS- (expressing reversal) + L. *similis* 'like, similar.']

dis·si·mil·i·tude /ˌdis-si'miliˌt(y)ōōd/ ▶n. formal dissimilarity or diversity. [ME: from L. *dissimilitudo*, from *dissimilis* 'unlike,' from *dis-* (expressing reversal) + *similis* 'like, similar.']

dis·sim·u·late /di'simyəˌlāt/ ▶v. [trans.] conceal or disguise (one's thoughts, feelings, or character): *he dissimulates his wealth beneath ragged pullovers* | [intrans.] *they no longer need to dissimulate.* —**dis·sim·u·la·tion** /-ˌsimyə'lāsHən/ n. **dis·sim·u·la·tor** /-ˌlātər/ n. [ME: from L. *dissimulat-* 'hidden, concealed,' from the v. *dissimulare*.]

dis·si·pate /'disəˌpāt/ ▶v. **1** [intrans.] disperse or scatter. ■ (of a feeling or other intangible thing) disappear or be dispelled. ■ [trans.] cause (a feeling or other intangible thing) to disappear or disperse. **2** [trans.] squander or fritter away (money, energy, or resources). ■ (usu. **be dissipated**) Physics cause (energy) to be lost, typically by converting it to heat. —**dis·si·pa·tive** /-ˌpātiv/ adj. **dis·si·pa·tor** /-ˌpātər/ (also **dis·si·pat·er**) n. [ME: from L. *dissipat-* 'scattered,' from the v. *dissipare*, from *dis-* 'apart, widely' + *supare* 'to throw.']

dis·si·pat·ed /'disəˌpātid/ ▶adj. (of a person or way of life) overindulging in sensual pleasures.

dis·si·pa·tion /ˌdisə'pāsHən/ ▶n. **1** dissipated living. **2** squandering of money, energy, or resources. ■ Physics loss of energy, esp. by its conversion into heat. ■ scattering or dispersion.

dis·so·ci·a·ble /di'sōsHəbəl/ ▶adj. able to be dissociated; separable.

dis·so·ci·ate /di'sōsHēˌāt; -'sōsē-/ ▶v. [trans.] **1** disconnect or separate (used esp. in abstract contexts). ■ (**dissociate oneself from**) declare that one is not connected with or a supporter of (someone or something). ■ [intrans.] become separated or disconnected: *the area would dissociate from the country.* ■ (usu. **be dissociated**) Psychiatry split off (a component of mental activity) to act as an independent part of mental life. **2** (usu. **be dissociated**) Chem. cause (a molecule) to split into separate smaller atoms, ions, or molecules, esp. reversibly. ■ [intrans.] (of a molecule) undergo this process. —**dis·so·ci·a·tive** /-shēˌātiv; -sHətiv/ adj. [16th C.: from L. *dissociat-* 'separated,' from the v. *dissociare*, from *dis-* (expressing reversal) + *sociare* 'join together' (from *socius* 'companion').]

dis·so·ci·at·ed per·son·al·i·ty ▶n. another term for MULTIPLE PERSONALITY.

dis·so·ci·a·tion /diˌsōsē'āsHən; -shē-/ ▶n. the disconnection or separation of something from something else or the state of being disconnected. ■ Chem. the splitting of a molecule into smaller molecules, atoms, or ions, esp. by a reversible process. ■ Psychiatry separation of normally related mental processes, resulting in one group functioning independently from the rest, leading in extreme cases to disorders such as multiple personality.

dis·sol·u·ble /di'sälyəbəl/ ▶adj. able to be dissolved, loosened, or disconnected. —**dis·sol·u·bil·i·ty** /-ˌsälyə'bilitē/ n. [16th C.: from L. *dissolubilis*, from the v. *dissolvere* (see DISSOLVE).]

dis·so·lute /'disəˌlōōt/ ▶adj. lax in morals; licentious. —**dis·so·lute·ly** adv. **dis·so·lute·ness** n. [ME: from L. *dissolutus* 'disconnected, loose,' from the v. *dissolvere* (see DISSOLVE).]

dis·so·lu·tion /ˌdisə'lōōsHən/ ▶n. **1** the closing down or dismissal of an assembly, partnership, or official body. ■ tech. the action or process of dissolving or being dissolved. ■ disintegration; decomposition. ■ formal death. **2** debauched living; dissipation.

dis·solve /di'zälv/ ▶v. **1** [intrans.] (of a solid) become incorporated into a liquid so as to form a solution. ■ [trans.] cause (a solid) to become incorporated into a liquid in this way. ■ (of something abstract, esp. a feeling) disappear. ■ deteriorate or degenerate. ■ subside uncontrollably into (an expression of strong feelings). ■ (in a movie) change gradually to (a different scene or picture). **2** [trans.] close down or dismiss (an assembly or official body). ■ annul or put an end to (a partnership or marriage). ▶n. (in a film) an act or instance of moving gradually from one picture to another. —**dis·solv·a·ble** adj. **dis·solv·er** n. [ME: from L. *dissolvere*, from *dis-* 'apart' + *solvere* 'loosen or solve.']

dis·sol·vent /di'zälvənt/ ▶n. a substance that dissolves something else.

dis·so·nance /'disənəns/ ▶n. Music lack of harmony among musical notes. ■ a tension or clash resulting from the combination of two disharmonious or unsuitable elements.

dis·so·nant /'disənənt/ ▶adj. Music lacking harmony. ■ unsuitable or unusual in combination; clashing. —**dis·so·nant·ly** adv. [ME: from OFr., or from L. *dissonant-* 'being discordant,' from the v. *dissonare*, from *dis-* 'apart' + *sonare* 'to sound.']

dis·suade /di'swād/ ▶v. [trans.] persuade (someone) not to take a particular course of action: *his friends tried to dissuade him from flying.* —**dis·suad·er** n. **dis·sua·sion** /-'swāzHən/ n. **dis·sua·sive** /-'swāsiv/ adj. [15th C.: from L. *dissuadere*, from *dis-* (expressing reversal) + *suadere* 'advise, persuade.']

dis·syl·la·ble /dī'siləbəl/ ▶n. var. of DISYLLABLE. —**dis·syl·lab·ic** /ˌdīsi'labik/ adj.

dis·sym·me·try /dis'simitrē/ ▶n. (pl. **-tries**) lack of symmetry. ■ tech. the symmetrical relation of mirror images, the left and right hands, or crystals with two corresponding forms. —**dis·sym·met·ric** /ˌdis-si'metrik/ **adj.** **dis·sym·met·ri·cal** /ˌdis-si'metrikəl/ **adj.**

dis·taff /'distaf/ ▶ **n.** a stick or spindle onto which wool or flax is wound for spinning. ■ [as adj.] of or concerning women. [OE *distæf*: the first element is appar. rel. to Mid. Low Ger. *dise, disene* 'distaff, bunch of flax'; the second is STAFF[1].]

dis·taff side ▶ **n.** the female side of a family. The opposite of SPEAR SIDE. ■ the female members of a group.

dis·tal /'distl/ ▶ **adj.** Anat. situated away from the center of the body or from the point of attachment. The opposite of PROXIMAL. — **dis·tal·ly** **adv.** [19th C.: from DISTANT.]

dis·tance /'distəns/ ▶ **n.** **1** an amount of space between two things or people. ■ the condition of being far off; remoteness. ■ a far-off point or place. ■ (**the distance**) the more remote part of what is visible or discernible. ■ an interval of time. ■ fig. the avoidance of familiarity; aloofness or reserve. **2** the full length of a race or bout. ▶ **v.** [trans.] make (someone or something) far off or remote in position or nature. ■ (**distance oneself from**) declare that one is not connected with or a supporter of (someone or something).
– PHRASES **go the distance** Boxing complete a fight without being knocked out. ■ (of a boxing match) last the scheduled length. ■ Baseball pitch for the entire length of a game. ■ last for a long time. **keep one's distance** stay far away. ■ maintain one's reserve. **within —— distance** near enough to reach by the means specified: *the parking lot is within easy walking distance.* **within spitting distance** within a very short distance. **within striking distance** near enough to hit or achieve something.

dis·tance learn·ing ▶ **n.** a method of studying in which lectures are broadcast or classes are conducted by correspondence or over the Internet, without the student's needing to attend a school or college. Also called **distance education**.

dis·tance run·ner ▶ **n.** an athlete who competes in long- or middle-distance races.

dis·tant /'distənt/ ▶ **adj.** **1** far away in space or time. ■ [predic.] (after a measurement) at a specified distance. ■ (of a sound) faint or vague because far away. ■ fig. remote or far apart in resemblance or relationship. ■ [attrib.] (of a person) not closely related. **2** (of a person) not intimate; cool or reserved. ■ remote; abstracted: *a distant look in his eyes.* [ME: from L. *distant-* 'standing apart,' from the v. *distare*, from *dis-* 'apart' + *stare* 'stand.']

dis·tant·ly /'distəntlē/ ▶ **adv.** far away. ■ not closely: *distantly related.* ■ coolly or remotely.

dis·taste /dis'tāst/ ▶ **n.** [in sing.] mild dislike or aversion.

dis·taste·ful /dis'tāstfəl/ ▶ **adj** causing dislike or disgust; offensive; unpleasant: *customers complained about the distasteful odor.* — **dis·taste·ful·ly** **adv.** **dis·taste·ful·ness** **n.**

dist. atty. ▶ **abbr.** district attorney.

dis·tem·per[1] /dis'tempər/ ▶ **n.** **1** a viral disease of some animals, esp. dogs, causing fever, coughing, and catarrh. **2** archaic political disorder. [16th C.: from ME *distemper* 'upset, derange,' from late L. *distemperare* 'soak, mix in the wrong proportions,' from *dis-* 'thoroughly' + *temperare* 'mingle.']

dis·tem·per[2] ▶ **n.** a kind of paint using glue or size instead of an oil base, for use on walls or for scene-painting. ■ a method of mural and poster painting using this. ▶ **v.** [trans.] [often as adj.] (**distempered**) paint (something) with distemper. [ME: from OFr. *destremper* or late L. *distemperare* 'soak.']

dis·tend /dis'tend/ ▶ **v.** [trans.] cause (something) to swell by stretching it from inside. ■ [intrans.] swell out because of pressure from inside. — **dis·ten·si·bil·i·ty** /-ˌtensə'bilitē/ **n.** **dis·ten·si·ble** /-'tensəbəl/ **adj.** **dis·ten·sion** /-'tenshən/ **n.** [ME: from L. *distendere*, from *dis-* 'apart' + *tendere* 'to stretch.']

dis·tich /'distik/ ▶ **n.** Pros. a pair of verse lines; a couplet. [16th C.: via L. from Gk. *distikhon (metron)* '(measure) of two lines,' neut. of *distikhos*, from *di-* 'twice' + *stikhos* 'line.']

dis·ti·chous /'distikəs/ ▶ **adj.** Bot. (of parts) arranged alternately in two opposite vertical rows. — **dis·ti·chous·ly** **adv.**

dis·till /dis'til/ (Brit. **distil**) ▶ **v.** [trans.] purify (a liquid) by vaporizing it, then condensing it by cooling the vapor, and collecting the resulting liquid. ■ (usu. **be distilled**) make (something, esp. liquor or an essence) in this way. ■ extract the essence of (something) by heating it with a solvent. ■ remove (a volatile constituent) of a mixture by using heat. ■ (often **be distilled**) fig. extract the essential meaning or most important aspects of. ■ [intrans.] literary emanate as a vapor or in minute drops. — **dis·til·la·tion** /ˌdistə'lāshən/ **n.** **dis·til·la·to·ry** /-əˌtôrē/ **adj.** [ME: from L. *distillare*, var. of *destillare*, from *de-* 'down, away' + *stillare* (from *stilla* 'a drop').]

dis·til·late /'distilit; -ˌlāt/ ▶ **n.** something formed by distilling.

dis·till·er /dis'tilər/ ▶ **n.** a person or company that manufactures liquor.

dis·till·er·y /dis'tilərē/ ▶ **n.** (pl. **-er·ies**) a place where liquor is manufactured.

dis·tinct /dis'tiNGkt/ ▶ **adj.** **1** recognizably different in nature from something else of a similar type. ■ physically separate. **2** readily distinguishable by the senses. ■ [attrib.] (used for emphasis) so clearly apparent as to be unmistakable; definite. — **dis·tinct·ly** **adv.** **dis·tinct·ness** **n.** [ME: from L. *distinctus* 'separated, distinguished,' from the v. *distinguere* (see DISTINGUISH).]

dis·tinc·tion /dis'tiNGkshən/ ▶ **n.** **1** a difference or contrast between similar things or people: *there is a sharp distinction between domestic and international politics* ■ the separation of things or people into different groups according to attributes or characteristics. **2** excellence that sets someone or something apart from others. ■ a decoration or honor awarded to someone in recognition of outstanding achievement. ■ recognition of outstanding achievement, as on an examination. Compare with MERIT.
– PHRASES **distinction without a difference** an artificially created distinction where no real difference exists. **have the distinction of** be different from others of a similar type by virtue of a notable characteristic or achievement.

dis·tinc·tive /dis'tiNGktiv/ ▶ **adj.** characteristic of one person or thing, and so serving to distinguish it from others. — **dis·tinc·tive·ly** **adv.** **dis·tinc·tive·ness** **n.**

dis·tin·gué /ˌdistaNG'gā/ ▶ **adj.** (fem. **dis·tin·guée** pronunc. same) having a distinguished manner or appearance. [19th C.: Fr., lit. 'distinguished.']

dis·tin·guish /dis'tiNGgwish/ ▶ **v.** [trans.] recognize or treat (someone or something) as different. ■ [intrans.] perceive or point out a difference. ■ manage to discern (something barely perceptible). ■ be an identifying or characteristic mark or property of. ■ (**distinguish oneself**) make oneself prominent and worthy of respect through one's behavior or achievements. — **dis·tin·guish·a·ble** **adj.** [16th C.: formed irregularly from Fr. *distinguer* or L. *distinguere*, from *dis-* 'apart' + *stinguere* 'put out' (from a base meaning 'prick').]

dis·tin·guished /dis'tiNGgwisht/ ▶ **adj.** successful, authoritative, and commanding great respect. ■ showing dignity or authority in one's appearance or manner.

Dis·tin·guished Fly·ing Cross (abbr.: **DFC**) ▶ **n.** a US or British military decoration for heroism or distinguished achievement while on aerial duty.

dis·tort /dis'tôrt/ ▶ **v.** [trans.] pull or twist out of shape. ■ [intrans.] become twisted out of shape. ■ fig. give a misleading or false account or impression of. ■ change the form of (an electrical signal or sound wave) during transmission, amplification, or other processing. — **dis·tort·ed·ly** **adv.** **dis·tort·ed·ness** **n.** **dis·tor·tion** /-'tôrshən/ **n.** **dis·tor·tion·al** /-'tôrshənl/ **adj.** **dis·tor·tion·less** /-'tôrshənlis/ **adj.** [15th C.: from L. *distort-* 'twisted apart,' from the v. *distorquere*, from *dis-* 'apart' + *torquere* 'to twist.']

distr. ▶ **abbr.** ■ distribution. ■ distributor. ■ district.

dis·tract /dis'trakt/ ▶ **v.** [trans.] prevent (someone) from giving full attention to something. ■ divert (attention) from something. ■ (**distract oneself**) divert one's attention from something worrying or unpleasant by doing something different or more pleasurable. ■ archaic perplex and bewilder. [ME: from L. *distract-* 'drawn apart,' from the v. *distrahere*, from *dis-* 'apart' + *trahere* 'to draw, drag.']

dis·tract·ed /dis'traktid/ ▶ **adj.** unable to concentrate because one's mind is preoccupied. ■ troubled or distraught: *distracted with grief.* — **dis·tract·ed·ly** **adv.**

dis·trac·tion /dis'trakshən/ ▶ **n.** **1** a thing that prevents someone from giving full attention to something else. ■ a diversion or recreation. **2** extreme agitation of the mind or emotions.
– PHRASES **drive someone to distraction** annoy someone intensely. **to distraction** (in hyperbolic use) intensely.

dis·train /dis'trān/ ▶ **v.** [trans.] Law seize (someone's property) to obtain payment of rent or other money owed. ■ seize the property of (someone) for this purpose. — **dis·train·er** **n.** **dis·train·ment** **n.** [ME: from OFr. *destreindre*, from L. *distringere* 'stretch apart,' from *dis-* 'apart' + *stringere* 'tighten.']

dis·traint /dis'trānt/ ▶ **n.** Law the seizure of someone's property in order to obtain payment of money owed, esp. rent. [18th C.: from DISTRAIN.]

dis·trait /dis'trā/ ▶ **adj.** (fem. **dis·traite** /dis'trāt/) [predic.] distracted or absentminded. [18th C.: Fr., from OFr. *destrait*, past part. of *destraire* 'distract,' from L. *distrahere* 'pull apart' (see DISTRACT).]

dis·traught /dis'trôt/ ▶ **adj.** deeply upset and agitated. [ME: alt. of the obs. adj. *distract* (from L. *distractus* 'pulled apart').]

dis·tress /dis'tres/ ▶ **n.** **1** extreme anxiety, sorrow, or pain. ■ the state of a ship or aircraft when in danger or difficulty and needing help: *vessels in distress.* ■ suffering caused by lack of money or the basic necessities of life. ■ Med. a state of physical strain, exhaustion, or, in particular, breathing difficulty. **2** Law another term for DISTRAINT. ▶ **v.** [trans.] cause (someone) anxiety, sorrow, or pain. ■ give (furniture, leather, or clothing) simulated marks of age and wear. — **dis·tress·ful** /-fəl/ **adj.** **dis·tress·ing·ly** **adv.** [ME: from OFr. *destresce* (n.), *destrecier* (v.), based on L. *distringere* 'stretch apart.']

dis·tressed /dis'trest/ ▶ **adj.** suffering from anxiety, sorrow, or pain. ■ dated impoverished. ■ (of furniture, leather, or clothing) having simulated marks of age and wear. ■ (of property) for sale, esp. below market value, due to mortgage foreclosure or because it is part of an insolvent estate. ■ (of goods) for sale at unusually low prices or at a loss because of damage or previous use.

dis·tress sale ▶ **n.** a sale of goods or assets at reduced prices to raise much-needed funds.

dis·trib·u·tar·y /dis'tribyo͝oˌterē/ ▶ **n.** (pl. **-tar·ies**) a branch of a river that does not return to the main stream after leaving it (as in a delta).

dis·trib·ute /dis'tribyo͞ot/ ▶ **v.** [trans.] **1** give shares of (something); deal out. ■ supply (goods) to stores and other businesses that sell to consumers. ■ (**be distributed**) occur throughout an area. ■ Print. separate (metal type that has been set up) and return the characters to their separate compartments in a type case. **2** Logic use (a term) to include every individual of the class to which it refers. — **dis·trib·ut·a·ble** adj. [ME: from L. *distribut-* 'divided up,' from the v. *distribuere*, from *dis-* 'apart' + *tribuere* 'assign.']

dis·tri·bu·tion /ˌdistrəˈbyo͞osHən/ (abbr.: **distr.**) ▶ n. the action of sharing something out among a number of recipients. ■ the way in which something is shared out among a group or spread over an area. ■ the action or process of supplying goods to stores and other businesses that sell to consumers. ■ Bridge the different number of cards of each suit in a player's hand. — **dis·tri·bu·tion·al** /-sHənl/ adj.

dis·tri·bu·tive /disˈtribyətiv/ ▶ adj. **1** concerned with the supply of goods to stores and other businesses that sell to consumers. ■ concerned with the way in which things are shared among people. **2** Gram. (of a determiner or pronoun) referring to each individual of a class, not to the class collectively, e.g., *each, either*. **3** Math. (of an operation) fulfilling the condition that, when it is performed on two or more quantities already combined by another operation, the result is the same as when it is performed on each quantity individually and the products then combined. ▶ n. Gram. a distributive word. — **dis·trib·u·tive·ly** adv.

dis·trib·u·tor /disˈtribyətər/ (abbr.: **distr.**) ▶ n. **1** an agent who supplies goods to stores and other businesses that sell to consumers. **2** a device in a gasoline engine for passing electric current to each spark plug in turn.

dis·trict /ˈdistrikt/ ▶ n. (abbr.: **distr.**) an area of a country or city, esp. one regarded as a distinct unit because of a particular characteristic. ■ a region defined for an administrative purpose. ■ (**the District**) the District of Columbia; Washington, DC. ▶ v. [trans.] divide into districts. [17th C.: from Fr., from med. L. *districtus* '(territory of) jurisdiction,' from L. *distringere* 'draw apart.']

dis·trict at·tor·ney (abbr.: **DA**) ▶ n. a public official who acts as prosecutor for the state or the federal government in court in a particular district.

dis·trict court ▶ n. a state of federal trial court.

Dis·trict of Co·lum·bi·a (abbr.: **DC** or **D.C.**) a federal district of the US, coextensive with the city of Washington.

dis·trust /disˈtrəst/ ▶ n. the feeling that someone or something cannot be relied on. ▶ v. [trans.] doubt the honesty or reliability of; regard with suspicion. — **dis·trust·er** n. **dis·trust·ful** /-fəl/ adj. **dis·trust·ful·ly** /-fəlē/ adv.

dis·turb /disˈtərb/ ▶ v. [trans.] interfere with the normal arrangement or functioning of. ■ destroy the sleep or relaxation of. ■ (often **be disturbed**) cause to feel anxious. ■ (often **be disturbed**) interrupt or intrude on (someone) when they want privacy or secrecy. — **dis·turb·er** n. **dis·turb·ing·ly** adv. [ME: from OFr. *destourber*, from L. *disturbare*, from *dis-* 'utterly' + *turbare* 'disturb' (from *turba* 'tumult').].

dis·tur·bance /disˈtərbəns/ ▶ n. the interruption of a settled and peaceful condition. ■ a breakdown of peaceful and law-abiding behavior; a riot. ■ the disruption of healthy functioning. ■ Meteorol. a local variation from normal or average wind conditions, usually a small tornado or cyclone. ■ Law interference with rights or property; molestation.

dis·turbed /disˈtərbd/ ▶ adj. having had its normal pattern or function disrupted. ■ suffering or resulting from emotional and mental problems.

di·sub·sti·tut·ed /dīˈsəbstiˌt(y)o͞otid/ ▶ adj. Chem. (of a molecule) having two substituent groups.

di·sul·fide /dīˈsəlfīd/ (Brit. **di·sul·phide**) ▶ n. Chem. a sulfide containing two atoms of sulfur in its molecule or empirical formula. ■ an organic compound containing the group –S–S– bonded to other groups.

di·sul·fir·am /dīˈsəlfəˌram/ ▶ n. Med. a synthetic compound, $(C_2H_5)_2$-$NCSSCN(C_2H_5)_2$, used in the treatment of alcoholics to make drinking alcohol produce unpleasant aftereffects. Also called **Antabuse** (trademark). [1940s: blend of **disulfide** and *thiuram*.]

dis·un·ion /disˈyo͞onyən/ ▶ n. the breaking up of something such as a federation.

dis·u·nit·ed /ˌdisyo͞oˈnītid/ ▶ adj. lacking unity.

dis·u·ni·ty /disˈyo͞onitē/ ▶ n. disagreement and conflict within a group.

dis·use /disˈyo͞os/ ▶ n. the state of not being used.
– PHRASES **fall into disuse** cease to be used.

dis·used /disˈyo͞ozd/ ▶ adj. no longer being used.

dis·u·til·i·ty /ˌdisyo͞oˈtilitē/ ▶ n. Econ. the adverse or harmful effects associated with a particular activity or process, esp. when carried out over a long period.

dis·val·ue /disˈvalyo͞o/ ▶ v. (**-val·ues, -val·ued, -val·u·ing**) [trans.] undervalue (something or someone). ▶ n. a negative value or worth. — **dis·val·u·a·tion** /-ˌvalyo͞oˈāsHən/ n.

di·syl·lab·ic /ˌdīsiˈlabik; ˌdisi-/ (also **dis·syl·lab·ic**) ▶ adj. (of a word or metrical foot) consisting of two syllables. ■ (of a bird's call) consisting of two distinct sounds, such as the call of the cuckoo.

di·syl·la·ble /dīˈsiləbəl; di-/ (also **dis·syl·la·ble**) ▶ n. Pros. a word or metrical foot consisting of two syllables.

dit /dit/ ▶ n. (in Morse code) another term for **dot**. [World War II: imitative.]

ditch /dicH/ ▶ n. a narrow channel dug in the ground, typically used for drainage alongside a road or the edge of a field. ▶ v. [trans.] **1** provide with ditches. ■ [intrans.] make or repair ditches. **2** informal get rid of; give up. ■ informal end a relationship with (someone) peremptorily; abandon. ■ informal be truant from (school or another obligation). **3** informal bring (an aircraft) down on water in an emergency: *he was picked up by a frigate after ditching his plane.* ■ [intrans.] (of an aircraft) make a forced landing on water. ■ derail (a train). — **ditch·er** n. [OE *dīc*, of Gmc. origin; rel. to Du. *dijk* 'ditch, dike' and Ger. *Teich* 'pond, pool,' also to **dike**[1].]

ditch·wa·ter /ˈdicHˌwôtər; -ˌwä-/ ▶ n. stagnant water in a ditch.
– PHRASES **dull as ditchwater** see **dull**.

di·the·ism /ˈdīTHēˌizəm; dīˈTHē-/ ▶ n. a belief in two gods, esp. as independent and opposed principles of good and evil. — **di·the·ist** n.

dith·er /ˈdiTHər/ ▶ v. [intrans.] **1** be indecisive. **2** [trans.] Comput. display or print (an image) without sharp edges so that there appear to be more colors in it than are really available. ▶ n. **1** informal indecisive behavior. **2** [in sing.] a state of agitation. — **dith·er·er** n. **dith·er·y** adj. [17th C. (in the dialect sense 'tremble, quiver'): var. of dial. *didder*; rel. to **dodder**[1].]

di·thi·o·nite /dīˈTHīəˌnīt/ ▶ n. Chem. a salt containing the anion S_2O_42-. [20th C.: from **di-**[1] 'two' + Gk. *theion* 'sulfur' + **-ite**[1].]

dith·y·ramb /ˈdiTHəˌram/ ▶ n. a wild choral hymn of ancient Greece, esp. one dedicated to Dionysus. ■ a passionate or inflated speech, poem, or other writing. — **dith·y·ram·bic** /ˌdiTHəˈrambik/ adj. [17th C.: via L. from Gk. *dithurambos*.]

di·tran·si·tive /dīˈtranzitiv/ ▶ adj. Gram. (of a verb) taking two objects, for example *give* as in *I gave her the book*.

dit·sy ▶ adj. var. of **ditzy**.

dit·ta·ny /ˈditn-ē/ ▶ n. any of a number of aromatic herbaceous or shrubby plants, in particular: ■ (also **dittany of Crete**) a dwarf shrub (*Origanum dictamnus*) of the mint family, with white woolly leaves and pink flowers, native to Crete and Greece. ■ (also **American dittany**) an American herb (genus *Cunila*) of the mint family, used in cooking and herbal medicine. ■ another term for **gas plant**. [ME: ult. from Gk. *diktamnon*, perh. from *Diktē*, the name of a mountain in Crete.]

dit·to /ˈditō/ **1** used in accounts and lists to indicate that an item is repeated (often indicated by ditto marks under the word or figure to be repeated). ■ informal used to indicate that something already said is applicable a second time. **2** a similar thing; a duplicate. [17th C. (in the sense 'in the aforesaid month'): from Tuscan dial., var. of Ital. *detto* 'said,' from L. *dictus* 'said.']

dit·tog·ra·phy /diˈtägrəfē/ ▶ n. (pl. **-phies**) a mistaken repetition of a letter, word, or phrase by a copyist. — **dit·to·graph·ic** /ˌditəˈgrafik/ adj. [19th C.: from Gk. *dittos* 'double' + **-graphy**.]

dit·to marks ▶ plural n. two apostrophes (") representing "ditto."

dit·ty /ˈditē/ ▶ n. (pl. **-ties**) a short simple song. [ME: from OFr. *dite* 'composition,' from L. *dictatum* (neut.) 'something dictated,' from *dictare* 'to dictate.']

dit·ty bag (also **ditty box**) ▶ n. a receptacle for odds and ends, esp. one used by sailors or fishermen. [19th C.: of unknown origin.]

dit·zy /ˈditsē/ (also **dit·sy**) ▶ adj. informal silly or scatterbrained: *don't tell me my ditzy secretary didn't send you an invitation!* — **ditz** /dits/ n. **dit·zi·ness** n. [1970s: of unknown origin.]

di·u·re·sis /ˌdīəˈrēsis/ ▶ n. Med. increased or excessive production of urine. Compare with **polyuria**.

di·u·ret·ic /ˌdīəˈretik/ Med. ▶ adj. (chiefly of drugs) causing increased passing of urine. ▶ n. a diuretic drug. [ME: from OFr. *diuretique*, or via late L. from Gk. *diourētikos*, from *diourein* 'urinate,' from *dia* 'through' + *ouron* 'urine.']

di·ur·nal /dīˈərnl/ ▶ adj. **1** of or during the day. ■ Zool. (of animals) active in the daytime. ■ Bot. (of flowers) open only during the day. **2** daily; of each day: *diurnal rhythms.* ■ Astron. of or resulting from the daily rotation of the earth. — **di·ur·nal·ly** adv. [ME: from late L. *diurnalis*, from L. *diurnus* 'daily,' from *dies* 'day.']

Div. ▶ abbr. ■ Division. ■ divorced.

div ▶ abbr. divergence (in mathematical equations).

di·va /ˈdēvə/ ▶ n. a famous female opera singer. ■ a female singer who has enjoyed great popular success. ■ an admired, glamorous, or distinguished woman. ■ a haughty, spoiled woman. [19th C.: via Ital. from L., lit. 'goddess.']

di·va·lent /dīˈvālənt/ ▶ adj. Chem. having a valence of two.

Di·va·li ▶ n. var. of **Diwali**.

di·van ▶ n. **1** /diˈvan; ˈdīvan/ a long low sofa without a back or arms, typically placed against a wall. **2** /diˈvan; -ˈvän/ hist. a legislative body, council chamber, or court of justice in the Ottoman Empire or elsewhere in the Middle East. [16th C. (sense 2): via Fr. or Ital. from Turk. *dīvān*, from Pers. *dīwān* 'anthology, bench.']

dive /dīv/ ▶ v. (past **dived** or **dove** /dōv/; past part. **dived**) [intrans.] **1** [with adverbial of direction] plunge head first into water. ■ move quickly or suddenly in a specified direction: *a bullet passed close to his head, and he dived for cover* | [as adj.] (**diving**) *he attempted a diving catch.* ■ (of an aircraft or bird) plunge steeply downward through the air. ■ (**dive into**) occupy oneself suddenly and enthusiastically with (a meal or an engrossing subject or activity): *dive into a barbecued beef burrito.* ■ fig. (of prices or profits) drop suddenly. ■ informal put one's hand quickly into something, esp. a pocket or purse, in order to find something: *she dived into her bag and extracted a card.* **2** swim under water using breathing equipment. ■ (of a fish, a submarine, or a vessel used for underwater exploration) go to a deeper level in water. ▶ n. **1** an act of diving, in particular: ■ a plunge head first into water, esp. from a diving board in a way prescribed for competition: *a high dive.* ■ an instance of swimming or exploring under water with breathing equipment. ■ an act of going deeper under water by a fish, submarine, or diving vessel. ■ a steep descent by an aircraft or bird. See also NOSEDIVE. ■ a sudden movement in a specified direction: *she made a dive for the fridge to quench her raging thirst.* ■ fig. a sudden and significant fall in prices or profits. **2** informal a disreputable nightclub or bar.

– PHRASES **take a dive** Boxing pretend to be knocked out. ■ (of prices, hopes, fortunes, etc.) fall suddenly: *profits could take a dive as easily as they could soar.* [OE *dūfan* 'dive, sink' and *dȳfan* 'immerse,' of Gmc. origin; rel. to DEEP and DIP.]

dive-bomb ▶ v. [trans.] bomb (a target) while diving steeply downward in an aircraft: *news that kamikazes had dive-bombed a US destroyer.* ■ (of a bird or flying insect) attack (something) by swooping down on it. — **dive-bomb·er** n.

div·er /'dīvər/ ▶ n. **1** a person or animal that dives, in particular: ■ a person who dives as a sport. ■ a person who wears a diving suit to work under water. **2** British term for LOON[1].

di·verge /di'vərj; dī-/ ▶ v. [intrans.] **1** (of a road, route, or line) separate from another route, esp. a main one, and go in a different direction. ■ develop in a different direction: *howler and spider monkeys **diverged from** a common ancestor.* ■ (of an opinion, theory, approach, etc.) differ markedly: [as adj.] (**diverging**) *studies from different viewpoints yield diverging conclusions.* ■ deviate from a set course or standard. **2** Math. (of a series) increase indefinitely as more terms are added. [17th C.: from med. L. *divergere*, from L. *dis-* 'in two ways' + *vergere* 'to turn or incline.']

di·ver·gence /di'vərjəns; dī-/ ▶ n. **1** the process or state of diverging. ■ a difference or conflict in opinions, interests, wishes, etc. ■ a place where airflows or ocean currents diverge, typically marked by downwelling (of air) or upwelling (of water). **2** Math. the inner product of the operator del and a given vector, which gives a measure of the quantity of flux emanating from any point of the vector field or the rate of loss of mass, heat, etc., from it.

di·ver·gent /di'vərjənt; dī-/ ▶ adj. **1** tending to be different or develop in different directions: *divergent interpretations* | *varieties of English can remain astonishingly **divergent from** one another.* **2** Math. (of a series) increasing indefinitely as more of its terms are added. — **di·ver·gen·cy** n. **di·ver·gent·ly** adv.

di·vers /'dīvərz/ ▶ adj. [attrib.] archaic, literary of varying types; several: *in divers places.* [ME: via OFr. from L. *diversus* 'diverse,' from *divertere*.]

di·verse /di'vərs; dī-/ ▶ adj. showing a great deal of variety: *a culturally diverse population.* ■ (of two or more things) markedly different from one another. — **di·verse·ly** adv. [ME: var. of DIVERS.]

di·ver·si·fy /di'vərsi͵fī; dī-/ ▶ v. (-fies, -fied) make or become more diverse or varied: [as adj.] (**diversified**). ■ [intrans.] (of a company) enlarge or vary its range of products or field of operation. ■ [trans.] [often as adj.] (**diversified**) enlarge or vary the range of products or the field of operation of (a company). ■ [trans.] spread (investment) over several enterprises or products in order to reduce the risk of loss: [as adj.] (**diversified**) *a diversified portfolio of assets.* — **di·ver·si·fi·ca·tion** /-͵vərsifi'kāsʜən/ n. [ME: via OFr. from med. L. *diversificare* 'make dissimilar,' from L. *diversus*, past part. of *divertere* (see DIVERT).]

di·ver·sion /di'vərzʜən; dī-/ ▶ n. **1** an instance of turning something aside from its course. **2** an activity that diverts the mind from tedious or serious concerns; a recreation or pastime. ■ something intended to distract someone's attention from something more important. — **di·ver·sion·ar·y** /-͵nerē/ adj.

di·ver·si·ty /di'vərsitē; dī-/ ▶ n. (pl. **-ties**) the state of being diverse; variety. ■ [usu. in sing.] a range of different things.

di·vert /di'vərt; dī-/ ▶ v. [trans.] **1** cause (someone or something) to change course or turn from one direction to another: *a scheme to **divert** water **from** the river **to** irrigate agricultural land.* ■ [intrans.] (of a vehicle or person) change course. ■ reallocate (something, esp. money or resources) to a different purpose. **2** distract (someone or their attention) from something. ■ [usu. as adj.] (**diverting**) draw the attention of (someone) away from tedious or serious concerns; entertain or amuse: *a diverting book.* — **di·vert·er** n. **di·vert·ing·ly** adv. [ME: via Fr. from L. *divertere*, from *di-* 'aside' + *vertere* 'to turn.']

di·ver·tic·u·la /͵dīvər'tikyələ/ plural form of DIVERTICULUM.

di·ver·tic·u·li·tis /͵dīvər͵tikyə'lītis/ ▶ n. Med. inflammation of a diverticulum, esp. in the colon, causing pain and disturbance of bowel function.

di·ver·tic·u·lo·sis /͵dīvər͵tikyə'lōsis/ ▶ n. Med. a condition in which diverticula are present in the intestine without signs of inflammation.

di·ver·tic·u·lum /͵dīvər'tikyələm/ ▶ n. (pl. **-la** /-lə/) Med. an abnormal sac or pouch formed at a weak point in the wall of the alimentary tract. [19th C.: from med. L., var. of L. *deverticulum* 'byway,' from *devertere* 'turn down or aside.']

di·ver·ti·men·to /di͵vərtə'mentō/ ▶ n. (pl. **-men·ti** /-'mentē/ or **-men·tos**) Music a light and entertaining composition, typically one in the form of a suite for chamber orchestra. [18th C.: Ital., lit. 'diversion.']

di·ver·tisse·ment /di'vərtismənt/ ▶ n. a minor entertainment or diversion: *as a Sunday divertissement Wittgenstein would play Schubert quartets.* [18th C.: Fr., from *divertiss-*, stem of *divertir*, from L. *divertere* 'turn in separate ways.']

Di·ves /'dīvēz/ ▶ n. literary used to refer to a typical or hypothetical rich man: *there must be rich and poor, Dives says, smacking his claret.* [ME: from late L.]

di·vest /di'vest; dī-/ ▶ v. [trans.] deprive (someone) of power, rights, or possessions. ■ deprive (something) of a particular quality: *he has **divested** the original play **of** its charm.* ■ [intrans.] rid oneself of something that one no longer wants or requires, such as a business interest or investment: *it appears easier to carry on in the business than to divest.* [17th C.: alt. of *devest*, from OFr. *desvestir*, from *des-* (expressing removal) + L. *vestire* (from *vestis* 'garment').]

di·vest·i·ture /di'vesticʜər; -͵cʜo͝or; dī-/ (also **di·ves·ture** /-'vescʜər; -cʜo͝or/) ▶ n. the action or process of selling off subsidiary business interests or investments. [17th C.: from med. L. *divestit-* 'divested' (from the v. *divestire*) + -URE.]

di·vest·ment /di'vestmənt; dī-/ ▶ n. another term for DIVESTITURE.

di·vide /di'vīd/ ▶ v. **1** separate or be separated into parts: [trans.] *consumer magazines can be **divided into** a number of different categories* | [intrans.] *the cell clusters began to divide rapidly.* ■ [trans.] separate (something) into portions and distribute a share to each of a number of people. ■ [trans.] allocate (different parts of one's time, attention, or efforts) to different activities or places. ■ [trans.] form a boundary between (two people or things). **2** disagree or cause to disagree. **3** [trans.] Math. find how many times (a number) contains another: *36 **divided by** 2 equals 18* | [intrans.] *the program helps children to multiply and divide quickly and accurately.* ■ [intrans.] (of a number) be susceptible to division without a remainder: *30 does not divide by 8.* ■ find how many times (a number) is contained in another: ***divide** 4 **into** 20.* ■ [intrans.] (of a number) be contained in a number without a remainder: *3 divides into 15.* ▶ n. a wide divergence between two groups, typically producing tension or hostility: *there was still a profound cultural **divide between** the parties.* ■ a boundary between two things. ■ a ridge or line of high ground forming the division between two valleys or river systems. [ME (as a v.): from L. *dividere* 'force apart, remove.']

di·vid·ed high·way ▶ n. a road with a median strip between the traffic in opposite directions and typically two or more lanes in each direction.

div·i·dend /'divi͵dend/ ▶ n. **1** a sum of money paid regularly (typically quarterly) by a company to its shareholders out of its profits (or reserves). ■ a payment divided among a number of people, e.g., members of a cooperative or creditors of an insolvent estate. ■ an individual's share of a dividend. ■ (**dividends**) a benefit from an action or policy: *persistence **pays dividends**.* See also PEACE DIVIDEND. **2** Math. a number to be divided by another number. [15th C.: from Anglo-Norman Fr. *dividende*, from L. *dividendum* 'something to be divided,' from the v. *dividere* (see DIVIDE).]

di·vid·er /di'vīdər/ ▶ n. **1** a person or thing that divides a whole into parts. ■ an issue on which opinions are divided: *the big divider was still nuclear weapons.* ■ (also **room divider**) a screen or piece of furniture that divides a room into two parts. **2** (**dividers**) a measuring compass, esp. one with a screw for making fine adjustments.

di·vid·ing line ▶ n. the boundary between two areas: ***the dividing line** between eastern and western zones.* ■ a distinction or set of distinctions marking the difference between two related things: ***the dividing line** between drama and reality.*

div·i-div·i /'divē'divē/ ▶ n. (pl. **div·i-div·is**) a tropical American tree (*Caesalpinia coriaria*) of the pea family, bearing curled pods. ■ these pods, used as a source of tannin. [19th C.: via Amer. Sp. from Carib.]

div·i·na·tion /͵divə'nāsʜən/ ▶ n. the practice of seeking knowledge of the future or the unknown by supernatural means. — **di·vin·a·to·ry** /di'vinə͵tôrē/ adj.

di·vine[1] /di'vīn/ ▶ adj. (**-vin·er, -vin·est**) **1** of, from, or like God or a god. ■ devoted to God; sacred: *divine liturgy.* **2** informal, dated excellent; delightful. ▶ n. **1** dated a cleric or theologian. **2** (**the Divine**) providence or God. — **di·vine·ly** adv. **di·vine·ness** n. [ME: via OFr. from L. *divinus*, from *divus* 'godlike' (rel. to *deus* 'god').]

di·vine[2] ▶ v. [trans.] discover (something) by guesswork or intuition: *his brother usually divined his ulterior motives.* ■ have supernatural or magical insight into (future events): *frauds who claimed to divine the future in chicken's entrails.* — **di·vin·er** n. [ME: from OFr. *deviner* 'predict,' from L. *divinare*, from *divinus* (see DIVINE[1]).]

Di·vine Of·fice ▶ n. see OFFICE (sense 4).

di·vine right of kings ▶ n. the doctrine that kings derive their authority from God, not from their subjects.

div·ing /'dīviɴɢ/ ▶ n. **1** the sport or activity of swimming or exploring under water. **2** the sport or activity of diving into water from a diving board.

div·ing bell ▶ n. an open-bottomed chamber supplied with compressed air, in which a person can be let down under water.

div·ing board ▶ n. an elevated board projecting over a swimming pool or other body of water, from which people dive or jump in.

div·ing duck ▶ n. a duck of a type that dives under water for food. Compare with DABBLING DUCK.

div·ing suit ▶ n. a watertight suit, typically with a helmet and an air supply, worn for working or exploring deep under water.

di·vin·ing rod ▶ n. a stick or rod used for dowsing.

di·vin·i·ty /di'vinitē/ ▶n. (pl. **-ties**) the state or quality of being divine: *Christ's divinity.* ■ the study of religion; theology: *a doctor of divinity.* ■ a divine being; a god or goddess. ■ (**the Divinity**) God.

di·vis·i·ble /di'vizəbəl/ ▶adj. capable of being divided: *the marine environment is divisible into a number of areas.* ■ Math. (of a number) capable of being divided by another number without a remainder: *24 is divisible by 4.* — **di·vis·i·bil·i·ty** /-,vizə'bilitē/ n.

di·vi·sion /di'vizʜən/ ▶n. **1** the action of separating something into parts, or the process of being separated. ■ the distribution of something separated into parts: *the **division** of his estates **between** the two branches of his family.* **2** disagreement between two or more groups, typically producing tension or hostility: *a growing sense of **division between** north and south.* **3** the process or skill of dividing one number by another. See also LONG DIVISION, SHORT DIVISION. ■ Math. the process of dividing a matrix, vector, or other quantity by another under specific rules to obtain a quotient. **4** each of the parts into which something is divided. ■ a major unit or section of an organization, typically one handling a particular kind of work. ■ a group of army brigades or regiments. ■ a part of a county, country, or city defined for administrative or political purposes: *a licensing division of a district.* **5** a partition that divides two groups or things.
– PHRASES **division of labor** the assignment of different parts of a manufacturing process or task to different people in order to improve efficiency. [ME: from OFr. *devisiun*, from L. *divisio(n-)*, from the v. *dividere* (see DIVIDE).]

di·vi·sion·al /di'vizʜənl/ ▶adj. of or relating to an organizational or administrative division: *a divisional manager.* — **di·vi·sion·al·ly** adv.

di·vi·sion sign ▶n. the sign ÷, placed between two numbers showing that the first is to be divided by the second, as in $6 \div 3 = 2$.

di·vi·sive /di'vīsiv/ ▶adj. tending to cause disagreement or hostility between people. — **di·vi·sive·ly** adv. **di·vi·sive·ness** n.

di·vi·sor /di'vīzər/ ▶n. Math. a number by which another number is to be divided. ■ a number that divides into another without a remainder: *the greatest common divisor.*

di·vorce /di'vôrs/ ▶n. the legal dissolution of a marriage by a court or other competent body: *her **divorce from** her first husband.* ■ a legal decree dissolving a marriage. ■ [in sing.] a separation between things that were or ought to be connected. ▶v. legally dissolve one's marriage with (someone). ■ separate or dissociate (something) from something else: *we knew how to **divorce** an issue **from** an individual.* ■ (**divorce oneself from**) distance or dissociate oneself from (something). — **di·vorce·ment** n. [ME: the n. from OFr. *divorce*, from L. *divortium*, based on *divertere* (see DIVERT).]

di·vor·cée /di,vôr'sā -'sē/ (also **di·vor·cee**) ▶n. a divorced woman. [19th C.: from Fr. *divorcée* 'divorced woman.']

div·ot /'divət/ ▶n. a piece of turf cut out of the ground by a golf club in making a stroke. [16th C.: of unknown origin.]

di·vulge /di'vəlj; dī-/ ▶v. [trans.] make known (private or sensitive information). — **di·vul·gence** /-'vəljəns/ n. [ME: from L. *divulgare*, from *di-* 'widely' + *vulgare* 'publish' (from *vulgus* 'common people').]

div·vy /'divē/ informal ▶v. (**div·vies, div·vied**) [trans.] divide up and share: *they divvied up the proceeds.*

Di·wa·li /di'wälē/ (also **Di·va·li** /di'välē/) ▶n. a Hindu festival of lights, held in the period October to November, to celebrate the new season at the end of the monsoon. [from Hindi *dīvālī*, from Sanskrit *dīpāvali* 'row of lights,' from *dīpa* 'lamp' + *vali* 'row.']

di·wan /di'wän/ (also **de·wan**) ▶n. **1** (in Islamic societies) a central finance department, chief administrative office, or regional governing body. **2** a chief treasury official, finance minister, or prime minister in some Indian states. [Urdu, from Pers. *dīwān* 'fiscal register'; cf. DIVAN.]

Dix /diks/, Dorothea Lynde (1802–87), US reformer. A pioneer in prison reform, she also supervised women army nurses during the American Civil War.

Dix·ie (also **Dixieland**) an informal name for the southern US states from the song "Dixie" (1859), popular with Confederate soldiers in the Civil War.
– PHRASES **whistle Dixie** engage in unrealistic fantasies; waste one's time: *until you nail down the facts, you're just whistling Dixie.*

Dix·ie·crat /'diksē,krat/ ▶n. informal any of the Southern Democrats who seceded from the party in 1948 in opposition to its policy of extending civil rights.

Dix·ie Cup ▶n. trademark a brand of disposable paper cup.

Dix·ie·land /'diksē,land/ ▶n. a kind of jazz with a strong two-beat rhythm and collective improvisation that originated in New Orleans in the early 20th century.

DIY ▶abbr. do-it-yourself.

Di·yar·ba·kir /di'yär,bəkər/ a city in southeastern Turkey; pop. 381,100.

diz·zy /'dizē/ ▶adj. (**-zi·er, -zi·est**) having or involving a sensation of spinning around and losing one's balance: *Jonathan had begun to suffer dizzy spells* | fig. *he looked around, dizzy with happiness.* ■ causing such a sensation: *a sheer, dizzy drop* | fig. *a dizzy range of hues.* ■ informal (of a woman) silly but attractive. ▶v. (**-zies, -zied**) [trans.] [usu. as adj.] (**dizzying**) make (someone) feel unsteady, confused, or amazed: *the dizzying rate of change* | *her nearness dizzied him.* — **diz·zi·ly** /'dizəlē/ adv. **diz·zi·ness** n. [OE *dysig* 'foolish,' of West Gmc. origin; rel. to Low Ger. *dusig, dösig* 'giddy.']

DJ ▶n. a disc jockey. ▶v. (**DJ's, DJ'ing, DJ'd**) [intrans.] perform as a disc jockey.

Dja·kar·ta var. of JAKARTA.

djeb·el ▶n. var. of JEBEL.

djel·la·ba /jə'läbə/ (also **djel·la·bah** or **jel·la·ba**) ▶n. a loose hooded cloak, typically woolen, of a kind traditionally worn by Arabs. [19th C.: from Moroccan Arab. *jellāba, jellābiyya*.]

djib·ba /'jibə/ (also **djib·bah**) ▶n. var. of JIBBA.

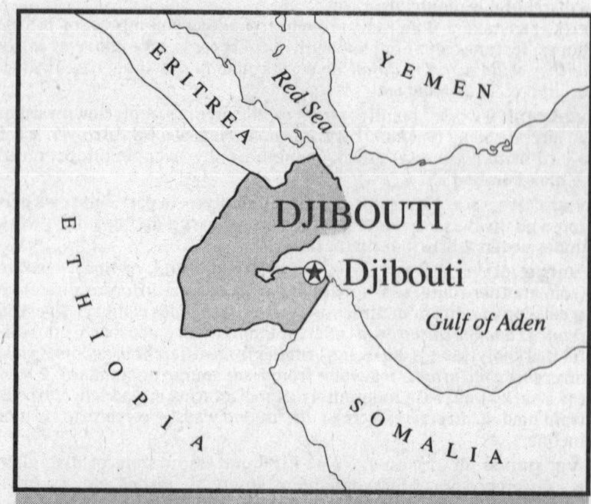

Djibouti
Official name: Republic of Djibouti
Location: northeastern coast of Africa, on the Gulf of Aden, between Eritrea and Somalia
Area: 8,500 square miles (22,000 sq km)
Population: 466,900
Capital: Djibouti
Languages: Arabic and French (both official), Somali, Afar
Currency: Djiboutian franc

Dji·bou·ti /jə'bōōtē/ (also **Ji·bu·ti**) a country on the northeastern coast of Africa. *See box.* — **Dji·bou·ti·an** /-tēən/ adj. & n.

djinn /jin/ ▶n. var. of JINN.

DL ▶abbr. ■ Football defensive lineman. ■ disabled list.

dl ▶abbr. deciliter(s).

DLitt (also **DLit**) ▶abbr. ■ Doctor of Letters. ■ Doctor of Literature. [from L. *Doctor Litterarum*.]

DLL Comput. ▶abbr. dynamic link library, a collection of subroutines stored on disk, which can be loaded into memory and executed when accessed by a running program.

DM (also **D-mark**) ▶abbr. Deutschmark.

dm ▶abbr. decimeter(s).

DMA ▶abbr. ■ Doctor of Musical Arts. ■ direct memory access, a method allowing a peripheral device to transfer data to or from the memory of a computer system using operations not under the control of the central processor.

D-mark ▶n. short for DEUTSCHMARK.

DMD ▶abbr. ■ Doctor of Dental Medicine. [from L. *Dentariae Medicinae Doctor* or *Doctor Medicinae Dentalis*] ■ Duchenne muscular dystrophy.

DMSO Chem. ▶abbr. dimethyl sulfoxide.

DMus ▶abbr. Doctor of Music.

DMV ▶abbr. Department of Motor Vehicles.

DMZ ▶abbr. demilitarized zone, an area from which warring parties agree to remove their military forces.

DNA ▶n. Biochem. deoxyribonucleic acid, a self-replicating material present in nearly all living organisms as the main constituent of chromosomes. It is the carrier of genetic information.

DNA fin·ger·print·ing (also **DNA pro·fil·ing**) ▶n. the analysis of DNA from samples of body tissues or fluids in order to identify individuals.

DNA vi·rus ▶n. a virus in which the genetic information is stored in the form of DNA (as opposed to RNA).

Dnie·per /'nēpər; də'nēpər/ a river that rises in Russia west of Moscow and flows south for about 1,370 miles (2,200 km) to the Black Sea. Ukrainian name DNIPRO.

Dnies·ter /'nēstər; də'nēstər/ a river that rises in western Ukraine and flows 876 miles (1,410 km) to the Black Sea. Russian name DNESTR, Ukrainian name DNISTER.

Dni·pro·dzer·zhinsk /də,nyēprōdzir'zʜēnsk/ a city in Ukraine, on the Dnieper River; pop. 283,600. Former name (until 1936) KAMENSKOYE.

Dni·pro·pe·trovsk /də,nyēprōpə'trôfsk/ a city in Ukraine, on the Dnieper River; pop. 1,187,000.

DNR ▶abbr. ■ do not resuscitate.

do[1] /do͞o/ ▶v. (**does** /dəz/; past **did** /did/; past part. **done** /dən/) **1** [trans.] perform (an action, the precise nature of which is often unspecified): *she knew what she was doing* | *what can I do for you?* ■ perform (a particular task). ■ work on (something) to bring it to completion or to a required state: *it takes them longer to do their hair than me.* ■ make or have available and provide: *he's doing bistro food* | [with two objs.] *he decided to do her a favor.* ■ solve; work out: *Joe was doing sums aloud.* ■ cook (food) to completion or to a specified degree: *if a knife inserted into the center comes out clean, then your pie is done.* ■ (often in questions) work at for a living: *what does she do?* ■ produce or give a performance of (a particular play, opera, etc.). ■ perform (a particular role, song, etc.) or imitate (a particular person) in order to entertain people: *he not only does Schwarzenegger and Groucho, he becomes them.* ■ informal take (a narcotic drug): *he doesn't smoke, drink, or do drugs.* ■ attend to (someone). ■ vulgar slang have sexual intercourse with. ■ (**do it**) informal have sexual intercourse. ■ (**do it**) informal urinate; defecate. **2** [trans.] achieve or complete, in particular: ■ travel (a specified distance): *one car I looked at had done 112,000 miles.* ■ travel at (a specified speed): *I was speeding, doing seventy-five.* ■ make (a particular journey). ■ achieve (a specified sales figure). ■ [trans.] informal visit as a tourist, esp. in a superficial or hurried way: *the tourists are allotted only a day to "do" Verona.* ■ spend (a specified period of time), typically in prison or in a particular occupation: *he did five years for manslaughter.* ■ [intrans.] informal finish: *you must sit there and wait till I'm done* | [with pres. part.] *we're done arguing.* ■ (**be done**) be over: *the special formula continues to beautify your tan when the day is done.* ■ (**be/have done with**) give up concern for; have finished with: *I should sell the place and **have done with it**.* **3** [intrans.] act or behave in a specified way. ■ make progress or perform in a specified way; get on: *when a team is doing badly, it's not easy for a new player to settle in.* ■ [trans.] have a specified effect on: *the walk will do me good.* ■ [trans.] result in: *the years of stagnation did a lot of harm to the younger generation.* **4** be suitable or acceptable: *if he's anything like you, he'll do.* ▶aux. v. **1** used before a verb (except *be, can, may, ought, shall, will*) in questions and negative statements: *do you have any pets?* | *did he see me?* ■ used to make tag questions: *you write poetry, don't you?* ■ used in negative commands: *don't be silly.* **2** used to refer to a verb already mentioned: *he looks better than he did before.* **3** used to give emphasis to a positive verb: *I do want to act on this.* ■ used in positive commands to give polite encouragement: *do tell me!* **4** used with inversion of a subject and verb when an adverbial phrase begins a clause for emphasis: *only rarely did they succumb.* ▶n. (pl. **dos** or **do's**) **1** (also **'do**) informal short for HAIRDO. **2** informal, esp. Brit. a party or other social event: *the soccer club Christmas do.*
– PHRASAL VERBS **do away with** informal put an end to; remove: *the desire to do away with racism.* ■ kill: *he didn't have the courage to do away with her.* **do by** dated treat or deal with in a specified way: *she did well by them.* **1 do for** informal defeat, ruin, or kill: *without that contract we're done for.* **2** suffice for: *the old version will do for now.* **do something** (or **nothing**) **for** informal enhance (or detract from) the appearance or quality of: *that scarf does nothing for you.* **do someone in** informal kill someone. ■ (usu. **be done in**) informal tire someone out: *after hiking in the hills all day, I was utterly done in.* **do someone out of** informal deprive someone of (something) in an underhanded or unfair way. **do something over 1** informal repeat something: *to absorb the lesson, I had to do it over and over.* **2** informal decorate or furnish a room or building. **do someone up** (usu. **be done up**) dress someone up, esp. in an elaborate or impressive way: *Agnes was all done up in a slinky black number.* **do something up** (usu. **be done up**) arrange one's hair in a particular way, esp. so as to be pulled back from one's face or shoulders: *her dark hair was done up in a pony tail.* ■ wrap something up: *unwieldy packages all done up with twine.* **do with** [with modal] would find useful or would like to have or do: *I could do with a cup of coffee.* **do without** (usu. **can do without**) manage without. ■ informal would prefer not to have: *I can do without your complaints first thing in the morning.* [OE *dōn*, of Gmc. origin; rel. to Ger. *tun*, from an Indo-Eur. root shared by Gk. *tithēmi* 'I place' and L. *facere* 'make, do.']

do[2] /dō/ ▶n. Music (in solmization) the first and eighth note of a major scale. ■ the note C in the fixed-do system. [18th C.: Ital.]

do. dated ▶abbr. ditto.

DOA ▶abbr. dead on arrival, used to describe a person who is declared dead immediately upon arrival at a hospital.

do·a·ble /'do͞oəbəl/ ▶adj. informal within one's powers; feasible: *none of the jobs were fun, but they were doable.*

dob·bin /'däbin/ ▶n. dated a pet name for a draft horse or a farm horse. [16th C.: nickname for the given name *Robert*.]

do·be /'dōbē/ ▶n. informal adobe.

Do·ber·man /'dōbərmən/ (also **Do·ber·man pin·scher** /'pinCHər/) ▶n. a large dog of a German breed with powerful jaws and a smooth coat, typically black with tan markings. [20th C.: from the name of Ludwig *Dobermann*, 19th-cent. German dog breeder (+ Ger. *Pinscher* 'terrier').]

Doberman

Do·brich /'dôbrēCH/ a city in northeastern Bulgaria, the center of an agricultural region; pop. 115,800. It was called Tolbukhin 1949–91.

do·bro /'dōbrō/ ▶n. (pl. **-bros**) trademark a type of acoustic guitar with steel resonating disks inside the body under the bridge. [1950s: from *Do(pěra) Bro(thers)*, the Czech-Amer. inventors of the instrument.]

dobro

Do·bru·ja /'dôbro͞ojä/ a district in eastern Romania and northeastern Bulgaria on the Black Sea coast.

dob·son·fly /'däbsən,flī/ ▶n. (pl. **-flies**) a large gray North American winged insect (family Corydalidae, order Neuroptera) related to the alderflies. See also HELLGRAMMITE [20th C.: of unknown origin.]

Dob·so·ni·an /däb'sōnēən/ ▶adj. relating to or denoting a low-cost Newtonian reflecting telescope with large aperture and short focal length, or the simple altazimuth mount used for it. [20th C.: from the name of John *Dobson*, Amer. amateur astronomer, + -IAN.]

doc /däk/ informal ▶abbr. ■ doctor. ■ Comput. document.

do·cent /'dōsənt/ ▶n. **1** a person who acts as a guide, typically on a voluntary basis, in a museum, art gallery, or zoo. **2** (in certain universities and colleges) a member of the teaching staff immediately below professorial rank. [19th C.: via Ger. from L. *docent-* 'teaching,' from *docere* 'teach.']

doc·ile /'däsəl/ ▶adj. ready to accept control or instruction; submissive. —**doc·ile·ly** adv. **do·cil·i·ty** /dä'silitē/ n. [15th C.: from L. *docilis*, from *docere* 'teach.']

dock[1] /däk/ ▶n. a structure extending alongshore or out from the shore into a body of water, to which boats may be moored. ■ an enclosed area of water in a port for the loading, unloading, and repair of ships. ■ (**docks**) a group of such enclosed areas of water along with the wharves and buildings near them. ■ short for DRY DOCK. ■ (also **loading dock**) a platform for loading or unloading trucks or freight trains. ▶v. [intrans.] (of a ship) tie up at a dock, esp. in order to load or unload passengers or cargo. ■ [trans.] bring (a ship or boat) into such a place. ■ (of a spacecraft) join with a space station or another spacecraft in space. ■ attach (a piece of equipment) to another. [ME: from MDu., Mid. Low Ger. *docke*, of unknown origin.]

dock[2] ▶v. [trans.] (usu. **be docked**) deduct (something, esp. an amount of money): *their wages are docked for public displays of affection.* ■ cut short (an animal's tail): *fifteen of the dogs had had their tails docked.* [ME: perh. rel. to Ger. *Docke* 'doll.']

dock[3] ▶n. (usu. **the dock**) Brit. the enclosure in a criminal court where a defendant is placed. [16th C.: prob. rel. to Flemish *dok* 'chicken coop.']

dock[4] ▶n. a coarse weed (genus *Rumex*, family Polygonaceae) of temperate regions, with inconspicuous greenish or reddish flowers. The leaves are popularly used to relieve nettle stings. [OE *docce*, of Gmc. origin; rel. to Du. dial. *dokke*.]

dock·age /'däkij/ ▶n. accommodation or berthing of ships at docks. ■ the charge made for using docks.

dock·er /'däkər/ ▶n. another term for LONGSHOREMAN.

dock·et /'däkit/ ▶n. **1** a calendar or list of cases for trial or people having cases pending. ■ an agenda or list of things to be done. **2** a document or label listing the contents of a package or delivery. ▶v. (**dock·et·ed, dock·et·ing**) [trans.] (usu. **be docketed**) enter (a case or suit) onto a list of those due to be heard: *the case will go to the Supreme Court, and may be docketed for the fall term.* [15th C.: perh. from DOCK[2].]

dock·hand /'däk,hand/ ▶n. a longshoreman.

dock·ing sta·tion ▶n. a device to which a portable computer is connected so that it can be used like a desktop computer, with an external power supply, monitor, data transfer capability, etc.

dock·side /'däk,sīd/ ▶n. [in sing.] the area immediately adjacent to a dock.

dock·work·er /'däk,wərkər/ ▶n. a longshoreman.

dock·yard /'däk,yärd/ ▶n. an area or establishment with docks and equipment for repairing and maintaining ships.

doc·tor /'däktər/ ▶n. **1** a qualified practitioner of medicine; a physician. ■ a qualified dentist or veterinary surgeon. ■ [with adj.] informal a person who gives advice or makes improvements: *the script doctor rewrote the original.* **2** (**Doctor**) a person who holds a doctorate. ▶v. [trans.] **1** change the content or appearance of (a document or picture) in order to deceive; falsify: *the reports could have been doctored.* ■ alter the content of (a drink, food, or substance) by adding strong or harmful ingredients. **2** [usu. as n.] (**doctoring**) informal treat (someone) medically: *he contemplated giving up doctoring.*
– PHRASES **be (just) what the doctor ordered** informal be very beneficial or desirable under the circumstances: *a 2-0 victory is just what the doctor ordered.* —**doc·tor·ly** adj. [ME: via OFr. from L. *doctor* 'teacher' (from *docere* 'teach').]

doc·tor·al /'däktərəl/ ▶adj. [attrib.] relating to or designed to achieve a doctorate: *a doctoral dissertation.*

doc·tor·ate /'däktərit/ ▶n. the highest degree awarded by a graduate school or other approved educational organization: *a doctorate in Classics.*

Doc·tor of Phi·los·o·phy (abbr.: **Ph.D.**) ▶n. a doctorate in any discipline except a few such as law, medicine, or sometimes theology. ■ a person holding such a degree.

Doc·tor of the Church ▶n. one of the early Christian theologians regarded as esp. authoritative in the Western Church. Compare with FATHERS OF THE CHURCH (see FATHER sense 3).

Doc·tor·ow /'däktə,rō/, E. L. (1931–), US writer; full name *Edgar Lawrence Doctorow.* His novels include *Ragtime* (1975) and *The March* (2005).

doc·tri·naire /,däktrə'ne(ə)r/ ▶adj. seeking to impose a doctrine in all circumstances without regard to practical considerations: *a doctrinaire socialist.* —**doc·tri·nair·ism** n. [19th C.: from Fr., from *doctrine* (see DOCTRINE).]

doc·tri·nal /'däktrənl/ ▶adj. concerned with a doctrine or doctrines: *doctrinal disputes.* —**doc·tri·nal·ly** adv.

doc·trine /'däktrin/ ▶n. a belief or set of beliefs held and taught by a church, political party, or other group. ■ a stated principle of government policy, mainly in foreign or military affairs: *the Monroe Doctrine.* [ME: from OFr., from L. *doctrina* 'teaching, learning,' from *doctor* 'teacher,' from *docere* 'teach.']

doc·u·dra·ma /'däkyə,drämə/ ▶n. a dramatized television movie based on real events. [1960s: blend of DOCUMENTARY and DRAMA.]

doc·u·ment ▶n. /'däkyəmənt/ a piece of written, printed, or electronic matter that provides information or evidence or that serves as an official record. ▶v. /'däkyə,ment/ [trans.] record (something) in written, photographic, or other form: *the photographer spent years documenting the lives of miners.* ■ support or accompany with documentation. —**doc·u·ment·a·ble** /,däkyə'mentəbəl/ adj. **doc·u·ment·al** /,däkyə'mentl/ adj. **doc·u·ment·er** /'däkyə,mentər/ n. [ME: from OFr., from L. *documentum* 'lesson, proof.']

doc·u·men·ta·ry /,däkyə'ment(ə)rē/ ▶adj. consisting of official pieces of written, printed, or other matter. ■ (of a movie, a television or radio program, or photography) using pictures or interviews with people involved in real events to provide a factual record or report. ▶n. (pl. **-ries**) a movie or a television or radio program that provides a factual record or report.

doc·u·men·ta·tion /,däkyəmen'tāsʜən/ ▶n. **1** material that provides official information or evidence or that serves as a record. ■ the written specification and instructions accompanying a computer program or hardware. **2** the process of classifying and annotating texts, photographs, etc.: *she arranged the collection and documentation of photographs.*

DOD ▶abbr. Department of Defense.

dod·der[1] /'dädər/ ▶v. [intrans.] tremble or totter, typically because of old age: *spent and nerve-weary, I doddered into the foyer of a third-rate hotel* | [as adj.] (**doddering**) *that doddering old fool.* —**dod·der·er** n. **dod·der·y** adj. [17th C.: var. of obs. dial. *dadder*; rel. to DITHER.]

dod·der[2] ▶n. a widely distributed parasitic climbing plant (genus *Cuscuta*) of the morning glory family, with leafless threadlike stems that are attached to the host plant by means of suckers. [ME: rel. to Mid. High Ger. *toter.*]

dodeca- ▶comb. form (used chiefly in scientific and musical terms) twelve; having twelve: *dodecahedron* | *dodecaphonic.* [from Gk.]

do·dec·a·gon /dō'dekə,gän/ ▶n. a plane figure with twelve sides. [17th C.: from Gk. *dōdekagōnon*, neut. of *dōdekagōnos* 'twelve-angled.']

do·dec·a·he·dron /dō,dekə'hēdrən/ ▶n. (pl. **-drons** or **-dra** /-drə/) a three-dimensional shape having twelve plane faces, in particular a regular solid figure with twelve equal pentagonal faces. —**do·dec·a·he·dral** /-drəl/ adj.

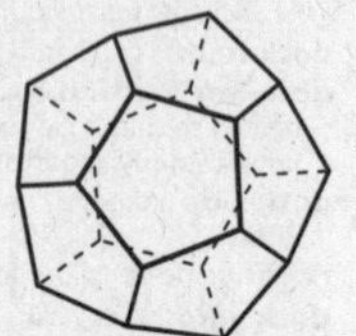
dodecahedron

Do·dec·a·nese /dō,dekə'nēz; -'nēs; ,dōdekə-/ a group of twelve Greek islands in the southeastern Aegean Sea.

dodge /däj/ ▶v. [trans.] avoid (someone or something) by a sudden quick movement: *we ducked inside our doorway to dodge shrapnel that was raining down.* ■ [intrans.] move quickly to one side or out of the way: *Adam dodged between the cars.* ■ avoid (something) in a cunning or dishonest way: *he went after people who had either dodged the war or invented a record in it.* ▶n. a sudden quick movement to avoid someone or something. ■ a cunning trick or dishonest act, in particular one intended to avoid something unpleasant: *bartering can be seen as a tax dodge.* [16th C. (in the senses 'dither' and 'haggle'): of unknown origin.]

dodge·ball /'däj,bôl/ ▶n. a game in which six players on each side of a court try to hit opponents on the opposite side, thus eliminating them, with an inflated ball.

Dodge Cit·y /däj/ a city in southwestern Kansas; a former shipping station and frontier town on the Santa Fe Trail; pop: 25,176.

dodg·er /'däjər/ ▶n. [often with adj.] a person who engages in cunning tricks or dishonest practices to avoid something unpleasant: *tax dodgers.*

do·do /'dōdō/ ▶n. (pl. **-dos** or **-does**) an extinct flightless bird (*Raphus cucullatus*, family Raphidae) with a stout body, stumpy wings, a large head, and a heavy hooked bill. It was found on Mauritius until the end of the 17th century. ■ informal an old-fashioned and ineffective person or thing. [17th C.: from Port. *doudo* 'simpleton.']

Do·do·ma /'dōdəmə; -,mä/ the capital of Tanzania, in the center of the country; pop. 203,830.

DOE ▶abbr. Department of Energy.

doe /dō/ ▶n. a female deer. ■ a female of certain other animal species, such as hare, rabbit, rat, ferret, or kangaroo. [OE *dā*, of unknown origin.]

doe-eyed ▶adj. having large, gentle, dark eyes: *portraits of doe-eyed young girls.*

do·er /'dōōər/ ▶n. the person who does something. ■ a person who acts rather than merely talking or thinking: *I'm a doer, not a moaner.*

does /dəz/ third person singular present of DO[1].

does·n't /'dəzənt/ ▶contr. does not.

doff /däf; dôf/ ▶v. [trans.] dated remove (an item of clothing): *he doffed his tie and jacket.* ■ tip (one's hat) as a greeting or token of respect. [ME: contr. of *do off.* Cf. DON[2].]

dog /dôg/ ▶n. **1** a domesticated carnivorous mammal (*Canis familiaris*) that typically has a long snout, an acute sense of smell, and a barking, howling, or whining voice. It is widely kept as a pet or for work or for hunting or fishing. The **dog family** (Canidae) also includes the wolves, coyotes, jackals, and foxes. ■ a wild animal of the dog family. ■ the male of an animal of the dog family, or of some other mammals such as the otter: [as adj.] *a dog fox.* ■ (in extended and metaphorical use) referring to behavior considered to be savage, dangerous, or wildly energetic: *he bit into it like a dog.* **2** [often with adj.] informal a person regarded as unpleasant, contemptible, or wicked (used as a term of abuse): *come out, Michael, you dog!* ■ [with adj.] used to refer to a person of a specified kind in a tone of playful reproof, commiseration, or congratulation: *you lucky dog!* ■ used in various phrases to refer to someone who is abject or miserable, esp. because they have been treated harshly: *I make him work like a dog.* ■ informal offens. a woman regarded as unattractive. ■ informal a thing of poor quality; a failure: *a dog of a movie.* **3** short for FIREDOG. **4** a mechanical device for gripping. **5** (**dogs**) informal feet: *my tired dogs.* ▶v. (**dogged, dog·ging**) [trans.] **1** follow (someone or their movements) closely and persistently: *photographers dog her every step.* ■ (of a problem) cause continual trouble for: *the committee has been dogged by controversy.* **2** (**dog it**) informal act lazily; fail to try one's hardest. **3** grip (something) with a mechanical device.

– PHRASES **dog eat dog** used to refer to a situation of fierce competition in which people are willing to harm each other in order to succeed: *in this business, it's always dog eat dog* | *popular music is a dog-eat-dog industry.* **a dog's age** informal a very long time. **a dog's life** an unhappy existence, full of problems or unfair treatment. **the dogs of war** literary the havoc accompanying military conflict. **every dog has its day** proverb everyone will have good luck or success at some point in their lives. **go to the dogs** informal deteriorate shockingly: *the country is going to the dogs.* **hair of the dog** see HAIR. **put on the dog** informal behave in a pretentious or ostentatious way. **rain cats and dogs** see RAIN. **(as) sick as a dog** see SICK[1]. **throw someone to the dogs** discard someone as worthless. **you can't teach an old dog new tricks** proverb you cannot make people change their established patterns of opinion and behavior. [OE *docga*, of unknown origin.]

dog and pon·y show ▶n. an elaborate display or presentation, esp. as part of a promotional campaign.

dog·bane /'dôg,bān/ ▶n. a shrubby North American plant (genus *Apocynum*, family Apocynaceae), typically having bell-shaped flowers and reputed to be poisonous to dogs.

dog bis·cuit ▶n. a hard thick biscuit for feeding to dogs.

dog·catch·er /'dôg,kacʜər; -,kecʜ-/ ▶n. an official or employee who rounds up and impounds stray dogs in a community. ■ fig. a low-level political official.

dog col·lar ▶n. a collar for a dog. ■ informal term for CLERICAL COLLAR.

dog days ▶plural n. the hottest period of the year (reckoned in antiquity from the heliacal rising of Sirius, the Dog Star). ■ a period of inactivity or sluggishness: *in August the baseball races are in the dog days.*

doge /dōj/ ▶n. hist. the chief magistrate of Venice or Genoa. [16th C.: from Fr., from Venetian Ital. *doze*, based on L. *dux, duc-* 'leader.']

dog-ear ▶v. [trans.] fold down the corner of (a book or magazine), typically to mark a place. ▶adj. (**dog-eared**) (of an object made from paper) with the corners worn or battered with use.

dog·fight /'dôg,fīt/ ▶n. a close combat between military aircraft. ■ a ferocious struggle for supremacy between interested parties: *the meeting deteriorated into a dogfight.* ■ a fight between dogs, esp. one organized illegally for public entertainment. ▶v. engage in a dogfight. —**dog·fight·er** n.

dog·fish /'dôg,fisʜ/ ▶n. (pl. same or **-fish·es**) **1** a small sand-colored, long-tailed bottom-dwelling shark (*Scyliorhinus canicula*, family Scyliorhinidae). **2** [with adj.] a small shark that resembles or is related to the dogfish, esp. of the families Scyliorhinidae, Squalidae, and Triakidae.

dog·ged /'dôgid/ ▶adj. having or showing tenacity and grim persistence: *success required dogged determination.* —**dog·ged·ly** adv. **dog·ged·ness** n.

dog·ger·el /'dôgərəl/ ▶n. comic verse composed in irregular rhythm. ■ verse or words that are badly written or expressed. [ME: appar. from DOG + -REL.]

dog·gie ▶ n. var. of DOGGY.

dog·gie bag ▶ n. a bag used by a restaurant customer or party guest to take home leftover food, supposedly for their dog.

dog·gone /ˈdôgˈgôn/ informal ▶ adj. [attrib.] used to express feelings of annoyance, surprise, or pleasure: *now just a doggone minute.* ▶ v. [trans.] used to express surprise, irritation, or anger: ***doggone it** if I didn't see a motivation in Joey!* [19th C.: prob. from *dog on it*, euphemism for *God damn it*.]

dog·gy /ˈdôgē/ ▶ n. (also **dog·gie**) (pl. **-gies**) a child's word for a dog. — **dog·gi·ness** n.

dog·house /ˈdôgˌhous/ ▶ n. a dog's kennel.
– PHRASES **(be) in the doghouse** informal, often humorous (be) in mild or temporary disfavor.

do·gie /ˈdōgē/ ▶ n. (pl. **-gies**) a motherless or neglected calf. [19th C.: of unknown origin.]

dog in the man·ger ▶ n. a person who has no need of, or ability to use, a possession that would be of use or value to others, but who prevents others from having it: *what a dog in the manger you must be!* [alluding to the fable of the dog that lay in a manger to prevent the ox and horse from eating the hay.]

dog Lat·in ▶ n. a debased form of Latin.

dog·leg /ˈdôgˌleg/ ▶ n. a thing that bends sharply, in particular a sharp bend in a road or route. ■ Golf a hole at which the player cannot aim directly at the green from the tee. ▶ adj. (also **dog-legged**) bent like a dog's hind leg: *the surf splashes over the dogleg concrete jetty.*

dog·ma /ˈdôgmə/ ▶ n. a principle or set of principles laid down by an authority as incontrovertibly true: *the Christian dogma of the Trinity.* [16th C.: via late L. from Gk. *dogma* 'opinion,' from *dokein* 'seem good, think.']

dog·mat·ic /dôgˈmatik/ ▶ adj. inclined to lay down principles as incontrovertibly true: *he gives his opinion without trying to be dogmatic.* — **dog·mat·i·cal·ly** /-ik(ə)lē/ adv. **dog·mat·ics** /-iks/ n.

dog·ma·tism /ˈdôgməˌtizəm/ ▶ n. the tendency to lay down principles as incontrovertibly true, without consideration of evidence or the opinions of others. — **dog·ma·tist** n.

dog·nap /ˈdôgˌnap/ ▶ v. (**-napped, -nap·ping** or **-naped, -nap·ing**) [trans.] informal steal (a dog), esp. in order to sell it. — **dog·nap·per** n.

do-good·er /ˈdo͞o ˌgo͝odər/ ▶ n. a well-meaning but unrealistic or interfering philanthropist or reformer. — **do-good** adj. & n. **do-good·er·y** /-ərē/ n. **do-good·ism** /-go͝odˌizəm/ n.

dog pad·dle ▶ n. an elementary swimming stroke like that of a swimming dog. ▶ v. (**dog-paddle**) [intrans.] swim using this stroke.

Dog·rib /ˈdôgˌrib/ ▶ n. **1** a member of a Dene people of northwestern Canada. **2** the Athabaskan language of this people. ▶ adj. of or relating to this people or their language.

dog rose ▶ n. a delicately scented Eurasian wild rose (genus *Rosa*) with pink or white flowers, esp. *R. canina*.

dogs·bod·y /ˈdôgzˌbädē/ ▶ n. (pl. **-bod·ies**) informal, esp. Brit. a person who is given boring, menial tasks to do. — **dogs·bod·y·ing** n.

dog·sled /ˈdôgˌsled/ (also **dog sled**) ▶ n. a sled designed to be pulled by dogs. ▶ v. [intrans.] [usu. as n.] (**dogsledding**) travel by dogsled: *winter activities include dogsledding.*

dogs·tail /ˈdôgzˌtāl/ (also **dog's-tail**) ▶ n. an Old World fodder grass (genus *Cynosurus*) with spiky flowerheads.

Dog Star the star Sirius.

dog tag ▶ n. a metal tag attached to a dog's collar, typically giving its name and owner's address. ■ informal a soldier's metal identity tag, worn on a chain around the neck.

dog-tired ▶ adj. extremely tired; worn out.

dog·tooth vi·o·let ▶ n. a plant (genus *Erythronium*) of the lily family that has backward-curving pointed petals, in particular the trout lily.

dog-trot ▶ n. **1** [in sing.] a gentle easy trot. **2** a breezeway connecting two cabins. ▶ v. [intrans.] move at such a pace.

dog vi·o·let ▶ n. a scentless wild violet, typically having purple or lilac flowers.

dog war·den ▶ n. another term for DOGCATCHER.

dog·watch /ˈdôgˌwäCH/ ▶ n. either of two short watches on a ship (4–6 or 6–8 p.m.).

dog·wood /ˈdôgˌwo͝od/ ▶ n. a shrub or small tree (genus *Cornus*, family Cornaceae) of north temperate regions that yields hard timber and is grown for its decorative foliage, red stems, and colorful berries. ■ used in names of trees that resemble the dogwood or yield similar hard timber.

flowering dogwood

Do·ha /ˈdōhə/ the capital of Qatar, in the eastern part of the country; pop 300,000.

doi·ly /ˈdoilē/ ▶ n. (pl. **-lies**) an ornamental mat, typically made of lace and placed under decorative objects. [17th C.: from *Doiley* or *Doyley*, the name of a 17th-cent. London draper.]

do·ing /ˈdo͞oiNG/ ▶ n. **1** (usu. **doings**) the activities in which a particular person engages. ■ deeds; accomplishments. ■ social events. **2** effort; activity: *it would take some doing to calm him down.*

do-it-your·self (abbr. **DIY**) ▶ adj. (of work, esp. building, painting, or decorating) done or to be done by an amateur at home: *easy-to-use materials and do-it-yourself kits for plumbing fittings.* — **do-it-your·self·er** n.

dol. ▶ abbr. dollar(s).

Dol·by /ˈdōlbē; ˈdôl-/ ▶ n. trademark an electronic noise-reduction system used in tape recording to reduce hiss. ■ an electronic system used to provide stereophonic sound for movie theaters and television sets. [1960s: named after Ray M. *Dolby* (born 1933), the Amer. engineer who devised it.]

dol·ce /ˈdōlCHā/ ▶ adv. & adj. Music (esp. as a direction) sweetly and softly. [Ital., lit. 'sweet.']

dol·ce vi·ta /ˌdōlCHā ˈvētə/ ▶ n. [in sing.] (usu. **la dolce vita**) a life of heedless pleasure and luxury. [Ital., lit. 'sweet life.']

dol·drums /ˈdōldrəmz; ˈdäl-; ˈdôl-/ ▶ plural n. (**the doldrums**) low spirits; a feeling of boredom or depression: *color catalogs will rid you of February doldrums.* ■ a period of inactivity or a state of stagnation: *the mortgage market has been **in the doldrums** for three years.* ■ an equatorial region of the Atlantic Ocean with calms, sudden storms, and light unpredictable winds. [18th C.: perh. from DULL.]

Dole /dōl/ US politicians. Robert Joseph (1923–), a Republican US senator from Kansas 1969–96, was defeated by Bill Clinton in the 1996 presidential election. His wife, Elizabeth Hanford (1936–) served as US secretary of transportation 1983–87, US secretary of labor 1989–90, and president of the American Red Cross 1991–2000 before her election to the US Senate in 2002 as a North Carolina Republican.

dole /dōl/ ▶ n. (usu. **the dole**) esp. Brit., informal benefit paid by the government to the unemployed: *she is drawing on the dole.* ▶ v. [trans.] (**dole something out**) distribute shares of something: *the scanty portions of food **doled out** to them.* [OE *dāl* 'division, portion, or share,' of Gmc. origin; rel. to DEAL[1].]

dole·ful /ˈdōlfəl/ ▶ adj. expressing sorrow; mournful: *a doleful look.* ■ causing grief or misfortune: *doleful consequences.* — **dole·ful·ly** adv. **dole·ful·ness** n.

dol·er·ite /ˈdäləˌrīt/ ▶ n. Geol. a dark, medium-grained igneous rock. Also called DIABASE. [19th C.: from Fr. *dolérite*, from Gk. *doleros* 'deceptive.']

dol·i·cho·ce·phal·ic /ˌdälikōsəˈfalik/ ▶ adj. Anat. having a relatively long skull (typically with the breadth less than 80 (or 75) percent of the length). Often contrasted with BRACHYCEPHALIC. — **dol·i·cho·ceph·a·ly** /-ˈsefəlē/ n. [19th C.: from Gk. *dolikhos* 'long' + -CEPHALIC.]

doll /däl/ ▶ n. a small model of a human figure, often one of a baby or girl, used as a child's toy. ■ informal an attractive young woman, often with connotations of unintelligence and frivolity. ■ informal an attractive young man. ■ a generous or considerate person. ■ informal used as an affectionate, sometimes offensive, form of address. ▶ v. [trans.] (**doll someone up**) informal dress someone or oneself smartly and attractively: *I got all **dolled up** for a party.* ■ (**doll something up**) informal decorate or dress up something. [16th C. (denoting a mistress): nickname for *Dorothy*.]

dol·lar /ˈdälər/ ▶ n. the basic monetary unit of the US, Canada, Australia, and certain countries in the Pacific, Caribbean, Southeast Asia, Africa, and South America. [from early Flemish or Low German *daler*, from Ger. *T(h)aler*, short for *Joachimsthaler*, a coin from the silver mine of *Joachimsthal* ('Joachim's valley'), now *Jáchymov* in the Czech Republic.]

dol·lar ar·e·a ▶ n. the area of the world in which currency is linked to the US dollar.

dol·lar di·plo·ma·cy ▶ n. the use of a country's financial power to extend its international influence.

dol·lar gap ▶ n. the amount by which a country's import trade with the dollar area exceeds the corresponding export trade.

dol·lar sign (also **dollar mark**) ▶ n. the sign $, representing a dollar.

doll·house /ˈdälˌhous/ ▶ n. a miniature toy house used for playing with dolls.

dol·lop /ˈdäləp/ ▶ n. informal a shapeless mass or blob of something, esp. soft food: ***great dollops of cream*** | fig. ***a dollop of romance here and there.*** ▶ v. (**-loped, -lop·ing**) [trans.] add (a shapeless mass or blob of something) casually and without measuring. [16th C.: perh. of Scand. origin and rel. to Norw. dial. *dolp* 'lump.']

dol·ly /ˈdälē/ ▶ n. (pl. **-lies**) **1** a child's word for a doll. ■ informal dated an attractive and stylish young woman, usually with connotations of unintelligence. **2** a small platform on wheels used for holding heavy objects, typically film or television cameras.

Dol·ly Var·den /ˌdälē ˈvärdn/ ▶ n. **1** (also **Dolly Varden hat**) a large hat with one side drooping and with a floral trimming, formerly worn by women. **2** a brightly spotted edible char (*Salvelinus malma*) occurring in fresh water on both sides of the North Pacific. [19th C.: after a character in Dickens's *Barnaby Rudge*.]

dol·ma /ˈdôlmə/ ▶ n. (pl. **dol·mas** or **dol·ma·des** /dôlˈmäT͟Hes/) a Greek and Turkish delicacy in which ingredients such as spiced rice, meat, and bread are wrapped in vine or cabbage leaves. [from mod. Gk. *ntolmas* or its source, Turk. *dolma*, from *dolmak* 'fill, be filled.']

dol·men /ˈdōlmən; ˈdäl-/ ▶ n. a megalithic tomb with a large flat stone laid on upright ones, found chiefly in Britain and France. [19th C.: from Fr., perh. via Breton from Cornish *tolmen* 'hole of a stone.']

dolmen

do·lo·mite /'dälə,mīt; 'dō-/ ▶ **n.** a translucent mineral consisting of a carbonate of calcium and magnesium. ■ a sedimentary rock formed chiefly of this mineral. — **dol·o·mit·ic** /,dälə'mitik/ **adj.** [18th C.: from French, from the name of *Dolomieu* (1750–1801), the Fr. geologist who discovered it, + -ITE[1].]

Do·lo·mite Moun·tains /'dōlə,mīt; 'däl-/ (also **the Do·lo·mites**) a range in northern Italy, part of the Alps; highest peak 10,965 feet (3,342 m).

dol·or·ous /'dōlərəs; 'däl-/ ▶ **adj.** literary feeling or expressing great sorrow or distress.

dol·phin /'dälfin; 'dôl-/ ▶ **n.** **1** a small gregarious and highly intelligent toothed whale that typically has a beaklike snout and a curved fin on the back. Dolphins inhabit seas (family Delphinidae) and rivers (family Platanistidae). ■ a dolphinlike creature depicted in heraldry or art, typically with an arched body and fins like a fish. **2** (also **dol·phin·fish**) another term for MAHIMAHI. **3** a bollard, pile, or buoy for mooring. **4** a structure for protecting the pier of a bridge or other structure from collision with ships. [ME: from OFr. *dauphin*, from Provençal *dalfin*, from L. *delphinus*, from Gk. *delphin*.]

dol·phin-safe ▶ **adj.** (on canned tuna labels) indicating that the tuna has been harvested using fishing methods that are not harmful to dolphins.

dolt /dōlt/ ▶ **n.** a stupid person. — **dolt·ish adj. dolt·ish·ly adv. dolt·ish·ness n.** [16th C.: perh. a var. of *dulled*, past part. of DULL.]

Dom /däm/ ▶ **n.** Portuguese form of DON[1] (sense 2). [from L. *dominus* 'master.']

-dom ▶ **suffix** forming nouns: **1** denoting a state or condition: *freedom.* **2** denoting rank or status: *earldom.* **3** denoting a domain: *fiefdom.* **4** denoting a class of people or the attitudes associated with them, regarded collectively: *officialdom.* [OE *-dōm*, orig. meaning 'decree, judgment.']

do·main /dō'mān/ ▶ **n.** an area of territory owned or controlled by a ruler or government: *the southwestern French domains of the Plantagenets.* ■ an estate or territory held in legal possession by a person or persons. ■ a specified sphere of activity or knowledge: fig. *visual communication is the domain of the graphic designer.* ■ Physics a discrete region of magnetism in ferromagnetic material. ■ Comput. a distinct subset of the Internet with addresses sharing a common suffix. ■ Math. the set of possible values of the independent variable or variables of a function. [ME: from Fr. *domaine*, alt. (by association with L. *dominus* 'lord') of OFr. *demeine* 'belonging to a lord' (see DEMESNE).]

do·main name ▶ **n.** a series of alphanumeric strings separated by periods, such as *www.oup-usa.org*, serving as an address for a computer network connection and identifying the owner of the address.

dome /dōm/ ▶ **n.** **1** a rounded vault forming the roof of a building or structure, typically with a circular base. ■ the revolving openable hemispherical roof of an observatory. ■ [in names] a sports stadium with a domed roof. **2** a thing shaped like such a roof, in particular: ■ the rounded summit of a hill or mountain. ■ a natural vault or canopy, such as that of the sky or trees. ▶ **v.** [trans.] [usu. as adj.] (**domed**) cover with or shape as a dome: *a domed stadium.* — **dome·like adj.** [16th C. (sense 3): from Fr. *dôme*, from Ital. *duomo* 'cathedral, dome,' from L. *domus* 'house.']

Dome of the Rock an Islamic shrine in Jerusalem.

Domes·day /'do͞omz,dā/ ▶ **n.** (also **Domesday Book, Doomsday Book**) a comprehensive record of the extent, value, ownership, and liabilities of land in England, made in 1086 by order of William I.

do·mes·tic /də'mestik/ ▶ **adj.** **1** of or relating to the running of a home or to family relations. ■ (of a person) fond of family life and running a home: *she was not at all domestic.* ■ (of an animal) tame and kept by humans: *domestic cattle.* **2** existing or occurring inside a particular country; not foreign or international. ▶ **n.** (also **domestic worker** or **domestic help**) a person who is paid to help with menial tasks such as cleaning. — **do·mes·ti·cal·ly adv.** [ME: from Fr. *domestique*, from L. *domesticus*, from *domus* 'house.']

do·mes·ti·cate /də'mesti,kāt/ ▶ **v.** [trans.] (usu. **be domesticated**) tame (an animal) and keep it as a pet or for farm produce. ■ cultivate (a plant) for food. ■ humorous make (someone) fond of and good at home life and the tasks that it involves: *you've quite domesticated him.* — **do·mes·ti·ca·ble** /-kəbəl/ **adj. do·mes·ti·ca·tion** /-,mesti'kāsʜən/ **n.**

do·mes·tic·i·ty /,dōme'stisitē/ ▶ **n.** home or family life: *the atmosphere is one of happy domesticity.*

do·mes·tic part·ner ▶ **n.** a person who shares a residence with a sexual partner, esp. without a legally recognized union. — **do·mes·tic part·ner·ship n.**

do·mes·tic pi·geon ▶ **n.** see PIGEON[1] (sense 1).

dom·i·cile /'dämə,sīl; 'dō-; 'däməsəl/ (also **dom·i·cil** /'däməsəl/) ▶ **n.** formal or Law the country that a person treats as their permanent home, or lives in and has a substantial connection with: *his wife has a domicile of origin in Germany.* ■ a person's residence or home. ■ the place at which a company or other body is registered, esp. for tax purposes. ▶ **v.** [with adverbial of place] (**be domiciled**) formal or Law treat a specified country as a permanent home: *the tenant is domiciled in the United States.* ■ reside; be based. [ME: via OFr. from L. *domicilium* 'dwelling,' from *domus* 'home.']

dom·i·nance /'dämənəns/ ▶ **n.** power and influence over others: *the worldwide dominance of Hollywood.* ■ Genet. the phenomenon whereby, in an individual containing two allelic forms of a gene, one is expressed to the exclusion of the other. — **dom·i·nan·cy** /-sē/ **n.**

dom·i·nant /'dämənənt/ ▶ **adj.** most important, powerful, or influential: *they are now in an even more dominant position in the market.* ■ (of a high place or object) overlooking others. ■ Genet. relating to or denoting heritable characteristics that are controlled by genes that are expressed in offspring even when inherited from only one parent. Often contrasted with RECESSIVE. ■ Ecol. denoting the predominant species in a plant (or animal) community. ▶ **n.** a dominant thing, in particular: ■ Genet. a dominant trait or gene. ■ Music the fifth note of the diatonic scale of any key, or the key based on this, considered in relation to the key of the tonic. — **dom·i·nant·ly adv.**

dom·i·nant sev·enth ▶ **n.** Music the common chord of the dominant note in a key, plus the minor seventh from that note (e.g., in the key of C, a chord of G-B-D-F). It is important in conventional harmony, as it naturally resolves to the tonic or subdominant.

dom·i·nate /'dämə,nāt/ ▶ **v.** [trans.] (often **be dominated**) have a commanding influence on; exercise control over. ■ be the most important or conspicuous person or thing in. ■ (of something tall or high) have a commanding position over; overlook. — **dom·i·na·tor** /-,nātər/ **n.** [17th C.: from L. *dominat-* 'ruled, governed,' from the v. *dominari*, from *dominus* 'lord, master.']

dom·i·na·tion /,dämə'nāsʜən/ ▶ **n.** the exercise of control or influence over someone or something, or the state of being so controlled.

dom·i·na·trix /,dämə'nātriks/ ▶ **n.** (pl. **-tri·ces** /-trə,sēz/ or **-trix·es**) a dominating woman, esp. one who takes the sadistic role in sadomasochistic sexual activities.

dom·i·neer /,dämə'ni(ə)r/ ▶ **v.** [intrans.] [usu. as adj.] (**domineering**) assert one's will over another in an arrogant way. — **dom·i·neer·ing·ly adv.** [16th C.: from Du. *dominieren*, from Fr. *dominer*, from L. *dominari* (see DOMINATE).]

Do·min·go /də'mɪɴgō/, Placido (1941–), Spanish opera singer.

Dom·i·nic, St. /'dämənik/ (*c.*1170–1221), Spanish priest and friar; Spanish name *Domingo de Guzmán*. In 1216, he founded the Order of Friars Preachers; its members became known as Dominicans.

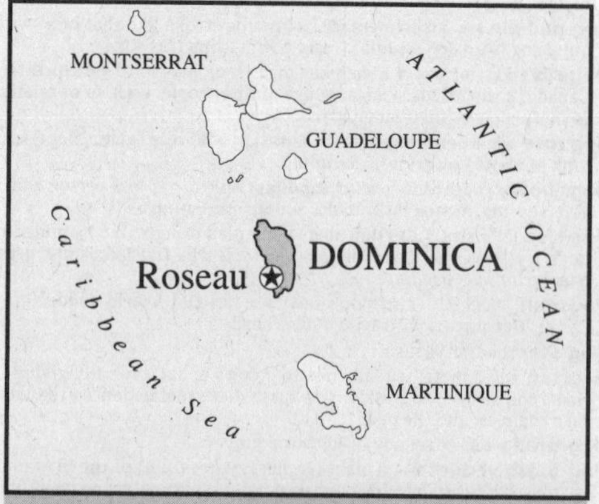

Dominica

Official name: Commonwealth of Dominica
Location: eastern West Indies, the most northern of the Windward Islands, in the Caribbean Sea, 320 miles (515 km) north of the Venezuelan coast
Area: 290 square miles (760 km)
Population: 71,790
Capital: Roseau
Languages: English (official), Creole
Currency: East Caribbean dollar

Dom·i·ni·ca /,dämə'nēkə; də'minikə/ a country in the eastern West Indies. *See box.*

Do·min·i·can[1] /də'minikən/ ▶ **n.** a member of the Roman Catholic order of preaching friars founded by St. Dominic, or of a religious order for women founded on similar principles. ▶ **adj.** of or relating to St. Dominic or the Dominicans.

Do·min·i·can[2] ▶ **adj.** of or relating to the Dominican Republic or its people. ▶ **n.** a native or national of the Dominican Republic.

Do·min·i·can[3] ▶ **adj.** of or relating to the island of Dominica or its people. ▶ **n.** a native or national of the island of Dominica.

Do·min·i·can Re·pub·lic /də'minəkən/ a country in the Caribbean Sea. *See box on next page.*

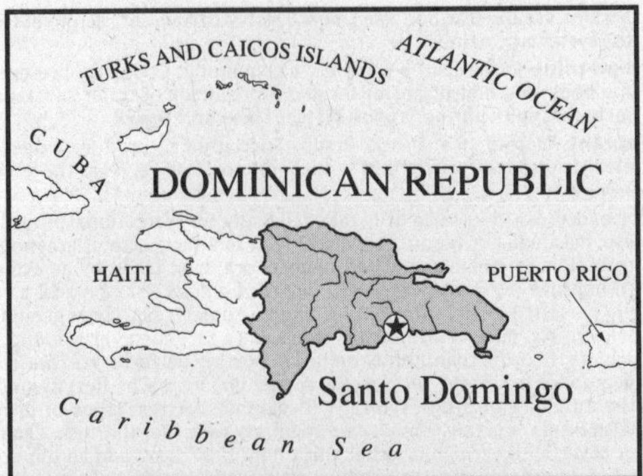

Dominican Republic

Location: the eastern two-thirds of the island of Hispaniola between the Caribbean Sea and the North Atlantic Ocean; bordering Haiti, which covers the western end of the island
Area: 18,700 square miles (48,400 sq km)
Population: 8,830,000
Capital: Santo Domingo
Language: Spanish
Currency: Dominican peso

do·min·ion /dəˈminyən/ ▶ **n.** **1** sovereignty; control: *man's attempt to establish **dominion** over nature.* **2** (usu. **dominions**) the territory of a sovereign or government: *the Angevin dominions.* ■ (**Dominion**) hist. each of the self-governing territories of the British Commonwealth. [ME: via OFr. from med. L. *dominio(n-)*, from L. *dominium*, from *dominus* 'lord, master.']

Do·min·ion Day former name for July 1, a national holiday observed in Canada to commemorate the formation of the Dominion in 1867. Since 1982, it has been known as **Canada Day**.

dom·i·no /ˈdäməˌnō/ ▶ **n.** (pl. **-noes** or **-nos**) **1** any of 28 small oblong pieces marked with 0–6 dots (pips) in each half. ■ (**dominoes**) [treated as sing.] the game played with such pieces, in which they are laid down to form a line, each player in turn trying to find and lay down a domino with a value matched by that of a piece at either end of the line already formed. **2** hist. a loose cloak, worn with a mask for the upper part of the face at masquerades. [17th C.: from Fr., denoting a hood worn by priests in winter, prob. based on L. *dominus* 'lord, master.']

dominoes

dom·i·no ef·fect ▶ **n.** the effect of the domino theory.

dom·i·no the·o·ry ▶ **n.** the theory that a political event in one country will cause similar events in neighboring countries, like a falling domino causing an entire row of upended dominoes to fall.

Do·mi·tian /dəˈmisʜən/ (AD 51–96), Roman emperor 81–96; son of Vespasian; full name *Titus Flavius Domitianus*.

Don /dän/ a river in Russia that rises southeast of Moscow and flows for 1,224 miles (1,958 km) to the Sea of Azov.

don[1] /dän/ ▶ **n.** **1** (**Don**) a Spanish title prefixed to a male forename. ■ a Spanish gentleman; a Spaniard. ■ informal a high-ranking member of the Mafia. **2** a university teacher, esp. a senior member of a college at Oxford or Cambridge. — **don·ship** **n.** [16th C.: from Sp., from L. *dominus* 'lord, master.' Cf. DONNA.]

don[2] ▶ **v.** (**donned, don·ning**) [trans.] put on (an item of clothing). [ME: contr. of *do on*. Cf. DOFF.]

do·nate /ˈdōnāt; dōˈnāt/ ▶ **v.** [trans.] give (money or goods) for a good cause, for example to a charity. ■ allow the removal of (blood or an organ) from one's body for transplantation, transfusion, or other use. — **do·na·tor** /ˈdōnātər/ **n.** [18th C.: back-form. from DONATION.]

Don·a·tel·lo /ˌdänəˈtelō/ (1386–1466), Italian sculptor; born *Donato di Betto Bardi*. His sculptures include the bronze *David* (c.1430–60).

do·na·tion /dōˈnāsʜən/ ▶ **n.** something that is given to a charity, esp. a sum of money. ■ the action of donating something. [ME: via OFr. from L. *donatio(n-)*, from the v. *donare*, based on *donum* 'gift.']

Do·nau /ˈdōnou/ German name for DANUBE.

Don·bas /dənˈbäs; ˈdänbas/ Ukrainian name for DONETS BASIN.

Don·cas·ter /ˈdäɴɢkəstər/ a town in northern England; pop. 284,300.

done /dən/ past participle of DO[1]. ▶ **v.** informal used as a nonstandard past tense of DO[1]. ■ informal used with a standard past tense verb to indicate absoluteness or completion: *I done told you.* ▶ **adj.** **1** carried out, completed, or treated in a particular way: *the path needed replacing and she wanted it done in asphalt.* ■ (of food) cooked thoroughly. ■ no longer happening or existing. **2** informal socially acceptable: *therapy was not the done thing then.* ▶ **exclam.** used to indicate that the speaker accepts the terms of an offer.
– PHRASES **a done deal** a plan or project that has been finalized. **done for** informal in a situation so bad that it is impossible to get out: *if he gets them, we'll all be done for.* **done in** informal extremely tired: *you look done in.* **over and done with** see OVER.

do·nee /dōˈnē/ ▶ **n.** a person who receives a gift. [16th C.: from DONOR + -EE.]

Don·e·gal /ˌdäniˈgôl/ a county in northwestern Republic of Ireland; capital, Lifford.

don·e·gal /ˈdänigəl; -ˌgôl/ (also **Donegal tweed**) ▶ **n.** a tweed characterized by bright flecks randomly distributed on a background usually of light gray, originally woven in County Donegal.

Do·nets /dəˈn(y)ets/ a river that rises near Belgorod in southern Russia and flows southeast for about 630 miles (1,000 km) to join the Don River near Rostov.

Do·nets Ba·sin an industrial region in southeastern Ukraine. Ukrainian name DONBAS.

Do·netsk /dəˈn(y)etsk/ a city in the Donets Basin in Ukraine; pop. 1,117,000.

dong[1] /dôɴɢ; däɴɢ/ ▶ **v.** [intrans.] (of a bell) make a deep resonant sound. ▶ **n.** **1** the deep resonant sound of a large bell. **2** vulgar slang a penis. [16th C.: imitative.]

dong[2] ▶ **n.** the basic monetary unit of Vietnam, equal to 100 xu. [from Vietnamese *đông* 'coin.']

Dong·nai Riv·er /ˈdôɴɢ ˈnī/ (also **Don·nai**) a river in south central Vietnam that flows for 300 miles (483 km) to the Saigon River.

dong quai /ˈdo͝oɴɢ ˈkwā; ˈkwī/ ▶ **n.** an aromatic herb (*Angelica sinersis*) of the parsley family, native to China and Japan, the root of which is used to treat gynecological complaints.

Don·i·zet·ti /ˌdänəˈzetē/, Gaetano (1797–1848), Italian composer. His operas include *Lucia di Lammermoor* (1835) and *Don Pasquale* (1843).

don·jon /ˈdänjən; ˈdən-/ ▶ **n.** the great tower or innermost keep of a castle. [ME: var. of DUNGEON.]

Don Juan /ˌdän ˈ(h)wän/ a legendary Spanish nobleman known for seducing women. ■ [as n.] (**a Don Juan**) a seducer of women; a libertine.

don·key /ˈdôɴɢkē; ˈdäɴɢ-/ ▶ **n.** (pl. **-keys**) **1** a domesticated hoofed mammal (*Equus asinus*) of the horse family with long ears and a braying call, used as a beast of burden; an ass. **2** informal a stupid or foolish person.
– PHRASES **donkey's years** informal a very long time. [18th C.: perh. from DUN[1].]

don·key en·gine ▶ **n.** a small or auxiliary engine, esp. on a ship.

don·na /ˈdänə; ˈdôn-nä/ ▶ **n.** an Italian lady. ■ (**Donna**) a courtesy title prefixed to the forename of such a lady. [17th C.: from Ital., from L. *domina* 'mistress,' fem. of *dominus* 'lord, master.' Cf. DON[1].]

Donne /dən/, John (1572–1631), English poet and preacher. He is noted for his *Satires* (c.1590–99), *Elegies* (c.1590–99), and love poems.

Don·ner Pass /ˈdänər/ a site in the Sierra Nevada in northeastern California where some members of an 1844 emigrant party survived a blizzard partly by eating the dead.

don·nish /ˈdänisʜ/ ▶ **adj.** thought to resemble or suit a college don, particularly because of a pedantic, scholarly manner.

don·ny·brook /ˈdänēˌbro͝ok/ ▶ **n.** a scene of uproar and disorder; a heated argument. [19th C.: from the name of a suburb of Dublin, Ireland, formerly famous for its annual fair.]

do·nor /ˈdōnər/ ▶ **n.** a person who donates something, esp. money to a fund or charity. ■ a person who provides blood for transfusion, semen for insemination, or an organ or tissue for transplantation. ■ Chem. an atom or molecule that provides electrons in forming a coordinate bond. ■ Physics an impurity atom in a semiconductor that contributes a conducting electron to the material. [ME: from OFr. *doneur*, from L. *donator*, from *donare* 'give.']

do-noth·ing ▶ **n.** a person who is idle or lacks ambition. ▶ **adj.** idle or lacking ambition.

Don Quix·o·te /ˌdän kēˈhōtē; -tā/ the hero of a romance (1605–15) by Cervantes, a satirical account of chivalric beliefs and conduct. Don Quixote is typified by a romantic vision and naive, unworldly idealism.

don't /dōnt/ ▶ **contr.** do not. ■ informal does not: *she don't drink tea.*

do·nut /ˈdōnət; -ˌnət/ ▶ **n.** var. of DOUGHNUT.

doo·dad /ˈdo͞oˌdad/ ▶ **n.** a fancy article or trivial ornament. ■ a gadget, esp. one whose name the speaker does not know or cannot recall. [20th C.: of unknown origin.]

doo·dle /ˈdo͞odl/ ▶ **v.** [intrans.] scribble absentmindedly. ■ engage in idle activity; dawdle: *they could plan another attack while we're just **doodling around**.* ▶ **n.** a rough drawing made absentmindedly. — **doo·dler** **n.** [17th C.: from Low Ger. *dudeltopf, dudeldopp* 'simpleton.']

doo·dly-squat /ˈdo͞odl-ē ˌskwät/ ▶ **n.** another term for DIDDLY-SQUAT.

doo-doo /ˈdo͞o ˌdo͞o/ ▶ **n.** a child's word for excrement, used euphemistically in other contexts: *when our fax machine isn't working, we're in deep doo-doo.*

doo·fus /ˈdo͞ofəs/ (also **du·fus**) ▶ **n.** (pl. **doo·fuses**) informal a stupid person. [1960s: perh. an alt. of GOOFUS.]

PRONUNCIATION KEY ə *ago, up*; ər *over, fur*; a *hat*; ā *ate*; ä *car*; e *let*; ē *see*; i *fit*; ī *by*; ɴɢ *sing*; ō *go*; ô *law, for*; oi *toy*; o͝o *good*; o͞o *goo*; ou *out*; ᴛʜ *thin*; ᴛ̲ʜ̲ *then*; ᴢʜ *vision*

doo·hick·ey /ˈdo͞oˌhikē/ ▶ **n.** (pl. **-eys**) informal a small object or gadget, esp. one whose name the speaker does not know or cannot recall. [20th C.: blend of DOODAD and HICKEY.]

Doo·lit·tle /ˈdo͞oˌlitl/, Hilda (1886–1961), US poet; pen name **H.D.** Her work shows the influence of imagist poets and classical mythology.

doom /do͞om/ ▶ **n.** death, destruction, or some other terrible fate. ▶ **v.** [trans.] (usu. **be doomed**) condemn to certain destruction or death: *fuel was spilling out of the damaged wing and the aircraft was doomed.* ■ cause to have an unfortunate and inescapable outcome: *her plan was doomed to failure* | [as adj.] (**doomed**) *the moving story of their doomed love affair.*
– PHRASES **doom and gloom** (also **gloom and doom**) a general feeling of pessimism or despondency: *the national feeling of doom and gloom.* [OE *dōm* 'statute, judgment,' of Gmc. origin, from a base meaning 'to put in place'; rel. to DO[1].]

doom·say·er /ˈdo͞omˌsāər/ ▶ **n.** a person who predicts disaster, esp. in politics or economics. — **doom·say·ing** /-ˌsāiNG/ **n.**

dooms·day /ˈdo͞omzˌdā/ (also **domes·day**) ▶ **n.** [in sing.] the last day of the world's existence. ■ (in Christian belief) the day of the Last Judgment. ■ fig. a time or event of crisis or great danger: [as adj.] *in all the concern over greenhouse warming, one **doomsday scenario** stands out.*
– PHRASES **till doomsday** informal forever: *we'll be here till doomsday if you don't hurry up.* [OE *dōmes dæg* (see DOOM, DAY).]

Dooms·day Book ▶ **n.** see DOMESDAY.

door /dôr/ ▶ **n.** a hinged, sliding, or revolving barrier at the entrance to a building, room, or vehicle, or in the framework of a cupboard. ■ a doorway. ■ used to refer to the distance from one building in a row to another: *they lived within three doors of each other.* ■ fig. a means of access, admission, or exit; a means to a specified end.
– PHRASES **close** (or **shut**) **the door on** (or **to**) exclude the opportunity for: *she had closed the door on ever finding out what he was feeling.* **(from) door to door 1** from start to finish of a journey: *the trip from door to door could take more than four hours.* **2** visiting all the houses in an area to sell or publicize something: *he went from door to door selling insurance policies* | [as adj.] *a door-to-door-salesman.* **lay something at someone's door** regard someone as responsible for something: *the failure is laid at the door of the government.* **leave the door open** ensure that there is still an opportunity for something: *he is leaving the door open for future change.* **out of doors** in or into the open air: *food tastes even better out of doors.* — **doored** **adj.** [in comb.] *a glass-doored desk.* [OE *duru, dor,* of Gmc. origin; rel. to Ger. *Tür* 'door'; from an Indo-Eur. root shared by L. *foris* 'gate' and Gk. *thura* 'door.']

door·bell /ˈdôrˌbel/ ▶ **n.** a bell in a building that can be rung by visitors outside to signal their arrival.

do-or-die /ˈdo͞o ər ˈdī/ ▶ **adj.** [attrib.] (of a person's attitude or a situation) showing or requiring a determination not to compromise or be deterred: *the mercenaries fought with a do-or-die resolution.*

door·frame /ˈdôrˌfrām/ (also **door frame**) ▶ **n.** the frame in a doorway into which a door is fitted.

door·jamb /ˈdôrˌjam/ ▶ **n.** each of the two upright parts of a doorframe, on one of which the door is hung.

door·knob /ˈdôrˌnäb/ ▶ **n.** a handle on a door that is turned to release the latch.

door knock·er ▶ **n.** a metal or wooden instrument hinged to a door and rapped by visitors to attract attention and gain entry.

door·man /ˈdôrˌman; -mən/ ▶ **n.** (pl. **-men**) a man such as a porter, bouncer, or janitor who is on duty at the entrance to a large building.

door·mat /ˈdôrˌmat/ ▶ **n.** a mat placed in a doorway, on which people can wipe their shoes on entering a building. ■ fig. a submissive person who allows others to dominate them: *to put up with such treatment you must be either a saint or a doormat.*

door·nail /ˈdôrˌnāl/ ▶ **n.** a stud set in a door for strength or as an ornament.
– PHRASES **(as) dead as a doornail** quite dead.

Door Peninsula a resort region in northeastern Wisconsin between Green Bay and Lake Michigan.

door·plate /ˈdôrˌplāt/ ▶ **n.** a plate on the door of a house or room that gives information about the occupant.

door·post /ˈdôrˌpōst/ ▶ **n.** another term for DOORJAMB.

door prize ▶ **n.** a prize awarded by lottery to the holder of a ticket purchased or distributed at a dance, party, or other function.

door·step /ˈdôrˌstep/ ▶ **n.** a step leading up to the outer door of a house.

door·stop /ˈdôrˌstäp/ (also **door·stop·per**) ▶ **n.** a fixed or heavy object that keeps a door open or stops it from banging against a wall. ■ fig. a heavy or bulky object (used esp. in reference to a thick book): *his sixth novel is a thumping 400-page doorstop.*

door·way /ˈdôrˌwā/ ▶ **n.** an entrance to a room or building through a door: *Beth stood there in the doorway* | fig. *the doorway to success.*

door·yard /ˈdôrˌyärd/ ▶ **n.** a yard or garden by the door of a house.

doo-wop /ˈdo͞o ˌwäp/ ▶ **n.** a style of pop music marked by the use of close harmony vocals using nonsense phrases, originating in the US in the 1950s. [imitative.]

doo·zy /ˈdo͞ozē/ (also **doo·zie**) ▶ **n.** (pl. **-zies**) informal something outstanding or unique of its kind. [20th C.: of unknown origin.]

do·pa /ˈdōpə/ ▶ **n.** Biochem. an amino acid, $C_9H_{11}NO_4$, that is present in nervous tissue as a precursor of dopamine, used in the treatment of Parkinson's disease. See also L-DOPA. [20th C.: from Ger., acronym from the systematic name.]

do·pa·mine /ˈdōpəˌmēn/ ▶ **n.** Biochem. a compound, $C_8H_{11}NO_2$, present in the body as a neurotransmitter and a precursor of other substances including epinephrine. [1950s: blend of DOPA and AMINE.]

dop·ant /ˈdōpənt/ ▶ **n.** Electron. a substance used to produce a desired electrical characteristic in a semiconductor. [1960s: from the v. DOPE + -ANT.]

dope /dōp/ ▶ **n. 1** informal a drug taken illegally for recreational purposes, esp. marijuana or heroin. ■ a drug given to a racehorse or greyhound to inhibit or enhance its performance. ■ a drug taken by an athlete to improve performance: [as adj.] *he failed a dope test.* **2** informal a stupid person. **3** informal information about a subject, esp. if not generally known. ▶ **v.** [trans.] **1** administer drugs to (a racehorse, greyhound, or athlete) in order to inhibit or enhance sporting performance: *the horse was doped before the race.* ■ (**be doped up**) informal be heavily under the influence of drugs, typically illegal ones. ■ treat (food or drink) with drugs. ■ [intrans.] informal, dated regularly take illegal drugs. **2** smear or cover with varnish or other thick liquid. **3** Electron. add an impurity to (a semiconductor) to produce a desired electrical characteristic. — **dop·er** **n.** [19th C. (in the sense 'thick liquid'): from Du. *doop* 'sauce,' from *doopen* 'to dip, mix.']

dope·y /ˈdōpē/ (also **dop·y**) ▶ **adj.** (**dop·i·er, dop·i·est**) informal stupefied by sleep or a drug: *she was under sedation and a bit dopey.* ■ idiotic: *did you ever hear such dopey names?* — **dop·i·ly** /ˈdōpəlē/ **adv.** **dop·i·ness** **n.**

dop·pel·gäng·er /ˈdäpəlˌgaNGər/ ▶ **n.** an apparition or double of a living person. [19th C.: from Ger., lit. 'double-goer.']

Dop·pler /ˈdäplər/, Johann Christian (1803–53), Austrian physicist. In 1842, he discovered what is now known as the Doppler effect.

Dop·pler ef·fect ▶ **n.** Physics an increase (or decrease) in the frequency of sound, light, or other waves as the source and observer move toward (or away from) each other. The effect causes the sudden change in pitch noticeable in a passing siren, as well as the redshift seen by astronomers.

Dop·pler ra·dar ▶ **n.** Meteorol. a radar tracking system using the Doppler effect to determine the location and velocity of a storm, clouds, precipitation, etc.

Dop·pler shift ▶ **n.** Physics a change in frequency due to the Doppler effect.

dop·y /ˈdōpē/ ▶ **adj.** var. of DOPEY.

dor /dôr/ (also **dor beetle**) ▶ **n.** a large black dung beetle (family Geotrupidae) that makes a droning sound in flight. [OE, prob. imitative.]

do·ra·do /dəˈrädō/ ▶ **n.** (pl. **-dos**) another term for MAHIMAHI. [17th C.: from Sp., lit. 'gilded,' from late L. *deauratus,* from *deaurare* 'to gild over' (see also DORY[1]).]

Do·ra·ti /ˈdôrätē; dôˈrätē/, Antal (1906–88), US conductor; born in Hungary. He served as the director of symphonies in Minneapolis 1949–60 and Washington, DC, 1970–77.

Dor·dogne /dôrˈdōnyə/ a river in southwestern France that flows west for 297 miles (472 km) to the Garonne River, forming the Gironde estuary. ■ a department in southwestern France, containing caves that have yielded remains of early humans.

Dor·drecht /ˈdôrˌdreKHt/ a city in the Netherlands, near the mouth of the Rhine (there called the Waal) River; pop. 110,500. Also called **Dort.**

Do·ri·an /ˈdôrēən/ ▶ **n.** a member of a Hellenic people speaking the Doric dialect of Greek, thought to have entered Greece from the north *c.*1100 BC. ▶ **adj.** of or relating to this people or to Doris in central Greece. [via L. from Gk. *Dōrios* 'of Doris' + -IAN.]

Dor·ic /ˈdôrik; ˈdär-/ ▶ **adj. 1** relating to or denoting a classical order of architecture characterized by a plain, sturdy column and a thick square abacus resting on a rounded molding. See illustration at CAPITAL[2]. **2** relating to or denoting the ancient Greek dialect of the Dorians. ▶ **n. 1** the Doric order of architecture. **2** the ancient Greek dialect of the Dorians.

dork /dôrk/ ▶ **n.** informal, derog. a dull, slow-witted, or socially inept person. ■ vulgar slang the penis. — **dork·y** **adj.** [1960s: perh. a var. of DIRK.]

dorm /dôrm/ ▶ **n.** informal a dormitory. [20th C.: abbrev.]

dor·mant /ˈdôrmənt/ ▶ **adj.** (of an animal) having normal physical functions suspended or slowed down for a period of time; in or as if in a deep sleep: *dormant butterflies* | fig. *the event evoked memories that she would rather had lain dormant.* ■ (of a plant or bud) alive but not actively growing. ■ (of a volcano) temporarily inactive. ■ (of a disease) causing no symptoms but not cured and liable to recur. — **dor·man·cy** **n.** [ME: from OFr., 'sleeping,' pres. part. of *dormir,* from L. *dormire* 'to sleep.']

dor·mer /ˈdôrmər/ (also **dormer window**) ▶ **n.** a window that projects vertically from a sloping roof. ■ the projecting structure that houses such a window. [16th C.: from OFr. *dormeor* 'dormitory,' from *dormir* 'to sleep.']

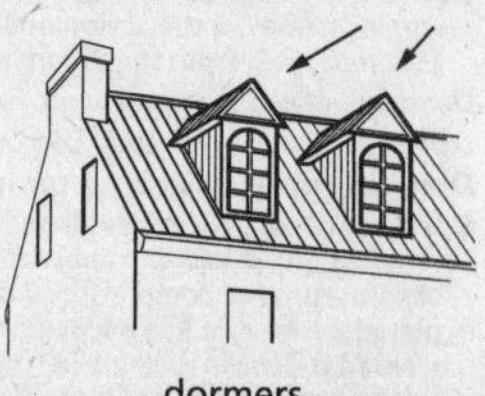
dormers

dor·mi·to·ry /ˈdôrmiˌtôrē/ ▶ **n.** (pl. **-ries**) a large bedroom for a number of people in a school or institution. ■ a university or college hall of residence or hostel. [ME: from L. *dormitorium,* neut.

(used as a n.) of *dormitorius*, from *dormire* 'to sleep.']

dor·mouse /'dôr,mous/ ▸ n. (pl. **-mice**) an agile mouselike rodent (family Gliridae) with a hairy or bushy tail, found in Africa and Eurasia. Some kinds are noted for spending long periods in hibernation. [ME: of unknown origin.]

dor·sal /'dôrsəl/ ▸ adj. Anat., Zool., & Bot. of, on, or relating to the upper side or back of an animal, plant, or organ: *a dorsal view of the body | the dorsal aorta.* Compare with VENTRAL. — **dor·sal·ly** adv. [ME: from late L. *dorsalis*, from L. *dorsum* 'back.']

dor·sal fin ▸ n. Zool. an unpaired fin on the back of a fish or whale, e.g., the tall triangular fin of a shark or killer whale.

Dor·set /'dôrsit/ a county of southwestern England; county town, Dorchester.

dorsi- ▸ comb. form **1** of, to, or on the back. **2** another term for DORSO-. [from L. *dorsum* 'back.']

dorso- ▸ comb. form **1** of, to, or on the back of (what is denoted by the second element). **2** another term for DORSI-. [from L. *dorsum* 'back.']

dor·sum /'dôrsəm/ ▸ n. (pl. **dor·sa**) Anat. Zool. the dorsal part of an organism or structure. [18th C.: from L., 'back.']

Dort /dôrt/ another name for DORDRECHT.

Dort·mund /'dôrtmənd/ a city in northwestern Germany; pop. 601,000.

do·ry[1] /'dôrē/ ▸ n. (pl. **-ries**) a narrow deep-bodied fish (families Zeidae and Oreosomatidae) with a mouth that can be opened very wide. See also JOHN DORY. [ME: from Fr. *dorée*, fem. past part. of *dorer* 'gild,' based on L. *aurum* 'gold.']

do·ry[2] ▸ n. (pl. **-ries**) a small flat-bottomed rowboat with a high bow and stern, of a kind originally used for fishing in New England. [18th C.: perh. from Miskito *dóri* 'dugout.']

DOS /dôs/ Comput. ▸ abbr. disk operating system, an operating system originally developed for IBM personal computers.

dos·age /'dōsij/ ▸ n. the size or frequency of a dose of a medicine or drug. ■ a level of exposure to or absorption of ionizing radiation.

dose /dōs/ ▸ n. a quantity of a medicine or drug taken or recommended to be taken at a particular time: *he took a dose of cough medicine.* ■ an amount of ionizing radiation received or absorbed at one time or over a specified period. ■ informal a venereal infection. ■ informal a quantity of something regarded as analogous to medicine in being necessary but unpleasant: *I wanted to give you a dose of the hell you put me through.* ▸ v. [trans.] administer a dose to (a person or animal): *he dosed himself with vitamins.*
– PHRASES **in small doses** informal when experienced or engaged in a little at a time: *computer games are great in small doses.* [ME: from Fr., via late L. from Gk. *dosis* 'gift,' from *didonai* 'give.']

do·sha /'dōsнə,/ ▸ n. (in Ayurvedic medicine) each of three energies believed to circulate in the body and govern physiological activity. [Sanskrit *doṣa*, lit. 'fault, disease.']

do-si-do /'dō sē 'dō/ ▸ n. (pl. **-dos**) (in square dancing, and other country dancing) a figure in which two dancers pass around each other back to back and return to their original positions. ▸ v. [intrans.] dance a do-si-do. [1920s: alt. of Fr. *dos-à-dos* 'back to back.']

do·sim·e·ter /dō'simitər/ ▸ n. a device used to measure an absorbed dose of ionizing radiation. — **do·si·met·ric** /,dōsə'metrik/ adj. **do·sim·e·try** /-'simitrē/ n.

Dos Pas·sos /däs 'pasəs/, John Roderigo (1896–1970), US writer. His novels include *USA* (1938).

dos·si·er /'dôsē,ā; 'dä-/ ▸ n. a collection of documents about a particular person, event, or subject: *we have a dossier on him | a dossier of complaints.* [19th C.: from Fr., denoting a bundle of papers, from *dos* 'back,' based on L. *dorsum*.]

dost /dəst/ archaic second person singular present of DO[1].

Do·sto·ev·sky /,dästə'yefskē/ (also **Do·sto·yev·sky**), Fyodor Mikhailovich (1821–81), Russian writer. His novels include *Crime and Punishment* (1866) and *The Brothers Karamazov* (1880).

DOT ▸ abbr. ■ Department of Transportation.

dot /dät/ ▸ n. a small round mark or spot. ■ such a mark written or printed as part of an *i* or *j*, as a diacritical mark, as one of a series of marks to signify omission, or as a period. ■ Music such a mark used to denote the lengthening of a note or rest by half, or to indicate staccato. ■ the shorter signal of the two used in Morse code. Compare with DASH (sense 3). ■ used to refer to an object that appears tiny because it is far away. ■ used in speech to indicate the punctuation separating parts of an electronic mail or Web site address. ▸ v. (**dot·ted, dot·ting**) [trans.] mark with a small spot or spots. ■ (of a number of items) be scattered over (an area): *churches dot the countryside.* ■ place a dot over (a letter). ■ Music mark (a note or rest) to show that the time value is increased by half: [as adj.] (**dotted**) *a dotted quarter note.*
– PHRASES **dot the i's and cross the t's** informal ensure that all details are correct. **on the dot** informal exactly on time: *he arrived on the dot at nine o'clock.* — **dot·ter** n. [OE *dott* 'head of a boil.']

dot·age /'dōtij/ ▸ n. [in sing.] the period of life in which a person is old and weak: *you could live here and look after me in my dotage.* ■ the state of having the intellect impaired, esp. through old age; senility. [ME: from DOTE + -AGE.]

do·tard /'dōtərd/ ▸ n. an old person, esp. one who has become weak or senile. [ME: from DOTE + -ARD.]

dot-com (also **dot.com**) ▸ n. a company that relies largely or exclusively on Internet commerce. ▸ adj. of or relating to business conducted on the Internet.

dote /dōt/ ▸ v. [intrans.] (**dote on/upon**) be extremely and uncritically fond of: *she doted on her two young children* | [as adj.] (**doting**) *she was spoiled outrageously by her doting father.* — **dot·er** n. **dot·ing·ly** adv. [ME: rel. to MDu. *doten* 'be silly.']

doth /dəтн/ archaic third person singular present of DO[1].

dot ma·trix print·er ▸ n. a printer that forms images of letters, numbers, etc., from a number of tiny dots.

dot prod·uct ▸ n. another term for INNER PRODUCT.

dot·ted line ▸ n. a line made up of dots or dashes (often used in reference to the space left for a signature on a contract): *Adam signed on the dotted line.*

dot·ted rhythm ▸ n. Music rhythm in which the beat is unequally subdivided into a long dotted note and a short note.

dot·ter·el /'dätərəl/ ▸ n. a small plover (genus *Eudromias*) of mountainous areas and the tundra. [ME: from DOTE + -REL.]

dot·ty /'dätē/ ▸ adj. (**dot·ti·er, dot·ti·est**) informal (of a person, action, or idea) somewhat mad or eccentric. — **dot·ti·ly** adv. **dot·ti·ness** n. [19th C.: perh. from obs. *dote* 'simpleton, fool,' appar. from Du. *dote* 'folly.']

Dou·a·la /dōō'älə/ a city in southwestern Cameroon; pop. 1,200,000.

Dou·ay Bi·ble /'dōō-ā/ (also **Douay version**) ▸ n. an English translation of the Bible formerly used in the Roman Catholic Church, completed at Douai in France early in the 17th century.

dou·ble /'dəbəl/ ▸ adj. **1** consisting of two equal, identical, or similar parts or things. ■ having twice the usual size, quantity, or strength. ■ designed to be used by two people. ■ having two different roles or interpretations, esp. in order to deceive or confuse. **2** having some essential part or feature twice, in particular: ■ (of a flower variety) having more than one circle of petals: *large double blooms.* ■ used to indicate that a letter or number occurs twice in succession: *"otter" is spelled with a double t.* ▸ predeterminer twice as much or as many. ▸ adv. at or to twice the amount or extent: *you have to be careful, and this counts double for older people.* ■ as two instead of the more usual one: *she thought she was seeing double.* ▸ n. **1** a thing that is twice as large as usual or is made up of two standard units or things: *join the two sleeping bags together to make a double.* ■ a double measure of liquor. ■ a thing designed to be used by two people, esp. a bed or a hotel room. ■ Baseball a hit that allows the batter to reach second base safely. ■ a system of betting in which the winnings and stake from the first bet are transferred to a second. **2** a person who looks exactly like another: *you could pass yourself off as his double.* ■ a person who stands in for an actor in a film. ■ an apparition of a living person. **3** (**doubles**) (esp. in tennis and badminton) a game or competition involving sides made up of two players. ▸ pron. a number or amount that is twice as large as a contrasting or usual number or amount: *he paid double and had a room all to himself.* ▸ v. **1** [intrans.] become twice as much or as many. ■ [trans.] make twice as much or as many of (something). ■ (**double up**) use the winnings from a bet as stake for another bet. ■ (**double up**) share a room. ■ Baseball (of a batter) get a two-base hit. ■ informal go out on a double date. **2** [trans.] fold or bend (paper, cloth, or other material) over on itself. ■ [intrans.] (**double up**) bend over or curl up, typically because one is overcome with pain or mirth. ■ [intrans.] (usu. **double back**) go back in the direction one has come: *he had to double back to pick them up.* **3** [intrans.] (of a person or thing) be used in or play another, different role: *a laser printer doubles as a photocopier.* ■ [trans.] (of an actor) play (two parts) in the same piece.
– PHRASES **on the double** at running speed; very fast: *he disappeared on the double.* ■ without hesitation; immediately *he summoned his officers on the double.* **double or nothing** a gamble to decide whether a loss or debt should be doubled or canceled. — **dou·bler** /-blər/ n. **dou·bly** /-blē/ adv. [ME: via OFr. from L. *duplus* (see DUPLE).]

dou·ble-act·ing ▸ adj. denoting a device or product that combines two different functions: *double-acting hydraulic shock absorbers | double-acting baking powder.* ■ (of an engine) having pistons pushed from both sides alternately.

dou·ble a·gent ▸ n. an agent who pretends to act as a spy for one country or organization while in fact acting on behalf of an enemy.

dou·ble-bar·reled ▸ adj. (of a gun) having two barrels. ■ having two parts or aspects.

dou·ble bass /bās/ ▸ n. the largest and lowest-pitched instrument of the violin family.

dou·ble bill ▸ n. a program of entertainment with two main items or personalities. ▸ v. [trans.] (**dou·ble-bill**) charge (different accounts) for the same expenses: *her two restaurants were double-billed for the one refrigerator* | [intrans.] *the previous accounting program had a tendency to double-bill.* — **dou·ble bill·ing** (also **dou·ble-bill·ing**) n.

dou·ble-bit·ted ax ▸ n. an ax with two blades.

dou·ble-blind ▸ adj. [attrib.] denoting a test or trial, esp. of a drug, in which any information that may influence the behavior of the tester or the subject is withheld until after the test.

dou·ble bo·gey Golf ▸ n. a score of two strokes over par for a hole. ▸ v. (**dou·ble-bo·gey**) [trans.] complete (a hole) in two strokes over par.

dou·ble boil·er ▶ n. a saucepan with a detachable upper compartment heated by boiling water in the lower one.

dou·ble bond ▶ n. a chemical bond in which two pairs of electrons are shared between two atoms.

dou·ble-book ▶ v. [trans.] (usu. **be double-booked**) inadvertently reserve (something, esp. a seat or a hotel room) for two different customers or parties at the same time: *the hotel was double-booked.* ■ book (someone) into a seat or room that is already reserved for another.

dou·ble-breast·ed ▶ adj. (of a jacket or coat) having a substantial overlap of material at the front and showing two rows of buttons when fastened.

dou·ble-check ▶ v. [trans.] go over (something) for a second time to ensure that it is accurate or safe.

dou·ble chin ▶ n. a roll of fatty flesh below a person's chin. — **dou·ble-chinned** adj.

dou·ble-click ▶ v. [intrans.] Comput. press a mouse button twice in quick succession to select a file, program, or function. ■ [trans.] select (a file) in this way.

dou·ble-clutch ▶ v. [intrans.] release and reengage the clutch of a vehicle twice when changing gear.

dou·ble con·cer·to ▶ n. a concerto for two solo instruments.

dou·ble-cross ▶ v. [trans.] deceive or betray (a person with whom one is supposedly cooperating). ▶ n. a betrayal of someone with whom one is supposedly cooperating. — **dou·ble-cross·er** n.

dou·ble dag·ger ▶ n. a symbol (‡) used in printed text to introduce an annotation.

dou·ble date ▶ n. a social outing in which two couples participate. ▶ v. [intrans.] (**double-date**) take part in a double date. ■ [trans.] accompany (someone) on a double date.

Dou·ble·day /ˈdəbəlˌdā/, Abner (1819–93), US general in the American Civil War. He is credited with creating the modern game of baseball, although this claim has been largely disputed.

dou·ble-deal·ing ▶ n. the practice of working to people's disadvantage behind their backs. ▶ adj. working deceitfully to injure others. — **dou·ble-deal·er** n.

dou·ble-deck·er ▶ n. something, esp. a bus, that has two floors or levels.

dou·ble-dig·it ▶ adj. [attrib.] (of a number, variable, or percentage) between 10 and 99: *double-digit inflation.* ▶ n. (**double digits**) another term for DOUBLE FIGURES.

dou·ble-dip ▶ v. [intrans.] informal obtain an income from two different sources, typically in an illicit way. — **dou·ble-dip·per** n. **dou·ble-dip·ping** n.

dou·ble dot ▶ n. (in musical composition or transcription) two dots placed side by side after a note to indicate that it is to be lengthened by three quarters of its value. ▶ v. (**dou·ble-dot**) [trans.] write or perform (music) with a rhythm of alternating long and short notes in a ratio of approximately seven to one, producing a more marked effect than ordinary dotted rhythm.

dou·ble drib·ble ▶ n. Basketball an illegal dribble that occurs when a player dribbles with both hands simultaneously or interrupts a dribble by holding the ball briefly in one or both hands. ▶ v. (**double-dribble**) commit or be charged with a double dribble.

dou·ble ea·gle ▶ n. **1** a gold coin worth twenty dollars. **2** Golf a score of three strokes under par at a hole.

dou·ble-edged ▶ adj. (of a knife or sword) having two cutting edges. ■ having two contradictory aspects or possible outcomes: *the consequences can be double-edged.*

– PHRASES **a double-edged sword** a situation or course of action having both positive and negative effects.

dou·ble-end·er ▶ n. a boat in which stern and bow are similarly tapered.

dou·ble en·ten·dre /änˈtändrə/ ▶ n. (pl. **dou·ble en·ten·dres** pronunc. same) a word or phrase open to two interpretations, one of which is usually risqué or indecent. ■ humor using such words or phrases. [17th C.: from obs. Fr., 'double understanding.']

dou·ble-en·try ▶ adj. [attrib.] denoting a system of bookkeeping in which each transaction is entered as a debit in one account and a credit in another.

dou·ble ex·po·sure ▶ n. the repeated exposure of a photographic plate or film to light, often producing ghost images. ■ the photograph that results from such exposure.

dou·ble fault ▶ n. Tennis an instance of two consecutive faults in serving, counting as a point against the server. ▶ v. (**dou·ble-fault**) [intrans.] serve a double fault.

dou·ble fea·ture ▶ n. a movie program with two full-length films.

dou·ble fig·ures ▶ plural n. a number or amount, esp. a percentage, between 10 and 99: *inflation was in double figures.*

dou·ble-head·er /ˌdəbəlˈhedər/ (also **dou·ble-head·er**) ▶ n. a sporting event in which two games or contests are played in succession at the same venue, typically between the same teams or players.

dou·ble he·lix ▶ n. a pair of parallel helices intertwined about a common axis, esp. that in the structure of the DNA molecule.

dou·ble-hung ▶ adj. (of a window) consisting of two sliding vertical sashes.

dou·ble in·dem·ni·ty ▶ n. provision for payment of double the death benefit of an insurance policy under certain conditions, e.g., when death occurs as a result of an accident.

dou·ble jeop·ard·y ▶ n. Law the prosecution of a person twice for the same offense. ■ risk or disadvantage incurred from two sources simultaneously.

dou·ble-joint·ed ▶ adj. (of a person) having unusually flexible joints, typically those of the fingers, arms, or legs.

dou·ble-knit ▶ adj. (of fabric) knit of two joined layers for extra thickness: *a green double-knit suit.*

dou·ble neg·a·tive ▶ n. Gram. a negative statement containing two negative elements (for example *didn't say nothing*). ■ a positive statement in which two negative elements are used to produce the positive force, usu. for some particular rhetorical effect (for example *there is not nothing to worry about!*).

dou·ble-park ▶ v. [trans.] (usu. **be double-parked**) park (a vehicle) alongside one that is already parked at the side of the road.

dou·ble play ▶ n. Baseball a defensive play in which two players are put out.

dou·ble pneu·mo·nia ▶ n. pneumonia affecting both lungs.

dou·ble-quick ▶ adj. & adv. informal very quick or quickly.

dou·ble reed ▶ n. Music a reed with two slightly separated blades, used for playing a wind instrument such as an oboe or bassoon.

dou·ble re·frac·tion ▶ n. Physics division of a single incident light ray or other electromagnetic wave into two separate rays in an anisotropic medium.

dou·ble salt ▶ n. Chem. a crystalline salt having the composition of a mixture of two simple salts but with a different crystal structure from either.

dou·ble sharp ▶ n. a sign (𝄪) placed before a musical note to indicate that it is to be raised two semitones. ■ a note so marked or raised.

dou·ble-space ▶ v. type or format with a full space between lines.

dou·ble-speak /ˈdəbəlˌspēk/ ▶ n. deliberately euphemistic, ambiguous, or obscure language: *the art of political doublespeak.*

dou·ble stand·ard ▶ n. a rule or principle that is unfairly applied in different ways to different people or groups: *the smaller pay received by black soldiers demonstrated a double standard.*

dou·ble star ▶ n. two stars physically very close together, as a binary star, or apparently so, as an optical double.

dou·blet /ˈdəblit/ ▶ n. **1** either of a pair of similar things, in particular: ■ either of two words of the same historical source, but with two different stages of entry into the language and different resultant meanings, for example *fashion* and *faction, cloak* and *clock.* ■ Physics & Chem. a pair of associated lines close together in a spectrum or electrophoretic gel. **2** a man's short close-fitting padded jacket, commonly worn from the 14th to the 17th century. [ME: from OFr., 'something folded,' from *double* 'double.']

dou·ble take ▶ n. a delayed reaction to something unexpected, immediately after one's first reaction: *Tony glanced at her, then did a double take.*

dou·ble-talk ▶ n. deliberately unintelligible speech combining nonsense syllables and actual words. ■ another term for DOUBLESPEAK.

dou·ble-team ▶ v. [trans.] (in ball games, esp. basketball) block (an opponent) with two players. ▶ n. an act of double-teaming.

dou·ble·think /ˈdəbəlˌTHiNGk/ ▶ n. the acceptance of or mental capacity to accept contrary opinions or beliefs at the same time, esp. as a result of political indoctrination. [1949: coined by George Orwell in his novel *Nineteen Eighty-Four.*]

dou·ble time ▶ n. **1** a rate of pay equal to double the standard rate, sometimes paid for working on holidays or outside normal working hours. **2** Mil. a regulation running pace. **3** Music a rhythm that is twice as fast as an earlier one.

dou·ble tongu·ing ▶ n. Music the use of two alternating movements of the tongue (usually as in sounding *t* and *k*) in playing rapid passages on a wind instrument. — **dou·ble-tongue** v.

dou·ble vi·sion ▶ n. the simultaneous perception of two images, usually overlapping, of a single scene or object.

dou·ble wham·my ▶ n. informal a twofold blow or setback: *a double whammy of taxation and price increases.*

dou·bloon /dəˈblo͞on/ ▶ n. hist. a Spanish gold coin. [from Fr. *doublon* or its source, Sp. *doblón*, from *doble* 'double.']

doubt /dout/ ▶ n. a feeling of uncertainty or lack of conviction. ▶ v. [trans.] feel uncertain about. ■ question the truth or fact of (something). ■ disbelieve (a person or their word). ■ [intrans.] feel uncertain, esp. about one's religious beliefs.

– PHRASES **beyond (a** or **a shadow of a) doubt** allowing no uncertainty. **in doubt** open to question. ■ feeling uncertain about something. **no doubt** used to indicate the speaker's firm belief that something is true even if evidence is not given or available. ■ used to introduce a concession that is subsequently dismissed as unimportant or irrelevant. **without (a) doubt** indisputably. — **doubt·a·ble** adj. **doubt·er** n. **doubt·ing·ly** adv. [ME: from OFr. *doute* (n.), *douter* (v.), from L. *dubitare* 'hesitate,' from *dubius* 'doubtful' (see DUBIOUS).]

doubt·ful /ˈdoutfəl/ ▶ adj. **1** feeling uncertain about something: *he looked doubtful, but gave a nod.* **2** not known with certainty. ■ improbable: [with clause] *it is doubtful whether these programs have any lasting effect.* ■ not established as genuine or acceptable: *of doubtful legality.* — **doubt·ful·ly** adv. **doubt·ful·ness** n.

doubt·ing Thom·as ▶**n.** a person who is skeptical and refuses to believe something without proof. [17th C.: with biblical allusion to the apostle Thomas (John 20: 24–29).]

doubt·less /ˈdoutlis/ ▶**adv.** [sentence adverb] used to indicate the speaker's belief that a statement is certain to be true given what is known about the situation: *the company would doubtless find the reduced competition to their liking.* ■ used to refer to a desirable outcome as though it were certain: *doubtless you'll solve the problem.* — **doubt·less·ly adv.**

dou·ceur /do͞oˈsər/ ▶**n.** a financial inducement; a bribe. ■ a gratuity or tip. [18th C.: Fr., lit. 'sweetness.']

douche /do͞osʜ/ ▶**n.** a shower of water: *a daily douche.* ■ a jet of liquid applied to part of the body for cleansing or medicinal purposes. ■ a device for washing out the vagina as a contraceptive measure. ▶**v.** [intrans.] use a douche as a method of contraception. [18th C. (as a n.): via Fr. from Ital. *doccia* 'conduit pipe,' from *docciare* 'pour by drops,' based on L. *ductus* 'leading' (see DUCT).]

douche bag ▶**n.** a small syringe for douching the vagina, esp. as a contraceptive measure. ■ informal a loathsome or contemptible person (used as a term of abuse).

dough /dō/ ▶**n. 1** a thick, malleable mixture of flour and liquid, used for baking into bread or pastry. **2** informal money: *lots of dough.* — **dough·i·ness n. dough·y adj.** (**dough·i·er, dough·i·est**). [OE *dāg*, of Gmc. origin; rel. to Du. *deeg* and Ger. *Teig*, from an Indo-Eur. root meaning 'smear, knead.']

dough·boy /ˈdō,boi/ ▶**n.** informal a US infantryman, esp. one in World War I.

dough·nut /ˈdōnət; -,nət/ (also **do·nut**) ▶**n.** a small fried cake of sweetened dough, typically in the shape of a ball or ring. ■ a ring-shaped object.

Doug·las[1] /ˈdəglis/, Stephen Arnold (1813–61), US politician; know as the **Little Giant**. A US senator 1847–61, he is best remembered for the Lincoln-Douglas debates.

Doug·las[2], William Orville (1898–1980), US Supreme Court associate justice 1939–75. He was appointed to the Court by President Franklin D. Roosevelt.

Doug·las fir ▶**n.** a tall, slender fir tree (genus *Pseudotsuga*) with soft foliage and, in mature trees, deeply fissured bark. [19th C.: David *Douglas* (1798–1834), Scot. botanist.]

Doug·las-Home /ˈhyo͞om/, Sir Alec (1903–95), prime minister of Britain 1963–64; born *Alexander Frederick Douglas-Home.*

Doug·lass /ˈdəgləs/, Frederick (1817–95), US abolitionist; born *Frederick Augustus Washington Bailey*. A former slave, he established an antislavery newspaper *North Star* (1847–64).

Doul·ton /ˈdōltən; ˈdôltən/ (also **Royal Doulton**) ▶**n.** trademark fine pottery or porcelain made at the factories of John Doulton (1793–1873) or his successors.

doum palm /do͞om/ ▶**n.** an Egyptian palm tree (*Hyphaene thebaica*) with a forked trunk, producing edible fruit and a vegetable ivory substitute. [18th C.: *doum* from Arab. *dawm, dūm.*]

dour /do͝or; dou(ə)r/ ▶**adj.** relentlessly severe, stern, or gloomy in manner or appearance. — **dour·ly adv. dour·ness n.** [ME (orig. Scots): prob. from Scot. Gael. *dúr* 'dull, obstinate, stupid,' perh. from L. *durus* 'hard.']

Dou·ro /ˈdōro͞o/ a river that rises in central Spain and flows west for 556 miles (900 km) through Portugal to the Atlantic Ocean. Spanish name **DUERO**.

douse /dous/ (also **dowse**) ▶**v.** [trans.] pour a liquid over; drench: *he doused the car with gasoline and set it on fire.* ■ extinguish (a fire or light): *stewards appeared and the fire was doused.* [17th C.: perh. imitative.]

Dove /dōv/, Rita (1952–), US poet. She was the first African-American woman poet laureate of the US 1993–95.

dove[1] /dəv/ ▶**n. 1** a stocky seed- or fruit-eating bird of the pigeon family, with a small head, short legs, and a cooing voice. **2** a person who advocates peaceful or conciliatory policies, esp. in foreign affairs. Compare with HAWK[1] (sense 2). — **dove·like adj. dov·ish adj.** (in sense 2). [ME: from ON *dúfa.*]

dove[2] /dōv/ past of DIVE.

dove·cote /ˈdəv,kōt/ (also **dove·cot**) ▶**n.** a shelter with nest holes for domesticated pigeons.

dove·kie /ˈdəvkē/ ▶**n.** a small, stubby short-billed auk (*Alle alle*) with black plumage and white underparts, breeding in the Arctic. [19th C.: from a Scots dimin. of DOVE[1].]

Do·ver /ˈdōvər/ **1** a ferry port in Kent, on the coast of the English Channel; pop. 34,300. **2** the capital of Delaware, in the central part of the state; pop. 32,135.

Do·ver, Strait of a sea passage between England and France.

dove·tail /ˈdəv,tāl/ ▶**n.** (also **dovetail joint**) a joint formed by one or more tapered projections (tenons) on one piece that interlock with corresponding notches or recesses (mortises) in another. ■ a tenon used in such a joint, typically wider at its extremity. ▶**v.** [trans.] join together by means of a dovetail. ■ fit or cause to fit together easily and conveniently: [trans.] *parents can dovetail career and family* | [intrans.] *flights that dovetail with the working day.*

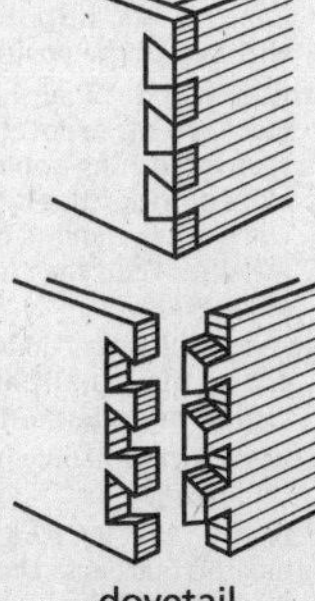
dovetail

Dow /dou/ short for DOW JONES INDUSTRIAL AVERAGE: *the Dow fell sharply that summer.*

dow·a·ger /ˈdouəjər/ ▶**n.** a widow with a title or property derived from her late husband: [as adj.] *the dowager duchess.* ■ informal a dignified elderly woman. [16th C.: from OFr. *douagiere*, from *douage* 'dower,' from *douer* 'endow,' from L. *dotare* 'endow' (see DOWER).]

dow·a·ger's hump ▶**n.** forward curvature of the spine resulting in a stoop, typically in women with osteoporosis, caused by collapse of the front edges of the thoracic vertebrae.

dow·dy /ˈdoudē/ ▶**adj.** (**dow·di·er, dow·di·est**) (of a person, typically a woman, or their clothes) unfashionable and without style in appearance. ▶**n.** (pl. **-dies**) a woman who is unfashionably and unattractively dressed. — **dow·di·ly adv. dow·di·ness n.** [16th C.: from *dowd* 'person of unfashionable appearance.']

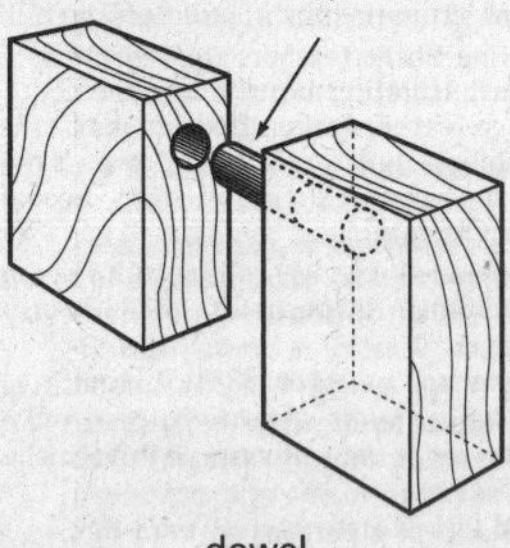
dowel

dow·el /ˈdouəl/ ▶**n.** a peg of wood, metal, or plastic without a distinct head, used for holding together components of a structure. ▶**v.** (**dow·eled, dow·el·ing** ; Brit. **dow·elled, dow·el·ling**) [trans.] fasten with a dowel or dowels. [ME: perh. from Mid. Low Ger. *dovel.*]

dow·el·ing /ˈdouəliɴɢ/ ▶**n.** cylindrical rods for cutting into dowels.

dow·er /ˈdou-ər/ ▶**n.** a widow's share for life of her husband's estate. [ME: from OFr. *douaire*, from med. L. *dotarium*, from L. *dotare* 'endow,' from *dos, dot-* 'dowry'; rel. to *dare* 'give.']

dow·itch·er /ˈdouicʜər/ ▶**n.** a wading bird (genus *Limnodromus*) of the sandpiper family, with a long straight bill, breeding in arctic and subarctic North America and eastern Asia. [19th C.: from Iroquoian.]

Dow Jones In·dus·tri·al Av·er·age /ˈdou ˈjōnz/ (also **Dow Jones Average**) an index of figures indicating the relative price of shares on the New York Stock Exchange, based on the average price of selected stocks. [Charles H. *Dow* (1851–1902) and Edward D. *Jones* (*c.*1855–1920).]

Down /doun/ one of the Six Counties of Northern Ireland; chief town, Downpatrick.

down[1] /doun/ ▶**adv. 1** toward or in a lower place or position, esp. to or on the ground or another surface. ■ at or to a specified distance below: *you can plainly see the bottom 35 feet down.* ■ downstairs. ■ expressing movement or position away from the north: *they're living down south.* ■ to or at a place perceived as lower (often expressing casualness or lack of hurry). ■ (with reference to food or drink swallowed) in or into the stomach: *she couldn't keep anything down.* ■ so as to lie or be fixed flush or flat. ■ [as exclam.] used as a command to a person or animal to sit or lie down: *down, boy!* ■ a crossword answer that reads vertically: *how many letters in fifteen down?* **2** to or at a lower level of intensity, volume, or activity: *keep the noise down.* ■ to or at a lower price, value, or rank. ■ to a finer consistency, a smaller amount or size, or a simpler or more basic state. ■ from an earlier to a later point in time or order. **3** in or into a weaker or worse position, mood, or condition: *the scandal brought down the government* | *he was **down with the flu.*** ■ losing or at a disadvantage by a specified amount. ■ used to express progress through a series of tasks or items: *one down and only six more to go.* ■ (of a computer system) out of action or unavailable for use (esp. temporarily). ■ (**down with ——**) shouted to express strong dislike of a specified person or thing: *crowds chanted "Down with bureaucracy!"* **4** in or into writing: *I just **write down** whatever comes into my head.* ■ on or on to a list, schedule, or record: *I'll **put you down for** the evening shift.* **5** (with reference to partial payment of a sum of money) made initially or on the spot: *pay $500 down and the rest at the end of the month.* **6** (of sailing) with the current or the wind. **7** Football (of the ball or a player in possession) not in play, typically because forward progress has been stopped. ▶**prep. 1** from a higher to a lower point of (something). ■ at or to a lower part of (a river or stream); nearer the sea. ■ at a point further along the course of (something): *he lived down the street.* ■ along the course or extent of. **2** throughout (a period of time): *astrologers down the ages.* ▶**adj. 1** [attrib.] directed or moving toward a lower place or position: *the down escalator.* ■ Physics denoting a flavor of quark having a charge of −1/3. Protons and neutrons are thought to be composed of combinations of up and down quarks. **2** [predic.] (of a person) unhappy; depressed: *he's been so down lately.* ■ [attrib.] informal (of a period of time) causing or characterized by unhappiness or depression. **3** [predic.] (of a

PRONUNCIATION KEY ə *ago, up*; ər *over, fur*; a *hat*; ā *ate*; ä *car*; e *let*; ē *see*; i *fit*; ī *by*; ɴɢ *sing*; ō *go*; ô *law, for*; oi *toy*; o͝o *good*; o͞o *goo*; ou *out*; ᴛʜ *thin*; T͟H *then*; ᴢʜ *vision*

computer system) temporarily out of action or unavailable. **4** [predic.] esp. slang supporting or going along with someone or something: *"You going to the movies?" "Yo, I'm down."* ▶**v.** [trans.] informal **1** knock or bring to the ground. **2** consume (something, typically a drink). ▶**n. 1** Football a chance for a team to advance the ball, ending when the ball carrier is tackled or the ball becomes out of play. A team must advance at least ten yards in a series of four downs in order to keep possession. **2** (**downs**) informal unwelcome experiences or events: *there had been more downs than ups during his years at the company.* **3** informal a feeling or period of unhappiness or depression: *everyone gets their downs, their depressive periods.*

– PHRASES **be down on** informal disapprove of; feel hostile or antagonistic toward. **down in the mouth** informal (of a person or their expression) unhappy; dejected. **down on one's luck** informal experiencing a period of bad luck. **down pat** (or **cold**) memorized or mastered perfectly: *she had the baby's medical routine down pat.* [OE *dūn, dūne*, shortened from *adūne* 'downward,' from the phr. *of dūne* 'off the hill' (see DOWN[3]).]

down[2] ▶**n.** soft fine fluffy feathers that form the first covering of a young bird or an insulating layer below the contour feathers of an adult bird. ■ such feathers taken from ducks or their nests and used for stuffing cushions, quilts, etc.; eiderdown. ■ fine soft hair on the face or body of a person. ■ short soft hairs on some leaves, fruit, or seeds. [ME: from ON *dúnn.*]

down[3] ▶**n.** (usu. **downs**) a gently rolling hill: *the gentle green contours of the downs.* [OE *dūn* 'hill,' perh. ult. of Celtic origin and rel. to Old Irish *dún* 'fort.']

down-and-dirt·y ▶**adj.** informal **1** highly competitive or unprincipled: *down-and-dirty hacker feuds.* **2** earthy, direct, and explicit: *the down-and-dirty realities about these diseases.* ■ unvarnished; in a raw or prototypical form.

down-and-out ▶**adj.** (of a person) without money, a job, or a place to live; destitute: *a down-and-out homeless vagrant.* ▶**n.** (also **down-and-out·er**) a person without money, a job, or a place to live.

down-at-the-heels (also **down-at-the-heel** or **down-at-heel**) ▶**adj.** (of a person, thing, or place) showing signs of neglect and deterioration; shabby.

down·beat /'doun,bēt/ ▶**adj.** pessimistic; gloomy: *the assessment of current economic prospects is downbeat.* ▶**n.** Music an accented beat, usually the first of the bar.

down·burst /'doun,bərst/ ▶**n.** a strong downward current of air from a cumulonimbus cloud, usually associated with intense rain or a thunderstorm.

down·cast /'doun,kast/ ▶**adj. 1** (of a person's eyes) looking downward. **2** (of a person) feeling despondent.

down·coun·try /'doun'kəntrē/ ▶**adj. & adv.** in, into, or relating to the low-lying and generally more densely settled part of a country as opposed to hilly regions: [as adj.] *even the downcountry conservatives support this reform* | [as adv.] *distant summer storms a hundred miles downcountry.*

down·draft /'doun,draft/ ▶**n.** a downward current or draft of air, esp. one down a chimney into a room.

Down East a name for northeastern New England esp. Maine, from an old term for sailing downwind, to the east.

down·er /'dounər/ ▶**n.** informal **1** (usu. **downers**) a depressant or tranquilizing drug, esp. a barbiturate. **2** a dispiriting or depressing experience or factor. ■ a period of consistent failure.

Dow·ney /'dounē/ a city in southwestern California; pop. 107,323.

down·fall /'doun,fôl/ ▶**n.** a loss of power, prosperity, or status: *the crisis led to the downfall of the government.* ■ the cause of such a loss.

down·field /'doun'fēld/ ▶**adv. adj.** Football in or to a position nearer to the opponents' end of a field.

down·grade ▶**v.** /'doun,grād/ [trans.] (usu. **be downgraded**) reduce to a lower grade, rank, or level of importance. ▶**n. 1** an instance of reducing someone or something's rank, status, or level of importance. **2** a downward gradient, typically on a railroad track or road.

down·heart·ed /'doun'härtid/ ▶**adj.** discouraged; in low spirits. — **down·heart·ed·ly adv. down·heart·ed·ness n.**

down·hill ▶**adv.** /'doun'hil/ toward the bottom of a slope. ■ fig. into a steadily worsening situation: *his marriage continued to slide downhill.* ■ [predic.] fig. used to describe easy or quick progress toward an objective after initial difficulties have been overcome. ▶**adj.** leading down toward the bottom of a slope: *the route is downhill for part of the way.* ■ fig. leading to a steadily worsening situation: ■ of or relating to the sport of skiing or cycling downhill. ▶**n.** Skiing a downhill race. ■ the activity of downhill skiing.

– PHRASES **go downhill** become worse; deteriorate: *the business is going downhill fast.*

down·hill·er /'doun'hilər/ ▶**n.** a skier or cyclist who takes part in downhill races.

down-home ▶**adj.** connected with an unpretentious way of life, esp. that of rural peoples or areas: *some good down-home cooking.*

Down·ing Street /'douniNG/ a street in London. No. 10 is the official residence of the prime minister. ■ used allusively for the British government or the prime minister.

down·link /'doun,liNGk/ ▶**n.** a telecommunications link for signals coming to the earth from a satellite, spacecraft, or aircraft. ▶**v.** [trans.] relay to the earth (a telecommunications signal or the information it conveys).

down·load Comput. /'doun,lōd/ ▶**v.** [trans.] copy (data) from one computer system to another or to a disk. ▶**n.** the act or process of copying data in such a way. ■ a computer file transferred in such a way. — **down·load·a·ble adj.**

down pay·ment ▶**n.** an initial payment made when something is bought on credit.

down·play /'doun,plā/ ▶**v.** [trans.] make (something) appear less important than it really is: *this report downplays the seriousness of global warming.*

down·pour /'doun,pôr/ ▶**n.** a heavy rainfall.

down·range /'doun,rānj/ ▶**adv. & adj.** (of a missile, space launch, etc.) traveling in a specified direction away from the launch site and toward the target.

down·right /'doun,rīt/ ▶**adj.** [attrib.] (of something bad or unpleasant) utter; complete (used for emphasis): *it's a downright disgrace.* ▶**adv.** [as submodifier] to an extreme degree; thoroughly: *he was downright rude.* — **down·right·ness n.**

down·riv·er /'doun'rivər/ ▶**adv. & adj.** toward or situated at a point nearer the mouth of a river: [as adv.] *the cabin cruiser started to drift downriver* | [as adj.] *the downriver side of the bridge.*

down·scale /'doun,skāl/ ▶**v.** [trans.] reduce in size, scale, or extent. ▶**adj.** at the lower end of a scale, esp. a social scale; downmarket.

down·shift /'doun,sHift/ ▶**v.** [intrans.] change to a lower gear in a motor vehicle or bicycle. ■ slow down; slacken off: *well before the country slipped into recession, business was downshifting.*

down·side /'doun,sīd/ ▶**n. 1** the negative aspect of something, esp. something regarded as in general good or desirable: *a magazine feature on the downside of fashion modeling.* **2** [often as adj.] a downward movement of share prices: *reduce the downside risk by using futures and options.*

down·size /'doun,sīz/ ▶**v.** [trans.] make (something) smaller. ■ make (a company or organization) smaller by eliminating staff positions. ■ [intrans.] (of a company) eliminate staff positions.

down·spout /'doun,spout/ ▶**n.** a pipe to carry rainwater from a roof to a drain or to ground level.

down·stage /'doun'stāj/ ▶**adj. & adv.** at or toward the front of a stage.

down·stairs ▶**adv.** /'doun'ste(ə)rz/ down a flight of stairs. ■ on or to a lower floor. ▶**adj.** [attrib.] situated downstairs: *the downstairs bathroom.* ▶**n.** the ground floor or lower floors of a building: *the downstairs was hardly damaged at all.*

down·state /'doun'stāt/ ▶**adj. & adv.** of, in, or to the southern part of a state. ▶**n.** such an area. — **down·stat·er n.**

down·stream /'doun'strēm/ ▶**adv. & adj.** situated or moving in the direction in which a stream or river flows: [as adv.] *the bridge spanned the river just downstream of the rail line.* ■ at a stage in the process of gas or oil extraction and production after the raw material is ready for refining.

down·stroke /'doun,strōk/ ▶**n.** a stroke made downward.

Down syn·drome /'doun 'sindrōm/ (also **Down's syn·drome**) ▶**n.** Med. a congenital disorder arising from a chromosome defect, causing intellectual impairment and physical abnormalities including short stature and a broad facial profile. It arises from a defect involving chromosome 21. [1960s: named after John L. H. *Down* (1828–96), the Engl. physician who first described it.]

down-the-line ▶**adj.** informal thorough and uncompromising: *the party avoids down-the-line support of unions.*

down·time /'doun,tīm/ (also **down time**) ▶**n.** time during which a machine, esp. a computer, is out of action or unavailable for use. ■ fig. a time of reduced activity or inactivity: *everyone needs downtime to unwind.*

down-to-earth ▶**adj.** with no illusions or pretensions; practical and realistic. — **down-to-earth·ness n.**

down·town /'doun'toun/ ▶**adj.** of, in, or characteristic of the central area or main business and commercial area of a city or town: *downtown Chicago.* ▶**adv.** in or into such an area. ▶**n.** such an area of a town or city. — **down·town·er n.**

down·trod·den /'doun,trädn/ ▶**adj.** oppressed or treated badly by people in power: *a downtrodden proletarian struggling for social justice.*

down·turn /'doun,tərn/ ▶**n.** a decline in economic, business, or other activity.

Down Un·der (also **down un·der**) informal ▶**adv.** in or to Australia or New Zealand. ▶**n.** informal term for Australia and New Zealand. [19th C.: with ref. to the position of these countries on a globe.]

down·ward /'dounwərd/ ▶**adv.** (also **down·wards**) toward a lower place, point, or level: *he was lying face downward.* ■ used to indicate that something applies to everyone in a certain hierarchy or set: *new rules on sick leave affect employees of all grades, from managers downward.* ▶**adj.** moving or leading toward a lower place or level: *the downward curve of the stairs.* — **down·ward·ly adv.** [ME: shortening of OE *adūnweard.*]

down·well·ing /'doun,weliNG/ ▶**n.** the downward movement of fluid, esp. in the sea, the atmosphere, or deep in the earth. ▶**adj.** characterized by or undergoing such movement.

down·wind /'doun'wind/ ▶**adv. & adj.** in the direction in which the wind is blowing.

down·y /'dounē/ ▶**adj.** (**down·i·er, down·i·est**) covered with fine soft hair or feathers: *the baby's downy cheek.* ■ filled with soft feathers. ■ soft and fluffy. — **down·i·ly adv. down·i·ness n.**

down·y mil·dew ▶ n. mildew on a plant that is marked by a whitish down composed of spore-forming hyphae.

down·y wood·peck·er ▶ n. a widespread small North American woodpecker (*Picoides pubescens*) with a short bill, black and white plumage, and (on the male) a red patch on the back of the head.

downy woodpecker

dow·ry /'dou(ə)rē/ ▶ n. (pl. **-ries**) property or money brought by a bride to her husband on their marriage. [ME: from Anglo-Norman Fr. *dowarie*, from med. L. *dotarium* (see DOWER).]

dowse[1] /douz/ ▶ v. [intrans.] practice dowsing: *water is easy to dowse for.* — **dows·er** n. [17th C.: of unknown origin.]

dowse[2] ▶ v. var. of DOUSE.

dows·ing /'douziNG/ ▶ n. a technique for searching for underground water, minerals, or anything invisible, by observing the motion of a pointer (traditionally a forked stick, now often paired bent wires) or the changes in direction of a pendulum, supposedly in response to unseen influences.

dox·ol·o·gy /däk'säləjē/ ▶ n. (pl. **-gies**) a liturgical formula of praise to God. — **dox·o·log·i·cal** /ˌdäksə'läjikəl/ adj. [17th C.: via med. L. from Gk. *doxologia*, from *doxa* 'appearance, glory' (from *dokein* 'seem') + *-logia* (see -LOGY).]

dox·y·cy·cline /ˌdäksē'sīklēn/ ▶ n. Med. a broad-spectrum antibiotic of the tetracycline group. [1960s: from *d(e)oxy-* + TETRACYCLINE.]

doy·en /doi'en; 'doi-en/ ▶ n. the most respected or prominent person in a particular field: *the doyen of Canadian poetry.* [17th C.: via Fr. from OFr. *deien* (see DEAN).]

doy·enne /doi'en/ ▶ n. a woman who is the most respected or prominent person in a particular field: *she's the doyenne of daytime TV.* [19th C.: from Fr., fem. of *doyen* (see DOYEN).]

Doyle /doil/, Sir Arthur Conan (1859–1930), Scottish writer. He is known for his creation of private detective Sherlock Holmes, who first appeared in the novel *A Study in Scarlet* (1887).

doy·ley ▶ n. dated var. of DOILY.

D'Oy·ly Carte /'doilē 'kärt/, Richard (1844–1901), English impresario. He brought together the librettist Sir W. S. Gilbert and the composer Sir Arthur Sullivan.

doz. ▶ abbr. dozen.

doze /dōz/ ▶ v. [intrans.] sleep lightly. ■ **(doze off)** fall lightly asleep. ▶ n. [in sing.] a short light sleep. [17th C.: perh. rel. to Dan. *døse* 'make drowsy.']

doz·en /'dəzən/ (abbr.: **dz.**) ▶ n. (pl. same) a group or set of twelve. ■ **(dozens)** informal a lot: *she has dozens of admirers.* — **doz·enth** /'dəzənTH/ adj. [ME: from OFr. *dozeine*, based on L. *duodecim* 'twelve.']

doz·er /'dōzər/ ▶ n. informal short for BULLDOZER.

do·zy /'dōzē/ ▶ adj. **(do·zi·er, do·zi·est)** drowsy and lazy. — **do·zi·ly** /-zəlē/ adv. **do·zi·ness** n.

DP ▶ abbr. ■ data processing. ■ dew point. ■ displaced person. ■ Baseball double play.

DPhil ▶ abbr. Doctor of Philosophy.

dpi Comput. ▶ abbr. dots per inch, a measure of the resolution of printers, scanners, etc.

DPT (also **DTP**) ▶ abbr. diphtheria, pertussis, and tetanus, a combined vaccine given to small children.

Dr. ▶ abbr. ■ (as a title) Doctor: *Dr. Michael Russell.* ■ (in street names) Drive.

dr. ▶ abbr. ■ debit. [formerly representing *debtor*.] ■ drachma(s). ■ dram(s).

drab /drab/ ▶ adj. **(drab·ber, drab·best) 1** lacking brightness or interest; drearily dull: *the landscape was drab and gray.* **2** of a dull light brown color. — **drab·ly** adv. **drab·ness** n. [16th C.: prob. from OFr. *drap* 'cloth' (see DRAPE).]

dra·cae·na /drə'sēnə/ ▶ n. a tropical palmlike shrub or tree (genera *Dracaena* and *Cordyline*) of the agave family, with ornamental foliage. [mod. L., from Gk. *drakaina*, fem. of *drakōn* 'serpent, dragon.']

drachm /dram/ (abbr.: **dr.**) ▶ n. a unit of weight formerly used by apothecaries, equivalent to 60 grains or one eighth of an ounce. [ME: from OFr. *dragme* or late L. *dragma*, via L. from Gk. *drakhmē* (see DRACHMA).]

drach·ma /'dräkmə/ ▶ n. (pl. **-mas** or **-mae** /-mē/) the basic monetary unit of Greece (until the introduction of the euro), notionally equal to 100 lepta. ■ a silver coin of ancient Greece. [via L. from Gk. *drakhmē*, an Attic weight and coin.]

Dra·co[1] /'drākō/ Astron. a large northern constellation (the Dragon), stretching around the north celestial pole. [L.]

Dra·co[2] (7th century BC), Athenian politician. His codification of Athenian law was notorious for its severity.

dra·co·ni·an /drə'kōnēən; drā-/ ▶ adj. (of laws or their application) excessively harsh and severe. — **dra·con·ic** /-'känik/ adj. [19th C.: from the Gk. name *Drakōn* (see DRACO[2]) + -IAN.]

Drac·u·la /'drakyələ/ the Transylvanian vampire in Bram Stoker's novel *Dracula* (1897).

draft /draft/ ▶ n. **1** a preliminary version of a piece of writing. ■ a plan, sketch, or rough drawing. ■ (in full **draft mode**) Comput. a mode of operation of a printer in which text is produced rapidly but with relatively low definition. **2 (the draft)** compulsory recruitment for military service. ■ a procedure whereby new or existing sports players are made available for selection or reselection by the teams in a league, usually with the earlier choices being given to the weaker teams. **3** a current of cool air in a room or other confined space. **4** the action or act of pulling something along, esp. a vehicle or farm implement. **5** a written order to pay a specified sum; a check. **6** a single act of drinking or inhaling. ■ the amount swallowed or inhaled in one such act. **7** the depth of water needed to float a ship. ▶ v. [trans.] **1** prepare a preliminary version of (a text). **2** select (a person or group of people) for a certain purpose. ■ conscript (someone) for military service. ■ select (a player) for a sports team through a draft. **3** pull or draw. **4** [intrans.] Auto Racing benefit from reduced wind resistance by driving very closely behind another vehicle. ▶ adj. [attrib.] **1** denoting beer or other drink that is kept in and served from a barrel or tank rather than from a bottle or can: *draft beer.* **2** denoting an animal used for pulling heavy loads: *draft oxen.*
– PHRASES **on draft** (of beer or other drink) on tap; ready to be drawn from a barrel or tank; not bottled or canned. — **draft·er** n. [16th C.: phonetic spelling of Brit. *draught*.]

draft board ▶ n. a board of civilians that is responsible for registering, classifying, and selecting people for compulsory military service.

draft dodg·er ▶ n. derog. a person who has avoided compulsory military service. — **draft dodg·ing** n.

draft·ee /draf'tē/ ▶ n. a person conscripted for military service.

draft horse ▶ n. a large horse used for pulling heavy loads, esp. a cart or plow.

draft pick ▶ n. the right of a sports team to select a player during the annual selection process. ■ a player selected during the draft.

drafts·man /'draftsmən/ ▶ n. (pl. **-men**) a person, esp. a man, who makes detailed technical plans or drawings. — **drafts·man·ship** n.

drafts·per·son /'drafts,pərsən/ ▶ n. (pl. **-peo·ple**) a draftsman or draftswoman.

drafts·wom·an /'drafts,wŏŏmən/ ▶ n. (pl. **-wom·en**) a woman who makes detailed technical plans or drawings.

draft·y /'draftē/ ▶ adj. **(draft·i·er, draft·i·est)** (of an enclosed space) cold and uncomfortable because of currents of cool air. ■ (of a door or window) ill-fitting, and so allowing currents of cool air in. — **draft·i·ly** adv. **draft·i·ness** n.

drag /drag/ ▶ v. **(dragged, drag·ging) 1** [trans.] pull (someone or something) along forcefully, roughly, or with difficulty. ■ take (someone) to or from a place or event, despite their reluctance: *my girlfriend is dragging me off to Atlantic City for a week.* ■ **(drag oneself)** go somewhere wearily, reluctantly, or with difficulty. ■ move (an icon or other image) across a computer screen using a tool such as a mouse. ■ [intrans.] (of a person's clothes or an animal's tail) trail along the ground. ■ [intrans.] engage in a drag race. ■ [trans.] (of a ship) trail (an anchor) along the seabed, causing the ship to drift. ■ [intrans.] (of an anchor) fail to hold, causing a ship or boat to drift. ■ [trans.] search the bottom of (a river, lake, or the sea) with grapnels or nets. **2** [trans.] **(drag something up)** informal deliberately mention an unwelcome or unpleasant fact: *pieces of evidence about his early life were dragged up.* ■ **(drag someone/something into)** involve someone or something in (a situation or matter), typically when such involvement is inappropriate or unnecessary. ■ **(drag something in/into)** introduce an irrelevant or inappropriate subject. ■ **(drag someone/something down)** bring someone or something to a lower level or standard. **3** [intrans.] (of time, events, or activities) pass slowly and tediously: *the day dragged.* ■ (of a process or situation) continue at tedious and unnecessary length: *the dispute between the two families dragged on for years.* ■ [trans.] **(drag something out)** protract something unnecessarily. **4** [intrans.] **(drag on)** informal (of a person) inhale the smoke from (a cigarette). ▶ n. **1** the action of pulling something forcefully or with difficulty: *the drag of the current.* ■ the longitudinal retarding force exerted by air or other fluid surrounding a moving object. ■ [in sing.] a person or thing that impedes progress or development: *Larry was turning out to be **a drag on** her career.* **2** [in sing.] informal a boring or tiresome person or thing: *working nine to five can be a drag.* **3** informal an act of inhaling smoke from a cigarette: *he **took a long drag on** his cigarette.* **4** clothing more conventionally worn by the opposite sex, esp. women's clothes worn by a man: *a fashion show, complete with men **in drag**.* **5** short for DRAG RACE. ■ informal a street or road: *the main drag.* ■ hist. a private vehicle like a stagecoach, drawn by four horses. **6** a thing that is pulled along the ground or through water, in particular: ■ an apparatus for dredging a river or for recovering the bodies of drowned people from a river, a lake, or the sea.
– PHRASES **drag one's feet** walk slowly and wearily or with difficulty. **drag someone/something through the mud** make damaging allegations about someone or something: *he felt enough loyalty to his old school not to drag its name through the mud.* **in drag** wearing the clothing of the opposite sex.

– PHRASAL VERBS **drag something out** extract information from someone against their will: *the truth was being dragged out of us.*

drag-and-drop Comput. ▶ **v.** [trans.] move (an icon or other image) to another part of the screen using a mouse or similar device, typically in order to perform some operation on a file or document. ▶ **adj.** of, relating to, or permitting the movement of images in this way.

drag·ger /ˈdragər/ ▶ **n.** a trawler.

drag·gle /ˈdragəl/ ▶ **v.** [trans.] make (something) dirty or wet, typically by trailing it through mud or water: [as adj.] (**draggled**) *she wore a draggled skirt.* ■ [intrans.] hang untidily: *red hairs draggled from under her cap.* [16th C.: dimin. and frequentative of DRAG.]

drag·line /ˈdrag,līn/ ▶ **n.** a large excavator with a bucket pulled in by a wire cable.

drag·net /ˈdrag,net/ ▶ **n.** a net drawn through a river or across ground to trap fish or game. ■ fig. a systematic search for someone or something, esp. criminals or criminal activity.

drag·o·man /ˈdragəmən/ ▶ **n.** (pl. **-mans** or **-men**) an interpreter or guide, esp. in countries speaking Arabic, Turkish, or Persian. [ME: from obs. Fr., based on Arab. *tarjumān* 'interpreter.']

drag·on /ˈdragən/ ▶ **n.** **1** a mythical monster like a giant reptile. In European tradition the dragon is typically fire-breathing and tends to symbolize chaos or evil, whereas in the Far East it is usually a beneficent symbol of fertility. ■ derog. a fierce and intimidating person, esp. a woman. **2** see KOMODO DRAGON. [ME (also denoting a large serpent): from OFr., via L. from Gk. *drakōn* 'serpent.']

drag·on ar·um ▶ **n.** any of a number of plants of the arum family, in particular the North American green dragon. See illustration at GREEN DRAGON.

drag·on·et /,dragəˈnet; ˈdragənit/ ▶ **n.** a marine fish (family Callionymidae) that often lies partly buried in the seabed. The male is brightly colored. [ME (denoting a small dragon): from OFr., dimin. of *dragon* 'dragon.']

drag·on·fly /ˈdragən,flī/ ▶ **n.** (pl. **-flies**) a fast-flying long-bodied predatory insect (suborder Anisoptera, order Odonata) with two pairs of large transparent wings that are spread out sideways at rest. Compare with DAMSELFLY.

drag·on's blood ▶ **n.** a red gum or powder that is derived from certain tropical trees and plants, esp. the dragon tree. It is used as an acid shield in photoengraving and to color varnishes.

drag·on tree ▶ **n.** a slow-growing palmlike tree (*Dracaena draco*) of the agave family, native to the Canary Islands.

dra·goon /drəˈgo͞on/ ▶ **n.** a member of any of several cavalry regiments in the household troops of the British army. ■ hist. a mounted infantryman armed with a short rifle or musket. ▶ **v.** [trans.] coerce (someone) into doing something: *she had been **dragooned into** helping with the housework.* [17th C.: from Fr. *dragon* 'dragon.']

drag queen ▶ **n.** a man who dresses up in women's clothes, typically for the purposes of entertainment. ■ a male homosexual transvestite.

drag race ▶ **n.** a race between two or more cars over a short distance, usually a quarter of a mile, as a test of acceleration. — **drag rac·er n. drag rac·ing n.**

drag·ster /ˈdragstər/ ▶ **n.** a car built or modified to take part in drag races.

drag strip ▶ **n.** a straight, paved track or section of road used for drag racing.

drain /drān/ ▶ **v.** [trans.] **1** cause the water or other liquid in (something) to run out, leaving it empty, dry, or drier. ■ cause or allow (liquid) to run off or out of something. ■ make (land) drier by providing channels for water to flow away in: *the land was drained and the boggy ground reclaimed.* ■ (of a river) carry off the superfluous water from (a district): *the stream drains a wide moorland above the waterfall.* ■ [intrans.] (of water or another liquid) flow away from, out of, or into something: *the river drains into the Pacific.* ■ [intrans.] become dry or drier as liquid runs off or away. ■ (of a person) drink the entire contents of (a glass or other container). ■ [intrans.] fig. (of a feeling or emotion) become progressively less strongly felt: *gradually the tension and stress **drained away**.* **2** deprive of strength or vitality: *his limbs were **drained of** all energy.* ■ cause (money, energy, or another valuable resource) to be lost, wasted, or used up: *my mother's hospital bills are draining my income.* ■ [intrans.] (of such a resource) be lost, wasted, or used up. ▶ **n.** **1** a channel or pipe carrying off surplus liquid, esp. rainwater or liquid waste. ■ a tube for drawing off accumulating fluid from a body cavity or an abscess. **2** [in sing.] a thing that uses up a particular resource: *nuclear power is **a serious drain on** the public purse.* [OE *drēahnian, drēhnian* 'strain (liquid),' of Gmc. origin; rel. to DRY.]

drain·age /ˈdrānij/ ▶ **n.** the action or process of draining something: *the drainage of wetlands.* ■ the means of removing surplus water or liquid waste; a system of drains.

drain·board /ˈdrān,bôrd/ ▶ **n.** a sloping grooved board or surface, on which washed dishes are left to drain, typically into a sink.

drain·pipe /ˈdrān,pīp/ ▶ **n.** a pipe for carrying off rainwater or liquid refuse from a building.

Drake /drāk/, Sir Francis (c.1540–96), English explorer. In his ship, the *Golden Hind*, he was the first Englishman to circumnavigate the globe (1577–80).

drake /drāk/ ▶ **n.** a male duck. [ME: of West Gmc. origin; rel. to Ger. *Enterich.*]

Drake e·qua·tion Astron. a speculative equation that gives an estimate of the likelihood of discovering intelligent extraterrestrial life in the galaxy.

Dra·kens·berg Moun·tains /ˈdräkənz,bərg/ a range in southern Africa that stretches 700 miles (1,126 km); highest peak, Thabana Ntlenyana (11,425 feet; 3,482 m).

Drake Pas·sage a strait that connects the South Atlantic Ocean with the South Pacific Ocean and separates Cape Horn from the Antarctic Peninsula.

DRAM /ˈdē,ram/ ▶ **n.** Electron. a memory chip that depends upon an applied voltage to keep the stored data. [acronym from *dynamic random-access memory.*]

dram /dram/ ▶ **n.** **1** a small drink of whiskey or other spirits (often used in humorous imitation of Scottish speech): *a wee dram to ward off the winter chill.* **2** another term for DRACHM. [ME (sense 2): from OFr. *drame* or med. L. *drama*, vars. of *dragme* and *dragma* (see DRACHM).]

dra·ma /ˈdrämə/ ▶ **n.** **1** a play for theater, radio, or television. ■ such works as a genre or style of literature. **2** an exciting, emotional, or unexpected series of events or set of circumstances: *a hostage drama.* [16th C.: via late L. from Gk. *drama*, from *dran* 'do, act.']

Dram·a·mine /ˈdramə,mēn/ ▶ **n.** trademark an antihistamine compound used to counter nausea (esp. travel sickness).

dra·mat·ic /drəˈmatik/ ▶ **adj.** **1** [attrib.] of or relating to drama or the performance or study of drama. **2** (of an event or circumstance) sudden and striking: *a dramatic increase in recorded crime.* ■ exciting or impressive: *he recalled his dramatic escape from the building.* ■ (of a person or their behavior) intending or intended to create an effect; theatrical. — **dra·mat·i·cal·ly adv.**

dra·mat·ic mon·o·logue ▶ **n.** a poem in the form of a speech or narrative by an imagined person, in which the speaker inadvertently reveals aspects of their character while describing a particular situation or event.

dra·mat·ics /drəˈmatiks/ ▶ **plural n.** **1** [often treated as sing.] the study or practice of acting in and producing plays: *amateur dramatics.* **2** theatrically exaggerated or overemotional behavior.

dram·a·tis per·so·nae /ˈdrämətis pərˈsōnē/ ▶ **plural n.** the characters of a play, novel, or narrative. ■ the participants in a series of events. [18th C.: L., lit. 'persons of the drama.']

dram·a·tist /ˈdrämə,tist/ ▶ **n.** a person who writes plays.

dram·a·tize /ˈdrämə,tīz/ ▶ **v.** [trans.] adapt (a novel) or present (a particular incident) as a play or movie: *Miss Akins intends to dramatize my book.* ■ present in a vivid or striking way: *he used scare tactics to dramatize the deficit.* ■ exaggerate the seriousness or importance of (an incident or situation). — **dram·a·ti·za·tion** /,drämətiˈzāshən/ **n.**

Dram·bu·ie /dramˈbo͞oē/ ▶ **n.** trademark a sweet Scotch whiskey liqueur.

dram·e·dy /ˈdrämidē/ ▶ **n.** (pl. **-dies**)a television program or motion picture in which the comic elements derive mainly from character and plot development. [20th C.: blend of DRAMA and COMEDY.]

Drang nach O·sten /ˈdräng näk ˈästən/ ▶ **n.** the former German policy of eastward expansion, esp. that espoused under Nazi rule. [20th C.: Ger., lit. 'pressure toward the east.']

drank /drangk/ past of DRINK.

drape /drāp/ ▶ **v.** [trans.] arrange (cloth or clothing) loosely or casually on or around something: *she draped a shawl around her shoulders.* ■ (usu. **be draped**) adorn, cover, or wrap (someone or something) loosely with folds of cloth: *the body was draped in a blanket.* ■ let (oneself or a part of one's body) rest somewhere in a casual or relaxed way: *he draped an arm around her shoulders.* ■ [intrans.] (of fabric) hang or be able to hang in loose, graceful folds. ▶ **n.** (**drapes**) long curtains. ■ a cloth for covering parts of a patient's body other than that part on which a surgical operation is being performed. [19th C.: back-form. from DRAPERY.]

dra·per·y /ˈdrāpərē/ ▶ **n.** (pl. **-per·ies**) cloth coverings hanging in loose folds. ■ (**draperies**) long curtains of heavy fabric.

dras·tic /ˈdrastik/ ▶ **adj.** likely to have a strong or far-reaching effect; radical and extreme: *a drastic reduction of staffing levels.* — **dras·ti·cal·ly adv.** [17th C.: from Gk. *drastikos*, from *dran* 'do.']

drat /drat/ ▶ **exclam.** (often **drat someone/something**) a mild expression of anger or annoyance: *"Drat!" said Mitchell, kicking the fence* | *"Drat you!"* — **drat·ted adj.** [19th C.: shortening of *od rat*, euphemism for *God rot.*]

Dra·va Riv·er /ˈdrävə/ (also **Drave**), a river that rises in northern Italy and flows for 456 miles (725 km) through to join the Danube River in Croatia.

Dra·vid·i·an /drəˈvidēən/ ▶ **adj.** of, relating to, or denoting a family of languages spoken in southern India and Sri Lanka, or the peoples who speak them. ▶ **n.** **1** this family of languages. **2** a member of any of the peoples speaking a Dravidian language. [from Sanskrit *drāviḍa* 'relating to the Tamils' (from *Dravida* 'Tamil') + -IAN.]

draw /drô/ ▶ **v.** (past **drew** /dro͞o/; past part. **drawn** /drôn/) [trans.] **1** produce (a picture or diagram) by making lines and marks, esp. with a pen or pencil, on paper. ■ produce an image of (someone or something) in such a way. ■ trace or produce (a line or mark) on a surface. **2** pull or drag (something such as a vehicle) so as to make it follow behind. ■ [trans.] pull or move (something) in a specified direction. ■ [trans.] gently pull or guide (someone) in a specified direction: *"David," she whispered, drawing him aside.* ■ [intrans.] move in a slow steady way: *the driver slowed as he drew even with me.* ■ [intrans.] come to or arrive at a point in time or a specified point in a process: *the time for the parade itself is **drawing near**.* ■ pull (curtains, blinds, or other such coverings) shut or open. ■ make (wire) by pulling a piece of metal through successively smaller holes. **3** extract (an object or liquid) from a container or receptacle: *he drew his gun* | [as adj.] (**drawn**) *he met them with a drawn sword.* ■ run (a bath): *she drew a hot bath.* ■ (**draw something from**) obtain something from (a particular source): *a panel drawn from members of the public.* ■ (**draw on**) use (one's experience, talents, or skills) as a resource. ■ obtain or withdraw (money) from a bank or other source: *this check **draws against** my personal account.* ■ [intrans.] suck smoke from (a cigarette or pipe). ■ [intrans.] (of a chimney, flue, or fire) allow air to flow in and upward freely, so that a fire can burn. ■ take in (a breath). ■ disembowel: *after the trial he was **hanged, drawn, and quartered**.* **4** be the cause of (a specified response): *he drew criticism for his lavish spending.* ■ attract (someone) to come to a place or an event: *you really drew the crowds.* ■ (usu. **be drawn**) induce (someone) to reveal or do something: ***drawn into** an argument.* ■ direct or attract (someone's attention) to something: *we had to draw people's attention to it.* ■ reach (a conclusion) by deduction or inference from a set of circumstances: *the moral to be drawn is that spending wins votes.* ■ formulate or perceive (a comparison or distinction): *the law drew a clear distinction.* **5** (of a ship) require (a specified depth of water) to float in; have (a certain draft): *boats that draw only a few inches of water.* **6** [intrans.] (of a sail) be filled with wind. ▶ **n. 1** an act of selecting names randomly, typically by extracting them from a bag or other container, to match competitors in a game or tournament: *the draw has been made for this year's tournament.* **2** a game that ends with the score even; a tie. **3** a person or thing that is very attractive or interesting: *the city was a powerful draw.* **4** an act of inhaling smoke from a cigar, cigarette, or pipe.

– PHRASES **draw a blank** see BLANK. **draw blood** cause someone to bleed, esp. in the course of a fight: *the blow drew blood from the corner of his mouth* | fig. *she knew she'd drawn blood when the smile faded from his face.* **draw fire** attract hostile criticism, usually away from a more important target: *the vaccination campaign continued to draw fire.* **draw the line at** set a limit of what one is willing to do or accept, beyond which one will not go: *she drew the line at prostitution.* **quick on the draw** very fast in taking one's gun from its holster. ■ fig. very fast in acting or reacting.

– PHRASAL VERBS **draw back** choose not to do something that one was expected to do: *the government has **drawn back from** attempting reform.* **draw on** (of a period of time) pass by and approach its end: *he remembered sitting in silence with his grandmother as evening drew on.* **draw something out** make something last longer: *the transition was long drawn out.* **draw something up** prepare a plan, proposal, agreement, or other document in detail: *they instructed an attorney to draw up a sales agreement.* [OE *dragan*, of Gmc. origin; rel. to Du. *dragen* and Ger. *tragen*, also to DRAFT.]

draw·back /'drô,bak/ ▶ **n.** a feature that renders something less acceptable; a disadvantage or problem.

draw·bar /'drô,bär/ ▶ **n.** a bar on a vehicle to which something can be attached to pull it or be pulled. ■ a coupler on a railroad car.

draw·bridge /'drô,brij/ ▶ **n.** hist. a bridge, esp. one over a castle's moat, that is hinged at one end so that it may be raised to prevent people's crossing or to allow vessels to pass under it.

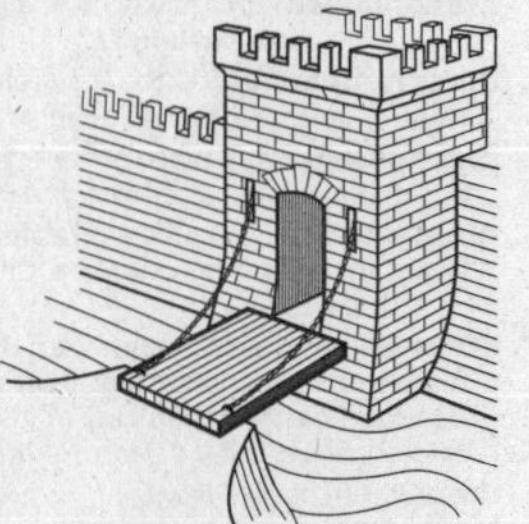
drawbridge

draw·down /'drô,doun/ ▶ **n.** a reduction in the size or presence of a military force. ■ a reduction in the volume of water in a lake or reservoir. ■ a withdrawal of oil or other commodity from stocks.

draw·ee /drô'ē/ ▶ **n.** the person or organization, typically a bank, who must pay a draft or bill.

draw·er /'drô(ə)r/ ▶ **n. 1** a boxlike storage compartment without a lid, made to slide horizontally in and out of a desk, chest, or other piece of furniture. **2** (**drawers**) dated humorous underpants. **3** a person who draws something, in particular: ■ a person who writes a check. ■ a person who produces a drawing or design. — **draw·er·ful** /-,fo͝ol/ **n.** (pl. **-fuls**).

draw·ing /'drô-iNG/ ▶ **n. 1** a picture or diagram made with a pencil, pen, or crayon rather than paint, esp. one drawn in monochrome. ■ the art or skill or making such pictures or diagrams. **2** the selection of a winner or winners in a lottery or raffle.

draw·ing board ▶ **n.** a large flat board on which paper may be spread for artists or designers to work on.

– PHRASES **back to the drawing board** used to indicate that an idea, scheme, or proposal has been unsuccessful and that a new one must be devised: *the government must go back to the drawing board and review the whole issue of youth training.* **on the drawing board** (of an idea, scheme, or proposal) under consideration and not yet ready to put into practice: *there are plans to enlarge the runway, but at present all this remains on the drawing board.*

draw·ing card /'drô-iNG/ ▶ **n.** informal a quality or feature that evokes interest or liking; an attraction: *rookie fireball flingers are the prime drawing cards of spring baseball.*

draw·ing room ▶ **n.** a room in a large private house in which guests can be received and entertained. ▶ **adj.** [attrib.] consciously refined, lighthearted, and elegant: *drawing-room small talk.* ■ (of a song or play) characterized by a polite observance of social proprieties: *a stock figure of Thirties drawing-room comedy.* [17th C.: abbrev. of 16th-cent. *withdrawing-room* 'a room to withdraw to.']

drawknife

draw·knife /'drô,nīf/ ▶ **n.** (pl. **-knives**) a knife consisting of a blade with a handle at each end at right angles to it, which is drawn over a surface, toward the user, with a paring effect.

drawl /drôl/ ▶ **v.** [intrans.] speak in a slow, lazy way with prolonged vowel sounds. ▶ **n.** [in sing.] a slow, lazy way of speaking or an accent with unusually prolonged vowel sounds: *a Texas drawl.* — **drawl·er n. drawl·y adj.** [16th C.: prob. from Low Ger. or Du. *dralen* 'delay, linger.']

drawn /drôn/ past participle of DRAW. ▶ **adj.** (of a person or a person's face) looking strained from illness, exhaustion, anxiety, or pain: *Cathy was pale and drawn and she looked tired out.*

drawn but·ter ▶ **n.** melted butter.

drawn-out ▶ **adj.** (often **long-drawn-out**) lasting or seeming to last longer than is necessary: *a long-drawn-out courtship.*

drawn·work /'drôn,wərk/ (also **drawn threadwork**) ▶ **n.** ornamental work on linen or other fabric, done by drawing out threads and usually with additional needlework.

draw pok·er ▶ **n.** a variety of poker in which each player is dealt five cards and, after the first round of betting, may discard some (usually up to three) of these cards and draw replacements from the dealer.

draw·string /'drô,striNG/ ▶ **n.** a string in the seam of the material of a garment or a bag, which can be pulled to tighten or close it.

dray horse ▶ **n.** a large, powerful horse used to pull heavy loads.

dread /dred/ ▶ **v.** [trans.] anticipate with great apprehension or fear: *Jane was dreading the party.* ▶ **n.** great fear or apprehension: *the thought of returning to New Jersey filled her with dread* | [in sing.] *I used to have a dread of Sunday afternoons.* ■ (**dreads**) dreadlocks. ▶ **adj.** [attrib.] greatly feared; dreadful: *he was stricken with the dread disease and died.* [OE *ādrǣdan, ondrǣdan*, of West Gmc. origin; rel. to Old High Ger. *intrātan*.]

dread·ed /'dredid/ ▶ **adj.** [attrib.] regarded with great fear or apprehension: *the dreaded news came that Joe had been wounded* | humorous *the dreaded fax machine.*

dread·ful /'dredfəl/ ▶ **adj.** causing or involving great suffering, fear, or unhappiness; extremely bad or serious: *there's been a dreadful accident.* ■ extremely disagreeable: *the weather was dreadful.* ■ [attrib.] used to emphasize the degree to which something is the case, esp. something regarded with sadness or disapproval: *you're a dreadful flirt.* ■ (of a person or their feelings) troubled: *I feel dreadful—I hate myself.* ■ (of a person or their appearance) feeling or looking ill. — **dread·ful·ness n.**

dread·ful·ly /'dredfəlē/ ▶ **adv. 1** [often as submodifier] extremely: *you're dreadfully thin.* ■ very much. **2** very badly.

dread·locks /'dred,läks/ ▶ **plural n.** a hairstyle in which the hair is washed, but not combed, and twisted while wet into tight braids or ringlets hanging down on all sides. — **dread·locked adj.**

dread·nought /'dred,nôt/ (also **dread·naught**) ▶ **n.** hist. a type of battleship introduced in the early 20th century, larger and faster than its predecessors and equipped entirely with large-caliber guns. [Britain's HMS *Dreadnought*.]

dream /drēm/ ▶ **n.** a series of thoughts, images, and sensations occurring in a person's mind during sleep. ■ [in sing.] a state of mind in which someone is or seems to be unaware of their immediate surroundings. ■ a cherished aspiration, ambition, or ideal: *the girl of **my dreams*** | [as adj.] *they'd found their dream home.* ■ an unrealistic or self-deluding fantasy. ■ a person or thing perceived as wonderful or perfect: *her new man's an absolute dream.* ▶ **v.** (past and past part. **dreamed** or **dreamt** /dremt/) [intrans.] **1** experience dreams during sleep: *I dreamed about her last night.* ■ [trans.] see, hear, or feel (something) in a dream: *maybe you dreamed it.* ■ indulge in daydreams or fantasies, typically about something greatly desired. **2** [with negative] contemplate the possibility of doing something or that something might be the case: *I wouldn't **dream of** foisting myself on you.*

– PHRASES **beyond one's wildest dreams** bigger or better than could be reasonably expected. **in your dreams** used in spoken English to assert that something much desired is not likely ever to happen. **in one's wildest dreams** [with negative] used to emphasize that a situation is beyond the scope of one's imagination. **like a dream** informal very well or successfully.

– PHRASAL VERBS **dream on** [in imper.] informal used, esp. in spoken English, as an ironic comment on the unlikely or impractical nature of a plan or aspiration: *Dean thinks he's going to get the job. Dream on, babe.* **dream something up** imagine or invent something: *he's been dreaming up new ways of attracting customers.* — **dream·ful** /-fəl/ **adj.** (literary) **dream·less adj. dream·like adj.** [ME: of Gmc. origin, rel. to Du. *droom* and Ger. *Traum*, and prob. also to OE *drēam* 'joy, music.']

dream·boat /'drēm,bōt/ ▶ **n.** informal a very attractive person, esp. a man.

dream·catch·er /'drēm,kacHər; -,kecH-/ ▶ **n.** a small hoop containing a horsehair mesh, or a similar construction of string or yarn, decorated with feathers and beads, believed to give its owner good dreams.

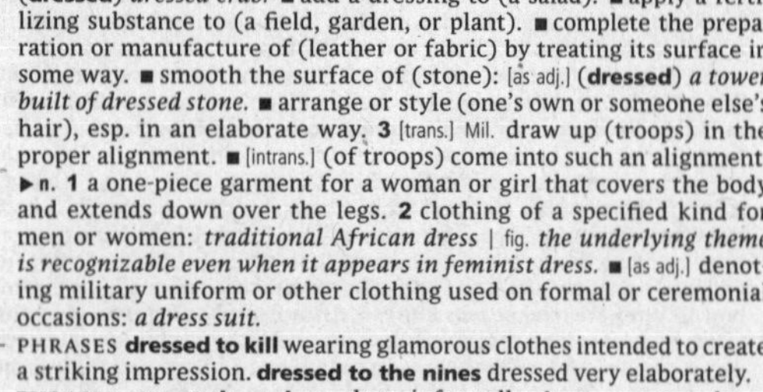

dreamcatcher

dream·er /'drēmər/ ▶ **n.** a person who dreams or is dreaming. ■ a person who is unpractical or idealistic.

dream·land /'drēm,land/ ▶ **n.** sleep regarded as a world of dreams. ■ an imagined and unrealistically ideal world.

dream·scape /'drēm,skāp/ ▶ **n.** a landscape or scene with the strangeness or mystery characteristic of dreams.

dream team ▶ **n.** a team of people perceived as the perfect combination for a particular purpose.

dream·time /'drēm,tīm/ ▶ **n.** [in sing.] (in the mythology of some Australian Aboriginals) the "golden age" when the first ancestors were created.

dream·world /'drēm,wərld/ ▶ **n.** a fantastic or idealized view of life.

dream·y /'drēmē/ ▶ **adj.** (**dream·i·er, dream·i·est**) reflecting a preoccupation with pleasant thoughts that distract one from one's present surroundings. ■ (of a person) not practical; given to daydreaming: *a dreamy boy who grew up absorbed in poetry.* ■ having a magical or dreamlike quality; peacefully gentle and relaxing: *a slow dreamy melody.* ■ informal delightful; gorgeous: *I bet he was really dreamy.* — **dream·i·ly adv. dream·i·ness n.**

drear /dri(ə)r/ ▶ **adj.** poetic/literary term for DREARY.

drear·y /'dri(ə)rē/ ▶ **adj.** (**drear·i·er, drear·i·est**) dull, bleak, and lifeless; depressing: *the dreary routine of working, eating, and trying to sleep.* — **drear·i·ly** /'dri(ə)rəlē/ **adv. drear·i·ness n.** [OE *drēorig* 'gory, cruel,' from *drēor* 'gore,' of Gmc. origin; rel. to Ger. *traurig* 'sorrowful,' also to DROWSY.]

dreck /drek/ (also **drek**) ▶ **n.** informal rubbish; trash: *this so-called art is pure dreck.* — **dreck·ish adj. dreck·y adj.** [20th C.: from Yiddish *drek* 'filth, dregs,' from a Gmc. base shared by OE *threax*.]

dredge[1] /drej/ ▶ **v.** [trans.] clean out the bed of (a harbor, river, or other area of water) by scooping out mud, weeds, and rubbish with a dredge. ■ bring up or clear (something) from a river, harbor, or other area of water with a dredge: *mud was dredged out of the harbor* | [intrans.] *they start to dredge for oysters in November.* ■ (**dredge something up**) fig. bring to people's attention an unpleasant or embarrassing fact or incident that had been forgotten: *I don't understand why you had to dredge up this story.* ▶ **n.** a dredger. [15th C.: perh. rel. to MDu. *dregghe* 'grappling hook.']

dredge[2] ▶ **v.** [trans.] sprinkle (food) with a powdered substance, typically flour or sugar. [16th C.: from obs. *dredge* 'sweetmeat, mixture of spices,' from OFr. *dragie*, perh. via L. from Gk. *tragēmata* 'spices.']

dredg·er /'drejər/ ▶ **n.** a barge or other vessel designed for dredging harbors or other bodies of water.

dregs /dregz/ ▶ **n.** the remnants of a liquid left in a container, together with any sediment or grounds. ■ fig. the most worthless part or parts of something. — **dreg·gy** /'dregē/ **adj.** [ME: prob. of Scand. origin and rel. to Swed. *drägg* (pl.).]

drei·del /'drādl/ ▶ **n.** a small four-sided spinning top with a Hebrew letter on each side, used by the Jews. [1930s: from Yiddish *dreydl*; cf. Ger. *drehen* 'to turn.']

Drei·ser /'drīzər/, Theodore Herman Albert (1871–1945), US writer. His novels include *Sister Carrie* (1900).

drek ▶ **n.** var. of DRECK.

drench /drencH/ ▶ **v.** [trans.] (usu. **be drenched**) wet thoroughly; soak: *I fell in the stream and got drenched* | [as n.] (**drenching**) *a severe drenching would kill his uncle.* ■ fig. cover (something) liberally or thoroughly: *cool patios drenched in flowers* | [as adj., in comb.] (**-drenched**) *a sun-drenched clearing.* [OE *drencan* 'force to drink,' *drenc* 'a drink or draft,' of Gmc. origin; rel. to Ger. *tränken* (v.), *Trank* (n.), also to DRINK.]

Dres·den[1] /'drezdən/ a city in eastern Germany, the capital of Saxony, on the Elbe River; pop. 485,130.

Dres·den[2] (also **Dresden china**) ▶ **n.** porcelain ware with elaborate decoration and delicate colorings, made originally at Dresden and (since 1710) at nearby Meissen: [as adj.] *a fine Dresden china cup.*

dress /dres/ ▶ **v.** 1 [intrans.] put on one's clothes. ■ [with adverbial] wear clothes in a particular way or of a particular type. ■ [trans.] put clothes on (someone). ■ put on clothes appropriate for a formal occasion: *we dressed for dinner.* ■ [trans.] design or supply clothes for (a celebrity): *he dressed the royal family.* ■ [trans.] decorate (something) in an artistic or attractive way. 2 [trans.] treat or prepare (something) in a certain way, in particular: ■ clean, treat, or apply a dressing to (a wound). ■ clean and prepare (food, esp. poultry or shellfish) for cooking or eating: [as adj.] (**dressed**) *dressed crab.* ■ add a dressing to (a salad). ■ apply a fertilizing substance to (a field, garden, or plant). ■ complete the preparation or manufacture of (leather or fabric) by treating its surface in some way. ■ smooth the surface of (stone): [as adj.] (**dressed**) *a tower built of dressed stone.* ■ arrange or style (one's own or someone else's hair), esp. in an elaborate way. 3 [trans.] Mil. draw up (troops) in the proper alignment. ■ [intrans.] (of troops) come into such an alignment. ▶ **n.** 1 a one-piece garment for a woman or girl that covers the body and extends down over the legs. 2 clothing of a specified kind for men or women: *traditional African dress* | fig. *the underlying theme is recognizable even when it appears in feminist dress.* ■ [as adj.] denoting military uniform or other clothing used on formal or ceremonial occasions: *a dress suit.*

– PHRASES **dressed to kill** wearing glamorous clothes intended to create a striking impression. **dressed to the nines** dressed very elaborately.

– PHRASAL VERBS **dress down** dress informally. **dress someone down** informal reprimand someone. **dress up** dress in smart or formal clothes. ■ dress in a special costume for fun or as part of an entertainment. **dress something up** present something in such a way that it appears better than it really is. [ME: from OFr. *dresser* 'arrange, prepare,' based on L. *directus* 'direct, straight.']

dres·sage /drə'säzH/ ▶ **n.** the art of riding and training a horse in a manner that develops obedience, flexibility, and balance. [1930s: from Fr., lit. 'training.']

dress code ▶ **n.** a set of rules, usually written and posted, specifying the required manner of dress at a school, office, club, restaurant, etc. ■ the customary style of dress of a specified group.

dress-down Fri·day ▶ **n.** another term for CASUAL FRIDAY.

dres·ser[1] /'dresər/ ▶ **n.** a chest of drawers. [ME: from OFr. *dresseur*, from *dresser* 'prepare' (see DRESS).]

dres·ser[2] ▶ **n.** 1 [usu. with adj.] a person who dresses in a specified way: *a snappy dresser.* ■ a person who habitually dresses in a smart or elegant way: *she's gorgeous—and she's a dresser.* 2 a person whose job is to look after theatrical costumes and help actors to dress. 3 a person who prepares, treats, or finishes a material or piece of equipment.

dress·ing /'dresiNG/ ▶ **n.** 1 (also **salad dressing**) a sauce for salads, typically one consisting of oil and vinegar mixed together with herbs or other flavorings: *vinaigrette dressing.* ■ stuffing: *turkey with apple dressing.* 2 a piece of material placed on a wound to protect it: *an antiseptic dressing.* 3 a fertilizing substance such as compost or manure spread over or plowed into land.

dress·ing-down ▶ **n.** [in sing.] informal a severe reprimand: *the secretary received a public dressing-down.*

dress·ing gown ▶ **n.** a long loose robe, typically worn after getting out of bed or bathing.

dress·ing room ▶ **n.** a room in which actors change clothes before and after their performance. ■ a small room or cubicle in a clothing store, used by customers to try on clothes.

dress·ing ta·ble ▶ **n.** a table with a mirror and drawers for cosmetics, etc., used while dressing or applying makeup.

dress·mak·er /'dres,mākər/ ▶ **n.** a person whose job is making women's clothes. — **dress·mak·ing n.**

dress re·hears·al ▶ **n.** the final rehearsal of a live show, in which everything is done as it would be in a real performance.

dress shield ▶ **n.** a piece of waterproof material fastened in the armpit of a dress to protect it from perspiration.

dress shirt ▶ **n.** a man's white shirt worn with a bow tie and a dinner jacket on formal occasions. ■ a man's long-sleeved shirt, suitable for wearing with a tie.

dress·y /'dresē/ ▶ **adj.** (**dress·i·er, dress·i·est**) (of clothes) suitable for a festive or formal occasion: *wear something dressy, Kate, we're going to a cocktail party.* ■ requiring or given to wearing such clothes: *this isn't a dressy place, but it's clean.* — **dress·i·ly adv. dress·i·ness n.**

drew /drōō/ past of DRAW.

Drex·el /'dreksəl/, Anthony Joseph (1826–93), US banker and philanthropist. His merger with J. P. Morgan in 1871 made Drexel, Morgan, and Co. the most powerful investment banking house in the US.

Drey·fus /'drāfəs; 'drī-/, Alfred (1859–1935), French army officer. In 1894, he was falsely accused of providing military secrets to the Germans; his trial and imprisonment caused a major political crisis in France.

drib·ble /'dribəl/ ▶ **v.** 1 [no obj. and usu. with adverbial of direction] (of a liquid) fall slowly in drops or a thin stream. ■ [with obj. and adverbial of direction] pour (a liquid) in such a way. ■ [intrans.] allow saliva to run from the mouth. 2 [with obj. and adverbial of direction] (chiefly in soccer, field hockey, and basketball) take (the ball) forward past opponents with slight touches of the feet or the stick, or (in basketball) by continuous bouncing. ▶ **n.** 1 a thin stream of liquid; a trickle. ■ saliva running from the mouth. 2 fig. foolish talk or ideas; nonsense. 3 (in soccer, hockey, and basketball) an act or instance of taking the ball forward with repeated slight touches or bounces. — **drib·bler n.** [16th C.: frequentative of obs. *drib*, var. of DRIP.]

dribs and drabs /'dribz ən 'drabz/ ▶ **plural n.** (**in dribs and drabs**) informal in small scattered or sporadic amounts: *doing the work in dribs and drabs.* [19th C.: from obs. *drib* (see DRIBBLE) and *drab* (by reduplication).]

dried /drīd/ past and past participle of DRY.

dri·er[1] /'drīər/ ▶ **adj.** comparative of DRY.

dri·er² ▶ n. var. of DRYER.

drift /drift/ ▶ v. [intrans.] **1** be carried slowly by a current of air or water. ■ [with adverbial of direction] (of a person) walk slowly, aimlessly, or casually. ■ [with adverbial] move passively, aimlessly, or involuntarily into a certain situation or condition. ■ (of a person or their attention) digress or stray to another subject. **2** (esp. of snow or leaves) be blown into heaps by the wind. ▶ n. **1** [in sing.] a continuous slow movement from one place to another. ■ the deviation of a vessel, aircraft, or projectile from its intended or expected course as the result of currents or winds. ■ a steady movement or development from one thing toward another, esp. one that is perceived as unwelcome. **2** [in sing.] the general intention or meaning of an argument or someone's remarks: *he didn't understand much Greek, but he got her drift.* **3** a large mass of snow, leaves, or other material piled up or carried along by the wind. ■ Geol. glacial and fluvioglacial deposits left by retreating ice sheets. **4** Mining a horizontal or inclined passage following a mineral deposit or coal seam. — **drift·y** adj. [ME: from ON *drift* 'snowdrift, something driven'; rel. to DRIVE.]

drift·er /'driftər/ ▶ n. **1** a person who continually moves from place to place, with no fixed home or job. **2** a fishing boat equipped with a drift net.

drift ice ▶ n. detached pieces of ice drifting with the wind or ocean currents.

drift net (also **drift·net**) ▶ n. a large net for herring and similar fish, kept upright by weights at the bottom and floats at the top and allowed to drift with the tide. — **drift net·ter** n. **drift net·ting** n.

drift pin ▶ n. a steel pin driven into a hole in a piece of metal to enlarge, shape, or align the hole.

drift·wood /'drift,wŏŏd/ ▶ n. pieces of wood that are floating on the sea or have been washed ashore.

drill¹ /dril/ ▶ n. **1** a hand tool, power tool, or machine with a rotating cutting tip or reciprocating hammer or chisel, used for making holes. ■ such a tool used by a dentist for cutting away part of a tooth before filling it. **2** instruction or training in military exercises. ■ intensive instruction or training in something, typically by means of repeated exercises. ■ a rehearsal of the procedure to be followed in an emergency. ■ (**the drill**) informal the correct or recognized procedure or way of doing something: *he didn't know the drill.* **3** a predatory mollusk (family Muricidae, class Gastropoda) that bores into the shells of other mollusks in order to feed on the soft tissue. ▶ v. [trans.] **1** produce (a hole) in something by or as if by boring with a drill. ■ make a hole in (something) by boring with a drill. ■ [intrans.] make a hole in or through something by using a drill: fig. *his eyes drilled into her.* ■ [intrans.] sink a borehole in order to obtain a certain substance, typically oil or water: *they are licensed to **drill for** oil in the area* | [as n.] (**drilling**) *drilling should begin next year.* ■ (of a dentist) cut away part of (a tooth) before filling it. ■ [trans.] informal (of a sports player) hit, throw, or kick (a ball or puck) hard and in a straight line. **2** subject (someone) to military training exercises. ■ [intrans.] (of a person) take part in such exercises. ■ instruct (someone) in something by the means of repeated exercises or practice. ■ (**drill something into**) cause (someone) to learn something by repeating it regularly. **3** [intrans.] (**drill down**) Computing access data that is in a lower level of a hierarchically structured database. — **drill·er** n. [17th C.: from MDu. *drillen* 'bore, turn in a circle.']

drill² ▶ n. a machine that makes small furrows, sows seed in them, and then covers the sown seed. ■ a small furrow, esp. one made by such a machine. ■ a ridge with such a furrow on top. ■ a row of plants sown in such a furrow: *drills of lettuces.* ▶ v. [trans.] (of a person or machine) sow (seed) with a drill. ■ plant (the ground) in furrows. [18th C.: perh. from DRILL¹.]

drill³ ▶ n. a dark brown baboon (*Mandrillus leucophaeus*) with a short tail, found in the rain forests of West Africa. Compare with MANDRILL. [17th C.: prob. a local word.]

drill⁴ ▶ n. a coarse twilled cotton or linen fabric. [18th C.: abbrev. of earlier *drilling*, from Ger. *Drillich*, from L. *trilix* 'triple-twilled,' from *tri-* 'three' + *licium* 'thread.']

drill·ing rig ▶ n. a large structure with equipment for drilling an oil well.

drill press ▶ n. a machine tool for drilling holes, set on a fixed stand.

drill ser·geant ▶ n. a noncommissioned officer who trains soldiers in basic military skills.

dri·ly ▶ adv. var. of DRYLY.

Dri·na Riv·er /'drēnə/ a river that flows north for 285 miles (459 km), along the border of Bosnia and Serbia, into the Sava River.

drink /driNGk/ ▶ v. (past **drank** /draNGk/; past part. **drunk** /drəNGk/) [trans.] take (a liquid) into the mouth and swallow. ■ [intrans.] consume or be in the habit of consuming alcohol, esp. to excess: *she doesn't drink or smoke* | [as n.] (**drinking**) *Les was ordered to cut down his drinking.* ■ [intrans.] (**drink up**) consume the rest of a drink, esp. in a rapid manner. ■ (**drink something in**) fig. watch or listen to something with eager pleasure or interest: *she strolled to the window to drink in the view.* ■ informal (of a plant or a porous substance) absorb (moisture). ▶ n. a liquid that can be swallowed as refreshment or nourishment. ■ a quantity of liquid swallowed. ■ alcohol, or the habitual or excessive consumption of alcohol: *they both **took to drink**.* ■ a glass of liquid, esp. when alcoholic: *we went for a drink.* ■ (**the drink**) informal the sea or another large area of water.
– PHRASES **drink and drive** drive a vehicle while under the influence of alcohol. **drink (a toast) to** celebrate or wish for the good fortune of someone or something by raising one's glass and drinking a small amount. **drink someone under the table** informal consume as much alcohol as one's drinking companion without becoming as drunk. **I'll drink to that** uttered to express one's agreement with or approval of a statement. — **drink·a·ble** adj. [OE *drincan* (v.), *drinc* (n.), of Gmc. origin; rel. to Du. *drinken* and Ger. *trinken*.]

drink·er /'driNGkər/ ▶ n. a person who drinks a particular drink: *coffee drinkers.* ■ a person who drinks alcohol, esp. to excess.

drink·ing foun·tain ▶ n. a device producing a small jet of water for drinking.

drip /drip/ ▶ v. (**dripped**, **drip·ping**) [intrans.] let fall or be so wet as to shed small drops of liquid: *the faucet won't stop dripping.* ■ [with adverbial] (of liquid) fall in small drops. ■ [trans.] cause or allow (a liquid) to fall in such a way. ■ fig. display a copious amount or degree of a particular quality or thing: *the women were **dripping with** gold and diamonds.* ▶ n. **1** a small drop of a liquid. ■ [in sing.] the action or sound of liquid falling steadily in small drops. ■ short for DRIP FEED. **2** informal a weak and ineffectual person. [OE *dryppan*, *dry̆pen*, of Gmc. origin; rel. to Dan. *dryppe*, also to DROP.]

drip-dry ▶ adj. (of a fabric or garment) capable of drying without creasing when hung up after washing. ▶ v. [intrans.] (of fabric or a garment) become dry without forming creases when hung up after washing. ■ [trans.] dry (fabric or a garment) by hanging it up in this way.

drip feed ▶ n. a device for introducing fluid drop by drop into a system, e.g., lubricating oil into an engine. ■ Med. a device that passes fluid, nutrients, or drugs drop by drop into a patient's body on a continuous basis, usually intravenously. ▶ v. (**drip-feed**) [trans.] introduce (fluid) drop by drop. ■ supply (a patient) with fluid, nutrients, or drugs through a drip feed.

drip·ping /'dripiNG/ ▶ n. (**drippings**) fat that has melted and dripped from roasting meat, used in cooking. ■ wax, fat, or other liquid produced from something by the effect of heat. ▶ adj. extremely wet: [as submodifier] ***dripping** wet hair.*

drip·py /'dripē/ ▶ adj. (**drip·pi·er**, **drip·pi·est**) **1** informal weak, ineffectual, or sloppily sentimental: *a drippy love song.* **2** tending to drip: *drippy food.* — **drip·pi·ly** adv. **drip·pi·ness** n.

drive /drīv/ ▶ v. (past **drove** /drōv/; past part. **driv·en** /'drivən/) **1** [intrans.] operate and control the direction and speed of a motor vehicle: *he got into his car and drove off.* ■ [trans.] own or use (a specified type of motor vehicle). ■ [intrans.] be licensed or competent to drive a motor vehicle. ■ [trans.] convey (someone) in a vehicle, esp. a private car. **2** [trans. and adverbial of direction] propel or carry along by force in a specified direction. ■ [intrans.] (of wind, water, or snow) move or fall with great force. ■ [trans.] (of a source of power) provide the energy to set and keep (an engine or piece of machinery) in motion. ■ Electron. (of a device) power or operate (another device): *the interface can be used to drive a printer.* ■ [trans.] force (a stake or nail) into place by hitting or pushing it. ■ [trans.] bore (a tunnel). ■ (in ball games) hit or kick (the ball) hard with a free swing of the bat, racket, or foot. ■ [trans.] Golf strike (a ball) from the tee, typically with a driver. **3** [trans.] urge or force (animals or people) to move in a specified direction. ■ [trans.] urge forward and direct the course of (an animal drawing a vehicle or plow). ■ [trans.] chase or frighten (wild animals) into nets, traps, or into a small area where they can be killed or captured. ■ compel to leave. **4** [trans.] (usu. **be driven**) (of a fact or feeling) compel (someone) to act in a particular way, esp. one that is considered undesirable or inappropriate: *he was driven by ambition* | [as adj.] (**driven**) *my husband is a driven man.* ■ [trans.] bring (someone) forcibly into a specified negative state: *the thought **drove** him **to despair*** | [trans.] *my laziness drives my wife crazy.* ■ [trans.] force (someone) to work to an excessive extent: *you're **driving yourself** too hard.* ▶ n. **1** a trip or journey in a car. ■ [in names] a street or road: *Hammond Drive.* ■ short for DRIVEWAY. **2** Psychol. an innate, biologically determined urge to attain a goal or satisfy a need. ■ the determination and ambition of a person to achieve something. **3** an organized effort by a number of people to achieve a particular purpose, often to raise money. ■ Football a series of offensive plays that advance the ball for the purpose of a score: *an 80-yard scoring drive.* **4** the transmission of power to machinery or to the wheels of a motor vehicle. ■ (in a car with automatic transmission) the position of the gear selector in which the car will move forward, changing gears automatically as required: *he threw the car into drive.* ■ Comput. short for DISK DRIVE. **5** (in ball games) a forceful stroke made with a free swing of the bat, racket, or foot against the ball. ■ Golf a shot from the tee. **6** an act of driving a group of animals to a particular destination. — **driv·a·bil·i·ty** /,drīvə'bilitē/ (also **drive·a·bil·i·ty**) n. **driv·a·ble** (also **drive·a·ble**) adj. [OE *drīfan* 'urge (a person or animal) to go forward,' of Gmc. origin; rel. to Du. *drijven* and Ger. *treiben*.]

drive belt ▶ n. a belt that transmits drive from a motor, engine, or line shaft to a moving part or machine tool.

drive-by ▶ adj. [attrib.] (of a shooting or other act) carried out from a passing vehicle: *a drive-by shooting.* ■ informal superficial or casual: *they practice drive-by journalism rather than trying to elevate the level of discussion.*

drive chain ▶ n. an endless chain with links that engage with toothed wheels in order to transmit power from one shaft to another in an engine or machine tool.

drive-in ▶ adj. [attrib.] denoting a facility such as a restaurant that one can visit without leaving one's car. ▶ n. a facility of this type.

driv·el /ˈdrivəl/ ▶ n. silly nonsense: *don't talk such drivel!* ▶ v. (**driv·eled, driv·el·ing**; Brit. **driv·elled, driv·el·ling**) [intrans.] talk nonsense: *he was **driveling on** about the glory days.* — **driv·el·er** n. [OE *dreflian*, of uncertain origin.]

driv·en /ˈdrivən/ past participle of DRIVE. ▶ adj. 1 [in comb.] operated, moved, or controlled by a specified person or source of power. ■ motivated or determined by a specified factor or feeling. 2 (of snow) piled into drifts or made smooth by the wind.

driv·er /ˈdrīvər/ ▶ n. 1 a person who drives a vehicle. ■ a person who drives a specified kind of animal. 2 a wheel or other part in a mechanism that receives power directly and transmits motion to other parts. ■ Electron. a device or part of a circuit that provides power for output. ■ Comput. a program that controls the operation of a device such as a printer or scanner. 3 a golf club with a nearly upright face and a large head, used for driving from the tee.

– PHRASES **in the driver's seat** in control of or dominating a situation: *the tax issue is back in the driver's seat of American politics.* — **driv·er·less** adj.

driv·er ant ▶ n. another term for ARMY ANT.

driv·er's li·cense ▶ n. a document permitting a person to drive a motor vehicle.

drive·shaft /ˈdrīvˌSHaft/ ▶ n. a rotating shaft that transmits torque in an engine.

drive-through (also informal **drive-thru**) ▶ adj. [attrib.] denoting a facility through or to which one can drive, esp. to be served without leaving one's car. ▶ n. a place or facility of this type.

drive time ▶ n. (esp. in broadcasting) the parts of the day when many people commute by car.

drive·train /ˈdrīvˌtrān/ ▶ n. the system in a motor vehicle that connects the transmission to the drive axles.

drive-up ▶ adj. & n. another term for DRIVE-THROUGH.

drive·way /ˈdrīvˌwā/ ▶ n. a short road leading from a public road to a house or garage.

driv·ing /ˈdrīviNG/ ▶ adj. [attrib.] (of rain or snow) falling and being blown by the wind with great force. ■ having a strong and controlling influence. ■ energetic; dynamic. ▶ n. the control and operation of a motor vehicle.

driv·ing range ▶ n. an area where golfers can practice drives.

driv·ing wheel ▶ n. any of the large wheels of a locomotive, to which power is applied either directly or via coupling rods.

driz·zle /ˈdrizəl/ ▶ n. light rain falling in very fine drops. ■ [in sing.] Cooking a thin stream of a liquid ingredient trickled over something. ▶ v. [intrans.] (**it drizzles, it is drizzling**, etc.) rain lightly. ■ [trans.] Cooking cause a thin stream of (a liquid ingredient) to trickle over food. ■ [trans.] cause a liquid ingredient to trickle over (food) in this way. — **driz·zly** adj. [16th C.: probably based on OE *drēosan* 'to fall,' of Gmc. origin; prob. rel. to DREARY.]

drogue /drōg/ ▶ n. a device, typically conical or funnel-shaped with open ends, towed behind a boat, aircraft, or other moving object to reduce speed or improve stability. ■ a similar object used as an aerial target for gunnery practice or as a windsock. ■ (in tanker aircraft) a funnel-shaped part on the end of the hose into which a probe is inserted by an aircraft being refueled in flight. ■ short for DROGUE PARACHUTE. [18th C.: perh. rel. to DRAG.]

drogue par·a·chute ▶ n. a small parachute used as a brake or to pull out a larger parachute or other object from an aircraft in flight or a fast-moving vehicle.

droid /droid/ ▶ n. (in science fiction) a robot. ■ fig. a person regarded as lifeless or mechanical. [1970s: shortening of ANDROID.]

droll /drōl/ ▶ adj. curious or unusual in a way that provokes dry amusement: *his unique brand of droll self-mockery.* — **droll·er·y** /ˈdrōlərē/ n. **droll·ness** n. **drol·ly** adv. [17th C. (as an adj.): from Fr. *drôle*, perh. from MDu. *drolle* 'imp, goblin.']

dro·mae·o·sau·rid /ˌdrōmēəˈsôrid/ (also **dro·mae·o·saur** /ˈdrōmēəˌsôr/) ▶ n. a carnivorous bipedal dinosaur (family Dromaeosauridae, suborder Theropoda) of a late Cretaceous family that included deinonychus and the velociraptors. They had a large slashing claw on each hind foot. [1970s: from mod. L. *Dromaeosauridae*, based on Gk. *dromaios* 'swift-running' + *sauros* 'lizard.']

-drome ▶ comb. form denoting a place for running or racing: *velodrome.* [from Gk. *dromos* 'course, running'.]

drom·e·dar·y /ˈdräməˌderē/ ▶ n. (pl. **-dar·ies**) an Arabian camel, esp. one of a light and swift breed trained for riding or racing. [ME: from OFr. *dromedaire* or late L. *dromedarius (camelus)* 'swift camel,' based on Gk. *dromas, dromad-* 'runner.']

drone /drōn/ ▶ v. [intrans.] make a continuous low humming sound. ■ speak tediously in a dull monotonous tone: *while Jim **droned on**.* ■ move with a continuous humming sound: *traffic droned up and down the street.* ▶ n. 1 a low continuous humming sound. ■ informal a monotonous speech. ■ a continuous musical note, typically of low pitch. ■ a musical instrument, or part of one, sounding such a continuous note, in particular (also **drone pipe**) a pipe in a bagpipe or (also **drone string**) a string in an instrument such as a hurdy-gurdy or a sitar. 2 a male bee in a colony of social bees, which does no work but can fertilize a queen. See illustration at HONEYBEE. ■ fig. a person who does no useful work and lives off others. 3 a remote-controlled pilotless aircraft or missile. [OE *drān, drǣn* 'male bee,' from a West Gmc. v. meaning 'resound, boom'; rel. to Ger. *dröhnen* 'to roar.']

drool /dro͞ol/ ▶ v. [intrans.] drop saliva uncontrollably from the mouth: *the baby begins to drool, then to cough.* ■ informal make an excessive and obvious show of pleasure or desire. ▶ n. saliva falling from the mouth. [19th C.: contr. of DRIVEL.]

droop /dro͞op/ ▶ v. [intrans.] bend or hang downward limply: *a long black cloak drooped from his shoulders.* ■ sag down from or as if from weariness or dejection. ■ [trans.] cause to bend or hang downward: *James drooped his head.* ▶ n. [in sing.] an act or instance of drooping; a limp or weary attitude. [ME: from ON *drúpa* 'hang the head'; rel. to DRIP and DROP.]

droop·y /ˈdro͞opē/ ▶ adj. (**droop·i·er, droop·i·est**) hanging down limply; drooping: *a droopy mustache.* ■ lacking strength or spirit: *the girls looked rather droopy* | fig. *a period of droopy sales.* — **droop·i·ly** adv. **droop·i·ness** n.

drop /dräp/ ▶ v. (**dropped, drop·ping**) [trans.] 1 let or make (something) fall vertically. ■ deliver (supplies or troops) by parachute. ■ (of an animal, esp. a mare, cow, or ewe) give birth to (young). ■ informal take (a drug, esp. LSD) orally: *he dropped a lot of acid in the Sixties.* 2 [intrans.] fall vertically. ■ (of a person) allow oneself to fall; let oneself down without jumping. ■ (of a person or animal) sink to or toward the ground: *he dropped to his knees in the mud.* ■ informal collapse or die from exhaustion: *he looked **ready to drop**.* ■ (of ground) slope steeply down. 3 make or become lower, weaker, or less: [trans.] *he dropped his voice as she came into the room* | [intrans.] *pretax profits dropped by 37 percent* | *tourism has **dropped off** in the last few years.* 4 abandon or discontinue (a course of action or study): *the charges against him were dropped last year* | *drop everything and get over here!* ■ discard or exclude (someone or something): *they were dropped from the team in the reshuffle.* ■ omit (a letter or syllable) in speech: *the drill sergeants are English—they drop their h's.* 5 set down or unload (a passenger or goods), esp. on the way to somewhere else: *he **dropped** the load **off** at a dealer's.* ■ [trans.] put or leave in a particular place without ceremony or formality: *just drop it in the mail when you've got time.* ■ mention in passing, typically in order to impress: *she dropped a remark about having been included in the selection.* 6 (in sports) fail to win (a point, game, or match). ■ informal lose (money), esp. through gambling. ▶ n. 1 a small round or pear-shaped portion of liquid that hangs or falls or adheres to a surface: ***drops of rain.*** ■ [often with negative] a very small amount of liquid. ■ [usu. with negative] a drink of alcoholic liquor: *he doesn't touch a drop during the week.* ■ (**drops**) liquid medicine to be measured or applied in very small amounts. 2 [usu. in sing.] an instance of falling or dropping. ■ an act of dropping supplies or troops by parachute. ■ a fall in amount, quality, or rate. ■ an abrupt fall or slope: *standing on the lip of a sixty-foot drop.* 3 something that drops or is dropped. 4 something resembling a drop of liquid in shape, in particular: ■ [usu. with adj.] a piece of candy or a lozenge: *a lemon drop.* ■ a pendant earring. 5 informal a delivery: *I got to the depot and made the drop.* ■ a mailbox. ■ a hiding place for stolen, illicit, or secret things: *the lavatory's water cistern could be used as a letter drop.*

– PHRASES **at the drop of a hat** informal without delay or good reason: *he used to be very bashful, blushing at the drop of a hat.* **drop the ball** informal make a mistake; mishandle things: *I really dropped the ball on this one.* **drop dead** die suddenly and unexpectedly: *she had seen her father drop dead of a heart attack.* ■ [in imper.] informal used as an expression of intense scorn or dislike.

– PHRASAL VERBS **drop back/behind** fall back or get left behind: *the colt was struggling to stay with the pace and started to drop back.* **drop by/in** call informally and briefly as a visitor: *they would unexpectedly drop in on us.* **drop off** fall asleep easily, esp. without intending to. **drop out 1** cease to participate in a race or competition. 2 abandon a course of study: *kids who had **dropped out of** college.* 3 reject conventional society to pursue an alternative lifestyle: *a child of the sixties who had temporarily dropped out.* — **drop·pa·ble** adj. [OE *dropa* (n.), *droppian* (v.), of Gmc. origin; rel. to Ger. *Tropfen* 'a drop,' also to DROOP.]

drop box ▶ n. a secured receptacle into which items such as returned books or videotapes, payments, keys, or donated clothing can be deposited.

drop cloth ▶ n. a large sheet for covering furniture or flooring to protect it from dust or while decorating.

drop cur·tain ▶ n. a curtain or painted cloth lowered vertically on to a theater stage.

drop-dead ▶ adj. informal used to emphasize how attractive someone or something is: *her drop-dead good looks.*

drop-down ▶ adj. [attrib.] dropping down or unfolding when required: *an RV with two drop-down beds.* ■ Comput. (of a menu) appearing below a menu title when it is selected, and remaining until used or dismissed. Compare with PULL-DOWN.

drop-forged ▶ adj. (of a metal object) made by forcing hot metal into or through a die with a drop hammer. — **drop-forg·ing** n.

drop ham·mer ▶ n. a large heavy weight raised mechanically and allowed to drop, as used in drop-forging and pile-driving.

drop han·dle·bars ▶ plural n. bicycle handlebars of which the handles are bent below the rest of the bar, used esp. on racing cycles.

drop-in ▶ adj. 1 visited on an informal basis without booking or appointments: *a drop-in disco.* 2 (of an object such as a chair seat) designed to drop into position.

drop-in cen·ter ▶ n. a place run by a welfare agency or charity where people may call casually for advice or assistance.

drop kick ▶ n. (formerly, in football) a kick for a goal made by dropping the ball and kicking after it touches the ground. ■ (chiefly in martial arts) a flying kick made against an opponent while dropping to the ground. ▶ v. (**drop-kick**) [trans.] kick using a drop kick.

drop leaf ▶ n. a hinged table leaf.

drop·let /'dräplit/ ▶ n. a very small drop of a liquid.

drop·light ▶ n. a light that is suspended from a reel so that it can be raised or lowered, typically over a work area.

drop-off ▶ n. **1** a decline or decrease. **2** a sheer downward slope; a cliff. ▶ adj. [attrib.] relating to or allowing the delivery or depositing of something: *drop-off points.*

drop·out /'dräp,out/ ▶ n. **1** a person who has abandoned a course of study or who has rejected conventional society to pursue an alternative lifestyle. **2** a momentary loss of recorded audio signal or an error in reading data on a magnetic tape or disk, usually due to a flaw in the coating.

drop·per /'dräpər/ ▶ n. a short glass tube with a rubber bulb at one end and a tiny hole at the other, for measuring out drops of medicine or other liquids.

drop·pings /'dräpiNGz/ ▶ plural n. the excrement of certain animals, such as rodents, sheep, birds, and insects.

drop ship·ment ▶ n. Commerce a shipment sent directly by a manufacturer to a customer, but billed through a wholesaler or distributor. — **drop-ship** v.

drop shot ▶ n. (chiefly in tennis or squash) a softly hit shot, usually with backspin, which drops abruptly to the ground.

drop-stitch ▶ adj. denoting an openwork pattern in knitted garments made by dropping a made stitch at intervals: *a drop-stitch cardigan.*

drop·sy /'dräpsē/ ▶ n. (pl. **-sies**) old-fashioned or less technical term for EDEMA. [ME: shortening of *idropesie*, based on Gk. *hudrōps* 'dropsy,' from *hudōr* 'water.']

drop waist (also **dropped waist**) ▶ n. a style of waistline on a dress cut so that the seam is positioned at the hips rather than the waist.

drop zone ▶ n. a designated area into which troops or supplies are dropped by parachute or in which skydivers land.

dros·er·a /'dräsərə/ ▶ n. a sundew. [mod. L., from Gk. *droseros* 'dewy.']

drosh·ky /'dräsHkē/ ▶ n. (pl. **-kies**) hist. a low four-wheeled open carriage of a kind formerly used in Russia. [19th C.: from Russ. *drozhki*, dimin. of *drogi* 'wagon,' from *droga* 'shaft, carriage pole.']

dro·soph·i·la /drə'säfələ/ ▶ n. a small fruit fly (genus *Drosophila*, family Drosophilidae), used extensively in genetic research because of its large chromosomes, numerous varieties, and rapid rate of reproduction. [mod. L., from Gk. *drosos* 'dew, moisture' + *philos* 'loving.']

dross /drôs; dräs/ ▶ n. something regarded as worthless; rubbish. ■ foreign matter, dregs, or mineral waste, in particular scum formed on the surface of molten metal. — **dross·y** adj. [OE *drōs*; rel. to Ger. *Drusen* 'dregs, lees.']

drought /drout/ ▶ n. a prolonged period of abnormally low precipitation; a shortage of water resulting from this. ■ [usu. with adj.] fig. a prolonged absence of something specified: *he ended a five-game hitting drought.* — **drought·i·ness** n. **drought·y** adj. [OE *drūgath* 'dryness,' of Gmc. origin; rel. to DRY.]

drove¹ /drōv/ past of DRIVE.

drove² ▶ n. a herd or flock of animals being driven in a body. ■ a large number of people or things doing or undergoing the same thing: *tourists stayed away in droves.* — **dro·ver** n. [OE *drāf*, rel. to *drīfan* 'to drive.']

drown /droun/ ▶ v. [intrans.] die through submersion in and inhalation of water. ■ [trans.] deliberately kill (a person or animal) in this way. ■ [trans.] submerge or flood (an area). ■ [trans.] (of a sound) make (another sound) inaudible by being much louder.
– PHRASAL VERBS **drowned in** be overwhelmed or enveloped by. ■ (of food) immersed in or covered by. [ME (orig. northern): rel. to ON *drukkna* 'to be drowned,' also to DRINK.]

drowse /drouz/ ▶ v. [intrans.] be half asleep; doze intermittently. ▶ n. [in sing.] a light sleep; a condition of being half asleep. [16th C.: back-form. from DROWSY.]

drow·sy /'drouzē/ ▶ adj. (**-si·er, -si·est**) sleepy and lethargic; half asleep. ■ causing sleepiness: *the drowsy heat of the meadows.* ■ (esp. of a place) very peaceful and quiet. — **drow·si·ly** /-zəlē/ adv. **drow·si·ness** n. [15th C.: prob. from the stem of OE *drūsian* 'be languid or slow,' of Gmc. origin; rel. to DREARY.]

drub /drəb/ ▶ v. (**drubbed, drub·bing**) [trans.] hit or beat (someone) repeatedly. ■ informal defeat thoroughly in a match or contest. [17th C.: prob. from Arab. *ḍaraba* 'to beat, bastinado.']

drub·bing /'drəbiNG/ ▶ n. a beating; a thrashing. ■ informal a resounding defeat in a match or contest.

drudge /drəj/ ▶ n. a person made to do hard, menial, or dull work. [ME (as a n.): perh. rel. to DRAG.]

drudg·er·y /'drəjərē/ ▶ n. hard, menial, or dull work.

drug /drəg/ ▶ n. a substance that has a physiological effect when ingested or otherwise introduced into the body, in particular: ■ a medicine, esp. a pharmaceutical preparation. ■ a substance taken for its narcotic or stimulant effects, often illegally: [as adj.] *a drug addict.* ▶ v. (**drugged, drug·ging**) [trans.] administer a drug to (someone) in order to induce stupor or insensibility. ■ add a drug to (food or drink). [ME: from OFr. *drogue*, possibly from MDu. *droge vate*, lit. 'dry vats.']

drug a·buse ▶ n. the habitual taking of addictive or illegal drugs.

drug ba·ron ▶ n. a person who controls an organization dealing in illegal drugs: *the deportation of a reputed drug baron.*

drug bust ▶ n. informal a seizure of illegal drugs by the police or other law-enforcement agency.

drug-free ▶ adj. (of a place or situation) where no illegal drugs are used or available. ■ (of a medical procedure or treatment) involving no administration of drugs. ■ (of a person) not taking drugs, esp. illegal ones. ■ (of a product) containing no drugs.

drug·gie /'drəgē/ (also **drug·gy**) ▶ n. informal a drug addict.

drug·gist /'drəgist/ ▶ n. a pharmacist or retailer of medicinal drugs.

drug·gy /'drəgē/ informal ▶ adj. caused by or involving drugs: *a druggy haze.* ■ given to taking drugs, esp. illegal ones: *the druggy world of rock and roll.* ▶ n. var. of DRUGGIE.

drug mule ▶ n. a person who transports illegal drugs by swallowing them or concealing them in a body cavity.

drug·store /'drəg,stôr/ ▶ n. a pharmacy that also sells toiletries and other articles.

Dru·id /'drōōid/ ▶ n. a priest, magician, or soothsayer in the ancient Celtic religion. ■ a member of a present-day group claiming to represent or be derived from this religion. — **Dru·id·ic** /drōō'idik/ adj. **Dru·id·i·cal** /drōō'idikəl/ adj. **Dru·id·ism** /-,izəm/ n. [from L. *druidae, druides* (pl.), from Gaulish; rel. to Irish *draoidh* 'magician, sorcerer.']

drum¹ /drəm/ ▶ n. **1** a percussion instrument sounded by being struck with sticks or the hands, typically cylindrical, barrel-shaped, or bowl-shaped with a taut membrane over one or both ends. ■ (**drums**) a set of drums. ■ (**drums**) the percussion section of a band or orchestra. ■ [in sing.] a sound made by or resembling that of a drum: *the drum of their feet.* ■ hist. a military drummer. **2** something resembling or likened to a drum in shape, in particular: ■ a cylindrical container or receptacle: *an oil drum.* ■ a rotating cylindrical part in a washing machine, in which the laundry is placed. ■ a similar cylindrical part in certain other appliances. ▶ v. (**drummed, drum·ming**) [intrans.] play on a drum. ■ make a continuous rhythmic noise: [as n.] (**drumming**) *the drumming of hooves.* ■ [trans.] beat (the fingers, feet, etc.) repeatedly on a surface, esp. as a sign of impatience or annoyance. ■ (of a woodpecker) strike the bill rapidly on a dead trunk or branch. ■ (of a snipe) vibrate the outer tail feathers in a diving display flight.
– PHRASAL VERBS **drum something into** drive a lesson into (someone) by constant repetition. **drum someone out** expel or dismiss someone with ignominy from a place or institution. **drum something up** attempt to obtain something by canvassing or soliciting. [ME: from MDu. or Low Ger. *tromme*, of imitative origin.]

drum² (also **drum·fish**) ▶ n. (pl. same or **drums**) a fish (family Sciaenidae) that makes a drumming sound by vibrating its swim bladder, found mainly in estuarine and shallow coastal waters.

drum and bass /bās/ ▶ n. a type of dance music characterized by bare instrumentation consisting largely of electronic drums and bass, originating in Britain during the early 1990s.

drum·beat /'drəm,bēt/ ▶ n. a stroke or pattern of strokes on a drum.

drum brake ▶ n. a type of vehicle brake in which brake shoes press against the inside of a drum on the wheel.

drum·head /'drəm,hed/ ▶ n. the membrane or skin of a drum. ▶ adj. [attrib.] carried out by or as if by an army in the field; improvised or summary.

drum kit (also **drum set**) ▶ n. a set of drums, cymbals, and other percussion instruments used with drumsticks in jazz and popular music. The most basic components are a foot-operated bass drum, a snare drum, a suspended cymbal, and one or more tom-toms. *See illustration on next page.*

drum·lin /'drəmlin/ ▶ n. Geol. a low oval mound or small hill, typically one of a group, consisting of compacted glacial till shaped by past glacial action.

drum ma·jor ▶ n. the male leader of a marching band, who often twirls a baton. ■ a male member of a baton-twirling parading group.

drum ma·jor·ette ▶ n. the female leader of a marching band. ■ a girl or woman who twirls a baton, typically with a marching band or drum corps.

drum·mer /'drəmər/ ▶ n. **1** a person who plays a drum or drums. **2** informal a traveling sales representative: *a drummer in electronic software.*

drum·roll /'drəm,rōl/ (also **drum roll**) ▶ n. a rapid succession of beats sounded on a drum, often used to introduce an announcement or event.

drum·stick /'drəm,stik/ ▶ n. a stick, typically with a shaped or padded head, used for beating a drum. ■ the lower joint of the leg of a cooked chicken, turkey, or other fowl.

drunk /drəNGk/ past participle of DRINK. ▶ adj. affected by alcohol to the extent of losing control of one's faculties or behavior. ■ [predic.] (**drunk with**) fig. overcome with (a strong emotion): *the crowd was drunk with patriotism.* ▶ n. a person who is drunk or who habitually drinks to excess. ■ informal a drinking bout; a period of drunkenness.

drum kit

drunk·ard /ˈdrəNGkərd/ ▸ n. a person who is habitually drunk.

drunk driv·ing (also **drunk·en driv·ing**) ▸ n. the crime of driving a vehicle with an excess of alcohol in the blood. — **drunk driv·er** n.

drunk·en /ˈdrəNGkən/ ▸ adj. [attrib.] drunk or intoxicated. ■ habitually or frequently drunk. ■ caused by or showing the effects of drink. — **drunk·en·ly** adv. **drunk·en·ness** n. [OE, archaic past part. of DRINK.]

drunk tank ▸ n. informal a large prison cell for the detention of drunks.

drupe /dro͞op/ ▸ n. Bot. a fleshy fruit with thin skin and a central stone containing the seed, e.g., a plum, cherry, almond, or olive. — **dru·pa·ceous** /dro͞oˈpāsHəs/ adj. [18th C.: from L. *drupa* 'overripe olive,' from Gk. *druppa* 'olive.']

drupe·let /ˈdro͞oplit/ ▸ n. Bot. any of the small individual drupes forming a fleshy aggregate fruit such as a blackberry or raspberry.

Dru·ry Lane /ˈdro͝orē/ the site in London of the Theatre Royal.

druth·er /ˈdrəT͟Hər/ informal ▸ n. (usu. **one's druthers**) a person's preference in a matter: *if I had my druthers, I would prefer to be a writer.* ▸ adv. rather; by preference. [19th C.: from a US regional pronunc. of *I'd rather*, contr. of *would rather*.]

Druze /dro͞oz/ (also **Druse**) ▸ n. (pl. same, **Druz·es** or **Drus·es** /ˈdro͞oziz/) a member of a political and religious sect of Islamic origin, living chiefly in Lebanon and Syria. [from Fr., from Arab. *durūz* (pl.), after Muhammad ibn Ismail *al-Darazī* (died 1019).]

dry /drī/ ▸ adj. (**dri·er, dri·est**) **1** free from moisture or liquid; not wet or moist. ■ having lost all wetness or moisture over a period of time. ■ for use without liquid: *the conversion of dry latrines into flush toilets.* ■ with little or no rainfall or humidity. ■ (of a river, lake, or stream) empty of water as a result of evaporation and lack of rainfall. ■ (of a source) not yielding a supply of water or oil: *a dry well.* ■ thirsty or thirst-making. ■ (of a cow or other domestic animal) having stopped producing milk. ■ without grease or other moisturizer or lubricator. ■ (of bread or toast) without butter or other spreads. **2** fig. bare or lacking adornment: *the dry facts.* ■ unexciting; dull. ■ unemotional, undemonstrative, or impassive. ■ (of a joke or sense of humor) subtle, expressed in a matter-of-fact way, and having the appearance of being unconscious or unintentional. **3** prohibiting the sale or consumption of alcoholic drink. ■ (of a person) no longer addicted to or drinking alcohol. **4** (of an alcoholic drink) not sweet. ▸ v. (**dries, dried**) [intrans.] become dry. ■ [trans.] cause to become dry. ■ [trans.] wipe tears from (the eyes). ■ wipe dishes dry with a cloth after they have been washed. ■ [trans.] [usu. as adj.] (**dried**) preserve by allowing or encouraging evaporation of moisture from: *dried flowers.* ▸ n. (pl. **dries** or **drys**) a person in favor of the prohibition of alcohol.
– PHRASES **come up dry** be unsuccessful: *experiments have so far come up dry.* (**as**) **dry as a bone** extremely dry. **there wasn't a dry eye (in the house)** (with reference to a play, film, or similar event) everyone in the audience was moved to tears.
– PHRASAL VERBS **dry out** informal (of an alcoholic) abstain from alcoholic drink, esp. as part of a detoxification program. **dry up 1** informal cease talking. **2** (of something perceived as a continuous flow or source) decrease and stop. — **dry·ish** adj. **dry·ness** n. [OE *drȳge* (adj.), *drȳgan* (v.), of Gmc. origin; rel. to Ger. *trocken*.]

dry·ad /ˈdrīˌad; -əd/ ▸ n. (in folklore and Greek mythology) a nymph inhabiting a forest or a tree, esp. an oak tree. [via OFr. and L. from Gk. *druas, druad-* 'tree nymph,' from *drus* 'tree.']

Dry·as /ˈdrīəs/ ▸ n. the first and third climatic stages of the late-glacial period in northern Europe. The **Older Dryas** (about 15,000 to 12,000 years ago) followed the last ice retreat, and the **Younger Dryas** (about 10,800 to 10,000 years ago) followed the Allerød stage. [mod. L., from Gk. *druas* (see DRYAD).]

dry·as·dust /ˈdrīəzˈdəst/ ▸ n. a boring, pedantic speaker or writer. ▸ adj. (also **dry-as-dust**) dull and boring.

dry bat·ter·y ▸ n. an electric battery consisting of one or more dry cells.

dry bulb ▸ n. an ordinary exposed thermometer bulb, esp. as used in conjunction with a wet bulb.

dry cell ▸ n. an electric cell in which the electrolyte is absorbed in a solid to form a paste, preventing spillage. Compare with WET CELL.

dry-clean ▸ v. [trans.] (usu. **be dry-cleaned**) clean (a garment) with an organic solvent, without using water: [as n.] (**dry cleaning**) *premises that offered dry cleaning.* — **dry clean·er** n.

dry cough ▸ n. a cough not accompanied by phlegm production.

Dry·den /ˈdrīdn/, John (1631–1700), English poet and playwright. His plays include *Marriage à la mode* (1673).

dry dock ▸ n. a dock that can be drained of water to allow the inspection and repair of a ship's hull. ▸ v. (**dry-dock**) [trans.] place (a ship) in a dry dock.

dry·er /ˈdrīər/ (also **dri·er**) ▸ n. **1** a machine or device for drying something, esp. the hair or laundry. **2** a substance mixed with oil paint or ink to promote drying.

dry-eyed ▸ adj. (of a person) not crying.

dry farm·ing ▸ n. another term for DRYLAND FARMING.

dry fly ▸ n. an artificial fishing fly that is made to float lightly on the water.

dry goods ▸ plural n. fabric, thread, clothing, and related merchandise, esp. as distinct from hardware and groceries.

dry hole ▸ n. a well drilled for oil or gas but yielding none.

dry hump (also **dry fuck**) ▸ v. [trans.] vulgar slang, simulate or unsuccessfully attempt sexual intercourse with (someone or something), usually while fully dressed.

dry ice ▸ n. solid carbon dioxide.

dry·ing oil ▸ n. an oil that thickens or hardens on exposure to air, esp. one used by artists in mixing paint.

dry land ▸ n. land as opposed to the sea or another body of water.

dry·land farm·ing /ˈdrīˌland/ (also **dry farm·ing**) ▸ n. a method of farming in semiarid areas without the aid of irrigation.

dry·lands /ˈdrīˌlandz/ ▸ plural n. an arid area; a region with low rainfall.

dry·ly /ˈdrīlē/ (also **dri·ly**) ▸ adv. **1** in a matter-of-fact or ironically humorous way. **2** in a dry way or condition.

dry mat·ter ▸ n. the part of a foodstuff or other substance that would remain if all its water content was removed.

dry meas·ure ▸ n. a measure of volume for loose dry commodities such as grain, tea, and sugar.

dry mount·ing ▸ n. Photog. a process in which a print is bonded to a mount using a layer of adhesive in a hot press. — **dry-mount** v. **dry-mount·ed** adj.

Dry·o·pith·e·cus /ˌdrīōˈpiTHikəs/ ▸ n. a fossil anthropoid ape (genus *Dryopithecus*, family Pongidae) of the middle Miocene to early Pliocene epochs, including the supposed common ancestor of gorillas, chimpanzees, and humans. — **dry·o·pith·e·cine** /-ˈpiTHiˌsēn/ n. & adj. [mod. L., from Gk. *drus* 'tree' + *pithēkos* 'ape.']

dry point ▸ n. a steel needle for engraving on a bare copper plate without acid. ■ an engraving or print so produced. ■ engraving by this means.

dry-roast·ed ▸ adj. roasted without fat or oil: *dry-roasted peanuts.*

dry rot ▸ n. **1** fungal timber decay occurring in poorly ventilated conditions in buildings, resulting in cracking and powdering of the wood. **2** (also **dry rot fungus**) the fungus (*Serpula lacrymans*, family Corticiaceae) that causes this.

dry run ▸ n. informal a rehearsal of a performance or procedure before the real one.

dry sink ▸ n. an antique kitchen cabinet with an inset basin, now generally used as an ornament rather than for practical purposes.

dry·stone /ˈdrīˌstōn/ ▸ adj. [attrib.] (of a stone wall) built without using mortar.

dry·suit /ˈdrīˌso͞ot/ ▸ n. a waterproof rubber suit worn for water sports and diving, under which warm clothes can be worn.

Dry Tor·tu·gas /tôrˈto͞ogəz/ islands in southwestern Florida. Also **the Tortugas** or **Tortugas Keys**.

dry·wall /ˈdrīˌwôl/ ▸ n. a type of board made from plaster, wood pulp, or other material, used esp. to form the interior walls of houses.

dry wash ▸ n. the dry bed of an intermittent stream.

dry well ▸ n. **1** a shaft or chamber constructed in the ground in order to aid drainage, sometimes containing pumping equipment. **2** another term for DRY HOLE.

Ds ▸ symb. the chemical element darmstadtium.

DSC ▸ abbr. Distinguished Service Cross, (in the US) an Army decoration for heroism in combat or (in the UK) a decoration for distinguished active service at sea.

DSc ▸ abbr. Doctor of Science.

DSL ▸ abbr. ■ deep scattering layer. ■ digital subscriber line.

DSM ▸ abbr. Distinguished Service Medal, (in the US) a military decoration for exceptionally meritorious performance of a duty of great responsibility during wartime.

DSO ▶ **abbr.** Distinguished Service Order, a British military decoration for distinguished service awarded to officers of the army and navy.

DSS ▶ **abbr.** ■ Department of Social Services. ■ digital satellite system; digital satellite services. ■ digital signature standard.

DST ▶ **abbr.** daylight saving time.

DTP ▶ **abbr.** desktop publishing.

DTs ▶ **plural n.** (usu. **the DTs**) informal delirium tremens.

du·al /ˈd(y)o͞oəl/ ▶ **adj.** [attrib.] consisting of two parts, elements, or aspects: *their dual role at work and home.* ■ Gram. (in some languages) denoting an inflection that refers to exactly two people or things (as distinct from singular and plural). ■ (in an aircraft) using dual controls: *a dual flight.* — **du·al·ize** /-əˌlīz/ **v.** **du·al·ly** **adv.** [ME: from L. *dualis*, from *duo* 'two.']

du·al cit·i·zen·ship ▶ **n.** citizenship in two countries concurrently.

du·al con·trol ▶ **adj.** (of an aircraft or a vehicle) having two sets of controls, one of which is used by the instructor: *a dual-control pilot trainer.* ▶ **n.** (usu. **dual controls**) two such sets of controls in an aircraft or vehicle.

du·al·ism /ˈd(y)o͞oəˌlizəm/ ▶ **n.** **1** the division of something conceptually into two opposed or contrasted aspects, or the state of being so divided: ■ Philos. a theory or system of thought that regards a domain of reality in terms of two independent principles, esp. mind and matter (**Cartesian dualism**). Compare with IDEALISM, MATERIALISM, and MONISM. ■ the religious doctrine that the universe contains opposed powers of good and evil, esp. seen as balanced equals. **2** the quality or condition of being dual; duality. — **du·al·ist** **n. & adj.** **du·al·is·tic** /ˌd(y)o͞oəˈlistik/ **adj.** **du·al·is·ti·cal·ly** /ˌd(y)o͞oəˈlistik(ə)lē/ **adv.**

du·al·i·ty /d(y)o͞oˈalitē/ ▶ **n.** (pl. **-ties**) **1** the quality or condition of being dual. ■ Physics the quantum-mechanical property of being regardable as both a wave and a particle. **2** an instance of opposition or contrast between two concepts or two aspects of something; a dualism: *the simple dualities of his youthful Marxism: capitalism against socialism, bourgeois against prole.*

du·al-pur·pose ▶ **adj.** serving two purposes or functions: *a dual-purpose hand and nail cream.*

du·al-use /yo͞os/ ▶ **adj.** (of technology or equipment) designed or suitable for both civilian and military purposes.

dub[1] /dəb/ ▶ **v.** (**dubbed, dub·bing**) [trans.] give an unofficial name or nickname to (someone or something): *the media dubbed anorexia "the slimming disease."* ■ make (someone) a knight by the ritual touching of the shoulder with a sword. [OE: from OFr. *adober* 'equip with armor.']

dub[2] ▶ **v.** (**dubbed, dub·bing**) [trans.] **1** provide (a film) with a soundtrack in a different language from the original. ■ add (sound effects or music) to a film or a recording. **2** make a copy of (a sound or video recording). ■ transfer (a recording) from one medium to another. ■ combine (two or more sound recordings) into one composite soundtrack. [1920s: abbrev. of DOUBLE.]

Du·bai /do͞oˈbī; də-/ a member state of the United Arab Emirates; pop. 674,100. ■ its capital city; pop. 265,700.

Du Bar·ry /d(y)o͞o ˈbarē/, Marie Jeanne Bécu, Comtesse (1743–93), French mistress of Louis XV. She was guillotined during the French Revolution.

Dub·ček /ˈdo͞obcʜek/, Alexander (1921–92), leader of Czechoslovakia 1968–69, noted for his political reforms of 1968.

dub-dub-dub /ˈdəb ˈdəb ˈdəb/ ▶ **n.** Comput., informal short form used instead of pronouncing the three letters in the abbreviation WWW (World Wide Web).

Du·bin·sky /do͞oˈbinskē/, David (1892–1982), US labor leader; born in Russia. He was president of the International Ladies' Garment Workers Union 1932–66.

du·bi·ous /ˈd(y)o͞obēəs/ ▶ **adj.** **1** hesitating or doubting. **2** not to be relied upon; suspect. ■ morally suspect. ■ of questionable value. — **du·bi·ous·ly** **adv.** **du·bi·ous·ness** **n.** [16th C. (sense 2): from L. *dubiosus*, from *dubium* 'a doubt,' neut. of *dubius* 'doubtful.']

Dub·lin /ˈdəblin/ the capital of the Republic of Ireland, on the Irish Sea; pop. 477,700. Irish name BAILE ÁTHA CLIATH. ■ a county in the Republic of Ireland, in the province of Leinster; county town, Dublin.

dub·ni·um /ˈdəbnēəm/ ▶ **n.** the chemical element of atomic number 105, a very unstable element made by high-energy atomic collisions. (Symbol: **Db**) [1967: mod. L., from *Dubna* in Russia.]

Du Bois /d(y)o͞o ˈbois/, W. E. B. (1868–1963), US political activist; full name *William Edward Burghardt Du Bois*. He co-founded the NAACP in 1909.

Du·bon·net /ˌd(y)o͞obəˈnā/ ▶ **n.** trademark a sweet French red wine.

Du·brov·nik /do͞oˈbrôvnik; ˈdo͞oˌbrôvnik/ a city on the Adriatic coast of Croatia; pop. 66,100. Italian name (until 1918) RAGUSA.

Du·buf·fet /ˌd(y)o͞obəˈfā/, Jean (1901–85), French artist. He incorporated sand and plaster in his paintings and produced sculptures made from garbage.

Du·buque /dəˈbyo͞ok/ a city in northeastern Iowa, on the Mississippi River; pop. 57,686.

Dub·ya a nickname for US president George W. Bush (from an informal pronunciation of his middle initial).

du·cal /ˈd(y)o͞okəl/ ▶ **adj.** [attrib.] of, like, or relating to a duke or dukedom: *the ducal palace in Rouen.* [15th C.: from OFr., from *duc* 'duke.']

duc·at /ˈdəkət/ ▶ **n.** a gold coin formerly current in most European countries. ■ (**ducats**) informal money: *their production of* Hamlet *has kept the ducats pouring in.* [from Ital. *ducato*, from med. L. *ducatus* (see DUCHY).]

Du·ce /ˈdo͞ocʜā/ (**Il Duce** /il/) the title assumed by Benito Mussolini in 1922. [Ital., lit. 'leader.']

Du·champ /d(y)o͞oˈsʜäɴ/, Marcel (1887–1968), US painter; born in France. A leading figure of the Dada movement, he originated conceptual art.

Du·chenne mus·cu·lar dys·tro·phy /do͞oˈsʜen/ (abbr.: **DMD**) ▶ **n.** a severe form of muscular dystrophy caused by a genetic defect and usually affecting boys. [19th C.: named after G. B. A. *Duchenne* (1806–75), the Fr. neurologist who first described it.]

duch·ess /ˈdəcʜis/ ▶ **n.** the wife or widow of a duke. ■ a woman holding a rank equivalent to duke in her own right. [ME: via OFr. from med. L. *ducissa*, from L. *dux, duc-* (see DUKE).]

duch·y /ˈdəcʜē/ ▶ **n.** (pl. **duch·ies**) the territory of a duke or duchess; a dukedom. [ME: from OFr. *duche*, from med. L. *ducatus*, from L. *dux, duc-* (see DUKE).]

duck[1] /dək/ ▶ **n.** (pl. same or **ducks**) **1** a waterbird with a broad blunt bill, short legs, webbed feet, and a waddling gait. The **duck family** (Anatidae) also includes geese and swans, from which ducks are distinguished by their generally smaller size and shorter necks. ■ the female of such a bird. Contrasted with DRAKE. ■ such a bird as food. **2** a pure white thin-shelled bivalve mollusk (genus *Anatina*, family Mactridae) found off the Atlantic coasts of America. **3** another term for **DUKW**.

– PHRASES **get** (or **have**) **one's ducks in a row** get (or have) one's facts straight; get (or have) everything organized. **take to something like a duck to water** take to something very readily: *he took to the trumpet like a duck to water.* **water off a duck's back** a potentially hurtful or harmful remark or incident that has no apparent effect on the person mentioned. [OE *duce*, from the Gmc. base of DUCK[2].]

duck[2] ▶ **v.** **1** [intrans.] lower the head or the body quickly to avoid a blow or so as not to be seen. ■ (**duck out**) depart quickly: *I thought I saw you duck out.* ■ [trans.] avoid (a blow) by moving down quickly. ■ [trans.] informal evade or avoid (an unwelcome duty or undertaking). **2** [intrans.] plunge one's head or body under water briefly. ▶ **n.** [in sing.] a quick lowering of the head. — **duck·er** **n.** [ME: of Gmc. origin; rel. to Ger. *tauchen* 'dive,' also to DUCK[1].]

duck[3] ▶ **n.** a strong untwilled linen or cotton fabric, used chiefly for casual or work clothes and sails. ■ (**ducks**) pants made of such a fabric. [17th C.: from MDu. *doek* 'linen, linen cloth'; rel. to Ger. *Tuch* 'cloth.']

duck·bill /ˈdəkˌbil/ ▶ **n.** an animal with jaws resembling a duck's bill, e.g., a platypus or a duck-billed dinosaur. ▶ **adj.** [attrib.] shaped like a duck's bill: *duckbill pliers.*

duck-billed di·no·saur ▶ **n.** another term for HADROSAUR.

duck·bill plat·y·pus (also **duck-billed plat·y·pus**) ▶ **n.** see PLATYPUS.

duck·board /ˈdəkˌbôrd/ ▶ **n.** (usu. **duckboards**) a board consisting of a number of wooden slats joined together, placed so as to form a path over muddy ground or in a trench.

duck·ing stool ▶ **n.** hist. a chair fastened to the end of a pole, used formerly to plunge offenders into a pond or river as a punishment.

duck·ling /ˈdəkliɴɢ/ ▶ **n.** a young duck. ■ the flesh of a young duck as food.

duck·pin /ˈdəkˌpin/ ▶ **n.** a short, squat bowling pin. ■ (**duckpins**) [treated as sing.] a game played with such pins.

ducks and drakes ▶ **n.** a game of throwing flat stones so that they skim along the surface of water.

duck's ass ▶ **n.** another term for DUCKTAIL.

duck soup ▶ **n.** informal an easy task, or someone easy to overcome.

duck·tail /ˈdəkˌtāl/ (also **duck's ass**) (abbr.: **DA**) ▶ **n.** informal a man's hairstyle, associated esp. with the 1950s, in which the hair is slicked back on both sides and tapered at the nape.

duck·walk /ˈdəkˌwôk/ ▶ **v.** [intrans.] walk with the body in a squatting posture. ▶ **n.** a walk with the body in this posture.

duck·weed /ˈdəkˌwēd/ ▶ **n.** a tiny aquatic flowering plant (family Lemnaceae, esp. the genus *Lemna*) that floats in large quantities on still water.

duck·y /ˈdəkē/ informal ▶ **adj.** charming; delightful: *everything here is just ducky.* [19th C.: from DUCK[1].]

duct /dəkt/ ▶ **n.** a channel or tube for conveying something, in particular: ■ (in a building or a machine) a tube or passageway for air, liquid, cables, etc. ■ (in the body) a vessel for conveying lymph or glandular secretions such as tears or bile. ■ (in a plant) a vessel for conveying water, sap, or air. ▶ **v.** [trans.] (usu. **be ducted**) convey through a duct. [17th C.: from L. *ductus* 'leading, aqueduct,' from *duct-* 'led,' from the v. *ducere*.]

duc·tile /ˈdəktl; -ˌtīl/ ▶ **adj.** (of a metal) able to be drawn out into a thin wire. ■ able to be deformed without losing toughness; pliable, not brittle. — **duc·til·i·ty** /dəkˈtilitē/ **n.** [ME: from L. *ductilis*, from *ducere*.]

duct·ing /ˈdəktiɴɢ/ ▶ **n.** a system of ducts. ■ tubing or piping forming such a system.

duct·less /ˈdəktlis/ ▸ **adj.** Anat. denoting a gland that secretes directly into the bloodstream, such as an endocrine gland or a lymph gland.

duct tape ▸ **n.** strong, cloth-backed, waterproof adhesive tape.

duct·work /ˈdəktˌwərk/ ▸ **n.** a system or network of ducts.

dud /dəd/ informal ▸ **n. 1** a thing that fails to work properly or is otherwise unsatisfactory or worthless. ■ an ineffectual person. **2** (**duds**) clothes: *buy yourself some new duds.* [ME: of unknown origin.]

dude /do͞od/ informal ▸ **n.** a man; a guy. ■ a stylish, fastidious man. ■ a city-dweller, esp. one vacationing on a ranch in the western US. ▸ **v.** [intrans.] (**dude up**) dress up elaborately: [as adj.] (**duded**) *my brother was all duded up in silver and burgundy.* — **dud·ish adj.** [19th C.: prob. from Ger. dial. *Dude* 'fool.']

dude ranch ▸ **n.** (in the western US) a cattle ranch converted to a vacation resort.

dudg·eon /ˈdəjən/ ▸ **n.** a feeling of offense or deep resentment: *the manager walked out* ***in high dudgeon.*** [16th C.: of unknown origin.]

due /d(y)o͞o/ ▸ **adj. 1** [predic.] expected at or planned for at a certain time: *the baby's due in August.* ■ (of a payment) required at a certain time. ■ (of a person) having reached a point where the thing mentioned is required or owed. ■ (of a thing) required or owed as a legal or moral obligation. **2** [attrib.] of the proper quality or extent; adequate: *driving without due care and attention.* ▸ **n. 1** (**one's due**) a person's right; what is owed to someone: *he attracts more criticism than is his due.* **2** (**dues**) an obligatory payment; a fee. ▸ **adv.** (with reference to a point of the compass) exactly; directly: *we'll head due south.*
– PHRASES **due to 1** caused by or ascribable to. **2** because of; owing to: *he had to withdraw due to a knee injury.* **give someone their due** be fair to someone. **in due course** at the appropriate time. **pay one's dues** fulfill one's obligations. ■ experience difficulties before achieving success: *this drummer has paid his dues with the best.* [ME (in the sense 'payable'): from OFr. *deu* 'owed,' based on L. *debitus* 'owed,' from *debere* 'owe'.]

due date ▸ **n.** the date on which something falls due, esp. the payment of a bill or the expected birth of a baby.

due dil·i·gence ▸ **n.** Law reasonable steps taken by a person in order to satisfy a legal requirement, esp. in buying or selling something.

du·el /ˈd(y)o͞oəl/ ▸ **n.** esp. hist. a contest with deadly weapons arranged between two people in order to settle a point of honor. ■ (in modern use) a contest or race between two parties: *two eminent critics engaged in a verbal duel.* ▸ **v.** (**du·eled, du·el·ing**; Brit. **du·elled, du·el·ling**) [intrans.] fight a duel or duels: [as n.] (**dueling**) *dueling had been forbidden for serving officers.* — **du·el·er n. du·el·ist n.** [15th C.: from L. *duellum*, archaic form of *bellum* 'war,' used in med. L. with the meaning 'combat between two persons,' partly influenced by *dualis* 'of two.']

duen·de /do͞oˈendā/ ▸ **n.** a quality of passion and inspiration. ■ a spirit. [1920s: from Sp., contr. of *duen de casa*, from *dueño de casa* 'owner of the house.']

du·en·na /d(y)o͞oˈenə/ ▸ **n.** an older woman acting as a governess and companion in charge of girls, esp. in a Spanish family; a chaperone. [17th C.: earlier form of Sp. *dueña*, from L. *domina* 'lady, mistress.']

due proc·ess (also **due process of law**) ▸ **n.** fair treatment through the normal judicial system, esp. as a citizen's entitlement.

Due·ro /ˈdwerō/ Spanish name for **Douro**.

du·et /d(y)o͞oˈet/ ▸ **n.** a performance by two people, esp. singers, instrumentalists, or dancers. ■ a musical composition for two performers. ▸ **v.** (**du·et·ted, du·et·ting**) [intrans.] perform a duet. — **du·et·tist n.** [18th C.: from Ital. *duetto*, dimin. of *duo* 'duet,' from L. *duo* 'two.']

duff[1] /dəf/ ▸ **n.** decaying vegetable matter covering the ground under trees. [18th C.: of unknown origin.]

duff[2] ▸ **n.** informal a person's buttocks: *I did not get where I am today by sitting on my duff.* [19th C.: of unknown origin.]

duf·fel /ˈdəfəl/ (also **duf·fle**) ▸ **n. 1** short for **duffel coat**. **2** sporting or camping equipment. ■ short for **duffel bag**. [17th C.: from *Duffel*, where the cloth was orig. made.]

duf·fel bag ▸ **n.** a cylindrical canvas bag carried over the shoulder.

duf·fel coat ▸ **n.** a heavy coat, typically hooded and fastened with toggles.

duf·fer /ˈdəfər/ ▸ **n.** informal an incompetent or stupid person, esp. an elderly one. ■ a person inexperienced at something, esp. at playing golf. [19th C.: from Scots *dowfart* 'stupid person,' from *douf* 'spiritless.']

du·fus ▸ **n.** var. of **doofus**.

Du·fy /d(y)o͞oˈfē/, Raoul (1877–1953), French painter. His characteristic style involved calligraphic outlines sketched on brilliant background washes.

dug[1] /dəg/ past and past participle of **dig**.

dug[2] ▸ **n.** (usu. **dugs**) the udder, teat, or nipple of a female animal. [16th C.: possibly of ON origin and rel. to Swed. *dägga* 'suckle.']

du·gong /ˈdo͞ogäNG; -gôNG/ ▸ **n.** (pl. same or **-gongs**) an aquatic mammal (*Dugong dugon*, family Dugongidae) found on the coasts of the Indian Ocean from eastern Africa to northern Australia. It is distinguished from the manatees by its forked tail. [19th C.: based on Malay *duyong*.]

dug·out /ˈdəgˌout/ ▸ **n. 1** a shelter that is dug in the ground and roofed over, esp. one used by troops in warfare. ■ a shelter at the side of a baseball field, with seating for a team's coaches and players not taking part. **2** (also **dugout canoe**) a canoe made from a hollowed tree trunk.

dugong

duh /də; do͞o/ ▸ **exclam.** informal used to comment on an action perceived as foolish or stupid: *they got back together—duh!*

DUI ▸ **abbr.** driving under the influence (of drugs or alcohol).

dui·ker /ˈdīkər/ ▸ **n.** (pl. same or **-kers**) a small African antelope (*Cephalophus* and other genera,) that typically has a tuft of hair between the horns, found mainly in the rain forest. [18th C.: from South Afr. Dutch, from Du., lit. 'diver'; rel. to **duck**[2].]

Duis·burg /ˈd(y)o͞ozˌbərg; -ˌbo͝ork; ˈd(y)o͞os-;/ a city in northwestern Germany; pop. 537,440.

du jour /də ˈZHo͝or; ˌd(y)o͞o/ ▸ **adj.** [postpositive] (of food in a restaurant) available and being served on this day. ■ informal used to describe something that is enjoying great but probably short-lived popularity or publicity: *attention deficit disorder is the disease du jour.* [Fr., lit. 'of the day.']

duke /d(y)o͞ok/ ▸ **n. 1** a male holding the highest hereditary title in the British and certain other peerages. ■ esp. hist. (in some parts of Europe) a male ruler of a small independent state. **2** (**dukes**) informal the fists, esp. when raised in a fighting attitude. [from rhyming slang *Duke of Yorks* 'forks' (= fingers).]
– PHRASES **duke it out** informal fight it out. [OE, from OFr. *duc*, from L. *dux, duc-* 'leader'; rel. to *ducere* 'to lead.']

duke·dom /ˈd(y)o͞okdəm/ ▸ **n.** a territory ruled by a duke. ■ the rank of duke.

DUKW ▸ **n.** an amphibious transport vehicle, esp. as used by the Allies during World War II. Also called **duck**[1]. [from factory-applied letters.]

dul·ce /ˈdəlsā/ ▸ **n.** a sweet food or drink, esp. a candy or jam. [Sp.] ▸ **adj.** sweet or mild. [from L. *dulcis*.]

dul·cet /ˈdəlsit/ ▸ **adj.** (esp. of sound) sweet and soothing (often used ironically): *record the* ***dulcet tones*** *of your family and friends.* [ME *doucet*, from OFr. *doucet*, dimin. of *doux*, from L. *dulcis* 'sweet.']

dul·ci·an /ˈdəlsēən/ ▸ **n.** an early type of bassoon made in one piece. ■ any of various organ stops, typically with 8-foot funnel-shaped flue pipes or 8- or 16-foot reed pipes. [19th C.: from Ger. *Dulzian*, or a var. of **dulciana**.]

dul·ci·an·a /ˌdəlsēˈanə; -ˈänə/ ▸ **n.** an organ stop, typically with small conical open metal pipes. [18th C.: via med. L. from L. *dulcis* 'sweet.']

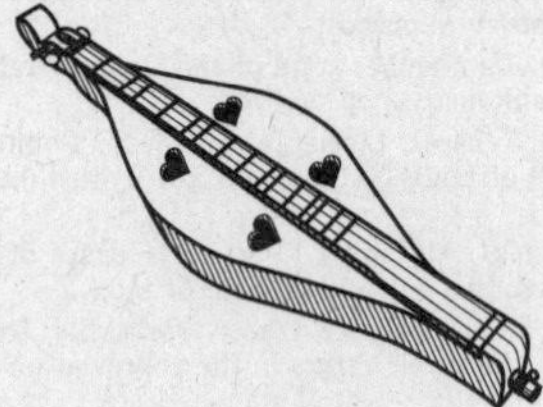

Appalachian dulcimer

dul·ci·mer /ˈdəlsəmər/ ▸ **n.** (also **hammered dulcimer**) a musical instrument with a sounding board or box, typically trapezoidal in shape, over which strings of graduated length are stretched, played by being struck with hand-held hammers. ■ (**Appalachian dulcimer**) a musical instrument with a long rounded body and a fretted fingerboard, played by bowing, plucking, and strumming. Also called **mountain dulcimer**. [15th C.: from OFr. *doulcemer*, prob. from L. *dulce melos* 'sweet melody.']

dull /dəl/ ▸ **adj. 1** lacking interest or excitement. **2** lacking brightness, vividness, or sheen: *his face glowed in the dull lamplight.* ■ (of the weather) overcast; gloomy. ■ (of sound) not clear; muffled: *a dull thud of hooves.* ■ (of pain) indistinctly felt; not acute: *there was a dull pain in his lower jaw.* ■ (of an edge or blade) blunt. **3** (of a person) slow to understand; stupid: *the voice of a teacher talking to a rather dull child.* ■ (of activity) sluggish, slow-moving: *gold closed lower in dull trading.* ▸ **v.** make or become dull or less intense: [trans.] *time dulls the memory* | [intrans.] *Albert's eyes dulled a little.*
– PHRASES **(as) dull as dishwater** extremely dull. **dull the edge of** cause to be less keenly felt; reduce the intensity or effectiveness of: *she'd have to find something to dull the edges of the pain.* — **dull·ish adj. dull·ness** (also **dul·ness**) **n. dul·ly adv.** [OE *dol* 'stupid,' of Gmc. origin; rel. to Du. *dol* 'crazy.']

dull·ard /ˈdələrd/ ▸ **n.** a slow or stupid person.

Dul·les /ˈdələs/, John Foster (1888–1959), US secretary of state 1953–59, noted for his aggressive anticommunism during the Cold War.

dulls·ville /ˈdəlzˌvil/ informal ▸ **n.** a dull or monotonous place or condition.

dull-wit·ted ▸ **adj.** slow to understand; stupid.

dulse /dəls/ ▸ **n.** a dark red edible seaweed (*Rhodymenia palmata*) with flattened branching fronds. [17th C.: from Irish and Scot. Gael. *duileasg*.]

Du·luth /də'lo͞oTH/ a city in northeastern Minnesota, on Lake Superior; pop. 86,918.

du·ly /'d(y)o͞olē/ ▶ **adv.** in accordance with what is required or appropriate; following proper procedure or arrangement: *a document duly signed and authorized by the inspector.* ■ as might be expected or predicted.

dum /dəm/ ▶ **adj.** Indian cooked with steam: *dum aloo.* [from Hindi *dam*.]

Du·ma /'do͞omə/ ▶ **n.** a legislative body in the ruling assembly of Russia and of some other republics of the former USSR.

Du·mas /d(y)o͞o'mä/ French writers. Alexandre (1802–70), known as **Dumas** *père* (father), wrote *The Three Musketeers* (1844–45) and *The Count of Monte Cristo* (1844–45). His son Alexandre (1824–95), known as **Dumas** *fils* (son), wrote *La Dame aux camélias* (1848).

Du Mau·ri·er /d(y)o͞o 'môrē,ā/, English writers. George Louis Palmella Busson (1834–96) wrote *Trilby* (1894). His granddaughter Daphne (1907–89) wrote *Rebecca* (1938) and *The Birds* (1952).

dumb /dəm/ ▶ **adj.** **1** chiefly offens. (of a person) unable to speak, most typically because of congenital deafness. ■ (of animals) unable to speak as a natural state and thus regarded as helpless or deserving pity. ■ [predic.] temporarily unable or unwilling to speak. ■ [attrib.] resulting in or expressed by speechlessness. **2** informal stupid: *a dumb question.* ■ (of a computer terminal) able only to transmit data to or receive data from a computer; having no independent processing capability. Often contrasted with **INTELLIGENT**. ▶ **v.** [trans.] (**dumb something down**) informal simplify or reduce the intellectual content of something so as to make it accessible to a larger number of people. — **dumb·ly adv. dumb·ness n.** [OE, of Gmc. origin; rel. to Ger. *dumm* 'stupid.']

dumb-ass ▶ **adj.** [attrib.] informal stupid; brainless.

dumb·bell /'dəm,bel/ ▶ **n.** **1** a short bar with a weight at each end, used typically in pairs for exercise or muscle-building. ■ [as adj.] shaped like a dumbbell: *a dumbbell molecule.* **2** informal a stupid person.

dumb blond (also **dumb blonde**) ▶ **n.** informal a blond-haired woman perceived in a stereotypical way as being attractive but unintelligent.

dumb cane ▶ **n.** a thick-stemmed plant (genus *Dieffenbachia*) of the arum family, with large variegated leaves, native to tropical America and widely grown as a houseplant. Its name is most associated with the Caribbean *D. seguine*, whose poisonous sap swells the tongue and temporarily disables the power of speech.

dumb cluck ▶ **n.** informal a stupid person.

dumb·found /'dəm,found/ (also **dum·found**) ▶ **v.** [trans.] (usu. **be dumbfounded**) greatly astonish or amaze: *they were dumbfounded at his popularity.* [17th C.: blend of **DUMB** and **CONFOUND**.]

dumb·head /'dəm,hed/ ▶ **n.** informal a stupid person.

dum·bo /'dəmbō/ ▶ **n.** (pl. **-bos**) informal a stupid person.

dumb·show /'dəm,SHō/ (also **dumb show**) ▶ **n.** gestures used to convey a meaning or message without speech; mime: *they demonstrated in dumbshow how the tea should be made.* ■ a piece of dramatic mime.

dumb·size /'dəm,sīz/ ▶ **v.** [intrans.] (of a company) reduce staff numbers to levels so low that work can no longer be carried out effectively. [1990s: humorously, on the pattern of *downsize*.]

dumb·struck /'dəm,strək/ ▶ **adj.** so shocked or surprised as to be unable to speak.

dumb wait·er ▶ **n.** a small elevator for carrying things, esp. food and dishes, between the floors of a building.

dum·dum /'dəm,dəm/ (also **dumdum bullet**) ▶ **n.** a kind of soft-nosed bullet that expands on impact and inflicts laceration. [19th C.: from *Dum Dum*, town near Calcutta, India.]

dum-dum ▶ **n.** informal a stupid person. [1970s: reduplication of **DUMB**.]

dum·found ▶ **v.** var. of **DUMBFOUND**.

Dum·fries and Gal·lo·way /dəm'frēs and 'galə,wā/ an administrative region in southwestern Scotland.

dum·ka /'do͝omkə/ ▶ **n.** (pl. **-kas** or **-ky** /-kē/) a piece of Slavic music, originating as a folk ballad or lament, typically melancholy with contrasting lively sections. [19th C.: via Czech and Pol. from Ukrainian.]

dumm·kopf /'do͝om,kôf; -,kôpf; 'dəm-/ ▶ **n.** a stupid person; a blockhead. [19th C.: from Ger. *dumm* 'dumb' + *Kopf* 'head.']

dum·my /'dəmē/ ▶ **n.** (pl. **-mies**) **1** a model or replica of a human being: *a waxwork dummy.* ■ a figure used for displaying or fitting clothes. ■ a ventriloquist's doll. ■ a person taking no real part or present only for appearances; a figurehead. **2** an object designed to resemble and serve as a substitute for the real or usual one. ■ a prototype or mock-up, esp. of a book or the layout of a page. ■ a blank round of ammunition. ■ [as adj.] Gram. denoting a word that has no semantic content but is used to maintain grammatical structure: *a dummy subject, as in "it is" or "there are."* **3** informal a stupid person. ▶ **v.** (**-mies, -mied**) [trans.] create a prototype or mock-up of a book or page: *officials **dummied up** a set of photos.* [16th C.: from **DUMB** + **-Y**[1].]

dump /dəmp/ ▶ **n.** **1** a site for depositing garbage. ■ [usu. with adj.] a place where a particular kind of waste, esp. dangerous waste, is left. ■ a heap of garbage left at a dump. ■ informal an unpleasant or dreary place. ■ informal an act of defecation. **2** Comput. a copying of stored data to a different location, performed typically as a protection against loss. ■ a printout or list of the contents of a computer's memory, occurring typically after a system failure. ▶ **v.** [trans.] **1** deposit or dispose of (garbage, waste, or unwanted material), typically in a careless or hurried way. ■ put down or abandon (something) hurriedly in order to make an escape. ■ put (something) down firmly or heavily and carelessly. ■ informal abandon or desert (someone). ■ send (goods unsalable in the home market) to a foreign market for sale at a low price. ■ informal sell off (assets) rapidly. **2** Comput. copy (stored data) to a different location, esp. so as to protect against loss. ■ print out or list the contents of (a store), esp. after a system failure.

– PHRASAL VERBS **dump on** informal criticize or abuse (someone); treat badly: *you get dumped on just because of your name.* — **dump·er** /'dəmpər/ **n.** [ME: perh. from ON and rel. to Dan. *dumpe* 'fall suddenly.']

dump·ing ground ▶ **n.** a place where garbage or unwanted material is left.

dump·ling /'dəmpliNG/ ▶ **n.** a small savory ball of dough (usually made with suet) that may be boiled, fried, or baked in a casserole. ■ a pudding consisting of apples or other fruit enclosed in a sweet dough and baked. ■ humorous a small, fat person. [17th C.: appar. from *dump* 'of the consistency of dough.']

dumps /dəmps/ ▶ **plural n.** (in phrase (**down**) **in the dumps**) informal (of a person) depressed or unhappy. [16th C.: prob. a figurative use of MDu. *domp* 'haze, mist.']

dump·ster /'dəmpstər/ (also **Dump·ster** trademark) trademark ▶ **n.** a large trash receptacle designed to be hoisted and emptied into a truck. [1930s: *Dempster Dumpster*, proprietary name.]

dump truck ▶ **n.** a truck with a body that tilts or opens at the back for unloading.

dump·y /'dəmpē/ ▶ **adj.** (**dump·i·er, dump·i·est**) **1** (of a person) short and stout: *her plain, dumpy sister.* **2** (of a room or building) ugly, dirty, and run-down. — **dump·i·ly adv. dump·i·ness n.** [18th C.: from **DUMPLING** + **-Y**[1].]

Dum·yat /do͝om'yät/ Arabic name for **DAMIETTA**.

dun[1] /dən/ ▶ **adj.** of a dull grayish-brown color: *a dun cow.* ▶ **n.** **1** a dull grayish-brown color. **2** a thing that is dun in color. [OE *dun, dunn*, of Gmc. origin; prob. rel. to **DUSK**.]

dun[2] ▶ **v.** (**dunned, dun·ning**) [trans.] make persistent demands on (someone), esp. for payment of a debt. [17th C. (as a n.): from obs. *Dunkirk privateer*, from the Fr. port of **DUNKIRK**.]

Dun·can /'dəNGkən/, Isadora (1878–1927), US dancer. A pioneer of modern dance, she was famous for her "free" barefoot dancing.

Dun·can I (*c.*1010–40), king of Scotland 1034–40. He was killed in battle by Macbeth.

dunce /dəns/ ▶ **n.** a person who is slow at learning; a stupid person. [16th C.: John **DUNS SCOTUS**.]

dunce cap ▶ **n.** a paper cone formerly put on the head of a dunce at school as a mark of disgrace.

Dun·dee /dən'dē/ a city in eastern Scotland, on the Firth of Tay; pop. 165,500.

dun·der·head /'dəndər,hed/ ▶ **n.** informal a stupid person. — **dun·der·head·ed adj.** [17th C.: cf. obs. Scots *dunder, dunner* 'resounding noise'; rel. to **DIN**.]

dune /d(y)o͞on/ ▶ **n.** a mound or ridge of sand or other loose sediment formed by the wind, esp. on the sea coast or in a desert: *a sand dune.* [18th C.: from Fr., from MDu. *dūne*; rel. to OE *dūn* 'hill' (see **DOWN**[3]).]

dune bug·gy ▶ **n.** a low, wide-wheeled motor vehicle for recreational driving on sand.

Dun·e·din /dən'ēdn/ a city and port on the South Island in New Zealand; pop. 113,900.

dung /dəNG/ ▶ **n.** the excrement of animals; manure. ▶ **v.** [trans.] drop or spread dung on (a piece of ground). [OE, of Gmc. origin; rel. to Ger. *Dung*.]

dun·ga·rees /,dəNGgə'rēz/ ▶ **plural n.** **1** blue jeans or overalls. **2** [in sing.] (**dungaree**) blue denim. [17th C.: from Hindi *duṅgrī*.]

dung bee·tle ▶ **n.** a beetle (esp. families Scarabaeidae and Geotrupidae) whose larvae feed on dung.

Dun·ge·ness crab /'dənjə,nes/ ▶ **n.** a large crab (*Cancer magister*, family Cancridae) found off the west coast of North America, where it is popular as food. [20th C.: *Dungeness*, village on the coast of Washington.]

dun·geon /'dənjən/ ▶ **n.** a strong underground prison cell, esp. in a castle. ■ (in fantasy role-playing games) a labyrinthine subterranean setting. ▶ **v.** [trans.] literary imprison (someone) in a dungeon. [ME): from OFr., based on L. *dominus* 'lord, master.']

dung·hill /'dəNG,hil/ (also **dung·heap**) ▶ **n.** a heap of dung or refuse, esp. in a farmyard.

du·nite /'dənīt/ ▶ **n.** Geol. a green to brownish coarse-grained igneous rock consisting largely of olivine. [19th C.: *Dun* Mountain, New Zealand, + **-ITE**[1].]

dunk /dəNGk/ ▶ **v.** **1** [trans.] dip (bread or other food) into a drink or soup before eating it. ■ immerse or dip in water: [as n.] (**dunking**) *the camera survived a dunking in a stream.* ■ baptize (someone) by immersion. **2** [intrans.] Basketball score by shooting the ball down through the basket with the hands above the rim. — **dunk·er n.** [20th C.: from Pennsylvania Du. *dunke* 'dip,' from Ger. *tunken* 'dip or plunge.']

Dunk·ard /'dəNGkərd/ ▶ **n.** another term for **DUNKER**.

Dunk·er /ˈdəNGkər/ ▶ **n.** a member of the German Baptist Brethren, a sect of Baptist Christians founded in 1708 but living in the US since the 1720s. [18th C.: from Pennsylvania Du., from *dunke* (see DUNK).]

Dun·kirk /ˈdən,kərk; dənˈkərk/ a port in northern France; pop. 71,070; scene of the evacuation of 335,000 Allied troops in 1940 while under constant German attack from the air. French name DUNKERQUE.

dun·lin /ˈdənlin/ ▶ **n.** (pl. same or **dun·lins**) a migratory sandpiper (*Calidris alpina*) with a down-curved bill and (in the breeding season) a red-dish-brown back and black belly. [16th C.: prob. from DUN¹ + -LING.]

dun·nage /ˈdənij/ ▶ **n.** pieces of wood, matting, or similar material used in stowing cargo in a ship's hold. ■ informal a person's belongings, esp. those brought on board ship. [ME: of unknown origin.]

dun·no /dəˈnō/ ▶ **contr.** (I) do not know.

Duns Sco·tus /dənz ˈskōtəs/, John (*c.*1265–1308), Scottish monk and theologian. He founded Scholasticism, also called Scotism.

Dun·stan, St. /ˈdənstən/ (*c.*909–988), Anglo-Saxon clergyman. As archbishop of Canterbury, he succeeded in restoring monastic life.

du·o /ˈd(y)o͞o-ō/ ▶ **n.** (pl. **du·os**) **1** a pair of people or things, esp. in music or entertainment: *the comedy duo Laurel and Hardy.* **2** Music a duet. [16th C. (sense 2): via Ital. from L. *duo* 'two.']

duo- ▶ **comb. form** two; having two: *duopoly* | *duotone.* [from L.]

du·o·dec·i·mal /,d(y)o͞oəˈdesəməl; ,d(y)o͞o-ō-/ ▶ **adj.** relating to or denoting a system of counting or numerical notation that has twelve as a base. ▶ **n.** the system of duodecimal notation. — **du·o·dec·i·mal·ly** **adv.** [17th C.: from L. *duodecimus* 'twelfth' (from *duodecim* 'twelve') + -AL.]

du·o·dec·i·mo /,d(y)o͞oəˈdesə,mō; ,d(y)o͞o-ō-/ (abbr.: **12mo**) ▶ **n.** (pl. **-mos**) a size of book page that results from the folding of each printed sheet into 12 leaves (24 pages). Also called TWELVEMO. ■ a book of this size. [17th C.: from L. *(in) duodecimo* 'in a twelfth,' from *duodecimus* 'twelfth.']

duodeno- (also **duoden-** before a vowel) ▶ **comb. form** Anat. Med. relating to the duodenum: *duodenitis.*

du·o·de·num /,d(y)o͞oəˈdēnəm; d(y)o͞oˈädn-əm/ ▶ **n.** (pl. **-nums** or **-na** /-nə/) Anat. the first part of the small intestine immediately beyond the stomach, leading to the jejunum. — **du·o·de·nal** /-ˈdēnl; -ˈädnəl/ **adj.** [ME: from med. L., from *duodeni* 'in twelves.']

duo·mo /ˈdwōmō/ ▶ **n.** (pl. **-mos**) an Italian cathedral. [Ital., lit. 'dome.']

du·op·o·ly /d(y)o͞oˈäpəlē/ ▶ **n.** (pl. **-lies**) a situation in which two suppliers dominate the market for a commodity or service. [1920s: from DUO-, on the pattern of *monopoly.*]

du·o·tone /ˈd(y)o͞oə,tōn/ ▶ **n.** a halftone illustration made from a single original with two different colors at different screen angles. ■ the technique or process of making such illustrations: *the best images that duotone can produce.*

dupe¹ /d(y)o͞op/ ▶ **v.** [trans.] deceive; trick. ▶ **n.** a victim of deception. — **dup·a·ble** **adj.** **dup·er** **n.** **dup·er·y** /ˈd(y)o͞opərē/ **n.** [17th C.: from dial. Fr. *dupe* 'hoopoe.']

dupe² ▶ **v.** & **n.** short for DUPLICATE, esp. in photography.

du·ple /ˈd(y)o͞opəl/ ▶ **adj.** Music (of rhythm) based on two main beats to the measure: *duple time.* [16th C.: from L. *duplus,* from *duo* 'two.']

du·plet /ˈd(y)o͞oplit/ ▶ **n.** a set of two things. ■ Music a pair of equal notes to be performed in the time of three. [17th C.: from L. *duplus* 'duple,' on the pattern of *doublet.*]

du·plex /ˈd(y)o͞opleks/ ▶ **n.** something having two parts, in particular: ■ a house divided into two apartments, with a separate entrance for each. ■ an apartment on two floors. ■ Biochem. a double-stranded polynucleotide molecule. ▶ **adj.** **1** having two parts, in particular: ■ (of a house) having two apartments. ■ (of an apartment) on two floors. ■ (of paper or board) having two differently colored layers or sides. ■ Biochem. consisting of two polynucleotide strands linked side by side. ■ (of a printer or its software) capable of printing on both sides of the paper. **2** (of a communications system, computer circuit, etc.) allowing the transmission of two signals simultaneously in opposite directions. [16th C. (as an adj.): from L. *duplex, duplic-,* from *duo* 'two' + *plicare* 'to fold.']

du·pli·cate ▶ **adj.** /ˈd(y)o͞opləkit/ [attrib.] **1** exactly like something else, esp. through having been copied. **2** having two corresponding or identical parts. ■ twice as large or many; doubled. ▶ **n.** /ˈd(y)o͞opləkit/ one of two or more identical things. ■ a copy of an original. ▶ **v.** /ˈd(y)o͞oplə,kāt/ [trans.] make or be an exact copy of. ■ make or supply copies of (a document): [as adj.] (**duplicating**) *a duplicating machine.* ■ multiply by two; double. ■ do (something) again unnecessarily.
– PHRASES **in duplicate** consisting of two exact copies: *forms to complete in duplicate.* — **du·pli·ca·ble** /-plikəbəl/ **adj.** **du·pli·ca·tive** /-,kātiv/ **adj.** [ME: from L. *duplicat-* 'doubled,' from the v. *duplicare,* from *duplic-* 'twofold' (see DUPLEX).]

du·pli·cate bridge ▶ **n.** a competitive form of bridge in which the same hands are played successively by different partnerships.

du·pli·ca·tion /,d(y)o͞opləˈkāsHən/ ▶ **n.** the action or process of duplicating something. ■ a copy. ■ Genet. a DNA segment in a chromosome which is a copy of another segment.

du·pli·ca·tor /ˈd(y)o͞oplə,kātər/ ▶ **n.** a machine or device for making copies of something, in particular a machine that makes copies of documents by means of fluid ink and a stencil.

du·plic·i·tous /d(y)o͞oˈplisitəs/ ▶ **adj.** deceitful: *treacherous, duplicitous behavior.*

du·plic·i·ty /d(y)o͞oˈplisitē/ ▶ **n.** deceitfulness; double-dealing. [ME: from OFr. *duplicite* or late L. *duplicitas,* from L. *duplic-* 'twofold' (see DUPLEX).]

du Pont /d(y)o͞o ˈpänt; ˈd(y)o͞o ,pänt/, E. I. (1771–1834), US industrialist; born in France; full name *Éleuthère Irénée du Pont.* His gunpowder manufacturing plant near Wilmington, Delaware, established in 1802, grew into a corporate giant.

Du·que de Ca·xi·as /ˈdo͞okē dā käˈsHēəs/ a city in southeastern Brazil; pop. 594,380.

du·ra¹ /ˈd(y)o͝orə/ (in full **dura mater**) ▶ **n.** Anat. the tough outermost membrane enveloping the brain and spinal cord. — **du·ral** **adj.** [19th C.: from med. L., lit. 'hard mother.']

du·ra² ▶ **n.** var. of DURRA.

du·ra·ble /ˈd(y)o͝orəbəl/ ▶ **adj.** able to withstand wear, pressure, or damage; hard-wearing. ■ informal (of a person) having endurance. ▶ **n.** (**durables**) short for DURABLE GOODS. — **du·ra·bil·i·ty** /,d(y)o͝orəˈbilitē/ **n.** **du·ra·ble·ness** **n.** **du·ra·bly** /-blē/ **adv.** [ME (in the sense 'steadfast'): via OFr. from L. *durabilis,* from *durare* 'to last' (see DURATION).]

du·ra·ble goods ▶ **plural n.** goods not for immediate consumption and able to be kept for a period of time.

du·ral·u·min /d(y)o͝orˈalyəmin/ ▶ **n.** a hard, light alloy of aluminum with copper and other elements. [20th C.: perh. from L. *durus* 'hard' + ALUMINUM.]

du·ra ma·ter /ˈd(y)o͝orə ˈmätər; ˈmā-/ ▶ **n.** see DURA¹.

Du·rand /dəˈrand/, Asher Brown (1796–1886), US painter, a member of the Hudson River School.

Du·ran·go /d(y)o͞oˈraNGgō/ a state in northern central Mexico; pop. 1,352,160. ■ its capital city; pop. 414,000. Full name VICTORIA DE DURANGO.

Du·ras /d(y)o͞oˈrä/, Marguerite (1914–96), French writer; pen name of *Marguerite Donnadieu.* Her works include *L'Amant* (1984).

du·ra·tion /d(y)o͞oˈrāsHən/ ▶ **n.** the time during which something continues. — **du·ra·tion·al** /-sHənl/ **adj.** [ME: via OFr. from med. L. *duratio (n-),* from *durare* 'to last,' from *durus* 'hard.']

dur·a·tive /ˈd(y)o͝orətiv/ ▶ **adj.** Gram. of or denoting continuing action. Contrasted with PUNCTUAL.

Dur·ban /ˈdərbən/ a city in South Africa, on the coast of KwaZulu-Natal; pop. 1,137,380. Former name (until 1835) PORT NATAL.

Dü·rer /ˈd(y)o͝orər/, Albrecht (1471–1528), German engraver and painter. He produced woodcuts, copper engravings, and watercolors.

du·ress /d(y)o͞oˈres/ ▶ **n.** threats, violence, constraints, or other action brought to bear on someone to do something against their will or better judgment: *confessions extracted* ***under duress.*** ■ Law constraint illegally exercised to force someone to perform an act. [ME: via OFr. from L. *duritia,* from *durus* 'hard.']

Dur·ga /ˈdo͝orgä/ Hinduism a fierce goddess, wife of Shiva, often identified with Kali.

Dur·ham /ˈdərəm; ˈdo͝or-/ a city in north central North Carolina; pop. 187,035.

du·ri·an /ˈdo͝orēən; -rē,än/ ▶ **n.** **1** an oval spiny tropical fruit containing a fetid-smelling, yet flavorful pulp. **2** (also **durian tree**) the large Malaysian tree (*Durio zibethinus,* family Bombaceae) that bears this fruit. [16th C.: from Malay *durian,* from *duri* 'thorn.']

dur·ing /ˈd(y)o͝oriNG/ ▶ **prep.** throughout the course or duration of (a period of time): *the restaurant is open during the day.* ■ used to indicate constant development throughout a period: *the period during which he grew to adulthood.* ■ at a particular point in the course of: *during an argument.* [ME: pres. part. of the obs. v. *dure* 'last, endure, extend,' via OFr. from L. *durare* 'to last' (see DURATION).]

Durk·heim /ˈdərk,hīm/, Émile (1858–1917), French sociologist. He was one of the founders of modern sociology.

dur·mast oak /ˈdər,mast/ ▶ **n.** a Eurasian oak tree (*Quercus petraea*) with stalkless, egg-shaped acorns. [18th C.: *durmast* perh. orig. an error for *dunmast,* from DUN¹ + MAST².]

durn /dərn/ ▶ **v., exclam., adj., & adv.** dialect form of DARN².

durned /dərnd/ ▶ **adj. & adv.** dialect form of DARNED.

dur·ra /ˈdo͝orə/ (also **du·ra**) ▶ **n.** grain sorghum (*Sorghum bicolor* var. *durra*) of the principal variety grown from northeastern Africa to India. [18th C.: from Arab. *ḍura, ḍurra.*]

Dur·rell /ˈdərəl/, Lawrence George (1912–90), English writer and poet. He wrote *Alexandria Quartet* (1957–60).

dur·rie /ˈdərē/ ▶ **n.** (pl. **-ries**) var. of DHURRIE.

durst /dərst/ archaic or regional past of DARE.

du·rum /ˈd(y)o͝orəm/ (also **durum wheat**) ▶ **n.** a kind of hard wheat (*Triticum durum*), having bearded ears and yielding flour that is used to make pasta. [20th C.: from L., neut. of *durus* 'hard.']

Du·shan·be /d(y)o͞oˈsHämbä; -bə/ the capital of Tajikistan; pop. 602,000. Former name (1929–61) STALINABAD.

dusk /dəsk/ ▶ **n.** the darker stage of twilight. [OE *dox* 'dark, swarthy' and *doxian* 'darken in color,' of Gmc. origin; rel. to Old High Ger. *tusin* 'darkish.']

dusk·y /ˈdəskē/ ▶ **adj.** (**dusk·i·er, dusk·i·est**) darkish in color. — **dusk·i·ly** **adv.** **dusk·i·ness** **n.**

Düs·sel·dorf /ˈd(y)o͞osəl,dôrf/ a city in northwestern Germany, on the Rhine River; pop. 577,560.

dust /dəst/ ▶ **n.** **1** fine, dry powder consisting of tiny particles of earth

or waste matter lying on the ground or on surfaces or carried in the air. ■ [with adj.] any material in the form of tiny particles: *coal dust.* ■ [in sing.] a fine powder. **2** [in sing.] an act of dusting. ▶**v.** [trans.] **1** remove the dust from the surface of (something) by wiping or brushing it. ■ (**dust something off**) bring something out for use again after a long period of neglect: *a number of aircraft will be dusted off and returned to flight.* **2** (usu. **be dusted**) cover lightly with a powdered substance: *roll out on a surface dusted with flour.* ■ sprinkle (a powdered substance) onto something. **3** informal beat up or kill someone: *the officers **dusted** him **up** a little bit.*
– PHRASES **the dust settles** things quiet down: *she hoped that the dust would settle quickly and the episode be forgotten.* **eat someone's dust** informal fall far behind someone in a competitive situation. **gather** (or **collect**) **dust** remain unused: *some professors let their computers gather dust.* — **dust·less** **adj.** [OE *dūst*, of Gmc. origin; rel. to Du. *duist* 'chaff.']

dust·ball /ˈdəstˌbôl/ ▶**n.** a ball of dust and fluff.

dust bowl ▶**n.** an area where vegetation has been lost and soil eroded, esp. as a consequence of drought or unsuitable farming practice. ■ (**the Dust Bowl**) an area, including parts of Oklahoma, Kansas, and northern Texas where windstorms caused severe soil erosion in the 1930s.

dust bun·ny ▶**n.** informal a ball of dust and fluff.

dust cov·er ▶**n.** a dust jacket.

dust dev·il ▶**n.** a small whirlwind over land, visible as a column of dust and debris.

dust·er /ˈdəstər/ ▶**n.** **1** a cloth or brush for dusting furniture. **2** a short, light housecoat. **3** informal a dust storm.

dust·heap /ˈdəstˌhēp/ ▶**n.** a heap of household refuse.

dust jack·et ▶**n.** a removable paper cover used to protect a book from dirt or damage.

dust mop ▶**n.** a long-handled mop with a soft, fluffy head, used to collect dust from floors and walls.

dust·pan /ˈdəstˌpan/ ▶**n.** a flat hand-held receptacle into which dust and waste can be swept from the floor.

dust ruf·fle ▶**n.** a sheet with a deep pleated or gathered border that is designed to hang down over the mattress and sides of a bed.

dust storm ▶**n.** a strong, turbulent wind that carries clouds of fine dust, soil, and sand over a large area.

dust trap ▶**n.** something on, in, or under which dust readily gathers.

dust-up ▶**n.** informal a fight; a quarrel.

dust·y /ˈdəstē/ ▶**adj.** (**dust·i·er**, **dust·i·est**) covered with, full of, or resembling dust. ■ (of a color) dull or muted: *patches of pale gold and dusty pink.* ■ fig. staid and uninteresting: *a dusty old bore.* — **dust·i·ly** **adv.** **dust·i·ness** **n.**

dust·y mill·er ▶**n.** a plant of the daisy family with whitish or grayish foliage, esp. the cultivated *Artemisia stellerana* of North America.

Dutch /dəCH/ ▶**adj.** of or relating to the Netherlands or its people or their language. ▶**n.** **1** the West Germanic language of the Netherlands. **2** [as pl. n.] (**the Dutch**) the people of the Netherlands collectively.
– PHRASES **go dutch** share the cost of something, esp. a meal, equally. **in dutch** informal dated in trouble: *he's been getting in dutch at school.* [from MDu. *dutsch* 'Dutch, Netherlandish, German.']

Dutch auc·tion ▶**n.** a method of selling in which the price is reduced until a buyer is found.

Dutch cap ▶**n.** a woman's lace cap with triangular flaps on each side, worn as part of Dutch traditional dress.

Dutch cour·age ▶**n.** strength or confidence gained from drinking alcohol.

Dutch door ▶**n.** a door divided into two parts horizontally, allowing one half to be shut and the other left open.

Dutch door

Dutch East In·di·a Com·pa·ny a Dutch trading company founded in 1602 to protect Dutch trading interests in the Indian Ocean. It was dissolved in 1799.

Dutch East In·dies former name (until 1949) of **INDONESIA**.

Dutch elm dis·ease ▶**n.** a disease of elm trees caused by the fungus *Ceratocystis ulmi* (phylum Ascomycota) and spread by bark beetles. A virulent strain of the fungus that arose in North America in the early 20th century has destroyed the majority of American elms in many areas.

Dutch Gui·an·a former name (until 1948) of **SURINAME**.

Dutch·man /ˈdəCHmən/ ▶**n.** (pl. **-men**) a native or national of the Netherlands, or a person of Dutch descent.

Dutch·man's breech·es ▶**n.** a plant (genus *Dicentra*, family Fumariaceae) closely related to bleeding heart, but typically having pale yellow or white flowers.

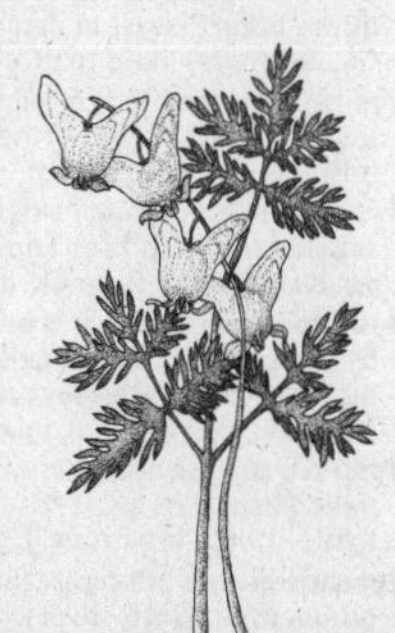

Dutchman's breeches

Dutch·man's pipe ▶**n.** a vigorous climbing vine (*Aristolochia durior*, family Aristolochiaceae) with hooked tubular flowers, native to eastern North America.

Dutch ov·en ▶**n.** a large, heavy cooking pot with a lid.

Dutch Re·formed Church a branch of the Protestant Church in the Netherlands, formed during the Reformation. ■ the dominant branch of the Protestant Church among Afrikaners in South Africa.

Dutch tile ▶**n.** a kind of glazed white tile painted with traditional Dutch motifs in blue or brown. ▶**v.** [trans.] [usu. as adj.] (**Dutch-tiled**) decorate with such tiles: *Dutch-tiled fireplaces.*

Dutch treat ▶**n.** an outing, meal, or other special occasion at which each participant pays for their share of the expenses.

Dutch un·cle ▶**n.** informal a person giving firm but benevolent advice.

Dutch West In·di·a Com·pa·ny a Dutch trading company founded in 1621 to develop Dutch trading interests in competition with Spain and Portugal and their colonies. It was dissolved in 1794.

Dutch·wom·an /ˈdəCHˌwo͝omən/ ▶**n.** (pl. **-wom·en**) a female native or national of the Netherlands, or a woman of Dutch descent.

du·ti·a·ble /ˈd(y)o͞otēəbəl/ ▶**adj.** liable to customs or other duties: *dutiable goods.*

du·ti·ful /ˈd(y)o͞otəfəl/ ▶**adj.** conscientiously or obediently fulfilling one's duty: *a dutiful daughter.* ■ motivated by duty rather than desire or enthusiasm. — **du·ti·ful·ly** **adv.** **du·ti·ful·ness** **n.**

du·ty /ˈd(y)o͞otē/ ▶**n.** (pl. **-ties**) **1** a moral or legal obligation; a responsibility: *it's my duty to uphold the law.* ■ [as adj.] (of a visit or other undertaking) done from a sense of moral obligation rather than for pleasure: *a fifteen-minute duty visit.* **2** (often **duties**) a task or action that someone is required to perform: *the queen's official duties.* ■ military service. ■ [as adj.] (of a person) engaged in their regular work. **3** a payment due and enforced by law or custom, in particular: ■ a payment levied on the import, export, manufacture, or sale of goods: *a 6 percent **duty on** imports.*
– PHRASES **do duty as** (or **for**) serve or act as a substitute for something else: *her mug was doing duty as a wine glass.* **on** (or **off**) **duty** engaged (or not engaged) in one's regular work: *the doorman had gone off duty and the lobby was unattended.* [ME: from Anglo-Norman Fr. *duete*, from OFr. *deu* (see **DUE**).]

du·ty-bound ▶**adj.** [predic., with infin.] morally or legally obliged to do something.

du·ty cy·cle ▶**n.** the cycle of operation of a machine or other device that operates intermittently rather than continuously. ■ the time occupied by this, esp. as a percentage of available time.

du·ty-free ▶**adj. & adv.** exempt from payment of duty: [as adj.] *the permitted number of duty-free goods* | [as adv.] *most EC goods enter almost duty-free.* ■ [as adj.] (of a shop or area) selling or trading in goods that are exempt from payment of duty.

du·ty of·fi·cer ▶**n.** an officer, esp. in the police or armed forces, who is on duty at a particular time.

du·um·vir /d(y)o͞oˈəmvər/ ▶**n.** (in ancient Rome) each of two magistrates or officials holding a joint office. [L., from *duum virum* 'of the two men.']

du·um·vi·rate /d(y)o͞oˈəmvərit/ ▶**n.** a coalition of two people having joint authority or influence. [17th C.: from L. *duumviratus.*]

Du·va·lier /do͞oˈvälyā; ˌdo͞ovälˈyā/ François (1907–71), president of Haiti 1957–71; known as **Papa Doc**. Upon his death, his oppressive dictatorship was continued by his son Jean-Claude (1951–), known as **Baby Doc**, who was deposed and exiled in 1986.

Du·vall /d(y)o͞oˈväl/, Gabriel (1752–1844), US Supreme Court associate justice 1811–35. He was appointed to the Court by President Madison.

du·vet /d(y)o͞oˈvā/ ▶**n.** a soft quilt filled with down, feathers, or a synthetic fiber, used instead of an upper sheet and blankets. [18th C.: from Fr., lit. 'down' (see **DOWN**²).]

DV formal ▶**abbr.** ■ Deo volente (God willing): *this time next week (DV) I shall be among the mountains.* ■ Bible Douay Version.

DVD ▶**n.** a high-density videodisc that stores large amounts of data, esp. high-resolution audio-visual material. [abbrev. of *digital videodisc* or *digital versatile disc.*]

Dvi·na Riv·er /d(ə)vēˈnä/ a river that rises in Russia's Valai Hills and flows southwest for 634 miles (1,020 km) to the Gulf of Riga; often called Western Dvina.

DVM ▶**abbr.** ■ Doctor of Veterinary Medicine.

Dvo·řák /ˈdvôrZHäk/, Antonín (1841–1904), Czech composer, noted for his ninth symphony ("From the New World," 1892–95).

DVR ▶**abbr.** digital video recorder.

dwarf /dwôrf/ ▶**n.** (pl. **dwarfs** or **dwarves** /dwôrvz/) **1** (in folklore or fantasy literature) a member of a mythical race of short, stocky humanlike creatures who are generally skilled in mining and metalworking. ■ often offensive an abnormally small person. ■ [as adj.] denoting something, esp. an animal or plant, that is much smaller than the usual size for its type or species: *a dwarf conifer.* **2** (also **dwarf star**) Astron. a star of relatively small size and low luminosity. ▶**v.** [trans.] cause to seem small or insignificant in comparison. ■ stunt the growth or development of: [as adj.]

(dwarfed) *the dwarfed but solid branch of a tree.* — **dwarf·ish** adj. [OE *dweorg, dweorh,* of Gmc. origin; rel. to Du. *dwerg* and Ger. *Zwerg.*]

dwarf·ism /ˈdwôrfizəm/ ▶ n. (in medical or technical contexts) unusually or abnormally low stature or small size.

dwarf le·mur ▶ n. a small Madagascan primate (family Cheirogaleidae), feeding primarily on fruit and gums.

dweeb /dwēb/ ▶ n. informal a boring, studious, or socially inept person. — **dweeb·ish** adj. **dweeb·y** adj. [1980s: perh. a blend of DWARF and early 20th-cent. *feeb* 'a feebleminded person' (from FEEBLE).]

dwell /dwel/ ▶ v. (past and past part. **dwelled** or **dwelt** /dwelt/) [intrans.] **1** [with adverbial of place] formal live in or at a specified place. **2 (dwell on/upon)** think, speak, or write at length about (a particular subject, esp. one that is a source of unhappiness, anxiety, or dissatisfaction). ■ **(dwell on/upon)** (of one's eyes or attention) linger on (a particular object or place). ▶ n. tech. a slight regular pause in the motion of a machine. — **dwell·er** n. [in comb.] *city-dwellers.* [OE *dwellan* 'lead astray, hinder, delay,' of Gmc. origin; rel. to ON *dvelja* 'delay.']

dwell·ing /ˈdweliNG/ (also **dwelling place**) ▶ n. formal a house, apartment, or other place of residence.

dwell·ing house ▶ n. Law a house used as a residence and not for business purposes.

DWI ▶ abbr. ■ driving while intoxicated.

dwin·dle /ˈdwindl/ ▶ v. [intrans.] diminish gradually in size, amount, or strength | [as adj.] **(dwindling)** *dwindling resources.* [16th C.: frequentative of *dwine* 'fade away,' from OE *dwīnan,* of Gmc. origin; rel. to ON *dvína.*]

DWM ▶ abbr. ■ (in personal ads) divorced white male.

dwt ▶ abbr. ■ dead-weight tonnage. ■ pennyweight.

Dy ▶ symb. the chemical element dysprosium.

dy·ad /ˈdīad/ ▶ n. tech. something that consists of two elements or parts: *the mother–child dyad.* ■ Math. an operator that is a combination of two vectors. ■ Chem. a divalent atom or radical. — **dy·ad·ic** /dīˈadik/ adj. [17th C.: from late L. *dyas, dyad,* from Gk. *duas,* from *duo* 'two.']

Dy·ak ▶ n. & adj. var. of DAYAK.

dy·ar·chy /ˈdī,ärkē/ ▶ n. (pl. **-chies**) var. of DIARCHY.

dyb·buk /ˈdibək/ ▶ n. (pl. **dyb·buks** or **dyb·bu·kim** /,dibŏŏˈkēm/) (in Jewish folklore) a malevolent wandering spirit that enters and possesses the body of a living person until exorcized. [from Yiddish *dibek,* from Heb. *dibbūq,* from *dāḇaq* 'cling.']

dye /dī/ ▶ n. a natural or synthetic substance used to add a color to or change the color of something. ▶ v. **(dyed, dye·ing)** [trans.] add a color to or change the color of (something) by soaking it in a solution impregnated with a dye. ■ [intrans.] take color well or badly during such a process.

– PHRASES **dyed in the wool** unchanging in a particular belief or opinion; inveterate: *she's a dyed-in-the-wool conservative.* [with allusion to the fact that yarn was dyed in the raw state, producing a more even and permanent color.] — **dye·a·ble** adj. [OE *dēag* (n.), *dēagian* (v.).]

dy·er /ˈdīər/ ▶ n. a person whose trade is the dyeing of cloth or other material.

dy·er's green·weed ▶ n. a bushy, yellow-flowered Eurasian plant (*Genista tinctoria*) of the pea family. The flowers were formerly used to make a yellow or green dye.

dye·stuff /ˈdī,stəf/ ▶ n. a substance that yields a dye or that can be used as a dye, esp. when in solution.

dy·ing /ˈdī-iNG/ ▶ adj. [attrib.] on the point of death. ■ occurring at or connected with the time that someone dies. ■ gradually ceasing to exist or function; in decline and about to disappear.

– PHRASES **to one's dying day** for the rest of one's life: *I shall remember that to my dying day.* [16th C.: pres. part. of DIE[1].]

dyke[1] ▶ n. var. of DIKE[1].

dyke[2] /dīk/ ▶ n. offens. a lesbian. — **dyke·y** adj. [1940s (earlier as BULLDYKE): of unknown origin.]

dyn ▶ abbr. dyne.

dy·nam·ic /dīˈnamik/ ▶ adj. **1** (of a process or system) characterized by constant change, activity, or progress. ■ (of a person) positive in attitude and full of energy and new ideas. ■ (of a thing) stimulating development or progress. ■ Physics of or relating to forces producing motion. Often contrasted with STATIC. ■ Ling. (of a verb) expressing an action, activity, event, or process. Contrasted with STATIVE. ■ Electron. (of a memory device) needing to be refreshed by the periodic application of a voltage. ■ Electron. of or relating to the volume of sound produced by a voice, instrument, or sound recording equipment. **2** Music relating to the volume of sound produced by an instrument, voice, or recording. ▶ n. **1** a force that stimulates change or progress within a system or process. **2** Music another term for DYNAMICS (sense 3). — **dy·nam·i·cal** adj. **dy·nam·i·cal·ly** adv. [19th C. (as a term in physics): from Fr. *dynamique,* from Gk. *dunamikos,* from *dunamis* 'power.']

dy·nam·ic e·qui·lib·ri·um ▶ n. a state of balance between continuing processes.

dy·nam·ic link li·brar·y ▶ n. see **DLL**.

dy·nam·ic range ▶ n. the range of acceptable or possible volumes of sound occurring in the course of a piece of music or a performance.

dy·nam·ics /dīˈnamiks/ ▶ plural n. **1** [treated as sing.] the branch of mechanics concerned with the motion of bodies under the action of forces. Compare with STATICS. ■ [usu. with adj.] the branch of any science in which forces or changes are considered: *chemical dynamics.* **2** the forces or properties that stimulate growth, development, or change within a system or process. **3** Music the varying levels of volume of sound in different parts of a musical performance. — **dy·nam·i·cist** /-ˈnaməsist/ n. (in sense 1).

dy·na·mism /ˈdīnə,mizəm/ ▶ n. the quality of being characterized by vigorous activity and progress. ■ the quality of being dynamic and positive in attitude. — **dy·na·mist** n.

dy·na·mite /ˈdīnə,mīt/ ▶ n. a high explosive consisting of nitroglycerine mixed with an absorbent material and typically molded into sticks. ■ fig. something that has the potential to generate extreme reactions or to have devastating repercussions. ■ informal an extremely impressive or exciting person or thing. ▶ v. [trans.] blow up (something) with dynamite. — **dy·na·mit·er** n. [19th C.: from Gk. *dunamis* 'power' + -ITE[1].]

dy·na·mo /ˈdīnə,mō/ ▶ n. (pl. **-mos**) a machine for converting mechanical energy into electrical energy; a generator. ■ informal an extremely energetic person. [19th C.: abbrev. of *dynamo-electric machine.*]

dy·na·mom·e·ter /,dīnəˈmämitər/ ▶ n. an instrument that measures the power output of an engine. [19th C.: from French *dynamomètre,* from Gk. *dunamis* 'power' + Fr. *-mètre* '(instrument) measuring.']

dy·nast /ˈdīnast; -nəst/ ▶ n. a member of a powerful family, esp. a hereditary ruler. [17th C.: via L. from Gk. *dunastēs,* from *dunasthai* 'be able.']

dy·nas·ty /ˈdīnəstē/ ▶ n. (pl. **-ties**) a line of hereditary rulers of a country: *the Tang dynasty.* ■ a succession of people from the same family who play a prominent role in a certain field. — **dy·nas·tic** /dīˈnastik/ adj. **dy·nas·ti·cal·ly** /dīˈnastik(ə)lē/ adv.

dyne /dīn/ ▶ n. Physics a unit of force that, acting on a mass of one gram, increases its velocity by one centimeter per second every second along the direction that it acts. [19th C.: from Fr., from Gk. *dunamis* 'force, power.']

dys- ▶ comb. form bad; difficult (used esp. in medical terms): *dyspepsia* | *dysphasia.* [from Gk. *dus-*; rel. to OE *to-*.]

dys·en·ter·y /ˈdisən,terē/ ▶ n. infection of the intestines resulting in severe diarrhea with the presence of blood and mucus in the feces. — **dys·en·ter·ic** /,disənˈterik/ adj. [ME: from OFr. *dissenterie,* or via L. from Gk. *dusenteria,* from *dusenteros* 'afflicted in the bowels,' from *dus-* 'bad' + *entera* 'bowels.']

dys·func·tion /disˈfəNGkSHən/ ▶ n. abnormality or impairment in the function of a specified bodily organ or system: *bowel dysfunction.* ■ deviation from the norms of social behavior in a way regarded as bad: *inner-city dysfunction.*

dys·func·tion·al /disˈfəNGkSHənl/ ▶ adj. not operating normally or properly. ■ deviating from the norms of social behavior in a way regarded as bad. — **dys·func·tion·al·ly** adv.

dys·gen·ic /disˈjenik/ ▶ adj. exerting a detrimental effect on later generations through the inheritance of undesirable characteristics: *dysgenic breeding.*

dys·ki·ne·sia /,diskiˈnēZHə/ ▶ n. Med. abnormality or impairment of voluntary movement. — **dys·ki·net·ic** /-ˈnetik/ adj.

dys·la·li·a /disˈlālēə/ ▶ n. Med. inability to articulate comprehensible speech, esp. when associated with the use of private words or sounds. [19th C.: from DYS- 'difficult' + Gk. *lalia* 'speech.']

dys·lex·i·a /disˈleksēə/ ▶ n. a general term for disorders that involve difficulty in learning to read or interpret words, letters, and other symbols, but that do not affect general intelligence. — **dys·lec·tic** /-ˈlektik/ adj. & n. **dys·lex·ic** /-ˈleksik/ adj. & n. [19th C.: coined in Ger. from DYS- 'difficult' + Gk. *lexis* 'speech.']

dys·men·or·rhe·a /dis,menəˈrēə/ ▶ n. Med. painful menstruation, typically involving abdominal cramps.

dys·pep·sia /disˈpepsēə; -ˈpepSHə/ ▶ n. indigestion. [18th C.: via L. from Gk. *duspepsia,* from *duspeptos* 'difficult to digest.']

dys·pep·tic /disˈpeptik/ ▶ adj. of or having indigestion or consequent irritability or depression. ▶ n. a person who suffers from indigestion or irritability.

dys·pha·sia /disˈfāZHə/ ▶ n. Med. language disorder marked by deficiency in the generation of speech, and sometimes also in its comprehension, due to brain disease or damage. — **dys·pha·sic** /-ˈfāzik/ adj. [19th C.: from Gk. *dusphatos* 'hard to utter,' from *dus-* 'difficult' + *phatos* 'spoken.']

dys·phe·mism /ˈdisfə,mizəm/ ▶ n. a derogatory or unpleasant term used instead of a pleasant or neutral one, such as "loony bin" for "mental hospital." The opposite of EUPHEMISM.

dys·pho·ri·a /disˈfôrēə/ ▶ n. Psychiatry a state of unease or generalized dissatisfaction with life. The opposite of EUPHORIA. — **dys·phor·ic** /-ˈfôrik/ adj. & n. [19th C.: from Gk. *dusphoria,* from *dusphoros* 'hard to bear.']

dys·pla·sia /disˈplāZHə/ ▶ n. Med. the enlargement of an organ or tissue by the proliferation of cells of an abnormal type, as a developmental disorder or an early stage in the development of cancer. — **dys·plas·tic** /-ˈplastik/ adj. [1930s: from DYS- 'bad' + Gk. *plasis* 'formation.']

dysp·ne·a /dispˈnēə/ ▶ n. Med. difficult or labored breathing. — **dysp·ne·ic** /dispˈnēik/ adj. [17th C.: via L. from Gk. *duspnoia,* from *dus-* 'difficult' + *pnoē* 'breathing.']

dys·pro·si·um /disˈprōzēəm/ ▶ n. the chemical element of atomic number 66, a soft, silvery-white metal of the lanthanide series. (Symbol: **Dy**) [19th C.: from Gk. *dusprositos* 'hard to get at' + -IUM.]

dys·rhyth·mi·a /disˈriT͟Hmēə/ ▶ n. Med. abnormality in a physiological rhythm, esp. in the activity of the brain or heart. — **dys•rhyth•mic** adj. **dys•rhyth•mi•cal** adj.

dys•to•ci•a /dis'tōsʜə/ ▶ n. Med. Vet. Med. difficult birth. [18th C.: from Gk. *dustokia*, from *dus-* 'difficult' + *tokos* 'childbirth.']

dys•to•ni•a /dis'tōnēə/ ▶ n. Med. a state of abnormal muscle tone resulting in muscular spasm and abnormal posture, typically due to neurological disease or a side effect of drug therapy. — **dys•ton•ic** /-'tänik/ adj.

dys•to•pi•a /dis'tōpēə/ ▶ n. an imagined place or state in which everything is unpleasant or bad, typically a totalitarian or environmentally degraded one. The opposite of UTOPIA. — **dys•to•pi•an** adj. & n. [18th C.: from DYS- 'bad' + UTOPIA.]

dys•troph•ic /dis'träfik/ ▶ adj. **1** Med. affected by or relating to dystrophy, esp. muscular dystrophy. **2** Ecol. (of a lake) having brown acidic water that is low in oxygen and supports little life, owing to high levels of dissolved humus. Compare with EUTROPHIC and OLIGOTROPHIC. [19th C.: from Gk. *dus-* 'bad' + *-trophia* 'nourishment' + -IC.]

dys•tro•phy /'distrəfē/ ▶ n. **1** Med. Vet. Med. a disorder in which an organ or tissue of the body wastes away. See also MUSCULAR DYSTROPHY. **2** Med. impaired nourishment of a bodily part. [19th C.: from mod. L. *dystrophia*, from Gk. *dus-* 'bad' + *-trophia* 'nourishment.']

dys•u•ri•a /dis'yo͝orēə/ ▶ n. Med. painful or difficult urination. [ME: via late L. from Gk. *dusouria*, from *dus-* 'difficult' + *ouron* 'urine.']

dz. ▶ abbr. ■ dozen.

Dzau•dzhi•kau /dzou'jē,kou/ former name (1944–54) of VLADIKAVKAZ.

Dzer•zhinsk /dzir'zʜēnsk/ a city in west central Russia; pop. 286,000. Former names CHERNORECHYE (until 1919) and RASTYAPINO (1919–29).

Dzong•kha /'zäɴɢkə/ ▶ n. the official language of Bhutan, closely related to Tibetan.

Ee

E[1] /ē/ (also **e**) ▶ **n.** (pl. **Es** or **E's**) **1** the fifth letter of the alphabet. ■ denoting the fifth in a set of items, categories, sizes, etc. **2** (**E**) a shape like that of a capital E. **3** (usu. **E**) Music the third note of the scale of C major. ■ a key based on a scale with E as its keynote.

E[2] ▶ **abbr.** ■ Earth. ■ East or Eastern. ■ Easter. ■ informal the drug Ecstasy or a tablet of Ecstasy. ■ Football end. ■ engineer or engineering. ■ English. ■ Baseball error. ■ [in comb.] (also **e**) electronic: *E-commerce.* ▶ **symb.** Physics ■ electric field strength. ■ electromotive force. ■ energy: $E = mc^2$.

E[3] ▶ **symbol** (€) euro(s).

e ▶ **symb.** ■ (also **e**−) Chem. an electron. ■ (*e*) Math. a transcendental number, the base of Napierian or natural logarithms, approximately equal to 2.71828.

e-[1] ▶ **prefix** var. of **EX-**[1] (as in *elect, emit*).

e-[2] ▶ **prefix** denoting anything in an electronic state, esp. data transferred in cyberspace, esp. through the Internet: *e-business.* [from **ELECTRONIC**, on the pattern of *e-mail.*]

ea. ▶ **abbr.** each: *T-shirts for $9.95 ea.*

each /ēCH/ ▶ **adj. & pron.** every one of two or more people or things, regarded and identified separately: [as adj.] *each battery is in a separate compartment* | ***each one of** us was asked what went on* | [as pron.] *got money from **each of** his five uncles* | *each has its own personality.* ▶ **adv.** to, for, or by every one of a group (used after a noun or an amount): *they cost $35 each* | *had a glass each.*

– PHRASES **each and every** every single (used for emphasis): *taking each and every opportunity.* [Old English *ǣlc*; related to German *jeglich*, based on a West Germanic phrase meaning 'ever alike' (see **AYE**[2], **ALIKE**).]

each oth·er ▶ **pron.** used to refer to each member of a group when each does something to or for other members: *they communicate with each other in French.*

Ea·gan /ˈēgən/ a city in southeastern Minnesota, just south of St. Paul; pop. 63,557.

ea·ger /ˈēgər/ ▶ **adj.** (of a person) wanting to do or have something very much: *the man was eager to please* | *young intellectuals **eager for** knowledge.* ■ (of a person's expression or tone of voice) characterized by keen expectancy or interest. — **ea·ger·ly adv. ea·ger·ness n.** [ME: from OFr. *aigre* 'keen,' from L. *acer, acr-* 'sharp.']

ea·ger bea·ver ▶ **n.** informal a keen and enthusiastic person who works very hard.

ea·gle /ˈēgəl/ ▶ **n. 1** a large bird of prey (family Accipitridae, esp. the genus *Aquila*) with a massive hooked bill and long broad wings, renowned for its keen sight and powerful soaring flight. See illustration at **BALD EAGLE**. ■ a figure of an eagle, esp. as a symbol of the US, or formerly as a Roman or French ensign. ■ one of a pair of officer's insignia in the shape of an eagle. **2** Golf a score of two strokes under par at a hole. [suggested by **BIRDIE**.] **3** in the US, a former gold coin worth ten dollars. ▶ **v.** [trans.] Golf play (a hole) in two strokes under par. [ME: from OFr. *aigle*, from L. *aquila*.]

ea·gle eye ▶ **n.** a keen or close watch: *she was **keeping an eagle eye on** Laura.* — **ea·gle-eyed** /ˈēgəl ˌīd/ **adj.**

ea·gle owl ▶ **n.** a very large Old World owl (genus *Bubo*, family Strigidae) with ear tufts and a deep hoot.

ea·gle ray ▶ **n.** a large marine ray (*Myliobatis* and *Aetobatus*, family Myliobatidae) with long pointed pectoral fins, a long tail, and a distinct head.

ea·glet /ˈēglit/ ▶ **n.** a young eagle.

ea·gre /ˈēgər/ ▶ **n.** dialect term for **BORE**[3]. [17th C.: of unknown origin.]

Ea·kins /ˈākinz/, Thomas (1844–1916), US painter and photographer. He is known for his portraits and genre pictures of life in Philadelphia.

-ean ▶ **suffix** forming adjectives and nouns such as *Antipodean, Joycean*, and *Pythagorean*. Compare with **-AN**. [from L. *-aeus, -eus* or Gk. *-aios, -eios*, + **-AN**.]

ear[1] /i(ə)r/ ▶ **n.** the organ of hearing and balance in humans and other vertebrates, esp. the external part of this. ■ an organ sensitive to sound in other animals. ■ [in sing.] an ability to recognize, appreciate, and reproduce sounds, esp. music or language: ***an ear for** rhythm and melody.* ■ a person's willingness to listen and pay attention to something: *offers a sympathetic ear to pet owners.* ■ an ear-shaped thing, esp. the handle of a jug.

– PHRASES **be all ears** informal be listening eagerly and attentively. **bring something (down) about one's ears** bring something, esp. misfortune, on oneself. **one's ears are burning** one is subconsciously aware of being talked about or criticized. **grin** (or **smile**) **from ear to ear** smile broadly. **have something coming out of one's ears** informal have a substantial or excessive amount of something: *he has money coming out of his ears.* **have someone's ear** have access to and influence with someone. **have** (or **keep**) **an ear to the ground** be well informed about events and trends. **in (at) one ear and out (at) the other** heard but disregarded or quickly forgotten: *advice seems to go in one ear and out the other.* **listen with half an ear** not give one's attention. **be out on one's ear** informal be dismissed or ejected ignominiously. **up to one's ears in** informal very busy with or deeply involved in: *I'm up to my ears in work.* — **eared adj.** [in comb.] *long-eared* **ear·less adj.** [OE *ēare*, of Gmc. origin; rel. to Ger. *Ohr*, from an Indo-Eur. root shared by L. *auris* and Gk. *ous*.]

ear[2] ▶ **n.** the seed-bearing head or spike of a cereal plant. ■ a head of corn. [OE *ēar*, of Gmc. origin; rel. to Du. *aar* and Ger. *Ähre*.]

ear·ache /ˈi(ə)rˌāk/ ▶ **n.** pain inside the ear. Also called **OTALGIA**.

ear·bud /ˈi(ə)rˌbəd/ ▶ **n.** a very small headphone, worn inside the ear.

ear can·dy ▶ **n.** light popular music that is pleasant and entertaining but intellectually unchallenging.

ear drops ▶ **plural n. 1** liquid medication to be applied in small amounts to the ear. **2** (**eardrops**) hanging earrings.

ear·drum /ˈi(ə)rˌdrəm/ ▶ **n.** the tympanic membrane of the middle ear, which vibrates in response to sound waves.

eared seal ▶ **n.** see **SEAL**[2].

ear·flap /ˈi(ə)rˌflap/ ▶ **n.** an ear-covering flap of material on a hat or cap.

ear·ful /ˈi(ə)rˌfo͝ol/ ▶ **n.** [in sing.] informal a loud blast of a noise. ■ a prolonged amount of talking, typically an angry reprimand: *he **gave** his players **an earful** at halftime.*

Ear·hart /ˈe(ə)rˌhärt/, Amelia Mary (1898–1937?), US aviator. In 1932, she became the first woman to fly an airplane across the Atlantic Ocean by herself. In 1937, her plane disappeared somewhere over the Pacific Ocean during an around-the-world flight.

ear·hole /ˈi(ə)rˌhōl/ ▶ **n.** the external opening of the ear. ■ informal a person's ear.

earl /ərl/ ▶ **n.** a British nobleman ranking above a viscount and below a marquess. [Old English *eorl*, of Germanic origin.]

earl·dom /ˈərldəm/ ▶ **n.** the rank or title of an earl. ■ hist. the territory governed by an earl.

ear·lobe /ˈi(ə)rˌlōb/ ▶ **n.** the soft, fleshy lower part of the external ear.

ear·lock /ˈi(ə)rˌläk/ ▶ **n.** a lock of hair over or above the ear.

earl pal·a·tine ▶ **n.** (pl. **earls pal·a·tine**) hist. an earl having royal authority within his country or domain.

Ear·ly /ˈərlē/, Jubal Anderson (1816–94), Confederate general in the American Civil War. He was defeated in the Shenandoah Valley and was relieved of his command in 1864.

ear·ly /ˈərlē/ ▶ **adj.** (**ear·li·er, ear·li·est**) **1** happening or done before the usual or expected time: *we ate an early lunch.* ■ (of a plant or crop) flowering or ripening before other varieties: *early potatoes.* **2** happening, belonging to, or done near the beginning of a particular period: *an early goal secured victory.* ■ denoting or belonging to the beginning or opening stages of a historical period, cultural movement, or sphere of activity: *early Impressionism.* ■ occurring at the beginning of a sequence: *the book's earlier chapters.* ▶ **adv.** before the usual or expected time: *I was planning to finish work early today.* ■ near the beginning of a particular time or period: *we lost a couple of games early in the season.* ■ (**earlier**) before the present time or before the time one is referring to: *you met my husband earlier.*

– PHRASES **at the earliest** not before the time or date specified: *the table won't be delivered until next week at the earliest.* **early bird** humorous a person who rises, arrives, or acts before the usual or expected time. **an early grave** a premature or untimely death. **the early hours** the time after midnight and before dawn. **an early night** an occasion when someone goes to bed before the usual time. **early** (or **earlier**) **on** at an early (or earlier) stage in a particular period: *problems discovered early on.* — **ear·li·ness n.** [OE *ǣrlīce* (see **ERE**, **-LY**[2]), influenced by ON *árliga*.]

ear·ly a·dopt·er ▶ **n.** a person who starts using a product or technology as soon as it becomes available.

ear·ly mu·sic ▶ **n.** medieval, Renaissance, and early baroque music, esp. as revived and played on period instruments.

ear·ly warn·ing sys·tem ▶ **n.** a network of radar stations established at the boundary of a region to provide advanced warning of an aircraft or missile attack. ■ a condition, system, or series of procedures indicating a potential development or impending problem.

ear·mark /ˈi(ə)rˌmärk/ ▶ **n.** a mark on the ear of a domesticated animal indicating ownership or identity. ■ a characteristic or identifying feature: *this car has all the earmarks of a classic.* ▶ **v.** [trans.] **1** (usu. **be earmarked**) designate (something, typically funds or resources) for a particular purpose: *the new money will be* ***earmarked for*** *cancer research.* **2** mark the ear of (an animal) to show ownership or identity.

ear·muffs /ˈi(ə)rˌməfs/ ▶ **plural n.** a pair of coverings, connected by a band across the top of the head, worn over the ears to protect them from cold or noise.

earn /ərn/ ▶ **v.** [trans.] obtain (money) in return for labor or services: *earns his living as a truck driver.* ■ [with two objs.] (of an activity or action) cause (someone) to obtain (money): *the win earned them $50,000 in prize money.* ■ (of capital invested) gain (money) as interest or profit. ■ gain or incur in return for one's behavior or achievements: *through the years she has earned affection and esteem.*

– PHRASES **earn one's keep** work in return for food and accommodations. ■ be worth the time, money, or effort spent on one. [Old Engl. *earnian*, of West Gmc. origin, from a base shared by OE *esne* 'laborer.']

earned in·come /ərnd/ ▶ **n.** money derived from paid work. Often contrasted with UNEARNED INCOME.

earned run ▶ **n.** Baseball a run scored without the aid of errors by the team in the field.

earned run av·er·age ▶ **n.** Baseball a statistic used to measure a pitcher's effectiveness, obtained by calculating the average number of earned runs scored against the pitcher in every nine innings pitched.

earn·er /ˈərnər/ ▶ **n.** [with adj.] a person who obtains money in return for labor or services: *high earners.* ■ an activity or product that brings in income of a specified kind or level: *a major foreign currency earner.*

ear·nest[1] /ˈərnist/ ▶ **adj.** resulting from or showing intense conviction: *an earnest student.*

– PHRASES **in earnest** occurring to a greater extent or more intensely than before: *after Labor Day the campaign begins in earnest.* ■ (of a person) sincere and serious in behavior or convictions. — **ear·nest·ly adv.** **ear·nest·ness n.** [OE *eornost*, of Gmc. origin; rel. to Ger. *Ernst.*]

ear·nest[2] ▶ **n.** [in sing.] a thing intended or regarded as a sign or promise of what is to come: *an earnest of the world's desire not to see the conflict repeated elsewhere.* [ME *ernes*, lit. 'installment paid to confirm a contract,' based on OFr. *erres*, from L. *arra*, shortened form of *arrabo* 'a pledge.']

ear·nest mon·ey ▶ **n.** money paid to confirm a contract.

Earn·hardt /ˈərnˌhärt/, Dale (1951–2001), US racecar driver; full name *Ralph Dale Earnhardt*. He died in an accident during the Daytona 500.

earn·ings /ˈərniNGz/ ▶ **plural n.** money obtained in return for labor or services. ■ income derived from an investment or product.

Earp /ərp/, Wyatt Berry Stapp (1848–1929), US marshal. He is best known for the gunfight at the OK Corral (1881) in Tombstone, Arizona.

ear·phone /ˈi(ə)rˌfōn/ ▶ **n.** (usu. **earphones**) an electrical device worn on the ear to receive radio or telephone communications or to listen to a radio or tape recorder without other people hearing.

ear·piece /ˈi(ə)rˌpēs/ ▶ **n.** **1** the part of a telephone, radio receiver, or other aural device that is applied to the ear. **2** the part of a pair of glasses that fits around the ear.

ear-pierc·ing ▶ **adj.** [attrib.] loud and shrill: *the alarm emits an ear-piercing screech.* ▶ **n.** the practice of making holes in the lobes or edges of the ears to allow the wearing of earrings.

ear·plug /ˈi(ə)rˌpləg/ ▶ **n.** (usu. **earplugs**) **1** something placed in the ear as protection against noise or water. **2** hist. an ornament worn in the lobe of the ear.

ear·ring /ˈi(ə)r(r)iNG/ ▶ **n.** a piece of jewelry worn on the lobe or edge of the ear.

ear·shot /ˈi(ə)rˌSHät/ ▶ **n.** the range or distance over which one can hear or be heard: *she waited until he was* ***out of earshot*** *before continuing.*

ear-split·ting ▶ **adj.** extremely loud.

earth /ərTH/ ▶ **n.** **1** (also **Earth**) the planet on which we live, the third planet from the sun in the solar system. ■ the surface of the world as distinct from the sky or the sea: *it plummeted back to earth.* ■ the present abode of humankind, as distinct from heaven or hell. **2** the substance of the land surface; soil: *a layer of earth.* ■ one of the four elements in ancient and medieval philosophy and in astrology. ■ literary the substance of the human body. **3** the underground lair or habitation of a badger or fox. **4** electrical British term for GROUND[1] (sense 7). ▶ **v.** [trans.] **1** (**earth something up**) cover the root and lower stem of a plant with heaped-up earth. **2** Hunting drive (a fox) to its underground lair. ■ [intrans.] (of a fox) run to its underground lair. **3** electrical British term for GROUND[1] (sense 5).

– PHRASES **come** (or **bring**) **back** (**down**) **to earth** return or cause to return to reality after a period of daydreaming or excitement. **go to earth** (of a hunted animal) hide in an underground burrow. ■ fig. go into hiding. **like nothing on earth** informal very strange. **on earth** used for emphasis: *who on earth would venture out in weather like this?* [OE *eorthe*, of Gmc. origin; rel. to Ger. *Erde.*]

earth·bound /ˈərTHˌbound/ ▶ **adj.** **1** attached or restricted to the earth: *a flightless earthbound bird.* ■ attached or limited to material existence as distinct from a spiritual or heavenly one. ■ fig. lacking in imaginative reach: *an earthbound performance.* **2** (also **earth-bound**) moving toward the earth: *an earthbound spaceship.*

earth·en /ˈərTHən/ ▶ **adj.** [attrib.] (of a floor or structure) made of compressed earth: *an earthen dam.* ■ (of a pot) made of baked or fired clay. ■ literary of, relating to, or characteristic of the earth or material existence.

earth·en·ware /ˈərTHənˌwer/ ▶ **n.** [often as adj.] pottery made of clay fired to a porous state, which can be made impervious to liquids by the use of a glaze.

earth·light /ˈərTHˌlīt/ ▶ **n.** another term for EARTHSHINE.

earth·ling /ˈərTHliNG/ ▶ **n.** an inhabitant of the earth (used esp. in science fiction).

earth·ly /ˈərTHlē/ ▶ **adj.** **1** of or relating to the earth or human life on the earth: *normal earthly temperatures.* ■ of or relating to humankind's material existence as distinct from a spiritual or heavenly one. **2** [with negative] informal used for emphasis: *there was* ***no earthly reason*** *why she should not come too.* — **earth·li·ness n.**

earth moth·er ▶ **n.** (in mythology and early religion) a goddess symbolizing fertility and the source of life. ■ an archetypically sensual and maternal woman.

earth·mov·er /ˈərthˌmo͞ovər/ ▶ **n.** a vehicle or machine designed to excavate large quantities of soil. — **earth·mov·ing n.**

earth·nut /ˈərTHˌnət/ ▶ **n.** **1** a Eurasian plant (*Conopodium majus*) of the parsley family, which has an edible roundish tuber, typically found in woodland and acid pasture. Also called PIGNUT. ■ the almond-flavored tuber of this plant. **2** esp. Brit. another term for PEANUT.

earth·quake /ˈərTHˌkwāk/ ▶ **n.** a sudden and violent shaking of the ground, sometimes causing great destruction, as a result of movements within the earth's crust or volcanic action. The intensity of earthquakes is expressed by the Richter scale, destructive earthquakes generally measuring between about 7 and 9. ■ fig. a great convulsion or upheaval: *a political earthquake.*

earth sci·ence ▶ **n.** the branch of science dealing with the constitution of the earth and its atmosphere. ■ (**earth sciences**) the various branches of this subject, e.g., geology, oceanography, and meteorology.

earth·shak·ing /ˈərTHˌSHākiNG/ ▶ **adj.** (of music or sound) loud and throbbing. ■ another term for EARTH-SHATTERING.

earth-shat·ter·ing ▶ **adj.** (in hyperbolic use) very important, momentous, or traumatic. — **earth-shat·ter·ing·ly adv.**

earth·shine /ˈərTHˌSHīn/ (also **earth·light**) ▶ **n.** Astron. the glow caused by sunlight reflected off the earth, esp. on the darker portion of a crescent moon.

earth·star /ˈərTHˌstär/ ▶ **n.** a brownish woodland fungus (family Geastraceae, class Gasteromycetes) with a spherical spore-containing fruiting body surrounded by a fleshy star-shaped structure, found in both Eurasia and North America.

earth sta·tion ▶ **n.** a radio station located on the earth and used for relaying signals from satellites.

earth tone ▶ **n.** a rich warm color with a brownish hue.

earth·ward /ˈərTHwərd/ (also **earth·wards**) ▶ **adv. & adj.** toward the earth.

earth·work /ˈərTHˌwərk/ ▶ **n.** **1** a large artificial bank of soil, esp. one made as a defense. **2** the process of excavating in civil engineering work. **3** a work of art that modifies a large piece of land.

earth·worm /ˈərTHˌwərm/ ▶ **n.** a burrowing annelid (*Lumbricus*, *Allolobophora*, and other genera, family Lumbricidae) that lives in the soil. Earthworms play an important role in aerating and draining the soil and in burying organic matter.

earth·y /ˈərTHē/ ▶ **adj.** (**earth·i·er**, **earth·i·est**) resembling or suggestive of earth or soil: *an earthy smell.* ■ (of a person) direct and uninhibited; hearty. ■ (of humor) somewhat coarse or crude. — **earth·i·ly adv.** **earth·i·ness n.**

ear trum·pet ▶ **n.** a trumpet-shaped device formerly used as a hearing aid.

ear tuft ▶ **n.** each of a pair of tufts of longer feathers on the top of the head of some owls. They are unconnected with the true ears.

ear·wax /ˈi(ə)rˌwaks/ ▶ **n.** the protective yellow waxy substance secreted in the outer ear. Also called CERUMEN.

ear·wig /ˈi(ə)rˌwig/ ▶ **n.** a small elongated insect (order Dermaptera) with a pair of terminal appendages that resemble pincers.

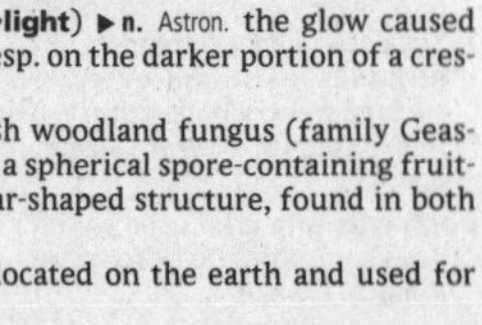

earwig

ear·wit·ness /ˈi(ə)rˈwitnis/ ▶ **n.** a witness whose testimony is based on what they personally heard.

ease /ēz/ ▶ **n.** absence of difficulty or effort: *he gave up tobacco with ease.* ■ absence of rigidity or discomfort; poise: *her self-contained ease.* ■ freedom from worries or problems, esp. about one's material situation: *a life of ease.* ▶ **v.** **1** [trans.] make (something unpleasant, painful, or intense) less serious or severe. ■ alleviate the mental or physical pain of: *unburdening herself was doing nothing to ease her misery.* ■ [intrans.] become less serious or severe: *the pain doesn't usually ease off for several hours.* ■ [intrans.] (**ease up**) relax one's efforts; do something with more moderation: *I'd ease up if I were you.* ■ (**ease something away/down/off**) Naut. slacken a rope. ■ (**ease something away/down/off**) Naut. sail slowly or gently. ■ make (something) happen more easily; facilitate. ■ [intrans.] Finance (of share prices, interest rates, etc.) decrease in value or amount: *interest rates eased.* **2** [no obj., with adverbial of direction] move carefully, gradually, or

gently: *I eased down the slope with care.* ■ [trans.] (**ease someone out**) gradually exclude someone from a post or place, esp. by subtle maneuvers: *he was eased out of his job.*
– PHRASES **at (one's) ease** free from worry, awkwardness, or problems; relaxed: *she was never quite at ease with Phil.* ■ (**at ease**) Mil. in a relaxed posture with the feet apart and the hands behind the back (often as a command): ***stand at ease!*** **ease someone's mind** alleviate someone's anxiety. — **eas•er** n. [ME: from OFr. *aise*, based on L. *adjacens* 'lying close by,' pres. part. of *adjacere*.]

ease•ful /'ēzfəl/ ▸ **adj.** literary providing or offering comfort or peace: *life was easeful at that time.*

ea•sel /'ēzəl/ ▸ **n.** a self-supporting frame for holding an artist's work while it is being painted or drawn. ■ a similar frame for displaying charts, promotional materials, announcements, etc. [16th C.: from Du. *ezel* 'ass.' The word "horse" is used in Engl. in a similar way to denote a supporting frame.]

ease•ment /'ēzmənt/ ▸ **n.** **1** Law a right to cross or otherwise use someone else's land for a specified purpose. **2** literary the state or feeling of comfort or peace.

eas•i•ly /'ēzəlē/ ▸ **adv.** **1** without difficulty or effort: *the area is easily accessible.* ■ in a relaxed manner: *he shrugged easily.* ■ more quickly or frequently than is usual: *I get bored easily.* **2** without doubt; by far: *English is easily the reigning language in the financial world.* ■ very probably: *events that could easily become routine.*

east /ēst/ ▸ **n.** (usu. **the east**) **1** the direction toward the point of the horizon where the sun rises at the equinoxes, on the right-hand side of a person facing north, or the point on the horizon itself: *a gale was blowing from the east.* ■ the compass point corresponding to this. **2** the eastern part of the world or of a specified country, region, or town: *a factory in the east of the city.* ■ (usu. **the East**) the regions or countries east of Europe, esp. China, Japan, and India: *the mysterious East.* ■ (usu. **the East**) the eastern part of the US, from the Alleghenies on the west, and north of the Mason-Dixon line. ■ (usu. **the East**) short for EAST COAST. ■ (usu. **the East**) hist. the former communist states of eastern Europe. **3** (**East**) [as name] Bridge the player sitting to the left of North and partnering West. ▸ **adj.** [attrib.] **1** lying toward, near, or facing the east. ■ (of a wind) blowing from the east. ■ situated in the part of a church containing the altar or high altar, usually the actual east. **2** of or denoting the eastern part of a specified area, city, or country or its inhabitants. ▸ **adv.** to or toward the east: *traveling east, he met two men.* [OE *ēast-*, of Gmc. origin; rel. to Ger. *ost*, from an Indo-Eur. root shared by L. *aurora*, Gk. *auōs* 'dawn.']

East Af•ri•ca the eastern part of the African continent, esp. the countries of Kenya, Uganda, and Tanzania.

East An•gli•a /'aNGglēə/ a region in eastern England.

East Ben•gal the part of Bengal that gained independence as Bangladesh in 1971.

East Ber•lin see BERLIN.

east•bound /'ēst,bound/ ▸ **adj.** leading or traveling toward the east: *the eastbound lane.*

east by north ▸ **n.** a direction or compass point midway between east and east-northeast.

east by south ▸ **n.** a direction or compass point midway between east and east-southeast.

East Chi•na Sea see CHINA SEA.

East Coast ▸ **n.** the eastern seaboard of the US, esp. the narrow corridor from Boston to Washington, DC.

Eas•ter /'ēstər/ ▸ **n.** the most important and oldest festival of the Christian Church, celebrating the resurrection of Christ and held (in the Western Church) between March 21 and April 25, on the first Sunday after the first full moon following the spring equinox. ■ the period in which this occurs, esp. the weekend from Good Friday to Easter Monday. [OE *ēastre*; of Gmc. origin and related to Ger. *Ostern* and EAST.]

Eas•ter bun•ny ▸ **n.** an imaginary rabbit said to bring gifts, esp. candy, to children at Easter.

Eas•ter egg ▸ **n.** an egg that is dyed and often decorated as part of the Easter celebration. ■ an artificial egg, typically chocolate, given at Easter.

Eas•ter Is•land an island in the southeastern Pacific Ocean, west of and administered by Chile; pop. 2,000. It is famous for its large monolithic statues of human heads that are believed to date from 1000–1600.

Eas•ter lil•y ▸ **n.** a spring-flowering lily, in particular the tall, white-flowered Japanese lily *Lilium longiflorum.*

east•er•ly /'ēstərlē/ ▸ **adj. & adv.** in an eastward position or direction: [as adj.] *an easterly course.* ■ (of a wind) blowing from the east: [as adj.] *the light easterly breeze.* ▸ **n.** (often **easterlies**) a wind blowing from the east.

Eas•ter Mon•day **n.** the day after Easter Sunday, a public holiday in some places.

east•ern /'ēstərn/ ▸ **adj.** **1** [attrib.] situated in the east, or directed toward or facing the east: *eastern Long Island.* ■ (of a wind) blowing from the east. **2** (usu. **Eastern**) living or originating in the east, esp. the regions or countries lying to the east of Europe: *an Eastern mystic.* ■ of, relating to, or characteristic of the East or its inhabitants: *an eastern religion.* — **east•ern•most** /'ēstərn,mōst/ **adj.**

East•ern bloc the countries of eastern and central Europe that were under Soviet domination from the end of World War II until the collapse of the Soviet communist system in 1989–91.

East•ern Church (also **Eastern Orthodox Church**) another name for ORTHODOX CHURCH. ■ any of the Christian Churches originating in eastern Europe and the Middle East.

East•ern Des•ert another name of the ARABIAN DESERT.

East•ern Em•pire the eastern part of the Roman Empire, after its division in AD 395. See also BYZANTINE EMPIRE.

east•ern e•quine en•ceph•a•li•tis ▸ **n.** a rare viral disease that affects horses and humans and is spread by mosquitoes, occurring mainly in eastern US states.

East•ern•er /'ēstərnər/ (also **east•ern•er**) ▸ **n.** a native or inhabitant of the east, esp. of the eastern US.

East•ern Eu•rope the portion of the European landmass that lies east of Germany and the Alps and west of the Ural Mountains.

East•ern Ghats see GHATS.

east•ern hem•i•sphere the half of the earth that contains Europe, Africa, Asia, and Australia.

East•ern Shore region of eastern Maryland on the east side of Chesapeake Bay.

East•ern time the standard time in a zone including the eastern states of the US and parts of Canada, specifically: ■ (**Eastern Standard Time**, abbrev.: **EST**), standard time based on the mean solar time at the meridian 75° W, five hours behind GMT. ■ (**Eastern Daylight Time**, abbrev.: **EDT**) Eastern time during daylight saving time, six hours behind GMT.

East•ern Zhou see ZHOU.

Eas•ter•tide /'ēstər,tīd/ ▸ **n.** the Easter period.

East Flan•ders a province in northern Belgium; capital, Ghent. See also FLANDERS.

East Fri•sian Is•lands see FRISIAN ISLANDS.

East Ger•man•ic ▸ **n.** the extinct eastern group of Germanic languages, including Gothic. ▸ **adj.** of or relating to this group of languages.

East Ger•many (official name **German Democratic Republic**) the former independent nation created in 1949 from the area of Germany occupied by the Soviet Union after World War II. German name **Deutsche Demokratische Republik**.

East Hart•ford an industrial town in central Connecticut, east of Hartford; pop. 50,452.

East In•di•a another name of EAST INDIES (sense 2).

East In•di•a Com•pa•ny a British trading company formed in 1600 to develop commerce in newly colonized areas of Southeast Asia and India. In the 18th century it controlled Bengal and other areas of India until the British Crown took over in 1858.

East In•dies **1** the islands in Southeast Asia, esp. those of the Malay Archipelago. **2** archaic the whole of Southeast Asia to the east of and including India. — **East In•di•an** **adj.**

east•ing /'ēstiNG/ ▸ **n.** distance traveled or measured eastward, esp. at sea. ■ a figure or line representing eastward distance on a map (expressed by convention as the first part of a grid reference, before northing).

East Lan•sing a city in south central Michigan, home to Michigan State University; pop. 50,677.

East Lon•don a port and resort in South Africa, on the southeastern coast; pop. 270,130.

East Los An•ge•les a city in southwestern California, east of Los Angeles; pop. 126,379.

East•man[1] /'ēstmən/, George (1854–1932), US inventor. He invented flexible roll film and, in 1888, the Kodak camera for use with it.

east-north•east ▸ **n.** the direction or compass point midway between east and northeast.

East Orange a city in northeastern New Jersey, northwest of Newark; pop. 69,824.

East Point a city in northwestern Georgia, south of Atlanta; pop. 39,595.

East•port /'ēst,pôrt/ a maritime city in eastern Maine, on an island in Passamaquoddy Bay, the easternmost US city; pop. 1,965.

East Prov•i•dence a city in eastern Rhode Island, east of Providence; pop. 48,688.

East Prus•sia the northeastern part of the former kingdom of Prussia, on the Baltic coast, later part of Germany and divided after World War II between the Soviet Union and Poland.

East Riv•er an arm of the Hudson River in New York City that separates the boroughs of Manhattan and the Bronx from the boroughs of Brooklyn and Queens.

east-south•east ▸ **n.** the direction or compass point midway between east and southeast.

East St. Lou•is a city in southwestern Illinois, across the Mississippi River from St. Louis; pop. 40,944.

East Ti•mor a state on the eastern part of the island of Timor in the southern part of the Malay Archipelago; pop. 1,019.252; capital, Dili. Formerly a Portuguese colony, the region declared itself independent in 1975. In 1976 it was invaded by Indonesia, which annexed and claimed it as their 27th state, a claim that was never recognized by the UN. After a bitter conflict, East Timor gained full independence in 1999 and a formal declaration by the United Nations in 2002. — **East Ti·mo·rese** /ˈtēmôˌrēz; -ˌrēs; ˈrēs/ **n. & adj.**

east·ward /ˈēstwərd/ ▶**adj.** in an easterly direction: *they followed an eastward course.* ▶**adv.** (also **east·wards**) toward the east. ▶**n.** (**the eastward**) the direction or region to the east. — **east·ward·ly adv.**

eas·y /ˈēzē/ ▶**adj.** (**eas·i·er, eas·i·est**) **1** achieved without great effort; presenting few difficulties. ■ [attrib.] (of an object of attack or criticism) having no defense; vulnerable: *he was an easy target.* ■ informal, derog. (of a woman) open to sexual advances; sexually available. **2** (of a period of time or way of life) free from worries or problems: *promises of an easy life in the New World.* ■ (of a person) lacking anxiety or awkwardness; relaxed. ▶**adv.** informal without difficulty or effort: *we all scared easy.* ▶**exclam.** be careful: *easy, girl—you'll knock me over!*

– PHRASES **be easier said than done** be more easily talked about than put into practice. (**as**) **easy as pie** see PIE[1]. **easy come, easy go** used to indicate that a relationship or possession acquired without effort may be abandoned or lost casually and without regret. **easy does it** used esp. in spoken English to advise someone to do something carefully and slowly. **easy on the eye** (or **ear**) informal pleasant to look at (or listen to). **go** (or **be**) **easy on someone** informal refrain from being harsh with or critical of someone. **go easy on something** informal be sparing or cautious in one's use or consumption of something: *go easy on fatty foods.* **have it easy** informal be free from difficulties; be fortunate. **I'm easy** informal said by someone offered a choice, to indicate no particular preference. **of easy virtue** dated humorous (of a woman) sexually promiscuous. **rest** (or **sleep**) **easy** be untroubled by (or go to sleep without) worries. **take the easy way out** extricate oneself from a difficult situation by choosing the simplest or most expedient course rather than the most honorable or ethical one. **take it easy** proceed calmly and in a relaxed manner. ■ make little effort; rest. — **eas·i·ness n.** [ME: from OFr. *aisie*, past part. of *aisier* 'put at ease, facilitate' (see EASE).]

eas·y chair ▶**n.** a large, comfortable chair, typically an armchair.

eas·y·go·ing /ˈēzēˌgōˈiNG/ (also **easy-go·ing**) ▶**adj.** relaxed and tolerant in approach or manner.

eas·y lis·ten·ing ▶**n.** popular music that is tuneful and undemanding.

eas·y mark ▶**n.** informal a person who is easy prey; a weakling or a sucker: *an easy mark for a grifter.*

eas·y mon·ey ▶**n.** money obtained by dubious means or for little work. ■ money available at relatively low interest.

eas·y street ▶**n.** informal a state of financial comfort or security.

eat /ēt/ ▶**v.** (past **ate** /āt/; past part. **eaten** /ˈētn/) [trans.] put (food) into the mouth and chew and swallow it: *he was eating a hot dog* | [intrans.] *she watched as he ate.* ■ have (a meal): *we ate dinner in a noisy cafe.* ■ [intrans.] (**eat out**) have a meal in a restaurant. ■ [intrans.] (**eat in**) have a meal at home rather than in a restaurant. ■ include (a particular food) in one's usual diet: *try to eat more greens.* ■ [no obj., with adverbial] follow a diet of a specified kind or quality: *she was very thin, although she was eating properly now.* ■ informal bother; annoy: *she knew what was eating him.* ■ vulgar slang perform fellatio or cunnilingus on (someone). ■ vulgar slang (**eat out**) perform cunnilingus or anilingus on (someone). ■ informal absorb (financial loss or cost). ▶**n.** (**eats**) informal food or snacks: *stop here for eats.*

– PHRASES **eat someone alive** informal (of insects) bite someone many times: *we were eaten alive by mosquitoes.* ■ exploit someone's weakness and completely dominate them: *they'll be eaten alive by lawyers in liability suits.* **eat crow** see CROW[1]. **eat dirt** see DIRT. **eat someone's dust** see DUST. **eat one's heart out** suffer from excessive longing, esp. for someone or something unattainable. ■ [in imper.] informal used to encourage feelings of jealousy or regret: *eat your heart out, I'm having a ball!* **eat humble pie** see HUMBLE. **eat like a bird** (or **a horse**) informal eat very little (or a lot). **eat someone out of house and home** informal eat a lot of someone else's food. **eat one's words** retract what one has said, esp. in a humiliated way. **have someone eating out of one's hand** have someone completely under one's control. **I'll eat my hat** informal used to indicate that one thinks a specified thing is extremely unlikely to happen.

– PHRASAL VERBS **eat away at something** (or **eat something away**) erode or destroy something gradually. ■ use up (profits, resources, or time), esp. when they are intended for other purposes: *inflation can eat away at the annuity's value over the years.* **eat into** another way of saying *EAT AWAY AT* above. **eat someone up** [usu. as adj.] (**eaten up**) dominate someone's thoughts completely: *I'm eaten up with guilt.* **eat something up** use resources or time in very large quantities: *a program that eats up 200Mb of disk space.* ■ encroach on something: *countryside eaten up by concrete.* [OE *etan*, from Gmc.; rel. to Ger. *essen*, from an Indo-Eur. root shared by L. *edere* and Gk. *edein*.]

eat·a·ble /ˈētəbəl/ ▶**adj.** fit to be consumed as food. ▶**n.** (**eatables**) items of food: *parcels of eatables and gifts.*

eat·er /ˈētər/ ▶**n.** [with adj.] a person who consumes food in a specified way or of a specified kind: *I'm still a big eater* | *they are meat eaters.*

eat·er·y /ˈētərē/ ▶**n.** (pl. **-er·ies**) informal a restaurant or other place where people can be served food.

eat-in ▶**adj.** [attrib.] (of a kitchen) designed for eating in as well as cooking.

eat·ing ap·ple ▶**n.** an apple that is suitable for eating raw.

eat·ing dis·or·der ▶**n.** any of a range of psychological disorders characterized by abnormal or disturbed eating habits (such as anorexia nervosa).

Eau Claire /ōˈkle(ə)r/ a city in west central Wisconsin; pop. 61,704.

eau de co·logne /ˌō də kəˈlōn/ ▶**n.** a toilet water with a strong scent, originally made in Cologne, Germany. [19th C.: Fr., literally 'water of Cologne.']

eau de toi·lette /ˌō də twäˈlet/ ▶**n.** (pl. **eaux de toi·lette** /ˌōz/) a dilute form of perfume; toilet water. [20th C.: Fr., literally 'toilet water.']

eau-de-vie /ˌō də ˈvē/ ▶**n.** (pl. **eaux-de-vie** /ˌōz/)brandy. [18th C.: from Fr. *eau-de-vie*, literally 'water of life.']

eaves /ēvz/ ▶**plural n.** the part of a roof that meets or overhangs the walls of a building. [OE *efes* (sing.); of Gmc. origin; rel. to Ger. dial. *Obsen*, also prob. to OVER.]

eaves·drop /ˈēvzˌdräp/ ▶**v.** (**-dropped, -drop·ping**) [intrans.] secretly listen to a conversation: *she opened the window enough to eavesdrop on the conversation.* — **eaves·drop·per n.** [17th C.: back-form. from *eavesdropper*, from the obs. n. *eavesdrop* 'the ground on to which water drips from the eaves,' prob. from ON *upsardropi*.]

ebb /eb/ ▶**n.** (usu. **the ebb**) the movement of the tide out to sea: *the tide was on the ebb* | [as adj.] *the ebb tide.* ▶**v.** [intrans.] (of tidewater) move away from the land; recede: *the tide began to ebb.* Compare with FLOW. ■ fig. (of an emotion or quality) gradually lessen or reduce: *my enthusiasm was ebbing away.*

– PHRASES **at a low ebb** in a poor state: *profits were at a low ebb.* **ebb and flow** a recurrent pattern of coming and going or decline and regrowth. [OE *ebba*, from West Gmc.; akin to Du. *ebbe* and OF.]

EBCDIC /ˈebsēˌdik/ ▶**abbr.** Extended Binary Coded Decimal Interchange Code, a standard eight-bit character code used in computing and data transmission.

Eb·la /ˈeblə; ˈēblə/ a city in ancient Syria that was southwest of Aleppo. It was very powerful in the mid-3rd millennium BC.

EbN ▶**abbr.** east by north.

Eb·o·la fe·ver /ēˈbōlə/ ▶**n.** an infectious and generally fatal disease marked by fever and internal bleeding, spread through contact with infected body fluids by a filovirus (**Ebola virus**), whose normal host is unknown. [1976: named after a river in the Democratic Republic of the Congo (formerly Zaire).]

eb·on /ˈebən/ ▶**n.** literary dark brown or black; ebony: [as adj.] *an ebon hue.*

eb·on·ite /ˈebəˌnīt/ ▶**n.** another term for VULCANITE. [19th C.: from EBONY + -ITE[1].]

eb·on·ize /ˈebəˌnīz/ ▶**v.** [trans.] [usu. as adj.] (**ebonized**) make (furniture) look like ebony: *an ebonized casket.*

eb·on·y /ˈebənē/ ▶**n.** heavy blackish or very dark brown timber from a mainly tropical tree (genera *Diospyros* and *Euclea*, family Ebenaceae). ■ a very dark brown or black color. [ME: from earlier *ebon* (via OFr. and L. from Gk. *ebenos* 'ebony tree'.]

e-book /ˈēˌbo͝ok/ ▶**n.** an electronic version of a printed book that can be read on a personal computer or hand-held device designed specifically for this purpose. ■ a dedicated device for reading electronic versions of printed books.

E·bro /ˈāvrō; ˈābrō/ a river in northeastern Spain that flows southeast for 570 miles (910 km) into the Mediterranean Sea.

EbS ▶**abbr.** east by south.

e·bul·lient /iˈbo͝olyənt; iˈbəl-/ ▶**adj.** **1** cheerful and full of energy: *she sounded ebullient and happy.* **2** archaic literary (of liquid or matter) boiling or agitated as if boiling: *misted and ebullient seas.* — **e·bul·lience n. e·bul·lient·ly adv.** [16th C.: from L. *ebullient-* 'boiling up,' from *ebullire*, from *e-* + *bullire* 'to boil.']

eb·ul·li·tion /ˌebəˈlisHən/ ▶**n.** tech. archaic the action of bubbling or boiling. ■ a sudden outburst of emotion or violence.

EBV ▶**abbr.** Epstein-Barr virus.

EC ▶**abbr.** ■ European Commission. ■ European Community. ■ executive committee.

é·car·té /ˌākärˈtā/ ▶**n.** **1** a card game for two players, in which thirty-two cards are used, and certain cards may be discarded in exchange for others. **2** Ballet a position in which the dancer, facing diagonally toward the audience, extends one leg to the side with the arm of the same side raised above the head and the other arm extended to the side. [19th C.: Fr., past part. of *écarter* 'discard, throw out,' from *é* 'out' + *carte* 'card.']

e-cash ▶**n.** electronic financial transactions conducted in cyberspace via computer networks.

ec·bol·ic /ekˈbälik/ Med. ▶**adj.** inducing contractions of the uterus leading to expulsion of a fetus. ▶**n.** an agent that induces such contractions. [18th C.: from Gk. *ekbolē* 'expulsion' + -IC.]

Ec·ce Ho·mo /ˈecHā ˈhōmō; ˈeksē; ˈekā/ ▶**n.** Art a painting of Jesus Christ wearing the crown of thorns. [17th C.: L., literally 'behold the man.']

ec·cen·tric /ikˈsentrik/ ▶**adj.** **1** (of a person or behavior) unconventional and slightly strange: *my eccentric aunt.* **2** tech. (of a thing) not placed centrally or not having its axis or other part placed centrally. ■ (of a circle) not centered on the same point as another. ■ (of an orbit) not circular. ▶**n.** **1** a person of unconventional and slightly strange views or behavior. **2** a disc or wheel mounted eccentrically on a revolving shaft in order to transform rotation into backward-and-forward motion, e.g., an automobile cam. — **ec·cen·tri·cal·ly adv.** [ME: via late L. from Gk. *ekkentros*, from *ek* 'out of' + *kentron* 'center.']

ec·cen·tric·i·ty /ˌeksenˈtrisitē/ ▶**n.** (pl. **-ties**) **1** the quality of being eccentric. ■ (usu. **eccentricities**) an eccentric act, habit, or thing. **2** tech.

deviation of a curve or orbit from circularity. ■ a measure of the extent of such deviation.

ec·chy·mo·sis /,ekə'mōsis/ ▶ **n.** (pl. **-ses** /,ekə'mōsēz/) Med. a discoloration of the skin resulting from bleeding underneath. [16th C.: mod. L., from Gk. *ekkhumōsis* 'escape of blood,' from *ekkhumonathai* 'force out blood.']

eccl. ▶ **abbr.** ■ ecclesiastic. ■ ecclesiastical.

Ec·cles /'ekəlz/, Sir John Carew (1903–97), Australian physiologist, who demonstrated the way in which nerve impulses are conducted. Nobel Prize for Physiology or Medicine (1963, shared with A. L. Hodgkin and A. F. Huxley).

Eccles. ▶ **abbr.** Bible Ecclesiastes.

ec·cle·si·al /i'klēzēəl/ ▶ **adj.** formal relating to or constituting a church or denomination. [17th C.: via OFr. from Gk. *ekklēsia*.]

ec·cle·si·arch /i'klēzē,ärk/ ▶ **n.** archaic a ruler of a church. [18th C.: from Gk. *ekklēsia* 'church' + *arkhos* 'leader.']

Ec·cle·si·as·tes /i,klēzē'astēz/ a book of the Bible traditionally attributed to Solomon, consisting largely of reflections on the vanity of human life.

ec·cle·si·as·tic /i,klēzē'astik/ formal ▶ **n.** a priest or clergyman. ▶ **adj.** another term for ECCLESIASTICAL. [ME: from Fr. *ecclésiastique*, or via late L. from Gk. *ekklēsiastikos*, from *ekklēsiastēs* 'member of an assembly,' from *ekklēsia* 'assembly, church,' based on *ekkalein* 'summon out.']

ec·cle·si·as·ti·cal /i,klēzē'astikəl/ ▶ **adj.** of or relating to the Christian Church or its clergy. — **ec·cle·si·as·ti·cal·ly adv.**

ec·cle·si·as·ti·cism /i,klēzē'asti,sizəm/ ▶ **n.** adherence or overattention to details of church practice.

Ec·cle·si·as·ti·cus /i,klēzē'astikəs/ a book of the Apocrypha containing moral and practical maxims, probably dating from the early 2nd century BC.

ec·cle·si·ol·o·gy /i,klēzē'äləjē/ ▶ **n. 1** the study of churches, esp. church building and decoration. **2** theology as applied to the nature and structure of the Christian Church. — **ec·cle·si·o·log·i·cal** /i,klēzēə'läjikəl/ **adj. ec·cle·si·ol·o·gist n.** [19th C.: from Gk. *ekklēsia*.]

Ec·clus ▶ **abbr.** Bible Ecclesiasticus.

ec·crine /'ekrən; 'ekrīn; 'ekrēn/ ▶ **adj.** Med. relating to or denoting multicellular glands that do not lose cytoplasm in their secretions, esp. the sweat glands distributed on the skin. Compare with APOCRINE. [1930s: from Gk. *ekkrinein* 'secrete,' from *ek-* 'out' + *krinein* 'sift, separate.']

ec·dys·i·ast /ek'dēzēəst/ ▶ **n.** humorous a striptease performer. [1940: Gk. *ekdusis* 'shedding.']

ec·dy·sis /'ekdəsis/ ▶ **n.** Zool. the process of shedding the old skin (in reptiles) or casting off the outer cuticle (in insects and other arthropods). — **ec·dys·i·al** /ek'dizēəl/ **adj.** [19th C.: from Gk. *ekdusis*, from *ekduein* 'put off,' from *ek-* 'out, off' + *duein* 'put.']

ec·dy·sone /'ekdi,sōn/ ▶ **n.** Biochem. a hormone that controls molting in insects and other arthropods. [1950s: from Gk. *ekdusis* 'shedding' + -ONE.]

ECG ▶ **abbr.** ■ electrocardiogram. ■ electrocardiograph.

é·chap·pé /,āshä'pā/ ▶ **adj.** [postpositive] Ballet (of a movement) progressing from a closed position to an open position of the feet. [French, literally 'escaped.']

ech·e·lon /'eshə,län/ ▶ **n. 1** a level or rank in an organization, a profession, or society. ■ [often with adj.] a part of a military force differentiated by battle position or function: *the rear echelon.* **2** Mil. a formation of troops, ships, aircraft, or vehicles in parallel rows with the end of each row projecting further than the one in front. ▶ **v.** [trans.] Mil. arrange in an echelon formation. [18th C.: from Fr. *échelon*, from *échelle* 'ladder,' from L. *scala*.]

ech·e·ve·ri·a /,echəvə'rēə/ ▶ **n.** a succulent plant (genus *Echeveria*) of the stonecrop family, with rosettes of fleshy colorful leaves, native to warm regions of America. [modern Latin, named after Anastasio *Echeveri* or *Echeverría*, 19th-cent. Mexican botanical illustrator.]

e·chid·na /i'kidnə/ ▶ **n.** a spiny insectivorous egg-laying mammal (family Tachyglossidae, order Monotremata) with a long snout and claws, native to Australia and New Guinea. Also called SPINY ANTEATER. [19th C.: mod. L., from Gk. *ekhidna* 'viper.']

ech·i·na·cea /,ekə'nāshə/ ▶ **n.** a North American coneflower (genus *Echinacea*), used in herbal medicine, largely for its antibiotic and wound-healing properties. [mod. L., from Gk. *ekhinos* 'hedgehog.']

Echi·no·der·ma·ta /i,kīnə'dərmətə; ,ekənə-/ Zool. a phylum of marine invertebrates that includes starfishes, sea urchins, crinoids, and sea cucumbers. They have fivefold radial symmetry, a calcareous skeleton, and tube feet operated by fluid pressure. — **echi·no·derm** /i'kīnə,dərm; 'ekənə,dərm/ **n.** [mod. L. (pl.), from Gk. *ekhinos* 'hedgehog, sea urchin' + *derma* 'skin.']

Ech·i·noi·de·a /,ekə'noidēə/ Zool. a class of echinoderms that comprises the sea urchins. — **echi·noid** /i'kīnoid; 'ekə,noid/ **n. & adj.** [mod. L. (pl.), from ECHINUS.]

e·chi·nus /i'kīnəs/ ▶ **n.** (pl. **-ni** /-nī/) **1** Zool. a sea urchin of the genus *Echinus*. **2** Archit. a rounded molding below an abacus on a Doric or Ionic capital. [ME: via L. from Gk. *ekhinos* 'hedgehog, sea urchin.']

Ech·o /'ekō/ Gk. Mythol. a nymph deprived of speech by Hera in order to stop her chatter, and left able only to repeat what others had said.

ech·o /'ekō/ ▶ **n. 1** (pl. **ech·oes**) a sound or series of sounds caused by the reflection of sound waves from a surface back to the listener: *the walls threw back echoes.* ■ a reflected radio or radar beam. ■ the deliberate introduction of reverberation into a sound recording. ■ Ling. the repetition in structure and content of one speaker's utterance by another. ■ a close parallel or repetition of an idea, feeling, style, or event. ■ (often **echoes**) a detail or characteristic suggestive of something else. ■ archaic a person who slavishly repeats the words or opinions of another. **2** Bridge a defender's play of a higher card in a suit followed by a lower one in a subsequent trick, used as a signal to request one's partner to lead that suit. **3** a radio code word representing the letter E. ▶ **v.** (**ech·oes, ech·oed**) [no obj., with adverbial] (of a sound) be repeated or reverberate after the original sound has stopped: *their footsteps echoed on the metal catwalks.* ■ (of a place) resound with or reflect back a sound or sounds: *the house* **echoed with** *shouts.* ■ fig. have a continued significance or influence: *illiteracy echoed through the fabric of society.* ■ [trans.] (often **be echoed**) repeat (someone's words or opinions), typically to express agreement: *these criticisms are echoed in other studies.* ■ [trans.] (of an object, movement, or event) be reminiscent of or have shared characteristics with: *a suit that echoed the color of her eyes.* ■ [trans.] Comput. send a copy of (an input signal or character) back to its source or to a screen for display: *the password will not be echoed to the screen.* ■ Bridge (of a defender) play a higher card followed by a lower one in the same suit, as a signal to request one's partner to lead that suit. — **ech·o·er n. ech·o·ey** /'ekō-ē/ **adj. ech·o·less adj.** [ME: from OFr. or L., from Gk. *ēkhō*, rel. to *ēkhē* 'a sound.']

ech·o·car·di·o·gram /,ekō'kärdēə,gram/ ▶ **n.** Med. a test of the action of the heart using ultrasound waves to produce a visual display.

ech·o·car·di·og·ra·phy /,ekō,kärdē'ägrəfē/ ▶ **n.** Med. the use of ultrasound waves to investigate the action of the heart. — **ech·o·car·di·o·graph** /,ekō'kärdēə,graf/ **n. ech·o·car·di·o·graph·ic** /-,kärdēə'grafik/ **adj.**

ech·o cham·ber ▶ **n.** an enclosed space for producing reverberation of sound.

ech·o·en·ceph·a·lo·gram /,ekōen'sefələ,gram/ ▶ **n.** Med. a record produced by echoencephalography.

ech·o·en·ceph·a·lo·graph /,ekōen'sefələ,graf/ (abbr.: **EEG**) ▶ **n.** an instrument used to examine the skull and brain by means of reflected ultrasonic waves as part of a painless and noninvasive procedure. — **ech·o·en·ceph·a·lo·graph·ic** /-,sefələ'grafik/ **adj.**

ech·o·en·ceph·a·log·ra·phy /,ekōen,sefə'lägrəfē/ ▶ **n.** Med. the use of ultrasound waves to investigate structures within the skull.

ech·o·gram /'ekō,gram/ ▶ **n.** a recording of depth or distance under water made by an echo sounder.

ech·o·graph /'ekō,graf/ ▶ **n.** an instrument for recording echograms; an automated echo sounder.

e·cho·ic /e'kō-ik/ ▶ **adj.** of or like an echo. ■ Ling. imitating a sound; onomatopoeic. — **e·cho·i·cal·ly adv.**

ech·o·la·li·a /,ekō'lālēə/ ▶ **n.** Psychiatry meaningless repetition of another person's spoken words as a symptom of psychiatric disorder. ■ repetition of speech by a child learning to talk. [19th C.: mod. L., from Gk. *ēkhō* 'echo' + *lalia* 'speech.']

ech·o·lo·ca·tion /,ekōlō'kāshən/ ▶ **n.** the location of objects by reflected sound, in particular that used by animals such as dolphins and bats.

ech·o sound·er ▶ **n.** a device for determining the depth of the seabed or detecting objects in water by measuring the time taken for echoes to return to the listener. — **ech·o sound·ing** (also **ech·o-sound·ing**) **n.**

ech·o·vi·rus /'ekō,vīrəs/ (also **ECHO vi·rus**) ▶ **n.** Med. any of a group of enteroviruses that can cause a range of diseases, including respiratory infections and a mild form of meningitis. [1950s: from *echo* (acronym from *enteric cytopathogenic human orphan*, because the virus was not orig. assignable to any known disease).]

echt /ekt/ ▶ **adj.** authentic and typical. ▶ **adv.** [as submodifier] authentically and typically: *echt-American writers like Hawthorne, Cooper, and Mark Twain.* [20th C.: Ger., literally 'genuine, real.']

ECL ▶ **abbr.** Computer Science emitter-coupled logic.

é·clair /ā'kler; i'kler/ (also **e·clair**) ▶ **n.** a small, log-shaped pastry filled with cream, topped with chocolate icing. [19th C.: from Fr., literally 'lightning.']

é·clair·cisse·ment /ā,klersēs'män/ ▶ **n.** archaic literary an enlightening explanation of something, typically someone's conduct, that has been hitherto inexplicable. [Fr., from *éclaircir* 'clear up,' from *é* + *clair* (see CLEAR).]

ec·lamp·si·a /i'klam(p)sēə/ ▶ **n.** Med. a condition in which one or more convulsions occur in a pregnant woman suffering from high blood pressure, often followed by coma and posing a threat to the health of mother and baby. See also PREECLAMPSIA. — **ec·lamp·tic** /i'klam(p)tik/ **adj.** [19th C.: mod. L., from Fr. *éclampsie*, from Gk. *eklampsis* 'sudden development,' from *eklampein* 'shine out.']

é·clat /ā'klä/ ▶ **n.** brilliant display or effect. ■ social distinction or conspicuous success: *such action bestows éclat upon a warrior.* [17th C.: from Fr., from *éclater* 'burst out.']

ec·lec·tic /i'klektik/ ▶ **adj. 1** deriving ideas, style, or taste from a broad and diverse range of sources. **2** (**Eclectic**) Philos. of, denoting, or belonging to a class of ancient philosophers who did not belong to or found any recognized school of thought but selected such doctrines as they wished from various schools. ▶ **n.** a person who derives ideas, style, or taste from a broad and diverse range of sources. — **ec·lec·ti·cal·ly** adv. **ec·lec·ti·cism** /iˈklektiˌsizəm/ **n.** [17th C.: from Gk. *eklektikos*, from *eklegein* 'pick out,' from *ek* 'out' + *legein* 'choose.']

e·clipse /iˈklips/ ▶ **n.** an obscuring of the light from one celestial body by the passage of another between it and the observer or between it and its source of illumination: *an eclipse of the sun.* ■ fig. a loss of significance, power, or prominence in relation to another person or thing. ■ Ornithol. a phase during which the distinctive markings of a bird are obscured by molting of the breeding plumage: [as adj.] *eclipse plumage.* ▶ **v.** [trans.] (often **be eclipsed**) (of a celestial body) obscure the light from or to (another celestial body). ■ literary obscure or block out (light): *a sea of blue sky violently eclipsed by showers.* ■ deprive (someone or something) of significance, power, or prominence.
– PHRASES **in eclipse 1** losing or having lost significance, power, or prominence: *his political power was in eclipse.* **2** Ornithol. in its eclipse plumage. [ME: from OFr. *e(s)clipse* (n.), *eclipser* (v.), via L. from Gk. *ekleipsis*, from *ekleipein* 'fail to appear, be eclipsed,' from *ek* 'out' + *leipein* 'to leave.']

e·clips·ing bi·na·ry ▶ **n.** Astron. a binary star whose brightness varies periodically as the two components pass one in front of the other.

e·clip·tic /iˈkliptik/ ▶ **n.** Astron. a great circle on the celestial sphere representing the sun's apparent path during the year, so called because lunar and solar eclipses can occur only when the moon crosses it. ▶ **adj.** of an eclipse or the ecliptic. [ME: via L. from Gk. *ekleiptikos*, from *ekleipein* 'fail to appear' (see ECLIPSE).]

ec·lo·gite /ˈekləˌjīt/ ▶ **n.** Geol. a metamorphic rock containing granular minerals, garnet and pyroxene. [19th C.: from Fr., from Gk. *eklogē* 'selection.']

ec·logue /ˈeklôg; -läg/ ▶ **n.** a short poem, esp. a pastoral dialogue. [ME: via L. from Gk. *eklogē* 'selection,' from *eklegein* 'pick out.']

e·close /iˈklōz/ ▶ **v.** [intrans.] Entomol. emerge as an adult from the pupa or as a larva from the egg. — **e·clo·sion** /iˈklōzʜən/ **n.** [19th C. (as *eclosion*): from Fr. *éclore* 'to hatch,' based on L. *ex-* 'out' + *claudere* 'to close.']

ECM ▶ **abbr.** electronic countermeasures.

eco- ▶ **comb. form** representing ECOLOGY.

ec·o·cide /ˈekōˌsīd; ˈēkō-/ ▶ **n.** destruction of the natural environment, esp. when willfully done.

ec·o·fem·i·nism /ˌekōˈfeməˌnizəm; ˌēkō-/ ▶ **n.** a philosophical and political movement that combines ecological concerns with feminist ones. — **ec·o·fem·i·nist** n.

ec·o·freak /ˈekōˌfrēk; ˈēkō-/ ▶ **n.** informal a person who is unusually enthusiastic about protecting and preserving the environment.

ec·o-friend·ly ▶ **adj.** not harmful to the environment.

ecol. ▶ **abbr.** ■ ecological. ■ ecology.

ec·o·la·bel·ing ▶ **n.** the practice of marking products with a distinctive label to show that their manufacture conforms to recognized environmental standards. — **ec·o·la·bel** n.

E. co·li /ē ˈkōlī/ ▶ **n.** a bacterium (*Escherichia coli*) commonly found in the intestines of humans and other animals, where it usually causes no harm. Some strains can cause severe food poisoning.

e·col·o·gy /iˈkäləjē/ ▶ **n. 1** the branch of biology that deals with the relations of organisms to one another and to their physical surroundings. ■ (also **human ecology**) the study of the interaction of people with their environment. **2** (also **Ecology**) the political movement that seeks to protect the environment, esp. from pollution. — **ec·o·log·i·cal** /ˌekəˈläjikəl; ˌēkə-/ **adj.** **ec·o·log·i·cal·ly** /ˌekəˈläjik(ə)lē; ˌēkə-/ **adv.** **e·col·o·gist** /-jist/ **n.** [19th C. (orig. as *oecology*): from Gk. *oikos* 'house' + -LOGY.]

e·con·o·met·rics /iˌkänəˈmetriks/ ▶ **plural n.** [treated as sing.] the branch of economics concerned with the use of mathematical methods (esp. statistics) in describing economic systems. — **e·con·o·met·ric** adj. **e·con·o·met·ri·cal** /iˌkänəˈmetrikəl/ **adj.** **e·con·o·me·tri·cian** /iˌkänəməˈtrisʜən/ **n.** **e·con·o·met·rist** /-ˈmetrist/ **n.** [1930s: from ECONOMY.]

ec·o·nom·ic /ˌekəˈnämik; ˌēkə-/ ▶ **adj.** of or relating to economics or the economy. ■ justified in terms of profitability. ■ requiring fewer resources or costing less money. ■ (of a subject) considered in relation to trade, industry, and the creation of wealth: *economic history.*

ec·o·nom·i·cal /ˌekəˈnämikəl; ˌēkə-/ ▶ **adj.** giving good value or service in relation to the amount of money, time, or effort spent. ■ (of a person or lifestyle) careful not to waste money or resources. ■ using no more of something than is necessary: *this chassis is economical in metal.*
– PHRASES **economical with the truth** used euphemistically to describe a person or statement that lies or deliberately withholds information.

ec·o·nom·i·cal·ly /ˌekəˈnämik(ə)lē; ˌēkə-/ ▶ **adv.** in a way that relates to economics or finance. ■ in a way that involves careful use of money or resources: *the new building was erected economically.* ■ in a way that uses no more of something than is necessary.

ec·o·nom·ic good ▶ **n.** Econ. a product or service that can command a price when sold.

ec·o·nom·ic rent ▶ **n.** Econ. the extra amount earned by a resource (e.g., land, capital, or labor) by virtue of its present use.

ec·o·nom·ics /ˌekəˈnämiks; ˌēkə-/ ▶ **plural n.** [often treated as sing.] the branch of knowledge concerned with the production, consumption, and transfer of wealth. ■ the condition of a region or group as regards material prosperity.

e·con·o·mism /iˈkänəˌmizəm/ ▶ **n.** belief in the primacy of economic causes or factors.

e·con·o·mist /iˈkänəmist/ ▶ **n.** an expert in economics.

e·con·o·mize /iˈkänəˌmīz/ ▶ **v.** [intrans.] spend less; reduce one's expenses. — **e·con·o·mi·za·tion** /iˌkänəməˈzāsʜən/ **n.** **e·con·o·miz·er** **n.**

e·con·o·my /iˈkänəmē/ ▶ **n.** (pl. **-mies**) **1** the wealth and resources of a country or region, esp. in terms of the production and consumption of goods and services. ■ a particular system or stage of an economy. **2** careful management of available resources: *even heat distribution and fuel economy.* ■ sparing or careful use of something: *economy of words.* ■ (usu. **economies**) a financial saving. ■ (also **economy class**) the cheapest class of air or rail travel. ▶ **adj.** [attrib.] (of a product) offering the best value for the money: [in comb.] *an economy pack.* ■ designed to be economical to use: *an economy car.*
– PHRASES **economy of scale** a proportionate saving in costs gained by an increased level of production. **economy of scope** a proportionate saving gained by producing two or more distinct goods, when the cost is less than that of producing each separately. [15th C.: from Fr. *économie*, or via L. from Gk. *oikonomia* 'household management,' based on *oikos* 'house' + *nemein* 'manage.']

e·con·o·my-size (also **e·con·o·my-sized**) ▶ **adj.** offering a large quantity for a proportionally lower cost.

ec·o·phys·i·ol·o·gy /ˌekōˌfizēˈäləjē; ˌēkō-/ ▶ **n.** Biol. the study of the interrelationship between the normal physical function of an organism and its environment.

é·cor·ché /ˌākôrˈsʜā/ ▶ **n.** (pl.**-chés** pronunc. same) a painting or sculpture of a human figure with the skin removed to display the musculature. [19th C.: Fr., literally 'flayed.']

ec·o·sphere /ˈekōˌsfi(ə)r; ˈēkō-/ ▶ **n.** the biosphere of the earth or another planet, esp. when the interaction between living and nonliving components is emphasized. ■ Astron. the region of space around a sun or star where conditions are such that planets are theoretically capable of sustaining life.

ec·o·sys·tem /ˈekōˌsistəm; ˈēkō-/ ▶ **n.** Ecol. a biological community of interacting organisms and their physical environment.

ec·o·tage /ˈekəˌtäzʜ; ēkə-/ ▶ **n.** sabotage carried out for ecological reasons. [1970s: blend of *ecological* (see ECOLOGY) and SABOTAGE.]

ec·o·ter·ror·ism /ˌekōˈterəˌrizəm; ˈekō-/ (also **ec·o-ter·ror·ism**) ▶ **n.** violence for environmentalist ends. ■ environmental damage for political ends. — **e·co·ter·ror·ist** **n.**

ec·o·tone /ˈekəˌtōn; ˈēkəˌtōn/ ▶ **n.** Ecol. a region of transition between two biological communities. — **ec·o·ton·al** **adj.**

ec·o·to·pi·a /ˌekəˈtōpēə; ˌēkə-/ ▶ **n.** an ecologically ideal region or form of society, generally viewed as imaginary. — **ec·o·to·pi·an** **adj.** [1975: from ECO-, on the pattern of *Utopia*.]

ec·o·tour·ism /ˌekōˈto͝orizəm; ˌēkō-/ ▶ **n.** tourism in exotic, often threatened, natural environments, esp. to support conservation efforts and observe wildlife. — **ec·o·tour** **n. & v.** **ec·o·tour·ist** **n.**

ec·o·tox·i·col·o·gy /ˌekōˌtäksiˈkäləjē; ˌēkō-/ ▶ **n.** the branch of science dealing with the nature, effects, and interactions of substances harmful to the environment. — **ec·o·tox·i·co·log·i·cal** /-kəˈläjikəl/ **adj.** **ec·o·tox·i·col·o·gist** **n.**

ec·o·type /ˈekōˌtīp; ˈēkō-/ ▶ **n.** a distinct form or race of a plant or animal species occupying a particular habitat.

ec·ru /ˈekro͞o/ ▶ **n.** the yellowish-brown color of unbleached linen. [19th C.: from Fr. *écru* 'unbleached.']

ec·sta·sy /ˈekstəsē/ ▶ **n.** (pl. **-sies**) **1** an overwhelming feeling of great happiness or joyful excitement. **2** esp. archaic an emotional or religious frenzy or trancelike state, originally one involving an experience of mystic self-transcendence. **3** (abbr.: **MDMA**) an illegal amphetamine-based synthetic drug with euphoric and hallucinatory effects, originally promoted as an adjunct to psychotherapy. Also called **MDMA**. [ME (sense 2): from OFr. *extasie*, via late L. from Gk. *ekstasis* 'standing outside oneself,' based on *ek-* 'out' + *histanai* 'to place.']

ec·stat·ic /ekˈstatik/ ▶ **adj. 1** feeling or expressing overwhelming happiness or joyful excitement. **2** involving an experience of mystic self-transcendence: *an ecstatic vision of God.* ▶ **n.** a person subject to mystical experiences. — **ec·stat·i·cal·ly** **adv.**

ECT ▶ **abbr.** electroconvulsive therapy.

ecto- ▶ **comb. form** outer; external; on the outside (used commonly in scientific terms): *ectoderm* | *ectoparasite.* [from Gk. *ektos* 'outside.']

ec·to·derm /ˈektəˌdərm/ ▶ **n.** Zool. Embryol. the outermost layer of cells or tissue of an embryo in early development, or the parts derived from this, which include the epidermis, nerve tissue, and nephridia. Compare with ENDODERM and MESODERM. — **ec·to·der·mal** /ˌektəˈdərməl/ **adj.** [19th C.: from ECTO- 'outside' + Gk. *derma* 'skin.']

ec·to·gen·e·sis /ˌektəˈjenəsis/ ▶ **n.** the development of embryos in artificial conditions outside the uterus. — **ec·to·gene** /ˈektəˌjēn/ **n.** **ec·to·ge·net·ic** /ˌektəjəˈnetik/ **adj.** **ec·to·ge·net·i·cal·ly** **adv.**

ec·to·morph /ˈektəˌmôrf/ ▶ **n.** Physiol. a person with a lean and delicate body build. Compare with ENDOMORPH and MESOMORPH. — **ec·to·mor·phic** /ˌektəˈmôrfik/ **adj.** **ec·to·morph·y** **n.** [1940s: *ecto-* from *ectodermal*.]

-ectomy ▶ **comb. form** denoting surgical removal of a specified part of the body: *appendectomy.* [from Gk. *ektomē* 'excision,' from *ek* 'out' + *temnein* 'to cut.']

ec·to·par·a·site /ˌektəˈparəˌsīt/ ▶ **n.** Biol. a parasite, such as a flea, that lives on the outside of its host. Compare with ENDOPARASITE. — **ec·to·**

par·a·sit·ic /-,parə'sitik/ **adj.**

ec·top·ic /ek'täpik/ ▶ **adj.** Med. in an abnormal place or position. [19th C.: from Gk. *ektopos* 'out of place.']

ec·top·ic beat ▶ **n.** another term for EXTRASYSTOLE.

ec·top·ic preg·nan·cy ▶ **n.** a pregnancy in which the fetus develops outside the uterus, typically in a Fallopian tube.

ec·to·plasm /'ektə,plazəm/ ▶ **n.** **1** Biol. the more viscous, clear outer layer of the cytoplasm in ameboid cells. Compare with ENDOPLASM. **2** a viscous substance supposed to exude from the body of a medium during a spiritualistic trance and to form the material for the manifestation of spirits. — **ec·to·plas·mic** /,ektə'plazmik/ **adj.**

Ec·to·proc·ta /,ektə'präktə/ Zool. another term for BRYOZOA. — **ec·to·proct** /'ektə,präkt/ **n.** [mod. L. (pl.), from Gk. *ektos* 'outside or external' + *prōktos* 'anus.']

ec·to·therm /'ektə,THərm/ ▶ **n.** Zool. an animal that is dependent on external sources of body heat. Often contrasted with ENDOTHERM. Compare with POIKILOTHERM. — **ec·to·ther·mic adj. ec·to·ther·my n.**

ECU /ā'k(y)o͞o/ (also **ecu**) ▶ **n.** (pl. same or **ecus**) the former monetary unit of the European Union, used to evaluate exchange rate. [acronym from *European currency unit.*]

Ec·ua·dor /'ekwə,dôr/ a republic in South America. *See box.* — **Ec·ua·dor·e·an** /,ekwə'dôrēən/ **adj. & n.**

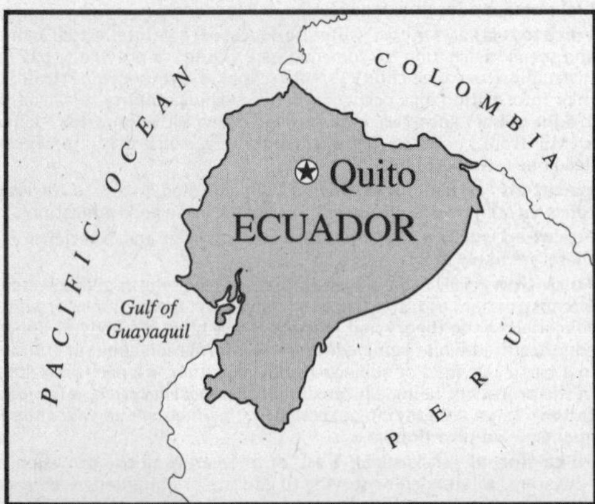

Ecuador

Official name: Republic of Ecuador
Location: northwestern South America, between Colombia and Peru, bordered on the west by the Pacific Ocean
Area: 106,900 square miles (276,800 sq km)
Population: 13,212,700
Capital: Quito
Languages: Spanish (official), Quechua
Currency: US dollar (formerly sucre)

ec·u·men·i·cal /,ekyə'menikəl/ ▶ **adj.** representing a number of different Christian churches. ■ promoting or relating to unity among the world's Christian churches: *ecumenical dialogue.* — **ec·u·men·i·cal·ly adv.** [16th C.: via late L. from Gk. *oikoumenikos*, from *oikoumenē* 'the (inhabited) earth.']

Ec·u·men·i·cal Pa·tri·arch ▶ **n.** a title of the Orthodox Patriarch of Constantinople.

ec·u·me·nism /'ekyəmə,nizəm; e'kyo͝omə-/ ▶ **n.** the principle or aim of promoting unity among the world's Christian churches.

ec·ze·ma /'egzəmə; 'eksə-; ig'zēmə/ ▶ **n.** a medical condition in which patches of skin become rough and inflamed, with itching and bleeding blisters, sometimes resulting from irritation (eczematous dermatitis) but more typically having no obvious external cause. — **ec·zem·a·tous** /ig'zemətəs; ik'sem-; ig'zē-/ **adj.** [18th C.: mod. L., from Gk. *ekzema*, from *ekzein* 'boil over, break out,' from *ek-* 'out' + *zein* 'boil.']

ED ▶ **abbr.** election district.

ed. ▶ **abbr.** ■ edited by. ■ edition. ■ editor. ■ education.

-ed[1] /d; t; id/ ▶ **suffix** forming adjectives: **1** (added to nouns) having; affected by: *talented* | *diseased.* ■ (added to nouns) characteristic of: *ragged.* **2** from phrases consisting of adjective and noun: *bad-tempered* | *three-sided.* [OE *-ede.*]

-ed[2] ▶ **suffix** forming: **1** the past tense and past participle of weak verbs: *landed* | *walked.* **2** participial adjectives: *wounded.* [OE *-ed, -ad, -od.*]

e·da·cious /i'dāSHəs/ ▶ **adj.** rare of, relating to, or given to eating. — **e·dac·i·ty** /i'dasitē/ **n.** [19th C.: from L. *edax, edac-* (from *edere* 'eat') + -IOUS.]

E·dam /'ēdəm/ ▶ **n.** a round Dutch cheese, typically pale yellow with a red wax coating. [19th C.: named after the town of *Edam* in the Netherlands.]

ed·a·ma·me /,edə'māmā/ ▶ **n.** a dish of green soybeans boiled or steamed in their pods. [Japanese, literally 'beans on a branch.']

e·daph·ic /i'dafik/ ▶ **adj.** Ecol. of, produced by, or influenced by the soil. [19th C.: coined in Ger. from Gk. *edaphos* 'floor' + -IC.]

Ed·da /'edə/ either of two 13th-century Icelandic books, the **Elder** or **Poetic Edda** (a collection of Old Norse poems on Norse legends) and the **Younger** or **Prose Edda** (a handbook to Icelandic poetry by Snorri Sturluson).

ed·do /'edō/ ▶ **n.** (pl. **-does**) a taro corm or plant (*Colocasia esculenta* var. *antiquorum*) of the arum family, esp. an edible West Indian variety. [17th C.: of West Afr. origin.]

Ed·dy /'edē/, Mary Baker (1821–1910), US religious leader. She founded the Christian Science movement.

ed·dy /'edē/ ▶ **n.** (pl. **-dies**) a movement of water, counter to a main current, causing a small whirlpool. ■ a movement of wind, fog, or smoke resembling this. ▶ **v.** (**-dies, -died**) [no obj., with adverbial of direction] (of water, air, or smoke) move in a circular way. [ME: prob. akin to OE *ed-* 'again, back.']

ed·dy cur·rent ▶ **n.** a localized electric current induced in a conductor by a varying magnetic field.

E·de /'ādə/ **1** an industrial city in eastern Netherlands; pop. 96,000. **2** an industrial town in southwestern Nigeria, northeast of Ibadan; pop. 271,000.

e·del·weiss /'ādl,wīs; -,vīs/ ▶ **n.** a European mountain plant (*Leontopodium alpinum*) of the daisy family that has woolly white bracts around its small flowers and downy gray-green leaves. [19th C.: from Ger., from *edel* 'noble' + *weiss* 'white.']

e·de·ma /i'dēmə/ (Brit. also **oe·de·ma**) ▶ **n.** a condition characterized by an excess of watery fluid collecting in the cavities or tissues of the body. Also called DROPSY. — **e·dem·a·tous** /i'dēmətəs/ **adj.** [ME: mod. L., from Gk. *oidēma*, from *oidein* 'to swell.']

E·den[1] /'ēdn/, Anthony (1897–1977), British prime minister 1955–57; full name Robert Anthony Eden, 1st Earl of Avon. His premiership was dominated by the Suez crisis of 1956.

E·den[2] (also **Garden of Eden**) the place where Adam and Eve lived in the biblical account of the Creation. ■ [as n.] (**an Eden**) a place or state of great happiness; an unspoiled paradise: *the lost Eden of childhood.* [from late L. (Vulgate), Gk. *Ēdēn* (Septuagint), and Heb. *'Ēḏen.*]

E·den Prai·rie a city in southeastern Minnesota, southwest of Minneapolis; pop. 54,901.

E·den·ta·ta /,ēden'tätə; -'tātə/ Zool. another term for XENARTHRA.

e·den·tate /ē'dentāt/ ▶ **n.** Zool. a mammal of an order (Xenarthra, or Edentata) distinguished by the lack of incisor and canine teeth. All edentates, including anteaters, sloths, and armadillos, are native to Central and South America. [19th C.: from L. *edentatus*, past part. of *edentare* 'make toothless,' from *e-* (var. of *ex-*) 'out' + *dens, dent-* 'tooth.']

e·den·tu·lous /ē'dencHələs/ ▶ **adj.** lacking teeth. [18th C.: from L. *edentulus*, from *e-* + *dens, dent-* 'tooth' + -ULOUS.]

E·der·le /'edərlē/, Gertrude Caroline (1906–2003), US swimmer. In 1926, she became the first woman to swim the English Channel.

edge /ej/ ▶ **n.** **1** the outside limit of an object, area, or surface; a place or part farthest away from the center of something: *a tree at the water's edge* | fig. *these measures are merely tinkering at the edges of a wider issue.* ■ an area next to a steep drop. ■ [in sing.] the point or state immediately before something unpleasant or momentous occurs. **2** the sharpened side of the blade of a cutting implement or weapon: *a knife with a razor-sharp edge.* ■ the line along which two surfaces of a solid meet. ■ [in sing.] a sharp, threatening, or bitter tone of voice, usually indicating the speaker's annoyance or tension: *there was an edge to her voice.* ■ [in sing.] an intense, sharp, or striking quality: *a primitive edge to the music.* ■ [in sing.] a quality or factor that gives superiority over close rivals or competitors. ▶ **v.** [trans.] **1** (often **be edged**) provide with a border or edge: *the pool is edged with paving.* **2** [no obj., with adverbial of direction] move gradually, carefully, or furtively in a particular direction: *she tried to edge away from him.* ■ [with obj. and adverbial of direction] cause to move in such a way: *Hazel edged him away from the others* | fig. *she was edged out of the organization.* ■ [trans.] informal defeat by a small margin: *Connecticut edged Yale 49–48.* **3** fig. give an intense or sharp quality to. **4** [intrans.] ski with one's weight on the edges of one's skis.

– PHRASES **on edge** tense, nervous, or irritable. **on the edge of one's seat** informal very excited and giving one's full attention to something. **set someone's teeth on edge** (esp. of an unpleasantly harsh sound) cause someone to feel intense discomfort or irritation. **take the edge off** reduce the intensity or effect of (something unpleasant or severe). — **edged adj.** [in comb.] *a black-edged handkerchief.* **edge·less adj. edg·er n.** [OE *ecg* 'sharpened side of a blade,' of Gmc. origin.]

edge cit·y ▶ **n.** a relatively large urban area situated on the outskirts of a city, typically along major roads.

edge tool ▶ **n.** any tool with a sharp cutting edge.

edge·wise /'ej,wīz/ (also **edge·ways**) ▶ **adv. & adj.** with the edge uppermost or toward the viewer: [as adv.] *could be inserted edgewise between the teeth* | [as adj.] *an edgewise view of our own galaxy.*

– PHRASES **get a word in edgewise** [usu. with negative] contribute to a conversation with difficulty because the other speaker talks almost without pause.

edg·ing /'ejiNG/ ▶ n. a thing forming an edge or border. ■ the process of providing something with an edge or border.

edg·y /'ejē/ ▶ adj. (**edg·i·er, edg·i·est**) tense, nervous, or irritable: *he became edgy and defensive.* ■ (of a musical performance or a piece of writing) having an intense or sharp quality. — **edg·i·ly** /'ejəlē/ adv. **edg·i·ness** n.

edh ▶ n. var. of ETH.

EDI ▶ abbr. electronic data interchange (a standard for exchanging information between computer systems).

ed·i·ble /'edəbəl/ ▶ adj. fit to be eaten (often used to contrast with unpalatable or poisonous examples). ▶ n. (**edibles**) items of food. — **ed·i·bil·i·ty** /,edə'bilitē/ n. [16th C.: from late L. *edibilis*, from L. *edere* 'eat.']

e·dict /'ēdikt/ ▶ n. an official order or proclamation. — **e·dic·tal** /i'diktl/ adj. [ME: from L. *edictum* 'something proclaimed,' neut. past part. of *edicere*, from *e-* (var. of *ex-*) 'out' + *dicere* 'say, tell.']

ed·i·fi·ca·tion /,edəfi'kāSHən/ ▶ n. formal the instruction or improvement of a person morally or intellectually: *the idea that art's main purpose is edification.*

ed·i·fice /'edəfis/ ▶ n. formal a building, esp. a large, imposing one. ■ fig. a complex system of beliefs. [ME: via OFr. from L. *aedificium*, from *aedis* 'dwelling' + *facere* 'make.']

ed·i·fy /'edə,fī/ ▶ v. (**-fies, -fied**) [trans.] formal instruct or improve (someone) morally or intellectually. [ME: from OFr. *edifier*, from L. *aedificare* 'build,' from *aedis* 'dwelling' + *facere* 'make' (cf. EDIFICE).]

ed·i·fy·ing /'edə,fī-iNG/ ▶ adj. providing moral or intellectual instruction: *edifying literature.* — **ed·i·fy·ing·ly** adv.

E·di·na /ē'dīnə/ a city in southeastern Minnesota, southwest of Minneapolis; pop. 47,425.

Ed·in·burgh /'edn,bərə/ the capital of Scotland, on the southern shore of the Firth of Forth; pop. 421,200. The city grew up around an 11th-century castle built by Malcolm III.

Ed·in·burgh, Duke of see PHILIP, PRINCE.

Ed·i·son[1] /'edəsən/ a township in eastern New Jersey; pop. 97,687. It is home to Thomas Edison's research laboratory in Menlo Park.

Ed·i·son[2], Thomas Alva (1847–1931), US inventor. His inventions include automatic telegraph systems, the carbon microphone for telephones, the phonograph, and the carbon filament lamp.

ed·it /'edit/ ▶ v. (**ed·it·ed, ed·it·ing**) [trans.] (often **be edited**) prepare (written material) for publication by correcting, condensing, or otherwise modifying it. ■ choose material for (a movie or a radio or television program) and arrange it to form a coherent whole: *the footage was edited into broadcast form* | [as adj.] (**edited**) *an edited version.* ■ be editor of (a newspaper or magazine). ■ (**edit something out**) remove unnecessary or inappropriate words, sounds, or scenes from a text, movie, or program. ▶ n. a change or correction made as a result of editing. [18th C.: partly a back-form. from EDITOR, reinforced by Fr. *éditer* 'to edit' (from *édition* 'edition').]

edit. ▶ abbr. ■ edited. ■ edition. ■ editor.

e·di·tion /i'diSHən/ ▶ n. a particular form or version of a published text: *a paperback edition.* ■ a particular version of a text that has been created or revised from a substantially new setting of type: *a first edition.* ■ the total number of copies of a book, newspaper, or other published material issued at one time. ■ a particular version or instance of a regular program or broadcast. ■ [in sing.] fig. a person or thing that is compared to another as a copy to an original. [ME: from Fr. *édition*, from L. *editio(n-)*, from *edere* 'put out,' from *e-* + *dare* 'give.']

e·di·ti·o prin·ceps /e'ditē,ō 'priNGkeps; i'diSHē,ō 'prinseps/ ▶ n. (pl. **e·di·ti·o·nes prin·ci·pes** /e,ditē'ōnes 'priNGkə,pes; i,diSHē'ōnēz 'prinsə,pēz/) the first printed edition of a book. [L., from *editio(n-)* 'edition' and *princeps* 'chief, leader' (from *primus* 'first').]

ed·i·tor /'editər/ ▶ n. a person who is in charge of and determines the final content of a text, particularly a newspaper or magazine. ■ a person who works for a publisher, commissioning or preparing material for publication. ■ a computer program enabling the user to alter or rearrange text. — **ed·i·tor·ship** n.

ed·i·to·ri·al /,edi'tôrēəl/ ▶ adj. **1** of or relating to the acquiring or preparing of material for publication. ■ of or relating to the part of a newspaper or magazine that contains news, information, or comment as opposed to advertising. **2** of or relating to a section in a newspaper, often written by the editor, that expresses an opinion. ▶ n. a newspaper article written by or on behalf of an editor that gives an opinion on a topical issue. ■ the parts of a newspaper, etc., that are not advertising. — **ed·i·to·ri·al·ist** n. **ed·i·to·ri·al·ly** adv.

ed·i·to·ri·al·ize /,edi'tôrēə,līz/ ▶ v. [intrans.] (of a newspaper, editor, or broadcaster) make comments or express opinions rather than just report the news. ■ offer one's opinion, as if in an editorial.

ed·it suite ▶ n. a room containing equipment for electronically editing video-recorded material.

Ed.M. ▶ abbr. master of education. [from L. *Educationis Magister.*]

Ed·mond /'edmənd/ a city in central Oklahoma, an oil center north of Oklahoma City; pop. 68,315.

Ed·mon·ton /'edməntən/ the capital of the province of Alberta, in western Canada; pop. 703,070.

Ed·mund /'edmənd/ the name of two kings of England: ■ Edmund I (921–946), reigned 939–946. He succeeded Athelstan. ■ Edmund II (*c.*980–1016), reigned 1016; known as **Edmund Ironside**; son of Ethelred the Unready.

Ed·mund, St. (*c.*1175–1240), archbishop of Canterbury 1234–40; born *Edmund Rich.*

Ed·mund Cam·pi·on, St. see CAMPION[2].

Ed·mund the Mar·tyr, St. (*c.*841–870), king of East Anglia 855–870. After his defeat by the Danes in 870, tradition holds that he was captured and shot with arrows for refusing to reject the Christian faith.

E·do[1] /'edō/ former name of TOKYO.

E·do[2] ▶ n. (pl. same or **E·dos**) **1** a member of a people inhabiting the district of Benin in Nigeria. **2** the Benue-Congo language of this people. ▶ adj. of or relating to this people or their language. [the name of Benin City in Edo.]

E·dom·ite /'ēdə,mīt/ ▶ adj. of or relating to Edom, an ancient region south of the Dead Sea, or its people. ▶ n. a member of an ancient people living in Edom in biblical times, traditionally descended from Esau.

EDP ▶ abbr. electronic data processing.

EDT ▶ abbr. Eastern Daylight Time (see EASTERN TIME).

EDTA Chem. ▶ abbr. ethylenediamine tetra-acetic acid, $(CH_2COOH)_2NCH_2CH_2N(CH_2COOH)_2$, a crystalline acid with a strong tendency to form chelates with metal ions.

educ. ▶ abbr. ■ educated. ■ education. ■ educational.

ed·u·cate /'ejə,kāt/ ▶ v. [trans.] (often **be educated**) give intellectual, moral, and social instruction to (someone, esp. a child). ■ provide or pay for instruction for (one's child), esp. at a school. ■ give (someone) training in or information on a particular field. — **ed·u·ca·bil·i·ty** /,ejəkə'bilitē/ n. **ed·u·ca·ble** /-kəbəl/ adj. **ed·u·ca·tive** /-,kātiv/ adj. **ed·u·ca·tor** /-,kātər/ n. [ME: from L. *educat-* 'led out,' from the v. *educare*, rel. to *educere* 'lead out' (see EDUCE).]

ed·u·cat·ed /'ejə,kātid/ ▶ adj. having been educated: [in comb.] *a Harvard-educated lawyer.* ■ resulting from or having had a good education.

ed·u·cat·ed guess ▶ n. a guess based on knowledge and experience and therefore likely to be correct.

ed·u·ca·tion /,ejə'kāSHən/ ▶ n. the process of receiving or giving systematic instruction, esp. at a school or university: *a new system of public education.* ■ the theory and practice of teaching. ■ a body of knowledge acquired while being educated. ■ information about or training in a particular field or subject: *health education.* ■ a particular stage in the process of being educated: *a high-school education.* ■ (**an education**) fig. an enlightening experience: *the shops are an education in quality.* — **ed·u·ca·tion·ist** n.

ed·u·ca·tion·al /,ejə'kāSHənl/ ▶ adj. of or relating to the provision of education. ■ intended or serving to educate or enlighten. — **ed·u·ca·tion·al·ist** n.

ed·u·ca·tion·al psy·chol·o·gy ▶ n. a branch of psychology that studies children in an educational setting and is concerned with teaching and learning methods, cognitive development, and aptitude assessment.

e·duce /i'd(y)o͞os/ ▶ v. [trans.] formal bring out or develop (something latent or potential). ■ infer (something) from data. — **e·duc·i·ble** /i'd(y)o͞osəbəl/ adj. **e·duc·tion** /i'dəkSHən/ n. [ME: from L. *educere* 'lead out,' from *e-* + *ducere* 'to lead.']

e·dul·co·rate /i'dəlkə,rāt/ ▶ v. [trans.] rare make (something) more acceptable or palatable. — **e·dul·co·ra·tion** /i,dəlkə'rāSHən/ n. [17th C.: from med. L. *edulcorat-* 'sweetened,' from the v. *edulcorare*, from L. *e-* (var. of *ex-*) 'out' + *dulcor* 'sweetness.']

ed·u·tain·ment /,ejə'tānmənt/ ▶ n. entertainment, esp. computer games, with an educational aspect. [1980s: blend of EDUCATION and ENTERTAINMENT.]

Edw. ▶ abbr. Edward.

Ed·ward /'edwərd/ the name of six kings of England and also one of Great Britain and Ireland and one of the United Kingdom: ■ Edward I (1239–1307), reigned 1272–1307; son of Henry III. His campaign against Prince Llewelyn ended with the annexation of Wales in 1284. ■ Edward II (1284–1327), reigned 1307–27; son of Edward I. He was deposed in favor of his son and murdered. ■ Edward III (1312–77), reigned 1327–77; son of Edward II. He started the Hundred Years War. ■ Edward IV (1442–83), reigned 1461–83; son of Richard, Duke of York. He became king after defeating the Lancastrian Henry VI. ■ Edward V (1470–*c.*1483), reigned 1483 but not crowned; son of Edward IV. Edward and his brother Richard were probably murdered. ■ Edward VI (1537–53), reigned 1547–53; son of Henry VIII. ■ Edward VII (1841–1910), reigned 1901–10; son of Queen Victoria. ■ Edward VIII (1894–1972), reigned 1936 but not crowned; son of George V. Edward abdicated the throne to marry US divorcée, Wallis Simpson.

Ed·ward, Lake a lake on the border between Uganda and the Democratic Republic of the Congo (formerly Zaire). It is linked to Lake Albert by the Semliki River.

Ed·ward, Prince of Wales see BLACK PRINCE.

Ed·ward·i·an /ed'wôrdēən; -'wär-/ ▶ adj. of, relating to, or characteristic of the reign of King Edward VII. ▶ n. a person who lived during this period.

Ed·ward·i·an·a /ed,wôrdē'anə; -,wär-/ ▶ plural n. articles, esp. collectors' items, from the Edwardian era.

Ed·ward the Con·fes·sor, St. (*c.*1003–66), king of England 1042–66; son of Ethelred the Unready. He founded Westminster Abbey, where he is buried.

Ed·ward the Mar·tyr, St. (*c.*963–978), king of England 975–978; son of Edgar. He was faced with a challenge for the throne by supporters of his half-brother, Ethelred, who eventually had him murdered.

EE ▶ abbr. ■ electrical engineer. ■ electrical engineering.

-ee ▶ suffix forming nouns: **1** denoting the person affected directly or indirectly by the action of the formative verb: *employee* | *lessee.* **2** denoting a person described as or concerned with: *absentee* | *patentee.* **3** denoting an object of relatively smaller size: *bootee.* [from Anglo-Norman French *-é*, from L. *-atus* (past participial ending). Some forms are anglicized mod. Fr. nouns (e.g., *refugee* from *réfugié*).]

EEC ▶ abbr. ■ European Economic Community. ■ echoencephalograph.

EEG ▶ abbr. ■ electroencephalogram. ■ electroencephalograph. ■ electroencephalography.

eek /ēk/ ▶ exclam. informal used as an expression of alarm, horror, or surprise.

eel /ēl/ ▶ n. a snakelike fish (order Anguilliformes, esp. the family Anguillidae) with a slender elongated body and poorly developed fins, proverbial for its slipperiness. ■ used in names of unrelated fishes that resemble the true eels, e.g., **electric eel, moray eel.** — **eel·like** adj. **eel·y** adj. [OE *ǣl*, of Gmc. origin; rel. to Du. *aal* and Ger. *Aal.*]

Ee·lam /'ēləm; 'ē,lam/ the proposed homeland of the Tamil people of Sri Lanka, for which the Tamil Tigers separatist group has been fighting since the 1980s.

eel·grass /'ēl,gras/ ▶ n. **1** a marine plant (*Zostera marina*, family Zosteraceae) with long ribbonlike leaves that grows in coastal waters and brackish inlets. **2** another term for TAPE GRASS.

eel·pout /'ēl,pout/ ▶ n. a fish (family Zoarcidae) of cool or cold seas, having a broad head with thick lips and an elongated body with the dorsal and anal fins continuous with the tail.

eel·worm /'ēl,wərm/ ▶ n. a nematode, esp. a small soil nematode that can be a serious plant and crop pest.

e'en /ēn/ literary ▶ contr. EVEN[1].

-een ▶ suffix Irish forming diminutive nouns like *colleen.* [from the Irish dimin. suffix *-ín.*]

een·sy /'ēn(t)sē/ (also **een·sy-ween·sy**) ▶ adj. informal extremely small; tiny.

EEO ▶ abbr. equal employment opportunity.

e'er /e(ə)r/ literary ▶ contr. ever.

-eer ▶ suffix **1** (forming nouns) denoting a person concerned with or engaged in an activity: *auctioneer* | *puppeteer.* **2** (forming verbs) denoting concern or involvement with an activity: *electioneer* | *profiteer.* [from Fr. *-ier*, from L. *-arius*; verbs (sense 2) are often back-formations (e.g., *electioneer* from *electioneering*).]

ee·rie /'i(ə)rē/ ▶ adj. (**ee·ri·er, ee·ri·est**) strange and frightening: *an eerie green glow in the sky.* — **ee·ri·ly** adv. [as submodifier] *it was eerily quiet.* **ee·ri·ness** n. [ME: prob. from OE *earg* 'cowardly,' of Gmc. origin; rel. to Ger. *arg.*]

ef- ▶ prefix var. of EX-[1] assimilated before *f* (as in *efface, effloresce*).

eff. ▶ abbr. efficiency.

ef·fa·ble /'efəbəl/ ▶ adj. rare describable in words. [17th C.: from L. *effabilis*, from *effari* 'utter.']

ef·face /i'fās/ ▶ v. [trans.] erase (a mark) from a surface: *words effaced by frost and rain* | fig. *his anger was effaced when he stepped into the open air.* ■ (**efface oneself**) fig. make oneself appear insignificant or inconspicuous. — **ef·face·ment** n. [15th C.: from Fr. *effacer*, from *e-* (from L. *ex-* 'away from') + *face* 'face.']

ef·fect /i'fekt/ ▶ n. **1** a change that is a result or consequence of an action or other cause. ■ used to refer to the state of being or becoming operative: ***putting strategies into effect*** | ***the ban is to take effect in six months.*** ■ the extent to which something succeeds or is operative. ■ [with adj.] Physics a physical phenomenon, typically named after its discoverer: *the Doppler effect.* ■ an impression produced in the mind of a person. **2** (**effects**) the lighting, sound, or scenery used in a play, movie, or broadcast. **3** (**effects**) personal belongings. ▶ v. [trans.] (often **be effected**) cause (something) to happen; bring about.
– PHRASES **for effect** in order to impress people. **in effect** in operation; in force. ■ used to convey that something is the case in practice even if it is not formally acknowledged to be so. **to the effect that** used to refer to the general sense of something written or spoken. **to that effect** having that result, purpose, or meaning: *she thought it a foolish rule and put a notice to that effect in a newspaper.* [ME: from OFr., or from L. *effectus*, from *efficere* 'accomplish,' from *ex-* 'out, thoroughly' + *facere* 'do, make.']

ef·fec·tive /i'fektiv/ ▶ adj. **1** successful in producing a desired or intended result. ■ (esp. of a law or policy) operative. **2** [attrib.] fulfilling a specified function in fact, though not formally acknowledged as such. ■ assessed according to actual rather than face value. ■ impressive; striking: *an effective finale.* ▶ n. a soldier fit and available for service. — **ef·fec·tive·ness** n. **ef·fec·tiv·i·ty** /,efek'tivitē; ,ēfek-/ n.

ef·fec·tive de·mand ▶ n. Econ. the level of demand that represents a real intention to purchase by people with the means to pay.

ef·fec·tive·ly /i'fektəvlē/ ▶ adv. in such a manner as to achieve a desired result: *resources used effectively.* ■ [sentence adverb] actually but not officially or explicitly: *they were effectively controlled by the people.* ■ [sentence adverb] the real fact or implication is that; in practice: *effectively, companies will be able to avoid regulations.*

ef·fec·tive tem·per·a·ture ▶ n. Physics the temperature of an object calculated from the radiation it emits, assuming black-body behavior.

ef·fec·tor /i'fektər/ ▶ n. Biol. an organ or cell that acts in response to a stimulus: [as adj.] *effector cells.*

ef·fec·tu·al /i'fekCHōōəl/ ▶ adj. (typically of something inanimate or abstract) successful in producing a desired or intended result; effective. — **ef·fec·tu·al·i·ty** /i,fekCHōō'alitē/ n. **ef·fec·tu·al·ly** adv. **ef·fec·tu·al·ness** n. [ME: from med. L. *effectualis*, from L. *effectus* (see EFFECT).]

ef·fec·tu·ate /i'fekCHōō,āt/ ▶ v. [trans.] formal put into force or operation: *effectuate a transfer of power.* — **ef·fec·tu·a·tion** /i,fekCHōō'āSHən/ n.

ef·fem·i·nate /i'femənit/ ▶ adj. derog. (of a man) having or showing characteristics regarded as typical of a woman; unmanly. — **ef·fem·i·na·cy** /i'femənəsē/ n. **ef·fem·i·nate·ly** adv. [ME: from L. *effeminatus*, past part. of *effeminare* 'make fem.,' from *ex-* + *femina* 'woman.']

ef·fen·di /i'fendē/ ▶ n. (pl. **-dis** /-dēz/) a man of high education or social standing in an eastern Mediterranean or Arab country. ■ hist. a title of respect or courtesy in Turkey. [17th C.: from Turk. *efendi*, from mod. Greek *aphentēs*, from Gk. *authentēs* 'lord, master.']

ef·fer·ent /'efərənt/ ▶ adj. Physiol. conducted or conducting outward or away from something (for nerves, the central nervous system; for blood vessels, the organ supplied). The opposite of AFFERENT. [19th C.: from L. *efferent-* 'carrying out,' from the v. *efferre*, from *ex-* 'out' + *ferre* 'carry.']

ef·fer·vesce /,efər'ves/ ▶ v. [intrans.] give off bubbles. ■ fig. (of a person) be vivacious and enthusiastic. [18th C.: from L. *effervescere*, from *ex-* 'out, up' + *fervescere* 'begin to boil' (from *fervere* 'be hot, boil').]

ef·fer·ves·cent /,efər'vesənt/ ▶ adj. (of a liquid) giving off bubbles; fizzy. ■ fig. (of a person or their behavior) vivacious and enthusiastic. — **ef·fer·ves·cence** n.

ef·fete /i'fēt/ ▶ adj. (of a person) affected, overrefined, and ineffectual: *effete trendies from art college.* ■ no longer capable of effective action. — **ef·fete·ness** n. [17th C.: from L. *effetus* 'worn out by bearing young,' from *ex-* 'out' + *fetus* 'breeding.']

ef·fi·ca·cious /,efi'kāSHəs/ ▶ adj. formal successful in producing a desired or intended result; effective. — **ef·fi·ca·cious·ly** adv. **ef·fi·ca·cious·ness** n. [16th C.: from L. *efficax, efficac-* (from *efficere* 'accomplish': see EFFECT) + -IOUS.]

ef·fi·ca·cy /'efikəsē/ ▶ n. the ability to produce a desired or intended result.

ef·fi·cien·cy /i'fiSHənsē/ ▶ n. (pl. **-cies**) the state or quality of being efficient: *greater energy efficiency.* ■ an action designed to achieve this. ■ tech. the ratio of the useful work performed by a machine or in a process to the total energy expended or heat taken in. ■ short for EFFICIENCY APARTMENT.

ef·fi·cien·cy a·part·ment (also **ef·fi·cien·cy**) ▶ n. an apartment in which one room typically contains the kitchen and living quarters, with a separate bathroom.

ef·fi·cient /i'fiSHənt/ ▶ adj. (esp. of a system or machine) achieving maximum productivity with minimum wasted effort or expense. ■ (of a person) working in a well-organized and competent way. ■ [in comb.] preventing the wasteful use of a particular resource: *energy-efficient.* — **ef·fi·cient·ly** adv. [ME: from L. *efficient-* 'accomplishing,' from the v. *efficere* (see EFFECT).]

ef·fi·cient cause ▶ n. Philos. an agent that brings a thing into being or initiates a change.

ef·fi·gy /'efijē/ ▶ n. (pl. **-gies**) a sculpture or model of a person: *coins bearing the effigy of Maria Theresa.* ■ a rough model of a particular person, damaged or destroyed as a protest or expression of anger. [16th C.: from L. *effigies*, from *effingere* 'to fashion (artistically),' from *ex-* 'out' + *fingere* 'to shape.']

ef·fing /'efiNG/ ▶ adj. informal a euphemistic substitute for the word FUCKING.

ef·fleu·rage /,eflə'räZH/ ▶ n. a form of massage using a circular stroking with the palm of the hand. ▶ v. [trans.] massage with such a circular stroking movement. [19th C.: from Fr., from *effleurer* lit. 'remove the flower of (something).']

ef·flo·resce /,eflə'res/ ▶ v. **1** [intrans.] (of a substance) lose moisture and turn to a fine powder upon exposure to air. ■ (of salts) come to the surface of brickwork, rock, or other material and crystallize there. ■ (of a surface) become covered with salt particles. **2** reach an optimum stage of development; blossom. — **ef·flo·res·cence** /-'resəns/ n. **ef·flo·res·cent** adj. [18th C.: from L. *efflorescere*, from *e-* 'out' + *florescere* 'begin to bloom.']

ef·flu·ence /'eflōōəns/ ▶ n. a substance that flows out from something. ■ the action of flowing out. [ME: from med. L. *effluentia*, from L. *effluere* 'flow out,' from *ex-* 'out' + *fluere* 'to flow.']

ef·flu·ent /'eflōōənt/ ▶ n. liquid waste or sewage discharged into a river or the sea. [ME: from L. *effluent-* 'flowing out,' from the v. *effluere* (see EFFLUENCE).]

ef·flu·vi·um /i'flōōvēəm/ ▶ n. (pl. **-vi·a** /-vēə/) an unpleasant or harmful odor, secretion, or discharge. [17th C.: from L., from *effluere* 'flow out.']

ef·flux /'ef,ləks/ ▶ n. tech. the flowing out of a particular substance or particle. ■ material flowing out. [16th C.: from med. L. *effluxus*, from *effluere* 'flow out.']

ef·flux·ion /e'flәksHәn/ ▶ **n.** **1** Law (**ef·flux**) the passing of time, in particular when leading to the expiration of an agreement or contract. **2** archaic the action of flowing out.

ef·fort /'efәrt/ ▶ **n.** a vigorous or determined attempt. ■ the result of an attempt. ■ strenuous physical or mental exertion. ■ tech. a force exerted by a machine or in a process. ■ [with adj.] the activities of a group of people with a common purpose: *the war effort.* — **ef·fort·ful adj. ef·fort·ful·ly adv.** [15th C.: from Fr., from OFr. *esforcier*, based on L. *ex-* 'out' + *fortis* 'strong.']

ef·fort·less /'efәrtlis/ ▶ **adj.** requiring no physical or mental exertion: *went up the steps in two effortless bounds.* ■ achieved with admirable ease: *her effortless style.* — **ef·fort·less·ly adv. ef·fort·less·ness n.**

ef·fron·ter·y /i'frәntәrē/ ▶ **n.** insolent or impertinent behavior: *had the effrontery to challenge the decision.* [17th C.: from Fr. *effronterie*, based on late L. *effrons, effront-* 'shameless, barefaced,' from *ex-* 'out' + *frons* 'forehead.']

ef·ful·gent /i'fo͝oljәnt; i'fәl-/ ▶ **adj.** literary shining brightly; radiant. ■ (of a person or expression) emanating joy or goodness. — **ef·ful·gence n. ef·ful·gent·ly adv.** [18th C.: from L. *effulgent-* 'shining brightly,' from the v. *effulgere*, from *ex-* 'out' + *fulgere* 'to shine.']

ef·fuse ▶ **v.** /i'fyo͞oz; i'fyo͞os/ [trans.] give off (a liquid, light, smell, or quality). ■ [intrans.] talk in an unrestrained, excited manner. [ME: from L. *effusus*, from *effundere* 'pour out,' from *ex-* 'out' + *fundere* 'pour.']

ef·fu·sion /i'fyo͞ozHәn/ ▶ **n.** an instance of giving off something such as a liquid, light, or smell. ■ Med. an escape of fluid into a body cavity. ■ talking or writing in an unrestrained or heartfelt way.

ef·fu·sive /i'fyo͞osiv/ ▶ **adj.** **1** expressing feelings of gratitude, pleasure, or approval in an unrestrained or heartfelt manner: *an effusive welcome.* **2** Geol. (of igneous rock) poured out when molten and later solidified. ■ of or relating to the eruption of large volumes of molten rock. — **ef·fu·sive·ly adv. ef·fu·sive·ness n.**

Ef·ik /'efik/ ▶ **n.** (pl. same) **1** a member of a people of southern Nigeria. **2** the Benue-Congo language of this people, closely related to Ibibio, and used as a lingua franca. ▶ **adj.** of or relating to this people or their language. [the name in Efik.]

EFL ▶ **abbr.** English as a foreign language.

EFM ▶ **abbr.** electronic fetal monitor.

eft /eft/ ▶ **n.** a newt. ■ Zool. the juvenile stage of a newt. [OE *efeta.*]

EFTA /'eftә/ ▶ **abbr.** European Free Trade Association.

EFTS ▶ **abbr.** electronic funds transfer system.

e.g. ▶ **abbr.** for example. [from L. *exempli gratia* 'for the sake of an example.']

e·gad /ē'gad/ (also **e·gads**) ▶ **exclam.** archaic expressing surprise, anger, or affirmation. [17th C.: representing earlier *A God.*]

e·gal·i·tar·i·an /i,galә'te(ә)rēәn/ ▶ **adj.** of, relating to, or believing in the principle that all people are equal and deserve equal rights and opportunities. ▶ **n.** a person who advocates or supports such a principle. — **e·gal·i·tar·i·an·ism n.** [19th C.: from Fr. *égalitaire*, from *égal* 'equal,' from L. *aequalis* (see **EQUAL**).]

Eg·bert /'egbәrt/ (died 839), king of Wessex 802–839. In 825, he won a decisive victory that temporarily brought Mercian supremacy to an end.

EGF ▶ **abbr.** epidermal growth factor.

egg[1] /eg/ ▶ **n.** **1** an oval or round object laid by a female bird, reptile, fish, or invertebrate, usually containing a developing embryo. The eggs of birds are enclosed in a chalky shell, those of reptiles in a leathery membrane. ■ an infertile egg, typically of the domestic hen, used for food. ■ Biol. the female reproductive cell in animals and plants; an ovum. ■ a thing resembling a bird's egg in shape. ■ Archit. a decorative oval molding, used alternately with triangular figures. **2** [with adj.] informal, dated a person possessing a specified quality: *she was a good egg.*
– PHRASES **don't put all your eggs in one basket** proverb don't risk everything on the success of one venture. **kill the goose that lays the golden egg** destroy a reliable and valuable source of income. **lay an egg** informal be completely unsuccessful; fail badly. **with egg on one's face** informal appearing foolish or ridiculous. — **egg·less adj.** [ME: from ON.]

egg[2] ▶ **v.** [trans.] (**egg someone on**) urge or encourage someone to do something, esp. something foolish or risky. [ME: from ON *eggja* 'incite.']

egg and dart ▶ **n.** Archit. a motif of alternating eggs and darts, used to enrich an ovolo molding.

egg·beat·er /'eg,bētәr/ ▶ **n.** a kitchen utensil used for beating ingredients such as eggs or cream. ■ informal a helicopter.

egg cream ▶ **n.** a drink consisting of milk and soda water, flavored with syrup.

egg·cup /'eg,kәp/ ▶ **n.** a small cup for holding a boiled egg upright while it is being eaten.

egg·head /'eg,hed/ ▶ **n.** informal a person who is highly academic or studious; an intellectual. — **egg·head·ed adj.**

egg·nog /'eg,näg; -,nôg/ ▶ **n.** a drink made from a mixture of eggs, cream, and flavorings, often with alcohol.

egg·plant /'eg,plant/ ▶ **n.** **1** the large egg-shaped fruit of a tropical Old World plant, eaten as a vegetable. ■ a dark purple color like the typical skin of this fruit. **2** the large plant (*Solanum melongena*) of the nightshade family that bears this fruit.

egg roll ▶ **n.** a Chinese-style snack consisting of diced meat or shrimp and shredded vegetables wrapped in a dough made with egg and deep-fried.

egg sac ▶ **n.** a protective silken pouch in which a female spider deposits her eggs.

eggs Ben·e·dict ▶ **plural n.** a dish consisting of poached eggs and sliced ham on toasted English muffins, covered with hollandaise sauce.

egg·shell /'eg,SHel/ ▶ **n.** the thin, hard outer layer of an egg, esp. a hen's egg. ■ used in similes and metaphors to refer to the fragile nature of something: *the truck would crush his car like an eggshell.* ■ [as adj.] (of china) of extreme thinness and delicacy: *eggshell porcelains.* ■ a pale yellowish-white color.

egg tem·per·a ▶ **n.** an emulsion of pigment and egg yolk, used in tempera painting.

egg tim·er ▶ **n.** a device for measuring the time required to cook a boiled egg, traditionally in the form of a miniature hourglass.

egg tooth ▶ **n.** a hard white protuberance on the beak or jaw of an embryo bird or reptile that is used for breaking out of the shell and is later lost.

egg white ▶ **n.** the clear, viscous substance around the yolk of an egg that turns white when cooked or beaten. Also called **ALBUMEN**.

egg·y /'egē/ ▶ **adj.** rich in or covered with egg.

eg·lan·tine /'eglәn,tēn; -,tīn/ ▶ **n.** another term for **SWEETBRIER**. [ME: from OFr. *eglantine*, based on L. *acus* 'needle' or *aculeus* 'prickle.']

e·go /'ēgō/ ▶ **n.** (pl. **e·gos**) a person's sense of self-esteem or self-importance: *a boost to my ego.* ■ Psychoanal. the part of the mind that mediates between the conscious and the unconscious and is responsible for reality testing and a sense of personal identity. Compare with **ID** and **SUPEREGO**. ■ an overly high opinion of oneself. ■ Philos. (in metaphysics) a conscious thinking subject. — **e·go·less adj.** [19th C.: from Latin, literally 'I.']

e·go·cen·tric /,ēgō'sentrik/ ▶ **adj.** thinking only of oneself, without regard for the feelings or desires of others; self-centered. ■ centered in or arising from a person's own existence or perspective: *egocentric spatial perception.* ▶ **n.** an egocentric person. — **e·go·cen·tric·al·ly** /-(ә)lē/ **adv. e·go·cen·tric·i·ty** /,ēgōsen'trisitē/ **n. e·go·cen·trism** /,ēgō'sentrizәm/ **n.** [20th C.: from **EGO**.]

e·go i·de·al ▶ **n.** (in Freudian theory) the part of the mind that imposes on itself concepts of ideal behavior developed from parental and social standards. ■ (in general use) an idealized conception of oneself.

e·go·ism /'ēgō,izәm/ ▶ **n.** Ethics an ethical theory that treats self-interest as the foundation of morality. ■ another term for **EGOTISM**. — **e·go·ist n. e·go·is·tic** /,ēgō'istik/ **adj. e·go·is·ti·cal** /,ēgō'istikәl/ **adj. e·go·is·ti·cal·ly** /,ēgō'istik(ә)lē/ **adv.**

e·go·ma·ni·a /,ēgō'mānēә/ ▶ **n.** obsessive egotism or self-centeredness. — **e·go·ma·ni·ac** /-nē,ak/ **n. e·go·ma·ni·a·cal** /,ēgōmә'nīәkәl/ **adj.**

e·go psy·chol·o·gy ▶ **n.** a system of psychoanalytic developmental psychology concerned esp. with personality. — **e·go psy·chol·o·gist n.**

e·go·tism /'ēgә,tizәm/ ▶ **n.** the practice of talking and thinking about oneself excessively because of an undue sense of self-importance. — **e·go·tist n. e·go·tis·tic** /,ēgә'tistik/ **adj. e·go·tis·ti·cal** /,ēgә'tistikәl/ **adj. e·go·tis·ti·cal·ly** /,ēgә'tistik(ә)lē/ **adv. e·go·tize** /-,tīz/ **v.** [18th C.: from Fr. *égoïste*, from L. *ego* 'I.']

e·go trip ▶ **n.** informal something done to increase one's sense of self-importance: *driving that car was one big ego trip.*

e·gre·gious /i'grējәs/ ▶ **adj.** **1** outstandingly bad; shocking. **2** archaic remarkably good. — **e·gre·gious·ly adv. e·gre·gious·ness n.** [16th C. (sense 2): from L. *egregius* 'illustrious,' lit. 'standing out from the flock,' from *ex-* 'out' + *grex, greg-* 'flock.']

e·gress /'ēgres/ ▶ **n.** the action of going out of or leaving a place: *direct means of access and egress.* ■ a way out: *a narrow egress.* ■ Law the right to come or go out. ■ Astron. another term for **EMERSION**. ▶ **v.** [trans.] go out of or leave (a place). [16th C.: from L. *egressus* 'gone out,' from the v. *egredi*, from *ex-* 'out' + *gradi* 'to step.']

e·gres·sive /i'gresiv/ ▶ **adj.** Phonet. (of a speech sound) produced using the normal outward-flowing airstream. Compare with **INGRESSIVE**.

e·gret /'ēgrit;'ē,gret; 'egrit/ ▶ **n.** a heron (genera *Egretta* and *Bubulcus*) with mainly white plumage, having long plumes in the breeding season. See illustration at **GREAT EGRET**. [ME: from OFr. *aigrette*, from Provençal *aigreta*, from the Gmc. base of **HERON**.]

E·gypt /'ējipt/ a country in northeastern Africa. *See box on next page.*

E·gyp·tian /i'jipsHәn/ ▶ **adj.** of or relating to Egypt or its people. ■ of or relating to Egyptian antiquities. ■ of or relating to the language of ancient Egypt. ▶ **n.** **1** a native of ancient or modern Egypt, or a person of Egyptian descent. **2** the Afro-Asiatic language used in ancient Egypt, attested from *c.*3000 BC. It is represented in its oldest stages by hieroglyphic inscriptions and in its latest form by Coptic; it has been replaced in modern use by Arabic. — **E·gyp·tian·i·za·tion** /i,jipsHәni'zāsHәn/ **n. E·gyp·tian·ize** /-,nīz/ **v.**

E·gyp·tian clo·ver ▶ **n.** another term for **BERSEEM CLOVER**.

E·gyp·tian co·bra ▶ **n.** a large nocturnal African cobra (*Naja haje*) with a thick body and large head. Also called **ASP**.

E·gyp·tian lo·tus ▶ **n.** see **LOTUS** (sense 1).

E·gyp·tian mon·goose ▶ **n.** a mongoose (*Herpestes ichneumon*) occurring over much of Africa and parts of southwestern Asia and Iberia, noted for its destruction of crocodile eggs. Also called **ICHNEUMON**.

E·gyp·tol·o·gy /,ējip'tälәjē/ ▶ **n.** the study of the language, history, and civilization of ancient Egypt. — **E·gyp·to·log·i·cal** /i,jiptә'läjikәl/ **adj. E·gyp·tol·o·gist** /-jist/ **n.**

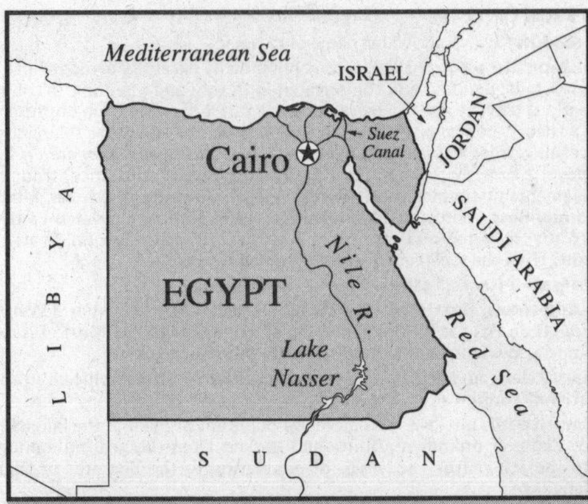

Egypt
Official name: Arab Republic of Egypt
Location: northeastern Africa, on the Mediterranean Sea, east of Libya
Area: 384,500 square miles (995,500 sq km)
Population: 76,117,000
Capital: Cairo
Languages: Arabic (official), English, French
Currency: Egyptian pound

eh /ā; e/ ▶ **exclam.** used to represent a sound made in speech in a variety of situations, in particular to ask for something to be repeated or explained or to elicit agreement: *"Eh? What's this?"* | *"Let's hope so, eh?"* [16th C.: natural utterance.]

EHF ▶ **abbr.** extremely high frequency.

EHP ▶ **abbr.** ■ effective horsepower. ■ electric horsepower.

EHV ▶ **abbr.** extra-high voltage.

Eich·mann /ˈīkmən/, Karl Adolf (1906–62), German Nazi administrator. He administered the concentration camps during World War II. In 1960, he was executed after trial in Israel.

Eid /ēd/ (also **Id**) ▶ **n.** a Muslim festival, in particular: ■ (in full **Eid ul-Fitr** /ēd o͝ol ˈfētr/) the feast marking the end of the fast of Ramadan. ■ (in full **Eid ul-A·dha** /ēd o͝ol ˈädə/) the festival marking the culmination of the annual pilgrimage to Mecca and commemorating the sacrifice of Abraham. [from Arab. *ʿīd* 'feast,' from Aramaic.]

ei·der /ˈīdər/ ▶ **n.** (also **ei·der duck**) (pl. same or **ei·ders**) a northern sea duck (genera *Somateria* and *Polysticta*), of which the male has mainly black and white plumage with a colored head, and the brown female has soft down feathers that are used to line the nest, in particular the **common eider** (*S. mollissima*). ■ another term for EIDERDOWN. [17th C.: from Icelandic *æthur*, from ON *æthr*.]

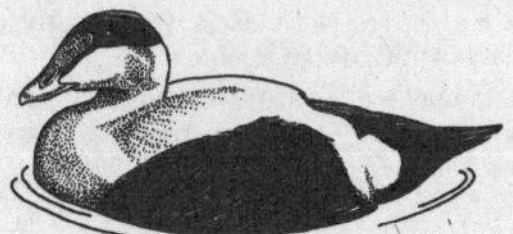
common eider

ei·der·down /ˈīdər,doun/ ▶ **n.** small, soft feathers from the breast of the female eider duck. ■ esp. Brit. a quilt filled with down (originally from the eider) or some other soft material.

ei·det·ic /īˈdetik/ ▶ **adj.** Psychol. relating to or denoting mental images having unusual vividness and detail, as if actually visible. ▶ **n.** a person able to form or recall eidetic images. — **ei·det·i·cal·ly** **adv.** [1920s: coined in Ger. from Gk. *eidētikos*, from *eidos* 'form.']

ei·do·lon /īˈdōlən/ ▶ **n.** (pl. **-lons** or **-la** /-lə/) **1** an idealized person or thing. **2** a specter or phantom. [19th C.: from Gk. *eidōlon*, from *eidos* 'form.']

ei·dos /ˈīdäs; ˈādäs/ ▶ **n.** (pl. **ei·de** /ˈīdē; ˈādā/) Anthropol. the distinctive expression of the cognitive or intellectual character of a culture or social group. [1930s: Greek, literally 'form, type, or idea.']

Eif·fel /ˈīfəl/, Alexandre Gustave (1832–1923), French engineer. He designed the Eiffel Tower and the inner structure of the Statue of Liberty.

Eif·fel Tow·er a wrought-iron structure erected in Paris in 1889. With a height of 984 feet (300 m), it was the tallest man-made structure for many years.

eigen- ▶ **comb. form** Math. Physics proper; characteristic: *eigenfunction.* [from the Ger. adj. *eigen* 'own.']

ei·gen·func·tion /ˈīgən,fəNG(k)SHən/ ▶ **n.** Math. Physics each of a set of independent functions that are the solutions to a given differential equation.

ei·gen·val·ue /ˈīgən,valyo͞o/ ▶ **n.** Math. Physics **1** each of a set of values of a parameter for which a differential equation has a nonzero solution under given conditions. **2** any number such that a given matrix minus that number times the identity matrix has a zero determinant.

ei·gen·vec·tor /ˈīgən,vektər/ ▶ **n.** Math. Physics a vector that when operated on by a given operator gives a scalar multiple of itself.

eight /āt/ ▶ **cardinal number** equivalent to the product of two and four; one more than seven, or two less than ten; 8: *a committee of eight members* | *eight of them were unemployed.* (Roman numeral: **viii** or **VIII.**) ■ a group or unit of eight people or things. ■ eight years old. *children as young as eight.* ■ eight o'clock. ■ short for FIGURE EIGHT. ■ a size of garment or other merchandise denoted by eight. ■ an eight-cylinder engine or a motor vehicle with such an engine. ■ a playing card with eight pips. [OE *ehta, eahta*, of Gmc. origin; rel. to Ger. *acht*, from an Indo-Eur. root shared by L. *octo* and Gk. *oktō*.]

eight ball ▶ **n.** Billiards the black ball, numbered eight. ■ a game of pool in which one side must pocket all of the striped or solid balls and finally the eight ball to win.
– PHRASES **behind the eight ball** informal at a disadvantage.

eight·een /āˈtēn; ˈā,tēn/ ▶ **cardinal number** equivalent to the product of two and nine; one more than seventeen, or eight more than ten; 18: *she wrote eighteen novels* | *out of sixty tested, eighteen passed.* (Roman numeral: **xviii** or **XVIII.**) ■ a set or team of eighteen individuals. ■ eighteen years old. ■ a size of garment or other merchandise denoted by eighteen. — **eight·eenth** /āˈtēnTH; ˈā,tēnTH/ **ordinal number.** [OE *e(a)htatēne* (see EIGHT, -TEEN).]

eight·een·mo /āˈtēnmō/ ▶ **n.** (pl. **-mos**) another term for OCTODECIMO.

eight·fold /ˈāt,fōld/ ▶ **adj.** eight times as great or as numerous: *an eightfold increase in expenditure.* ■ having eight parts or elements: *an eightfold shape.* ▶ **adv.** by eight times; to eight times the number or amount: *claims have grown eightfold in ten years.*

eight·fold path Buddhism the path to nirvana, comprising eight aspects in which an aspirant must become practiced: right views, intention, speech, action, livelihood, effort, mindfulness, and concentration.

eighth /ˈā(t)TH/ ▶ **ordinal number** constituting number eight in a sequence; 8th: *in the eighth century* | *the eighth of September* | *seven men were caught, an eighth escaped.* ■ (**an eighth/one eighth**) each of eight equal parts into which something is or may be divided. ■ the eighth finisher or position in a race or competition. ■ the eighth grade of a school. — **eighth·ly** **adv.**

eighth note (Brit. **qua·ver**) ▶ **n.** Music a note having the time value of an eighth of a whole note or half a quarter note, represented by a large dot with a hooked stem.

eight·pen·ny nail /ˈāt,penē/ ▶ **n.** a nail that is 2.5 inches (64 mm) long.

8vo /ākˈtāvō/ ▶ **abbr.** octavo.

eight·y /ˈātē/ ▶ **cardinal number** (pl. **eight·ies**) equivalent to the product of eight and ten; ten less than ninety; 80: *eighty miles north* | *a buffet for eighty.* (Roman numeral: **lxxx** or **LXXX.**) ■ (**eighties**) the numbers from 80 to 89, esp. the years of a century or of a person's life: *she was in her eighties.* ■ eighty years old. ■ eighty miles an hour. — **eight·i·eth** /ˈātēiTH/ **ordinal number** **eight·y·fold** /ˈātē,fōld/ **adj. & adv.** [OE *hunde(a)htatig*, from *hund* (of uncert. origin) + *e(a)hta* 'eight' + *-tig* (see -TY²).]

eigh·ty-six /,ātēˈsiks/ (also **86**) ▶ **v.** [trans.] **1** refuse to serve (someone): *He got 86ed from a reservation casino.* **2** reject, discard, or cancel: *the passwords will be 86ed by next October.* ▶ **n.** informal someone regarded as undesirable as a restaurant or bar patron. [1930s: perh. rhyming sl. for NIX.]

Eijk·man /ˈīkmən/, Christiaan (1858–1930), Dutch physician. His work led to the discovery of the vitamin thiamine. Nobel Prize for Physiology or Medicine (1929, shared with F. G. Hopkins).

Ei·lat /āˈlät/ (also **E·lat**) the southernmost town in Israel; pop. 36,000. Founded in 1949, it is Israel's only outlet to the Red Sea.

Eind·ho·ven /ˈīnt,hōvən; ˈānt-/ a city in southern Netherlands; pop. 193,000.

Ein·fühl·ung /ˈīnfo͞o,ləNG/ ▶ **n.** empathy. [Ger., from *ein-* 'into' + *Fühlung* 'feeling.']

ein·korn /ˈīn,kôrn/ ▶ **n.** an old kind of Mediterranean wheat (*Triticum monococcum*) with small bearded ears and spikelets that each contain one slender grain, used as fodder in prehistoric times but now rarely grown. Compare with EMMER, SPELT². [20th C.: from Ger., from *ein* 'one' + *Korn* 'seed.']

Ein·stein /ˈīn,stīn/, Albert (1879–1955), US physicist; born in Germany. He founded the theory of relativity in 1905. Often regarded as the greatest scientist of the 20th century, he was influential in the decision to build an atomic bomb. ■ [as n.] (**an Einstein**) a genius. — **Ein·stein·i·an** /īnˈstīnēən/ **adj.**

ein·stein·i·um /īnˈstīnēəm/ ▶ **n.** the chemical element of atomic number 99, a radioactive metal of the actinide series. Einsteinium does not occur naturally and was discovered in 1953 in debris from the first hydrogen bomb explosion. (Symbol: **Es**) [1950s: from EINSTEIN.]

Ei·re /'e(ə)rə; 'īrə/ the Gaelic name for Ireland; the official name 1937–49 of the Republic of Ireland.

Ei·rene /ī'rēnē/ Gk. Mythol. the goddess of peace. Roman equivalent **PAX**.

ei·ren·ic /ī'renik; -'rē-/ ▶ **adj.** var. of **IRENIC**.

Ei·sen·how·er /'īzən,hou-ər/, Dwight David (1890–1969), 34th president of the US 1953–61; nicknamed **Ike**. A Kansas Republican, he was a celebrated military leader before entering politics. In World War II, he was Supreme Commander of Allied Expeditionary Forces in western Europe 1943–45. As president, he adopted a hard line toward communism.

Ei·sen·stein /'īzən,SHtīn/, Sergei Mikhailovich (1898–1948), Soviet film director; born in Latvia. He is noted for *The Battleship Potemkin* (1925).

eis·tedd·fod /ī'steTH,väd/ ▶ **n.** (pl. **-fods** or **-fo·dau** /-'vädī/) a competitive festival of music and poetry in Wales, in particular the annual National Eisteddfod. — **eis·tedd·fod·ic** /,īsteTH'vädik/ **adj.** [Welsh, lit. 'session,' from *eistedd* 'sit.']

Eis·wein /'īs,vīn/ ▶ **n.** (pl. **-wei·ne** /-,vīnə/ or **-weins**) wine made from ripe grapes picked while covered with frost. [from Ger., from *Eis* 'ice' + *Wein* 'wine.']

ei·ther /'ēTHər; 'īTHər/ ▶ **conj. & adv. 1** used before the first of two (or occasionally more) alternatives that are being specified (the other being introduced by "or"). **2** [adv., with negative] used to indicate a similarity or link with a statement just made: *it won't do any harm, but won't help, either.* ■ for that matter; moreover (used to add information): *I was too tired to go. And I couldn't have paid, either.* ▶ **adj. & pron.** one or the other of two people or things: [as adj.] *there were no children of either marriage* | [as pron.] *a mortgage that will be repaid if* ***either of*** *them dies.* ■ [adj.] each of two: *with fields of grass on either side.*

– PHRASES **either way** whichever of two given alternatives is the case: *I'm not sure whether he is trying to be clever or controversial, but either way, it smacks of racism.* [OE *ǣgther*, contracted form of *ǣg(e)hwæther*, of Gmc. origin; ult. rel. to **AYE**[1] and **WHETHER**.]

ei·ther/or /'ēTHər'ôr; 'īTHər'ôr/ (also **ei·ther-or**) ▶ **n.** an unavoidable choice between two alternatives: *you can give him an ultimatum—an either/or.* ▶ **adj.** involving such a choice.

e·jac·u·late ▶ **v.** /i'jakyə,lāt/ **1** [intrans.] (of a man or male animal) eject semen from the body at the moment of sexual climax. **2** dated utter suddenly (a short prayer). ■ [with direct speech] say something quickly and suddenly: *"Indeed?" ejaculated the stranger.* ▶ **n.** /-,lit/ semen that has been ejected from the body. — **e·jac·u·la·tion** /i,jakyə'lāSHən/ **n.** **e·jac·u·la·to·ry** /-lə,tôrē/ **adj.** [16th C.: from L. *ejaculat-* 'darted out,' from the v. *ejaculari*, from *e-* 'out' + *jaculari* 'to dart' (from *jaculum* 'dart,' from *jacere* 'to throw').]

e·jac·u·la·tor /i'jakyə,lātər/ ▶ **n.** a muscle that causes ejaculation of semen.

e·ject /i'jekt/ ▶ **v.** [trans.] (often **be ejected**) force or throw (something) out, typically in a violent or sudden way: *many types of rock are* ***ejected*** *from volcanoes.* ■ cause (something) to drop out or be removed, usually mechanically. ■ [intrans.] (of a pilot) escape from an aircraft by being explosively propelled out of it. ■ compel (someone) to leave a place. ■ dismiss (someone), esp. from political office. ■ emit; give off. ■ dispossess (a tenant) by legal process. — **e·jec·tion** /i'jekSHən/ **n.** [ME: from L. *eject-* 'thrown out,' from the v. *eicere*, from *e-* + *jacere* 'to throw.']

e·jec·ta /i'jektə/ ▶ **plural n.** [often treated as sing.] material that is forced or thrown out, esp. as a result of volcanic eruption, meteoritic impact, or stellar explosion. [19th C.: from Latin, 'things thrown out.']

e·jec·tion seat /i'jekSHən/ ▶ **n.** a device that causes the ejection of a pilot from an aircraft in an emergency.

e·jec·tive /i'jektiv/ Phonet. ▶ **adj.** denoting a type of consonant in some languages, e.g., Hausa, produced by sudden release of pressure from the glottis. ▶ **n.** an ejective consonant.

e·ject·ment /i'jektmənt/ ▶ **n.** Law the action or process of evicting a tenant from property. ■ the action or process in which a person evicted from property seeks to recover possession and damages.

e·jec·tor /i'jektər/ ▶ **n.** a device that causes something to be removed or to drop out: *a built-in drill ejector.*

e·ji·do /e'hēdō/ ▶ **n.** (pl. **-dos**) (in Mexico) a piece of land farmed communally under a system supported by the state. [Mex. Sp., from Sp., denoting common land on the road leading out of the village.]

Eka·te·rin·burg /yi,kətyərin'boork; i'katərin,bərg/ (also **Yekaterinburg**) a city in central Russia; pop. 1,372,000. From 1924 until 1991, it was known as **Sverdlovsk**. [*Ekaterina* (1684–1727), the wife of Peter the Great.]

eke[1] /ēk/ ▶ **v.** [trans.] **(eke something out)** manage to support oneself with difficulty: *they eked out a living from the soil.* ■ make an amount of something last longer by using or consuming it frugally: *the remains could be eked out to make another meal.* ■ obtain or create, but just barely: *Tennessee eked out a 74–73 overtime victory.* [OE *ēacian, ēcan* (in the sense 'increase'), of Gmc. origin; rel. to ON *auka*.]

eke[2] ▶ **adv.** archaic term for **ALSO**. [OE, of Gmc. origin.]

EKG ▶ **abbr.** ■ electrocardiogram. ■ electrocardiograph. ■ electrocardiography.

el /el/ ▶ **n.** **(the El)** an elevated railroad or section of railroad, esp. that in Chicago. ■ a train running on such a railroad.

el. ▶ **abbr.** elevation.

-el ▶ **suffix** var. of **-LE**[2].

El Aa·iún /,el ä'yōōn/ Arabic name of **LA'YOUN**.

e·lab·o·rate ▶ **adj.** /i'lab(ə)rit/ involving many carefully arranged parts or details; detailed and complicated in design and planning. ■ (of an action) lengthy and exaggerated. ▶ **v.** /-,rāt/ **1** [trans.] develop or present (a theory, policy, or system) in detail. ■ [intrans.] add more detail concerning what has already been said: *he would not* ***elaborate on*** *his news.* **2** [trans.] Biol. (of a natural agency) produce (a substance) from its elements or simpler constituents. — **e·lab·o·rate·ly** /-ritlē/ **adv.** **e·lab·o·rate·ness** /-ritnis/ **n.** **e·lab·o·ra·tion** /i,labə'rāSHən/ **n.** **e·lab·o·ra·tive** /-,rātiv/ **adj.** **e·lab·o·ra·tor** /-rātər/ **n.** [16th C.: from L. *elaborat-* 'worked out,' from the v. *elaborare*, from *e-* + *labor* 'work.']

El·a·gab·a·lus /,elə'gabələs/ var. of **HELIOGABALUS**.

El A·la·mein, Battle of /el ,älə'mān; ,alə'mān/ a battle of World War II fought in 1942 at El Alamein in Egypt, 60 miles (90 km) west of Alexandria, in which British forces defeated the Germans.

E·lam /'ēləm/ an ancient state in southwestern Iran, established in the 4th millennium BC.

E·lam·ite /'ēlə,mīt/ ▶ **n. 1** a native or inhabitant of Elam. **2** the language of Elam, of unknown affinity and spoken from the 3rd millennium to the 4th century BC. ▶ **adj.** of or relating to the Elamites or their language.

é·lan /ā'län; ā'lan/ ▶ **n.** energy, style, and enthusiasm. [19th C.: from Fr. *élan*, from *élancer* 'to dart,' from *é-* 'out' + *lancer* 'to throw.']

e·land /'ēlənd/ ▶ **n.** a spiral-horned African antelope (genus *Taurotragus*) that lives in open woodland and grassland. It is the largest of the antelopes. [18th C.: via Afrik. from Du. 'elk,' from obsolete Ger. *Elend*, from Lith. *élnis*.]

e·lapse /i'laps/ ▶ **v.** [intrans.] (of time) pass or go by: *weeks elapsed before anyone was charged* | [as adj.] **(elapsed)** *a display tells you the elapsed time.* [16th C.: from L. *elaps-* 'slipped away,' from *elabi*, from *e-* + *labi* 'to glide, slip.']

e·las·mo·branch /ə'lazmə,braNGk/ ▶ **n.** Zool. a cartilaginous fish of a group (subclass Elasmobranchii, class Chondrichthyes) that comprises the sharks, rays, and skates. [19th C.: from mod. L. *Elasmobranchii* (pl.), from Gk. *elasmos* 'beaten metal' + *brankhia* 'gills.']

e·las·tase /i'lastās; -tāz/ ▶ **n.** Biochem. a pancreatic enzyme that digests elastin. [1940s: from **ELASTIC** + **-ASE**.]

e·las·tic /i'lastik/ ▶ **adj.** (of an object or material) able to resume its normal shape spontaneously after contraction, dilatation, or distortion. ■ able to encompass variety and change; flexible and adaptable. ■ springy and buoyant: *Annie returned with elastic step.* ■ Econ. (of demand or supply) sensitive to changes in price or income. ■ Physics (of a collision) involving no decrease of kinetic energy. ▶ **n.** cord, tape, or fabric, typically woven with strips of rubber, that returns to its original length or shape after being stretched. — **e·las·ti·cal·ly** /-(ə)lē/ **adv.** **e·las·tic·i·ty** /i,la'stisitē; ,ēla-/ **n.** **e·las·ti·cize** /i'lastə,sīz/ **v.** [17th C.: from mod. L. *elasticus*, from Gk. *elastikos* 'propulsive,' from *elaunein* 'to drive.']

e·las·tic band ▶ **n.** a rubber band.

e·las·tic fi·ber ▶ **n.** Anat. a yellowish fiber composed chiefly of elastin and occurring in networks or sheets that give elasticity to tissues in the body.

e·las·tic lim·it ▶ **n.** Physics the maximum extent to which a solid may be stretched without permanent alteration of size or shape.

e·las·tic mod·u·lus ▶ **n.** Physics the ratio of the force exerted upon a substance or body to the resultant deformation.

e·las·tin /i'lastin/ ▶ **n.** Biochem. an elastic, fibrous glycoprotein found in connective tissue. [19th C.: from **ELASTIC** + **-IN**[1].]

e·las·to·mer /i'lastəmər/ ▶ **n.** a natural or synthetic polymer having elastic properties, e.g., rubber. — **e·las·to·mer·ic** /i,lastə'merik/ **adj.** [1930s: from **ELASTIC** + **-MER**.]

E·lat var. of **EILAT**.

e·late /i'lāt/ ▶ **v.** [trans.] [usu. as adj.] **(elated)** make (someone) ecstatically happy: *I felt elated at winning.* ▶ **adj.** archaic in high spirits; exultant or proud. — **e·lat·ed·ly** **adv.** **e·lat·ed·ness** **n.** [ME: from L. *elat-* 'raised,' from the v. *efferre*, from *ex-* 'out, from' + *ferre* 'to bear.']

e·la·tion /i'lāSHən/ ▶ **n.** great happiness and exhilaration.

E lay·er ▶ **n.** a layer of the ionosphere able to reflect medium-frequency radio waves.

Ela·zig /,elä'zi/ a commercial city in east central Turkey, east of the upper Euphrates River; pop. 205,000.

El·ba /'elbə/ a small island off the western coast of Italy, where Napoleon was first exiled 1814–15.

El·be /elb(ə)/ a river in central Europe that flows for 720 miles (1,159 km) from the Czech Republic through Germany to the North Sea.

El·bert, Mount /'elbərt/ a mountain in Colorado, east of Aspen. Rising to 14,431 feet (4,399 m), it is the highest peak in the Rocky Mountains.

el·bow /'elbō/ ▶ **n.** the joint between the forearm and the upper arm: *she propped herself up on one elbow.* ■ the part of the sleeve of a garment covering the elbow. ■ a thing resembling an elbow, in particular a piece of piping bent through an angle. ▶ **v.** [with obj. and adverbial] strike (someone) with one's elbow: *one player had elbowed another in the face.* ■ [adverbial of direction] move by pushing past people with one's elbows: *people* ***elbowed past*** *each other to the door.* ■ fig. get rid of or disregard in a cursory and dismissive way: *his new show was elbowed aside in the ratings war.*

– PHRASES **at one's elbow** close at hand; nearby. **elbow-to-elbow** very close together. **up to one's elbows in** informal with one's hands plunged in (something). ■ fig. deeply involved in (a task or undertaking). [OE *elboga, elnboga*, of Gmc. origin; rel. to Ger. *Ellenbogen* (see also ELL[1], BOW[1]).]

el·bow grease ▶ n. informal hard physical work, esp. vigorous polishing or cleaning.

el·bow room ▶ n. informal adequate space to move or work in: *the car has elbow room for four adults* | fig. *Quebec wants more elbow room within the federation.*

El·brus /el'brōōs; 'el,brōōs/ a peak in the Caucasus Mountains, on the border between Russia and Georgia. Rising to 18,481 feet (5,642 m), it is the highest mountain in Europe.

El·burz Moun·tains /el'bŏŏrz/ a mountain range in northwestern Iran. Damavand is the highest peak, rising to 18,386 feet (5,604 m).

El Ca·jon /,el kə'hōn/ a city in southwestern California, east of San Diego; pop. 88,693.

El Cap·i·tan /el ,kapi'tan/ a peak in Yosemite National Park in California, known for its sheer walls that rise over 3,000 feet (1,000 m) above its base.

El·che /'elCHā/ a town in southeastern Spain, in the province of Alicante; pop. 181,200.

el cheap·o /el 'CHēpō/ informal ▶ adj. & n. another way of saying CHEAPO. [1960s: from CHEAP, on the pattern of Sp. phrs. such as *El Dorado* and *El Greco*.]

El Cid /el 'sid/, see CID, EL.

eld /eld/ ▶ n. literary old age. ■ former times; the past. [OE *ieldu, eldu*, of Gmc. origin; rel. to ELDER[1] and OLD.]

eld·er[1] /'eldər/ ▶ adj. (of one or more out of a group of related or otherwise associated people) of a greater age: *my elder daughter.* ■ (**the Elder**) used to distinguish between related famous people with the same name: *Pliny the Elder.* ▶ n. (usu. **elders**) a person of greater age than someone specified: *children no less fascinated than their elders.* ■ a person of advanced age. ■ (often **elders**) a leader or senior figure in a tribe or other group: *a council of village elders.* ■ an official in the early Christian Church, or of various Protestant Churches and sects. — **el·der·ship** n. [OE *ieldra, eldra*, of Gmc. origin; rel. to Ger. *älter*, also to ELD and OLD.]

eld·er[2] ▶ n. (also **el·der·ber·ry**) a small tree or shrub (genus *Sambucus*) of the honeysuckle family, with pithy stems, typically having white flowers and bluish-black or red berries. [OE *ellærn*; rel. to Mid. Low Ger. *ellern, elderne*.]

eld·er·ber·ry /'eldər,berē; -bərē/ ▶ n. the bluish-black or red berry of the elder, used esp. for making jelly or wine. ■ an elder tree or shrub.

el·der·care /'eldər,ke(ə)r/ ▶ n. care of the elderly or infirm, provided by residential institutions, by paid daily help in the home, or by family members.

eld·er·ly /'eldərlē/ ▶ adj. (of a person) old or aging: *she was an elderly lady* | [as pl. n.] (**the elderly**) *volunteers carried out home repairs for the elderly.* ■ (of a machine or similar object) showing signs of age. — **eld·er·li·ness** n.

eld·er states·man ▶ n. a person who is experienced and well-respected, esp. a politician.

eld·est /'eldist/ ▶ adj. (of one out of a group of related or otherwise associated people) of the greatest age; oldest. [OE *ieldest, eldest*, of Gmc. origin; rel. to Ger. *ältest*, also to ELD and OLD.]

eld·est hand ▶ n. (in card games) the player who is the first to receive a complete hand, usually the player immediately to the left of the dealer.

El Do·ra·do /,el də'rädō/ the name of a fictitious country or city abounding in gold, formerly believed to exist somewhere in South America. ■ [as n.] (**an El Dorado** or **eldorado**) (pl. **-dos**) a place of great abundance. [Spanish, literally 'the gilded one.']

el·dritch /'eldriCH/ ▶ adj. weird and sinister or ghostly. [16th C. (originally Scots): perh. rel. to ELF.]

El·ea·nor of Aq·ui·taine /'elənər əv 'akwi,tān/ (*c.*1122–1204), queen of France 1137–52 and of England 1154–89; daughter of the duke of Aquitaine. She was married to Louis VII of France and then to Henry II of England.

El·e·at·ic /,elē'atik/ ▶ adj. of or relating to Elea, an ancient Greek city in southwestern Italy, or the school of philosophers that flourished there in the 5th century BC, including Xenophanes, Parmenides, and Zeno. ▶ n. an Eleatic philosopher.

elec. ▶ abbr. ■ electric, electrical. ■ electrician. ■ electricity.

el·e·cam·pane /,elikam'pān/ ▶ n. an Asian plant (*Inula helenium*) of the daisy family with long slender yellow petals and bitter aromatic roots that are used in herbal medicine. [ME: from med. L. *enula* (from Gk. *helenion* 'elecampane') + *campana* prob. meaning 'of the fields' (from *campus* 'field').]

e·lect /i'lekt/ ▶ v. [trans.] (often **be elected**) choose (someone) to hold public office or some other position by voting. ■ opt for or choose to do (something). ■ Christian Theol. (of God) choose (someone) in preference to others for salvation. ▶ adj. [usu. as pl. n.] (**the elect**) (of a person) chosen or singled out: *one of the century's elect.* ■ [postpositive, in comb.] elected to or chosen for a position but not yet in office: *the president-elect.* ■ Christian Theol. chosen by God for salvation. — **e·lect·a·ble** adj. [ME: from L. *elect-* 'picked out,' from *eligere*, from *e-* + *legere* 'to pick.']

e·lec·tion /i'lekSHən/ ▶ n. **1** a formal and organized process of electing or being elected, esp. of members of a political body: *the 1860 presidential election* | [as adj.] *an election year.* ■ the act or an instance of electing or of being elected: *his election to the House of Representatives.* **2** (in Calvinist theology) predestined salvation.

e·lec·tion·eer /i,lekSHə'ni(ə)r/ ▶ v. [intrans.] [usu. as n.] (**electioneering**) (of a politician or political campaigner) take part actively and energetically in the activities of an election campaign. ▶ n. a campaigning politician during an election.

e·lec·tive /i'lektiv/ ▶ adj. **1** related to or working by means of election: *an elective democracy.* ■ (of a person or office) appointed or filled by election. ■ (of a body or position) possessing or giving the power to elect. **2** (of a course of study) chosen by the student rather than compulsory. ■ (of surgical or medical treatment) chosen by the patient rather than urgently necessary. ▶ n. an optional course of study. — **e·lec·tive·ly** adv. [ME: from OFr. *electif, -ive*, from late L. *electivus*, from *elect-* 'picked out,' from the v. *eligere* (see ELECT).]

e·lec·tor /i'lektər; -tôr/ ▶ n. **1** a person who has the right to vote in an election. ■ (in the US) a member of the electoral college. **2** [usu. as title] hist. a German prince entitled to take part in the election of the Holy Roman Emperor. — **e·lec·tor·ship** n.

e·lec·tor·al /i'lektərəl/ ▶ adj. of or relating to elections or electors: *electoral reform.* — **e·lec·tor·al·ly** adv.

e·lec·tor·al col·lege ▶ n. (also **E·lec·tor·al Col·lege**) (in the US) a body of people representing the states of the US, who formally cast votes for the election of the president and vice president. ■ a body of electors chosen by a larger group.

e·lec·tor·ate /i'lektərit/ ▶ n. **1** [treated as sing. or pl.] all the people entitled to vote in an election. **2** hist. the office or territories of a German elector.

E·lec·tra /i'lektrə/ Gk. Mythol. the daughter of Agamemnon and Clytemnestra. She persuaded her brother Orestes to kill Clytemnestra and Aegisthus (their mother's lover) in revenge for the murder of Agamemnon.

E·lec·tra com·plex ▶ n. Psychoanal., dated the Oedipus complex as manifested in young girls. [20th C.: named after ELECTRA.]

e·lec·tress /i'lektris/ ▶ n. [usu. as title] hist. the wife of a German elector.

e·lec·tret /i'lektrit/ ▶ n. Physics a permanently polarized piece of dielectric material, analogous to a permanent magnet. [19th C.: blend of ELECTRICITY and MAGNET.]

e·lec·tric /i'lektrik/ ▶ adj. of, worked by, charged with, or producing electricity: *an electric stove.* ■ fig. having or producing a sudden sense of thrilling excitement: *the atmosphere was electric.* ■ (of a musical instrument) amplified through a loudspeaker: *electric guitar.* ■ (of a color) brilliant and vivid: *images shot through with streaks of electric blue* ▶ n. an electric train or other vehicle. [17th C.: from mod. L. *electricus*, from L. *electrum* 'amber,' from Gk. *ēlektron*.]

e·lec·tri·cal /i'lektrikəl/ ▶ adj. operating by or producing electricity: *an electrical appliance.* ■ concerned with electricity: *an electrical engineer.* — **e·lec·tri·cal·ly** adv.

e·lec·tri·cal storm ▶ n. a thunderstorm or other disturbance of the electrical condition of the atmosphere.

e·lec·tric arc /ə'lektrik; ē'lektrik ärk/ ▶ n. see ARC.

e·lec·tric blan·ket ▶ n. a blanket that can be heated electrically by an internal element.

e·lec·tric chair ▶ n. a chair in which criminals sentenced to death are executed by electrocution.

e·lec·tric eel ▶ n. an eellike freshwater fish (*Electrophorus electricus*) of South America, using pulses of electricity to kill prey, to assist in navigation, and for defense.

e·lec·tric eye ▶ n. informal a photoelectric cell operating a relay when the light illuminating it is obscured.

e·lec·tric fence ▶ n. a fence through which an electric current can be passed, giving an electric shock to any person or animal touching it.

e·lec·tric field ▶ n. Physics a region around a charged particle or object within which a force would be exerted on other charged particles or objects.

e·lec·tric gui·tar ▶ n. a guitar with a built-in pickup or pickups that convert sound vibrations into electrical signals for amplification.

e·lec·tri·cian /ilek'triSHən; ,ēlek-/ ▶ n. a person who installs and maintains electrical equipment.

e·lec·tric in·ten·si·ty ▶ n. the strength of an electric field at any point, equal to the force per unit charge experienced by a small charge placed at that point.

e·lec·tric·i·ty /ilek'trisitē; ,ēlek-/ ▶ n. a form of energy resulting from the existence of charged particles (such as electrons or protons), either statically as an accumulation of charge or dynamically as a current. ■ the supply of electric current to a house or other building for heating, lighting, or powering appliances. ■ fig. a state or feeling of thrilling excitement: *an atmosphere charged with sexual electricity.*

e·lec·tric mo·ment ▶ n. the product of the distance separating the charges of a dipole and the magnitude of either charge.

e·lec·tric or·gan ▶ n. **1** Music an organ in which the sound is made electrically rather than by pipes. **2** Zool. an organ in certain fishes that is used to produce an electrical discharge for stunning prey, for sensing the surroundings, or as a defense.

e·lec·tric ray ▶**n.** a sluggish bottom-dwelling marine ray (*Torpedo* and other genera, family Torpedinidae) that typically lives in shallow water and can produce an electric shock to capture prey and for defense.

e·lec·tric shock ▶**n.** a sudden discharge of electricity through a part of the body.

e·lec·tri·fy /i'lektrə,fī/ ▶**v.** (**-fies, -fied**) [trans.] charge with electricity; pass an electric current through: [as adj.] (**electrified**) *an electrified fence.* ■ (often **be electrified**) convert (a machine or system, esp. a railroad line) to the use of electrical power. ■ fig. impress greatly; thrill. — **e·lec·tri·fi·ca·tion** /i,lektrəfi'kāsHən/ **n.** **e·lec·tri·fi·er n.**

e·lec·tro /i'lektrō/ ▶**n.** (pl. **-tros**) short for ELECTROTYPE or ELECTROPLATE.

electro- ▶**comb. form** of, relating to, or caused by electricity; involving electricity and ...: *electromagnetic.*

e·lec·tro·a·cous·tic /i,lektrōə'ko͞ostik/ ▶**adj.** involving the direct conversion of electrical into acoustic energy or vice versa. ■ (of a guitar) having both a pickup and a reverberating hollow body. ▶**n.** an electroacoustic guitar.

e·lec·tro·ac·u·punc·ture (also **e·lec·tro·ac·u·punc·ture**) ▶**n.** acupuncture in which the needles used carry a mild electric current.

e·lec·tro·car·di·o·gram /i,lektrō'kärdēə,gram/ (abbr.: **ECG** or **EKG**) ▶**n.** Med. a record or display of a person's heartbeat produced by electrocardiography.

e·lec·tro·car·di·o·graph /i,lektrō'kärdiə,graf/ (abbr.: **ECG** or **EKG**) ▶**n.** a machine used for electrocardiography.

e·lec·tro·car·di·og·ra·phy /i,lektrō,kärdē'ägrəfē/ (abbr.: **ECG** or **EKG**) ▶**n.** the measurement of electrical activity in the heart and the recording of such activity as a visual trace (on paper or on an oscilloscope screen), using electrodes placed on the skin. — **e·lec·tro·car·di·o·graph·ic** /-,kärdiə'grafik/ **adj.**

e·lec·tro·chem·is·try /i,lektrō'kemistrē/ ▶**n.** the branch of chemistry that deals with the relations between electrical and chemical phenomena. — **e·lec·tro·chem·i·cal** /-'kemikəl/ **adj.** **e·lec·tro·chem·i·cal·ly** /-'kemik(ə)lē/ **adv.** **e·lec·tro·chem·ist n.**

e·lec·tro·chrom·ism /i,lektrō'krōmizəm/ ▶**n.** Chem. the property of certain dyes of changing color when placed in an electric field. — **e·lec·tro·chro·mic adj.**

e·lec·tro·con·vul·sive /i,lektrōkən'vəlsiv/ ▶**adj.** of or relating to the treatment of mental illness by the application of electric shocks to the brain.

e·lec·tro·cor·ti·co·gram /i,lektrō'kôrtikō,gram/ ▶**n.** Physiol. a chart or record of the electrical activity of the brain made using electrodes in direct contact with it.

e·lec·tro·cute /i'lektrə,kyo͞ot/ ▶**v.** [trans.] (often **be electrocuted**) injure or kill someone by electric shock: *a man was electrocuted when he switched on the lights.* ■ execute (a criminal) by means of the electric chair. — **e·lec·tro·cu·tion** /i,lektrə'kyo͞osHən/ **n.** [19th C.: from ELECTRO-, on the pattern of *execute.*]

e·lec·trode /i'lektrōd/ ▶**n.** a conductor through which electricity enters or leaves an object, substance, or region.

e·lec·tro·der·mal /i,lektrō'dərməl/ ▶**adj.** of or relating to measurement of the electrical conductivity of the skin, esp. as an indicator of emotional responses.

e·lec·tro·di·al·y·sis /i,lektrōdī'aləsis/ ▶**n.** Chem. dialysis in which the movement of ions is aided by an electric field applied across the semipermeable membrane.

e·lec·tro·dy·nam·ics /i,lektrōdī'namiks/ ▶**plural n.** [usu. treated as sing.] the branch of mechanics concerned with the interaction of electric currents with magnetic fields or with other electric currents. — **e·lec·tro·dy·nam·ic adj.**

e·lec·tro·dy·na·mom·e·ter /i,lektrō,dīnə'mämitər/ ▶**n.** an instrument that measures electric current by indicating the strength of repulsion or attraction between the magnetic fields of two sets of coils, one fixed and one movable.

e·lec·tro·en·ceph·a·lo·gram /i,lektrōən'sefələ,gram/ (abbr.: **EEG**) ▶**n.** a test or record of brain activity produced by electroencephalography.

e·lec·tro·en·ceph·a·lo·graph /i,lektrōən'sefələ,graf/ (abbr.: **EEG**) ▶**n.** a machine used for electroencephalography.

e·lec·tro·en·ceph·a·log·ra·phy /i,lektrōən,sefə'lägrəfē/ (abbr.: **EEG**) ▶**n.** the measurement of electrical activity in different parts of the brain and the recording of such activity as a visual trace (on paper or on an oscilloscope screen).

e·lec·tro·gen·ic /i,lektrō'jenik/ ▶**adj.** Physiol. producing a change in the electrical potential of a cell.

e·lec·tro·jet /i'lektrə,jet/ ▶**n.** an intense electric current that occurs in a narrow belt in the lower ionosphere, esp. in the region of strong auroral displays.

e·lec·tro·ki·net·ic /i,lektrōkə'netik/ ▶**adj.** of or relating to the flow of electricity.

e·lec·trol·o·gist /ilek'träləjist/ ▶**n.** a person trained to remove unwanted hair on the body or face or small blemishes on the skin by a method that involves the application of heat using an electric current.

e·lec·tro·lu·mi·nes·cence /i,lektrō,lo͞omə'nesəns/ ▶**n.** Chem. luminescence produced electrically, esp. in a phosphor by the application of a voltage. — **e·lec·tro·lu·mi·nes·cent adj.**

e·lec·trol·y·sis /ilek'träləsis; ,ēlek-/ ▶**n.** **1** Chem. chemical decomposition produced by passing an electric current through a liquid or solution containing ions. **2** the removal of hair roots or small skin blemishes by the application of heat using an electric current. — **e·lec·tro·lyt·ic** /i,lektrə'litik/ **adj.** **e·lec·tro·lyt·i·cal** /i,lektrə'litikəl/ **adj.** **e·lec·tro·lyt·i·cal·ly** /i,lektrə'litik(ə)lē/ **adv.**

e·lec·tro·lyte /i'lektrə,līt/ ▶**n.** a liquid or gel that contains ions and can be decomposed by electrolysis, e.g., that present in a battery. ■ (usu. **electrolytes**) Physiol. the ionized or ionizable constituents of a living cell, blood, or other organic matter. [19th C.: from ELECTRO- + Gk. *lutos* 'released' (from *luein* 'loosen').]

e·lec·tro·lyt·ic cell /i,lektə'litik/ ▶**n** **1** a cell in which electrolysis occurs, consisting of an electrolyte through which current from an external source is passed, by a system of electrodes, in order to produce an electrochemical reaction. **2** a cell consisting of an electrolyte, its container, and two electrodes, in which the electrochemical reaction between the electrodes and the electrolyte produces an electric current.

e·lec·tro·lyze /i'lektrə,līz/ ▶**v.** [trans.] subject to or treat by electrolysis. — **e·lec·tro·lyz·er n.**

e·lec·tro·mag·net /i,lektrō'magnit/ ▶**n.** Physics a soft metal core made into a magnet by the passage of electric current through a coil surrounding it.

e·lec·tro·mag·net·ic /i,lektrōmag'netik/ ▶**adj.** of or relating to the interrelation of electric currents or fields and magnetic fields. — **e·lec·tro·mag·net·i·cal·ly** /-(ə)lē/ **adv.**

e·lec·tro·mag·net·ic field ▶**n.** a field of force that consists of both electric and magnetic components, resulting from the motion of an electric charge and containing a definite amount of electromagnetic energy.

e·lec·tro·mag·net·ic pulse ▶**n.** an intense pulse of electromagnetic radiation, esp. one generated by a nuclear explosion and occurring high above the earth's surface.

e·lec·tro·mag·net·ic ra·di·a·tion ▶**n.** Physics a kind of radiation including visible light, radio waves, gamma rays, and X-rays, in which electric and magnetic fields vary simultaneously.

e·lec·tro·mag·net·ic spec·trum ▶**n.** Physics the range of wavelengths or frequencies over which electromagnetic radiation extends.

e·lec·tro·mag·net·ic u·nits ▶**plural n.** Physics a largely obsolete system of electrical units derived primarily from the magnetic properties of electric currents.

e·lec·tro·mag·net·ism /i,lektrō'magnə,tizəm/ ▶**n.** the interaction of electric currents or fields and magnetic fields. ■ the branch of physics concerned with this.

e·lec·tro·me·chan·i·cal /i,lektrōmə'kanikəl/ ▶**adj.** of, relating to, or denoting a mechanical device that is electrically operated.

e·lec·trom·e·ter /ilek'trämitər; ,ēlek-/ ▶**n.** Physics an instrument for measuring electrical potential without drawing any current from the circuit. — **e·lec·tro·met·ric** /i,lektrə'metrik/ **adj.** **e·lec·trom·e·try** /-'trämitrē/ **n.**

e·lec·tro·mo·tive /i,lektrə'mōtiv/ ▶**adj.** Physics producing or tending to produce an electric current.

e·lec·tro·mo·tive force (abbr.: **emf**) ▶**n.** Physics a difference in potential that tends to give rise to an electric current.

e·lec·tro·my·o·gram /i,lektrō'mīə,gram/ ▶**n.** Med. a record or display produced by electromyography.

e·lec·tro·my·og·ra·phy /i,lektrōmī'ägrəfē/ ▶**n.** the recording of the electrical activity of muscle tissue, or its visual or audible representation, using electrodes attached to the skin or inserted into the muscle. — **e·lec·tro·my·o·graph** /-'mīə,graf/ **n.** **e·lec·tro·my·o·graph·ic** /-,mīə'grafik/ **adj.** **e·lec·tro·my·o·graph·i·cal·ly** /-,mīə'grafik(ə)lē/ **adv.**

e·lec·tron /i'lekträn/ ▶**n.** Physics a stable subatomic particle with a charge of negative electricity, found in all atoms and acting as the primary carrier of electricity in solids. [19th C.: from ELECTRIC + -ON.]

e·lec·tron beam ▶**n.** Physics a stream of electrons in a gas or vacuum.

e·lec·tron dif·frac·tion ▶**n.** Physics the diffraction of a beam of electrons by atoms or molecules, used esp. for determining crystal structures.

e·lec·tro·neg·a·tive /i,lektrə'negətiv/ ▶**adj.** **1** Physics electrically negative. **2** Chem. (of an element) tending to acquire electrons and form negative ions in chemical reactions. — **e·lec·tro·neg·a·tiv·i·ty** /i,lektrō,negə'tivitē/ **n.** (sense 2).

e·lec·tron gun ▶**n.** Physics a device for producing a narrow stream of electrons from a heated cathode.

e·lec·tron·ic /ilek'tränik; ,ēlek-/ ▶**adj.** **1** (of a device) having, or operating with the aid of, many small components, esp. microchips and transistors, that control and direct an electric current: *an electronic calculator.* ■ (of music) produced by electronic instruments. ■ of or relating to electronics. **2** of or relating to electrons. **3** relating to or carried out using a computer or other electronic device, esp. over a network. — **e·lec·tron·i·cal·ly** /-ik(ə)lē/ **adv.** [20th C.: from ELECTRON + -IC.]

e·lec·tron·ic flash ▶**n.** Photog. a flash from a gas-discharge tube, used in high-speed photography.

e·lec·tron·ic mail ▶**n.** another term for E-MAIL.

e·lec·tron·ic mu·sic ▶**n.** music created using synthesizers and other electronic instruments.

e·lec·tron·ic or·gan·iz·er ▶**n.** a pocket-sized computer used for storing and retrieving information such as addresses and appointments.

e·lec·tron·ic pub·lish·ing ▶**n.** the issuing of books and other material in machine-readable form.

e·lec·tron·ics /ilek'träniks; ˌēlek-/ ▶ **plural n.** [usu. treated as sing.] the branch of physics and technology concerned with the design of circuits using transistors and microchips, and with the behavior and movement of electrons in a semiconductor, conductor, vacuum, or gas. ■ [treated as pl.] circuits or devices using transistors, microchips, and other components.

e·lec·tron·ic tag·ging ▶ **n.** the attaching of electronic markers to people or goods for monitoring purposes.

e·lec·tron lens ▶ **n.** Physics a device for focusing a stream of electrons by means of electric or magnetic fields.

e·lec·tron mi·cro·scope ▶ **n.** Physics a microscope with high magnification and resolution, employing electron beams in place of light and using electron lenses.

e·lec·tron op·tics ▶ **plural n.** [treated as sing.] the branch of physics that deals with the behavior of electrons and electron beams in magnetic and electric fields.

e·lec·tron spin res·o·nance (abbr.: **ESR**) ▶ **n.** Physics a spectroscopic method of locating electrons within the molecules of a paramagnetic substance.

e·lec·tron tube ▶ **n.** Physics an evacuated or gas-filled tube in which a current of electrons flows between electrodes.

e·lec·tron volt (abbr.: **eV**) ▶ **n.** Physics a unit of energy equal to the work done on an electron in accelerating it through a potential difference of one volt.

e·lec·tro·op·tics /iˌlektrō'äptiks/ ▶ **plural n.** [treated as sing.] the branch of science that deals with the effect of electric fields on light and on optical properties. — **e·lec·tro·op·tic adj. e·lec·tro·op·ti·cal** /-'äptikəl/ **adj.**

e·lec·tro·os·mo·sis /iˌlektrō-äz'mōsis; -äs-/ ▶ **n.** osmosis under the influence of an electric field. — **e·lec·tro·os·mot·ic** /-'mätik/ **adj.**

e·lec·tro·phil·ic /iˌlektrə'filik/ ▶ **adj.** Chem. (of a molecule or group) having a tendency to attract or acquire electrons. Often contrasted with NUCLEOPHILIC. — **e·lec·tro·phile** /i'lektrəˌfīl/ **n.**

e·lec·tro·pho·re·sis /iˌlektrəfə'rēsis/ ▶ **n.** Physics Chem. the movement of charged particles in a fluid or gel under the influence of an electric field. — **e·lec·tro·pho·rese** /-'rēs/ **v. e·lec·tro·pho·ret·ic** /-'retik/ **adj. e·lec·tro·pho·ret·i·cal·ly** /-'retik(ə)lē/ **adv.** [20th C.: from ELECTRO- + Gk. *phorēsis* 'being carried.']

e·lec·troph·o·rus /iˌlek'träfərəs/ ▶ **n.** Physics a device for generating static electricity by induction. [18th C.: from ELECTRO- + Gk. *-phoros* 'bearing.']

e·lec·tro·phys·i·ol·o·gy /iˌlektrōˌfizē'äləjē/ ▶ **n.** the branch of physiology that deals with the electrical phenomena associated with nervous and other activity. — **e·lec·tro·phys·i·o·log·i·cal** /-ˌfizēə'läjikəl/ **adj. e·lec·tro·phys·i·o·log·i·cal·ly** /-ˌfizēə'läjik(ə)lē/ **adv. e·lec·tro·phys·i·ol·o·gist** /-jist/ **n.**

e·lec·tro·plate /i'lektrəˌplāt/ ▶ **v.** [trans.] [usu. as n.] (**electroplating**) coat (a metal object) by electrolytic deposition with chromium, silver, or another metal. ▶ **n.** electroplated articles. — **e·lec·tro·plat·er n.**

e·lec·tro·pol·ish /iˌlektrō'pälisн/ ▶ **v.** [trans.] [often as n.] (**electropolishing**) give a shiny surface to (metal) using electrolysis.

e·lec·tro·pos·i·tive /iˌlektrə'päzitiv/ ▶ **adj.** **1** Physics electrically positive. **2** Chem. (of an element) tending to lose electrons and form positive ions in chemical reactions.

e·lec·tro·re·cep·tion /iˌlektrō-ri'sepsнən/ ▶ **n.** the detection by an aquatic animal of electric fields or currents. — **e·lec·tro·re·cep·tor** /-'septər/ **n.**

e·lec·tro·ret·i·no·gram /iˌlektrō'retn-ōˌgram/ ▶ **n.** a record of the electrical activity of the retina, used in medical diagnosis and research.

e·lec·tro·scope /i'lektrəˌskōp/ ▶ **n.** Physics an instrument for detecting and measuring electricity, esp. as an indication of the ionization of air by radioactivity. — **e·lec·tro·scop·ic** /iˌlektrə'skäpik/ **adj.**

e·lec·tro·shock /i'lektrəˌsнäk/ ▶ **adj.** [attrib.] of or relating to medical treatment by means of electric shocks.

e·lec·tro·stat·ic /iˌlektrə'statik/ ▶ **adj.** Physics of or relating to stationary electric charges or fields as opposed to electric currents.

e·lec·tro·stat·ic gen·er·a·tor ▶ **n.** any of various devices used to build up an electric charge to an extreme potential in order to generate electricity, esp. the Van de Graaf generator.

e·lec·tro·stat·ic pre·cip·i·ta·tor ▶ **n.** a device that removes suspended dust particles from a gas or exhaust by applying a high-voltage electrostatic charge and collecting the particles on charged plates.

e·lec·tro·stat·ics /iˌlektrə'statiks/ ▶ **plural n.** [treated as sing.] Physics the study of stationary electric charges or fields as opposed to electric currents.

e·lec·tro·stat·ic u·nits ▶ **plural n.** a system of units based primarily on the forces between electric charges.

e·lec·tro·sur·ger·y /iˌlektrō'sərjərē/ ▶ **n.** surgery using an electric current to heat and cut tissue. — **e·lec·tro·sur·gi·cal** /-'sərjikəl/ **adj.**

e·lec·tro·tech·nol·o·gy /iˌlektrōtek'näləjē/ (also **e·lec·tro·tech·nics** /-'tekniks/) ▶ **n.** the science of the application of electricity in technology. — **e·lec·tro·tech·nic** /-'teknik/ **adj. e·lec·tro·tech·ni·cal** /-'teknikəl/ **adj.**

e·lec·tro·ther·a·py /iˌlektrō'тнerəpē/ ▶ **n.** the use of electric currents passed through the body to stimulate nerves and muscles, chiefly in the treatment of various forms of paralysis. — **e·lec·tro·ther·a·peu·tic** /-ˌтнerə'pyōōtik/ **adj. e·lec·tro·ther·a·peu·ti·cal** /-ˌтнerə'pyōōtikəl/ **adj. e·lec·tro·ther·a·pist n.**

e·lec·tro·ther·mal /iˌlektrə'тнərməl/ ▶ **adj.** Physics of or relating to heat derived from electricity.

e·lec·tro·type /i'lektrəˌtīp/ ▶ **v.** [trans.] [often as n.] (**electrotyping**) make a copy of (something) by the electrolytic deposition of copper on a mold. ▶ **n.** a copy made in such a way. — **e·lec·tro·typ·er n.**

e·lec·tro·va·lent /iˌlektrə'vālənt/ ▶ **adj.** Chem. (of bonding) resulting from electrostatic attraction between positive and negative ions; ionic. — **e·lec·tro·va·lence n. e·lec·tro·va·len·cy n.** [1920s: from ELECTRO- + *-valent*, on the pattern of *trivalent*.]

e·lec·tro·weak /i'lektrōˌwēk/ ▶ **adj.** Physics relating to or denoting electromagnetic and weak interactions regarded as manifestations of the same interaction.

e·lec·trum /i'lektrəm/ ▶ **n.** a natural or artificial alloy of gold with at least 20 percent silver. [ME: via L. from Gk. *ēlektron* 'amber, electrum.']

e·lec·tu·ar·y /i'lekcнōōˌerē/ ▶ **n.** (pl. **-ar·ies**) archaic a medicine mixed with honey or another sweet substance. [ME: from late L. *electuarium*, prob. from Gk. *ekleikton*, from *ekleikhein* 'lick up.']

el·ee·mos·y·nar·y /ˌelə'mäsəˌnerē; ˌelēə-/ ▶ **adj.** of, relating to, or dependent on charity; charitable. [16th C.: from med. L. *eleemosynarius*, from late L. *eleemosyna* 'alms,' from Gk. *eleēmosunē* 'compassion' (see ALMS).]

el·e·gan·cy /'eligənsē/ ▶ **n.** **1** graceful and stylish appearance or manner; elegance. **2** something that is elegant: *the elegancies of life.*

el·e·gant /'eligənt/ ▶ **adj.** pleasingly graceful and stylish in appearance or manner. ■ (of a scientific theory or solution to a problem) pleasingly ingenious and simple. — **el·e·gance n. el·e·gant·ly adv.** [15th C.: from Fr., or from L. *elegans, elegant-*, rel. to *eligere* 'choose, select' (see ELECT).]

el·e·gi·ac /ˌelə'jīək; i'lējēˌak/ ▶ **adj.** (esp. of a work of art) having a mournful quality. ■ (of a poetic meter) used for elegies. ▶ **plural n.** (**elegiacs**) verses in an elegiac meter. — **el·e·gi·a·cal·ly** /ˌelə'jīək(ə)lē/ **adv.**

el·e·gi·ac cou·plet ▶ **n.** a pair of lines consisting of a dactylic hexameter and a pentameter, esp. in Greek and Latin verse.

el·e·gi·ac stan·za ▶ **n.** a quatrain in iambic pentameter rhymed *abab*. Compare with HEROIC STANZA.

el·e·gize /'eləˌjīz/ ▶ **v.** [intrans.] write in a wistfully mournful way about someone or something. — **el·e·gist** /-jist/ **n.**

el·e·gy /'eləjē/ ▶ **n.** (pl. **-gies**) **1** a poem of serious reflection, typically a lament for the dead. ■ a piece of music in a mournful style. **2** (in Greek and Roman poetry) a poem written in elegiac couplets, as notably by Catullus and Propertius. [16th C.: from Fr. *élégie*, or via L., from Gk. *elegeia*, from *elegos* 'mournful poem.']

elem. ▶ **abbr.** elementary.

el·e·ment /'eləmənt/ ▶ **n.** **1** a part or aspect of something, esp. one that is essential or characteristic. ■ a small but significant presence of a feeling or abstract quality: *it was the element of danger he loved in flying.* ■ (**elements**) *legal training may include the elements of economics and political science.* ■ [usu. with adj.] (often **elements**) a group of people of a particular kind within a larger group or organization. ■ Math. Logic an entity that is a single member of a set. **2** (also **chemical element**) each of more than one hundred substances that cannot be chemically interconverted or broken down into simpler substances and are primary constituents of matter. Each element is distinguished by its atomic number, i.e., the number of protons in the nuclei of its atoms. ■ any of the four substances (earth, water, air, and fire) regarded as the fundamental constituents of the world in ancient and medieval philosophy. ■ one of these substances considered as a person's or animal's natural environment: *the sea is their kingdom, water their element* | fig. *she* ***was in her element*** *with hospitals.* ■ (**the elements**) the weather, esp. winds, heavy rain, and other kinds of bad weather. ■ (**elements**) (in church use) the bread and wine of the Eucharist. **3** a part in an electric pot, heater, or stove that contains a wire through which current is passed to provide heat. [ME: via OFr. from L. *elementum* 'principle, rudiment.']

el·e·men·tal /ˌelə'mentl/ ▶ **adj.** **1** primary or basic: *elemental features from which structures are compounded.* ■ concerned with chemical elements or other basic components: *elemental analysis.* ■ consisting of a single chemical element. **2** related to or embodying the powers of nature. ■ (of a human emotion or action) having the primitive and inescapable character of a force of nature. ▶ **n.** a supernatural entity or force thought to be physically manifested by occult means. — **el·e·men·tal·ism n.**

el·e·men·ta·ry /ˌelə'ment(ə)rē/ ▶ **adj.** of or relating to the most rudimentary aspects of a subject. ■ easily dealt with; straightforward and uncomplicated: *a lot of the work is elementary.* ■ not decomposable into elements or other primary constituents. — **el·e·men·tar·i·ly adv. el·e·men·ta·ri·ness n.**

el·e·men·ta·ry par·ti·cle ▶ **n.** another term for PARTICLE (sense 1).

el·e·men·ta·ry school ▶ **n.** a school for the first four to eight grades, and usually including kindergarten.

el·e·mi /'eləmē/ ▶ **n.** an oleoresin obtained from a tropical tree and used in varnishes, ointments, and aromatherapy. This resin is obtained from several trees in the family Burseraceae, in particular *Bursera simaruba* (producing **American elemi**) and *Canarium luzanicum* (producing **Manila elemi**). [16th C.: perh. from Arab. *al-lāmī*.]

e·len·chus /iˈleNGkəs/ ▶**n.** (pl. **-chi** /-kī; -kē/) Logic a logical refutation. ■ (also **Socratic elenchus**) the Socratic method of eliciting truth by question and answer, esp. as used to refute an argument. [17th C.: via L. from Gk. *elenkhos*.]

el·e·phant /ˈeləfənt/ ▶**n.** (pl. same or **-phants**) a heavy plant-eating mammal (family Elephantidae, order Proboscidea) with a prehensile trunk, long curved ivory tusks, and large ears, native to Africa and southern Asia. It is the largest living land animal. See **African elephant, Indian elephant.**
– PHRASES **the elephant in the room** a major problem or controversial issue that is obviously present but avoided as a subject for discussion because it is more comfortable to do so. [ME: from OFr. *elefant*, via L. from Gk. *elephas, elephant-* 'ivory, elephant.']

Indian elephant

African elephant

elephants

el·e·phant bird ▶**n.** a heavily built, giant flightless bird (genera *Aepyornis* and *Mullerornis*, family Aepyornithidae), found in Madagascar until its extermination about AD 1000. The eggs are the largest known.

el·e·phant ear ▶**n.** any of a number of plants with large heart-shaped leaves.

el·e·phan·ti·a·sis /ˌeləfənˈtīəsis/ ▶**n.** Med. a condition in which a limb or other body part becomes grossly enlarged due to obstruction of lymphatic vessels, typically by the parasitic nematodes that cause filariasis.

el·e·phan·tine /ˌeləˈfantēn; -tīn; ˈeləfənˌtēn; -ˌtīn/ ▶**adj.** of, resembling, or characteristic of an elephant or elephants, esp. in being large, clumsy, or awkward.

el·e·phant seal ▶**n.** a large true seal (genus *Mirounga*) that breeds on the west coast of North America and the islands around Antarctica. The male, much larger than the female, has a very thick neck and an inflatable snout.

El·eu·sin·i·an mys·ter·ies /ˌelyo͞oˈsinēən/ ▶**plural n.** the annual rites performed by the ancient Greeks at Eleusis, near Athens, in honor of Demeter and Persephone.

elev. ▶**abbr.** elevation.

el·e·vate /ˈeləˌvāt/ ▶**v.** [trans.] raise or lift (something) up to a higher position. ■ raise to a more important or impressive level: *he was **elevated to** secretary of state.* ■ (of a priest) hold up (a consecrated host or chalice) for adoration. ■ increase the level or amount of (something, esp. the level of a component of a person's blood): *the drug can elevate blood pressure.* ■ raise the axis of (a piece of artillery) to increase its range. — **el·e·va·to·ry** /-vəˌtôrē/ **adj.** [ME: from L. *elevat-* 'raised,' from the v. *elevare*, from *e-* (var. of *ex-*) 'out, away' + *levare* 'lighten' (from *levis* 'light').]

el·e·vat·ed /ˈeləˌvātid/ ▶**adj.** situated or placed higher than the surrounding area. ■ (of a road or railroad) raised on supports above the surrounding area: *the elevated section of the freeway.* ■ (of a level or amount) higher or greater than what is considered normal: *an elevated temperature.* ■ of a high intellectual or moral standard or level. ■ having a high rank or social standing. ▶**n.** an elevated railroad.

el·e·va·tion /ˌeləˈvāSHən/ ▶**n.** **1** the action or fact of elevating or being elevated. ■ augmentation of or increase in the amount or level of something: ■ (in a Christian Mass) the raising of the consecrated elements for adoration. **2** height above a given level, esp. sea level. ■ a high place or position. ■ the angle of something with the horizontal, esp. of a gun or of the direction of a celestial object. ■ Ballet the ability of a dancer to attain height in jumps. **3** a particular side of a building: *the front elevation.* ■ a drawing of the front, side, or back of a house or other building: *a set of plans and elevations.* ■ a drawing or diagram, esp. of a building, made by projection on a vertical plane. Compare with **plan** (sense 3). — **el·e·va·tion·al** /-SHənl/ **adj.**

el·e·va·tor /ˈeləˌvātər/ ▶**n.** **1** a platform or compartment housed in a shaft for raising and lowering people or things to different floors or levels. ■ a machine consisting of an endless belt with scoops attached, used typically for raising grain for storage. ■ a tall building used for storing grain. **2** a hinged flap on the horizontal stabilizer of an aircraft, used to control the motion of the aircraft about its lateral axis. **3** a muscle whose contraction raises a part of the body. **4** (also **elevator shoe**) a shoe with a raised insole designed to make the wearer appear taller.

e·lev·en /iˈlevən/ ▶**cardinal number** equivalent to the sum of six and five; one more than ten; 11: *the room was about eleven feet wide* | *eighteen schools, eleven of them in Los Angeles.* (Roman numeral: **xi** or **XI**.) ■ eleven years old. ■ eleven o'clock. ■ a size of garment or other merchandise. ■ a group of eleven people or things. — **e·lev·en·fold adj. & adv.** [OE *endleofon*, from the base of **one** + a second element (prob. 'left over').]

e·lev·enth /iˈlevənTH/ ▶**ordinal number** constituting number eleven in a sequence; 11th: *the eleventh century* | *February the eleventh* | *the eleventh fairway.* ■ (**an eleventh/one eleventh**) each of eleven equal parts into which something is or may be divided. ■ the eleventh grade of a school.
– PHRASES **the eleventh hour** the latest possible moment: *refused to make a decision until the eleventh hour.*

el·e·von /ˈeləˌvän/ ▶**n.** Aeron. the movable part of the trailing edge of a delta wing. [1940s: blend of **elevator** and **aileron.**]

ELF ▶**abbr.** extremely low frequency.

elf /elf/ ▶**n.** (pl. **elves** /elvz/) a supernatural creature of folk tales, typically represented as a small, elusive figure in human form with pointed ears, magical powers, and a capricious nature. — **elf·ish adj. elv·en** /ˈelvin/ **adj.** (literary) **elv·ish** /ˈelviSH/ **adj.** [OE, of Gmc. origin; rel. to Ger. *Alp* 'nightmare.']

El Fai·yum /ˌel fāˈ(y)o͞om; fī-/ (also **Fayum** or **Al Fayyum**) a historic oasis town in northern Egypt, southwest of Cairo; pop. 244,000.

elf·in /ˈelfin/ ▶**adj.** small and delicate, typically with an attractively mischievous or strange charm. ▶**n.** archaic an elf. [16th C.: from **elf.**]

elf·locks /ˈelfˌläks/ ▶**plural n.** a tangled mass of hair.

elf owl ▶**n.** a tiny owl (*Micrathene whitneyi*, family Strigidae) that nests in cacti and trees in the arid country of the southern US and Mexico.

El·gar /ˈelˌgär; -gər/, Sir Edward William (1857–1934), British composer, noted for his five *Pomp and Circumstance* marches (1901–30).

El·gin /ˈeljin/ a in northeastern Illinois, west of Chicago; pop. 94,487.

El·gin Mar·bles /ˈelgin ˈmärbəlz; ˈeljin/ a collection of classical Greek marble sculptures and architectural fragments, chiefly from the Parthenon in Athens, brought to England by the diplomat and art connoisseur Thomas Bruce (1766–1841), the 7th Earl of Elgin.

El Gi·za /el ˈgēzə/ another name for **Giza.**

El Gre·co /el ˈgrekō/ (1541–1614), Spanish painter; born on Crete; born *Domenikos Theotokopoulos.* His works are characterized by distorted perspective, elongated figures, and strident use of color.

el·hi /ˈelˈhī/ ▶**adj.** informal of, relating to, or intended for use in grades 1 to 12.

E·li /ˈēlī/ (in the Bible) a priest who acted as a teacher to the prophet Samuel.

E·li·a /ˈēlēə/ the pen name used by Charles Lamb.

e·lic·it /iˈlisit/ ▶**v.** (**-it·ed, -it·ing**) [trans.] evoke or draw out (a response or fact) from someone by actions or questions: *their moves elicit exclamations of approval.* ■ archaic draw forth (something that is latent or potential) into existence: *war elicits all that is bad in us.* — **e·lic·i·ta·tion** /iˌlisiˈtāSHən/ **n. e·lic·i·tor** /-tər/ **n.** [17th C.: from L. *elicit-* 'drawn out,' from *elicere*, from *e-* + *lacere* 'entice, deceive.']

e·lide /iˈlīd/ ▶**v.** [trans.] omit (a sound or syllable) when speaking: [as adj.] (**elided**) *elided consonants or vowels.* ■ join together; merge: *whole periods are **elided into** a few seconds of screen time* | [intrans.] *the two things elided in his mind.* [16th C.: from L. *elidere* 'crush out,' from *e-* + *laedere* 'to dash.']

el·i·gi·ble /ˈeləjəbəl/ ▶**adj.** having the right to do or obtain something; satisfying the appropriate conditions. ■ (of a person) desirable or suitable as a partner in marriage: *the world's most eligible bachelor.* — **el·i·gi·bil·i·ty** /ˌeləjəˈbilitē/ **n. el·i·gi·bly adv.** [ME: via Fr. from late L. *eligibilis*, from L. *eligere* 'choose, select' (see **elect**).]

E·li·jah /iˈlījə/ (9th century BC), a Hebrew prophet in the time of Jezebel who maintained the worship of Jehovah against that of Baal and other pagan gods.

e·lim·i·nate /iˈliməˌnāt/ ▶**v.** [trans.] completely remove or get rid of (something). ■ exclude (someone or something) from consideration. ■ murder (a rival or political opponent). ■ (usu. **be eliminated**) exclude (a person or team) from further participation in a sporting competition following defeat or inadequate results. ■ Math. remove (a variable) from an equation, typically by substituting another that is shown by another equation to be equivalent. ■ Chem. generate or remove (a simple substance) as a product in the course of a reaction involving larger molecules. ■ Physiol. expel (waste matter) from the body. — **e·lim·i·na·ble** /-nəbəl/ **adj. e·lim·i·na·tion** /iˌliməˈnāSHən/ **n. e·lim·i·na·tor** /-ˌnātər/ **n. e·lim·i·na·to·ry** /-nəˌtôrē/ **adj.** [16th C.: from L. *eliminat-* 'turned out of doors,' from *eliminare*, from *e-* 'out' + *limen, limin-* 'threshold.']

El·i·ot[1] /ˈelēət/, A. D., see **Jewett.**

El·i·ot[2], Alice, see **Jewett.**

El·i·ot[3], George (1819–80), English writer; pen name of *Mary Ann Evans.* Her novels include *Adam Bede* (1859), *The Mill on the Floss* (1860), and *Middlemarch* (1871–72).

El·i·ot[4], T. S. (1888–1965), British poet, critic, and playwright; born in the US; full name *Thomas Stearns Eliot.* Associated with the rise of literary modernism, he wrote *The Waste Land* (1922). Nobel Prize for Literature (1948).

ELISA /iˈlīzə; iˈlīsə/ ▶**n.** Biochem. enzyme-linked immunosorbent assay, an immunological assay technique making use of an enzyme bonded to a particular antibody or antigen.

E·li·sha /iˈlīSHə/ (9th century BC), a Hebrew prophet.

e·li·sion /iˈliZHən/ ▶**n.** the omission of a sound or syllable when speaking (as in *I'm, let's, e'en*). ■ an omission of a passage in a book, speech, or film. ■ the process of joining together or merging things, esp. abstract ideas: *the elision of vital questions.* [16th C.: from late L. *elision-*, from

L. *elidere* 'crush out' (see ELIDE).]

e·lite /i'lēt; ā'lēt/ ▶ n. **1** a group of people considered to be the best in a particular society or category, esp. because of their power, talent, or wealth: *China's educated elite* | [as adj.] *an elite combat force.* **2** a size of letter in typewriting, with 12 characters to the inch (about 4.7 to the centimeter). [18th C.: from Fr. *élite* 'selection, choice,' from *élire* 'to elect,' from a var. of L. *eligere* (see ELECT).]

e·lit·ism /i'lē,tizəm; ā'lē-/ ▶ n. the advocacy or existence of an elite as a dominating element in a system or society. ■ the attitude or behavior of a person or group who regard themselves as belonging to an elite.

e·lit·ist /i'lētist; ā'lētist/ ▶ n. a person who believes that a system or society should be ruled or dominated by an elite. ■ a person who believes that they belong to an elite. ▶ adj. favoring, advocating, or restricted to an elite.

e·lix·ir /i'liksər/ ▶ n. a magical or medicinal potion. ■ a preparation that was supposedly able to change metals into gold, sought by alchemists. ■ (also **elixir of life**) a preparation supposedly able to prolong life indefinitely. ■ a medicinal solution of a specified type: *a natural herbal cough elixir.* [ME: via med. L. from Arab. *al-'iksīr*, from *al* 'the' + *'iksīr* from Gk. *xērion* 'powder for drying wounds' (from *xēros* 'dry').]

Eliz·a·beth /i'lizəbəTH/ a port city in northeastern New Jersey, on Newark Bay; pop. 120,568.

E·liz·a·beth I /ə'lizəbəTH/ (1533–1603), queen of England and Ireland 1558–1603; daughter of Henry VIII. She reestablished Protestantism as the state religion.

E·liz·a·beth II (1926–), daughter of George VI; queen of the United Kingdom since 1952; born *Princess Elizabeth Alexandra Mary.* She married Prince Philip in 1947; they have four children: Prince Charles, Princess Anne, Prince Andrew, and Prince Edward.

E·liz·a·be·than /i,lizə'bēTHən/ ▶ adj. of, relating to, or characteristic of the reign of Queen Elizabeth I. ▶ n. a person, esp. a writer, of that time.

E·liz·a·be·than son·net ▶ n. a type of sonnet much used by Shakespeare, written in iambic pentameter and consisting of three quatrains and a final couplet with the rhyme scheme abab cdcd efef gg.

elk /elk/ ▶ n. **1** (pl. same or **elks**) a red deer (*Cervus canadensis*) of a large race native to North America. Also called WAPITI. ■ British term for MOOSE. **2** (**Elk**) (pl. **Elks**) a member of a fraternal organization, the Benevolent and Protective Order of Elks. [15th C.: prob. from OE *elh, eolh.*]

Elk·hart /'elkärt; 'elk,härt/ a city in northern Indiana; pop. 51,847.

Elk Hills a range in south central California, near Bakersfield, the site of an oil reserve that was involved in the 1920s Teapot Dome scandal.

elk·hound /'elk,hound/ (in full **Norwegian elkhound**) ▶ n. a large hunting dog of a Scandinavian breed with a shaggy gray coat.

ell[1] /el/ ▶ n. a former measure of length (equivalent to six hand breadths) used mainly for textiles, locally variable but typically about 45 inches. [OE *eln*, of Gmc. origin; from an Indo-Eur. root shared by L. *ulna* (see ULNA).]

ell[2] ▶ n. something that is L-shaped or that creates an L shape, in particular: ■ an extension of a building or room that is at right angles to the main part. ■ a bend or joint for connecting two pipes at right angles.

el·lag·ic ac·id /ə'lajik/ ▶ n. Chem. a compound, $C_{14}H_6O_8$, extracted from oak galls and various fruits and nuts. It has some ability to inhibit blood flow and inhibit the growth of cancer cells. [19th C.: *ellagic* from Fr. *ellagique* (an anagram of *galle* 'gallnut' + *-ique*).]

Elles·mere Is·land /'elz,mi(ə)r/ the most northern of the islands in the Canadian Arctic.

El·lice Is·lands /'eləs/ former name of TUVALU.

El·li·cott Cit·y /'elikət/ a historic community in north central Maryland; pop. 41,396.

El·ling·ton /'eliNGtən/, Duke (1899–1974), US pianist, composer, and bandleader; born *Edward Kennedy Ellington.* He wrote over 900 compositions, including *Mood Indigo* (1930).

el·lipse /i'lips/ ▶ n. a regular oval shape, traced by a point moving in a plane so that the sum of its distances from two other points (the foci) is constant, or resulting when a cone is cut by an oblique plane that does not intersect the base.

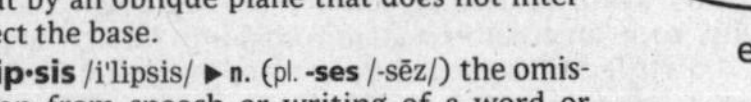
ellipse

el·lip·sis /i'lipsis/ ▶ n. (pl. **-ses** /-sēz/) the omission from speech or writing of a word or words that are superfluous or be understood from contextual clues. ■ a set of dots indicating such an omission. [16th C.: via L. from Gk. *elleipsis*, from *elleipein* 'leave out.']

el·lip·soid /i'lipsoid/ ▶ n. a three-dimensional figure symmetrical around each of three perpendicular axes, whose plane sections normal to one axis are circles and all the other plane sections are ellipses. — **el·lip·soi·dal** /i,lip'soidl; ,elip-/ adj.

el·lip·tic /i'liptik/ ▶ adj. **1** of, relating to, or having the form of an ellipse. **2** (of speech or writing) lacking a word or words, esp. when the sense is understandable from contextual clues. — **el·lip·ti·cal** adj. **el·lip·ti·cal·ly** /-(ə)lē/ adv.

el·lip·tic·i·ty /i,lip'tisitē; ,elip-/ ▶ n. the condition of being elliptic. ■ the degree of deviation from circularity (or sphericity).

El·lis Is·land /'eləs/ an island in the bay of New York that served as an entry point for immigrants 1892–1943 and as a detention center for deportation until 1954. It is now part of a national monument.

El·li·son /'eləsən/, Ralph Waldo (1914–94), US writer. He is noted for his novel *Invisible Man* (1952).

Ells·berg, Daniel, (1931–), US political activist. A former adviser to President Nixon on policy in Southeast Asia, he became an avid opponent of the Vietnam War and was indicted for leaking classified Vietnam-related papers (the "Pentagon Papers") to the press in 1971.

Ells·worth[1] /'elz,wərTH/, Lincoln (1880–1951), US explorer. He was the first person to fly over both the North (1926) and South (1935) poles.

Ells·worth[2], Oliver (1745–1807), Chief Justice of the US 1796–1800.

Ells·worth Land a plateau region in Antarctica between the Walgreen Coast and Palmer Land. It rises at the Vinson Massif to 16,863 feet (5,140 m), the highest point in Antarctica.

elm /elm/ (also **elm tree**) ▶ n. a tall deciduous tree (genus *Ulmus*, family Ulmaceae) that typically has rough serrated leaves and propagates from root suckers. ■ (also **elmwood**) the wood of this tree. [OE, of Gmc. origin; rel. to Ger. dial. *Ilm.*]

El Ma·hal·la el Ku·bra /,el mə'halə ,el 'ko͞obrə/ a city in northern Egypt; pop. 400,000.

El Man·su·ra /,el män'so͞orə/ (also **Al Mansurah**) a city in northeastern Egypt, in the Nile Delta, on the Damietta branch; pop. 362,000.

El Mon·te /el 'mäntē/ a city in southwestern California, east of Los Angeles; pop. 106,209.

El Ni·ño /el 'nēnyō/ ▶ n. (pl. **-ños**) an irregularly occurring and complex series of climatic changes affecting the equatorial Pacific region and beyond every few years, characterized by the appearance of unusually warm, nutrient-poor water off northern Peru and Ecuador, typically in late December.

el·o·cu·tion /,elə'kyo͞oSHən/ ▶ n. the skill of clear and expressive speech, esp. of distinct pronunciation and articulation. ■ a particular style of speaking. — **el·o·cu·tion·ar·y** /-SHə,nerē/ adj. **el·o·cu·tion·ist** n. [ME: from L. *elocutio(n-)*, from *eloqui* 'speak out' (see ELOQUENCE).]

e·lo·de·a /i'lōdēə/ ▶ n. an aquatic plant (family Hydrocharitaceae) of the genus *Elodea*, which includes the ornamental waterweeds. [mod. L., from Gk. *helōdēs* 'marshy.']

E·lo·him /e'lōhim; ,elō'hēm; ,elō'him/ ▶ n. a name for God used frequently in the Hebrew Bible. [from Heb. *'ĕlōhīm* (pl.).]

E·lo·hist /e'lōhist; 'elō,hist/ the postulated author or authors of parts of the Hexateuch in which God is regularly named Elohim. Compare with YAHWIST. [from Hebrew *'ĕlōhīm* (see ELOHIM) + -IST.]

e·lon·gate /i'lôNGgāt; i'läNG-/ ▶ v. [trans.] make (something) longer, esp. unusually so in relation to its width. ■ prolong (a sound). ■ [intrans.] esp. Biol. grow longer. ▶ adj. esp. Biol. long in relation to width; elongated: *elongate, fishlike creatures.* [ME: from late L. *elongat-* 'placed at a distance,' from *elongare*, from L. *e-* 'away' + *longus* 'long.']

e·lon·gat·ed /i'lôNG,gātid; i'läNG-/ ▶ adj. unusually long in relation to its width. ■ having grown or been made longer.

e·lon·ga·tion /i,lôNG'gāSHən; ē,lôNG-; i,läNG-; ē,läNG-/ ▶ n. the lengthening of something. ■ a part of a line formed by lengthening; a continuation. ■ the amount of extension of an object under stress, usually expressed as a percentage of the original length. ■ Astron. the angular separation of a planet from the sun or of a satellite from a planet, as seen by an observer.

e·lope /i'lōp/ ▶ v. [intrans.] run away secretly in order to get married, esp. without parental consent. ■ run away with a lover. — **e·lope·ment** n. **e·lop·er** n. [16th C.: from Anglo-Norman Fr. *aloper*, perh. rel. to LEAP.]

el·o·quence /'eləkwəns/ ▶ n. fluent or persuasive speaking or writing. ■ the art or manner of such speech or writing. [ME: via OFr. from L. *eloquentia*, from *eloqui* 'speak out,' from *e-* 'out' + *loqui* 'speak.']

el·o·quent /'eləkwənt/ ▶ adj. fluent or persuasive in speaking or writing. ■ clearly expressing or indicating something: *the touches of fatherliness are* ***eloquent of*** *the real man.* — **el·o·quent·ly** adv.

El Pas·o /el 'pasō/ a city in western Texas, on the Rio Grande, opposite Ciudad Juárez in Mexico; pop. 563,662.

El Qa·hi·ra /el kä'hērə/ var. of AL QAHIRA.

El Sal·va·dor /el 'salvə,dôr; ,sälvä'dôr/ a country in Central America. *See box on next page.*

else /els/ ▶ adv. **1** [with indefinite pron. or adv.] in addition; besides: ***anything else*** *you need?* | *I wasn't sure* ***what else*** *you'd want* | *offering low prices* ***but little else.*** **2** [with indefinite pron. or adv.] different; instead: *isn't there* ***anyone else?*** | *it's fate, or* ***whatever else*** *you call it.* **3** short for OR ELSE below.

– PHRASES **or else** used to introduce the second of two alternatives: *tempted to shout or else leave.* ■ in circumstances different from those mentioned; if it were not the case: *they can't want it, or else they'd request it.* ■ used to warn what will happen if something is not carried out: *you go along with this or else you're going to jail.* ■ used after a demand as a threat: *shape up, or else.* [OE *elles*, of Gmc. origin; rel. to MDu. *els* and Swed. *eljest.*]

else·where /'els,(h)we(ə)r/ ▶ adv. in, at, or to some other place or other places: *he is seeking employment elsewhere.* ▶ pron. some other place: *plants originally from elsewhere.* [OE *elles hwǣr* (see ELSE, WHERE).]

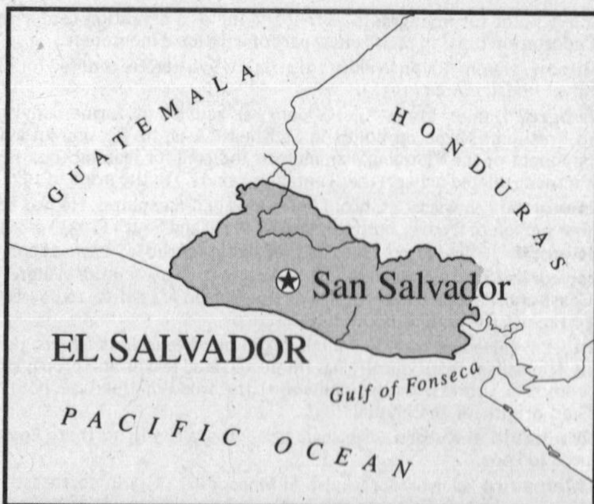

El Salvador

Official name: Republic of El Salvador
Location: Central America, between Guatemala and Honduras, bordered on the south by the Pacific Ocean
Area: 8,000 square miles (20,700 sq km)
Population: 6,587,000
Capital: San Salvador
Language: Spanish
Currency: Salvadoran colon, US dollar

El·si·nore /'elsə,nôr/ a port on the northeastern coast of the island of Zealand in Denmark; pop. 56,750. It is the site of the 16th-century Kronborg Castle, which is the setting for Shakespeare's *Hamlet.* Danish name HELSINGØR.

ELSS ▶ abbr. extravehicular life support system.

el·u·ant /'elyo͞oənt/ ▶ n. Chem. a fluid used to elute a substance. [1940s: from L. *eluent-* 'washing out,' from the v. *eluere* (see ELUTE).]

el·u·ate /'elyo͞oit; -,āt/ ▶ n. Chem. a solution obtained by elution.

e·lu·ci·date /i'lo͞osi,dāt/ ▶ v. [trans.] make (something) clear; explain: *work that will help to elucidate this matter* | [intrans.] *they would not elucidate further.* — **e·lu·ci·da·tion** /i,lo͞osi'dāsHən/ n. **e·lu·ci·da·tive** adj. **e·lu·ci·da·tor** /-,dātər/ n. **e·lu·ci·da·to·ry** /-də,tôrē/ adj. [16th C.: from late L. *elucidat-* 'made clear,' from *elucidare,* from *e-* 'out' + *lucidus* 'lucid.']

e·lude /i'lo͞od/ ▶ v. [trans.] evade or escape from (a danger, enemy, or pursuer), typically in a skillful or cunning way: *he managed to elude his pursuer.* ■ (of an idea or fact) fail to be grasped or remembered by (someone). ■ (of an achievement, or something desired or pursued) fail to be attained by (someone). ■ avoid compliance with or subjection to (a law, demand, or penalty). — **e·lu·sion** /i'lo͞ozHən/ n. [16th C.: from L. *eludere,* from *e-* 'out, away from' + *ludere* 'to play.']

el·u·ent /'elyo͞oənt/ ▶ n. var. of ELUANT.

E·lul /'eləl; e'lo͞ol/ ▶ n. (in the Jewish calendar) the twelfth month of the civil and sixth of the religious year, usually coinciding with parts of August and September. [from Heb. *'ĕlūl.*]

El Uq·sur /el 'o͝oksoor/ (also **Al Uq·sur** /äl/) Arabic name for LUXOR.

e·lu·sive /i'lo͞osiv/ (also rare **e·lu·so·ry** /-sərē; -zə-/) ▶ adj. difficult to find, catch, or achieve. ■ difficult to remember or recall. — **e·lu·sive·ly** adv. **e·lu·sive·ness** n. [18th C.: from L. *elus-* 'eluded' (from *eludere*).]

e·lute /i'lo͞ot/ ▶ v. [trans.] Chem. remove (an adsorbed substance) by washing with a solvent, esp. in chromatography. — **e·lu·tion** /i'lo͞osHən/ n. [1920s: from L. *elut-* 'washed out,' from *eluere,* suggested by Ger. *eluieren.*]

e·lu·tri·ate /i'lo͞otrē,āt/ ▶ v. [trans.] Chem. separate (lighter and heavier particles in a mixture) by suspension in an upward flow of liquid or gas. ■ purify by straining. — **e·lu·tri·a·tion** /i,lo͞otrē'āsHən/ n. [18th C.: from L. *elutriat-* 'washed out,' from *elutriare,* from *e-* 'out' + *lutriare* 'to wash.']

el·ver /'elvər/ ▶ n. a young eel, esp. when undergoing mass migration upriver from the sea. [17th C.: based on EEL + FARE.]

elves /elvz/ plural form of ELF.

Elyr·ia /i'li(ə)rēə/ a city in northern Ohio; pop. 55,953.

E·ly·sée Pal·ace /,elē'zā/ a building in Paris, erected in 1718, that has been the official residence of the French president since 1870.

E·ly·sian /i'lizHən; i'lē-/ ▶ adj. of, relating to, or characteristic of heaven or paradise: *Elysian visions.*
– PHRASES **the Elysian Fields** another name for ELYSIUM.

E·ly·si·um /i'lizHēəm; i'lizēəm; i'lē-/ Gk. Mythol. the place at the ends of the earth to which certain favored heroes were conveyed by the gods after death. ■ [as n.] **(an Elysium)** a place or state of perfect happiness.

el·y·tron /'elə,trän/ ▶ n. (pl. **-tra** /-trə/) Entomol. each of the two wing cases of a beetle. — **el·y·trous** /-trəs/ adj. [18th C.: from Gk. *elutron* 'sheath.']

EM ▶ abbr. ■ electromagnetic. ■ Engineer of Mines. ■ enlisted man (men).

em /em/ ▶ n. Print. a unit for measuring the width of printed matter, equal to the height of the type size being used. ■ a unit of measurement equal to twelve points. [18th C.: the width of the letter M.]

em- ▶ prefix var. of EN-[1], EN-[2] assimilated before *b, p* (as in *emblazon, emplacement*).

'em /əm/ ▶ pron. short for THEM, esp. in informal use: *let 'em know who's boss.* [ME.: a form of *hem,* dative and accusative third person pl. pronoun in ME.]

e·ma·ci·ate /i'māsHē,āt/ ▶ v. [trans.] [usu. as adj.] **(emaciated)** make abnormally thin or weak, esp. because of illness or a lack of food. — **e·ma·ci·a·tion** /i,māsHē'āsHən/ n. [17th C.: from L. *emaciat-* 'made thin,' from *emaciare,* from *e-* (expressing a change of state) + *macies* 'leanness.']

e-mail /'ē ,māl/ (also **e·mail**) ▶ n. messages distributed from one computer user to one or more others via a network: *reading e-mail* | [as adj.] *e-mail messages.* ■ the system of sending such messages: *communicated by e-mail.* ▶ v. [trans.] send an e-mail to (someone). ■ send (a message) by e-mail. [20th C.: abbrev. of ELECTRONIC MAIL.]

em·a·lan·gen·i /,eməläNG'genē/ plural form of LILANGENI.

em·a·nate /'emə,nāt/ ▶ v. [intrans.] **(emanate from)** issue or spread out from (a source): *warmth emanated from the fireplace* | *she felt charm emanating from him.* ■ originate from; be produced by. ■ [trans.] give out or emit (something): *he emanated a powerful brooding air.* — **em·a·na·tive** /-,nātiv/ adj. **em·a·na·tor** /-,nātər/ n. [18th C.: from L. *emanat-* 'flowed out,' from *emanare,* from *e-* + *manare* 'to flow.']

em·a·na·tion /,emə'nāsHən/ ▶ n. something that issues or originates from a source. ■ the action or process of issuing from a source. ■ a tenuous substance or form of radiation given off by something. ■ Chem., archaic a radioactive gas formed by radioactive decay of a solid. ■ a body or organization that has its source or takes its authority from another: *the commission is an emanation of the state.* ■ (in various mystical traditions) a being or force that is a manifestation of God.

e·man·ci·pate /i'mansə,pāt/ ▶ v. [trans.] set free, esp. from legal, social, or political restrictions: *the citizen must be emancipated from obsessive government secrecy* | [as adj.] **(emancipated)** *emancipated young women.* ■ Law set (a child) free from the authority of its father or parents. ■ free from slavery. — **e·man·ci·pa·tion** /i,mansə'pāsHən/ n. **e·man·ci·pa·tor** /-,pātər/ n. **e·man·ci·pa·to·ry** /-pə,tôrē/ adj. [17th C.: from L. *emancipat-* 'transferred as property,' from *emancipare,* from *e-* 'out' + *mancipium* 'slave.']

E·man·ci·pa·tion Proc·la·ma·tion /i,mansə'pāsHən/ the announcement made by President Lincoln during the Civil War on September 22, 1862, emancipating all slaves in states still engaged in rebellion against the Union.

e·mas·cu·late /i'maskyə,lāt/ ▶ v. [trans.] make (a person, idea, or piece of legislation) weaker or less effective. ■ [usu. as adj.] **(emasculated)** deprive (a man) of his male role or identity: *he feels emasculated because he cannot control his sons' behavior.* ■ archaic castrate (a man or male animal). ■ Bot. remove the anthers from a flower. — **e·mas·cu·la·tion** /i,maskyə'lāsHən/ n. **e·mas·cu·la·tor** /-,lātər/ n. **e·mas·cu·la·to·ry** /-lə,tôrē/ adj. [17th C.: from L. *emasculat-* 'castrated,' from *emasculare,* from *e-* (expressing a change of state) + *masculus* 'male.']

em·balm /em'bä(l)m/ ▶ v. [trans.] **1** [often as n.] **(embalming)** preserve (a corpse) from decay, originally with spices and now usually by arterial injection of a preservative: *the Egyptian method of embalming.* ■ fig. preserve (someone or something) in an unaltered state. **2** archaic give a pleasant fragrance to. — **em·balm·er** n. **em·balm·ment** n. [ME: from OFr. *embaumer,* from *em-* 'in' + *baume* 'balm,' var. of *basme* (see BALM).]

em·bank /em'baNGk/ ▶ v. [trans.] construct a wall or bank of earth or stone in order to confine (a river) within certain limits. ■ construct a bank of earth or stone to carry (a road or railroad) over an area of low ground.

em·bank·ment /em'baNGkmənt/ ▶ n. a wall or bank of earth or stone built to prevent a river flooding an area. ■ a bank of earth or stone built to carry a road or railroad over an area of low ground.

em·bar·go /em'bärgō/ ▶ n. (pl. **-goes**) an official ban on trade or other commercial activity with a particular country. ■ an official prohibition on any activity. ■ hist. an order of a state forbidding foreign ships to enter, or any ships to leave, its ports. ■ archaic a stoppage, prohibition, or impediment. ▶ v. **(-goes, -goed)** [trans.] **1** (usu. **be embargoed**) impose an official ban on (trade or a country or commodity). ■ officially ban the publication of. **2** archaic seize (a ship or goods) for state service. [17th C.: from Sp., from *embargar* 'arrest,' based on L. *in-* 'in, within' + *barra* 'a bar.']

em·bark /em'bärk/ ▶ v. [intrans.] go on board a ship, aircraft, or other vehicle: *he embarked for India in 1817.* ■ [trans.] put or take on board a ship or aircraft. ■ **(embark on/upon)** begin (a course of action, esp. one that is important or demanding). — **em·bar·ka·tion** /,embär'kāsHən/ n. **em·bark·ment** n. [16th C.: from Fr. *embarquer,* from *em-* 'in' + *barque* 'bark, ship.']

em·bar·ras de ri·chesses /äNbä'rä də rē'sHes/ (also **em·bar·ras de choix** /'sHwä/) ▶ n. more options or resources than one knows what to do with. [18th C.: Fr., literally 'embarrassment of riches (or choice).']

em•bar•rass /em'barəs/ ▶ **v.** [trans.] cause (someone) to feel awkward, self-conscious, or ashamed. ■ (**be embarrassed**) be caused financial difficulties. ■ archaic hamper or impede (a person, movement, or action). ■ archaic make difficult or intricate; complicate. ■ create difficulties for (someone, esp. a public figure or political party) by drawing attention to their failures or shortcomings. [17th C.: from Fr. *embarrasser*, from Sp. *embarazar*, prob. from Port. *embaraçar* (from *baraço* 'halter').]

em•bar•rassed /em'barəst/ ▶ **adj.** feeling or showing embarrassment. ■ having or showing financial difficulties. — **em•bar•rassed•ly** /-əstlē; -əsidlē/ **adv.**

em•bar•rass•ing /em'barəsiNG/ ▶ **adj.** causing embarrassment: *an embarrassing muddle.* ■ creating difficulties, esp. for a political party or public figure. — **em•bar•rass•ing•ly adv.**

em•bar•rass•ment /em'barəsmənt/ ▶ **n.** a feeling of self-consciousness, shame, or awkwardness. ■ a person or thing causing such feelings. ■ financial difficulty.

– PHRASES **embarrassment of riches** see EMBARRAS DE RICHESSES.

em•bas•sage /'embəsij/ ▶ **n.** archaic the business or message of an envoy. ■ a body of people sent as a deputation to or on behalf of a head of state. ■ archaic term for EMBASSY.

em•bas•sy /'embəsē/ ▶ **n.** (pl. **-sies**) **1** the official residence or offices of an ambassador. ■ the staff working in such a building. ■ the position or function of an ambassador. **2** esp. hist. a deputation or mission sent by one ruler or state to another. [16th C.: from OFr. *ambasse*, based on L. *ambactus* 'servant.']

em•bat•tle /em'batl/ ▶ **v.** [trans.] archaic set (an army) in battle array. ■ fortify (a building or place) against attack. [ME: from OFr. *embataillier*.]

em•bat•tled /em'batld/ ▶ **adj. 1** (of a place or people) involved in or prepared for war, esp. because surrounded by enemy forces. ■ (of a person) beset by problems or difficulties. **2** [postpositive] Heraldry divided or edged by a line of square notches like battlements in outline.

em•bay /em'bā/ ▶ **v.** [trans.] (usu. **be embayed**) (chiefly of the wind) confine (a sailing vessel) to a bay. ■ [as adj.] (**embayed**) formed into bays; hollowed out by or as if by the sea: *the embayed island.* ■ esp. Geol. enclose (something) in a recess or hollow.

em•bay•ment /em'bāmənt/ ▶ **n.** a recess in a coastline forming a bay.

em•bed /em'bed/ (also **im•bed** /im-/) ▶ **v.** (**-bed•ded, -bed•ding**) [trans.] (often **be embedded**) fix (an object) firmly and deeply in a surrounding mass: *he had an operation to remove a nail* **embedded in** *his chest.* ■ figurative implant (an idea or feeling) within something else so it becomes an ingrained or essential characteristic of it: *the Victorian values* **embedded in** *Tennyson's poetry.* ■ Linguistics place (a phrase or clause) within another clause or sentence. ■ Computing incorporate (a text or code) within the body of a file or document. ■ [often as adj.] (**embedded**) design and build (a microprocessor) as an integral part of a system or device. ■ permit a (journalist) to travel with a military unit. ▶ **n.** /'em,bed/ an embedded journalist. — **em•bed•ment n.**

em•bel•lish /em'belisH/ ▶ **v.** [trans.] make (something) more attractive by the addition of decorative details or features: *blue silk embellished with golden embroidery.* ■ make (a statement or story) more interesting or entertaining by adding extra details, esp. ones that are not true. — **em•bel•lish•er n.** [ME: from OFr. *embelliss-*, based on *bel* 'handsome,' from L. *bellus*.]

em•bel•lish•ment /em'belisHmənt/ ▶ **n.** a decorative detail or feature added to something to make it more attractive: *architectural embellishments.* ■ a detail, esp. one not true, added to a statement or story to make it more interesting or entertaining. ■ the action of adding such details or features.

em•ber /'embər/ ▶ **n.** (usu. **embers**) a small piece of burning or glowing coal or wood in a dying fire: fig. *the flickering embers of nationalism.* [OE *ǣmyrge*, of Gmc. origin; rel. to Old High Ger. *eimuria* 'pyre.']

Em•ber day ▶ **n.** any of a number of days reserved for fasting and prayer in the Western Christian Church, esp. the Wednesday, Friday, and Saturday following St. Lucy's Day (December 13), the first Sunday in Lent, Pentecost (Whitsun), and Holy Cross Day (September 14). [OE *ymbren*, perh. an alt. of *ymbryne* 'period,' from *ymb* 'around' + *ryne* 'course.']

em•bez•zle /em'bezəl/ ▶ **v.** [trans.] steal or misappropriate (money placed in one's trust or belonging to the organization for which one works). — **em•bez•zle•ment n. em•bez•zler** /em'bezlər/ **n.** [ME: from Anglo-Norman Fr. *embesiler*.]

em•bit•ter /em'bitər/ ▶ **v.** [trans.] [usu. as adj.] (**embittered**) cause (someone) to feel bitter or resentful. ■ literary give a sharp or pungent taste or smell to. — **em•bit•ter•ment n.**

em•bla•zon /em'blāzən/ ▶ **v.** [with obj. and adverbial of place] (often **be emblazoned**) conspicuously inscribe or display (a design) on something. ■ depict (a heraldic device). ■ archaic celebrate or extol publicly: *their success was emblazoned.* — **em•bla•zon•ment n.**

em•blem /'embləm/ ▶ **n.** a heraldic device or symbolic object as a distinctive badge of a nation, organization, or family: *America's national emblem, the bald eagle.* ■ (**emblem of**) a thing serving as a symbolic representation of a particular quality or concept. — **em•blem•at•ic** /,emblə'matik/ **adj. em•blem•at•i•cal** /,emblə'matikəl/ **adj. em•blem•at•i•cal•ly** /,emblə'matik(ə)lē/ **adv.** [16th C.: from L. *emblema* 'inlaid work,' from Gk. *emblēma* 'insertion,' from *emballein* 'insert,' from *em-* 'in' + *ballein* 'to throw.']

em•blem•a•tist /em'blemətist/ ▶ **n.** a creator or user of emblems, esp. in allegorical pictures.

em•blem•a•tize /em'blemə,tīz/ ▶ **v.** [trans.] formal serve as a symbolic representation of (a quality or concept).

em•ble•ments /'embləmənts/ ▶ **plural n.** Law the profit from growing crops that have been sown, regarded as personal property. [15th C.: from OFr. *emblaement*, from *emblaier* 'sow with wheat' (based on *blé* 'wheat').]

em•bod•i•ment /em'bädēmənt/ ▶ **n.** a tangible or visible form of an idea, quality, or feeling. ■ the representation or expression of something in such a form.

em•bod•y /em'bädē/ ▶ **v.** (**-bod•ies, -bod•ied**) [trans.] **1** be an expression of or give a tangible or visible form to (an idea, quality, or feeling). ■ provide (a spirit) with a physical form. **2** include or contain (something) as a constituent part: *the changes* **embodied in** *the Freedom of Information Act.* **3** archaic form (people) into a body, esp. for military purposes. — **em•bod•i•er** /-'bädēər/ **n.** [16th C.: from EM- + BODY.]

em•bold•en /em'bōldən/ ▶ **v.** [trans.] **1** (often **be emboldened**) give (someone) the courage or confidence to do something or to behave in a certain way. **2** cause (a piece of text) to appear in a bold typeface.

em•bo•lec•to•my /,embə'lektəmē/ ▶ **n.** (pl. **-mies**) surgical removal of an embolus.

em•bo•lism /'embə,lizəm/ ▶ **n. 1** Med. obstruction of an artery, typically by a clot of blood or an air bubble. **2** the periodic intercalation of days or a month to correct the accumulating discrepancy between the calendar year and the solar year, as in a leap year. [19th C.: via late L. from Gk. *embolismos*, from *emballein* 'insert.']

em•bo•li•za•tion /,embəli'zāsHən/ ▶ **n.** Med. the formation or development of an embolus.

em•bo•lus /'embələs/ ▶ **n.** (pl. **-li** /-,lī; -lē/) a blood clot, air bubble, piece of fatty deposit, or other object that has been carried in the bloodstream to lodge in a vessel and cause an embolism. — **em•bol•ic** /em'bälik/ **adj.** [17th C.: from L., literally 'piston,' from Greek *embolos* 'peg.']

em•bon•point /,äNbôN'pwaN/ ▶ **n.** archaic the plump or fleshy part of the body, in particular a woman's bosom. [17th C.: from Fr. *en bon point* 'in good condition.']

em•bos•om /em'bo͝ozəm/ ▶ **v.** [trans.] (usu. **be embosomed**) literary take or press to one's bosom; embrace. ■ enclose or surround (something) protectively.

em•boss /em'bôs; -'bäs/ ▶ **v.** [trans.] [usu. as adj.] (**embossed**) carve or mold a design on (a surface) so that it stands out in relief: *an embossed brass dish.* ■ decorate (a surface) with a raised design. — **em•boss•er n. em•boss•ment n.** [ME: from OFr. *embosser*, from *em-* 'into' + *boce* 'protuberance.']

em•bou•chure /,ämbo͞o'sHo͝or/ ▶ **n. 1** Music the way in which a player applies the mouth to the mouthpiece of a brass or wind instrument. ■ the mouthpiece of a flute or a similar instrument. **2** archaic the mouth of a river or valley. [18th C.: Fr., from *s'emboucher* 'discharge itself by the mouth,' from *emboucher* 'put in or to the mouth,' from *em-* 'into' + *bouche* 'mouth.']

em•bour•geoise•ment /em'bo͝orzHwäzmənt; -,mänt/ ▶ **n.** the proliferation in a society of values perceived as characteristic of the middle class, esp. of materialism. [1930s: Fr., from *embourgeoiser* 'become or make bourgeois.']

em•bowed /em'bōd/ ▶ **adj.** literary bent, arched, or vaulted.

em•bow•er /em'bouər/ ▶ **v.** [trans.] (usu. **be embowered**) literary surround or shelter (a place or a person), esp. with trees or climbing plants.

em•brace /em'brās/ ▶ **v.** [trans.] hold (someone) closely in one's arms, esp. as a sign of affection: *Aunt Sophie embraced her warmly* | [intrans.] *the two embraced, holding each other tightly.* ■ accept or support (a belief, theory, or change) willingly and enthusiastically. ■ include or contain (something) as a constituent part: *his career embraced composing, playing, and acting.* ▶ **n.** an act of holding someone closely in one's arms. ■ fig. used to refer to something that is regarded as surrounding or holding someone securely, esp. in a restrictive or comforting way. ■ [in sing.] an act of accepting or supporting something willingly or enthusiastically. — **em•brace•a•ble adj. em•brace•ment n. em•brac•er n.** [ME: from OFr. *embracer*, based on L. *in-* 'in' + *bracchium* 'arm.']

em•bra•sure /em'brāzHər/ ▶ **n.** the beveling or splaying of a wall at the sides of a door or window. ■ a small opening in a parapet of a fortified building, splayed on the inside. — **em•bra•sured adj.** [18th C.: from Fr. *embraser* 'widen a door opening,' of unknown ultimate origin.]

em•brit•tle /em'britl/ ▶ **v.** make or become brittle. — **em•brit•tle•ment n.**

em•bro•ca•tion /,embrə'kāsHən/ ▶ **n.** a liquid rubbed on the body to relieve pain from sprains and strains. [ME: from med. L. *embrocatio(n-)*, from the v. *embrocare*, based on Gk. *embrokhē* 'lotion.']

em•broi•der /em'broidər/ ▶ **v.** [trans.] decorate (cloth) by sewing patterns on it with thread: *she embroidered nighties for the babies* | [intrans.] *teaching us how to embroider.* ■ produce (a design) on cloth in this way: [as adj.] (**embroidered**) *a sweater with embroidered flowers.* ■ fig. add fictitious or exaggerated details to (an account) to make it more interesting. — **em•broi•der•er n.** [ME: from Anglo-Norman Fr. *enbrouder*, from *en-* 'in' + OFr. *broisder* 'embroider,' of Gmc. origin.]

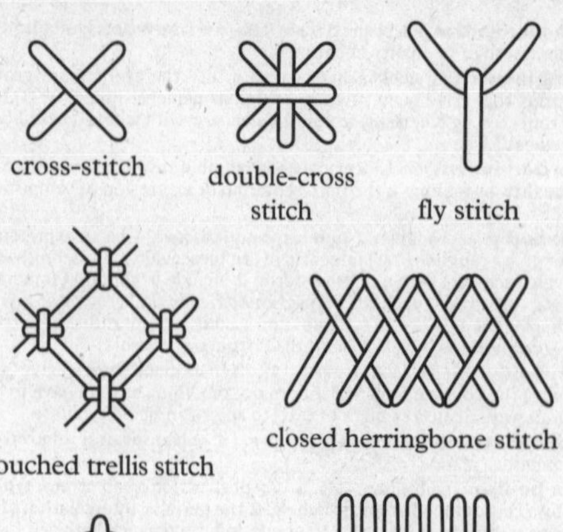

embroidery stitches

em·broi·der·y /em'broid(ə)rē/ ▶n. (pl. **-der·ies**) the art or pastime of embroidering cloth. ■ cloth decorated in this way. ■ fig. embellishment or exaggeration in describing or reporting an event.

em·broil /em'broil/ ▶v. [trans.] [often as adj.] (**embroiled**) involve (someone) deeply in an argument, conflict, or difficult situation. ■ bring into a state of confusion or disorder. —**em·broil·ment** n. [17th C.: from Fr. *embrouiller* 'to muddle,' from *em-* 'in' + *brouiller* 'confuse.']

em·bry·ec·to·my /ˌembrē'ektəmē/ ▶n. (pl.**-mies**) the surgical removal of an embryo, esp. one implanted outside the uterus in an ectopic pregnancy.

em·bry·o /'embrē,ō/ ▶n. (pl. **-os**) an unborn or unhatched offspring in the process of development. ■ an unborn human baby, esp. in the first eight weeks from conception, after implantation but before all the organs are developed. Compare with FETUS. ■ Bot. the part of a seed that develops into a plant, consisting (in the mature embryo of a higher plant) of a plumule, a radicle, and one or two cotyledons. ■ fig. a thing at a rudimentary stage that shows potential for development.
– PHRASES **in embryo** at a rudimentary stage with the potential for further development. [ME: via late L. from Gk. *embruon* 'fetus,' from *em-* 'into' + *bruein* 'swell, grow.']

embryo- ▶comb. form representing EMBRYO.

em·bry·o·gen·e·sis /ˌembrē-ō'jenəsis/ ▶n. Biol. the formation and development of an embryo. —**em·bry·o·ge·net·ic** /-jə'netik/ **adj. em·bry·o·gen·ic** /-'jenik/ **adj. em·bry·og·e·ny** /ˌembrē'äjənē/ **n.**

em·bry·ol·o·gy /ˌembrē'äləjē/ ▶n. the branch of biology and medicine concerned with the study of embryos and their development. —**em·bry·o·log·ic** /ˌembrēə'läjik/ **adj. em·bry·o·log·i·cal** /ˌembrēə'läjikəl/ **adj. em·bry·o·log·i·cal·ly** /ˌembrēə'läjik(ə)lē/ **adv. em·bry·ol·o·gist** /-jist/ **n.**

em·bry·on·ic /ˌembrē'änik/ ▶adj. (also **em·bry·o·nal** /'embrēənl/) of or relating to an embryo. ■ fig. in a rudimentary stage with potential for further development. —**em·bry·on·i·cal·ly** /-ik(ə)lē/ **adv.** [19th C.: from late L. *embryo, embryon-* 'embryo' + -IC.]

em·bry·op·a·thy /ˌembrē'äpəTHē/ ▶n. (pl. **-thies**) a developmental defect in an embryo or fetus.

em·bry·o sac ▶n. a cell inside the ovule of a flowering plant where fertilization occurs and which becomes the female gametophyte, containing the endosperm nucleus and the ovum that develops into the embryo.

em·cee /'em'sē/ informal ▶n. a master of ceremonies. ▶v. (**em·cees, em·ceed, em·cee·ing**) [trans.] perform the role of a master of ceremonies at (a public entertainment or a large social occasion). [1930s.]

em dash ▶n. a long dash used in punctuation.

-eme ▶suffix Ling. forming nouns denoting linguistic units that are in systemic contrast with one other: *grapheme* | *phoneme.* [abstracted from PHONEME.]

e·mend /i'mend/ ▶v. [trans.] make corrections and improvements to (a text). ■ alter (something) in such a way as to correct it. —**e·mend·a·ble adj. e·men·da·tion** /ˌēmən'dāSHən; ˌemən-/ **n. e·mend·er n.** [ME: from L. *emendare*, from *e-* 'out of' + *menda* 'a fault.' Cf. AMEND.]

emer. ▶abbr. emerita or emeritus.

em·er·ald /'em(ə)rəld/ ▶n. **1** a bright green precious stone consisting of a chromium-rich variety of beryl. **2** a bright green color like that of an emerald. ▶adj. bright green in color. [ME: from OFr. *e(s)meraud*, ult. via L. from Gk. *(s)maragdos*, via Prakrit from Semitic.]

em·er·ald-cut ▶adj. (of a gem) cut in a rectangular shape with stepped facets.

Em·er·ald Isle a name for Ireland.

e·merge /i'mərj/ ▶v. [intrans.] move out of or away from something and come into view. ■ become apparent, important, or prominent: *Philadelphia has emerged as the favorite* | [as adj.] (**emerging**) *a world of emerging economic giants.* ■ (of facts or circumstances) become known. ■ recover from or survive a difficult or demanding situation: *the economy has started to emerge from recession.* ■ (of an insect or other invertebrate) break out from an egg, cocoon, or pupal case. [16th C.: from L. *emergere*, from *e-* 'out, forth' + *mergere* 'to dip.']

e·mer·gence /i'mərjəns/ ▶n. the process of coming into being, or of becoming important or prominent. ■ the process of coming into view or becoming exposed after being concealed. ■ the escape of an insect or other invertebrate from an egg, cocoon, pupal case, etc. ■ an outgrowth from a stem or leaf composed of epidermal and subepidermal tissue, as the prickles on a thistle plant.

e·mer·gen·cy /i'mərjənsē/ ▶n. (pl. **-cies**) a serious, unexpected, and often dangerous situation requiring immediate action. ■ [as adj.] arising from or needed or used in an emergency. ■ a person with a medical condition requiring immediate treatment. ■ short for EMERGENCY ROOM.

e·mer·gen·cy med·i·cal tech·ni·cian (abbr.: **EMT**) ▶n. a person trained and certified to administer emergency care to victims of trauma or acute illness before and during transportation to a medical facility.

e·mer·gen·cy room ▶n. a hospital department providing immediate treatment for acute illness and trauma.

e·mer·gent /i'mərjənt/ ▶adj. in the process of coming into being or becoming prominent. ■ Philos. (of a property) arising as an effect of complex causes and not analyzable simply as the sum of their effects. ■ Bot. of or denoting a plant that is taller than the surrounding vegetation, esp. a tall tree in a forest. ■ Bot. of or denoting a water plant with leaves and flowers that appear above the surface. ▶n. Philos. an emergent property. ■ Bot. an emergent tree or other plant.

e·mer·i·ta /i'meritə/ ▶adj. [postpositive] (of a woman who is the former holder of an office, esp. a female professor) having retired but retaining her title as an honor.

e·mer·i·tus /i'meritəs/ ▶adj. (of the former holder of an office, esp. a professor) having retired but retaining his title as an honor. [18th C.: from L. *emereri* 'earn one's discharge by service,' from *e-* 'out of, from' + *mereri* 'earn.']

e·mersed /i'mərst/ ▶adj. Bot. denoting or characteristic of an aquatic plant reaching above the surface of the water. Contrasted with SUBMERSED (see SUBMERSE).

e·mer·sion /i'mərZHən/ ▶n. the process or state of emerging from or being out of water after being submerged. ■ Astron. the reappearance of a celestial body after its eclipse or occultation. [17th C.: from late L. *emersio(n-)*, from L. *emergere* (see EMERGE).]

Em·er·son /'emərsən/, Ralph Waldo (1803–82), US philosopher and poet. Associated with German idealism, he evolved the concept of transcendentalism, which found expression in his essay *Nature* (1836).

em·er·y /'em(ə)rē/ ▶n. a grayish-black powdered mixture of corundum and magnetite, used as an abrasive. ■ [as adj.] denoting materials coated with emery for polishing, smoothing, or grinding: *emery paper.* [15th C.: from Fr. *émeri*, from OFr. *esmeri*, from Ital. *smeriglio*, based on Gk. *smuris, smiris* 'polishing powder.']

em·er·y board ▶n. a strip of thin wood or card coated with emery or another abrasive and used as a nail file.

em·e·sis /'eməsis/ ▶n. tech. the action or process of vomiting. [19th C.: from Gk., from *emein* 'to vomit.']

e·met·ic /i'metik/ ▶adj. causing vomiting. ■ informal nauseating or revolting. ▶n. a medicine or other substance that causes vomiting. [17th C.: from Gk. *emetikos*, from *emein* 'to vomit.']

em·e·tine /'emi,tēn/ ▶n. an alkaloid present in ipecac and formerly used in the treatment of amebic infections and as an emetic in aversion therapy.

EMF ▶abbr. ■ electromagnetic field(s). ■ (**emf**) electromotive force. ■ European Monetary Fund.

EMG ▶abbr. ■ electromyogram. ■ electromyography.

-emia (also **-hemia**, Brit. **-aemia** or **-haemia**) ▶comb. form in nouns denoting that a substance is present in the blood, esp. in excess: *septicemia* | *leukemia.* [from mod. L. *-aemia*, from Gk. *-aimia*, from *haima* 'blood.']

e·mic /'ēmik/ Anthropol. ▶adj. relating to or denoting an approach to the study or description of a particular language or culture in terms of its internal elements and their functioning rather than in terms of any existing external scheme. Often contrasted with ETIC. ▶plural n. (**emics**) [treated as sing.] study adopting this approach. [1950s: abstracted from such words as *phonemic* (see PHONEME) and SYSTEMIC.]

em·i·grant /'emigrənt/ ▶n. a person who leaves their own country to settle permanently in another. ▶adj. used by emigrants: *an emigrant ship.*

em·i·grate /'emi,grāt/ ▶v. [intrans.] leave one's own country in order to settle permanently in another. —**em·i·gra·tion** /ˌemi'grāSHən/ **n.** [18th C.: from L. *emigrare*, from *e-* 'out of' + *migrare* 'migrate.']

é·mi·gré /'emə,grā/ (also **emigre**) ▶n. a person who has left their own country in order to settle in another. [18th C.: Fr., past part. of *émigrer* 'emigrate.']

em·i·nence /'emənəns/ ▶n. **1** fame or recognized superiority, esp. within a particular sphere or profession: *her eminence in cinematog-*

raphy. ■ an important, influential, or distinguished person: *the Attorney General canvassed the views of various legal eminences.* ■ (**His/Your Eminence**) a title given to a Roman Catholic cardinal, or used in addressing him. **2** formal literary a piece of rising ground: *an eminence commanding the River Emme.* ■ Anat. a slight projection from the surface of a part of the body.

é·mi·nence grise /ˈāmēnäns ˈgrēz/ ▶ **n.** (pl. **é·mi·nences grises** pronunc. same) a person who exercises power or influence without holding an official position. [1930s: French, literally 'gray eminence.']

em·i·nent /ˈemənənt/ ▶ **adj.** (of a person) famous and respected within a particular sphere or profession. ■ [attrib.] used to emphasize the presence of a positive quality: *the guitar's eminent suitability for studio work.* — **em·i·nent·ly** **adv.** [as submodifier] *an eminently readable textbook.* [ME: from L. *eminent-* 'jutting, projecting,' from the v. *eminere.*]

em·i·nent do·main ▶ **n.** Law the right of a government or its agent to expropriate private property for public use, with payment of compensation.

e·mir /əˈmi(ə)r; āˈmi(ə)r/ (also **a·mir**) ▶ **n.** a title of various Muslim (mainly Arab) rulers: *the emir of Kuwait.* ■ hist. a Muslim (usually Arab) military commander or local chief. [16th C.: from French *émir*, from Arabic *ʼamīr* (see **AMIR**).]

e·mir·ate /əˈmi(ə)rāt; əˈmi(ə)rit; ˈemərit/ ▶ **n.** the rank, lands, or reign of an emir.

em·is·sar·y /ˈeməˌserē/ ▶ **n.** (pl. **-sar·ies**) a person sent on a special mission, e.g., as a diplomatic representative. [17th C.: from L. *emissarius* 'scout, spy,' from *emittere* 'send out' (see **EMIT**).]

e·mis·sion /iˈmisHən/ ▶ **n.** the production and discharge of something, esp. gas or radiation. ■ a thing emitted. ■ an ejaculation of semen. ■ the action of giving off radiation or particles; a flow of electrons from a cathode-ray tube or other source.

e·mis·sion spec·trum ▶ **n.** a spectrum of the electromagnetic radiation emitted by a source. Compare with **ABSORPTION SPECTRUM.**

e·mis·sive /iˈmisiv/ ▶ **adj.** tech. having the power to radiate something, esp. light, heat, or radiation. — **em·is·siv·i·ty** /ˌeməˈsivitē; ˌēmə-/ **n.**

e·mit /iˈmit/ ▶ **v.** (**e·mit·ted, e·mit·ting**) [trans.] produce and discharge (something, esp. gas or radiation). ■ make (a sound). ■ issue formally; put into circulation, esp. currency. [17th C.: from L. *emittere*, from *e-* 'out of' + *mittere* 'send.']

e·mit·ter /iˈmitər/ ▶ **n.** a thing that emits something. ■ Electron. a region in a bipolar transistor producing carriers of current.

Em·man·u·el /iˈmanyo͞oəl/ (also **Im·man·u·el**) the name given to Christ as the deliverer of Judah prophesied by Isaiah (Isa. 7:14, 8:8; Matt. 1:23).

em·men·a·gogue /əˈmenəˌgôg; -ˌgäg; -ˈmēnə-/ ▶ **n.** Med. a substance that stimulates or increases menstrual flow. [18th C.: from Gk. *emmēna* 'menses' + *agōgos* 'eliciting.']

Em·men·tal /ˈemənˌtäl/ (also **Em·men·thal**) ▶ **n.** a kind of hard Swiss cheese with many holes in it. [from German *Emmental*, the name of a Swiss valley.]

em·mer /ˈemər/ ▶ **n.** an old kind of Eurasian wheat (*Triticum dicoccum*) with bearded ears and spikelets that each contain two grains, now grown mainly for fodder and breakfast cereals. Compare with **EINKORN, SPELT²**. [20th C.: from Ger., from Old High Ger. *amer* 'spelt.']

em·met /ˈemit/ ▶ **n.** archaic an ant. [OE *ǣmete* (see **ANT**).]

Em·my /ˈemē/ ▶ **n.** (pl. **Em·mys**) a statuette awarded annually to an outstanding television program or performer.

e·mol·lient /iˈmälyənt/ ▶ **adj.** having the quality of softening or soothing the skin. ■ attempting to avoid confrontation or anger; soothing or calming. ▶ **n.** a preparation that softens the skin. — **e·mol·lience** **n.** [17th C.: from L. *emollient-* 'softening,' from *emollire*, from *e-* 'out' + *mollis* 'soft.']

e·mol·u·ment /iˈmälyəmənt/ ▶ **n.** (usu. **emoluments**) formal a salary, fee, or profit from employment or office. [ME: from L. *emolumentum*, from *emolere* 'grind up,' from *e-* + *molere* 'grind.']

e·mote /iˈmōt/ ▶ **v.** [intrans.] (esp. of an actor) portray emotion in a theatrical manner. — **e·mot·er** **n.** [20th C. (orig.US): back-form. from **EMOTION.**]

e·mo·ti·con /iˈmōtəˌkän/ ▶ **n.** a representation of a facial expression such as :-) (for a smile), formed by combinations of keyboard characters and used in electronic communications to convey the writer's tone. [1990s: blend of **EMOTION** and **ICON.**]

e·mo·tion /iˈmōsHən/ ▶ **n.** a natural instinctive state of mind deriving from one's circumstances, mood, or relationships with others. ■ any of the particular feelings that characterize such a state of mind, such as joy, anger, love, hate, horror, etc. ■ instinctive or intuitive feeling as distinguished from reasoning or knowledge. — **e·mo·tion·less** **adj.** [16th C.: from Fr. *émotion*, based on L. *emovere*, from *e-* 'out' + *movere* 'move.']

e·mo·tion·al /iˈmōsHənl/ ▶ **adj.** of or relating to a person's emotions. ■ arousing or characterized by intense feeling. ■ (of a person) having feelings that are easily excited and openly displayed. ■ based on emotion rather than reason. — **e·mo·tion·al·ism** **n.** **e·mo·tion·al·ist** **n.** & **adj.** **e·mo·tion·al·i·ty** /iˌmōsHəˈnalitē/ **n.** **e·mo·tion·al·ize** /-nl-ˌīz/ **v.** **e·mo·tion·al·ly** **adv.**

e·mo·tive /iˈmōtiv/ ▶ **adj.** arousing or able to arouse intense feeling. ■ expressing a person's feelings rather than being neutrally or objectively descriptive. — **e·mo·tive·ly** **adv.** **e·mo·tive·ness** **n.** **e·mo·tiv·i·ty** /ˌēmōˈtivitē/ **n.**

EMP ▶ **abbr.** electromagnetic pulse.

emp. ▶ **abbr.** ■ emperor. ■ empire. ■ empress.

em·pa·na·da /empəˈnädə/ ▶ **n.** a Spanish or Latin American pastry turnover filled with a variety of savory ingredients and baked or fried. [Sp., past part. of *empanar* 'roll in pastry,' based on L. *panis* 'bread.']

em·pan·el /emˈpanl/ ▶ **v.** var. of **IMPANEL.** — **em·pan·el·ment** **n.**

em·pa·thize /ˈempəˌTHīz/ ▶ **v.** [intrans.] understand and share the feelings of another: *counselors need to be able to empathize with people.*

em·pa·thy /ˈempəTHē/ ▶ **n.** the ability to understand and share the feelings of another. — **em·pa·thet·ic** /ˌempəˈTHetik/ **adj.** **em·pa·thet·i·cal·ly** /ˌempəˈTHetik(ə)lē/ **adv.** **em·path·ic** /emˈpaTHik/ **adj.** **em·path·i·cal·ly** /emˈpaTHik(ə)lē/ **adv.** [20th C.: from Gk. *empatheia* (from *em-* 'in' + *pathos* 'feeling.')]

Em·ped·o·cles /emˈpedəˌklēz/ (*c.*493–*c.*433 BC), Greek philosopher; born in Sicily. He taught that the universe is composed of fire, air, water, and earth, which mingle and separate under the influence of the opposing principles of Love and Strife.

em·pen·nage /ˌämpəˈnäzH; ˌem-/ ▶ **n.** Aeron. an arrangement of stabilizing surfaces at the tail of an aircraft. [20th C.: from Fr., from *empenner* 'to feather an arrow,' from *em-* 'in' + *penne* 'a feather' (from L. *penna*).]

em·per·or /ˈemp(ə)rər/ ▶ **n.** **1** a sovereign ruler of great power and rank, esp. one ruling an empire. **2** (also **emperor butterfly**) an orange and brown North American butterfly (genus *Asterocampa*, family Nymphalidae) with a swift dodging flight. — **em·per·or·ship** **n.** [ME: from OFr. *emperere*, from L. *imperator* 'military commander,' from *imperare* 'to command.']

em·per·or moth ▶ **n.** a large silkworm moth (*Saturnia* and other genera, family Saturniidae) with eyespots on all four wings.

em·per·or pen·guin ▶ **n.** the largest species of penguin (*Aptenodytes forsteri*). It has a yellow patch on each side of the head and rears its young during the Antarctic winter.

em·pha·sis /ˈemfəsis/ ▶ **n.** (pl. **-ses** /-ˌsēz/) importance, value, or prominence given to something. ■ stress laid on a word or words to indicate special meaning or particular importance. ■ vigor or intensity of expression. [16th C.: via L. from Gk., 'appearance, show,' from *emphainein* 'exhibit,' from *em-* 'in, within' + *phainein* 'to show.']

em·pha·size /ˈemfəˌsīz/ ▶ **v.** [trans.] give special importance or prominence to (something) in speaking or writing: *pounded the tabletop to emphasize his point.* ■ lay stress on (a word or phrase) when speaking. ■ make (something) more clearly defined: *a one-piece bathing suit that emphasized her build.*

em·phat·ic /emˈfatik/ ▶ **adj.** showing or giving emphasis; expressing something forcibly and clearly. ■ (of an action or event or its result) definite and clear. ■ (of word or syllable) bearing the stress.

em·phat·i·cal·ly /emˈfatik(ə)lē/ ▶ **adv.** in a forceful way. ■ [as submodifier] without doubt; clearly: *Jane, though born in California, feels emphatically Canadian.* ■ [sentence adverb] used to give emphasis to a statement: *Greg is emphatically not a slacker.*

em·phy·se·ma /ˌemfəˈsēmə; -ˈzēmə/ ▶ **n.** Med. **1** (also **pulmonary emphysema**) a condition in which the air sacs of the lungs are damaged and enlarged, causing breathlessness. **2** a condition in which air is abnormally present within the body tissues. — **em·phy·sem·a·tous** /ˌemfəˈsemətəs; -ˈsēmə-; -ˈzemə-; -ˈzēmə-/ **adj.** **em·phy·se·mic** **adj.** [17th C. (sense 2): via late L. from Gk. *emphusēma*, from *emphusan* 'puff up.']

em·pire /ˈempī(ə)r/ ▶ **n.** **1** an extensive group of states or countries under a single supreme authority, formerly esp. an emperor or empress. ■ a government in which the head of state is an emperor or empress. ■ a large commercial organization owned or controlled by one person or group. ■ an extensive operation or sphere of activity controlled by one person or group. ■ supreme political power over several countries when exercised by a single authority: *the Greeks' dream of empire in Asia Minor.* ■ archaic absolute control over a person or group. **2** a variety of apple. ▶ **adj.** /**also** ämˈpi(ə)r/ (usu. **Empire**) [attrib.] denoting a style of furniture, decoration, or dress fashionable during the First or the Second Empire in France. The decorative style was neoclassical but incorporated Egyptian and other ancient motifs probably inspired by Napoleon's Egyptian campaigns. ■ (of a dress) having a high waist and a low neckline. [ME: via OFr. from L. *imperium*, rel. to *imperare* 'to command' (see **EMPEROR**).]

empire dress

em·pire build·er ▶ **n.** a person who adds to or strengthens an empire. ■ a person who seeks more power, responsibility, or staff within an organization for the purposes of self-aggrandizement. — **em·pire-build·ing** **n.**

Em·pire State Build·ing a skyscraper on Fifth Avenue, New York City, which was once the tallest building in the world. When erected in 1930–31, it measured 1,250 feet (381 m); the addition of a television mast in 1951 brought its height to 1,472 feet (449 m).

em·pir·ic /em'pirik/ ▶ **adj.** another term for EMPIRICAL. ▶ **n.** archaic a person who, in medicine or other branches of science, relies solely on observation and experiment. ■ a quack doctor. [ME: via L. from Gk. *empeirikos*, from *empeiria* 'experience,' from *empeiros* 'skilled' (based on *peira* 'trial, experiment').]

em·pir·i·cal /em'pirikəl/ ▶ **adj.** based on, concerned with, or verifiable by observation or experience rather than theory or pure logic. — **em·pir·i·cal·ly adv.**

em·pir·i·cal for·mu·la ▶ **n.** Chem. a formula giving the proportions of the elements present in a compound but not the actual numbers or arrangement of atoms.

em·pir·i·cism /em'pirə,sizəm/ ▶ **n.** Philos. the theory that all knowledge is derived from sense-experience. Compare with PHENOMENALISM. ■ practice based on experiment and observation. ■ dated ignorant or unscientific practice; quackery. — **em·pir·i·cist n. & adj.**

em·place·ment /em'plāsmənt/ ▶ **n.** **1** a structure on or in which something is firmly placed. ■ a position where a gun is placed for firing. **2** esp. Geol. the process or state of setting something in place or being set in place. [19th C.: from Fr., from *em-* 'in' + *place* 'a place.']

em·plane /em'plān/ ▶ **v.** var. of ENPLANE.

em·ploy /em'ploi/ ▶ **v.** [trans.] **1** give work to (someone) and pay them for it. ■ keep occupied: ***employed in** developing products.* **2** make use of. ▶ **n.** [in sing.] the state or fact of being employed for wages or a salary: ***in the employ of** a grocer and wine merchant.* ■ archaic employment: *her place of employ.* — **em·ploy·a·bil·i·ty** /em,ploi-ə'bilitē/ **n.** **em·ploy·a·ble adj.** [ME: from OFr. *employer*, based on L. *implicari* 'be involved in,' (see IMPLY).]

em·ploy·ee /em'ploi-ē; ,emploi'ē/ ▶ **n.** a person employed for wages or salary, esp. a nonexecutive.

em·ploy·er /em'ploi-ər/ ▶ **n.** a person or organization that employs people.

em·ploy·ment /em'ploimənt/ ▶ **n.** the condition of having paid work. ■ a person's trade or profession. ■ the action of giving work to someone: *employment of a full-time tutor.*

em·ploy·ment a·gen·cy ▶ **n.** an agency that finds employers or employees for those seeking them.

em·po·ri·um /em'pôrēəm/ ▶ **n.** (pl. **-po·ri·ums** or **-po·ri·a** /-'pôrēə/) a large retail store selling a wide variety of goods. ■ a business establishment that specializes in products or services on a large scale (often used for humorously formal effect). ■ archaic a principal center of commerce; a market. [16th C.: from L., from Gk. *emporion*, from *emporos* 'merchant.']

em·pow·er /em'pouər/ ▶ **v.** [with obj. and infin.] give (someone) the authority or power to do something: *nobody was empowered to sign checks on her behalf.* ■ enable (someone) to do something. ■ [trans.] make (someone) stronger and more confident, esp. in controlling their life and claiming their rights: *movements to empower the poor.* — **em·pow·er·ment n.**

em·press /'empris/ ▶ **n.** a female emperor. ■ the wife or widow of an emperor. [ME: from OFr. *emperesse*, fem. of *emperere* (see EMPEROR).]

em·presse·ment /,änpres'män/ ▶ **n.** archaic animated eagerness or friendliness; effusion. [from Fr., from *empresser* 'rush eagerly.']

emp·ty /'em(p)tē/ ▶ **adj.** (**-ti·er, -ti·est**) containing nothing; not filled or occupied. ■ fig. (of words or a gesture) having no meaning or likelihood of fulfillment; insincere. ■ fig. having no value or purpose. ■ informal hungry. ■ Math. (of a set) containing no members or elements. ■ emotionally exhausted. ▶ **v.** (**-ties, -tied**) [trans.] remove all the contents of (a container). ■ remove (the contents) from a container. ■ [intrans.] (of a place) be vacated by people in it. ■ [intrans.] (**empty into**) (of a river) discharge itself into (the sea or a lake). ▶ **n.** (pl. **-ties**) (usu. **empties**) informal a container (esp. a bottle or glass) left empty of its contents.

– PHRASES **running on empty** exhausted of all one's resources or sustenance. **on an empty stomach** see STOMACH. — **emp·ti·ly adv.** **emp·ti·ness n.** [OE *ǣmtig* 'at leisure,' from *ǣmetta* 'leisure,' perh. from *ā* 'no' + *mōt* 'meeting'.]

emp·ty nest·er ▶ **n.** informal a parent whose children have grown up and left home.

Emp·ty Quar·ter another name for RUB' AL KHALI.

em·pur·ple /em'pərpəl/ ▶ **v.** make or become purple.

em·py·e·ma /,empī'ēmə/ ▶ **n.** Med. the collection of pus in a cavity in the body, esp. in the pleural cavity. [ME: via late L. from Gk. *empuēma*, from *empuein* 'suppurate,' from *em-* 'in' + *puon* 'pus.']

em·py·re·an /em'pirēən; ,empə'rēən/ (also **em·py·re·al** /-əl/) ▶ **adj.** belonging to or deriving from heaven. ▶ **n.** (**the empyrean**) heaven, in particular the highest part of heaven. ■ literary the visible heavens; the sky. [ME: via med. L. from Gk. *empurios*, from *en-* 'in' + *pur* 'fire.']

EMS ▶ **abbr.** ■ emergency medical service. ■ European Monetary System.

EMT ▶ **abbr.** emergency medical technician.

EMU ▶ **abbr.** European Monetary Union.

e·mu /'ēm(y)o͞o/ ▶ **n.** a large flightless fast-running Australian bird (*Dromaius novaehollandiae*) resembling the ostrich, with shaggy gray or brown plumage, bare blue skin on the head and neck, and three-toed feet. [17th C.: from Port. *ema*.]

em·u·late /'emyə,lāt/ ▶ **v.** [trans.] match or surpass (a person or achievement), typically by imitation. ■ imitate. ■ Comput. reproduce the function or action of (a different computer or software system). — **em·u·la·tion** /,emyə'lāsʜən/ **n.** **em·u·la·tive** /-,lātiv/ **adj.** **em·u·la·tor** /-,lātər/ **n.** [16th C.: from L. *aemulat-* 'rivaled, equaled,' from the v. *aemulari*, from *aemulus* 'rival.']

em·u·lous /'emyələs/ ▶ **adj.** (often **emulous of**) formal seeking to emulate or imitate someone or something. ■ motivated by a spirit of rivalry: *emulous young writers.* — **em·u·lous·ly adv.** **em·u·lous·ness n.**

e·mul·si·fi·er /i'məlsə,fīər/ ▶ **n.** a substance that stabilizes an emulsion, in particular a food additive used to stabilize processed foods. ■ an apparatus used for making an emulsion by stirring or shaking a substance.

e·mul·si·fy /i'məlsə,fī/ ▶ **v.** (**-fies, -fied**) make into or become an emulsion. — **e·mul·si·fi·a·ble** /-,fīəbəl/ **adj.** **e·mul·si·fi·ca·tion** /i,məlsəfi'kāsʜən/ **n.**

e·mul·sion /i'məlsʜən/ ▶ **n.** a fine dispersion of minute droplets of one liquid in another in which it is not soluble or miscible. ■ a light-sensitive coating for photographic films and plates, containing crystals of a silver compound dispersed in a medium such as gelatin. — **e·mul·sive** /-siv/ **adj.** [17th C.: from mod. L. *emulsio(n-)*, from *emulgere* 'milk out,' from *e-* 'out' + *mulgere* 'to milk.']

en /en/ ▶ **n.** Print. a unit of measurement equal to half an em and approximately the average width of typeset characters, used esp. for estimating the total amount of space a text will require. [18th C.: the width of the letter *N*.]

en-[1] (also **em-**) ▶ **prefix** **1** forming verbs (added to nouns) expressing entry into the specified state or location: *engulf* | *embed.* **2** forming verbs (added to nouns and adjectives) expressing conversion into the specified state (as in *ennoble*). ■ often forming verbs having the suffix *-en* (as in *embolden, enliven*). **3** (added to verbs) in; into; on: *ensnare.* ■ as an intensifier: *entangle.* [from Fr., from L. *in-*.]

en-[2] (also **em-**) ▶ **prefix** within; inside: *encyst* | *endemic* | *embolism* | *empyema.* [from Gk.]

-en[1] ▶ **suffix** forming verbs: **1** (from adjectives) denoting the development, creation, or intensification of a state: *widen* | *deepen* | *loosen.* **2** from nouns (such as *strengthen* from *strength*). [OE *-nian*, of Gmc. origin.]

-en[2] ▶ **suffix** (also **-n**) forming adjectives from nouns: **1** made or consisting of: *earthen* | *woolen.* **2** resembling: *golden* | *silvern.* [OE, of Gmc. origin.]

-en[3] (also **-n**) ▶ **suffix** forming past participles of strong verbs: **1** as a regular inflection: *spoken.* **2** as an adjective: *mistaken* | *torn.* ■ often with a restricted adjectival sense: *drunken* | *sunken.* [OE, of Gmc. origin.]

-en[4] ▶ **suffix** forming the plural of a few nouns such as *children, oxen.* [ME reduction of the earlier suffix *-an*.]

-en[5] ▶ **suffix** forming diminutives of nouns (such as *chicken, maiden*). [OE, of Gmc. origin.]

-en[6] ▶ **suffix** **1** forming feminine nouns such as *vixen.* **2** forming abstract nouns such as *burden.* [OE, of Gmc. origin.]

en·a·ble /en'ābəl/ ▶ **v.** [with obj. and infin.] give (someone or something) the authority or means to do something. ■ [trans.] make possible. ■ [trans.] esp. Comput. make (a device or system) operational; activate. ■ [as adj. **-enabled**] adapted for use with the specified application or system: *WAP-enabled cell phones.* — **en·a·ble·ment n.** **en·a·bler n.**

en·a·bling act ▶ **n.** a statute empowering a person or body to take certain action, esp. to make regulations, rules, or orders.

en·act /en'akt/ ▶ **v.** [trans.] **1** (often **be enacted**) make (a bill or other proposal) law. ■ put into practice (a belief, idea, or suggestion). **2** act out (a role or play) on stage. — **en·act·a·ble adj.** **en·ac·tion** /en'aksʜən/ **n.** **en·ac·tor** /-tər/ **n.**

en·act·ment /en'aktmənt/ ▶ **n.** **1** the process of passing legislation. ■ a law that is passed. **2** a process of acting something out. — **en·ac·tive adj.**

e·nam·el /i'naməl/ ▶ **n.** an opaque or semitransparent glassy substance applied to metallic or other hard surfaces for ornament or as a protective coating. ■ a work of art executed in such a substance. ■ the hard glossy substance that covers the crown of a tooth. ■ (also **enamel paint**) a paint that dries to give a smooth, hard coat. ■ dated nail polish. ▶ **v.** (**-eled, -el·ing**; Brit. **-elled, -el·ling**) [trans.] [often as adj.] (**enameled**) coat or decorate (a metallic or hard object) with enamel. ■ dated apply nail polish to (fingernails or toenails). — **e·nam·el·er n.** **e·nam·el·ist n.** [ME: from Anglo-Norman Fr. *enamailler*, from *en-* 'in, on' + *amail* 'enamel,' ult. of Gmc. origin.]

e·nam·el·ware /i'naməl,we(ə)r/ ▶ **n.** enameled kitchenware.

en·am·or /i'namər/ (esp. Brit. **en·am·our**) ▶ **v.** (**be enamored of/with/by**) be filled with a feeling of love for: *it is not difficult to see why Edward is enamored of her.* ■ have a liking or admiration for: *enamored of New York.* [ME: from OFr. *enamourer*, from *en-* 'in' + *amour* 'love.']

en·an·ti·o·mer /i'nantēəmər/ ▶ **n.** Chem. each of a pair of molecules that are mirror images of each other. — **en·an·ti·o·mer·ic** /i,nantēə'merik/ **adj.** **en·an·ti·o·mer·i·cal·ly** /-ik(ə)lē/ **adv.** [1930s: from Gk. *enantios* 'opposite' + -MER.]

en·an·ti·o·morph /i'nantēə,môrf/ ▶ **n.** each of two crystalline or other geometric forms that are mirror images of each other. — **en·an·ti·o·mor·phic** /i,nantēə'môrfik/ **adj.** **en·an·ti·o·mor·phism** /i,nantēə'môrfizəm/ **n.** **en·an·ti·o·mor·phous** /i,nantēə'môrfəs/ **adj.**

en·ar·thro·sis /,enär'tʜrōsis/ ▶ **n.** (pl. **-ses** /-sēz/) Anat. a ball-and-socket joint. [16th C.: from Gk. *enarthrōsis*, from *enarthros* 'jointed,' from *en-* 'inside' + *arthron* 'joint.']

e·na·tion /ē'nāshən/ ▶ **n.** Bot. an outgrowth from the surface of a leaf or other part of a plant. [19th C.: from L. *enatio(n-)*, from *enasci* 'issue forth.']

en bloc /äN 'bläk/ ▶ **adv.** all together or all at the same time. [19th C.: Fr.]

en bro·chette /äN brō'shet/ ▶ **adj.** Cooking (of a dish) cooked on a skewer. [Fr.]

en brosse /äN 'brôs/ ▶ **adj.** [postpositive] (of a person's hair) cut in a short and bristly style. [20th C.: French, literally 'in the form of a brush.']

enc. ▶ **abbr.** ■ enclosed. ■ enclosure.

en·cage /en'kāj/ ▶ **v.** [trans.] literary confine in or as in a cage.

en·camp /en'kamp/ ▶ **v.** [intrans.] settle in or establish a camp, esp. a military one.

en·camp·ment /en'kampmənt/ ▶ **n.** a place with temporary accommodations consisting of huts or tents, typically for troops or nomads. ■ the process of setting up a camp.

en·cap·su·late /en'kaps(y)ə,lāt/ ▶ **v.** [trans.] enclose (something) in or as if in a capsule. ■ express the essential features of (someone or something) succinctly. ■ Comput. enclose (a message or signal) in a set of codes that allow use by or transfer through different computer systems or networks. ■ Comput. provide an interface for (a piece of software or hardware) to allow or simplify access for the user. ■ [as adj.] (**encapsulated**) enclosed by a protective coating or membrane. — **en·cap·su·la·tion** /en,kaps(y)ə'lāshən/ **n.**

en·case /en'kās/ (also dated **in·case**) ▶ **v.** [trans.] (often **be encased**) enclose or cover in a case or close-fitting surround. — **en·case·ment n.**

en·caus·tic /en'kôstik/ ▶ **adj.** (esp. in painting and ceramics) using pigments mixed with hot wax that are burned in as an inlay. ■ (of bricks and tiles) decorated with colored clays inlaid into the surface and burned in. ▶ **n.** the art or process of encaustic painting. [16th C.: via L. from Gk. *enkaustikos*, from *enkaiein* 'burn in,' from *en-* 'in' + *kaiein* 'to burn.']

-ence /əns; ns/ ▶ **suffix** forming nouns: **1** denoting a quality or an instance of it: *impertinence.* **2** denoting an action or its result: *reference.* [from Fr. *-ence*, from L. *-entia, -antia.*]

en·ceinte[1] /en'sānt; än'sant/ ▶ **n.** archaic an enclosure or the enclosing wall of a fortified place. [18th C.: from Fr., from L. *incincta*, fem. past part. of *incingere* 'gird in,' from *in-* 'in' + *cingere* 'to gird.']

en·ceinte[2] ▶ **adj.** archaic pregnant. [17th C.: from Fr.]

En·cel·a·dus /en'selədəs/ Astron. a satellite of Saturn, the eighth closest to the planet, discovered by W. Herschel in 1789.

en·ce·phal·ic /,ensə'falik/ ▶ **adj.** Anat. relating to, affecting, or situated in the brain. [19th C.: from Gk. *enkephalos* 'brain' (from *en-* 'in' + *kephalē* 'head') + -IC.]

en·ceph·a·li·tis /en,sefə'lītis/ ▶ **n.** inflammation of the brain, caused by infection or an allergic reaction. — **en·ceph·a·lit·ic** /-'litik/ **adj.**

en·ceph·a·li·tis le·thar·gi·ca /li'thärjikə/ ▶ **n.** a form of encephalitis caused by a virus and characterized by headache and drowsiness leading to coma. Also called SLEEPING SICKNESS.

encephalo- ▶ **comb. form** of or relating to the brain: *encephalopathy.* [from Gk. *enkephalos.*]

en·ceph·a·lo·gram /en'sefələ,gram/ ▶ **n.** Med. an image, trace, or other record of the structure or electrical activity of the brain.

en·ceph·a·log·ra·phy /en,sefə'lägrəfē/ ▶ **n.** Med. any of various techniques for recording the structure or electrical activity of the brain. — **en·ceph·a·lo·graph** /en'sefələ,graf/ **n.** **en·ceph·a·lo·graph·ic** /-lə'grafik/ **adj.**

en·ceph·a·lo·my·e·li·tis /en,sefələ,mīə'lītis/ ▶ **n.** Med. inflammation of the brain and spinal cord, typically due to acute viral infection.

en·ceph·a·lon /en'sefə,län; -lən/ ▶ **n.** Anat. the brain. [18th C.: from Gk. *enkephalon*, from *en-* 'inside' + *kephalē* 'head.']

en·ceph·a·lop·a·thy /en,sefə'läpəthē/ ▶ **n.** (pl. **-thies**) Med. any disease in which the functioning of the brain is affected by some agent or condition.

en·chain /en'chān/ ▶ **v.** [trans.] literary bind with or as with chains. — **en·chain·ment n.**

en·chant /en'chant/ ▶ **v.** [trans.] (often **be enchanted**) fill (someone) with great delight; charm. ■ put (someone or something) under a spell. — **en·chant·ed·ly adv.** **en·chant·ment n.** [ME: from Fr. *enchanter*, from L. *incantare*, from *in-* 'in' + *cantare* 'sing.']

en·chant·er /en'chantər/ ▶ **n.** a person who uses magic or sorcery, esp. to put someone or something under a spell.

en·chant·ing /en'chantiNG/ ▶ **adj.** delightfully charming or attractive: *Dinah looked enchanting.* — **en·chant·ing·ly adv.**

en·chant·ress /en'chantris/ ▶ **n.** a woman who uses magic or sorcery, esp. to put someone or something under a spell. ■ a very attractive and beguiling woman.

en·chase /en'chās/ ▶ **v.** [trans.] decorate (a piece of jewelry or work of art) by inlaying, engraving, or carving. ■ place (a jewel) in a setting. [ME: from OFr. *enchasser* 'set gems,' from *en-* 'in' + *chasse* 'a case.']

en·chi·la·da /,enchə'lädə/ ▶ **n.** a rolled tortilla with a filling typically of meat and served with a chili sauce.

– PHRASES **the big enchilada** informal a person or thing of great importance. **the whole enchilada** informal the whole situation; everything. [L. Amer. Sp., fem. past part. of *enchilar* 'season with chili.']

en·chi·rid·i·on /,eNGkə'ridēən; ,enkī-/ ▶ **n.** (pl. **-rid·i·ons** or **-rid·i·a** /-'ridēə/) formal a book containing essential information on a subject. [ME: via late L. from Gk. *enkheiridion*, from *en-* 'within' + *kheir* 'hand' + the dimin. suffix *-idion.*]

En·ci·ni·tas /,ensi'nētəs/ a city in southwestern California, northwest of San Diego; pop. 55,386.

en·ci·pher /en'sīfər/ ▶ **v.** [trans.] convert (a message or piece of text) into a coded form; encrypt. — **en·ci·pher·ment n.**

en·cir·cle /en'sərkəl/ ▶ **v.** [trans.] form a circle around; surround: *the town is encircled by fortified walls.* — **en·cir·cle·ment n.**

encl. (also **enc.**) ▶ **abbr.** ■ enclosed. ■ enclosure.

en clair /äN 'kler/ ▶ **adj. & adv.** (esp. of a telegram or official message) in ordinary language, rather than in code or cipher. [Fr., lit. 'in clear.']

en·clasp /en'klasp/ ▶ **v.** [trans.] formal hold tightly in one's arms.

en·clave /'enklāv; 'äNG-/ ▶ **n.** a portion of territory within or surrounded by a larger territory whose inhabitants are culturally or ethnically distinct. ■ fig. a place or group that is different in character from those surrounding it. ▶ **v.** [trans.] rare surround and isolate; make an enclave of. [19th C.: from Fr. *enclaver* 'enclose,' based on L. *clavis* 'key.']

en·clit·ic /en'klitik/ Ling. ▶ **n.** a word pronounced with so little emphasis that it is shortened and forms part of the preceding word, e.g., *n't* in *can't.* Compare with PROCLITIC. ▶ **adj.** denoting or relating to such a word. — **en·clit·i·cal·ly** /-ik(ə)lē/ **adv.** [17th C.: via late L. from Gk. *enklitikos*, from *enklinein* 'lean on,' from *en-* 'in, on' + *klinein* 'to lean.']

en·close /en'klōz/ (also dated **in·close**) ▶ **v.** [trans.] **1** (often **be enclosed**) surround or close off on all sides. ■ hist. fence in (common land) so as to make it private property. ■ [usu. as adj.] (**enclosed**) seclude (a religious or other community) from the outside world. ■ esp. Math. bound on all sides; contain. **2** place (something) in an envelope with a letter. [ME: from OFr. *enclos*, based on L. *includere* 'shut in.']

en·clo·sure /en'klōzhər/ (also dated **in·clo·sure**) ▶ **n.** **1** an area sealed off artificially or naturally. ■ an artificial or natural barrier that seals off an area. **2** the state of being enclosed, esp. in a religious community: *the nuns kept strict enclosure.* **3** a document or object placed in an envelope together with a letter.

en·code /en'kōd/ ▶ **v.** [trans.] convert into a coded form. ■ Comput. convert (information or an instruction) into a digital form. ■ Biochem. (of a gene) be responsible for producing (a substance or behavior). — **en·cod·a·ble adj.** **en·cod·er n.** **en·code·ment n.**

en·co·mi·ast /en'kōmē,ast/ ▶ **n.** formal a person who publicly praises or flatters someone else. — **en·co·mi·as·tic** /en,kōmē'astik/ **adj.** **en·co·mi·as·ti·cal·ly** /en,kōmē'astik(ə)lē/ **adv.** [17th C.: from Gk. *enkōmiastēs*, from *enkōmiazein* 'to praise,' from *enkōmion* (see ENCOMIUM).]

en·co·mi·en·da /en,kōmē'endə; -,kämē-/ ▶ **n.** hist. a grant by the Spanish Crown to a colonist in America conferring the right to demand tribute and forced labor from the Indian inhabitants of an area. [19th C.: Spanish, literally 'commission, charge.']

en·co·mi·um /en'kōmēəm/ ▶ **n.** (pl. **-mi·ums** or **-mi·a** /-mēə/) formal a speech or piece of writing that praises someone or something highly. [16th C.: L., from Gk. *enkōmion* 'eulogy,' from *en-* 'within' + *komos* 'revel.']

en·com·pass /en'kəmpəs/ ▶ **v.** **1** [trans.] surround and have or hold within: *a vast halo encompassing the galaxy.* ■ include comprehensively. **2** archaic cause (something) to take place. — **en·com·pass·ment n.**

en·core /'äNGkôr; 'än-/ ▶ **n.** a repeated or additional performance of an item at the end of a concert, as called for by an audience. ▶ **exclam.** called out by an audience as such a request. ▶ **v.** [trans.] (often **be encored**) give or call for an encore. [18th C.: French, literally 'still, again.']

en·coun·ter /en'kountər/ ▶ **v.** [trans.] unexpectedly experience or face (something difficult or hostile). ■ meet unexpectedly and confront (an adversary). ■ meet (someone) unexpectedly. ▶ **n.** an unexpected or casual meeting. ■ a confrontation or unpleasant struggle. [ME: from OFr. *encontrer*, based on L. *in-* 'in' + *contra* 'against.']

en·coun·ter group ▶ **n.** a group of people who meet to gain psychological benefit through close contact with one another.

en·cour·age /en'kərij; -'kə-rij/ ▶ **v.** [trans.] give support, confidence, or hope to (someone): [as adj.] (**encouraging**) *encouraging results* | [as adj.] (**encouraged**) *I feel encouraged.* ■ give support and advice to (someone) to do or continue something: [with obj. and infin.] *pupils are encouraged to be creative.* ■ help or stimulate (an activity, state, or view) to develop. — **en·cour·age·ment n.** **en·cour·ag·er n.** **en·cour·ag·ing·ly adv.** [ME: from Fr. *encourager*, from *en-* 'in' + *corage* 'courage.']

en·croach /en'krōch/ ▶ **v.** [intrans.] (**encroach on/upon**) intrude on (a person's territory or a thing considered to be a right). ■ advance gradually and in a way that causes damage. — **en·croach·er n.** **en·croach·ment n.** [ME: from OFr. *encrochier* 'seize,' from *en-* 'in' + *crochier* (from *croc* 'hook,' from ON *krókr*).]

en·croach·ment /en'krōchmənt/ ▶ **n.** Football a penalty in which a defensive player is positioned in the neutral zone at the start of a play.

en croute /äN 'kroot/ ▶ **adj. & adv.** in a pastry crust. [Fr. *en croûte.*]

en·crust /en'krəst/ (also **in·crust**) ▶ **v.** [trans.] cover (something) with a hard surface layer. ■ overlay (something) with an ornamental crust of gems or other precious material. ■ [intrans.] form a crust.

[17th C.: from Fr. *incruster*, from L. *incrustare*, from *in-* 'into' + *crusta* 'a crust.']

en·crus·ta·tion /ˌenkrəsˈtāsʜən/ (also **in·crus·ta·tion**) ▶ **n.** the action of encrusting or state of being encrusted. ■ a crust or hard coating on the surface of something. ■ an outer layer or crust of ornamentation. ■ Archit. a facing of marble on a building.

en·crypt /enˈkript/ ▶ **v.** [trans.] convert (information or data) into a cipher or code. ■ (**encrypt something in**) conceal information or data in something by this means. — **en·cryp·tion** /-ˈkripsʜən/ **n.** [1950s (orig. US): from EN-[1] 'in' + Gk. *kruptos* 'hidden.']

en·cul·tu·ra·tion /enˌkəlcʜəˈrāsʜən/ (also **in·cul·tu·ra·tion**) ▶ **n.** the gradual acquisition of the characteristics and norms of a culture or group.

en·cum·ber /enˈkəmbər/ ▶ **v.** [trans.] (often **be encumbered**) restrict or burden (someone or something) in such a way that free action or movement is difficult. ■ saddle (a person or estate) with a debt or mortgage. ■ fill or block up (a place). [ME: from OFr. *encombrer* 'block up,' from *en-* 'in' + *combre* 'river barrage.']

en·cum·brance /enˈkəmbrəns/ ▶ **n.** a burden or impediment. ■ Law a mortgage or other charge on property or assets. ■ archaic a person, esp. a child, who is dependent on someone else for support.

ency. ▶ **abbr.** encyclopedia.

-ency /ənsē; n-sē/ ▶ **suffix** forming nouns: **1** denoting a quality: *efficiency.* **2** denoting a state: *presidency.* [from L. *-entia* (cf. -ENCE).]

encyc. ▶ **abbr.** encyclopedia.

en·cyc·li·cal /enˈsiklikəl/ ▶ **n.** a papal letter sent to all bishops of the Roman Catholic Church. ▶ **adj.** of or relating to such a letter. [17th C.: via late L. from Gk. *enkuklios* 'general,' from *en-* 'in' + *kuklos* 'a circle.']

en·cy·clo·pe·di·a /enˌsīkləˈpēdēə/ (also esp. Brit. **en·cy·clo·pae·di·a**) ▶ **n.** a book or set of books giving information on many subjects or on many aspects of one subject and typically arranged alphabetically. [16th C.: mod. L., from pseudo-Gk. *enkuklopaideia* 'all-around education.']

en·cy·clo·pe·dic /enˌsīkləˈpēdik/ (also esp. Brit. **en·cy·clo·pae·dic**) ▶ **adj.** comprehensive in terms of information: *an almost encyclopedic knowledge of food.* ■ relating to or containing information about words that is not simply linguistic. — **en·cy·clo·pe·di·cal·ly** /-dik(ə)lē/ **adv.**

en·cy·clo·pe·dism /enˌsīkləˈpēdizəm/ (also esp. Brit. **en·cy·clo·pae·dism**) ▶ **n.** comprehensive learning or knowledge.

en·cy·clo·pe·dist /enˌsīkləˈpēdist/ (also esp. Brit. **en·cy·clo·pae·dist**) ▶ **n.** a person who writes, edits, or contributes to an encyclopedia.

en·cyst /enˈsist/ ▶ **v.** Zool. enclose or become enclosed in a cyst. — **en·cys·ta·tion** /ˌensiˈstāsʜən/ **n.** **en·cyst·ment n.**

end /end/ ▶ **n.** **1** a final part of something, esp. a period of time, an activity, or a story. ■ a termination of a state or situation. ■ used to emphasize that something, typically a subject of discussion, is considered finished: *you will go and that's the end of it.* ■ death or ruin: *another injury will be the end of her career.* ■ archaic an ultimate state or condition: *the end of that man is peace.* **2** the furthest or most extreme part or point of something. ■ a small piece that is left after something has been used: *a box of candle ends.* ■ a specified extreme point on a scale. ■ the part or share of an activity with which someone is concerned: *honor your end of the deal.* ■ a place that is linked to another by a telephone call, letter, or journey. ■ the part of an athletic field or court defended by one team or player. **3** a goal or result that one seeks to achieve: *each would use the other to further his own ends.* **4** Football an offensive or defensive lineman positioned nearest to the sideline. ▶ **v.** come or bring to a final point; finish. ■ [intrans.] reach a point and go no further: *where agnosticism ends and atheism begins.* ■ [intrans.] perform a final act: *he ended by attacking an officer.* ■ [intrans.] (**end in**) have as its final part, point, or result: *one in three marriages now ends in divorce.* ■ [intrans.] (**end up**) eventually reach or come to a specified place, state, or course of action: *I ended up in Connecticut.*

– PHRASES **at the end of the day** informal when everything is taken into consideration: *at the end of the day, I'm responsible.* **be at** (or **have come to**) **an end** be finished or completed. ■ (of a supply of something) become exhausted: *our patience has come to an end.* **be at the end of** be close to having no more of (something): *he was at the end of his ability to cope.* **come to** (or **meet**) **a bad end** be led by one's own actions to ruin or an unpleasant death. **end one's days** (or **life**) spend the final part of one's existence in a specified place or state: *the last passenger pigeon ended her days in the Cincinnati Zoo.* **an end in itself** a goal that is pursued in its own right to the exclusion of others. **end in tears** have an unhappy or painful outcome (often as a warning): *this treaty will end in tears.* **end it all** commit suicide. **the end of the road** (or **line**) the point beyond which progress or survival cannot continue. **the end of one's rope** (or **tether**) having no patience or energy left to cope with something. **end on** with the furthest point of an object facing toward one: *seen end on, their sharp, rocky summits point like arrows.* ■ with the furthest point of an object touching that of another. **end to end** in a row with the furthest point of one object touching that of another object. **in the end** eventually or on reflection: *in the end, I saw that she was right.* **keep** (or **hold**) **one's end up** informal perform well in a difficult or competitive situation. **make an end of** cause (someone or something) to stop existing. **make** (**both**) **ends meet** earn enough money to live without getting into debt. **never** (or **not**) **hear the end of** be continually reminded of (an unpleasant topic or cause of annoyance). **no end** informal to a great extent; very much: *this cheered me up no end.* **no end of** informal a vast number or amount of (something): *we shared no end of good times.* **on end 1** continuing without stopping for a specified period of time: *sometimes they'll be gone for days on end.* **2** in an upright position. **put an end to** cause someone or something to stop existing: *injury put an end to his career.* **a —— to end all ——s** informal used to emphasize how impressive or successful something is of its kind: *it was a party to end all parties.* **without end** without a limit or boundary: *a war without end.* [OE *ende*, of Gmc. origin; rel. to Ger. *Ende.*]

-end ▶ **suffix** denoting a person or thing to be treated in a specified way: *dividend* | *reverend.* [from L. *-endus*, gerundive ending.]

end-all ▶ **n.** (**the end-all**) the thing that is final or definitive.

en·dan·ger /enˈdānjər/ ▶ **v.** [trans.] put (someone or something) at risk or in danger. — **en·dan·ger·ment n.**

en·dan·gered /enˈdānjərd/ ▶ **adj.** (of a species) seriously at risk of extinction.

end-a·round ▶ **n.** Football a play in which an end carries the ball around the side of the line of scrimmage. ▶ **adj.** Comput. involving the transfer of a digit from one end of a register to the other.

end·ar·ter·ec·to·my /ˌendärtəˈrektəmē/ ▶ **n.** (pl. **-mies**) surgical removal of part of the inner lining of an artery, with obstructive deposits, most often carried out on the carotid artery or on vessels supplying the legs.

end·ar·te·ri·tis /ˌendärtəˈrītis/ ▶ **n.** Med. inflammation of the inner lining of an artery.

en dash ▶ **n.** a short dash, the width of an en, used in punctuation.

en·dear /enˈdi(ə)r/ ▶ **v.** [trans.] cause to be loved or liked: *Flora's spirit and character endeared her to everyone.* — **en·dear·ing adj.** **en·dear·ing·ly adv.**

en·dear·ment /enˈdi(ə)rmənt/ ▶ **n.** a word or phrase expressing love or affection. ■ love or affection: *a term of endearment.*

en·deav·or /enˈdevər/ (Brit. **en·deav·our**) ▶ **v.** [no obj., with infin.] try hard to do or achieve something. ▶ **n.** an attempt to achieve a goal. ■ earnest and industrious effort, esp. when sustained over a period of time. ■ an enterprise or undertaking. [ME: from the phr. *put oneself in devoir* 'do one's utmost' (see DEVOIR).]

en·dem·ic /enˈdemik/ ▶ **adj.** **1** (of a disease or condition) regularly found among particular people or in a certain area. ■ [attrib.] denoting an area in which a particular disease is regularly found. **2** (of a plant or animal) native or restricted to a certain country or area: *a marsupial endemic to Australia.* ▶ **n.** an endemic plant or animal. ■ an endemic disease. — **en·dem·i·cal·ly** /-ik(ə)lē/ **adv.** **en·de·mic·i·ty** /ˌendəˈmisitē/ **n.** **en·de·mism** /ˈendəˌmizəm/ **n.** (in sense 2 of the **adjective**). [17th C.: from Fr. *endémique* or mod. L. *endemicus*, from Gk. *endēmios* 'native' (based on *dēmos* 'people').]

En·der·by Land /ˈendərbē/ a part of Antarctica that is claimed by Australia.

end·er·gon·ic /ˌendərˈgänik/ ▶ **adj.** Biochem. (of a metabolic or chemical process) accompanied by or requiring the absorption of energy, the products being of greater free energy than the reactants. The opposite of EXERGONIC. [20th C.: from ENDO- 'within' + Gk. *ergon* 'work' + -IC.]

En·ders /ˈendərz/, John Franklin (1897–1985), US virologist. He helped devise a method of growing viruses in tissue cultures. Nobel Prize for Physiology or Medicine (1954, shared Frederick C. Robbins (1916–92) and Thomas H. Weller (1915–92)).

end·game /ˈendˌgām/ (also **end game**) ▶ **n.** the final stage of a game such as chess or bridge, when few pieces or cards remain.

end·ing /ˈendiɴɢ/ ▶ **n.** an end or final part of something, esp. a period, an activity, or a book or movie. ■ the furthest part or point of something: *a nerve ending.* ■ the final part of a word, constituting a grammatical inflection or formative element.

en·dive /ˈendīv; änˈdēv/ ▶ **n.** **1** an edible Mediterranean plant (*Cichorium endivia*) of the daisy family whose bitter leaves may be blanched and used in salads. **2** (also **Belgian endive**) a young, typically blanched chicory plant, eaten as a cooked vegetable or in salads. [ME (also denoting the sow thistle): via OFr. from med. L. *endivia*, based on Gk. *entubon.*]

end·less /ˈendlis/ ▶ **adj.** having or seeming to have no end or limit: *the list is endless.* ■ countless; innumerable: *endless cigarettes.* ■ (of a belt, chain, or tape) having the ends joined to form a loop allowing continuous action. — **end·less·ly adv.** **end·less·ness n.**

end·less screw ▶ **n.** the threaded cylinder in a worm gear.

end line ▶ **n.** Football the line that marks the back of the end zone.

end·long /ˈendˌlôɴɢ; -ˌläɴɢ/ ▶ **adv.** archaic from end to end; lengthwise.

end man ▶ **n.** **1** a man at the end of a row, line, or series. **2** hist. a man at the end of a line of minstrel show performers who engaged in repartee with the interlocutor.

end·most /ˈendˌmōst/ ▶ **adj.** nearest to the end.

end·note /ˈendˌnōt/ ▶ **n.** a note printed at the end of a book or section of a book.

endo- ▶ **comb. form** internal; within: *endoderm* | *endogenous.* [from Gk. *endon* 'within.']

en·do·car·di·al /ˌendōˈkärdēəl/ ▶ **adj.** Anat. Med. **1** of or relating to the endocardium. **2** situated inside the heart.

en·do·car·di·tis /ˌendōkärˈdītis/ ▶ **n.** Med. inflammation of the endocardium. — **en·do·car·dit·ic** /-ˈditik/ **adj.**

en·do·car·di·um /ˌendōˈkärdēəm/ ▶ **n.** the thin, smooth membrane that lines the inside of the chambers of the heart and forms the surface of the valves. [19th C.: mod. L., from ENDO- 'within' + Gk. *kardia* 'heart.']

en·do·carp /'endə,kärp/ ▶ n. Bot. the innermost layer of the pericarp that surrounds a seed in a fruit. It may be membranous (as in apples) or woody (as in the stone of a peach or cherry). — **en·do·car·pic** /,endō'kärpik/ adj. [19th C.: from ENDO- 'within' + a shortened form of PERICARP.]

en·do·cen·tric /,endō'sentrik/ ▶ adj. Ling. denoting or being a construction in which the whole has the same syntactic function as the head, for example *big black dogs*. Contrasted with EXOCENTRIC.

en·do·crine /'endəkrin/ ▶ adj. Physiol. of, relating to, or denoting glands that secrete hormones or other products directly into the blood: *the endocrine system*. ▶ n. an endocrine gland. [20th C.: from ENDO- 'within' + Gk. *krinein* 'sift.']

en·do·cri·nol·o·gy /,endəkrə'näləjē/ ▶ n. the branch of physiology and medicine concerned with endocrine glands and hormones. — **en·do·crin·o·log·i·cal** /-,krinə'läjikəl/ adj. **en·do·cri·nol·o·gist** /-jist/ n.

en·do·cy·to·sis /,endōsī'tōsis/ ▶ n. Biol. the taking in of matter by a living cell by invagination of its membrane to form a vacuole. — **en·do·cy·tose** /-'tōs; -'tōz/ v. **en·do·cy·tot·ic** /-'tätik/ adj.

en·do·derm /'endə,dərm/ (also **en·to·derm**) ▶ n. Zool. Embryol. the innermost layer of cells or tissue of an embryo in early development, or the parts derived from this, which include the lining of the gut and associated structures. Compare with ECTODERM and MESODERM. — **en·do·der·mal** /,endə'dərməl; ,endō-/ adj. **en·do·der·mic** /,endə'dərmik; ,endō-/ adj. [19th C.: from ENDO- 'within' + Gk. *derma* 'skin.']

en·do·der·mis /,endō'dərməs/ ▶ n. Bot. an inner layer of cells in the cortex of a root and of some stems, surrounding a vascular bundle. [20th C.: from ENDO- 'within' + mod. L. *dermis* 'skin.']

en·dog·a·my /en'dägəmē/ ▶ n. Anthropol. the custom of marrying only within the limits of a local community, clan, or tribe. Compare with EXOGAMY. ■ Biol. the fusion of reproductive cells from related individuals; inbreeding; self-pollination. — **en·do·gam·ic** /,endō'gamik/ adj. **en·dog·a·mous** /-gəməs/ adj. [19th C.: from ENDO- 'within' + Gk. *gamos* 'marriage.']

en·do·ge·net·ic /,endōjə'netik/ ▶ adj. another term for ENDOGENIC.

en·do·gen·ic /,endō'jenik/ ▶ adj. Geol. formed or occurring beneath the surface of the earth. Often contrasted with EXOGENIC.

en·dog·e·nous /en'däjənəs/ ▶ adj. having an internal cause or origin. Often contrasted with EXOGENOUS. ■ Biol. growing or originating from within an organism. ■ esp. Psychiatry (of a disease or symptom) not attributable to any external or environmental factor. ■ confined within a group or society. — **en·dog·e·nous·ly** adv.

en·do·lith·ic /,endō'liᴛʜik/ ▶ adj. Biol. living in or penetrating into stone: *endolithic algae*.

en·do·lymph /'endə,limf/ ▶ n. Anat. the fluid in the membranous labyrinth of the ear.

en·do·me·tri·o·sis /,endō,mētrē'ōsis/ ▶ n. Med. a condition resulting from the appearance of endometrial tissue outside the uterus and causing pelvic pain.

en·do·me·tri·tis /,endōmi'trītis/ ▶ n. Med. inflammation of the endometrium.

en·do·me·tri·um /,endō'mētrēəm/ ▶ n. Anat. the mucous membrane lining the uterus, which thickens during the menstrual cycle in preparation for possible implantation of an embryo. — **en·do·me·tri·al** /-trēəl/ adj. [19th C.: mod. L., from ENDO- 'within' + Gk. *mētra* 'womb.']

en·do·morph /'endə,môrf/ ▶ n. **1** Physiol. a person with a round body build and a high proportion of fat. Compare with ECTOMORPH and MESOMORPH. **2** Mineral. a mineral or crystal enclosed within another. — **en·do·mor·phic** /,endə'môrfik/ adj. **en·do·mor·phy** /-,môrfē/ n. [1940s: *endo-* from *endodermal* + -MORPH.]

en·do·nu·cle·ase /,endō'n(y)o͞oklē,ās; -,āz/ ▶ n. Biochem. an enzyme that cleaves a polynucleotide chain by separating nucleotides other than the two end ones.

en·do·par·a·site /,endō'parə,sīt/ ▶ n. Biol. a parasite, such as a tapeworm, that lives inside its host. Compare with ECTOPARASITE. — **en·do·par·a·sit·ic** /-,parə'sitik/ adj.

en·do·pep·ti·dase /,endō'pepti,dās/ ▶ n. Biochem. an enzyme that breaks peptide bonds other than terminal ones in a peptide chain.

en·do·phyte /'endə,fīt/ ▶ n. Bot. a plant, esp. a fungus, that lives inside another plant. — **en·do·phyt·ic** /,endə'fitik/ adj. **en·do·phyt·i·cal·ly** /,endə'fitik(ə)lē/ adv.

en·do·plasm /'endō,plazəm/ ▶ n. Biol., dated the more fluid, granular inner layer of the cytoplasm in ameboid cells. Compare with ECTOPLASM (sense 1).

en·do·plas·mic re·tic·u·lum /,endō'plazmik ri'tikyələm/ ▶ n. Biol. a network of membranous tubules within the cytoplasm of a eukaryotic cell, continuous with the nuclear membrane. It usually has ribosomes attached and is involved in protein and lipid synthesis.

end or·gan ▶ n. Anat. a specialized, encapsulated ending of a peripheral sensory nerve, which acts as a receptor for a stimulus.

en·dor·phin /en'dôrfin/ ▶ n. Biochem. any of a group of hormones secreted within the brain and nervous system and having a number of physiological functions. They are peptides that activate the body's opiate receptors, causing an analgesic effect. [1970s: blend of ENDOGENOUS and MORPHINE.]

en·dorse /en'dôrs/ (also dated **in·dorse**) ▶ v. [trans.] **1** declare one's public approval or support of. ■ recommend (a product) in an advertisement. **2** sign (a check or bill of exchange) on the back to make it payable to someone other than the stated payee or to accept responsibility for paying it. ■ (usu. **be endorsed on**) write (a comment) on the front or back of a document. — **en·dors·a·ble** adj. **en·dors·er** n. [15th C.: from med. L. *indorsare*, from L. *in-* 'on' + *dorsum* 'back.']

en·dor·see /,endôr'sē/ ▶ n. a person to whom a check or bill of exchange is made payable instead of the stated payee.

en·dorse·ment /en'dôrsmənt/ (also dated **in·dorse·ment**) ▶ n. **1** an act of giving one's public approval or support to someone or something. ■ a recommendation of a product in an advertisement. **2** a clause in an insurance policy detailing an exemption from or change in coverage. **3** the action of endorsing a check or bill of exchange.

en·do·scope /'endə,skōp/ ▶ n. Med. an instrument that can be introduced into the body to give a view of its internal parts. — **en·do·scop·ic** /,endə'skäpik/ adj. **en·do·scop·i·cal·ly** /,endə'skäpik(ə)lē/ adv. **en·dos·co·pist** /en'däskəpist/ n. **en·dos·co·py** /en'däskəpē/ n.

en·do·skel·e·ton /,endō'skelitn/ ▶ n. Zool. an internal skeleton, such as the bony or cartilaginous skeleton of vertebrates. Compare with EXOSKELETON. — **en·do·skel·e·tal** /-'skelitl/ adj.

en·do·sperm /'endə,spərm/ ▶ n. Bot. the part of a seed that acts as a food store for the developing plant embryo, usually containing starch with protein and other nutrients.

en·do·spore /'endə,spôr/ ▶ n. Biol. a resistant asexual spore that develops inside some bacteria cells. ■ the inner layer of the membrane or wall of some spores and pollen grains. — **en·dos·por·ous** /en'däspərəs; ,endə'spôrəs/ adj.

en·do·sym·bi·o·sis /,endō,simbē'ōsis; -,simbī-/ ▶ n. Biol. symbiosis in which one of the symbiotic organisms lives inside the other. — **en·do·sym·bi·ont** /-'simbē,änt; -'simbī-/ n. **en·do·sym·bi·ot·ic** /-'ätik/ adj.

en·do·the·li·um /,endə'ᴛʜēlēəm/ (pl. **-li·a** /-lēə/) ▶ n. the tissue that forms a single layer of cells lining various organs and cavities of the body, esp. the blood vessels, heart, and lymphatic vessels. It is formed from the embryonic mesoderm. Compare with EPITHELIUM. — **en·do·the·li·al** /-lēəl/ adj. [19th C.: mod. L., from ENDO- 'within' + Gk. *thēlē* 'nipple.']

en·do·therm /'endə,ᴛʜərm/ ▶ n. Zool. an animal that can generate internal heat; a warm-blooded animal. Often contrasted with ECTOTHERM. Compare with HOMEOTHERM. — **en·do·ther·my** n. [1940s: from ENDO- 'within,' on the pattern of *homoiotherm*.]

en·do·ther·mic /,endə'ᴛʜərmik/ ▶ adj. **1** (also **en·do·ther·mal**) Chem. (of a reaction or process) accompanied by or requiring the absorption of heat. The opposite of EXOTHERMIC. ■ (of a compound) requiring a net input of heat for its formation from its constituent elements. **2** Zool. (of an animal) capable of generating internal heat. — **en·do·ther·mi·cal·ly** /-mik(ə)lē/ adv.

en·do·tox·in /'endə,täksin/ ▶ n. Microbiol. a toxin present inside a bacterial cell and released when the cell disintegrates, and sometimes responsible for the symptoms of a disease, e.g., in botulism. Compare with EXOTOXIN. — **en·do·tox·ic** /,endō'täksik/ adj.

en·do·tra·che·al /,endō'trākēəl/ ▶ adj. situated or occurring within or performed by way of the trachea. — **en·do·tra·che·al·ly** adv.

en·dow /en'dou/ ▶ v. [trans.] give or bequeath an income or property to (a person or institution): *he endowed the church with lands*. ■ establish (a college post, annual prize, or project) by donating the funds needed to maintain it. ■ (usu. **be endowed with**) provide with a quality, ability, or asset: *he was endowed with tremendous strength*. — **en·dow·er** n. [ME: from legal Anglo-Norman Fr. *endouer*, from *en-* 'toward' + OFr. *douer* 'give as a gift' (from L. *dotare*: see DOWER).]

en·dow·ment /en'doumənt/ ▶ n. the action of endowing something or someone. ■ an income or form of property given or bequeathed to someone. ■ (usu. **endowments**) a quality or ability possessed or inherited by someone. ■ [usu. as adj.] a form of life insurance involving payment of a fixed sum to the insured person on a specified date, or to their estate should they die before this date.

end·pa·per /'end,pāpər/ (also **end pa·per**) ▶ n. a blank or decorated leaf of paper at the beginning or end of a book, esp. one fixed to the inside of the cover.

end plate ▶ n. a flattened piece at or forming the end of something such as a motor or generator. ■ Anat. each of the discoid expansions of a motor nerve where its branches terminate on a muscle fiber.

end·play /'end,plā/ Bridge ▶ n. a way of playing the last few tricks that forces an opponent to make a disadvantageous lead. ▶ v. [trans.] force (an opponent) to make such a lead.

end·point /'end,point/ (also **end point**) ▶ n. the final stage of a period or process. ■ Chem. the point in a titration at which a reaction is complete, often marked by a color change. ■ Math. a point or value that marks the end of a ray or one of the ends of a line segment or interval.

end prod·uct ▶ n. that which is produced as the final result of an activity or process, esp. the finished article in a manufacturing process.

en·drin /'endrin/ ▶ n. a toxic insecticide that is a stereoisomer of dieldrin. [20th C.: from ENDO- 'within' + a shortened form of DIELDRIN.]

end run ▶ n. Football an attempt by the ballcarrier to run around the end of the defensive line. ■ an evasive tactic or maneuver. ▶ v. (**end-run**) [trans.] evade; circumvent.

end-stopped ▸ **adj.** (of verse) having a pause at the end of each line.

en·due /en'd(y)o͞o/ ▸ **v.** (**-dues, -dued, -du·ing**) [trans.] literary endow or provide with a quality or ability: *our sight endued with a far greater sharpness.* [ME: from OFr. *enduire*, partly from L. *inducere* 'lead in' (see INDUCE).]

en·dur·ance /en'd(y)o͝orəns/ ▸ **n.** the fact or power of enduring an unpleasant or difficult process or situation without giving way. ■ the capacity of something to last or to withstand wear and tear.

en·dure /en'd(y)o͝or/ ▸ **v. 1** [trans.] suffer (something painful or difficult) patiently. ■ tolerate (someone or something). **2** [intrans.] remain in existence; last. — **en·dur·a·ble** /-əbəl/ **adj.** **en·dur·er n.** [ME: from OFr. *endurer*, from L. *indurare* 'harden,' from *in-* 'in' + *durus* 'hard.']

en·dur·ing /en'd(y)o͝oriNG/ ▸ **adj.** continuing or long-lasting. — **en·dur·ing·ly adv.**

end use ▸ **n.** the application or function for which something is designed or for which it is ultimately used.

end us·er (also **end-us·er**) ▸ **n.** the person who actually uses a particular product.

end·ways /'en(d),wāz/ (also **end·wise**) ▸ **adv.** with its end facing upward, forward, or toward the viewer. ■ in a row with the end of one object touching that of another: *strips of rubber cemented endways.*

En·dym·i·on /en'dimēən/ Gk. Mythol. a remarkably beautiful young man, loved by the Moon (Selene).

end zone ▸ **n. 1** Football the rectangular area at each end of the field into which the ball must be carried or passed and caught to score a touchdown. **2** Hockey the area at either end of the rink, extending from the blue line to the boards behind the goal.

ENE ▸ **abbr.** east-northeast.

-ene ▸ **suffix 1** denoting an inhabitant: *Nazarene.* **2** Chem. forming names of unsaturated hydrocarbons containing a double bond: *benzene | ethylene.* [from Gk. *-ēnos.*]

en·e·ma /'enəmə/ ▸ **n.** (pl. **en·e·mas** or rare **en·em·a·ta** /ə'nemətə/) a procedure in which liquid or gas is injected into the rectum, typically to expel its contents, but also to introduce drugs or permit X-ray imaging. ■ a quantity of fluid or a syringe for such a procedure. [ME: via late L. from Gk., from *enienai* 'send or put in,' from *en-* 'in' + *hienai* 'send.']

en·e·my /'enəmē/ ▸ **n.** (pl. **-mies**) a person who is actively opposed or hostile to someone or something. ■ (**the enemy**) [treated as sing. or pl.] a hostile nation or its armed forces or citizens, esp. in time of war. ■ a thing that harms or weakens something else.
– PHRASES **be one's own worst enemy** act in a way contrary to one's own interests. [ME: from OFr. *enemi*, from L. *inimicus*, from *in-* 'not' + *amicus* 'friend.']

en·er·get·ic /,enər'jetik/ ▸ **adj.** showing or involving great activity or vitality: *energetic exercise.* ■ powerfully operative; forceful. ■ Physics characterized by a high level of energy. ■ of or relating to energy. — **en·er·get·i·cal·ly** /-ik(ə)lē/ **adv.** [17th C.: from Gk. *energētikos*, from *energein* 'operate' (based on *ergon* 'work').]

en·er·get·ics /,enər'jetiks/ ▸ **plural n. 1** the properties of something in terms of energy. **2** [treated as sing.] the branch of science dealing with the properties of energy and the way it is redistributed in physical, chemical, or biological processes. — **en·er·get·i·cist** /-'jetisist/ **n.**

en·er·gize /'enər,jīz/ ▸ **v.** [trans.] give vitality and enthusiasm to: *people were energized by his ideas.* ■ supply energy, typically kinetic or electrical energy, to (something). — **en·er·giz·er n.**

en·er·gy /'enərjē/ ▸ **n.** (pl. **-gies**) **1** the strength and vitality required for sustained physical or mental activity. ■ a feeling of possessing such strength and vitality. ■ force or vigor of expression. ■ (**energies**) a person's physical and mental powers, typically as applied to a particular task or activity. **2** power derived from the utilization of physical or chemical resources, esp. to provide light and heat or to work machines. **3** Physics the property of matter and radiation that is manifest as a capacity to perform work (such as causing motion or the interaction of molecules). ■ a degree or level of this capacity possessed by something or required by a process. [16th C.: from Fr. *énergie*, or via late L. from Gk. *energeia*, from *en-* 'in, within' + *ergon* 'work.']

en·er·gy au·dit ▸ **n.** an assessment of the energy needs and efficiency of a building or buildings.

en·er·gy lev·el ▸ **n.** Physics the fixed amount of energy that a system described by quantum mechanics, such as a molecule, atom, electron, or nucleus, can have.

en·er·vate ▸ **v.** /'enər,vāt; -vit/ [trans.] cause (someone) to feel drained of energy or vitality; weaken. ▸ **adj.** literary lacking in energy or vitality. — **en·er·va·tion** /,enər'vāSHən/ **n.** **en·er·va·tor** /-,vātər/ **n.** [17th C.: from L. *enervat-* 'weakened,' from *enervare*, from *e-* 'out of' + *nervus* 'sinew.']

en·er·vat·ing /'enər,vātiNG/ ▸ **adj.** causing one to feel drained of energy or vitality.

En·e·we·tak var. of ENIWETOK.

en fa·mille /,äN fä'mē/ ▸ **adv.** with one's family. ■ as or like a member or members of a family. [18th C.: French, literally 'in family.']

en·fant ter·ri·ble /äN,fäN te'rēbl(ə)/ ▸ **n.** (pl. **en·fants ter·ri·bles** pronunc. same) a person whose behavior or ideas shock, embarrass, or annoy others. [19th C.: French, literally 'terrible child.']

en·fee·ble /en'fēbəl/ ▸ **v.** [trans.] make weak or feeble. — **en·fee·ble·ment n.** **en·fee·bler n.** [ME: from OFr. *enfeblir*, from *en-* (expressing a change of state) + *feble* 'feeble.']

en·fet·ter /en'fetər/ ▸ **v.** [trans.] literary restrain (someone) with shackles.

en·fi·lade /'enfə,lād; -,läd/ ▸ **n. 1** a volley of gunfire directed along a line from end to end. **2** a suite of rooms with doorways in line with each other. ▸ **v.** [trans.] direct a volley of gunfire along the length of (a target). [18th C.: from Fr., from *enfiler* 'thread on a string,' from *en-* 'on' + *fil* 'thread.']

en·fleu·rage /,äNflə'räZH/ ▸ **n.** the extraction of essential oils and perfumes from flowers using odorless animal or vegetable fats. [19th C.: Fr., from *enfleurer* 'saturate with the perfume from flowers.']

en·flu·rane /en'flo͝orān/ ▸ **n.** Med. a volatile organic liquid, CHF_2OCF_2CHFCl, used as a general anesthetic. [1970s: from *en-* (of unknown origin) + FLUORO- + -ANE[2].]

en·fold /en'fōld/ (also dated **in·fold**) ▸ **v.** [trans.] **1** surround; envelop. ■ hold or clasp (someone) lovingly in one's arms. **2** fold or shape into folds. — **en·fold·ment n.**

en·force /en'fôrs/ ▸ **v.** [trans.] compel observance of or compliance with (a law, rule, or obligation). ■ cause (something) to happen by necessity or force. — **en·force·a·bil·i·ty** /-,fôrsə'bilitē/ **n.** **en·force·a·ble adj.** **en·forc·ed·ly** /-'fôrsidlē/ **adv.** **en·force·ment n.** **en·forc·er n.** [ME: from OFr. *enforcir*, based on L. *in-* 'in' + *fortis* 'strong.']

en·fran·chise /en'franCHīz/ ▸ **v.** [trans.] give the right to vote to. ■ hist. free (a slave). — **en·fran·chise·ment n.** [ME: from OFr. *enfranchiss-*, lengthened stem of *enfranchir*, from *en-* + *franc, franche* 'free.']

ENG ▸ **abbr.** electronic news gathering.

eng. ▸ **abbr.** ■ engine. ■ engineer. ■ engineering. ■ engraved. ■ engraver. ■ engraving.

en·gage /en'gāj/ ▸ **v. 1** [trans.] occupy, attract, or involve (someone's interest or attention). ■ (**engage someone in**) cause someone to become involved in (a conversation or discussion). ■ arrange to employ or hire (someone). ■ [with infin.] pledge or enter into a contract to do something: *he engaged to pay them $10,000 in July.* ■ dated reserve (accommodations, a place, etc.) in advance. **2** [intrans.] (**engage in**) participate or become involved in. ■ (**engage with**) establish a meaningful contact or connection with: *the teams needed to engage with local communities.* ■ (of a part of a machine or engine) move into position so as to come into operation. ■ [trans.] cause (a part of a machine or engine) to do this. ■ [trans.] (of fencers or swordsmen) bring (weapons) together preparatory to fighting. ■ [trans.] enter into conflict or combat with (an adversary). [ME: from Fr. *engager*, ult. from the base of GAGE[1].]

en·ga·gé /,äNgä'ZHā/ ▸ **adj.** (of a writer, artist, or works) committed to a particular aim or cause.

en·gaged /en'gājd/ ▸ **adj. 1** [predic.] busy; occupied. ■ (of a toilet) already in use. **2** having formally agreed to marry. **3** Archit. (of a column) attached to or partly let into a wall.

en·gage·ment /en'gājmənt/ ▸ **n. 1** a formal agreement to get married. ■ the duration of such an agreement. **2** an arrangement to do something or go somewhere at a fixed time: *a dinner engagement.* ■ a period of paid employment. **3** the action of engaging or being engaged. **4** a fight or battle between armed forces.

en·gag·ing /en'gājiNG/ ▸ **adj.** charming and attractive. — **en·gag·ing·ly adv.** **en·gag·ing·ness n.**

en garde /än 'gärd; äN/ ▸ **interj.** Fencing a direction to be ready to fence, taking the opening position for action. [Fr. *en garde* '(be) on guard.']

En·gel·mann spruce /'eNGgəlmən/ (also **En·gel·mann's spruce**) ▸ **n.** a tall spruce (*Picea engelmannii*) found in the mountains of western North America and Mexico. [19th C.: named after George *Engelmann* (1809–84), American botanist.]

En·gels /'eNGgəlz/, Friedrich (1820–95), German socialist and philosopher. He collaborated with Karl Marx in the writing of the *Communist Manifesto* (1848).

en·gen·der /en'jendər/ ▸ **v.** [trans.] cause or give rise to (a feeling, situation, or condition). ■ archaic beget (offspring). ■ [intrans.] come into being; arise. [ME: from OFr. *engendrer*, from L. *ingenerare*, from *in-* 'in' + *generare* 'beget' (see GENERATE).]

en·gine /'enjən/ ▸ **n. 1** a machine with moving parts that converts power into motion. ■ a thing that is the agent or instrument of a particular process: *exports used to be the engine of growth.* **2** a railroad locomotive. ■ short for FIRE ENGINE. ■ hist. a mechanical device, esp. one used in warfare: *a siege engine.* — **en·gined adj.** [in comb.] **en·gine·less adj.** [ME: from OFr. *engin*, from L. *ingenium* 'talent, device,' from *in-* 'in' + *gignere* 'beget.']

en·gine block ▸ **n.** see BLOCK (sense 1).

en·gi·neer /,enjə'ni(ə)r/ ▸ **n.** a person who designs, builds, or maintains engines, machines, or public works. ■ a person trained in a branch of engineering, esp. as a professional. ■ the operator or supervisor of an engine, esp. a locomotive or an aircraft or ship. ■ a skillful contriver or originator of something. ▸ **v.** [trans.] design and build (a machine or structure). ■ skillfully or artfully arrange for (an event or situation) to occur: *she engineered another meeting with him.* ■ modify (an organism) by manipulating its genetic material. [ME: from OFr. *engigneor*, from med. L. *ingeniator*, from *ingeniare* 'devise,' from L. *ingenium* (see ENGINE).]

en·gi·neer·ing /,enjə'ni(ə)riNG/ ▸ **n.** the branch of science and technology concerned with the design, building, and use of engines, machines, and structures. ■ the work done by, or the occupation of, an engineer. ■ the action of working artfully to bring something about.

en·gi·neer·ing sci·ence (also **en·gi·neer·ing sci·enc·es**) ▸ **n.** the parts of science concerned with the physical and mathematical basis of engineering and machine technology.

en·gine·ry /'enjənrē/ ▶ **n.** archaic engines collectively; machinery.

en·gir·dle /en'gərdl/ (also **en·gird**) ▶ **v.** [trans.] literary surround; encircle.

en·gla·cial /en'glāshəl/ ▶ **adj.** situated, occurring, or formed inside a glacier. — **en·gla·cial·ly adv.**

Eng·land /'iNG(g)lənd/ a country in the southern and eastern part of Great Britain, forming part of the United Kingdom; pop. 46,170,300; capital, London. See map at UNITED KINGDOM.

Eng·lish /'iNG(g)lish/ ▶ **adj.** of or relating to England or its people or language. ▶ **n.** **1** the West Germanic language of England, now widely used in many varieties throughout the world. **2** [as pl. n.] (**the English**) the people of England. **3** spin given to a ball, esp. in pool or billiards. — **Eng·lish·man n.** (pl. **-men**) **Eng·lish·ness n. Eng·lish·wom·an n.** (pl. **-wom·en**) [OE *Englisc* (see ANGLE, -ISH[1]).]

Eng·lish bond ▶ **n.** Building a brickwork bond consisting of alternate courses of stretchers and headers.

Eng·lish Chan·nel a sea channel that separates southern England from northern France. It is 22 miles (35 km) wide at its narrowest point. A railroad tunnel (the Channel Tunnel) under the channel opened in 1994.

Eng·lish Civ·il War the war between Charles I and his Parliamentary opponents, 1642–49.

Eng·lish horn ▶ **n.** Music a woodwind instrument of the oboe family, having a bulbous bell and sounding a fifth lower than the oboe.

English horn

Eng·lish i·vy ▶ **n.** see IVY.

Eng·lish muf·fin ▶ **n.** a flat circular spongy roll made from yeast dough and eaten toasted and buttered.

Eng·lish Pale (also **the Pale**) that part of Ireland, centered in Dublin and varying in extent, which England controlled from 1089 until the whole country was conquered under Elizabeth I. [*Pale* from PALE[2].]

Eng·lish set·ter ▶ **n.** a setter of a breed of dog with a long white or partly white coat.

Eng·lish spar·row ▶ **n.** another term for HOUSE SPARROW.

en·gorge /en'gôrj/ ▶ **v.** **1** [trans.] cause to swell with blood, water, or another fluid. ■ [intrans.] become swollen in this way. **2** (**engorge oneself**) archaic eat to excess. — **en·gorge·ment n.** [15th C.: from OFr. *engorgier* 'feed to excess,' from *en-* 'into' + *gorge* 'throat.']

engr. ▶ **abbr.** ■ engineer. ■ engraved. ■ engraver. ■ engraving.

en·graft /en'graft/ (also **in·graft**) ▶ **v.** another term for GRAFT[1]. — **en·graft·ment n.**

en·grailed /en'grāld/ ▶ **adj.** esp. Heraldry having semicircular indentations along the edge.

en·grain /en'grān/ ▶ **v.** var. of INGRAIN.

en·grained /en'grānd/ ▶ **adj.** var. of INGRAINED.

en·gram /'engram/ ▶ **n.** a hypothetical permanent change in the brain accounting for the existence of memory; a memory trace. — **en·gram·mat·ic** /,engrə'matik/ **adj.** [20th C.: coined in Ger. from Gk. *en-* 'within' + *gramma* 'letter of the alphabet.']

en·grave /en'grāv/ ▶ **v.** [trans.] (usu. **be engraved**) cut or carve (a text or design) on the surface of a hard object: *my name was engraved on the ring.* ■ cut or carve a text or design on (such an object). ■ cut (a design) as lines on a metal plate for printing. ■ (**be engraved on** or **in**) be permanently fixed in (one's memory or mind).
– PHRASES **be engraved in stone** see STONE. — **en·grav·er n.** [15th C.: from EN-[1], IN-[2] 'in, on' + GRAVE[3].]

en·grav·ing /en'grāviNG/ ▶ **n.** a print made from an engraved plate, block, or other surface. ■ the process or art of cutting or carving a design on a hard surface, esp. so as to make a print.

en·gross /en'grōs/ ▶ **v.** [trans.] **1** absorb all the attention or interest of: *the notes totally engrossed him.* ■ archaic gain or keep exclusive possession of (something). **2** Law produce (a legal document) in its final or definitive form. — **en·gross·ment n.** [ME: based on EN-[1], IN-[2] 'in' + late L. *grossus* 'large.']

en·grossed /en'grōst/ ▶ **adj.** [predic.] having all one's attention or interest absorbed by someone or something.

en·gross·ing /en'grōsiNG/ ▶ **adj.** absorbing all one's attention or interest: *the most engrossing parts of the book.* — **en·gross·ing·ly adv.**

en·gulf /en'gəlf/ ▶ **v.** [trans.] (often **be engulfed**) (of a natural force) sweep over (something) so as to surround or cover it completely. ■ eat or swallow (something) whole. — **en·gulf·ment n.**

en·hance /en'hans/ ▶ **v.** [trans.] intensify, increase, or further improve the quality, value, or extent of. — **en·hance·ment n. en·hanc·er n.** [ME: from Anglo-Norman Fr. *enhauncer*, based on L. *in-* (expressing intensive force) + *altus* 'high.']

en·har·mon·ic /,enhär'mänik/ ▶ **adj.** Music of or relating to notes that are the same in pitch (in modern tuning) though bearing different names (e.g., F sharp and G flat or B and C flat). ■ of or having intervals smaller than a semitone (e.g., between notes such as F sharp and G flat, in systems of tuning that distinguish them). — **en·har·mon·i·cal·ly** /-(ə)lē/ **adv.** [17th C.: via late L. from Gk. *enarmonikos*, from *en-* 'in' + *harmonia* 'harmony.']

E·nid /'ēnid/ a city in north central Oklahoma; pop. 47,045.

e·nig·ma /i'nigmə/ ▶ **n.** (pl. **-mas** or **-ma·ta** /-mətə/) a person or thing that is mysterious, puzzling, or difficult to understand. ■ a riddle or paradox. [16th C.: via L. from Gk. *ainigma*, from *ainissesthai* 'speak allusively,' from *ainos* 'fable.']

en·ig·mat·ic /,enig'matik/ (also **en·ig·mat·i·cal**) ▶ **adj.** difficult to interpret or understand; mysterious. — **en·ig·mat·i·cal·ly** /-ik(ə)lē/ **adv.**

en·isle /en'īl/ ▶ **v.** [trans.] literary isolate on or as if on an island.

En·i·we·tok /,enə'wētäk; ə'nēwi-/ (also **En·e·we·tak**) an uninhabited island in the North Pacific Ocean, one of the Marshall Islands. It was used by the US as a testing ground for atom bombs 1948–54.

en·jambed /en'jamd/ ▶ **adj.** (of a line, couplet, or stanza of verse) ending partway through a sentence or clause that continues in the next. — **en·jamb·ment** /en'jam(b)mənt/ (also **enjambement**) **n.** [19th C.: from Fr. *enjamber* 'stride over' + -ED[2].]

en·join /en'join/ ▶ **v.** [with obj. and infin.] instruct or urge (someone) to do something. ■ [trans.] prescribe (an action or attitude) to be performed or adopted: *the charitable deeds enjoined on him by religion.* ■ [trans.] (**enjoin someone from**) Law prohibit someone from performing (a particular action) by issuing an injunction. — **en·join·er n. en·join·ment n.** [ME: from OFr. *enjoindre*, from L. *injungere* 'attach,' from *in-* 'in' + *jungere* 'to join.']

en·joy /en'joi/ ▶ **v.** [trans.] **1** take delight or pleasure in (an activity or occasion). ■ (**enjoy oneself**) have a pleasant time. ■ [no obj., in imper.] informal used to urge someone to take pleasure in what is about happen or be done: *here's your ticket—enjoy!* **2** possess and benefit from. — **en·joy·er n. en·joy·ment n.** [ME: from OFr. *enjoier enjoïr* 'enjoy,' both based on L. *gaudere* 'rejoice.']

en·joy·a·ble /en'joi-əbəl/ ▶ **adj.** (of an activity or occasion) giving delight or pleasure. — **en·joy·a·bil·i·ty** /en,joi-ə'bilitē/ **n. en·joy·a·ble·ness n. en·joy·a·bly adv.**

en·keph·al·in /en'kefəlin/ ▶ **n.** Biochem. either of two compounds that occur naturally in the brain. They are peptides related to the endorphins, with similar physiological effects. [1970s: from Gk. *enkephalos* 'brain' (from *en-* 'in' + *kephalē* 'head') + -IN[1].]

en·kin·dle /en'kindl/ ▶ **v.** [trans.] literary set on fire. ■ arouse or inspire (an emotion). ■ inflame with passion.

enl. ▶ **abbr.** ■ enlarge. ■ enlarged. ■ enlisted.

en·lace /en'lās/ ▶ **v.** [trans.] literary entwine or entangle: *a web of green enlaced the thorn trees.* ■ encircle tightly; embrace. [ME: from OFr. *enlacier*, based on L. *laqueus* 'noose.']

en·large /en'lärj/ ▶ **v.** make or become bigger or more extensive. ■ [trans.] (often **be enlarged**) develop a bigger print of (a photograph).
– PHRASAL VERBS **enlarge on/upon** speak or write about (something) in greater detail: *I would like to enlarge on this theme.* [ME: from OFr. *enlarger*, from *en-* + *large* 'large.']

en·large·ment /en'lärjmənt/ ▶ **n.** the action or state of enlarging or being enlarged. ■ a photograph that is larger than the negative from which it is produced or than a print that has already been made from it.

en·larg·er /en'lärjər/ ▶ **n.** Photog. an apparatus for enlarging or reducing negatives or positives.

en·light·en /en'lītn/ ▶ **v.** [trans.] give (someone) greater knowledge and understanding about a subject or situation. ■ give (someone) spiritual knowledge or insight. ■ fig. illuminate or make clearer (a problem or area of study). ■ archaic shed light on (an object). — **en·light·en·er n.**

en·light·ened /en'lītnd/ ▶ **adj.** having or showing a rational, modern, and well-informed outlook. ■ spiritually aware.

en·light·en·ment /en'lītnmənt/ ▶ **n.** **1** the action of enlightening or the state of being enlightened. ■ the attainment of spiritual knowledge or insight, esp. (in Buddhism) that which frees a person from the cycle of rebirth. **2** (**the Enlightenment**) a European intellectual movement of the late 17th and 18th centuries emphasizing reason and individualism rather than tradition.

en·list /en'list/ ▶ **v.** enroll or be enrolled in the armed services. ■ [trans.] engage (a person or their help or support). — **en·list·er n. en·list·ment n.**

en·list·ed man ▶ **n.** a member of the armed forces below the rank of NCO.

en·liv·en /en'līvən/ ▶ **v.** [trans.] make (something) more entertaining, interesting, or appealing. ■ make (someone) more cheerful or animated. — **en·liv·en·er n. en·liv·en·ment n.** [17th C.: from *enlive*, from EN-[1], IN-[2] (as an intensifier) + LIFE.]

en masse /än 'mas/ ▶ **adv.** in a group; all together. [18th C.: French, literally 'in a mass.']

en·mesh /en'mesh/ ▶ **v.** [trans.] (usu. **be enmeshed in**) cause to become entangled in something. — **en·mesh·ment n.**

en·mi·ty /'enmitē/ ▶ **n.** (pl. **-ties**) the state or feeling of being actively opposed or hostile to someone or something. [ME: from OFr. *enemi(s)tie*, based on L. *inimicus* (see ENEMY).]

en·ne·ad /'enē,ad/ ▶ **n.** rare a group or set of nine. [16th C.: from Gk. *enneas, ennead-*, from *ennea* 'nine.']

en·ne·a·gram /'enēə,gram/ ▶ **n.** a nine-sided figure used in a particular system of analysis to represent the spectrum of possible personality types. [from Gk. *ennea* 'nine' + -GRAM[1].]

en·no·ble /en'nōbəl/ ▶ **v.** [trans.] give (someone) a noble rank or title. ■ lend greater dignity or nobility of character to. — **en·no·ble·ment n.**

en·nui /än'wē/ ▶ **n.** listlessness and dissatisfaction arising from a lack of occupation or excitement. [18th C.: Fr., from L. *mihi in odio est* 'it is hateful to me.']

E·noch /'ēnək; 'ēnäk/ **1** (in the Bible) the eldest son of Cain. ■ the first city, built by Cain. **2** a Hebrew patriarch, father of Methuselah.

e·nol·o·gy /ē'näləjē/ (also **oe·nol·o·gy**) ▶ **n.** the study of wines. — **e·no·log·i·cal** /,ēnə'läjikəl/ **adj. e·nol·o·gist** /-jist/ **n.** [19th C.: from Gk. *oinos* 'wine' + -LOGY.]

e·nor·mi·ty /i'nôrmitē/ ▶ **n.** (pl. **-ties**) **1** (**the enormity of**) the great or extreme scale, seriousness, or extent of something perceived as bad or morally wrong. ■ (in neutral use) the large size or scale of something: *the enormity of his intellect.* **2** a grave crime or sin: *the enormities of the Hitler regime.* [ME: via OFr. from L. *enormitas*, from *enormis*, from *e-* (var. of *ex-*) 'out of' + *norma* 'pattern, standard.']

e·nor·mous /i'nôrməs/ ▶ **adj.** very large in size, quantity, or extent. — **e·nor·mous·ly adv.** [as submodifier] *she has been enormously successful* **e·nor·mous·ness n.**

e·nough /i'nəf/ ▶ **adj. & pron.** as much or as many as required. ■ used to indicate that one is unwilling to tolerate any more of something undesirable. ▶ **adv. 1** to the required degree or extent (used after an adjective, adverb, or verb); adequately: *old enough to shave.* **2** to a moderate degree; fairly: *he seems nice enough.* **3** [with sentence adverb] used for emphasis: *curiously enough, there is no mention of him.* ▶ **exclam.** used to express impatient desire for an end to undesirable behavior or speech: *Enough! No more arguing!*
– PHRASES **enough is enough** no more will be tolerated. **enough said** there is no need to say more; all is understood. [OE *genōg*, of Gmc. origin; rel. to Ger. *genug*.]

en pas·sant /,än pä'sänt; äɴ pä'säɴ/ ▶ **adv.** by the way; incidentally. ■ Chess by the en passant rule.
– PHRASES **en passant rule** (or **law**) Chess the rule that a pawn making a first move of two squares instead of one may nevertheless be immediately captured by an opposing pawn on the fifth rank. [17th C.: French, literally 'in passing.']

en·plane /en'plān/ (also **em·plane**) ▶ **v.** go or put on board an aircraft.

en pointe /äɴ 'pwaɴt/ ▶ **adj. & adv.** see *ON POINTE* at POINTE. [Fr.]

en prise /än 'prēz/ ▶ **adj.** [predic.] Chess (of a piece or pawn) in a position to be taken. [19th C.: Fr.]

en·quire /en'kwī(ə)r/ ▶ **v.** esp. Brit. another term for INQUIRE. — **en·quir·er n. en·quir·ing adj. en·quir·y n.**

en·rage /en'rāj/ ▶ **v.** [trans.] (usu. **be enraged**) make very angry. [15th C.: from Fr. *enrager*.]

en rap·port /,än ra'pôr/ ▶ **adv.** having a close and harmonious relationship. [Fr. (see RAPPORT).]

en·rapt /en'rapt/ ▶ **adj.** fascinated; enthralled: *the enrapt audience.*

en·rap·ture /en'rapchər/ ▶ **v.** [trans.] (usu. **be enraptured**) give intense pleasure or joy to.

en·rich /en'rich/ ▶ **v.** [trans.] **1** improve or enhance the quality or value of: *her exposure to museums enriched her life in France.* ■ (often **be enriched**) add to the nutritive value of (food) by adding vitamins or nutrients: *cereal enriched with extra oat bran.* ■ add to the cultural, intellectual, or spiritual wealth of: *the collection was enriched by a bequest of graphic works.* ■ [usu. as adj.] (**enriched**) increase the proportion of a particular isotope in (an element), esp. that of the fissile isotope U-235 in uranium so as to make it more powerful or explosive. ■ Archit. embellish a molding by carving or otherwise forming a sculpted, ornamental pattern, such as egg and dart: *one may enrich the echinus of a Doric capital with the egg and dart motif.* **2** make (someone) wealthy or wealthier: *top party members had enriched themselves.* — **en·rich·ment n.** [ME (in the sense 'make wealthy'): from OFr. *enrichir*, from *en-* 'in' + *riche* 'rich.']

en·robe /en'rōb/ ▶ **v.** [trans.] formal dress in a robe or vestment.

en·roll /en'rōl/ (Brit. **en·rol**) ▶ **v.** (**-rolled, -rol·ling**) [intrans.] officially register as a member of an institution or a student on a course: *he enrolled in drama school.* ■ [trans.] register (someone) as a member or student. ■ [trans.] recruit (someone) to perform a service. ■ [trans.] Law, hist. enter (a document) among the rolls of a court of justice. ■ archaic write the name of (someone) on a list or register. — **en·roll·ee** /,enrō'lē/ **n.** [ME: from OFr. *enroller*, from *en-* 'in' + *rolle* 'a roll.']

en·roll·ment /en'rōlmənt/ (Brit. **en·rol·ment**) ▶ **n.** the action of enrolling or being enrolled. ■ the number of people enrolled, typically at a school or college.

en route /än 'ro͞ot; en; äɴ/ ▶ **adv.** during the course of a journey; on the way. [18th C.: Fr. (see ROUTE).]

ENS ▶ **abbr.** ensign.

En·sche·de /'enskə,dā/ a city in eastern Netherlands; pop. 146,500.

en·sconce /en'skäns/ ▶ **v.** [with obj. and adverbial of place] establish or settle (someone) in a comfortable, safe, or secret place. [16th C.: from EN-[1], IN-[2] 'in' + SCONCE[2].]

en·sem·ble /än'sämbəl/ ▶ **n. 1** a group of musicians, actors, or dancers who perform together. ■ a scene or passage written for performance by a whole cast, choir, or group of instruments. ■ the coordination between performers executing such a passage. **2** a group of items viewed as a whole rather than individually. ■ [usu. in sing.] a set of clothes chosen to harmonize when worn together. ■ esp. Physics a group of similar systems, or different states of the same system, often considered statistically. [ME: from Fr., based on L. *insimul*, from *in-* 'in' + *simul* 'at the same time.']

En·se·na·da /,ensə'nädə/ a city in northwestern Mexico; pop. 260,000.

en·sheathe /en'shēth/ (also **en·sheath**) ▶ **v.** [trans.] esp. Biol. enclose (an organism, tissue, structure, etc.) in or as in a sheath. — **en·sheath·ment n.**

en·shrine /en'shrīn/ ▶ **v.** [with obj. and adverbial of place] (usu. **be enshrined**) place (a revered or precious object) in an appropriate receptacle. ■ preserve (a right, tradition, or idea) in a form that ensures it will be protected and respected. — **en·shrine·ment n.**

en·shroud /en'shroud/ ▶ **v.** [trans.] literary envelop completely and hide from view.

en·si·form /'ensə,fôrm/ ▶ **adj.** esp. Bot. shaped like a sword blade; long and narrow with sharp edges and a pointed tip. [16th C.: from L. *ensis* 'sword' + -FORM.]

en·sign ▶ **n. 1** /'ensən; 'ensīn/ a flag or standard, esp. a military or naval one indicating nationality. ■ archaic a sign or emblem of a particular thing. **2** /'ensən/ a commissioned officer of the lowest rank in the US Navy and Coast Guard, ranking above chief warrant officer and below lieutenant. ■ hist. the lowest rank of commissioned infantry officer in the British army. ■ hist. a standard-bearer. [ME: from OFr. *enseigne*, from L. *insignia* 'signs of office' (see INSIGNIA).]

en·si·lage /'ensəlij/ ▶ **n.** another term for SILAGE. ▶ **v.** another term for ENSILE.

en·sile /en'sīl/ ▶ **v.** [trans.] put (grass or another crop) into a silo or silage clamp to preserve it as silage. [19th C.: from Fr. *ensiler*, from Sp. *ensilar*, from *en-* 'in' + *silo* 'silo.']

en·slave /en'slāv/ ▶ **v.** [trans.] make (someone) a slave. ■ cause (someone) to lose freedom of choice or action. — **en·slave·ment n. en·slav·er n.**

en·snare /en'sne(ə)r/ ▶ **v.** [trans.] catch in or as in a trap. — **en·snare·ment n.**

en·snarl /en'snärl/ ▶ **v.** [trans.] cause to become caught up in complex difficulties or problems.

En·sor /'ensôr/, James Sydney, Baron (1860–1949), Belgian painter and engraver. His work is significant for its symbolism.

en·sor·cell /en'sôrsəl/ (also **en·sor·cel**) ▶ **v.** (**-celled, -cel·ling**; also **-celed, -cel·ing**) [trans.] literary enchant; fascinate. — **en·sor·cell·ment** (also **en·sor·cel·ment**) **n.** [16th C.: from OFr. *ensorceler*, alt. of *ensorcerer*, from *sorcier* 'sorcerer.']

en·soul /en'sōl/ ▶ **v.** [trans.] endow with a soul. — **en·soul·ment n.**

en·sta·tite /'enstə,tīt/ ▶ **n.** a translucent crystalline mineral of the pyroxene group, occurring in some igneous rocks and stony meteorites. — **en·sta·tit·ic** /,enstə'titik/ **adj.** [19th C.: from Gk. *enstatēs* 'adversary' + -ITE[1].]

en·sue /en'so͞o/ ▶ **v.** (**en·sues, en·sued, en·su·ing**) [intrans.] happen or occur afterward or as a result. [ME: from OFr. *ensivre*, from L. *insequi*, based on *sequi* 'follow.']

en suite /än 'swēt/ ▶ **adj. & adv.** immediately adjoining or connected. [18th C.: from French, literally 'in sequence.']

en·sure /en'sho͝or/ ▶ **v.** [trans.] make certain that (something) shall occur or be the case. ■ make certain of obtaining or providing (something). ■ [intrans.] (**ensure against**) make sure that (a problem) shall not occur. [ME: from Anglo-Norman Fr. *enseurer*, alt. of OFr. *assurer* (see ASSURE).]

en·swathe /en'swä<u>th</u>; -'swā<u>th</u>/ ▶ **v.** [trans.] literary envelop or wrap in a garment or piece of fabric.

ENT ▶ **abbr.** ear, nose, and throat (as a department in a hospital).

-ent /ənt; nt/ ▶ **suffix 1** (forming adjectives) denoting an occurrence of action: *refluent.* ■ denoting a state: *convenient.* **2** (forming nouns) denoting an agent: *coefficient.* [from Fr., or from the L. present participial v. stem *-ent-* (see also -ANT).]

en·tab·la·ture /en'tablәchәr; -,cho͝or/ ▶ **n.** Archit. a horizontal, continuous lintel on a classical building supported by columns or a wall, comprising the architrave, frieze, and cornice. [17th C.: from Ital. *intavolatura* 'boarding,' from *intavolare* 'board up' (based on *tavola* 'table').]

en·ta·ble·ment /en'tābəlmənt/ ▶ **n.** Archit. a platform supporting a statue, above the dado and base.

en·tail /en'tāl/ ▶ **v.** [trans.] **1** involve (something) as a necessary or inevitable part or consequence. ■ Logic have as a logically necessary consequence. **2** Law settle the inheritance of (property) over a number of generations so that ownership remains within a group, usually on family. ▶ **n.** /'en,tāl/ Law a settlement of the inheritance of property over a number of generations so that it remains within a family or other group. ■ a property that is bequeathed under such conditions. — **en·tail·ment n.** [ME: from EN-[1], IN-[2] 'into' + OFr. *taille* 'notch, tax' (see TAIL[2]).]

ent·a·me·ba /,entə'mēbə/ (also **ent·a·moe·ba**) ▶ **n.** (pl. **-me·bae** /-'mēbē/ or **-me·bas**) an ameba (genus *Entamoeba*) that typically lives harmlessly in the gut, although one kind can cause amebic dysentery. [mod. L., from Gk. *entos* 'within' + AMEBA.]

en·tan·gle /en'taNGgəl/ ▶ **v.** [trans.] (usu. **be entangled**) cause to become twisted together with or caught in. ■ involve (someone) in difficulties or complicated circumstances.

en·tan·gle·ment /en'taNGgəlmənt/ ▶ **n.** the action or fact of entangling or being entangled. ■ a complicated or compromising relationship or situation.

en·ta·sis /'entəsis/ ▶ **n.** (pl. **-ses** /-sēz/) Archit. a slight convex curve in the shaft of a column, introduced to correct the visual illusion of concavity produced by a straight shaft. [17th C.: mod. L., from Gk., from *enteinein* 'to stretch or strain.']

en·tel·e·chy /en'teləkē/ ▸**n.** (pl. **-chies**) Philos. the realization of potential. ■ the supposed vital principle that guides the development and functioning of an organism or other system or organization. ■ Philos. the soul. [ME: via late Latin from Greek *entelekheia* (used by Aristotle), from *en-* 'within' + *telos* 'end, perfection' + *ekhein* 'be in a certain state.']

en·tente /än'tänt/ ▸**n.** (also **en·tente cor·diale** /kôr'dyäl/) a friendly understanding or informal alliance between states or factions. ■ a group of states in such an alliance. [19th C.: French *entente (cordiale)* '(friendly) understanding.']

en·ter /'entər/ ▸**v.** **1** come or go into (a place): [trans.] *she entered the kitchen* | [intrans.] *the door opened and Karl entered.* ■ [intrans.] used as a stage direction to indicate when a character comes on stage: *enter Hamlet.* ■ [trans.] penetrate (something). ■ [trans.] insert the penis into the vagina of (a woman). ■ [trans.] come or be introduced into: *the thought never entered my head.* **2** [trans.] begin to be involved in: *in 1941 America entered the war.* ■ become a member of or start working in (an institution or profession). ■ register as a competitor or participant in (a tournament, race, or examination). ■ register (a person, animal, or thing) to compete or participate in a tournament, race, or examination. ■ start or reach (a stage or period of time) in an activity or situation. ■ [intrans.] (of a performer in an ensemble) start or resume playing or singing. **3** write or key (information) in a book, computer, etc., so as to record it. ■ Law submit (a statement) in an official capacity, usually in a court of law: *entered a plea of guilty.* ▸**n.** (also **enter key**) a key on a computer keyboard that is used to perform various functions, such as executing a command or selecting options on a menu.

– PHRASAL VERBS **enter into** become involved in (an activity, situation, or matter). ■ undertake to bind oneself by (an agreement or other commitment). ■ form part of or be a factor in: *medical ethics also enter into the question.* **enter on/upon 1** formal begin (an activity or job); start to pursue (a particular course in life). **2** Law (as a legal entitlement) go freely into property as or as if the owner. [ME: from OFr. *entrer*, from L. *intrare*, from *intra* 'within.']

en·ter·al /'entərəl/ ▸**adj.** Med. (chiefly of nutrition) involving or passing through the intestine, either naturally via the mouth and esophagus, or through an artificial opening. Often contrasted with PARENTERAL. — **en·ter·al·ly** adv. [20th C.: from Gk. *enteron* 'intestine.']

en·ter·ic /en'terik/ ▸**adj.** of, relating to, or occurring in the intestines.

en·ter·ic fe·ver ▸**n.** another term for TYPHOID or PARATYPHOID.

en·ter·i·tis /,entə'rītis/ ▸**n.** Med. inflammation of the intestine, esp. the small intestine, usually accompanied by diarrhea.

entero- ▸**comb. form** of or relating to the intestine: *enterovirus.* [from Gk. *enteron.*]

en·ter·o·coc·cus /'entərō,käkəs/ ▸**n.** (pl. **-coc·ci** /-,käk(s)ī; -,käk(s)ē/) a streptococcus (genus *Streptococcus*, or *Enterococcus*) of a group that occurs naturally in the intestine but causes inflammation and blood infection if introduced elsewhere in the body (e.g., by injury or surgery). — **en·ter·o·coc·cal** /,entərō'käkəl/ adj.

en·ter·o·coele /'entərō,sēl/ (also **en·ter·o·coel**) ▸**n.** Zool. a coelom or coelomic cavity developed from the wall of the archenteron in some invertebrates. — **en·ter·o·coe·lic** /,entərō'sēlik/ adj. **en·ter·o·coe·ly** /-,sēlē/ n.

en·ter·o·co·li·tis /,entə,rō-kə'lītis/ ▸**n.** Med. inflammation of both the small intestine and the colon.

en·ter·op·a·thy /,entə'räpəTHē/ ▸**n.** (pl. **-thies**) Med. a disease of the intestine, esp. the small intestine.

en·ter·os·to·my /,entə'rästəmē/ ▸**n.** (pl. **-mies**) an ileostomy or similar surgical operation in which the small intestine is diverted to an artificial opening in the abdominal wall or in another part of the intestine. ■ an opening in the abdominal wall formed in this way.

en·ter·o·tox·in /,entərō'täksin/ ▸**n.** Med. a toxin produced in or affecting the intestines, such as those causing food poisoning or cholera.

en·ter·o·vi·rus /,entərō'vīrəs/ ▸**n.** Med. any of a group of RNA viruses (including those causing polio and hepatitis A) that typically occur in the gastrointestinal tract, sometimes spreading to the central nervous system or other parts of the body.

en·ter·prise /'entər,prīz/ ▸**n.** **1** a project or undertaking, typically one that is difficult or requires effort. ■ initiative and resourcefulness. **2** a business or company. ■ entrepreneurial economic activity. — **en·ter·pris·er** n. [ME: from Old French, 'something undertaken,' past participle of *entreprendre*, based on Latin *prendere* 'to take.']

en·ter·prise zone ▸**n.** an impoverished area in which incentives such as tax concessions are offered to encourage investment and provide jobs for residents.

en·ter·pris·ing /'entər,prīziNG/ ▸**adj.** having or showing initiative and resourcefulness. — **en·ter·pris·ing·ly** adv.

en·ter·tain /,entər'tān/ ▸**v.** [trans.] **1** provide (someone) with amusement or enjoyment. ■ receive (someone) as a guest and provide food and drink. **2** give attention or consideration to (an idea, suggestion, or feeling). [ME: from Fr. *entretenir*, based on L. *inter* 'among' + *tenere* 'to hold.']

en·ter·tain·er /,entər'tānər/ ▸**n.** a person, such as a singer, dancer, or comedian, whose job is to entertain others.

en·ter·tain·ing /,entər'tāniNG/ ▸**adj.** providing amusement or enjoyment. — **en·ter·tain·ing·ly** adv.

en·ter·tain·ment /,entər'tānmənt/ ▸**n.** the action of providing or being provided with amusement or enjoyment. ■ an event, performance, or activity designed to entertain others. ■ the action of receiving a guest or guests and providing them with food and drink.

en·thal·py /'enTHalpē; en'THalpē/ ▸**n.** Physics a thermodynamic quantity equivalent to the total heat content of a system, equal to the internal energy of the system plus the product of pressure and volume. (Symbol: **H**) ■ the change in this quantity associated with a particular chemical process. [1920s: from Gk. *enthalpein* 'warm in,' from *en-* 'within' + *thalpein* 'to heat.']

en·thrall /en'THrôl/ (Brit. also **en·thral**) ▸**v.** (**-thralled, -thrall·ing**) [trans.] (often **be enthralled**) capture the fascinated attention of. ■ (also **in·thrall**) archaic enslave. — **en·thrall·ment** (Brit also **en·thral·ment**) **n.** [ME: from EN-[1], IN-[2] + THRALL.]

en·throne /en'THrōn/ ▸**v.** [trans.] (usu. **be enthroned**) install (a monarch) on a throne. ■ fig. give or ascribe a position of authority to. — **en·throne·ment** n.

en·thuse /en'THōōz/ ▸**v.** [reporting verb] say something that expresses one's eager enjoyment, interest, or approval: [intrans.] *they both enthused over my new look.* ■ [trans.] make (someone) interested and eagerly appreciative.

en·thu·si·asm /en'THōōzē,azəm/ ▸**n.** **1** intense and eager enjoyment, interest, or approval. ■ a thing that arouses such feelings. **2** archaic, derog. religious fervor supposedly resulting directly from divine inspiration, typically involving speaking in tongues and wild, uncoordinated body movements. [17th C.: from Fr. *enthousiasme*, or via late L. from Gk. *enthousiasmos*, from *enthous* 'possessed by a god' (based on *theos* 'god').]

en·thu·si·ast /en'THōōzē,ast/ ▸**n.** a person who is highly interested in a particular activity or subject. ■ archaic, derog. a person of intense and visionary Christian views.

en·thu·si·as·tic /en,THōōzē'astik/ ▸**adj.** having or showing intense and eager enjoyment, interest, or approval. — **en·thu·si·as·ti·cal·ly** adv.

en·thy·meme /'enTHə,mēm/ ▸**n.** Logic an argument in which one premise is not explicitly stated. [16th C.: via L. from Gk. *enthumēma*, from *enthumeisthai* 'consider,' from *en-* 'within' + *thumos* 'mind.']

en·tice /en'tīs/ ▸**v.** [trans.] attract or tempt by offering pleasure or advantage. — **en·tice·ment** n. **en·tic·er** n. **en·tic·ing·ly** adv. [ME: from OFr. *enticier*, prob. based on L. *titio* 'firebrand.']

en·tire /en'tī(ə)r/ ▸**adj.** [attrib.] with no part left out; whole. ■ not broken or decayed. ■ without qualification or reservations; absolute. ■ (of a male horse) not castrated. ■ Bot. (of a leaf) without indentations or division into leaflets. [ME: from OFr. *entier*, based on L. *integer* 'untouched,' from *in-* 'not' + *tangere* 'to touch.']

en·tire·ly /en'tī(ə)rlē/ ▸**adv.** completely (often used for emphasis). ■ solely: *eight coaches entirely for passenger transport.*

en·tire·ty /en'tī(ə)rtē; -'tīritē/ ▸**n.** the whole of something.

– PHRASES **in its entirety** as a whole; completely.

en·ti·tle /en'tītl/ ▸**v.** [trans.] (usu. **be entitled**) **1** give (someone) a legal right or a just claim to receive or do something. **2** give (something, esp. a text or work of art) a particular title. ■ [with obj. and complement] archaic give (someone) a specified title expressing rank, office, or character. [ME: via OFr. from late L. *intitulare*, from *in-* 'in' + L. *titulus* 'title.']

en·ti·tle·ment /en'tītlmənt/ ▸**n.** the fact of having a right to something. ■ the amount to which a person has a right.

en·ti·tle·ment pro·gram ▸**n.** a government program that guarantees certain benefits to a particular group or segment of the population.

en·ti·ty /'entitē/ ▸**n.** (pl. **-ties**) a thing with distinct and independent existence. ■ existence; being: *entity and nonentity.* — **en·ti·ta·tive** /-,tātiv/ adj. (esp. Philos.) [15th C.: from Fr. *entité* or med. L. *entitas*, from late L. *ens, ent-* 'being' (from *esse* 'be').]

entom. ▸**abbr.** entomology.

en·tomb /en'tōōm/ ▸**v.** [trans.] (usu. **be entombed**) place (a dead body) in a tomb. ■ bury or trap in or under something. — **en·tomb·ment** n.

entomo- ▸**comb. form** of an insect; of or relating to insects: *entomophagous.* [from Gk. *entomon*, neut. (denoting an insect) of *entomos* 'cut up, segmented.']

en·to·mol·o·gy /,entə'mäləjē/ ▸**n.** the branch of zoology concerned with the study of insects. — **en·to·mo·log·i·cal** /-mə'läjikəl/ adj. **en·to·mol·o·gist** /-jist/ n.

en·to·moph·a·gy /,entə'mäfəjē/ ▸**n.** the practice of eating insects, esp. by people. — **en·to·moph·a·gist** /-jist/ n. **en·to·moph·a·gous** /-'mäfəgəs/ adj.

en·to·moph·i·lous /,entə'mäfələs/ ▸**adj.** Bot. pollinated by insects. — **en·to·moph·i·ly** /-'mäfəlē/ n.

en·to·par·a·site /,entō'parə,sīt/ ▸**n.** Biol. another term for ENDOPARASITE. [19th C.: from Gk. *entos* 'within' + PARASITE.]

En·to·proc·ta /,entə'präktə/ Zool. a small phylum of sedentary aquatic invertebrates having a rounded body on a long stalk, bearing a ring of tentacles for filtering food from the water. — **en·to·proct** /'entə,präkt/ n. [mod. L., from Gk. *entos* 'within' + *prōktos* 'anus.']

en·tou·rage /,äntōō'räzH/ ▸**n.** a group of people attending or surrounding an important person. [19th C.: Fr., from *entourer* 'to surround.']

en·tr'acte /'än,trakt; än'trakt/ ▶ n. an interval between two acts of a play or opera. ■ a piece of music or a dance for such an interval. [19th C.: Fr., from *entre* 'between' + *acte* 'act.']

en·trails /'enträlz; -trəlz/ ▶ plural n. a person or animal's intestines or internal organs, esp. when removed or exposed. ■ fig. the innermost parts of something. [ME: from OFr. *entrailles*, from med. L. *intralia*, alt. of L. *interanea* 'internal things,' based on *inter* 'among.']

en·train¹ /en'trān/ ▶ v. [intrans.] board a train. ■ [trans.] put or allow (someone or something) on board a train.

en·train² ▶ v. [trans.] **1** (of a current or fluid) incorporate and sweep along in its flow. ■ cause or bring about as a consequence. **2** Biol. (of a rhythm or something that varies rhythmically) cause (another) gradually to fall into synchronism with it. ■ [intrans.] **(entrain to)** fall into synchronism with (something) in such a way. — **en·train·ment** n. [16th C.: from Fr. *entraîner*, from *en-* 'in' + *traîner* 'to drag.']

en·trance¹ /'entrəns/ ▶ n. an opening, such as a door, passage, or gate, that allows access to a place. ■ [usu. in sing.] an act or instance of going or coming in. ■ [usu. in sing.] the coming of an actor or performer onto a stage. ■ [usu. in sing.] an act of becoming involved in something. ■ the right, means, or opportunity to enter somewhere or be a member of an institution, society, or other body. ■ Music another term for ENTRY.
– PHRASES **make an** (or **one's**) **entrance** (of an actor or performer) come on stage. ■ enter somewhere in a conspicuous or impressive way. [15th C.: from OFr., from *entrer* 'enter.']

en·trance² /en'trans/ ▶ v. [trans.] (often **be entranced**) fill (someone) with wonder and delight, holding their entire attention. ■ cast a spell on. — **en·trance·ment** n. **en·tranc·ing·ly** adv.

en·trance·way /'entrəns,wā/ ▶ n. a way into a place or thing, esp. a doorway or corridor leading into a building.

en·trant /'entrənt/ ▶ n. a person or group that enters, joins, or takes part in something.

en·trap /en'trap/ ▶ v. (**-trapped, -trap·ping**) [trans.] catch (someone or something) in or as in a trap. ■ trick or deceive (someone), esp. by inducing commission of a crime to secure prosecution. — **en·trap·ment** n. **en·trap·per** n.

en·treat /en'trēt/ ▶ v. **1** [reporting verb] ask someone earnestly or anxiously to do something. ■ [trans.] ask earnestly or anxiously for (something). **2** [with obj. and adverbial] archaic treat (someone) in a specified manner. — **en·treat·ing·ly** adv. **en·treat·ment** n. [ME: from OFr. *entraitier*, based on *traitier* 'to treat,' from L. *tractare* 'to handle.']

en·treat·y /en'trētē/ ▶ n. (pl. **-treat·ies**) an earnest or humble request: *turned a deaf ear to his entreaties.*

en·tre·chat /,äntrə'SHä/ ▶ n. Ballet a vertical jump during which the dancer repeatedly crosses the feet and beats them together. [Fr., from Ital. *(capriola) intrecciata* 'complicated (caper).']

en·tre·côte /'äntrə,kōt/ ▶ n. a boned steak cut off the sirloin. [Fr., from *entre* 'between' + *côte* 'rib.']

en·trée /'äntrā; än'trā/ (also **en·tree**) ▶ n. **1** the main course of a meal. ■ Brit. a dish served between the fish and meat courses at a formal dinner. **2** the right or opportunity to enter a domain or join a particular social group. ■ an entrance, esp. of performers onto a stage. [18th C.: Fr., fem. past part. of *entrer* 'enter' (see ENTRY).]

en·tre·mets /,äntrə'mā/ ▶ n. a light dish served between two courses of a formal meal. [Fr., from *entre* 'between' + *mets* 'dish.']

en·trench /en'trencH/ (also dated **in·trench**) ▶ v. **1** [trans.] (often **be entrenched**) establish (an attitude, habit, or belief) so firmly that change is very difficult or unlikely. ■ establish (a person or authority) in a position of great strength or security. ■ establish (a military force, camp, etc.) in trenches or other fortified positions. **2** [intrans.] **(entrench on/upon)** archaic encroach or trespass upon. — **en·trench·ment** n.

en·tre nous /,äntrə 'nōō/ ▶ adv. between ourselves; privately: *entre nous, the old man's a bit of a problem.* [17th C.: Fr.]

en·tre·pôt /'äntrə,pō/ ▶ n. (pl. **-pôts** pronunc. same or /-,pōz/) a port, city, or other center to which goods are brought for import and export, and for collection and distribution. [18th C.: Fr., from *entreposer* 'to store,' from *entre* 'among' + *poser* 'to place.']

en·tre·pre·neur /,äntrəprə'nōōr; -'nər/ ▶ n. a person who organizes and operates a business or businesses, taking on financial risk to do so. ■ a promoter in the entertainment industry. — **en·tre·pre·neur·i·al** /-'nərēəl; -'nōōrēəl/ adj. **en·tre·pre·neur·i·al·ism** /-'nərēə,lizəm; -'nōōrēə,lizəm/ n. **en·tre·pre·neur·i·al·ly** /-'nərēəlē; 'nōōrēəlē/ adv. **en·tre·pre·neur·ism** n. **en·tre·pre·neur·ship** n. [19th C.: from Fr., from *entreprendre* 'undertake' (see ENTERPRISE).]

en·tre·sol /'entər,säl; 'äntrə,säl; -,sôl/ ▶ n. a low story above the ground floor of a building; a mezzanine. [18th C.: Fr., from Sp. *entresuelo*, from *entre* 'between' + *suelo* 'story.']

en·tro·pi·on /en'trōpē,än; -pēən/ ▶ n. Med. a condition in which the eyelid is rolled inward against the eyeball, typically caused by muscle spasm or by inflammation or scarring of the conjunctiva (as in diseases such as trachoma), and resulting in irritation of the eye by the lashes (trichiasis). [19th C.: from EN-² 'inside,' on the pattern of *ectropion*.]

en·tro·py /'entrəpē/ ▶ n. Physics a thermodynamic quantity representing the unavailability of a system's thermal energy for conversion into mechanical work, often interpreted as the degree of disorder or randomness in the system. (Symbol: **S**) ■ fig. lack of order or predictability; gradual decline into disorder. ■ (in information theory) a logarithmic measure of the rate of transfer of information in a particular message or language. — **en·tro·pic** /en'träpik/ adj. **en·tro·pi·cal·ly** /en'träpik(ə)lē/ adv. [19th C.: from EN-² 'inside' + Gk. *tropē* 'transformation.']

en·trust /en'trəst/ ▶ v. [trans.] assign the responsibility for doing something to (someone): *I've been entrusted with the task of getting him safely back.* ■ put (something) into someone's care or protection: *you persuade people to entrust their savings to you.* — **en·trust·ment** n.

en·try /'entrē/ ▶ n. (pl. **-tries**) **1** an act of going or coming in: *the door was locked, but he forced an entry.* ■ a place of entrance, such as a door or lobby. ■ the right, means, or opportunity to enter a place or be a member of something. ■ the action of undertaking something or becoming a member of something. ■ Bridge a card providing an opportunity to transfer the lead to a particular hand. ■ Law the action of taking up the legal right to property. ■ Music the point in a piece of ensemble music at which a particular performer starts or resumes playing or singing. **2** an item written or printed in a diary, list, ledger, or reference book. ■ the action of recording such an item: *sophisticated features to help ensure accurate data entry.* **3** a person or thing competing in a race or competition: *from the hundreds of entries we received, twelve winners were finally chosen.* ■ [in sing.] the number of competitors in a particular race or competition. ■ the action of participating in a race or competition. **4** the forward part of a ship's hull below the waterline, considered in terms of breadth or narrowness. [ME: from OFr. *entree*, based on L. *intrata*, fem. past part. of *intrare* (see ENTER).]

en·try-lev·el ▶ adj. at the lowest level in an employment hierarchy. ■ (of a product) suitable for a beginner or first-time user; basic.

en·try·way /'entrē,wā/ ▶ n. a way in to somewhere or something; an entrance.

en·try word ▶ n. a word, name, or phrase that is the subject of and heading for an entry in a dictionary, glossary, or encyclopedia.

en·twine /en'twīn/ ▶ v. [trans.] (often **be entwined**) wind or twist together; interweave. — **en·twine·ment** n.

e·nu·cle·ate /i'n(y)ōōklē,āt/ ▶ v. [trans.] **1** Biol. remove the nucleus from (a cell). **2** surgically remove (a tumor or gland, or the eyeball) intact from its surrounding capsule. ▶ adj. Biol. (of a cell) lacking a nucleus. — **e·nu·cle·a·tion** /i,n(y)ōōklē'āsHən/ n. [16th C.: from L. *enucleat-* 'extracted,' from *enucleare*, from *e-* 'out of' + *nucleus* 'kernel' (see NUCLEUS).]

E·nu·gu /ā'nōōgōō/ a city in southeastern Nigeria; pop. 293,000. It was the capital of BIAFRA.

e·nu·mer·a·ble /i'n(y)ōōmərəbəl/ ▶ adj. Math. able to be counted by one-to-one correspondence with the set of all positive integers.

e·nu·mer·ate /i'n(y)ōōmə,rāt/ ▶ v. [trans.] mention (a number of things) one by one. ■ formal establish the number of. — **e·nu·mer·a·tion** /i,n(y)ōōmə'rāsHən/ n. **e·nu·mer·a·tive** /-rətiv; -,rātiv/ adj. [17th C.: from L. *enumerat-* 'counted out,' from *enumerare*, from *e-* 'out' + *numerus* 'number.']

e·nun·ci·ate /i'nənsē,āt/ ▶ v. [trans.] say or pronounce clearly. ■ express (something) in clear or definite terms. ■ proclaim. — **e·nun·ci·a·tion** /i,nənsē'āsHən/ n. **e·nun·ci·a·tive** /i'nənsēətiv; -,ātiv/ adj. **e·nun·ci·a·tor** /-,ātər/ n. [16th C.: from L. *enuntiat-* 'announced clearly,' from *enuntiare*, from *e-* 'out' + *nuntiare* 'announce' (from *nuntius* 'messenger').]

en·ure /i'n(y)ōōr/ ▶ v. var. of INURE.

en·u·re·sis /,enyə'rēsis/ ▶ n. Med. involuntary urination, esp. by children at night. — **en·u·ret·ic** /-'retik/ adj. & n. [19th C.: mod. L., from Gk. *enourein* 'urinate in,' from *en-* 'in' + *ouron* 'urine.']

en·vel·op /en'veləp/ ▶ v. (**-vel·oped, -vel·op·ing**) [trans.] wrap up, cover, or surround completely. ■ make obscure; conceal. ■ (of troops) surround (an enemy force). — **en·vel·op·ment** n. [ME: from OFr. *envoluper*, from *en-* 'in' + a second element of unknown origin.]

en·vel·ope /'envə,lōp; 'änvə-/ ▶ n. **1** a flat paper container with a sealable flap, used to enclose a letter or document. **2** a covering or containing structure or layer. ■ the outer metal or glass housing of a vacuum tube, electric light, etc. ■ the structure within a balloon or airship containing the gas. ■ Microbiol. a membrane forming the outer layer of certain viruses. ■ Electron. a curve joining the successive peaks of a modulated wave. ■ Math. a curve or surface tangent to each of a family of curves or surfaces. ■ Astron. the nebulous covering of the head of a comet; coma.
– PHRASES **push the envelope** informal approach or extend the limits of what is possible. [16th C.: from Fr. *enveloppe*, from *envelopper* 'envelop.']

en·ven·om /en'venəm/ ▶ v. [trans.] archaic put poison on or into; make poisonous. ■ fig. infuse with hostility or bitterness.

en·vi·a·ble /'envēəbəl/ ▶ adj. arousing or likely to arouse envy. — **en·vi·a·bly** adv.

en·vi·ous /'envēəs/ ▶ adj. feeling or showing envy: *I'm envious of their happiness* | *an envious glance.* — **en·vi·ous·ly** adv.

en·vi·ron /en'vīrən; -'vī(ə)rn/ ▶ v. [trans.] formal surround; enclose. [ME: from OFr. *environer*, from *environ* 'surroundings,' from *en* 'in' + *viron* 'circuit' (from *virer* 'to turn, veer').]

en·vi·ron·ment /en'vīrənmənt; -'vī(ə)rn-/ ▶ n. **1** the surroundings or conditions in which a person, animal, or plant lives or operates. ■ [usu. with adj.] the setting or conditions in which a particular activity is carried on. ■ [with adj.] Comput. the overall structure within which a user, computer, or program operates. **2** (**the environment**) the natural world, as a whole or in a particular area, esp. as affected by human activity.

en·vi·ron·men·tal /en,vīrən'men(t)l; -,vī(ə)rn-/ ▶ adj. **1** relating to the natural world and the impact of human activity on its condition: *acid rain may have caused major environmental damage.* ■ aiming or designed to promote the protection of the natural world: *environmental tourism.* **2** relating to or arising from a person's surroundings: *environmental noise.* — **en·vi·ron·men·tal·ly** adv.

en·vi·ron·men·tal art ▶ n. **1** the production of artistic works intended to enhance or become part of an urban or other outdoor environment. ■ the production of works of art by manipulation of the natural landscape. **2** the production of works of art in the form of installations or assemblages that surround the observer.

en·vi·ron·men·tal au·dit ▶ n. an assessment of the extent to which an organization is observing practices that seek to minimize harm to the environment.

en·vi·ron·men·tal·ist /en,vīrən'men(t)l-ist; -,vī(ə)rn-/ ▶ n. **1** a person who is concerned with or advocates the protection of the environment. **2** a person who considers that environment, as opposed to heredity, has the primary influence on the development of a person or group. — **en·vi·ron·men·tal·ism** n.

en·vi·ron·ment-friend·ly ▶ adj. another term for ECO-FRIENDLY.

en·vi·rons /en'vīrənz; -'vī(ə)rnz/ ▶ plural n. the surrounding area or district. [17th C.: from Fr., pl. of *environ* (see ENVIRON).]

en·vis·age /en'vizij/ ▶ v. [trans.] contemplate or conceive of as a possibility or a desirable future event. ■ form a mental picture of (something not yet existing or known). [19th C.: from Fr. *envisager*, from *en-* 'in' + *visage* 'face.']

en·vi·sion /en'vizHən/ ▶ v. [trans.] imagine as a future possibility; visualize.

en·voi /'envoi; 'änvoi/ (also **en·voy**) ▶ n. **1** a short stanza concluding a ballade. **2** archaic an author's concluding words. [ME: from OFr. *envoi*, from *envoyer* 'send' (see ENVOY).]

en·voy /'envoi; 'änvoi/ ▶ n. a messenger or representative, esp. one on a diplomatic mission. [17th C.: from Fr. *envoyé*, past part. of *envoyer* 'send,' from *en voie* 'on the way,' based on L. *via* 'way.']

en·voy ex·traor·di·nar·y ▶ n. (pl. **en·voys ex·traor·di·nar·y**) a minister plenipotentiary, ranking below an ambassador and above a chargé d'affaires.

en·vy /'envē/ ▶ n. (pl. **-vies**)a feeling of discontented or resentful longing aroused by someone else's possessions, qualities, or luck. ■ (**the envy of**) a person or thing that inspires such a feeling: *their health service is the envy of Europe.* ▶ v. (**-vies, -vied**) [trans.] desire to have a quality, possession, or other attribute belonging to (someone else): *he envied tall people* | [with two objs.] *I envy Jane her happiness.* ■ desire for oneself (something possessed or enjoyed by another): *a lifestyle that most would envy.* — **en·vi·er** n. [ME: from OFr. *envier*, from L. *invidere* 'grudge,' from *in-* 'into' + *videre* 'to see.']

en·wrap /en'rap/ ▶ v. (**-wrapped, -wrap·ping**) [trans.] wrap; envelop. ■ (usu. **be enwrapped**) engross or absorb (someone): *they were enwrapped in conversation.*

en·wreathe /en'rēTH/ ▶ v. [trans.] (usu. **be enwreathed**) literary surround or envelop (something).

en·zo·ot·ic /,enzō'ätik/ ▶ adj. of, relating to, or denoting a disease that regularly affects animals in a particular district or at a particular season. Compare with EPIZOOTIC, ENDEMIC (sense 1). [19th C.: from EN-[2] 'within' + Gk. *zōion* 'animal' + -IC.]

en·zyme /'enzīm/ ▶ n. Biochem. a substance produced by a living organism that acts as a catalyst to bring about a specific biochemical reaction. Most enzymes are proteins; some enzymes control reactions within cells and some, such as the enzymes involved in digestion, outside them. — **en·zy·mat·ic** /,enzə'matik/ adj. **en·zy·mat·i·cal·ly** /,enzə'matik(ə)lē/ adv. **en·zy·mic** /en'zīmik; -'zimik/ adj. **en·zy·mi·cal·ly** /en'zīmik(ə)lē; -'zim-/ adv. [19th C.: coined in Ger. from mod. Greek *enzumos* 'leavened,' from *en-* 'within' + Gk. *zumē* 'leaven.']

en·zy·mol·o·gy /,enzə'mäləjē/ ▶ n. the branch of biochemistry concerned with enzymes. — **en·zy·mo·log·i·cal** /-mə'läjikəl/ adj. **en·zy·mol·o·gist** n.

EO ▶ abbr. executive order.

e.o. ▶ abbr. ex officio.

eo- ▶ comb. form. early, primeval: *eohippus.* [from Gk. *ēōs*, 'dawn.']

E·o·cene /'ēə,sēn/ ▶ adj. Geol. of, relating to, or denoting the second epoch of the Tertiary period (between the Paleocene and Oligocene epochs, 56.5 million to 35.4 million years ago), a time when the first horses, bats, and whales appeared. ■ [as n.] (**the Eocene**) the Eocene epoch or the system of rocks deposited during it. [19th C.: from Gk. *ēōs* 'dawn' + *kainos* 'new.']

e·o·hip·pus /,ē-ō'hipəs/ ▶ n. (pl. **-pus·es**)another term for HYRACOTHERIUM. [19th C.: from Gk. *ēōs* 'dawn' + *hippos* 'horse.']

e·o·li·an /ē'ōlēən/ ▶ adj. (also **ae·o·li·an**) esp. Geol. relating to or arising from the action of the wind.

e·o·lith /'ēə,liTH/ ▶ n. Archaeol. a roughly chipped flint found in Tertiary strata, originally thought to be an early artifact but probably of natural origin.

E·o·lith·ic /,ēə'liTHik/ ▶ adj. dated of, relating to, or denoting a period at the beginning of the Stone Age, preceding the Paleolithic and characterized by early stone tools. ■ [as n.] (**the Eolithic**) the Eolithic period.

e.o.m. ▶ abbr. end of the month.

e·on /'ēən; 'ēän/ (esp. Brit. also **ae·on**) ▶ n. (often **eons**) an indefinite and very long period of time, often a period exaggerated for humorous or rhetorical effect: *he reached the crag eons before I arrived.* ■ Astron. & Geol. a unit of time equal to a billion years. ■ Geol. a major division of geological time, subdivided into eras: *the Precambrian eon.* [17th C.: via eccles. L. from Gk. *aiōn* 'age.']

E·os /'ēäs/ Gk. Mythol. the Greek goddess of the dawn. Roman equivalent AURORA[2].

e·o·sin /'ēəsin/ ▶ n. a red fluorescent dye that is a bromine derivative of fluorescein, or one of its salts or other derivatives. [19th C.: from Gk. *ēōs* 'dawn' + -IN[1].]

e·o·sin·o·phil /,ēə'sinə,fil/ ▶ n. Physiol. a white blood cell containing granules readily stained by eosin.

e·o·sin·o·phil·i·a /,ēə,sinə'filēə/ ▶ n. Med. an increase in the number of eosinophils in the blood, occurring in response to some allergens, drugs, and parasites, and in some types of leukemia.

e·o·sin·o·phil·ic /,ēə,sinə'filik/ ▶ adj. **1** Physiol. (of a cell or its contents) readily stained by eosin. **2** Med. relating to or marked by eosinophilia.

-eous ▶ suffix (forming adjectives) resembling; displaying the nature of: *aqueous* | *erroneous.* [from the L. suffix *-eus* + -OUS.]

EP ▶ abbr. ■ electroplate. ■ European Parliament. ■ European plan. ■ extended-play (of a record or compact disc): *an EP of remixes.*

Ep. ▶ abbr. Epistle.

ep- ▶ prefix var. of EPI- before a vowel or *h* (as in *eparch, ephemeral*).

EPA ▶ abbr. Environmental Protection Agency.

e·pact /'ēpakt/ ▶ n. [in sing.] the number of days by which the solar year differs from the lunar year. ■ the number of days into the moon's phase cycle at the beginning of the solar (calendar) year. [16th C.: from Fr. *épacte*, via late L. from Gk. *epaktai (hēmerai)* 'intercalated (days),' from *epagein* 'bring in,' from *epi* 'in addition' + *agein* 'bring.']

ep·arch /'epärk/ ▶ n. the chief bishop of an eparchy. [17th C.: from Gk. *eparkhos*, from *epi* 'above' + *arkhos* 'ruler.']

ep·ar·chy /'epärkē/ ▶ n. (pl. **-chies**) a province of the Orthodox Church.

é·pa·ter /ā'pätā/ ▶ v. (in phrase **épater les bourgeois**) shock people who are conventional or complacent. [20th C.: Fr., literally 'startle, shock.']

ep·au·let /'epə,let; ,epə'let/ (also **ep·au·lette**) ▶ n. an ornamental shoulder piece on an item of clothing, typically on the coat or jacket of a military uniform. [18th C.: from Fr. *épaulette*, dimin. of *épaule* 'shoulder,' from L. *spatula* in the late L. sense 'shoulder blade.']

epaulet

é·pée /,e'pā/ ▶ n. a sharp-pointed dueling sword, designed for thrusting and used, blunted, in fencing. — **é·pée·ist** /-ist/ n. [19th C.: Fr., 'sword,' from OFr. *espee* (see SPAY).]

ep·ei·rog·e·ny /,epī'räjənē/ ▶ n. Geol. the regional uplift of an extensive area of the earth's crust. — **e·pei·ro·gen·e·sis** /i,pīrə'jenəsis/ n. **e·pei·ro·gen·ic** /i,pīrə'jenik/ adj. [19th C.: from Gk. *ēpeiros* 'mainland' + -GENY.]

ep·en·dy·ma /ə'pendəmə/ ▶ n. Anat. the thin membrane of glial cells lining the ventricles of the brain and the central canal of the spinal cord. — **ep·en·dy·mal** adj. [19th C.: from Gk. *ependuma*, from *ependuein* 'put on over.']

ep·en·the·sis /i'penTHəsis/ ▶ n. (pl. **-ses** /-,sēz/) the insertion of a sound or an unetymological letter within a word, e.g., the *b* in *thimble.* — **ep·en·thet·ic** /,epen'THetik/ adj. [16th C.: via late L. from Gk., from *epentithenai* 'insert,' from *epi* 'in addition' + *en-* 'within' + *tithenai* 'to place.']

e·pergne /i'pərn; ā'pərn/ ▶ n. an ornamental centerpiece for a table, typically used to hold fruit or flowers. [18th C.: perh. an alt. form of Fr. *épargne* 'saving, economy.']

ep·ex·e·ge·sis /e,peksə'jēsis/ ▶ n. (pl. **-ses** /-sēz/)the addition of words to clarify meaning. ■ words added for such a purpose. — **ep·ex·e·get·ic** /-'jetik/ adj. **ep·ex·e·get·i·cal** /-'jetikəl/ adj. **ep·ex·e·get·i·cal·ly** /-'jetik(ə)lē/ adv. [16th C.: from Gk. *epexēgēsis*, from *epi* 'in addition' + *exēgēsis* 'explanation' (see EXEGESIS).]

Eph. ▶ abbr. Bible Ephesians.

e·phah /'ēfə; 'efä/ ▶ n. an ancient Hebrew dry measure equivalent to a bushel (35 l). [from Heb. *ēpāh*.]

e·phebe /'efēb; i'fēb/ ▶ n. (in ancient Greece) a young man of 18–20 years undergoing military training. — **e·phe·bic** /i'fēbik/ adj. [via L. from Gk. *ephēbos*, from *epi* 'near to' + *hēbē* 'early manhood.']

e·phed·rine /ə'fedrin; 'efə,drēn/ ▶ n. Med. a crystalline alkaloid drug, $C_{10}H_{15}NO$, obtained from certain Asiatic shrubs of the genus *Ephedra.* It causes constriction of the blood vessels and widening of the bronchial passages and is used to relieve asthma and hay fever. [19th C.: from *Ephedra* + -INE[4].]

e·phem·er·a /ə'fem(ə)rə/ ▶ plural n. things that exist or are used or enjoyed for only a short time. ■ items of collectible memorabilia, typically written or printed ones, that were originally expected to have only short-term usefulness or popularity. [16th C.: pl. of EPHEMERON.]

e·phem·er·al /ə'fem(ə)rəl/ ▶ adj. lasting for a very short time: *fashions are ephemeral.* ■ (chiefly of plants) having a very short life cycle. ▶ n. an ephemeral plant. — **e·phem·er·al·i·ty** /ə,femə'ralitē/ n. **e·phem·er·al·ly** adv. **e·phem·er·al·ness** n. [16th C.: from Gk. *ephēmeros* (see EPHEMERA) + -AL.]

PRONUNCIATION KEY ə *ago, up*; ər *over, fur*; a *hat*; ā *ate*; ä *car*; e *let*; ē *see*; i *fit*; ī *by*; NG *sing*; ō *go*; ô *law, for*; oi *toy*; o͝o *good*; o͞o *goo*; ou *out*; TH *thin*; T͟H *then*; ZH *vision*

e·phem·er·is /iˈfem(ə)ris/ ▶ **n.** (pl. **-er·i·des** /-ərəˌdēz/) Astron. Astrol. a table or data file giving the calculated positions of a celestial object at regular intervals throughout a period. ▪ a book or set of such tables or files. [16th C.: from L., from Gk. *ephēmeros* 'lasting only a day.']

e·phem·er·is time ▶ **n.** time on a scale defined by the orbital period rather than the axial rotation of the earth.

e·phem·er·on /iˈfeməˌrän,/ ▶ **n.** (pl. **ephemerons**) an insect that lives only for a day or a few days. [from Gk., neut. of *ephēmeros* 'lasting only a day.']

E·phe·sians /iˈfēzHənz/ a book of the New Testament ascribed to St. Paul, consisting of an epistle to the Church at Ephesus.

Eph·e·sus /ˈefəsəs/ an ancient Greek city on the western coast of Asia Minor, in modern Turkey, site of the temple of Diana. St. Paul preached here, and St. John is said to have lived here.

eph·od /ˈefäd; ˈēfäd/ ▶ **n.** (in ancient Israel) a sleeveless garment worn by Jewish priests. [ME: from Heb. *ēpōd*.]

eph·or /ˈefôr; ˈefər/ ▶ **n.** (in ancient Greece) one of five senior Spartan magistrates. — **eph·or·ate** /ˈefəˌrāt; -rit/ **n.** [from Gk. *ephoros* 'overseer,' from *epi* 'above' + the base of *horan* 'see.']

epi- (also **ep-**) ▶ **prefix 1** on; upon: *epicycle* | *epigraph*. **2** above: *epicotyl* | *epicontinental*. **3** in addition: *epigenesis* | *epiphenomenon*. [from Gk. *epi* 'upon, near to, in addition.']

ep·i·ben·thos /ˌepəˈbenTHäs/ ▶ **n.** Ecol. the flora and fauna living on the bottom of a sea or lake. — **ep·i·ben·thic** /-ˈbenTHik/ **adj.** [20th C.: from Gk. *epi* 'upon' + *benthos* 'depth of the sea.']

ep·i·blast /ˈepəˌblast/ ▶ **n.** Embryol. the outermost layer of an embryo before it differentiates into ectoderm and mesoderm.

ep·ic /ˈepik/ ▶ **n.** a long poem, typically derived from oral tradition, narrating the deeds and adventures of heroic or legendary figures or the history of a nation. ▪ the genre of such poems. ▪ a long film, book, or other work portraying heroic deeds and adventures or covering an extended period of time. ▶ **adj.** of, relating to, or characteristic of an epic or epics. ▪ heroic or grand in scale or character. — **ep·i·cal adj.** **ep·i·cal·ly** /-k(ə)lē/ **adv.** [16th C.: via L. from Gk. *epikos*, from *epos* 'word, song,' rel. to *eipein* 'say.']

ep·i·can·thic /ˌepiˈkanTHik/ ▶ **adj.** denoting a fold of skin from the upper eyelid covering the inner angle of the eye, typical in many peoples of eastern Asia and found as a congenital abnormality elsewhere.

ep·i·car·di·um /ˌepiˈkärdēəm/ ▶ **n.** Anat. a serous membrane that forms the innermost layer of the pericardium and the outer surface of the heart. — **ep·i·car·di·al** /-dēəl/ **adj.** [19th C.: from **EPI-** 'above' + Gk. *kardia* 'heart.']

ep·i·ce·di·um /ˌepiˈsēdēəm/ ▶ **n.** (pl. **-di·a** /-dēə/) formal a funeral ode. — **ep·i·ce·di·an** /-dēən/ **adj.** [16th C.: from L., from Gk. *epikēdeion*, neut. of *epokēdeios* 'of a funeral' (based on *kēdos* 'care, grief').]

ep·i·cene /ˈepiˌsēn/ ▶ **adj.** having characteristics of both sexes or no characteristics of either sex; of indeterminate sex. ▪ effeminate; effete. ▪ Gram. (of a noun or pronoun) denoting either sex without change of gender. ▶ **n.** an epicene person. [ME: via late L. from Gk. *epikoinos* (based on *koinos* 'common').]

ep·i·cen·ter /ˈepiˌsentər/ (Brit. **ep·i·cen·tre**) ▶ **n.** the point on the earth's surface vertically above the focus of an earthquake. ▪ fig. the central point of something, typically a difficult or unpleasant situation. — **ep·i·cen·tral** /ˌepiˈsentrəl/ **adj.** [19th C.: from Gk. *epikentros* 'situated on a center,' from *epi* 'upon' + *kentron* 'center.']

ep·i·con·ti·nen·tal /ˌepiˌkäntəˈnentl/ ▶ **adj.** denoting areas of sea or ocean overlying the continental shelf.

ep·i·cot·yl /ˌepiˈkätl/ ▶ **n.** Bot. the region of an embryo or seedling stem above the cotyledon.

ep·i·crit·ic /ˌepiˈkritik/ ▶ **adj.** Physiol. relating to or denoting those sensory nerve fibers of the skin that are capable of fine discrimination of touch or temperature stimuli. Often contrasted with **PROTOPATHIC.** [20th C.: from Gk. *epikritikos* 'giving judgment over,' from *epi* 'upon or over' + *krinein* 'to judge.']

Ep·ic·te·tus /ˌepikˈtētəs/ (*c.*AD55–*c.*135), Greek philosopher. He preached the common brotherhood of man and advocated a Stoic philosophy.

ep·i·cure /ˈepiˌkyo͝or/ ▶ **n.** a person who takes particular pleasure in fine food and drink. — **ep·i·cur·ism n.** [ME: via med. L. from Gk. *Epikouros* 'Epicurus.']

Ep·i·cu·re·an /ˌepikyəˈrēən; ˌepiˈkyo͝orēən/ ▶ **n.** a disciple or student of the Greek philosopher Epicurus. ▪ **(epicurean)** a person devoted to sensual enjoyment, esp. that derived from fine food and drink. ▶ **adj.** of or concerning Epicurus or his ideas: *Epicurean philosophers*. ▪ **(epicurean)** relating to or suitable for an epicure.

Ep·i·cu·re·an·ism /ˌepəkyəˈrēəˌnizəm; -ˈkyo͝orēə-/ ▶ **n.** a school of philosophy founded in Athens by Epicurus, who taught that pleasure, particularly mental pleasure, was the highest good.

Ep·i·cu·rus /ˌepəˈkyo͝orəs/ (341–270 BC), Greek philosopher. He founded Epicureanism.

ep·i·cu·ti·cle /ˌepiˈkyo͞otikəl/ ▶ **n.** Bot. Zool. the thin, waxy, protective outer layer covering the surfaces of some plants, fungi, insects, and other arthropods. — **ep·i·cu·tic·u·lar** /-kyo͞oˈtikyələr/ **adj.**

ep·i·cy·cle /ˈepiˌsīkəl/ ▶ **n.** Geom. a small circle whose center moves around the circumference of a larger one. ▪ hist. a circle of this type used to describe planetary orbits in the Ptolemaic system. — **ep·i·cy·clic** /ˌepiˈsīklik/ **adj.** [ME: from OFr., or via late L. from Gk. *epikuklos*, from *epi* 'upon' + *kuklos* 'circle.']

ep·i·cy·cloid /ˌepiˈsīkloid/ ▶ **n.** Math. a curve traced by a point on the circumference of a circle rolling on the exterior of another circle. — **ep·i·cy·cloi·dal** /-sīˈkloidl/ **adj.**

ep·i·deic·tic /ˌepiˈdīktik/ ▶ **adj.** formal characterized by or designed to display rhetorical or oratorical skill. [18th C.: from Gk. *epideiktikos* (based on *deiknunai* 'to show').]

ep·i·dem·ic /ˌepiˈdemik/ ▶ **n.** a widespread occurrence of an infectious disease in a community at a particular time: *a flu epidemic*. ▪ a disease occurring in such a way. ▪ a sudden, widespread occurrence of a particular undesirable phenomenon: *an epidemic of violent crime*. ▶ **adj.** of, relating to, or of the nature of an epidemic. Compare with **ENDEMIC, PANDEMIC, EPIZOOTIC.** [17th C.: from Fr. *épidémie*, via late L. from Gk. *epidēmia* 'prevalence of disease,' from *epidēmios* 'prevalent,' from *epi* 'upon' + *dēmos* 'the people.']

ep·i·de·mi·ol·o·gy /ˌepiˌdēmēˈäləjē/ ▶ **n.** the branch of medicine that deals with the incidence, distribution, and control of diseases. — **ep·i·de·mi·o·log·i·cal** /-əˈläjikəl/ **adj.** **ep·i·de·mi·ol·o·gist** /-jist/ **n.** [19th C.: from Gk. *epidēmia* 'prevalence of disease' + **-LOGY.**]

ep·i·der·mis /ˌepiˈdərmis/ ▶ **n.** Biol. the outer layer of cells covering an organism, in particular: ▪ Zool. Anat. the surface epithelium of the skin of an animal, overlying the dermis. ▪ Bot. the outer layer of tissue in a plant, except where it is replaced by periderm. — **ep·i·der·mal** /-ˈdərməl/ **adj.** **ep·i·der·mic adj.** **ep·i·der·moid** /-ˈdərˌmoid/ **adj.** [17th C.: via late L. from Gk., from *epi* 'upon' + *derma* 'skin.']

ep·i·di·a·scope /ˌepiˈdīəˌskōp/ ▶ **n.** an optical projector capable of giving images of both opaque and transparent objects.

ep·i·did·y·mis /ˌepiˈdidəməs/ ▶ **n.** (pl. **-did·y·mi·des** /-ˈdidəmiˌdēz; -diˈdimiˌdēz/) Anat. a highly convoluted duct behind the testis, along which sperm passes to the vas deferens. — **ep·i·did·y·mal** /-məl/ **adj.** [17th C.: from Gk. *epididumis*, from *epi* 'upon' + *didumos* 'testicle' (from *duo* 'two').]

ep·i·dote /ˈepiˌdōt/ ▶ **n.** a yellow-green crystalline mineral, common in metamorphic rocks, consisting of a hydroxyl silicate of calcium, aluminum, and iron. [19th C.: from Fr. *épidote*, from Gk. *epididonai* 'give additionally.']

ep·i·du·ral /ˌepiˈd(y)o͝orəl/ ▶ **adj.** Anat. Med. on or around the dura mater, in particular, (of an anesthetic) introduced into the space around the dura mater of the spinal cord. ▶ **n.** an epidural anesthetic, used esp. in childbirth to produce loss of sensation below the waist.

ep·i·fau·na /ˌepəˈfônə/ ▶ **n.** Ecol. animals living on the surface of the seabed or a riverbed, or attached to submerged objects or aquatic animals or plants. Compare with **INFAUNA.** — **ep·i·fau·nal** /-ˈfônl/ **adj.**

ep·i·gas·tri·um /ˌepiˈgastrēəm/ ▶ **n.** (pl. **-tri·a** /-trēə/) Anat. the part of the upper abdomen immediately over the stomach. — **ep·i·gas·tric adj.** [17th C.: via late L. from Gk. *epigastrion*, neut. of *epigastrios* 'over the belly,' from *epi* 'upon' + *gastēr* 'belly.']

ep·i·ge·al /ˌepiˈjēəl/ ▶ **adj.** Bot. growing on or close to the ground. Compare with **HYPOGEAL.** ▪ (of seed germination) with one or more seed leaves appearing above the ground. [19th C.: from Gk. *epigeios* (from *epi* 'upon' + *gē* 'earth') + **-AL.**]

ep·i·gene /ˈepiˌjēn/ ▶ **adj.** Geol. taking place or produced on the surface of the earth. [19th C.: from Fr. *épigène*, from Gk. *epigenēs*, from *epi* 'upon' + *genēs* (see **-GEN**).]

ep·i·gen·e·sis /ˌepiˈjenəsis/ ▶ **n.** Biol. the theory, now generally held, that an embryo develops progressively from an undifferentiated egg cell. Often contrasted with **PREFORMATION.** — **ep·i·gen·e·sist n. & adj.**

ep·i·ge·net·ic /ˌepijəˈnetik/ ▶ **adj.** Biol. resulting from external rather than genetic influences. ▪ Biol. of, relating to, or of the nature of epigenesis. ▪ Geol. formed later than the surrounding or underlying rock formation. — **ep·i·ge·net·i·cal·ly** /-k(ə)lē/ **adv.** **ep·i·ge·net·i·cist** /-ˈnetəsist/ **n.**

ep·i·glot·tis /ˌepiˈglätis/ ▶ **n.** a flap of cartilage at the root of the tongue, which is depressed during swallowing to cover the opening of the windpipe. — **ep·i·glot·tal** /-ˈglätl/ **adj.** **ep·i·glot·tic adj.** [ME: from Gk. *epiglōttis*, from *epi* 'upon, near to' + *glōtta* 'tongue.']

ep·i·gone /ˈepiˌgōn/ ▶ **n.** (pl. **ep·i·gones** /ˈepiˌgōnz/ or **e·pig·o·ni** /iˈpigəˌnī/) a less distinguished follower or imitator, esp. of an artist or philosopher. [18th C.: plurals from Fr. *épigones* and L. *epigoni*, from Gk. *epigonoi* 'those born afterward' (based on *gignesthai* 'be born').]

ep·i·gram /ˈepiˌgram/ ▶ **n.** a pithy saying or remark expressing an idea in a clever and amusing way. ▪ a short poem, esp. a satirical one, having a witty or ingenious ending. — **ep·i·gram·ma·tist** /ˌepiˈgramətist/ **n.** **ep·i·gram·ma·tize** /ˌepiˈgraməˌtīz/ **v.** [ME: from Fr. *épigramme*, or L. *epigramma*, from Gk., from *epi* 'upon, in addition' + *gramma* (see **-GRAM**).]

ep·i·gram·mat·ic /ˌepigrəˈmatik/ ▶ **adj.** like or in the style of an epigram; concise, clever, and amusing. — **ep·i·gram·mat·i·cal·ly** /-k(ə)lē/ **adv.**

ep·i·graph /ˈepiˌgraf/ ▶ **n.** an inscription on a building, statue, or coin. ▪ a short quotation or saying at the beginning of a book or chapter, intended to suggest its theme. [16th C.: from Gk. *epigraphē*, from *epigraphein* 'write on.']

e·pig·ra·phy /iˈpigrəfē/ ▶ **n.** the study and interpretation of ancient inscriptions. ▪ epigraphs collectively. — **e·pig·ra·pher n.** **ep·i·graph·ic** /ˌepiˈgrafik/ **adj.** **ep·i·graph·i·cal** /ˌepiˈgrafikəl/ **adj.** **ep·i·graph·i·cal·ly** /ˌepiˈgrafik(ə)lē/ **adv.** **e·pig·ra·phist n.**

e·pig·y·nous /iˈpijənəs/ ▶ **adj.** Bot. (of a plant or flower) having the ovary enclosed in the receptacle, with the stamens and other floral parts situated above. Compare with **HYPOGYNOUS, PERIGYNOUS.** — **e·pig·y·ny** /iˈpijənē/ **n.** [19th C.: from mod. L. *epigynus*, from **EPI-** 'upon, above' +

Gk. *gunē* 'woman' + **-ous.**]

ep·i·lep·sy /'epəˌlepsē/ ▶ **n.** a neurological disorder marked by sudden recurrent episodes of sensory disturbance, loss of consciousness, or convulsions, associated with abnormal electrical activity in the brain. [16th C.: from Fr. *épilepsie*, or via late L. from Gk. *epilēpsia*, from *epilambanein* 'seize, attack,' from *epi* 'upon' + *lambanein* 'take hold of.']

ep·i·lep·tic /ˌepə'leptik/ ▶ **adj.** of, relating to, or having epilepsy: *he had an epileptic fit.* ▶ **n.** a person who has epilepsy.

ep·i·lim·ni·on /ˌepə'limnēˌän; -nēən/ ▶ **n.** (pl. **-ni·a** /-nēə/) the upper layer of water in a stratified lake. [20th C.: from **EPI-** 'above' + Gk. *limnion* (dimin. of *limnē* 'lake').]

ep·i·logue /'epəˌlôg; -ˌläg/ (also **ep·i·log**) ▶ **n.** a section or speech at the end of a book or play that serves as a comment on or a conclusion to what has happened. [ME: from Fr. *épilogue*, via L. from Gk. *epilogos*, from *epi* 'in addition' + *logos* 'speech.']

ep·i·my·si·um /ˌepə'mizēəm; -'mizHēəm/ ▶ **n.** Anat. a sheath of fibrous elastic tissue surrounding a muscle. [mod. L., from **EPI-** 'upon' + Gk. *mus* 'muscle.']

ep·i·neph·rine /ˌepi'nefrin/ ▶ **n.** Biochem. a hormone secreted by the adrenal glands, esp. in conditions of stress, increasing rates of blood circulation, breathing, and carbohydrate metabolism and preparing muscles for exertion. Also called **ADRENALINE.** [19th C.: from **EPI-** 'above' + Gk. *nephros* 'kidney' + **-INE[4]**.]

e·piph·a·ny /i'pifənē/ ▶ **n.** (pl. **-nies**) (also **E·piph·a·ny**) the manifestation of Christ to the Gentiles as represented by the Magi (Matthew 2:1–12). ■ the festival commemorating this on January 6. ■ a manifestation of a divine or supernatural being. ■ a moment of sudden revelation or insight. — **ep·i·phan·ic** /ˌepə'fanik/ **adj.** [ME: from Gk. *epiphainein* 'reveal.']

ep·i·phe·nom·e·non /ˌepəfə'näməˌnän; -'nämənən/ ▶ **n.** (pl. **-nom·e·na** /-'nämənə/) a secondary effect or byproduct that arises from but does not causally influence a process, in particular: ■ Med. a secondary symptom, occurring simultaneously with a disease or condition but not directly related to it. ■ a mental state regarded as a byproduct of brain activity. — **ep·i·phe·nom·e·nal** /-'nämənl/ **adj.**

e·piph·y·sis /ə'pifəsis/ ▶ **n.** (pl. **-ses** /-sēz/) **1** the end part of a long bone, initially growing separately from the shaft. Compare with **DIAPHYSIS.** **2** another term for **PINEAL.** [17th C.: mod. L., from Gk. *epiphusis*, from *epi* 'upon, in addition' + *phusis* 'growth.']

ep·i·phyte /'epəˌfīt/ ▶ **n.** Bot. a plant that grows on another plant but is not parasitic, such as the numerous ferns, bromeliads, air plants, and orchids growing on tree trunks in tropical rain forests. — **ep·i·phyt·al** /ˌepə'fītl/ **adj.** **ep·i·phyt·ic** /ˌepə'fitik/ **adj.** [19th C.: from **EPI-** 'in addition' + Gk. *phuton* 'plant.']

E·pi·rus /i'pīrəs/ a coastal region in northwestern Greece; capital, Ioánnina. Greek name **IPIROS.** ■ an ancient country that included the modern region of Epirus and extended north to Illyria and east to Macedonia and Thessaly.

Epis. ▶ **abbr.** ■ Episcopal. ■ Episcopalian. ■ Epistle.

Episc. ▶ **abbr.** ■ Episcopal. ■ Episcopalian.

e·pis·co·pa·cy /i'piskəpəsē/ ▶ **n.** (pl. **-cies**)government of a church by bishops. ■ **(the episcopacy)** the bishops of a region or church collectively. ■ another term for **EPISCOPATE.**

e·pis·co·pal /i'piskəpəl/ ▶ **adj.** of a bishop or bishops. ■ (of a church) governed by or having bishops. — **e·pis·co·pal·ism n.** **e·pis·co·pal·ly adv.** [ME: from Fr. *épiscopal* or eccles. L. *episcopalis*, from *episcopus* 'bishop,' from Gk. *episkopos* 'overseer' (see **BISHOP**).]

E·pis·co·pal Church the Anglican Church in the US and Scotland.

e·pis·co·pa·lian /iˌpiskə'pālēən/ ▶ **adj.** of or advocating government of a church by bishops. ■ of or belonging to an episcopal church. ■ **(Episcopalian)** of or belonging to the Episcopal Church. ▶ **n.** an adherent of episcopacy. ■ **(Episcopalian)** a member of the Episcopal Church. — **e·pis·co·pa·lian·ism n.**

e·pis·co·pate /i'piskəpit; -ˌpāt/ ▶ **n.** the office or term of office of a bishop. ■ **(the episcopate)** the bishops of a church or region collectively.

ep·i·scope /'epəˌskōp/ ▶ **n.** an optical projector that gives images of opaque objects.

e·pi·si·ot·o·my /iˌpēzē'ätəmē/ ▶ **n.** (pl. **-mies**) a surgical cut made at the opening of the vagina during childbirth, to aid delivery and prevent rupture of tissues. [19th C.: from Gk. *epision* 'pubic region' + **-TOMY.**]

ep·i·sode /'epiˌsōd/ ▶ **n.** an event or a group of events occurring as part of a larger sequence; an incident or period considered in isolation. ■ each of the separate installments into which a serialized story or radio or television program is divided. ■ a finite period in which someone is affected by a specified illness. ■ Music a passage containing distinct material or introducing a new subject. [17th C.: from Gk. *epeisodion*, from *epi* 'in addition' + *eisodos* 'entry.']

ep·i·sod·ic /ˌepə'sädik/ ▶ **adj.** containing or consisting of a series of loosely connected parts or events. ■ occurring occasionally and at irregular intervals. ■ (of a television or radio program or magazine story) broadcast or published as a series of installments. — **ep·i·sod·i·cal·ly** /-k(ə)lē/ **adv.**

ep·i·some /'epiˌsōm/ ▶ **n.** Microbiol. a genetic element inside some bacterial cells, esp. the DNA of some bacteriophages, that can replicate independently of the host and also in association with a chromosome with which it becomes integrated. Compare with **PLASMID.**

Epist. ▶ **abbr.** Epistle.

e·pis·ta·sis /ə'pistəsis/ ▶ **n.** Genet. the interaction of genes that are not alleles, in particular the suppression of the effect of one such gene by another. — **ep·i·stat·ic** /ˌepi'statik/ **adj.** [19th C.: from Greek, literally 'stoppage,' from *ephistanai* 'to stop.']

ep·i·stax·is /ˌepə'staksis/ ▶ **n.** Med. nosebleed. [18th C.: mod. L., from Gk., from *epistazein* 'bleed from the nose,' from *epi* 'upon, in addition' + *stazein* 'to drip.']

ep·i·ste·mic /ˌepə'stemik; -'stē-/ ▶ **adj.** of or relating to knowledge or to the degree of its validation. — **ep·i·ste·mi·cal·ly** /-k(ə)lē/ **adv.**

e·pis·te·mol·o·gy /iˌpistə'mäləjē/ ▶ **n.** Philos. the theory of knowledge, esp. with regard to its methods, validity, and scope. — **e·pis·te·mo·log·i·cal** /-mə'läjikəl/ **adj.** **e·pis·te·mo·log·i·cal·ly** /-mə'läjik(ə)lē/ **adv.** **e·pis·te·mol·o·gist** /-jist/ **n.** [19th C.: from Gk. *epistēmē* 'knowledge,' from *epistasthai* 'know, know how to do.']

ep·i·ster·num /ˌepi'stərnəm/ ▶ **n.** (pl. **-nums** or **-na** /-nə/) Zool. a bone between the clavicles, esp. (in mammals) the upper part of the sternum. ■ Entomol. (in insects) the anterior part of the sidewall of a thoracic segment.

e·pis·tle /i'pisəl/ ▶ **n.** formal humorous a letter. ■ a poem or other literary work in the form of a letter or series of letters. ■ (also **Epistle**) a book of the New Testament in the form of a letter from an Apostle. ■ an extract from an Epistle (or another New Testament book not a Gospel) that is read in a church service. [OE, via L. from Gk. *epistolē*, from *epistellein* 'send news,' from *epi* 'upon, in addition' + *stellein* 'send.']

e·pis·to·lar·y /i'pistəˌlerē/ ▶ **adj.** relating to or denoting the writing of letters or literary works in the form of letters: *an epistolary novel.*

e·pis·tro·phe /ə'pistrəfē/ ▶ **n.** Rhet.the repetition of a word at the end of successive clauses or sentences. [16th C.: from Gk. *epistrophē*, from *epistrephein* 'to turn around,' from *epi* 'in addition' + *strephein* 'to turn.']

ep·i·style /'epiˌstīl/ ▶ **n.** Archit. an architrave. [16th C.: from Fr. *épistyle* or via L., from Gk. *epistulion*, from *epi* 'upon' + *stulos* 'pillar.']

ep·i·taph /'epiˌtaf/ ▶ **n.** a phrase or statement written in memory of a person, esp. on a tombstone. [ME: from OFr. *epitaphe*, via L. from Gk. *epitaphion* 'funeral oration,' neut. of *ephitaphios* 'over or at a tomb,' from *epi* 'upon' + *taphos* 'tomb.']

ep·i·tax·y /'epiˌtaksē/ ▶ **n.** Crystallog. the natural or artificial growth of crystals on a crystalline substrate determining their orientation. — **ep·i·tax·i·al** /ˌepi'taksēəl/ **adj.** [1930s: from Fr. *épitaxie*, from Gk. *epi* 'upon' + *taxis* 'arrangement.']

ep·i·tha·la·mi·um /ˌepəTHə'lāmēəm/ (also **ep·i·tha·la·mi·on** /-mēən/) ▶ **n.** (pl. **-mi·ums** or **-mi·a** /-mēə/ also **-mi·ons**) a song or poem celebrating a marriage. — **ep·i·tha·lam·ic** /-'lamik/ **adj.** [16th C.: via L. from Gk. *epithalamion*, from *epi* 'upon' + *thalamos* 'bridal chamber.']

ep·i·thal·a·mus /ˌepə'THaləməs/ ▶ **n.** (pl. **-mi** /-ˌmī/) Anat. a part of the dorsal forebrain including the pineal gland and a region in the roof of the third ventricle.

ep·i·the·li·al·ize /ˌepə'THēlēəˌlīz/ ▶ **v.** [trans. & intrans.] cover or become covered with epithelial tissue, e.g. during the healing of a wound. — **ep·i·the·li·al·i·za·tion** /ˌepəˌTHēlēəli'zāSHən/ **n.**

ep·i·the·li·um /ˌepə'THēlēəm/ ▶ **n.** (pl. **-li·a** /-lēə/) Anat. the thin tissue forming the outer layer of a body's surface and lining the alimentary canal and other hollow structures. ■ more specifically, the part of this derived from embryonic ectoderm and endoderm, as distinct from endothelium and mesothelium. — **ep·i·the·li·al** /-lēəl/ **adj.** [18th C.: mod. L., from **EPI-** 'above' + Gk. *thēlē* 'teat.']

ep·i·thet /'epəˌTHet/ ▶ **n.** an adjective or descriptive phrase expressing a quality regarded as characteristic of the person or thing mentioned. ■ such a word or phrase as a term of abuse. ■ a descriptive title: *the epithet "Father of Waters," used of the Mississippi River.* — **ep·i·thet·ic** /epə'THetik/ **adj.** **ep·i·thet·i·cal** /epə'THetikəl/ **adj.** **ep·i·thet·i·cal·ly** /epə'THetik(ə)lē/ **adv.** [16th C.: from Fr. *épithète*, or via L. from Gk. *epitheton*, neut. of *epithetos* 'attributed,' from *epitithenai* 'add,' from *epi* 'upon' + *tithenai* 'to place.']

e·pit·o·me /i'pitəmē/ ▶ **n.** **1** **(the epitome of)** a person or thing that is a perfect example of a particular quality or type: *she is the epitome of elegance and taste.* **2** a summary of a written work; an abstract. ■ archaic a miniature representation of something. — **e·pit·o·mist n.** [16th C.: via L. from Gk. *epitomē*, from *epitemnein* 'abridge,' from *epi* 'in addition' + *temnein* 'to cut.']

e·pit·o·mize /i'pitəˌmīz/ ▶ **v.** [trans.] **1** be a perfect example of. **2** archaic give a summary of (a written work). — **e·pit·o·mi·za·tion** /iˌpitəmi'zāSHən/ **n.**

ep·i·tope /'epiˌtōp/ ▶ **n.** Biochem. the part of an antigen molecule to which an antibody attaches itself. [1960s: from **EPI-** 'upon' + Gk. *topos* 'place.']

ep·i·zo·ic /ˌepi'zō-ik/ ▶ **adj.** Biol. (of a plant or animal) growing or living nonparasitically on the exterior of a living animal. — **ep·i·zo·ite** /ˌepi'zōˌīt/ **n.**

ep·i·zo·on /ˌepi'zōän/ ▶ **n.** (pl. **-zo·a** /-'zōə/) Zool. an animal that lives on the body of another animal, esp. as a parasite. [19th C.: from **EPI-** 'upon' + Gk. *zōion* 'animal.']

ep·i·zo·ot·ic /ˌepizō'ätik/ ▶ **adj.** of, relating to, or denoting a disease that is temporarily prevalent and widespread in an animal population. Compare with ENZOOTIC, EPIDEMIC. ▶ n. an outbreak of such a disease. [18th C.: from Fr. *épizootique*, from Gk. *epi* 'upon' + *zōion* 'animal.']

e plu·ri·bus u·num /'ē 'plŏŏrəbəs '(y)ōōnəm/ ▶ n. out of many, one (the motto of the US).

ep·och /'epək/ ▶ n. a period of time in history or a person's life, typically one marked by notable events or particular characteristics. ■ the beginning of a distinctive period in the history of someone or something. ■ Geol. a division of time that is a subdivision of a period and is itself divided into ages, corresponding to a series in chronostratigraphy. ■ Astron. an arbitrarily fixed date relative to which planetary or stellar measurements are expressed. [17th C.: from mod. L. *epocha*, from Gk. *epokhē* 'stoppage,' from *epekhein* 'stop,' from *epi* 'upon' + *ekhein* 'stay.']

ep·och·al /'epəkəl/ ▶ adj. forming or characterizing an epoch; epochmaking.

ep·och-mak·ing ▶ adj. of major importance; likely to have a significant effect on a particular period of time.

ep·ode /'epōd/ ▶ n. **1** a lyric poem written in couplets, in which a long line is followed by a shorter one. **2** the third section of an ancient Greek choral ode, or of one division of such an ode. Compare with STROPHE and ANTISTROPHE. [17th C.: from Fr. *épode*, or via L. *epodos*, from Gk. *epōidos*, from *epi* 'upon' + *ōidē* (see ODE).]

ep·o·nym /'epə,nim/ ▶ n. a person after whom a discovery, invention, place, etc., is named. ■ a name or noun formed in such a way. — **e·pon·y·mous** /ə'pänəməs/ adj. **e·pon·y·my** /ə'pänəmē/ n. [19th C.: from Gk. *epōnumos* 'given as a name,' from *epi* 'upon' + *onoma* 'name.']

ep·ox·ide /e'päk,sīd/ ▶ n. Chem. an organic compound whose molecule contains a three-membered ring involving an oxygen atom and two carbon atoms. [1930s: from EPI- 'in addition' + OXIDE.]

ep·ox·y /i'päksē/ ▶ n. (pl. **-ox·ies**) (also **ep·ox·y res·in**) an adhesive, plastic, paint, or other material made from a class of synthetic thermosetting polymers containing epoxide groups. ▶ adj. [attrib.] consisting of or denoting such a material. ▶ v. (**-ox·ies, -ox·ied**) [trans.] glue (something) using epoxy. [20th C.: from EPI- 'in addition' + OXY-[2].]

EPROM /'ēpräm/ ▶ n. Electron. a read-only memory whose contents can be erased and reprogrammed. [1970s: acronym from *erasable programmable ROM*.]

ep·si·lon /'epsi,län/ ▶ n. the fifth letter of the Greek alphabet (Ε, ε), transliterated as 'e.' ■ [as adj.] denoting the fifth in a series of items, categories, etc. ▶ symb. Physics (e) permittivity. [18th C.: Greek, 'plain or simple E,' from *psilos* 'plain.']

Ep·som /'epsəm/ a town in southeastern England; pop. 68,500. Its natural mineral waters were used in the production of Epsom salts. The annual Derby horse race is held at its racecourse on Epsom Downs.

Ep·som salts ▶ plural n. crystals of hydrated magnesium sulfate, $MgSO_4.7H_2O$, used as a purgative or for other medicinal use. [18th C.: named after the town of EPSOM, where it was first found occurring naturally.]

Ep·stein /'ep,stīn/, Sir Jacob (1880–1959), British sculptor; born in the US. He was noted for his portrait busts of well-known people.

Ep·stein–Barr vi·rus /'epstīn 'bär/ (abbr.: **EBV**) ▶ n. Med. a herpesvirus causing infectious mononucleosis and associated with certain cancers, for example Burkitt's lymphoma. [1960s: named after Michael A. *Epstein* (1921–), British virologist, and Y. M. *Barr* (1932–), Irish virologist.]

EQ ▶ abbr. ■ educational quotient ■ emotional quotient.

eq. ▶ abbr. ■ equal. ■ equation. ■ equivalent.

eq·ua·ble /'ekwəbəl/ ▶ adj. (of a person) not easily disturbed or angered; calm and even-tempered. ■ not varying or fluctuating greatly: *an equable climate*. — **eq·ua·bil·i·ty** /,ekwə'bilitē/ n. **eq·ua·bly** adv. [17th C.: from L. *aequabilis*, from *aequare* 'make equal' (see EQUATE).]

e·qual /'ēkwəl/ ▶ adj. **1** being the same in quantity, size, degree, or value. ■ (of people) having the same status, rights, or opportunities. ■ uniform in application or effect; without discrimination on any grounds. ■ evenly or fairly balanced: *an equal contest*. **2** [predic.] (**equal to**) having the ability or resources to meet (a challenge): *the players proved equal to the task*. ▶ n. a person or thing considered to be the same as another in status or quality. ▶ v. (**e·qualed, e·qual·ing** ; also esp. Brit. **e·qualled, e·qual·ling**) [trans.] be the same as in number or amount. ■ match or rival in performance or extent. ■ be equivalent to.
– PHRASES (**the**) **first among equals** the person or thing having the highest status in a group. **other** (or **all**) **things being equal** provided that other factors or circumstances remain the same. [ME: from L. *aequalis*, from *aequus* 'even, level, equal.']

e·qual·i·tar·i·an /i,kwäli'te(ə)rēən/ ▶ n. another term for EGALITARIAN. — **e·qual·i·tar·i·an·ism** n.

e·qual·i·ty /i'kwälitē/ ▶ n. the state of being equal, esp. in status, rights, and opportunities. ■ Math. the condition of being equal in number or amount. ■ Math. a symbolic expression of the fact that two quantities are equal; an equation.

e·qual·ize /'ēkwə,līz/ ▶ v. [trans.] make the same in quantity, size, or degree throughout a place or group. ■ [intrans.] become equal to a specified or standard level. ■ make uniform in application or effect. ■ [trans.] Electron. correct or modify (a signal, etc.) with an equalizer ■ [trans.] Electron. compensate for by means of an equalizer. — **e·qual·i·za·tion** /,ēkwəli'zāsHən/ n.

e·qual·iz·er /'ēkwə,līzər/ ▶ n. a thing that has an equalizing effect: *education is the **great equalizer***. ■ informal a weapon, esp. a gun. ■ Electron. a passive network designed to modify a frequency response, esp. to compensate for distortion.

e·qual·ly /'ēkwəlē/ ▶ adv. **1** in the same manner. ■ in amounts or parts that are the same in size. **2** to the same extent or degree. ■ [sentence adverb] in addition and having the same importance (used to introduce a further comment on a topic): *not all who live in inner cities are poor; equally, many poor people live outside inner cities*.

e·qual op·por·tu·ni·ty ▶ n. the policy of treating employees and others without discrimination, esp. on the basis of their sex, race, or age.

E·qual Rights A·mend·ment (abbr.: **ERA**) ▶ n. a proposed amendment to the US Constitution stating that civil rights may not be denied on the basis of one's sex.

e·quals sign (also **e·qual sign**) ▶ n. the symbol =.

e·qual tem·per·a·ment ▶ n. Musicsee TEMPERAMENT (sense 2).

e·qual time ▶ n. (in broadcasting) a principle of allowing equal air time to opposing points of view, esp. to political candidates for two or more parties.

e·qua·nim·i·ty /,ēkwə'nimitē; ,ekwə-/ ▶ n. mental calmness, composure, and evenness of temper, esp. in a difficult situation. — **e·quan·i·mous** /i'kwänəməs/ adj. [17th C.: from L. *aequanimitas*, from *aequus* 'equal' + *animus* 'mind.']

e·quate /i'kwāt/ ▶ v. [trans.] consider (one thing) to be the same as or equivalent to another: *customers **equate** their name **with** quality*. ■ [intrans.] (**equate to/with**) (of one thing) be the same as or equivalent to (another). ■ cause (two or more things) to be the same in quantity or value. — **e·quat·a·ble** adj. [ME: from L. *aequat-* 'made equal,' from *aequare*, from *aequus* (see EQUAL).]

e·qua·tion /i'kwāzHən/ ▶ n. **1** Math. a statement that the values of two mathematical expressions are equal (indicated by the sign =). **2** the process of equating one thing with another. ■ (**the equation**) a situation or problem in which several factors must be taken into account. **3** Chem. a symbolic representation of the changes that occur in a chemical reaction, in terms of the formulae of the molecules or other species involved.

e·qua·tion·al /i'kwāzHənl/ ▶ adj. another term for EQUATIVE.

e·qua·tion of time ▶ n. the difference between mean solar time (as shown by clocks) and apparent solar time (indicated by sundials), which varies with the time of year.

eq·ua·tive /i'kwātiv/ ▶ adj. Gram. denoting a sentence or other structure in which one term is identified with another, as in *the winner is Jill*. ■ denoting a use of the verb *to be* that equates one term with another. — **eq·ua·tive·ly** adv.

e·qua·tor /i'kwātər/ ▶ n. an imaginary line drawn around the earth equally distant from both poles, dividing the earth into northern and southern hemispheres and constituting the parallel of latitude 0°. ■ a corresponding line on a planet or other body. ■ Astron.short for CELESTIAL EQUATOR. [ME: from med. L. *aequator*, from L. *aequare* 'make equal' (see EQUATE).]

e·qua·to·ri·al /,ekwə'tôrēəl/ ▶ adj. of, at, or near the equator: *equatorial regions*. — **e·qua·to·ri·al·ly** adv.

E·qua·to·ri·al Guin·ea a country in West Africa. *See box on next page.* — **E·qua·to·ri·al Guin·e·an** adj. & n.

e·qua·to·ri·al mount (also **equatorial mounting**) ▶ n. Astron. a telescope mounting with one axis aligned to the celestial pole, which allows the movement of celestial objects to be followed by motion about this axis alone. Compare with ALTAZIMUTH.

e·qua·to·ri·al tel·e·scope ▶ n. an astronomical telescope on an equatorial mount.

eq·uer·ry /'ekwərē; ə'kwerē/ ▶ n. (pl. **-ries**) an officer of the British royal household who attends or assists members of the royal family. ■ hist. an officer of the household of a prince or noble who had charge over the stables. [16th C.: from OFr. *esquierie* 'company of squires.']

e·ques /'ekwes/ singular form of EQUITES.

e·ques·tri·an /i'kwestrēən/ ▶ adj. of or relating to horse riding: *his amazing equestrian skills*. ■ depicting or representing a person on horseback. ▶ n. (fem. **e·ques·tri·enne** /i,kwestrē'en/)a rider or performer on horseback. [17th C.: from L. *equester* 'belonging to a horseman' (from *eques* 'horseman,' from *equus* 'horse') + -IAN.]

e·ques·tri·an·ism /i'kwestrēə,nizəm/ ▶ n. the skill or sport of horse riding. In the Olympics it is divided into show jumping, dressage, and the three-day event (combining show jumping, dressage, and cross-country riding).

equi- ▶ comb. form equal; equally: *equiangular* | *equidistant*. [from L. *aequi-*, from *aequus* 'equal.']

e·qui·an·gu·lar /,ēkwē'aNGgyələr; ,ekwē-/ ▶ adj. having equal angles.

eq·uid /'ēkwid; 'ekwid/ ▶ n. Zool. a mammal of the horse family (Equidae). [19th C.: from mod. Latin *Equidae* (pl.), from L. *equus* 'horse.']

e·qui·dis·tant /,ēkwi'distənt; ,ekwi-/ ▶ adj. at equal distances: *he wants to be **equidistant from** both political parties*. — **e·qui·dis·tance** n. **e·qui·dis·tant·ly** adv.

e·qui·fi·nal /,ēkwə'fīnəl; ,ekwə-/ ▶ adj. tech. having the same end or result. — **e·qui·fi·nal·i·ty** /,ēkwəfī'nalitē; ,ekwə-/ n. **e·qui·fi·nal·ly** adv.

e·qui·lat·er·al /,ēkwə'latərəl; ,ekwə-/ ▶ adj. having all its sides of the same length: *an equilateral triangle*.

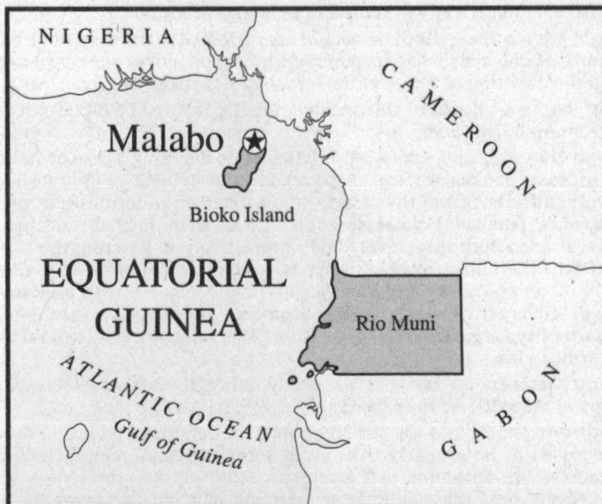

Equatorial Guinea

Official name: Republic of Equatorial Guinea
Location: West Africa, on the Gulf of Guinea, including several offshore islands and a coastal settlement between Cameroon and Gabon
Area: 10,900 square miles (28,100 sq km)
Population: 523,000
Capital: Malabo (on the island of Bioko)
Languages: Spanish and French (both official), pidgin English, Fang, Ibo
Currency: CFA franc

e·quil·i·brate /iˈkwilə,brāt/ ▶ v. [trans.] tech. bring into or keep in equilibrium. ■ [intrans.] approach or attain a state of equilibrium. — **e·quil·i·bra·tion** /i,kwiləˈbrāsʜən/ n. [17th C.: from late L. *aequilibrat-* 'balanced,' from *aequilibrare*, from *aequi-* 'equal' + *libra* 'balance.']

e·quil·i·brist /iˈkwilə,brist/ ▶ n. esp. archaic an acrobat who performs balancing feats, esp. a tightrope walker.

e·qui·lib·ri·um /,ēkwəˈlibrēəm; ,ekwə-/ ▶ n. (pl. **-lib·ri·a** /-ˈlibrēə/) a state in which opposing forces or influences are balanced. ■ a state of physical balance. ■ a calm state of mind. ■ Chem. a state in which a process and its reverse are occurring at equal rates so that no overall change is taking place. ■ Econ. a situation in which supply and demand are matched and prices stable. — **e·qui·lib·ri·al** /-ˈlibrēəl/ adj. [17th C.: from L. *aequilibrium*, from *aequi-* 'equal' + *libra* 'balance.']

e·quine /ˈekwīn; ˈēkwīn/ ▶ adj. of, relating to, or affecting horses or other members of the horse family. ■ resembling a horse. ▶ n. a horse or other member of the horse family. [18th C.: from L. *equinus*, from *equus* 'horse.']

e·quine en·ceph·a·li·tis ▶ n. a category of viral diseases that affects horses and, in some cases, humans. See also EASTERN EQUINE ENCEPHALITIS.

e·qui·noc·tial /,ēkwəˈnäksʜəl; ,ekwə-/ ▶ adj. happening at or near the time of an equinox. ■ of or relating to equal day and night. ■ at or near the equator. ▶ n. (also **equinoctial line** or **equinoctial circle**) another term for CELESTIAL EQUATOR.

e·qui·noc·tial point ▶ n. either of two points at which the ecliptic cuts the celestial equator.

e·qui·noc·tial year ▶ n. see YEAR (sense 1).

e·qui·nox /ˈēkwə,näks; ˈekwə-/ ▶ n. the time or date (twice each year) at which the sun crosses the celestial equator, when day and night are of equal length (about September 22 and March 20). ■ another term for EQUINOCTIAL POINT. [ME: from OFr. *equinoxe* or L. *aequinoctium*, from *aequi-* 'equal' + *nox*, *noct-* 'night.']

e·quip /iˈkwip/ ▶ v. (**e·quipped**, **e·quip·ping**) [trans.] supply with the necessary items for a particular purpose. ■ prepare (someone) mentally for a particular situation or task: *I don't think he's equipped for the modern age.* — **e·quip·per** n. [16th C.: from Fr. *équiper*, prob. from ON *skipa* 'to man (a ship),' from *skip* 'ship.']

equip. ▶ abbr. equipment.

eq·ui·page /ˈekwəpij/ ▶ n. **1** archaic the equipment for a particular purpose. **2** hist. a carriage and horses with attendants.

e·quip·ment /iˈkwipmənt/ ▶ n. the necessary items for a particular purpose. ■ the process of supplying someone or something with such necessary items. ■ mental resources. ■ informal a man's penis and testicles.

e·qui·poise /ˈekwə,poiz/ ▶ n. balance of forces or interests. ■ a counterbalance or balancing force: *capital flows act as an **equipoise to** international savings imbalances.* ▶ v. [trans.] balance or counterbalance (something).

e·qui·pol·lent /,ēkwəˈpälənt; ,ekwə-/ archaic ▶ adj. equal or equivalent in power, effect, or significance. ▶ n. a thing that has equal or equivalent power, effect, or significance. — **e·qui·pol·lence** n. **e·qui·pol·len·cy** n. [ME: from OFr. *equipolent*, from L. *aequipollent-* 'of equal value,' from *aequi-* 'equally' + *pollere* 'be strong.']

e·qui·po·tent /,ēkwəˈpōtnt; ,ekwə-/ ▶ adj. tech. equally powerful; having equal potencies.

e·qui·po·ten·tial /,ēkwəpəˈtencʜəl; ,ekwə-/ ▶ adj. [attrib.] Physics (of a surface or line) composed of points all at the same potential. ▶ n. an equipotential line or surface.

e·qui·prob·a·ble /,ēkwəˈpräbəbəl; ,ekwə-/ ▶ adj. (of two or more things) equally likely to occur; having equal probability. — **e·qui·prob·a·bil·i·ty** /-,präbəˈbilitē/ n.

eq·ui·se·tum /,ekwiˈsētəm/ ▶ n. (pl. **-se·ta** /-ˈsētə/ or **-se·tums**) Bot. a plant of the genus *Equisetum*, family Equisetaceae, which comprises the horsetails. [mod. Latin, from L. *equus* 'horse' + *saeta* 'bristle.']

eq·ui·ta·ble /ˈekwitəbəl/ ▶ adj. **1** fair and impartial. **2** Law valid in equity as distinct from law. — **eq·ui·ta·bil·i·ty** /,ekwitəˈbilitē/ n. **eq·ui·ta·ble·ness** n. **eq·ui·ta·bly** adv.

eq·ui·tant /ˈekwitənt/ ▶ adj. Bot. (of a leaf) having its base folded and partly enclosing the leaf next above it, as in an iris.

eq·ui·ta·tion /,ekwiˈtāsʜən/ ▶ n. formal the art and practice of horsemanship and horse riding.

eq·ui·tes /ˈekwə,tās; -,tēz/ ▶ plural n. (sing. **eq·ues** /ˈekwes; -wēz/) a class of citizens who originally formed the cavalry of the Roman army and at a later period were a wealthy class of great political importance. [L., pl. of *eques* 'horseman.']

eq·ui·ty /ˈekwitē/ ▶ n. (pl. **-ties**) **1** the quality of being fair and impartial: *equity of treatment.* ■ Law a branch of law that developed alongside common law in order to remedy some of its defects in fairness and justice, formerly administered in special courts. ■ (**Equity**) (in the US, UK, and several other countries) a trade union to which most professional actors belong. **2** the value of the shares issued by a company. ■ (**equities**) stocks and shares that carry no fixed interest. **3** the value of a mortgaged property after deduction of charges against it. [ME: from OFr. *equité*, from L. *aequitas*, from *aequus* 'equal.']

eq·ui·ty of re·demp·tion ▶ n. Law the right of a mortgagor over property, esp. the right to redeem the property on payment of the principal, interest, and costs.

equiv. ▶ abbr. equivalent.

e·quiv·a·lence class /iˈkwivələns/ ▶ n. Math. Logic the class of all members of a set that are in a given equivalence relation.

e·quiv·a·lence prin·ci·ple ▶ n. Physics a basic postulate of general relativity, stating that at any point of space-time the effects of a gravitational field cannot be experimentally distinguished from those due to an accelerated frame of reference.

e·quiv·a·lence re·la·tion ▶ n. Math. Logic a relation between elements of a set that is reflexive, symmetric, and transitive. It thus defines exclusive classes whose members bear the relation to each other and not to those in other classes (e.g., "having the same value of a measured property").

e·quiv·a·len·cy /iˈkwivələnsē/ ▶ n. (pl. **-cies**) another term for EQUIVALENCE (see EQUIVALENT).

e·quiv·a·lent /iˈkwivələnt/ ▶ adj. equal in value, amount, function, etc.: *a unit **equivalent to** one glass.* ■ [predic.] (**equivalent to**) having the same or a similar effect as: *some regulations are equivalent to censorship.* ■ Math. belonging to the same equivalence class. ▶ n. a person or thing that is equal to or corresponds with another in value, amount, function, meaning, etc. ■ (also **equivalent weight**) Chem. the mass of a particular substance that can combine with or displace one gram of hydrogen or eight grams of oxygen, used in expressing combining powers, esp. of elements. — **e·quiv·a·lence** n. **e·quiv·a·lent·ly** adv. [ME: via OFr. from late L. *aequivalent-* 'being of equal worth,' from the v. *aequivalere*, from *aequi-* 'equally' + *valere* 'be worth.']

e·quiv·o·cal /iˈkwivəkəl/ ▶ adj. open to more than one interpretation; ambiguous. ■ uncertain or questionable in nature. — **e·quiv·o·cal·i·ty** /i,kwivəˈkalitē/ n. **e·quiv·o·cal·ly** adv. **e·quiv·o·cal·ness** n. [16th C.: from late L. *aequivocus*, from L. *aequus* 'equally' + *vocare* 'to call.']

e·quiv·o·cate /iˈkwivə,kāt/ ▶ v. [intrans.] use ambiguous language so as to conceal the truth or avoid committing oneself. — **e·quiv·o·ca·tion** /i,kwivəˈkāsʜən/ n. **e·quiv·o·ca·tor** /-,kātər/ n. **e·quiv·o·ca·to·ry** /-kə,tôrē/ adj.

eq·ui·voque /ˈekwə,vōk; ˈēkwə-/ (also **eq·ui·voke**) ▶ n. an expression capable of having more than one meaning; a pun. ■ the fact of having more than one meaning or possible interpretation; ambiguity. [ME: from OFr. *equivoque* or late L. *aequivocus* (see EQUIVOCAL).]

ER ▶ abbr. ■ emergency room.

Er ▶ symb. the chemical element erbium.

er /ə; ər/ ▶ exclam. expressing hesitation. [19th C.: natural utterance.]

-er[1] /ər/ ▶ suffix **1** denoting a person, animal, or thing that performs a specified action or activity: *farmer* | *baler.* **2** denoting a person or thing that has a specified attribute or form: *foreigner* | *two-wheeler.* **3** denoting a person concerned with a specified thing or subject: *milliner* | *philosopher.* **4** denoting a person belonging to a specified place or group: *city-dweller* | *New Yorker.* [OE *-ere*, of Gmc. origin.]

-er[2] ▶ suffix forming the comparative of adjectives (as in *bigger*) and adverbs (as in *faster*). [OE suffix *-ra* (adjectival), *-or* (adverbial), of Gmc. origin.]

-er[3] ▸ **suffix** forming frequentative verbs such as *glimmer, patter*. [OE *-erian, -rian*, of Gmc. origin.]

-er[4] ▸ **suffix** forming nouns: **1** such as *sampler*. Compare with **-AR**[1]. ■ such as *butler, danger*. ■ such as *border*. ■ such as *laver*. See **LAVER**[2]. **2** equivalent to **-OR**[1]. [via OFr. or Anglo-Norman Fr.]

-er[5] ▸ **suffix** esp. Law (forming nouns) denoting verbal action or a document effecting such action: *disclaimer* | *misnomer*. [from Anglo-Norman Fr. (infinitive ending).]

ERA ▸ **abbr.** ■ Baseball earned run average. ■ Equal Rights Amendment.

e·ra /'i(ə)rə; 'erə/ ▸ **n.** a long and distinct period of history with a particular feature or characteristic. ■ a system of chronology dating from a particular noteworthy event. ■ Geol. a major division of time that is a subdivision of an eon and is itself divided into periods. ■ archaic a date or event marking the beginning of a new and distinct period of time. [17th C.: from late L. *aera*, denoting a number used as a basis of reckoning, pl. of *aes, aer-* 'money, counter.']

e·rad·i·cate /i'radi,kāt/ ▸ **v.** [trans.] put an end to; destroy. — **e·rad·i·ca·ble** /-kəbəl/ **adj.** **e·rad·i·cant** /-kənt/ **n.** **e·rad·i·ca·tion** /i,radi'kāsHən/ **n.** **e·rad·i·ca·tor** /-,kātər/ **n.** [ME: from L. *eradicat-* 'torn up by the roots,' from *eradicare*, from *e-* 'out' + *radic-* 'root.']

e·rase /i'rās/ ▸ **v.** [trans.] rub out or remove (writing or marks). ■ remove all traces of (a thought, feeling, or memory). ■ destroy or obliterate (someone or something) so as to leave no trace. ■ remove recorded material from (a magnetic tape or medium); delete (data) from a computer's memory. — **e·ras·a·ble adj.** **e·ra·sure** /i'rāsHər/ **n.** [16th C.: from L. *eras-* 'scraped away,' from *eradere*, from *e-* 'out' + *radere* 'scrape.']

e·ras·er /i'rāsər/ ▸ **n.** an object, typically a piece of soft rubber or plastic, used to rub out something written.

E·ras·mus /i'razməs/, Desiderius (*c.*1469–1536), Dutch scholar; Dutch name *Gerhard Gerhards*. He paved the way for the Reformation with his satires on the Church.

E·ras·tian·ism /i'rastēə,nizəm; i'rascHə-/ ▸ **n.** the doctrine that the state should have supremacy over the Church in ecclesiastical matters (wrongly attributed to Erastus). — **E·ras·tian n. & adj.**

E·ras·tus /i'rastəs/ (1524–83), Swiss theologian; Swiss name *Thomas Lieber*, also *Liebler* or *Lüber*. He opposed the imposition of a Calvinistic system of church government in the city.

Er·a·to /'erə,tō/ Greek Rom. Mythol. the Muse of lyric poetry and hymns.

Er·a·tos·the·nes /,erə'tästHə,nēz/ (*c.*275–194 BC), Greek scholar, geographer, and astronomer. He was the first systematic geographer of antiquity.

er·bi·um /'ərbēəm/ ▸ **n.** the chemical element of atomic number 68, a soft, silvery-white metal of the lanthanide series. (Symbol: **Er**) [19th C.: modern Latin, from *(Ytt)erb(y)*, in Sweden.]

ere /e(ə)r/ ▸ **prep. & conj.** literary archaic before (in time): [as prep.] *we hope you will return ere long* | [as conj.] *I was driven for some half mile ere we stopped.* [OE *ǣr*, from Gmc.; akin to Du. *eer*.]

Er·e·bus /'erəbəs/ Gk. Mythol. the primeval god of darkness, son of Chaos.

Er·e·bus, Mount a volcanic peak on Ross Island, Antarctica. It rises to 12,452 feet (3,794 m).

E·rech·the·um /i'rektHēəm; ,erik'tHēəm/ a temple on the Acropolis in Athens *c.*421–406 BC. It is famous for its southern portico, where six caryatids support the entablature.

e·rect /i'rekt/ ▸ **adj.** rigidly upright or straight. ■ (of the penis, clitoris, or nipples) enlarged and rigid, esp. in sexual excitement. ■ (of hair) standing up from the skin; bristling. ▸ **v.** [trans.] construct (a building, wall, or other upright structure). ■ put into position and set upright (a barrier, statue, or other object). ■ create or establish (a theory or system). — **e·rect·a·ble adj.** **e·rect·ly adv.** **e·rect·ness n.** [ME: from L. *erect-* 'set up,' from *erigere*, from *e-* 'out' + *regere* 'to direct.']

e·rec·tile /i'rektl; -,tīl/ ▸ **adj.** able to become erect: *erectile spines*. ■ denoting tissues that are capable of becoming temporarily engorged with blood, particularly those of the penis or other sexual organs. ■ relating to this process: *men with erectile dysfunction*.

e·rec·tile dys·func·tion ▸ **n.** inability of a man to maintain an erection sufficient for satisfying sexual activity: *a treatment proven safe for erectile dysfunction*.

e·rec·tion /i'reksHən/ ▸ **n.** **1** the action of erecting a structure or object. ■ a building or other upright structure. **2** an enlarged and rigid state of the penis, typically in sexual excitement.

e·rec·tor /i'rektər/ ▸ **n.** a person or thing that erects. ■ a muscle that maintains an erect state of a part of the body or an erect posture of the body.

ere·long /e(ə)r'lôNG; -'läNG/ ▸ **adv.** archaic before long; soon.

er·e·mite /'erə,mīt/ ▸ **n.** a Christian hermit or recluse. — **er·e·mit·ic** /,erə'mitik/ **adj.** **er·e·mit·i·cal** /,erə'mitikəl/ **adj.** [ME: from OFr. *eremite*, from late L. *eremita* (see **HERMIT**).]

er·e·thism /'erə,tHizəm/ ▸ **n.** **1** excessive sensitivity or rapid reaction to stimulation of a part of the body, esp. the sexual organs. **2** a state of abnormal mental excitement or irritation. [19th C.: from Fr. *éréthisme*, from Gk. *erethismos*, from *erethizein* 'irritate.']

E·re·van /,yeri'vän/ another name for **YEREVAN**.

ere·while /er'(h)wīl/ ▸ **adv.** archaic a while before; some time ago. [ME: from **ERE** + **WHILE**.]

Er·furt /'er,fo͝ort/ a city in central Germany; pop. 205,000.

erg[1] /ərg/ ▸ **n.** Physics a unit of work or energy, equal to the work done by a force of one dyne when its point of application moves one centimeter in the direction of action of the force. [19th C.: from Gk. *ergon* 'work.']

erg[2] /erg/ ▸ **n.** an area of shifting dunes in the Sahara. [19th C.: from Fr., from Arab. *irq, erg*.]

er·ga·tive /'ərgətiv/ Gram. ▸ **adj.** relating to or denoting a case of nouns (in some languages, e.g., Basque) for the subject of a transitive verb, different from the case for the subject of an intransitive verb. ■ (of a language) possessing this case. ■ (in English) denoting verbs used both transitively and intransitively to describe the same action, the object in the former case being the subject in the latter, as in *I fired the gun* and *the gun fired*. Compare with **INCHOATIVE**. ▸ **n.** an ergative word. ■ (**the ergative**) the ergative case. — **er·ga·tiv·i·ty** /,ərgə'tivitē/ **n.** [1950s: from Gk. *ergatēs* 'worker' (from *ergon* 'work') + **-IVE**.]

er·go /'ərgō; 'ergō/ ▸ **adv.** [sentence adverb] therefore: *she was the sole beneficiary of the will, ergo the prime suspect.* [ME: L.]

er·god·ic /ər'gädik/ ▸ **adj.** Math. relating to or denoting systems or processes with the property that, given sufficient time, they include or impinge on all points in a given space and can be represented statistically by a reasonably large selection of points. — **er·go·dic·i·ty** /,ərgə'disitē/ **n.** [20th C.: from Ger. *ergoden*, from Gk. *ergon* 'work' + *hodos* 'way' + **-IC**.]

er·go·graph /'ərgə,graf/ ▸ **n.** an instrument for measuring and recording the work done by a particular muscle group.

er·gom·e·ter /ər'gämitər/ ▸ **n.** an apparatus that measures work or energy expended during a period of physical exercise.

er·go·nom·ic /ərgə'nämik/ ▸ **adj.** (esp. of workplace design) intended to provide optimum comfort and to avoid stress or injury.

er·go·nom·ics /,ərgə'nämiks/ ▸ **plural n.** [treated as sing.] the study of efficiency in working environments. — **er·gon·o·mist** /ər'gänəmist/ **n.** [1950s: from Gk. *ergon* 'work,' on the pattern of *economics*.]

er·gos·ter·ol /ər'gästə,rôl; -,räl/ ▸ **n.** Biochem. a steroid alcohol in ergot and other fungi, converted to vitamin D_2 when irradiated with ultraviolet light. [20th C.: from **ERGOT**, on the pattern of *cholesterol*.]

er·got /'ərgət; -gät/ ▸ **n.** a disease of rye and other cereals in which black, elongated, fruiting bodies grow in the ears of the cereal, caused by the fungus *Claviceps purpurea*. ■ a fruiting body of this fungus. ■ these fruiting bodies used as a source of certain medicinal alkaloids, esp. for inducing uterine contractions or controlling postpartum bleeding. [17th C.: from Fr., from OFr. *argot* 'cock's spur.']

er·got·a·mine /ər'gätə,mēn; -min/ ▸ **n.** Med. an alkaloid present in some kinds of ergot, used to treat migraine.

er·got·ism /'ərgə,tizəm/ ▸ **n.** poisoning produced by eating food affected by ergot, resulting in headache, vomiting, and gangrene of the fingers and toes.

er·i·ca /'erikə/ ▸ **n.** a plant of the heath family belonging to the genus *Erica*, esp. (in gardening) heather. [mod. L., from Gk. *ereikē*.]

er·i·ca·ceous /,eri'kāsHəs/ ▸ **adj.** Bot. of, relating to, or denoting plants of the heath family (Ericaceae).

Er·ics·son[1] /'eriksən/, John (1803–89), Swedish engineer. He built the ironclad *Monitor* 1862, a ship used in a battle on the Union side in the American Civil War.

Er·ics·son[2] (also **Er·ic·son** or **Er·iks·son**), Leif (fl. 1000), Norse explorer; son of Eric the Red. He reputedly discovered land (variously identified as Labrador, Newfoundland, or New England), which he named Vinland.

Er·ic the Red /'erik/ (*c.* 940–*c.* 1010), Norse explorer. He explored Greenland, establishing a Norse settlement there in 986.

E·rid·a·nus /ə'ridn-əs/ Astron. a long, straggling southern constellation (the River), said to represent the river into which Phaethon fell.

Erie /'i(ə)rē/ a port city in northwestern Pennsylvania, on Lake Erie; pop. 103,717.

Erie Canal a historic canal that connects the Hudson River at Albany in eastern New York with the Niagara River and the Great Lakes. It opened in 1825.

E·rie, Lake /'irē/ one of the five Great Lakes in North America, on the border between Canada and the US.

e·rig·er·on /ə'rijərən; -,rän/ ▸ **n.** a widely distributed, often cultivated herbaceous plant (genus *Erigeron*) of the daisy family. [17th C.: from L., from Gk. *ērigerōn*, from *ēri* 'early' + *gerōn* 'old man.']

Er·in /'erən/ ▸ **n.** archaic or poetic/literary name for Ireland.

E·rin·ys /i'rinəs/ ▸ **n.** (pl. **E·rin·y·es** /i'rinē-ēz/) (in Greek mythology) a Fury.

er·is·tic /i'ristik/ formal ▸ **adj.** of or characterized by debate or argument. ■ (of an argument or arguer) aiming at winning rather than at reaching the truth. ▸ **n.** a person given to debate or argument. ■ the art or practice or debate or argument. — **er·is·ti·cal·ly** /-k(ə)lē/ **adv.** [17th C.: from Gk. *eristikos*, from *erizein* 'to wrangle,' from *eris* 'strife.']

Er·i·tre·a /,erə'trēə; -'trāə/ a country in northeastern Africa. *See box on next page.* — **Er·i·tre·an adj. & n.**

Er·lan·ger /'ər,laNGər/, Joseph (1874–1965), US physiologist. Collaborating with Herbert Gasser, he showed that the velocity of a nerve impulse is proportional to the diameter of the fiber. Nobel Prize for Physiology or Medicine (1944, shared with Gasser).

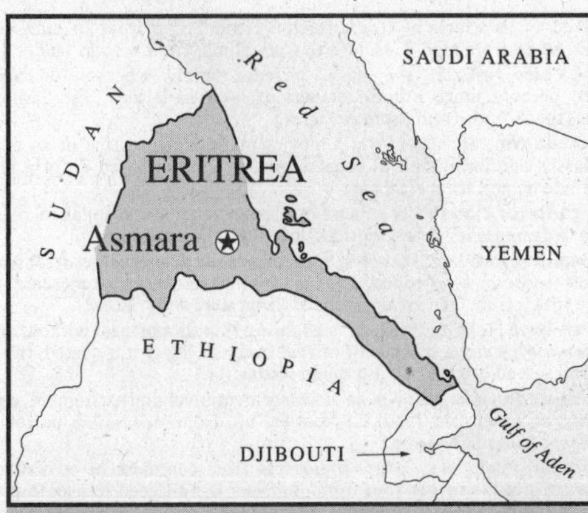

Eritrea

Official name: State of Eritrea
Location: northeastern Africa, bordered on the east by the Red Sea and on the south by Ethiopia
Area: 46,800 square miles (121,200 sq km)
Population: 4,447,000
Capital: Asmara
Languages: Afar, Amharic, Arabic, Tigre, and Cushitic
Currency: nakfa

Er·len·mey·er flask /ˈərlən,mīər; ˈerlən-/ ▶ **n.** a conical, flat-bottomed laboratory flask with a narrow neck. [19th C.: named after Emil *Erlenmeyer* (1825–1909), German chemist.]

erl-king /ˈərl,kiNG/ ▶ **n.** (in Germanic mythology) a bearded giant or goblin who lures little children to the land of death. [18th C.: from Ger. *Erlkönig* 'alder king,' a mistranslation of Dan. *ellerkonge* 'king of the elves.']

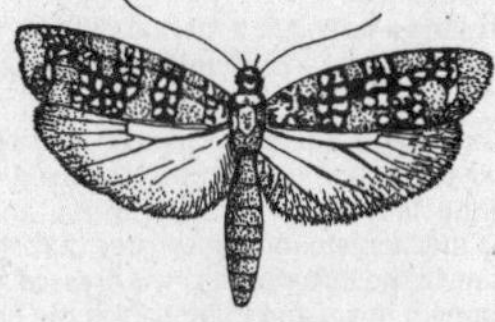
ermine moth

er·mine /ˈərmən/ ▶ **n.** (pl. same or **er·mines**) **1** a stoat, esp. when in its white winter coat. ■ the white fur of the stoat, used for trimming garments, esp. ceremonial robes. ■ Heraldry fur represented as black spots on a white ground, as a heraldic tincture. **2** (also **ermine moth**) a stout-bodied moth (family Arctiidae) that has cream or white wings with black spots. — **er·mined adj.** [ME: from OFr. *hermine*, prob. from med. L. *(mus) Armenius* 'Armenian (mouse).']

-ern ▶ **suffix** forming adjectives such as *northern*. [OE *-erne*, of Gmc. origin.]

erne /ərn/ ▶ **n.** literary the sea eagle. [OE *earn* 'eagle,' of Gmc. origin; rel. to Du. *arend*.]

Ernst /ərnst/, Max (1891–1976), German painter. He was a leader of the Dada movement.

e·rode /iˈrōd/ ▶ **v.** [trans.] (often **be eroded**) (of wind, water, or other natural agents) gradually wear away (soil, rock, or land). ■ [intrans.] (of soil, rock, or land) be gradually worn away by such natural agents. ■ fig. gradually destroy or be gradually destroyed. ■ Med. (of a disease) gradually destroy (bodily tissue). — **e·rod·i·ble** /iˈrōdəbəl/ **adj.** [17th C.: from Fr. *éroder* or L. *erodere*, from *e-* 'away' + *rodere* 'gnaw.']

e·rog·e·nous /iˈräjənəs/ ▶ **adj.** (of a part of the body) sensitive to sexual stimulation: *erogenous zones.* [19th C.: from **Eros** + **-genous**.]

E·ros /ˈeräs; ˈi(ə)räs/ Gk. Mythol. the god of love, son of Aphrodite. Roman equivalent **Cupid**. ■ [as n.] sexual love or desire. ■ (in Freudian theory) the life instinct. Often contrasted with **Thanatos**. ■ (in Jungian psychology) the principle of personal relatedness in human activities, associated with the anima. Often contrasted with **Logos**. [Latin, from Greek, literally 'sexual love.']

e·ro·sion /iˈrōZHən/ ▶ **n.** the process of eroding or being eroded by wind, water, or other natural agents. ■ fig. the gradual destruction or diminution of something: *the erosion of support for the party.* ■ Med. the gradual destruction of tissue or tooth enamel by physical or chemical action. ■ Med. a place where surface tissue has been gradually destroyed. — **e·ro·sion·al adj. e·ro·sive** /iˈrōsiv/ **adj.**

e·rot·ic /iˈrätik/ ▶ **adj.** of, relating to, or tending to arouse sexual desire or excitement. — **e·rot·i·cal·ly** /-ik(ə)lē/ **adv.** [17th C.: from Fr. *érotique*, from Gk. *erōtikos*, from *erōs, erōt-* 'sexual love.']

e·rot·i·ca /iˈrätikə/ ▶ **n.** literature or art intended to arouse sexual desire.

e·rot·i·cism /iˈrätə,sizəm/ ▶ **n.** the quality or character of being erotic. ■ sexual desire or excitement.

e·rot·i·cize /iˈrätə,sīz/ ▶ **v.** [trans.] give (something or someone) erotic qualities. — **e·rot·i·ci·za·tion** /i,rätəsəˈzāSHən/ **n.**

er·o·tism /ˈerə,tizəm/ ▶ **n.** sexual desire or excitement; eroticism.

eroto- ▶ **comb. form** relating to eroticism: *erotomania.*

e·ro·to·gen·ic /i,rätəˈjenik; -rōtə-/ (also **e·ro·tog·e·nous** /erəˈtäjənəs/) ▶ **adj.** another term for **erogenous**.

er·o·tol·o·gy /,erəˈtäləjē/ ▶ **n.** the study of sexual love and behavior.

e·ro·to·ma·ni·a /i,rätəˈmānēə; -,rōtə-/ ▶ **n.** excessive sexual desire. ■ Psychiatry a delusion in which a person (typically a woman) believes that another person (typically of higher social status) is in love with them. — **e·ro·to·ma·ni·ac** /-nē,ak/ **n.**

err /ər; er/ ▶ **v.** [intrans.] formal be mistaken or incorrect; make a mistake: *the judge erred in so ruling.* ■ [often as adj.] (**erring**) sin; do wrong. [ME: from OFr. *errer*, from L. *errare* 'to stray.']

er·rand /ˈerənd/ ▶ **n.** a short journey undertaken in order to deliver or collect something, often on someone else's behalf. ■ archaic the purpose or object of such a journey. [OE *ǣrende* 'message, mission,' of Gmc. origin; rel. to Old High Ger. *ārunti*.]

er·rant /ˈerənt/ ▶ **adj. 1** [attrib.] erring or straying from the proper course or standards: *he could never forgive his daughter's errant ways.* ■ Zool. (of a polychaete worm) of a predatory kind that moves about actively and is not confined to a tube or burrow. **2** [often postpositive] archaic literary traveling in search of adventure. See also **knight-errant**. — **er·ran·cy** /ˈerənsē/ **n.** (in sense 1) **er·rant·ry n.** (in sense 2). [ME (sense 2): sense 1 from L. *errant-* 'erring,' from the v. *errare*; sense 2 from OFr. *errant* 'traveling,' pres. part. of *errer*, from late L. *iterare* 'go on a journey,' from *iter* 'journey.']

er·rat·ic /iˈratik/ ▶ **adj.** not even or regular in pattern or movement; unpredictable. ■ deviating from the normal or conventional in behavior or opinions. ▶ **n.** (also **erratic block** or **boulder**) Geol. a rock or boulder that differs from the surrounding rock and is believed to have been brought from a distance by glacial action. — **er·rat·i·cal·ly** /-k(ə)lē/ **adv.** **er·rat·i·cism** /-,sizəm/ **n.** [ME: from OFr. *erratique*, from L. *erraticus*, from *errare* 'to stray, err.']

er·ra·tum /iˈrätəm; -ˈrā-; -ˈrat-/ ▶ **n.** (pl. **-ta** /-tə/) an error in printing or writing. ■ (**errata**) a list of corrected errors appended to a book or published in a subsequent issue of a journal. [16th C.: from Latin, 'error,' neuter past participle of *errare* 'err.']

Er Rif /ər ˈrif/ another name for **Rif Mountains**.

er·ro·ne·ous /iˈrōnēəs/ ▶ **adj.** wrong; incorrect. — **er·ro·ne·ous·ly adv.** **er·ro·ne·ous·ness n.** [ME: from L. *errare* 'to stray, err') + **-ous**.]

er·ror /ˈerər/ ▶ **n.** a mistake. ■ the state or condition of being wrong in conduct or judgment: *the money had been paid in error.* ■ Baseball a misplay by a fielder that allows a batter to reach base or a runner to advance. ■ tech. a measure of the estimated difference between the observed or calculated value of a quantity and its true value. ■ Law a mistake of fact or of law in a court's opinion, judgment or order. — **er·ror·less adj.** [ME: via OFr. from L. *error*, from *errare* 'to stray, err.']

er·ror mes·sage ▶ **n.** Comput. a message displayed on a monitor screen or printout, indicating that an incorrect instruction has been given, or that there is an error resulting from faulty software or hardware.

er·satz /ˈersäts; -zäts; erˈzäts/ ▶ **adj.** (of a product) made or used as a substitute, typically an inferior one, for something else. ■ not real or genuine. [19th C.: from German, literally 'replacement.']

Erse /ərs/ ▶ **n.** the Scottish or Irish Gaelic language. [early Scots form of **Irish**.]

erst /ərst/ ▶ **adv.** archaic long ago; formerly. [OE *ǣrest*, superlative of *ǣr* (see **ere**).]

erst·while /ˈərst,(h)wīl/ ▶ **adj.** [attrib.] former. ▶ **adv.** archaic formerly.

e·ru·cic ac·id /iˈro͞osik/ ▶ **n.** Chem. an unsaturated fatty acid, $C_{21}H_{41}COOH$, present in mustard and rape seeds. [19th C.: *erucic* from L. *eruca* 'rocket' (denoting the plant) + **-ic**.]

e·ruct /iˈrəkt/ ▶ **v.** [intrans.] tech. emit stomach gas noisily through the mouth; belch. — **e·ruc·ta·tion n.** [ME: from L. *eructare*, from *e-* 'out' + *ructare* 'belch.']

er·u·dite /ˈer(y)ə,dīt/ ▶ **adj.** having or showing great knowledge or learning. — **er·u·dite·ly adv. er·u·di·tion** /,er(y)o͞oˈdiSHən/ **n.** [ME: from L. *eruditus*, past part. of *erudire* 'instruct, train' (based on *rudis* 'rude, untrained').]

e·rum·pent /iˈrəmpənt/ ▶ **adj.** Biol. bursting forth or through a surface. [17th C.: from L. *erumpent-* 'bursting out,' from *erumpere*.]

e·rupt /iˈrəpt/ ▶ **v.** [intrans.] (of a volcano) become active and eject lava, ash, and gases. ■ be ejected from an active volcano. ■ (of an object) explode with fire and noise resembling an active volcano. ■ break out or burst forth suddenly and dramatically. ■ give vent to anger, enthusiasm, amusement, or other feelings in a sudden and noisy way. ■ (of a pimple, rash, or other prominent mark) suddenly appear on the skin. ■ (of the skin) suddenly develop such a pimple, rash, or mark. ■ (of a tooth) break through the gums during normal development.

[17th C.: from L. *erupt-* 'broken out,' from the v. *erumpere*, from *e-* 'out' + *rumpere* 'break.']

e·rup·tion /i'rəpsHən/ ▶ **n.** an act or instance of erupting. ■ a sudden outpouring of a particular substance from somewhere. ■ a sudden outbreak of something, typically something unwelcome or noisy. ■ a spot, rash, or other prominent and reddish mark appearing suddenly on the skin.

e·rup·tive /i'rəptiv/ ▶ **adj.** of, relating to, or formed by volcanic activity. ■ producing or characterized by eruptions.

er·uv /'eroo͝v/ ▶ **n.** (pl. usu. **er·u·vim** /,eroo͝'vēm/) Judaism an urban area enclosed by a wire boundary that symbolically extends the private domain of Jewish households into public areas, permitting activities within it that are normally forbidden in public on the Sabbath. [from Heb. *ērûḇ*, from a base meaning 'mixture.']

Er·ving /'ərviNG/, Julius Winfield (1950–), US basketball player; nickname **Dr. J.** During his professional career 1971–87, he was famed for his acrobatics and powerful offense.

-ery (also **-ry**) ▶ **suffix** forming nouns: **1** denoting a class or kind: *confectionery* | *greenery.* **2** denoting an occupation, a state, a condition, or behavior: *archery* | *bravery* | *slavery.* ■ with depreciatory reference: *knavery* | *tomfoolery.* **3** denoting a place set aside for an activity or a grouping of things, animals, etc.: *orangery* | *rookery.* [from Fr. *-erie*, based on L. *-arius* and *-ator.*]

e·ryn·gi·um /i'rinjēəm/ ▶ **n.** (pl. **-ums**) a plant of the genus *Eryngium* in the parsley family, esp. (in gardening) sea holly. [16th C.: mod. Latin, from L. *eryngion*, from Gk. *ērungos* 'sea holly.']

e·ryn·go /ə'riNGgō/ ▶ **n.** (pl. **-gos** or **-goes**)another term for SEA HOLLY or ERYNGIUM. [16th C.: from Ital. and Sp. *eringio*, from L. *eryngion* (see ERYNGIUM).]

er·y·sip·e·las /,erə'sipələs/ ▶ **n.** Med. an acute, sometimes recurrent disease caused by the bacterium *Streptococcus pyogenes*. It is characterized by fever and large, raised red patches on the skin. [ME: via L. from Gk. *erusipelas.*]

er·y·sip·e·loid /,erə'sipə,loid/ ▶ **n.** Med. dermatitis of the hands caused by the bacterium *Erysipelothrix rhusiopathiae*, occurring mainly among handlers of meat and fish products.

er·y·the·ma /,erə'THēmə/ ▶ **n.** Med. superficial reddening of the skin, usually in patches, as a result of injury or irritation causing dilatation of the blood capillaries. — **er·y·the·mal** /-məl/ **adj.** **er·y·them·a·tous** /-'THemətəs; -'THēmətəs/ **adj.** [18th C.: from Gk. *eruthēma*, from *eruthainein* 'be red,' from *eruthros* 'red.']

e·ryth·rism /'erə,THrizəm; i'riTH,rizəm/ ▶ **n.** Zool. a congenital condition of abnormal redness in an animal's fur, plumage, or skin. [19th C.: from Gk. *eruthros* 'red.']

e·ryth·ri·tol /ə'riTHrə,tôl; -,täl/ ▶ **n.** Chem. a sweet substance, $C_4H_{10}O_4$, extracted from certain lichens and algae, used medicinally as a vasodilator. [19th C.: from *erythrite* (earlier name for *erythritol*) + -OL.]

erythro- ▶ **comb. form** (used commonly in zoological and medical terms) red: *erythrocyte.* [from Gk. *eruthros* 'red.']

e·ryth·ro·blast /i'riTHrō,blast/ ▶ **n.** Physiol. an immature erythrocyte containing a nucleus. — **e·ryth·ro·blas·tic** /i,riTHrō'blastik/ **adj.**

e·ryth·ro·blas·to·sis /i,riTHrōbla'stōsis/ ▶ **n.** Med. the abnormal presence of erythroblasts in the blood. ■ (also **erythroblastosis fetalis**) another term for HEMOLYTIC DISEASE OF THE NEWBORN.

e·ryth·ro·cyte /i'riTHrə,sīt/ ▶ **n.** a red blood cell that (in humans) is typically a biconcave disk without a nucleus. Erythrocytes contain the pigment hemoglobin, which imparts the red color to blood, and transport oxygen and carbon dioxide to and from the tissues. — **e·ryth·ro·cyt·ic** /i,riTHrə'sitik/ **adj.**

er·y·throid /i'riTHroid/ ▶ **adj.** Physiol. of or relating to erythrocytes.

e·ryth·ro·my·cin /i,riTHrə'mīsin/ ▶ **n.** Med. an antibiotic obtained from the bacterium *Streptomyces erythreus* and used to treat infections caused by Gram-positive bacteria. [1950s: from elements of the mod. L. taxonomic name (see above) + -IN[1].]

e·ryth·ro·poi·e·sis /i,riTHrōpoi'ēsis/ ▶ **n.** Physiol. the production of red blood cells. — **e·ryth·ro·poi·et·ic** /-'etik/ **adj.**

e·ryth·ro·poi·e·tin /i,riTHrō'poi-itn/ ▶ **n.** Biochem. a hormone secreted by the kidneys that increases the rate of production of red blood cells in response to falling levels of oxygen in the tissues.

Erz·ge·bir·ge /'ertsgə,birgə/ a mountain range on the border between Germany and the Czech Republic. Also called the **ORE MOUNTAINS.**

Er·zu·rum /,erzoo͝'roo͞m/ a city in northeastern Turkey; pop. 242,400.

Es ▶ **symb.** the chemical element einsteinium.

-es[1] ▶ **suffix** **1** forming plurals of nouns ending in sibilant sounds: *boxes* | *kisses.* **2** forming plurals of certain nouns ending in *-o*: *potatoes* | *heroes.* [var. of **-s[1]**.]

-es[2] ▶ **suffix** forming the third person singular of the present tense: **1** in verbs ending in sibilant sounds: *pushes.* **2** in verbs ending in *-o* (but not *-oo*): *goes.* [var. of **-s[2]**.]

E·sa·ki /e'säkē/, Leo (1925–), Japanese physicist. He designed the tunnel diode (also called Esaki diode). Nobel Prize for Physics (1973, shared with Ivar Giaever 1929– and Brian D. Josephson 1940–).

E·sau /'ēsô/ (in the Bible) the elder of the twin sons of Isaac and Rebecca.

es·ca·drille /'eskə,dril; ,eskə'dril/ ▶ **n.** a European, typically French, aircraft squadron. [20th C.: French, literally 'flotilla, flight.']

es·ca·lade /,eskə'lād; 'eskə,lād/ ▶ **n.** hist. the scaling of fortified walls using ladders, as a form of attack. [16th C.: from Fr., or from Sp. *escalada, escalado*, from med. L. *scalare* 'to scale, climb,' from L. *scala* 'ladder.']

es·ca·late /'eskə,lāt/ ▶ **v.** [intrans.] increase rapidly. ■ become or cause to become more intense or serious. — **es·ca·la·tion** /,eskə'lāsHən/ **n.** [1920s: back-form. from ESCALATOR.]

es·ca·la·tor /'eskə,lātər/ ▶ **n.** a moving staircase consisting of an endlessly circulating belt of steps driven by a motor. [20th C. (orig.as a trade name): from *escalade.*]

es·ca·la·tor clause ▶ **n.** a clause in a contract that allows for an increase or a decrease in wages or prices under certain conditions.

es·cal·lop /i'skäləp; i'skal-/ ▶ **n.** **1** var. of ESCALOPE. **2** another term for SCALLOP (sense 2). ▶ **v.** (**-loped**, **-lop·ing**) another term for SCALLOP (sense 3). [15th C.: from OFr. *escalope* 'shell.' Cf. ESCALOPE and SCALLOP.]

es·ca·lope /,eskə'lōp; i'skäləp; -'skal-/ ▶ **n.** a thin slice of meat without any bone, typically a special cut of veal from the leg that is coated, fried, and served in a sauce. Also called SCALLOP. [Fr.]

es·ca·pade /'eskə,pād/ ▶ **n.** an act or incident involving excitement, daring, or adventure. [17th C.: from Fr., ult. from med. L. *ex-* 'out of' + *cappa* 'cloak.' Cf. ESCAPE.]

es·cape /i'skāp/ ▶ **v.** [intrans.] break free from confinement or control. ■ [trans.] elude or get free from (someone). ■ succeed in avoiding or eluding something dangerous, unpleasant, or undesirable: *the driver escaped with a broken knee* | [trans.] *a baby boy narrowly escaped death.* ■ [trans.] fail to be noticed or remembered by (someone). ■ (of a gas, liquid, or heat) leak from a container. ■ [trans.] (of words or sounds) issue involuntarily or inadvertently from (someone or their lips). ▶ **n.** an act of breaking free from confinement or control. ■ an act of successfully avoiding something dangerous, unpleasant, or unwelcome. ■ a means of escaping from somewhere: [as adj.] *escape route.* ■ a form of temporary distraction from reality or routine. ■ a leakage of gas, liquid, or heat from a container. ■ (also **escape key**) Comput. a key on a computer keyboard that either interrupts the current operation or converts subsequent characters to a control sequence. ■ a garden plant or pet animal that has gone wild and (esp. in plants) become naturalized. — **es·cap·a·ble adj.** **es·cap·er n.** [ME: from OFr. *eschaper*, based on med. L. *ex-* 'out' + *cappa* 'cloak.' Cf. ESCAPADE.]

es·cape clause ▶ **n.** a clause in a contract that specifies the conditions under which one party can be freed from an obligation.

es·cap·ee /i,skā'pē; ,eskā'pē/ ▶ **n.** a person who has escaped from somewhere, esp. prison.

es·cape hatch ▶ **n.** a hatch for use as an emergency exit, esp. from a submarine, ship, or aircraft.

es·cape mech·an·ism ▶ **n.** Psychol. a mental process such as daydreaming that enables a person to avoid unpleasant or threatening aspects of reality.

es·cape·ment /i'skāpmənt/ ▶ **n.** a mechanism in a clock or watch that alternately checks and releases the train by a fixed amount and transmits a periodic impulse from the spring or weight to the balance wheel or pendulum. ■ a mechanism in a typewriter that shifts the carriage a small fixed amount to the left after a key is pressed and released. ■ the part of the mechanism in a piano that enables the hammer to fall back as soon as it has struck the string. [18th C.: from Fr. *échappement*, from *échapper* 'to escape.']

es·cape ve·loc·i·ty ▶ **n.** the lowest velocity that a body must have in order to escape the gravitational attraction of a particular planet or other object.

es·cap·ism /i'skāpizəm/ ▶ **n.** the tendency to seek distraction and relief from unpleasant realities, esp. by seeking entertainment or engaging in fantasy. — **es·cap·ist n. & adj.**

es·cap·ol·o·gist /i,skā'päləjist; ,eskā-/ ▶ **n.** an entertainer specializing in escaping from the confinement of such things as ropes, handcuffs, and chains. — **es·cap·ol·o·gy** /-'päləjē/ **n.**

es·car·got /,eskär'gō/ ▶ **n.** a snail, esp. as an item on a menu. [Fr., from OFr. *escargol*, from Provençal *escaragol.*]

es·ca·role /'eskə,rōl/ ▶ **n.** an endive of a variety with broad leaves and a slightly bitter flavor, used in salads. [20th C.: from Fr., from Ital. *scar(i)ola*, based on L. *esca* 'food.']

es·carp·ment /i'skärpmənt/ ▶ **n.** a long, steep slope, esp. one at the edge of a plateau or separating areas of land at different heights. [19th C.: from Fr. *escarpement*, *escarpe* 'scarp,' from Ital. *scarpa* 'slope.' Cf. SCARP.]

Es·caut /es'kō/ French name for **SCHELDT.**

-esce ▶ **suffix** forming verbs, often denoting the initiation of action: *coalesce* | *effervesce.* [from or suggested by L. verbs ending in *-escere.*]

-escent ▶ **suffix** forming adjectives denoting a developing state or action: *coalescent* | *fluorescent.* — **-escence suffix** forming corresponding nouns. [from Fr., or from L. *-escent-* (present participial stem of verbs ending in *-escere*).]

es·char /'eskär/ ▶ **n.** Med. a dry, dark scab or falling away of dead skin, typically caused by a burn or as a result of anthrax infection. [ME: from Fr. *eschare* or late L. *eschara* 'scab,' from Gk. (see also SCAR).]

es·cha·tol·o·gy /,eskə'täləjē/ ▶ **n.** the part of theology concerned with death, judgment, and the final destiny of the soul and of humankind. — **es·cha·to·log·i·cal** /e,skatl'äjikəl; ,eskətl-/ **adj.** **es·cha·tol·o·gist** /-jist/ **n.** [19th C.: from Gk. *eskhatos* 'last.']

es·cheat /es'CHēt/ esp. hist. ▶ **n.** the reversion of property to the state, or (in feudal law) to a lord, on the owner's dying without legal heirs. ■ an item of property affected by this. ▶v. [intrans.] (of land) revert to a lord or the state by escheat. ■ [trans.] [usu. as adj.] (**escheated**) hand over (land) as an escheat. [ME: from OFr. *eschete*, based on L. *excidere* 'fall away,' from *ex-* 'out of, from' + *cadere* 'to fall.']

Esch·er /'esHər/, M. C. (1898–1972), Dutch graphic artist; full name *Maurits Corneille Escher*. His prints are characterized by their use of visual illusion.

es·chew /es'CHōō/ ▶v. [trans.] deliberately avoid using; abstain from: *he appealed to the crowd to eschew violence.* — **es·chew·al** n. [ME: from OFr. *eschiver*, ult. of Gmc. origin and rel. to Ger. *scheuen* 'shun,' also to SHY[1].]

Es·cof·fier /,eskäf'yā/, Georges-Auguste (1846–1935), French chef.

es·co·lar /,eskə'lär/ ▶n. a large, elongated predatory fish (family Gempylidae) occurring in tropical and temperate oceans throughout the world. Also called SNAKE MACKEREL. [19th C.: from Spanish, literally 'scholar.']

Es·con·di·do /,eskən'dēdō/ a city in southwestern California, north of San Diego; pop. 108,635.

Es·co·ri·al /e'skôrēəl; ,eskôr'yäl/ a monastery and palace in central Spain, near Madrid, built in the late 16th century by Philip II.

es·cort ▶n. /'eskôrt/ a person, vehicle, ship, or aircraft, or a group of these, accompanying another for protection, security, or as a mark of rank. ■ a man who accompanies a woman to a particular social event. ■ a person, typically a woman, who may be hired to accompany someone socially. ▶v. /i'skôrt/ [trans.] accompany (someone or something) somewhere, esp. for protection or security, or as a mark of rank. [16th C.: from Fr. *escorte*, from Ital. *scorta*, fem. past part. of *scorgere* 'to guide,' based on L. *ex-* 'out of' + *corrigere* 'set right' (see CORRECT).]

es·cri·toire /,eskri'twär/ ▶n. a small writing desk with drawers and compartments. [16th C.: from Fr., from med. L. *scriptorium* 'writing room' (see SCRIPTORIUM).]

es·crow /'eskrō/ Law ▶n. a bond, deed, or other document kept in the custody of a third party, taking effect only when a specified condition has been fulfilled. ■ [usu. as adj.] a deposit or fund held in trust or as a security: *an escrow account.* ■ the state of being kept in custody or trust in this way: *funds held in escrow.* ▶v. [trans.] place in custody or trust in this way. [16th C.: from OFr. *escroe* 'scrap, scroll,' from med. L. *scroda*, of Gmc. origin; rel. to SHRED.]

es·cu·do /i'skōōdō/ ▶n. (pl. **-dos**) the basic monetary unit of Portugal (until the introduction of the euro) and Cape Verde, equal to 100 centavos. [Sp. and Port., from L. *scutum* 'shield.']

es·cu·lent /'eskyələnt/ formal ▶adj. fit to be eaten; edible. ▶n. a thing, esp. a vegetable, fit to be eaten. [17th C.: from L. *esculentus*, from *esca* 'food,' from *esse* 'eat.']

es·cutch·eon /i'skəCHən/ ▶n. **1** a shield or emblem bearing a coat of arms. **2** (also **escutcheon plate**) a flat piece of metal for protection and often ornamentation, around a keyhole, door handle, or light switch.
– PHRASES **a blot on one's escutcheon** a stain on one's reputation or character. — **es·cutch·eoned** adj. [15th C.: from Anglo-Norman Fr. *escuchon*, based on L. *scutum* 'shield.']

Esd. ▶abbr. Esdras.

Es·dras /'ezdrəs/ **1** either of two books of the Apocrypha, one mainly a compilation from Chronicles, Nehemiah, and Ezra, the other a record of angelic revelation. **2** (in the Vulgate) the books of Ezra and Nehemiah.

ESE ▶abbr. east-southeast.

-ese ▶suffix forming adjectives and nouns: **1** denoting an inhabitant or language of a country or city: *Taiwanese* | *Viennese.* **2** often derog. (esp. with reference to language) denoting character or style: *journalese* | *officialese.* [from OFr. *-eis*, based on L. *-ensis.*]

es·em·plas·tic /,esem'plastik/ ▶adj. rare molding into one; unifying. — **es·em·plas·ti·cal·ly** /-k(ə)lē/ adv. [19th C.: from Greek *es* 'into' + *hen* 'one' + PLASTIC.]

es·er·ine /'esə,rēn; -rin/ ▶n. Chem. another term for PHYSOSTIGMINE. [19th C.: from Fr. *ésérine*, from Efik *esere.*]

Es·fa·han /,esfə'hän/ var. of ISFAHAN.

Esk. ▶abbr. Eskimo.

es·ker /'eskər/ ▶n. Geol. a long ridge of gravel and other sediment, typically winding, deposited by meltwater from a retreating glacier or ice sheet. [19th C.: from Irish *eiscir.*]

Es·ki·mo /'eskə,mō/ ▶n. (pl. same or **-mos**) **1** a member of an indigenous people inhabiting northern Canada, Alaska, Greenland, and eastern Siberia, traditionally living by hunting (esp. of seals) and by fishing. **2** either of the two main languages of this people (Inuit and Yupik), forming a major division of the Eskimo-Aleut family. ▶adj. of or relating to the Eskimos or their languages. [from Fr. *Esquimaux*, possibly from Sp. *esquimao, esquimal*, from Montagnais *ayas̆kimew* 'netter of snowshoes.']
– USAGE **1** In recent years, **Eskimo** has come to be regarded as offensive because of one of its possible etymologies (Abnaki *askimo* 'eater of raw meat'), but this descriptive name is accurate since Eskimos traditionally derived their vitamins from eating raw meat. This dictionary gives another possible etymology above, but the etymological problem is still unresolved. **2** The peoples inhabiting the regions from northwestern Canada to western Greenland call themselves **Inuit** (see usage at INUIT). Since there are no Inuit living in the US, **Eskimo** is the only term that can be properly applied to all of the peoples as a whole, and it is still widely used in anthropological and archaeological contexts. The broader term **Native American** is sometimes used to refer to Eskimo and Aleut peoples. See usage at NATIVE AMERICAN.

Es·ki·mo-Al·eut ▶n. the family of languages comprising Inuit, Yupik, and Aleut. ▶adj. of or relating to this family of languages.

Es·ki·mo roll ▶n. a complete rollover in kayaking, from upright to capsized to upright.

Es·ki·se·hir /,eskisHə'hi(ə)r/ a spa city in west central Turkey, the capital of Eskisehir province; pop. 413,000.

ESL ▶abbr. English as a second language.

ESOL /'ēsäl/ ▶abbr. English for speakers of other languages.

ESOP ▶abbr. employee stock ownership plan; a plan by which a company's capital stock is bought by its employees or workers.

e·soph·a·gi·tis /i,säfə'jītis/ ▶n. Med. inflammation of the esophagus.

e·soph·a·gus /i'säfəgəs/ (Brit. **oe·soph·a·gus**) ▶n. (pl. **-gi** /-,gī; -jī/ or **-gus·es**) the part of the alimentary canal that connects the throat to the stomach; the gullet. In humans and other vertebrates it is a muscular tube lined with mucous membrane. — **e·soph·a·ge·al** /i,säfə'jēəl/ adj. [ME: mod. L., from Gk. *oisophagos.*]

es·o·ter·ic /,esə'terik/ ▶adj. intended for or likely to be understood by only a small number of people with a specialized knowledge or interest. — **es·o·ter·i·cal·ly** /-k(ə)lē/ adv. **es·o·ter·i·cism** /-'terə,sizəm/ n. **es·o·ter·i·cist** /-'terəsist/ n. [17th C.: from Gk. *esōterikos*, from *esōterō*, compar. of *esō* 'with-in,' from *es, eis* 'into.' Cf. EXOTERIC.]

espadrille

es·o·ter·i·ca /,esə'terikə/ ▶n. esoteric or highly specialized subjects or publications. [20th C.: from Gk. *esōterika*, neut: pl. of *esōterikos* 'esoteric.']

ESP ▶abbr. ■ extrasensory perception.

esp. ▶abbr. especially.

es·pa·drille /'espə,dril/ ▶n. a light canvas shoe with a plaited fiber sole. [19th C.: from Fr., from Provençal *espardi(l)hos*, from *espart* 'esparto,' from L. *spartum* (see ESPARTO).]

es·pal·ier /i'spalyər; -yā/ ▶n. a fruit tree or shrub whose branches are trained to grow flat against a wall, supported on a lattice or a framework of stakes. ■ a lattice or framework of this type. ▶v. [trans.] train (a tree or shrub) in such a way. [17th C.: from Fr., from Ital. *spalliera*, from *spalla* 'shoulder,' from L. *spatula* (see SPATULA).]

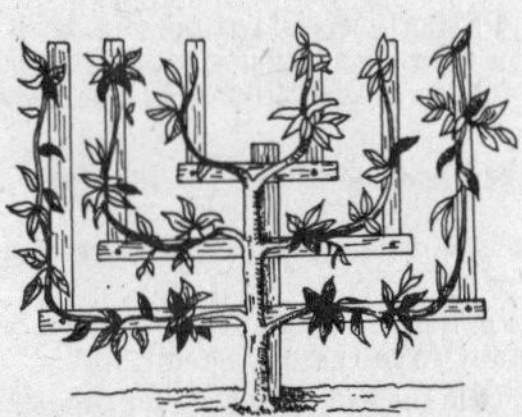
espalier

Es·pa·ña /es'pänyə/ Spanish name for SPAIN.

es·par·to /i'spärtō/ (also **esparto grass**) ▶n. (pl. **-tos**) a coarse long-leaved grass (*Stipa tenacissima*), native to Spain and North Africa, used to make ropes, wickerwork, and high-quality paper. [19th C.: from Sp., via L. from Gk. *sparton* 'rope.']

es·pe·cial /i'spesHəl/ ▶adj. [attrib.] better or greater than usual; special. ■ for or belonging chiefly to one person or thing. [ME: via OFr. from L. *specialis* 'special,' from *species* (see SPECIES).]

es·pe·cial·ly /i'spesHəlē/ ▶adv. **1** used to single out one person, thing, or situation over all others. **2** to a great extent; very much.

Es·pe·ran·to /,espə'räntō/ ▶n. an artificial language devised in 1887 as an international medium of communication, based on roots from the chief European languages. — **Es·pe·ran·tist** n. [from the name *Dr. Esperanto*, pen name of its inventor, Ludwik L. Zamenhof (1858–1917), Polish physician.]

es·pi·al /i'spī(ə)l/ ▶n. archaic the action of watching or catching sight of or the fact of being seen. [ME: from OFr. *espiaille*, from *espier* 'espy.']

es·pi·o·nage /'espēə,näzH; -,näj/ ▶n. the practice of spying or of using spies, typically by governments. [18th C.: from Fr. *espionnage*, from *espionner* 'to spy,' from *espion* 'a spy.']

es·pla·nade /'esplə,näd; -,nād/ ▶n. a long, open, level area, typically beside the sea. ■ an open, level space separating a fortress from a town. [16th C.: from Fr., from Ital. *spianata*, from L. *explanatus* 'flattened, leveled,' from *explanare* (see EXPLAIN).]

Es·poo /'espō/ the second-largest city in Finland, in the southern part of the country, a western suburb of Helsinki; pop. 173,000.

es·pous·al /i'spouzəl; -səl/ ▶n. **1** [in sing.] an act of adopting or supporting a cause, belief, or way of life. **2** archaic a marriage or engagement.

es·pouse /i'spouz/ ▶v. [trans.] **1** adopt or support (a cause, belief, or way of life). **2** archaic marry. ■ (**be espoused to**) (of a woman) be engaged

PRONUNCIATION KEY ə *ago, up*; ər *over, fur*; a *hat*; ā *ate*; ä *car*; e *let*; ē *see*; i *fit*; ī *by*; NG *sing*; ō *go*; ô *law, for*; oi *toy*; ōō *good*; ōō *goo*; ou *out*; TH *thin*; TH *then*; ZH *vision* to (a particular man). — **es·pous·er** n. [ME: from OFr. *espouser*, from L. *sponsare*, from *sponsus* 'betrothed,' past part. of *spondere*.]

es·pres·so /e'spresō/ ▶ n. (pl. **-sos**) strong black coffee made by forcing steam through ground coffee beans. [1940s: from Ital. *(caffè) espresso*, lit. 'pressed out (coffee).']

es·prit /e'sprē/ ▶ n. the quality of being lively, vivacious, or witty. [Fr., from L. *spiritus* 'spirit.']

es·prit de corps /e,sprē də 'kôr/ ▶ n. a feeling of pride, fellowship, and common loyalty shared by the members of a particular group. [18th C.: Fr., literally 'spirit of the body.']

es·prit de l'es·ca·lier /e,sprē də ,leskal'yā/ ▶ n. used to refer to the fact that a witticism or retort often comes to mind after the opportunity to make it has passed. [20th C.: Fr., literally 'wit of the staircase.']

es·py /i'spī/ ▶ v. (**-pies, -pied**) [trans.] literary catch sight of. [ME: from OFr. *espier*, ult. of Gmc. origin and rel. to Ger. *spähan*.]

Esq. ▶ abbr. Esquire.

-esque ▶ suffix (forming adjectives) in the style of; resembling: *carnivalesque* | *Reaganesque*. [from Fr., via Ital. *-esco* from med. L. *-iscus*.]

es·quire /'eskwī(ə)r; i'skwī(ə)r/ ▶ n. **1** (**Esquire**) (abbr.: **Esq.**) a title appended to a lawyer's surname. ■ Brit. a polite title appended to a man's name when no other title is used, typically in the address of a letter or other documents. **2** hist. a young nobleman who, in training for knighthood, acted as an attendant to a knight. ■ an officer in the service of a king or nobleman. ■ [as title] a landed proprietor or country squire. [ME: from OFr. *esquier*, from L. *scutarius* 'shield-bearer,' from *scutum* 'shield.']

es·qui·val·i·ence /eskwə'vālēəns/ ▶ n. the willful avoidance of one's official responsibilities; the shirking of duties: *after three subordinates attested to his esquivalience, Lieutenant Claiborne was dismissed.* ■ an unwillingness to work, esp. as part of a group effort: *Bovich was chided by teammates for her esquivalience.* ■ lack of interest or motivation: *a teenager's esquivalience is not necessarily symptomatic of depression.* — **es·qui·val·i·ent** adj. **es·qui·val·i·ent·ly** adv. [19th C.: perh. from Fr. *esquiver* 'dodge, slink away.']

ess /es/ ▶ n. a thing shaped like the letter S.

-ess[1] ▶ suffix forming nouns denoting female gender: *abbess* | *adulteress* | *tigress*. [from Fr. *-esse*, via late L. from Gk. *-issa*.]

-ess[2] ▶ suffix forming abstract nouns from adjectives, such as *largess*. [ME via Fr. *-esse* from L. *-itia*.]

es·say ▶ n. /'esā/ **1** a short piece of writing on a particular subject. **2** formal an attempt or effort. ■ a trial design of a postage stamp yet to be accepted. ▶ v. /e'sā/ [trans.] formal attempt or try: *essay a smile.* [15th C.: alt. of **ASSAY**.]

es·say·ist /'esā-ist/ ▶ n. a person who writes essays, esp. as a literary genre.

es·say·is·tic /,esā'istik/ ▶ adj. characteristic of or used in essays; discursive; informal.

es·se /'esē; 'ese/ ▶ n. Philos. essential nature or essence. See also **IN ESSE**. [16th C.: L., literally 'to be' (used as a noun).]

Es·sen /'esən/ a city in the Ruhr valley, in northwestern Germany; pop. 627,000.

es·sence /'esəns/ ▶ n. the intrinsic nature or indispensable quality of something, esp. something abstract, that determines its character. ■ Philos. a property or group of properties of something without which it would not exist or be what it is. ■ something that exists; in particular, a spiritual entity. ■ an extract or concentrate obtained from a plant or other matter and used for flavoring or scent.

– PHRASES **in essence** basically and without regard for peripheral details; fundamentally. **of the essence** critically important: *time will be of the essence.* [ME: via OFr. from L. *essentia*, from *esse* 'be.']

Es·sene /i'sēn; 'esēn/ ▶ n. a member of an ancient Jewish ascetic sect of the 2nd century BC–2nd century AD in Palestine. [from L. *Esseni* (pl.), from Gk. *Essēnoi*, perh. from Aramaic.]

es·sen·tial /i'sensHəl/ ▶ adj. **1** absolutely necessary; extremely important. ■ [attrib.] fundamental or central to the nature of something or someone. ■ Biochem. (of an amino acid or fatty acid) required for normal growth but not synthesized in the body and therefore necessary in the diet. **2** Med. (of a disease) with no known external stimulus or cause; idiopathic: *essential hypertension.* ▶ n. (usu. **essentials**) something absolutely necessary. ■ (**essentials**) the fundamental elements or characteristics of something. — **es·sen·ti·al·i·ty** /i,sensHē'alitē/ n. **es·sen·tial·ness** n.

es·sen·tial·ism /i'sensHə,lizəm/ ▶ n. Philos. a belief that things have a set of characteristics that make them what they are, and that the task of science and philosophy is their discovery and expression; the doctrine that essence is prior to existence. Compare with **EXISTENTIALISM**. ■ the view that all children should be taught on traditional lines the ideas and methods regarded as essential to the prevalent culture. ■ the view that categories of people, such as women and men, or members of ethnic groups, have intrinsically different and characteristic natures or dispositions. — **es·sen·tial·ist** n. & adj.

es·sen·tial·ly /i'sensHəlē/ ▶ adv. used to emphasize the basic, fundamental, or intrinsic nature of a someone or something: [sentence adverb] *essentially, they are amateurs.*

es·sen·tial oil ▶ n. a natural oil typically obtained by distillation and having the characteristic fragrance of the plant or other source from which it is extracted.

Es·se·qui·bo /,esə'kwēbō;-'kēbō/ a river in Guyana that rises in the Guiana Highlands and flows north for about 600 miles (965 km) to the Atlantic Ocean.

Es·sex /'esiks/ a county in eastern England; county town, Chelmsford.

EST ▶ abbr. Eastern Standard Time (see **EASTERN TIME**).

est. ▶ abbr. ■ established. ■ estimated.

-est[1] /əst; ist/ ▶ suffix forming the superlative of adjectives (such as *shortest*), and of adverbs (such as *soonest*). [OE *-ost-*, *-ust-*, *-ast-*.]

-est[2] /əst; ist/ (also **-st** /st/) ▶ suffix archaic forming the second person singular of verbs: *canst* | *goest*. [OE *-est*, *-ast*, *-st*.]

es·tab·lish /i'stablisH/ ▶ v. [trans.] **1** set up (an organization, system, or set of rules) on a firm or permanent basis. ■ initiate or bring about (contact or communication). **2** achieve permanent acceptance for (a custom, belief, practice, or institution). ■ achieve recognition or acceptance for (someone) in a particular capacity: *he established himself as a star.* ■ [intrans.] (of a plant) take root and grow. ■ introduce (a character, or location) into a film or play and allow its identification. **3** show (something) to be true or certain by determining the facts. **4** Bridge ensure that one's remaining cards in (a suit) will be winners (if not trumped). — **es·tab·lish·er** n. [ME: from OFr. *establiss-*, from L. *stabilire* 'make firm,' from *stabilis* 'stable.']

es·tab·lished /i'stablisHt/ ▶ adj. **1** (of a custom, belief, practice, or institution) having been in existence for a long time and therefore generally accepted. ■ (of a person) recognized and accepted in a particular capacity. ■ (of a plant) having taken root; growing well. **2** (of a church or religion) recognized by the government as the national church or religion.

– PHRASES **the Established Church** the Church of England or of Scotland.

es·tab·lish·ment /i'stablisHmənt/ ▶ n. **1** the action of establishing something or being established. ■ the recognition by the state of a national church or religion. ■ archaic a marriage. **2** a business organization, public institution, or household. ■ [usu. in sing.] the premises or staff of such an organization. **3** (usu. **the Establishment**) a group in a society exercising power and influence over matters of policy or taste, and seen as resisting change. ■ [with adj.] an influential group within a specified profession or area of activity.

es·tab·lish·men·tar·i·an /i,stablisHmən'te(ə)rēən/ ▶ adj. adhering to, advocating, or relating to the principle of an established church. ▶ n. a person adhering to or advocating this. — **es·tab·lish·men·tar·i·an·ism** n.

Es·tab·lish·ment Clause ▶ n. Law the clause in the First Amendment of the US Constitution that prohibits the establishment of religion by Congress.

es·ta·mi·net /es,tamē'nā/ ▶ n. a small cafe selling alcoholic drinks. [Fr., from Walloon *staminé* 'cowshed,' from *stamo* 'a pole for tethering a cow,' prob. from Ger. *Stamm* 'stem.']

es·tan·cia /e'stänsēə/ ▶ n. a cattle ranch in Latin America or the southwestern US. [17th C.: from Sp., lit. 'station,' from med. L. *stantia*, based on L. *stare* 'to stand.']

es·tate /i'stāt/ ▶ n. **1** an area or amount of land or property, in particular: ■ an extensive area of land in the country, usually with a large house, owned by one person or organization. ■ all the money and property owned by a particular person, esp. at death. ■ a property where coffee, rubber, grapes, or other crops are cultivated. ■ Brit. a housing or commercial development. **2** (also **estate of the realm**) a class or order regarded as forming part of the body politic, in particular (in Britain), one of the three groups constituting Parliament, now the Lords spiritual (the heads of the Church), the Lords temporal (the peerage), and the Commons. They are also known as **the three estates**. ■ dated a particular class or category of people in society: *the spiritual welfare of all estates of men.* **3** archaic literary a particular state, period, or condition in life: *programs for the improvement of man's estate* | *the holy estate of matrimony.* ■ grandeur, pomp, or state: *a chamber without a chair of estate.* [ME: from OFr. *estat*, from L. *status* 'state, condition,' from *stare* 'to stand.']

Es·tates Gen·er·al /i'stāts/ another term for **STATES-GENERAL**.

es·tate tax ▶ n. a tax levied on the net value of the estate of a deceased person before distribution to the heirs. Also called **DEATH TAX**.

es·teem /i'stēm/ ▶ n. respect and admiration, typically for a person: *he was held in high esteem by colleagues.* ▶ v. [trans.] (usu. **be esteemed**) respect and admire. ■ formal consider; deem. [ME: from OFr. *estimer*, from L. *aestimare* 'to estimate.']

es·ter /'estər/ ▶ n. Chem. an organic compound made by replacing the hydrogen of an acid by an alkyl or other organic group. Many naturally occurring fats and essential oils are esters of fatty acids. — **es·ter·i·fy** /i'sterə,fī/ v. (**-fies, -fied**). [19th C.: from Ger., prob. from a blend of *Essig* 'vinegar' and *Äther* 'ether.']

es·ter·ase /'estə,rās; -,rāz/ ▶ n. Biochem. an enzyme that hydrolyzes particular esters into acids and alcohols or phenols.

es·ter·i·fi·ca·tion /es,terəfi'kāsHən/ ▶ n. Chem. a reaction of an alcohol with an acid to produce an ester and water.

Esth. ▶ abbr. Bible Esther.

Es·ther /'estər/ (in the Bible) a woman chosen on account of her beauty by the Persian king Ahasuerus (generally supposed to be Xerxes I) to be his queen. ■ a book of the Bible containing an account of these events.

es·thet·ic, etc. ▶ adj. var. of **AESTHETIC**, etc.

es·ti·ma·ble /'estəməbəl/ ▶ **adj.** worthy of respect. — **es·ti·ma·bly adv.**

es·ti·mate ▶ **v.** /'estə,māt/ [trans.] roughly calculate or judge the value, number, quantity, or extent of. ▶ **n.** /-mit/ an approximate calculation or judgment of the value, number, quantity, or extent of something. ■ a written statement indicating the likely price that will be charged for specified work or repairs. ■ a judgment of the worth or character of someone or something. — **es·ti·ma·tive** /'estə,mātiv/ **adj.** [ME: from L. *aestimat-* 'appraised,' from *aestimare.*]

es·ti·ma·tion /,estə'māsHən/ ▶ **n.** a rough calculation of the value, number, quantity, or extent of something. ■ [usu. in sing.] a judgment of the worth or character of someone or something: *the pop star rose in my estimation.*

es·ti·ma·tor /'estə,mātər/ ▶ **n.** **1** Stat. a rule, method, or criterion for arriving at an estimate of the value of a parameter. ■ a quantity used or evaluated as such an estimate. **2** a person who estimates the price, value, number, quantity, or extent of something.

es·ti·val /'estəvəl; e'stī- ;/ (also **aes·ti·val**) ▶ **adj.** tech. belonging to or appearing in summer. [ME: from L. *aestivalis*, from *aestivus*, from *aestus* 'heat.']

es·ti·vate /'estə,vāt/ (also **aes·ti·vate**) ▶ **v.** [intrans.] Zool. (of an animal, particularly an insect, fish, or amphibian) spend a hot or dry period in a prolonged state of torpor or dormancy. [17th C.: from L. *aestivat-*, from *aestivare* 'spend the summer,' from *aestus* 'heat.']

es·ti·va·tion /,estə'vāsHən/ (also **aes·ti·va·tion**) ▶ **n.** **1** Zool. prolonged torpor or dormancy of an animal during a hot or dry period. **2** Bot. the arrangement of petals and sepals in a flower bud before it opens. Compare with **VERNATION**.

Es·to·ni·a /e'stōnēə/ a country in eastern Europe. *See box.*

Estonia

Official name: Republic of Estonia
Location: eastern Europe, bordering the Baltic Sea and the Gulf of Finland
Area: 16,700 square miles (43,200 sq km)
Population: 1,341,000
Capital: Tallinn
Languages: Estonian (official), Russian, Ukrainian, English, Finnish
Currency: Estonian kroon

Es·to·ni·an /e'stōnēən/ ▶ **adj.** of or relating to Estonia or its people or their language. ▶ **n.** **1** a native or national of Estonia, or a person of Estonian descent. **2** the Finno-Ugric language of Estonia, closely related to Finnish.

es·top /e'stäp/ ▶ **v.** (**es·topped**, **es·top·ping**) [trans.] (usu. **be estopped from**) Law bar or preclude by estoppel. [ME: from OFr. *estopper* 'impede,' from late L. *stuppare*, from L. *stuppa* 'tow, oakum.']

es·top·pel /e'stäpəl/ ▶ **n.** Law the principle that precludes a person from asserting something contrary to what is implied by a previous action or statement of that person or by a previous pertinent judicial determination.

es·tra·di·ol /,estrə'dīôl; -äl/ (Brit. **oes·tra·di·ol**) ▶ **n.** Biochem. a major estrogen produced in the ovaries, controlling the growth of the female sexual organs and some functions of the uterus, and used to treat menopausal symptoms. [1930s: from **ESTRUS** + **DI-**[1] + **-OL.**]

es·trange /i'strānj/ ▶ **v.** [trans.] cause (someone) to be no longer close or affectionate to someone; alienate. — **es·trange·ment n.** [15th C.: from OFr. *estranger*, from L. *extraneare* 'treat as a stranger,' from *extraneus* 'not belonging to the family.']

es·tranged /i'strānjd/ ▶ **adj.** (of a person) no longer close or affectionate to someone; alienated. ■ (of a wife or husband) no longer living with their spouse.

es·tri·ol /'estrī,ôl; - ,äl; e'strīôl; e'strīäl/ (also **oes·tri·ol**) ▶ **n.** Biochem. an estrogen that is one of the metabolic products of estradiol. Measurement of estriol secretion serves as a guide to the health of the fetus and placenta. [1930s: from *estrane* (the parent molecule of most estrogens) + **TRI-** + **-OL.**]

es·tro·gen /'estrəjən/ (Brit. **oes·tro·gen**) ▶ **n.** any of a group of steroid hormones that promote the development and maintenance of female characteristics of the body. Such hormones are also produced artificially for use in oral contraceptives or to treat menopausal and menstrual disorders. — **es·tro·gen·ic** /,estrə'jenik/ **adj.** [1920s: from **ESTRUS** + **-GEN.**]

es·trone /'estrōn/ (Brit. **oes·trone**) ▶ **n.** Biochem. an estrogen similar to but less potent than estradiol. [1930s: from *estrane* (parent molecule of most estrogens) + **-ONE.**]

es·trous cy·cle /'estrəs/ ▶ **n.** the recurring reproductive cycle in many female mammals, including estrus, ovulation, and changes in the uterine lining.

es·trus /'estrəs/ (also **es·trum** /'estrəm/ or esp. Brit. **oes·trus**) ▶ **n.** a recurring period of sexual receptivity and fertility in many female mammals; heat: *a mare in estrus.* — **es·trous** /'estrəs/ **adj.** [17th C.: from Gk. *oistros* 'gadfly or frenzy.']

es·tu·ar·y /'escHōō,erē/ ▶ **n.** (pl. **-ar·ies**) the tidal mouth of a river, where the tide meets the stream. — **es·tu·ar·i·al** /,escHōō'e(ə)rēəl/ **adj.** **es·tu·a·rine** /'escHōōə,rīn; -ə,rēn/ **adj.** [16th C.: from L. *aestuarium* 'tidal part of a shore,' from *aestus* 'tide.']

esu ▶ **abbr.** electrostatic unit(s).

e·su·ri·ent /i'sŏŏrēənt/ ▶ **adj.** archaic hungry or greedy. — **e·su·ri·ent·ly adv.** [17th C.: from L. *esurient-* 'being hungry,' from the v. *esurire*, from *esse* 'eat.']

ET ▶ **abbr.** ■ Eastern time. ■ extraterrestrial.

-et[1] ▶ **suffix** forming nouns that were originally diminutives: *baronet* | *hatchet* | *tablet.* [from OFr. *-et, -ete.*]

-et[2] (also **-ete**) ▶ **suffix** forming nouns such as *comet*, and often denoting people: *athlete* | *poet.* [from Gk. *-ētēs.*]

ETA[1] ▶ **abbr.** estimated time of arrival, in particular the time at which an aircraft or ship is expected to arrive at its destination.

ETA[2] /'etə/ a separatist movement in Spain, founded in 1959 to promote an independent Basque state. [Basque acronym, from *Euzkadi ta Azkatasuna* 'Basque homeland and liberty.']

e·ta /'ātə; 'ētə/ ▶ **n.** the seventh letter of the Greek alphabet (Η, η), transliterated as 'e' or 'ē.'

é·ta·gère /,ātä'zHer/ (also **e·ta·gere**) ▶ **n.** (pl. **é·ta·gères** /,ātä'zHer(z)/) a piece of furniture with a number of open shelves for displaying ornaments. [Fr. *étagère*, from *étage* 'shelf.']

et al. /,et 'al; ,et 'äl/ ▶ **abbr.** and others: *the conclusions of Gardner et al.* [from L. *et alii.*]

e·ta·lon /'ātl,än/ ▶ **n.** Physics a device consisting of two reflecting plates for producing interfering light beams. [20th C.: from Fr. *étalon*, lit. 'standard of measurement.']

etc. ▶ **abbr.** et cetera.

et cet·er·a /et 'set(ə)rə/ (also **et·cet·er·a**) ▶ **adv.** used at the end of a list to indicate that further, similar items are included. ■ indicating that a list is too tedious or clichéd to give in full: *Dancer, Prancer, et cetera, et cetera.* [L., from *et* 'and' and *cetera* 'the rest' (neut. pl. of *ceterus* 'left over').]

et·cet·er·as /et'set(ə)rəz/ ▶ **plural n.** dated unspecified or typical extra items.

etch /ecH/ ▶ **v.** [trans.] **1** engrave (metal, glass, or stone) by coating it with a protective layer, drawing on it with a needle, and then covering it with acid to attack the parts the needle has exposed, esp. in order to produce prints from it: [as adj.] (**etched**) *etched windows.* ■ use such a process to produce (a print or design). ■ (of an acid or other solvent) corrode or eat away the surface of (something). ■ selectively dissolve the surface of (a semiconductor or printed circuit) with a solvent, laser, or stream of electrons. **2** (usu. **be etched**) cut or carve (a text or design) on a surface. ■ mark (a surface) with a carved text or design. ■ cause to stand out or be clearly defined or visible. ▶ **n.** the action or process of etching something. — **etch·er n.** [17th C.: from Du. *etsen*, from a base meaning 'cause to eat'; rel. to **EAT.**]

etch·ant /'ecHənt/ ▶ **n.** an acid or corrosive chemical used in etching; a mordant.

etch·ing /'ecHiNG/ ▶ **n.** a print produced by the process of etching. ■ the art or process of producing etched plates or objects.

ETD ▶ **abbr.** estimated time of departure.

-ete ▶ **suffix** var. of **-ET**[2] (as in *athlete*).

e·ter·nal /i'tərnl/ ▶ **adj.** lasting or existing forever; without end or beginning. ■ (of truths, values, or questions) valid for all time; essentially unchanging. ■ informal seeming to last or persist forever, esp. on account of being tedious or annoying. ■ (**the Eternal**) used to refer to an everlasting or universal spirit, as represented by God.
– PHRASES **the Eternal City** the city of Rome. **eternal triangle** a relationship among three people, typically a couple and the lover of one of them, involving sexual rivalry. — **e·ter·nal·i·ty** /,ētər'nalitē/ **n.** **e·ter·nal·ize** /i'tərnl,īz/ **v.** **e·ter·nal·ly adv.** **e·ter·nal·ness n.** [ME: via OFr. from late L. *aeternalis*, from L. *aeternus*, from *aevum* 'age.']

e·ter·ni·ty /iˈtərnitē/ ▸ **n.** (pl. **-ties**) infinite or unending time. ▪ a state to which time has no application; timelessness. ▪ Theol. endless life after death. ▪ used euphemistically to refer to death. ▪ **(an eternity)** informal a period of time that seems very long, esp. on account of being tedious or annoying.

e·ter·nize /iˈtərˌnīz/ ▸ **v.** [trans.] literary make eternal; cause to live or last forever.

Eth. ▸ **abbr.** Ethiopia.

eth /e*TH*/ (also **edh**) ▸ **n.** an Old English letter, ð or Ð, representing the dental fricatives /*TH*/ and /TH./ Compare with THORN (sense 3). [from Dan. *edh*.]

-eth[1] ▸ **suffix** var. of -TH[1] (as in *fiftieth*).

-eth[2] (also **-th**) ▸ **suffix** archaic forming the third person singular of the present tense of verbs: *doeth* | *saith*. [OE *-eth, -ath, -th*.]

eth·a·nal /ˈeTHəˌnäl/ ▸ **n.** systematic chemical name for ACETALDEHYDE. [19th C.: blend of ETHANE and ALDEHYDE.]

eth·ane /ˈeTHˌān/ ▸ **n.** Chem. a colorless, odorless, flammable gas, C_2H_6, that is a constituent of petroleum and natural gas. It is the second member of the alkane series. [19th C.: from ETHER + -ANE[2].]

eth·a·nol /ˈeTHəˌnôl; -ˌnäl/ ▸ **n.** systematic chemical name for ETHYL ALCOHOL (see ALCOHOL). [20th C.: blend of ETHANE and ALCOHOL.]

Eth·el·red /ˈeTHəlˌred/ the name of two English kings: ▪ Ethelred I (died 871), king of Wessex and Kent 865–871; elder brother of Alfred. ▪ Ethelred II (*c.*969–1016), king of England 978–1016; known as **Ethelred the Unready**. His inability to confront the Danes after he took the throne led to his payment of tribute to prevent their attacks.

eth·ene /ˈeTHēn/ ▸ **n.** systematic chemical name for ETHYLENE. [19th C.: from ETHER + -ENE.]

e·ther /ˈēTHər/ ▸ **n. 1** Chem. a pleasant-smelling, highly flammable, colorless, volatile liquid, $C_2H_5OC_2H_5$, used as an anesthetic and as a solvent or intermediate in industrial processes. ▪ any organic compound with a similar structure to this, having an oxygen atom linking two alkyl or other organic groups. **2** (also **ae·ther**) esp. literary the clear sky; the upper regions of air beyond the clouds. **3** (also **ae·ther**) Physics, archaic a very rarefied and highly elastic substance formerly believed to permeate all space, including the interstices between the particles of matter, and to be the medium whose vibrations constituted light and other electromagnetic radiation. ▪ **(the ether)** informal air regarded as a medium for radio. — **e·ther·ic** /iˈTHerik; iˈTHi(ə)rik/ **adj.** [ME: from OFr., or via L. from Gk. *aithēr* 'upper air,' from the base of *aithein* 'burn, shine.']

e·the·re·al /iˈTHi(ə)rēəl/ ▸ **adj. 1** extremely delicate and light in a way that seems too perfect for this world. ▪ heavenly or spiritual: *ethereal, otherworldly visions.* **2** Chem. (of a solution) having diethyl ether as a solvent. — **e·the·re·al·i·ty** /iˌTHi(ə)rēˈalitē/ **n.** **e·the·re·al·ize** /-əˌlīz/ **v.** **e·the·re·al·ly** **adv.**

e·ther·ize /ˈēTHəˌrīz/ ▸ **v.** [trans.] esp. hist. anesthetize (a person or animal) with ether. — **e·ther·i·za·tion** /ˌēTHəriˈzāSHən/ **n.**

E·ther·net /ˈēTHərˌnet/ ▸ **n.** Comput., trademark a system for connecting a number of computer systems to form a local area network, with protocols to control the passing of information and to avoid simultaneous transmission by two or more systems. ▪ a network using this. [1970s: blend of ETHER and NETWORK.]

eth·ic /ˈeTHik/ ▸ **n.** [in sing.] a set of moral principles, esp. ones relating to or affirming a specified group, field, or form of conduct: *the puritan ethic.* ▸ **adj.** rare of or relating to moral principles or the branch of knowledge dealing with these. [ME: from OFr. *éthique*, from L. *ethice*, from Gk. *(hē) ēthikē (tekhnē)* '(the science of) morals,' based on *ēthos* (see ETHOS).]

eth·i·cal /ˈeTHikəl/ ▸ **adj.** of or relating to moral principles or the branch of knowledge dealing with these. ▪ morally correct. ▪ [attrib.] (of a medicine) legally available only on a doctor's prescription and usually not advertised to the general public. — **eth·i·cal·i·ty** /ˌeTHəˈkalitē/ **n.** **eth·i·cal·ly** /-ik(ə)lē/ **adv.**

eth·ics /ˈeTHiks/ ▸ **plural n. 1** [usu. treated as pl.] moral principles that govern a person's or group's behavior. ▪ the moral correctness of specified conduct. **2** [usu. treated as sing.] the branch of knowledge that deals with moral principles. — **eth·i·cist** /ˈeTHisist/ **n.**

E·thi·o·pi·a /ˌēTHēˈōpēə/ a country in northeastern Africa. Former name ABYSSINIA. *See box.*

E·thi·o·pi·an /ˌēTHēˈōpēən/ ▸ **n.** a native or national of Ethiopia, or a person of Ethiopian descent. ▪ archaic a black person. ▸ **adj. 1** of or relating to Ethiopia or its people. **2** Zool. of, relating to, or denoting a zoogeographical region comprising Africa south of the Sahara, together with the tropical part of the Arabian peninsula and (usually) Madagascar.

E·thi·op·ic /ˌēTHēˈäpik; -ˈōpik/ ▸ **n.** another term for GE'EZ. ▸ **adj.** of, in, or relating to Ge'ez.

eth·moid /ˈeTHmoid/ (also **ethmoid bone**) ▸ **n.** Anat. a square bone at the root of the nose, forming part of the cranium, and having many perforations through which the olfactory nerves pass to the nose. — **eth·moi·dal** /eTHˈmoidl/ **adj.** [18th C.: from Gk. *ēthmoeidēs*, from *ēthmos* 'a sieve.']

eth·nic /ˈeTHnik/ ▸ **adj.** of or relating to a population subgroup (within a larger or dominant national or cultural group) with a common national or cultural tradition. ▪ of or relating to national and cultural origins. ▪ denoting origin by birth or descent rather than by present nationality. ▪ characteristic of or belonging to a non-Western cultural tradition. ▪ archaic neither Christian nor Jewish; pagan or heathen. ▸ **n.** a member of an ethnic minority. — **eth·ni·cal·ly** /-k(ə)lē/ **adv.** [ME: via eccles. L. from Gk. *ethnikos* 'heathen,' from *ethnos* 'nation.']

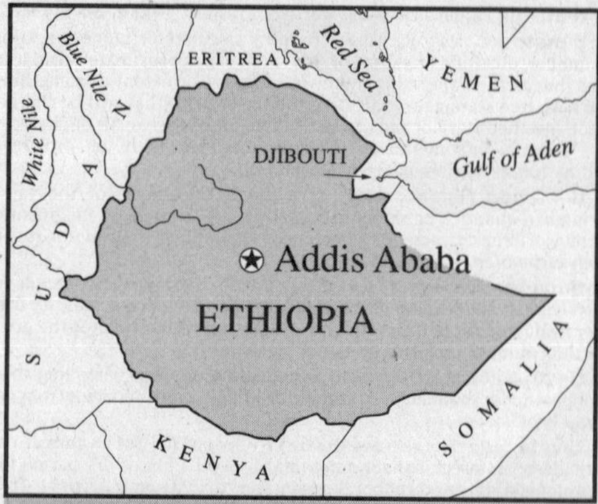

Ethiopia

Official name: Federal Democratic Republic of Ethiopia
Location: northeastern Africa, west of Somalia and north of Kenya
Area: 432,400 square miles (1,119,700 sq km)
Population: 67,251,000
Capital: Addis Ababa
Languages: Amharic (official), Arabic, English, and several other Afro-Asiatic languages
Currency: birr

eth·nic cleans·ing ▸ **n.** the mass expulsion or killing of members of an ethnic or religious group in a society.

eth·nic·i·ty /eTHˈnisitē/ ▸ **n.** (pl. **-ties**) the fact or state of belonging to a social group that has a common national or cultural tradition.

eth·nic mi·nor·i·ty ▸ **n.** a group that has different national or cultural traditions from the main population.

ethno- ▸ **comb. form** ethnic; ethnological: *ethnocentric* | *ethnology.* [from Gk. *ethnos* 'nation.']

eth·no·bot·a·ny /ˌeTHnōˈbätn-ē/ ▸ **n.** the scientific study of the traditional knowledge and customs of a people concerning plants and their medical, religious, and other uses. — **eth·no·bo·tan·ic** /-bəˈtanik/ **adj.** **eth·no·bo·tan·i·cal** /-bəˈtanikəl/ **adj.** **eth·no·bot·a·nist** /-ˈbätn-ist/ **n.**

eth·no·cen·tric /ˌeTHnōˈsentrik/ ▸ **adj.** evaluating other peoples and cultures according to the standards of one's own culture. — **eth·no·cen·tri·cal·ly** /-k(ə)lē/ **adv.** **eth·no·cen·tric·i·ty** /-senˈtrisitē/ **n.** **eth·no·cen·trism** **n.**

eth·no·cide /ˈeTHnəˌsīd/ ▸ **n.** the deliberate and systematic destruction of the culture of an ethnic group.

eth·no·cul·tur·al /ˌeTHnōˈkəlCHərəl/ ▸ **adj.** relating to or denoting a particular ethnic group.

eth·nog·ra·phy /eTHˈnägrəfē/ ▸ **n.** the scientific description of the customs of peoples and cultures. — **eth·nog·ra·pher** **n.** **eth·no·graph·ic** /ˌeTHnəˈgrafik/ **adj.** **eth·no·graph·i·cal** /ˌeTHnəˈgrafikəl/ **adj.** **eth·no·graph·i·cal·ly** /ˌeTHnəˈgrafik(ə)lē/ **adv.**

eth·no·his·to·ry /ˌeTHnōˈhist(ə)rē/ ▸ **n.** the branch of anthropology concerned with the history of peoples and cultures, esp. non-Western ones. — **eth·no·his·to·ri·an** /-hiˈstôrēən/ **n.** **eth·no·his·tor·ic** /-hiˈstôrik; -ˈstär-/ **adj.** **eth·no·his·tor·i·cal** /-hiˈstôrikəl; -ˈstär-/ **adj.** **eth·no·his·tor·i·cal·ly** /-hiˈstôrik(ə)lē; -stär-/ **adv.**

eth·no·lin·guis·tics /ˌeTHnōliNGˈgwistiks/ ▸ **plural n.** [treated as sing.] the branch of linguistics concerned with the relations between linguistic and cultural behavior. — **eth·no·lin·guist** /-ˈliNGgwist/ **n.** **eth·no·lin·guis·tic** **adj.**

eth·nol·o·gy /eTHˈnäləjē/ ▸ **n.** the study of the characteristics of various peoples and the differences and relationships among them. — **eth·no·log·ic** /ˌeTHnəˈläjik/ **adj.** **eth·no·log·i·cal** /ˌeTHnəˈläjikəl/ **adj.** **eth·no·log·i·cal·ly** /ˌeTHnəˈläjik(ə)lē/ **adv.** **eth·nol·o·gist** /-jist/ **n.**

eth·no·meth·od·ol·o·gy /ˌeTHnōˌmeTHəˈdäləjē/ ▸ **n.** a method of sociological analysis that examines how individuals use everyday conversation and gestures to construct a common-sense view of the world. — **eth·no·meth·od·o·log·i·cal** /-dəˈläjikəl/ **adj.** **eth·no·meth·od·ol·o·gist** /-jist/ **n.**

eth·no·mu·si·col·o·gy /ˌeTHnōˌmyo͞oziˈkäləjē/ ▸ **n.** the study of the music of different cultures, esp. non-Western ones. — **eth·no·mu·si·co·log·ic** /-kəˈläjik/ **adj.** **eth·no·mu·si·co·log·i·cal** /-kəˈläjikəl/ **adj.** **eth·no·mu·si·col·o·gist** /-jist/ **n.**

eth·no·sci·ence /ˌeTHnōˈsīəns/ ▸ **n.** the study of the different ways the world is perceived and categorized in different cultures.

e·tho·gram /'ēTHə,gram/ ▶ **n.** Zool. a catalog or table of all the different kinds of behavior or activity observed in an animal. [1930s: from Gk. *ēthos* 'nature, disposition' + -GRAM[1].]

e·thol·o·gy /ē'THäləjē/ ▶ **n.** the science of animal behavior. ■ the study of human behavior and social organization from a biological perspective. — **e·tho·log·i·cal** /,ēTHə'läjikəl/ **adj.** **e·thol·o·gist** /-jist/ **n.** [19th C.: via L. from Gk. *ēthologia*, from *ēthos* (see ETHOS).]

e·thos /'ēTHäs/ ▶ **n.** the characteristic spirit of a culture, era, or community as seen in its beliefs and aspirations. [19th C.: from mod. L., from Gk. *ēthos* 'nature, disposition.']

eth·ox·y·eth·ane /ə,THäksē'eTHān/ ▶ **n.** systematic chemical name for DIETHYL ETHER (see ETHER (sense 1)).

eth·yl /'eTHəl/ ▶ **n.** [usu. as adj.] Chem. of or denoting the hydrocarbon radical $-C_2H_5$, derived from ethane and present in many organic compounds: *an ethyl group.* [19th C.: from Ger., from *Äther* 'ether' + -YL.]

eth·yl ac·e·tate ▶ **n.** Chem. a colorless, volatile liquid, $CH_3COOC_2H_5$, with a fruity smell, used as a plastics solvent and in flavorings and perfumes.

eth·yl al·co·hol ▶ **n.** see ALCOHOL.

eth·yl·ene /'eTHə,lēn/ ▶ **n.** Chem. a flammable hydrocarbon gas, C_2H_4, of the alkene series, occurring in natural gas, coal gas, and crude oil and given off by ripening fruit. It is used in chemical synthesis, esp. in the manufacture of polyethylene.

eth·yl·ene gly·col ▶ **n.** Chem. a colorless viscous hygroscopic liquid, $CH_2(OH)CH_2OH$, used as an antifreeze, in the manufacture of polyesters, and in the preservation of ancient waterlogged timbers.

eth·yl·ene ox·ide ▶ **n.** Chem. a flammable toxic gas, $(CH_2)_2O$, used as an intermediate and fumigant.

eth·yne /'eTHīn; e'THīn/ ▶ **n.** systematic chemical name for ACETYLENE.

et·ic /'etik/ Anthropol. ▶ **adj.** relating to or denoting an approach to the study of a particular language or culture that is general, nonstructural, and objective in its perspective. Often contrasted with EMIC. ▶ **plural n.** (**etics**) [treated as sing.] study adopting this approach. [1950s: abstracted from PHONETIC.]

-etic ▶ **suffix** forming adjectives and nouns such as *pathetic, peripatetic.* [from Gk. -*ētikos* or -*etikos*.]

e-tick·et ▶ **n.** trademark a reservation for an airline flight for which the details are recorded electronically without the issuing of a paper ticket.

e·ti·o·lat·ed /'ētēə,lātid/ ▶ **adj.** (of a plant) pale and drawn out due to a lack of light. ■ having lost vigor or substance; feeble. — **e·ti·o·la·tion** /,ētēə'lāsHən/ **n.** [18th C.: from the v. *etiolate* (from French *étioler*, from Norman Fr. *étieuler* 'grow into haulm') + -ED[2].]

e·ti·ol·o·gy /,ētē'äləjē/ (Brit. **ae·ti·ol·o·gy**) ▶ **n.** (pl. **-gies**) **1** Med. the cause, set of causes, or manner of causation of a disease or condition. ■ the causation of diseases and disorders as a subject of investigation. **2** the investigation or attribution of the cause or reason for something, often expressed in terms of historical or mythical explanation. — **e·ti·o·log·ic** /,ētēə'läjik/ **adj.** **e·ti·o·log·i·cal** /,ētēə'läjikəl/ **adj.** **e·ti·o·log·i·cal·ly** /,ētēə'läjik(ə)lē/ **adv.** [16th C.: via med. L. from Gk. *aitiologia*, from *aitia* 'a cause' + -LOGY).]

et·i·quette /'etikit; -,ket/ ▶ **n.** the customary code of polite behavior in society or among members of a particular profession or group. [18th C.: from Fr. 'label,' from OFr. *estiquette* (see TICKET).]

Et·na, Mount /'etnə/ a volcano in eastern Sicily that rises to 10,902 feet (3,323 m). It is the highest and most active volcano in Europe.

ETO ▶ **abbr.** (in World War II) European Theater of Operations.

E·ton col·lar /'ētn/ ▶ **n.** a broad, stiff white collar worn outside the coat collar, esp. with an Eton jacket.

E·ton Col·lege a preparatory school in southern England, on the Thames opposite Windsor, founded in 1440 to prepare boys for King's College, Cambridge.

E·ton jack·et ▶ **n.** a short jacket reaching only to the waist, typically black and having a point at the back, formerly worn by students at Eton College.

é·touf·fée /ātoo'fā/ ▶ **n.** a spicy Cajun stew made with vegetables and seafood.

E·tru·ri·a /i'troorēə/ an ancient region in central Italy, between the Arno and Tiber rivers. — **E·tru·ri·an** **n. & adj.**

E·trus·can /i'trəskən/ ▶ **adj.** of or relating to ancient Etruria, its people, or their language. The Etruscan civilization was at its height c.500 BC and was an important influence on the Romans, who subdued the Etruscans by the end of the 3rd century BC. ▶ **n. 1** a native of ancient Etruria. **2** the language of ancient Etruria, of unknown affinity, written in an alphabet derived from Greek. [from L. *Etruscus* + -AN.]

et seq. (also **et seqq.**) ▶ **adv.** and what follows (used in page references). [from L. *et sequens* 'and the following,' or from *et sequentes, et sequentia* 'and the following things.']

-ette ▶ **suffix** forming nouns: **1** denoting relatively small size: *kitchenette.* **2** denoting an imitation or substitute: *flannelette.* **3** denoting female gender: *suffragette.* [from OFr. *-ette*, fem. of -ET[1].]

é·tude /ā't(y)ood/ ▶ **n.** a short musical composition, typically for one instrument, designed as an exercise to improve the technique or demonstrate the skill of the player. [19th C.: from French, literally 'study.']

e·tui /ā'twē/ ▶ **n.** (pl. **e·tuis**) dated a small ornamental case for holding needles, cosmetics, and other articles. [17th C.: from Fr. *étui*, from OFr. *estui* 'prison,' from *estuier* 'shut up, keep.']

-etum ▶ **suffix** (forming nouns) denoting a collection or plantation of trees or other plants: *arboretum* | *pinetum.* [from L.]

et ux. ▶ **abbr.** Latin et uxor (and wife).

ETV ▶ **abbr.** educational television.

etym. ▶ **abbr.** ■ etymological. ■ etymology.

et·y·mol·o·gize /,etə'mälə,jīz/ ▶ **v.** [trans.] (usu. **be etymologized**) give or trace the etymology of (a word).

et·y·mol·o·gy /,etə'mäləjē/ ▶ **n.** (pl. **-gies**)the study of the origin of words and the way in which their meanings have changed throughout history. ■ the origin of a word and the historical development of its meaning. — **et·y·mo·log·i·cal** /-mə'läjikəl/ **adj.** **et·y·mo·log·i·cal·ly** /-mə'läjik(ə)lē/ **adv.** **et·y·mol·o·gist** /-jist/ **n.** [ME: from OFr. *ethimologie*, via L. from Gk. *etumologia*, from *etumon*, neut. sing. of *etumos* 'true.']

et·y·mon /'etə,män/ ▶ **n.** (pl. **-mons** or **-ma** /-mə/) a word or morpheme from which a later word is derived. [16th C.: via L. from Gk. *etumon* 'true thing' (see ETYMOLOGY).]

EU ▶ **abbr.** European Union.

Eu ▶ **symb.** the chemical element europium.

eu- ▶ **comb. form** good; well; easily; normal: *eupeptic* | *euphony.* [from Gk. *eu* 'well,' from *eus* 'good.']

eu·bac·te·ri·um /,yoobak'ti(ə)rēəm/ ▶ **n.** (pl. **-ter·i·a** /-'ti(ə)rēə/) **1** a bacterium of a large group (kingdom Eubacteria) typically having simple cells with rigid cell walls and often flagella for movement. The group comprises the "true" bacteria and cyanobacteria, as distinct from archaebacteria. **2** a bacterium (genus *Eubacterium*) found mainly in the intestines of vertebrates and in the soil. — **eu·bac·te·ri·al** /-ti(ə)rēəl/ **adj.**

Eu·boe·a /yoo'bēə/ an island in Greece in the western Aegean Sea. Greek name ÉVVOIA.

eu·ca·lyp·tus /,yookə'liptəs/ (also **eu·ca·lypt** /'yookə,lipt/) ▶ **n.** (pl. **-tus·es** or **-ti** /-tī/) a fast-growing evergreen Australasian tree (genus *Eucalyptus*) of the myrtle family that has been widely introduced elsewhere. It is valued for its timber, oil, gum, and resin, and as an ornamental tree. Also called GUM[1], GUM TREE. ■ (also **eucalyptus oil**) the oil from eucalyptus leaves, chiefly used for its medicinal properties. [mod. L., from EU- + *kaluptos* 'covered.']

eu·car·y·ote /yoo'karē,ōt/ ▶ **n.** var. of EUKARYOTE.

Eu·cha·rist /'yookərist/ ▶ **n.** the Christian ceremony commemorating the Last Supper, in which bread and wine are consecrated and consumed. ■ the consecrated elements, esp. the bread. — **Eu·cha·ris·tic** /,yookə'ristik/ **adj.** **Eu·cha·ris·ti·cal** /,yookə'ristikəl/ **adj.** [ME: from OFr. *eucariste*, based on Greek *eukharistia* 'thanksgiving,' from Gk. *eukharistos* 'grateful,' from EU- + *kharizesthai* 'offer graciously' (from *kharis* 'grace').]

eu·chre /'yookər/ ▶ **n.** a card game for two to four players, usually played with the thirty-two highest cards. ▶ **v.** [trans.] (in this game) gain the advantage over (another player) by preventing them from taking three tricks. ■ informal deceive, outwit, or cheat (someone): *he was euchred out of his rent money.* [19th C.: from Ger. dial. *Jucker(spiel)*.]

eu·chro·ma·tin /yoo'krōmətin/ ▶ **n.** Genet. chromosome material that does not stain strongly except during cell division. It represents the major genes and is involved in transcription. Compare with HETEROCHROMATIN. — **eu·chro·mat·ic** /,yookrə'matik/ **adj.**

Eu·clid[1] /'yooklid/ a city in northeastern Ohio, northeast of Cleveland; pop. 54,875.

Eu·clid[2] (c.300 BC), Greek mathematician. His *Elements of Geometry* was the standard work until the 19th century.

Eu·clid·e·an /yoo'klidēən/ ▶ **adj.** of or relating to Euclid, in particular: ■ of or denoting the system of geometry based on the work of Euclid and corresponding to the geometry of ordinary experience. ■ of such a nature that the postulates of this system of geometry are valid. Compare with NON-EUCLIDEAN.

eu·crite /'yookrīt/ ▶ **n.** Geol. a highly basic form of gabbro containing anorthite or bytownite with augite. ■ a stony meteorite that contains no chondrules and consists mainly of anorthite and augite. [19th C.: from Gk. *eukritos* 'easily discerned,' from *eu-* 'well' + *kritos* 'separated' (from *krinein* 'to separate').]

eu·dae·mon·ic /,yoodə'mänik/ (also **eu·de·mon·ic**) ▶ **adj.** formal conducive to happiness. — **eu·dae·mo·ni·a** /-'mōnēə/ **n.**

eu·dae·mon·ism /yoo'dēmə,nizəm/ (also **eu·de·mon·ism**) ▶ **n.** a system of ethics that bases moral value on the likelihood that actions will produce happiness. — **eu·dae·mon·ist** **n.** **eu·dae·mon·is·tic** /-,dēmə'nistik/ **adj.** [19th C.: from Gk. *eudaimonismos* 'system of happiness,' from *eudaimōn* 'happy,' from EU- + *daimōn* 'guardian spirit.']

eu·di·om·e·ter /,yoodē'ämitər/ ▶ **n.** Chem. a graduated glass tube in which mixtures of gases can be made to react by an electric spark, used to measure changes in volume of gases during chemical reactions. — **eu·di·o·met·ric** /,yoodēə'metrik/ **adj.** **eu·di·o·met·ri·cal** /,yoodēə'metrikəl/ **adj.** **eu·di·om·e·try** **n.** [18th C.: from Gk. *eudios* 'clear, fine', from EU- + *dios* 'heavenly.']

Eu·gene /yoo'jēn/ a city in west central Oregon, on the Willamette River, home to the University of Oregon; pop. 137,893.

eu·gen·ics /yoo'jeniks/ ▶ **plural n.** [treated as sing.] the science of improving a human population by controlled breeding to increase the occurrence of desirable heritable characteristics. Developed in the 19th century, it fell into disfavor only after the perversion of its doctrines by the Nazis. — **eu·gen·ic** adj. **eu·gen·i·cal·ly** /-ik(ə)lē/ adv. **eu·gen·i·cist** /-isist/ n. & adj. **eu·gen·ist** n. & adj.

Eu·gé·nie /yo͞oZHā'nē/ (1826–1920), Spanish empress of France 1853–70 and wife of Napoleon III; born *Eugénia María de Montijo de Guzmán.* She was an important influence on her husband's foreign policy.

eu·ge·nol /'yo͞ojə,nôl; -,näl/ ▶ n. Chem. a colorless or pale yellow liquid compound, $C_{10}H_{12}O_2$, present in oil of cloves and other essential oils and used in perfumery. [19th C.: from *Eugenia,* named in honor of Prince *Eugene* of Savoy (1663–1736).]

eu·gle·na /yo͞o'glēnə/ ▶ n. Biol. a green, single-celled, freshwater organism (genus *Euglena*) with a flagellum, sometimes forming a green scum on stagnant water. [mod. L., from EU- + Gk. *glēnē* 'eyeball.']

eu·gle·noid /yo͞o'glēnoid/ Biol. ▶ n. a flagellated single-celled organism of a group that comprises euglena and its relatives. ▶ adj. of or relating to organisms of this group. ■ (of cell locomotion) achieved by peristaltic waves that pass along the cell, characteristic of the euglenoids.

eu·kar·y·ote /yo͞o'karē,ōt; -ēət/ (also **eu·car·y·ote**) ▶ n. Biol. an organism consisting of a cell or cells in which the genetic material is DNA in the form of chromosomes contained within a distinct nucleus. Eukaryotes include all living organisms other than the eubacteria and archaebacteria. Compare with PROKARYOTE. — **eu·kar·y·ot·ic** /-,karē'ätik/ adj. [1960s: from EU- + KARYO- 'kernel' + *-ote* as in *zygote.*]

eu·la·chon /'yo͞olə,kän/ ▶ n. (pl. same) another term for CANDLEFISH. [19th C.: from Lower Chinook *ulâkân.*]

Eu·ler[1] /'oilər/, Leonhard (1707–83), Swiss mathematician. His study of infinite series led his successors to introduce ideas of convergence and rigorous argument into mathematics.

Eu·ler[2], Ulf Svante von (1905–83), Swedish physiologist; son of Hans Euler-Chelpin. He was the first to discover a prostaglandin and also identified norepinephrine as the principal chemical neurotransmitter. Nobel Prize for Physiology or Medicine (1970, shared with Bernard Katz 1911– and Julius Axelrod 1912–).

Eu·ler-Chel·pin /'kelpin/, Hans Karl August Simon von (1873–1964), Swedish biochemist; born in Germany. He worked mainly on enzymes and vitamins. Nobel Prize for Chemistry (1929, shared with Arthur Harden 1865–1940).

eu·lo·gi·um /yo͞o'lōjēəm/ ▶ n. (pl. **-gi·a** /-jēə/ or **-gi·ums**) another term for EULOGY. [17th C.: from medieval Latin, 'praise.']

eu·lo·gize /'yo͞olə,jīz/ ▶ v. [trans.] praise highly in speech or writing. — **eu·lo·gist** /-jist/ n. **eu·lo·gis·tic** /,yo͞olə'jistik/ adj. **eu·lo·gis·ti·cal·ly** /'yo͞olə'jistik(ə)lē/ adv.

eu·lo·gy /'yo͞oləjē/ ▶ n. (pl. **-gies**) a speech or piece of writing that praises someone or something highly, typically someone who has just died. [ME: from med. L. *eulogium, eulogia* (from Greek *eulogia* 'praise'), appar. influenced by L. *elogium* 'inscription on a tomb' (from Gk. *elegia* 'elegy').]

Eu·men·i·des /yo͞o'meni,dēz/ Gk. Mythol. a name given to the Furies. The Eumenides probably originated as well-disposed deities of fertility, whose name was given to the Furies either by confusion or euphemistically. [via L. from Gk., from *eumenēs* 'well disposed,' from EU- + *menos* 'spirit.']

eu·nuch /'yo͞onək/ ▶ n. a castrated man, esp. one who guards the women's living areas at an oriental court. ■ an ineffectual person: *a nation of political eunuchs.* [OE, via L. from Gk. *eunoukhos,* lit. 'bedroom guard,' from *eunē* 'bed' + *ekhein* 'to hold.']

eu·on·y·mus /yo͞o'änəməs/ ▶ n. a shrub or small tree (genus *Euonymus,* family Celastraceae), widely cultivated for its autumn colors and bright fruit. [mod. L., from L. *euonymos,* from Gk. *euōnumos* 'having a good name,' from EU- + *onoma* 'name.']

eu·pep·tic /yo͞o'peptik/ ▶ adj. of or having good digestion or a consequent air of healthy good spirits. [17th C.: from Gk. *eupeptos,* from EU- + *peptein* 'to digest.']

eu·phau·si·id /yo͞o'fôzēid/ ▶ n. Zool. a shrimplike, planktonic marine crustacean of an order (Euphausiaceae) that includes krill. Many kinds are luminescent. [19th C.: from mod. L. *Euphausia* (genus name from EU- + *phainein* 'to show' + *ousia* 'substance') + -ID[2].]

eu·phe·mism /'yo͞ofə,mizəm/ ▶ n. a mild or indirect word or expression for one too harsh or blunt when referring to something unpleasant or embarrassing: *"downsizing" as* ***a euphemism for*** *layoffs.* The opposite of DYSPHEMISM. [16th C.: from Gk. *euphēmismos,* from *euphēmizein* 'use auspicious words,' from EU- + *phēmē* 'speaking.']

eu·phe·mis·tic /,yo͞ofə'mistik/ ▶ adj. using or of the nature of a euphemism. — **eu·phe·mis·ti·cal·ly** /-k(ə)lē/ adv.

eu·phe·mize /'yo͞ofə,mīz/ ▶ v. [trans.] refer to (something unpleasant or embarrassing) by means of a euphemism.

eu·pho·ni·ous /yo͞o'fōnēəs/ ▶ adj. (of sound, esp. speech) pleasing to the ear. — **eu·pho·ni·ous·ly** adv.

eu·pho·ni·um /yo͞o'fōnēəm/ ▶ n. a valved brass musical instrument resembling a small tuba of tenor pitch, played mainly in military and brass bands. [19th C.: from Gk. *euphōnos.*]

eu·pho·ny /'yo͞ofənē/ ▶ n. (pl. **-nies**) the quality of being pleasing to the ear, esp. through a harmonious combination of words. ■ the tendency to make phonetic change for ease of pronunciation. — **eu·phon·ic** /yo͞o'fänik/ adj. **eu·pho·nize** /-,nīz/ v. [ME: from Fr. *euphonie,* via late L. from Gk. *euphōnia,* from *euphōnos* 'well sounding' (based on *phōnē* 'sound').]

eu·phor·bi·a /yo͞o'fôrbēə/ ▶ n. a plant of a genus (*Euphorbia*) that comprises the spurges. [ME: from L. *euphorbea,* named after *Euphorbus,* Greek physician.]

eu·pho·ri·a /yo͞o'fôrēə/ ▶ n. a feeling or state of intense excitement and happiness. [17th C.: mod. L., from Gk., from *euphoros* 'healthy,' from EU- + *pherein* 'to bear.']

eu·pho·ri·ant /yo͞o'fôrēənt/ ▶ adj. (chiefly of a drug) producing a feeling of euphoria. ▶ n. a euphoriant drug.

eu·phor·ic /yo͞o'fôrik; -'fär-/ ▶ adj. characterized by or feeling intense excitement and happiness. — **eu·phor·i·cal·ly** /-k(ə)lē/ adv.

eu·phra·sia /yo͞o'frāZHə/ ▶ n. a plant of the genus *Euphrasia* in the figwort family, esp. eyebright. ■ a preparation of eyebright used in herbal medicine and homeopathy, esp. for treating eye problems. [18th C.: via medieval Latin from Greek, literally 'cheerfulness'.]

Eu·phra·tes /yo͞o'frātēz/ a river of southwestern Asia that rises in Turkey and flows for 1,700 miles (2,736 km) through Syria and Iraq to join the Tigris River to form the Shatt al-Arab waterway.

eu·phu·ism /'yo͞ofyo͞o'izəm/ ▶ n. formal an artificial, highly elaborate way of writing or speaking. — **eu·phu·ist** n. **eu·phu·is·tic** /,yo͞ofyo͞o'istik/ adj. **eu·phu·is·ti·cal·ly** /,yo͞ofyo͞o'istik(ə)lē/ adv. [16th C.: from *Euphues,* a character in John Lyly's prose romance of the same name (1578–80).]

Eur·a·sia /yo͞o'rāZHə/ a term used to describe the combined continental landmass of Europe and Asia.

Eur·a·sian /yo͞o'rāZHən/ ▶ adj. **1** of mixed European (or European-American) and Asian parentage. **2** of or relating to Eurasia. ▶ n. a person of mixed European (or European-American) and Asian parentage.

eu·re·ka /yo͞o'rēkə; yə-/ ▶ exclam. a cry of joy or satisfaction when one finds or discovers something. [17th C.: from Greek *heurēka* 'I have found it' (from *heuriskein* 'find').]

eu·rhyth·mics ▶ plural n. var. of EURYTHMICS.

eu·rhyth·my ▶ n. var. of EURYTHMY.

Eu·rip·i·des /yo͞o'ripə,dēz/ (480–*c.*406 BC), Greek tragedian. Notable works include *Medea, Hippolytus, Electra, Trojan Women,* and *Bacchae.*

eu·ro /'yərō; 'yo͞orō/ ▶ n. (pl. **eu·ros** or **eu·ro**) (also **Eu·ro**) the single European currency that was introduced into some of the states of the European Union countries in 1999 as an alternative currency in non-cash transactions and replaced national currencies in 2002. ▶ adj. (usu. **Euro**) [attrib.] informal European, esp. concerned with the European Union. [independent usage of EURO-.]

Euro- ▶ comb. form European; European and ...: *Euro-American.* ■ relating to Europe or the European Union: *Eurocommunism | a Euro-MP.*

Eu·ro·bond /'yərə,bänd; 'yo͞orō-/ ▶ n. an international bond issued in Europe or elsewhere outside the country in whose currency its value is stated (usually the US or Japan).

Eu·ro·cen·tric /,yərō'sentrik; ,yo͞orō-/ ▶ adj. focusing on European culture or history to the exclusion of a wider view of the world; implicitly regarding European culture as preeminent. — **Eu·ro·cen·tric·i·ty** /-sen'trisitē/ n. **Eu·ro·cen·trism** /-'sen,trizəm/ n.

Eu·ro·com·mu·nism /,yərō'kämyə,nizəm; ,yo͞orō-/ ▶ n. a political system formerly advocated by some communist parties in western European countries, stressing independence from the Soviet Communist Party and preservation of many elements of Western liberal democracy. — **Eu·ro·com·mu·nist** adj. & n.

Eu·ro·crat /'yərə,krat; 'yo͞orə-/ ▶ n. informal, esp. derog. a European Union bureaucrat.

Eu·ro·cur·ren·cy /'yərō,kərənsē; 'yo͞orō-/ ▶ n. a form of money held or traded outside the country in whose currency its value is stated (originally US dollars held in Europe).

Eu·ro·dol·lar /'yərō,dälər; 'yo͞orō-/ ▶ n. a US dollar deposit held in Europe or elsewhere outside the US.

Eu·ro·mar·ket /'yərō,märkit; 'yo͞orō-/ ▶ n. **1** a financial market that deals with Eurocurrencies. **2** the European Union regarded as a single commercial or financial market.

Eu·ro·pa /yə'rōpə; yo͞o-/ **1** Gk. Mythol. a princess of Tyre who was courted by Zeus in the form of a bull. She was carried off by him to Crete. **2** Astron. one of the Galilean moons of Jupiter, the sixth closest satellite to the planet, having a diameter of 1,951 miles (3,140 km).

Eu·rope /'yərəp; 'yo͞or-/ a continent in the northern hemisphere, separated from Africa on the south by the Mediterranean Sea and from Asia on the east roughly by the Bosporus, the Caucasus Mountains, and the Ural Mountains.

Eu·ro·pe·an /,yərə'pēən; ,yo͞orə-/ ▶ adj. of, relating to, or characteristic of Europe or its inhabitants. ■ of or relating to the European Union. ▶ n. a native or inhabitant of Europe. ■ a national of a state belonging to the European Union. ■ a person who is committed to the European Union: *they claimed to be the party of good Europeans.* ■ a person who is white or of European parentage, esp. in a country with a large nonwhite population. — **Eu·ro·pe·an·ism** n.

Eu·ro·pe·an Com·mu·ni·ty (abbr.: EC) an economic and political association of certain European countries, incorporated since 1993 in the European Union.

Eu·ro·pe·an Ec·o·nom·ic Com·mu·ni·ty (abbr.: EEC) an institution of the European Union, an economic association of western European countries set up by the Treaty of Rome (1957). The original members

were France, West Germany, Italy, Belgium, the Netherlands, and Luxembourg. See also **European Community** and **European Union**.

Eu·ro·pe·an·ize /ˌyərəˈpēəˌnīz; ˌyo͝orə-/ ▶v. [trans.] [often as adj.] (**Europeanized**) give (someone or something) a European character or scope. ▪ transfer to the control or responsibility of the European Union. —**Eu·ro·pe·an·i·za·tion** /ˌyərəˌpēəniˈzāshən; ˌyo͝orə-/ n.

Eu·ro·pe·an Par·lia·ment the Parliament of the European Community, originally established in 1952.

Eu·ro·pe·an plan ▶n. a system of charging for a hotel room only, without meals. Often contrasted with **American plan**.

Eu·ro·pe·an Space A·gen·cy (abbr.: **ESA**) an organization set up in 1975 to coordinate the national space programs of the collaborating countries.

Eu·ro·pe·an Un·ion (abbr.: **EU**) an economic and political association of certain European countries with internal free trade and common external tariffs. It was created on November 1, 1993, with the coming into force of the Maastricht Treaty and encompasses the old European Community (EC) and two intergovernmental 'pillars' dealing with foreign affairs and with immigration and justice.

eu·ro·pi·um /yəˈrōpēəm/ ▶n. the chemical element of atomic number 63, a soft silvery-white metal of the lanthanide series. Europium oxide is used with yttrium oxide as a red phosphor in color television screens. (Symbol: **Eu**) [20th C.: mod. L., based on **Europe**.]

Eu·ro·trash /ˈyərōˌtrash; ˈyo͝orō-/ ▶n. informal rich European socialites, esp. those living or working in the United States.

eury- ▶comb. form denoting a wide variety or range of something specified: *eurytopic*. [from Gk. *eurus* 'wide.']

Eu·ryd·i·ce /yəˈridəsē/ Gk. Mythol. the wife of Orpheus. After she died, Orpheus secured her release from the underworld on the condition that he not look back at her on their way back to the world of the living. But Orpheus did look back, whereupon Eurydice disappeared.

eu·ry·ha·line /ˌyərəˈhālīn; -ˈhal-/ ▶adj. Ecol. (of an aquatic organism) able to tolerate a wide range of salinity. Often contrasted with **stenohaline**. [19th C.: from Gk. *eurus* 'wide' + *halinos* 'of salt.']

eu·ryp·ter·id /yəˈriptərid/ ▶n. an extinct marine arthropod of a group (subclass Eurypterida, class Merostomata, subphylum Chelicerata) occurring in the Paleozoic era. They are related to horseshoe crabs and resemble large scorpions with a terminal pair of paddle-shaped swimming appendages. [19th C.: from mod. L. *Eurypterus* (genus name), from **eury-** + Gk. *pteron* 'wing' + **-id²**.]

eu·ry·ther·mal /ˌyo͝orəˈthərməl/ (also **eu·ry·ther·mic**) ▶adj. Ecol. (of an organism) able to tolerate a wide range of temperatures. Often contrasted with **stenothermal**.

eu·ryth·mic /yəˈrit͟hmik; yo͞o-/ ▶adj. rare (esp. of architecture or art) in or relating to harmonious proportion.

eu·ryth·mics /yəˈrit͟hmiks; yo͞o-/ ▶plural n. [treated as sing.] a system of rhythmical physical movements to music used to teach musical understanding or for therapeutic purposes. [20th C.: from **eu-** 'well' + **rhythm** + **-ics**.]

eu·ryth·my /yo͞oˈrit͟hmē/ ▶n. another term for **eurythmics**. [17th C.: via L. from Gk. *euruthmia*, from **eu-** + *rhuthmos* 'proportion, rhythm.']

eu·ry·top·ic /ˌyərəˈtäpik; yo͝orə-/ ▶adj. Ecol. (of an organism) able to tolerate a wide range of habitats or ecological conditions. Often contrasted with **stenotopic**.

Eu·se·bi·us /yo͞oˈsēbēəs/ (c.AD 264–c.340), bishop and church historian; known as **Eusebius of Caesaria**. His *Ecclesiastical History* traces Christianity (esp. in the Eastern Church) from the age of the Apostles until 324.

eu·so·cial /yo͞oˈsōshəl/ ▶adj. Zool. (of an animal species, esp. an insect) showing an advanced level of social organization, in which a single female or caste produces the offspring and nonreproductive individuals cooperate in caring for the young. —**eu·so·ci·al·i·ty** /-ˌsōshēˈalitē/ n.

Eu·sta·chian tube /yo͞oˈstāsh(ē)ən; -kēən/ ▶n. Anat. a narrow passage leading from the pharynx to the cavity of the middle ear, permitting the equalization of pressure on each side of the eardrum. [18th C.: named after Bartolomeo *Eustachio* (died 1574), Italian anatomist.]

eu·sta·sy /ˈyo͞ostəsē/ ▶n. a change of sea level throughout the world, caused typically by movements of parts of the earth's crust or melting of glaciers. —**eu·sta·tic** /yo͞oˈstatik/ adj. [1940s: back-form. from *eustatic*, coined in Ger. from **eu-** 'well' + Gk.*statikos* 'static.']

eu·tec·tic /yo͞oˈtektik/ Chem. ▶adj. relating to or denoting a mixture of substances (in fixed proportions) that melts and solidifies at a single temperature that is lower than the melting points of the separate constituents or of any other mixture of them. [19th C.: from Gk. *eutēktos* 'easily melting,' from **eu-** + *tēkein* 'melt.']

eu·tec·toid /yo͞oˈtektoid/ Metallurgy ▶adj. relating to or denoting an alloy that has a minimum transformation temperature between a solid solution and a simple mixture of metals. ▶n. a eutectoid mixture or alloy.

Eu·ter·pe /yo͞oˈtərpē/ Greek Rom. Mythol. the Muse of flute playing and lyric poetry. [Greek, literally 'well-pleasing.']

eu·tha·na·sia /ˌyo͞oTHəˈnāZHə/ ▶ **n.** the painless killing of a patient suffering from an incurable and painful disease or in an irreversible coma. The practice is illegal in most countries. [17th C.: from EU- + Gk. *thanatos* 'death.']

eu·tha·nize /ˈyo͞oTHəˌnīz/ ▶ **v.** [trans.] (usu. **be euthanized**) put (a living being, esp. a dog or cat) to death humanely.

Eu·the·ri·a /yo͞oˈTHi(ə)rēə/ Zool. a major group of mammals that comprises the placentals. Compare with METATHERIA. — **eu·the·ri·an n. & adj.** [mod. L. (pl.), from EU- + Gk. *thērion* 'wild beast.']

eu·thy·roid /yo͞oˈTHīroid/ ▶ **adj.** Med. having a normally functioning thyroid gland.

eu·troph·ic /yo͞oˈträfik; -ˈtrō-/ ▶ **adj.** Ecol. (of a lake or other body of water) rich in nutrients and so supporting a dense plant population, the decomposition of which kills animal life by depriving it of oxygen. Compare with DYSTROPHIC and OLIGOTROPHIC. [18th C.: from Gk. *eutrophia*, from EU- + *trephein* 'nourish.']

eu·troph·i·ca·tion /yo͞oˌträfiˈkāSHən/ ▶ **n.** excessive richness of nutrients in a lake or other body of water, frequently due to runoff from the land, which causes a dense growth of plant life. — **eu·troph·i·cate** /yo͞oˈträfiˌkāt/ **v.**

eV ▶ **abbr.** electron volt(s).

EVA ▶ **abbr.** ■ (in space) extravehicular activity.

e·vac·u·ant /iˈvakyo͞oənt/ ▶ **n.** a medicine that induces some kind of bodily discharge, such as an emetic, a sudorific, or esp. a laxative. ▶ **adj.** (of a medicine or treatment) acting to induce some kind of bodily discharge.

e·vac·u·ate /iˈvakyo͞oˌāt/ ▶ **v.** [trans.] **1** remove (someone) from a place of danger to a safe place. ■ leave or cause the occupants to leave (a place of danger). ■ (of troops) withdraw from (a place). **2** tech. remove air, water, or other contents from (a container). ■ empty (the bowels or another bodily organ). ■ discharge (feces or other matter) from the body. [ME: from L. *evacuat-* 'emptied,' from *evacuare*, from *e-* 'out of' + *vacuus* 'empty.']

e·vac·u·a·tion /iˌvakyo͞oˈāSHən/ ▶ **n.** **1** the action of evacuating a person or a place. **2** the action of emptying the bowels or another bodily organ. ■ a quantity of matter discharged from the bowels or another bodily organ. ■ tech. the action of emptying a container of air, water, or other contents.

e·vac·u·a·tive /iˈvakyo͞oˌātiv/ ▶ **adj. & n.** another term for EVACUANT.

e·vac·u·ee /iˌvakyo͞oˈē/ ▶ **n.** a person evacuated from a place of danger to somewhere safe. [20th C.: from Fr. *évacué*, past part. of *évacuer*, from L. *evacuare* (see EVACUATE).]

e·vade /iˈvād/ ▶ **v.** [trans.] escape or avoid, esp. by cleverness or trickery. ■ (of an abstract thing) elude (someone). ■ avoid giving a direct answer to (a question). ■ avoid dealing with or accepting; contrive not to do (something morally or legally required). ■ escape paying (tax or duty), esp. by illegitimate presentation of one's finances. ■ defeat the intention of (a law or rule), esp. while complying with its letter. — **e·vad·a·ble adj. e·vad·er n.** [15th C.: from Fr. *évader*, from L. *evadere*, from *e-* 'out of' + *vadere* 'go.']

e·vag·i·nate /iˈvajəˌnāt/ ▶ **v.** [trans.] Biol. Physiol. turn (a tubular or pouch-shaped organ or structure) inside out. ■ [intrans.] (of such a structure or organ) turn inside out. — **e·vag·i·na·tion** /iˌvajəˈnāSHən/ **n.** [17th C.: from L. *evaginat-* 'unsheathed,' from *evaginare*, from *e-* 'out of' + *vagina* 'sheath.']

e·val·u·ate /iˈvalyo͞oˌāt/ ▶ **v.** [trans.] form an idea of the amount, number, or value of; assess. ■ Math. find a numerical expression or equivalent for (an equation, formula, or function). — **e·val·u·a·tion** /iˌvalyo͞oˈāSHən/ **n. e·val·u·a·tive** /-yo͞oˌātiv; -ətiv/ **adj. e·val·u·a·tor** /-yo͞oˌātər/ **n.** [19th C.: back-form. from *evaluation*, from Fr. *évaluer*, from *es-* (from L. *ex-*) 'out, from' + OFr. *value* 'value.']

ev·a·nesce /ˌevəˈnes/ ▶ **v.** [intrans.] literary pass out of sight, memory, or existence. [19th C.: from L. *evanescere*, from *e-* 'out of' + *vanus* 'empty.']

ev·a·nes·cent /ˌevəˈnesənt/ ▶ **adj.** esp. literary soon passing out of sight, memory, or existence; quickly fading or disappearing. ■ Physics denoting a field or wave that extends into a region where it cannot propagate and whose amplitude therefore decreases with distance. — **ev·a·nes·cence n. ev·a·nes·cent·ly adv.**

evang. (or **Evang.**) ▶ **abbr.** ■ evangelical. ■ evangelist.

e·van·gel /iˈvanjəl/ ▶ **n.** **1** archaic the Christian gospel. ■ any of the four Gospels. **2** another term for EVANGELIST. [ME: from OFr. *evangile*, via eccles. L. from Gk. *euangelion* 'good news,' from *euangelos* 'bringing good news,' from EU- + *angelein* 'announce.']

e·van·gel·i·cal /ˌēvanˈjelikəl/ ▶ **adj.** of or according to the teaching of the gospel or the Christian religion. ■ of or denoting a tradition within Protestant Christianity emphasizing the authority of the Bible, personal conversion, and salvation by faith in the Atonement. ■ zealous in advocating something. ▶ **n.** a member of the evangelical tradition in the Christian Church. — **e·van·gel·ic adj. e·van·gel·i·cal·ism n. e·van·gel·i·cal·ly adv.**

e·van·ge·lism /iˈvanjəˌlizəm/ ▶ **n.** the spreading of the Christian gospel by preaching or personal witness. ■ zealous advocacy of a cause.

e·van·ge·list /iˈvanjəlist/ ▶ **n.** **1** a person who seeks to convert others to the Christian faith, esp. by preaching. ■ a layperson engaged in Christian missionary work. ■ a zealous advocate of something. **2** the writer of one of the four Gospels (Matthew, Mark, Luke, or John): *St. John the Evangelist.* — **e·van·ge·lis·tic** /iˌvanjəˈlistik/ **adj.**

e·van·ge·lize /iˈvanjəˌlīz/ ▶ **v.** [trans.] convert or seek to convert (someone) to Christianity. ■ [intrans.] preach the Christian gospel. — **e·van·ge·li·za·tion** /iˌvanjəliˈzāSHən/ **n. e·van·ge·liz·er n.**

Ev·ans[1] /ˈevənz/, Sir Arthur John (1851–1941), English archaeologist. His excavations at Knossos (1899–1935) resulted in the discovery of the Bronze Age civilization of Crete, which he named Minoan.

Ev·ans[2], Mary Ann, see ELIOT[3].

Ev·ans·ton /ˈevənstən/ **1** a city in northeastern Illinois, just north of Chicago; pop. 74,239. **2** a city in southwestern Wyoming, next to the Utah border, southwest of Green River; pop. 11,507.

Ev·ans·ville /ˈevənzˌvil/ a port city in southwestern Indiana, on the Ohio River; pop. 121,582.

evap. ▶ **abbr.** evaporate.

e·vap·o·rate /iˈvapəˌrāt/ ▶ **v.** turn from liquid into vapor. ■ lose or cause to lose moisture or solvent as vapor. ■ [intrans.] (of something abstract) cease to exist: *militancy evaporated in the wake of defeat.* — **e·vap·o·ra·ble** /-rəbəl/ **adj. e·vap·o·ra·tion** /iˌvapəˈrāSHən/ **n. e·vap·o·ra·tor** /-ˌrātər/ **n.** [ME: from L. *evaporat-* 'changed into vapor,' from *evaporare*, from *e-* 'out of' + *vapor* 'steam.']

e·vap·o·rat·ed milk ▶ **n.** thick, sweetened milk that has had some of the liquid removed by evaporation.

e·vap·o·ra·tive /iˈvapəˌrātiv/ ▶ **adj.** relating to or involving evaporation: *evaporative water loss.*

e·vap·o·ra·tive cool·ing ▶ **n.** reduction in temperature resulting from the evaporation of a liquid, which removes latent heat from the surface from which evaporation takes place. This process is employed in industrial and domestic cooling systems, and is also the physical basis of sweating.

e·vap·o·rite /iˈvapəˌrīt/ ▶ **n.** Geol. a natural salt or mineral deposit left after the evaporation of a body of water. [1920s: alt. of EVAPORATE (see also -ITE[1]).]

e·vap·o·tran·spi·ra·tion /iˌvapōˌtranspəˈrāSHən/ ▶ **n.** the process by which water is transferred from the land to the atmosphere by evaporation from the soil and other surfaces and by transpiration from plants.

e·va·sion /iˈvāZHən/ ▶ **n.** the action of evading something. ■ an indirect answer; a prevaricating excuse. [ME (in the sense 'prevaricating excuse'): via OFr. from L. *evasio(n-)*, from *evadere* (see EVADE).]

e·va·sive /iˈvāsiv/ ▶ **adj.** tending to avoid commitment or self-revelation, esp. by responding only indirectly. ■ directed toward avoidance or escape. — **e·va·sive·ly adv. e·va·sive·ness n.**

Eve /ēv/ (in the Bible) the first woman, wife of Adam and mother of Cain and Abel.

eve /ēv/ ▶ **n.** the day or period of time immediately before an event or occasion. ■ the evening or day before a religious festival. ■ esp. literary evening: *a bitter winter's eve.* [ME (in the sense 'close of day'): short form of EVEN[2].]

e·vec·tion /iˈvekSHən/ ▶ **n.** Astron. regular variation in the eccentricity of the moon's orbit around the earth, caused mainly by the sun's attraction. [17th C. (in the sense 'elevation, exaltation'): from L. *evectio(n-)*, from *evehere* 'carry out or up,' from *e-* (var. of *ex-*) 'out' + *vehere* 'carry.']

e·ven[1] /ˈēvən/ ▶ **adj.** (**e·ven·er, e·ven·est**) **1** flat and smooth. ■ in the same plane or line; level. ■ having little variation in quality; regular. ■ equal in number, amount, or value. ■ equally balanced. ■ exactly equal to a round number; not having any fractions. ■ (of a person's temper or disposition) equable; calm. **2** (of a number, such as 2, 6, or 108) divisible by two without a remainder. ■ bearing such a number: *odd or even pages.* ▶ **v.** make or become even. ▶ **adv.** used to emphasize something surprising or extreme. ■ used in comparisons for emphasis: *he knows even less about it than I do.*

— PHRASES **even as** at the very same time as: *even as he spoke, their baggage was being unloaded.* **an even break** informal a fair chance. **even if** despite the possibility that; no matter whether: *always try, even if you think you can't.* ■ despite the fact that. **even now** (or **then**) **1** now (or then) as well as before. **2** in spite of what has (or had) happened. **3** at this (or that) very moment. **even so** in spite of that; nevertheless. **even though** despite the fact that: *even though he was bigger, he never looked down on me.* **get** (or **be**) **even** informal inflict trouble or harm on someone similar to that which they have inflicted on oneself. **of even date** Law formal of the same date. **on an even keel** (of a ship or aircraft) having the same draft forward and aft. ■ fig. (of a person or situation) functioning normally after a period of difficulty. — **e·ven·ly adv. e·ven·ness n.** [OE *efen* (adj.), *efne* (adv.), of Gmc. origin; rel. to Du. *even, effen* and Ger. *eben.*]

e·ven[2] ▶ **n.** archaic literary the end of the day; evening: *bring it to my house this even.* [OE *ǣfen*, of Gmc. origin; rel. to Du. *avont* and Ger. *Abend.*]

e·ven-aged ▶ **adj.** Forestry (of woodland) composed of trees of approximately the same age. ■ (of trees) of approximately the same age.

eve·ning /ˈēvniNG/ ▶ **n.** the period of time at the end of the day, usually from about 6 p.m. to bedtime. ■ this time characterized by a specified type of activity or particular weather conditions. ■ [as adj.] prescribed by fashion as suitable for relatively formal social events held in the evening: *evening dress.* ▶ **adv.** (**evenings**) informal in the evening; every evening. ▶ **exclam.** informal short for GOOD EVENING. [OE *ǣfnung* 'dusk falling, the time around sunset,' from *ǣfnian* 'approach evening,' from *ǣfen* (see EVEN[2]).]

eve·ning gown ▶ **n.** a long, elegant dress suitable for wearing on formal occasions.

eve·ning gros·beak ▸**n.** a North American grosbeak (*Coccothraustes vespertinus*), with yellow coloring.

eve·ning prayer ▸**n.** a prayer said in the evening. ■ (usu. **evening prayers**) a formal act of worship held in the evening. ■ [in sing.] (in the Anglican Church) the service of evensong.

eve·ning prim·rose ▸**n.** a yellow-flowered plant (genus *Oenothera*, family Onagraceae) yielding seeds from which a medicinal oil is extracted.

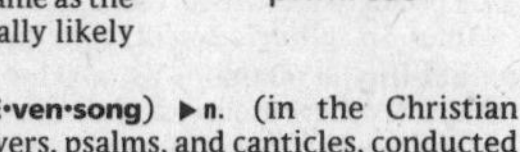

common evening primrose

eve·ning star ▸**n.** (**the evening star**) the planet Venus, seen shining in the western sky after sunset.

eve·ning wear ▸**n.** clothing, esp. for women, that is suitable for wearing on formal social occasions.

E·ven·ki /i'weNGkē; i'veNGkē/ ▸**n.** (pl. same or **-kis**) **1** a member of a native people of northern Siberia. Also called **TUNGUS.** **2** the Tungusic language of this people. ▸**adj.** of or relating to this people or their language.

e·ven mon·ey ▸**n.** (in betting) odds offering an equal chance of winning or losing, with the amount won being the same as the stake. ■ [as adj.] (of a chance) equally likely to happen or not; fifty-fifty.

e·ven·song /'ēvən,sôNG/ (also **E·ven·song**) ▸**n.** (in the Christian Church) a service of evening prayers, psalms, and canticles, conducted according to a set form, esp. that of the Anglican Church [OE *ǣfensang* (see **EVEN**², **SONG**).]

e·ven-ste·ven /'stēvən/ ▸**adj. & adv.** informal used in reference to fair and equal competition or distribution of resources. [19th C.: rhyming phr., used as an intensive.]

e·vent /i'vent/ ▸**n.** a thing that happens, esp. one of importance. ■ a planned public or social occasion. ■ each of several contests making up a sports competition. ■ Physics a single occurrence of a process, e.g., the ionization of one atom.

– PHRASES **in any event** (or **at all events**) whatever happens or may have happened. **in the event** as it turns (or turned) out: *this important and, in the event, quite fruitless mission.* **in the event of —** if — happens: *the chance of serious injury in the event of an accident.* **in the event that** if; should it happen that. **in that event** if that happens. — **e·vent·less adj. e·vent·less·ness n.** [16th C.: from L. *eventus*, from *evenire* 'result, happen,' from *e-* (var. of *ex-*) 'out of' + *venire* 'come.']

e·ven-tem·pered ▸**adj.** not easily annoyed or angered.

e·vent·ful /i'ventfəl/ ▸**adj.** marked by interesting or exciting events. — **e·vent·ful·ly adv. e·vent·ful·ness n.**

e·vent ho·ri·zon ▸**n.** Astron. a theoretical boundary around a black hole beyond which no light or other radiation can escape.

e·ven·tide /'ēvən,tīd/ ▸**n.** archaic literary the end of the day; evening: *the moon flower opens its white, trumpetlike flowers at eventide.* [OE *ǣfentīd* (see **EVEN**², **TIDE**).]

e·vent·ive /i'ventiv/ ▸**adj.** Ling. (of the subject or object of a sentence) denoting an event.

e·ven-toed un·gu·late ▸**n.** a hoofed mammal of an order (Artiodactyla) that includes the ruminants, camels, pigs, and hippopotamuses. Mammals of this group have either two or four toes on each foot. Compare with **ODD-TOED UNGULATE.**

even-toed ungulate

e·ven·tu·al /i'venCHōōəl/ ▸**adj.** [attrib.] occurring at the end of or as a result of a series of events; final; ultimate. [17th C.: from L. *eventus*.]

e·ven·tu·al·i·ty /i,venCHōō'alitē/ ▸**n.** (pl. **-ties**) a possible event or outcome.

e·ven·tu·al·ly /i'venCHōōəlē/ ▸**adv.** [sentence adverb] in the end, esp. after a long delay, dispute, or series of problems: *eventually, after midnight, I arrived at the hotel.*

e·ven·tu·ate /i'venCHōō,āt/ ▸**v.** [intrans.] formal occur as a result. ■ (**eventuate in**) lead to as a result: *circumstances that eventuate in crime.* — **e·ven·tu·a·tion** /i,venCHōō'āSHən/ **n.**

ev·er /'evər/ ▸**adv. 1** [usu. with negative or in questions] at any time. ■ used in comparisons for emphasis: *they felt better than ever before.* **2** at all times; always. **3** [with comparative] increasingly; constantly. **4** used for emphasis in questions expressing astonishment or outrage: *who ever heard of such a thing?*

– PHRASES **ever and anon** archaic occasionally. **ever since** throughout the period since. **ever so** very: *I am ever so grateful.* **for ever** see **FOREVER.** [OE *ǣfre*, of unknown origin.]

ev·er·bloom·ing /'evər'blōōmiNG/ ▸**adj.** (of a plant) in bloom throughout most or all of the growing season.

Ev·er·est, Mount /'ev(ə)rəst/ a mountain in the Himalayas, on the border between Nepal and Tibet. Rising to 29,028 feet (8,848 m), it is the highest mountain in the world.

Ev·er·ett /'ev(ə)rit/ **1** a city in northeastern Massachusetts, just north of Boston; pop. 35,701. **2** a port in northwestern Washington, north of Seattle; pop. 91,488.

ev·er·glade /'evər,glād/ ▸**n.** a marshy tract of land that is mostly under water and covered with tall grass.

Ev·er·glades /'evər,glādz/ a vast area of marshland and coastal mangrove in southern Florida, part of which is protected as a national park.

ev·er·green /'evər,grēn/ ▸**adj.** of or denoting a plant that retains green leaves throughout the year. Often contrasted with **DECIDUOUS.** ▸**n.** a plant that retains green leaves throughout the year.

ev·er·green oak ▸**n.** another term for **HOLM OAK.**

ev·er·last·ing /,evər'lastiNG/ ▸**adj.** lasting forever or for a very long time. ▸**n. 1** literary eternity. **2** (also **everlasting flower**) a flower of the daisy family with a papery texture, retaining its shape and color after being dried, esp. a helichrysum. Also called **IMMORTELLE.** — **ev·er·last·ing·ly adv. ev·er·last·ing·ness n.**

ev·er·more /,evər'môr/ ▸**adv.** (chiefly used for rhetorical effect or in ecclesiastical contexts) always.

Ev·ers /'evərz/, Medgar Wiley (1925–63), US civil rights activist. He was Mississippi field secretary of the NAACP 1954–63. His assassination prompted a call for new civil rights legislation.

E·vert /'evərt/, Chris (1954–), US tennis player; full name *Christine Marie Evert.* During 1974–86, she won 18 major women's singles championships.

e·vert /i'vərt/ ▸**v.** [trans.] Biol. Physiol. turn (a structure or organ) outward or inside out. — **e·ver·si·ble** /i'vərsəbəl/ **adj. e·ver·sion** /i'vərZHən; -SHən/ **n.** [16th C.: from L. *evertere*, from *e-* 'out' + *vertere* 'to turn.']

eve·ry /'evrē/ ▸**adj.** (preceding a singular noun) used to refer to all the individual members of a set without exception. ■ used before an amount to indicate something happening at specified intervals: *tours every thirty minutes.* ■ (used for emphasis) all possible; the utmost: *you have every reason to be disappointed.*

– PHRASES **every bit as** (in comparisons) equally as: *the planning should be every bit as enjoyable as the event itself.* **every inch** see **INCH**¹. **every last** (or **every single**) used to emphasize that every member of a group is included. **every now and then** (or **now and again**) from time to time; occasionally. **every other** each second in a series; each alternate. **every so often** from time to time; occasionally. **every time** without exception. **every which way** informal in all directions. ■ by all available means: *he has tried every which way to avoid contact.* [OE *ǣfre ǣlc* (see **EVER, EACH**).]

eve·ry·bod·y /'evrē,bädē; -,bədē/ ▸**pron.** every person: *everybody agrees with his views | it's not everybody's cup of tea.*

eve·ry·day /'evrē,dā/ ▸**adj.** [attrib.] happening or used every day; daily: *everyday chores.* ■ commonplace: *everyday drugs like aspirin.*

Eve·ry·man /'evrē,man/ ▸**n.** [in sing.] an ordinary or typical human being. [20th C.: the name of the principal character in a 15th-cent. morality play.]

eve·ry·one /'evrē,wən/ ▸**pron.** every person. See usage at **EVERYBODY.**

eve·ry one ▸**pron.** each one. See usage at **EVERYBODY.**

eve·ry·place /'evrē,plās/ ▸**adv.** informal term for **EVERYWHERE.**

eve·ry·thing /'evrē,THiNG/ ▸**pron. 1** all things; all the things of a group or class. ■ all things of importance; a great deal. ■ the most important thing or aspect. **2** the current situation; life in general: *how's everything?*

– PHRASES **and everything** informal used to refer vaguely to other things associated with what has been mentioned: *you'll still get paid and everything.* **have everything** informal possess every attraction or advantage.

eve·ry·where /'evrē,(h)we(ə)r/ ▸**adv.** in or to all places. ■ in many places; common or widely distributed. ▸**n.** all places or directions: *everywhere was in darkness.*

– PHRASES **everywhere else** in all other places.

eve·ry·wom·an /'evrē,wōōmən/ (also **Eve·ry·wom·an**) ▸**n.** the ordinary or typical woman.

evg. ▸**abbr.** evening.

e·vict /i'vikt/ ▸**v.** [trans.] expel (someone) from a property, esp. with the support of the law. — **e·vic·tion** /i'vikSHən/ **n. e·vic·tor** /-tər/ **n.** [ME: from L. *evict-* 'defeated,' from *evincere*, from *e-* 'out' + *vincere* 'conquer.']

ev·i·dence /'evədəns/ ▸**n.** the available body of facts or information indicating whether a belief or proposition is true or valid. ■ Law information given personally, drawn from a document, or in the form of material objects, tending or used to establish facts in a legal investigation or admissible as testimony in a law court. ■ signs; indications. ▸**v.** [trans.] (usu. **be evidenced**) be or show evidence of.

– PHRASES **give evidence** Law give information and answer questions formally and in person in a law court or at an inquiry. **in evidence** noticeable; conspicuous. **turn state's** (or Brit. **King's** or **Queen's**) **evidence** Law (of a criminal) give information in court against one's accomplices in order to receive a less severe punishment oneself.

ev·i·dent /'evədənt/ ▸**adj.** plain or obvious; clearly seen or understood.

[ME: from OFr., or from L. *evidens, evident-* 'obvious to the eye or mind,' from *e-* (var. of *ex-*) 'out' + *videre* 'to see.']

ev·i·den·tial /ˌeviˈdenCHəl/ ▶ adj. formal of or providing evidence: *the evidential value of the record.* — **ev·i·den·ti·al·i·ty** /ˌeviˌdenCHēˈalitē/ n. **ev·i·den·tial·ly** adv.

ev·i·den·tia·ry /ˌeviˈdensHərē/ ▶ adj. esp. Law another term for EVIDENTIAL.

ev·i·dent·ly /ˈevidəntlē; ˈeviˌdentlē; ˌeviˈdentlē/ ▶ adv. 1 plainly or obviously; in a way that is clearly seen or understood. 2 [sentence adverb] it is plain that; it would seem that: *evidently Mrs. Smith thought differently.* ■ used as an affirmative response or reply: *"Were they old pals or something?" "Evidently."*

e·vil /ˈēvəl/ ▶ adj. profoundly immoral and malevolent. ■ (of a force or spirit) embodying or associated with the forces of the devil. ■ harmful or tending to harm. ■ (of something seen or smelled) extremely unpleasant. ▶ n. profound immorality, wickedness, and depravity, esp. when regarded as a supernatural force. ■ a manifestation of this, esp. in people's actions. ■ something that is harmful or undesirable.

– PHRASES **the evil eye** a gaze or stare superstitiously believed to cause material harm. **the Evil One** archaic the Devil. **put off the evil day** (or **hour**) postpone something unpleasant for as long as possible. **speak evil of** slander. — **e·vil·ly** /ˈēvəl(l)ē/ adv. **e·vil·ness** n. [OE *yfel*, of Gmc. origin; rel. to Du. *euvel* and Ger. *Übel*.]

e·vil·do·er /ˈēvəlˌdo͞oər/ ▶ n. a person who commits profoundly immoral and malevolent deeds. — **e·vil·do·ing** /ˈēvəlˌdo͞oiNG/ n.

e·vil-mind·ed ▶ adj. having wicked thoughts, ideas, or intentions.

e·vince /iˈvins/ ▶ v. [trans.] formal reveal the presence of (a quality or feeling). ■ be evidence of; indicate: *man's inhumanity to man as evinced in the use of torture.* [16th C.: from L. *evincere* 'overcome' (see EVICT).]

e·vis·cer·ate /iˈvisəˌrāt/ ▶ v. [trans.] formal disembowel (a person or animal). ■ fig. deprive (something) of its essential content. ■ Surg. remove the contents of (a body organ). — **e·vis·cer·a·tion** /iˌvisəˈrāsHən/ n. [16th C.: from L. *eviscerat-* 'disemboweled,' from the v. *eviscerare*, from *e-* (var. of *ex-*) 'out' + *viscera* 'internal organs.']

e·voc·a·tive /iˈväkətiv/ ▶ adj. bringing strong images, memories, or feelings to mind. — **e·voc·a·tive·ly** adv. **e·voc·a·tive·ness** n. [17th C.: from L. *evocativus*, from *evocat-* 'called forth,' from the v. *evocare* (see EVOKE).]

e·voke /iˈvōk/ ▶ v. [trans.] 1 bring or recall to the conscious mind. ■ elicit (a response). 2 invoke (a spirit or deity). — **e·vo·ca·tion** /ˌēvōˈkāsHən; ˌevə-/ n. **e·vok·er** n. [17th C. (sense 2): from L. *evocare*, from *e-* (var. of *ex-*) 'out of, from' + *vocare* 'to call.']

ev·o·lute /ˈevəˌlo͞ot/ (also **evolute curve**) ▶ n. Math. a curve that is the locus of the centers of curvature of another curve (its involute). [18th C.: from L. *evolutus*, past part. of *evolvere* 'roll out' (see EVOLVE).]

ev·o·lu·tion /ˌevəˈlo͞osHən/ ▶ n. 1 the process by which different kinds of living organisms are thought to have developed and diversified from earlier forms during the history of the earth. 2 the gradual development of something, esp. from a simple to a more complex form. 3 Chem. the giving off of a gaseous product, or of heat. 4 a pattern of movements or maneuvers. 5 Math., dated the extraction of a root from a given quantity. — **ev·o·lu·tion·al** /-sHənl/ adj. **ev·o·lu·tion·al·ly** /-sHənl-ē/ adv. **ev·o·lu·tion·ar·i·ly** /ˌevəˌlo͞osHəˈne(ə)rəlē/ adv. **ev·o·lu·tion·ar·y** /-ˌnerē/ adj. **ev·o·lu·tive** /-ˈlo͞otiv/ adj. [17th C.: from L. *evolutio(n-)* 'unrolling,' from the v. *evolvere* (see EVOLVE).]

ev·o·lu·tion·ist /ˌevəˈlo͞osHənist/ ▶ n. a person who believes in the theories of evolution and natural selection. ▶ adj. of or relating to the theories of evolution and natural selection. — **ev·o·lu·tion·ism** n.

e·volve /iˈvälv/ ▶ v. 1 develop gradually, esp. from a simple to a more complex form: [intrans.] *the Gothic style evolved steadily and naturally from the Romanesque* | [trans.] *each school must evolve its own way of working.* ■ (with reference to an organism or biological feature) develop over successive generations, esp. as a result of natural selection. 2 [trans.] Chem. give off (gas or heat). — **e·volv·a·ble** adj. **e·volve·ment** n. [17th C.: from L. *evolvere*, from *e-* 'out of' + *volvere* 'to roll.']

EVOO ▶ abbr. extra-virgin olive oil.

Év·ros /ˈevrôs/ Greek name for the MARITSA.

e·vul·sion /iˈvəlsHən/ ▶ n. the action of plucking something out by force; violent or forcible extraction.

Év·voi·a /ˈeveä/ Greek name for EUBOEA.

ev·zone /ˈevzōn/ ▶ n. a kilted soldier belonging to a select Greek infantry regiment. [19th C.: from modern Greek *euzōnos*, from Greek, 'dressed for exercise' (from EU- + *zōnē* 'belt').]

EW ▶ abbr. enlisted woman (women).

E·we /ˈāwā; ˈāvā/ ▶ n. (pl. same) 1 a member of a people of Ghana, Togo, and Benin. 2 the Kwa language of this people. ▶ adj. of, relating to, or denoting this people or their language. [the name in Ewe.]

ewe /yo͞o/ ▶ n. a female sheep. [OE *eowu*, of Gmc. origin; rel. to Du. *ooi* and Ger. *Aue*.]

ew·er /ˈyo͞oər/ ▶ n. a large jug with a wide mouth, formerly used for carrying water for someone to wash in. [ME: from Anglo-Norman Fr. *ewer*, var. of OFr. *aiguiere*, based on L. *aquarius* 'of water,' from *aqua* 'water.']

Ex. ▶ abbr. Bible Exodus.

ex[1] /eks/ ▶ prep. 1 (of goods) sold direct from: *carpet tiles offered at a special price, ex stock.* 2 without; excluding: *the discount and market price are ex dividend.* [19th C. (sense 2): from Latin, 'out of.']

ex[2] ▶ n. informal a former husband, wife, or partner in a relationship. [19th C.: independent usage of EX-[1].]

ex-[1] (also **e-**) ▶ prefix 1 out; outside of: *expand* | *express.* 2 up and away; upward: *excel* | *extol.* 3 thoroughly: *exacerbate* | *excruciate.* 4 removal or release: *excommunicate* | *exculpate* | *expel.* 5 forming verbs expressing inducement of a state: *exasperate* | *excite.* 6 forming nouns (from titles of office, status, etc.) expressing a former state: *ex-husband* | *ex-convict.* [from L. *ex* 'out of.']

ex-[2] ▶ prefix out: *exodus* | *exorcism.* [from Gk. *ex* 'out of.']

exa- ▶ comb. form (used in units of measurement) denoting a factor of 10^{18}: *exajoule.* [from *(h)exa-* (see HEXA-), based on the supposed analogy of *tera-* and *tetra-*.]

ex·ac·er·bate /igˈzasərˌbāt/ ▶ v. [trans.] make (a problem, bad situation, or negative feeling) worse. — **ex·ac·er·ba·tion** /igˌzasərˈbāsHən/ n. [17th C. from L. *exacerbat-* 'made harsh,' from *exacerbare*, from *ex-* 'out' + *acerbus* 'harsh, bitter.']

ex·act /igˈzakt/ ▶ adj. not approximated in any way; precise. ■ accurate or correct in all details. ■ (of a person) tending to be accurate and careful about minor details. ■ (of a subject of study) permitting precise or absolute measurements as a basis for rigorously testable theories: *an exact science.* ▶ v. [trans.] demand and obtain (something, esp. a payment) from someone. ■ inflict (revenge) on someone. — **ex·act·a·ble** adj. **ex·ac·ti·tude** /-tiˌt(y)o͞od/ n. **ex·act·ness** n. **ex·ac·tor** /-tər/ n. [ME: from L. *exact-* 'completed,' from *exigere*, from *ex-* 'thoroughly' + *agere* 'perform.']

ex·act·a /igˈzaktə/ ▶ n. a bet in which the first two places in a race must be predicted in the correct order. Compare with QUINELLA. [1960s: from Amer. Sp. *quiniela exacta* 'exact quinella.']

ex·act·ing /igˈzaktiNG/ ▶ adj. making great demands on one's skill, attention, or other resources. — **ex·act·ing·ly** adv. **ex·act·ing·ness** n.

ex·ac·tion /igˈzaksHən/ ▶ n. formal the action of demanding and obtaining something from someone, esp. a payment or service. ■ a sum of money demanded in such a way. ■ an act of demanding unfair and exorbitant payment; extortion.

ex·act·ly /igˈzaktlē/ ▶ adv. 1 without discrepancy (used to emphasize the accuracy of a figure or description). 2 in exact terms; without vagueness. 3 used as a reply to confirm or agree with what has just been said.

– PHRASES **not exactly** informal 1 not at all. 2 not quite but close to being.

ex·ag·ger·ate /igˈzajəˌrāt/ ▶ v. [trans.] represent (something) as being larger, greater, better, or worse than it really is. ■ [as adj.] (**exaggerated**) enlarged or altered beyond normal or due proportions. — **ex·ag·ger·at·ed·ly** adv. **ex·ag·ger·a·tion** /igˌzajəˈrāsHən/ n. **ex·ag·ger·a·tive** /-ˌrātiv/ adj. **ex·ag·ger·a·tor** /-ˌrātər/ n. [16th C.: from L. *exaggerat-* 'heaped up,' from the v. *exaggerare*, from *ex-* 'thoroughly' + *aggerare* 'heap up.']

ex·alt /igˈzôlt/ ▶ v. [trans.] hold (someone or something) in very high regard; think or speak very highly of. ■ raise to a higher rank or a position of greater power. ■ make noble in character; dignify. [ME: from L. *exaltare*, from *ex-* 'out, upward' + *altus* 'high.']

ex·al·ta·tion /ˌegzôlˈtāsHən; ˌeksôl-/ ▶ n. 1 a feeling or state of extreme happiness. 2 the action of elevating someone in rank, power, or character. ■ the action of praising someone or something highly.

ex·alt·ed /igˈzôltid; eg-/ ▶ adj. 1 (of a person or their rank or status) placed at a high or powerful level; held in high regard. ■ (of an idea) noble; lofty. 2 in a state of extreme happiness. — **ex·alt·ed·ly** adv. **ex·alt·ed·ness** n.

ex·am /igˈzam/ ▶ n. 1 short for EXAMINATION (sense 2). 2 [with adj.] a medical test of a specified kind.

ex·a·men /igˈzāmən/ ▶ n. a formal examination of the soul or conscience, made usually daily by Jesuits and some other Roman Catholics. [17th C.: from Latin, literally 'tongue of a balance,' from *exigere* 'weigh accurately.']

ex·am·i·na·tion /igˌzaməˈnāsHən/ ▶ n. 1 a detailed inspection or investigation. ■ the action or process of conducting such an inspection or investigation. 2 a formal test of a person's knowledge or proficiency in a particular subject or skill. 3 Law the formal questioning of a defendant or witness in court.

ex·am·i·na·tion-in-chief ▶ n. another term for DIRECT EXAMINATION.

ex·am·ine /igˈzamən/ ▶ v. [trans.] 1 inspect (someone or something) in detail to determine their nature or condition; investigate thoroughly. 2 test the knowledge or proficiency of (someone) by requiring them to answer questions or perform tasks. ■ Law formally question (a defendant or witness) in court. Compare with CROSS-EXAMINE. — **ex·am·in·a·ble** adj. **ex·am·i·nee** /igˌzaməˈnē/ n. **ex·am·in·er** n. [ME: from OFr. *examiner*, from L. *examinare* 'weigh, test,' from *examen* (see EXAMEN).]

ex·am·ple /igˈzampəl/ ▶ n. 1 a thing characteristic of its kind or illustrating a general rule. ■ a printed or written problem or exercise designed to illustrate a rule. 2 a person or thing regarded in terms of their fitness to be imitated or the likelihood of their being imitated. ▶ v. (**be exampled**) be illustrated or exemplified.

– PHRASES **for example** used to introduce something chosen as a typical case. **make an example of** punish as a warning to others. [ME: from OFr., from L. *exemplum*, from *eximere* 'take out,' from *ex-* 'out' + *emere* 'take.' Cf. SAMPLE.]

ex·an·the·ma /ˌegzanˈTHēmə/ ▶ n. (pl. **-them·a·ta** /-ˈTHemətə/) Med. a skin rash accompanying a disease or fever. — **ex·an·the·mat·ic**

/eg,zanTHə'matik/ **adj.** **ex·an·them·a·tous** /-'THemətəs/ **adj.** [17th C.: via late L. from Gk. *exanthēma* 'eruption,' from *ex-* 'out' + *antheein* 'to blossom' (from *anthos* 'flower').]

ex·arch /'eksärk/ ▶ **n.** **1** (in the Orthodox Church) a bishop lower in rank than a patriarch and having jurisdiction wider than the metropolitan of a diocese. **2** hist. a governor of a distant province under the Byzantine emperors. [16th C.: via eccles. L. from Gk. *exarkhos*, from *ex-* 'out of' + *arkhos* 'ruler.']

ex·ar·chate /'eksär,kāt/ ▶ **n.** hist. a distant province governed by an exarch under the Byzantine emperors.

ex·as·per·ate /ig'zaspə,rāt/ ▶ **v.** [trans.] irritate intensely; infuriate. — **ex·as·per·at·ed·ly** **adv.** **ex·as·per·at·ing·ly** **adv.** **ex·as·per·a·tion** /ig,zaspə'rāSHən/ **n.** [16th C.: from L. *exasperat-* 'irritated to anger,' from the v. *exasperare* (based on *asper* 'rough').]

Exc. ▶ **abbr.** Excellency.

exc. ▶ **abbr.** ■ except. ■ exception. ■ excursion.

Ex·cal·i·bur /ek'skaləbər/ (in Arthurian legend) King Arthur's magic sword.

ex ca·the·dra /,eks kə'THēdrə/ ▶ **adv. & adj.** with the full authority of office (esp. of the pope's infallibility as defined in Roman Catholic doctrine). [19th C.: Latin, 'from the (teacher's) chair,' from *ex* 'from' and *cathedra* 'seat' (from Greek *kathedra*).]

ex·ca·vate /'ekskə,vāt/ ▶ **v.** [trans.] **1** make (a hole or channel) by digging. ■ dig out material from (the ground). ■ extract (material) from the ground by digging. **2** remove earth carefully and systematically from (an area) in order to find buried remains. ■ reveal or extract (buried remains) in this way. [16th C.: from L. *excavat-* 'hollowed out,' from the v. *excavare*, from *ex-* 'out' + *cavare* 'make or become hollow' (from *cavus* 'hollow').]

ex·ca·va·tion /,ekskə'vāSHən/ ▶ **n.** the action of excavating something, esp. an archaeological site. ■ a site that is being or has been excavated.

ex·ca·va·tor /'ekskə,vātər/ ▶ **n.** a person who removes earth carefully and systematically from an archaeological site in order to find buried remains. ■ a large machine for removing soil from the ground, esp. on a building site.

ex·ceed /ik'sēd/ ▶ **v.** [trans.] be greater in number or size than (a quantity, number, or other measurable thing). ■ go beyond what is allowed or stipulated by (a set limit, esp. of one's authority). ■ be better than; surpass. [ME: from OFr. *exceder*, from L. *excedere*, from *ex-* 'out' + *cedere* 'go.']

ex·ceed·ing /ik'sēdiNG/ archaic literary ▶ **adj.** very great: *she spoke warmly of his exceeding kindness.* ▶ **adv.** [as submodifier] extremely; exceedingly: *an ale of exceeding poor quality.*

ex·ceed·ing·ly /ik'sēdiNGlē/ ▶ **adv.** **1** [as submodifier] extremely: *the team played exceedingly well.* **2** to a great extent.

ex·cel /ik'sel/ ▶ **v.** (**ex·celled, ex·cel·ling**) [intrans.] be exceptionally good at or proficient in an activity or subject. [ME: from L. *excellere*, from *ex-* 'out, beyond' + *celsus* 'lofty.']

ex·cel·lence /'eksələns/ ▶ **n.** the quality of being outstanding or extremely good. ■ archaic an outstanding feature or quality.

ex·cel·len·cy /'eksələnsē/ ▶ **n.** (pl. **-cies**) **1** (**His, Your,** etc., **Excellency**) a title given to certain high officials of state, esp. ambassadors, or of the Roman Catholic Church, or used in addressing them. **2** archaic an outstanding feature or quality.

ex·cel·lent /'eksələnt/ ▶ **adj.** extremely good; outstanding. ▶ **exclam.** used to indicate approval or pleasure. — **ex·cel·lent·ly** **adv.**

ex·cel·si·or /ik'selsēər/ ▶ **n.** used in the names of hotels, newspapers, and other products to indicate superior quality. ■ softwood shavings used for packing fragile goods or stuffing furniture. [18th C. (as an exclamation): from L., compar. of *excelsus*, from *ex-* 'out, beyond' + *celsus* 'lofty.']

ex·cen·tric /ik'sentrik/ ▶ **adj.** not centrally placed or not having its axis or other part placed centrally. — **ex·cen·tri·cal·ly** /-k(ə)lē/ **adv.**

ex·cept /ik'sept/ ▶ **prep.** not including; other than. ▶ **conj.** used before a statement that forms an exception to one just made: *I didn't tell him anything, except that I needed the money.* ■ archaic unless. ▶ **v.** [trans.] formal specify as not included in a category or group; exclude. [ME: from L. *except-* 'taken out,' from the v. *excipere*, from *ex-* 'out of' + *capere* 'take.']

ex·cept·ed /ik'septid/ ▶ **adj.** [postpositive] not included in the category or group specified.

ex·cept·ing /ik'septiNG/ ▶ **prep.** formal except for; apart from.

ex·cep·tion /ik'sepSHən/ ▶ **n.** a person or thing that is excluded from a general statement or does not follow a rule.

– PHRASES **take exception to** object strongly to; be offended by. **with the exception of** except; not including. **without exception** with no one or nothing excluded.

ex·cep·tion·a·ble /ik'sepSHənəbəl/ ▶ **adj.** formal open to objection; causing disapproval or offense.

ex·cep·tion·al /ik'sepSHənəl/ ▶ **adj.** unusual; not typical. ■ unusually good; outstanding. ■ (of a child) mentally or physically disabled so as to require special schooling. — **ex·cep·tion·al·i·ty** /ik,sepSHə'nalitē/ **n.** **ex·cep·tion·al·ly** **adv.**

ex·cep·tion·al·ism /ik'sepSHənl,izəm/ ▶ **n.** the belief that something is exceptional, esp. the theory that the peaceful capitalism of the US constitutes an exception to the general economic laws governing national historical development.

ex·cerpt ▶ **n.** /'eksərpt/ a short extract from a film, broadcast, or piece of music or writing. ▶ **v.** /ik'sərpt/ [trans.] take (a short extract) from a text. ■ take an excerpt or excerpts from (a text). — **ex·cerpt·i·ble** /ek'sərptəbəl; ik-/ **adj.** **ex·cerp·tion** /ek'sərpSHən; ik-/ **n.** [16th C. (as a verb): from L. *excerpt-* 'plucked out,' from the v. *excerpere*, from *ex-* 'out of' + *carpere* 'to pluck.']

ex·cess /ik'ses; 'ekses/ ▶ **n.** **1** an amount of something that is more than necessary, permitted, or desirable. ■ the amount by which one quantity or number exceeds another. **2** lack of moderation in an activity, esp. eating or drinking. ■ (**excesses**) outrageous or immoderate behavior. **3** the action of exceeding a permitted limit. ▶ **adj.** [attrib.] exceeding a prescribed or desirable amount: *trim any excess fat off the meat.*

– PHRASES **in** (or **to**) **excess** exceeding the proper amount or degree. **in excess of** more than; exceeding. [ME: via OFr. from L. *excessus*, from *excedere* 'go out, surpass' (see EXCEED).]

ex·ces·sive /ik'sesiv/ ▶ **adj.** more than is necessary, normal, or desirable; immoderate. — **ex·ces·sive·ly** **adv.** [as submodifier] *excessively high taxes.* **ex·ces·sive·ness** **n.** [ME: from OFr. *excessif, -ive*, from med. L. *excessivus*, from L. *excedere* 'surpass' (see EXCEED).]

exch. ▶ **abbr.** ■ exchange. ■ exchequer.

ex·change /iks'CHānj/ ▶ **n.** an act of giving one thing and receiving another (esp. of the same type or value) in return. ■ a visit or visits in which two people or groups from different countries stay with each other or do each other's jobs. ■ a short conversation; an argument. ■ the giving of money for its equivalent in the money of another country. ■ the fee or percentage charged for converting the currency of one country into that of another. ■ a system or market in which commercial transactions involving currency, shares, commodities, etc., can be carried out within or between countries. See also FOREIGN EXCHANGE. ■ a central office or station of operations providing telephone service. ■ Chess a move or short sequence of moves in which both players capture material of comparable value, or particularly (**the exchange**) in which one captures a rook in return for a knight or bishop (and is said to *win the exchange*). ■ a building or institution used for the trading of a particular commodity or commodities. ▶ **v.** [trans.] give something and receive something of the same kind in return. ■ give or receive one thing in place of another.

– PHRASES **in exchange** as a thing exchanged. — **ex·change·a·bil·i·ty** /iks,CHānjə'bilitē/ **n.** **ex·change·a·ble** **adj.** **ex·chang·er** **n.** [ME: from OFr. *eschangier*, based on *changer* (see CHANGE).]

ex·change rate ▶ **n.** (also **rate of exchange**) the value of one currency for the purpose of conversion to another.

ex·cheq·uer /eks'CHekər; iks-/ ▶ **n.** a royal or national treasury. ■ (**Exchequer**) Brit. the bank account into which tax receipts and other public monies are paid; the funds of the British government. ■ (**Exchequer**) Brit., hist. the former government office responsible for collecting revenue and making payments on behalf of the sovereign, auditing official accounts, and trying legal cases relating to revenue. [ME: from OFr. *eschequier*, from med. L. *scaccarium* 'chessboard,' from *scaccus* (see CHECK[1]).]

ex·ci·mer /'eksəmər/ ▶ **n.** Chem. an unstable molecule that is formed in an excited state by the combination of two smaller molecules or atoms and rapidly dissociates with emission of radiation. Such species are utilized in some kinds of lasers. [1960s: blend of EXCITED and DIMER.]

ex·cip·i·ent /ik'sipēənt/ ▶ **n.** an inactive substance that serves as the vehicle or medium for a drug or other active substance. [18th C.: from L. *excipient-* 'taking out,' from the v. *excipere*.]

ex·cise[1] ▶ **n.** /'eksīz/ [usu. as adj.] a tax levied on certain goods and commodities produced or sold within a country and on licenses granted for certain activities. ▶ **v.** /ik'sīz; ek'sīz/ [trans.] [usu. as adj.] (**excised**) charge excise on (goods): *excised goods.* [15th C. (in the general sense 'a tax or toll'): from MDu. *excijs, accijs*, perh. based on L. *accensare* 'to tax,' from *ad-* 'to' + *census* 'tax' (see CENSUS).]

ex·cise[2] /ik'sīz/ ▶ **v.** [trans.] cut out surgically. ■ remove (a section) from a text or piece of music: *the clauses were excised from the treaty.* — **ex·ci·sion** /-'siZHən/ **n.** [16th C. (in the sense 'notch or hollow out'): from L. *excis-* 'cut out,' from the v. *excidere*, from *ex-* 'out of' + *caedere* 'to cut.']

ex·cise·man /'eksīzmən; -man/ ▶ **n.** (pl. **-men**) Brit., hist. an official responsible for collecting excise tax and enforcing excise laws (esp. against smuggling).

ex·cit·a·ble /ik'sītəbəl/ ▶ **adj.** responding rather too readily to something new or stimulating; too easily excited. ■ (of tissue or a cell) responsive to stimulation. — **ex·cit·a·bil·i·ty** /ik,sītə'bilitē/ **n.** **ex·cit·a·bly** /-əblē/ **adv.**

ex·cit·ant /ik'sītnt/ ▶ **n.** Biol. a substance that elicits an active physiological or behavioral response.

ex·ci·ta·tion /,eksī'tāSHən/ ▶ **n.** **1** tech. the application of energy to a particle, object, or physical system, in particular: ■ Physics the process in which an atom or other particle adopts a higher energy state when energy is supplied. ■ Physiol. the state of enhanced activity or potential activity of a cell, organism, or tissue that results from its stimulation. ■ the process of applying current to the winding of an electromagnet to produce a magnetic field. ■ the process of applying a signal voltage to the control electrode of an electron tube or the base of a transistor. **2** the action or state of exciting or being excited; excitement.

ex·cit·a·tive /ik'sītətiv/ ▶ **adj.** rare causing excitation.

ex·cit·a·to·ry /ik'sītə,tôrē/ ▶ **adj.** esp. Physiol. characterized by, causing, or constituting excitation.

ex·cite /ik'sīt/ ▶ **v.** [trans.] **1** cause strong feelings of enthusiasm and eagerness in (someone). ■ arouse (someone) sexually. **2** bring out or give rise to (a feeling or reaction). **3** produce a state of increased energy or activity in (a physical or biological system). [ME: from OFr. *exciter* or L. *excitare*, frequentative of *exciere* 'call out or forth.']

ex·cit·ed /ik'sītid/ ▶ **adj.** **1** very enthusiastic and eager. ■ sexually aroused. **2** Physics of or in an energy state higher than the normal or ground state. — **ex·cit·ed·ly adv.**

ex·cite·ment /ik'sītmənt/ ▶ **n.** a feeling of great enthusiasm and eagerness. ■ something that arouses such a feeling; an exciting incident. ■ sexual arousal.

ex·cit·er /ik'sītər/ ▶ **n.** a thing that produces excitation, in particular a device that provides a magnetizing current for the electromagnets in a motor or generator.

ex·cit·ing /ik'sītiNG/ ▶ **adj.** causing great enthusiasm and eagerness. ■ sexually arousing. — **ex·cit·ing·ly adv. ex·cit·ing·ness n.**

ex·ci·ton /'eksi,tän; ik'sītän/ ▶ **n.** Physics a mobile concentration of energy in a crystal formed by an excited electron and an associated hole. [1930s: from EXCITATION + -ON.]

excl. ▶ **abbr.** ■ exclamation. ■ excluding. ■ exclusive.

ex·claim /ik'sklām/ ▶ **v.** [intrans.] [often with direct speech] cry out suddenly, esp. in surprise, anger, or pain. [16th C.: from Fr. *exclamer* or L. *exclamare*, from *ex-* 'out' + *clamare* 'to shout.']

ex·cla·ma·tion /,ekskləˈmāSHən/ ▶ **n.** a sudden cry or remark, esp. expressing surprise, anger, or pain.

ex·cla·ma·tion point (Brit. **exclamation mark**) ▶ **n.** a punctuation mark (!) indicating an exclamation.

ex·clam·a·to·ry /ik'sklamə,tôrē/ ▶ **adj.** of or relating to a sudden cry or remark, esp. one expressing surprise, anger, or pain.

ex·clave /'eksklāv/ ▶ **n.** a portion of territory of one state completely surrounded by territory of another or others, as viewed by the home territory. Compare with ENCLAVE. [19th C.: from EX-[1] 'out' + a shortened form of ENCLAVE.]

ex·clo·sure /ik'sklōZHər/ ▶ **n.** Forestry an area from which unwanted animals are excluded. [1920s: from EX-[1] 'out' + CLOSURE, on the pattern of *enclosure*.]

ex·clude /ik'sklōōd/ ▶ **v.** [trans.] deny (someone) access to or bar (someone) from a place, group, or privilege. ■ keep (something) out of a place. ■ (often **be excluded**) remove from consideration; rule out. ■ prevent the occurrence of; preclude.

– PHRASES **law** (or **principle**) **of the excluded middle** Logic the principle that one (and one only) of two contradictory propositions must be true. — **ex·clud·a·ble adj. ex·clud·er n.** [ME: from L. *excludere*, from *ex-* 'out' + *claudere* 'to shut.']

ex·clud·ing /ik'sklōōdiNG/ ▶ **prep.** not taking someone or something into account; apart from; except.

ex·clu·sion /ik'sklōōZHən/ ▶ **n.** the process or state of excluding or being excluded. ■ an item or risk specifically not covered by an insurance policy or other contract.

– PHRASES **to the exclusion of** so as to exclude something specified. — **ex·clu·sion·ar·y** /-ZHə,nerē/ **adj.** [ME: from L. *exclusio(n-)*, from *excludere* 'shut out' (see EXCLUDE).]

ex·clu·sion·ar·y rule /ik'sklōōZHə,nerē/ ▶ **n.** a law that prohibits the use of illegally obtained evidence in a criminal trial.

ex·clu·sion clause ▶ **n.** (in a contract) a clause disclaiming liability for a particular risk.

ex·clu·sion·ist /ik'sklōōZHənist/ ▶ **adj.** acting to shut out or bar someone from a place, group, or privilege. ▶ **n.** a person favoring the exclusion of someone from a place, group, or privilege.

ex·clu·sion prin·ci·ple (in full **Pauli exclusion principle**) ▶ **n.** see PAULI.

ex·clu·sion zone ▶ **n.** an area into which entry is forbidden, esp. by ships or aircraft of particular nationalities.

ex·clu·sive /ik'sklōōsiv/ ▶ **adj.** **1** excluding or not admitting other things. ■ unable to exist or be true if something else exists or is true. *mutually exclusive political views.* ■ (of terms) excluding all but what is specified. **2** restricted or limited to the person, group, or area concerned. ■ (of an item or story) not published or broadcast elsewhere. ■ (of a commodity) not obtainable elsewhere. **3** catering or available to only a few, select persons; high class and expensive. **4** [predic.] (**exclusive of**) not including; excepting. ▶ **n.** an item or story published or broadcast by only one source. — **ex·clu·sive·ness n. ex·clu·siv·i·ty** /,eksklōō'sivitē/ **n.**

ex·clu·sive·ly /ik'sklōōsivlē/ ▶ **adv.** to the exclusion of others; only; solely.

ex·clu·siv·ism /ik'sklōōsə,vizəm/ ▶ **n.** the action or policy of excluding a person or group from a place, group, or privilege. — **ex·clu·siv·ist adj. & n.**

ex·cog·i·tate /ek'skäji,tāt/ ▶ **v.** [trans.] formal think out, plan, or devise. — **ex·cog·i·ta·tion** /ek,skäji'tāSHən/ **n.** [16th C.: from L. *excogitat-* 'found by process of thought,' from the v. *excogitare*, from *ex-* 'out' + *cogitare* 'think.']

ex·com·mu·ni·cate ▶ **v.** /,ekskə'myōōni,kāt/ [trans.] officially exclude (someone) from participation in the sacraments and services of the Christian Church. ▶ **adj.** excommunicated: *all were pronounced excommunicate.* ▶ **n.** an excommunicated person. — **ex·com·mu·ni·ca·tion** /,ekskə,myōōni'kāSHən/ **n. ex·com·mu·ni·ca·tive** /-,kātiv/ **adj. ex·com·mu·ni·ca·tor** /-,kātər/ **n. ex·com·mu·ni·ca·to·ry** /-kə,tôrē/ **adj.** [ME: from Latin *excommunicat-* 'excluded from communication with the faithful,' from *excommunicare*, from *ex-* 'out' + L. *communis* 'common to all.']

ex-con ▶ **n.** informal an ex-convict; a former inmate of a prison.

ex·co·ri·ate /ik'skôrē,āt/ ▶ **v.** [trans.] **1** formal censure or criticize severely. **2** esp. Med. damage or remove part of the surface of (the skin). — **ex·co·ri·a·tion** /ik,skôrē'āSHən/ **n.** [ME: from L. *excoriat-* 'skinned,' from the v. *excoriare*, from *ex-* 'out, from' + *corium* 'skin, hide.']

ex·cre·ment /'ekskrəmənt/ ▶ **n.** waste matter discharged from the bowels; feces. — **ex·cre·men·tal** /,ekskrə'men(t)l/ **adj.** [16th C.: from Fr. *excrément* or L. *excrementum*, from *excernere* 'to sift out' (see EXCRETE).]

ex·cres·cence /ik'skresəns/ ▶ **n.** a distinct outgrowth on a human or animal body or on a plant, esp. one that is the result of disease or abnormality. ■ an unattractive or superfluous addition or feature. [ME: from L. *excrescentia*, from *excrescere* 'grow out,' from *ex-* 'out' + *crescere* 'grow.']

ex·cres·cent /ik'skresənt/ ▶ **adj.** **1** forming or constituting an excrescence. **2** (of a speech sound) added without etymological justification (e.g., the *-t* at the end of the surname *Bryant*).

ex·cre·ta /ik'skrētə/ ▶ **n.** [treated as sing. or pl.] waste matter discharged from the body, esp. feces and urine. [19th C.: from L., 'things sifted out,' neut. pl. of *excretus*, past part. of *excernere* (see EXCRETE).]

ex·crete /ik'skrēt/ ▶ **v.** [trans.] (of a living organism or cell) separate and expel as waste (a substance, esp. a product of metabolism): *excess bicarbonate is excreted by the kidney* | [intrans.] *the butterfly pupa neither feeds nor excretes.* — **ex·cret·er n. ex·cre·tive** /'ekskritiv; ik'skrētiv/ **adj.** [17th C. (in the sense 'cause to excrete'): from L. *excret-* 'sifted out,' from the v. *excernere*, from *ex-* 'out' + *cernere* 'sift.']

ex·cre·tion /ik'skrēSHən/ ▶ **n.** (in living organisms and cells) the process of eliminating or expelling waste matter. ■ a product of this process.

ex·cre·to·ry /'ekskri,tôrē/ ▶ **adj.** of, relating to, or concerned with excretion.

ex·cru·ci·ate /ik'skrōōSHē,āt/ ▶ **v.** [trans.] rare torment (someone) physically or mentally. — **ex·cru·ci·a·tion** /ik,skrōōSHē,āSHən/ **n.** [16th C.: from L. *excruciat-* 'tormented,' from the v. *excruciare* (based on *crux, cruc-* 'a cross').]

ex·cru·ci·at·ing /ik'skrōōSHē,ātiNG/ ▶ **adj.** intensely painful. ■ mentally agonizing; very embarrassing, awkward, or tedious. — **ex·cru·ci·at·ing·ly adv.**

ex·cul·pate /'ekskəl,pāt/ ▶ **v.** [trans.] formal show or declare that (someone) is not guilty of wrongdoing. — **ex·cul·pa·tion** /,ekskəl'pāSHən/ **n. ex·cul·pa·to·ry** /ek'skəlpə,tôrē/ **adj.** [17th C.: from med. L. *exculpat-* 'freed from blame,' from the v. *exculpare*, from *ex-* 'out, from' + L. *culpa* 'blame.']

ex·cur·rent /ek'skərənt; -'skə-rənt/ ▶ **adj.** esp. Zool. (of a vessel or opening) conveying fluid outward. The opposite of INCURRENT.

ex·cur·sion /ik'skərZHən/ ▶ **n.** **1** a short journey or trip, esp. one engaged in as a leisure activity. ■ [usu. as adj.] a trip at reduced rates. **2** tech. an instance of the movement of something along a path or through an angle. ■ a deviation from a regular pattern, path, or level of operation. **3** archaic a digression. **4** archaic a military sortie (see ALARUM). — **ex·cur·sion·ist n.** [16th C.: from L. *excursio(n-)*, from *excurrere* 'run out,' from *ex-* 'out' + *currere* 'to run.']

ex·cur·sive /ik'skərsiv/ ▶ **adj.** formal of the nature of an excursion; ranging widely; digressive. — **ex·cur·sive·ly adv. ex·cur·sive·ness n.**

ex·cur·sus /ek'skərsəs/ ▶ **n.** (pl. same or **-sus·es**) a detailed discussion of a particular point in a book, usually in an appendix. ■ a digression in a written text. [19th C.: from Latin, 'excursion,' from *excurrere* 'run out.']

ex·cuse ▶ **v.** /ik'skyōōz/ [trans.] **1** attempt to lessen the blame attaching to (a fault or offense); seek to defend or justify. ■ forgive (someone) for a fault or offense. ■ overlook or forgive (a fault or offense). ■ (of a fact or circumstance) serve in mitigation of (a person or act). **2** release (someone) from a duty or requirement. ■ (used in polite formulas) allow (someone) to leave a room or gathering. ■ (**excuse oneself**) say politely that one is leaving. ▶ **n.** /ik'skyōōs/ **1** a reason or explanation put forward to defend or justify a fault or offense. ■ a reason put forward to conceal the real reason for an action; a pretext. **2** (**an excuse for**) informal a poor or inadequate example of: *that pathetic excuse for a man!*

– PHRASES **make one's excuses** say politely that one is leaving or cannot be present. — **ex·cus·a·ble adj. ex·cus·a·bly adv. ex·cus·a·to·ry** /-zə,tôrē/ **adj.** [ME: from OFr. *escuser* (v.), from L. *excusare* 'to free from blame,' from *ex-* 'out' + *causa* 'accusation, cause.']

ex div·i·dend (abbr.: **ex div.**) ▶ **adj. & adv.** (of stocks or shares) not including the next dividend.

ex·ec /eg'zek/ ▶ **n.** informal an executive: *top execs.* [19th C.: abbrev.]

ex·e·cra·ble /'eksikrəbəl/ ▶ **adj.** extremely bad or unpleasant. — **ex·e·cra·bly adv.**

ex·e·crate /'eksi,krāt/ ▶ **v.** [trans.] feel or express great loathing for. ■ [intrans.] archaic curse; swear. — **ex·e·cra·tion** /,eksi'krāSHən/ **n. ex·e·cra·tive** /-,krātiv/ **adj. ex·e·cra·to·ry** /-krə,tôrē/ **adj.** [16th C.: from L. *exsecrat-* 'cursed,' from the v. *exsecrari*, based on *sacrare* 'dedicate' (from *sacer* 'sacred').]

ex•e•cut•a•ble /'eksi,kyōōtəbəl/ Comput. ▶ **adj.** (of a file or program) able to be run by a computer. ▶ **n.** an executable file or program.

ex•ec•u•tant /ig'zekyətənt/ formal ▶ **n.** a person who carries something into effect. ■ a person who performs music or makes a work of art or craft. ▶ **adj.** of or relating to the performance of music or the making of works of art or craft.

ex•e•cute /'eksi,kyōōt/ ▶ **v.** [trans.] **1** carry out or put into effect (a plan, order, or course of action). ■ produce (a work of art). ■ perform (an activity or maneuver requiring care or skill). ■ Law make (a legal instrument) valid by signing or sealing it. ■ Law carry out (a judicial sentence, the terms of a will, or other order). ■ Comput. carry out an instruction or a program. **2** (often **be executed**) carry out a sentence of death on (a legally condemned person). ■ kill (someone) as a political act. [ME: from OFr. *executer*, from med. L. *executare*, from L. *exsequi* 'follow up, carry out, punish,' from *ex-* 'out' + *sequi* 'follow.']

ex•e•cu•tion /,eksi'kyōōsHən/ ▶ **n.** **1** the carrying out or putting into effect of a plan, order, or course of action. ■ the technique or style with which an artistic work is produced or carried out. ■ Law the putting into effect of a legal instrument or order. ■ Law seizure of the property or person of a debtor in default of payment. ■ Law short for WRIT OF EXECUTION. ■ Comput. the performance of an instruction or a program. **2** the carrying out of a sentence of death on a condemned person. ■ the killing of someone as a political act.

ex•e•cu•tion•er /,eksi'kyōōsHənər/ ▶ **n.** an official who carries out a sentence of death on a legally condemned person.

ex•ec•u•tive /ig'zekyətiv; eg-/ ▶ **adj.** [attrib.] having the power to put plans, actions, or laws into effect. ■ relating to managing an organization or political administration and putting into effect plans, policies, or laws. Often contrasted with LEGISLATIVE. ▶ **n.** **1** a person with senior managerial responsibility in a business organization. ■ [as adj.] suitable or appropriate for a senior business executive. ■ an executive committee or other body within an organization. **2** (**the executive**) the person or branch of a government responsible for putting policies or laws into effect. — **ex•ec•u•tive•ly adv.**

ex•ec•u•tive a•gree•ment ▶ **n.** an international agreement, usu. regarding routine administrative matters not warranting a formal treaty, made by the executive branch of the US government without ratification by the Senate.

ex•ec•u•tive of•fi•cer ▶ **n.** an officer with executive power. ■ (in naval vessels and some other military contexts) the officer who is second in command to the captain or commanding officer.

ex•ec•u•tive or•der ▶ **n.** a rule or order issued by the president to an executive branch of the government and having the force of law.

ex•ec•u•tive priv•i•lege ▶ **n.** the privilege, claimed by the president for the executive branch of the US government, of withholding information in the public interest.

ex•ec•u•tive sec•re•tar•y ▶ **n.** a secretary with administrative responsibilities, esp. one managing the business affairs and activities of an executive or an organization.

ex•ec•u•tive ses•sion ▶ **n.** a meeting, esp. a private one, of a legislative body for executive business.

ex•ec•u•tor ▶ **n.** **1** /ig'zekyətər/ Law a person or institution appointed by a testator to carry out the terms of their will. **2** /'eksə,kyōōtər/ a person who produces something or puts something into effect. — **ex•ec•u•to•ri•al** /ig,zekyə'tôrēəl/ **adj.** (rare) **ex•ec•u•tor•ship n. ex•ec•u•to•ry** /-,tôrē/ **adj.**

ex•ec•u•trix /ig'zekyə,triks/ ▶ **n.** (pl. **-tri•ces** /ig,zekyə'trīsēz/ or **-trix•es** /-,triksiz/) Law a female executor of a will.

ex•e•dra /'eksidrə; ik'sēdrə/ ▶ **n.** (pl. **-drae** /-drē/) Archit. a room, portico, or arcade with a bench or seats where people may converse, esp. in ancient Roman and Greek houses and gymnasia, typically semicircular in plan. ■ an outdoor recess containing a seat. [L., from Gk. *ex-* 'out of' + *hedra* 'seat.']

ex•e•ge•sis /,eksi'jēsis/ ▶ **n.** (pl. **-ses** /-sēz/) critical explanation or interpretation of a text, esp. of scripture. — **ex•e•get•ic** /-'jetik/ **adj. ex•e•get•i•cal** /-'jetikəl/ **adj.** [17th C.: from Gk. *exēgēsis*, from *exēgeisthai* 'interpret,' from *ex-* 'out of' + *hēgeisthai* 'to guide, lead.']

ex•e•gete /'eksi,jēt/ ▶ **n.** an expounder or textual interpreter, esp. of scripture. ▶ **v.** [trans.] expound or interpret (a text, esp. scripture). [18th C.: from Gk. *exēgētēs*, from *exēgeisthai* 'interpret.']

ex•em•plar /ig'zemplər; -plär/ ▶ **n.** a person or thing serving as a typical example or excellent model. [ME: from OFr. *exemplaire*, from late L. *exemplarium*, from L. *exemplum* 'sample, imitation' (see EXAMPLE).]

ex•em•pla•ry /ig'zemplərē/ ▶ **adj.** **1** serving as a desirable model; representing the best of its kind. ■ characteristic of its kind or illustrating a general rule. **2** (of a punishment) serving as a warning or deterrent. ■ Law (of damages) exceeding the amount needed for simple compensation. — **ex•em•pla•ri•ly** /-rəlē/ **adv. ex•em•pla•ri•ness n. ex•em•plar•i•ty** /,egzem'plaritē/ **n.**

ex•em•pli•fy /ig'zemplə,fī/ ▶ **v.** (**-fies, -fied**) [trans.] be a typical example of. ■ give an example of; illustrate by giving an example. ■ Law make an attested copy of (a document) under an official seal. — **ex•em•pli•fi•ca•tion** /ig,zempləfi'kāsHən/ **n.**

ex•em•plum /ig'zempləm/ ▶ **n.** (pl. **-pla** /-plə/) an example, esp. a moralizing or illustrative one. [19th C.: Latin, literally 'example.']

ex•empt /ig'zem(p)t/ ▶ **adj.** free from an obligation or liability imposed on others. ▶ **v.** [trans.] free (a person or organization) from an obligation or liability imposed on others. ▶ **n.** a person who is exempt from something, esp. the payment of tax. [ME: from L. *exemptus* 'taken out, freed,' past part. of *eximere*.]

ex•emp•tion /ig'zem(p)sHən/ ▶ **n.** the process of freeing or state of being free from an obligation or liability imposed on others. ■ (also **personal exemption**) the process of exempting a person from paying taxes on a specified amount of income for themselves and their dependents. ■ a dependent exempted in this way.

ex•en•ter•a•tion /ig,zentə'rāsHən/ ▶ **n.** Med. complete surgical removal of a body organ, esp. the eyeball and other contents of the eye socket, usually in cases of malignant cancer. [17th C.: from L. *exenterat-* 'removed,' from *exenterare*, from *ex-* 'out of' + *enteron* 'intestine.']

ex•e•quy /'eksikwē/ ▶ **n.** (**exequies**) formal funeral rites; obsequies: *exequies for the dead pope.* [ME: via OFr. from L. *exsequias*, accusative of *exsequiae* 'funeral ceremonies,' from *exsequi* 'follow after.']

ex•er•cise /'eksər,sīz/ ▶ **n.** **1** activity requiring physical effort, carried out esp. to sustain or improve health and fitness. ■ a task or activity done to practice or test a skill. ■ a process or activity carried out for a specific purpose, esp. one concerned with a specified area or skill. ■ (often **exercises**) a military drill or training maneuver. ■ (**exercises**) ceremonies. **2** the use or application of a faculty, right, or process. ▶ **v.** [trans.] **1** use or apply (a faculty, right, or process). **2** [intrans.] engage in physical activity to sustain or improve health and fitness; take exercise. ■ exert (part of the body) to promote or improve muscular strength. ■ cause (an animal) to engage in exercise. **3** occupy the thoughts of; worry or perplex. — **ex•er•cis•a•ble adj.** [ME: via OFr. from L. *exercitium*, from *exercere* 'keep busy, practice,' from *ex-* 'thoroughly' + *arcere* 'keep in or away.']

ex•er•cise book ▶ **n.** a book containing printed exercises for the use of students.

ex•er•cise price ▶ **n.** Stock Market the price per share at which the owner of a traded option is entitled to buy or sell the underlying security.

ex•er•cis•er /'eksər,sīzər/ ▶ **n.** a person who exercises. ■ an apparatus used to exercise.

ex•er•gon•ic /,eksər'gänik/ ▶ **adj.** Biochem. (of a metabolic or chemical process) accompanied by the release of energy. The opposite of ENDERGONIC. [20th C.: from EX-[2] 'out of' + Gk. *ergon* 'work' + -IC.]

ex•ergue /ig'zərg; 'eksərg; 'egzərg/ ▶ **n.** a small space or inscription below the principal emblem on a coin or medal, usually on the reverse side. [17th C.: from Fr., from med. L. *exergum*, from *ex-* 'out' + Gk. *ergon* 'work.']

ex•ert /ig'zərt/ ▶ **v.** [trans.] **1** apply or bring to bear (a force, influence, or quality). **2** (**exert oneself**) make a physical or mental effort. [17th C. (in the sense 'perform, practice'): from L. *exserere* 'put forth,' from *ex-* 'out' + *serere* 'bind.']

ex•er•tion /ig'zərsHən/ ▶ **n.** **1** physical or mental effort. **2** the application of a force, influence, or quality.

Ex•e•ter /'eksətər; 'egzətər/ the county town of Devon, in southwestern England, on the Exe River; pop. 101,000.

ex•e•unt /'eksēənt; -,ōōnt/ ▶ **v.** used as a stage direction in a printed play to indicate that a group of characters leave the stage: *exeunt Hamlet and Polonius.* See also EXIT.
– PHRASES **exeunt omnes** used in this way to indicate that all the actors leave the stage. [15th C.: Latin, literally 'they go out.']

ex•fo•li•ant /eks'fōlēənt/ ▶ **n.** a cosmetic product designed to remove dead cells from the surface of the skin.

ex•fo•li•ate /eks'fōlē,āt/ ▶ **v.** [intrans.] (of a material) come apart or be shed from a surface in scales or layers. ■ [trans.] cause to do this. ■ [trans.] wash or rub (a part of the body) with a granular substance to remove dead cells from the surface of the skin. ■ [trans.] (often **be exfoliated**) shed (material) in scales or layers. — **ex•fo•li•a•tion** /eks,fōlē'āsHən/ **n. ex•fo•li•a•tive** /-,ātiv/ **adj. ex•fo•li•a•tor** /-,ātər/ **n.** [17th C.: from late L. *exfoliat-* 'stripped of leaves,' from the v. *exfoliare*, from *ex-* 'out, from' + *folium* 'leaf.']

ex gra•ti•a /eks 'grāsHēə/ ▶ **adv. & adj.** (esp. with reference to the paying of money) done from a sense of moral obligation rather than because of any legal requirement. [18th C.: Latin, literally 'from favor.']

ex•ha•la•tion /,eks(h)ə'lāsHən/ ▶ **n.** the process or action of exhaling. ■ an expiration of air from the lungs. ■ an amount of vapor or fumes given off.

ex•hale /eks'hāl; 'ekshāl/ ▶ **v.** breathe out in a deliberate manner: [intrans.] *she sat back and exhaled deeply* | [trans.] *he exhaled the smoke toward the ceiling.* ■ [trans.] give off (vapor or fumes). — **ex•hal•a•ble adj.** [ME (in the sense 'be given off as vapor'): from OFr. *exhaler*, from L. *exhalare*, from *ex-* 'out' + *halare* 'breathe.']

ex•haust /ig'zôst/ ▶ **v.** [trans.] **1** drain (someone) of their physical or mental resources; tire out. **2** use up (resources or reserves) completely. ■ expound on, write about, or explore (a subject or options) so fully that there is nothing further to be said or discovered. **3** expel (gas or steam) from or into a particular place. ▶ **n.** waste gases or air expelled from an engine, turbine, or other machine in the course of its operation. ■ the system through which such gases are expelled: [as adj.] *an exhaust pipe.* — **ex•haust•er n. ex•haust•i•bil•i•ty** /ig,zôstə'bilitē/ **n. ex•haust•i•ble adj. ex•haust•ing•ly adv.** [16th C. (in the general sense 'draw off or out'): from L. *exhaust-* 'drained out,' from the

v. *exhaurire*, from *ex-* 'out' + *haurire* 'draw (water), drain.']

ex·haust·ed /ig'zôstid/ ▶ **adj.** **1** drained of one's physical or mental resources; very tired. **2** (of resources or reserves) completely used up. — **ex·haust·ed·ly** **adv.**

ex·haus·tion /ig'zôsCHən/ ▶ **n.** **1** a state of extreme physical or mental fatigue. **2** the action or state of using something up or of being used up completely: *exhaustion of fossil fuel reserves.* ■ the action of exploring a subject or options so fully that there is nothing further to be said or discovered. ■ Logic the process of establishing a conclusion by eliminating all the alternatives.

ex·haus·tive /ig'zôstiv/ ▶ **adj.** examining, including, or considering all elements or aspects; comprehensive. — **ex·haus·tive·ly** **adv.** **ex·haus·tive·ness** **n.**

ex·hib·it /ig'zibit/ ▶ **v.** [trans.] **1** publicly display (a work of art or item of interest) in an art gallery or museum or at a trade fair. ■ [intrans.] (of an artist) display one's work to the public in an art gallery or museum. ■ (usu. **be exhibited**) publicly display the work of (an artist) in an art gallery or museum. **2** manifest or deliberately display (a quality or a type of behavior). ■ show as a sign or symptom. ▶ **n.** an object or collection of objects on public display in an art gallery or museum or at a trade fair. ■ an exhibition. ■ Law a document or other object produced in a court as evidence. [ME: from L. *exhibit-* 'held out,' from *exhibere*, from *ex-* 'out' + *habere* 'hold.']

ex·hi·bi·tion /,eksə'bisHən/ ▶ **n.** **1** a public display of works of art or other items of interest, held in an art gallery or museum or at a trade fair. **2** a display or demonstration of a particular skill. ■ [in sing.] an ostentatious or insincere display of a particular quality or emotion. **3** Brit. a scholarship awarded to a student at a school or college, usually after a competitive examination.

– PHRASES **make an exhibition of oneself** behave in a conspicuously foolish way in public.

ex·hi·bi·tion·er /,eksə'bisHənər/ ▶ **n.** Brit. a student who has been awarded an exhibition (scholarship).

ex·hi·bi·tion·ism /,eksə'bisHə,nizəm/ ▶ **n.** extravagant behavior intended to attract attention to oneself. ■ Psychiatry a mental condition characterized by the compulsion to display one's genitals in public. — **ex·hi·bi·tion·ist** **n.** **ex·hi·bi·tion·is·tic** /-,bisHə'nistik/ **adj.** **ex·hi·bi·tion·is·ti·cal·ly** /-,bisHə'nistik(ə)lē/ **adv.**

ex·hib·i·tor /ig'zibitər/ ▶ **n.** a person who displays works of art or other items of interest at an exhibition.

ex·hil·a·rate /ig'zilə,rāt/ ▶ **v.** (usu. **be exhilarated**) make (someone) feel very happy, animated, or elated. — **ex·hil·a·rat·ing·ly** **adv.** **ex·hil·a·ra·tion** /ig,zilə'rāsHən/ **n.** [16th C.: from L. *exhilarat-* 'made cheerful,' from *exhilarare*, from *ex-* + *hilaris* 'cheerful.']

ex·hort /ig'zôrt/ ▶ **v.** [trans.] strongly encourage or urge (someone) to do something. — **ex·hort·a·tive** /-zôrtətiv/ **adj.** **ex·hort·a·to·ry** /-zôrtə,tôrē/ **adj.** **ex·hort·er** **n.** [ME: from OFr. *exhorter* or L. *exhortari*, from *ex-* 'thoroughly' + *hortari* 'encourage.']

ex·hor·ta·tion /,egzôr'tāsHən; ,eksôr-/ ▶ **n.** an address or communication emphatically urging someone to do something.

ex·hume /ig'z(y)o͞om; eks'(y)o͞om/ ▶ **v.** [trans.] dig out (something buried, esp. a corpse) from the ground. — **ex·hu·ma·tion** /,egz(y)o͞o'māsHən; ,eks(h)yo͞o-/ **n.** [ME: from med. L. *exhumare*, from *ex-* 'out of' + *humus* 'ground.']

ex hy·poth·e·si /,eks hī'päTHə,sī/ ▶ **adv.** according to the hypothesis proposed. [mod. L., from *ex* 'from' and *hypothesi*, ablative of late L. *hypothesis* (see **HYPOTHESIS**).]

ex·i·gence /'eksijəns/ ▶ **n.** another term for **EXIGENCY**.

ex·i·gen·cy /'eksijənsē; ig'zijənsē/ ▶ **n.** (pl. **-cies**) an urgent need or demand.

ex·i·gent /'eksijənt/ ▶ **adj.** formal pressing; demanding. [17th C.: from L. *exigent-* 'completing, ascertaining,' from the v. *exigere* (see **EXACT**).]

ex·i·gi·ble /'eksijəbəl/ ▶ **adj.** (of a tax, duty, or other payment) able to be charged or levied.

ex·ig·u·ous /ig'zigyo͞oəs; ik'sig-/ ▶ **adj.** formal very small in size or amount. — **ex·i·gu·i·ty** /,eksi'gyo͞oitē/ **n.** **ex·ig·u·ous·ly** **adv.** **ex·ig·u·ous·ness** **n.** [17th C.: from L. *exiguus* 'scanty' (from *exigere* 'weigh exactly') + **-OUS**.]

ex·ile /'egzīl; 'eksīl/ ▶ **n.** the state of being barred from one's native country, typically for political or punitive reasons. ■ a person who lives away from their native country, either from choice or compulsion. ■ (**the Exile**) another term for **BABYLONIAN CAPTIVITY**. ▶ **v.** [trans.] (usu. **be exiled**) expel and bar (someone) from their native country, typically for political or punitive reasons. [ME: from OFr. *exil* 'banishment' and *exile* 'banished person', based on L. *exilium* 'banishment,' from *exul* 'banished person.']

ex·il·ic /eg'zilik; ek'silik/ ▶ **adj.** of or relating to a period of exile, esp. that of the Jews in Babylon in the 6th century BC.

ex·ine /'eksēn; -sīn/ ▶ **n.** Bot. the decay-resistant outer coating of a pollen grain or spore. [19th C.: perh. from **EX-**[2] 'out' + Gk. *is, in-* 'fiber.']

ex·ist /ig'zist/ ▶ **v.** [intrans.] **1** have objective reality or being. ■ be found, esp. in a particular place or situation. **2** live, esp. under adverse conditions. [17th C.: prob. a back-form. from **EXISTENCE**.]

ex·ist·ence /ig'zistəns/ ▶ **n.** the fact or state of living or having objective reality. ■ continued survival. ■ a way of living. ■ any of a person's supposed current, future, or past lives on this earth. ■ archaic a being or entity. ■ all that exists. [ME: from OFr., or from late L. *existentia*, from L. *exsistere* 'come into being,' from *ex-* 'out' + *sistere* 'take a stand.']

ex·ist·ent /ig'zistənt/ ▶ **adj.** formal having reality or existence.

ex·is·ten·tial /,egzi'stencHəl/ ▶ **adj.** of or relating to existence. ■ Philos. concerned with existence, esp. human existence as viewed in the theories of existentialism. ■ Logic (of a proposition) affirming or implying the existence of a thing. — **ex·is·ten·tial·ly** **adv.**

ex·is·ten·tial·ism /,egzi'stencHə,lizəm/ ▶ **n.** a philosophical theory or approach that emphasizes the existence of the individual person as a free and responsible agent determining their own development through acts of the will. — **ex·is·ten·tial·ist** **n. & adj.**

ex·is·ten·tial quan·ti·fi·er ▶ **n.** Logic a formal expression used in asserting that something exists of which a stated general proposition can be said to be true.

ex·ist·ing /ig'zistiNG/ ▶ **adj.** [attrib.] in existence or operation at the time under consideration; current.

ex·it /'egzit; 'eksit/ ▶ **n.** **1** a way out, esp. of a public building, room, or passenger vehicle. ■ a ramp where traffic can leave a highway, major road, or traffic circle. **2** an act of going out of or leaving a place. ■ a departure of an actor from the stage. ■ a departure from a particular situation. ▶ **v.** (**ex·it·ed**, **ex·it·ing**) [intrans.] go out of or leave a place: *they exited from the aircraft* | [trans.] *elephants enter and exit the forest on narrow paths.* ■ (of an actor) leave the stage. ■ (**exit**) used as a stage direction in a printed play to indicate that a character leaves the stage. See also **EXEUNT**. ■ leave a particular situation. ■ Comput. terminate a process or program, usually returning to an earlier or more general level of interaction. ■ Bridge relinquish the lead. [16th C. (as a stage direction): from L. *exit* 'he or she goes out,' third person sing. present tense of *exire*, from *ex-* 'out' + *ire* 'go.']

ex·it line ▶ **n.** a line spoken by an actor immediately before leaving the stage. ■ a parting remark.

ex·it poll ▶ **n.** a poll of people leaving a polling place, asking how they voted.

ex li·bris /eks 'lēbris; 'lībris/ ▶ **adv.** used as an inscription on a bookplate to show the name of the book's owner. ▶ **n.** (pl. same) a bookplate inscribed in such a way, esp. a decorative one. [19th C.: Latin, literally 'out of the books or library (of someone).']

ex ni·hi·lo /'eks 'nē(h)ə,lō; 'nī(h)ə,lō/ ▶ **adv.** formal out of nothing. [16th C.: L.]

exo- ▶ **prefix** external; from outside: *exodermis.* [from Gk. *exō* 'outside.']

ex·o·bi·ol·o·gy /,eksōbī'äləjē/ ▶ **n.** the branch of science that deals with the possibility and likely nature of life on other planets or in space. — **ex·o·bi·o·log·i·cal** /-,bīə'läjikəl/ **adj.** **ex·o·bi·ol·o·gist** /-jist/ **n.**

ex·o·carp /'eksō,kärp/ ▶ **n.** Bot. the outer layer of the pericarp of a fruit.

ex·o·cen·tric /,eksō'sentrik/ ▶ **adj.** Ling. denoting or being a construction that has no explicit head, for example *John slept*. Contrasted with **ENDOCENTRIC**.

ex·o·crine /'eksə,krin; -,krēn/ ▶ **adj.** Physiol. relating to or denoting glands that secrete their products through ducts opening onto an epithelium rather than directly into the bloodstream. Often contrasted with **ENDOCRINE**. [20th C.: from **EXO-** 'outside' + Gk. *krinein* 'sift.']

ex·o·cy·to·sis /'eksōsī'tōsis/ ▶ **n.** Biol. a process by which the contents of a cell vacuole are released to the exterior through fusion of the vacuole membrane with the cell membrane. — **ex·o·cy·tot·ic** /-'tätik/ **adj.**

Ex·o·dus /'eksədəs/ the second book of the Bible, which recounts the departure of the Israelites from slavery in Egypt. [OE, via eccles. L. from Gk. *exodos*, from *ex-* 'out of' + *hodos* 'way.']

ex·o·dus /'eksədəs/ ▶ **n.** a mass departure of people, esp. emigrants. ■ (**the Exodus**) the departure of the Israelites from Egypt. [17th C.: from Gk. (see **EXODUS**).]

ex·o·en·zyme /,eksō'enzīm/ ▶ **n.** Biochem. an enzyme that acts outside the cell that produces it.

ex of·fi·ci·o /'eks ə'fisHē,ō/ ▶ **adv. & adj.** by virtue of one's position or status: [as adj.] *an ex officio committee member.* [L., from *ex* 'out of, from' + *officium* 'duty.']

ex·og·a·my /ek'sägəmē/ ▶ **n.** Anthropol. the custom of marrying outside a community, clan, or tribe. Compare with **ENDOGAMY**. ■ Biol. the fusion of reproductive cells from distantly related or unrelated individuals; outbreeding; cross-pollination. — **ex·og·a·mous** /-məs/ **adj.** [19th C.: from **EXO-** + Gk. *gamos* 'marriage.']

ex·o·gen·ic /,eksə'jenik/ ▶ **adj.** Geol. formed or occurring on the surface of the earth. Often contrasted with **ENDOGENIC**.

ex·og·e·nous /ek'säjənəs/ ▶ **adj.** of, relating to, or developing from external factors. Often contrasted with **ENDOGENOUS**. ■ Biol. growing or originating from outside an organism. ■ esp. Psychiatry (of a disease, symptom, etc.) caused by an agent or organism outside the body. ■ relating to an external group or society. — **ex·og·e·nous·ly** **adv.** [19th C.: from mod. L. *exogena* (denoting an exogenous plant, suggested by classical L. *indigena* 'native') + **-OUS**.]

ex·on /'eksän/ ▶ **n.** Biochem. a segment of a DNA or RNA molecule containing information coding for a protein or peptide sequence. Compare with **INTRON**. — **ex·on·ic** /ek'sänik/ **adj.** [20th C.: from *expressed* (see **EXPRESS**[1]) + **-ON**.]

ex·on·er·ate /ig'zänə,rāt/ ▶ **v.** [trans.] **1** (esp. of an official body) absolve (someone) from blame for a fault or wrongdoing, esp. after due consideration of the case. **2** (**exonerate someone from**) release someone from (a duty or obligation). — **ex·on·er·a·tion** /ig,zänə'rāsHən/ **n.** **ex·on·er·a·tive** /-,rātiv/ **adj.** [ME: from L. *exonerat-* 'freed from a burden,' from the v. *exonerare*, from *ex-* 'from' + *onus, oner-* 'a burden.']

ex·o·nu·cle·ase /ˌeksō'n(y)o͞oklēˌās/ ▸ **n.** Biochem. an enzyme that removes successive nucleotides from the end of a polynucleotide molecule.

ex·o·pep·ti·dase /ˌeksō'peptiˌdās/ ▸ **n.** Biochem. an enzyme that breaks the terminal peptide bond in a peptide chain.

ex·oph·thal·mic /ˌeksäf'THalmik/ ▸ **adj.** Med. having or characterized by protruding eyes.

ex·oph·thal·mic goi·ter ▸ **n.** another term for GRAVES' DISEASE.

ex·oph·thal·mos /ˌeksäf'THalməs/ (also **ex·oph·thal·mus** or **ex·oph·thal·mi·a** /-mēə/) ▸ **n.** Med. abnormal protrusion of the eyeball or eyeballs. [17th C.: from mod. L. *exophthalmus*, from Gk. *exophthalmos* 'having prominent eyes,' from *ex-* 'out' + *ophthalmos* 'eye.']

exor. ▸ **abbr.** an executor (of a will).

ex·or·bi·tant /ig'zôrbitənt/ ▸ **adj.** (of a price or amount charged) unreasonably high. — **ex·or·bi·tance** /eg'zôrbətns/ **n.** **ex·or·bi·tant·ly** **adv.** [ME: from late L. *exorbitant-* 'going off the track,' from *exorbitare*, from *ex-* 'out from' + *orbita* 'course, track.']

ex·or·cise /'eksôrˌsīz; 'eksər-/ (also **ex·or·cize**) ▸ **v.** [trans.] drive out or attempt to drive out (an evil spirit) from a person or place. ■ (often **be exorcised**) rid (a person or place) of an evil spirit. [ME: from Fr. *exorciser* or eccles. L. *exorcizare*, from Gk. *exorkizein*, from *ex-* 'out' + *horkos* 'oath.']

ex·or·cism /'eksôrˌsizəm; 'eksər-/ ▸ **n.** the expulsion or attempted expulsion of an evil spirit. — **ex·or·cist** **n.**

ex·or·di·um /ig'zôrdēəm; ik'sôr-/ ▸ **n.** (pl. **-di·ums** or **-di·a** /-dēə/) formal the beginning or introductory part, esp. of a discourse or treatise. — **ex·or·di·al** /-dēəl/ **adj.** [16th C.: from L., from *exordiri* 'begin,' from *ex-* 'out, from' + *ordiri* 'begin.']

ex·o·skel·e·ton /ˌeksō'skelitn/ ▸ **n.** Zool. a rigid external covering for the body in some invertebrate animals, esp. arthropods. Compare with ENDOSKELETON. — **ex·o·skel·e·tal** /ˌeksō'skelətl/ **adj.**

ex·o·sphere /'eksōˌsfi(ə)r/ ▸ **n.** Astron. the outermost region of a planet's atmosphere. — **ex·o·spher·ic** /ˌeksō'sfi(ə)rik; -'sferik/ **adj.**

ex·o·spore /'eksōˌspôr/ ▸ **n.** **1** the outer layer of the membrane in some spores. **2** a spore formed by separation and release from a sporophore, the spore-bearing structure of a fungus. — **ex·o·spor·al** /ˌeksə'spôrəl/ **adj.**

ex·o·spor·i·um /ˌeksō'spôrēəm/ ▸ **n.** (pl. **-spor·i·a**) Bot. another term for EXINE. — **ex·o·spor·ial** /-'spôrēəl/ **adj.**

ex·os·to·sis /ˌeksä'stōsis/ ▸ **n.** (pl. **-ses** /-sēz/) Med. a benign outgrowth of cartilaginous tissue on a bone. [16th C.: from Gk., from *ex-* 'out' + *osteon* 'bone.']

ex·o·ter·ic /ˌeksə'terik/ ▸ **adj.** formal (esp. of a doctrine or mode of speech) intended for or likely to be understood by the general public. The opposite of ESOTERIC. ■ relating to the outside world; external. ■ current or popular among the general public. [17th C.: via L. from Gk. *exōterikos*, from *exōterō* 'outer,' compar. of *exō* 'outside.']

ex·o·ther·mic /ˌeksə'THərmik/ ▸ **adj.** Chem. (of a reaction or process) accompanied by the release of heat. The opposite of ENDOTHERMIC (sense 1). ■ (of a compound) formed from its constituent elements with a net release of heat. — **ex·o·ther·mi·cal·ly** /-k(ə)lē/ **adv.**

ex·ot·ic /ig'zätik/ ▸ **adj.** originating in or characteristic of a distant foreign country. ■ attractive or striking because colorful or out of the ordinary. | [as n.] (**the exotic**). ■ of a kind not used for ordinary purposes or not ordinarily encountered. ▸ **n.** an exotic plant or animal. ■ a thing that is imported or unusual. — **ex·ot·i·cal·ly** /-k(ə)lē/ **adv.** **ex·ot·i·cism** /-əˌsizəm/ **n.** [16th C.: via L. from Gk. *exōtikos* 'foreign,' from *exō* 'outside.']

ex·ot·i·ca /ig'zätikə/ ▸ **plural n.** objects considered strange or interesting because out of the ordinary, esp. because they originated in a distant foreign country. [19th C.: from L., neut. pl. of *exoticus* 'foreign' (see EXOTIC).]

ex·ot·ic danc·er ▸ **n.** a striptease dancer.

ex·o·tox·in /'eksōˌtäksin/ ▸ **n.** Microbiol. a toxin released by a living bacterial cell into its surroundings. Compare with ENDOTOXIN.

exp. ▸ **abbr.** ■ expenses. ■ experience (usually in the context of job advertisements). ■ (**Exp.**) experimental (in titles of periodicals). ■ expiration. ■ exposures (in the context of photography). ■ express.

ex·pand /ik'spand/ ▸ **v.** become or make larger or more extensive. ■ [intrans.] Physics (of the universe) undergo a continuous change whereby all the galaxies recede from one another. ■ [intrans.] (**expand on**) give a fuller version or account of. — **ex·pand·a·ble** **adj.** **ex·pand·er** **n.** **ex·pan·si·bil·i·ty** /ikˌspansə'bilitē/ **n.** **ex·pan·si·ble** /-'spansəbəl/ **adj.** [ME: from L. *expandere* 'to spread out,' from *ex-* 'out' + *pandere* 'to spread.']

ex·pand·ed /ik'spandid/ ▸ **adj.** being or having been enlarged, extended or broadened, in particular: ■ denoting materials which have a light cellular structure. ■ denoting sheet metal slit and stretched into a mesh, used to reinforce concrete and other brittle materials. ■ relatively broad in shape.

ex·panse /ik'spans/ ▸ **n.** an area of something, typically land or sea, presenting a wide continuous surface. ■ the distance to which something expands or can be expanded. [17th C.: from mod. L. *expansum* 'something expanded,' neut. past part. of *expandere* (see EXPAND).]

ex·pan·sile /ik'spansəl; -sīl/ ▸ **adj.** Physics of, relating to, or capable of expansion.

ex·pan·sion /ik'spanSHən/ ▸ **n.** the action of becoming larger or more extensive. ■ extension of a state's territory by encroaching on that of other nations, pursued as a political strategy. ■ a thing formed by the enlargement, broadening, or development of something. ■ the increase in the volume of fuel on combustion in the cylinder of an engine, or the piston stroke in which this occurs.

ex·pan·sion·ar·y /ik'spanSHəˌnerē/ ▸ **adj.** (of a policy or action) intended to result in economic or political expansion.

ex·pan·sion bolt ▸ **n.** a bolt that expands when inserted, no thread being required in the surrounding material.

ex·pan·sion·ism /ik'spanSHəˌnizəm/ ▸ **n.** the policy of territorial or economic expansion. — **ex·pan·sion·ist** **n.** & **adj.** **ex·pan·sion·is·tic** /ikˌspanSHə'nistik/ **adj.**

ex·pan·sion joint ▸ **n.** a joint that makes allowance for thermal expansion of the parts joined without distortion.

ex·pan·sive /ik'spansiv/ ▸ **adj.** **1** covering a wide area in terms of space or scope; extensive or wide-ranging. **2** (of a person or their manner) open, demonstrative, and communicative. **3** tending toward economic or political expansion. — **ex·pan·sive·ly** **adv.** **ex·pan·sive·ness** **n.**

ex·pan·siv·i·ty /ˌekspan'sivitē/ ▸ **n.** Physics the amount a material expands or contracts per unit length due to a one-degree change in temperature.

ex par·te /eks 'pärtē/ ▸ **adj.** & **adv.** Law with respect to or in the interests of one side only or of an interested outside party. [17th C.: Latin, literally 'from a side.']

ex·pat /eks'pat/ ▸ **n.** & **adj.** informal short for EXPATRIATE.

ex·pa·ti·ate /ik'spāSHēˌāt/ ▸ **v.** [intrans.] speak or write at length or in detail. — **ex·pa·ti·a·tion** /ikˌspāSHē'āSHən/ **n.** [16th C. (in the sense 'roam freely'): from L. *exspatiari* 'move beyond one's usual bounds,' from *ex-* 'out, from' + *spatiari* 'to walk' (from *spatium* 'space').]

ex·pa·tri·ate ▸ **n.** /eks'pātrēit/ a person who lives outside their native country. ■ archaic a person exiled from their native country. ▸ **adj.** [attrib.] living outside one's native country. ■ archaic expelled from one's native country. ▸ **v.** /-ˌāt/ [intrans.] settle oneself abroad. — **ex·pa·tri·a·tion** /eksˌpātrē'āSHən/ **n.** [18th C. (as a verb): from med. L. *expatriat-* 'gone out from one's country,' from the v. *expatriare*, from *ex-* 'out' + *patria* 'native country.']

ex·pect /ik'spekt/ ▸ **v.** [trans.] regard (something) as likely to happen. ■ regard (someone) as likely to do or be something. ■ believe that (someone or something) will arrive soon. ■ look for (something) from someone as rightfully due or requisite in the circumstances. ■ require (someone) to fulfill an obligation. ■ (**I expect**) informal used to indicate that one supposes something to be so, but has no firm evidence or knowledge.

– PHRASES **be expecting** (**a baby**) informal be pregnant. **to be expected** completely normal. **what can** (or **do**) **you expect?** used to emphasize that there was nothing unexpected about a person or event, however disappointed one might be. — **ex·pect·a·ble** **adj.** [16th C. (in the sense 'defer action, wait'): from L. *exspectare* 'look out for,' from *ex-* 'out' + *spectare* 'to look' (frequentative of *specere* 'see').]

ex·pect·an·cy /ik'spektənsē/ ▸ **n.** (pl. **-cies**) the state of thinking or hoping that something, esp. something pleasant, will happen or be the case.

ex·pect·ant /ik'spektənt/ ▸ **adj.** having or showing an excited feeling that something is about to happen, esp. something pleasant and interesting. ■ [attrib.] (of a woman) pregnant. ▸ **n.** archaic a person who anticipates receiving something, esp. high office. — **ex·pect·ant·ly** **adv.**

ex·pec·ta·tion /ˌekspek'tāSHən/ ▸ **n.** a strong belief that something will happen or be the case in the future. ■ a belief that someone will or should achieve something. ■ (**expectations**) archaic one's prospects of inheritance. ■ Math. another term for EXPECTED VALUE.

ex·pect·ed val·ue ▸ **n.** Math. a predicted value of a variable, calculated as the sum of all possible values each multiplied by the probability of its occurrence.

ex·pec·to·rant /ik'spektərənt/ ▸ **n.** a medicine that promotes the secretion of sputum by the air passages, used esp. to treat coughs.

ex·pec·to·rate /ik'spektəˌrāt/ ▸ **v.** [intrans.] cough or spit out phlegm from the throat or lungs. ■ [trans.] spit out (phlegm) in this way. — **ex·pec·to·ra·tion** /ikˌspektə'rāSHən/ **n.** [17th C.: from L. *expectorat-* 'expelled from the chest,' from *expectorare*, from *ex-* 'out' + *pector-* 'breast.']

ex·pe·di·ent /ik'spēdēənt/ ▸ **adj.** (of an action) convenient and practical, although possibly improper or immoral. ■ (of an action) suitable or appropriate. ▸ **n.** a means of attaining an end, esp. one that is convenient but considered improper or immoral. — **ex·pe·di·ence** **n.** **ex·pe·di·en·cy** **n.** **ex·pe·di·ent·ly** **adv.** [ME: from L. *expedient-* 'putting in order,' from *expedire* (see EXPEDITE).]

ex·pe·dite /'ekspəˌdīt/ ▸ **v.** [trans.] make (an action or process) be accomplished more quickly. — **ex·pe·dit·er** (also **ex·pe·di·tor** /-ˌdītər/) **n.** [15th C.: from L. *expedire* 'put in order,' from *ex-* 'out' + *ped-* 'foot.']

ex·pe·di·tion /ˌekspə'diSHən/ ▸ **n.** **1** a journey or voyage undertaken by a group of people with a particular purpose, esp. that of exploration, research, or war. ■ the people involved in such a journey or voyage. **2** formal promptness or speed in doing something.

ex·pe·di·tion·ar·y /ˌekspə'diSHəˌnerē/ ▸ **adj.** [attrib.] of or forming an expedition, esp. a military expedition.

ex·pe·di·tious /ˌekspəˈdisHəs/ ▶ **adj.** done with speed and efficiency. — **ex·pe·di·tious·ly** adv. **ex·pe·di·tious·ness** n. [15th C.: from EXPEDITION + -OUS.]

ex·pel /ikˈspel/ ▶ v. (**ex·pelled, ex·pel·ling**) [trans.] (often **be expelled**) deprive (someone) of membership of or involvement in a school or other organization. ■ force (someone) to leave a place, esp. a country. ■ force out or eject (something), esp. from the body. — **ex·pel·la·ble** adj. **ex·pel·lee** /ˌekspelˈlē/ n. **ex·pel·ler** n. [ME: from L. *expellere*, from *ex-* 'out' + *pellere* 'to drive.']

ex·pend /ikˈspend/ ▶ v. [trans.] spend or use up (a resource such as money, time, or energy). [ME: from L. *expendere*, from *ex-* 'out' + *pendere* 'weigh, pay.' Cf. SPEND.]

ex·pend·a·ble /ikˈspendəbəl/ ▶ **adj.** (of an object) designed to be used only once and then abandoned or destroyed. ■ of little significance when compared to an overall purpose, and therefore able to be abandoned. — **ex·pend·a·bil·i·ty** /ikˌspendəˈbilitē/ n. **ex·pend·a·bly** adv.

ex·pend·i·ture /ikˈspendicHər/ ▶ n. the action of spending funds. ■ an amount of money spent. [18th C.: from EXPEND.]

ex·pense /ikˈspens/ ▶ n. the cost required for something; the money spent on something. ■ (**expenses**) the costs incurred in the performance of one's job or a specific task, esp. one undertaken for another person. ■ a thing on which one is required to spend money. ▶ v. [trans.] (usu. **be expensed**) offset (an item of expenditure) as an expense against taxable income.
– PHRASES **at someone's expense** paid for by someone. ■ with someone as the victim, esp. of a joke. **at the expense of** so as to cause harm to or neglect of. [ME: based on late L. *expensa (pecunia)* '(money) spent,' from L. *expendere* 'pay out' (see EXPEND).]

ex·pense ac·count ▶ n. an arrangement under which sums of money spent in the course of business by an employee are later reimbursed by an employer.

ex·pen·sive /ikˈspensiv/ ▶ adj. costing a lot of money. — **ex·pen·sive·ly** adv. **ex·pen·sive·ness** n.

ex·pe·ri·ence /ikˈspi(ə)rēəns/ ▶ n. practical contact with and observation of facts or events. ■ the knowledge or skill acquired by such means over a period of time, esp. that gained in a particular profession by someone at work. ■ an event or occurrence that leaves an impression on someone. ▶ v. [trans.] encounter or undergo (an event or occurrence). ■ feel (an emotion). — **ex·pe·ri·ence·a·ble** adj. **ex·pe·ri·enc·er** n. [ME: via OFr. from L. *experientia*, from *experiri* 'try.']

ex·pe·ri·enced /ikˈspi(ə)rēənst/ ▶ adj. having knowledge or skill in a particular field, esp. a profession or job, gained over a period of time.

ex·pe·ri·en·tial /ekˌspi(ə)rēˈencHəl/ ▶ adj. involving or based on experience and observation. — **ex·pe·ri·en·tial·ly** adv.

ex·per·i·ment /ikˈsperəmənt/ ▶ n. a scientific procedure undertaken to make a discovery, test a hypothesis, or demonstrate a known fact. ■ a course of action tentatively adopted without being sure of the eventual outcome. ▶ v. /-ˌment/ [intrans.] perform a scientific procedure, esp. in a laboratory, to determine something. ■ try out new concepts or ways of doing things. — **ex·per·i·men·ta·tion** /ikˌsperəmənˈtāsHən/ n. **ex·per·i·ment·er** n. [ME: from OFr., or from L. *experimentum*, from *experiri* 'try.']

ex·per·i·men·tal /ikˌsperəˈmen(t)l/ ▶ adj. (of a new invention or product) based on untested ideas or techniques and not yet established or finalized. ■ (of a work of art or an artistic technique) involving a radically new and innovative style. ■ of or relating to scientific experiments. ■ archaic based on experience as opposed to authority or conjecture. — **ex·per·i·men·tal·ism** n. **ex·per·i·men·tal·ist** n. **ex·per·i·men·tal·ly** adv.

ex·per·i·men·tal psy·chol·o·gy ▶ n. the branch of psychology concerned with the scientific investigation of basic psychological processes such as learning, memory, and cognition in humans and animals.

ex·pert /ˈekspərt/ ▶ n. a person who has a comprehensive and authoritative knowledge of or skill in a particular area. ▶ adj. having or involving such knowledge or skill. — **ex·pert·ly** adv. **ex·pert·ness** n. [ME: from Fr., from L. *expertus*, past part. of *experiri* 'try.']

ex·per·tise /ˌekspərˈtēz; -ˈtēs/ ▶ n. expert skill or knowledge in a particular field: *technical expertise.*

ex·pert sys·tem ▶ n. Comput. a piece of software programmed using artificial intelligence techniques. Such systems use databases of expert knowledge to offer advice or make decisions.

ex·pi·ate /ˈekspēˌāt/ ▶ v. [trans.] atone for (guilt or sin). — **ex·pi·a·ble** /-əbəl/ adj. **ex·pi·a·tion** /ˌekspēˈāsHən/ n. **ex·pi·a·tor** /-ˌātər/ n. **ex·pi·a·to·ry** /ˈekspēəˌtôrē/ adj. [16th C.: from L. *expiat-* 'appeased by sacrifice,' from *expiare*, from *ex-* 'out' + *piare* (from *pius* 'pious').]

ex·pi·ra·tion /ˌekspəˈrāsHən/ ▶ n. **1** the ending of the fixed period for which a contract is valid. ■ the end of a period of time. **2** tech. exhalation of breath.

ex·pir·a·to·ry /ikˈspīrəˌtôrē/ ▶ adj. of or relating to the exhalation of air from the lungs.

ex·pire /ikˈspī(ə)r/ ▶ v. **1** [intrans.] (of a document, authorization, or agreement) cease to be valid, typically after a fixed period of time. ■ (of a period of time) come to an end. ■ (of a person) die. **2** [trans.] tech. exhale (air) from the lung. [ME: from OFr. *expirer*, from L. *exspirare* 'breathe out,' from *ex-* 'out' + *spirare* 'breathe.']

ex·pi·ry /ikˈspī(ə)rē; ek-/ ▶ n. Brit. Canadian the end of the period for which something is valid. ■ the end of a fixed period of time. ■ archaic death.

ex·plain /ikˈsplān/ ▶ v. [reporting verb] make (an idea, situation, or problem) clear to someone by describing it in more detail or revealing relevant facts or ideas. ■ [trans.] account for (an action or event) by giving a reason as excuse or justification. ■ (**explain something away**) minimize the significance of an embarrassing fact or action by giving an excuse or justification.
– PHRASES **explain oneself** expand on what one has said in order to make one's meaning clear. ■ give an account of one's motives or conduct in order to excuse or justify oneself. — **ex·plain·a·ble** adj. **ex·plain·er** n. [ME: from L. *explanare*, based on *planus* 'plain.']

ex·pla·na·tion /ˌeksplәˈnāsHən/ ▶ n. a statement or account that makes something clear. ■ a reason or justification given for an action or belief. [ME: from L. *explanatio(n-)*, from the v. *explanare* (see EXPLAIN).]

ex·plan·a·to·ry /ikˈsplanəˌtôrē/ ▶ adj. serving to explain something. — **ex·plan·a·to·ri·ly** /ikˌsplanəˈtôrəlē/ adv.

ex·plant Biol. ▶ v. /ekˈsplant/ [trans.] [often as adj.] (**explanted**) transfer (living cells, tissues, or organs) from animals or plants to a nutrient medium. ▶ n. /ˈeksˌplant/ a cell, organ, or piece of tissue that has been transferred in this way. — **ex·plan·ta·tion** /ˌeksplanˈtāsHən/ n. [20th C.: from mod. L. *explantare*, from *ex-* 'out' + *plantare* 'to plant.']

ex·ple·tive /ˈeksplitiv/ ▶ n. an oath or swear word. ■ Gram. a word or phrase used to fill out a sentence or a line of verse without adding to the sense. ▶ adj. Gram. (of a word or phrase) serving to fill out a sentence or line of verse. [ME (as an adj.): from late L. *expletivus*, from *explere* 'fill out.']

ex·pli·ca·ble /ekˈsplikəbəl; ˈeksplik-/ ▶ adj. able to be accounted for or understood.

ex·pli·cate /ˈekspliˌkāt/ ▶ v. [trans.] analyze and develop (an idea or principle) in detail. ■ analyze (a literary work) in order to reveal its meaning. — **ex·pli·ca·tion** /ˌeksplіˈkāsHən/ n. **ex·pli·ca·tive** /-ˌkātiv/ adj. **ex·pli·ca·tor** /-ˌkātər/ n. **ex·pli·ca·to·ry** /ikˈsplikəˌtôrē/ adj. [16th C.: from L. *explicat-* 'unfolded,' from the v. *explicare*, from *ex-* 'out' + *plicare* 'to fold.']

ex·plic·it /ikˈsplisit/ ▶ adj. stated clearly and in detail, leaving no room for confusion or doubt. ■ (of a person) stating something in such a way. ■ describing or representing sexual activity in a graphic fashion. ▶ n. the closing words of a text, manuscript, early printed book, or chanted liturgical text. Compare with INCIPIT. — **ex·plic·it·ly** adv. **ex·plic·it·ness** n. [17th C.: from Fr. *explicite* or L. *explicitus*, past part. of *explicare* 'unfold' (see EXPLICATE).]

ex·plode /ikˈsplōd/ ▶ v. [intrans.] **1** burst or shatter violently and noisily as a result of rapid combustion, decomposition, excessive internal pressure, or other process, typically scattering fragments widely. ■ [trans.] cause (a bomb) to do this. ■ tech. undergo a violent expansion in which much energy is released as a shock wave. ■ (of a person) suddenly give expression to violent and uncontainable emotion, esp. anger. ■ (of a violent emotion or a situation) arise or develop suddenly. ■ (**explode into**) suddenly begin to move or start a new activity. ■ increase suddenly or rapidly in size, number, or extent. ■ [as adj.] (**exploded**) (of a diagram or drawing) showing the components of a mechanism as if separated by an explosion but in the normal relative positions. **2** [trans.] (often **be exploded**) show (a belief or theory) to be false or unfounded. — **ex·plod·er** n. [16th C.: from L. *explodere* 'drive out by clapping,' from *ex-* 'out' + *plaudere* 'to clap.']

ex·ploit ▶ v. /ikˈsploit/ [trans.] make full use of and derive benefit from (a resource): *500 companies sprang up to exploit this new technology.* ■ use (a situation or person) in an unfair or selfish way: *the company was exploiting a legal loophole | accusations that he exploited a wealthy patient.* ■ benefit unfairly from the work of (someone), typically by overworking or underpaying them: *making money does not always mean exploiting others.* ▶ n. /ˈeksploit/ a bold or daring feat: *the most heroic and secretive exploits of the war.* — **ex·ploit·a·ble** adj. **ex·ploi·ta·tion** /ˌeksploiˈtāsHən/ n. **ex·ploit·a·tive** /ikˈsploitətiv/ adj. **ex·ploit·er** /ikˈsploitər/ n. **ex·ploit·ive** /ikˈsploitiv/ adj. [ME: from OFr. *esploit* (n.), based on L. *explicare* 'unfold' (see EXPLICATE).]

ex·plo·ra·tion /ˌeksplәˈrāsHən/ ▶ n. the action of traveling in or through an unfamiliar area in order to learn about it. ■ thorough analysis of a subject or theme. — **ex·plo·ra·tion·al** /-sHənl/ adj.

ex·plor·a·to·ry /ikˈsplôrəˌtôrē/ ▶ adj. relating to or involving exploration or investigation.

ex·plore /ikˈsplôr/ ▶ v. [trans.] travel in or through (an unfamiliar country or area) in order to learn about or familiarize oneself with it. ■ [intrans.] (**explore for**) search for resources such as mineral deposits. ■ inquire into or discuss (a subject or issue) in detail. ■ examine or evaluate (an option or possibility). ■ examine by touch. ■ Med. surgically examine (a wound or body cavity) in detail. — **ex·plor·a·tive** /-ˈplôrətiv/ adj. [16th C. (in the sense 'investigate (why)'): from Fr. *explorer*, from L. *explorare* 'search out,' from *ex-* 'out' + *plorare* 'utter a cry.']

ex·plo·sion /ikˈsplōzHən/ ▶ n. a violent and destructive shattering or blowing apart of something, as is caused by a bomb. ■ tech. a violent expansion in which energy is transmitted outward as a shock wave. ■ a sudden outburst of something such as noise, light, or violent emotion, esp. anger. ■ a sudden political or social upheaval. ■ a rapid or sudden increase in amount or extent. ■ Phonet. another term for PLOSION. [17th C.: from L. *explosio(n-)* 'scornful rejection,' from the v. *explodere* (see EXPLODE).]

ex·plo·sive /ikˈsplōsiv/ ▶ adj. able or likely to shatter violently or burst apart, as when a bomb explodes. ■ likely to cause an eruption of anger or controversy. ■ of or relating to a sudden and dramatic increase in amount or extent. ■ (of a vocal sound) produced with a sharp release of air. ■ Phonet. another term for PLOSIVE. ▶ n. (often **explosives**) a substance that can be made to explode, esp. any of those used in bombs or shells. — **ex·plo·sive·ly** adv. **ex·plo·sive·ness** n.

ex·po /'ekspō/ ▶ n. (pl. **-pos**) a large exhibition. [1960s: abbreviation of EXPOSITION.]

ex·po·nent /ik'spōnənt; 'ekspōnənt/ ▶ n. **1** a person who believes in and promotes the truth or benefits of an idea or theory. ■ a person who has and demonstrates a particular skill, esp. to a high standard. **2** Math. a quantity representing the power to which a given number or expression is to be raised, usually expressed as a raised symbol beside the number or expression (e.g., 3 in 23 = 2 × 2 × 2). **3** Ling. a linguistic unit that realizes another, more abstract unit. [16th C.: from L. *exponent-* 'putting out,' from *exponere* (see EXPOUND).]

ex·po·nen·tial /,ekspə'nenCHəl/ ▶ adj. Math. of or expressed by a mathematical exponent. ■ (of an increase) becoming more and more rapid. — **ex·po·nen·tial·ly** adv.

ex·po·nen·tial func·tion ▶ n. Math. a function whose value is a constant raised to the power of the argument, esp. the function where the constant is *e*.

ex·po·nen·tial growth ▶ n. growth whose rate becomes ever more rapid in proportion to the growing total number or size.

ex·po·nen·ti·a·tion /,ekspə,nenCHē'āSHən/ ▶ n. Math. the operation of raising one quantity to the power of another. — **ex·po·nen·ti·ate** /-'nenCHē,āt/ v.

ex·port ▶ v. /ik'spôrt; 'ekspôrt/ [trans.] send (goods or services) to another country for sale. ■ spread or introduce (ideas and beliefs) to another country. ■ Comput. transfer (data) in a format that can be used by other programs. ▶ n. /'ekspôrt/ (usu. **exports**) a commodity, article, or service sold abroad. ■ (**exports**) sales of goods or services to other countries, or the revenue from such sales. ■ the selling and sending out of goods or services to other countries. ■ [as adj.] of a high standard suitable for export. — **ex·port·a·bil·i·ty** /ik,spôrtə'bilitē/ n. **ex·port·a·ble** /ik'spôrtəbəl/ adj. **ex·por·ta·tion** /,ekspôr'tāSHən/ n. **ex·port·er** n. [15th C.: from L. *exportare*, from *ex-* 'out' + *portare* 'carry.']

ex·pose /ik'spōz/ ▶ v. [trans.] (often **be exposed**) make (something) visible, typically by uncovering it. ■ [often as adj.] (**exposed**) leave (something) uncovered or unprotected, esp. from the weather. ■ subject (photographic film) to light, esp. when operating a camera. ■ (**expose oneself**) publicly and indecently display one's genitals. ■ [usu. as adj.] (**exposed**) leave or put (someone) in an unprotected and vulnerable state. ■ (**expose someone to**) cause someone to experience or be at risk of. ■ make (something embarrassing or damaging) public. ■ reveal the true and typically objectionable nature of (someone or something). ■ (**expose someone to**) introduce (someone) to (a subject or area of knowledge). ■ leave (a child) in the open to die. — **ex·pos·er** n. [ME: from OFr. *exposer*, from Latin *exponere* (see EXPOUND), but influenced by L. *expositus* 'put or set out.']

ex·po·sé /,ekspō'zā/ ▶ n. a report of the facts about something, esp. a journalistic report that reveals something scandalous. [19th C.: from French, 'shown, set out,' past participle of *exposer* (see EXPOSE).]

ex·po·si·tion /,ekspə'ziSHən/ ▶ n. **1** a comprehensive description and explanation of an idea or theory. ■ Music the part of a movement, esp. in sonata form, in which the principal themes are first presented. ■ the part of a play or work of fiction in which the background to the main conflict is introduced. **2** a large public exhibition of art or trade goods. ■ archaic the action of making public; exposure. — **ex·po·si·tion·al** /-'ziSHənl/ adj.

ex·pos·i·tor /ik'späzitər/ ▶ n. a person or thing that explains complicated ideas or theories.

ex·pos·i·to·ry /ik'späzi,tôrē/ ▶ adj. intended to explain or describe something: *expository prose*.

ex post fac·to /,eks ,pōst 'faktō/ ▶ adj. & adv. with retroactive effect or force: [as adj.] *ex post facto laws*. [erroneous division of L. *ex postfacto* 'in the light of subsequent events.']

ex·pos·tu·late /ik'späsCHə,lāt/ ▶ v. [intrans.] express strong disapproval or disagreement. — **ex·pos·tu·la·tion** /ik,späsCHə'lāSHən/ n. **ex·pos·tu·la·tor** /-lātər/ n. **ex·pos·tu·la·to·ry** /ik,späsCHələ,tôrē/ adj. [16th C.: from L. *expostulat-* 'demanded,' from *expostulare*, from *ex-* 'out' + *postulare* 'demand.']

ex·po·sure /ik'spōZHər/ ▶ n. **1** the state of being exposed to contact with something. ■ an act or instance of being uncovered or unprotected. ■ a physical condition resulting from being outside in severe weather conditions without adequate protection. ■ experience of something. ■ the action of exposing a photographic film to light or other radiation. ■ the quantity of light or other radiation reaching a photographic film, as determined by shutter speed and lens aperture. ■ the action of placing oneself at risk of financial losses. **2** the revelation of an identity or fact, esp. one that is concealed or likely to arouse disapproval. ■ the publicizing of information or an event. **3** the direction in which a building faces; an outlook.

ex·po·sure me·ter ▶ n. another term for LIGHT METER.

ex·pound /ik'spound/ ▶ v. present and explain (a theory or idea) systematically and in detail. ■ explain the meaning of (a literary or doctrinal work). — **ex·pound·er** n. [ME *expoune*: from OFr. *espon-*, present tense stem of *espondre*, from L. *exponere* 'expose,' from *ex-* 'out' + *ponere* 'put.']

ex·press[1] /ik'spres/ ▶ v. [trans.] **1** convey (a thought or feeling) in words or by gestures and conduct. ■ (**express oneself**) say what one thinks or means. ■ esp. Math. represent (a number, relation, or property) by a figure, symbol, or formula. ■ (usu. **be expressed**) Genet. cause (an inherited characteristic or gene) to appear in a phenotype. **2** squeeze out (liquid or air). — **ex·press·er** n. **ex·press·i·ble** adj. [ME: from OFr. *expresser*, based on L. *ex-* 'out' + *pressare* 'to press.']

ex·press[2] ▶ adj. operating at high speed. ■ (of a train or other vehicle of public transportation) making few intermediate stops and so reaching its destination quickly. Compare with LOCAL. ■ denoting a company undertaking the transportation of letters and packages, esp. one promising overnight or other rapid delivery. ■ esp. Brit. denoting a service in which messages or goods are delivered by a special messenger to ensure speed or security. ▶ adv. by express train or delivery service. ▶ n. **1** an express train or other vehicle of public transportation. **2** an overnight or rapid delivery service. ■ used in names of delivery services, trains, and newspapers to denote speed of service. ■ used in names of airlines to denote nonstop regional service on small planes. **3** an express rifle. ▶ v. [trans.] send by express delivery or messenger. [18th C. (in the sense of the v.): extension of EXPRESS[3].]

ex·press[3] ▶ adj. definitely stated, not merely implied. ■ precisely and specifically identified to the exclusion of anything else. — **ex·press·ly** adv. [ME: from OFr. *expres*, from L. *expressus* 'distinctly presented,' past part. of *exprimere* 'press out, express,' from *ex-* 'out' + *primere* 'press.']

ex·pres·sion /ik'spreSHən/ ▶ n. **1** the process of making known one's thoughts or feelings. ■ the conveying of opinions publicly without interference by the government: *freedom of expression*. ■ the look on someone's face that conveys a particular emotion. ■ the ability to put an emotion into words. ■ a word or phrase, esp. an idiomatic one, used to convey an idea. ■ the style or phrasing of written or spoken words. ■ the conveying of feeling in the face or voice, in a work of art, or in the performance of a piece of music. ■ Math. a collection of symbols that jointly express a quantity. ■ Genet. the appearance in a phenotype of a characteristic or effect attributed to a particular gene. ■ (also **gene expression**) Genet. the process by which possession of a gene leads to the appearance in the phenotype of the corresponding character. **2** the production of something, esp. by pressing or squeezing it out. — **ex·pres·sion·al** /ek'spreSHənəl/ adj. **ex·pres·sion·less** adj. **ex·pres·sion·less·ly** adv. **ex·pres·sion·less·ness** n.

ex·pres·sion·ism /ik'spreSHə,nizəm/ ▶ n. a style of painting, music, or drama in which the artist or writer seeks to express emotional experience rather than impressions of the external world. — **ex·pres·sion·ist** n. & adj. **ex·pres·sion·is·tic** /ik,spreSHə'nistik/ adj. **ex·pres·sion·is·ti·cal·ly** /ik,spreSHə'nistik(ə)lē/ adv.

ex·pres·sive /ik'spresiv/ ▶ adj. effectively conveying thought or feeling. ■ [predic.] (**expressive of**) conveying (the specified quality or idea): *spires expressive of religious aspiration*. — **ex·pres·sive·ly** adv. **ex·pres·sive·ness** n. **ex·pres·siv·i·ty** /,ekspre'sivitē/ n.

ex·press lane ▶ n. (on a highway) a lane for through traffic, having fewer exits. ■ (in a grocery store) a checkout aisle for shoppers buying only a few items.

Ex·press Mail ▶ n. trademark a service of the US Postal Service that guarantees overnight delivery.

ex·pres·so /ik'spresō/ ▶ n. var. of ESPRESSO.

ex·press ri·fle ▶ n. a rifle that discharges a bullet at high speed and is used in big-game hunting.

ex·press·way /ik'spres,wā/ ▶ n. a highway designed for fast traffic, with controlled entrance and exit, a dividing strip between the traffic in opposite directions, and typically two or more lanes in each direction.

ex·pro·pri·ate /eks'prōprē,āt/ ▶ v. [trans.] (esp. of the state) take away (property) from its owner. ■ dispossess (someone) of property. — **ex·pro·pri·a·tion** /eks,prōprē'āSHən/ n. **ex·pro·pri·a·tor** /-,ātər/ n. [16th C.: from med. L. *expropriat-* 'taken from the owner,' from the v. *expropriare*, from *ex-* 'out, from' + *proprium* 'property,' neut. sing. of *proprius* 'own.']

expt. ▶ abbr. experiment.

exptl. ▶ abbr. experimental.

ex·pul·sion /ik'spəlSHən/ ▶ n. the action of depriving someone of membership in an organization. ■ the process of forcing someone to leave a place, esp. a country. ■ the process of forcing something out of the body. — **ex·pul·sive** adj. [ME: from L. *expulsio(n-)*, from *expellere* 'drive out' (see EXPEL).]

ex·punge /ik'spənj/ ▶ v. [trans.] erase or remove completely (something unwanted or unpleasant). — **ex·punc·tion** /ik'spəNG(k)SHən/ n. **ex·punge·ment** n. **ex·pung·er** n. [17th C.: from L. *expungere* 'mark for deletion by means of points,' from *ex-* 'out' + *pungere* 'to prick.']

ex·pur·gate /'ekspər,gāt/ ▶ v. [trans.] [often as adj.] (**expurgated**) remove matter thought to be objectionable or unsuitable from (a book or account). — **ex·pur·ga·tion** /,ekspər'gāSHən/ n. **ex·pur·ga·tor** /-,gātər/ n. **ex·pur·ga·to·ry** /ik'spərgə,tôrē/ adj. [17th C.: from L. *expurgat-* 'thoroughly cleansed,' from *expurgare*, from *ex-* 'out' + *purgare* 'cleanse.']

ex·quis·ite /ek'skwizit; 'ekskwizit/ ▶ adj. extremely beautiful and, typically, delicate. ■ intensely felt: *exquisite agony*. ■ highly sensitive or discriminating: *exquisite taste*. ▶ n. a person who is affectedly concerned with appearance. — **ex·quis·ite·ly** adv. **ex·quis·ite·ness** n. [ME:

from L. *exquisit-* 'sought out,' from *exquirere*, from *ex-* 'out' + *quaerere* 'seek.']

exr. ▶ abbr. executor.

exrx. ▶ abbr. executrix.

ex·san·gui·na·tion /ek,saNGgwə'nāsHən/ ▶ n. Med. the action of draining a person, animal, or organ of blood. ■ severe loss of blood. — **ex·san·gui·nate** /ek'saNGgwə,nāt/ v.

ex·san·guine /eks'saNGgwin/ ▶ adj. literary bloodless; anemic. [17th C.: from EX-[1] 'out' + L. *sanguis, sanguin-* 'blood.']

ex·sert /ek'sərt/ ▶ v. [trans.] Biol. cause to protrude; push out: [as adj.] (**exserted**) *an exserted stigma.* [17th C.: from L. *exsert-* 'put forth,' from the v. *exserere* (see EXERT).]

ext. ▶ abbr. ■ extension (in a telephone number). ■ exterior. ■ external. ■ extra.

ex·tant /'ekstənt; ek'stant/ ▶ adj. (esp. of a document) still in existence; surviving. [16th C.: from L. *exstant-* 'existing,' from *exstare*, from *ex-* 'out' + *stare* 'to stand.']

ex·tem·po·ra·ne·ous /ik,stempə'rānēəs/ ▶ adj. spoken or done without preparation. — **ex·tem·po·ra·ne·ous·ly** adv. **ex·tem·po·ra·ne·ous·ness** n.

ex·tem·po·rar·y /ik'stempə,rerē/ ▶ adj. another term for EXTEMPORANEOUS. — **ex·tem·po·rar·i·ly** /ik,stempə'rerəlē/ adv. **ex·tem·po·rar·i·ness** n.

ex·tem·po·re /ik'stempərē/ ▶ adj. & adv. spoken or done without preparation. [16th C.: from L. *ex tempore* 'on the spur of the moment' (lit. 'out of the time').]

ex·tem·po·rize /ik'stempə,rīz/ ▶ v. compose, perform, or produce something such as music or a speech without preparation; improvise. — **ex·tem·po·ri·za·tion** /ik,stempəri'zāsHən/ n.

ex·tend /ik'stend/ ▶ v. [trans.] **1** cause to cover a larger area; make longer or wider. ■ expand in scope, effect, or meaning. ■ cause to last longer. ■ postpone (a starting or ending time) beyond the original limit. ■ straighten or spread out (the body or a limb) at full length. ■ [intrans.] spread from a central point to cover a wider area. ■ [intrans.] occupy a specified area or stretch to a specified point. ■ [intrans.] (**extend to**) include within one's scope; be applicable to. ■ increase the volume or bulk of (something) by adding a cheaper substance. ■ (**extend oneself**) exert or exercise oneself to the utmost. **2** hold (something) out toward someone. ■ offer. ■ make (a resource) available to someone. — **ex·tend·a·bil·i·ty** /ik,stendə'bilitē/ n. **ex·tend·a·ble** adj. **ex·tend·i·bil·i·ty** /ik,stendə'bilitē/ n. **ex·tend·i·ble** /-əbəl/ adj. **ex·ten·si·bil·i·ty** /ik,stensə'bilitē/ n. **ex·ten·si·ble** /-'stensəbəl/ adj. [ME: from L. *extendere* 'stretch out,' from *ex-* 'out' + *tendere* 'stretch.']

ex·tend·ed fam·i·ly ▶ n. a family that extends beyond the nuclear family, including grandparents, aunts, uncles, and other relatives, who typically all live nearby or in one household.

ex·tend·ed-play ▶ adj. denoting a record that plays for longer than most singles. ■ denoting an audio- or videotape that is thinner and longer than standard.

ex·tend·er /ik'stendər/ ▶ n. a person or thing that extends something. ■ a substance added to a product such as paint, ink, or glue, to dilute its color or increase its bulk.

ex·ten·sile /ik'stensəl; -sīl/ ▶ adj. capable of being stretched out or protruded.

ex·ten·sion /ik'stensHən/ ▶ n. **1** a part that is added to something to enlarge or prolong it; a continuation. ■ a room or set of rooms added to an existing building. ■ the action or process of becoming or making something larger. ■ an application of an existing system or activity to a new area. ■ an increase in the length of time given to someone to fulfill an obligation. ■ Comput. an optional suffix to a file name, typically consisting of a period followed by several characters, indicating the file's content or function. **2** (also **extension cord**) a length of electric cord that permits the use of appliances at some distance from a fixed socket. ■ an extra telephone on the same line as the main one. ■ a subsidiary telephone in a set of offices or similar building, on a line leading from the main switchboard but having its own additional number. **3** [usu. as adj.] instruction by a university or college for students who do not attend full time: *extension courses.* **4** (**extensions**) long lengths of artificial hair woven into a person's own hair. **5** the action of moving a limb from a bent to a straight position. ■ the muscle action controlling this. ■ Ballet the ability of a dancer to raise one leg above the waist. **6** Logic the range of a term or concept as measured by the objects that it denotes or contains, as opposed to its internal content. Often contrasted with INTENSION. ■ Physics Philos. the property of occupying space; spatial magnitude.

– PHRASES **by extension** taking the same line of argument further. — **ex·ten·sion·al** /-sHənl/ adj. [ME: from late L. *extensio(n-)*, from *extendere* 'stretch out' (see EXTEND).]

ex·ten·sion lad·der ▶ n. a ladder that can be extended by means of sliding sections.

ex·ten·sion tube ▶ n. Photog. a tube fitted to a camera between the body and lens to shorten the distance of closest focus of an object so that close-up pictures can be taken.

ex·ten·sive /ik'stensiv/ ▶ adj. **1** covering or affecting a large area. ■ large in amount or scale. **2** (of agriculture) obtaining a relatively small crop from a large area with a minimum of attention and expense: *extensive farming techniques.* Often contrasted with INTENSIVE (sense 1). — **ex·ten·sive·ly** adv. **ex·ten·sive·ness** n.

ex·ten·som·e·ter /eksten'sämitər/ ▶ n. an instrument for measuring the deformation of a material under stress.

ex·ten·sor /ik'stensər; -sôr/ (also **extensor muscle**) ▶ n. Anat. a muscle whose contraction extends or straightens a limb or other part of the body. Often contrasted with FLEXOR. ■ any of a number of specific muscles in the arm, hand, leg, and foot. [18th C.: from late L., from *extens-* 'stretched out,' from the v. *extendere* (see EXTEND).]

ex·tent /ik'stent/ ▶ n. [in sing.] the area covered by something: *an enclosure ten acres in extent.* ■ the degree to which something has spread; the size or scale of something. ■ the amount to which something is or is believed to be the case. ■ a large space or area. [ME: from Anglo-Norman Fr. *extente*, from med. L. *extenta*, fem. past part. of L. *extendere* 'stretch out' (see EXTEND).]

ex·ten·u·ate /ik'stenyoo͞,āt/ ▶ v. [trans.] **1** [usu. as adj.] (**extenuating**) make (guilt or an offense) seem less serious or more forgivable: *there were extenuating circumstances that caused me to say the things I did.* **2** [usu. as adj.] (**extenuated**) literary make (someone) thin. — **ex·ten·u·a·tion** /ik,stenyoo͞'āsHən/ n. **ex·ten·u·a·to·ry** /-ə,tôrē/ adj. [ME: from L. *extenuat-* 'made thin,' from *extenuare* (based on *tenuis* 'thin').]

ex·te·ri·or /ik'sti(ə)rēər/ ▶ adj. forming, situated on, or relating to the outside of something. ■ coming from outside. ■ (in filming) outdoor. ▶ n. the outer surface or structure of something. ■ the outer structure of a building. ■ a person's behavior and appearance, often contrasted with their true character ■ (in filming) an outdoor scene. — **ex·te·ri·or·i·ty** /ik,sti(ə)rē'ôritē; -'äritē/ n. **ex·te·ri·or·ize** /-ə,rīz/ v. **ex·te·ri·or·ly** adv. [16th C.: from L., compar. of *exter* 'outer.']

ex·te·ri·or an·gle ▶ n. Geom. the angle between a side of a rectilinear figure and an adjacent side extended outward.

ex·ter·mi·nate /ik'stərmə,nāt/ ▶ v. [trans.] (often **be exterminated**) destroy completely. ■ kill (a pest). — **ex·ter·mi·na·tion** /ik,stərmə'nāsHən/ n. **ex·ter·mi·na·tor** /-,nātər/ n. **ex·ter·mi·na·to·ry** /-nə,tôrē/ adj. [ME: from L. *exterminat-* 'banished,' from *exterminare*, from *ex-* 'out' + *terminus* 'boundary.']

ex·tern /'ekstərn/ ▶ n. a person working in but not living in an institution. — **ex·tern·ship** n. [16th C.: from French *externe* or Latin *externus*, from *exter* 'outer.']

ex·ter·nal /ik'stərnl/ ▶ adj. **1** belonging to or forming the outer surface or structure of something. ■ relating to or denoting a medicine or similar substance for use on the outside of the body. **2** coming or derived from a source outside the subject affected. ■ coming from or relating to a foreign country or an outside institution. ■ existing outside the mind. ■ Comput. (of hardware) not contained in the main computer; peripheral. ■ Comput. (of storage) using a disk or tape drive rather than the main memory. ▶ n. (**externals**) the outward features of something. ■ features that are only superficial; inessentials. — **ex·ter·nal·ly** adv.

ex·ter·nal au·di·to·ry me·a·tus ▶ n. see MEATUS.

ex·ter·nal ear ▶ n. the parts of the ear outside the eardrum, esp. the pinna.

ex·ter·nal·ism /ik'stərnl,izəm/ ▶ n. **1** excessive regard for outward form in religion. **2** Philos. the view that mental events and acts are essentially dependent on the world external to the mind. — **ex·ter·nal·ist** n. & adj.

ex·ter·nal·i·ty /,ekstər'nalitē/ ▶ n. (pl. **-ties**) **1** Econ. a side effect or consequence of an industrial or commercial activity that affects other parties without this being reflected in the cost of the goods or services involved, such as the pollination of surrounding crops by bees kept for honey. **2** Philos. the fact of existing outside the perceiving subject.

ex·ter·nal·ize /ik'stərnl,īz/ ▶ v. [trans.] (usu. **be externalized**) give external existence or form to. ■ express (a thought or feeling) in words or actions. ■ Psychol. project (a mental image or process) onto a figure outside oneself. — **ex·ter·nal·i·za·tion** /ik,stərnl-i'zāsHən/ n.

ex·ter·o·cep·tive /,ekstərō'septiv/ ▶ adj. Physiol. relating to stimuli that are external to an organism. Compare with INTEROCEPTIVE. — **ex·ter·o·cep·tion** /-'sepsHən/ n. **ex·ter·o·cep·tiv·i·ty** /-sep'tivitē/ n. [20th C.: prob. a blend of EXTERIOR or EXTERNAL and RECEPTIVE.]

ex·ter·o·cep·tor /,ekstərō'septər/ ▶ n. Physiol. a sensory receptor that receives external stimuli. Compare with INTEROCEPTOR.

ex·tinct /ik'stiNG(k)t/ ▶ adj. (of a species, family, or other larger group) having no living members. ■ often humorous no longer in existence. ■ (of a volcano) not having erupted in recorded history. ■ no longer burning. ■ (of a title of nobility) having no qualified claimant. [ME (in the sense 'no longer alight'): from L. *exstinct-* 'extinguished,' from the v. *exstinguere* (see EXTINGUISH).]

ex·tinc·tion /ik'stiNG(k)sHən/ ▶ n. **1** the state or process of a species, family, or larger group being or becoming extinct. ■ the state or process of ceasing or causing something to cease to exist. ■ the wiping out of a debt. **2** Physics reduction in the intensity of light or other radiation as it passes through a medium or object, due to absorption, reflection, and scattering.

ex·tin·guish /ik'stiNGgwisH/ ▶ v. [trans.] cause (a fire or light) to cease to burn or shine. ■ (often **be extinguished**) put an end to; annihilate. ■ (often **be extinguished**) cancel (a debt) by full payment. ■ Law render (a right or obligation) void. — **ex·tin·guish·a·ble** adj. **ex·tin·guish·ment** n. (Law). [16th C.: from L. *exstinguere*, from *ex-* 'out' + *stinguere* 'quench.' Cf. DISTINGUISH.]

ex·tin·guish·er /ik'stiNGgwisHər/ ▶ n. short for FIRE EXTINGUISHER.

ex·tir·pate /'ekstər,pāt/ ▶ v. [trans.] root out and destroy completely. — **ex·tir·pa·tion** /,ekstər'pāsHən/ n. **ex·tir·pa·tor** /-,pātər/ n. [ME (as *extirpation*): from L. *exstirpare*, from *ex-* 'out' + *stirps* 'a stem.']

ex·tol /ik'stōl/ ▶ v. (**ex·tolled, ex·tol·ling**) [trans.] praise enthusiastically.

—**ex·tol·ler** n. **ex·tol·ment** n. [ME: from L. *extollere*, from *ex-* 'out, upward' + *tollere* 'raise.']

ex·tort /ik'stôrt/ ▶v. obtain (something) by force, threats, or other unfair means. —**ex·tort·er** n. **ex·tor·tive** adj. [16th C.: from L. *extort-* 'wrested,' from the v. *extorquere*, from *ex-* 'out' + *torquere* 'to twist.']

ex·tor·tion /ik'stôrsHən/ ▶n. the practice of obtaining something, esp. money, through force or threats. —**ex·tor·tion·er** n. **ex·tor·tion·ist** /-ist/ n.

ex·tor·tion·ate /ik'stôrsHənit/ ▶adj. **1** (of a price) much too high; exorbitant. **2** using or given to extortion. —**ex·tor·tion·ate·ly** adv.

ex·tra /'ekstrə/ ▶adj. added to an existing or usual amount or number. ▶adv. **1** [as submodifier] to a greater extent than usual; especially: *he is trying to be extra good.* **2** in addition: *installation will cost about $60 extra.* ▶n. an item in addition to what is usual or strictly necessary. ■ an item for which an additional charge is made. ■ a person engaged temporarily to fill out a scene in a movie or play, esp. as one of a crowd. ■ dated a special issue of a newspaper. [17th C.: prob. a shortening of EXTRAORDINARY.]

extra- ▶prefix outside; beyond. ■ beyond the scope of: *extracurricular.* [via med. L. from L. *extra* 'outside.']

ex·tra-base hit ▶n. Baseball a base hit that allows a batter to safely reach second base, third base, or home without the benefit of a fielding error; a double, triple, or home run.

ex·tra·cel·lu·lar /,ekstrə'selyələr/ ▶adj. Biol. situated or taking place outside a cell or cells. —**ex·tra·cel·lu·lar·ly** adv.

ex·tra·chro·mo·so·mal /,ekstrə,krōmə'sōməl/ ▶adj. Biol. situated or operating outside the chromosome.

ex·tra·con·sti·tu·tion·al /,ekstrə,känstə't(y)o͞osHənl/ ▶adj. not based on or authorized by a political constitution.

ex·tra·cor·po·re·al /'ekstrəkôr'pôrēəl/ ▶adj. esp. Surg. situated or occurring outside the body. ■ denoting a technique of lithotripsy using shock waves generated externally.

ex·tract ▶v. /ik'strakt/ [trans.] (often **be extracted**) remove or take out, esp. by effort or force. ■ obtain (something such as money or an admission) from someone in the face of initial unwillingness. ■ obtain (a substance or resource) from something by a special method. ■ select (a passage from a piece of writing, music, or film) for quotation, performance, or reproduction. ■ derive (an idea or the evidence for it) from a body of information. ■ Math. calculate (a root of a number). ▶n. /'ekstrakt/ **1** a short passage taken from a piece of writing, music, or film. **2** [with adj.] a preparation containing the active ingredient of a substance in concentrated form. —**ex·tract·a·bil·i·ty** /ik,straktə'bilitē/ n. **ex·tract·a·ble** adj. [ME: from L. *extract-* 'drawn out,' from the v. *extrahere*, from *ex-* 'out' + *trahere* 'draw.']

ex·trac·tion /ik'straksHən/ ▶n. **1** the action of taking out something, esp. using effort or force. **2** [with adj.] the ethnic origin of someone's family.

ex·trac·tive /ik'straktiv/ ▶adj. of or involving extraction, esp. the extensive extraction of natural resources without provision for their renewal.

ex·trac·tor /ik'straktər/ ▶n. [often with adj.] a machine or device used to extract something.

ex·tra·cur·ric·u·lar /,ekstrəkə'rikyələr/ ▶adj. (of an activity at a school or college) pursued in addition to the normal course of study. ■ often humorous outside the normal routine, esp. that provided by a job or marriage. —**ex·tra·cur·ric·u·lar·ly** adv.

ex·tra·dit·a·ble /'ekstrə,dītəbəl; ,ekstrə'dītəbəl/ ▶adj. (of a crime) making a criminal liable to extradition. ■ (of a criminal) liable to extradition.

ex·tra·dite /'ekstrə,dīt/ ▶v. [trans.] hand over (a person accused or convicted of a crime) to the jurisdiction of the foreign state in which the crime was committed. [19th C.: back-form. from EXTRADITION.]

ex·tra·di·tion /,ekstrə'disHən/ ▶n. the action of extraditing a person accused or convicted of a crime. [19th C.: from Fr., from *ex-* 'out, from' + *tradition* 'delivery.']

ex·tra·dos /'ekstrə,däs/ ▶n. (pl. same or **-dos·es**) Archit. the upper or outer curve of an arch. Often contrasted with INTRADOS. [18th C.: from French, from Latin *extra* 'outside' + Fr. *dos* 'back' (from L. *dorsum*).]

ex·tra·flo·ral /,ekstrə'flôrəl/ ▶adj. Bot. (of a nectary) situated outside a flower, esp. on a leaf or stem.

ex·tra·ga·lac·tic /,ekstrəgə'laktik/ ▶adj. Astron. situated, occurring, or originating outside the Milky Way galaxy.

ex·tra in·nings ▶n. Baseball the continuation of a tie game beyond the usual nine innings. ■ any continuation beyond the expected or scheduled time.

ex·tra·ju·di·cial /,ekstrəjo͞o'disHəl/ ▶adj. Law (of a sentence) not legally authorized. ■ (of a settlement, statement, or confession) not made in court; out-of-court. —**ex·tra·ju·di·cial·ly** adv.

ex·tra·le·gal /,ekstrə'lēgəl/ ▶adj. (of an action or situation) beyond the authority of the law; not regulated by the law.

ex·tra·lim·it·al /,ekstrə'limitl/ ▶adj. esp. Biol. situated, occurring, or derived from outside a particular area.

ex·tra·lin·guis·tic /,ekstrəliNG'gwistik/ ▶adj. not involving or beyond the bounds of language.

ex·tra·mar·i·tal /,ekstrə'maritl/ ▶adj. (esp. of sexual relations) occurring outside marriage. —**ex·tra·mar·i·tal·ly** adv.

ex·tra·mun·dane /,ekstrəmən'dān/ ▶adj. rare outside or beyond the physical world.

ex·tra·mu·ral /,ekstrə'myo͝orəl/ ▶adj. outside the walls or boundaries of a town, college, or institution. ■ additional to one's work or course of study and typically not connected with it. —**ex·tra·mu·ral·ly** adv. [19th C.: from L. *extra muros* 'outside the walls' + -AL.]

ex·tra·mu·si·cal /,ekstrə'myo͞ozikəl/ ▶adj. extrinsic to a piece of music or outside the field of music.

ex·tra·ne·ous /ik'strānēəs/ ▶adj. irrelevant or unrelated to the subject being dealt with. ■ of external origin. ■ separate from the object to which it is attached. —**ex·tra·ne·ous·ly** adv. **ex·tra·ne·ous·ness** n. [17th C.: from L. *extraneus* + -OUS.]

ex·tra·nu·cle·ar /,ekstrə'n(y)o͞oklēər/ ▶adj. **1** situated in or affecting parts of a cell outside the nucleus. **2** situated or occurring outside the nucleus of an atom.

ex·tra·oc·u·lar mus·cle /,ekstrə'äkyələr/ ▶n. each of six small voluntary muscles controlling movement of the eyeball within the socket.

ex·tra·or·di·naire /,ekstrə,ôrdn'er/ ▶adj. [postpositive] informal outstanding or remarkable in a particular capacity: *memories of a gardener extraordinaire.* [1940s: French, 'extraordinary.']

ex·traor·di·nar·y /ik'strôrdn,erē; ,ekstrə'ôrdn-/ ▶adj. very unusual or remarkable. ■ unusually great. ■ [attrib.] (of a meeting) specially convened. ■ [postpositive] (of an official) additional; specially employed. —**ex·traor·di·nar·i·ly** /-,erəlē/ adv. **ex·traor·di·nar·i·ness** n. [ME: from L. *extraordinarius*, from *extra ordinem* 'outside the normal course of events.']

ex·traor·di·nar·y ren·di·tion ▶n. another term for RENDITION (sense 2).

ex·tra point ▶n. Football a point awarded for a successful placekick following a touchdown.Also called POINT AFTER TOUCHDOWN.

ex·trap·o·late /ik'strapə,lāt/ ▶v. [trans.] extend the application of (a method or conclusion, esp. one based on statistics) to an unknown situation by assuming that existing trends will continue or similar methods will be applicable: *results extrapolated to other groups.* | [intrans.] *it is always dangerous to **extrapolate from** a sample.* ■ estimate or conclude (something) in this way: *attempts to extrapolate likely human cancers from laboratory studies.* ■ Math. extend (a graph, curve, or range of values) by inferring unknown values from trends in the known data: [as adj.] (**extrapolated**) *a set of extrapolated values.* —**ex·trap·o·la·tion** /ik,strapə'lāsHən/ n. **ex·trap·o·la·tive** /-,lātiv/ adj. **ex·trap·o·la·tor** /-,lātər/ n. [19th C.: from EXTRA- 'outside' + a shortened form of INTERPOLATE.]

ex·tra·po·si·tion /,ekstrəpə'zisHən/ ▶n. Gram. the placing of a word or group of words outside or at the end of a clause, while retaining the sense. The subject is often postponed and replaced by *it* at the start, as in *it's no use crying over spilt milk* rather than *crying over spilt milk is no use.*

ex·tra·py·ram·i·dal /,ekstrəpə'ramidl/ ▶adj. Anat. Med. relating to or denoting nerves concerned with motor activity that descend from the cortex to the spine and are not part of the pyramidal system.

ex·tra·sen·so·ry per·cep·tion /,ekstrə'sensərē/ (abbr.: **ESP**) ▶n. the faculty of perceiving things by means other than the known senses, e.g., by telepathy or clairvoyance.

ex·tra·sys·to·le /,ekstrə'sistəlē/ ▶n. Med. a heartbeat outside the normal rhythm, as often occurs in normal individuals.

ex·tra·ter·res·tri·al /,ekstrətə'restrēəl/ ▶adj. of or from outside the earth or its atmosphere. ▶n. a hypothetical or fictional being from outer space, esp. an intelligent one.

ex·tra·ter·ri·to·ri·al /,ekstrə,terə'tôrēəl/ ▶adj. (of a law or decree) valid outside a country's territory. ■ denoting the freedom of an ambassador or other embassy staff from the jurisdiction of the territory of residence. ■ situated outside a country's territory. —**ex·tra·ter·ri·to·r i·al·i·ty** /-,tôrē'alitē/ n.

ex·tra·trop·i·cal /,ekstrə'träpikəl/ ▶adj. esp. Meteorol. situated, existing, or occurring outside the tropics.

ex·tra·u·ter·ine /,ekstrə'yo͞otərin; -,rīn/ ▶adj. Med. existing, formed, or occurring outside the uterus.

ex·trav·a·gance /ik'stravəgəns/ ▶n. lack of restraint in spending money or use of resources. ■ a thing on which too much money has been spent or which has used up too many resources. ■ excessive elaborateness of style, speech, or action. —**ex·trav·a·gan·cy** /-gənsē/ n.

ex·trav·a·gant /ik'stravəgənt/ ▶adj. lacking restraint in spending money or using resources. ■ costing too much money. ■ exceeding what is reasonable or appropriate; absurd. ■ excessively elaborate in style, speech, or action. —**ex·trav·a·gant·ly** adv. [ME: from med. L. *extravagant-* 'diverging greatly,' from the v. *extravagari*, from L. *extra-* 'outside' + *vagari* 'wander.']

ex·trav·a·gan·za /ik,stravə'ganzə/ ▶n. an elaborate and spectacular entertainment or production. [18th C.: from Ital. *estravaganza* 'extravagance.']

ex·trav·a·sate /ik'stravə,sāt/ ▶v. [trans.] [usu. as adj.] (**extravasated**) esp. Med. let or force out (a fluid, esp. blood) from the vessel that naturally contains it into the surrounding area. —**ex·trav·a·sa·tion** /ik,stravə'sāsHən/ n. [17th C.: from EXTRA- 'outside' + L. *vas* 'vessel' + -ATE[3].]

ex·tra·vas·cu·lar /ˌekstrəˈvaskyələr/ ▶ **adj.** Med. situated or occurring outside the vascular system.

ex·tra·ve·hic·u·lar /ˌekstrəvēˈhikyələr/ ▶ **adj.** of or relating to work performed in space outside a spacecraft.

ex·tra·vert ▶ **n.** var. of EXTROVERT.

ex·tra-vir·gin ▶ **adj.** denoting a particularly fine grade of olive oil made from the first pressing of the olives.

ex·tre·ma /ikˈstrēmə/ plural form of EXTREMUM.

ex·treme /ikˈstrēm/ ▶ **adj.** **1** reaching a high or the highest degree; very great: *extreme cold.* ■ not usual; exceptional. ■ very severe or serious. ■ (of a person or their opinions) advocating severe or drastic measures; far from moderate, esp. politically. ■ denoting or relating to a sport performed in a hazardous environment and involving great physical risk, such as parachuting or white-water rafting. **2** [attrib.] furthest from the center or a given point; outermost. ▶ **n.** **1** either of two abstract things that are as different from each other as possible. ■ the highest or most extreme degree of something. ■ a very severe or serious act. **2** Logic the subject or predicate in a proposition, or the major or minor term in a syllogism (as contrasted with the middle term).
– PHRASES **go** (or **take something**) **to extremes** take an extreme course of action; do something to an extreme degree. **in the extreme** to an extreme degree. — **ex·treme·ly** adv. **ex·treme·ness** n. [ME: via OFr. from L. *extremus* 'outermost, utmost,' superlative of *exterus* 'outer.']

ex·treme unc·tion ▶ **n.** (in the Roman Catholic Church) a former name for the sacrament of anointing of the sick, esp. when administered to the dying.

ex·trem·ist /ikˈstrēmist/ ▶ **n.** esp. derog. a person who holds extreme or fanatical political or religious views, esp. one who resorts to or advocates extreme action. — **ex·trem·ism** n.

ex·trem·i·ty /ikˈstremitē/ ▶ **n.** (pl. **-ties**) **1** the furthest point or limit of something. ■ (**extremities**) the hands and feet. **2** the extreme degree or nature of something. ■ a condition of extreme adversity or difficulty: *the terror of an animal in extremity.*

ex·tre·mum /ikˈstrēməm/ ▶ **n.** (pl. **-mums** or **-ma** /-mə/) [usu. as adj.] Math. the maximum or minimum value of a function. [20th C.: from L., neut. of *extremus* 'utmost' (see EXTREME).]

ex·tri·cate /ˈekstriˌkāt/ ▶ **v.** [trans.] free (someone or something) from a constraint or difficulty. — **ex·tri·ca·ble** /ˈekstrikəbəl; ikˈstrik-/ adj. **ex·tri·ca·tion** /ˌekstriˈkāsHən/ n. [17th C. (in the sense 'unravel, untangle'): from L. *extricat-* 'unraveled,' from the v. *extricare*, from *ex-* 'out' + *tricae* 'perplexities.']

ex·trin·sic /ikˈstrinzik; -sik/ ▶ **adj.** not part of the essential nature of someone or something; coming or operating from outside. ■ (of a muscle, such as any of the eye muscles) having its origin some distance from the part that it moves. — **ex·trin·si·cal·ly** /-k(ə)lē/ adv. [16th C.: from late L. *extrinsecus* 'outward,' from L. *extrinsecus* 'outwardly,' based on *exter* 'outer.']

Ex·tro·py /ˈekstrəpē/ ▶ **n.** the pseudoscientific principle that life will expand indefinitely and in an orderly, progressive way throughout the entire universe by the means of human intelligence and technology. — **Ex·tro·pi·an** /ekˈstrōpēən/ adj. & n. [1980s: from EX-[1] 'out' + a shortened form of ENTROPY.]

ex·trorse /ˈekstrôrs/ ▶ **adj.** Bot. Zool. turned outward. The opposite of INTRORSE. ■ (of anthers) releasing their pollen on the outside of the flower. — **ex·trorse·ly** adv. [19th C.: from late L. *extrorsus* 'outward'(adv.).]

ex·tro·vert /ˈekstrəˌvərt/ (also **extravert**) ▶ **n.** an outgoing, overtly expressive person. ■ Psychol. a person predominantly concerned with external things or objective considerations. Compare with INTROVERT. ▶ **adj.** of, denoting, or typical of an extrovert. — **ex·tro·ver·sion** /ˌekstrəˈvərZHən/ n. **ex·tro·vert·ed** adj. [20th C.: from *extro-* (var. of EXTRA-, on the pattern of *intro-*) + L. *vertere* 'to turn.']

ex·trude /ikˈstrōōd/ ▶ **v.** [trans.] (usu. **be extruded**) thrust or force out. ■ shape (a material such as metal or plastic) by forcing it through a die. — **ex·trud·a·ble** adj. **ex·tru·sile** /ikˈstrōōsəl; -sīl/ adj. **ex·tru·sion** /ikˈstrōōZHən/ n. [16th C.: from L. *extrudere*, from *ex-* 'out' + *trudere* 'to thrust.']

ex·tru·sive /ikˈstrōōsiv/ ▶ **adj.** Geol. relating to or denoting rock that has been extruded at the earth's surface as lava or other volcanic deposits. [19th C.: from L. *extrus-* 'thrust out', past part. of *extrudere*.]

ex·u·ber·ant /igˈzōōbərənt/ ▶ **adj.** filled with or characterized by a lively energy and excitement. ■ growing luxuriantly or profusely: *exuberant foliage.* — **ex·u·ber·ance** n. **ex·u·ber·ant·ly** adv. [ME: from Fr. *exubérant*, from L. *exuberant-* 'abundantly fruitful,' from *exuberare* (based on *uber* 'fertile').]

ex·u·date /ˈeksyōōˌdāt; ˈeksə-/ ▶ **n.** an exuded substance, in particular: ■ Med. a mass of cells and fluid that has seeped out of blood vessels or an organ, esp. in inflammation. ■ Bot. Entomol. a substance secreted by a plant or insect.

ex·ude /igˈzōōd/ ▶ **v.** [trans.] discharge (moisture or a smell) slowly and steadily. ■ [intrans.] (of moisture or a smell) be discharged by something in such a way. ■ fig. (of a person) display (an emotion or quality) strongly and openly. ■ [intrans.] fig. (of an emotion or quality) be displayed by someone in such a way. ■ fig. (of a place) have a strong atmosphere of. — **ex·u·da·tion** /ˌeksyōōˈdāsHən; ˌeksə-/ n. **ex·u·da·tive** /igˈzōōdətiv; ˈeksəˌdātiv; ˈeksyōō-/ adj. [16th C.: from L. *exsudare*, from *ex-* 'out' + *sudare* 'to sweat.']

ex·ult /igˈzəlt/ ▶ **v.** [intrans.] show or feel elation or jubilation, esp. as the result of a success. — **ex·ul·ta·tion** /ˌeksəlˈtāsHən; ˌegzəl-/ n. **ex·ult·ing·ly** adv. [16th C.: from L. *exsultare*, frequentative of *exsilire* 'leap up,' from *ex-* 'out, upward' + *salire* 'to leap.']

ex·ult·ant /igˈzəltnt/ ▶ **adj.** triumphantly happy. — **ex·ult·an·cy** /-ˈzəltnsē/ n. **ex·ult·ant·ly** adv.

ex·urb /ˈeksərb/ ▶ **n.** a district outside a city, esp. a prosperous area beyond the suburbs. — **ex·ur·ban** /ekˈsərbən/ adj. **ex·ur·ban·ite** /ekˈsərbəˌnīt/ n. & adj. [1955: perhaps from Latin *ex* 'out of' + *urbs* 'city.']

ex·ur·bi·a /ekˈsərbēə/ ▶ **n.** the exurbs collectively; the region beyond the suburbs. [1955: from EX-[1] 'out of' + *-urbia*, on the pattern of *suburbia*. See EXURB.]

ex·u·vi·ae /igˈzōōvēˌē/ ▶ **plural n.** [also treated as sing.] Zool. an animal's cast or sloughed skin, esp. that of an insect larva. — **ex·u·vi·al** /-vēəl/ adj. [17th C.: from Latin, literally 'animal skins, spoils of the enemy,' from *exuere* 'divest oneself of.']

ex·u·vi·ate /igˈzōōvēˌāt/ ▶ **v.** [trans.] tech. shed (a skin or shell). — **ex·u·vi·a·tion** /igˌzōōvēˈāsHən/ n. [19th C.: from EXUVIAE + -ATE[3].]

ex-vo·to /eks ˈvōtō/ ▶ **n.** (pl. **-vo·tos**) a religious offering given in order to fulfill a vow. [18th C.: from L. *ex voto* 'from a vow.']

-ey ▶ **suffix** var. of -Y[2] (as in *Charley*, *Limey*).

ey·as /ˈīəs/ (also **ey·ass**) ▶ **n.** (pl. **ey·as·ses**) a young hawk, esp. (in falconry) an unfledged nestling taken from the nest for training. [15th C. (originally *nyas*): from Fr. *niais*, based on L. *nidus* 'nest.' The initial *n* was lost by wrong division of *a nyas*.]

eye /ī/ ▶ **n.** **1** each of a pair of globular organs in the head through which people and vertebrate animals see. ■ the corresponding visual or light-detecting organ of many invertebrate animals. ■ the region of the face surrounding an eye or the eyes. ■ a person's eye as characterized by the color of the iris. ■ used to refer to someone's power of vision and in descriptions of the manner or direction of someone's gaze: *I couldn't take my eyes off him.* ■ used to refer to someone's opinion or attitude toward something: *in the eyes of his colleagues he was an eccentric.* **2** a thing resembling an eye in appearance, shape, or relative position, in particular: ■ the small hole in a needle through which the thread is passed. ■ a small metal loop into which a hook is fitted as a fastener on a garment. See also HOOK AND EYE. ■ Naut. a loop at the end of a rope, esp. one at the top end of a shroud or stay. ■ a rounded eyelike marking on an animal, such as those on the tail of a peacock; an eyespot. ■ a round, dark spot on a potato from which a new shoot can grow. ■ a center cut of meat: *eye of round.* ■ the center of a flower, esp. when distinctively colored. ■ the calm region at the center of a storm or hurricane. See also THE EYE OF THE STORM below. ■ (**eyes**) Naut. the extreme forward part of a ship: *it was hanging in the eyes of the ship.* ▶ **v.** (**eye·ing** or **ey·ing**) [trans.] look at or watch closely or with interest: *Rose eyed him warily.*
– PHRASES **all eyes** used to convey that a particular person or thing is currently the focus of public interest or attention: *all eyes are on eastern Europe.* **be all eyes** be watching eagerly and attentively. **before** (or **under**) **one's** (**very**) **eyes** right in front of one (used for emphasis, esp. in the context of something surprising or unpleasant). **close** (or **shut**) **one's eyes to** refuse to notice or acknowledge something unwelcome or unpleasant. **the eye of the storm** the calm region at the center of a storm. ■ the most intense part of a tumultuous situation. **eyes front** (or **left** or **right**) a military command to turn the head in the particular direction stated. **a ——'s-eye view** a view from the position or standpoint of a ——. See also BIRD'S-EYE VIEW, WORM'S-EYE VIEW. **give someone the eye** informal look at someone in a way that clearly indicates sexual interest in them. **half an eye** used in reference to a slight degree of perception or attention. **have an eye for** be able to recognize, appreciate, and make good judgments about. **have** (or **keep**) **one's eye on** keep under careful observation. ■ (**have one's eye on**) hope or plan to acquire. **have** (or **with**) **an eye to** have (or having) as one's objective. ■ consider (or be considering) prudently; look (or be looking) ahead to. **one's eyes are bigger than one's stomach** one has asked for or taken more food than one can actually eat. (**only**) **have eyes for** be (exclusively) interested in or attracted to. **have eyes in the back of one's head** know what is going on around one even when one cannot see it. **hit someone between the eyes** (or **in the eye**) informal be very obvious or impressive. **keep an eye out** (or **a sharp eye**) **on** keep under careful observation: **keep an eye out** (or **open**) look out for something with particular attention. **keep one's eyes open** (or **peeled** or Brit. **skinned**) be on the alert; watch carefully or vigilantly for something. **lay** (or **set** or **clap**) **eyes on** informal see. **make eyes at someone** look at someone in a way that indicates one's sexual interest. **my eye** informal dated used esp. in spoken English to indicate surprise or disbelief. **open someone's eyes** enlighten someone about certain realities; cause someone to realize or discover something. **see eye to eye** have similar views or attitudes to something; be in full agreement. **a twinkle** (or **gleam**) **in someone's eye** something that is as yet no more than an idea or dream. **with one's eyes open** fully aware of the possible difficulties or consequences. **with one's eyes shut** (or **closed**) **1** without having to make much effort; easily. **2** without considering the possible difficulties or consequences. **with one eye on** giving some but not all one's attention to. — **eyed** /īd/ adj. [in comb.] *a brown-eyed girl.* **eye·less** adj. [OE *ēage*, of Gmc. origin; rel. to Du. *oog* and Ger. *Auge*.]

eye·ball /ˈīˌbôl/ ▶ **n.** the round part of the eye of a vertebrate, within the eyelids and socket. In mammals it is typically a firm, mobile, spherical structure enclosed by the sclera and the cornea. ▶ **v.** [trans.] informal look or stare at closely.
– PHRASES **eyeball to eyeball** face to face with someone, esp. in an aggressive way. **up to the** (or **one's**) **eyeballs** informal used to emphasize

the extreme degree of an undesirable situation or condition.

eye·black /ˈī,blak/ ▶ n. old-fashioned term for MASCARA.

eye·bolt /ˈī,bōlt/ ▶ n. a bolt or bar with an eye at the end for attaching a hook or ring to.

eye·bright /ˈī,brīt/ ▶ n. a small plant (genus *Euphrasia*) of the figwort family with little snapdragonlike flowers, formerly used as a remedy for eye problems.

eye·brow /ˈī,brou/ ▶ n. the strip of hair growing on the ridge above a person's eye socket.
– PHRASES **raise one's eyebrows** (or **an eyebrow**) show surprise, disbelief, or mild disapproval.

eye·brow pen·cil ▶ n. a cosmetic pencil for defining or accentuating the eyebrows.

eye can·dy ▶ n. informal visual images that are superficially attractive and entertaining but intellectually undemanding.

eye-catch·ing ▶ adj. immediately appealing or noticeable; striking. — **eye-catch·er** n. **eye-catch·ing·ly** adv.

eye con·tact ▶ n. the state in which two people are aware of looking directly into one another's eyes.

eye·cup /ī,kəp/ ▶ n. **1** a piece of an optical device such as a microscope, camera, or pair of binoculars that is contoured to provide a comfortable rest against the user's eye. **2** a small container used for applying cleansing solutions to the eye.

eye·ful /ˈī,fo͝ol/ ▶ n. [in sing.] informal a long, steady look at something. ■ a visually striking person or thing. ■ a quantity or piece of something thrown or blown into the eye.

eye·glass /ˈī,glas/ ▶ n. a single lens for correcting or assisting defective eyesight, esp. a monocle. ■ (**eyeglasses**) another term for GLASSES. ■ another term for EYEPIECE.

eye·hole /ˈī,hōl/ ▶ n. a hole to look through, esp. in a curtain or mask. ■ the eye socket. ■ an eyelet.

eye·lash /ˈī,lasн/ ▶ n. each of the short curved hairs growing on the edges of the eyelids, serving to protect the eyes from dust particles.

eye·let /ˈīlit/ ▶ n. a small round hole in leather or cloth for threading a lace, string, or rope through. ■ a metal ring used to reinforce such a hole. ■ a small hole ornamented with stitching around its edge, used as a form of decoration in embroidery. ■ a fabric pierced with these holes in an ornamental pattern. ■ a small hole or slit in a wall for looking through. ▶ v. (**eye·let·ed, eye·let·ing**) [trans.] make eyelets in (fabric). [ME *oilet*, from OFr. *oillet*, dimin. of *oil* 'eye,' from L. *oculus*.]

eye lev·el ▶ n. the level of the eyes looking straight ahead.

eye·lid /ˈī,lid/ ▶ n. each of the upper and lower folds of skin that cover the eye when closed.

eye·lin·er /ˈī,līnər/ ▶ n. a cosmetic applied as a line around the eyes to make them appear larger or more noticeable.

eye-o·pen·er ▶ n. informal **1** [in sing.] an event or situation that proves to be unexpectedly enlightening. **2** an alcoholic drink taken early in the day. — **eye-o·pen·ing** adj.

eye·patch /ˈī,pacн/ ▶ n. a patch worn to protect an injured eye.

eye pen·cil ▶ n. a pencil for applying makeup around the eyes.

eye·piece /ˈī,pēs/ ▶ n. the lens or group of lenses that is closest to the eye in a microscope, telescope, or other optical instrument. Also called EYEGLASS or OCULAR.

eye-pop·ping ▶ adj. informal astonishingly large, impressive, or blatant.

eye rhyme ▶ n. a similarity between words in spelling but not in pronunciation, e.g., *love* and *move*.

eye·shade /ˈī,sнād/ ▶ n. a translucent visor used to protect the eyes from strong light.

eye·shad·ow /ˈī,sнadō/ ▶ n. a colored cosmetic, typically in powder form, applied to the eyelids or to the skin around the eyes to accentuate them.

eye·shot /ˈī,sнät/ ▶ n. the distance one can see.

eye·sight /ˈī,sīt/ ▶ n. a person's ability to see.

eye sock·et ▶ n. the cavity in the skull that encloses an eyeball with its surrounding muscles. Also called ORBIT.

eyes-on·ly ▶ adj. intended to be seen or read only by the person addressed; confidential, secret.

eye·sore /ˈī,sôr/ ▶ n. a thing that is very ugly, esp. a building that disfigures a landscape.

eye splice ▶ n. a splice made by turning the end of a rope back on itself and interlacing the strands, thereby forming a loop. See illustration at SPLICE.

eye·spot /ˈī,spät/ ▶ n. Zool. **1** a light-sensitive pigmented spot on the bodies of invertebrate animals such as flatworms, starfishes, and microscopic crustaceans, and also in some unicellular organisms. **2** a rounded eyelike marking, esp. on the wing of a butterfly or moth.

eye·stalk /ī,stôk/ ▶ n. Zool. a movable stalk that bears an eye near its tip, esp. in crabs, shrimps, and related crustaceans, and in some mollusks.

eye strain ▶ n. fatigue of the eyes, such as that caused by reading or looking at a computer screen for too long.

eye·stripe /ī,strīp/ ▶ n. a stripe on a bird's head that encloses or appears to run through the eye.

eye·tooth /ˈī'to͞oтн/ ▶ n. a canine tooth, esp. one in the upper jaw.
– PHRASES **give one's eyeteeth for** (or **to be**) do anything in order to have or be something.

eye·wash /ˈī,wôsн; -,wäsн/ ▶ n. **1** cleansing solution for a person's eye. **2** informal insincere talk; nonsense.

eye·wear /ī,we(ə)r/ ▶ n. things worn on the eyes, such as spectacles and contact lenses.

eye·wit·ness /ˈī'witnəs/ ▶ n. [often as adj.] a person who has personally seen something happen and so can give a first-hand description of it.

ey·ra /ˈe(ə)rə/ ▶ n. a reddish-brown form of the jaguarundi. [17th C.: from Sp., from Tupi *eirara, irara*.]

eyre /e(ə)r/ ▶ n. hist. a circuit court held in medieval England by a judge (a **justice in eyre**) who rode from county to county for that purpose. [ME: from OFr. *eire*, from L. *iter* 'journey.']

Eyre, Lake /er/ a lake in southern Australia, the country's largest salt lake.

ey·rie /ˈe(ə)rē; ˈi(ə)rē/ ▶ n. var. of AERIE.

ey·rir /ˈāri(ə)r/ ▶ n. (pl. **au·rar** /ˈoirär/) a monetary unit of Iceland, equal to one hundredth of a krona.

E·ze·ki·el /iˈzēkēəl/ a Hebrew prophet of the 6th century BC who prophesied the forthcoming destruction of Jerusalem and the Jewish nation. ■ a book of the Bible containing his prophecies.

e-zine /ˈē,zēn/ ▶ n. a magazine published only in electronic form on a computer network.

Ez·ra /ˈezrə/ a Jewish priest and scribe who played a central part in the reform of Judaism in the 5th or 4th century BC. ■ a book of the Bible telling of Ezra, the return of the Jews from Babylon, and the rebuilding of the Temple.

Ff

F[1] /ef/ (also **f**) ▸ **n.** (pl. **Fs** or **F's**) **1** the sixth letter of the alphabet. ▪ denoting the next after E in a set of items, categories, etc. ▪ the sixth highest or lowest class of academic marks (also used to represent "Fail"). **2** (usu. **F**) Music the fourth note of the diatonic scale of C major. ▪ a key based on a scale with F as its keynote.

F[2] ▸ **abbr.** ▪ Fahrenheit. ▪ failure. ▪ false. ▪ farad(s). ▪ Chem. faraday(s). ▪ February. ▪ Fellow. ▪ female. ▪ fighter (in designations of US aircraft): *the F-117 Stealth fighter.* ▪ forint. ▪ (in auto racing) formula: *an F1 driver.* ▪ Franc(s). ▸ **symb.** ▪ the chemical element fluorine. ▪ Physics force: *F=ma.*

f ▸ **abbr.** ▪ farad. ▪ farthing. ▪ father. ▪ fathom. ▪ feet. ▪ Gram. feminine. ▪ female. ▪ [in comb.] (in units of measurement) femto- (10–15). ▪ fine. ▪ (in textual references) folio. ▪ following. ▪ foot. ▪ form. ▪ Music forte. ▪ (in racing results) furlong(s). ▪ franc. ▪ from. ▸ **symb.** ▪ focal length: *apertures of f/5.6 to f/11.* See also F-NUMBER. ▪ Math. a function of a specified variable: *the value of f(x).* ▪ Electron. frequency.

f/ ▸ **abbr.** Symbol f-number.

F_1 (also **F1**) Biol. ▸ **abbr.** the first filial generation, i.e., the generation of hybrids arising from a first cross. The second filial generation is designated F_2 (or **F2**), etc.

fa /fä/ ▸ **n.** Music the fourth note of a major scale. ▪ the note F in the fixed-do system. [ME: *famuli* from L.]

FAA ▸ **abbr.** Federal Aviation Administration.

fab[1] /fab/ ▸ **adj.** informal fabulous; wonderful.

fab[2] ▸ **n.** Electron. a microchip fabrication plant. ▪ a particular fabrication process in such a plant.

Fa·ber·gé /ˌfabərˈzhā/ , Peter Carl (1846–1920), Russian goldsmith and jeweler. He is known for his intricate Easter eggs.

Fa·bi·an /ˈfābēən/ ▸ **n.** a member or supporter of the Fabian Society, an organization of socialists aiming at the gradual achievement of socialism. ▸ **adj.** relating to or characteristic of the Fabians. ▪ employing a cautiously persistent and dilatory strategy to wear out an enemy. — **Fa·bi·an·ism n. Fa·bi·an·ist n.** [18th C.: from the name of *Quintus Fabius Maximus Verrucosus* (see FABIUS).]

Fa·bi·us /ˈfābēəs/ (died 203 BC), Roman general; full name *Quintus Fabius Maximus Verrucosus*; known as **Fabius Cunctator** (Fabius the Delayer). He defeated Hannibal in 209 BC.

fa·ble /ˈfābəl/ ▸ **n.** a short story, typically with animals as characters, conveying a moral. ▪ a story, typically a supernatural one incorporating elements of myth and legend. ▪ myth and legend. ▪ a false statement or belief. ▸ **v.** [trans.] fabricate or invent (an incident, person, or story). — **fa·bler n.** [ME: from OFr. *fable* (n.), from L. *fabula* 'story,' from *fari* 'speak.']

fa·bled /ˈfābəld/ ▸ **adj.** [attrib.] well known for being of great quality or rarity; famous. ▪ mythical; imaginary.

fab·li·au /ˈfablēˌō/ ▸ **n.** (pl. **-aux** /-ˌōz/) a metrical tale, typically a bawdily humorous one, of a type found chiefly in early French poetry. [from OFr. (Picard dial.) *fabliaux*, pl. of *fablel* 'short fable,' dimin. of *fable*.]

fab·ric /ˈfabrik/ ▸ **n. 1** cloth, typically produced by weaving or knitting textile fibers. **2** the walls, floor, and roof of a building. ▪ the body of a car or aircraft. ▪ fig. the essential structure of anything, esp. a society or culture. [15th C.: from Fr. *fabrique*, from L. *fabrica* 'something skillfully produced,' from *faber* 'worker in metal, stone, etc.']

fab·ri·cate /ˈfabriˌkāt/ ▸ **v.** [trans.] invent or concoct (something), typically with deceitful intent. ▪ construct or manufacture (something, esp. an industrial product), esp. from prepared components. — **fab·ri·ca·tion** /ˌfabriˈkāshən/ **n. fab·ri·ca·tor** /-ˌkātər/ **n.**

fab·ric soft·en·er ▸ **n.** any product used to soften clothes when washed or dried.

fab·u·late /ˈfabyəˌlāt/ ▸ **v.** [trans.] relate (an event or events) as a fable or story. ▪ [intrans.] relate untrue or invented stories. — **fab·u·la·tion** /ˌfabyəˈlāshən/ **n. fab·u·la·tor** /-ˌlātər/ **n.**

fab·u·list /ˈfabyəlist/ ▸ **n.** a person who composes or relates fables. ▪ a person who invents elaborate, dishonest stories.

fab·u·lous /ˈfabyələs/ ▸ **adj.** extraordinary, esp. extraordinarily large. ▪ informal amazingly good; wonderful. ▪ having no basis in reality; mythical. — **fab·u·los·i·ty** /ˌfabyəˈläsitē/ **n. fab·u·lous·ly adv. fab·u·lous·ness n.** [ME: from Fr. *fabuleux* or L. *fabulosus* 'celebrated in fable,' from *fabula* (see FABLE).]

fac. ▸ **abbr.** ▪ facsimile. ▪ faculty.

fa·cade /fəˈsäd/ (also **fa·çade**) ▸ **n.** the front of a building that looks onto a street or open space. ▪ fig. an outward appearance that is maintained to conceal a less pleasant or creditable reality. [17th C.: from Fr. *façade*, from *face* 'face,' on the pattern of Ital. *facciata*.]

face /fās/ ▸ **n. 1** the front part of a person's head from the forehead to the chin, or the corresponding part in an animal. ▪ an expression shown on the face. ▪ a manifestation or outward aspect of something: *the unacceptable face of social drinking.* **2** the surface of a thing, esp. one that is presented to the view or has a particular function, in particular: ▪ Geom. each of the surfaces of a solid. ▪ a vertical or sloping side of a mountain or cliff. ▪ the side of a planet or moon facing the observer. ▪ the front of a building. ▪ the plate of a clock or watch bearing the digits or hands. ▪ the distinctive side of a playing card. ▪ short for TYPEFACE. ▪ the side of a coin showing the head or principal design. ▸ **v.** [trans.] **1** be positioned with the face or front toward (someone or something): *he turned to face her.* ▪ [intrans.] have the face or front pointing in a specified direction. ▪ [intrans.] (of a soldier) turn in a particular direction: *they immediately faced about.* **2** confront and deal with or accept: *honesty forced her to face facts* | [intrans.] *face up to the issues.* ▪ (**face someone/something down**) overcome by a show of determination: *he faced down persistent hecklers.* ▪ have (a difficult event or situation) in prospect: *they faced a sentence of 10 years.* ▪ (of a problem or difficult situation) present itself to and require action from (someone): *faced with an emergency.* **3** (usu. **be faced with**) cover the surface of (a thing) with a layer of a different material: *the walls were faced with granite.*
– PHRASES **face the music** be confronted with the unpleasant consequences of one's actions. **get out of someone's face** [usu. as imper.] informal stop harassing or annoying someone. **in one's face** directly at or against one; as one approaches. **in the face of** when confronted with. ▪ in spite of. **in your face** see IN-YOUR-FACE. **lose face** suffer a loss of respect; be humiliated. **make a face** (or **faces**) produce an expression on one's face that shows dislike, disgust, or some other negative emotion, or that is intended to be amusing. **on the face of it** without knowing all of the relevant facts; at first glance. **put a good** (or **brave** or **bold**) **face on something** act as if something unpleasant or upsetting is not as bad as it really is. **put one's face on** informal apply makeup to one's face. **save face** retain respect; avoid humiliation. **throw something back in someone's face** reject something in a brusque or ungracious manner. **to one's face** openly in one's presence.
– PHRASAL VERBS **face off** take up an attitude of confrontation: *close to a million soldiers face off in the desert.* ▪ Ice Hockey start or restart play with a face-off. — **faced** /fāst/ **adj.** [in comb.] *red-faced.* [ME: from OFr., based on L. *facies* 'form, appearance, face.']

face card ▸ **n.** a playing card that is a king, queen, or jack of a suit.

face·cloth /ˈfāsˌklôth/ ▸ **n.** a washcloth.

face·less /ˈfāslis/ ▸ **adj.** (of a person) remote and impersonal; anonymous. ▪ (of a building or place) characterless and dull. — **face·less·ness n.**

face-lift (also **face·lift**) ▸ **n.** cosmetic surgery to remove wrinkles by tightening the skin of the face. ▪ fig. a procedure carried out to improve the appearance of something.

face mask ▸ **n.** a protective mask covering the nose and mouth or nose and eyes.

face-off ▸ **n.** a direct confrontation between two people or groups. ▪ Ice Hockey the start or restart of play, in which the referee drops the puck between two opposing players.

face·plate /ˈfāsˌplāt/ ▸ **n. 1** an enlarged end or attachment on the end of the mandrel on a lathe, with slots and holes on which work can be mounted. ▪ a plate protecting a piece of machinery, a light switch, or an electrical outlet. ▪ the part of a cathode-ray tube that carries the phosphor screen. **2** the window of a diver's or astronaut's helmet.

face pow·der ▸ **n.** flesh-tinted cosmetic powder used to improve the appearance of the face.

face-sav·ing ▸ **adj.** preserving one's reputation, credibility, or dignity. — **face-sav·er n.**

fac·et /ˈfasit/ ▸ **n.** one side of something many-sided, esp. of a cut gem. ▪ a particular aspect or feature of something. ▪ Zool. any of the individual units (ommatidia) that make up the compound eye of an insect or crustacean. — **fac·et·ed adj.** [in comb.] *multifaceted.* [early 17th cent.: from Fr. *facette*, dimin. of *face* 'face, side' (see FACE).]

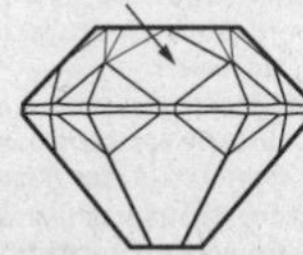

facet of a gem

fa·ce·ti·ae /fəˈsēshēˌē; -shēˌī/ ▸ **plural n.** dated pornographic literature. [16th C.: from L., pl. of *facetia* 'jest,' from *facetus* 'witty.']

face time ▶ n. informal time spent in face-to-face contact. ■ time spent being filmed or photographed by the media.

fa·ce·tious /fəˈsēsʜəs/ ▶ adj. treating serious issues with deliberately inappropriate humor; flippant. — **fa·ce·tious·ly** adv. **fa·ce·tious·ness** n. [16th C.: from Fr. *facétieux*, from *facétie*, from L. *facetia* 'jest,' from *facetus* 'witty.']

face to face ▶ adv. & adj. with the people involved being close together and looking directly at each other. ■ [as adv.] in direct confrontation: *he came face to face with a tiger.*

face val·ue ▶ n. the value printed or depicted on a coin, banknote, postage stamp, ticket, etc. ■ fig. the superficial appearance of something.

fa·ci·a /ˈfasʜ(ē)ə; ˈfā-/ ▶ n. esp. Brit. var. of FASCIA (sense 1).

fa·cial /ˈfāsʜəl/ ▶ adj. of or affecting the face. ▶ n. a beauty treatment for the face. — **fa·cial·ly** adv.

fa·cial nerve ▶ n. Anat. each of the seventh pair of cranial nerves, supplying the facial muscles and the tongue.

fa·cial tis·sue ▶ n. tissue that is used to blow one's nose, contain a sneeze, etc.

-facient ▶ comb. form producing a specified action or state: *abortifacient.* [from L. *facient-* 'doing, making.']

fa·cies /ˈfāsʜēz; ˈfāsʜē,ēz/ ▶ n. (pl. same) **1** Med. the appearance or facial expression of an individual that is typical of a particular disease or condition. **2** Geol. the character of a rock expressed by its formation, composition, and fossil content. **3** Ecol. the characteristic set of dominant species in a habitat. [17th C. (denoting the face): from Latin, 'form, appearance, face.']

fac·ile /ˈfasəl/ ▶ adj. **1** (esp. of a theory or argument) appearing neat and comprehensive by ignoring the complexities of an issue; superficial. ■ (of a person) having a superficial or simplistic knowledge or approach. **2** (of success, esp. in sports) easily achieved; effortless. ■ acting or done in a quick, fluent, and easy manner. — **fac·ile·ly** adv. **fac·ile·ness** n. [15th C. (in the sense 'easily accomplished'): from Fr., or from L. *facilis* 'easy,' from *facere* 'do, make.']

fa·cil·i·tate /fəˈsili,tāt/ ▶ v. [trans.] make (an action or process) easy or easier. — **fa·cil·i·ta·tive** /-,tātiv/ adj. **fa·cil·i·ta·tor** /-,tātər/ n. **fa·cil·i·ta·to·ry** /-tə,tôrē/ adj.

fa·cil·i·ta·tion /fə,siliˈtāsʜən/ ▶ n. the action of facilitating something. ■ Physiol. the enhancement of the response of a neuron to a stimulus following prior stimulation.

fa·cil·i·ty /fəˈsilitē/ ▶ n. (pl. **-ties**) **1** space or equipment necessary for doing something. ■ an amenity or resource. ■ **(the facilities)** a public toilet. ■ an establishment set up to fulfill a particular function or provide a particular service, typically an industrial or medical one. **2** [usu. in sing.] a natural aptitude. ■ absence of difficulty or effort.

fac·ing /ˈfāsiɴɢ/ ▶ n. **1** a layer of material covering part of a garment and providing contrast, decoration, or strength. ■ **(facings)** the cuffs, collar, and lapels of a military jacket. **2** an outer layer covering the surface of a wall. ▶ adj. [attrib.] positioned with the front toward a certain direction; opposite: *Italian and English lyrics printed on facing pages* | [in comb.] *a south-facing garden.*

fac·sim·i·le /fakˈsiməlē/ ▶ n. an exact copy, esp. of written or printed material. ■ another term for FAX. ▶ v. (**-led, -le·ing**) [trans.] make a copy of.

– PHRASES **in facsimile** as an exact copy. [late 16th cent.: mod. Latin, from L. *fac!* (imper. of *facere* 'make') and *simile* (neut. of *similis* 'like').]

fact /fakt/ ▶ n. a thing that is indisputably the case. ■ (usu. **facts**) information used as evidence or as part of a report or news article. ■ esp. Law the truth about events as opposed to interpretation or application of law.

– PHRASES **before** (or **after**) **the fact** before (or after) the committing of a crime. **a fact of life** something that must be accepted as true and unchanging, even if unpleasant. **facts and figures** precise details. **the facts of life** information about sexual functions, esp. as given to children. **the fact of the matter** the truth. **in (point of) fact** used to emphasize the truth of an assertion, esp. one contrary to what might be expected or what has been asserted. [15th C.: from L. *factum*, neut. past part. of *facere* 'do.']

fact-find·ing ▶ adj. [attrib.] having the purpose of discovering and establishing the facts of an issue. ▶ n. the discovery and establishment of the facts of an issue. — **fact-find·er** n.

fac·tic·i·ty /fakˈtisitē/ ▶ n. the quality or condition of being fact.

fac·tion[1] /ˈfaksʜən/ ▶ n. a small, organized, dissenting group within a larger one, esp. in politics. ■ a state of conflict within an organization; dissension. — **fac·tion·al** /-sʜənl/ adj. **fac·tion·al·ism** n. **fac·tion·al·ize** /-sʜənl,īz/ v. **fac·tion·al·ly** adv. [15th C.: via Fr. from L. *factio(n-)*, from *facere* 'do, make.']

fac·tion[2] ▶ n. a literary and cinematic genre in which real events are used as a basis for a fictional narrative or dramatization. [1960s: blend of FACT and FICTION.]

-faction ▶ comb. form in nouns of action derived from verbs ending in *-fy* (such as *satisfaction* from *satisfy*). [from L. *factio(n)-*, from *facere* 'do, make.']

fac·tious /ˈfaksʜəs/ ▶ adj. relating or inclined to a state of faction. — **fac·tious·ly** adv. **fac·tious·ness** n. [16th C.: from Fr. *factieux* or L. *factiosus*, from *factio* (see FACTION[1]).]

fac·ti·tious /fakˈtisʜəs/ ▶ adj. artificially created or developed. — **fac·ti·tious·ly** adv. **fac·ti·tious·ness** n. [17th C.: from L. *facticius* 'made by art,' from *facere* 'do, make.']

fac·ti·tive /ˈfaktitiv/ ▶ adj. Ling. (of a verb) having a sense of causing a result and taking a complement as well as an object, as in *he appointed me captain.* [19th C.: from mod. Latin *factitivus*, formed irregularly from L. *factitare*, frequentative of *facere* 'do, make.']

fac·toid /ˈfaktoid/ ▶ n. a brief or trivial item of news or information. ■ an assumption or speculation that is reported and repeated so often that it becomes accepted as fact.

fac·tor /ˈfaktər/ ▶ n. **1** a circumstance, fact, or influence that contributes to a result or outcome. ■ Biol. a gene that determines a hereditary characteristic: *the Rhesus factor.* **2** a number or quantity that when multiplied with another produces a given number or expression. ■ Math. a number or algebraic expression by which another is exactly divisible. **3** Physiol. any of a number of substances in the blood, mostly identified by numerals, which are involved in coagulation. See FACTOR VIII. **4** a business agent; a merchant buying and selling on commission. ■ a company that buys a manufacturer's invoices at a discount and takes responsibility for collecting the payments due on them. ▶ v. [trans.] **1** Math. another term for FACTORIZE. **2** sell (one's receivable debts) to a factor.

– PHRASAL VERBS **factor something in** (or **out**) include (or exclude) something as a relevant element. — **fac·tor·a·ble** adj. [ME: from Fr. *facteur* or L. *factor*, from *fact-* 'done,' from the v. *facere.*]

fac·tor VIII (also **fac·tor eight**) ▶ n. Physiol. a blood protein (a beta globulin) involved in clotting. A deficiency of this causes one of the main forms of hemophilia.

fac·tor·age /ˈfaktərij/ ▶ n. the commission or charges payable to a factor.

fac·to·ri·al /fakˈtôrēəl/ ▶ n. Math. the product of an integer and all the integers below it; e.g., factorial four (*4!*) is equal to 24. (Symbol: **!**) ■ the product of a series of factors in an arithmetic progression. ▶ adj. esp. Math. relating to a factor or such a product. — **fac·to·ri·al·ly** adv.

fac·tor·ize /ˈfaktə,rīz/ ▶ v. [trans.] Math. express (a number or expression) as a product of factors. ■ [intrans.] (of a number) be capable of resolution into factors. — **fac·tor·i·za·tion** /,faktərəˈzāsʜən/ n.

fac·to·ry /ˈfakt(ə)rē/ ▶ n. (pl. **-ries**) **1** a building or buildings where goods are manufactured or assembled. ■ fig. a person, group, or institution that produces a great quantity of something: *a factory of bad English.* **2** hist. an establishment for traders carrying on business in a foreign country.

fac·to·ry out·let ▶ n. a store in which goods are sold directly by the manufacturers at a discount.

fac·to·ry ship ▶ n. a fishing or whaling ship with facilities for immediate processing of the catch.

fac·to·tum /fakˈtōtəm/ ▶ n. (pl. **-tums**) an employee who does all kinds of work. [16th C.: from med. L., from L. *fac!* 'do!' (imper. of *facere*) + *totum* 'the whole thing' (neut. of *totus*).]

fac·tu·al /ˈfakcʜo͞oəl/ ▶ adj. concerned with what is actually the case rather than interpretations of or reactions to it. ■ actually occurring. — **fac·tu·al·i·ty** /,fakcʜo͞oˈalitē/ n. **fac·tu·al·ly** adv. **fac·tu·al·ness** n. [19th C.: from FACT, on the pattern of *actual.*]

fac·ture /ˈfakcʜər/ ▶ n. the quality of the execution of a painting; an artist's characteristic handling of the paint. [ME: via OFr. from L. *factura* 'formation, manufacture,' from *facere* 'do, make.']

fac·u·la /ˈfakyələ/ ▶ n. (pl. **-lae** /-,lē/) Astron. a bright region on the surface of the sun, linked to the subsequent appearance of sunspots in the same area. ■ a bright spot on the surface of a planet. — **fac·u·lar** /-lər/ adj. [18th C.: from L., dimin. of *fax, fac-* 'torch.']

fac·ul·ta·tive /ˈfakəl,tātiv/ ▶ adj. occurring optionally in response to circumstances rather than by nature: *prison-style, facultative homosexuality.* ■ Biol. capable of but not restricted to a particular function or mode of life: *a facultative parasite.* Often contrasted with OBLIGATE. — **fac·ul·ta·tive·ly** adv.

fac·ul·ty /ˈfakəltē/ ▶ n. (pl. **-ties**) **1** an inherent mental or physical power. ■ an aptitude or talent for doing something. **2** the teaching staff of a university or college, or of one of its departments or divisions, viewed as a body. ■ a group of university departments concerned with a major division of knowledge: *the Faculty of Arts and Sciences.* **3** a license or authorization, esp. from a church authority. [ME: from OFr. *faculte*, from L. *facultas*, from *facilis* 'easy,' from *facere* 'make, do.']

FAD Biochem. ▶ abbr. flavin adenine dinucleotide, a coenzyme derived from riboflavin and important in various metabolic reactions.

fad /fad/ ▶ n. an intense and widely shared enthusiasm for something, esp. one that is short-lived; a craze. — **fad·dish** adj. **fad·dish·ly** adv. **fad·dish·ness** n. **fad·dism** n. **fad·dist** n. [19th C. (orig.dial.): prob. the second element of *fidfad*, contr. of FIDDLE-FADDLE.]

fade /fād/ ▶ v. [intrans.] **1** gradually grow faint and disappear. ■ lose or cause to lose color or brightness. ■ (of a flower) lose freshness and wither. ■ gradually become thin and weak, esp. to the point of death. ■ (of a racehorse, runner, etc.) lose strength or drop back, esp. after a promising start. ■ (of a radio signal) gradually lose intensity. ■ (of a vehicle brake) become temporarily less efficient as a result of frictional heating. **2** [with adverbial] (with reference to film and television images) come or cause to come gradually into or out of view, or to merge into another shot. ■ (with reference to recorded sound) increase or decrease in volume or merge into another recording. **3** Golf (of the ball) deviate to the right (or, for a left-handed golfer, the left), typically as a result of spin given to the ball. ■ [trans.] (of a golfer) cause (the ball) to move in such a way. Compare with DRAW. ▶ n. **1** the process of becom-

ing less bright. ▪ an act of causing a film or television picture to darken and disappear gradually. Compare with FADE-OUT. 2 Golf a shot causing the ball to deviate to the right (or, for a left-handed golfer, the left), usually purposely.
– PHRASAL VERBS **fade back** Football move back from the scrimmage line. [ME: from OFr. *fader*, from *fade* 'dull, insipid,' prob. based on a blend of L. *fatuus* 'silly, insipid' and *vapidus* 'vapid.']

fade·a·way /'fādə,wā/ ▶ adj. Basketball another term for FALLAWAY.

fade-in ▶ n. a filmmaking and broadcasting technique whereby an image is made to appear gradually or the volume of sound is gradually increased from zero.

fade-out ▶ n. a filmmaking and broadcasting technique whereby an image is made to disappear gradually or the sound volume is gradually decreased to zero. ▪ a gradual and temporary loss of a broadcast signal.

fade-up ▶ n. an instance of increasing the brightness of an image or the volume of a sound.

fa·do /'fäTHōō/ ▶ n. (pl. **-dos**) a type of popular Portuguese song, usually with a melancholy theme and accompanied by mandolins or guitars. [20th C.: Portuguese, literally 'fate.']

fae·ces ▶ n. British spelling of FECES.

fa·er·ie /'fe(ə)rē/ (also **fa·er·y**) ▶ n. a fairy. ▪ [as adj.] imaginary; mythical. [16th C. (introduced by Spenser): pseudoarchaic variant of FAIRY.]

Faer·oe Is·lands /'fe(ə)rō/ (also **Far·oe** or **the Faer·oes**) islands in the North Atlantic Ocean that belong to Denmark but are partly autonomous; pop. 43,000; capital, Tórshavn.

Faer·o·ese /,fe(ə)rō'ēz; -'ēs/ (also **Far·o·ese**) ▶ adj. of or relating to the Faeroe Islands or their people or language. ▶ n. (pl. same) 1 a native or national of the Faeroes, or a person of Faeroese descent. 2 the official language of the Faeroes, a North Germanic language closely related to Icelandic.

fag[1] /fag/ ▶ n. informal, offens. a male homosexual. — **fag·gy** adj. [1920s: short for FAGGOT.]

fag[2] ▶ n. Brit., informal a cigarette. [19th C.: elliptically from FAG END.]

fag end ▶ n. an inferior and useless remnant of something: *the fag ends of rope* | fig. *a culture reaching the fag end of its existence.* ▪ informal, esp. Brit. a cigarette butt. [17th C. (in the sense 'remnant'): from 15th-cent. *fag* 'a flap.']

fag·got /'fagət/ ▶ n. informal offens. a male homosexual. — **fag·got·y** adj. [20th C.: perh. from the obs. sense of *fagot* 'contemptible woman.']

fag hag ▶ n. derog. a heterosexual woman who spends much of her time with homosexual men.

fag·ot·ing /'fagətiNG/ (Brit. **fag·got·ing**) ▶ n. embroidery in which threads are fastened together in bundles.

Fahd /fäd/ (1923–2005), king of Saudi Arabia 1982–2005; full name *Fahd ibn Abdul-Aziz al Saud.*

Fahr. ▶ abbr. Fahrenheit.

Fahr·en·heit /'farən,hīt/ (abbr.: **F**) ▶ adj. [postpositive when used with a numeral] of or denoting a scale of temperature on which water freezes at 32° and boils at 212° under standard conditions. ▶ n. (also **Fahrenheit scale**) this scale of temperature. [18th C.: named after Gabriel Daniel *Fahrenheit* (1686–1736), German physicist.]

fa·ience /fī'äns; fā-/ ▶ n. glazed ceramic ware, in particular decorated tin-glazed earthenware. [17th C. (originally denoting pottery made at Faenza, Italy): from French *faïence*, from *Faïence*, the French name for *Faenza*.]

fail /fāl/ ▶ v. [intrans.] 1 be unsuccessful in achieving one's goal: *he failed in his attempt to secure election.* ▪ [trans.] be unsuccessful in (an examination, test, or interview). ▪ [trans.] (of a person or a commodity) be unable to meet the standards set by (a test of quality or eligibility). ▪ [trans.] judge (a candidate) not to have passed. 2 neglect to do something. ▪ [with infin.] behave in a way contrary to hopes or expectations by not doing something: *commuter chaos has again failed to materialize.* ▪ [trans.] desert or let down (someone). 3 break down; cease to work well. ▪ become weaker or of poorer quality; die away. ▪ (esp. of rain or a crop or supply) be lacking or insufficient when needed or expected. ▪ (of a business or a person) be obliged to cease trading because of lack of funds; become bankrupt. ▶ n. a grade that is not high enough to pass an examination or test.
– PHRASES **without fail** absolutely predictably; with no exception. [ME: from OFr. *faillir* (v.), *faille* (n.), based on L. *fallere* 'deceive.']

failed /fāld/ ▶ adj. [attrib.] 1 (of an undertaking or a relationship) not achieving its end or not lasting; unsuccessful. ▪ (of a person) unsuccessful in a particular activity. ▪ (of a business) unable to continue owing to financial difficulties. 2 (of a mechanism) not functioning properly; broken-down.

fail·ing /'fāliNG/ ▶ n. a weakness, esp. in character; a shortcoming. ▶ prep. in default of; in the absence of: *she longed to be with him and, failing that, to be on her own.*

faille /fīl/ ▶ n. a soft, light-woven fabric having a ribbed texture and originally made of silk. [16th C.: from OFr.]

fail-safe ▶ adj. causing a piece of machinery to revert to a safe condition in the event of a breakdown or malfunction. ▪ unlikely or unable to fail. ▶ n. [usu. in sing.] a system or plan that comes into operation in the event of something going wrong or that is there to prevent such an occurrence.

fail·ure /'fālyər/ ▶ n. 1 lack of success. ▪ an unsuccessful person, enterprise, or thing. ▪ lack of success in passing a test. ▪ a grade that is not high enough to pass a test. 2 the omission of expected or required action. ▪ a lack or deficiency of a desirable quality. 3 the action or state of not functioning. ▪ a sudden cessation of power. ▪ the collapse of a business.

faint /fānt/ ▶ adj. 1 (of a sight, smell, or sound) barely perceptible. ▪ (of a hope, chance, or possibility) slight; remote. 2 [predic.] weak and dizzy; close to losing consciousness. ▪ appearing feeble or lacking in strength. ▶ v. [intrans.] lose consciousness for a short time because of an insufficient supply of oxygen to the brain. ▶ n. [in sing.] a sudden loss of consciousness.
– PHRASES **not have the faintest** informal have no idea. — **faint·ly** adv. **faint·ness** n. [ME: from OFr. *faint*, past part. of *faindre* (see FEIGN).]

faint-heart·ed ▶ adj. lacking courage; timid. — **faint-heart·ed·ly** adv. **faint-heart·ed·ness** n.

fair[1] /fe(ə)r/ ▶ adj. 1 in accordance with the rules or standards; legitimate. ▪ just or appropriate in the circumstances. ▪ Baseball (of a batted ball) within the field of play marked by the first and third baselines. ▪ Baseball pertaining to this part of the field. 2 (of hair or complexion) light; blond. ▪ (of a person) having such a complexion or hair. 3 considerable though not outstanding in size or amount. ▪ moderately good though not outstandingly so. 4 (of weather) fine and dry. ▪ (of the wind) favorable. 5 archaic, literary beautiful: attractive: *the fairest of her daughters.* ▪ (of words, a speech, or a promise) false, despite being initially attractive or pleasing; specious. 6 (of handwriting) easy to read. ▶ adv. without cheating or trying to achieve unjust advantage: *he played fair.*
– PHRASES **fair and square** honestly and straightforwardly. **a fair deal** equitable treatment. **fair enough** informal used to admit that something is reasonable or acceptable. **fair-to-middling** slightly above average. **the fair sex** (also **the fairer sex**) dated or humorous women. **fair's fair** informal used to request just treatment or assert that an arrangement is just. **no fair** informal unfair (often used in or as a petulant protestation): *no fair—we don't get to watch TV on school nights.* — **fair·ish** adj. **fair·ness** n. [OE *fæger* 'pleasing, attractive,' of Gmc. origin; rel. to Old High Ger. *fagar*.]

fair[2] ▶ n. a gathering of stalls and amusements for public entertainment. ▪ (also **agricultural fair**) a competitive exhibition of livestock, agricultural products, and household skills held annually by a town, county, or state and also featuring entertainment and educational displays. ▪ a periodic gathering for the sale of goods. ▪ an exhibition to promote particular products. [ME: from OFr. *feire*, from late L. *feria*, sing. of L. *feriae* 'holy days' (on which fairs were often held).]

fair[3] ▶ v. [trans.] [usu. as adj.] (**faired**) streamline (a vehicle, boat, or aircraft) by adding fairings. [OE in the senses 'beautify' and 'appear or become clean.']

Fair·banks /'fe(ə)r,baNGks/ the second-largest city in Alaska, in the central part of the state; pop. 30,224.

fair catch ▶ n. Football a catch of a punt in which a player first raises a hand and does not advance the ball.

fair cop·y ▶ n. written or printed matter transcribed or reproduced after final correction.

fair game ▶ n. a person or thing that is considered a reasonable target for criticism, exploitation, or attack.

fair·ground /'fe(ə)r,ground/ (often **fair·grounds**) ▶ n. an outdoor area where a fair is held.

fair-haired ▶ adj. 1 having light-colored hair. 2 (of a person) favorite; cherished.

fair·ing /'fe(ə)riNG/ ▶ n. an external structure added to increase streamlining and reduce drag, esp. on a high-performance car, motorcycle, boat, or aircraft.

Fair Isle one of the Shetland Islands. ▪ [usu. as adj.] traditional multicolored geometric designs used in woolen knitwear.

fair·lead /'fe(ə)r,lēd/ ▶ n. a ring mounted on a boat or ship to guide a rope, keeping it clear of obstructions and preventing it from cutting or chafing.

fair·ly /'fe(ə)rlē/ ▶ adv. 1 with justice: *he could not fairly be accused.* 2 [usu. as submodifier] to quite a high degree: *I was fairly certain she was innocent.* ▪ to an acceptable extent: *I get along fairly well with everybody.* ▪ actually (used to emphasize something surprising or extreme): *he fairly snarled at her.*
– PHRASES **fairly and squarely** another term for *FAIR AND SQUARE* (see FAIR[1]).

fair-mar·ket val·ue ▶ n. a selling price for an item to which a buyer and seller can agree.

fair-mind·ed ▶ adj. impartial in judgment; just. — **fair-mind·ed·ly** adv. **fair-mind·ed·ness** n.

fair·ness doc·trine ▶ n. a former federal policy requiring television and radio broadcasters that presented one side of a controversy to also present opposing points of view.

fair play ▶ n. respect for the rules or equal treatment of all concerned.

fair-spo·ken ▶ adj. archaic (of a person) courteous and pleasant.

fair trade ▶ n. 1 trade carried on legally. 2 trade in which fair prices are paid to producers in developing countries.

EF

fair-trade a·gree·ment ▶ n. an agreement, typically illegal, between a manufacturer of a trademarked item in the US and its retail distributors to sell the item at a price at or above the manufacturer's price.

fair use ▶ n. (in US copyright law) the doctrine that copyright material may be quoted verbatim, provided that attribution is clearly given and that the material quoted is reasonably brief in extent.

fair·way /ˈfe(ə)r,wā/ ▶ n. **1** the part of a golf course between a tee and the corresponding green. **2** a navigable channel in a river or harbor.

fair-weath·er friend ▶ n. a person who stops being a friend in times of difficulty.

fair·y /ˈfe(ə)rē/ ▶ n. (pl. **fair·ies**) **1** a small imaginary being of human form that has magical powers. **2** informal, offens. a male homosexual. ▶ adj. belonging to, resembling, or associated with fairies. [ME: from OFr. *faerie*, from *fae* 'a fairy,' from L. *fata* 'the Fates,' pl. of *fatum* (see FATE).]

fair·y ar·ma·dil·lo ▶ n. a very small burrowing armadillo (genus *Clamyphorus*) found in southern South America.

fair·y·land /ˈfe(ə)rē,land/ ▶ n. the imaginary home of fairies. ■ a beautiful or seemingly enchanted place: [as adj.] *a fairyland castle.* ■ an imagined ideal place; a utopia.

fair·y ring ▶ n. a circular area of grass that is darker in color than the surrounding grass due to the growth of certain fungi. Such rings were popularly believed to have been caused by fairies dancing.

fair·y shrimp ▶ n. a small, transparent crustacean (order Anostraca, class Branchiopoda) that typically swims on its back, using its legs to filter food particles from the water.

fair·y tale (also **fairy story**) ▶ n. a children's story about magical and imaginary beings and lands. ■ [as adj.] denoting something regarded as resembling a fairy story in being magical, idealized, or extremely happy.

Fai·sal /ˈfīsəl/ the name of two kings of Iraq: ■ Faisal I (1885–1933); reigned 1921–33. He was supported by the British and by fervent Arab nationalists. Under his rule, Iraq achieved full independence in 1932. ■ Faisal II (1935–58), reigned 1939–58; grandson of Faisal I. He was assassinated in a military coup.

Fai·sa·la·bad /fī,sälə'bäd; -'bad/ a city in Punjab, Pakistan; pop. 1,092,000. Formerly Lyallpur.

fait ac·com·pli /ˈfet əkäm'plē; ˈfāt/ ▶ n. [in sing.] a thing that has already happened or been decided. [19th C.: from French, literally 'accomplished fact.']

faith /fāTH/ ▶ n. **1** complete trust or confidence in someone or something. **2** strong belief in God or in the doctrines of a religion, based on spiritual apprehension rather than proof. ■ a system of religious belief. ■ a strongly held belief or theory.
– PHRASES **break** (or **keep**) **faith** be disloyal (or loyal). [ME: from OFr. *feid*, from L. *fides*.]

faith·ful /ˈfāTHfəl/ ▶ adj. **1** loyal, constant, and steadfast: *remain faithful to the principles* | [as pl. n.] (**the faithful**) *the struggle to please the party faithful.* ■ (of a spouse or partner) never having a sexual relationship with anyone else. ■ (of an object) reliable. **2** [usu. as pl. n.] (**the faithful**) having a strong belief in a particular religion, esp. Islam. **3** true to the facts or the original. — **faith·ful·ness** n.

faith·ful·ly /ˈfāTHfəlē/ ▶ adv. **1** in a loyal manner. **2** in a manner that is true to the facts or the original: *she translated the novel as faithfully as possible.*

faith heal·ing ▶ n. healing achieved by religious belief and prayer, rather than by medical treatment. — **faith heal·er** n.

faith·less /ˈfāTHlis/ ▶ adj. **1** disloyal, esp. to a spouse or partner; untrustworthy. **2** without religious faith. — **faith·less·ly** adv. **faith·less·ness** n.

fa·ji·ta /fəˈhētə/ ▶ n. a dish of Mexican origin consisting of strips of spiced beef or chicken, chopped vegetables, and grated cheese, wrapped in a soft tortilla. [20th C.: Mexican Spanish, literally 'little strip or belt.']

fake¹ /fāk/ ▶ n. a thing that is not genuine; a forgery or sham. ■ a person who appears or claims to be something that they are not. ■ a pretense or trick. ▶ adj. not genuine; counterfeit. ■ (of a person) claiming to be something that one is not. ▶ v. [trans.] forge or counterfeit (something). ■ pretend to feel or suffer from (an emotion or illness). ■ make (an event) appear to happen. ■ accomplish (a task) by improvising. ■ Music improvise. — **fak·er** n. **fak·er·y** n. [18th C.: perh. ult. rel. to Ger. *fegen* 'sweep, thrash.']

fake² ▶ n. & v. var. of FLAKE⁴. [ME (as a v.): of unknown origin.]

fake book ▶ n. Music a book of music containing the basic chord sequences of jazz or other tunes.

fak·ie /ˈfākē/ ▶ n. (pl. **-ies**) (in skateboarding or snowboarding) a movement in which the board is ridden backward. ▶ adv. with such a movement.

fa·kir /fəˈki(ə)r; ˈfākər/ (also **fa·keer**, **fa·qir**, **fa·quir**) ▶ n. a Muslim (or, loosely, a Hindu) religious ascetic who lives solely on alms. [17th C.: via Fr. from Arab. *faḳīr* 'needy man.']

fa·la·fel /fəˈläfəl/ (also **fe·la·fel**) ▶ n. a Middle Eastern dish of spiced mashed chickpeas or other pulses formed into balls and deep-fried. [from colloq. Egyptian Arabic *falāfil*, pl. of Arab. *fulful, filfil* 'pepper.']

Fa·lange /fəˈlanj; ˈfālanj/ the Spanish Fascist movement that merged with traditional right-wing elements in 1937 to form the ruling party under General Franco. — **Fa·lan·gism** n. **Fa·lan·gist** n. & adj. [Sp., from L. *phalanx, phalang-* (see PHALANX).]

Fa·la·sha /fəˈläsHə/ ▶ n. (pl. same or **-shas**) often offens. Ethiopians who hold the Jewish faith but use Ge'ez rather than Hebrew as a liturgical language. [18th C.: Amharic, literally 'exile, immigrant.']

fal·cate /ˈfalkāt; ˈfôl-/ ▶ adj. Bot. Zool. curved like a sickle; hooked. [19th C.: from L. *falcatus*, from *falx, falc-* 'sickle.']

fal·chion /ˈfôlcHən; -sHən/ ▶ n. hist. a broad, slightly curved sword with the cutting edge on the convex side. [ME *fauchon*, from OFr., based on L. *falx, falc-* 'sickle.']

fal·ci·form /ˈfalsə,fôrm/ ▶ adj. Anat. Zool. curved like a sickle; hooked. [18th C.: from L. *falx, falc-* 'sickle' + -IFORM.]

fal·con /ˈfalkən; ˈfôl-/ ▶ n. a diurnal bird of prey (family Falconidae, esp. the genus *Falco*) with long pointed wings and a notched beak, typically catching prey by diving on it from above. Compare with HAWK¹ (sense 1). See illustration at PEREGRINE. ■ one of these birds kept and trained to hunt small game for sport. ■ Falconry the female of such a bird, esp. a peregrine. Compare with TERCEL. [ME *faucon*: from OFr., from late L. *falco*, from L. *falx, falc-* 'sickle,' or of Gmc. origin and rel. to Ger. *Falke*.]

fal·con·er /ˈfalkənər; ˈfôl-/ ▶ n. a person who keeps, trains, or hunts with falcons or other birds of prey.

fal·co·net /,falkəˈnet; ,fôl-/ ▶ n. **1** hist. a light cannon. **2** a very small South Asian or South American falcon (genera *Microhierax* and *Spiziapteryx*), typically having bold black-and-white plumage.

fal·con·ry /ˈfalkənrē; ˈfôl-/ ▶ n. the sport of hunting with falcons or other birds of prey; the keeping and training of such birds.

fal·de·ral ▶ n. var. of FOLDEROL.

fald·stool /ˈfôld,stōōl/ ▶ n. **1** a folding chair used by a bishop when not occupying the throne or when officiating in a church other than his own. **2** a small folding desk or stool for kneeling at prayer. [OE *fældestōl*, of Gmc. origin, from the base of FOLD¹ and STOOL.]

Falk·land Is·lands /ˈfôklənd/ (also **the Falk·lands**) a group of more than 100 islands in the South Atlantic Ocean, forming an overseas territory of the UK, about 300 miles (500 km) east of the Strait of Magellan; pop. 2,121; capital, Stanley (on East Falkland). They were colonized by Britain in 1832–33. Argentina has contested British sovereignty, and in 1982, an Argentine invasion led to the Falklands War.

Falk·land Is·lands De·pen·den·cies an overseas territory of the UK in the South Atlantic Ocean that consists of the South Sandwich Islands and South Georgia.

Falk·lands War an armed conflict between Britain and Argentina in 1982.

fall /fôl/ ▶ v. (past **fell** ; past part. **fall·en**) [intrans.] **1** move downward, typically rapidly and freely without control, from a higher to a lower level. ■ (**fall off**) become detached accidentally and drop to the ground: *my glasses fell off and broke.* ■ hang down. ■ (of land) slope downward; drop away. ■ (**fall into**) (of a river) flow or discharge itself into. ■ [intrans.] (of someone's eyes or glance) be directed downward. ■ [intrans.] (of someone's face) show dismay or disappointment by appearing to sag or droop. ■ fig. occur, arrive, or become apparent as if by dropping suddenly: *when night fell we crawled back to our lines* | *the information might fall into the wrong hands.* **2** (of a person) lose one's balance and collapse. ■ throw oneself down, typically in order to worship or implore someone. ■ (of a tree, building, or other structure) collapse to the ground. ■ (of a building or place) be captured or defeated. ■ die in battle. ■ [intrans.] archaic commit sin; yield to temptation. ■ [intrans.] (of a government or leader) lose office. ■ (in sports) lose or be eliminated from play. **3** decrease in number, amount, intensity, or quality. ■ find a lower level; subside or abate. ■ (of a measuring instrument) show a lower reading. **4** pass into a specified state: *many buildings fell into disrepair.* ■ (**fall to doing something**) begin to do something: *he fell to musing about it.* ■ be drawn accidentally into. ■ occur at a specified time: *Mother's birthday fell on Flag Day.* ■ be classified or ordered in the way specified: *that falls under the general heading of corruption.* ▶ n. **1** [usu. in sing.] an act of falling or collapsing; a sudden uncontrollable descent. ■ a controlled act of falling, esp. as a stunt or in martial arts. ■ Wrestling a move that pins the opponent's shoulders on the ground for a count of three. ■ a state of hanging downward. ■ a downward difference in height between parts of a surface. ■ a sudden onset or arrival as if by dropping: *the fall of darkness.* **2** a thing that falls or has fallen. ■ (usu. **falls**) a waterfall or cascade. ■ (**falls**) the parts or petals of a flower that bend downward, esp. the outer perianth segments of an iris. **3** a decrease in size, number, rate, or level; a decline. **4** a loss of office. ■ the loss of a city or fortified place during battle. ■ a person's moral descent, typically through succumbing to temptation. ■ (**the Fall** or **the Fall of Man**) the lapse of humankind into a state of sin, ascribed in traditional Jewish and Christian theology to the disobedience of Adam and Eve as described in Genesis. **5** (also **Fall**) autumn.
– PHRASES **fall foul** (or **afoul**) **of** come into conflict with and be undermined by. **fall in** (or **into**) **line** conform with others or with accepted behavior. **fall into place** (of a series of events or facts) begin to make sense or cohere. **fall over oneself to do something** informal be excessively eager to do something. **fall short** (**of**) (of a missile) fail to reach its target. ■ fig. be deficient or inadequate; fail to reach a required goal. **fall victim to** see VICTIM. **take the fall** informal receive blame or punishment, typically in the place of another person.
– PHRASAL VERBS **fall apart** (or **to pieces**) break up, come apart, or disintegrate: *their marriage is likely to fall apart.* ■ (of a person) lose one's capacity to cope. **fall back** move or turn back; retreat. **fall back on** have recourse to when in difficulty. **fall behind** fail to keep up with one's competitors. ■ fail to meet a commitment to make a regular payment. **fall down** be shown to be inadequate or false; fail. **fall for** informal **1** be captivated by; fall in love with. **2** be deceived by (something). **fall in 1** take one's place in a military formation. **2** (of a structure)

collapse inward. **fall in with 1** meet by chance and become involved with. **2** act in accordance with (someone's ideas or suggestions); agree to. **fall on** (or **upon**) **1** attack fiercely or unexpectedly. ■ seize enthusiastically. **2** (of someone's eyes or gaze) be directed toward. **3** (of a burden or duty) be borne or incurred by. **fall out 1** (of the hair, teeth, etc.) become detached and drop out. **2** have an argument. **3** leave one's place in a military formation, or on parade. **4** happen; turn out. **fall through** come to nothing; fail. **fall to** (of a task) become the duty or responsibility of. ■ (of property) revert to the ownership of. [OE *fallan, feallan*, of Gmc. origin; rel. to Ger. *fallen*.]

fal·la·cy /'faləsē/ ▶ **n.** (pl. **-cies**) a mistaken belief, esp. one based on unsound argument. ■ Logic a failure in reasoning that renders an argument invalid. ■ faulty reasoning; misleading or unsound argument. — **fal·la·cious** /fə'lāsʜəs/ **adj. fal·la·cious·ly** /fə'lāsʜəslē/ **adv. fal·la·cious·ness** /fə'lāsʜəsnis/ **n.** [15th C.: from L. *fallacia*, from *fallax, fallac-* 'deceiving,' from *fallere* 'deceive.']

fal·la·way /'fôlə,wā/ ▶ **n.** [usu. as adj.] made or done while moving or falling away, esp. (in basketball) from the basket: *he hit a **fallaway jumper**.*

fall·back /'fôl,bak/ ▶ **n. 1** an alternative plan that may be used in an emergency. **2** a reduction or retreat.

Fall Clas·sic ▶ **n.** Baseball a nickname for the World Series.

fall·en /'fôlən/ past participle of **FALL.** ▶ **adj.** [attrib.] **1** Theol. subject to sin or depravity. ■ dated (of a woman) regarded as having lost her honor through engaging in a sexual relationship outside marriage. **2** (of a soldier) killed in battle. — **fall·en·ness n.**

fall·en an·gel ▶ **n.** (in Christian, Jewish, and Muslim tradition) an angel who rebelled against God and was cast out of heaven.

fall·fish /'fôl,fisʜ/ ▶ **n.** (pl. same or **-fish·es**) a North American freshwater fish (*Semotilus corporalis*) of the minnow family, resembling the chub and often found near rapids or waterfalls.

fall guy ▶ **n.** informal a scapegoat.

fal·li·ble /'faləbəl/ ▶ **adj.** capable of making mistakes or being erroneous. — **fal·li·bil·i·ty** /,falə'bilətē/ **n. fal·li·bly** /-blē/ **adv.** [ME: from med. L. *fallibilis*, from L. *fallere* 'deceive.']

fall·ing-out ▶ **n.** [in sing.] a quarrel or disagreement.

fall·ing star ▶ **n.** a meteor or shooting star.

fall line ▶ **n. 1** a narrow zone that marks the geological boundary between an upland region and a plain, distinguished by the occurrence of falls and rapids where rivers and streams cross it. ■ **(the Fall Line)** (in the US) the zone demarcating the Piedmont from the Atlantic coastal plain. **2** (**the fall line**) Skiing the route leading straight down any particular part of a slope.

fall·off /'fôl,ôf/ ▶ **n.** [in sing.] a decrease in something.

fal·lo·pi·an tube /fə'lōpēən/ (also **Fal·lo·pi·an**) ▶ **n.** Anat. (in a female mammal) either of a pair of tubes along which eggs travel from the ovaries to the uterus. [18th C.: named after Gabriello *Fallopio* (1523–62), the Italian anatomist who first described them.]

fall·out /'fôl,out/ ▶ **n.** radioactive particles that are carried into the atmosphere after a nuclear explosion or accident and fall back as dust or in precipitation. ■ fig. the adverse side effects or results of a situation. ■ [usu. with adj.] airborne substances resulting from an industrial process or accident.

fal·low¹ /'falō/ ▶ **adj.** (of farmland) plowed and harrowed but left unsown for a period in order to restore its fertility as part of a crop rotation or to avoid surplus production. ■ fig. inactive. ■ (of a sow) not pregnant. ▶ **n.** a piece of fallow or uncultivated land. ▶ **v.** [trans.] leave (land) fallow. — **fal·low·ness n.** [OE *fealgian* 'to break up land for sowing,' of Gmc. origin; rel. to Low Ger. *falgen*.]

fal·low² ▶ **n.** a pale brown or reddish yellow color. [OE *falu, fealu*, of Gmc. origin; rel. to Du. *vaal* and Ger. *fahl, falb*.]

fal·low deer ▶ **n.** a Eurasian deer (*Cervus dama*, or *Dama dama*) with branched palmate antlers, typically having a white-spotted reddish-brown coat in summer.

Fall Riv·er a city in southeastern Massachusetts, a textile center; pop. 91,938.

false /fôls/ ▶ **adj. 1** not according with truth or fact; incorrect. ■ not according with rules or law. **2** appearing to be the thing denoted; deliberately made or meant to deceive. ■ artificial. ■ feigned. **3** illusory; not actually so. ■ [attrib.] used in names of plants, animals, and gems that superficially resemble the thing properly so called, e.g., **false oat, false killer whale. 4** treacherous; unfaithful.

– PHRASES **false position** a situation in which one acts in a manner inconsistent with one's nature or principles. **play someone false** deceive or cheat someone. — **false·ly adv. false·ness n. fal·si·ty** /'fôlsətē/ **n.** [OE *fals* 'fraud, deceit,' from L. *falsum* 'fraud,' neut. past part. of *fallere* 'deceive.']

false a·ca·cia ▶ **n.** a tree of the pea family, as are "true" acacias, but of a different genus (*Robinia*), in particular the black locust of North America.

false a·larm ▶ **n.** a false report of a fire to a fire department. ■ a warning given about something that fails to happen.

false beech·drops ▶ **n.** see **PINESAP.**

false col·or ▶ **n.** color added during the processing of a photographic or computer image to aid interpretation of the subject.

false cy·press ▶ **n.** a conifer of a genus (*Chamaecyparis*) that includes Lawson cypress (see **PORT ORFORD CEDAR**).

false dawn ▶ **n.** a transient light that precedes the rising of the sun by about an hour. ■ fig. a promising sign that comes to nothing.

false face ▶ **n.** a mask, usually wooden, traditionally worn ceremonially by some North American Indian peoples to cure the sick.

false fruit ▶ **n.** a fruit formed from other parts of the plant as well as the ovary, esp. the receptacle, as occurs in the strawberry or fig. Also called **PSEUDOCARP.**

false gha·ri·al /'ge(ə)rēəl/ ▶ **n.** a rare, narrow-snouted crocodile (*Tomistoma schlegelii*) that resembles the gharial, native to Indonesia and Malaysia.

false hel·le·bore /'helə,bôr/ ▶ **n.** a herbaceous plant (genus *Veratrum*) of the lily family, with pleated leaves and a tall spike of densely packed yellow-green flowers, found in damp soils in north temperate regions.

false·hood /'fôls,ho͝od/ ▶ **n.** the state of being untrue. ■ a lie. ■ lying.

false move ▶ **n.** an unwise or careless action that could have dangerous consequences.

false ox·lip ▶ **n.** see **OXLIP.**

false preg·nan·cy ▶ **n.** Med. an abnormal condition in which signs of pregnancy are present in a woman who is not pregnant.

false pre·tens·es ▶ **plural n.** behavior intended to deceive others.

false rib ▶ **n.** another term for **FLOATING RIB.**

false scor·pi·on ▶ **n.** another term for **PSEUDOSCORPION.**

false start ▶ **n.** an invalid or disallowed start to a race. ■ an unsuccessful attempt to begin something.

false step ▶ **n.** [usu. in sing.] a slip or stumble. ■ a careless or unwise act; a mistake.

false teeth ▶ **plural n.** another term for ***DENTURES*** (see **DENTURE**).

fal·set·to /fôl'setō/ ▶ **n.** (pl. **-tos**) Music a method of voice production used by male singers, esp. tenors, to sing notes higher than their normal range. ■ a singer using this method. ■ a voice or sound that is unusually or unnaturally high. [18th C.: from Ital., dimin. of *falso* 'false,' from L. *falsus* (see **FALSE**).]

false·work /'fôls,wərk/ ▶ **n.** temporary framework used to support a building during its construction.

fals·ies /'fôlsēz/ ▶ **plural n.** informal pads of material in women's bras used to make the breasts appear larger.

fal·si·fy /'fôlsə,fī/ ▶ **v.** (**-fies, -fied**) [trans.] **1** alter (information or evidence) so as to mislead. ■ forge or alter fraudulently: [as adj.] (**falsified**) *falsified documents.* **2** prove to be false: *the hypothesis is falsified by the evidence.* ■ fail to fulfill (a hope, fear, etc.); remove the justification for: *changes falsify individual expectations.* — **fal·si·fi·a·bil·i·ty** /,fôlsə,fīə'bilitē/ **n. fal·si·fi·a·ble** /,fôlsə'fīəbəl/ **adj. fal·si·fi·ca·tion** /,fôlsəfə'kāsʜən/ **n.** [ME (sense 2): from Fr. *falsifier* or med. L. *falsificare*, from L. *falsificus* 'making false,' from *falsus* 'false.']

Fal·staff·i·an /fôl'stafēən/ ▶ **adj.** of or resembling Shakespeare's character Sir John Falstaff in being fat, jolly, and debauched: *a Falstaffian gusto for life.*

fal·ter /'fôltər/ ▶ **v.** [intrans.] start to lose strength or momentum: *her smile faltered* | [as adj.] (**faltering**) *his faltering career.* ■ speak or move in a hesitant or unsteady manner. — **fal·ter·er n. fal·ter·ing·ly adv.** [ME: perh. from the v. **FOLD¹** + *-ter* as in *totter*.]

Fa·lun Gong /'fälo͞on 'go͝oɴɢ; 'gäɴɢ/ (also **Fa·lun Da·fa** /'däfä/) ▶ **n.** a spiritual exercise and meditation regime with similarities to t'ai chi ch'uan, practiced predominantly in China. ■ a Taoist-Buddhist sect practicing Falun Gong. [1990s: Chin., literally 'wheel of law,' from *fǎ* 'law' + *lún* 'wheel' (+ *gōng* 'skill' or *dàfǎ* 'great method').]

fam. ▶ **abbr.** ■ familiar. ■ family.

fame /fām/ ▶ **n.** the condition of being known or talked about by many people, esp. on account of notable achievements. [ME: via OFr. from L. *fama*.]

famed /fāmd/ ▶ **adj.** known about by many people; renowned: *he is **famed for** his eccentricities.* [ME: past part. of archaic *fame* (v.), from OFr. *famer*, from L. *fama*.]

fa·mil·ial /fə'milēəl; -'milyəl/ ▶ **adj.** of, relating to, or occurring in a family: *the familial Christmas dinner.*

fa·mil·iar /fə'milyər/ ▶ **adj. 1** well known from long or close association: *a familiar voice.* ■ often encountered or experienced; common. ■ [predic.] (**familiar with**) having a good knowledge of: *you are familiar with the controls.* **2** in close friendship; intimate. ■ informal to an inappropriate degree. ▶ **n. 1** (also **familiar spirit**) a demon supposedly attending a witch, often said to assume the form of an animal. **2** (in the Roman Catholic Church) a person rendering certain services in a pope's or bishop's household. **3** a close friend or associate. — **fa·mil·iar·ly adv.** [ME: from OFr. *familier*, from L. *familiaris*, from *familia* 'household servants, household, family,' from *famulus* 'servant.']

fa·mil·iar·i·ty /fə,milē'aritē; -mil'yar-/ ▶ **n.** (pl. **-ties**)close acquaintance with or knowledge of something. ■ the quality of being well known; recognizability based on long or close association. ■ relaxed friendliness or intimacy between people. ■ inappropriate and often offensive informality of behavior or language.

fa·mil·iar·ize /fə'milyə,rīz/ ▶ **v.** [trans.] give (someone) knowledge or understanding of something. ■ make (something) better known or more easily grasped. — **fa·mil·iar·i·za·tion** /fə,milyərə'zāsʜən/ **n.**

fam·i·list /'faməlist/ ▶ **adj.** of, relating to, or advocating a social framework centered on family relationships rather than on the needs of the individual. — **fam·i·lism** n. **fam·i·lis·tic** /ˌfamə'listik/ adj.

fam·i·ly /'fam(ə)lē/ ▶ n. (pl. **-lies**) **1** [treated as sing. or pl.] a group consisting of parents and children living together in a household. ■ a group of people related to one another by blood or marriage. ■ the children of a person or couple. ■ a person or people related to one and so to be treated with a special loyalty or intimacy. ■ a group of people united in criminal activity. ■ Biol. a principal taxonomic category that ranks above genus and below order, usually ending in *-idae* (in zoology) or *-aceae* (in botany). ■ a group of objects united by a significant shared characteristic. ■ Math. a group of curves or surfaces obtained by varying the value of a constant in the equation generating them. **2** all the descendants of a common ancestor. ■ a race or group of peoples from a common stock. ■ all the languages ultimately derived from a particular early language, regarded as a group. ▶ adj. [attrib.] designed to be suitable for children as well as adults.

– PHRASES **the** (or **one's**) **family jewels** informal a man's genitals. **in the family way** informal pregnant. [ME: from L. *familia* 'household servants, household, family,' from *famulus* 'servant.']

fam·i·ly Bi·ble ▶ n. a Bible designed to be used at family prayers, typically one with space on its flyleaves for recording important family events.

fam·i·ly hour ▶ n. a period in the evening during which many children and their families watch television, esp. 8 to 9 p.m.

fam·i·ly leave ▶ n. an excused absence from work for the purpose of dealing with family matters, esp. a birth, adoption, or care of a dependent.

fam·i·ly man ▶ n. a man who lives with his wife and children, esp. one who enjoys home life.

fam·i·ly name ▶ n. a surname. ■ a first or middle name that is frequently given in a family. ■ a family's good reputation.

fam·i·ly plan·ning ▶ n. [often as adj.] the practice of controlling the number of children in a family and the intervals between their births, particularly by means of artificial contraception or voluntary sterilization. ■ artificial contraception.

fam·i·ly style ▶ adj. **1** designating a style of preparation or serving of food in which diners help themselves from plates of food that have been put on the table. **2** suitable for an entire family, including children. ▶ adv. with plates of food from which individual diners can serve themselves.

fam·i·ly tree ▶ n. a diagram showing the relationships between people in several generations of a family. ■ all of the descendants and ancestors in a family.

fam·ine /'famən/ ▶ n. extreme scarcity of food. ■ a shortage. [ME: from OFr., from *faim* 'hunger,' from L. *fames*.]

fam·ished /'famisʜt/ ▶ adj. informal extremely hungry. [ME: past part. of the v. *famish*, from ME *fame* 'starve,' from OFr. *afamer*, based on L. *fames* 'hunger.']

fa·mous /'fāməs/ ▶ adj. known about by many people.

– PHRASES **famous last words** said as an ironic comment on an overconfident assertion that may well be proved wrong by events: *"I'll be OK on my own." "Famous last words," she thought to herself.* — **fa·mous·ness** n. [ME: from OFr. *fameus*, from L. *famosus* 'famed,' from *fama* (see FAME).]

fa·mous·ly /'fāməslē/ ▶ adv. **1** informal excellently. **2** indicating that the fact asserted is widely known.

fam·u·lus /'famyələs/ ▶ n. (pl. **-li** /-ˌlē; -ˌlī/) hist. an assistant or servant, esp. one working for a magician or scholar. [19th C.: from L., 'servant.']

Fan /fan; fän/ ▶ n. & adj. var. of FANG.

fan¹ /fan/ ▶ n. **1** an apparatus with rotating blades that creates a current of air for cooling or ventilation. **2** a device, typically folding and shaped like a segment of a circle when spread out, that is held in the hand and waved so as to cool the person by moving air. ■ a thing or shape resembling such a device when open. ■ an alluvial or talus deposit spread out in such a shape at the foot of a slope. ■ a small sail for keeping the head of a windmill toward the wind. **3** a device for winnowing grain. ▶ v. (**fanned, fan·ning**) **1** [trans.] cool (esp. a person or a part of the body) by waving something to create a current of air. ■ (of breath or a breeze) blow gently on: *his breath fanned her skin.* ■ [trans.] brush or drive away with a waving movement. ■ [intrans.] Baseball Ice Hockey swing at and miss the ball or puck. ■ [intrans.] Baseball (of a batter) strike out. ■ Baseball (of a pitcher) strike out (a batter). **2** [trans.] increase the strength of (a fire) by blowing on it or stirring up the air near it. ■ cause (a belief or emotion) to become stronger or more widespread. **3** [intrans.] disperse or radiate from a central point to cover a wide area. ■ spread out or cause to spread out into a semicircular shape. — **fan·like** adj. **fan·ner** n. [OE *fann* (as a n. denoting a device for winnowing grain), *fannian* (v.), from L. *vannus* 'winnowing fan.' Cf. VANE.]

fan¹ 2

fan² ▶ n. a person who has a strong interest in or admiration for a particular sport, art or entertainment form, or famous person. — **fan·dom** /'fandəm/ n. [19th C. (orig.US): abbrev. of FANATIC.]

fa·nat·ic /fə'natik/ ▶ n. a person filled with excessive and single-minded zeal, esp. for an extreme religious or political cause. ■ [often with adj.] informal a person with an obsessive interest in and enthusiasm for something, esp. an activity. ▶ adj. [attrib.] filled with or expressing excessive zeal. — **fa·nat·i·cism** /-əˌsizəm/ n. **fa·nat·i·cize** /-əˌsīz/ v. [16th C. (as an adj.): from Fr. *fanatique* or L. *fanaticus* 'of a temple, inspired by a god,' from *fanum* 'temple.']

fa·nat·i·cal /fə'natikəl/ ▶ adj. filled with excessive and single-minded zeal. ■ obsessively concerned with something. — **fa·nat·i·cal·ly** /-k(ə)lē/ adv.

fan belt ▶ n. (in a motor-vehicle engine) a belt that transmits motion from the driveshaft to the radiator fan and the generator or alternator.

fan·ci·er /'fansēər/ ▶ n. [with adj.] a connoisseur or enthusiast of something, esp. someone who has a special interest in or breeds a particular animal.

fan·ci·ful /'fansəfəl/ ▶ adj. (of a person or their thoughts and ideas) overimaginative and unrealistic. ■ existing only in the imagination or fancy. ■ designed to be exotically ornamental rather than practical. — **fan·ci·ful·ly** adv. **fan·ci·ful·ness** n.

fan·cy /'fansē/ ▶ adj. (**-ci·er, -ci·est**) elaborate in structure or decoration. ■ designed to impress. ■ (esp. of foodstuffs) of high quality. ■ (of flowers) of two or more colors. ■ (of an animal) bred to develop particular points of appearance. ▶ v. (**-cies, -cied**) [trans.] **1** feel a desire or liking for: *do you fancy a drink?* ■ find sexually attractive: *he saw a woman he fancied.* ■ (**fancy oneself**) informal have an unduly high opinion of oneself, or of one's ability in a particular area: *he fancied himself an amateur psychologist.* **2** [with clause] imagine; think: *he fancied he could smell roses.* ■ [in imper.] used to express one's surprise at something: *fancy meeting all those actors!* ▶ n. (pl. **-cies**) **1** a feeling of liking or attraction, typically one that is superficial or transient. **2** the faculty of imagination: *my research assistant is prone to flights of fancy.* ■ a thing that one supposes or imagines, typically an unfounded or tentative belief or idea; notion or whim.

– PHRASES **take someone's fancy** appeal to someone. **take a fancy to** become fond of, esp. without an obvious reason. — **fan·ci·ly** adv. **fan·ci·ness** n. [ME: contr. of FANTASY.]

fan·cy dress ▶ n. an unusual or amusing costume worn as part of a theme at a party.

fan·cy-free ▶ adj. free from emotional involvement or commitment to anyone.

fan·cy man ▶ n. dated a woman's lover. ■ archaic a pimp.

fan·cy wom·an ▶ n. dated a married man's mistress. ■ a prostitute.

fan·cy·work /'fansēˌwərk/ (also **fan·cy-work**) ▶ n. ornamental needlework, crochet, or knitting.

fan·dan·go /fan'daNGgō/ ▶ n. (pl. **-goes** or **-gos**) **1** a lively Spanish dance for two people, typically accompanied by castanets or tambourine. **2** a foolish or useless act or thing. [18th C.: Sp., of unknown origin.]

fan·fare /'fanˌfe(ə)r/ ▶ n. a short ceremonial tune or flourish played on brass instruments. ■ fig. an ostentatious or noisy display. [18th C.: from Fr., ult. of imitative origin.]

fan·fa·ron·ade /ˌfanˌfarə'nād/ ▶ n. arrogant or boastful talk. [17th C.: from Fr. *fanfaronnade*, from *fanfaron* 'braggart,' from *fanfare* (see FANFARE).]

Fang /faNG; fäNG/ (also **Fan** /fan; fän/) ▶ n. (pl. same or **Fangs**) **1** a member of a people inhabiting parts of Cameroon, Equatorial Guinea, and Gabon. **2** the Bantu language of this people. ▶ adj. of or relating to this people or their language. [Fr., prob. from Fang *Pangwe*.]

fang

fang /faNG/ ▶ n. a large, sharp tooth, esp. a canine tooth of a dog or wolf. ■ the tooth of a venomous snake, by which poison is injected. ■ the biting mouthpart of a spider. — **fanged** adj. [also in comb.] [OE (denoting booty or spoils), from ON *fang* 'capture, grasp'; cf. VANG.]

fan·jet /'fanˌjet/ ▶ n. another term for TURBOFAN.

fan·light /'fanˌlīt/ ▶ n. a small semicircular or rectangular window over a door or another window.

fan mail ▶ n. letters from fans to a famous person they admire.

Fan·nie Mae /'fanē 'mā/ ▶ n. informal the Federal National Mortgage Association, a corporation (now privately owned) that trades in mortgages. [1940s: elaboration of the abbrev. FNMA.]

fan·ny /'fanē/ ▶ n. (pl. **-nies**) informal a person's buttocks. [19th C.: of unknown origin.]

fan·ny pack ▶ n. a small pouch on a belt, for money and other valuables, worn around the waist or hips.

fan palm ▶ n. a palm (*Chamaerops* and other genera) with large, lobed, fan-shaped leaves.

fanlight

fan·tab·u·lous /fan'tabyələs/ ▸ **adj.** informal excellent; wonderful. [1950s: blend of FANTASTIC and FABULOUS.]

fan·tail /'fan,tāl/ ▸ **n.** a fan-shaped tail or end. ■ the rounded overhanging part of the stern of a boat, esp. a warship. ■ (also **fantail pigeon**) a broad-tailed domestic pigeon. — **fan-tailed adj.**

fan-tan ▸ **n.** **1** a Chinese gambling game in which players try to guess the remainder after the banker has divided a number of hidden objects into four groups. **2** a card game in which players build on sequences of sevens. [19th C.: from Chin. *fān tān*, literally 'repeated divisions.']

fan·ta·sia /fan'tāzHə; ,fantə'zēə/ ▸ **n.** a musical composition with a free form and often an improvisatory style. ■ a musical composition that is based on several familiar tunes. ■ a thing that is composed of a mixture of different forms or styles. [18th C.: from Ital., 'fantasy,' from L. *phantasia* (see FANTASY).]

fan·ta·size /'fantə,sīz/ ▸ **v.** [intrans.] indulge in daydreaming about something desired. ■ [trans.] imagine (something that one wants to happen). — **fan·ta·sist n.**

fan·tast /'fantast/ (also **phan·tast**) ▸ **n.** an impractical, impulsive person; a dreamer. [16th C.: orig.via med. L. from Gk. *phantastēs* 'boaster,' from *phantazein* or *phantazesthai* (see FANTASTIC); in mod. use from Ger. *Phantast*.]

fan·tas·tic /fan'tastik/ ▸ **adj.** **1** imaginative or fanciful; remote from reality. ■ of extraordinary size or degree. ■ (of a shape or design) bizarre or exotic. **2** informal extraordinarily good or attractive. — **fan·tas·ti·cal adj.** (in sense 1) **fan·tas·ti·cal·i·ty** /fan,tasti'kalitē/ **n.** (in sense 1) **fan·tas·ti·cal·ly** /-k(ə)lē/ **adv.** [ME: from OFr. *fantastique*, via med. L. from Gk. *phantastikos*, from *phantazein* 'make visible,' from *phantos* 'visible.']

fan·ta·sy /'fantəsē; -zē/ ▸ **n.** (pl. **-sies**) **1** the faculty or activity of imagining things that are impossible or improbable. ■ the product of this faculty or activity. ■ a fanciful mental image, typically one that reflects a person's conscious or unconscious wishes. ■ an idea with no basis in reality. ■ a genre of imaginative fiction involving magic and adventure, esp. in a setting other than the real world. **2** a musical composition, free in form, typically involving variation on an existing work or the imaginative representation of a situation or story; a fantasia. ▸ **v.** (**-sies, -sied**) [trans.] literary imagine the occurrence of; fantasize about. [late ME: from OFr. *fantasie*, from L. *phantasia*, from Gk., 'imagination,' from *phantazein* 'make visible.']

fan·ta·sy·land /'fantəsē,land/ ▸ **n.** a fantastic place exciting wonder, esp. one with imaginary creatures.

Fan·te /'fäntē; 'fantē/ (also **Fan·ti**) ▸ **n.** (pl. same or **-tis** /-tēz/) **1** a member of a people of southern Ghana. **2** the dialect of Akan spoken by this people. ▸ **adj.** of or relating to this people or their language. [the name in Akan.]

fan·tod /'fantäd/ ▸ **n.** informal a state or attack of uneasiness or unreasonableness. [19th C.: of unknown origin.]

fan vault ▸ **n.** Archit. a type of vault consisting of a set of concave ribs spreading out from a central point like the ribs of an opened umbrella. — **fan vault·ing n.**

fan·zine /'fan,zēn; ,fan'zēn/ ▸ **n.** a magazine, usually produced by amateurs, for fans of a particular performer, group, or form of entertainment. [1940s (orig.US): blend of FAN[2] and MAGAZINE.]

FAO ▸ **abbr.** Food and Agriculture Organization.

FAQ /fak/ ▸ **n.** Comput. a text file containing a list of questions and answers relating to a particular subject. [1990s: acronym from *frequently asked questions*.]

fa·quir ▸ **n.** var. of FAKIR.

far /fär/ ▸ **adv.** (**far·ther, far·thest** or **fur·ther, fur·thest**) **1** [often with adverbial] at, to, or by a great distance (used to indicate the extent to which one thing is distant from another): *it was not too far away.* **2** over a large expanse of space or time: *he had not traveled far.* **3** by a great deal: *he is able to function far better than usual.* ▸ **adj.** [attrib.] situated at a great distance in space or time: *the far reaches of the universe.* ■ more distant than another object of the same kind: *standing in the far corner.* ■ distant from a point seen as central; extreme: *brought up in the far north of Scotland.*

– PHRASES **as far as** for as great a distance as. ■ for a great enough distance to reach: *I decided to walk as far as the village.* ■ to the extent that: *as far as I am concerned, it is no big deal.* **be a far cry from** be very different from. **by far** by a great amount. **far and away** by a great amount. **far and near** (also **near and far**) everywhere. **far and wide** over a large area. **far be it from me to** used to express reluctance, esp. to do something that one thinks may be resented: *far be it from me to speculate.* **far from** very different from being; tending to the opposite of. **far gone** in a bad or worsening state, esp. so as to be beyond recovery. ■ advanced in time. **go far 1** achieve a great deal. **2** contribute greatly. **3** be worth or amount to much. **go so far as to do something** do something regarded as extreme. **go too far** exceed the limits of what is reasonable or acceptable. **so far 1** to a certain limited extent. **2** (of a trend that seems likely to continue) up to this time. **so far, so good** progress has been satisfactory up to now: *"How's the job?" "So far, so good."* [OE *feorr*, of Gmc. origin; rel. to Du. *ver*, from an Indo-Eur. root shared by Sanskrit *para* and Gk. *pera* 'further.']

Far. ▸ **abbr.** faraday.

far·ad /'farəd; -ad/ (abbr.: **F**) ▸ **n.** the SI unit of electrical capacitance, equal to the capacitance of a capacitor in which one coulomb of charge causes a potential difference of one volt. [19th C.: shortening of FARADAY. The term was orig. proposed as a unit of electrical charge.]

far·a·da·ic /,farə'dāik/ ▸ **adj.** another term for FARADIC.

Far·a·day /'farə,dā; -dē/, Michael (1791–1867), English scientist. He worked with electromagnetism and also discovered the laws of electrolysis.

far·a·day /'farə,dā; -dē/ (abbr.: **F**) ▸ **n.** Chem. a unit of electric charge equal to Faraday's constant. [20th C.: coined in German from the name of M. FARADAY.]

Far·a·day's con·stant Chem. the quantity of electric charge carried by one mole of electrons (equal to 96.49 coulombs). Compare with FARADAY.

fa·rad·ic /fə'radik/ (also **far·a·da·ic** /,farə'dāik/) ▸ **adj.** produced by or associated with electrical induction. [19th C.: from the name of M. FARADAY + -IC.]

Far·al·lon Is·lands /'farə,län/ a small, uninhabited island group in the Pacific Ocean, west of San Francisco in California. Also called the **Farallones.**

far·an·dole /,farən'dōl;'farən,dōl/ ▸ **n.** hist. a lively Provençal dance in which the dancers join hands and wind in and out in a chain. [19th C.: Fr., from mod. Provençal *farandoulo*.]

far·a·way /'färə,wā/ ▸ **adj.** distant in space or time. ■ seeming remote from the immediate surroundings; dreamy.

farce /färs/ ▸ **n.** a comic dramatic work using buffoonery and horseplay and typically including crude characterization and ludicrously improbable situations. ■ the genre of such works. ■ an absurd event. — **far·ci·cal** /'färsikəl/ **adj.** **far·ci·cal·ly** /'färsik(ə)lē/ **adv.** [16th C.: from Fr., literally 'stuffing,' from *farcir* 'to stuff,' from L. *farcire*.]

far·ceur /fär'sər/ ▸ **n.** a writer of or performer in farces. ■ a joker or comedian. [17th C.: Fr.]

far·cy /'färsē/ ▸ **n.** glanders in horses (or a similar disease in cattle) in which there is inflammation of the lymph vessels, causing nodules. [ME: from OFr. *farcin*, from late L. *farciminum*, from *farcire* 'to stuff.']

fare /fe(ə)r/ ▸ **n.** **1** the money a passenger on public transportation has to pay. ■ a passenger paying to travel in a vehicle, esp. a taxicab. **2** a range of food, esp. of a particular type. ■ fig. performance or entertainment of a particular style. ▸ **v.** [intrans.] [with adverbial] perform in a specified way in a particular situation or over a particular period of time: *the party fared badly in the elections.* [OE *fær, faru* 'traveling, a journey or expedition,' *faran* 'to travel,' also 'get on (well or badly'), of Gmc. origin; rel. to Ger. *fahren* 'to travel,' also to FORD.]

Far East the countries in eastern Asia. — **Far East·ern adj.**

fare-thee-well (also **fare-you-well**) ▸ **n.** (in phrase **to a fare-thee-well**) to perfection; thoroughly.

fare·well /,fe(ə)r'wel/ ▸ **exclam.** used to express good wishes on parting. ▸ **n.** an act of parting or of marking someone's departure. ■ parting good wishes. [ME: from the imper. of FARE + the adv. WELL[1].]

far·fal·le /fär'fälā; -'falē/ ▸ **n.** small pieces of pasta shaped like bows or butterflies' wings. [Ital., pl. of *farfalla* 'butterfly.']

far·fel /'färfəl/ ▸ **n.** ground noodle dough formed into small pellets that are used in soups.

far-fetched ▸ **adj.** (of an explanation or theory) contrived and unconvincing; unlikely. ■ (of a story or idea) implausible, silly, or exaggerated.

far-flung ▸ **adj.** distant or remote. ■ widely distributed.

Far·go[1] /'färgō/ the largest city in North Dakota, in the southeastern part of the state, on the Red River of the North; pop. 90,599.

Far·go[2], William, see WELLS, FARGO & CO.

fa·ri·na /fə'rēnə/ ▸ **n.** flour or meal made of cereal grains, nuts, or starchy roots. — **far·i·na·ceous** /,farə'nāsHəs/ **adj.** [ME: from L., from *far* 'grain.']

far·kle·ber·ry /'färkəl,berē/ ▸ **n.** a shrub or small tree (*Vaccinium arboreum*) of the heath family, with thick leathery leaves and inedible black berries, native to the southeastern US.

farm /färm/ ▸ **n.** an area of land and its buildings used for growing crops and rearing animals, typically under the control of one owner or manager. ■ the main dwelling place on such a site; a farmhouse. ■ [with adj.] a place for breeding a particular type of animal or producing a specified crop. ■ [with adj.] an establishment at which something is produced or processed. ▸ **v.** **1** [intrans.] make one's living by growing crops or keeping livestock: *he has farmed organically for years.* ■ [trans.] use (land) for growing crops and rearing animals, esp. commercially. ■ [trans.] breed or grow commercially (a type of livestock or crop, esp. one not normally domesticated or cultivated). **2** [trans.] (**farm someone/something out**) send out or subcontract work to others. ■ arrange for a child or other dependent person to be looked after by someone, usually for payment. **3** [trans.] hist. allow someone to collect and keep the revenues from (a tax) on payment of a fee: *the customs had been farmed to the collector for a fixed sum.*

– PHRASES **buy the farm** see BUY. — **farm·a·ble** /'färməbəl/ **adj.** [ME: from OFr. *ferme*, from med. L. *firma* 'fixed payment,' from L. *firmare* 'fix, settle,' from *firmus* 'constant, firm.']

Farm Belt the agricultural states of the US Midwest, esp. Iowa, Kansas, Minnesota, Nebraska, North Dakota, and South Dakota.

Far·mer /'färmər/, Fannie Merritt (1857–1915), US educator and culinary expert. Her *Boston Cooking School Cook Book* (1896) was known as "the mother of level measurements."

farm·er /ˈfärmər/ ▶ **n.** **1** the owner or manager of a farm. **2** [with adj.] hist. a person to whom the collection of taxes was contracted for a fee.

farm·er cheese ▶ **n.** a mild unripened cheese that is somewhat crumbly in texture. Also called **farm cheese**.

farm·ers' mar·ket ▶ **n.** a food market, often held in a public place outdoors at regular intervals, at which local farmers sell their produce directly to consumers.

farm·hand /ˈfärm,hand/ ▶ **n.** a worker on a farm.

farm·house /ˈfärm,hous/ ▶ **n.** a house attached to a farm, esp. the main house in which the farmer lives.

farm·ing /ˈfärmiNG/ ▶ **n.** the activity or business of growing crops and raising livestock.

farm·land /ˈfärm,land/ ▶ **n.** (also **farmlands**) land used for farming.

farm·stead /ˈfärm,sted/ ▶ **n.** a farm and its buildings.

farm team ▶ **n.** Baseball a minor league team that prepares players for an affiliated major league team.

farm·yard /ˈfärm,yärd/ ▶ **n.** a yard or enclosure attached to a farmhouse.

Farne Is·lands /färn/ a group of 17 small islands off the coast of Northumberland, England, noted for their wildlife.

Far·ne·se /färˈnāzā/, Alessandro, see **PAUL III**.

Farn·ham /ˈfärnəm/, Eliza Wood (1815–64), US reformer. She instituted major prison reforms.

far·o /ˈfe(ə)rō/ ▶ **n.** a gambling card game in which players bet on the order in which the cards will appear. [18th C. (orig. as *pharaoh* or *pharo*): from Fr. *pharaon* (see **PHARAOH**), perh. because a pharaoh was pictured on the cards.]

Far·oe Is·lands var. of **FAEROE ISLANDS**

Far·o·ese ▶ **adj. & n.** var. of **FAEROESE**.

far-off ▶ **adj.** remote in time or space.

fa·ro·li·to /,farəˈlētō; ,fär-/ another term for **LUMINARIA**.

fa·rouche /fəˈro͞osH/ ▶ **adj.** sullen or shy in company. [18th C.: from Fr., alt. of OFr. *forache*, based on L. *foras* 'out of doors.']

Fa·rouk /fəˈro͞ok/ (1920–65), king of Egypt 1936–52. His defeat in the Arab–Israeli conflict of 1948, together with the general corruption of his reign, led to a military coup in 1952.

far-out ▶ **adj.** unconventional or avant-garde. ■ [often as exclam.] informal excellent.

Far·quhar /ˈfärkwər/, George (1678–1707), Irish playwright. He was a principal figure in Restoration comedy.

far·ra·go /fəˈrägō; -ˈrā-/ ▶ **n.** (pl. **-goes**) a confused mixture. — **far·rag·i·nous** /fəˈrajənəs/ **adj.** [17th C.: from L., literally 'mixed fodder,' from *far* 'corn.']

Far·ra·gut /ˈfarəgət/, David Glasgow (1801–70), US admiral. During the American Civil War, he captured the city of New Orleans in April 1862 and extended Union control of the Mississippi River north to Vicksburg.

far-reach·ing ▶ **adj.** having important and widely applicable effects or implications.

Far·rell[1] /ˈfarəl/, J. T. (1904–79), US writer; full name *James Thomas Farrell*. His trilogy about Studs Lonigan began with *Young Lonigan* (1932).

Far·rell[2], Suzanne (1945–), US dancer; born *Roberta Sue Ficker*. She performed with the New York City Ballet 1961–69 and was principal dancer 1965–69.

far·ri·er /ˈfarēər/ ▶ **n.** a craftsman who trims and shoes horses' hooves. — **far·ri·er·y** **n.** [16th C.: from OFr. *ferrier*, from L. *ferrarius*, from *ferrum* 'iron, horseshoe.']

far·row /ˈfarō/ ▶ **n.** a litter of pigs. ■ an act of giving birth to a litter of pigs. ▶ **v.** [trans.] (of a sow) give birth to (piglets). [OE *fearh*, *færh* 'young pig,' of West Gmc. origin, from an Indo-Eur. root shared by Gk. *porkos* and L. *porcus* 'pig.']

far-see·ing ▶ **adj.** having shrewd judgment and an ability to predict and plan for future eventualities.

Far·si /ˈfärsē/ ▶ **n.** the modern Persian language that is the official language of Iran. [from Arab. *fārsī*, from *Fārs*, from Pers. *Pārs* 'Persia.' Cf. **PARSEE**.]

far·sight·ed /ˈfär,sītid; -ˈsītid/ ▶ **adj.** unable to see things clearly, esp. if they are relatively close to the eyes; hyperopic. ■ seeing or able to see for a great distance. ■ fig. having imagination or foresight. — **far·sight·ed·ly** **adv.** **far·sight·ed·ness** **n.**

fart /färt/ informal ▶ **v.** [intrans.] emit gas from the anus. ■ (**fart about/around**) waste time. ▶ **n.** an emission of gas from the anus. ■ a boring or contemptible person. [OE (recorded in the verbal n. *feorting* 'farting') of Gmc. origin; rel. to Ger. *farzen*, *furzen*.]

far·ther /ˈfärTHər/ used as comparative of **FAR**. ▶ **adv.** (also **fur·ther**) **1** at, to, or by a greater distance (used to indicate the extent to which one thing or person is or becomes distant from another): *the farther away you are from home, the better you should behave.* **2** over a greater expanse of space or time; for a longer way: fig. *get their food dollars to go farther.* ▶ **adj.** more distant in space than another item of the same kind. ■ more remote from a central point.

far·ther·most /ˈfärTHər,mōst/ (also **fur·ther·most**) ▶ **adj.** (of an edge or extreme) at the greatest distance from a central point or implicit standpoint.

far·thest /ˈfärTHist/ (also **fur·thest**) used as superlative of **FAR**. ▶ **adj.** [attrib.] situated at the greatest distance from a specified or understood point. ■ covering the greatest area or distance. ■ extremely remote. ▶ **adv.** **1** at or by the greatest distance (used to indicate how far one thing or person is or becomes distant from another). **2** over the greatest distance or area. ■ used to indicate the most distant point reached in a specified direction. ■ to the most extreme or advanced point. [ME: formed as a superlative of **FURTHER**.]

far·thing /ˈfärTHiNG/ ▶ **n.** a former monetary unit and coin of the UK, equal to a quarter of an old penny. [OE *fēorthing*, from *fēortha* 'fourth.']

far·thin·gale /ˈfärTHiNG,gāl/ ▶ **n.** hist. a hooped petticoat or circular pad of fabric around the hips, worn under women's skirts to extend and shape them. [16th C. (formerly also as *vardingale*): from Fr. *verdugale*, alt. of Sp. *verdugado*, from *verdugo* 'rod, stick,' from *verde* 'green.']

farthingale

fart·lek /ˈfärtlik/ ▶ **n.** Track & Field a system of training for distance runners in which the terrain and pace are varied to enhance conditioning. [1940s: from Swed., from *fart* 'speed' + *lek* 'play.']

Far West the region of North America west of the Great Plains.

FAS ▶ **abbr.** ■ fetal alcohol syndrome. ■ Foreign Agricultural Service.

fasc. ▶ **abbr.** fascicle.

fas·ces /ˈfasēz/ ▶ **plural n.** hist. (in ancient Rome) a bundle of rods with a projecting ax blade, carried by a lictor as a symbol of a magistrate's power. ■ (in Fascist Italy) such items used as emblems of authority. [L., pl. of *fascis* 'bundle.']

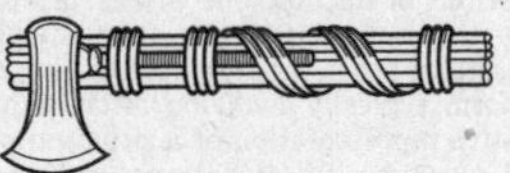

fasces

fas·ci·a /ˈfasH(ē)ə; ˈfā-/ ▶ **n.** **1** (esp. Brit. also **fa·ci·a**) a wooden board or other flat piece of material covering the ends of rafters or other fittings. ■ (in classical architecture) a long flat surface between moldings on an architrave. **2** (pl. **fas·ci·ae** /-sHē,ē/) Anat. a thin sheath of fibrous tissue enclosing a muscle or other organ. — **fas·ci·al** **adj.** (in sense 2). [16th C.: from L., 'band, doorframe,' related to **FASCES**. Compare with **FESS**[1].]

fas·ci·at·ed /ˈfasHē,ātid; ˈfā-/ (also **fas·ci·ate**) ▶ **adj.** **1** Bot. showing abnormal fusion of parts or organs, resulting in a flattened, ribbonlike structure. **2** Zool. striped or banded. — **fas·ci·a·tion** /,fasHēˈāsHən; ,fā-/ **n.**

fas·ci·cle /ˈfasikəl/ ▶ **n.** **1** (also **fas·ci·cule** /-,kyo͞ol/) a separately published installment of a printed work. **2** (also **fas·cic·u·lus** /fəˈsikyələs/) Anat. Biol. a bundle of structures, such as nerve or muscle fibers or conducting vessels in plants. — **fas·ci·cled** **adj.** **fas·cic·u·lar** /fəˈsikyələr/ **adj.** **fas·cic·u·late** /fəˈsikyə,lāt; -yəlit/ **adj.** [15th C. (sense 2): from L. *fasciculus*, dimin. of *fascis* 'bundle.']

fas·cic·u·la·tion /fə,sikyəˈlāsHən/ ▶ **n.** **1** Med. a brief, spontaneous contraction affecting muscle fibers, often causing a flicker of movement under the skin. **2** esp. Biol. arrangement in bundles.

fas·ci·i·tis /,fasēˈītəs; ,fasHē-/ ▶ **n.** Med. inflammation of the fascia of a muscle or organ.

fas·ci·nate /ˈfasə,nāt/ ▶ **v.** [trans.] (usu. **be fascinated**) draw irresistibly the attention and interest of (someone): *I've always been fascinated by other cultures.* — **fas·ci·na·tion** /,fasəˈnāsHən/ **n.** **fas·ci·na·tor** /-,nātər/ **n.** [16th C.: from L. *fascinat-* 'bewitched,' from the v. *fascinare*, from *fascinum* 'spell, witchcraft.']

fas·ci·nat·ing /ˈfasə,nātiNG/ ▶ **adj.** extremely interesting: *fascinating facts.* — **fas·ci·nat·ing·ly** **adv.**

fas·cism /ˈfasHizəm/ (also **Fas·cism**) ▶ **n.** an authoritarian and nationalistic right-wing system of government and social organization. ■ (in general use) extreme right-wing, authoritarian, or intolerant views or practice. — **fas·cist** **n. & adj.** **fas·cis·tic** /faˈsHistik/ **adj.** [from Ital. *fascismo*, from *fascio* 'bundle, political group,' from L. *fascis* (see **FASCES**).]

fash·ion /ˈfasHən/ ▶ **n.** **1** a popular trend, esp. in styles of dress, ornament, or behavior. ■ the production and marketing of new styles of goods, esp. clothing and cosmetics. **2** a manner of doing something. ▶ **v.** [trans.] (often **be fashioned**) make into a particular form. ■ (**fashion something into**) use materials to make into.
– PHRASES **after a fashion** to a certain extent but not perfectly or satisfactorily: *he could read after a fashion.* — **fash·ion·er** **n.** [ME: from OFr. *façon*, from L. *factio(n-)*, from *facere* 'do, make.']

-fashion ▶ **comb. form** in the manner of something specified: *dog-fashion.* ■ in the style associated with a specified place or people: *American-fashion.*

fash·ion·a·ble /ˈfasH(ə)nəbəl/ ▶ **adj.** characteristic of, influenced by, or representing a current popular trend or style. ■ (of a person) dressing or behaving according to the current trend. — **fash·ion·a·bil·i·ty** /,fasH(ə)nəˈbilitē/ **n.** **fash·ion·a·ble·ness** **n.** **fash·ion·a·bly** **adv.**

fash·ion·is·ta /,fasHəˈnēstə/ ▶ **n.** informal **1** a designer of haute couture. **2** a devoted follower of fashion: *sleek designs that press all the fashionistas' buttons.* [1990s: from *fashion* + Sp. suffix *-ista*, as in *Sandinista, turista*.]

fash·ion plate ▸ n. a picture showing a fashion, esp. in dress. ▪ fig. a person who dresses very fashionably.

Fast /fast/, Howard Melvin (1914–2003), US writer. A member of the Communist party 1943–56, he was imprisoned in 1950 for refusing to cooperate with the House Committee on Un-American Activities. His works include *Spartacus* (1951) and *The Immigrants* (1977).

fast[1] /fast/ ▸ adj. **1** moving or capable of moving at high speed. ▪ performed or taking place at high speed; taking only a short time. ▪ [attrib.] allowing people or things to move at high speed. ▪ performing or able to perform a particular type of action quickly. ▪ Sports (of a playing field) likely to make the ball bounce or run quickly or to allow competitors to reach a high speed. ▪ (of a person or their lifestyle) engaging in or involving exciting or shocking activities. **2** [predic. or as complement] (of a clock or watch) showing a time ahead of the correct time. **3** firmly fixed or attached: *he made a rope fast to each corner.* ▪ (of friends) close and loyal. ▪ (of a dye) not fading. **4** Photog. (of a film) needing only a short exposure. ▪ (of a lens) having a large aperture and therefore suitable for use with short exposure times. ▸ adv. **1** at high speed: *he was driving too fast.* ▪ within a short time. **2** so as to be hard to move; firmly or securely: *the ship was held fast by the anchor chain.* ▪ (of sleeping) so as to be hard to wake.
– PHRASES **pull a fast one** informal try to gain an unfair advantage. [OE *fæst* 'firmly fixed, steadfast' and *fæste* 'firmly, securely,' of Gmc. origin; rel. to Ger. *fest* 'firm, solid.']

fast[2] ▸ v. [intrans.] abstain from all or some kinds of food or drink, esp. as a religious observance. ▸ n. an act or period of fasting. [OE *fæstan* (v.), of Gmc. origin; rel. to ON *fasta*, the source of the n.]

fast·back /'fast,bak/ ▸ n. a car with a roofline that slopes continuously down at the back.

fast·ball /'fast,bôl/ ▸ n. a baseball pitch thrown at or near a pitcher's maximum speed.

fast break ▸ n. a swift attack from a defensive position in basketball, soccer, and other ball games. ▸ v. **(fast-break)** [intrans.] make such an attack.

fast buck ▸ n. see BUCK[2].

fas·ten /'fasən/ ▸ v. [trans.] close or join securely. ▪ [intrans.] be closed or done up in a particular place or part or in a particular way: *a nightie that fastens down the back.* ▪ [trans.] fix or hold in place. ▪ **(fasten something on/upon)** direct one's eyes, thoughts, feelings, etc., intently at. ▪ **(fasten something on/upon)** ascribe responsibility to. ▪ [intrans.] **(fasten on/upon)** single out (someone or something) and concentrate on them or it obsessively: *the critics fastened on two sections of the report.* — **fas·ten·er** n. [OE *fæstnian* 'make sure, confirm,' also 'immobilize,' of West Gmc. origin; rel. to FAST[1].]

fast·en·ing /'fasəniNG/ ▸ n. a device that closes or secures something.

fast food ▸ n. food that can be prepared quickly and easily and is sold in restaurants and snack bars as a quick meal or to be taken out.

fast for·ward ▸ n. a control on a tape or video player for advancing the tape rapidly. ▪ a facility for cueing audio equipment by allowing the tape to be played at high speed and stopped when the desired place is reached. ▸ v. **(fast-for·ward)** [trans.] advance (a tape) rapidly, sometimes while simultaneously playing it at high speed. ▪ [intrans.] fig. move speedily forward in time: *the text fast-forwards to 1990.*

fast ice ▸ n. ice that covers seawater but is attached to land.

fas·tid·i·ous /fas'tidēəs/ ▸ adj. very attentive to and concerned about accuracy and detail. ▪ very concerned about matters of cleanliness. — **fas·tid·i·ous·ly** adv. **fas·tid·i·ous·ness** n. [ME: from L. *fastidiosus*, from *fastidium* 'loathing.']

fas·tig·i·ate /fə'stijēit/ ▸ adj. Bot. (of a tree or shrub) having the branches sloping upward more or less parallel to the main stem. [17th C.: from L. *fastigium* 'tapering point, gable' + -ATE[2].]

fast lane ▸ n. [usu. in sing.] a lane of a highway for use by traffic that is moving more quickly than the rest. ▪ a hectic or highly pressured lifestyle: *his face showed the strain of a life lived **in the fast lane**.*

fast·ness /'fastnis/ ▸ n. **1** a secure refuge, esp. a place well protected by natural features. **2** the ability of a material or dye to maintain its color without fading or washing away. [OE *fæstnes* (see FAST[1], -NESS).]

fast re·ac·tor ▸ n. a nuclear reactor in which fission is caused mainly by fast neutrons.

fast-talk ▸ v. [trans.] informal pressure (someone) into doing something using rapid or misleading speech: *heroin dealers tried to fast-talk him into a quick sale.*

fast track ▸ n. [in sing.] a route, course, or method that provides for more rapid results than usual. ▸ v. **(fast-track)** [trans.] accelerate the development or progress of (a person or project).

fat /fat/ ▸ n. a natural oily or greasy substance occurring in animal bodies, esp. when deposited as a layer under the skin or around certain organs. ▪ a substance of this type, or a similar one made from plant products, used in cooking. ▪ the presence of an excessive amount of such a substance in a person or animal, causing them to appear corpulent. ▪ Chem. any of a group of natural esters of glycerol and various fatty acids, which are solid at room temperature and are the main constituents of animal and vegetable fat. Compare with OIL. ▪ something excessive or unnecessary. ▸ adj. **(fat·ter, fat·test)** (of a person or animal) having a large amount of excess flesh. ▪ (of an animal bred for food) made plump for slaughter. ▪ containing much fat. ▪ large in bulk or circumference. ▪ informal (of an asset or opportunity) financially substantial or desirable. ▪ informal used ironically to express the belief that there is none or very little of something: ***fat chance** she had of influencing him.* ▪ (of coal) containing a high proportion of volatile oils. ▪ (of wood) containing a high proportion of resin. ▸ v. **(fat·ted, fat·ting)** archaic make or become fat: [trans.] *numbers of cattle are fatted here.*
– PHRASES **the fat is in the fire** trouble has been caused and is beginning. **kill the fatted calf** produce one's best food to celebrate, esp. at a prodigal's return. **live off** (or **on**) **the fat of the land** have the best of everything. — **fat·ly** adv. **fat·ness** n. **fat·tish** adj. [OE *fætt* 'well fed, plump,' also 'fatty, oily,' of West Gmc. origin; rel. to Du. *vet* and Ger. *feist*.]

Fa·tah, Al /,äl fə'tä; äl 'fätə/ a Palestinian organization founded in 1958 by Yasser Arafat to bring about the establishment of a Palestinian state. [Arab., literally 'victory.']

fa·tal /'fātl/ ▸ adj. causing death. ▪ leading to failure or disaster. — **fa·tal·ly** adv. [ME: from OFr., or from L. *fatalis*, from *fatum* (see FATE).]

fa·tal·ism /'fātl,izəm/ ▸ n. the belief that all events are predetermined and therefore inevitable. ▪ a submissive attitude to events, resulting from such a belief. — **fa·tal·ist** n. **fa·tal·is·tic** /,fātl'istik/ adj. **fa·tal·is·ti·cal·ly** /,fātl'istik(ə)lē/ adv.

fa·tal·i·ty /fā'talitē; fə-/ ▸ n. (pl. **-ties**) **1** an occurrence of death by accident, in war, or from disease. ▪ a person killed in this way. **2** helplessness in the face of fate.

Fa·ta Mor·ga·na /'fätə môr'gänə/ ▸ n. a mirage. [Ital., literally 'fairy Morgan'; originally a mirage attributed to MORGAN LE FAY.]

fat·back /'fat,bak/ ▸ n. **1** fat from the upper part of a side of pork, esp. when dried and salted in strips. **2** informal term for MENHADEN.

fat cat ▸ n. derog. a wealthy and powerful person, esp. a businessman or politician.

fat cit·y ▸ n. (often **Fat City**) informal **1** a condition of great prosperity or good fortune. **2** the condition of being overweight.

fate /fāt/ ▸ n. **1** the development of events outside a person's control, regarded as determined by a supernatural power. ▪ the course of someone's life, or the outcome of a particular situation for someone or something, seen as outside their control. ▪ [in sing.] the inescapable death of a person. **2** **(the Fates)** Greek Rom. Mythol. the three goddesses (Clotho, Lachesis, and Atropos) who preside over the birth and life of humans. Also called the MOIRAI and the PARCAE. ▪ **(Fates)** another term for NORNS. ▸ v. **(be fated)** be destined to happen, turn out, or act in a particular way: [with infin.] *it was fated to end badly.*
– PHRASES **a fate worse than death** see DEATH. **seal someone's fate** make it inevitable that something unpleasant will happen to someone. [ME: from Ital. *fato* or (later) from its source, L. *fatum* 'that which has been spoken,' from *fari* 'speak.']

fate·ful /'fātfəl/ ▸ adj. having far-reaching and typically disastrous consequences or implications. — **fate·ful·ly** adv. **fate·ful·ness** n.

fat farm ▸ n. informala residential establishment where people who are overweight seek improved health by a regimen of dieting, exercise, and treatment.

fat-free ▸ adj. (of a food) not containing animal or vegetable fats.

fat·head /'fat,hed/ ▸ n. informal a stupid person. — **fat·head·ed** adj. **fat·head·ed·ness** n.

fa·ther /'fäT͟Hər/ ▸ n. **1** a man in relation to his natural child or children. ▪ a man who has continuous care of a child, esp. by adoption; an adoptive father, stepfather, or foster father. ▪ a father-in-law. ▪ a male animal in relation to its offspring. ▪ (usu. **fathers**) literary an ancestor. ▪ (also **founding father**) an important figure in the origin and early history of something. ▪ a man who gives care and protection to someone or something. ▪ the oldest or most respected member of a society or other body. ▪ **(the Father)** (in Christian belief) the first person of the Trinity; God. ▪ **(Father)** literary used in proper names, esp. when personifying time or a river, to suggest an old and venerable character: *Father Time.* **2** (also **Father**) (often as a title or form of address) a priest. **3** **(the Fathers** or **the Church Fathers)** early Christian theologians (in particular of the first five centuries) whose writings are regarded as especially authoritative. ▸ v. [trans.] be the father of: *he fathered three children.* ▪ [usu. as n.] **(fathering)** treat with the protective care usually associated with a father. ▪ be the source or originator of. ▪ **(father someone/something on)** assign the paternity of a child or responsibility for a book, idea, or action to: *a collection of Irish stories was fathered on him.* — **fa·ther·hood** n. **fa·ther·li·ness** n. **fa·ther·ly** adj. [OE *fæder*, of Gmc. origin; rel. to Du. *vader* and Ger. *Vater*, from an Indo-Eur. root shared by L. *pater* and Gk. *patēr*.]

Fa·ther Christ·mas Brit.another name for SANTA CLAUS.

fa·ther con·fes·sor ▸ n. a priest or minister who hears confessions. ▪ fig. someone with whom one seeks comfort by trusting with one's confidences.

fa·ther fig·ure ▸ n. an older man who is respected for his paternal qualities and may be an emotional substitute for a father.

fa·ther-in-law ▸ n. (pl. **fa·thers-in-law**) the father of one's spouse.

fa·ther·land /'fäT͟Hər,land/ ▸ n. (often **the Fatherland**) a person's native country, esp. when referred to in patriotic terms. ▪ esp. hist. Germany, esp. during the period of Hitler's control.

Fa·ther's Day n. a day of the year on which fathers are particularly honored by their children. It is observed on the third Sunday in June in the US.

Fa·ther Time ▶ **n.** see TIME (sense 1).

fath·om /ˈfa*TH*əm/ ▶ **n.** a unit of length equal to six feet (approximately 1.8 m), chiefly used in reference to the depth of water. ▶ **v.** [trans.] **1** [usu. with negative] understand (a difficult problem or an enigmatic person) after much thought: *he could scarcely fathom the idea.* **2** measure the depth of (water). — **fath·om·a·ble adj.** [OE *fæthm*, of Gmc. origin; rel. to Du. *vadem, vaam* and Ger. *Faden* 'six feet.']

Fa·thom·e·ter /faˈ*TH*ämitər; ˈfa*TH*ə,mētər/ ▶ **n.** trademark a type of echo sounder.

fa·tigue /fəˈtēg/ ▶ **n. 1** extreme tiredness, typically resulting from mental or physical exertion or illness. ■ a reduction in the efficiency of a muscle or organ after prolonged activity. ■ weakness in materials, esp. metal, caused by repeated variations of stress. ■ [with adj.] a lessening in one's response to or enthusiasm for something, typically as a result of overexposure to it: *museum fatigue.* **2** (also **fa·tigue de·tail**) a group of soldiers ordered to perform menial, nonmilitary tasks. ■ **(fatigues)** loose-fitting clothing, typically khaki, olive drab, or camouflaged, of a sort worn by soldiers. ▶ **v.** **(-tigues, -tigued, -ti·guing)** [trans.] (often **be fatigued**) cause (someone) to feel tired or exhausted: *they were fatigued by their journey.* ■ reduce the efficiency of (a muscle or organ) by prolonged activity. ■ weaken (a material, esp. metal) by repeated variations of stress. — **fa·tigu·a·bil·i·ty** /fə,tēgəˈbilitē/ **n. fa·tigu·a·ble** (also **fat·i·ga·ble**) **adj.** [17th C.: from Fr. *fatigue* (n.), *fatiguer* (v.), from L. *fatigare* 'tire out,' from *ad fatim, affatim* 'to satiety.']

Fat·i·ma /ˈfatəmə/ (*c.* AD 606–632), daughter of the prophet Muhammad and wife of Ali. The descendants of Muhammad trace their lineage through her; she is revered, especially by Shiite Muslims, as the mother of the imams Hasan and Husayn.

Fá·ti·ma /ˈfatəmə; ˈfätēmä/ a village in west central Portugal, northeast of Lisbon; pop. 5,000. It became a center of Roman Catholic pilgrimage after the reported sighting of the Virgin Mary in 1917.

Fat·i·mid /ˈfatəmid/ ▶ **n.** a member of a dynasty that ruled in parts of northern Africa and Syria 909–1171. ▶ **adj.** of or relating to the Fatimids. — **Fat·i·mite** /-,mīt/ **n. & adj.** [from Arab. *Fāṭima* (see FATIMA) + -ID[3].]

fat·ling /ˈfatliNG/ ▶ **n.** a young animal that has been fattened for slaughter.

fat·so /ˈfatsō/ ▶ **n.** (pl. **-sos**) informal, offens. a fat person.

fat·ten /ˈfatn/ ▶ **v.** [trans.] make (a person or animal) fat or fatter. ■ [intrans.] become fat or fatter.

fat·ten·ing /ˈfatn-iNG/ ▶ **adj.** (of a food) causing an increase in the weight of someone who eats it.

fat·ty /ˈfatē/ ▶ **adj.** **(-ti·er, -ti·est)** containing a large amount of fat. ■ Med. (of a disease or lesion) marked by abnormal deposition of fat in cells. ▶ **n.** (pl. **-ties**) informal a fat person (esp. as a nickname). — **fat·ti·ness n.**

fat·ty ac·id ▶ **n.** Chem. a carboxylic acid consisting of a hydrocarbon chain and a terminal carboxyl group, esp. any of those occurring as esters in fats and oils.

fat·u·ous /ˈfacHōōəs/ ▶ **adj.** silly and pointless. — **fa·tu·i·ty** /fəˈt(y)ōōitē/ **n.** (pl. **-ties**) **fat·u·ous·ly adv. fat·u·ous·ness n.** [17th C.: from L. *fatuus* 'foolish' + -OUS.]

fat·wa /ˈfätwä/ ▶ **n.** a ruling on a point of Islamic law given by a recognized authority. [17th C.: from Arab. *fatwā*, from *afta'ā* 'decide a point of law.' Cf. MUFTI[1].]

fau·bourg /ˈfōbōōr; -bərg/ ▶ **n.** [usu. in place names] a suburb, esp. one in Paris: *the Faubourg Saint-Germain.* [Fr., perh. an alt. of *forsborc*, lit. 'outside the town.']

fau·cet /ˈfôsit/ ▶ **n.** a device by which a flow of liquid or gas from a pipe or container can be controlled; a tap. [ME: from OFr. *fausset*, from Provençal *falset*, from *falsar* 'to bore.']

Faulk·ner /ˈfôknər/, William (1897–1962), US writer. His works include *The Sound and the Fury* (1929) and *Absalom! Absalom!* (1936). Nobel Prize for Literature (1949).

fault /fôlt/ ▶ **n. 1** an unattractive or unsatisfactory feature, esp. in a piece of work or in a person's character. ■ a break or other defect in an electrical circuit or piece of machinery. ■ a misguided or dangerous action or habit. ■ (in tennis and similar games) a service of the ball not in accordance with the rules. **2** responsibility for an accident or misfortune. **3** Geol. an extended break in a rock formation, marked by the relative displacement and discontinuity of strata on either side of a particular plane. ▶ **v.** [trans.] **1** criticize for inadequacy or mistakes. **2** (**be faulted**) Geol. (of a rock formation) be broken by a fault or faults.

– PHRASES **at fault 1** responsible for an undesirable situation or event; in the wrong. **2** mistaken or defective. **find fault** make an adverse criticism or objection, sometimes unfairly or destructively. **to a fault** (of someone who displays a particular commendable quality) to an extent verging on excess. [ME *faut(e)* 'lack, failing,' from OFr., based on L. *fallere* 'deceive.']

fault-find·ing ▶ **n. 1** continual criticism, typically concerning trivial things. **2** the investigation of the cause of malfunction in machinery, esp. electronic equipment. — **fault-find·er n.**

fault·less /ˈfôltlis/ ▶ **adj.** free from defect or error. — **fault·less·ly adv. fault·less·ness n.**

fault·y /ˈfôltē/ ▶ **adj.** **(fault·i·er, fault·i·est)** working badly or unreliably because of imperfections. ■ (of reasoning and other mental processes) mistaken or misleading because of flaws. ■ having or displaying weaknesses. — **fault·i·ly adv. fault·i·ness n.**

faun /fôn/ ▶ **n.** Rom. Mythol. one of a class of lustful rural gods, represented as a man with a goat's horns, ears, legs, and tail. [ME: from the name of the pastoral god FAUNUS.]

fau·na /ˈfônə/ ▶ **n.** (pl. **-nas** or **-nae** /-nē/) the animals of a particular region, habitat, or geological period. Compare with FLORA. ■ a book or other work describing or listing the animal life of a region. — **fau·nal** /ˈfônl/ **adj. fau·nis·tic** /fôˈnistik/ **adj.** [18th C.: mod. L. application of *Fauna*, the name of a rural goddess, sister of FAUNUS.]

Faun·tle·roy /ˈfôntlə,roi/ (also **Little Lord Fauntleroy**) ▶ **n.** an excessively well-mannered or elaborately dressed young boy. [from the name of the boy hero of Frances Hodgson Burnett's novel *Little Lord Fauntleroy* (1886).]

Fau·nus /ˈfônəs/ Rom. Mythol. an ancient Italian pastoral god, grandson of Saturn, associated with wooded places.

Faust /foust/ (also **Faus·tus** /ˈfoustəs; ˈfô-/) (died *c.*1540), German astronomer. Reputed to have sold his soul to the Devil, he became the subject of dramas, operas, and novels. — **Faus·ti·an** /ˈfoustēən/ **adj.**

faute de mieux /,fōt də ˈmyœ/ ▶ **adv.** for want of a better alternative. [18th C.: Fr., literally 'for want of (something) better.']

fau·teuil /ˈfōtil; fōˈtœyə/ ▶ **n.** a wooden seat in the form of an armchair with open sides and upholstered arms. [Fr., from OFr. *faudestuel*, from med. L. *faldistolium* (see FALDSTOOL).]

Fauv·ism /ˈfōvizəm/ (also **fauv·ism**) ▶ **n.** a style of painting with vivid expressionistic use of color that flourished in Paris in the early 20th century. Matisse was its leading figure. — **fauv·ist n. & adj.** [from Fr. *fauvisme*, from *fauve* 'wild beast.']

faux /fō/ ▶ **adj.** [attrib.] artificial or imitation; false. [20th C.: Fr., literally 'false.']

faux-na·ïf /,fō näˈēf/ ▶ **adj.** (of a work of art or a person) artificially or affectedly simple or naive. ▶ **n.** **(faux naif)** a person who pretends to be ingenuous. [20th C.: from Fr. *faux* 'false' + *naïf* 'naive.']

faux pas /fō ˈpä; ˈfō ,pä/ ▶ **n.** (pl. same) an embarrassing or tactless act or remark in a social situation. [17th C.: Fr., literally 'false step.']

fa·va bean /ˈfävə/ ▶ **n.** another term for BROAD BEAN. [Ital. *fava*, from L. *faba* 'bean.']

fave /fāv/ ▶ **n. & adj.** informal short for FAVORITE.

fa·ve·la /fəˈvelə/ ▶ **n.** a Brazilian shanty town; a slum.

fa·vor /ˈfāvər/ (Brit. **fa·vour**) ▶ **n. 1** an attitude of approval or liking. ■ support or advancement given as a sign of approval. ■ preferential treatment. ■ a small gift or souvenir. **2** an act of kindness beyond what is due or usual. ■ **(one's favors)** dated used with reference to a woman allowing a man to have sexual intercourse with her. ▶ **v.** [trans.] **1** feel or show approval or preference for: *a policy that few politicians favor.* ■ give unfairly preferential treatment to: *the policy favored the private sector.* ■ work to the advantage of: *natural selection has favored bats.* **2** (**favor someone with**) (often used in polite requests) give someone (something that they want): *please favor me with an answer.* **3** informal resemble (a parent or relative) in facial features. **4** treat (an injured limb) gently, not putting one's full weight on it.

– PHRASES **in favor 1** meeting with approval. **2** having or showing approval: *the court ruled 2-1* ***in favor of*** *his extradition.* **in one's favor** to one's advantage. **in favor of 1** to be replaced by: *he stepped down as leader in favor of his rival.* **2** to the advantage of. **out of favor** lacking or having lost approval or popularity. [ME (in the n. sense 'liking, preference'): via OFr. from L. *favor*, from *favere* 'show kindness to' (rel. to *fovere* 'cherish').]

fa·vor·a·ble /ˈfāv(ə)rəbəl/ (Brit. **fa·vour·a·ble**) ▶ **adj. 1** expressing approval. ■ giving consent. **2** to the advantage of someone or something: *a settlement favorable to the unions.* ■ (of a wind) blowing in the direction of travel. ■ (of weather, or a period of time judged in terms of its weather) fine. ■ suggesting a good outcome. — **fa·vor·a·ble·ness n. fa·vor·a·bly adv.**

fa·vor·ite /ˈfāv(ə)rit/ (Brit. **fa·vour·ite**) ▶ **adj.** [attrib.] preferred before all others of the same kind. ▶ **n.** a person or thing that is especially well liked. ■ the competitor thought most likely to win a game or contest, esp. by people betting on the outcome.

– PHRASES **favorite son** a famous man who is particularly popular in his native area. ■ a person supported as a presidential candidate by delegates from the candidate's home state. [16th C. (as a n.): from obs. Fr. *favorit*, from Ital. *favorito*, past part. of *favorire* 'to favor,' from L. *favor* (see FAVOR).]

fa·vor·it·ism /ˈfāv(ə)ri,tizəm/ ▶ **n.** the practice of giving unfair preferential treatment to one person or group at the expense of another.

Fawkes /fôks/, Guy (1570–1606), English conspirator. He was hanged for his part in the Gunpowder Plot of November 5, 1605. The occasion is commemorated annually in Britain on November 5.

fawn[1] /fôn/ ▶ **n. 1** a young deer in its first year. **2** a light yellowish-brown color. ▶ **v.** [intrans.] (of a deer) produce young. [ME: from OFr. *faon*, based on L. *fetus* 'offspring'; cf. FETUS.]

fawn[2] ▶ **v.** [intrans.] (of a person) give a servile display of exaggerated flattery or affection, typically in order to gain favor. ■ (of an animal, esp. a dog) show slavish devotion, esp. by crawling and rubbing against someone. — **fawn·ing·ly adv.** [OE *fagnian* 'make or be glad,' of Gmc. origin.]

fax /faks/ ▶ **n.** an image of a document made by electronic scanning and transmitted as data by telecommunication links. ■ the production or transmission of documents in this way. ■ (also **fax machine**) a machine for transmitting and receiving such documents. ▶ **v.** [trans.] send (a document) by such means. ■ contact (someone) by such means. [abbrev. of FACSIMILE.]

fay /fā/ ▶ **n.** literary a fairy. [ME: from OFr. *fae, faie*, from L. *fata* 'the Fates,' pl. of *fatum* (see FATE). Cf. FAIRY.]

Fay·ette·ville /'fāit,vil/ a city in south central North Carolina; pop. 121,015.

faze /fāz/ ▶ **v.** [trans.] [usu. with negative] (often **be fazed**) informal disturb or disconcert (someone): *she was not fazed by his show of anger.* [19th C.: var. of dial. *feeze* 'drive or frighten off,' from OE *fēsian*, of unknown origin.]

FB ▶ **abbr.** ■ foreign body. ■ freight bill.

fb (also **f.b.**) ▶ **abbr.** Sports fullback.

FBI ▶ **abbr.** Federal Bureau of Investigation.

f.c. ▶ **abbr.** ■ fielder's choice. ■ follow copy.

fcap. ▶ **abbr.** foolscap.

FCC ▶ **abbr.** Federal Communications Commission.

FD ▶ **abbr.** ■ Fire Department.

FDA ▶ **abbr.** Food and Drug Administration.

FDDI ▶ **abbr.** fiber-distributed data interface, a communications, cabling, and hardware standard for high-speed optical-fiber networks.

FDIC ▶ **abbr.** Federal Deposit Insurance Corporation, a body that underwrites most private bank deposits.

FDR nickname of President Franklin Delano Roosevelt (see ROOSEVELT[2]).

Fe ▶ **symb.** the chemical element iron. [from L. *ferrum*.]

fe·al·ty /'fēəltē/ ▶ **n.** hist. a feudal tenant's or vassal's sworn loyalty to a lord: *they owed fealty to the Earl.* ■ formal acknowledgment of this: *a property for which she did fealty.* [ME: from OFr. *feau(l)te, fealte*, from L. *fidelitas* (see FIDELITY).]

fear /fi(ə)r/ ▶ **n.** an unpleasant emotion caused by the belief that someone or something is dangerous, likely to cause pain, or a threat. ■ archaic a mixed feeling of dread and reverence: *the love and fear of God.* ■ (**fear for**) a feeling of anxiety concerning the outcome of something or the safety and well-being of someone: *a search for the family amid fears for their safety.* ■ the likelihood of something unwelcome happening. ▶ **v.** [trans.] be afraid of (someone or something) as likely to be dangerous, painful, or threatening: *farmers fear that they will lose business.* ■ [intrans.] (**fear for**) feel anxiety or apprehension on behalf of: *I fear for the city.* ■ used to express regret or apology. ■ archaic regard (God) with reverence and awe.
– PHRASES **for fear of** (or **that**) to avoid the risk of (or that): *no one dared refuse the order for fear of losing their job.* **without fear or favor** impartially. [OE *fǣr* 'calamity, danger,' *fǣran* 'frighten,' also 'revere,' of Gmc. origin; rel. to Du. *gevaar* and Ger. *Gefahr* 'danger.']

fear·ful /'fi(ə)rfəl/ ▶ **adj.** **1** feeling afraid; showing fear or anxiety. ■ causing or likely to cause people to be afraid; horrifying. **2** informal very great. — **fear·ful·ly adv. fear·ful·ness n.**

fear·less /'fi(ə)rlis/ ▶ **adj.** showing a lack of fear; intrepid. — **fear·less·ly adv. fear·less·ness n.**

fear·some /'fi(ə)rsəm/ ▶ **adj.** frightening, esp. in appearance. — **fear·some·ly adv. fear·some·ness n.**

fea·si·bil·i·ty /,fēzə'bilitē/ ▶ **n.** the state or degree of being easily or conveniently done.

fea·si·ble /'fēzəbəl/ ▶ **adj.** possible to do easily or conveniently. ■ informal likely; probable. — **fea·si·bly** /-zəblē/ **adv.** [ME: from OFr. *faisible*, from *fais-*, stem of *faire* 'do, make,' from L. *facere*.]

feast /fēst/ ▶ **n.** a large meal, typically one in celebration of something. ■ a plentiful supply of something enjoyable, esp. for the mind or senses. ■ an annual religious celebration. ■ a day dedicated to a particular saint. ▶ **v.** [intrans.] eat and drink sumptuously. ■ (**feast on**) eat large quantities of. ■ [trans.] give (someone) a plentiful and delicious meal: *he was feasted and invited to all the parties.*
– PHRASES **feast one's eyes on** gaze at with pleasure. **feast or famine** either too much of something or too little. [ME: from OFr. *feste* (n.), *fester* (v.), from L. *festa*, neut. pl. of *festus* 'joyous.']

feast day ▶ **n.** a day on which a celebration, esp. an annual Christian one, is held.

Feast of Ded·i·ca·tion ▶ **n.** another name for HANUKKAH.

Feast of Tab·er·nac·les ▶ **n.** another name for SUCCOTH.

Feast of Weeks ▶ **n.** another name for SHAVUOTH.

feat /fēt/ ▶ **n.** an achievement that requires great courage, skill, or strength. [ME: from OFr. *fait*, from L. *factum* (see FACT).]

feath·er /'feT͟Hər/ ▶ **n.** any of the flat appendages forming a bird's plumage, consisting of a partly hollow horny shaft fringed with vanes of barbs. ■ (often **feathers**) one of these appendages as decoration. ■ one of the feathers or featherlike vanes fastened to the shaft of an arrow or a dart. ■ (**feathers**) a fringe of long hair on the legs of a dog, horse, or other animal. ■ a small side branch on a tree. ▶ **v.** **1** [trans.] rotate the blades of (a propeller) about their own axes in such a way as to lessen the air or water resistance. ■ vary the angle of attack of (rotor blades). ■ Rowing turn (an oar) so that it passes through the air edgeways. **2** [intrans.] float, move, or wave like a feather. ■ [with obj. and adverbial] touch (someone or something) very lightly. **3** [trans.] shorten or taper the hair by cutting or trimming.
– PHRASES **a feather in one's cap** an achievement to be proud of. **feather one's (own) nest** make money illicitly and at someone else's expense. — **feath·er·i·ness n. feath·er·y adj.** [OE *fether*, rel. to Ger. *Feder*, from an Indo-Eur. root shared by L. *penna* 'feather,' and Gk. *pteron, pterux* 'wing.']

feath·er·bed /'feT͟Hər,bed/ ▶ **n.** (also **feath·er bed**) a bed that has a mattress stuffed with feathers. ▶ **v.** (also **feath·er-bed**) [trans.] provide (someone) with advantageous economic or working conditions. ■ [usu. as n.] (**featherbedding**) deliberately limit production or retain excess staff in (a business) in order to prevent unemployment, typically as a result of a union contract.

feath·er·brain /'feT͟Hər,brān/ (also **feath·er-brain** or **feath·er·head**) ▶ **n.** a silly or absentminded person. — **feath·er·brained** (also **feath·er-brained** or **feath·er·head·ed**) **adj.**

feath·ered /'feT͟Hərd/ ▶ **adj.** (of a bird) covered with feathers: [in comb.] *black-feathered ostriches.* ■ decorated with feathers: *a feathered hat.*

feath·er edge ▶ **n.** a fine edge produced by tapering a board, plank, or other object.

feath·er·ing /'feT͟HəriNG/ ▶ **n.** **1** the plumage of a bird or part of a bird. ■ featherlike markings or structure. ■ the feathers of an arrow. ■ fringes of hairs on the appendages or body of a dog. **2** the action of varying the angle of propellers, rotor blades, or oars so as to reduce air or water resistance.

feath·er star ▶ **n.** an echinoderm (order Comatulida, class Crinoidea) with a small disklike body, long feathery arms for feeding and movement, and short appendages for grasping the surface.

feath·er·stitch /'feT͟Hər,stiCH/ ▶ **n.** ornamental zigzag sewing. ▶ **v.** [trans.] [usu. as n.] (**feath·er·stitch·ing**) sew (something) with such a stitch.

feath·er·weight /'feT͟Hər,wāt/ ▶ **n.** a weight in boxing and other sports between bantamweight and lightweight. It ranges from 118 to 126 pounds (54 to 57 kg). ■ a boxer or other competitor of this weight. ■ a very light person or thing. ■ a person or thing not worth serious consideration.

fea·ture /'fēCHər/ ▶ **n.** **1** a distinctive attribute or aspect of something. ■ (usu. **features**) a part of the face, such as the mouth or eyes, making a significant contribution to its overall appearance. **2** a newspaper or magazine article or a broadcast program that treats a topic at length. ■ (also **feature film**) a full-length film intended as the main item in a movie theater program. ▶ **v.** [trans.] have as a prominent attribute or aspect: *the hotel features a sauna.* ■ have as an important actor or participant: *the film featured Jimmy Stewart.* ■ [intrans.] (often **be featured**) be a significant characteristic of or take an important part in. ■ [intrans.] be apparent: *women rarely feature in writing on land settlement.* — **fea·tured adj.** [in comb.] *fine-featured women.* [ME: from OFr. *faiture* 'form,' from L. *factura* (see FACTURE).]

fea·ture-length ▶ **adj.** of the length of a typical feature film or program: *a feature-length documentary.*

Feb. ▶ **abbr.** February.

feb·ri·fuge /'febrə,fyo͞oj/ ▶ **n.** a medicine used to reduce fever. — **fe·brif·u·gal** /,fəbrə'f(y)o͞ogəl/ **adj.** [17th C.: from Fr. *fébrifuge*, from L. *febris* 'fever' + *fugare* 'drive away.' Cf. FEVERFEW.]

fe·brile /'febrīl; 'fēbrīl/ ▶ **adj.** having or showing the symptoms of a fever. ■ having or showing a great deal of nervous excitement or energy. — **fe·bril·i·ty** /fē'brilitē/ **n.** [17th C.: from Fr. *fébrile* or med. L. *febrilis*, from L. *febris* 'fever.']

Feb·ru·ar·y /'febro͞o,erē; 'febyo͞o-/ ▶ **n.** (pl. **-ar·ies**) the second month of the year, in the northern hemisphere usually considered the last month of winter. [ME *feverer*, from OFr. *feverier*, based on L. *februarius*, from *februa*, a purification feast.]

Feb·ru·ar·y Rev·o·lu·tion the first phase of the Russian Revolution. See RUSSIAN REVOLUTION.

fe·ces /'fēsēz/ (Brit. **fae·ces**) ▶ **plural n.** waste matter discharged from the bowels; excrement. — **fe·cal** /'fēkəl/ **adj.** [ME: from L., pl. of *faex* 'dregs.']

feck·less /'feklis/ ▶ **adj.** (of a person) lacking in efficiency or vitality. ■ unthinking and irresponsible. — **feck·less·ly adv. feck·less·ness n.** [16th C.: from Scots and north. Engl. dial. *feck* (from *effeck*, var. of EFFECT) + -LESS.]

fec·u·lent /'fekyələnt/ ▶ **adj.** of or containing dirt, sediment, or waste matter. — **fec·u·lence n.** [15th C.: from Fr. *féculent* or L. *faeculentus*, from *faex, faec-* 'dregs.']

fe·cund /'fekənd; 'fē-/ ▶ **adj.** producing or capable of producing an abundance of offspring or new growth; fertile. — **fe·cun·di·ty** /fe'kəndətē; fi'kən-/ **n.** [ME: from Fr. *fécond* or L. *fecundus* 'fruitful'.]

fe·cun·date /'fekən,dāt; 'fē-/ ▶ **v.** [trans.] fertilize: *there were no insects to fecundate flowering plants.* ■ literary make fruitful. — **fe·cun·da·tion** /,fekən'dāSHən; ,fē-/ **n.**

Fed /fed/ ▶ **n.** informal **1** a federal agent or official, esp. a member of the FBI. **2** (usu. **the Fed**) short for FEDERAL RESERVE.

fed /fed/ past and past participle of FEED.

fed. ▶ **abbr.** ■ federal. ■ federated. ■ federation.

fe·da·yeen /,fedä'ēn; -dī'ēn/ ▶ **plural n.** Arab guerrillas operating esp. against Israel. [1950s: from colloq. Arab. *fidā'iyīn*, pl. of classical Arab. *fidā'ī* 'one who gives his life for another or for a cause,' from *fadā* 'to ransom someone.']

fed·er·al /'fed(ə)rəl/ ▶ **adj.** having or relating to a system of government in which several states form a unity but remain independent in internal affairs. ■ of, relating to, or denoting the central government as distinguished from the separate units constituting a federation. ■ of, relating to, or denoting the central government of the US. ■ (**Federal**) hist. of the Northern States in the Civil War. — **fed·er·al·i·za·tion** /ˌfed(ə)rələˈzāSHən/ **n.** **fed·er·al·ize v.** **fed·er·al·ly adv.** [17th C.: from L. *foedus, foeder-* 'league, covenant' + -AL.]

Fed·er·al Bu·reau of In·ves·ti·ga·tion (abbr.: **FBI**) a branch of the US Department of Justice that deals principally with internal security and counterintelligence and that also conducts investigations in federal law enforcement.

fed·er·al case ▶ **n.** Law a criminal case that falls under the jurisdiction of a federal court. ■ fig. a matter of great concern or with dire consequences.

fed·er·al·ism /ˈfed(ə)rəˌlizəm/ ▶ **n.** the federal principle or system of government. ■ (**Federalism**) the principles of the Federalist Party.

fed·er·al·ist /ˈfed(ə)rəlist/ ▶ **n.** **1** an advocate or supporter of federalism. **2** (**Federalist**) a member or supporter of the Federalist Party. ▶ **adj.** **1** of, pertaining to, or favoring federalism or federalists. **2** (**Federalist**) designating or pertaining to the Federalist Party.

Fed·er·al·ist Pa·pers (also **The Federalist**) a collection of essays written under the pseudonym "Publius" by Alexander Hamilton, John Jay, and James Madison that sought to persuade New Yorkers to ratify the Constitution.

Fed·er·al·ist Par·ty an early political party in the US that advocated a strong central government. It was joined by George Washington during his presidency (1789–97) and in power until 1801.

Fed·er·al O·pen Mar·ket Com·mit·tee ▶ **n.** a committee of the Federal Reserve Board that meets regularly to set monetary policy, including the interest rates that are charged to banks.

Fed·er·al Reg·is·ter ▶ **n.** a daily publication of the US federal government that issues proposed and final administrative regulations of federal agencies.

Fed·er·al Re·pub·lic of Ger·ma·ny former name of West Germany.

Fed·er·al Re·serve the federal banking authority in the US that performs the functions of a central bank and is used to implement the country's monetary policy, providing a national system of reserve cash available to banks. Created in 1913, it consists of twelve Federal Reserve Districts, each having a Federal Reserve Bank. These are controlled by the Federal Reserve Board, which consists of governors appointed by the president with Senate approval.

Fed·er·al Un·ion see UNION (sense 3).

fed·er·ate ▶ **v.** /ˈfedəˌrāt/ [intrans.] (of a number of states or organizations) form a single centralized unit, within which each keeps some internal autonomy. ■ [trans.] [usu. as adj.] (**federated**) form (states or organizations) into such a centralized unit. ▶ **adj.** /-rit/ of or relating to such an arrangement. — **fed·er·a·tive** /-ˌrātiv; -rətiv/ **adj.** [18th C. (as an adj.): from late L. *foederatus*, based on *foedus, foeder-* 'league, covenant.']

Fed·er·at·ed States of Mi·cro·ne·sia full name for MICRONESIA (sense 2).

fed·er·a·tion /ˌfedəˈrāSHən/ ▶ **n.** a group of states with a central government but independence in internal affairs. ■ an organization or group within which smaller divisions have some degree of internal autonomy: [in names] *World Wrestling Federation.* ■ the action of forming states or organizations into a single group with centralized control. — **fed·er·a·tion·ist n.**

fe·do·ra /fəˈdôrə/ ▶ **n.** a low, soft felt hat with a curled brim and the crown creased lengthwise. [19th C. (orig.US): from *Fédora*, the title of a drama (1882) written by the Fr. dramatist Victorien Sardou (1831–1908).]

fedora

fed up ▶ **adj.** [predic.] annoyed or upset at a situation or treatment: *he was* **fed up with** *doing all the work.*

fee /fē/ ▶ **n.** **1** a payment made for professional advice or services. ■ money paid as part of a special transaction, e.g., for a privilege or for admission to something. ■ (usu. **fees**) money regularly paid (esp. to a school or similar institution) for continuing services. **2** Law, hist. an estate of land, esp. one held on condition of feudal service. [ME: from an Anglo-Norman Fr. var. of OFr. *feu, fief*, from med. L. *feodum, feudum*, ult. of Gmc. origin.]

feeb /fēb/ informal ▶ **n.** **1** a feebleminded person. **2** an FBI agent.

fee·ble /ˈfēbəl/ ▶ **adj.** (**-bler, -blest**) lacking physical strength, esp. as a result of age or illness. ■ (of a sound) faint. ■ lacking strength of character. ■ failing to convince or impress. — **fee·ble·ness n.** **fee·bly adv.** [ME: from OFr. *fieble*, earlier *fleible*, from L. *flebilis* 'lamentable,' from *flere* 'weep.']

fee·ble·mind·ed /ˈfēbəlˌmīndəd/ (also **fee·ble-mind·ed**) ▶ **adj.** (of a person) unable to make intelligent decisions. ■ (of an idea or proposal) lacking in sense or clear direction. ■ dated (of a person) having less than average intelligence. — **fee·ble·mind·ed·ly** (also **fee·ble-mind·ed·ly**) **adv.** **fee·ble·mind·ed·ness** (also **fee·ble-mind·ed·ness**) **n.**

feed /fēd/ ▶ **v.** (past **fed**) [trans.] **1** give food to. ■ [intrans.] (esp. of an animal or baby) take food; eat something: *morays emerge at night to feed.* ■ provide an adequate supply of food for. ■ [intrans.] (**feed on/off**) derive regular nourishment from (a particular substance). ■ encourage the growth of: *I could feed my melancholy by reading Romantic poetry.* ■ give fertilizer to (a plant). ■ put fuel on (a fire). **2** supply (a machine) with material or power: *the programs are fed into the computer.* ■ [with two objs.] supply (someone) with (information, ideas, etc.): *he is feeding his old employer commercial secrets.* ■ supply water to (a body of water): *the pond is fed by a small stream.* ■ insert coins into (a meter) to extend the time for which it operates. ■ [with two objs.] prompt (an actor) with (a line). ■ (in ball games) pass (the ball) to a player. ■ distribute (a broadcast) to local television or radio stations via satellite or network. **3** [trans.] cause to move gradually and steadily, typically through a confined space. ▶ **n.** **1** an act of giving food, esp. to animals or a baby, or of having food given to one. ■ informal a meal. ■ food for domestic animals. **2** a device or pipe for supplying material to a machine. ■ the supply of raw material to a machine or device: [as adj.] *a feed pipe.* ■ a broadcast distributed by satellite or network from a central source to a large number of radio or television stations. [OE *fēdan* (v.), of Gmc. origin; rel. to Du. *voeden* and FOOD.]

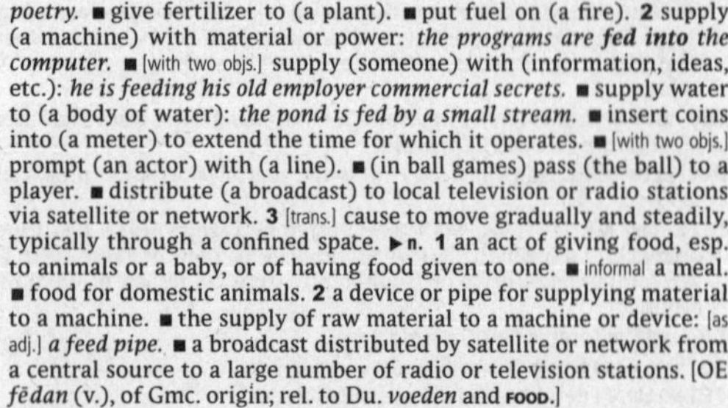

feed·back /ˈfēdˌbak/ ▶ **n.** **1** information about reactions to a product, a person's performance of a task, etc., used as a basis for improvement. **2** the modification or control of a process or system by its results or effects, e.g., in a biochemical pathway or behavioral response. See also NEGATIVE FEEDBACK, POSITIVE FEEDBACK. ■ the return of part of the output signal from an amplifier, microphone, or other device to the input of the same device; sound distortion produced by this.

feed dog ▶ **n.** the mechanism in a sewing machine that feeds the material under the needle.

feed·er /ˈfēdər/ ▶ **n.** **1** a person or animal that eats a particular food or in a particular manner. **2** a container filled with food for birds or mammals. **3** a person or thing that supplies something, in particular: ■ a device supplying material to a machine. ■ a tributary stream. ■ [usu. as adj.] a branch road or railroad line linking outlying districts with a main communication system. ■ a main carrying electricity to a distribution point. ■ [usu. as adj.] a school, sports team, etc., from which members move on to one more advanced.

feed·ing fren·zy ▶ **n.** an aggressive and competitive group attack on prey by sharks or piranhas. ■ fig. an episode of frantic competition or rivalry for something: *his remark caused a media feeding frenzy.*

feed·lot /ˈfēdˌlät/ ▶ **n.** an area or building where livestock are fed or fattened up.

feed·stock /ˈfēdˌstäk/ ▶ **n.** raw material to supply or fuel a machine or industrial process.

feed·stuff /ˈfēdˌstəf/ ▶ **n.** (usu. **feedstuffs**) a food provided for cattle and other livestock.

feed·through /ˈfēdˌTHro͞o/ ▶ **n.** an electrical connector used to join two parts of a circuit on opposite sides of something, such as a circuit board.

feel /fēl/ ▶ **v.** (past **felt** /felt/) [trans.] **1** be aware of (a person or object) through touching or being touched. ■ be aware of (something happening) through physical sensation. ■ examine or search by touch. ■ [intrans.] be capable of sensation: *the dead cannot feel.* ■ [intrans., with complement] give a sensation of a particular physical quality when touched. ■ (**feel one's way**) find one's way by touch rather than sight. ■ (**feel one's way**) fig. act cautiously, esp. in an area with which one is unfamiliar: *she was new in the job, still feeling her way.* ■ (**feel something out**) informal investigate something cautiously. ■ (**feel someone up**) informal fondle someone surreptitiously and without their consent. **2** experience (an emotion or sensation). ■ [intrans.] consider oneself to be in a particular state or exhibiting particular qualities: *he doesn't feel obliged to visit.* ■ (**feel up to**) have the strength and energy to do or deal with. ■ [usu. with negative] (**feel oneself**) be healthy and well: *Ruth was not quite feeling herself.* ■ be emotionally affected by. ■ [intrans.] have a specified reaction or attitude, esp. an emotional one, toward something: *we feel strongly about freedom of expression.* ■ (**feel for**) have compassion for. **3** have a belief or impression, esp. without an identifiable reason: *she felt that the woman disliked her.* ■ hold an opinion: *I felt I could make a contribution.* ▶ **n.** [usu. in sing.] **1** an act of touching something to examine it. ■ the sense of touch. **2** a sensation given by an object or material when touched. ■ the impression given by something.

– PHRASES **feel one's age** become aware that one is growing older and less energetic. **feel like (doing) something** be inclined to have or do: *I feel like celebrating.* **feel one's oats** see OAT. **feel the pinch** see PINCH. **get a** (or **the**) **feel for** (or **of**) become accustomed to. **have a feel for** have a sensitive appreciation or an intuitive understanding of. **make oneself** (or **one's presence**) **felt** make people keenly aware of one; have a noticeable effect. [OE *fēlan*, of West Gmc. origin; rel. to Du. *voelen* and Ger. *fühlen.*]

feel·er /ˈfēlər/ ▶ **n.** an animal organ such as an antenna or palp that is used for testing things by touch or for searching for food. ■ fig. a tentative proposal intended to ascertain someone's attitude or opinion: *he put out feelers about seeking the party nomination.*

feel-good ▶ **adj.** [attrib.] causing a feeling of happiness and well-being: *a feel-good movie.* — **feel-good·ism n.**

feel·ing /ˈfēliNG/ ▶ **n.** **1** an emotional state or reaction. ■ (**feelings**) the emotional side of someone's character; emotional responses or tendencies to respond. ■ strong emotion. **2** a belief, esp. a vague or irrational one. ■ an opinion, typically one shared by several people. **3** the capacity to experience the sense of touch. ■ the sensation of touching or being touched by a particular thing. **4** (**feeling for**) a sensitivity to or intuitive understanding of. ▶ **adj.** showing emotion or sensitivity.

feel·ing·ly /ˈfēliNGlē/ ▶ **adv.** (of the expression of a feeling or opinion) in a heartfelt way.

fee sim·ple ▶ **n.** (pl. **fees sim·ple**) Law a permanent and absolute tenure of an estate in land with freedom to dispose of it at will, esp. (in full **fee simple absolute**) a freehold tenure, which is the main type of land ownership.

feet /fēt/ plural form of FOOT.

fee tail ▶ **n.** (pl. **fees tail**) Law, hist. a former type of tenure of an estate in land with restrictions or entailment regarding the line of heirs to whom it may be willed. [ME: from Anglo-Norman Fr. *fee tailé* (see FEE, TAIL[2]).]

Feif·fer /'fīfər/, Jules (1929–), US cartoonist. His satirical cartoons appeared in *The Village Voice* and the *New Yorker*.

feign /fān/ ▶ **v.** [trans.] pretend to be affected by (a feeling, state, or injury): *she feigned nervousness.* [ME: from OFr. *feign-*, stem of *feindre*, from L. *fingere* 'mold, contrive.']

feint /fānt/ ▶ **n.** a deceptive or pretended blow, thrust, or other movement, esp. in boxing or fencing. ■ a mock attack or movement in warfare, made in order to distract or deceive an enemy. ▶ **v.** [intrans.] make a deceptive or distracting movement, typically during a fight. ■ [trans.] pretend to throw a (punch or blow) in order to deceive or distract an opponent. [17th C.: from Fr. *feinte*, past part. (used as a n.) of *feindre* 'feign.']

feist·y /'fīstē/ ▶ **adj.** (**feist·i·er**, **feist·i·est**) informal having or showing exuberance and strong determination. ■ touchy and aggressive. — **feist·i·ly adv.** **feist·i·ness n.** [19th C.: from earlier *feist*, *fist* 'small dog,' from *fisting cur*, a lapdog, from ME *fist* 'break wind,' of West Gmc. origin.]

fe·la·fel ▶ **n.** var. of FALAFEL.

feld·spar /'fel(d),spär/ ▶ **n.** an abundant rock-forming mineral typically occurring as colorless or pale-colored crystals and consisting of aluminosilicates of potassium, sodium, and calcium. — **feld·spath·ic** /fel(d)'spaTHik/ **adj.** [18th C.: alt. of Ger. *Feldspat*, *Feldspath*, from *Feld* 'field' + *Spat*, *Spath* 'spar' (see SPAR[3]).]

feld·spath·oid /fel(d)'spaTHoid/ ▶ **n.** Geol. any of a group of minerals chemically similar to feldspar but containing less silica, such as nepheline and leucite. — **feld·spath·oid·al** /,fel(d)spaTH'oidl/ **adj.**

fe·li·cif·ic /,felə'sifik/ ▶ **adj.** Ethics relating to or promoting increased happiness. [19th C.: from L. *felicificus*, from *felix*, *felic-* 'happy.']

fe·lic·i·tate /fə'lisi,tāt/ ▶ **v.** [trans.] congratulate. [17th C.: from late L. *felicitat-* 'made happy,' from the v. *felicitare*, from L. *felix*, *felic-* 'happy.']

fe·lic·i·ta·tion /fə,lisi'tāSHən/ ▶ **n.** (**felicitations**) words expressing praise for an achievement or good wishes on a special occasion.

fe·lic·i·tous /fə'lisitəs/ ▶ **adj.** well chosen or suited to the circumstances. ■ pleasing and fortunate. — **fe·lic·i·tous·ly adv.** **fe·lic·i·tous·ness n.**

fe·lic·i·ty /fə'lisitē/ ▶ **n.** (pl. **-ties**) **1** intense happiness. **2** the ability to find appropriate expression for one's thoughts. ■ a particularly effective feature of a work of literature or art. [ME: from OFr. *felicite*, from L. *felicitas*, from *felix*, *felic-* 'happy.']

fe·lid /'fēlid/ ▶ **n.** Zool. a mammal of the cat family (Felidae); a wild cat. [19th C.: from mod. L. *Felidae* (pl.), from L. *feles* 'cat.']

fe·line /'fēlīn/ ▶ **adj.** of, relating to, or affecting cats or other members of the cat family. ■ catlike, esp. in beauty or slyness. ▶ **n.** a cat or other member of the cat family. — **fe·lin·i·ty** /fē'linitē/ **n.** [17th C.: from L. *felinus*, from *feles* 'cat.']

fell[1] /fel/ past of FALL.

fell[2] ▶ **v.** [trans.] **1** (usu. **be felled**) cut down (a tree). ■ knock down. **2** (also **flat-fell**) stitch down (the edge of a seam) to lie flat: [as adj.] (**flat-felled**) *a flat-felled seam.* ▶ **n.** an amount of timber cut. [OE *fellan*, of Gmc. origin; rel. to Du. *vellen* and Ger. *fällen*, also to FALL.]

fell[3] ▶ **n.** a hill or stretch of high moorland, esp. in northern England. [ME: from ON *fjall*, *fell* 'hill'; prob. rel. to Ger. *Fels* 'rock.']

fell[4] ▶ **adj.** literary of terrible evil or ferocity; deadly.
– PHRASES **in** (or **at**) **one fell swoop** all at one time. [from Shakespeare's *Macbeth* (IV. iii. 219).] [ME: from OFr. *fel*, nominative of *felon* 'wicked (person)' (see FELON).]

fel·la /'felə/ (also **fel·lah**) ▶ **n.** nonstandard spelling of FELLOW.

fel·lah /'felə; fe'lä/ ▶ **n.** (pl. **fel·la·hin** /,felə'hēn/) an Egyptian peasant. [from Arab. *fallāḥ* 'tiller of the soil,' from *falaḥa* 'till the soil.']

fel·late /fe'lāt/ ▶ **v.** [trans.] perform fellatio on (a man). [19th C.: from L. *fellat-* 'sucked,' from the v. *fellare*.]

fel·la·ti·o /fə'lāSH(ē),ō/ ▶ **n.** oral stimulation of a man's penis. — **fel·la·tor** /fe'lātər/ **n.** [19th C.: mod. L., from L. *fellare* 'to suck.']

fell·er[1] /'felər/ ▶ **n.** nonstandard spelling of FELLOW.

fell·er[2] ▶ **n.** a person who cuts down trees.

fel·lies /'felēz/ ▶ **plural n.** another term for FELLOES.

Fel·li·ni /fə'lēnē/, Federico (1920–93), Italian director, noted for the movie *La Strada* (1954).

fel·loes /'felōz/ (also **fel·lies**) ▶ **plural n.** the outer rim of a wheel, to which the spokes are fixed. [OE *felg* (sing.); rel. to Du. *velg* and Ger. *Felge*; of unknown ultimate origin.]

fel·low /'felō/ ▶ **n. 1** informal a man or boy. ■ a boyfriend or lover. **2** (usu. **fellows**) a person in the same position, involved in the same activity, or otherwise associated with another. ■ a thing of the same kind as or otherwise associated with another. **3** a member of a learned society. ■ (also **research fellow**) a student or graduate receiving a fellowship for a period of research. ■ a member of the governing body in some universities. ▶ **adj.** [attrib.] sharing a particular activity, quality, or condition with someone or something. [OE *fēolaga* 'a partner or colleague,' from ON *félagi*, from *fé* 'cattle, property, money' + the Gmc. base of LAY[1].]

fel·low·ship /'felō,SHip/ ▶ **n. 1** friendly association, esp. with people who share one's interests. ■ a group of people meeting to pursue a shared interest or aim. ■ a guild or corporation. **2** an endowment established or a sum of money awarded to support a scholar or student engaged in advanced research in a particular field. ■ the status of a fellow of a college or society.

fel·low trav·el·er ▶ **n.** a person who travels with another. ■ a person who is not a member of a particular group or political party (esp. the Communist Party), but who sympathizes with the group's aims and policies. — **fel·low trav·el·ing adj.**

fe·lo-de-se /,felōdə 'sā/ ▶ **n.** (pl. **fe·los-de-se** /,felōz/) suicide. [from Anglo-L., lit. 'felon of himself.']

fel·on /'felən/ ▶ **n.** a person who has been convicted of a felony. [ME: from OFr., literally 'a wicked person' (oblique case of *fel* 'evil'), from medieval L. *fello*, *fellon-*.]

fe·lo·ni·ous /fə'lōnēəs/ ▶ **adj.** of, relating to, or involved in crime. ■ Law relating to or of the nature of felony. — **fe·lo·ni·ous·ly adv.**

fel·o·ny /'felənē/ ▶ **n.** (pl. **-nies**) a crime, typically one involving violence, regarded as more serious than a misdemeanor, and usually punishable by imprisonment for more than one year or by death.

fel·sic /'felsik/ ▶ **adj.** Geol. of, relating to, or denoting a group of light-colored minerals including feldspar, feldspathoids, quartz, and muscovite. [20th C.: from FELDSPAR + a contr. of SILICA.]

fel·spar /'fel,spär/ ▶ **n.** Brit.var. of FELDSPAR.

felt[1] /felt/ ▶ **n.** a kind of cloth made by rolling and pressing wool or another suitable textile while applying moisture or heat, causing the fibers to mat together to create a smooth surface. ▶ **v.** [trans.] make into felt; mat together: *the wood fibers are felted together.* ■ cover with felt: [as adj.] (**felted**) *felted goat hair.* ■ [intrans.] become matted: *wool can shrink and felt.* — **felt·y adj.** [OE, of West Gmc. origin; rel. to Du. *vilt*, also to FILTER.]

felt[2] past and past participle of FEEL.

fe·luc·ca /fə'lōōkə; -'ləkə/ ▶ **n.** a small boat propelled by oars or lateen sails or both, used on the Nile and formerly more widely in the Mediterranean region. [17th C.: from Ital. *feluc(c)a*, prob. from obs. Sp. *faluca*, of Arab. origin.]

fem /fem/ ▶ **n.** var. of FEMME.

fem. ▶ **abbr.** ■ female. ■ feminine.

FEMA /'fēmə/ ▶ **abbr.** Federal Emergency Management Agency.

fe·male /'fēmāl/ ▶ **adj.** of or denoting the sex that can bear offspring or produce eggs, distinguished biologically by the production of gametes (ova) that can be fertilized by male gametes. ■ relating to or characteristic of women or female animals. ■ (of a plant or flower) having a pistil but no stamens. ■ (of parts of machinery, fittings, etc.) manufactured hollow so that a corresponding male part can be inserted. ▶ **n.** a female person, animal, or plant. — **fe·male·ness n.** [ME: from OFr. *femelle*, from L. *femella*, dimin. of *femina* 'a woman.']

fe·male cir·cum·ci·sion ▶ **n.** (among some peoples) the action or traditional practice of cutting off the clitoris and sometimes the labia of girls or young women.

fem·i·nine /'femənin/ ▶ **adj. 1** having qualities or appearance traditionally associated with women, esp. delicacy and prettiness. ■ of or relating to women; female. **2** Gram. of or denoting a gender of nouns and adjectives, conventionally regarded as female. **3** Music (of a cadence) occurring on a metrically weak beat. ▶ **n.** (**the feminine**) the female sex or gender. ■ Gram. a feminine word or form. — **fem·i·nine·ly adv.** **fem·i·nine·ness n.** **fem·i·nin·i·ty** /,femə'ninitē/ **n.** [ME: from L. *femininus*, from *femina* 'woman.']

fem·i·nine rhyme ▶ **n.** Pros. a rhyme between stressed syllables followed by one or more unstressed syllables (e.g., *stocking/shocking*, *glamorous/amorous*). Compare with MASCULINE RHYME.

fem·i·nism /'femə,nizəm/ ▶ **n.** the advocacy of women's rights on the grounds of political, social, and economic equality to men.

fem·i·nist /'femənist/ ▶ **n.** a person who supports feminism. ▶ **adj.** of, relating to, or supporting feminism.

fem·i·nize /'femə,nīz/ ▶ **v.** [trans.] make (something) more characteristic of or associated with women. ■ induce female sexual characteristics in (a male). — **fem·i·ni·za·tion** /,femənə'zāSHən/ **n.**

femme /fem/ (also **fem**) ▶ **n.** informal a lesbian or a male homosexual who takes a traditionally feminine sexual role. [1960s: Fr., 'woman.']

femme fa·tale /,fem fə'tal; fə'täl/ ▶ **n.** (pl. **femmes fa·tales** pronunc. same) an attractive and seductive woman, esp. one who will ultimately bring disaster to a man who becomes involved with her. [20th C.: Fr., literally 'disastrous woman.']

femto- ▶ **comb. form** (used in units of measurement) denoting a factor of 10^{-15}: *femtosecond.* [from Dan. or Norw. *femten* 'fifteen.']

fe·mur /'fēmər/ ▶ **n.** (pl. **fe·murs** or **fem·o·ra** /'femərə/) Anat. the bone of the thigh or upper hind limb, articulating at the hip and the knee. ■ Zool. the third segment of the leg in insects and some other arthropods, typically the longest and thickest segment. — **fem·o·ral** /'femərəl/ **adj.** [15th C.: from L. *femur*, *femor-* 'thigh.']

fen[1] /fen/ ▶ **n.** a low and marshy or frequently flooded area of land. ▪ (**the Fens**) flat low-lying areas of eastern England. ▪ Ecol. wetland with alkaline, neutral, or only slightly acid peaty soil. Compare with BOG. — **fen·ny** **adj.** [OE *fen(n)*, of Gmc. origin; rel. to Du. *veen* and Ger. *Fenn*.]

fen[2] ▶ **n.** (pl. same) a monetary unit of China, equal to one hundredth of a yuan. [from Chin. *fēn* 'a hundredth part.']

fence /fens/ ▶ **n.** **1** a barrier, railing, or other upright structure, typically of wood or wire, enclosing an area of ground to mark a boundary, control access, or prevent escape. ▪ a large upright obstacle used in equestrian jumping events. ▪ a guard or guide on a plane, saw, or other tool. **2** informal a person who deals in stolen goods. ▶ **v. 1** [trans.] (often **be fenced**) surround or protect with a fence. ▪ (**fence something in/off**) enclose or separate with a fence for protection or to prevent escape. ▪ (**fence someone/something out**) use a barrier to exclude someone or something. **2** [trans.] informal deal in (stolen goods). **3** [intrans.] fight with swords, esp. as a sport. See also FENCING. ▪ fig. conduct a discussion or argument so as to avoid the direct mention of something.
– PHRASES **mend (one's) fences** see MEND. **side of the fence** used to refer to either of the opposing positions involved in a conflict. **sit on the fence** avoid making a decision or choice. — **fenc·er n.** [ME: shortening of DEFENSE.]

fence·row /'fens,rō/ ▶ **n.** an uncultivated strip of land on each side of and below a fence.

fenc·ing /'fensiNG/ ▶ **n.** **1** the sport of fighting with swords, esp. foils, épées, or sabers, according to a set of rules, in order to score points against an opponent. ▪ fig. the action of conducting a discussion or argument so as to avoid the direct mention of something. **2** a series of fences. ▪ material used for the construction of fences. ▪ the erection of fences.

fend /fend/ ▶ **v. 1** [intrans.] (**fend for oneself**) look after and provide for oneself, without any help from others. **2** [trans.] (**fend someone/something off**) defend oneself from a blow, attack, or attacker. ▪ evade someone or something in order to protect oneself. [ME: shortening of DEFEND.]

Fend·er /'fendər/, Leo (1907–91), US guitar maker. He designed and produced electric guitars.

fend·er /'fendər/ ▶ **n.** **1** a thing used to keep something off or prevent a collision, in particular: ▪ the mudguard or area around the wheel well of a vehicle. ▪ a plastic cylinder, tire, etc., hung over a ship's side to protect it against impact. ▪ a metal frame at the front of a locomotive or streetcar for pushing aside obstacles on the line; a cowcatcher. **2** a low frame bordering a fireplace to contain burning materials.

fend·er bend·er ▶ **n.** informal a minor collision between motor vehicles.

fe·nes·tra /fə'nestrə/ ▶ **n.** (pl. **-trae** /-trē; -trī/) **1** Anat. Zool. a small natural hole or opening, esp. in a bone. The mammalian middle ear is linked by the **fenestra ovalis** to the vestibule of the inner ear, and by the **fenestra rotunda** to the cochlea. **2** Med. an artificial opening. [19th C.: from L., literally 'window.']

fe·nes·trate /'fenə,strāt/ ▶ **adj.** Bot. Zool. having small windowlike perforations or transparent areas.

fe·nes·trat·ed /'fenə,strātid/ ▶ **adj.** provided with a window or windows. ▪ esp. Anat. having perforations, apertures, or transparent areas.

fen·es·tra·tion /,fenə'strāSHən/ ▶ **n.** Archit. the arrangement of windows and doors on the elevations of a building. ▪ Bot. Zool. the condition of being fenestrate. ▪ Med. a surgical operation in which a new opening is formed, esp. in the bony labyrinth of the inner ear to treat certain types of deafness.

fen·flu·ra·mine /fen'flo͝orə,mēn/ ▶ **n.** Med. a prescription drug once prescribed for obesity, withdrawn from the US market in 1997 because of safety concerns. Also called FEN-PHEN.

feng shui /'fəNG 'SHwē; 'SHwā/ ▶ **n.** (in Chinese thought) a system of laws considered to govern spatial arrangement and orientation in relation to the flow of energy (qi), and whose effects are taken into account when siting and designing buildings. [Chin., from *fēng* 'wind' and *shuǐ* 'water.']

Fe·ni·an /'fēnēən/ ▶ **n.** a member of a 19th-century revolutionary nationalist organization among the Irish in the US and Ireland. — **Fe·ni·an·ism n.** [from Old Irish *féne*, the name of an ancient Irish people, confused with *fiann*, *fianna* (see FIANNA FÁIL).]

fen·land /'fenlənd/ ▶ **n.** (also **fenlands**) land consisting of fens.

fen·nec /'fenik/ (also **fennec fox**) ▶ **n.** a small pale fox (*Vulpes zerda*) with large pointed ears, native to the deserts of North Africa and Arabia. [18th C.: via Arab. from Pers. *fanak*, *fanaj*.]

fen·nel /'fenl/ ▶ **n.** an aromatic yellow-flowered European plant (*Foeniculum vulgare*) of the parsley family, with feathery leaves. The seeds and leaves of the perennial fennel (subsp. dulce) are used as culinary herbs. The swollen leaf bases of **sweet fennel** (subsp. azoricum), an annual, are eaten as a vegetable. [OE *finule*, *fenol*, from L. *faeniculum*, dimin. of *faenum* 'hay.']

fen-phen /'fen ,fen/ ▶ **n.** a shortened form of FENFLURAMINE.

fen·u·greek /'fen(y)ə,grēk/ ▶ **n.** a white-flowered herbaceous plant (*Trigonella foenum-graecum*) of the pea family, with aromatic seeds that are used for flavoring. [OE *fenogrecum*, from L. *faenugraecum*, from *faenum graecum* 'Gk. hay.']

Fen·way, the /'fen,wā/ a park system that incorporates the wetlands in Boston, Massachusetts.

FEPC ▶ **abbr.** Fair Employment Practices Commission.

FERA ▶ **abbr.** Federal Emergency Relief Administration.

fe·ral /'fi(ə)rəl; 'ferəl/ ▶ **adj.** (esp. of an animal) in a wild state, esp. after escape from captivity or domestication: *a feral cat.* ▪ resembling a wild animal. [17th C.: from L. *fera* 'wild animal' (from *ferus* 'wild') + -AL.]

Fer·ber /'fərbər/, Edna (1887–1968), US writer. Her novels include *So Big* (1924) and *Giant* (1952).

fer de lance /,fer dl'ans; -'äns/ ▶ **n.** (pl. **fers de lance** pronunc. same or /,ferz;/ or **fer de lances**) a large and dangerous pit viper (genus *Bothrops*) native to Central and South America. [19th C.: from Fr., literally 'iron (head) of a lance.']

Fer·di·nand /'fərdn,and/ (1452–1516), king of Castile 1474–1516 and of Aragon 1479–1516; known as **Ferdinand the Catholic**. He and his wife Isabella instituted the Spanish Inquisition in 1478 and supported the expedition of Chistopher Columbus in 1492.

fe·ri·a /'fi(ə)rēə; 'fer-/ ▶ **n.** (in Spanish-speaking regions) a local fair or festival, usually in honor of a patron saint. [19th C.: Sp., from L., literally 'holiday.']

fe·ri·al /'fi(ə)rēəl; 'fer-/ ▶ **adj.** Christian Church denoting an ordinary weekday, as opposed to a festival. [ME: from med. L. *ferialis*, from L. *feria* 'holiday.']

Fer·lin·ghet·ti /,fərliNG'getē/, Lawrence Monsanto (1919–), US poet; born *Lawrence Ferling*. Identified with San Francisco's beat movement, his poems are collected in volumes such as *A Coney Island of the Mind* (1958).

Ferm. **abbr.** Fermanagh.

Fer·man·agh /fər'manə/ one of the Six Counties of Northern Ireland; chief town, Enniskillen.

Fer·mat /fer'mä/, Pierre de (1601–65), French mathematician. His work on curves led directly to the general methods of calculus introduced by Isaac Newton and Gottfried Leibniz.

fer·ma·ta /fer'mätə; fər-/ ▶ **n.** Music a pause of unspecified length on a note or rest. ▪ a mark (8) designating such a pause. [Ital., from *fermare* 'to stop.']

fer·ment ▶ **v.** /fər'ment/ **1** [intrans.] (of a substance) undergo fermentation. ▪ [trans.] cause the fermentation of (a substance). **2** [trans.] incite or stir up (trouble or disorder). ▪ [intrans.] (of a negative feeling or memory) fester and develop into something worse. ▶ **n.** /'fərment/ agitation and excitement among a group of people, typically concerning major change and leading to trouble or violence. — **fer·ment·a·ble adj.** [ME: from OFr. *ferment* (n.), *fermenter* (v.), based on L. *fermentum* 'yeast,' from *fervere* 'to boil.']

fer·men·ta·tion /,fərmən'tāSHən/ ▶ **n.** the chemical breakdown of a substance by bacteria, yeasts, or other microorganisms, typically involving effervescence and the giving off of heat. ▪ the process of this kind involved in the making of beer, wine, and liquor, in which sugars are converted to ethyl alcohol. — **fer·ment·a·tive** /fər'mentətiv/ **adj.**

fer·ment·er /fər'mentər/ ▶ **n.** a container in which fermentation takes place. ▪ an organism that causes fermentation.

Fer·mi /'fermē; 'fər-/, Enrico (1901–54), US physicist; born in Italy. He directed the first controlled nuclear chain reaction in 1942 and worked on the atom bomb. Nobel Prize for Physics (1938).

fer·mi /'fermē; 'fər-/ ▶ **n.** (pl. same) a unit of length equal to 10–15 meter (one femtometer), used in nuclear physics. It is similar to the diameter of a proton. [20th C.: named after E. FERMI.]

Fer·mi-Di·rac sta·tis·tics /də'rak/ ▶ **plural n.** [treated as sing.] Physics a type of quantum statistics used to describe systems of fermions. [1920s: named after E. FERMI and P. A. M. DIRAC.]

fer·mi·on /'fərmē,än/ ▶ **n.** Physics a subatomic particle, such as a nucleon, that has half-integral spin and follows the statistical description given by Fermi and Dirac. [1940s: from the name of E. FERMI + -ON.]

fer·mi·um /'fərmēəm-/ ▶ **n.** the chemical element of atomic number 100, a radioactive metal of the actinide series. Fermium does not occur naturally and was discovered in 1953 in the debris of the first hydrogen bomb explosion. (Symbol: **Fm**) [1950s: from the name of E. FERMI + -IUM.]

fern /fərn/ ▶ **n.** (pl. same or **ferns**) a flowerless plant (class Filicopsida, division Pteridophyta) that has feathery or leafy fronds and reproduces by spores released from the undersides of the fronds. Ferns have a vascular system for the transport of water and nutrients. See illustration at WOODFERN. — **fern·y adj.** [OE *fearn*, of West Gmc. origin; rel. to Du. *varen* and Ger. *Farn*.]

Fer·nan·do Pó·o /fər'nandō 'pō-ō/ former name (until 1973) for BIOKO.

fern bar ▶ **n.** informal a barroom in a contemporary design that includes ferns and other plants.

fe·ro·cious /fə'rōSHəs/ ▶ **adj.** savagely fierce, cruel, or violent. ▪ (of a conflict) characterized by or involving aggression, bitterness, and determination. ▪ extreme and unpleasant. — **fe·ro·cious·ly adv.** **fe·ro·cious·ness n.** [17th C.: from L. *ferox*, *feroc-* 'fierce' + -IOUS.]

fe·roc·i·ty /fə'räsitē/ ▶ **n.** (pl. **-ties**) the state or quality of being ferocious.

-ferous (usu. **-iferous**) ▶ **suffix** having, bearing, or containing (a specified thing): *Carboniferous*. — **-ferously comb. form** in corresponding adverbs **-ferousness comb. form** in corresponding nouns. [from Fr. *-fère* or L. *-fer* 'producing,' from *ferre* 'to bear.']

Fer·ra·ra /fə'rärə/ a city in northern Italy, capital of a province of the same name; pop. 141,000.

Fer·ra·ri /fə'rärē/, Enzo (1898–1988), Italian businessman. In 1929, he founded the automobile company named for him.

fer·rate /ˈferāt/ ▶ **n.** Chem. a salt in which the anion contains both iron (typically ferric iron) and oxygen. [19th C.: from L. *ferrum* 'iron' + -ATE[1].]

ferret

fer·ret /ˈferit/ ▶ **n.** a domesticated polecat (*Mustela putorius furo*), typically albino or brown in coloration. ▶ **v.** (**-ret·ed, -ret·ing**) [intrans.] (of a person) hunt with ferrets, typically for rabbits. ■ clear (a hole or area of ground) of rabbits with ferrets. ■ look around in a place or container in search of something: *he went to the desk and ferreted around.* ■ [trans.] (**ferret something out**) search tenaciously for and find something: *ferret out the facts.* — **fer·ret·er** n. [ME: from OFr. *fuiret*, alt. of *fuiron*, based on late L. *furo* 'thief, ferret,' from L. *fur* 'thief.']

fer·ri- ▶ **comb. form** Chem. of iron with a valence of three; ferric. Compare with FERRO-. [from L. *ferrum* 'iron.']

fer·ric /ˈferik/ ▶ **adj.** of or relating to iron. ■ Chem. of iron with a valence of three; of iron(III). Compare with FERROUS. [18th C.: from L. *ferrum* 'iron' + -IC.]

fer·ri·cy·a·nide /ˌferiˈsīəˌnīd/ ▶ **n.** Chem. a salt containing the anion $Fe(CN)_6{}^{3-}$.

Fer·ris wheel /ˈferis/ ▶ **n.** an amusement-park or fairground ride consisting of a giant vertical revolving wheel with passenger cars suspended on its outer edge. [19th C.: named after George W. G. *Ferris* (1859–96), the American engineer who invented it.]

fer·rite /ˈferīt/ ▶ **n.** **1** a ceramic compound consisting of a mixed oxide of iron and one or more other metals. It is used in high-frequency electrical components such as antennas. **2** Metallurgy a form of pure iron, occurring in low-carbon steel. — **fer·rit·ic** /fəˈritik/ **adj.** (in sense 2). [19th C.: from L. *ferrum* 'iron' + -ITE[1].]

fer·ri·tin /ˈferitn/ ▶ **n.** Biochem. a protein that stores iron in the tissues of mammals. [1930s: from FERRI- + -t- + -IN[1].]

fer·ro- ▶ **comb. form** containing iron: *ferroconcrete.* ■ Chem. of iron with a valence of two; ferrous. Compare with FERRI-. [from L. *ferrum* 'iron.']

fer·ro·al·loy /ˌferōˈaloi; -əˈloi/ ▶ **n.** an alloy of iron with one or more other metals, used in making steel.

fer·ro·con·crete /ˌferōˈkänkrēt/ ▶ **n.** another term for REINFORCED CONCRETE.

fer·ro·cy·a·nide /ˌferōˈsīəˌnīd/ ▶ **n.** Chem. a salt containing the anion $Fe(CN)_6{}^{4-}$.

fer·ro·e·lec·tric /ˌferō-iˈlektrik/ Physics ▶ **adj.** (of a substance) exhibiting permanent electric polarization that varies in strength with the applied electric field. ▶ **n.** a ferroelectric substance. — **fer·ro·e·lec·tric·i·ty** /ˌferō-iˌlekˈtrisətē/ **n.**

fer·ro·flu·id /ˈferōˌflo͞oid/ ▶ **n.** [often as adj.] a fluid containing a magnetic suspension: *ferrofluid cooling.*

fer·ro·mag·ne·sian /ˌferōmagˈnēzhən; -zēən/ ▶ **adj.** Geol. (of a rock or mineral) containing iron and magnesium as major components.

fer·ro·mag·net·ic /ˌferōmagˈnetik/ ▶ **adj.** Physics (of a body or substance) having a high susceptibility to magnetization, the strength of which depends on that of the applied magnetizing field, and that may persist after removal of the applied field. This is the kind of magnetism displayed by iron. — **fer·ro·mag·ne·tism** /ˌferōˈmagniˌtizəm/ **n.**

fer·ro·man·ga·nese /ˌferōˈmaNGgəˌnēz; -ˌnēs/ ▶ **n.** an alloy of iron and manganese used in making steel.

fer·ro·sil·i·con /ˌferōˈsilikən; -ˌkän/ ▶ **n.** an alloy of iron and silicon used in making steel and some types of iron.

fer·rous /ˈferəs/ ▶ **adj.** (chiefly of metals) containing or consisting of iron. ■ Chem. of iron with a valence of two; of iron(II). Compare with FERRIC. [19th C.: from L. *ferrum* 'iron' + -OUS.]

fer·rous ox·ide ▶ **n.** a black powder, FeO, used in making steel and glass.

fer·rous sul·fate ▶ **n.** a pale green iron salt, $FeSO_4 7H_2O$, used in inks, tanning, water purification, and treatment of anemia.

fer·ru·gi·nous /fəˈro͞ojənəs/ ▶ **adj.** containing iron oxides or rust. ■ reddish brown; rust-colored. [17th C.: from L. *ferrugo, ferrugin-* 'rust, dark red' (from *ferrum* 'iron') + -OUS.]

fer·rule /ˈferəl/ ▶ **n.** a ring or cap, typically a metal one, that strengthens the end of a handle, stick, or tube and prevents it from splitting or wearing. ■ a metal band strengthening or forming a joint. [17th C.: alt. of obs. *verrel*, from OFr. *virelle*, from L. *viriola*, dimin. of *viriae* 'bracelets.']

fer·ry /ˈferē/ ▶ **n.** (pl. **-ries**) (also **fer·ry·boat**) a boat or ship for conveying passengers and goods, esp. over a relatively short distance and as a regular service. ■ a service for conveying passengers or goods in this way. ■ the place where such a service operates from. ■ a similar service using another mode of transportation, esp. aircraft. ▶ **v.** (**-ries, -ried**) [trans.] convey in a boat, esp. across a short stretch of water. ■ transport (someone or something) from one place to another. — **fer·ry·man** /ˈferēmən/ (pl. **-men**) **n.** [ME: from ON *ferja* 'ferryboat,' of Gmc. origin and rel. to FARE.]

fer·tile /ˈfərtl/ ▶ **adj.** (of soil) producing or capable of producing abundant vegetation or crops. ■ (of a seed or egg) capable of becoming a new individual. ■ (of a person, animal, or plant) able to conceive young or produce seed. ■ (of a person's mind or imagination) producing many new and inventive ideas with ease. ■ (of a situation or subject) being fruitful and productive in generating new ideas. ■ Physics (of nuclear material) able to become fissile by the capture of neutrons. — **fer·til·i·ty** /fərˈtilitē/ **n.** [ME: via Fr. from L. *fertilis*, from *ferre* 'to bear.']

Fer·tile Cres·cent a crescent-shaped area of fertile land in the Middle East that extends from the eastern Mediterranean coast through the valley of the Tigris and Euphrates rivers to the Persian Gulf. It was the cradle of the Assyrian, Sumerian, and Babylonian civilizations.

fer·til·i·za·tion /ˌfərtl-əˈzāSHən/ ▶ **n.** Biol. the action or process of fertilizing an egg, female animal, or plant, involving the fusion of male and female gametes to form a zygote. ■ the action or process of applying a fertilizer to soil.

fer·ti·lize /ˈfərtlˌīz/ ▶ **v.** [trans.] cause (an egg, female animal, or plant) to develop a new individual by introducing male reproductive material. ■ make (soil) more fertile or productive by adding suitable substances to it. — **fer·ti·liz·a·ble adj.**

fer·ti·liz·er /ˈfərtlˌīzər/ ▶ **n.** a chemical or natural substance added to soil to increase its fertility.

fer·u·la /ˈfer(y)ələ/ ▶ **n.** **1** a tall large-leaved Eurasian parsley-family plant of a genus (*Ferula*) that includes asafetida and its relatives. **2** rare term for FERULE. [late ME: from L., 'giant fennel, rod.']

fer·ule /ˈferəl/ ▶ **n.** hist. a flat ruler with a widened end, formerly used for punishing children. [ME (denoting the giant fennel): from L. *ferula* (see FERULA).]

fer·vent /ˈfərvənt/ ▶ **adj.** having or displaying a passionate intensity. — **fer·ven·cy n. fer·vent·ly adv.** [ME: via OFr. from L. *fervent-* 'boiling,' from the v. *fervere*.]

fer·vid /ˈfərvid/ ▶ **adj.** intensely enthusiastic or passionate. ■ literary burning, hot, or glowing. — **fer·vid·ly adv.** [16th C.: from L. *fervidus*, from *fervere* 'to boil.']

fer·vor /ˈfərvər/ (Brit. **fer·vour**) ▶ **n.** intense and passionate feeling. [ME: via OFr. from L. *fervor*, from *fervere* 'to boil.']

Fès /fes/ var. of FEZ.

fes·cue /ˈfeskyo͞o/ ▶ **n.** any of a number of narrow-leaved grasses, esp. a perennial grass (genus *Festuca*) used for lawns, pasture, and fodder, and an annual grass (genus *Vulpia*) of drier soils such as dunes and wasteland. [ME *festu, festue* 'straw, twig,' from OFr. *festu*, based on L. *festuca* 'stalk, straw.']

fess[1] /fes/ (also **fesse**) ▶ **n.** Heraldry an ordinary in the form of a broad horizontal stripe across the middle of the shield.
– PHRASES **in fess** across the middle third of the field. [15th C.: from OFr. *fesse*, alt. of *faisse*, from L. *fascia* 'band.' Cf. FASCIA.]

fess[2] ▶ **v.** [intrans.] (**fess up**) informal confess; own up.

fess point ▶ **n.** Heraldry a point at the center of a shield.

-fest ▶ **comb. form** in nouns denoting a festival or large gathering of a specified kind: *gabfest* | *slugfest.* [from Ger. *Fest* 'festival.']

fes·ta /ˈfestə/ ▶ **n.** (in Italy and other Mediterranean countries) a religious or other festival. [19th C.: from Ital., 'festival,' from L.]

fes·tal /ˈfestəl/ ▶ **adj.** of, like, or relating to a celebration or festival. — **fes·tal·ly adv.** [15th C.: via OFr. from late L. *festalis*, from L. *festum*, (pl.) *festa* 'feast.']

fes·ter /ˈfestər/ ▶ **v.** [intrans.] (of a wound or sore) become septic; suppurate. ■ (of food or garbage) become rotten and offensive to the senses. ■ (of a negative feeling or a problem) become worse or more intense, esp. through long-term neglect or indifference. ■ (of a person) undergo physical and mental deterioration in isolated inactivity. [ME: based on OFr. *festre* 'a sore,' from L. *fistula* 'pipe, reed, fistula.']

fes·ti·val /ˈfestəvəl/ ▶ **n.** a day or period of celebration, typically a religious commemoration. ■ an annual celebration or anniversary. ■ an organized series of concerts, plays, or movies. [ME (as an adj.): via OFr. from med. L. *festivalis*, from L. *festivus*, from *festum*, (pl.) *festa* 'feast.']

fes·ti·val of lights ▶ **n.** **1** another term for HANUKKAH. **2** another term for DIWALI.

fes·tive /ˈfestiv/ ▶ **adj.** of or relating to a festival. ■ cheerful and jovially celebratory. — **fes·tive·ly adv. fes·tive·ness n.** [mid 17th cent.: from L. *festivus*, from *festum*, (pl.) *festa* 'feast.']

fes·tiv·i·ty /feˈstivitē/ ▶ **n.** (pl. **-ties**) the celebration of something in a joyful and exuberant way. ■ a festive celebration. ■ (**festivities**) activities or events celebrating a special occasion.

fes·toon /fesˈto͞on/ ▶ **n.** a chain or garland of flowers, leaves, or ribbons, hung in a curve as a decoration. ■ a carved or molded ornament representing such a garland. ▶ **v.** [trans.] (often **be festooned with**) adorn (a place) with chains, garlands, or other decorations: *the room was festooned with balloons.* [17th C.: from Fr. *feston*, from Ital. *festone* 'festal ornament,' from *festum*, (pl.) *festa* 'feast.']

Fest·schrift /ˈfes(t),SHrift/ (also **fest·schrift**) ▶**n.** (pl. **-schrift·en** /-,SHriftən/ or **-schrifts**) a collection of writings published in honor of a scholar. [19th C.: from Ger., from *Fest* 'celebration' + *Schrift* 'writing.']

FET ▶**abbr.** field-effect transistor.

fet·a /ˈfetə/ (also **fet·a cheese**) ▶**n.** a white salty Greek cheese made from the milk of ewes or goats. [from mod. Gk. *pheta.*]

fe·tal /ˈfētl/ ▶**adj.** of or relating to a fetus. ■ denoting a posture characteristic of a fetus, with the back curved forward and the limbs folded in front of the body.

fe·tal al·co·hol syn·drome (abbr.: **FAS**) ▶**n.** Med. a congenital syndrome caused by excessive consumption of alcohol by the mother during pregnancy, characterized by retardation of both mental and physical development.

fetch /fecH/ ▶**v.** [trans.] **1** go for and then bring back (someone or something). **2** achieve (a particular price) when sold. **3** [with two objs.] informal inflict (a blow or slap) on (someone). **4** informal, dated cause great interest or delight in (someone). ▶**n. 1** [in sing.] an act of going for something and then bringing it back. **2** the distance traveled by wind or waves across open water. ■ the distance a vessel must sail to reach open water.
– PHRASES **fetch and carry** run backward and forward bringing things to someone in a servile fashion.
– PHRASAL VERBS **fetch up** informal arrive or come to rest somewhere, typically by accident or unintentionally. — **fetch·er n.** [OE *fecc(e)an,* var. of *fetian,* prob. related to *fatian* 'grasp,' of Gmc. origin and rel. to Ger. *fassen.*]

fetch·ing /ˈfecHiNG/ ▶**adj.** attractive. — **fetch·ing·ly adv.**

fête /fāt; fet/ (also **fete**) ▶**n.** a celebration or festival. ▶**v.** [trans.] (usu. **be fêted**) honor or entertain (someone) lavishly. [ME (in the sense 'festival, fair'): from Fr., from OFr. *feste* (see **FEAST**).]

fête cham·pê·tre /ˈfāt SHänˈpetr(ə); ˈfet/ ▶**n.** (pl. **fêtes cham·pê·tres** pronunc. same) an outdoor entertainment; a rural festival. [18th C.: Fr., literally 'rural festival.']

fe·ti·cide /ˈfētə,sīd/ ▶**n.** destruction or abortion of a fetus.

fet·id /ˈfetid; ˈfē-/ (Brit. also **foet·id**) ▶**adj.** smelling extremely unpleasant. — **fet·id·ly adv. fet·id·ness n.** [ME: from L. *fetidus,* from *fetere* 'to stink.']

fet·ish /ˈfetisH/ ▶**n.** an inanimate object worshiped for its supposed magical powers or because it is considered to be inhabited by a spirit. ■ a course of action to which one has an excessive and irrational commitment. ■ a form of sexual desire in which gratification is linked to an abnormal degree to a particular object, part of the body, etc. — **fet·ish·ism n. fet·ish·ist n. fet·ish·is·tic** /,fetiˈsHistik/ **adj.** [17th C. (originally denoting an object used by the peoples of West Africa as an amulet or charm): from Fr. *fétiche,* from Port. *feitiço* 'charm, sorcery.']

fet·ish·ize /ˈfeti,SHīz/ ▶**v.** [trans.] have an excessive and irrational commitment to (something). ■ make (something) the object of a sexual fetish. — **fet·ish·i·za·tion** /,fetisHiˈzāSHən/ **n.**

fet·lock /ˈfet,läk/ (also **fetlock joint**) ▶**n.** the joint of a horse's or other quadruped's leg between the cannon bone and the pastern. ■ the tuft of hair that grows at this joint. [ME: ult. of Gmc. origin; rel. to Ger. *Fessel* 'fetlock,' also to **FOOT**.]

fetlock

feto- ▶**comb. form** representing **FETUS**.

fe·tor /ˈfētər/ (Brit. also **foe·tor**) ▶**n.** a strong, foul smell. [15th C.: from L., from *fetere* 'to stink.' Cf. **FETID**.]

fet·ter /ˈfetər/ ▶**n.** (usu. **fetters**) a chain or manacle used to restrain a prisoner, typically placed around the ankles. ■ a restraint or check on someone's freedom, typically one considered unfair or overly restrictive. ▶**v.** [trans.] restrain with chains or manacles, typically around the ankles. ■ (often **be fettered**) restrict or restrain (someone) in an unfair or undesirable fashion: *fettered by tradition.* [OE *feter,* of Gmc. origin; rel. to Du. *veter* 'a lace,' from an Indo-Eur. root shared by **FOOT**.]

fet·tle /ˈfetl/ ▶**n.** condition, esp. physical; trim. ▶**v.** [trans.] trim or clean the rough edges of (a metal casting or a piece of pottery) before firing. — **fet·tler n.** [ME: from dial. *fettle* 'strip of material, girdle,' from OE *fetel,* of Gmc. origin; rel. to Ger. *Fessel* 'chain, band.']

fet·tuc·ci·ne /,fetəˈcHēnē/ (also **fet·tu·ci·ni**) ▶**n.** pasta made in ribbons. [from Ital., pl. of *fettucina,* dimin. of *fetta* 'slice, ribbon.']

fe·tus /ˈfētəs/ (Brit. (in nontechnical use) also **foe·tus**) ▶**n.** (pl. **-tus·es**) an unborn or unhatched offspring of a mammal, in particular an unborn human baby more than eight weeks after conception. [ME: from L., 'pregnancy, childbirth, offspring.']

feud /fyo͞od/ ▶**n.** a state of prolonged mutual hostility, typically between two families or communities, characterized by murderous assaults in revenge for previous injuries. ■ a prolonged and bitter quarrel or dispute. ▶**v.** [intrans.] take part in such a quarrel or violent conflict: *they have been feuding since the Civil War.* [ME *fede* 'hostility, ill will,' from OFr. *feide,* from MDu., Mid. Low Ger. *vēde,* of Gmc. origin; rel. to **FOE**.]

feud. ▶**abbr.** ■ feudal. ■ feudalism.

feu·dal /ˈfyo͞odl/ ▶**adj.** according to, resembling, or denoting the system of feudalism. ■ absurdly outdated or old-fashioned. — **feu·dal·i·za·tion** /,fyo͞odl-iˈzāSHən/ **n. feu·dal·ize v. feu·dal·ly adv.** [17th C.: from med. L. *feudalis,* from *feudum* (see **FEE**).]

feu·dal·ism /ˈfyo͞odl,izəm/ ▶**n.** hist. the dominant social system in medieval Europe, in which land granted by the Crown to the nobility was in turn held by vassals and worked by peasants, with each group owing homage and service to that above it. — **feu·dal·ist n. feu·dal·is·tic** /,fyo͞odlˈistik/ **adj.**

feu·dal·i·ty /fyo͞oˈdalitē/ ▶**n.** archaic the principles and practice of the feudal system.

feu·da·to·ry /ˈfyo͞odə,tôrē/ hist. ▶**adj.** owing feudal allegiance to: *they had for a long period been feudatory to the Norwegian Crown.* ▶**n.** (pl. **-ries**) a person who holds land under the conditions of the feudal system.

feud·ist /ˈfyo͞odist/ ▶**n.** a person taking part in a feud.

feuil·le·ton /ˈfoi-itn; ,fœyəˈtôN/ ▶**n.** a part of a newspaper or magazine devoted to fiction, criticism, or light literature. ■ an article printed in such a part. [19th C.: Fr., from *feuillet,* dimin. of *feuille* 'leaf.']

fe·ver /ˈfēvər/ ▶**n.** an abnormally high body temperature, usually accompanied by shivering, headache, and in severe instances, delirium. ■ a state of nervous excitement or agitation. ■ [with adj.] the excitement felt by a group of people about a particular event: *election fever.* [OE *fēfor,* from L. *febris.*]

fe·vered /ˈfēvərd/ ▶**adj.** having or showing the symptoms associated with a dangerously high temperature. ■ feeling or displaying an excessive degree of nervous excitement, agitation, or energy.

fe·ver·few /ˈfēvər,fyo͞o/ ▶**n.** a bushy aromatic plant (*Tanacetum parthenium*) of the daisy family, with feathery leaves and daisylike flowers. It is used in herbal medicine to treat headaches. [OE *feferfuge,* from L. *febrifuga,* from *febris* 'fever' + *fugare* 'drive away.' Cf. **FEBRIFUGE**.]

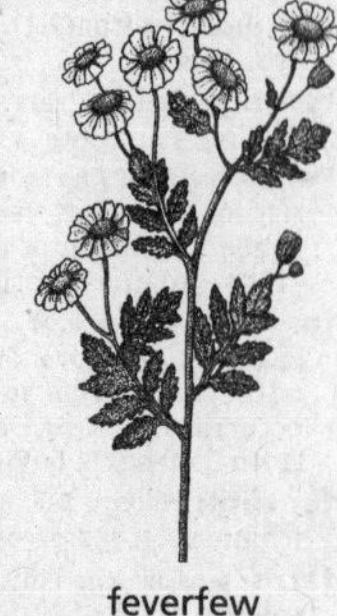
feverfew

fe·ver·ish /ˈfēv(ə)risH/ ▶**adj.** having or showing the symptoms of a fever. ■ displaying a frenetic excitement or energy. — **fe·ver·ish·ly adv. fe·ver·ish·ness n.**

fe·ver pitch ▶**n.** a state of extreme excitement.

few /fyo͞o/ ▶**adj. & pron. 1** (**a few**) a small number of: [as adj.] *may I ask a few questions?* | [as pron.] *I will recount a few of the stories told me.* **2** used to emphasize how small a number of people or things is: [as adj.] *he had few friends* | [as pron.] *few thought to ask.* ▶**n.** [as pl. n.] (**the few**) the minority of people; the elect: *a world that increasingly belongs to the few.*
– PHRASES **every few** once in every small group of (typically units of time): *she visits every few weeks.* **few and far between** scarce; infrequent. **have a few** informal drink enough alcohol to be slightly drunk. **no fewer than** used to emphasize a surprisingly large number. **not a few** a considerable number. [OE *fēawe, fēawa,* of Gmc. origin; rel. to Old High Ger. *fao,* from an Indo-Eur. root shared by L. *paucus* and Gk. *pauros* 'small.']

fey /fā/ ▶**adj.** giving an impression of vague unworldliness: *a strange, fey woman.* ■ having supernatural powers of clairvoyance. — **fey·ly adv. fey·ness n.** [OE *fǣge* (in the sense 'fated to die soon'), of Gmc. origin; rel. to Du. *veeg* and to Ger. *feige* 'cowardly.']

Feyn·man /ˈfīnmən/, Richard Phillips (1918–88), US physicist. He worked on quantum electrodynamics. Nobel Prize for Physics (1965, shared with Julian Schwinger 1918–94 and Sin-Itiro Tomonaga 1906–97).

Fez /fez/ (also **Fès** /fes/) a city in northern Morocco; pop. 564,000.

fez /fez/ ▶**n.** (pl. **fez·zes**) a flat-topped conical red hat with a black tassel on top, worn by men in some Muslim countries (formerly the Turkish national headdress). — **fezzed adj.** [19th C.: from Turk. *fes,* named after **FEZ**.]

fez

ff Music ▶**abbr.** fortissimo.

ff. ▶**abbr.** ■ folios. ■ following pages.

FFA ▶**abbr.** ■ Future Farmers of America.

FG ▶**abbr.** ■ Football & Basketball field goal. ■ fine grain.

FHA ▶**abbr.** ■ Federal Housing Administration. ■ Future Homemakers of America.

FHLBB ▶**abbr.** Federal Home Loan Bank Board.

f-hole /ˈef ,hōl/ ▶**n.** either of a pair of sound holes resembling an d and a reversed d in shape, cut in the front of some stringed musical instruments.

fi·a·cre /fēˈäkər; -kr(ə)/ ▶**n.** (pl. **-cres** /-kərz; -kr(ə)/) hist. a small four-wheeled carriage for public hire. [17th C.: from Fr., named after the Hôtel de St. *Fiacre* in Paris.]

fi·an·cé /,fēänˈsā; fēˈänsā/ ▶**n.** a man who is engaged to be married. [19th C.: from Fr., past part. of *fiancer* 'betroth,' from OFr. *fiance* 'a promise,' based on L. *fidere* 'to trust.']

fi·an·cée /,fēänˈsā; fēˈänsā/ ▶**n.** a woman who is engaged to be married. [19th C.: Fr., fem. of *fiancé.*]

fi·an·chet·to /,fēänˈcHetō; -ˈketō/ Chess ▶**n.** (pl. **-toes**) the development of a bishop by moving it one square to a long diagonal of the board.

▶ v. (-toes, -toed) [trans.] develop (a bishop) in such a way. [19th C.: from Ital., dimin. of *fianco* 'flank,' ult. of Gmc. origin.]

Fi·an·na Fáil /'fēənə 'foil/ one of the two main political parties of the Republic of Ireland. Larger and traditionally more republican than its rival Fine Gael, it was formed in 1926 by Eamon de Valera together with some of the moderate members of Sinn Fein. [Irish, from *fianna* 'band of warriors' and *Fáil*, genitive of *Fál*, an ancient name for Ireland.]

fi·as·co /fē'askō/ ▶ n. (pl. -cos) a thing that is a complete failure, esp. in a ludicrous or humiliating way. [19th C.: from Ital., literally 'bottle, flask.']

fi·at /'fēät; 'fēət/ ▶ n. a formal authorization or proposition; a decree. ■ an arbitrary order. [late ME: from L., 'let it be done,' from *fieri* 'be done or made.']

fi·at mon·ey ▶ n. inconvertible paper money made legal tender by a government decree.

fib /fib/ ▶ n. a lie, typically an unimportant one. ▶ v. (**fibbed, fib·bing**) [intrans.] tell such a lie. — **fib·ber** n. [16th C.: perh. a shortening of obs. *fible-fable* 'nonsense,' reduplication of FABLE.]

fi·ber /'fībər/ (Brit. **fi·bre**) ▶ n. **1** a thread or filament formed from a vegetable tissue, mineral substance, or textile. ■ a substance formed of such threads or filaments. ■ a threadlike structure forming part of the muscular, nervous, connective, or other tissue in the human or animal body. ■ fig. strength of character. **2** dietary material containing substances which are resistant to the action of digestive enzymes. — **fi·bered** adj. [in comb.] *natural-fibered.* [ME: via Fr. from L. *fibra* 'fiber, filament, entrails.']

fi·ber·board /'fībər,bôrd/ (Brit. **fi·bre·board**) ▶ n. a building material made of wood or other plant fibers compressed into boards.

fi·ber·fill /'fībər,fil/ ▶ n. synthetic material used for padding and insulation in garments, cushions, etc.

fi·ber·glass /'fībər,glas/ (Brit. **fi·bre·glass**) (also trademark **Fi·ber·glas**) ▶ n. **1** a reinforced plastic material composed of glass fibers embedded in a resin matrix. **2** a woollike mass of glass filaments, used in insulation. **3** a textile fabric made from woven glass filaments.

fi·ber op·tics ▶ plural n. [treated as sing.] the use of thin flexible fibers of glass or other transparent solids to transmit light signals, chiefly for telecommunications or for internal examination of the body. ■ [treated as pl.] the fibers and associated devices so used. — **fi·ber-op·tic** adj.

fi·ber·scope /'fībər,skōp/ (Brit. **fi·bre·scope**) ▶ n. a fiber-optic device for viewing inaccessible internal structures, esp. in the human body.

Fi·bo·nac·ci /,fēbə'näCHē/, Leonardo (*c.*1170–*c.*1250), Italian mathematician; known as **Fibonacci of Pisa**. He pioneered number theory and indeterminate analysis, discovering the Fibonacci series.

Fi·bo·nac·ci se·ries (also **Fibonacci sequence**) ▶ n. Math. a series of numbers in which each number (**Fibonacci number**) is the sum of the two preceding numbers. The simplest is the series 1, 1, 2, 3, 5, 8, etc.

fi·bre ▶ n. British spelling of FIBER.

fi·bril /'fībrəl; 'fib-/ ▶ n. tech. a small or slender fiber. — **fi·bril·lar** /-lər/ adj. **fi·bril·lar·y** /-,lerē/ adj. [17th C.: from mod. L. *fibrilla*, dimin. of L. *fibra* (see FIBER).]

fi·bril·late /'fibrə,lāt/ ▶ v. [intrans.] **1** (of a muscle, esp. in the heart) make a quivering movement due to uncoordinated contraction of the individual fibrils. **2** (of a fiber) split up into fibrils. ■ [trans.] break (a fiber) into fibrils. — **fi·bril·la·tion** /,fibrə'lāSHən/ n.

fi·brin /'fībrin/ ▶ n. Biochem. an insoluble protein formed from fibrinogen during the clotting of blood. — **fi·brin·oid** /'fībrə,noid; 'fib-/ adj. **fi·brin·ous** /'fībrənəs; 'fib-/ adj. [19th C.: from FIBER + -IN[1].]

fi·brin·o·gen /fī'brinəjən/ ▶ n. Biochem. a soluble protein present in blood plasma, from which fibrin is produced by the action of the enzyme thrombin. — **fi·brin·o·gen·ic** /,fībrənō'jenik/ adj.

fi·bri·nol·y·sis /,fībrə'näləsis/ ▶ n. Physiol. the enzymatic breakdown of the fibrin in blood clots. — **fi·bri·no·lyt·ic** /'fībrənə'litik/ adj.

fibro- ▶ comb. form of, relating to, or characterized by fibers: *fibroblast* | *fibroma.* [from L. *fibra* 'fiber.']

fi·bro·blast /'fībrə,blast; 'fib-/ ▶ n. Physiol. a cell in connective tissue that produces collagen and other fibers.

fi·broid /'fībroid/ ▶ adj. of or characterized by fibers or fibrous tissue. ▶ n. Med. a benign tumor of muscular and fibrous tissues, typically developing in the wall of the uterus.

fi·bro·in /'fībrō-in; 'fib-/ ▶ n. a protein that is the chief constituent of silk and spider webs. [19th C.: from FIBRO- + -IN[1].]

fi·bro·ma /fī'brōmə/ ▶ n. (pl. **-mas** or **-ma·ta** /-mətə/) Med. a benign fibrous tumor of connective tissue. [19th C.: from L. *fibra* (see FIBER) + -OMA.]

fi·bro·my·al·gia /,fībrōmī'alj(ē)ə/ ▶ n. a chronic disorder characterized by widespread musculoskeletal pain, fatigue, and tenderness in localized areas.

fi·bro·sis /fī'brōsis/ ▶ n. Med. the thickening and scarring of connective tissue, usually as a result of injury. — **fi·brot·ic** /fī'brätik/ adj. [19th C.: from L. *fibra* (see FIBER) + -OSIS.]

fi·bro·si·tis /,fībrə'sītis/ ▶ n. Med. inflammation of fibrous connective tissue. — **fi·bro·sit·ic** /-'sitik/ adj.

fi·brous /'fībrəs/ ▶ adj. consisting of or characterized by fibers. — **fi·brous·ly** adv. **fi·brous·ness** n.

fib·u·la /'fibyələ/ ▶ n. (pl. **-lae** /-,lē; -,lī/ or **-las**) **1** Anat. the outer and usually smaller of the two bones between the knee and the ankle in humans (or the equivalent joints in other terrestrial vertebrates), parallel with the tibia. **2** Archaeol. a brooch or clasp. — **fib·u·lar** /-lər/ adj. [16th C.: from L., 'brooch,' perhaps related to *figere* 'to fix.']

-fic (usu. as **-ific**) ▶ suffix (forming adjectives) producing; making: *prolific* | *soporific.* — **-fically** suffix forming corresponding adverbs. [from Fr. *-fique* or L. *-ficus* from *facere* 'do, make.']

FICA ▶ abbr. Federal Insurance Contributions Act.

-fication (usu. as **-ification**) ▶ suffix forming nouns of action from verbs ending in *-fy*. [from Fr., or from L. *-fication-* (from verbs ending in *-ficare*).]

fiche /fēSH/ ▶ n. short for MICROFICHE.

Fich·te /'fiktə/, Johann Gottlieb (1762–1814), German philosopher. He postulated that the world is posited by the ego in defining and delimiting itself.

fich·u /'fishōō; 'fē-/ ▶ n. a small triangular shawl, worn around a woman's shoulders and neck. [18th C.: from Fr., from *ficher* 'to fix, pin.']

fick·le /'fikəl/ ▶ adj. changing frequently, esp. as regards one's loyalties, interests, or affection. — **fick·le·ness** n. **fick·ly** adv. [OE *ficol* 'deceitful,' of Gmc. origin.]

fict. ▶ abbr. ■ fiction. ■ fictitious.

fic·tile /'fiktl; -,tīl/ ▶ adj. made of earth or clay by a potter. ■ of or relating to pottery or its manufacture. ■ capable of being molded; plastic. [17th C.: from L. *fictilis*, from *fict-* 'formed, contrived,' from the v. *fingere*.]

fic·tion /'fikSHən/ ▶ n. prose literature, esp. short stories and novels, about imaginary events and people. ■ invention or fabrication as opposed to fact. ■ [in sing.] a belief or statement that is false, but that is often held to be true because it is expedient to do so. — **fic·tion·al** /-SHənl/ adj. **fic·tion·al·i·ty** /,fikSHə'nalətē/ n. **fic·tion·al·i·za·tion** /,fikSHənl-ə'zāSHən/ n. **fic·tion·al·ize** v. **fic·tion·al·ly** adv. **fic·tion·ist** n. [ME: via OFr. from L. *fictio(n-)*, from *fingere* 'form, contrive.']

fic·ti·tious /fik'tiSHəs/ ▶ adj. not real or true, being imaginary or having been fabricated. ■ of, relating to, or denoting the imaginary characters and events found in fiction. — **fic·ti·tious·ly** adv. **fic·ti·tious·ness** n. [17th C.: from L. *ficticius* (from *fingere* 'contrive, form').]

fic·tive /'fiktiv/ ▶ adj. creating or created by imagination: *the novel's fictive universe.* — **fic·tive·ness** n.

fi·cus /'fīkəs/ ▶ n. (pl. same) a chiefly tropical tree, shrub, or climbing plant of a large genus (*Ficus*) in the mulberry family that includes the figs and the rubber plant. [19th C.: from L., 'fig, fig tree.']

fid /fid/ ▶ n. Naut. a thick peg, wedge, or supporting pin, in particular: ■ a square wooden or iron bar that supports a topmast. ■ a conical pin or spike used in splicing rope. [17th C.: of unknown origin.]

fid. ▶ abbr. fiduciary.

fid·dle /'fidl/ ▶ n. **1** informal a violin, esp. when used to play folk music. **2** Naut. a contrivance, such as a raised rim, that prevents things from falling off a table in bad weather. ▶ v. informal**1** [intrans.] play the fiddle: *he fiddled with the band* | (**fiddling**) *lots of fiddling and banjo playing.* ■ [trans.] play (a tune) on the fiddle. **2** [intrans.] touch or fidget with something in a restless or nervous way: *Laura fiddled with her cup.* ■ tinker with something: *never fiddle with an electric machine that's plugged in.* ■ (**fiddle around**) pass time aimlessly.
– PHRASES **(as) fit as a fiddle** in good health. **play second fiddle to** take a subordinate role to someone or something in a way often considered demeaning. [OE *fithele*, denoting a violin or similar instrument, based on L. *vitulari* 'celebrate a festival, be joyful,' perh. from *Vitula*, a Roman goddess.]

fid·dle·back /'fidl,bak/ ▶ n. **1** [usu. as adj.] a thing shaped like the back of a violin, with the sides deeply curved inward, in particular the back of a chair. **2** a rippled effect in the grain of fine wood, often exploited when making the backs of violins. **3** (also **fiddleback spider**) another term for BROWN RECLUSE.

fid·dle-de-dee /,fidl dē 'dē/ ▶ n. [often as exclam.] dated nonsense. [18th C.: from FIDDLE + a reduplication without meaning.]

fid·dle-fad·dle /'fidl ,fadl/ ▶ n. trivial matters: nonsense. ▶ v. [intrans.] bother with trifles; fuss: *no time to fiddle-faddle.* [16th C.: reduplication of FIDDLE.]

fid·dle·head /'fidl,hed/ ▶ n. **1** (also **fiddlehead fern**) the young, curled, edible frond of certain ferns. **2** a scroll-like carving at a ship's bow.

fid·dler /'fidlər; 'fidl-ər/ ▶ n. informal a person who plays the violin, esp. one who plays folk music.

fid·dler crab ▶ n. a small amphibious crab (genus *Uca*, family Ocypodidae), the males of which have one greatly enlarged claw that they wave in territorial display and courtship.

fid·dle·stick /'fidl,stik/ ▶ exclam. (**fiddlesticks**) nonsense. ▶ n. informal a violin bow.

fid·dling /'fidliNG; 'fidl-iNG/ ▶ adj. annoyingly trivial or petty.

fi·de·ism /'fēdā,izəm/ ▶ n. the doctrine that knowledge depends on faith or revelation. — **fi·de·ist** n. **fi·de·is·tic** /,fēdā'istik/ adj. [19th C.: from L. *fides* 'faith' + -ISM.]

fi·del·i·ty /fə'delitē/ ▶ n. faithfulness to a person, cause, or belief, demonstrated by continuing loyalty and support. ■ sexual faithfulness to a spouse or partner. ■ the degree of exactness with which something is

PRONUNCIATION KEY ə *ago, up*; ər *over, fur*; a *hat*; ā *ate*; ä *car*; e *let*; ē *see*; i *fit*; ī *by*; NG *sing*; ō *go*; ô *law, for*; oi *toy*; ŏŏ *good*; ōō *goo*; ou *out*; TH *thin*; T͟H *then*; ZH *vision*

copied or reproduced. [ME: from OFr. *fidelite* or L. *fidelitas*, from *fidelis* 'faithful,' from *fides* 'faith.' Cf. FEALTY.]

fidg·et /'fijit/ ▶v. (**fidg·et·ed, fidg·et·ing**) [intrans.] make small movements, esp. of the hands and feet, through nervousness or impatience. ■ [trans.] make (someone) uneasy or uncomfortable: *she fidgets me with her never-ending cleaning.* ▶n. a quick, small movement, typically a repeated one, caused by nervousness or impatience. ■ a person given to such movements, esp. one whom other people find irritating. ■ (usu. **fidgets**) a state of mental or physical restlessness or uneasiness. —**fidg·et·er** n. **fidg·et·i·ness** /'fijitēnis/ n. **fidg·et·y** /'fijitē/ adj. [17th C.: from obs. or dial. *fidge* 'to twitch'; perh. rel. to ON *fikja* 'move briskly, be restless or eager.']

fi·du·cial /fə'do͞oSHəl/ ▶adj. tech. (esp. of a point or line) assumed as a fixed basis of comparison.

fi·du·ci·ar·y /fə'do͞oSHē,erē; -SHərē/ ▶adj. Law involving trust, esp. with regard to the relationship between a trustee and a beneficiary. ■ archaic held or given in trust. ■ Finance (of a paper currency) depending for its value on securities (as opposed to gold) or the reputation of the issuer. ▶n. (pl. **-ar·ies**) a trustee. [16th C.: from L. *fiduciarius*, from *fiducia* 'trust,' from *fidere* 'to trust.']

fie /fī/ ▶exclam. archaic humorous used to express disgust or outrage: *fie on those boors!* [ME: via OFr. from L. *fi*.]

Fied·ler /'fēdlər/, Arthur (1894–1979), US conductor. He conducted the Boston Pops Orchestra 1930–74.

fief /fēf/ ▶n. **1** hist. an estate of land, esp. one held on condition of feudal service. **2** a person's sphere of operation or control. [17th C.: from Fr. (see FEE).]

fief·dom /'fēfdəm/ ▶n. a fief.

Field[1] /fēld/, Marshall (1834–1906), US merchant and philanthropist. In 1881, he organized Marshall Field & Co., which became the largest retail store in the world.

Field[2], Stephen Johnson (1816–99), US Supreme Court associate justice 1863–97.

field /fēld/ ▶n. **1** an area of open land, esp. one planted with crops or pasture. ■ a piece of land used for a particular purpose, esp. an area marked out for a game or sport. ■ Baseball defensive play or the defensive positions collectively. ■ a large area of land or water completely covered in a particular substance, esp. snow or ice. ■ an area rich in a natural product, typically oil or gas. ■ an area on which a battle is fought. ■ an area on a flag with a single background color. ■ a place where a subject of scientific study or artistic representation can be observed in its natural location or context. **2** a particular branch of study or sphere of activity or interest. ■ Comput. a part of a record, representing an item of data. ■ a space or range within which objects are visible from a particular viewpoint or through a piece of apparatus: *the telescope's field of view.* See also FIELD OF VISION. ■ Heraldry the surface of an escutcheon or of one of its divisions. **3** (usu. **the field**) all the participants in a contest or sport. **4** Physics the region in which a particular condition prevails, esp. one in which a force or influence is effective regardless of the presence or absence of a material medium. ■ the force exerted or potentially exerted in such an area. ■ Math. a system subject to two binary operations analogous to those for the multiplication and addition of real numbers, and having similar commutative and distributive laws. ▶v. **1** [intrans.] Baseball play as a fielder. ■ [trans.] catch or stop (the ball). **2** [trans.] send out (a team or individual) to play in a game: *a school that fielded mediocre teams.* ■ (of a political party) put up (a candidate) to stand in an election. ■ deploy (an army). **3** [trans.] deal with (a difficult question, telephone call, etc.). ▶adj. [attrib.] carried out or working in the natural environment, rather than in a laboratory or office. ■ (of an employee or work) away from the home office; remote. ■ (of military equipment) light and mobile for use on campaign. ■ used in names of animals or plants found in the open country, rather than among buildings or as cultivated varieties. ■ denoting a game played outdoors on a marked field.

– PHRASES **in the field** on campaign; (while) engaged in combat or maneuvers. ■ away from the laboratory or studio; engaged in practical work in a natural environment. ■ (of an employee) away from the home office; working while traveling. **play the field** informal indulge in a series of sexual relationships without committing oneself to anyone. **take the field** (of a sports team) go onto a field to begin a game. ■ Baseball begin one's turn on defense in an inning. ■ start a military campaign. [OE *feld*, of West Gmc. origin; rel. to Ger. *Feld*.]

field corn ▶n. corn grown to feed livestock.

field·craft /'fēld ,kraft/ ▶n. the techniques involved in living, traveling, or making military or scientific observations in the field, esp. while remaining undetected.

field crick·et ▶n. a cricket that lives in a burrow in grassland and has a musical birdlike chirp.

field day ▶n. **1** Mil. a review or an exercise, esp. in maneuvering. **2** a day devoted to athletic contests or other sporting events, typically at a school. **3** [in sing.] an opportunity for action, success, or excitement, esp. at the expense of others: *shoplifters are having a field day in the store.*

field cricket

field-ef·fect tran·sis·tor (abbr.: **FET**) ▶n. Electron. a transistor in which most current is carried along a channel whose effective resistance can be controlled by a transverse electric field.

field·er /'fēldər/ ▶n. Baseball Cricket a player who occupies a defensive position in the field while the other side is batting.

field·er's choice ▶n. Baseball a play in which the fielding team's decision to put out another player allows the batter to reach first base safely.

field e·vents ▶plural n. track-and-field contests other than races, such as throwing and jumping events. Compare with TRACK EVENTS.

field·fare /'fēld,fe(ə)r/ ▶n. a large migratory thrush (*Turdus pilaris*) with a gray head, breeding in northern Eurasia. [OE *feldefare*, perh. from *feld* 'field' + the base of *faran* 'to travel' (see FARE).]

field glass·es ▶plural n. binoculars for outdoor use.

field goal ▶n. **1** Football a goal scored by a placekick, scoring three points. **2** Basketball a basket scored while the clock is running and the ball is in play.

field-grade of·fi·cer ▶n. Mil.a major, lieutenant colonel, or colonel.

field guide ▶n. a book for the identification of birds, flowers, minerals, etc. in their natural environment.

field hand ▶n. a person employed as a farm laborer.

field hock·ey ▶n. a game played between two teams of eleven players who use hooked sticks to drive a small hard ball toward goals at opposite ends of a field.

field hol·ler ▶n. see HOLLER.

field hos·pi·tal ▶n. a temporary hospital set up near a combat zone to provide emergency care.

field house ▶n. a building usually adjacent to an athletic field and equipped with changing rooms, lockers, showers, etc.

Field·ing /'fēldiNG/, Henry (1707–54), English writer. His novels include *Joseph Andrews* (1742) and *Tom Jones* (1749).

field lens ▶n. in a multiple lens optical system, the lens farthest from the eye.

field mark ▶n. a visible mark or characteristic used in identifying a bird or other animal in the field.

field mar·shal ▶n. an officer of the highest rank in the British and other armies.

field mouse ▶n. a dark brown mouse (genus *Apodemus*) with a long tail and large eyes.

field mush·room ▶n. another term for CHAMPIGNON.

field of·fi·cer ▶n. another term for FIELD-GRADE OFFICER.

field of hon·or ▶n. the place where a duel or battle is fought.

field of vi·sion ▶n. the entire area that a person or animal is able to see when their eyes are fixed in one position.

field pea ▶n. a pea plant of a variety grown chiefly for fodder or as green manure.

field·stone /'fēld,stōn/ ▶n. [often as adj.] stone used in its natural form.

field test ▶n. a test carried out in the environment in which a product or device is to be used. ▶v. (**field-test**) [trans.] test (something) in the environment in such a way.

field the·o·ry ▶n. Physics a theory that explains physical phenomena in terms of a field and the manner in which it interacts with matter or with other fields.

field tri·al ▶n. **1** a field test. **2** a competition for hunting dogs to test their levels of skill and training in retrieving or pointing.

field trip ▶n. a trip made by students or research workers to study something at first hand.

field·work /'fēld,wərk/ ▶n. practical work conducted by a researcher in the natural environment, rather than in a laboratory or office. —**field·work·er** n.

fiend /fēnd/ ▶n. an evil spirit or demon. ■ (**the fiend**) archaic the Devil. ■ a wicked or cruel person. ■ a person causing mischief or annoyance. ■ informal a person who is excessively fond of or addicted to something. [OE *fēond* 'an enemy, the devil, a demon,' of Gmc. origin; rel. to Du. *vijand* and Ger. *Feind* 'enemy.']

fiend·ish /'fēndiSH/ ▶adj. extremely cruel or unpleasant; devilish. ■ extremely awkward or complex. —**fiend·ish·ly** adv. **fiend·ish·ness** n.

fierce /fi(ə)rs/ ▶adj. (**fierc·er, fierc·est**) having or displaying an intense or ferocious aggressiveness. ■ (of a feeling, emotion, or action) showing a heartfelt and powerful intensity. ■ (of the weather) powerful and destructive.

– PHRASES **something fierce** informal to a great and almost overwhelming extent: *he missed me something fierce.* —**fierce·ly** adv. **fierce·ness** n. [ME: from OFr. *fiers* 'fierce, brave, proud,' from L. *ferus* 'untamed.']

fier·y /'fī(ə)rē/ ▶adj. (**fier·i·er, fier·i·est**) consisting of fire or burning strongly and brightly. ■ having the bright color of fire. ■ (of a person) having a passionate, quick-tempered nature. ■ (of behavior or words) passionately angry and deeply felt. —**fier·i·ly** /'fī(ə)rəlē/ adv. **fier·i·ness** n. [ME: from FIRE.]

fier·y cross ▶n. a burning wooden cross used as a symbol by the Ku Klux Klan. ■ hist. a wooden cross, charred and dipped in blood, used among Scottish clans to summon men to battle.

fi·es·ta /fē'estə/ ▶n. (in Spanish-speaking regions) a religious festival. ■ an event marked by festivities or celebration. [Sp., from L. *festum*, (pl.) *festa* (see FEAST).]

fife /fīf/ ▶n. a kind of small shrill flute used esp. with the drum in military bands. —**fif·er** n. [16th C.: from Ger. *Pfeife* 'pipe,' or from Fr. *fifre*, from Swiss Ger. *Pfifre* 'piper.']

fife

fife rail (also **fife-rail**) ▶ **n.** esp. hist. a rail around the mainmast of a sailing ship, holding belaying pins. [18th C.: of unknown origin.]

FIFO /ˈfīˌfō/ ▶ **abbr.** first in, first out (chiefly with reference to methods of stock valuation and data storage). Compare with **LIFO**.

fif·teen /fifˈtēn; ˈfifˌtēn/ ▶ **cardinal number** equivalent to the product of three and five; one more than fourteen, or five more than ten; 15. (Roman numeral: **xv** or **XV**.) ■ fifteen years old. [OE *fiftēne, fiftīene* (see FIVE, -TEEN).]

fif·teenth /fifˈtēnTH; ˈfifˌtēnTH/ ▶ **ordinal number** constituting number fifteen in a sequence; 15th. ■ (**a fifteenth/one fifteenth**) each of fifteen equal parts into which something is or may be divided.

fifth /fifTH/ ▶ **ordinal number** constituting number five in a sequence; 5th. ■ (**a fifth/one fifth**) each of five equal parts into which something is or may be divided. ■ the fifth finisher or position in a race or competition. ■ (in some vehicles) the fifth (and typically highest) in a sequence of gears. ■ fifthly (used to introduce a fifth point or reason). ■ Music an interval spanning five consecutive notes in a diatonic scale, in particular (also **perfect fifth**) an interval of three whole steps and a half step (e.g., C to G). ■ Music the note that is higher by such an interval than the root of a diatonic scale. ■ (**a fifth of**) a fifth of a gallon, as a measure of liquor, or a bottle of this capacity. ■ the fifth grade of a school.
– PHRASES **take the Fifth** exercise the right guaranteed by the Fifth Amendment to the US Constitution of refusing to answer questions in order to avoid incriminating oneself. — **fifth·ly adv.** [OE: *fifta.*]

fifth col·umn ▶ **n.** a group within a country at war who are sympathetic to or working for its enemies. — **fifth col·umn·ist n.** [from the Spanish Civil War, when General Mola, leading four columns of troops toward Madrid, declared that he had a fifth column inside the city.]

fifth-gen·er·a·tion ▶ **adj.** denoting a proposed new class of computer or programming language employing artificial intelligence.

Fifth Re·pub·lic the republican regime established in France in 1958.

fifth wheel ▶ **n. 1** an extra wheel for a four-wheeled vehicle. ■ informal a superfluous person or thing. **2** a coupling between a trailer and a vehicle used for towing. ■ (also **fifth-wheel trailer**) a trailer with accommodations for camping out. ■ hist. a horizontal turntable over the front axle of a carriage as an extra support to prevent its tipping.

fif·ty /ˈfiftē/ ▶ **cardinal number** (pl. **-ties**) the number equivalent to the product of five and ten; half of one hundred; 50. (Roman numeral: **l** or **L**.) ■ (**fifties**) the numbers from 50 to 59, esp. the years of a century or of a person's life. ■ fifty years old. ■ fifty miles an hour. — **fif·ti·eth** /ˈfiftēiTH/ **ordinal number fif·ty·fold adj. & adv.** [OE *fiftig* (see FIVE, -TY²).]

fif·ty-fif·ty ▶ **adj.** the same in share or proportion; equal. ▶ **adv.** equally; half and half: *they divided the spoils fifty-fifty.*

fig /fig/ ▶ **n. 1** a soft pear-shaped fruit with sweet dark flesh and many small seeds, eaten fresh or dried. **2** (also **figtree**) the deciduous Old World tree or shrub (*Ficus carica*) of the mulberry family that bears this fruit. ■ used in names of other plants of this genus, or in names of nonrelated plants that bear a similar fruit. [ME: from OFr. *figue*, from Provençal *fig(u)a*, based on L. *ficus*.]

fig. ▶ **abbr.** figure: *see fig.34.*

fight /fīt/ ▶ **v.** (past and past part. **fought**) [intrans.] take part in a violent struggle involving the exchange of physical blows or the use of weapons. ■ [trans.] engage in (a war or battle). ■ quarrel or argue. ■ [trans.] struggle to put out (a fire, esp. a large one). ■ [trans.] endeavor vigorously to win (an election or other contest). ■ campaign determinedly for or against something. ■ [trans.] struggle or campaign against (something). ■ [trans.] attempt to repress (a feeling or an expression of a feeling): *she had to fight back tears.* ■ [trans.] take part in a boxing match against (an opponent). ■ (**fight one's way**) move forward with difficulty, esp. by pushing through a crowd or overcoming physical obstacles: *fight his way across the room.* ▶ **n.** a violent confrontation or struggle. ■ a boxing match. ■ a battle or war. ■ a vigorous struggle or campaign for or against something. ■ an argument or quarrel. ■ the inclination or ability to fight or struggle.
– PHRASES **fight fire with fire** use the weapons or tactics of one's enemy or opponent, even if one finds them distasteful. **fight or flight** the instinctive physiological response to a threatening situation, which readies one either to resist forcibly or to run away. **put up a fight** offer resistance to an attack.
– PHRASAL VERBS **fight back** counterattack or retaliate. **fight it out** settle a dispute by fighting or competing aggressively. **fight someone/something off** defend oneself against an attack by someone or something. [OE *feohtan* (v.), *feoht(e)*, *gefeoht* (n.), of West Gmc. origin; rel. to Ger. *fechten, Gefecht.*]

fight·er /ˈfītər/ ▶ **n. 1** a person or animal that fights, esp. as a soldier or a boxer. ■ a person who does not easily admit defeat in spite of difficulties or opposition. **2** a fast military aircraft designed for attacking other aircraft.

fight·er-bomb·er ▶ **n.** an aircraft serving as both a fighter and bomber.

fight·ing chance ▶ **n.** a possibility of success if great effort is made.

fight·ing fish (also **Siamese fighting fish**) ▶ **n.** a small Thai labyrinth fish (*Betta splendens*, family Belontiidae), the males of which fight vigorously. It has been bred in a variety of colors, esp. for aquariums.

fight·ing words ▶ **plural n.** informal words indicating a willingness to fight or challenge someone. ■ words expressing an insult, esp. of an ethnic, racial, or sexist nature.

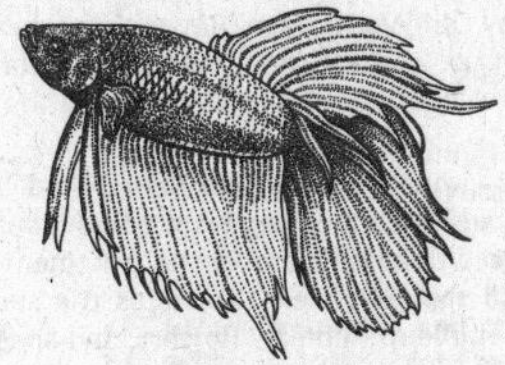
fighting fish

fig leaf ▶ **n.** a leaf of a fig tree, often depicted as concealing the genitals in paintings and sculpture. ■ fig. a thing designed to conceal a difficulty or embarrassment.

fig·ment /ˈfigmənt/ ▶ **n.** a thing that someone believes to be real but that exists only in their imagination. [ME: from L. *figmentum*, rel. to *fingere* 'form, contrive.']

fig·ur·al /ˈfigyərəl/ ▶ **adj. 1** another term for FIGURATIVE (sense 1). **2** Art another term for FIGURATIVE (sense 2).

fig·u·rant /ˈfigyərənt; ˌfigyəˈränt/ ▶ **n.** (fem. **fig·u·ran·te** /ˌfigyəˈräntē; -ˈränt/) a supernumerary actor.

fig·u·ra·tion /ˌfigyəˈrāSHən/ ▶ **n. 1** ornamentation by means of figures or designs. ■ Music use of florid counterpoint. **2** allegorical representation.

fig·ur·a·tive /ˈfigyərətiv/ ▶ **adj. 1** departing from a literal use of words; metaphorical. **2** (of an artist or work of art) representing forms that are recognizably derived from life. — **fig·ur·a·tive·ly adv. fig·ur·a·tive·ness n.**

fig·ure /ˈfigyər/ ▶ **n. 1** a number, esp. one that forms part of official statistics or relates to the financial performance of a company. ■ a numerical symbol, esp. any of the ten in Arabic notation. ■ one of a specified number of digits making up a larger number, used to give a rough idea of the order of magnitude: [in comb.] *a six-figure salary.* ■ an amount of money. ■ (**figures**) arithmetical calculations. **2** a person's bodily shape, esp. that of a woman and when considered to be attractive. ■ a person seen indistinctly, esp. at a distance: *a backpacked figure.* ■ a person of a particular kind, esp. one who is important or distinctive in some way: *a cult figure.* ■ a representation of a human or animal form in drawing or sculpture. **3** a shape defined by one or more lines in two dimensions (such as a circle or a triangle), or one or more surfaces in three dimensions (such as a sphere or a cuboid). ■ a diagram or illustrative drawing, esp. in a book or magazine. ■ Figure Skating a movement or series of movements following a prescribed pattern. ■ a pattern formed by the movements of a group of people, for example in square dancing or synchronized swimming. **4** Music a short succession of notes producing a single impression. **5** Logic the form of a syllogism, classified according to the position of the middle term. ▶ **v.** [intrans.] **1** be a significant and noticeable part of something: *nuclear policy figured prominently in the talks.* ■ (of a person) play a significant role in a situation or event. **2** [trans.] calculate or work out (an amount or value) arithmetically. **3** informal think, consider, or expect to be the case. ■ (of a recent event or newly discovered fact) be logical and unsurprising: *well, that figured.* **4** [trans.] represent (something) in a diagram or picture. ■ [usu. as adj.] (**figured**) embellish (something) with a pattern: *figured linoleum.*
– PHRASES **figure of speech** a word or phrase used in a nonliteral sense to add rhetorical force to a spoken or written passage.
– PHRASAL VERBS **figure on** informal count or rely on something happening or being the case in the future. **figure something out** informal solve or discover the cause of a problem. **figure someone out** reach an understanding of a person's actions, motives, or personality. [ME: from OFr. *figure* (n.), *figurer* (v.), from L. *figura* 'shape, figure, form'; rel. to *fingere* 'form, contrive.']

fig·ured bass ▶ **n.** Music a bass line with the intended harmonies indicated by figures rather than written out as chords, typical of continuo parts in baroque music.

fig·ure eight ▶ **n.** an object or movement having the shape of the number eight.

fig·ure·head /ˈfigyərˌhed/ ▶ **n. 1** a nominal leader or head without real power. **2** a carving, typically a bust or a full-length figure, set at the prow of an old-fashioned sailing ship.

fig·ure skat·ing ▶ **n.** the competitive sport of ice skating in prescribed patterns and choreographed free skating. — **fig·ure skat·er n.**

fig·ur·ine /ˌfigyəˈrēn/ ▶ **n.** a statuette, esp. one of a human form. [19th C.: from Fr., from Ital. *figurina*, dimin. of *figura*, from L. *figura* (see FIGURE).]

figurehead 2

PRONUNCIATION KEY ə *ago, up*; ər *over, fur*; a *hat*; ā *ate*; ä *car*; e *let*; ē *see*; i *fit*; ī *by*; NG *sing*; ō *go*; ô *law, for*; oi *toy*; o͝o *good*; o͞o *goo*; ou *out*; TH *thin*; T͟H *then*; ZH *vision*

fig wasp ▶ **n.** a tiny Old World wasp (*Blastophaga psenes*, family Agaonidae) that lays its eggs inside the flower of the wild fig. It was introduced into the New World to effect cross-fertilization of the cultivated fig.

fig·wort /'fig,wərt; -,wôrt/ ▶ **n.** a widely distributed herbaceous plant (genus *Scrophularia*) with purplish-brown two-lobed flowers. It was formerly considered to be effective in the treatment of scrofula. The **figwort family** (Scrophulariaceae) includes the snapdragons, toadflaxes, foxgloves, mulleins, monkey flowers, and speedwells. [16th C.: from obs. *fig* 'piles' + WORT.]

Fi·ji /'fējē/ a republic in the South Pacific. *See box.*

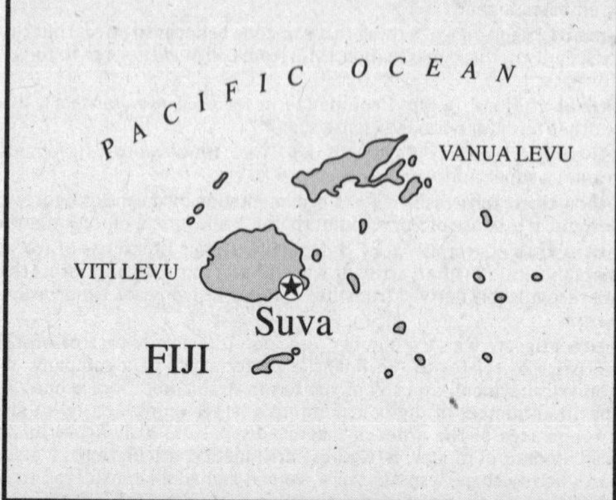

Fiji

Official name: Republic of the Fiji Islands
Location: south Pacific Ocean, consisting of a group of more than 800 islands, of which about 100 are inhabited
Area: 7,100 square miles (18,300 sq km)
Population: 800,000
Capital: Suva
Languages: English (official), Fijian, Hindi
Currency: Fijian dollar

Fi·ji·an /,fējēən; fi'jēən/ ▶ **adj.** of or relating to Fiji, its people, or its language. ▶ **n.** **1** a native or national of Fiji, or a person of Fijian descent. **2** the Austronesian language of the indigenous people of Fiji.

fil·a·gree /'filə,grē/ ▶ **n.** var. of FILIGREE.

fil·a·ment /'filəmənt/ ▶ **n.** a slender threadlike object or fiber, esp. one found in animal or plant structures. ■ a conducting wire or thread with a high melting point, forming part of an electric bulb or vacuum tube and heated or made incandescent by an electric current. ■ Bot. the slender part of a stamen that supports the anther. — **fil·a·men·ta·ry** /,filə'ment(ə)rē/ **adj.** **fil·a·ment·ed adj.** **fil·a·men·tous** /-,mentəs/ **adj.** [16th C.: from Fr., or from mod. L. *filamentum*, from late L. *filare* 'to spin,' from L. *filum* 'thread.']

fi·lar·i·a /fə'le(ə)rēə/ ▶ **n.** (pl. **-lar·i·ae** /-'le(ə)rē,ē; -ē,ī/) a threadlike parasitic nematode (superfamily Filarioidea, class Phasmida) transmitted by biting flies and mosquitoes, causing filariasis and related diseases. — **fi·lar·i·al** /-'le(ə)rēəl/ **adj.** [19th C.: from mod. L. *Filaria* (former genus name), from L. *filum* 'thread.']

fil·a·ri·a·sis /,filə'rīəsəs/ ▶ **n.** Med. a tropical disease caused by the presence of filarial worms, esp. in the lymph vessels.

fil·a·ture /'filəcHər; -,cHŏŏr/ ▶ **n.** the process of obtaining silk thread from silkworm cocoons. ■ an establishment where such activity takes place. [18th C.: from Fr., from Ital. *filatura*, from *filare* 'to spin.']

fil·bert /'filbərt/ ▶ **n.** **1** a cultivated hazel tree (genus *Corylus*) that bears edible oval nuts. ■ the nut of this tree. **2** (also **filbert brush**) a brush with bristles forming a flattened oval head, used in oil painting. [ME *fylberd*, from Anglo-Norman Fr. *philbert*, dial. Fr. *noix de filbert* (named after *St. Philibert*).]

filch /filcH/ ▶ **v.** [trans.] informal pilfer or steal (something, esp. a thing of small value) in a casual way. — **filch·er n.** [ME: of unknown origin.]

file[1] /fīl/ ▶ **n.** a folder or box for holding loose papers that are typically arranged in a particular order for easy reference. ■ the contents of such a folder or box. ■ Comput. a collection of data, programs, etc., stored in a computer's memory or on a storage device under a single identifying name. ▶ **v.** [trans.] place (a document) in a cabinet, box, or folder in a particular order for preservation and easy reference. ■ submit (a document) to be placed on record by the appropriate authority: *criminal charges were filed against the firm.* ■ (of a reporter) send (a story) to a newspaper or news organization.
– PHRASES **on file** in a file or filing system. — **fil·er n.** [ME: from Fr. *filer* 'to string,' *fil* 'a thread,' both from L. *filum* 'a thread.']

file[2] ▶ **n.** a line of people or things one behind another. ■ Mil. a small detachment of men. ■ Chess each of the eight rows of eight squares on a chessboard running away from the player toward the opponent. Compare with RANK[1] (sense 2). ▶ **v.** [intrans.] (of a group of people) walk one behind the other, typically in an orderly and solemn manner. [16th C.: from Fr. *file*, from *filer* 'to string.']

file[3] ▶ **n.** a tool with a roughened surface or surfaces, typically of steel, used for smoothing or shaping a hard material. ▶ **v.** [trans.] smooth or shape (something) with such a tool. ■ **(file something away/off)** remove something by grinding it off with a file. — **fil·er n.** [OE *fīl*, of West Gmc. origin; rel. to Du. *vijl* and Ger. *Feile*.]

fi·lé /fi'lā; 'fēlā/ ▶ **n.** pounded or powdered sassafras leaves used to flavor and thicken soup, esp. gumbo. [19th C.: from Fr., past part. of *filer* 'to twist.']

file ex·ten·sion ▶ **n.** Comput. a group of letters occurring after a period in a file name, indicating the purpose or contents of the file.

file·fish /'fīl,fisH/ ▶ **n.** (pl. same or **-fish·es**) a fish (family Balistidae or Monacanthidae) with a dorsal spine and rough scales, related to the triggerfishes and occurring in tropical and sometimes temperate seas. [18th C.: from FILE[3].]

Fi·lene /fi'lēn/, Edward Albert (1860–1937), US merchant. As the president of Wm. Filene & Sons, he brought about many retail marketing innovations, including the bargain basement and charge accounts.

file serv·er ▶ **n.** Comput. a device that controls access to separately stored files, as part of a multiuser system.

fi·let /fi'lā; 'filā/ ▶ **n.** **1** French spelling of FILLET, used esp. in the names of French dishes: *filet de boeuf.* **2** a kind of net or lace with a square mesh. [19th C.: from Fr., 'net.']

fi·let mi·gnon /fi,lā mēn'yôN; -min'yän/ ▶ **n.** (pl. **fi·lets mi·gnons** pronunc. same or /-min'yänz/) a small tender piece of beef from the end of the tenderloin. [20th C.: Fr., literally 'dainty fillet.']

fil·i·al /'filēəl; 'filyəl/ ▶ **adj.** of or due from a son or daughter. ■ Biol. denoting the generation or generations after the parental generation. See also F_1. — **fil·i·al·ly adv.** [ME: from OFr., or from eccles. L. *filialis*, from *filius* 'son,' *filia* 'daughter.']

fil·i·a·tion /,filē'āsHən/ ▶ **n.** the fact of being or of being designated the child of a particular parent or parents. ■ the manner in which a thing is related to another from which it is derived or descended in some respect. ■ a branch of a society or language.

fil·i·bus·ter /'filə,bəstər/ ▶ **n.** **1** an action such as a prolonged speech that obstructs progress in a legislative assembly while not technically contravening the required procedures. **2** hist. a person engaging in unauthorized warfare against a foreign country. ▶ **v.** [intrans.] [often as n.] **(filibustering)** act in an obstructive manner in a legislature, esp. by speaking at inordinate length. ■ [trans.] obstruct (a measure) in such a way. [18th C.: from Fr. *flibustier*, first applied to pirates.]

fil·i·cide /'filə,sīd/ ▶ **n.** the killing of one's child. ■ a person who kills their child. [17th C. from L. *filius* 'son,' *filia* 'daughter' + -CIDE.]

fil·i·form /'filə,fôrm/ ▶ **adj.** Biol. threadlike. [18th C.: from L. *filum* 'thread' + -IFORM.]

fil·i·gree /'filə,grē/ (also **fil·a·gree**) ▶ **n.** ornamental work of fine (typically gold or silver) wire formed into delicate tracery. ■ a thing resembling such fine ornamental work. [17th C. (earlier as *filigreen, filigrane*): from Fr. *filigrane*, from Ital. *filigrana* (from L. *filum* 'thread' + *granum* 'seed').]

fil·i·greed /'filə,grēd/ (also **fil·a·greed**) ▶ **adj.** ornamented with or resembling filigree work.

fil·ing /'fīliNG/ ▶ **n.** (usu. **filings**) a small particle rubbed off by a file when smoothing or shaping something.

Fil·i·pi·no /,filə'pēnō/ (also **Pil·i·pi·no**) ▶ **adj.** of or relating to the Philippines, the Filipinos, or their language. ▶ **n.** (pl. **-nos**) **1** (fem. **Fil·i·pi·na** /,filə'pēnə/) a native or national of the Philippines, or a person of Filipino descent. **2** the national language of the Philippines, a standardized form of Tagalog. [Sp., from *las Islas Filipinas* 'the Philippine Islands.']

Fí·lip·poi /'fēlē,pē/ Greek name for PHILIPPI.

fill /fil/ ▶ **v.** [trans.] put someone or something into (a space or container) so that it is completely or almost completely full: *I filled the bottle with water.* ■ [intrans.] **(fill with)** become full of: *her eyes filled with tears.* ■ become an overwhelming presence in. ■ cause (someone) to have an intense experience of an emotion or feeling. ■ appoint a person to hold (a vacant position). ■ hold and perform the expected duties of (a position or role). ■ occupy or take up (a period of time): *the days were filled with meetings.* ■ be supplied with the items described in (a prescription or order). ■ block up (a cavity in a tooth) with cement, amalgam, or gold. ■ [intrans.] (of a sail) curve out tautly as the wind blows into it. ■ [trans.] (of the wind) blow into (a sail), causing it to curve outward. ■ Poker complete (a good hand) by drawing the necessary cards. ▶ **n.** **(one's fill)** an amount of something that is as much as one wants or can bear. ■ an amount of something that will occupy all the space in a container. ■ material, typically loose or compacted, that fills a space, esp. in building or engineering work. ■ the action of filling something, esp. of shading in a region of a computer graphics display. ■ (in popular music) a short interjected phrase on a particular instrument.
– PHRASES **fill the bill** see BILL[1]. **fill someone's shoes** informal take over someone's function or duties and fulfill them satisfactorily.
– PHRASAL VERBS **fill in** act as a substitute for someone. **fill someone in** inform someone more fully of a matter. **fill something in** put material into a hole, trench, or space so that it is completely full. ■ complete a

drawing by adding color or shade to the spaces within an outline. **fill out** (of a person) put on weight to a noticeable extent. **fill something out** add information to complete an official form or document. ■ give more details to add to someone's understanding of something. **fill up** become completely full. ■ fill the fuel tank of a car. [OE *fyllan* (verb), *fyllu* (n.) of Gmc. origin; rel. to Ger. *füllen* (v.), also to FULL.]

fille de joie /ˌfē(yə) də ˈZHwä/ ▶n. used euphemistically to refer to a prostitute. [18th C.: Fr., literally 'girl of pleasure.']

filled gold ▶n. a relatively inexpensive metal with a layer of gold applied over it.

fill·er¹ /ˈfilər/ ▶n. **1** [usu. in comb.] a thing put in a space or container to fill it: *these plants are attractive gap-fillers.* ■ a substance used for filling cracks or holes in a surface, esp. before painting it. ■ material used to fill a cavity or increase bulk. ■ an item serving only to fill space or time, esp. in a newspaper, broadcast, or recording. ■ a word or sound filling a pause in an utterance or conversation (e.g., *er, well, you know*). ■ the tobacco blend used in a cigar. **2** [in comb.] a person or thing that fills a space or container: *supermarket shelf-fillers.*

fill·er² ▶n. (pl. same) a monetary unit of Hungary, equal to one hundredth of a forint. [from Hungarian *fillér.*]

fil·let ▶n. **1** /fiˈlā; ˈfilā/ (also **fi·let**) a fleshy boneless piece of meat from near the loins or the ribs of an animal. ■ (also **fillet steak**) a beef steak cut from the lower part of a sirloin. ■ a boned side of a fish. **2** /ˈfilit/ a band or ribbon worn around the head, esp. for binding the hair. ■ Archit. a narrow flat band separating two moldings. ■ Archit. a small band between the flutes of a column. ■ a plain or decorated line impressed on the cover of a book. ■ a roller used to impress such a line. **3** /ˈfilit/ a concave strip of material roughly triangular in cross section that rounds off an interior angle between two surfaces. ▶v. /fiˈlā/ (**-leted** /-ˈlād/, **-let·ing** /-ˈlāiNG/) [trans.] remove the bones from (a fish). ■ cut (fish or meat) into boneless strips. — **fil·let·er** /fiˈlāər/ n. [ME (denoting a band worn around the head): from OFr. *filet* 'thread,' based on L. *filum* 'thread.']

fill·ing /ˈfiliNG/ ▶n. a quantity of material that fills or is used to fill something. ■ a piece of material used to fill a cavity in a tooth. ■ an edible substance placed between the layers of a sandwich, cake, etc. ■ another term for WEFT. ▶adj. (of food) leaving one with a pleasantly satiated feeling.

fill·ing sta·tion ▶n. a service station.

fil·lip /ˈfiləp/ ▶n. **1** something that acts as a stimulus or boost to an activity. **2** archaic a movement made by bending the last joint of a finger against the thumb and suddenly releasing it; a flick of the finger. ■ a slight smart stroke or tap given in such a way. ▶v. (**-liped, -lip·ing**) [trans.] archaic propel (a small object) with a flick of the finger. ■ strike (someone or something) slightly and smartly. ■ stimulate or urge (someone or something). [ME: symbolic.]

Fill·more /ˈfilmôr/, Millard (1800–74), 13th president of the US 1850–53. A New York Whig; he served in the US House of Representatives 1833–35, 1837–43 and as US vice president in 1849–50, succeeding to the presidency upon the death of President Taylor. Fillmore was an advocate of compromise on the slavery issue, but his unpopular enforcement of the 1850 Fugitive Slave Act hastened the end of the Whig Party.

fill-up ▶n. an instance of making something completely full, esp. the fuel tank of an automobile.

fil·ly /ˈfilē/ ▶n. (pl. **-lies**) a young female horse, esp. one less than four years old. ■ dated a lively girl or young woman. [ME: from ON *fylja*, of Gmc. origin; rel. to FOAL.]

film /film/ ▶n. **1** a thin flexible strip of plastic or other material coated with light-sensitive emulsion for exposure in a camera, used to produce photographs or motion pictures. ■ material in the form of a thin flexible sheet. ■ a thin layer covering a surface. **2** a motion picture; a movie. ■ movies considered as an art or industry. ▶v. **1** [trans.] capture on film as part of a series of moving images; make a movie of (a story or event). ■ make a movie of (a book). ■ [intrans.] (**film well/badly**) be well or badly suited to portrayal in a film: *a story that would film well.* **2** [intrans.] become or appear to become covered with a thin layer of something: *his eyes had filmed over.* [OE *filmen* 'membrane,' of West Gmc. origin.]

film badge ▶n. a device containing photographic film that registers the wearer's exposure to radiation.

film·go·er /ˈfilm,gōər/ ▶n. a person who goes to the movies, esp. regularly. — **film·go·ing** /-ˌgōiNG/ n.

film·ic /ˈfilmik/ ▶adj. of or relating to movies or cinematography.

film·mak·er /ˈfilm,mākər/ ▶n. a person who directs or produces movies for the theater or television. — **film·mak·ing** n.

film noir /ˌfilm ˈnwär/ ▶n. a style or genre of motion picture marked by a mood of pessimism, fatalism, and menace. The term was originally applied to American thriller or detective films made 1944–54. ■ a film of this genre. [20th C.: Fr., literally 'black film.']

film·og·ra·phy /filˈmägrəfē/ ▶n. (pl: **-phies**) a list of films by one director or actor, or on one subject.

film stock ▶n. see STOCK (sense 1).

film·strip /ˈfilm,strip/ ▶n. a series of transparencies in a strip for projection, used esp. as a teaching aid.

film·y /ˈfilmē/ ▶adj. (**film·i·er, film·i·est**) (esp. of fabric) thin and translucent. ■ covered with or forming a thin layer of something. — **film·i·ly** adv. **film·i·ness** n.

fi·lo /ˈfēlō/ ▶n. var. of PHYLLO.

Fi·lo·fax /ˈfīlō,faks; ˈfīlə,-/ ▶n. trademark a loose-leaf notebook for recording appointments, addresses, and notes.

fil·o·po·di·um /ˌfiləˈpōdēəm; ˌfī-/ ▶n. (pl. **-di·a** /-dēə/) Biol. a long, slender, tapering pseudopodium, as found in some protozoans and in embryonic cells. — **fil·o·po·di·al** /-dēəl/ adj. [20th C.: from L. *filium* 'thread' + PODIUM.]

fi·lo·vi·rus /ˈfēlō,vīrəs; ˈfī-/ ▶n. a filamentous RNA virus of a genus that causes severe hemorrhagic fevers in humans and primates. It includes the Ebola virus.

fils¹ /fils/ ▶n. (pl. same) a monetary unit of Iraq, Bahrain, Jordan, Kuwait, and Yemen, equal to one hundredth of a riyal in Yemen and one thousandth of a dinar elsewhere. [from Arab. *fals*, a coin.]

fils² /fēs/ ▶n. used after a surname to distinguish a son from a father of the same name: *Alexandre Dumas fils.* Compare with PÈRE. [19th C.: Fr., literally 'son.']

fil·ter /ˈfiltər/ ▶n. a porous device for removing impurities or solid particles from a liquid or gas passed through it. ■ short for FILTER TIP. ■ a screen, plate, or layer of a substance that absorbs light or other radiation or selectively absorbs some of its components. ■ a device for suppressing electrical or sound waves of frequencies not required. ■ Comput. a piece of software that processes text, for example to remove unwanted spaces or to format it for use in another application. ▶v. [trans.] pass (a liquid, gas, light, or sound) through a device to remove unwanted material. ■ [intrans.] move slowly or in small quantities or numbers through something or in a specified direction: *people filtered out of the concert.* ■ [intrans.] (of information) gradually become known: *the news began to filter in.* — **fil·ter·a·ble** adj. [ME (denoting a piece of felt): from Fr. *filtre*, from med. L. *filtrum* 'felt used as a filter,' of West Gmc. origin and rel. to FELT¹.]

fil·ter bed ▶n. a tank or pond containing a layer of sand or gravel, used for filtering large quantities of liquid.

fil·ter feed·ing ▶n. Zool. (of an aquatic animal) feeding by filtering out plankton or other nutrients. — **fil·ter-feed** v. **fil·ter feed·er** n.

fil·ter pa·per ▶n. a piece of porous paper for filtering liquids.

fil·ter tip ▶n. a filter attached to a cigarette for removing impurities from the inhaled smoke. ■ a cigarette with such a filter. — **fil·ter-tipped** adj.

filth /filTH/ ▶n. disgusting dirt. ■ obscene and offensive language or printed material. ■ corrupt behavior; decadence. ■ used as a term of abuse for a person or people one greatly despises. [OE *fy¯lth* 'rotting matter,' of Gmc. origin; rel. to Du. *vuilte*, also to FOUL.]

filth·y /ˈfilTHē/ ▶adj. (**filth·i·er, filth·i·est**) disgustingly dirty. ■ obscene and offensive. ■ informal used to express one's anger and disgust. ■ (of a mood) bad-tempered and aggressive. ▶adv. [as submodifier] informal to an extreme and often disgusting extent: *he is filthy rich.* — **filth·i·ly** adv. **filth·i·ness** n.

filth·y lu·cre ▶n. money, esp. when gained in a dishonest or dishonorable way.

fil·trate /ˈfiltrāt/ ▶n. a liquid that has passed through a filter. ▶v. [trans.] filter: *the alkali is filtrated.*

fil·tra·tion /filˈtrāSHən/ ▶n. the action or process of filtering something.

fim·bri·a /ˈfimbrēə/ ▶n. (pl. **-bri·ae** /-brē,ē; -brē,ī/) esp. Anat. a series of threads or other projections resembling a fringe. ■ [usu. in pl.] an individual thread in such a structure, esp. a fingerlike projection at the end of the Fallopian tube near the ovary. — **fim·bri·al** /-brēəl/ adj. [18th C.: from late L., literally 'border, fringe.']

fim·bri·at·ed /ˈfimbrē,ātid/ (also **fim·bri·ate** /-it; -,āt/) ▶adj. Biol. having a fringe or border of hairlike or fingerlike projections.

fin /fin/ ▶n. a flattened appendage on various parts of the body of many aquatic vertebrates and some invertebrates, including fish and cetaceans, used for propelling, steering, and balancing. ■ an underwater swimmer's flipper. ■ a small flattened projecting surface or attachment on an aircraft, rocket, or automobile, providing aerodynamic stability or serving as a design element. ■ a flattened projection on a device, such as a radiator, used for increasing heat transfer. ▶v. (**finned, fin·ning**) [intrans.] swim underwater by means of flippers: *I finned for the surface.* — **finned** adj. [in comb.] *ray-finned fishes.* [OE *finn, fin*, of Gmc. origin; rel. to Du. *vin.*]

fin. ▶abbr. ■ finance. ■ financial. ■ finish.

fi·na·gle /fəˈnāgəl/ ▶v. [trans.] informal obtain (something) by devious or dishonest means. ■ [intrans.] act in a devious or dishonest manner: *they finagled over the fine points.* — **fi·na·gler** n. [1920s (orig.US): from dial. *fainaigue* 'cheat'; perh. from OFr. *fornier* 'deny.']

fi·nal /ˈfīnl/ ▶adj. coming at the end of a series. ■ reached or designed to be reached as an outcome: *the final cost will run high.* ■ allowing no further doubt or dispute: *the decision is final.* ▶n. **1** the last game in a sports tournament or other competition, which decides the winner of the tournament. ■ (**finals**) a series of games constituting the final stage of a competition. **2** (**final**) an examination at the end of a term, academic year, or particular class.

– PHRASES **the final straw** see STRAW. [ME: from OFr., or from L. *finalis*, from *finis* 'end.']

fi·na·le /fə'nalē; -'nälē/ ▶ **n.** the last part of a piece of music, a performance, or a public event, esp. when particularly dramatic or exciting. [18th C.: from Ital., from L. *finalis* (see FINAL).]

Fi·nal Four ▶ **n.** the four teams that qualify for the championship round in the annual NCAA men's or women's college basketball tournament.

fi·nal·ist /'fīnl-ist/ ▶ **n.** a competitor or team in the final or finals of a competition.

fi·nal·i·ty /fī'nalətē; fi-/ ▶ **n.** (pl. **-ties**) the fact or impression of being an irreversible ending: *the finality of death.* ■ a tone or manner that indicates that no further comment or argument is possible. ■ the quality of being complete or conclusive.

fi·nal·ize /'fīnl,īz/ ▶ **v.** [trans.] complete (a transaction, esp. in commerce or diplomacy) after discussion of the terms. ■ produce or agree on a finished and definitive version of. — **fi·nal·i·za·tion** /,fīnl-ə'zāsHən/ **n.**

fi·nal·ly /'fīnl-ē/ ▶ **adv.** after a long time, typically involving difficulty or delay: *he finally arrived.* ■ as the last in a series of related events or objects: *a referendum followed by local, legislative, and, finally, presidential elections.* ■ used to introduce a final point or reason. ■ in such a way as to put an end to doubt and dispute.

fi·nal so·lu·tion ▶ **n.** the Nazi policy of exterminating European Jews 1941–45.

fi·nance /'fīnans; fə'nans/ ▶ **n.** the management of large amounts of money, esp. by governments or large companies. ■ monetary support for an enterprise. ■ (**finances**) the monetary resources and affairs of a country, organization, or person. ▶ **v.** [trans.] provide funding for (a person or enterprise). [ME: from OFr., from *finer* 'make an end, settle a debt,' from *fin* 'end' (see FINE[2]).]

fi·nance com·pa·ny ▶ **n.** a company concerned primarily with providing money, e.g., for short-term loans.

fi·nan·cial /fə'nancHəl; fī-/ ▶ **adj.** of or relating to finance. — **fi·nan·cial·ly adv.**

fin·an·cier /,finən'si(ə)r; fə'nansi(ə)r/ ▶ **n.** a person concerned with the management of large amounts of money on behalf of governments or other large organizations. [17th C.: from Fr., from *finance* (see FINANCE).]

fin·back /'fin,bak/ (also **finback whale**) ▶ **n.** a large rorqual (*Balaenoptera physalus*) with a small dorsal fin, a dark gray back, and white underparts.

fin·ca /'fiNGkə/ ▶ **n.** (in Spanish-speaking regions) a country estate; a ranch.

finch /fincH/ ▶ **n.** a seed-eating songbird that typically has a stout bill and colorful plumage. The true finches belong to the family Fringillidae (the **finch family**), which includes chaffinches, canaries, linnets, and crossbills. Other finches belong to the bunting, waxbill, or sparrow families. [OE *finc*, of West Gmc. origin; rel. to Du. *vink* and Ger. *Fink*.]

find /fīnd/ ▶ **v.** (past **found** /found/) [trans.] **1** discover or perceive by chance or unexpectedly. ■ discover (someone or something) after a deliberate search: *hard to find a buyer.* ■ (**find oneself**) discover oneself to be in a surprising or unexpected situation. ■ succeed in obtaining (something). ■ summon up (a quality, esp. courage) with an effort. ■ recover the use of (an ability or faculty). **2** (often **be found**) recognize or discover (something) to be present: *vitamin B12 is found in dairy products.* ■ become aware of; discover to be the case. ■ ascertain (something) by study, calculation, or inquiry. ■ [trans.] perceive or experience (something) to be the case. ■ (**find oneself**) discover the fundamental truths about one's own character and identity. ■ Law (of a court) officially declare to be the case: [trans.] *he was found guilty of speeding.* **3** (of a thing) reach or arrive at, either of its own accord or without the human agent being known: *water finds its own level.* ■ (**find one's way**) reach one's destination by one's own efforts, without knowing in advance how to get there: *he found his way to the door.* ■ (**find one's way**) come to be in a certain situation: *he found his way into a suitable occupation.* ■ (of a letter) reach (someone). ▶ **n.** a discovery of something valuable, typically something of archaeological interest. ■ a person who is discovered to be useful or interesting in some way: *Paul had been a real find.*

– PHRASES **find fault** see FAULT. **find favor** be liked or prove acceptable. **find one's feet** stand up and become able to walk. ■ establish oneself in a particular field. **find God** experience a religious conversion or awakening. **find in favor of** see FIND FOR below.

– PHRASAL VERBS **find against** Law (of a court) make a decision against or judge to be guilty. **find for** (or **find in favor of**) Law (of a court) make a decision in favor of or judge to be innocent. **find someone out** detect a person's offensive or immoral actions. **find something out** (or **find out about something**) discover a fact. — **find·a·ble** /'fīndəbəl/ **adj.** [OE *findan*, of Gmc. origin; rel. to Du. *vinden* and Ger. *finden*.]

find·er /'fīndər/ ▶ **n.** a person who finds someone or something. ■ (in full **finder-scope**) a small telescope attached to a large one to locate an object for observation. ■ the viewfinder of a camera.

– PHRASES **finders keepers** (**losers weepers**) informal used, often humorously, to assert that whoever finds something by chance is entitled to keep it.

find·er's fee ▶ **n.** a fee paid by a business to a person or organization for bringing potential new business to its attention.

fin de siè·cle /,fan də 'syekl(ə); faN/ ▶ **adj.** relating to or characteristic of the end of a century, esp. the 19th century: *fin-de-siècle art.* ■ decadent: *a fin-de-siècle air in the club.* ▶ **n.** the end of a century, esp. the 19th century. [Fr., 'end of century.']

find·ing /'fīndiNG/ ▶ **n. 1** the action of finding someone or something: *the finding of numerous dead rats.* ■ (often **findings**) a conclusion reached as a result of an inquiry, investigation, or trial. **2** (**findings**) small articles or tools used in making garments, shoes, or jewelry.

fine[1] /fīn/ ▶ **adj. 1** of high quality. ■ (of a person) worthy of or eliciting admiration. ■ good; satisfactory. ■ used to express one's agreement with or acquiescence to something: *anything you want is fine by me.* ■ in good health and feeling well. ■ (of the weather) bright and clear. ■ of imposing and dignified appearance or size: *a very fine mansion.* ■ (of speech or writing) sounding impressive and grand but ultimately insincere. ■ (of gold or silver) containing a specified high proportion of pure metal. **2** (of a thread, filament, or person's hair) thin. ■ (of a point) sharp. ■ consisting of small particles. ■ having or requiring an intricate delicacy of touch. ■ (of something abstract) subtle and therefore perceived only with difficulty and care: *the fine distinctions between definitions.* ■ (of feelings) refined; elevated: *you might appeal to their finer feelings.* ▶ **n.** (**fines**) very small particles found in mining, milling, etc. ▶ **adv.** informal in a satisfactory or pleasing manner; very well: *"And how's the job?" "Oh, fine."* ▶ **v. 1** [trans.] clarify (beer or wine) by causing the precipitation of sediment during production. ■ [intrans.] (of liquid) become clear: *the ale hadn't had time to fine down.* **2** make or become thinner.

– PHRASES **do fine** be entirely satisfactory: *an omelet will do fine.* ■ be healthy or well. **the finer points of** the more complex or detailed aspects of: *he went on to discuss the finer points of his work.* **——'s finest** informal the police of a particular city: *New York's finest.* **one's finest hour** the time of one's greatest success. **not to put too fine a point on it** to speak bluntly: *not to put too fine a point on it, your Emily is a liar.* **one fine day** at some unspecified or unknown time. — **fine·ly adv. fine·ness n.** [ME: from OFr. *fin*, based on L. *finire* 'to finish' (see FINISH).]

fine[2] /fīn/ ▶ **n.** a sum of money exacted as a penalty by a court of law or other authority. ▶ **v.** [trans.] (often **be fined**) punish (someone) by making them pay a sum of money, typically as a penalty for breaking the law. — **fine·a·ble adj.** [ME: from OFr. *fin* 'end, payment,' from L. *finis* 'end.']

fine[3] /fēn/ ▶ **n.** French brandy of high quality made from distilled wine rather than from pomace.

fi·ne[4] /'fēnā/ ▶ **n.** (in musical directions) the place where a piece of music finishes (when this is not at the end of the score but at the end of an earlier section that is repeated at the end of the piece). [Ital., from L. *finis* 'end.']

fine art ▶ **n. 1** (also **fine arts**) creative art, esp. visual art, whose products are to be appreciated primarily or solely for their imaginative, aesthetic, or intellectual content. **2** an activity requiring great skill or accomplishment: *the fine art of persuasion.*

fine chem·i·cals ▶ **plural n.** chemical substances prepared to a very high degree of purity for use in research and industry.

Fi·ne Gael /,fēnə 'gāl/ one of the two major political parties of the Republic of Ireland (the other being Fianna Fáil). [Irish, literally 'tribe of Gaels.']

fine-grained ▶ **adj.** (chiefly of wood) having a fine or delicate arrangement of fibers. ■ (chiefly of rock) consisting of small particles. ■ involving great attention to detail.

fine print ▶ **n.** printed matter in small type. ■ inconspicuous details or conditions printed in an agreement or contract that may prove unfavorable.

fin·er·y[1] /'fīnərē/ ▶ **n.** expensive or ostentatious clothes or decoration.

fin·er·y[2] ▶ **n.** (pl. **-er·ies**) hist. a hearth where pig iron was converted into wrought iron. [16th C.: from Fr. *finerie*, from OFr. *finer* 'refine.']

fines herbes /,fēn'(z)erb/ ▶ **plural n.** mixed herbs used in cooking, esp. as a flavoring for omelets. [19th C.: Fr., literally 'fine herbs.']

fine-spun ▶ **adj.** (esp. of fabric) fine or delicate in texture. ■ subtle; overly refined.

fi·nesse /fi'nes/ ▶ **n. 1** intricate and refined delicacy. ■ artful subtlety, typically that needed for tactful handling of a difficulty. ■ subtle or delicate manipulation. **2** (in bridge and whist) an attempt to win a trick with a card that is not a certain winner. ▶ **v.** [trans.] **1** do (something) in a subtle and delicate manner. ■ slyly attempt to avoid blame or censure when dealing with (a situation or action). **2** (in bridge and whist) play (a card that is not a certain winner) in the hope of winning a trick with it. [ME (in the sense 'purity, delicacy': from Fr., rel. to FINE[1].]

fine-tooth comb (also **fine-toothed comb**) ▶ **n.** a comb with narrow teeth that are close together. ■ [in sing.] used with reference to a very thorough search or analysis of something.

fine-tune ▶ **v.** [trans.] make small adjustments to (something) in order to achieve the best or a desired performance.

fin·ger /'fiNGgər/ ▶ **n.** each of the four slender jointed parts attached to either hand (or five, if the thumb is included). ■ a part of a glove intended to cover a finger. ■ a measure of liquor in a glass, based on the breadth of a finger. ■ an object that has roughly the long, narrow shape of a finger. ▶ **v.** [trans.] **1** touch or feel (something) with the fingers. ■ play (a musical instrument) with the fingers, esp. in a tentative or casual manner. **2** informal inform on (someone) to the police: *you fingered me for those burglaries.* ■ (**finger someone for**) identify or choose someone for (a particular purpose): *a biologist was fingered for team leader.* **3** Music play (a passage) with a particular sequence of positions of the fingers. See also FINGERING. ■ mark (music) with signs showing which fingers are to be used.

– PHRASES **give someone the finger** informal make an obscene gesture with the middle finger raised as a sign of contempt. **have a finger in every pie** be involved in a large and varied number of activities or enterprises. **have** (or **keep**) **one's finger on the pulse** be aware of all the latest news or developments. **keep one's fingers crossed** see CROSS. **lay a finger on someone** touch someone, esp. with the intention of harming them. **lift a finger** see LIFT. **put one's finger on something** identify something exactly. **twist** (or **wind** or **wrap**) **someone around one's little finger** see LITTLE FINGER. **work one's fingers to the bone** see BONE. — **fin·gered adj.** [in comb.] *a two-fingered whistle* [OE, of Gmc. origin; rel. to Du. *vinger* and Ger. *Finger*.]

fin·ger·board /ˈfiNGgər,bôrd/ ▶ **n.** a flat or roughly flat strip on the neck of a stringed instrument, against which the strings are pressed to shorten the vibrating length and produce notes of higher pitches.

fin·ger bowl ▶ **n.** a small bowl holding water for rinsing the fingers during or after a meal.

fin·ger food ▶ **n.** food served in such a form and style that it can conveniently be eaten with the fingers.

fin·ger·ing /ˈfiNGgəriNG/ ▶ **n.** a manner or technique of using the fingers, esp. to play a musical instrument. ■ an indication of this in a musical score.

Fin·ger Lakes a region in central New York that is named for its series of narrow glacial lakes. Canandaigua, Keuka, Seneca, and Cayuga lakes are among the better known.

fin·ger-lick·ing ▶ **adj.** tasty; delicious.

fin·ger·ling /ˈfiNGgərliNG/ ▶ **n. 1** a small young fish, esp. a salmon parr. **2** a variety of potato.

fin·ger·nail /ˈfiNGgər,nāl/ ▶ **n.** the flattish horny part on the upper surface of the tip of each finger.

fin·ger paint ▶ **n.** thick paint designed to be applied with the fingers, used esp. by young children. ▶ **v.** (**fin·ger-paint**) [intrans.] (esp. of children) apply paint with the fingers. — **fin·ger paint·ing n.**

fin·ger·pick /ˈfiNGgər,pik/ ▶ **v.** [trans.] play (a guitar or similar instrument) using the fingernails or small plectrums worn on the fingertips to pluck the strings. ▶ **n.** a plectrum worn on a fingertip. — **fin·ger·pick·er n.**

fin·ger-point·ing ▶ **n.** informal actions or words that bring accusatory attention to a particular person or issue.

fin·ger·post /ˈfiNGgər,pōst/ ▶ **n.** a post at a road junction from which signs project in the direction of the place or route indicated.

fin·ger·print /ˈfiNGgər,print/ ▶ **n.** an impression or mark made on a surface by a person's fingertip, esp. as used for identifying individuals from the unique pattern of whorls and lines. ■ fig. a distinctive identifying characteristic. ▶ **v.** [trans.] (usu. **be fingerprinted**) record the fingerprints of (someone).

fin·ger·spell·ing /ˈfiNGgər,speliNG/ ▶ **n.** a form of sign language in which individual letters are formed by the fingers to spell out words.

fin·ger·tip /ˈfiNGgər,tip/ ▶ **n.** the tip of a finger. ▶ **adj.** [attrib.] using or operated by the fingers. ■ reaching to the fingertips.
– PHRASES **at one's fingertips** (esp. of information) readily available; accessible. **by one's fingertips** only with difficulty; precariously. **to one's fingertips** completely.

fin·ger wave ▶ **n.** a wave set in wet hair using the fingers.

fin·i·al /ˈfinēəl/ ▶ **n.** a distinctive ornament at the apex of a roof, pinnacle, canopy, or similar structure. ■ an ornament at the top, end, or corner of an object such as a post, piece of furniture, etc. [ME: from OFr. *fin* or L. *finis* 'end.']

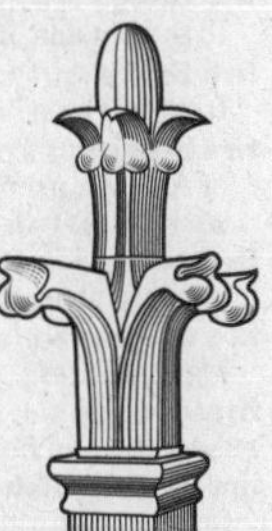
finial

fin·i·cal /ˈfinikəl/ ▶ **adj.** another term for FINICKY. — **fin·i·cal·i·ty** /,finiˈkalitē/ **n.** **fin·i·cal·ly adv.** **fin·i·cal·ness n.** [16th C.: prob. from FINE[1] + -ICAL.]

fin·ick·ing /ˈfinikiNG/ ▶ **adj.** another term for FINICKY.

fin·ick·y /ˈfinikē/ ▶ **adj.** (of a person) fussy about one's needs or requirements. ■ showing or requiring great attention to detail. — **fin·ick·i·ness n.** [19th C.: based on FINICAL.]

fin·ing /ˈfīniNG/ ▶ **n.** (usu. **finings**) a substance used for clarifying liquid, esp. beer or wine. ■ the process of clarifying wine or beer.

fin·is /ˈfinis; fiˈnē/ ▶ **n.** the end (printed at the end of a book or shown at the end of a film). [ME: from L.]

fin·ish /ˈfinisH/ ▶ **v. 1** bring (a task or activity) to an end; complete: [trans.] *straining to finish the job* | [with pres. part.] *we finished eating our meal* | [intrans.] *the musician finished to thunderous applause.* ■ consume or get through the final amount or portion of (something, esp. food or drink). ■ [intrans.] (of an activity) come to an end. ■ [intrans.] (**finish with**) have no more need for or nothing more to do with: *"I've finished with Tom," Gloria said.* ■ reach the end of a race or other sporting competition, typically in a particular position. **2** (usu. **be finished**) complete the manufacture or decoration of (a material, object, or place) by giving it an attractive surface appearance. ▶ **n. 1** [usu. in sing.] an end or final part or stage of something. ■ a point or place at which a race or competition ends. **2** the manner in which the manufacture of an article is completed in detail. ■ the surface appearance of a manufactured material or object, or the material used to produce this. ■ the final taste impression of a wine or beer.
– PHRASES **a fight to the finish** a fight or contest that ends only with the complete defeat of one of the parties involved.
– PHRASAL VERBS **finish someone off** kill, destroy, or comprehensively defeat someone. **finish up** complete an action or process. ■ end a period of time or course of action by doing something or being in a particular position. [ME: from OFr. *feniss-*, lengthened stem of *fenir*, from L. *finire*, from *finis* 'end.']

fin·ished /ˈfinisHt/ ▶ **adj.** (of an action, activity, or piece of work) having been completed or ended. ■ [predic.] (of a person) having completed or ended an action or activity: *they'll be finished here in an hour.* ■ [predic.] having lost effectiveness, power, or prestige. ■ (of an object or room) having been given a particular decorative surface as the final stage in its manufacture or decoration: [in comb.] *plastic-finished lining paper.*

fin·ish·er /ˈfinisHər/ ▶ **n.** a person or thing that finishes something, in particular: ■ a person who reaches the end of a race or other sporting competition: *a third-place finisher.* ■ a worker or machine performing the last operation in a manufacturing process.

fin·ish·ing school ▶ **n.** a private school where girls are prepared for entry into fashionable society.

fin·ish·ing touch ▶ **n.** (usu. **finishing touches**) a final detail or action completing and enhancing a piece of work.

fin·ish line ▶ **n.** a line marking the end of a race.

fi·nite /ˈfīnīt/ ▶ **adj. 1** having limits or bounds. ■ not infinitely small. **2** Gram. (of a verb form) having a specific tense, number, and person. Contrasted with NONFINITE. — **fi·nite·ly adv.** **fi·nite·ness n.** [ME: from L. *finitus* 'finished,' past part. of *finire* (see FINISH).]

fi·nit·ism /ˈfīnə,tizəm/ ▶ **n.** Philos. Math. rejection of the belief that anything can actually be infinite. — **fi·nit·ist n.**

fi·ni·to /fəˈnētō/ ▶ **adj.** [predic.] informal finished. [Ital.]

fin·i·tude /ˈfini,t(y)o͞od; ˈfī-/ ▶ **n.** formal the state of having limits.

Fink /fiNGk/, Mike (*c.*1770–*c.*1823), US frontiersman. His exploits as a keelboatman on the Ohio and Mississippi Rivers were legendary.

fink /fiNGk/ informal ▶ **n.** an unpleasant or contemptible person, in particular: ■ a person who informs on people to the authorities. ■ dated a strikebreaker. ▶ **v.** [intrans.] **1** (**fink on**) inform on to the authorities. **2** (**fink out**) fail to do something promised or expected because of a lack of courage or commitment. ■ cease to function. [19th C.: perh. from Ger., lit. 'finch.']

Fin·land /ˈfinlənd/ a country in northern Europe. *See box on next page.* Finnish name SUOMI.

Fin·land, Gulf of an arm of the Baltic Sea between Finland and Estonia.

Fin·land·i·za·tion /,finləndiˈzāsHən/ ▶ **n.** hist. the process or result of being obliged for economic reasons to favor the interests of the former Soviet Union despite not being politically allied to it. — **Fin·land·ize** /ˈfinlən,dīz/ **v.**

Finn /fin/ ▶ **n.** a native or national of Finland or a person of Finnish descent. [OE *Finnas* (pl.).]

fin·nan /ˈfinən/ (also **fin·nan had·die** /ˈhadē/) ▶ **n.** haddock cured with the smoke of green wood, turf, or peat. [18th C.: alt. of *Findon*, a village in Scotland.]

Finn·ic /ˈfinik/ ▶ **adj. 1** of, relating to, or denoting the group of Finno-Ugric languages that includes Finnish and Estonian. **2** of, relating to, or denoting the group of peoples that includes the Finns and the Estonians.

Finn·ish /ˈfinisH/ ▶ **adj.** of or relating to the Finns or their language. ▶ **n.** the Finno-Ugric language of the Finns, spoken in Finland and in parts of Russia and Sweden.

Fin·no-U·gric /ˈfinō ˈ(y)o͞ogrik/ (also **Fin·no-U·gri·an** /ˈ(y)o͞ogrēən/) ▶ **adj.** of or relating to the major group of Uralic languages, whose main branches are Finnic and Ugric (Hungarian and the Ob-Ugric languages). ▶ **n.** this group of languages.

fin·ny /ˈfinē/ ▶ **adj.** literary of, relating to, or resembling a fish: *it transfixes its finny prey.*

fi·no /ˈfēnō/ ▶ **n.** (pl. **-nos**) a light-colored dry sherry. [19th C.: Sp., literally 'fine,' based on L. *finire* 'to finish' (see FINISH).]

fi·noc·chi·o /fəˈnōkē,ō/ ▶ **n.** another term for *SWEET FENNEL* (see FENNEL). [18th C.: from Ital., from a pop. L. var. of L. *faeniculum* (see FENNEL).]

fin ray ▶ **n.** see RAY[1] (sense 2).

fin whale ▶ **n.** another term for FINBACK.

fiord ▶ **n.** var. of FJORD.

fio·ri·tu·ra /fē,ôriˈto͝orə/ ▶ **n.** (pl. **-tu·re** /-ˈto͝orā/) Music an embellishment of a melody, esp. as improvised by an operatic singer. [Ital., literally 'flowering,' from *fiorire* 'to flower.']

fip·ple /ˈfipəl/ ▶ **n.** the mouthpiece of a recorder or similar wind instrument that is blown endwise, in which a thin channel cut through a block directs a stream of air against a sharp edge. [17th C.: perh. rel. to Icelandic *flipi* 'horse's lip.']

fip·ple flute ▶ **n.** a flute, such as a recorder, played by blowing endwise.

fir /fər/ ▶ **n.** (also **fir tree**) an evergreen coniferous tree (genus *Abies*, family Pinaceae) with upright cones and flat needle-shaped leaves, typically arranged in two rows. Firs are an important source of timber and resins. — **fir·ry adj.** [ME: prob. from ON *fyri-* (recorded in *fyriskógr* 'fir-wood').]

Finland

Official name: Republic of Finland
Location: northern Europe, on the Baltic Sea, between Sweden and Russia
Area: 118,000 square miles (305,500 sq km)
Population: 5,214,000
Capital: Helsinki
Languages: Finnish and Swedish (both official), also Lapp- and Russian-speaking minorities
Currency: euro

fire /fī(ə)r/ ▶ **n.** **1** combustion or burning, in which substances combine chemically with oxygen from the air and typically give out bright light, heat, and smoke. ■ one of the four elements in ancient and medieval philosophy and in astrology. ■ a destructive burning of something. ■ a collection of fuel, esp. wood or coal, burned in a controlled way to provide heat or a means for cooking. ■ a burning sensation in the body. ■ fervent or passionate emotion or enthusiasm. ■ literary luminosity; glow. **2** the shooting of projectiles from weapons, esp. bullets from guns. ■ strong criticism or antagonism. ▶ **v.** [trans.] **1** discharge a gun or other weapon in order to explosively propel (a bullet or projectile). ■ discharge (a gun or other weapon). ■ [intrans.] (of a gun) be discharged. ■ direct (questions or statements, esp. unwelcome ones) toward someone in rapid succession. ■ (**fire something off**) send a message aggressively, esp. as one of a series. **2** informal dismiss (an employee) from a job. **3** supply (a furnace, engine, boiler, or power station) with fuel. ■ [intrans.] (of an internal combustion engine, or a cylinder in one) undergo ignition of its fuel when started. **4** stimulate or excite (the imagination or an emotion). ■ fill (someone) with enthusiasm: *in the locker room they were really fired up.* ■ [intrans.] (**fire up**) archaic show sudden anger: *I would fire up in a flash.* **5** bake or dry (pottery, bricks, etc.) in a kiln. **6** start (an engine or other device).
— PHRASES **breathe fire** be extremely angry. **catch fire** begin to burn. ■ fig. become interesting or exciting. **fire and brimstone** the torments of hell. **fire away** informal used to give someone permission to begin speaking, typically to ask questions. **fire in the** (or **one's**) **belly** a powerful sense of ambition or determination. **firing on all (four) cylinders** working or functioning at a peak level. **go through fire (and water)** face any peril. **light a fire under someone** stimulate someone to work or act more quickly or enthusiastically. **on fire** in flames; burning. ■ in a state of excitement. **open fire** see OPEN. **play with fire** see PLAY. **set fire to** (or **set something on fire**) cause to burn; ignite. **set the world on fire** do something remarkable or sensational. **take fire** start to burn. **under fire** being shot at. ■ being rigorously criticized. **where's the fire?** informal used to ask someone why they are in such a hurry or state of excitement. [OE *fȳr* (n.), *fȳrian* 'supply with material for a fire,' of West Gmc. origin; rel. to Du. *vuur* and Ger. *Feuer*.]

fire a·larm ▶ **n.** a device making a loud noise that gives warning of a fire.

fire-and-for·get ▶ **adj.** [attrib.] (of a missile) able to guide itself to its target once fired.

fire ant ▶ **n.** a tropical American ant (genus *Solenopsis*) that has a painful and sometimes dangerous sting.

fire·arm /'fī(ə)r,ärm/ ▶ **n.** a rifle, pistol, or other portable gun.

fire·back /'fī(ə)r,bak/ ▶ **n.** the back wall of a fireplace. ■ a metal plate covering such a wall.

fire·ball /'fī(ə)r,bôl/ ▶ **n.** a ball of flame or fire. ■ an extremely hot, luminous ball of gas generated by a nuclear explosion. ■ a large bright meteor. ■ hist. a ball filled with combustibles or explosives, fired at an enemy or enemy fortifications. ■ fig. a person with a fiery temper or a great deal of energy.

fire·base /'fī(ə)r,bās/ ▶ **n.** an area in a war zone in which artillery can be massed to provide heavy firepower.

fire·blight /'fī(ə)r,blīt/ ▶ **n.** a serious disease of plants of the rose family, esp. fruit trees, giving the leaves a scorched appearance, caused by the bacterium *Erwinia amylovora.*

fire·bomb /'fī(ə)r,bäm/ ▶ **n.** a bomb designed to cause a fire. ▶ **v.** [trans.] attack or destroy (something) with such a bomb.

fire·box /'fī(ə)r,bäks/ ▶ **n.** the chamber of a steam engine or boiler in which the fuel is burned.

fire·brand /'fī(ə)r,brand/ ▶ **n.** **1** a person who is passionate about a particular cause, typically inciting change and taking radical action. **2** a piece of burning wood.

fire·brat /'fī(ə)r,brat/ ▶ **n.** a fast-moving brownish insect (*Thermobia domestica*, family Lepismatidae), a type of true bristletail, that frequents warm places indoors.

fire·break /'fī(ə)r,brāk/ ▶ **n.** an obstacle to the spread of fire. ■ a strip of open space in a forest or other area of dense vegetation.

fire·brick /'fī(ə)r,brik/ ▶ **n.** a brick capable of withstanding intense heat, used esp. to line furnaces and fireplaces.

fire bri·gade ▶ **n.** esp. Brit. an organized body of people trained and employed to extinguish fires.

fire·bug /'f(ə)r,bəg/ ▶ **n.** informal an arsonist or pyromaniac.

fire·clay /'fī(ə)r,klā/ ▶ **n.** clay capable of withstanding high temperatures, chiefly used for making firebricks.

fire com·pa·ny ▶ **n.** another term for FIRE DEPARTMENT.

fire con·trol ▶ **n.** **1** the process of targeting and firing heavy weapons. **2** the prevention and monitoring of forest fires and grass fires. ■ the containment and extinguishing of fires in buildings, ships, etc.

fire cor·al ▶ **n.** a colonial corallike hydrozoan (genus *Millepora*, order Hydroida), the heavy external skeleton of which forms reefs. The polyps bear nematocysts that can inflict painful stings.

fire·crack·er /'fī(ə)r,krakər/ ▶ **n.** a loud, explosive firework, typically wrapped in paper and lit with a fuse.

fire·damp /'fī(ə)r,damp/ ▶ **n.** methane, esp. as forming an explosive mixture with air in coal mines.

fire de·part·ment ▶ **n.** the department of a local or municipal authority in charge of preventing and fighting fires.

fire·dog /'fī(ə)r,dôg/ ▶ **n.** another term for ANDIRON.

fire door ▶ **n.** a fire-resistant door to prevent the spread of fire. ■ a door to the outside of a building used only as an emergency exit.

fire·drake /'fī(ə)r,drāk/ ▶ **n.** Germanic Mythol. a fiery dragon. [OE *fȳr-draca*, from *fȳr* (see FIRE) + *draca* 'dragon,' from L. *draco*.]

fire drill ▶ **n.** **1** a practice of the emergency procedures to be used in case of fire. **2** a primitive device for kindling fire, consisting of a pointed stick that is twirled in a hole in a flat piece of soft wood.

fire-eat·er ▶ **n.** **1** an entertainer who appears to eat fire. **2** dated a person prone to quarreling or fighting.

fire en·gine ▶ **n.** a vehicle carrying firefighters and equipment for fighting large fires.

fire es·cape ▶ **n.** a staircase or other apparatus used for escaping from a building on fire.

fire ex·tin·guish·er ▶ **n.** a portable device that discharges a jet of water, foam, gas, or other material to extinguish a fire.

fire·fight /'fī(ə)r,fīt/ ▶ **n.** Mil. a battle using guns rather than bombs or other weapons.

fire·fight·er /'fī(ə)r,fītər/ ▶ **n.** a person whose job is to extinguish fires. — **fire·fight·ing** **n.**

firefly

fire·fly /ˈfī(ə)rˌflī/ ▶ n. (pl. **-flies**) a soft-bodied beetle (family Lampyridae) related to the glowworm, the winged male and flightless female of which both have luminescent organs. The light is chiefly produced as a signal between the sexes, esp. in flashes.

fire·guard /ˈfī(ə)rˌgärd/ ▶ n. **1** a protective screen or grid placed in front of an open fire. **2** a firebreak in a forest.

fire·house /ˈfī(ə)rˌhous/ ▶ n. a fire station.

fire i·rons ▶ plural n. implements for tending a fireplace, typically tongs, a poker, and a shovel.

Fire Is·land a barrier island on the southern shore of Long Island in New York.

fire·light /ˈfī(ə)rˌlīt/ ▶ n. light from a fire in a fireplace.

fire line ▶ n. a firebreak in a forest.

fire·lock /ˈfī(ə)rˌläk/ ▶ n. hist. a firearm in which the priming is ignited by sparks.

fire·man /ˈfī(ə)rmən/ ▶ n. (pl. **-men** /-mən/) **1** a firefighter. **2** a person who tends a furnace or the fire of a steam engine or steamship; a stoker. ■ an enlisted person in the US navy who maintains and operates a ship's machinery.

Fi·ren·ze /fēˈrentsā/ Italian name of FLORENCE.

fire o·pal ▶ n. another term for GIRASOL (sense 1).

fire·place /ˈfī(ə)rˌplās/ ▶ n. a place for a domestic fire, esp. a grate or hearth at the base of a chimney. ■ a structure surrounding such a place.

fire·plug /ˈfī(ə)rˌpləg/ ▶ n. a hydrant for a fire hose.

fire·pow·er /ˈfī(ə)rˌpouər/ ▶ n. the destructive capacity of guns, missiles, or a military force (used with reference to the number and size of guns available).

fire·proof /ˈfī(ə)rˌpro͞of/ ▶ adj. able to withstand fire or great heat. ▶ v. [trans.] make (something) fireproof.

fire sale ▶ n. a sale of goods remaining after the destruction of commercial premises by fire. ■ a sale of goods or assets at a very low price.

fire screen ▶ n. a screen or grid placed in front of an open fire to deflect the direct heat or to protect against sparks. ■ an ornamental screen placed in front of a fireplace when the fire is unlit.

fire·ship /ˈfī(ə)rˌSHip/ ▶ n. hist. a ship loaded with burning material and explosives and set adrift to ignite and blow up an enemy's ships.

fire·side /ˈfī(ə)rˌsīd/ ▶ n. the area around a fireplace (used esp. with reference to a person's home or family life).

fire sta·tion ▶ n. the headquarters of a fire department, where fire engines and other equipment are housed.

Fire·stone /ˈfī(ə)rˌstōn/, Harvey Samuel (1868–1938), US industrialist. He headed the Firestone Tire & Rubber Company 1903–38.

fire·stone /ˈfī(ə)rˌstōn/ ▶ n. stone that can withstand fire and great heat, used esp. for lining furnaces and ovens.

fire·storm /ˈfī(ə)rˌstôrm/ ▶ n. an intense and destructive fire (typically one caused by bombing) in which strong currents of air are drawn into the blaze from the surrounding area, making it burn more fiercely.

fire·thorn /ˈfī(ə)rˌT͟Hôrn/ ▶ n. another term for PYRACANTHA.

fire tow·er ▶ n. a tower, often at a high elevation, that especially in former years was staffed by a lookout for the detection of fires occurring over a wide area.

fire·trap /ˈfī(ə)rˌtrap/ ▶ n. a building without proper provision for escape in case of fire.

fire truck ▶ n. another term for FIRE ENGINE.

fire·wall /ˈfī(ə)rˌwôl/ ▶ n. a wall or partition designed to inhibit or prevent the spread of fire. ■ any barrier that is intended to thwart the spread of a destructive agent. ■ Comput. a part of a computer system or network that is designed to block unauthorized access while permitting outward communication.

fire ward·en ▶ n. a person employed to prevent or extinguish fires, esp. in a town, camp, or forest.

fire·wa·ter /ˈfī(ə)rˌwôtər; -ˌwätər/ ▶ n. informal strong liquor.

fire·weed /ˈfī(ə)rˌwēd/ ▶ n. **1** a plant that springs up on burned land, esp. the pink-flowered *Epilobium angustifolium*, a widespread willow herb. **2** another term for PILEWORT (sense 1).

fire·wood /ˈfī(ə)rˌwo͝od/ ▶ n. wood burned as fuel.

fire·work /ˈfī(ə)rˌwərk/ ▶ n. a device containing gunpowder and other combustible chemicals that causes a spectacular explosion when ignited, used typically for display or in celebrations. ■ (**fireworks**) a display of fireworks. ■ (**fireworks**) fig. an outburst of anger or other emotion, or a display of brilliance or energy.

fir·ing /ˈfī(ə)riNG/ ▶ n. the action of setting fire to something. ■ the discharging of a gun or other weapon. ■ the dismissal of an employee from a job. ■ the baking or drying of pottery or bricks in a kiln.

fir·ing line ▶ n. the line of positions from which gunfire is directed at targets. ■ the front line of troops in a battle. ■ a position where one is subject to criticism or blame because of one's responsibilities or position.

fir·ing pin ▶ n. a movable pin in a firearm that strikes the primer of a cartridge to set off the charge.

fir·ing squad ▶ n. a group of soldiers detailed to shoot a condemned person. ■ a group of soldiers detailed to fire the salute at a military funeral.

fir·kin /ˈfərkin/ ▶ n. esp. hist. a small cask used chiefly for liquids, butter, or fish. ■ a unit of liquid volume equal to half a kilderkin (about 11 gallons or 41 liters). [ME *ferdekyn*, prob. from the MDu. dimin. of *vierde* 'fourth.']

firm¹ /fərm/ ▶ adj. **1** having a solid, almost unyielding surface or structure. ■ solidly in place and stable. ■ having steady but not excessive power or strength. ■ (of a person, action, or attitude) showing resolute determination and strength of character. **2** strongly felt and unlikely to change. ■ (of a person) steadfast and constant. ■ decided upon and fixed or definite. ■ (of a currency, a commodity, or shares) having a steady value or price that is more likely to rise than fall. ▶ v. [trans.] make (something) physically solid or resilient. ■ fix (a plant) securely in the soil. ■ [intrans.] (of a price) rise slightly to reach a level considered secure. ■ make (an agreement or plan) explicit and definite: *archaeologists have **firmed up** this new view.* ▶ adv. in a resolute and determined manner: *she will **stand firm** against the proposal.*
– PHRASES **be on firm ground** be sure of one's facts or secure in one's position, esp. in a discussion. **a firm hand** strict discipline or control.
— **firm·ly** adv. **firm·ness** n. [ME: from OFr. *ferme*, from L. *firmus*.]

firm² ▶ n. a business concern, esp. one involving a partnership of two or more people. [16th C.: from Sp. and Ital. *firma*, from med. L., from L. *firmare* 'fix, settle,' from *firmus* 'firm.']

fir·ma·ment /ˈfərməmənt/ ▶ n. literary the heavens or the sky, esp. when regarded as a tangible thing. ■ fig. a sphere or world viewed as a collection of people. — **fir·ma·men·tal** /ˌfərməˈmentl/ adj. [ME: via OFr. from L. *firmamentum*, from *firmare* 'fix, settle.']

firm·ware /ˈfərmˌwe(ə)r/ ▶ n. Comput. permanent software programmed into a read-only memory.

firn /fi(ə)rn/ ▶ n. crystalline or granular snow, esp. on the upper part of a glacier, where it has not yet been compressed into ice. [19th C.: from Ger., from Old High Ger. *firni* 'old'; rel. to Swed. *forn* 'former.']

first /fərst/ ▶ ordinal number **1** coming before all others in time or order; earliest; 1st. ■ never previously done or occurring: *her first day at school.* ■ coming next after a specified or implied time or occurrence. ■ met with or encountered before any others. ■ originally. ■ before doing something else specified or implied: *do you mind if I take a shower first?* ■ firstly; in the first place (used to introduce a first point or reason). ■ in preference; rather (used when strongly rejecting a suggestion or possibility): *go abroad?—she'd die first!* ■ with a specified part or person in a leading position: *it plunged nose first into the river.* ■ informal the first occurrence of something notable: *we traveled by air, a first for both of us.* ■ the first in a sequence of a vehicle's gears. ■ Baseball first base. ■ the first grade of a school. ■ a first edition of a book. **2** foremost in position, rank, or importance. ■ [often with infin.] the most likely, pressing, or suitable: *his first problem is where to live.* ■ **the first finisher or position in a race or competition.** ■ Music performing the highest or chief of two or more parts for the same instrument or voice: *the first violins.* ■ (**firsts**) goods of the best quality: *factory firsts, seconds, and discontinued styles.*
– PHRASES **at first** at the beginning; in the initial stage or stages. **at first glance** see GLANCE. **at first hand** see FIRSTHAND. **at first sight** see SIGHT. **(the) first among equals** see EQUAL. **first blood** see BLOOD. **first and foremost** most importantly; more than anything else: *I'm first and foremost a writer.* **first and last** fundamentally; on the whole. **first of all** before doing anything else; at the beginning. ■ most importantly. **first off** informal as a first point; first of all. **first thing** early in the morning; before anything else. **first things first** used to assert that important matters should be dealt with before other things. **from the (very) first** from the beginning or the early stages. **from first to last** from beginning to end; throughout. **get to first base** see BASE¹. **in the first place** as the first consideration or point. ■ at the beginning; to begin with (esp. in reference to the time when an action was being planned or discussed). **of the first order** (or **magnitude**) used to denote something that is excellent or considerable of its kind. **of the first water** see WATER. [OE *fyr(e)st*; rel. to Ger. *Fürst* 'prince,' from an Indo-Eur. root shared by L. *primus*, Gk. *prōtos*.]

First A·dar /äˈdär/ see ADAR.

first aid ▶ n. help given to a sick or injured person until full medical treatment is available.

first·born /ˈfərstˌbôrn/ ▶ adj. (of a person's child) the first to be born; the eldest. ▶ n. a person's first child.

First Cause ▶ n. Philos. a supposed ultimate cause of all events, which does not itself have a cause, identified with God.

first class ▶ n. a set of people or things grouped together as the best. ■ the best accommodations in a plane, train, or ship. ▶ adj. & adv. of the best quality. ■ of or relating to the best accommodations in a train, ship, or plane: [as adj.] *first-class air transportation* | [as adv.] *you can travel first class.* ■ of or relating to a class of mail given priority.

first cous·in ▶ n. see COUSIN.

first-day cov·er (also **first day cover**) ▶ n. an envelope bearing a stamp or stamps postmarked on their day of issue.

first-de·gree ▶ adj. [attrib.] **1** Med. denoting burns that affect only the surface of the skin and cause reddening. **2** Law denoting the most serious category of a crime, esp. murder.
– PHRASES **first-degree relative** a person's parent, sibling, or child.

first down ▶ n. Football a gain of ten yards or more in field position during a series of downs, permitting the offensive team to attempt another series of downs.

first fam·i·ly ▶ n. a family considered to rank first in social prestige or pedigree in a particular place. ■ the family of the president of the United States or of the governor of a US state.

first fin·ger ▶ n. the finger next to the thumb; the forefinger; the index finger.

first floor ▶ n. the ground floor of a building.

first fruits ▶ plural n. the first agricultural produce of a season, esp. when given as an offering to God. ■ the initial results of an enterprise or endeavor.

first-gen·er·a·tion ▶ adj. **1** designating the first of a generation to become a citizen in a new country. ■ designating the first of a generation to be born in a country of parents who had immigrated. **2** designating the first version of a type made available.

first·hand /ˈfərstˈhand/ ▶ adj. & adv. (of information or experience) from the original source or personal experience; direct: [as adj.] *no firsthand knowledge of Andean culture* | [as adv.] *this is something you have to hear firsthand.*

– PHRASES **at first hand** directly or from personal experience.

first in·ten·tion ▶ n. Med. the healing of a wound by natural contact of the parts involved: *healing by first intention.* Compare with SECOND INTENTION.

First In·ter·na·tion·al see INTERNATIONAL (sense 2).

first la·dy ▶ n. (**First La·dy**) the wife of the president of the US or other head of state. ■ the leading woman in a particular activity or profession.

first lan·guage ▶ n. a person's native language.

first lieu·ten·ant ▶ n. a commissioned officer in the US Army, Air Force, or Marine Corps ranking above second lieutenant and below captain.

first light ▶ n. the time when light first appears in the morning; dawn.

first·ling /ˈfərstliNG/ ▶ n. (usu. **firstlings**) archaic the first agricultural produce or animal offspring of a season.

first·ly /ˈfərstlē/ ▶ adv. used to introduce a first point or reason.

first mate ▶ n. the deck officer second in command to the master of a merchant ship.

first name ▶ n. a personal name given to someone at birth or baptism and used before a family name.

– PHRASES **on a first-name basis** having a friendly and informal relationship.

first night ▶ n. the first public performance of a play or show: [as adj.] *first-night nerves.*

first-night·er ▶ n. a person who attends a first night.

first of·fend·er ▶ n. a person who is convicted of a criminal offense for the first time.

first of·fi·cer ▶ n. the first mate on a merchant ship. ■ the second in command to the captain on an aircraft.

first-or·der ▶ adj. of or relating to the simplest or most fundamental level of organization, experience, or analysis; primary or immediate: *for a teacher, of course, drama must be a first-order experience.* ■ tech. having an order of one, esp. denoting mathematical equations involving only the first power of the independent variable or only the first derivative of a function.

first per·son ▶ n. see PERSON (sense 2).

First Pres·i·den·cy ▶ n. see PRESIDENCY.

first-rate ▶ adj. of the best class or quality; excellent. ■ in good health or condition; very well.

first re·fus·al ▶ n. the privilege of deciding whether to accept or reject something before it is offered to others.

First Reich see REICH.

First Re·pub·lic the republican regime in France from the abolition of the monarchy in 1792 until Napoleon's accession as emperor in 1804.

first re·spond·er ▶ n. a person whose job entails being the first on the scene of an emergency, such as a firefighter.

first ser·geant ▶ n. (in the US Army or Marine Corps) the highest-ranking noncommissioned officer in a company or equivalent unit.

first strike ▶ n. an attack with nuclear weapons designed to destroy the enemy's nuclear capability.

first string ▶ n. Sports the best players on a team, the ones that normally play the most. ■ fig. the best or most talented individuals in any endeavor.

First World ▶ n. the industrialized capitalist countries of western Europe, North America, Japan, Australia, and New Zealand. Compare with SECOND WORLD and THIRD WORLD.

First World War another term for WORLD WAR I.

Firth /fərTH/, J. R. (1890–1960), English linguist; full name *John Rupert Firth.* He contributed to linguistic semantics and prosodic phonology.

firth /fərTH/ ▶ n. a narrow inlet of the sea; an estuary. [ME (originally Scots), from ON *fjǫrthr* (see FJORD).]

fir tree ▶ n. see FIR.

fis·cal /ˈfiskəl/ ▶ adj. of or relating to government revenue, esp. taxes. ■ of or relating to financial matters. ■ used to denote a fiscal year. — **fis·cal·ly** /ˈfiskəlē/ adv. [16th C.: from Fr., or from L. *fiscalis,* from *fiscus* 'purse, treasury.']

fis·cal year ▶ n. a year as reckoned for taxing or accounting purposes.

Fisch·er[1] /ˈfisHər/, Bobby (1943–), Icelandic chess player; born in the US; full name *Robert James Fischer.* The first US-born world chess champion (1972–75), he became a citizen of Iceland in 2005 to avoid extradition to the US for tax evasion.

Fisch·er[2], Emil Hermann (1852–1919), German chemist. He studied the structure of sugars, other carbohydrates, and purines and synthesized many of them. Nobel Prize for Chemistry (1902).

Fisch·er[3], Hans (1881–1945), German chemist. He determined the structure of the porphyrin group of many natural pigments. Nobel Prize for Chemistry (1930).

Fish /fisH/ a family of US politicians from New York. Hamilton (1808–93), US secretary of state 1869–77, was a Whig who served as governor of New York 1849–50 and a US senator 1851–57. The next three generations served as Republicans in the US House of Representatives, including his son Hamilton (1849–1936), in the House 1909–11, his grandson Hamilton (1888–1991), in the House 1920–45, and his great-grandson Hamilton, Jr. (1926–1996), in the House 1969–95.

fish[1] /fisH/ ▶ n. (pl. same or **fish·es**) a limbless cold-blooded vertebrate animal with gills and fins and living wholly in water. ■ the flesh of such animals as food. ■ (**the Fish** or **Fishes**) the zodiacal sign or constellation Pisces. ■ used in names of invertebrate animals living wholly in water, e.g., **cuttlefish, shellfish, jellyfish.** ■ [with adj.] informal a person who is strange in a specified way: *he is thought to be a cold fish.* ■ informal a torpedo. ▶ v. [intrans.] catch or try to catch fish, typically by using a net or hook and line. ■ [trans.] catch or try to catch fish in (a particular body of water). ■ search, typically by groping or feeling for something concealed. ■ try subtly or deviously to elicit a response or some information from someone: *I was not fishing for compliments.* ■ [trans.] (**fish something out**) pull or take something out of water or a container.

– PHRASES **a big fish** an important or influential person. **a big fish in a small** (or **little**) **pond** a person seen as important and influential only within a limited scope. **drink like a fish** drink excessive amounts of alcohol. **fish or cut bait** see BAIT. **a fish out of water** a person in a completely unsuitable environment or situation. **have other** (or **bigger**) **fish to fry** have other (or more important) matters to attend to. **like shooting fish in a barrel** extremely easy. **neither fish nor fowl** (**nor good red herring**) of indefinite character and difficult to identify or classify. [OE *fisc* (n.), *fiscian* (v.), of Gmc. origin.]

fish[2] /fisH/ ▶ n. a flat plate of metal, wood, or another material that is fixed on a beam or across a joint in order to give additional strength, esp. on a ship's damaged mast or spar as a temporary repair. ▶ v. [trans.] mend or strengthen (a beam, joint, mast, etc.) with a fish. ■ join (rails in a railroad track) with a fishplate. [16th C.: prob. from Fr. *fiche,* from *ficher* 'to fix,' based on L. *figere.*]

fish·bowl /ˈfisH,bōl/ ▶ n. a round glass bowl for keeping pet fish in. ■ fig. a place open to public view and criticism.

fish cake ▶ n. a patty of shredded fish and mashed potato, typically coated and fried.

fish·er /ˈfisHər/ ▶ n. **1** a fisherman. **2** a large brown marten (*Martes pennanti*) valued for its fur, found in North American woodland where it frequently preys on porcupines.

fish·er·folk /ˈfisHər,fōk/ ▶ plural n. people who catch fish for a living.

fish·er·man /ˈfisHərmən/ ▶ n. (pl. **-men**) a person who catches fish for a living or for sport. ■ a fishing boat.

fish·er·man knit (also **fish·er·man's knit**) ▶ n. a type of thick ribbed knitting.

fish·er·man's bend ▶ n. a knot tied by making a full turn around something (typically the ring of an anchor), a half hitch through the turn, and a half hitch around the standing part of the rope.

Fish·er, St. John /ˈfisHər/ (1469–1535), English bishop of Rochester 1504–35. Because he refused to accept Henry VIII as supreme head of the English church, he was condemned to death.

fish·er·wom·an /ˈfisHər,wo͝omən/ ▶ n. (pl. **-wom·en**) a woman who catches fish, esp. for a living.

fish·er·y /ˈfisHərē/ ▶ n. (pl. **-er·ies**) a place where fish are reared for commercial purposes. ■ a fishing ground or area where fish are caught. ■ the occupation or industry of catching or rearing fish.

fish·eye /ˈfisH,ī/ ▶ n. **1** (also **fisheye lens**) a wide-angle lens with a field of vision covering up to 180°, the scale being reduced toward the edges. **2** informal a suspicious or unfriendly look.

fish farm ▶ n. a place where fish are artificially bred or cultivated, e.g., for food, to restock lakes for angling, or to supply aquariums. — **fish farm·er** n. **fish farm·ing** n.

fish hawk ▶ n. another term for OSPREY.

fish·hook /ˈfisH,ho͝ok/ ▶ n. see HOOK (sense 1).

fish·ing /ˈfisHiNG/ ▶ n. the activity of catching fish, either for food or as a sport.

– PHRASES **fishing expedition** a search or investigation undertaken with the hope, though not the stated purpose, of discovering information.

fish·ing fly ▶ n. a natural or artificial flying insect used as bait in fishing.

fish·ing line ▶ n. a long thread, esp. of nylon, attached to a baited hook, with a sinker or float, and used for catching fish.

fish·ing pole ▶ n. a fishing rod, esp. a simple one with no reel.

fish·ing reel ▶ n. a device for winding and unwinding fishing line, designed to be attached to a fishing rod. *See illustration on next page.*

fish·ing rod ▶ n. a long, tapering rod to which a fishing line is attached, typically on a reel.

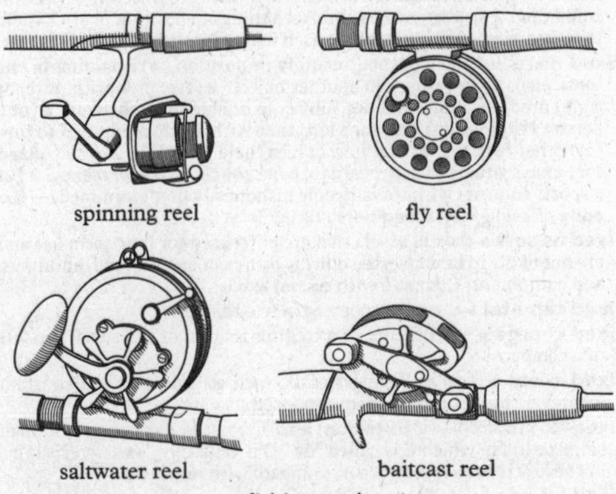

fishing reels

fish lad·der ▶ **n.** a series of pools built like steps to enable fish to ascend a dam or waterfall.

fish louse ▶ **n.** an aquatic crustacean that is a parasite of fish, typically attached to the skin or gills.

fish meal (also **fish·meal**) ▶ **n.** ground dried fish used as fertilizer or animal feed.

fish·mon·ger /ˈfisн,məNGgər; -,mäNGgər/ ▶ **n.** a person or store that sells fish for food.

fish·net /ˈfisн,net/ ▶ **n.** a fabric with an open mesh resembling a fishing net.

fish·plate /ˈfisн,plāt/ ▶ **n.** a flat piece of metal used to connect adjacent rails in a railroad track. ■ a flat piece of metal with ends like a fish's tail, used to position masonry.

fish stick ▶ **n.** a small, oblong piece of fish fillet, usually breaded and fried.

fish sto·ry ▶ **n.** an incredible or far-fetched story.

fish·tail /ˈfisн,tāl/ ▶ **n.** [usu. as adj.] an object that is forked like a fish's tail. ■ an uncontrolled sideways movement of the back of a motor vehicle. ▶ **v.** [intrans.] (of a vehicle) make such a movement. ■ [trans.] cause (a vehicle) to make such a movement.

fish·way /ˈfisн,wā/ ▶ **n.** another term for FISH LADDER.

fish·wife /ˈfisн,wīf/ ▶ **n.** (pl. **-wives**) **1** a coarse-mannered woman who is prone to shouting. **2** archaic a woman who sells fish.

fish·y /ˈfisнē/ ▶ **adj.** (**fish·i·er, fish·i·est**) **1** of, relating to, or resembling fish or a fish. **2** informal arousing feelings of doubt or suspicion. — **fish·i·ly adv. fish·i·ness n.**

Fisk /fisk/, James (1834–72), US financier. He made his fortune by stock manipulation and, with Jay Gould, engineered the Black Friday attempt to corner the gold market in 1869.

fis·sile /ˈfisəl; ˈfisīl/ ▶ **adj.** (of an atom or element) able to undergo nuclear fission. ■ (chiefly of rock) easily split. — **fis·sil·i·ty** /fiˈsilitē/ **n.** [17th C. (in the sense 'easily split'): from L. *fissilis*, from *fiss-* 'split, cracked,' from the v. *findere*.]

fis·sion /ˈfisнən; ˈfizн-/ ▶ **n.** the action of dividing or splitting something into two or more parts. ■ short for NUCLEAR FISSION. ■ Biol. reproduction by means of a cell or organism dividing into two or more new cells or organisms. ▶ **v.** [intrans.] (chiefly of atoms) undergo fission. [17th C.: from L. *fissio(n-)*, from *findere* 'to split.']

fis·sion·a·ble /ˈfisнənəbəl; ˈfizн-/ ▶ **adj.** another term for FISSILE.

fis·sion bomb ▶ **n.** another term for ATOM BOMB.

fis·sip·a·rous /fiˈsipərəs/ ▶ **adj.** inclined to cause or undergo division into separate parts or groups. ■ Biol. (of an organism) reproducing by fission. — **fis·sip·a·rous·ness n.** [19th C.: from L. *fissus*, past part. of *findere* 'split,' on the pattern of *viviparous*.]

fis·sure /ˈfisнər/ ▶ **n.** a long, narrow opening or line of breakage made by cracking or splitting, esp. in rock or earth. ■ esp. Anat. a long narrow opening in the form of a crack or groove, e.g., any of the spaces separating convolutions of the brain. ■ a state of incompatibility or disagreement. ▶ **v.** [trans.] [usu. as adj.] (**fissured**) split or crack (something) to form a long narrow opening: *the skin becomes dry, fissured, and cracked.* [ME: from OFr., or from L. *fissura*, from *findere* 'to split.']

fist /fist/ ▶ **n.** a person's hand when the fingers are bent in toward the palm and held there tightly, typically in order to strike a blow or grasp something. ▶ **v. 1** [trans.] hit with or as with the fists or a fist. **2** (also **fist-fuck**) [trans.] vulgar slang penetrate (a person's anus or vagina) with one's fist. — **fist·ed adj.** [in comb.] *bare-fisted* **fist·ful** /-,fo͝ol/ **n.** [OE *fȳst*, of West Gmc. origin; rel. to Du. *vuist* and Ger. *Faust*.]

fist·fight /ˈfist,fīt/ ▶ **n.** a fight with bare fists.

fist·ic /ˈfistik/ ▶ **adj.** of or relating to boxing; pugilistic.

fist·i·cuffs /ˈfisti,kəfs/ ▶ **plural n.** fighting with the fists. [17th C.: prob. from obs. *fisty* 'relating to the fists or to fistfighting' + CUFF².]

fis·tu·la /ˈfiscнələ/ ▶ **n.** (pl. **-las** or **-lae** /-lē/) Med. an abnormal or surgically made passage between a hollow or tubular organ and the body surface, or between two hollow or tubular organs. — **fis·tu·lar** /-lər/ **adj. fis·tu·lous** /-ləs/ **adj.** [late ME: from L., 'pipe, flute, fistula.' Compare with FESTER.]

fit¹ /fit/ ▶ **adj.** (**fit·ter, fit·test**) **1** [predic.] (of a thing) of a suitable quality, standard, or type to meet the required purpose: *the meat is fit for human consumption.* ■ (of a person) having the requisite qualities or skills to undertake something competently. ■ Biol. possessing or conferring the ability to survive and reproduce in a particular environment: *survival of the fittest.* ■ suitable and correct according to accepted social standards. ■ [with infin.] informal (of a person or thing) having reached such an extreme condition as to be on the point of doing the thing specified: *he baited them until they were fit to kill him.* **2** in good health, esp. because of regular physical exercise. ▶ **v.** (**fit·ted** or **fit** /fit/, **fit·ting**) [trans.] **1** be of the right shape and size for: *those jeans still fit me.* ■ (usu. **be fitted for**) try clothing on (someone) in order to make or alter it to the correct size: *be fitted for her costume.* ■ [intrans.] be of the right size, shape, or number to occupy a particular position or place: *we can all fit in her car.* **2** fix or put (something) into place: *they fitted smoke alarms to their home.* ■ (often **be fitted with**) provide (something) with a particular component or article. ■ join or cause to join together to form a whole. **3** be in agreement or harmony with; match. ■ (of an attribute, qualification, or skill) make (someone) suitable to fulfill a particular role or undertake a particular task. ▶ **n.** the particular way in which something, esp. a garment or component, fits around or into something. ■ the particular way in which a thing matches something else.

– PHRASES (**as**) **fit as a fiddle** see FIDDLE. **fit the bill** see BILL¹. **fit like a glove** see GLOVE. **fit to be tied** informal very angry. **see** (or **think**) **fit** consider it correct or acceptable to do something.

– PHRASAL VERBS **fit in** (of a person) be socially compatible with other members of a group. ■ (of a thing) be in harmony with other things within a larger structure. ■ (also **fit into**) (of a person or thing) constitute part of a particular situation or larger structure. **fit someone/something in** (or **into**) find room or have sufficient space for someone or something: *can you fit any more books into the box?* ■ find time to see someone or do something: *too busy to fit exercise into your life.* — **fit·ly adv.** [ME: of unknown origin.]

fit² ▶ **n.** a sudden uncontrollable outbreak of intense emotion, laughter, coughing, or other action or activity: *in a fit of temper.* ■ a sudden attack of convulsions and/or loss of consciousness, typical of epilepsy and some other medical conditions.

– PHRASES **have** (or **throw**) **a fit** informal be very angry. **in fits** (**of laughter**) informal highly amused. **in** (or **by**) **fits and starts** with irregular bursts of activity. [OE *fitt* 'conflict.']

fitch /ficн/ ▶ **n.** old-fashioned term for POLECAT. ■ (also **fitch fur**) the fur of a polecat. [ME (denoting the fur of a polecat): from MDu. *visse* 'polecat.']

fit·ful /ˈfitfəl/ ▶ **adj.** active or occurring spasmodically or intermittently; not regular or steady. — **fit·ful·ly adv. fit·ful·ness n.**

fit·ness /ˈfitnis/ ▶ **n.** the condition of being physically fit and healthy. ■ the quality of being suitable to fulfill a particular role or task. ■ Biol. an organism's ability to survive and reproduce in a particular environment.

fit·ted /ˈfitid/ ▶ **adj. 1** made or shaped to fill a space or to cover something closely or exactly. **2** attached to or provided with a particular component or article: *a pistol fitted with a match-grade barrel.* **3** [predic.] having the appropriate qualities or skills to do something.

fit·ter /ˈfitər/ ▶ **n. 1** a person who puts together or installs machinery, engine parts, or other equipment. **2** a person who supervises the cutting, fitting, or alteration of garments or shoes.

fit·ting /ˈfitiNG/ ▶ **n. 1** (often **fittings**) a small part on or attached to a piece of furniture or equipment. ■ (**fittings**) items, such as a stove or shelves, that are fixed in a building but can be removed when the owner moves. Compare with FIXTURE. **2** the action of fitting something, in particular: ■ the installing, assembling, and adjusting of machine parts. ■ an occasion when one tries on a garment that is being made or altered. ▶ **adj. 1** suitable or appropriate under the circumstances; right or proper. **2** [in comb.] fitted around or to something or someone in a specified way: *loose-fitting trousers.* — **fit·ting·ly adv. fit·ting·ness n.**

fit·ting room ▶ **n.** a room in a store in which one can try on clothes before deciding whether to purchase them.

Fitz·ger·ald¹ /fitsˈjerəld/, Ella (1917–96), US singer; full name *Ella Jane Fitzgerald.* She is known for her distinctive style of scat singing.

Fitz·ger·ald², F. Scott (1896–1940), US writer; full name *Francis Scott Key Fitzgerald.* His novels, in particular *The Great Gatsby* (1925), provide a vivid portrait of the jazz era of the 1920s.

Fiu·me /ˈfyo͞omā/ Italian name of RIJEKA.

five /fīv/ ▶ **cardinal number** equivalent to the sum of two and three; one more than four, or half of ten; 5. (Roman numeral: **v** or **V.**) ■ a group or unit of five people or things. ■ five years old. ■ five o'clock. ■ a size of garment or other merchandise denoted by five. ■ a playing card or domino with five spots or pips. ■ a five-dollar bill. [OE *fīf*, of Gmc. origin; rel. to Du. *vijf* and Ger. *fünf*, from an Indo-Eur. root shared by L. *quinque* and Gk. *pente*.]

five-a·larm ▶ **adj.** [attrib.] informal (of a fire) very large or fierce. ■ (of food, such as chilies) extremely pungent; hot.

five-and-dime (also **five-and-dime store** or **five-and-ten**) ▶ **n.** a store selling a wide variety of inexpensive household and personal goods. ■ hist. a store where all the articles were priced at five or ten cents.

five-fin·ger (also **five·fin·ger**) ▶ **n.** any of a number of plants with leaves that are divided into five leaflets or with flowers that have five petals, such as cinquefoil.

five·fold /ˈfīvˌfōld/ ▶ **adj.** five times as great or as numerous. ■ having five parts or elements. ▶ **adv.** by five times; to five times the number or amount.

five hun·dred ▶ **n.** a form of euchre in which making 500 points wins a game.

Five Na·tions ▶ **plural n.** hist. the original Iroquois confederacy, comprising the Mohawk, Oneida, Onondaga, Cayuga and Seneca peoples. Compare with **Six Nations**.

five o'clock shad·ow ▶ **n.** a dark appearance on a man's face caused by the slight growth of beard that has occurred since he shaved in the morning.

Five Pil·lars of Is·lam the five duties expected of every Muslim—profession of the faith in a prescribed form, observance of ritual prayer, giving alms to the poor, fasting during the month of Ramadan, and performing a pilgrimage to Mecca.

fiv·er /ˈfīvər/ ▶ **n.** informal a five-dollar bill. ■ Brit. a five-pound note.

five-star ▶ **adj.** (esp. of a hotel or restaurant) given five stars in a grading system, typically one in which this denotes the highest class or quality. ■ (in the US armed forces) having or denoting the highest military rank (awarded only in wartime), distinguished by five stars on the uniform.

fix /fiks/ ▶ **v.** [trans.] **1** [trans.] fasten (something) securely in a particular place or position. ■ fig. lodge or implant (an idea, image, or memory) firmly in a person's mind. **2** (**fix something on/upon**) direct one's eyes, attention, or mind steadily or unwaveringly toward. ■ [intrans.] (**fix on/upon**) (of a person's eyes, attention, or mind) be directed steadily or unwaveringly toward: *her gaze fixed on Jess.* ■ attract and hold (a person's attention or gaze). ■ (**fix someone with**) look at someone unwaveringly. **3** mend; repair. ■ (**fix something up**) do the necessary work to improve or adapt something. ■ make arrangements for (something); organize. ■ informal restore order or tidiness to (something, esp. one's hair, clothes, or makeup). ■ informal prepare or arrange for the provision of (food or drink): [with two objs.] *Ruth fixed herself a cold drink.* ■ (**fix someone up**) informal arrange for someone to have something; provide someone with something. ■ (**fix someone up**) informal arrange for someone to meet or date someone. ■ (**be fixing to do something**) informal be intending or planning to do something. **4** decide or settle on (a specific price, date, course of action, etc.): *no date has been fixed for a hearing.* ■ discover the exact location of (something) by using radar or visual bearings or astronomical observation: *he fixed his position.* ■ settle the form of (a language). ■ assign or determine (a person's liability or responsibility) for legal purposes: *there are no facts that fix the defendant with liability.* **5** make (something) permanent or static in nature. ■ make (a dye, photographic image, or drawing) permanent. ■ Biol. preserve or stabilize (a specimen) with a chemical substance prior to microscopy or other examination. ■ (of a plant or microorganism) assimilate (nitrogen or carbon dioxide) by forming a nongaseous compound. **6** informal influence the outcome of (something, esp. a race, contest, or election) by illegal or underhanded means. ■ put (an enemy or rival) out of action, esp. by killing them: *I'll fix you good!* **7** informal [intrans.] take an injection of a narcotic drug. **8** castrate or spay (an animal); neuter. ▶ **n. 1** [in sing.] informal a difficult or awkward situation from which it is hard to extricate oneself; a predicament. **2** informal a dose of a narcotic drug to which one is addicted. ■ fig. a thing or activity that gives a person a feeling of euphoria or pleasure and that it is difficult to do without. **3** informal a solution to a problem, esp. one that is hastily devised or makeshift. **4** a position determined by visual or radio bearings or astronomical observations. **5** [in sing.] informal a dishonest or underhanded arrangement.
– PHRASES **get a fix on** determine the position of (something) by visual or radio bearings or astronomical observation. ■ informal assess or determine the nature or facts of; obtain a clear understanding of. — **fix·a·ble adj.** [ME: partly from OFr. *fix* 'fixed,' partly from med. L. *fixare* 'to fix,' both from L. *fixus*, past part. of *figere* 'fix, fasten.']

fix·ate /ˈfiksāt/ ▶ **v.** [trans.] **1** (usu. **be fixated on/upon**) cause (someone) to acquire an obsessive attachment to someone or something: *fixated on photography.* ■ [intrans.] (**fixate on/upon**) acquire such an obsessive attachment to: *it is important not to fixate on an imosity.* ■ (in Freudian theory) arrest (a person or their libidinal energy) at an immature stage, causing an obsessive attachment. **2** tech. direct one's eyes toward.

fix·a·tion /fikˈsāsHən/ ▶ **n. 1** an obsessive interest in or feeling about someone or something. ■ Psychoanal. the arresting of part of the libido at an immature stage, causing an obsessive attachment. **2** the action of making something firm or stable. ■ Biochem. the process by which some plants and microorganisms incorporate gaseous nitrogen or carbon dioxide to form nongaseous compounds. ■ Biol. the process of preserving or stabilizing (a specimen) with a chemical substance prior to microscopy or other examination. **3** tech. the action of concentrating the eyes directly on something.

fix·a·tive /ˈfiksətiv/ ▶ **n. 1** a chemical substance used to preserve or stabilize biological material prior to microscopy or other examination. ■ a substance used to stabilize the volatile components of perfume. ■ a liquid sprayed on to a pastel or charcoal drawing to fix colors or prevent smudging. **2** a substance used to keep things in position or stick them together. ▶ **adj.** (of a substance) used to fix or stabilize something.

fixed /fikst/ ▶ **adj. 1** fastened securely in position. ■ remaining in the same place with respect to another object. ■ (esp. of a price, rate, or time) predetermined and not subject to or able to be changed. ■ (of a person's expression) held for a long time without changing, esp. to conceal other feelings. ■ (of a view or idea) held inflexibly. **2** [predic.] (**fixed for**) informal situated with regard to: *how's the club fixed for money?* **3** (of a sports contest) with the outcome dishonestly predetermined. — **fix·ed·ly** /ˈfiksidlē/ **adv.** **fix·ed·ness** /ˈfiksidnis/ **n.**

fixed as·sets ▶ **plural n.** assets that are purchased for long-term use and are not likely to be converted quickly into cash, such as land, buildings, and equipment. Compare with **current assets**.

fixed cap·i·tal ▶ **n.** capital invested in fixed assets.

fixed charge ▶ **n.** a liability to a creditor that relates to specific assets of a company.

fixed costs ▶ **plural n.** business costs, such as rent, that are constant whatever the amount of goods produced.

fixed-do /ˈfikst ˈdō/ (Brit. **fixed-doh**) ▶ **adj.** [attrib.] Music denoting a system of solmization in which C is called "do," D is called "re," etc., irrespective of the key in which they occur. Compare with **movable-do**.

fixed i·de·a ▶ **n.** another term for **idée fixe**.

fixed in·come ▶ **n.** an income from a pension or investment that is set at a particular figure and does not vary (as a dividend) or rise with the rate of inflation.

fixed oil ▶ **n.** a nonvolatile oil of animal or plant origin.

fixed point ▶ **n.** Physics a well-defined reproducible temperature that can be used as a reference point, e.g., one defined by a change of phase. ▶ **adj.** (**fixed-point**) Comput. denoting a mode of representing a number by a single sequence of digits whose values depend on their location relative to a predetermined radix point: *fixed-point binary format.* Often contrasted with **floating-point**.

fixed star ▶ **n.** see **star** (sense 1).

fixed-wing ▶ **adj.** [attrib.] denoting aircraft of the conventional type as opposed to those with rotating wings, such as helicopters.

fix·er /ˈfiksər/ ▶ **n. 1** a person who makes arrangements for other people, esp. of an illicit or devious kind. **2** a substance used for fixing a photographic image.

fix·er-up·per ▶ **n.** informal a house in need of repairs (used chiefly in connection with the purchase of such a house).

fix·ing /ˈfiksiNG/ ▶ **n. 1** the action of fixing something: *artificial price fixing.* **2** (**fixings**) apparatus or equipment for a particular purpose: *picnic fixings.* ■ the ingredients necessary to make a dish or meal.

fix·it /ˈfiksit/ ▶ **n.** informal a person known for repairing things or putting things in order: *a Mr. Fixit.* ■ [usu. as adj.] an act of repairing or putting something right: *a fixit shop.* [20th C.: from *Little Miss Fixit*, the title of a musical show.]

fix·i·ty /ˈfiksitē/ ▶ **n.** the state of being unchanging or permanent: *the fixity of his stare.*

fix·ture /ˈfiksCHər/ ▶ **n.** a piece of equipment or furniture that is fixed in position in a building or vehicle. ■ (**fixtures**) articles attached to a house or land and considered legally part of it so that they normally remain in place when an owner moves. Compare with **fitting** (sense 1). ■ informal a person or thing that is established in a particular place or situation. [16th C.: alt. of obs. *fixure* (from late L. *fixura*, from L. *figere* 'to fix').]

fizz /fiz/ ▶ **v.** [intrans.] (of a liquid) produce bubbles of gas and make a hissing sound: *the mixture fizzed like mad.* ■ make a buzzing or crackling sound. ■ fig. move with or display excitement, exuberance, or liveliness. ▶ **n.** effervescence. ■ informal an effervescent drink, esp. sparkling wine. ■ fig. exuberance; liveliness. ■ a buzzing or crackling sound. [17th C.: imitative.]

fiz·zle /ˈfizəl/ ▶ **v.** [intrans.] end or fail in a weak or disappointing way: *their revolt fizzled out.* ■ make a feeble hissing or spluttering sound. ▶ **n.** a failure. ■ a feeble hissing or spluttering sound. [ME (in the sense 'break wind quietly'): prob. imitative.]

fizz·y /ˈfizē/ ▶ **adj.** (**fizz·i·er, fizz·i·est**) (of a beverage) containing bubbles of gas; effervescent. — **fizz·i·ly adv. fizz·i·ness n.**

fjord /fēˈôrd; fyôrd/ (also **fiord**) ▶ **n.** a long, narrow, deep inlet of the sea between high cliffs, as in Norway and Iceland, typically formed by submergence of a glaciated valley. [17th C.: Norw., from ON *fjǫrthr*. Cf. **firth**.]

FL ▶ **abbr.** Florida (in official postal use).

fl. ▶ **abbr.** ■ floor. ■ floruit. ■ fluid.

Fla. ▶ **abbr.** Florida.

flab /flab/ ▶ **n.** informal soft loose flesh on a person's body; fat. [1950s: back-form. from **flabby**.]

flab·ber·gast /ˈflabərˌgast/ ▶ **v.** [trans.] [usu. as adj.] (**flabbergasted**) informal surprise (someone) greatly; astonish. [18th C.: of unknown origin.]

flab·by /ˈflabē/ ▶ **adj.** (**-bi·er, -bi·est**) (of a part of a person's body) soft, loose, and fleshy. ■ (of a person) having soft loose flesh. ■ fig. not tightly controlled, powerful, or effective. — **flab·bi·ly** /ˈflabəlē/ **adv.** **flab·bi·ness n.** [17th C.: alt. of earlier *flappy*.]

fla·bel·lum /fləˈbeləm/ ▶ **n.** (pl. **-bel·la** /-ˈbelə/) a fan, esp. an elegant, ornamental one used in Christian ritual. ■ Biol. hist. a fan-shaped organ, part, or anatomical structure.

flac·cid /ˈfla(k)sid/ ▶ **adj.** (of part of the body) soft and hanging loosely or limply. ■ (of plant tissue) drooping or inelastic through lack of water. ■ fig. lacking force or effectiveness. — **flac·cid·i·ty** /fla(k)ˈsiditē/ **n.** **flac·cid·ly adv.** [17th C.: from Fr. *flaccide* or L. *flaccidus*, from *flaccus* 'flabby.']

flack[1] /flak/ informal ▶ **n.** a publicity agent. ▶ **v.** [trans.] publicize or promote (something or someone). — **flack·er·y n.** [1940s: of unknown origin.]

flack[2] ▶ **n.** var. of FLAK.

flac·on /ˈflakən; flaˈkôN/ ▶ **n.** (pl. **flac·ons** pronunc. same or /-kənz/) a small stoppered bottle, esp. one for perfume. [19th C.: Fr., 'flask.']

flag[1] /flag/ ▶ **n.** **1** a piece of cloth or similar material, typically oblong or square, attachable by one edge to a pole or rope and used as the symbol or emblem of a country or institution. ■ used in reference to the country to which a person has allegiance. ■ a small piece of cloth, typically attached at one edge to a pole, used as a marker or signal in various sports. ■ the ensign carried by a flagship as an emblem of an admiral's rank. **2** a device, symbol, or drawing typically resembling a flag, used as a marker. ■ Comput. a variable used to indicate a particular property of the data in a record. **3** a hook attached to the stem of a musical note, determining the rhythmic value of the note. ▶ **v.** (**flagged, flag·ging**) [trans.] **1** (often **be flagged**) mark (an item) for attention or treatment in a specified way. ■ fig. draw attention to. **2** [trans.] direct (someone) to go in the specified direction by waving a flag or using hand signals. ■ (**flag someone/something down**) signal to a vehicle or driver to stop, esp. by waving one's arm. ■ [intrans.] (of an official in some sports) raise or throw a flag to indicate a breach of the rules. **3** provide or decorate with a flag or flags. ■ register (a vessel) in a specific country, under whose flag it then sails.
– PHRASES **wrap oneself in the flag** make an excessive show of one's patriotism, esp. for political ends. — **flag·ger n.** [16th C.: perh. from obs. *flag* 'drooping.']

flag[2] ▶ **n.** another term for FLAGSTONE. — **flagged adj.** [often in comb.] *stone-flagged steps.* [ME: prob. of Scand. origin and rel. to ON *flaga* 'slab of stone.']

flag[3] ▶ **n.** a plant with sword-shaped leaves that grow from a rhizome, in particular: ■ a plant of the iris family, esp. blue flag or yellow flag. ■ **sweet flag.** [ME: rel. to MDu. *flag*.]

flag[4] ▶ **v.** (**flagged, flag·ging**) [intrans.] (of a person) become tired, weaker, or less enthusiastic. ■ [often as adj.] (**flagging**) (esp. of an activity or quality) become weaker or less dynamic. [16th C.: rel. to obs. *flag* 'hanging down.']

Flag Day n. June 14, the anniversary of the adoption of the Stars and Stripes as the official US flag in 1777.

flag·el·lant /ˈflajələnt; fləˈjelənt/ ▶ **n.** a person who subjects themselves or others to flogging, either as a religious discipline or for sexual gratification. [16th C.: from L. *flagellant-* 'whipping,' from the v. *flagellare*, from *flagellum* 'whip' (see FLAGELLUM).]

flag·el·late[1] /ˈflajəˌlāt/ ▶ **v.** [trans.] flog (someone), either as a religious discipline or for sexual gratification. — **flag·el·la·tion** /ˌflajəˈlāsHən/ **n.** **flag·el·la·tor** /-ˌlātər/ **n.** **flag·el·la·to·ry** /fləˈjeləˌtôrē/ **adj.**

flag·el·late[2] /ˈflajəlit; -ˌlāt/ Zool. ▶ **n.** a protozoan that has one or more flagella used for swimming. ▶ **adj.** (of a cell or single-celled organism) bearing one or more flagella: *motile flagellate cells.*

fla·gel·lin /fləˈjelən/ ▶ **n.** the structural protein of bacterial flagella.

fla·gel·lum /ˌfləˈjeləm/ ▶ **n.** (pl. **-gel·la** /-ˈjelə/) Biol. a slender threadlike structure, esp. a microscopic whiplike appendage that enables many protozoa, bacteria, spermatozoa, etc., to swim. — **fla·gel·lar** /fləˈjelər; ˈflajələr/ **adj.** [19th C. (denoting a whip or scourge): from L., dimin. of *flagrum* 'scourge.']

flag·eo·let[1] /ˌflajəˈlet; -ˈlā/ ▶ **n.** a small flutelike instrument resembling a recorder but with four finger holes on top and two thumb holes below. ■ another term for TIN WHISTLE. [17th C.: from Fr., dimin. of OFr. *flageol*, from Provençal *flaujol*, of unknown origin.]

flag·eo·let[2] ▶ **n.** a French kidney bean of a small variety used in cooking. [19th C.: from Fr., based on L. *phaseolus* 'bean.']

flag foot·ball ▶ **n.** a modified form of football in which ballcarriers are downed by pulling off a marker, or flag, loosely attached to a belt, rather than by tackling.

Flagg /flag/, James Montgomery (1877–1960), US painter. He created the World War I recruiting poster that features Uncle Sam and the caption "I Want You."

fla·gi·tious /fləˈjisHəs/ ▶ **adj.** (of a person or their actions) criminal; villainous. — **fla·gi·tious·ly adv.** **fla·gi·tious·ness n.** [ME: from L. *flagitiosus*, from *flagitium* 'importunity, shameful crime,' from *flagitare* 'demand earnestly.']

Flag·ler /ˈflaglər/, Henry Morrison (1830–1913), US financier. He helped to develop the Standard Oil Company in 1870 and organized the Florida East Coast Railway in 1886.

flag·man /ˈflagmən/ ▶ **n.** (pl. **-men**) a person who gives signals with a flag, esp. on railroad lines.

flag of con·ven·ience ▶ **n.** a flag of a country under which a ship is registered in order to avoid taxes or regulations in the owner's country.

flag of·fi·cer ▶ **n.** an admiral, vice admiral, or rear admiral. ■ the commodore of a yacht club.

flag of truce ▶ **n.** a white flag indicating a desire for a truce.

flag·on /ˈflagən/ ▶ **n.** a large container in which drink is served, typically with a handle and spout. ■ the amount of liquid held in such a container. ■ a similar container used to hold the wine for the Eucharist. [ME: from OFr. *flacon*, based on late L. *flasco, flascon-*.]

flag·pole /ˈflagˌpōl/ ▶ **n.** a pole used for flying a flag.
– PHRASES **run something up the flagpole (to see who salutes)** test the popularity of a new idea or proposal: *the idea was first run up the flagpole in 1997.*

flag rank ▶ **n.** the rank attained by flag officers.

fla·grant /ˈflāgrənt/ ▶ **adj.** (of something considered wrong or immoral) conspicuously or obviously offensive. — **fla·gran·cy n.** **fla·grant·ly adv.** [15th C.: from Fr., or from L. *flagrant-* 'blazing,' from the v. *flagrare*.]

flag·ship /ˈflagˌsHip/ ▶ **n.** the ship in a fleet that carries the commanding admiral. ■ the best or most important thing owned or produced by a particular organization.

flag·staff /ˈflagˌstaf/ ▶ **n.** another term for FLAGPOLE.

flag·stick /ˈflagˌstik/ ▶ **n.** Golf another term for PIN (sense 2).

flag·stone /ˈflagˌstōn/ ▶ **n.** a flat stone slab, typically rectangular or square, used for paving. — **flag·stoned adj.**

flag stop ▶ **n.** hist. a station at which trains stop only if signaled to do so. ■ a small town or a place of no consequence.

flag-wav·ing ▶ **n.** the expression of patriotism in a populist and emotional way. — **flag-wav·er n.**

flail /flāl/ ▶ **n.** a threshing tool consisting of a wooden staff with a short heavy stick swinging from it. ■ a similar device used as a weapon or for flogging. ■ a machine for threshing or slashing. ▶ **v.** **1** wave or swing or cause to wave or swing wildly. ■ [intrans.] flounder; struggle uselessly: *I was flailing about in the water.* **2** [trans.] beat; flog. [OE, of West Gmc. origin, based on L. *flagellum* 'whip' (see FLAGELLUM).]

flair /fle(ə)r/ ▶ **n.** **1** [in sing.] a special or instinctive aptitude or ability for doing something well. **2** stylishness and originality. [19th C.: from Fr., from *flairer* 'to smell,' based on L. *fragrare* 'smell sweet.' Cf. FRAGRANT.]

flak /flak/ (also **flack**) ▶ **n.** antiaircraft fire. ■ fig., informal strong criticism. [1930s: from Ger., abbrev. of *Fliegerabwehrkanone*, lit. 'aviator-defense gun.']

flake[1] /flāk/ ▶ **n.** **1** a small, flat, thin piece of something, typically one that has broken away or been peeled off from a larger piece. ■ a snowflake. ■ Archaeol. a piece of hard stone chipped off for use as a tool by prehistoric humans. **2** informal a crazy or eccentric person. ▶ **v.** **1** [intrans.] come or fall away from a surface in thin pieces: *the paint had been flaking off for years.* ■ lose small fragments from the surface. **2** [trans.] break or divide (food) into thin pieces. ■ [intrans.] (of food) come apart in thin pieces. [ME: senses perh. from different words; prob. of Gmc. origin and rel. to FLAG[2] and FLAW[1].]

flake[2] ▶ **n.** a rack or shelf for storing or drying food such as fish. [ME: perh. of Scand. origin and rel. to ON *flaki, fleki* 'wicker shield.']

flake[3] ▶ **v.** [intrans.] (**flake out**) informal fall asleep; drop from exhaustion. [15th C.: var. of obs. *flack* and the v. FLAG[4].]

flake[4] (also **fake** /fāk/) Naut. ▶ **n.** a single turn of a coiled rope or hawser. ▶ **v.** [trans.] lay (a rope) in loose coils in order to prevent it tangling: *a cable had to be flaked out.* ■ lay (a sail) down in folds on either side of the boom. [17th C. (as a n.): of unknown origin; cf. Ger. *Flechte* in the same sense.]

flak jack·et (also **flak vest**) ▶ **n.** a sleeveless jacket made of heavy fabric reinforced with metal or Kevlar, worn as protection against bullets and shrapnel.

flak·y /ˈflākē/ (also **flak·ey**) ▶ **adj.** (**flak·i·er, flakiest**) **1** breaking or separating easily into small thin pieces. ■ (esp. of skin or paint) tending to crack and come away from a surface in small pieces. **2** informal crazy or eccentric. ■ informal (of a device or software) prone to break down; unreliable. — **flak·i·ness n.** **flak·i·ly adv.**

flam /flam/ ▶ **n.** Music one of the basic patterns (rudiments) of drumming, consisting of a stroke preceded by a grace note. [18th C.: prob. imitative.]

flam·bé /flämˈbā/ ▶ **adj.** [postpositive] (of food) covered with liquor and set alight briefly: *crêpes flambé.* ▶ **v.** (**-béed** /-ˈbād/, **-bé·ing**) [trans.] cover (food) with liquor and set it alight briefly. [19th C.: Fr., literally 'singed,' past participle of *flamber*, from *flambe* 'a flame.']

flam·beau /ˈflambō/ ▶ **n.** (pl. **-beaus** or **-beaux** /-bōz/) hist. a flaming torch. ■ a large candlestick with several branches. [17th C.: from Fr., from *flambe* 'a flame.']

flam·boy·ant /flamˈboiənt/ ▶ **adj.** **1** (of a person or their behavior) tending to attract attention because of their exuberance, confidence, and stylishness. ■ (esp. of clothing) noticeable because brightly colored, highly patterned, or unusual in style. **2** Archit. of or denoting a style of French Gothic architecture marked by wavy flamelike tracery and ornate decoration. — **flam·boy·ance n.** **flam·boy·an·cy** /-ˈboiənsē/ **n.** **flam·boy·ant·ly adv.** [19th C.: from Fr., literally 'flaming, blazing,' present participle of *flamboyer*, from *flambe* 'a flame.']

flame /flām/ ▶ **n.** **1** a hot glowing body of ignited gas that is generated by something on fire. **2** fig. used in similes and metaphors to refer to something resembling a flame in various respects, in particular: ■ a thing resembling a flame in heat, shape, or brilliance. ■ a brilliant orange-red color: [in comb.] *a flame-red trench coat.* ■ a thing compared

to a flame's ability to burn fiercely or be extinguished: *the flame of hope.* ■ a very intense emotion. ■ a cause that generates passionate feelings. ■ Comput. a vitriolic or abusive message sent via electronic mail. ▶ v. [intrans.] burn and give off flames. ■ [trans.] set (something) alight. ■ fig. shine or glow like a flame: *her hair flamed against the light.* ■ fig. (of an intense emotion) appear suddenly and fiercely. ■ (of a person's face) suddenly become red with intense emotion, esp. anger or embarrassment. ■ [trans.] Comput. send (someone) abusive or vitriolic electronic mail messages.
– PHRASES **old flame** informal a former lover.
– PHRASAL VERBS **flame out** (of a jet engine) lose power through the extinction of the flame in the combustion chamber. ■ informal fail, esp. conspicuously. — **flam·er** n. (Comput.) **flam·y** /ˈflāmē/ adj. [ME: from OFr. *flame* (n.), *flamer* (v.), from L. *flamma* 'a flame.']

fla·men /ˈflāmən/ ▶ n. (pl. **fla·mens** or **flam·i·nes** /ˈflaməˌnēz/) Roman History a priest serving a particular deity. [ME: L., literally 'priest.']

fla·men·co /fləˈmeNGkō/ ▶ n. a style of Spanish music, played esp. on the guitar and accompanied by singing and dancing. ■ a style of spirited, rhythmical dance performed to such music, often with castanets. [19th C.: Sp., 'like a gypsy,' literally 'Fleming,' from MDu. *Vlaminc.*]

flame·out /ˈflāˌmout/ ▶ n. an instance of the flame in the combustion chamber of a jet engine being extinguished, with a resultant loss of power. ■ informal a complete or conspicuous failure.

flame·proof /ˈflāmˌpro͞of/ ▶ adj. (esp. of a fabric) treated so as to be nonflammable. ■ (of cookware) able to be used either in an oven or on a stove. ▶ v. [trans.] make (something) flameproof.

flame stitch another term for **BARGELLO**.

flame·throw·er /ˈflāmˌTHrōər/ ▶ n. a weapon that sprays out burning fuel.

flame tree ▶ n. any of a number of trees with brilliant red flowers, including an Australian bottle tree (*Brachychiton acerifolius*, family Sterculiaceae).

flam·ing /ˈflāmiNG/ ▶ adj. [attrib.] **1** burning fiercely and emitting flames. ■ very hot. ■ glowing with a bright orange or red color. ■ (of red or orange) brilliant or intense. ■ (esp. of an argument) passionate. **2** informal used for emphasis to express annoyance: *a flaming nuisance.* — **flam·ing·ly** adv.

fla·min·go /fləˈmiNGgō/ ▶ n. (pl. **-gos** or **-goes**) a tall wading bird (family Phoenicopteridae) with mainly pink or scarlet plumage. It has a heavy bent bill used to filter-feed on small organisms. Its four species include the **greater flamingo** (*Phoenicopterus ruber*). [16th C.: from Sp. *flamengo*, earlier form of *flamenco* (see **FLAMENCO**).]

greater flamingo

flam·ma·ble /ˈflaməbəl/ ▶ adj. easily set on fire. — **flam·ma·bil·i·ty** /ˌflaməˈbilitē/ n. [19th C.: from L. *flammare*, from *flamma* 'a flame.']

flam·mu·lat·ed owl /ˈflamyəˌlātəd/ ▶ n. a small reddish-gray migratory American owl (*Otus flammeolus*) that sometimes occurs in loose colonies.

flan /flan/ ▶ n. **1** a baked dish consisting of an open-topped pastry case with a savory or sweet filling. ■ a sponge base with a sweet topping. **2** a disk of metal such as one from which a coin is made. [19th C.: from Fr., from OFr. *flaon*, from med. L. *flado, fladon-*, of West Gmc. origin; rel. to Du. *vlade* 'custard.']

Flan·ders /ˈflandərz/ a region in the southwestern part of the Low Countries, now divided between Belgium, France, and the Netherlands.

flâ·ne·rie /ˌflän(ə)ˈrē/ ▶ n. aimless idle behavior. [Fr., from *flâner* 'saunter, lounge.']

flâ·neur /fläˈnər; -ˈnœr/ (also **fla·neur**) ▶ n. (pl. **flâ·neurs** pronunc. same) an idler or lounger. [Fr., from *flâner* 'saunter, lounge.']

flange /flanj/ ▶ n. a projecting flat rim, collar, or rib on an object, serving to strengthen or attach or (on a wheel) to maintain position on a rail. — **flanged** adj. [17th C.: perh. based on OFr. *flanchir* 'to bend.']

flang·er /ˈflanjər/ ▶ n. an electronic device that alters a sound signal, used esp. in popular music.

flang·ing /ˈflanjiNG/ ▶ n. **1** the provision of a flange or flanges on an object. **2** the alteration of sound using a flanger.

flank /flaNGk/ ▶ n. **1** the side of a person's or animal's body between the ribs and the hip. ■ a cut of meat from such a part of an animal. ■ the side of something large, such as a mountain, building, or ship. **2** the right or left side of a body of people such as an army, a naval force, or a soccer team. ■ the right or left side of a game board such as a chessboard. ▶ v. [trans.] (often **be flanked**) be situated on each side of or on one side of (someone or something). ■ [usu. as adj.] (**flanking**) guard or strengthen (a military force or position) from the side: *flanking towers.* ■ [usu. as adj.] (**flanking**) attack down or from the sides, or rake with gunfire from the sides: *a flanking attack.* [late OE, from OFr. *flanc*, of Gmc. origin.]

flank·er /ˈflaNGkər/ ▶ n. a person or thing situated on the flank of something, in particular: ■ Football an offensive back who lines up to the outside of an end. ■ Mil. a fortification guarding or menacing the side of a force or position.

flan·nel /ˈflanl/ ▶ n. a kind of soft-woven fabric, typically made of wool or cotton and slightly milled and raised. ■ (**flannels**) men's trousers made of such material. ■ short for **FLANNELETTE**. [ME: prob. from Welsh *gwlanen* 'woolen article,' from *gwlân* 'wool.']

flan·nel·board /ˈflanlˌbôrd/ ▶ n. a board covered with flannel to which paper or cloth cutouts will stick, used as a toy or a teaching aid.

flan·nel·ette /ˌflanlˈet/ ▶ n. a napped cotton fabric resembling flannel.

flan·nel·mouth /ˈflanlˌmouTH/ ▶ n. informal a person who talks too much, esp. in a boastful or deceitful way.

flap /flap/ ▶ v. (**flapped, flap·ping**) [trans.] (of a bird) move (its wings) up and down when flying or preparing to fly. ■ [intrans.] (of something attached at one point or loosely fastened) flutter or wave around: *the corners flapped furiously.* ■ move (one's arms or hands) up and down or back and forth. ■ [trans.] strike or attempt to strike (something) loosely with one's hand, a cloth, or a broad implement, esp. to drive it away. ■ wave (something, esp. a cloth) around or at something or someone. ▶ n. **1** a piece of something thin, such as cloth, paper, or metal, hinged or attached only on one side, that covers an opening or hangs down from something. ■ a hinged or sliding section of an aircraft wing used to control lift. ■ the part of a dust jacket that folds inside a book's cover. ■ a large broad mushroom. ■ Phonet. a type of consonant produced by allowing the tip of the tongue to strike the alveolar ridge very briefly. **2** a movement of a wing or an arm from side to side or up and down. ■ [in sing.] the sound of something making such a movement. **3** [in sing.] informal a state of agitation; a panic: *they're in a flap over who's going to take Henry's lectures.* — **flap·py** adj. [ME: prob. imitative.]

flap·doo·dle /ˈflapˌdo͞odl/ ▶ n. informal nonsense. [19th C.: an arbitrary formation.]

flap·jack /ˈflapˌjak/ ▶ n. a pancake. [from **FLAP** (in the dial. sense 'toss a pancake') + **JACK**[1].]

flap·pa·ble /ˈflapəbəl/ ▶ adj. excitable and quick to lose one's composure.

flap·per /ˈflapər/ ▶ n. **1** informal (in the 1920s) a fashionable young woman intent on enjoying herself and flouting conventional standards of behavior. **2** a thing that flaps, esp. a movable seal inside a toilet tank.

flare /fle(ə)r/ ▶ n. **1** a sudden brief burst of bright flame or light. ■ a device producing a bright flame, used esp. as a signal or marker. ■ [in sing.] a sudden burst of intense emotion. ■ Astron. a sudden explosion in the chromosphere and corona of the sun or another star, resulting in an intense burst of radiation. See also **SOLAR FLARE**. ■ Photog. extraneous illumination on film caused by internal reflection in the camera. **2** [in sing.] a gradual widening, esp. of a skirt or pants. ■ an upward and outward curve of a vessel's bow, designed to throw the water outward when under way. ▶ v. [intrans.] **1** burn with a sudden intensity: *the blaze across the water flared.* ■ (of a light or a person's eyes) glow with a sudden intensity: *her eyes flared at the stinging insult.* ■ (of an emotion) suddenly become manifest in a person or their expression. ■ (**flare up**) (of an illness or chronic medical complaint) recur unexpectedly and cause further discomfort. ■ (esp. of an argument, conflict, or trouble) suddenly become more violent or intense. ■ (**flare up**) (of a person) suddenly become angry. **2** [often as adj.] (**flared**) gradually become wider at one end: *a flared skirt.* ■ (of a person's nostrils) dilate. ■ [trans.] (of a person) cause (the nostrils) to dilate. [16th C.: of unknown origin.]

flare-up ▶ n. a sudden outburst of something, esp. violence or a medical condition.

flash /flaSH/ ▶ v. **1** [intrans.] (of a light or something that reflects light) shine in a bright but brief, sudden, or intermittent way: *the lights started flashing* | [as adj.] (**flashing**) *a flashing light.* ■ [trans.] cause to shine briefly or suddenly. ■ [trans.] shine or show a light to send (a signal). ■ [trans.] give (a swift or sudden look). **2** [trans.] display (an image, words, or information) suddenly on a television or computer screen or electronic sign, typically briefly or repeatedly: *the screen flashes a message.* ■ [intrans.] (of an image or message) be displayed in such a way. ■ informal hold up or show (something, often proof of one's identity) quickly: *she flashed her ID card.* ■ informal make a conspicuous display of (something) so as to impress or attract attention. ■ [intrans.] [often as n.] (**flashing**) informal (esp. of a man) show one's genitals briefly in public. **3** [intrans.] move or pass very quickly: *the scenery flashed by.* ■ (of a thought or memory) suddenly come into or pass through the mind. ■ [trans.] send (news or information) swiftly by means of telegraphy or telecommunications: *the story was flashed around the world.* ▶ n. **1** a sudden brief burst of bright light or a sudden glint from a reflective surface. ■ a bright patch of color, often one used for decoration or identification. **2** a thing that occurs suddenly and within a brief period of time, in particular: ■ a sudden instance or manifestation of a quality, understanding, or humor. ■ a fleeting glimpse of something, esp. something vivid or eye-catching. ■ a news flash. **3** a camera attachment that produces a brief very bright light, used for taking photographs in poor light. **4** a rush of water, esp. down a weir to take a boat over shallows. ■ a device for producing such a rush of water.
– PHRASES **flash in the pan** a thing or person whose sudden but brief success is not repeated or repeatable. **in** (or **like**) **a flash** very quickly; immediately. (**as**) **quick as a flash** (esp. of a person's response or reaction) very quickly.
– PHRASAL VERBS **flash back** (of a person's thoughts or mind) briefly and suddenly recall a previous time or incident. **flash over** make an electric circuit by sparking across a gap. ■ (of a fire) spread instantly across a gap because of intense heat. [ME: prob. imitative.]

flash·back /ˈflaSHˌbak/ ▶ n. a scene in a movie, novel, etc., set in a time earlier than the main story. ■ a sudden and disturbing vivid memory of an event in the past, typically as the result of psychological trauma or taking LSD.

flash·board /ˈflasH,bôrd/ ▶ n. a board used for increasing the depth of water behind a dam.

flash·bulb /ˈflasH,bəlb/ ▶ n. a light bulb that flashes in order to illuminate a photographic subject, of a type that is used only once.

flash burn ▶ n. a burn caused by sudden intense heat, e.g., from a nuclear explosion.

flash card ▶ n. a card containing a small amount of information, held up for students to see, as an aid to learning.

flash·cube /ˈflasH,kyo͞ob/ ▶ n. esp. hist. a set of four flashbulbs arranged in a cube and operated in turn.

flash drive ▶ n. Computing a data storage device containing flash memory that has no moving parts and does not need batteries or a power supply.

flash·er /ˈflasHər/ ▶ n. **1** an automatic device causing a light to flash on and off rapidly. ■ a signal using such a device, for example a car's turn signal. **2** informal a person, esp. a man, who exposes their genitals in public.

flash flood ▶ n. a sudden local flood, typically due to heavy rain.

flash-freeze ▶ v. [trans.] freeze (food or other material) rapidly so as to prevent the formation of ice crystals. — **flash-freez·er** n.

flash·gun /ˈflasH,gən/ ▶ n. a device that gives a brief flash of intense light, used for taking photographs indoors or in poor light.

flash·ing /ˈflasHiNG/ ▶ n. a strip of metal used to stop water from penetrating a junction, typically of a roof with another surface. [18th C.: from the earlier synonym *flash* (of unknown origin) + -ING[1].]

flash·light /ˈflasH,līt/ ▶ n. **1** a battery-operated portable light. **2** a flashing light used for signals and in lighthouses. **3** a light giving an intense flash, used for photographing at night or indoors.

flash mem·o·ry ▶ n. Comput. memory that retains data in the absence of a power supply.

flash·o·ver /ˈflasH,ōvər/ ▶ n. **1** a high-voltage electric short circuit made through the air between exposed conductors. **2** an instance of a fire spreading very rapidly through the air because of intense heat.

flash point (also **flash·point**) ▶ n. **1** a place, event, or time at which trouble, such as violence or anger, flares up. **2** Chem. the temperature at which a particular organic compound gives off sufficient vapor to ignite in air.

flash tube ▶ n. a gas discharge tube used, esp. in photography, to provide an electronic flash when a current is suddenly passed through it.

flash·y /ˈflasHē/ ▶ adj. (**flash·i·er**, **flash·i·est**) ostentatiously attractive or impressive. — **flash·i·ly** adv. **flash·i·ness** n.

flask /flask/ ▶ n. a container or bottle, in particular: ■ a narrow-necked glass container, typically conical or spherical, used in a laboratory to hold reagents or samples. ■ a metal container for storing a small amount of liquor, typically to be carried in one's pocket. ■ a narrow-necked bulbous glass container, typically with a covering of wickerwork, for storing wine or oil. ■ a small glass bottle for perfume. ■ a vacuum flask. ■ the contents of any of these containers. [ME (in the sense 'cask'): from med. L. *flasca*.]

flat[1] /flat/ ▶ adj. (**flat·ter**, **flat·test**) **1** smooth and even; without marked lumps or indentations. ■ (of land) without hills. ■ (of an expanse of water) calm and without waves. ■ not sloping. ■ having a broad level surface but little height or depth; shallow. ■ (of shoes) without heels or with very low heels. **2** lacking interest or emotion; dull and lifeless. ■ (of a person) without energy; dispirited. ■ (of a market, prices, etc.) not showing much activity; sluggish. ■ (of a sparkling drink) having lost its effervescence. ■ (of something kept inflated, esp. a tire) having lost some or all of its air, typically because of a puncture. ■ (of a color) uniform. ■ (of a photographic print or negative) lacking contrast. **3** [attrib.] (of a fee, wage, or price) the same in all cases, not varying with changed conditions or in particular cases. See also FLAT RATE. ■ (of a denial, contradiction, or refusal) completely definite and firm; absolute. **4** (of musical sound) below true or normal pitch. ■ [postpositive, in comb.] (of a note) a semitone lower than a specified note: *B-flat major*. ■ (of a key) having a flat or flats in the signature. ▶ adv. **1** in or to a horizontal position: *lying flat on his back*. ■ lying in close juxtaposition, esp. against another surface. ■ so as to become smooth and even. **2** informal completely; absolutely. ■ after a phrase expressing a period of time to emphasize how quickly something can be done or has been done: *a healthy meal **in ten minutes flat***. **3** below the true or normal pitch of musical sound. ▶ n. **1** [in sing.] the flat part of something. **2** a flat object, in particular: ■ (often **flats**) an upright section of painted stage scenery mounted on a frame. ■ informal a flat tire. ■ a shallow container in which seedlings are grown and sold. ■ (often **flats**) a shoe with a very low heel or no heel. ■ a railroad car with a flat floor and no sides or roof; a flatcar. **3** (usu. **flats**) an area of low level ground, esp. near water. See also MUDFLAT. **4** a musical note lowered a semitone below natural pitch. ■ the sign (♭) indicating this. ▶ v. (**flat·ted**, **flat·ting**) [trans.] [usu. as adj.] (**flatted**) Music lower (a note) by a semitone.

– PHRASES **fall flat** fail completely to produce the intended or expected effect. **fall flat on one's face** fall over forward. ■ fig. fail in an embarrassingly obvious way. (**Flat**) **flat as a pancake** see PANCAKE. **flat out** **1** as fast or as hard as possible. **2** informal without hesitation or reservation; unequivocally: *I'd just flat out vote against foreign aid* | [as adj.] (**flat-out**) *flat-out perjury*. **3** lying completely stretched out, esp. asleep or exhausted. — **flat·ness** n. **flat·tish** adj. [ME: from ON *flatr*.]

flat[2] ▶ n. British term for APARTMENT. — **flat·let** /-lit/ n. [19th C. (denoting a floor or story): alt. of obs. *flet* 'floor, dwelling,' of Gmc. origin and rel. to FLAT[1].]

flat·bed /ˈflat,bed/ ▶ n. a long flat area or structure. ■ a vehicle with a flat load-carrying area: [as adj.] *a flatbed truck*. ■ Comput. a scanner, plotter, or other device that keeps paper flat during use.

flat-bed press ▶ n. a press in which a rotating cylinder equipped with paper makes contact with a horizontal printing surface.

flat·boat /ˈflat,bōt/ ▶ n. a cargo boat with a flat bottom for use in shallow water.

flat·bread /ˈflat,bred/ ▶ n. flat, thin, often unleavened bread.

Flat·bush /ˈflat,bo͝osH/ a section of central Brooklyn in New York City.

flat·car /ˈflat,kär/ ▶ n. a railroad freight car without a roof or sides.

flat-chest·ed ▶ adj. (of a woman) having small breasts.

flat-fell ▶ v. see FELL[2] (sense 2).

flat file ▶ n. Comput. a file having no internal hierarchy. ■ [as adj.] denoting a system using such files.

flat·fish /ˈflat,fisH/ ▶ n. (pl. same or **-fish·es**) a flattened marine fish (order Pleuronectiformes) that swims on its side with both eyes on the upper side. They live typically on the seabed and are colored to resemble it. Its several families include Bothidae (left-eye flounders), Pleuronectidae (right-eye flounders), and Soleidae (soles).

flat·foot /ˈflat,fo͝ot/ ▶ n. (also **flat foot**) a condition in which the foot has an arch that is lower than usual. ■ (pl. **flatfoots** or **flatfeet** /ˈflatˈ,fēt/) informal, dated a police officer.

flat-foot·ed ▶ adj. **1** having flat feet. **2** having one's feet flat on the ground. ■ informal unable to move quickly and smoothly; clumsy. ■ informal not clever or imaginative; uninspired.

– PHRASES **catch someone flat-footed** informal take someone by surprise. — **flat-foot·ed·ly** adv. **flat-foot·ed·ness** n.

flat·head /ˈflat,hed/ ▶ n. **1** [often as adj.] (**Flathead**) a member of a native people of western Montana. ■ the Salishan language spoken by those people. ■ a member of certain other North American Indian peoples, such as the Chinook and Choctaw, who practiced or were thought to practice head-flattening. **2** [as adj.] (of a screw) countersunk.

Flat·head Range a range of the Rocky Mountains in northwestern Montana.

flat·i·ron /ˈflat,īərn/ ▶ n. hist. an iron that was heated externally and used for pressing clothes.

flat·land /ˈflat,land/ ▶ n. (also **flatlands**) land with no hills, valleys, or mountains. — **flat·land·er** n.

flat-leafed pars·ley (also **flat-leaf pars·ley**) ▶ n. parsley of a variety with large flat leaves. Also called ITALIAN PARSLEY.

flat·line /ˈflat,līn/ ▶ v. [intrans.] informal **1** (of a person) die. **2** fail to increase; remain static: *their share of the vote flatlined at 3%*. — **flat·lin·er** n. [1980s: from FLAT[1] + LINE[1].]

flat·ly /ˈflatlē/ ▶ adv. **1** showing little interest or emotion: *"You'd better go," she said flatly*. **2** in a firm and unequivocal manner; absolutely: *they flatly refused to play*. **3** in a smooth and even way. ■ Photog. without marked contrast of light and dark.

flat·pack ▶ n. Electron. a package for an integrated circuit consisting of a rectangular sealed unit with a number of horizontal metal pins protruding from its sides.

flat rate ▶ n. a charge that is the same in all cases, not varying in proportion with something. ■ a rate of taxation that is not progressive, but remains at the same proportion on all amounts.

flat sheet ▶ n. an ordinary sheet for a bed as distinct from a fitted one.

flat·ten /ˈflatn/ ▶ v. **1** make or become flat or flatter. ■ [trans.] press (oneself or one's body) against a surface, typically to get away from something or to let someone pass: ***they flattened themselves on the pavement***. ■ [trans.] Music lower (a note) in pitch by a half step. **2** [trans.] raze (a building or settlement) to the ground. ■ informal knock someone down with power and vigor: *I know I can flatten him*. ■ informal defeat (someone) completely, esp. in a sports contest.

– PHRASAL VERBS **flatten out** **1** (of an increasing quantity or rate) show a less marked rise; slow down. **2** make an aircraft fly horizontally after a dive or climb. — **flat·ten·er** n.

flat·ter /ˈflatər/ ▶ v. [trans.] lavish insincere praise and compliments upon (someone), esp. to further one's own interests. ■ give an unrealistically favorable impression of. ■ (usu. **be flattered**) make (someone) feel honored and pleased: [trans.] *I was flattered to be given the commission*. ■ (**flatter oneself**) make oneself feel pleased by believing something favorable about oneself, typically something that is unfounded. ■ (of a color or a style of clothing) make (someone) appear more attractive or to the best advantage. — **flat·ter·er** n. [ME: perh. a back-form. from FLATTERY.]

flat·ter·ing /ˈflatəriNG/ ▶ adj. (of a person or their remarks) full of praise and compliments. ■ pleasing; gratifying. ■ (esp. of a garment or color) enhancing someone's appearance. ■ (of a picture or portrait) giving an unrealistically favorable impression of someone or something. — **flat·ter·ing·ly** adv.

flat·ter·y /ˈflatərē/ ▶ n. (pl. **-ter·ies**) excessive and insincere praise, esp. that given to further one's own interests. [ME: from OFr. *flaterie*, from *flater* 'stroke, flatter,' prob. of Gmc. origin and rel. to FLAT[1].]

flat·top /'flat,täp/ ▶ n. 1 informal an aircraft carrier. 2 a man's hairstyle in which the hair is cropped short so that it bristles up into a flat surface.

flat·u·lent /'flacHələnt/ ▶ adj. suffering from or marked by an accumulation of gas in the alimentary canal. ■ related to or causing this condition. ■ fig. inflated or pretentious in speech or writing. — **flat·u·lence** n. **flat·u·len·cy** n. **flat·u·lent·ly** adv. [16th C.: via Fr. from mod. L. *flatulentus*, from L. *flatus* 'blowing' (see FLATUS).]

fla·tus /'flātəs/ ▶ n. formal gas in or from the stomach or intestines, produced by swallowing air or by bacterial fermentation. [17th C.: from L., literally 'blowing,' from *flare* 'to blow.']

flat·ware /'flat,we(ə)r/ ▶ n. eating utensils such as knives, forks, and spoons. ■ relatively flat dishes such as plates and saucers. The opposite of HOLLOWWARE.

flat·worm /'flat,wərm/ ▶ n. a worm of a phylum (Platyhelminthes) that includes the planarians together with the parasitic flukes and tapeworms. They are distinguished by having a simple flattened body that lacks blood vessels, and a digestive tract that, if present, has a single opening.

flat-wo·ven ▶ adj. (of a carpet or rug) woven so as not to form a projecting pile. — **flat-weave** n.

Flau·bert /flō'ber/, Gustave (1821–80), French writer. A dominant figure in the French realist school, he is best known for *Madame Bovary* (1857).

flaunt /flônt; flänt/ ▶ v. [trans.] display (something) ostentatiously, esp. in order to provoke envy or admiration or to show defiance: *consumers eager to flaunt their prosperity.* ■ (**flaunt oneself**) dress or behave in a sexually provocative way.
– PHRASES **if you've got it, flaunt it** informal one should make a conspicuous and confident show of one's wealth or attributes rather than be modest about them. — **flaunt·er** n. **flaunt·y** adj. [16th C.: of unknown origin.]

flau·tist /'flôtist; 'flou-/ ▶ n. a flutist. [19th C.: from Ital. *flautista*, from *flauto* 'flute.']

fla·va·none /'flāvə,nōn/ ▶ n. a colorless, crystalline derivative of flavone.

fla·ves·cent /flə'vesənt/ ▶ adj. yellowish or turning yellow. [19th C.: from L. *flavescent-* 'turning yellow,' from the v. *flavescere*, from *flavus* 'yellow.']

Fla·vi·an /'flāvēən/ ▶ adj. of or relating to a dynasty (AD 69–96) of Roman emperors including Vespasian and his sons Titus and Domitian. ▶ n. a member of this dynasty. [from L. *Flavianus*, from *Flavius*, a given name used by this dynasty.]

fla·vin /'flāvin/ ▶ n. Biochem. any of a group of naturally occurring pigments including riboflavin. They have a tricyclic aromatic molecular structure. [19th C.: from L. *flavus* 'yellow' + -IN[1].]

fla·vine /'flāvēn/ ▶ n. 1 Med. an antiseptic derived from acridine. 2 Chem. another term for QUERCETIN. [20th C.: from L. *flavus* 'yellow' + -INE[4].]

fla·vi·vi·rus /'flāvə,vīrəs/ ▶ n. a virus (Family Flaviviridae, three genera) whose genome consists of positive RNA, that is capable of reproducing in its arthropod vector, and that causes a number of serious human diseases including yellow fever, dengue, Japanese encephalitis, and West Nile virus.

fla·vone /'flāvōn/ ▶ n. Chem. a colorless crystalline compound, $C_{15}H_{10}O_2$, that is the basis of a number of white or yellow plant pigments. ■ any of these pigments. [19th C.: from L. *flavus* 'yellow' + -ONE.]

fla·vo·noid /'flāvə,noid/ ▶ n. Chem. any of a large class of plant pigments having a structure based on or similar to that of flavone.

fla·vo·pro·tein /,flāvə'prōtēn; -'prōtēən/ ▶ n. Biochem. any of a class of conjugated proteins that contain flavins and are involved in oxidation reactions in cells. [1930s: blend of FLAVIN and PROTEIN.]

fla·vor /'flāvər/ (Brit. **fla·vour**) ▶ n. 1 the distinctive quality of a particular food or drink as perceived by the taste buds and the sense of smell. ■ the general quality of taste in a food. ■ a substance used to alter or enhance the taste of food or drink; a flavoring. ■ [in sing.] fig. an indefinable distinctive quality of something: *a European flavor.* ■ [in sing.] fig. an indication of the essential character of something. 2 Physics a quantized property of quarks that differentiates them into at least six varieties (up, down, charmed, strange, top, bottom). Compare with COLOR. ▶ v. [trans.] alter or enhance the taste of (food or drink) by adding a particular ingredient: *they use spices to flavor their foods.* ■ fig. give a distinctive quality to. — **fla·vor·ful** /-fəl/ adj. **fla·vor·some** adj. [ME: from OFr. *flaor*, perh. based on a blend of L. *flatus* 'blowing' and *foetor* 'stench.']

fla·vored /'flāvərd/ (Brit. **fla·voured**) ▶ adj. (of food or drink) having a particular type of taste: [in comb.] *the peanut oil is full-flavored.* ■ (of food or drink) having been given a particular taste by the addition of a flavoring. ■ [in comb.] fig. having a particular distinctive quality: *rock 'n' roll-flavored singles.*

fla·vor en·hanc·er ▶ n. a chemical additive, e.g., monosodium glutamate, used to intensify the flavor of food.

fla·vor·ing /'flāvəriNG/ (Brit. **flavouring**) ▶ n. a substance used to give a different, stronger, or more agreeable taste to food or drink.

flaw[1] /flô/ ▶ n. a mark, fault, or other imperfection that mars a substance or object. ■ a fault or weakness in a person's character. ■ a mistake or shortcoming in a plan, theory, or legal document that causes it to fail or reduces its effectiveness. ▶ v. [trans.] (usu. **be flawed**) (of an imperfection) mar, weaken, or invalidate (something): *the computer game was flawed by poor programming.* [ME: perh. from ON *flaga* 'slab.']

flaw[2] ▶ n. literary a squall of wind; a short storm. [16th C.: prob. from MDu. *vlāghe*, Mid. Low Ger. *vlāge*.]

flawed /flôd/ ▶ adj. (of a substance or object) blemished, damaged, or imperfect in some way. ■ (of something abstract) containing a mistake, weakness, or fault. ■ (of a person) having a weakness in character.

flaw·less /'flôlis/ ▶ adj. without any blemishes or imperfections; perfect. ■ without any mistakes or shortcomings. ■ (of a person) lacking any faults or weaknesses of character. — **flaw·less·ly** adv. **flaw·less·ness** n.

flax /flaks/ ▶ n. a blue-flowered herbaceous plant (*Linum usitatissimum*, family Linaceae) that is cultivated for its seed (linseed) and for textile fiber made from its stalks. ■ textile fiber obtained from this plant. ■ used in names of other plants of the flax family or plants that yield similar fiber. [OE *flæx*, rel. to Ger. *Flachs*, from an Indo-Eur. root shared by L. *plectere* and Gk. *plekein* 'to plait, twist.']

flax·en /'flaksən/ ▶ adj. of flax. ■ (esp. of hair) of the pale yellow color of dressed flax.

flax·seed /'flak(s),sēd/ ▶ n. another term for LINSEED.

flay /flā/ ▶ v. [trans.] peel the skin off (a corpse or carcass). ■ peel (the skin) off a corpse or carcass. ■ whip or beat (someone) so harshly as to remove their skin. ■ fig. criticize severely and brutally. ■ fig. extort or exact money or belongings from (someone). — **flay·er** n. [OE *flēan*, of Gmc. origin; rel. to MDu. *vlaen*.]

F lay·er ▶ n. the highest and most strongly ionized region of the ionosphere.

fld. ▶ abbr. ■ field. ■ fluid.

flea /flē/ ▶ n. a small wingless jumping insect (order Siphonaptera) that feeds on the blood of mammals and birds, including the **human flea** (*Pulex irritans*) and the **cat flea** (*Ctenocephalides felis*). ■ **a water flea** (see DAPHNIA). [OE *flēa*, *flēah*, of Gmc. origin; rel. to Du. *vlo* and Ger. *Floh*.]

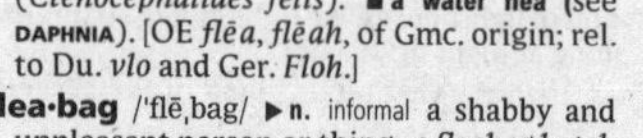
cat flea

flea·bag /'flē,bag/ ▶ n. informal a shabby and unpleasant person or thing: *a fleabag hotel.*

flea·bane /'flē,bān/ ▶ n. a herbaceous plant (*Erigeron*, *Pulicaria*, and other genera) of the daisy family, reputed to drive away fleas.

flea bee·tle ▶ n. a small jumping leaf beetle (*Phyllotreta* and other genera) that can be a pest of plants such as crucifers.

flea·bite /'flē,bīt/ ▶ n. a small red mark caused by the bite of a flea. ■ fig. a trivial injury or cost: *the proposed energy tax amounted to little more than a fleabite.*

flea-bit·ten ▶ adj. bitten by or infested with fleas. ■ sordid, shabby, or disreputable: *this flea-bitten gross-out movie seems to believe that it's about something.*

flea cir·cus ▶ n. a novelty show of performing fleas.

flea col·lar ▶ n. a collar for a cat or dog that is impregnated with insecticide in order to keep the pet free of fleas.

flea-flick·er ▶ n. Football a designed play in which a pass is thrown to a receiver who then laterals to a teammate.

flea mar·ket ▶ n. a market, typically outdoors, selling secondhand goods.

fle·chette /flā'sHet; flesH'et/ (also **flé·chette**) ▶ n. a type of ammunition resembling a small dart, shot from a gun. [20th C.: from Fr. *fléchette*, dimin. of *flèche* 'arrow.']

fleck /flek/ ▶ n. a very small patch of color or light: *his blue eyes had gray flecks in them* | *flecks of sunshine.* ■ a small particle or speck of something: *brushing a few flecks of dandruff from his suit.* ▶ v. [trans.] (often **be flecked**) mark or dot with small patches of color or particles of something: *the minarets are flecked with gold leaf.* [ME (as a verb): perh. from ON *flekkr* (n.), *flekka* (v.).]

flec·tion /'fleksHən/ ▶ n. var. of FLEXION.

fled /fled/ past and past participle of FLEE.

fledge /flej/ ▶ v. 1 [intrans.] (of a young bird) develop wing feathers that are large enough for flight. ■ [trans.] bring up (a young bird) until its wing feathers are developed enough for flight. 2 [trans.] provide (an arrow) with feathers. [16th C.: from the obs. adj. *fledge* 'ready to fly,' from OE, of Gmc. origin; rel. to Du. *vlug* 'quick, agile,' also to FLY[1].]

fledged /flejd/ ▶ adj. (of a young bird) having wing feathers that are large enough for flight; able to fly. See also FULL-FLEDGED. ■ fig. (of a person or thing) having just taken on the role specified: *our discipline is so new fledged that the FBI had to take its cases to the Smithsonian for analysis.* ■ esp. literary (of an arrow) provided with feathers.

fledg·ling /'flejliNG/ (also **fledge·ling**) ▶ n. a young bird that has just fledged. ■ [usu. as adj.] a person or organization that is immature, inexperienced, or underdeveloped: *the fledgling democracies of eastern Europe.*

flee /flē/ ▶ v. (**flees, flee·ing** ; past and past part. **fled**) [intrans.] run away from a place or situation of danger: *a man was shot twice as he fled from five masked youths.* ■ [trans.] run away from (someone or something): *he was forced to flee the country* | fig. *all remaining doubt that he was a guerrilla began to flee my mind.* [OE *flēon*, of Gmc. origin; rel. to Du. *vlieden* and Ger. *fliehen*.]

fleece /flēs/ ▶ n. 1 the woolly coat of a sheep or goat. ■ the amount of wool shorn from a sheep in a single piece at one time. 2 a thing resembling a sheep's woolly covering, in particular: ■ a soft warm fabric with a texture similar to sheep's wool, used as a lining material. ▶ v. [trans.] 1 informal obtain a great deal of money from (someone), typically by overcharging or swindling them: *money that authorities say he fleeced from well-to-do acquaintances.* **2** fig. cover as if with a fleece. — **fleeced** adj. [OE *flēos, flēs,* of West Gmc. origin; rel. to Du. *vlies* and Ger. *Vlies.*]

fleec·y /'flēsē/ ▶ adj. (**fleec·i·er, fleec·i·est**) **1** (esp. of a towel or garment) made of or lined with a soft, warm fabric: *a fleecy sweatshirt.* **2** (esp. of a cloud) white and fluffy. — **fleec·i·ly** adv. **fleec·i·ness** n.

fleet[1] /flēt/ ▶ n. the largest group of naval vessels under one commander, organized for specific tactical or other purposes: *an invasion fleet.* ■ (**the fleet**) a country's navy. ■ a group of ships sailing together, engaged in the same activity, or under the same ownership. ■ a number of vehicles or aircraft operating together or under the same ownership. *a fleet of ambulances.* [OE *flēot* 'ship, shipping,' from *flēotan* 'float, swim.']

fleet[2] ▶ adj. fast and nimble in movement: *a man of advancing years, but fleet of foot.* [16th C.: prob. from ON *fljótr,* of Gmc. origin.]

Fleet Ad·mi·ral ▶ n. an admiral of the highest rank in the US Navy (awarded only in wartime).

fleet-foot·ed ▶ adj. nimble and fast on one's feet: *the fleet-footed sprinter captured his third gold medal.*

fleet·ing /'flētiNG/ ▶ adj. lasting for a very short time: *hoping to get a fleeting glimpse.*

Fleet Street a street in central London in which the offices of national newspapers were located until the mid-1980s (often used to refer to the British press).

Flem. ▶ abbr. Flemish.

Flem·ing[1] /'flemiNG/, Sir Alexander (1881–1955), Scottish bacteriologist. In 1928, he discovered the effect of penicillin on bacteria. Nobel Prize for Physiology or Medicine (1945, shared with Florey and Chain).

Flem·ing[2], Ian Lancaster (1908–64), English writer. He is known for his spy novels whose hero is the secret agent James Bond.

Flem·ing[3] ▶ n. **1** a native of Flanders. **2** a member of the Flemish-speaking people inhabiting northern and western Belgium. Compare with WALLOON. [late OE *Flæmingi,* from ON.]

Flem·ish /'flemisH/ ▶ adj. of or relating to Flanders, its people, or their language. ▶ n. **1** the Dutch language as spoken in Flanders, one of the two official languages of Belgium. **2** (**the Flemish**) [as pl. n.] the people of Flanders. [ME: from MDu. *Vlāmisch,* rel. to *Vlaanderen* 'Flanders.']

Flem·ish bond ▶ n. Building a pattern of bricks in a wall in which each course consists of alternate headers and stretchers.

flense /flens/ (also **flench** /flencH/, **flinch** /flincH/) ▶ v. [trans.] slice the skin or fat from (a carcass, esp. that of a whale). [19th C.: from Dan. *flensa.*]

flesh /flesH/ ▶ n. the soft substance consisting of muscle and fat that is found between the skin and bones of an animal or a human. ■ this substance in an animal or fish, regarded as food: *boned lamb flesh* | [in comb.] *a flesh-eater.* ■ the pulpy substance of a fruit or vegetable, esp. the part that is eaten. ■ fat: *he carries no spare flesh.* ■ the skin or surface of the human body with reference to its color, appearance, or sensual properties. ■ (**the flesh**) the human body and its physical needs and desires, esp. as contrasted with the mind or the soul: *the pleasures of the flesh.* ▶ v. [intrans.] (**flesh out**) put weight on: *he had fleshed out to a solid 220 pounds.* ■ [trans.] (**flesh something out**) add more details to something that exists only in a draft or outline form: *the theorists have fleshed out a variety of scenarios.*
– PHRASES **all flesh** all human and animal life. **go the way of all flesh** die or come to an end. **in the flesh** in person rather than via a telephone, a movie, the written word, or other means: *they should meet Alexander in the flesh.* **make someone's flesh creep** (or **crawl**) see MAKE SOMEONE'S SKIN CRAWL at SKIN. **one flesh** used to refer to the spiritual and physical union of two people in a relationship, esp. marriage: *my body is his, his is mine: one flesh.* [with biblical allusion to Gen. 2:24.] **put flesh on (the bones of) something** add more details to something that exists only in a draft or outline form: *put flesh on his "big idea."* **put on flesh** put on weight. **sins of the flesh** archaic humorous sins related to physical indulgence, esp. sexual gratification: *the bible-bashing chiefs lectured her on "sins of the flesh"* — **fleshed** /flesHt/ adj. [usu. in comb.] *a white-fleshed fish* **flesh·less** adj. [OE *flǣsc,* of Gmc. origin; rel. to Du. *vlees* and Ger. *Fleisch.*]

flesh and blood ▶ n. used to emphasize that a person is a physical, living being with human emotions or frailties, often in contrast to something abstract, spiritual, or mechanical: *the customer is flesh and blood, not just a sales statistic* | [as adj.] *he seemed more like a creature from a dream than a flesh-and-blood father.*
– PHRASES **one's (own) flesh and blood** a near relative: *he felt for that girl as if she was his own flesh and blood.*

flesh col·or ▶ n. a light brownish pink. — **flesh-col·ored** adj.

flesh fly ▶ n. a fly (*Sarcophaga* and other genera, family Sarcophagidae) that breeds in carrion, typically producing live young.

flesh·ings /'flesHiNGz/ ▶ plural n. flesh-colored tights worn by actors.

flesh·ly /'flesHlē/ ▶ adj. (**-li·er, -li·est**) **1** of or relating to human desire or bodily appetites; sensual: *fleshly pleasures.* **2** having an actual physical presence: *we will shed the lofty metaphysical Cage and incorporate the earlier dynamic and fleshly Cage.*

flesh·pots /'flesH,päts/ ▶ plural n. places providing luxurious or hedonistic living: *he had lived the life of a roué in the fleshpots of London and Paris.*

flesh side ▶ n. the side of a hide that adjoins the flesh.

flesh wound /,wo͞ond/ ▶ n. a wound that breaks the skin but does not damage bones or vital organs.

flesh·y /'flesHē/ ▶ adj. (**flesh·i·er, flesh·i·est**) **1** (of a person or part of the body) having a substantial amount of flesh; plump: *her torso was full, fleshy, and heavy.* ■ (of plant or fruit tissue) soft and thick: *fleshy, greeny-gray leaves.* ■ (of a wine) full-bodied. **2** resembling flesh in appearance or texture. — **flesh·i·ness** n.

fletch /flecH/ ▶ v. [trans.] provide (an arrow) with feathers for flight: *most arrows are fletched with feathers.* ▶ n. each of the feathered vanes of an arrow: [in comb.] *a four-fletch arrow.* [17th C.: alt. of FLEDGE.]

Fletch·er /'flecHər/, John (1579–1625), English playwright. He wrote some 15 plays with Francis Beaumont and is also believed to have collaborated with William Shakespeare on certain plays.

fleur-de-lis /,flər dl'ē; ,flo͝or-/ (also **fleur-de-lys**) ▶ n. (pl. **fleurs-de-lis** pronunc. same or /-dl'ēz/) **1** Art Heraldry a stylized lily composed of three petals bound together near their bases. **2** a European iris (genus *Iris*). [ME: from OFr. *flour de lys* 'flower of the lily.']

fleur-de-lis 1

flew /flo͞o/ past of FLY[1].

flews /flo͞oz/ ▶ plural n. the thick hanging lips of a bloodhound or similar dog. [16th C.: of unknown origin.]

flex /fleks/ ▶ v. [trans.] bend (a limb or joint): *she saw him flex his ankle and wince.* ■ [intrans.] (of a limb or joint) become bent: *prevent the damaged wrist from flexing.* ■ cause (a muscle) to stand out by contracting or tensing it: *bodybuilders flexing their muscles.* ■ [intrans.] (of a muscle) contract or be tensed: *a muscle flexed in his jaw.* ■ [intrans.] (of a material) be capable of warping or bending and then reverting to shape: *set windows in rubber so they flex during an earthquake.*
– PHRASES **flex one's muscles** see MUSCLE.

flex·i·ble /'fleksəbəl/ ▶ adj. capable of bending easily without breaking: *flexible rubber seals.* ■ able to be easily modified to respond to altered circumstances or conditions: *flexible forms of retirement.* ■ (of a person) ready and able to change so as to adapt to different circumstances: *you can save money if you're flexible about where your room is located.* — **flex·i·bil·i·ty** /,fleksə'bilitē/ n. **flex·i·bly** adv. [ME: from OFr., or from L. *flexibilis,* from *flectere* 'to bend.']

flex·ion /'flekSHən/ (also **flec·tion**) ▶ n. the action of bending or the condition of being bent, esp. the bending of a limb or joint: *flexion of the fingers* | *these protozoans can move by body flexions.* [17th C.: from L. *flexio(n-),* from *flectere* 'to bend.']

flex·og·ra·phy /flek'sägrəfē/ ▶ n. a rotary relief printing method using rubber or plastic plates and fluid inks or dyes for printing on fabrics and impervious materials such as plastics, as well as on paper. — **flex·o·graph·ic** /,fleksə'grafik/ adj. [1950s: from L. *flexus* 'a bending' (from the v. *flectere*) + -GRAPHY.]

flex·or /'fleksər; -sôr/ (also **flexor muscle**) ▶ n. Anat. a muscle whose contraction bends a limb or other part of the body. Often contrasted with EXTENSOR.

flex·time /'fleks,tīm/ ▶ n. a system of working a set number of hours with the starting and finishing times chosen within agreed limits by the employee. [1970s: blend of FLEXIBLE and TIME.]

flex·wing /'fleks,wiNG/ ▶ n. a collapsible fabric delta wing, as used in hang gliders.

flib·ber·ti·gib·bet /'flibərtē,jibit/ ▶ n. a frivolous, flighty, or excessively talkative person. [ME: prob. imitative of idle chatter.]

flick /flik/ ▶ n. **1** a sudden sharp movement. ■ the sudden release of a bent finger or thumb, esp. to propel a small object. ■ a light, sharp, quickly retracted blow, esp. with a whip. **2** informal a motion picture: *an action flick.* ▶ v. [with obj. and adverbial of direction] propel (something) with a sudden sharp movement, esp. of the fingers: *Emily **flicked** some ash **off** her sleeve.* ■ (**flick something on/off**) turn something electrical on or off by means of a switch. ■ [no obj., with adverbial of direction] make a sudden sharp movement: *the finch's tail flicks up and down.* ■ [trans.] move (a whip) so as to strike. [ME: symbolic.]

flick·er[1] /'flikər/ ▶ v. [intrans.] **1** (of light or a source of light) shine unsteadily; vary rapidly in brightness: *the interior lights flickered and came on.* ■ (of a flame) burn fitfully, alternately flaring up and dying down: *the candle flickered again* | [as adj.] (**flickering**) *the flickering flames of the fire.* ■ [with adverbial of place] fig. (of a feeling or emotion) be experienced or show itself briefly and faintly, esp. in someone's eyes: *amusement flickered briefly in his eyes.* **2** make small, quick movements; flutter rapidly: *her eyelids flickered* | [with complement] *the injured killer's eyes flickered open.* ■ [with adverbial of direction] (of someone's eyes) move quickly in a particular direction in order to look at something: *her alert hazel eyes flickered around the room.* ■ [with adverbial] (of a facial expression) appear briefly: *a look of horror flickered across his face.* ▶ n. **1** an unsteady movement of a flame or light that causes rapid variations in brightness. ■ fluctuations in the brightness of a movie or television image. **2** a tiny movement. ■ a faint indication of a facial expression. ■ fig. a very brief and faint experience of an emotion or feeling.
– PHRASAL VERBS **flicker out** (of a flame or light) die away and go out after a series of flickers. ■ fig. (of a feeling) die away and finally

disappear: *the swift burst of curiosity and eagerness flickered out.* [OE *flicorian, flycerian* 'to flutter,' prob. of Gmc. origin and rel. to Low Ger. *flickern* and Du. *flikkeren.*]

flick·er[2] ▶ n. an American woodpecker (genus *Colaptes*) that often feeds on ants on the ground, esp. the **common flicker** (*C. auratus*), occurring in two forms that are distinguished by the underside of the tail and wings, which may be yellow (**yellow-shafted flicker**) or salmon red (**red-shafted flicker**). [19th C.: imitative of its call.]

fli·er /ˈflīər/ (also **fly·er**) ▶ n. **1** a person or thing that flies, esp. in a particular way: *a nervous flier.* ■ a person who flies something, esp. an aircraft. ■ informal **2** a small handbill advertising an event or product. **3** a speculative investment.
– PHRASES **take a flyer** take a chance.

flight /flīt/ ▶ n. **1** the action or process of flying through the air: *an eagle in flight* | *the history of space flight.* ■ an act of flying; a journey made through the air or in space, esp. a scheduled journey made by an airline. ■ the movement or trajectory of a projectile or ball through the air. ■ literary swift passage of time: *the never-ending flight of future days.* **2** a group of creatures or objects flying together, in particular: ■ a flock or large body of birds or insects in the air, esp. when migrating. ■ a group of aircraft operating together, esp. an air force unit of about six aircraft. **3** the action of fleeing or attempting to escape. **4** a series of steps between floors or levels. **5** an extravagant or far-fetched idea or account: *ignoring such ridiculous flights of fancy.*
– PHRASES **in full flight** escaping as fast as possible. ■ having gained momentum in a run or activity: *when this jazz pianist is in full flight he can be mesmerizing.* **put someone/something to flight** cause someone or something to flee: *a soldier who held off, and eventually put to flight, waves of attackers.* **take flight 1** (of a bird) take off and fly: *the whole flock took flight* | fig. *my celebrityhood took flight.* **2** flee: *noise that would prompt a spooked horse to take flight.* [OE *flyht* 'action or manner of flying,' of Gmc. origin; rel. to Du. *vlucht* and FLY[1].]

flight at·tend·ant ▶ n. an airline steward or stewardess.

flight bag ▶ n. a small zippered bag carried by air travelers.

flight con·trol ▶ n. the activity of directing the movement of aircraft: *automatic flight control* | [as adj.] *the flight-control computer.* ■ a control surface on an aircraft.

flight crew ▶ n. [treated as sing. or pl.] the personnel responsible for the operation of an aircraft during flight.

flight deck ▶ n. **1** the cockpit of a large aircraft, from which the pilot and crew fly it. **2** the deck of an aircraft carrier, used for takeoff and landing.

flight en·gi·neer ▶ n. a member of a flight crew responsible for the aircraft's engines and other systems during flight.

flight feath·er ▶ n. any of the large primary or secondary feathers in a bird's wing, supporting it in flight. Also called REMEX.

flight·less /ˈflītlis/ ▶ adj. (of a bird or an insect) naturally unable to fly. — **flight·less·ness** n.

flight line ▶ n. **1** the part of an airport around the hangars where aircraft can be parked and serviced. **2** a line of flight.

flight path ▶ n. the actual or planned course of an aircraft or spacecraft.

flight plan ▶ n. Aeron. a written account of the details of a particular proposed flight.

flight re·cord·er (also **flight data recorder**) ▶ n. a device in an aircraft that records technical data during a flight, used in case of an accident to discover its cause.

flight sim·u·la·tor ▶ n. a machine designed to resemble the cockpit of an aircraft, with computer-generated images that mimic the pilot's view and mechanisms that move the entire structure in imitation of an aircraft's motion, used for training pilots.

flight test ▶ n. a flight of an aircraft, rocket, or equipment to see how well it functions. ▶ v. (**flight-test**) [trans.] test by flying: [as n.] (**flight-testing**).

flight·y /ˈflītē/ ▶ adj. (**flight·i·er, flight·i·est**) fickle and irresponsible: *you may be seen as too flighty and lightweight for real responsibility.* — **flight·i·ly** adv. **flight·i·ness** n.

flim·flam /ˈflimˌflam/ informal ▶ n. nonsensical or insincere talk. ■ a confidence game. ▶ v. (**-flammed, -flam·ming**) [trans.] swindle (someone) with a confidence game: *the tribe was flimflammed out of its land.* — **flim·flam·mer** n. [16th C.: symbolic reduplication.]

flim·sy /ˈflimzē/ ▶ adj. (**-si·er, -si·est**) comparatively light and insubstantial; easily damaged. ■ (of clothing) light and thin. ■ (of a pretext or account) weak and unconvincing. — **flim·si·ly** adv. **flim·si·ness** n. [18th C.: prob. from FLIMFLAM.]

flinch[1] /flincH/ ▶ v. [intrans.] make a quick, nervous movement of the face or body as an instinctive reaction to fear or pain: *he had faced death without flinching.* ■ (**flinch from**) fig. avoid doing or becoming involved in (something) through fear or anxiety: *I rarely flinch from a fight when I'm sure of myself.* ▶ n. [in sing.] an act of flinching. — **flinch·er** n. **flinch·ing·ly** adv. [16th C.: from OFr. *flenchir* 'turn aside,' of West Gmc. origin and rel. to Ger. *lenken* 'to guide, steer.']

flinch[2] ▶ v. var. of FLENSE.

Flin·ders /ˈflindərz/, Matthew (1774–1814), English explorer. He circumnavigated Australia (1801–03).

fling /fliNG/ ▶ v. (past **flung**) [with obj. and adverbial of direction] throw or hurl forcefully: *he picked up the debris and flung it away* | fig. *I was flung into jail.* ■ move or push (something) suddenly or violently: *he flung back the bedclothes* | [with obj. and complement] *Jennifer flung open a door.* ■ (**fling oneself**) throw oneself headlong: *he flung himself down at her feet with a laugh.* ■ (**fling oneself into**) wholeheartedly engage in or begin on (an enterprise): *the producer flung himself into an ugly battle with the studio.* ■ (**fling something on/off**) put on or take off clothes carelessly or rapidly. ■ utter (words) forcefully: *the words were flung at her like an accusation.* ▶ n. a short period of enjoyment or wild behavior: *one final fling before a tranquil retirement.* ■ a short, spontaneous sexual relationship: *I had a fling with someone when I was at college.* — **fling·er** n. [ME (in the sense 'go violently'): perh. rel. to ON *flengja* 'flog.']

Flint /flint/ a city in southeastern Michigan; pop. 124,943.

flint /flint/ ▶ n. a hard gray rock consisting of nearly pure silica (chert), occurring chiefly as nodules in chalk. ■ a piece of this stone, esp. as flaked or ground in ancient times to form a tool or weapon. ■ a piece of flint used with steel to produce an igniting spark, e.g., in a flintlock gun, or (in modern use) a piece of an alloy used similarly, esp. in a cigarette lighter. ■ used to express how hard and unyielding something or someone is: *mean faces with eyes like flints.* [OE; rel. to MDu. *vlint* and Old High Ger. *flins.*]

flint glass ▶ n. a pure lustrous kind of glass originally made with flint.

flint·lock /ˈflintˌläk/ ▶ n. **1** an old-fashioned type of gun fired by a spark from a flint. **2** [usu. as adj.] the lock on such a gun: *a flintlock pistol.*

flintlock 2

flint·y /ˈflintē/ ▶ adj. (**flint·i·er, flint·i·est**) of, containing, or reminiscent of flint: *flinty soil.* ■ (of a person or their expression) very hard and unyielding: *a flinty stare.* — **flint·i·ly** adv. **flint·i·ness** n.

flip /flip/ ▶ v. (**flipped, flip·ping**) **1** turn over or cause to turn over with a sudden sharp movement: [trans.] *the yacht was flipped by a huge wave* | [intrans.] *the plane flipped over and then exploded.* **2** [with obj. and adverbial] move, push, or throw (something) with a sudden sharp movement: *she flipped a few coins on to the bar.* ■ [trans.] turn (an electrical appliance or switch) on or off: *he flipped a switch and the front door opened.* ■ [trans.] toss (a coin) to decide an issue: *given those odds, one may as well flip a coin* | [intrans.] *you want to flip for it?* **3** [intrans.] informal suddenly become deranged or very angry: *he had clearly flipped under the pressure.* ■ suddenly become very enthusiastic: *I walked into a store, saw it on the wall, and just flipped.* ▶ n. a sudden sharp movement. ■ (**a flip through**) a quick look or search through a volume or a collection of papers. ▶ adj. glib; flippant. ▶ exclam. used to express mild annoyance.
– PHRASES **flip one's lid** (or **one's wig**) informal suddenly become deranged or lose one's self-control.
– PHRASAL VERBS **flip through** look or search quickly through (a volume or a collection of papers): *just flip through the phone book.* [16th C.: prob. a contr. of FILLIP.]

flip chart ▶ n. a large pad of paper bound so that each page can be turned over at the top to reveal the next.

flip-flop ▶ n. **1** a light sandal, typically of plastic or rubber, with a thong between the big and second toes. **2** a backward somersault or handspring. **3** informal an abrupt reversal of policy: *his flip-flop on taxes.* ▶ v. [intrans.] **1** move with a flapping sound or motion. **2** perform a backward somersault or handspring: **3** informal make an abrupt reversal of policy: *she flip-flopped on a number of issues.* [17th C.: imitative reduplication of FLOP.]

flip-flop 1

flip·pant /ˈflipənt/ ▶ adj. not showing a serious or respectful attitude: *a flippant remark.* — **flip·pan·cy** /ˈflipənsē/ n. **flip·pant·ly** adv. [17th C.: from FLIP[1].]

flip·per /ˈflipər/ ▶ n. a broad flat limb without fingers, used for swimming by various sea animals such as seals, whales, and turtles. ■ a flat rubber attachment worn on the foot for underwater swimming. ■ a pivoted arm in a pinball machine, controlled by the player and used for sending the ball back up the table. ■ informal a hand.

flip side ▶ n. informal the less important side of a pop single record; the B-side. ■ another aspect or version of something, esp. its reverse or its unwanted concomitant: *virtues are the flip side of vices.*

flip-top ▶ adj. [attrib.] denoting or having a lid or cover that can be easily opened by pulling, pushing, or flicking it with the fingers. ▶ n. a lid or cover of this kind.

flirt /flərt/ ▶ v. [intrans.] behave as though attracted to or trying to attract someone, but without serious intentions: *it amused him to flirt with her.* ■ (**flirt with**) experiment with or show a superficial interest in (an idea, activity, or movement) without committing oneself to it seriously: *a painter who had flirted briefly with Cubism.* ■ (**flirt with**) deliberately expose oneself to (danger or difficulty): *the need of some individuals to flirt with death.* ▶ n. a person who habitually flirts. — **flir·ta·tion** /flərˈtāsHən/ n. **flir·ta·tious** /flərˈtāsHəs/ adj. **flir·ta·tious·ly**

/flərˈtāsʜəslē/ **adv.** **flir·ta·tious·ness** /flərˈtāsʜəsnəs/ **n.** **flirt·y adj.** (**flirt·i·er, flirt·i·est**). [16th C.: appar. symbolic.]

flit /flit/ ▶ **v.** (**flit·ted, flit·ting**) [no obj., with adverbial of direction] move swiftly and lightly: *small birds flitted about in the branches* | fig. *the idea had flitted through his mind.* [ME: from ON *flytja.*]

flitch beam ▶ **n.** a compound beam made of an steel plate between two slabs of wood.

flit·ter /ˈflitər/ ▶ **v.** [no obj., with adverbial of direction] move quickly in an apparently random or purposeless manner: *flittering around the countryside.* ▶ **n.** a fluttering movement. ■ (in science fiction) a small personal aircraft. [ME: frequentative of FLIT.]

fliv·ver /ˈflivər/ ▶ **n.** informal, dated a cheap car or aircraft, esp. one in bad condition. [20th C.: of unknown origin.]

FLN ▶ **abbr.** Front de Libération Nationale.

float /flōt/ ▶ **v.** [intrans.] **1** rest or move on or near the surface of a liquid without sinking: *she relaxed, floating gently in the water.* ■ [with obj. and adverbial] cause (a buoyant object) to rest or move in such a way: *trees were felled and floated downstream.* ■ be suspended freely in a liquid or gas: *fragments of chipped cartilage floated in the joint.* **2** [with adverbial of direction] move or hover slowly and lightly in a liquid or the air; drift: *clouds floated across a brilliant blue sky* | fig. *through the open window floated the sound of traffic.* ■ (**float about/around**) (of a rumor, idea, or substance) circulate: *the notion was floating around Capitol Hill.* ■ (of a sight or idea) come before the eyes or mind: *the advice his father had given him floated into his mind.* **3** [trans.] put forward (an idea) as a suggestion or test of reactions. ■ [trans.] offer the shares of (a company) for sale on the stock market for the first time. **4** (of a currency) fluctuate freely in value in accordance with supply and demand in the financial markets: *a policy of letting the pound float.* ■ [trans.] allow (a currency) to fluctuate in such a way. ▶ **n.** **1** a thing that is buoyant in water, in particular: ■ a small object attached to a fishing line to indicate by moving when a fish bites. ■ a cork or buoy supporting the edge of a fishing net. ■ a hollow or inflated organ enabling an organism (such as the Portuguese man-of-war) to float in the water. ■ each of the hollow structures fixed underneath an aircraft enabling it to take off and land on water. ■ a device floating on the surface of a liquid that forms part of a valve apparatus controlling flow in and out of the enclosing container, e.g., in a toilet tank or a carburetor. **2** a platform mounted on a truck and carrying a display in a parade. **3** a hand tool with a rectangular blade used for smoothing plaster. **4** a soft drink with a scoop of ice cream floating in it.
– PHRASES **float someone's boat** informal appeal to or excite someone, esp. sexually: *Kevin doesn't exactly float her boat.* [OE *flotian* (v.), of Gmc. origin.]

float·a·tion /flōˈtāsʜən/ ▶ **n.** var. of FLOTATION.

float·el /flōˈtel/ (also **flot·el**) ▶ **n.** a floating hotel, esp. a boat used as a hotel. ■ a vessel providing housing for workers on an offshore oil rig. [1950s: blend of FLOAT and HOTEL.]

float·er /ˈflōtər/ ▶ **n.** **1** a person or thing that floats, in particular: ■ a worker who is required to do a variety of tasks as the need for each arises. ■ informal a person who frequently changes occupation or residence. ■ a fishing float. ■ a loose particle within the eyeball that is apparent in one's field of vision. **2** an insurance policy covering loss of articles without specifying a location.

float glass ▶ **n.** glass made by allowing it to solidify on molten metal.

float·ing /ˈflōtiɴɢ/ ▶ **adj.** [attrib.] **1** buoyant or suspended in water or air: *a massive floating platform.* **2** not settled in a definite place; fluctuating or variable: *the floating population that is migrating to the cities.*

float·ing debt ▶ **n.** a debt that is repayable in the short term. Compare with FUNDED DEBT.

float·ing dock ▶ **n.** a submersible floating structure used as a dry dock.

float·ing kid·ney ▶ **n.** a condition in which the kidneys are abnormally movable. ■ such a kidney.

float·ing-point ▶ **adj.** Comput. denoting a mode of representing numbers as two sequences of bits, one representing the digits in the number and the other an exponent that determines the position of the radix point: *speeds of more than one million **floating-point operations** per second.* Often contrasted with FIXED POINT.

float·ing rib ▶ **n.** any of the lower ribs that are not attached directly to the breastbone. Also called FALSE RIB.

float·plane /ˈflōtˌplān/ ▶ **n.** an aircraft equipped with floats for landing on water; a seaplane.

float valve ▶ **n.** another term for BALL VALVE.

floc /fläk/ ▶ **n.** tech. a loosely clumped mass of fine particles.

floc·ci·nau·ci·ni·hil·i·pil·i·fi·ca·tion /ˌfläksəˌnôsəˌnīhiləˌpiləfiˈkāsʜən/ ▶ **n.** the action or habit of estimating something as worthless. (The word is used chiefly as a curiosity.) [18th C.: from L. *flocci, nauci, nihili, pili* (words meaning 'at little value') + -FICATION.]

floc·cu·lant /ˈfläkyələnt/ ▶ **n.** a substance that promotes the clumping of particles, esp. one used in treating waste water.

floc·cu·late /ˈfläkyəˌlāt/ ▶ **v.** tech. form or cause to form into small clumps or masses: [intrans.] *it tends to flocculate in high salinities* | [trans.] *its ability to flocculate suspended silt.* — **floc·cu·la·tion** /ˌfläkyəˈlāsʜən/ **n.** [19th C.: from mod. L. *flocculus* 'small clump,' dimin. of *floccus* 'flock.']

flock[1] /fläk/ ▶ **n.** a number of birds feeding, resting, or traveling together. ■ a number of domestic animals, esp. sheep, goats, or geese, that are kept together. ■ (**flocks**) large crowds of people. ■ a group of children or students in someone's charge. ■ a Christian congregation or body of believers, esp. one under the charge of a particular minister. ▶ **v.** [no obj., with adverbial] congregate or mass in a flock or large group: *students flocked to spring break sites.* [OE *flocc*, of unknown origin.]

flock[2] (also **flock·ing**) ▶ **n.** [often as adj.] a soft material for stuffing cushions, quilts, and other soft furnishings, made of wool refuse or torn-up cloth: *flock mattresses.* ■ powdered wool or cloth, sprinkled on wallpaper, cloth, or metal to make a raised pattern. ■ a lock or tuft of wool or cotton. — **flock·y adj.** [ME: from OFr. *floc*, from L. *floccus.*]

Flod·den, Battle of /ˈflädn/ (also **Flodden Field**) a decisive battle for the English in the Anglo-Scottish war of 1513, at Flodden, a hill in northeastern England.

floe /flō/ (also **ice floe**) ▶ **n.** a sheet of floating ice. [19th C.: prob. from Norw. *flo*, from ON *fló* 'layer.']

flog /fläg/ ▶ **v.** (**flogged, flog·ging**) [trans.] beat (someone) with a whip or stick to punish or torture them: *the stolen horses will be returned and the thieves flogged* | [as n.] (**flogging**) *public floggings.* ■ informal promote or talk about (something) repetitively or at excessive length: *rather than **flogging** one idea **to death**, they should be a lighthearted pop group.* — **flog·ger n.** [17th C. (orig. slang): perh. imitative, or from L. *flagellare* 'to whip,' from *flagellum* 'whip.']

flood /fləd/ ▶ **n.** **1** an overflowing of a large amount of water beyond its normal confines, esp. over what is normally dry land. [as adj.] *a flood barrier.* ■ (**the Flood**) the biblical flood brought by God upon the earth because of the wickedness of the human race (Gen. 6 ff.). ■ the inflow of the tide. ■ literary a river, stream, or sea. **2** an outpouring of tears or emotion. ■ a very large quantity of people or things that appear or need to be dealt with. **3** short for FLOODLIGHT. ▶ **v.** **1** [trans.] cover or submerge (a place or area) with water: *the dam burst, flooding a small town* | *watching her father flood their backyard skating rink* | [as n.] (**flooding**) *a serious risk of flooding.* ■ [intrans.] become covered or submerged in this way: *part of the vessel flooded* | fig. *Sarah's eyes **flooded with** tears.* ■ (usu. **be flooded out**) drive someone out of their home or business with a flood: *most of the families who have been flooded out will receive compensation.* ■ (of a river or sea) become swollen and overflow (its banks): *the river flooded its banks* | [intrans.] *the river will flood if it gets much worse.* ■ overfill the carburetor of (an engine) with fuel, causing the engine to fail to start. **2** [no obj., with adverbial of direction] arrive in overwhelming amounts or quantities: *congratulatory messages flooded in* | *his old fears came flooding back.* ■ [trans.] overwhelm or swamp with large amounts or quantities: *our switchboard was **flooded with** calls.* ■ [trans.] fill or suffuse completely: *she flooded the room with light.* [OE *flōd*, of Gmc. origin; rel. to Du. *vloed* and Ger. *Flut*, also to FLOW.]

flood·gate /ˈflədˌgāt/ ▶ **n.** a gate that can be opened or closed to admit or exclude water, esp. the lower gate of a lock. ■ (usu. **the floodgates**) fig. a last restraint holding back an outpouring of something powerful or substantial: *his lawsuit could **open the floodgates** for thousands of similar claims.*

flood·light /ˈflədˌlīt/ ▶ **n.** a large, powerful light, typically one of several used to illuminate a sports field, a stage, or the exterior of a building. ■ the illumination provided by such a light. ▶ **v.** (past and past part. **-lit**) [trans.] [usu. as adj.] (**floodlit**) illuminate (a building or outdoor area) with such lights: *floodlit football fields.*

flood·plain /ˈflədˌplān/ ▶ **n.** an area of low-lying ground adjacent to a river, formed mainly of river sediments and subject to flooding.

flood tide ▶ **n.** an incoming tide. ■ a powerful surge or flow of something: *the trickle of tourists has become a flood tide.*

flood·wa·ter /ˈflədˌwôtər; -ˌwätər/ (also **flood·wa·ters**) ▶ **n.** water overflowing as the result of a flood.

floor /flôr/ ▶ **n.** **1** the lower surface of a room, on which one may walk: *he dropped the cup and it smashed on **the floor*** | *the kitchen floor.* ■ all the rooms or areas on the same level of a building; a story: *his office was on the twenty-second floor* | [as adj., in comb.] *a third-floor apartment.* ■ a level area or space used or designed for a particular activity. ■ fig. the minimum level of prices or wages: *the dollar's floor against the yen.* ■ the bottom of the sea, a cave, or an area of land. **2** (**the floor**) (in a legislative assembly) the part in which members sit and from which they speak. ■ the right or opportunity to speak next in debate: *other speakers **have the floor**.* ■ (of the stock exchange) the large central hall where trading takes place. ▶ **v.** [trans.] informal knock (someone) to the ground, esp. with a punch. ■ baffle or confound (someone) completely: *that question floored him.*
– PHRASES **from the floor** (of a speech or question) delivered by an individual member at a meeting, not by a representative on the platform: *questions from the floor will be invited.* **take the floor 1** begin to dance on a dance floor. **2** speak in a debate or assembly. [OE *flōr*, of Gmc. origin; rel. to Du. *vloer* and Ger. *Flur.*]

floor·board /ˈflôrˌbôrd/ ▶ **n.** a long plank making up part of a wooden floor. ■ the floor of a motor vehicle.

floor·cloth /ˈflôrˌklôᴛʜ/ ▶ **n.** a thin canvas rug or similar light floor covering.

floor ex·er·cise ▶ **n.** a routine of gymnastic exercises performed without the use any of apparatus.

floor·ing /ˈflôriNG/ ▶ n. the boards or other material of which a floor is made.

floor lamp ▶ n. a tall lamp designed to stand on the floor.

floor plan ▶ n. a scale diagram of the arrangement of rooms in one story of a building.

floor sam·ple ▶ n. an article of merchandise that has been displayed in a store and that is offered for sale at a reduced price.

floor show ▶ n. an entertainment, such as singing or comedy, presented at a nightclub, restaurant, or similar venue.

floor·walk·er /ˈflôr,wôkər/ ▶ n. a senior employee of a large store who assists customers and supervises salespeople.

floo·zy /ˈflo͞ozē/ (also **floo·zie, floo·sie**) ▶ n. (pl. **-zies**) informal a girl or a woman who has a reputation for promiscuity. [20th C.: perh. rel. to FLOSSY or to dial. *floosy* 'fluffy.']

flop /fläp/ ▶ v. (**flopped, flop·ping**) **1** [no obj., with adverbial] fall, move, or hang in a heavy, loose, and ungainly way: *black hair flopped across his forehead.* ■ sit or lie down heavily or suddenly in a specified place, esp. when very tired: *Liz flopped down into the armchair.* ■ informal rest or sleep in a specified place: *I'm going to flop here for the night.* **2** [intrans.] informal (of a performer or show) be completely unsuccessful; fail totally: *prime-time dramas that flopped in the US market.* **3** [trans.] Photog. invert (a negative) so that the right and left sides of a photograph are reversed. ▶ n. **1** a heavy, loose, and ungainly movement, or a sound made by it: *they hit the ground with a flop.* **2** informal a total failure. [17th C.: var. of FLAP.]

-flop ▶ comb. form Comput. floating-point operations per second (used as a measure of computing power): *a gigaflop computer.* [acronym; orig. spelled *-flops* (*s* = second) but shortened to avoid misinterpretation as pl.]

flop·house /ˈfläp,hous/ ▶ n. informal a cheap hotel or rooming house.

flop·py /ˈfläpē/ ▶ adj. (**flop·pi·er, flop·pi·est**) tending to hang or move in a limp, loose, or ungainly way: *the dog had floppy ears.* ▶ n. (pl. **-pies**) (also **flop·py disk**) Comput. short for FLOPPY DISK. — **flop·pi·ly** adv. **flop·pi·ness** n.

flop·py disk ▶ n. Comput. a flexible removable magnetic disk, typically encased in hard plastic, used for storing data. Also called DISKETTE. Compare with HARD DISK.

flor. ▶ abbr. floruit.

flo·ra /ˈflôrə/ ▶ n. (pl. **flo·ras** or **flo·rae** /ˈflôrē; ˈflôrī/) the plants of a particular region, habitat, or geological period: *the desert flora give way to oak woodlands* | *the river's **flora and fauna** have been inventoried and protected.* Compare with FAUNA. ■ a treatise on or list of such plant life. [18th C.: from L. *flos, flor-* 'flower.']

flo·ral /ˈflôrəl/ ▶ adj. of flowers: *celebrations of the season's floral abundance.* ■ decorated with or depicting flowers: *a floral pattern.* ■ Bot. of flora or floras: *faunal and floral evolution.* — **flo·ral·ly** adv. [18th C.: from L. *flos, flor-* 'flower' + -AL.]

Flor·ence /ˈflôrəns; ˈflär-/ a city in west central Italy; pop. 408,000. It was a leading center of the Italian Renaissance, esp. under the rule of the Medici family during the 15th century. Italian name FIRENZE.

Flor·en·tine /ˈflôrən,tēn; -,tīn/ ▶ adj. **1** of or relating to Florence. **2** (**florentine**) [postpositive] (of food) served or prepared on a bed of spinach: *eggs florentine.* ▶ n. **1** a native or citizen of Florence. **2** (**florentine**) a cookie consisting mainly of nuts and preserved fruit, coated on one side with chocolate.

Flo·res /ˈflôrəs/ the largest of the Lesser Sunda Islands in Indonesia.

flo·res·cence /flôˈresəns; fləˈres-/ ▶ n. the process of flowering: *the Hieracia are erect throughout florescence* | fig. *a spectacular cultural florescence.* [18th C.: from mod. L. *florescentia*, from L. *florescere* 'begin to flower,' based on *flos, flor-* 'flower.']

flo·ret /ˈflôrit/ ▶ n. Bot. one of the small flowers making up a composite flowerhead. ■ one of the flowering stems making up a head of cauliflower or broccoli. [17th C.: from L. *flos, flor-* 'flower' + -ET¹.]

Flo·rey /ˈflôrē/, Howard Walter, Baron (1898–1968), Australian pathologist. With Ernst Chain he isolated and purified penicillin. Nobel Prize for Physiology or Medicine (1945, shared with Chain and Fleming).

Flo·ri·a·nóp·o·lis /,flôrēəˈnôpəlis/ a city in southern Brazil; pop. 293,000.

flo·ri·bun·da /,flôrəˈbəndə/ ▶ n. a plant, esp. a rose, that bears dense clusters of flowers. [19th C.: mod. L., fem. of *floribundus* 'freely flowering,' from L. *flos, flor-* 'flower.']

flor·id /ˈflôrid; ˈflär-/ ▶ adj. **1** having a red or flushed complexion: *a stout man with a florid face.* **2** elaborately or excessively intricate or complicated: *florid operatic-style music was out.* ■ (of language) using unusual words or complicated rhetorical constructions: *the florid prose of the nineteenth century.* **3** Med. (of a disease or its manifestations) occurring in a fully developed form: *florid symptoms of psychiatric disorder.* — **flo·rid·i·ty** /fləˈriditē/ n. **flor·id·ly** adv. **flor·id·ness** n. [17th C.: from L. *floridus*, from *flos, flor-* 'flower.']

Flor·i·da /ˈflôridə; ˈflär-/ a state in the southeastern US, on a peninsula that extends into the Atlantic Ocean and the Gulf of Mexico; pop. 15,982,378; capital, Tallahassee; statehood, Mar. 3, 1845 (27). Explored by Ponce de León in 1513, it was purchased from Spain by the US in 1819. — **Flo·rid·i·an** /fləˈridēən/ adj. & n.

Flor·i·da Keys a chain of small islands off the tip of the Florida peninsula. They extend southwest over a distance of 100 miles (160 km).

Flor·i·da room ▶ n. another term for SUNROOM.

flor·in /ˈflôrin; ˈflär-/ ▶ n. **1** a former British coin and monetary unit worth two shillings. **2** a foreign coin of gold or silver, esp. a Dutch guilder. **3** the basic monetary unit of Aruba, equal to 100 cents. [via OFr. from Ital. *fiorino*, dimin. of *fiore* 'flower,' from L. *flos, flor-*.]

flo·rist /ˈflôrist/ ▶ n. a person who sells and arranges cut flowers. — **flo·rist·ry** n. [17th C.: from L. *flos, flor-* 'flower.']

flo·ris·tic /fləˈristik/ ▶ adj. Bot. relating to the study of the distribution of plants. — **flo·ris·ti·cal·ly** /-k(ə)lē/ adv.

flo·ru·it /ˈflôr(y)o͞oit/ (abbr.: **fl.** or **flor.**) ▶ v. used in conjunction with a specified period or set of dates to indicate when a particular historical figure lived, worked, or was most active. [19th C.: L., literally 'he or she flourished'.]

floss /flôs; fläs/ ▶ n. the rough silk enveloping a silkworm's cocoon. ■ (also **floss silk**) untwisted silk fibers used in embroidery. ■ the silky down in corn and other plants: *milkweed floss.* ■ short for DENTAL FLOSS. ▶ v. [trans.] clean between (one's teeth) with dental floss. [18th C.: from Fr. *(soie) floche* 'floss (silk),' from OFr. *flosche* 'down, nap of velvet,' of unknown origin.]

floss·y /ˈflôsē; ˈfläsē/ ▶ adj. (**floss·i·er, floss·i·est**) **1** of or like floss: *short flossy curls.* **2** informal excessively showy: *the flossy gleam of a cheap suit* | *she cultivated flossy friends.*

flo·ta·tion /flōˈtāsHən/ (also **float·a·tion**) ▶ n. the action of floating in a liquid or gas: *the body form is modified to assist in flotation and propulsion.* ■ the process of offering a company's shares for sale on the stock market for the first time. ■ the separation of small particles of a solid by their different capacities to float. ■ the capacity to float; buoyancy. [19th C.: alt. of *floatation*.]

flo·tel ▶ n. var. of FLOATEL.

flo·til·la /flōˈtilə/ ▶ n. a fleet of ships or boats: ***a flotilla of** cargo boats.* [18th C.: from Sp., dimin. of *flota* 'fleet.']

flot·sam /ˈflätsəm/ ▶ n. the wreckage of a ship or its cargo found floating on or washed up by the sea. Compare with JETSAM. ■ fig. people or things that have been rejected and are regarded as worthless: *the room was cleared of boxes and other flotsam.*

– PHRASES **flotsam and jetsam** useless or discarded objects. [17th C.: from Anglo-Norman Fr. *floteson*, from *floter* 'to float.']

flounce¹ /flouns/ ▶ v. [no obj., with adverbial of direction] go or move in an exaggeratedly impatient or angry manner: *he stood up in a fury and flounced out.* ▶ n. [in sing.] an exaggerated action, typically intended to express one's annoyance or impatience. [16th C.: perh. of Scand. origin and rel. to Norw. *flunsa* 'hurry.']

flounce² /ˈflounsē/ ▶ n. a wide ornamental strip of material gathered and sewn to a piece of fabric; a frill. ▶ v. [as adj.] (**flounced**) trimmed with a flounce or flounces. [18th C.: from an alt. of obs. *frounce* 'a fold or pleat,' from OFr. *fronce*, of Gmc. origin; rel. to RUCK².]

floun·der¹ /ˈfloundər/ ▶ v. [intrans.] struggle or stagger helplessly or clumsily in water or mud: *he was **floundering about** in the shallow offshore waters.* ■ fig. struggle mentally; show or feel great confusion: *she floundered, not knowing quite what to say.* ■ fig. be in serious difficulty: *many firms are floundering.* — **floun·der·er** n. [16th C.: perh. a blend of FOUNDER and BLUNDER.]

floun·der² ▶ n. a small flatfish (families Pleuronectidae and Bothidae) that typically occurs in shallow coastal water. ■ (**flounders**) a collective term for flatfishes other than soles. See FLATFISH. [ME: from OFr. *flondre*, prob. of Scand. origin and rel. to Dan. *flynder*.]

flour /ˈflou(ə)r/ ▶ n. a powder obtained by grinding grain, typically wheat, and used to make bread, cakes, and pastry. ■ fine soft powder obtained by grinding the seeds or roots of starchy vegetables: *manioc flour.* ▶ v. [trans.] sprinkle with a thin layer of flour. [ME: from FLOWER.]

flour·ish /ˈflərisH/ ▶ v. **1** [intrans.] (of a person, animal, or other living organism) grow or develop in a healthy or vigorous way, esp. as the result of a particularly congenial environment. ■ develop rapidly and successfully. ■ [with adverbial] (of a person) be working or at the height of one's career during a specified period: *the caricaturist and wit who flourished in the early years of this century.* **2** [trans.] (of a person) wave (something) around to attract the attention of others: *"Happy New Year!" he yelled, flourishing a bottle of whiskey.* ▶ n. **1** a bold or extravagant gesture or action, made esp. to attract the attention of others. ■ an instance of suddenly performing or developing in an impressively successful way. ■ an elaborate rhetorical or literary expression. ■ an ornamental flowing curve in handwriting or scrollwork. **2** Music a fanfare played by brass instruments. ■ an ornate musical passage. ■ an improvised addition played esp. at the beginning or end of a composition. — **flour·ish·er** n. [ME: from OFr. *floriss-*, lengthened stem of *florir*, based on L. *florere*, from *flos, flor-* 'a flower.']

flour moth (in full **Mediterranean flour moth**) ▶ n. a grayish-yellow moth (*Ephestia kuehniella*, family Pyralidae), the caterpillar of which is a pest of flour and other cereal products.

flour·y /ˈflou(ə)rē/ ▶ adj. covered with flour. ■ of or resembling flour.

flout /flout/ ▶ v. [trans.] openly disregard (a rule, law or convention): *these same companies still flout basic ethical practices.* [16th C.: perh. from Du. *fluiten* 'whistle, play the flute, hiss (in derision).']

flow /flō/ ▶ v. [intrans.] (esp. of a liquid) move along or out steadily and continuously in a current or stream: *from here the river flows north* | *a cross-current of electricity seemed to flow between them.* ■ (of the sea or a tidal river) move toward the land; rise. Compare with EBB. ■ [with adverbial of direction] (of clothing or hair) hang loosely in an easy and graceful manner: *her red hair **flowed over** her shoulders.* ■ circulate continuously within a particular system: *ventilation channels keep the air flowing* | *an electric current flows through it.* ■ [with adverbial of direction]

(of people or things) go from one place to another in a steady stream, typically in large numbers: *the firm is hoping the orders will keep flowing in.* ■ proceed or be produced smoothly, continuously, and effortlessly: *talk flowed freely around the table.* ■ (**flow from**) result from; be caused by: *there are certain advantages that may flow from that decision.* ■ be available in copious quantities: *their talk and laughter grew louder as the excellent brandy flowed.* ■ (of a solid) undergo a permanent change of shape under stress, without melting. ▶ **n.** [in sing.] the action or fact of moving along in a steady, continuous stream. ■ the rate or speed at which such a stream moves. ■ the rise of a tide or a river. Compare with EBB. ■ a steady, continuous stream of something. ■ menstrual discharge. ■ the gradual permanent deformation of a solid under stress, without melting.
– PHRASES **go with the flow** informal be relaxed and accept a situation, rather than trying to alter or control it. [OE *flōwan*, of Gmc. origin; rel. to Du. *vloeien*, also to FLOOD.]

flow chart (also **flow·chart** or **flow diagram**) ▶ **n.** a diagram of the sequence of movements or actions of people or things involved in a complex system or activity. ■ a graphical representation of a computer program in relation to its sequence of functions (as distinct from the data it processes).

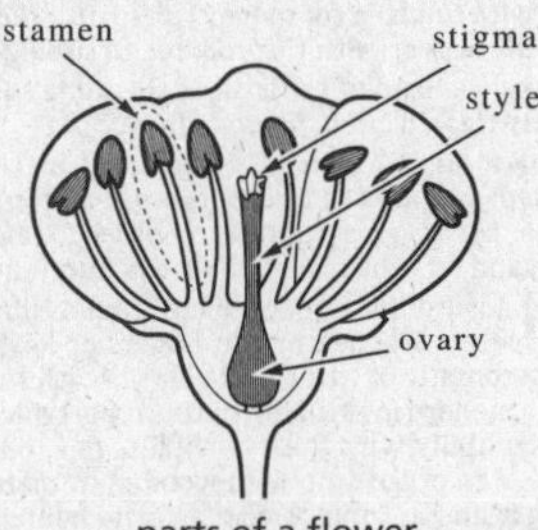

parts of a flower

flow·er /ˈflouər/ ▶ **n.** Bot. the seed-bearing part of a plant, consisting of reproductive organs (stamens and carpels) that are typically surrounded by a brightly colored corolla (petals) and a green calyx (sepals). ■ a brightly colored and conspicuous example of such a part of a plant together with its stalk. ■ the state or period in which a plant's flowers have developed and opened: *the roses were coming into flower.* ▶ **v.** [intrans.] (of a plant) produce flowers; bloom. ■ fig. be in or reach an optimum stage of development; develop fully and richly.
– PHRASES **the flower of 1** the finest individuals out of a number of people or things. **2** the period of optimum development: *in the flower of his life.* [ME *flour*, from OFr. *flour, flor*, from L. *flos, flor-*.]

flow·er bed ▶ **n.** a garden where flowers are grown.

flow·er child ▶ **n.** hist. a hippie who wore flowers as symbols of peace and love.

flow·ered /ˈflouərd/ ▶ **adj. 1** (esp. of fabric or a garment) having a floral design: *flowered curtains.* **2** [in comb.] (of a plant) bearing flowers of a specified kind or number: *yellow-flowered japonica.*

flow·er girl ▶ **n.** a young girl who carries flowers or scatters them in front of the bride at a wedding.

flow·er head (also **flow·er·head**) ▶ **n.** a compact mass of flowers at the top of a stem, esp. a capitulum.

flow·er·ing /ˈflouəriNG/ ▶ **adj.** (of a plant) in bloom: *a basket of flowering plants.* ■ capable of producing flowers, esp. in contrast to a similar plant with the flowers inconspicuous or absent: *flowering dogwood.* ■ [in comb.] producing flowers at a specified time or of a specified type: *winter-flowering heathers.*

flow·er·ing plum ▶ **n.** another term for MYROBALAN (sense 1).

flow·er·ing quince ▶ **n.** an Asian shrub (genus *Chaenomeles*) of the rose family, with bright red flowers followed by round white, green, or yellow edible fruits. Also called JAPANESE QUINCE, JAPONICA.

flow·er·ing rush ▶ **n.** a tall rushlike plant (*Butomus umbellatus*, family Butomaceae.) with long narrow leaves and pinkish flowers, living in shallow slow-moving water. Native to Eurasia, it has become established in North America.

flow·er·pot /ˈflouər,pät/ ▶ **n.** a small container, used for growing a plant in.

flow·er pow·er ▶ **n.** hist. the ideas of the flower children, esp. the promotion of peace and love.

flow·ers of sul·fur ▶ **plural n.** [treated as sing.] Chem. a fine yellow powdered form of sulfur produced by sublimation.

flow·er·y /ˈflouərē/ ▶ **adj.** full of, resembling, or smelling of flowers: *a flowery meadow | flowery wallpaper.* ■ (of a style of speech or writing) full of elaborate or literary words and phrases: *flowery language.* — **flow·er·i·ness n.**

flow·ing /ˈflōiNG/ ▶ **adj.** (esp. of long hair or clothing) hanging or draping loosely and gracefully. ■ (of a line or contour) smoothly continuous: *the flowing curves of the lawn.* ■ (of language, movement, or style) graceful and fluent. — **flow·ing·ly adv.**

flow·me·ter /ˈflō,mētər/ ▶ **n.** an instrument for measuring the rate of flow of water, gas, or fuel, esp. through a pipe.

flown /flōn/ past participle of FLY[1].

flow·sheet /ˈflō,SHēt/ ▶ **n.** another term for FLOW CHART.

fl. oz. ▶ **abbr.** fluid ounce.

flu /flo͞o/ ▶ **n.** influenza: *I had a bad case of the flu.*

flub /fləb/ informal ▶ **v.** (**flubbed, flub·bing**) [trans.] botch or bungle (something): *she glanced at her notes and flubbed her lines* | [intrans.] *don't flub again.* ▶ **n.** a thing badly or clumsily done; a blunder. [1920s: of unknown origin.]

fluc·tu·ate /ˈfləkCHo͞o,āt/ ▶ **v.** [intrans.] rise and fall irregularly in number or amount. | [as adj.] (**fluctuating**) — **fluc·tu·a·tion** /,fləkCHo͞oˈāSHən/ **n.** [17th C.: from L. *fluctuat-* 'undulated,' from the v. *fluctuare*, from *fluctus* 'flow, current, wave,' from *fluere* 'to flow.']

flue /flo͞o/ ▶ **n.** a duct for smoke and waste gases produced by a fire, a gas heater, a power station, or other fuel-burning installation: *no air rises up the chimney, usually because the flue is blocked* | [as adj.] *flue gases.* [ME: of unknown origin.]

flu·en·cy /ˈflo͞oənsē/ ▶ **n.** the quality or condition of being fluent, in particular: ■ the ability to speak or write a foreign language easily and accurately. ■ the ability to express oneself easily and articulately. ■ gracefulness and ease of movement or style.

flu·ent /ˈflo͞oənt/ ▶ **adj.** (of a person) able to express oneself easily and articulately: *a fluent speaker and writer on technical subjects.* ■ (of a person) able to speak or write a particular foreign language easily and accurately: *she became fluent in French and German.* ■ (of a foreign language) spoken accurately and with facility: *he spoke fluent Spanish.* ■ (of speech, language, movement, or style) smoothly graceful and easy: *his style of play was fast and fluent.* — **flu·ent·ly adv.** [16th C.: from L. *fluent-* 'flowing,' from the v. *fluere*.]

flue pipe ▶ **n. 1** a pipe acting as a flue. **2** an organ pipe into which the air enters directly without striking a reed.

fluff /fləf/ ▶ **n. 1** soft fibers from fabrics such as wool or cotton that accumulate in small light clumps: *he brushed his sleeve to remove the fluff.* ■ any soft downy substance, esp. the fur or feathers of a young mammal or bird. ■ fig. entertainment or writing perceived as trivial or superficial. **2** informal a mistake made in speaking or playing music, or by an actor in delivering lines. ▶ **v.** [trans.] **1** make (something) appear fuller and softer, typically by shaking or brushing it: *I fluffed up the pillows.* **2** informal fail to perform or accomplish (something) successfully or well (used esp. in a sporting or acting context): *the extra fluffed his only line.* [18th C.: prob. a dial. alt. of 16th-cent. *flue* 'down, nap, fluff,' appar. from Flemish *vluwe*.]

fluff·y /ˈfləfē/ ▶ **adj.** (**fluff·i·er, fluff·i·est**) **1** of, like, or covered with fluff: *fluffy white clouds | a fluffy towel.* ■ (of food) light in texture and containing air. **2** informal lacking substance, depth, or seriousness. ■ (of a person, esp. a woman) frivolous, silly, or vague. — **fluff·i·ness n.**

flu·gel·horn /ˈflo͞ogəl,hôrn/ (also **flü·gel·horn, flue·gel·horn**) ▶ **n.** a valved brass musical instrument like a cornet but with a mellower tone. [19th C.: from Ger. *Flügelhorn*, from *Flügel* 'wing' + *Horn* 'horn.']

flu·id /ˈflo͞oid/ ▶ **n.** a substance that has no fixed shape and yields easily to external pressure; a gas or (esp.) a liquid. ▶ **adj.** (of a substance) able to flow easily: *the paint is more fluid than tube watercolors | a fluid medium.* ■ not settled or stable; likely or able to change: *our plans are still fluid | the fluid political situation of the 1930s.* ■ smoothly elegant or graceful: *her movements were fluid and beautiful to watch.* ■ (of a clutch or coupling) using a liquid to transmit power. — **flu·id·i·ty** /flo͞oˈiditē/ **n. flu·id·ly adv.** [ME (as an adj.): from Fr. *fluide* or L. *fluidus*, from *fluere* 'to flow.']

flu·id drachm ▶ **n.** see DRACHM.

flu·id·ize /ˈflo͞oi,dīz/ ▶ **v.** [trans.] tech. cause (a finely divided solid) to acquire the characteristics of a fluid by passing a gas upward through it. — **flu·id·i·za·tion** /,flo͞oidiˈzāSHən/ **n.**

flu·id ounce (abbr.: **fl. oz.**) ▶ **n. 1** a unit of capacity equal to one sixteenth of a US pint (approximately 0.03 liter). **2** Brit. a unit of capacity equal to one twentieth of a pint (approximately 0.028 liter).

fluke[1] /flo͝ok/ ▶ **n.** unlikely chance occurrence, esp. a surprising piece of luck: *their triumph was no fluke.* [19th C.: perh. a dial. word.]

fluke[2] ▶ **n. 1** a parasitic flatworm (classes Trematoda and Monogenea, phylum Platyhelminthes) that typically has suckers and hooks for attachment to the host. **2** a flatfish, esp. a flounder. [OE *flōc* (sense 2), of Gmc. origin; rel. to Ger. *flach* 'flat.']

fluke[3] ▶ **n.** a broad triangular plate on the arm of an anchor. See illustration at ANCHOR. ■ either of the lobes of a whale's tail. [16th C.: perh. from FLUKE[2] (because of the shape).]

fluk·y /ˈflo͞okē/ (also **fluk·ey**) ▶ **adj.** (**fluk·i·er, fluk·i·est**) obtained or achieved more by chance than skill: *a fluky goal.* ■ subject to chance; unpredictable. — **fluk·i·ly adv. fluk·i·ness n.**

flume /flo͞om/ ▶ **n.** a deep narrow channel or ravine with a stream running through it. ■ an artificial channel conveying water, typically used for transporting logs or timber. ■ a water-chute ride at an amusement park. [ME: from OFr. *flum*, from L. *flumen* 'river,' from *fluere* 'to flow.']

flum·mer·y /ˈfləmərē/ ▶ **n.** (pl. **-mer·ies**) empty compliments; nonsense: *she hated the flummery of public relations.* [17th C. (denoting a dish made with oatmeal or wheatmeal boiled to a jelly): from Welsh *llymru*; perh. rel. to *llymrig* 'soft, slippery.']

flum·mox /ˈfləməks/ ▶**v.** [trans.] (usu. **be flummoxed**) informal perplex (someone) greatly; bewilder: *he was completely flummoxed by the question.* [19th C.: prob. of dialect origin; cf. dial. *flummock* 'to make untidy, confuse.']

flung /fləNG/ past and past participle of FLING.

flunk /fləNGk/ informal ▶**v.** [trans.] fail to reach the required standard in (an examination, test, or course of study). ■ judge (a student or examination candidate) to have failed to reach the required standard. ■ [intrans.] (**flunk out**) (of a student) leave or be dismissed from school or college as a result of failing to reach the required standard. [19th C.: perh. rel. to FUNK[1].]

flun·ky /ˈfləNGkē/ (also **flun·key**) ▶**n.** (pl. **-kies** or **-keys**) a person who performs relatively menial tasks for someone else, esp. obsequiously. [18th C. (originally Scots): perh. from FLANK.]

fluo·resce /flo͝o(ə)ˈres; flôˈres/ ▶**v.** [intrans.] shine or glow brightly due to fluorescence: *the molecules fluoresce when excited by ultraviolet radiation.* [19th C.: back-form. from FLUORESCENCE.]

fluo·res·ce·in /flo͝o(ə)ˈresēən; flôˈresē-/ ▶**n.** Chem. an orange dye, $C_{20}H_{12}O_5$, with a yellowish-green fluorescence, used as an indicator and tracer. [19th C.: from FLUORESCENCE + -IN[1].]

fluo·res·cence /flo͝o(ə)ˈresəns; flôˈres-/ ▶**n.** the visible or invisible radiation produced from certain substances as a result of incident radiation of a shorter wavelength such as X-rays or ultraviolet light. ■ the property of absorbing light of short wavelength and emitting light of longer wavelength. [19th C.: from FLUORSPAR.]

fluo·res·cent /ˌflo͝o(ə)ˈresənt; flôˈres-/ ▶**adj.** (of a substance) having or showing fluorescence. ■ containing a fluorescent tube: *fluorescent lighting.* ■ vividly colorful. ▶**n.** a fluorescent tube or lamp.

fluo·res·cent screen ▶**n.** a transparent screen coated with fluorescent material to show images from X-rays.

fluo·res·cent tube (also **fluorescent bulb** or **fluorescent lamp**) ▶**n.** a glass tube that radiates light when phosphor on its inside surface is made to fluoresce by ultraviolet radiation from mercury vapor.

fluor·i·date /ˈflo͝orəˌdāt; ˈflôr-/ ▶**v.** [trans.] add traces of fluorides to (something, esp. a water supply): — **fluor·i·da·tion** /ˌflo͝orəˈdāSHən; ˌflôr-/ **n.**

fluor·ide /ˈflo͝orˌīd; ˈflôr-/ ▶**n.** Chem. a compound of fluorine with another element or group, esp. a salt of the anion F− or an organic compound with fluorine bonded to an alkyl group. ■ sodium fluoride or another fluorine-containing salt added to water supplies or toothpaste in order to reduce tooth decay. [19th C.: from FLUORINE + -IDE.]

fluor·i·nate /ˈflo͝orəˌnāt; ˈflôr-/ ▶**v.** [trans.] Chem. introduce fluorine into (a compound). ■ another term for FLUORIDATE. — **fluor·i·na·tion** /ˌflo͝orəˈnāSHən; ˌflôr-/ **n.**

fluor·ine /ˈflo͝orˌēn; ˈflôr-/ ▶**n.** the chemical element of atomic number 9, a poisonous pale yellow gas of the halogen series. It is the most reactive of all the elements. (Symbol: **F**) [19th C.: from *fluor* (see FLUORSPAR) + -INE[4].]

fluo·rite /ˈflo͝orīt; ˈflôr-/ ▶**n.** a mineral consisting of calcium fluoride that typically occurs as cubic crystals, colorless when pure but often colored by impurities. [19th C.: from *fluor* (see FLUORSPAR) + -ITE[1].]

fluoro- ▶**comb. form 1** representing FLUORINE. **2** representing FLUORESCENCE.

fluor·o·car·bon /ˌflo͝oroˈkärbən; ˌflôrō-/ ▶**n.** Chem. a compound formed by replacing one or more of the hydrogen atoms in a hydrocarbon with fluorine atoms.

fluor·o·scope /ˈflo͝orəˌskōp; ˈflôr-/ ▶**n.** an instrument with a fluorescent screen used for viewing X-ray images without taking and developing X-ray photographs.

fluo·ro·sis /flo͝oˈrōsəs; flô-/ ▶**n.** Med. a chronic condition caused by excessive intake of fluorine compounds, marked by mottling of the teeth and, if severe, calcification of the ligaments.

flu·or·spar /ˈflo͝orˌspär; ˈflôr-/ ▶**n.** another term for FLUORITE. [18th C.: from *fluor* 'a flow, a mineral used as a flux, fluorspar' (from L. *fluor*, from *fluere* 'to flow') + SPAR[3].]

flu·ox·e·tine /flo͞oˈäksəˌtīn/ ▶**n.** Med. a synthetic compound that inhibits the uptake of serotonin in the brain and is taken to treat depression. Also called PROZAC (trademark). [1970s: from *fluo(rine)* + *ox(y)* + *-etine* (perh. from *e* + a blend of TOLUENE and AMINE).]

flur·ried /ˈflərēd; ˈflə-rēd/ ▶**adj.** (of a person) agitated, nervous, or anxious: *I sat down, feeling a little flurried and excited.*

flur·ry /ˈflərē; ˈflə-rē/ ▶**n.** (pl. **-ries**) a small swirling mass of something, esp. snow or leaves, moved by sudden gusts of wind: *a flurry of snow.* ■ a sudden short period of commotion or excitement. ■ a number of things arriving or happening during the same period. ▶**v.** (**-ries, -ried**) [no obj., with adverbial of direction] (esp. of snow or leaves) be moved in small swirling masses by sudden gusts of wind: *gusts of snow flurried through the door.* [17th C.: from obs. *flurr* 'fly up, flutter, whir' (imitative), prob. influenced by HURRY.]

flush[1] /fləSH/ ▶**v. 1** [intrans.] (of a person's skin or face) become red and hot, typically as the result of illness or strong emotion: *Mr. Cunningham flushed angrily* | [as adj.] (**flushed**) *her flushed cheeks.* ■ [trans.] cause (a person's skin or face) to become red and hot. ■ glow or cause to glow with warm color or light: [intrans.] *the ash in the center of the fire flushed up* | [trans.] *the sky was flushed with the gold of dawn.* ■ (**be flushed with**) fig. be excited or elated by: *flushed with success, I was getting into my stride.* **2** [trans.] cleanse (something, esp. a toilet) by causing large quantities of water to pass through it. ■ [intrans.] (of a toilet) be cleansed in such a way: *Cally heard the toilet flush.* ■ [with obj. and adverbial of direction] remove or dispose of (an object or substance) in such a way: *I flushed the pills down the toilet.* ■ [with obj. and adverbial of direction] cause (a liquid) to flow through something: *0.3 ml of saline is gently flushed through the tube.* **3** [with obj. and adverbial of direction] drive (a bird, esp. a game bird, or an animal) from its cover: *the grouse were flushed from the woods.* ■ fig. cause to be revealed; force into the open: *they're trying to flush Tilton out of hiding.* **4** [intrans.] (of a plant) send out fresh shoots: *the plant had started to flush by late March.* ▶**n. 1** a reddening of the face or skin that is typically caused by illness or strong emotion. ■ an area of warm color or light. **2** [in sing.] a sudden rush of intense emotion. ■ fig. a period when something is new or particularly fresh and vigorous: *he is no longer in the first flush of youth.* **3** an act of cleansing something, esp. a toilet, with a sudden flow of water: ■ the device used for producing such a flow of water in a toilet: *he pressed the flush absentmindedly.* ■ [as adj.] denoting a type of toilet that has such a device: *a flush toilet.* — **flush·er n.** [ME 'move rapidly': symbolic, *fl-* frequently beginning words connected with sudden movement.]

flush[2] ▶**adj. 1** completely level or even with another surface: *the gates are flush with the adjoining fencing.* ■ (of printed text) not indented or protruding: *each line is flush with the left-hand margin.* ■ (of a door) having a smooth surface, without indented or protruding panels or moldings. **2** [predic.] informal having plenty of something, esp. money: *the banks are flush with funds.* ■ (of money) plentiful: *the years when cash was flush.* — **flush·ness n.** [16th C.: prob. rel. to FLUSH[1].]

flush[3] ▶**n.** (in poker) a hand of cards all of the same suit. [16th C.: from Fr. *flux* (formerly *flus*), from L. *fluxus* 'a flow.']

flust·er /ˈfləstər/ ▶**v.** [trans.] [often as adj.] (**flustered**) make (someone) agitated or confused: *you need to be able to work under pressure and not get flustered.* ▶**n.** [in sing.] an agitated or confused state. [17th C.: perh. of Scand. origin and rel. to Icelandic *flaustra* 'hurry, bustle.']

flute /flo͞ot/ ▶**n. 1** a wind instrument made from a tube with holes along it that are stopped by the fingers or keys, held vertically or horizontally so that the player's breath strikes a narrow edge. ■ a modern instrument of this type, typically of metal, held horizontally, with the mouthpiece near one end, which is closed. ■ an organ stop with wooden or metal flue pipes producing a similar tone. **2** Archit. an ornamental vertical groove in a column. ■ a trumpet-shaped frill on a dress or other garment. ■ any similar cylindrical groove, as on pastry. **3** a tall, narrow wine glass. ▶**v. 1** [with direct speech] speak in a melodious way reminiscent of the sound of a flute. ■ literary play a flute or pipe. **2** [trans.] [often as adj.] (**fluted**) make flutes or grooves in: *fluted columns.* ■ make trumpet-shaped frills on (a garment). [ME: from OFr. *flahute*, prob. from Provençal *flaüt*, perh. a blend of *flaujol* 'flageolet' + *laüt* 'lute.']

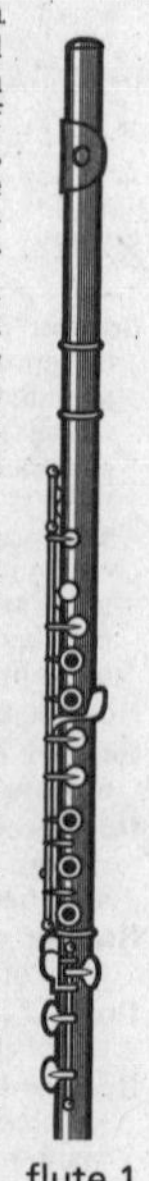

flute 1

flut·ing /ˈflo͞otiNG/ ▶**n.** a groove or set of grooves forming a surface decoration: *a hollow stem with vertical flutings* | *pieces decorated with fluting.* ▶**adj.** reminiscent of the sound of a flute: *the golden, fluting voice filled the room.*

flut·ist /ˈflo͞otist/ (also esp. Brit. **flaut·ist**) ▶**n.** a flute player.

flut·ter /ˈflətər/ ▶**v.** [intrans.] (of a bird or other winged creature) fly unsteadily or hover by flapping the wings quickly and lightly: *a couple of butterflies fluttered around the garden.* ■ (with reference to a bird's wings) flap in such a way: | [trans.] *the lark fluttered its wings, hovering.* ■ [with adverbial] move or fall with a light irregular or trembling motion: *the remaining petals fluttered to the ground.* ■ (of a pulse or heartbeat) beat feebly or irregularly. ▶**n.** an act of fluttering. ■ a state or sensation of tremulous excitement: *Sandra felt a flutter in the pit of her stomach* | *her insides were in a flutter.* ■ Med. disturbance of the rhythm of the heart that is less severe than fibrillation. ■ Electron. rapid variation in the pitch or amplitude of a signal, esp. of recorded sound. Compare with WOW[2].

– PHRASES **flutter one's eyelashes** open and close one's eyes rapidly in a coyly flirtatious manner. — **flut·ter·er n. flut·ter·y adj.** [OE *floterian, flotorian.*]

flut·ter kick ▶**n.** a brisk, alternating, up-and-down movement of the legs when swimming with certain strokes, such as the crawl.

flut·ter-tongu·ing ▶**n.** the action of vibrating the tongue (as if rolling an *r*) in playing a wind instrument to produce a whirring effect.

flut·y /ˈflo͞otē/ (also **flut·ey**) ▶**adj.** (**flut·i·er, flut·i·est**) reminiscent of the sound of a flute: *a drawn-out fluty whistle.*

flu·vi·al /ˈflo͞ovēəl/ ▶**adj.** esp. Geol. of or found in a river. [ME: from L. *fluvialis*, from *fluvius* 'river,' from *fluere* 'to flow.']

flu·vi·a·tile /ˈflo͞ovēəˌtīl/ ▶**adj.** of, found in, or produced by a river: *fluviatile sediments.* [16th C.: from Fr., from L. *fluviatilis*, from *fluviatus* 'moistened,' from *fluvius* 'river.']

flu·vi·o·gla·cial /ˌflo͞ovēōˈglāSHəl/ ▶**adj.** Geol. relating to or denoting erosion or deposition caused by flowing meltwater from glaciers or ice sheets.

flux /fləks/ ▶**n. 1** the action or process of flowing or flowing out. ■ Med. an abnormal discharge of blood or other matter from or within the body. ■ (usu. **the flux**) archaic diarrhea or dysentery. **2** continuous change. **3** Physics the rate of flow of a fluid, radiant energy, or particles across a given area. ■ the amount of radiation or particles incident on an area in a given time. ■ the total electric or magnetic field passing through a surface. **4** a substance mixed with a solid to lower its melting point, used esp. in soldering and brazing metals or to promote vitrification in glass or ceramics. ■ a substance added to a furnace during metal smelting or glassmaking that combines with impurities to form slag. ▶v. [trans.] treat (a metal object) with a flux to promote melting. [ME: from L. *fluxus*, from *fluere* 'to flow.']

flux den·si·ty ▶n. the amount of magnetic, electric, or other flux passing through a unit area.

fly[1] /flī/ ▶v. (**flies** /flīz/; past **flew**; past part. **flown**) [intrans.] **1** (of a bird or other winged creature) move through the air under control: *close the door or the moths will fly in* | *the bird can fly enormous distances.* ■ (of an aircraft or its occupants) travel through the air: *I fly back to New York this evening.* ■ [trans.] control the flight of (an aircraft); pilot. ■ [with obj. and adverbial of direction] transport in an aircraft: *helicopters flew the injured to a hospital.* ■ [trans.] accomplish (a purpose) in an aircraft: *pilots trained to fly combat missions.* **2** move or be hurled quickly through the air: *balls kept flying over her hedge* | *he was sent flying by the tackle.* ■ [with adverbial of direction] (past **flied**) Baseball hit a ball high into the air: *Gwynn flied to left.* ■ (past **flied**) (**fly out**) Baseball (of a batter) be put out by hitting a fly ball that is caught. ■ [with adverbial of direction] go or move quickly: *she flew along the path.* ■ (of time) pass swiftly: *how time flies!* ■ (of a report) be circulated among many people: *rumors were flying around Chicago.* ■ (of accusations or insults) be exchanged swiftly and heatedly: *the accusations flew thick and fast.* **3** [with adverbial] (esp. of hair) wave or flutter in the wind: *they were running, hair flying everywhere.* ■ (of a flag) be displayed, esp. on a flagpole: *flags were flying at half-mast.* ■ [trans.] display (a flag). ▶n. (pl. **flies**) **1** (Brit. often **flies**) an opening at the crotch of a pair of pants, closed with a zipper or buttons and typically covered with a flap. ■ a flap of material covering the opening or fastening of a garment or of a tent: [as adj., in comb.] *a fly-fronted shirt.* **2** (**the flies**) the space over the stage in a theater. **3** Baseball short for FLY BALL.

– PHRASES **fly the coop** informal make one's escape. **fly the flag** see FLAG[1]. **fly high** be very successful; prosper: *that young man is the sort to fly high.* **fly in the face of** be openly at variance with (what is usual or expected): *a need to fly in the face of convention.* **fly into a rage** (or **temper**) become suddenly or violently angry. **fly the nest** ■ informal (of a young person) leave their parents' home to set up home elsewhere. **fly off the handle** informal lose one's temper suddenly and unexpectedly. **go fly a kite** [in imper.] informal go away. **on the fly** while in motion or progress: *his deep shot was caught on the fly.* ■ Comput. during the running of a computer program without interrupting the run. [OE *flēogan*, of Gmc. origin; rel. to Du. *vliegen* and Ger. *fliegen*, also to FLY[2].]

fly[2] ▶n. (pl. **flies** /flīz/) a flying insect (order Diptera) of a large order characterized by a single pair of transparent wings and sucking (and often also piercing) mouthparts. Flies are noted as vectors of disease. ■ [usu. in comb.] used in names of flying insects of other orders, e.g., **butterfly, dragonfly, firefly.** ■ an infestation of flying insects on a plant or animal: *cattle treated for warble fly.* ■ a natural or artificial flying insect used as bait in fishing, esp. a mayfly.

– PHRASES **die** (or **drop**) **like flies** die or collapse in large numbers. **a fly in the ointment** a minor irritation that spoils the success or enjoyment of something. **fly on the wall** an unnoticed observer of a particular situation. [OE *flȳge*, *flēoge*, denoting any winged insect, of West Gmc. origin; rel. to Du. *vlieg* and Ger. *Fliege*, also to FLY[1].]

fly ag·a·ric ▶n. a poisonous toadstool (*Amanita muscaria*, family Amanitaceae) that has a red cap with fluffy white spots, growing particularly among birch trees.

fly ash ▶n. ash produced in small dark flecks, typically from a furnace, and carried into the air.

fly·a·way /ˈflīəˌwā/ ▶adj. (of a person's hair) fine and difficult to control.

fly ball ▶n. Baseball a ball batted high into the air.

fly·blown /ˈflīˌblōn/ ▶adj. dirty or contaminated, esp. through contact with flies and their eggs and larvae: *the room was filthy and flyblown.*

fly·boy /ˈflīˌboi/ ▶n. informal a pilot, esp. one in the air force.

fly·by /ˈflīˌbī/ (also **fly-by**) ▶n. (pl. **-bys**) a flight past a point, esp. the close approach of a spacecraft to a planet or moon for observation.

fly-by-night ▶adj. [attrib.] unreliable or untrustworthy, esp. in business or financial matters. ▶n. (also **fly-by-nighter**) an unreliable or untrustworthy person.

fly-by-wire ▶n. [often as adj.] a semiautomatic and typically computer-regulated system for controlling the flight of an aircraft or spacecraft.

fly·catch·er /ˈflīˌkacHər; -ˌkecHər/ ▶n. a bird that catches flying insects, esp. in short flights from a perch. Old World flycatchers belong to the families Muscicapidae and Monarchidae. Most New World species belong to the family Tyrannidae (**tyrant flycatchers**).

fly·er /ˈflīˈər/ ▶n. var. of FLIER.

fly-fish·ing ▶n. the sport of fishing using a rod and an artificial fly as bait. — **fly-fish** v.

fly gal·ler·y ▶n. a raised platform at the side of a stage that contains ropes and equipment for moving props and scenery. Also called **fly floor.**

fly-in ▶n. a meeting for pilots who arrive by air: *they are holding a helicopter fly-in.* ■ an act of transporting people or goods by air: *one or two fly-ins to remote lakes.* ■ [as adj.] denoting a place or activity that is reached using an aircraft.

fly·ing /ˈflī-iNG/ ▶adj. moving or able to move through the air with wings: *a flying ant.* ■ relating to airplanes or aviators: *a flying ace* | *a flying career.* ■ done while hurling oneself through the air: *he took a flying kick at a policeman.* ■ moving rapidly, esp. through the air: *one passenger was cut by flying glass.* ■ hasty; brief: *a flying visit.* ■ used in names of animals that can glide by using winglike membranes or other structures, e.g., **flying squirrel.** ▶n. flight, esp. in an aircraft: *she hates flying.*

– PHRASES **with flying colors** with distinction.

fly·ing boat ▶n. a large seaplane that lands with its fuselage in the water.

fly·ing bomb ▶n. a small pilotless aircraft with an explosive warhead, esp. a V-1.

fly·ing bridge ▶n. an open deck above the main bridge of a vessel such as a yacht or cabin cruiser, typically equipped with duplicate controls.

fly·ing but·tress ▶n. Archit. a buttress slanting from a separate pier, typically forming an arch with the wall it supports.

Fly·ing Dutch·man a legendary spectral ship supposedly seen in the region of the Cape of Good Hope and presaging disaster. ■ the captain of this ship

fly·ing fish ▶n. a fish (family Exocoetidae, in particular *Exocoetus volitans*) of warm seas that leaps out of the water and uses its winglike pectoral fins to glide over the surface for some distance.

flying fish

fly·ing fox ▶n. a large fruit bat (*Pteropus* and other genera, family Pteropodidae) with a foxlike face, found in Madagascar, Southeast Asia, and northern Australia.

fly·ing frog ▶n. a nocturnal arboreal Asian frog (*Polypedates leucomystax*, family Rhacophoridae) that is able to glide between trees using the large webs between its extended toes.

fly·ing gur·nard ▶n. a bottom-dwelling marine fish (family Dactylopteridae) that has bony armor on the skull, spines behind the head, and large brightly colored pectoral fins. It moves through the water with a gliding or flying motion.

fly·ing le·mur ▶n. a tree-dwelling lemurlike mammal (genus *Cynocephalus*, family Cynocephalidae) of Southeast Asia, with a membrane between the fore and hind limbs for gliding from tree to tree.

fly·ing ma·chine ▶n. an aircraft, esp. an early or unconventional one.

fly·ing pha·lan·ger ▶n. a small Australasian marsupial (genera *Petaurus* and *Petauroides*, family Petauridae) with a membrane between the fore and hind limbs for gliding.

fly·ing sau·cer ▶n. a disk-shaped flying craft supposedly piloted by aliens; a UFO.

southern flying squirrel

fly·ing squir·rel ▶n. a small squirrel that has skin joining the fore and hind limbs for gliding from tree to tree. The two common North American species are the **northern flying squirrel** (*Glaucomys sabrinus*) and the **southern flying squirrel** (*G. volans*).

fly·ing start ▶n. a start of a race or time trial in which the starting point is passed at speed. ■ a good beginning, esp. one giving an advantage over competitors: *the team got off to a flying start.*

fly·ing tra·peze ▶n. another term for TRAPEZE (sense 1).

fly·ing wedge ▶n. a fast-moving group, as of police officers, linked together closely in a V-shaped formation, sometimes used to force a way through a crowd or to protect someone behind them.

fly·ing wing ▶n. an aircraft with little or no fuselage and no vertical airfoil.

fly·leaf /ˈflīˌlēf/ ▶n. (pl. **-leaves** /-ˌlēvz/) a blank page at the beginning or end of a book.

fly·o·ver /ˈflīˌōvər/ ▶n. a low flight by one or more aircraft over a specific location: *there were artillery platforms in the hills, making a flyover too risky.* ■ a ceremonial flight of an aircraft past a person or a place.

fly·pa·per /'flī,pāpər/ ▶ n. sticky, poison-treated strips of paper that are hung indoors to catch and kill flies.

Fly River /flī/ a river in Papua New Guinea that flows for 750 miles (1,200 km) into the Gulf of Papua.

fly rod ▶ n. a lightweight flexible rod used in fly-fishing.

fly·speck /'flī,spek/ ▶ n. a tiny stain made by the excrement of an insect. ■ a thing that is contemptibly small or insignificant: *a sleepy flyspeck of a town.*

fly spray ▶ n. a substance sprayed from an aerosol that kills flying insects.

fly swat·ter (also **fly·swat·ter**) ▶ n. an implement used for swatting insects, typically a square of plastic mesh attached to a wire handle.

fly-through ▶ n. a computer-animated simulation of what would be seen by one flying through a particular real or imaginary region.

fly-ty·ing ▶ n. the making of artificial flies used in fly-fishing.

fly·way /'flī,wā/ ▶ n. Ornithol. a route regularly used by large numbers of migrating birds.

fly·weight /'flī,wāt/ ▶ n. a weight in boxing and other sports intermediate between light flyweight and bantamweight. In boxing it ranges from 108 to 112 pounds (48 to 51 kg). ■ a boxer or other competitor of this weight.

fly·wheel /'flī,(h)wēl/ ▶ n. a heavy revolving wheel in a machine that is used to increase the machine's momentum and thereby provide greater stability or a reserve of available power.

fly whisk ▶ n. see WHISK (sense 3).

FM ▶ abbr. frequency modulation: [as adj.] *an FM radio station.*

Fm ▶ symb. the chemical element fermium.

fm. ▶ abbr. fathom(s).

FMB ▶ abbr. Federal Maritime Board.

FMCG ▶ abbr. fast-moving consumer goods: [as adj.] *the FMCG sector.*

FMCS ▶ abbr. Federal Mediation and Conciliation Service.

FMN ▶ abbr. flavin mononucleotide.

FMV ▶ abbr. full-motion video.

FN ▶ abbr. foreign national.

fn. ▶ abbr. footnote.

FNMA ▶ abbr. Federal National Mortgage Association. Also called FANNIE MAE.

f-num·ber ▶ n. Photog. the ratio of the focal length of a camera lens to the diameter of the aperture being used for a particular shot (e.g., *f8*, indicating that the focal length is eight times the diameter). [20th C.: from *f* (denoting the focal length) and NUMBER.]

FO ▶ abbr. ■ field officer. ■ Foreign Office.

Fo /fō/, Dario (1926–), Italian playwright. His works include *Accidental Death of an Anarchist* (1970). Nobel Prize for Literature (1997).

fo. ▶ abbr. folio.

foal /fōl/ ▶ n. a young horse or related animal. ▶ v. [intrans.] (of a mare) give birth to a foal. [OE *fola*, of Gmc. origin; rel. to Du. *veulen* and Ger. *Fohlen*, also to FILLY.]

foam /fōm/ ▶ n. a mass of small bubbles formed on or in liquid, typically by agitation or fermentation. ■ a similar mass formed from saliva or sweat. ■ a thick preparation containing many small bubbles. ■ a lightweight form of rubber or plastic made by solidifying such a liquid. ■ (**the foam**) literary the sea. ▶ v. [intrans.] form or produce a mass of small bubbles; froth: *the sea foamed beneath them.* ■ fig., informal be very angry: *the audience was* ***foaming at the mouth****, venting their outrage.* — **foam·less** adj. **foam·y** adj. [OE *fām* (noun), *fǣman* (verb), of West Gmc. origin; rel. to Old High Ger. *feim* (n.), *feimen* (v.).]

foam rub·ber ▶ n. a spongy material made of rubber or plastic in the form of foam, used for cushioning and in upholstery.

fob[1] /fäb/ ▶ n. (also **fob chain**) a chain attached to a watch for carrying in a waistcoat or waistband pocket. [17th C.: prob. rel. to Ger. dial. *Fuppe* 'pocket.']

fob[2] ▶ v. (**fobbed, fob·bing**) [trans.] (**fob someone off**) deceitfully attempt to satisfy someone by making excuses or giving them something inferior. ■ (**fob something off on**) give (someone) something inferior to or different from what they want. [ME: perh. rel. to Ger. *foppen* 'deceive, cheat, banter.']

f.o.b. ▶ abbr. free on board. See FREE.

fo·cac·cia /fō'kächē(ē)ə/ ▶ n. a type of flat Italian bread made with yeast and olive oil and flavored with herbs. [Ital.]

fo·cal /'fōkəl/ ▶ adj. of or relating to the center or main point of interest: *tapestries in which birds or animals provide the focal interest.* ■ Optics of or relating to the focus of a lens. — **fo·cal·ly** adv. [17th C.: from mod. L. *focalis*, from L. *focus*, or directly from FOCUS.]

fo·cal length ▶ n. the distance between the center of a lens or curved mirror and its focus. ■ the equivalent distance in a compound lens or telescope.

fo·cal point ▶ n. the point at which rays or waves meet after reflection or refraction, or the point from which diverging rays or waves appear to proceed. ■ the center of interest or activity: *almost every sizable city can have a junior college that can act as a focal point for cultural activity.*

Foch /fôsh/, Ferdinand (1851–1929), French general. He led the French troops and eventually the Allied troops in France during World War I.

fo'c'sle /'fōksəl/ (also **fo'c's'le**) ▶ n. var. of FORECASTLE.

fo·cus /'fōkəs/ ▶ n. (pl. **fo·cus·es** or **fo·ci** /'fōsī; -kī/) **1** the center of interest or activity. ■ an act of concentrating interest or activity on something. ■ Geol. the point of origin of an earthquake. Compare with EPICENTER. ■ Med. the principal site of an infection or other disease. **2** the state or quality of having or producing clear visual definition. ■ another term for FOCAL POINT. ■ the point at which an object must be situated with respect to a lens or mirror for an image of it to be well defined. ■ a device on a lens that can be adjusted to produce a clear image. **3** Geom. one of the fixed points from which the distances to any point of a given curve, such as an ellipse or parabola, are connected by a linear relation. ▶ v. (**fo·cused, fo·cus·ing** or **fo·cussed, fo·cus·sing**) [intrans.] **1** (of a person or their eyes) adapt to the prevailing level of light and become able to see clearly: *try to focus on a stationary object.* ■ [trans.] bring (one's eyes) into such a state: *trying to* ***focus*** *his bleary eyes* ***on*** *Corbett.* ■ [trans.] adjust the focus of (a telescope, camera, or other instrument): *they were* ***focusing*** *a telescope* ***on*** *a star.* ■ [trans.] (of a lens) make (rays or waves) meet at a single point. ■ [intrans.] (of light, radio waves, or other energy) become concentrated into a sharp beam of light or energy. ■ [trans.] (of a lens) concentrate (light, radio waves, or energy) into a sharp beam. **2** (**focus on**) pay particular attention to. ■ [trans.] concentrate: *the course helps to focus and stimulate your thoughts.* [17th C. (as a term in geometry and physics): from L., literally 'domestic hearth.']

fo·cus group ▶ n. a demographically diverse group of people assembled to participate in a guided discussion about a particular product before it is launched, or to provide ongoing feedback.

fod·der /'fädər/ ▶ n. food, esp. dried hay or feed, for cattle and other livestock. [OE *fōdor*, of Gmc. origin; rel. to Du. *voeder* and Ger. *Futter*, also to FOOD.]

FoE ▶ abbr. Friends of the Earth.

foe /fō/ ▶ n. an enemy or opponent. [OE *fāh* 'hostile' and *gefā* 'enemy,' of West Gmc. origin; rel. to FEUD.]

foehn /fān; fœn/ (also **föhn**) ▶ n. Meteorol. a warm dry wind developing in the lee of any mountain range. [19th C.: from Ger. *Föhn*, based on L. *(ventus) Favonius* 'mild west wind.']

foet·id ▶ adj. var. of FETID.

foe·tus /'fētəs/ ▶ n. var. of FETUS (chiefly in British nontechnical use). — **foe·tal** /'fētl/ adj. **foe·ti·cide** /'fētə,sīd/ n.

fog /fôg; fäg/ ▶ n. a thick cloud of water droplets suspended in the atmosphere at or near the earth's surface that obscures or restricts visibility (strictly, reducing visibility to below 1 km). ■ [in sing.] an opaque mass of something in the atmosphere. ■ [in sing.] fig. something that obscures and confuses a situation or someone's thought processes: *lost in a fog of detail.* ■ Photog. cloudiness that obscures the image on a developed negative or print. ▶ v. (**fogged, fog·ging**) [trans.] **1** cause (a glass surface) to become covered with steam. ■ [intrans.] (of a glass surface) become covered with steam: *the windshield was starting to* ***fog up****.* ■ fig. bewilder or puzzle (someone). ■ Photog. make (a film, negative, or print) obscure or cloudy. **2** treat with something, esp. an insecticide, in the form of a spray.

– PHRASES **in a fog** in a state of perplexity; unable to think clearly or understand something. [16th C.: perh. a back-form. from FOGGY.]

fog bank ▶ n. a dense mass of fog, esp. at sea.

fog·bound /'fôg,bound; 'fäg-/ ▶ adj. unable to travel or function normally because of thick fog. ■ enveloped or obscured by fog: *a fogbound forest.*

fo·gey /'fōgē/ (also **fo·gy**) ▶ n. (pl. **-geys** or **-gies**) a person, typically an old one, who is considered to be old-fashioned or conservative in attitude or tastes: — **fo·gey·dom** n. **fo·gey·ish** adj. **fo·gey·ism** n. [18th C.: rel. to earlier slang *fogram*, of unknown origin.]

Fog·gia /'fôjə; 'fôdjä/ a town in southeastern Italy; pop. 160,000.

fog·gy /'fôgē; 'fägē/ ▶ adj. (**fog·gi·er, fog·gi·est**) full of or accompanied by fog. ■ unable to think clearly; confused. ■ indistinctly expressed or perceived; obscure.

– PHRASES **not have the foggiest** (**idea** or **notion**) informal have no idea at all. — **fog·gi·ness** n. [15th C.: perhaps from *fog* 'grass,' perh. akin to Norw. *fogg*.]

fog·horn /'fôg,hôrn; 'fäg-/ ▶ n. a device making a loud, deep sound as a warning to ships in fog. ■ informal a loud penetrating voice.

fog lamp (also **fog·light**) ▶ n. a bright light on a motor vehicle, used in foggy conditions to improve road visibility or warn other drivers of one's presence.

fo·gy /'fōgē/ ▶ n. var. of FOGEY.

föhn ▶ n. var. of FOEHN.

foi·ble /'foibəl/ ▶ n. a minor weakness or eccentricity in someone's character: *they have to tolerate each other's little foibles.* [16th C.: from obs. Fr., in OFr. *fieble* (see FEEBLE).]

foil[1] /foil/ ▶ v. [trans.] prevent (something considered wrong or undesirable) from succeeding. ■ frustrate the efforts or plans of. [ME: perh. from OFr. *fouler* 'to full cloth, trample,' based on L. *fullo* 'fuller.']

foil[2] ▶ n. **1** metal hammered or rolled into a thin flexible sheet, used chiefly for covering or wrapping food. **2** a person or thing that contrasts with and so emphasizes and enhances the qualities of another: *the earthy taste is a foil for the tartness.* ■ a thin leaf of metal placed under a precious stone to increase its brilliance. [ME: via OFr. from L. *folium* 'leaf.']

foil³ ▸ **n.** a light fencing sword without cutting edges but with a button on its point. — **foil·ist n.** [16th C.: of unknown origin.]

foil⁴ ▸ **n.** each of the structures fitted to a hydrofoil's hull to lift it clear of the water at speed.

foist /foist/ ▸ **v.** [trans.] (**foist someone/something on**) impose an unwelcome or unnecessary person or thing on: *don't let anyone foist inferior goods on you.* [16th C.: from Du. dial. *vuisten* 'take in the hand,' from *vuist* (see FIST).]

Fo·kine /fô'kēn/, Michel (1880–1942), US dancer and choreographer; born in Russia; born *Mikhail Mikhailovich Fokin.* He was chief choreographer at the Ballets Russes 1909–14.

Fok·ker /'fäkər/, Anthony Herman Gerard (1890–1939), US aviation pioneer; born in Java. He designed German fighter planes in World War I.

fol. ▸ **abbr.** ■ folio. ■ following.

fold¹ /fōld/ ▸ **v.** [trans.] **1** bend (something flexible and relatively flat) over on itself so that one part of it covers another: *she folded all her clothes and packed all her bags.* ■ (**fold something in/into**) mix an ingredient gently with (another ingredient), esp. by lifting a mixture with a spoon so as to enclose it without stirring or beating: *fold the egg whites into the chocolate mixture.* ■ [intrans.] (of a piece of furniture or equipment) be able to be bent or rearranged into a flatter or more compact shape, typically in order to make it easier to store or carry: [with complement] *the deck chair folds flat* | [as adj.] (**folding**) *a folding chair.* ■ bend or rearrange (a piece of furniture or equipment) in such a way: *he folded up his tripod.* ■ [intrans.] (**fold out**) be able to be opened out; unfold: *the sofa folds out.* ■ (of a bird) collapse (its wings) and lay them flat against its body. **2** [with adverbial] cover or wrap something in (a soft or flexible material). ■ hold or clasp (someone) closely in one's arms with passion or deep affection. **3** [intrans.] informal (of an enterprise or organization) cease operating as a result of financial problems or a lack of support. ■ (esp. of a sports player or team) suddenly stop performing well or effectively. ■ (of a poker player) drop out of a hand. ▸ **n. 1** (usu. **folds**) a form or shape produced by the gentle draping of a loose, full garment or piece of cloth. ■ an area of skin that sags or hangs loosely. ■ Geol. a bend or curvature of strata. **2** a line or crease produced in paper or cloth as the result of folding it.
– PHRASES **fold one's arms** bring one's arms together and cross them over one's chest. **fold one's hands** bring or hold one's hands together. — **fold·a·ble adj.** [OE *falden, fealden,* of Gmc. origin; rel. to Du. *vouwen* and Ger. *falten.*]

fold² ▸ **n.** a pen or enclosure in a field where livestock, esp. sheep, can be kept. ■ (**the fold**) a group or community, esp. when perceived as the locus of a particular set of aims and values: *he's performing a ritual to be accepted into the fold.* [OE *fald,* of Gmc. origin; rel. to Du. *vaalt.*]

-fold ▸ **suffix** forming adjectives and adverbs from cardinal numbers: **1** in an amount multiplied by: *threefold.* **2** consisting of so many parts or facets: *twofold.* [OE *-fald, -feald;* rel. to FOLD¹.]

fold·er /'fōldər/ ▸ **n.** a folding cover or holder, typically made of stiff paper, for storing loose papers. ■ an icon on a computer screen that can be used to access a directory. ■ a folded leaflet or a booklet made of folded sheets of paper.

fol·de·rol /'fäldə,räl; 'fōldə,rôl/ (also **fal·de·ral**) ▸ **n.** trivial or nonsensical fuss: *all the folderol of the athletic contests and the cheerleaders.* [19th C.: first used as a meaningless refrain in popular songs.]

fold·ing door ▸ **n.** a door with vertical jointed sections that can be folded together to one side to allow access to a room or building.

fold·ing mon·ey ▸ **n.** informal paper money; banknotes.

fold·out /'fōl,dout/ ▸ **adj.** [attrib.] (of a page in a book or magazine or a piece of furniture) designed to be opened out for use and then folded away. ▸ **n.** a page or piece of furniture designed in such a way.

fo·li·a /'fōlēə/ plural form of FOLIUM.

fo·li·age /'fōlēij/ ▸ **n.** plant leaves, collectively: *healthy green foliage.* [ME *foilage:* from OFr. *feuillage,* from *feuille* 'leaf,' from L. *folium.*]

fo·li·age leaf ▸ **n.** Bot. a normal leaf, as opposed to petals and other modified leaves.

fo·li·ar /'fōlēər/ ▸ **adj.** [attrib.] tech. of or relating to leaves: *foliar color and shape.* [19th C.: from mod. L. *foliaris,* from L. *folium* 'leaf.']

fo·li·at·ed /'fōlē,ātid/ ▸ **adj.** decorated with leaves or leaflike motifs: *ten columns foliated at the capitals.* [17th C.: based on L. *foliatus* 'leaved,' from *folium* 'leaf.']

fo·li·a·tion /,fōlē'āsHən/ ▸ **n.** the process of numbering the leaves of a book.

fo·lic ac·id /'fōlik; 'fä-/ ▸ **n.** Biochem. a vitamin of the B complex, found esp. in leafy green vegetables, liver, and kidney. A deficiency causes megaloblastic anemia. Also called PTEROYLGLUTAMIC ACID, VITAMIN M. — **fo·late** /'fōlāt/ **n.** [1940s: *folic* from L. *folium* 'leaf' + -IC.]

Fo·lies-Ber·gère /fô,lē bər'zHer; ber-/ a variety theater in Paris, opened in 1869, known for its lavish productions.

fo·li·o /'fōlē,ō/ ▸ **n.** (pl. **-os**) an individual leaf of paper or parchment, numbered on the recto or front side only, occurring either loose as one of a series or forming part of a bound volume. ■ Print. the leaf number in a printed book. ■ a sheet of paper folded once to form two leaves (four pages) of a book. ■ a size of book made up of such sheets: *copies in folio.* ■ a book or manuscript made up of sheets of paper folded in such a way; a volume of the largest standard size: | [as adj.] *a folio volume.* [ME: from L., ablative of *folium* 'leaf.']

fo·li·um /'fōlēəm/ ▸ **n.** (pl. **-li·a** /-lēə/) tech. a thin leaflike structure, e.g., in some rocks or in the cerebellum of the brain. [18th C.: from L., literally 'leaf.']

folk /fōk/ (also **folks**) ▸ **plural n. 1** informal people in general: *some folk will do anything for money.* ■ a specified group of people: *city folks.* ■ (**folks**) used as a friendly form of address to a group of people. ■ (**one's folks**) the members of one's family, esp. one's parents. **2** folk music: *a mixture of folk and reggae.* **1 adj.** [attrib.] of or relating to the traditional art or culture of a community or nation: *a folk museum.* ■ relating to or originating from the beliefs and opinions of ordinary people: *a folk hero* | *folk wisdom.* **2** of or relating to folk music.
– PHRASES **just (plain) folks** ordinary, down-to-earth, unpretentious people. [OE *folc,* of Gmc. origin; rel. to Du. *volk* and Ger. *Volk.*]

folk dance ▸ **n.** a popular dance, considered as part of the tradition or custom of a particular people: *well-known folk dances.* — **folk danc·er n. folk danc·ing n.**

folk et·y·mol·o·gy ▸ **n.** a popular but mistaken account of the origin of a word or phrase. ■ the process by which the form of an unfamiliar or foreign word is adapted to a more familiar form through popular usage.

folk·life /'fōk,līf/ ▸ **n.** the way of life of a rural or traditional community.

folk·lore /'fōk,lôr/ ▸ **n.** the traditional beliefs, customs, and stories of a community, passed through the generations by word of mouth. ■ a body of popular myth and beliefs relating to a particular place, activity, or group of people. — **folk·lor·ic** /-,lôrik/ **adj. folk·lor·ist n. folk·lor·is·tic** /,fōklə'ristik/ **adj.**

folk mass ▸ **n.** a mass in which folk music is used instead of traditional liturgical music.

folk med·i·cine ▸ **n.** treatment of disease or injury based on tradition, esp. on oral tradition, often utilizing indigenous plants as remedies.

folk mu·sic ▸ **n.** music that originates in traditional popular culture or that is written in such a style. Folk music is typically of unknown authorship and is transmitted orally from generation to generation.

folk rock ▸ **n.** popular music resembling or derived from folk music but incorporating the stronger beat of rock music and using electric instruments.

folk sing·er (also **folk·sing·er**) ▸ **n.** a person who sings folk songs, typically accompanying themselves on a guitar.

folk song ▸ **n.** a song that originates in traditional popular culture or that is written in such a style.

folks·on·o·my /fōk'sänəmē/ ▸ **n.** the activity of sorting information into categories derived from the consensus of the information users. ■ a taxonomy so derived. [21st C.: blend of FOLK and TAXONOMY.]

folk·sy /'fōksē/ ▸ **adj.** (**-si·er, -si·est**) having the characteristics of traditional culture and customs, esp. in a contrived or artificial way: *the shop's folksy, small-town image.* ■ (of a person) informal and unpretentious: *his tireless energy and folksy oratory.* — **folk·si·ness n.**

folk tale ▸ **n.** a story originating in popular culture, typically passed on by word of mouth.

folk·ways /'fōk,wāz/ ▸ **plural n.** the traditional behavior or way of life of a particular community or group.

fol·li·cle /'fälikəl/ ▸ **n.** Anat. a small secretory cavity, sac, or gland, in particular: ■ (also **hair follicle**) the sheath of cells and connective tissue that surrounds the root of a hair. — **fol·lic·u·lar** /fə'likyələr/ **adj. fol·lic·u·late** /fə'likyəlit; -,lāt/ **adj. fol·lic·u·lat·ed** /fə'likyə,lātid/ **adj.** [ME: from L. *folliculus* 'little bag,' dimin. of *follis* 'bellows.']

fol·li·cle mite ▸ **n.** a parasitic mite (genus *Demodex,* family Demodicidae) that burrows into the hair follicles, causing demodectic mange.

fol·li·cle-stim·u·lat·ing hor·mone (abbr.: **FSH**) ▸ **n.** Biochem. a hormone secreted by the anterior pituitary gland that promotes the formation of ova or sperm.

fol·low /'fälō/ ▸ **v.** [trans.] **1** go or come after (a person or thing proceeding ahead); move or travel behind: *she went back into the house, and Ben followed her* | [intrans.] *he was following behind in his car.* ■ go after (someone) in order to observe or monitor. ■ go along (a route or path). ■ (of a route or path) go in the same direction as or parallel to (another). **2** come after in time or order: [intrans.] *the rates are as follows.* ■ happen after (something else) as a consequence: *raucous laughter followed the ribald remark* | [intrans.] *retribution soon followed.* ■ [intrans.] be a logical consequence. ■ [with obj. and adverbial] (of a person) do something after (something else). **3** act according to (an instruction or precept): *following written instructions.* ■ conform to: *the film faithfully follows Shakespeare's plot.* ■ act according to the lead or example of (someone): *he follows Aristotle in believing this.* ■ treat as a teacher or guide: *those who seek to follow Jesus Christ.* **4** pay close attention to (something). ■ keep track of; trace the movement or direction of: *she followed his gaze.* ■ maintain awareness of the current state or progress of (events in a particular sphere or account). ■ (of a person or account) be concerned with the development of (something): *the book follows the life and career of Henry Clay.* ■ understand the meaning or tendency of (a speaker or argument): *I still don't follow you.* **5** practice (a trade or profession). ■ undertake or carry out (a course of action or study).
– PHRASES **follow in someone's footsteps** (or **steps**) do as another person did before, esp. in following a particular career. **follow one's nose**

PRONUNCIATION KEY ə *ago, up;* ər *over, fur;* a *hat;* ā *ate;* ä *car;* e *let;* ē *see;* i *fit;* ī *by;* NG *sing;* ō *go;* ô *law, for;* oi *toy;* o͝o *good;* o͞o *goo;* ou *out;* TH *thin;* T͟H *then;* ZH *vision*

1 trust to one's instincts: *you are on the right track so follow your nose.* **2** move along guided by one's sense of smell. **3** go straight ahead. **follow suit** (in bridge, whist, and other card games) play a card of the suit led. ■ conform to another's actions: *Spain cut its rates by half a percent but no other country has followed suit.*
– PHRASAL VERBS **follow through** (in golf, baseball, and other sports) continue one's movement after the ball has been struck or thrown. **follow something through** continue an action or task to its conclusion. **follow something up** pursue or investigate something further: *I decided to follow up the letters with phone calls.* [OE *folgian*, of Gmc. origin; rel. to Du. *volgen* and Ger. *folgen*.]

fol·low·er /'fälōər/ ▶ **n.** an adherent or devotee of a particular person, cause, or activity. ■ a person who moves or travels behind someone or something.

fol·low·ing /'fälōiNG/ ▶ **prep.** coming after or as a result of. ▶ **n. 1** a body of supporters or admirers. **2** (**the following**) [treated as sing. or pl.] what follows or comes next: *the following are both correct sentences.* ▶ **adj.** [attrib.] **1** next in time. ■ about to be mentioned: *you are required to provide us with the following information.* **2** (of a wind or sea) blowing or moving in the same direction as a vehicle or vessel.

fol·low-the-lead·er ▶ **n.** a children's game in which the participants copy the actions and words of a person who has been chosen as leader. ■ fig. the copying of the actions of others. | [as adj.] *a follow-the-leader effect in the investments market.*

fol·low-through ▶ **n.** the continuing of an action or task to its conclusion. ■ a continuation of the movement of an arm, bat, racket, or club after a ball has been thrown or struck: *he has a characteristic swing and follow-through.*

fol·low-up ▶ **n.** a continuation or repetition of something that has already been started or done, in particular: ■ an activity carried out as part of a study in order to monitor or further develop earlier work: [as adj.] *follow-up interviews.* ■ further observation or treatment of a patient, esp. to monitor earlier treatment: *patients who require proper medical follow-up.*

fol·ly /'fälē/ ▶ **n.** (pl. **-lies**) **1** lack of good sense; foolishness: *an act of sheer folly.* ■ a foolish act, idea, or practice: *the follies of youth.* **2** (**Follies**) a theatrical revue, typically with glamorous female performers: [in names] *the Ziegfeld Follies.* [ME: from OFr. *folie* 'madness.']

Fol·som ▶ **n.** [usu. as adj.] Archaeol. a Paleo-Indian culture of Central and North America, dated to about 10,500–8,000 years ago. The culture is distinguished by fluted stone projectile points. Compare with **CLOVIS**[2]. [20th C.: *Folsom*, New Mexico.]

fo·ment /'fōment; fō'ment/ ▶ **v.** [trans.] instigate or stir up (an undesirable or violent sentiment or course of action): *they accused him of fomenting political unrest.* — **fo·ment·er n.** [ME (sense 2): from Fr. *fomenter*, from late L. *fomentare*, from L. *fomentum* 'poultice, lotion,' from *fovere* 'to heat, cherish.']

fo·men·ta·tion /,fōmen'tāSHən; -mən-/ ▶ **n.** the action of instigating or stirring up undesirable sentiment or actions.

Fon /fän/ ▶ **n.** (pl. same or **Fons**) **1** a member of a people inhabiting the southern part of Benin. **2** the Kwa language of this people. ▶ **adj.** of or relating to this people or their language. [the name in Fon.]

fond /fänd/ ▶ **adj.** [predic.] (**fond of**) having an affection or liking for: *I'm very fond of Mike | he was not too fond of dancing.* ■ [attrib.] affectionate; loving. ■ [attrib.] (of a hope or belief) foolishly optimistic; naive. — **fond·ly adv. fond·ness n.** [ME: from obs. *fon* 'a fool, be foolish.']

fon·dle /'fändl/ ▶ **v.** [trans.] stroke or caress lovingly or erotically: *the dog came over to have his ears fondled.* ▶ **n.** an act of fondling. — **fon·dler n.** [17th C.: back-form. from obs. *fondling* 'much-loved or petted person,' from **FOND** + **-LING**.]

fon·due /fän'd(y)ōō/ ▶ **n.** a dish in which small pieces of food are dipped into a hot sauce or a hot cooking medium such as oil or broth: *a Swiss cheese fondue.* [Fr., fem. past part. of *fondre* 'to melt.']

Fon·se·ca, Gulf of /fän'sākə/ an inlet of the Pacific Ocean in western Central America, surrounded on three sides by El Salvador, Honduras, and Nicaragua.

font[1] /fänt/ ▶ **n. 1** a receptacle in a church for the water used in baptism, typically a freestanding stone structure. **2** a fount: *they dip down into the font of wisdom.* — **font·al** /'fäntl/ **adj.** [late OE: from L. *fons, font-* 'spring, fountain.']

font[2] (Brit. also **fount** /fount/) ▶ **n.** Print. a set of type of one particular face and size. [16th C.: from Fr. *fonte*, from *fondre* 'to melt.']

Fon·taine /fän'tān/, Joan de Beauvoir (1917–), US actress; born in Japan; born *Joan de Havilland*; sister of Olivia de Havilland. Her movies include *Rebecca* (1940) and *Suspicion* (Academy Award, 1941).

Fon·taine·bleau /,fônten'blō; 'fäntin,blō/ a town in north central France, southeast of Paris, where King Louis XIV revoked the Edict of Nantes; pop. 20,000.

Fon·tana /fän'tanə/ a city in southwestern California, east of Los Angeles; pop. 87,535.

fon·ta·nel /,fäntn'el/ (also **fon·ta·nelle**) ▶ **n.** a space between the bones of the skull in an infant or fetus, where ossification is not complete and the sutures not fully formed. The main one is between the frontal and parietal bones. [16th C.: from Fr., from mod. L. *fontanella*, from an OFr. dimin. of *fontaine* (see **FOUNTAIN**).]

Fon·tanne /fän'tan/, Lynn (1887–1983), US actress; born in England. She married actor Alfred Lunt (1892–1977) in 1922. They appeared in many plays together, including *The Guardsman* (1924) and *The Visit* (1958).

Fon·teyn /fän'tān/, Dame Margot (1919–91), English ballet dancer; born *Margaret Hookham*. In 1962, she began a dancing partnership with Rudolf Nureyev.

Foo·chow /'fōō'jō/ variant of **FUZHOU**.

food /fōōd/ ▶ **n.** any nutritious substance that people or animals eat or drink, or that plants absorb, in order to maintain life and growth: *cans of cat food | baby foods.*
– PHRASES **food for thought** something that warrants serious consideration. [late OE *fōda*, of Gmc. origin; rel. to **FODDER**.]

Food and Ag·ri·cul·ture Or·gan·i·za·tion (abbr.: **FAO**) an agency of the United Nations established in 1945 to secure improvements in the production and distribution of all food and agricultural products, and in nutrition.

food chain ▶ **n.** a series of organisms each dependent on the next as a source of food.

food court ▶ **n.** an area, typically in a shopping mall, where fast-food outlets, tables, and chairs are located.

food fish ▶ **n.** a species of fish that is used as food by humans or forms a major part of the diet of a particular predator.

food mile ▶ **n.** a mile over which a food item is transported from producer to consumer, as a unit of measurement of the fuel used to do this.

food poi·son·ing ▶ **n.** illness caused by bacteria or other toxins in food.

food proc·es·sor ▶ **n.** an electric kitchen appliance used for chopping, mixing, or puréeing foods.

food pyr·a·mid ▶ **n. 1** a nutritional diagram in the shape of a pyramid. **2** Ecol. a graphic representation of predatory relationships in the food chain, in which various forms of life are shown on different levels, with each level preying on the one below it, so that as the pyramid narrows toward the apex, the number of types decreases as the reliance on predation grows.

food stamp ▶ **n.** a voucher issued by the government to those on low income, exchangeable for food.

food·stuff /'fōōd,stəf/ ▶ **n.** a substance suitable for consumption as food.

food val·ue ▶ **n.** the nutritional value of a foodstuff.

food web ▶ **n.** Ecol. a system of interlocking and interdependent food chains.

foo·fa·raw /'fōōfə,rô/ informal ▶ **n. 1** a great deal of fuss or attention given to a minor matter. **2** showy frills added unnecessarily.

fool /fōōl/ ▶ **n.** a person who acts unwisely or imprudently; a silly person: *what a fool I was to do this.* ■ hist. a jester or clown, esp. one retained in a noble household. ■ informal a person devoted to a particular activity: *he is a running fool.* ▶ **v.** [trans.] trick or deceive (someone); dupe. ■ [intrans.] act in a joking, frivolous, or teasing way: *I shouted at him impatiently to stop fooling around.* ■ [intrans.] (**fool around**) engage in casual or extramarital sexual activity. ▶ **adj.** [attrib.] informal foolish or silly.
– PHRASES **be no** (or **nobody's**) **fool** be a shrewd or prudent person. **a fool and his money are soon parted** proverb a foolish person spends money carelessly and will soon be penniless. **fools rush in where angels fear to tread** proverb people without good sense or judgment will have no hesitation in tackling a situation that even the wisest would avoid. **make a fool of** trick or deceive (someone) so that they look foolish. ■ (**make a fool of oneself**) behave in an incompetent or inappropriate way that makes one appear foolish. **play** (or **act**) **the fool** behave in a playful or silly way. **there's no fool like an old fool** proverb the foolish behavior of an older person seems especially foolish as they are expected to think and act more sensibly than a younger one. **you could have fooled me!** used to express cynicism or doubt about an assertion.
– PHRASAL VERBS **fool with** toy with; play idly with: *I like fooling with cameras.* ■ tease (a person): *we've just been fooling with you.* [ME: from OFr. *fol* 'fool, foolish,' from L. *follis* 'bellows, bag.']

fool·er·y /'fōōlərē/ ▶ **n.** silly or foolish behavior.

fool·har·dy /'fōōl,härdē/ ▶ **adj.** (**-di·er**, **-di·est**) recklessly bold or rash. — **fool·har·di·ly adv. fool·har·di·ness n.** [ME: from OFr. *folhardi*, from *fol* 'foolish' + *hardi* 'bold' (see **HARDY**).]

fool·ish /'fōōliSH/ ▶ **adj.** (of a person or action) lacking good sense or judgment; unwise. ■ [as complement] silly; ridiculous: *he'd been made to look foolish.* — **fool·ish·ly adv. fool·ish·ness n.**

fool·proof /'fōōl,prōōf/ ▶ **adj.** incapable of going wrong or being misused.

fools·cap /'fōōlz,kap/ ▶ **n.** a size of paper, now standardized at about 13 × 8 (or 15.75) inches (300 × 200 [or 400] mm). ■ paper of this size: *several sheets of foolscap.* [17th C.: said to be named from a former watermark representing a fool's cap.]

fool's er·rand ▶ **n.** a task or activity that has no hope of success.

fool's gold ▶ **n.** a brassy yellow mineral, esp. pyrite, that can be mistaken for gold.

fool's par·a·dise ▶ **n.** [in sing.] a state of happiness based on a person's not knowing about or denying the existence of potential trouble.

fool's pars·ley ▶ **n.** a poisonous white-flowered plant (*Aethusa cynapium*) of the parsley family, with fernlike leaves and an unpleasant smell.

foos·ball /'fōōs,bôl/ ▶ **n.** trademarka tabletop version of soccer in which players turn rods fixed on top of a playing box and attached to miniature figures of players, in order to flick the ball and strike it toward the goal. [20th C.: from Ger. *Fussball* 'football.']

foot /fo͝ot/ ▶**n.** (pl. **feet**) **1** the lower extremity of the leg below the ankle, on which a person stands or walks. ■ a corresponding part of the leg in vertebrate animals. ■ Zool. a locomotory or adhesive organ of an invertebrate. ■ the part of a sock or stocking that covers the foot. ■ literary a person's manner or speed of walking or running: *fleet of foot.* ■ [treated as pl.] **2** the lower or lowest part of something standing or perceived as standing vertically; the base or bottom. ■ the end of a table that is furthest from where the host sits. ■ the end of a bed, couch, or grave where the occupant's feet normally rest. ■ a device on a sewing machine for holding the material steady as it is sewn. ■ the lower edge of a sail. **3** a unit of linear measure equal to 12 inches (30.48 cm): *shallow water no more than a foot deep.* **4** Pros. a group of syllables constituting a metrical unit. In English poetry it consists of stressed and unstressed syllables, while in ancient classical poetry it consists of long and short syllables. ▶**v.** [trans.] **1** informal pay (the bill) for something, esp. when the bill is considered large or unreasonable. **2** (**foot it**) cover a distance, esp. a long one, on foot: *the rider was left to foot it ten or twelve miles back to camp.*

– PHRASES **at someone's feet** as someone's disciple or subject: *you would like to sit at my feet and thus acquire my wisdom.* **get one's feet wet** begin to participate in an activity. **get** (or **start**) **off on the right** (or **wrong**) **foot** make a good (or bad) start at something, esp. a task or relationship. **have something at one's feet** have something in one's power or command: *the world at their feet.* **have** (or **keep**) **one's** (or **both**) **feet on the ground** be (or remain) practical and sensible. **have a foot in both camps** have an interest or stake concurrently in two parties or sides. **have** (or **get**) **a foot in the door** gain or have a first introduction to a profession or organization. **have one foot in the grave** informal often humorous be near death through old age or illness. **my foot!** informal said to express strong contradiction: *Efficient, my foot!* **off one's feet** so as to be no longer standing. **on one's feet** standing. ■ well enough after an illness or injury to walk around: *back on your feet in no time.* **on** (or **by**) **foot** walking rather than traveling by car or using other transport. **put one's best foot forward** embark on an undertaking with as much effort and determination as possible. **put one's feet up** informal take a rest, esp. when reclining with one's feet raised and supported. **put one's foot down** informal adopt a firm policy when faced with opposition or disobedience. **put one's foot in it** (or **put one's foot in one's mouth**) informal say or do something tactless or embarrassing; commit a blunder or indiscretion. **set foot on** (or **in**) [often with negative] enter; go into. **sweep someone off their feet** quickly and overpoweringly charm someone. **think on one's feet** react to events decisively, effectively, and without prior thought or planning. — **foot·ed** /'fo͝otəd/ **adj.** [in comb.] *the black-footed ferret.* [OE *fōt*; rel. to Ger. *Fuss*, from an Indo-Eur. root shared by Gk. *pous, pod-* and L. *pes, ped-* 'foot.']

foot·age /'fo͝otij/ ▶**n. 1** a length of film made for movies or television: *film footage of the riot.* **2** size or length measured in feet.

foot-and-mouth dis·ease ▶**n.** a contagious viral disease of cattle and sheep, causing ulceration of the hoofs and around the mouth.

foot·ball /'fo͝ot,bôl/ ▶**n. 1** a team game played in North America with an oval ball on a field marked out as a gridiron. ■ play in such a game, esp. when stylish and entertaining: *his team played some impressive football.* ■ British term for **SOCCER**. **2** an oval ball used in such a game, made of leather and filled with compressed air. ■ fig. a topical issue or problem that is the subject of continued argument or controversy: *the use of education as a **political football**.* ■ Brit. a soccer ball. — **foot·ball·er n. foot·ball·ing adj.**

foot·ball pool ▶**n.** a form of gambling on the results of football games, the winners receiving amounts accumulated from entry money.

foot·board /'fo͝ot,bôrd/ ▶**n. 1** an upright panel forming the foot of a bed. **2** a board serving as a step up to a vehicle such as a train.

foot·brake /'fo͝ot,brāk/ ▶**n.** a brake lever in a motor vehicle, operated by pressing down with the foot.

foot·bridge /'fo͝ot,brij/ ▶**n.** a bridge designed to be used by pedestrians.

foot-drag·ging ▶**n.** reluctance or deliberate delay concerning a decision or action. — **foot-drag·ger n.**

foot·er /'fo͝otər/ ▶**n. 1** [in comb.] a person or thing of a specified number of feet in length or height. **2** a line or block of text appearing at the foot of each page of a book or document. Compare with **HEADER**.

foot·fall /'fo͝ot,fôl/ ▶**n.** the sound of a footstep or footsteps: *you will recognize his footfall on the stairs.*

foot·gear /'fo͝ot,gi(ə)r/ ▶**n.** another term for **FOOTWEAR**.

foot·hill /'fo͝ot,hil/ ▶**n.** (usu. **foothills**) a low hill at the base of a mountain or mountain range.

foot·hold /'fo͝ot,hōld/ ▶**n.** a place where a person's foot can be lodged to support them securely, esp. while climbing. ■ [usu. in sing.] fig. a secure position from which further progress may be made.

foot·ing /'fo͝otiNG/ ▶**n. 1** (**one's footing**) a secure grip with one's feet: *he suddenly lost his footing.* ■ the condition of a piece of ground for walking or running: *paths with enough variety to give you practice with uneven footing.* **2** [in sing.] the basis on which something is established or operates: *on a firm financial footing.* ■ the position or status of a person in relation to others: *the suppliers are **on an equal footing with** the buyers.* **3** (usu. **footings**) the bottommost part of a foundation wall, with a course of concrete wider than the base of the wall.

foot·lights /'fo͝ot,līts/ ▶**plural n.** (usu. **the footlights**) a row of spotlights along the front of a stage.

foot·lock·er /'fo͝ot,läkər/ ▶**n.** a small trunk or storage chest, typically stored at the foot of a bed.

foot·long /'fo͝ot,lôNG; -,läNG/ ▶**adj.** measuring one foot in length. ▶**n.** a hot dog one foot long.

foot·loose /'fo͝ot,lo͞os/ ▶**adj.** able to travel freely and do as one pleases due to a lack of responsibilities or commitments: *I am **footloose and fancy-free**—I can follow my job wherever it takes me.*

foot·man /'fo͝otmən/ ▶**n.** (pl. **-men**) **1** a liveried servant whose duties include admitting visitors and waiting at table. **2** hist. a soldier in the infantry.

foot·note /'fo͝ot,nōt/ ▶**n.** an additional piece of information printed at the bottom of a page. ■ fig. a thing that is additional or less important. ▶**v.** [trans.] add a footnote or footnotes to (a piece of writing).

foot·path /'fo͝ot,paTH/ ▶**n.** a path for people to walk along, esp. one in the countryside.

foot-pound ▶**n.** a unit of energy equal to the amount required to raise 1 lb a distance of 1 foot.

foot-pound-sec·ond sys·tem ▶**n.** a system of measurement with the foot, pound, and second as basic units.

foot·print /'fo͝ot,print/ ▶**n. 1** the impression left by a foot or shoe on the ground or a surface. **2** the area covered by something, in particular: ■ the area in which a broadcast signal from a particular source can be received. ■ the space taken up on a surface by a piece of computer hardware. ■ the area beneath an aircraft or a land vehicle that is affected by its noise or weight. ■ the area of ground taken up by the floor of a building. **3** the impact on the environment of human activity in terms of pollution, damage to ecosystems, and the depletion of natural resources.

foot·rest /'fo͝ot,rest/ ▶**n.** a support for the feet or a foot, used when sitting.

foot rope ▶**n.** Sailing **1** a rope to which the lower edge of a sail is sewn. **2** a rope below a yard on which a sailor can stand while furling or reefing a sail.

foot rot ▶**n.** a disease of the feet in hoofed animals, esp. sheep, caused by bacteria of the genera *Bacteroides* and *Fusobacterium.* ■ any of a number of fungal diseases of plants in which the base of the stem rots.

foot·sie /'fo͝otsē/ ▶**n.** (also **foot·sy**) informal the action of touching someone's feet with one's own feet, esp. under a table, as a playful expression of romantic interest.

– PHRASES **play footsie** touch someone's feet in such a way. ■ work with someone in a close but covert way. [1940s: humorous dimin. of **FOOT**.]

foot sol·dier ▶**n.** a soldier who fights on foot; an infantryman. ■ a person who carries out important work but does not have a role of authority in an organization or field.

foot·sore /'fo͝ot,sôr/ ▶**adj.** (of a person or animal) having painful or tender feet from much walking.

foot·stalk /'fo͝ot,stôk/ ▶**n.** the short supporting stalk of a leaf or flower.

foot·step /'fo͝ot,step/ ▶**n.** a step taken by a person in walking, esp. as heard by another person.

foot·stool /'fo͝ot,sto͞ol/ ▶**n.** a low stool for resting the feet on when sitting.

foot valve ▶**n.** a one-way valve at the inlet of a pipe or the base of a suction pump.

foot·wear /'fo͝ot,we(ə)r/ ▶**n.** outer coverings for the feet, such as shoes, boots, and sandals.

foot·work /'fo͝ot,wərk/ ▶**n.** the manner in which one moves one's feet in various activities such as sports and dancing. ■ [usu. with adj.] adroit response to sudden danger or new opportunities: *the company had to do a lot of nimble footwork to stay alive.*

foo yong /'fo͞o 'yəNG/ ▶**n.** a Chinese dish or sauce made with egg as a main ingredient. [from Chin. (Cantonese dial.) *foō yung*, lit. 'hibiscus.']

fop /fäp/ ▶**n.** a man who is concerned with his clothes and appearance in an affected and excessive way; a dandy. — **fop·per·y n. fop·pish adj. fop·pish·ness n.** [ME (in the sense 'fool'): perh. rel. to **FOB**[2].]

for /fôr; fər/ ▶**prep. 1** in support of or in favor of (a person or policy). **2** affecting, with regard to, or in respect of (someone or something): *she is responsible for the efficient running of their department* | *the demand for money.* **3** on behalf of or to the benefit of (someone or something): *these parents aren't speaking for everyone.* ■ employed by: *it was a good firm to work for.* **4** having (the thing mentioned) as a purpose or function: *she is searching for enlightenment* | *the necessary tools for making a picture frame.* **5** having (the thing mentioned) as a reason or cause: *Aileen is proud of her family for their support.* **6** having (the place mentioned) as a destination: *they are leaving for Swampscott tomorrow.* **7** representing (the thing mentioned): *the "F" is for Fascinating.* **8** in place of or in exchange for (something): *swap these two bottles for that one.* ■ charged as (a price): *copies are available for only a buck.* **9** in relation to the expected norm of (something): *she was tall for her age.* **10** indicating the length of (a period of time): *he was in prison for 12 years.* **11** indicating the extent of (a distance): *he crawled for 300 yards.* **12** indicating an occasion in a series: *the camcorder failed for the third time.* ▶**conj.** literary because; since: *he felt guilty, for he knew that he bore a share of responsibility for Fanny's death.*

– PHRASES **for all ——** see **ALL**. **for why** informal for what reason: *you're* *going to and I'll tell you for why.* **oh for ——** I long for ——: *oh for a strong black coffee!* **there's** (or **that's**) **—— for you** used ironically to indicate a particularly poor example of (a quality mentioned): *there's gratitude for you.* [OE, prob. a reduction of a Gmc. prep. meaning 'before' (in place or time); rel. to Ger. *für*, also to FORE.]

for- ▶ **prefix** **1** denoting prohibition: *forbid.* **2** denoting abstention, neglect, or renunciation: *forgive* | *forget* | *forgo.* **3** denoting extremity of negative state expressed: *forlorn* | *forsake.* [OE.]

f.o.r. ▶ **abbr.** free on rail. See FREE.

for. ▶ **abbr.** ■ foreign. ■ forest. ■ forester. ■ forestry.

fo·ra /'fôrə/ plural form of FORUM (sense 3).

for·age /'fôrij; 'fär-/ ▶ **v.** [intrans.] (of a person or animal) search widely for food or provisions: *gulls are equipped by nature to forage for food.* ■ [trans.] obtain (food or provisions): *a girl foraging grass for oxen.* ▶ **n.** **1** bulky food such as grass or hay for horses and cattle; fodder. **2** [in sing.] a wide search over an area in order to obtain something, esp. food or provisions: *the nightly forage produces things that can be sold.* — **for·ag·er** **n.** [ME: from OFr. *fourrage* (n.), *fourrager* (v.), from *fuerre* 'straw,' of Gmc. origin and rel. to FODDER.]

fo·ra·men /fə'rāmən/ ▶ **n.** (pl. **-ram·i·na** /-'ramənə/) Anat. an opening, hole, or passage, esp. in a bone. [17th C.: from L., from *forare* 'bore a hole.']

fo·ra·men mag·num ▶ **n.** Anat. the hole in the base of the skull through which the spinal cord passes. [19th C.: L., 'large opening.']

for·a·min·i·fer /ˌfôrə'minəfər; ˌfär-/ ▶ **n.** (pl. **for·a·min·i·fers** or **fo·ram·i·nif·e·ra** /fəˌramə'nifərə/) Zool. a single-celled planktonic animal (order Foraminiferida, phylum Rhizopoda) with a perforated chalky shell through which slender protrusions of protoplasm extend. Most kinds are marine, and when they die, their shells form thick ocean-floor sediments. — **fo·ram·i·nif·er·al** /fəˌramə'nifərəl/ **adj.** **fo·ram·i·nif·er·an** /fəˌramə'nifərən/ **n. & adj.** **fo·ram·i·nif·er·ous** /fəˌramə'nifərəs/ **adj.** [19th C.: from L. *foramen, foramin-* (see FORAMEN) + *-fer* 'bearing' (from *ferre* 'to bear').]

for·ay /'fôrā; 'färā/ ▶ **n.** a sudden attack or incursion into enemy territory, esp. to obtain something; a raid: *the garrison made a foray against Richard's camp* ■ an attempt to become involved in a new activity or sphere: *my first foray into journalism.* ▶ **v.** [no obj., with adverbial of direction] make or go on a foray: *the place into which they were forbidden to foray.* [ME: back-form. from *forayer* 'a person who forays,' from OFr. *forrier* 'forager,' from *fuerre* 'straw' (see FORAGE).]

forb /fôrb/ ▶ **n.** Bot. a herbaceous flowering plant other than a grass. [1920s: from Gk. *phorbē* 'fodder,' from *phorbein* 'to feed.']

for·bade /fər'bad; -'bād; fôr-/ (also **for·bad** /-'bad/) past of FORBID.

for·bear[1] /fôr'be(ə)r; fôr-/ ▶ **v.** (past **-bore**; past part. **-borne**) [intrans.] literary formal politely or patiently restrain an impulse to do something; refrain: *the boy forbore from touching anything* | [with infin.] *he modestly forbears to include his own work.* ■ [trans.] refrain from doing or using (something): *Rebecca could not forbear a smile.* [OE *forberan* (see FOR-, BEAR[1]).]

for·bear[2] ▶ **n.** var. of FOREBEAR.

for·bear·ance /fôr'be(ə)rəns; fər-/ ▶ **n.** formal patient self-control; restraint and tolerance. ■ Law the action of refraining from exercising a legal right, esp. enforcing the payment of a debt.

for·bear·ing /fôr'be(ə)riNG; fər-/ ▶ **adj.** (of a person) patient and restrained.

for·bid /fər'bid; fôr-/ ▶ **v.** (**-bid·ding**; past **-bade** or **forbad**; past part. **-bid·den**) [trans.] refuse to allow (something). ■ order (someone) not to do something: | [with obj. and infin.] *my doctor has forbidden me to eat sugar.* ■ refuse (someone or something) entry to a place or area. ■ (of a circumstance or quality) make (something) impossible; prevent: *the cliffs forbid any easy turning movement.*

– PHRASES **God** (or **Heaven**) **forbid** used to express a fervent wish that something does not happen: [with clause] *God forbid that this should happen to anyone ever again.* [OE *forbēodan* (see FOR-, BID[2]).]

for·bid·den /fər'bidn; fôr-/ ▶ **adj.** not allowed; banned: *a list of forbidden books.*

– PHRASES **forbidden fruit** a thing that is desired all the more because it is not allowed.

For·bid·den Cit·y **1** an area of Beijing, China, that contains the former imperial palaces, to which entry was forbidden to all except imperial family members. **2** a name given to Lhasa, Tibet.

for·bid·ding /fər'bidiNG; fôr-/ ▶ **adj.** unfriendly or threatening in appearance. — **for·bid·ding·ly** **adv.**

for·bore /fər'bôr; fôr-/ past of FORBEAR[1].

for·borne /fər'bôrn; fôr-/ past participle of FORBEAR[1].

force /fôrs/ ▶ **n.** **1** strength or energy as an attribute of physical action or movement: *he was thrown backward by the force of the explosion.* ■ Physics an influence tending to change the motion of a body or produce motion or stress in a stationary body. The magnitude of such an influence is often calculated by multiplying the mass of the body and its acceleration. ■ a person or thing regarded as exerting power or influence: *he might still be a force for peace and unity.* **2** coercion or compulsion, esp. with the use or threat of violence: *they ruled by law and not by force.* **3** mental or moral strength or power: *the force of popular opinion.* ■ the state of being in effect or valid: *the law came into force in January.* ■ the powerful effect of something: *the force of her writing is undiminished.* **4** an organized body of military personnel or police. ■ (**forces**) troops and weaponry. | fig. *a battle between the forces of good and evil.* ■ a group of people brought together and organized for a particular activity. ■ (**the force**) informal the police. ▶ **v.** [trans.] **1** make a way through or into by physical strength; break open by force: *they broke into Fred's house and forced every cupboard door with ax or crowbar.* ■ [with obj. and adverbial] drive or push into a specified position or state using physical strength or against resistance: *she forced her feet into sandals* | fig. *Fields was forced out as director.* ■ achieve or bring about (something) by coercion or effort: *Sabine forced a smile.* ■ push or strain (something) to the utmost: *she knew if she forced it she would rip it.* ■ artificially hasten the development or maturity of (a plant). **2** (often **be forced**) make (someone) do something against their will: *she was forced into early retirement* ■ Baseball put out (a runner), or cause (a runner) to be put out, at the base to which they are advancing when they are forced to run on a batted ball: *I was forced at second base.*

– PHRASES **by force of** by means of: *exercising authority by force of arms.* **force someone's hand** make someone do something: *the exchange markets may force the Fed's hand.* **force the issue** compel the making of an immediate decision. **in force** **1** in great strength or numbers: *birdwatchers were out in force.* **2** in effect; valid: *the United States has over $8 trillion worth of life insurance in force.*

– PHRASAL VERBS **force something down** **1** manage to swallow food or drink when one does not want to: *I forced down a slice of toast.* **2** compel an aircraft to land: *the plane might have been forced down by fighters.* **force something on/upon** impose or press something on (a person or organization): *economic cutbacks were forced on the government.* — **force·a·ble** **adj.** **forc·er** **n.** [ME: from OFr. *force* (n.), *forcer* (v.), based on L. *fortis* 'strong.']

forced /fôrst/ ▶ **adj.** obtained or imposed by coercion or physical power: *the brutal regime of forced labor.* ■ (of a gesture or expression) produced or maintained with effort; affected or unnatural. ■ (of a plant) having its development or maturity artificially hastened.

– PHRASES **forced march** a fast march by soldiers, typically over a long distance.

forced land·ing ▶ **n.** an act of abruptly bringing an aircraft to the ground or water in an emergency. — **force-land** **v.**

force-feed ▶ **v.** [trans.] force (a person or animal) to eat food. ■ [with two objs.] fig. impose or force (information or ideology) upon (someone): *no group has the right to force-feed its beliefs on her.*

force field ▶ **n.** (chiefly in science fiction) an invisible barrier of exerted strength or impetus: *combat vehicles will deflect enemy shells with an electromagnetic force field.*

force·ful /'fôrsfəl/ ▶ **adj.** (esp. of a person or argument) strong and assertive; vigorous and powerful: *she was a forceful personality* | *forceful, imaginative marketing.* — **force·ful·ly** **adv.** **force·ful·ness** **n.**

force ma·jeure /ˌfôrs mä'ZHər/ ▶ **n.** **1** unforeseeable circumstances that prevent someone from fulfilling a contract. **2** irresistible compulsion or superior strength. [19th C.: Fr., literally 'superior strength.']

force out ▶ **n.** Baseball an out made by holding the ball and touching the base to which a base runner must advance.

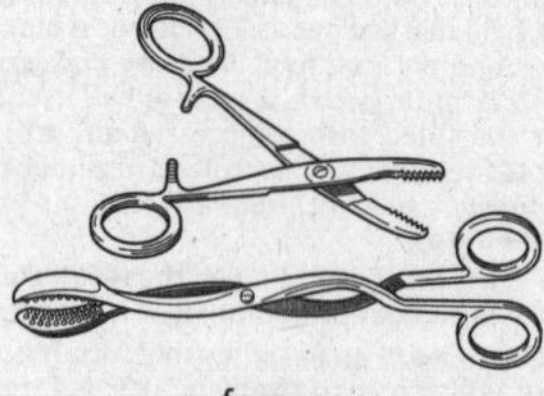

forceps

for·ceps /'fôrsəps; -seps/ (also **a pair of forceps**) ▶ **plural n.** a pair of pincers or tweezers used in surgery or in a laboratory. ■ a large instrument of such a type with broad blades, used to encircle a baby's head and assist in birth. ■ Zool. an organ or structure resembling forceps, esp. the cerci of an earwig. [16th C.: from L., 'tongs, pincers.']

force pump ▶ **n.** a pump used to move water or other liquid under pressure.

for·ci·ble /'fôrsəbəl/ ▶ **adj.** done by force: *signs of forcible entry.* ■ vigorous and strong; forceful. — **for·ci·bly** **adv.**

Ford[1] /fôrd/, Ford Madox (1873–1939), English writer; born *Ford Hermann Hueffer.* He wrote *The Good Soldier* (1915).

Ford[2], Gerald Rudolph, Jr. (1913–2006), 38th president of the US 1974–77; born *Leslie Lynch King, Jr.* (renamed by his stepfather in 1916). He served in the US House of Representatives 1949–73 and as vice president 1973–74 before succeeding to the presidency upon the resignation of President Nixon.

Ford[3], Henry (1863–1947), US industrialist. A pioneer of large-scale mass production, he founded the Ford Motor Company, which produced the Model T automobile in 1909.

ford /fôrd/ ▶ **n.** a shallow place in a river or stream allowing one to walk or drive across. ▶ **v.** [trans.] (of a person or vehicle) cross (a river or stream) at a shallow place. — **ford·a·ble** **adj.** [OE, of West Gmc. origin; rel. to Du. *voorde*, also to FARE.]

fore /fôr/ ▶ **adj.** [attrib.] situated or placed in front: *the fore and hind pairs of wings.* ▶ **exclam.** called out as a warning to people in the path of a golf ball.

– PHRASES **to the fore** in or to a conspicuous or leading position: *his* *effort brought this issue to the fore.* [OE (prep.): of Gmc. origin; rel. to Ger. *vor.*]

fore- ▶ comb. form **1** (added to verbs) in front: *foreshorten.* ■ beforehand; in advance: *foreshadow.* **2** (added to nouns) situated in front of: *forecourt.* ■ the front part of: *forebrain.* ■ of or near the bow of a ship: *forecastle.* ■ preceding; going before: *forefather.* [OE (see FORE).]

fore and aft ▶ adv. at the front and rear (often used with reference to a ship or plane): *we're moored fore and aft.* ▶ adj. [attrib.] backward and forward: *the fore-and-aft motion of the handles.* ■ (of a sail or rigging) set lengthwise, not on yards: *a fore-and-aft-rigged yacht.*

fore·arm /ˈfôr,ärm/ ▶ n. the part of a person's arm extending from the elbow to the wrist or the fingertips.

fore·bear /ˈfôr,be(ə)r/ (also **for·bear**) ▶ n. (usu. **one's forebears**) an ancestor. [15th C.: from FORE + *bear*, var. of obs. *beer* 'someone who exists' (from BE + -ER[1]).]

fore·bod·ing /fôrˈbōdiNG/ ▶ n. fearful apprehension; a feeling that something bad will happen. ▶ adj. implying or seeming to imply that something bad is going to happen. — **fore·bod·ing·ly** adv.

fore·brain /ˈfôr,brān/ ▶ n. Anat. the anterior part of the brain. Also called PROSENCEPHALON.

fore·cast /ˈfôr,kast/ ▶ v. (past **-cast** or **-cast·ed**) [trans.] predict or estimate (a future event or trend). ▶ n. a prediction or estimate of future events, esp. coming weather or a financial trend. — **fore·cast·er** n.

fore·cas·tle /ˈfōksəl; ˈfôr,kasəl/ (also **fo'c's'le**) ▶ n. the forward part of a ship below the deck, traditionally used as the crew's living quarters. ■ a raised deck at the bow of a ship.

fore·check /ˈfôr,CHek/ ▶ v. [intrans.] Ice Hockey play an aggressive style of defense, checking opponents in their own defensive zone, before they can attack. — **fore·check·er** n.

fore·close /fôrˈklōz/ ▶ v. **1** [intrans.] take possession of a mortgaged property as a result of someone's failure to keep up their mortgage payments. ■ [trans.] take away someone's power of redeeming (a mortgage) and take possession of the mortgaged property. **2** [trans.] rule out or prevent (a course of action): *the decision effectively foreclosed any possibility of his early rehabilitation.* [ME: from OFr. *forclos*, past part. of *forclore*, from *for-* 'out' (from L. *foras* 'outside') + *clore* 'to close.']

fore·clo·sure /fôrˈklōZHər/ ▶ n. the process of taking possession of a mortgaged property as a result of someone's failure to keep up mortgage payments.

fore·court /ˈfôr,kôrt/ ▶ n. **1** an open area in front of a large building. **2** Tennis the part of the court between the service line and the net.

fore·deck /ˈfôr,dek/ ▶ n. the deck at the bow of a ship.

fore·fa·ther /ˈfôr,fäT͟Hər/ ▶ n. (usu. **one's forefathers**) a member of the past generations of one's family or people; an ancestor. ■ a precursor of a particular movement: *the forefathers of rock 'n' roll.*

fore·fend ▶ v. var. of FORFEND (sense 2).

fore·fin·ger /ˈfôr,fiNGgər/ ▶ n. the finger next to the thumb.

fore·foot /ˈfôr,fo͝ot/ ▶ n. (pl. **-feet**) each of the front feet of a four-footed animal. ■ the forward end of a vessel's keel where it joins the stern.

fore·front /ˈfôr,frənt/ ▶ n. (**the forefront**) the leading or most important position or place: *we are at the forefront of developments.*

fore·go[1] ▶ v. var. of FORGO.

fore·go[2] ▶ v. (**fore·goes**; past **fore·went**; past part. **fore·gone**) [trans.] archaic precede in place or time.

fore·go·ing /fôrˈgōiNG/ formal ▶ adj. [attrib.] just mentioned or stated; preceding. ▶ n. (**the foregoing**) [treated as sing. or pl.] the things just mentioned or stated.

fore·gone /ˈfôr,gôn/ past participle of FOREGO[2]. ▶ adj. [often postpositive] archaic past: *poets dream of lives foregone in worlds fantastical.*
– PHRASES **a foregone conclusion** a result that can be predicted with certainty.

fore·ground /ˈfôr,ground/ ▶ n. (**the foreground**) the part of a view that is nearest to the observer, esp. in a picture or photograph: *the images show vegetation in the foreground.* ■ the most prominent or important position or situation: *whenever books are chosen for children, meaning should always be in the foreground.* ▶ v. [trans.] make (something) the most prominent or important feature: *his negative characteristics are foregrounded as the journey unfolds.*

fore·hand /ˈfôr,hand/ ▶ n. (in tennis and other racket sports) a stroke played with the palm of the hand facing in the direction of the stroke: [as adj.] *a good forehand drive.*

fore·head /ˈfôrəd; ˈfôr,hed/ ▶ n. the part of the face above the eyebrows.

for·eign /ˈfôrin; ˈfär-/ ▶ adj. **1** of, from, in, or characteristic of a country or language other than one's own: *a foreign language.* ■ dealing with or relating to other countries: *foreign policy.* ■ of or belonging to another district or area. ■ coming or introduced from outside: *the quotation is a foreign element imported into the work.* **2** strange and unfamiliar: *I suppose this all feels pretty foreign to you.* ■ (**foreign to**) not belonging to or characteristic of: *crime and brutality are foreign to our nature and our country.* — **for·eign·ness** n. [ME *foren, forein*, from OFr. *forein, forain*, based on L. *foras, foris* 'outside,' from *fores* 'door.']

for·eign aid ▶ n. money, food, or other resources given or lent by one country to another.

for·eign bill ▶ n. a bill of exchange payable in another country.

for·eign bod·y ▶ n. an object or piece of extraneous matter that has entered the body.

for·eign·er /ˈfôrinər; ˈfär-/ ▶ n. a person born in or coming from a country other than one's own. ■ informal a person not belonging to a particular place or group; a stranger or outsider.

for·eign ex·change ▶ n. the currency of other countries. ■ an institution or system for dealing in such currency.

For·eign Le·gion a unit of the French army founded in the 1830s to fight France's colonial wars. Composed, except for the higher ranks, of non-Frenchmen, the Legion was famed for its audacity and endurance. Its most famous campaigns were in French North Africa in the late 19th and early 20th centuries.

for·eign min·is·ter ▶ n. (in many countries) a government minister in charge of relations with other countries.

for·eign mis·sion ▶ n. **1** a permanent office established by a nation to represent its interests in a foreign country. **2** a group sent by a church to live in a foreign country for a period of time, esp. to seek converts.

for·eign of·fice in some countries, the department of government in charge of foreign affairs.

for·eign sec·re·tar·y ▶ n. (in the UK) a foreign minister.

for·eign serv·ice ▶ n. the government department concerned with the representation of a country abroad. ■ (**Foreign Service**) a division of the US State Department staffed by diplomatic and consular personnel.

fore·knowl·edge /fôrˈnäləj/ ▶ n. awareness of something before it happens or exists.

fore·leg /ˈfôr,leg/ ▶ n. either of the front legs of a four-footed animal.

fore·limb /ˈfôr,lim/ ▶ n. either of the front limbs of an animal.

fore·lock /ˈfôr,läk/ ▶ n. a lock of hair growing just above the forehead. ■ the part of the mane (of a horse or similar animal) that grows from the poll and hangs down over the forehead.

Fore·man /ˈfôrmən/, George (1949–), US boxer. He was world heavyweight champion 1973–74, 1994–95, the oldest man to hold the title.

fore·man /ˈfôrmən/ ▶ n. (pl. **-men**) a worker, esp. a man, who supervises and directs other workers. ■ (in a court of law) a person, esp. a man, who presides over a jury and speaks on its behalf.

fore·mast /ˈfôr,mast; -məst/ ▶ n. the mast of a ship nearest the bow.

fore·most /ˈfôr,mōst/ ▶ adj. the most prominent in rank, importance, or position: *one of the foremost art collectors of his day.* ▶ adv. before anything else in rank, importance, or position; in the first place: *O'Keeffe's work was, foremost, an expression of the feelings of a woman.*
– PHRASES **first and foremost** see FIRST. [OE *formest, fyrmest*, from *forma* 'first' (ult. a superlative formed from the Gmc. base of FORE) + -EST[1].]

fore·name /ˈfôr,nām/ ▶ n. another term for FIRST NAME.

fore·noon /ˈfôr,no͞on/ ▶ n. [in sing.] the morning.

fo·ren·sic /fəˈrenzik; -sik/ ▶ adj. of, relating to, or denoting the application of scientific methods and techniques to the investigation of crime: *forensic evidence.* ■ of or relating to courts of law. ▶ n. (**forensics**) scientific tests or techniques used in connection with the detection of crime. — **fo·ren·si·cal·ly** /-k(ə)lē/ adv. [17th C.: from L. *forensis* 'in open court, public,' from *forum* (see FORUM).]

fore·or·dain /,fôrôrˈdān/ ▶ v. [trans.] (of God or fate) appoint or decree (something) beforehand: *progress is not foreordained.*

fore·paw /ˈfôr,pô/ ▶ n. either of the front paws of a quadruped.

fore·play /ˈfôr,plā/ ▶ n. sexual activity that precedes intercourse.

fore·run·ner /ˈfôr,rənər/ ▶ n. a person or thing that precedes the coming or development of someone or something else: *the icebox was a forerunner of today's refrigerator.* ■ a sign or warning of something to come: *overcast mornings are the sure forerunners of steady rain.*

fore·sail /ˈfôr,sāl; -səl/ ▶ n. the principal sail on a foremast.

fore·see /fôrˈsē/ ▶ v. (**-sees**, **-see·ing**; past **-saw**; past part. **-seen**) [trans.] be aware of beforehand; predict: *we did not foresee any difficulties* | [with clause] *it is impossible to foresee how life will work out.* — **fore·se·er** /-ˈsēər/ n.

fore·see·a·ble /fôrˈsēəbəl/ ▶ adj. able to be foreseen or predicted: *the situation is unlikely to change in the foreseeable future.* — **fore·see·a·bly** adv.

fore·shad·ow /fôrˈSHadō/ ▶ v. [trans.] be a warning or indication of (a future event).

fore·short·en /fôrˈSHôrtn/ ▶ v. [trans.] portray or show (an object or view) as closer than it is or as having less depth or distance, as an effect of perspective or the angle of vision: *seen from the road, the mountain is greatly foreshortened.* ■ prematurely or dramatically shorten or reduce (something) in time or scale: [as adj.] (**foreshortened**) *foreshortened reports.*

fore·sight /ˈfôr,sīt/ ▶ n. the ability to predict or the action of predicting what will happen or be needed in the future: *he had the foresight to check that his escape route was clear.*

fore·sight·ed /ˈfôr,sītid/ ▶ adj. having or using foresight. — **fore·sight·ed·ness** n.

fore·skin /ˈfôr,skin/ ▶ n. the retractable roll of skin covering the end of the penis. Also called PREPUCE.

for·est /ˈfôrəst; ˈfär-/ ▶ n. a large area covered chiefly with trees and undergrowth: *a pine forest.* ■ a large number or dense mass of vertical or tangled objects: *a forest of connecting wires.* ▶ v. [trans.] [usu. as adj.] (**forested**) cover (land) with forest; plant with trees: *a forested area.*

– PHRASES **cannot see the forest for the trees** fail to grasp the main issue because of overattention to details. — **for·est·a·tion** /ˌfôrəˈstāsHən; ˌfär-/ n. [ME: via OFr. from late L. *forestis (silva)*, lit. '(wood) outside,' from L. *foris* 'outside' (see FOREIGN).]

fore·stall /fôrˈstôl/ ▶v. [trans.] prevent or obstruct (an anticipated event or action) by taking action ahead of time: *vitamins may forestall many diseases of aging.* ■ act in advance of (someone) in order to prevent them from doing something. — **fore·stal·ment** n. [OE *foresteall* 'an ambush' (see FORE- and STALL).]

For·est·er /ˈfôrəstər/, C. S. (1899–1966), English writer; pen name of *Cecil Lewis Troughton Smith.* His seafaring novels feature Captain Horatio Hornblower. He also wrote *The African Queen* (1935).

for·est·er /ˈfôrəstər; ˈfär-/ ▶n. **1** a person in charge of a forest or skilled in planting, managing, or caring for trees. **2** a small, black, day-flying moth (family Agaristidae) with two white or yellow spots on each wing, including the **eight-spotted forester** (*Alypia octomaculata*) of the northeastern US.

eight-spotted forester

for·est·land /ˈfôrəstˌland; ˈfär-/ ▶n. an area of land covered by forests.

for·est·ry /ˈfôrəstrē; ˈfär-/ ▶n. the science or practice of planting, managing, and caring for forests.

fore·taste ▶n. /ˈfôrˌtāst/ [in sing.] a sample or suggestion of something that lies ahead: *the freezing rain was a foretaste of winter.*

fore·tell /fôrˈtel/ ▶v. (past and past part. **-told**) [trans.] predict (the future or a future event): *as he foretold, thousands lost their lives* | [with clause] *a seer had foretold that she would assume the throne.* — **fore·tell·er** n.

fore·thought /ˈfôrˌTHôt/ ▶n. careful consideration of what will be necessary or may happen in the future: *Jim had the forethought to book in advance.*

fore·to·ken /fôrˈtōkin/ ▶v. [trans.] literary be a sign of (something to come): *a shiver in the night air foretokening December.* [OE *foretācn* (n.: see FORE-, TOKEN).]

fore·told /fôrˈtōld/ past and past participle of FORETELL.

for·ev·er /fəˈrevər; fô-/ ▶adv. **1** for all future time; for always. ■ a very long time (used hyperbolically). ■ used in slogans of support after the name of something or someone: *Elvis Forever!* **2** continually: *the heater is forever running.*

for·ev·er·more /fəˌrevərˈmôr/ ▶adv. forever (used for rhetorical effect): *our military will be invincible forevermore.*

fore·warn /fôrˈwôrn/ ▶v. [trans.] inform (someone) of a possible future danger or problem.

– PHRASES **forewarned is forearmed** proverb prior knowledge of possible dangers or problems gives one a tactical advantage. — **fore·warn·er** n.

fore·went /fôrˈwent/ past of FOREGO[1], FOREGO[2].

fore·wing /ˈfôrˌwiNG/ ▶n. either of the two front wings of a four-winged insect.

fore·wom·an /ˈfôrˌwo͝omən/ ▶n. (pl. **-wom·en**) a female worker who supervises and directs other workers. ■ (in a court of law) a woman who presides over a jury and speaks on its behalf.

fore·word /ˈfôrˌwərd/ ▶n. a short introduction to a book, typically by a person other than the author.

fore·yard /ˈfôrˌyärd/ ▶n. the lowest yard on a sailing ship's foremast.

for·feit /ˈfôrfit/ ▶v. (**-feit·ed, -feit·ing**) [trans.] lose or be deprived of (property or a right or privilege) as a penalty for wrongdoing: *those unable to meet their taxes were liable to forfeit their property.* ■ lose or give up (something) as a necessary consequence of something else: *she didn't mind forfeiting an extra hour in bed to get up and clean the stables.* ▶n. a fine or penalty for wrongdoing or for a breach of the rules in a club or game. ■ Law an item of property or a right or privilege lost as a legal penalty. ■ (**forfeits**) a game in which trivial penalties are exacted. ■ the action of forfeiting something. ▶adj. [predic.] lost or surrendered as a penalty for wrongdoing or neglect: *the lands which he had acquired were automatically forfeit.* — **for·fei·ture** /ˈfôrfiCHər/ n. [ME: from OFr. *forfet, forfait*, past part. of *forfaire* 'transgress,' from *for-* 'out' + *faire* 'do' (from L. *facere*).]

for·fend /fôrˈfend/ ▶v. [trans.] **1** archaic avert, keep away, or prevent (something evil or unpleasant): *"The fiend forfend" said the grim Earl.* **2** (also **fore·fend**) protect (something) by precautionary measures: *the sacrifice of Mississippi was forfended against even the treason of Wilkinson.*

– PHRASES **Heaven** (or **God**) **forfend** archaic or humorous used to express dismay or horror at the thought of something happening: *Invite him back? Heaven forfend!*

for·gave /fərˈgāv/ past of FORGIVE.

forge[1] /fôrj/ ▶v. [trans.] **1** make or shape (a metal object) by heating it in a fire or furnace and beating or hammering it. ■ fig. create (a relationship or new conditions): *the two women forged a close bond.* **2** produce a copy or imitation of (a document, signature, banknote, or work or art) for the purpose of deception. ▶n. a blacksmith's workshop; a smithy. ■ a furnace or hearth for melting or refining metal. ■ a workshop or factory containing such a furnace. — **forge·a·ble** adj. **forg·er** n. [ME: from OFr. *forger*, from L. *fabricare* 'fabricate,' from *fabrica* 'manufactured object, workshop.']

forge[2] ▶v. [no obj., with adverbial of direction] move forward gradually or steadily.

– PHRASAL VERBS **forge ahead** move forward or take the lead in a race. ■ continue or make progress with a course or undertaking: *the government is forging ahead with reforms.* [18th C.: perh. from FORCE.]

for·ger·y /ˈfôrjərē/ ▶n. (pl. **-ger·ies**) the action of forging or producing a copy of a document, signature, banknote, or work of art. ■ a forged or copied document, signature, banknote, or work of art.

for·get /fərˈget/ ▶v. (**-get·ting**; past **-got**; past part. **-got·ten** or **-got**) [trans.] fail to remember. ■ inadvertently neglect to attend to, do, or mention something: [with infin.] *she forgot to lock her door* | [intrans.] *I'm sorry, I just forgot.* ■ inadvertently omit to bring or retrieve. ■ put out of one's mind; cease to think of or consider. ■ (**forget it**) said when insisting to someone that there is no need for apology or thanks. ■ (**forget it**) said when telling someone that their idea or aspiration is impracticable. ■ (**forget oneself**) act improperly or unbecomingly.

– PHRASES **not forgetting ——** (at the end of a list) and also ——: *we depend on them for food and shelter and clothing, not forgetting heat in the wintertime.* — **for·get·ter** n. [OE *forgietan*, of West Gmc. origin; rel. to FOR- and GET.]

for·get·ful /fərˈgetfəl/ ▶adj. apt or likely not to remember: *I'm a bit forgetful these days.* — **for·get·ful·ly** adv. **for·get·ful·ness** n.

for·get-me-not ▶n. a low-growing plant (*Myosotis* and other genera) of the borage family that typically has blue flowers.

for·get·ta·ble /fərˈgetəbəl/ ▶adj. easily forgotten, esp. through being uninteresting or mediocre.

for·give /fərˈgiv/ ▶v. (past **-gave** ; past part. **-giv·en**) [trans.] stop feeling angry or resentful toward (someone) for an offense, flaw, or mistake. ■ (usu. **be forgiven**) stop feeling angry or resentful toward someone for (an offense, flaw, or mistake). ■ used in polite expressions as a request to excuse or regard indulgently one's foibles, ignorance, or impoliteness. ■ cancel (a debt).

– PHRASES **one could** (or **may**) **be forgiven** it would be understandable (if one mistakenly did a particular thing): *the arrangements are so complex that you could be forgiven for feeling confused.* — **for·giv·a·ble** adj. [OE *forgiefan*, of Gmc. origin, rel. to FOR- and GIVE.]

for·give·ness /fərˈgivnis/ ▶n. the action or process of forgiving or being forgiven.

for·giv·ing /fərˈgiviNG/ ▶adj. ready and willing to forgive: *Taylor was in a forgiving mood.* ■ tolerant: *these flooring planks are more durable and forgiving of heavy traffic than real wood.* — **for·giv·ing·ly** adv.

for·go /fôrˈgō/ (also **fore·go**) ▶v. (**for·goes**; past **for·went**; past part. **for·gone**) [trans.] omit or decline to take (something pleasant or valuable); go without. ■ refrain from. [OE *forgān* (see FOR-, GO[1]).]

for·got /fərˈgät/ past of FORGET.

for·got·ten /fərˈgätn/ past participle of FORGET.

for·int /ˈfôrint/ ▶n. the basic monetary unit of Hungary, equal to 100 fillér. [Hungarian, from Ital. *fiorino* (see FLORIN).]

fork /fôrk/ ▶n. **1** an implement with two or more prongs used for lifting food to the mouth or holding it when cutting. ■ a tool of larger but similar form used for digging or lifting in a garden or farm. **2** a device, component, or part with two or more prongs. ■ a unit consisting of a pair of supports in which a bicycle or motorcycle wheel revolves. **3** the point where something, esp. a road or river, divides into two parts. ▶v. **1** [intrans.] (esp. of a road or other route) divide into two parts: *the place where the road forks.* **2** [trans.] dig, lift, or manipulate (something) with a fork: *fork in some compost.*

– PHRASAL VERBS **fork something over/out/up** (or **fork over/out/up**) informal pay money for something, esp. reluctantly. — **fork·ful** /-ˌfo͝ol/ n. (pl. **-fuls**). [OE *forca, force*, based on L. *furca* 'pitchfork, forked stick.';]

Fork·beard /ˈfôrkˌbi(ə)rd/, Sweyn, see SWEYN I.

forked /fôrkt/ ▶adj. having a divided or pronged end or branches; bifurcated: *a deeply forked tail.*

– PHRASES **with forked tongue** humorous untruthfully; deceitfully.

forked light·ning ▶n. lightning that is visible in the form of a branching line across the sky.

fork·lift /ˈfôrkˌlift/ ▶n. (also **fork·lift truck**) a vehicle with a pronged device in front for lifting and carrying heavy loads. ▶v. lift and carry (a heavy load) with such a vehicle.

forklift

for·lorn /fər'lôrn; fôr-/ ▶ **adj.** **1** pitifully sad and abandoned or lonely: *forlorn figures at bus stops.* **2** (of an aim or endeavor) unlikely to succeed or be fulfilled; hopeless: *a forlorn attempt to escape.*
– PHRASES **forlorn hope** a persistent or desperate hope that is unlikely to be fulfilled. [16th C.: from Du. *verloren hoop* 'lost troop,' from *verloren* (past part. of *verliezen* 'lose') and *hoop* 'company' (rel. to HEAP).] — **for·lorn·ly** adv. **for·lorn·ness** /fər'lôrn,nəs/ n. [OE *forloren*, past part. of *forlēosan* 'lose,' of Gmc. origin; rel. to FOR- and LOSE.]

form /fôrm/ ▶ **n.** **1** the visible shape or configuration of something. ■ arrangement of parts; shape: *the entities underlying physical form.* ■ the body or shape of a person or thing. ■ arrangement and style in literary or musical composition: *these videos are a triumph of form over content.* ■ Philos. the essential nature of a species or thing, esp. (in Plato's thought) regarded as an abstract ideal that real things imitate or participate in. **2** a mold, frame, or block in or on which something is shaped. ■ a temporary structure for holding fresh concrete in shape while it sets. **3** a particular way in which a thing exists or appears; a manifestation: *her obsession has taken the form of compulsive exercise.* ■ any of the ways in which a word may be spelled, pronounced, or inflected: *an adjectival rather than adverbial form.* **4** a type or variety of something: *sponsorship is a form of advertising.* ■ an artistic or literary genre. **5** the customary or correct method or procedure; what is usually done. ■ a formality or item of mere ceremony: *the outward forms of religion.* **6** a printed document with blank spaces for information to be inserted: *an application form.* **7** the state of an athlete or sports team with regard to their current standard of performance: *illness has affected his form.* ■ details of previous performances by a racehorse or greyhound: *an interested bystander studying the form.* ▶ **v.** [trans.] **1** bring together parts or combine to create (something): *the company was formed in 1982.* ■ (**form people/things into**) organize people or things into (a group or body). ■ go to make up or constitute: *the precepts that form the basis of the book.* ■ [intrans.] gradually appear or develop: *a thick mist was forming all around.* ■ conceive (an idea or plan) in one's mind. ■ enter into or contract (a relationship). **2** make or fashion into a certain shape or form: *form the dough into balls.* ■ [intrans.] (**form into**) be made or fashioned into a certain shape or form. ■ (**be formed**) have a specified shape. ■ influence or shape (something abstract): *the role of the news media in forming public opinion.* — **form·a·bil·i·ty** n. /,fôrmə'bilətē/ **form·a·ble** adj. [ME: from OFr. *forme* (n.), *fo(u)rmer* (v.), based on L. *forma* 'a mold or form.']

-form (usu. as **-iform**) ▶ **comb. form** **1** having the form of: *cruciform.* **2** having a particular number of: *multiform.* [from Fr. *-forme*, from L. *-formis*, from *forma* 'form.']

for·mal /'fôrməl/ ▶ **adj.** **1** done in accordance with rules of convention or etiquette; suitable for or constituting an official or important situation or occasion: *a formal dinner party.* ■ (of a person or their manner) prim or stiff. ■ of or denoting a style of writing or public speaking characterized by more elaborate grammatical structures and more conservative and technical vocabulary. ■ (esp. of a house or garden) arranged in a regular, classical, and symmetrical manner. **2** officially sanctioned or recognized. ■ having a conventionally recognized form, structure, or set of rules: *he had little formal education.* **3** of or concerned with outward form or appearance, esp. as distinct from content or matter: *I don't know enough about art to appreciate the purely formal qualities.* ■ having the form or appearance without the spirit: *his sacrifice will be more formal than real.* ▶ **n.** an evening gown. ■ an occasion on which evening dress is worn. [ME: from L. *formalis*, from *forma* 'shape, mold' (see FORM).]

form·al·de·hyde /fôr'maldə,hīd; fər-/ ▶ **n.** Chem. a colorless pungent gas, CH_2O, in solution made by oxidizing methanol. [19th C.: blend of FORMIC ACID and ALDEHYDE.]

for·ma·lin /'fôrməlin/ ▶ **n.** a colorless solution of formaldehyde in water, used chiefly as a preservative. [19th C.: from FORMALDEHYDE + -IN[1].]

for·mal·ism /'fôrmə,lizəm/ ▶ **n.** **1** excessive adherence to prescribed forms: *academic dryness and formalism.* **2** a description of something in formal mathematical or logical terms. — **for·mal·ist** n. **for·mal·is·tic** /,fôrmə'listik/ adj.

for·mal·i·ty /fôr'malitē/ ▶ **n.** (pl. **-ties**) the rigid observance of rules of convention or etiquette. ■ stiffness of behavior or style: *with disconcerting formality, the brothers shook hands.* ■ (usu. **formalities**) a thing that is done simply to comply with requirements of etiquette, regulations, or custom: *legal formalities.* ■ (**a formality**) something that is done as a matter of course and without question; an inevitability.

for·mal·ize /'fôrmə,līz/ ▶ **v.** [trans.] give (something) legal or formal status. ■ give (something) a definite structure or shape: *we became able to formalize our thoughts.* — **for·mal·i·za·tion** /,fôrməli'zāsHən/ n.

for·mal·ly /'fôrməlē/ ▶ **adv.** **1** in accordance with the rules of convention or etiquette: *he was formally attired.* **2** officially: *the mayor will formally open the new railroad station.* **3** [sentence adverb] in outward form or appearance; in theory: *all Javanese are formally Muslims.*

for·mal·wear /,fôrməl,we(ə)r/ ▶ **n.** clothing, such as tuxedos and evening gowns, for formal social occasions.

For·man /'fôrmən/, Milos (1932–), US director; born in Czechoslovakia. He directed *One Flew Over the Cuckoo's Nest* (1975) and *Amadeus* (1983).

for·mat /'fôrmat/ ▶ **n.** the way in which something is arranged or set out. ■ the shape, size, and presentation of a book or periodical. ■ the medium in which a sound recording is made available. ■ Comput. a defined structure for the processing, storage, or display of data: *a data file in binary format.* ▶ **v.** (**-mat·ted, -mat·ting**) [trans.] (esp. in computing) arrange or put into a format. ■ prepare (a storage medium) to receive data. [19th C.: via Fr. and Ger. from L. *formatus (liber)* 'shaped (book),' past part. of *formare* 'to form.']

for·ma·tion /fôr'māsHən/ ▶ **n.** **1** the action of forming or process of being formed. **2** a structure or arrangement of something. ■ a formal arrangement of aircraft in flight or troops: *the helicopters hovered overhead in formation.* ■ Geol. an assemblage of rocks or series of strata having some common characteristic. — **for·ma·tion·al** /-sHənl/ adj.

for·ma·tive /'fôrmətiv/ ▶ **adj.** serving to form something, esp. having a profound and lasting influence on a person's development: *his formative years.* ■ of or relating to a person's development: *a formative assessment.* — **for·ma·tive·ly** adv.

forme /fôrm/ ▶ **n.** Print. a body of type secured in a chase for printing. ■ a quantity of film arranged for making a plate.

form·er /'fôrmər/ ▶ **adj.** [attrib.] **1** having previously filled a particular role or been a particular thing. ■ of or occurring in the past or an earlier period. **2** (**the former**) denoting the first or first mentioned of two people or things. [ME: from OE *forma* (see FOREMOST) + -ER[2].]

for·mer·ly /'fôrmərlē/ ▶ **adv.** in the past; in earlier times: *Bangladesh, formerly East Pakistan* | [sentence adverb] *the building formerly housed their accounting offices.*

form·fit·ting /'fôrm,fitiNG/ ▶ **adj.** (of clothing) fitting the body snugly, so that its shape is clearly visible: said of clothing: *she wore a formfitting dress.*

For·mi·ca /fôr'mīkə; fər-/ ▶ **n.** trademark a hard durable plastic laminate used for countertops, cupboard doors, and other surfaces.

for·mic ac·id /'fôrmik/ ▶ **n.** Chem. a colorless irritant volatile acid, HCOOH, made catalytically from carbon monoxide and steam. It is present in the fluid emitted by some ants. [18th C.: *formic* from L. *formica* 'ant.']

for·mi·da·ble /'fôrmidəbəl; fôr'mid-; fər'mid-/ ▶ **adj.** inspiring fear or respect through being impressively large, powerful, intense, or capable: *a formidable opponent.* [ME: from Fr., or from L. *formidabilis*, from *formidare* 'to fear.']

form·less /'fôrmlis/ ▶ **adj.** without a clear or definite shape or structure: *a dark and formless idea.*

form let·ter ▶ **n.** a standardized letter to deal with frequently occurring matters.

For·mo·sa /fôr'mōsə/ former name of TAIWAN.

for·mu·la /'fôrmyələ/ ▶ **n.** **1** (pl. **-las** or **-lae** /-,lē; -,lī/) a mathematical relationship or rule expressed in symbols. ■ (also **chemical formula**) a set of chemical symbols showing the elements present in a compound and their relative proportions. **2** (pl. **-las**) a fixed form of words, esp. one used in particular contexts or as a conventional usage: *a legal formula.* ■ a method, statement, or procedure for achieving something, esp. reconciling different aims or positions. ■ a rule or style unintelligently or slavishly followed: [as adj.] *one of those formula tunes.* ■ a stock epithet, phrase, or line repeated for various effects in literary composition, esp. epic poetry. **3** (pl. **-las**) a list of ingredients for or constituents of something. ■ a formulation. ■ an infant's liquid food preparation based on cow's milk or soy protein, given as a substitute for breast milk. [17th C.: from L., dimin. of *forma* 'shape, mold.']

for·mu·la·ic /,fôrmyə'lāik/ ▶ **adj.** constituting or containing a verbal formula or set form of words. ■ produced in accordance with a slavishly followed rule or style; predictable: *much romantic fiction is stylized, formulaic, and unrealistic.* — **for·mu·la·i·cal·ly** /-k(ə)lē/ adv.

For·mu·la One ▶ **n.** an international form of auto racing, whose races are called Grand Prix.

for·mu·lar·y /'fôrmyə,lerē/ ▶ **n.** (pl. **-lar·ies**) an official list giving details of prescribable medicines. ▶ **adj.** relating to or using officially prescribed formulas.

for·mu·late /'fôrmyə,lāt/ ▶ **v.** [trans.] create or devise methodically (a strategy or a proposal): *economists and statisticians were needed to help formulate economic policy.* ■ express (an idea) in a concise or systematic way: *the argument is sufficiently clear that it can be formulated mathematically.* — **for·mu·la·ble** /-ləbəl/ adj. **for·mu·la·tor** /-,lātər/ n.

for·mu·la·tion /,fôrmyə'lāsHən/ ▶ **n.** **1** the action of devising or creating something. ■ a particular expression of an idea, thought, or theory. **2** a material or mixture prepared according to a particular formula.

for·ni·cate /'fôrni,kāt/ ▶ **v.** [intrans.] formal humorous (of people not married to each other) have sexual intercourse. — **for·ni·ca·tion** /,fôrni'kāsHən/ n. **for·ni·ca·tor** /-,kātər/ n. [ME (as *fornication*): from eccles. L. *fornicat-* 'arched,' from *fornicari*, from L. *fornix, fornic-* 'vaulted chamber,' later 'brothel.']

for-prof·it ▶ **adj.** [attrib.] denoting an organization that operates to make a profit, esp. one (such as a hospital or school) that would more typically be nonprofit.

For·rest /'fôrəst; 'fär-/, Nathan Bedford (1821–77), Confederate general in the American Civil War. He led a massacre of 300 black Union soldiers in 1864 and was revered by the Ku Klux Klan, who named him first Grand Wizard in 1867.

for·sake /fər'sāk; fôr-/ ▶ **v.** (past **-sook** /-'so͝ok/; past part. **-sak·en** /-'sākən/) [trans.] esp. literary abandon (someone or something). | [as adj.] (**forsaken**) fig. | *a tiny, forsaken island.* ■ renounce or give up (something valued or pleasant): *I won't forsake my vegetarian principles.* — **for·sak·en·ness** n. **for·sak·er** n. [OE *forsacan* 'renounce, refuse,' of West Gmc. origin; rel. to FOR- and SAKE[1].]

for·sooth /fər'sōōTH/ ▶ **adv.** [sentence adverb] archaic humorous indeed (often used ironically or to express surprise or indignation): *forsooth, there is no one I trust more.* ■ used to give an ironic politeness to questions. [OE *forsōth* (see FOR, SOOTH).]

For·ster /'fôrstər/, E. M. (1879–1970), English writer; full name *Edward Morgan Forster.* His novels include *A Room with a View* (1908) and *A Passage to India* (1924).

for·swear /fôr'swe(ə)r/ ▶ **v.** (past **-swore**; past part. **-sworn**) [trans.] formal agree to give up or do without (something). ■ (**forswear oneself/be forsworn**) swear falsely; commit perjury: *I swore that I would lead us safely home and I do not mean to be forsworn.* [OE *forswerian* (see FOR-, SWEAR).]

For·syth /'fôrsīTH/, Frederick (1938–), English writer. His novels include *The Day of the Jackal* (1971) and *The Fourth Protocol* (1984).

for·syth·i·a /fər'siTHēə/ ▶ **n.** a widely cultivated ornamental Eurasian shrub (genus *Forsythia*) of the olive family, whose bright yellow flowers appear in early spring before the leaves. [mod. L., after William *Forsyth* (1737–1804), Scot. botanist.]

fort /fôrt/ ▶ **n.** a fortified building or strategic position. ■ a permanent army post. ■ hist. a trading post.
– PHRASES **hold the fort** see HOLD[1]. [ME: from Old Fr. *fort* or Ital. *forte*, from L. *fortis* 'strong.']

fort. ▶ **abbr.** ■ fortification. ■ fortified.

For·ta·le·za /ˌfôrtl'äzə/ a port in northeastern Brazil; pop. 1,769,000.

For·tas /'fôrtəs/, Abe (1910–82), US Supreme Court associate justice 1965–69. He was the first justice ever forced to resign due to public criticism.

Fort Col·lins /'kälinz/ a city in north central Colorado; pop. 118,652.

Fort-de-France /ˌfôr də 'fräNs/ the capital of Martinique; pop. 102,000.

for·te[1] /'fôrtā; fôrt/ ▶ **n.** [in sing.] a thing at which someone excels: *small talk was not his forte.* [17th C.: from Fr. *fort* (masc.), *forte* (fem.) 'strong,' from L. *fortis.*]

for·te[2] /'fôrtā/ Music ▶ **adv. & adj.** (esp. as a direction) loud or loudly. [Ital., literally 'strong, loud,' from L. *fortis.*]

for·te·pi·an·o /ˌfôrtāpē'anō; -pē'änō/ ▶ **n.** (pl. **-an·os**) Music a piano, esp. of the kind made in the 18th and early 19th centuries. [18th C.: from FORTE[2] + PIANO[2].]

Forth /fôrTH/ a river in central Scotland that rises on Ben Lomond and flows east into the North Sea.

forth /fôrTH/ ▶ **adv.** esp. archaic out from a starting point and forward or into view. ■ onward in time: *from that day forth he gave me endless friendship.*
– PHRASES **and so forth** and so on: *particular services like education, housing, and so forth.* [OE, from an Indo-Eur. root shared by FORE-.]

Forth, Firth of the estuary of the Forth River in Scotland.

forth·com·ing /ˌfôrTH'kəmiNG; 'fôrTHˌkəmiNG/ ▶ **adj.** **1** planned for or about to happen in the near future: *the forthcoming baseball season.* **2** [predic.] [often with negative] (of something required) ready or made available when wanted or needed: *financial support was not forthcoming.* ■ (of a person) willing to divulge information: *their daughter had never been forthcoming about her time in Europe.*

forth·right /'fôrTHˌrīt/ ▶ **adj.** (of a person or their manner or speech) direct and outspoken; straightforward and honest: *his most forthright attack yet on the reforms.* — **forth·right·ly** adv. **forth·right·ness** n. [OE *forthriht* 'straightforward, directly' (see FORTH, RIGHT).]

forth·with /ˌfôrTH'wiTH/ ▶ **adv.** (esp. in official use) immediately; without delay. [ME ('along with'): based on *forth with.*]

for·ti·fi·ca·tion /ˌfôrtəfi'kāSHən/ ▶ **n.** (often **fortifications**) a defensive wall or other reinforcement built to strengthen a place against attack. ■ the action of fortifying or process of being fortified.

for·ti·fy /'fôrtəˌfī/ ▶ **v.** (**-fies, -fied**) [trans.] strengthen (a place) with defensive works. | [as adj.] (**fortified**) *a fortified manor house.* ■ strengthen or invigorate (someone) mentally or physically. ■ [often as adj.] (**fortified**) strengthen (a drink) with alcohol. ■ increase the nutritive value of (food), esp. with vitamins. — **for·ti·fi·a·ble** adj. **for·ti·fi·er** n. [ME: from Fr. *fortifier*, from late L. *fortificare*, from L. *fortis* 'strong.']

for·tis·si·mo /fôr'tisəˌmō/ Music ▶ **adv. & adj.** (esp. as a direction) very loud or loudly. ▶ **n.** (pl. **-mos** or **-mi** /-ˌmē/) a passage marked to be performed very loudly. [Ital., from L. *fortissimus* 'very strong.']

for·ti·tude /'fôrtiˌtōōd/ ▶ **n.** courage in pain or adversity: *she endured her illness with great fortitude.* [ME: via Fr. from L. *fortitudo*, from *fortis* 'strong.']

Fort Knox /näks/ a US military reservation in Kentucky, noted as the site of the depository that holds the bulk of the nation's gold bullion in its vaults.

Fort La·my /ˌfôr lə'mē/ former name (until 1973) for N'DJAMENA.

Fort Lau·der·dale /'lôdərˌdāl/ a city in southeastern Florida, north of Miami; pop. 152,397.

Fort Mc·Hen·ry /mək'henrē/ a historic site in the harbor of Baltimore in Maryland, scene of an 1812 British siege that inspired Francis Scott Key to write what eventually became "The Star-Spangled Banner."

Fort My·ers /'mī-ərz/ a city in southwestern Florida; pop. 45,206.

fort·night /'fôrtˌnīt/ ▶ **n.** esp. Brit. a period of two weeks. [OE *fēowertīene niht* 'fourteen nights.']

For·tran /'fôrˌtran/ (also **FORTRAN**) ▶ **n.** a high-level computer programming language used esp. for scientific calculations. [1950s: contr. of *formula translation.*]

for·tress /'fôrtris/ ▶ **n.** a military stronghold. ■ a heavily protected and impenetrable building. ■ fig. a person or thing not susceptible to outside influence or disturbance. [ME: from OFr. *forteresse* 'strong place,' based on L. *fortis* 'strong.']

Fort Sum·ter /'səmtər/ a historic site in the harbor of Charleston in South Carolina. It is the site of the beginning of the Civil War 1861.

for·tu·i·tous /fôr't(y)ōōitəs/ ▶ **adj.** happening by accident or chance rather than design. ■ informal happening by a lucky chance; fortunate. — **for·tu·i·tous·ly** adv. **for·tu·i·tous·ness** n. [17th C.: from L. *fortuitus*, from *forte* 'by chance,' from *fors* 'chance, luck.']

for·tu·nate /'fôrCHənit/ ▶ **adj.** favored by or involving good luck or fortune; lucky. ■ auspicious or favorable. ■ materially well off; prosperous.

for·tu·nate·ly /'fôrCHənitlē/ ▶ **adv.** [sentence adverb] it is fortunate that.

for·tune /'fôrCHən/ ▶ **n.** **1** chance or luck as an external, arbitrary force affecting human affairs: *some malicious act of fortune keeps them separate.* ■ luck, esp. good luck. ■ (**fortunes**) the success or failure of a person or enterprise over a period of time or in the course of a particular activity. **2** a large amount of money or assets. ■ (**a fortune**) informal a surprisingly high price or amount of money: *I spent a fortune on drink and drugs.*
– PHRASES **the fortunes of war** the unpredictable, haphazard events of war. **make a** (or **one's**) **fortune** acquire great wealth by one's own efforts. **a small fortune** informal a large amount of money. **tell someone's fortune** make predictions about a person's future by palmistry, using a crystal ball, reading tarot cards, or similar divining methods. [ME: via OFr. from L. *Fortuna*, the name of a goddess personifying luck or chance.]

For·tune 500 ▶ **n.** trademark an annual list of the five hundred most profitable US industrial corporations.

for·tune cook·ie ▶ **n.** a thin folded cookie containing a slip of paper with a prediction or aphorism written on it, served in Chinese restaurants.

for·tune-tell·er (also **for·tune tell·er**) ▶ **n.** a person who tells fortunes. — **for·tune-tell·ing** n.

Fort Wayne /'wān/ a city in northeastern Indiana; pop. 205,727.

Fort Worth /'wərTH/ a city in northern Texas; pop. 534,694.

for·ty /'fôrtē/ ▶ **cardinal number** (pl. **-ties**) the number equivalent to the product of four and ten; ten less than fifty; 40. (Roman numeral: **xl** or **XL.**) ■ (**forties**) the numbers from forty to forty-nine, esp. the years of a century or of a person's life. ■ forty years old. ■ forty miles an hour.
– PHRASES **forty winks** informal a short sleep or nap, esp. during the day. — **for·ti·eth** /-tēiTH/ **ordinal number** [OE *fēowertig* (see FOUR, -TY[2]).]

for·ty-five ▶ **n.** **1** a phonograph record played at 45 rpm. **2** (often. **45**) a 45-caliber revolver.

for·ty-nin·er /'nīnər/ ▶ **n.** a prospector in the California gold rush of 1849.

fo·rum /'fôrəm/ ▶ **n.** (pl. **fo·rums**) **1** a place, meeting, or medium where ideas and views on a particular issue can be exchanged. **2** a court or tribunal. **3** (pl. **fo·ra** /'fôrə/) (in an ancient Roman city) a public square or marketplace used for judicial and other business. [late ME (sense 3): from L., literally 'what is out of doors'; related to *fores* '(outside) door.']

for·ward /'fôrwərd/ ▶ **adv.** (also **for·wards**) **1** toward the front; in the direction that one is facing or traveling. ■ in, near, or toward the bow or nose of a ship or aircraft. ■ in the normal order or sequence: *the number was the same backward as forward.* **2** onward so as to make progress; toward a successful conclusion: *there's no way forward for the relationship.* ■ into a position of prominence or notice. **3** toward the future; ahead in time. ■ to an earlier time. ▶ **adj.** **1** directed or facing toward the front or the direction that one is facing or traveling: *forward flight.* ■ positioned near the enemy lines: *troops moved to the forward areas.* ■ (in sports) moving toward the opponents' goal: *a forward pass.* ■ in, near, or toward the bow or nose of a ship or aircraft. **2** (of a person) bold or familiar in manner, esp. in a presumptuous way. ▶ **n.** an attacking player in basketball, hockey, or other sports. ■ Football an offensive or defensive lineman. ▶ **v.** [trans.] **1** send (a letter) on to a further destination: [as adj.] (**forwarding**) *a forwarding address.* ■ hand over or send (an official document): *their final report was forwarded to the Commanding Officer.* ■ dispatch (goods): [as adj.] (**forwarding**) *a freight forwarding company.* **2** help to advance (something); promote. — **for·ward·ly** adv. **for·ward·ness** n. [OE *forweard*, var. of *forthweard* (see FORTH, -WARD).]

for·ward con·tract ▶ **n.** Finance an informal agreement traded through a broker-dealer network to buy and sell specified assets, typically currency, at a specified price at a certain future date. Compare with FUTURES CONTRACT.

for·ward-look·ing ▶ **adj.** favoring innovation and development; progressive.

for·ward pass ▶ **n.** Football a pass thrown forward from behind the line of scrimmage, toward the opponent's goal.

for·wards /'fôrwərdz/ ▶ **adv.** var. of FORWARD.

for·went /fôr'went/ past of FORGO.

Fos·bur·y /'fäzˌberē; -bərē/, Dick (1947–), US track and field athlete; full name *Richard Douglas Fosbury.* An Olympic gold medalist for the high jump 1968, he popularized the "Fosbury flop," in which the high jumper clears the bar head first and backward.

fos·sa ▶ n. a large nocturnal reddish-brown catlike mammal (*Cryptoprocta ferox*) of the civet family, found in the rain forests of Madagascar. [19th C.: from Malagasy *fosa*.]

Fos·se /ˈfôsē; ˈfäsē/, Bob (1927–87), US choreographer; full name *Robert Louis Fosse*. His work includes the Broadway musical *All That Jazz* (1979) and the movie *Cabaret* (1972).

fos·sil /ˈfäsəl/ ▶ n. the remains or impression of a prehistoric organism preserved in petrified form or as a mold or cast in rock: *sites rich in fossils* | fig. *the buildings are still intact, fossils of another culture* | [as adj.] *a fossil fish.* ■ derog. humorous an antiquated or stubbornly unchanging person or thing: *he can be a cantankerous old fossil at times.* ■ a word or phrase that has become obsolete except in set phrases or forms, e.g., *hue* in *hue and cry*. [16th C.: from Fr. *fossile*, from L. *fossilis* 'dug up,' from *fodere* 'dig.']

fos·sil fu·el ▶ n. a natural fuel such as coal or gas, formed in the geological past from the remains of living organisms.

fos·sil·ize /ˈfäsəˌlīz/ ▶ v. [trans.] (usu. **be fossilized**) preserve (an organism) so that it becomes a fossil. | [as adj.] (**fossilized**) *the fossilized remains of a dinosaur.* ■ [intrans.] become a fossil: *flowers do not readily fossilize.* ■ become antiquated, fixed, or incapable of change or development. — **fos·sil·i·za·tion** /ˌfäsəliˈzāsʜən/ n.

Fos·ter /ˈfôstər; ˈfäs-/, Stephen Collins (1826–64), US composer. His songs include "Oh! Susannah" (1848), "Camptown Races" (1850), and "Old Folks at Home" (1851).

fos·ter /ˈfôstər; ˈfäs-/ ▶ v. [trans.] **1** encourage or promote the development of (something, typically something regarded as good). ■ develop (a feeling or idea) in oneself: *appropriate praise helps a child foster a sense of self-worth.* **2** bring up (a child that is not one's own by birth). ▶ adj. denoting someone that has a specified family connection through fostering rather than birth. ■ involving or concerned with fostering a child. — **fos·ter·age** /-tərij/ n. **fos·ter·er** n. [OE *fōstrian* 'feed, nourish,' from *fōster* 'food, nourishment,' of Gmc. origin; rel. to FOOD.]

Fou·cault[1] /fo͞oˈkō/, Jean Bernard Léon (1819–68), French physicist. He is chiefly remembered for his demonstration with a pendulum of the earth's rotation.

Fou·cault[2], Michel Paul (1926–84), French philosopher. He was concerned with how society defines categories of abnormality.

fought /fôt/ past and past participle of FIGHT.

Fou-hsin var. of FUXIN.

foul /foul/ ▶ adj. **1** offensive to the senses, esp. through having a disgusting smell or taste or being unpleasantly soiled. ■ informal very disagreeable or unpleasant. ■ (of the weather) wet and stormy. **2** wicked or immoral: *murder most foul.* ■ (of language) obscene or profane. ■ done contrary to the rules of a sport: *a foul tackle.* **3** containing or charged with noxious matter; polluted. ▶ n. (in sports) an unfair or invalid stroke or play, esp. one involving interference with an opponent. ■ a collision or entanglement in riding, rowing, or running. ■ short for FOUL BALL. ▶ adv. unfairly; contrary to the rules. ■ (in sports) in foul territory. ▶ v. [trans.] **1** make foul or dirty; pollute. ■ disgrace or dishonor. ■ (of an animal) make (something) dirty with excrement. ■ (**foul oneself**) (of a person) defecate involuntarily. **2** (in sports) commit a foul against (an opponent). ■ Baseball hit a foul ball.

– PHRASES **fall foul of** see FALL. **foul one's (own) nest** do something damaging or harmful to oneself or one's own interests.

– PHRASAL VERBS **foul out** Basketball be put out of the game for exceeding the permitted number of fouls. ■ Baseball (of a batter) be made out by hitting a foul ball that is caught by an opposing player. **foul something up** (or **foul up**) make a mistake with or spoil something: *leaders should admit when they completely foul things up.* — **foul·ly** adv. **foul·ness** n. [OE *fūl*, rel. to Ger. *faul* 'rotten, lazy,' from an Indo-Eur. root shared by L. *pus*, Gk. *puos* 'pus.']

foul ball ▶ n. Baseball a ball struck so that it falls or will fall outside the lines extending from home plate past first and third bases.

foul brood ▶ n. a fatal disease of larval honeybees, caused by the bacterium *Paenibacillus larvae* or *Melissococcus pluton*.

foul line ▶ n. Sports a line marking the boundary of permissible movement or play, in particular: ■ Baseball either of the straight lines extending from home plate past first and third bases into the outfield and marking the limit of the area within which a hit is deemed to be fair. ■ Basketball either of the lines 15 feet in front of each backboard, from which free throws are made. Also called FREE-THROW LINE. ■ (in bowling) a line on the alley, perpendicular to the gutters and 60 feet from the head pin.

foul mouth ▶ n. a tendency to use bad language. — **foul-mouthed** adj.

foul play ▶ n. **1** unfair play in a game or sport. **2** unlawful or dishonest behavior.

foul tip ▶ n. Baseball a pitched ball that tips off the bat and travels directly to the catcher's hands. Unlike a foul ball, a foul tip can be a batter's third strike. — **foul-tip** v.

foul-up ▶ n. a mistake resulting in confusion.

found[1] /found/ past and past participle of FIND. ▶ adj. having been discovered by chance or unexpectedly, in particular: ■ (of an object or sound) collected in its natural state and presented in a new context as part of a work of art or piece of music: *collages of found photos.*

found[2] ▶ v. [trans.] **1** establish or originate (a continuing institution or organization), esp. by providing an endowment: *the monastery was founded in 1665* | [as adj.] (**founding**) *the three founding partners.* ■ plan and begin the building of (a town or colony). **2** (usu. **be founded on/upon**) construct or base (a principle or other abstract thing) according to a particular principle or grounds. ■ (of a thing) serve as a basis for. [ME: from OFr. *fonder*, from L. *fundare*, from *fundus* 'bottom, base.']

foun·da·tion /founˈdāsʜən/ ▶ n. **1** (often **foundations**) the lowest load-bearing part of a building, typically below ground level. ■ fig. a body or ground on which other parts rest or are overlaid: *he starts playing melody lines on the bass instead of laying the foundation down.* ■ (also **foundation garment**) a woman's supporting undergarment, such as a girdle. ■ a cream or powder used as a base to even out facial skin tone before applying other cosmetics. **2** an underlying basis or principle for something. ■ [often with negative] justification or reason: *distorted and misleading accusations with no foundation.* **3** the action of establishing an institution or organization on a permanent basis, esp. with an endowment. ■ an institution established with an endowment, for example a college. — **foun·da·tion·al** /-sʜənl/ adj.

foun·da·tion stone ▶ n. a stone laid with ceremony to celebrate the founding of a building. ■ fig. a basic or essential element.

found·er[1] ▶ n. a person who establishes an institution or settlement.

found·er[2] ▶ v. [no obj., with adverbial] (of a ship) fill with water and sink: *six drowned when the yacht foundered off the Florida coast.* ■ fig. (of a plan or undertaking) fail or break down, typically as a result of a particular problem or setback: *the talks **foundered on** the issue of reform.* [ME: from OFr. *fondrer, esfondrer* 'submerge, collapse,' based on L. *fundus* 'bottom, base.']

found·ing fa·ther ▶ n. a person who starts or helps to start a movement or institution. ■ (**Founding Father**) a member of the convention that drew up the US Constitution in 1787.

found·ling /ˈfoundliɴɢ/ ▶ n. an infant abandoned by its parents and cared for by others. [ME: from FOUND[1] (past part.).]

found·ry /ˈfoundrē/ ▶ n. (pl. **-ries**) a workshop or factory for casting metal. [17th C.: from *found* 'melt,' from Fr. *fondre*, from L. *fundere*.]

fount /fount/ ▶ n. a source of a desirable quality or commodity: *our courier was a fount of knowledge.* [16th C.: back-form. from FOUNTAIN.]

foun·tain /ˈfountn/ ▶ n. an ornamental structure in a pool or lake from which one or more jets of water are pumped into the air. ■ short for DRINKING FOUNTAIN. ■ fig. a thing that spurts or cascades into the air: *little fountains of dust.* [ME: from OFr. *fontaine*, from late L. *fontana*, fem. of L. *fontanus*, adj. from *fons, font-* 'a spring.']

foun·tain·head /ˈfountnˌhed/ ▶ n. the headwaters or source of a stream. ■ an original source of something.

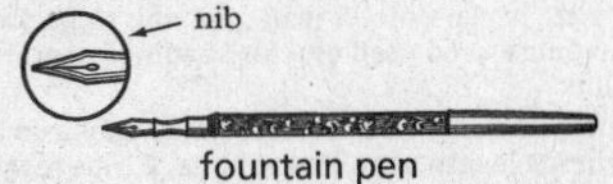

fountain pen

foun·tain pen ▶ n. a pen with a reservoir or cartridge from which ink flows continuously to the nib.

four /fôr/ ▶ cardinal number equivalent to the product of two and two; one more than three, or six less than ten; 4. (Roman numeral: **iv**, **IV**, archaic **iiii** or **IIII**.) ■ a group or unit of four people or things. ■ four years old. ■ four o'clock. ■ a size of garment or other merchandise denoted by four. ■ a playing card or domino with four spots or pips. [OE *fēower*, rel. to Ger. *vier*, L. *quattuor*.]

four-by-four (also **4X4**) ▶ n. informal a vehicle with four-wheel drive.

Four Can·tons, Lake of the another name for Lake Lucerne (see LUCERNE, LAKE).

four-col·or ▶ adj. denoting a color printing process using red, cyan (greenish blue), yellow, and black inks on separate plates that are serially transferred to the same sheet to produce images in full color.

Four Cor·ners the point in the US where Arizona, New Mexico, Colorado, and Utah meet.

four-di·men·sion·al ▶ adj. having four dimensions, typically the dimensions of length, breadth, depth, and time.

four-eyes ▶ n. derog. a person who wears glasses.

four flush ▶ v. (**four-flush**) [intrans.] informal (in poker) bluff when holding a weak hand. — **four-flush·er** n.

four·fold /ˈfôrˌfōld/ ▶ adj. four times as great. ■ having four parts or elements: *fourfold symmetry.* ▶ adv. by four times; to four times the number or amount.

four free·doms (usu. **the four freedoms**) the four essential human freedoms as proclaimed in a speech to Congress by President Franklin D. Roosevelt in 1941: freedom of speech and expression, freedom of worship, freedom from want, and freedom from fear.

Fou·rier /ˈfo͝orēˌā; fo͝orˈyā/, Jean Baptiste Joseph (1768–1830), French mathematician. He analyzed the series and integrals that are now known by his name.

Fou·rier a·nal·y·sis ▶ n. Math. the analysis of a complex waveform expressed as a series of sinusoidal functions, the frequencies of which form a harmonic series.

four-in-hand ▶ n. 1 a vehicle with four horses driven by one person. 2 hist. a necktie tied in a loose knot with two hanging ends, popular in the late 19th and early 20th centuries.

four-leaf clo·ver (also **four-leafed clo·ver**) ▶ n. a clover leaf with four leaflets, rather than the typical three, thought to bring good luck.

four-let·ter word ▶ n. any of several short words regarded as coarse or offensive.

four no·ble truths (usu. **the Four Noble Truths**) the four central beliefs containing the essence of Buddhist teaching. See BUDDHISM.

four-o'clock ▶ n. a tropical American herbaceous plant (*Mirabilis jalapa*, family Nyctaginaceae) with fragrant trumpet-shaped flowers that open late in the afternoon.

four-post·er (also **four-poster bed**) ▶ n. a bed with a post at each corner, sometimes supporting a canopy.

four·score /ˈfôrˈskôr/ ▶ cardinal number archaic eighty.

four·some /ˈfôrsəm/ ▶ n. a group of four people. ▪ a golf match between two pairs of players, with partners playing the same ball.

four-square ▶ adj. (of a building or structure) having a square shape and solid appearance. ▪ (of a person or quality) firm and resolute: *a four-square and formidable hero.* ▶ adv. squarely and solidly. ▪ firmly or resolutely, esp. in support of someone or something.

four-star ▶ adj. (esp. of a hotel or restaurant) given four stars in a grading system, typically one in which this denotes the highest class or quality or the next standard to the highest. ▪ (in the US armed forces) having or denoting the second-highest military rank.

four-stroke ▶ adj. denoting an internal combustion engine having a cycle of four strokes (intake, compression, combustion, and exhaust). ▪ denoting a vehicle having such an engine. ▶ n. an engine or vehicle of this type.

four·teen /ˌfôrˈtēn; ˈfôrˌtēn/ ▶ cardinal number equivalent to the product of seven and two; one more than thirteen, or six less than twenty; 14. (Roman numeral: **xiv** or **XIV**.) ▪ a size of garment or other merchandise denoted by fourteen. ▪ fourteen years old. — **four·teenth** /ˌfôrˈtēnTH; ˈfôrˌtēnTH/ ordinal number. [OE *fēowertiene* (see FOUR, -TEEN).]

fourth /fôrTH/ ▶ ordinal number constituting number four in a sequence; 4th. ▪ (**a fourth**/**one fourth**) a quarter: *nearly three fourths of that money is now gone.* ▪ the fourth finisher or position in a race or competition. ▪ the fourth (and often highest) in a sequence of a vehicle's gears. ▪ the fourth grade of a school. ▪ fourthly (used to introduce a fourth point or reason). ▪ Music an interval spanning four consecutive notes in a diatonic scale, in particular (also **perfect fourth**) an interval of two tones and a semitone (e.g., C to F).

fourth-class ▶ adj. a class of US mail applying to packages weighing more than 16 ounces and used esp. for sending general merchandise, books and films.

fourth di·men·sion ▶ n. 1 a postulated spatial dimension additional to those determining length, area, and volume. 2 time regarded as analogous to linear dimensions.

fourth es·tate ▶ n. (**the fourth estate**) the press; journalism.

fourth·ly /ˈfôrTHlē/ ▶ adv. in the fourth place (used to introduce a fourth point or reason).

Fourth of Ju·ly ▶ n. (in the US) a national holiday celebrating the anniversary of the adoption of the Declaration of Independence in 1776. Also called INDEPENDENCE DAY.

Fourth World ▶ n. 1 those countries and communities considered to be the poorest and most underdeveloped of the Third World. 2 those communities that form politically and economically disadvantaged minorities within societies.

4to /ˈkwôrtō/ ▶ abbr. quarto.

4WD ▶ abbr. four-wheel drive.

four-wheel drive ▶ n. a transmission system that provides power to all four wheels of a vehicle. ▪ a vehicle with such a system, typically designed for off-road driving.

fo·ve·a /ˈfōvēə/ (also **fo·ve·a cen·tra·lis** /senˈtrālis/) ▶ n. (pl. **-ve·ae** /-vēˌē; -vēˌī/) Anat. a small depression in the retina of the eye where visual acuity is highest. The center of the field of vision is focused in this region, where retinal cones are particularly concentrated. — **fo·ve·al** /-vēəl/ adj. [17th C.: from L., literally 'small pit.']

fowl /foul/ ▶ n. (pl. same or **fowls**) (also **domestic fowl**) a gallinaceous bird kept chiefly for its eggs and flesh; a domestic cock or hen. ▪ any other domesticated bird kept for its eggs or flesh, e.g., the turkey, duck, goose, and guineafowl. ▪ the flesh of birds, esp. of the domestic cock or hen, as food; poultry. ▪ birds collectively, esp. as the quarry of hunters. ▪ archaic a bird. [OE *fugol*, of Gmc. origin; rel. to Ger. *Vogel*, also to FLY[1].]

Fowl·er /ˈfoulər/ English lexicograhers. Brothers H. W. (1858–1933), full name *Henry Watson Fowler*, and F. G. (1871–1918), full name *Francis George Fowler*, compiled the first edition of the *Concise Oxford Dictionary* (1911).

Fowles /foulz/, John Robert (1926–2005), English writer. His novels include *The French Lieutenant's Woman* (1969).

Fox[1] /fäks/, George (1624–91), English clergyman. He founded the Society of Friends (Quakers).

Fox[2] ▶ n. (pl. same) 1 a member of an American Indian people formerly living in southern Wisconsin, and now mainly in Iowa, Nebraska, and Kansas. 2 the Algonquian language of this people. ▶ adj. of or relating to this people or their language.

fox /fäks/ ▶ n. 1 a carnivorous mammal (*Vulpes* and other genera) of the dog family with a pointed muzzle and bushy tail, proverbial for its cunning. See illustration at RED FOX. ▪ the fur of a fox. 2 informal a cunning or sly person. ▪ a sexually attractive woman. ▶ v. 1 [trans.] informal baffle or deceive (someone). ▪ [intrans.] dated behave in a cunning or sly way. 2 [trans.] repair (a boot or shoe) by renewing the upper leather. ▪ ornament (the upper of a boot or shoe) with a strip of leather. [OE, of Gmc. origin; rel. to Du. *vos* and Ger. *Fuchs*.]

foxed /fäkst/ ▶ adj. (of the paper of old books or prints) discolored with brown spots. — **fox·ing** /ˈfäksiNG/ n.

fox·fire /ˈfäksˌfī(ə)r/ ▶ n. the phosphorescent light emitted by certain fungi on decaying timber.

fox·glove /ˈfäksˌgləv/ ▶ n. a tall Eurasian plant (genus *Digitalis*) of the figwort family, with erect spikes of flowers, typically pinkish-purple or white, shaped like the fingers of gloves. It is a source of the drug digitalis.

fox grape ▶ n. a wild grape-bearing vine native to the eastern US. Also called LABRUSCA, ISABELLA.

fox·hole /ˈfäksˌhōl/ ▶ n. a hole in the ground used as a shelter against enemy fire or as a firing point. ▪ a place of refuge or concealment.

fox·hound /ˈfäksˌhound/ ▶ n. a dog of a smooth-haired breed with drooping ears, often trained to hunt foxes in packs over long distances.

fox·tail /ˈfäksˌtāl/ ▶ n. a common meadow grass (genus *Alopecurus*) that has soft brushlike flowering spikes.

fox ter·ri·er ▶ n. a terrier of a short-haired or wire-haired breed originally used for unearthing foxes.

fox·trot /ˈfäksˌträt/ ▶ n. 1 a ballroom dance having an uneven rhythm with alternation of slow and quick steps. ▪ a piece of music written for such a dance. ▪ a gait in which a horse walks with its front legs and trots with its hind legs. 2 a code word representing the letter F, used in radio communication. ▶ v. (**-tro·tted, -tro·tting**) [intrans.] perform such a ballroom dance.

Fox·woods /ˈfäksˌwo͝odz/ a gambling resort on the Mashantucket Pequot reservation in Ledyard, Connecticut, north of New London.

foxglove

fox·y /ˈfäksē/ ▶ adj. (**fox·i·er, fox·i·est**) resembling or likened to a fox: *a terrier with a foxy expression.* ▪ informal cunning or sly in character. ▪ informal (chiefly of a woman) sexually attractive. ▪ reddish brown in color. ▪ (of wine) having a musky flavor. ▪ (of paper or other material) marked with spots; foxed. — **fox·i·ly** adv. **fox·i·ness** n.

foy·er /ˈfoiər; ˈfoiˌā/ ▶ n. an entrance hall or other open area in a building used by the public, esp. a hotel or theater, or in a house or an apartment. [18th C.: from Fr., 'hearth, home,' based on L. *focarius* 'kitchen servant,' from *focus* 'domestic hearth.']

Foyt /foit/, A. J. (1935–) US race car driver; full name *Anthony Joseph Foyt, Jr.* He won the Indy 500 four times during 1961–77.

fp ▶ abbr. ▪ (**FP**) Fabricated Plate. ▪ fireplace. ▪ forte-piano. ▪ freezing point.

FPC ▶ abbr. ▪ Federal Power Commission. ▪ fish protein concentrate. ▪ Friends Peace Committee.

fpl ▶ abbr. fireplace.

fpm ▶ abbr. feet per minute.

FPO ▶ abbr. ▪ Field post office. ▪ Fleet post office.

fps (also **f.p.s.**) ▶ abbr. ▪ feet per second. ▪ foot-pound-second. ▪ frames per second.

FPU ▶ abbr. Comput. floating-point unit, a processor that performs arithmetic operations.

Fr. ▶ abbr. ▪ Father (as a courtesy title of priests): *Fr. Buckley.* [from Fr. *frère*, lit. 'brother.'] ▪ France. ▪ French. ▪ Friday. ▶ symb. the chemical element francium.

fr. ▶ abbr. franc(s).

f.r. ▶ abbr. folio recto (right-hand page). [L.]

Fra /frä/ ▶ n. a prefixed title given to an Italian monk or friar: *Fra Angelico.* [Ital., abbrev. of *frate* 'brother.']

fra·cas /ˈfrākəs; ˈfrak-/ ▶ n. (pl. **-cas·es**) a noisy disturbance or quarrel. [18th C.: Fr., from *fracasser*, from Ital. *fracassare* 'make an uproar.']

frac·tal /ˈfraktl/ Math. ▶ n. a curve or geometric figure, each part of which has the same statistical character as the whole. ▶ adj. relating to or of the nature of a fractal or fractals: *fractal geometry.* [1970s: from Fr., from L. *fract-* 'broken,' from the v. *frangere*.]

frac·tion /ˈfrakSHən/ ▶ n. a numerical quantity that is not a whole number (e.g., 12, 0.5). ▪ a small or tiny part, amount, or proportion of something. ▪ a dissenting group within a larger one. ▪ each of the portions into which a mixture may be separated by a process in which the individual components behave differently according to their physical properties. [ME: via OFr. from eccles. L. *fractio(n-)* 'breaking (bread),' from L. *frangere* 'to break.']

frac·tion·al /ˈfrakSHənl/ ▶ **adj.** of, relating to, or expressed as a numerical value that is not a whole number, esp. a fraction less than one. ■ small or tiny in amount. ■ Chem. relating to or denoting the separation of components of a mixture by making use of their differing physical properties: *fractional crystallization.* — **frac·tion·al·ly** adv.

frac·tious /ˈfrakSHəs/ ▶ **adj.** easily irritated; bad-tempered: *they fight and squabble like fractious children.* ■ (of an organization) difficult to control; unruly: *the fractious coalition of Social Democrats.* — **frac·tious·ly** adv. **frac·tious·ness** n. [17th C.: from FRACTION.]

frac·ture /ˈfrakCHər/ ▶ **n.** the cracking or breaking of a hard object or material. ■ a crack or break in a hard object or material, typically a bone or a rock stratum. ■ the physical appearance of a freshly broken rock or mineral, esp. as regards the shape of the surface formed. ▶ **v.** break or cause to break. ■ [trans.] sustain a fracture of (a bone). [as adj.] (**fractured**) ■ fig. (with reference to an organization or other abstract thing) split or fragment so as to no longer function or exist: [intrans.] *the movement had fractured without his leadership.* ■ [as adj.] (**fractured**) (of speech or a language) broken. [ME: from Fr., or from L. *fractura*, from *frangere* 'to break.']

frag /frag/ military slang ▶ **n.** a hand grenade. ▶ **v.** (**fragged, frag·ging**) [trans.] deliberately kill (an unpopular senior officer), typically with a hand grenade. [20th C.: from *fragmentation grenade.*]

frag·ile /ˈfrajəl; -jīl/ ▶ **adj.** (of an object) easily broken or damaged. ■ flimsy or insubstantial; easily destroyed. ■ (of a person) not strong or sturdy; delicate and vulnerable. — **frag·ile·ly** adv. **fra·gil·i·ty** /frəˈjilitē/ n. [15th C.: from L. *fragilis*, from *frangere* 'to break.']

frag·ment ▶ **n.** /ˈfragmənt/ a small part broken or separated from something. ■ an isolated or incomplete part of something. ▶ **v.** /ˈfragment; fragˈment/ break or cause to break into fragments: [intrans.] *his followers fragmented into sects.* [ME: from Fr., or from L. *fragmentum*, from *frangere* 'to break.']

frag·men·tar·y /ˈfragmənˌterē/ ▶ **adj.** consisting of small parts that are disconnected or incomplete. — **frag·men·tar·i·ly** /ˌfragmənˈterəlē/ adv.

frag·men·ta·tion /ˌfragmənˈtāSHən/ ▶ **n.** the process or state of breaking or being broken into small or separate parts. ■ Comput. the storing of a file in separate areas of memory scattered throughout a hard disk.

Fra·go·nard /ˌfragəˈnär/, Jean-Honoré (1732–1806), French painter. He is known for landscapes and erotic canvases.

fra·grance /ˈfrāgrəns/ ▶ **n.** a pleasant, sweet smell. ■ a perfume or aftershave.

fra·grant /ˈfrāgrənt/ ▶ **adj.** having a pleasant or sweet smell. — **fra·grant·ly** adv. [ME: from Fr., or from L. *fragrant-* 'smelling sweet,' from the v. *fragrare.*]

'fraid /frād/ ▶ **v.** informal nonstandard contraction of "afraid" or "I'm afraid," expressing regret.

fraid·y cat /ˈfrādē/ ▶ **n.** a child's term for a timid or fearful person, often used as a taunt.

frail /frāl/ ▶ **adj.** (of a person) weak and delicate. ■ easily damaged or broken; fragile or insubstantial. ■ weak in character or morals. — **frail·ly** adv. **frail·ness** n. [ME: from OFr. *fraile*, from L. *fragilis* (see FRAGILE).]

frail·ty /ˈfrāltē/ ▶ **n.** (pl. **-ties**) the condition of being weak and delicate. ■ weakness in character or morals.

Frak·tur /fräkˈto͝or/ ▶ **n.** a German style of black-letter type. [19th C.: Ger., from L. *fractura* 'fracture' (because of its angularity).]

fram·be·sia /framˈbēZH(ē)ə/ ▶ **n.** another term for YAWS. [19th C.: mod. L., from Fr. *framboise* 'raspberry,' so named because of the red swellings caused by the disease, likened to raspberries.]

frame /frām/ ▶ **n.** **1** a rigid structure that surrounds or encloses something such as a door or window. ■ (**frames**) a metal or plastic structure holding the lenses of a pair of glasses. ■ a case or border enclosing a mirror or picture. ■ the rigid supporting structure of an object such as a vehicle, building, or piece of furniture: *the wooden frame of the huge bed | an old bicycle frame.* ■ a person's body with reference to its size or build: *his muscular frame.* ■ a boxlike structure of glass or plastic in which seeds or young plants are grown. ■ an apparatus with a surrounding structure, esp. one used in weaving, knitting, or embroidery. ■ [in sing.] archaic literary the universe, or part of it, regarded as an embracing structure. *this goodly frame the Earth.* ■ a removable box of slats for the building of a honeycomb in a beehive. **2** [usu. in sing.] a basic structure that underlies or supports a system, concept, or text. ■ tech. short for FRAME OF REFERENCE: *the Earth's motion relative to the frame of the distant galaxies.* ■ the genre or form of a literary text determining its expected style and content. ■ [often as adj.] an enclosing section of narrative, esp. one which foregrounds or comments on the primary narrative of a text: *a frame narrator reports the narrative spoken by an inner narrator.* **3** a single complete picture in a series forming a movie, television, or video film. ■ a single picture in a comic strip. **4** another term for RACK[1] (sense 4). ■ a round of play in bowling. ■ informal an inning in a baseball game: *he closed out the game by pitching two hitless frames.* ▶ **v.** [trans.] **1** place (a picture or photograph) in a frame. ■ surround so as to create a sharp or attractive image. **2** create or formulate (a concept, plan, or system). ■ form or articulate (words). **3** informal produce false evidence against (an innocent person) so that they appear guilty.
– PHRASES **frame of mind** a particular mood that influences one's attitude or behavior. — **fram·a·ble** /-məbəl/ adj. **frame·less** adj. **fram·er** n. [OE *framian* 'be useful,' of Gmc. origin and rel. to FROM.]

framed /frāmd/ ▶ **adj.** **1** (of a picture or similar) held in a frame: *a framed photograph of her father.* **2** [in comb.] (of a building) having a frame of a specified material: *a traditional oak-framed house.*

frame house ▶ **n.** a house constructed from a wooden skeleton.

frame of ref·er·ence ▶ **n.** a set of criteria or stated values in relation to which measurements or judgments can be made. ■ (also **reference frame**) a system of geometric axes in relation to which measurements of size, position, or motion can be made.

frame-up ▶ **n.** [in sing.] informal a conspiracy to falsely incriminate someone.

frame·work /ˈfrāmˌwərk/ ▶ **n.** an essential supporting structure of a building, vehicle, or object. ■ a basic structure underlying a system, concept, or text: *the theoretical framework of political sociology.*

fram·ing /ˈfrāmiNG/ ▶ **n.** the action of framing something. ■ frames collectively. ■ framework.

franc /fraNGk/ ▶ **n.** the basic monetary unit of Switzerland and several other countries (including France, Belgium, and Luxembourg until the introduction of the euro), equal to 100 centimes. [from OFr., from L. *Francorum Rex* 'king of the Franks.']

Fran·ca /ˈfräNGkə/ a city in southern Brazil; pop. 267,000.

France[1] /frans; fräNs/ a country in western Europe. *See box.*

France

Official name: French Republic
Location: western Europe, bordered on the north by the English Channel, on the west by the Bay of Biscay, and on the southeast by the Mediterranean Sea
Area: 210,700 square miles (545,600 sq km)
Population: 60,424,000
Capital: Paris
Language: French
Currency: euro

France[2] /frans/, Anatole (1844–1924), French writer; pen name of *Jacques-Anatole-François Thibault.* His works include *Le Crime de Sylvestre Bonnard* (1881). Nobel Prize for Literature (1921).

fran·chise /ˈfranCHīz/ ▶ **n.** **1** an authorization granted by a government or company to an individual or group enabling them to carry out specified commercial activities, e.g., providing a broadcasting service or acting as an agent for a company's products. ■ a business or service given such authorization to operate. ■ an authorization given by a league to own a sports team. ■ informal a professional sports team. **2** (usu. **the franchise**) the right to vote. ■ the rights of citizenship. ▶ **v.** [trans.] grant a franchise to (an individual or group). ■ grant a franchise for the sale of (goods) or the operation of (a service): *all the catering was franchised out.* — **fran·chi·see** /ˌfranCHīˈzē/ n. **fran·chis·er** n. [ME: from OFr., based on *franc, franche* 'free' (see FRANK[1]).]

Fran·cis /ˈfransis/, Dick (1920–), English writer; full name *Richard Stanley Francis.* A champion jockey, he wrote thrillers, mostly set in the world of horse racing.

Fran·cis I (1494–1547), king of France 1515–47. Much of his reign 1521–44 was spent at war with Charles V of Spain. A supporter of the arts, he commissioned the building of the Louvre.

Fran·cis·can /franˈsiskən/ ▶ **n.** a friar, sister, or lay member of a Christian religious order founded in 1209 by St. Francis of Assisi or based on its rule. ▶ **adj.** of, relating to, or denoting St. Francis or the Franciscans.

[from Fr. *franciscain*, from mod. L. *Franciscanus*, from *Franciscus* 'Francis.']

Fran·cis of As·si·si, St. (*c.*1181–1226), Italian monk; born *Giovanni di Bernardone.* He founded the Franciscan order in 1209.

Fran·cis of Sales, St. /säl/ (1567–1622), French bishop of Geneva 1602–22. The Salesian order, founded in 1859, is named after him.

Fran·cis Xa·vi·er, St., see **Xavier, St. Francis.**

fran·ci·um /'fransēəm/ ▶ **n.** the chemical element of atomic number 87, a radioactive member of the alkali metal group. (Symbol: **Fr**) [1940s: from **France**[1] (the discoverer's native country) + **-ium.**]

Franck[1] /fräNGk/, César Auguste (1822–90), French composer and organist; born in Belgium. His works include the *D minor Symphony* (1886–88).

Franck[2], James (1882–1964), US physicist; born in Germany. He worked on the bombardment of atoms by electrons and became involved in the US atom bomb project.

Fran·co /'fraNGkō/, Francisco (1892–1975), dictator of Spain 1939–75. Leader of the Nationalists in the Spanish Civil War, he became head of the Falange Party in 1937 and took control of the government.

Franco- (also **franco-**) ▶ **comb. form** French; French and ...: *francophone* | *Franco-German.* ■ relating to France. [from med. L. *Francus* 'Frank.']

fran·co·lin /'fraNGkəlin/ ▶ **n.** a large game bird (genus *Francolinus*, family Phasianidae) resembling a partridge, with bare skin on the head or neck, found in Africa and South Asia. [17th C.: from Fr., from Ital. *francolino*, of unknown origin.]

Fran·co·ni·a /fraNG'kōnēə/ a medieval duchy in southern Germany, inhabited by the Franks.

Fran·co·ni·a Notch a valley in the White Mountains of northern New Hampshire, noted for a rock formation called the Old Man of the Mountains.

Fran·co·phile /'fraNGkə,fīl/ ▶ **n.** a person who is fond of or greatly admires France or the French.

fran·co·phone /'fraNGkə,fōn/ (also **Fran·co·phone**) ▶ **adj.** French-speaking: *a summit of francophone countries.* ▶ **n.** a person who speaks French. [20th C.: from **Franco-** 'French' + Gk. *phōnē* 'voice.']

Fran·co-Prus·sian War /'fraNGkō/ the war of 1870–71 between France (under Napoleon III) and Prussia, in which Prussian troops advanced into France and decisively defeated the French.

fran·gi·ble /'franjəbəl/ ▶ **adj.** formal fragile; brittle. [ME: from OFr., or from med. L. *frangibilis*, from L. *frangere* 'to break.']

fran·gi·pane /'franjə,pān; ,fränji'pän/ **1 n.** an almond-flavored cream or paste. ■ a pastry filled with this. **2** var. of **frangipani.** [17th C.: from Fr., named after the Marquis Muzio *Frangipani* (see **frangipani**).]

fran·gi·pan·i /,franjə'panē; -'pänē/ (also **fran·gi·pane** /'franjə,pān/) ▶ **n.** (pl. same or **-pan·is**) a tropical American tree or shrub (genus *Plumeria*) of the dogbane family, with clusters of fragrant white, pink, or yellow flowers. ■ perfume obtained from this plant. [19th C.: named after the Marquis Muzio *Frangipani*, a 16th-cent. Italian nobleman who invented a perfume for scenting gloves.]

fran·glais /frän'glā/ (also **Fran·glaise** /-'glāz/) ▶ **n.** a corrupt form of French, borrowing from English. [1960s: coined in French, from a blend of *français* 'Fr.' and *anglais* 'Engl.']

Frank[1] /fraNGk/, Anne (1929–45), German Jewish girl noted for her diary (*The Diary of a Young Girl*, 1953) that records the experiences of her Jewish family, who hid from the Nazis for two years in occupied Amsterdam before they were betrayed and died in concentration camps.

Frank[2] ▶ **n.** a member of a Germanic people that conquered Gaul in the 6th century and controlled much of western Europe for several centuries afterward. ■ (in the eastern Mediterranean region) a person of western European nationality or descent. [OE. *Franca*, of Gmc. origin; perh. rel. to OE *franca* 'javelin.')]

frank[1] /fraNGk/ ▶ **adj.** open, honest, and direct in speech or writing, esp. when dealing with unpalatable matters. ■ open, sincere, or undisguised in manner or appearance. ■ Med. unmistakable; obvious: *frank ulceration.* — **frank·ness n.** [ME: from OFr. *franc*, from med. L. *francus* 'free,' from *Francus* (see **Frank**[2].]

frank[2] ▶ **v.** [trans.] (often **be franked**) stamp an official mark on (a letter or parcel), esp. to indicate that postage has been paid or does not need to be paid. ▶ **n.** an official mark or signature on a letter or parcel, esp. to indicate that postage has been paid or does not need to be paid. [18th C.: from **frank**[1].]

frank[3] ▶ **n.** short for **frankfurter.**

Frank·en·stein /'fraNGkin,stīn/ a character in the novel *Frankenstein, or the Modern Prometheus* (1818) by Mary Shelley. He is a scientist who creates and brings to life a manlike monster that eventually turns on him and destroys him. ■ (also **Frankenstein's monster**) [as n.] a thing that becomes terrifying or destructive to its maker.

Frank·fort /'fraNGkfərt/ the capital of Kentucky, in the northern part of the state; pop. 25,968.

Frank·furt /'fraNGkfərt; 'fräNGkfoort/ a city in western Germany; pop. 654,000. Full name **Frankfurt am Main.**

Frank·fur·ter /'fraNGk,fərtər/, Felix (1882–1965), US Supreme Court associate justice 1939–62; born in Austria. He was a founder of the American Civil Liberties Union in 1920 and was awarded the Presidential Medal of Freedom in 1963.

frank·furt·er /'fraNGkfərtər; -,fərtər/ ▶ **n.** a seasoned smoked sausage typically made of beef and pork. [from Ger. *Frankfurter Wurst* 'Frankfurt sausage.']

frank·in·cense /'fraNGkin,sens/ ▶ **n.** an aromatic gum resin obtained from an African tree (*Boswellia sacra*, family Burseraceae) and burned as incense. [ME: from OFr. *franc encens*, lit. 'high-quality incense.' (see **frank**[1]).]

Frank·ish /'fraNGkisH/ ▶ **adj.** of or relating to the ancient Franks or their language. ▶ **n.** the West Germanic language of the ancient Franks.

Frank·lin /'fraNGklin/, Benjamin (1706–90), American statesman, inventor, and scientist. He was the only individual to sign all three principal documents of the new nation: the Declaration of Independence, the treaty with Great Britain that ended the American Revolution, and the US Constitution. As a scientist, he demonstrated the electrical nature of lightning.

Frank·lin stove ▶ **n.** a large cast-iron stove for heating a room. [18th C.: named after Benjamin *Franklin*.]

Franklin stove

frank·ly /'fraNGklē/ ▶ **adv.** in an open, honest, and direct manner: *she talks very frankly about herself.* ■ [sentence adverb] used to emphasize the truth of a statement, however unpalatable or shocking this may be: *frankly, I was pleased to leave.*

fran·tic /'frantik/ ▶ **adj.** wild or distraught with fear, anxiety, or other emotion: *she was frantic with worry.* ■ conducted in a hurried, excited, and chaotic way, typically because of the need to act quickly: *frantic attempts to resuscitate the girl.* — **fran·ti·cal·ly** /-k(ə)lē/ **adv.** **fran·tic·ness n.** [ME *frentik* 'insane, violently mad,' from OFr. *frenetique* (see **frenetic**).]

Franz Jo·sef /,fränz 'jōzəf; ,fränts 'yōzəf/ (1830–1916), emperor of Austria 1848–1916 and king of Hungary 1867–1916. The assassination in Sarajevo of his heir apparent, Archduke Franz Ferdinand (1863–1914), precipitated World War I.

Franz Jo·sef Land /,land; ,länt/ a group of islands in the Arctic Ocean, annexed by the Soviet Union in 1928.

frap·pé /fra'pā/ ▶ **adj.** [postpositive] (of a drink) iced or chilled: *a crème de menthe frappé.* ▶ **n.** a drink served with ice or frozen to a slushy consistency. ■ (usu. **frappe** /frap/) (chiefly in New England) a milk shake, esp. one made with ice cream. [19th C.: Fr., literally 'iced.']

Fra·ser /'frāzər 'frāzər/, Malcolm (1930–), prime minister of Australia 1975–83; full name *John Malcolm Fraser.*

Fras·er fir ▶ **n.** a North American fir (*Abies fraseri*), occurring primarily in the mountains of Virginia, Tennessee, and North Carolina.

frat /frat/ ▶ **n.** [usu. as adj.] informal a students' fraternity.

fra·ter·nal /frə'tərnl/ ▶ **adj.** **1** of or like a brother or brothers: *his lack of fraternal feeling shocked me.* ■ of or denoting an organization or order for people, esp. men, that have common interests or beliefs. **2** (of twins) developed from separate ova and therefore genetically distinct and not necessarily of the same sex or more similar than other siblings. Compare with **identical.** — **fra·ter·nal·ism n. fra·ter·nal·ly adv.** [ME: from med. L. *fraternalis*, from L. *fraternus*, from *frater* 'brother.']

fra·ter·ni·ty /frə'tərnitē/ ▶ **n.** (pl. **-ties**) **1** [treated as sing. or pl.] a group of people sharing a common profession or interests: *members of the hunting fraternity.* ■ a male students' society in a university or college. ■ a religious or masonic society or guild. **2** the state or feeling of friendship and mutual support within a group.

frat·er·nize /'fratər,nīz/ ▶ **v.** [intrans.] associate or form a friendship with someone, esp. when one is not supposed to. — **frat·er·ni·za·tion** /,fratərni'zāsHən/ **n.**

frat·ri·cid·al /,fratrə'sīdl/ ▶ **adj.** relating to or denoting conflict within a single family or organization.

frat·ri·cide /'fratrə,sīd/ ▶ **n.** the killing of one's brother or sister. ■ a person who kills their brother or sister. [15th C.: current sense comes via Fr. from late L. *fratricidium*, from *frater* 'brother' + *-cidium* (see **-cide**).]

Frau /frou/ ▶ **n.** (pl. **Frau·en** /'frouən/) a title or form of address for a married or widowed German-speaking woman: *Frau Nordern.* [19th C.: Ger., literally 'wife.']

fraud /frôd/ ▶ **n.** wrongful or criminal deception intended to result in financial or personal gain. ■ a person or thing intended to deceive others, typically by unjustifiably claiming or being credited with accomplishments or qualities: *mediums exposed as tricksters and frauds.* [ME: from OFr. *fraude*, from L. *fraus, fraud-* 'deceit, injury.']

fraud·u·lent /'frôjələnt/ ▶ **adj.** obtained, done by, or involving deception, esp. criminal deception: *the fraudulent copying of American software.* ■ unjustifiably claiming or being credited with particular accomplishments or qualities. — **fraud·u·lence** n. **fraud·u·lent·ly** adv. [ME: from OFr., or from L. *fraudulentus*, from *fraus, fraud-* 'deceit, injury.']

fraught /frôt/ ▶ adj. [predic.] **(fraught with)** (of a situation or course of action) filled with or destined to result in (something undesirable): *marketing any new product is fraught with danger.* [ME, past part. of obs. *fraught* 'load with cargo,' from MDu. *vrachten*, from *vracht* 'ship's cargo.']

Fräu·lein /ˈfroiˌlīn/ ▶ n. a title or form of address for an unmarried German-speaking woman. [Ger., dimin. of FRAU.]

Fraun·ho·fer /ˈfrounˌhōfər/, Joseph von (1787–1826), German optician. He mapped the dark lines in the solar spectrum (**Fraunhofer lines**) that result from the absorption of particular frequencies of light by elements present in the outer layers.

frax·i·nel·la /ˌfraksəˈnelə/ ▶ n. another term for GAS PLANT. [17th C.: mod. L. (former specific epithet), dimin. of L. *fraxinus* 'ash tree' (because of its leaves, thought to resemble those of the ash).]

fray[1] /frā/ ▶ v. [intrans.] (of a fabric, rope, or cord) unravel or become worn at the edge, typically through constant rubbing: *cheap fabric soon frays* | [as adj.] **(frayed)** *the frayed collar of her old coat.* ■ fig. (of a person's nerves or temper) show the effects of strain. [ME: from OFr. *freiier*, from L. *fricare* 'to rub.']

fray[2] ▶ n. **(the fray)** a situation of intense activity, typically one incorporating an element of aggression or competition. ■ a battle or fight. [ME: from archaic *fray* 'to quarrel,' from *affray* 'startle,' from Anglo-Norman Fr. *afrayer* (see AFFRAY).]

Fra·zier /ˈfrāzʜər/, Joe (1944–), US boxer; full name *Joseph Frazier*. He won the world heavyweight title in 1968.

fraz·zle /ˈfrazəl/ informal ▶ v. [trans.] [usu. as adj.] **(frazzled)** cause to feel completely exhausted; wear out. ■ fray: fig. *it's enough to frazzle the nerves.* ▶ n. **(a frazzle)** the state of being completely exhausted or worn out: *I'm tired, worn to a frazzle.* [19th C. (orig. dial.): perh. a blend of FRAY[1] and obs. *fazle* 'ravel out,' of Gmc. origin.]

FRB ▶ abbr. ■ Federal Reserve Bank. ■ Federal Reserve Board.

freak /frēk/ ▶ n. a very unusual and unexpected event or situation: | [as adj.] *a freak storm.* ■ (also **freak of nature**) a person, animal, or plant with an unusual physical abnormality. ■ informal a person regarded as strange because of their unusual appearance or behavior. ■ [with adj.] informal a person who is obsessed with or unusually enthusiastic about a specified interest: *a fitness freak.* ■ [usu. with adj.] informal a person addicted to a drug of a particular kind: *the twins were cocaine freaks.* ▶ v. [intrans.] informal react or behave in a wild and irrational way, typically because of the effects of extreme emotion, mental illness, or drugs: *I could have* ***freaked out*** *and started smashing the place up.* [16th C.: perh. from *freck* 'eager,' from OE *frec*, rel. to Old High Ger. *freh* 'greedy.']

freak·ing /ˈfrēkin; -kɪɴɢ/ ▶ adj. informal used as a euphemism for "fucking": *I'm going out of my freaking mind!*

freak·ish /ˈfrēkɪsʜ/ ▶ adj. bizarre or grotesque; abnormal: *freakish and mischievous elves.* ■ capricious or whimsical; unpredictable: *freakish weather.* — **freak·ish·ly** adv. **freak·ish·ness** n.

freak-out ▶ n. informal a wildly irrational reaction or spell of behavior.

freak show ▶ n. a sideshow at a fair, featuring abnormally developed people or animals. ■ an unusual or grotesque event viewed for pleasure, esp. when in bad taste.

freak·y /ˈfrēkē/ ▶ adj. **(freak·i·er, freak·i·est)** informal very odd, strange, or eccentric. — **freak·i·ly** adv. **freak·i·ness** n.

freck·le /ˈfrekəl/ ▶ n. a small patch of light brown color on the skin, often becoming more pronounced through exposure to the sun. ▶ v. cover or become covered with freckles: [intrans.] *skin that freckles easily* | [as adj.] **(freckled)** *a freckled face.* — **freck·ly** adj. [ME: alt. of dial. *frecken*, from ON *freknur* (pl.).]

freck·le-faced ▶ adj. having freckles on the face (often used to suggest innocence or wholesomeness).

Fred·er·ick /ˈfred(ə)rik/ a city in northern Maryland; pop. 52,767.

Fred·er·ick I /ˈfred(ə)rik/ (*c.*1123–90), king of Germany and Holy Roman Emperor 1152–90; known as **Frederick Barbarossa** ("Redbeard"). He made a sustained effort to subdue Italy and the papacy, but was defeated at the battle of Legnano in 1176.

Fred·er·ick II (1712–86), king of Prussia 1740–86; known as **Frederick the Great**. He strengthened Prussia's position; by the end of his reign he had doubled the area of his country.

Fred·er·icks·burg /ˈfred(ə)riksˌbərg/ a city in northeastern Virginia, site of a Confederate victory 1862; pop. 19,027.

Fred·er·ick Wil·liam (1620–88), elector of Brandenburg 1640–88; known as **the Great Elector**. His program of reconstruction and reorganization following the Thirty Years War brought stability to his country.

Fred·er·ic·ton /ˈfred(ə)riktən/ the capital of New Brunswick, Canada; pop. 46,466.

free /frē/ ▶ adj. **(fre·er, fre·est) 1** not under the control or in the power of another; able to act or be done as one wishes: ■ (of a state or its citizens or institutions) subject neither to foreign domination nor to despotic government. ■ [often as complement] not or no longer confined or imprisoned. ■ hist. not a slave. ■ [with infin.] able or permitted to take a specified action. **2** [often as complement] not physically restrained, obstructed, or fixed; unimpeded: *she lifted the cat free.* ■ Physics Chem. not bound in an atom, a molecule, or a compound. See also FREE RADICAL. ■ Ling. (of syntax) not constrained by word order. **3** not subject to or constrained by engagements or obligations: *she spent her free time shopping.* ■ (of a facility or piece of equipment) not occupied or in use: *the bathroom was free.* **4** [predic.] **(free of/from)** not subject to or affected by (a specified thing, typically an undesirable one). **5** given or available without charge: *free health care.* **6** using or expending something without restraint; lavish. ■ frank or unrestrained in speech, expression, or action. **7** (of a literary style) not observing the strict laws of form. ■ (of a translation) conveying only the broad sense; not literal. ▶ adv. without cost or payment: *ladies were admitted free.* ▶ v. **(frees, freed, free·ing)** [trans.] make free, in particular: ■ from captivity, confinement, or slavery: *they were freed from jail.* ■ from physical obstruction, restraint, or entanglement: *I had to tug hard and at last freed him.* ■ from restriction or excessive regulation: *his inheritance freed him from financial constraints.* ■ from something undesirable: *free your mind and body of excess tension.* ■ so as to become available for a particular purpose: *this will free up funds for development elsewhere.*

– PHRASES **for free** informal without cost or payment: *these professionals were giving their time for free.* **free and easy** informal and relaxed. **a free hand** freedom to act at one's own discretion. **free on board** (abbr.: **f.o.b.**) including or assuming delivery without charge to the buyer's named destination. **(a) free rein** see REIN. **a free ride** used in reference to a situation in which someone benefits without having to make a fair contribution: *people have been having a free ride, paying so little rent that there is no money for maintenance.* **the free world** the noncommunist countries of the world, as formerly opposed to the Soviet bloc. **it's a free country** said when asserting that a course of action is not illegal or forbidden, often in justification of it. **make free with** treat without ceremony or proper respect: *he'll have something to say about your making free with his belongings.* — **free·ness** n. [OE *frēo* (adj.), *frēon* (v.), rel. to Ger. *frei*, from an Indo-Eur. root meaning 'to love,' shared by FRIEND.]

-free ▶ comb. form free of or from: *smoke-free.*

free a·gent ▶ n. a person who does not have any commitments that restrict their actions. ■ a sports player who is not bound by a contract and so is eligible to join any team.

free as·so·ci·a·tion ▶ n. **1** Psychol. the mental process by which one word or image may spontaneously suggest another without logical connection. ■ a psychoanalytic technique for investigation of the unconscious mind, in which a relaxed subject reports all passing thoughts without reservation. **2** the forming of a group, political alliance, or other organization without any constraint or external restriction. — **free-as·so·ci·ate** (usu. in sense 1) v.

free·base /ˈfrēˌbās/ (also **freebase cocaine**) ▶ n. cocaine that has been converted from its salt to its base form by heating with ether or boiling with sodium bicarbonate. ▶ v. [trans.] prepare or take (cocaine) in such a way.

free·bie /ˈfrēbē/ (also **free·bee**) ▶ n. informal a thing given free of charge. [1940s: an arbitrary formation from FREE.]

free·board /ˈfrēˌbôrd/ ▶ n. the height of a ship's side between the waterline and the deck.

free·boot·er /ˈfrēˌbo͞otər/ ▶ n. a pirate or lawless adventurer. — **free·boot** v. [16th C.: from Du. *vrijbuiter*, from *vrij* 'free' + *buit* 'booty,' + the n. suffix *-er*. Cf. FILIBUSTER.]

free·born /ˈfrēˌbôrn/ ▶ adj. not born in slavery. ■ of or befitting a freeborn person.

freed·man /ˈfrēdmən; -ˌman/ ▶ n. (pl. **-men**) hist. an emancipated slave.

free·dom /ˈfrēdəm/ ▶ n. the power or right to act, speak, or think as one wants without hindrance or restraint. ■ absence of subjection to foreign domination or despotic government. ■ the state of not being imprisoned or enslaved. ■ the state of being physically unrestricted and able to move easily. ■ **(freedom from)** the state of not being subject to or affected by (a particular undesirable thing). ■ the power of self-determination attributed to the will; the quality of being independent of fate or necessity. ■ unrestricted use of something: *the dog is happy having the freedom of the house when we are out.*

free·dom fight·er ▶ n. a person who takes part in a violent struggle to achieve a political goal.

free·dom of con·science ▶ n. the right to follow one's own beliefs in matters of religion and morality.

free·dom of speech (also **free speech**) ▶ n. the right to express any opinions without censorship or restraint.

free·dom rid·er ▶ n. a person who challenged racial laws in the American South in the 1960s, originally by refusing to abide by the laws designating that seating in buses be segregated by race.

Free·dom Trail a walking tour in Boston, Massachusetts, that takes visitors past American Revolution sites.

free en·er·gy ▶ n. Physics a thermodynamic quantity equivalent to the capacity of a system to do work.

free en·ter·prise ▶ n. an economic system in which private business operates in competition and largely free of state control.

free fall ▶ n. downward movement under the force of gravity only: *the path of a body in free fall.* ■ the part of a parachute descent before the parachute opens. ▶ v. **(free-fall)** [intrans.] move under the force of gravity only; fall rapidly.

free fire zone ▶ **n.** a military combat zone in which there are no restrictions on the use of fire power. ■ fig. an area of activity apparently without rules.

free-float·ing ▶ **adj.** not attached to anything and able to move freely: *free-floating aquatic plants.* ■ fig. not assigned to a fixed or particular position, category, or level: *free-floating exchange rates.* ■ (of a person) not committed to a particular cause or political party. — **free-float v. free-float·er n.**

free-for-all ▶ **n.** a disorganized or unrestricted situation or event in which everyone may take part.

free-form ▶ **adj.** not conforming to a regular or formal structure or shape: *a free-form jazz improvisation.*

Free French ▶ **plural n.** an organization of French troops and volunteers in exile formed under General de Gaulle in 1940. Based in London, the movement organized forces that opposed the Axis powers in French Equatorial Africa, Lebanon, and elsewhere, and cooperated with the French Resistance.

free·hand /'frē,hand/ ▶ **adj. & adv.** (esp. with reference to drawing) done manually without the aid of instruments such as rulers.

free-hand·ed ▶ **adj.** generous, esp. with money. — **free-hand·ed·ly adv. free-hand·ed·ness n.**

free·hold /'frē,hōld/ ▶ **n.** permanent and absolute tenure of land or property with freedom to dispose of it at will. Often contrasted with LEASEHOLD. ■ (**the freehold**) the ownership of a piece of land or property by such tenure. ■ a piece of land or property held by such tenure. ▶ **adj.** held by or having the status of freehold. — **free·hold·er n.**

free jazz ▶ **n.** an improvised style of jazz characterized by the absence of set chord patterns or time patterns.

free·lance /'frē,lans/ (also **free-lance**) ▶ **adj.** working for different companies at different times rather than being permanently employed by one company. ■ independent or uncommitted in politics or personal life. ▶ **adv.** earning one's living in such a way. ▶ **v.** [intrans.] earn one's living as a freelance. [19th C. (denoting a mercenary): orig. as two words.]

free·lanc·er /'frē,lansər/ ▶ **n.** a person who works freelance.

free-liv·ing ▶ **adj.** Biol. living freely and independently, not as a parasite or attached to a substrate.

free·load·er /'frē,lōdər/ ▶ **n.** informal a person who takes advantage of others' generosity without giving anything in return. — **free·load** /'frē,lōd/ **v.**

free love ▶ **n.** the idea or practice of having sexual relations according to choice, without being restricted by marriage or long-term relationships.

free·ly /'frēlē/ ▶ **adv.** not under the control of another; as one wishes. ■ without restriction or interference. ■ in copious or generous amounts. ■ openly and honestly. ■ willingly and readily; without compulsion.

free·man /'frēmən; -,man/ ▶ **n.** (pl. **-men**) **1** a person who is entitled to full political and civil rights. **2** hist. a person who is not a slave or serf.

free mar·ket ▶ **n.** an economic system in which prices are determined by unrestricted competition between privately owned businesses. — **free mar·ket·eer** (also **free-mar·ket·eer**) **n.**

Free·ma·son /'frē'māsən/ ▶ **n.** a member of an international order established for mutual help and fellowship that holds elaborate secret ceremonies. The original **freemasons** were itinerant skilled stonemasons of the 14th century, who are said to have recognized fellow craftsmen by secret signs.

free·ma·son·ry /'frē'māsənrē/ ▶ **n.** **1** (**Freemasonry**) the system and institutions of the Freemasons. **2** instinctive sympathy or fellowship between people with something in common.

free path see MEAN FREE PATH.

Free·port /'frē,pôrt/ a city in the northern Bahamas, on Grand Bahama Island; pop. 27,000.

free port ▶ **n.** a port open to all traders. ■ a port area where goods in transit are exempt from customs duty.

fre·er /'frēər/ ▶ **adj.** comparative of FREE.

free rad·i·cal ▶ **n.** Chem. an uncharged molecule (typically highly reactive and short-lived) having an unpaired valence electron.

free-range ▶ **adj.** (of livestock, esp. poultry) kept in natural conditions, with freedom of movement. ■ (of eggs) produced by birds reared under such conditions.

free·sia /'frēZHə/ ▶ **n.** a small southern African plant (genus *Freesia*) of the iris family, with fragrant, colorful, tubular flowers, many varieties of which are cultivated for use by florists. [mod. L., named after Friedrich H. T. *Freese* (died 1876), Ger. physician.]

free skat·ing ▶ **n.** the sport of performing variable skating figures and jumps to music. — **free skate n.**

free speech ▶ **n.** another term for FREEDOM OF SPEECH.

free spir·it ▶ **n.** an independent or uninhibited person.

fre·est /'frēist/ ▶ **adj.** superlative of FREE.

free·stand·ing /'frē'standiNG/ (also **free-stand·ing**) ▶ **adj.** not supported by another structure. ■ not relying on or linked to anything else; independent.

Free State ▶ **n.** **1** hist. (before the Civil War) a state of the US in which legal slavery did not exist. **2** a province in central South Africa, situated to the north of the Orange River; capital, Bloemfontein. Formerly (until 1995) called ORANGE FREE STATE.

free·stone /'frē,stōn/ ▶ **n.** a stone fruit in which the pit is easily separated from the flesh when the fruit is ripe: [as adj.] *freestone peaches.* Contrasted with CLINGSTONE.

free·style /'frē,stīl/ ▶ **adj.** denoting a contest or version of a sport in which there are few restrictions on the moves or techniques that competitors employ. ▶ **n.** a contest of such a kind, in particular a swimming race in which competitors may use any stroke. — **free·styl·er n.**

free·think·er /'frē'THiNGkər/ ▶ **n.** a person who rejects accepted opinions. — **free·think·ing** /'frē'THiNGkiNG/ **n. & adj.**

free throw ▶ **n.** Basketball an unimpeded attempt at a basket following a foul or other infringement.

free-throw line (also **free throw line**) ▶ **n.** Basketball another term for FOUL LINE.

Free·town /'frē,toun/ the capital of Sierra Leone, in the western part of the country; pop. 505,000.

free trade ▶ **n.** international trade left to its natural course without tariffs, quotas, or other restrictions.

free verse ▶ **n.** poetry that does not rhyme or have a regular meter. Also called VERS LIBRE.

free·ware /'frē,we(ə)r/ ▶ **n.** software that is free of charge.

free·way /'frē,wā/ ▶ **n.** an express highway. ■ a toll-free highway.

free·wheel /'frē,(h)wēl/ ▶ **n.** a device in a motor vehicle transmission allowing the drive shaft to spin faster than the engine. ■ a device that allows a bicycle wheel to revolve forward while the crank is stationary. ▶ **v.** [intrans.] ride a bicycle with the pedals at rest, esp. downhill: *he had come freewheeling down the road.* ■ [usu. as adj.] (**freewheeling**) act without concern for rules, conventions, or the consequences of one's actions: *the freewheeling drug scene of the sixties.*

free will ▶ **n.** the power of acting without the constraint of necessity or fate; the ability to act at one's own discretion. ▶ **adj.** [attrib.] (esp. of a donation) given readily; voluntary: *free-will offerings.*

freeze /frēz/ ▶ **v.** (past **froze**; past part. **fro·zen**) **1** [intrans.] (of a liquid) be turned into ice or another solid as a result of extreme cold. ■ [trans.] turn (a liquid) into ice or another solid in such a way. ■ (of something wet or containing liquid) become blocked, covered, or rigid with ice. ■ [trans.] cause (something wet or containing liquid) to become blocked, covered, or rigid with ice: [with complement] *the ground was frozen hard.* ■ be or feel so cold that one is near death (often used hyperbolically). ■ [trans.] (of the weather) cause (someone) to feel so cold that they are near death. ■ (of the weather) be at or below freezing. ■ [trans.] deprive (a part of the body) of feeling, esp. by the application of a chilled anesthetic substance. ■ [trans.] treat (someone) with a cold manner; stare coldly at (someone). **2** [trans.] store (something) at a very low temperature in order to preserve it: *the cake can be frozen.* ■ [no obj., with complement] (of food) be able to be preserved in such a way: *this soup freezes well.* **3** [intrans.] become suddenly motionless or paralyzed with fear or shock. ■ stop moving when ordered or directed. **4** [trans.] hold (something) at a fixed level or in a fixed state for a period of time. ■ prevent (assets) from being used for a period of time. ■ stop (a moving image) at a particular frame when filming or viewing. ■ [intrans.] (of a computer screen) become temporarily locked because of system problems. ▶ **n.** **1** an act of holding or being held at a fixed level or in a fixed state: *workers faced a pay freeze.* **2** informal a period of frost or very cold weather.
– PHRASAL VERBS **freeze someone out** informal behave in a hostile or obstructive way so as to exclude someone from something. — **freez·a·ble adj.** [OE *frēosan* of Gmc. origin.]

freeze-dry ▶ **v.** [trans.] [usu. as adj.] (**freeze-dried**) preserve (something) by rapidly freezing it and then subjecting it to a high vacuum that removes ice.

freeze-frame ▶ **n.** the facility of stopping a film or videotape in order to view a motionless image. ■ a motionless image obtained with such a facility.

freez·er /'frēzər/ ▶ **n.** a refrigerated compartment, cabinet, or room for preserving food at low temperatures. ■ a device for making frozen desserts such as ice cream or sherbet.

freeze-up ▶ **n.** the freezing over of a body of water.

freez·ing /'frēziNG/ ▶ **adj.** below 32°F (0°C). ■ (used hyperbolically) very cold: *he was freezing and miserable* | [as submodifier] *it was freezing cold outside.* ■ (of fog or rain) consisting of droplets that freeze rapidly on contact with a surface to form ice crystals. ▶ **n.** the freezing point of water.

freez·ing point ▶ **n.** the temperature at which a liquid turns into a solid when cooled.

Fre·ge /'frāgə/, Gottlob (1848–1925), German philosopher. He founded modern logic.

Frei·burg /'frībərg; -,bŏŏrk/ a city in southwestern Germany, on the edge of the Black Forest; pop. 194,000. Full name FREIBURG IM BREISGAU.

freight /frāt/ ▶ **n.** **1** goods transported by truck, train, ship, or aircraft. ■ a charge for the transport of goods. **2** (in full **freight train**) a train of freight cars. ▶ **v.** [trans.] transport (goods) in bulk by truck, train, ship, or aircraft. ■ (**be freighted with**) fig. be laden or burdened with: *each word was freighted with anger.* [LME: from MDu., Mid. Low Ger. *vrecht*, var. of *vracht* 'ship's cargo.']

freight car ▶ **n.** a railroad car for carrying freight.

freight·er /'frātər/ ▶ **n.** a large ship or aircraft designed to carry goods in bulk.

freight ton ▶ **n.** see TON[1] (sense 1).

Fre·man·tle /'frē,mantl/ a city in southwestern Australia, the port for

Perth; pop. 24,000.

Fre·mont /ˈfrēˌmänt/ a city in north central California; pop. 203,413.

Fré·mont /ˈfrēˌmänt/, John Charles (1813–90), US explorer. He discovered several viable routes to the Pacific Ocean in the 1840s, and during the Mexican War he fought to win California.

French¹ /frencH/ ▶ **adj.** of or relating to France or its people or language. ▶ **n.** **1** the Romance language of France. **2** [as pl. n.] (**the French**) the people of France collectively.

– PHRASES (**if you'll**) **excuse** (or **pardon**) **my French** informal used to apologize for swearing. — **French·ness** **n.** [OE *Frencisc*, of Gmc. origin, from the base of FRANK².]

French² /frencH/, Daniel Chester (1850–1931), US sculptor. His works include the Minute Man statue (1873) at Concord, Massachusetts, and the Abraham Lincoln figure (1922) in the Lincoln Memorial in Washington, DC.

French and In·di·an War North American war (1754–63) between France and Great Britain.

French braid ▶ **n.** a hairstyle in which all the hair is gathered into one large braid down the back of the head, starting from the forehead. ▶ **v.** (also **French-braid**) [trans.] create such a hairstyle.

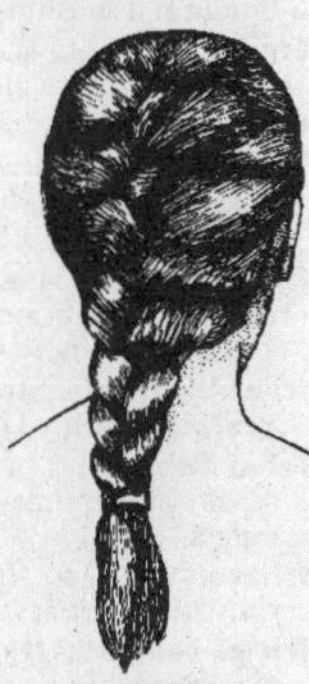
French braid

French bread ▶ **n.** white bread in a long, crisp loaf.

French Ca·na·di·an ▶ **n.** **1** a Canadian whose principal language is French. **2** the form of French spoken in Canada. ▶ **adj.** of or relating to French-speaking Canadians or their language.

French Con·go former name (until 1910) of FRENCH EQUATORIAL AFRICA.

French cuff ▶ **n.** a shirt cuff that is folded back before fastening, creating a double-layered cuff.

French curve ▶ **n.** a template used for drawing curved lines.

French curve

French-cut ▶ **adj.** **1** Cooking sliced obliquely. **2** (of women's panties) cut so as to reveal much of the upper thigh.

French door ▶ **n.** a door with glass panes throughout its length. ■ a French window.

French doors

French dress·ing ▶ **n.** a salad dressing of vinegar, oil, and seasonings. ■ a sweet, creamy salad dressing commercially prepared from oil, tomato purée, and spices.

French E·qua·to·ri·al Af·ri·ca a former federation of French territories in west central Africa 1910–58. It was previously called French Congo.

French fries (also **French fried potatoes**) ▶ **plural n.** potatoes cut into strips and deep-fried.

French Gui·an·a /gēˈänə; gīˈanə/ an overseas department of France, in northern South America; pop. 96,000; capital, Cayenne.

french heel ▶ **n.** a high, curved heel on a woman's shoe.

French horn ▶ **n.** a brass instrument with a coiled tube, valves, and a wide bell.

French horn

French·ie /ˈfrencHē/ ▶ **n.** (pl. **-ies**) var. of FRENCHY.

French·i·fy /ˈfrencHiˌfī/ ▶ **v.** (**-fies, -fied**) [trans.] [usu. as adj.] (**Frenchified**) often derog. make French in form, character, or manners.

French kiss ▶ **n.** a kiss with contact between tongues. — **French kiss·ing** **n.**

French knot ▶ **n.** (in embroidery) a stitch that forms a small, raised dot.

French·man /ˈfrencHmən/ ▶ **n.** (pl. **-men**) a person, esp. a man, who is French by birth or descent.

French pas·try ▶ **n.** a rich pastry, often with a filling of fruit or custard.

French Pol·y·ne·sia /ˌpäləˈnēzHə/ an overseas territory of France in the South Pacific; pop. 200,000; capital, Papeete (on the island of Tahiti).

French Re·pub·li·can cal·en·dar ▶ **n.** a reformed calendar officially introduced by the French Republican government on October 5, 1793.

French Rev·o·lu·tion the overthrow of the Bourbon monarchy in France 1789–99.

French seam ▶ **n.** a seam with the raw edges enclosed.

French So·ma·li·land /səˈmälēˌland/ former name (until 1967) of DJIBOUTI.

French South·ern and Ant·arc·tic Ter·ri·to·ries an overseas territory of France, comprised of Adélie Land in Antarctica, the Kerguelen and Crozet archipelagos, and the islands of Amsterdam and St. Paul in the southern Indian Ocean.

French Su·dan former name of MALI.

French toast ▶ **n.** bread coated in egg and milk and fried.

French twist ▶ **n.** a hairstyle in which the hair is tucked into a vertical roll down the back of the head.

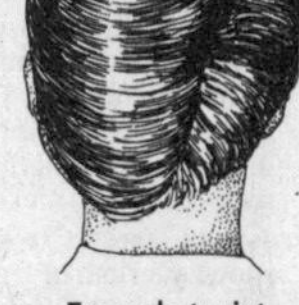
French twist

French Wars of Re·li·gion a series of religious and political conflicts in France 1562–98 involving the Protestant Huguenots on one side and Catholic groups on the other. The wars were finally settled by the Edict of Nantes.

French West Af·ri·ca a former federation of French territories in northwestern Africa 1895–1959.

French win·dow ▶ **n.** (usu. **French windows**) each of a pair of casement windows extending to the floor in an outside wall, serving as a window and door.

French·wom·an /ˈfrencHˌwoomən/ ▶ **n.** (pl. **-wom·en**) a female who is French by birth or descent.

French·y /ˈfrencHē/ (also **French·ie**) ▶ **adj.** informal esp. derog. perceived as characteristically French: *a perfect example of that kind of progressive Frenchy art.* ▶ **n.** (pl. **French·ies**) informal, esp. derog. a French person. ■ Canadian a French Canadian.

fre·net·ic /frəˈnetik/ ▶ **adj.** fast and energetic in a rather wild and uncontrolled way: *a frenetic pace of activity.* — **fre·net·i·cal·ly** /-ik(ə)lē/ **adv.** [LME: from OFr. *frenetique*, via L. from Gk. *phrenitikos*, from *phrenitis* 'delirium,' from *phrēn* 'mind.']

fren·zied /ˈfrenzēd/ ▶ **adj.** wildly excited or uncontrolled: *a frenzied attack.* — **fren·zied·ly** **adv.**

fren·zy /ˈfrenzē/ ▶ **n.** (pl. **-zies**) [usu. in sing.] a state or period of uncontrolled excitement or wild behavior. [ME: from OFr. *frenesie*, from med. L. *phrenesia*, from L. *phrenesis*, from Gk. *phrēn* 'mind.']

Fre·on /ˈfrēän/ (also **fre·on**) ▶ **n.** trademark an aerosol propellant, refrigerant, or organic solvent consisting of one or more of a group of chlorofluorocarbons and related compounds.

freq. ▶ **abbr.** ■ frequency. ■ frequent. ■ Gram. frequentative. ■ frequently.

fre·quen·cy /ˈfrēkwənsē/ ▶ **n.** (pl. **-cies**) **1** the rate at which something occurs or is repeated over a particular period of time or in a given sample. ■ the fact of being frequent or happening often. ■ Stat. the ratio of the number of actual to possible occurrences of an event. ■ Stat. the (relative) number of times something occurs in a given sample. **2** the rate at which a vibration occurs that constitutes a wave, either in a material (as in sound waves), or in an electromagnetic field (as in radio waves and light), usually measured per second. (Symbol: **f** or) ■ the particular waveband at which a radio station or other system broadcasts or transmits signals.

fre·quen·cy dis·tri·bu·tion ▶ **n.** Stat. a mathematical function showing the number of instances in which a variable takes each of its possible values.

fre·quen·cy mod·u·la·tion (abbr.: **FM**) ▶ **n.** the modulation of a radio or other wave by variation of its frequency, esp. to carry an audio signal. Often contrasted with AMPLITUDE MODULATION. ■ the system of radio transmission using such modulation.

fre·quen·cy re·sponse ▶ **n.** Electron. the dependence on signal frequency of the output–input ratio of an amplifier or other device.

fre·quent ▶ **adj.** /ˈfrēkwənt/ occurring or done on many occasions, in many cases, or in quick succession. ■ [attrib.] (of a person) doing something often; habitual. ■ found at short distances apart. ▶ **v.** /frēˈkwent/

[trans.] visit (a place) often or habitually: *bars frequented by soldiers* | [as adj., with submodifier] **(frequented)** *one of the most frequented sites.* — **fre·quen·ta·tion** /ˌfrēkwənˈtāsHən; ˌfrēkwen-/ **n.** **fre·quent·ly** /ˈfrēkwəntlē/ **adv.** [ME: from Fr., or from L. *frequens, frequent-* 'crowded, frequent.']

fre·quen·ta·tive /frēˈkwentətiv/ Gram. ▶ **adj.** (of a verb or verbal form) expressing frequent repetition or intensity of action.

fre·quent fli·er ▶ **n.** a person who regularly travels by air on commercial flights, esp. one who is enrolled in a promotional program for such travelers.

fres·co /ˈfreskō/ ▶ **n.** (pl. **-coes** or **-cos**) a painting done rapidly in watercolor on wet plaster on a wall or ceiling, so that the colors penetrate the plaster and become fixed as it dries. ■ this method of painting, used in Roman times and by the great masters of the Italian Renaissance. ▶ **v.** [trans.] paint in fresco. [16th C.: Ital., lit. 'cool, fresh.']

fres·co sec·co /ˈfreskō ˈsekō/ ▶ **n.** see SECCO.

fresh /fresH/ ▶ **adj.** **1** not previously known or used; new or different: *the court had heard fresh evidence.* **2** recently created or experienced and not faded or impaired: *the memory was still fresh in their minds.* ■ (of food) recently made or obtained; not canned, frozen, or otherwise preserved. ■ [predic.] (of a person) full of energy and vigor. ■ (of a color or a person's complexion) bright or healthy in appearance. ■ (of a person) attractively youthful and inexperienced. ■ [predic.] **(fresh from/out of)** (of a person) having just had (a particular experience) or come from (a particular place): *we were fresh out of art school.* **3** (of water) not salty. ■ pleasantly clean, pure, and cool. **4** (of the wind) cool and fairly strong. **5** informal presumptuous or impudent toward someone, esp. in a sexual way. **6** (of a cow) yielding a renewed or increased supply of milk following the birth of a calf. ▶ **adv.** [usu. in comb.] newly; recently.
– PHRASES **be fresh out of** informal have just sold or run out of a supply of (something). **(as) fresh as a daisy** see DAISY. **fresh blood** see BLOOD.
— **fresh·ness n.** [OE *fersc* 'not salt, fit for drinking,' ult. of Gmc. origin and rel. to Du. *vers* and Ger. *frisch.*]

fresh·en /ˈfresHən/ ▶ **v.** **1** [trans.] make (something) newer, cleaner, or more attractive. ■ add more liquid to (a drink); top off. **2** [intrans.] (of wind) become stronger and colder. **3** [intrans.] (of a cow) give birth and come into milk.
– PHRASAL VERBS **freshen up** revive oneself by washing oneself or changing into clean clothes: *I freshened up by having a shower.* ■ **(freshen something up)** make something look newer or more attractive.

fresh·et /ˈfresHit/ ▶ **n.** the flood of a river from heavy rain or melted snow. ■ a rush of fresh water flowing into the sea. [16th C.: prob. from OFr. *freschete,* dimin. of *freis* 'fresh.']

fresh-faced ▶ **adj.** having a clear and young-looking complexion.

fresh·ly /ˈfresHlē/ ▶ **adv.** [usu. as submodifier] newly; recently: *freshly ground black pepper.*

fresh·man /ˈfresHmən/ ▶ **n.** (pl. **-men**) a first-year student at a university, college, or high school. ■ a newcomer or novice, esp. someone newly elected to Congress.

fresh·wa·ter /ˈfresHˈwôtər; -ˈwätər/ ▶ **adj.** **1** of or found in fresh water; not of the sea: *freshwater and marine fish.* **2** informal (esp. of a school or college) situated in a remote or obscure area; provincial.

Fres·nel /frāˈnel/, Augustin Jean (1788–1827), French physicist. He deduced that light moves in a wavelike motion transverse to the direction of propagation.

fres·nel /frāˈnel/ (also **fresnel lens**) ▶ **n.** Photog. a flat lens made of a number of concentric rings, to reduce spherical aberration. [19th C.: named after A. J. FRESNEL.]

Fres·no /ˈfreznō/ a city in central California; pop. 427,652.

fret[1] /fret/ ▶ **v.** **(fret·ted, fret·ting)** [intrans.] be constantly or visibly worried or anxious. [OE *fretan* 'devour, consume,' of Gmc. origin; rel. to FOR- and EAT.]

fret[2] ▶ **n.** Art Archit. a repeating ornamental design of interlaced vertical and horizontal lines, such as the Greek key pattern. ▶ **v.** **(fret·ted, fret·ting)** [trans.] [usu. as adj.] **(fretted)** decorate with fretwork: *intricately carved and fretted balustrades.* [ME: from OFr. *frete* 'trelliswork' and *freter* (v.), of unknown origin.]

fret[3] ▶ **n.** each of a sequence of bars or ridges on the fingerboard of some stringed musical instruments (such as the guitar), used for fixing the positions of the fingers to produce the desired notes. ▶ **v.** **(fret·ted, fret·ting)** [trans.] [often as adj.] **(fretted)** **1** provide (a stringed instrument) with frets. **2** play (a note) while pressing the string down against a fret. — **fret·less adj.** [16th C.: of unknown origin.]

fret[3]

fret·ful /ˈfretfəl/ ▶ **adj.** feeling or expressing distress or irritation: *the baby was crying with a fretful whimper.* — **fret·ful·ly adv.** **fret·ful·ness n.**

fret·saw /ˈfretˌsô/ ▶ **n.** a saw with a narrow blade stretched vertically on a frame, for cutting thin wood in patterns.

fret·work /ˈfretˌwərk/ ▶ **n.** ornamental design in wood, typically openwork, done with a fretsaw.

Freud[1] /froid/, Lucian (1922–), British painter; born in Germany; grandson of Sigmund Freud. His subjects are painted in a powerful naturalistic style.

Freud[2] a family of psychoanalysts. Sigmund (1856–1939), an Austrian neurologist, founded psychoanalysis and was the first to emphasize the significance of unconscious processes in normal and neurotic behavior. His daughter Anna (1895–1982), a naturalized Briton, pioneered the field of child developmental psychology.

Freud·i·an /ˈfroidēən/ Psychol. ▶ **adj.** relating to or influenced by Sigmund Freud and his methods of psychoanalysis, esp. with reference to the importance of sexuality in human behavior. ■ susceptible to analysis in terms of unconscious desires: *he wasn't sure whether his passion for water power had some deep Freudian significance.* — **Freud·i·an·ism n.**

Freud·i·an slip ▶ **n.** an unintentional error regarded as revealing subconscious feelings.

Frey /frā/ (also **Freyr** /frār/) Scand. Mythol. the god of fertility and dispenser of rain and sunshine.

Frey·a /ˈfrāə/ Scand. Mythol. the goddess of love and of the night; sister of Frey. She is often identified with Frigga.

Fri. ▶ **abbr.** Friday.

fri·a·ble /ˈfrīəbəl/ ▶ **adj.** easily crumbled: *the soil was friable between her fingers.* — **fri·a·bil·i·ty** /ˌfrīəˈbilətē/ **n.** **fri·a·ble·ness n.** [16th C.: from Fr., or from L. *friabilis,* from *friare* 'to crumble.']

fri·ar /ˈfrīər/ ▶ **n.** a member of any of certain religious orders of men, esp. the four mendicant orders (Augustinians, Carmelites, Dominicans, and Franciscans). [ME: from OFr. *frere,* from L. *frater* 'brother.']

fri·ar·bird /ˈfrīərˌbərd/ ▶ **n.** a large Australasian honeyeater (genus *Philemon*) with a dark, partly naked head and a long curved bill.

Fri·ar Mi·nor ▶ **n.** a Franciscan friar. [so named because the Franciscans regarded themselves as of humbler rank than members of other orders.]

fri·ar·y /ˈfrīərē/ ▶ **n.** (pl. **-ar·ies**) a building or community occupied by or consisting of friars.

fric·as·see /ˈfrikəˌsē; ˌfrikəˈsē/ ▶ **n.** a dish of stewed or fried pieces of meat served in a thick white sauce. ▶ **v.** **(-sees, -seed, -see·ing)** [trans.] make a fricassee of (something). [from Fr. *fricassée,* fem. past part. of *fricasser* 'cut up and cook in sauce' (prob. a blend of *frire* 'to fry' and *casser* 'to break').]

fric·a·tive /ˈfrikətiv/ Phonet. ▶ **adj.** denoting a type of consonant made by the friction of breath in a narrow opening, producing a turbulent air flow. ▶ **n.** a consonant made in this way, e.g., *f* and *th.* [19th C.: from mod. L. *fricativus,* from L. *fricare* 'to rub.']

Frick /frik/, Henry Clay (1849–1919), US industrialist. He was chairman of the Carnegie Steel Company 1889–1900 and is known for his art collection.

fric·tion /ˈfriksHən/ ▶ **n.** the resistance that one surface or object encounters when moving over another. ■ the action of one surface or object rubbing against another. ■ conflict or animosity caused by a clash of wills, temperaments, or opinions. — **fric·tion·less adj.** [16th C.: via Fr. from L. *frictio(n-),* from *fricare* 'to rub.']

fric·tion·al /ˈfriksHənl/ ▶ **adj.** of or produced by the action of one surface or object rubbing against or moving over another: *frictional drag.*

fric·tion clutch ▶ **n.** a clutch in which friction between two moving surfaces is increased until they move in unison.

fric·tion tape ▶ **n.** adhesive tape used chiefly to cover exposed electric wires.

Fri·day /ˈfrīdā; -dē/ ▶ **n.** the day of the week before Saturday and following Thursday. ▶ **adv.** on Friday: *we'll try again Friday.* ■ **(Fridays)** on Fridays; each Friday. [OE *Frīgedæg,* named after the Germanic goddess FRIGGA.]

fridge /frij/ ▶ **n.** informal a refrigerator. [1920s: abbrev.]

fried /frīd/ past and past participle of FRY[1]. ▶ **adj.** **1** (of food) cooked in hot fat or oil. **2** [predic.] informal exhausted or worn out. ■ intoxicated with drugs or alcohol.

Frie·dan /friˈdan/, Betty (1921–2006), US feminist and writer. She wrote *The Feminine Mystique* (1963) and founded the National Organization for Women in 1966.

Fried·man /ˈfrēdmən/, Milton (1912–2006), US economist. As a policy adviser to President Ronald Reagan 1981–89, he advocated free market forces to produce balanced economic growth. Nobel Prize for Economics (1976).

friend /frend/ ▶ **n.** a person whom one knows and with whom one has a bond of mutual affection, typically exclusive of sexual or family relations: *she's a friend of mine* | *we were close friends* | *he made friends easily.* ■ a person who acts as a supporter of a cause, organization, or country by giving financial or other help. ■ a person who is not an enemy or who is on the same side. ■ a familiar or helpful thing: *the fog had crept in like an old friend.* ■ (often as a polite form of address or in ironic reference) an acquaintance or a stranger one comes across. ■ **(Friend)** a member of the Religious Society of Friends; a Quaker.
– PHRASES **be** (or **make**) **friends with** be (or become) on good or affectionate terms with (someone). **be no friend of** (or **to**) show no support or sympathy for: *he is no friend of the Republican Party* | *the policy revealed itself as no friend to the utilities.* **a friend at court** a person in a position to use their influence on one's behalf. **a friend in need is a friend indeed** proverb a person who helps at a difficult time is a person who you can really rely on. **friends in high places** people in senior positions who are able and willing to use their influence on one's behalf.
— **friend·less adj.** [OE *frēond,* of Gmc. origin; rel. to Du. *vriend* and Ger. *Freund,* from an Indo-Eur. root meaning 'to love,' shared by FREE.]

friend·ly /ˈfrendlē/ ▶ **adj.** (**-li·er, -li·est**) kind and pleasant. ■ [predic.] (of a person) on good or affectionate terms: *I was **friendly with** one of the local farmers.* ■ (of a contest) not seriously or unpleasantly competitive or divisive. ■ [in comb.] denoting something that is adapted for or is not harmful to a specified thing: *an environment-friendly agronomic practice.* ■ favorable or serviceable: *trees providing a friendly stage on which seedlings begin to grow.* ■ Mil. (of troops or equipment) of, belonging to, or in alliance with one's own forces. — **friend·li·ness n.**

friend·ly fire ▶ **n.** Mil. weapon fire coming from one's own side.

Friend·ly Is·lands another name for **TONGA**.

friend·ship /ˈfrend,SHip/ ▶ **n.** the emotions or conduct of friends; the state of being friends. ■ a relationship between friends. ■ a state of mutual trust and support between allied nations.

Friends of the Earth (abbr.: **FoE**) an international pressure group established in 1971 to campaign for a better awareness of and response to environmental problems.

fri·er ▶ **n.** var. of **FRYER**.

Fries·land /ˈfrēzlənd/ the western part of the ancient region of Frisia. ■ a northern province in the Netherlands; capital, Leeuwarden.

frieze /frēz/ ▶ **n.** a broad horizontal band of sculpted or painted decoration, esp. on a wall near the ceiling. ■ a horizontal paper strip mounted on a wall to give a similar effect. ■ Archit. the part of an entablature between the architrave and the cornice. [16th C.: from Fr. *frise*, from med. L. *frisium*, var. of *frigium*, from L. *Phrygium (opus)* '(work) of Phrygia.']

frig[1] /frig/ vulgar slang ▶ **v.** (**frigged, frig·ging**) [trans.] used as a euphemism for 'fuck.' [ME: of unknown origin. The original sense was 'move restlessly, wriggle,' later 'rub, chafe,' hence 'masturbate' (17th C.).]

frig[2] /frij/ (also **'frig**) ▶ **n.** informal short for **REFRIGERATOR**.

frig·ate /ˈfrigit/ ▶ **n.** a warship with a mixed armament, generally heavier than a destroyer (in the US Navy) and of a kind originally introduced for convoy escort work. ■ hist. a sailing warship of a size and armament just below that of a ship of the line. [16th C.: from Fr. *frégate*, from Ital. *fregata*, of unknown origin.]

frig·ate bird ▶ **n.** a predatory tropical seabird (genus *Fregata*, family Fregatidae) with dark plumage, long narrow wings, a deeply forked tail, and a long hooked bill.

Frig·ga /ˈfrigə/ Scand. Mythol. the wife of Odin and goddess of married love and of the hearth, often identified with Freya. Friday is named after her.

frig·ging /ˈfrigən; -iNG/ (often **frig·gin'**) ▶ **adj. & adv.** vulgar slang used for emphasis, esp. to express anger, annoyance, contempt, or surprise.

fright /frīt/ ▶ **n. 1** a sudden intense feeling of fear. ■ an experience that causes one to feel sudden intense fear. **2** a person or thing looking grotesque or ridiculous.

– PHRASES **look a fright** informal have a disheveled or grotesque appearance. **take fright** suddenly become frightened or panicked. [OE *fryhto*, *fyrhto* (n.), of Gmc. origin; rel. to Du. *furcht* and Ger. *Furcht*.]

fright·en /ˈfrītn/ ▶ **v.** [trans.] make (someone) afraid or anxious. ■ (**frighten someone/something off**) deter someone or something from involvement or action by making them afraid. ■ [intrans.] (of a person) become afraid or anxious. — **fright·en·ing·ly** /ˈfrītn-iNGlē/ **adv.**

fright·ened /ˈfrītnd/ ▶ **adj.** afraid or anxious.

fright·ful /ˈfrītfəl/ ▶ **adj.** very unpleasant, serious, or shocking. ■ informal used for emphasis, esp. of something bad. — **fright·ful·ness n.**

frig·id /ˈfrijid/ ▶ **adj.** very cold in temperature. ■ (esp. of a woman) unable or unwilling to be sexually aroused and responsive. ■ showing no friendliness or enthusiasm; stiff or formal in behavior or style. — **fri·gid·i·ty** /frəˈjidətē/ **n. frig·id·ly adv. frig·id·ness n.** [ME: from L. *frigidus*, from *frigere* 'be cold,' from *frigus* (n.) 'cold.']

frig·id zone ▶ **n.** (also **Frig·id Zone**) each of the two areas of the earth respectively north of the Arctic Circle and south of the Antarctic Circle. ■ informal a range of extremely cold temperatures.

fri·jo·les /frēˈhōlēz; -ˈhōles/ ▶ **plural n.** (in Mexican cooking) beans. [Sp., pl. of *frijol* 'bean.']

frill /fril/ ▶ **n.** a strip of gathered or pleated material sewn by one side onto a garment or larger piece of material as a decorative edging or ornament. ■ a thing resembling such a strip in appearance or function. ■ a natural fringe of feathers or hair on a bird or other animal. ■ (usu. **frills**) fig. an unnecessary extra feature or embellishment. — **frilled adj. frill·er·y** /ˈfrilərē/ **n.** [16th C.: from or rel. to Flemish *frul*.]

frilled liz·ard (also **frill-necked lizard**) ▶ **n.** a large northern Australian lizard (*Chlamydosaurus kingii*, family Agamidae) with a neck membrane that forms an erect ruff for defensive display. When disturbed, it runs away on its hind legs.

frilled lizard

frill·y /ˈfrilē/ ▶ **adj.** (**frill·i·er, frill·i·est**) decorated with frills or similar ornamentation: *a frilly apron.* ■ overelaborate or showy in character or style. ▶ **plural n.** (**frillies**) informal an item of women's underwear. — **frill·i·ness** /ˈfrilēnis/ **n.**

fringe /frinj/ ▶ **n. 1** an ornamental border of threads left loose or formed into tassels or twists, used to edge clothing or material. **2** a natural border of hair or fibers in an animal or plant. **3** (often **the fringes**) the outer, marginal, or extreme part of an area, group, or sphere of activity. ■ (**the fringe**) the unconventional, extreme, or marginal wing of a group or sphere of activity. **4** short for **FRINGE BENEFIT**. ▶ **adj.** [attrib.] not part of the mainstream; unconventional, peripheral, or extreme: *fringe theater.* ▶ **v.** [trans.] decorate (clothing or material) with a fringe. ■ (often **be fringed**) form a border around (something). — **fringe·less adj. fring·y** /ˈfrinjē/ **adj.** [ME: from OFr. *frenge*, based on late L. *fimbria*, earlier a pl. n. meaning 'fibers, shreds.']

fringe ben·e·fit ▶ **n.** an extra benefit supplementing an employee's salary.

fringed or·chid ▶ **n.** a North American orchid (genus *Habenaria*) with a flower that has a fringed lip.

frip·per·y /ˈfripərē/ ▶ **n.** (pl. **-per·ies**) showy or unnecessary ornament in architecture, dress, or language. ■ a tawdry or frivolous thing. [16th C.: from Fr. *friperie*, from OFr. *freperie*, from *frepe* 'rag.']

Fris. ▶ **abbr.** Frisian.

Fris·bee /ˈfrizbē/ (also **fris·bee**) ▶ **n.** trademark a concave plastic disk designed for skimming through the air. ■ the game or amusement of skimming such a disk.

Frisch[1] /friSH/, Karl von (1886–1982), Austrian zoologist. He worked mainly on honeybees, studying particularly their vision, navigation, and communication. Nobel Prize in Physiology or Medicine (1973, shared with Konrad Lorenz and Nikolaas Tinbergen).

Frisch[2], Otto Robert (1904–79), British physicist; born in Austria. With his aunt, Lise Meitner, he recognized a new type of nuclear reaction, which he called nuclear fission.

Frisch[3], Ragnar Anton Kittil (1895–1973), Norwegian economist. He was a pioneer of econometrics. Nobel Prize for Economics (1969, shared with Jan Tinbergen).

Fri·sia /ˈfriZHə; ˈfrēZHə/ an ancient region in northwestern Europe. It included the Frisian Islands and parts of the mainland in the Netherlands and Germany.

Fri·sian /ˈfriZHən; ˈfrē-/ ▶ **adj.** of or relating to Frisia or Friesland, its people, or language. ▶ **n. 1** a native or inhabitant of Frisia or Friesland. **2** the West Germanic language of Frisia or Friesland, the language most closely related to English.

Fri·sian Is·lands a chain of islands off the coast of northwestern Europe. The **West Frisian Islands** form part of the Netherlands, the **East Frisian Islands** form part of Germany, and the **North Frisian Islands** are divided between Germany and Denmark.

frisk /frisk/ ▶ **v. 1** [trans.] (of a police officer or other official) pass the hands over (someone) in a search for hidden weapons, drugs, or other items. **2** [no obj., with adverbial of direction] (of an animal or person) skip or leap playfully; frolic. ■ [trans.] (of an animal) move or wave (its tail or legs) playfully. ▶ **n.** a playful skip or leap. — **frisk·er n.** [16th C. (sense 2): from obs. *frisk* 'lively, frisky,' from OFr. *frisque* 'alert, lively, merry,' perh. of Gmc. origin.]

frisk·y /ˈfriskē/ ▶ **adj.** (**frisk·i·er, frisk·i·est**) playful and full of energy: *he bounds about like a frisky pup.* — **frisk·i·ly adv. frisk·i·ness n.**

fris·son /frēˈsôN/ ▶ **n.** a sudden strong feeling of excitement or fear; a thrill: *a frisson of excitement.* [18th C.: Fr., lit. 'a shiver or thrill.']

frit /frit/ ▶ **n.** the mixture of silica and fluxes that is fused at high temperature to make glass. ■ a similar calcined and pulverized mixture used to make soft-paste porcelain or ceramic glazes. ▶ **v.** (**frit·ted, frit·ting**) [trans.] make into frit. [17th C.: from Ital. *fritta*, fem. past part. of *friggere* 'to fry.']

frites /frēt(s)/ ▶ **plural n.** short for **POMMES FRITES**.

frit fly ▶ **n.** a very small black fly (*Oscinella frit*, family Chloropidae) whose larvae are a serious pest of cereal crops and golf-course turf. [19th C.: from L. *frit* 'particle on an ear of grain.']

frit·il·lar·y /ˈfritl,erē/ ▶ **n. 1** a Eurasian plant (genus *Fritillaria*) of the lily family, with hanging bell-like flowers. **2** a butterfly (*Argynnis*, *Speyeria*, and other genera, family Nymphalidae) with orange-brown wings that are checkered with black, including the North American

great spangled fritillary

great spangled fritillary (*S. cybele*). [17th C.: from mod. L. *fritillaria*, from L. *fritillus* 'dice box.']

frit·ta·ta /frē'tätə/ ▶ n. an Italian dish made with fried beaten eggs, resembling a Spanish omelet. [Ital., from *fritto*, past part. of *friggere* 'to fry.' Cf. FRITTER².]

frit·ter¹ /'fritər/ ▶ v. [trans.] (**fritter something away**) waste time, money, or energy on trifling matters. ■ [intrans.] dwindle; diminish. —**frit·ter·er** n. [18th C.: based on obs. *fitter* 'break into fragments, shred'; perh. rel. to Ger. *Fetzen* 'rag, scrap.']

frit·ter² ▶ n. a piece of fruit, vegetable, or meat that is coated in batter and deep-fried. [ME: from OFr. *friture*, based on L. *frigere* (see FRY¹). Cf. FRITTATA.]

fritz /frits/ ▶ n. (in phrase **go** or **be on the fritz**) informal (of a machine) stop working properly. [20th C.: said to be a use of *Fritz*, with allusion to cheap Ger. imports into the US before World War I.]

Fri·u·li /frē'o͞olē/ a region in southeastern Europe now divided between Slovenia and Italy. —**Fri·u·li·an** /-lēən/ adj. & n.

Fri·u·li-Ve·ne·zia Giu·lia /frē'o͞olē vä'netsēə 'jo͞olyə/ a region in northeastern Italy.

friv·o·lous /'frivələs/ ▶ adj. not having any serious purpose or value: *rules to stop frivolous lawsuits.* ■ (of a person) carefree and not serious. —**fri·vol·i·ty** /fri'välətē/ n. **friv·o·lous·ly** adv. **friv·o·lous·ness** n. [ME: from L. *frivolus* 'silly, trifling' + -OUS.]

frizz /friz/ ▶ v. [trans.] form (hair) into a mass of small, tight curls or tufts. ■ [intrans.] (of hair) form itself into such a mass. ▶ n. the state of being formed into such a mass of curls or tufts: *a perm designed to add curl without frizz.* [ME (in the sense 'dress leather with pumice'): from Fr. *friser*.]

friz·zle ▶ v. [trans.] form (hair) into tight curls. ▶ n. a tight curl in hair. —**friz·zly** /'friz(ə)lē/ adj. [16th C.: from FRIZZ + -LE⁴.]

friz·zy /'frizē/ ▶ adj. (-**zi·er**, -**zi·est**) formed of a mass of small, tight curls or tufts: *frizzy red hair.* —**friz·zi·ness** n.

fro /frō/ ▶ adv. see TO AND FRO. [ME: from ON *frá* (see FROM).]

Fro·bish·er /'frōbisHər/, Sir Martin (*c.*1535–94), English explorer. In 1576, he led an unsuccessful expedition in search of the Northwest Passage.

frock /fräk/ ▶ n. **1** a woman's or girl's dress. **2** a loose outer garment, in particular: ■ a long gown with flowing sleeves worn by monks, priests, or clergy. ■ short for FROCK COAT. ▶ v. [trans.] provide with or dress in a frock. [ME: from OFr. *froc*, of Gmc. origin.]

frock coat ▶ n. a man's double-breasted, long-skirted coat, now worn chiefly on formal occasions.

froe /frō/ ▶ n. a cleaving tool with a handle at right angles to the blade. [16th C.: abbrev. of obs. *frower*, from FROWARD in the sense 'turned away.']

Froe·bel /'frəbəl/, Friedrich Wilhelm August (1782–1852), German educator. He founded the kindergarten system.

frog¹ /frôg; fräg/ ▶ n. **1** a tailless amphibian with a short squat body, moist smooth skin, and very long hind legs for leaping. Frogs are found in most families of the order Anura, but the 'true frogs' are confined to the large family Ranidae. **2** (**Frog**) derog. a French person. ▶ v. [intrans.] hunt for or catch frogs.
– PHRASES **have a frog in one's throat** informal lose one's voice or find it hard to speak because of hoarseness. [OE *frogga*, of Gmc. origin; rel. to Du. *vors* and Ger. *Frosch*.]

frog² ▶ n. a thing used to hold or fasten something, in particular: ■ an ornamental coat fastener or braid consisting of a spindle-shaped button and a loop through which it passes. ■ a perforated or spiked device for holding the stems of flowers in an arrangement. ■ a grooved metal plate for guiding the wheels of a railroad vehicle at an intersection. [18th C.: perh. a use of FROG¹.]

frog·fish /'frôg,fisH/ ▶ n. (pl. same or -**fish·es**) an anglerfish (families Antennariidae and Brachionichthyidae) that typically lives on the seabed, where its warty skin and color provide camouflage.

frog·hop·per /'frôg,häpər; fräg-/ ▶ n. a jumping, plant-sucking bug (family Cercopidae), the larva of which produces a frothy mass on plants. Also called SPITTLEBUG.

frog kick ▶ n. a movement used in swimming, esp. in the breast stroke, in which the legs are brought toward the body with the knees bent and the feet together and then kicked outward before being brought together again, all in one continuous movement.

frog·man /'frôg,man; 'fräg-; -mən/ ▶ n. (pl. -**men**) a person who swims underwater wearing a rubber suit, flippers, and an oxygen supply.

frog·march /'frôg,märcH; 'fräg-/ ▶ v. [with obj. and adverbial of direction] force (someone) to walk forward by holding and pinning their arms from behind.

frog·mouth /'frôg,moutH; 'fräg-/ ▶ n. a nocturnal bird (family Podargidae) resembling a nightjar, occurring in Southeast Asia and Australasia.

frog's-bit ▶ n. a floating freshwater plant (family Hydrocharitaceae) with creeping stems that bear clusters of small rounded leaves.

frol·ic /'frälik/ ▶ v. (**frol·icked, frol·ick·ing**) [no obj., with adverbial of place] (of an animal or person) play and move about cheerfully, excitedly, or energetically. ■ play about with someone in a flirtatious or sexual way. ▶ n. (often **frolics**) a playful action or movement. ■ flirtatious or sexual activity or actions. [16th C. (as an adj.): from Du. *vrolijk* 'merry, cheerful.']

frol·ic·some /'fräliksəm/ ▶ adj. lively and playful.

from /frəm/ ▶ prep. **1** indicating the point in space at which a journey, motion, or action starts: *she began to walk away from him.* ■ indicating the distance between a particular place and another place used as a point of reference: *50 yards from a checkpoint.* **2** indicating the point in time at which a particular process, event, or activity starts. **3** indicating the source or provenance of someone or something: *I'm from Hartford.* ■ indicating the date at which something was created. **4** indicating the starting point of a specified range on a scale. ■ indicating one extreme in a range of conceptual variations: *anything from geography to literature.* **5** indicating the point at which an observer is placed. **6** indicating the raw material out of which something is manufactured: *a varnish made from copal.* **7** indicating separation or removal. **8** indicating prevention. **9** indicating a cause. **10** indicating a source of knowledge or the basis for one's judgment. **11** indicating a distinction.
– PHRASES **as from** see AS¹. **from day to day** (or **hour to hour**, etc.) daily (or hourly, etc.); as the days (or hours, etc.) pass. **from now** (or **then**, etc.) **on** now (or then, etc.) and in the future: *they were friends from that day on.* **from time to time** occasionally. [OE *fram, from*, of Gmc. origin; rel. to ON *frá* (see FRO).]

Fromm /främ/, Erich (1900–80), US psychoanalyst and philosopher; born in Germany. His works, including *The Sane Society* (1955), emphasize the role of culture in neurosis.

frond /fränd/ ▶ n. the leaf or leaflike part of a palm, fern, or similar plant: *fronds of bracken.* —**frond·ed** adj. [18th C.: from L. *frons, frond-* 'leaf.']

front /frənt/ ▶ n. **1** the side or part of an object that presents itself to view or that is normally seen or used first; the most forward part of something. ■ [in sing.] the position directly ahead of someone or something; the most forward position or place: ■ the forward-facing part of a person's body, on the opposite side to their back. ■ the part of a garment covering this. ■ informal a woman's bust or cleavage. ■ any face of a building, esp. that of the main entrance. **2** the foremost line or part of an armed force; the furthest position that an army has reached and where the enemy is or may be engaged. ■ the direction toward which a line of troops faces when formed. ■ a particular formation of troops for battle. ■ a particular situation or sphere of operation. ■ [often in names] an organized political group. ■ Meteorol. the forward edge of an advancing mass of air. See COLD FRONT, WARM FRONT. **3** [in sing.] an appearance or form of behavior assumed by a person to conceal their genuine feelings. ■ a person or organization serving as a cover for subversive or illegal activities. ■ a well-known or prestigious person who acts as a representative, rather than an active member, of an organization. See also FRONTMAN. ▶ adj. [attrib.] **1** of or at the front: *she was in the front yard.* **2** Phonet. (of a vowel sound) formed by raising the body of the tongue, excluding the blade and tip, toward the hard palate. ▶ v. [trans.] **1** (of a building or piece of land) have the front facing or directed toward: *the houses that front Beacon Street.* | [intrans.] *we sold the uphill land that fronted on the road.* ■ be or stand in front of: *they reached the hedge fronting the garden.* **2** (usu. **be fronted**) provide (something) with a front or facing of a particular type or material: *a metal box fronted by an alloy panel* | [as adj., in comb.] (**-fronted**) *a glass-fronted bookcase.* **3** lead or be the most prominent member in (an organization, activity, or group of musicians). ■ present or host (a television or radio program). ■ [intrans.] act as a front or cover for someone or something acting illegally or wishing to conceal something. **4** Phonet. articulate (a vowel sound) with the tongue further forward: [as adj.] (**fronted**) *all speakers use raised and fronted variants more in spontaneous speech.* ▶ exclam. used to summon someone to the front or to command them to assume a forward-facing position, as in calling a bellhop to the front desk or giving orders to troops on parade: *scouts, front and center!*
– PHRASES **in front 1** in a position just ahead of or further forward than someone or something else. ■ in the lead in a game or contest. **2** on the part or side that normally first presents itself to view. **in front of 1** in a position just ahead or at the front part of someone or something else. ■ in a position facing someone or something. **2** in the presence of. **out front** at or to the front; in front. ■ in the auditorium of a theater. **up front 1** at or near the front. **2** in advance. **3** open and direct; frank. —**front·less** adj. **front·ward** /-wərd/ adj. & adv. **front·wards** /-wərdz/ adv. [ME (denoting the forehead): from OFr. *front* (n.), *fronter* (v.), from L. *frons, front-* 'forehead, front.']

front·age /'frəntij/ ▶ n. the facade of a building. ■ the direction this faces: *beautiful homes with river frontage.* ■ a strip or extent of land abutting on a street or water.

front·age road ▶ n. a subsidiary road running parallel to a main road and giving access to houses, stores, and businesses. Also called SERVICE ROAD.

fron·tal /'frəntl/ ▶ adj. of or at the front. ■ (of an attack) delivered directly on the front, not the side or back. ■ of or relating to the forehead or front part of the skull.

fron·tal bone ▶ n. the bone that forms the front part of the skull and the upper part of the eye sockets.

fron·tal lobe ▶ n. each of the paired lobes of the brain lying immediately behind the forehead, including areas concerned with behavior, learning, personality, and voluntary movement.

fron·tal lo·bot·o·my ▶ n. lobotomy of the frontal lobe of the cerebrum to sever the white connecting fibers.

front burn·er ▶ n. fig. the focus of attention: *the 1872 Mining Law is next up on the front burner.*

Front de Lib·ér·a·tion Na·tion·ale /,frôN də ,libē,räs'yôN ,näsyə'näl/ (abbr.: **FLN**) a revolutionary political party in Algeria that supported the war of independence against France 1954–62. [Fr., 'National Liberation Front.']

front desk ▸ n. the main desk at a hotel or motel, for checking in or out and handling requests from guests.

Fron·te·nac /'frontəˌnak; frônt(ə)'näk/, Louis de Buade, Comte de (1622–98), colonial administrator. He was governor of New France 1672–82, 1689–98.

front-end ▸ adj. [attrib.] of or relating to the front of a car or other vehicle: *front-end styling.* ■ informal (of money) paid or charged at the beginning of a transaction: *a front-end fee.* ■ Comput. (of a device or program) directly accessed by the user and allowing access to further devices or programs. ▸ n. Comput. a part of a computer or program that allows access to other parts.

front-end load ▸ n. the deduction of commission fees and expenses from mutual fund shares at the time of purchase.

front-end load·er ▸ n. a machine with a scoop or bucket on an articulated arm at the front for digging and loading earth.

front-fanged ▸ adj. (of a snake such as a cobra or viper) having the front pair of teeth modified as fangs, with grooves or canals to conduct the venom. Compare with BACK-FANGED.

fron·tier /ˌfrən'ti(ə)r/ ▸ n. a line or border separating two countries. ■ the district near such a line. ■ the extreme limit of settled land beyond which lies wilderness, esp. referring to the western US before Pacific settlement. ■ the extreme limit of understanding or achievement in a particular area. [ME: from OFr. *frontiere*, based on L. *frons, front-* 'front.']

fron·tiers·man /ˌfrən'ti(ə)rzmən/ ▸ n. (pl. **-men**) a person, esp. a man, living in the region of a frontier.

fron·tiers·wom·an /ˌfrən'ti(ə)rzˌwo͝omən/ ▸ n. (pl. **-wom·en**) a woman living in the region of a frontier.

fron·tis·piece /'frəntisˌpēs/ ▸ n. an illustration facing the title page of a book. [16th C. (sense 2): from Fr. *frontispice* or late L. *frontispicium* 'facade,' from L. *frons, front-* 'front' + *specere* 'to look.']

front line (also **front-line**) ▸ n. (usu. **the front line**) the military line or part of an army that is closest to the enemy: [as adj.] *the front-line troops.* ■ the most important or influential position in a debate or movement.

front-line state ▸ n. a country that borders on an area troubled by a war or other crisis: *Germany will no longer be a front-line state with little strategic depth.*

front-load ▸ v. [trans.] to incur the greater share of expenses in (a project) at the beginning or early stages.

front·man /'frəntˌman; -mən/ ▸ n. (pl. **-men**) a person who leads or represents a group or organization, in particular: ■ the leader of a group of musicians, esp. the lead singer of a pop group. ■ (also **front**) a person who represents an illegal or disreputable organization to give it an air of legitimacy.

front mat·ter ▸ n. the pages preceding the main text of a book, including the title, table of contents, and preface.

front mon·ey ▸ n. money received at the beginning of the period of a contract, or money spent in advance of a business operation before income can be obtained.

front of·fice ▸ n. the management or administrative officers of a business or other organization.

front-page ▸ adj. appearing on the first page of a newspaper or similar publication and containing important or remarkable news. ■ worthy of being printed on the first page of a newspaper, etc. ▸ v. [trans.] print (a story) on the first page of a newspaper, etc.

Front Range the easternmost mountain range of the Rockies, chiefly in Colorado, that reaches 14,270 feet (4,349 m) at Grays Peak; also home to Pikes Peak.

front run·ner ▸ n. the contestant that is leading in a race or other competition.

front-run·ning ▸ adj. ahead in a race or other competition. ▸ n. Stock Market the practice by market makers of dealing on advance information provided by their brokers and investment analysts, before their clients have been given the information.

front-wheel drive ▸ n. a transmission system that provides power to the front wheels of a motor vehicle.

Frost /frôst/, Robert Lee (1874–1963), US poet. Much of his poetry reflects his ties to New England, as in the collection *New Hampshire* (1923).

frost /frôst/ ▸ n. a deposit of small white ice crystals formed on the ground or other surfaces when the temperature falls below freezing. ■ a period of cold weather when such deposits form. ■ fig. a chilling or dispiriting quality, esp. one conveyed by a cold manner. ▸ v. [trans.] cover (something) with or as if with small ice crystals; freeze. ■ [intrans.] become covered with small ice crystals: *a mustache that* ***frosts up*** *when he's ice-climbing.* ■ decorate (a cake, cupcake, or other baked item) with icing. ■ tint hair strands to change the color of isolated strands. ■ injure (a plant) by freezing weather. ■ informal anger or annoy: *such discrimination frosted her.* — **frost·less** adj. [OE *frost, forst*, of Gmc. origin; rel. to Du. *vorst* and Ger. *Frost*, also to FREEZE.]

frost·bite /'frôstˌbīt/ ▸ n. injury to body tissues caused by exposure to extreme cold, often resulting in gangrene.

frost·ed /'frôstid/ ▸ adj. covered with or as if with frost. ■ (of glass or a window) having a translucent textured surface so that it is difficult to see through. ■ (of food) decorated or dusted with icing or sugar. ■ (of hair) having isolated strands tinted a light color.

frost-free ▸ adj. free of a buildup of ice without defrosting: *a frost-free freezer.*

frost heave ▸ n. the uplift of soil or other surface deposits due to expansion of groundwater on freezing. ■ a mound formed in this way, esp. when broken through the pavement of a road. — **frost heav·ing** n.

frost·ing /'frôstiNG/ ▸ n. icing.

frost line ▸ n. [in sing.] the maximum depth of ground below which the soil does not freeze in winter.

frost·y /'frôstē/ ▸ adj. (**frost·i·er**, **frost·i·est**) **1** (of the weather) very cold with frost forming on surfaces. ■ covered with or as if with frost. **2** cold and unfriendly in manner. — **frost·i·ly** /'frôstəlē/ adv. **frost·i·ness** /-stēnis/ n.

froth /frôTH/ ▸ n. a mass of small bubbles in liquid caused by agitation, fermentation, etc.; foam. ■ impure matter that rises to the surface of liquid. ■ fig. a thing that rises or overflows in a soft, light mass. ■ worthless or insubstantial talk, ideas, or activities. ▸ v. [intrans.] form or contain a rising or overflowing mass of small bubbles: *he took a quick sip of beer as it frothed out of the can* | [as adj.] (**frothing**) *scooping salmon out of the frothing gorge.*

– PHRASES **froth at the mouth** emit a large amount of saliva from the mouth in a bodily seizure. ■ fig. display intense anger. [ME: from ON *frotha, frauth.*]

froth·y /'frôTHē; -T͟Hē/ ▸ adj. (**froth·i·er**, **froth·i·est**) full of or covered with a mass of small bubbles. ■ light and entertaining but of little substance. — **froth·i·ly** /-THəlē; T͟Həlē/ adv. **froth·i·ness** /-THēnis; T͟Hēnis/ n.

frot·tage /frô'täZH/ ▸ n. **1** Art the technique or process of taking a rubbing from an uneven surface to form the basis of a work of art. ■ a work of art produced in this way. **2** the practice of touching or rubbing against the clothed body of another person in a crowd as a means of obtaining sexual gratification. — **frot·teur** /-'tər/ n. (pl. same) (in sense 2) **frot·teur·ism** /-'tərˌizəm/ n. (in sense 2). [1930s: Fr., 'rubbing, friction.']

frou·frou /'fro͞oˌfro͞o/ (also **frou-frou**) ▸ n. a rustling noise made by someone walking in a dress. ■ frills or other ornamentation, particularly of women's clothes: [as adj.] *a little froufrou skirt.* [19th C.: from Fr., imitative.]

fro·ward /'frō(w)ərd/ ▸ adj. (of a person) difficult to deal with; contrary. — **fro·ward·ly** adv. **fro·ward·ness** n. [OE *frāward* 'leading away from, away,' based on ON *frá* (see FRO, FROM).]

frown /froun/ ▸ v. [intrans.] furrow one's brow in an expression indicating disapproval, displeasure, or concentration. ■ (**frown on/upon**) disapprove of: *the old Russian rural system frowned on private enterprise.* ▸ n. a facial expression or look characterized by such a furrowing of one's brows: *a frown of disapproval.* — **frown·er** n. **frown·ing·ly** adv. [ME: from OFr. *froignier*, from *froigne* 'surly look,' of Celtic origin.]

frowz·y /'frouzē/ (also **frows·y**) ▸ adj. (**frowz·i·er**, **frowz·i·est**) scruffy and neglected in appearance. ■ dingy and stuffy: *a frowzy nightclub.* — **frowz·i·ness** /-zēnis/ n. [17th C. (orig. dial.): of unknown origin.]

froze /frōz/ past of FREEZE.

fro·zen /'frōzən/ past participle of FREEZE.

FRS ▸ abbr. ■ Federal Reserve System. ■ (in the UK) Fellow of the Royal Society.

frt. ▸ abbr. freight.

fruc·tose /'frəktōs; -tōz; 'fro͝ok-/ ▸ n. Chem. a sugar of the hexose class found esp. in honey and fruit. [19th C.: from L. *fructus* 'fruit' + -OSE[2].]

frug /fro͞og/ ▸ n. a vigorous dance to pop music, popular in the mid-1960s. ▸ v. (**frugged**, **frug·ging**) [intrans.] perform such a dance. [of unknown origin.]

fru·gal /'fro͞ogəl/ ▸ adj. sparing or economical with regard to money or food. ■ simple and plain and costing little: *a frugal meal.* — **fru·gal·i·ty** /fro͞o'galitē/ n. **fru·gal·ly** adv. **fru·gal·ness** n. [16th C.: from L. *frugalis*, from *frugi* 'economical, thrifty,' from *frux, frug-* 'fruit.']

fruit /fro͞ot/ ▸ n. **1** the sweet and fleshy product of a tree or other plant that contains seed and can be eaten as food. ■ Bot. the seed-bearing structure of a plant, e.g., an acorn. ■ the result or reward of work or activity. ■ archaic literary natural produce that can be used for food: *the fruits of the earth.* ■ archaic offspring: *the fruit of her womb.* **2** derog. a male homosexual. ▸ v. [intrans.] (of a tree or other plant) produce fruit, typically at a specified time: *the trees fruit very early* | [as n.] (**fruiting**) *cover strawberries with cloches to encourage early fruiting.*

– PHRASES **bear fruit** have good results. **in fruit** (of a tree or plant) at the stage of producing fruit. [ME: from OFr., from L. *fructus* 'enjoyment of produce, harvest,' from *frui* 'enjoy.']

fruit·ar·i·an /fro͞o'te(ə)rēən/ ▸ n. a person who eats only fruit. — **fruit·ar·i·an·ism** n.

fruit bat ▸ n. a bat (family Pteropodidae) with a long snout and large eyes, feeding chiefly on fruit or nectar and found mainly in the Old World tropics.

fruit·cake /'fro͞otˌkāk/ ▸ n. a cake containing dried fruit and nuts. ■ informal an eccentric or insane person. [cf. *nutty as a fruitcake* (see NUTTY).]

fruit cock·tail ▸ n. a finely chopped fruit salad, often commercially produced in cans.

fruit cup ▸ n. a salad made of chopped fruit and served in a glass dish as an appetizer or dessert.

fruit·ed /'fro͞otid/ ▸ adj. [usu. in comb.] (of a tree or plant) producing fruit, esp. of a specified kind: *heavy-fruited plants like tomatoes.*

fruit fly ▸ n. a small fly (families Drosophilidae and Tephritidae) that feeds on fruit in both its adult and larval stages.

fruit·ful /ˈfro͞otfəl/ ▶ **adj.** (of a tree, a plant, or land) producing much fruit; fertile. ■ producing good or helpful results; productive: *years of fruitful collaboration | the two days of talks had been fruitful.* ■ (of a person) producing many offspring. — **fruit·ful·ly adv. fruit·ful·ness n.**

fruit·ing bod·y ▶ **n.** Bot. the spore-producing organ of a fungus, often seen as a toadstool.

fru·i·tion /fro͞oˈisʜən/ ▶ **n.** the point at which a plan or project is realized: *the plans have* ***come to fruition*** *sooner than expected.* ■ [in sing.] the realization of a plan or project: *new methods will come with the fruition of that research.* [ME (in the sense 'enjoyment'): via OFr. from late L. *fruitio(n-)*, from *frui* 'enjoy.']

fruit·less /ˈfro͞otlis/ ▶ **adj. 1** failing to achieve the desired results; unproductive or useless: *his fruitless attempts to publish poetry.* **2** (of a tree or plant) not producing fruit. — **fruit·less·ly adv. fruit·less·ness n.**

fruit sal·ad ▶ **n.** a mixture of different types of chopped fruit served in syrup or juice. ■ military slang a display of medals and other decorations.

fruit sug·ar ▶ **n.** another term for FRUCTOSE.

fruit tree ▶ **n.** a tree grown for its edible fruit.

fruit·wood /ˈfro͞otˌwo͝od/ ▶ **n.** [usu. as adj.] the wood of a fruit tree, esp. when used in furniture: *a fruitwood dressing table.*

fruit·y /ˈfro͞otē/ ▶ **adj.** (**fruit·i·er, fruit·i·est**) **1** (esp. of food or drink) of, resembling, or containing fruit: *a light and fruity Beaujolais.* **2** (of a voice or sound) mellow, deep, and rich: *Jeff had a wonderfully fruity voice.* **3** derog. relating to or associated with homosexuals. **4** informal eccentric or crazy: *a kind of fruity professor.* — **fruit·i·ly adv. fruit·i·ness n.**

frump /frəmp/ ▶ **n.** an unattractive woman who wears dowdy old-fashioned clothes. — **frump·i·ly** /ˈfrəmpəlē/ **adv. frump·i·ness** /ˈfrəmpēnis/ **n. frump·ish adj. frump·ish·ly adv. frump·y adj.** [16th C.: prob. a contr. of ME *frumple* 'wrinkle,' from MDu. *verrompelen*.]

Frun·ze /ˈfro͞onzə/ former name of BISHKEK.

frus·ta /ˈfrəstə/ plural form of FRUSTUM.

frus·trate /ˈfrəstrāt/ ▶ **v.** [trans.] prevent (a plan or attempted action) from progressing, succeeding, or being fulfilled: *his attempt to frustrate the merger.* ■ prevent (someone) from doing or achieving something. ■ cause (someone) to feel upset or annoyed, typically as a result of being unable to change or achieve something. [as adj.] (**frustrating**) — **frus·trat·er n. frus·trat·ing·ly adv.** [as submodifier] *progress turned out to be frustratingly slow.* [ME: from L. *frustrat-* 'disappointed,' from the v. *frustrare*, from *frustra* 'in vain.']

frus·trat·ed /ˈfrəsˌtrātid/ ▶ **adj.** feeling or expressing distress and annoyance, esp. because of inability to change or achieve something. ■ [attrib.] (of a person) unable to follow or be successful in a particular career. ■ [attrib.] prevented from progressing, succeeding, or being fulfilled. ■ (of a person or sexual desire) unfulfilled sexually. — **frus·trat·ed·ly adv.**

frus·tra·tion /frəˈstrāsʜən/ ▶ **n.** the feeling of being upset or annoyed, esp. because of inability to change or achieve something. ■ an event or circumstance that causes one to have such a feeling. ■ the prevention of the progress, success, or fulfillment of something.

frus·tum /ˈfrəstəm/ ▶ **n.** (pl. **-ta** /-tə/ or **-tums**) Geom. the portion of a cone or pyramid that remains after its upper part has been cut off by a plane parallel to its base, or that is intercepted between two such planes. [17th C.: from L., 'piece cut off.']

Fry /frī/, Christopher Harris (1907–2005), English playwright, noted for his comic verse dramas, such as *The Lady's Not for Burning* (1948).

fry¹ /frī/ ▶ **v.** (**fries, fried**) [trans.] cook (food) in hot fat or oil, typically in a shallow pan. ■ [intrans.] (of food) be cooked in such a way: *put half a dozen steaks to fry in a pan.* ■ [intrans.] informal (of a person) burn or overheat. ■ informal execute or be executed by electrocution. ▶ **n.** (pl. **fries**) [in sing.] a meal of meat or other food cooked in such a way. ■ a social gathering where fried food is served: *you'll explore islands and stop for a fish fry.* ■ (**fries**) another term for FRENCH FRIES. [ME: from OFr. *frire*, from L. *frigere*.]

fry² ▶ **plural n.** young fish, esp. when newly hatched. [ME: from ON *frjó*.]

fry·er /ˈfrīər/ (also **fri·er**) ▶ **n. 1** a large, deep container for frying food. **2** a small young chicken suitable for frying.

fry·ing pan (also **fry·pan**) ▶ **n.** a shallow pan with a long handle, used for cooking food in hot fat or oil.

– PHRASES **out of the frying pan into the fire** from a bad situation to one that is worse.

FSH ▶ **abbr.** follicle-stimulating hormone.

FSLIC ▶ **abbr.** Federal Savings and Loan Insurance Corporation.

FST ▶ **abbr.** flat-screen television.

f-stop ▶ **n.** Photog. a camera setting corresponding to a particular f-number.

FT ▶ **abbr.** ■ Basketball free throw. ■ full-time.

Ft. ▶ **abbr.** Fort: *Ft. Lauderdale.*

ft. ▶ **abbr.** foot; feet.

FTA ▶ **abbr.** Free Trade Agreement, used to refer to that signed in 1988 between the US and Canada.

FTC ▶ **abbr.** Federal Trade Commission.

fth. ▶ **abbr.** fathom.

ft-lb ▶ **abbr.** foot-pound.

FTP Comput. ▶ **abbr.** file transfer protocol, a standard for the exchange of program and data files across a network. ▶ **v.** (**FTP'd** or **FTPed, FTPing**) [trans.] informal transfer (a file) from one computer or system to another, esp. on the Internet.

Fu·ad /fo͞oˈäd/ the name of two kings of Egypt: ■ Fuad I (1868–1936), reigned 1922–36. ■ Fuad II (1952–), reigned 1952–53; grandson of Fuad I.

fu·bar /ˈfo͞oˌbär/ ▶ **adj.** informal out of working order; seriously, perhaps irreparably, damaged: *the clock in the hall is fubar.* [1940s: acronym from *fucked up beyond all recognition* (or *repair*).]

Fuchs¹ /fyo͝oks; fo͝oks/, Emil Klaus Julius (1911–88), British physicist; born in Germany. He passed secret information regarding the atom bomb to the Soviet Union during the 1940s.

Fuchs² /fyo͝oks/, Sir Vivian Ernest (1908–99), English explorer. He made the first overland crossing of the Antarctic 1955–58.

fuch·sia /ˈfyo͞osʜə/ ▶ **n. 1** a shrub (genus *Fuchsia*, family Onagraceae) with pendulous tubular flowers that are typically of two contrasting colors. Native to America and New Zealand, they are commonly grown as ornamentals. **2** a vivid purplish-red color. ▶ **adj.** purplish red. [mod. L., named in honor of Leonhard *Fuchs* (1501–66), German botanist.]

fuch·sin /ˈfyo͞oksən; -ˌsēn/ (also **fuch·sine**) ▶ **n.** a deep red synthetic dye ($C_{20}H_{20}N_3Cl$) used as a biological stain and disinfectant. [19th C.: from Ger. *Fuchs* 'fox.']

fu·ci /ˈfyo͞osī; -sē/ plural form of FUCUS.

fuck /fək/ vulgar slang ▶ **v.** [trans.] **1** have sexual intercourse with (someone). ■ [intrans.] (of two people) have sexual intercourse. **2** ruin or damage (something). ▶ **n.** an act of sexual intercourse. ■ [with adj.] a sexual partner. ▶ **exclam.** used alone or as a noun (**the fuck**) or a verb in various phrases to express anger, annoyance, contempt, impatience, or surprise, or simply for emphasis.

– PHRASES **go fuck yourself** an exclamation expressing anger or contempt for, or rejection of, someone. **not give a fuck** (**about**) used to emphasize indifference or contempt.

– PHRASAL VERBS **fuck around** spend time doing unimportant or trivial things. ■ have sexual intercourse with a variety of partners. ■ (**fuck around with**) meddle with. **fuck off** [usu. in imper.] (of a person) go away. **fuck someone over** treat someone in an unfair or humiliating way. **fuck someone up** damage or confuse someone emotionally. **fuck something up** (or **fuck up**) do something badly or ineptly. [16th C.: of Gmc. origin (compare Swed. dial. *focka*); possibly from an Indo-Eur. root meaning 'strike,' shared by L. *pugnus* 'fist.']

fuck·er /ˈfəkər/ ▶ **n.** vulgar slang a contemptible or stupid person (often used as a general term of abuse).

fuck·head /ˈfəkˌhed/ ▶ **n.** vulgar slang a stupid or contemptible person (often used as a general term of abuse).

fuck·ing /ˈfəkiNG/ ▶ **adj.** [attrib.] & **adv.** [as submodifier] vulgar slang used for emphasis or to express anger, annoyance, contempt, or surprise.

fuck-up ▶ **n.** vulgar slang a mess or muddle. ■ a person who has a tendency to make a mess of things.

fu·coid /ˈfyo͞okoid/ Bot. ▶ **n.** a brown seaweed or fossil plant (order Fucales) of a group to which bladderwrack belongs. ▶ **adj.** of, relating to, or resembling a brown seaweed, esp. a fucoid. [19th C.: from FUCUS + -OID.]

fu·cus /ˈfyo͞okəs/ ▶ **n.** (pl. **fu·ci** /ˈfyo͞osī; -sē/) a seaweed of a large genus (genus *Fucus*) of brown algae having flat leathery fronds. — **fu·coid** /-ˌkoid/ **adj.** [17th C. (denoting a cosmetic): from L., 'rock lichen, red dye, rouge,' from Gk. *phukos* 'seaweed,' of Semitic origin.]

fud·dle /ˈfədl/ ▶ **v.** [trans.] [usu. as adj.] (**fuddled**) confuse or stupefy (someone), esp. with alcohol. ▶ **n.** [in sing.] a state of confusion or intoxication. [16th C. (in the sense 'go on a drinking bout'): of unknown origin.]

fud·dy-dud·dy /ˈfədē ˌdədē/ ▶ **n.** (pl. **-dies**) informal a person who is old-fashioned and fussy. [20th C. (orig. dial.): of unknown origin.]

fudge /fəj/ ▶ **n. 1** a soft candy made from sugar, butter, and milk or cream. ■ rich chocolate, used esp. as a filling for cakes or a sauce on ice cream. **2** an instance of faking or ambiguity: *the new settlement is a fudge rushed out to win cheers at the conference.* **3** a piece of late news inserted in a newspaper page. ▶ **v.** [trans.] present or deal with (something) in a vague, noncommittal, or inadequate way, esp. so as to conceal the truth or mislead: *a temptation to fudge the issue.* ■ adjust or manipulate (facts or figures) so as to present a desired picture. ▶ **exclam.** dated nonsense (expressing disbelief or annoyance). [17th C.: prob. an alt. of obs. *fadge* 'to fit.']

fudge fac·tor ▶ **n.** informal a figure included in a calculation to account for error or unanticipated circumstances, or to ensure a desired result.

fueh·rer /ˈfyo͝orər/ ▶ **n.** var. of FÜHRER.

fu·el /ˈfyo͞oəl/ ▶ **n.** material such as coal, gas, or oil that is burned to produce heat or power. ■ short for NUCLEAR FUEL. ■ food, drink, or drugs as a source of energy. ■ a thing that sustains or inflames passion, argument, or other emotion or activity: *the remuneration packages will add fuel to the debate.* ▶ **v.** (**fu·eled, fu·el·ing**; Brit. **fu·elled, fu·el·ling**) [trans.] **1** supply or power (an industrial plant, vehicle, or machine) with fuel: fig. *a big novel that is fueled by anger and revenge.* ■ fill up (a vehicle, aircraft, or ship) with oil or gasoline. ■ [intrans.] (**fuel up**) (of a person) eat a meal: *arrive straight from work and fuel up on the complimentary buffet.* **2** cause (a fire) to burn more intensely. ■ sustain or inflame (a feeling or activity): *his rascal heart and private pain fuel his passion as an actor.*

– PHRASES **add fuel to the fire** (or **flames**) fig. cause a situation or conflict to become more intense, esp. by provocative comments. [ME: from OFr. *fouaille*, based on L. *focus* 'hearth' (in late L. 'fire').]

fu·el cell ▶ n. a cell producing an electric current directly from a chemical reaction.

fu·el el·e·ment ▶ n. an element consisting of nuclear fuel and other materials for use in a reactor.

fu·el in·jec·tion ▶ n. the direct introduction of fuel under pressure into the combustion units of an internal combustion engine. — **fu·el-in·ject·ed** adj.

fu·el oil ▶ n. oil used as fuel in an engine or furnace.

fu·el rod ▶ n. a rod-shaped fuel element in a nuclear reactor.

Fuen·tes /'fwentās/, Carlos (1928–), Mexican writer. His works include *The Old Gringo* (1984).

fu·gac·i·ty /fyo͞o'gasitē/ ▶ n. Chem. a thermodynamic property of a real gas that, if substituted for the pressure or partial pressure in the equations for an ideal gas, gives equations applicable to the real gas. [17th C.: from L. *fugax, fugac-*, from *fugere* 'flee.']

fu·gal /'fyo͞ogəl/ ▶ adj. of the nature of a fugue: *the virtuosity of the fugal finale.* — **fu·gal·ly** adv.

-fuge ▶ comb. form expelling or dispelling either a specified thing or in a specified way: *vermifuge* | *centrifuge.* [from mod. L. *-fugus*, from L. *fugare* 'cause to flee.']

fu·gi·tive /'fyo͞ojətiv/ ▶ n. a person who has escaped from a place or is in hiding, esp. to avoid arrest or persecution. ■ [as adj.] fig. quick to disappear; fleeting. [ME: from OFr. *fugitif, -ive*, from L. *fugitivus*, from *fugere* 'flee.']

fu·gu /'f(y)o͞ogo͞o/ ▶ n. a puffer fish that is eaten as a Japanese delicacy, after some highly poisonous parts have been removed by an authorized chef. [20th C.: from Japanese.]

fugue /fyo͞og/ ▶ n. **1** Music a contrapuntal composition in which a short melody or phrase (the subject) is introduced by one part and successively taken up by others and developed by interweaving the parts. **2** Psychiatry a state or period of loss of awareness of one's identity, often coupled with flight from one's usual environment, associated with certain forms of hysteria and epilepsy. [16th C.: from Fr., or from Ital. *fuga*, from L. *fuga* 'flight,' rel. to *fugere* 'flee.']

füh·rer /'fyo͝orər/ (also **fueh·rer**) ▶ n. a ruthless, tyrannical leader. [20th C.: from Ger. *Führer* 'leader.']

Fu·jai·rah /fo͞o'jīrə/ (also **Al Fu·jay·rah**) a member state of the United Arab Emirates; pop. 76,000.

Fu·ji, Mount /'fo͞ojē/ a dormant volcano on the island of Honshu in Japan. Japan's highest mountain, it rises to 12,385 feet (3,776 m) and is regarded as sacred by the Japanese. Also called FUJIYAMA /,fo͞ojē'ämə/.

Fu·jian /'fo͞o'jyän/ (also **Fu·kien** /'fo͞o'kyen/) a province in southeastern China; capital, Fuzhou.

Fu·ku·o·ka /,fo͞oko͞o'ōkə/ a city in southern Japan, capital of Kyushu island; pop. 1,237,000.

-ful ▶ suffix **1** (forming adjectives from nouns) full of: *sorrowful.* ■ having the qualities of: *masterful.* **2** forming adjectives from adjectives or from Latin stems with little change of sense: *grateful.* **3** (forming adjectives from verbs) apt to; able to; accustomed to: *forgetful* | *watchful.* **4** (pl. **-fuls**) forming nouns denoting the amount needed to fill the specified container, holder, etc.: *bucketful* | *handful.* [from FULL.]

Fu·la /'fo͞olə/ ▶ n. the Benue-Congo language of the Fulani people, spoken as a first language by about 10 million people and widely used in West Africa as a lingua franca. Also called FUL, FULANI.

Fu·la·ni /fo͞o'länē/ ▶ n. (pl. same) **1** a member of a people living in a region of West Africa from Senegal to northern Nigeria and Cameroon. They are traditionally nomadic cattle herders of Muslim faith. **2** another term for FULA. ▶ adj. of or relating to this people or their language. [the name in Hausa.]

Ful·bright /'fo͝ol,brīt/, James William (1905–95), US politician. A US senator 1945–74, he sponsored the Fulbright Act of 1946, which finances exchange programs of students and teachers between the US and other countries.

ful·crum /'fo͝olkrəm; 'fəl-/ ▶ n. (pl. **-cra** /-krə/ or **-crums**) the point on which a lever rests or is supported. See illustration at LEVER. ■ a thing that plays a central or essential role in an activity, event, or situation: *research is the fulcrum of the academic community.* [17th C.: from L., lit. 'post of a couch,' from *fulcire* 'to prop up.']

ful·fill /fo͝ol'fil/ (Brit. **ful·fil**) ▶ v. **1** bring to completion or reality; achieve or realize (something desired, promised, or predicted). ■ (**fulfill oneself**) gain happiness or satisfaction by fully developing one's abilities or character. ■ archaic complete (a period of time or piece of work). **2** carry out (a task, duty, or role) as required, pledged, or expected. ■ satisfy or meet (a requirement or condition). — **ful·fill·a·ble** adj. **ful·fill·er** n. [OE *fullfyllan* 'fill up, make full' (see FULL, FILL).]

ful·filled /fo͝ol'fild/ ▶ adj. satisfied or happy because of fully developing one's abilities or character.

ful·fill·ing /fo͝ol'filiNG/ ▶ adj. making someone satisfied or happy because of fully developing their character or abilities: *a fulfilling and rewarding career.*

ful·fill·ment /fo͝ol'filmənt/ (Brit. **ful·fil·ment**) ▶ n. **1** satisfaction or happiness as a result of fully developing one's abilities or character: *she did not believe that marriage was the key to happiness and fulfillment.* **2** the achievement of something desired, promised, or predicted: *winning the championship was the fulfillment of a childhood dream.* ■ the meeting of a requirement or condition: *the fulfillment of statutory requirements.* ■ the performance of a task, duty, or role as required, pledged, or expected.

Fu·ling /'fo͞o'liNG/ a city in Sichuan province, in central China; pop. 986,000.

full /fo͝ol/ ▶ adj. **1** containing or holding as much or as many as possible; having no empty space: *wastebaskets full of rubbish* | *she could only nod, for her mouth was full.* ■ having eaten or drunk to one's limits or satisfaction. See also FULL UP below. ■ [predic.] (**full of**) containing or holding much or many; having a large number of: *his diary is full of entries about her.* ■ [predic.] (**full of**) having a lot of (a particular quality): *she was full of confidence.* ■ [predic.] (**full of**) completely engrossed with; unable to stop talking or thinking about: *Anna had been full of her day, saying how Mitch had described England to her.* ■ filled with intense emotion: *she picked at her food, her heart too full to eat.* ■ involving a lot of activities: *he lived a full life.* **2** [attrib.] not lacking or omitting anything; complete: *fill in your full name below* | *full details on request.* ■ (often used for emphasis) reaching the utmost limit; maximum: *he reached for the engine control and turned it up to full power* | *John made full use of all the tuition provided.* ■ having all the privileges and status attached to a particular position: *the country applied for full membership in the European Community.* ■ (of a report or account) containing as much detail or information as possible. ■ used to emphasize an amount or quantity: *he kept his fast pace going for the full 14-mile distance.* **3** (of a person or part of their body) plump or rounded: *she had full lips* | *the fuller figure.* ■ (of the hair) having body. ■ (of a garment) made using much material arranged in folds or gathers, or generously cut so as to fit loosely: *the dress has a square neck and a full skirt.* ■ (of a sound) strong and resonant. ■ (of a flavor or color) rich or intense. ▶ adv. **1** straight; directly: *she turned her head and looked full into his face.* **2** very: *he knew full well she was too polite to barge in.* ■ archaic entirely (used to emphasize an amount or quantity): *they talked for full half an hour.* ▶ n. the state or time of full moon. ▶ v. **1** [trans.] black English make (something) full; fill up: *he full up the house with bawling.* **2** [trans.] gather or pleat (fabric) so as to make a garment full.

– PHRASES **full of beans** see BEAN. **full of oneself** very self-satisfied and with an exaggerated sense of self-worth. **full on 1** running at or providing maximum power or capacity: *he had the heater full on.* **2** so as to make a direct or significant impact: *the recession has hit us full on.* ■ (**full-on**) informal (of an activity or thing) not diluted in nature or effect: *this is full-on ballroom boogie.* **full out** as much or as far as possible; with maximum effort or power: *he held his foot to the floor until the car raced full out.* **full steam** (or **speed**) **ahead** used to indicate that one should proceed with as much speed or energy as possible. **full to the brim** see BRIM. **full up** filled to capacity. ■ having eaten or drunk so much that one is replete. **in full** with nothing omitted: *I shall expect your life story in full.* ■ to the full amount due: *their relocation costs would be paid in full.* ■ to the utmost; completely: *the textbooks have failed to exploit in full the opportunities offered.* **to the full** to the greatest possible extent: *enjoy your free trip to Europe to the full.* [OE, of Gmc. origin; rel. to Du. *vol* and Ger. *voll.*]

full·back /'fo͝ol,bak/ ▶ n. **1** Football an offensive player in the backfield. ■ an offensive position in the backfield. **2** (in a game such as soccer or field hockey) a player in a defensive position near the goal. ■ a defensive position near the goal.

full-blood·ed ▶ adj. **1** [attrib.] of unmixed race. ■ fig. genuine; pure. **2** vigorous, enthusiastic, and without compromise. — **full blood** n. (in sense 1) **full-blood·ed·ly** adv. **full-blood·ed·ness** n.

full-blown ▶ adj. fully developed. ■ (of a flower) in full bloom.

full-bod·ied ▶ adj. rich and satisfying in flavor or sound.

full bore ▶ adv. at full speed or maximum capacity: *the boat came full bore toward us.* ■ fig. complete; thoroughgoing: *a full-bore leftist.*

full col·or ▶ n. the full range of colors.

full-court press ▶ n. Basketball a defensive tactic in which members of a team cover their opponents throughout the court and not just near their own basket. ■ fig. an instance of aggressive pressure: *if the president mounts a full-court press for the space station.*

full dress ▶ n. clothes worn on ceremonial or formal occasions. ▶ adj. [attrib.] denoting an event, activity, or process that is treated with complete seriousness or that possesses all the characteristics of a genuine example of the type: *shuttle diplomacy is better than a full-dress conference.*

full dress u·ni·form ▶ n. a military uniform worn on ceremonial occasions.

full em·ploy·ment ▶ n. the condition in which virtually all who are able and willing to work are employed.

Ful·ler[1] /'fo͝olər/, Melville Weston (1833–1910), Chief Justice of the US 1888–1910.

Ful·ler[2] /'fo͝olər/, Sarah Margaret (1810–50), US literary critic and social activist. She advocated cultural education for women and was literary critic of the *New York Tribune* 1844–46.

Full·er[3] /'fo͝olər/, R. Buckminster (1895–1983), US architect; full name *Richard Buckminster Fuller.* He is best known for his invention of the geodesic dome.

full·er·ene /,fo͝olə'rēn/ ▶ n. Chem. a form of carbon having a large spheroidal molecule consisting of a hollow cage of atoms, of which buckminsterfullerene was the first known example. [20th C.: contr. of BUCKMINSTERFULLERENE.]

ful·ler's earth ▶ n. a type of clay used in fulling cloth and as an adsorbent.

[*fuller* 'person who shrinks cloth,' from OE *fullere*, from L. *fullo*.]

ful·ler's tea·sel ▶ n. a teasel (*Dipsacus sativus*) with stiff bracts that curve backward from the prickly flowerhead.

Ful·ler·ton /'fo͝olərtən/ a city in southwestern California; pop. 114,144.

full face ▶ adv. with all of the face visible; facing directly at someone or something: *she looked full face at the mirror.* ▶ adj. [attrib.] **1** showing all of the face: *a full-face mug shot.* **2** covering all of the face: *a full-face motorcycle helmet.*

full-fash·ioned ▶ adj. (of women's clothing, esp. hosiery) shaped and seamed to fit the body: *full-fashioned stockings.* ▪ (of a knitted garment) shaped by increasing or decreasing the number of loops made along the fabric length without alteration of the stitch.

full-fig·ured ▶ adj. (of women's clothing) designed for larger women.

full-fledged ▶ adj. completely developed or established; of full status.

full flood ▶ n. the tide or a river at its highest. ▪ (**in full flood**) speaking enthusiastically and volubly: *she was in full flood about the glories of bicycling.*

full-fron·tal ▶ adj. (of nudity or a nude figure) with full exposure of the front of the body. ▪ with nothing concealed or held back: *they put a full-frontal guitar assault to clever lyrics.*

full-grown ▶ adj. having reached maturity.

full-heart·ed ▶ adj. with great enthusiasm and commitment; full of sincere feeling: *full-hearted consent of the electorate.* — **full-heart·ed·ly** adv. **full-heart·ed·ness** n.

full house ▶ n. [in sing.] **1** an audience, or a group of people attending a meeting, that fills the venue for the event to capacity. **2** a poker hand with three of a kind and a pair, beating a flush and losing to four of a kind. ▪ a winning card at bingo in which all the numbers have been successfully marked off.

full-length ▶ adj. of the standard length. ▪ (of a garment or curtain) extending to, or almost to, the ground. ▪ (of a mirror or portrait) showing the whole human figure. ▶ adv. (usu. **full length**) (of a person) with the body lying stretched out and flat.

full marks ▶ plural n. the maximum award in an examination or assessment. ▪ praise for someone's intelligence, hard work, or other quality: *she had to give him full marks for originality.*

full meas·ure ▶ n. the total amount or extent.

full moon ▶ n. the phase of the moon in which its whole disk is illuminated. ▪ the time when this occurs.

full-mo·tion vid·e·o (abbr.: **FMV**) ▶ n. digital video data that is transmitted or stored on video discs for real-time reproduction on a computer (or other multimedia system) at a rate of not less than 25 frames per second.

full·ness /'fo͝olnis/ (also **ful·ness**) ▶ n. **1** the state of being filled to capacity. ▪ the state of having eaten enough or more than enough and feeling full. ▪ the state of being complete or whole. ▪ (in or alluding to biblical use) all that is contained in the world. **2** (of a person's body or part of it) the state of being filled out so as to produce a rounded shape: *the childish fullness of his cheeks.* ▪ (of a garment or the hair) the condition of having been cut or designed to give a full shape. ▪ richness or intensity of flavor, sound, or color.
– PHRASES **in the fullness of time** after a due length of time has elapsed; eventually: *he'll tell us in the fullness of time.*

full page ▶ n. [usu. as adj.] an entire page of a newspaper or magazine: *full-page advertisements.*

full pro·fes·sor ▶ n. see PROFESSOR. — **full pro·fes·sor·ship** n.

full-scale ▶ adj. of the same size as the thing represented: *a huge tank containing two full-scale pirate ships.* ▪ unrestricted in size, extent, or intensity; complete and thorough: *a full-scale invasion of the mainland.*

full score ▶ n. a score of a musical composition giving the parts for all performers on separate staves.

full-size ▶ adj. **1** of normal size for its type. ▪ (of a bed) having the dimensions suitable for two people, specifically 54 inches by 75 inches. **2** enlarged: *click on any item to see a full-size picture.* (Also **full-sized.**)

full term ▶ n. see TERM (sense 2).

full tilt ▶ adv. see TILT.

full-time ▶ adj. occupying or using the whole of someone's available working time, typically 40 hours in a week: *a full-time job.* ▶ adv. on a full-time basis.

full-tim·er ▶ n. a person who does a full-time job.

ful·ly /'fo͝olē/ ▶ adv. **1** completely or entirely; to the furthest extent: *I fully understand the fears of the workers.* ▪ without lacking or omitting anything: [as submodifier] *a fully equipped gymnasium.* **2** no less or fewer than (used to emphasize an amount): *fully 65 percent of all funerals are by cremation.*

-fully ▶ suffix forming adverbs corresponding to adjectives ending in *-ful* (such as *sorrowfully* corresponding to *sorrowful*).

ful·mar /'fo͝olmər; -mär/ ▶ n. a gull-sized gray and white seabird (genus *Fulmarus*) of the petrel family, with a stocky body and tubular nostrils. [17th C.: from Hebridean Norn dial., from ON *fúll* 'stinking, foul.']

ful·mi·nate /'fo͝olmə,nāt; 'fəl-/ ▶ v. [intrans.] express vehement protest. ▪ Med. (**fulminating**) (of a disease or symptom) develop suddenly and severely: *fulminating appendicitis.* [ME: from L. *fulminat-* 'struck by lightning,' from *fulmen, fulmin-* 'lightning.']

ful·mi·nate of mer·cu·ry ▶ n. a white or grayish crystalline powder that when dry is volatile when exposed to heat or pressure and is used as an explosive.

ful·mi·na·tion /,fo͝olmə'nāshən; -fəl-/ ▶ n. (usu. **fulminations**) an expression of vehement protest: ▪ a violent explosion or a flash like lightning.

ful·min·ic ac·id /fo͝ol'minik; fəl-/ ▶ n. Chem. a very unstable acid, HONC, isomeric with cyanic acid. [19th C.: *fulminic* from L. *fulmen, fulmin-* 'lightning' + -IC.]

ful·ness /'fo͝olnəs/ ▶ n. var. of FULLNESS.

ful·some /'fo͝olsəm/ ▶ adj. **1** complimentary or flattering to an excessive degree: *they are almost embarrassingly fulsome in their appreciation.* **2** of large size or quantity; generous or abundant. — **ful·some·ly** adv. **ful·some·ness** n. [ME (in the sense 'abundant'): from FULL + -SOME[1].]

Ful·ton /'fo͝oltn/, Robert (1765–1815), US inventor. In 1800, he constructed a steam-propelled "diving-boat," the first submarine. In 1806, he built the first successful paddle steamer, the *Clermont*.

Fu Man·chu /'fo͞o man'cho͞o/ (in full **Fu Manchu mustache**) ▶ n. a long narrow mustache in which the ends taper and droop down to the chin. [20th C.: *Fu Manchu*, a master criminal in the novels of British writer Sax Rohmer (1883–1959).]

Fu Manchu

fu·mar·ic ac·id /fyo͞o'marik/ ▶ n. Chem. a crystalline acid, HOOCCH=CHCOOH, isomeric with maleic acid, present in fumitory and many other plants. — **fu·ma·rate** /'fyo͞omə,rāt/ n. [19th C.: *fumaric* from mod. L. *Fumaria* 'fumitory' + -IC.]

fu·ma·role /'fyo͞omə,rōl/ ▶ n. an opening in or near a volcano, through which hot sulfurous gases emerge. — **fu·ma·rol·ic** /,fyo͞omə'rōlik/ adj. [19th C.: from obs. Ital. *fumaruolo*, from late L. *fumariolum* 'vent, hole for smoke,' a dimin. based on L. *fumus* 'smoke.']

fum·ble /'fəmbəl/ ▶ v. [no obj., with adverbial] use the hands clumsily while doing or handling something. ▪ (of the hands) do or handle something clumsily. ▪ (**fumble around/about**) move clumsily in various directions using the hands to find one's way. ▪ [with obj. and adverbial] use the hands clumsily to move (something) as specified: *she fumbled a cigarette from her bag.* ▪ [trans.] Football drop or lose control of (the ball), sometimes causing a turnover. ▪ [trans.] (in other ball games) fail to catch or field (the ball, a pass, a shot, etc.) cleanly. ▪ express oneself or deal with something clumsily or nervously. ▶ n. [usu. in sing.] an act of using the hands clumsily while doing or handling something. ▪ Football an act of dropping or losing control of the ball, sometimes causing a turnover. ▪ (in other ball games) an act of failing to catch or field the ball cleanly. ▪ an act of managing or dealing with something clumsily. — **fum·bler** n. **fum·bling·ly** adv. [ME: from Low Ger. *fommeln* or Du. *fommelen*.]

fume /fyo͞om/ ▶ n. (usu. **fumes**) gas, smoke, or vapor that smells strongly or is dangerous to inhale. ▪ a pungent odor of a particular thing or substance. ▶ v. [intrans.] **1** emit gas, smoke, or vapor: *fragments of lava hit the ground, fuming and sizzling.* ▪ [trans.] [usu. as adj.] (**fumed**) expose (esp. wood) to ammonia fumes in order to produce dark tints: *the fumed oak sideboard.* **2** feel, show, or express great anger. — **fum·ing·ly** adv. **fum·y** adj. [ME: from OFr. *fumer* (v.), from L. *fumare* 'to smoke.']

fume hood ▶ n. a ventilated enclosure in a chemistry laboratory, in which harmful volatile chemicals can be used or kept.

fu·mi·gate /'fyo͞omə,gāt/ ▶ v. [trans.] apply the fumes of certain chemicals to (an area) to disinfect it or to rid it of vermin. — **fu·mi·gant** /-gənt/ n. **fu·mi·ga·tion** /,fyo͞omə'gāshən/ n. **fu·mi·ga·tor** /-,gātər/ n. [16th C. (in the sense 'to perfume'): from L. *fumigat-* 'fumigated,' from the v. *fumigare*, from *fumus* 'smoke.']

fu·mi·to·ry /'fyo͞omə,tôrē/ ▶ n. an Old World plant (genus *Fumaria*, family Fumariaceae) with spikes of small tubular pink or white flowers and finely divided grayish leaves. [ME: from OFr. *fumeterre*, from med. L. *fumus terrae* 'smoke of the earth' (because of its grayish leaves).]

fun /fən/ ▶ n. enjoyment, amusement, or lighthearted pleasure: *anyone who turns up can join in the fun.* ▪ a source of this: *people-watching is great fun.* ▪ playful behavior or good humor: *she's full of fun.* ▪ behavior or an activity that is intended purely for amusement and should not be interpreted as having serious or malicious purposes. ▪ [attrib.] (of a place or event) providing entertainment or leisure activities for children. ▶ adj. (**fun·ner, fun·nest**) informal amusing, entertaining, or enjoyable: *it was a fun evening.* ▶ v. informal joke or tease: [intrans.] *no need to get sore—I was only funning* | [trans.] *they are just funning you.*
– PHRASES **for fun** (or **for the fun of it**) in order to amuse oneself and not for any more serious purpose. **fun and games** amusing and enjoyable activities: *teaching isn't all fun and games.* **someone's idea of fun** used to emphasize one's dislike for an activity or to mock someone else's liking for it: *being stuck behind a desk all day isn't my idea of fun.* **in fun** not intended seriously; as a joke: *remember when you meet the press to say that your speech was all in fun.* **make fun of** (or **poke fun at**) tease, laugh at, or joke about (someone) in a mocking or unkind way. **not much** (or **a lot of**) **fun** used to indicate that something strikes one as extremely unpleasant and depressing: *it can't be much fun living next door to him.* **what fun!** used to convey that an activity or situation sounds amusing or enjoyable. [17th C.: from obs. *fun* 'to cheat or hoax,' dial. var. of ME *fon* 'be a fool,' rel. to *fon* 'a fool.']

Fu·na·ba·shi /,fo͞onä'bäshē/ a city in central Japan, on eastern Honshu Island; pop. 533,000.

Fu·na·fu·ti /,f(y)o͞onə'f(y)o͞otē/ the capital of Tuvalu, on an island of the same name; pop. 2,500.

fu·nam·bu·list /fyo͞oˈnambyəlist/ ▶ **n.** a tightrope walker. [18th C.: from Fr. *funambule* or L. *funambulus* (from *funis* 'rope' + *ambulare* 'to walk') + -IST.]

Fun·chal /ˌfo͞onˈsʜäl; ˌfən-/ the capital of Madeira, on the south coast of the island; pop. 110,000.

func·tion /ˈfəNGksʜən/ ▶ **n.** **1** an activity or purpose natural to or intended for a person or thing. ■ practical use or purpose in design. ■ a basic task of a computer, esp. one that corresponds to a single instruction from the user. **2** Math. a relationship or expression involving one or more variables: *the function (bx + c).* ■ a variable quantity regarded in relation to one or more other variables in terms of which it may be expressed or on which its value depends. **3** a thing dependent on another factor or factors: *class shame is a function of social power.* **4** a large or formal social event or ceremony. ▶ **v.** [intrans.] work or operate in a proper or particular way. ■ (**function as**) fulfill the purpose or task of (a specified thing). — **func·tion·less adj.** [16th C.: from Fr. *fonction*, from L. *functio(n-)*, from *fungi* 'perform.']

func·tion·al /ˈfəNGksʜənl/ ▶ **adj.** of or having a special activity, purpose, or task; relating to the way in which something works or operates: *there are important functional differences between left and right brain.* ■ designed to be practical and useful, rather than attractive. ■ working or operating. ■ (of a disease) affecting the operation, rather than the structure, of an organ: *functional diarrhea.* ■ (of a mental illness) having no discernible organic cause: *functional psychosis.* — **func·tion·al·ly adv.**

func·tion·al group ▶ **n.** Chem. a group of atoms responsible for the characteristic reactions of a particular compound.

func·tion·al il·lit·er·ate ▶ **n.** a person whose level of ability to read and write is below that needed to do the ordinary tasks required to function normally in society.

func·tion·al·ism /ˈfəNGksʜənlˌizəm/ ▶ **n.** belief in or stress on the practical application of a thing, in particular: ■ (in the arts) the doctrine that an object's design determined solely by its function will be inherently beautiful. ■ (in the social sciences) the theory that all aspects of a society serve a function and are necessary for the survival of that society. ■ (in the philosophy of mind) the theory that mental states are defined by their cause and their effect on other mental states and behavior. — **func·tion·al·ist n. & adj.**

func·tion·al·i·ty /ˌfəNGksʜəˈnalətē/ ▶ **n.** **1** the quality of being suited to serve a purpose well; practicality: *I like the feel and functionality of this bakeware.* ■ the purpose that something is designed or expected to fulfill: *manufacturing processes may be affected by the functionality of the product.* **2** the range of operations that can be run on a computer or other electronic system.

func·tion·ar·y /ˈfəNGksʜəˌnerē/ ▶ **n.** (pl. **-ar·ies**) a person who performs official functions or duties; an official.

func·tion key ▶ **n.** Comput. a button on a computer keyboard, distinct from the main alphanumeric keys, to which software can assign a particular function.

func·tion word ▶ **n.** Ling. a word whose purpose is more to signal grammatical relationship in a sentence than to convey lexical meaning, e.g., *do* in *do you live here?*

fund /fənd/ ▶ **n.** a sum of money saved or made available for a particular purpose. ■ (**funds**) financial resources: *the misuse of public funds.* ■ a large stock or supply of something. ■ an organization set up for the administration and management of a monetary fund. ▶ **v.** [trans.] provide with money for a particular purpose: [in comb.] *government-funded research.* [17th C.: from L. *fundus* 'bottom, piece of landed property.']

fun·da·ment /ˈfəndəmənt/ ▶ **n.** **1** the foundation or basis of something. **2** humorous a person's buttocks. [ME: from OFr. *fondement*, from L. *fundamentum*, from *fundare* 'to found.']

fun·da·men·tal /ˌfəndəˈmentl/ ▶ **adj.** forming a necessary base or core; of central importance. ■ affecting or relating to the essential nature of something or the crucial point about an issue. ■ so basic as to be hard to alter, resolve, or overcome. ▶ **n.** (usu. **fundamentals**) a central or primary rule or principle on which something is based. ■ a fundamental note, tone, or frequency. — **fun·da·men·tal·i·ty** /-mənˈtalətē/ **n.**

fun·da·men·tal fre·quen·cy ▶ **n.** Physics the lowest frequency produced by the oscillation of the whole of an object, as distinct from the harmonics of higher frequency.

fun·da·men·tal·ism /ˌfəndəˈmentlˌizəm/ ▶ **n.** a form of Protestant Christianity that upholds belief in the strict and literal interpretation of the Bible. ■ strict maintenance of ancient or fundamental doctrines of any religion or ideology, notably Islam. — **fun·da·men·tal·ist n. & adj.**

fun·da·men·tal·ly /ˌfəndəˈmentl-ē/ ▶ **adv.** [often as submodifier] in central or primary respects: *two fundamentally different concepts of democracy.* ■ [sentence adverb] used to make an emphatic statement about the basic truth of something.

fun·da·men·tal note ▶ **n.** Music the lowest note of a chord in its original (uninverted) form.

fun·da·men·tal par·ti·cle ▶ **n.** another term for ELEMENTARY PARTICLE.

fun·da·men·tal tone ▶ **n.** Music the tone that represents the fundamental frequency of a vibrating object such as a string or bell.

fun·da·men·tal u·nit ▶ **n.** one of a set of unrelated units of measurement, which are arbitrarily defined and from which other units are derived. For example, in the SI system the fundamental units are the meter, kilogram, and second. ■ a thing that is or is perceived as being the smallest part into which a complex whole can be analyzed.

fund·ed debt ▶ **n.** debt in the form of securities with long-term or indefinite redemption. Compare with FLOATING DEBT.

fun·di /ˈfəndī; -dē/ plural form of FUNDUS.

fund·ing /ˈfəndiNG/ ▶ **n.** money provided, esp. by an organization or government, for a particular purpose. ■ the action or practice of providing such money.

fund-rais·er ▶ **n.** a person whose job or task is to seek financial support for a charity or other enterprise. ■ an event held to generate financial support for such an enterprise. — **fund-raise v. fund-rais·ing n.**

fun·dus /ˈfəndəs/ ▶ **n.** (pl. **-di** /-dī; -dē/) Anat. the part of a hollow organ (such as the uterus or the gallbladder) that is farthest from the opening. [18th C.: from L., lit. 'bottom.']

Fun·dy, Bay of /ˈfəndē/ an arm of the Atlantic Ocean between the Canadian provinces of New Brunswick and Nova Scotia. Its fast-running tides are the highest in the world and reach 40–48 feet (12–15 m).

fu·ner·al /ˈfyo͞on(ə)rəl/ ▶ **n.** the ceremonies honoring a dead person, typically involving burial or cremation: *in the afternoon, he'd attended a funeral* | [as adj.] *a funeral service.*

– PHRASES **it's** (or **that's**) **someone's funeral** informal used to warn someone that an unwise act or decision is their responsibility: *Don't then—it's your funeral."* [ME: from OFr. *funeraille*, from med. L. *funeralia*, neut. pl. of late L. *funeralis*, from L. *funus, funer-* 'funeral, death, corpse.']

fu·ner·al di·rec·tor ▶ **n.** an undertaker.

fu·ner·al home (also **funeral parlor**) ▶ **n.** a place where the dead are prepared for burial or cremation.

fu·ner·al pyre ▶ **n.** a pile of wood on which a corpse is burned as part of a funeral ceremony in some traditions.

fu·ner·ar·y /ˈfyo͞onəˌrerē/ ▶ **adj.** relating to a funeral or the commemoration of the dead: *funerary ceremonies.* [17th C.: from late L. *funerarius*, from *funus, funer-* 'funeral.']

fu·ne·re·al /fyəˈni(ə)rēəl; fyo͞o-/ ▶ **adj.** having the mournful, somber character appropriate to a funeral.

fun·gal /ˈfəNGgəl/ ▶ **adj.** of or caused by a fungus or fungi: *fungal diseases such as mildew.*

fun·gi /ˈfənjī; -gī/ plural form of FUNGUS.

fun·gi·ble /ˈfənjəbəl/ ▶ **adj.** Law (of goods contracted for without an individual specimen being specified) able to replace or be replaced by another identical item; mutually interchangeable. — **fun·gi·bil·i·ty** /ˌfənjəˈbilitē/ **n.** [17th C.: from med. L. *fungibilis*, from *fungi* 'perform, enjoy.']

fun·gi·cide /ˈfənjəˌsīd; ˈfəNGgə-/ ▶ **n.** a chemical that destroys fungus. — **fun·gi·cid·al** /ˌfənjəˈsīdl; ˌfəNGgə-/ **adj.**

fun·go /ˈfəNGgō/ ▶ **n.** (also **fun·go fly**) (pl. **-goes** or **-gos**) Baseball a fly ball hit for fielding practice. ■ (also **fungo bat** or **stick**) a long lightweight bat for hitting practice balls to fielders. [19th C.: of unknown origin.]

fun·gus /ˈfəNGgəs/ ▶ **n.** (pl. **-gi** /-jī; -gī/ or **-gus·es**) any of a group of unicellular, multicellular, or syncytial spore-producing organisms feeding on organic matter, including molds, yeast, and mushrooms. ■ fungal infection (esp. on fish). ■ [in sing.] used to describe something that has appeared or grown rapidly and is considered unpleasant or unattractive: *there was a fungus of outbuildings behind the house.* [ME: from L., perh. from Gk. *spongos* (see SPONGE).]

fun·house /ˈfənˌhous/ ▶ **n.** (in an amusement park) a building equipped with trick mirrors, shifting floors, and other devices designed to scare or amuse people as they walk through.

fu·nic·u·lar /fyo͞oˈnikyələr; fə-/ ▶ **adj.** (of a railroad, esp. one on a mountainside) operating by cable with ascending and descending cars counterbalanced. ▶ **n.** a railroad operating in such a way. [17th C.: from L. *funiculus* (dimin. of *funis* 'rope') + -AR[1].]

Funk /fo͞oNGk; fəNGk/, Casimir (1884–1967), US biochemist; born in Poland. He showed that certain diseases, including scurvy, rickets, beriberi, and pellagra, were caused by the deficiency of a particular vitamin.

funk[1] /fəNGk/ informal ▶ **n.** (also **blue funk**) [in sing.] a state of depression: *I sat absorbed in my own blue funk.* ■ esp. Brit. a state of great fear or panic: *are you in a blue funk about running out of things to say?* [18th C.: perh. from FUNK[2].]

funk[2] ▶ **n.** **1** a style of popular dance music of US black origin, based on elements of blues and soul and having a strong rhythm that typically accentuates the first beat in the bar. **2** [in sing.] informal, dated a strong musty smell as of sweat or tobacco.

– PHRASAL VERBS **funk something up** give music elements of such a style. [17th C. (in the sense 'musty smell'): perh. from Fr. dial. *funkier* 'blow smoke on,' based on L. *fumus* 'smoke.']

funk·y /ˈfəNGkē/ ▶ **adj.** (**funk·i·er, funk·i·est**) informal **1** (of music) having or using a strong dance rhythm, in particular that of funk: *some excellent funky beats.* ■ modern and stylish in an unconventional or striking way: *she likes wearing funky clothes.* **2** strongly musty: *cooked greens make the kitchen smell really funky.* — **funk·i·ly adv. funk·i·ness** /-kēnis/ **n.** [18th C.: from FUNK[2].]

fun·nel /ˈfənl/ ▶ **n.** a tube or pipe that is wide at the top and narrow at the bottom, used for guiding liquid or powder into a small opening.

■ a thing resembling such a tube or pipe in shape or function: ■ a metal chimney on a ship or steam engine. ▶ **v.** (**funneled, funneling** ; Brit. **funnelled, funnelling**) [with obj. and adverbial of direction] guide or channel (something) through or as if through a funnel: *some $12.8 billion was funneled through the Marshall Plan.* ■ [no obj., with adverbial of direction] move or be guided through or as if through a funnel. ■ [intrans.] assume the shape of a funnel by widening or narrowing at the end: *the crevice funneled out.* [ME: appar. via OFr. from Provençal *fonilh*, from late L. *fundibulum*, from L. *infundibulum*, from *infundere*, from *in-* 'into' + *fundere* 'pour.']

fun·nel cake ▶ **n.** a cake made of batter that is poured through a funnel into hot fat or oil, deep-fried until crisp, and served sprinkled with sugar.

fun·nel cloud ▶ **n.** a rotating funnel-shaped cloud forming the core of a tornado or waterspout.

fun·nel-web spi·der ▶ **n.** any of a number of spiders that build a funnel-shaped web.

fun·ni·ly /ˈfənl-ē/ ▶ **adv.** in a strange or amusing way. ■ [sentence adverb] (**funnily enough**) used to admit that a situation or fact is surprising or curious.

fun·ny /ˈfənē/ ▶ **adj.** (**-ni·er, -ni·est**) **1** causing laughter or amusement; humorous. ■ [predic.] expressing a speaker's objection to another's laughter or mockery: *She started to laugh. "What's so funny?" he asked.* ■ [predic.] [with negative] informal used to emphasize that something is unpleasant or wrong and should be regarded seriously or avoided: *stealing other people's work isn't funny.* **2** difficult to explain or understand; strange. ■ unusual or odd; curious: *Bev has a funny little stammer.* ■ unusual in such a way as to arouse suspicion: *there was something funny going on.* ■ used to draw attention to or express surprise at a curious or interesting fact or occurrence: *that's funny!—that vase of flowers has been moved.* ■ informal (of a person or part of the body) not in wholly good health or order; slightly ill: *suddenly my stomach felt funny.* ▶ **n.** (pl. **-nies**) (**funnies**) informal the comic strips in newspapers: *I read the sports page, funnies, and editorial.*

– PHRASES **see the funny side** (**of something**) appreciate the humorous aspect of a situation or experience. (**oh**) **very funny!** informal used ironically to indicate that a speaker does not share another's joke or amusement. — **fun·ni·ness** /ˈfənēnis/ **n.**

fun·ny bone ▶ **n.** informal the part of the elbow over which the ulnar nerve passes. A knock on the funny bone may cause numbness and pain along the forearm and hand. ■ a person's sense of humor, as located in an imaginary physical organ: *photographs to jostle the mind and the funny bone.*

fun·ny busi·ness ▶ **n.** deceptive, disobedient, or lecherous behavior.

fun·ny farm ▶ **n.** informal, offens. a psychiatric hospital.

fun·ny man ▶ **n.** a professional comedian or clown.

fun·ny mon·ey ▶ **n.** informal currency that is forged or otherwise worthless.

fun·ny pa·pers ▶ **plural n.** a section of a newspaper containing comics and humorous matter.

fun run ▶ **n.** informal a noncompetitive run, esp. for sponsored runners in support of a charity.

fur /fər/ ▶ **n.** **1** the short, fine, soft hair of certain animals: *a long, lean, muscular cat with sleek fur.* ■ the skin of an animal with such hair on it. ■ skins of this type, or fabrics resembling these, used as material for making, trimming, or lining clothes: *jackets made out of yak fur* | [as adj.] *a fur coat.* ■ a garment made of, trimmed, or lined with fur: *she pulled the fur around her* **2** a coating formed on the tongue as a symptom of sickness. ▶ **v.** (**furred, fur·ring**) [trans.] **1** [as adj., often in comb.] (**furred**) covered with or made from a particular type of fur: *silky-furred lemurs.* **2** level (floor or wall timbers) by inserting strips of wood.

– PHRASES **fur and feather** game mammals and birds. **make the fur fly** informal cause serious, perhaps violent, trouble. [ME (as a v.): from OFr. *forrer* 'to line, sheathe,' from *forre* 'sheath,' of Gmc. origin.]

fur. ▶ **abbr.** furlong(s).

fu·ran /ˈfyo͝oran; fyo͝oˈran/ ▶ **n.** Chem. a colorless volatile liquid, C_4H_4O, with a planar unsaturated five-membered ring in its molecule. ■ any substituted derivative of this. [19th C.: from synonymous *furfuran.*]

fur·bear·er /ˈfərˌbe(ə)rər/ ▶ **n.** an animal whose fur is valued commercially.

fur·bish /ˈfərbisʜ/ ▶ **v.** [trans.] [usu. as adj.] (**furbished**) give a fresh look to (something old or shabby); renovate: *the newly furbished church.* — **fur·bish·er n.** [ME: from OFr. *forbiss-*, lengthened stem of *forbir*, of Gmc. origin.]

fur·cu·la /ˈfərkyələ/ ▶ **n.** (pl. **-lae** /-ˌlē; -ˌlī/) Zool. a forked organ or structure, in particular: ■ the wishbone of a bird. ■ the forked appendage at the end of the abdomen in a springtail, by which the insect jumps. — **fur·cu·lar** /ˈfərkyələr/ **adj.** [19th C.: from L., dimin. of *furca* 'fork.']

fur·fur·al /ˈfərf(y)əˌral/ ▶ **n.** Chem. a colorless liquid, C_4H_3OCHO, used in synthetic resin manufacture, originally obtained by distilling bran. [19th C.: from obs. *furfurol* (in the same sense) + **-AL**.]

fur·fur·al·de·hyde /ˌfərf(y)əˈraldəˌhīd/ ▶ **n.** Chem. another term for **FURFURAL**.

fu·ri·o·so /ˌfyo͝orēˈōsō; -zō/ ▶ **adv. & adj.** Music (esp. as a direction) furiously and wildly. [Ital.]

fu·ri·ous /ˈfyo͝orēəs/ ▶ **adj.** extremely angry. ■ full of anger or energy; violent or intense. — **fu·ri·ous·ly adv. fu·ri·ous·ness n.** [ME: from OFr. *furieus*, from L. *furiosus*, from *furia* 'fury.']

furl /fərl/ ▶ **v.** [trans.] roll or fold up and secure neatly (a flag, sail, umbrella, or other piece of fabric). — **furl·a·ble adj.** [16th C.: from Fr. *ferler*, from OFr. *fer, ferm* 'firm' + *lier* 'bind' (from L. *ligare*).]

fur·long /ˈfərˌlôɴɢ; -ˌläɴɢ/ ▶ **n.** an eighth of a mile, 220 yards. [OE *furlang*, from *furh* 'furrow' + *lang* 'long.']

fur·lough /ˈfərlō/ ▶ **n.** leave of absence, esp. that granted to a member of the armed services. ■ a temporary release of a convict from prison. ■ a layoff, esp. a temporary one, from a place of employment. ▶ **v.** [trans.] grant such leave of absence to. ■ lay off (workers), esp. temporarily. [17th C.: from Du. *verlof*, modeled on Ger. *Verlaub*, of West Gmc. origin and rel. to **LEAVE**[2].]

furn. ▶ **abbr.** furnished.

fur·nace /ˈfərnəs/ ▶ **n.** an enclosed structure in which material can be heated to very high temperatures, e.g., for smelting metals. ■ an appliance fired by gas or oil in which air or water is heated to be circulated throughout a building in a heating system. ■ used to describe a very hot place. [ME: from OFr. *fornais(e)*, from L. *fornax, fornac-*, from *fornus* 'oven.']

Fur·neaux Is·lands /ˈfərnō/ a group of islands in Australia, in the Bass Strait.

fur·nish /ˈfərnisʜ/ ▶ **v.** [trans.] provide (a house or room) with furniture and fittings. ■ (**furnish someone with**) supply someone with (something); give (something) to someone. ■ be a source of; provide. — **fur·nish·er n.** [ME: from OFr. *furniss-*, lengthened stem of *furnir*, ult. of West Gmc. origin.]

fur·nished /ˈfərnisʜt/ ▶ **adj.** (of accommodations) available to be rented with furniture.

fur·nish·ing /ˈfərnisʜiɴɢ/ ▶ **n.** **1** (usu. **furnishings**) furniture, fittings, and other decorative accessories, such as curtains and carpets, for a house or room. **2** the action of decorating a house or room and providing it with furniture and fittings.

fur·ni·ture /ˈfərnicʜər/ ▶ **n.** **1** large movable equipment, such as tables and chairs, used to make a house, office, or other space suitable for living or working. ■ fig. a person's habitual attitude, outlook, and way of thinking: *the mental furniture of the European.* **2** [usu. with adj.] small accessories or fittings for a particular use or piece of equipment: *computer hardware, software, and furniture.*

– PHRASES **part of the furniture** informal a person or thing that has been somewhere so long as to seem a permanent, unquestioned, or invisible feature of the landscape. [16th C. (denoting the action of furnishing): from Fr. *fourniture*, from *fournir*, from OFr. *furnir* 'to furnish.']

fu·ror /ˈfyo͝orôr; -ər/ ▶ **n.** [in sing.] an outbreak of public anger or excitement: *the article raised a furor among mathematicians.* [18th C.: from Ital. *furore*, from L. *furor*, from *furere* 'be mad, rage.']

fu·ro·se·mide /fyo͝oˈrōsəˌmīd/ (esp. Brit. also **fru·se·mide**) ▶ **n.** Med. a synthetic compound, $C_{12}H_{11}ClN_2O_5S$, with a strong diuretic action, used to treat edema. [1960s: from *fur-* (alt. of *fur(yl)*) + **-O-** + *sem-* + **-IDE**.]

fur·ri·er /ˈfərēər/ ▶ **n.** a person who prepares or deals in furs. [ME: from OFr. *forreor*, from *forrer* 'to line, sheathe' (see **FUR**).]

fur·ring strip /ˈfəriɴɢ/ ▶ **n.** a length of wood tapering to nothing, used in roofing and other construction work.

fur·row /ˈfərō; ˈfə-rō/ ▶ **n.** a long narrow trench made in the ground by a plow, esp. for planting seeds or for irrigation. ■ a rut, groove, or trail in the ground or another surface. ■ a line or wrinkle on a person's face. ▶ **v.** [trans.] make a rut, groove, or trail in (the ground or the surface of something). ■ (with reference to the forehead or face) mark or be marked with lines or wrinkles caused by frowning, anxiety, or concentration: [as adj.] (**furrowed**) *he stroked his furrowed brow.* ■ (with reference to the eyebrows) tighten or be tightened and lowered in anxiety, concentration, or disapproval, so wrinkling the forehead. ■ [usu. as adj.] (**furrowed**) use a plow to make a long narrow trench in (land or earth): *furrowed fields.* [OE *furh*, rel. to Ger. *Furche*, L. *porca* 'ridge between furrows.']

fur·ry /ˈfərē/ ▶ **adj.** (**-ri·er, -ri·est**) covered with fur. ■ having a soft surface like fur. — **fur·ri·ness** /ˈfərēnis/ **n.**

fur seal ▶ **n.** a gregarious thick-furred eared seal (genera *Callorhinus* and *Arctocephalus*) that frequents the coasts of the Pacific and southern oceans.

fur·ther /ˈfərT͟Hər/ used as comparative of **FAR.** ▶ **adv.** **1** (also **far·ther** /ˈfärT͟Hər/) at, to, or by a greater distance (used to indicate the extent to which one thing or person is or becomes distant from another). ■ [with negative] used to emphasize the difference between a supposed or suggested fact or state of mind and the truth: *as for her being a liar, nothing could be further from the truth.* **2** (also **far·ther** /ˈfär-/) over a greater expanse of space or time; for a longer way: *we had walked further than I realized.* ■ beyond the point already reached or the distance already covered. **3** beyond or in addition to what has already been done: *this theme will be developed further in Chapter 6.* ■ [sentence adverb] used to introduce a new point relating to or reinforcing a previous statement. ■ at or to a more advanced, successful, or desirable stage. ▶ **adj.** **1** (also **far·ther** /ˈfär-/) more distant in space than another item of the same kind: *two men were standing at the further end of the clearing.* ■ more remote from a central point: *the museum is in the further reaches of the town.* **2** additional to what already exists or has already taken place, been done, or been accounted for. ▶ **v.** [trans.] help the progress or development of (something); promote.

– PHRASES **not go any further** (of a secret) not be told to anyone else. **until further notice** used to indicate that a situation will not change until another announcement is made. **until further orders** used to indicate that a situation is only to change when another command is received. [OE *furthor* (adv.), *furthra* (adj.), *fyrthrian* (v.), of Gmc. origin; rel. to FORTH.]

fur·ther·ance /ˈfərT͟Hərəns/ ▶ n. the advancement of a scheme or interest: *acts in furtherance of an industrial dispute.*

fur·ther·more /ˈfərT͟Hərˌmôr/ ▶ adv. [sentence adverb] in addition; besides (used to introduce a fresh consideration in an argument).

fur·ther·most /ˈfərT͟Hərˌmōst/ ▶ adj. var. of FARTHERMOST.

fur·thest /ˈfərT͟Hist/ ▶ adj. & adv. var. of FARTHEST.

fur·tive /ˈfərtiv/ ▶ adj. attempting to avoid notice or attention, typically because of guilt or a belief that discovery would lead to trouble; secretive. ■ suggestive of guilty nervousness. —**fur·tive·ly** adv. **fur·tive·ness** n. [17th C.: from Fr. *furtif, -ive* or L. *furtivus*, from *furtum* 'theft.']

fu·ry /ˈfyo͝orē/ ▶ n. (pl. **-ries**) **1** wild or violent anger. ■ (**a fury**) a surge of violent anger or other feeling. ■ [in sing.] violence or energy displayed in natural phenomena or in someone's actions. **2** (**Fury**) Gk. Mythol. a spirit of punishment, often represented as one of three goddesses who executed the curses pronounced upon criminals, tortured the guilty with stings of conscience, and inflicted famines and pestilences. The Furies were identified at an early date with the Eumenides. ■ dated used to convey a woman's anger or aggression by comparing her to such a spirit: *she turned on him like a vengeful fury.*

– PHRASES **like fury** informal with great energy or effort: *she fought like fury in his arms.* [ME: from OFr. *furie*, from L. *furia*, from *furiosus* 'furious,' from *furere* 'be mad, rage.']

fu·sar·i·um /fyo͝oˈze(ə)rēəm/ ▶ n. a mold of a large genus (*Fusarium*), many of which cause plant diseases, esp. wilting. ■ infestation with any of these or related molds. [20th C.: mod. L., from L. *fusus* 'spindle.']

fuse[1] /fyo͞oz/ ▶ n. a safety device consisting of a thin strip of metal that melts and breaks an electric circuit if the current exceeds a safe level. ▶ v. **1** [trans.] join or blend to form a single entity. ■ [intrans.] (of groups of atoms or cellular structures) join or coalesce. ■ melt (a material or object) with intense heat, esp. so as to join it with something else. **2** [trans.] provide (a circuit or electrical appliance) with a fuse: [as adj.] (**fused**) *a fused plug.*

– PHRASES **blow a fuse** use too much power in an electrical circuit, causing a fuse to melt. ■ informal lose one's temper: *it was only a suggestion—there's no need to blow a fuse.* [16th C.: from L. *fus-* 'poured, melted,' from the v. *fundere*.]

fuse[2] (also **fuze**) ▶ n. a length of material along which a small flame moves to explode a bomb or firework, meanwhile allowing time for those who light it to move to a safe distance. ■ a device in a bomb, shell, or mine that makes it explode on impact, after an interval, at set distance from the target, or when subjected to magnetic or vibratory stimulation. ▶ v. [trans.] fit a fuse to (a bomb, shell, or mine).

– PHRASES **light the** (or **a**) **fuse** set something tense or exciting in motion: *the event lit the fuse for the revolution.* **a short fuse** a tendency to lose one's temper quickly. ■ (**on a short fuse**) likely to lose one's temper or explode. —**fuse·less** adj. [17th C.: from Ital. *fuso*, from L. *fusus* 'spindle.']

fuse box ▶ n. a box housing the fuses for circuits in a building.

fu·see /fyo͞oˈzē/ (also **fu·zee**) ▶ n. **1** a conical pulley or wheel, esp. in a watch or clock. **2** a railroad signal flare. [16th C. (denoting a spindle-shaped figure): from Fr. *fusée* 'spindleful,' based on L. *fusus* 'spindle.']

fu·se·lage /ˈfyo͞osəˌläzH; -zə-/ ▶ n. the main body of an aircraft. [20th C.: from Fr., from *fuseler* 'shape into a spindle,' from *fuseau* 'spindle.']

fu·sel oil /ˈfyo͞ozəl/ ▶ n. a mixture of several alcohols (chiefly amyl alcohol) produced as a byproduct of alcoholic fermentation. [19th C.: from Ger. *Fusel* 'bad liquor,' prob. rel. to *fuseln* 'to bungle.']

Fu·shun /ˈfo͞oˈsHo͞on/ a city in northeastern China; pop. 1,330,000.

fu·si·ble /ˈfyo͞ozəbəl/ ▶ adj. able to be fused or melted. —**fu·si·bil·i·ty** /ˌfyo͞ozəˈbilətē/ n. [ME: from OFr., or from med. L. *fusibilis*, from *fundere* 'pour, melt.']

fu·sil /ˈfyo͞ozəl/ ▶ n. hist. a light flintlock musket. [16th C. (denoting a flint in a tinderbox): from Fr., based on L. *focus* 'hearth, fire.']

fu·sil·ier /ˌfyo͞ozəˈli(ə)r/ (also **fu·sil·eer**) ▶ n. (usu. **Fusiliers**) a member of any of several British regiments formerly armed with fusils. ■ hist. a soldier armed with a fusil.

fu·sil·lade /ˈfyo͞osəˌläd; -ˌlād/ ▶ n. a series of shots fired or missiles thrown all at the same time or in quick succession: fig. *a fusillade of accusations.* [19th C.: from Fr., from *fusiller* 'to shoot,' from *fusil* (see FUSIL).]

fu·sil·li /fyo͞oˈsilē; -ˈsēlē/ ▶ n. pasta pieces in the form of short spirals. [Ital., lit. 'little spindles,' dimin. of *fuso*.]

fu·sion /ˈfyo͞ozHən/ ▶ n. the process or result of joining two or more things together to form a single entity. ■ Physics short for NUCLEAR FUSION. ■ the process of causing a material or object to melt, esp. so as to join with another: *the fusion of resin and glass fiber in the molding process.* ■ music that is a mixture of different styles, esp. jazz and rock. ▶ adj. (of food or cooking) that incorporates elements of diverse cuisines: *Latin/Japanese fusion cuisine.* —**fu·sion·al** /-zHənl/ adj. [16th C.: from L. *fusio(n-)*, from *fundere* 'pour, melt.']

fu·sion bomb ▶ n. a bomb deriving its energy from nuclear fusion, esp. a hydrogen bomb.

fuss /fəs/ ▶ n. [in sing.] a display of unnecessary or excessive excitement, activity, or interest. ■ a protest or dispute of a specified degree or kind: *he didn't put up too much of a fuss.* ■ elaborate or complex procedures; trouble or difficulty: *they settled in with very little fuss.* ▶ v. [intrans.] show unnecessary or excessive concern about something. ■ move around or busy oneself restlessly.

– PHRASES **make a fuss** become angry and complain. **make a fuss over** treat (a person or animal) with excessive attention or affection. —**fuss·er** n. [18th C.: perh. Anglo-Irish.]

fuss·y /ˈfəsē/ ▶ adj. (**fuss·i·er, fuss·i·est**) (of a person) fastidious about one's needs or requirements; hard to please: *he is very fussy about what he eats.* ■ showing excessive or anxious concern about detail. ■ full of unnecessary detail or decoration. —**fuss·i·ly** adv. **fuss·i·ness** n.

fus·tian /ˈfəsCHən/ ▶ n. **1** thick, durable twilled cloth with a short nap, usually dyed in dark colors. **2** pompous or pretentious speech or writing: *a smoke screen of fustian and fantasy.* [ME: from OFr. *fustaigne*, from med. L. *fustaneum*, from *(pannus) fustaneus* 'cloth from *Fostat*,' a suburb of Cairo.]

fus·tic /ˈfəstik/ ▶ n. **1** archaic a yellow dye obtained from either of two kinds of timber, esp. that of old fustic. **2** (also **old fustic**) a tropical American tree (*Madura Chlorophora*) of the mulberry family with heartwood that yields dyes and other products. [ME: via Fr. from Sp. *fustoc*, from Arab. *fustuk*, from Gk. *pistakē* 'pistachio tree.']

fus·ty /ˈfəstē/ ▶ adj. (**fus·ti·er, fus·ti·est**) smelling stale, damp, or stuffy: *the fusty odor of decay.* ■ old-fashioned in attitude or style. —**fus·ti·ly** /ˈfəstəlē/ adv. **fus·ti·ness** n. [15th C.: from OFr. *fuste* 'smelling of the cask,' from *fust* 'cask, tree trunk,' from L. *fustis* 'cudgel.']

fut. ▶ abbr. future.

fu·thark /ˈfo͞oˌTHärk/ (also **fu·thorc** /-ˌTHôrk/, **fu·thork**) ▶ n. the runic alphabet. [19th C.: from its first six letters: *f, u, th, a* (or *o*), *r, k*.]

fu·tile /ˈfyo͞otl; -til/ ▶ adj. incapable of producing any useful result; pointless. [16th C.: from L. *futilis* 'leaky, futile,' appar. from *fundere* 'pour.']

fu·ton /ˈfo͞oˌtän/ ▶ n. a Japanese quilted mattress rolled out on the floor for use as a bed. ■ a type of low wooden sofa bed having such a mattress.

fu·ture /ˈfyo͞oCHər/ ▶ n. **1** (usu. **the future**) the time or a period of time following the moment of speaking or writing; time regarded as still to come: ■ events that will or are likely to happen in the time to come. ■ used to refer to what will happen to someone or something in the time to come. ■ a prospect of success or happiness. ■ Gram. a tense of verbs expressing events that have not yet happened. **2** (**futures**) Finance short for FUTURES CONTRACT. ▶ adj. [attrib.] at a later time; going or likely to happen or exist: *the needs of future generations.* ■ (of a person) planned or destined to hold a specified position. ■ existing after death. ■ Gram. (of a tense) expressing an event yet to happen.

– PHRASES **in future** esp. Brit. from now on. [ME: via OFr. from L. *futurus*, future part. of *esse* 'be.']

fu·ture life ▶ n. a future state or existence, esp. seen as very different from the present: *he became confident of a future life as a student.* ■ (in Hinduism and some other religions) a reincarnated existence. ■ [in sing.] (in Christianity and some other religions) the afterlife.

fu·ture per·fect ▶ n. Gram. a tense of verbs expressing expected completion in the future, in English exemplified by *will have done.*

fu·tures con·tract ▶ n. Finance an agreement traded on an organized exchange to buy or sell assets, esp. commodities or shares, at a fixed price but to be delivered and paid for later. Compare with FORWARD CONTRACT.

fu·ture shock ▶ n. a state of distress or disorientation due to rapid social or technological change.

fu·tur·ism /ˈfyo͞oCHəˌrizəm/ ▶ n. concern with events and trends of the future or which anticipate the future. ■ (**Futurism**) an artistic movement begun in Italy in 1909 that violently rejected traditional forms so as to celebrate and incorporate into art the energy and dynamism of modern technology. [from FUTURE + -ISM, translating Ital. *futurismo*, Fr. *futurisme*.]

fu·tur·ist /ˈfyo͞oCHərist/ ▶ n. a person who studies the future and makes predictions about it based on current trends. ▶ adj. relating to a vision of the future, esp. one involving the development of technology: *the grim urban setting of the novel would have been a futurist nightmare.*

fu·tur·is·tic /ˌfyo͞oCHəˈristik/ ▶ adj. having or involving modern technology or design. ■ (of a film or book) set in the future, typically in a world of advanced or menacing technology. ■ dated of or characteristic of Futurism. —**fu·tur·is·ti·cal·ly** /-ik(ə)lē/ adv.

fu·tu·ri·ty /fyo͝oˈto͝oritē; -ˈCHo͝or-/ ▶ n. (pl. **-ties**) the future time. ■ a future event. ■ renewed or continuing existence.

futz /fəts/ ▶ v. [intrans.] informal waste time; idle or busy oneself aimlessly: *mother futzed around in the kitchen.* ■ (**futz around with**) deal with (something) in a trifling way; fiddle with. [1930s: perh. an alt. of Yiddish *arumfartzen* 'fart around.']

Fu·xin /ˈfo͞oˈsHin/ (also **Fou-hsin**) a city in northeastern China; pop. 743,000.

fuze /fyo͞oz/ ▶ n. var. of FUSE[2].

fu·zee ▶ n. var. of FUSEE.

Fu·zhou /ˈfo͞oˈjō/ (also **Foo·chow**) a city in southeastern China; pop. 1,270,000.

fuzz[1] /fəz/ ▶ n. a fluffy or frizzy mass of hair or fiber. ■ a blurred image or area. ■ a buzzing or distorted sound, esp. one deliberately produced as an effect on an electric guitar. ▶ v. **1** make or become blurred or indistinct. **2** [intrans.] (of hair) become fluffy or frizzy. [16th C.: prob. of Low German or Du. origin; cf. Du. *voos*, Low Ger. *fussig* 'spongy.']

fuzz[2] ▶ n. (**the fuzz**) informal the police. [1920s: of unknown origin.]

fuzz·ball /ˈfəz,bôl/ ▶ n. a ball of fuzz. ■ another term for PUFFBALL (sense 1).

fuzz·y /ˈfəzē/ ▶ adj. (**fuzz·i·er, fuzz·i·est**) **1** having a frizzy, fluffy, or frayed texture or appearance. **2** difficult to perceive clearly or understand and explain precisely; indistinct or vague. ■ (of a person or the mind) unable to think clearly; confused: *my mind felt fuzzy.* **3** Comput. Logic of or relating to a form of set theory and logic in which predicates may have degrees of applicability, rather than simply being true or false. It has important uses in artificial intelligence and the design of control systems.
– PHRASES **warm fuzzy** (or **warm and fuzzy**) informal used to refer to a sentimentally emotional response or something designed to evoke such a response. — **fuzz·i·ly** adv. **fuzz·i·ness** n.

fuz·zy·head·ed /ˈfəzē,hedid/ ▶ adj. **1** muddled in thought or conception: *fuzzyheaded liberals.* **2** slightly dizzy or giddy.

f.v. ▶ abbr. Latin folio verso (on the back of the page).

FWD ▶ abbr. ■ four-wheel drive. ■ front-wheel drive.

fwd. ▶ abbr. forward.

F-word ▶ n. informal used instead of or in reference to the word "fuck" because of its taboo nature.

FX ▶ abbr. ■ foreign exchange. ■ unusual (visual or sound) effects: *computer FX may allow him to redefine cinema.* [from the pronunc. of *effects*.]

FY ▶ abbr. fiscal year.

-fy ▶ suffix **1** (added to nouns) forming verbs denoting making or producing: *speechify.* ■ denoting transformation or the process of making into: *deify* | *petrify.* **2** forming verbs denoting the making of a state defined by an adjective: *amplify* | *falsify.* **3** forming verbs expressing a causative sense: *horrify.* [from Fr. *-fier*, from L. *-ficare*, *-facere*, from *facere* 'do, make.']

FYI ▶ abbr. for your information.

FZS ▶ abbr. Fellow of the Zoological Society.

Gg

G¹ /jē/ (also **g**) ▶ **n.** (pl. **Gs** or **G's**) **1** the seventh letter of the alphabet. ■ denoting the next after F in a set of items, categories, etc. **2** Music the fifth note in the diatonic scale of C major. ■ a key based on a scale with G as its keynote.

G² ▶ **abbr.** ■ Physics gauss. ■ German. ■ [in comb.] (in units of measurement) giga- (109). ■ good. ■ informal grand (a thousand dollars). ■ a unit of gravitational force equal to that exerted by the earth's gravitational field. ▶ **symb.** ■ Chem. Gibbs free energy. ■ general audiences, a rating in the Voluntary Movie Rating System that all ages may be admitted. ■ Physics the gravitational constant, equal to 6.67 × 10–11N m2 kg–2.

g ▶ **abbr.** ■ Chem. gas. ■ gram(s). ▶ **symb.** Physics the acceleration due to gravity, equal to 9.81 m s–2.

G7 ▶ **abbr.** Group of Seven.

GA ▶ **abbr.** ■ Gamblers Anonymous. ■ General Assembly. ■ general aviation. ■ General of the Army. ■ Georgia (in official postal use).

Ga¹ /gä/ ▶ **symb.** the chemical element gallium.

Ga² ▶ **abbr.** Bible Galatians.

Ga. ▶ **abbr.** Georgia.

gab /gab/ informal ▶ **v.** (**gabbed, gab•bing**) [intrans.] talk, typically at length, about trivial matters. ▶ **n.** talk; chatter. [18th C.: var. of **GOB¹**.]

GABA ▶ **abbr.** gamma-aminobutyric acid.

gab•ar•dine /ˈgabərˌdēn/ (esp. Brit. also **gab•er•dine**) ▶ **n.** a smooth, durable twill-woven cloth, typically of worsted or cotton. [16th C.: from OFr. *gauvardine*, earlier *gallevardine*, perh. from Mid. High Ger. *wallevart* 'pilgrimage' and orig. 'a garment worn by a pilgrim.']

gab•ble /ˈgabəl/ ▶ **v.** [intrans.] talk rapidly and unintelligibly; utter meaningless sounds. ▶ **n.** rapid, unintelligible talk. — **gab•bler n.** [16th C.: from Du. *gabbelen*, of imitative origin.]

gab•bro /ˈgabrō/ ▶ **n.** (pl. **-bros**) Geol. a dark, coarse-grained plutonic rock of crystalline texture, consisting mainly of pyroxene, plagioclase feldspar, and often olivine. — **gab•bro•ic** /gəˈbrō-ik/ **adj.** [19th C.: from Ital., from L. *glaber, glabr-* 'smooth.']

gab•by /ˈgabē/ ▶ **adj.** (**gab•bi•er, gab•bi•est**) informal excessively or annoyingly talkative.

gab•fest /ˈgabˌfest/ ▶ **n.** informal a conference or other gathering with prolonged talking. ■ a prolonged conversation.

ga•bi•on /ˈgābēən/ ▶ **n.** a wirework container filled with rock, broken concrete, or other material, used in the construction of dams, retaining walls, etc. ■ hist. a similar container of wickerwork, filled with earth or stone and used in fortifications. [16th C.: via Fr. from Ital. *gabbione*.]

gable

ga•ble /ˈgābəl/ ▶ **n.** the part of a wall that encloses the end of a pitched roof. ■ (also **gable end**) a wall topped with a gable. ■ a gable-shaped canopy over a window or door. — **ga•bled adj.** [ME: via OFr. from ON *gafl*, of Gmc. origin; rel. to Ger. *Gabel* 'fork.']

ga•ble roof ▶ **n.** a roof with two sloping sides and a gable at each end. See illustration at **ROOF**.

Ga•bon /gäˈbôN/ a country in West Africa. *See box.* — **Gab•o•nese** /ˌgabəˈnēz; -ˈnēs/ **adj. & n.**

Ga•bor /gəˈbôr; ˈgäbôr/, Dennis (1900–79), British engineer; born in Hungary. He conceived the idea of holography. Nobel Prize for Physics (1971).

Ga•bo•ro•ne /ˌgäbəˈrōnā/ the capital of Botswana, in the southern part of the country; pop. 133,000.

Ga•bri•el /ˈgābrēəl/ (in the Bible) the archangel who foretold the birth of Jesus to the Virgin Mary, and who also appeared to Zacharias and to Daniel; (in Islam) the archangel who revealed the Koran to the Prophet Muhammad.

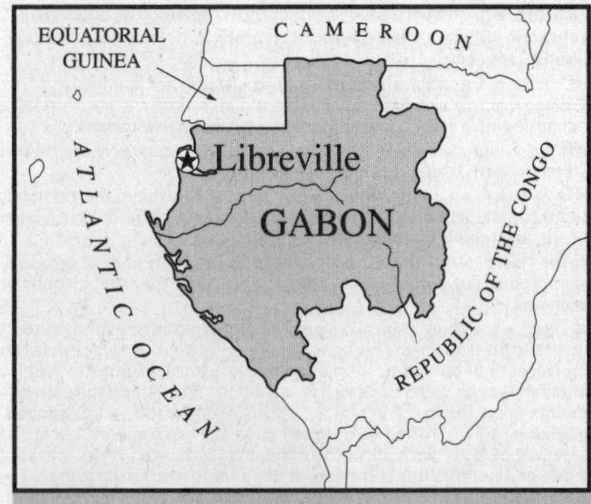

Gabon

Official name: Gabonese Republic
Location: West Africa, bordered on west by Atlantic Ocean, east and south by the Republic of the Congo
Area: 99,500 square miles (257,700 sq km)
Population: 1,355,000
Capital: Libreville
Languages: French (official), other West African languages
Currency: CFA franc

Gad¹ /gad/ (in the Bible) a Hebrew patriarch, son of Jacob and Zilpah. ■ the tribe of Israel traditionally descended from him.

Gad² ▶ **interj.** used to express dismay or surprise. [alt. of **GOD**.]

gad¹ /gad/ ▶ **v.** (**gad•ded, gad•ding**) [intrans.] informal go around from one place to another, in the pursuit of pleasure or entertainment. [ME: back-form. from obs. *gadling* 'wanderer, vagabond,' (earlier) 'companion,' of Gmc. origin.]

gad² ▶ **exclam.** archaic an expression of surprise or emphatic assertion. [15th C.: euphemistic alt. of **GOD**.]

gad•a•bout /ˈgadəˌbout/ ▶ **n.** a habitual pleasure-seeker.

Gad•da•fi /gəˈdäfē/ (also **Qad•da•fi** /kə-/), Mu'ammer Muhammad al (1942–), de facto chief of state of Libya 1969– . He established the Libyan Arab Republic and pursued a policy of Islamic fundamentalism blended with Arab nationalism.

Gad•dis /ˈgadis/, William (1922–98) US writer. His novels include *JR* (1975) and *Carpenter's Gothic* (1985).

gad•fly /ˈgadˌflī/ ▶ **n.** (pl. **-flies**) a fly that bites livestock, esp. a horsefly, warble fly, or botfly. ■ fig. an annoying person, esp. one who provokes others into action by criticism. [16th C.: from **GAD¹**, or obs. *gad* 'goad, spike,' from ON *gaddr*, of Gmc. origin; rel. to **YARD¹**.]

gadg•et /ˈgajit/ ▶ **n.** a small mechanical device or tool, esp. an ingenious or novel one. — **gadg•et•ry** /-trē/ **n.** [19th C.: prob. from Fr. *gâchette* 'lock mechanism.']

ga•doid /ˈgādoid/ ▶ **n.** Zool. a bony fish of an order (Gadiformes) that comprises the cods, hakes, and their relatives. [19th C.: from mod. L. *gadus* (from Gk. *gados* 'cod') + **-OID**.]

gad•o•lin•ite /ˈgadl-əˌnīt/ ▶ **n.** a rare dark brown or black mineral, consisting of a silicate of iron, beryllium, and rare earths. [19th C.: after Johan *Gadolin* (1760–1852), Finnish mineralogist.]

gad•o•lin•i•um /ˌgadlˈinēəm/ ▶ **n.** the chemical element of atomic number 64, a soft silvery-white metal of the lanthanide series. (Symbol: **Gd**) [19th C.: from *gadolinite*, a mineral, after Johan Gadolin (1760–1852), Finnish mineralogist.]

Gads•den /ˈgadzdən/ a city in northeastern Alabama; pop. 38,978.

Gads•den Pur•chase /ˈgadzdən/ an area in New Mexico and Arizona, near the Rio Grande, that covers more than 30,000 square miles (77,700 sq km). It was purchased from Mexico in 1853 by US diplomat James Gadsden (1788–1858).

gad·wall /'gad,wôl/ ▶ **n.** (pl. same or **-walls**) a brownish-gray freshwater duck (*Anas strepera*) found across Eurasia and North America.

Gad·zooks /gad'zo͝oks/ (also **gad·zooks**) ▶ **exclam.** dated or humorous an exclamation of surprise or annoyance. [17th C.: alt. of *God's hooks*.]

Gae·a /'jēə/ var. of **Gaia**.

Gael /gāl/ ▶ **n.** a Gaelic-speaking person. ■ a person whose ancestors spoke Gaelic. — **Gael·dom** /-dəm/ **n.** [from Scot. Gael. *Gaidheal*.]

Gael·ic /'gālik/ ▶ **adj.** of or relating to the Goidelic languages, particularly the Celtic language of Scotland, and the culture associated with speakers of these languages and their descendants. ▶ **n.** (also **Scottish Gaelic**) a Goidelic language brought from Ireland in the 5th and 6th centuries AD and spoken in the highlands and islands of western Scotland. ■ (also **Irish Gaelic**) another term for **Irish** (the language).

Gael·tacht /'gāltəkнt/ (**the Gaeltacht**) regions in Ireland where the vernacular language is Irish.

gaff[1] /gaf/ ▶ **n. 1** a stick with a hook, or a barbed spear, for landing large fish. **2** Sailing a spar to which the head of a fore-and-aft sail is bent. ▶ **v.** [trans.] seize or impale with a gaff. [ME: from Provençal *gaf* 'hook'; rel. to **gaffe**.]

gaff[2] ▶ **n.** rough treatment; criticism: *if wages increase, perhaps we can stand the gaff.* [19th C.: of unknown origin.]

gaffe /gaf/ ▶ **n.** an unintentional act or remark causing embarrassment to its originator; a blunder: *an unforgivable social gaffe.* [20th C.: from Fr., lit. 'boat hook' (from Provençal *gaf*: see **gaff**[1]).]

gaf·fer /'gafər/ ▶ **n. 1** the chief electrician in a motion-picture or television production unit. **2** informal an old man. [16th C.: prob. a contr. of **godfather**.]

gag[1] /gag/ ▶ **n.** a thing, typically a piece of cloth, put in or over a person's mouth to prevent them from speaking or crying out. ■ fig. a restriction on freedom of speech or dissemination of information: *they lobbied hard for a gag on doctors and nurses.* ■ a device for keeping the patient's mouth open during a dental or surgical operation. ▶ **v.** (**gagged, gag·ging**) **1** [trans.] (often **be gagged**) put a gag on (someone). ■ fig. (of a person or body with authority) prevent (someone) from speaking freely or disseminating information: *the administration is trying to gag its critics.* **2** [intrans.] choke or retch. [ME: perh. rel. to ON *gagháls* 'with the neck thrown back.']

gag[2] ▶ **n.** a joke or an amusing story or scene, esp. one forming part of a comedian's act or in a film or play. [19th C. (orig. theatrical slang): of unknown origin.]

ga·ga /'gä,gä/ ▶ **adj.** informal overexcited or irrational, typically as a result of infatuation or excessive enthusiasm; mentally confused; senile. [20th C.: from Fr., 'senile, a senile person,' reduplication based on *gâteux*, var. of *gâteur* 'bed wetter.']

Ga·ga·rin /gə'gärin/, Yury Alekseyevich (1934–68), Russian cosmonaut. In 1961, he made the first manned space flight, completing a single orbit of the earth in 108 minutes.

gage[1] /gāj/ archaic ▶ **n.** a valued object deposited as a guarantee of good faith. ■ a pledge, esp. a glove, thrown down as a symbol of a challenge to fight. ▶ **v.** [trans.] offer (a thing or one's life) as a guarantee of good faith. [ME: from OFr. *gage* (n.), *gager* (v.), of Gmc. origin; rel. to **wage** and **wed**.]

gage[2] ▶ **n. & v.** var. of **gauge**.

gage[3] ▶ **n.** another term for **greengage**.

gag·gle /'gagəl/ ▶ **n.** a flock of geese. ■ informal a disorderly or noisy group of people. [ME: imitative of the noise that a goose makes.]

gag or·der ▶ **n.** Law a judge's order that a case may not be discussed in public.

gag rule ▶ **n.** a regulation or directive that prohibits public discussion of a particular matter, in particular: ■ a regulation preventing the staff of government-funded family-planning clinics from offering patients information about abortion. ■ a US government policy preventing US aid to foreign family-planning organizations unless they agree not to promote or perform abortions.

Gai·a /'gīə/ (also **Gae·a, Ge**) Gk. Mythol. the Earth personified as a goddess, daughter of Chaos. [Gk., 'Earth.']

Gai·a hy·poth·e·sis the theory, put forward by James Lovelock, that living matter on the earth collectively regulates the conditions necessary for the continuance of life, likening the planet to a vast self-regulating organism.

gai·e·ty /'gāitē/ (also **gay·e·ty**) ▶ **n.** (pl. **-ties**) the state or quality of being lighthearted or cheerful: *the gaiety of children's laughter.* ■ merrymaking or festivity. [17th C.: from Fr. *gaieté*, from *gai* (see **gay**).]

gail·lar·di·a /gə'lärdēə/ ▶ **n.** an American plant (genus *Gaillardia*) of the daisy family, cultivated for its bright red and yellow flowers. [mod. L., named in memory of *Gaillard* de Marentonneau, 18th-cent. French amateur botanist.]

gai·ly /'gālē/ ▶ **adv.** in a cheerful or lighthearted way. ■ without thinking of the consequences: *she plunged gaily into the stock market.* ■ [as submodifier] with a bright or cheerful appearance: *gaily colored sailboats.*

gain /gān/ ▶ **v. 1** [trans.] obtain or secure (something desired, favorable, or profitable): *gain confidence.* ■ reach or arrive at (a desired destination): *we gained the ridge.* ■ [intrans.] (**gain on**) come closer to (a person or thing pursued): *a huge bear gaining on him.* **2** [trans.] increase the amount or rate of (something, typically weight or speed): *she had gradually gained weight.* ■ [intrans.] increase in value: *stocks gained for the third day in a row.* ■ [intrans.] (**gain in**) improve or advance in some respect: *canoeing is gaining in popularity.* ■ (of a clock or watch) become fast by (a specific amount of time): *this clock will neither gain nor lose a second.* ▶ **n.** an increase in wealth or resources: *using municipal funds for personal gain.* ■ a thing that is achieved or acquired. ■ the factor by which power or voltage is increased in an amplifier or other electronic device, usually expressed as a logarithm. [15th C.: from OFr. *gaigne* (n.), *gaignier* (v.), of Gmc. origin.]

Gaines·ville /'gānz,vil; -vəl/ a city in north central Florida; pop. 95,447.

gain·ful /'gānfəl/ ▶ **adj.** [attrib.] serving to increase wealth or resources: *he soon found gainful employment.* — **gain·ful·ly adv. gain·ful·ness n.**

gain·say /,gān'sā; 'gān,sā/ ▶ **v.** (past and past part. **-said**) [trans.] [with negative] formal deny or contradict (a fact or statement): *the impact of the railroads cannot be gainsaid.* ■ speak against or oppose (someone). — **gain·say·er n.** [ME: from obs. *gain-* 'against' + **say**.]

Gains·bor·ough /'gānzbərə/, Thomas (1727–88), English painter, noted for his portraits, including *The Blue Boy* (*c.*1770), and for landscapes.

'gainst /genst/ ▶ **prep.** literary short for **against**.

gait /gāt/ ▶ **n.** a person's manner of walking. ■ the paces of an animal, esp. a horse or dog. ▶ **v.** [intrans.] (of a dog or horse) walk in a trained gait, as at a show: *the dogs are gaiting in a circle.* [ME (orig. Scots).]

gait·er /'gātər/ ▶ **n.** (usu. **gaiters**) a garment similar to leggings, worn to cover or protect the ankle and lower leg. ■ a shoe or overshoe extending to the ankle or above. — **gait·ered adj.** [18th C.: from Fr. *guêtre*, prob. of Gmc. origin and rel. to **wrist**.]

Gai·thers·burg /'gāᴛʜərz,bərg/ a city in west central Maryland; pop. 52,613.

Gal. ▶ **abbr.** Bible Galatians.

gal[1] /gal/ ▶ **n.** informal a girl or young woman. [18th C.: representing a pronunc.]

gal[2] ▶ **n.** Physics a unit of gravitational acceleration equal to one centimeter per second per second. [20th C.: after **Galileo Galilei**.]

gal. ▶ **abbr.** gallon(s).

ga·la /'gālə; 'galə/ ▶ **n.** a social occasion with special entertainments or performances. [17th C. (in the sense 'showy dress'): via Ital. and Sp. from OFr. *gale* 'rejoicing.']

ga·lac·tic /gə'laktik/ ▶ **adj.** of or relating to a galaxy or galaxies, esp. the Milky Way galaxy. ■ Astron. measured relative to the galactic equator. [19th C.: from Gk. *galaktias* (var. of *galaxias* 'galaxy') + **-ic**.]

ga·lac·tic e·qua·tor ▶ **n.** Astron. the great circle passing as closely as possible through the densest parts of the Milky Way.

ga·lac·tor·rhe·a /gə,laktə'rēə/ ▶ **n.** Med. excessive or inappropriate production of milk. [19th C.: from Gk. *gala, galakt-* 'milk' + *rhoia* 'flux, flow.']

ga·lac·tose /gə'laktōs/ ▶ **n.** Chem. a sugar of the hexose class that is a constituent of lactose and many polysaccharides. [19th C.: from Gk. *gala, galakt-* 'milk' + **-ose**[2].]

ga·lah /gə'lä/ ▶ **n.** a small Australian cockatoo (*Eulophus roseicapillus*) with a gray back and rosy pink head and underparts. [19th C.: from Yuwaalaraay (an Aboriginal language).]

Gal·a·had /'galə,had/ (also **Sir Galahad**) the noblest of King Arthur's legendary knights.

ga·lan·gal /gə'laNGgəl/ (also **ga·lin·gale** /'galin,gāl/) ▶ **n.** an Asian plant (genera *Alpinia* and *Kaempferia*) of the ginger family, with an aromatic rhizome used in cooking and herbal medicine. [ME *galingale*, via OFr. from Arab. *ḵalanjān*, perh. from Chin. *gāoliángjiāng*, from *gāoliáng* (the name of a district in Guangdong Province, China) + *jiāng* 'ginger.']

gal·an·tine /'galən,tēn/ ▶ **n.** a dish of white meat or fish that is boned, cooked, pressed, and served cold in aspic. [ME (in the sense 'sauce for fish'): from OFr., alt. of *galatine*, from med. L. *galatina*; the current sense dates from the early 18th C.]

Ga·la·pa·gos Is·lands /gə'läpəgəs; -'lap-/ a Pacific Ocean archipelago on the equator, about 650 miles (1,045 km) west of Ecuador, to which it belongs; pop. 9,750. It is noted for giant tortoises and many other endemic species. Spanish name **Archipiélago de Colón**.

Gal·a·te·a /,galə'tēə/ **1** Gk. Mythol. a sea nymph courted by the Cyclops Polyphemus, who in jealousy killed his rival Acis. **2** the name given to the statue fashioned by Pygmalion and brought to life.

Ga·la·ţi /gä'läts; -'lätsē/ a city in eastern Romania, a port on the lower Danube River; pop. 324,000.

Ga·la·tia /gə'lāsʜ(ē)ə/ an ancient region in central Asia Minor, settled by the Galatians in the 3rd century BC. It later became a province of the Roman Empire. — **Ga·la·tian adj. & n.**

Ga·la·tians /gə'lāsʜənz/ a book of the New Testament, an epistle of St. Paul to the Church in Galatia.

gal·ax·y /'galəksē/ ▶ **n.** (pl. **-ax·ies**) a system of millions or billions of stars, together with gas and dust, held together by gravitational attraction. ■ (**the Galaxy**) the galaxy of which the solar system is a part; the Milky Way. ■ fig. a large or impressive group of people or things: *a galaxy of talent.* [ME (orig. referring to the Milky Way): via OFr. from med. L. *galaxia*, from Gk. *galaxias (kuklos)* 'milky (vault),' from *gala, galakt-* 'milk.']

Gal·ba /'galbə/ (*c.*3 BC–AD 69), Roman emperor AD 68–69; full name *Servius Sulpicius Galba*. The successor to Nero, he aroused hostility because of his severity and parsimony and was murdered.

Gal·braith /'galbrāᴛʜ/, John Kenneth (1908–2006), US economist; born in Canada. He wrote *The Affluent Society* (1958) and *The Economics of Innocent Fraud* (2004).

gale /gāl/ ▶ **n.** a very strong wind. ■ Meteorol. a wind of force 7 to 10 on the Beaufort scale (28–55 knots or 32–63 mph). ■ a storm at sea. ■ **(a gale of/gales of)** fig. a burst of sound, esp. of laughter: ***gales of laughter.*** [16th C.: perh. rel. to ON *galinn* 'mad, frantic.']

ga·le·a /'gālēə/ ▶ **n.** (pl. **-le·ae** /-lē,ē/ or **-le·as**) Bot. Zool. a structure shaped like a helmet. [19th C.: from L., 'helmet.']

Ga·len /'gālən/ (129–199), Greek physician; full name *Claudios Galenos*; Latin name *Claudius Galenus*. He made important discoveries in anatomy and physiology. — **Ga·len·ism n. Ga·len·ist adj. & n.**

ga·le·na /gə'lēnə/ ▶ **n.** a bluish, gray, or black mineral of metallic appearance, consisting of lead sulfide. It is the chief ore of lead. [17th C.: from L., 'lead ore' (in a partly purified state).]

ga·len·i·cal /gā'lenikəl; gə-/ Med. ▶ **adj.** (of a medicine) made of natural rather than synthetic components. ■ (usu. **Galenical**) of or relating to Galen or his methods. ▶ **n.** a medicine of this type.

gal Fri·day ▶ **n.** informal term for GIRL FRIDAY.

Ga·li·bi /gə'lēbē/ ▶ **n.** another term for CARIB (sense 2). [Carib, lit. 'strong man.']

Ga·li·cia /gə'lisнə/ **1** an autonomous region in northwestern Spain; capital, Santiago de Compostela. **2** a region in east central Europe. A former province of Austria, it now forms part of southeastern Poland and western Ukraine.

Ga·li·ci·an /gə'lisнən/ ▶ **adj.** **1** of or relating to Galicia in northwestern Spain, its people, or their language. **2** of or relating to Galicia in east central Europe. ▶ **n.** **1** a native or inhabitant of Galicia in northwestern Spain. **2** the Romance language of Galicia in northwestern Spain, closely related to Portuguese. **3** a native or inhabitant of Galicia in east central Europe.

Gal·i·le·an[1] /,galə'lēən/ ▶ **adj.** of or relating to Galileo or his methods.

Gal·i·le·an[2] ▶ **adj.** of or relating to Galilee. ▶ **n.** a native of Galilee.

Gal·i·le·an sat·el·lites Astron. the four largest moons of Jupiter (Callisto, Europa, Ganymede, and Io), discovered by Galileo in 1610 and independently by the German astronomer Simon Marius (1573–1624).

Gal·i·lee /'galə,lē/ a region of ancient Palestine, associated with the ministry of Jesus. It is now part of Israel.

gal·i·lee /'galə,lē/ ▶ **n.** a chapel or porch at the entrance to some English churches. [ME: from OFr., from med. L. *galilea* 'Galilee.' Cf. GALLERY.]

Gal·i·lee, Sea of a lake in northern Israel. The Jordan River flows through it from north to south. Also called TIBERIAS, LAKE, KINNERET, LAKE.

Gal·i·le·o /,galə'lāō/ an American space probe to Jupiter launched in 1989.

Gal·i·le·o Ga·li·lei /,galə'lāō ,galə'lā/ (1564–1642), Italian astronomer and physicist. He discovered the constancy of a pendulum's swing, formulated the law of uniform acceleration of falling bodies, and described the parabolic trajectory of projectiles. He applied the telescope to astronomy and observed the moon and planets.

gal·in·gale /'galin,gāl/ ▶ **n.** var. of GALANGAL.

gall[1] /gôl/ ▶ **n.** **1** bold, impudent behavior: *the gall to demand a fee.* **2** the contents of the gallbladder; bile (proverbial for its bitterness). ■ an animal's gallbladder. ■ used to refer to something bitter or cruel: *accept life's gall.* [OE *gealla* (denoting bile): rel. to Ger. *Galle* 'gall,' from an Indo-Eur. root shared by L. *fel* 'bile.']

gall[2] ▶ **n.** **1** annoyance; irritation. **2** (esp. of a horse) a sore on the skin made by chafing. ▶ **v.** [trans.] **1** make (someone) feel annoyed: *losing galled him.* **2** make sore by rubbing. [OE *gealle* 'sore on a horse,' superseded by forms from Mid. Low Ger. or MDu.]

gall[3] ▶ **n.** an abnormal growth formed in response to the presence of insect larvae, mites, or fungi on plants and trees, esp. oaks. ■ [as adj.] denoting insects or mites that produce such growths: *gall flies.* [ME: via OFr. from L. *galla.*]

gal·lant ▶ **adj.** **1** /'galənt/ (of a person or their behavior) brave; heroic. **2** /'galənt/ (of a man or his behavior) giving special attention and respect to women; chivalrous. ▶ **n.** /gə'lant; -'länt; 'galənt/ dated or literary a man who pays special attention to women. ■ a dashing man of fashion; a fine gentleman. — **gal·lant·ly** /'galəntlē/ **adv.** [ME (in the sense 'finely dressed'): from OFr. *galant*, from *galer* 'have fun, make a show,' from *gale* 'pleasure, rejoicing.']

gal·lant·ry /'galəntrē/ ▶ **n.** (pl. **-ries**) **1** courageous behavior, esp. in battle: ***outstanding gallantry during the raid.*** **2** polite attention or respect given by men to women. ■ **(gallantries)** actions or words used when paying such attention.

Gal·lau·det /,galə'det/, Thomas Hopkins (1787–1851) US educator. In 1817, he founded the first free US school for the deaf in Hartford, Connecticut. Gallaudet College in Washington, DC, is named for him.

gall·ber·ry /'gôl,berē/ (also **gallberry holly**) ▶ **n.** (pl. **-ries**) a North American holly (genus *Ilex*) with white flowers, including the **low gallberry** (*I. glabra*), with black berries and nearly spineless shiny leaves.

gall·blad·der /'gôl,bladər/ (also **gall blad·der**) ▶ **n.** the small sac-shaped organ beneath the liver, in which bile is stored after secretion by the liver and before release into the intestine.

gal·le·on /'galēən; 'galyən/ ▶ **n.** a sailing ship in use (esp. by Spain) from the 15th through 17th centuries, originally as a warship, later for trade. Galleons were mainly square-rigged and usually had three or more decks and masts. [16th C.: either via MDu. from Fr. *galion*, from *galie* 'galley,' or from Sp. *galeón.*]

galleon

gal·le·ri·a /,galə'rēə/ ▶ **n.** a covered or enclosed area, esp. one with commercial establishments for shopping, dining, etc. [Ital. (see GALLERY).]

gal·ler·y /'galərē/ ▶ **n.** (pl. **-ler·ies**) **1** a room or building for the display or sale of works of art. **2** a balcony, esp. a platform or upper floor, projecting from the back or sidewall inside a church or hall, providing space for an audience or musicians. ■ **(the gallery)** the highest of such balconies in a theater, containing the cheapest seats. ■ a group of spectators, esp. those at a golf tournament. **3** a horizontal underground passage, esp. in a mine. [ME (sense 3): via OFr. from Ital. *galleria* 'gallery,' formerly also 'church porch,' from med. L. *galeria*, perh. an alt. of *galilea* (see GALILEE).]

gal·ley /'galē/ ▶ **n.** (pl. **-leys**) **1** hist. a low, flat ship with one or more sails and up to three banks of oars. ■ a long rowboat used as a ship's boat. **2** the kitchen in a ship or aircraft. **3** (also **galley proof**) a printer's proof in the form of long single-column strips, not in sheets or pages. [*galley* from Fr. *galée* denoting an oblong tray for holding setup type.] [ME: via OFr. from med. L. *galea*, from med. Gk. *galaia*, of unknown origin.]

gal·ley slave ▶ **n.** hist. a person condemned to row in a galley.

Gal·lia·no /gal'yänō/ ▶ **n.** a golden-yellow Italian liqueur flavored with herbs. [named after Major Giuseppe *Galliáno*, noted for halting Ethiopian forces in the war of 1895–96.]

gal·liard /'galyərd/ ▶ **n.** hist. a lively dance in triple time for two people, including complicated turns and steps. [ME: from OFr. *gaillard* 'valiant,' of Celtic origin.]

Gal·lic /'galik/ ▶ **adj.** **1** French or typically French. **2** of or relating to the Gauls. — **Gal·li·cize** /'galə,sīz/ **v.** [17th C.: from L. *Gallicus*, from *Gallus* 'a Gaul.']

gal·lic ac·id /'galik/ ▶ **n.** Chem. an acid, $C_6H_2(OH)_3COOH$, extracted from oak galls and other vegetable products, formerly used in making ink.

Gal·li·can /'galikən/ ▶ **adj.** of or relating to the ancient Church of Gaul or France. — **Gal·li·can·ism n.**

Gal·li·cism /'gali,sizəm/ ▶ **n.** a French expression, esp. one adopted by speakers of another language.

Gal·lic Wars Julius Caesar's campaigns 58–51 BC, which established Roman control over Gaul north of the Alps and west of the Rhine River.

gal·li·mau·fry /,galə'môfrē/ ▶ **n.** (pl. **-fries**) a confused jumble or medley of things. ■ a hash made from diced or minced meat. [16th C.: from archaic Fr. *galimafrée* 'unappetizing dish,' perh. from OFr. *galer* 'have fun' + Picard *mafrer* 'eat copious quantities.']

gal·li·na·ceous /,galə'nāsнəs/ ▶ **adj.** dated relating to birds of an order (Galliformes) which includes domestic poultry and game birds. [18th C.: from L. *gallinaceus* (from *gallina* 'hen,' from *gallus* 'cock') + **-ous**.]

gall·ing /'gôliɴɢ/ ▶ **adj.** annoying; humiliating: *the loss was particularly galling.* — **gall·ing·ly adv.**

gal·li·nule /'galə,n(y)o͞ol/ ▶ **n.** a marsh bird (genera *Porphyrio* and *Porphyrula*) of the rail family, with mainly black, purplish-blue, or dark green plumage, and a red bill. See also MOORHEN. [18th C.: from mod. L. *Gallinula* (genus term), dimin. of L. *gallina* 'hen,' from *gallus* 'cock.']

gal·li·ot /'galēət/ ▶ **n.** hist. a single-masted Dutch cargo boat or fishing vessel. ■ a small fast galley, esp. in the Mediterranean. [ME: from OFr. *galiote* or Du. *galjoot*, from a dimin. of med. L. *galea* 'galley.']

Gal·lip·o·li /gə'lipəlē/ a major campaign of World War I that took place on the Gallipoli peninsula, on the European side of the Dardanelles in 1915–16.

gal·li·pot /'galə,pät/ ▶ **n.** hist. a small earthenware pot, used by pharmacists to hold medicines. [ME: prob. from GALLEY + POT[1] (because gallipots were brought from the Mediterranean in galleys).]

gal·li·um /'galēəm/ ▶ **n.** the chemical element of atomic number 31, a soft, silvery-white metal that melts at about 30°C, just above room temperature. (Symbol: **Ga**) [19th C.: mod. L., from L. *Gallia* 'France' or *gallus* 'cock.']

gal·li·um ar·sen·ide ▶ **n.** a dark-gray crystalline compound containing gallium and arsenic, used in the manufacture of microelectronic components.

gal·li·vant /'galə,vant/ ▶**v.** [intrans.] informal go around from one place to another in the pursuit of pleasure or entertainment.

gal·li·wasp /'galə,wäsp/ ▶**n.** a marsh lizard (genus *Diploglossus*, family Anguidae) of Central America and the Caribbean.

gall midge ▶**n.** a small, delicate midge (family Cecidomyiidae) that induces gall formation in plants or may cause other damage to crops.

gall mite ▶**n.** a minute mite (family Eriophyidae) that is parasitic on plants, typically living inside buds and causing them to form hard galls.

Gallo- ▶**comb. form** French; French and ...: *Gallo-German.* ■ relating to France. [from L. *Gallus* 'a Gaul.']

gal·lon /'galən/ ▶**n. 1** a unit of volume for liquid measure equal to four quarts, in particular: ■ US equivalent to 3.79 liters. ■ (also **imperial gallon**) Brit. (also used for dry measure) equivalent to 4.55 liters. **2** (**gallons of**) informal a large volume. — **gal·lon·age** /'galənij/ **n.** [ME: from Anglo-Norman Fr. *galon*, from the base of med. L. *galleta*, *galletum* 'pail, liquid measure.']

gal·loon /gə'lo͞on/ ▶**n.** a narrow ornamental strip of fabric used to trim clothing or upholstery. [17th C.: from Fr. *galon*, from *galonner* 'to trim with braid,' of unknown ultimate origin.]

gal·lop /'galəp/ ▶**n.** [in sing.] the fastest pace of a horse or other quadruped, with all the feet off the ground together in each stride. ■ a ride on a horse at this pace. ■ a very fast pace of running or moving. ▶**v.** (**gal·loped, gal·lop·ing**) [intrans.] (of a horse) go at the pace of a gallop. ■ [trans.] make (a horse) gallop. ■ (of a person) run fast and rather boisterously. ■ fig. (of a process or time) progress rapidly in a seemingly uncontrollable manner: *the deadline galloping toward them* | [as adj.] (**galloping**) *galloping inflation.* [16th C.: from OFr. *galop* (n.), *galoper* (v.), vars. of Old North. Fr. *walop*, *waloper* (see **WALLOP**).]

gal·lows /'galōz/ ▶**plural n.** [usu. treated as sing.] a structure, typically of two uprights and a crosspiece, for the hanging of criminals. ■ (**the gallows**) execution by hanging. [OE *galga*, *gealga*, of Gmc. origin; rel. to Ger. *Galgen*.]

gal·lows hu·mor ▶**n.** grim and ironic humor in a desperate or hopeless situation.

gall·stone /'gôl,stōn/ ▶**n.** a small, hard crystalline mass formed abnormally in the gallbladder, often causing severe pain and blockage of the bile duct.

Gal·lup poll /'galəp/ ▶**n.** trademark an assessment of public opinion by the questioning of a statistically representative sample. [1940s: named after George H. *Gallup* (1901–84), US statistician who devised the method.]

gal·lus·es /'galəsiz/ ▶**plural n.** informal suspenders for trousers. [19th C.: pl. of *gallus*, var. of **GALLOWS**.]

gall wasp ▶**n.** a small winged insect (superfamily Cynipoidea, order Hymenoptera) of antlike appearance. The female lays its egg in plant tissue, which swells to form a gall when the larva hatches.

Ga·lois the·o·ry /gäl'wä/ **n.** Math. a method of applying group theory to the solution of algebraic equations. [named for Évariste Galois (1811–32).]

ga·loot /gə'lo͞ot/ ▶**n.** informal a clumsy or oafish person (often as a term of abuse). [19th C.: of unknown origin.]

ga·lore /gə'lôr/ ▶**adj.** [postpositive] in abundance: *prizes galore.* [17th C.: from Irish *go leor*, lit. 'to sufficiency.']

ga·losh /gə'läsн/ ▶**n.** (usu. **galoshes**) a waterproof overshoe, typically made of rubber. [ME: via OFr. from late L. *gallicula*, dimin. of L. *gallica (solea)* 'Gallic (shoe).']

Gals·wor·thy /'gôlz,wər<u>TH</u>ē/, John (1867–1933), British writer. He wrote *The Forsyte Saga* (1906–28), a series of novels. Nobel Prize for Literature (1932).

Gal·ton /'gôltn/, Sir Francis (1822–1911), English scientist. He founded eugenics and introduced methods of measuring human mental and physical abilities.

ga·lumph /gə'ləmf/ ▶**v.** [intrans.] informal move in a clumsy, ponderous, or noisy manner. [1871: coined by Lewis Carroll in *Through the Looking Glass*; perh. a blend of **GALLOP** and **TRIUMPH**.]

galv. ▶**abbr.** galvanic.

Gal·va·ni /gäl'vänē/, Luigi (1737–98), Italian anatomist. He is noted for his work with electric fields.

gal·van·ic /gal'vanik/ ▶**adj. 1** relating to or involving electric currents produced by chemical action. **2** sudden and dramatic: *hurry with awkward galvanic strides.* — **gal·van·i·cal·ly adv.** [18th C.: from Fr. *galvanique*, from **GALVANI**.]

gal·van·ic skin re·sponse (also **galvanic skin reflex**) (abbr.: **GSR**) ▶**n.** a change in the electrical resistance of the skin caused by emotional stress, measurable with a sensitive galvanometer, e.g., in lie-detector tests.

gal·va·nize /'galvə,nīz/ ▶**v.** [trans.] **1** shock or excite (someone), typically into taking action: *his voice galvanized them into action.* **2** [often as adj.] (**galvanized**) coat (iron or steel) with a protective layer of zinc. — **gal·va·ni·za·tion** /,galvəni'zāsнən/ **n. gal·va·niz·er n.** [19th C.: from Fr. *galvaniser* (see **GALVANI**).]

gal·va·nom·e·ter /,galvə'nämitər/ ▶**n.** an instrument for detecting and measuring small electric currents. — **gal·va·no·met·ric** /-nə'metrik/ **adj.**

Gal·ves·ton /'galvəstən/ a city in southeastern Texas, southeast of Houston; pop. 59,070.

Gal·way /'gôl,wā/ a county in the Republic of Ireland. ■ its county town, on Galway Bay; pop. 51,000.

Gal·way Bay an inlet of the Atlantic Ocean on the western coast of Ireland.

gam¹ /gam/ ▶**n.** informal a leg, esp. in reference to the shapeliness of a woman's leg. [18th C.: prob. based on Old North. Fr. *gambe* 'leg.']

gam² ▶**n. 1** a school of whales, porpoises, or dolphins. **2** a social meeting or informal conversation (originally one among whalers at sea).

Ga·ma, Vas·co da see **DA GAMA**.

Ga·may /ga'mā; 'gamā/ ▶**n.** a variety of black wine grape native to the Beaujolais district of France. ■ a fruity red wine made from this grape. [hamlet in Burgundy, France.]

gam·ba /'gämbə; 'gam-/ ▶**n.** short for **VIOLA DA GAMBA**.

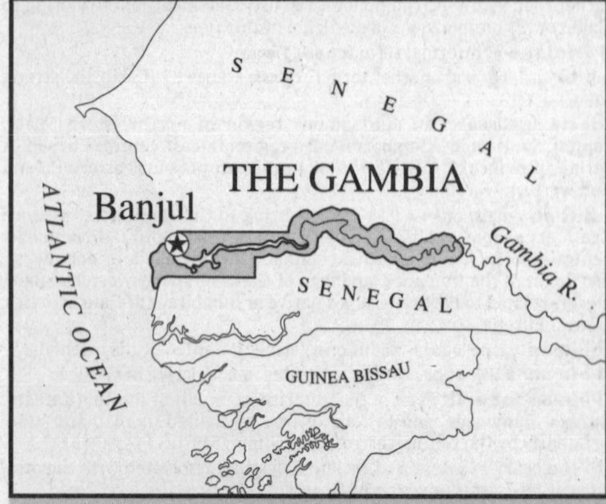

Gambia, The

Official name: Republic of the Gambia
Location: West Africa, a strip of land on either side of the Gambia River, bordered on the north, east, and south by Senegal, and on the west by the Atlantic Ocean
Area: 3,900 square miles (10,000 sq km)
Population: 900,000
Capital: Banjul
Languages: English (official), Mandinka, Creole, and other indigenous African languages
Currency: dalasi

Gam·bi·a /'gambēə; 'gäm-/ **1** (also **the Gambia**) a country in West Africa. *See box.* **2** a river in West Africa that rises near Labé in Guinea and flows for 500 miles (800 km) through Senegal and Gambia to the Atlantic. — **Gam·bi·an adj. & n.**

gam·bier /'gambi(ə)r/ (also **gam·bir**) ▶**n.** an astringent extract of a tropical Asiatic plant (esp. *Uncaria gambier*) of the bedstraw family, used in tanning.

Gam·bier Is·lands /'gambi(ə)r/ a group of islands in the South Pacific Ocean, part of French Polynesia.

gam·bit /'gambit/ ▶**n.** (in chess) an opening in which a player makes a sacrifice, typically of a pawn, for the sake of some compensating advantage. ■ a device, action, or opening remark, typically one entailing a degree of risk, that is calculated to gain an advantage: *his resignation was a tactical gambit.* [17th C.: orig. *gambett*, from Ital. *gambetto*, lit. 'tripping up,' from *gamba* 'leg.']

gam·ble /'gambəl/ ▶**v.** [intrans.] play games of chance for money; bet. ■ [trans.] bet (a sum of money) in such a way. ■ fig. take risky action in the hope of a desired result. ▶**n.** [usu. in sing.] an act of gambling; an enterprise undertaken or attempted with a risk of loss and a chance of profit or success. — **gam·bler n.** [18th C.: from obs. *gamel* 'play games,' or from the v. **GAME¹**.]

gam·boge /gam'bōj; -'bo͞ozн/ ▶**n.** a gum resin produced by various eastern Asian trees, used as a yellow pigment and as a purgative. [18th C. (earlier in the L. form): from mod. L. *gambaugium*, from **CAMBODIA**.]

gam·bol /'gambəl/ ▶**v.** (**-boled, -bol·ing**; Brit. **-bolled, -bol·ling**) run or jump about playfully. [16th C.: alt. of obs. *gambade*, via Fr. from Ital. *gambata* 'trip up,' from *gamba* 'leg.']

gam·brel /'gambrəl/ (also **gambrel roof**) ▶**n.** a roof with two sides, each of which has a shallower slope above a steeper one. See illustration at **ROOF**. [16th C.: from Old North. Fr. *gamberel*, from *gambier* 'forked stick,' from *gambe* 'leg.']

game¹ /gām/ ▶**n. 1** a form of play or sport, esp. a competitive one played according to rules and decided by skill, strength, or luck. ■ a complete episode or period of play, typically ending in a definite result: *a baseball game.* ■ a single portion of play forming a scoring unit in a match, esp. in tennis. ■ a person's performance in a game; a person's standard or method of play: *he will attempt to raise his game to another level.* ■ (**games**) a meeting for sporting contests, esp.

track and field: *the Olympic Games.* ■ the equipment for a game, esp. a board game or a computer game. **2** a type of activity or business, esp. when regarded as a game: *a game of diplomacy.* ■ a secret and clever plan or trick: *I was on to his little game.* **3** wild mammals or birds hunted for sport or food. ■ the flesh of these mammals or birds, used as food. ▶**adj.** eager and willing to do something new or challenging: *they were* ***game for anything.*** ▶**v.** [intrans.] [often as adj.] (**gaming**) play games of chance for money: *the gaming tables of Monte Carlo.* ■ play video or computer games.

– PHRASES **ahead of the game** ahead of one's competitors or peers in the same sphere of activity. **beat someone at their own game** use someone's own methods to outdo them in their chosen activity. **off** (or **on**) **one's game** playing badly (or well). **the only game in town** informal the best, the most important, or the only thing worth considering. **play the game** behave in a fair or honorable way. **play games** deal with someone or something in a way that lacks due seriousness or respect: *Don't* ***play games*** *with me!* — **game·ly adv.** [OE *gamen* 'amusement, fun,' *gamenian* 'play, amuse oneself,' of Gmc. origin.]

game² ▶**adj.** dated (of a person's leg) permanently injured; lame. [18th C.: orig. dial., of unknown origin.]

game bird ▶**n.** **1** a bird hunted for sport or food. **2** a bird of a large group (order Galliformes) that includes pheasants, grouse, quails, guineafowl, guans, etc.

game·cock /'gām,käk/ ▶**n.** a rooster bred and trained for cockfighting. Also called **game fowl**.

game fish (also **game·fish** /'gām,fiSH/) ▶**n.** (pl. same) a fish caught by anglers for sport.

game·keep·er /'gām,kēpər/ ▶**n.** a person employed to breed and protect game, typically for a large estate. — **game·keep·ing** /-,kēpiNG/ **n.**

gam·e·lan /'gamə,lan/ ▶**n.** a traditional instrumental ensemble of Indonesia, typically including many bronze percussion instruments. [19th C.: from Javanese.]

game plan ▶**n.** a strategy worked out in advance, esp. in sports, politics, or business.

game point ▶**n.** (in tennis and other sports) a point that, if won by one contestant, will also win the game.

gam·er /'gāmər/ ▶**n.** a person who plays a game or games, typically a participant in a computer or role-playing game.

game show ▶**n.** a television program in which people compete to win prizes.

games·man·ship /'gāmzmən,SHip/ ▶**n.** the art of winning games by using various ploys and tactics to gain a psychological advantage. — **games·man n.** (pl. **-men**).

gam·ete /'gamēt; gə'mēt/ ▶**n.** Biol. a mature haploid male or female germ cell that is able to unite with another of the opposite sex in sexual reproduction to form a zygote. — **ga·met·ic** /gə'metik/ **adj.** [19th C.: from mod. L. *gameta*, from Gk. *gametē* 'wife,' *gametēs* 'husband,' from *gamos* 'marriage.']

game the·o·ry (also **games the·o·ry**) ▶**n.** the branch of mathematic analysis dealing with competitive situations where the outcome of a participant's choice of action depends critically on the actions of other participants, applied to war, business, and biology. Compare with DECISION THEORY.

gameto- ▶**comb. form** Biol. representing GAMETE.

ga·me·to·cyte /gə'mētə,sīt/ ▶**n.** Biol. a cell that divides (by meiosis) to form gametes.

gam·e·to·gen·e·sis /gə,mētə'jenəsis/ ▶**n.** Biol. the process in which cells undergo meiosis to form gametes. — **ga·me·to·gen·ic** /-'jenik/ **adj.** **gam·e·tog·e·ny** /,gamə'täjənē/ **n.**

ga·me·to·phyte /gə'mētə,fīt/ ▶**n.** Bot. (in the life cycle of plants with alternating generations) the gamete-producing and usually haploid phase, producing the zygote from which the sporophyte arises. — **ga·me·to·phyt·ic** /gə,mētə'fitik/ **adj.**

game war·den ▶**n.** a person who is employed to supervise game and hunting in a particular area.

gam·ey ▶**adj.** var. of GAMY.

gam·in /'gamin/ ▶**n.** dated a street urchin. [19th C.: Fr., orig. an eastern dial. word, of unknown origin.]

gam·ine /'gamēn/ ▶**n.** a girl with mischievous or boyish charm. ▶**adj.** characteristic of or relating to such a girl. [19th C.: Fr., fem. of *gamin* (see GAMIN).]

gam·ma /'gamə/ ▶**n.** the third letter of the Greek alphabet (Γ, γ), transliterated as 'g.' ■ [as adj.] denoting the third in a series of items, categories, etc. ■ [as adj.] relating to gamma rays: *gamma detector.* ■ Physics (pl. same) a unit of magnetic field strength equal to 10–5 oersted.

gam·ma-a·mi·no·bu·tyr·ic ac·id /ə,mēnōbyōō'tirik/ ▶**n.** Biochem. an amino acid, $H_2NCH_2CH_2CH_2COOH$, that acts to inhibit the transmission of nerve impulses in the central nervous system. [20th C.: *gamma* indicating the relative position of amino on the third carbon away from the acid group.]

gam·ma glob·u·lin /'gläbyələn/ ▶**n.** see GLOBULIN.

gam·ma ra·di·a·tion ▶**n.** gamma rays.

gam·ma rays ▶**plural n.** penetrating electromagnetic radiation of shorter wavelength than X-rays.

gam·mon¹ /'gamən/ ▶**n.** ham that has been cured or smoked like bacon. ■ the bottom piece of a side of bacon, including a hind leg. [15th C. (denoting the haunch of a pig): from Old North. Fr. *gambon*, from *gambe* 'leg.']

gam·mon² ▶**n.** a victory in backgammon (carrying a double score) in which the winner removes all their pieces before the loser has removed any. ▶**v.** [trans.] defeat (a backgammon opponent) in such a way. [18th C.: appar. from OE *gamen* or *gamenian* (see GAME¹).]

Gam·ow /'gamôf/, George (1904–68), US physicist; born in Russia. A proponent of the big bang theory, he also worked with genetics.

gamp /gamp/ ▶**n.** Brit., dated an umbrella, esp. a large unwieldy one. [19th C.: Mrs. *Gamp* in Charles Dickens's *Martin Chuzzlewit*.]

gam·ut /'gamət/ ▶**n.** (**the gamut**) **1** the complete range or scope of something: *the whole gamut of human emotion.* **2** Music a complete scale of musical notes; the compass or range of a voice or instrument.

– PHRASES **run the gamut** experience, display, or perform the complete range of something. [ME: from med. L. *gamma ut*; the Gk. letter γ (gamma) was used for bass G, with *ut* indicating that it was the first note in the lowest of the hexachords.]

gam·y /'gāmē/ (also **gam·ey**) ▶**adj.** (**gam·i·er, gam·i·est**) (of meat) having the strong flavor or smell of game, esp. when it is slightly tainted. ■ racy; disreputable: *gamy language.* — **gam·i·ly** /'gāməlē/ **adv.** **gam·i·ness n.**

Ga·na·pa·ti /,gənə'pətē/ Hinduism another name for GANESH.

Gän·cä /gän'jä/ a city in Azerbaijan; pop. 281,000. It was formerly called Elizavetpol 1804–1918 and Kirovabad 1935–89.

Gand /gän/ French name of GHENT.

Gan·da /'gändə/ ▶**n. & adj.** another term for BAGANDA.

Gan·der /'gandər/ a town on the island of Newfoundland; pop. 10,339. Its airport served the first regular transatlantic flights during World War II.

gan·der /'gandər/ ▶**n.** **1** a male goose. **2** [in sing.] informal a look or glance: *take a gander at that luggage.* [OE *gandra*, of Gmc. origin; rel. to Du. *gander*, also to GANNET.]

Gan·dhi¹ /'gändē/ a family of Indian politicians. Indira (1917–84), daughter of Jawaharlal Nehru, was prime minister of India 1966–77, 1980–84. She was assassinated by her own Sikh bodyguards following prolonged religious disturbance. Her son, Rajiv (1944–91), prime minister 1984–89, was assassinated during an election campaign.

Gan·dhi², Mahatma (1869–1948), Indian nationalist and spiritual leader; full name *Mohandas Karamchand Gandhi.* Prominent in the opposition to British rule in India, he pursued a policy of nonviolent civil disobedience. He was assassinated following his agreement to the creation of Pakistan.

Gan·dhi·na·gar /,gəndi'nəgər/ a city in western India, capital of the state of Gujarat; pop. 122,000.

gan·dy danc·er /'gandē/ ▶**n.** informal a track maintenance worker on a railroad. [20th C.: of unknown origin.]

ga·nef /'gänəf/ ▶**n.** var. of GONIF.

Ga·nesh /gə'näsH/ (also **Ga·ne·sha** /-'näsHə/) Hinduism an elephant-headed deity, son of Shiva and Parvati. Also called GANAPATI. [from Sanskrit *Gaṅeśa* 'lord of the ganas' (Shiva's attendants).]

gang¹ /gaNG/ ▶**n.** **1** an organized group of criminals. ■ a group of young people involved in petty crime or violence. ■ informal a group of people, esp. young people, who regularly associate together. ■ an organized group of people doing manual work. **2** a set of switches, sockets, or other electrical or mechanical devices grouped together. ▶**v.** **1** [intrans.] (**gang together**) (of a number of people) form a group or gang. ■ (**gang up**) (of a number of people) join together, typically in order to intimidate someone. **2** [trans.] (often **be ganged**) arrange (electrical devices or machines) together to work in coordination. [OE, from ON *gangr*, *ganga* 'gait, course, going,' of Gmc. origin; rel. to GANG².]

gang² ▶**v.** [intrans.] Scot. go; proceed.

– PHRASAL VERBS **gang agley** (of a plan) go wrong. [OE *gangan*, of Gmc. origin; rel. to GO¹.]

Gan·ga /'gəNGgə/ Hindi name for GANGES.

gang·bang /'gaNG,baNG/ ▶**n.** informal **1** the successive rape of a person by a group of other people. ■ a sexual orgy involving changes of partner. **2** an instance of violence, esp. a shooting, involving members of a criminal gang. ▶**v.** [intrans.] participate in a gangbang. ■ [trans.] victimize (someone) by such participation. — **gang·bang·er n.**

gang·bust·er /'gaNG,bəstər/ ▶**n.** informal a police officer or other person who takes part in breaking up criminal gangs. ■ [as adj.] very successful, esp. commercially: *the restaurant did a gangbuster business.*

– PHRASES **go** (or **like**) **gangbusters** used to refer to great vigor, speed, or success: *it's growing like gangbusters.*

Gan·ges /'ganjēz/ a river in northern India and Bangladesh that rises in the Himalayas and flows southwest for about 1,678 miles (2,700 km) to the Bay of Bengal. It is regarded by Hindus as sacred. Hindi name GANGA. — **Gan·get·ic** /gan'jetik/ **adj.**

gang·land /'gaNG,land/ ▶**n.** the world of criminal gangs: *a gangland shooting.*

gan·gling /'gaNGgliNG/ ▶**adj.** (of a person) tall, thin, and awkward in movements or bearing. [19th C.: from the v. GANG² + -LE⁴ + -ING².]

gan·gli·on /'gaNGglēən/ ▶**n.** (pl. **-gli·a** /-glēə/ or **-gli·ons**) **1** Anat. a structure containing a number of nerve cell bodies, typically linked by synapses, and often forming a swelling on a nerve fiber. ■ a network of cells forming a nerve center in the nervous system of an invertebrate. ■ a well-defined mass of gray matter within the central nervous system. See also **BASAL GANGLIA**. **2** Med. an abnormal benign swelling on a tendon sheath. — **gan·gli·on·ic** /ˌgaNGglēˈänik/ **adj.** [17th C.: from Gk. *ganglion* 'tumor on or near sinews or tendons.']

gan·gli·o·side /ˈgaNGglēəˌsīd/ ▶ **n.** Biochem. any of a group of complex lipids that are present in the gray matter of the human brain. [1940s: from **GANGLION** + *-oside* (see **-OSE**[2], **-IDE**).]

gan·gly /ˈgaNGglē/ ▶ **adj.** (**gan·gl·ier**, **gan·gl·iest**) another term for **GANGLING**.

Gang of Four (in China) a group of four associates, including Mao Zedong's wife, involved in implementing the Cultural Revolution. They were among the groups competing for power on Mao's death in 1976, but were arrested and imprisoned.

gang·plank /ˈgaNGˌplaNGk/ ▶ **n.** a movable plank used as a ramp to board or disembark from a ship or boat.

gang rape ▶ **n.** the rape of one person by a group. — **gang-rape v.**

gan·grene /ˈgaNGgrēn; gaNGˈgrēn/ ▶ **n.** Med. localized death and decomposition of body tissue, resulting from either obstructed circulation or bacterial infection. — **gan·gre·nous** /ˈgaNGgrənəs/ **adj.** [16th C.: via Fr. from L. *gangraena*, from Gk. *gangraina*.]

gang·sta /ˈgaNGstə/ ▶ **n. 1** black slang a gang member. **2** (also **gangsta rap**) a type of rap music featuring aggressive lyrics, often with reference to gang violence. [1980s: alt. of **GANGSTER**.]

gang·ster /ˈgaNGstər/ ▶ **n.** a member of a gang of violent criminals. — **gang·ster·ism** /-ˌrizəm/ **n.**

Gang·tok /ˈgəNGtôk/ a city in northern India, capital of the state of Sikkim; pop. 25,000.

gangue /gaNG/ ▶ **n.** the commercially valueless material in which ore is found. [19th C.: from Fr., from Ger. *Gang* 'course, lode'; rel. to **GANG**[1].]

gang·way /ˈgaNGˌwā/ ▶ **n.** a raised platform or walkway providing a passage. ■ a movable bridge linking a ship to the shore. ■ an opening in the bulwarks by which a ship is entered or left. ■ a temporary arrangement of planks for crossing muddy or difficult ground on a building site. ▶ **exclam.** /ˈgaNGˈwā/ make way!; get out of the way!

gan·is·ter /ˈganəstər/ ▶ **n.** a hard siliceous rock, or a similar synthetic product, used esp. for lining furnaces. [19th C.: of unknown origin.]

gan·ja /ˈgänjə/ ▶ **n.** marijuana. [19th C.: from Hindi *gāṃjā*.]

gan·net /ˈganit/ ▶ **n.** a large seabird (genus *Morus*, family Sulidae) with mainly white plumage, known for catching fish by plunge-diving. [OE *ganot*, of Gmc. origin; rel. to Du. *gent* 'gander,' also to **GANDER**.]

gan·oid /ˈganoid/ Zool. ▶ **adj.** (of fish scales) hard and bony with a shiny enamellike surface. Compare with **CTENOID** and **PLACOID**. ■ (of a fish) having ganoid scales. ▶ **n.** a primitive fish that has ganoid scales, e.g., sturgeon or freshwater garfish. [19th C.: from Fr. *ganoïde*, from Gk. *ganos* 'brightness.']

Gan·su /ˈgänˈsōō; ˈgan-/ (also **Kan·su**) a province in northwest central China, between Mongolia and Tibet; capital, Lanzhou.

gant·let /ˈgantlit; ˈgônt-/ ▶ **n.** var. of **GAUNTLET**[2].

gan·try /ˈgantrē/ ▶ **n.** (pl. **-tries**) a bridgelike overhead structure with a platform supporting equipment such as a crane, railroad signals, lights, or cameras. ■ a movable framework for supporting and servicing a rocket prior to launching. [ME (denoting a wooden stand for barrels): prob. from dial. *gawn* (contr. of **GALLON**) + **TREE**.]

Gan·y·mede /ˈganəˌmēd/ **1** Gk. Mythol. a Trojan youth who was so beautiful that he was carried off by Zeus to be the cupbearer for the Olympic gods. **2** Astron. one of the Galilean moons of Jupiter, the seventh closest satellite to the planet.

ganz·feld /ˈgänzˌfeld; ˈgans-/ (also **Ganz·feld**) ▶ **n.** a technique of controlled sensory input used in parapsychology with the aim of improving results in tests of telepathy and other paranormal phenomena. [20th C.: from Ger., lit. 'whole field.']

GAO ▶ **abbr.** General Accounting Office, a body that undertakes investigations for Congress.

gaol ▶ **n.** Brit. var. of **JAIL**. — **gaol·er n.**

gap /gap/ ▶ **n. 1** a break or hole in an object or between two objects: *he came through the gap in the hedge.* ■ a pass or way through a range of hills. **2** an unfilled space or interval; a break in continuity: *there are many gaps in our understanding of what happened.* ■ a difference, esp. an undesirable one, between two views or situations: *the media were bridging the gap between government and people.* — **gapped adj. gap·py adj.** [ME: from ON, 'chasm'; rel. to **GAPE**.]

gape /gāp/ ▶ **v.** [intrans.] stare with one's mouth open wide, typically in amazement or wonder. ■ be or become wide open: [with complement] *a large duffel bag gaped open by her feet* | [as adj.] (**gaping**) *there was a gaping hole in the wall.* ▶ **n.** a wide opening or breach. ■ an open-mouthed stare. ■ a widely open mouth or beak. ■ (**the gapes**) a disease of birds with gaping of the mouth as a symptom, caused by infestation with gapeworm. — **gap·ing·ly adv.** [ME: from ON *gapa*; rel. to **GAP**.]

gape·worm /ˈgāpˌwərm/ ▶ **n.** a parasitic nematode (*Syngamus trachea*, class Phasmida) that infests the trachea and bronchi of birds, causing the gapes.

gap-toothed ▶ **adj.** having or showing gaps between the teeth.

gar /gär/ ▶ **n.** the freshwater garfish of North America.

ga·rage /gəˈräzн; -ˈräj/ ▶ **n. 1** a building or shed for housing a motor vehicle or vehicles. ■ an establishment that provides services and repairs for motor vehicles. **2** (also **garage rock**) [mass noun] a style of unpolished energetic rock music associated with suburban amateur bands: [as adj.] *garage band.* ▶ **v.** [trans.] put or keep (a motor vehicle) in a garage. [20th C.: from Fr., from *garer* 'to shelter.']

ga·rage sale ▶ **n.** a sale of miscellaneous household goods, often held in the garage or front yard of someone's house.

ga·ram ma·sa·la /ˌgärəm məˈsälə/ ▶ **n.** a spice mixture used in Indian cooking. [from Urdu *garam maṣālaḥ*, from *garam* 'hot, pungent' + *maṣālaḥ* 'spice.']

Gar·a·mond /ˈgarəˌmänd/ ▶ **n.** a typeface much used in books. [19th C.: named after Claude *Garamond* (1499–1561), French type founder.]

garb /gärb/ ▶ **n.** clothing or dress, esp. of a distinctive or special kind. ▶ **v.** [trans.] (usu. **be garbed**) dress in distinctive clothes: ***garbed in shawls.*** [16th C.: via Fr. from Ital. *garbo* 'elegance,' of Gmc. origin; rel. to **GEAR**.]

gar·bage /ˈgärbij/ ▶ **n.** wasted or spoiled food and other refuse, as from a kitchen or household. ■ a thing that is considered worthless or meaningless.

– PHRASES **garbage in, garbage out** (abbr.: **GIGO**) used to express the idea that in computing and other spheres, incorrect or poor quality input will always produce faulty output. [ME (in the sense 'offal'): from Anglo-Norman Fr.]

gar·ban·zo /gärˈbänzō/ (also **garbanzo bean**) ▶ **n.** (pl. **-zos**) a chickpea. [18th C.: from Sp.]

gar·ble /ˈgärbəl/ ▶ **v.** [trans.] reproduce (a message, sound, or transmission) in a confused and distorted way: [as adj.] (**garbled**) *I got a garbled set of directions.* ▶ **n.** a garbled account or transmission. — **gar·bler n.** [ME: from Anglo-Latin and Ital. *garbellare*, from Arab. *ġarbala* 'sift' perh. from late L. *cribellare* 'to sieve,' from L. *cribrum* 'sieve.']

gar·board /ˈgärˌbôrd/ (also **garboard strake**) ▶ **n.** the first range of planks or plates laid on a ship's bottom next to the keel. [17th C.: from Du. *gaarboord*, perh. from *garen* 'gather' + *boord* 'board.']

Gar·cí·a Lor·ca /gärˈsēə ˈlôrkə/ see **LORCA**.

Gar·cí·a Már·quez /gärˈsēə ˈmärkes/, Gabriel (1928–), Colombian writer. His works include *One Hundred Years of Solitude* (1967). Nobel Prize for Literature (1982).

gar·çon /gärˈsôN/ ▶ **n.** a waiter in a French restaurant or hotel. [Fr., lit. 'boy.']

Gar·da, Lake /ˈgärdə/ a lake in northeastern Italy.

gar·den /ˈgärdn/ ▶ **n. 1** a piece of ground, often near a house, used for growing flowers, fruit, or vegetables. ■ (**gardens**) ornamental grounds laid out for public enjoyment and recreation: *botanical gardens.* ■ a similar place with the service of refreshments: *tea gardens.* **2** [in names] a large public hall: *Madison Square Garden.* ▶ **v.** [intrans.] cultivate or work in a garden. [ME: from Old North. Fr. *gardin*, var. of OFr. *jardin*, of Gmc. origin.]

Gar·de·na /gärˈdēnə/ a city in southwestern California, south of Los Angeles; pop. 49,847.

gar·den a·part·ment ▶ **n. 1** a low-rise apartment complex with landscaped gardens or lawns. **2** a ground-floor unit of an apartment building, with access to a garden or lawn.

gar·den cress ▶ **n.** a type of cress (*Lepidium sativum*) that is usually grown as a sprouting vegetable, often used in salads.

gar·den·er /ˈgärdnər; -dn-ər/ ▶ **n.** a person who tends and cultivates a garden as a pastime or for a living. — **gar·den·ing** /ˈgärdniNG; -dn-iNG/ **n.** [ME: from OFr. *gardinier*, from *gardin* (see **GARDEN**).]

Gar·den Grove a city in southwestern California, southeast of Los Angeles; pop. 143,050.

gar·de·nia /gärˈdēnyə/ ▶ **n.** a widely cultivated tree or shrub (genus *Gardenia*) of the bedstraw family, with large fragrant white or yellow flowers. [mod. L., named in honor of Dr. Alexander *Garden* (1730–91), Scottish naturalist.]

Gar·den of E·den see **EDEN**[2].

Gar·den of Geth·sem·a·ne see **GETHSEMANE, GARDEN OF.**

gar·den-va·ri·e·ty ▶ **adj.** [attrib.] of the usual or ordinary type; commonplace.

Gard·ner /ˈgärdnər/, Erle Stanley (1899–1970), US writer. He practiced as a defense lawyer before writing novels that feature lawyer-detective Perry Mason.

Gar·field /ˈgärˌfēld/, James Abram (1831–81), 20th president of the US 1881. He fought for the Union during the Civil War, resigning his command to serve as an Ohio Republican in the US House of Representatives 1863–80. After four months in the presidency, he was shot by an assassin and died nearly 12 weeks later.

gar·fish /ˈgärˌfiSH/ ▶ **n.** (pl. same or **-fish·es**) any of a number of long, slender fish with elongated beaklike jaws containing sharply pointed teeth, in particular: ■ a North American freshwater fish (genus *Lepisosteus*, family Lepisosteidae). ■ a common European marine fish (*Belone belone*, family Belonidae). Also called **NEEDLEFISH**. [ME: appar. from OE *gār* 'spear' + **FISH**[1].]

gar·ga·ney /ˈgärgənē/ ▶ **n.** (pl. same or **-neys**) a small Eurasian duck (*Anas querquedula*), the male of which has a dark brown head with a white stripe from the eye to the neck. [17th C.: from Ital. dial. *garganei*, of imitative origin.]

gar·gan·tu·a /gärˈganCHōōə/ ▶ **n.** a person of great size; a giant. — **gar·gan·tu·an adj.** [16th C.: from *Gargantua*, a voracious giant in Rabelais' book of the same name (1534).]

gar·gle /ˈgärgəl/ ▶ **v.** [intrans.] wash one's mouth and throat with a liquid kept in motion by exhaling through it. ▶n. an act or instance or the sound of gargling. ■ [usu. in sing.] a liquid used for gargling. [16th C.: from Fr. *gargouiller* 'gurgle, bubble,' from *gargouille* 'throat' (see GARGOYLE).]

gar·goyle /'gärgoil/ ▶n. a grotesque carved human or animal face or figure projecting from the gutter of a building, typically acting as a water spout. [ME: from OFr. *gargouille* 'throat,' also 'gargoyle,' rel. to Gk. *gargarizein* 'to gargle.']

Gar·i·bal·di /ˌgarə'bôldē/, Giuseppe (1807–82), Italian patriot. The leader of the Risorgimento, he captured Sicily and southern Italy from the Austrians in 1860–61. His volunteer force was known as the "Red Shirts."

gar·i·bal·di /ˌgarə'bôldē/ ▶n. (pl. **-dis**) **1** hist. a woman's or children's loose blouse, originally bright red in imitation of the shirts worn by Garibaldi and his followers. **2** a small bright orange marine fish (*Hypsypops rubicundus*, family Pomacentridae) found off California.

gar·ish /'ge(ə)risн; 'gar-/ ▶adj. obtrusively bright and showy; lurid. —**gar·ish·ly** adv. **gar·ish·ness** n. [16th C.: of unknown origin.]

Gar·land /'gärlənd/ a city in northeastern Texas; pop. 215,768.

gar·land /'gärlənd/ ▶n. a wreath of flowers and leaves, worn on the head or hung as a decoration. ▶v. [trans.] adorn or crown with a garland. [ME: from OFr. *garlande*, of unknown origin.]

gar·lic /'gärlik/ ▶n. **1** a strong-smelling pungent-tasting bulb, used as a flavoring in cooking and in herbal medicine. **2** the plant (*Allium sativum*) of the lily family that produces this bulb. —**gar·lick·y** adj. [OE *gārlēac*, from *gār* 'spear' + *lēac* 'leek.']

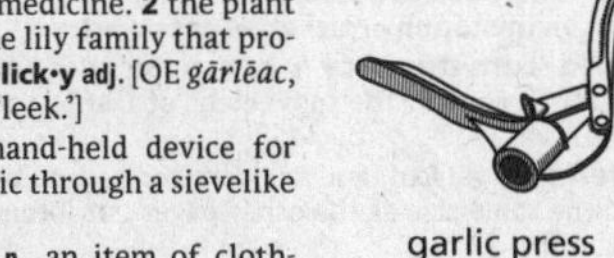
garlic press

gar·lic press ▶n. a hand-held device for crushing cloves of garlic through a sievelike receptacle.

gar·ment /'gärmənt/ ▶n. an item of clothing. [ME: from OFr. *garnement* 'equipment,' from *garnir* 'equip' (see GARNISH).]

Gar·mo, Mount /'gärmō/ former name (until 1933) of COMMUNISM PEAK.

Gar·ner /'gärnər/, John Nance (1868–1967) vice president of the US 1933–41. A Texas Democrat, he served in the US House of Representatives 1903–33.

gar·ner /'gärnər/ ▶v. [trans.] gather or collect (something, esp. information or approval): *garner evidence.* [ME: from OFr. *gernier*, from L. *granarium* 'granary,' from *granum* 'grain.']

gar·net /'gärnit/ ▶n. a precious stone consisting of a deep red vitreous silicate mineral. ■ Mineral. any of a class of silicate minerals that have the general chemical formula $A_3B_2(SiO_4)_3$, used as abrasives. [ME: prob. via MDu. from OFr. *grenat*, from med. L. *granatus*, perh. from *granatum* (see POMEGRANATE).]

gar·nish /'gärnisн/ ▶v. [trans.] **1** decorate or embellish (something, esp. food). **2** Law serve notice of garnishment. ■ seize (money, esp. part of a person's salary) to settle a debt or claim: *the IRS garnished his earnings.* ▶n. a decoration or embellishment for something, esp. food. [ME: from OFr. *garnir*, prob. of Gmc. origin and rel. to WARN.]

gar·nish·ee /ˌgärni'sнē/ Law ▶n. a third party who is served notice by a court to surrender money in settlement of a debt or claim: [as adj.] *a garnishee order.* ▶v. (**-ees, -eed**) another term for GARNISH (sense 2).

gar·nish·ment /'gärnisнmənt/ ▶n. **1** a decoration or embellishment. **2** Law a court order directing that money or property of a third party (usually wages paid by an employer) be seized to satisfy a debt owed.

Ga·ronne /gə'rän; gə'rôn/ a river in southwestern France that rises in the Pyrenees Mountains and flows for 400 miles (645 km) to the Dordogne River.

ga·rotte ▶v. & n. var. of GARROTE.

gar·ret /'garit/ ▶n. a top-floor or attic room, esp. a small dismal one (traditionally inhabited by an artist). [ME: from OFr. *garite*, from *garir* (see GARRISON).]

Gar·rick /'garik/, David (1717–79), English actor and playwright. He managed the Drury Lane Theatre.

Gar·ri·son /'garəsən/, William Lloyd (1805–79) US abolitionist. He published *The Liberator* 1831–65 and was a founder of the American Anti-Slavery Society in 1833.

gar·ri·son /'garəsən/ ▶n. the troops stationed in a fortress or town to defend it. ■ the building occupied by such troops. ▶v. [trans.] provide (a place) with a body of troops: *troops are garrisoned in the various territories.* ■ [trans.] station (troops) in a particular place: *Soviet forces were garrisoned in Lithuania.* [ME: from OFr. *garison*, from *garir* 'defend, provide,' of Gmc. origin.]

gar·ri·son town ▶n. a town that has troops permanently stationed in it.

gar·rote /gə'rät; -'rōt/ (also **gar·rotte** or **ga·rotte**) ▶v. [trans.] kill (someone) by strangulation, typically with an iron collar or a length of wire or cord. ▶n. a wire, cord, or apparatus used for such a killing. [17th C.: via Fr. from Sp., 'a cudgel, a garrote,' perh. of Celtic origin.]

gar·ru·lous /'gar(y)ələs/ ▶adj. excessively talkative, esp. on trivial matters. —**gar·ru·li·ty** /gə'ro͞olitē/ n. **gar·ru·lous·ly** adv. **gar·ru·lous·ness** n. [17th C.: from L. *garrulus* (from *garrire* 'to chatter, prattle') + -OUS.]

gar·ter /'gärtər/ ▶n. **1** a band worn around the leg to keep up a stocking or sock. ■ a band worn on the arm to keep a shirtsleeve up. ■ a suspender for a sock or stocking. **2** (**the Garter**) short for ORDER OF THE GARTER. ■ the badge or membership of this order. —**gar·tered** adj. [ME: from OFr. *gartier*, from *garet* 'bend of the knee, calf of the leg,' prob. of Celtic origin.]

gar·ter belt ▶n. a belt with attached garters or fasteners, worn as an undergarment to hold up stockings.

gar·ter snake ▶n. a harmless North American snake (genus *Thamnophis*, family Colubridae) that typically has well-defined longitudinal stripes.

Gar·vey /'gärvē/, Marcus Mosiah (1887–1940), Jamaican political activist and nationalist. He advocated the establishment of an African homeland for black Americans.

Gar·y /'garē; 'ge(ə)rē/ a city in northwestern Indiana, on Lake Michigan; pop. 102,746.

gas /gas/ ▶n. (pl. **gas·es** or **gas·ses**) **1** an airlike fluid substance which expands freely to fill any space available, irrespective of its quantity. ■ Physics a substance of this type that cannot be liquefied by the application of pressure alone. Compare with VAPOR. ■ a flammable substance of this type used as a fuel. ■ a gaseous anesthetic such as nitrous oxide, used in dentistry. ■ gas or vapor used as a poisonous agent to kill or disable an enemy in warfare. ■ gas generated in the alimentary canal; flatulence. **2** informal short for GASOLINE. **3** (**a gas**) informal a person or thing that is entertaining or amusing: *the party would be a gas.* ▶v. (**gas·es, gassed, gas·sing**) [trans.] **1** attack with or expose to poisonous gas. ■ kill by exposure to poisonous gas. ■ [intrans.] (of a storage battery or dry cell) give off gas. **2** fill the tank of (an engine or motor vehicle) with gasoline.

– PHRASES **run out of gas** informal run out of energy; lose momentum. [17th C.: suggested by Gk. *khaos* 'chaos.']

gas·bag /'gasˌbag/ ▶n. **1** informal a person who talks too much, typically about unimportant things. **2** the container holding the gas in a balloon or airship.

gas burn·er ▶n. a nozzle or jet through which gas is released to burn, e.g., on a stove.

gas cham·ber ▶n. an airtight room that can be filled with poisonous gas as a means of execution.

gas chro·mat·o·graph ▶n. a device or apparatus used in gas chromatography to separate the constituents of a volatile substance.

gas·con·ade /ˌgaskə'nād/ ▶n. literary extravagant boasting. [17th C.: from Fr. *gasconnade*, from *gasconner* 'talk like a Gascon, brag.']

Gas·co·ny /'gaskənē/ a region and former province in southwestern France. French name GASCOGNE.

gas·e·ous /'gasēəs; 'gasнəs/ ▶adj. of, relating to, or having the characteristics of a gas. —**gas·e·ous·ness** n.

gas-fired ▶adj. using a combustible gas as its fuel: *gas-fired central heating.*

gas gan·grene ▶n. rapidly spreading gangrene occurring in wounds infected by bacteria (esp. genus *Clostridium*) that give off a foul-smelling gas.

gas gi·ant ▶n. Astron. a large planet of relatively low density consisting predominantly of hydrogen and helium, such as Jupiter, Saturn, Uranus, or Neptune.

gas guz·zler ▶n. informal an automobile with high fuel consumption.

gash /gasн/ ▶n. a long deep slash, cut, or wound. ■ a cleft made as if by a slashing cut: *the blast ripped a 25-foot gash in the hull.* ▶v. [trans.] make a gash in; cut deeply. [ME *garse*, from OFr. *garcer* 'to chap, crack,' perh. based on Gk. *kharassein* 'sharpen.']

gas·i·fy /'gasəˌfī/ ▶v. (**-fies, -fied**) [trans.] (often **be gasified**) convert (a solid or liquid, esp. coal) into gas. ■ [intrans.] become a gas. —**gas·i·fi·ca·tion** /ˌgasəfi'kāsнən/ n.

Gas·kell /'gaskəl/, Mrs. Elizabeth Cleghorn (1810–65), English writer. She wrote *Mary Barton* (1848).

gas·ket /'gaskit/ ▶n. **1** a shaped piece or ring of rubber or other material sealing the junction between two surfaces in an engine or other device. **2** a cord securing a furled sail to the yard, boom, or gaff of a sailing vessel.

– PHRASES **blow a gasket 1** informal lose one's temper. **2** suffer a leak in a gasket of an engine. [17th C.: perh. from Fr. *garcette* 'thin rope,' dimin. of *garce*, fem. of *gars* 'boy.']

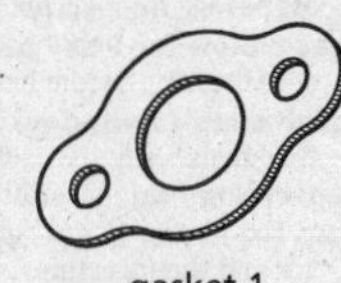
gasket 1

gas·kin /'gaskin/ ▶n. the muscular part of the hind leg of a horse between the stifle and the hock. [16th C.]

gas·light /'gasˌlīt/ ▶n. a type of lamp in which an incandescent mantle is heated by a jet of burning gas. ■ the light produced by such a lamp. —**gas·lit** adj.

gas log ▶n. a gas-burning appliance consisting of a gas burner made to resemble a log, used in a fireplace to simulate the effect of a burning log.

gas man·tle ▶n. see MANTLE[1] (sense 1).

gas mask ▶n. a protective mask used to cover a person's face as a defense against poisonous gas. *See illustration on next page.*

gas·o·hol /'gasəˌhôl; -ˌhäl/ ▶n. a mixture of gasoline and ethyl alcohol used as fuel in internal combustion engines. [1970s: blend of GAS and ALCOHOL.]

PRONUNCIATION KEY ə *ago, up*; ər *over, fur*; a *hat*; ā *ate*; ä *car*; e *let*; ē *see*; i *fit*; ī *by*; NG *sing*; ō *go*; ô *law, for*; oi *toy*; o͝o *good*; o͞o *goo*; ou *out*; TH *thin*; T͟H *then*; ZH *vision*

gas oil ▶ **n.** a type of fuel oil distilled from petroleum.

gas·o·line /ˌgasəˈlēn; ˈgasəˌlēn/ (dated also **gas·o·lene**) ▶ **n.** refined petroleum used as fuel for internal combustion engines.

gas·om·e·ter /gaˈsämitər/ ▶ **n.** a tank for storing and measuring gas.

gasp /gasp/ ▶ **v.** [intrans.] inhale suddenly with the mouth open, out of pain or astonishment. ■ [trans.] say (something) while catching one's breath, esp. as a result of strong emotion: *gasp out an apology.* ■ strain to take a deep breath: *gasp for air.* ▶ **n.** a convulsive catching of breath: *his breath was coming in gasps.*

– PHRASES **one's** (or **the**) **last gasp** the point of exhaustion, death, or completion. [ME: from ON *geispa* 'to yawn.']

gas mask

Gas·pé Pen·in·su·la /gasˈpā/ a region in southeastern Quebec in Canada.

gas-per·me·a·ble ▶ **adj.** (of a contact lens) allowing the diffusion of gases into and out of the cornea.

gas plant ▶ **n.** an aromatic Eurasian plant (*Dictamnus albus*) of the rue family, with showy white flowers and fragrant leaves that emit a flammable vapor, which can sometimes be ignited without harming the plant. Also called BURNING BUSH, DITTANY, FRAXINELLA.

Gas·ser /ˈgasər/, Herbert Spencer (1888–1963), US physiologist. He and Joseph Erlanger showed that the velocity of a nerve impulse is proportional to the diameter of the fiber. Nobel Prize for Physiology or Medicine (1944, shared with Erlanger).

gas·ser /ˈgasər/ ▶ **n.** informal **1** an idle talker; a chatterbox. **2** a very attractive or impressive person or thing: *that story you wrote for me is a gasser!*

gas sta·tion ▶ **n.** a service station.

gas·sy /ˈgasē/ ▶ **adj.** (**-si·er**, **-si·est**) **1** of, like, or full of gas. **2** informal (of people or language) inclined to be verbose: *a long and gassy book.* — **gas·si·ness n.**

Gast·ar·beit·er /ˈgästˌärbītər/ ▶ **n.** (pl. same or **-beit·ers**) German term for GUEST WORKER. [Ger., from *Gast* 'guest' + *Arbeiter* 'worker.']

gast·haus /ˈgästˌhous/ (also **Gast·haus**) ▶ **n.** (pl. **-haus·es** or **-häus·er** /-ˌhoizər/) a small inn or hotel in a German-speaking country or region. [from Ger., from *Gast* 'guest' + *Haus* 'house.']

Gas·to·nia /gaˈstōnēə/ a city in southwestern North Carolina; pop. 66,277.

gastr- ▶ **comb. form** var. of GASTRO- shortened before a vowel (as in *gastrectomy*).

gas·trec·to·my /gaˈstrektəmē/ ▶ **n.** (pl. **-mies**) surgical removal of a part or the whole of the stomach.

gas·tric /ˈgastrik/ ▶ **adj.** of the stomach. [17th C.: from mod. L. *gastricus*, from Gk. *gastēr, gastr-* 'stomach.']

gas·tric juice ▶ **n.** a thin, clear, virtually colorless acidic fluid secreted by the stomach glands and active in promoting digestion.

gas·trin /ˈgastrin/ ▶ **n.** Biochem. a hormone that stimulates secretion of gastric juice into the bloodstream by the stomach.

gas·tri·tis /gaˈstrītis/ ▶ **n.** Med. inflammation of the lining of the stomach.

gastro- (also **gastr-** before a vowel) ▶ **comb. form** of or relating to the stomach: *gastrectomy* | *gastroenteritis.* [from Gk. *gastēr, gastr-* 'stomach.']

gas·troc·ne·mi·us /ˌgasträ(k)ˈnēmēəs/ (also **gastrocnemius muscle**) ▶ **n.** (pl. **-mi·i** /-mēˌī/) Anat. the chief muscle of the calf of the leg, which flexes the knee and foot. [17th C.: mod. L., from Gk. *gastroknēmia* 'calf of the leg,' from *gastēr, gastr-* 'stomach' + *knēmē* 'leg.']

gas·tro·en·ter·i·tis /ˌgastrōˌentəˈrītis/ ▶ **n.** inflammation of the stomach and intestines, from bacterial toxins or viral infection.

gas·tro·en·ter·ol·o·gy /ˌgastrōˌentəˈräləjē/ ▶ **n.** the branch of medicine that deals with disorders of the stomach and intestines. — **gas·tro·en·ter·o·log·i·cal** /-tərəˈläjikəl/ **adj.** **gas·tro·en·te·rol·o·gist n.**

gas·tro·in·tes·ti·nal /ˌgastrōinˈtestənl/ ▶ **adj.** of or relating to the stomach and the intestines.

gas·tro·lith /ˈgastrəˌliTH/ ▶ **n.** Med. a hard concretion in the stomach.

gas·tro·nome /ˈgastrəˌnōm/ (also **gas·tron·o·mer** /gaˈstränəmər/ or **gas·tron·o·mist** /gaˈstränəˌmist/) ▶ **n.** a gourmet.

gas·tron·o·my /gaˈstränəmē/ ▶ **n.** the practice or art of choosing, cooking, and eating good food. ■ the cooking of a particular area: *traditional American gastronomy.* — **gas·tro·nom·ic** /ˌgastrəˈnämik/ **adj.** **gas·tro·nom·i·cal** /ˌgastrəˈnämikəl/ **adj.** **gas·tro·nom·i·cal·ly** /ˌgastrəˈnämik(ə)lē/ **adv.** [19th C.: from Fr. *gastronomie*, from Gk. *gastronomia*, alt. of *gastrologia* (see GASTRO-, -LOGY).]

Gas·trop·o·da /ˌgastrəˈpōdə/ Zool. a large class of mollusks which includes snails, slugs, and whelks, having a large muscular foot for movement and (in many kinds) a single asymmetrical spiral shell. — **gas·tro·pod** /ˈgastrəˌpäd/ **n.** [mod. L. (pl.), from Gk. *gastēr, gastr-* 'stomach' + *pous, pod-* 'foot.']

Gas·trot·ri·cha /gasˈträtrikə/ Zool. a small phylum of minute aquatic wormlike animals that bear bristles and cilia. — **gas·tro·trich** /ˈgastrəˌtrik/ **n.** [mod. L. (pl.), from Gk. *gastēr, gastr-* 'stomach' + *thrix, trikh-* 'hair.']

gas·tru·la /ˈgastrŏŏlə/ ▶ **n.** (pl. **-lae** /-lē/) Embryol. an embryo at the stage following the blastula, when it is a hollow cup-shaped structure having three layers of cells. — **gas·tru·la·tion** /ˌgastrəˈlāSHən/ **n.** [19th C.: mod. L., from Gk. *gastēr, gastr-* 'stomach' + the L. dimin. ending *-ula.*]

gas tur·bine ▶ **n.** a turbine driven by expanding hot gases produced by burning fuel, as in a jet engine.

gas·works /ˈgasˌwərks/ ▶ **plural n.** [treated as sing.] a place where gas is manufactured and processed.

gat /gat/ ▶ **n.** informal a revolver or pistol. [20th C.: abbrev. of GATLING GUN.]

gate /gāt/ ▶ **n. 1** a hinged barrier used to close an opening in a wall, fence, or hedge. ■ a gateway: *she went out through the gate.* ■ fig. a means of entrance or exit: *opening the gates of their country.* ■ an exit from an airport building to an aircraft. **2** the number of people who pay to enter a sports facility, exhibition hall, etc., for any one event: [as adj.] *gate receipts.* ■ the money taken for admission. **3** a device resembling a gate in structure or function, in particular: ■ a hinged or sliding barrier for controlling the flow of water: *a sluice gate.* ■ Skiing an opening through which a skier must pass in a slalom course, typically marked by upright poles. **4** an electric circuit with an output that depends on the combination of several inputs: *a logic gate.* [OE *gæt, geat*, pl. *gatu*, of Gmc. origin; rel. to Du. *gat* 'gap, hole, breach.']

-gate ▶ **comb. form** in nouns denoting an actual or alleged scandal, esp. one involving a cover-up: *Irangate.* [1970s: suggested by the *Watergate* scandal, 1972.]

gate-crash·er ▶ **n.** a person who attends a party or other gathering without an invitation or ticket. — **gate-crash v.**

gat·ed com·mu·ni·ty ▶ **n.** a residential area with roads that have gates to control the movement of traffic and people into and out of the area.

gate·fold /ˈgātˌfōld/ ▶ **n.** an oversized page in a book or magazine folded to the same size as the other pages but intended to be opened out for reading.

gate·house /ˈgātˌhous/ ▶ **n.** a house or enclosure near a gateway.

gate·keep·er /ˈgātˌkēpər/ ▶ **n.** an attendant at a gate who is employed to control who goes through it.

gateleg table

gate·leg ta·ble /ˈgātˌleg/ ▶ **n.** a table with hinged legs that swing out from the frame to support the drop leaves that make the surface of the table larger.

gate·post /ˈgātˌpōst/ ▶ **n.** a post on which a gate is hinged, or against which it shuts.

Gates[1] /gāts/, Bill (1955–), US entrepreneur and philanthropist; full name *William Henry Gates.* He cofounded Microsoft, a computer software company, becoming the youngest multibillionaire in US history.

Gates[2], Horatio (1728–1806), American army officer; born in England. Siding with the colonials when the American Revolution broke out, he commanded the Saratoga campaign 1777.

Gates[3], Robert Michael (1943–), US secretary of defense 2006– .

Gates·head /ˈgātsˌhed/ a town in northeastern England, opposite Newcastle; pop. 196,000.

gate·way /ˈgātˌwā/ ▶ **n.** an opening that can be closed by a gate: *a gateway leading to a small cottage.* ■ a frame or arch built around or over a gate. ■ a means of access or entry to a place: *Mombasa, the gateway to East Africa.* ■ Comput. a device used to connect two different networks, esp. a connection to the Internet.

Gate·way Arch a stainless steel arch built along the west bank of the Mississippi River in St. Louis, Missouri. The arch, 630 feet (192 m) wide and rising to 630 feet (192 m) high, was designed by Eero Saarinen and built 1963–65.

gath·er /ˈgaT͟Hər/ ▶ **v. 1** [intrans.] come together; assemble or accumulate: *a crowd gathered.* **2** [trans.] bring together and take in from scattered places or sources: *gather information.* ■ pick up from the ground or a surface: *they gathered up the dirty plates.* ■ collect grain or other crops as a harvest. ■ collect plants, fruits, etc., for food. ■ draw together or toward oneself: *she gathered the child in her arms.* ■ draw and hold together (fabric or a part of a garment) by running thread through it: *the front is gathered at the waist.* **3** [trans.] infer; understand: *her clients were, I gathered, a prosperous group.* **4** [trans.] develop a higher degree of: *the green movement is gathering pace.* **5** [trans.] summon up (a mental or physical attribute such as one's thoughts or strength) for a purpose: *he gathered himself for a tremendous leap.* — **gath·er·er n.** [OE *gaderian*, of West Gmc. origin; rel. to Du. *gaderen*, also to TOGETHER.]

gath·er·ing /ˈgaT͟HəriNG/ ▶ **n.** an assembly or meeting, esp. a social or festive one or one held for a specific purpose: *a family gathering.*

Gat·i·neau /ˌgatnˈō; gatēˈnō/ a city in southwestern Quebec in Canada; pop. 92,284.

Gat·ling gun /ˈgatliNG/ ▶ **n.** a rapid-fire, crank-driven gun with a cylindrical cluster of several barrels. The first practical machine gun, it was officially adopted by the US Army in 1866. [named after Richard J. *Gatling* (1818–1903), its American inventor.]

Gatling gun

ga·tor /ˈgātər/ ▶ **n.** informal an alligator.

Ga·tor·ade /ˈgātəˌrād/ ▶ **n.** trademark a fruit-flavored drink esp. for athletes, designed to supply the body with carbohydrates and to replace fluids and sodium lost during exercise.

GATT /gat/ General Agreement on Tariffs and Trade, an international treaty (1948–94) to promote trade and economic development by reducing tariffs and other restrictions. It was superseded by the World Trade Organization in 1995.

gauche /gōsH/ ▶ **adj.** lacking ease or grace; unsophisticated and socially awkward. — **gauche·ly adv. gauche·ness n.** [18th C.: Fr., lit. 'left.']

gau·che·rie /ˌgōsHəˈrē/ ▶ **n.** awkward, embarrassing, or unsophisticated ways: *she had long since gotten over gaucheries such as blushing.* [18th C.: Fr., from *gauche* (see GAUCHE).]

Gau·cher's dis·ease /gōˈsHāz/ ▶ **n.** a hereditary disease in which the metabolism and storage of fats is abnormal. It results in bone fragility, neurological disturbance, anemia, and enlargement of the liver and spleen. [20th C.: named after Phillippe C. E. *Gaucher* (1854–1918), French physician.]

gau·cho /ˈgouCHō/ ▶ **n.** (pl. **-chos**) a cowboy of the South American pampas. [L. Amer. Sp., prob. from Araucanian *kauču* 'friend.']

Gau·dí /ˈgoudē/, Antonio (1853–1926), Spanish architect; full name *Antonio Gaudí y Cornet.* He is known for his design of La Sagrada Familia, a basilica in Barcelona.

gaud·y /ˈgôdē/ ▶ **adj.** (**gaud·i·er, gaud·i·est**) extravagantly bright or showy, typically so as to be tasteless. — **gaud·i·ly adv. gaud·i·ness n.** [15th C.: prob. from *gaud* 'showy, ornament, a jest,' perh. based on L. *gaudere* 'rejoice.']

gauge /gāj/ (esp. tech. also **gage**) ▶ **n. 1** an instrument or device for measuring the magnitude, amount, or contents of something, typically with a visual display of such information. ■ a tool for checking whether something conforms to a desired dimension. ■ fig. a means of estimating something; a criterion or test: *emigration is a gauge of public unease.* **2** the thickness, size, or capacity of something, esp. as a standard measure, in particular: ■ the diameter of a string, fiber, tube, etc.: [as adj.] *a fine 0.018-inch gauge wire.* ■ [in comb.] a measure of the diameter of a gun barrel, or of its ammunition, expressed as the number of spherical pieces of shot of the same diameter as the barrel that can be made from 1 pound (454 g) of lead: [as adj.] *a 12-gauge shotgun.* ■ [in comb.] the thickness of sheet metal or plastic: [as adj.] *500-gauge polyethylene.* ■ the distance between the rails of a line of railroad track: *the line was laid to a gauge of 2 ft. 9 in.* ▶ **v.** [trans.] **1** estimate or determine the magnitude, amount, or volume of. ■ form a judgment or estimate of (a situation, mood, etc.): *she is unable to gauge his mood.* **2** measure the dimensions of (an object) with a gauge. — **gauge·a·ble adj. gaug·er n.** [ME: from OFr. *gauge* (n.), *gauger* (v.), var. of Old North. Fr. *jauge* (n.), *jauger* (v.).]

gauge the·o·ry ▶ **n.** Physics a quantum theory using mathematical functions to describe subatomic interactions in terms of particles that are not directly detectable.

Gau·guin /gōˈgaN/, Paul (1848–1903), French painter; full name *Eugène Henri Paul Gauguin.* He lived mainly in Tahiti from 1891, painting in a post-Impressionist style that was influenced by primitive art.

Gau·ha·ti /gouˈhätē/ a city in northeastern India, a port on the Brahmaputra River; pop. 578,000.

Gaul[1] /gôl/ an ancient region in Europe that is now France, Belgium, the southern Netherlands, southwestern Germany, and northern Italy.

Gaul[2] ▶ **n.** a native or inhabitant of ancient Gaul. [from L. *Gallus*, prob. of Celtic origin.]

Gau·lei·ter /ˈgouˌlītər/ ▶ **n.** hist. a political official governing a district under Nazi rule. [1930s: Ger., from *Gau* 'administrative district' + *Leiter* 'leader.']

Gaulle, Charles de, see DE GAULLE.

Gaull·ism /ˈgôlizəm/ ▶ **n.** the policies of Charles de Gaulle, characterized by conservatism and nationalism. — **Gaull·ist n. & adj.**

Gaunt[1] /gônt/ former name of GHENT.

Gaunt[2], John of, see JOHN OF GAUNT.

gaunt /gônt/ ▶ **adj.** (of a person) lean and haggard, esp. because of suffering, hunger, or age. — **gaunt·ly adv. gaunt·ness n.** [ME: of unknown origin.]

gaunt·let[1] /ˈgôntlit; ˈgänt-/ ▶ **n.** a stout glove with a long loose wrist. ■ hist. an armored glove, as worn by a medieval knight.
– PHRASES **take up** (or **throw down**) **the gauntlet** accept (or issue) a challenge. [ME: from OFr. *gantelet*, dimin. of *gant* 'glove,' of Gmc. origin.]

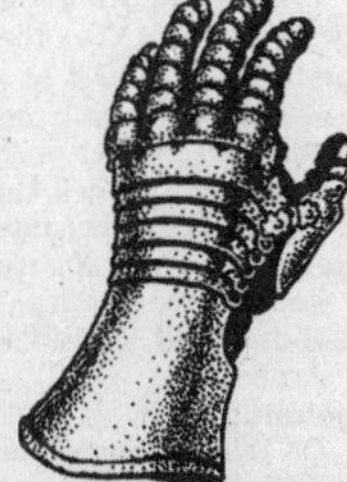
knight's gauntlet

gaunt·let[2] (also **gant·let** /ˈgantlit; ˈgônt-/) ▶ **n.** (in phrase **run the gauntlet**) **1** go through an intimidating or dangerous crowd, place, or experience in order to reach a goal. **2** hist. undergo the military punishment of receiving blows while running between two rows of men with sticks. [17th C.: alt. of *gantlope* (from Swed. *gatlopp*, from *gata* 'lane' + *lopp* 'course').]

Gauss /gous/, Karl Friedrich (1777–1855), German mathematician. He laid the foundations of number theory.

gauss /gous/ (abbr.: **G**) ▶ **n.** (pl. same or **gauss·es**) a unit of magnetic induction, equal to one ten-thousandth of a tesla. [19th C.: named after K. GAUSS.]

Gau·ta·ma /ˈgôtəmə; ˈgou-/, Siddhartha, see BUDDHA.

gauze /gôz/ ▶ **n.** a thin translucent fabric of silk, linen, or cotton. ■ (also **wire gauze**) a very fine wire mesh. ■ Med. thin, loosely woven cloth used for dressing and swabs. ■ [in sing.] fig. a transparent haze or film. — **gauz·i·ness n. gauz·y adj.** [16th C.: from Fr. *gaze*, perh. from *Gaza*, town in Palestine.]

gave /gāv/ past of GIVE.

gav·el /ˈgavəl/ ▶ **n.** a small mallet with which an auctioneer, a judge, or the chair of a meeting hits a surface to call for attention or order. ▶ **v.** (**gav·eled, gav·el·ing**; Brit. **gav·elled, gav·el·ling**) [trans.] bring (a hearing or person) to order by use of such a mallet: *he gaveled the convention to order.* [19th C.: of unknown origin.]

ga·vi·al /ˈgāvēəl/ ▶ **n.** var. of GHARIAL. [from Fr.]

ga·votte /gəˈvät/ ▶ **n.** a medium-paced French dance, popular in the 18th century. ■ a piece of music accompanying or in the rhythm of such a dance, composed in common time beginning on the third beat of the bar. [Fr., from Provençal *gavoto* 'dance of the mountain people,' from *Gavot* 'a native of the Alps.']

Ga·wain /gəˈwān; ˈgäwän; ˈgäwən/ (in Arthurian legend) one of the knights of the Round Table who quested after the Holy Grail.

gawk /gôk/ ▶ **v.** [intrans.] stare openly and stupidly: *they were gawking at some pinup.* — **gawk·er n.** [17th C. (as a n.): perh. rel. to obs. *gaw* 'to gaze,' from ON *gá* 'heed.']

gawk·y /ˈgôkē/ ▶ **adj.** (**gawk·i·er, gawk·i·est**) nervously awkward and ungainly: *a gawky teenager.* — **gawk·i·ly adv. gawk·i·ness n.**

gawp /gôp/ ▶ **v.** [intrans.] informal stare openly in a stupid or rude manner: *what are you gawping at?* [17th C.: perh. an alt. of GAPE.]

Gay /gā/, John (1685–1732), English poet and playwright. He wrote *The Beggar's Opera* (1728).

gay /gā/ ▶ **adj.** (**gay·er, gay·est**) **1** (of a person, esp. a man) homosexual. ■ relating to or used by homosexuals. **2** lighthearted and carefree: *Nan had a gay disposition.* ■ characterized by cheerfulness or pleasure: *we had a gay old time.* ■ brightly colored; showy; brilliant. **3** informal, offens. foolish; stupid: *making students wait for the light is kind of a gay rule.* ▶ **n.** a homosexual, esp. a man. — **gay·ness n.** [ME (sense 2): from OFr. *gai*, of unknown origin.]
– USAGE **Gay** meaning 'homosexual,' dating back to the 1930s (if not earlier), became established in the 1960s as the term preferred by homosexual men to describe themselves. It is now the standard accepted term throughout the English-speaking world. As a result, the centuries-old other senses of **gay** meaning either 'carefree' or 'bright and showy,' once common in speech and literature, are much less frequent. The word **gay** cannot be readily used unselfconsciously today in these older senses without sounding old-fashioned or arousing a sense of double entendre, despite concerted attempts by some to keep them alive. **Gay** in its modern sense typically refers to men (**lesbian** being the standard term for homosexual women), but in some contexts it can be used of both men and women.

Ga·ya /gəˈyä/ a city in northeastern India; pop. 291,000. It is a place of Hindu pilgrimage.

gay·dar /ˈgādär/ ▶ **n.** informal, humorous the putative ability of homosexuals to recognize one another intuitively or by means of very slight indications. [1990s: blend of *gay* and *radar.*]

gay·e·ty ▶ **n.** var. of GAIETY.

gay pride ▶ **n.** a sense of dignity and satisfaction in connection with the public acknowledgment of one's own homosexuality.

gay rights ▶ **plural n.** equal civil and social rights for homosexuals compared with heterosexuals.

gaz. ▶ **abbr.** ■ gazette. ■ gazetteer.

ga·za·ni·a /gəˈzānēə/ ▶ **n.** a tropical herbaceous plant (genus *Gazania*) of the daisy family, with showy flowers that are typically orange or yellow. [mod. L., named after Theodore of *Gaza* (1398–1478), Greek scholar.]

Ga·za Strip /ˈgäzə; ˈgazə/ a strip of territory in Palestine, on the southeastern Mediterranean coast, including the town of Gaza; pop. 748,000. Administered by Egypt from 1949 and occupied by Israel from 1967, it became a self-governing enclave under the PLO–Israeli accord of 1994.

gaze /gāz/ ▶ **v.** [no obj., with adverbial of direction] look steadily and intently, esp. in admiration, surprise, or thought. ▶ **n.** a steady intent look. — **gaz·er n.** [ME: perh. rel. to obs. *gaw* (see GAWK).]

ga·ze·bo /gəˈzēbō/ ▶ **n.** (pl. **-bos** or **-boes**) a roofed structure that offers an open view of the surrounding area, typically used for relaxation or entertainment. [18th C.: perh. from GAZE.] *See illustration on next page.*

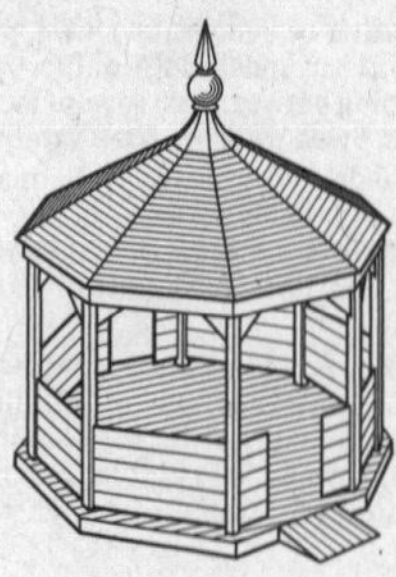
gazebo

ga·zelle /gə'zel/ ▶ **n.** (pl. same or **-zelles**) a small slender antelope (*Gazella* and other genera) that typically has curved horns and a yellowish-brown coat with white underparts, found in open country in Africa and Asia. [17th C.: from Fr., prob. via Sp. from Arab. *ghazāl*.]

ga·zette /gə'zet/ ▶ **n.** (used in the names of periodicals) a journal or newspaper. [17th C.: via Fr. from Ital. *gazzetta*, orig. Venetian *gazeta de la novità* 'a halfpennyworth of news' (because the news-sheet sold for a *gazeta*, a Venetian coin of small value).]

gaz·et·teer /ˌgazi'ti(ə)r/ ▶ **n.** a geographical index or dictionary.

Ga·zi·an·tep /ˌgäzē-än'tep/ a city in southern Turkey; pop. 603,000. Former name (until 1921) AINTAB.

ga·zil·lion /gə'zilyən/ (also **ka·zil·lion**) ▶ **cardinal number** informal a very large number or quantity (used humorously or for emphasis): *I'd like to sell **gazillions** of books.* [20th C.: fanciful formation on the pattern of *billion* and *million*.]

gaz·pa·cho /gä'späCHō/ ▶ **n.** (pl. **-chos**) a Spanish-style soup made from tomatoes and other vegetables and spices, served cold.

GB ▶ **abbr.** ■ Comput. (also **Gb**) gigabyte(s). ■ Great Britain.

Gbyte ▶ **abbr.** gigabyte(s).

gcd ▶ **abbr.** Math. greatest common divisor.

gcf ▶ **abbr.** Math. greatest common factor.

Gd ▶ **symb.** the chemical element gadolinium.

gd. ▶ **abbr.** ■ good. ■ guard.

Gdańsk /gə'dänsk; -'dansk/ a city in northern Poland; pop. 465,000. German name DANZIG.

g'day /gə'dā/ ▶ **exclam.** Austral./NZ good day.

GDP ▶ **abbr.** gross domestic product.

GDR hist. ▶ **abbr.** German Democratic Republic.

Gdy·nia /gə'dinēə/ a city in northern Poland, on the Baltic Sea; pop. 251,500.

Ge[1] ▶ **symb.** the chemical element germanium.

Ge[2] /gā/ Gk. Mythol. another name for GAIA.

gear /gi(ə)r/ ▶ **n. 1** (often **gears**) one of a set of toothed wheels that work together to alter the relation between the speed of a driving mechanism (such as the engine of a vehicle or the crank of a bicycle) and the speed of the driven parts (the wheels). ■ a particular function or state of adjustment of engaged gears: *he was tooling along in fifth gear.* **2** informal equipment that is used for a particular purpose. ■ a person's personal possessions and clothes. ■ clothing, esp. of a specified kind: *combat gear.* ■ Naut. a ship's rigging. ▶ **v.** [trans.] design or adjust the gears in a machine to give a specified speed or power output: *it's geared too high.*
– PHRASES **in gear** with a gear engaged. ■ fig. done with more energy or effort: *I've got to get my act in gear.*
– PHRASAL VERBS **gear down** (or **up**) change to a lower (or higher) gear. **gear for** make ready or prepared: *geared for war.* **gear up** equip or prepare oneself. [ME: of Scand. origin; cf. ON *gervi*.]

gear·box /'gi(ə)rˌbäks/ ▶ **n.** a set of gears with its casing, esp. in a motor vehicle; the transmission.

gear·ing /'gi(ə)riNG/ ▶ **n.** the set or arrangement of gears in a machine.

gear ra·ti·o ▶ **n.** (in a gearbox, transmission, etc.) the ratio between the rates at which the last and first gears rotate.

gear·shift /'gi(ə)rˌSHift/ ▶ **n.** a device used to engage or disengage gears in a transmission or similar mechanism.

gear·wheel /'gi(ə)rˌ(h)wēl/ ▶ **n.** a toothed wheel in a set of gears. ■ (on a bicycle) a cogwheel driven directly by the chain.

geck·o /'gekō/ ▶ **n.** (pl. **-os** or **-oes**) a nocturnal and often highly vocal lizard (Gekkonidae and related families) that has adhesive pads on the feet to assist in climbing on smooth surfaces. [18th C.: from Malay dial. *geko, gekok*, imitative of its cry.]

GED ▶ **abbr.** general equivalency degree (or diploma).

gee[1] /jē/ (also **gee-whiz** /'jē '(h)wiz/) ▶ **exclam.** informal a mild expression, typically of surprise, enthusiasm, or sympathy: *Gee, Linda looks great at fifty!* [19th C.: perh. an abbrev. of JESUS.]

gee[2] ▶ **n.** informal a thousand dollars: *we paid five gees.* [1930s: representing the initial letter of GRAND.]

Gee·chee /'gēCHē/ ▶ **n.** term used of the Gullah dialect, or a speaker of this dialect. [possibly from the name of the Ogeechee River, in Georgia.]

geek /gēk/ ▶ **n.** informal **1** an unfashionable or socially inept person. ■ [with adj.] a person with an eccentric devotion to a particular interest: *a computer geek.* **2** a carnival performer who does wild or disgusting acts. — **geek·y adj.** [19th C.: from dial. *geck* 'fool,' of Gmc. origin; rel. to Du. *gek* 'mad, silly.']

Gee·long /jē'lôNG/ a city in southern Australia; pop. 126,000.

geese /gēs/ plural form of GOOSE.

gee-string ▶ **n.** var. of G-STRING.

gee-whiz informal ▶ **exclam.** another term for GEE[1]. ▶ **adj.** [attrib.] characterized by or causing naive astonishment or wonder, in particular at new technology: *this era of gee-whiz gadgetry.*

Ge'ez /gē'ez/ ▶ **n.** an ancient Semitic language of Ethiopia, which survives as the liturgical language of the Ethiopian Orthodox Church. Also called ETHIOPIC. [of Ethiopic origin.]

geez ▶ **exclam.** var. of JEEZ.

gee·zer /'gēzər/ ▶ **n.** informal an old man (used as a disparaging term). [19th C.: representing a dial. pronunc. of earlier *guiser* 'mummer.']

ge·fil·te fish /gə'filtə/ ▶ **n.** a dish of stewed or baked stuffed fish, or of fish cakes boiled in a fish or vegetable broth and usually served chilled. [19th C.: Yiddish, 'stuffed fish,' from *filn* 'to fill' + FISH[1].]

ge·gen·schein /'gāgənˌSHīn/ ▶ **n.** Astron. a patch of very faint nebulous light sometimes seen in the night sky opposite the sun, thought to be sunlight reflected from gas and dust. [19th C.: Ger. *Gegenschein*, from *gegen* 'opposite' + *Schein* 'glow, shine.']

Ge·hen·na /gə'henə/ (in Judaism and the New Testament) hell. [via eccles. L. from Gk. *geenna*, from Heb. *gē' hinnōm* 'hell,' lit. 'valley of Hinnom,' a place near Jerusalem where children were sacrificed to Baal (Jer. 19:5,6).]

Geh·rig /'gerig/, Lou (1903–41), US baseball player; full name *Henry Louis Gehrig*; known as **the Iron Horse**. He played for the New York Yankees 1925–39. He died from amyotrophic lateral sclerosis (ALS), often called Lou Gehrig's disease.

Gei·ger /'gīgər/, Hans Johann Wilhelm (1882–1945), German physicist. In 1908, he developed a prototype radiation counter for detecting alpha particles.

Gei·ger count·er (also **Gei·ger-Mül·ler count·er** /'mələr; 'myōōlər/) ▶ **n.** a device for measuring radioactivity by detecting and counting ionizing particles.

G8 ▶ **abbr.** Group of Eight, the eight leading industrial nations (US, Japan, Germany, France, UK, Italy, Canada, and Russia) whose heads of government meet regularly.

Gei·sel /'gīzəl/, Theodor Seuss (1904–91) US writer and illustrator; known as Dr. Seuss. His children's books include *The Cat in the Hat* (1957) and *Green Eggs and Ham* (1960).

gei·sha /'gāSHə; 'gē-/ (also **geisha girl**) ▶ **n.** (pl. same or **-shas**) a Japanese hostess trained to entertain men with conversation, dance, and song. [19th C.: Japanese, 'entertainer,' from *gei* 'performing arts' + *sha* 'person.']

Geist /gīst/ ▶ **n.** [in sing.] the spirit of an individual or group. [Ger.; rel. to GHOST.]

Ge·jiu /'ge'jōō/ (also **Ge·ju**) a city in southern China; pop. 384,000.

gel[1] /jel/ ▶ **n.** a gelatinous substance containing a cosmetic, medicinal, or other preparation. ■ a substance of this consistency used for setting the hair. ■ Chem. a semisolid colloidal suspension of a solid dispersed in a liquid. ▶ **v. (gelled, gel·ling)** [intrans.] Chem. form into a gel. ■ [trans.] treat (the hair) with gel. [19th C.: abbrev. of GELATIN.]

gel[2] ▶ **v. (gelled, gel·ling)** esp. Brit. var. of JELL. [19th C.: from GEL[1].]

gel·a·da /jə'lädə/ (also **gelada baboon**) ▶ **n.** (pl. same or **-das**) a brownish baboon (*Theropithecus gelada*) with a long mane and naked red rump, native to Ethiopia. [19th C.: from Amharic *č̣äallada*.]

ge·la·ti /jə'lätē/ plural form of GELATO.

gel·a·tin /'jelətn/ (also esp. dated **gel·a·tine**) ▶ **n.** a virtually colorless and tasteless water-soluble protein prepared from collagen and used in food preparation as the basis of jellies, in photographic processes, and in glue. [19th C.: from Fr. *gélatine*, from Ital. *gelatina*, from *gelata*, from L. (see JELLY).]

ge·lat·i·nize /jə'latnˌīz; 'jelətnˌīz/ ▶ **v.** make or become gelatinous or jellylike. ■ [trans.] [usu. as adj.] (**gelatinized**) coat with gelatin. — **ge·lat·i·ni·za·tion** /jeˌlatni'zāSHən/ **n.**

ge·lat·i·nous /jə'latn-əs/ ▶ **adj.** having a jellylike consistency. — **ge·lat·i·nous·ly adv.**

ge·la·tion[1] /je'lāSHən/ ▶ **n.** tech. solidification by freezing. [19th C.: from L. *gelatio(n-)*, from *gelare* 'freeze.']

ge·la·tion[2] ▶ **n.** Chem. the process of forming a gel.

ge·la·to /jə'lätō/ ▶ **n.** (pl. **-ti** /-tē/) an Italian-style ice cream.

gel·cap ▶ **n.** a gelatin capsule containing liquid medication or other substance to be taken orally.

gel·coat /'jelˌkōt/ ▶ **n.** the smooth, hard surface layer of polyester resin in a fiberglass structure.

geld /geld/ ▶ **v.** [trans.] castrate (a male animal). [ME: from ON *gelda*, from *geldr* 'barren.']

Gel·der·land /'geldərˌlänt; 'KHel-/ a province in the Netherlands; capital, Arnhem.

geld·ing /'geldiNG/ ▶ **n.** a castrated animal, esp. a male horse. [ME: from ON *geldingr*, from *geldr* 'barren.']

gel·id /'jelid/ ▶ **adj.** icy; extremely cold. [17th C.: from L. *gelidus*, from *gelu* 'frost, intense cold.']

gel·ig·nite /ˈjelig,nīt/ ▶ **n.** an explosive made from a gel of nitroglycerine and nitrocellulose. [19th C.: prob. from GELATIN + L. *(l)ignis* 'wood' + -ITE[1].]

Gell-Mann /,gel ˈmän/, Murray (1929–), US physicist. He coined the word *quark*. Nobel Prize for Physics (1969).

gel·se·mi·um /jelˈsēmēəm/ ▶ **n.** 1 a preparation of the rhizome of yellow jasmine, used in homeopathy to treat flulike symptoms. 2 a plant of the genus *Gelsemium* (family Loganiaceae), which includes the yellow jasmine. [19th C.: mod. L., from Ital. *gelsomino* 'jasmine.']

Gel·sen·kir·chen /,gelzənˈki(ə)rKHən/ a city in western Germany, northeast of Essen; pop. 294,000.

gelt /gelt/ ▶ **n.** informal money. [16th C.: from Ger. *Geld*.]

gem /jem/ ▶ **n.** a precious or semiprecious stone, esp. when cut and polished or engraved. ■ a person or thing considered to be outstandingly good or special in some respect: *an architectural gem.* ▶ **v.** (**gemmed, gem·ming**) [trans.] [usu. as adj.] (**gemmed**) rare decorate with or as with gems. — **gem·like adj.** [OE *gim*, from L. *gemma* 'bud, jewel'.]

Ge·mein·schaft /gəˈmīn,sHäft; -,sHaft/ ▶ **n.** social relations between individuals, based on close personal and family ties; community. Contrasted with GESELLSCHAFT. [Ger., from *gemein* 'common' + *-schaft* (see -SHIP).]

gem·i·nate Phonet. ▶ **adj.** /ˈjemənit/ consisting of identical adjacent speech sounds, esp. consonants; doubled. ▶ **v.** /ˈjemə,nāt/ [trans.] double or repeat (a speech sound). — **gem·i·na·tion** /jeməˈnāsHən/ **n.** [ME: from L. *geminatus*, past part. of *geminare* 'double, pair with,' from *geminus* 'twin.']

Gem·i·ni /ˈjemə,nī; -,nē/ 1 Astron. a northern constellation (the Twins), said to represent the mythological twins Castor and Pollux, whose names are given to its two brightest stars. See DIOSCURI. 2 Astrol. the third sign of the zodiac, which the sun enters about May 21. ■ (**a Gemini**) (pl. **-nis**) a person born when the sun is in this sign. 3 a series of twelve manned orbiting space missions, launched by the US in the 1960s. — **Gem·i·ni·an** /-,nīən/ **n. & adj.** (in sense 2).

Gem·i·nids /ˈjeməˈnidz/ Astron. an annual meteor shower with a radiant in the constellation Gemini, reaching a peak about December 13.

gem·ma /ˈjemə/ ▶ **n.** (pl. **gem·mae** /ˈjemē/) Biol. a small cellular body or bud that can separate to form a new organism. [18th C.: from L., lit. 'bud, jewel.']

gem·mule /ˈjemyōōl/ ▶ **n.** Zool. a dormant cluster of embryonic cells produced by a freshwater sponge for development in more favorable conditions. — **gem·mu·la·tion** /jemyəˈlāsHən/ **n.** [19th C.: from Fr., from L. *gemmula*, dimin. of *gemma* 'bud, jewel.']

gem·ol·o·gy /jeˈmäləjē/ (also **gem·mol·ogy**) ▶ **n.** the study of precious stones. — **gem·o·log·i·cal** /jeməˈläjikəl/ **adj. gem·ol·o·gist n.** [19th C.: from L. *gemma* 'bud, jewel' + -LOGY.]

gems·bok /ˈgemz,bäk/ ▶ **n.** a large antelope (*Oryx gazella*) that has a gray coat, distinctive black-and-white head markings, and long straight horns, native to southwestern and East Africa. [18th C.: via Afrik. from Du., lit. 'chamois,' from *gems* 'chamois' + *bok* 'buck.']

gem·stone /ˈjem,stōn/ ▶ **n.** a precious or semiprecious stone, esp. one cut, polished, and used in a piece of jewelry.

ge·müt·lich /gəˈmōōtlik/ ▶ **adj.** pleasant and cheerful. [19th C.: Ger.]

ge·müt·lich·keit /gəˈmōōtlik,kīt/ (also **Ge·müt·lich·keit**) ▶ **n.** geniality; friendliness.

Gen. ▶ **abbr.** ■ General: *Gen. Eisenhower.* ■ Bible Genesis.

-gen ▶ **comb. form** 1 Chem. denoting a substance that produces something: *oxygen* | *allergen.* 2 Bot. denoting a substance or plant that is produced: *cultigen.* [via Fr. *-gène* from Gk. *genēs* '-born, of a specified kind,' from *gen-* (root of *gignomai* 'be born, become,' *genos* 'a kind').]

gen·darme /ˈZHändärm/ ▶ **n.** an armed police officer in France and other French-speaking countries. [16th C.: Fr., from *gens d'armes* 'men of arms.']

gen·dar·me·rie /ZHänˈdärmərē/ ▶ **n.** a force of gendarmes. ■ the headquarters of such a force. [16th C.: Fr.]

gen·der /ˈjendər/ ▶ **n.** 1 Gram. (in languages such as Latin, Greek, Russian, and German) each of the classes (typically masculine, feminine, common, neuter) of nouns and pronouns distinguished by the different inflections that they have and require in words syntactically associated with them. ■ the property (in nouns and related words) of belonging to such a class: *adjectives usually agree with the noun in gender and number.* 2 the state of being male or female (typically used with reference to social and cultural differences rather than biological ones): *traditional concepts of gender.* ■ the members of one or other sex. [ME: from OFr. *gendre*, based on L. *genus* 'birth, family, nation.']

gen·der bend·er ▶ **n.** informal a person who dresses and behaves in a way characteristic of the opposite sex.

gen·dered /ˈjendərd/ ▶ **adj.** of, specific to, or biased toward the male or female sex: *gendered occupations.*

gen·der gap ▶ **n.** the discrepancy in opportunities, status, attitudes, etc. between men and women.

gen·der-neu·tral ▶ **adj.** 1 denoting a word that cannot be taken to refer to one sex only, e.g., *firefighter* (as opposed to *fireman*). 2 (of language or a piece of writing) using gender-neutral words wherever appropriate.

gene /jēn/ ▶ **n.** Biol. (in informal use) a unit of heredity that is transferred from a parent to offspring and is held to determine some characteristic of the offspring: *proteins coded directly by genes.* ■ (in technical use) a distinct sequence of nucleotides forming part of a chromosome. [20th C.: from Ger. *Gen*, from *Pangen* (from Gk. *pan-* 'all' + *genos* 'race, kind, offspring').]

ge·ne·a·log·i·cal /jēnēəˈläjikəl/ ▶ **adj.** of or relating to the study or tracing of lines of family descent: *genealogical research.* — **ge·ne·a·log·i·cal·ly adv.**

ge·ne·al·o·gy /jēnēˈäləjē; -ˈal-/ ▶ **n.** (pl. **-gies**) a line of descent traced continuously from an ancestor: *combing through the birth records and genealogies.* ■ the study and tracing of lines of descent or development. ■ a plant's or animal's line of evolutionary development from earlier forms. — **ge·ne·al·o·gist n. ge·ne·al·o·gize** /-,jīz/ **v.** [ME: via OFr. and late L. from Gk. *genealogia*, from *genea* 'race, generation' + *-logia* (see -LOGY).]

gene fre·quen·cy ▶ **n.** the ratio of a particular allele to the total of all other alleles of the same gene in a given population.

gene pool ▶ **n.** the stock of different genes in an interbreeding population.

gen·er·a /ˈjenərə/ plural form of GENUS.

gen·er·al /ˈjenərəl/ ▶ **adj.** 1 affecting or concerning all or most people, places, or things; widespread: *books of general interest.* ■ not specialized or limited in range of subject, application, activity, etc.: *general knowledge.* ■ (of a rule, principle, etc.) true for all or most cases. ■ normal or usual: *general practice.* 2 considering or including the main features or elements of something, and disregarding exceptions; overall: *they fired in the general direction of the enemy.* 3 [often in titles] chief or principal: *a general manager.* ▶ **n.** a commander of an army, or an army officer of very high rank. ■ an officer in the US Army, Air Force, or Marine Corps ranking above lieutenant general.
– PHRASES **as a general rule** in most cases. **in general** 1 usually; mainly: *in general, a peaceful man.* 2 as a whole: *our understanding of culture in general.* [ME: via OFr. from L. *generalis*, from *genus, gener-* 'class, race, kind.']

gen·er·al an·es·the·sia ▶ **n.** anesthesia that affects the whole body and usually induces a loss of consciousness: *he had the operation under general anesthesia.* Compare with LOCAL ANESTHESIA.

gen·er·al court-mar·tial ▶ **n.** a court-martial for trying serious offenses.

gen·er·al·cy /ˈjenərəlsē/ ▶ **n.** the rank, office, or tenure of a general.

gen·er·al de·liv·er·y ▶ **n.** mail delivery to a post office for pickup by the addressee.

gen·er·al e·lec·tion ▶ **n.** a regular election of candidates for office, as opposed to a primary election.

gen·er·al e·quiv·a·len·cy de·gree (also **gen·er·al e·quiv·a·len·cy di·plo·ma**) (abbr.: **GED**) ▶ **n.** a certificate attesting that the holder has passed examinations considered equivalent to the completion of high school.

gen·er·al head·quar·ters ▶ **n.** [treated as sing. or pl.] the headquarters of a military commander.

gen·er·al·is·si·mo /jenərəˈlisə,mō/ ▶ **n.** (pl. **-mos**) the commander of a combined military force consisting of army, navy, and air force units. [17th C.: Ital., 'having greatest authority,' superlative of *generale* (see GENERAL).]

gen·er·al·ist /ˈjenərəlist/ ▶ **n.** a person competent in several different fields or activities: *with a generalist's education and some specific skills.* ▶ **adj.** able to carry out a range of activities, or adapt to different situations: *a generalist doctor.*

gen·er·al·i·ty /jenəˈralitē/ ▶ **n.** (pl. **-ties**) a statement or principle having general rather than specific validity or force: *he confined his remarks to generalities.* ■ the quality or state of being general.

gen·er·al·i·za·tion /jenərəliˈzāsHən/ ▶ **n.** a general statement or concept obtained by inference from specific cases. ■ the action of generalizing: *such anecdotes cannot be a basis for generalization.*

gen·er·al·ize /ˈjenərə,līz/ ▶ **v.** 1 [intrans.] infer general principles from: *it is tempting to generalize from these conclusions.* ■ make general or broad statements: *it is not easy to **generalize about** the poor.* ■ make or become more widely or generally applicable: [trans.] *most of what we have observed in this field can be generalized to other fields.* 2 [trans.] make (something) more widespread or common. ■ make for wide general use or application: [as adj.] (**generalized**) *generalized information pertinent to anyone.* ■ [as adj.] (**generalized**) Med. (of a disease) affecting much or all of the body; not localized. — **gen·er·al·iz·a·ble adj.**

gen·er·al·ly /ˈjenərəlē/ ▶ **adv.** 1 [sentence adverb] in most cases; usually. 2 in general terms; without regard to particulars or exceptions. 3 widely: *generally reckoned.*

gen·er·al of·fi·cer ▶ **n.** an officer ranking above colonel in the US Army, Air Force, or Marine Corps.

gen·er·al of the air force ▶ **n.** an officer of the highest rank in the US Air Force, ranking above general (awarded only in wartime).

gen·er·al of the ar·my ▶ **n.** an officer of the highest rank in the US Army, above general (awarded only in wartime).

gen·er·al prac·ti·tion·er (abbr.: **GP**) ▶ **n.** a medical doctor who is trained to provide primary health care to patients of either sex and any age.

gen·er·al-pur·pose ▶ adj. having a range of potential uses; not specialized in function or design.

Ge·ne·ral San Mar·tín /ˌkhānäˈräl ˌsän märˈtēn/ (also **San Martín**) a city in eastern Argentina; pop. 408,000.

Ge·ne·ral San·tos /ˌkhānäˈräl ˈsäntōs/ (also called **Dadiangas**) a city in the Philippines, on southern Mindanao Island; pop. 250,000.

Ge·ne·ral Sar·mien·to /ˌkhānäˈräl ˌsärˈmyentō/ (also **Sar·mien·to** or **San Mi·guel**) a city in eastern Argentina; pop. 647,000.

gen·er·al staff ▶ n. [treated as sing. or pl.] the staff assisting a military commander in planning and executing operations.

gen·er·al strike ▶ n. a strike of workers in all or most industries.

gen·er·ate /ˈjenəˌrāt/ ▶ v. [trans.] cause (something, esp. an emotion or situation) to arise or come about: *generate more jobs in the economy.* ■ produce (energy, esp. electricity). ■ produce (a set or sequence of items) by performing specified mathematical or logical operations on an initial set. ■ Ling. produce (a sentence or other unit, esp. a well-formed one) by the application of a finite set of rules to lexical or other linguistic input. ■ Math. form (a line, surface, or solid) by notionally moving a point, line, or surface. [16th C.: from L. *generat-* 'created,' from the v. *generare,* from *genus, gener-* 'stock, race.']

gen·er·a·tion /ˌjenəˈrāshən/ ▶ n. **1** all of the people born and living at about the same time, regarded collectively: *one of his generation's finest songwriters.* ■ the average period, generally considered to be about thirty years, during which children are born and grow up, become adults, and begin to have children of their own. ■ a set of members of a family regarded as a single step or stage in descent: [as adj., in comb.] *a third-generation Canadian.* ■ a single stage in the development of a type of product: *a new generation of sports cars.* **2** the production of something: *the generation of wealth.* ■ the propagation of living organisms; procreation. — **gen·er·a·tion·al** /-shənl/ adj. **gen·er·a·tion·al·ly** /-shənl-ē/ adv.

gen·er·a·tion gap ▶ n. (usu. **the generation gap**) differences of outlook or opinion between people of different generations.

Gen·er·a·tion X ▶ n. the generation born after that of the baby boomers (roughly from the early 1960s to mid 1970s), often perceived to be disaffected and directionless. — **Gen·er·a·tion X·er** /ˈeksər/ n.

gen·er·a·tive /ˈjenərətiv; -ˌrātiv;/ ▶ adj. of or relating to reproduction. ■ able to produce: *the generative power of the life force.* ■ Ling. applying principles of generative grammar.

gen·er·a·tive gram·mar ▶ n. Ling. a type of grammar that describes a language in terms of a set of logical rules formulated so as to be capable of generating the infinite number of possible sentences of that language. ■ a set of rules of this kind.

gen·er·a·tor /ˈjenəˌrātər/ ▶ n. a thing that generates something, in particular: ■ a dynamo or similar machine for converting mechanical energy into electricity. ■ an apparatus for producing gas, steam, or another product. ■ a facility that generates electrical power. ■ [with adj.] Comput. a routine that constructs other routines or subroutines using given parameters, for specific applications: *a report generator.* ■ Math. a point, line, or surface regarded as moving and so notionally forming a line, surface, or solid.

ge·ner·ic /jəˈnerik/ ▶ adj. **1** characteristic of or relating to a class or group of things; not specific: *chèvre is a generic term for all goat's milk cheese.* ■ (of goods, esp. medicinal drugs) having no brand name; not protected by a registered trademark: *generic aspirin.* **2** Biol. of or relating to a genus. ▶ n. a consumer product having no brand name or registered trademark: *substituting generics for brand-name drugs.* — **ge·ner·i·cal·ly** adv. [17th C.: from Fr. *générique,* from L. *genus, gener-* 'stock, race.']

gen·er·os·i·ty /ˌjenəˈräsitē/ ▶ n. the quality of being kind and generous. ■ the quality or fact of being plentiful or large.

gen·er·ous /ˈjenərəs/ ▶ adj. (of a person) showing a readiness to give more of something, as money or time, than is strictly necessary or expected: *generous with her money.* ■ showing kindness toward others. ■ (of a thing) larger or more plentiful than is usual or necessary: *a generous sprinkle of pepper.* — **gen·er·ous·ly** adv. [16th C.: via OFr. from L. *generosus* 'noble, magnanimous,' from *genus, gener-* 'stock, race.']

Gen·e·see Riv·er /ˌjenəˈsē; ˈjenəˌsē/ a river that flows for 144 miles (232 km) from northwestern Pennsylvania into Lake Ontario at Rochester, New York.

Gen·e·sis /ˈjenəsis/ the first book of the Bible. [OE, via L. from Gk., 'creation,' from the base of *gignesthai* 'be born or produced.']

gen·e·sis /ˈjenəsis/ ▶ n. [in sing.] the origin or mode of formation of something. [17th C.: from Gk. (see **Genesis**).]

Ge·net /jəˈnā/, Jean (1910–86), French writer. His works include *Our Lady of the Flowers* (1944).

gen·et /ˈjenit/ ▶ n. a nocturnal, catlike mammal (genus *Genetta*) of the civet family, with short legs, spotted fur, and a long bushy ringed tail, found in Africa, southwestern Europe, and Arabia. ■ the fur of the genet. [ME: from OFr. *genete,* prob. via Catalan, Port., or Sp. from Arab. *jarnait.*]

gene ther·a·py ▶ n. the transplantation of normal genes into cells in place of missing or defective ones in order to correct genetic disorders.

ge·net·ic /jəˈnetik/ ▶ adj. **1** of or relating to genes or heredity. ■ of or relating to genetics: *an attempt to control mosquitoes by genetic techniques.* **2** of or relating to origin; arising from a common origin: *the genetic relations between languages.* — **ge·net·i·cal** adj. **ge·net·i·cal·ly** adv. [19th C. (sense 2): from **genesis**, on the pattern of pairs such as *antithesis, antithetic.*]

ge·net·ic code ▶ n. the nucleotide triplets of DNA and RNA molecules that carry genetic information in living cells. See **triplet code**.

ge·net·ic en·gi·neer·ing ▶ n. the deliberate modification of the characteristics of an organism by manipulating its genetic material.

ge·net·ic fin·ger·print·ing (also **genetic profiling**) ▶ n. another term for **DNA fingerprinting**.

ge·net·ics /jəˈnetiks/ ▶ plural n. [treated as sing.] the study of heredity and the variation of inherited characteristics. ■ [treated as sing. or pl.] the genetic properties or features of an organism, characteristic, etc.: *the effects of family genetics on the choice of career.* — **ge·net·i·cist** /-ˈnetəsist/ n.

Ge·ne·va /jəˈnēvə/ a city in southwestern Switzerland, on Lake Geneva; pop. 167,000. French name **Genève**.

Ge·ne·va, Lake a lake in southwest central Europe. It forms part of the border between France and Switzerland. French name **Lac Léman**.

Ge·ne·va Bi·ble ▶ n. an English translation of the Bible published in 1560 by Protestant scholars working in Europe.

Ge·ne·va Con·ven·tion an international agreement first made at Geneva in 1864 and later revised, governing the status and treatment of captured and wounded military personnel and civilians in wartime.

Ge·nève /zhəˈnev; -ˈnāv/ French name for **Geneva**.

Gen·ghis Khan /ˌgengis ˈkän; jeng-/ (1162–1227), leader of the Mongol empire; born *Temujin.* He took the name Genghis Khan ("ruler of all") in 1206 after uniting the nomadic Mongol tribes.

ge·nial /ˈjēnyəl; -nēəl/ ▶ adj. friendly and cheerful. ■ (esp. of air or climate) pleasantly mild and warm. — **ge·ni·al·i·ty** /ˌjēnēˈalitē/ n. **gen·ial·ly** adv. [16th C.: from L. *genialis* 'nuptial, productive,' from *genius* (see **genius**).]

-genic ▶ comb. form **1** producing: *carcinogenic.* ■ produced by: *iatrogenic.* **2** well suited to: *mediagenic.* — **-genically** suffix forming corresponding adverbs. [from **-gen** + **-ic**.]

ge·nic·u·late /jəˈnikyəlit; -ˌlāt/ ▶ adj. Anat. bent at a sharp angle. [17th C.: from L. *geniculatus,* from *geniculum* 'small knee, joint (of a plant).']

ge·nie /ˈjēnē/ ▶ n. (pl. **-nies** or **-ni·i** /-nēˌī/) a spirit of Arabian folklore, as traditionally depicted imprisoned within a bottle or oil lamp, and capable of granting wishes when summoned. Compare with **jinn**. [17th C.: from Fr. *génie,* from L. *genius* (see **genius**).]

ge·ni·i /ˈjēnēˌī/ plural form of **genie, genius**.

ge·nip /gəˈnip/ ▶ n. **1** the edible fruit of a tropical American tree. **2** (also **gen·i·pap tree** /ˈjenəˌpap/) either of two tropical American trees that yield this fruit: ■ (also **gui·nep** /giˈnep/) a large spreading tree (*Melicoccus bijugatus*) of the soapberry family. ■ another term for **genipapo**. [18th C.: from Amer. Sp. *quenepo* 'guinep tree,' *quenepa,* denoting the fruit.]

gen·i·pa·po /ˌjenəˈpapō/ (also **gen·i·pap tree** /ˈjenəˌpap/) ▶ n. a tropical American tree (*Genipa americana*) of the bedstraw family that yields useful timber. Its fruit has a jellylike pulp that is used for flavoring drinks and to make a black dye. Also called **genip**. ■ a drink, flavoring, or dye made from this fruit. [17th C.: from Port. *jenipapo,* from Tupi.]

genit. ▶ abbr. Gram. genitive.

gen·i·tal /ˈjenitl/ ▶ adj. of or relating to the human or animal reproductive organs. ■ Psychoanal. (in Freudian theory) relating to or denoting the final stage of psychosexual development reached in adulthood. ▶ n. (**genitals**) a person or animal's external organs of reproduction. [ME: from OFr., or from L. *genitalis,* from *genitus,* past part. of *gignere* 'beget.']

gen·i·tal her·pes ▶ n. a disease characterized by blisters in the genital area, caused by a variety of the herpes simplex virus.

gen·i·ta·li·a /ˌjeniˈtālēə; -ˈtālyə/ ▶ plural n. formal tech. the genitals. [19th C.: from L., neut. pl. of *genitalis* (see **genital**).]

gen·i·tal wart ▶ n. a small growth occurring in the anal or genital areas, caused by a virus that is spread esp. by sexual contact.

gen·i·tive /ˈjenitiv/ Gram. ▶ adj. relating to or denoting a case of nouns and pronouns (and words in grammatical agreement with them) indicating possession or close association. ▶ n. a word in the genitive case. ■ (**the genitive**) the genitive case. [ME: from OFr. *genitif, -ive* or L. *genitivus (casus)* '(case) of production or origin,' from *gignere* 'beget.']

gen·i·tor /ˈjenitər/ ▶ n. Anthropol. a person's biological father. Often contrasted with **pater**. [ME (in the sense 'father'): from OFr. *geniteur* or L. *genitor,* from the root of *gignere* 'beget.' The current sense dates from the mid 20th cent.]

gen·i·to·u·ri·nar·y /ˌjenitōˈyo͝orəˌnerē/ ▶ adj. [attrib.] esp. Med. of or relating to the genital and urinary organs.

gen·ius /ˈjēnyəs/ ▶ n. (pl. **geniuses** or **genii** /ˈjēnēˌī/) **1** exceptional intellectual or creative power or other natural ability. **2** a person who is exceptionally intelligent or creative, either generally or in some particular respect: *musical genius.* **3** (pl. **genii**) (in some mythologies) a guardian spirit associated with a person, place, or institution. ■ a person regarded as exerting a powerful influence over another for good or evil. **4** the prevalent character or spirit of something such as a nation or age: *the austere genius of neoclassicism.* [ME: from L., 'attendant spirit present from one's birth, innate ability or inclination,' from the root of *gignere* 'beget.']

ge·ni·us lo·ci /ˈjēnēəs ˈlōsī; -kī/ ▶ n. [in sing.] the prevailing character or atmosphere of a place. [17th C.: L., lit. 'spirit of the place.']

genl. ▶ abbr. general.

gen·lock /ˈjenˌläk/ ▶ **n.** a device for maintaining synchronization between two different video signals, or between a video signal and a computer or audio signal, enabling video images and computer graphics to be mixed. ▶ **v.** [intrans.] maintain synchronization between two signals using the genlock technique. [1960s: from GENERATOR + the v. LOCK[1].]

Gen·o·a /ˈjenōə/ a city on the northwestern coast of Italy; pop. 701,000. Italian name GENOVA. — **Gen·o·ese** /ˌjenōˈēz; -ˈēs/ **adj. & n.**

gen·o·a /ˈjenōə/ ▶ **n.** (also **genoa jib**) Sailing a large jib or foresail whose foot extends aft of the mast, used esp. on racing yachts. [19th C.: so named because of association with the city of GENOA.]

gen·o·cide /ˈjenəˌsīd/ ▶ **n.** the deliberate killing of a large group of people, esp. those of a particular ethnic group or nation. — **gen·o·cid·al** /ˌjenəˈsīdl/ **adj.** [1940s: from Gk. *genos* 'race' + -CIDE.]

ge·nome /ˈjēnōm/ ▶ **n.** Biol. the haploid set of chromosomes in a gamete or microorganism, or in each cell of a multicellular organism. ■ the complete set of genes or genetic material present in a cell or organism. — **ge·no·mic** /jēˈnämik; -ˈnō-; ji-/ **adj.** [1930s: blend of GENE and CHROMOSOME.]

ge·no·mics /jēˈnōmiks; -ˈnä-,/ ▶ **plural n.** [treated as sing.] the branch of molecular biology concerned with the structure, function, evolution, and mapping of genomes.

gen·o·type /ˈjenəˌtīp; ˈjē-/ ▶ **n.** Biol. the genetic constitution of an individual organism. Often contrasted with PHENOTYPE. — **gen·o·typ·ic** /ˌjenəˈtipik; ˌjē-/ **adj.** [20th C.: from Ger. *Genotypus*, from Gk. *genos* 'race, offspring' + *-tupos* 'type.']

-genous ▶ **comb. form** **1** producing; inducing: *erogenous.* **2** originating in: *endogenous.* [from -GEN + -OUS.]

Ge·no·va /ˈjenəvə/ Italian name for GENOA.

gen·re /ˈZHänrə/ ▶ **n.** a category of artistic composition, as in music or literature, characterized by similarities in form, style, or subject matter. [19th C.: Fr., lit. 'a kind' (see GENDER).]

gen·re paint·ing ▶ **n.** a style of painting depicting scenes from everyday life, associated particularly with 17th-century Dutch and Flemish artists.

gens /jenz/ ▶ **n.** (pl. **gen·tes** /ˈjentēz/) **1** a group of families in ancient Rome who shared a name and claimed a common origin. **2** Anthropol. a group of people who are related through their male ancestors. [L., from the root of *gignere* 'beget.']

Gent /KHent/ Flemish name for GHENT.

gent /jent/ ▶ **n.** informal a gentleman.

gen·ta·mi·cin /ˌjentəˈmīsin/ ▶ **n.** a broad-spectrum antibiotic, derived from bacteria of the genus *Micromonospora* and used chiefly for severe systemic infections. [20th C.: from *genta-* (of unknown origin) + *-micin* (alt. of -MYCIN).]

gen·teel /jenˈtēl/ ▶ **adj.** polite, refined, or respectable, often in an affected or ostentatious way. — **gen·teel·ly adv. gen·teel·ness n.** [16th C. (in the sense 'fashionable, stylish'): from Fr. *gentil* 'well-born.']

gen·teel·ism /jenˈtēlizəm/ ▶ **n.** a word or expression used because it is thought to be socially more acceptable than the everyday word: *in German usage "sister" was the accepted genteelism for "mistress."*

gen·tes /ˈjentēz/ plural form of GENS.

gen·tian /ˈjenCHən/ ▶ **n.** a plant (genera *Gentiana* and *Gentianella*, family Gentianaceae) of temperate and mountainous regions, typically with violet or vivid blue trumpet-shaped flowers, including the four-petaled **fringed gentian** (*Gentiana crinita*) of North America. [ME: from L. *gentiana*, after *Gentius*, king of Illyria, who is said to have discovered the plant's medicinal properties.]

fringed gentian

gen·tian vi·o·let ▶ **n.** a synthetic violet dye derived from rosaniline, used as an antiseptic.

gen·tile /ˈjentīl/ ▶ **adj.** (**Gentile**) not Jewish. ■ (of a person) not belonging to one's own religious community. ▶ **n.** (**Gentile**) a person who is not Jewish. [ME: from L. *gentilis* 'of the same clan,' from *gens, gent-* 'family, race,' from the root of *gignere* 'beget.']

gen·til·i·ty /jenˈtilitē/ ▶ **n.** genteel manners, behavior, or appearances. [ME (in the sense 'honorable birth'): from OFr. *gentilite*, from *gentil* (see GENTLE).]

gen·tle /ˈjentl/ ▶ **adj.** (**gen·tler, gen·tlest**) **1** (of a person) mild in temperament or behavior; kind or tender. **2** moderate in action, effect, or degree; not harsh or severe: *a gentle breeze.* ■ (of a slope) gradual. ▶ **v.** make or become gentle; calm or pacify. ■ [trans.] make (an animal) docile by gentle handling. — **gen·tle·ness n. gen·tly adv.** [ME: from OFr. *gentil* 'highborn, noble,' from L. *gentilis* (see GENTILE).]

gent·le·folk /ˈjentlˌfōk/ ▶ **plural n.** archaic people of high social position.

gen·tle·la·dy /ˈjentlˌlādē/ ▶ **n.** a polite form of address for a woman, used esp. to a congresswoman during a congressional debate.

gent·le·man /ˈjentlmən/ ▶ **n.** (pl. **-men**) **1** a chivalrous, courteous, or honorable man. ■ a man of good social position, esp. one of wealth and leisure. ■ (in the UK) a man of noble birth attached to a royal household. **2** a polite or formal way of referring to a man: *an old gentleman sat reading.* ■ (**gentlemen**) used as a polite form of address to a group of men: *"Can I help you, gentlemen?"* [ME: from GENTLE + MAN.]

gen·tle·man·ly /ˈjentlmənlē/ ▶ **adj.** (of a man) befitting a gentleman; chivalrous, courteous, or honorable.

gen·tle·man's a·gree·ment (also **gen·tle·men's a·gree·ment**) ▶ **n.** an arrangement or understanding which is based upon the trust of both or all parties, rather than being legally binding.

gen·tle·man's gen·tle·man ▶ **n.** a valet.

gen·too /ˈjentoo/ (also **gentoo penguin**) ▶ **n.** a tall penguin (*Pygoscelis papua*) with a white triangular patch above the eye, breeding on subantarctic islands. [19th C.: perh. from Anglo-Ind. *Gentoo* 'a Hindu,' from Port. *gentio* 'gentile.']

gen·tri·fy /ˈjentrəˌfī/ ▶ **v.** (**-fies, -fied**) [trans.] renovate and improve (esp. a house or district) so that it conforms to middle-class taste. ■ [usu. as adj.] (**gentrified**) make (someone or their way of life) more refined or dignified. — **gen·tri·fi·ca·tion** /ˌjentrəfiˈkāSHən/ **n. gen·tri·fi·er n.**

gen·try /ˈjentrē/ ▶ **n.** (often **the gentry**) people of good social position, specifically (in the UK) the class of people next below the nobility in position and birth: *a member of the landed gentry.* [ME: from Anglo-Norman Fr. *genterie*, based on *gentil* (see GENTLE).]

gen·u·flect /ˈjenyəˌflekt/ ▶ **v.** [intrans.] lower one's body briefly by bending one knee to the ground, typically in worship or as a sign of respect. ■ [with adverbial] fig. show deference or servility. — **gen·u·flec·tion** /ˌjenyəˈflekSHən/ **n.** [17th C. (in the sense 'bend (the knee)'): from eccles. L. *genuflectere*, from L. *genu* 'knee' + *flectere* 'to bend.']

gen·u·ine /ˈjenyooin/ ▶ **adj.** truly what something is said to be; authentic: *genuine leather.* ■ (of a person, emotion, or action) sincere. — **gen·u·ine·ly adv. gen·u·ine·ness n.** [16th C.: from L. *genuinus* 'native,' from the base of *gignere* 'beget.']

ge·nus /ˈjēnəs/ ▶ **n.** (pl. **gen·e·ra** /ˈjenərə/ or **ge·nus·es**) Biol. a grouping of organisms having common characteristics distinct from those of other such groupings. The genus is a principal taxonomic category that ranks above species and below family, and is denoted by a capitalized Latin name, e.g., *Leo.* ■ (in philosophical and general use) a class of things that have common characteristics and that can be divided into subordinate kinds. [16th C.: from L., 'birth, race, stock.']

-geny ▶ **comb. form** denoting the mode by which something develops or is produced: *orogeny.* [rel. to Fr. *-génie*; from Gk. *-geneia*, from *gen-* (root of *gignomai* 'be born').]

Geo. dated ▶ **abbr.** George.

geo- ▶ **comb. form** of or relating to the earth: *geocentric* | *geochemistry.* [from Gk. *gē* 'earth.']

ge·o·cen·tric /ˌjēōˈsentrik/ ▶ **adj.** having or representing the earth as the center, as in former astronomical systems. Compare with HELIOCENTRIC. — **ge·o·cen·tri·cal·ly** /-trik(ə)lē/ **adv. ge·o·cen·trism n.**

ge·o·chem·is·try /ˌjēōˈkemistrē/ ▶ **n.** the study of the chemical composition of the earth and its rocks and minerals. — **ge·o·chem·i·cal** /-ˈkemikəl/ **adj. ge·o·chem·ist** /-ˈkemist/ **n.**

ge·o·chro·nol·o·gy /ˌjēōkrəˈnäləjē/ ▶ **n.** the branch of geology concerned with the dating of rock formations and geological events. — **ge·o·chron·o·log·i·cal** /-ˌkränəˈläjikəl/ **adj. ge·o·chro·nol·o·gist n.**

ge·o·chron·o·met·ric /ˌjēōˌkränəˈmetrik/ ▶ **adj.** of or relating to geochronological measurement. — **ge·o·chro·nom·e·try** /-krəˈnämətrē/ **n.**

ge·ode /ˈjēōd/ ▶ **n.** a small cavity in rock lined with crystals or other mineral matter. ■ a rock containing such a cavity. — **ge·od·ic** /jēˈädik/ **adj.** [17th C.: via L. from Gk. *geōdēs* 'earthy,' from *gē* 'earth.']

ge·o·des·ic /ˌjēəˈdesik; -ˈdē-/ ▶ **adj.** **1** of, relating to, or denoting the shortest possible line between two points on a sphere or other curved surface. **2** another term for GEODETIC. ▶ **n.** a geodesic line or structure.

geodesic dome

ge·o·des·ic dome ▶ **n.** a dome constructed of short struts following geodesic lines and forming an open framework of triangles or polygons.

ge·od·e·sy /jēˈädəsē/ ▶ **n.** the branch of mathematics dealing with the shape and area of the earth or large portions of it. [16th C.: from mod. L. *geodaesia*, from Gk. *geōdaisia*, from *gē* 'earth' + *daiein* 'to divide.']

ge·o·det·ic /ˌjēəˈdetik/ ▶ **adj.** of or relating to geodesy, esp. as applied to land surveying. [17th C.: from Gk. *geōdaitēs* 'land surveyor,' from *geōdaisia* (see GEODESY).]

ge·o·det·ic sur·vey ▶ **n.** a land survey with corrections made to account for the curvature of the earth's surface.

ge·o·duck /ˈgōoēˌdək/ ▶ **n.** a giant mud-burrowing bivalve mollusk (*Panopea generosa*, family Hyatellidae) occurring on the west coast of North America, where it is collected for food. [19th C.: from Puget Sound Salish.]

Geof·frey of Mon·mouth /ˈjefrē əv ˈmänməTH/ (*c.*1100–*c.*54), Welsh chronicler. His *Historia Regum Britanniae* (*c.*1139; first printed in 1508), is an account of the kings of Britain.

geog. ▶ abbr. ■ geographer. ■ geographic. ■ geographical. ■ geography.

ge·o·graph·i·cal /jēəˈgrafikəl/ ▶ adj. of or relating to geography. — **ge·o·graph·ic** adj. **ge·o·graph·i·cal·ly** adv.

ge·og·ra·phy /jēˈägrəfē/ ▶ n. the study of the physical features of the earth and its atmosphere, and of human activity as it affects and is affected by these. ■ [usu. in sing.] the nature and relative arrangement of places and physical features: *the geography of the battlefield.* — **ge·og·ra·pher** n. [15th C.: from Fr. *géographie* or L. *geographia*, from Gk. *geōgraphia*, from *gē* 'earth' + *-graphia* 'writing.']

ge·oid /ˈjē-oid/ ▶ n. (**the geoid**) the hypothetical shape of the earth, coinciding with mean sea level and its imagined extension under (or over) land areas. [19th C.: from Gk. *geoeidēs*, from *gē* 'earth' + *-oeidēs* (see -OID).]

geol. ▶ abbr. ■ geologic. ■ geological. ■ geologist. ■ geology.

ge·ol·o·gy /jēˈäləjē/ ▶ n. the science that deals with the earth's physical structure and substance, its history, and the processes that act on it. ■ the geological features of an area: *the geology of the Outer Hebrides.* ■ the geological features of a planetary body: *the geology of the surface of Mars.* — **ge·o·log·ic** /jēəˈläjik/ adj. **ge·o·log·i·cal** /jēəˈläjikəl/ adj. **ge·o·log·i·cal·ly** /jēəˈläjik(ə)lē/ adv. **ge·ol·o·gist** n. [18th C.: from mod. L. *geologia*, from Gk. *gē* 'earth' + *-logia* (see -LOGY).]

geom. ▶ abbr. ■ geometric. ■ geometrical. ■ geometry.

ge·o·mag·net·ism /jēōˈmagniˌtizəm/ ▶ n. the branch of geology concerned with the magnetic properties of the earth. — **ge·o·mag·net·ic** /-magˈnetik/ adj. **ge·o·mag·net·i·cal·ly** /-magˈnetik(ə)lē/ adv.

ge·o·man·cy /ˈjēəˌmansē/ ▶ n. divination from configurations seen in a handful of earth thrown on the ground, or by interpreting lines or textures on the ground. — **ge·o·man·cer** n. **ge·o·man·tic** /jēəˈmantik/ adj.

ge·om·e·ter /jēˈämitər/ ▶ n. a person skilled in geometry.

Circles

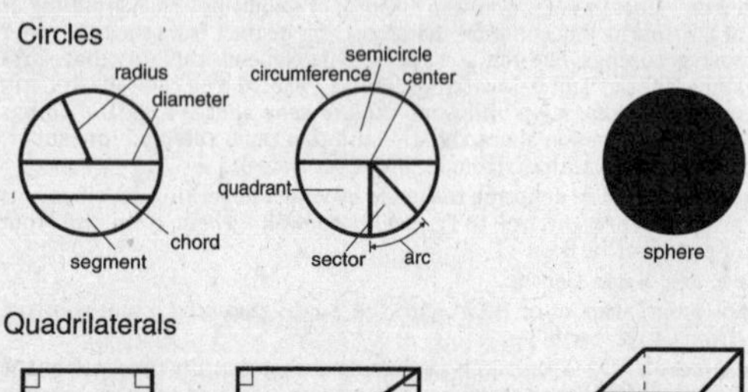

Quadrilaterals

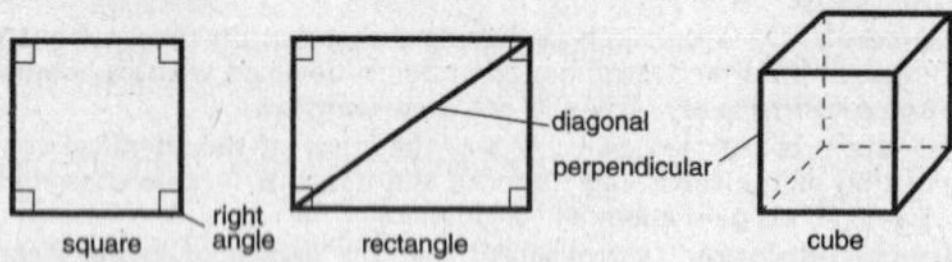

Triangles

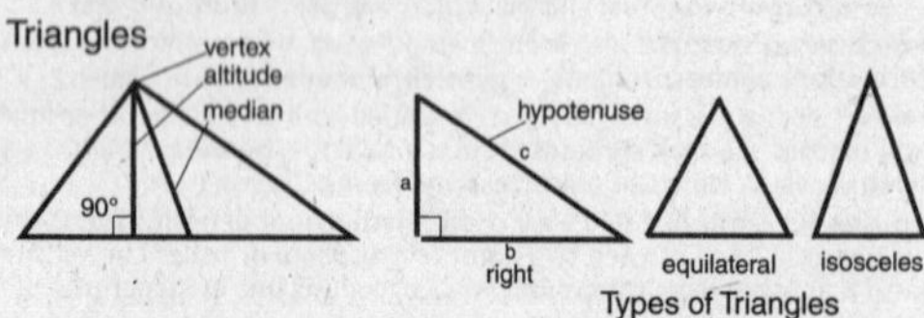

Types of Triangles

Conic Sections

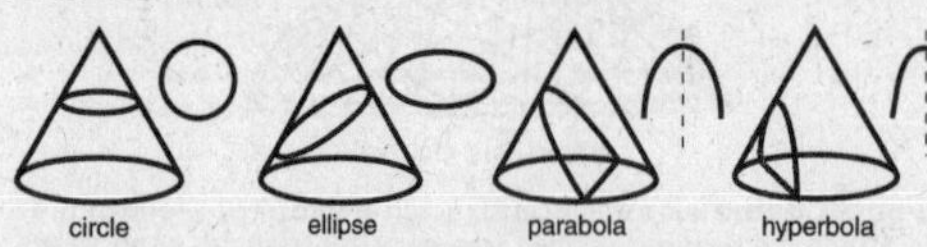

geometric shapes and forms

ge·o·met·ric /jēəˈmetrik/ ▶ adj. **1** of or relating to geometry, or according to its methods. **2** (of a design) characterized by or decorated with regular lines and shapes. ■ (**Geometric**) Archaeol. of or denoting a period of Greek culture (around 900–700 BC) characterized by geometrically decorated pottery. — **ge·o·met·ri·cal** adj. **ge·o·met·ri·cal·ly** adv.

ge·o·met·ric mean ▶ n. the central number in a geometric progression (e.g., *9* in *3, 9, 27*), also calculable as the *n*th root of a product of *n* numbers.

ge·o·met·ric pro·gres·sion ▶ n. a progression of numbers with a constant ratio between each number and the one before (e.g., each subsequent number is increased by a factor of 3 in the progression *1, 3, 9, 27, 81*).

ge·o·met·rics /jēəˈmetriks/ ▶ plural n. straight lines and simple geometric shapes, e.g. circles and squares, used together to form a design or pattern.

ge·o·met·ric se·ries ▶ n. a series of numbers or quantities in geometric progression.

ge·om·e·trid /jēˈämitrid/ ▶ n. a moth of a large family (Geometridae), distinguished by having twiglike caterpillars that move by arching and straightening the body. [19th C.: from mod. L. *Geometridae* (pl.), from the genus name *Geometra*, from L. *geometres*, based on Gk. *gē* 'earth' + *metrēs* 'measurer.']

ge·om·e·try /jēˈämitrē/ ▶ n. the branch of mathematics concerned with the properties and relations of points, lines, surfaces, solids, and higher dimensional analogs. ■ (pl. **-tries**) a particular mathematical system describing such properties: *non-Euclidean geometries.* ■ [in sing.] the shape and relative arrangement of the parts of something: *the geometry of spiders' webs.* [ME: via OFr. from L. *geometria*, from Gk., from *gē* 'earth' + *metria* (see -METRY).]

ge·o·mor·phol·o·gy /ˌjēōmôrˈfäləjē/ ▶ n. the study of the physical features of the surface of the earth and their relation to its geological structures. — **ge·o·mor·pho·log·i·cal** /-ˌmôrfəˈläjikəl/ adj. **ge·o·mor·phol·o·gist** n.

ge·oph·a·gy /jēˈäfəjē/ ▶ n. the practice of eating earth, esp. chalk or clay in famine-stricken regions. [19th C.: from GEO- 'earth' + Gk. *phagia* 'eating, feeding' (from *phagein* 'eat').]

ge·o·phys·ics /jēōˈfiziks/ ▶ plural n. [treated as sing.] the physics of the earth. — **ge·o·phys·i·cal** /-ˈfizikəl/ adj. **ge·o·phys·i·cist** /-ˈfizisist/ n.

ge·o·pol·i·tics /jēōˈpäləˌtiks/ ▶ plural n. [treated as sing. or pl.] politics, esp. international relations, as influenced by geographical factors. ■ [treated as sing.] the study of politics of this type. — **ge·o·po·lit·i·cal** /-pəˈlitikəl/ adj. **ge·o·po·lit·i·cal·ly** /-pəˈlitik(ə)lē/ adv. **ge·o·pol·i·ti·cian** /-ˌpäləˈtisHən/ n.

George /jôrj/ the name of four kings of Great Britain and Ireland, one of Great Britain and Ireland (from 1920, of the United Kingdom), and one of the United Kingdom: ■ George I (1660–1727), reigned 1714–27; great-grandson of James I. ■ George II (1683–1760), reigned 1727–60; son of George I. ■ George III (1738–1820), reigned 1760–1820; grandson of George II. He reigned during the time of the American Revolution and the War of 1812. ■ George IV (1762–1830), reigned 1820–30; son of George III. ■ George V (1865–1936), reigned 1910–36; son of Edward VII. ■ George VI (1895–1952), reigned 1936–52; son of George V. He came to the throne when his older brother Edward VIII abdicated.

George, St., patron saint of England. He is reputed to have slain a dragon and may have been martyred near Lydda in Palestine.

George, Lake /jôrj/ a lake in northeastern New York, near the Vermont border.

Georges Bank /ˈjôrjiz/ an underwater rise in the Atlantic Ocean, between Massachusetts and Nova Scotia, site of important fishing grounds.

George·town /ˈjôrjˌtoun/ **1** the capital of Guyana, a port on the Demerara River; pop. 188,000. **2** a section of northwestern Washington, DC.

George Town **1** the capital of the Cayman Islands, on the island of Grand Cayman; pop. 12,000. **2** the chief port of Malaysia, on Penang Island; pop. 219,000. Also called PENANG.

geor·gette /jôrˈjet/ ▶ n. a thin silk or crepe dress material. [20th C.: named after *Georgette* de la Plante (*c.*1900), French dressmaker.]

Georgia

Location: southwestern Asia, on the eastern shore of the Black Sea

Area: 26,900 square miles (69,700 sq km)

Population: 4,693,000

Capital: Tbilisi

Languages: Georgian (official), Russian, Armenian, Azerbaijani

Currency: lari

Geor·gia /ˈjôrjə/ **1** a country in southwestern Asia. *See box.* **2** a state in the southeastern US, on the Atlantic coast; pop. 8,186,453; capital, Atlanta; statehood, Jan. 2, 1788 (4). Founded as an English colony in 1732 and named after George II, it was one of the original thirteen states.

Geor·gian[1] /ˈjôrjən/ ▶ adj. **1** of or characteristic of the reigns of the British kings George I–IV (1714–1830). ■ of or relating to British architecture of this period. **2** of or characteristic of the reigns of the British kings George V and VI (1910–52). ■ of or relating to British literature of 1910–20.

Geor·gian[2] ▶ **adj.** of or relating to the country of Georgia, its people, or their language. ▶ **n. 1** a native or national of Georgia, or a person of Georgian descent. **2** the South Caucasian (or Kartvelian) language, the official language of Georgia.

Geor·gian[3] ▶ **adj.** of or relating to the state of Georgia in the US. ▶ **n.** a native of Georgia.

Geor·gia, Strait of /ˈjôrjə/ an ocean passage between Vancouver Island and British Columbia and Washington.

geor·gic /ˈjôrjik/ ▶ **n.** a poem or book dealing with agriculture or rural topics. [16th C.: via L. from Gk. *geōrgikos*, from *geōrgos* 'farmer.']

ge·o·sci·ence /ˌjēōˈsīəns; ˈjēōˌsīəns/ ▶ **n.** (also **geosciences**) earth sciences, esp. geology. — **ge·o·sci·en·tist** /ˌjēōˈsīəntist; ˈjēōˌsīəntist/ **n.**

ge·o·sta·tion·ar·y /ˌjēōˈstāsHəˌnerē/ ▶ **adj.** (of an artificial satellite of the earth) moving in a geosynchronous orbit in the plane of the equator, so that it remains stationary in relation to a fixed point on the surface.

ge·o·syn·chro·nous /ˌjēōˈsiNGkrənəs/ ▶ **adj.** (of an earth satellite or its orbit) having a period of rotation synchronous with that of the earth's rotation.

ge·o·syn·cline /ˌjēōˈsinklīn/ ▶ **n.** Geol. a large-scale depression in the earth's crust containing a thick series of sediments.

ge·o·ther·mal /ˌjēōˈTHərməl/ (also **ge·o·ther·mic** /-ˈTHərmik/) ▶ **adj.** of, relating to, or produced by the internal heat of the earth: *some 70% of Iceland's energy needs are met from geothermal sources.*

ge·ot·ro·pism /jēˈätrəˌpizəm/ ▶ **n.** Bot. the growth of the parts of plants with respect to the force of gravity. — **ge·o·trop·ic** /ˌjēəˈträpik; -ˈtrō-/ **adj.** [19th C.: from GEO- 'earth' + Gk. *tropē* 'turning' + -ISM.]

ger. ▶ **abbr.** Gram. ■ gerund. ■ gerundive.

Ge·ra /ˈgārä/ a city in east central Germany; pop. 127,000.

ge·ra·ni·al /jəˈrānēəl/ ▶ **n.** Chem. a fragrant oil, $C_{10}H_{16}O$, present in lemongrass oil and used in perfumery. [19th C.: from Ger., contr. of *Geraniumaldehyde*.]

ge·ra·ni·ol /jəˈrānēˌôl; -ˌäl/ ▶ **n.** Chem. a fragrant liquid, $C_{10}H_{18}O$, present in some floral oils and used in perfumery. [19th C.: from Ger., from GERANIUM + -OL.]

ge·ra·ni·um /jəˈrānēəm/ ▶ **n.** a herbaceous plant or small shrub of the genus *Geranium* (family Geraniaceae), which comprises the cranesbills and their relatives. Geraniums bear a long narrow fruit that is said to be shaped like the bill of a crane. ■ (in general use) a cultivated pelargonium. ■ the scarlet color of many cultivated pelargoniums. [mod. L., from Gk. *geranion*, from *geranos* 'crane.']

ger·ber·a /ˈgərbərə/ ▶ **n.** a tropical plant (genus *Gerbera*) of the daisy family, native to Asia and Africa, with large brightly colored flowers. [mod. L., named after Traugott *Gerber* (died 1743), German naturalist.]

ger·bil /ˈjərbəl/ ▶ **n. 1** a burrowing mouselike rodent (subfamily Gerbillinae) that is specially adapted to living in arid conditions, found in Africa and Asia. **2** another term for JIRD. [19th C.: from Fr. *gerbille*, from mod. L. *gerbillus*, dimin. of *gerboa* (see JERBOA).]

ger·e·nuk /ˈgerəˌno͝ok/ ▶ **n.** a slender East African antelope (*Litocranius walleri*) with a long neck, often browsing on tall bushes by standing on its hind legs. [19th C.: from Somali.]

ger·i·at·ric /ˌjerēˈatrik/ ▶ **adj.** [attrib.] of or relating to old people, esp. with regard to their health care. ▶ **n.** an old person, esp. one receiving special care. [1920s: from Gk. *gēras* 'old age' + *iatros* 'doctor.']

ger·i·at·rics /ˌjerēˈatriks/ ▶ **plural n.** [treated as sing. or pl.] the branch of medicine or social science dealing with the health and care of old people. — **ger·i·a·tri·cian** /ˌjerēəˈtrisHən/ **n.**

Gé·ri·cault /ˌZHerēˈkō/, Théodore (1791–1824), French painter; full name *Jean Louis André Théodore Gericault*. His work includes *The Raft of the Medusa* (1819).

germ /jərm/ ▶ **n. 1** a microorganism, esp. one that causes disease. **2** a portion of an organism capable of developing into a new one or part of one. Compare with GERM CELL. ■ the embryo in a cereal grain or other plant seed. Compare with WHEAT GERM. ■ an initial stage from which something may develop: *the germ of a brilliant idea.* — **germ·y adj.** (informal, in sense 1). [ME (sense 2): via OFr. from L. *germen* 'seed, sprout.']

Ger·man /ˈjərmən/ ▶ **n. 1** a native or national of Germany. ■ a person of German descent. **2** a West Germanic language used in Germany, Austria, and parts of Switzerland, and by communities in the US and elsewhere. See also HIGH GERMAN, LOW GERMAN. ▶ **adj.** of or relating to Germany, its people, or their language. [from L. *Germanus*.]

ger·man /ˈjərmən/ ▶ **adj.** [postpositive] (of a sibling) having the same parents: *my brothers-german.* [ME: from OFr. *germain*, from L. *germanus* 'genuine, of the same parents.']

Ger·man cock·roach ▶ **n.** a small, brown, common indoor cockroach (*Blatella germanica*) found worldwide.

Ger·man Dem·o·crat·ic Re·pub·lic (abbr.: **GDR, DDR**) official name for the former state of East Germany.

ger·man·der /jərˈmandər/ ▶ **n.** a widely distributed plant (genus *Teucrium*) of the mint family. Some kinds are cultivated as ornamentals and some are used in herbal medicine. [ME: from med. L. *germandra*, based on Gk. *khamaidrus*, lit. 'ground oak,' from *khamai* 'on the ground' + *drus* 'oak.']

ger·man·der speed·well ▶ **n.** a Eurasian speedwell (*Veronica chamaedrys*) with bright blue flowers and leaves resembling those of the germander, now common in North America.

ger·mane /jərˈmān/ ▶ **adj.** relevant to a subject under consideration: *that is not germane to our theme.* — **ger·mane·ly adv. ger·mane·ness n.** [17th C.: var. of GERMAN.]

Ger·man East Af·ri·ca a former German protectorate in East Africa 1891–1918.

Ger·man Em·pire an empire in German-speaking central Europe, created by Bismarck in 1871 after the Franco-Prussian War by the union of twenty-five German states under the Hohenzollern king of Prussia. Also called **Second Reich**.

Ger·man·ic /jərˈmanik/ ▶ **adj.** of, relating to, or denoting the branch of the Indo-European language family that includes English, German, Dutch, Frisian, the Scandinavian languages, and Gothic. ■ of, relating to, or denoting the peoples of ancient northern and western Europe speaking such languages. ▶ **n.** the Germanic languages collectively. See also EAST GERMANIC, NORTH GERMANIC, WEST GERMANIC. ■ the unrecorded ancient language from which these developed.

ger·ma·ni·um /jərˈmānēəm/ ▶ **n.** the chemical element of atomic number 32, a shiny gray semimetal. (Symbol: **Ge**) [19th C.: mod. L., from L. *Germanus* (see GERMAN).]

Ger·man·ize /ˈjərməˌnīz/ ▶ **v.** [trans.] make German; cause to adopt German language and customs. — **Ger·man·i·za·tion** /ˌjərməniˈzāsHən/ **n.**

Ger·man mea·sles ▶ **plural n.** [usu. treated as sing.] another term for RUBELLA.

Germano- ▶ **comb. form** German; German and ...: *Germanophile.* ■ relating to Germany: *Germanocentric.*

German shepherd

Ger·man shep·herd (also **German shepherd dog**) ▶ **n.** a large dog of a breed often used as guard dogs or guide dogs or for police work.

Ger·man·town /ˈjərmənˌtoun/ **1** a city in southwestern Tennessee; pop. 37,348. **2** a historic section of northwestern Philadelphia, Pennsylvania; scene of a 1777 battle.

Ger·ma·ny /ˈjərmənē/ a country in central Europe. German name DEUTSCHLAND. *See box on next page.*

germ cell ▶ **n.** Biol. a cell containing half the number of chromosomes of a somatic cell and able to unite with one from the opposite sex to form a new individual; a gamete. ■ an embryonic cell with the potential of developing into a gamete.

ger·mi·cide /ˈjərməˌsīd/ ▶ **n.** a substance or other agent that destroys harmful microorganisms; an antiseptic. — **ger·mi·cid·al** /ˌjərməˈsīdl/ **adj.**

ger·mi·nal /ˈjərmənl/ ▶ **adj.** [attrib.] relating to or of the nature of a germ cell or embryo. ■ in the earliest stage of development. ■ providing material for future development: *the subject was revived in a germinal article by Charles Ferguson.* — **ger·mi·nal·ly adv.** [19th C.: from L. *germen, germin-* 'sprout, seed' + -AL.]

ger·mi·nate /ˈjərməˌnāt/ ▶ **v.** [intrans.] (of a seed or spore) begin to grow and put out shoots after a period of dormancy. *See illustration on next page.* ■ [trans.] cause (a seed or spore) to sprout in such a way. ■ fig. come into existence and develop. — **ger·mi·na·tion** /ˌjərməˈnāsHən/ **n. ger·mi·na·tive** /-ˌnātiv/ **adj. ger·mi·na·tor** /-ˌnātər/ **n.** [16th C.: from L. *germinat-* 'sprouted forth, budded,' from the v. *germinare*, from *germen, germin-* 'sprout, seed.']

Ger·mis·ton /ˈjərməstən/ a city in South Africa, southeast of Johannesburg; pop. 134,000. It is the site of a large gold refinery.

germ plasm ▶ **n.** Biol. germ cells, collectively. ■ the genetic material of such cells.

germ war·fare ▶ **n.** another term for BIOLOGICAL WARFARE.

Ge·ron·i·mo[1] /jəˈränəˌmō/ (*c.*1829–1909), Apache chief. He resisted white encroachment on tribal lands in Arizona by leading his people in raids on settlers and US troops before he surrendered in 1886.

Ge·ron·i·mo[2] ▶ **exclam.** used to express exhilaration, esp. when leaping from a great height or moving at a high speed. [World War II: GERONIMO[1].]

ger·on·toc·ra·cy /ˌjerənˈtäkrəsē/ ▶ **n.** a state, society, or group governed by old people. — **ge·ron·to·crat** /jəˈräntəˌkrat/ **n. ge·ron·to·crat·ic** /jəˌräntəˈkratik/ **adj.** [19th C.: from Gk. *gerōn, geront-* 'old man' + -CRACY.]

ger·on·tol·o·gy /ˌjerənˈtäləjē/ ▶ **n.** the scientific study of old age, the process of aging, and the particular problems of old people. — **ge·ron·to·log·i·cal** /jəˌräntlˈäjikəl/ **adj. ger·on·tol·o·gist n.**

PRONUNCIATION KEY ə *ago, up*; ər *over, fur*; a *hat*; ā *ate*; ä *car*; e *let*; ē *see*; i *fit*; ī *by*; NG *sing*; ō *go*; ô *law, for*; oi *toy*; o͝o *good*; o͞o *goo*; ou *out*; TH *thin*; T͟H *then*; ZH *vision*

Germany

Official name: Federal Republic of Germany
Location: central Europe, bordered on the north by the North and Baltic seas
Area: 134,900 square miles (349,200 sq km)
Population: 84,424,000
Capital: Berlin
Language: German
Currency: euro

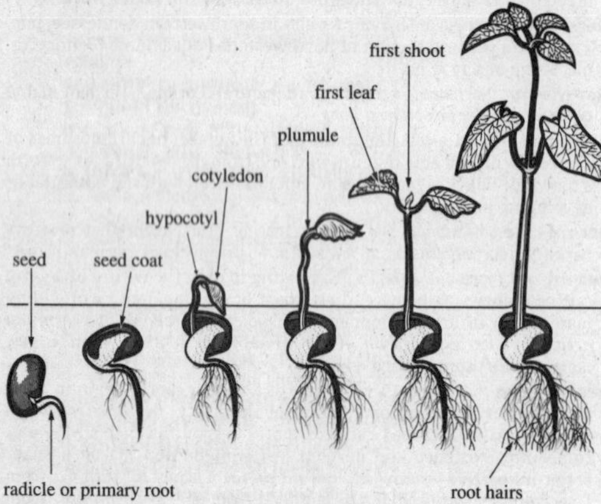

germination of a bean

-gerous ▶ **comb. form** bearing (a specified thing): *armigerous.* [from L. *-ger* 'bearing' (from the root of *gerere* 'to bear, carry') + **-ous**.]

Ger·ry /'jerē/, Elbridge (1744–1814), vice president of the US 1813–14. His political maneuvering in Massachusetts gave rise to the term "gerrymander."

ger·ry·man·der /'jerē,mandər/ ▶ **v.** [trans.] [often as n.] (**gerrymandering**) manipulate the boundaries of (an electoral constituency) so as to favor one party or class. ■ achieve (a result) by such manipulation: *a total freedom to gerrymander the results they want.* ▶ **n.** an instance of such a practice. — **ger·ry·man·der·er n.** [19th C.: from the name of Governor Elbridge *Gerry* of Massachusetts + **salamander**, from the supposed similarity between a salamander and the shape of a new voting district on a map drawn when he was in office, which was felt to favor his party.]

Gersh·win /'gər,sʜwin/, George (1898–1937), US composer; born *Jacob Gershovitz.* Often with his brother Ira (1896–1983) writing the lyrics, he composed numerous works, including *Rhapsody in Blue* (1924) for orchestra, and the opera *Porgy and Bess* (1935).

ger·und /'jerənd/ ▶ **n.** Gram. a form that is derived from a verb but that functions as a noun, in English ending in *-ing*, e.g., *asking* in *do you mind my asking you?.* [16th C.: from late L. *gerundium*, from *gerundum*, var. of *gerendum*, the gerund of L. *gerere* 'do.']

ger·un·dive /jə'rəndiv/ ▶ **n.** Gram. (in Latin) a form that is derived from a verb, but that functions as an adjective, denoting something "that should or must be done." [ME (in the sense 'gerund'): from late L. *gerundivus (modus)* 'gerundive (mood),' from *gerundium* (see **gerund**).]

Ge·sell·schaft /gə'zel,sʜäft; -,sʜaft/ ▶ **n.** social relations based on impersonal ties, as duty to a society or organization. Contrasted with **Gemeinschaft**. [Ger., from *Gesell(e)* 'companion' + *-schaft* (see **-ship**).]

ges·ne·ri·ad /ges'ni(ə)rē,ad; jes-/ ▶ **n.** a tropical plant of a family (Gesneriaceae) that includes African violets and gloxinias. [19th C.: from mod. L. *Gesneria*, after Conrad von *Gesner* (1516–65), Swiss naturalist.]

ges·so /'jesō/ ▶ **n.** (pl. **-soes**) a hard compound of plaster of Paris or whiting in glue, used in sculpture or as a base for gilding or painting on wood. — **ges·soed adj.** [16th C.: Ital., from L. *gypsum* (see **gypsum**).]

ge·stalt /gə'sʜtält; -'sʜtôlt/ (also **Ge·stalt**) ▶ **n.** (pl. **-stalt·en** /-'sʜtältn; -'sʜtôltn/ or **-stalts**) Psychol. an organized whole that is perceived as more than the sum of its parts. — **ge·stalt·ism** /-,tizəm/ **n.** **ge·stalt·ist** /-tist/ **n.** [1920s: from Ger. *Gestalt*, lit. 'form, shape.']

Ge·stalt ther·a·py ▶ **n.** a psychotherapeutic approach that focuses on insight into gestalts in patients and their relations to the world, and often uses role-playing to aid the resolution of past conflicts.

Ge·sta·po /gə'stäpō/ the German secret police under Nazi rule. It ruthlessly suppressed opposition to the Nazis in Germany and occupied Europe and sent Jews and others to concentration camps. [Ger., from *Geheime Staatspolizei* 'secret state police.']

ges·tate /'jestāt/ ▶ **v.** [trans.] carry (a fetus) in the womb from conception to birth: [intrans.] *rabbits gestate for approximately twenty-eight days.* ■ [intrans.] (of a fetus) undergo gestation. [19th C.: from L. *gestat-* 'carried in the womb,' from the v. *gestare*.]

ges·ta·tion /je'stāsʜən/ ▶ **n.** the process of carrying or being carried in the womb between conception and birth. ■ the duration of such a process. ■ fig. the development of something over a period of time. — **ges·ta·tion·al** /-sʜənl/ **adj.**

ges·tic·u·late /je'stikyə,lāt/ ▶ **v.** [intrans.] use gestures, esp. dramatic ones, instead of speaking or to emphasize one's words. — **ges·tic·u·la·tion** /je,stikyə'lāsʜən/ **n.** **ges·tic·u·la·tor** /-,lātər/ **n.** [17th C.: from L. *gesticulat-* 'gesticulated,' from the v. *gesticulari*, from *gesticulus*, dimin. of *gestus* 'action.']

ges·ture /'jescʜər/ ▶ **n.** a movement of part of the body, esp. a hand or the head, to express an idea or meaning: *so much is conveyed by gesture.* ■ an action performed to convey one's feelings or intentions: *Maggie was touched by the kind gesture.* ■ an action performed for show in the knowledge that it will have no effect: *I hope the amendment will not be just a gesture.* ▶ **v.** [intrans.] make a gesture: *she gestured meaningfully with the pistol.* ■ [trans.] express (something) with a gesture or gestures: *he gestured his dissent at this.* ■ [trans.] direct or invite (someone) to move somewhere specified: *he gestured her to a chair.* [ME: from med. L. *gestura*, from L. *gerere* 'bear, wield, perform.']

ge·sund·heit /gə'zo͝ontīt/ ▶ **exclam.** used to wish good health to a person who has just sneezed. [from Ger. *Gesundheit* 'health.']

get /get/ ▶ **v.** (**get·ting** ; past **got** /gät/; past part. **got** or **got·ten** /'gätn/) **1** [trans.] come to have or hold (something); receive: *I got the impression that she wasn't happy.* ■ experience, suffer, or be afflicted with (something bad): *I got a sudden pain in my eye.* ■ receive as a punishment or penalty: *he got five years for the robbery.* ■ contract (a disease or ailment): *I might be getting the flu.* ■ receive (a communication): *I got a letter.* **2** [trans.] succeed in attaining, achieving, or experiencing; obtain: *I need all I can get.* ■ move in order to pick up or bring (something); fetch: *get another chair.* ■ [trans.] tend to meet with or find in a specified place or situation: *the winters we get in Florida.* ■ travel by or catch (a bus, train, or other form of transport): *I'll get a taxi.* ■ obtain (a figure or answer) as a result of calculation. ■ respond to a ring of (a telephone or doorbell) or the knock on (a door): *I'll get it!* ■ [in imper.] informal said as an invitation to notice or look at someone, esp. to criticize or ridicule them: *get her!* **3** [intrans.] enter or reach a specified state or condition; become: *he got very worried.* ■ [as auxiliary v.] used with past participle to form the passive mood: *the cat got groomed.* ■ [trans.] cause to be treated in a specified way: *get the form signed.* ■ [trans.] induce or prevail upon (someone) to do something: *Sophie got Beth to make a fire.* ■ [intrans.] have the opportunity to do: *he got to try out a new car.* ■ [intrans.] begin to be or do something, esp. gradually or by chance: *we got talking.* **4** [intrans.] come, go, or make progress eventually or with some difficulty: *I got to the airport.* ■ [intrans.] move or come into a specified position, situation, or state: *she got into the car.* ■ [trans.] succeed in making (someone or something) come, go, or make progress: *my honesty often gets me into trouble.* ■ [intrans.] informal reach a specified point or stage: *it's getting so I can't even think.* ■ [usu. in imper.] informal go away. **5** (**have got**) see **have**. **6** [trans.] catch or apprehend (someone). ■ strike or wound (someone) with a blow or missile: *you got me in the eye!* ■ informal punish, injure, or kill (someone), esp. as retribution. ■ (**get it**) informal be punished, injured, or killed: *when Dad comes home you'll get it!* ■ informal annoy or amuse (someone) greatly: *cleaning the same things all the time, that's what gets me.* ■ informal baffle (someone): *"What's a 'flowery boundary tree'?" "You got me."* **7** [trans.] informal understand (an argument or the person making it): *I don't get it.*

– PHRASES **be out to get someone** be determined to punish or harm someone, esp. in retaliation.

– PHRASAL VERBS **get something across** manage to communicate an idea clearly. **get ahead** become successful in one's life or career: *how to get ahead in advertising.* **get along 1** have a harmonious or friendly relationship: *they seem to get along pretty well.* **2** manage to live or survive: *don't worry, we'll get along without you.* **get around** deal successfully with (a problem). ■ evade (a regulation or restriction) without contravening it: *the company changed its name to get around the law.* **get around to** deal with (a task) in due course. **get at 1** reach or gain access to (something). ■ bribe or unfairly influence (someone): *he had been got at by government officials.* **2** informal imply (something): *I see what you're getting at.* **get away** escape. ■ leave one's home or work for a time of rest or recreation; go on a vacation. **get away with** escape blame, punishment, or undesirable consequences for (an act that is wrong or mistaken). **get back at** take revenge on (someone); retaliate against. **get back to** contact (someone) later to give a reply or return a message. **get by** manage with difficulty to live or accomplish something: *just enough to get by.* **get something down 1** write something down. **2** swallow food or drink, esp. with difficulty. **get down to** begin to do or give serious attention to: *get down to business.* **get in** (of a train, aircraft, or other transport) arrive at its destination. ■ (of a person) arrive at one's destination. **get in on** become involved in (a profitable or exciting activity). **get into** (of a feeling) affect, influence, or take control of (someone). **get in with** become friendly with (someone), esp. in order to gain an advantage. **get off** informal escape a punishment; be acquitted. *she got off lightly.* **get off on** informal be excited or aroused by (something). **get on 1** perform or make progress in a specified way: *how are you getting on?* ■ continue doing something, esp. after an interruption: *I've got to get on with this job.* **2** (**be getting on**) informal be old or comparatively old: *we are both getting on a bit.* **get out 1** (of something previously secret) become known. **2** (also **get out of here**) informal [in imper.] used to express disbelief: *get out, you're a liar.* ■ [usu. in imper.] informal go away; leave. **get out of** contrive to avoid or escape (a duty or responsibility). **get something out of** achieve benefit from (an undertaking or exercise). **get over 1** recover from (an ailment or an upsetting or startling experience). **2** overcome (a difficulty). **get something over 1** manage to communicate an idea or theory: *the company is keen to get the idea over.* **2** complete an unpleasant or tedious but necessary task promptly: *Come on, let's get it over with.* **get through 1** (also **get someone through**) pass or assist someone in passing (a difficult or testing experience or period): *I need these lessons to get me through my exam.* ■ (also **get something through**) (with reference to a piece of legislation) make or become law. **2** make contact by telephone: *after an hour of busy signals, I finally got through.* ■ succeed in communicating with someone in a meaningful way: *I don't think anyone can get through to these kids.* **get to 1** informal annoy or upset (someone) by persistent action: *he started crying—we were getting to him.* **2** another way of saying GET AROUND TO above. **get up** (also **get someone up**) rise or cause to rise from bed after sleeping. [ME: from ON *geta* 'obtain, beget, guess'; rel. to OE *forgietan* 'forget,') L. *praeda* 'booty, prey.']

ge·ta /'getə; 'getä/ ▶ **adj.** (pl. same or **ge·tas**) a Japanese wooden shoe with a thong to pass between the first (big) toe and the second toe.

geta

get·a·way /'getə,wā/ ▶ **n.** **1** an escape or quick departure, esp. after committing a crime. ■ a fast start by a racecar. **2** informal a vacation. ■ the destination or accommodations for a vacation: *a popular getaway.*

get-go (also **git-go**) ▶ **n.** the very beginning: *he knew from the get-go that he could count on me.*

Geth·sem·a·ne, Gar·den of /geᴛʜ'semənē/ a garden between Jerusalem and the Mount of Olives, where Jesus was betrayed (Matt. 26:36–46).

get·ter /'getər/ ▶ **n.** [usu. in comb.] a person or thing that gets a specified desirable thing: *an attention-getter.*

get-to·geth·er ▶ **n.** an informal gathering. ■ a sociable meeting or conference.

get-tough ▶ **adj.** informal designating an approach or attitude characterized by assertiveness, firmness, or aggressiveness: *implementing get-tough changes.*

Get·ty /'getē/, J. Paul (1892–1976), US industrialist; full name *Jean Paul Getty.* He made a fortune in the oil industry and was also a noted art collector.

Get·tys·burg /'getēz,bərg; -iz-/ a historic borough in south central Pennsylvania, scene of a critical Civil War battle in July 1863; pop. 7,025.

Get·tys·burg Ad·dress a speech delivered on November 18, 1863, by President Abraham Lincoln at the dedication of the national cemetery on the site of the Battle of Gettysburg.

get·up /'getəp/ (also **get-up**) ▶ **n.** informal a style or arrangement of dress, esp. an elaborate or unusual one: *she looks ridiculous in that getup.*

Getz /gets/, Stan (1927–91), US saxophonist; born *Stanley Gayetsky.* A leader of the "cool" school of jazz, his recordings include "Early Autumn" (1948).

ge·um /'jēəm/ ▶ **n.** a plant of the rose family belonging to the genus *Geum,* which comprises the avens. [mod. L., var. of L. *gaeum.*]

GeV ▶ **abbr.** gigaelectronvolt, equivalent to 109 electron-volts.

gew·gaw /'g(y)o͞o,gô/ ▶ **n.** (usu. **gewgaws**) a showy thing, esp. one that is useless or worthless. [ME: of unknown origin.]

gey·ser /'gīzər/ ▶ **n.** a hot spring in which water intermittently boils, sending a tall column of water and steam into the air. ■ a jet or stream of liquid. [18th C.: from Icelandic *Geysir,* spring in Iceland; rel. to *geysa* 'to gush.']

gey·ser·ite /'gīzə,rīt/ ▶ **n.** a hard opaline siliceous deposit occurring around geysers and hot springs. [19th C.: from GEYSER + -ITE[1].]

Gha·ga·ra Ri·ver /gə'gärə; 'gägərə/ (also **Gogra**; Nepalese **Karnali**) a river in south central Asia that flows for 570 miles (900 km) to join the Ganges River.

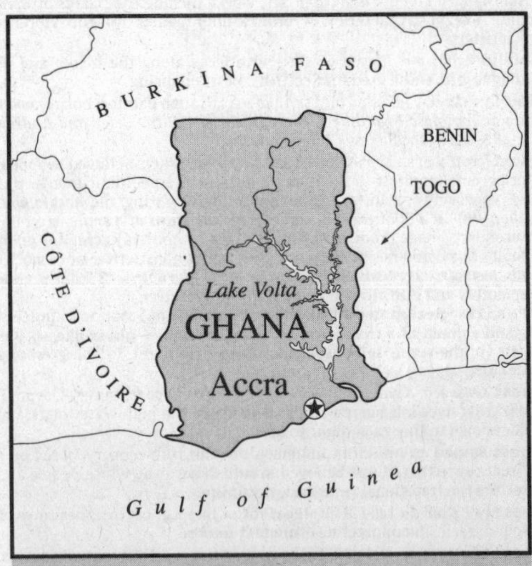

Ghana

Official name: Republic of Ghana
Location: West Africa, on the Gulf of Guinea, east of Côte d'Ivoire and west of Togo
Area: 88,800 square miles (230,000 sq km)
Population: 20,750,000
Capital: Accra
Languages: English (official), West African languages
Currency: cedi

Gha·na /'gänə/ a country in West Africa. Former name (until 1957) **Gold Coast.** *See box.* — **Gha·na·ian** /gə'nāən; gə'nīən/ **adj. & n.**

gha·ri·al /'gərēəl/ (also **ga·vi·al** /'gāvēəl/) ▶ **n.** a large fish-eating crocodile (*Gavialis gangeticus,* family Gavialidae) with a long narrow snout that widens at the nostrils, native to the Indian subcontinent. See also FALSE GHARIAL. [19th C.: from Hindi *ghaṛiyāl*; see also GAVIAL.]

ghast·ly /'gastlē/ ▶ **adj.** (**-li·er, -li·est**) **1** causing great horror or fear; frightful or macabre. ■ informal objectionable; unpleasant: *ghastly old-fashioned dresses.* **2** extremely unwell: *he felt ghastly in the morning.* ■ deathly white or pallid. — **ghast·li·ness** **n.** [ME: from obs. *gast* 'terrify,' from OE *gǣstan,* of Gmc. origin; rel. to GHOST.]

ghat /gôt; gät/ (also **ghaut**) ▶ **n.** **1** (in the Indian subcontinent) a flight of steps leading down to a river. **2** (in the Indian subcontinent) a mountain pass. [from Hindi *ghāṭ.*]

Ghats /gôts/ two mountain ranges in central and southern India. Known as **the Eastern Ghats** and **the Western Ghats,** they run parallel to the coast on either side of the Deccan plateau.

gha·zi /'gäzē/ (also, esp. as an honorific title, **Gha·zi**) ▶ **n.** (pl. **gha·zis**) a Muslim fighter against non-Muslims. [from Arab. *al-ġāzī,* part. of *ġazā* 'invade, raid.']

Gha·zi·a·bad /'gäzēə,bäd/ a city in northern India, east of Delhi; pop. 461,000.

GHB ▶ **abbr.** (sodium) gamma-hydroxybutyrate, $CH_2OH(CH_2)_2COONa$, a designer drug with anesthetic properties.

ghee /gē/ ▶ **n.** clarified butter made from the milk of a buffalo or cow, used in Indian cooking. [from Hindi *ghī,* from Sanskrit *ghṛtá* 'sprinkled.']

Ghent /gent/ a city in Belgium, on the Scheldt River; pop. 230,200. Flemish name GENT, French name GAND.

gher·kin /'gərkin/ ▶ **n.** **1** a small variety of cucumber, or a young green cucumber used for pickling. ■ a pickle made from such a cucumber. **2** a trailing plant (*Cucumis anguria*) of the gourd family with cucumber-like fruits used for pickling. ■ the fresh or pickled fruit of this plant. [17th C.: from Du. *augurkje, gurkje,* dimin. of *augurk, gurk,* from Slavic, based on med. Gk. *angourion* 'cucumber.']

ghet·to /'getō/ ▶ **n.** (pl. **-tos** or **-toes**) a part of a city, esp. a slum area, occupied by a minority group or groups. ■ hist. the Jewish quarter in a city: *the Warsaw Ghetto.* ■ an isolated or segregated group or area: *the relative security of the gay ghetto.* [17th C.: perh. from Ital. *getto* 'foundry' (because the first ghetto was established in 1516 on the site of a foundry in Venice).]

Ghi·ber·ti /gē'bertē/, Lorenzo (1378–1455), Italian sculptor and goldsmith; born *Lorenzo di Bartolo.* His works include the "Gates of Paradise" (1425–52), a series of bronze door panels for the Florence Baptistery.

ghil·lie /'gilē/ ▶ **n.** a type of shoe with laces along the instep and no tongue, esp. those used for Scottish country dancing.

Ghir·lan·da·io /,gi(ə)rlən'dīō/ (*c.*1448–94), Italian painter; born *Domenico di Tommaso Bigordi.* He painted *Christ Calling Peter and Andrew* (1482–84) in the Sistine Chapel in Rome.

ghost /gōst/ ▶ **n.** an apparition of a dead person that is believed to appear or become manifest to the living, typically as a nebulous image. ■ [as adj.] appearing or manifesting but not actually existing: *the most famous ghost ship.* ■ a faint trace of something: *the **ghost of** a smile.* ■ a faint secondary image produced by a fault in a cathode-ray screen, e.g., by faulty television reception. ▶ **v. 1** [trans.] act as ghostwriter of (a work): *his memoirs were smoothly ghosted by a journalist.* **2** [intrans.] glide smoothly and effortlessly: *they ghosted up the river.*
– PHRASES **give up the ghost** die. ■ (of a machine) stop working. **not stand a ghost of a chance** have no chance at all. — **ghost·like adj.** [OE *gāst* (in the sense 'spirit, soul'), of Gmc. origin; rel. to Du. *geest* and Ger. *Geist.*]

ghost crab ▶ **n.** a pale yellowish crab (genus *Ocypode,* family Ocypodidae) that lives in a burrow in the sand above the high-water mark and goes down to the sea at night to feed.

Ghost Dance an American Indian cult of the 19th century, based on a ritual dance that, it was believed, would drive away white people and restore the traditional lands and way of life.

ghost·ly /'gōstlē/ ▶ **adj.** (**-li·er, -li·est**) of or like a ghost in appearance or sound; eerie and unnatural. — **ghost·li·ness n.**

ghost sto·ry ▶ **n.** a story involving ghosts or ghostly circumstances, intended to be suspenseful and scary.

ghost town ▶ **n.** a deserted town with few or no remaining inhabitants.

ghost·writ·er /'gōst,rītər/ ▶ **n.** a person whose job it is to write material for someone else who is the named author. — **ghost·write v.**

ghoul /go͞ol/ ▶ **n.** an evil spirit or phantom, esp. one supposed to rob graves and feed on dead bodies. ■ a person morbidly interested in death or disaster. — **ghoul·ish adj. ghoul·ish·ly adv. ghoul·ish·ness n.** [18th C.: from Arab. *ġūl,* a desert demon believed to rob graves and devour corpses.]

GHQ ▶ **abbr.** general headquarters.

Ghul·ghu·leh /go͞ol'go͞ole/ an ancient city in central Afghanistan; destroyed by Genghis Khan *c.*1221.

Ghz (or **GHz**) ▶ **abbr.** gigahertz.

GI[1] ▶ **n.** (pl. **GIs**) a private soldier in the US Army. [US Military: orig. (1930s) an abbrev. of *galvanized iron;* now of *government issue.*]

GI[2] ▶ **abbr.** glycemic index.

gi /gē/ ▶ **n.** (pl. **gis**) a lightweight two-piece white garment worn in judo and other martial arts, typically consisting of loose-fitting pants and a jacket that is closed with a cloth belt. [Japanese.]

Gia·co·met·ti /,jäkə'metē/, Alberto (1901–66), Swiss sculptor and painter. His typical works are of extremely elongated human forms, such as *Pointing Man* (1947).

gi·ant /'jīənt/ ▶ **n. 1** an imaginary or mythical being of human form but superhuman size. ■ (in Greek mythology) any of the beings of this kind who rebelled unsuccessfully against the gods of Olympus. ■ an abnormally tall or large person, animal, or plant. ■ a very large company or organization. ■ a person of exceptional talent or qualities: *musical giant.* **2** Astron. a star of relatively great size and luminosity compared to ordinary stars of the main sequence, and 10–100 times the diameter of the sun. ▶ **adj.** [attrib.] of very great size or force; gigantic: *giant multinational corporations.* ■ used in names of very large animals and plants. [ME *geant,* from OFr., via L. from Gk. *gigas, gigant-.*]

gi

gi·ant ant·eat·er ▶ **n.** a large anteater (*Myrmecophaga tridactyla*) of Central and South America, with long coarse fur and large claws.

gi·ant clam ▶ **n.** a very large bivalve mollusk (family Tridacnidae) that occurs in the tropical Indo-Pacific, including *Tridacna gigas,* the largest living shelled mollusk.

gi·ant deer ▶ **n.** another term for IRISH ELK.

gi·ant or·der ▶ **n.** Archit. an order whose columns extend through more than one story.

gi·ant pan·da ▶ **n.** see PANDA.

gi·ant pet·rel ▶ **n.** the largest petrel (genus *Macronectes,* family Procellariidae), which is found around southern oceans, has a massive bill, and scavenges from carcasses.

gi·ant se·quoi·a ▶ **n.** another term for giant redwood (see REDWOOD).

gi·ant squid ▶ **n.** a deep-sea squid (genus *Architeuthis,* order Teuthoidea) that is the largest known invertebrate, reaching a length of 59 feet (18 m) or more.

gi·ant tor·toise ▶ **n.** a very large tortoise (genus *Geochelone,* family Testudinidae) with a long lifespan, occurring on several tropical oceanic islands.

gi·ar·di·a·sis /,jēär'dīəsis; jär'dī-/ ▶ **n.** infection of the intestine with a flagellate protozoan (*Giardia lamblia,* phylum Metamonada), which causes diarrhea and other symptoms. [20th C.: from mod. L. *Giardia* (from the name of Alfred M. *Giard* (1846–1908), French biologist) + -ASIS.]

gib /gib/ ▶ **n.** a wood or metal bolt, wedge, or pin for holding part of a machine or structure in place, usually adjusted by a screw or key: [as adj.] *gib screws.* ▶ **v.** [trans.] fasten (parts) together with a gib. [18th C.: of unknown origin.]

gib·ber /'jibər/ ▶ **v.** [intrans.] speak rapidly and unintelligibly, typically through fear or shock: [as adj.] (**gibbering**) *a gibbering idiot.* [17th C.: imitative.]

gib·ber·el·lin /,jibə'relin/ ▶ **n.** any of a group of plant hormones that stimulate stem elongation, germination, and flowering. [1930s: from mod. L. *Gibberella,* dimin. of *Gibbera,* from L. *gibber* 'hump,' + -IN[1].]

gib·ber·ish /'jibərish/ ▶ **n.** unintelligible or meaningless speech or writing; nonsense. [16th C.: perh. from GIBBER + the suffix -ISH[1].]

gib·bet /'jibit/ hist. ▶ **n.** a gallows. ■ an upright post with an arm on which the bodies of executed criminals were left hanging as a warning or deterrent to others. [ME: from OFr. *gibet* 'staff, cudgel, gallows,' dimin. of *gibe* 'club, staff,' prob. of Gmc. origin.]

Gib·bon /'gibən/, Edward (1737–94), English historian. He wrote *The History of the Decline and Fall of the Roman Empire* (1776–88).

gib·bon /'gibən/ ▶ **n.** a small, slender tree-dwelling ape (genus *Hylobates,* family Hylobatidae) with long powerful arms and loud hooting calls, native to the forests of Southeast Asia. [18th C.: from Fr., from an Ind. dial. word.]

gib·bous /'gibəs/ ▶ **adj.** (of the moon) having the observable illuminated part greater than a semicircle and less than a circle. — **gib·bos·i·ty** /gi'bäsitē/ **n. gib·bous·ly adv. gib·bous·ness n.** [ME: from late L. *gibbosus,* from L. *gibbus* 'hump.']

Gibbs /gibz/, Josiah Willard (1839–1903), US physical chemist. He pioneered in chemical thermodynamics and statistical mechanics.

Gibbs free en·er·gy ▶ **n.** Chem. a thermodynamic quantity equal to the enthalpy (of a system or process) minus the product of the entropy and the absolute temperature. (Symbol: **G**) [named after J. W. *Gibbs* (see GIBBS).]

gibe /jīb/ (also **jibe**) ▶ **n.** an insulting or mocking remark; a taunt: *a gibe at his old rivals.* ▶ **v.** [intrans.] make insulting or mocking remarks; jeer: *some cynics in the media might gibe.* [16th C. (as a v.): perh. from OFr. *giber* 'handle roughly.']

gib·lets /'jiblits/ ▶ **plural n.** the liver, heart, gizzard, and neck of a chicken or other fowl, usually removed before the bird is cooked, and often used to make gravy, stuffing, or soup. [ME from OFr. *gibelet* 'game bird stew,' prob. from *gibier* 'birds or mammals hunted for sport.']

Gi·bral·tar /jə'brôltər/ a British dependency near the southern tip of the Iberian peninsula, at the eastern end of the Strait of Gibraltar; pop. 28,000. Occupying a site of great strategic importance, Gibraltar consists of a fortified town and a military base at the foot of a rocky headland called the **Rock of Gibraltar.** — **Gi·bral·tar·i·an** /jə,brôl'te(ə)rēən; ,jibrôl-/ **adj. & n.**

Gi·bral·tar, Strait of a channel between the southern tip of the Iberian peninsula and North Africa that forms the only outlet of the Mediterranean Sea to the Atlantic Ocean.

Gib·ran /ji'brän/ (also **Jub·ran**), Khalil (1883–1931), US writer; born in Lebanon. His writings in both Arabic and English are deeply romantic.

Gib·son[1] /'gibsən/, Althea (1927–2003), US tennis player. The first black player in the US Nationals and at Wimbledon, she won 11 Grand Slam titles in the late 1950s.

Gib·son[2] ▶ **n.** a dry martini cocktail garnished with a pickled onion.

Gib·son Des·ert /'gibsən/ a desert region in western Australia, southeast of the Great Sandy Desert.

Gib·son Girl ▶ **n.** a girl typifying the fashionable ideal of the late 19th and early 20th centuries, characterized as tall and slender, yet curvaceous. [represented in the work of US illustrator Charles D. *Gibson* (1867–1944).]

gid·dy /'gidē/ ▶ **adj.** (**-di·er, -di·est**) having a sensation of whirling and a tendency to fall or stagger; dizzy. ■ excitable and frivolous. ▶ **v.** (**-dies, -died**) [trans.] make (someone) feel excited to the point of disorientation. — **gid·di·ly adv. gid·di·ness n.** [OE *gidig* 'insane,' lit. 'possessed by a god,' from the base of GOD.]

gid·dy-up /,gidē 'əp/ (also **gid·dap**) ▶ **exclam.** used to get a horse to start moving or go faster. [1920s (: from *get up.*]

Gide /zhēd/, André Paul Guillaume (1869–1951), French writer. Known as the father of modern French literature, his works include *The Immoralist* (1902) and *The Counterfeiters* (1927). Nobel Prize for Literature (1947).

Gid·e·on /'gidēən/ **1** (in the Bible) an Israelite leader. **2** a member of Gideons International.

Gid·e·ons In·ter·na·tion·al a Christian organization of business people, founded in 1899 in the US with the aim of placing bibles in hotel rooms and hospital wards.

gie /gē/ ▶v. (**gies, gie·ing**; past **gied**; past part. **gied** or **gien** /gēn/) Scottish form of GIVE.

GIF /jif/ ▶n. Comput. a popular format for image files, with built-in data compression. ■ (also **gif**) a file in this format. [20th C.: acronym from *graphic interchange format.*]

gift /gift/ ▶n. **1** a thing given willingly to someone without payment; a present: [as adj.] *a gift shop.* ■ an act of giving something as a present: *his mother's gift of a pen.* **2** a natural ability or talent: *a gift for comedy.* ▶v. [trans.] give (something) as a gift, esp. formally or as a donation or bequest: *the company gifted 2,999 shares to a charity.* ■ present (someone) with a gift or gifts: *the director gifted her with a brooch.* ■ (**gift someone with**) endow with (something): *she was gifted with clairvoyance.*
– PHRASES **look a gift horse in the mouth** find fault with something that has been received as a gift or favor. [ME: from ON *gipt*; rel. to GIVE.]

gift cer·tif·i·cate ▶n. a voucher given as a present that is exchangeable for a specified cash value of goods or services from a particular place of business.

gift·ed /ˈgiftid/ ▶adj. having exceptional talent or natural ability: *a gifted musician.* ■ having exceptional intelligence: *gifted students.*

gift of gab ▶n. the ability to speak with eloquence and fluency.

gift wrap ▶n. decorative paper for wrapping presents. ▶v. (also **gift-wrap**) [trans.] [usu. as adj.] (**gift-wrapped**) wrap (a present) in decorative paper.

Gi·fu /ˈgēfo͞o/ a city in central Japan; pop. 410,000.

gig[1] /gig/ ▶n. **1** esp. hist. a light two-wheeled carriage pulled by one horse. **2** a light, fast, narrow boat adapted for rowing or sailing. ▶v. [intrans.] travel in a gig. [18th C.: appar. a transferred sense of obs. *gig* 'a flighty girl,' which was also applied to various objects or devices that whirled.]

gig[2] informal ▶n. a live performance by or engagement for a musician or group playing popular music. ■ a job, esp. one that is temporary or that has an uncertain future: *his first gig as a coach.* ▶v. (**gigged, gig·ging**) [intrans.] perform a gig or gigs.

gig[3] ▶n. a harpoonlike device used for catching fish or frogs. ▶v. (**gigged, gig·ging**) [intrans.] catch fish or frogs using such a device. [18th C.: shortening of *fizgig*, prob. from Sp. *fisga* 'harpoon.']

gig[4] ▶n. Comput., informal short for GIGABYTE.

giga- ▶comb. form used in units of measurement: **1** denoting a factor of 10^9: *gigahertz.* **2** Comput. denoting a factor of 2^{30}. [from Gk. *gigas* 'giant.']

gig·a·bit /ˈgigəˌbit; ˈjig-/ ▶n. Comput. a unit of information equal to one billion (10^9) or, strictly, 2^{30} bits.

gig·a·byte /ˈgigəˌbīt; ˈjig-/ (abbr.: **GB**) ▶n. Comput. a unit of information equal to one billion (10^9) or, strictly, 2^{30} bytes.

gig·a·flop /ˈgigəˌfläp/ ▶n. Comput. a unit of computing speed equal to one billion floating-point operations per second. [1970s: back-form. from *gigaflops* (see GIGA-, -FLOP).]

gi·gan·tesque /ˌjīgənˈtesk/ ▶adj. like or appropriate to a giant: *a gigantesque feat.* [19th C.: from Fr., from Ital. *gigantesco*, from Gk. *gigas, gigant-* (see GIANT).]

gi·gan·tic /jīˈgantik/ ▶adj. of very great size or extent; huge or enormous. [17th C. (in the sense 'like or suited to a giant'): from L. *gigas, gigant-* (see GIANT) + -IC.]

gi·gan·tism /jīˈgantizəm/ ▶n. esp. Biol. unusual or abnormal largeness. ■ Med. excessive growth due to hormonal imbalance.

Gi·gan·to·pi·the·cus /jīˌgantəˈpiTHikəs/ ▶n. a very large fossil Asian ape (genus *Gigantopithecus*, family Pongidae) of the late Miocene to early Pleistocene epochs. [mod. L., from Gk. *gigas, gigant-* (see GIANT) + *pithēkos* 'ape.']

gig·a·ton /ˈgigəˌtən; ˈjig-/ ▶n. a unit of explosive force equal to one billion (10^9) tons of trinitrotoluene (TNT).

gig·a·watt /ˈgigəˌwät; ˈjig-/ ▶n. (abbr. **GW**) a unit of electric power equal to one billion (10^9) watts.

gig·gle /ˈgigəl/ ▶v. [intrans.] laugh lightly in a nervous, affected, or silly manner: [as adj.] (**giggling**) *three giggling girls.* ▶n. a laugh of such a kind. ■ (**the giggles**) continuous uncontrollable giggling. — **gig·gler** /ˈgig(ə)lər/ n. **gig·gly** /ˈgig(ə)lē/ adj. [16th C.: imitative.]

GIGO /ˈgiˌgō/ esp. Comput. ▶abbr. garbage in, garbage out. See GARBAGE.

gig·o·lo /ˈjigəˌlō/ ▶n. (pl. **-los**) often derog. a young man paid or financially supported by an older woman to be her escort or lover. ■ a professional male dancing partner or escort. [1920s: from Fr., masc. of *gigole* 'dance hall woman,' from colloq. *gigue* 'leg.']

gigue /ZHēg/ ▶n. Music a lively piece of music in the style of a dance, typically of the Renaissance or baroque period, and usually in compound time. [17th C.: Fr., lit. 'jig.']

Gi·jón /KHēˈKHōn/ a city in northern Spain; pop. 260,000.

Gi·la mon·ster /ˈhēlə/ ▶n. a venomous lizard (*Heloderma suspectum*, family Helodermatidae) native to the southwestern US and Mexico. [19th C.: named after *Gila*, a river in New Mexico and Arizona.]

Gi·la River a river that flows for 645 miles (1,045 km) from New Mexico to the Colorado River.

Gil·bert[1] /ˈgilbərt/, Cass (1859–1934), US architect. His designs include the US Supreme Court Building 1932–35, completed by his son.

Gil·bert[2], Sir Humphrey (c.1539–83), English explorer. He claimed Newfoundland for England in 1583.

Gila monster

Gil·bert[3], William (1544–1603), English physician and physicist. He coined the term *magnetic pole.*

Gil·bert[4], Sir W. S. (1836–1911), English playwright; full name *William Schwenck Gilbert.* He is best known as a librettist who collaborated on light operas with composer Sir Arthur Sullivan.

Gil·bert and El·lice Is·lands /ˈelis/ a former British colony 1915–75 in the central Pacific Ocean that consisted of the Gilbert Islands, now a part of Kiribati, and the Ellice Islands, now Tuvalu.

Gil·bert Is·lands a group of islands in the central Pacific Ocean that forms part of Kiribati.

gild[1] /gild/ ▶v. [trans.] cover thinly with gold. ■ give a specious or false brilliance to: *the useless martyrs' deaths of the pilots gilded the operation.*
– PHRASES **gild the lily** try to improve what is already beautiful or excellent. — **gild·er** n. [OE *gyldan*, of Gmc. origin; rel. to GOLD.]

gild[2] ▶n. archaic spelling of GUILD.

gild·ed /ˈgildid/ ▶adj. covered thinly with gold leaf or gold paint.

gild·ing /ˈgildiNG/ ▶n. the process of applying gold leaf or gold paint. ■ the material used in, or the surface produced by, this process.

Gil·ga·mesh /ˈgilgəˌmeSH/ a legendary king of the Sumerian city-state of Uruk who supposedly ruled during the first half of the 3rd millennium BC. He is the hero of the Babylonian epic of Gilgamesh, one of the best-known works of ancient literature.

gill[1] /gil/ ▶n. (often **gills**) **1** the paired respiratory organ of fishes and some amphibians, by which oxygen is extracted from water flowing over surfaces within or attached to the walls of the pharynx. ■ an organ of similar function in an invertebrate animal. **2** the vertical plates arranged radially on the underside of mushrooms and many toadstools. **3** (**gills**) the flesh below a person's jaws and ears: *we stuffed ourselves to the gills.*
– PHRASES **green around** (or **at**) **the gills** (of a person) sickly-looking. — **gilled** adj. [ME: from ON.]

gill[2] /jil/ ▶n. a unit of liquid measure, equal to a quarter of a pint. [ME: from OFr. *gille*, from late L. *gillo* 'water pot.']

gill cov·er ▶n. a flap of skin protecting a fish's gills, typically stiffened by bony plates. Also called OPERCULUM.

Gil·les·pie /gəˈlespē/, Dizzy (1917–93), US trumpeter; born *John Birks Gillespie.* He was a leading exponent of bebop style.

gil·lie /ˈgilē/ (also **ghil·lie**) ▶n. **1** (in Scotland) a man or boy who attends someone hunting or fishing. **2** ghillie. [16th C.: from Scot. Gael. *gille* 'lad, servant.']

gill net ▶n. a fishing net that is hung vertically so that fish get trapped in it by their gills. — **gill-net·ter** n.

gil·ly·flow·er /ˈjilēˌflouər/ (also **gil·li·flow·er**) ▶n. any of a number of fragrant flowers, such as the wallflower, clove pink, or white stock. [ME *gilofre* (in the sense 'clove'), from OFr. *gilofre, girofle*, via med. L. from Gk. *karuophullon* (from *karuon* 'nut' + *phullon* 'leaf').]

gilt /gilt/ ▶adj. covered thinly with gold leaf or gold paint. ■ gold-colored. ▶n. gold leaf or gold paint applied in a thin layer to a surface. [ME: archaic past part. of GILD[1].]

gilt-edged ▶adj. (esp. of paper or a book) having a gilded edge or edges. ■ relating to or denoting stocks or securities that are regarded as extremely reliable investments. ■ of very high quality.

gim·bal /ˈgimbəl; ˈjim-/ ▶n. (often **gimbals**) a mechanism, typically consisting of rings pivoted at right angles, for keeping an instrument such as a compass horizontal in a moving vessel. — **gim·baled** (or **gim·balled**) adj. [16th C.: variant of *gimmal*, var. of *gemel* 'twin, hinge,' from OFr. *gemel* 'twin,' from L. *gemellus*, dimin. of *geminus*.]

gim·crack /ˈjimˌkrak/ ▶adj. flimsy or poorly made but deceptively attractive: *plastic gim-crack cookware.* ▶n. a cheap and showy ornament; a knickknack. — **gim·crack·er·y** /-ˌkrakərē/ n. [ME *gibecrake*, of unknown origin.]

gim·let /ˈgimlit/ ▶n. **1** a small T-shaped tool with a screw-tip for boring holes. **2** a cocktail of gin (or sometimes vodka) and lime juice. [ME: from OFr. *guimbelet*, dimin. of *guimble* 'drill,' ult. of Gmc. origin.]

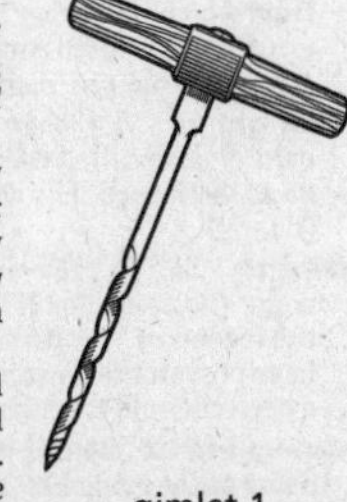

gimlet 1

gim·me /'gimē/ informal ▶ contr. give me (not acceptable in standard use): *just gimme the damn thing.*

gim·me cap (also **gim·me hat**) ▶ n. informal a cap that bears a company name and is given away for publicity.

gim·mick /'gimik/ ▶ n. a trick or device intended to attract attention, publicity, or business. ▶ v. [trans.] provide with a gimmick; alter or tamper with: *restaurants gimmicked up like barns.* — **gim·mick·y** adj. [1920s: possibly an anagram of *magic.*]

gim·mick·ry /'gimikrē/ ▶ n. gimmicks collectively; the use of gimmicks.

gimp[1] /gimp/ ▶ n. twisted silk or cotton with cord or wire running through it, used chiefly in upholstery. ■ (in lacemaking) coarser thread that forms the outline of the design in some techniques. [17th C.: from Du., of unknown ultimate origin.]

gimp[2] informal, often offens. ▶ n. a physically handicapped or lame person. ■ a limp. ■ a feeble or contemptible person. ▶ v. [no obj., with adverbial of direction] limp; hobble: *she gimped around.* — **gimp·y** adj. [1920s (orig. US): of unknown origin.]

gin[1] /jin/ ▶ n. **1** a clear alcoholic spirit distilled from grain or malt and flavored with juniper berries. **2** (also **gin rummy**) a two-handed form of the card game rummy. [18th C.: from Du., from OFr. *genevre*, alt. of L. *juniperus.*]

gin[2] ▶ n. a machine for separating cotton from its seeds. ▶ v. (**ginned, gin·ning**) [trans.] treat (cotton) in a gin. — **gin·ner** n. [ME (in the sense 'a tool or device, a trick'): from OFr. *engin* (see ENGINE).]

gin·ger /'jinjər/ ▶ n. **1** a hot fragrant spice made from the rhizome of a plant. It is chopped or powdered for cooking, preserved in syrup, or candied. ■ spirit; mettle. **2** the Southeast Asian plant (*Zingiber officinale*, family Zingiberaceae) from which this rhizome is taken. **3** a light reddish-yellow color. ▶ adj. (chiefly of hair or fur) of a light reddish-yellow color. ▶ v. [trans.] **1** flavor with ginger. **2** stimulate; enliven: *she slapped his hand lightly to ginger him up.* — **gin·ger·y** adj. [OE *gingifer*, based on Gk. *zingiberis*, from Pali *siṅgivera*, of Dravidian origin.]

gin·ger ale ▶ n. a clear, effervescent nonalcoholic drink flavored with ginger extract.

gin·ger beer ▶ n. a cloudy, effervescent mildly alcoholic drink, made by fermenting a mixture of ginger and syrup. ■ a nonalcoholic commercial variety of this.

gin·ger·bread /'jinjər,bred/ ▶ n. cake made with molasses and flavored with ginger. ■ fancy decoration, esp. on a building: [as adj.] *a high-gabled gingerbread house.* [ME ('preserved ginger'), from OFr. *gingembrat*, from med. L. *gingibratum*, from *gingiber* (see GINGER).]

gin·ger jar ▶ n. a small ceramic jar with a high rim over which a lid fits.

gin·ger·ly /'jinjərlē/ ▶ adv. in a careful or cautious manner: *Jackson sat down gingerly.* ▶ adj. showing great care or caution: *a gingerly pace.* — **gin·ger·li·ness** n. [16th C.: perh. from OFr. *gensor* 'delicate,' compar. of *gent* 'graceful,' from L. *genitus* 'well-born.']

gin·ger snap ▶ n. a thin brittle cookie flavored with ginger.

ging·ham /'giNGəm/ ▶ n. lightweight plain-woven cotton cloth, typically checked in white and a color: [as adj.] *gingham curtains.* [17th C.: from Du. *gingang*, from Malay *genggang* (orig. an adj. meaning 'striped').]

gin·gi·va /jin'jīvə; 'jinjəvə/ ▶ n. (pl. **-vae** /-vē/) Med. the gum. — **gin·gi·val** adj. [17th C.: L., 'gum.']

gin·gi·vi·tis /,jinjə'vītis/ ▶ n. Med. inflammation of the gums.

ging·ko ▶ n. var. of GINKGO.

gink·go /'giNGkō/ (also **ging·ko**) ▶ n. (pl. **-goes** or **-gos**) a deciduous Chinese tree (*Ginkgo biloba*, family Ginkgoaceae) related to the conifers, with fan-shaped leaves and yellow flowers. [18th C.: from Japanese *ginkyō*, from Chin. *yinxing.*]

gin mill ▶ n. informal a run-down or seedy nightclub or bar.

gin rum·my ▶ n. see GIN[1].

Gins·berg /'ginzbərg/, Allen (1926–97), US poet, part of the beat generation and later influential in the hippie movement of the 1960s.

Gins·burg /'ginzbərg/, Ruth Bader (1933–), US Supreme Court associate justice 1993– .

gin·seng /'jinseNG/ ▶ n. **1** a plant tuber credited with various tonic and medicinal properties. **2** the plant (genus *Panax*, family Araliaceae) from which this tuber is obtained, native to eastern Asia and North America. [17th C.: from Chin. *rénshēn*, from *rén* 'man' + *shēn*, a kind of herb.]

Gior·gio·ne /jôr'jōnē/ (*c.*1478–1510), Italian painter; also called **Giorgio Barbarelli** or **Giorgio da Castelfranco**. His works include *The Tempest* (*c.*1505).

Giot·to /'jôtō/ (*c.*1267–1337), Italian painter; full name *Giotto di Bondone.* He is associated with the legend of "Giotto's O," in which he is said to have proven his mastery to the pope by drawing a perfect circle freehand.

Gio·van·ni de' Me·di·ci /jō'vänē də 'medicHē/ the name of the Pope Leo X (see LEO[1]).

gip /jip/ ▶ n. var. of GYP.

gip·sy ▶ n. var. of GYPSY.

gi·raffe /jə'raf/ ▶ n. (pl. same or **-raffes**) a large African mammal (*Giraffa camelopardalis*, family Giraffidae) with a very long neck and forelegs, having a coat patterned with brown patches separated by lighter lines. It is the tallest living animal. [16th C.: from Fr. *girafe*, Ital. *giraffa*, or Sp. and Port. *girafa*, based on Arab. *zarāfa.*]

giraffe

gir·an·dole /'jirən,dōl/ ▶ n. **1** a branched support for candles or other lights, which either stands on a surface or projects from a wall. **2** an earring or pendant with a large central stone surrounded by small ones. [17th C. (denoting a revolving cluster of fireworks): from Fr., from Ital. *girandola*, from *girare* 'gyrate, turn,' from L. *gyrare* (see GYRATE).]

gir·a·sol /'jirə,sôl; -,säl/ (also **gir·a·sole** /-,sōl/) ▶ n. **1** a kind of opal reflecting a reddish glow. **2** another term for JERUSALEM ARTICHOKE. [16th C.: from Fr., or from Ital. *girasole*, from *girare* 'to turn' + *sole* 'sun.']

gird /gərd/ ▶ v. (past and past part. **gird·ed** or **girt** /gərt/) [trans.] literary encircle (a person or part of the body) with a belt or band: *girded with the belt of knighthood.* ■ secure (a garment or sword) on the body with a belt or band: *girded with a sash.* ■ surround; encircle.
– PHRASAL VERBS **gird oneself for** prepare oneself for (dangerous or difficult future actions). [OE *gyrdan*, of Gmc. origin; rel. to Ger. *gürten*, also to GIRTH.]

gird·er /'gərdər/ ▶ n. a large iron or steel beam or compound structure used for building bridges and the framework of large buildings. [17th C.: from GIRD.]

gir·dle /'gərdl/ ▶ n. a belt or cord worn around the waist. ■ a woman's elasticized corset extending from waist to thigh. ■ a thing that surrounds something like a belt or girdle: *a communications girdle around the world.* ■ a ring around a tree made by removing bark. ▶ v. [trans.] **1** encircle (the body) with or as a girdle or belt. ■ surround; encircle. **2** cut through the bark all the way around (a tree or branch), typically in order to kill it or to kill a branch. [OE *gyrdel*, of Gmc. origin; rel. to Ger. *Gürtel*, also to GIRTH.]

girl /gərl/ ▶ n. **1** a female child. ■ a person's daughter, esp. a young one. **2** a young or relatively young woman. ■ [with adj.] a young woman of a specified kind or having a specified job: *a career girl.* ■ (**girls**) informal women who mix socially or belong to a particular group, team, or profession: *lunch with the girls.* ■ a person's girlfriend. [ME (denoting a child or young person of either sex): perh. rel. to Low Ger. *gör* 'child.']

girl Fri·day ▶ n. a female helper, esp. a junior office worker or a personal assistant to a business executive. [1940s: on the pattern of *man Friday.*]

girl·friend /'gərl,frend/ ▶ n. a regular female companion with whom a person has a romantic relationship. ■ a woman's female friend.

girl·hood /'gərl,ho͝od/ ▶ n. the state or time of being a girl: *friends since girlhood.*

girl·ie /'gərlē/ ▶ n. (also **girl·y**) (pl. **-ies**) informal a girl or young woman (often used as a term of address). ▶ adj. **1** (usu. **girly**) often derog. like, characteristic of, or appropriate to a girl or young woman: *men aren't afraid to be soft, girly, and foppish.* **2** [attrib.] depicting or featuring nude or partially nude young women in erotic poses: *girlie magazines.*

girl·ish /'gərlisH/ ▶ adj. of, like, or characteristic of a girl. — **girl·ish·ly** adv. **girl·ish·ness** n.

Girl Scout ▶ n. a member of an organization of girls, esp. the **Girl Scouts of America**, that promotes character and good citizenship.

Gi·ronde /zHə'rôNd/ an estuary in southwestern France, formed at the junction of the Garonne and Dordogne rivers.

girt /gərt/ past participle of GIRD.

girth /gərTH/ ▶ n. **1** the measurement around the middle of something, esp. a person's waist. ■ a person's middle or stomach, esp. when large. **2** a band attached to a saddle, used to secure it on a horse by being fastened around its belly. [ME (sense 2): from ON *gjǫrth.*]

GIS ▶ abbr. geographic information system, a system for storing and manipulating geographical information on computer.

Gis·card d'Es·taing /zHē'skär de'stanG/, Valéry (1926–), president of France 1974–81. He later served as a member of the European Parliament 1989–93.

gis·mo ▶ n. var. of GIZMO.

gist /jist/ ▶ n. [in sing.] the substance or essence of a speech or text: *she noted the gist of each message.* [18th C.: from OFr., third person sing. present tense of *gesir* 'to lie,' from L. *jacere.*]

Gi·te·ga /gē'tāgə/ a commercial town in central Burundi, east of Bujumbura; pop. 102,000.

git·tern /'gitərn/ ▶ n. hist. a lutelike medieval stringed instrument, forerunner of the guitar. [ME: from OFr. *guiterne*; perh. rel. to CITTERN and GUITAR.]

Giu·li·a·ni /,jo͞olē'änē/, Rudolph (1944–), US politician. The mayor of New York City 1994–2001. He earned worldwide recognition for his leadership following the terrorist attacks on the World Trade Center on September 11, 2001.

give /giv/ ▶ v. (past **gave** /gāv/; past part. **giv·en** /'givən/) **1** [with two objs.] freely transfer the possession of (something) to (someone); hand over to: *they gave her water.* ■ bestow (love, affection, or other emotional support): *his parents gave him encouragement* | [as adj.] (**giving**) *he was very giving and supportive.* ■ administer (medicine): *give antibiotics.* ■ hand over (an amount) in exchange or payment; pay. ■ [trans.] used hyperbolically to express how greatly one wants to have or do something: *I'd give anything for a cup of tea.* ■ communicate or impart (a message) to (someone): *give my love to all.* ■ [trans.] commit, consign, or entrust: *a baby given into their care.* ■ freely devote, set aside, or sacrifice for a purpose: [intrans.] *committee members who give so generously of their time.* ■ [trans.] (of a man) sanction the marriage of (his daughter) to someone: *he gave her in marriage to a noble.* ■ pass on (an illness or infection) to (someone): *I hope I don't give you my cold.* ■ [usu. in imper.] make a connection to allow (someone) to speak to (someone else) on the telephone: *give me the police.* ■ cite or present when making a toast or introducing a speaker or entertainer: *I give you ... Mr. Albert DeNero!* **2** [with two objs.] cause or allow (someone or something) to have (something, esp. something abstract); provide or supply with: *you gave me such a fright.* ■ allot or assign (a score) to: *I gave it five out of ten.* ■ sentence (someone) to (a specified penalty): *I was given a fine.* ■ concede or yield (something) as valid or deserved in respect of (someone): *give him his due.* ■ allow (someone) to have (a specified amount of time) for an activity or undertaking: *give me a second.* ■ [trans.] (**give something off/out/forth**) emit odor, vapor, or similar substances: *giving off fumes.* **3** [trans.] carry out or perform (a specified action): *I gave a bow.* ■ utter or produce (a sound): *he gave a gasp.* ■ provide (a party or social meal) as host: *a dinner given in honor of a Canadian diplomat.* **4** [trans.] state or put forward (information or argument): *he did not give his name.* ■ pledge or assign as a guarantee: [with two objs.] *I give you my word.* ■ present (an appearance or impression): *he gave no sign of life.* ■ [intrans.] informal tell what one knows: *okay, give—what's that all about?* **5** [intrans.] alter in shape under pressure rather than resist or break: *that chair doesn't give.* ■ yield or give way to pressure: *the heavy door didn't give.* ▶ **n.** capacity to bend or alter in shape under pressure; elasticity: *pots that have enough give to accommodate the roots.* ■ fig. ability to adapt or comply; flexibility: *there is no give at all in the British position.*

– PHRASES **give and take** mutual concessions and compromises. **give the (whole) game** (or **show**) **away** inadvertently reveal something secret or concealed. **give it to someone** informal scold or punish someone. **give me ——** I prefer or admire ——: *give me the mainland any day!* **give me a break** informal used to express exasperation, protest, or disbelief. **give or take ——** informal to within —— (used to express the degree or accuracy of a figure): *three hundred and fifty years ago, give or take a few.* **give rise to** cause or induce to happen: *decisions which give rise to arguments.* **give someone to understand** (or **believe** or **know**) inform someone in a formal and rather indirect way: *I was given to understand that I had been invited.* **not give a damn** (or **hoot**, etc.) informal not care at all. **what gives?** informal what's happening? (frequently used as a friendly greeting).

– PHRASAL VERBS **give someone away 1** reveal the true identity of someone. ■ reveal information that incriminates someone. **2** hand over a bride ceremonially to her bridegroom as part of a wedding. **give something away** reveal something secret or concealed. **give in** cease fighting or arguing; yield; surrender. **give out** stop functioning; break down: *he swears till his voice gives out.* **give up** cease making an effort; resign oneself to failure. **give oneself up to 1** surrender oneself to law-enforcement agents. **2** dated allow oneself to be taken over by (an emotion or addiction): *he gave himself up to pleasure.* **give someone up** deliver a wanted person to authority. **give something up** part with something that one would prefer to keep: *she would have given up everything for love.* ■ stop the habitual doing or consuming of something: *give up drinking.* **give up on** stop having faith in: *they weren't about to give up on their heroes.* — **giv•er n.** [OE *giefan, gefan*, of Gmc. origin; rel. to Du. *geven* and Ger. *geben*.]

give•a•way /ˈgivəˌwā/ informal ▶ **n. 1** a thing that is given free, esp. for promotional purposes: *a preelection tax giveaway.* **2** a thing that makes an inadvertent revelation: *the shape of the parcel was a dead giveaway.* ▶ **adj.** [attrib.] **1** free of charge: *giveaway goodies.* ■ (of prices) very low. **2** revealing: *small giveaway mannerisms.*

give•back /ˈgivˌbak/ ▶ **n.** an agreement by workers to surrender benefits and conditions previously agreed upon in return for new concessions or awards.

giv•en /ˈgivən/ past participle of **GIVE**. ▶ **adj. 1** specified or stated: *our level of knowledge on any given subject.* **2** [predic.] (**given to**) inclined or disposed to: *she was not often given to anger.* **3** conferred or bestowed as a gift: *she squandered what was a given opportunity.* **4** Law, archaic (of a document) signed and dated: *given under my hand this eleventh day of April.* ▶ **prep.** taking into account: *given the complexity of the task, they were able to do a good job.* ▶ **n.** a known or established fact or situation: *at a couture house, attentive service is a given.*

giv•en name ▶ **n.** another term for **FIRST NAME**.

Gi•za /ˈgēzə/ a city in northern Egypt, on the Nile River, site of the Pyramids and the Sphinx; pop. 2,156,000. Also called **EL GIZA**; Arabic name **AL JIZAH**.

giz•mo /ˈgizmō/ (also **gis•mo**) ▶ **n.** (pl. **-mos**) informal a gadget, esp. one whose name the speaker does not know. [1940s (orig. US): of unknown origin.]

giz•zard /ˈgizərd/ ▶ **n.** a muscular, thick-walled part of a bird's stomach for grinding food, typically with grit. Also called **VENTRICULUS**. ■ a muscular stomach of some fish, insects, mollusks, and other invertebrates. ■ informal a person's stomach or throat. [ME *giser*: from OFr., based on L. *gigeria* 'cooked entrails of fowl.']

gla•bel•la /gləˈbelə/ ▶ **n.** (pl. **-bel•lae** /-ˈbelē/) Anat. the smooth part of the forehead above and between the eyebrows. — **gla•bel•lar** /-ˈbelər/ **adj.** [19th C.: mod. L., from L. *glabellus* (adj.), dimin. of *glaber* 'smooth.']

gla•brous /ˈglābrəs/ ▶ **adj.** tech. (chiefly of the skin or a leaf) free from hair or down; smooth. [17th C.: from L. *glaber, glabr-* 'hairless, smooth' + **-OUS**.]

gla•cé /glaˈsā/ ▶ **adj.** [attrib.] **1** (of fruit) having a glossy surface due to preservation in sugar. **2** (of cloth or leather) smooth and highly polished. ▶ **v.** (**-céed** or **-céd**, **-cé•ing**) [trans.] glaze with a thin sugar-based coating. [19th C.: Fr., lit. 'iced,' past part. of *glacer*, from *glace* 'ice.']

gla•cial /ˈglāsʜəl/ ▶ **adj. 1** relating to, resulting from, or denoting the presence or agency of ice, esp. in the form of glaciers: *a glacial lake.* **2** of ice; icy: fig. *glacial blue eyes.* ■ extremely cold. ■ Chem. denoting pure organic acids (esp. acetic acid) that form icelike crystals on freezing. — **gla•cial•ly adv.** [17th C.: from Fr., or from L. *glacialis* 'icy,' from *glacies* 'ice.']

gla•cial pe•ri•od ▶ **n.** a period in the earth's history when polar and mountain ice sheets were unusually extensive across the earth's surface.

gla•ci•at•ed /ˈglāsʜēˌātid/ ▶ **adj.** covered or having been covered by glaciers or ice sheets.

gla•ci•a•tion /ˌglāsʜēˈāsʜən/ ▶ **n.** Geol. the process, condition, or result of being covered by glaciers.

gla•cier /ˈglāsʜər/ ▶ **n.** a slowly moving mass or river of ice formed by the accumulation and compaction of snow on mountains or near the poles. [18th C.: from Fr., from *glace* 'ice,' based on L. *glacies*.]

Gla•cier Bay Na•tion•al Park a national park in southeastern Alaska, on the Pacific coast.

gla•ci•ol•o•gy /ˌglāsʜēˈäləjē/ ▶ **n.** the study of the internal dynamics and effects of glaciers. — **gla•ci•o•log•i•cal** /-sʜēəˈläjikəl/ **adj.** **gla•ci•ol•o•gist n.**

gla•cis /ˈglāsis; ˈglas-/ ▶ **n.** (pl. same or **-cis•es**) a gently sloping bank, in particular one that slopes down from a fort, exposing attackers to the defenders' missiles. [17th C.: from Fr., from OFr. *glacier* 'to slip,' from *glace* 'ice,' based on L. *glacies*.]

glad[1] /glad/ ▶ **adj.** (**glad•der, glad•dest**) [predic.] pleased; delighted. ■ happy for someone's good fortune: *I'm so glad for you.* ■ [attrib.] causing happiness: *glad tidings.* ■ grateful: *he was glad for the excuse.* ■ [with infin.] willing and eager (to do something): *he will be glad to carry your bags.* — **glad•ly adv.** **glad•ness n.** [OE *glæd* ('bright, shining'), of Gmc. origin; rel. to Ger. *glatt* 'smooth.']

glad[2] ▶ **n.** informal a gladiolus. [1920s: abbrev.]

glad•den /ˈgladn/ ▶ **v.** [trans.] make glad: *it was a sound that gladdened her heart.*

glade /glād/ ▶ **n.** an open space in a forest. [ME: perh. rel. to **GLAD**[1] or **GLEAM**.]

glad-hand ▶ **v.** [trans.] (esp. of a politician) greet warmly or with the appearance of warmth: *glad-hand loyal supporters.* — **glad-hand•er n.**

glad•i•a•tor /ˈgladēˌātər/ ▶ **n. 1** (in ancient Rome) a man trained to fight with weapons against other men or wild animals in an arena. **2** a person defending or opposing a cause; a controversialist: *a gladiator in the presidential arena.* — **glad•i•a•to•ri•al** /ˌgladēəˈtôrēəl/ **adj.** [ME: from L., from *gladius* 'sword.']

glad•i•o•lus /ˌgladēˈōləs/ ▶ **n.** (pl. **-li** /-lī/ or **-lus•es**) a widely cultivated plant (genus *Gladiolus*) of the iris family, with sword-shaped leaves and spikes of brightly colored flowers. [OE: from L., dimin. of *gladius* 'sword.']

glad rags ▶ **plural n.** informal clothes for a special occasion; one's best clothes.

Glad•stone /ˈgladˌstōn/, William Ewart (1809–98), prime minister of Britain 1868–74, 1880–85, 1886, 1892–94. At first a Conservative, he later joined the Liberal Party.

Glad•stone bag ▶ **n.** a bag like a briefcase having two equal compartments joined by a hinge. [19th C.: named after W. E. **GLADSTONE**, who was noted for the amount of traveling he undertook when electioneering.]

Glag•o•lit•ic /ˌglagəˈlitik/ ▶ **adj.** denoting or relating to an alphabet based on Greek minuscules, formerly used in writing some Slavic languages. ▶ **n.** this alphabet. [from mod. L. *glagoliticus*, based on Old Church Slavic *glagolŭ* 'word.']

glair /gle(ə)r/ ▶ **n.** a preparation made from egg white, esp. as an adhesive for bookbinding and gilding. [ME: from OFr. *glaire*, based on L. *clara*, fem. of *clarus* 'clear.']

glam /glam/ informal ▶ **adj.** glamorous. ■ relating to or denoting glam rock. ▶ **n.** glamour. ▶ **v.** (**glammed, glamming**) [intrans.] (**glam up**) make oneself look glamorous.

glam•or•ize /ˈglaməˌrīz/ (also **glam•our•ize**) ▶ **v.** [trans.] make (something) seem glamorous or desirable, esp. spuriously so: *the lyrics glamorize drugs.* — **glam•or•i•za•tion** /ˌglaməriˈzāsʜən/ **n.**

glam•or•ous /ˈglamərəs/ ▶ **adj.** having glamour. — **glam•or•ous•ly adv.**

glam•our /ˈglamər/ (also **glam•or**) ▶ **n.** the attractive or exciting quality that makes certain people or things seem appealing or special: *the glamour of Monte Carlo.* ■ beauty or charm that is sexually attractive. [18th C. ('enchantment, magic'): alt. of **GRAMMAR**.]

glam rock ▶ **n.** a style of rock music first popular in the early 1970s, characterized by male performers wearing flamboyant clothes and makeup.

glance /glans/ ▶ **v.** [no obj., with adverbial of direction] **1** take a brief or hurried look. ■ (**glance at/through**) read quickly or cursorily. **2** hit something at an angle and bounce off obliquely: *he saw a stone glance off a crag.* ■ (esp. of light) reflect off (something) with a brief flash: *sunlight glanced off the dolphin.* ■ [with obj. and adverbial of direction] (in ball games) deflect (the ball) slightly with a delicate contact: *he glanced the ball*

into the right corner. ▶ **n.** a brief or hurried look.
– PHRASES **at a glance** immediately upon looking. **at first glance** when seen or considered for the first time, esp. briefly. [ME: prob. from obs. *glace*, from OFr. *glacier* 'to slip,' from *glace* 'ice,' based on L. *glacies*.]

glanc·ing /ˈglansiNG/ ▶ **adj.** [attrib.] striking someone or something at an angle rather than directly and with full force: *he was struck a glancing blow.*

gland[1] /gland/ ▶ **n.** an organ in the human or animal body that secretes particular chemical substances for use in the body or for discharge into the surroundings. ■ a structure resembling this, esp. a lymph node. [17th C.: from Fr. *glande*, alt. of OFr. *glandre*, from L. *glandulae* 'throat glands.']

gland[2] ▶ **n.** a sleeve used to produce a seal around a piston rod or other shaft. [19th C.: prob. a var. of Scots *glam* 'a vice or clamp'; rel. to CLAMP.]

gland·ers /ˈglandərz/ ▶ **plural n.** [usu. treated as sing.] a rare contagious disease that mainly affects horses, characterized by swellings below the jaw and mucous discharge from the nostrils, caused by the bacterium *Pseudomonas mallei*. [15th C.: from OFr. *glandre* (see GLAND[1]).]

glan·du·lar /ˈglanjələr/ ▶ **adj.** of, relating to, or affecting a gland or glands.

glans /glanz/ ▶ **n.** (pl. **glan·des** /ˈglandēz/) Anat. the rounded part forming the end of the penis (**glans penis**) or clitoris (**glans clitoris**). [17th C.: from L., lit. 'acorn.']

glare /gle(ə)r/ ▶ **v.** [intrans.] **1** stare in an angry or fierce way. ■ [trans.] express (a feeling, esp. defiance) by staring in such a way: *he glared defiance.* **2** [with adverbial] (of the sun or an electric light) shine with a strong or dazzling light: *the sun glared out of a clear sky.* ▶ **n. 1** a fierce or angry stare. **2** strong and dazzling light: *the glare of the sun.* ■ fig. oppressive public attention or scrutiny: *in the full glare of publicity.* [ME: from MDu. and Mid. Low Ger. *glaren* 'to gleam, glare': perh. rel. to GLASS.]

glare ice ▶ **n.** smooth, glassy ice. [19th C.: prob. from obs. *glare* 'frost'; perh. rel. to GLARE.]

glar·ing /ˈgle(ə)riNG/ ▶ **adj. 1** [attrib.] giving out or reflecting a strong or dazzling light. ■ staring fiercely or fixedly. **2** highly obvious or conspicuous: *a glaring omission.* — **glar·ing·ly adv.**

Glas·gow /ˈglasgō; ˈglaz-/ a city in Scotland, on the Clyde River; pop. 655,000.

Glash·ow /ˈglasHō/, Sheldon Lee (1932–), US theoretical physicist. He independently developed a unified theory to explain electromagnetic interactions and the weak nuclear force. Nobel Prize for Physics (1979).

glas·nost /ˈglaznōst; ˈglas-; ˈgläz-; ˈgläs-/ ▶ **n.** (in the former Soviet Union) the policy or practice of more open government and wider dissemination of information, initiated by Mikhail Gorbachev in the 1980s. [from Russ. *glasnost'*, from *glasnyy* 'public, open' + *-nost'* '-ness.']

glass shapes

glass /glas/ ▶ **n. 1** a hard, brittle substance, typically transparent or translucent, made by fusing sand with soda, lime, and sometimes other ingredients and cooling rapidly. It is used to make windows, drinking containers, and other articles. ■ any similar substance that has solidified from a molten state without crystallizing. **2** a thing made from, or partly from, glass, in particular: ■ a container to drink from. ■ glassware. ■ esp. Brit. a mirror. **3** a lens, or an optical instrument containing a lens or lenses, in particular a monocle or a magnifying lens. **4** the liquid or amount of liquid contained in a glass; a glassful: *a glass of lemonade.* ▶ **v.** [trans.] **1** cover or enclose with glass: *we glassed in the porch.* **2** (esp. in hunting) scan (one's surroundings) with binoculars. **3** literary reflect in or as if in a mirror.
– PHRASES **people (who live) in glass houses shouldn't throw stones** proverb you shouldn't criticize others when you have similar faults of your own. — **glass·ful** /-ˌfo͝ol/ **n.** (pl. **-fuls.**) [OE *glæs*, of Gmc. origin; rel. to Du. *glas* and Ger. *Glas*.]

glass·blow·ing /ˈglasˌblō-iNG/ ▶ **n.** the craft of making glassware by blowing air through a tube into a mass of semimolten glass. — **glass·blow·er n.**

glass ceil·ing ▶ **n.** [usu. in sing.] an unofficially acknowledged barrier to advancement in a profession, esp. affecting women and members of minorities.

glass cut·ter ▶ **n.** a tool that scores a line on a piece of glass, allowing the glass to be snapped along the line. ■ a person who cuts glass. — **glass cut·ting n.**

glass·es /ˈglasiz/ ▶ **plural n.** a pair of lenses set in a frame resting on the nose and ears, used to correct or assist defective eyesight or protect the eyes. ■ a pair of binoculars.

glass eye ▶ **n.** an artificial eye made from glass.

glass har·mon·i·ca ▶ **n.** a musical instrument in which the sound is made by pressing the moistened rims of rotating glass bowls, graduated in size.

glass·ine /glaˈsēn/ ▶ **n.** [usu. as adj.] a glossy transparent paper: *glassine envelopes.* [20th C.: from GLASS + -INE[4].]

glass jaw ▶ **n.** informal Boxing a weak jaw that is easily broken.

glass liz·ard ▶ **n.** a legless burrowing lizard (genus *Ophisaurus*, family Anguidae) of snakelike appearance, with smooth shiny skin and an easily detached tail. Also called **glass snake**.

glass·ware /ˈglasˌwe(ə)r/ ▶ **n.** ornaments and articles made from glass.

glass wool ▶ **n.** glass in the form of fine fibers used for packing and insulation.

glass·work /ˈglasˌwərk/ ▶ **n. 1** the business or technique of cutting and installing glass for windows and doors; glazing. **2** the manufacture of glass and glassware. **3** ornaments and articles made of glass; glassware.

glass·works /ˈglasˌwərks/ ▶ **n.** [treated as sing. or pl.] a factory where glass and glass articles are made.

glass·wort /ˈglasˌwərt; -ˌwôrt/ ▶ **n.** a widely distributed salt-marsh plant (genus *Salicornia*) of the goosefoot family, with fleshy scalelike leaves. The ashes of the burned plant were formerly used in glassmaking. Also called SAMPHIRE.

glass·y /ˈglasē/ ▶ **adj.** (**glass·i·er, glass·i·est**) **1** of or resembling glass in some way, in particular: ■ having the physical properties of glass; vitreous. ■ (of water) having a smooth surface. **2** (of a person's eyes or expression) showing no interest or animation; dull and glazed. — **glass·i·ly adv. glass·i·ness n.**

Glas·we·gian /glazˈwējən; -jēən; glas-/ ▶ **adj.** of or relating to Glasgow. ▶ **n.** a native of Glasgow. [from GLASGOW.]

Glat·zer Neisse /ˈglätsər ˌnīsə/ German name for NEISSE (sense 2).

Glau·ber's salt /ˈgloubərz/ ▶ **n.** (also **Glau·ber's salts**) a crystalline hydrated form of sodium sulfate, used chiefly as a laxative. [18th C.: Johann R. *Glauber* (1604–1668), German chemist.]

glau·co·ma /glôˈkōmə/ ▶ **n.** Med. a condition of increased pressure within the eyeball, causing gradual loss of sight. — **glau·co·ma·tous** /-mətəs/ **adj.** [17th C.: via L. from Gk. *glaukōma*, based on *glaukos* 'bluish-green, bluish-gray.']

glau·co·nite /ˈglôkəˌnīt/ ▶ **n.** a greenish clay mineral of the illite group, found chiefly in marine sands.

glau·cous /ˈglôkəs/ ▶ **adj.** tech., literary **1** of a dull grayish-green or blue color. **2** covered with a powdery bloom like that on grapes.

glaze /glāz/ ▶ **v.** [trans.] **1** fit panes of glass into (a window or doorframe or similar structure). **2** (often **be glazed**) cover with a glaze or similar finish: *glazed in butter.* **3** [intrans.] lose brightness and animation: [as adj.] (**glazed**) *that glazed look in her eyes.* ▶ **n.** [usu. in sing.] **1** a substance used to give a smooth, shiny surface to something, in particular: ■ a vitreous substance fused on to the surface of pottery to form a hard, decorative coating. ■ a liquid such as milk or egg, used to form a shiny coating on food. ■ esp. Art a thin topcoat of transparent paint used to modify an underlying color. **2** a smooth, shiny surface formed esp. by glazing. ■ a thin, glassy coating of ice on the ground or the surface of water. — **glaz·er n.** [ME *glase*, from GLASS.]

gla·zier /ˈglāzHər/ ▶ **n.** a person whose profession is fitting glass into windows and doors.

glazier's point ▶ **n.** a small triangle of sheet metal, used to hold glass in a window frame until the putty dries.

glaz·ing /ˈglāziNG/ ▶ **n.** the action of installing windows. ■ glass windows: *sealed protective glazing.* ■ a material used to produce a glaze.

GLBT ▶ **abbr.** gay, lesbian, bisexual, and transgendered.

GLC ▶ **abbr.** Chem. gas–liquid chromatography.

gleam /glēm/ ▶ **v.** [intrans.] shine brightly, esp. with reflected light: ■ (of a smooth surface or object) reflect light because well polished: [as adj.] (**gleaming**) *gleaming limousines.* ■ (of an emotion or quality) appear or be expressed through the brightness of someone's eyes or expression: *mischief gleaming in her eyes.* ▶ **n.** [usu. in sing.] a faint or brief light, esp. one reflected from something. ■ a brief or faint instance of a quality or emotion: *gleam of hope.* [OE *glǣm* 'brilliant light,' of Gmc. origin.]

glean /glēn/ ▶ **v.** [trans.] extract (information) from various sources. ■ collect gradually and bit by bit. ■ hist. gather (leftover grain or other produce) after a harvest. — **glean·er n. glean·ing n.** [ME: from OFr. *glener*, from late L. *glennare*, prob. of Celtic origin.]

glean·ings /ˈglēniNGz/ ▶ **plural n.** things, esp. facts, that are gathered or collected from various sources. ■ hist. grain or other produce that is gathered after a harvest.

glebe /glēb/ ▶ **n.** hist. a piece of land serving as part of a clergyman's benefice and providing income. [ME: from L. *gleba*, *glaeba* 'clod, land, soil.']

glee /glē/ ▶**n.** great delight or pleasure. [OE *glēo* 'entertainment, fun,' of Gmc. origin.]

glee club ▶**n.** a group organized to sing short choral works, esp. part-songs.

glee·ful /'glēfəl/ ▶**adj.** exuberantly or triumphantly joyful. — **glee·ful·ly adv. glee·ful·ness n.**

gleet /glēt/ ▶**n.** Med. an abnormal discharge from a bodily orifice in humans or animals, esp. (in humans) a discharge from the urethra caused by gonorrhea. [ME: from OFr. *glette* 'slime, secretion.']

glen /glen,dal/ ▶**n.** a narrow valley. [ME: from Scot. Gael. and Irish *gleann* (earlier *glenn*).]

Glen·dale /'glen,dāl/ **1** a city in south central Arizona; pop. 218,812. **2** a city in southwestern California; pop. 194,973.

Glen·do·ra /glen'dôrə/ a city in southwestern California; pop. 47,828.

glen·gar·ry /glen'garē/ ▶**n.** (pl. **-ries**) a brimless boat-shaped hat with a cleft down the center, typically having two ribbons hanging at the back, worn as part of Scottish Highland dress. [19th C.: from *Glengarry*, valley in Scotland.]

glengarry

Glenn /glen/, John Herschel, Jr. (1921–), US astronaut and politician. In 1962, he became the first American to orbit the earth. An Ohio Democrat, he served in the US Senate 1975–99. In 1998, he joined the crew of the space shuttle to help study the effects of space travel on older people.

gli·a /'glēə; 'glīə/ ▶**n.** Anat. the connective tissue of the nervous system, consisting of several different types of cell associated with neurons. Also called **NEUROGLIA.** — **gli·al adj.** [19th C.: from Gk., lit. 'glue.']

glib /glib/ ▶**adj.** (**glib·ber, glib·best**) (of words or the person speaking them) fluent and voluble but insincere and shallow. — **glib·ly adv. glib·ness n.** [16th C.: ult. of Gmc. origin; rel. to Ger. *glibberig* 'slimy.']

glide /glīd/ ▶**v. 1** [no obj., with adverbial of direction] move with a smooth continuous motion, typically with little noise: *gondolas glided past.* ■ [with obj. and adverbial of direction] cause to move with a smooth continuous motion. **2** [intrans.] make an unpowered flight, either in a glider or in an aircraft with engine failure. ■ (of a bird) fly through the air with very little movement of the wings. ▶**n.** [in sing.] **1** a smooth continuous movement. ■ an unpowered maneuver in an aircraft. ■ a flight in a glider or unpowered aircraft. ■ a smooth continuous step in ballroom dancing. **2** Phonet. a sound produced as the vocal organs move toward or away from articulation of a vowel or consonant, for example /y/ in *mute* /myo͞ot/. [OE *glīdan*, of Gmc. origin; rel. to Du. *glijden* and Ger. *gleiten*.]

glid·er /'glīdər/ ▶**n. 1** a light aircraft designed to fly for long periods without using an engine. **2** a person or thing that glides. **3** a long swinging seat suspended from a frame in a porch.

glim·mer /'glimər/ ▶**v.** [intrans.] shine faintly with a wavering light: [as adj.] (**glimmering**) *pools of glimmering light.* ▶**n.** a faint or wavering light. ■ a faint sign of a feeling or quality, esp. a desirable one: *glimmer of hope.* — **glim·mer·ing·ly adv.** [ME: prob. of Scand. origin; rel. to Swed. *glimra* and Dan. *glimre*.]

glim·mer·ing /'glimərinɢ/ ▶**n.** a glimmer: *the glimmering of an idea.*

glimpse /glimps/ ▶**n.** a momentary or partial view: *she caught a glimpse of the ocean.* ▶**v.** [trans.] see or perceive briefly or partially. [ME: prob. of Gmc. origin; rel. to Mid. High Ger. *glimsen*, also to **GLIMMER.**]

Glin·ka /'glinɢkə/, Mikhail Ivanovich (1804–57), Russian composer. His operas include *A Life for the Czar* (1836) and *Russlan and Ludmilla* (1842).

glint /glint/ ▶**v.** [intrans.] give out or reflect small flashes of light; *her glasses were glinting.* ■ (of a person's eyes) shine with a particular emotion: *his eyes glinted angrily.* ▶**n.** a small flash of light, esp. as reflected from a shiny surface. [ME: var. of dialect *glent*, prob. of Scand. origin and rel. to Swed. dial. *glänta, glinta* 'to slip.']

gli·o·ma /glī'ōmə/ ▶**n.** (pl. **-mas** or **-ma·ta** /-mətə/) Med. a malignant tumor of the glial tissue of the nervous system. [19th C.: from Gk. *glia* 'glue' + **-OMA.**]

glis·sade /gli'säd; -'sād/ ▶**n. 1** a way of sliding down a steep slope of snow or ice with the support of an ice ax. **2** Ballet a movement in which one leg is brushed outward from the body, which then takes the weight while the second leg is brushed in to meet it. [19th C.: Fr., from *glisser* 'to slip, slide.']

glis·san·do /gli'sändō/ ▶**n.** (pl. **-di** /-dē/ or **-dos**) Music a continuous slide upward or downward between two notes. [Ital., from Fr. *glissant*, pres. part. of *glisser* 'to slip, slide.']

glis·ten /'glisən/ ▶**v.** [intrans.] (of something wet or greasy) shine; glitter: *his cheeks glistened with tears* | [as adj.] (**glistening**) *the glistening swimming pool.* ▶**n.** [in sing.] a sparkling light reflected from something wet: *there was a glisten of perspiration across her top lip.* — **glis·ten·ing·ly adv.** [OE *glisnian*, of Gmc. origin; rel. to Mid. Low Ger. *glisen*.]

glitch /gliCH/ informal ▶**n.** a sudden, usually temporary malfunction or irregularity of equipment: *a computer glitch.* ■ an unexpected setback in a plan; a hitch, a snag. — **glitch·y adj.** [1960s: of unknown origin.]

glit·ter /'glitər/ ▶**v.** [intrans.] shine with a bright, shimmering, reflected light. ▶**n.** [in sing.] bright, shimmering, reflected light. ■ tiny pieces of sparkling material used for decoration: *sneakers trimmed with glitter.* ■ fig. an attractive, exciting, often superficial, quality: *the glitter of show business.*
– PHRASES **all that glitters is not gold** proverb the attractive external appearance of something is not a reliable indication of its true nature. — **glit·ter·y adj.** [ME: from ON *glitra*.]

glit·te·ra·ti /,glitə'rätē/ ▶**plural n.** informal the fashionable set of people engaged in show business or some other glamorous activity. [1950s (orig. US): blend of **GLITTER** and **LITERATI.**]

glit·ter·ing /'glitəriNG/ ▶**adj.** [attrib.] shining with a shimmering or sparkling light: *glittering chandeliers.* ■ fig. impressively successful or elaborate: *a glittering military career.* — **glit·ter·ing·ly adv.**

glitz /glits/ informal ▶**n.** extravagant but superficial display. ▶**v.** [trans.] make (something) glamorous or showy: *we need to glitz up the program.* [1970s: back-form. from **GLITZY.**]

glitz·y /'glitsē/ ▶**adj.** (**glitz·i·er, glitz·i·est**) informal ostentatiously attractive (often used to suggest superficial glamour). [1960s: from **GLITTER,** suggested by **RITZY.**]

Gli·wi·ce /gli'vētsə/ a city in southern Poland; pop. 214,000.

gloam·ing /'glōmiNG/ ▶**n.** (**the gloaming**) literary twilight; dusk. [OE *glōmung*, from *glōm* 'twilight,' of Gmc. origin; rel. to **GLOW.**]

gloat /glōt/ ▶**v.** [intrans.] contemplate or dwell on one's own success or another's misfortune with malignant pleasure: *his enemies gloated over his death.* ▶**n.** [in sing.] informal an act of gloating. [16th C.: perh. rel. to Mid. High Ger. *glotzen* 'to stare.']

glob /gläb/ ▶**n.** informal a lump of a semiliquid substance: *thick globs of cheese.* [20th C.: perh. a blend of **BLOB** and **GOB**[1].]

glob·al /'glōbəl/ ▶**adj.** of or relating to the whole world; worldwide: *global economy.* ■ of or relating to the entire earth as a planet: *global environmental change.* ■ relating to or embracing the whole of something, or of a group of things: *a global picture of what is involved.* ■ Comput. operating or applying through the whole of a file, program, etc.: *global searches.* — **glob·al·ly adv.**

glob·al·ist /'glōbəlist/ ▶**n.** a person who advocates the interpretation or planning of economic and foreign policy in relation to events and developments throughout the world. ■ a person or organization advocating or practicing operations across national divisions. — **glob·al·ism** /-,lizəm/ **n.**

glob·al·ize /'glōbə,līz/ ▶**v.** develop or be developed so as to make possible international influence or operation: [trans.] *communication globalizes capital markets.* — **glob·al·i·za·tion** /,glōbəli'zāSHən/ **n.**

glob·al vil·lage ▶**n.** the world considered as a single community linked by telecommunications.

glob·al warm·ing ▶**n.** the gradual increase in the temperature of the earth's atmosphere, believed to be due to the greenhouse effect, caused by increased levels of carbon dioxide, chlorofluorocarbons, and other pollutants.

globe /glōb/ ▶**n. 1** (**the globe**) the earth. ■ a spherical representation of the earth or of the constellations with a map on the surface. **2** a spherical or rounded object: *trees clipped into globes.* ■ a glass sphere protecting a lamp. — **globe·like adj. glo·boid** /'glōboid/ **adj. & n. glo·bose** /'glōbōs/ **adj.** [ME: from OFr., or from L. *globus*.]

globe·flow·er /'glōb,flouər/ ▶**n.** a plant (genus *Trollius*) of the buttercup family with globular yellow or orange flowers, native to north temperate regions.

Globe The·a·tre a theater in Southwark, London, erected in 1599, where many of Shakespeare's plays were first publicly performed.

globe this·tle ▶**n.** a thistle (genus *Echinops*) with globe-shaped heads of metallic blue-gray flowers.

globe-trot·ter (also **globe·trot·ter**) ▶**n.** informal a person who travels widely. — **globe-trot v. globe-trot·ting n. & adj.**

glo·big·er·i·na /glō,bijə'rīnə; -'rēnə/ ▶**n.** (pl. **-nas** or **-nae** /-nē/) a planktonic marine protozoan (genus *Globigerina*, order Foraminiferida) with a calcareous shell. The shells collect as a deposit (**globigerina ooze**) over much of the ocean floor. [mod. L., from L. *globus* 'spherical object, globe' + *-ger* 'carrying.']

glob·u·lar /'gläbyələr/ ▶**adj. 1** globe-shaped; spherical. **2** composed of globules.

glob·u·lar clus·ter ▶**n.** Astron. a large compact spherical star cluster, typically of old stars in the outer regions of a galaxy.

glob·ule /'gläbyo͞ol/ ▶**n.** a small round particle of a substance; a drop: *globules of fat.* — **glob·u·lous** /-yələs/ **adj.** [17th C.: from Fr., or from L. *globulus*, dimin. of *globus* 'spherical object, globe.']

glob·u·lin /'gläbyəlin/ ▶**n.** Biochem. any of a group of simple proteins soluble in salt solutions and forming a large fraction of blood serum protein.

glo·chid·i·um /glō'kidēəm/ ▶**n.** (pl. **-chid·i·a** /-'kidēə/) Zool. a parasitic larva of certain freshwater bivalve mollusks, which attaches itself by hooks and suckers to the fins or gills of fish. [19th C.: mod. L., based on Gk. *glōkhis* 'arrowhead.']

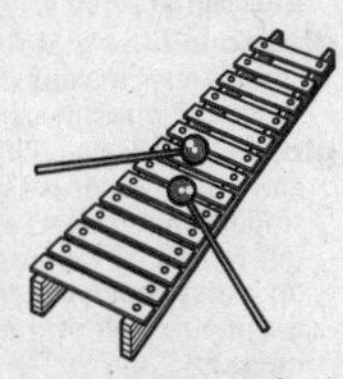
glockenspiel

glock·en·spiel /'gläkən,spēl; -,SHpēl/ ▶**n.** a musical percussion instrument having a set of tuned metal pieces mounted in a frame and struck with small hammers. [19th C.: from Ger. *Glockenspiel*, lit. 'bell-play.']

glom /gläm/ ▶v. (**glommed, glom·ming**) informal [trans.] steal: *I thought he was about to glom my wallet.* ■ [intrans.] (**glom onto**) become stuck or attached to. [20th C.: var. of Scots *glaum*, of unknown origin.]

glo·mer·u·lo·ne·phri·tis /glō,meryəlō-nə'frītis/ ▶n. Med. acute inflammation of the kidney, typically caused by an immune response.

glo·mer·u·lus /glō'meryələs/ ▶n. (pl. **-li** /-,lī/) Anat. Biol. a cluster of nerve endings or blood vessels, esp. the capillaries around the end of a kidney tubule, where waste products are filtered from the blood. —**glo·mer·u·lar** /-lər/ adj. [19th C.: mod. L., dimin. of L. *glomus, glomer-* 'ball of thread.']

gloom /glo͞om/ ▶n. **1** partial or total darkness. **2** a state of depression or despondency: *economic gloom.*
– PHRASES **gloom and doom** see DOOM. [ME (as a v.): of unknown origin.]

gloom·y /'glo͞omē/ ▶adj. (**gloom·i·er, gloom·i·est**) dark or poorly lit, esp. so as to appear depressing. ■ feeling distressed or pessimistic: *gloomy about prospects for industry.* ■ causing distress or depression. —**gloom·i·ly** /-məlē/ adv. **gloom·i·ness** n.

glop /gläp/ ▶n. informal a sticky and amorphous substance. ■ a soft, shapeless lump of something: *a glop of dressing.* ■ fig. worthless or overly sentimental writing, music, or other material: *commercialized glop.* [1940s: symbolic.]

Glo·ri·a /'glôrēə/ ▶n. a Christian liturgical hymn or formula beginning (in the Latin text) with *Gloria*, in particular: ■ the hymn beginning *Gloria in excelsis Deo* (Glory be to God in the highest), forming a set part of the Mass. ■ a musical setting of this: *Vivaldi's Gloria.* [ME: L., 'glory.']

Glo·ri·a·na /,glôrē'änə/ the nickname of Queen Elizabeth I.

glo·ri·fied /'glôrə,fīd/ ▶adj. [attrib.] (esp. of something or someone ordinary or unexceptional) represented in such a way as to appear more elevated or special: *a glorified secretary.*

glo·ri·fy /'glôrə,fī/ ▶v. (**-fies, -fied**) [trans.] **1** reveal or make clearer the glory of (God) by one's actions. ■ give praise to (God). **2** describe or represent as admirable, esp. unjustifiably or undeservedly: *a football video glorifying violence.* —**glo·ri·fi·ca·tion** /,glôrəfi'kāshən/ n. **glo·ri·fi·er** n. [ME: from OFr. *glorifier*, from eccles. Latin *glorificare*, from late L. *glorificus*, from L. *gloria* 'glory.']

glo·ri·ous /'glôrēəs/ ▶adj. **1** having, worthy of, or bringing fame or admiration: *glorious victory.* **2** having a striking beauty or splendor that evokes feelings of delighted admiration. —**glo·ri·ous·ly** adv.

glo·ry /'glôrē/ ▶n. (pl. **-ries**) **1** high renown or honor won by notable achievements. ■ praise, worship, and thanksgiving offered to God. **2** magnificence; great beauty: *restored to its former glory.* ■ (often **glories**) a thing that is beautiful or distinctive; a special cause for pride, respect, or delight: *the glories of Paris.* ▶v. [intrans.] (**glory in**) take great pride or pleasure in.
– PHRASES **glory be!** expressing enthusiastic piety. ■ informal used as an exclamation of surprise or delight. **in one's glory** informal in a state of extreme joy or exaltation. [ME: from OFr. *glorie*, from L. *gloria*.]

glo·ry days ▶plural n. a time in the past regarded as being better than the present: *the glory days of tourism.*

glo·ry hole ▶n. a small furnace used to keep glass malleable for handworking. [19th C.: of unknown origin.]

gloss[1] /gläs; glôs/ ▶n. shine or luster on a smooth surface. ■ see LIPGLOSS. ■ (also **gloss paint**) a type of paint that dries to a bright shiny surface. ■ [in sing.] a superficially attractive appearance or impression: *the gloss of success hid a tragic life.* ▶v. [trans.] apply a cosmetic gloss to. ■ apply gloss paint to. ■ (**gloss over**) try to conceal or disguise (something embarrassing or unfavorable) by treating it briefly or representing it misleadingly: *the social costs of this growth are glossed over.*

gloss[2] ▶n. a translation or explanation of a word or phrase. ■ an explanation, interpretation, or paraphrase: *the chapter acts as a helpful gloss on Pynchon's general method.* ▶v. [trans.] (usu. **be glossed**) provide an explanation, interpretation, or paraphrase for (a text, word, etc.). [16th C.: alt. of the n. *gloze*, from OFr. *glose*, suggested by med. L. *glossa* 'explanation of a difficult word,' from Gk. *glōssa* 'word needing explanation, language, tongue.']

gloss. ▶abbr. glossary.

glos·sa·ry /'gläsərē; 'glô-/ ▶n. (pl. **-ries**) an alphabetical list of terms or words found in or relating to a specific subject, text, or dialect, with explanations; a brief dictionary. —**glos·sar·i·al** /glä'se(ə)rēəl; glô-/ adj. **glos·sa·rist** /-rist/ n.

glos·so·la·li·a /,gläsə'lālēə; ,glô-/ ▶n. the speaking of unintelligible sounds, esp. in religious worship. [19th C.: from Gk. *glōssa* 'language, tongue' + *lalia* 'speech.']

gloss·y /'gläsē; 'glô-/ ▶adj. (**gloss·i·er, gloss·i·est**) shiny and smooth: *glossy hair.* ■ (of a magazine or photograph) printed on high-quality smooth shiny paper. ■ superficially attractive and stylish, and suggesting wealth or expense. ▶n. (pl. **gloss·ies**) informal a magazine printed on glossy paper, expensively produced with many color photographs. ■ a photograph printed on glossy paper. —**gloss·i·ly** /-səlē/ adv. **gloss·i·ness** n.

glot·tal /'glätl/ ▶adj. [attrib.] of or produced by the glottis.

glot·tal stop ▶n. a consonant formed by the audible release of the airstream after complete closure of the glottis.

glot·tis /'glätis/ ▶n. the part of the larynx consisting of the vocal cords and the slitlike opening between them. It affects voice modulation through expansion or contraction. —**glot·tic** /'glätik/ adj. [16th C.: mod. L., from Gk. *glōttis*, from *glōtta*, var. of *glōssa* 'tongue.']

glot·to·chro·nol·o·gy /,glätōkrə'näləjē/ ▶n. the use of statistical data to date the divergence of languages from their common sources. —**glot·to·chron·o·log·i·cal** /-,känə'läjikəl/ adj.

Glouces·ter /'glôstər; 'gläs-/ a city in southwestern England; pop. 93,000.

Glouces·ter·shire /'glôstərshər; 'gläs-; -,shi(ə)r/ a county in southwestern England; county town, Gloucester.

glove /gləv/ ▶n. a covering for the hand worn for protection against cold or dirt and typically having separate parts for each finger and the thumb. ■ a padded protective covering for the hand used in boxing, baseball, and other sports. ▶v. [trans.] informal (of a baseball catcher) catch, deflect, or touch (the ball) with one's glove.
– PHRASES **fit like a glove** (of clothes) fit exactly. —**gloved** adj. **glove·less** adj. [OE *glōf*, of Gmc. origin.]

glove box (also **glove·box**) ▶n. **1** another term for GLOVE COMPARTMENT. **2** a closed chamber into which a pair of gloves projects from openings in the side, used esp. in laboratories and incubators in hospitals to prevent contamination.

glove com·part·ment ▶n. a recess with a hinged door in the dashboard of a motor vehicle, used for storing small items.

glow /glō/ ▶v. [intrans.] give out steady light without flame: *their cigarettes glowed.* ■ have an intense color and a slight shine: [with complement] *faces that glowed red with the cold.* ■ have a heightened color as a result of warmth or health: *glowing with health.* ■ feel deep pleasure or satisfaction and convey it through one's expression and bearing. ▶n. [in sing.] a steady radiance of light or heat: *the sun cast a red glow.* ■ a feeling of warmth in the face or body; the visible effects of this as a redness of the cheeks. [OE *glōwan*, of Gmc. origin; rel. to Du. *gloeien* and Ger. *glühen*.]

glow·er /'glouər/ ▶v. [intrans.] have an angry or sullen look on one's face; scowl. ▶n. [in sing.] an angry or sullen look. —**glow·er·ing** adj. [15th C.: perh. a Scots var. of dial. *glore*, possibly of Scand. origin.]

glow·ing /'glōiNG/ ▶adj. [attrib.] expressing great praise: *a glowing report.*

glow·worm /'glō,wərm/ ▶n. a soft-bodied beetle (families Lampyridae and Phengodidae) with luminescent organs in the abdomen, esp. the larvalike wingless female, which emits light to attract the flying male.

glox·in·i·a /gläk'sinēə/ ▶n. a tropical American plant (genera *Gloxinia* and *Sinningia*, family Gesneriaceae) with large, velvety, bell-shaped flowers. [mod. L., named after Benjamin P. *Gloxin*, the 18th-cent. German botanist who first described it.]

glu·ca·gon /'glo͞okə,gän/ ▶n. Biochem. a hormone formed in the pancreas that promotes the breakdown of glycogen to glucose in the liver. [1920s: from Gk. *glukus* 'sweet' + *agōn* 'leading, bringing.']

Gluck /glo͞ok/, Christoph Willibald von (1714–87), German composer. His operas include *Orfeo ed Euridice* (1762).

glu·co·sa·mine /glo͞o'kōsə,mēn; -min/ ▶n. a natural component of human cartilage. ■ a synthesized form of this, taken as a dietary supplement to relieve arthritis pain.

glu·cose /'glo͞okōs/ ▶n. Biochem. a simple sugar, $C_6H_{12}O_6$, that is an important energy source in living organisms and is a component of many carbohydrates. ■ a syrup containing glucose and other sugars, used in the food industry. [19th C.: from Fr., from Gk. *gleukos* 'sweet wine,' rel. to *glukus* 'sweet.']

glu·co·side /'glo͞okə,sīd/ ▶n. Biochem. a glycoside derived from glucose. —**glu·co·sid·ic** /,glo͞okə'sidik/ adj.

glue /glo͞o/ ▶n. an adhesive substance used for sticking objects or materials together. ▶v. (**glues, glued, glu·ing** or **glue·ing**) [trans.] fasten or join with or as if with glue: *small pieces are glued together.* ■ (**be glued to**) informal be paying very close attention to (something, esp. a television or computer screen). —**glue·like** adj. [ME: from OFr. *glu* (n.), *gluer* (v.), from late L. *glus, glut-*, from L. *gluten*.]

glue sniff·ing ▶n. the practice of inhaling intoxicating fumes from the solvents in adhesives. —**glue sniff·er** n.

glug /gləg/ informal ▶v. (**glugged, glug·ging**) [trans.] drink or pour (liquid) with a gurgling sound: *he glugs down his beer.* ▶n. a hollow gurgling sound or series of sounds as of liquid being poured from a bottle. [17th C.: imitative.]

glum /gləm/ ▶adj. (**glum·mer, glum·mest**) looking or feeling dejected; morose. —**glum·ly** adv. **glum·ness** n. [16th C.: rel. to dial. *glum* 'to frown,' var. of GLOOM.]

glume /glo͞om/ ▶n. Bot. each of two bracts surrounding the spikelet of a grass (forming the husk of a cereal grain) or one surrounding the florets of a sedge. [18th C.: from L. *gluma* 'husk.']

glu·on /'glo͞oän/ ▶n. Physics a subatomic particle of a class that is thought to bind quarks together. [1970s: from GLUE + -ON.]

glut /glət/ ▶n. an excessively abundant supply of something: *a glut of cars on the market.* ▶v. (**glut·ted, glut·ting**) [trans.] (usu. **be glutted**) supply or fill to excess: *the factories for recycling paper are glutted.* [ME: prob. via OFr. from L. *gluttire* 'to swallow'; rel. to GLUTTON.]

glu·ta·mate /'glo͞otə,māt/ ▶n. Biochem. a salt or ester of glutamic acid. ■ glutamic acid, its salts, or its anion. ■ short for MONOSODIUM GLUTAMATE.

glu·tam·ic ac·id /glo͞o'tamik/ ▶n. Biochem. an acidic amino acid, $HOOC(CH_2)_2(NH_2)COOH$, that is a constituent of many proteins. [19th C.: from GLUTEN + AMINE + -IC.]

glu·ta·mine /'glo͞otə,mēn/ ▶n. Biochem. a hydrophilic amino acid,

$H_2NCOCH_2CH_2(NH_2)COOH$, that is a constituent of most proteins. [19th C.: blend of GLUTAMIC ACID and AMINE.]

glute /glo͞ot/ ▶ **n.** (usu. **glutes**) informal short for GLUTEUS.

glu·ten /ˈglo͞otn/ ▶ **n.** a substance present in cereal grains, esp. wheat, that is responsible for the elastic texture of dough. [16th C.: via Fr. from L., lit. 'glue.']

glu·te·us /ˈglo͞otēəs/ (also **gluteus muscle**) ▶ **n.** (pl. **-te·i** /-tē,ī/) any of three muscles in each buttock that move the thigh, the largest of which is the **gluteus maximus**. — **glu·te·al** /-tēəl/ **adj.** [17th C.: mod. L., from Gk. *gloutos* 'buttock.']

glu·ti·nous /ˈglo͞otn-əs/ ▶ **adj.** like glue in texture; sticky. [ME: from OFr. *glutineux* or L. *glutinosus*, from *gluten* 'glue.']

glut·ton /ˈglətn/ ▶ **n.** an excessively greedy eater. ■ a person who is excessively fond of or always eager for something: ***a glutton for adventure.***
– PHRASES **a glutton for punishment** a person who is always eager to undertake hard or unpleasant tasks. — **glut·ton·ize** /-,īz/ **v.** **glut·ton·ous** /-əs/ **adj.** **glut·ton·ous·ly** /-əslē/ **adv.** **glut·ton·y** **n.**

gly·ce·mic in·dex /glīˈsēmik/ ▶ **n.** a number representing the ability of a food, relative to that of glucose, to increase the level of glucose in the blood.

glyc·er·ide /ˈglisə,rīd/ ▶ **n.** a fatty acid ester of glycerol.

glyc·er·in /ˈglisərin/ (also **glyc·er·ine** /-rin; -,rēn; ,glisəˈrēn/) ▶ **n.** another term for GLYCEROL. [19th C.: from Fr. *glycerin*, from Gk. *glukeros* 'sweet.']

glyc·er·ol /ˈglisə,rôl; -,räl/ ▶ **n.** a colorless, sweet, viscous liquid, $CH_2(OH)CH(OH)CH_2(OH)$, formed as a by-product in soap manufacture. It is used as an emollient and laxative, and for making explosives and antifreeze. [19th C.: from GLYCERIN + -OL.]

glyc·er·yl /ˈglisə,ril/ ▶ **n.** [as adj.] Chem. of or denoting a radical derived from glycerol by replacement of one or more hydrogen atoms: *glyceryl trinitrate.* [19th C.: from GLYCERIN + -YL.]

gly·cine /ˈglīsēn/ ▶ **n.** Biochem. the simplest naturally occurring amino acid, H_2NCH_2COOH. It is a constituent of most proteins. [19th C.: from Gk. *glukus* 'sweet' + -INE[4].]

glyco- ▶ **comb. form** of, relating to, or producing sugar: *glycogenesis* | *glycoside.* [from Gk. *glukus* 'sweet.']

gly·co·gen /ˈglīkəjən/ ▶ **n.** Biochem. a substance deposited in bodily tissues as a store of carbohydrates; a polysaccharide that yields glucose on hydrolysis. — **gly·co·gen·ic** /,glīkəˈjenik/ **adj.**

gly·col /ˈglīkôl; -kōl/ ▶ **n.** short for ETHYLENE GLYCOL. ■ Chem. another term for DIOL. [19th C. (applied to ethylene glycol): from GLYCERIN + -OL (orig. intended to designate a substance intermediate between glycerine and alcohol).]

gly·col·ic ac·id /glīˈkälik/ ▶ **n.** a colorless, translucent, crystalline compound, $C_2H_4O_3$, that occurs in cane sugar, unripe grapes, and sugar beets and has numerous industrial uses.

gly·col·y·sis /glīˈkäləsis/ ▶ **n.** Biochem. the breakdown of glucose by enzymes, releasing energy and pyruvic acid. — **gly·co·lyt·ic** /,glīkəˈlitik/ **adj.**

gly·co·side /ˈglīkə,sīd/ ▶ **n.** Biochem. a compound formed from a simple sugar and another compound by replacement of a hydroxyl group in the sugar molecule. — **gly·co·sid·ic** /,glīkəˈsidik/ **adj.** [19th C.: from GLYCO-.]

gly·cos·u·ri·a /,glīkōsyo͝oˈrēə/ ▶ **n.** Med. a condition characterized by an excess of sugar in the urine, typically associated with diabetes or kidney disease. — **gly·cos·u·ric** /-ˈsyo͝orik/ **adj.**

glyph /glif/ ▶ **n. 1** a hieroglyphic character or symbol; a pictograph. ■ strictly, a sculptured symbol (e.g., as forming the ancient Mayan writing system). ■ Comput. a small graphic symbol. **2** Archit. an ornamental carved groove or channel, as on a Greek frieze. — **glyph·ic** /ˈglifik/ **adj.** [18th C. (sense 2): from Fr. *glyphe*, from Gk. *gluphē* 'carving.']

glyp·tic /ˈgliptik/ ▶ **adj.** of or concerning carving or engraving. ▶ **n.** (usu. **glyptics**) the art of carving or engraving, esp. on precious stones. [19th C.: from Fr. *glyptique* or Gk. *gluptikos*, from *gluptēs* 'carver,' from *gluphein* 'carve.']

glyp·to·dont /ˈgliptə,dänt/ ▶ **n.** a fossil South American edentate mammal (*Glyptodon* and other genera, family Glyptodontidae) of the Cenozoic era, related to armadillos but much larger. Glyptodonts had fluted teeth and a body covered in a thick bony carapace. [19th C.: from Gk. *gluptos* 'carved' (from *gluphein* 'carve') + *odous, odont-* 'tooth.']

GM ▶ **abbr.** ■ general manager.

gm ▶ **abbr.** gram(s).

G-man ▶ **n.** (pl. **G-men**) informal an FBI agent. [1930s: prob. an abbrev. of *Government man.*]

GMT ▶ **abbr.** Greenwich Mean Time.

GMW ▶ **abbr.** gram-molecular weight.

gnarl /närl/ ▶ **n.** a rough, knotty protuberance, esp. on a tree. [19th C.: back-form. from GNARLED.]

gnarled /närld/ ▶ **adj.** knobbly, rough, and twisted, esp. with age.

gnarl·y /ˈnärlē/ ▶ **adj.** (**gnarl·i·er**, **gnarl·i·est**) **1** gnarled. **2** informal difficult, dangerous, or challenging.

gnash /nash/ ▶ **v.** [trans.] grind (one's teeth) together, typically as a sign of anger. ■ [intrans.] (of teeth) strike together; grind. [ME: perh. rel. to ON *gnastan* 'a gnashing.']

gnat /nat/ ▶ **n.** a small two-winged fly (Simuliidae, Ceratopogonidae, and other families). Gnats include both biting and nonbiting forms, and they typically form large swarms. ■ a person or thing seen as tiny or insignificant, esp. in comparison with something larger or more important. [OE *gnætt*, of Gmc. origin; rel. to Ger. *Gnitze*.]

gnat·catch·er /ˈnat,kachər; -,kechər/ ▶ **n.** a tiny gray-backed New World songbird (genus *Polioptila*, family Polioptilidae), with a long tail that is often cocked.

gnaw /nô/ ▶ **v.** [intrans.] bite at or nibble something persistently. ■ [trans.] bite at or nibble (something). ■ fig. (of something painful to the mind or body) cause persistent and wearing distress or anxiety: ***the doubts continued to gnaw at me*** | [as adj.] (**gnawing**) ***that gnawing pain.*** [OE *gnagan*, of Gmc. origin; rel. to Ger. *nagen*, ult. imitative.]

gneiss /nīs/ ▶ **n.** a metamorphic rock with a banded or foliated structure, typically coarse-grained and consisting mainly of feldspar, quartz, and mica. — **gneiss·ic** **adj.** **gneiss·oid** **adj.** [18th C.: from German, from Old High Ger. *gneisto* 'spark.']

gnoc·chi /ˈnäkē/ ▶ **plural n.** (in Italian cooking) small dumplings made from potato, semolina, or flour, usually served with a sauce. [Ital., pl. of *gnocco*, alt. of *nocchio* 'knot in wood.']

gnome[1] /nōm/ ▶ **n.** a legendary dwarfish creature supposed to guard the earth's treasures underground. ■ informal a small ugly person. ■ informal a person regarded as having secret or sinister influence, esp. in financial matters: *the gnomes of Zurich.* — **gnom·ish** **adj.** [17th C.: from Fr., from mod. L. *gnomus*.]

gnome[2] ▶ **n.** a short statement encapsulating a general truth; a maxim. [16th C.: from Gk. *gnōmē* 'thought, opinion' (rel. to *gignōskein* 'know').]

gno·mic /ˈnōmik/ ▶ **adj.** expressed in or of the nature of aphorisms: *that most gnomic form, the aphorism.* ■ enigmatic; ambiguous. — **gno·mi·cal·ly** **adv.** [19th C.: from Gk. *gnōmikos*, from *gnōmē* 'thought, judgment,' (pl.) *gnōmai* 'sayings, maxims,' rel. to *gignōskein* 'know.']

gno·mon /ˈnōmän/ ▶ **n.** the projecting piece on a sundial that shows the time by the position of its shadow. [16th C.: via L. from Gk. *gnōmōn* 'indicator, carpenter's square' (rel. to *gignōskein* 'know').]

gno·sis /ˈnōsis/ ▶ **n.** knowledge of spiritual mysteries. [16th C.: from Gk. *gnōsis* 'knowledge' (rel. to *gignōskein* 'know').]

gnos·tic /ˈnästik/ ▶ **adj.** of or relating to knowledge, esp. esoteric mystical knowledge. ■ (**Gnostic**) of or relating to Gnosticism. ▶ **n.** (**Gnostic**) an adherent of Gnosticism. [16th C.: via eccles. L. from Gk. *gnōstikos*, from *gnōstos* 'known.']

Gnos·ti·cism /ˈnästə,sizəm/ ▶ **n.** a heretical movement of the 2nd-century Christian Church, teaching that esoteric knowledge (gnosis) of the supreme divine being enabled the redemption of the human spirit.

GNP ▶ **abbr.** gross national product.

gnu /n(y)o͞o/ ▶ **n.** a large dark antelope (genus *Connochaetes*) with a long head, a beard and mane, and a sloping back. Also called WILDEBEEST. [18th C.: from Khoikhoi and San, perh. imitative.]

go[1] /gō/ ▶ **v.** (**goes**, **go·ing**; past **went** /went/; past part. **gone** /gôn; gän/) **1** [no obj., usu. with adverbial of direction] move from one place or point to another; travel. ■ travel a specified distance or time. ■ travel or move in order to engage in a specified activity or course of action. ■ (**go to**) attend or visit for a particular purpose. ■ (**go to**) provide access to. ■ [in imper.] begin motion (used in a starter's order to begin a race). ■ (**go to**) (of a rank or honor) be allotted or awarded. ■ (**go into/to/towards**) (of a thing) contribute to or be put into (a whole); be used for or devoted to. ■ pass a specified amount of time in a particular way or under particular circumstances. ■ used to indicate how many people a supply of food, money, or another resource is sufficient for or how much can be achieved using it. ■ (of a thing) lie or extend in a certain direction. ■ change in level, amount, or rank in a specified direction. ■ informal used to emphasize the speaker's annoyance at a specified action or event: ***then he goes and spoils it all.*** ■ informal said in various expressions when angrily or contemptuously dismissing someone: ***go jump in the lake.*** **2** [intrans.] leave; depart. ■ (of time) pass or elapse. ■ come to an end; cease to exist. ■ leave or resign from a post. ■ be lost or stolen. ■ die (used euphemistically). ■ (of a thing) be sold. ■ (of money) be spent, esp. in a specified way. **3** (**be going to be/do something**) intend or be likely or intended to be or do something; be about to (used to express a future tense): ***I'm going to be late for work.*** **4** [no obj., with complement] pass into a specified state, esp. an undesirable one: ***the food is going bad.*** ■ (**go to/into**) enter into a specified state, institution, or course of action. ■ happen, proceed, or be for a time in a specified condition: *no one went hungry.* ■ make a sound of a specified kind. ■ (of a bell or similar device) make a sound in functioning: *I heard the buzzer go four times.* ■ [with direct speech] informal say: *the kids go, "Yeah, sure."* ■ (**go by/under**) be known or called by (a specified name). **5** [intrans.] proceed in a specified way or have a specified outcome; turn out. ■ be successful, esp. in being enjoyable or exciting. ■ be acceptable or permitted. ■ (of a song, account, or similar) have a specified content or wording. **6** [intrans.] be harmonious, complementary, or matching. ■ be found in the same place or situation; be associated: ***cooking and eating go together.*** **7** [intrans.] (of a machine or device) function. ■ continue in operation or existence. **8** [intrans.] (of an article) be regularly kept or put in a particular place. ■ fit or be able to be accommodated in a particular place or space. **9** [intrans.] informal use a toilet; urinate or defecate. ▶ **n.** (pl. **goes**) informal **1** an attempt or trial at something: ***give it a go.*** ■ esp.

Brit. a state of affairs: *this seems a rum sort of go.* ■ esp. Brit. an attack of illness: *a nasty go of dysentery.* ■ a project or undertaking that has been approved: *the project is a go.* ■ esp. Brit. used in reference to a single item, action, or spell of activity: *he knocked it back in one go.* **2** dated spirit, animation, or energy. ■ vigorous activity: *it's **all go** around here.* ▶ **adj.** [predic.] informal functioning properly: *all systems go.*

– PHRASES **as** (or **so**) **far as it goes** bearing in mind its limitations (said when qualifying praise of something). **as —— go** compared to the average or typical one of the specified kind: *as castles go, it is small and old.* **from the word go** informal from the very beginning. **go figure!** informal said to express the speaker's belief that something is amazing or incredible. **go great guns** see GUN. **go halves** share something equally. **going!, (going!,) gone!** an auctioneer's announcement that bidding is closing or closed. **going on ——** (Brit. also **going on for ——**) approaching a specified time, age, or amount: *I was going on fourteen.* **go (to) it** informal act in a vigorous, energetic, or dissipated way: *Go it, Dad! Give him what for!* **go it alone** see ALONE. **go to show** (or **prove**) (of an occurrence) serve as evidence or proof of something specified. **have a go at 1** make an attempt at; try. **2** esp. Brit. attack or criticize (someone): *she's always having a go at me.* **have —— going for one** informal used to indicate how much someone has in their favor or to their advantage. *She had so much going for her.* **make a go of** informal be successful in (something). **on the go** informal very active or busy. **to go** (of food or drink from a restaurant or cafe) to be eaten or drunk off the premises. **who goes there?** said by a sentry as a challenge.

– PHRASAL VERBS **go about 1** begin or carry on work at (an activity); busy oneself with. **2** Sailing change to the opposite tack. **go against** oppose or resist. ■ be contrary to (a feeling or principle). ■ (of a judgment, decision or result) be unfavorable for. **go ahead** proceed or be carried out without hesitation. **go along with** give one's consent or agreement to (a person, decision, or opinion). **go around 1** (esp. Brit. **go round**) spin: revolve. **2** (esp. Brit. **go round**) (esp. of food) be sufficient to supply everybody present. **3** (of an aircraft) abort an approach to landing and prepare to make a fresh approach. **go around with** be regularly in the company of. **go at** energetically attack or tackle. **go back** (of two people) have known each each for a specified, typically long, period of time: *Victor and I go back a long way.* **go back on** fail to keep (a promise). **go down 1** (of a ship or aircraft) sink or crash. ■ be defeated in a contest. **2** (of a person, period, or event) be recorded or remembered in a particular way. **3** be swallowed. **4** (of a person, action, or work) elicit a specified reaction. **5** informal happen. **go down on** vulgar slang perform oral sex on. **go for 1** decide on; choose. ■ tend to find (a person or a particular type of person) attractive. **2** attempt to gain or attain. ■ **(go for it)** strive to the utmost to gain or achieve something (frequently said as an exhortation). **3** launch oneself at (someone); attack. **4** end up having a specified value or effect. **5** apply to; have relevance for. **go in for** like or habitually take part in (something, esp. an activity). **go into 1** take up in study or as an occupation. **2** investigate or inquire into (something). **3** (of a whole number) be capable of dividing another, typically without a remainder. **go off** (of a gun, bomb, or similar device) explode or fire. ■ (of an alarm) begin to sound. **go on 1** [often with pres. part.] continue or persevere. ■ talk at great length, esp. tediously or angrily. ■ continue speaking or doing something after a short pause. ■ informal said when encouraging someone or expressing disbelief. **2** happen; take place. **3** [often with infin.] proceed to do. **go out 1** (of a fire or light) be extinguished. ■ cease operating or functioning. **2** (of the tide) ebb; recede to low tide. **3** leave one's home to go to an entertainment or social event, typically in the evening. ■ carry on a regular romantic, and sometimes sexual, relationship. **4** used to convey someone's deep sympathy or similar feeling: *the boy's heart went out to the pitiful figure.* **5** Golf play the first nine holes in a round of eighteen holes. **6** (in some card games) be the first to dispose of all the cards in one's hand. **go over 1** examine, consider, or check the details of (something). **2** change one's allegiance or religion: *he went over to the Democratic Party.* **3** (esp. of an action or performance) be received in a specified way. **go through 1** undergo (a difficult or painful period or experience). **2** search through or examine carefully or in sequence. **3** (of a proposal or contract) be officially approved or completed. **4** informal use up or spend (available money or other resources). **5** (of a book) be successively published in (a specified number of editions). **go through with** perform (an action or process) to completion despite difficulty or unwillingness. **go under** (of a business) become bankrupt. ■ (of a person) die or suffer an emotional collapse. **go up 1** (of a building or other structure) be built. **2** explode or suddenly burst into flames. **3** Brit., informal begin one's studies at a university, esp. Oxford or Cambridge. **go with 1** give one's consent or agreement to (a person or their views). **2** have a romantic or sexual relationship with (someone). **go without** suffer lack or deprivation. [OE *gān*, of Gmc. origin; rel. to Du. *gaan* and Ger. *gehen*; the form *went* was orig. the past tense of WEND.]

go² ▶ **n.** a Japanese board game of territorial possession and capture. [19th C.: Japanese, lit. 'small stone,' also the name of the game.]

Go·a /'gōə/ a state on the western coast of India; capital, Panaji. Formerly a Portuguese territory, it was seized by India in 1961 and made a state in 1987. — **Go·an adj. & n. Go·a·nese** /gōə'nēz; -'nēs/ **adj. & n.**

goad /gōd/ ▶ **n.** a spiked stick used for driving cattle. ■ a thing that stimulates someone into action. ▶ **v.** [trans.] provoke or annoy (someone) so as to stimulate some action or reaction. ■ [with obj. and adverbial of direction] drive or urge (an animal) on with a goad. [OE *gād*, of Gmc. origin.]

go-a·head informal ▶ **n.** (usu. **the go-ahead**) permission to proceed. ▶ **adj. 1** enthusiastic about new projects; enterprising. **2** [attrib.] denoting the run, score, etc., that gives a team the lead in a game.

goal /gōl/ ▶ **n. 1** (in football, soccer, rugby, hockey, and some other games) a pair of posts linked by a crossbar and often with a net attached behind it, forming a space into or over which the ball or puck has to be sent in order to score. ■ an instance of sending the ball or puck into or over this space, esp. as a unit of scoring in a game. ■ a cage or basket used similarly in other sports. **2** the object of a person's ambition or effort; an aim or desired result. ■ the destination of a journey. ■ literary a point marking the end of a race.

– PHRASES **in goal** in the position of goalkeeper. — **goal·less adj.** [ME: of unknown origin.]

goal·ie /'gōlē/ ▶ **n.** informal term for GOALKEEPER or GOALTENDER.

goal·keep·er /'gōl,kēpər/ ▶ **n.** chiefly Brit. another term for GOALTENDER — **goal·keep·ing** /-,kēpiNG/ **n.**

goal kick ▶ **n.** Soccer a free kick taken by the defending side from within their goal area after attackers send the ball over the end line outside the goal.

goal line ▶ **n.** Sports a line between each pair of goals or goalposts, extended across the playing field to form the end boundary of the field of play. ■ Football either of two lines, one at each end of the football field, across which the ball must be carried or caught for a touchdown.

goal·mouth /'gōl,mouTH/ ▶ **n.** the area just in front of a goal in soccer, lacrosse, or hockey.

goal·post /'gōl,pōst/ ▶ **n.** either of the two upright posts of a goal.

– PHRASES **move the goalposts** unfairly alter the conditions or rules of a procedure during its course.

goal·tend·er /'gōl,tendər/ ▶ **n.** a player in soccer or hockey whose special role is to stop the ball from entering the goal.

goal·tend·ing /'gōl,tendiNG/ ▶ **n. 1** Basketball a violation in which a defensive player interferes with a shot when it is on its downward arc or is on, within, or over the rim. **2** the activity of playing the position of goaltender.

go·an·na /gō'anə/ ▶ **n.** Australian term for MONITOR (sense 4). [19th C.: alt. of IGUANA.]

go-a·round (also **go-round**) ▶ **n. 1** a flight path typically taken by an aircraft after an aborted approach to landing. **2** informal a confrontation; an argument: *they had one go-around after another.*

goat /gōt/ ▶ **n. 1** a hardy domesticated ruminant (*Capra hircus*) of the cattle family that has backward curving horns and (in the male) a beard. Kept for its milk and meat, it is noted for its frisky behavior. ■ a wild mammal related to this, such as the ibex. ■ **(the Goat)** the zodiacal sign Capricorn or the constellation Capricornus. **2** a person likened to a goat, in particular: ■ a lecherous man. ■ a scapegoat.

– PHRASES **get someone's goat** informal irritate someone: *I've tried to get along with her, but sometimes she really gets my goat.* — **goat·ish adj. goat·y adj.** [OE *gāt* 'nanny goat,' of Gmc. origin; rel. to Du. *geit*.]

goat·an·te·lope ▶ **n.** a ruminant of the cattle family that belongs to a group (subfamily Caprinae) that combines the characteristics of both goats and antelopes.

goat·ee /gō'tē/ (also **goatee beard**) ▶ **n.** a small, sometimes pointed, beard. ■ a small, trimmed beard covering the chin. — **goat·eed adj.** [19th C.: so named because of its resemblance to the tuft on a goat's chin.]

goatee

goat·fish /'gōt,fisH/ ▶ **n.** (pl. same or **-fish·es**) an elongated fish (family Mullidae) with long barbels on the chin, living in warmer seas and widely valued as a food fish.

goat·herd /'gōt,hərd/ ▶ **n.** a person who tends goats. [OE, from GOAT + obs. *herd* 'herdsman.']

goat's-beard (also **goats·beard**) ▶ **n. 1** a plant (*Tragopogon pratensis*) of the daisy family, with slender grasslike leaves, yellow flowers, and downy fruits that resemble those of a dandelion. **2** a plant (*Aruncus vulgaris*) of the rose family, with long plumes of white flowers.

goat·skin /'gōt,skin/ ▶ **n.** the skin of a goat. ■ such a skin, or leather made from it, as a material. ■ a garment or object made out of goatskin.

goat's-rue ▶ **n.** a herbaceous plant of the pea family, which was formerly used in medicine, esp. the North American *Tephrosia virginiana*, which has pink and yellow flowers and smells of goats.

goat·suck·er /'gōt,səkər/ ▶ **n.** another term for NIGHTJAR.

gob¹ /gäb/ informal ▶ **n. 1** a lump or clot of a slimy or viscous substance: *a gob of phlegm.* ■ a small lump. **2** (**gobs of**) a lot of. [ME: from OFr. *gobe* 'mouthful, lump,' from *gober* 'to swallow, gulp,' perh. of Celtic origin.]

gob² ▶ **n.** informal, dated an American sailor. [20th C.: of unknown origin.]

gob³ ▶ **n.** informal, esp. Brit. a person's mouth: *shut your big gob.* [16th C.: perh. from Scot. Gael. *gob* 'beak, mouth.']

gob·bet /'gäbit/ ▶ **n.** a piece or lump of flesh, food, or other matter. [ME: from OFr. *gobet*, dimin. of *gobe* (see GOB¹).]

gob·ble¹ /'gäbəl/ ▶ **v.** eat (something) hurriedly and noisily. ■ use a large amount of (something) very quickly. ■ (of a large organization or other body) incorporate or take over (a smaller one). [17th C.: prob. from GOB².]

gob·ble² ▶ **v.** [intrans.] (of a male turkey) make a characteristic swallowing sound in the throat. ■ (of a person) make such a sound when speaking, esp. when excited or angry. ▶ **n.** the gurgling sound made by a male turkey. [17th C.: imitative.]

gob·ble·dy·gook /ˈgäbəldē,go͝ok; -,go͞ok/ (also **gob·ble·de·gook**) ▸ **n.** informal language that is meaningless or is made unintelligible by excessive use of abstruse technical terms; nonsense. [1940s (orig. US): prob. imitating a turkey's gobble.]

gob·bler[1] /ˈgäb(ə)lər/ ▸ **n.** a person who eats greedily and noisily.

gob·bler[2] ▸ **n.** informal a turkey cock.

Gob·e·lin /ˈgōbəlin; ˈgä-/ (also **Gobelin tapestry**) ▸ **n.** a tapestry made at the Gobelins factory in Paris, or in imitation of one.

Gob·e·lins /ˈgōbəlinz; ˈgä-/ a tapestry and textile factory in Paris, established by the Gobelin family *c.*1440.

go-be·tween ▸ **n.** an intermediary or negotiator.

Go·bi Des·ert /ˈgōbē/ a barren plateau in southern Mongolia and northern China.

Go·bin·eau /ˈgäbə,nō/, Joseph Arthur, Comte de (1816–82), French anthropologist. He viewed races as innately unequal and the white race as superior.

gob·let /ˈgäblit/ ▸ **n.** a drinking glass with a foot and a stem. ■ archaic a metal or glass bowl-shaped drinking cup, sometimes with a foot and a cover. [ME: from OFr. *gobelet*, dimin. of *gobel* 'cup,' of unknown origin.]

gob·let cell ▸ **n.** Anat. a column-shaped cell found in the respiratory and intestinal tracts, which secretes the main component of mucus.

gob·lin /ˈgäblin/ ▸ **n.** a mischievous, ugly, dwarflike creature of folklore. [ME: from OFr. *gobelin*, possibly rel. to Ger. *Kobold* (see KOBOLD).]

go·bo /ˈgōbō/ ▸ **n.** (pl. **-bos**) a dark plate or screen used to shield a lens from light. ■ Theater a partial screen used in front of a spotlight to project a shape. ■ a shield used to mask a microphone from extraneous noise. [1930s: of unknown origin, perh. from *go between.*]

go·by /ˈgōbē/ ▸ **n.** (pl. **-bies**) a small, usually marine fish (family Gobiidae) that typically has a suction disk on the underside. [18th C.: from L. *gobius*, from Gk. *kōbios*, a small fish.]

go-by ▸ **n.** (in phrase **give someone the go-by**) informal, dated avoid or snub someone. ■ end a romantic relationship with someone.

go-cart ▸ **n.** **1** var. of GO-KART. **2** a handcart. ■ a stroller. ■ archaic a baby walker.

God /gäd/ ▸ **n.** **1** [without article] (in Christianity and other monotheistic religions) the creator and ruler of the universe and source of all moral authority; the Supreme Being. **2** (**god**) (in certain other religions) a superhuman being or spirit worshiped as having power over nature or human fortunes; a deity. ■ an image, idol, animal, or other object worshiped as divine or symbolizing a god. ■ used as a conventional personification of fate. **3** (**god**) an adored, admired, or influential person. ■ a thing accorded the supreme importance appropriate to a god. **4** (**the gods**) informal the gallery in a theater. ■ the people sitting in this area. ▸ **exclam.** used to express a range of emotions such as surprise, anger, and distress: *my God! Why didn't you tell us?* ■ used to give emphasis to a statement or declaration.
– PHRASES **for God's sake!** see SAKE[1] (sense 3). **God bless** an expression of good wishes on parting or sneezing. **God damn** (**you, him,** etc) may (you, he, etc.) be damned. **God the Father** (in Christian doctrine) the first person of the Trinity, God as creator and supreme authority. **God forbid** see FORBID. **God grant** used to express a wish that something should happen. **God help** (**you, him,** etc.) used to express the belief that someone is in a difficult, dangerous, or hopeless situation. **God the Son** (in Christian doctrine) Christ regarded as the second person of the Trinity; God as incarnate and resurrected savior. **God willing** used to express the wish that one will be able to do as one intends or that something will happen as planned. **in God's name** used in questions to emphasize anger or surprise. **play God** behave as if all-powerful or supremely important. **please God** used to emphasize a strong wish or hope. **thank God** see THANK. **to God** used after a verb to emphasize a strong wish or hope: *I hope to God you've got something else.* **with God** dead and in heaven. — **god·hood** **n.** **god·ship** **n.** **god·ward** /-wərd/ **adj.** **& adv.** **god·wards** /-wərdz/ **adv.** [OE, of Gmc. origin; rel. to Du. *god* and Ger. *Gott.*]

God Al·might·y (also **God·al·might·y**) ▸ **exclam.** used to express esp. surprise, anger, or exasperation.

Go·dard /gōˈdär(d)/, Jean-Luc (1930–), French movie director. A leading figure of the *nouvelle vague*, his movies include *Breathless* (1960).

Go·da·va·ri /gəˈdävərē/ a river in India that flows southeast for 900 miles (1,440 km) from the state of Maharashtra to the Bay of Bengal.

god·aw·ful /ˈgädˈôfəl/ (also **god-aw·ful** or **God-aw·ful**) ▸ **adj.** informal extremely unpleasant:.

god·child /ˈgäd,CHīld/ ▸ **n.** (pl. **-child·ren** /-,CHildrən/) a person in relation to a godparent.

god·damn /ˈgädˈdam/ (also **god·dam** or **god·damned**) ▸ **adj., adv., & n.** informal used for emphasis, esp. to express anger or frustration. [17th C.: abbrev. of *God damn (me).*]

God·dard /ˈgädərd/, Robert Hutchings (1882–1945), US physicist. He designed and built the first successful liquid-fueled rocket.

god·daugh·ter /ˈgäd,dôtər/ ▸ **n.** a female godchild.

god·dess /ˈgädis/ ▸ **n.** a female deity. ■ a woman who is adored, esp. for her beauty.

Gö·del /ˈgōdl/, Kurt (1906–78), US mathematician and logician; born in Austria. Among his important contributions to mathematical logic is Gödel's incompleteness theorem.

go·det /gōˈdet/ ▸ **n.** a triangular piece of material inserted in a dress, shirt, or glove to make it flared or for ornamentation. [19th C.: from Fr.]

go-dev·il ▸ **n.** esp. hist. a gadget used in farming, logging, or drilling for oil, in particular: ■ a crude sled, used chiefly for dragging logs. ■ a jointed apparatus for cleaning pipelines.

god·fa·ther /ˈgäd,fäTHər/ ▸ **n.** **1** a male godparent. **2** a man who is influential in a movement or organization, through providing support for it or through playing a leading or innovative part in it. ■ a person directing an illegal organization, esp. a leader of a Mafia family.

God-fear·ing ▸ **adj.** earnestly religious.

god·for·sak·en /ˈgädfər,sākən/ ▸ **adj.** lacking any merit or attraction; dismal.

God-giv·en ▸ **adj.** received from God. ■ possessed without question, as if by divine authority.

God·havn /ˈgôTH,houn/ a town in western Greenland, on the south coast of the island of Disko.

god·head /ˈgäd,hed/ ▸ **n.** (usu. **the Godhead**) God. ■ divine nature. ■ informal an adored, admired, or influential person; an idol.

Go·di·va /gəˈdīvə/, Lady (died 1080), English noblewoman, wife of Leofric, Earl of Mercia. According to legend, her husband agreed to reduce unpopular taxes if she rode naked on horseback through Coventry's marketplace, which she did.

god·less /ˈgädlis/ ▸ **adj.** not recognizing or obeying God. ■ without a god. ■ profane; wicked. — **god·less·ness** **n.**

god·like /ˈgäd,līk/ ▸ **adj.** resembling God or a god in qualities such as power, beauty, or benevolence. ■ befitting or appropriate to a god.

god·ly /ˈgädlē/ ▸ **adj.** (**-li·er, -li·est**) devoutly religious; pious. — **god·li·ness** **n.**

god·moth·er /ˈgäd,məTHər/ ▸ **n.** a female godparent. ■ a woman who is influential in a movement or organization, through providing support for it or through playing a leading or innovative part in it.

go·down /ˈgōdoun; gōˈdoun/ ▸ **n.** (in eastern Asia, esp. India) a warehouse. [16th C.: from Port. *guda-o*, from Tamil *kiṭaṅku*, Malayalam *kiṭaṅṅu*, or Kannada *gadaṅgu* 'store, warehouse.']

god·par·ent /ˈgäd,pe(ə)rənt; -,par-/ ▸ **n.** a person who presents a child at baptism and responds on the child's behalf, promising to take responsibility for the child's religious education.

God's a·cre ▸ **n.** archaic a churchyard. [17th C.: from Ger. *Gottesacker*, Du. *Godsakker.*]

God Save the Queen (or **King**) ▸ **n.** the British national anthem.

God's coun·try (also **God's own country**) ▸ **n.** [in sing.] an area or region, esp. a peaceful, rural one, supposedly favored by God.

god·send /ˈgäd,send/ ▸ **n.** a very helpful or valuable event, person, or thing. [19th C.: from *God's send* 'what God has sent.']

God's gift ▸ **n.** the ideal or best possible person or thing for someone or something (used chiefly ironically or negatively): *he thought he was God's gift to women.*

god·son /ˈgäd,sən/ ▸ **n.** a male godchild.

God·speed /ˈgädˈspēd/ ▸ **exclam.** dated an expression of good wishes to a person starting a journey. [ME: from *God speed you* 'may God help you prosper.']

God Squad ▸ **n.** informal used to refer to evangelical Christians, typically suggesting intrusive moralizing and proselytizing.

God's truth ▸ **n.** the absolute truth.

Godt·håb /ˈgôt,hôp/ former name (until 1979) of NUUK.

Go·du·nov /ˈgädn,ôf/, Boris (1550–1605), czar of Russia 1598–1605.

God·win /ˈgädwin/, William (1756–1836), English philosopher and writer; the father of Mary Wollstonecraft Shelley.

God·win-Aus·ten, Mount /ˈgädwən ˈôstən/ former name for K2.

god·wit /ˈgädwit/ ▸ **n.** a large, long-legged wader (genus *Limosa*) of the sandpiper family, with a long, slightly upturned or straight bill, and typically a reddish-brown head and breast in the breeding male. [16th C.: of unknown origin.]

Goeb·bels /ˈgəbəlz/ (also **Göb·bels**), (Paul) Joseph (1897–1945), German Nazi administrator. From 1933, he was Adolf Hitler's minister of propaganda.

go·er /ˈgōər/ ▸ **n.** **1** a person or thing that goes. **2** [in comb.] a person who attends a specified place or event, esp. regularly. **3** [with adj.] informal a person or thing that goes in a specified way. ■ a project likely to be accepted or to succeed.

Goe·ring /ˈgəriNG/, Hermann Wilhelm (1893–1946), German Nazi administrator. He was responsible for the German rearmament program, founder of the Gestapo, and director of the German economy.

goes /gōz/ third person singular present of GO[1].

go·est /ˈgō-ist/ archaic second person singular present of GO[1].

go·eth /ˈgō-iTH/ archaic third person singular present of GO[1].

Goe·thals /ˈgōTHəlz/, George Washington (1858–1928), US engineer. As chief engineer and chairman of the Panama Canal Commission 1907, he oversaw construction of the canal.

Goe·the /ˈgə(r)tə; ˈgœtə/, Johann Wolfgang von (1749–1832), German playwright and poet. His plays include *Faust* (1808–32).

goe·thite /ˈgōTHīt/ ▸ **n.** a dark reddish-brown or yellowish-brown

PRONUNCIATION KEY ə *ago, up*; ər *over, fur*; a *hat*; ā *ate*; ä *car*; e *let*; ē *see*; i *fit*; ī *by*; NG *sing*; ō *go*; ô *law, for*; oi *toy*; o͝o *good*; o͞o *goo*; ou *out*; TH *thin*; T͟H *then*; ZH *vision*

mineral consisting of oxyhydroxide iron, occurring typically as masses of fibrous crystals. [19th C.: from the name of J.W. von GOETHE + -ITE[1].]

go·fer /ˈgōfər/ (also **go·pher**) ▸ n. informal a person who runs errands, esp. on a movie set or in an office. [1960s: from *go for* (i.e., go and fetch).]

gof·fer /ˈgäfər/ (also **gauf·fer** /ˈgôfər; ˈgä-/) ▸ v. [trans.] [usu. as adj.] (**goffered**) treat (a lace edge or frill) with heated irons in order to crimp or flute it: *a goffered frill.* ■ [as adj.] (**goffered**) (of the gilt edges of a book) embossed with a repeating design. ▸ n. an iron used to crimp or flute lace. [16th C.: from Fr. *gaufrer* 'stamp with a patterned tool,' from *gaufre* 'honeycomb,' from Mid. Low Ger. *wâfel* (see WAFFLE[2]).]

Gog and Ma·gog /gôg and məˈgäg/ 1 in the Bible, the names of enemies of God's people. In Ezek. 38–9, Gog is apparently a ruler from the land of Magog, while in Rev. 20:8, Gog and Magog are nations under the dominion of Satan. 2 (in medieval legend) opponents of Alexander the Great, living north of the Caucasus.

go-get·ter ▸ n. informal an aggressively enterprising person. — **go-get·ting** adj.

gog·gle /ˈgägəl/ ▸ v. [intrans.] look with wide open eyes, typically in amazement or wonder. ■ (of the eyes) protrude or open wide. ▸ adj. [attrib.] (of the eyes) protuberant or rolling. ▸ n. 1 (**goggles**) close-fitting eyeglasses with side shields, for protection from glare, dust, water, etc. ■ informal eyeglasses. 2 [in sing.] a stare with protruding eyes. — **gog·gled** adj. [ME: prob. symbolic.]

gog·gle-eye ▸ n. any of a number of large-eyed edible fishes that occur widely on reefs in tropical and subtropical seas.

gog·gle-eyed ▸ adj. having staring or protuberant eyes, esp. through astonishment.

go-go ▸ adj. [attrib.] 1 relating to or denoting an unrestrained and erotic style of dancing to popular music. 2 assertively dynamic. [1960s: reduplication of GO[1].]

Go·gol /ˈgōgəl/, Nikolai Vasilevich (1809–52), Russian writer; born in Ukraine. His novels are satirical and often explore themes of fantasy and the supernatural.

Goi·â·nia /goiˈanēə/ a city in southern central Brazil, capital of the state of Goiás; pop. 998,000.

Goi·del·ic /goiˈdelik/ ▸ adj. of, relating to, or denoting the northern group of Celtic languages, including Irish, Scottish Gaelic, and Manx. Compare with BRYTHONIC. Also called Q-CELTIC. ▸ n. these languages collectively.

go·ing /ˈgō-iNG/ ▸ n. 1 an act or instance of leaving a place; a departure. 2 [in sing.] the condition of the ground viewed in terms of suitability for walking, riding, or other travel (used esp. in the context of horse racing). ■ progress affected by such a condition. ■ conditions for, or progress in, an endeavor. ▸ adj. [attrib.] (esp. of a price) generally accepted as fair or correct; current: *willing to work for the going rate.*

go·ing a·way ▸ adj. [attrib.] marking or celebrating a departure: *a going-away party.* ▸ adv. informal with victory assured before the end of a contest: *Jordan rested as Chicago won going away.*

go·ing-o·ver ▸ n. [in sing.] informal a thorough treatment, esp. in cleaning or inspection: *give the place a going-over with the vacuum cleaner.* ■ a beating.

go·ings-on ▸ plural n. events or behavior, esp. of an unusual or suspect nature.

goi·ter /ˈgoitər/ (Brit. **goi·tre**) ▸ n. a swelling of the neck resulting from enlargement of the thyroid gland. — **goi·tered** adj. **goi·trous** /ˈgoitrəs/ adj. [17th C.: from Fr. *goitre*, based on L. *guttur* 'throat.']

go-kart (also **go-cart**) ▸ n. a small racecar with a lightweight or skeleton body. — **go-kart·ing** n. [1950s: *kart*, alt. of CART.]

Go·lan Heights /ˈgōlän; -lən/ a region between Syria and Israel, northeast of the Sea of Galilee. Formerly under Syrian control, the area was occupied by Israel in 1967 and annexed in 1981.

Gol·con·da /gälˈkändə/ ▸ n. a source of wealth, advantages, or happiness. [19th C.: from the name of a city near Hyderabad, India, famous for its diamonds.]

gold /gōld/ ▸ n. 1 a yellow precious metal, the chemical element of atomic number 79, valued esp. for use in jewelry and decoration, and to guarantee the value of currencies. Used in electrical contacts and as a filling for teeth. (Symbol: **Au**) ■ [with adj.] an alloy of this: *9-carat gold.* 2 a deep lustrous yellow or yellow-brown color. 3 coins or articles made of gold. ■ money in large sums; wealth. ■ a thing that is precious, beautiful, or brilliant. ■ short for GOLD MEDAL.
– PHRASES **go gold** (of a recording) achieve sales (over 1 million copies) meriting a gold disk award. **pot** (or **crock**) **of gold** a large but distant or imaginary reward. [with allusion to the story of a crock of gold supposedly to be found by anyone reaching the end of a rainbow.] [OE, of Gmc. origin; rel. to Ger. *Gold*, from an Indo-Eur. root shared by YELLOW.]

gold·beat·er /ˈgōld,bētər/ ▸ n. a person who beats gold out into gold leaf.

gold bee·tle (also **gold·bug**) ▸ n. a leaf beetle (esp. *Metriona bicolor*) with metallic gold coloration.

Gold·berg[1] /ˈgōld,bərg/, Arthur Joseph (1908–90), US Supreme Court associate justice 1962–65.

Gold·berg[2], Rube (1883–1970), US cartoonist; full name *Reuben Lucius Goldberg.* He is noted for his designs of ridiculously complex devices.

gold brick informal ▸ n. a thing that looks valuable, but is in fact worthless. ■ (also **gold·brick** or **gold·brick·er**) a con man. ■ a lazy person. ▸ v. (usu. **goldbrick**) [intrans.] invent excuses to avoid a task; shirk.

gold·bug /ˈgōld,bəg/ (also **gold bug**) ▸ n. 1 informal an advocate of a single gold standard for currency. ■ a person favoring gold as an investment. 2 another term for GOLD BEETLE.

Gold Coast former name (until 1957) of GHANA. ■ (also **gold coast**) informal a coastal or urban area noted for luxurious living and expensive homes.

gold dig·ger ▸ n. informal a person who dates others purely to extract money from them, in particular a woman who strives to marry a wealthy man.

gold dust ▸ n. 1 fine particles of gold. 2 another term for BASKET-OF-GOLD.

gold·en /ˈgōldən/ ▸ adj. 1 colored or shining like gold. 2 made or consisting of gold. 3 rare and precious, in particular: ■ (of a period) very happy and prosperous. ■ (of an opportunity) very favorable. ■ (of a person) popular, talented, and successful. 4 (of a voice) rich and smooth. 5 denoting the fiftieth year of something. — **gold·en·ly** adv.

gold·en age ▸ n. an idyllic, often imaginary past time of peace, prosperity, and happiness. ■ the period when a specified art, skill, or activity is at its peak.

gold·en ag·er ▸ n. used euphemistically or humorously to refer to an old person.

gold·en calf ▸ n. (in the Bible) an image of gold in the shape of a calf, made by Aaron in response to the Israelites' plea for a god while they awaited Moses' return from Mount Sinai, where he was receiving the Ten Commandments (Exod. 32). ■ a false god, esp. wealth as an object of worship.

Gold·en De·li·cious ▸ n. a widely grown dessert apple of a greenish-yellow, soft-fleshed variety.

gold·en ea·gle ▸ n. a large Eurasian and North American eagle (*Aquila chrysaetos*) with yellow-tipped head feathers in the mature adult.

gold·en·eye /ˈgōldən,ī/ ▸ n. (pl. same or **-eyes**) a migratory northern diving duck (genus *Bucephala*), the male of which has a dark head with a white cheek patch and yellow eyes.

Gold·en Fleece Gk. Mythol. the fleece of a golden ram that was sought and won by Jason with the help of Medea. ■ a goal that is highly desirable but difficult to achieve.

Gold·en Gate a deep channel that connects San Francisco Bay with the Pacific Ocean; spanned by the Golden Gate suspension bridge, which was completed in 1937.

gold·en glow ▸ n. a yellow-petaled coneflower with a greenish disk.

gold·en goose ▸ n. a continuing source of wealth or profit that may be exhausted if it is misused. See also *KILL THE GOOSE THAT LAYS THE GOLDEN EGG* at EGG[1].

gold·en ham·ster ▸ n. see HAMSTER.

gold·en hand·cuffs ▸ plural n. informal used to refer to benefits, typically deferred payments, provided by an employer to discourage an employee from taking employment elsewhere.

gold·en hand·shake ▸ n. informal a payment given to someone who is laid off or retires early.

Gold·en Horde the Tartar and Mongol army, led by descendants of Genghis Khan, that overran Asia and parts of eastern Europe in the 13th century and maintained an empire until around 1500 (so called from the richness of the leader's camp).

Gold·en Horn a curved inlet of the Bosporus that forms the harbor of Istanbul. Turkish name HALIÇ.

gold·en hour ▸ n. Med. the first hour after the occurrence of a traumatic injury, considered the most critical for successful emergency treatment.

gold·en ju·bi·lee ▸ n. the fiftieth anniversary of a significant event.

gold·en mean ▸ n. [in sing.] 1 the ideal moderate position between two extremes. 2 another term for GOLDEN SECTION.

gold·en old·ie ▸ n. informal an old song or movie that is still well known and popular.

gold·en par·a·chute ▸ n. informal a large payment or other financial compensation guaranteed to an executive dismissed as a result of a merger or takeover.

gold·en plov·er ▸ n. a northern Eurasian and North American plover (genus *Pluvialis*), with a gold-speckled back and black face and underparts in the breeding season.

golden retriever

gold·en re·triev·er ▸ n. a retriever of a breed with a thick golden-colored coat.

gold·en·rod /ˈgōldən,räd/ ▸ n. a plant (genus *Solidago*) of the daisy family that bears tall spikes of small bright yellow flowers.

gold·en rule ▸ n. a basic principle that should be followed to ensure success in general or in a particular activity. ■ (often **Golden Rule**) the biblical rule "do unto others as you would have them do unto you" (Matt. 7:12).

gold·en·seal /'gōldən,sēl/ ▶ **n.** a North American woodland plant (*Hydrastis canadensis*) of the buttercup family, with a bright yellow root that is used in herbal medicine.

gold·en sec·tion ▶ **n.** the division of a line so that the whole is to the greater part as that part is to the smaller part (i.e., in a ratio of 1 to ½ (√5 + 1)), a proportion that is considered to be particularly pleasing to the eye.

gold·en wed·ding (also **golden wedding anniversary**) ▶ **n.** the fiftieth anniversary of a wedding.

gold·field /'gōld,fēld/ ▶ **n.** a district in which gold is found as a mineral.

gold-filled ▶ **adj.** (esp. of jewelry) consisting of a base metal covered in a thin layer of gold.

gold·finch /'gōld,finCH/ ▶ **n.** a brightly colored finch (genus *Carduelis*) with yellow feathers in the plumage. [OE *goldfinc* (see GOLD, FINCH).]

gold·fish /'gōld,fiSH/ ▶ **n.** (pl. same or **-fish·es**) a small reddish-golden Eurasian carp (*Carassius auratus*), popular in ponds and aquariums.

gold·fish bowl ▶ **n.** a spherical glass container for goldfish. ■ fig. a place or situation lacking privacy. *a goldfish bowl of publicity.*

gold·i·locks /'gōldē,läks/ ▶ **n.** informal a person with golden hair.

Gold·ing /'gōldiNG/, Sir William Gerald (1911–93), English writer. His novels include *Lord of the Flies* (1954). Nobel Prize for Literature (1983).

gold leaf ▶ **n.** gold that has been beaten into a very thin sheet, used in gilding.

Gold·man /'gōldmən/, Emma (1869–1940), US political activist; born in Lithuania. She was involved in the anarchist movement and opposed US conscription.

gold med·al ▶ **n.** a medal made of or colored gold, as awarded for first place in a race or competition. — **gold med·al·ist n.**

gold mine ▶ **n.** a place where gold is mined. ■ fig. a source of wealth, valuable information, or resources: *this book is a gold mine of information.* — **gold min·er n.**

gold plate ▶ **n.** a thin layer of gold, electroplated or otherwise applied as a coating to another metal. ■ objects coated with gold. ■ plates, dishes, etc., made of gold. ▶ **v.** (**gold-plate**) [trans.] cover (something) with a thin layer of gold.

gold-plat·ed ▶ **adj.** covered with a thin layer of gold. ■ fig. likely to prove profitable; secure.

gold re·serve ▶ **n.** a quantity of gold held by a central bank to support the issue of currency.

gold rush ▶ **n.** a rapid movement of people to a newly discovered goldfield. The first major gold rush, to California in 1848–49, was followed by others in the US, Australia (1851–53), South Africa (1884), and Canada (Klondike, 1897–98).

Golds·bor·o /'gōldz,bərō/ a city in eastern North Carolina; pop. 39,043.

Gold·smith /'gōld,smiTH/, Oliver (1728–74), Irish writer. His works include *The Vicar of Wakefield* (1766) and *She Stoops to Conquer* (1773).

gold·smith /'gōld,smiTH/ ▶ **n.** a person who makes gold articles.

gold stand·ard ▶ **n.** hist. the system by which the value of a currency was defined in terms of gold, for which it could be exchanged. The gold standard was generally abandoned in the 1930s Depression. ■ fig. the best, most reliable, or most prestigious thing of its type.

gold·stone /'gōld,stōn/ ▶ **n.** a variety of aventurine containing sparkling gold-colored particles.

gold·thread /'gōld,THred/ ▶ **n.** a plant (genus *Coptis*) of the buttercup family that yields a yellow dye and is used in herbal medicine as a treatment for mouth ulcers.

Gold·wa·ter /'gōld,wôtər; -,wä-/, Barry Morris (1909–98) US politician. A member of the US Senate from Arizona 1953–65, 1969–87, he was the Republican presidential candidate in 1964.

Gold·wyn /'gōldwin/, Samuel (1882–1974), US producer; born in Poland; born *Schmuel Gelbfisz*, changed to *Samuel Goldfish*. With Louis B. Mayer, he founded MGM in 1924.

go·lem /'gōləm/ ▶ **n.** (in Jewish legend) a clay figure brought to life by magic. ■ an automaton or robot. [19th C.: from Yiddish *goylem*, from Heb. *gōlem* 'shapeless mass.']

golf /gälf; gôlf/ ▶ **n.** **1** a game played on a large open-air course, in which a small hard ball is struck with a club into a series of small holes in the ground, the object being to use the fewest possible strokes. **2** a radio code word representing the letter G. ▶ **v.** [intrans.] play golf. — **golf·er n.** [ME: perh. rel. to Du. *kolf* 'club, bat.']

golf club ▶ **n.** **1** a club used to hit the ball in golf, with a heavy wooden or metal head on a slender shaft. **2** an organization of members for playing golf. ■ the premises used by such an organization.

golf links ▶ **plural n.** see LINKS.

Gol·gi /'gôljē/, Camillo (1844–1926), Italian histologist and anatomist. He classified types of nerve cells, and described the structure in the cytoplasm of most cells. Nobel Prize for Physiology or Medicine (1906, shared with Ramón y Cajal).

Gol·gi ap·pa·rat·us (also **Golgi body**) ▶ **n.** Biol. a complex of vesicles and folded membranes within the cytoplasm of most eukaryotic cells, involved in secretion and intracellular transport.

Gol·go·tha /'gälgəTHə; gôl'gäTHə/ the site of the crucifixion of Jesus; Calvary.

Go·li·ath /gə'līəTH/ (in the Bible) a Philistine giant, according to legend slain by David, but according to another tradition slain by Elhanan.

go·li·ath bee·tle ▶ **n.** a very large, boldly marked tropical beetle (genus *Goliathus*) related to the chafers, the male of which has a forked horn on the head.

gol·li·wog /'gälē,wäg/ (also **gol·li·wogg**) ▶ **n.** **1** a soft doll with bright clothes, a black face, and fuzzy hair. **2** derog. a grotesque person. [19th C.: from *Golliwogg*, a character in books by Bertha Upton (died 1912), American writer, and Florence K. Upton (died 1922), Amer. illustrator.]

gol·ly /'gälē/ (also **by golly**) ▶ **exclam.** informal, dated used to express surprise or delight: *"Golly! Is that the time?"* [18th C.: euphemism for GOD.]

Go·mel /gô'm(y)el/ Russian name for HOMEL.

Go·mor·rah /gə'môrə/ see SODOM.

Gom·pers /'gämpərz/, Samuel (1850–1924) US labor leader; born in England. He was president of the American Federation of Labor 1886–1924.

-gon ▶ **comb. form** in nouns denoting plane figures with a specified number of angles: *hexagon* | *pentagon.* [from Gk. *-gōnos* '-angled.']

go·nad /'gōnad/ ▶ **n.** Physiol. Zool. an organ that produces gametes; a testis or ovary. — **go·nad·al** /gō'nadl/ **adj.** [19th C.: from mod. L. *gonades*, pl. of *gonas*, from Gk. *gonē* 'generation, seed.']

go·nad·o·trop·ic hor·mone /gō,nadə'träpik; -'trōpik/ (esp. Brit. also **gonadotrophic hormone** /-'träfik; -'trōfik/) ▶ **n.** another term for GONADOTROPIN.

go·nad·o·tro·pin /gō,nadə'trōpin/ (esp. Brit. also **go·nad·o·tro·phin** /-'trōfin/) ▶ **n.** Biochem. any of a group of hormones secreted by the pituitary that stimulate the activity of the gonads.

Gon·court /gôn'ko͝or/, Edmond de (1822–96) and Jules de (1830–70), French writers and critics. The brothers collaborated on works such as *Madame Gervaisais* (1869).

Gond /gänd/ (also **Gon·di** /'gändē/) ▶ **n.** (pl. same) **1** a member of an indigenous people living in the hill forests of central India. **2** the Dravidian language of this people. ▶ **adj.** of or relating to the Gonds or their language. [from Sanskrit *goṇḍa.*]

Gon·dar /'gändər/ (also **Gonder**) a city in northwestern Ethiopia, in Amhara province; pop. 112,000.

gondola

gon·do·la /'gändələ; gän'dōlə/ ▶ **n.** a light flat-bottomed boat used on Venetian canals, having a high point at each end and worked by one oar at the stern. ■ a cabin on a suspended ski lift. ■ (also **gondola car**) an open railroad freight car. ■ an enclosed compartment suspended from an airship or balloon. [16th C.: from Venetian Ital., from Rhaeto-Romanic *gondolà* 'to rock, roll.']

gon·do·lier /,gändl'i(ə)r/ ▶ **n.** a person who propels and steers a gondola.

Gond·wa·na /gän'dwänə/ (also **Gond·wa·na·land**) a landmass believed to have existed in the southern hemisphere in Mesozoic times, comprising the present Africa, South America, Antarctica, Australia, and peninsular India.

gone /gôn; gän/ past participle of GO¹. ▶ **adj.** [predic.] **1** no longer present; departed. ■ no longer in existence; dead or extinct. ■ no longer available. ■ informal in a trance or stupor, esp. through exhaustion, drink, or drugs. ■ [attrib.] lost; hopeless. **2** informal having reached a specified time in a pregnancy: *she is now four months gone.*

– PHRASES **be gone on** informal be infatuated with.

gon·er /'gônər/ ▶ **n.** informal a person or thing that is doomed or cannot be saved.

gon·fa·lon /'gänfələn/ ▶ **n.** a banner or pennant, esp. one with streamers, hung from a crossbar. ■ hist. such a banner as the standard of some Italian republics. [16th C.: from Ital. *gonfalone*, from a Gmc. compound whose second element is rel. to VANE.]

gon·fa·lon·ier /,gänfələ'ni(ə)r/ ▶ **n.** the bearer of a gonfalon, a standard-bearer.

gong /gäNG; gôNG/ ▶ **n.** a metal disk with a turned rim, giving a resonant note when struck: *a dinner gong.* ▶ **v.** [intrans.] sound a gong or make a sound like that of a gong being struck. [17th C.: from Malay *gong, gung*, of imitative origin.]

gon·if /'gänəf/ (also **gon·iff, gan·ef**) ▶ **n.** informal a disreputable or dishonest person. [19th C.: from Yiddish *ganev*, from Heb. *gannāḇ* 'thief.']

go·ni·om·e·ter /,gōnē'ämitər/ ▶ **n.** an instrument for the precise measurement of angles, esp. one used to measure the angles between the faces of crystals. — **go·ni·o·met·ric** /-nēə'metrik/ **adj.** **go·ni·om·e·try** /-trē/ **n.** [18th C.: from Fr. *goniomètre*, from Gk. *gōnia* 'angle.']

gon·na /ˈgônə; ˈgənə/ informal ▶ **contr.** going to: *we're gonna win this game.*

gon·o·coc·cus /ˌgänəˈkäkəs/ ▶ **n.** (pl. **-coc·ci** /-ˈkäksī/) a bacterium (*Neisseria gonorrhoeae*) that causes gonorrhea. — **gon·o·coc·cal** /-ˈkäkəl/ **adj.** [19th C.: from *gono-* (as in GONORRHEA) + COCCUS.]

go-no-go /ˈgō ˈnō ˌgō/ ▶ **adj. 1** designating a situation in which one must decide whether or not to continue with a particular course of action, or the moment when such a decision must be made. **2** designating the decision to continue with or abandon a course of action.

gon·or·rhe·a /ˌgänəˈrēə/ (Brit. **gon·or·rhoe·a**) ▶ **n.** a venereal disease involving inflammatory discharge from the urethra or vagina. — **gon·or·rhe·al adj.** [16th C.: via late L. from Gk. *gonorrhoia*, from *gonos* 'semen' + *rhoia* 'flux.']

Gon·za·les /gənˈzäləs/, Alberto R. (1955–), US attorney general 2005– .

gon·zo /ˈgänzō/ ▶ **adj.** informal of or associated with journalistic writing of an exaggerated, subjective, and fictionalized style. ■ bizarre or crazy. [1970s: perh. from Ital. *gonzo* 'foolish' or Sp. *ganso* 'goose, fool.']

goo /go͞o/ ▶ **n.** informal **1** a sticky or slimy substance. **2** sickly sentiment. [20th C. (orig. US): perh. from *burgoo*, a nautical slang term for porridge, based on Pers. *bulgūr* 'bruised grain.']

goo·ber /ˈgo͞obər/ informal **1** (also **goo·ber pea**) a peanut. **2** often offens. a person from the southeastern United States, esp. Georgia or Arkansas. ■ offens. an unsophisticated person; a yokel. [19th C.: perh. of Bantu origin; compare Kimbundu *nguba* 'peanut.']

good /go͝od/ ▶ **adj.** (**bet·ter, best**) **1** to be desired or approved of. ■ pleasing and welcome. ■ expressing approval. **2** having the qualities required for a particular role. ■ functioning or performed well. ■ appropriate to a particular purpose. ■ (of language) with correct grammar and pronunciation. ■ strictly adhering to or fulfilling all the principles of a particular cause, religion, or party. ■ (of a ticket) valid. **3** possessing or displaying moral virtue. ■ showing kindness. ■ obedient to rules or conventions. ■ used to address or refer to people, esp. in a patronizing or humorous way: *the good people of the city were disconcerted.* ■ commanding respect. ■ belonging or relating to a high social class. **4** giving pleasure; enjoyable or satisfying. ■ pleasant to look at; attractive. ■ (of food and drink) having a pleasant taste. ■ (of clothes) smart and suitable for formal wear. **5** [attrib.] thorough. ■ used to emphasize that a number is at least as great as one claims: *they're a good twenty years younger.* ■ used to emphasize a following adjective: *we had a good long hug.* ■ fairly large. **6** used in conjunction with the name of God or a related expression as an exclamation of extreme surprise or anger: *good heavens!* ▶ **n. 1** that which is morally right; righteousness. **2** benefit or advantage to someone or something. **3** (**goods**) merchandise or possessions. ■ Brit. things to be transported, as distinct from passengers. ■ (**the goods**) informal the genuine article. ▶ **adv.** informal well: *my mother could never cook this good.*
– PHRASES **all to the good** to be welcomed without qualification: **as good as —** very nearly —: *she's as good as here.* ■ used of a result which will inevitably follow. **be any** (or **no** or **much**) **good** have some (or none or much) merit. ■ be of some (or none or much) help in dealing with a situation. **be so good as** (or **be good enough**) **to do something** used to make a polite request. **be — to the good** have a specified net profit or advantage. **come up with** (or **deliver**) **the goods** informal do what is expected or required of one. **do good 1** act virtuously, esp. by helping others. **2** make a helpful contribution to a situation. **do someone good** be beneficial to someone, esp. to their health. **for good** (**and all**) forever; definitively. **get** (or **have**) **the goods on** informal obtain (or possess) information about (someone) that may be used to their detriment. **good and —** informal used as an intensifier before an adjective or adverb: *it'll be good and dark by then.* (**as**) **good as gold** (esp. of a child) extremely well behaved. (**as**) **good as new** in a very good condition or state, close to the original state again after damage, injury, or illness. **the Good Book** the Bible. **good for 1** having a beneficial effect on. **2** reliably providing. ■ sufficient to pay for. **good for you** (or **him, her**, etc.)! used as an exclamation of approval toward a person, esp. for something that they have achieved. **the Good Shepherd** a name for Jesus. **a good word** words in recommendation or defense of a person: *I hoped you might put in a good word for me.* **have a good mind to do something** see MIND. **in someone's good books** see BOOK. **in good time 1** with no risk of being late. **2** (also **all in good time**) in due course but without haste. **make good** be successful. **make something good 1** compensate for loss, damage, or expense. ■ repair or restore after damage. **2** fulfill a promise or claim. **put a good face on something** see FACE. **take something in good part** not be offended by something. **up to no good** doing something wrong. [OE *gōd*, of Gmc. origin; rel. to Du. *goed* and Ger. *gut*.]

good af·ter·noon ▶ **exclam.** expressing good wishes on meeting or parting in the afternoon.

Good·all /ˈgo͝odôl/, Jane (1934–), English zoologist. After working with Louis Leakey in Tanzania from 1957, she made prolonged studies of chimpanzees.

good·bye /ˌgo͝odˈbī/ (also **good-bye** or **good·by** or **good-by**) ▶ **exclam.** used to express good wishes when parting or at the end of a conversation. ▶ **n.** (pl. **-byes** or **-bys**) an instance of saying "goodbye"; a parting: *a final goodbye.* [16th C.: contr. of *God be with you!*]

good eve·ning ▶ **exclam.** expressing good wishes on meeting or parting during the evening.

good faith ▶ **n.** honesty or sincerity of intention.

good·fel·la /ˈgo͝odˌfelə/ ▶ **n.** informal a gangster, esp. a member of a Mafia family.

good form ▶ **n.** what complies with current social conventions.

good-for-noth·ing ▶ **adj.** (of a person) worthless. ▶ **n.** a worthless person.

Good Fri·day ▶ **n.** the Friday before Easter Sunday, on which the Crucifixion of Christ is commemorated in the Christian Church. It is traditionally a day of fasting and penance. [from GOOD, in the sense 'holy.']

good-heart·ed ▶ **adj.** kind and well meaning. — **good-heart·ed·ly adv. good-heart·ed·ness n.**

Good Hope, Cape of see CAPE OF GOOD HOPE.

good hu·mor ▶ **n.** a genial disposition or mood.

good-hu·mored ▶ **adj.** genial; cheerful. — **good-hu·mored·ly adv.**

good·ie ▶ **n.** var. of GOODY[1].

good-look·ing ▶ **adj.** (chiefly of a person) attractive. — **good-look·er n.**

good·ly /ˈgo͝odlē/ ▶ **adj.** (**-li·er, -li·est**) **1** considerable in size or quantity: *we ran up a goodly bar bill.* **2** archaic attractive, excellent, or admirable. — **good·li·ness n.**

Good·man /ˈgo͝odmən/, Benny (1909–86), US clarinetist and bandleader; full name *Benjamin David Goodman*; known as **the King of Swing**.

good·man /ˈgo͝odmən/ ▶ **n.** (pl. **-men**) archaic the male head of a household.

good morn·ing ▶ **exclam.** expressing good wishes on meeting or parting during the morning.

good na·ture ▶ **n.** a kind and unselfish disposition. — **good-na·tured adj. good-na·tured·ly adv.**

good·ness /ˈgo͝odnis/ ▶ **n.** the quality of being good, in particular: ■ virtue; moral excellence. ■ kindness; generosity. ■ the beneficial or nourishing element of food. ▶ **exclam.** (as a substitution for "God") expressing surprise, anger, etc.: *goodness knows!*
– PHRASES **for goodness' sake** see SAKE[1]. **goodness of fit** Stat. the extent to which observed data match the values predicted by theory. **have the goodness to do something** used in exaggeratedly polite requests.

good night (also **good-night** or **good-night**) ▶ **exclam.** expressing good wishes on parting at night or before going to bed.

good old boy ▶ **n.** a man who embodies some or all of the qualities considered characteristic of white men of the southern US, including an unpretentious, convivial manner, conservative or intolerant attitudes, and a strong sense of fellowship with and loyalty to other members of his peer group.

goods and chat·tels ▶ **plural n.** esp. Law all kinds of personal possessions.

good-sized ▶ **adj.** of ample size; fairly large.

good-tem·pered ▶ **adj.** not easily irritated or made angry. — **good-tem·pered·ly adv.**

good-time ▶ **adj.** [attrib.] (of a person) recklessly pursuing pleasure.

good·wife /ˈgo͝odˌwīf/ ▶ **n.** (pl. **-wives**) archaic the female head of a household.

good·will /ˈgo͝odˈwil/ (also **good will**) ▶ **n. 1** friendly, helpful, or cooperative feelings or attitude. **2** the established reputation of a business regarded as a quantifiable asset, e.g., as represented by the excess of the price paid at a takeover for a company over its fair market value.

good works ▶ **plural n.** charitable acts.

good·y[1] /ˈgo͝odē/ ▶ **n.** (also **good·ie**) (pl. **good·ies**) informal (usu. **goodies**) something attractive or desirable, esp. something tasty or pleasant to eat. ▶ **exclam.** expressing childish delight.

good·y[2] ▶ **n.** (pl. **good·ies**) archaic (often as a title prefixed to a surname) an elderly woman of humble station. [16th C.: pet form of GOODWIFE.]

Good·year /ˈgo͝odˌyi(ə)r/, Charles (1800–60), US inventor. He developed the process of the vulcanization of rubber.

good·y-good·y informal ▶ **n.** a smug or obtrusively virtuous person. ▶ **adj.** smug or obtrusively virtuous.

good·y two-shoes ▶ **n.** a smugly or obtrusively virtuous person; a goody-goody.

goo·ey /ˈgo͞oē/ ▶ **adj.** (**goo·i·er, goo·i·est**) informal soft and sticky. ■ mawkishly sentimental. — **goo·ey·ness n.**

goof /go͞of/ informal ▶ **n. 1** a mistake. **2** a foolish or stupid person. ▶ **v.** [intrans.] **1** spend time idly or foolishly; fool around. ■ (**goof off**) evade a duty; idle or shirk. ■ (**goof on**) make fun of; ridicule. **2** make a mistake; blunder: *you're scared you'll goof up.* [20th C.: of unknown origin.]

goof·ball /ˈgo͞ofˌbôl/ ▶ **n.** informal **1** a naive, silly, or stupid person. **2** a narcotic drug in pill form, esp. a barbiturate. ▶ **adj.** informal foolish; silly.

goof-off ▶ **n.** informal a person who is habitually lazy or does less than a fair share of work.

goof·proof /ˈgo͞ofˌpro͞of/ ▶ **adj.** (of a product, procedure, etc.) designed to be simple enough for anyone to use or implement. ▶ **v.** [trans.] design or adapt (a product, procedure, etc.) so that it is simple for anyone to use.

goof-up ▶ **n.** informal a stupid mistake.

goof·us /ˈgo͞ofəs/ ▶ **n.** informal a foolish or stupid person (often used as a general term of abuse). [1920s: based on GOOF.]

goof·y /ˈgo͞ofē/ ▶ **adj.** (**goof·i·er, goof·i·est**) informal **1** foolish; harmlessly eccentric. **2** (in surfing and other board sports) with the right leg in front of the left on the board. — **goof·i·ly** /-fəlē/ **adv. goof·i·ness n.**

goo·gle /ˈgo͞ogəl/ (also **Goo·gle**) ▶ **v.** informal [intrans.] use an Internet search engine, particularly Google.com: *she spent the afternoon googling aim-*

lessly. ■ [trans.] search for the name of (someone) on the Internet to find out information about them. [from *Google*, a trademark for a popular Internet search engine.]

goo·gol /'go͞ogôl/ ▶ **cardinal number** equivalent to ten raised to the power of a hundred (10^{100}). [1940s: said to have been coined by the nine-year-old nephew of E. Kasner (1878–1955), American mathematician, at Kasner's request.]

goo·gol·plex /'go͞ogôl,pleks/ ▶ **cardinal number** equivalent to ten raised to the power of a googol. [1940s: from GOOGOL + *-plex* as in *multiplex*.]

goo-goo informal ▶ **adj. 1** amorously adoring. **2** (of speech or vocal sounds) childish or meaningless. [20th C.: possibly rel. to GOGGLE.]

gook[1] /go͝ok; go͞ok/ ▶ **n.** offens. a foreigner, esp. a person of Philippine, Korean, or Vietnamese descent. [1930s: of unknown origin.]

gook[2] ▶ **n.** informal a sloppy wet or viscous substance. [1970s: var. of GUCK.]

Goo·la·gong /'go͞olə,gäNG/, Evonne, see CAWLEY.

goom·bah /'go͞ombä; go͞om'bä/ ▶ **n.** informal an associate or accomplice, esp. a senior member of a criminal gang. [1960s: prob. a dial. alt. of Ital. *compàre* 'godfather, friend, accomplice.']

goon /go͞on/ ▶ **n.** informal **1** a silly, foolish, or eccentric person. **2** a bully or thug, esp. one hired to terrorize or do away with opposition. [19th C.: perh. from dial. *gooney* 'booby.']

goon·ey bird /'go͞onē/ (also **goon·y bird**) ▶ **n. 1** another term for an albatross (genus *Diomedea*) of the North Pacific. **2** informal a foolish or inept person; a goon. [19th C.: of unknown origin.]

goop /go͞op/ ▶ **n.** informal sloppy or sticky semifluid matter, typically something unpleasant. ■ mawkish sentiment. —**goop·i·ness** /-pēnis/ **n.** **goop·y adj.**

goose /go͞os/ ▶ **n.** (pl. **geese**) **1** a large waterbird (esp. the genera *Anser* and *Branta*), with a long neck, short legs, webbed feet, and a short broad bill. Generally geese are larger than ducks and have longer necks and shorter bills. ■ the female of such a bird. ■ the flesh of a goose as food. **2** informal a foolish person. ▶ **v.** [trans.] informal **1** poke (someone) between the buttocks. **2** give (something) a boost; invigorate; increase: *goosing up ticket sales.*
– PHRASES **cook someone's goose** see COOK. [OE *gōs*, of Gmc. origin.]

goose bar·na·cle (also **goose·neck bar·na·cle**) ▶ **n.** a stalked barnacle (genus *Lepas*) that hangs down from driftwood or other slow-moving floating objects, catching passing prey with its feathery legs.

goose·ber·ry /'go͞os,berē; -bərē/ ▶ **n.** (pl. **-ries**) **1** a round edible yellowish-green or reddish berry with a thin translucent hairy skin. **2** the thorny shrub (*Ribes grossularia*, family Grossulariaceae) that bears this fruit. [16th C.: perh. from GOOSE.]

goose·bumps /'go͞os,bəmps/ ▶ **plural n.** another term for GOOSE PIMPLES.

goose egg informal ▶ **n. 1** zero, esp. a zero score in a game. **2** a lump, typically on the head, from a blow.

goose·fish /'go͞os,fisH/ ▶ **n.** (pl. same or **-fish·es**) a bottom-dwelling anglerfish (family Lophiidae). Also called MONKFISH.

goose·flesh /'go͞os,flesH/ ▶ **n.** a pimply state of the skin with the hairs erect, produced by cold or fright.

goose·foot /'go͞os,fo͝ot/ ▶ **n.** (pl. **-foots**) a plant (genus *Chenopodium*, family Chenopodiaceae) of temperate regions with divided leaves that are said to resemble the foot of a goose. Some kinds are edible and many are common weeds.

goose·grass /'go͞os,gras/ ▶ **n.** another term for CLEAVERS.

goose·neck /'go͞os,nek/ ▶ **n.** a support or pipe curved like a goose's neck: [as adj.] *a gooseneck lamp.* ■ Sailing a metal fitting at the end of a boom, connecting it to a pivot or ring near the base of the mast.

goose pim·ples ▶ **plural n.** the pimples that form gooseflesh.

goose step ▶ **n.** a military marching step in which the legs are not bent at the knee. ▶ **v.** (**goose-step**) [no obj., with adverbial] march with such a step.

goose·y /'go͞osē/ (also **goos·y**) ▶ **adj.** (**goos·i·er, goos·i·est**) having or showing a quality considered to be characteristic of a goose, esp. foolishness or nervousness. ■ informal exhibiting gooseflesh: *I've gone all goosey.*

GOP ▶ **abbr.** Grand Old Party (the Republican Party).

go·pher[1] /'gōfər/ ▶ **n. 1** (also **pocket gopher**) a burrowing rodent (family Geomyidae) with fur-lined pouches on the outside of the cheeks, found in North and Central America. ■ informal another term for GROUND SQUIRREL. **2** (also **gopher tortoise**) a tortoise (*Gopherus polyphemus*, family Testudinidae) of dry sandy regions that excavates tunnels as shelter from the sun, native to the southern US. [18th C.: perh. from Canad. Fr. *gaufre* 'honeycomb.']

go·pher[2] ▶ **n.** var. of GOFER.

go·pher ball ▶ **n.** Baseball a pitch that is hit for a home run.

go·pher snake ▶ **n.** a large harmless yellowish-cream bull snake (*Pituophis catenifer*) with dark markings, native to western North America. ■ (also **blue gopher snake**) another term for INDIGO SNAKE.

go·pher wood ▶ **n.** (in biblical use) the timber from which Noah's ark was made, from an unidentified tree (Gen. 6:14). [17th C.: *gopher* from Heb. *gōper*.]

go·pik /'gōpik/ ▶ **n.** (pl. same or **-piks**) a monetary unit of Azerbaijan, equal to one hundredth of a manat.

Go·rakh·pur /'gôrək,po͝or/ a city in northeastern India, in Uttar Pradesh; pop. 490,000.

go·ral /'gôrəl/ ▶ **n.** a long-haired goat-antelope (genus *Nemorhaedus*) with backward curving horns, found in mountainous regions of eastern Asia. [19th C.: a local word in the Himalayas.]

Gor·ba·chev /'gôrbə,cHôf/, Mikhail Sergeyevich (1931–), president of the Soviet Union 1988–91. His foreign policy helped bring about an end to the Cold War.

Gor·di·an knot /'gôrdēən/ ▶ **n.** an extremely difficult or involved problem.
– PHRASES **cut the Gordian knot** solve or remove a problem in a direct or forceful way, rejecting gentler or more indirect methods. [16th C.: from the legend that *Gordius*, king of Gordium, tied an intricate knot and prophesied that whoever untied it would become the ruler of Asia. It was cut through with a sword by Alexander the Great.]

gor·di·an worm ▶ **n.** another term for HORSEHAIR WORM.

Gor·di·mer /'gôrdəmər/, Nadine (1923–), South African writer. Her novels include *Burger's Daughter* (1979) and *Get a Life* (2005). Nobel Prize for Literature (1991).

Gor·don /'gôrdn/, Charles George (1833–85), British colonial administrator. He crushed the Taiping Rebellion (1863–64) in China.

Gor·don set·ter ▶ **n.** a setter of a black-and-tan breed, used as a gun dog. [19th C.: named after the 4th Duke of *Gordon* (1743–1827), who promoted the breed.]

Gore /gôr/ Albert Arnold, Jr. (1948–) vice president of the US 1993–2001. The Democratic nominee in the 2000 presidential election, he bowed to George W. Bush in one of the closest and most controversial elections in US history.

gore[1] /gôr/ ▶ **n.** blood that has been shed, esp. as a result of violence. [OE *gor* 'dung, dirt,' of Gmc. origin; rel. to Swed. *gorr* 'muck, filth.']

gore[2] ▶ **v.** [trans.] (of an animal such as a bull) pierce or stab with a horn or tusk. [ME (in the sense 'stab, pierce'): of unknown origin.]

gore[3] ▶ **n.** a triangular or tapering piece of material used in making a garment, sail, or umbrella. ■ a small, triangular piece of land, esp. one lying in the fork of a road. ▶ **v.** [trans.] make with a gore-shaped piece of material. [OE *gāra* 'triangular piece of land,' of Gmc. origin; rel. to Ger. *Gehre*.]

Gore-Tex /'gôr ,teks/ ▶ **n.** trademark a synthetic waterproof fabric permeable to air and water vapor, used in outdoor and sports clothing.

gorge /gôrj/ ▶ **n. 1** a narrow valley between hills or mountains, typically with steep rocky walls and a stream running through it. **2** archaic the throat. ■ the contents of the stomach. **3** Archit. the neck of a bastion or other outwork; the rear entrance to a fortification. **4** a mass of ice obstructing a narrow passage, esp. a river. ▶ **v.** eat a large amount greedily; fill oneself with food: *we used to go to all the little restaurants and gorge ourselves.*
– PHRASES **one's gorge rises** one is sickened or disgusted: *looking at it, Wendy felt her gorge rise.* —**gorg·er n.** [ME: from OFr. *gorge* 'throat,' based on L. *gurges* 'whirlpool.']

gor·geous /'gôrjəs/ ▶ **adj.** beautiful; very attractive. ■ informal very pleasant. —**gor·geous·ly adv. gor·geous·ness n.** [15th C.: from OFr. *gorgias* 'fine, elegant,' of unknown origin.]

gor·get /'gôrjit/ ▶ **n. 1** hist. an article of clothing that covered the throat. ■ a piece of armor for the throat. ■ a wimple. **2** a patch of color on the throat of a bird or other animal, esp. a hummingbird. [ME: from OFr. *gorgete*, from *gorge* 'throat' (see GORGE).]

Gor·gon /'gôrgən/ (also **gor·gon**) ▶ **n.** Gk. Mythol. each of three sisters, Stheno, Euryale, and Medusa, with snakes for hair, who had the power to turn anyone who looked at them to stone. ■ a fierce, frightening, or repulsive woman. [via L. from Gk. *Gorgō*, from *gorgos* 'terrible.']

gor·go·ni·an /gôr'gōnēən/ Zool. ▶ **n.** a colonial coral of an order (Gorgonacea) distinguished by a horny, treelike skeleton, including the sea fans and precious red coral. ▶ **adj.** of or relating to Gorgons or gorgonians. [19th C.: from mod. L. *Gorgonia*, from L. *Gorgo* (see GORGON).]

Gor·gon·zo·la /,gôrgən'zōlə/ ▶ **n.** a type of rich, strong-flavored Italian cheese with bluish-green veins. [named after *Gorgonzola*, a village in northern Italy, where it was orig. made.]

go·ril·la /gə'rilə/ ▶ **n.** a powerfully built great ape (*Gorilla gorilla*) with a large head and short neck, found in the forests of central Africa. It is the largest living primate. ■ informal a heavily built, aggressive-looking man. [19th C.: from Gk., representing an alleged African word for a wild or hairy person.]

Gor·ky[1] /'gôrkē/ former name (1932–91) for NIZHNI NOVGOROD.

Gor·ky[2], Arshile (1904–48), US painter; born in Turkey. He was an exponent of abstract expressionism.

Gor·ky[3], Maxim (1868–1936), Russian writer and revolutionary; pen name of *Aleksei Maksimovich Peshkov*. After the Russian Revolution, he was proclaimed the founder of the new, officially sanctioned socialist realism.

Gor·no-Al·tai /'gôrnə äl'tī/ an autonomous republic in south central Russia; pop. 192,000; capital, Gorno-Altaisk.

gorp /gôrp/ ▶ **n.** informal another term for TRAIL MIX.

gorse /gôrs/ ▶ **n.** a yellow-flowered shrub (genus *Ulex*) of the pea family, the leaves of which are modified to form spines, native to western Europe and North Africa. —**gors·y adj.** [OE *gors, gorst*, akin to Ger. *Gerste* and L. *hordeum* 'barley.']

gor·y /'gôrē/ ▶ **adj.** (**gor·i·er, gor·i·est**) involving or showing violence and bloodshed: *a gory horror film.* ■ covered in blood.

– PHRASES **the gory details** humorous the explicit details of something: *she told him the gory details of her past.* — **gor·i·ly** adv. **gor·i·ness** n.

gosh /gäsн/ ▶ exclam. informal used to express surprise or give emphasis: *gosh, we envy you.* ■ used as a euphemism for "God": *a gosh-awful team.*

gos·hawk /ˈgäs,hôk/ ▶ n. a large, short-winged hawk (genus *Accipiter*) resembling a large sparrow hawk. [OE *gōshafoc*, from *gōs* 'goose' + *hafoc* 'hawk.']

gos·ling /ˈgäzlinG/ ▶ n. a young goose. [ME (orig. *gesling*): from ON *gǽslingr*, from *gás* 'goose' + -LING.]

go-slow ▶ adj. (of a proposal or course of action) cautious and prudent. ▶ n. esp. Brit. a strategy or tactic, esp. a form of protest, in which work or progress is delayed or slowed down.

gos·pel /ˈgäspəl/ ▶ n. **1** the teaching or revelation of Christ. ■ (also **gospel truth**) a thing that is absolutely true. ■ a set of principles or beliefs. **2** (**Gospel**) the record of Jesus' life and teaching in the first four books of the New Testament. ■ each of these books. ■ a portion from one of these read at a church service. **3** (also **gospel music**) a fervent style of black American evangelical singing, developed from spirituals sung in Southern Baptist and Pentecostal churches. [OE *gōdspel*, from *gōd* 'good' + *spel* 'news, a story' (see SPELL[2]).]

gos·pel·er /ˈgäspələr/ (Brit. **gos·peller**) ▶ n. a person who zealously teaches or professes faith in the gospel. ■ (in church use) the reader of the Gospel in a Communion service.

gos·pel·ize /ˈgäspə,līz/ ▶ v. **1** [trans.] rare preach the Gospel to; convert to Christianity. **2** convert (a piece) to the style of gospel music.

Gos·pel side ▶ n. (in a church) the north side of the altar, at which the Gospel is read.

gos·sa·mer /ˈgäsəmər/ ▶ n. a fine, filmy substance consisting of cobwebs spun by small spiders, which is seen esp. in autumn. ■ used to refer to something very light, thin, and insubstantial or delicate. ▶ adj. [attrib.] made of or resembling gossamer. — **gos·sa·mer·y** adj. [ME: appar. from GOOSE + SUMMER[1].]

gos·san /ˈgäsən; ˈgäz-/ ▶ n. Geol. Mining an iron-containing secondary deposit, largely consisting of oxides and typically yellowish or reddish, occurring above a deposit of a metallic ore. [18th C.: of unknown origin.]

gos·sip /ˈgäsip/ ▶ n. casual or unconstrained conversation or reports about other people, typically involving details that are not confirmed as being true. ■ a person who likes talking about others' private lives. ▶ v. (**-siped, -sip·ing**) [intrans.] engage in gossip. — **gos·sip·er** n. **gos·sip·y** adj. [OE *godsibb* 'godfather, godmother,' lit. 'a person rel. to one in God,' from *god* 'God' + *sibb* 'a relative' (see SIB).]

gos·sip·mon·ger /ˈgäsip,mənGgər; -,mäNG-/ ▶ n. derog. a person who habitually passes on confidential information or spreads rumors.

gos·soon /gäˈso͞on/ ▶ n. Irish a lad. [17th C.: from Fr. *garçon* 'boy.']

gos·sy·pol /ˈgäsə,pôl; -,päl/ ▶ n. Chem. a toxic crystalline compound, $C_{30}H_{30}O_8$, present in cotton-seed oil. [19th C.: from mod. L. *Gossypium*, from L. *gossypinum* 'cotton plant' + -OL.]

got /gät/ past and past participle of GET.

got·cha /ˈgächə/ informal ▶ exclam. I have got you (used to express satisfaction at having captured or defeated someone or uncovered their faults). ▶ n. an instance of publicly tricking someone or exposing them to ridicule, esp. by deception.

Gö·te·borg /ˈyœtə,bôr(yə)/ Swedish name of GOTHENBURG.

Goth /gäтн/ ▶ n. **1** a member of a Germanic people that invaded the Roman Empire from the east between the 3rd and 5th centuries. The eastern division, the Ostrogoths, founded a kingdom in Italy, while the Visigoths went on to found one in Spain. **2** (**goth**) a style of rock music derived from punk, typically with apocalyptic or mystical lyrics. ■ a member of a subculture favoring black clothing, white and black makeup, and goth music. [OE *Gota*, superseded by late L. *Gothi*, from Gk. *Gothoi*, from Gothic *Gutthiuda* 'the Gothic people.']

Goth. ▶ abbr. Gothic.

Go·tham /ˈgäтнəm/ a nickname for New York City, used originally by Washington Irving.

Goth·en·burg /ˈgäтнən,bərg/ a seaport in southwestern Sweden, on the Kattegat strait; pop. 433,000. Swedish name GÖTEBORG.

Goth·ic /ˈgäтнik/ ▶ adj. **1** of or relating to the Goths or their extinct East Germanic language. **2** of or in the style of architecture prevalent in western Europe in the 12th–16th centuries, characterized by pointed arches, rib vaults, and flying buttresses. **3** belonging to or redolent of the Dark Ages; portentously gloomy or horrifying. **4** (of lettering) of or derived from the angular style of handwriting with broad vertical downstrokes used in western Europe from the 13th century. **5** (also pseudoarchaic **Gothick**) of or relating to goths or their rock music. ▶ n. **1** the language of the Goths. **2** the Gothic style of architecture. **3** Gothic type. — **Goth·i·cal·ly** adv. **Goth·i·cism** /-ə,sizəm/ n.

goth·ic nov·el ▶ n. a genre of fiction developed in the 18th and early 19th centuries, characterized by an atmosphere of mystery and horror and having a pseudomedieval setting.

Got·land /ˈgät,land; ˈgôt,länt/ an island and province of Sweden, in the Baltic Sea; pop. 57,000

got·ta /ˈgätə/ ▶ contr. ■ have got to (not acceptable in standard use): *you gotta be careful.*

got·ten /ˈgätn/ past participle of GET.

Göt·ter·däm·mer·ung /,gätərˈdaməro͝oNG/ (in Germanic mythology) the downfall of the gods. [Ger., lit. 'twilight of the gods.']

Göt·ting·en /ˈgœtiNGən/ a town in northern central Germany, on the Leine River; pop. 124,000.

gouache /gwäsн; go͞oˈäsн/ ▶ n. a method of painting using opaque pigments ground in water and thickened with a gluelike substance. ■ paint of this kind; opaque watercolor. ■ a picture painted in this way. [19th C.: Fr., from Ital. *guazzo*.]

Gou·da /ˈgo͞odə/ ▶ n. a flat round cheese with a yellow rind, originally made in Gouda, in the Netherlands.

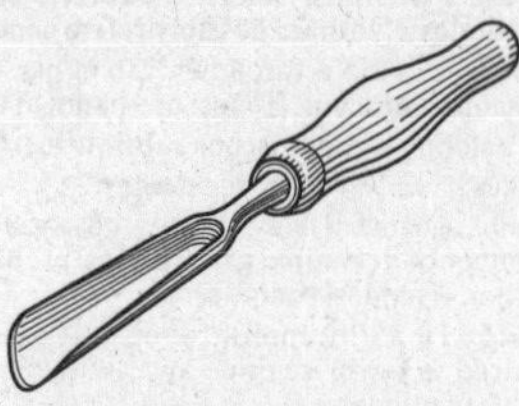

gouge 1

gouge /gouj/ ▶ n. **1** a chisel with a concave blade, used in carpentry, sculpture, and surgery. **2** an indentation or groove made by gouging. ▶ v. [trans.] **1** make (a groove, hole, or indentation) with or as if with a gouge: *a channel gouged out by water.* ■ make a rough hole or indentation in (a surface), esp. so as to mar or disfigure it. ■ (**gouge something out**) cut or force something out roughly or brutally. **2** informal overcharge; swindle. — **goug·er** n. [ME: from OFr., from late L. *gubia*, *gulbia*, perh. of Celtic origin; cf. Old Irish *gulba* 'beak.']

gou·lash /ˈgo͞oläsн/ ▶ n. a highly seasoned Hungarian soup or stew of meat and vegetables, flavored with paprika. [from Hungarian *gulyás-hús*, from *gulyás* 'herdsman' + *hús* 'meat.']

Gould[1], Jay (1836–92) US financier. With James Fisk, he attempted to corner the gold market, an effort that created the Black Friday panic on September 24, 1869.

Gould[2], Stephen Jay (1941–), US paleontologist. He wrote on the social context of scientific theory in works such as *Bully for Brontosaurus* (1992).

Gou·nod /go͞oˈnō/, Charles François (1818–93), French composer, noted for his opera *Faust* (1859).

gou·ra·mi /go͞oˈrämē/ ▶ n. (pl. same or **-mis**) a small, brightly colored Asian labyrinth fish (Belontiidae and related families), popular in aquariums. It builds a nest of bubbles, typically guarded by the male. [19th C.: from Malay *gurami*.]

gourd /gôrd; go͝ord/ ▶ n. **1** a fleshy, typically large fruit with a hard skin, some varieties of which are edible. ■ a container or ornament made from the hollowed and dried skin of this fruit. **2** a climbing or trailing plant that bears this fruit. The **gourd family** (Cucurbitaceae) also includes the squashes, pumpkins, melons, and cucumbers.

– PHRASES **out of one's gourd** informal out of one's mind; crazy. — **gourd·ful** /-,fo͝ol/ n. (pl. **-fuls**). [ME: from OFr. *gourde*, based on L. *cucurbita*.]

gourde /go͝ord/ ▶ n. the basic monetary unit of Haiti, equal to 100 centimes. [the Franco-Amer. name for a dollar.]

gour·mand /go͝orˈmänd/ ▶ n. a person who enjoys eating and often eats too much. ■ a connoisseur of good food. — **gour·man·dize** /ˈgo͝ormən,dīzəm/ n. & v. [ME: from OFr., of unknown origin.]

gour·met /gôrˈmā; go͝or-/ ▶ n. a connoisseur of good food; a person with a discerning palate. ■ [as adj.] of a kind or standard suitable for a gourmet. [19th C.: Fr., 'wine taster.']

gout /gout/ ▶ n. **1** a disease in which defective metabolism of uric acid causes arthritis, esp. in the smaller bones of the feet, and episodes of acute pain. **2** literary a drop or spot, esp. of blood, smoke, or flame. — **gout·i·ness** n. **gout·y** adj. [ME: from OFr. *goute*, from med. L. *gutta*, lit. 'drop.']

gov. ▶ abbr. ■ government. ■ governor.

gov·ern /ˈgəvərn/ ▶ v. [trans.] **1** conduct the policy, actions, and affairs of (a state, organization, or people). ■ control, influence, or regulate (a person, action, or course of events). ■ (**govern oneself**) conduct oneself, esp. with regard to controlling one's emotions. ■ regulate the speed of (a motor or engine) by a governor. **2** constitute a law, rule, standard, or principle for. ■ serve to decide (a legal case). **3** Gram. (of a word) require that (another word or group of words) be in a particular case. **4** regulate the speed of (a motor or machine) with a governor. — **gov·ern·a·bil·i·ty** /,gəvərnəˈbilitē/ n. **gov·ern·a·ble** adj. [ME: from OFr. *governer*, from L. *gubernare* 'to steer, rule,' from Gk. *kubernan* 'to steer.']

gov·ern·ance /ˈgəvərnəns/ ▶ n. the action or manner of governing. ■ archaic sway; control.

gov·ern·ess /ˈgəvərnis/ ▶ n. a woman employed to teach children in a private household. — **gov·ern·ess·y** adj.

gov·ern·ing bod·y ▶ n. a group of people who formulate the policy and direct the affairs of an institution in partnership with the managers, esp. on a voluntary or part-time basis: *the school's governing body.*

gov·ern·ment /ˈgəvər(n)mənt/ ▶ n. [treated as sing. or pl.] the governing body of a nation, state, or community. ■ the system by which a nation, state, or community is governed. ■ the action or manner of controlling or regulating a nation, organization, or people. ■ the group of persons in office at a particular time; administration. ■ another term for POLITICAL SCIENCE. ■ (**governments**) all bonds issued by the US Treasury or other federal agencies. — **gov·ern·men·tal** /ˌgəvər(n)ˈmentl/ **adj.** **gov·ern·men·tal·ly** /ˌgəvər(n)ˈmentl-ē/ **adv.**

gov·ern·ment-is·sue ▶ **adj.** (of equipment) provided by the government.

gov·er·nor /ˈgəvə(r)nər/ ▶ **n.** **1** the elected executive head of a state of the US. ■ an official appointed to govern a town or region. ■ the representative of the British Crown in a colony or in a Commonwealth state that regards the monarch as head of state. **2** Brit. the head of a public institution. ■ a member of a governing body. **3** Brit., informal the person in authority; one's employer. **4** a device automatically regulating the supply of fuel, steam, or water to a machine, ensuring uniform motion or limiting speed. — **gov·er·nor·ship** **n.**

gov·er·nor gen·er·al ▶ **n.** (pl. **gov·er·nors gen·er·al**) the chief representative of the Crown in a Commonwealth country of which the British monarch is head of state.

govt. ▶ **abbr.** government: *local govt.*

gowk /gouk/ ▶ **n.** dialect **1** an awkward or foolish person (often as a general term of abuse). **2** a cuckoo. [ME (sense 2): from ON *gaukr*.]

gown /goun/ ▶ **n.** a long dress, typically having a close-fitting bodice and a flared or flowing skirt, worn on formal occasions. ■ a nightgown. ■ a dressing gown. ■ a protective garment worn in a hospital, either by a staff member during surgery or by a patient. ■ a loose cloak indicating one's profession or status, worn by a lawyer, teacher, academic, or college student. ■ the members of a college as distinct from the permanent residents of the college town. Often contrasted with TOWN. ▶ **v.** (**be gowned**) be dressed in a gown. [ME: from OFr. *goune*, from late L. *gunna* 'fur garment.']

goy /goi/ ▶ **n.** (pl. **goy·im** /ˈgoi-im/ or **goys**) informal, often offens. a Jewish name for a non-Jew. — **goy·ish** **adj.** [from Heb. *gōy* 'people, nation.']

Go·ya /ˈgoiə/ (1746–1828), Spanish painter; full name *Francisco José de Goya y Lucientes*. Many of his works concerned the French occupation of Spain 1808–14.

GP ▶ **abbr.** general practitioner.

GPA ▶ **abbr.** grade point average.

g.p.d. (also **GPD** or **gpd**) ▶ **abbr.** gallons per day.

gph ▶ **abbr.** gallons per hour.

gpm ▶ **abbr.** gallons per minute.

GPO ▶ **abbr.** Government Printing Office.

GPRS ▶ **abbr.** general packet radio services, a technology for radio transmission of small packets of data, especially between cellular phones and the Internet.

GPS ▶ **abbr.** Global Positioning System, an accurate worldwide navigational and surveying facility based on the reception of signals from an array of orbiting satellites.

g.p.s. (also **GPS** or **gps**) ▶ **abbr.** gallons per second.

GQ ▶ **abbr.** general quarters.

gr (also **gr.**) ▶ **abbr.** ■ grain(s). ■ gram(s). ■ gray. ■ gross.

Graaf·i·an fol·li·cle /ˈgräfēən/ ▶ **n.** Physiol. a fluid-filled structure in the mammalian ovary within which an ovum develops before ovulation. [19th C.: named after R. de *Graaf* (1641–73), Du. anatomist.]

grab /grab/ ▶ **v.** (**grabbed, grab·bing**) [trans.] **1** grasp or seize suddenly and roughly. ■ [intrans.] (**grab at/for**) make a sudden snatch at. ■ informal obtain or get (something) quickly or opportunistically, sometimes unscrupulously. ■ [intrans.] (of a brake on a vehicle) grip the wheel harshly or jerkily. **2** [usu. with negative or in questions] informal attract the attention of; impress: *how does that grab you?* ▶ **n.** **1** [in sing.] a quick, sudden clutch or attempt to seize. ■ an act of obtaining something opportunistically or unscrupulously: *they use the law to effect a land grab.* **2** a mechanical device for clutching, lifting, and moving things, esp. materials in bulk. ■ [as adj.] denoting a bar or strap to hold on to for support or in a moving vehicle. **3** a frame of video or television footage, digitized and stored as a still image in a computer memory for subsequent display, printing, or editing.
– PHRASES **up for grabs** informal available; obtainable, esp. by the quickest or most aggressive person. — **grab·ber** **n.** [16th C.: from Mid. Low Ger. and MDu. *grabben*; perh. rel. to GRIP.]

grab bag ▶ **n.** a container from which a person chooses a wrapped item at random, without knowing the contents. ■ an assortment of miscellaneous items.

grab·by /ˈgrabē/ ▶ **adj.** informal having or showing a selfish desire for something; greedy. ■ attracting attention; arousing interest.

gra·ben /ˈgräbən/ ▶ **n.** (pl. same or **gra·bens**) Geol. an elongated block of the earth's crust lying between two faults and displaced downward relative to the blocks on either side, as in a rift valley. [19th C.: from Ger. *Graben* 'a ditch.']

grace /grās/ ▶ **n.** **1** simple elegance or refinement of movement. ■ courteous goodwill. ■ (**graces**) an attractively polite manner: *she has all the social graces.* **2** (in Christian belief) the free and unmerited favor of God, as manifested in the salvation of sinners and the bestowal of blessings. ■ a divinely given talent or blessing. ■ the condition or fact of being favored by someone. **3** (also **grace period**) a period officially allowed for payment of a sum due or for compliance with a law or condition, esp. an extension granted as a special favor. **4** a short prayer of thanks said before or after a meal. **5** (**His, Her,** or **Your Grace**) used as forms of description or address for a duke, duchess, or archbishop. ▶ **v.** [with obj. and adverbial] do honor or credit to (someone or something) by one's presence. ■ [trans.] (of a person or thing) be an attractive presence in or on; adorn.
– PHRASES **be in someone's good** (or **bad**) **graces** be regarded by someone with favor (or disfavor). **there but for the grace of God (go I)** used to acknowledge one's good fortune in avoiding another's mistake or misfortune. **the (Three) Graces** Gk. Mythol. three beautiful goddesses (Aglaia, Thalia, and Euphrosyne), daughters of Zeus. They were believed to personify and bestow charm, grace, and beauty. **with good** (or **bad**) **grace** in a willing and happy (or reluctant and resentful) manner. [ME: via OFr. from L. *gratia*, from *gratus* 'pleasing, thankful'; rel. to GRATEFUL.]

grace·ful /ˈgrāsfəl/ ▶ **adj.** having or showing grace or elegance. — **grace·ful·ly** **adv.** **grace·ful·ness** **n.**

grace·less /ˈgrāslis/ ▶ **adj.** lacking grace, elegance, or charm. — **grace·less·ly** **adv.** **grace·less·ness** **n.**

grace note ▶ **n.** Music an extra note added as an embellishment and not essential to the harmony or melody.

grac·ile /ˈgrasəl/ ▶ **adj.** Anthropol. (of a hominid species) of slender build. ■ (of a person) slender or thin, esp. in a charming or attractive way. [17th C.: from L. *gracilis* 'slender.']

gra·cil·i·ty /graˈsilitē; grə-/ ▶ **n.** formal **1** the state of being gracefully slender. **2** (with reference to a literary style) plain simplicity.

gra·ci·o·so /ˌgräsʜēˈōsō; ˌgräsē-/ ▶ **n.** (pl. **-sos**) (in Spanish comedy) a buffoon or clown. [Sp., lit. 'gracious.']

gra·cious /ˈgrāsʜəs/ ▶ **adj.** **1** courteous, kind, and pleasant, esp. toward someone of lower social status. ■ elegant and tasteful, esp. as exhibiting wealth or high social status. **2** (in Christian belief) showing divine grace. ▶ **exclam.** expressing polite surprise. — **gra·cious·ly** **adv.** **gra·cious·ness** **n.** [ME: via OFr. from L. *gratiosus*, from *gratia* 'esteem, favor' (see GRACE).]

grack·le /ˈgrakəl/ ▶ **n.** **1** a songbird (esp. *Quiscalus quiscula*) of the American blackbird family, the male of which has shiny black plumage with a blue-green sheen. **2** another term for an Asian mynah or starling (*Gracula* and other genera), with mainly black plumage. [18th C.: from mod. L. *Gracula*, from L. *graculus* 'jackdaw.']

grad /grad/ ▶ **n.** informal term for GRADUATE.

grad. ▶ **abbr.** ■ gradient. ■ graduate. ■ graduated.

grad·a·ble /ˈgrādəbəl/ ▶ **adj.** Gram. denoting an adjective that can be used in the comparative and superlative and take a submodifier. — **grad·a·bil·i·ty** /ˌgrādəˈbilitē/ **n.**

gra·date /ˈgrādāt/ ▶ **v.** pass or cause to pass by gradations from one shade of color to another. ■ [trans.] arrange in steps or grades of size, amount, or quality. [18th C.: back-form. from GRADATION.]

gra·da·tion /grāˈdāsʜən/ ▶ **n.** a scale or a series of successive changes, stages, or degrees. ■ a stage or change in a such a scale or series. ■ a minute change from one shade, tone, or color to another. ■ (in historical linguistics) another term for ABLAUT. — **gra·da·tion·al** /-sʜənl/ **adj.** **gra·da·tion·al·ly** /-sʜənl-ē/ **adv.** [16th C.: from L. *gradatio(n-)*, based on *gradus* 'step.']

grade /grād/ ▶ **n.** **1** a particular level of rank, quality, proficiency, intensity, or value. ■ a level in a salary or employment structure. ■ a mark indicating the quality of a student's work. ■ (with specifying ordinal number) those students in a school or school system who are grouped by age or ability for teaching at a particular level for a year. ■ a level of quality or size for food or other products. ■ (in historical linguistics) one in a series of related root forms exhibiting ablaut. ■ Zool. a group of animals at a similar evolutionary level. **2** a gradient or slope: *a long seven percent grade.* **3** [usu. as adj.] a variety of cattle produced by crossing with a superior breed: *grade stock.* ▶ **v.** [trans.] (usu. **be graded**) **1** arrange in or allocate to grades; class or sort. ■ give a mark to (a student or a piece of work). **2** [intrans.] pass gradually from one level, esp. a shade of color, into another. **3** reduce (a road) to an easy gradient. **4** cross (livestock) with a superior breed.
– PHRASES **at grade** on the same level. **make the grade** informal succeed; reach the desired standard. [16th C.: from Fr., or from L. *gradus* 'step.']

grade cross·ing ▶ **n.** a place where a railroad and a road, or two railroad lines, cross at the same level.

grade point ▶ **n.** a numerical value assigned to a letter grade received in an academic course, multiplied by the number of credits awarded for the course.

grade point av·er·age ▶ **n.** an indication of a student's academic achievement, calculated as the total number of grade points received over a given period divided by the total number of credits awarded.

grad·er /ˈgrādər/ ▶ **n.** **1** a person or thing that grades. ■ a wheeled machine for leveling the ground, esp. in making roads. **2** [in comb.] a pupil of a specified grade in a school: *first-grader.*

grade school ▶ **n.** an elementary school. — **grade school·er** **n.**

gra·di·ent /ˈgrādēənt/ ▶ **n.** **1** an inclined part of a road or railway; a slope. ■ the degree of such a slope. ■ Math. the degree of steepness of a graph at any point. **2** Physics an increase or decrease in the magnitude of a property (e.g., temperature, pressure, or concentration) observed in passing from one point or moment to another. ■ the rate of such a change. ■ Math. the vector formed by the operator ∇ acting on a scalar function at a given point in a scalar field. [19th C.: from GRADE, on the pattern of *salient*.]

gra·di·om·e·ter /ˌgrādēˈämitər/ ▶n. a surveying instrument used for setting out or measuring the gradient of a slope. ■ Physics an instrument for measuring the gradient of an energy field, esp. the horizontal gradient of the earth's gravitational or magnetic field.

grad·u·al /ˈgrajo͞oəl/ ▶adj. taking place or progressing slowly or by degrees. ■ (of a slope) not steep or abrupt. ▶n. (in the Western Christian Church) a response sung or recited between the Epistle and Gospel in the Mass. ■ a book of plainsong for the Mass. — **grad·u·al·ly** adv. **grad·u·al·ness** n. [ME: from med. L. *gradualis*, from L. *gradus* 'step.']

grad·u·al·ism /ˈgrajo͞oəˌlizəm/ ▶n. a policy of gradual reform rather than sudden change or revolution. ■ Biol. the hypothesis that evolution proceeds chiefly by the accumulation of gradual changes (in contrast to the punctuationist model). — **grad·u·al·ist** n. **grad·u·al·is·tic** /ˌgrajo͞oəˈlistik/ adj.

grad·u·ate ▶n. /ˈgrajo͞oit/ **1** a person who has successfully completed a course of study or training, esp. a person who has been awarded an undergraduate academic degree. ■ a person who has received a high school diploma. **2** a graduated cup, tube, flask, or measuring glass, used esp. by chemists and pharmacists. ▶v. /ˈgrajo͞oˌāt/ **1** [intrans.] successfully complete an academic degree, course of training, or high school. ■ [trans.] confer a degree or other academic qualification on. ■ (**graduate to**) move up to (a more advanced level or position). **2** [trans.] arrange in a series or according to a scale. ■ mark out (an instrument or container) in degrees or other proportionate divisions. **3** [trans.] change (something, typically color or shade) gradually or step by step. ▶adj. /ˈgrajo͞oit/ [attrib.] relating to graduate school education. ■ having graduated from a school or academic program. [ME: from med. L. *graduat-* 'graduated,' from *graduare* 'take a degree,' from L. *gradus* 'degree, step.']

grad·u·ate school ▶n. a division of a university offering advanced programs beyond the bachelor's degree.

grad·u·a·tion /ˌgrajo͞oˈāsʜən/ ▶n. **1** the receiving or conferring of an academic degree or diploma. ■ the ceremony at which degrees are conferred. **2** the action of dividing into degrees or other proportionate divisions on a graduated scale. ■ a mark on a container or instrument indicating a degree of quantity.

Grae·cism ▶n. esp. Brit. var. of GRECISM.

Graeco- ▶comb. form esp. Brit. var. of GRECO-. [from L. *Graecus* (see GREEK).]

Grae·co-Ro·man ▶adj. esp. Brit. var. of GRECO-ROMAN.

Graf /graf/, Steffi (1969–), German tennis player; full name *Stefanie Maria Graf*. She won 22 Grand Slam singles titles before retiring in 1999.

graf·fi·ti /grəˈfētē/ ▶plural n. (sing. **-to** /-tō/) [treated as sing. or pl.] writing or drawings scribbled, scratched, or sprayed illicitly on a wall or other surface in a public place. ▶v. [trans.] write or draw graffiti on (something): *they graffitied an entire train.* ■ write (words or drawings) as graffiti. — **graf·fi·tist** n. [19th C.: from Ital. (pl.), from *graffio* 'a scratch.']

graft[1] /graft/ ▶n. **1** Horticulture a shoot or scion inserted into a slit of stock, from which it receives sap. ■ an instance of inserting a shoot or scion in this way. **2** Med. a piece of living tissue that is transplanted surgically. ■ a surgical operation in which tissue is transplanted. ▶v. [with obj. and adverbial] **1** Horticulture insert (a scion) as a graft. ■ insert a graft on (a stock). **2** Med. transplant (living tissue) as a graft. ■ fig. insert or fix (something) permanently to something else, typically in a way considered inappropriate. [ME *graff*, from OFr. *grafe*, via L. from Gk. *graphion* 'stylus, writing implement.' (with ref. to the tapered tip of the scion), from *graphein* 'write.']

graft[2] ▶n. practices, esp. bribery, used to secure illicit gains in politics or business; corruption. ■ such gains. ▶v. [intrans.] make money by shady or dishonest means. — **graft·er** n. [19th C.: of unknown origin.]

Gra·ham[1] /gram; ˈgrāəm/, Billy (1918–), US clergyman; full name *William Franklin Graham*. A minister of the Southern Baptist Church, he is known for his large evangelistic crusades.

Gra·ham[2], Katherine Meyer (1917–2001) US publisher. She headed the communications empire that included *Newsweek* magazine.

Gra·ham[3], Martha (1893–1991), US dancer and choreographer. She evolved a new style of dance intended to express psychological complexities and emotional power.

gra·ham /gram; ˈgrāəm/ (also **Gra·ham**) ▶adj. [attrib.] denoting unsieved whole-wheat flour, or cookies or bread made from this: *a box of graham crackers.* [19th C.: named after Sylvester *Graham* (1794–1851), an American advocate of dietary reform.]

Gra·hame /ˈgrāəm; gram/, Kenneth (1859–1932), Scottish writer. He wrote *The Wind in the Willows* (1908).

Gra·ham Land /ˈgrāəm; gram/ the northern part of the Antarctic Peninsula. Discovered in 1831–32 by English navigator John Biscoe (1794–1843), it forms part of British Antarctic Territory.

Grail /grāl/ (also **Holy Grail**) n. (in medieval legend) the cup or platter used by Jesus at the Last Supper, and in which Joseph of Arimathea received Christ's blood at the Cross. Quests for it undertaken by medieval knights are described in versions of the Arthurian legends written from the early 13th century onward. ■ fig. a thing that is earnestly pursued or sought after. [from OFr. *graal*, from med. L. *gradalis* 'dish.']

grain /grān/ ▶n. **1** wheat or any other cultivated cereal crop used as food. ■ the seeds of such cereals. **2** a single fruit or seed of a cereal. ■ a small hard particle of a substance such as salt or sand. ■ the smallest possible quantity or amount of a quality. ■ a discrete particle or crystal in a metal, igneous rock, etc., typically visible only when a surface is magnified. ■ a piece of solid propellant for use in a rocket engine. **3** (abbr.: **gr.**) the smallest unit of weight in the troy and avoirdupois systems, equal to $\frac{1}{5760}$ of a pound troy and $\frac{1}{7000}$ of a pound avoirdupois (approximately 0.0648 grams). **4** the longitudinal arrangement or pattern of fibers in wood, paper, etc. ■ roughness in texture of wood, stone, etc.; the arrangement and size of constituent particles. ■ the rough or textured outer surface of leather, or of a similar artificial material. ■ Photog. a granular appearance of a photograph or negative, which is in proportion to the size of the emulsion particles composing it. **5** archaic a person's character or natural tendency. **6** kermes or cochineal, or dye made from either of these. ▶v. [trans.] **1** (usu. **be grained**) give a rough surface or texture to. ■ [intrans.] form into grains. **2** [usu. as n.] (**graining**) paint (esp. furniture or interior surfaces) in imitation of the grain of wood or marble. **3** remove hair from (a hide).
– PHRASES **against the grain** contrary to the natural inclination or feeling of someone or something. — **grained** adj. [usu. in comb.] **grain·er** n. **grain·less** adj. [ME: from OFr. *grain*, from L. *granum*.]

grain wee·vil ▶n. a weevil (*Sitophilus granarius*, family Curculionidae) that is a common pest of stored grain, which is eaten by the larvae.

grain whis·key ▶n. whiskey made mainly from corn and malted and unmalted barley.

grain·y /ˈgrānē/ ▶adj. (**grain·i·er**, **grain·i·est**) **1** granular. ■ Photog. showing visible grains of emulsion, as characteristic of old photographs or modern high-speed film. ■ (of sound, esp. recorded music or a voice) having a rough or gravelly quality. ■ (of food) containing whole grains. **2** (of wood) having prominent grain. — **grain·i·ness** n.

gram[1] /gram/ (Brit. also **gramme**) (abbr.: **g**) ▶n. a metric unit of mass equal to one thousandth of a kilogram. [18th C.: from Fr. *gramme*, from late L. *gramma* 'a small weight,' from Gk.]

gram[2] ▶n. chickpeas or other legumes used as food. [18th C.: from Port. *grão*, from L. *granum* 'grain.']

gram[3] ▶n. short for GRANDMA.

-gram[1] ▶comb. form in nouns denoting something written or recorded (esp. in a certain way): *cryptogram*. — **-grammatic** comb. form in corresponding adjectives. [from Gk. *gramma* 'thing written, letter of the alphabet,' from *graphein* 'write.']

-gram[2] ▶comb. form in nouns denoting a novelty greeting or message as a humorous or embarrassing surprise for the recipient: *kissogram*. [on the pattern of *telegram*.]

gram·i·niv·o·rous /ˌgraməˈnivərəs/ ▶adj. Zool. (of an animal) feeding on grass.

gram·ma /ˈgramə/ ▶n. informal one's grandmother (often as a form of address).

gram·mar /ˈgramər/ ▶n. the whole system and structure of a language or of languages in general, usually taken as consisting of syntax and morphology (including inflections) and sometimes also phonology and semantics. ■ [usu. with adj.] a particular analysis of the system and structure of language or of a specific language. ■ a book on grammar. ■ a set of actual or presumed prescriptive notions about correct use of a language. ■ the basic elements of an area of knowledge or skill. ■ Comput. a set of rules governing what strings are valid or allowable in a language or text. [ME: from OFr. *gramaire*, via L. from Gk. *grammatikē (tekhnē)* '(art) of letters,' from *gramma*, *grammat-* 'letter of the alphabet, thing written.']

gram·mar·i·an /grəˈme(ə)rēən/ ▶n. a person who studies and writes about grammar.

gram·mar school ▶n. **1** another term for ELEMENTARY SCHOOL. **2** (in the UK) a state secondary school to which pupils are admitted on the basis of ability.

gram·mat·i·cal /grəˈmatikəl/ ▶adj. of or relating to grammar. ■ well formed; in accordance with the productive rules of the grammar of a language. — **gram·mat·i·cal·i·ty** /-ˌmatiˈkalitē/ n. **gram·mat·i·cal·ly** adv. **gram·mat·i·cal·ness** n.

gram·mat·i·cal·ize /grəˈmatikəˌlīz/ ▶v. [trans.] Ling. change (an element) from one having lexical meaning into one having a largely grammatical function. — **gram·mat·i·cal·i·za·tion** /-ˌmatikəliˈzāsʜən/ n.

gramme ▶n. Brit. var. of GRAM[1].

gram-mo·lec·u·lar weight (abbr.: **GMW**) ▶n. the quantity of a chemical compound equal to its molecular weight in grams; now usu. replaced by the mole. Also called **gram molecule.** See MOLE[4])

Gram·my /ˈgramē/ ▶n. (pl. **-mys** or **-mies**) each of a number of annual awards given by the American National Academy of Recording Arts and Sciences for achievement in the record industry.

Gram-neg·a·tive /gram/ ▶adj. see GRAM STAIN.

gram·o·phone /ˈgraməˌfōn/ ▶n. old-fashioned term for RECORD PLAYER. [19th C.: formed by inversion of elements of *phonogram* 'sound recording.']

gram·o·phone rec·ord ▶n. old-fashioned term for RECORD (sense 4).

gramp /gramp/ (also **gramps**, **gramp·y** /ˈgrampē/) ▶n. dialect informal one's grandfather. [19th C.: contr. of GRANDPAPA.]

Gram·pi·an /ˈgrampēən/ a former local government region in northeastern Scotland, dissolved in 1996.

Gram·pi·an Moun·tains (also **the Gram·pi·ans**) a mountain range in northern central Scotland. Its southern edge forms a natural boundary between the Highlands and the Lowlands.

Gram-pos·i·tive ▶adj. see GRAM STAIN.

gram·pus /ˈgrampəs/ ▶n. (pl. **-pus·es**) a cetacean of the dolphin family, in particular: ■ another term for RISSO'S DOLPHIN. ■ another term for ORCA. [16th C.: alt. (by association with GRAND 'big') of OFr. *grapois*, from med. L. *craspiscis*, from L. *crassus piscis* 'fat fish.']

Gram stain ▶ n. Med. a staining technique for the preliminary distinction of bacteria between two categories (**Gram-positive** and **Gram-negative**). [19th C.: named after Hans C. J. *Gram* (1853–1938), the Danish physician who devised the method.]

Gra·na·da /grə'nädə/ **1** a city in southern Spain; pop. 287,000. Founded in the 8th century, it became the capital of the Moorish kingdom of Granada in 1238. **2** a city in Nicaragua, on the northwestern shore of Lake Nicaragua; pop. 89,000.

gran·a·dil·la /,granə'dilə; -'dēyə/ (also **gren·a·dil·la**) ▶ n. a passion fruit, or the fruit of a related plant (genus *Passiflora*, family Passifloraceae). [16th C.: Sp., dimin. of *granada* 'pomegranate.']

gra·na·ry /'grānərē; 'gran-/ ▶ n. (pl. **-ries**) a storehouse for threshed grain. ■ a region producing large quantities of grain. [16th C.: from L. *granarium*, from *granum* 'grain.']

Gran Ca·na·ria /,grän kə'näryə/ an island off the northwestern coast of Africa, one of the Canary Islands; pop. 715,000.

Gran Cha·co /grän 'CHäkō/ (also **Cha·co**) a lowland plain in central South America, extending from southern Bolivia through Paraguay to northern Argentina.

grand /grand/ ▶ adj. **1** magnificent and imposing in appearance, size, or style. ■ designed to impress through scale or splendor. ■ (of a person) of high rank and with an appearance and manner appropriate to it. ■ large or ambitious in scope or scale. ■ used in names of places or buildings to suggest size or splendor. **2** [attrib.] denoting the largest or most important item of its kind. ■ of the highest rank (used esp. in official titles). ■ Law (of a crime) serious. Compare with PETTY (sense 2). **3** informal very good or enjoyable; excellent. **4** [in comb.] (in names of family relationships) denoting one generation removed in ascent or descent. ▶ n. **1** (pl. same) informal a thousand dollars or pounds. **2** a grand piano.
– PHRASES **a** (or **the**) **grand old man of** a man long and highly respected in (a particular field). — **grand·ly** adv. **grand·ness** n. [ME: from OFr. *grant, grand*, from L. *grandis* 'full-grown, big, great.']

gran·dad /'gran,dad/ ▶ n. var. of GRANDDAD.

grand·dad·dy /'gran,dadē/ (also **grandaddy**) ▶ n. (pl. **-ies**) another term for GRANDDAD. ■ (**the granddaddy of**) used to denote a person or thing that is considered to be the best, largest, or most notable of a particular kind.

gran·dam /'gran,dam; -dəm/ (also **grand·dam, gran·dame**) ▶ n. archaic term for GRANDMOTHER. ■ an old woman. ■ a female ancestor. [ME: from Anglo-Norman Fr. *graund dame* (see GRAND, DAME).]

grand·aunt /'grand,ant; -,änt/ ▶ n. another term for GREAT-AUNT.

grand·ba·by /'gran(d),bābē/ ▶ n. (pl. **-bies**) a grandchild who is still a baby.

Grand Banks a shallow area off the southeastern coast of Newfoundland, Canada; important fishing waters.

Grand Ca·nal **1** a series of waterways in eastern China that extend south 1,060 miles (1,700 km) from Beijing to Hangzhou; built between 486 BC and AD 1327. **2** the main waterway of Venice, Italy.

Grand Can·yon a deep gorge formed by the Colorado River in Arizona; about 277 miles (440 km) long, 5–15 miles (8–24 km) wide, and, in places, 6,000 feet (1,800 m) deep.

grand·child /'gran(d),CHīld/ ▶ n. (pl. **-child·ren** /-,CHildrən/) a child of one's son or daughter.

Grand Cou·lee Dam /'kōōlē/ a dam on the Columbia River in east central Washington, completed in 1942.

grand cru /,gräN 'krY/ ▶ n. (pl. **grands crus** pronunc. same) (chiefly in French official classifications) a wine of the highest grade, or the vineyard that produces it. Compare with PREMIER CRU. [20th C.: Fr., lit. 'great growth.']

grand·dad /'gran,dad/ (also **gran·dad**) ▶ n. informal one's grandfather.

grand·daugh·ter /'gran,dôtər/ ▶ n. a daughter of one's son or daughter.

grand duch·ess ▶ n. the wife or widow of a grand duke. ■ a princess or noblewoman ruling over a territory in certain European countries. ■ hist. a daughter (or son's daughter) of a Russian czar.

grand duch·y ▶ n. a state or territory ruled by a grand duke or duchess.

grand duke ▶ n. a prince or nobleman ruling over a territory in certain European countries. ■ hist. a son (or son's son) of a Russian czar.

grande dame /gran 'dam; 'grän 'däm/ ▶ n. a woman of influential position within a particular sphere. [18th C.: Fr., lit. 'grand lady.']

gran·dee /gran'dē/ ▶ n. a Spanish or Portuguese nobleman of the highest rank. ■ a person of high rank or eminence. [16th C.: from Sp. and Port. *grande* 'grand.']

gran·deur /'granjər; 'grandyŏŏr/ ▶ n. splendor and impressiveness, esp. of appearance or style. ■ high rank or social importance. [16th C. (denoting tall stature): from Fr., from *grand* 'great, grand' (see GRAND).]

grand·fa·ther /'gran(d),fäT͟Hər/ ▶ n. the father of one's father or mother. ■ the person who founded or originated something. ▶ v. [trans.] informal exempt (someone or something) from a new law or regulation. — **grand·fa·ther·ly** adj.

grand·fa·ther clause ▶ n. informal a clause exempting certain classes of people or things from the requirements of a piece of legislation affecting their previous rights, privileges, or practices. [20th C.: because in some southern states the descendants of those voting before 1867 did not have to meet stringent conditions for voting.]

grand·fa·ther clock ▶ n. a clock in a tall freestanding wooden case, driven by weights.

Grand Forks a city in northeastern North Dakota, on the Red River of the North; pop. 49,321.

gran·di·flo·ra /,grandə'flôrə/ ▶ adj. [attrib.] (of a cultivated plant) bearing large flowers. ▶ n. a grandiflora plant. [20th C.: mod. L., from L. *grandis* 'great' + *flos, flor-* 'flower.']

gran·dil·o·quent /gran'diləkwənt/ ▶ adj. pompous or extravagant in language, style, or manner, esp. in a way that is intended to impress. — **gran·dil·o·quence** n. **gran·dil·o·quent·ly** adv. [16th C.: from L. *grandiloquus*, lit. 'grand-speaking,' from *grandis* 'grand' + *loqui* 'speak.']

Grand In·quis·i·tor ▶ n. hist. the director of the court of Inquisition, esp. in Spain and Portugal.

gran·di·ose /'grandē,ōs; ,grandē'ōs/ ▶ adj. impressive or magnificent in appearance or style, esp. pretentiously so. ■ excessively grand or ambitious. — **gran·di·ose·ly** adv. **gran·di·os·i·ty** /,grandē'äsitē/ n. [19th C.: from Fr., from Ital. *grandioso*, from *grande* 'grand.']

Grand Is·land a city in south central Nebraska; pop. 42,940.

Grand Junction a city in western Colorado; pop. 41,986.

grand ju·ry ▶ n. Law a jury, normally of twenty-three jurors, selected to examine the validity of an accusation before trial.

grand lar·ce·ny ▶ n. Law (in many US states and formerly in Britain) theft of personal property having a value above a legally specified amount.

grand·ma /'gran(d),mä; 'gram-/ ▶ n. informal one's grandmother.

grand mal /,gran(d) 'mäl; 'mal/ ▶ n. a serious form of epilepsy with muscle spasms and prolonged loss of consciousness. Compare with PETIT MAL. ■ an epileptic fit of this kind. [19th C.: from Fr., lit. 'great sickness.']

grand·ma·ma /'gran(d),mämə; -mə,mä; 'gram-/ (also **grand·mam·ma**) ▶ n. archaic form of GRANDMA.

Grand·ma Mo·ses see MOSES[2].

grand man·ner ▶ n. (**the grand manner**) a style considered appropriate for noble and stately matters.

grand mas·ter ▶ n. **1** (usu. **grandmaster**) a chess player of the highest class, esp. one who has won an international tournament. **2** (**Grand Master**) the head of an order of chivalry or of Freemasons.

grand·moth·er /'gran(d),məT͟Hər/ ▶ n. the mother of one's father or mother. — **grand·moth·er·ly** adj.

grand·moth·er clock ▶ n. a clock similar to a grandfather clock but about two-thirds the size.

grand·neph·ew /'gran(d),nefyōō/ ▶ n. another term for GREAT-NEPHEW.

grand·niece /'gran(d),nēs/ ▶ n. another term for GREAT-NIECE.

grand op·er·a ▶ n. an opera on a serious theme in which the entire libretto (including dialogue) is sung. ■ the genre of such opera.

grand·pa /'gran(d),pä; 'gram-/ ▶ n. informal one's grandfather.

grand·pa·pa /'gran(d),päpə; -pə,pä; 'gram-/ ▶ n. old-fashioned term for GRANDFATHER.

grand·pap·py /'gran(d),papē; 'gram-/ ▶ n. (pl. **-pies**) dialect term for GRANDFATHER.

grand·par·ent /'gran(d),pe(ə)rənt; -,par-/ ▶ n. a parent of one's father or mother; a grandmother or grandfather. — **grand·pa·ren·tal** /,gran(d)pə'rentl/ adj. **grand·par·ent·hood** n.

grand pi·an·o ▶ n. a large, full-toned piano that has the body, strings, and soundboard arranged horizontally and in line with the keys and is supported by three legs.

Grand Prairie a city in northeastern Texas; pop. 99,616.

Grand Prix /,gräN 'prē; ,gran/ (in full **Grand Prix de Paris**) ▶ n. (pl. **Grands Prix** pronunc. same) an important sporting event in which participants compete for a major prize. ■ any of a series of auto-racing or motorcycling contests forming part of a world championship series, held in various countries under international rules. [19th C.: Fr., lit. 'great or chief prize.']

Grand Rapids a city in southwestern Michigan, on the Grand River; pop. 197,800.

grand sei·gneur /,gräN sān'yər/ ▶ n. a man whose rank or position allows him to command others. [17th C.: Fr., lit. 'great lord.']

grand siè·cle /'grän sē'eklə/ ▶ n. the reign of Louis XIV, seen as France's period of political and cultural preeminence. [19th C.: Fr., lit. 'great century or age.']

grand·sire /'grand,sī(ə)r/ ▶ n. archaic term for GRANDFATHER.

grand slam ▶ n. the winning of each of a group of major championships or matches in a particular sport in the same year, in particular in tennis or golf. ■ Bridge the bidding and winning of all thirteen tricks. ■ Baseball a home run hit when each of the three bases is occupied by a runner, thus scoring four runs. [19th C. (as a term in cards, esp. bridge): from SLAM[2].]

grand·son /'gran(d),sən/ ▶ n. the son of one's son or daughter.

grand·stand /'gran(d),stand/ ▶ n. the main seating area, usually roofed, commanding the best view for spectators at racetracks or sports stadiums. ▶ v. [intrans.] [usu. as n.] (**grandstanding**) derog. seek to attract applause or favorable attention from spectators or the media.

Grand Strand a name for the northeastern coast of South Carolina, site of many resorts.

Grand Te·ton National Park /'tē,tän/ a preserve in northwestern Wyoming, south of Yellowstone National Park, named for the highest of its peaks.

grand to·tal ▶n. the final amount after everything is added up; the sum of other totals.

grand tour ▶n. hist. a cultural tour of Europe conventionally undertaken, esp. in the 18th century, by a young, upper-class man as a part of his education. ■ a guided inspection or tour of a building, exhibit, or institution.

grand·un·cle /'grand,əNGkəl/ ▶n. another term for GREAT-UNCLE.

grand u·ni·fied the·o·ry ▶n. Physics a theory attempting to give a single explanation of the strong, weak, and electromagnetic interactions among subatomic particles.

Grange /grānj/, Red (1903–91) US football player; born *Harold Edward Grange*; known as the **Galloping Ghost**. He played professionally 1925–34, mostly as halfback for the Chicago Bears.

grange /grānj/ ▶n. 1 [usu. in names] Brit. a country house with farm buildings attached: *Biddulph Grange*. ■ hist. an outlying farm with tithe barns, belonging to a monastery or feudal lord. ■ archaic a barn. 2 (**the Grange**) (in the US) a farmers' association organized in 1867. The Grange sponsors social activities, community service, and political lobbying. ■ a local lodge of this association. [ME: from OFr., from med. L. *granica (villa)* 'grain house or farm,' based on L. *granum* 'grain.']

gran·i·fer·ous /grə'nifərəs/ ▶adj. Bot. (of a plant) producing grain or a grainlike seed. [17th C.: from L. *granum* 'grain' + -FEROUS.]

gran·ite /'granit/ ▶n. a very hard, granular, crystalline, intrusive igneous rock consisting mainly of quartz, mica, and feldspar and often used as a building stone. ■ used in similes and metaphors to refer to something very hard and impenetrable. — **gra·nit·ic** /grə'nitik/ adj. **gran·it·oid** /'grani,toid/ adj. & n. [17th C.: from Ital. *granito*, lit. 'grained,' from *grano* 'grain,' from L. *granum*.]

gran·ite·ware /'granit,we(ə)r/ ▶n. a speckled form of earthenware imitating the appearance of granite. ■ a kind of enameled ironware.

gra·niv·o·rous /grə'nivərəs/ ▶adj. Zool. (of an animal) feeding on grain. — **gra·ni·vore** /'granə,vôr/ n. [17th C.: from L. *granum* 'grain' + -VOROUS.]

gran·ny /'granē/ (also **gran·nie**) ▶n. (pl. **-nies**) informal one's grandmother. [17th C.: from *grannam*, from GRANDAM) + -Y².]

gran·ny glass·es ▶plural n. informal round, metal-rimmed glasses.

gran·ny knot ▶n. a square knot with the ends crossed the wrong way and therefore liable to slip or jam. See illustration at KNOT¹.

Gran·ny Smith ▶n. a bright green apple with crisp, sharp-flavored flesh, originating in Australia. [19th C.: named after Maria Ann (*Granny*) *Smith* (*c.*1801–1870), who first produced such apples.]

gran·o·di·or·ite /,granə'dīə,rīt/ ▶n. Geol. a coarse-grained, plutonic rock containing quartz and plagioclase, between granite and diorite in composition. [19th C.: from GRANITE + DIORITE.]

gra·no·la /grə'nōlə/ ▶n. a kind of breakfast cereal consisting typically of rolled oats, brown sugar or honey, dried fruit, and nuts. ■ [as adj.] esp. derog. denoting those with liberal or environmentalist political views, typified as eating health foods. [19th C. (as a trademark): from *gran-* (representing GRANULAR or GRAIN) + *-ola*.]

gran·o·lith·ic /,granə'liTHik/ ▶adj. (of concrete) containing fine granite chippings or crushed granite, used to render floors and surfaces. ■ (of a floor or surface) rendered with such concrete. ▶n. granolithic concrete or rendering. [19th C.: from *grano-* from L. *granum* 'grain' + Gk. *lithos* 'stone' + -IC.]

Grant /grant/, Ulysses Simpson (1822–85), 18th president of the US 1869–77; born *Hiram Ulysses Grant*. Named supreme commander of Union forces in 1863, he defeated the Confederacy in 1865 with a policy of attrition. As president, he lacked political experience and was unable to check widespread corruption and inefficiency.

grant /grant/ ▶v. [with two objs.] 1 agree to give or allow (something requested) to. ■ give (a right, power, property, etc.) formally or legally to. 2 agree or admit to (someone) that (something) is true. 1 n. a sum of money given by an organization, esp. a government, for a particular purpose. ■ formal the action of granting something. ■ Law a legal conveyance or formal conferment. 2 a geographical subdivision in New Hampshire, Vermont, and Maine.

– PHRASES **take someone or something for granted** fail to appreciate someone or something that is very familiar or obvious. ■ (**take something for granted**) assume that something is true without questioning it. — **grant·a·ble** adj. **grant·er** n. [ME: from OFr. *granter* 'consent to support,' var. of *creanter* 'to guarantee,' based on L. *credere* 'entrust.']

grant·ed /'grantid/ ▶adv. [sentence adverb] admittedly; it is true (used to introduce a factor that is opposed to the main line of argument but is not regarded as so strong as to invalidate it): *granted, life can be hard, but consider the alternative.* ▶conj. (**granted that**) even assuming that.

gran·tee /gran'tē/ ▶n. esp. Law a person to whom a grant or conveyance is made.

grant-in-aid ▶n. (pl. **grants-in-aid**) an amount of money given to a local government, an institution, or a particular scholar.

gran·tor /gran'tôr; 'grantər/ ▶n. esp. Law a person or institution that makes a grant or conveyance.

grants·man·ship /'grantsmən,SHip/ ▶n. the skill or practice of obtaining grants-in-aid, esp. for research. — **grants·man** n.

gran·u·lar /'granyələr/ ▶adj. resembling or consisting of small grains or particles. ■ having a roughened surface or structure. — **gran·u·lar·i·ty** /,granyə'laritē/ n. [18th C.: from late L. *granulum* (see GRANULE) + -AR¹.]

gran·u·late /'granyə,lāt/ ▶v. 1 [trans.] [usu. as adj.] (**granulated**) form (something) into grains or particles. ■ [intrans.] (of a substance) take the form of grains or particles. 2 [intrans.] [often as adj.] (**granulating**) Med. (of a wound or lesion) form a grainy surface as part of the healing process. ■ [as adj.] (**granulated**) esp. Biol. having a roughened surface. — **gran·u·la·tion** /,granyə'lāSHən/ n. **gran·u·la·tor** /-,lātər/ n.

gran·ule /'granyo͞ol/ ▶n. 1 a small compact particle of a substance. 2 a small convective cell on the surface of the sun with temperatures a few hundred degrees hotter than the surrounding regions, and lasting a few minutes. [17th C.: from late L. *granulum*, dimin. of L. *granum* 'grain.']

gran·u·lite /'granyə,līt/ ▶n. Geol. a fine-grained, granular metamorphic rock in which the main component minerals are typically feldspars and quartz. — **gran·u·lit·ic** /,granyə,litik/ adj.

gran·u·lo·cyte /'granyələ,sīt/ ▶n. Physiol. a white blood cell with secretory granules in its cytoplasm, e.g., an eosinophil or a basophil. — **gran·u·lo·cyt·ic** /,granyələ'sitik/ adj.

gran·u·lo·ma /,granyə'lōmə/ ▶n. (pl. **-mas** or **-ma·ta** /-mətə/) Med. a mass of granulation tissue, typically produced in response to infection, inflammation, or the presence of a foreign substance. — **gran·u·lom·a·tous** /-'lämətəs/ adj.

gran·u·lose /'granyə,lōs/ ▶adj. consisting of or covered with small grains or granules.

grape /grāp/ ▶n. 1 a berry, typically green, purple, or black, growing in clusters on a grapevine, eaten as fruit, and used in making wine. ■ (**the grape**) informal wine. 2 a dark purplish red color. 3 short for GRAPESHOT. — **grap·ey** (also **grap·y**) adj. [ME: from OFr., 'bunch of grapes,' prob. from *graper* 'gather (grapes),' from *grap* 'hook,' of Gmc. origin.]

grape·fruit /'grāp,fro͞ot/ ▶n. (pl. same) 1 a large, round, yellow citrus fruit with an acid, juicy pulp. 2 the tree (*Citrus paradisi*) bearing this fruit.

grape hy·a·cinth ▶n. a small Eurasian plant (genus *Muscari*) of the lily family, with clusters of small, globular blue flowers, cultivated as an ornamental or for use in perfume.

grape i·vy ▶n. an evergreen climbing plant (genus *Cissus*) of the grape family that is grown as a houseplant.

grape·shot /'grāp,SHät/ ▶n. hist. ammunition consisting of a number of small iron balls fired together from a cannon.

grape sug·ar ▶n. dextrose present in or derived from grapes.

grape·vine /'grāp,vīn/ ▶n. 1 a vine (genus *Vitis*, family Vitaceae) native to both Eurasia and North America, esp. one bearing fruit (grapes) used for eating or winemaking. 2 informal used to refer to the circulation of rumors and unofficial information. *I heard it through the grapevine.*

graph¹ /graf/ ▶n. a diagram showing the relation between typically two variable quantities, each measured along one of a pair of axes at right angles. ■ Math. a collection of points whose coordinates satisfy a given relation. ▶v. [trans.] plot or trace on a graph. [19th C.: abbrev. of *graphic formula*.]

graph² ▶n. Ling. a visual symbol representing a unit of sound or other feature of speech. Graphs include not only letters of the alphabet but also punctuation marks. [1930s: from Gk. *graphē* 'writing.']

-graph ▶comb. form 1 in nouns denoting something written or drawn in a specified way: *autograph*. 2 in nouns denoting an instrument that records: *seismograph*. [from Fr. *-graphe*, based on Gk. *graphos* 'written, writing.']

graph·eme /'grafēm/ ▶n. Ling. the smallest meaningful contrastive unit in a writing system. Compare with PHONEME. — **gra·phe·mic** /grə'fēmik/ adj. **gra·phe·mi·cal·ly** /grə'fēmik(ə)lē/ adv. **gra·phe·mics** /grə'fēmiks/ n.

-grapher ▶comb. form indicating a person concerned with a subject denoted by a noun ending in *-graphy* (such as *geographer* corresponding to *geography*). [from Gk. *-graphos* 'writer' + -ER¹.]

graph·ic /'grafik/ ▶adj. 1 of or relating to visual art, esp. involving drawing, engraving, or lettering. ■ giving a vivid picture with explicit detail. ■ Comput. of, relating to, or denoting a visual image. 2 of or in the form of a graph. 3 [attrib.] Geol. of or denoting rocks having a surface texture resembling cuneiform writing. ▶n. Comput. a graphical item displayed on a screen or stored as data. — **graph·i·cal·ly** adv. [17th C.: via L. from Gk. *graphikos*, from *graphē* 'writing, drawing.']

-graphic ▶comb. form in adjectives corresponding to nouns ending in *-graphy* (such as *demographic* corresponding to *demography*). — **-graphically** comb. form in corresponding adverbs. [from or suggested by Gk. *-graphikos*, from *graphē* 'writing, drawing.']

graph·i·cal /'grafikəl/ ▶adj. 1 of, relating to, or in the form of a graph. 2 of or relating to visual art or computer graphics. — **graph·i·cal·ly** adv.

-graphical ▶comb. form equivalent to -GRAPHIC.

graph·i·cal us·er in·ter·face (abbr.: **GUI**) ▶n. Comput. a visual way of interacting with a computer using items such as windows, icons, and menus.

graph·ic arts ▶plural n. the visual arts based on the use of line and tone on paper and other surfaces. ■ (**graphic art**) the activity of practicing these arts, esp. as a subject of study. — **graph·ic art·ist** n.

graph·ic de·sign ▶n. the art or skill of combining text and pictures in advertisements, magazines, or books. — **graph·ic de·sign·er** n.

graph·ic e·qual·iz·er ▶ n. an electronic device or computer program that allows the separate control of the strength and quality of selected frequency bands.

graph·ic nov·el ▶ n. a novel in comic-strip format.

graph·ics /ˈgrafiks/ ▶ **plural** n. [usu. treated as sing.] **1** the products of the graphic arts, esp. commercial design or illustration. **2** the use of diagrams in calculation and design. **3** (also **computer graphics**) [treated as pl.] visual images produced by computer processing. ■ [treated as sing.] the use of computers linked to display screens to generate and manipulate images.

graph·ics card ▶ n. Comput. a printed circuit board that controls the output to a display screen.

graph·ics tab·let ▶ n. Comput. an input device consisting of a flat, pressure-sensitive pad that the user draws on or points at with a special stylus, to guide a pointer displayed on the screen.

graph·ite /ˈgrafīt/ ▶ n. a gray, crystalline, allotropic form of carbon that occurs as a mineral in some rocks and can be made from coke. It is used as a solid lubricant, in pencils, and as a moderator in nuclear reactors. [18th C.: coined in Ger. (*Graphit*), from Gk. *graphein* 'write.']

graph·ol·o·gy /graˈfäləjē/ ▶ n. **1** the study of handwriting, for example as used to infer a person's character. **2** Ling. the study of written and printed symbols and of writing systems. — **graph·o·log·i·cal** /ˌgrafəˈläjikəl/ adj. **graph·ol·o·gist** n. [19th C.: from Gk. *graphē* 'writing' + -LOGY.]

graph pa·per ▶ n. paper printed with a network of small squares to assist the drawing of graphs or other diagrams.

graph the·o·ry ▶ n. the mathematical theory of the properties and applications of graphs.

-graphy ▶ comb. form in nouns denoting: **1** a descriptive science: *geography.* **2** a technique of producing images: *radiography.* **3** a style or method of writing or drawing: *calligraphy.* ■ writing about (a specified subject): *hagiography.* ■ a written or printed list: *filmography.* [from or suggested by Gk. *-graphia* 'writing.']

grap·nel /ˈgrapnəl/ ▶ n. a grappling hook. ■ a small anchor with several flukes. [ME: from an Anglo-Norman Fr. dimin. of OFr. *grapon*, of Gmc. origin.]

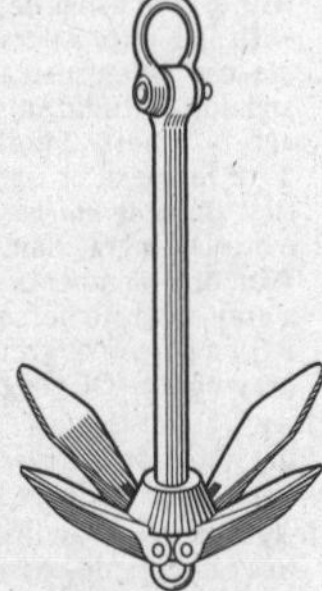
grapnel (anchor)

grap·pa /ˈgräpə/ ▶ n. a brandy distilled from the fermented residue of grapes after they have been pressed in winemaking. [Ital., lit. 'grape stalk,' of Gmc. origin.]

grap·ple /ˈgrapəl/ ▶ v. **1** [intrans.] engage in a close fight or struggle without weapons; wrestle. ■ [trans.] seize hold of (someone). ■ (**grapple with**) struggle with or work hard to deal with or overcome (a difficulty or challenge). **2** [trans.] archaic seize or hold with a grapnel. ▶ n. an act of grappling. ■ informal a wrestling match. ■ an instrument for catching hold of or seizing something; a grappling hook. — **grap·pler** /ˈgraplər/ n. [ME: from OFr. *grapil*, from Provençal, dimin. of *grapa* 'hook,' of Gmc. origin; rel. to GRAPE.]

grap·pling hook /ˈgrapliNG/ (also **grappling iron**) ▶ n. a device with iron claws, attached to a rope and used for dragging or grasping.

grap·to·lite /ˈgraptəˌlīt/ ▶ n. a fossil marine invertebrate (class Graptolithina, phylum Hemichordata) of the Paleozoic era, forming mainly planktonic colonies. [19th C.: from Gk. *graptos* 'marked with letters' + -LITE.]

GRAS ▶ abbr. generally recognized as safe; an FDA label for substances not known to be health hazards.

grasp /grasp/ ▶ v. [trans.] seize and hold firmly. ■ [intrans.] (**grasp at**) try to seize hold of. ■ get mental hold of; comprehend fully. ■ act decisively to take advantage of (something). ▶ n. [in sing.] a firm hold or grip. ■ a person's power or capacity to attain something. ■ a person's understanding.
– PHRASES **grasp at straws** (or **a straw**) see STRAW. — **grasp·a·ble** adj. **grasp·er** n. [ME: perh. rel. to GROPE.]

grasp·ing /ˈgraspiNG/ ▶ adj. greedy; avaricious. — **grasp·ing·ly** adv. **grasp·ing·ness** n.

Grass /gräs/, Günter Wilhelm (1927–), German writer. His works of fiction include *The Tin Drum* (1959) and *Crabwalk* (2002). Nobel Prize for Literature (1999).

grass /gras/ ▶ n. **1** vegetation consisting of typically short plants with long narrow leaves, growing wild or cultivated on lawns and pasture, and as a fodder crop. ■ ground covered with grass. ■ pastureland. **2** the mainly herbaceous plant that constitutes such vegetation, which has jointed stems and spikes of small, wind-pollinated flowers. The numerous members of the **grass family** (Gramineae, or Poaceae) form the dominant vegetation of many areas of the world. **3** informal marijuana. ▶ v. [trans.] (usu. **be grassed**) cover (an area of ground) with grass.
– PHRASES **not let the grass grow under one's feet** not delay in acting or taking an opportunity. — **grass·less** adj. **grass·like** adj. [OE *græs*, of Gmc. origin; rel. to Ger. *Gras*, also to GREEN and GROW.]

grass carp ▶ n. a large Chinese freshwater carp (*Ctenopharyngodon idella*), farmed for food in Southeast Asia and introduced elsewhere to control the growth of vegetation in waterways.

grass·cloth /ˈgrasˌklôTH/ ▶ n. a fine, light cloth resembling linen, woven from the fibers of the inner bark of the ramie plant.

American grasshopper

grass·hop·per /ˈgrasˌhäpər/ ▶ n. a plant-eating insect (family Acrididae, order Orthoptera) with long hind legs that are used for jumping and for producing a chirping sound.

grass·land /ˈgrasˌland/ ▶ n. (also **grasslands**) a large open area of country covered with grass, esp. one used for grazing: *rough grassland.*

grass roots (also **grass·roots** /ˈgrasˌro͞ots/) ▶ plural n. the most basic level of an activity or organization: *a campaign conducted **at the grass roots**.* ■ ordinary people regarded as the main body of an organization's membership.

grass skirt ▶ n. a skirt made of long grass and leaves fastened to a waistband, associated esp. with female dancers from some Pacific islands.

grass tet·a·ny ▶ n. a disease of livestock caused by magnesium deficiency, occurring esp. when there is a change from indoor feeding to outdoor grazing.

grass wid·ow ▶ n. a woman whose husband is away often or for a prolonged period.

grass·y /ˈgrasē/ ▶ adj. (**grass·i·er, grass·i·est**) of or covered with grass. ■ characteristic of grass. ■ tasting or smelling like grass. — **grass·i·ness** n.

grate[1] /grāt/ ▶ v. **1** [trans.] reduce (something, esp. food) to small shreds by rubbing it on a grater. **2** [intrans.] make an unpleasant rasping sound. ■ (**grate against**) rub against something with such a sound. ■ have an irritating effect: *a juvenile streak that **grated on** her nerves.* [ME: from OFr. *grater*, of Gmc. origin; rel. to Ger. *kratzen* 'to scratch.']

grate[2] ▶ n. **1** the recess of a fireplace or furnace. ■ a metal frame confining fuel in a fireplace or furnace. **2** a grating. [ME (meaning 'a grating'): from OFr., based on L. *cratis* 'wickerwork.']

grate·ful /ˈgrātfəl/ ▶ adj. feeling or showing an appreciation of kindness; thankful. — **grate·ful·ly** adv. **grate·ful·ness** n. [16th C.: from obs. *grate* 'pleasing, agreeable, thankful' (from L. *gratus*) + -FUL.]

grat·er /ˈgrātər/ ▶ n. a device having a surface covered with holes edged by slightly raised cutting edges, used for grating cheese and other foods. ■ a device in which blades are moved manually (by turning a handle), used for grating cheese and other foods.

grat·i·fy /ˈgratəˌfī/ ▶ v. (**-fies, -fied**) [trans.] (often **be gratified**) give (someone) pleasure or satisfaction. ■ indulge or satisfy (a desire). — **grat·i·fi·ca·tion** /ˌgratəfiˈkāsHən/ n. **grat·i·fi·er** n. **gra·ti·fy·ing·ly** adv. [ME (in the sense 'make pleasing'): from Fr. *gratifier* or L. *gratificari* 'give or do as a favor,' from *gratus* 'pleasing, thankful.']

grat·in /ˈgrätn; ˈgratn/ ▶ n. a dish with a light browned crust of breadcrumbs or melted cheese. [Fr., from *gratter*, earlier *grater* 'to grate.']

gra·ti·né /ˌgrätnˈā; ˌgra-/ (also **gra·ti·née**) ▶ adj. [postpositive] another term for AU GRATIN. — **gra·ti·néed** adj. [Fr., past part. of *gratiner* 'cook au gratin.']

grat·ing[1] /ˈgrātiNG/ ▶ adj. sounding harsh and unpleasant. ■ irritating. — **grat·ing·ly** adv.

grat·ing[2] ▶ n. a framework of parallel or crossed bars, typically preventing access through an opening while permitting communication or ventilation. ■ Optics shortened form of DIFFRACTION GRATING.

grat·is /ˈgratis/ ▶ adv. without charge; free. ▶ adj. given or done for nothing; free. [ME: from L., contr. of *gratiis* 'as a kindness,' from *gratia* 'grace, kindness.']

grat·i·tude /ˈgratəˌt(y)o͞od/ ▶ n. the quality of being thankful; readiness to show appreciation for and to return kindness. [ME: from OFr., or from med. L. *gratitudo*, from L. *gratus* 'pleasing, thankful.']

gra·tu·i·tous /grəˈt(y)o͞oitəs/ ▶ adj. **1** uncalled for; lacking good reason; unwarranted. **2** given or done free of charge. — **gra·tu·i·tous·ly** adv. **gra·tu·i·tous·ness** n. [17th C.: from L. *gratuitus* 'given freely, spontaneous' + -OUS.]

gra·tu·i·ty /grəˈt(y)o͞oitē/ ▶ n. (pl. **-ties**) money given in return for some service or favor, in particular: ■ formal a tip given to a waiter, taxicab driver, etc.

gra·va·men /grəˈvāmən/ ▶ n. (pl.**-vam·i·na** /-ˈvamənə/) esp. Law the essence or most serious part of a complaint or accusation. ■ a grievance. [17th C.: from late L., lit. 'physical inconvenience,' from L. *gravare* 'to load,' from *gravis* 'heavy.']

grave[1] /grāv/ ▶ n. a place of burial for a dead body, typically a hole dug in the ground and marked by a stone or mound. ■ (**the grave**) used as an allusive term for death. ■ a place where a broken piece of machinery or other discarded object lies.
– PHRASES **dig one's own grave** do something foolish that causes one to fail or be ruined. (**as**) **silent** (or **quiet**) **as the grave** extremely quiet.

take the (or **one's**, etc.) **secret to the grave** die without revealing a secret. **turn** (also **turn over**) **in one's grave** used to express the opinion that something would have caused anger or distress to someone who is now dead: *he must be turning in his grave at today's politics.* [OE *græf*, of Gmc. origin; rel. to Du. *graf* and Ger. *Grab*.]

grave[2] ▶ **adj.** giving cause for alarm; serious. ■ serious or solemn in manner or appearance; somber. ▶ **n.** /**also** gräv/ another term for GRAVE ACCENT. — **grave·ly adv. grave·ness n.** [15th C.: from OFr. *grave* or L. *gravis* 'heavy, serious.']

grave[3] ▶ **v.** (past part. **grav·en** /'grāvən/ or **graved**) [trans.] archaic engrave (an inscription or image) on a surface. ■ literary fix (something) indelibly in the mind. [OE *grafan* 'dig,' of Gmc. origin; rel. to Ger. *graben* and GROOVE.]

grave[4] ▶ **v.** [trans.] hist. clean (a ship's bottom) by burning off the accretions and then tarring it. [ME: perh. from Fr. dial. *grave*, var. of OFr. *greve* 'shore.']

grave[5] /'grävā/ ▶ **adj.** Music slowly; with solemnity. [Ital.: *grave* 'slowly.']

grave ac·cent /gräv; grāv/ ▶ **n.** a mark (`) placed over certain letters in some languages to indicate an alteration of a sound, as of quality, quantity, stress, or pitch. [17th C.: Fr. *grave* (see GRAVE[2]).]

grave·dig·ger /'grāv,digər/ ▶ **n.** a person who digs graves.

grav·el /'gravəl/ ▶ **n.** a loose aggregation of small water-worn or pounded stones. ■ a mixture of such stones with coarse sand, used for paths and roads and as an aggregate. ■ Med. aggregations of crystals formed in the urinary tract. ▶ **v.** (**grav·eled, grav·el·ing** ; Brit. **grav·elled, grav·el·ling**) [trans.] **1** cover (an area of ground) with gravel. **2** informal make (someone) angry or annoyed. [ME: from OFr., dimin. of *grave* (see GRAVE[4]).]

gra·vel·ly /'gravəlē/ ▶ **adj.** resembling, containing, or consisting of gravel. ■ (of a voice) deep and rough-sounding.

grav·en /'grāvən/ past participle of GRAVE[3].

grav·en im·age ▶ **n.** a carved idol or representation of a god used as an object of worship.

Gra·ven·stein /'grävən,stīn/ ▶ **n.** a widely grown apple of a large variety having yellow, red-streaked skin. [19th C.: the Ger. form of *Graasten*, a village in Denmark.]

grav·er /'grāvər/ ▶ **n.** a burin or other engraving tool. ■ archaic a person who engraves or carves.

Graves[1] /'grāvz/, Robert Ranke (1895–1985), English writer. His works include *I, Claudius* (1934).

Graves[2] /'grävz; gräv/ ▶ **n.** a red or white wine from the district of Graves, south of Bordeaux in France.

Graves' dis·ease ▶ **n.** a swelling of the neck and protrusion of the eyes resulting from an overactive thyroid gland. Also called EXOPHTHALMIC GOITER. [19th C.: named after Robert J. *Graves* (1796–1853), the Irish physician who first identified it.]

grave·side /'grāv,sīd/ ▶ **n.** the area around the edge of a grave.

grave·site /'grāv,sīt/ ▶ **n.** the location of a person's grave.

grave·stone /'grāv,stōn/ ▶ **n.** an inscribed headstone marking a grave.

grave·yard /'grāv,yärd/ ▶ **n.** a burial ground, esp. one beside a church.

grave·yard shift ▶ **n.** a work shift that runs through the early morning hours, typically covering the period between midnight and 8 a.m. ■ a group of employees working such a shift.

grav·id /'gravid/ ▶ **adj.** tech. pregnant; carrying eggs or young. ■ fig. full of meaning or a specified quality. [16th C.: from L. *gravidus* 'laden, pregnant,' from *gravis* 'heavy.']

gra·vim·e·ter /grə'vimitər/ ▶ **n.** an instrument for measuring the difference in the force of gravity from one place to another. [18th C.: from Fr. *gravimètre*, from *grave* 'heavy.']

grav·i·met·ric /,gravə'metrik/ ▶ **adj.** of or relating to the measurement of weight. ■ (of chemical analysis) based on weighing reagents and products.

gra·vim·e·try /grə'vimətrē/ ▶ **n.** Physics the measurement of weight.

grav·i·tas /'gravi,täs/ ▶ **n.** dignity, seriousness, or solemnity of manner. [L., from *gravis* 'serious.']

grav·i·tate /'gravi,tāt/ ▶ **v.** [no obj., with adverbial] move toward or be attracted to a place, person, or thing. ■ Physics move, or tend to move, toward a center of gravity or other attractive force. ■ archaic descend or sink by the force of gravity.

grav·i·ta·tion /,gravi'tāsHən/ ▶ **n.** movement, or a tendency to move, toward a center of attractive force, as in the falling of bodies to the earth. ■ Physics a force of attraction exerted by each particle of matter in the universe on every other particle. Compare with GRAVITY. ■ fig. movement toward or attraction to something. — **grav·i·ta·tion·al adj. grav·i·ta·tion·al·ly** /-sHənl-ē/ **adv.**

grav·i·ta·tion·al field ▶ **n.** Physics the region of space surrounding a body in which another body experiences a force of gravitational attraction.

grav·i·ta·tion·al lens ▶ **n.** Astron. a region of space containing a massive object whose gravitational field distorts electromagnetic radiation passing through it in a similar way to a lens, sometimes producing a multiple image of a remote object.

grav·i·ton /'gravi,tän/ ▶ **n.** Physics a hypothetical quantum of gravitational energy, regarded as a particle. [1940s: from GRAVITATION + -ON.]

grav·i·ty /'gravitē/ ▶ **n. 1** Physics the force that attracts a body toward the center of the earth, or toward any other physical body having mass. For most purposes Newton's laws of gravity apply, with minor modifications to take the general theory of relativity into account. ■ the degree of intensity of this, measured by acceleration. **2** extreme or alarming importance; seriousness. ■ seriousness or solemnity of manner. [15th C.: from OFr., or from L. *gravitas* 'weight, seriousness,' from *gravis* 'heavy.']

grav·i·ty feed ▶ **n.** a supply system making use of gravity to maintain the flow of material. — **grav·i·ty-fed adj.**

grav·i·ty wave ▶ **n.** Physics **1** a hypothetical wave carrying gravitational energy, postulated by Einstein to be emitted when a massive body is accelerated. **2** a wave propagated on a liquid surface or in a fluid through the effects of gravity.

grav·lax /'gräv,läks/ ▶ **n.** a Scandinavian dish of dry-cured salmon marinated in herbs. [Swed., from *grav* 'trench' + *lax* 'salmon.']

gra·vure /grə'vyŏŏr/ ▶ **n.** an image produced from etching a plate through an intaglio process and producing a print from it. ■ the production of prints in this way.

gra·vy /'grāvē/ ▶ **n.** (pl. **-vies**) **1** the fat and juices exuding from meat during cooking. ■ a sauce made from these juices together with stock and other ingredients. **2** informal unearned or unexpected money. [ME: perh. from OFr. *grave*, a misreading of *grané*, prob. from *grain* 'spice,' from L. *granum* 'grain.']

gra·vy boat ▶ **n.** a boat-shaped vessel used for serving gravy or sauce; a sauceboat.

gra·vy train ▶ **n.** informal used to refer to a situation in which someone can make a lot of money for very little effort: *come to Hollywood and get on the gravy train.*

Gray[1] /grā/, Asa (1810–88), US botanist. He is noted for popularizing the study of botany.

Gray[2], Elisha (1835–1901) US inventor. A rival of Alexander Graham Bell for the telephone patent, his small business eventually became Western Electric.

Gray[3], Horace (1828–1902) US Supreme Court associate justice 1881–1902.

Gray[4], Thomas (1716–71), English poet. He wrote "Elegy Written in a Country Church-Yard" (1751).

gray[1] /grā/ (Brit. **grey**) ▶ **adj. 1** of a color intermediate between black and white, as of ashes or an overcast sky. ■ (of hair) turning gray or white with age. ■ (of a person) having gray hair. ■ informal relating to old people, esp. when seen as an oppressed group. ■ (of the weather) cloudy and dull; without sun. ■ (of a person's face) pale, as through tiredness, age, or illness. **2** dull and nondescript; without interest or character. **3** (of financial or trading activity) not accounted for in official statistics: *the gray market.* ▶ **n. 1** gray color or pigment. ■ gray clothes or material. ■ gray hair. ■ (usu. **Gray**) the Confederate army in the Civil War, or a member of that army. **2** a gray thing or animal, in particular a gray or white horse. ▶ **v.** [intrans.] (esp. of hair) become gray with age. ■ (of a person or group) become older; age. — **gray·ish adj. gray·ly adv. gray·ness n.** [OE *grǣg*, of Gmc. origin; rel. to Du. *grauw* and Ger. *grau*.]

gray[2] (abbr.: **Gy**) ▶ **n.** Physics the SI unit of the absorbed dose of ionizing radiation, corresponding to one joule per kilogram. [1970s: named after Louis H. *Gray* (1905–65), Engl. radiobiologist.]

gray a·re·a ▶ **n.** an ill-defined situation or field not readily conforming to a category or existing set of rules.

gray·beard /'grā,bi(ə)rd/ ▶ **n.** humorous derog. an old man.

gray em·i·nence ▶ **n.** another term for ÉMINENCE GRISE.

Gray Fri·ar ▶ **n.** a Franciscan friar. [ME: so named because of the color of the order's habit.]

gray jay ▶ **n.** a fluffy, long-tailed jay (*Perisoreus canadensis*) with dark gray upper parts and a whitish face, found in Canada and the northwestern US.

gray·lag /'grā,lag/ (also **graylag goose**) ▶ **n.** a large goose (*Anser anser*) with mainly gray plumage, which is native to Eurasia and is the ancestor of the domestic goose. [18th C.: prob. from GRAY[1] + dial. *lag* 'goose,' of unknown origin.]

gray·ling /'grāliNG/ ▶ **n. 1** an edible freshwater fish (genus *Thymallus*) of the salmon family that is silvery-gray with horizontal violet stripes and has a long, high dorsal fin. **2** a mainly brown European butterfly (*Hipparchia semele*, family Nymphalidae) that has wings with bright eyespots and grayish undersides.

gray·mail /'grā,māl/ ▶ **n.** a tactic used by the defense in a spy trial, involving the threat to expose government secrets unless charges against the defendant are dropped.

gray mar·ket ▶ **n.** an unofficial market or trade in something, esp. unissued shares or controlled or scarce goods.

gray mat·ter ▶ **n.** the darker tissue of the brain and spinal cord, consisting mainly of nerve cell bodies and branching dendrites. Compare with WHITE MATTER. ■ informal intelligence.

gray·scale /'grā,skāl/ ▶ **n.** Comput. a range of gray shades from white to black, as used in a monochrome display or printout.

gray squir·rel ▶ **n.** an American tree squirrel (genus *Sciurus*) with mainly gray fur.

gray·wacke /'grā,wak; -,wakə/ (Brit. **grey·wacke**) ▶ **n.** Geol. a dark coarse-grained sandstone containing more than 15 percent clay. [18th C.: from Ger. *Grauwacke*, from *grau* 'gray' + *Wacke* 'large stone.']

gray wa·ter ▶ **n.** tech. the relatively clean waste water from baths, sinks, washing machines, and other kitchen appliances. Compare with BLACK WATER.

gray whale ▶ **n.** a mottled gray baleen whale (*Eschrichtius robustus*, family Eschrichtiidae) that typically has heavy encrustations of barnacles on the skin, commonly seen in coastal waters of the northeastern Pacific.

gray wolf ▶ **n.** another term for TIMBER WOLF.

Graz /gräts/ a city in southern Austria, on the Mur River; pop. 232,000.

graze¹ /grāz/ ▶ **v.** [intrans.] (of cattle, sheep, etc.) eat grass in a field. ■ [trans.] (of an animal) feed on (grass or land covered by grass). ■ [trans.] put (cattle, sheep, etc.) to feed on land covered by grass. ■ informal (of a person) eat small quantities of food at frequent but irregular intervals. ■ informal casually sample something. — **graz·er n.** [OE *grasian*, from *græs* 'grass.']

graze² ▶ **v.** [trans.] scrape the skin of (a part of the body) so as to break the surface but cause little or no bleeding. ■ touch or scrape lightly in passing. ▶ **n.** a slight injury where the skin is scraped. [16th C.: perh. a specific use of GRAZE¹.]

graz·ing /'grāziNG/ ▶ **n.** grassland suitable for pasturage.

grease ▶ **n.** /grēs/ oily or fatty matter, in particular: ■ a thick oily substance used as a lubricant. ■ oil or fat used or produced in cooking. ■ oily matter in the hair, esp. when used for styling. ■ the oily matter in unprocessed wool; lanolin. ▶ **v.** /grēs; grēz/ [trans.] smear or lubricate with grease.

– PHRASES **grease the palm of** informal bribe (someone). **grease the skids** informal help matters run smoothly. **grease the wheels** help something go smoothly. **like greased lightning** informal extremely fast. — **grease·less adj.** [ME: from OFr. *graisse*, based on L. *crassus* 'thick, fat.']

grease·ball /'grēs,bôl/ ▶ **n.** offens. a foreigner, esp. one of Mediterranean or Latin American origin.

grease gun ▶ **n.** a device for pumping grease under pressure to a lubrication point.

grease mon·key ▶ **n.** informal, derog. a mechanic.

grease·paint /'grēs,pānt/ ▶ **n.** a waxy substance used as makeup by actors.

grease pen·cil ▶ **n.** a pencil made of grease colored with a pigment, used esp. for marking glossy surfaces.

greas·er /'grēsər; -zər/ ▶ **n.** **1** a mechanic. ■ an unskilled member of a ship's engine-room crew. ■ informal a rough young man, esp. one who greases his hair back and is a member of a motorcycle gang. **2** informal, offens. a Hispanic American, esp. a Mexican.

grease·wood /'grēs,wood/ ▶ **n.** **1** a resinous dwarf shrub (*Sarcobatus vermiculatus*) of the goosefoot family, which yields hard yellow wood used chiefly for fuel. It grows in dry areas of the western US and can be toxic to livestock. **2** Another term for CHAMISE.

greas·y /'grēsē; -zē/ ▶ **adj.** (**greas·i·er, greas·i·est**) covered with an oily substance. ■ producing more body oils than average. ■ containing or cooked with too much oil or fat. ■ of or like grease. ■ slippery. ■ fig. (of a person or their manner) effusively polite in a way that is felt to be insincere and repulsive. — **greas·i·ly adv. greas·i·ness n.**

greas·y spoon ▶ **n.** informal a cheap, run-down cafe or restaurant serving fried foods.

great /grāt/ ▶ **adj.** **1** of an extent, amount, or intensity considerably above the normal or average. ■ very large and imposing. ■ [attrib.] used to reinforce another adjective of size or extent: *a great big grin.* ■ [attrib.] used to express surprise, admiration, or contempt, esp. in exclamations: *you great oaf!* ■ (also **greater**) [attrib.] used in names of animals or plants that are larger than similar kinds, e.g., **great auk, greater flamingo.** ■ (**Greater**) [attrib.] (of a city) including adjacent urban areas. **2** of ability, quality, or eminence considerably above the normal or average: *the great Italian conductor* | *we obeyed our great men and leaders* | *great art has the power to change lives.* ■ (**the Great**) a title denoting the most important person of the name: *Alexander the Great.* ■ informal very good or satisfactory; excellent. ■ [predic.] informal (of a person) very skilled or capable in a particular area. **3** [attrib.] denoting the element of something that is the most important or the most worthy of consideration. ■ used to indicate that someone or something particularly deserves a specified description. **4** [in comb.] (in names of family relationships) denoting one degree further removed upward or downward: *great-grandson* | *great-great-grandfather.* ▶ **n.** a great or distinguished person. ■ [as pl. n.] (**the great**) great people collectively. ▶ **adv.** informal excellently; very well.

– PHRASES **great and small** of all sizes, classes, or types. **a great deal** see DEAL¹. **a great many** see MANY. **a great one for** a habitual doer of; an enthusiast for. **Great Scott!** expressing surprise or amazement. **to a great extent** in a substantial way; largely. [OE *grēat* 'big,' of West Gmc. origin; rel. to Du. *groot* and Ger. *gross*.]

great ape ▶ **n.** a large ape of a family (Pongidae) closely related to humans, including the gorilla, orangutan, and chimpanzees, but excluding the gibbons; an anthropoid ape.

great auk ▶ **n.** a large, extinct, flightless auk (*Alca impennis*) of the North Atlantic. The last great auks were killed on an islet off Iceland in 1844.

great-aunt ▶ **n.** an aunt of one's father or mother.

Great Aus·tra·lian Bight a wide bay on the southern coast of Australia, part of the southern Indian Ocean.

Great Bar·ri·er Reef a coral reef in the western Pacific, off the coast of Queensland, Australia; extending about 1,250 miles (2,000 km).

Great Ba·sin an arid region in the western US between the Sierra Nevada and the Rocky Mountains that includes most of Nevada and parts of the adjacent states.

Great Bear Astron. the constellation Ursa Major.

Great Bear Lake a large lake in western Northwest Territories, Canada. It drains into the Mackenzie River via the Great Bear River.

Great Brit·ain /'britn/ England, Wales, and Scotland considered as a unit. The name is also often used loosely to refer to the United Kingdom.

great circle ▶ **n.** a circle on the surface of a sphere that lies in a plane passing through the sphere's center. As it represents the shortest distance between any two points on a sphere, a great circle of the earth is the preferred route taken by a ship or aircraft.

great·coat /'grāt,kōt/ ▶ **n.** a long heavy overcoat.

Great Dane

Great Dane ▶ **n.** a dog of a very large, powerful, short-haired breed.

Great De·pres·sion see DEPRESSION.

Great Dis·mal Swamp (also **Dismal Swamp**) an area of swampland in southeastern Virginia and northeastern North Carolina.

Great Di·vide another name for CONTINENTAL DIVIDE or GREAT DIVIDING RANGE.

great di·vide ▶ **n.** a distinction regarded as significant and very difficult to ignore or overcome. ■ an event, date, or place seen as the point at which significant and irrevocable change occurs. ■ the boundary between life and death. ■ (**Great Divide**) another term for CONTINENTAL DIVIDE.

Great Di·vid·ing Range a mountain system along the coast of eastern Australia; extending from eastern Victoria to northern Queensland. Also called GREAT DIVIDE.

great e·gret ▶ **n.** a large white heron (*Casmerodius albus*) of North and South America. Its yellow bill turns orange when breeding. Also called AMERICAN EGRET.

Great·er An·til·les /an'tilēz/ see ANTILLES.

great·er cel·an·dine /'selən,dīn; -,dēn/ ▶ **n.** a yellow-flowered Eurasian plant (*Chelidonium majus*) of the poppy family. Its toxic orange sap is used in herbal medicine, esp. for disorders of the eyes and skin.

Great·er Sun·da Is·lands /'sandə; 'soondə/ see SUNDA ISLANDS.

great egret

Great Falls a city in north central Montana, on the Missouri River; pop. 56,690.

great-heart·ed ▶ **adj.** dated having a noble, generous, and courageous spirit. — **great-heart·ed·ness n.**

great horned owl ▶ **n.** a large owl (*Bubo virginianus*, family Strigidae) found throughout North and South America, with hornlike ear tufts.

Great In·di·an Des·ert another name for THAR DESERT.

Great Lakes a group of five freshwater lakes in central North America, between Canada and the US, that consist of lakes Superior, Michigan, Huron, Erie, and Ontario.

great·ly /'grātlē/ ▶ **adv.** by a considerable amount; very much.

Great Moth·er ▶ **n.** another name for MOTHER GODDESS.

Great Neb·u·la Astron. **1** (also **Great Nebula in Andromeda**) the Andromeda Galaxy. **2** (also **Great Nebula in Orion**) a bright emission nebula in Orion, visible to the naked eye.

great-neph·ew ▶ **n.** a son of one's nephew or niece.

great·ness /'grātnis/ ▶ **n.** the quality of being great, distinguished, or eminent.

great-niece ▶ **n.** a daughter of one's nephew or niece.

Great Ouse /ooz/ another name of OUSE (sense 1).

Great Plains a vast area of plains east of the Rocky Mountains in North America that extend from the valleys of the Mackenzie River in Canada to southern Texas.

Great Pyr·e·nees ▶ **n.** a large heavily built dog of a white breed, with a thick shaggy double coat.

Great Rift Val·ley a geologic depression in eastern Africa and the Middle East that runs for about 3,000 miles (4,285 km) from the Jordan valley in Syria into Mozambique.

Great Rus·sian ▶ **adj. & n.** former term for RUSSIAN (language and people), as distinguished from other peoples and languages of the Russian Empire.

Great St. Ber·nard Pass see St. Bernard Pass.

Great Salt Lake a salt lake in northern Utah; the size varies greatly due to precipitation and water use.

Great Sand·y Des·ert 1 a large desert in northwestern Australia, in north central Western Australia. **2** another name for Rub' al Khali.

Great Schism /'s(k)izəm/ **1** the breach between the Eastern and Western Christian churches, traditionally dated to 1054 and becoming final in 1472. **2** the period 1378–1417, when the Western (Roman) Church was divided by the creation of antipopes.

Great Seal ▶ n. a seal used for the authentication of state documents of the highest importance, held by the Secretary of State.

Great Slave Lake a large lake in southwestern Northwest Territories, Canada; area 10,980 square miles (28,438 sq km).

Great Smok·y Moun·tains (also **Smoky Mountains** or **Smokies**) a range of the Appalachian Mountains in southwestern North Carolina and eastern Tennessee.

Great So·ci·e·ty ▶ n. a domestic program in the administration of President Lyndon B. Johnson that instituted federally sponsored social welfare programs.

Great Trek the migration 1835–37 of large numbers of Boers, discontented with British rule in the Cape of Good Hope, northward where they founded the Transvaal Republic and Orange Free State.

great-un·cle ▶ n. an uncle of one's mother or father.

Great Vic·to·ri·a Des·ert /vik'tôrēə/ a desert region in southwestern Australia.

Great Wall of Chi·na a fortified wall in northern China, extending some 1,500 miles (2,400 km) from Kansu province to the Yellow Sea north of Beijing.

Great War another name for World War I.

great white shark ▶ n. a large, aggressive shark (*Carcharodon carcharias*, family Lamnidae) of warm seas, with a brownish or gray back, white underparts, and large triangular teeth.

Great White Way a nickname for Broadway.

greave /grēv/ ▶ n. hist. a piece of armor used to protect the shin. [ME: from OFr. *greve* 'shin, greave,' of unknown origin.]

pied-billed grebe

grebe /grēb/ ▶ n. a diving waterbird (family Podicipedidae) with a long neck, lobed toes, and almost no tail, typically having bright breeding plumage used in display. The several North American species include the **western grebe** (*Aechmorphorus occidentalis*) and the **pied-billed grebe** (*Podilymbus podiceps*). [18th C.: from Fr. *grèbe*.]

Gre·cian /'grēsHən/ ▶ adj. of or relating to ancient Greece, esp. its architecture. [ME: from OFr. *grecien*, from L. *Graecia* 'Greece.']

Gre·cian nose ▶ n. a straight nose that continues the line of the forehead without a dip.

Gre·cism /'grēsizəm/ (also esp. Brit. **Grae·cism**) ▶ n. a Greek idiom or grammatical feature, esp. as imitated in another language. ■ the Greek spirit, style, or mode of expression, esp. as imitated in a work of art.

Greco- (also esp. Brit. **Graeco-**) ▶ comb. form Greek; Greek and ...: *Grecophile* | *Greco-Turkish*. ■ relating to Greece.

Gre·co, El see El Greco.

Gre·co-Ro·man /'grekō/ (also esp. Brit. **Grae·co-Ro·man**) ▶ adj. of or relating to the ancient Greeks and Romans. ■ denoting a style of wrestling in which holds below the waist are prohibited.

Greece /grēs/ a country in southeastern Europe. *See box.*

greed /grēd/ ▶ n. intense and selfish desire for something, esp. wealth, power, or food. [16th C.: back-form. from greedy.]

greed·y /'grēdē/ ▶ adj. (**greed·i·er**, **greed·i·est**) having or showing an intense and selfish desire for something, esp. wealth or power. ■ having an excessive desire or appetite for food. — **greed·i·ly** adv. **greed·i·ness** n. [OE *grǣdig*, of Gmc. origin.]

Greek /grēk/ ▶ adj. of or relating to Greece, its people, or their language. Compare with Hellenic. ▶ n. **1** a native or national of modern Greece, or a person of Greek descent. ■ a Greek-speaking person in the ancient world, typically a native of one of the city-states of Greece and the eastern Mediterranean. **2** the ancient or modern language of Greece, the only representative of the Hellenic branch of the Indo-European family. **3** a member of a fraternity or sorority having a Greek-letter name.

– PHRASES **it's (all) Greek to me** informal I can't understand it at all.
— **Greek·ness** n. [OE *Grēcas* 'the Greeks,' from L. *Graeci*, from Gk. *Graikoi*.]

Greek Cath·o·lic ▶ n. **1** a member of the Eastern Orthodox Church. **2** a Uniate member of a church observing the Greek rite.

Greek Church another term for Greek Orthodox Church.

Greece

Official name: Hellenic Republic
Location: southeastern Europe, consisting of the southern tip of the Balkan Peninsula with borders on the Aegean, Mediterranean, and Ionian Seas; includes the Ionian Islands, the Aegean Islands, and Crete
Area: 50,500 square miles (130,800 sq km)
Population: 10,647,000
Capital: Athens
Languages: Greek (official), English, French
Currency: euro

Greek cross ▶ n. a cross of which all four arms are of equal length. See illustration at cross.

Greek fire ▶ n. hist. a combustible compound emitted by a flame-throwing weapon and used to set fire to enemy ships. First used by the Greeks besieged in Constantinople (673–78), it ignited on contact with water, and was probably based on naphtha and quicklime.

Greek key ▶ n. a pattern of interlocking right-angled spirals.

Greek Or·tho·dox Church (also **Greek Church**) the Eastern Orthodox Church, which uses the Byzantine rite in Greek, in particular the national Church of Greece. See Orthodox Church.

Greek re·vi·val ▶ n. a neoclassical style of architecture inspired by and incorporating features of Greek temples from the 5th century BC, popular in the US and Europe in the first half of the 19th century.

Gree·ley[1] /'grēlē/ a city in north central Colorado; pop. 76,930.

Gree·ley[2], Horace (1811–72) US journalist and reformer. He was founding editor of the *New York Tribune* 1841–72 and a founder of the Republican party in 1854.

green /grēn/ ▶ adj. **1** of the color between blue and yellow in the spectrum; colored like grass or emeralds. ■ consisting of fresh vegetables of this color. ■ denoting a light or flag of this color used as a signal to proceed. ■ Physics denoting one of three colors of quark. **2** covered with grass, trees, or other plants. ■ (usu. **Green**) concerned with or supporting protection of the environment as a political principle. ■ (of a product) not harmful to the environment. **3** (of a plant or fruit) young or unripe. ■ (of wood) unseasoned. ■ (of food or leather) not dried, smoked, or tanned. ■ (of a person) inexperienced, naive, or gullible. ■ (of a memory) not fading. ■ still strong or vigorous. **4** (of the complexion or a person) pale and sickly-looking. ■ as a sign of jealousy or envy. ▶ n. **1** green color or pigment. ■ green clothes or material. ■ green foliage or growing plants. ■ informal dated money: *you'll save yourself some green.* **2** a green thing, in particular: ■ a green light. **3** a piece of public or common grassy land, esp. in the center of a town. ■ an area of smooth, very short grass immediately surrounding a hole on a golf course. **4** (**greens**) green leafy vegetables. **5** (usu. **Green**) a member or supporter of an environmentalist group or party. ▶ v. make or become green, in particular: ■ [trans.] make (an urban or desert area) more verdant by planting or encouraging trees or other greenery. ■ [trans.] make less harmful or more sensitive to the environment. ■ [intrans.] become green in color, through age or by becoming covered with plants. — **green·ish** adj. **green·ly** adv. **green·ness** n. [OE *grēne* (adj.), *grēnian* (v.), of Gmc. origin; rel. to Du. *groen*, Ger. *grün*, also to grass and grow.]

green al·gae ▶ plural n. photosynthetic algae that contain chlorophyll and store starch in discrete chloroplasts. They are eukaryotic, and most live in fresh water, ranging from unicellular flagellates to more complex multicellular forms.

Green·a·way /'grēnə,wā/, Kate (1846–1901), English artist; full name *Catherine Greenaway*. She illustrated children's books.

green·back /'grēn,bak/ ▶ n. informal a dollar bill.

Green Bay a port city in northeastern Wisconsin, on Green Bay; pop. 102,313.

green belt ▶ n. **1** a symbol of a level of proficiency in judo, karate, or other martial arts below that of a brown belt. ■ a person qualified to wear this. **2** (**greenbelt**) an area of open land around a city, on which building is restricted.

Green Be·ret ▶ n. informal a member of the US Army Special Forces.

green·bot·tle /'grēn,bätl/ ▶ n. a metallic green fly (genus *Lucilia*, family Calliphoridae) that sometimes lays eggs in the wounds of animals.

green·bri·er /'grēn,brīər/ (also **green·bri·ar**) ▶ n. a green-stemmed North American vine (genus *Smilax*) of the lily family, typically prickly and with blue-black berries. Also called CATBRIER.

green card ▶ n. (in the US) a permit allowing a foreign national to live and work permanently in the US.

green corn ▶ n. the tender ears of young sweet corn, suitable for cooking and eating.

green drag·on ▶ n. a North American arum (*Arisaema dracontium*) with a large divided leaf, a greenish-cream spathe, and a very long white spadix. Also called DRAGON ARUM.

green dragon

Greene[1] /grēn/, Graham (1904–91), English writer; full name *Henry Graham Greene*. His novels include *The Power and the Glory* (1940) and *The Quiet American* (1955).

Greene[2], Nathanael (1742–86), American Revolution general. Noted as a military strategist, he forced the British out of Georgia and the Carolinas in 1781.

green earth ▶ n. another term for TERRE VERTE.

green·er·y /'grēnərē/ ▶ n. green foliage, growing plants, or vegetation.

green-eyed mon·ster ▶ n. (**the green-eyed monster**) informal, humorous jealousy personified.

green fee ▶ n. another term for GREENS FEE.

green·field /'grēn,fēld/ ▶ adj. [attrib.] relating to or denoting previously undeveloped sites for commercial development or exploitation. Compare with BROWNFIELD. ▶ n. an undeveloped site, esp. one being evaluated and considered for commercial development or exploitation.

green·finch /'grēn,fincH/ ▶ n. a Eurasian finch (genus *Carduelis*) with green and yellow plumage.

green·fly /'grēn,flī/ ▶ n. (pl. same or **-flies**) a green aphid that is a common pest of crops and garden plants.

green·gage /'grēn,gāj/ ▶ n. **1** (also **greengage plum**) a sweet, greenish fruit resembling a small plum. Also called GAGE[3]. **2** the tree (*Prunus domestica* subsp. *italica*) of the rose family bearing this fruit. [18th C.: named after Sir William *Gage* (1657–1727), English botanist.]

green·heart /'grēn,härt/ ▶ n. a South American evergreen tree (*Ocotea rodiaei*) of the laurel family, yielding hard greenish timber that is used for marine work because of its resistance to marine borers. ■ this timber, or similar timber from various other tropical trees.

green·horn /'grēn,hôrn/ ▶ n. informal a person who is new to or inexperienced at a particular activity.

green·house /'grēn,hous/ ▶ n. a glass building in which plants are grown that need protection from cold weather.

green·house ef·fect ▶ n. the trapping of the sun's warmth in a planet's lower atmosphere due to the greater transparency of the atmosphere to visible radiation from the sun than to infrared radiation emitted from the planet's surface. See also GLOBAL WARMING.

green·house gas ▶ n. a gas that contributes to the greenhouse effect by absorbing infrared radiation, e.g., carbon dioxide and chlorofluorocarbons.

Green·ing /'grēniNG/ (also **Rhode Island Greening**) ▶ n. an apple of a variety that is green when ripe. [17th C.: prob. from MDu. *groeninc*, a kind of apple, from *groen* 'green.']

green·keep·er /'grēn,kēpər/ ▶ n. another term for GREENSKEEPER.

Green·land /'grēnlənd/ a large island that lies to the northeast of North America, mostly within the Arctic Circle; pop. 55,100; capital, Godthåb (Nuuk). Danish name GRØNLAND; called in Inuit KALAALLIT NUNAAT. — **Green·land·er** n.

Green·land·ic /grēn'landik/ ▶ n. a dialect of the Inuit (Eskimo) language that is one of the official languages of Greenland, the other being Danish. See also usage at INUIT.

Green·land Sea a sea that lies off the east coast of Greenland.

green·let /'grēnlit/ ▶ n. a small warblerlike vireo (genus *Hylophilus*) with drab plumage, found in Central and South America.

green light ▶ n. a green traffic light giving permission to proceed. ■ fig. permission to go ahead with a project. ▶ v. (**green-light**) [trans.] give permission to go ahead with (a project, esp. a movie).

green·ling /'grēnliNG/ ▶ n. (pl. same or **-lings**) a spiny-finned, edible fish (family Hexagrammidae) of the North Pacific.

green·mail /'grēn,māl/ ▶ n. Stock Market the practice of buying enough shares in a company to threaten a takeover, forcing the owners to buy them back at a higher price in order to retain control. — **green·mail·er** n. [1980s: blend of GREEN and BLACKMAIL.]

green ma·nure ▶ n. a fertilizer consisting of growing plants that are plowed back into the soil.

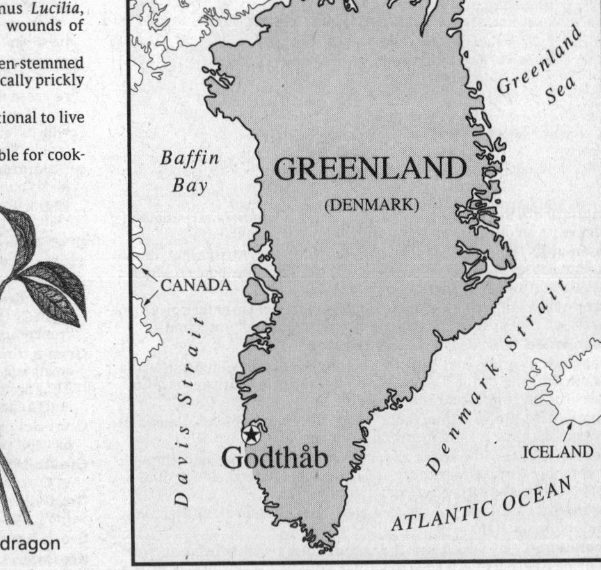

green mon·key ▶ n. a common African guenon (*Cercopithecus aethiops*) with greenish-brown upper parts and a black face, esp. the race *C. a. sabaeus* of West Africa. Compare with GRIVET, VERVET.

Green Moun·tains a range of the Appalachian Mountains that extends through Vermont and reaches 4,393 feet (1,340 m) at Mount Mansfield.

green·ock·ite /'grēnə,kīt/ ▶ n. a mineral consisting of cadmium sulfide and typically occurring as a yellow crust on zinc ores. [19th C.: from the name of Lord *Greenock*, who later became Earl Cathcart (1783–1859), + -ITE[1].]

green on·ion ▶ n. an onion taken from the ground before the bulb has formed, typically eaten raw in salad; a scallion.

Green Par·ty ▶ n. an environmentalist political party.

green pep·per ▶ n. the unripe fruit of a sweet pepper, which is mild in flavor and widely used in cooking. ■ the plant that yields this fruit. See CAPSICUM.

green rev·o·lu·tion ▶ n. a large increase in crop production in developing countries achieved by the use of fertilizers, pesticides, and high-yield crop varieties.

Green Riv·er a river that flows for 730 miles (1,130 km) from Wyoming through Colorado and Utah into the Colorado River

green room ▶ n. a room in a theater or studio in which performers can relax when they are not performing.

green·sand /'grēn,sand/ ▶ n. Geol. a greenish kind of sandstone, often loosely consolidated.

Greens·bor·o /'grēnz,bərō; -,bə-rō/ a city in north central North Carolina; pop. 223,891.

greens fee (also **green fee**) ▶ n. a charge for playing one round or session on a golf course.

green·shank /'grēn,sHaNGk/ ▶ n. a large sandpiper (genus *Tringa*) with long, greenish legs and gray plumage, breeding in northern Eurasia and North America.

greens·keep·er /'grēnz,kēpər/ (also **green·keep·er**) ▶ n. a person employed to look after a golf course.

green snake ▶ n. a harmless American snake (genus *Opheodrys*, family Colubridae) with a green back and white or yellowish underparts.

Green·span /'grēn,span/, Alan (1926–) US economist. He served as chairman of the Federal Reserve Board 1987–2006.

green·stick frac·ture /'grēn,stik/ ▶ n. a fracture of the bone, occurring typically in children, in which one side of the bone is broken and the other only bent.

green·stone /'grēn,stōn/ ▶ n. Geol. a greenish igneous rock containing feldspar and hornblende.

green·sward /'grēn,swôrd/ ▶ n. archaic literary grass-covered ground.

green tea ▶ n. tea that is made from unfermented leaves and is pale in color and slightly bitter in flavor. Compare with BLACK TEA.

green thumb ▶ n. informal natural talent for growing plants: *you don't need a green thumb to grow them.*

green turtle

green tur·tle ▶ n. an edible sea turtle (*Chelonia mydas*, family Cheloniidae) with an olive-brown shell, often living close to the coast.

Green·ville /ˈgrēnˌvil; -vəl/ **1** a city in northwestern Mississippi, in the Delta; pop. 41,633. **2** a city in eastern North Carolina; pop. 60,476. **3** a city in northwestern South Carolina; pop. 56,002.

green·way /ˈgrēnˌwā/ ▶ n. a strip of undeveloped land in or near an urban area, set aside for recreational use or environmental protection.

green·weed /ˈgrēnˌwēd/ see DYER'S GREENWEED.

Green·wich /ˈgrinij; -ICH; ˈgren-;/ **1** a borough of London, England, on the southern bank of the Thames River. **2** a town in southwestern Connecticut, on Long Island Sound; pop. 61,101.

Green·wich Mean Time (abbr.: **GMT**) (also **Green·wich time**) the mean solar time at the Greenwich meridian.

Green·wich me·rid·i·an ▶ n. the prime meridian, which passes through the former Royal Observatory at Greenwich, England, adopted internationally as the earth's zero of longitude in 1884.

Green·wich Vil·lage a district of New York City on the lower West Side of Manhattan.

green·wood /ˈgrēnˌwo͝od/ ▶ n. **1** wood that has recently been cut from a living tree and thus is slow to burn or resistant to burning. **2** archaic a wood or forest in leaf (regarded as the typical scene of medieval outlaw life).

green·y /ˈgrēnē/ ▶ adj. [often in comb.] slightly green.

Greer /gri(ə)r/, Germaine (1939–), Australian feminist and writer. She wrote *The Female Eunuch* (1970) and *The Beautiful Boy* (2003).

greet /grēt/ ▶ v. [trans.] give a polite word or sign of welcome or recognition to (someone) on meeting. ■ [with obj. and adverbial] receive or acknowledge (something) in a specified way. ■ (of a sight or sound) become apparent to or be noticed by (someone) on arrival somewhere. [OE *grētan* 'approach, attack, or salute,' of West Gmc. origin; rel. to Du. *groeten* and Ger. *grüssen* 'greet.']

greet·er /ˈgrētər/ ▶ n. a person who greets people entering a store, church service, or other public place.

greet·ing /ˈgrētiNG/ ▶ n. a polite word or sign of welcome or recognition. ■ the action of giving such a sign. ■ (usu. **greetings**) a formal expression of goodwill, said on meeting or in a written message.

greet·ing card (Brit. **greet·ings card**) ▶ n. a decorative card sent to convey good wishes on some occasion.

greg·a·rine /ˈgregəˌrīn/ Zool. ▶ adj. of or relating to a group of microscopic, wormlike protozoans that are internal parasites of insects, annelids, and other invertebrates. ■ (of movement) slow and gliding, as seen in these protozoans. ▶ n. a gregarine protozoan (class Gregarina, phylum Sporozoa). [19th C.: from mod. L. *Gregarina*, from L. *gregarius* (see GREGARIOUS).]

gre·gar·i·ous /griˈge(ə)rēəs/ ▶ adj. (of a person) fond of company; sociable. ■ (of animals) living in flocks or loosely organized communities. ■ (of plants) growing in open clusters or in pure associations. — **gre·gar·i·ous·ly** adv. **gre·gar·i·ous·ness** n. [17th C.: from L. *gregarius* (from *grex, greg-* 'a flock') + -OUS.]

Gre·go·ri·an cal·en·dar /griˈgôrēən/ n. the calendar introduced in 1582 by Pope Gregory XIII, as a modification of the Julian calendar.

Gre·go·ri·an chant ▶ n. church music sung as a single vocal line in free rhythm and a restricted scale (plainsong), in a style developed for the medieval Latin liturgy. [18th C.: named after St. Gregory the Great (in L. *Gregorius*).]

Greg·o·ry, St. /ˈgregərē/ (*c.*540–604), pope (as Gregory I) 590–604; known as **St. Gregory the Great**. He is credited with the introduction of Gregorian chant.

Greg·o·ry VIII (1502–85) pope 1572–85; born in Italy. The Gregorian calendar was introduced in 1582 as a result of his efforts to correct the errors in the Julian calendar.

Greg·o·ry of Nys·sa, St. /ˈnisə/ (*c.*330–*c.*395), bishop of Nyssa in Cappadocia; brother of St. Basil.

Greg·o·ry of Tours, St. /to͝or/ (*c.*540–594), Frankish bishop of Tours in 573–94.

grei·sen /ˈgrīzən/ ▶ n. Geol. a light-colored rock containing quartz, mica, and fluorine-rich minerals, resulting from the alteration of granite by hot vapor from magma. [19th C.: from Ger., prob. a dial. word, from *greis* 'gray with age.']

grem·lin /ˈgremlin/ ▶ n. an imaginary mischievous sprite regarded as responsible for an unexplained problem or fault, esp. a mechanical or electronic one. ■ such a problem or fault. [1940s: perh. suggested by GOBLIN.]

Gre·nache /grəˈnäsH/ ▶ n. a variety of black wine grape native to the Languedoc-Roussillon region of France. ■ a sweet red dessert wine made from this grape. [Fr.]

Gre·na·da /grəˈnādə/ a country in the southern Windward Islands, in the Caribbean Sea, that consists of the island of Grenada and the southern Grenadine Islands; pop. 84,800; capital, St. George's. — **Gre·na·di·an** /-dēən/ adj. & n.

gre·nade /grəˈnād/ ▶ n. a small bomb thrown by hand or launched mechanically. ■ a glass receptacle containing chemicals that are released when the receptacle is thrown and broken, used for testing drains and extinguishing fires. [16th C. (in the sense 'pomegranate,' which the bomb supposedly resembled in shape): from Fr., alt. of OFr. *(pome) grenate* (see POMEGRANATE), on the pattern of Sp. *granada*.]

gren·a·dier /ˌgrenəˈdi(ə)r/ ▶ n. **1** a soldier armed with grenades or a grenade launcher. **2** a common bottom-dwelling fish (family Macrouridae) with a large head, a long tapering tail, and typically a luminous gland on the belly.

gren·a·dil·la /ˌgrenəˈdilə; -ˈdēyə/ ▶ n. var. of GRANADILLA.

gren·a·dine[1] /ˈgrenəˌdēn; ˌgrenəˈdēn/ ▶ n. a sweet syrup made from pomegranates. [Fr., from *grenade* 'pomegranate' (see GRENADE).]

gren·a·dine[2] ▶ n. dress fabric of loosely woven silk or silk and wool. [19th C.: from Fr. (earlier *grenade*), 'grained silk,' from *grenu* 'grained,' from *grain* 'grain.']

Gren·a·dine Is·lands /ˌgrenəˈdēn/ (also **the Gren·a·dines**) a chain of small islands in the Caribbean Sea, part of the Windward Islands. They are divided administratively between the islands of St. Vincent and Grenada.

Gren·del /ˈgrendl/ the water monster killed by Beowulf in the Old English epic poem *Beowulf*.

Gre·no·ble /grəˈnōbəl; grəˈnôbl(ə)/ a city in southeastern France; pop. 153,970.

Gren·ville /ˈgrenvil/, George (1712–70), prime minister of Britain 1763–65.

Gresh·am /ˈgresHəm/ a city in northwestern Oregon; pop. 90,205.

Gresh·am's law Econ. the tendency for money of lower intrinsic value to circulate more freely than money of higher intrinsic and equal nominal value (often expressed as "Bad money drives out good").

Gret·na Green /ˈgretnə/ a village in Scotland just north of the English border, formerly (until 1939), a place for runaway couples from England to elope.

Gretz·ky /ˈgretskē/, Wayne Douglas (1961–), Canadian hockey player. The leading career scorer in the National Hockey League, he was voted most valuable player nine times.

grew /gro͞o/ past of GROW.

Grey[1] /grā/, Charles, 2nd Earl (1764–1845), prime minister of Britain 1830–34.

Grey[2], Lady Jane (1537–54), queen of England July 9–19, 1553; great-niece of Henry VIII. Named as monarch by Edward VI to ensure a Protestant succession, she was deposed by the Catholic Mary I.

Grey[3], Zane (1872–1939), US writer; born *Pearl Zane Gray*. He wrote nearly 100 books, most of them adventure novels about the Old West.

grey ▶ adj. British spelling of GRAY[1].

grey·hen /ˈgrāˌhen/ ▶ n. the female of the black grouse.

grey·hound /ˈgrāˌhound/ ▶ n. a dog of a tall, slender breed having keen sight and capable of high speed, used since ancient times for hunting small game and now chiefly in racing and coursing. [OE *grīghund*; first element rel. to ON *grey* 'bitch.']

grey·lag ▶ n. var. of GRAYLAG.

grey·wacke ▶ n. British spelling of GRAYWACKE.

grib·ble /ˈgribəl/ ▶ n. a small marine isopod (*Limnoria lignorum*) that bores into submerged wooden structures, often causing damage to pier timbers. [18th C.: perh. rel. to the v. GRUB.]

grid /grid/ ▶ n. **1** a framework of spaced bars that are parallel to or cross each other; a grating. **2** a network of lines that cross each other to form a series of squares or rectangles. ■ a football field. ■ a network of cables or pipes for distributing power, esp. high-voltage transmission lines for electricity. ■ a network of regularly spaced lines on a map that cross one another at right angles and are numbered to enable the precise location of a place. ■ a pattern of lines marking the starting places on a auto-racing track. ■ Electron. an electrode placed between the cathode and anode of a thermionic tube or cathode-ray tube, serving to control or modulate the flow of electrons. ▶ v. [trans.] [usu. as adj.] (**gridded**) put into or set out as a grid. [19th C.: back-form. from GRIDIRON.]

grid·der /ˈgridər/ ▶ n. a football player.

grid·dle /ˈgridl/ ▶ n. a heavy, flat iron plate that is heated and used for cooking food. ▶ v. [trans.] cook on a griddle. [ME: from OFr. *gredil*, from L. *craticula*, dimin. of *cratis* 'wickerwork.']

grid·i·ron /ˈgridˌīərn/ ▶ n. **1** a frame of parallel bars or beams, typically in two sets arranged at right angles, in particular: ■ a frame of parallel metal bars used for grilling meat or fish over an open fire. ■ (in the theater) a framework over a stage supporting scenery and lighting. **2** a field for football, marked with regularly spaced parallel lines. ■ the game of football. **3** another term for GRID (sense 2). [ME *gredire*, alt. of *gredile* 'griddle' by association with IRON.]

grid·lock /ˈgridˌläk/ ▶ n. **1** a traffic jam affecting a whole network of intersecting streets. **2** another term for DEADLOCK. — **grid·locked** adj.

grid ref·er·ence ▶ **n.** a map reference indicating a location in terms of a series of vertical and horizontal grid lines identified by numbers or letters.

grief /grēf/ ▶ **n.** deep sorrow, esp. that caused by someone's death. ■ informal trouble or annoyance.
– PHRASES **come to grief** have an accident; meet with disaster. **good grief!** an exclamation of irritation, frustration, or surprise. [ME: from OFr. *grief*, from *grever* 'to burden' (see GRIEVE).]

grief-strick·en ▶ **adj.** overcome with deep sorrow.

Grieg /grēg/, Edvard (1843–1907), Norwegian composer. His works include the *Piano Concerto in A Minor* (1869) and the *Peer Gynt Suites* (1876).

Grier /gri(ə)r/, Robert Cooper (1794–1870) US Supreme Court associate justice 1846–70.

griev·ance /'grēvəns/ ▶ **n.** a real or imagined wrong or other cause for complaint or protest, esp. unfair treatment. ■ an official statement of a complaint over something believed to be wrong or unfair. ■ a feeling of resentment over something believed to be wrong or unfair.

grieve /grēv/ ▶ **v.** [intrans.] suffer grief: *she grieved for her father.* ■ [trans.] feel grief for or because of. ■ [trans.] cause great distress to (someone). — **griev·er** n. [ME: from OFr. *grever* 'burden, encumber,' based on L. *gravare*, from *gravis* 'heavy, grave.']

griev·ous /'grēvəs/ ▶ **adj.** formal (of something bad) very severe or serious. — **griev·ous·ly** adv. **griev·ous·ness** n.
– USAGE Do not pronounce this word as though it had an extra syllable, as /'grēvē-əs/.

griffin

grif·fin /'grifin/ (also **gryph·on**, **grif·fon** /'grifən/) ▶ **n.** a mythical creature with the head and wings of an eagle and the body of a lion, typically depicted with pointed ears and with the eagle's legs taking the place of the forelegs. [ME: from OFr. *grifoun*, based on late L. *gryphus*, via L. from Gk. *grups, grup-*.]

Grif·fith /'grifiTH/, D. W. (1875–1948), US director; full name *David Llewelyn Wark Griffith*. He introduced many cinematic techniques, notably in his controversial white-supremacy film, *The Birth of a Nation* (1915).

Grif·fith Joy·ner /'joinər/, Florence (1959–98), US track and field athlete; called *Flo-Jo*. She won three gold medals at the 1988 Olympic Games, where she set the world records for the 100-meter and 200-meter events.

grif·fon /'grifən/ ▶ **n.** **1** a dog of any of several terrierlike breeds originating in northwestern Europe. ■ (also **Brussels griffon**) a dog of a toy breed with a flat face and upturned chin. **2** (also **griffon vulture**) a large Old World vulture (genus *Gyps*) with predominantly pale brown plumage. **3** var. of GRIFFIN. [ME: var. of GRIFFIN.]

grift /grift/ informal ▶ **v.** [intrans.] engage in petty swindling. ▶ **n.** a petty swindle. — **grift·er** n. [20th C.: alt. of GRAFT[2].]

grill[1] /gril/ ▶ **n.** a metal framework used for cooking food over an open fire; a gridiron. ■ a portable device for cooking outdoors, consisting of such a framework placed over charcoal or gas fuel. ■ a large griddle. ■ a dish of food, esp. meat, cooked using a grill. ■ (also **grill room**) a restaurant serving grilled food. ▶ **v.** **1** [trans.] cook (something) using a grill. **2** [trans.] informal subject (someone) to intense questioning or interrogation. — **grill·er** n. [17th C.: from Fr. *gril* (n.), *griller* (v.), from OFr. *graille* 'grille.']

grill[2] ▶ **n.** var. of GRILLE.

gril·lage /'grilij/ ▶ **n.** a heavy framework of cross-timbering or metal beams forming a foundation for building, esp. on soft, wet, or unstable ground. [18th C.: from Fr. (see GRILLE, -AGE).]

grille /gril/ (also **grill**) ▶ **n.** a grating or screen of metal bars or wires, placed in front of something as protection or to allow ventilation or discreet observation. ■ a grating at the front of a motor vehicle allowing air to circulate to the radiator to cool it. [17th C.: from Fr., from med. L. *craticula*, dimin. of *cratis* 'wickerwork.']

grill room ▶ **n.** see GRILL[1].

grill·work /'gril,wərk/ ▶ **n.** metal bars or wires arranged to form a grille.

grilse /grils/ ▶ **n.** a salmon that has returned to fresh water after a single winter at sea. [ME: of unknown origin.]

grim /grim/ ▶ **adj.** (**grim·mer, grim·mest**) forbidding or uninviting. ■ (of humor) lacking genuine levity; mirthless; black. ■ depressing or worrying to consider. ■ allowing no compromise; stern; relentless. ■ unrelentingly harsh; merciless or severe. — **grim·ly** adv. **grim·ness** n. [OE, of Gmc. origin; rel. to Du. *grim* and Ger. *grimm*.]

grim·ace /'griməs; gri'mās/ ▶ **n.** a twisted expression on a person's face, typically expressing disgust, pain, or wry amusement. ▶ **v.** [intrans.] make a grimace. [17th C.: from Fr., from Sp. *grimazo* 'caricature,' from *grima* 'fright.']

gri·mal·kin /gri'môlkin; -'mal-/ ▶ **n.** archaic a cat (used esp. in reference to its characteristically feline qualities). ■ a spiteful old woman. [16th C.: from GRAY[1] + *Malkin* (nickname for the given name *Matilda*).]

grime /grīm/ ▶ **n.** dirt ingrained on the surface of something, esp. clothing, a building, or the skin. ▶ **v.** [trans.] (usu. **be grimed**) blacken or make dirty with grime. [ME: from Mid. Low Ger. and MDu.]

Grim·ke /'grimkē/ a family of US reformers and abolitionists. Sisters Sarah Moore (1792–1872) and Angelina Emily (1805–79) wrote for the American Anti-Slavery Society.

Grimm /grim/, German folklorists. Brothers Jacob Ludwig Carl (1785–1863) and Wilhelm Carl (1786–1859) compiled an anthology of German fairy tales, which appeared in three volumes 1812–22.

Grimm's law Ling. the observation that certain Indo-European consonants (mainly stops) undergo regular changes in the Germanic languages that are not seen in non-Germanic languages such as Greek or Latin. The principle was set out by Jacob Grimm (1822).

gri·moire /grim'wär/ ▶ **n.** a book of magic spells and invocations. [19th C.: Fr., alt. of *grammaire* 'grammar.']

Grim Reap·er ▶ **n.** a personification of death in the form of a cloaked skeleton wielding a large scythe.

grim·y /'grīmē/ ▶ **adj.** (**grim·i·er, grim·i·est**) covered with or characterized by grime. — **grim·i·ly** adv. **grim·i·ness** n.

grin /grin/ ▶ **v.** (**grinned, grin·ning**) [intrans.] smile broadly, esp. in an unrestrained manner and with the mouth open. ■ grimace or appear to grimace grotesquely in a way that reveals the teeth. ▶ **n.** a broad smile.
– PHRASES **grin and bear it** suffer pain or misfortune in a stoical manner. — **grin·ner** n. **grin·ning·ly** adv. [OE *grennian* 'bare the teeth in pain or anger,' of Gmc. origin.]

grinch /grinCH/ ▶ **n.** informal a person who is mean-spirited and unfriendly. [20th C.: from the name of the title character in Dr. Seuss's book *How the Grinch Stole Christmas!* (1957).]

grind /grīnd/ ▶ **v.** (past **ground** /ground/) **1** [trans.] reduce (something) to small particles or powder by crushing it. ■ [intrans.] (of a mill or machine) work with a crushing action. ■ sharpen, smooth, or produce (something) by crushing or by friction. ■ operate (a mill or machine) by turning the handle. **2** rub or cause to rub together gratingly. ■ [no obj., with adverbial] move noisily and laboriously, esp. against a countering force. **3** [intrans.] informal (of a dancer) rotate the hips. ▶ **n.** [in sing.] **1** a crushing or grating sound or motion. ■ hard dull work. ■ informal an excessively hard-working student. ■ the size of ground particles. **2** informal a dancer's rotary movement of the hips.
– PHRASES **grind to a halt** (or **come to a grinding halt**) move more and more slowly and then stop.
– PHRASAL VERBS **grind someone down** wear someone down with continuous harsh or oppressive treatment. **grind on** continue for a long time in a wearying or tedious way. **grind something out** produce something dull or tedious slowly and laboriously. [OE *grindan*, prob. of Gmc. origin.]

grind·er /'grīndər/ ▶ **n.** **1** a machine used for grinding something. ■ a person employed to grind cutlery, tools, or cereals. **2** a molar tooth. ■ (**grinders**) informal the teeth. **3** informal another term for SUBMARINE SANDWICH.

grind·ing /'grīndiNG/ ▶ **adj.** [attrib.] **1** (of a condition) oppressive, tedious, and seemingly without end. **2** (of a sound or motion) harsh and grating. — **grind·ing·ly** adv.

grind·ing wheel ▶ **n.** a wheel used for cutting, grinding, or finishing metal or other objects, and typically made of abrasive particles bonded together.

grind·stone /'grīnd,stōn/ ▶ **n.** a thick disk of stone or other abrasive material mounted so as to revolve, used for grinding, sharpening, or polishing metal objects.
– PHRASES **keep one's nose to the grindstone** work hard and continuously.

grin·go /'griNGgō/ ▶ **n.** (pl. **-gos**) informal, often offens. a white person from an English-speaking country (used in Spanish-speaking regions, chiefly Latin America). [19th C.: Sp., lit. 'foreign, foreigner, or gibberish,' perh. an alt. of *griego* 'Greek.']

gri·ot /grē'ō; 'grēō/ ▶ **n.** a member of a class of traveling poets, musicians, and storytellers who maintain a tradition of oral history in parts of West Africa. [Fr., earlier *guiriot*, perh. from Port. *criado*.]

grip /grip/ ▶ **v.** (**gripped, grip·ping**) [trans.] **1** take and keep a firm hold of; grasp tightly. ■ [intrans.] maintain a firm contact, esp. by friction. **2** (of a feeling or emotion) deeply affect (someone). ■ (of an illness or unwelcome situation) afflict strongly. ■ compel the attention or interest of: [as adj.] (**gripping**) *a gripping thriller.* ▶ **n.** **1** [in sing.] a firm hold; a tight grasp or clasp. ■ a manner of grasping or holding something. ■ the ability of something, esp. a wheel or shoe, to maintain a firm contact with a surface. ■ [in sing.] an effective form of control over something. ■ [in sing.] an intellectual understanding of something. **2** a part or attachment by which something is held in the hand. **3** a traveling bag. **4** an assistant in a theater; a stagehand. ■ a member of a camera crew responsible for moving and setting up equipment.

– PHRASES **come** (or **get**) **to grips with** engage in combat with. ■ begin to deal with or understand. **get a grip** [usu. in imper.] informal keep or recover one's self-control. **get a grip on** take control of. **in the grip of** dominated or affected by something undesirable or adverse. **lose one's grip** become unable to understand or control one's situation. — **grip·per** n. **grip·ping·ly** adv. [OE *grippa* (v.), *gripe* 'grasp, clutch' (n.), *gripa* 'handful, sheath'; rel. to GRIPE.]

gripe /grīp/ ▶ v. **1** [reporting verb] informal express a complaint or grumble about something, esp. something trivial. ■ [trans.] dated distress; annoy. **2** [trans.] affect with gastric or intestinal pain. ▶ n. **1** informal a complaint, esp. a trivial one. **2** (usu. **gripes**) gastric or intestinal pain; colic. **3** (**gripes**) Naut. lashings securing a boat in its place on deck or in davits. — **grip·er** n. [OE *grīpan* 'grasp, clutch,' of Gmc. origin; rel. to Ger. *greifen* 'seize,' and to GROPE.]

grippe /grip/ ▶ n. old-fashioned term for INFLUENZA. — **grip·py** /'gripē/ adj. [18th C.: Fr., from *gripper* 'seize.']

Gris /grēs/, Juan (1887–1927), Spanish painter; born *José Victoriano Gonzales*. His work features the use of collage and paint in simple fragmented shapes.

gri·saille /gri'zī; -'zāl/ ▶ n. Art a method of painting in gray monochrome, typically to imitate sculpture. ■ a painting or stained-glass window in this style. [19th C.: Fr., from *gris* 'gray.']

gris·e·o·ful·vin /,grizēə'fo͝olvin/ ▶ n. Med. an antibiotic obtained from the mold *Penicillium griseofulvum* and used against fungal infections of the hair and skin. [1930s: from the mod. L. binomial, from med. L. *griseus* 'grayish' + L. *fulvus* 'reddish yellow.']

gri·sette /gri'zet/ ▶ n. **1** an edible woodland mushroom (*Amanita vaginata* and *A. fulva*, family Amanitaceae) with a brown or gray cap, a slender stem, and white gills. **2** dated a young working-class Frenchwoman. [Fr., from *gris* 'gray' + the dimin. suffix *-ette*.]

gris-gris /'grē,grē/ ▶ n. (pl. same) an African or Caribbean charm or amulet. ■ the use of such charms esp. in voodoo. [17th C.: from Fr. *grisgris*, of West Afr. origin.]

Grish·am /'grishəm/, John (1955–) US writer. His legal thrillers include the novel *The Firm* (1991) and the nonfictional *The Innocent Man* (2006).

gris·ly /'grizlē/ ▶ adj. (**-li·er**, **-li·est**) causing horror or disgust. — **gris·li·ness** n. [OE *grislic* 'terrifying,' of Gmc. origin; rel. to Du. *griezelig*.]

Gris·som /'grisəm/, Gus (1926–67) US astronaut; full name *Virgil Ivan Grissom*. He flew the second manned space flight in 1961. The first NASA astronaut to fly a second mission, he was killed while commanding a training exercise for the Apollo program.

grist /grist/ ▶ n. grain that is ground to make flour. ■ malt crushed to make mash for brewing. ■ fig. useful material, esp. to back up an argument.

– PHRASES **grist for the mill** useful experience, material, or knowledge. [OE, 'grinding,' of Gmc. origin; rel. to GRIND.]

gris·tle /'grisəl/ ▶ n. cartilage, esp. when found as tough, inedible tissue in meat. — **gris·tly** /'gris(ə)lē/ adj. [OE, of unknown origin.]

grist·mill /'grist,mil/ ▶ n. a mill for grinding grain.

grit /grit/ ▶ n. **1** small, loose particles of stone or sand. ■ [as adj.] (with numeral) indicating the fineness of an abrasive: *220-grit paper.* ■ (also **grit·stone**) a coarse sandstone. **2** courage and resolve; strength of character. ▶ v. (**grit·ted**, **grit·ting**) [trans.] **1** clench (the teeth), esp. in order to keep one's resolve when faced with an unpleasant or painful duty. **2** [intrans.] move with or make a grating sound. [OE *grēot* 'sand, gravel,' of Gmc. origin; rel. to Ger. *Griess*, also to GROATS.]

grits /grits/ ▶ plural n. [also treated as sing.] a dish of coarsely ground corn kernels boiled with water or milk. ■ the kernels from which this dish is made. [OE *grytt*, *grytte* 'bran, mill dust,' of Gmc. origin: rel. to GROATS.]

grit·ty /'gritē/ ▶ adj. (**grit·ti·er**, **grit·ti·est**) **1** containing or covered with grit. **2** showing courage and resolve: *a gritty pioneer woman.* ■ tough and uncompromising: *a gritty look at urban life.* — **grit·ti·ly** adv. **grit·ti·ness** n.

griv·et /'grivit/ (also **grivet monkey**) ▶ n. a common African guenon (*Cercopithecus aethiops*) with greenish-brown upper parts and a black face, esp. the race *C. a. aethiops* of Ethiopia and Sudan, with long white cheek tufts. Compare with GREEN MONKEY, VERVET. [19th C.: from Fr., of unknown origin.]

griz·zle /'grizəl/ ▶ adj. [often in comb.] (esp. of hair or fur) having dark and white hairs mixed. ▶ n. a mixture of dark and white hairs. [ME: from OFr. *grisel*, from *gris* 'gray.']

griz·zled /'grizəld/ ▶ adj. having or streaked with gray hair. [ME: from the adj. GRIZZLE + -ED[1].]

griz·zly /'grizlē/ ▶ n. (pl. **-zlies**) (also **griz·zly bear**) a bear (*Ursus arctos horribilis*) of a large race of the North American brown bear. [19th C.: from GRIZZLE.]

gro. ▶ abbr. gross.

groan /grōn/ ▶ v. [intrans.] make a deep inarticulate sound in response to pain or despair. ■ [with direct speech] say something in a despairing or miserable tone. ■ complain; grumble. ■ (of a thing) make a low creaking or moaning sound when pressure or weight is applied. ■ (**groan under/beneath**) fig. be oppressed by. ■ (**groan with/under**) be heavily loaded with. ▶ n. a deep, inarticulate sound made in pain or despair. ■ a complaint. ■ a low creaking or moaning sound made by an object or device under pressure.

– PHRASES **groan inwardly** feel like groaning at something but remain silent. — **groan·er** n. **groan·ing·ly** adv. [OE *grānian*, of Gmc. origin.]

groat /grōt/ ▶ n. hist. any of various medieval European coins, in particular an English silver coin worth four old pence, issued between 1351 and 1662. [from MDu. *groot* or Mid. Low Ger. *grōte* 'great, thick.']

groats /grōts/ ▶ plural n. hulled or crushed grain, esp. oats. [OE *grotan* (pl.): rel. to GRIT and GRITS.]

gro·cer /'grōsər/ ▶ n. a person who sells food and small household goods. [ME: from OFr. *grossier*, from med. L. *grossarius*, from late L. *grossus* 'gross.']

gro·cer·y /'grōs(ə)rē/ ▶ n. (pl. **-cer·ies**) (also **grocery store**) a grocer's store or business. ■ (**groceries**) items of food sold in such a store.

grog /gräg/ ▶ n. spirits (originally rum) mixed with water. ■ informal, alcoholic drink, esp. beer. ■ crushed unglazed pottery or brick used as an additive in plaster or clay. [18th C.: said to be from *Old Grog*, the reputed nickname of Admiral Vernon (1684–1757).]

grog·gy /'grägē/ ▶ adj. (**-gi·er**, **-gi·est**) dazed, weak, or unsteady, esp. from illness, intoxication, sleep, or a blow: *the sleeping pills had left her feeling groggy.* — **grog·gi·ly** adv. **grog·gi·ness** n.

grog·ram /'grägrəm/ ▶ n. a coarse fabric made of silk, often combined with mohair or wool and stiffened with gum. [16th C.: from Fr. *gros grain* 'coarse grain' (see also GROSGRAIN).]

groin[1] /groin/ ▶ n. **1** the area between the abdomen and the thigh on either side of the body. ■ informal the region of the genitals. **2** Archit. a curved edge formed by two intersecting vaults. [ME *grynde*, perh. from OE *grynde* 'depression, abyss.']

groin[2] (also **groyne**) ▶ n. a low wall or sturdy timber barrier built out into the sea from a beach to check erosion and drifting. [16th C.: from dial. *groin* 'snout,' from OFr. *groign*, from late L. *grunium* 'pig's snout,' from L. *grunnire* 'to grunt.']

grok /gräk/ ▶ v. (**grokked**, **grok·king**) [trans.] informal understand (something) intuitively or by empathy. ■ [intrans.] empathize or communicate sympathetically; establish a rapport. [20th C.: coined by Robert Heinlein (1907–88), US science fiction writer, in *Stranger in a Strange Land*.]

grom·met /'grämit/ ▶ n. an eyelet placed in a hole in a sheet or panel to protect or insulate a rope or cable passed through it or to prevent the sheet or panel from being torn. [17th C.: from obs. Fr. *grommette*, from *gourmer* 'to curb,' of unknown ultimate origin.]

Gro·my·ko /grə'mēkō/, Andrei Andreevich (1909–89), president of the Soviet Union 1985–88.

Gro·ning·en /'grōniNGən/ a city in the northern Netherlands, capital of a province with the same name; pop. 169,000.

Grøn·land /'grœn,län/ Danish name for GREENLAND.

groom /gro͞om; gro͝om/ ▶ v. [trans.] **1** look after the coat of (a horse, dog, or other animal) by brushing and cleaning it. ■ (of an animal) clean the fur or skin of. ■ give a neat and tidy appearance to (someone). ■ look after (a lawn, ski slope, or other surface). **2** prepare or train (someone) for a particular purpose or activity. ▶ n. **1** a person employed to take care of horses. **2** a bridegroom. **3** Brit. any of various officials of the royal household. [ME (in the sense 'boy,' later 'man, male servant'): of unknown origin.]

grooms·man /'gro͞omzmən; 'gro͝omz-/ ▶ n. (pl. **-men**) a male friend officially attending the bridegroom at a wedding.

groove /gro͞ov/ ▶ n. **1** a long, narrow cut or depression, esp. one made to guide motion or receive a corresponding ridge. ■ a spiral track cut in a phonograph record, into which the stylus fits. **2** an established routine or habit. **3** informal a rhythmic pattern in popular or jazz music. ▶ v. **1** [trans.] make a groove or grooves in. **2** [intrans.] informal dance or listen to popular or jazz music, esp. that with an insistent rhythm. ■ dated play such music in an accomplished and stylish manner. ■ enjoy oneself. **3** [trans.] Baseball, informal pitch (a ball) in the center of the strike zone. ■ (in the context of other sports) kick or throw (the ball) successfully; score (a goal) with stylish ease.

– PHRASES **in** (or **into**) **the groove** informal performing consistently well or confidently: *it might take me a couple of races to get back into the groove.* ■ indulging in relaxed and spontaneous enjoyment, esp. dancing: *get into the groove!* [ME (denoting a mine or shaft): from Du. *groeve* 'furrow, pit'; rel. to GRAVE[1].]

grooved /gro͞ovd/ ▶ adj. provided with or having a groove or grooves.

groov·y /'gro͞ovē/ ▶ adj. (**groov·i·er**, **groov·i·est**) informal, dated humorous fashionable and exciting. ■ enjoyable and excellent. — **groov·i·ly** adv. **groov·i·ness** n.

grope /grōp/ ▶ v. **1** [no obj., with adverbial] feel about or search blindly or uncertainly with the hands. ■ (**grope for**) search mentally with hesitation or uncertainty for (a word or answer). ■ move along with difficulty by feeling objects as one goes. **2** [trans.] informal feel or fondle (someone) for sexual pleasure, esp. against their will. ▶ n. an act of fondling someone for sexual pleasure. — **grop·ing·ly** adv. [OE *grāpian*, of West Gmc. origin; rel. to GRIPE.]

Gro·pi·us /'grōpēəs/, Walter (1883–1969), US architect; born in Germany. He founded the Bauhaus school of art and architecture, as exemplified in his design of the Harvard Graduate Center (1948–50).

gros·beak /'grōs,bēk/ ▶ n. a finch or related songbird with a stout conical bill and typically brightly colored plumage. [17th C.: from Fr. *grosbec*, from *gros* 'big, fat' + *bec* 'beak.']

gro·schen /'grōsHən/ ▶ n. (pl. same) a monetary unit in Austria (until the introduction of the euro), equal to one hundredth of a schilling. ■ hist. a small German silver coin. ■ informal a German ten-pfennig piece.

[Ger., from Mid. High Ger. *grosse*, from med. L. *(denarius) grossus* 'thick (penny)'; cf. GROAT.]

gros·grain /'grō,grān/ ▶ **n.** a heavy, ribbed fabric, typically of silk or rayon. [19th C.: Fr., 'coarse grain' (see also GROGRAM).]

gros point /grō/ ▶ **n.** a type of needlepoint embroidery consisting of stitches crossing two or more threads of the canvas in each direction. [19th C.: Fr., lit. 'large stitch.']

gross /grōs/ ▶ **adj.** **1** unattractively large or bloated. ■ large-scale; not fine or detailed. ■ derog. complete; blatant. ■ vulgar; unrefined. ■ informal very unpleasant; repulsive. **2** (of income, profit, or interest) without deduction of tax or other contributions; total. Often contrasted with NET[2] (sense 1). ■ (of weight) including all contents, fittings, wrappings, or other variable items; overall. ■ (of a score in golf) as actually played, without taking handicap into account. ▶ **adv.** without tax or other contributions having been deducted. ▶ **v.** [trans.] produce or earn (an amount of money) as gross profit or income. ▶ **n.** **1** (pl. same) an amount equal to twelve dozen; 144. [From Fr. *grosse douzaine*, lit. 'large dozen.'] **2** (pl. **gross·es**) a gross profit or income.

– PHRASES **by the gross** fig. in large numbers or amounts.

– PHRASAL VERBS **gross someone out** informal disgust someone, typically with repulsive or obscene behavior or appearance. — **gross·ly** **adv.** [as submodifier] *Freda was grossly overweight.* **gross·ness** **n.** [ME: from OFr. *gros, grosse* 'large,' from late L. *grossus*.]

gross a·nat·o·my ▶ **n.** the branch of anatomy that deals with the structure of organs and tissues that are visible to the naked eye.

gross do·mes·tic prod·uct (abbr.: **GDP**) ▶ **n.** the total value of goods produced and services provided in a country during one year. Compare with GROSS NATIONAL PRODUCT.

gross na·tion·al prod·uct (abbr.: **GNP**) ▶ **n.** the total value of goods produced and services provided by a country during one year, equal to the gross domestic product plus the net income from foreign investments.

gross-out ▶ **n.** informal something disgusting or repellent.

gross ton ▶ **n.** see TON[1] (sense 1).

gros·su·lar /'gräsyələr/ ▶ **n.** a mineral of the garnet group, consisting essentially of calcium aluminum silicate. [19th C.: from mod. L. *grossularia* 'gooseberry.']

Gros Ventre /'grō ,vänt/ ▶ **n.** (pl. **Gros Ventres** pronunc. same) (also **Gros Ventres of the Missouri**) another term for HIDATSA. [Fr., lit. 'big belly.']

grosz /grôsh/ ▶ **n.** (pl. **groszy** /-shē/) a monetary unit in Poland, equal to one hundredth of a zloty. [Pol.; cf. GROSCHEN.]

grot /grät/ ▶ **n.** literary a grotto. [16th C.: from Fr. *grotte*, from Ital. *grotta*.]

gro·tesque /grō'tesk/ ▶ **adj.** comically or repulsively ugly or distorted. ■ incongruous or inappropriate to a shocking degree. ▶ **n.** a very ugly or comically distorted figure, creature, or image. ■ (**the grotesque**) that which is grotesque. ■ a style of decorative painting or sculpture consisting of the interweaving of human and animal forms with flowers and foliage. — **gro·tesque·ly** **adv.** **gro·tesque·ness** **n.** [16th C. (as n.): from Fr. *crotesque*, from Ital. *grottesca*, from *opera* or *pittura grottesca* 'work or painting resembling that found in a grotto'.]

gro·tes·quer·ie /grō'teskərē/ (also **gro·tes·quer·y**) ▶ **n.** (pl. **-quer·ies**) grotesque quality or grotesque things collectively. ■ a grotesque figure, object, or action. [17th C.: Fr. (see GROTESQUE).]

Gro·ti·us /'grōsh(ē)əs/, Hugo (1583–1645), Dutch jurist; Latinized name of *Huig de Groot*. His *De Jure Belli et Pacis* (1625) established the basis of modern international law.

Grot·on /'grätn/ a town in southeastern Connecticut, a submarine building center; pop. 39,907.

grot·to /'grätō/ ▶ **n.** (pl. **-toes** or **-tos**) a small picturesque cave, esp. an artificial one in a park or garden. ■ an indoor structure resembling a cave. — **grot·toed** **adj.** [17th C.: from Ital. *grotta*, via L. from Gk. *kruptē* (see CRYPT).]

grot·ty /'grätē/ ▶ **adj.** (**-ti·er**, **-ti·est**) Brit., informal unpleasant and of poor quality. ■ [as complement] unwell. — **grot·ti·ness** **n.** [1960s: from GROTESQUE + -Y[1].]

grouch /grouch/ ▶ **n.** a habitually grumpy person. ■ a complaint or grumble. ■ a fit of grumbling or sulking. ▶ **v.** [intrans.] voice one's discontent in an ill-tempered manner; grumble. [19th C.: var. of obs. *grutch*, from OFr. *grouchier* 'to grumble, murmur.']

grouch·y /'grouchē/ ▶ **adj.** (**grouch·i·er**, **grouch·i·est**) irritable and bad-tempered; grumpy; complaining. — **grouch·i·ly** **adv.** **grouch·i·ness** **n.**

ground[1] /ground/ ▶ **n.** **1** [in sing.] the solid surface of the earth. ■ a limited or defined extent of the earth's surface; land. ■ land of a specified kind. ■ an area of land or sea used for a specified purpose. ■ (**grounds**) an area of enclosed land surrounding a large house or other building. ■ [as adj.] (in aviation) of or relating to the ground rather than the air (with particular reference to the maintenance and servicing of an aircraft on the ground). ■ [as adj.] (of an animal) living on or in the ground. ■ [as adj.] (of a fish) bottom-dwelling. ■ [as adj.] (of a plant) low-growing, esp. in relation to similar plants. **2** an area of knowledge or subject of discussion or thought. **3** (**grounds**) factors forming a basis for action or the justification for a belief. **4** esp. Art a prepared surface to which paint is applied. ■ a substance used to prepare a surface for painting. ■ (in embroidery or ceramics) a plain surface to which decoration is applied. ■ a piece of wood fixed to a wall as a base for boards, plaster, or woodwork. **5** Music short for GROUND BASS. **6** (**grounds**) solid particles, esp. of ground coffee, that form a residue; sediment. **7** electrical connection of a circuit or conductor to the earth. ▶ **v.** [trans.] **1** (often **be grounded**) prohibit or prevent (a pilot or an aircraft) from flying. ■ informal (of a parent) refuse to allow (a child) to go out socially as a punishment. **2** run (a ship) aground. ■ [intrans.] (of a ship) go aground. **3** (usu. **be grounded in**) give (something abstract) a firm theoretical or practical basis. ■ instruct (someone) thoroughly in a subject. **4** place or lay (something) on the ground or hit the ground with it. **5** connect (an electrical device) with the ground. **6** [intrans.] Baseball (of a batter) hit a pitched ball so that it bounces on the ground. ■ (**ground out**) (of a batter) be put out by hitting a ball on the ground to a fielder who throws it to or touches first base before the batter touches that base.

– PHRASES **be thick** (or **thin**) **on the ground** existing (or not existing) in large numbers or amounts. **break ground 1** do preparatory digging or other work prior to building or planting something. **2** another term for *BREAK NEW GROUND* below. **break new** (or **fresh**) **ground** do something innovative that is considered an advance or positive benefit. **cut the ground from under someone's feet** do something that leaves someone without a reason or justification for their actions or opinions. **from the ground up** informal completely or complete. **gain ground** become more popular or accepted. **gain ground on** get closer to someone or something one is pursuing or with whom one is competing. **get off the ground** (or **get something off the ground**) start or cause to start happening or functioning successfully. **give** (or **lose**) **ground** retreat or lose one's advantage during a conflict or competition. **go to ground** (of a fox or other animal) enter its earth or burrow. ■ fig. (of a person) hide or become inaccessible, esp. for a long time. **hold** (or **stand**) **one's ground** not retreat or lose one's advantage during a conflict or competition. **make up ground** get closer to someone ahead in a race or competition. **on the ground** in a place where real, practical work is done. **on one's own ground** in one's own territory or concerning one's own range of knowledge or experience. **prepare the ground** make it easier for something to occur or be developed. **run someone/something to ground** see RUN. **work** (or **run**) **oneself into the ground** exhaust oneself by working or running very hard. [OE *grund*, of Gmc. origin; rel. to Du. *grond* and Ger. *Grund*.]

ground[2] past and past participle of GRIND. ▶ **adj.** [attrib.] reduced to fine particles by crushing or mincing. ■ shaped, roughened, or polished by grinding.

– PHRASES **ground down** exhausted or worn down.

ground ball ▶ **n.** Baseball a ball hit along the ground.

ground bass /bās/ ▶ **n.** Music a short theme, usually in the bass, that is constantly repeated as the other parts of the music vary.

ground bee·tle ▶ **n.** any of a number of beetles that live mainly on or near the ground, in particular a fast-running predatory beetle of the family Carabidae.

ground·break·ing /'ground,brāking/ ▶ **adj.** breaking new ground; innovative; pioneering. — **ground·break·er** **n.**

ground cher·ry ▶ **n.** an American plant (genus *Physalis*) of the nightshade family that resembles the cape gooseberry.

ground cloth (also **ground·cloth**) ▶ **n.** a waterproof cloth spread under a sleeping bag, directly on the ground or inside a tent. Also called GROUNDSHEET.

ground con·trol ▶ **n.** [treated as sing. or pl.] the ground-based personnel and equipment that monitor and direct the flight and landing of aircraft or spacecraft. — **ground con·trol·ler** **n.**

ground cov·er ▶ **n.** low-growing, spreading plants that help to stop weeds growing.

ground crew ▶ **n.** [treated as sing. or pl.] a team of people who maintain and service an aircraft on the ground.

ground ef·fect ▶ **n.** the effect of added aerodynamic buoyancy produced by a cushion of air below a vehicle moving close to the ground.

ground·er /'groundər/ ▶ **n.** Baseball a ground ball.

ground floor ▶ **n.** the floor of a building at ground level.

– PHRASES **get in on the ground floor** informal become part of an enterprise in its early stages.

ground glass ▶ **n.** **1** glass with a smooth ground surface that renders it nontransparent while retaining its translucency. **2** glass ground into an abrasive powder.

ground·hog /'ground,häg; -,hôg/ ▶ **n.** another term for WOODCHUCK.

Ground·hog Day **n.** February 2, when the groundhog is said to come out of its hole at the end of hibernation. If the animal sees its shadow (that is, if the weather is sunny), it is said to portend six weeks more of winter weather.

ground·ing /'grounding/ ▶ **n.** [in sing.] basic training or instruction in a subject.

ground i·vy ▶ **n.** a creeping plant (*Glechoma hederacea*) of the mint family, with bluish-purple flowers. Native to Europe, it has become established in eastern North America. Also called **gill-over-the-ground**.

ground·less /'groundlis/ ▶ **adj.** not based on any good reason. — **ground·less·ly** **adv.** **ground·less·ness** **n.**

ground lev·el ▶ **n.** **1** the level of the ground: [as adj.] *ground-level ozone pollution.* ■ the ground floor of a building. **2** Physics another term for GROUND STATE.

ground·ling /'groundling/ ▶ **n.** **1** a spectator or reader of inferior taste, such as a member of a theater audience who traditionally stood in the pit beneath the stage. **2** a person on the ground as opposed to one in a spacecraft or aircraft. **3** a fish that lives at the bottom of lakes and streams, esp. a gudgeon or loach. **4** a creeping or dwarf plant. [17th C. (denoting a fish): from GROUND[1].]

ground loop ▶n. a violent, uncontrolled swinging movement of an aircraft while landing, taking off, or taxiing. ▶v. (**ground-loop**) [intrans.] (of an aircraft) make a ground loop.

ground·mass /'ground,mas/ ▶n. [in sing.] Geol. the compact, finer-grained material in which the crystals are embedded in a porphyritic rock.

ground·nut /'ground,nət/ ▶n. **1** another term for PEANUT. **2** a North American twining vine (genus *Apios*) of the pea family. It bears clusters of fragrant brownish or maroon flowers and yields a sweet edible tuber.

ground·out /'ground,out/ ▶n. Baseball a play in which a batter is put out by hitting a ball on the ground to a fielder who throws it to or touches first base before the batter touches that base.

ground pine ▶n. **1** a small, yellow-flowered Eurasian plant (*Ajuga chamaepitys*) of the mint family that resembles a pine seedling in appearance and smell. **2** a North American club moss (genus *Lycopodium*) with small, shiny leaves, resembling a miniature conifer and growing typically in coniferous woodland.

ground plan ▶n. the plan of a building at ground level as imagined seen from above. ■ the general outline or basis of a plan.

ground rule ▶n. (usu. **ground rules**) a basic principle. ■ Baseball a rule pertaining to the limits of play on a particular field.

ground·sel /'groun(d)səl/ ▶n. **1** a widely distributed plant (genus *Senecio*) of the daisy family, with yellow rayless flowers. **2** var. of GROUNDSILL. [OE *gundæswelgiæ* (later *grundeswylige*), prob. from *gund* 'pus' + *swelgan* 'to swallow.']

ground·sheet /'groun(d),shēt/ ▶n. another term for GROUND CLOTH.

ground·sill (also **ground·sel**) ▶n. the horizontal beam or timber in a building that is secured to the foundation and is the base for the rest of the structure.

grounds·keep·er /'groun(d)z,kēpər/ ▶n. a person who maintains an athletic field, a park, or the grounds of a school or other institution.

ground·speed /'ground,spēd/ ▶n. an aircraft's speed relative to the ground. Compare with AIRSPEED.

ground squir·rel ▶n. a burrowing squirrel (*Spermophilus* and other genera) that is typically highly social, found chiefly in North America and northern Eurasia, where it usually hibernates in winter.

ground state ▶n. Physics the lowest energy state of an atom or other particle.

ground·stroke /'ground,strōk/ ▶n. Tennis a stroke played after the ball has bounced, as opposed to a volley.

ground·swell /'groun(d),swel/ ▶n. [in sing.] **1** a buildup of opinion or feeling in a large section of the population. **2** a large or extensive swell in the sea.

ground·wa·ter /'ground,wôtər; -,wätər/ ▶n. water held underground in the soil or in pores and crevices in rock.

ground wave ▶n. a radio wave that reaches a receiver from a transmitter directly, without reflection from the ionosphere.

ground·work /'ground,wərk/ ▶n. preliminary or basic work.

ground ze·ro ▶n. [in sing.] the point on the earth's surface directly above or below an exploding nuclear bomb. ■ (**Ground Zero**) the 16-acre site of the Twin Towers and other buildings of the World Trade Center in lower Manhattan, destroyed by terrorists on September 11, 2001. ■ fig. a starting point or base for some activity.

group /groōp/ ▶n. [treated as sing. or pl.] a number of people or things that are located close together or are considered or classed together. ■ a number of people who work together or share certain beliefs. ■ a commercial organization consisting of several companies under common ownership. ■ a number of musicians who play popular music together. ■ Mil. a unit of the US Air Force, consisting of two or more squadrons. ■ Mil. a unit of the US Army, consisting of two or more battalions. ■ Art two or more figures or objects forming a design. ■ Chem. a set of elements occupying a column in the periodic table and having broadly similar properties arising from their similar electronic structure. ■ Chem. a combination of atoms having a recognizable identity in a number of compounds. ■ Math. a set of elements, together with an associative binary operation, that contains an inverse for each element and an identity element. ■ Geol. a stratigraphic division consisting of two or more formations. ▶v. [with obj. and adverbial] (often **be grouped**) put together or place in a group or groups. ■ put into categories; classify. ■ [no obj., with adverbial] form a group or groups. [17th C.: from Fr. *groupe*, from Ital. *gruppo*, of Gmc. origin; rel. to CROP.]

group dy·nam·ics ▶plural n. [also treated as sing.] Psychol. the processes involved when people in a group interact with each other, or the study of these.

Nassau grouper

group·er /'groōpər/ ▶n. a large heavy-bodied fish (*Epinephelus, Mycteroperca*, and other genera) of the sea bass family, with a big head and wide mouth, found in warm seas. The **Nassau grouper** (*E. striatus*) is the most economically important fish of the Bahamas. [17th C.: from Port. *garoupa*, prob. from a local term in South America.]

group home ▶n. a home where a small number of unrelated people in need of care, support, or supervision, such as the elderly or the mentally ill, can live together.

group·ie /'groōpē/ ▶n. informal a person, esp. a young woman, who regularly follows a pop music group or other celebrity in the hope of meeting or getting to know them. ■ [with adj.] often derog. an enthusiastic or uncritical follower.

group·ing /'groōpiNG/ ▶n. a set of people acting together with a common interest or purpose, esp. within a larger organization. ■ the arrangement or formation of people or things in a group or groups.

Group of Sev·en (abbr.: **G7**) a group of seven leading industrial nations outside the former communist bloc, consisting of the US, Japan, Germany (originally West Germany), France, the UK, Italy, and Canada.

group prac·tice ▶n. a medical practice run by several doctors.

group ther·a·py ▶n. a form of psychotherapy in which a group of patients meet to describe and discuss their problems together under the supervision of a therapist.

group·think /'groōp,THiNGk/ ▶n. the practice of thinking or making decisions as a group in a way that discourages creativity or individual responsibility. [20th C.: on the pattern of *doublethink*.]

group·ware /'groōp,we(ə)r/ ▶n. Comput. software designed to facilitate collaboration by a number of different users.

grouse[1] /grous/ ▶n. (pl. same) a game bird (*Lagopus, Tetrao*, and other genera) with a plump body and feathered legs, the male being larger and more conspicuously colored than the female. The **grouse family** (Tetraonidae, or Phasianidae) also includes ptarmigans, capercaillies, and prairie chickens. [16th C.: perh. rel. to med. L. *gruta* or to OFr. *grue* 'crane.']

grouse[2] ▶v. [intrans.] complain pettily; grumble. ▶n. a grumble or complaint. — **grous·er** n. [19th C.: of unknown origin; cf. GROUCH.]

grout /grout/ ▶n. a mortar or paste for filling crevices, esp. the gaps between wall or floor tiles. ▶v. [trans.] fill in with grout. [17th C.: perh. from obs. *grout* 'sediment,' (pl.) 'dregs.']

grout·er /'groutər/ ▶n. a tool used for grouting tiles.

grove /grōv/ ▶n. a small wood, orchard, or group of trees. — **grovy** adj. [OE *grāf*, of Gmc. origin.]

grov·el /'grävəl; 'grə-/ ▶v. (**grov·eled, grov·el·ing** ; Brit. **grov·elled, grov·el·ling**) [intrans.] lie or move abjectly on the ground with one's face downward. ■ act in an obsequious manner in order to obtain someone's forgiveness or favor. — **grov·el·er** n. **grov·el·ing·ly** adv. [ME: *groof, grufe* 'the face or front,' from ON *á grúfu* 'face downward').]

groves of Ac·a·deme ▶plural n. the academic world. [translating Horace's *silvas Academi*.]

grow /grō/ ▶v. (past **grew** /groō/; past part. **grown** /grōn/) [intrans.] **1** (of a living thing) undergo natural development by increasing in size and changing physically; progress to maturity. ■ (of a plant) germinate and develop. ■ [trans.] produce by cultivation. ■ [trans.] allow or cause (a part of the body) to grow or develop. ■ (of something abstract) come into existence and develop. **2** become larger or greater over a period of time; increase. ■ [trans.] cause (something, esp. a business) to expand or increase. **3** [with complement] become gradually or increasingly: *sharing our experiences, we grew braver.* ■ [with infin.] (of a person) come to feel or know something over time. ■ (**grow apart**) (of two or more people) become gradually estranged.

– PHRASES **grow on trees** [usu. with negative] informal be plentiful or easily obtained: *money doesn't grow on trees.*

– PHRASAL VERBS **grow into** become as a result of natural development or gradual increase. ■ become large enough to wear (a garment) comfortably. **grow on** become gradually more appealing to (someone). **grow out of** become too large to wear (a garment). ■ become too mature to retain (a childish habit). **grow up** advance to maturity; spend one's childhood and adolescence. ■ [often in imper.] begin to behave or think sensibly and realistically. ■ arise; develop. — **grow·a·ble** adj. [OE *grōwan*, of Gmc. origin.]

grow·er /'grōər/ ▶n. **1** a person who grows a particular type of crop. **2** [with adj.] a plant that grows in a specified way.

grow·ing pains ▶plural n. neuralgic pains that occur in the limbs of some young children. ■ fig. the difficulties experienced in the early stages of an enterprise.

grow·ing point ▶n. the point at which growth originates. ■ Bot. the meristem region at the apex of a plant shoot at which continuous cell division and differentiation occur.

grow·ing sea·son ▶n. the part of the year during which rainfall and temperature allow plants to grow.

growl /groul/ ▶v. [intrans.] (of an animal, esp. a dog) make a low guttural sound of hostility in the throat. ■ [with direct speech] (of a person) say something in a low grating voice, typically in a threatening manner. ■ (of a thing) make a low or harsh rumbling sound, typically one that is felt to be threatening. ▶n. a low guttural sound made in the throat, esp. by a dog. ■ a similar sound made by a person, esp. to express hostility or anger. ■ [in sing.] a low throaty sound made by a machine or engine. — **growl·ing·ly** adv. [17th C.: prob. imitative.]

growl·er /'groulər/ ▶n. **1** a person or thing that growls. **2** a small iceberg that rises little above the water. **3** informal a pail or other container used for carrying drink, esp. draft beer.

grown /grōn/ past participle of GROW.

grown-up ▶ **adj.** adult. ■ suitable for or characteristic of an adult. ▶ **n.** an adult (esp. a child's word).

growth /grōTH/ ▶ **n. 1** the process of increasing in physical size. ■ the process of developing or maturing physically, mentally, or spiritually. ■ the increase in number and spread of small or microscopic organisms. ■ the process of increasing in amount, value, or importance. ■ increase in economic value or activity. **2** something that has grown or is growing. ■ Med. Biol. a tumor or other abnormal formation. **3** a vineyard or crop of grapes of a specified classification of quality, or a wine from it.

growth fac·tor ▶ **n.** Biol. a substance, such as a vitamin or hormone, that is required for the stimulation of growth in living cells.

growth fund ▶ **n.** a mutual fund that invests primarily in stocks that are expected to increase in capital value rather than yield high income.

growth hor·mone ▶ **n.** a hormone that stimulates growth in animal or plant cells, esp. (in animals) a hormone secreted by the pituitary gland.

growth ring ▶ **n.** a concentric layer of wood, shell, or bone developed during an annual or other regular period of growth.

groyne ▶ **n.** var. of GROIN[2].

Groz·ny /'grôznē; 'gräznē/ a city in southwestern Russia, capital of Chechnya; pop. 401,000.

grrrl ▶ **n.** see RIOT GIRL.

grub /grəb/ ▶ **n. 1** the larva of an insect, esp. a beetle. ■ a maggot or small caterpillar. **2** informal food. ▶ **v.** **(grubbed, grub·bing)** [no obj., with adverbial] **1** dig or poke superficially at the earth; dig shallowly in soil. ■ [trans.] remove (something) from the earth by digging it up. ■ [trans.] clear (the ground) of roots and stumps. **2** search for something in a clumsy and unmethodical manner; rummage. ■ do demeaning or humiliating work in order to achieve something. ■ [trans.] achieve or acquire (something) in such a way. — **grub·ber** **n.** [ME: perh. rel. to Du. *grobbelen*, also to GRAVE[1].]

grub·by /'grəbē/ ▶ **adj.** **(-bi·er, -bi·est)** dirty; grimy. ■ fig. disreputable; sordid. — **grub·bi·ly** **adv.** **grub·bi·ness** **n.**

grub·stake /'grəb,stāk/ informal ▶ **n.** an amount of material, provisions, or money supplied to an enterprise (originally a prospector for ore) in return for a share in the resulting profits. ▶ **v.** [trans.] provide with a grubstake.

Grub Street /grəb/ ▶ **n.** used in reference to a world or class of impoverished journalists and hack writers. [a street (later Milton Street) in London, England.]

grudge /grəj/ ▶ **n.** a persistent feeling of ill will or resentment resulting from a past insult or injury. ▶ **v.** [trans.] be resentfully unwilling to give, grant, or allow (something). ■ [with two objs.] [usu. with negative] feel resentful that (someone) has achieved (something).

– PHRASES **bear** (or **owe**) **someone a grudge** maintain a feeling of ill will or resentment toward someone. — **grudg·er** **n.** [ME: var. of obs. *grutch* 'complain, murmur, grumble,' from OFr. *grouchier*.]

grudge match ▶ **n.** a contest or other competitive situation involving personal antipathy between the participants.

grudg·ing /'grəjiNG/ ▶ **adj.** given, granted, or allowed only reluctantly or resentfully. ■ (of a person) reluctant or resentfully unwilling to give, grant, or allow something. — **grudg·ing·ly** **adv.** **grudg·ing·ness** **n.**

gruel /'grōōəl/ ▶ **n.** a thin liquid food of oatmeal or other meal boiled in milk or water. [ME: from OFr., of Gmc. origin.]

gruel·ing /'grōōəliNG/ (Brit. **gruel·ling**) ▶ **adj.** extremely tiring and demanding. — **gruel·ing·ly** **adv.** [19th C.: from the v. *gruel* 'exhaust, punish,' from an old phr. *get one's gruel* 'receive one's punishment.']

grue·some /'grōōsəm/ ▶ **adj.** causing repulsion or horror; grisly. ■ informal extremely unpleasant. — **grue·some·ly** **adv.** **grue·some·ness** **n.** [16th C.: from Scots *grue* 'to feel horror, shudder' (of Scand. origin) + -SOME[1].]

gruff /grəf/ ▶ **adj.** abrupt or taciturn in manner. ■ (of a voice) rough and low in pitch. — **gruff·ly** **adv.** **gruff·ness** **n.** [15th C.: from Flemish and Du. *grof* 'coarse, rude,' of West Gmc. origin.]

grum·ble /'grəmbəl/ ▶ **v.** [reporting verb] complain or protest about something in a bad-tempered but typically muted way. ■ [intrans.] make a low rumbling sound. ■ [intrans.] (of an internal organ) give intermittent discomfort. ▶ **n.** a complaint. ■ a low rumbling sound. — **grum·bler** **n.** **grum·bling·ly** **adv.** **grum·bly** **adj.** [16th C.: from obs. *grumme* (prob. of Gmc. origin and rel. to Du. *grommen*) + -LE[4].]

grump /grəmp/ informal ▶ **n.** a grumpy person. ■ a fit of sulking. ▶ **v.** [intrans.] act in a sulky, grumbling manner. — **grump·ish** **adj.** **grump·ish·ly** **adv.** [18th C.: imitative.]

grump·y /'grəmpē/ ▶ **adj.** **(grump·i·er, grump·i·est)** bad-tempered and sulky. — **grump·i·ly** **adv.** **grump·i·ness** **n.**

Grun·dy /'grəndē/ ▶ **n.** see MRS. GRUNDY.

Grü·ne·wald /'grōōn,väld/, Mathias (*c.*1460–1528), German painter; born **Mathis Nithardt**; also called *Mathis Gothardt*. His most noted work is the nine-panel *Isenheim Altar* (completed 1516).

grunge /grənj/ ▶ **n. 1** grime; dirt. **2** (also **grunge rock**) a style of rock music characterized by a raucous guitar sound and lazy vocal delivery. ■ the fashion associated with this music, including loose, layered clothing and ripped jeans. — **grun·gi·ness** **n.** **grun·gy** **adj.** [1970s: back-form. from *grungy*.]

grun·ion /'grənyən/ ▶ **n.** a small, slender Californian fish (*Leuresthes tenuis*, family Atherinidae) that swarms onto beaches at night to spawn. The eggs are buried in the sand, and the young fish are swept out to sea on the following spring tide. [20th C.: prob. from Sp. *gruñón* 'grunter.']

grunt /grənt/ ▶ **v.** [intrans.] (of an animal, esp. a pig) make a low, short guttural sound. ■ (of a person) make a low inarticulate sound resembling this, typically to express effort or indicate assent. ▶ **n. 1** a low, short guttural sound made by an animal or a person. **2** informal a low-ranking or unskilled soldier or other worker. ■ a common soldier. **3** an edible shoaling fish (family Pomadasyidae) of tropical inshore waters and coral reefs, able to make a loud noise by grinding its teeth and amplifying the sound in the swim bladder. [OE *grunnettan*, of Gmc. origin and rel. to Ger. *grunzen*; prob. orig. imitative.]

grunt·er /'grəntər/ ▶ **n.** a fish that makes a grunting noise, esp. when caught, in particular: ■ a mainly marine fish (family Theraponidae) of warm waters. ■ another term for GRUNT (sense 3).

Gru·yère /grōō'yer; grē-/ ▶ **n.** a firm, tangy cheese. [named after *Gruyère*, a district in Switzerland, where it was first made.]

gr. wt. ▶ **abbr.** gross weight.

gryph·on ▶ **n.** var. of GRIFFIN.

GSA ▶ **abbr.** ■ General Services Administration. ■ Girl Scouts of America.

GSC ▶ **abbr.** General Staff Corps.

G-spot ▶ **n.** a sensitive area of the anterior wall of the vagina believed by some to be highly erogenous and capable of ejaculation. [1944: *G* from *Gräfenberg*, because first described by Gräfenberg and Dickinson in the *Western Journal of Surgery*.]

GSR ▶ **abbr.** galvanic skin response.

Gstaad /gə'SHtät/ a winter-sports resort in western Switzerland.

G-string (also **gee-string**) ▶ **n.** a garment consisting of a narrow strip of cloth that covers the genitals and is attached to a waistband, worn as underwear or by striptease performers.

G-suit (also **an·ti-G suit**) ▶ **n.** a garment with pressurized pouches that are inflatable with air or fluid, worn by fighter pilots and astronauts to enable them to withstand high forces of acceleration. [1940s: from *g* (symbol of *gravity*) + SUIT.]

GT ▶ **adj.** denoting a high-performance car: *GT cars*. ▶ **n.** a high-performance car. [1960s: abbrev. of Ital. *gran tourismo*.]

gt. ▶ **abbr.** ■ gilt. ■ great.

G.T.C. ▶ **abbr.** ■ good till canceled. ■ good till countermanded.

gtd. ▶ **abbr.** guaranteed.

GTP ▶ **abbr.** guanosine triphosphate.

GU ▶ **abbr.** ■ genitourinary. ■ Guam.

gua·ca·mo·le /,gwäkə'mōlē/ ▶ **n.** a dish of mashed avocado mixed with chopped onion, tomatoes, chili peppers, and seasoning. [L. Amer. Sp., from Nahuatl *ahuacamolli*, from *ahuacatl* 'avocado' + *molli* 'sauce.']

gua·cha·ro /'gwäCHə,rō/ ▶ **n.** (pl. **-ros**) a large, nocturnal, fruit-eating bird (*Steatornis caripensis*, family Steatornithidae) that resembles a nightjar and lives in caves in Central and South America. [19th C.: from Sp. *guácharo*, of South Amer. origin.]

Gua·da·la·ja·ra /,gwädl-ə'härə/ a city in western central Mexico, capital of the state of Jalisco; pop. 2,846,720.

Gua·dal·ca·nal /,gwädlkə'nal/ an island in the southwestern Pacific Ocean, the largest of the Solomon Islands; pop. 71,000.

Gua·dal·quiv·ir /,gwädlki'vi(ə)r/ a river in southern Spain. Flowing 410 miles (657 km) through Cordoba and Seville to the Atlantic.

Gua·da·lu·pe Moun·tains /'gwädl,ōōp; -'ōōpē; -'ōōpā/ a range in western Texas and southern New Mexico. Guadalupe Peak at 8,749 feet (2,668 m) is the highest point.

Gua·de·loupe /,gwädl-'ōōp/ a group of islands in the Lesser Antilles, an overseas department of France; pop. 426,493; capital, Basse-Terre. — **Gua·de·lou·pi·an** /-pēən/ **adj. & n.**

Gua·di·a·na /gwäd'yänə/ a river in Spain and Portugal. Rising southeast of Madrid, it flows southwest for about 350 miles (580 km) to the Atlantic Ocean at the Gulf of Cadiz.

guai·ac /'gwīak/ ▶ **n.** brown resin obtained from guaiacum trees, used as a flavoring and in varnishes. It was formerly used medicinally and as a test for traces of blood.

guai·a·col /'gwīə,kôl; -,kōl/ ▶ **n.** Chem. an oily yellow liquid, $HOC_6H_4OCH_3$, with a penetrating odor, obtained by distilling wood tar or guaiac, used as a flavoring and an expectorant. [19th C.: from GUAIACUM + -OL.]

guai·a·cum /'gwīəkəm/ ▶ **n.** an evergreen tree (*Guaiacum officinale* and *G. sanctum*, family Zygophyllaceae) of the Caribbean and tropical America, formerly important for its hard, heavy, oily timber but now scarce. Also called LIGNUM VITAE. ■ another term for GUAIAC. [16th C.: mod. L., via Sp. from Taino *guayacan*.]

Guam /gwäm/ the largest and most southern of the Mariana Islands, administered as an unincorporated territory of the US; pop. 166,000; capital, Hagåtña (or Agaña). — **Gua·ma·ni·an** /gwä'mānēən/ **adj. & n.**

guan /gwän/ ▶ **n.** a large, pheasantlike, tree-dwelling bird (*Penelope* and other genera) of tropical American rain forests. The **guan family** (Cracidae) also includes curassows and chachalacas. [17th C.: via Amer. Sp. from Miskito *kwamu*.]

gua·na·co /gwə'näkō/ ▶ **n.** (pl. **-cos**) a wild Andean mammal (*Lama* *guanicoe*) of the camel family, similar to the domestic llama. [17th C.: via Sp. from Quechua *huanacu*.]

Gua·na·jua·to /ˌgwänə'(h)wätō/ a state in central Mexico. ■ its capital city; pop. 45,000.

Guang·dong /'gwäNG'dōōNG/ (also **Kwang·tung**) a province in southern China, on the South China Sea; capital, Guangzhou (Canton).

Guang·xi Zhuang /'gwäNG'SHē 'jwäNG/ (also **Kwang·si Chuang**) an autonomous region in southern China, on the Gulf of Tonkin; capital, Nanning.

Guang·zhou /'gwäNG'jō/ (also **Kwang·chow**) a city in southern China, the capital of Guangdong province; pop. 3,918,000. Also called CANTON[1].

guan·i·dine /'gwänəˌdēn/ ▶n. Chem. a strongly basic crystalline compound, $HNC(NH_2)_2$, used in organic synthesis. [19th C.: from GUANO + -IDE + -INE[4].]

gua·nine /'gwänēn/ ▶n. Biochem. a compound, $C_5H_5N_5O$, that occurs in guano and fish scales, and is one of the four constituent bases of nucleic acids. A purine derivative, it is paired with cytosine in DNA.

gua·no /'gwänō/ ▶n. (pl. **-nos**) the excrement of seabirds, occurring in thick deposits notably on the islands off Peru and Chile, and used as fertilizer. ■ an artificial fertilizer resembling natural guano, esp. one made from fish. [17th C.: from Sp., or from L. Amer. Sp. *huano*, from Quechua *huanu* 'dung.']

gua·no·sine /'gwänəˌsēn/ ▶n. Biochem. a compound consisting of guanine combined with ribose, a nucleoside unit in RNA. [20th C.: from GUANINE, with the insertion of -OSE[2].]

gua·no·sine tri·phos·phate /trī'fäsfāt/ (abbr.: **GTP**) ▶n. a nucleotide composed of guanine, ribose, and three phosphate groups, which participates in various metabolic reactions, including protein synthesis.

Guan·tá·na·mo Bay /gwän'tänəˌmō/ a bay on the southeastern coast of Cuba, site of a US naval base.

Gua·po·ré /ˌgwäpə'rā/ a river that flows northwest for 1,090 miles (1,745 km) from southwestern Brazil to the Mamoré River.

guar /gwär/ ▶n. a drought-resistant plant (*Cyamopsis tetragonoloba*) of the pea family, which is grown as a vegetable and fodder crop and as a source of guar gum, native to dry regions of Africa and Asia. ■ (also **guar gum** or **guar flour**) a fine powder obtained by grinding guar seeds, which has numerous commercial applications, esp. as a thickener and a binder. [19th C.: from Hindi *guār*.]

guar. ▶abbr. guaranteed.

gua·ra·che ▶n. var. of HUARACHE.

Gua·ra·ni /gwärə'nē/ ▶n. (pl. same) **1** a member of an American Indian people of Paraguay and adjacent regions. **2** the language of this people, one of the main divisions of the Tupi-Guarani language family and a national language of Paraguay. **3** (**gua·ra·ni**) the basic monetary unit of Paraguay, equal to 100 centimos. ▶adj. of or relating to the Guarani or their language. [Sp.]

guar·an·tee /ˌgarən'tē/ ▶n. a formal promise or assurance (typically in writing) that certain conditions will be fulfilled, esp. that a product will be repaired or replaced if not of a specified quality and durability. ■ something that gives a certainty of outcome. ■ var. of GUARANTY. ■ less common term for GUARANTOR. ▶v. (**-tees, -teed, -tee·ing**) [intrans.] provide a formal assurance or promise, esp. that certain conditions shall be fulfilled relating to a product, service, or transaction. ■ [trans.] provide such an assurance regarding (something, esp. a product). ■ [trans.] provide financial security for; underwrite. ■ [trans.] promise with certainty. [17th C.: perh. from Sp. *garante*, corresponding to Fr. *garant* (see WARRANT).]

guar·an·tor /ˌgarən'tôr; 'garəntər/ ▶n. a person, organization, or thing that guarantees something. ■ Law a person or organization providing a guaranty.

guar·an·ty /'garənˌtē/ (also **guar·an·tee**) ▶n. (pl. **-ties**) a formal pledge to pay another person's debt or to perform another person's obligation in the case of default. ■ a thing serving as security for a such a pledge. [16th C.: from OFr. *garantie*, from *garantir*; rel. to WARRANT.]

guard /gärd/ ▶v. [trans.] watch over to keep safe. ■ watch over in order to control entry and exit. ■ watch over (someone) to prevent them from escaping. ■ [intrans.] (**guard against**) take precautions against. ■ protect against damage or harm. ■ Basketball stay close to (an opponent) in order to prevent a good shot, pass, or drive. ■ cover or equip (a part of a machine) with a device to protect the operator. ▶n. **1** a person who keeps watch, esp. a soldier or other person formally assigned to protect a person or to control access to a place. ■ [treated as sing. or pl.] a body of soldiers serving to protect a place or person. ■ (**Guards**) the household troops of the British army. ■ a prison warder. ■ Brit. an official who rides on and is in general charge of a train. ■ Football each of two offensive players positioned either side of the center. ■ Basketball each of two backcourt players chiefly responsible for running the team's offense. **2** a device worn or fitted to prevent injury or damage. ■ a chain attached to a watch or bracelet to prevent loss. ■ a ring worn to prevent another ring from falling off the finger. ■ a piece of metal placed to protect an operator from the dangerous parts of a machine. **3** a defensive posture adopted in a boxing, fencing, or martial arts contest or in a fight. ■ a state of caution, vigilance, or preparedness against adverse circumstances.

– PHRASES **keep** (or **stand**) **guard** act as a guard. **lower** (or **let down**) **one's guard** relax one's defensive posture, leaving oneself vulnerable to attack. ■ reduce one's level of vigilance or caution. **off guard** unprepared for some surprise or difficulty. **on guard** on duty to protect or defend something. ■ (also **on one's guard**) prepared for any contingency; vigilant. **put up one's guard** adopt a defensive posture. **under guard** being guarded. [ME: from OFr. *garde*, of West Gmc. origin.]

guard·ant /'gärdnt/ ▶adj. [usu. postpositive] Heraldry (esp. of an animal) depicted with the body sideways and the face toward the viewer: *three lions guardant*. [16th C.: from Fr. *gardant* 'guarding,' from *garder* 'to guard.']

guard cell ▶n. Bot. each of a pair of curved cells that surround a stoma, becoming larger or smaller according to the pressure within the cells.

guard·ed /'gärdid/ ▶adj. cautious and having possible reservations. ■ (of a person's medical condition) serious and of uncertain outcome. — **guard·ed·ly** adv. **guard·ed·ness** n.

guard hair ▶n. long, coarse hair forming an animal's outer fur.

guard·house /'gärdˌhous/ ▶n. a building used to accommodate a military guard or to detain military prisoners. ■ a building accommodating a guard who controls entrance to the grounds of a house, housing development, school, or other facility.

guard·i·an /'gärdēən/ ▶n. a defender, protector, or keeper. ■ a person who looks after and is legally responsible for someone who is unable to manage their own affairs, esp. an incompetent or disabled person or a child whose parents have died. — **guard·i·an·ship** n. [ME: from OFr. *garden*, of Gmc. origin.]

guard·i·an an·gel ▶n. a spirit that is believed to watch over and protect a person or place.

guard of hon·or ▶n. a group of soldiers ceremonially welcoming an important visitor or escorting a casket in a funeral. Also called HONOR GUARD.

guard·rail /'gärdˌrāl/ ▶n. a rail that prevents people from falling off or being hit by something. ■ a strong fence at the side of a road or in the middle of an expressway, intended to reduce the risk of serious accidents.

guard·room /'gärdˌrōōm; -ˌrŏŏm/ ▶n. a room in a military base used to accommodate a guard or detain prisoners.

guards·man /'gärdzmən/ ▶n. (pl. **-men**) (in the US) a member of the National Guard. ■ (in the UK) a soldier of a regiment of Guards.

Guar·ne·ri /gwär'ne(ə)rē/, Giuseppe (1687–1744), Italian violin-maker; known as **del Gesù**.

Guar·ne·ri·us /gwär'ne(ə)rēəs/ ▶n. a violin made by a member of the Guarneri family of Cremona, Italy, during the 17th and 18th centuries.

Gua·ru·lhos /gwä'rōōlyŏŏs/ a city in southeastern Brazil; pop. 973,000.

Gua·te·ma·la /ˌgwätə'mälə/ a country in Central America. *See box.* — **Gua·te·ma·lan** adj. & n.

Guatemala

Official name: Republic of Guatemala
Location: Central America, bordered on the west and north by Mexico, and on the south by the Pacific Ocean
Area: 41,900 square miles (108,400 sq km)
Population: 14,280,200
Capital: Guatemala City
Languages: Spanish (official), many Amerindian languages
Currency: quetzal

Gua·te·ma·la Cit·y the capital of Guatemala; pop. 1,167,000.

gua·va /'gwävə/ ▶n. **1** an edible pale orange tropical fruit with pink, juicy flesh and a strong, sweet aroma. **2** the small tropical American tree (genus *Psidium*) of the myrtle family that bears this fruit. [16th C.: from Sp. *guayaba*, prob. from Taino.]

Gua·via·re Riv·er /gwäv'yärā/ a river that flows east for 650 miles (1,040 km) from the Andes Mountains in Colombia to the Orinoco River at the Venezuelan border.

Gua·ya·quil /,gīə'kēl/ a seaport in western Ecuador; pop. 1,877,000.

Guay·na·bo /gwī'näbō/ a community in northeastern Puerto Rico; pop. 73,385.

gua·yu·le /(g)wä'yoolē/ ▶ **n.** a silver-leaved Mexican shrub (*Parthenium argentatum*) of the daisy family that yields latex. ■ a rubber substitute made from this latex. [20th C.: via L. Amer. Sp. from Nahuatl *cuauhuli*.]

gu·ber·na·to·ri·al /,goobərnə'tôrēəl/ ▶ **adj.** of or relating to a state governor or the office of state governor. [18th C.: from L. *gubernator* 'governor' (from *gubernare* 'steer, govern,' from Gk. *kubernan* 'to steer') + -IAL.]

guck /gək/ ▶ **n.** informal a slimy, dirty, or otherwise unpleasant substance. [possibly a blend of GOO and MUCK.]

gudg·eon[1] /'gəjən/ ▶ **n.** a small, edible, European freshwater fish (*Gobio gobio*) of the minnow family, often used as fishing bait. [ME: from OFr. *goujon*, from L. *gobio(n-)*, from *gobius* 'goby.']

gudg·eon[2] ▶ **n.** a pivot or spindle on which a bell or other object swings or rotates. ■ the tubular part of a hinge into which the pin fits to unite the joint. ■ a socket at the stern of a vessel, into which a rudder is fitted. ■ a pin holding two blocks of stone together. [ME: from OFr. *goujon*, dimin. of *gouge* (see GOUGE).]

Gud·run /'goodroon/ (in Norse legend) the Norse equivalent of Kriemhild, wife of Sigurd and later of Atli (Attila the Hun).

guel·der rose /'geldər/ ▶ **n.** a deciduous Eurasian shrub (*Viburnum opulus*) of the honeysuckle family with flattened heads of fragrant, creamy-white flowers, followed by clusters of bitter translucent red berries. [16th C.: from Du. *geldersche roos* 'rose of *Gelderland*.']

gue·non /gə'nōn/ ▶ **n.** an African monkey (genus *Cercopithecus*, family Cercopithecidae) found mainly in forests, with a long tail and typically a brightly colored coat. [19th C.: from Fr., of unknown origin.]

guer·don /'gərdn/ esp. archaic ▶ **n.** a reward or recompense. ▶ **v.** [trans.] give a reward to (someone). [ME: from OFr., from med. L. *widerdonum*, alt. of a West Gmc. compound represented by Old High Ger. *widarlōn* 'repayment.']

Gue·rick·e /'gerikə/, Otto von (1602–86), German physicist. He devised the Magdeburg hemispheres to demonstrate atmospheric pressure.

gue·ril·la the·a·ter (also **guerrilla theater**) ▶ **n.** the dramatization of political and social issues, typically performed outdoors, e.g. in the street or a park, as a means of protest or propaganda.

Guern·sey[1] /'gərnzē/ an island in the English Channel; pop. 59,000; capital, St. Peter Port.

Guern·sey[2] ▶ **n.** (pl. **-seys**) **1** an animal of a breed of cattle from Guernsey producing rich, creamy milk. **2** (**guernsey**) a thick sweater made with oiled navy blue wool and originally worn by fishermen.

Guer·re·ro /gə're(ə)rō/ a state in southwestern central Mexico; capital, Chilpancingo.

guer·ril·la /gə'rilə/ (also **gue·ril·la**) ▶ **n.** a member of a small independent group taking part in irregular fighting, typically against larger regular forces. [19th C.: from Sp., dimin. of *guerra* 'war.']

Guess /ges/, George, see SEQUOYA.

guess /ges/ ▶ **v.** [trans.] estimate or suppose (something) without sufficient information to be sure of being correct. ■ (**guess at**) make a conjecture about. ■ correctly conjecture or perceive. ■ [in imper.] used to introduce something considered surprising or exciting: *guess what I've just seen!* ■ (**I guess**) informal used to indicate that although one thinks or supposes something, it is without any great conviction or strength of feeling. ▶ **n.** an estimate or conjecture.
– PHRASES **anybody's** (or **anyone's**) **guess** very difficult or impossible to determine. **keep someone guessing** informal leave someone uncertain or in doubt as to one's intentions or plans. — **guess·a·ble adj. guess·er n.** [ME: origin uncert.; perh. from Du. *gissen*, and prob. rel. to GET.]

guess·ti·mate (also **gues·ti·mate**) informal ▶ **n.** /'gestəmit/ an estimate based on a mixture of guesswork and calculation. ▶ **v.** /'gestə,māt/ [trans.] form such an estimate of. [1930s (orig. US): blend of GUESS and ESTIMATE.]

guess·work /'ges,wərk/ ▶ **n.** the process or results of guessing.

guest /gest/ ▶ **n.** a person who is invited to visit the home of or take part in a function organized by another. ■ a person invited to participate in an official event. ■ a person invited to take part in a radio or television program, sports event, or other entertainment. ■ a person lodging at a hotel or boardinghouse. ■ a customer at a restaurant. ■ Entomol. a small invertebrate that lives unharmed within an ants' nest. ▶ **v.** [intrans.] informal appear as a guest.
– PHRASES **be my guest** informal please do. **guest of honor** the most important guest at an occasion. [ME: from ON *gestr*; from an Indo-Eur. root shared by L. *hostis* 'enemy' (orig. 'stranger').]

guest book ▶ **n.** a book in which visitors to a public building or to a private home write their names and addresses, and sometimes remarks. ■ (also **guest·book**) Comput. a page on a website that allows visitors to the website to record their name, e-mail address, comments, or other information.

guest house (also **guest·house**) ▶ **n.** a private house offering accommodations to paying guests. ■ a small, separate house on the grounds of a larger house or establishment, used for accommodating guests.

gues·ti·mate ▶ **n. & v.** var. of GUESSTIMATE.

guest work·er ▶ **n.** a person with temporary permission to work in another country, esp. in Germany.

Gue·va·ra /gə'värə/, Che (1928–67), Argentine revolutionary; full name *Ernesto Guevara de la Serna*. A leader in the Cuban revolution 1956–59, he became a government minister under Fidel Castro.

guff /gəf/ ▶ **n.** informal trivial, worthless, or insolent talk or ideas. [19th C. (in the sense 'puff, whiff of a bad smell'): imitative.]

guf·faw /gə'fô/ ▶ **n.** a loud and boisterous laugh. ▶ **v.** [intrans.] laugh in such a way. [18th C. (orig. Scots): imitative.]

Gug·gen·heim /'googən,hīm; 'goo-/, Meyer (1828–1905), US industrialist; born in Switzerland. With his seven sons he established large mining and metal-processing companies.

GUI /'gooē/ Comput. ▶ **abbr.** graphical user interface.

Gui·a·na /gē'änə; gī'anə/ a region in northern South America, including Guyana, Suriname, French Guiana, and the Guiana Highlands.

Gui·a·na High·lands a mountainous plateau region in northern South America, largely in southeastern Venezuela and northern Brazil.

guid·ance /'gīdns/ ▶ **n.** **1** advice or information aimed at resolving a problem or difficulty, esp. as given by someone in authority. **2** the directing of the motion or position of something, esp. a missile.

guide /gīd/ ▶ **n.** **1** a person who advises or shows the way to others. ■ a professional mountain climber in charge of a group. **2** a thing that helps someone to form an opinion or make a decision or calculation. ■ a principle or standard of comparison. ■ a book, document, or display providing information on a subject or about a place. **3** a structure or marking that directs the motion or positioning of something. **4** a soldier, vehicle, or ship whose position determines the movements of others. ▶ **v.** **1** [with obj. and adverbial of direction] show or indicate the way to (someone). ■ [trans.] direct the motion or positioning of (something). **2** [trans.] direct or have an influence on the course of action of (someone or something). — **guid·a·ble adj. guid·er n.** [ME: from OFr. *guide* (n.), *guider* (v.), of Gmc. origin; rel. to WIT[2].]

guide·book /'gīd,book/ ▶ **n.** a book of information about a place, designed for the use of visitors or tourists.

guid·ed /'gīdid/ ▶ **adj.** conducted by a guide. ■ directed by remote control or by internal equipment.

guide dog ▶ **n.** a dog trained to lead a blind person.

guide·line /'gīd,līn/ ▶ **n.** a general rule, principle, or piece of advice.

guide·way /'gīd,wā/ ▶ **n.** a groove or track along which something moves.

gui·don /'gīdn/ ▶ **n.** a pennant that narrows to a point or fork at the free end, esp. one used as the standard of a light cavalry regiment. [16th C.: from Fr., from Ital. *guidone*, from *guida* 'a guide.']

guild /gild/ (also **gild**) ▶ **n.** a medieval association of craftsmen or merchants, often having considerable power. ■ an association of people for mutual aid or the pursuit of a common goal. ■ Ecol. a group of species that have similar requirements and play a similar role within a community. [OE: prob. from Mid. Low Ger. and MDu. *gilde*, of Gmc. origin; rel. to YIELD.]

guild·er /'gildər/ ▶ **n.** (pl. same or **-ers**) the basic monetary unit of the Netherlands (until the introduction of the euro), equal to 100 cents. ■ hist. a gold or silver coin formerly used in the Netherlands, Germany, and Austria. [alt. of Du. *gulden* (see GULDEN).]

guild·hall /'gild,hôl/ ▶ **n.** a building used as the meeting place of a guild or corporation.

guile /gīl/ ▶ **n.** sly or cunning intelligence. — **guile·ful** /-fəl/ **adj. guile·ful·ly** /-fəlē/ **adv.** [ME: from OFr., prob. from ON; cf. WILE.]

guile·less /'gīl(l)is/ ▶ **adj.** devoid of guile; innocent and without deception: *his face, once so open and guileless.* — **guile·less·ly adv. guile·less·ness n.**

Gui·lin /'gwā'lin/ (also **Kwei·lin**) a city in southern China in Guangxi Zhuang; pop. 552,000.

Guil·lain–Bar·ré syn·drome /gē'yan bə'rā/ ▶ **n.** Med. an acute form of polyneuritis, often preceded by a respiratory infection, causing weakness and often paralysis of the limbs. [1916: named after Georges *Guillain* (1876–1961) and Jean *Barré* (1880–1967), two of those who first described the syndrome.]

guil·le·mot /'gilə,mät/ ▶ **n.** a black-breasted auk (genus *Cepphus*) with a long narrow pointed bill, typically nesting on cliff ledges. [17th C.: from Fr., dimin. of *Guillaume* 'William.']

guil·loche /gi'lōsʜ/ ▶ **n.** architectural ornamentation resembling braided or interlaced ribbons. [19th C.: from Fr. *guillochis*, denoting the ornamentation, or *guilloche*, a carving tool.]

guil·lo·tine /'gilə,tēn; 'gēə-/ ▶ **n.** a machine with a heavy blade sliding vertically in grooves, used for beheading people. ■ a device for cutting that incorporates a descending or sliding blade, used typically for cutting paper, card, or sheet metal. ▶ **v.** [trans.] execute (someone) by guillotine. [18th C.: from Fr., named after Joseph-Ignace *Guillotin* (1738–1814), the

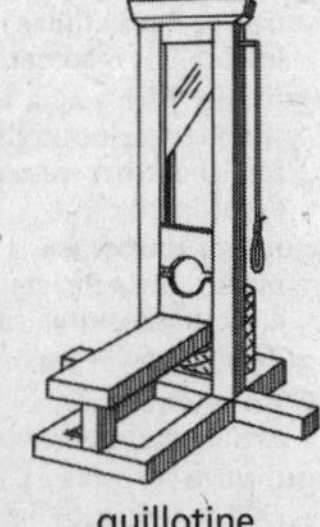

guillotine

PRONUNCIATION KEY ə *ago, up*; ər *over, fur*; a *hat*; ā *ate*; ä *car*; e *let*; ē *see*; i *fit*; ī *by*; NG *sing*; ō *go*; ô *law, for*; oi *toy*; oo *good*; oo *goo*; ou *out*; TH *thin*; TH *then*; ZH *vision*

French physician who recommended its use for executions in 1789.]

guilt /gilt/ ▶ n. the fact of having committed a specified or implied offense or crime. ■ a feeling of having committed wrong or failed in an obligation. ▶ v. [trans.] informal make (someone) feel guilty, esp. in order to induce them to do something.
– PHRASES **guilt by association** guilt ascribed to someone not because of any evidence but because of their association with an offender. [OE *gylt*, of unknown origin.]

guilt·less /'giltlis/ ▶ adj. having no guilt; innocent. — **guilt·less·ly** adv. **guilt·less·ness** n.

guilt trip ▶ n. an experience of feeling guilty about something, esp. when such guilt is excessive, self-indulgent, or unfounded. ▶ v. (**guilt-trip**) [trans.] make (someone) feel guilty, esp. in order to induce them to do something.

guilt·y /'giltē/ ▶ adj. (**guilt·i·er, guilt·i·est**) culpable of or responsible for a specified wrongdoing. See also FIND, PLEAD. ■ justly chargeable with a particular fault or error. ■ conscious of or affected by a feeling of guilt. ■ involving a feeling or a judgment of guilt.
– PHRASES **not guilty** innocent, esp. of a formal charge. — **guilt·i·ly** adv. **guilt·i·ness** n.

Guin·ea /'ginē/ a country on the western coast of Africa. *See box.* — **Guin·e·an** /-ēən/ adj. & n.

Guinea
Official name: Republic of Guinea
Location: western coast of Africa, south of Senegal and Mali
Area: 95,000 square miles (245,900 sq km)
Population: 9,246,000
Capital: Conakry
Languages: French (official), Fulani, Malinke, and others
Currency: Guinean franc

guin·ea /'ginē/ (abbr.: **gn.**) ▶ n. Brit. the sum of £1.05 (21 shillings in predecimal currency), now used mainly for determining professional fees and auction prices. ■ hist. a former British gold coin that was first minted in 1663 from gold imported from West Africa, with a value that was later fixed at 21 shillings. It was replaced by the sovereign from 1817. [named after GUINEA in West Africa.]

Guin·ea, Gulf of a large inlet of the Atlantic Ocean that borders on the southern coast of West Africa.

Guin·ea-Bis·sau /'ginē bi'sou/ a country on the western coast of Africa. *See box.*

guin·ea fowl ▶ n. (pl. same) a large African game bird (family Numididae, or Phasianidae) with slate-colored, white-spotted plumage and a loud call. It is sometimes domesticated.

guin·ea pig ▶ n. a tailless South American cavy (*Cavia porcellus*). It no longer occurs in the wild and is now typically kept as a pet or for laboratory research. ■ a person or thing used as a subject for experiment.

guin·ea worm ▶ n. a very long parasitic nematode (*Dracunculus medinensis*, class Phasmida) that lives under the skin of infected humans and other mammals in rural Africa and Asia.

gui·nep /gi'nep/ ▶ n. variant spelling of GENIP (sense 2).

Guin·e·vere /'gwinə,vi(ə)r/ (in Arthurian legend) the wife of King Arthur and mistress of Lancelot.

gui·pure /gi'pyo͝or/ ▶ n. a heavy lace consisting of embroidered motifs held together by large connecting stitches. [19th C.: from Fr., from *guiper* 'cover with silk,' of Gmc. origin.]

gui·ro /'gwi(ə)rō/ ▶ n. (pl. **-ros**) a musical instrument with a serrated surface that gives a rasping sound when scraped with a stick, originally made from an elongated gourd and used in Latin American music. [19th C.: Sp., lit. 'gourd.']

guise /gīz/ ▶ n. an external form, appearance, or manner of presentation, typically concealing the true nature of something: *telemarketing under the guise of market research.* [ME: from OFr., of Gmc. origin; rel. to WISE[2].]

electric guitar acoustic guitar
guitars

gui·tar /gi'tär/ ▶ n. a stringed musical instrument with a fretted fingerboard, typically incurved sides, and usually six or twelve strings, played by plucking or strumming with the fingers or a plectrum. See also ELECTRIC GUITAR. — **gui·tar·ist** n. [17th C.: from Sp. *guitarra* (partly via Fr.), from Gk. *kithara*, denoting an instrument similar to the lyre.]

gui·tar·fish /gi'tär,fisʜ/ ▶ n. (pl. same or **-fish·es**) a fish (families Rhinobatidae and Platyrhinidae) of shallow warm seas, related to the rays and having a guitarlike body shape.

Gui·yang /'gwē'yäɴɢ/ (also **Kwei·yang**) a city in southern China, capital of Guizhou province; pop. 1,490,000.

Gui·zhou /'gwē'jō/ (also **Kwei·chow**) a province in southern China; capital, Guiyang.

Gu·ja·rat /,go͞ojə'rät; ,go͝oj-/ a state in western India, on the Arabian Sea; capital, Gandhinagar.

Gu·ja·ra·ti /,go͞ojə'rätē; ,go͝oj-/ (also **Gu·je·ra·ti**) ▶ n. (pl. **-tis** /-tēz/) **1** a native or inhabitant of Gujarat. **2** the Indic language of the Gujaratis. ▶ adj. of or relating to this people or their language.

Guj·ran·wa·la /,go͞ojrən'wälə; ,go͝oj-/ a city in northeastern Pakistan, in Punjab province; pop. 597,000.

Gu·lag /'go͞oläg/ ▶ n. [in sing.] a system of labor camps maintained in the Soviet Union from 1930 to 1955 in which many people died. ■ (**gulag**) such a camp, or any political labor camp. [Russ., from *G(lavnoe) u(pravlenie ispravitel'no-trudovykh) lag(ereĭ)* 'Chief Administration for Corrective Labor Camps.']

gu·lar /'g(y)o͞olər/ Zool. ▶ adj. of, relating to, or situated on the throat of an animal, esp. a reptile, fish, or bird. ▶ n. a plate or scale on the throat of a reptile or fish. [19th C.: from L. *gula* 'throat' + -AR[1].]

Guinea-Bissau
Official name: Republic of Guinea-Bissau
Location: western coast of Africa, south of Senegal and north of Guinea
Area: 10,800 square miles (28,000 sq km)
Population: 1,300,000
Capital: Bissau
Languages: Portuguese (official), Creole, West African languages
Currency: CFA franc

Gul·bar·ga /ˈgo͝olbərˌgä/ a city in southern central India, in the state of Karnataka; pop. 303,000.

gulch /gəlCH/ ▶ **n.** a narrow and steep-sided ravine marking the course of a fast stream. [19th C.: perh. from dial. *gulch* 'to swallow.']

gul·den /ˈgo͞oldən/ ▶ **n.** (pl. same or **-dens**) another term for GUILDER. [19th C.: Du. and Ger., lit. 'golden.']

gules /gyo͞olz/ ▶ **n.** red, as a heraldic tincture. [ME: from OFr. *goles* (pl. of *gole* 'throat,' from L. *gula*), pieces of red-dyed fur.]

gulf /gəlf/ ▶ **n. 1** a deep inlet of the sea almost surrounded by land, with a narrow mouth. ■ (**the Gulf**) informal name for GULF OF MEXICO or PERSIAN GULF. **2** a deep ravine, chasm, or abyss. ■ fig. a large difference or division between two people or groups, or between viewpoints, concepts, or situations: *a wide gulf between theory and practice.* [ME: from OFr. *golfe*, from Ital. *golfo*, based on Gk. *kolpos* 'bosom, gulf.']

Gulf of A·den, Gulf of Boo·thia, etc. see ADEN, GULF OF; BOOTHIA, GULF OF, etc.

Gulf·port /ˈgəlfˌpôrt/ a city in southern Mississippi, on the Gulf of Mexico; pop. 71,127.

Gulf States 1 the countries bordering on the Persian Gulf (Iran, Iraq, Kuwait, Saudi Arabia, Bahrain, Qatar, the United Arab Emirates, and Oman). **2** the US states that border on the Gulf of Mexico (Florida, Alabama, Mississippi, Louisiana, and Texas).

Gulf Stream a warm ocean current that flows from the Gulf of Mexico along the east coast of the US toward Newfoundland, Canada, and then across the Atlantic toward northwestern Europe.

Gulf War 1 another name for IRAN–IRAQ WAR. **2** the war of January–February 1991 in which an international coalition of forces assembled in Saudi Arabia under UN auspices forced the withdrawal of Saddam Hussein's Iraqi forces from Kuwait, which they had invaded and occupied in August 1990.

Gulf War syn·drome ▶ **n.** a medical condition affecting many veterans of the 1991 Gulf War, causing fatigue, chronic headaches, and skin and respiratory disorders. Its origin is uncertain, though it has been attributed to exposure to a combination of pesticides, vaccines, and other chemicals.

gulf·weed /ˈgəlfˌwēd/ ▶ **n.** another term for SARGASSUM.

gull¹ /gəl/ ▶ **n.** a long-winged, web-footed seabird (*Larus* and other genera, family Laridae) with a raucous call, typically having white plumage with a gray or black mantle. [ME: of Celtic origin; rel. to Welsh *gwylan* and Breton *gwelan*.]

gull² ▶ **v.** [trans.] fool or deceive (someone). ▶ **n.** a person who is fooled or deceived. [16th C.: of unknown origin.]

Gul·lah /ˈgələ/ ▶ **n. 1** a member of a black people living on the coast of South Carolina and nearby islands. **2** the Creole language of this people, having an English base with elements from various West African languages. It has about 125,000 speakers. ▶ **adj.** of or relating to this people or their language. [perh. a shortening of *Angola*, or from *Gola*, the name of an agricultural people of Liberia and Sierra Leone.]

gul·let /ˈgəlit/ ▶ **n.** the passage by which food passes from the mouth to the stomach; the esophagus. [ME: from OFr. *goulet*, dimin. of *goule* 'throat,' from L. *gula*.]

gul·ley /ˈgəlē/ ▶ **n.** (pl. **-leys**) var. of GULLY.

gul·li·ble /ˈgələbəl/ ▶ **adj.** easily persuaded to believe something; credulous. — **gul·li·bil·i·ty** /ˌgələˈbilitē/ **n.** **gul·li·bly** /-blē/ **adv.**

gull-wing ▶ **adj.** (of a door on a car or aircraft) opening upward: *gull-wing doors.*

gul·ly /ˈgəlē/ (also **gul·ley**) ▶ **n.** (pl. **-lies**) a water-worn ravine. ▶ **v.** [trans.] [usu. as adj.] (**gullied**) erode gullies into (land) by water action. [16th C. (in the sense 'gullet'): from Fr. *goulet* (see GULLET).]

gulp /gəlp/ ▶ **v.** [trans.] swallow (drink or food) quickly or in large mouthfuls, often audibly. ■ breathe (air) deeply and quickly. ■ [intrans.] make effortful breathing or swallowing movements, typically in response to strong emotion. ▶ **n.** an act of gulping food or drink. ■ a large mouthful of liquid hastily drunk. ■ a large quantity of air breathed in. ■ a swallowing movement of the throat.
– PHRASES **at a gulp** with one gulp. — **gulpy adj.** [ME: prob. from MDu. *gulpen*, of imitative origin.]

gum¹ /gəm/ ▶ **n. 1** a viscous secretion of some trees and shrubs that hardens on drying but is soluble in water, and from which adhesives and other products are made. Compare with RESIN. ■ glue that is used for sticking paper or other light materials together. ■ short for CHEWING GUM or BUBBLEGUM. ■ a gum tree, esp. a eucalyptus. See also SWEET GUM. **2** dated a long rubber boot. ▶ **v.** (**gummed, gum·ming**) [trans.] cover with gum or glue. ■ [with obj. and adverbial] fasten with gum or glue. ■ (**gum something up**) clog up a mechanism and prevent it from working properly. [ME: from OFr. *gomme*, based on L. *gummi*, from Gk. *kommi*, from Egyptian *kemai*.]

gum² ▶ **n.** the firm area of flesh around the roots of the teeth in the upper or lower jaw. ▶ **v.** (**gummed, gum·ming**) [trans.] chew with toothless gums. [OE *gōma* 'inside of the mouth or throat,' of Gmc. origin.]

gum ar·a·bic ▶ **n.** a gum exuded by some kinds of acacia and used as an emulsifier, in glue, as the binder for watercolor paints, and in incense.

gum ben·ja·min /ˈbenjəmin/ ▶ **n.** another term for BENZOIN (sense 1).

gum ben·zo·in ▶ **n.** see BENZOIN (sense 1).

gum·bo /ˈgəmbō/ ▶ **n.** (pl. **-bos**) **1** okra, esp. the gelatinous pods used in cooking. ■ (in Cajun cooking) a spicy chicken or seafood soup thickened typically with okra or rice. **2** (**Gumbo**) a French-based patois spoken by some blacks and Creoles in Louisiana. **3** a fine, clayey soil that becomes sticky and impervious when wet. [19th C.: from the Angolan word *kingombo* 'okra.']

gum·boil /ˈgəmˌboil/ ▶ **n.** a small swelling formed on the gum over an abscess at the root of a tooth.

gum·drop /ˈgəmˌdräp/ ▶ **n.** a firm, jellylike, translucent candy made with gelatin or gum arabic.

gum·ma /ˈgəmə/ ▶ **n.** (pl. **gum·mas** or **gum·ma·ta** /ˈgəmətə/) Med. a small, soft swelling that is characteristic of the late stages of syphilis and occurs in the connective tissue of the liver, brain, testes, and heart. — **gum·ma·tous** /ˈgəmətəs/ **adj.** [18th C.: mod. L., from L. *gummi* (see GUM¹).]

gum·mo·sis /gəˈmōsis/ ▶ **n.** the copious production and exudation of gum by a diseased or damaged tree, esp. as a symptom of a disease of fruit trees.

gum·my /ˈgəmē/ ▶ **adj.** (**-mi·er, -mi·est**) viscous; sticky. ■ covered with or exuding a viscous substance. — **gum·mi·ness n.**

gum o·lib·a·num /ōˈlibənəm/ ▶ **n.** another term for FRANKINCENSE.

gump·tion /ˈgəmpSHən/ ▶ **n.** informal shrewd or spirited initiative and resourcefulness. [18th C. (orig. Scots): of unknown origin.]

gum res·in ▶ **n.** a plant secretion consisting of resin mixed with gum.

gum san·da·rac ▶ **n.** see SANDARAC.

gum·shoe /ˈgəmˌSHo͞o/ ▶ **n.** informal a detective. [20th C.: from *gumshoes* in the sense 'sneakers,' suggesting stealth.]

gum trag·a·canth ▶ **n.** see TRAGACANTH.

gum tree ▶ **n.** a tree that exudes gum, esp. a eucalyptus.

gum tur·pen·tine ▶ **n.** see TURPENTINE.

gun /gən/ ▶ **n.** a weapon incorporating a metal tube from which bullets, shells, or other missiles are propelled by explosive force, typically making a characteristic loud, sharp noise. ■ a device for discharging something (e.g., insecticide, grease, or electrons) in a required direction. ■ a gunman. ■ a starting pistol used in track and field events. ■ the firing of a piece of artillery as a salute or signal. ▶ **v.** (**gunned, gun·ning**) [trans.] **1** (**gun someone down**) shoot someone with a gun. **2** informal cause (an engine) to race. ■ [with obj. and adverbial of direction] accelerate (a vehicle).
– PHRASES **go great guns** informal proceed forcefully, vigorously, or successfully. **jump the gun** informal act before the proper time. **stick to one's guns** informal refuse to compromise or change, despite criticism. **top gun** a (or the) most important person. **under the gun** informal under great pressure.
– PHRASAL VERBS **gun for** pursue or act against (someone) with hostility. ■ seek out or strive for (something) determinedly. — **gun·less adj.** **gunned adj.** [in comb.] *a heavy-gunned ship.* [ME *gunne, gonne*, perh. from the name *Gunnhildr*, from *gunnr* + *hildr*, both meaning 'war.']

gun·boat /ˈgənˌbōt/ ▶ **n.** a small, fast ship mounting guns, for use in shallow coastal waters and rivers.

gun·boat di·plo·ma·cy ▶ **n.** foreign policy that is supported by the use or threat of military force.

gun car·riage ▶ **n.** a wheeled support for a piece of artillery.

gun·cot·ton /ˈgənˌkätn/ ▶ **n.** a highly nitrated form of nitrocellulose, used as an explosive.

gun deck ▶ **n.** a deck on a vessel on which guns are placed.

gun dog ▶ **n.** a dog trained to retrieve game for a hunter.

gun·fight /ˈgənˌfīt/ ▶ **n.** a fight involving an exchange of gunfire. — **gun·fight·er n.**

gun·fire /ˈgənˌfī(ə)r/ ▶ **n.** the repeated firing of a gun or guns.

gun·flint /ˈgənˌflint/ ▶ **n.** a small piece of flint that is used to ignite the gunpowder in a flintlock gun.

gung-ho /ˈgəNG ˈhō/ ▶ **adj.** unthinkingly enthusiastic and eager, esp. about taking part in fighting or warfare. [World War II: from Chin. *gōnghé*, taken to mean 'work together' and adopted as a slogan by US Marines.]

gun·ite /ˈgənīt/ ▶ **n.** a mixture of cement, sand, and water applied through a pressure hose, producing a dense hard layer of concrete used in building for lining tunnels and structural repairs. [20th C.: from GUN + -ITE¹.]

gunk /gəNGk/ ▶ **n.** informal unpleasantly sticky or messy substance. [1930s (orig. US): the proprietary name of a detergent.]

gunk·hole /ˈgəNGkˌhōl/ informal ▶ **n.** a shallow inlet or cove that is difficult or dangerous to navigate. ▶ **v.** [no obj., with adverbial of direction] cruise in and out of such inlets or coves. [20th C.: of unknown origin.]

gun·lock /ˈgənˌläk/ ▶ **n.** a mechanism by which the charge of a gun is exploded.

gun·man /ˈgənmən/ ▶ **n.** (pl. **-men**) a man who uses a gun to commit a crime or terrorist act.

gun·met·al /ˈgənˌmetl/ ▶ **n.** a gray, corrosion-resistant form of bronze containing zinc, formerly used for making cannon. ■ (also **gunmetal gray**) a dark blue-brown gray color.

gun mi·cro·phone ▶ **n.** a highly directional microphone with an elongated barrel that can be directed from a distance at a localized sound source.

gun moll ▶ **n.** informal another term for MOLL (sense 1).

gun·nel¹ /'gənl/ ▶n. an elongated laterally compressed fish (family Pholidae) of the northern hemisphere, with a dorsal fin that runs along most of the back and reduced or absent pelvic fins. [17th C.: of unknown origin.]

gun·nel² ▶n. var. of GUNWALE.

gun·ner /'gənər/ ▶n. **1** a serviceman who operates or specializes in guns, in particular: ■ hist. a naval warrant officer in charge of a ship's guns, gun crews, and ordnance stores. ■ a member of an aircraft crew who operates a gun, esp. (formerly) in a gun turret on a bomber. **2** a person who hunts game with a gun.

gun·ner·y /'gənərē/ ▶n. the design, manufacture, or firing of heavy guns: *a pioneer of naval gunnery.*

gun·ner·y ser·geant ▶n. a noncommissioned officer in the US Marine Corps ranking above staff sergeant and below master sergeant.

Gun·ni·son Riv·er /'gənəsən/ a river that flows for 180 miles (290 km) through western Colorado to the Colorado River.

gun·ny /'gənē/ ▶n. coarse fabric, typically made of jute fiber and used esp. for sacks. [18th C.: from Marathi *gōnī*, from Sanskrit *goṇī* 'sack.']

gun·play /'gən,plā/ ▶n. the use of guns, esp. by two or more people exchanging shots.

gun·point /'gən,point/ ▶n. (in phrase **at gunpoint**) while threatening someone or being threatened with a gun.

gun·port /'gən,pôrt/ ▶n. see PORT⁴.

gun·pow·der /'gən,poudər/ ▶n. **1** an explosive consisting of a powdered mixture of saltpeter, sulfur, and charcoal. **2** (also **gunpowder tea**) a fine green China tea of granular appearance.

Gun·pow·der Plot a conspiracy by a small group of Catholic extremists to blow up James I of England and his Parliament on November 5, 1605.

gun·room /'gən,ro͞om; -,ro͝om/ ▶n. a room used for storing sporting guns in a house.

gun·run·ner /'gən,rənər/ ▶n. a person engaged in the illegal sale or importing of firearms. — **gun·run·ning** n.

gun·sel /'gənsəl/ ▶n. informal, dated a criminal carrying a gun. [20th C. (denoting a homosexual youth): from Yiddish *gendzel* 'little goose,' influenced in sense by GUN.]

gun·ship /'gən,sHip/ ▶n. an airplane or a helicopter heavily armed with machine guns or with machine guns and cannon, providing air support for ground troops in combat.

gun·shot /'gən,sHät/ ▶n. a shot fired from a gun. ■ the range of a gun.

gun-shy ▶adj. (esp. of a hunting dog) alarmed at the report of a gun. ■ fig. nervous and apprehensive.

gun·sight /'gən,sīt/ ▶n. a device on a gun that enables it to be aimed accurately.

gun·sling·er /'gən,sliNGər/ ▶n. informal a man who carries a gun and shoots well. ■ fig. a forceful and adventurous participant in a particular sphere. — **gun·sling·ing** adj.

gun·smith /'gən,smiTH/ ▶n. a person who makes, sells, and repairs small firearms.

gun·stock /'gən,stäk/ ▶n. the stock or support to which the barrel of a gun is attached.

gun·ter /'gəntər/ ▶n. Sailing a fore-and-aft sail whose spar is nearly vertical, so that the sail is nearly triangular. [18th C.: named after Edmund *Gunter* (1581–1626), English mathematician.]

Gun·ther /'go͝ontər/ (in the Nibelungenlied) the husband of Brunhild and brother of Kriemhild, by whom he was beheaded in revenge for Siegfried's murder.

Gun·tur /go͝on'to͝or/ a city in eastern India, in Andhra Pradesh; pop. 471,000.

gun·wale /'gənl/ (also **gun·nel**) ▶n. (often **gunwales**) the upper edge of the side of a boat or ship.

– PHRASES **to the gunwales** informal so as to be almost overflowing. [ME: from GUN + WALE.]

Guo·min·dang /'gwō'min'däNG/ var. of KUOMINTANG.

gup·py /'gəpē/ ▶n. (pl. **-pies**) a small, livebearing freshwater fish (*Poecilia reticulata*, family Poeciliidae) native to tropical America and widely kept in aquariums. [1920s: named after R. J. Lechmere *Guppy* (1836–1916), a Trinidadian clergyman who sent the first specimen to the British Museum.]

Gup·ta /'go͝optə/ a Hindu dynasty established in AD 320 by Chandragupta I in Bihar. At one stage it ruled most of the north of the Indian subcontinent, but it began to disintegrate toward the end of the 5th century. — **Gup·tan** adj.

Gur /go͝or/ ▶n. a branch of the Niger–Congo family of languages spoken in parts of West Africa. Also called VOLTAIC. ▶adj. of, relating to, or denoting this group of languages.

gur·gle /'gərgəl/ ▶v. [intrans.] make a hollow bubbling sound like that made by water running out of a bottle. ■ [with adverbial of direction] (of a liquid) run or flow with such a sound. ▶n. a gurgling sound. [ME: imitative, or based on L. *gurgulio* 'gullet.']

Gur·kha /'go͝orkə/ ▶n. a member of any of several peoples of Nepal noted for their military prowess. ■ a member of units of the British army established specifically for Nepalese recruits in the mid 19th century. [name of a locality.]

gur·nard /'gərnərd/ ▶n. a bottom-dwelling fish (family Triglidae) of coastal waters, with a heavily boned head and three fingerlike pectoral rays which it uses for searching for food and for walking on the seabed. [ME: from OFr. *gornart*, from *grondir* 'to grunt,' from L. *grundire, grunnire*.]

gur·ney /'gərnē/ ▶n. (pl. **-eys**) a wheeled stretcher used for transporting hospital patients. [19th C.: appar. named after J. T. *Gurney* of Boston, Massachusetts, patentee of a new cab design in 1883.]

gur·ry /'gərē/ ▶n. fish or whale offal. [18th C.: of unknown origin.]

gu·ru /'go͞oro͞o; go͞o'ro͞o/ ▶n. (pl. **-rus**) (in Hinduism and Buddhism) a spiritual teacher, esp. one who imparts initiation. ■ each of the ten first leaders of the Sikh religion. ■ an influential teacher or popular expert. [from Hindi and Punjabi, from Sanskrit *guru*, lit. 'weighty, grave.']

gush /gəsH/ ▶v. [intrans.] **1** [with adverbial of direction] (of a liquid) flow out in a rapid and plentiful stream, often suddenly. ■ [with obj. and adverbial of direction] send out in a rapid and plentiful stream. **2** speak or write with effusiveness or exaggerated enthusiasm. ▶n. **1** a rapid and plentiful stream or burst. **2** exaggerated effusiveness or enthusiasm. — **gush·ing·ly** adv. [ME: prob. imitative.]

gush·er /'gəsHər/ ▶n. **1** an oil well from which oil flows profusely without being pumped. ■ a thing from which a liquid flows profusely. **2** an effusive person.

gush·y /'gəsHē/ ▶adj. (**gush·i·er, gush·i·est**) excessively effusive: *her gushy manner.* — **gush·i·ly** /-sHəlē/ adv. **gush·i·ness** n.

gus·set /'gəsit/ ▶n. a piece of material sewn into a garment to strengthen or enlarge a part of it, such as the collar of a shirt or the crotch of an undergarment. ■ a bracket strengthening an angle of a structure. — **gusseted** adj. [ME: from OFr. *gousset*, dimin. of *gousse* 'pod, shell,' of unknown origin.]

gus·sy /'gəsē/ ▶v. (**-sies, -sied**) [trans.] (**gussy someone/something up**) informal make more attractive, esp. in a showy or gimmicky way. [1940s: perh. from *Gussie*, nickname for *Augustus*.]

gust /gəst/ ▶n. a brief, strong rush of wind. ■ a burst of something such as rain, sound, or emotion. ▶v. [intrans.] (of the wind) blow in gusts. [16th C.: from ON *gustr*, rel. to *gjósa* 'to gush.']

gus·ta·tion /gə'stāsHən/ ▶n. formal the action or faculty of tasting. — **gus·ta·tive** /'gəstətiv/ adj. [16th C.: from L. *gustatio(n-)*, from *gustare* 'to taste,' from *gustus* 'taste.']

gus·ta·to·ry /'gəstə,tôrē/ ▶adj. formal concerned with tasting or the sense of taste: *gustatory delights.*

Gus·ta·vus Adol·phus /gə'stävəs ə'dôlfəs/ (1594–1632), king of Sweden 1611–32.

gus·to /'gəstō/ ▶n. (pl. **-tos** or **-toes**) enjoyment or vigor in doing something; zest. [17th C.: from Ital., from L. *gustus* 'taste.']

gust·y /'gəstē/ ▶adj. (**gust·i·er, gust·i·est**) **1** characterized by or blowing in gusts. **2** having or showing gusto. — **gust·i·ly** adv. **gust·i·ness** n.

gut /gət/ ▶n. **1** (also **guts**) the stomach or belly. ■ Med. Biol. the lower alimentary canal or a part of this; the intestine. ■ (**guts**) entrails that have been removed or exposed in violence or by a butcher. ■ (**guts**) the internal parts or essence of something. **2** (**guts**) informal personal courage and determination; toughness of character. ■ [as adj.] informal (of a feeling or reaction) based on a deep-seated emotional response rather than considered thought; instinctive. **3** fiber made from the intestines of animals, used esp. for violin or racket strings or for surgical use. **4** a narrow passage or strait. ▶v. (**gut·ted, gut·ting**) [trans.] take out the intestines and other internal organs of (a fish or other animal) before cooking it. ■ remove or destroy completely the internal parts of (a building or other structure). ■ remove or extract the most important parts of (something) in a damaging or destructive manner.

– PHRASES **bust a gut** informal make a strenuous effort. —— **one's guts out** used to indicate that the specified action is done or performed as hard as possible. **hate someone's guts** informal feel strong hatred for someone. [OE *guttas* (pl.), prob. rel. to *gēotan* 'pour.']

gut·buck·et /'gət,bəkit/ informal ▶n. [as adj.] informal (of jazz or blues) raw and spirited in style. [20th C.: perh. from the earlier denotation of a one-stringed plucked instrument.]

gut course ▶n. informal a college or university course requiring little work or intellectual ability.

Gu·ten·berg /'go͞otn,bərg/, Johannes (*c.*1400–68), German printer. He was the first in the West to print by using movable type and to use a press.

Gu·ten·berg Bi·ble ▶n. the edition of the Bible (Vulgate version) completed by Johannes Gutenberg in about 1455 in Mainz, Germany. It is the first complete book extant in the West and is also the earliest to be printed from movable type.

Guth·rie /'gəTHrē/, Woody (1912–67), US folk singer and songwriter; full name *Woodrow Wilson Guthrie*. His anti-injustice ballads include *"This Land Is Your Land"* (1940).

gut·less /'gətlis/ ▶adj. informal lacking courage or determination. — **gut·less·ly** adv. **gut·less·ness** n.

guts·y /'gətsē/ ▶adj. (**guts·i·er, guts·i·est**) informal showing courage, determination, and spirit. ■ (of food or drink) strongly flavorsome. — **guts·i·ly** adv. **guts·i·ness** n.

gut·ta-per·cha /,gətə 'pərcHə/ ▶n. a hard, tough thermoplastic substance that is the coagulated latex of certain Malaysian trees (genus *Palaquium*) of the sapodilla family. It consists chiefly of a hydrocarbon isomeric with rubber and is used chiefly in dentistry and for electrical insulation. [19th C.: from Malay *getah perca*, from *getah* 'gum' + *perca* 'strips of cloth.']

gut·tate /'gətāt/ ▶adj. esp. Biol. having drops or droplike markings. ■ in the form of or resembling drops. [19th C.: from L. *guttatus* 'speckled,' from *gutta* 'a drop.']

gut·ta·tion /gə'tāsHən/ ▶ n. the secretion of droplets of water from the pores of plants.

gut·ter /'gətər/ ▶ n. a shallow trough fixed beneath the edge of a roof for carrying off rainwater. ■ a channel at the side of a street for carrying off rainwater. ■ (**the gutter**) used to refer to a poor or squalid background or environment. ■ tech. a groove or channel for flowing liquid. ■ the blank space between facing pages of a book or between adjacent columns of type or stamps in a sheet. ■ a channel on either side of a lane in a bowling alley. ▶ v. **1** [intrans.] (of a candle or flame) flicker and burn unsteadily. **2** [trans.] archaic channel or furrow with something such as streams or tears. ■ [intrans.] (**gutter down**) stream down. [ME: from OFr. *gotiere*, from L. *gutta* 'a drop.']

gut·ter ball ▶ n. (in tenpin bowling) a nonscoring ball that enters the gutter before reaching the pins.

gut·ter·snipe /'gətər,snīp/ ▶ n. derog. a street urchin. ■ an ill-bred person.

gut·tur·al /'gətərəl/ ▶ adj. (of a speech sound) produced in the throat; harsh-sounding. ■ (of a manner of speech) characterized by the use of such sounds. ▶ n. a guttural consonant (e.g., *k*, *g*) or other speech sound. — **gut·tur·al·ly** adv. [16th C.: from Fr., or from med. L. *gutturalis*, from L. *guttur* 'throat.']

gut·tur·al·ize /'gətərə,līz/ ▶ v. [trans.] **1** say or pronounce in a harsh-sounding guttural manner. **2** articulate (a speech sound) by moving the back of the tongue toward the velum.

gut·ty /'gətē/ ▶ adj. (**-ier, -iest**) informal gutsy.

guy[1] /gī/ ▶ n. **1** informal a man: *he's a nice guy.* ■ (**guys**) people of either sex. **2** Brit. a figure representing Guy Fawkes, burned on a bonfire on Guy Fawkes' Night, and often displayed by children begging for money for fireworks. ▶ v. [trans.] make fun of; ridicule. [19th C. (sense 2): named after *Guy* Fawkes (see GUNPOWDER PLOT).]

guy[2] ▶ n. a rope or line fixed to the ground to secure a tent or other structure. ▶ v. [trans.] secure with a line or lines. [ME: prob. of Low German origin; rel. to Du. *gei* 'brail' and Ger. *Geitaue* 'brails.']

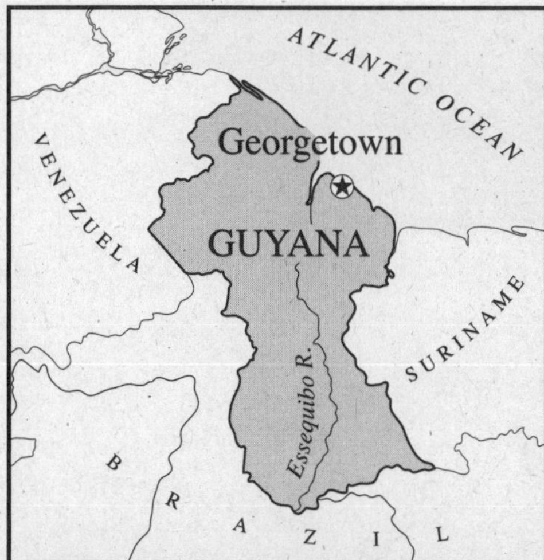

Guyana

Official name: Cooperative Republic of Guyana
Location: northeastern coast of South America, north of Brazil between Venezuela and Suriname
Area: 76,000 square miles (196,900 sq km)
Population: 705,000
Capital: Georgetown
Languages: English (official), English Creole, Hindi, Urdu, and Amerindian languages
Currency: Guyanese dollar

Guy·a·na /gī'änə; -anə/ a country on the northeastern coast of South America. *See box.* — **Guy·a·nese** /,gīə'nēz; -'nēs/ adj. & n.

guy·ot /gē'ō/ ▶ n. Geol. a seamount with a flat top. [1940s: named after Arnold H. *Guyot* (1807–84), Swiss geographer.]

guz·zle /'gəzəl/ ▶ v. [trans.] eat or drink (something) greedily. — **guz·zler** n. [16th C.: perh. from OFr. *gosillier* 'chatter, vomit,' from *gosier* 'throat,' from late L. *geusiae* 'cheeks.']

Gvozdena Vrata /'gvôzdənə 'vrätə/ Serbo-Croat name for IRON GATE.

GVW ▶ abbr. gross vehicle weight.

GW ▶ abbr. gigawatt.

Gwa·li·or /'gwälē,ôr/ a city in central India, in a district of the same name in Madhya Pradesh; pop. 693,000.

Gwyn /gwin/, Nell (1650–87), English actress; full name *Eleanor Gwyn.* She was a mistress of Charles II.

Gy Physics ▶ abbr. gray(s).

gybe ▶ v. & n. var. of JIBE[2].

gym /jim/ ▶ n. informal **1** a gymnasium. **2** a membership organization that provides a range of facilities designed to improve and maintain physical fitness and health. **3** physical education.

gym·kha·na /jim'känə/ ▶ n. an event comprising races and other competitions between horse riders or car drivers. [19th C.: from Urdu *gendkānah* 'racket court,' from Hindi *gemd* 'ball' + Pers. *kānah* 'house,' alt. by association with GYMNASTIC.]

gym·na·si·um /jim'nāzēəm/ ▶ n. (pl. **-si·ums** or **-si·a** /-zēə/) **1** a room or building equipped for gymnastics, games, and other physical exercise. **2** /gim'näzē,ŏŏm/ a preparatory school in Germany, Scandinavia, or central Europe. [16th C.: via L. from Gk. *gumnasion*, from *gumnazein* 'exercise naked,' from *gumnos* 'naked.']

gym·nast /'jimnist/ ▶ n. a person trained in or skilled in gymnastics. [16th C.: from Fr. *gymnaste* or Gk. *gumnastēs* 'trainer of athletes,' from *gumnazein* 'exercise naked' (see GYMNASIUM).]

gym·nas·tics /jim'nastiks/ ▶ plural n. [also treated as sing.] exercises developing or displaying physical agility and coordination. The modern sport of gymnastics typically involves exercises on uneven bars, balance beam, floor, and vaulting horse (for women), and horizontal and parallel bars, rings, floor, and pommel horse (for men). ■ [with adj.] other physical or mental agility of a specified kind. — **gym·nas·tic** adj. **gym·nas·ti·cal·ly** /-tik(ə)lē/ adv.

gymno- ▶ comb. form bare; naked: *gymnosophist.* [from Gk. *gumnos* 'naked.']

gym·nos·o·phist /jim'näsəfist/ ▶ n. a member of an ancient Indian sect that wore very little clothing and was given to asceticism and contemplation. — **gym·nos·o·phy** n. [ME: from Fr. *gymnosophiste*, via L. from Gk. *gumnosophistai* (pl.), from *gumnos* 'naked' + *sophistēs* 'teacher of philosophy, sophist.']

gym·no·sperm /'jimnə,spərm/ ▶ n. Bot. a plant that has seeds unprotected by an ovary or fruit. Gymnosperms include the conifers, cycads, and ginkgo.

gyn. ▶ abbr. ■ gynecological. ■ gynecologist. ■ gynecology.

gynaeco- esp. Brit. var. of GYNECO-.

gy·nan·dro·morph /gī'nandrə,môrf; ji'nan-/ ▶ n. Zool. Med. an abnormal individual, esp. an insect, having some male and some female characteristics. — **gy·nan·dro·mor·phic** /gī,nandrə'môrfik; ji,nan-/ adj. **gy·nan·dro·mor·phy** n. [19th C.: from Gk. *gunandros* 'of doubtful sex' (see GYNANDROUS) + *morphē* 'form.']

gy·nan·drous /gī'nandrəs; ji'nan-/ ▶ adj. Bot. (of a flower) having stamens and pistil united in one column, as in orchids. ■ (of a person or animal) hermaphrodite. [19th C.: from Gk. *gunandros* 'of doubtful sex' (from *gunē* 'woman' + *anēr, andr-* 'man, male') + -OUS.]

gyn·ar·chy /'gī,närkē; 'jin,är-/ ▶ n. (pl. **-chies**) rule by women or a woman.

gyneco- ▶ comb. form comb. form relating to women; female: *gynecocracy* | *gynecophobia.* [from Gk. *gunē, gunaik-* 'woman, female.']

gyn·e·coc·ra·cy /,gīnə'käkrəsē; jinə-/ (Brit. **gyn·ae·coc·ra·cy**) ▶ n. another term for GYNARCHY.

gy·ne·coid /'jini,koid; 'gīni-; 'jīni-/ ▶ adj. relating to or characteristic of a woman.

gynecol. ▶ abbr. ■ gynecological. ■ gynecology.

gy·ne·col·o·gy /,gīnə'käləjē; jinə-/ (Brit. **gy·nae·col·o·gy**) ▶ n. the branch of physiology and medicine that deals with the functions and diseases specific to women and girls, esp. those affecting the reproductive system. — **gyn·e·co·log·ic** /-kə'läjik/ adj. **gyn·e·co·log·i·cal** /-kə'läjikəl/ adj. **gyn·e·co·log·i·cal·ly** /-kə'läjik(ə)lē/ adv. **gy·ne·col·o·gist** n.

gyn·e·co·mas·ti·a /,gīnəkō'mastēə/ (Brit. **gyn·ae·co·mas·ti·a**) ▶ n. Med. enlargement of a man's breasts, usually due to hormone imbalance or hormone therapy.

gyn·e·co·pho·bi·a /,gīnəkō'fōbēə/ (Brit. **gyn·ae·co·pho·bi·a**) ▶ n. another term for GYNOPHOBIA.

gy·no·cen·tric /,gīnə'sentrik/ ▶ adj. centered on or concerned exclusively with women; taking a female (or specifically a feminist) point of view.

gy·noe·ci·um /ji'nēsHēəm; -sēəm; gī-/ ▶ n. (pl. **-ci·a** /-sHēə; -sēə/) Bot. the female part of a flower, consisting of one or more carpels. [19th C.: mod. L., from Gk. *gunaikeion* 'women's apartments,' from *gunē, gunaik-* 'woman, female' + *oikos* 'house.']

gy·no·pho·bi·a /,gīnə'fōbēə; jinə-/ ▶ n. extreme or irrational fear of women or of the female. — **gy·no·pho·bic** adj.

-gynous ▶ comb. form Bot. having female organs or pistils of a specified kind or number: *epigynous.* [based on mod. L. *-gynus* (from Gk. *-gunos*, from *gunē* 'woman') + -OUS.]

gyp /jip/ informal ▶ v. (**gypped, gyp·ping**) [trans.] cheat or swindle (someone). ▶ n. (also **gip**) an act of cheating; a swindle. [19th C.: of unknown origin.]

gyp joint ▶ n. informal **1** a business establishment, esp. a store, that has a reputation for cheating customers by charging high prices for inferior goods or services. **2** a gambling establishment in which the games are run dishonestly.

gyp·soph·i·la /jip'säfələ/ ▶ **n.** a plant of the genus *Gypsophila* in the pink family, esp. (in gardening) baby's breath. [mod. L., from Gk. *gupsos* 'chalk, gypsum' + *philos* 'loving.']

gyp·sum /'jipsəm/ ▶ **n.** a soft white or gray mineral consisting of hydrated calcium sulfate. It occurs chiefly in sedimentary deposits and is used to make plaster of Paris and fertilizers, and in the building industry. — **gyp·sif·er·ous** /jip'sifərəs/ **adj.** [ME: from L., from Gk. *gupsos*.]

gyp·sum board ▶ **n.** another term for PLASTERBOARD.

gyp·sy /'jipsē/ (also **gip·sy**) ▶ **n.** (pl. **-sies**) a member of a traveling people with dark skin and hair who speak Romany and traditionally live by seasonal work, itinerant trade, and fortune-telling. Gypsies are believed to have originated in the Indian subcontinent. ■ the language of the gypsies; Romany. ■ a person who leads an unconventional life. ■ a person who moves from place to place as required by employment. ▶ **adj.** (of a business or business person) nonunion or unlicensed. — **gyp·sy·ish** **adj.** [16th C.: orig. *gipcyan*, short for EGYPTIAN (because gypsies were popularly supposed to have come from Egypt).]

gyp·sy moth ▶ **n.** a tussock moth (*Lymantria dispar*) having a brown male and larger white female. The caterpillar can be a serious pest of orchards and woodland.

gy·ral /'jīrəl/ ▶ **adj.** esp. Anat. of or relating to a gyrus or gyri.

gy·rate /'jīrāt/ ▶ **v.** move or cause to move in a circle or spiral, esp. quickly. ■ [intrans.] dance in a wild or suggestive manner. — **gy·ra·tion** /jī'rāsʜən/ **n.** **gy·ra·tor** /-,rātər/ **n.** [19th C.: from L. *gyrat-* 'revolved,' from the v. *gyrare*, from Gk. *guros* 'a ring.']

gy·ra·to·ry /'jīrə,tôrē/ ▶ **adj.** of or involving circular or spiral motion.

gyre /jī(ə)r/ ▶ **v.** [intrans.] literary whirl; gyrate. ▶ **n.** a spiral; a vortex. ■ Geog. a circular pattern of currents in an ocean basin. [ME: from late L. *gyrare*, from L. *gyrus* 'a ring,' from Gk. *guros*.]

gyr·fal·con /'jər,falkən; -,fôl-/ ▶ **n.** the largest falcon (*Falco rusticolus*), found in arctic regions and occurring in several color forms, one of which is mainly white. [ME: from OFr. *gerfaucon*, of Gmc. origin. The first element is prob. rel. to Old High Ger. *gēr* 'spear.']

gy·ri /'jīrī/ plural form of GYRUS.

gy·ro[1] /'jīrō/ ▶ **n.** (pl. **-ros**) short for GYROSCOPE or GYROCOMPASS.

gy·ro[2] /'yērō; 'jīrō/ ▶ **n.** (pl. **-ros**) a sandwich made with slices of spiced meat cooked on a spit, served with salad in pita bread. [1970s: from mod. Gk. *guros* 'turning.']

gyro- ▶ **comb. form** **1** relating to rotation: *gyromagnetic*. **2** gyroscopic: *gyrostabilizer*. [from Gk. *guros* 'a ring.']

gy·ro·com·pass /'jīrō,kəmpəs/ ▶ **n.** a nonmagnetic compass in which the direction of true north is maintained by a continuously driven gyroscope whose axis is parallel to the earth's axis of rotation.

gy·ro·mag·net·ic /,jīrōmag'netik/ ▶ **adj.** **1** Physics of or relating to the magnetic and mechanical properties of a rotating charged particle. **2** (of a compass) combining a gyroscope and a normal magnetic compass.

gy·ro·pi·lot /'jīrə,pīlət/ ▶ **n.** a gyrocompass used to provide automatic steering for a ship or aircraft.

gy·ro·plane /'jīrə,plān/ ▶ **n.** an autogiro or similar aircraft.

gy·ro·scope /'jīrə,skōp/ ▶ **n.** a device, used to provide stability or maintain a fixed orientation, consisting of a wheel or disk mounted so that it can spin rapidly about an axis that is itself free to change direction. — **gy·ro·scop·ic** /,jīrə'skäpik/ **adj.** **gy·ro·scop·i·cal·ly** /,jīrə'skäpik(ə)lē/ **adv.**

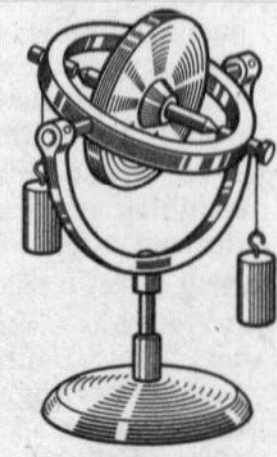

gyroscope

gy·ro·sta·bi·liz·er /,jīrō'stābə,līzər/ ▶ **n.** a gyroscopic device for maintaining the equilibrium of something such as a ship, aircraft, or platform.

gy·rus /'jīrəs/ ▶ **n.** (pl. **gy·ri** /'jīrī/) Anat. a ridge or fold between two clefts on the cerebral surface in the brain. [19th C.: from L., from Gk. *guros* 'a ring.']

GySgt ▶ **abbr.** gunnery sergeant.

gyt·tja /'yicнä/ ▶ **n.** Geol. sediment rich in organic matter deposited at the bottom of a eutrophic lake. [19th C.: Swed., lit. 'mud, ooze.']

H¹ /āCH/ (also **h**) ▶ **n.** (pl. **Hs** or **H's** /'āCHiz/) **1** the eighth letter of the alphabet. ■ denoting the next after G in a set of items, categories, etc. **2** (**H**) a shape like that of a capital H. **3** (**H**) Music (in the German system) the note B natural.

H² ▶ **abbr.** ■ hard (used in describing grades of pencil lead): *a 2H pencil.* ■ height (in giving the dimensions of an object). ■ Physics henry(s). ■ informal heroin. ▶ **symb.** ■ Chem. enthalpy. ■ the chemical element hydrogen. ■ Physics magnetic field strength.

h /āCH/ ▶ **abbr.** ■ (in measuring the height of horses) hand(s). ■ [in comb.] (in units of measurement) hecto-: *wine production reached 624,000 hl last year.* ■ horse. ■ (esp. with reference to water) hot: *nine rooms, all with h & c.* ■ hour(s): *breakfast at 0700 h.* ▶ **symb.** ■ Physics Planck's constant. ■ (ħ) Physics Planck's constant divided by 2π.

ha¹ /hä/ (also **hah**) ▶ **exclam.** used to express surprise, suspicion, triumph, or some other emotion. [natural utterance: first recorded in ME.]

ha² ▶ **abbr.** hectare(s).

Haar·lem /'härləm/ a city in western Netherlands, near Amsterdam; pop. 148,000.

Hab. ▶ **abbr.** Bible Habakkuk.

Ha·bak·kuk /'habə,ko͝ok; hə'bakək/ a Hebrew prophet. ■ a book of the Bible containing his prophecies.

ha·ba·ne·ra /,häbə'ne(ə)rə; -'ny(ə)rə/ ▶ **n.** a Cuban dance. [19th C.: Sp., short for *danza habanera* 'dance of Havana.']

Ha·ba·ne·ro /,häbə'ne(ə)rō; -'nye(ə)rō/ (also **ha·ba·ne·ro**) ▶ **n.** a small hot chili pepper. Also called **Scotch bonnet**. [Sp., lit. 'of Havana.']

ha·be·as cor·pus /'hābēəs 'kôrpəs/ ▶ **n.** Law a writ requiring a person under arrest to be brought before a judge or into court. ■ the legal right to apply for such a writ. [ME: L., lit. 'you shall have the body (in court).']

ha·ben·dum /hə'bendəm/ ▶ **n.** Law the part of a deed or conveyance that states the estate or quantity of interest to be granted, e.g., the term of a lease. [17th C.: L., lit. '(that is) to be had'.]

hab·er·dash·er /'habər,dasHər/ ▶ **n.** a dealer in men's clothing. [ME: prob. based on Anglo-Norman Fr. *hapertas*, perh. a fabric.]

hab·er·dash·er·y /'habər,dasHərē/ ▶ **n.** (pl. **-er·ies**) the shop and its goods and wares of a haberdasher.

hab·er·geon /'habərjən; hə'bərjən/ ▶ **n.** hist. a sleeveless coat of mail or scale armor. [ME: from OFr. *haubergeon*, from *hauberc* (see **hauberk**).]

Ha·ber proc·ess /'häbər/ (also **Ha·ber–Bosch proc·ess** /'bäsH/) ▶ **n.** an industrial process for producing ammonia from nitrogen and hydrogen, using an iron catalyst. [named after Fritz *Haber* (1868–1934) and Carl *Bosch* (1874–1940), German chemists.]

hab·ile /'habəl/ ▶ **adj.** rare deft; skillful. [ME: var. of **able**.]

ha·bil·i·ment /hə'biləmənt/ ▶ **n.** (usu. **habiliments**) archaic clothing. [ME: from OFr. *habillement*, from *habiller* 'fit out,' from L. *habilis* (see **able**).]

ha·bil·i·tate /hə'bilə,tāt/ ▶ **v.** [trans.] fit out the workings of (a mine). — **ha·bil·i·ta·tion** /hə,bilə'tāsHən/ **n.** [17th C.: from med. L. *habilitat-* 'made able,' from the v. *habilitare*, from *habilitas* (see **ability**).]

hab·it /'habit/ ▶ **n.** **1** a settled or regular tendency or practice, esp. one that is hard to give up. ■ informal an addictive practice, esp. one of taking drugs. ■ Psychol. an automatic reaction to a specific situation. ■ general shape or mode of growth, esp. of a plant or a mineral: *a shrub of spreading habit.* **2** a long, loose garment worn by a member of a religious order or congregation. ■ short for **riding habit**. ■ archaic dress; attire. ▶ **v.** [trans.] (usu. **be habited**) archaic dress; clothe: *a boy habited as a serving lad.*
- PHRASES **break** (or informal **kick**) **the habit** stop engaging in a habitual practice. [ME: from OFr. *abit*, *habit*, from L. *habitus* 'condition, appearance,' from *habere* 'have, consist of.']

hab·it·a·ble /'habitəbəl/ ▶ **adj.** suitable to live in. — **hab·it·a·bil·i·ty** /,habətə'bilətē/ **n.**

hab·i·tant /'habitənt; -itnt/ ▶ **n.** **1** [often as adj.] an early French settler in Canada (esp. Quebec) or Louisiana: *the habitant farmhouses of old Quebec.* **2** archaic an inhabitant. [ME (sense 2): from OFr., from *habiter*, from L. *habitare* 'inhabit.']

hab·i·tat /'habi,tat/ ▶ **n.** the natural home or environment of an animal, plant, or other organism. ■ a particular type of environment regarded as a home for organisms. ■ informal a person's usual or preferred surroundings. [18th C.: from L., lit. 'it dwells,' from *habitare* 'inhabit.']

hab·i·ta·tion /,habi'tāsHən/ ▶ **n.** the state or process of living in a particular place. ■ formal a place in which to live; a house or home. — **hab·i·ta·tive** /'habitə,tiv/ **adj.**

hab·it-form·ing ▶ **adj.** (of a drug or activity) addictive.

ha·bit·u·al /hə'biCHo͞oəl/ ▶ **adj.** done as a habit. ■ regular; usual: *his habitual dress.* — **ha·bit·u·al·ly** **adv.**

ha·bit·u·ate /hə'biCHo͞o,āt/ ▶ **v.** make or become accustomed or used to something. — **ha·bit·u·a·tion** /hə,biCHo͞o'āsHən/ **n.**

hab·i·tude /'habi,t(y)o͞od/ ▶ **n.** rare a habitual tendency or way of behaving.

ha·bit·u·é /hə'biCHo͞o,ā/ ▶ **n.** a resident of or frequent visitor to a particular place. [19th C.: Fr., lit. 'accustomed,' past part. of *habituer*.]

hab·i·tus /'habitəs/ ▶ **n.** esp. Med. Psychol. general constitution, esp. bodily build. [19th C.: from L.]

ha·boob /hə'bo͞ob/ ▶ **n.** a violent and oppressive wind blowing in summer, esp. in Sudan. [19th C.: from Arab. *habūb* 'blowing furiously.']

Habs·burg /'haps,bərg; 'häps,bo͝ork/ (also **Haps·burg**) one of the principal dynasties of central Europe.

ha·ček /'ha,CHek/ (also **há·ček**) ▶ **n.** a diacritic mark (ˇ) placed over a letter to indicate modification of the sound in Slavic and other languages. [Czech, dimin. of *hák* 'hook.']

ha·cen·da·do /,äsen'dädō/ (also **ha·cien·da·do** /,äsyen-/) ▶ **n.** (pl. **-dos**) the owner of a hacienda. [Sp.]

Ha·chi·o·ji /,häCHē'ōjē/ a city in east central Japan, on east central Honshu; pop. 466,000.

ha·chures /ha'sHo͝orz; 'hasHərz/ ▶ **plural n.** short parallel lines used in hill-shading on maps, their closeness indicating steepness of gradient. — **ha·chured** /ha'sHo͝ord; 'hasHərd/ **adj.** [19th C.: from Fr., from *hacher* (see **hatch³**).]

ha·ci·en·da /,häsē'endə/ ▶ **n.** (in Spanish-speaking regions) a large estate or plantation. ■ the main house on such an estate. [Sp., from L. *facienda* 'things to be done,' from *facere* 'make, do.']

hack¹ /hak/ ▶ **v.** **1** [trans.] cut with rough or heavy blows. **2** [intrans.] use a computer to gain unauthorized access to data in a system. ■ [trans.] gain unauthorized access to computer data. **3** [usu. with negative] (**hack it**) informal manage; cope. ▶ **n.** **1** a rough cut, blow, or stroke. ■ (in sports) a kick or hit inflicted on another player. ■ a cut or gash. ■ a tool for rough striking or cutting. **2** informal an act of computer hacking. ■ a piece of computer code that performs some function, esp. an unofficial alternative or addition to a commercial program: *freeware and shareware hacks.*
- PHRASES **hacking cough** a short, dry cough.
- PHRASAL VERBS **hack around** pass one's time idly. [OE *haccian* 'cut in pieces,' of West Gmc. origin; rel. to Du. *hakken* and Ger. *hacken*.]

hack² ▶ **n.** **1** a writer or journalist producing dull, unoriginal work: [as adj.] *a hack scriptwriter.* ■ a person who does dull routine work. **2** a horse for ordinary riding. ■ a ride on a horse. ■ an inferior or worn-out horse. ■ a horse rented out for riding. **3** a taxicab. ▶ **v.** [intrans.] [usu. as n.] (**hacking**) ride a horse for pleasure or exercise. — **hack·er·y** /'hakərē/ **n.** (in sense 1) [ME: abbrev. of **hackney**.]

hack³ ▶ **n.** **1** Falconry a board on which a hawk's meat is laid. **2** a wooden frame for drying bricks, cheeses, etc. ■ a pile of bricks stacked up to dry before firing. [ME (denoting the lower half of a divided door): var. of **hatch¹**.]

hack·a·more /'hakə,môr/ ▶ **n.** a bitless bridle that operates by exerting pressure on the horse's nose. [19th C.: perh. from Sp. *jaquima*, earlier *xaquima* 'halter.']

hack·ber·ry /'hak,berē/ ▶ **n.** (pl. **-ries**) a tree (genus *Celtis*) of the elm family that has leaves resembling those of nettles, found in both tropical and temperate regions. ■ the berry of this tree. [18th C.: var. of dial. *hagberry*, of Scand. origin.]

hack·er /'hakər/ ▶ **n.** **1** informal an enthusiastic and skillful computer programmer or user. ■ a person who uses computers to gain unauthorized access to data. **2** a person or thing that hacks or cuts roughly. **3** a person who plays amateur sports without skill.

hack·ing jack·et ▶ **n.** a riding jacket, often tweed, with slits at the side or back, and slanted pockets with flaps.

hack·le /'hakəl/ ▶ **n.** **1** (**hackles**) hairs along the back of an animal that rise when it is angry or alarmed. ■ the hairs on the back of a person's neck, thought of as being raised when the person is angry or hostile. **2** (often **hackles**) a long, narrow feather on the neck or saddle of a domestic rooster or other bird. ■ Fishing a feather wound around a fishing fly so that its filaments are splayed out. ■ such feathers collectively. ■ a bunch of feathers in a military headdress. **3** a steel comb for separating flax fibers. ▶ **v.** [trans.] dress or comb with a hackle. [ME (sense 2): var. of **hatchel**.]

hack·ma·tack /ˈhakməˌtak/ ▶ **n.** any of a number of North American coniferous trees, in particular the tamarack. [18th C.: perh. from Western Abnaki *akemantak* 'snowshoe-conifer.']

hack·ney /ˈhaknē/ ▶ **n.** (pl. **-neys**) hist. a horse or pony with a high-stepping trot, used in harness. ■ [usu. as adj.] a horse-drawn vehicle kept for hire. [ME: prob. from *Hackney* in East London, England, where horses were pastured.]

hack·neyed /ˈhaknēd/ ▶ **adj.** (of a phrase or idea) lacking significance through having been overused.

hack·saw /ˈhakˌsô/ ▶ **n.** a saw with a narrow fine-toothed blade set in a frame, used esp. for cutting metal. ▶ **v.** (past part. **-sawn** or **-sawed**) [trans.] cut (something) using a hacksaw.

had /had/ past and past participle of **HAVE**.

ha·dal /ˈhādl/ ▶ **adj.** of or relating to the zone of the sea greater than about 20,000 feet (6,000 m) deep. [20th C.: from **HADES** + **-AL**.]

had·da /ˈhadə/ informal ▶ **contr.** had to.

had·dock /ˈhadək/ ▶ **n.** (pl. same) a silvery-gray bottom-dwelling food fish (*Melanogrammus aeglefinus*) of the cod family, inhabiting North Atlantic coastal waters. [ME: from Anglo-Norman Fr. *hadoc*, from OFr. *hadot*, of unknown origin.]

hade /hād/ Geol. ▶ **n.** the inclination of a mineral vein or fault from the vertical. ▶ **v.** [intrans.] (of a shaft, vein, or fault) incline from the vertical: *it was hading one inch for every fathom in depth.* [17th C.: perh. a dial. form of the v. **HEAD**.]

Ha·des /ˈhādēz/ Gk. Mythol. the underworld. ■ the god of the underworld, one of the sons of Cronus. Also called **PLUTO**. — **Ha·de·an** /ˈhādēən/ **adj.**

Ha·dith /həˈdēTH/ ▶ **n.** (pl. same or **-diths**) a collection of traditions containing sayings of the prophet Muhammad. ■ one of these sayings. [from Arab. *ḥadīṯ* 'tradition.']

hadj ▶ **n.** var. of **HAJJ**.

hadj·i ▶ **n.** var. of **HAJI**.

Had·ley cell /ˈhadlē/ ▶ **n.** Meteorol. a large-scale atmospheric convection cell in which air rises at the equator and sinks at medium latitudes. [1950s: named after George *Hadley* (1685–1768), English scientific writer.]

had·n't /ˈhadnt/ ▶ **contr.** had not.

Ha·dri·an /ˈhādrēən/ (AD 76–138), Roman emperor 117–138; full name *Publius Aelius Hadrianus*.

Ha·dri·an's Wall /ˈhādrēənz/ a Roman defensive wall across northern England, from the Solway Firth to the Tyne River (about 74 miles; 120 km), begun in AD 122.

had·ron /ˈhadrän/ ▶ **n.** Physics a subatomic particle of a type including the baryons and mesons that can take part in the strong interaction. — **ha·dron·ic** /hadˈränik/ **adj.** [1960s: from Gk. *hadros* 'bulky' + **-ON**.]

had·ro·saur /ˈhadrəˌsôr/ (also **had·ro·sau·rus** /ˌhadrəˈsôrəs/) ▶ **n.** a large, herbivorous, mainly bipedal dinosaur (family Hadrosauridae, infraorder Ornithopoda) of the middle to late Cretaceous period, with jaws flattened like the bill of a duck. Also called **DUCK-BILLED DINOSAUR**. — **had·ro·sau·ri·an** **adj.** [19th C.: from mod. L. *Hadrosaurus* (genus name), from Gk. *hadros* 'thick, stout' + *sauros* 'lizard.']

haec·ce·i·ty /hakˈsēitē/ ▶ **n.** Philos. that property or quality of a thing by virtue of which it is unique. ■ the property of being a unique and individual thing. [17th C.: from med. L. *haecceitas*, from L. *haec*, fem. of *hic* 'this.']

haem ▶ **n.** British spelling of **HEME**.

hae·mag·glu·ti·na·tion, etc. ▶ **n.** British spelling of **HEMAGGLUTINATION**, etc.

hae·mal ▶ **adj.** British spelling of **HEMAL**.

haemato- ▶ **comb. form** British spelling of **HEMATO-**.

-haemia ▶ **comb. form** esp. Brit. var. of **-EMIA**.

haemo- ▶ **comb. form** British spelling of **HEMO-**.

ha·fiz /ˈhäfiz/ ▶ **n.** a Muslim who knows the Koran by heart. [Pers., from Arab. *ḥāfiẓ* 'guardian,' from *ḥāfiẓa* 'guard, know by heart.']

haf·ni·um /ˈhafnēəm/ ▶ **n.** the chemical element of atomic number 72, a hard silver-gray metal, resembling and often occurring with zirconium. (Symbol: **Hf**) [1920s: mod. L., from *Hafnia* Copenhagen.]

haft /haft/ ▶ **n.** the handle of a knife, ax, or spear. ▶ **v.** [trans.] [often as adj.] (**hafted**) provide (a blade, ax head, or spearhead) with a haft. [OE *hæft*, of Gmc. origin: rel. to Ger. *Heft*, also to **HEAVE**.]

Haf·to·rah /ˌhäftäˈrä; häfˈtôrə/ (also **Haph·ta·rah** or **Haph·to·rah**) ▶ **n.** (pl. **-to·roth** /-täˈrôt, -ˈtôrōs/) Judaism a short reading from the Prophets that follows the reading from the Law in a synagogue. [from Heb. *hapṭārāh* 'dismissal.']

Hag. ▶ **abbr.** Bible Haggai.

hag[1] /hag/ ▶ **n.** a witch, esp. one in the form of an ugly old woman (often used to disparage a woman). — **hag·gish** **adj.** [ME: perh. from OE *hægtesse*, *hegtes*, rel. to Ger. *Hexe* 'witch.']

hag[2] ▶ **n.** Scot. N. English **1** (also **peat hag**) an overhang of peat. **2** a soft place on a moor or a firm place in a bog. [ME (denoting a gap in a cliff): from ON *hǫgg* 'gap,' from *hǫggva* 'hack, hew.']

Ha·gar /ˈhägər/ (in the Bible and in Islamic tradition) the mother of Ishmael (Ismail), son of Abraham.

Ha·gen /ˈhägən/ a city in northwestern Germany, in North Rhine-Westphalia; pop. 214,000.

hag·fish /ˈhagˌfisH/ ▶ **n.** (pl. same or **-fish·es**) a primitive jawless marine vertebrate (*Myxine* and other genera, family Myxinidae) distantly related to the lampreys, with a slimy eellike body, a slitlike mouth surrounded by barbels, and a rasping tongue used for feeding on dead or dying fish.

Hag·ga·dah /hägäˈdä; həˈgädə/ (also **Ag·ga·dah** /ägäˈdä; əˈgädə/) ▶ **n.** (pl. **-doth** or **-dot** /-ˈdôt/) Judaism **1** the text recited at the Seder on the first two nights of the Jewish Passover, including a narrative of the Exodus. **2** a legend, parable, or anecdote used to illustrate a point of the Law in the Talmud. ■ this (nonlegal) element of the Talmud. Compare with **HALACHA**. — **Hag·gad·ic** /həˈgädik/ **adj.** **Hag·ga·dist** /həˈgädist/ **n.** [18th C.: from Heb. *Haggāḏāh* 'tale, parable,' from *higgîḏ* 'tell, expound.']

Hag·gai /ˈhagēˌī; ˈhagī/ a Hebrew minor prophet. ■ a book of the Bible.

hag·gard /ˈhagərd/ ▶ **adj.** **1** looking exhausted and unwell, esp. from fatigue, worry, or suffering. **2** (of a hawk) caught for training as a wild adult. Compare with **PASSAGE HAWK**. ▶ **n.** a haggard hawk. — **hag·gard·ly** **adv.** **hag·gard·ness** **n.** [16th C.: from Fr. *hagard*; perh. rel. to **HEDGE**.]

hag·gis /ˈhagis/ ▶ **n.** (pl. same) a Scottish dish of a sheep's or calf's offal, suet, oatmeal, and seasoning, boiled in a bag. [ME: prob. from earlier *hag* 'hack, hew,' from ON *hǫggva*.]

hag·gle /ˈhagəl/ ▶ **v.** [intrans.] dispute or bargain persistently, esp. over the cost of something. ▶ **n.** a period of such bargaining. — **hag·gler** /ˈhaglər/ **n.** [16th C. (in the sense 'hack, mangle'): from ON *hǫggva* 'hew.']

hagio- ▶ **comb. form** relating to saints or holiness: *hagiographer*. [from Gk. *hagios* 'holy.']

Hag·i·og·ra·pha /ˌhagēˈägrəfə; ˌhāgē-/ ▶ **plural n.** the books of the Bible comprising the last of the three major divisions of the Hebrew scriptures, other than the Law and the Prophets. Also called ***THE WRITINGS*** (see **WRITING**).

hag·i·og·ra·pher /ˌhagēˈägrəfər; ˌhāgē-/ ▶ **n.** a writer of the lives of the saints.

hag·i·og·ra·phy /ˌhagēˈägrəfē; ˌhāgē-/ ▶ **n.** the writing of the lives of saints. — **hag·i·o·graph·ic** /ˌhagēəˈgrafik; ˌhāgēə-/ **adj.** **hag·i·o·graph·i·cal** /ˌhagēəˈgrafəkəl; ˌhāgēə-/ **adj.**

hag·i·ol·a·try /ˌhagēˈälətrē; ˌhāgē-/ ▶ **n.** the worship of saints. ■ derog. undue veneration of a famous person.

hag·i·ol·o·gy /ˌhagēˈäləjē; ˌhāgē-/ ▶ **n.** literature dealing with saints. — **hag·i·o·log·i·cal** /ˌhagēəˈläjəkəl; ˌhāgēə-/ **adj.** **hag·i·ol·o·gist** **n.**

hag·rid·den /ˈhagˌridn/ ▶ **adj.** afflicted by nightmares or anxieties: *it once made parents and doctors hagridden.*

Hague /hāg/ (**The Hague**) the seat of government and administrative center of the Netherlands, on the North Sea coast; pop. 444,000. Dutch name **DEN HAAG**; also called **'S-GRAVENHAGE**.

hah ▶ **exclam.** var. of **HA**[1].

ha-ha /ˈhä ˌhä; ˌhä ˈhä/ ▶ **n.** a ditch with a wall on its inner side below ground level. [18th C.: from Fr., said to be from a cry of surprise.]

ha ha ▶ **exclam.** used to represent laughter. [natural utterance: OE.]

Hahn /hän/, Otto (1879–1968), German chemist. He codiscovered nuclear fission. Nobel Prize for Chemistry (1944, shared with Fritz Strassmann (1902–80)).

Hai·da /ˈhīdə/ ▶ **n.** (pl. same or **-das**) **1** a member of an American Indian people of coastal British Columbia and southeastern Alaska. **2** the language of this people, of unknown affinity. ▶ **adj.** of or relating to this people or their language. [19th C.: the name in Haida, lit. 'people.']

Hai·fa /ˈhīfə/ a city in northwestern Israel; pop. 248,000.

Haight-Ash·bury /ˈhāt ˈasHˌberē/ a section of San Francisco, California.

haik /hīk/ (also **haick**) ▶ **n.** a large outer wrap, typically white, worn by people from North Africa. [18th C.: from Arab. *ḥā'ik*.]

hai·ku /ˈhīˌko͞o; ˌhīˈko͞o/ ▶ **n.** (pl. same or **-kus**) a Japanese poem of seventeen syllables, in three lines of five, seven, and five. ■ an English imitation of this. [Japanese, contracted form of *haikai no ku* 'light verse.']

hail[1] /hāl/ ▶ **n.** pellets of frozen rain. ■ [in sing.] a large number of things hurled forcefully through the air: ***a hail of bullets.*** ▶ **v.** [intrans.] (**it hails, it is hailing**, etc.) hail falls. [OE *hagol*, *hægl* (n.), *hagalian* (v.), of Gmc. origin; rel. to Du. *hagel* and Ger. *Hagel*.]

hail[2] ▶ **v.** **1** [trans.] call out to (someone). ■ signal to stop: *hail a cab.* **2** [trans.] (often **be hailed**) acclaim enthusiastically as being a specified thing. **3** [intrans.] (**hail from**) have one's home or origins in. ▶ **exclam.** archaic expressing greeting or acclaim: *hail, Caesar!* ▶ **n.** a shout or call used to attract attention. — **hail·er** **n.** [ME: from the obs. adj. *hail* 'healthy,' from ON *heill*, rel. to **WHOLE**.]

Hai·le Se·las·sie /ˈhīlē səˈlasē/ (1892–1975), emperor of Ethiopia 1930–74; born *Tafari Makonnen*. In exile in Britain during the Italian occupation 1936–41, he was restored to the throne by the Allies.

hail-fel·low-well-met ▶ **adj.** showing excessive familiarity: *hail-fellow-well-met salesmen.*

Hail Mar·y ▶ **n.** (pl. **Hail Ma·rys**) **1** a prayer to the Virgin Mary. Also called **AVE MARIA**. ■ a recitation of such a devotional phrase or prayer. **2** [usu. as adj.] Football a desperation long pass late in the game. ■ any attempt with a small chance of success: *a Hail Mary plan.*

hail·stone /ˈhālˌstōn/ ▶ **n.** a pellet of hail.

hail·storm /ˈhālˌstôrm/ ▶ **n.** a storm of heavy hail.

Hai·nan /ˈhīˈnän/ an island province of China in the South China Sea; pop. 6,420,000; capital, Haikou.

Hai·phong /ˈhīˈfôNG; -ˈfäNG/ a city in northern Vietnam, on the Gulf of Tonkin; pop. 783,000.

hair /he(ə)r/ ▶ **n.** **1** any of the fine threadlike strands growing from the skin of mammals and other animals. ■ a similar strand growing from

the epidermis of a plant, or forming part of a living cell. ■ **(a hair)** a very small quantity or extent: *a hair above the competition.* **2** such strands collectively, esp. those growing on a person's head: [as adj.] *a hair salon.* ■ the styling or dressing of a person's hair.
– PHRASES **hair of the dog** informal an alcoholic drink taken to cure a hangover. **a hair's breadth** a very small amount or margin: *you escaped death by a hair's breadth.* **in** (or **out of**) **someone's hair** informal annoying (or ceasing to annoy) someone. **let one's hair down** informal behave in an uninhibited or relaxed manner. **not a hair out of place** (of a person) extremely neat and tidy. **put hair on one's chest** informal (of an alcoholic drink) be very strong. **split hairs** make small and overfine distinctions. — **haired** adj. [in comb.] *a curly-haired boy.* **hair·less** adj. [OE *hǣr*, of Gmc. origin; rel. to Du. *haar* and Ger. *Haar.*]

hair·breadth /'he(ə)r,bre(d)TH/ ▶ n. see A HAIR'S BREADTH at HAIR.

hair·brush /'he(ə)r,brəSH/ ▶ n. a brush for arranging or smoothing a person's hair.

hair·cloth /'he(ə)r,klôTH/ ▶ n. stiff cloth woven with a cotton or linen warp and horsehair weft.

hair·cut /'he(ə)r,kət/ ▶ n. the style in which a person's hair is cut. ■ an act of cutting a person's hair.

hair·do /'he(ə)r,do͞o/ ▶ n. (pl. **-dos**) informal the style of a person's hair. ■ an act of styling a person's hair (used esp. of a woman's hair).

hair·dress·er /'he(ə)r,dresər/ ▶ n. a person who cuts and styles hair as an occupation. — **hair·dress·ing** n.

hair·line /'he(ə)r,līn/ ▶ n. **1** the edge of a person's hair. **2** a very thin or fine line: [as adj.] *a hairline fracture.*

hair·net /'he(ə)r,net/ ▶ n. a piece of fine mesh fabric for confining the hair.

hair·piece /'he(ə)r,pēs/ ▶ n. a quantity or switch of detached hair used to augment a person's natural hair.

hair·pin /'he(ə)r,pin/ ▶ n. a U-shaped pin to fasten hair. ■ a sharp U-shaped curve in a road. ▶ adj. shaped like a hairpin: *a slippery hairpin path.*

hair-rais·ing ▶ adj. extremely alarming or frightening. — **hair-rais·er** n.

hair shirt ▶ n. a shirt of haircloth. ▶ adj. (**hair-shirt** or **hair-shirt·ed**) austere and self-sacrificing: *a hair-shirted existence.*

hair space ▶ n. Print. a very thin space between letters or words.

hair·split·ting /'he(ə)r,splitiNG/ ▶ adj. (also **hair-split·ting**) characterized by or fond of small and overfine distinctions. ▶ n. the action of making small distinctions; quibbling. — **hair·split·ter** n.

hair spray /'he(ə)r,sprā/ (also **hair·spray**) ▶ n. a solution to keep hair in place.

hair·spring /'he(ə)r,spriNG/ ▶ n. a slender flat coiled spring that regulates a watch's balance wheel.

hair·streak /'he(ə)r,strēk/ ▶ n. a butterfly (family Lycaenidae) with a narrow streak or row of dots on the underside of the hind wing and a small taillike projection on the hind wing.

hair·style /'he(ə)r,stīl/ ▶ n. the way hair is cut or arranged. — **hair·styl·ist** n. (also **hair stylist**)

hair trig·ger ▶ n. a trigger of a firearm set for release at the slightest pressure. ■ [as adj.] fig. liable to change suddenly and violently: *a hair-trigger temper.*

hair worm ▶ n. another term for HORSEHAIR WORM.

hair·y /'he(ə)rē/ ▶ adj. (**hair·i·er, hair·i·est**) **1** covered with hair, esp. thick or long hair: *a hairy chest.* ■ having a rough feel or appearance. **2** informal alarming and difficult: *a hairy road.* — **hair·i·ly** adv. **hair·i·ness** n.

Hai·ti /'hātē/ a country in the West Indies. *See box.*

Hai·tian /'hāSHən/ ▶ adj. of or relating to Haiti, its inhabitants, or their language. ▶ n. **1** a native or inhabitant of Haiti. **2** (also **Haitian Creole**) the French-based Creole language spoken in Haiti.

haj·i /'hajē/ (also **haj·ji** or **had·ji**) ▶ n. (pl. **haj·is**) a Muslim who has been to Mecca as a pilgrim. [from Pers. and Turk. *ḥājjī, ḥājī*, from Arab. *ḥajj* (see HAJJ).]

hajj /haj/ (also **haj** or **hadj**) ▶ n. the Muslim pilgrimage to Mecca that takes place in the last month of the year, expected once of all Muslims. [from Arab. *(al-) ḥajj* '(the Great) Pilgrimage.']

hake /hāk/ (pl. same or **hakes**) ▶ n. **1** a large-headed elongated food fish (genus *Merluccius*, family Merlucciidae) with long jaws and strong teeth. **2** any of a number of similar fishes related to the true hakes, esp. those of the northwestern Atlantic genus *Urophycis* (family Phycidae). [ME: perh. from OE *haca* 'hook.']

ha·kim /hə'kēm/ ▶ n. **1** a physician in India and Muslim countries. [from Arab. *ḥakīm* 'wise man, physician.'] **2** a judge or ruler in India and Muslim countries. [from Arab. *ḥākim* 'ruler.']

Hak·ka /'häkə/ ▶ n. **1** a member of a people of southeastern China, esp. Canton, Taiwan, and Hong Kong. **2** the dialect of Chinese spoken by this people. ▶ adj. of or relating to this people or their language. [from Chin. (Cantonese dial.) *haak ka* 'stranger.']

Ha·ko·da·te /,häkō'dätā/ a city on the southwestern coast of Hokkaido, Japan; pop. 307,000.

Ha·la·cha /,hälä'KHä; hä'lôKHə/ (also **Ha·la·kah**) ▶ n. Jewish law and jurisprudence, based on the Talmud. — **Ha·la·chic** /hə'läKHik; hə'lakik/ adj. [from Heb. *hălākāh* 'law.']

ha·lal /hə'läl; -'lal/ ▶ adj. denoting or relating to meat prepared as prescribed by Muslim law. ■ religiously acceptable according to Muslim law. ▶ n. halal meat. [19th C.: from Arab. *ḥalāl* 'according to religious law.']

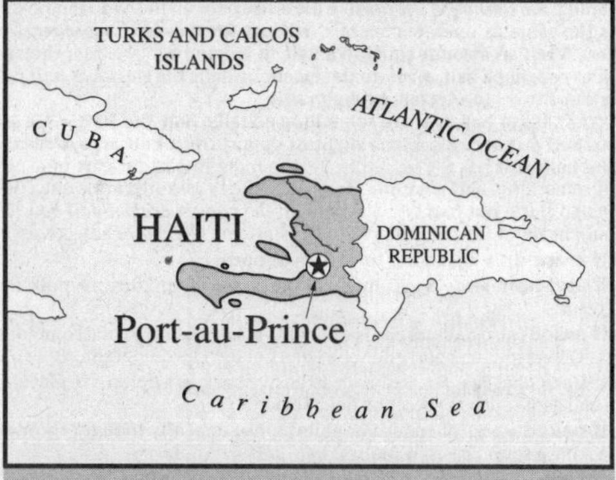

Haiti

Official name: Republic of Haiti
Location: West Indies, the western third of the island of Hispaniola, in the Caribbean Sea
Area: 10,700 square miles (27,600 sq km)
Population: 7,600,000
Capital: Port-au-Prince
Languages: French and Creole (both official)
Currency: gourde

ha·la·la /hə'lälə/ ▶ n. (pl. same or **-las**) a monetary unit of Saudi Arabia, equal to one hundredth of a riyal. [Arab.]

Hal·as /'haləs/, George Stanley (1895–1983), US football coach; known as **Papa Bear**. He founded the Chicago Bears in 1920.

ha·la·tion /hā'lāSHən/ ▶ n. the spreading of light beyond its boundaries to form a fog around a bright image in a photograph or on a television screen. [19th C.: formed irregularly from HALO + -ATION.]

hal·berd /'halbərd; 'hôl-/ (also **hal·bert** /-bərt/) ▶ n. hist. a combined spear and battle-ax. — **hal·berd·ier** /,halbər'di(ə)r; ,hôlbər-/ n. [15th C.: from Fr. *hallebarde*, from Ital. *alabarda*, from Mid. High Ger. *helmbarde* (from *helm* 'handle' + *barde* 'hatchet').]

halberd

hal·cy·on /'halsēən/ ▶ adj. denoting a period of time in the past that was idyllically happy and peaceful. ▶ n. **1** a tropical Asian and African kingfisher (genus *Halcyon*) with brightly colored plumage. **2** a mythical bird said by ancient writers to breed in a nest floating at sea at the winter solstice, charming the wind and waves into calm. [ME: via L. from Gk. *alkuōn* 'kingfisher.']

Hale¹ /hāl/, Edward Everett (1822–1909) US clergyman and writer. He wrote the story "The Man Without a Country" (1863).

Hale², George Ellery (1868–1938), US astronomer. He invented the spectroheliograph and initiated the construction of the 200-inch (5-meter) Hale reflector at Mount Palomar in California.

Hale³, Nathan (1755–76), American patriot, hanged by the British as a spy during the American Revolution.

hale¹ /hāl/ ▶ adj. (of a person) strong and healthy. [OE, var. of *hāl* 'whole.']

hale² ▶ v. [trans.] archaic drag or draw forcibly: *he haled an old man out of the audience.* [ME: from OFr. *haler*, from ON *hala.*]

Ha·le·a·ka·la /,hälā,äkə'lä/ a volcano on Maui in Hawaii.

Hale–Bopp /'hāl'bäp/ a periodic comet that passed close to the sun in the spring of 1997. [Alan *Hale* and Thomas *Bopp*, US astronomers.]

ha·ler /'hälər/ ▶ n. (pl. same or **-le·ru** /-lə,ro͞o/) a monetary unit of the Czech Republic and Slovakia, equal to one hundredth of a koruna. [from Czech *haléř*, from Mid. High Ger. *haller*, from *Schwäbisch Hall*, a town in Germany.]

Ha·ley /'hālē/, Alexander Murray Palmer (1921–92), US writer. His novel *Roots: The Saga of an American Family* (1976) chronicled the ancestors of his African-American family.

half /haf/ ▶ n. (pl. **halves** /havz/) either of two equal or corresponding parts into which something is or can be divided: *the northern half of the island.* ■ either of two equal periods of time into which a sports game or a performance is divided. ■ Baseball either of the two parts of one inning: *the top half of the third.* ■ Golf a score for an individual hole that is the same as one's opponent's. ■ short for HALFBACK. ▶ **predeterminer, pron. & adj.** an amount equal to a half. ■ amounting to a part thought of as roughly a half. ▶ **adv.** to the extent of half: *the glass was half full.* ■ [often in comb.] to a certain extent; partly.

– PHRASES **go halves** share something equally. **half the battle** see BATTLE. **half a chance** informal the slightest opportunity. **half an eye** see EYE. **the half of it** [usu. with negative] informal the most important part or aspect of something. **half past one (two,** etc.) thirty minutes after one (two, etc.) o'clock. **not half** informal not at all: *the players are not half bad.* [OE *half, healf,* of Gmc. origin; rel. to Du. *half* and Ger. *halb* (adjectives).]

half a doz·en ▶ **n.** another term for HALF-DOZEN.

half-and-half ▶ **adv. & adj.** in equal parts. ▶ **n.** a mixture of milk and cream.

half-assed (also **half-ass,** Brit. **half-arsed**) ▶ **adj.** vulgar slang (of a completed task) inadequate; poorly done. ■ (of a person) incompetent.

half·back /'haf,bak/ ▶ **n.** Football an offensive back. ■ a defensive player in a ball game such as soccer or field hockey.

half-baked ▶ **adj.** (of an idea or philosophy) not fully thought through; lacking a sound basis. ■ foolish: *half-baked visionaries.*

half·beak /'haf,bēk/ ▶ **n.** a slender shoaling fish (family Exocoetidae) of coastal areas, with small pectoral fins and the lower jaw lengthened into a beak. It is related to the flying fishes and often skitters along the surface.

half bind·ing ▶ **n.** a type of bookbinding in which the spine and corners are bound in one material (typically leather) and the rest of the cover in another. — **half-bound adj.**

half blood ▶ **n. 1** dated the relationship between people having one parent in common. ■ a person related to another in this way. **2** (**half-blood**) offens. another term for HALF-BREED. — **half-blood·ed adj.** (in sense 2).

half boot ▶ **n.** a boot that reaches up to the calf.

half-bot·tle ▶ **n.** a bottle that is half the standard size.

half-breed offens. ▶ **n.** a person whose parents are of different races. ▶ **adj.** denoting such a person.

half-broth·er (also **half broth·er**) ▶ **n.** a brother with whom one has only one parent in common.

half-caste offens. ▶ **n.** a person whose parents are of different races. ▶ **adj.** denoting such a person.

half cock ▶ **n.** the partly raised position of a gun cock.

half-cocked ▶ **adj.** (of a gun) with the cock partly raised. ▶ **adv.** fig. when only partly ready; prematurely.

half crown (also **half-crown** or **half a crown**) ▶ **n.** a former British coin equal to two shillings and sixpence.

half dol·lar (also **half-dol·lar**) ▶ **n.** a US or Canadian coin worth fifty cents. ■ the sum of fifty cents.

half-door ▶ **n.** a door of half the usual size, typically covering the bottom half of an opening (e.g., in a stable).

half-doz·en (also **half a dozen**) ▶ **n.** a group of six.

half-du·plex ▶ **adj.** (of a communications system or computer circuit) allowing the transmission of signals in both directions but not simultaneously.

half gain·er ▶ **n.** a dive in which the diver does a half-somersault backward, and enters the water head first facing the board.

half-heart·ed /'haf'härtid/ (also **half-heart·ed**) ▶ **adj.** without enthusiasm or energy. — **half·heart·ed·ly adv. half·heart·ed·ness n.**

half hitch ▶ **n.** a knot formed by passing the end of a rope around its standing part and then through the loop, often used in pairs. See illustration at KNOT[1].

half hour ▶ **n.** (also **half an hour**) thirty minutes. ■ a point in time thirty minutes after any full hour of the clock. — **half-hour·ly adj. & adv.**

half-in·te·ger ▶ **n.** a number obtained by dividing an odd integer by two (1/2, 1 1/2, 2 1/2, etc.). — **half-in·te·gral adj.**

half-length ▶ **adj.** of half the normal length. ■ (of a painting or sculpture) showing a person down to the waist. ▶ **n.** a painting or sculpture of a person down to the waist.

half-life ▶ **n.** the time taken for the radioactivity of a specified isotope to fall to half its original value. ■ the time required for any specified property to decrease by half.

half-light ▶ **n.** dim light such as at dusk.

half-mast ▶ **n.** the position of a flag that is being flown some way below the top of its staff as a mark of respect for a person who has died. ■ esp. humorous a position lower than normal or acceptable: *his zipper was always riding at half-mast.*

half meas·ure ▶ **n.** (usu. **half measures**) an action or policy that is not forceful or decisive enough.

half-moon ▶ **n.** the moon when only half of its illuminated surface is visible from the earth; the first or last quarter. ■ the time when this occurs. ■ a semicircular or crescent-shaped object.

half-move ▶ **n.** Chess a move made by one player (esp. in the context of the analysis of play made by a chess-playing computer program).

half nel·son ▶ **n.** see NELSON.

half note (Brit. **min·im**) ▶ **n.** Music a note having the time value of two quarter notes or half of a whole note, represented by a ring with a stem.

half pay ▶ **n.** half of a person's salary or wages.

half·pen·ny /'hāp(ə)nē; 'haf,penē/ (also **ha'pen·ny**) ▶ **n.** (pl. for separate coins **-pen·nies,** for a sum of money **-pence** /-pəns/) a former British coin, used until 1984, equal to half an old or new penny.

half pint (also **half-pint**) ▶ **n. 1** half of a pint. **2** informal a small or insignificant person or animal. ▶ **adj.** informal very small; diminutive.

half-pipe ▶ **n.** a channel with a U-shaped cross section, made of concrete or cut into the snow, used by skateboarders, snowboarders, etc. to perform jumps and other maneuvers.

half-price ▶ **adj. & adv.** costing half the normal price. ▶ **n.** half the usual price.

half-sis·ter (also **half sis·ter**) ▶ **n.** a sister with whom one has only one parent in common.

half sov·er·eign (also **half-sov·er·eign**) ▶ **n.** a former British gold coin worth ten shillings.

half step ▶ **n. 1** Music a semitone. **2** a military marching pace approximately half the speed of the quick march.

half-tim·bered ▶ **adj.** having walls with a timber frame and a brick or plaster filling. — **half-tim·ber·ing** /'timb(ə)riNG/ **n.**

half-time /'haf,tīm/ ▶ **n.** the time when half of a game or contest is completed, esp. with an intermission.

half ti·tle ▶ **n.** the title of a book, printed on the right-hand page before the title page. ■ the title of a section of a book printed on the right-hand page before the section begins.

half·tone /'haf,tōn/ ▶ **n.** [usu. as adj.] a reproduction of an image in which the various tones of gray or color are produced by dots of ink.

half-track ▶ **n.** a military or other vehicle with wheels at the front and caterpillar tracks at the rear.

half-truth ▶ **n.** a statement that conveys only part of the truth.

half-vol·ley ▶ **n.** (in ball games, esp. tennis) a stroke made just after the ball bounces off the ground.

half·way /'haf'wā/ ▶ **adv. & adj.** at or to a point equidistant between two others. ■ in the middle of a period of time. ■ [as adv.] to some extent.

– PHRASES **meet someone halfway** compromise; concede some points in order to gain others.

half·way house ▶ **n.** a center for helping former drug addicts, prisoners, or others to adjust to life in society. ■ the halfway point in a progression. ■ hist. an inn midway between two towns.

half·wit /'haf,wit/ ▶ **n.** informal, derog. a foolish or stupid person. — **half·wit·ted adj. half·wit·ted·ly adv. half·wit·ted·ness n.**

hal·i·but /'haləbət/ ▶ **n.** (pl. same) a northern marine food fish (genus *Hippoglossus,* family Pleuronectidae) that is the largest of the flatfishes. [ME: from *haly* 'holy' + obs. *butt* 'flatfish.']

Ha·liç /hä'lēCH/ Turkish name of GOLDEN HORN.

Hal·i·car·nas·sus /,halikär'nasəs/ an ancient Greek city on the Aegean coast of Asia Minor (now the Turkish city of Bodrum).

hal·ide /'halīd; 'hā-/ ▶ **n.** Chem. a binary compound of a halogen with another element or group.

Hal·i·fax /'halə,faks/ the capital of Nova Scotia, Canada, on the Atlantic coast; pop. 67,800.

hal·ite /'halīt; 'hālīt/ ▶ **n.** sodium chloride as a mineral, typically occurring as colorless cubic crystals; rock salt. [19th C.: from Gk. *hals* 'salt' + -ITE[1].]

hal·i·to·sis /,hali'tōsis/ ▶ **n.** technical term for BAD BREATH. [19th C.: from L. *halitus* 'breath' + -OSIS.]

Hall[1] /hôl/, Gus (1910–2000), US leader of the Communist Party; born *Arvo Custa Halberg.* He was the party's presidential candidate in four elections 1972–84.

Hall[2], Lyman (1724–90), American patriot and politician. He signed the Declaration of Independence in 1776.

hall /hôl/ ▶ **n. 1** an area in a building onto which rooms open; a corridor. ■ the room or space just inside the front entrance of a house or apartment. **2** a large room for meetings, concerts, or other events. ■ a large public room used for receptions and banquets. ■ a college or university building containing classrooms, residences, or rooms for other purposes. ■ the principal living room of a medieval house. **3** [usu. in names] Brit. a large country house, esp. one with a landed estate: *Darlington Hall.* [OE *hall, heall*; of Gmc. origin and rel. to Ger. *Halle.*]

Hal·le /'hälə/ a city in east central Germany; pop. 303,000.

Hal·lel /hä'lāl; 'hälāl/ ▶ **n.** (usu. **the Hallel**) a portion of the service for certain Jewish festivals, consisting of Psalms 113–118. [from Heb. *hallēl* 'praise.']

hal·le·lu·jah /,halə'lo͞oyə/ (also **al·le·lu·ia**) ▶ **exclam.** God be praised. ▶ **n.** an expression of worship or rejoicing. ■ (usu. **alleluia**) a piece of music containing this. [OE, via eccles. L. *alleluia* from Gk. *allēlouia,* or directly from Heb. *hallĕlūyāh* 'praise ye the Lord.']

Hal·ley's Com·et /'halēz; 'hā-/ a periodical comet with an orbital period of about 76 years, its reappearance in 1758–59 having been predicted by the English astronomer Edmond Halley (1656–1742).

hall·mark /'hôl,märk/ ▶ **n.** a mark stamped on articles of precious metals in Britain, certifying their purity. ■ a distinctive feature, esp. one of excellence. ▶ **v.** [trans.] stamp with a hallmark. ■ designate as distinctive, esp. for excellence. [18th C. (as a n.): from *Goldsmiths' Hall* in London, England.]

hal·lo /hə'lō/ ▶ **exclam., n. & v.** var. of HELLO. ■ variant of HALLOO.

hal·loa /hə'lō; ha-/ ▶ **exclam, n. & v.** variant of HALLOO.

Hall of Fame a national memorial in New York City honoring the achievements of famous Americans. ■ [as n.] a similar establishment commemorating the achievements of a particular group of people. — **Hall of Fam·er** n.

hal·loo /hə'lo͞o/ ▶ exclam. used to attract attention. ■ used to incite dogs to the chase during a hunt. ▶ n. a cry of "halloo." ▶ v. (**-loos, -looed**) [intrans.] shout "halloo" to attract attention or to give encouragement to hunting dogs. ■ [trans.] shout to (someone) to attract their attention. [16th C.: prob. from the rare v. *hallow* 'pursue or urge on with shouts,' from imitative OFr. *haloer*.]

hal·low /'halō/ ▶ v. [trans.] honor as holy. ■ formal make holy; consecrate. ■ [as adj.] (**hallowed**) greatly revered or respected. [OE *hālgian* (v.), *hālga* (n.), of Gmc. origin; rel. to Du. and Ger. *heiligen*, also to HOLY.]

Hal·low·een /ˌhalə'wēn; -ō'ēn; ˌhälə-/ (also **Hal·low·e'en**) ▶ n. the night of October 31, celebrated by children who dress in costume and solicit treats door-to-door. [18th C.: contr. of *All Hallow Even* (see HALLOW, EVEN[2]).]

Hall·statt /'hälˌshtät/ ▶ n. [usu. as adj.] Archaeol. a cultural phase of the late Bronze Age and early Iron Age in Europe (*c.*1200–600 BC). [19th C.: a village in Austria.]

hal·lu·ces /'hal(y)əˌsēz/ plural form of HALLUX.

hal·lu·ci·nate /hə'lo͞osəˌnāt/ ▶ v. [intrans.] experience a seemingly real perception of something not actually present, typically as a result of a mental disorder or of taking drugs. ■ [trans.] experience a hallucination of (something). — **hal·lu·ci·nant** /-sənənt/ adj. & n. **hal·lu·ci·na·tor** /-ˌnātər/ n. [17th C.: from L. *hallucinat-* 'gone astray in thought,' from the v. *hallucinari*, from Gk. *alussein* 'be uneasy.']

hal·lu·ci·na·tion /həˌlo͞osə'nāshən/ ▶ n. an experience involving the perception of something not present.

hal·lu·ci·na·to·ry /hə'lo͞osənəˌtôrē/ ▶ adj. of or resembling a hallucination. ■ inducing hallucinations.

hal·lu·ci·no·gen /hə'lo͞osənəjən/ ▶ n. a drug such as LSD that causes hallucinations. — **hal·lu·ci·no·gen·ic** /həˌlo͞osənə'jenik/ adj.

hal·lux /'haləks/ ▶ n. (pl. **hal·lu·ces** /'hal(y)əˌsēz/) Anat. a person's big toe. ■ Zool. the innermost digit of the hind foot of vertebrates. [19th C.: mod. L. alt. of med. L. *allex*, L. *hallus*.]

hall·way /'hôlˌwā/ ▶ n. another term for HALL (sense 1).

ha·lo /'hālō/ ▶ n. (pl. **-loes** or **-los**) a circle of light surrounding the head of a saint or holy person. ■ fig. the glory associated with an idealized person or thing. ■ a circle or ring of something resembling a halo. ■ a circle of white or colored light around the sun, moon, or other luminous body caused by refraction through ice crystals in the atmosphere. ■ Astron. a tenuous sphere of hot gas and old stars surrounding a spiral galaxy. ▶ v. (**-loes, -loed**) [trans.] (usu. **be haloed**) surround with or as if with a halo. [16th C.: from med. L., from L. *halos*, from Gk. *halōs* 'disk of the sun or moon.']

halo- ▶ comb. form **1** relating to salinity: *halophile*. [from Gk. *hals, halo-* 'salt.'] **2** representing HALOGEN.

hal·o·car·bon /'haləˌkärbən/ ▶ n. Chem. a chlorofluorocarbon or other compound in which the hydrogen of a hydrocarbon is replaced by halogens.

ha·lo ef·fect ▶ n. the tendency for an impression created in one area to influence opinion in another area: *the convertible furnishes a sporty image and provides a halo effect for other cars in the showrooms.*

hal·o·gen /'haləjən/ ▶ n. Chem. any of the elements fluorine, chlorine, bromine, iodine, and astatine, occupying group VIIA (17) of the periodic table. ■ [as adj.] denoting lamps and radiant heat sources using a filament surrounded by the vapor of iodine or another halogen. — **hal·o·gen·ic** /ˌhalə'jenik/ adj. [19th C.: from Gk. *hals, halo-* 'salt' + -GEN.]

hal·o·gen·ate /'haləjəˌnāt; ha'läjə-/ ▶ v. [trans.] [usu. as adj.] (**halogenated**) Chem. introduce one or more halogen atoms into (a compound or molecule). — **hal·o·gen·a·tion** /ˌhaləjə'nāshən; həˌläjə-/ n.

hal·o·per·i·dol /ˌhalō'perəˌdôl; -däl/ ▶ n. Med. a synthetic antidepressant drug. [1960s: blend of HALOGEN and PIPERIDINE + -OL.]

hal·o·phile /'haləˌfīl/ ▶ n. Ecol. an organism, esp. a microorganism, that grows in saline conditions. — **hal·o·phil·ic** /ˌhalə'filik/ adj.

hal·o·phyte /'haləˌfīt/ ▶ n. Bot. a plant adapted to growing in saline conditions, as in a salt marsh.

hal·o·thane /'haləˌthān/ ▶ n. Med. a volatile synthetic organic compound, $CF_3CHBrCl$, used as a general anesthetic. [1950s: blend of HALOGEN and ETHANE.]

Hals /hälz/, Frans (*c.*1580–1666), Dutch painter. His works include *The Laughing Cavalier* (1624).

Hal·sey /'hôlzē/, William Frederick (1882–1959), US admiral; known as **Bull**. He was commander of Allied naval forces in the South Pacific 1942–44 and of the US Third Fleet 1944–45.

halt[1] /hôlt/ ▶ v. bring or come to an abrupt stop. ■ [in imper.] used as a military command to bring marching soldiers to a stop: *company, halt!* ▶ n. a suspension of movement or activity, typically a temporary one.
– PHRASES **call a halt** demand or order a stop. [16th C.: orig. in the phr. *make halt*, from Ger. *haltmachen*, from *halten* 'to hold.']

halt[2] archaic ▶ adj. lame. ▶ v. [intrans.] walk with a limp: *he halted slightly in his walk.* ■ hesitate; waver. [OE *healtian* (v.), *halt, healt* (adj.), of Gmc. origin.]

hal·ter[1] /'hôltər/ ▶ n. **1** a rope or strap with a noose or headstall placed around the head of a horse or other animal, used for leading or tethering it. ■ archaic a rope with a noose for hanging a person. **2** [usu. as adj.] a strap by which the bodice of a sleeveless dress or top is fastened or held behind at the neck, leaving the shoulders and back bare. ■ a top with such a neck. ▶ v. [trans.] put a halter on (an animal). [OE *hælftre*, of Gmc. origin, meaning 'something to hold things by'; rel. to Ger. *Halfter*, also to HELVE.]

hal·ter[2] /'halˌti(ə)r/ (also **hal·tere**) ▶ n. (usu. **halteres**) Entomol. the balancing organ of a two-winged fly. [16th C.: from Gk. *haltēres* (pl.), from *hallesthai* 'to leap.']

halt·ing /'hôltiNG/ ▶ adj. slow and hesitant, esp. through lack of confidence; faltering. — **halt·ing·ly** adv.

hal·vah /'hälvä/ (also **hal·va**) ▶ n. a Middle Eastern confection made of sesame flour and honey. [Yiddish, or from Turk. *helva*, from Arab. and Pers. *ḥalwā* 'sweetmeat.']

halve /hav/ ▶ v. [trans.] **1** divide into two parts of equal or roughly equal size: *peel and halve the pears.* ■ reduce or be reduced by half. ■ share (something) equally with another person. ■ Golf use the same number of strokes as one's opponent and thus tie (a hole or match). **2** [usu. as n.] (**halving**) fit (crossing timbers) together by cutting out half the thickness of each. [ME: from HALF.]

halves /havz/ plural form of HALF.

hal·yard /'halyərd/ ▶ n. a rope used for raising and lowering a sail, spar, flag, or yard on a sailing ship. [ME *halier*, from HALE[2] + -IER.]

Ham /ham/ (in the Bible) a son of Noah (Gen. 10:1).

ham[1] /ham/ ▶ n. **1** meat from the upper part of a pig's leg salted and dried or smoked. **2** (**hams**) the backs of the thighs or the thighs and buttocks. [OE *ham, hom* (orig. denoting the back of the knee), from a Gmc. base meaning 'be crooked.']

ham[2] ▶ n. **1** an excessively theatrical actor. ■ excessively theatrical acting. **2** informal an amateur radio operator. ▶ v. (**hammed, ham·ming**) [intrans.] informal overact: *he was **hamming it up**.* [19th C.: perh. from the first syllable of AMATEUR.]

Ha·ma /'hämə/ (also **Ha·mah**) a city in western Syria, on the Orontes River; pop. 229,000.

Ha·ma·da /hə'mädə/, Shoji (1894–1978), Japanese potter. He worked mainly in stoneware.

Ha·ma·dan /ˌhämä'dän; 'haməˌdan/ a city in western Iran, in the Zagros Mountains; pop. 350,000.

ham·a·dry·ad /ˌhamə'drīəd/ ▶ n. **1** (also **Ham·a·dry·ad**) Greek & Rom. Mythol. a nymph who lives in a tree and dies when the tree dies. **2** another term for KING COBRA. [via L. from Gk. *Hamadruas*, from *hama* 'together' + *drus* 'tree.']

ham·a·dry·as ba·boon /ˌhamə'drīəs/ ▶ n. a large Arabian and northeastern African baboon (*Papio hamadryas*), the male of which has a silvery-gray cape of hair and a naked red face and rump. It was held sacred in ancient Egypt. Also called SACRED BABOON. [1930s: mod. L. (see HAMADRYAD).]

ham·a·mel·is /ˌhamə'mēlis/ ▶ n. technical name for witch hazel. [18th C.: mod. L. (genus name), from Gk. *hamamēlis* 'medlar.']

ha·mar·ti·a /ˌhämär'tēə/ ▶ n. a fatal flaw. [18th C.: Gk., 'fault, failure, guilt.']

Ha·mas /hä'mäs/ a Palestinian Islamic fundamentalist movement that has become a focus for Arab resistance in the Israeli-occupied territories. In 2006 Hamas was victorious in the elections for the Palestinian National Authority.

ha·mate /'hāmāt/ (also **hamate bone**) ▶ n. Anat. a carpal bone on the lower outside edge of the hand. [18th C.: from L. *hamatus* 'hooked,' from *hamus* 'hook.']

ham·bone /'hamˌbōn/ ▶ n. informal an inferior actor.

Ham·burg /'hamˌbərg; 'hämˌbo͝ork/ a port in northern Germany, on the Elbe River; pop. 1,669,000.

ham·burg /'hambərg/ ▶ n. (also **Hamburg steak**) another term for HAMBURGER.

ham·burg·er /'hamˌbərgər/ ▶ n. a round patty of ground beef, fried or grilled. ■ ground beef. [19th C. (orig. US): from Ger., from HAMBURG.]

hames /hāmz/ ▶ plural n. two curved pieces of iron or wood forming or attached to the collar of a draft horse, to which the traces are attached. See illustration at HARNESS. [ME: from MDu.]

ham·fat·ter /'hamˌfatər/ (also **ham·fat**) ▶ n. informal an inexpert or amateurish performer, esp. a mediocre jazz musician. [19th C.: perh. an alt. of AMATEUR.]

ham-hand·ed ▶ adj. informal clumsy; bungling. Also called **ham-fisted**. — **ham-hand·ed·ly** adv. **ham-hand·ed·ness** n.

Ham·hung /'hämˌho͝ong/ a city in eastern North Korea; pop. 775,000.

Ha·mil·car /hə'milkär/ (*c.*270–229 BC), Carthaginian general; father of Hannibal.

Ham·il·ton[1] /'hamәltәn; -әltn/ **1** the capital of Bermuda; pop. 1,100. **2** a city in southern Ontario, Canada, on Lake Ontario; pop. 318,499. **3** a city on North Island in New Zealand; pop. 149,000. **4** a town in southern Scotland; pop. 50,000.

Ham·il·ton[2], Alexander (*c.*1757–1804), US politician. He established the US central banking system as secretary of the treasury 1789–95. He was killed in a duel with Aaron Burr.

Ham·il·ton[3], Sir William Rowan (1806–65), Irish mathematician and theoretical physicist. Hamilton made influential contributions to optics and to the foundations of algebra and quantum mechanics.

Ham·il·to·ni·an /ˌhaməlˈtōnēən/ ▶**adj.** of or relating to the American statesman Alexander Hamilton or his doctrines. ▶**n.** a follower or adherent of Alexander Hamilton or his doctrines. —**Ham·il·to·ni·an·ism n.**

Ham·ite /ˈhamīt/ ▶**n.** a member of a group of North African peoples, including the ancient Egyptians and Berbers, supposedly descended from Ham.

Ham·it·ic /həˈmitik/ ▶**adj.** hist. of or denoting a hypothetical language family formerly proposed to comprise Berber, ancient Egyptian, the Cushitic languages, and the Chadic languages. [from *Ham* (a son of Noah).]

Ham·i·to-Se·mit·ic /ˈhamiˌtō səˈmitik/ ▶**adj.** former term for AFRO-ASIATIC.

Ham·let /ˈhamlit/ a legendary prince of Denmark, hero of a tragedy by Shakespeare.

ham·let /ˈhamlit/ ▶**n.** a small settlement, generally one smaller than a village. [ME: from OFr. *hamelet*, dimin. of *hamel* 'little village'; rel. to HOME (*hām* in OE).]

Ham·mar·skjöld /ˈhamərˌSHōld; -ˌSHəld; ˈhä-/, Dag Hjalmar Agne Carl (1905–61), Swedish diplomat. He served as secretary-general of the UN 1953–61. Nobel Peace Prize (1961).

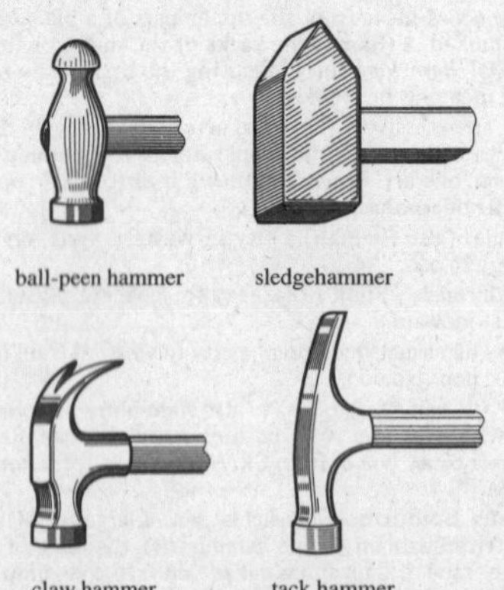

hammer 1

ham·mer /ˈhamər/ ▶**n.** **1** a tool with a heavy metal head mounted at right angles at the end of a handle. ■ a machine with a metal block for giving a heavy blow to something. ■ an auctioneer's mallet. ■ a part of a mechanism that hits another part to make it work. **2** a metal ball, typically weighing 16 pounds (7.3 kg), attached to a wire for throwing in an athletic contest. ■ (**the hammer**) the sport of throwing such a ball. **3** another term for MALLEUS. ▶**v.** [trans.] **1** hit or beat (something) with a hammer or similar object. ■ [intrans.] strike or knock at or on something violently with one's hand or with a hammer or other object. ■ [intrans.] (**hammer away**) work hard and persistently. ■ [trans.] drive or secure (something) by striking with or as if with a hammer. ■ (**hammer something in/into**) instill (an attitude, idea, or habit) forcefully or repeatedly. **2** informal attack or criticize forcefully and relentlessly. ■ utterly defeat in a game or contest.
– PHRASES **come** (or **go**) **under the hammer** be sold at an auction. **hammer something home** see HOME.
– PHRASAL VERBS **hammer something out** **1** make something by shaping metal with a hammer. **2** laboriously work out details. **3** play a tune loudly or clumsily, esp. on the piano. —**ham·mer·er n. ham·mer·ing n.** [OE *hamor, hamer*, of Gmc. origin: rel. to ON *hamarr* 'rock.']

ham·mer and sick·le ▶**n.** the symbols of the industrial worker and the peasant used as the emblem of the former Soviet Union and of international communism.

hammer and sickle

Ham·mer·fest /ˈhämərˌfest/ a port in northern Norway, on North Kvaløy island; pop. 7,000; the most northern town in Europe.

ham·mer·head /ˈhamərˌhed/ ▶**n.** **1** (also **hammerhead shark**) a shark (genus *Sphyrna*, family Sphyrnidae) of tropical and temperate oceans that has flattened bladelike extensions on either side of the head, with the eyes and nostrils placed at or near the ends. **2** a brown African marsh bird (*Scopus umbretta*, family Scopidae) related to the storks, having a crest that looks like a backward projection of the head, and constructing an enormous nest. **3** the striking head of a hammer.

ham·mer·lock /ˈhamərˌläk/ ▶**n.** an armlock in which a person's arm is bent up behind the back.

ham·mer price ▶**n.** the price realized by an item sold at auction.

Ham·mer·stein /ˈhamərˌstīn/, Oscar II (1895–1960), US librettist. He wrote *Showboat* (1927) with Jerome Kern and *Oklahoma!* (1943) with Richard Rogers.

ham·mer·toe /ˈhamərˌtō/ ▶**n.** a toe that is bent downward, typically as a result of pressure from footwear.

Ham·mett /ˈhamət/, Dashiell (1894–1961), US writer; full name *Samuel Dashiell Hammett*. His novels include *The Maltese Falcon* (1930) and *The Thin Man* (1932).

ham·mock /ˈhamək/ ▶**n.** a bed made of canvas or of rope mesh and suspended by cords at the ends. [16th C.: via Sp. from Taino *hamaka*.]

Ham·mu·ra·bi /ˌhaməˈräbē; ˌhä-/ (died 1750 BC), the sixth king of the first dynasty of Babylonia, reigned 1792–50 BC. He instituted one of the earliest known collections of laws.

ham·my /ˈhamē/ ▶**adj.** (**-mi·er, -mi·est**) **1** informal (of acting or an actor) overtheatrical. **2** (of a hand or thigh) thick and solid. —**ham·mi·ly adv. ham·mi·ness n.**

ham·per[1] /ˈhampər/ ▶**n.** a lidded basket for laundry. ■ a basket with a carrying handle and a hinged lid, used for food, cutlery, and plates on a picnic. [ME: from Anglo-Norman Fr. *hanaper* 'case for a goblet,' from OFr. *hanap* 'goblet,' of Gmc. origin.]

ham·per[2] ▶**v.** [trans.] (often **be hampered**) hinder or impede the movement or progress of. ▶**n.** Naut. necessary but cumbersome equipment on a ship. [ME: perh. rel. to Ger. *hemmen* 'restrain.']

Hamp·shire /ˈham(p)SHər/ a county on the coast of southern England; county town, Winchester.

Hamp·ton[1] /ˈham(p)tən/ a city in southeastern Virginia, on Chesapeake Bay; pop. 146,437.

Hamp·ton[2], Lionel Leo (1909–2002), US jazz vibraphonist, drummer, pianist, singer, and bandleader.

Hamp·ton Roads a deep-water estuary in southeastern Virginia.

ham·ster /ˈhamstər/ ▶**n.** a solitary burrowing rodent (subfamily Cricetinae, family Muridae) with a short tail and large cheek pouches for carrying food, native to Europe and northern Asia; several species, including the **golden hamster** (*Mesocricetus auratus*), often kept as a pet. [17th C.: from German, from Old High Ger. *hamustro* 'weevil.']

ham·string /ˈhamˌstriNG/ ▶**n.** any of five tendons at the back of a person's knee. ■ the great tendon at the back of a quadruped's hock. ▶**v.** (past and past part. **-strung**) [trans.] cripple (a person or animal) by cutting their hamstrings. ■ (usu. **be hamstrung**) severely restrict the efficiency or effectiveness of.

Ham·sun /ˈhämsən/, Knut (1859–1952), Norwegian writer; pen name of *Knut Pedersen*. He wrote *Hunger* (1890). Nobel Prize for Literature (1920).

ham·u·lus /ˈhamyələs/ ▶**n.** (pl. **-li** /-ˌlī; -ˌlē/) Anat. Zool. a small hook or hooklike projection, esp. one linking the fore- and hind wings of a bee or wasp. [18th C.: from L., dimin. of *hamus* 'hook.']

ham·za /ˈhamzə/ ▶**n.** (in Arabic script) a symbol representing a glottal stop. ■ such a sound. [19th C.: Arab., lit. 'compression.']

Han /han/ **1** the Chinese dynasty that ruled from 206 BC until AD 220 with only a brief interruption. **2** the dominant ethnic group in China.

Han·cock[1] /ˈhanˌkäk/, John (1737–93), American revolutionary and politician. He was the first to sign the Declaration of Independence in 1776.

Han·cock[2], Winfield Scott (1824–86), Union general in the American Civil War. He defended Cemetery Ridge at the Battle of Gettysburg 1863.

Hand /hand/, Learned (1872–1961), US jurist; full name *Billings Learned Hand*. He wrote over 2,000 opinions as a judge of the US Court of Appeals 1924–51.

hand /hand/ ▶**n.** **1** the end part of a person's arm beyond the wrist, including the palm, fingers, and thumb. ■ a similar prehensile organ forming the end part of a limb of various mammals, such as that on all four limbs of a monkey. ■ [as adj.] operated by or held in the hand. ■ [as adj. or in comb.] done or made manually: *hand signals.* ■ [in sing.] informal a round of applause. ■ dated a pledge of marriage by a woman: *request her hand in marriage.* **2** something resembling a hand in form or position, in particular: ■ a pointer on a clock or watch indicating the passing of units of time. ■ a bunch of bananas. **3** (**hands**) used in reference to the power to direct something: *the running of the house was in her hands.* ■ (usu. **a hand**) an active role in influencing something. ■ (usu. **a hand**) help in doing something. ■ (usu. **hands**) (in sports) skill and dexterity. ■ a person's handwriting: *he inscribed the statement in a bold hand.* ■ [with adj.] a person who does something to a specified standard: *I'm a great* ***hand at*** *inventing.* **4** a person who engages in manual labor, esp. in a factory, on a farm, or on board a ship. **5** the set of cards dealt to a player in a card game. ■ a round or short spell of play in a card game: *a* ***hand*** *of bridge.* **6** a unit of measurement of a horse's height, equal to 4 inches (10.16 cm). ▶**v.** **1** [with two objs.] pick (something) up and give to (someone): *he handed each man a glass.* ■ informal make (abusive, untrue, or otherwise objectionable) remarks to (someone): *all the yarns she'd been handing me.* ■ informal make (something) easily obtainable for (someone): *it was a win handed to him.* **2** [trans.] hold the hand of (someone) in order to help them move in the specified direction: *he handed him into a carriage.*
– PHRASES **at hand** nearby. ■ readily accessible when needed. ■ close in time; about to happen. **at** (or **by**) **the hands** (or **hand**) **of** through the agency of: *at the hands of a neurologist.* **bind** (or **tie**) **someone hand and foot** tie someone's hands and feet together. **by hand** by a person and not a machine. **give** (or **lend**) **a hand** assist in an action or enterprise. **hand in glove** in close collusion or association: *working* ***hand in glove*** *with our enemies.* **hand in hand** (of two people) with hands joined. ■ fig. closely associated. (**from**) **hand to mouth** satisfying only one's immediate needs because of lack of money for future plans and invest-

ments: *they were flat broke and living hand to mouth.* **hands down** easily and decisively; without question: *winning hands down.* **hands off** used as a warning not to touch or interfere with something. ■ [as adj.] (**hands-off**) not involving or requiring direct control or intervention: *a hands-off management style.* **hands-on** involving or offering active participation rather than theory: *hands-on practice.* ■ Comput. involving or requiring personal operation at a keyboard. **hands up!** used as an instruction to raise one's hands in surrender or to signify assent or participation. **have one's hands full** have as much work as one can do. **have one's hands tied** informal be unable to act freely. **have to hand it to someone** informal used to acknowledge the merit or achievement of someone. **in hand 1** receiving or requiring immediate attention: *he threw himself into the work in hand.* ■ in progress: *negotiations are now well in hand.* **2** ready for use if required; in reserve: *he had $1,000 in hand.* **3** under one's control: *the police had the situation well in hand.* **in safe hands** protected by someone trustworthy from harm or damage. **keep one's hand in** become (or remain) practiced in something. **make** (or **lose** or **spend**) **money hand over fist** informal make (or lose or spend) money very rapidly. **off someone's hands** not having to be dealt with or looked after by the person specified. **on hand** present, esp. for a specified purpose. ■ readily available. ■ needing to be dealt with. **on someone's hands** used to indicate that someone is responsible for dealing with someone or something. ■ used to indicate that someone is to blame for something: *he has my son's blood on his hands.* ■ at someone's disposal: *I've had more time on my hands.* **on the one** (or **the other**) **hand** used to present factors that are opposed or that support opposing opinions. **out of hand 1** not under control. **2** without taking time to think: *they rejected negotiations out of hand.* **the right hand doesn't know what the left hand is doing** used to convey that there is a state of confusion within a group or organization. **set** (or **put**) **one's hand to** start work on. **turn one's hand to** undertake (an activity different from one's usual occupation). **wait on someone hand and foot** attend to all needs or requests. **with one hand (tied) behind one's back** with serious limitations or restrictions. ■ used to indicate that one could do something without any difficulty: *I could do her job with one hand tied behind my back.*

– PHRASAL VERBS **hand something down 1** pass something on to a younger person or a successor. **2** announce something, esp. a judgment or sentence, formally or publicly. **hand over** pass responsibility to someone else: *he will soon **hand over** to a new director.* [OE *hand, hond,* of Gmc. origin; rel. to Du. *hand* and Ger. *Hand.*]

Han·dan /'hän'dän/ a city in eastern China; pop. 1,110,000.

hand·bag /'han(d),bag/ ▶ **n.** a woman's purse.

hand·ball /'han(d),bôl/ ▶ **n. 1** a game similar to squash in which a ball is hit with the hand in a walled court. ■ (also **team handball**) a team game similar to soccer in which the ball is thrown or hit with the hands rather than kicked. ■ the ball used in these games. **2** (**hand ball**) Soccer touching of the ball with the hand or arm, constituting a foul.

hand·bar·row /'han(d),barō/ ▶ **n.** a rectangular frame with poles at each end for being carried by two people.

hand·bell /'han(d),bel/ ▶ **n.** a small bell with a handle.

hand·bill /'han(d),bil/ ▶ **n.** a small printed advertisement or other notice distributed by hand.

hand·blown /'han(d),blōn/ ▶ **adj.** (of glassware) made by a glassblower with a hand-held blowpipe.

hand·book /'han(d),bo͝ok/ ▶ **n.** a book giving information such as facts on a particular subject.

hand·car /'han(d),kär/ ▶ **n.** a light railroad vehicle propelled by pushing cranks or levers and used by workers for inspecting the track.

hand·cart /'han(d),kärt/ ▶ **n.** a small cart pushed or drawn by hand.

hand·clap /'han(d),klap/ ▶ **n.** a clap of the hands: *the switch is sensitive enough to be activated by a handclap.*

hand·craft /'han(d),kraft/ ▶ **v.** [trans.] [usu. as adj.] (**handcrafted**) make skillfully by hand. ▶ **n.** another term for HANDICRAFT.

hand·cuff /'han(d),kəf/ ▶ **n.** (**handcuffs**) a pair of lockable linked rings for securing a prisoner's wrists. ▶ **v.** [trans.] put handcuffs on (someone). ■ fig. restrain; hamper.

-handed ▶ **comb. form 1** for or involving a specified number of hands: *a two-handed backhand.* **2** chiefly using or designed for use by the hand specified: *a right-handed batter | a left-handed guitar.* **3** relating to capability, means, or result, esp. of failure: *empty-handed | heavy-handed.* — **-handedly adv. -handedness n.**

Han·del /'handl/, George Frederick (1685–1759), German composer; born *Georg Friedrich Händel.* He is best known for his oratorio *Messiah* (1742).

hand·ful /'han(d),fo͝ol/ ▶ **n.** (pl. **-fuls**) **1** a quantity that fills the hand. ■ a small number or amount: *one of **a handful of** attorneys.* **2** informal a person who is very difficult to deal with.

hand gre·nade ▶ **n.** a hand-thrown grenade.

hand·grip /'han(d),grip/ ▶ **n. 1** a handle for holding onto something. **2** a grasp with the hand, as in a handshake.

hand·gun /'han(d),gən/ ▶ **n.** a gun designed for use by one hand, chiefly either a pistol or a revolver.

hand-held (also **hand·held**) ▶ **adj.** designed to be held in the hand: *a hand-held computer.*

hand·hold /'han(d),hōld/ ▶ **n.** something for a hand to grip: *the rock is steep and there are few handholds.* ■ a secure grip with a hand or the hands.

hand·hold·ing /'han(d),hōldiNG/ ▶ **n.** the provision of careful attention, support, or reassurance to another. ■ the giving of step-by-step instructions.

hand·i·cap /'handē,kap/ ▶ **n.** a condition that markedly restricts a person's ability to function physically, mentally, or socially. ■ a circumstance that makes progress or success difficult. ■ a disadvantage imposed on a superior competitor in sports such as golf, horse racing, and sailing in order to make the chances more equal. ■ a race or contest in which such a disadvantage is imposed. ■ the extra weight to be carried in a race by a racehorse on the basis of its previous performance to make its chances of winning the same as those of the other horses. ■ the number of strokes by which a golfer normally exceeds par for a course (used so that players of unequal ability can compete with each other). ▶ **v.** (**-capped, -cap·ping**) [trans.] act as an impediment to. ■ place (someone) at a disadvantage. [17th C.: *hand in cap,* a pastime in which three players deposited forfeit money in a cap.]

hand·i·capped /'handē,kapt/ ▶ **adj.** having a condition that markedly restricts one's ability to function physically, mentally, or socially: [as pl. n.] (**the handicapped**) *a home for the handicapped.*

– USAGE **Handicapped** in the sense referring to a person's mental or physical disabilities is first recorded in the early 20th century. For a brief period in the second half of the 20th century, it looked as if **handicapped** would be replaced by **disabled**, but both words are now acceptable and interchangeable in standard American English, and neither word has been overtaken by newer coinages such as *differently abled* or *physically challenged.* See also usage at LEARNING DISABILITY.

hand·i·cap·per /'handē,kapər/ ▶ **n.** a person appointed to assign or assess a competitor's handicap, esp. in golf or horse racing. ■ [usu. in comb.] a person or horse having a specified handicap.

hand·i·craft /'handē,kraft/ ▶ **n.** (often **handicrafts**) a particular skill of making decorative objects by hand. ■ an object made using a skill of this kind. [ME: alt. of HANDCRAFT, on the pattern of *handiwork.*]

hand·i·work /'handē,wərk/ ▶ **n. 1** (**one's handiwork**) something that one has made or done. **2** making things by hand, considered as a subject of instruction. [OE *handgeweorc,* from HAND + *geweorc* 'something made'.]

hand·ker·chief /'haNGkər,CHif; -,CHēf/ ▶ **n.** a square of material, intended for wiping one's nose.

han·dle /'handl/ ▶ **v.** [trans.] **1** feel or manipulate with the hands. ■ drive or control (a vehicle). ■ [intrans.] (of a vehicle) respond in a specified manner when being driven or controlled. **2** manage (a situation or problem). ■ informal deal with (someone or something). ■ have the resources to cope with. ■ control or manage commercially. ■ [with adverbial] (**handle oneself**) conduct oneself in a specified manner. **3** process: *the airport handled 250,000 passengers.* ▶ **n. 1** the part by which a thing is held or carried. ■ (**a handle on**) fig. a means of understanding, controlling, or approaching a person or situation: *it'll give people some kind of handle on these issues.* **2** informal the name of a person or place. — **han·dle·a·bil·i·ty** /,handl-ə'bilitē/ **n. han·dle·a·ble adj. han·dled adj.** [in comb.] *a rope-handled canvas bag.* [OE *handle* (n.), *handlian* (v.), from HAND.]

han·dle·bar /'handl,bär/ ▶ **n.** (usu. **handlebars**) the steering bar of a vehicle, with a handgrip at each end.

han·dle·bar mus·tache ▶ **n.** a wide, thick mustache with the ends curving slightly upward.

handlebar mustache

han·dler /'handlər/ ▶ **n. 1** [usu. with adj.] a person who handles or deals with certain articles or commodities. ■ a device that handles certain articles or substances. **2** a person who trains or has charge of an animal. **3** a person who trains or manages another person, in particular: ■ a person who trains and acts as second to a boxer. ■ a publicity agent. ■ a person who advises on and directs the activities of a public figure.

hand·ling /'handl-iNG/ ▶ **n.** the act of taking or holding something in the hands. ■ the packaging and labeling of something to be shipped.

hand·made /'han(d)'mād/ ▶ **adj.** made by hand, not by machine.

hand·maid·en /'han(d),mādn/ (also **hand·maid**) ▶ **n.** a female servant. ■ a subservient partner or element: *shipping will continue to be the handmaiden of world trade.*

hand-me-down ▶ **n.** (often **hand-me-downs**) something that has been passed on from another person. ▶ **adj.** [attrib.] (of a garment or other item) passed on from another person: *he wore a hand-me-down coat.*

hand·off /'hand,ôf; -,äf/ ▶ **n.** Football an exchange made by handing the ball to a teammate.

hand·out /'hand,out/ ▶ **n. 1** something given free to a needy person or organization. **2** printed information provided free of charge.

hand·o·ver /'hand,ōvər/ ▶ **n.** esp. Brit. an act or instance of handing something over.

hand·pick /'han(d)'pik/ (also **hand-pick**) ▶ **v.** [trans.] select carefully with a particular purpose in mind.

hand press ▶ **n.** a hand-operated press.

hand·print /'han(d),print/ ▶ n. the mark left by the impression of a hand.

hand·print·ed /'han(d)'printid/ ▶ adj. **1** written by hand. **2** of or bearing a design printed by hand.

hand pup·pet ▶ n. a puppet operated by putting one's hand inside it.

hand·rail /'han(d),rāl/ ▶ n. a rail fixed to posts or a wall for people to hold onto for support.

hand·saw /'han(d),sô/ ▶ n. a wood saw worked by one hand.

hand·set /'han(d),set/ ▶ n. the part of a telephone that is held up to speak into and listen to.

hand·shake /'han(d),SHāk/ ▶ n. an act of shaking a person's hand with one's own. ■ a person's particular way of doing this. ■ Comput. an exchange of standardized signals between devices. — **hand·shak·ing** /-SHākiNG/ n.

hand·some /'han(d)səm/ ▶ adj. (**-som·er, -som·est**) **1** (of a man) good-looking. ■ (of a woman) striking and imposing in good looks rather than conventionally pretty. ■ (of a thing) well made, imposing, and of obvious quality. **2** (of a number, sum of money, or margin) substantial. ■ generous; liberal: *a handsome gift.* — **hand·some·ly** adv. **hand·some·ness** n. [ME: from HAND + -SOME[1]. The original sense was 'easy to handle or use.']

hand·spike /'han(d),spīk/ ▶ n. hist. a wooden rod with an iron tip, used as a lever on board ship and by artillery soldiers.

hand·spring /'han(d),spriNG/ ▶ n. an acrobatic jump onto one's hands followed by springing onto one's feet.

hand·stand /'han(d),stand/ ▶ n. an act of balancing on one's hands with one's feet in the air or against a wall.

hand-to-hand ▶ adj. (of fighting) at close quarters.

hand tool ▶ n. a tool held in the hand and operated without electricity or other power.

hand·work /'han(d),wərk/ ▶ n. work done by hand. — **hand·worked** adj.

hand·wo·ven /'han(d)'wōvən/ ▶ adj. made on a hand-operated loom: *handwoven linens.* ■ woven by hand.

hand·wring·ing /'han(d),riNGiNG/ ▶ n. the clasping together and squeezing of one's hands, esp. when distressed or worried. ■ an excessive display of concern or distress.

hand·writ·ing /'han(d),rītiNG/ ▶ n. writing with a pen or pencil. ■ a person's particular style of writing.

hand·writ·ten /'han(d),ritn/ ▶ adj. written with a pen, pencil, or other hand-held implement.

Han·dy /'handē/, W. C. (1873–1958), US composer; full name *William Christopher Handy.* His works include "Memphis Blues" (1909) and "St. Louis Blues" (1912).

hand·y /'handē/ ▶ adj. (**hand·i·er, hand·i·est**) **1** convenient to handle or use; useful. **2** close at hand: *keep credit cards handy.* ■ placed or occurring conveniently: *in a handy central location.* **3** skillful: *he's handy with a needle.*
– PHRASES **come in handy** informal turn out to be useful: *junk that might come in handy one day.* — **hand·i·ly** /'handl-ē/ adv. **hand·i·ness** n.

hand·y·man /'handē,man/ ▶ n. (pl. **-men**) a person able or employed to do occasional repairs.

hang /haNG/ ▶ v. (past **hung** /həNG/ except in sense 2) **1** suspend or be suspended from above with the lower part dangling free. ■ attach or be attached to a wall. ■ (**be hung with**) be adorned with pictures or other decorations. ■ exhibit or be exhibited, as in a museum. ■ attach or be attached so as to allow free movement about the point of attachment: [trans.] *hanging a door.* ■ [intrans., with complement] droop: *she sat with her mouth hanging open.* ■ [intrans.] (of fabric or a garment) be arranged in folds so as to droop in a specified way. ■ [trans.] paste (wallpaper) to a wall. ■ informal way of saying HANG AROUND (sense 2) or HANG OUT (sense 3). **2** (past **hanged**) [trans.] kill (someone) by tying a rope attached from above around the neck and removing the support from beneath. ■ [intrans.] be killed in such a way. ■ dated used in expressions as a mild oath: *I'm hanged if I know.* **3** [intrans.] remain static in the air: *a haze of smoke hung below the ceiling.* ■ be present or imminent, esp. oppressively or threateningly: *a sense of dread hung over him for days.* ■ [trans.] Baseball deliver (a breaking pitch) that does not change direction as intended. **4** [trans.] (of a juror) prevent (a jury) from reaching a verdict by a dissenting vote. **5** Comput. come or cause to come unexpectedly to a state in which no further operations can be carried out. ▶ n. [in sing.] a downward droop or bend: *the bullish hang of his head.* ■ the way in which something hangs. ■ the way in which pictures are displayed in an exhibition.
– PHRASES **get the hang of** informal learn how to operate or do (something). **hang by a thread** see THREAD. **hang one's hat** informal be resident. **hang heavily** (or **heavy**) (of time) pass slowly. **hang in the air** remain unresolved. **hang a left** (or **right**) informal make a left (or right) turn. **hang loose** see LOOSE. **hang someone out to dry** informal leave someone in a difficult or vulnerable situation. **hang ten** Surfing ride a surfboard with all ten toes curled over the board's front edge. **hang tough** be or remain inflexible or firmly resolved. **let it all hang out** informal be very relaxed or uninhibited.
– PHRASAL VERBS **hang around 1** loiter; wait around. **2** (**hang around with**) associate with (someone). **hang back** remain behind. ■ show reluctance to act or move. **hang in** informal remain persistent and determined. **hang on 1** hold tightly. ■ informal remain firm or persevere, esp. in difficult circumstances. ■ (**hang on to**) keep; retain. **2** informal wait for a short time: *hang on a minute.* ■ (on the telephone) remain connected until one is able to talk to a particular person. **3** be contingent or dependent on. **4** listen closely to: *she hung on his every word.* **hang something on** informal attach the blame for something to (someone). **hang out 1** (of laundry) hang from a clothesline to dry. **2** protrude and hang loosely downward. **3** informal spend time relaxing or enjoying oneself. **hang together 1** make sense; be consistent. **2** (of people) remain associated; help or support each other. **hang up 1** hang from a hook, hanger, etc. **2** end a telephone conversation by cutting the connection. ■ (**hang up on**) end a telephone conversation by abruptly cutting the connection. **hang up something** hang something on a hook. ■ informal cease or retire from the activity associated with the garment or object specified. [OE *hangian* (intransitive v.), of West Gmc. origin, rel. to Du. and Ger. *hangen.*]

hang·ar /'haNGər/ ▶ n. a large building with extensive floor area, typically for housing aircraft. ▶ v. [trans.] (usu. **be hangared**) place or store in a hangar. — **hang·ar·age** /-ərij/ n. [17th C. (in the sense 'shelter'): from Fr.; prob. from Gmc. bases meaning 'hamlet' and 'enclosure.']

Hang·chow /'haNG'CHou; 'häNG'jō/ variant of HANGZHOU.

hang·dog /'haNG,dôg; -,däg/ ▶ adj. having a dejected or guilty appearance; shamefaced.

hang·er /'haNGər/ ▶ n. **1** [in comb.] a person who hangs something: *a wallpaper hanger.* **2** (also **coat hanger**) a shaped piece of wood, plastic, or metal with a hook at the top, from which clothes may be hung. **3** something from which another thing hangs, such as a hook. **4** hist. a short sword that hung from a belt.

hang·er-on ▶ n. (pl. **hang·ers-on**) a person who associates with another person or a group in a sycophantic manner or to gain some personal advantage.

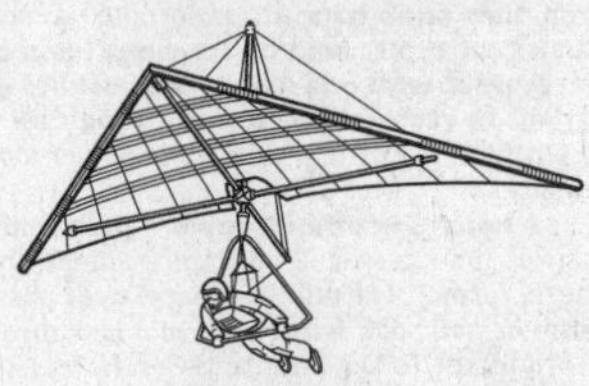

hang glider

hang glid·er ▶ n. an unpowered flying apparatus for a single person, consisting of a frame with a fabric airfoil stretched over it. The operator is suspended from a harness below and controls flight by body movement. ■ a person flying such an apparatus. — **hang-glide** v. **hang glid·ing** n.

hang·ing /'haNGiNG/ ▶ n. **1** the practice of hanging condemned people as a form of capital punishment. **2** a decorative piece of fabric or curtain hung on the wall of a room or around a bed. ▶ adj. [attrib.] suspended in the air: *hanging palls of smoke.* ■ situated or designed so as to appear to hang down: *hanging gardens.*

Hang·ing Gar·dens of Bab·y·lon legendary terraced gardens at Babylon (*c.*600 BC), one of the Seven Wonders of the World.

hang·ing in·dent ▶ n. indentation of a paragraph in which all lines except the first are indented.

hang·man /'haNGmən; -,man/ ▶ n. (pl. **-men**) an executioner who hangs condemned people. ■ a game for two in which one player tries to guess the letters of a word, and failed attempts are recorded by drawing a gallows and someone hanging on it.

hang·nail /'haNG,nāl/ ▶ n. a piece of torn cuticle. [17th C.: alt. of *agnail* 'painful swelling around a nail' (from OE *angnægl,* denoting a corn on the toe), influenced by HANG.]

hang·out /'haNG,out/ ▶ n. informal a place one frequently visits: *a favorite college hangout.*

hang·o·ver /'haNG,ōvər/ ▶ n. ill effects caused by drinking an excess of alcohol. ■ a thing that has survived from the past.

hang time ▶ n. Football the number of seconds during which a punted ball is in the air.

hang-up ▶ n. informal an emotional problem or inhibition.

Hang·zhou /'häNG'jō/ (also **Hang·chow**) a city in eastern China, on an inlet of the Yellow Sea; pop. 2,589,500.

hank /haNGk/ ▶ n. **1** a coil or skein of yarn, hair, rope, or other material: *a thick* **hank** *of her blonde hair.* **2** a measurement of the length per unit mass of cloth or yarn, which varies according to the type being measured. For example, a hank is equal to 840 yards for cotton yarn and 560 yards for worsted. **3** Sailing a ring for securing a staysail to the stay. [ME: from ON *hǫnk*; cf. Swed. *hank* 'string' and Dan. *hank* 'handle.']

hank·er /'haNGkər/ ▶ v. [intrans.] (**hanker after/for/to do something**) feel a strong desire to do something. — **hank·er·er** n. [17th C.: prob. rel. to HANG.]

han·ky /'haNGkē/ (also **han·kie**) ▶ n. (pl. **-kies**) informal a handkerchief.

han·ky-pan·ky /'paNGkē/ ▶ n. informal, humorous behavior, in particular sexual or legally dubious behavior, considered improper but not seriously so. [19th C.: perh. an alt. of HOKEY-POKEY.]

Han·ni·bal /'hanəbəl/ (247–182 BC), Carthaginian general. In the second Punic War he attacked Italy by crossing the Alps.

Ha·noi /ha'noi; hə-/ the capital of Vietnam, in the northern part of the country; pop. 1,090,000.

Han·o·ver /'han,ōvər; 'hän-/ a city in northwestern Germany; pop. 517,000. German name **Hannover**. ■ a former state and province in northern Germany. ■ the British royal house from 1714–1901.

Han·o·ve·ri·an /,hanə've(ə)rēən/ ▶ **adj.** of or relating to the royal house of Hanover. ▶ **n. 1** (usu. **the Hanoverians**) any of the British sovereigns from George I to Victoria. **2** a medium-built horse of a German breed.

Han Riv·er /hän/ **1** (Chinese name **Han Shui**) a river in eastern China that flows southeast to the Yangtze River. **2** (Chinese name **Han Jiang**) river in south China that flows south to the South China Sea.

Hans·ber·ry /'hanz,berē/, Lorraine (1930–65) US playwright. She wrote *A Raisin in the Sun* (1959).

Hanse /hans; 'hänzə/ ▶ **n.** a medieval merchant's guild. ■ (**the Hanse**) the Hanseatic League. ■ a fee payable to a guild of merchants. [ME: from OFr. *hanse* 'guild, company,' from Old High Ger. *hansa* 'company, troop.']

Han·se·at·ic League /,hansē'atik/ a medieval association of northern German cities.

Han·sen's dis·ease /'hansənz/ ▶ **n.** another name for **leprosy**. [1930s: Gerhard H. A. *Hansen* (1841–1912), Norwegian physician.]

hansom

han·som /'hansəm/ (also **han·som cab**) ▶ **n.** hist. a two-wheeled horse-drawn carriage accommodating two inside, with the driver seated behind outside. [19th C.: named after Joseph A. *Hansom* (1803–82), English architect, patentee of such a cab in 1834.]

han·ta·vi·rus /'hantə,vīrəs/ ▶ **n.** a virus of a genus carried by rodents and causing various febrile hemorrhagic diseases, often with kidney damage or failure. [1980s: from *Hantaan* (a river in Korea).]

Ha·nuk·kah /'KHänəkə; 'hä-/ (also **Cha·nu·kah**) ▶ **n.** a Jewish festival, lasting eight days from the 25th day of Kislev (in December) and commemorating the rededication of the Temple in 165 BC by the Maccabees after its desecration by the Syrians. [from Heb. *ḥănukkāh* 'consecration.']

han·u·man /'hanŏŏ,män/ ▶ **n. 1** (also **hanuman langur**) a pale-colored langur monkey (*Presbytis entellus*) of India, venerated by Hindus. **2** Hinduism (**Hanuman**) a semidivine being of monkeylike form, whose exploits are described in the Ramayana. [from Sanskrit *hanumant* 'large-jawed.']

Hao·ra var. of **Howrah**.

hap /hap/ archaic ▶ **n.** luck; fortune. ■ a chance occurrence, esp. an unlucky event. ▶ **v.** (**happed, hap·ping**) [intrans.] come about by chance. ■ [with infin.] have the fortune or luck to do something: *where'er I happ'd to roam.* [ME: from ON *happ.*]

hap·ax le·go·me·non /'hapaks lə'gämə,nän/ ▶ **n.** (pl. **hap·ax le·go·me·na** /lə'gämənə/) a term of which only one instance of use is recorded. [17th C.: Gk., 'a thing said once,' from *hapax* 'once' and the passive part. of *legein* 'to say.']

ha'·pen·ny ▶ **n.** var. of **halfpenny**.

hap·haz·ard /hap'hazərd/ ▶ **adj.** lacking any obvious principle of organization. — **hap·haz·ard·ly** **adv.** **hap·haz·ard·ness** **n.** [16th C.: from **hap** + **hazard**.]

Haph·ta·rah /,häftä'rä; häf'tôrə/ (also **Haph·to·rah**) ▶ **n.** (pl. **-ta·roth** /-tä'rôt; -'tôrōs/) var. of **Haftorah**.

hap·less /'haplis/ ▶ **adj.** (esp. of a person) unfortunate. — **hap·less·ly** **adv.** **hap·less·ness** **n.** [ME: from **hap**.]

haplo- ▶ **comb. form** single; simple: *haploid.* [from Gk. *haploos* 'single.']

hap·lo·dip·loid /,haplō'diploid/ ▶ **adj.** Biol. denoting or possessing a genetic system in which females develop from fertilized (diploid) eggs and males from unfertilized (haploid) ones.

hap·loid /'haploid/ Genet. ▶ **adj.** (of a cell or nucleus) having a single set of unpaired chromosomes. Compare with **diploid**. ■ (of an organism or part) composed of haploid cells. ▶ **n.** a haploid organism or cell. — **hap·loi·dy** **n.** [20th C.: from Gk. *haploos* 'single' + **-oid**.]

hap·lol·o·gy /hap'läləjē/ ▶ **n.** the omission of an occurrence of a sound or syllable that is repeated within a word, e.g., in *probly* for *probably*

hap·lon·tic /hap'läntik/ ▶ **adj.** Genet. (chiefly of an alga or other lower plant) having a life cycle in which the main form is haploid, with a diploid zygote being formed only briefly. Compare with **diplontic**. — **hap·lont** /'haplänt/ **n.**

hap·lo·sis /hap'lōsis/ ▶ **n.** Biol. the halving of the number of chromosomes in a diploid cell during meiosis, resulting in two haploid cells.

hap·pen /'hapən/ ▶ **v.** [intrans.] **1** take place; occur. ■ ensue as an effect or result of an action or event. ■ [with infin.] chance to do something or come about: *we just happened to meet Paul.* ■ [with clause] come about by chance. ■ (**happen on**) find or come across by chance. ■ [with infin.] used as a polite formula in questions: *do you happen to know?* **2** (**happen to**) be experienced by (someone); befall. ■ become of: *I don't care what happens to the money.*
– PHRASES **as it happens** actually; as a matter of fact. [ME: from the n. **hap**.]

hap·pen·ing /'hapəniNG/ ▶ **n. 1** an event or occurrence. ■ a noteworthy or exciting event. **2** an ostensibly spontaneous piece of artistic performance, typically involving audience participation. ▶ **adj.** informal fashionable; trendy: *the happening thing.*

hap·pen·stance /'hapən,stans/ ▶ **n.** coincidence. [19th C.: blend of **happen** and **circumstance**.]

hap·pi·ly /'hapəlē/ ▶ **adv.** in a happy way. ■ [sentence adverb] it is fortunate that.

hap·py /'hapē/ ▶ **adj.** (**-pi·er, -pi·est**) **1** feeling or showing pleasure or contentment. ■ [predic.] (**happy about**) having a sense of confidence in or satisfaction with (a person, arrangement, or situation). ■ [predic.] (**happy with**) satisfied with the quality or standard of. ■ [with infin.] willing to do something. ■ (of an event or situation) characterized by happiness. ■ [attrib.] used in greetings: *happy birthday.* ■ [attrib.] fortunate and convenient: *he had the happy knack of making people like him.* **2** [in comb.] informal inclined to use a specified thing excessively or at random: *our litigation-happy society.*
– PHRASES (**as**) **happy as a clam** (**at high tide**) extremely happy. **happy hunting ground** a place where success or enjoyment is obtained. — **hap·pi·ness** **n.** [ME (in the sense 'lucky'): from the n. **hap** + **-y**[1].]

hap·py-go-luck·y ▶ **adj.** cheerfully unconcerned about the future: *a happy-go-lucky, relaxed attitude.*

hap·py hour ▶ **n.** a period of the day when drinks are sold at reduced prices in a bar or restaurant.

hap·py me·di·um ▶ **n.** a satisfactory compromise.

Haps·burg /'hapsbərg; 'häps,bŏŏrk/ var. of **Habsburg**.

hap·ten /'hapten/ ▶ **n.** Physiol. a small molecule that, when combined with a larger carrier such as a protein, can elicit the production of antibodies that bind specifically to it (in the free or combined state). [20th C.: from Gk. *haptein* 'fasten.']

hap·tic /'haptik/ ▶ **adj.** tech. of or relating to the sense of touch. [19th C.: from Gk. *haptikos* 'able to touch or grasp,' from *haptein* 'fasten.']

hap·to·glo·bin /,haptə'glōbən/ ▶ **n.** Biochem. a protein present in blood serum that binds to and removes free hemoglobin from the bloodstream. [1940s: from Gk. *haptein* 'fasten' + *(hemo)globin.*]

ha·ra-ki·ri /,härə 'ki(ə)rē; ,harə-; ,harē 'karē/ ▶ **n.** ritual suicide by disembowelment with a sword, formerly practiced in Japan by samurai as an honorable alternative to disgrace or execution. ■ fig. ostentatious or ritualized self-destruction. [19th C.: colloq. Japanese, from *hara* 'belly' + *kiri* 'cutting.']

ha·rangue /hə'raNG/ ▶ **n.** a lengthy and aggressive speech. ▶ **v.** [trans.] lecture (someone) at length in an aggressive and critical manner. — **ha·rangu·er** **n.** [ME: from OFr. *arenge*, from med. L. *harenga*, perh. of Gmc. origin.]

Ha·rap·pa /hə'rapə/ an ancient city (*c.*2600–1700 BC), in northern Pakistan.

Ha·ra·re /hə'rärē; -'rärā/ the capital of Zimbabwe; pop. 1,184,000. Former name (until 1982) **Salisbury**[2].

ha·rass /hə'ras; 'harəs/ ▶ **v.** [trans.] subject to aggressive pressure or intimidation. ■ make repeated small-scale attacks on (an enemy). ■ [as adj.] (**harassed**) feeling or looking strained by having too many demands made on one. — **ha·rass·er** **n.** **ha·rass·ing·ly** **adv.** **ha·rass·ment** **n.** [17th C.: from Fr. *harasser*, from *harer* 'set a dog on,' from Gmc. *hare*, a cry urging a dog to attack.]

Har·bin /här'bin; 'härbin/ a city in northeastern China; pop. 3,597,000.

har·bin·ger /'härbənjər/ ▶ **n.** a person or thing that announces or signals the approach of another. ■ a forerunner of something. [ME: from OFr. *herbergere*, from *herbergier* 'provide lodging for,' from *herberge* 'lodging,' from Old Saxon *heriberga*, (from *heri* 'army' + a Gmc. base meaning 'fortified place'), rel. to **harbor**.]

har·bor /'härbər/ (Brit. **har·bour**) ▶ **n.** a place on the coast where vessels may find shelter, esp. one protected from rough water by piers, jetties, and other artificial structures. ■ fig. a place of refuge: *the offered harbor of his arms.* ▶ **v.** [trans.] **1** keep (a thought or feeling, typically a negative one) in one's mind, esp. secretly. **2** give a home or shelter to. ■ shelter or hide (a criminal or wanted person). ■ carry the germs of (a disease). — **har·bor·er** **n.** **har·bor·less** **adj.** [OE *herebeorg* 'shelter, refuge,' of Gmc. origin; rel. to Ger. *Herberge.*]

har·bor·mas·ter /'härbər,mastər/ (also **har·bor mas·ter**) ▶ **n.** an official in charge of a harbor.

har·bor seal ▶ **n.** a true seal (*Phoca vitulina*) with a mottled gray-brown coat and a concave profile, found along North Atlantic and North Pacific coasts.

hard /härd/ ▶ **adj. 1** solid, firm, and resistant to pressure; not easily broken, bent, or pierced. ■ (of a person) not showing any signs of weakness; tough. ■ (of information) reliable, esp. because based on something true or substantiated: *hard facts.* ■ (of a subject of study) dealing with precise and verifiable facts: *turn psychology into hard science.* ■ (of water) containing mineral salts that make lathering difficult. ■ (of prices of stock, commodities, etc.) stable or firm in value. ■ (of science fiction) scientifically accurate rather than purely fantastic or whimsical. ■ (of a consonant) pronounced as *c* in *cat* or *g* in *go.* **2** requiring a great deal of endurance or physical or mental effort. ■ putting a lot of energy into an activity: *hard worker.* ■ difficult to bear; causing suffering. ■ not showing sympathy or affection; strict: *a hard taskmaster.* ■ (of a season or the weather) severe: *a hard winter.* ■ harsh or unpleasant to the senses: *the hard light of morning.* ■ (of wine) harsh or sharp to the taste. **3** done with a great deal of force or strength. **4** potent, powerful, or intense, in particular: ■ (of liquor) strongly alcoholic; denoting distilled spirits rather than beer or wine. ■ (of apple cider) having alcoholic content from fermentation. ■ (of a drug) potent and addictive. ■ denoting an extreme or dogmatic faction within a political party: *the hard left.* ■ (of radiation) highly penetrating. ■ (of pornography) highly obscene and explicit. ▶ **adv. 1** with a great deal of effort. ■ with a great deal of force; violently. **2** so as to be solid or firm: *the mortar has set hard.* **3** to the fullest extent possible: *put the wheel* ***hard*** *over.*

– PHRASES **be hard on 1** treat or criticize (someone) severely. **2** be difficult for or unfair to. **3** be likely to hurt or damage: *the monitor flickers, which is hard on the eyes.* **be hard put** [usu. with infin.] find it very difficult. **give someone a hard time** informal deliberately make a situation difficult for someone. **hard and fast** (of a rule or a distinction made) fixed and definitive. **hard as nails** see NAIL. **hard at it** informal busily working or occupied. **hard feelings** [usu. with negative] feelings of resentment. **hard going** difficult to understand or enjoy: *the studying is hard going.* **hard hit** badly affected. **a hard nut to crack** informal a person or thing that is difficult to understand or influence. **hard of hearing** not able to hear well. **hard up** informal short of money. **the hard way** through suffering or learning from the unpleasant consequences of mistakes. **play hard to get** informal deliberately adopt an aloof or uninterested attitude. — **hard•ish** adj. **hard•ness** n. [OE *hard, heard,* of Gmc. origin; rel. to Du. *hard* and Ger. *hart.*]

hard•back /'härd,bak/ ▶ adj. & n. another term for HARDCOVER.

hard•ball /'härd,bôl/ ▶ n. baseball, esp. as contrasted with softball. ■ Baseball a very competitive pitching and playing style. ■ informal uncompromising and ruthless methods: *the leadership* ***played hardball*** *to win the vote.*

hard-bit•ten (also **hard•bit•ten**) ▶ adj. tough and cynical.

hard•board /'härd,bôrd/ ▶ n. stiff board made of compressed and treated wood pulp.

hard-boiled ▶ adj. **1** (of an egg) boiled until the white and the yolk are solid. **2** (of a person) tough and cynical. ■ denoting a tough, realistic style of detective fiction set in a world permeated by corruption and deceit. — **hard-boil** v. (in sense 1).

hard case ▶ n. informal a tough or intractable person.

hard cash ▶ n. negotiable coins and paper money as opposed to other forms of payment.

hard cheese ▶ n. see CHEESE[1].

hard clam ▶ n. another term for QUAHOG.

hard coal ▶ n. another term for ANTHRACITE.

hard-code ▶ v. [trans.] Comput. fix (data or parameters) in a program in such a way that they cannot easily be altered by the user.

hard cop•y ▶ n. a printed version on paper of data held in a computer.

hard core ▶ n. the most active, committed, or doctrinaire members of a group or movement. ■ popular music that is experimental in nature and typically characterized by high volume and aggressive presentation. ■ pornography of an explicit kind.

hard•cov•er /'härd,kəvər/ ▶ adj. (of a book) bound between rigid boards covered in cloth, paper, leather, or film: *hardcover and paperback editions.* ▶ n. a hardcover book.

hard cur•ren•cy ▶ n. currency that is not likely to depreciate suddenly or to fluctuate greatly in value.

hard disk ▶ n. Comput. a rigid nonremovable magnetic disk with a large data storage capacity.

hard drive ▶ n. Comput. a high-capacity, self-contained storage device containing a read-write mechanism plus one or more hard disks, inside a sealed unit. Also called HARD DISK DRIVE.

hard-earned ▶ adj. having taken a great deal of effort to earn or acquire.

hard-edged ▶ adj. **1** having sharply defined edges. **2** having an intense, tough, or sharp quality.

hard•en /'härdn/ ▶ v. make or become hard or harder. ■ make or become more severe and less sympathetic. ■ make or become tougher and more clearly defined: [intrans.] *suspicion* ***hardened into*** *certainty.* ■ [intrans.] (of prices of stocks, commodities, etc.) rise and remain steady at a higher level.

– PHRASES **hardening of the arteries** another term for ARTERIOSCLEROSIS. — **hard•en•er** n.

hard•ened /'härdnd/ ▶ adj. **1** having become or been made hard or harder: *hardened steel.* ■ strengthened or made secure against attack, esp. by nuclear weapons: *the silos are* ***hardened against*** *air attack.* **2** [attrib.] experienced in a particular job or activity and therefore not easily upset by its more unpleasant aspects: *hardened police officers.* ■ utterly fixed in a habit or way of life seen as bad.

hard er•ror ▶ n. Comput. an error or hardware fault causing failure of a program or operating system.

hard hat ▶ n. a rigid protective helmet. ■ informal a worker who wears a hard hat. ■ informal a person with reactionary or conservative views.

hard•head /'härd,hed/ ▶ n. (also **hardhead catfish**) a marine catfish (*Arius felis,* family Ariidae), the male of which incubates the eggs inside its mouth. It occurs along the Atlantic coast of North America.

hard•head•ed /'härd,hedid/ ▶ adj. practical and realistic; not sentimental: *hardheaded legislators.* — **hard•head•ed•ly** adv. **hard•head•ed•ness** n.

hard•heads /'härd,hedz/ ▶ plural n. [treated as sing.] another term for KNAPWEED, esp. the black knapweed.

hard-heart•ed ▶ adj. incapable of being moved to pity or tenderness; unfeeling. — **hard-heart•ed•ly** adv. **hard-heart•ed•ness** n.

hard-hit•ting ▶ adj. **1** uncompromisingly direct and honest, esp. in revealing unpalatable facts. **2** (of an athlete or athletes) aggressive and physical. ■ Baseball denoting a power hitter.

har•di•hood /'härdē,ho͝od/ ▶ n. dated boldness; daring.

Har•ding /'härdiNG/, Warren Gamaliel (1865–1923), 29th president of the US 1921–23. A Republican, he served in the US Senate 1915–21. As president, his administration was marred by the Teapot Dome scandal.

hard la•bor ▶ n. heavy manual work as a punishment.

hard land•ing ▶ n. a clumsy or rough landing of an aircraft. ■ an uncontrolled landing in which a spacecraft crashes onto the surface of a planet or moon and is destroyed.

hard line ▶ n. an uncompromising adherence to a firm policy. ▶ adj. uncompromising; strict: *a hard-line party activist.*

hard-lin•er ▶ n. a member of a group that adheres uncompromisingly to a set of ideas or policies.

hard-luck sto•ry ▶ n. an account of one's problems intended to gain sympathy or help.

hard•ly /'härdlē/ ▶ adv. scarcely (used to qualify a statement by saying that it is true to an insignificant degree): *it is hardly bigger than a credit card.* ■ only a very short time before: *the party had hardly started.* ■ only with great difficulty: *she could hardly sit up.* ■ no or not (suggesting surprise at or disagreement with a statement): *I hardly think so.*

– PHRASES **hardly any** almost no. ■ almost none. **hardly ever** very rarely.

hard-nosed ▶ adj. informal realistic and determined; tough-minded: *the hard-nosed, tough approach.*

hard-on ▶ n. vulgar slang an erection of the penis.

hard pal•ate ▶ n. the bony front part of the palate.

hard•pan /'härd,pan/ ▶ n. a hardened impervious layer, typically of clay, occurring in or below the soil.

hard-paste ▶ adj. denoting true porcelain made of fusible and infusible materials (usually kaolin and china stone) fired at a high temperature.

hard-pressed ▶ adj. **1** closely pursued. **2** burdened with urgent business. ■ (also **hard pressed**) in difficulties: *creating jobs in the hard-pressed construction industry.*

hard rock ▶ n. highly amplified rock music.

hard sauce ▶ n. a sauce of butter and sugar, typically with brandy, rum, or vanilla added.

hard•scrab•ble /'härd,skrabəl/ ▶ adj. **1** returning little in exchange for great effort: *her uncle's hardscrabble peanut farm.* **2** characterized by chronic poverty and hardship.

hard sell ▶ n. a policy or technique of aggressive salesmanship or advertising.

hard•shell ▶ adj. [attrib.] **1** having a hard shell or outer casing: *hard-shell helmets.* **2** rigid or uncompromising: *a hard-shell Baptist.*

hard-shell clam ▶ n. another term for QUAHOG.

hard•ship /'härd,SHip/ ▶ n. severe suffering or privation: *intolerable levels of hardship.*

hard•tack /'härd,tak/ ▶ n. hard dry bread or biscuit.

hard•top /'härd,täp/ ▶ n. a motor vehicle with a rigid roof that in some cases is detachable. ■ a roof of this type.

hard•ware /'härd,we(ə)r/ ▶ n. tools, machinery, and other durable equipment: *tanks and other military hardware.* ■ the machines, wiring, and other physical components of a computer or other electronic system. Compare with SOFTWARE. ■ tools, implements, and other items used in home life and activities such as gardening.

hard•wear•ing /'härd,we(ə)riNG/ (also **hard-wear•ing**) ▶ adj. able to stand much wear.

hard wheat ▶ n. wheat of a variety having a hard grain rich in gluten.

hard-wired ▶ adj. Electron. involving or achieved by permanently connected circuits. ■ informal genetically determined or compelled. — **hard-wire** v. & adj.

hard•wood /'härd,wo͝od/ ▶ n. **1** the wood from a broad-leaved tree rather than from conifers. ■ a tree producing such wood. **2** (in gardening) mature growth on shrubs and other plants from which cuttings may be taken.

hard-work•ing (also **hard•work•ing**) ▶ adj. (of a person) working with energy and commitment; diligent.

Har•dy /'härdē/, Thomas (1840–1928), English writer. His works include

Tess of the D'Urbervilles (1891) and *Jude the Obscure* (1896).

har·dy /ˈhärdē/ ▶ **adj.** (**-di·er**, **-di·est**) robust; capable of enduring difficult conditions. ■ (of a plant) able to survive outside during winter. — **har·di·ly** adv. **har·di·ness** n. [ME (in the sense 'bold, daring'): from OFr. *hardi*, past part. of *hardir* 'become bold,' of Gmc. origin; rel. to HARD.]

hare /he(ə)r/ ▶ **n.** a fast-running, long-eared rabbitlike mammal (*Lepus* and other genera, family Leporidae), having long hind legs and occurring typically in grassland or open woodland. [OE *hara*, rel. to Du. *haas* and Ger. *Hase*.]

hare·bell /ˈhe(ə)rˌbel/ ▶ **n.** a widely distributed bellflower (*Campanula rotundifolia*) with slender stems and pale blue flowers. Also called BLUEBELL.

hare·brained /ˈhe(ə)rˌbrānd/ (also **hair-brained**) ▶ **adj.** rash; ill-judged.

Ha·re·di /ᴋʜäreˈdē; häˈrādē/ ▶ **n.** (pl. **-dim** /-ˈdēm/) a member of any of various Orthodox Jewish sects that adhere to the traditional form of Jewish law and reject modern secular culture. [Heb., lit. 'one who trembles (in awe at the word of God).']

Hare·foot /ˈhe(ə)rˌfo͝ot/, Harold, see HAROLD.

Ha·re Krish·na /ˌhärē ˈkrisʜnə; ˌharē/ ▶ **n.** a member of the International Society for Krishna Consciousness, a religious sect based mainly in the US and other Western countries. ■ this sect. [1960s: Sanskrit, lit. 'O Vishnu Krishna.']

harebell

hare·lip /ˈhe(ə)rˌlip/ ▶ **n.** another term for CLEFT LIP. — **hare·lipped** adj. [16th C.: from a perceived resemblance to the mouth of a hare.]

har·em /ˈhe(ə)rəm; ˈhar-/ ▶ **n.** **1** the part of a Muslim household reserved for wives, concubines, and female servants. **2** the wives (or concubines) of a polygamous man. ■ a group of female animals sharing a single mate. [17th C. (sense 1): from Arab. *ḥaram*, *ḥarīm*, lit. from *ḥarama* 'be prohibited.']

Har·gei·sa /härˈgāsə/ (also **Har·gey·sa**) a city in northwestern Somalia; pop. 400,000.

Har·greaves /ˈhärˌgrēvz/, James (1720–78), English inventor. He invented the spinning jenny in 1764.

har·i·cot /ˈhariˌkō/ (also **har·i·cot bean**) ▶ **n.** **1** a bean with small white seeds, esp. the kidney bean. **2** the dried seed of this bean used as a vegetable. [17th C.: Fr., perh. from Aztec *ayacotli*.]

Har·i·jan /ˈharəjan/ ▶ **n.** a member of a hereditary Hindu group of the lowest social and ritual status. See UNTOUCHABLE. [from Sanskrit *harijana*, lit. 'a person dedicated to Vishnu,' from *Hari* 'Vishnu' + *jana* 'person.']

hark /härk/ ▶ **v.** [intrans.] literary listen: *Hark! He knocks.*
– PHRASAL VERBS **hark back** mention or remember something from the past. **hark back to** evoke (an older style or genre). [ME: of Gmc. origin; rel. to Ger. *horchen*, also to HEARKEN.]

hark·en ▶ **v.** var. of HEARKEN.

Har·lan /ˈhärlən/ US Supreme Court associate justices. John Marshall Harlan (1833–1911) served on the Court 1877–1911. His grandson, John Marshall Harlan (1899–1971) served 1955–71.

Har·lem /ˈhärləm/ a district in New York City, north of 96th Street in northeastern Manhattan.

Har·lem Ren·ais·sance a literary movement in the 1920s that centered on Harlem.

har·le·quin /ˈhärlik(w)ən/ ▶ **n.** **1** (**Harlequin**) a mute character in traditional pantomime, typically masked and dressed in a diamond-patterned costume. ■ hist. a stock comic character in Italian *commedia dell'arte*. **2** (also **harlequin duck**) a small duck (*Histrionicus histrionicus*) of fast-flowing streams around the Arctic and North Pacific, the male having mainly gray-blue plumage with bold white markings. ▶ **adj.** in varied colors; variegated. [16th C.: from obs. Fr., from *Herlequin*, leader of a legendary troop of demon horsemen.]

har·le·quin·ade /ˌhärlik(w)əˈnād/ ▶ **n.** hist. the section of a traditional pantomime in which Harlequin played a leading role. ■ dated a piece of buffoonery.

har·lot /ˈhärlət/ ▶ **n.** archaic a prostitute or promiscuous woman. — **har·lot·ry** n. [ME: from OFr. *harlot*, *herlot* 'young man, knave, vagabond.']

harm /härm/ ▶ **n.** physical injury, esp. that which is deliberately inflicted. ■ material damage. ■ actual or potential ill effect or danger: *I can't see any harm in it.* ▶ **v.** [trans.] physically injure: *the villains didn't harm him.* ■ damage the health of. ■ have an adverse effect on.
– PHRASES **come to no harm** be unhurt or undamaged. **do more harm than good** inadvertently make a situation worse rather than better. **do (someone) no harm** used to indicate that a situation or action will not hurt someone, whether or not it will provide any benefit. **mean no harm** not intend to cause damage or insult. **no harm done** used to reassure someone that what they have done has caused no real damage. **out of harm's way** in a safe place. [OE *hearm* (n.), *hearmian* (v.), of Gmc. origin; rel. to Ger. *Harm* and ON *harmr* 'grief, sorrow.']

har·mat·tan /ˌhärməˈtän/ ▶ **n.** a dry, dusty easterly or northeasterly wind on the West African coast, occurring from December to February. [17th C.: from Twi *haramata*.]

harm·ful /ˈhärmfəl/ ▶ **adj.** causing harm. — **harm·ful·ly** adv. **harm·ful·ness** n.

harm·less /ˈhärmlis/ ▶ **adj.** not able or likely to cause harm. ■ inoffensive. — **harm·less·ly** adv. **harm·less·ness** n.

har·mon·ic /härˈmänik/ ▶ **adj.** **1** of, relating to, or characterized by musical harmony. ■ Music relating to or denoting a harmonic or harmonics. **2** Math. of or relating to a harmonic progression. ■ Physics of or relating to component frequencies of a complex oscillation or wave. ■ Astrol. using or produced by the application of a harmonic. ▶ **n.** **1** Music an overtone accompanying a fundamental tone at a fixed interval, produced by vibration of a string, column of air, etc., in a fraction of its length. ■ a note produced on a musical instrument as an overtone. **2** Physics a component frequency of an oscillation or wave. ■ Astrol. a division of the zodiacal circle by a specified number, used in the interpretation of a birth chart. — **har·mon·i·cal·ly** /-ik(ə)lē/ adv.

har·mon·i·ca /härˈmänikə/ ▶ **n.** a small rectangular wind instrument with a row of metal reeds along its length. Also called MOUTH ORGAN. [18th C.: from L., fem. sing. or neut. pl. of *harmonicus* 'musical.' from *harmonia*.]

har·mon·ic mo·tion ▶ **n.** Physics oscillatory motion under a retarding force proportional to the amount of displacement from an equilibrium position.

har·mon·ic pro·gres·sion ▶ **n.** **1** Music a series of chord changes forming the underlying harmony of music. **2** Math. a sequence of quantities whose reciprocals are in arithmetic progression (e.g., 1, 13, 15, 17, etc.).

har·mon·ic se·ries ▶ **n.** **1** Music a set of frequencies consisting of a fundamental and the harmonics related to it by an exact fraction. **2** Math. a series of values in harmonic progression.

har·mo·ni·ous /härˈmōnēəs/ ▶ **adj.** not discordant; tuneful. ■ forming a pleasing whole: *the decor is a harmonious blend.* ■ free from disagreement or dissent. — **har·mo·ni·ous·ly** adv. **har·mo·ni·ous·ness** n.

har·mo·nist /ˈhärmənist/ ▶ **n.** a person skilled in musical harmony.

har·mo·ni·um /härˈmōnēəm/ ▶ **n.** a keyboard instrument in which the notes are produced by air driven through metal reeds by foot-operated bellows. [19th C.: from Fr., from L. *harmonia* (see HARMONY) or Gk. *harmonios* 'harmonious.']

har·mo·nize /ˈhärməˌnīz/ ▶ **v.** [trans.] add notes to (a melody) to produce harmony. ■ [intrans.] sing in harmony. ■ [intrans.] produce a pleasing visual combination. ■ make consistent. — **har·mo·ni·za·tion** /ˌhärmənəˈzāsʜən/ n.

har·mo·ny /ˈhärmənē/ ▶ **n.** (pl. **-nies**) **1** the combination of simultaneously sounded musical notes to produce chords and chord progressions with a pleasing effect. ■ the study or composition of musical harmony. ■ the quality of forming a pleasing and consistent whole. ■ an arrangement of the four Gospels, or of any parallel narratives, that presents a single continuous narrative text. **2** agreement or concord. [ME: via OFr. from L. *harmonia* 'joining, concord,' from Gk., from *harmos* 'joint.']

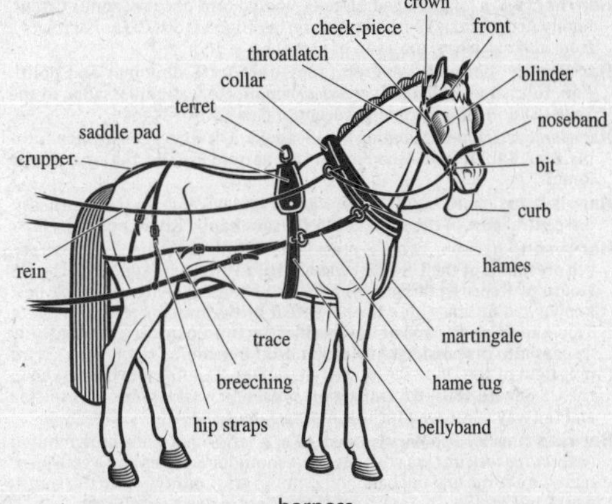

harness

har·ness /ˈhärnis/ ▶ **n.** a set of straps and fittings by which a horse or other draft animal is fastened to a cart, plow, etc., and is controlled by its driver. ■ an arrangement of straps for fastening something to a person's body, such as a parachute. ▶ **v.** [trans.] **1** put a harness on. **2** control and make use of (natural resources), esp. to produce energy: *attempts to harness solar energy.* — **har·ness·er** n. [ME: from OFr. *harneis* 'military equipment,' from ON, from *herr* 'army' + *nest* 'provisions.']

har·ness rac·ing ▶ **n.** racing for trotting horses pulling a sulky and driver. Also called TROTTING. — **har·ness race** n.

Har·old /ˈharəld/ the name of two kings of England: ■ Harold I (died

1040), reigned 1035–40; known as **Harold Hare·foot** /ˈhe(ə)rˌfo͝ot./ ■ Harold II (*c.*1019–66), reigned 1066; the last Anglo-Saxon king of England.

Ha·roun-al-Ra·schid /häˈro͞on äl räˈsнēd/ var. of HARUN AR-RASHID.

harp /härp/ ▶ n. **1** a musical instrument, roughly triangular in shape, consisting of a frame supporting a graduated series of parallel strings, played by plucking with the fingers. The modern orchestral harp has an upright frame, with pedals that enable the strings to be retuned to different keys. **2** informal short for HARMONICA. ▶ v. [intrans.] **1** talk or write persistently and tediously on a particular topic. **2** archaic play on a harp. [OE *hearpe*, of Gmc. origin; rel. to Du. *harp* and Ger. *Harfe*.]

Har·per /ˈhärpər/, Stephen (1959–), prime minister of Canada 2006– .

Har·pers Fer·ry /ˈhärpərz/ a town in northeastern West Virginia. It is noted for a raid in October 1859 in which John Brown and a group of abolitionists captured a Federal arsenal here.

harp·ist /ˈhärpist/ ▶ n. a musician who plays a harp.

Har·poc·ra·tes /härˈpäkrəˌtēz/ Greek name for HORUS.

har·poon /härˈpo͞on/ ▶ n. a barbed spearlike missile attached to a long rope and thrown by hand or fired from a gun, used mainly for catching whales. ▶ v. [trans.] spear (something) with a harpoon. — **har·poon·er** n. [17th C.: from Fr. *harpon*, from *harpe* 'dog's claw, clamp,' via L. from Gk. *harpē* 'sickle.']

harp seal ▶ n. a slender North Atlantic true seal (*Phoca groenlandica*) that typically has a dark harp-shaped mark on its gray back.

harp·si·chord /ˈhärpsiˌkôrd/ ▶ n. a keyboard instrument with horizontal strings that run perpendicular to the keyboard in a long tapering case, and are plucked by points of quill, leather, or plastic operated by depressing the keys. — **harp·si·chord·ist** n. [17th C.: from obs. Fr. *harpechorde*, from late L. *harpa* 'harp' + *chorda* 'string.']

har·py /ˈhärpē/ ▶ n. (pl. **-pies**) Greek Rom. Mythol. a rapacious monster described as having a woman's head and body and a bird's wings and claws or depicted as a bird of prey with a woman's face. ■ a grasping, unscrupulous woman. [ME: from L. *harpyia*, from Gk. *harpuiai* 'snatchers.']

har·py ea·gle ▶ n. a large crested eagle of tropical rain forests, esp. *Harpia harpyja* of South America, the largest eagle.

har·que·bus /ˈ(h)ärk(w)əbəs/ (also **ar·que·bus**) ▶ n. hist. an early type of portable gun supported on a tripod or a forked rest. [16th C.: from Fr. *harquebuse*, based on Mid. Low Ger. *hakebusse*, from *hake* 'hook' + *busse* 'gun.']

har·ri·dan /ˈharidn/ ▶ n. a strict, bossy, or belligerent old woman: *a bullying old harridan.* [17th C. (orig. slang): perh. from Fr. *haridelle* 'old horse.']

har·ri·er¹ /ˈharēər/ ▶ n. a person who engages in attacks on others or incursions into their land.

har·ri·er² ▶ n. a hound used for hunting hares. ■ a cross-country runner. [ME *hayrer*, from HARE + -ER¹.]

har·ri·er³ ▶ n. a long-winged, slender-bodied bird of prey (genus *Circus*, family Accipitridae) with low quartering flight. [16th C. (as *harrower*): from *harrow* 'harry, rob' (var. of HARRY).]

Har·ri·man /ˈharəmən/, Averell (1891–1986), US diplomat and politician; full name *William Averell Harriman.* He was ambassador to the Soviet Union 1943–46 and governor of New York 1955–59.

Har·ris /ˈharis/, Joel Chandler (1848–1908), US writer, best known for his Brer Rabbit and Brer Fox stories as told by the fictional Uncle Remus.

Har·ris·burg /ˈharisˌbərg/ the capital of Pennsylvania, in the southeastern central part of the state, on the Susquehanna River; pop. 52,376.

Har·ri·son /ˈharisən/ two US presidents. William Henry (1773–1841), 9th president of the US 1841, was an Ohio Whig who served in the US House of Representatives 1817–19 and the US Senate 1825–28. Best known as a military hero for his defeat of the Indians at the Battle of Tippecanoe in 1811 and of Indian chief Tecumseh in 1813, he died only 32 days into his presidency. His grandson Benjamin (1833–1901), 23rd president of the US 1889–93, was an Indiana Republican who served in the US Senate 1881–87. During his presidency, Oklahoma was settled and the way was paved for the annexation of Hawaii.

Har·ris's hawk (also **Har·ris hawk**) ▶ n. a large chocolate-brown buteo (*Parabuteo unicinctus*) with chestnut shoulder patches and a conspicuous white rump and tail band. It occurs in arid country from the southwestern US to South America and frequently nests in tall cacti.

Har·ris tweed ▶ n. trademark handwoven tweed made in the Outer Hebrides in Scotland.

har·row /ˈharō/ ▶ n. an implement consisting of a heavy frame set with teeth or tines that is dragged over plowed land. ▶ v. [trans.] **1** draw a harrow over (land). **2** cause distress to: [as adj.] (**harrowing**) *a harrowing film.* — **har·row·er** n. **har·row·ing·ly** adv. [ME: from ON *herfi*; obscurely rel. to Du. *hark* 'rake.']

har·rumph /həˈrəmf/ ▶ v. [intrans.] clear the throat noisily. ■ grumpily express dissatisfaction or disapproval. ▶ n. a noisy clearing of the throat. ■ a grumpy expression of dissatisfaction or disapproval. [1930s: imitative.]

har·ry /ˈharē/ ▶ v. (**-ries, -ried**) [trans.] persistently carry out attacks on. ■ persistently harass. [OE *herian, hergian*, from Gmc. 'army.']

harsh /härsн/ ▶ adj. **1** unpleasantly rough or jarring to the senses: *drenched in a harsh white neon light.* **2** cruel or severe: *a time of harsh military discipline.* ■ (of a climate or conditions) difficult to survive in; hostile. ■ (of reality or a fact) grim and unpalatable. ■ having an undesirably strong effect. — **harsh·en** v. **harsh·ly** adv. **harsh·ness** n. [ME: from Mid. Low Ger. *harsch* 'rough,' lit. 'hairy,' from *haer* 'hair.']

hars·let /ˈhärslit/ ▶ n. var. of HASLET.

Hart¹ /härt/, Frederick E. (1943–99), US sculptor. His work includes the statue of soldiers (1984) at the Vietnam Veterans Memorial in Washington, DC.

Hart², Lorenz Milton (1895–1943), US lyricist. He wrote *Babes in Arms* (1937) and *Pal Joey* (1940) with Richard Rodgers.

Hart³, Moss (1904–61), US playwright. His collaborations with George S. Kaufman include the play *The Man Who Came to Dinner* (1939).

hart /härt/ ▶ n. an adult male deer, esp. a red deer. [OE *heorot, heort*, of Gmc. origin; rel. to Du. *hert* and Ger. *Hirsch*.]

Harte /härt/, Bret (1836–1902), US writer; full name *Francis Bret Harte*. He is chiefly remembered for his stories about life in a California gold-mining town.

har·te·beest /ˈhärt(ə)ˌbēst/ ▶ n. a large African antelope (genera *Alcelaphus, Damaliscus*, and *Sigmoceros*) with a long head and sloping back, related to the gnus. [18th C.: from South Afr. Dutch, from Du. *hert* 'hart' + *beest* 'beast.']

Hart·ford /ˈhärtfərd/ the capital of Connecticut, in the center of the state; pop. 121,578.

harts·horn /ˈhärtsˌhôrn/ (also **spirit of hartshorn**) ▶ n. archaic an aqueous ammonia solution used as smelling salts, formerly prepared from the horns of deer. [OE *heortes horn* (see HART, HORN).]

hart's tongue (also **hart's tongue fern**) ▶ n. a common European fern (*Phyllitis scolopendrium*, family Aspleniaceae) whose long, narrow undivided fronds are said to resemble the tongues of deer.

har·um-scar·um /ˈhe(ə)rəm ˈske(ə)rəm/ ▶ adj. reckless; impetuous. ▶ n. such a person. ▶ adv. in a harum-scarum manner. [17th C. (as an adv.): reduplication based on HARE and SCARE.]

Ha·run ar-Ra·shid /häˈro͞on är räˈsнēd/ (also **Ha·roun-al-Ras·chid** /äl/) (763–809), fifth Abbasid caliph of Baghdad 786–809.

ha·rus·pex /həˈrəsˌpeks; ˈharəˌspeks/ ▶ n. (pl. **ha·rus·pi·ces** /həˈrəspəˌsēz/) (in ancient Rome) a religious official who interpreted omens by inspecting the entrails of sacrificial animals. — **ha·rus·pi·cy** /həˈrəspəsē/ n. [L., from an unrecorded element meaning 'entrails' (rel. to Sanskrit *hirā* 'artery') + *-spex* (from *specere* 'look at').]

Har·vard clas·si·fi·ca·tion /ˈhärvərd/ ▶ n. Astron. a system of classifying stars based on their spectral types. [1960s: HARVARD UNIVERSITY.]

Har·vard U·ni·ver·si·ty an Ivy League university in Cambridge, Massachusetts, founded in 1636.

har·vest /ˈhärvist/ ▶ n. the process or period of gathering in crops: *helping with the harvest.* ■ the season's yield or crop. ■ a quantity of animals caught or killed for human use: *a harvest of wild mink.* ■ fig. the product or result of an action. ▶ v. [trans.] gather (a crop) as a harvest. ■ catch or kill (animals) for human consumption or use. ■ remove (cells, tissue, or an organ) from a person or animal for transplantation or experimental purposes. ■ fig. gain (something) as the result of an action. — **har·vest·a·ble** adj. **har·vest·er** n. [OE *hærfest* 'autumn,' rel. to Ger. *Herbst*, from an Indo-Eur. root shared by L. *carpere* 'pluck' and Gk. *karpos* 'fruit.']

har·vest·man /ˈhärvistmən/ ▶ n. (pl. **-men**) another term for DADDY LONGLEGS.

har·vest mite ▶ n. another term for CHIGGER (sense 1).

har·vest moon ▶ n. the full moon that is seen nearest to the time of the autumnal equinox.

har·vest mouse ▶ n. **1** a nocturnal mouse (genus *Reithrodontomys*) found in North and Central America. **2** a small northern Eurasian mouse (*Micromys minutus*) with a prehensile tail.

Har·vey /ˈhärvē/, William (1578–1657), English physician. He first described how blood circulates.

Ha·ry·a·na /ˌhärēˈänə/ a state in northern India; capital, Chandigarh.

harz·burg·ite /ˈhärtsbərˌgīt/ ▶ n. Geol. a plutonic rock of the peridotite group consisting largely of orthopyroxene and olivine. [19th C.: from *Harzburg*, the name of a town in Germany, + -ITE¹.]

Harz Moun·tains /härts/ a range of mountains in central Germany, the highest of which is the Brocken.

has /haz/ third person singular present of HAVE.

has-been ▶ n. informal, derog. a person or thing considered to be outmoded or no longer significant.

hash¹ /hasн/ ▶ n. a dish of cooked meat cut into small pieces and recooked, usually with potatoes. ■ a finely chopped mixture. ■ a mixture of jumbled incongruous things; a mess. ▶ v. [trans.] **1** make (meat or other food) into a hash. **2** (**hash something out**) come to agreement on something after lengthy and vigorous discussion.
– PHRASES **make a hash of** informal make a mess of; bungle: *listening to other board members make a hash of things.* **sling hash** see SLING¹. [16th C. (as a v.): from Fr. *hacher*, from *hache* (see HATCHET).]

hash² ▶ n. informal short for HASHISH.

hash³ (also **hash sign**) ▶ n. the sign #. [1980s: prob. from HATCH³, alt. by folk etymology.]

hash browns (also **hashed browns**) ▶ plural n. a dish of cooked potatoes that have been chopped into small pieces and fried until brown.

Hash·e·mite /ˈhasнəˌmīt/ ▶ n. a member of an Arab princely family claiming descent from Hashim, great-grandfather of Muhammad. ▶ adj. of or relating to this family.

Hash·e·mite King·dom of Jor·dan official name for JORDAN[1] (sense 1).

hash·ish /ˈhaˌSHēSH; haˈSHēSH/ ▶n. an extract of the cannabis plant, containing psychoactive resins. [16th C.: from Arab. *ḥašīš* 'dry herb, powdered hemp leaves.']

hash mark ▶n. **1** a service stripe worn on the left sleeve of an enlisted person's uniform to indicate three years of service in the army or four years in the navy. ■ a similar stripe on any uniform. **2** Football one of a series of marks made along parallel lines that delineate the middle of the field. **3** the symbol #, used esp. for tallying.

Ha·sid /KHäˈsēd; ˈKHäsid; ˈhäsid/ (also **Cha·sid**, **Chas·sid**, or **Has·sid**) ▶n. (pl. **Ha·si·dim** /ˌKHäsēˈdēm; häˈsēdim/) **1** a member of a strictly orthodox Jewish sect in Palestine 3rd–2nd centuries BC. **2** an adherent of Hasidism. —**Ha·sid·ic** /KHäˈsēdik; häˈsēdik/ **adj.** [from Heb. *ḥāsīd* 'pious.']

Has·i·dism /ˈhasiˌdizəm/ (also **Cha·s·idism**, **Chas·si·dism**, or **Has·si·dism**) ▶n. an influential mystical Jewish movement founded in Poland in the 18th century in reaction to the rigid academicism of rabbinical Judaism.

has·let /ˈhaslit; ˈhāz-/ (also **hars·let**) ▶n. a cold meat preparation of chopped or minced pork offal. [ME: from OFr. *hastelet*, dimin. of *haste* 'roast meat, spit,' prob. of Gmc. origin and rel. to Du. *harst* 'sirloin.']

has·n't /ˈhaznt/ ▶contr. has not.

hasp /hasp/ ▶n. a slotted hinged metal plate that forms part of a fastening for a door or lid and is fitted over a metal loop and secured by a pin or padlock. ■ a similar metal plate on a trunk or suitcase with a projecting piece that is secured by the lock. ▶v. [trans.] archaic lock (a door, window, or lid) by securing the hasp over the loop of the fastening. [OE *hæpse*, *hæsp*, of Gmc. origin; rel. to Du. *haspel* and Ger. *Haspe*.]

hasp

Has·sid ▶n. var. of HASID.

Has·sid·ism ▶n. var. of HASIDISM.

has·si·um /ˈhasēəm/ ▶n. the chemical element of atomic number 108, a very unstable element made by high-energy atomic collisions. (Symbol: **Hs**) [mod. L., from L. *Hassias* 'Hesse' (the German state).]

has·sle /ˈhasəl/ informal ▶n. irritating inconvenience. ■ deliberate harassment. ■ a disagreement; a quarrel. ▶v. [trans.] harass; pester. [19th C.: perh. a blend of HAGGLE and TUSSLE.]

has·sock /ˈhasək/ ▶n. **1** a thick, firmly padded cushion, esp. a footstool. **2** a firm clump of grass in marshy or boggy ground. [OE *hassuc* (sense 2), of unknown origin.]

hast /hast/ archaic second person singular present of HAVE.

has·tate /ˈhastāt/ ▶adj. Bot. (of a leaf) having a narrow triangular shape like that of a spearhead. [18th C.: from L. *hastatus*, from *hasta* 'spear.']

haste /hāst/ ▶n. excessive speed or urgency of movement or action; hurry: *working with feverish haste.*
– PHRASES **make haste** dated hurry; hasten. [ME: from OFr. *haste* (n.), *haster* (v.), of Gmc. origin.]

has·ten /ˈhāsən/ ▶v. [intrans.] be quick to do something. ■ [with adverbial of direction] move or travel hurriedly. ■ [trans.] cause (something) to happen sooner than it otherwise would: *a move that could hasten peace talks.* [16th C.: extended form of HASTE, on the pattern of verbs in -EN[1].]

Has·tings, Bat·tle of /ˈhāstiNGz/ a battle that took place in 1066 north of the town of Hastings, East Sussex, England, in which William the Conqueror defeated the forces of the Anglo-Saxon king Harold II.

hast·y /ˈhāstē/ ▶adj. (**hast·i·er**, **hast·i·est**) done or acting with excessive speed or urgency; hurried. —**hast·i·ly** adv. **hast·i·ness** n. [ME: from OFr. *hasti*, *hastif*, from *haste* (see HASTE).]

hast·y pud·ding ▶n. a boiled mush containing cornmeal or (in Britain) wheat flour and milk or water.

hat /hat/ ▶n. a shaped covering for the head. ■ used to refer to a particular role or occupation of someone who has more than one: *wearing her scientific hat, she is director of a research group.*
– PHRASES **hat in hand** used to indicate an attitude of humility. **keep something under one's hat** keep something a secret. **pass the hat** collect contributions of money. **pick something out of a hat** select something, esp. the winner of a contest, at random. **take one's hat off to** (or **hats off to**) used to state one's admiration for (someone who has done something praiseworthy). **talk through one's hat** see TALK. **throw one's hat in** (or **into**) **the ring** express willingness to take up a challenge, esp. to enter a political race. —**hat·ful** /-ˌfo͝ol/ n. (pl. **-fuls.**) **hat·less** adj. **hat·ted** adj. [in comb.] *a white-hatted cowboy.* [OE *hætt*, of Gmc. origin; rel. to ON *hǫttr* 'hood,' also to HOOD[1].]

hat·band /ˈhatˌband/ ▶n. a decorative ribbon encircling a hat, held in position above the brim.

hatch[1] /haCH/ ▶n. an opening of restricted size allowing for passage from one area to another, in particular: ■ a door in an aircraft, spacecraft, or submarine. ■ an opening in the deck of a boat or ship leading to the cabin or a lower level, esp. a hold. ■ an opening in a ceiling leading to a loft. ■ an opening in a kitchen wall for serving or selling food through. ■ the rear door of a hatchback car. ■ short for HATCHBACK.
– PHRASES **down the hatch** informal used in a toast; drink up. [OE *hæcc* (denoting the lower half of a divided door), of Gmc. origin; rel. to Du. *hek* 'paling, screen.']

hatch[2] ▶v. **1** [intrans.] (of a young bird, fish, or reptile) emerge from its egg: *ten little chicks **hatched out**.* ■ (of an egg) open and produce a young animal. ■ [trans.] incubate (an egg). ■ [trans.] cause (a young animal) to emerge from its egg. **2** [trans.] conspire to devise (a plot or plan). ▶n. a newly hatched brood: *a hatch of mayflies.* [ME *hacche*; rel. to Swed. *häcka* and Dan. *hække*.]

hatch[3] ▶v. [trans.] (in fine art and technical drawing) shade (an area) with closely drawn parallel lines: [as n.] (**hatching**) *the miniaturist's use of hatching and stippling.* [15th C. (in the sense 'inlay with strips of metal'): from OFr. *hacher*, from *hache* (see HATCHET).]

hatch·back /ˈhaCHˌbak/ ▶n. a car with a door across the full width at the back end that opens upward.

hat·check /ˈhatˌCHek/ ▶adj. of or employed in a checkroom for hats, coats, and other personal items.

hatch·el /ˈhaCHəl/ ▶n. another term for HACKLE (sense 3). ▶v. another term for HACKLE. [ME *hechele*, of West Gmc. origin, rel. to HOOK.]

hatch·er·y /ˈhaCHərē/ ▶n. (pl. **-er·ies**) a place where the hatching of fish or poultry eggs is artificially controlled.

hatch·et /ˈhaCHit/ ▶n. a small ax with a short handle. ■ a tomahawk. [ME: from OFr. *hachette*, dimin. of *hache* 'ax,' from med. L. *hapia*, of Gmc. origin.]

hatch·et-faced ▶adj. informal with a narrow face and sharp features.

hatch·et·fish /ˈhaCHitˌfiSH/ ▶n. (pl. same or **-fish·es**) a deep-bodied laterally compressed tropical freshwater fish (*Gasteropelecus* and other genera, family Gasteropelecidae) of the New World. It is able to fly short distances above the surface of the water by beating its broad pectoral fins.

hatch·et job ▶n. informal a fierce attack on someone or their work, esp. in print.

hatch·et man ▶n. informal a person employed to carry out controversial or disagreeable tasks. ■ a person who writes fierce attacks on others.

hatch·ling /ˈhaCHliNG/ ▶n. a young animal that has recently emerged from its egg.

hatch·way /ˈhaCHˌwā/ ▶n. an opening or hatch.

hate /hāt/ ▶v. [trans.] feel intense or passionate dislike for (someone): *the boys hate each other.* ■ have a strong aversion to (something). ■ [with infin.] used politely to express one's regret or embarrassment at doing something: *I hate to bother you.* ▶n. intense or passionate dislike: *feelings of hate.* ■ [as adj.] denoting hostile actions motivated by intense dislike or prejudice: *a hate campaign.* —**hat·a·ble** (also **hate·a·ble**) adj. **hat·er** n. [OE *hatian* (verb), *hete* (n.), of Gmc. origin; rel. to Ger. *hassen* (v.).]

hate crime ▶n. a crime motivated by racial, sexual, or other prejudice, typically one involving violence.

hate·ful /ˈhātfəl/ ▶adj. arousing, deserving of, or filled with hatred: *hateful letters of abuse.* ■ informal very unpleasant: *this hateful place.* —**hate·ful·ly** adv. **hate·ful·ness** n.

hate mail ▶n. hostile and sometimes threatening letters.

hath /haTH/ archaic third person singular present of HAVE.

Hath·a·way /ˈhaTHəˌwā/, Anne (*c.*1557–1623), the wife of Shakespeare. She married him in 1582.

hath·a yo·ga /ˈhäTHə/ ▶n. a yoga system of physical exercises and breathing control. [from Sanskrit *haṭha* 'force' and YOGA.]

Hath·or /ˈhaTHər/ Egyptian Mythol. a sky goddess, the patron of love and joy, usually represented as a cow.

hat·pin /ˈhatˌpin/ ▶n. a long pin that holds a woman's hat in position by securing it to her hair.

hat·rack /ˈhatˌrak/ ▶n. a tall freestanding post fitted with large hooks for hanging hats on.

ha·tred /ˈhātrid/ ▶n. intense dislike or ill will. [ME: from HATE + -*red* (from OE *rǣden* 'condition').]

Hat·shep·sut /hatˈSHepˌso͞ot/ (died 1482 BC), queen of Egypt; reigned *c.*1503–1482 BC.

hat·ter /ˈhatər/ ▶n. a person who makes and sells hats.

Hat·ter·as, Cape /ˈhatərəs/ a peninsula in eastern North Carolina.

hat trick ▶n. three successes of the same kind, esp. consecutive ones within a limited period: *the band completes the trilogy, making for a dubious musical hat trick.* ■ (chiefly in ice hockey or soccer) the scoring of three goals in a game by one player. [19th C.: orig. referring to a cricket club's presentation of a new hat (or some equivalent) to a bowler taking three wickets successively.]

hau·berk /ˈhôbərk/ ▶n. hist. a piece of armor originally covering only the neck and shoulders but later consisting of a full-length coat of mail or military tunic. [ME: from OFr. *hauberc*, *hausberc*, orig. denoting protection for the neck, of Gmc. origin.]

haugh·ty /ˈhôtē/ ▶adj. (**haugh·ti·er**, **haugh·ti·est**) arrogantly superior and disdainful: *a look of haughty disdain.* —**haugh·ti·ly** adv. **haugh·ti·ness** n. [16th C.: extended form of obs. *haught*, earlier *haut*, from OFr., from L. *altus* 'high.']

haul /hôl/ ▶v. **1** [trans.] (of a person) pull or drag with effort or force. ■ Naut. pull on (a rope). ■ (**haul oneself**) propel or pull oneself with difficulty. ■ informal force (someone) to appear for reprimand or trial. ■ [intrans.] (of a person) pull hard. **2** [trans.] (of a vehicle) pull (an attached trailer) behind it. ■ transport in a truck or cart: *haul trash.* **3** [intrans.] (esp. of a sailing ship) make an abrupt change of course. ▶n. **1** an

amount of something gained or acquired. ■ a quantity of something that was stolen or is possessed illegally. ■ the number of points, medals, or titles won by a person or team in a sporting event or over a period. ■ a number of fish caught. **2** a distance to be traversed: *the thirty-mile haul to Tallahassee.* See also LONG HAUL, SHORT HAUL.
– PHRASES **haul ass** informal move or leave fast. **haul off** informal leave; depart. ■ withdraw a little in preparation for some action: *he hauled off and smacked the kid.* [16th C.: var. of HALE².]

haul·age /'hôlij/ ▶ **n.** the action or process of hauling. ■ the commercial transport of goods: *road haulage.* ■ a charge for such transport.

haul·er /'hôlər/ ▶ **n.** a person or company employed in the transport of goods or materials by road. ■ a truck used for the transport of goods or materials.

haulm /hôm/ esp. Brit. ▶ **n.** a stalk or stem. ■ the stalks or stems collectively of peas, beans, or potatoes without the pods or tubers. [OE *healm, halm*, of Gmc. origin; rel. to Ger. *Halm*, L. *culmus* 'stalk.']

haunch /hônch; hänch/ ▶ **n. 1** a buttock and thigh considered together, in a human or animal. ■ the leg and loin of an animal as food. **2** Archit. the side of an arch, between the crown and the pier.
– PHRASES **sit on one's haunches** squat with the haunches resting on the backs of the heels. [ME: from OFr. *hanche*, of Gmc. origin.]

haunt /hônt; hänt/ ▶ **v.** [trans.] (of a ghost) manifest itself at (a place) regularly. ■ (of a person) frequent (a place). ■ be persistently and disturbingly present, esp. in someone's mind. ▶ **n.** a place frequented: *I revisited my old haunts.* — **haunt·er n.** [ME (in the sense 'frequent (a place)'): from OFr. *hanter*, of Gmc. origin; distantly rel. to HOME.]

haunt·ed /'hôntid; 'hän-/ ▶ **adj.** (of a place) frequented by a ghost: *it looked like a classic haunted mansion.* ■ showing signs of mental anguish or torment.

haunt·ing /'hônting; 'hän-/ ▶ **adj.** poignant and evocative; difficult to ignore or forget: *haunting beauty.* — **haunt·ing·ly adv.**

Haupt·mann /'houpt,män/, Gerhart (1862–1946), German playwright. He wrote *Before Sunrise* (1889). Nobel Prize for Literature (1912).

Hau·sa /'housə; 'houzə/ ▶ **n.** (pl. same or **-sas**) **1** a member of a people in and around Nigeria. **2** the Chadic language of this people, spoken mainly in Nigeria and Niger, and widely used as a lingua franca in parts of West Africa. ▶ **adj.** of or relating to this people or their language. [the name in Hausa.]

haus·frau /'hous,frou/ ▶ **n.** a German housewife. ■ informal a woman regarded as overly efficient. [18th C.: from Ger., from *Haus* 'house' + *Frau* 'woman, wife.']

haus·tel·lum /hô'steləm/ ▶ **n.** (pl. **haus·tel·la** /hô'stelə/) Zool. the sucking organ or proboscis of an insect or crustacean. — **haus·tel·late** /hô'stelit; 'hôstə,lāt/ **adj.** [19th C.: mod. L. dimin. of *haustrum* 'scoop,' from *haust-* 'drawn in,' from the v. *haurire*.]

haus·to·ri·um /hô'stôrēəm/ ▶ **n.** (pl. **haus·to·ri·a** /hô'stôrēə/) Bot. a slender projection from the root of a parasitic plant, such as a dodder, or from the hyphae of a parasitic fungus, enabling the parasite to penetrate the tissues of its host and absorb nutrients from it. — **haus·to·ri·al** /hôstôrēəl/ **adj.** [19th C.: mod. L., from L. *haustor* 'thing that draws in,' from the v. *haurire*.]

haute /ōt/ (or **haut**) ▶ **adj.** elegant or high-class.

haute bour·geoi·sie /,ōt bo͝ozhwä'zē/ ▶ **n.** (**the haute bourgeoisie**) [treated as sing. or pl.] the upper middle class. [19th C.: Fr., lit. 'high bourgeoisie.']

haute cou·ture /,ōt ko͞o'to͝or/ ▶ **n.** the designing and making of high-quality fashionable clothes by leading fashion houses, esp. to order. ■ fashion houses that engage in such work. ■ clothes of this kind. [20th C.: Fr., lit. 'high dressmaking.']

haute cui·sine /,ōt kwə'zēn/ ▶ **n.** the preparation and cooking of high-quality food. ■ food produced in such a way. [20th C.: Fr., lit. 'high cookery.']

Haute-Nor·man·die /,ōt ,nôrmäN'dē/ a region in northern France, on the coast of the English Channel.

hau·teur /hō'tər/ ▶ **n.** haughtiness of manner; disdainful pride. [Fr., from *haut* 'high.']

haut monde /ō 'mônd; 'mänd/ ▶ **n.** (**the haut monde**) fashionable society. [19th C.: Fr., lit. 'high world.']

Ha·va·na¹ /hə'vanə/ the capital of Cuba, on the northern coast; pop. 2,160,000. Spanish name LA HABANA.

Ha·van·a² /hə'vanə; hə'vänə/ ▶ **n.** a cigar made in Cuba or from Cuban tobacco.

have /hav/ **v.** (**has** ; past **had**) ▶ **v.** [trans.] **1** (also **have got**) possess, own, or hold. ■ possess or be provided with (a quality, characteristic, or feature). ■ (**have oneself**) informal provide or indulge oneself with (something): *he had himself two highballs.* ■ be made up of; comprise. ■ used to indicate a particular relationship: *he's got three children.* ■ be able to make use of (something available or at one's disposal): *how much time have I got?* ■ have gained (a qualification): *he's got a BA in English.* ■ possess as an intellectual attainment; know (a language or subject): *I had only a little French.* **2** experience; undergo. ■ (also **have got**) suffer from (an illness, ailment, or disability). ■ (also **have got**) let (a feeling or thought) come into one's mind; hold in the mind: *he had the strong impression that someone was watching him.* ■ [with past part.] experience or suffer the specified action happening or being done to (something): *she had her bag stolen.* ■ [trans.] cause (someone or something) to be in a particular state or condition: *I want to have everything ready in good time.* ■ (also **have got**) informal have put (someone) at a disadvantage in an argument (said either to acknowledge that one has no answer to a point or to show that one knows one's opponent has no answer): *"Why are your dreams full of violence?' She had me there.* ■ [with past part.] cause (something) to be done for one by someone else: *have your carpet laid by a professional.* ■ tell or arrange for something to be done: [trans.] *she had her long hair cut.* ■ (usu. **be had**) informal cheat or deceive (someone): *I'd been had.* ■ vulgar slang engage in sexual intercourse with (someone). **3** (**have to do something** or **have got to do something**) be obliged or find it necessary to do the specified thing: *we've got to plan for the future.* ■ [trans.] need or be obliged to do (something): *he's got a lot to do.* ■ be strongly recommended to do something: *you have to try our summer house.* ■ be certain or inevitable to happen or be the case: *there has to be a catch.* **4** perform the action indicated by the noun specified (used esp. in spoken English as an alternative to a more specific verb): *he had a look around.* ■ organize and bring about: *have a party.* ■ eat or drink. ■ give birth to or be due to give birth to. **5** (also **have got**) show (a personal attribute or quality) by one's actions or attitude: *he had little patience.* ■ [often in imper.] exercise or show (mercy, pity, etc.) toward another person: *God have mercy on me!* ■ [with negative] not accept; refuse to tolerate. **6** (also **have got**) [trans.] place or keep (something) in a particular position. ■ hold or grasp (someone or something) in a particular way: *he had me by the throat.* **7** be the recipient of (something sent, given, or done). ■ take or invite into one's home so as to provide care or entertainment, esp. for a limited period. ▶ **aux. v.** used with a past participle to form the perfect, pluperfect, and future perfect tenses, and the conditional mood: *I have finished | he had asked her | she will have left by now | I could have helped, had I known | "Have you seen him?" "Yes, I have."* ▶ **n.** /hav/ (**the haves**) informal people with plenty of money and possessions.
– PHRASES **have a care** (or **an eye**, etc.) see CARE, EYE, etc. **have got it bad** informal be very powerfully affected emotionally, esp. by love. ■ be in a situation where one is treated badly or exploited. **have had it** informal **1** be in a very poor condition; be beyond repair or past its best. ■ be extremely tired. ■ have lost all chance of survival. **2** be unable to tolerate someone or something any longer: ***I've had it with him—!*** **have it 1** [with clause] express the view that (used to indicate that the speaker is reporting something that they do not necessarily believe to be fact): *rumor had it.* **2** win a decision, esp. after a vote: *the ayes have it.* **3** have found the answer to something: *"I have it!"* **have it both ways** see BOTH. **have it coming** deserve punishment or downfall. **have (got) it in for** informal feel a particular dislike of (someone) and behave in a hostile manner toward them. **have (got) it in one (to do something)** informal have the capacity or potential (to do something). **have it out** informal attempt to resolve a contentious matter by confronting someone and engaging in a frank discussion or argument. **have (got) nothing on** informal **1** be not nearly as good as: *bright as they were, they had nothing on Sally.* **2 have nothing** (or **something**) **on someone** know nothing (or something) discreditable or incriminating about someone. **have nothing to do with** see DO¹. **have one too many** see MANY. **have —— to do with** see DO¹.
– PHRASAL VERBS **have at** attempt or attack forcefully or aggressively. **have (got) something on** be wearing something. **have something out** undergo an operation to extract the part of the body specified. [OE *habban*, of Gmc. origin; rel. to Du. *hebben* and Ger. *haben*, also prob. to HEAVE.]

Ha·vel /'hävəl/, Václav (1936–), Czech playwright and president of Czechoslovakia 1989–92 and of the Czech Republic 1993–2003. His plays include *The Garden Party* (1963).

have·lock /'hav,läk/ ▶ **n.** a cloth covering for a military cap that extends downward to protect the neck from sun and weather. [19th C.: named after Sir Henry *Havelock* (1795–1857), an English general who served in India.]

havelock

ha·ven /'hāvən/ ▶ **n.** a place of safety or refuge. ■ an inlet providing shelter for ships or boats; a harbor. [OE *hæfen*, from ON *hǫfn*; rel. to Du. *haven*, Ger. *Hafen* 'harbor.']

have-nots ▶ **plural n.** (usu. **the have-nots**) informal economically disadvantaged people.

have·n't /'havənt/ ▶ **contr.** have not.

ha·ver /'hāvər/ ▶ **v.** [intrans.] Scot. talk foolishly; babble. ▶ **n.** (also **havers**) Scot. foolish talk; nonsense. [18th C.: of unknown origin.]

hav·er·sack /'havər,sak/ ▶ **n.** a small, sturdy bag carried on the back or over the shoulder. [18th C.: from Fr. *havresac*, from obs. Ger. *Habersack*, 'a bag for oats,' from dial. *Haber* 'oats' + *Sack* 'sack, bag.']

Ha·ver·sian ca·nal /hə'vərzhən/ ▶ **n.** Anat. any of the minute tubes that form a network in bone and contain blood vessels. [19th C.: named after Clopton *Havers* (1650–1702), English anatomist.]

hav·oc /'havək/ ▶ **n.** widespread destruction. ■ great confusion or disorder. ▶ **v.** (**hav·ocked, hav·ock·ing**) [trans.] archaic lay waste to; devastate.
– PHRASES **play havoc with** completely disrupt; cause serious damage to. [ME: from Anglo-Norman Fr. *havok*, signal for plundering.]

haw¹ /hô/ ▶ **n.** the red fruit of the hawthorn. [OE *haga*, of Gmc. origin; prob. rel. to HEDGE.]

haw² ▶ **n.** the third eyelid or nictitating membrane in certain mammals, esp. dogs and cats. [ME (denoting a discharge from the eye): of unknown origin.]

Ha·wai·i /hə'wī,ē; -'wä,ē/ a state in the US, comprising most of a group of islands in the North Pacific Ocean, about 3,000 miles (4,830 km) west of mainland US; pop. 1,211,537; capital, Honolulu (on Oahu); statehood, Aug. 21, 1959 (50). First settled by Polynesians, Hawaii was discovered by Captain James Cook in 1778. It was annexed by the US in 1898. Former name **Sandwich Islands.** ■ the largest island in the state of Hawaii.

Hawaii-Aleutian Standard Time (abbr.: **HST**) ▶ **n.** the standard time in a zone including the Hawaiian Islands and the western Aleutian Islands. Also called **Hawaiian Standard Time**

Ha·wai·ian /hə'wīən; -'woi-ən/ ▶ **n. 1** a native or inhabitant of Hawaii. **2** the Austronesian language of Hawaii. ▶ **adj.** of or relating to Hawaii, its people, or their language.

Ha·wai·ian goose ▶ **n.** a rare goose (*Branta sandvicensis*) native to Hawaii, now breeding chiefly in captivity. Also called **nene.**

Ha·wai·ian gui·tar ▶ **n.** a steel-stringed guitar in which a characteristic glissando effect is produced by sliding a metal bar along the strings as they are plucked.

Ha·wai·ian hon·ey·creep·er ▶ **n.** see **honeycreeper** (sense 2).

haw·finch /'hô,finCH/ ▶ **n.** a large Old World finch (genus *Coccothraustes*) with a massive bill for cracking open cherrystones and other hard seeds. [17th C.: from **haw**[1] + **finch.**]

hawk[1] /hôk/ ▶ **n. 1** a diurnal bird of prey (*Accipiter* and other genera, family Accipitridae) with broad rounded wings and a long tail, typically taking prey by surprise with a short chase. Compare with **falcon.** ■ Falconry any diurnal bird of prey used in falconry. **2** a person who advocates an aggressive or warlike policy, esp. in foreign affairs. Compare with **dove**[1] (sense 2). ▶ **v.** [intrans.] **1** (of a person) hunt game with a trained hawk. **2** (of a bird or dragonfly) hunt on the wing for food.
– PHRASES **have eyes like a hawk** miss nothing of what is going on around one. **watch someone like a hawk** keep a vigilant eye on someone, esp. to check that they do nothing wrong. — **hawk·ish adj. hawk·ish·ly adv. hawk·ish·ness n.** [OE *hafoc, heafoc*, of Gmc. origin; rel. to Du. *havik* and Ger. *Habicht*.]

hawk[2] ▶ **v.** [trans.] carry around and offer (goods) for sale, typically advertising them by shouting. [15th C.: back-form. from **hawker**[1].]

hawk[3] ▶ **v.** [intrans.] clear the throat noisily. ■ [trans.] (**hawk something up**) bring phlegm up from the throat. [16th C.: prob. imitative.]

hawk[4] ▶ **n.** a plasterer's square board with a handle underneath for carrying plaster or mortar. [ME: of unknown origin.]

Hawke /hôk/, Bob (1929–), prime minister of Australia 1983–91; full name *Robert James Lee Hawke*.

hawk·er[1] /'hôkər/ ▶ **n.** a person who travels around selling goods, typically advertising them by shouting. [16th C.: prob. from Low Ger. or Du. and rel. to **huckster.**]

hawk·er[2] ▶ **n.** a falconer.

hawk-eyed ▶ **adj.** having very good eyesight. ■ watching carefully; vigilant.

Hawk·ing /'hôkiNG/, Stephen William (1942–), English physicist. He worked with space-time, quantum mechanics, and black holes.

hawk moth

hawk moth (also **hawk·moth**) ▶ **n.** a large swift-flying moth (family Sphingidae) with a stout body and narrow forewings, typically feeding on nectar while hovering. Also called **sphinx.** See also **hornworm.**

hawks·beard /'hôks,bi(ə)rd/ (also **hawk's beard**) ▶ **n.** a plant (genus *Crepis*) of the daisy family that resembles a dandelion but has a branched stem with several flowers.

hawksbill

hawks·bill /'hôks,bil/ (also **hawksbill turtle**) ▶ **n.** a small tropical sea turtle (*Eretmochelys imbricata*, family Cheloniidae) with hooked jaws and overlapping horny plates on the shell, extensively hunted as the traditional source of tortoiseshell.

hawk·weed /'hôk,wēd/ ▶ **n.** a widely distributed plant (genus *Hieracium*) of the daisy family, typically having small yellow dandelionlike flowerheads and often growing as a weed. [OE, rendering L. *hieracium*, based on Gk. *hierax* 'hawk.']

Ha·worth /'hou,wərTH; 'ô-/, Sir Walter Norman (1883–1950), English chemist. He was the first to make a vitamin artificially. Nobel Prize for Chemistry (1937, shared with Paul Karrer 1889-1971).

hawse /hôz/ ▶ **n.** the part of a ship's bows through which the anchor cables pass. ■ the space between the head of an anchored vessel and the anchors. [ME *halse*, prob. from ON *háls* 'neck, ship's bow.']

hawse·hole /'hôz,hōl/ ▶ **n.** a hole in the bow of a ship through which an anchor cable passes.

hawse·pipe /'hôz,pīp/ ▶ **n.** an inclined pipe leading from a hawsehole to the side of a ship, containing the shank of the anchor when the anchor is raised.

haw·ser /'hôzər/ ▶ **n.** a thick rope or cable for mooring or towing a ship. [ME: from Anglo-Norman Fr. *haucer*, from OFr. *haucier* 'to hoist,' based on L. *altus* 'high.']

haw·ser-laid ▶ **adj. 1** another term for **cable-laid. 2** esp. hist. denoting the ordinary type of rope commonly used in ships' rigging.

haw·thorn /'hô,THôrn/ ▶ **n.** a thorny shrub or tree (genus *Crataegus*) of the rose family, with white, pink, or red blossoms and small dark red fruits (haws). Native to north temperate regions, it is commonly used for hedges. [OE *hagathorn*, prob. meaning lit. 'hedge thorn' (see **haw**[1], **thorn**).]

Haw·thorne /'hô,THôrn/, Nathaniel (1804–64), US writer. His novels include *The Scarlet Letter* (1850) and *The House of the Seven Gables* (1851).

Haw·thorne ef·fect ▶ **n.** the alteration of behavior by the subjects of a study because they are being observed. [1960s: from *Hawthorne*, one of the Western Electric Company's plants in Chicago.]

Hay /hā/, John Milton (1838–1905), US diplomat. As US secretary of state 1898–1905, he negotiated the Hay–Pauncefote Treaty 1901, which made construction of the Panama Canal possible.

hay /hā/ ▶ **n.** grass that has been mown and dried for use as fodder.
– PHRASES **hit the hay** informal go to bed. **make hay (while the sun shines)** proverb make good use of an opportunity while it lasts. [OE *hēg, hieg, hig*, of Gmc. origin; rel. to Du. *hooi* and Ger. *Heu*, also to **hew.**]

hay·cock /'hā,käk/ ▶ **n.** a conical heap of hay in a field.

Hay·dn /'hīdn/, Franz Joseph (1732–1809), Austrian composer. His work includes the oratorio *The Creation* (1796–98).

Ha·yek /'hīək/, Friedrich August von (1899–1992), British economist; born in Austria. He was a leading advocate of the free market. Nobel Prize for Economics (1974, shared with Gunnar Myrdal).

Hayes[1] /hāz/, Helen (1900–93), US actress; born *Helen Hayes Brown*; known as **the first lady of the American theater.** Her Broadway career spanned seven decades and included *Happy Birthday* (1946). She also appeared in movies such as *The Sin of Madelon Claudet* (1932) and *Airport* (1970).

Hayes[2], Rutherford Birchard (1822–93), 19th president of the US 1877–81. A Republican, he served in the US House of Representatives 1865–68 and as governor of Ohio 1868–72, 1876–77. While president, Reconstruction in the South came to an end. His use of federal troops during the railroad strikes of 1877 cost him popular support.

hay fe·ver ▶ **n.** an allergy caused by pollen or dust in which the mucous membranes of the eyes and nose are itchy and inflamed.

hay·field /'hā,fēld/ ▶ **n.** a field where hay is being or is to be made.

hay·fork /'hā,fôrk/ ▶ **n.** a hand tool for lifting hay; pitchfork. ■ a machine for lifting hay.

hay·loft /'hā,lôft/ ▶ **n.** a loft over a stable or barn used for storing hay or straw.

hay·mak·er /'hā,mākər/ ▶ **n. 1** a person who is involved in making hay. ■ an apparatus for shaking and drying hay. **2** informal a forceful blow: *a stinging haymaker.* — **hay·mak·ing n.**

Hay·mar·ket Square /'hā,märkit/ a site in Chicago, Illinois, where an 1886 bombing during a labor demonstration took place.

hay·mow /'hā,mō/ ▶ **n.** a stack of hay. ■ a part of a barn in which hay is stored.

hay·rick /'hā,rik/ ▶ **n.** another term for **haystack.**

hay·ride /'hā,rīd/ ▶ **n.** a ride taken for pleasure in a wagon carrying hay.

hay·seed /'hā,sēd/ ▶ **n. 1** grass seed obtained from hay. **2** informal a simple, unsophisticated person.

hay·stack /'hā,stak/ ▶ **n.** a packed pile of hay, typically with a pointed or ridged top.

Hay·ward /'hāwərd/ a city in north central California; pop. 111,498.

hay·wire /'hā,wī(ə)r/ ▶ **adj.** informal erratic; out of control. [20th C.: from **hay** + **wire.**]

haz·ard /'hazərd/ ▶ **n. 1** a danger or risk. ■ a potential source of danger: *a fire hazard | a health hazard.* ■ a permanent feature of a golf course that presents an obstruction to playing a shot, such as a bunker or stream. **2** literary chance; probability. **3** a gambling game using two dice, in which the chances are complicated by arbitrary rules. ▶ **v.** [trans.] **1** venture to say (something). **2** put (something) at risk of being lost. [ME (sense 3): from OFr. *hasard*, from Sp. *azar*, from Arab. *az-zahr* 'chance, luck,' from Pers. *zār* or Turk. *zar* 'dice.']

haz·ard·ous /'hazərdəs/ ▶ **adj.** risky; dangerous. — **haz·ard·ous·ly adv. haz·ard·ous·ness n.**

haze¹ /hāz/ ▶ **n.** a slight obscuration of the lower atmosphere, typically caused by fine suspended particles. ■ a tenuous cloud of something such as vapor or smoke in the air: *a faint haze of steam.* ■ [in sing.] fig. a state of mental obscurity or confusion. [18th C. (orig. denoting fog or hoarfrost): prob. a back-form. from HAZY.]

haze² ▶ **v. 1** [trans.] force (a new or potential recruit to the military, a college fraternity, etc.) to perform strenuous, humiliating, or dangerous tasks. **2** [trans.] drive (cattle) in a specified direction while on horseback. — **haz·ing n.** [17th C.: perh. rel. to obs. Fr. *haser* 'tease or insult.']

ha·zel /ˈhāzəl/ ▶ **n. 1** a temperate shrub or small tree (genus *Corylus*) of the birch family, with broad leaves, bearing prominent male catkins in spring and round hard-shelled edible nuts in autumn. **2** a reddish-brown or greenish-brown color, esp. of someone's eyes. [OE *hæsel*, rel. to Ger. *Hasel*, L. *corylus*.]

ha·zel·nut /ˈhāzəlˌnət/ ▶ **n.** a round brown hard-shelled nut that is the edible fruit of the hazel.

Haz·litt /ˈhazlit/, William (1778–1830), English writer. His works include *Table Talk* (1821).

haz·mat /ˈhazˌmat/ (also **haz·mats**) ▶ **n.** dangerous substances; hazardous material.

ha·zy /ˈhāzē/ ▶ **adj.** (**ha·zi·er, ha·zi·est**) covered by a haze. ■ vague, indistinct, or ill-defined: *hazy memories.* — **ha·zi·ly adv. ha·zi·ness n.** [17th C. (in nautical use in the sense 'foggy'): of unknown origin.]

haz·zan /KHäˈzän; ˈKHäzən/ ▶ **n.** (pl. **haz·za·nim** /ˌKHäzäˈnēm; KHäˈzônim/) another term for CANTOR (sense 1). [17th C.: from Heb. *ḥazzān* 'cantor,' possibly from Assyrian *hazannu* 'mayor, village headman.']

Hb ▶ **symb.** hemoglobin.

H-bomb ▶ **n.** another term for HYDROGEN BOMB.

HBP ▶ **abbr.** Baseball (in box scores, of a batter) hit by a pitch.

HC ▶ **abbr.** ■ Holy Communion. ■ (in the UK) House of Commons. ■ hydrocarbon.

h.c. ▶ **abbr.** honoris causa.

HCF ▶ **abbr.** Math. highest common factor.

HCFC ▶ **abbr.** hydrochlorofluorocarbon.

HCG ▶ **abbr.** human chorionic gonadotropin.

H.D. see DOOLITTLE.

hd. ▶ **abbr.** ■ hand. ■ head.

hdbk. ▶ **abbr.** handbook.

HDD Comput. ▶ **abbr.** hard disk drive.

HDL ▶ **abbr.** high-density lipoprotein.

hdqrs. ▶ **abbr.** headquarters.

HDTV ▶ **abbr.** high-definition television.

hdwe. ▶ **abbr.** hardware.

HE ▶ **abbr.** ■ high explosive. ■ His Eminence. ■ His or Her Excellency.

He ▶ **symb.** the chemical element helium.

he /hē/ ▶ **pron.** [third person sing.] used to refer to a man, boy, or male animal previously mentioned or easily identified. ■ used to refer to a person or animal of unspecified sex (in modern use, now chiefly replaced by "he or she" or "they": *every child needs to know that he is loved.* ■ any person (in modern use, now chiefly replaced by "anyone" or "the person"): *he who is silent consents.* ▶ **n.** [in sing.] a male; a man: *is that a he or a she?* ■ [in comb.] male: *a he-goat.* [OE *he, hē*, of Gmc. origin; rel. to Du. *hij*.]

head /hed/ ▶ **n. 1** the upper part of the human body, or the front or upper part of the body of an animal, typically separated from the rest of the body by a neck, and containing the brain, mouth, and sense organs. ■ the head regarded as the location of intellect, imagination, and memory: *whatever comes into my head.* ■ (**head for**) an aptitude for or tolerance of. ■ informal a headache, esp. one resulting from intoxication. ■ the height or length of a head as a measure: *half a head taller than he was.* ■ [usu. in comb.] a habitual user of an illicit drug: *pothead.* ■ [usu. in comb.] a fan or enthusiast: *metalheads.* ■ (**heads**) the obverse side of a coin (used when tossing a coin): *heads or tails?* ■ the antlers of a deer. **2** a thing having the appearance of a head either in form or in relation to a whole, in particular: ■ the cutting, striking, or operational end of a tool, weapon, or mechanism. ■ the flattened or knobbed end of a nail, pin, screw, or match. ■ the ornamented top of a pillar or column. ■ a compact mass of leaves or flowers at the top of a stem, esp. a capitulum. ■ the edible leafy part at the top of the stem of such green vegetables as cabbage and lettuce. ■ one salable unit of certain vegetables, such as cabbage or cauliflower. **3** the front, forward, or upper part or end of something, in particular: ■ the upper end of a table or bed. ■ the flat end of a cask or drum. ■ the front of a line or procession. ■ the top of a page. ■ short for HEADLINE. ■ the top of a flight of stairs or steps. ■ the source of a river or stream. ■ the end of a lake or inlet at which a river enters. ■ [usu. in place names] a promontory. ■ the top of a ship's mast. ■ the bows of a ship. ■ the fully developed top of a pimple, boil, or abscess. ■ the foam on top of a glass of beer. ■ short for CYLINDER HEAD. **4** a person in charge of something; a director or leader. ■ Brit. short for HEADMASTER, or HEADMISTRESS. **5** Gram. the word that governs all the other words in a phrase in which it is used, having the same grammatical function as the whole phrase. **6** a person considered as a numerical unit. ■ [treated as pl.] a number of cattle or game as specified: *seventy head of dairy cattle.* **7** a component in an audio, video, or information system by which information is transferred from an electrical signal to the recording medium, or vice versa. ■ short for PRINTHEAD. **8** a body of water kept at a particular height in order to provide a supply at sufficient pressure: *an 8m head of water in the shafts.* ■ the pressure exerted by such water or by a confined body of steam: *a good head of steam on the gauge.* **9** Naut., slang a toilet, esp. on a boat or ship. **10** Geol. a superficial deposit of rock fragments, formed at the edge of an ice sheet by repeated freezing and thawing and then moved downhill. ▶ **adj.** [attrib.] chief; principal: *the head waiter.* ▶ **v.** [trans.] **1** be in the leading position on. ■ be in charge of: *she headed up the Centennial program.* **2** (usu. **be headed**) give a title or caption to. ■ [as adj.] (**headed**) having a printed heading. **3** [intrans.] (also **be headed**) move in a specified direction: *he was heading for the exit.* ■ (**head for**) appear to be moving inevitably toward (something, esp. something undesirable). ■ [trans.] direct or steer in a specified direction. **4** Soccer shoot or pass (the ball) with the head. **5** lop off the upper part or branches of (a plant or tree). **6** [intrans.] (of a lettuce or cabbage) form a head.

– PHRASES **be banging** (or **knocking**) **one's head against a brick wall** be doggedly attempting the impossible and suffering in the process. **bang** (or **knock**) **people's heads together** reprimand people severely, esp. in an attempt to stop their arguing. **be hanging over someone's head** (of something unpleasant) threaten to affect someone at any moment. **be on someone's** (**own**) **head** be someone's sole responsibility. **bite** (or **snap**) **someone's head off** reply sharply and brusquely to someone. **come to a head** reach a crisis. ■ suppurate, fester. **enter someone's head** [usu. with negative] occur to someone: *such an idea never entered my head.* **from head to toe** (or **foot**) all over one's body. **go to someone's head** (of alcohol) make someone dizzy or slightly drunk. ■ (of success) make someone conceited. **get something into one's** (or **someone's**) **head** come or cause (someone) to realize or understand. **—— one's head off** talk, laugh, etc., unrestrainedly: *singing his head off.* **head over heels 1** turning over completely in forward motion, as in a somersault. **2** (also **head over heels in love**) madly in love. **a head start** an advantage granted or gained at the beginning of something. **heads will roll** people will be dismissed or forced to resign. **head to head** in open, direct conflict or competition. **keep one's head** remain calm. **keep one's head above water** avoid succumbing to difficulties, typically debt. **keep one's head down** remain inconspicuous in difficult or dangerous times. **lose one's head** lose self-control; panic. **make head or tail of** (or **heads or tails**) [usu. with negative] understand at all. **off the top of one's head** without careful thought or investigation. **over someone's head 1** (also **above someone's head**) beyond someone's ability to understand. **2** without someone's knowledge or involvement, esp. when they have a right to it. ■ with disregard for someone else's (stronger) claim. **put their** (or **our** or **your**) **heads together** consult and work together. **put something into someone's head** suggest something to someone. **take it into one's head to do something** impetuously decide to do something. **turn someone's head** make someone conceited. **turn heads** attract a great deal of attention or interest.

– PHRASAL VERBS **head someone/something off** intercept and turn aside: *he ran up the road to head off approaching cars.* ■ forestall. **head up** Sailing steer toward the wind. — **head·ed adj.** [in comb.] *bald-headed men.* **head·less adj.** [OE *hēafod*, of Gmc. origin; rel. to Du. *hoofd* and Ger. *Haupt*.]

-head¹ ▶ **suffix** equivalent to -HOOD. [ME *-hed, -hede*.]

-head² ▶ **comb. form 1** denoting the front, forward, or upper part or end of a specified thing: *masthead.* **2** in nouns used informally to express disparagement of a person: *airhead.* **3** in nouns used informally to denote an addict or habitual user of a specified drug: *crackhead.* ■ forming informal nouns denoting an enthusiast of a particular thing: *geeky tech-heads.*

head·ache /ˈhedˌāk/ ▶ **n.** a continuous pain in the head. ■ informal a thing or person that causes worry or trouble; a problem: *an administrative headache.* — **head·ach·y adj.**

head·band /ˈhedˌband/ ▶ **n. 1** a band of fabric worn around the head. **2** an ornamental strip of colored silk fastened to the top of the spine of a book.

head·bang·er /ˈhedˌbaNGər/ ▶ **n.** informal a fan or performer of heavy metal music. Also called METALHEAD.

head·board /ˈhedˌbôrd/ ▶ **n.** an upright panel forming or placed behind the head of a bed.

head-butt /ˈhedˌbət/ ▶ **n.** a forceful thrust with the top of the head, esp. into another person. ▶ **v.** [trans.] attack (someone) with a thrust of the head.

head case ▶ **n.** informal a mentally ill or unstable person.

head·cheese /ˈhedˌCHēz/ ▶ **n.** cooked meat from a pig's or calf's head that is made into a loaf with aspic.

head cold ▶ **n.** a common cold.

head count ▶ **n.** an instance of counting the number of people present. ■ a total number of people, esp. the number of people employed in a particular organization: *by reducing your head count you can reach this quarter's goals.*

head·dress /ˈhedˌdres/ ▶ **n.** an ornamental covering or band for the head, esp. for ceremonial occasions.

head·er /ˈhedər/ ▶ **n. 1** Soccer a shot or pass made with the head. **2** informal a headlong fall or dive. **3** a brick or stone laid at right angles to the face of a wall. Compare with STRETCHER (sense 4). **4** a line or block of text

American Indian headdress

appearing at the top of each page of a book or document. Compare with FOOTER (sense 2). **5** (also **header tank**) a raised tank of water maintaining pressure in a plumbing system. **6** a beam crossing and supporting the ends of joists, studs, or rafters.

head first ▶ adj. & adv. with the head in front of the rest of the body: [as adv.] *she dived head first into the water.* ▪ without sufficient forethought.

head·ful /ˈhed,fo͝ol/ ▶ n. **1** a quantity sufficient to cover the head: *a headful of tight curls.* **2** a great amount (of knowledge or information).

head gas·ket ▶ n. the gasket that fits between the cylinder head and the cylinders or cylinder block in an internal combustion engine.

head·gear /ˈhed,gi(ə)r/ ▶ n. hats, helmets, and other items worn on the head: *protective headgear.* ▪ orthodontic equipment worn on the head and attached to braces on the teeth. ▪ the parts of a harness around a horse's head.

head·hunt·er /ˈhed,həntər/ ▶ n. a person who searches for suitable candidates to fill business positions. ▪ a member of a society that collects the heads of dead enemies as trophies. — **head·hunt** v. **head·hunt·ing** n.

head·ing /ˈhediNG/ ▶ n. **1** a title at the head of a page or section of a book: *chapter headings.* ▪ a division or section of a subject; a class or category. **2** a direction or bearing: *a heading of 90 degrees.* **3** a horizontal passage made in preparation for building a tunnel. ▪ Mining another term for DRIFT (sense 4). **4** a strip of cloth at the top of a curtain above the hooks or wire that suspend the curtain.

head·land /ˈhedlənd; -,land/ ▶ n. **1** a narrow piece of land that projects from a coastline into the sea. **2** a strip of land left unplowed at the end of a field.

head·light /ˈhed,līt/ (also **head·lamp**) ▶ n. a powerful light at the front of a motor vehicle or railroad engine.

head·line /ˈhed,līn/ ▶ n. a heading at the top of an article or page in a newspaper or magazine. ▪ (**the headlines**) the most important items of news in a newspaper or in a broadcast news bulletin. ▶ v. **1** [trans.] provide with a headline. **2** [trans.] appear as the star performer at (a concert).

head·lin·er /ˈhed,līnər/ ▶ n. a performer or act that is promoted as the star attraction.

head·lock /ˈhed,läk/ ▶ n. a method of restraining someone by holding an arm firmly around their head.

head·long /ˈhed,lôNG; -,läNG/ ▶ adv. & adj. **1** [as adv.] with the head foremost: *he fell headlong into the tent.* **2** in a rush; with reckless haste. [ME *headling* (from HEAD + the adverbial suffix *-ling*), alt. by association with -LONG.]

head louse ▶ n. a louse (*Pediculus humanus capitis*) that infests the scalp and hair of the human head and is especially common among schoolchildren.

head·mas·ter /ˈhed,mastər/ ▶ n. (esp. in private schools) the man in charge of a school; the principal. — **head·mas·ter·ly** adj.

head·mis·tress /ˈhed,mistris/ ▶ n. (esp. in private schools) the woman in charge of a school; the principal.

head·note /ˈhed,nōt/ ▶ n. a note inserted at the head of an article or document, commenting on the content. ▪ Law a summary of a decided case prefixed to the case report, setting out the principles behind the decision and an outline of the facts.

head-on ▶ adj. & adv. **1** with or involving the front of a vehicle: [as attrib. adj.] *a head-on collision* | [as adv.] *they hit a bus head-on.* **2** with or involving direct confrontation.

head·phones /ˈhed,fōnz/ ▶ plural n. a pair of earphones typically joined by a band placed over the head, for listening to audio signals such as music or speech.

head·piece /ˈhed,pēs/ ▶ n. **1** a device worn on the head as an ornament or to serve a function. **2** an illustration or ornamental motif printed at the head of a chapter in a book. **3** the part of a halter or bridle that fits over the top of a horse's head behind the ears.

head·quar·ter /ˈhed,kwôrtər/ ▶ v. [trans.] (usu. **be headquartered**) provide (an organization) with headquarters at a specified location.

head·quar·ters /ˈhed,kwôrtərz/ ▶ n. [treated as sing. or pl.] the premises occupied by a military commander and the commander's staff. ▪ the place or building serving as the managerial and administrative center of an organization.

head·rail /ˈhed,rāl/ ▶ n. a horizontal rail at the top of something.

head·rest /ˈhed,rest/ ▶ n. an extension fixed to the back of a seat or chair, designed to support the head.

head·room /ˈhed,ro͞om; -,ro͝om/ ▶ n. the space above a driver's or passenger's head in a vehicle. ▪ the space or clearance between the top of a vehicle and the structure above it.

head·sail /ˈhed,sāl/ ▶ n. a sail on a ship's foremast or bowsprit.

head·scarf /ˈhed,skärf/ ▶ n. (pl. **-scarves**) a square of fabric worn as a covering for the head, often folded into a triangle and knotted under the chin.

head·set /ˈhed,set/ ▶ n. a set of headphones, typically with a microphone attached.

head shop ▶ n. a store that sells drug-related paraphernalia.

head·shrink·er /ˈhed,SHriNGkər/ ▶ n. hist. a headhunter who preserved and shrank the heads of his dead enemies. ▪ informal a clinical psychiatrist, psychologist, or psychotherapist. Compare with SHRINK.

heads·man /ˈhedzmən/ ▶ n. (pl. **-men**) hist. a man responsible for beheading condemned prisoners.

head·space /ˈhed,spās/ ▶ n. the unfilled space above the contents of a closed container.

head·spring /ˈhed,spriNG/ ▶ n. a spring that is the main source of a stream.

head·stall /ˈhed,stôl/ ▶ n. **1** the part of a bridle or halter that fits around a horse's head. **2** another term for HEADPIECE (sense 3).

head·stand /ˈhed,stand/ ▶ n. the act of balancing on one's head and hands with the feet in the air.

head·stay /ˈhed,stā/ ▶ n. a forestay, esp. in a small vessel.

head·stock /ˈhed,stäk/ ▶ n. **1** a set of bearings in a machine, supporting a revolving part. **2** the widened piece at the end of the neck of a guitar, to which the tuning pegs are fixed. **3** the horizontal end member of the underframe of a railroad vehicle.

head·stone /ˈhed,stōn/ ▶ n. a slab of stone set up at the head of a grave, typically inscribed with the name of the dead person.

head·stream /ˈhed,strēm/ ▶ n. a headwater stream.

head·strong /ˈhed,strôNG/ ▶ adj. self-willed; obstinate.

heads-up informal ▶ n. an advance warning of something. ▶ adj. [attrib.] showing alertness or perceptiveness. ▶ exclam. (**heads up**) used as a warning against danger, esp. from overhead, or to make a passageway.

head-to-head ▶ adj. & adv. involving two parties confronting each other. ▶ n. a conversation, confrontation, or contest between two parties.

head-trip ▶ n. an intellectually stimulating experience.

head-turn·ing ▶ adj. extremely noticeable or attractive.

head-up dis·play (also **heads-up dis·play**) ▶ n. a display of instrument readings in an aircraft or vehicle that can be seen without lowering the eyes, typically through being projected onto the windshield or visor.

head·ward /ˈhedwərd/ ▶ adj. in the region or direction of the head. ▪ Geol. denoting erosion by a stream or river occurring progressively upstream from the original source. ▶ adv. (also **head·wards**) toward the head.

head·wa·ter /ˈhed,wôtər; -,wätər/ ▶ n. (usu. **headwaters**) a tributary stream of a river close to or forming part of its source.

head·way /ˈhed,wā/ ▶ n. **1** forward movement or progress. **2** the average interval of time between vehicles moving in the same direction on the same route.

head·wind /ˈhed,wind/ ▶ n. a wind blowing from directly in front, opposing forward motion.

head·word /ˈhed,wərd/ ▶ n. a word that begins a separate entry in a reference work such as a dictionary.

head·work /ˈhed,wərk/ ▶ n. **1** activities taxing the mind; mental work. **2** (**headworks**) apparatus for controlling the flow of water in a river or canal.

head·y /ˈhedē/ ▶ adj. (**head·i·er, head·i·est**) (of liquor) potent; intoxicating: *several bottles of heady local wine.* ▪ having a strong or exhilarating effect. — **head·i·ly** adv. **head·i·ness** n.

heal /hēl/ ▶ v. [trans.] (of a person or treatment) cause (a wound, injury, or person) to become sound or healthy again. | [as adj.] (**healing**) *a healing effect on the body* | [as n.] (**healing**) *the gift of healing.* ▪ [intrans.] become sound or healthy again. ▪ alleviate (a person's distress or anguish). ▪ correct or put right (an undesirable situation). — **heal·a·ble** adj. **heal·er** n. [OE *hǣlan*, of Gmc. origin; rel. to Ger. *heilen*, also to WHOLE.]

heal-all ▶ n. a universal remedy; a panacea. ▪ informal any of a number of medicinal plants.

health /helTH/ ▶ n. the state of being free from illness or injury: *he was restored to health* | [as adj.] *a health risk.* ▪ a person's mental or physical condition. ▪ fig. soundness, esp. financial or moral. ▪ used to express friendly feelings toward one's companions before drinking. [OE *hǣlth*, of Gmc. origin; rel. to WHOLE.]

health·care /ˈhelTH,ke(ə)r/ (also **health care**) ▶ n. the maintenance and improvement of physical and mental health, esp. through the provision of medical services: [as adj.] *healthcare workers.*

health club ▶ n. a membership organization having exercise facilities and also offering health and beauty treatments.

health food ▶ n. natural food that is thought to have health-giving qualities.

health·ful /ˈhelTHfəl/ ▶ adj. having or conducive to good health: *healthful methods of cooking vegetables.* — **health·ful·ly** adv. **health·ful·ness** n.

health main·te·nance or·ga·ni·za·tion (abbr.: **HMO**) ▶ n. a health insurance organization to which subscribers pay a predetermined fee in return for a range of medical services from physicians and healthcare workers registered with the organization.

health phys·ics ▶ plural n. [treated as sing.] the branch of radiology that deals with the health of people working with radioactive materials.

health serv·ice ▶ n. a public service providing medical care.

health·y /ˈhelTHē/ ▶ adj. (**health·i·er, health·i·est**) in good health: *feeling fit and healthy.* ▪ (of a part of the body) not diseased. ▪ indicative of, conducive to, or promoting good health. ▪ (of a person's attitude) sensible and well balanced. ▪ fig. in a good condition. ▪ desirable; beneficial. ▪ of a satisfactory size or amount. — **health·i·ly** adv. **health·i·ness** n.

Hea·ney /ˈhēnē/, Seamus Justin (1939–), Irish poet; born in Northern Ireland. His works include *North* (1975). Nobel Prize for Literature (1995).

heap /hēp/ ▶ **n.** an untidy collection of things piled up haphazardly. ■ a mound or pile of a particular substance. ■ informal an untidy or dilapidated place or vehicle. ■ (**a heap of/heaps of**) informal a large amount or number of something. ▶ **adv.** (**heaps**) informal a great deal. ▶ **v.** [trans.] put in a pile or mound. ■ (**heap something with**) load something copiously with. ■ (**heap something on/upon**) bestow praise, abuse, or criticism liberally on. ■ [intrans.] form a heap: *clouds heaped higher in the west.*
– PHRASES **at the top** (or **bottom**) **of the heap** (of a person) at the highest (or lowest) point of a society or organization. [OE *hēap* (n.), *hēapian* (v.), of Gmc. origin; rel. to Du. *hoop* and Ger. *Haufen*.]

hear /hi(ə)r/ ▶ **v.** (past **heard** /hərd/) [trans.] perceive with the ear the sound made by (someone or something). ■ be told or informed of. ■ [intrans.] (**have heard of**) be aware of; know of the existence of. ■ [intrans.] (**hear from**) be contacted by (someone), esp. by letter or telephone: *we would love to hear from you.* ■ listen or pay attention to: [with clause] *she just doesn't hear what I'm telling her.* ■ (**hear someone out**) listen to all that someone has to say. ■ [intrans.] (**will/would not hear of**) will or would not allow or agree to. ■ Law listen to and judge (a case or plaintiff): *a jury heard the case.* ■ listen to and grant (a prayer).
– PHRASES **be hearing things** see THING. **be unable to hear oneself think** informal used to complain about very loud noise. **hear! hear!** used to express one's wholehearted agreement, esp. with something said in a speech. **hear tell of** (or **that**) be informed of (or that). — **hear·a·ble** adj. **hear·er** n. [OE *hīeran, hēran*, of Gmc. origin; rel. to Du. *hooren* and Ger. *hören*.]

hear·ing /ˈhi(ə)riNG/ ▶ **n.** **1** the faculty of perceiving sounds. ■ the range within which sounds may be heard; earshot: *she had moved out of hearing.* **2** an opportunity to state one's case. ■ Law an act of listening to evidence in a court of law or before an official, esp. a trial before a judge without a jury.

hear·ing aid ▶ **n.** a small device that fits in or on the ear, worn by a partially deaf person to amplify sound.

hear·ing dog ▶ **n.** a dog trained to alert the deaf or hard of hearing to sounds such as a doorbell or telephone.

heark·en /ˈhärkən/ (also **hark·en**) ▶ **v.** [intrans.] archaic listen: *he refused to hearken to Thomas's words of wisdom.*
– PHRASAL VERBS **hearken back** another way of saying HARK BACK (see HARK). [OE *heorcnian*; prob. rel. to HARK.]

hear·say /ˈhi(ə)rˌsā/ ▶ **n.** information received from other people that cannot be adequately substantiated; rumor. ■ Law the report of another person's words by a witness, usually disallowed as evidence in a court of law.

hearse /hərs/ ▶ **n.** a vehicle for conveying the coffin at a funeral. [ME: from Anglo-Norman Fr. *herce* 'harrow, frame,' from L. *hirpex* 'a kind of large rake,' from Oscan *hirpus* 'wolf' (with ref. to the teeth).]

Hearst /hərst/, William Randolph (1863–1951), US newspaper publisher. His large headlines and sensational crime reporting revolutionized US journalism. He was the model for the title character of Orson Welles's movie *Citizen Kane* (1941).

heart /härt/ ▶ **n.** **1** a hollow muscular organ that pumps the blood through the circulatory system by rhythmic contraction and dilation. In vertebrates there may be up to four chambers (as in humans), with two atria and two ventricles. ■ the region of the chest above the heart. ■ the heart regarded as the center of a person's thoughts and emotions, esp. love or compassion: *he has no heart.* ■ one's mood or feeling: *a change of heart.* ■ courage or enthusiasm: *Mary took heart from the encouragement.* **2** the central or innermost part of something. ■ the vital part or essence: *the heart of the matter.* ■ the close compact head of a cabbage or lettuce. **3** a conventional representation of a heart with two equal curves meeting at a point at the bottom and a cusp at the top. ■ (**hearts**) one of the four suits in a conventional pack of playing cards, denoted by a red figure of such a shape. ■ a card of this suit. ■ (**hearts**) a card game similar to whist, in which players attempt to avoid taking tricks containing a card of this suit. **4** the condition of agricultural land as regards fertility.
– PHRASES **after one's own heart** of the type that one likes or understands best; sharing one's tastes. **at heart** in one's real nature, in contrast to how one may appear: *he's a good lad at heart.* **break someone's heart** overwhelm someone with sadness. **by heart** from memory. **close** (or **dear**) **to** (or **near**) **one's heart** of deep interest and concern to one. **from the** (**bottom of one's**) **heart** with sincere feeling. **give** (or **lose**) **one's heart to** fall in love with. **have a heart** [often in imper.] be merciful; show pity. **have a heart of gold** have a generous nature. **have the heart to do something** [usu. with negative] be insensitive or hard-hearted enough to do something. **have** (or **put**) **one's heart in** be (or become) keenly involved in or committed to (an enterprise). **have one's heart in one's mouth** be greatly alarmed or apprehensive. **have one's heart in the right place** be sincere or well intentioned. **hearts and flowers** used in allusion to extreme sentimentality. **hearts and minds** used in reference to emotional and intellectual support or commitment: *the hearts and minds of college students.* **one's heart's desire** a person or thing that one greatly wishes for. **one's heartstrings** used in reference to one's deepest feelings of love or compassion: *the kitten's pitiful little squeak tugged at her heartstrings.* **in one's heart of hearts** in one's inmost feelings. **take something to heart** take criticism seriously and be affected or upset by it. **wear one's heart on one's sleeve** make one's feelings apparent. **with all one's heart** (or **one's whole heart**) sincerely; completely. — **heart·ed** adj. [in comb.] *a generous-hearted woman.* [OE *heorte*, of Gmc. origin; rel. to Du. *hart* and Ger. *Herz*, from an Indo-Eur. root shared by L. *cor, cord-* and Gk. *kēr, kardia*.]

heart·ache /ˈhärtˌāk/ ▶ **n.** emotional anguish or grief, typically caused by the absence of someone loved.

heart at·tack ▶ **n.** a sudden and sometimes fatal occurrence of coronary thrombosis, typically resulting in the death of part of a heart muscle.

heart·beat /ˈhärtˌbēt/ ▶ **n.** the pulsation of the heart. ■ (usu. **heartbeats**) a single pulsation of the heart. ■ fig. a person or thing providing or representing an animating or vital unifying force: *conflict is the essential heartbeat of fiction.*
– PHRASES **a heartbeat away from** very close to; on the verge of.

heart·break /ˈhärtˌbrāk/ ▶ **n.** overwhelming distress.

heart·break·er /ˈhärtˌbrākər/ ▶ **n.** a story or event that causes overwhelming distress.

heart·break·ing /ˈhärtˌbrākiNG/ ▶ **adj.** causing overwhelming distress; very upsetting. — **heart·break·ing·ly** adv. [as submodifier] *a heartbreakingly lonely place.*

heart·bro·ken /ˈhärtˌbrōkən/ ▶ **adj.** (of a person) suffering from overwhelming distress; very upset.

heart·burn /ˈhärtˌbərn/ ▶ **n.** a form of indigestion caused by acid regurgitation into the esophagus.

heart·en /ˈhärtn/ ▶ **v.** [trans.] (usu. **be heartened**) make more cheerful or confident. — **heart·en·ing·ly** adv.

heart fail·ure ▶ **n.** severe failure of the heart to function properly, esp. as a cause of death.

heart·felt /ˈhärtˌfelt/ ▶ **adj.** (of a feeling or its expression) sincere; deeply and strongly felt.

hearth /härTH/ ▶ **n.** the floor of a fireplace. ■ the area in front of a fireplace. ■ used as a symbol of one's home: *he left hearth and home.* ■ the base or lower part of a furnace, where molten metal collects. [OE *heorth*, of West Gmc. origin; rel. to Du. *haard* and Ger. *Herd*.]

hearth·stone /ˈhärTHˌstōn/ ▶ **n.** a flat stone forming a hearth or part of a hearth.

heart·i·ly /ˈhärtl-ē/ ▶ **adv.** **1** in a hearty manner. **2** [as submodifier] very; to a great degree (esp. with reference to personal feelings): *heartily sick of the subject.*

heart·land /ˈhärtˌland/ ▶ **n.** the central or most important part of a country, area, or field of activity. ■ the center of support for a belief or movement. ■ (**the heartland**) the central part of the US; the Midwest.

heart·less /ˈhärtlis/ ▶ **adj.** displaying a complete lack of feeling or consideration. — **heart·less·ly** adv. **heart·less·ness** n.

heart line ▶ **n.** (in palmistry) the upper of the two horizontal lines that cross the palm of the hand.

heart mas·sage ▶ **n.** another term for cardiac massage.

heart of palm ▶ **n.** the edible bud of a palm tree.

heart-rend·ing ▶ **adj.** (of a story or event) causing great sadness or distress. — **heart-rend·ing·ly** adv.

heart-search·ing ▶ **n.** thorough, typically painful examination of one's feelings and motives.

hearts·ease /ˈhärtsˌēz/ (also **heart's-ease**) ▶ **n.** a wild European pansy (*Viola tricolor*) that typically has purple and yellow flowers. Most garden pansies were developed from its hybrids.

heart·sick /ˈhärtˌsik/ ▶ **adj.** despondent, typically from grief or loss of love. — **heart·sick·ness** n.

heart·sore /ˈhärtˌsôr/ ▶ **adj.** literary grieving; heartsick.

heart-stop·ping ▶ **adj.** thrilling; full of suspense. — **heart-stop·per** n. **heart-stop·ping·ly** adv.

heart·throb /ˈhärtˌTHräb/ ▶ **n.** informal a man, typically a celebrity, whose good looks excite immature romantic feelings in women.

heart-to-heart ▶ **adj.** (of a conversation) candid, intimate, and personal: *a heart-to-heart chat.* ▶ **n.** such a conversation.

heart ur·chin ▶ **n.** a heart-shaped burrowing sea urchin that has a thick covering of fine spines on the shell, giving it a furry appearance.

heart·warm·ing /ˈhärtˌwôrmiNG/ ▶ **adj.** emotionally rewarding or uplifting.

heart·wood /ˈhärtˌwo͝od/ ▶ **n.** the dense inner part of a tree trunk, yielding the hardest timber.

heart·y /ˈhärtē/ ▶ **adj.** (**heart·i·er, heart·i·est**) **1** (of a person or their behavior) loudly vigorous and cheerful. ■ (of a feeling or an opinion) heartfelt. ■ (of a person) strong and healthy. **2** (of food) wholesome and substantial. ■ (of a person's appetite) robust and healthy. — **heart·i·ness** n.

heat /hēt/ ▶ **n.** **1** the quality of being hot; high temperature: *it is sensitive to both heat and cold.* ■ hot weather conditions. ■ a source or level of heat for cooking. ■ a spicy quality in food that produces a burning sensation in the mouth. ■ Physics heat seen as a form of energy arising from the random motion of the molecules of bodies, which may be transferred by conduction, convection, or radiation. ■ tech. the amount of heat that is needed to cause a specific process or is evolved in such a process: *the heat of formation.* ■ tech. a single operation of heating something. **2** intensity of feeling, esp. of anger or excitement. ■ (**the heat**) informal intensive and unwelcome pressure or criticism, esp. from the authorities. **3** a preliminary round in a race or contest. ▶ **v.** make or become hot or warm. ■ [intrans.] (**heat up**) (of a person) become excited or impassioned. ■ [intrans.] (**heat up**) become more intense and exciting: *the action really begins to heat up.*

– PHRASES **if you can't stand the heat, get out of the kitchen** proverb if you can't deal with the pressures and difficulties of a situation or task, you should leave others to deal with it rather than complain. **in the heat of the moment** while temporarily angry, excited, or engrossed, and without stopping for thought. **in heat** (of a female mammal) in the receptive period of the sexual cycle; in estrus. [OE *hǣtu* (noun), *hǣtan* (verb), of Gmc. origin; rel. to Du. *hitte* (n.) and Ger. *heizen* (v.), also to HOT.]

heat bar·ri·er ▶ n. the limitation of the speed of an aircraft or other flying object by heat from air friction.

heat ca·pac·i·ty ▶ n. the number of heat units needed to raise the temperature of a body by one degree.

heat death ▶ n. Physics a state of uniform distribution of energy, esp. viewed as a possible fate of the universe. It is a corollary of the second law of thermodynamics.

heat·ed /ˈhētid/ ▶ adj. **1** made warm or hot. **2** inflamed with passion or conviction. — **heat·ed·ly** adv.

heat en·gine ▶ n. a device for producing motive power from heat, such as a gasoline engine or steam engine.

heat·er /ˈhētər/ ▶ n. **1** a person or thing that heats, in particular a device for warming the air or water. ■ Electron. a conductor used for indirect heating of the cathode of a thermionic tube. **2** Baseball a fastball. **3** informal, dated a gun.

heat ex·chang·er ▶ n. a device for transferring heat from one medium to another.

Heath /hēTH/, Sir Edward Richard George (1916–2005), prime minister of Britain 1970–74.

heath /hēTH/ ▶ n. **1** an area of open uncultivated land, esp. in Britain, with characteristic vegetation of heather, gorse, and coarse grasses. ■ Ecol. vegetation dominated by dwarf shrubs of the heath family: [as adj.] *heath vegetation.* **2** a dwarf shrub (*Erica* and related genera) with small leathery leaves and small pink or purple bell-shaped flowers, characteristic of heathland and moorland. The **heath family** (Ericaceae) also includes the rhododendrons and azaleas as well as the blueberries and many other berry-bearing dwarf shrubs. [OE *hǣth*, of Gmc. origin; rel. to Du. *heide* and Ger. *Heide*.]

heat haze ▶ n. an obscuration of the atmosphere in hot weather, esp. a shimmering in the air near the ground.

heath·en /ˈhēTHən/ ▶ n. esp. derog. a person who does not belong to a widely held religion (esp. one who is not a Christian, Jew, or Muslim) as regarded by those who do: *bringing Christianity to the heathens.* ■ a follower of a polytheistic religion; a pagan. ■ (**the heathen**) heathen people collectively, esp. (in biblical use) those who did not worship the God of Israel. ■ informal an unenlightened person; a person regarded as lacking culture or moral principles. ▶ adj. of or relating to heathens: *heathen gods.* ■ informal unenlightened or uncivilized. — **heath·en·dom** /-dəm/ n. **heath·en·ish** adj. **heath·en·ism** n. [OE *hǣthen*, of Germanic origin; rel. to Du. *heiden* and Ger. *Heide*; from Gmc., 'inhabiting open country,' from the base of HEATH.]

heath·er /ˈheTHər/ ▶ n. a purple-flowered Eurasian heath (*Calluna vulgaris*) that grows abundantly on moorland and heathland. Many ornamental varieties have been developed. ■ informal any similar plant of this family; a heath. [OE *hadre, hedre* (in place names).]

heath·land /ˈhēTH,land/ ▶ n. (also **heathlands**) an extensive area of heath: *1,000 acres of heathland.*

heat in·dex ▶ n. a quantity expressing the discomfort because of the temperature and humidity of the air.

heat·ing /ˈhētiNG/ ▶ n. the imparting or generation of heat. ■ equipment or devices used to provide heat.

heat light·ning ▶ n. a flash or flashes of light seen near the horizon, esp. on warm evenings, believed to be the reflection of distant lightning on high clouds.

heat·proof /ˈhēt,pro͞of/ ▶ adj. able to resist great heat.

heat pump ▶ n. a device that transfers heat from a colder area to a hotter area by using mechanical energy.

heat rash ▶ n. another term for PRICKLY HEAT.

heat-re·sist·ant ▶ adj. another term for HEATPROOF. ■ not easily becoming hot: *heat-resistant handles.*

heat-seek·ing /ˈhēt,sēkiNG/ ▶ adj. (of a missile) able to detect and home in on infrared radiation emitted by a target, such as the exhaust vent of a jet aircraft.

heat shield ▶ n. a device or coating for protection from excessive heat.

heat sink ▶ n. a device or substance for absorbing excessive or unwanted heat.

heat·stroke /ˈhēt,strōk/ ▶ n. a condition caused by failure of the body's temperature-regulating mechanism when exposed to excessively high temperatures.

heat treat·ment ▶ n. **1** the use of heat for therapeutic purposes in medicine. **2** the use of heat to modify the properties of a material, esp. in metallurgy. — **heat-treat** v.

heat wave ▶ n. a prolonged period of hot weather.

heave /hēv/ ▶ v. (past **heaved** or esp. Naut. **hove** /hōv/) **1** [trans.] lift or haul (a heavy thing) with great effort. ■ Naut. pull, raise, or move (a boat or ship) by hauling on a rope or ropes. ■ informal throw (something heavy): *she heaved half a brick at him.* **2** [trans.] produce (a sigh): *he heaved a euphoric sigh of relief.* **3** [intrans.] rise and fall rhythmically or spasmodically. ■ make an effort to vomit; retch: *my stomach heaved.* ▶ n. **1** an act of heaving, esp. a strong pull. ■ Geol. a sideways displacement in a fault. **2** (**the heaves**) informal a case of retching or vomiting. **3** (**heaves**) a disease of horses.

– PHRASAL VERBS **heave to** Naut. (of a boat or ship) come to a stop, esp. by turning across the wind leaving the headsail backed. — **heav·er** n. [OE *hebban*, of Gmc. origin; rel. to Du. *heffen* and Ger. *heben* 'lift up.']

heave-ho ▶ exclam. a cry emitted when doing in unison actions that take physical effort. ▶ n. such an exclamation. ■ (**the heave-ho**) expulsion or elimination from an institution, association, or contest: *get the heave-ho.* [ME: from *heave!* (imper.) + HO².]

heav·en /ˈhevən/ ▶ n. **1** a place regarded in various religions as the abode of God (or the gods) and the angels, and of the good after death, often traditionally depicted as being above the sky. ■ God (or the gods). ■ Theol. a state of being eternally in the presence of God after death. ■ informal a place, state, or experience of supreme bliss. ■ used in various exclamations as a substitute for "God": *Heaven knows!* **2** (often **heavens**) literary the sky, esp. perceived as a vault in which the sun, moon, stars, and planets are situated: *Galileo used a telescope to observe the heavens.*

– PHRASES **the heavens open** it suddenly starts to rain heavily. **in seventh heaven** in a state of ecstasy. **move heaven and earth to do something** make extraordinary efforts to do a specified thing. **stink** (or **smell**) **to high heaven** have a very strong and unpleasant odor. — **heav·en·ward** /-wərd/ adj. & adv. **heav·en·wards** /-wərdz/ adv. [OE *heofon*, of Gmc. origin; rel. to Du. *hemel* and Ger. *Himmel*.]

heav·en·ly /ˈhevənlē/ ▶ adj. **1** of heaven; divine. **2** of the heavens or sky: *heavenly constellations.* **3** informal very pleasing; wonderful. — **heav·en·li·ness** n.

heav·en-sent ▶ adj. (of an event or opportunity) occurring at a favorable time; opportune.

heav·i·er-than-air ▶ adj. (of an aircraft) weighing more than the air it displaces.

heav·ing line ▶ n. a lightweight line with a weight at the end, made to be thrown between a ship and the shore, or from one ship to another, and used to pull a heavier line across.

heav·y /ˈhevē/ ▶ adj. (**heav·i·er, heav·i·est**) **1** of great weight; difficult to lift or move. ■ used in questions about weight: *how heavy is it?* ■ [attrib.] (of a class of thing) above the average weight; large of its kind. ■ [predic.] weighed down; full of something. ■ (of a person's head or eyes) feeling weighed down by weariness. ■ Physics of or containing atoms of an isotope of greater than the usual mass. See also HEAVY WATER. **2** of great density; thick or substantial: *heavy gray clouds.* ■ (of food or a meal) hard to digest; too filling. ■ (of ground or soil) hard to travel over or work with because muddy or full of clay. ■ not delicate or graceful; coarse. ■ moving slowly or with difficulty. ■ aviation slang (of a large aircraft) leaving a large amount of turbulence behind in its flight. ■ (of a smell) overpowering. ■ (of the sky) full of dark clouds; oppressive. **3** of more than the usual size, amount, or force. ■ doing something to excess. ■ (**heavy on**) using a lot of. **4** striking or falling with force: *a heavy blow to the head.* ■ causing a strong impact: *a heavy fall.* ■ (of music, esp. rock) having a strong bass component and a forceful rhythm. **5** needing much physical effort: *heavy work.* ■ mentally oppressive; hard to endure: *a heavy burden.* ■ important or serious: *a heavy discussion.* ■ (of a literary work) hard to read or understand because overly serious or difficult. ■ feeling or expressing grief. ■ informal (of a situation) serious and hard to deal with. ■ informal (of a person) strict or harsh: *the police were really getting heavy.* ▶ n. (pl. **heav·ies**) **1** a thing that is large or heavy of its kind. ■ informal a large, strong man, esp. one hired for protection. ■ an important person. **2** a villainous role or actor in a book, movie, etc. ▶ adv. heavily: *his words hung heavy in the air.*

– PHRASES **heavy with child** pregnant. **make heavy weather of** see WEATHER. — **heav·i·ly** adv. **heav·i·ness** n. **heav·y·ish** adj. [OE *hefig*, of Gmc. origin; rel. to Du. *hevig*, also to HEAVE.]

heav·y breath·ing ▶ n. breathing that is audible through being deep or labored, esp. in sleep or as a result of exertion. ■ fig. sexual desire or arousal.

heav·y cream ▶ n. thick cream that contains a lot of butterfat.

heav·y-du·ty ▶ adj. (of material or an article) designed to withstand the stresses of demanding use. ■ informal intense, important, or abundant.

heav·y-foot·ed ▶ adj. slow and laborious in movement.

heav·y go·ing ▶ n. a person or situation that is difficult.

heav·y-hand·ed ▶ adj. clumsy or insensitive. ■ overly forceful or oppressive. — **heav·y-hand·ed·ly** adv. **heav·y-hand·ed·ness** n.

heav·y-heart·ed ▶ adj. feeling depressed or melancholy.

heav·y hy·dro·gen ▶ n. another term for DEUTERIUM.

heav·y in·dus·try ▶ n. the manufacture of large, heavy articles and materials in bulk.

heav·y-lift ▶ adj. [attrib.] (of a vehicle) capable of lifting or transporting extremely heavy loads: *a heavy-lift helicopter.*

heav·y lift·ing ▶ n. the lifting of heavy objects. ■ fig. hard or difficult work: *the heavy lifting in this business is in designing external distribution systems.*

heav·y met·al ▶ n. **1** a type of highly amplified harsh-sounding rock music with a strong beat, characteristically using violent or fantastic imagery. **2** a metal of relatively high density, or of high relative atomic weight.

heav·y oil ▶ **n.** any of the relatively dense hydrocarbons (denser than water) derived from petroleum, coal tar, and similar materials.

heav·y pet·ting ▶ **n.** erotic contact between two people stopping short of intercourse.

heav·y·set /ˈhevēˌset/ ▶ **adj.** having a stocky build.

heav·y wa·ter ▶ **n.** water in which the hydrogen in the molecules is partly or wholly replaced by the isotope deuterium, used esp. as a moderator in nuclear reactors.

heav·y·weight /ˈhevēˌwāt/ ▶ **n. 1** a weight in boxing and other sports, typically the heaviest category. ■ a boxer or other competitor of this weight. **2** a person or thing of above-average weight. ■ [often with adj.] a person of influence or importance, esp. in a particular sphere. ▶ **adj.** of above-average weight. ■ serious, important, or influential.

Heb. ▶ **abbr.** ■ Bible Hebrews. ■ Hebrew.

heb·dom·a·dal /hebˈdämədl/ ▶ **adj.** formal weekly (used esp. of organizations that meet weekly). [17th C.: from late L. *hebdomadalis*, from Gk. *hebdomas, hebdomad-* 'the number seven, seven days,' from *hepta* 'seven.']

He·be[1] /ˈhēbē/ Gk. Mythol. the daughter of Hera and Zeus, and cupbearer of the gods.

Hebe[2] /hēb/ ▶ **n.** informal, offens. a Jewish person. [20th C.: abbrev. of HEBREW.]

He·bei /ˈhəˈbā/ (also **Ho·peh** /ˈhəˈbā; ˈhō-/) a province in northeast central China; capital, Shijiazhuang.

he·be·phre·ni·a /ˌhēbəˈfrēnēə/ ▶ **n.** a form of chronic schizophrenia involving disordered thought, inappropriate emotions, hallucinations, and bizarre behavior. — **he·be·phren·ic** /-ˈfrenik/ **adj. & n.** [19th C.: from HEBE[1] + Gk. *phrēn* 'mind' + -IA[1].]

heb·e·tude /ˈhebəˌt(y)o͞od/ ▶ **n.** literary the state of being dull or lethargic. [17th C.: from late L. *hebetudo*, from *hebes, hebet-* 'blunt.']

Hebr. ▶ **abbr.** Hebrew or Hebrews.

He·bra·ic /hēˈbrāik/ ▶ **adj.** of Hebrew or the Hebrews. — **He·bra·i·cal·ly** /-ik(ə)lē/ **adv.** [via Christian L. from late Gk. *Hebraikos*, from *Hebraios* (see HEB.).]

He·bra·ism /ˈhēbrāˌizəm/ ▶ **n. 1** a Hebrew idiom or expression. **2** the Jewish religion, culture, or character. — **He·bra·is·tic** /ˌhēbrāˈistik/ **adj. He·bra·ize** /-ˌīz/ **v.**

He·bra·ist /ˈhēbrāist/ ▶ **n.** a scholar of the Hebrew language. ■ a student or adherent of the Jewish religion, culture, or character.

He·brew /ˈhēbro͞o/ ▶ **n. 1** a member of an ancient people living in what is now Israel and Palestine and, according to biblical tradition, descended from the patriarch Jacob, grandson of Abraham. ■ old-fashioned and often offensive term for JEW. **2** the Semitic language of this people. ▶ **adj. 1** of the Hebrews or the Jews. **2** of or in Hebrew. [from OFr. *Ebreu*, via L. from late Gk. *Hebraios*, from Aramaic *ʿibray*, based on Heb. *ʿibrî* understood to mean 'one from the other side (of the river).']

He·brew Bi·ble the sacred writings of Judaism (the Old Testament to Christians), including the Law (Torah), the Prophets, and the Hagiographa or Writings.

He·brews /ˈhēbro͞oz/ a book of the New Testament.

Heb·ri·des /ˈhebrəˌdēz/ a group of about 500 islands off the northwestern coast of Scotland. The **Inner Hebrides** are separated from the **Outer Hebrides** by the Little Minch Strait. Also called WESTERN ISLES. — **Heb·ri·de·an** /ˌhebrəˈdēən/ **n. & adj.**

He·bron /ˈhēbrən/ a Palestinian city on the West Bank of the Jordan River; pop. 75,000.

Heb·ros /ˈhēbrəs/ (also **Heb·rus**) ancient Greek name for MARITSA.

Hec·a·te /ˈhekətē/ Gk. Mythol. a goddess of dark places, often associated with ghosts and sorcery.

hec·a·tomb /ˈhekəˌtōm/ ▶ **n.** (in ancient Greece or Rome) a great public sacrifice. ■ fig. an extensive loss of life for some cause. [16th C.: via L. from Gk. *hekatombē* (from *hekaton* 'hundred' + *bous* 'ox').]

heck /hek/ ▶ **exclam.** expressing surprise, frustration, or dismay: *oh heck, I can't for the life of me remember.* ■ **(the heck)** used for emphasis in questions and exclamations.

– PHRASES **a heck of a ——** used for emphasis in various statements or exclamations: *it was a heck of a lot of money.* [19th C. (orig. dial.): euphemistic alt. of HELL.]

heck·el·phone /ˈhekəlˌfōn/ ▶ **n.** a woodwind instrument resembling a large oboe. [20th C.: from German *Heckelphon*, after Wilhelm *Heckel* (1856–1909), German instrument maker.]

heck·le /ˈhekəl/ ▶ **v.** [trans.] **1** (often **be heckled**) interrupt (a public speaker) with derisive or aggressive comments or abuse. **2** dress (flax or hemp) to split and straighten the fibers for spinning. ▶ **n.** a heckling comment. — **heck·ler n.** [ME (sense 2): from *heckle* 'flax comb,' a northern and eastern form of HACKLE.]

heck·uv·a /ˈhekəvə/ nonstandard spelling of *HECK OF A* (see HECK).

hec·tare /ˈhekˌte(ə)r/ (abbr.: **ha**) ▶ **n.** a metric unit of square measure, equal to 100 ares (2.471 acres or 10,000 square meters). — **hec·tar·age** /ˈhektərij/ **n.** [19th C.: from Fr., formed irregularly from Gk. *hekaton* 'hundred' + ARE[2].]

hec·tic /ˈhektik/ ▶ **adj. 1** full of frantic activity. **2** Med., archaic relating to or denoting a regularly recurrent fever typically accompanying tuberculosis. — **hec·ti·cal·ly** /-tik(ə)lē/ **adv.** [ME *etik*, via OFr. from late L. *hecticus*, from Gk. *hektikos* 'habitual,' from *hexis* 'habit.']

hecto- ▶ **comb. form** (used commonly in units of measurement) a hundred: *hectometer.* [from Fr., formed irregularly by contr. of Gk. *hekaton* 'hundred.']

hec·to·cot·y·lus /ˌhektōˈkätl-əs/ ▶ **n.** (pl. **-cot·y·li** /-ˈkätlˌī/) Zool. a modified arm used by male octopuses and some other cephalopods to transfer sperm to the female. [19th C.: mod. L., from HECTO- 'hundred' + Gk. *kotulē* 'hollow thing.']

hec·to·gram /ˈhektəˌgram/ (Brit. also **hec·to·gramme**) (abbr.: **hg**) ▶ **n.** a metric unit of mass equal to one hundred grams.

hec·to·graph /ˈhektəˌgraf/ ▶ **n.** an apparatus for copying documents by the use of a gelatin plate that receives an impression of the master copy.

hec·to·li·ter /ˈhektəˌlētər/ (Brit. **hec·to·li·tre**) ▶ **n.** a metric unit of capacity equal to one hundred liters.

hec·to·me·ter /ˈhektəˌmētər/ (Brit. **hec·to·me·tre**) (abbr.: **hm**) ▶ **n.** a metric unit of length equal to one hundred meters.

Hec·tor /ˈhektər/ Gk. Mythol. a Trojan warrior, son of Priam and Hecuba and husband of Andromache.

hec·tor /ˈhektər/ ▶ **v.** [trans.] talk to (someone) in a bullying way. — **hec·tor·ing·ly** /ˈhekt(ə)riNGlē/ **adv.** [ME: from HECTOR.]

Hec·u·ba /ˈhekyəbə/ Gk. Mythol. the queen of Troy, wife of Priam and mother of children including Hector, Paris, Cassandra, and Troilus.

he'd /hēd/ ▶ **contr.** ■ he had. ■ he would.

hed·dle /ˈhedl/ ▶ **n.** one of a set of looped wires or cords in a loom, with an eye in the center through which a warp yarn is passed before going through the reed to control its movement and divide the threads. [16th C.: appar. from an alt. of OE *hefeld*.]

he·der /ˈKHādər; ˈhā-/ ▶ **n.** (pl. **he·da·rim** /KHəˈdärim/ or **he·ders**) var. of CHEDER.

hedge /hej/ ▶ **n.** a fence or boundary formed by closely growing bushes or shrubs. ■ a contract entered into or asset held as a protection against possible financial loss. ■ a word or phrase used to avoid overprecise commitment, for example, *etc., often,* or *usually.* ▶ **v.** [trans.] **1** (often **be hedged**) surround or bound with a hedge: *a garden hedged with yews.* ■ **(hedge something in)** enclose. **2** limit or qualify by conditions or exceptions. ■ [intrans.] avoid making a definite decision, statement, or commitment: *she hedged around the question.* **3** protect against loss by making balancing or compensating contracts or transactions. — **hedg·er n.** [OE *hegg*, of Gmc. origin; rel. to Du. *heg* and Ger. *Hecke*.]

hedge fund ▶ **n.** a limited partnership of investors that uses high risk methods.

hedge·hog /ˈhejˌhôg; -ˌhäg/ ▶ **n.** a nocturnal insectivorous Old World mammal (family Erinaceidae) with a spiny coat and short legs, able to roll itself into a ball for defense. Its several species include the **common hedgehog** (*Erinaceus europaeus*) of western and northern Europe. ■ any other animal covered with spines, esp. a porcupine.

commmon hedgehog

hedge·hop /ˈhejˌhäp/ ▶ **v.** fly an aircraft at a very low altitude. — **hedge·hop·per n.**

hedge·row /ˈhejˌrō/ ▶ **n.** a hedge of wild shrubs and trees, typically bordering a road or field. [OE: from HEDGE + obs. *rew* 'hedgerow,' assimilated to ROW[1].]

he·don·ic /hēˈdänik/ ▶ **adj.** tech. considered in terms of pleasant (or unpleasant) sensations.

he·don·ism /ˈhēdnˌizəm/ ▶ **n.** the pursuit of pleasure. ■ the ethical theory that pleasure is the highest good and proper aim of human life. — **he·don·ist n. he·don·is·tic** /ˌhēdnˈistik/ **adj. he·don·is·ti·cal·ly** /ˌhēdnˈistik(ə)lē/ **adv.** [19th C.: from Gk. *hēdonē* 'pleasure' + -ISM.]

-hedron ▶ **comb. form** (pl. **-hedra** or **-hedrons**) in nouns denoting geometric solids having a specified number of plane faces: *decahedron.* ■ denoting geometric solids having faces of a specified shape: *rhombohedron.* — **-hedral comb. form** in corresponding adjectives. [from Gk. *hedra* 'seat, base.']

hee·bie-jee·bies /ˈhēbē ˈjēbēz/ ▶ **plural n.** **(the heebie-jeebies)** informal a state of nervous fear or anxiety. [1920s: coined by W. B. DeBeck (1890–1942), US cartoonist.]

heed /hēd/ ▶ **v.** [trans.] pay attention to; take notice of. ▶ **n.** careful attention: *if he heard, he* **paid no heed.** [OE *hēdan* (orig. intransitive), of West Gmc. origin; rel. to Du. *hoeden* and Ger. *hüten*.]

heed·ful /ˈhēdfəl/ ▶ **adj.** aware of and attentive to. — **heed·ful·ly adv. heed·ful·ness n.**

heed·less /ˈhēdlis/ ▶ **adj.** showing a reckless lack of care or attention: *his heedless impetuosity.* — **heed·less·ly adv. heed·less·ness n.**

hee-haw /ˈhēˌhô/ ▶ **n.** the cry of a donkey or mule. ▶ **v.** [intrans.] make the loud, harsh cry of a donkey or mule. [19th C.: imitative.]

heel[1] /hēl/ ▶ **n. 1** the back part of the foot below the ankle. ■ a corresponding part of the foot in vertebrate animals. ■ the part of the palm of the hand next to the wrist. ■ the part of a shoe or boot supporting the heel. ■ the part of a sock covering the heel. ■ **(heels)** high-heeled shoes. **2** a thing resembling a heel in form or position, in particular:

■ the end of a violin bow at which it is held. ■ the part of the head of a golf club nearest the shaft. ■ a crusty end of a loaf of bread, or the rind of a cheese. ■ a piece of the main stem of a plant left attached to the base of a cutting. **3** informal an inconsiderate or untrustworthy person. **4** [as exclam.] a command to a dog to walk close behind. ▶ **v.** [trans.] **1** fit or renew a heel on (a shoe or boot). **2** [intrans.] (of a dog) follow closely behind its owner. **3** [intrans.] touch the ground with the heel when dancing. **4** Golf strike (the ball) with the heel of the club.

– PHRASES **at** (or **to**) **heel** (of a dog) close to and slightly behind its owner. **at the heels of** following closely behind. **bring someone to heel** bring someone under control. **down at heel** (of a shoe) with the heel worn down. ■ having a poor, shabby appearance. **kick up one's heels** have a lively, enjoyable time. **on the heels of** following closely after. **set someone back on their heels** astonish or discomfit someone. **turn on one's heel** turn sharply around. **under the heel of** dominated or controlled by. — **heeled** adj. **heel·less** adj. [OE *hēla*, *hǣla*, of Gmc. origin; rel. to Du. *hiel*.]

heel² ▶ **v.** [intrans.] (of a boat or ship) be tilted temporarily by the pressure of wind or by an uneven distribution of weight on board. Compare with LIST². ■ [trans.] cause (a boat or ship) to lean over in such a way. ▶ **n.** an instance of a ship leaning over in such a way. ■ the degree of incline of a ship's leaning measured from the vertical. [16th C.: from obs. *heeld*, *hield* 'incline,' of Gmc. origin; rel. to Du. *hellen*.]

heel bone ▶ **n.** the calcaneus.

heel·tap /'hēl,tap/ ▶ **n. 1** one of the layers of leather or other material of which a shoe heel is made. **2** dated liquor left at the bottom of a glass after drinking.

He·fei /'hə'fā/ (also **Ho·fei**) an industrial city in eastern China, capital of Anhui province; pop. 1,541,000.

heft /heft/ ▶ **v.** [trans.] lift or carry (something heavy). ■ lift or hold (something) in order to test its weight. ▶ **n.** the weight of someone or something. ■ fig. ability or influence: *intellectual heft*. [ME (as a n.): prob. from HEAVE.]

heft·y /'heftē/ ▶ **adj.** (**heft·i·er**, **heft·i·est**) large, heavy, and powerful. ■ (of a number or amount) impressively large. — **heft·i·ly** adv. **heft·i·ness** n.

He·gel /'hāgəl/, Georg Wilhelm Friedrich (1770–1831), German philosopher. In *Science of Logic* (1812–16) he described dialectical reasoning. — **He·ge·li·an** /hə'gālēən/ adj. & n. **He·ge·li·an·ism** /hə'gālēə,nizəm/ n.

heg·e·mon·ic /,hegə'mänik/ ▶ **adj.** ruling or dominant in a political or social context.

he·gem·o·ny /hə'jemənē; 'hejə,mōnē/ ▶ **n.** leadership or dominance, esp. by one country or social group. [16th C.: from Gk. *hēgemonia*, from *hēgemōn* 'leader,' from *hēgeisthai* 'to lead.']

He·gi·ra /hi'jīrə; 'hejərə/ (also **He·ji·ra** or **Hij·ra** /'hijrə/) ▶ **n.** Muhammad's departure from Mecca to Medina in AD 622. ■ the Muslim era reckoned from this date: *the second century of the Hegira*. See also **AH**. ■ (**hegira**) an exodus or migration. [via med. L. from Arab. *hijra* 'departure,' from *hajara* 'emigrate.']

Hei·deg·ger /'hīdəgər/, Martin (1889–1976), German philosopher. In *Being and Time* (1927), he examined the ontology of being.

Hei·del·berg /'hīdl,bərg/ a city in southwestern Germany, in Baden-Württemberg; pop. 139,000. Its university is the oldest in Germany.

Hei·del·berg man ▶ **n.** a fossil hominid of the early middle Pleistocene period, an early form of *Homo erectus* (formerly *H. heidelbergensis*), family Hominidae.

Hei·den /'hīdn/, Eric (1958–), US speed skater. He won five gold medals at the 1980 Olympic Games.

heif·er /'hefər/ ▶ **n.** a young female cow that has not borne a calf. [OE *heahfore*, of unknown origin.]

Hei·fetz /'hīfits/, Jascha (1901–87), US violinist; born in Lithuania.

heigh-ho ▶ **exclam.** informal expressing boredom, resignation, or jollity.

height /hīt/ ▶ **n. 1** the measurement from base to top or (of a standing person) from head to foot. ■ elevation above ground or a recognized level (typically sea level). ■ the quality of being tall or high. **2** a high place or area: *he's terrified of heights*. **3** the most intense part or period of something. ■ an extreme instance or example of something. [OE *hēhthu* (in the sense 'top of something'), of Gmc. origin; rel. to Du. *hoogte*, also to HIGH.]

height·en /'hītn/ ▶ **v.** [trans.] make (something) higher. ■ make or become more intense.

height of land ▶ **n.** a watershed.

Heil·bronn /'hīl,brän; -,brôn/ a city in southwestern Germany; pop. 117,000.

Hei·long /'hā'lông/ Chinese name of **AMUR**.

Hei·long·jiang /'hā'lôngjē'äng/ (also **Hei·lung·kiang** /-'lŏŏng-/) a province in northeastern China; capital, Harbin.

Heim·lich ma·neu·ver /'hīmlik; 'hīmlikh/ ▶ **n.** a first-aid procedure for dislodging an obstruction from a person's windpipe. [1970s: named after Henry J. *Heimlich* (1920–), the US doctor who developed the procedure.]

hei·nie /'hīnē/ ▶ **n.** informal a person's buttocks. [1960s: alt. of HINDER², var. of HIND¹.]

hei·nous /'hānəs/ ▶ **adj.** (of a person or wrongful act, esp. a crime) utterly odious or wicked. — **hei·nous·ly** adv. **hei·nous·ness** n. [ME: from OFr. *haineus*, from *hair* 'to hate,' of Gmc. origin.]

heir /e(ə)r/ ▶ **n.** a person legally entitled to the property or rank of another on that person's death. ■ fig. a person inheriting and continuing the legacy of a predecessor. — **heir·dom** n. **heir·less** adj. **heir·ship** n. [ME: via OFr. from L. *heres*.]

heir ap·par·ent ▶ **n.** (pl. **heirs ap·par·ent**) an heir whose claim cannot be set aside by the birth of another heir. Compare with HEIR PRESUMPTIVE. ■ fig. a person who is most likely to succeed to the place of another.

heir-at-law ▶ **n.** (pl. **heirs-at-law**) an heir by right of blood, esp. to property of a person who dies intestate.

heir·ess /'e(ə)ris/ ▶ **n.** a female heir, esp. to vast wealth.

heir·loom /'e(ə)r,lōōm/ ▶ **n.** a valuable object that has belonged to a family for several generations. [ME: from HEIR + LOOM¹ (which formerly had the senses 'tool, heirloom').]

heir pre·sump·tive ▶ **n.** (pl. **heirs pre·sump·tive**) an heir whose claim could be set aside by the birth of another heir. Compare with HEIR APPARENT.

Hei·sen·berg /'hīzən,bərg/, Werner Karl (1901–76), German physicist. He developed a system of quantum mechanics. Nobel Prize for Physics (1932).

Heis·man Tro·phy /'hīsmən/ ▶ **n.** an annual award given to the outstanding college football player in the US by the Downtown Athletic Club of New York City.

heist /hīst/ informal ▶ **n.** a robbery. ▶ **v.** [trans.] steal. [19th C.: representing a local pronunc. of HOIST.]

He·jaz /hē'jaz; -'zhäz/ (also **Hi·jaz**) a coastal region in western Saudi Arabia that borders the Red Sea.

He·ji·ra ▶ **n.** var. of **HEGIRA**.

held /held/ past and past participle of HOLD¹.

hel·den·ten·or /'heldəntā,nôr; 'heldn,tenər/ ▶ **n.** a powerful tenor voice suitable for heroic roles in opera. ■ a singer with such a voice. [1920s: Ger., lit. 'hero tenor.']

Hel·en /'helən/ Gk. Mythol. the daughter of Zeus and Leda, born from an egg. In the Homeric poems she was the wife of Menelaus, and her abduction by Paris led to the Trojan War.

Hel·e·na /'helənə/ the capital of Montana, in the western central part of the state; pop. 25,780.

Hel·e·na, St. (*c.*255–*c.*330), Roman empress; mother of Constantine the Great. She is credited with finding the crucifixion cross of Christ.

heli- ▶ **comb. form** relating to helicopters: *helipad*.

he·li·a·cal /hə'līəkəl/ ▶ **adj.** Astron. relating to the sun. [16th C.: via late L. from Gk. *hēliakos* (from *hēlios* 'sun') + -AL.]

he·li·a·cal ris·ing ▶ **n.** the rising of a celestial object at the same time or just before the sun, or its first visible rising after a period of invisibility due to conjunction with the sun. The last setting before such a period is the **heliacal setting**. [17th C.: *heliacal*, via late L. from Gk. *hēliakos* (from *hēlios* 'sun') + -AL.]

he·li·an·the·mum /,hēlē'anthəməm/ ▶ **n.** a rockrose of the genus *Helianthemum*. [mod. L., from Gk. *hēlios* 'sun' + *anthemon* 'flower.']

he·li·an·thus /,hēlē'anthəs/ ▶ **n.** a plant of the genus *Helianthus* in the daisy family, esp. (in gardening) a sunflower. [mod. L., from Gk. *hēlios* 'sun' + *anthos* 'flower.']

hel·i·cal /'helikəl; 'hē-/ ▶ **adj.** having the shape or form of a helix; spiral: *helical molecules*. — **hel·i·cal·ly** adv.

hel·i·ces /'helə,sēz/ plural form of HELIX.

hel·i·chry·sum /,helə'krīsəm/ ▶ **n.** an Old World plant (genus *Helichrysum*) of the daisy family. Some kinds are grown as everlastings, retaining their shape and color when dried. [L., from Gk. *helikhrusos*, a yellow-flowered plant, from *helix* 'spiral' + *khrusos* 'gold.']

hel·i·coid /'heli,koid/ ▶ **n.** an object of spiral or helical shape. ■ Geom. a surface formed by simultaneously moving a straight line along an axis and rotating it around it (like a screw thread). ▶ **adj.** of the form of a helix or helicoid. — **hel·i·coi·dal** /,heli'koidəl/ adj.

hel·i·con /'heli,kän; -kən/ ▶ **n.** a large spiral bass tuba played encircling the player's head. [19th C.: from L., associated with HELIX.]

hel·i·co·nia /,heli'kōnēə/ ▶ **n.** a large-leaved tropical American plant (genus *Heliconia*, family Heliconiaceae) that bears spectacular flowers with brightly colored bracts.

Hel·i·con, Mount /'heli,kän; -kən/ a mountain in Boeotia, in central Greece.

hel·i·cop·ter /'heli,käptər/ ▶ **n.** a type of aircraft that derives both lift and propulsion from one or two sets of horizontally revolving overhead rotors. Compare with AUTOGIRO. ▶ **v.** [trans.] transport by helicopter: *the Coast Guard helicoptered a compressor to one ship*. ■ [intrans.] fly somewhere in a helicopter: *the inspection team helicoptered ashore*. [19th C.: from Fr. *hélicoptère*, from Gk. *helix* 'spiral' + *pteron* 'wing.']

he·lic·tite /hə'liktīt; 'helik,tīt/ ▶ **n.** Geol. a distorted form of stalactite, typically resembling a twig. [19th C.: from Gk. *heliktos* 'twisted,' on the pattern of *stalactite*.]

helio- ▶ **comb. form** of or relating to the sun: *heliogravure*. [from Gk. *hēlios* 'sun.']

he·li·o·cen·tric /,hēlēə'sentrik/ ▶ **adj.** having the sun as the center. Compare with GEOCENTRIC. ■ Astron. measured from or considered in relation to the center of the sun: *heliocentric distance*. — **he·li·o·cen·tri·cal·ly** /-trik(ə)lē/ adv.

He·li·o·gab·a·lus /ˌhēlēō'gabələs/ (also **El·a·gab·a·lus** /ˌelə'gabələs/) (AD 204–222), Roman emperor 218–222; born *Varius Avitus Bassianus*.

he·li·o·gram /'hēlēəˌgram/ ▶ **n.** a message sent by reflecting sunlight in flashes from a movable mirror.

he·li·o·graph /'hēlēəˌgraf/ ▶ **n.** **1** a signaling device by which sunlight is reflected in flashes from a mirror. ▪ a message sent in such a way; a heliogram. **2** a telescopic apparatus for photographing the sun. **3** hist. a type of early photographic engraving. ▶ **v.** [trans.] **1** dated send (a message) by heliograph. **2** hist. take a heliographic photograph of. — **he·li·o·graph·ic** /ˌhēlēə'grafik/ **adj.** **he·li·og·ra·phy** /ˌhēlē'ägrəfē/ **n.**

he·li·o·gra·vure /ˌhēlēˌōgrə'vyo͝or/ ▶ **n.** another term for **PHOTOGRAVURE**.

he·li·om·e·ter /ˌhēlē'ämitər/ ▶ **n.** hist. Astron. a refracting telescope with a split objective lens, used for finding the angular distance between two stars. [18th C.: from **HELIO-** 'of the sun' + **-METER** (because it was orig. used for measuring the diameter of the sun).]

he·li·o·pause /'hēlēəˌpôz/ ▶ **n.** Astron. the boundary of the heliosphere.

He·li·op·o·lis /ˌhēlē'äpəlis/ **1** an ancient Egyptian city near what is now Cairo. **2** ancient Greek name for **BAALBEK**.

He·li·os /'hēlēˌäs/ Gk. Mythol. the sun personified as a god, father of Phaethon represented as a charioteer.

he·li·o·sphere /'hēlēəˌsfi(ə)r/ ▶ **n.** Astron. the region of space, encompassing the solar system, in which the solar wind has a significant influence. — **he·li·o·spher·ic** /ˌhēlēə'sferik; -'sfi(ə)rik/ **adj.**

he·li·o·stat /'hēlēəˌstat/ ▶ **n.** an apparatus containing a movable or driven mirror, used to reflect sunlight in a fixed direction. See also **COELOSTAT**.

he·li·o·ther·a·py /ˌhēlēə'THerəpē/ ▶ **n.** the therapeutic use of sunlight.

he·li·o·trope /'hēlēəˌtrōp/ ▶ **n.** a plant (genus *Heliotropium*) of the borage family, cultivated for its fragrant purple or blue flowers, which are used in perfume. ▪ a light purple color, similar to that typical of heliotrope flowers. [OE *eliotropus* various plants, via L. from Gk. *hēliotropion* 'plant turning its flowers to the sun,' from *hēlios* 'sun' + *trepein* 'to turn.']

he·li·ot·ro·pism /ˌhēlē'ätrəˌpizəm; ˌhēlēə'trōpizəm/ ▶ **n.** Bot. the directional growth of a plant in response to sunlight. Compare with **PHOTOTROPISM**. ▪ Zool. the tendency of an animal to move toward light. — **he·li·o·trop·ic** /ˌhēlēə'träpik; -'trōpik/ **adj.**

He·li·o·zo·a /ˌhēlēə'zōə/ Zool. a class of single-celled aquatic animals that have a spherical shell with fine radiating needlelike projections. — **he·li·o·zo·an** /-ən/ **n. & adj.** [mod. L. (pl.), from Gk. *hēlios* 'sun' + *zōion* 'animal.']

hel·i·pad /'heləˌpad/ ▶ **n.** a landing and takeoff area for helicopters.

hel·i·port /'heləˌpôrt/ ▶ **n.** an airport or landing place for helicopters.

hel·i·ski·ing /'heləˌskē-iNG/ ▶ **n.** skiing in which the skier is taken up the mountain by helicopter. — **hel·i·ski** **v.** **hel·i·ski·er** **n.**

he·li·um /'hēlēəm/ ▶ **n.** the chemical element of atomic number 2, an inert gas that is the lightest member of the noble gas series. (Symbol: **He**) [19th C.: mod. L., from Gk. *hēlios* 'sun.']

he·lix /'hēliks/ ▶ **n.** (pl. **-li·ces** /-ləˌsēz/) an object having a three-dimensional shape like that of a wire wound uniformly around a cylinder or cone. ▪ Geom. a curve on a conical or cylindrical surface that would become a straight line if the surface were unrolled into a plane. ▪ Biochem. an extended spiral chain of atoms in a protein, nucleic acid, or other polymeric molecule. ▪ Archit. a spiral ornament. ▪ Anat. the rim of the external ear. [16th C.: via L. from Gk.]

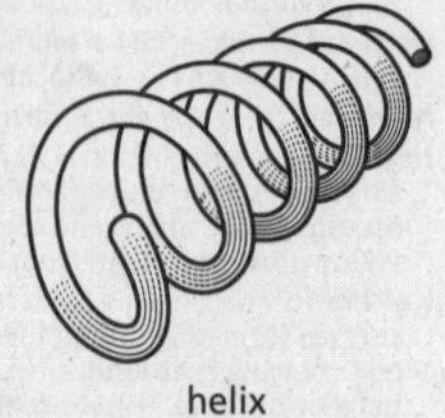
helix

hell /hel/ ▶ **n.** a place regarded in various religions as a spiritual realm of evil and suffering. ▪ a state or place of great suffering. ▶ **exclam.** used to express annoyance or surprise. ▪ (**the hell**) informal expressing anger or contempt.

– PHRASES **all hell broke loose** informal suddenly there was pandemonium. **(as) —— as hell** informal used for emphasis: *he's as guilty as hell.* **catch** (or **get**) **hell** informal be severely reprimanded. **come hell or high water** whatever difficulties may occur. **for the hell of it** informal just for fun. **get the hell out (of)** informal escape quickly from (a place or situation). **give someone hell** informal severely reprimand or make things very unpleasant for someone. **go to hell** informal used to express angry rejection of someone or something. **go to** (or **through**) **hell and back** endure an extremely unpleasant or difficult experience. **go to hell in a handbasket** informal undergo a rapid process of deterioration. **a** (or **one**) **hell of a ——** informal used to emphasize something very bad or great: *a hell of a lot of money.* **hell on wheels** a disastrous situation. **like hell** informal **1** very fast, much, hard, etc. (used for emphasis): *it hurts like hell.* **2** used in ironic expressions of scorn or disagreement: *like hell, he thought.* **not a hope in hell** informal no chance at all. **there will be hell to pay** informal serious trouble will occur as a result of a previous action. **to hell** used for emphasis: *damn it to hell.* **to hell with** informal expressing one's scorn or lack of concern for (someone or something): *to hell with the consequences.* **until** (or **till**) **hell freezes over** for an extremely long time or forever. **what the hell** informal it doesn't matter. — **hell·ward** /-wərd/ **adv. & adj.** [OE *hel, hell*, of Gmc. origin; rel. to Du. *hel* and Ger. *Hölle*, from an Indo-Eur. root meaning 'to cover or hide.']

he'll /hēl/ ▶ **contr.** he shall; he will.

hel·la·cious /he'lāSHəs/ ▶ **adj.** informal very great, bad, or overwhelming: *there was this hellacious hailstorm.* — **hel·la·cious·ly** **adv.** [1930s: from **HELL**.]

Hel·lad·ic /he'ladik/ ▶ **adj.** Archaeol. of, relating to, or denoting the Bronze Age cultures of mainland Greece (*c.*3000–1050 BC). [19th C.: from Gk. *Helladikos*, from *Hellas, Hellad-* 'Greece.']

Hel·las /'heləs/ Greek name for **GREECE**.

hellbender

hell·bend·er /'helˌbendər/ ▶ **n.** a very large aquatic North American salamander (*Cryptobranchus alleganiensis*, family Cryptobranchidae) with grayish skin and a flattened head.

hell-bent ▶ **adj.** [predic.] determined to achieve something at all costs: *why are you hell-bent on leaving?*

hell·cat /'helˌkat/ ▶ **n.** a spiteful, violent woman.

hel·le·bore /'heləˌbôr/ ▶ **n.** a poisonous winter-flowering Eurasian plant (genus *Helleborus*) of the buttercup family, typically having coarse divided leaves and large white, green, or purplish flowers. ▪ another term for **FALSE HELLEBORE**. [OE, from OFr. *ellebre, elebore* or med. L. *eleborus*, via L. from Gk. *helleboros*.]

Hel·len /'helən/ Gk. Mythol. the son or brother of Deucalion and ancestor of all the Hellenes or Greeks.

Hel·lene /'helēn/ ▶ **n.** an ancient Greek. ▪ a native of modern Greece. [from Greek *Hellēn* 'a Greek.' Cf. **HELLEN**.]

Hel·len·ic /he'lenik/ ▶ **adj.** Greek. ▪ Archaeol. relating to or denoting Iron Age and Classical Greek culture. ▶ **n.** the branch of the Indo-European language family comprising classical and modern Greek. ▪ the Greek language.

Hel·len·ism /'heləˌnizəm/ ▶ **n.** the national character or culture of Greece, esp. ancient Greece. ▪ the study or imitation of ancient Greek culture. — **Hel·len·ist** **n.** **Hel·len·i·za·tion** /ˌheləni'zāSHən/ **n.** **Hel·len·ize** /-ˌnīz/ **v.** **Hel·len·iz·er** /-ˌnīzər/ **n.**

Hel·len·is·tic /ˌhelə'nistik/ ▶ **adj.** of or relating to Greek history, language, and culture from the death of Alexander the Great to the defeat of Cleopatra and Mark Antony by Octavian in 31 BC.

Hel·ler /'helər/, Joseph (1923–99), US writer. He wrote *Catch-22* (1961).

Hel·les·pont /'heləˌspänt/ ancient name for the Dardanelles.

hell·fire /'helˌfī(ə)r/ ▶ **n.** the fire or fires of hell.

hell·gram·mite /'helgrəˌmīt/ ▶ **n.** the aquatic larva of a dobsonfly, often used as fishing bait. [19th C.: of unknown origin.]

hell·hole /'helˌhōl/ ▶ **n.** an oppressive place.

hell·hound /'helˌhound/ ▶ **n.** a demon in the form of a dog.

hel·lion /'helyən/ ▶ **n.** informal a rowdy, mischievous, or troublemaking person, esp. a child. [19th C.: perh. from dial. *hallion* 'a worthless fellow.']

hell·ish /'heliSH/ ▶ **adj.** of or like hell. ▪ informal extremely difficult or unpleasant. — **hell·ish·ly** **adv.** [as submodifier] *a hellishly dull holiday.* **hell·ish·ness** **n.**

Hell·man /'helmən/, Lillian Florence (1907–84), US playwright. She wrote *The Children's Hour* (1934), *The Little Foxes* (1939), and *Watch on the Rhine* (1941).

hel·lo /hə'lō; he'lō; 'helō/ (also **hal·lo** or esp. Brit. **hul·lo**) ▶ **exclam.** used as a greeting: *hello there, Katie!* ▪ used to begin a telephone conversation. ▪ used as a cry to attract someone's attention. ▪ /hə'lō; he'lō/ [often pronounced with a rising–falling intonation pattern and a prolonged final vowel] expressing sarcasm or anger. ▶ **n.** (pl. **-los**) an utterance of "hello"; a greeting. [19th C.: var. of earlier *hollo*; rel. to **HOLLA**.]

hell-rais·er ▶ **n.** a person who causes trouble. — **hell-rais·ing** **adj. & n.**

Hell's Can·yon canyon of the Snake River, Idaho, deepest in the US; maximum depth 7,900 feet (2,433 m).

hell·uv·a /'heləvə/ nonstandard spelling of ***HELL OF A*** (see **HELL**).

helm /helm/ ▶ **n.** (**the helm**) a tiller or wheel and any associated equipment for steering a ship or boat. ▪ fig. a position of leadership. ▪ Naut. a helmsman. ▶ **v.** [trans.] steer (a boat or ship). ▪ fig. manage the running of. [OE *helma*; prob. rel. to **HELVE**.]

Hel·mand /'helmənd/ a river in southwestern Afghanistan, flowing southwest for 700 miles (1,125 km) to the Iran–Afghanistan frontier.

hel·met /'helmit/ ▶ **n.** **1** a hard or padded protective hat, various types of which are worn by soldiers, police officers, firefighters, motorcyclists, athletes, and others. **2** Bot. the arched upper part (galea) of the corolla in some flowers, esp. those of the mint and orchid families. **3** (also **helmet shell**) a predatory mollusk (family Cassidae) with a squat heavy shell, living in tropical and temperate seas and preying chiefly on sea urchins. — **hel·met·ed** **adj.** [ME: from OFr., dimin. of *helme*, of Gmc. origin.]

helmet 1

hel·minth /'helminTH/ ▶ **n.** a parasitic worm; a fluke, tapeworm, or nematode. — **hel·min·thic** /hel'minTHik/ **adj.** [19th C.: from Gk. *helmins, helminth* 'intestinal worm.']

hel•min•thi•a•sis /ˌhelmənˈTHīəsis/ ▶ **n.** Med. infestation with parasitic worms.

hel•min•thol•o•gy /ˌhelmənˈTHäləjē/ ▶ **n.** the study of parasitic worms. — **hel•min•tho•log•i•cal** /helˌminTHəˈläjikəl/ **adj.** **hel•min•thol•o•gist** **n.**

helms•man /ˈhelmzmən/ ▶ **n.** (pl. **-men**) a person who steers a ship or boat.

Hé•lo•ïse /ˈ(h)eləˌwēz/ (1098–1164), French abbess. She had a love affair with theologian Abelard.

hel•ot /ˈhelət/ ▶ **n.** a member of a class of serfs in ancient Sparta. ■ a serf or slave. — **hel•ot•age** /-ˌtij/ **n.** **hel•ot•ism** **n.** **hel•ot•ry** **n.** [via L. from Gk. *Heilōtes* (pl.), traditionally taken as referring to *Helos*, a Laconian town whose inhabitants were enslaved.]

help /help/ ▶ **v.** [trans.] **1** make it easier for (someone) to do something by offering aid. ■ improve (a situation or problem); be of benefit to. ■ assist (someone) to move in a specified direction: *help her up.* ■ (**help someone on/off with**) assist someone to put on or take off (a garment). ■ relieve the symptoms of (an ailment). **2** (**help someone to**) serve someone with. ■ (**help oneself**) take something without permission. **3** (**can/could not help**) cannot or could not avoid. ■ (**can/could not help oneself**) cannot or could not stop oneself from acting in a certain way. ▶ **n.** assistance. ■ [in sing.] a person or thing that helps. ■ a domestic servant or employee. ■ [as pl. n.] (**the help**) a group of such employees. ■ [as adj.] giving displayed instructions to a computer user. ▶ **exclam.** used as an appeal for urgent assistance: *Help!*
– PHRASES **so help me (God)** used to emphasize that one means what one is saying. — **help•er** **n.** [OE *helpan* (v.), *help* (n.), of Gmc. origin; rel. to Du. *helpen* and Ger. *helfen.*]

help desk ▶ **n.** a service providing information and support to the users of a computer network.

help•er cell /ˈhelpər/ (also **helper T cell**) ▶ **n.** Physiol. a T cell that influences or controls the differentiation or activity of other cells of the immune system.

help•ful /ˈhelpfəl/ ▶ **adj.** giving or ready to give help. ■ useful: *we find it very helpful to receive comments.* — **help•ful•ly** **adv.** **help•ful•ness** **n.**

help•ing /ˈhelpiNG/ ▶ **n.** a portion of food served.

help•ing hand ▶ **n.** (**a helping hand**) assistance.

help•less /ˈhelplis/ ▶ **adj.** unable to defend oneself or to act without help: *the cubs are born blind and helpless.* ■ uncontrollable: *helpless laughter.* — **help•less•ly** **adv.** **help•less•ness** **n.**

help•mate /ˈhelpˌmāt/ (also **help•meet** /-ˌmēt/) ▶ **n.** a helpful companion or partner, esp. one's husband or wife. [17th C. (as *helpmeet*): from an erroneous reading of Gen. 2:18, 20, "an help meet for him."]

Hel•sing•fors /ˈhelsiNGˌfôrz/ Swedish name of HELSINKI.

Hel•sing•ør /ˌhelsiNGˈœr/ Danish name of ELSINORE.

Hel•sin•ki /helˈsiNGkē; ˈhelsiNGkē/ the capital of Finland, a port on the Gulf of Finland; pop. 492,000. Swedish name HELSINGFORS.

hel•ter-skel•ter /ˈheltər ˈskeltər/ ▶ **adj. & adv.** in disorderly haste or confusion. ▶ **n.** [in sing.] disorder; confusion. [16th C.: perh. from ME *skelte* 'hasten.']

helve /helv/ ▶ **n.** the handle of a weapon or tool. [OE *helfe*, of Gmc. origin; rel. to HALTER[1].]

Hel•ve•tia /helˈvēSHə/ Latin name of SWITZERLAND.

Hel•ve•tian /helˈvēSHən/ esp. hist. ▶ **adj.** Swiss. ▶ **n.** a native of Switzerland.

Hel•vet•ic /helˈvetik/ ▶ **adj. & n.** another term for HELVETIAN.

Hel•ve•ti•i /helˈvēSHēˌī/ ▶ **plural n.** an ancient Celtic people living in what is now western Switzerland.

hem[1] /hem/ ▶ **n.** the edge of a piece of cloth or clothing that has been turned under and sewn. ▶ **v.** (**hemmed, hem•ming**) [trans.] **1** turn under and sew the edge of (a piece of cloth or clothing). **2** (**hem someone/something in**) (usu. **be hemmed in**) surround and restrict the space or movement of. [OE, 'the border of a piece of cloth,' of West Gmc. origin.]

hem[2] ▶ **exclam.** used to indicate a sound made when clearing the throat to attract someone's attention.
– PHRASES **hem and haw** hesitate; be indecisive. [15th C.: imitative.]

he•mag•glu•ti•na•tion /ˌhēməˌglo͞otnˈāSHən/ (Brit. **haemag•glu•ti•na•tion**) ▶ **n.** Med. Biol. the clumping together of red blood cells. — **he•mag•glu•ti•nate** /-ˈglo͞otnˌāt/ **v.**

he•mag•glu•ti•nin /ˌhēməˈglo͞otn-in/ (Brit. **haemag•glu•ti•nin**) ▶ **n.** Med. Biol. a substance, such as a viral protein, that causes hemagglutination.

he•mal /ˈhēməl/ (Brit. **hae•mal**) ▶ **adj.** Physiol. of or concerning the blood. ■ Zool. situated on the same side of the body as the heart and major blood vessels (i.e., in chordates, ventral). [19th C.: from Gk. *haima* 'blood' + -AL.]

he-man ▶ **n.** informal a muscular man.

he•man•gi•o•ma /hiˌmanjēˈōmə/ ▶ **n.** (pl. **-o•mas** or **-o•ma•ta** /-ˈōmətə/) Med. a benign tumor of blood vessels.

he•ma•te•in /ˌhēməˈtē-in; ˈhēməˌtēn/ ▶ **n.** a reddish-brown crystalline dye, $C_{16}H_{12}O_6$, obtained from logwood and used as a stain and indicator.

he•mat•ic /hēˈmatik/ ▶ **adj.** Med., dated of, relating to, or affecting the blood. [19th C.: from Gk. *haimatikos*, from *haima, haimat-* 'blood.']

he•ma•tin /ˈhēməˌtin/ ▶ **n.** Biochem. a bluish-black compound derived from hemoglobin by removal of the protein part and oxidation of the iron atom. [19th C.: from Gk. *haima, haimat-* 'blood' + -IN[1].]

he•ma•tin•ic /ˌhēməˈtinik/ ▶ **n.** any substance that tends to increase hemoglobin in the blood. ▶ **adj.** tending to increase hemoglobin in the blood.

he•ma•tite /ˈhēməˌtīt/ (Brit. **hae•ma•tite**) ▶ **n.** a reddish-black mineral consisting of ferric oxide. [ME: via L. from Gk. *haimatitēs (lithos)* 'bloodlike (stone),' from *haima, haimat-* 'blood.']

hemato- (esp. Brit. **haemato-**) ▶ **comb. form** of or relating to the blood: *hematoma.* [from Gk. *haima, haimat-* 'blood.']

he•mat•o•blast /hiˈmatəˌblast/ ▶ **n.** an immature blood cell.

he•mat•o•cele /hiˈmatəˌsēl/ ▶ **n.** Med. a swelling caused by blood collecting in a body cavity.

he•mat•o•crit /hiˈmatəˌkrit/ ▶ **n.** Physiol. the ratio of red blood cells to the total volume of blood. ■ an instrument for measuring this, by centrifugation. [19th C.: from HEMATO- 'of blood' + Gk. *kritēs* 'judge.']

he•mat•o•gen•e•sis /ˌhēmətəˈjenəsis; hiˌmatə-/ ▶ **n.** another term for HEMOPOIESIS.

he•ma•tol•o•gy /ˌhēməˈtäləjē/ ▶ **n.** the study of the physiology of the blood. — **he•ma•to•log•ic** /-təˈläjik/ **adj.** **he•ma•to•log•i•cal** /-təˈläjikəl/ **adj.** **he•ma•tol•o•gist** **n.**

he•ma•to•ma /ˌhēməˈtōmə/ ▶ **n.** (pl. **-to•mas** or **-to•ma•ta** /-ˈtōmətə/) Med. a solid swelling of clotted blood within the tissues.

he•ma•toph•a•gous /ˌhēməˈtäfəgəs/ (Brit. **hae•ma•toph•a•gous**) ▶ **adj.** (of an animal, esp. an insect or tick) feeding on blood.

he•mat•o•poi•e•sis /ˌhēməˌtōpoiˈēsis; hiˌmatə-/ (Brit. **hae•mat•o•poi•e•sis**) ▶ **n.** another term for HEMOPOIESIS. — **he•ma•to•poi•et•ic** /-poiˈetik/ **adj.**

he•ma•tox•y•lin /ˌhēməˈtäksəlin/ (Brit. **hae•ma•tox•y•lin**) ▶ **n.** Chem. a colorless compound, $C_{16}H_{14}O_6$, present in logwood that is easily converted into blue, red, or purple dyes and is used as a biological stain. [19th C.: from mod. L. *Haematoxylum* (genus name), from *haemato-*, var. of HEMATO- 'of blood,' + Gk. *xulon* 'wood.']

he•mat•o•zo•on /hiˌmatəˈzōən; ˌhēmətə-/ ▶ **n.** (pl. **-zo•a** /-ˈzōə/) any parasitic organism that lives in the blood.

he•ma•tu•ri•a /ˌhēməˈt(y)o͝orēə/ ▶ **n.** Med. the presence of blood in urine.

heme /hēm/ (Brit. **haem**) ▶ **n.** Biochem. an iron-containing compound of the porphyrin class that forms the nonprotein part of hemoglobin and some other biological molecules. [1920s: back-form. from HEMOGLOBIN.]

hemi- ▶ **prefix** half: *hemiplegia.* [from Gk. *hēmi-*; rel. to L. *semi-*.]

-hemia ▶ **comb. form** var. of -EMIA.

he•mic /hēmik/ ▶ **adj.** of or relating to the blood or the circulatory system.

hem•i•cel•lu•lose /ˌhemiˈselyəlōs; -lōz/ ▶ **n.** Biochem. any of a class of substances that occur as constituents of the cell walls of plants and are polysaccharides of simpler structure than cellulose.

Hem•i•chor•da•ta /ˌhemikôrˈdātə/ Zool. a small phylum of wormlike marine invertebrates. — **hem•i•chor•date** /-ˈkôrdāt; -ˈkôrdit/ **n. & adj.**

hem•i•cy•cle /ˈhemiˌsīkəl/ ▶ **n.** a semicircular shape or structure.

hem•i•he•dral /ˌheməˈhēdrəl/ ▶ **adj.** Crystallog. having half the number of planes required for symmetry of the holohedral form.

hem•i•hy•drate /ˌhemiˈhīdrāt/ ▶ **n.** Chem. a crystalline hydrate containing one molecule of water for every two molecules of the compound in question.

hem•i•me•tab•o•lous /ˌheməməˈtabələs/ ▶ **adj.** Entomol. (of an insect) having no pupal stage. — **hem•i•met•a•bol•ic** /ˌheməˌmetəˈbälik/ **adj.**

hem•i•mor•phite /ˌheməˈmôrfīt/ ▶ **n.** a mineral consisting of hydrated zinc silicate.

Hem•ings /ˈhemiNGz/, Sally (1773–1835), US slave, reported to be the mistress of Thomas Jefferson.

Hem•ing•way /ˈhemiNGˌwā/, Ernest Miller (1899–1961), US writer. He wrote *A Farewell to Arms* (1929) and *For Whom the Bell Tolls* (1940). Nobel Prize for Literature (1954).

hem•i•o•la /ˌhemēˈōlə/ ▶ **n.** Music a musical figure in which, typically, two groups of three beats are replaced by three groups of two beats. [ME: via med. L. from Gk. *hēmiolia* 'in the ratio of one and a half to one' (from *hēmi-* 'half' + *holos* 'whole').]

hem•i•par•a•site /ˌheməˈparəˌsīt/ ▶ **n.** Bot. a plant that may obtain part of its food by parasitism.

hem•i•ple•gi•a /ˌheməˈplēj(ē)ə/ ▶ **n.** Med. paralysis of one side of the body. — **hem•i•ple•gic** **n. & adj.** [17th C.: mod. L., from Gk. *hēmiplēgia*, from *hemi-* 'half' + *plēgē* 'stroke.']

He•mip•ter•a /həˈmiptərə/ Entomol. a large order of insects that comprises the true bugs. See also HETEROPTERA, HOMOPTERA. ■ [as pl. n.] (**hemiptera**) insects of this order. — **he•mip•ter•an** **n. & adj.** **he•mip•ter•ous** /-tərəs/ **adj.** [mod. L. (pl.), from Gk. *hemi-* 'half' + *pteron* 'wing.']

hem•i•sphere /ˈheməˌsfi(ə)r/ ▶ **n.** a half of a sphere. ■ a half of the earth, usually as divided into northern and southern halves by the equator, or into western and eastern halves by an imaginary line passing through the poles. ■ a half of the celestial sphere. ■ (also **cerebral hemisphere**) each of the two parts of the cerebrum in the brain of a vertebrate. — **hem•i•spher•ic** /ˌheməˈsfi(ə)rik; -ˈsferik/ **adj.** **hem•i•spher•i•cal** /ˌheməˈsfi(ə)rikəl; -ˈsfer-/ **adj.** **hem•i•spher•i•cal•ly** /ˌheməˈsfi(ə)rik(ə)lē; -ˈsfer-/ **adv.** [ME: from OFr. *emisphere*, via L. from Gk. *hēmisphairion*, from *hēmi-* 'half' + *sphaira* 'sphere.']

hem•line /ˈhemˌlīn/ ▶ **n.** the level of the lower edge of a garment such as a skirt, dress, or coat.

hem•lock /ˈhemˌläk/ ▶ **n.** **1** a highly poisonous European plant (*Conium* *maculatum*) of the parsley family, with a purple-spotted stem, fernlike leaves, small white flowers, and an unpleasant smell. ■ a sedative or poisonous potion obtained from this plant. **2** (also **hemlock fir** or **spruce**) a coniferous North American tree (genus *Tsuga*) of the pine family with dark green foliage that is said to smell like the hemlock plant when crushed, grown chiefly for timber and pulp production. [OE *hymlice, hemlic*, of unknown origin.]

hemo- (esp. Brit. **haemo-**) ▶ **comb. form** equivalent to HEMATO-. [from Gk. *haima* 'blood.']

he·mo·chro·ma·to·sis /ˌhēməˌkrōmə'tōsis/ ▶ **n.** Med. a hereditary disorder in which iron salts are deposited in the tissues.

he·mo·coel /'hēməˌsēl/ ▶ **n.** Zool. the primary body cavity of most invertebrates, containing circulatory fluid. [19th C.: from HEMO- 'of blood' + Gk. *koilos* 'hollow, cavity.']

he·mo·cy·a·nin /ˌhēmə'sīənin/ ▶ **n.** Biochem. a protein responsible for transporting oxygen in the blood plasma of arthropods and mollusks.

he·mo·cyte /'hēməˌsīt/ ▶ **n.** a blood cell.

he·mo·cy·tom·e·ter /ˌhēməsī'tämitər/ (also **he·ma·cy·tom·e·ter**) ▶ **n.** an instrument for counting of cells in a blood sample or other fluid under a microscope.

he·mo·di·al·y·sis /ˌhēməˌdī'aləsis/ ▶ **n.** (pl. **-ses** /-ˌsēz/) Med. kidney dialysis.

he·mo·dy·nam·ic /ˌhēmōdī'namik/ ▶ **adj.** Physiol. of or relating to the flow of blood within a body. — **he·mo·dy·nam·i·cal·ly adv. he·mo·dy·nam·ics n.**

he·mo·flag·el·late /ˌhēmə'flajəˌlāt; -lit/ ▶ **n.** any parasitic flagellate protozoan that lives in the bloodstream.

he·mo·glo·bin /'hēməˌglōbin/ ▶ **n.** Biochem. a red protein responsible for transporting oxygen in the blood of vertebrates. [19th C.: a contracted form of *hematoglobulin*, in the same sense.]

he·mo·lymph /'hēməˌlimf/ ▶ **n.** a fluid equivalent to blood in most invertebrates.

he·mol·y·sin /hi'mälisin; ˌhēmə'lī-/ ▶ **n.** a substance in the blood that destroys red blood cells and liberates hemoglobin.

he·mol·y·sis /hē'mäləsis/ (Brit. **hae·mol·y·sis**) ▶ **n.** the rupture or destruction of red blood cells.

he·mo·lyt·ic /ˌhēmə'litik/ ▶ **adj.** Med. relating to the rupture or destruction of red blood cells.

he·mo·lyt·ic dis·ease of the new·born ▶ **n.** Med. a severe form of anemia caused in a fetus or newborn infant by incompatibility with the mother's blood type. Also called ERYTHROBLASTOSIS.

he·mo·phil·i·a /ˌhēmə'filēə/ ▶ **n.** a medical condition in which the ability of the blood to clot is severely reduced, often due to lack of factor VIII. — **he·mo·phil·i·ac** /-'filēˌak/ **n. he·mo·phil·ic** /-'filik/ **adj.**

he·mo·poi·e·sis /ˌhēməpoi'ēsis/ ▶ **n.** the production of blood cells and platelets, which occurs in the bone marrow. Also called HEMATOGENESIS. — **he·mo·poi·et·ic** /-poi'etik/ **adj.** [20th C.: from HEMO- 'of blood' + Gk. *poiēsis* 'making.']

he·mop·ty·sis /hē'mäptəsis/ ▶ **n.** the coughing up of blood. [17th C.: mod. L., from HEMO- 'of blood' + Gk. *ptusis* 'spitting.']

hem·or·rhage /'hem(ə)rij/ ▶ **n.** an escape of blood from a ruptured blood vessel. ■ a damaging loss of valuable people or resources. ▶ **v.** [intrans.] (of a person) suffer a hemorrhage. ■ [trans.] expend (money) in large amounts in a seemingly uncontrollable manner. [17th C. (as a n.): alt. of obs. *hemorrhagy*, via L. *haemorrhagia* from Gk. *haimorrhagia*, from *haima* 'blood' + the stem of *rhēgnunai* 'burst.']

hem·or·rhag·ic /ˌhemə'rajik/ ▶ **adj.** accompanied by or produced by hemorrhage.

hem·or·rhoid /'hem(ə)ˌroid/ ▶ **n.** (usu. **hemorrhoids**) a swollen vein or group of veins in the region of the anus. Also (collectively) called PILES. — **hem·or·rhoi·dal** /ˌhemə'roidl/ **adj.** [ME: via OFr. and L. from Gk. *haimorrhoides (phlebes)* 'bleeding (veins),' from *haima* 'blood' + an element rel. to *rhein* 'to flow.']

he·mos·ta·sis /ˌhēmə'stāsəs; heme-/ ▶ **n.** Med. the stopping of blood flow. — **he·mo·stat·ic** /-'statik/ **adj.**

he·mo·stat /'hēməˌstat/ ▶ **n.** Med. an instrument for preventing the flow of blood from an open blood vessel by compression of the vessel.

hemp /hemp/ ▶ **n.** (also **Indian hemp**) the cannabis plant, esp. when grown for fiber. ■ the fiber of this plant, extracted from the stem. ■ used in names of other plants that yield fiber, e.g., **Manila hemp**. ■ marijuana. [OE *henep, hænep*, of Gmc. origin; rel. to Du. *hennep* and Ger. *Hanf*, also to Gk. *kannabis*.]

hemp ag·ri·mo·ny ▶ **n.** an erect Eurasian plant (*Eupatorium cannabinum*) of the daisy family, resembling a valerian, with clusters of pale purple flowers and hairy stems.

hemp·en /'hempən/ ▶ **adj.** [attrib.] made from hemp fiber: *hempen rope*.

hemp net·tle ▶ **n.** a nettlelike plant (genus *Galeopsis*) of the mint family, native to Eurasia but introduced elsewhere.

Hemp·stead /'hem(p)ˌsted/ a town on western Long Island, New York; pop. 725,639.

hen /hen/ ▶ **n.** a female bird, esp. of a domestic fowl. ■ (**hens**) domestic fowls of either sex. ■ used in names of birds, esp. waterbirds of the rail family, e.g., **moorhen**. ■ a female lobster, crab, or salmon.
– PHRASES **as rare** (or **scarce**) **as hen's teeth** extremely rare. [OE *henn*, of Gmc. origin; rel. to Du. *hen* and Ger. *Henne*.]

He·nan /'hə'nän/ (also **Ho·nan** /'hō'nän/) a province in northeast central China; capital, Zhengzhou.

hen and chick·ens ▶ **n.** any of a number of plants, esp. the houseleeks, producing small flowerheads or offshoots.

hen·bane /'henˌbān/ ▶ **n.** a coarse and poisonous Eurasian plant (*Hyoscyamus niger*) of the nightshade family, with sticky hairy leaves and an unpleasant smell. ■ a psychoactive drink prepared from this plant.

hen·bit /'henˌbit/ ▶ **n.** a dead-nettle (genus *Lamium*) with purple flowers and partly prostrate stems.

hence /hens/ ▶ **adv. 1** as a consequence; for this reason. **2** in the future (used after a period of time). **3** (also **from hence**) archaic from here: *hence, be gone*. [ME *hennes* (sense 3): from earlier *henne* (from OE *heonan*, of Gmc. origin, rel. to HE) + -S³.]

hence·forth /'hensˌfôrTH/ (also **hence·for·ward** /hens'fôrwərd/) ▶ **adv.** from this time on or from that time on.

hench·man /'henCHmən/ ▶ **n.** (pl. **-men**) esp. derog. a faithful follower or political supporter, esp. one prepared to engage in crime or dishonest practices. [ME, from OE *hengest* 'male horse' + MAN.]

hen·coop /'henˌko͞op/ ▶ **n.** a cage or pen for keeping poultry in.

hendeca- ▶ **comb. form** eleven; having eleven. [from Gk. *hendeka* 'eleven.']

hen·dec·a·gon /hen'dekəˌgän/ ▶ **n.** a plane figure with eleven straight sides and angles. — **hen·de·cag·o·nal** /ˌhendə'kagənl/ **adj.**

hen·dec·a·syl·la·ble /hen'dekəˌsiləbəl; -ˌdekə'siləbəl/ ▶ **n.** Pros. a line of verse with eleven syllables. — **hen·dec·a·syl·lab·ic** /henˌdekəsə'labik/ **adj.**

Hen·der·son /'hendərsən/ a city in southeastern Nevada; pop. 175,381.

Hen·der·son·ville /'hendərsənˌvil/ a city in north central Tennessee, a northeastern suburb of Nashville; pop. 40,620.

hen·di·a·dys /hen'dīədəs/ ▶ **n.** Rhet. the expression of a single idea by two words connected with "and," e.g., *nice and warm*, when one could be used to modify the other, as in *nicely warm*. [16th C.: via med. L. from Gk. *hen dia duoin* 'one thing by two.']

hen·e·quen /'henik(w)ən/ ▶ **n. 1** a fiber resembling sisal, chiefly used for twine and paper pulp. **2** a Central American agave (*Agave fourcroydes*) from which such fiber is obtained. [17th C.: from Sp. *jeniquen*, from a local word.]

henge /henj/ ▶ **n.** a prehistoric monument consisting of a circle of stone or wooden uprights. [18th C.: back-form. from STONEHENGE.]

hen·house /'henˌhous/ ▶ **n.** a small shed for keeping poultry in.

hen·na /'henə/ ▶ **n. 1** the powdered leaves of a tropical shrub, used as a dye to color the hair and decorate the body. **2** the Old World shrub (*Lawsonia inermis*, family Lythraceae) that produces these leaves, with small pink, red, or white flowers. ▶ **v.** (**hen·nas, hen·naed** /'henəd/, **hen·na·ing**) [trans.] dye (hair) with henna. ▶ **adj.** reddish-brown. [17th C.: from Arab. *ḥinnā'*.]

Hen·ne·pin /'henəpən/, Louis (1640–c. 1701), French explorer. He accompanied La Salle as his chaplain through the Great Lakes in 1679 and explored the surrounding territory.

hen·o·the·ism /'henōTHēˌizəm; ˌhenō'THē-/ ▶ **n.** adherence to one particular god out of several. [19th C.: from Gk. *heis, heno-* 'one' + *theos* 'god' + -ISM.]

hen par·ty ▶ **n.** informal a social gathering of women.

hen·peck /'henˌpek/ ▶ **v.** [trans.] [usu. as adj.] (**henpecked**) (of a woman) continually criticize and give orders to (her husband or other male partner).

Hen·ri /'henrē/, Robert (1865–1929), US painter. The Ashcan School of painters was formed largely as a result of his influence.

Hen·ri·cian /hen'risHēən/ ▶ **adj.** of or relating to the reign and policies of Henry VIII of England.

Hen·ry¹ /'henrē/ the name of eight kings of England: ■ Henry I (1068–1135), reigned 1100–35; son of William I. He conquered Normandy in 1105. ■ Henry II (1133–89), reigned 1154–89; son of Matilda. He was the first Plantagenet king. ■ Henry III (1207–72), reigned 1216–72; son of John. ■ Henry IV (1367–1413), reigned 1399–1413; son of John of Gaunt; known as **Henry Bolingbroke**. ■ Henry V (1387–1422), reigned 1413–22; son of Henry IV. He defeated the French at Agincourt in 1415. ■ Henry VI (1421–71), reigned 1422–61, 1470–71; son of Henry V. ■ Henry VII (1457–1509), reigned 1485–1509; son of Edmund Tudor, Earl of Richmond; known as **Henry Tudor**. He was the first Tudor king. ■ Henry VIII (1491–1547), reigned 1509–47; son of Henry VII. Henry had six wives (Catherine of Aragon, Anne Boleyn, Jane Seymour, Anne of Cleves, Catherine Howard, Katherine Parr). His first divorce led to England's break with the Roman Catholic Church.

Hen·ry² (1394–1460), Portuguese explorer; known as **Henry the Navigator**. The third son of John I of Portugal, he laid the foundation for Portuguese imperial expansion around Africa to the Far East.

Hen·ry³ the name of seven kings of the Germans, six of whom were also Holy Roman Emperors: ■ Henry I (*c.*876–936), reigned 919–936; known as **Henry the Fowler**. ■ Henry II (973–1024), reigned 1002–24; Holy Roman Emperor 1014–24; also known as **Saint Henry**. ■ Henry III (1017–56), reigned 1039–56; Holy Roman Emperor 1046–56. He defeated the Czechs and fixed the frontier between Austria and Hungary. ■ Henry IV (1050–1106), reigned 1056–1105; Holy Roman Emperor 1084–1105; son of Henry III. ■ Henry V (1086–1125), reigned 1099–1125; Holy Roman Emperor 1111–25. ■ Henry VI (1165–97), reigned 1169–97; Holy Roman Emperor 1191–97. ■ Henry VII (*c.*1269/74–1313), reigned 1308–13; Holy Roman Emperor 1312–13.

Hen·ry⁴, O. (1862–1910), US writer; pen name of *William Sydney Porter*. Collections of his short stories include *Cabbages and Kings* (1904) and

The Voice of the City (1908).

Hen·ry[5], Patrick (1736–99) American patriot. His speech in which he urged the colonies into readiness concluded with "Give me liberty, or give me death."

hen·ry /ˈhenrē/ (abbr.: **H**) ▶ **n.** (pl. **hen·ries** or **hen·rys**) Physics the SI unit of inductance, equal to one volt in a closed circuit with a uniform rate of change of current of one ampere per second. [19th C.: named after Joseph *Henry* (1797–1878), the American physicist who discovered the phenomenon.]

Hen·ry Bo·ling·broke /ˈbôliNG,bro͝ok; ˈbōliNG,brōk/, Henry IV of England (see **Henry**[1]).

Hen·ry IV (1553–1610), king of France 1589–1610; known as **Henry of Navarre**. He established religious freedom with the Edict of Nantes 1598.

Hen·ry the Fow·ler /ˈfoulər/, Henry I, king of the Germans (see **Henry**[3]).

Hen·ry Tu·dor /ˈto͞odər/, Henry VII of England (see **Henry**[1]).

Hen·son /ˈhensən/, Matthew Alexander (1866–1955) US explorer. He accompanied Peary as his valet when the North Pole was reached in 1909.

hep /hep/ ▶ **adj.** dated term for **hip**[3].

hep·a·rin /ˈhepərin/ ▶ **n.** Biochem. a compound in the liver and other tissues that inhibits blood coagulation. [20th C.: via late L. from Gk. *hēpar* 'liver' + **-in**[1].]

hep·a·rin·ize /ˈhepərə,nīz/ ▶ **v.** [trans.] add heparin to. —**hep·a·rin·i·za·tion** /,hepərənəˈzāSHən/ **n.**

he·pat·ic /həˈpatik/ ▶ **adj.** of or relating to the liver. ▶ **n.** Bot. less common term for **liverwort**. [ME: via L. from Gk. *hēpatikos*, from *hēpar*, *hēpat-* 'liver.']

he·pat·i·ca /həˈpatikə/ ▶ **n.** a plant (genus *Hepatica*) of the buttercup family, with anemonelike flowers, native to north temperate regions. [from med. L. *hepatica (herba)* 'liverwort,' fem. of *hepaticus* (see **hepatic**).]

hep·a·ti·tis /,hepəˈtītis/ ▶ **n.** a disease characterized by inflammation of the liver. [18th C.: mod. L., from Gk. *hēpar*, *hēpat-* 'liver' + **-itis**.]

hep·a·ti·tis A ▶ **n.** a form of viral hepatitis transmitted in food.

hep·a·ti·tis B ▶ **n.** a severe form of viral hepatitis transmitted in infected blood.

hep·a·ti·tis C ▶ **n.** a form of viral hepatitis transmitted in infected blood, causing chronic liver disease.

hepato- ▶ **comb. form** of or relating to the liver. [from Gk. *hēpar*, *hēpat-* 'liver.']

hep·a·to·ma /,hepəˈtōmə/ ▶ **n.** (pl. **-to·mas** or **-to·ma·ta** /-ˈtōmətə/) Med. a cancer of the cells of the liver.

hep·cat /ˈkep,kat/ ▶ **n.** informal, dated a stylish or fashionable person, esp. in the sphere of jazz. [1930s: from **hep** + **cat**[1].]

He·phaes·tus /hiˈfestəs/ Gk. Mythol. the god of fire and of craftsmen, son of Zeus and Hera. Roman equivalent **Vulcan**.

Hep·ple·white /ˈhepəl,(h)wīt/, George (died 1786), English cabinetmaker.

hepta- ▶ **comb. form** seven; having seven: *heptagon.* [from Gk. *hepta* 'seven.']

hep·ta·chlor /ˈheptə,klôr/ ▶ **n.** a chlorinated hydrocarbon, $C_{10}H_5Cl_7$, used as an insecticide.

hep·tad /ˈhep,tad/ ▶ **n.** tech. a group or set of seven. [17th C.: from Gk. *heptas*, *heptad-*, from *hepta* 'seven.']

hep·ta·gon /ˈheptə,gän/ ▶ **n.** a plane figure with seven straight sides and angles. —**hep·tag·o·nal** /hepˈtagənl/ **adj.** [16th C.: from Gk. *heptagonon*, neut. (used as a n.) of *heptagonos* 'seven-angled.']

hep·ta·he·dron /,heptəˈhēdrən/ ▶ **n.** (pl. **-he·drons** or **-he·dra** /-ˈhēdrə/) a solid figure with seven plane faces. —**hep·ta·he·dral** /-ˈhēdrəl/ **adj.**

hep·tam·er·ous /hepˈtamərəs/ ▶ **adj.** Bot. Zool. having parts arranged in groups of seven. ■ consisting of seven joints or parts.

hep·tam·e·ter /hepˈtamitər/ ▶ **n.** Pros. a line of verse consisting of seven metrical feet.

hep·tane /ˈhep,tān/ ▶ **n.** Chem. a colorless liquid hydrocarbon, C_7H_{16}, of the alkane series, obtained from petroleum. [19th C.: from **hepta-**.]

hep·tar·chy /ˈhep,tärkē/ ▶ **n.** (pl. **-chies**) a country or region consisting of seven smaller, autonomous regions. ■ the seven kingdoms of the Angles and the Saxons. ■ government by seven rulers. —**hep·tar·chic** /hepˈtärkik/ **adj.** **hep·tar·chi·cal** /hepˈtärkikəl/ **adj.** [16th C.: from **hepta-** 'seven' + Gk. *arkhia* 'rule,' on the pattern of *tetrarchy*.]

Hep·ta·teuch /ˈheptə,t(y)o͞ok/ ▶ **n.** the first seven books of the Bible (Genesis to Judges) collectively. [17th C.: via late L. from Gk. *heptateukhos*, from *hepta* 'seven' + *teukhos* 'book, volume.']

hep·tath·lon /hepˈtaTHlän/ ▶ **n.** a track and field event, in particular one for women, in which each competitor takes part in the same prescribed seven events. —**hep·tath·lete** /-ˈtaTHlēt/ **n.** [1970s: from **hepta-** 'seven' + Gk. *athlon* 'contest.']

hep·ta·va·lent /ˈheptəvālənt/ ▶ **adj.** Chem. having a valence of seven.

Hep·worth /ˈhep,wərTH/, Dame Jocelyn Barbara (1903–75), English sculptor. Her work includes *The Family of Man* (1972).

her /hər/ ▶ **pron.** [third person sing.] used as the object of a verb or preposition to refer to a female person or animal previously mentioned. Compare with **she**. ■ referring to a ship, country, or other inanimate thing regarded as female. ■ used after the verb "to be" and after "than" or "as" to refer to a female person or animal. ▶ **possessive adj.** **1** belonging to or associated with a female person or animal previously mentioned. ■ belonging to or associated with a ship, country, or other inanimate thing regarded as female. **2** (**Her**) used in titles: *Her Royal Highness.* [OE *hire*, genitive and dative of *hīo*, *hēo* 'she.']

He·ra /ˈherə/ Gk. Mythol. a powerful goddess, the wife and sister of Zeus and the daughter of Cronus and Rhea. Roman equivalent **Juno**. [from Gk. *Hēra* 'lady,' fem. of *hērōs* 'hero,' perh. used as a title.]

Her·a·cles /ˈherəklēz/ (also **Her·a·kles**) Greek equivalent of **Hercules**.

Her·a·cli·tus /,herəˈklītəs/ (*c.*500 BC), Greek philosopher. He believed that fire is the origin of all things.

He·rak·li·on /heˈraklēən/ the capital of Crete, on the northern coast; pop. 117,000. Greek name **Iráklion**.

her·ald /ˈherəld/ ▶ **n.** **1** an official messenger of news. **2** a person or thing viewed as a sign that something is about to happen. **3** hist. an official who oversees state ceremony. ▶ **v.** [trans.] be a sign that (something) is about to happen. ■ (usu. **be heralded**) acclaim. [ME: from OFr. *herault* (n.), *herauder* (v.), of Gmc. origin.]

he·ral·dic /həˈraldik/ ▶ **adj.** of or relating to heraldry. —**he·ral·di·cal·ly** **adv.**

her·ald·ry /ˈherəldrē/ ▶ **n.** the system by which coats of arms and other armorial bearings are devised. ■ armorial bearings or other heraldic symbols. ■ colorful ceremony. —**her·ald·ist** **n.**

He·rat /həˈrät; he-/ a city in western Afghanistan; pop. 177,000.

herb /(h)ərb/ ▶ **n.** **1** any plant with leaves, seeds, or flowers used for flavoring, food, medicine, or perfume. ■ a part of such a plant as used in cooking. **2** Bot. any seed-bearing plant without a woody stem that dies down to the ground after flowering. [ME: via OFr. from L. *herba* 'grass, green crops, herb.']

her·ba·ceous /(h)ərˈbāSHəs/ ▶ **adj.** of, denoting, or relating to herbs (in the botanical sense).

herb·age /ˈ(h)ərbij/ ▶ **n.** herbaceous vegetation. ■ the succulent part of this vegetation, used as pasture. ■ hist. the right of pasture on another's land.

herb·al /ˈ(h)ərbəl/ ▶ **adj.** relating to or made from herbs, esp. those used in cooking and medicine. ▶ **n.** a book about herbs.

her·bal·ism /ˈ(h)ərbə,lizəm/ ▶ **n.** the study or practice of the medicinal and therapeutic use of plants.

herb·al·ist /ˈ(h)ərbəlist/ ▶ **n.** a practitioner of herbalism. ■ a dealer in medicinal herbs.

her·bar·i·um /(h)ərˈbe(ə)rēəm/ ▶ **n.** (pl. **-bar·i·ums** or **-bar·i·a** /-ˈbe(ə)rēə/) a collection of dried plants. ■ a room or building housing such a collection.

herbed /(h)ərbd/ ▶ **adj.** (of food) seasoned with herbs.

Her·bert /ˈhərbərt/, Victor (1859–1924), US composer; born in Ireland. His operettas include *Babes in Toyland* (1903) and *Naughty Marietta* (1910).

herb·i·cide /ˈ(h)ərbə,sīd/ ▶ **n.** a substance that is toxic to plants and is used to destroy unwanted vegetation.

her·biv·ore /ˈ(h)ərbə,vôr/ ▶ **n.** an animal that feeds on plants. —**her·biv·o·rous** /(h)ərˈbiv(ə)rəs/ **adj.** [19th C.: from L. *herba* 'herb' + *-vore* (see **-vorous**).]

herb Par·is ▶ **n.** a European woodland plant (*Paris quadrifolia*) of the lily family, with a single unbranched stem bearing a green and purple flower above four unstalked leaves. [translating med. L. *herba paris*, prob. lit. 'herb of a pair.']

herb Rob·ert ▶ **n.** a common cranesbill (*Geranium robertianum*) with pungent-smelling red-stemmed leaves and pink flowers, native to north temperate regions. [supposed to refer to *Robert* Duke of Normandy, St. Robert, or St. Rupert.]

herb·y /ˈ(h)ərbē/ ▶ **adj.** (**herb·i·er**, **herb·i·est**) (of food or drink) containing or tasting or smelling of herbs.

Her·ce·go·vi·na var. of **Herzegovina**.

Her·cu·la·ne·um /,hərkyəˈlānēəm/ an ancient Roman town, buried on the slopes of Mount Vesuvius.

Her·cu·le·an /,hərkyəˈlēən; hərˈkyo͞olēən/ ▶ **adj.** requiring great strength or effort: *a Herculean task.* ■ (of a person) muscular and strong.

Her·cu·les /ˈhərkyə,lēz/ **1** Greek Rom. Mythol. a hero of superhuman strength and courage who performed twelve immense tasks or "labors." ■ [as n.] (**a Hercules**) a man of exceptional strength. **2** Astron. a large northern constellation, said to represent the kneeling figure of Hercules. [L., from Gk. *Hēraklēs*.]

Her·cu·les bee·tle ▶ **n.** a large tropical American rhinoceros beetle (genus *Dynastes*), the male of which has two long curved horns extending from the head and one from the thorax.

Her·cu·les-club ▶ **n.** either of two tall prickly shrubs or small trees of the US: ■ the **southern prickly-ash** (*Zanthoxylum clava-herculis*), a tree of the rue family, with knobby, corky protrusions on its trunk. ■ the **devil's walking stick** (*Aralia spinosa*), a tree of the ginseng family, with large leaves and black berries. Also called **angelica tree**.

herd /hərd/ ▶ **n.** a large group of animals that live together or are kept together as livestock. ■ derog. a large group of people, typically with a shared characteristic: *I dodged herds of joggers.* ▶ **v.** [intrans.] move in a particular direction. ■ [trans.] keep or look after (livestock). [OE *heord*, of Gmc. origin; rel. to Ger. *Herde*.]

herd·er /ˈhərdər/ ▶ **n.** a person who looks after a herd.

herds·man /ˈhərdzmən/ ▶ **n.** (pl. **-men**) the owner or keeper of a herd of domesticated animals. ■ (**the Herdsman**) the constellation Boötes.

here /hi(ə)r/ ▶ **adv.** **1** in, at, or to this place or position. ■ used when pointing or gesturing to indicate the place in mind: *sign here.* ■ used to draw attention to someone or something that has just arrived. ■ [with infin.] used to indicate one's role in a particular situation: *I'm here to help you.* ■ used to refer to existence in the world in general. **2** (usu. **here is/are**) used when introducing something or someone: *here's what you have to do.* ■ used when giving something to someone. **3** used when indicating a time or situation that has arrived or is happening: *here is your opportunity.* ■ used to refer to a particular point or aspect reached in an argument, situation, or activity: *here lies the key to the recovery.* ▶ **exclam.** **1** used to attract someone's attention: *here, hold it.* **2** indicating one's presence in a roll call.

– PHRASES **here and now** at this very moment; at the present time. **here and there** in various places. **here goes** an expression indicating that one is about to start something difficult or exciting. **here's to someone/something** used to wish health or success before drinking. **here today, gone tomorrow** soon over or forgotten; short-lived. **here we go again** said to indicate that the same events, typically undesirable ones, are recurring. **neither here nor there** of no importance or relevance. [OE *hēr*, of Gmc. origin; rel. to Du. and Ger. *hier*, also to **HE**.]

here·a·bouts /ˈhi(ə)rəˌbouts/ (also **here·a·bout**) ▶ **adv.** near this place: *there is little water hereabouts.*

here·af·ter /hi(ə)rˈaftər/ ▶ **adv.** formal from now on. ■ at some time in the future. ■ after death: *hope of life hereafter.* ▶ **n.** (**the hereafter**) life after death.

here·by /ˌhi(ə)rˈbī; ˈhi(ə)rˌbī/ ▶ **adv.** formal as a result of this document or utterance.

he·red·i·tar·y /həˈrediˌterē/ ▶ **adj.** (of a title, office, or right) conferred by or based on inheritance. ■ [attrib.] (of a person) holding a position by inheritance. ■ (of a characteristic or disease) determined by genetic factors and therefore able to be passed on from parents to their offspring or descendants. ■ of or relating to inheritance. ■ Math. (of a set) defined such that every element that has a given relation to a member of the set is also a member of the set. — **he·red·i·tar·i·ly** /həˌrediˈte(ə)rəlē/ **adv.** **he·red·i·tar·i·ness** **n.** [ME: from L. *hereditarius*, from *hereditas* (see **HEREDITY**).]

he·red·i·ty /həˈreditē/ ▶ **n.** **1** the passing on of physical or mental characteristics genetically from one generation to another. ■ a person's ancestry. **2** inheritance of title, office, or right. [18th C.: from Fr. *hérédité*, from L. *hereditas* 'heirship,' from *heres, hered-* 'heir.']

Her·e·ford /ˈhərfərd; ˈherə-/ ▶ **n.** an animal of a breed of red and white beef cattle. [19th C.: named after *Hereford*, England, where it originated.]

here·in /ˌhi(ə)rˈin/ ▶ **adv.** formal in this document or book. ■ in this matter; arising from this: *the statues are sensual and herein lies their interest.*

here·in·af·ter /ˌhi(ə)rinˈaftər/ ▶ **adv.** formal further on in this document: *grievous bodily harm (hereinafter GBH).*

here·in·be·fore /ˌhi(ə)rinbiˈfôr/ ▶ **adv.** formal before this point in this document.

here·of /ˌhi(ə)rˈəv/ ▶ **adv.** formal of this document.

He·re·ro /həˈre(ə)rō/ ▶ **n.** (pl. same or **-ros**) **1** a member of a people living in Namibia, Angola, and Botswana. **2** the Bantu language of this people. ▶ **adj.** of or relating to the Herero or their language. [a local name, from *Otshi-Herero*, the Herero word for the language.]

he·re·si·arch /həˈrēzēˌärk; ˈherəsē-/ ▶ **n.** the founder of a heresy or the leader of a heretical sect. [16th C.: via ecclesiastical L. from eccles. Gk. *hairesiarkhēs* 'leader of a sect,' from *hairesis* 'heretical sect, heresy' + *arkhēs* 'ruler.']

her·e·sy /ˈherəsē/ ▶ **n.** (pl. **-sies**) belief or opinion contrary to orthodox religious (esp. Christian) doctrine. ■ opinion profoundly at odds with what is generally accepted: *cutting capital gains taxes is heresy.* [ME: from OFr. *heresie*, based on L. *haeresis*, from Greek *hairesis* 'choice' (in eccles. Gk. 'heretical sect'), from *haireisthai* 'choose.']

her·e·tic /ˈherətik/ ▶ **n.** a person believing in or practicing religious heresy. ■ a person holding an opinion at odds with what is generally accepted. — **he·ret·i·cal** /həˈretikəl/ **adj.** **he·ret·i·cal·ly** /həˈretiklē/ **adv.**

here·to /ˌhi(ə)rˈto͞o/ ▶ **adv.** formal to this matter or document: *the written consent of each of the parties hereto.*

here·to·fore /ˈhi(ə)rtəˌfôr/ ▶ **adv.** formal before now.

here·un·der /ˌhi(ə)rˈəndər/ ▶ **adv.** formal as provided for under the terms of this document. ■ further on in a document.

here·up·on /ˌhi(ə)rəˈpän/ ▶ **adv.** after or as a result of this.

here·with /ˌhi(ə)rˈwiᴛʜ; -ˈwiᴛʜ/ ▶ **adv.** formal with this letter: *I send you herewith fifteen dollars.*

her·i·ot /ˈherēət/ ▶ **n.** Brit., hist. a tribute paid to a lord out of the belongings of a tenant who died, often consisting of a live animal or, originally, military equipment that he had been lent during his lifetime. [OE *heregeatwa*, from *here* 'army' + *geatwa* 'trappings.']

her·it·a·ble /ˈheritəbəl/ ▶ **adj.** able to be inherited. — **her·it·a·bil·i·ty** /ˌheritəˈbilitē/ **n.** **her·it·a·bly** **adv.**

her·it·age /ˈheritij/ ▶ **n.** [in sing.] property that is or may be inherited; an inheritance. ■ valued objects and qualities such as cultural traditions, unspoiled countryside, and historic buildings that have been passed down from previous generations. ■ [as adj.] (of a plant variety) not hybridized with another; old-fashioned. [ME: from OFr. *heritage*, from *heriter* 'inherit' (see **HERITABLE**).]

her·i·tor /ˈheritər/ ▶ **n.** a person who inherits.

herk·y-jerk·y /ˈhərkē ˈjərkē/ ▶ **adj.** informal characterized by or moving in sudden stops and starts. [20th C.: reduplication of **JERKY**[1].]

herl /hərl/ ▶ **n.** a barb or filament of a feather used in dressing a fishing fly. [ME: appar. of Gmc. origin and rel. to Mid. Low Ger. *harle*.]

herm /hərm/ ▶ **n.** a squared stone pillar with a carved head on top (typically of Hermes), used in ancient Greece as a boundary marker or a signpost. [from the Gk. name **HERMES**.]

her·maph·ro·dite /hərˈmafrədīt/ ▶ **n.** a person or animal having both male and female sex organs or other sexual characteristics, either abnormally or naturally. ■ Bot. a plant with stamens and pistils in the same flower. ▶ **adj.** of or denoting a person, animal, or plant of this kind. — **her·maph·ro·dit·ic** /-ˌmafrəˈditik/ **adj.** **her·maph·ro·dit·ism** /hərˈmafrədiˌtizəm/ (or **her·maph·ro·dism** /-ˌdizəm/) **n.** [ME: via L. from Gk. *hermaphroditos* (see **HERMAPHRODITUS**).]

her·maph·ro·dite brig ▶ **n.** a two-masted sailing ship with a square-rigged foremast and a mainmast with a square topsail and a fore-and-aft mainsail.

Her·maph·ro·dit·us /hərˌmafrəˈdītəs/ Gk. Mythol. a son of Hermes and Aphrodite. Hermaphroditus and the nymph Salmacis became joined in a single body that retained characteristics of both sexes.

her·me·neu·tic /ˌhərməˈn(y)o͞otik/ ▶ **adj.** concerning hermeneutics; interpretative. — **her·me·neu·ti·cal** **adj.** **her·me·neu·ti·cal·ly** /-(ə)lē/ **adv.**

her·me·neu·tics /ˌhərməˈn(y)o͞otiks/ ▶ **plural n.** [usu. treated as sing.] the branch of knowledge that deals with interpretation, esp. of the Bible or literary texts.

Her·mes /ˈhərmēz/ Gk. Mythol. the son of Zeus and Maia, the messenger of the gods, and god of merchants, thieves, and oratory. Roman equivalent **MERCURY**.

her·met·ic /hərˈmetik/ ▶ **adj.** **1** (of a seal or closure) complete and airtight. ■ insulated or protected from outside influences. **2** (also **Her·met·ic**) of or relating to an ancient occult tradition including alchemy, astrology, and theosophy. ■ esoteric; cryptic. — **her·met·i·cal·ly** **adv.** **her·met·i·cism** /-iˌsizəm/ **n.** [17th C. (sense 2): from mod. L. *hermeticus*, from **HERMES**.]

her·mit /ˈhərmit/ ▶ **n.** **1** a person living in solitude as a religious discipline. ■ any person living in solitude or seeking to do so. **2** a hummingbird (*Phaethornis* and other genera) found in the shady lower layers of tropical forests. — **her·mit·ic** /hərˈmitik/ **adj.** [ME: from OFr. *hermite*, from late L. *eremita*, from Gk. *erēmitēs*, from *erēmos* 'solitary.']

her·mit·age /ˈhərmitij/ ▶ **n.** **1** a hermit's dwelling. **2** (**the Hermitage**) a major art museum in St. Petersburg, Russia. **3** (**the Hermitage**) an estate, the home of Andrew Jackson, in central Tennessee, northeast of Nashville.

her·mit crab ▶ **n.** a crab with a soft asymmetrical abdomen that lives in a castoff mollusk shell for protection.

her·mit thrush ▶ **n.** a small migratory North American thrush (*Catharus guttatus*) noted for its melodious song.

hermit thrush

Her·mo·sil·lo /ˌermōˈsē(y)ō/ a city in northwestern Mexico, capital of Sonora; pop. 449,000.

her·ni·a /ˈhərnēə/ ▶ **n.** (pl. **-ni·as** or **-ni·ae** /-nēˌē/) a condition in which part of an organ is displaced and protrudes through the wall of the cavity containing it. — **her·ni·al** **adj.** [ME: from L.]

her·ni·ate /ˈhərnēˌāt/ ▶ **v.** [intrans.] [usu. as adj.] (**herniated**) (of an organ) suffer a hernia: *a herniated bowel.* — **her·ni·a·tion** /hərnēˈāsʜən/ **n.**

He·ro[1] /ˈhi(ə)rō/ Gk. Mythol. a priestess of Aphrodite.

He·ro[2] (1st century), Greek mathematician and inventor; known as **Hero of Alexandria**. He described a number of hydraulic, pneumatic, and other mechanical devices.

he·ro /ˈhi(ə)rō/ ▶ **n.** (pl. **-roes**) a person, typically a man, who is admired for courage or noble qualities. ■ the chief male character in a book, play, or movie, who is typically identified with good qualities. ■ (in mythology and folklore) a person of superhuman qualities and often semidivine origin. ■ (also **hero sandwich**) another term for **SUBMARINE SANDWICH**. [ME (with mythological ref.): via L. from Gk. *hērōs*.]

Her·od /ˈherəd/ the name of four rulers of ancient Palestine: ■ Herod the Great (*c.*74–04 BC), ruled 37–04 BC. Jesus was born during his reign, and he ordered the massacre of the innocents (Matt. 2:16). ■ Herod Antipas (22 BC–*c.*AD 40), tetrarch of Galilee and Peraea 4 BC–AD 40; son of Herod the Great. He was responsible for the beheading of John the Baptist. ■ Herod Agrippa I (10 BC–AD 44), king of Judaea AD 41–44; grandson of Herod the Great. ■ Herod Agrippa II (AD 27–*c.*93), king of various territories in northern Palestine 50–*c.*93; son of Herod Agrippa I. — **He·ro·di·an** /həˈrōdēən/ **adj.** & **n.**

He·rod·o·tus /heˈrädətəs/ (5th century BC), Greek historian. He was the first historian to collect materials systematically and test their accuracy.

he·ro·ic /həˈrōik/ ▶ **adj.** having the characteristics of a hero or heroine; very brave. ■ of or representing heroes or heroines. ■ (of language or a work of art) grand or grandiose in scale or intention. ■ Sculpture (of a statue) larger than life-size but not colossal. ▶n. (**heroics**) **1** behavior or talk that is bold or dramatic. **2** short for HEROIC VERSE. — **he·ro·i·cal·ly** adv.

he·ro·ic cou·plet ▶n. (in verse) a pair of rhyming iambic pentameters, much used by Chaucer.

he·ro·ic stan·za ▶n. a rhyming quatrain in heroic verse. Also called **heroic quatrain**. ■ (in English poetry) a quatrain in iambic pentameter rhyming *abab* or *abba*. Compare with ELEGIAC STANZA.

he·ro·ic verse ▶n. a type of verse used for epic or heroic subjects. Also called **heroic meter**.

her·o·in /'herō-in/ ▶n. a highly addictive analgesic drug, $C_{17}H_{17}NO(C_2H_3O_2)_2$, derived from morphine, often used illicitly as a narcotic producing euphoria. [19th C.: from Ger. *Heroin*, from L. *heros* 'hero.']

her·o·ine /'herō-in/ ▶n. a woman admired or idealized for her courage or noble qualities. ■ the chief female character in a book, play, or movie, who is typically identified with good qualities. ■ (in mythology and folklore) a woman of superhuman qualities and often semidivine origin.

her·o·ism /'herō,izəm/ ▶n. great bravery.

her·o·ize /'hi(ə)rō,īz/ ▶v. [trans.] (often **be heroized**) treat or represent as a hero.

her·on /'herən/ ▶n. a large fish-eating wading bird (family Ardeidae) with long legs, a long S-shaped neck, and a long pointed bill. Its numerous species include the **great blue heron** (*Ardea herodias*). [ME: from OFr., of Gmc. origin.]

her·on·ry /'herənrē/ ▶n. (pl. **-ries**) a breeding colony of herons, typically in a group of trees.

he·ro-wor·ship ▶n. excessive admiration for someone. ▶v. [trans.] admire (someone) excessively. — **he·ro-wor·ship·er** n.

her·pes /'hərpēz/ ▶n. any of a group of viral diseases caused by herpes viruses affecting the skin or nervous system. — **her·pet·ic** /hər'petik/ adj. [ME: via L. from Gk. *herpēs* 'shingles,' lit. 'creeping,' from *herpein* 'to creep.']

her·pes sim·plex ▶n. a viral infection, caused by a group of herpes viruses, that may produce cold sores, genital inflammation, or conjunctivitis.

her·pes·vi·rus /'hərpēz,vīrəs/ ▶n. Med. any of a group of DNA viruses, esp. those causing herpes.

her·pes zos·ter /'zästər/ ▶n. medical name for SHINGLES. ■ a herpesvirus that causes shingles and chicken pox. [ME: from HERPES and L. *zoster*, from Gk. *zōstēr* 'girdle, shingles.']

her·pe·tol·o·gy /,hərpə'täləjē/ ▶n. the branch of zoology concerned with reptiles and amphibians. — **her·pe·to·log·i·cal** /-tə'läjəkəl/ adj. **her·pe·tol·o·gist** n. [19th C.: from Gk. *herpeton* 'reptile' (from *herpein* 'to creep') + -LOGY.]

Herr /he(ə)r/ ▶n. (pl. **Herr·en** /'he(ə)rən/) a title or form of address used of or to a German-speaking man, corresponding to *Mr.* and also used before a rank or occupation. ■ a German man. [German, from Old High Ger. *hērro*, compar. of *hēr* 'exalted.']

her·ring /'heriNG/ ▶n. a silvery fish (*Clupea* and other genera) that is most abundant in coastal waters and is of great commercial importance as a food fish in many parts of the world. The **herring family** (Clupeidae) also includes the sprats, shads, and pilchards. [OE *hǣring, hēring*, of West Gmc. origin; rel. to Du. *haring* and Ger. *Hering*.]

her·ring·bone /'heriNG,bōn/ ▶n. [usu. as adj.] **1** an arrangement or design resembling the bones in a fish, used esp. in the weave of cloth or the placing of bricks. ■ (also **herringbone stitch**) a cross-stitch with a pattern resembling such an arrangement. See illustration at EMBROIDERY. **2** Skiing a method of ascending a slope by walking forward in alternate steps with each ski angled outward. ▶v. **1** [trans.] mark with a herringbone pattern. ■ work with a herringbone stitch. **2** [intrans.] Skiing ascend a slope using the herringbone technique.

herringbone 1

her·ring gull ▶n. a gull (*Larus argentatus*) with gray black-tipped wings, abundant and widespread in both Eurasia and North America.

Her·ri·ot /'herēət/, James (1916–95), English veterinarian and writer; pen name of *James Alfred Wight*. He wrote *All Creatures Great and Small* (1972).

hers /hərz/ ▶possessive pron. used to refer to a thing or things belonging to or associated with a female person or animal previously mentioned.

Her·schel /'hərsHəl/, Sir (Frederick) William (1738–1822), English astronomer; born in Germany. He discovered the planet Uranus.

her·self /hər'self/ ▶pron. [third person sing.] **1** [reflexive] used as the object of a verb or preposition to refer to a female person or animal previously mentioned as the subject of the clause. **2** [emphatic] she or her personally.
– PHRASES (**not**) **be herself** see *BE ONESELF, NOT BE ONESELF* at BE. **by herself** see *BY ONESELF* at BY. [OE (see HER, SELF).]

Her·sey /'hərsē/, John Richard (1914–93), US writer; born in China of missionary parents. He wrote *A Bell for Adano* (1944) and *Hiroshima* (1946).

her·sto·ry /'hərstərē/ ▶n. (pl. **-ries**) history viewed from a female or specifically feminist perspective. [1970s: from HER, based on *history*.]

Hertz /hərts/, Heinrich Rudolf (1857–94), German physicist. He pioneered in radio communication.

hertz /hərts/ (abbr.: **Hz**) ▶n. (pl. same) the SI unit of frequency, equal to one cycle per second. [19th C.: named after H. R. HERTZ.]

Hertz·ian wave /'hərtsēən/ ▶n. former term for RADIO WAVE.

Her·ze·go·vi·na /,hərtsə'gōvənə; -gō'vēnə; ,hert-/ (also **Her·ce·go·vi·na**) a region in the Balkans that forms the southern part of Bosnia–Herzegovina. — **Her·ze·go·vi·ni·an** /-gō'vinēən; -'vēnē-/ adj. & n.

Her·zl /'hərtsəl/, Theodor (1860–1904), Hungarian journalist. He founded the Zionist movement in 1897.

he's /hēz/ ▶contr. ■ he is. ■ he has.

Hesh·van /'KHesHvän; 'hesHvən/ ▶n. var. of HESVAN.

He·si·od /'hesēəd/ (c.700 BC), Greek poet. One of the earliest known Greek poets, he wrote the *Theogony*.

hes·i·tant /'hezitənt/ ▶adj. tentative, unsure, or slow in acting or speaking: *clients are hesitant about buying*. — **hes·i·tance** n. **hes·i·tan·cy** n. **hes·i·tant·ly** adv.

hes·i·tate /'hezi,tāt/ ▶v. [intrans.] pause before saying or doing something, esp. through uncertainty. ■ [with infin.] be reluctant to do something. — **hes·i·tat·er** n. **hes·i·tat·ing·ly** /-,tātiNGlē/ adv. [17th C.: from L. *haesitat-* 'stuck fast, left undecided,' from the v. *haesitare*, from *haerere* 'stick, stay.']

hes·i·ta·tion /,hezi'tāsHən/ ▶n. the action of pausing or hesitating before saying or doing something.

Hes·pe·ri·an /he'spi(ə)rēən/ ▶adj. Gk. Mythol. of or concerning the Hesperides. ■ literary western. [15th C.: from L. *hesperius* (from Gk. *hesperios*, from *Hesperia* 'land of the west,' from *hesperos* 'western' (see HESPERUS)) + -AN.]

Hes·per·i·des /he'sperə,dēz/ Gk. Mythol. a group of nymphs who were guardians of a tree of golden apples in a garden at the western border of Oceanus.

hes·per·id·i·um /,hespə'ridēəm/ ▶n. (pl. **-i·a** /-ēə/) Bot. a fruit with sectioned pulp inside a separable rind, e.g., an orange or grapefruit. [19th C.: based on the HESPERIDES.]

Hes·per·us /'hespərəs/ ▶n. literary the planet Venus. [L., from Gk. *hesperos* 'western,' (as a n.) 'the evening star.']

Hess[1] /hes/, Victor Francis (1883–1964), US physicist; born in Austria. He showed that some cosmic rays are extraterrestrial in origin. Nobel Prize for Physics (1936, shared with C. D. Anderson).

Hess[2], Rudolf (1894–1987), German Nazi administrator; full name *Walther Richard Rudolf Hess*. In 1941, he secretly parachuted into Scotland to negotiate peace with Britain. He was sentenced to life imprisonment at the Nuremberg war trials.

Hes·se[1] /hes; 'hesə/ a state in western Germany; capital, Wiesbaden. German name HESSEN. — **Hes·sian** /'hesHən/ adj. & n.

Hes·se[2] /'hesə/, Hermann (1877–1962), Swiss writer; born in Germany. His works include *Der Steppenwolf* (1927) and *The Glass Bead Game* (1943). Nobel Prize for Literature (1946).

Hes·sian /'hesHən/ ▶adj. of or relating to Hesse, its people, or their language. ▶n. **1** a native or inhabitant of Hesse. ■ a German mercenary fighting for the British during the American Revolution. ■ a mercenary soldier. **2** (**hessian**) British term for BURLAP.

Hes·sian boot ▶n. a high tasseled leather boot, originally worn by Hessian troops.

Hes·sian fly ▶n. a gall midge (*Mayetiola destructor*) whose larvae are a pest of cereal crops, occurring in wheat-growing areas.

Hes·van /'KHesHvän; 'hesvən/ (also **Ches·van**, **Hesh·van**) ▶n. (in the Jewish calendar) the second month of the civil and eighth of the religious year. [from Heb. *ḥešwān*.]

he·tae·ra /hi'ti(ə)rə/ (also **he·tai·ra** /-'tīrə/) ▶n. (pl. **-tae·ras** or **-tae·rae** /-'ti(ə)rē/) a courtesan or mistress, esp. one in ancient Greece. [from Gk. *hetaira*, fem. of *hetairos* 'companion.']

het·er·o /'hetə,rō/ ▶adj. & n. informal short for HETEROSEXUAL.

hetero- ▶comb. form other; different: *heterosexual*. Often contrasted with HOMO-. [from Gk. *heteros* 'other.']

het·er·o·ar·o·mat·ic /,hetərō,arə'matik/ ▶adj. Chem. denoting an organic compound with a ring structure that is both heterocyclic and aromatic.

het·er·o·chro·mat·ic /,hetə,rōkrə'matik/ ▶adj. **1** of several different colors or (in physics) wavelengths. **2** Biochem. of or relating to heterochromatin.

het·er·o·chro·ma·tin /,hetərō'krōmətin/ ▶n. Biol. chromosome material of different density from normal (usually greater), in which the activity of the genes is modified or suppressed. Compare with EUCHROMATIN.

het·er·o·chro·mo·some /,hetərō'krōmə,sōm/ ▶n. another term for SEX CHROMOSOME.

het·er·o·clite /'hetərə,klīt/ formal ▶adj. abnormal or irregular. ▶n. an abnormal thing or person. ■ an irregularly declined word, esp. a Greek or Latin noun. — **het·er·o·clit·ic** /,hetərə'klitik/ adj. [15th C.: via late L. from Gk. *heteroklitos*, from *heteros* 'other' + *-klitos* 'inflected' (from *klinein* 'to lean, inflect').]

het·er·o·cy·clic /,hetərō'sīklik; -'siklik/ ▶adj. Chem. denoting a compound whose molecule contains a ring of atoms of at least two elements (one

PRONUNCIATION KEY ə *ago, up*; ər *over, fur*; a *hat*; ā *ate*; ä *car*; e *let*; ē *see*; i *fit*; ī *by*; NG *sing*; ō *go*; ô *law, for*; oi *toy*; o͝o *good*; o͞o *goo*; ou *out*; TH *thin*; TH *then*; ZH *vision*

of which is generally carbon).

het·er·o·dox /ˈhetərəˌdäks/ ▶ **adj.** not conforming with accepted or orthodox standards or beliefs. — **het·er·o·dox·y** **n.** [17th C.: via late L. from Gk. *heterodoxos*, from *heteros* 'other' + *doxa* 'opinion.']

het·er·o·dyne /ˈhetərəˌdīn/ Electron. ▶ **adj.** of or relating to the production of a lower frequency from the combination of two almost equal high frequencies, as used in radio transmission. ▶ **v.** [trans.] combine (a high-frequency signal) with another to produce a lower frequency in this way. [20th C.: from HETERO- 'other' + *-dyne*, from Gk. *dunamis* 'power.']

het·er·oe·cious /ˌhetəˈrēsHəs/ ▶ **adj.** parasitic on different and often unrelated species of host at different stages of life. Compare with HOMOECIOUS.

het·er·o·ga·met·ic /ˌhetəˌrōgəˈmetik/ ▶ **adj.** Biol. denoting the sex that has sex chromosomes that differ in morphology, resulting in two different kinds of gamete, e.g., (in mammals) the male and (in birds) the female. The opposite of HOMOGAMETIC.

het·er·og·a·my /ˌhetəˈrägəmē/ ▶ **n.** **1** esp. Zool. the alternation of generations, esp. between sexual and parthenogenetic generations. **2** Bot. a state in which the flowers of a plant are of two or more types. Compare with HOMOGAMY (sense 2). ■ another term for ANISOGAMY. **3** marriage between people from different sociological or educational backgrounds. Compare with HOMOGAMY (sense 1). — **het·er·og·a·mous** /-ˈrägəməs/ **adj.** [19th C.: from HETERO- + Gk. *gamos* 'marriage.']

het·er·o·ge·ne·ous /ˌhetərəˈjēnēəs/ ▶ **adj.** diverse in character or content: *a large and heterogeneous collection.* ■ Chem. of or denoting a process involving substances in different phases (solid, liquid, or gaseous). ■ Math. incommensurable through being of different kinds, degrees, or dimensions. — **het·er·o·ge·ne·i·ty** /-jəˈnēitē/ **n.** **het·er·o·ge·ne·ous·ly** **adv.** **het·er·o·ge·ne·ous·ness** **n.** [17th C.: from med. L. *heterogeneus*, from Gk. *heterogenēs*, from *heteros* 'other' + *genos* 'a kind.']

het·er·og·e·nous /ˌhetəˈräjənəs/ ▶ **adj.** Med. originating outside the organism.

het·er·o·graft /ˈhetərōˌgraft/ ▶ **n.** another term for XENOGRAFT.

het·er·og·y·nous /ˌhetəˈräjənəs/ ▶ **adj.** having females of two kinds, fertile and neuter, as in bees and ants.

het·er·ol·o·gous /ˌhetəˈräləgəs/ ▶ **adj.** esp. Med. Biol. not homologous. — **het·er·ol·o·gy** /-ˈräləjē/ **n.**

het·er·ol·y·sis /ˌhetəˈräləsis; -rōˈlīsis/ ▶ **n.** **1** Biol. the dissolution of cells by lysins or enzymes from different species. **2** Chem. the breakdown of a compound into oppositely charged ions. — **het·er·o·lyt·ic** /ˌhetərōˈlitik/ **adj.**

het·er·om·er·ous /ˌhetəˈrämərəs/ ▶ **adj.** Biol. having or composed of parts that differ in number or position.

het·er·o·mor·phic /ˌhetərəˈmôrfik/ ▶ **adj.** Biol. occurring in two or more different forms. — **het·er·o·morph** /ˈhetərəˌmôrf/ **n.** **het·er·o·mor·phy** /ˈhetərəˌmôrfē/ **n.**

het·er·o·mor·phism /ˌhetərəˈmôrfizəm/ ▶ **n.** Biol. the quality or condition of existing in various forms.

het·er·on·o·mous /ˌhetəˈränəməs/ ▶ **adj.** subject to a law or standard external to itself. ■ (in Kantian moral philosophy) acting in accordance with one's desires rather than reason or moral duty. Compare with AUTONOMOUS. ■ subject to different laws. — **het·er·on·o·my** /-ˈränəmē/ **n.**

het·er·o·nym /ˈhetərəˌnim/ ▶ **n.** Ling. **1** each of two or more words that are spelled identically but have different sounds and meanings, such as *tear* meaning "rip" and *tear* meaning "liquid from the eye." **2** each of two or more words that are used to refer to the identical thing in different geographical areas of a speech community, such as *hoagie* and *grinder*. **3** each of two words having the same meaning but derived from unrelated sources, for example *preface* and *foreword*. Contrasted with PARONYM. — **het·er·o·nym·ic** /ˌhetərəˈnimik/ **adj.** **het·er·on·y·mous** /ˌhetəˈränəməs/ **adj.**

het·er·o·phyte /ˈhetərəˌfīt/ ▶ **n.** Bot. a plant that derives its nourishment from other organisms. — **het·er·o·phyt·ic** **adj.** /ˌhetərəˈfitik/

het·er·o·plas·ty /ˈhetərəˌplastē/ ▶ **n.** the operation of grafting tissue between two individuals of the same or different species. — **het·er·o·plas·tic** **adj.** /ˈhetərəˈplastik/

Het·er·op·ter·a /ˌhetəˈräptərə/ Entomol. a group of true bugs (suborder Heteroptera, order Hemiptera) in which the forewings are nonuniform, having a thickened base and membranous tip. The predatory and water bugs belong to this group, as well as many plant bugs. Compare with HOMOPTERA. ■ [as pl. n.] (**heteroptera**) bugs of this group. — **het·er·op·ter·an** /-tərən/ **n.** & **adj.** **het·er·op·ter·ous** /-tərəs/ **adj.** [mod. L. (pl.), from Gk. *heteros* 'other' + *pteron* 'wing.']

het·er·o·sex·ism /ˌhetərōˈseksizəm/ ▶ **n.** discrimination or prejudice against homosexuals on the assumption that heterosexuality is the norm. — **het·er·o·sex·ist** **adj.**

het·er·o·sex·u·al /ˌhetərōˈsekSHo͞oəl/ ▶ **adj.** (of a person) sexually attracted to people of the opposite sex. ▶ **n.** a heterosexual person. — **het·er·o·sex·u·al·i·ty** /-ˌsekSHo͞oˈalitē/ **n.** **het·er·o·sex·u·al·ly** **adv.**

het·er·o·sis /ˌhetəˈrōsis/ ▶ **n.** Genet. the tendency of a crossbred individual to show qualities superior to those of both parents. Also called HYBRID VIGOR. — **het·er·ot·ic** /-ˈrätik/ **adj.** [20th C.: from Gk. *heterōsis* 'alteration,' from *heteros* 'other.']

het·er·os·po·rous /ˌhetəˈräspərəs; -ərəˈspôrəs/ ▶ **adj.** Biol. producing two different kinds of spores. — **het·er·os·po·ry** **n.** /-ˈspôrē/

het·er·o·sty·ly /ˈhetərəˌstīlē/ ▶ **n.** Bot. the condition (e.g., in primroses) of having styles of different lengths relative to the stamens in the flowers of different individual plants, to reduce self-fertilization. — **het·er·o·sty·lous** /ˌhetərəˈstīləs/ **adj.** [19th C.: from HETERO- 'different' + Gk. *stulos* 'column' + -Y³.]

het·er·o·troph /ˈhetərəˌträf; -ˌtrōf/ ▶ **n.** Biol. an organism deriving its nutritional requirements from complex organic substances. Compare with AUTOTROPH. — **het·er·o·troph·ic** /ˌhetərəˈträfik; -ˈtrō-/ **adj.** **het·er·ot·ro·phy** /ˌhetəˈrätrəfē/ **n.** [20th C.: from HETERO- 'other' + Gk. *trophos* 'feeder.']

het·er·o·typ·ic /ˌhetərōˈtipik/ ▶ **adj.** different in form, arrangement, or type. ■ Biol. of or relating to the first of the two nuclear divisions of meiosis.

het·er·o·zy·go·sis /ˌhetərōzīˈgōsis/ ▶ **n.** Genet. the state of being a heterozygote. ■ Biol. the formation of a zygote through the fusion of genetically different gametes.

het·er·o·zy·gote /ˌhetərōˈzīgət; -gōt/ ▶ **n.** Genet. an individual having two different alleles of a particular gene or genes, and so giving rise to varying offspring. Compare with HOMOZYGOTE. — **het·er·o·zy·gos·i·ty** /-zīˈgäsitē/ **n.** **het·er·o·zy·gous** /-ˈzīgəs/ **adj.**

het·man /ˈhetmən/ ▶ **n.** (pl. **-men**) a Polish or Cossack military commander. [Pol., prob. from Ger. *Hauptmann* 'captain.']

het up /het/ ▶ **adj.** [predic.] informal angry and agitated. [19th C.: from dial. *het* 'heated, hot,' surviving in Scots.]

heu·cher·a /ˈhyo͞okərə/ ▶ **n.** a North American plant (genus *Heuchera*, family Saxifragaceae) with dark green round or heart-shaped leaves and slender stems of tiny flowers. [mod. L., named after Johann H. von *Heucher* (1677–1747), German botanist.]

heu·ris·tic /hyo͞oˈristik/ ▶ **adj.** enabling a person to discover or learn something for themselves. ■ Comput. proceeding to a solution by trial and error or by rules that are only loosely defined. ▶ **n.** a heuristic process or method. ■ (**heuristics**) [usu. treated as sing.] the study and use of heuristic techniques. — **heu·ris·ti·cal·ly** **adv.** [19th C.: formed irregularly from Gk. *heuriskein* 'find.']

He·ve·sy /ˈhevəSHē/, George Charles de (1885–1966), Hungarian chemist. He invented the technique of labeling with isotopic tracers. Nobel Prize for Chemistry (1943).

HEW ▶ **abbr.** (Department of) Health, Education, and Welfare.

hew /hyo͞o/ ▶ **v.** (past part. **hewn** /hyo͞on/ or **hewed**) **1** [trans.] chop or cut (something, esp. wood) with an ax, pick, or other tool. ■ (usu. **be hewn**) make or shape (something) by cutting or chopping a material such as wood or stone. **2** [intrans.] (**hew to**) conform or adhere to. [OE *hēawan*, of Gmc. origin; rel. to Du. *houwen* and Ger. *hauen*.]

hex¹ /heks/ ▶ **v.** [trans.] cast a spell on; bewitch. ▶ **n.** a magic spell; a curse. ■ a witch. [19th C. (as a verb): from Pennsylvania Du. *hexe* (verb), *Hex* (noun), from Ger. *hexen* (v.), *Hexe* (n.).]

hex² ▶ **adj.** & **n.** **1** short for HEXADECIMAL. **2** short for HEXAGONAL.

hexa- (also **hex-** before a vowel) ▶ **comb. form** six; having six. [from Gk. *hex* 'six.']

hex·a·chlor·o·phene /ˌheksəˈklôrəˌfēn/ ▶ **n.** a white, odorless compound used as an antibacterial agent. Chem. formula: $(C_6HCl_3OH)_2CH_2$.

hex·a·chord /ˈheksəˌkôrd/ ▶ **n.** a musical scale of six notes with a half step between the third and fourth.

hex·ad /ˈheksad/ ▶ **n.** tech. a group or set of six. [17th C. (denoting a series of six numbers): from Gk. *hexas, hexad-*, from *hex* 'six.']

hex·a·dec·i·mal /ˌheksəˈdes(ə)məl/ ▶ **adj.** Comput. relating to or using a system of numerical notation that has 16 rather than 10 as its base. — **hex·a·dec·i·mal·ly** **adv.**

hex·a·gon /ˈheksəˌgän/ ▶ **n.** a plane figure with six straight sides and angles. [16th C.: via late L. from Gk. *hexagōnon*, neut. (used as a n.) of *hexagōnos* 'six-angled.']

hex·ag·o·nal /hekˈsagənl/ ▶ **adj.** of or pertaining to a hexagon. ■ (of a solid) having a section that is a hexagon; constructed on a base that is a hexagon. ■ designating or pertaining to a crystal system in which three coplanar axes of equal length are separated by 60° and a fourth axis of a different length is at right angles to these. ■ (of a mineral) crystallizing in this system. — **hex·ag·o·nal·ly** **adv.**

hex·a·gram /ˈheksəˌgram/ ▶ **n.** a figure formed of six straight lines, in particular: ■ a star-shaped figure formed by two intersecting equilateral triangles. ■ any of a set of sixty-four figures made up of six parallel whole or broken lines, occurring in the ancient Chinese *I Ching*. [19th C.: from HEXA- 'six' + Gk. *gramma* 'line.']

hex·a·he·dron /ˌheksəˈhēdrən/ ▶ **n.** (pl. **-drons** or **-dra** /-drə/) a solid figure with six plane faces. — **hex·a·he·dral** /-drəl/ **adj.**

hex·am·er·ous /hekˈsamərəs/ ▶ **n.** Bot. Zool. having parts arranged in groups of six. ■ consisting of six joints or parts.

hex·am·e·ter /hekˈsamitər/ ▶ **n.** Pros. a line of verse consisting of six metrical feet, esp. of six dactyls. — **hex·a·met·ric** /ˌheksəˈmetrik/ **adj.**

hex·ane /ˈheksān/ ▶ **n.** Chem. a colorless liquid hydrocarbon, C_6H_{14}, of the alkane series. [19th C.: from HEXA-.]

hex·a·pla /ˈheksəplə/ ▶ **n.** a sixfold text in parallel columns, esp. of the Old Testament. [17th C.: from Gk., neut. pl. of *hexaploos* 'sixfold,' from *hex* 'six' + *ploos* '-fold.']

Hex·ap·o·da /ˌheksəˈpōdə/ Entomol. a class of six-legged arthropods that comprises the true insects. — **hex·a·pod** /ˈheksəˌpäd/ **n.** [mod. L. (pl.), from Gk. *hexapous, hexapod-*, from *hex* 'six' + *pous* 'foot.']

Hex·a·teuch /ˈheksəˌt(y)o͞ok/ ▶ **n.** the first six books of the Bible (Genesis to Joshua) collectively. [19th C.: from HEXA- 'six' + Gk. *teukhos* 'book.']

hex·a·va·lent /ˌheksəˈvālənt/ ▶ **adj.** Chem. having a valence of six.

hex·ose /ˈheksōs/ ▶ **n.** Chem. any of the class of simple sugars whose molecules contain six carbon atoms, such as glucose and fructose. They generally have the chemical formula $C_6H_{12}O_6$. [19th C.: from HEXA- 'six' + -OSE[2].]

hex sign ▶ n. a design usually in the shape of a star, wheel, or rosette on a circular field. They were thought to ward off evil.

hex·yl /'heksəl/ ▶ n. [as adj.] Chem. of or denoting an alkyl radical $-C_6H_{13}$, derived from hexane.

hey /hā/ ▶ exclam. used to attract attention, to express surprise, interest, or annoyance, or to elicit agreement. ■ hi; hello: *hey, how you doing?*
– PHRASES **what the hey** informal used as a euphemism for "what the hell." [natural exclamation: first recorded in ME.]

hey·day /'hā,dā/ ▶ n. (usu. **one's heyday**) the period of a person's or thing's greatest success or popularity. [16th C. (denoting good spirits or passion): from archaic *heyday!*, an exclamation of joy, surprise, etc.]

Hey·er·dahl /'hāər,däl/, Thor (1914–2002), Norwegian anthropologist. He made ocean voyages in primitive craft to demonstrate his theories of cultural diffusion, such as on the balsa raft *Kon-Tiki* from Peru to the islands east of Tahiti in 1947.

Hez·bol·lah /,hezbə'lä; hez'bälə/ (also **Hiz·bul·lah**) an extremist Shiite Muslim group that has close links with Iran, created after the Iranian revolution of 1979 and active esp. in Lebanon. [from Arab. *ḥizbullāh* 'Party of God,' from *ḥezb* 'party' + *allāh* (see ALLAH).]

HF Physics ▶ abbr. high frequency.

Hf ▶ symb. the chemical element hafnium.

hf ▶ abbr. half.

HFC ▶ abbr. hydrofluorocarbon.

hfs ▶ abbr. hyperfine structure.

Hg ▶ symb. the chemical element mercury. [abbrev. of mod. L. *hydrargyrum*.]

hg ▶ abbr. hectogram(s).

hgb. ▶ abbr. hemoglobin.

HGH ▶ abbr. human growth hormone.

hgt. ▶ abbr. height.

hgwy. ▶ abbr. highway.

hh. ▶ abbr. hands (as a unit of measurement of a horse's height).

H-hour ▶ n. the time of day at which an attack, landing, or other military operation is scheduled to begin. [World War I: from *H* (for *hour*) + HOUR.]

HHS ▶ abbr. (Department of) Health and Human Services.

HI ▶ abbr. Hawaii (in official postal use).

hi /hī/ ▶ exclam. informal used as a friendly greeting or to attract attention: *"Hi there. How was the flight?"* [natural exclamation: first recorded in ME.]

Hi·a·le·ah /,hīə'lēə/ a city in southeastern Florida; pop. 226,419.

hi·a·tus /hī'ātəs/ ▶ n. (pl. **-tus·es**) [usu. in sing.] a pause or gap in a sequence, series, or process. — **hi·a·tal** /-'ātl/ adj. [16th C. (orig. denoting a physical gap or opening): from L., lit. 'gaping,' from *hiare* 'gape.']

hi·a·tus her·ni·a (also **hi·a·tal her·ni·a**) ▶ n. Med. the protrusion of an organ, typically the stomach, through the esophageal opening in the diaphragm.

Hi·a·wath·a[1] /,hīə'wäTHə/ (fl. c. 1570) Mohawk Indian chief; meaning of name "He Makes Rivers." He is credited with establishing an Iroquois confederacy, the Five Nations League.

Hi·a·wath·a[2] a fictional Chippewa Indian who was the hero of a poem by Henry Wadsworth Longfellow.

hi·ba·chi /hi'bächē/ ▶ n. (pl. **-chis**) a portable cooking apparatus consisting of a small grill over a brazier. [19th C.: Japanese *hibachi*, *hi-hachi*, from *hi* 'fire' + *hachi* 'bowl, pot.']

hi·ber·nate /'hībər,nāt/ ▶ v. [intrans.] (of an animal or plant) spend the winter in a dormant state. ■ fig. (of a person) remain inactive or indoors for an extended period. — **hi·ber·na·tion** /,hībər'nāSHən/ n. **hi·ber·na·tor** /-,nātər/ n. [19th C.: from L. *hibernare*, from *hiberna* 'winter quarters,' from *hibernus* 'wintry.']

Hi·ber·ni·an /hī'bərnēən/ ▶ adj. of or concerning Ireland (now chiefly used in names). ▶ n. a native of Ireland (now chiefly used in names). [from L. *Hibernia* 'Ireland.']

Hiberno- ▶ comb. form Irish; Irish and ...: *Hiberno-English*. [from med. L. *Hibernus*.]

hi·bis·cus /hī'biskəs/ ▶ n. a plant (genus *Hibiscus*) of the mallow family, grown in warm climates esp. for its large brightly colored flowers. [L., from Gk. *hibiskos*, the marsh mallow.]

hic /hik/ ▶ exclam. used in writing to express the sound of a hiccup, esp. a drunken one.

hic·cup /'hik,əp/ (also **hic·cough**) ▶ n. an involuntary spasm of the diaphragm and respiratory organs, with a sudden closure of the glottis and a sound like a cough. ■ (**hiccups**) an attack of such spasms occurring repeatedly for some time. ■ a temporary or minor difficulty or setback. ▶ v. (**-cuped, -cup·ing**) [intrans.] suffer from or make the sound of a hiccup or series of hiccups. — **hic·cup·y** adj. [16th C.: imitative.]

hick /hik/ ▶ n. informal a person who lives in the country, regarded as being unintelligent or provincial. [16th C.: nickname for the given name *Richard*.]

hick·ey /'hikē/ ▶ n. (pl. **-eys**) **1** informal a gadget. **2** informal a skin blemish, esp. a mark caused by a lover biting or sucking the skin. [20th C.: of unknown origin.]

Hick·ok /'hikäk/, James Butler (1837–76), US frontiersman and marshal; known as **Wild Bill Hickok**. The legend of his invincibility became a challenge to gunmen, and he was eventually murdered at Deadwood, South Dakota.

hick·o·ry /'hik(ə)rē/ ▶ n. a chiefly North American tree (genus *Carya*) of the walnut family that yields useful timber and typically bears edible nuts. ■ a stick made of hickory wood. [17th C.: abbrev. of *pohickery*, the local Virginian name, from Algonquian *pawcohiccora*.]

Hicks /hiks/, Sir John Richard (1904–89), English economist. He did pioneering work on general economic equilibrium. Nobel Prize in Economics (1972, shared with K. J. Arrow).

Hicks·ville /'hiks,vil/ a village in central Long Island in New York; pop. 40,174.

hid /hid/ past of HIDE[1].

Hi·dal·go /ē'dälgō/ a state in southern Mexico; capital, Pachuca de Soto.

hi·dal·go /hi'dälgō/ ▶ n. (pl. **-gos**) (in Spanish-speaking regions) a gentleman. [16th C.: Sp., from *hijo de algo*, lit. 'son of something.']

Hi·dat·sa /hē'dätsä/ ▶ n. (pl. same or **-sas**) **1** a member of an American Indian people living on the upper Missouri River in North Dakota. **2** the Siouan language of this people. ▶ adj. of or relating to this people or their language. [a Hidatsa village name.]

hid·den /'hidn/ past participle of HIDE[1]. ▶ adj. kept out of sight; concealed. — **hid·den·ness** n.

hid·den a·gen·da ▶ n. a secret or ulterior motive for something.

hid·den·ite /'hidn,īt/ ▶ n. a rare green gem variety of spodumene. [19th C.: named after William E. *Hidden* (1832–1918), US mineralogist.]

hide[1] /hīd/ ▶ v. (past **hid** ; past part. **hid·den**) [trans.] put or keep out of sight; conceal from the view or notice of others. ■ (of a thing) prevent (someone or something) from being seen. ■ keep secret or unknown. ■ [intrans.] conceal oneself. ■ [intrans.] (**hide behind**) use (someone or something) to protect oneself from criticism or punishment, esp. in a way considered cowardly or unethical: *companies with poor security can hide behind the law*. ▶ n. Brit. a camouflaged shelter used to get a close view of wildlife; a blind. — **hid·er** n. [OE *hȳdan*, of West Gmc. origin.]

hide[2] ▶ n. the skin of an animal, esp. when tanned or dressed. ■ used to refer to a person's ability to withstand criticisms or insults.
– PHRASES **hide or hair of someone** [with negative] the slightest sight or trace of someone. **tan** (or **whip**) **someone's hide** beat or flog someone. ■ punish someone severely. [OE *hȳd*, of Gmc. origin; rel. to Du. *huid* and Ger. *Haut*.]

hide[3] ▶ n. a former measure of land used in England, typically equal to between 60 and 120 acres, being the amount that would support a family and its dependents. [OE *hīd*, *hīgid*, from the base of *hīgan*, *hīwan* 'household members,' of Gmc. origin.]

hide-and-seek ▶ n. a children's game in which one player tries to find other players who have hidden themselves.

hide·a·way /'hīdə,wā/ ▶ n. a place used as a retreat or a hiding place: *an intimate hideaway overlooking the bay*. ▶ adj. designed to be concealed when not in use: *a hideaway bed*.

hide·bound /'hīd,bound/ ▶ adj. unwilling or unable to change because of tradition or convention: *you are hidebound by your petty laws*. ■ (of cattle) with their skin clinging close to their back and ribs as a result of bad feeding. ■ (of a tree) having the bark so tightly adherent as to impede growth. [16th C.: from HIDE[2] + BOUND[4].]

hid·e·ous /'hidēəs/ ▶ adj. ugly or disgusting to look at. ■ extremely unpleasant. — **hid·e·ous·ly** adv. **hid·e·ous·ness** n. [ME. from OFr. *hidos*, *hideus*, from *hide*, *hisde* 'fear,' of unknown origin.]

hide·out /'hīd,out/ ▶ n. a hiding place, esp. one used by someone who has broken the law.

hid·ey-hole /'hīdē,hōl/ ▶ n. informal a place for hiding something or oneself in, esp. as a retreat from other people.

hid·ing[1] /'hīdiNG/ ▶ n. informal a physical beating. ■ fig. a severe defeat. [19th C.: from HIDE[2] + -ING[1].]

hid·ing[2] ▶ n. the action of concealing someone or something. ■ the state of being hidden. [ME: from HIDE[1] + -ING[1].]

hi·dro·sis /hi'drōsis; hī-/ ▶ n. Med. sweating. — **hi·drot·ic** /hi'drätik; hī-/ adj. [19th C.: from Gk. *hidrōsis*, from *hidrōs* 'sweat.']

hie /hī/ ▶ v. (**hies, hied, hie·ing** or **hy·ing**) [no obj., with adverbial of direction] go quickly: *I hied down to New Orleans | I hied myself to a screenwriters' conference*. [ME: from OE *hīgian* 'strive, pant,' of unknown origin.]

hi·er·arch /'hī(ə),rärk/ ▶ n. a chief priest, archbishop, or other leader. [ME: via med. L. from Gk. *hierarkhēs*, from *hieros* 'sacred' + *arkhēs* 'ruler.']

hi·er·ar·chi·cal /,hī(ə)'rärkikəl/ ▶ adj. of the nature of a hierarchy; arranged in order of rank. — **hi·er·ar·chi·cal·ly** adv.

hi·er·ar·chy /'hī(ə),rärkē/ ▶ n. (pl. **-chies**) a system or organization in which people or groups are ranked one above the other according to status or authority. ■ (**the hierarchy**) the upper echelons of a hierarchical system; those in authority. ■ an arrangement or classification of things according to relative importance or inclusiveness. ■ (**the hierarchy**) the clergy of the Catholic or Anglican Church; the religious authorities. — **hi·er·ar·chic** /,hī(ə)'rärkik/ adj. [ME: via OFr. and med. L. from Gk. *hierarkhia*, from *hierarkhēs* 'sacred ruler' (see HIERARCH).]

hi·er·at·ic /,hī(ə)'ratik/ ▶ adj. of or concerning priests. ■ of or in the ancient Egyptian writing of abridged hieroglyphics used by priests. Compare with DEMOTIC. — **hi·er·at·i·cal·ly** adv. [17th C. (earlier as *hieratical*): via L. from Gk. *hieratikos*, from *hierasthai* 'be a priest,' from *hiereus* 'priest,' *hieros* 'sacred.']

hiero- ▶ comb. form sacred; holy. [from Gk. *hieros* 'sacred.']

hi·er·oc·ra·cy /ˌhī(ə)'räkrəsē/ ▶ n. (pl. **-cies**) rule by priests. ■ a ruling body composed of priests. — **hi·er·o·crat·ic** /ˌhī(ə)rə'kratik/ adj.

hi·er·o·glyph /'hī(ə)rəˌglif/ ▶ n. a stylized picture of an object representing a word, syllable, or sound, as found in ancient Egyptian and other writing systems. [16th C.: back-form. from HIEROGLYPHIC.]

hi·er·o·glyph·ic /ˌhī(ə)rə'glifik/ ▶ n. (**hieroglyphics**) writing consisting of hieroglyphs. ■ enigmatic or incomprehensible symbols or writing. ▶ adj. of or written in hieroglyphs. ■ (esp. in art) stylized, symbolic, or enigmatic in effect. — **hi·er·o·glyph·i·cal·ly** adv. [16th C.: from Fr. *hiéroglyphique*, from Gk. *hieroglyphikos*, from *hieros* 'sacred' + *gluphē* 'carving.']

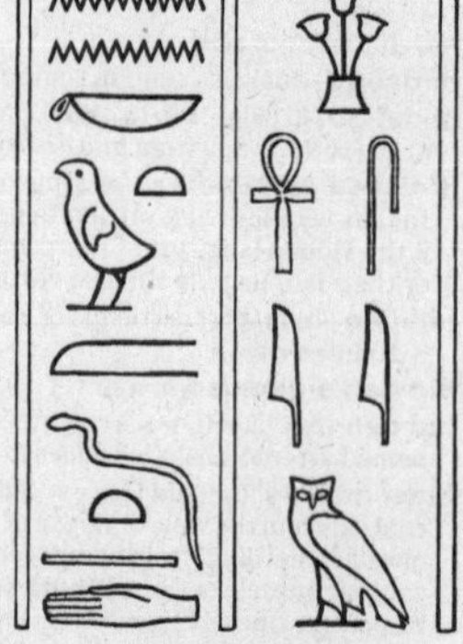
hieroglyphics

hi·er·o·phant /'hī(ə)rəˌfant/ ▶ n. a person, esp. a priest in ancient Greece, who interprets sacred mysteries or esoteric principles. — **hi·er·o·phan·tic** /ˌhī(ə)rə'fantik/ adj. [17th C.: via late L. from Gk. *hierophantēs*, from *hieros* 'sacred' + *phainein* 'show, reveal.']

hi-fi /'hī 'fī/ informal ▶ adj. of or relating to the reproduction of sound or music with high fidelity. ▶ n. (pl. **-fis**) a set of equipment for high-fidelity sound reproduction, esp. a radio or phonograph. [1950s: abbrev. of HIGH FIDELITY.]

hig·gle /'higəl/ ▶ v. archaic spelling of HAGGLE.

hig·gle·dy-pig·gle·dy /'higəldē 'pigəldē/ ▶ adv. & adj. in confusion or disorder. [16th C.: prob. with ref. to pigs.]

Higgs /higz/ (also **Higgs boson** or **Higgs particle**) ▶ n. Physics a subatomic particle whose existence is predicted by the theory that unified the weak and electromagnetic interactions. [1970s: named after Peter W. Higgs (1929–), English physicist.]

high /hī/ ▶ adj. **1** of great vertical extent: *the top of a high mountain.* ■ (after a measurement and in questions) measuring a specified distance from top to bottom: *a tree forty feet high.* ■ far above ground, sea level, or another point of reference: *a fortress high up on a hill.* ■ extending above the normal or average level: *a high forehead.* ■ [attrib.] (of territory or landscape) inland and well above sea level: *high prairies.* ■ near to the top of a real or notional list in order of rank or importance: *a high priority on security.* ■ [attrib.] performed at, to, or from a considerable height: *high diving.* ■ Baseball (of a pitched ball) above a certain level, such as the batter's armpits, as it crosses home plate, and thus outside the strike zone. **2** great, or greater than normal, in quantity, size, or intensity: *a high temperature.* ■ of large numerical or monetary value: *playing for high stakes.* ■ very favorable: *a high opinion of himself.* ■ extreme in religious or political views: *the high Christology of the Christian creeds.* ■ (of a period or movement) at its peak: *high summer.* ■ (of latitude) close to 90°; near the North or South Pole: *high southern latitudes.* **3** great in rank or status: *he held high office.* ■ ranking above others of the same kind: *the High Commissioner's retirement.* ■ morally or culturally superior: *driven by something higher than selfishness.* **4** (of a sound or note) having a frequency at the upper end of the auditory range: *a high, squeaky voice.* ■ (of a singer or instrument) producing notes of relatively high pitch: *a high soprano voice.* **5** [predic.] informal excited; euphoric: *he was high on an idea.* ■ intoxicated with drugs: ***high on** Ecstasy.* **6** [predic.] unpleasantly strong-smelling, in particular (of food) beginning to go bad. ■ (of game) slightly decomposed and so ready to cook. **7** Phonet. (of a vowel) produced with the tongue relatively near the palate. ▶ n. **1** a high point, level, or figure: *prices were at a high.* ■ a notably happy or successful moment: *the highs and lows of life.* ■ a high-frequency sound or musical note. ■ an area of high atmospheric pressure; an anticyclone. **2** [usu. in sing.] informal a state of high spirits or euphoria: *we're still **on a high** from our victory.* **3** informal high school (chiefly used in names): *my years at McKinley High.* **4** a high power setting: *the blower **on high**.* ■ top gear in a motor vehicle. ▶ adv. **1** at or to a considerable or specified height: *the sculpture stood about five feet high.* **2** highly: *he ranked high among twentieth-century novelists.* ■ at a high price: *buying shares low and selling them high.* **3** (of a sound) at or to a high pitch.

– PHRASES **from on high** from a very high place. ■ from remote high authority or heaven. **high and dry** out of the water, esp. the sea as it retreats. ■ in a difficult position, esp. without resources. **high and low** in many different places. **high and mighty** usu. derog. important and influential. ■ informal thinking or acting as though one is more important than others. **a high old time** informal a most enjoyable time. **high, wide, and handsome** informal expansive and impressive. **it is high time that ——** it is past the time when something should have happened or been done. **on high** in or to heaven or a high place. **on one's high horse** informal behaving in an arrogant or pompous manner. **run high** (of a river) be full and close to overflowing, with a strong current. ■ (of feelings) be intense. [OE *hēah*, of Gmc. origin; rel. to Du. *hoog* and Ger. *hoch*.]

high·ball /'hīˌbôl/ ▶ n. **1** a drink consisting of whiskey and a mixer such as soda or ginger ale, served with ice in a tall glass. **2** informal a railroad signal to proceed. ▶ v. [no obj., with adverbial of direction] informal travel fast.

high-band ▶ adj. relating to or denoting a video system using a relatively high carrier frequency, which allows more bandwidth for the signal.

high beam ▶ n. the brightest setting of a vehicle's headlights. ■ (**high beams**) the headlights of a vehicle when set on high beam.

high·born /'hīˌbôrn/ (also **high-born**) ▶ adj. having noble parents.

high·boy /'hīˌboi/ ▶ n. a tall chest of drawers on legs.

high·bred /'hīˌbred/ ▶ adj. **1** bred from superior stock. **2** having or showing good manners; well-bred.

high·brow /'hīˌbrou/ ▶ adj. often derog. scholarly or rarefied in taste. ▶ n. a person of this type.

high·bush cran·ber·ry /'hīˌbo͝osh/ ▶ n. a shrub (*Viburnum trilobum*) of the honeysuckle family, with round clusters of white flowers followed by red berries. Compare with GUELDER ROSE.

high chair ▶ n. a small chair with long legs for a baby, fitted with a tray used as a table at mealtimes.

High Church ▶ adj. of or adhering to a tradition within the Anglican Church emphasizing ritual, priestly authority, sacraments, and historical continuity with Catholic Christianity. Compare with LOW CHURCH, BROAD CHURCH. ▶ n. [treated as sing. or pl.] the principles or adherents of this tradition.

high-class ▶ adj. of a high standard, quality, or social class.

high com·e·dy ▶ n. comedy employing sophisticated wit and often satirizing the upper classes. Compare with LOW COMEDY.

high com·mand ▶ n. the commander in chief and associated senior staff of an army, navy, or air force.

high com·mis·sion ▶ n. an embassy of one British Commonwealth country in another. — **high com·mis·sion·er** n.

high-coun·try ▶ adj. of or relating to land above the piedmont and below the timberline.

high court ▶ n. a supreme court of justice. ■ the US Supreme Court. ■ (in the US) the supreme court in a state. ■ (in some US states) a superior court.

high-den·si·ty li·po·pro·tein (abbr.: **HDL**) ▶ n. a lipoprotein that removes cholesterol from the blood and is associated with a reduced risk of atherosclerosis and heart disease. Compare with LOW-DENSITY LIPOPROTEIN.

high-end ▶ adj. [attrib.] denoting the most expensive of a range of products.

high·er court ▶ n. Law a court that can overrule the decision of another.

high·er crit·i·cism ▶ n. the study of the literary methods and sources discernible in a text, esp. as applied to biblical writings.

high·er ed·u·ca·tion ▶ n. education beyond high school, esp. at a college or university.

high·er law ▶ n. a moral or religious principle that is believed to overrule secular constitutions and laws.

high·er learn·ing ▶ n. education and learning at the college or university level.

high·er plants ▶ plural n. plants of relatively complex or advanced characteristics, esp. vascular plants (including flowering plants).

high·er-up ▶ n. informal a senior person in an organization.

high·est com·mon fac·tor (abbr.: **HCF**) ▶ n. the highest number that can be divided exactly into each of two or more numbers.

high ex·plo·sive ▶ n. a chemical explosive that is rapid and destructive, used in shells and bombs.

high·fa·lu·tin /ˌhīfə'lo͞otn/ (also **high·fa·lu·ting** /-'lo͞otiNG/) ▶ adj. informal (esp. of speech, writing, or ideas) pompous or pretentious. [19th C.: perh. from HIGH + *fluting* (pres. part. of FLUTE).]

high fash·ion ▶ n. another term for HAUTE COUTURE.

high fi·del·i·ty ▶ n. the reproduction of sound with little distortion, giving a result very similar to the original.

high five informal ▶ n. a gesture of celebration or greeting in which two people slap each other's palms with their arms raised. ▶ v. (**high-five**) [trans.] greet with such a gesture.

high·fli·er /'hī'flīər/ (also **high-fli·er, high·fly·er, high-fly·er**) ▶ n. a person who is or has the potential to be very successful, esp. academically or in business. — **high·fly·ing** /-'flī-iNG/ adj.

high-flown ▶ adj. (esp. of language or ideas) extravagant and lofty.

high fre·quen·cy ▶ n. (in radio) a frequency of 3–30 megahertz.

high gear ▶ n. a gear that causes a wheeled vehicle to move fast, owing to a high ratio between the speed of the wheels and that of the mechanism driving them.

High Ger·man ▶ n. the standard literary and spoken form of German, originally used in the highlands in the south of Germany. See also MIDDLE HIGH GERMAN, OLD HIGH GERMAN.

high-grade ▶ adj. of very good quality.

high ground ▶ n. **1** land that is higher than the surrounding area, esp. that which stays dry. **2** (**the high ground**) a position of superiority in a debate.

high-hand·ed ▶ adj. using power or authority without considering the feelings of others. — **high-hand·ed·ly** adv. **high-hand·ed·ness** n.

high hat ▶ n. **1** a tall hat, esp. a top hat. ■ informal a snobbish or supercilious person. **2** (**high-hat**) var. of HI-HAT. ▶ adj. (**high-hat**) informal snobbish. ▶ v. (**high-hat**) (**-hat·ted, -hat·ting**) [trans.] informal act in a snobbish or supercilious manner toward (someone).

high heels ▶ plural n. tall, thin heels on women's shoes. ■ women's shoes with heels of this type. — **high-heeled** adj.

High Hol·i·days (also **High Holy Days**) ▶ plural n. the Jewish holy days of Yom Kippur and Rosh Hashanah. Also called DAYS OF AWE.

high-im·pact ▶ adj. [attrib.] **1** (of plastic or a similar substance) able to withstand great impact without breaking. **2** denoting exercises, typically aerobics, that place a great deal of harmful stress on the body.

high·jack ▶ v. var. of HIJACK.

high jinks /ˈjiNGks/ (also **hi·jinks** /ˈhīˌjiNGls/) ▶ plural n. boisterous fun. [17th C.: see JINK.]

high jump ▶ n. (**the high jump**) an athletic event in which competitors jump over a bar that is raised until only one competitor can jump over it without dislodging it. — **high jump·er** n.

high-key (also **high-keyed**) ▶ adj. emotionally taut; high-strung.

high·land /ˈhīlənd/ ▶ n. **1** (also **highlands**) an area of high or mountainous land. **2** (**the Highlands**) the mountainous part of Scotland, north of Glasgow, often associated with Gaelic culture. — **high·land·er** n. **high·land·man** n. (pl. **-men**).

High·land dress ▶ n. clothing in the traditional style of the Scottish Highlands, including the kilt, now chiefly worn on formal occasions.

High·land fling ▶ n. a vigorous Scottish dance consisting of a series of complex steps performed solo, originally to celebrate victory.

high-lev·el ▶ adj. at or of a level above normal or average. ■ relating to or involving people of high administrative rank or great authority. ■ Comput. denoting a programming language (e.g., BASIC or Pascal) that is relatively accessible to the user, having instructions that resemble an existing language such as English. ■ (of nuclear waste) highly radioactive and requiring long-term storage in isolation.

high life ▶ n. (also **high liv·ing**) an extravagant social life as enjoyed by the wealthy.

high·light /ˈhīˌlīt/ ▶ n. **1** an outstanding part of an event or period of time. ■ (**highlights**) the best parts of a sporting or other event edited for broadcasting or recording. **2** a bright or reflective area in a painting, picture, or design. ■ (usu. **highlights**) a bright tint in the hair, esp. one produced by bleaching or dyeing. ▶ v. [trans.] **1** (often **be highlighted**) pick out and emphasize: *the issues highlighted by the report.* ■ make visually prominent. ■ mark with a highlighter. **2** create highlights in (hair).

high·light·er /ˈhīˌlītər/ ▶ n. **1** a broad felt-tipped pen used to overlay transparent fluorescent color on text or a part of an illustration, leaving it legible and emphasized. **2** a cosmetic that is lighter than the wearer's foundation or skin, used to emphasize features such as the eyes or cheekbones.

high-low ▶ n. a poker game in which the high and low hands split the pot.

high·ly /ˈhīlē/ ▶ adv. to a high degree: *highly paid people.* ■ high in a hierarchy: *a highly placed official.* ■ favorably: *he was highly regarded by his colleagues.*

high-main·te·nance ▶ adj. needing a lot of work to keep in good condition. ■ informal (of a person or relationship) demanding a lot of attention.

High Mass ▶ n. (in the Roman Catholic Church) formerly, a mass with full ceremonial.

high-mind·ed ▶ adj. having strong moral principles. — **high-mind·ed·ly** adv. **high-mind·ed·ness** n.

high muck-a-muck /ˈhī ˈmək ə ˌmək/ (also **high muck·e·ty-muck**) ▶ n. informal a person in a position of authority, esp. one who is overbearing or conceited. [19th C.: perh. from Chinook *hiyu* 'plenty' + *muckamuck* 'food,' from Nootka *ḥayo* 'ten' + *maḥ̣ṃaq-* 'choice wheatmeal.']

high·ness /ˈhīnis/ ▶ n. **1** the state of being high. **2** (**His/Your**, etc., **Highness**) a title given to a person of royal rank, or used in addressing them: *I am most grateful, Your Highness.*

high noon ▶ n. **1** noon exactly. **2** an event or confrontation that is likely to decide the final outcome of a situation.

high note ▶ n. a successful point in an event or period of time.

high-oc·tane ▶ adj. denoting gasoline having a high octane number and thus good anti-knock properties. ■ fig. powerful or dynamic.

high-pitched ▶ adj. **1** (of a sound) high in pitch. **2** (of a roof) steep. **3** (of a battle or dispute) intense.

high plac·es ▶ plural n. positions of power or authority: *people in high places were taking note.*

High Point a city in north central North Carolina; pop. 85,839.

high point ▶ n. the most enjoyable or significant part of an experience or period of time.

high-pow·ered (also **high-pow·er**) ▶ adj. (of a machine or device) having greater than normal strength or capabilities. ■ dynamic and capable.

high-pres·sure ▶ adj. **1** involving a high degree of activity and exertion; stressful. ■ (of a salesperson or sales pitch) employing a high degree of coercion; insistent. **2** involving or using much physical force. **3** denoting a condition of the atmosphere with the pressure above average.

high priest ▶ n. a chief priest of a non-Christian religion, in particular: ■ the chief priest of the historic Jewish religion. ■ the head of a religious cult or similar group. ■ fig. a chief advocate of a belief or practice: *the high priest of the drug culture.*

high priest·ess ▶ n. a female high priest.

high pro·file ▶ n. [in sing.] a position attracting much attention or publicity. ▶ adj. attracting much attention or publicity.

high re·lief ▶ n. see RELIEF (sense 4).

high-res ▶ adj. var. of HI-RES.

high-rise ▶ adj. (of a building) having many stories. ■ taller or set higher than normal. ▶ n. a building with many stories.

high road ▶ n. Brit. a main road. ■ fig. a morally superior approach toward something.

high roll·er ▶ n. informal a person who gambles or spends large amounts of money. — **high-roll·ing** adj. [with ref. to rolling dice.]

high school ▶ n. a school that typically comprises grades 9 through 12. — **high school·er** n.

high seas ▶ plural n. (**the high seas**) the open ocean, esp. that not within any country's jurisdiction.

high sign ▶ n. informal a surreptitious gesture, often prearranged, giving warning or indicating that all is well.

High·smith /ˈhīˌsmiTH/, Patricia (1921–95), US writer; born *Patricia Plangman.* Her novels include *The Talented Mr. Ripley* (1956), and *Ripley Under Water* (1991).

high so·ci·e·ty ▶ n. see SOCIETY (sense 1).

high-sound·ing ▶ adj. (of language or ideas) extravagant and lofty.

high-speed ▶ adj. moving, operating, or happening very quickly. ■ (of photographic film) needing little light or only short exposure.

high spir·its ▶ plural n. lively and cheerful behavior or mood. — **high-spir·it·ed** adj. **high-spir·it·ed·ness** n.

high spot ▶ n. the most enjoyable or significant part of an experience or period of time.

– PHRASES **hit the high spots** informal visit the most exciting places in town.

high-stick ▶ v. [intrans.] [usu. as n.] (**high-sticking**) Ice Hockey strike an opponent on or above the shoulders with one's stick, for which a penalty may be assessed.

high-strung ▶ adj. nervous and easily upset.

hight /hīt/ ▶ adj. [predic.] archaic literary named: *a little pest, hight Tommy Moore.* [ME, from OE *heht*, past tense of *hātan* 'command, call, or name,' of Gmc. origin; rel. to Du. *heten* and Ger. *heissen.*]

high·tail /ˈhīˌtāl/ ▶ v. [no obj., with adverbial of direction] informal move or travel fast: *I hightailed it home.*

high tea ▶ n. Brit. a meal eaten in the late afternoon or early evening.

high-tech (also **hi-tech**) ▶ adj. employing, requiring, or involved in high technology. ■ (chiefly in architecture and interior design) using styles and materials, such as steel, glass, and plastic, that are more usual in industry. ▶ n. (**high tech**) short for HIGH TECHNOLOGY.

high tech·nol·o·gy ▶ n. advanced technological development, esp. in electronics.

high-ten·sile ▶ adj. (of metal) very strong under tension: *high-tensile steel.*

high ten·sion ▶ n. another term for HIGH VOLTAGE.

high-test ▶ adj. (of gasoline) high-octane. ■ meeting very high standards: *a high-test office.*

high tide ▶ n. the state of the tide when at its highest level. ■ the highest point of something: *the high tide of nationalism.*

high-toned ▶ adj. stylish or superior.

high-top (also **high·top**) ▶ adj. denoting a sneaker with a laced upper that extends some distance above the wearer's ankle. ▶ n. (**high-tops**) a pair of such sneakers.

high trea·son ▶ n. see TREASON.

high-up ▶ n. informal a senior person in an organization.

high volt·age ▶ n. an electrical potential large enough to cause injury or damage.

high wa·ter ▶ n. **1** another term for HIGH TIDE. **2** the highest level reached by any body of water, esp. a river.

high-wa·ter mark ▶ n. the level reached by the sea at high tide, or by a lake or river at its highest stand. ■ a maximum recorded level or value.

high·way /ˈhīˌwā/ ▶ n. a main road, esp. one connecting major towns or cities. ■ another term for EXPRESSWAY. ■ (chiefly in official use) a public road.

high·way·man /ˈhīˌwāmən/ ▶ n. (pl. **-men**) hist. a man, typically on horseback, who held up travelers at gunpoint in order to rob them.

high wire ▶ n. a high tightrope. ■ [as adj.] fig. requiring great skill or judgment.

high yel·low offens. ▶ adj. denoting a mulatto or a light-skinned black person. ▶ n. person of this kind.

HIH Brit. ▶ abbr. Her or His Imperial Highness.

hi-hat (also **high-hat**) ▶ n. a pair of foot-operated cymbals forming part of a drum kit.

hi·jab /hi'jäb/ ▶ **n.** a head covering worn in public by some Muslim women. ▪ the religious code that governs the wearing of such clothing. [from Persian, from Arabic *ḥajaba* 'to veil.']

hi·jack /'hī,jak/ (also **high·jack**) ▶ **v.** [trans.] illegally seize (an aircraft, ship, or vehicle) in transit and force it to go to a different destination or use it for one's own purposes. ▪ steal (goods) by seizing them in transit. ▪ take over (something) and use it for a different purpose. ▶ **n.** an incident or act of hijacking. — **hi·jack·er n.** [1920s (orig. US): of unknown origin.]

Hi·jaz var. of HEJAZ.

Hij·ra /'hijrə/ ▶ **n.** var. of HEGIRA.

hike /hīk/ ▶ **n. 1** a long walk, esp. in the country or wilderness. ▪ informal a long distance. **2** a sharp increase, esp. in price. **3** Football a snap. ▶ **v. 1** [no obj., with adverbial of direction] walk for a long distance, esp. across country or in the woods. **2** [trans.] pull or lift up (something, esp. clothing): *he hiked up his sweatpants and marched to the door.* ▪ increase (something, esp. a price) sharply. **3** Football snap (a football).
– PHRASES **take a hike** [usu. in imper.] informal go away (used as an expression of irritation or annoyance). — **hik·er n.** [19th C. (orig. dial., as a v.): of unknown origin.]

hi·la /'hīlə/ plural form of HILUM.

hi·lar /'hīlər/ ▶ **adj.** Anat. Bot. of or relating to a hilus or hilum.

hi·lar·i·ous /hə'le(ə)rēəs/ ▶ **adj.** extremely amusing. ▪ boisterously merry. — **hi·lar·i·ous·ly adv.** [19th C.: from L. *hilaris* (from Gk. *hilaros* 'cheerful') + -OUS.]

hi·lar·i·ty /hə'le(ə)ritē/ ▶ **n.** extreme amusement, esp. when expressed by laughter. ▪ boisterous merriment.

Hil·bert space /'hilbərt/ ▶ **n.** Math. an infinite-dimensional analog of Euclidean space. [20th C.: named after David *Hilbert* (1862–1943), German mathematician.]

Hil·des·heim /'hildəs,hīm/ a city in northwestern Germany, in Lower Saxony; pop. 106,000.

Hil·i·gay·non /,hili'gīnən/ ▶ **n.** (pl. same or **-nons**) **1** a member of a people inhabiting islands in the central Philippines. **2** the Austronesian language of this people. ▶ **adj.** of or relating to this people or their language.

hill /hil/ ▶ **n. 1** a naturally raised area of land, not as high or craggy as a mountain. ▪ a sloping piece of road or trail. ▪ a heap or mound of something. **2** (**the Hill**) informal short for CAPITOL HILL. ▶ **v.** [trans.] form (something) into a heap. ▪ bank up (a plant) with soil.
– PHRASES **a hill of beans** [with negative] informal a thing of little value. **over the hill** informal old and past one's prime. **up hill and down dale** see UP. [OE *hyll*, of Gmc. origin; from an Indo-Eur. root shared by L. *collis* and Gk. *kolōnos* 'hill.']

Hil·la·ry /'hilərē/, Sir Edmund Percival (1919–), New Zealand explorer. In 1953, Hillary and Tenzing Norgay were the first people to reach the summit of Mount Everest.

hill·bil·ly /'hil,bilē/ ▶ **n.** (pl. **-lies**) informal, usu. derog. an unsophisticated country person, associated originally with the remote regions of the Appalachians. [20th C.: from HILL + *Billy* (nickname for the given name *William*).]

hill climb ▶ **n.** a race for vehicles up a steep, often winding, hill.

hill·ock /'hilək/ ▶ **n.** a small hill or mound. — **hill·ock·y adj.**

Hills·bo·ro /'hilz,bərō/ a city in northwestern Oregon; pop. 70,186.

hill·side /'hil,sīd/ ▶ **n.** the sloping side of a hill.

hill sta·tion ▶ **n.** a town in the low mountains of the Indian subcontinent, popular as a holiday resort during the hot season.

hill·top /'hil,täp/ ▶ **n.** the summit of a hill.

hill·y /'hilē/ ▶ **adj.** (**hill·i·er, hill·i·est**) having many hills. — **hill·i·ness n.**

Hi·lo /'hēlō/ a port community on the northern coast of the island of Hawaii; pop. 40,759.

hilt /hilt/ ▶ **n.** the handle of a weapon or tool, esp. a sword, dagger, or knife.
– PHRASES (**up**) **to the hilt** completely. — **hilt·ed adj.** [OE *hilt, hilte*, of Gmc. origin.]

Hil·ton Head Is·land a resort town in southeastern South Carolina; pop. 33,862.

hi·lum /'hīləm/ ▶ **n.** (pl. **hi·la** /'hīlə/) Bot. the scar on a seed marking the point of attachment to its seed vessel. ▪ a point in a starch granule around which the layers of starch are deposited. ▪ Anat. another term for HILUS. [17th C. (in the Latin sense): from L., lit. 'little thing, trifle,' once thought to mean 'that which sticks to a bean,' hence the current sense (18th C.).]

hi·lus /'hīləs/ ▶ **n.** (pl. **hi·li** /'hīlī; -lē/) Anat. an indentation in the surface of a kidney, spleen, or other organ, where blood vessels, ducts, nerve fibers, etc., enter or leave it. [19th C.: mod. L., alt. of HILUM.]

HIM Brit. ▶ **abbr.** Her or His Imperial Majesty.

him /him/ ▶ **pron.** [third person sing.] **1** used as the object of a verb or preposition to refer to a male person or animal previously mentioned or easily identified: *his wife survived him* | *he took the children with him.* Compare with HE. ▪ referring to a person or animal of unspecified sex (in modern use chiefly replaced by "him or her" or "them"): *withdrawing your child from school to educate him at home may seem drastic.* ▪ often used in place of "he" after the verb "to be" and after "than" or "as": *that's him all right* | *I could never be as good as him.* **2** archaic dialect himself: *in the depths of him, he too didn't want to go.* [OE, dative sing. form of *he, hē* 'he' and *hit* 'it.']

Hi·ma·chal Pra·desh /hə'mächəl prə'dāsh; -'desh/ a state in northern India.

Him·a·la·yan /,himə'lāən/ ▶ **adj.** of or relating to the Himalayas: *the Himalayan foothills.* ▶ **n.** a cat of a long-haired breed having blue eyes and a pale coat with dark points.

Hi·ma·la·yas /,himə'lāəz; hə'mäl(ə)yəz/ a vast mountain system in southern Asia that extends for 1,500 miles (2,400 km) and forms the northeastern border of the Indian subcontinent; highest peak, Mount Everest 29,028 feet (8,848 m).

hi·mat·i·on /hə'matē,än/ ▶ **n.** an outer garment worn by the ancient Greeks over the left shoulder and under the right. [Gk.]

Himm·ler /'himlər/, Heinrich (1900–45), German Nazi administrator. He was chief of the SS (Nazi special police force) 1929–45 and of the Gestapo 1936–45.

Hims /himz; hims/ var. of HOMS.

him·self /him'self/ ▶ **pron.** [third person sing.] **1** [reflexive] used as the object of a verb or preposition to refer to a male person or animal previously mentioned as the subject of the clause: *the steward introduced himself as Pete* | *he ought to be ashamed of himself.* **2** [emphatic] he or him personally (used to emphasize a particular male person or animal mentioned): *Thomas himself laid down what we should do* | *he said so himself.* ▪ esp. Irish a third party of some importance, esp. the master of the house: *I'll mention it to himself.*
– PHRASES (**not**) **be himself** see BE ONESELF, NOT BE ONESELF at BE. **by himself** see BY ONESELF at BY.

Him·yar·ite /'himyə,rīt/ ▶ **n.** a member of an ancient people of the southwestern part of the Arabian peninsula. [from the name *Himyar* (the name of a traditional king of Yemen) + -ITE[1].]

hin /hin/ ▶ **n.** a Hebrew unit of liquid capacity equal to approximately 5.5 quarts (5 l). [ME: from biblical Heb. *hīn*.]

Hi·na·ya·na /,hēnə'yänə/ (also **Hinayana Buddhism**) ▶ **n.** a pejorative name given by the followers of Mahayana Buddhism to the more conservative schools of early Buddhism. See THERAVADA. [from Sanskrit *hīna* 'lesser' + *yāna* 'vehicle.']

Hind. ▶ **abbr.** ▪ Hindi. ▪ Hindu. ▪ Hindustan. ▪ Hindustani.

hind[1] /hīnd/ ▶ **adj.** [attrib.] (esp. of a bodily part) situated at the back; posterior: *he snagged a calf by the hind leg.* [ME: perh. shortened from OE *behindan* (see BEHIND).]

hind[2] ▶ **n. 1** a female deer, esp. a red deer or sika in and after its third year. **2** any of several large edible groupers with spotted markings. [OE, of Gmc. origin; rel. to Du. *hinde* and Ger. *Hinde*, from an Indo-Eur. root meaning 'hornless,' shared by Gk. *kemas* 'young deer.']

hind[3] ▶ **n.** archaic, esp. Scot. a skilled farm worker. ▪ a peasant or rustic. [OE *hīne* 'household servants,' appar. from *hīgna, hīna*, genitive pl. of *hīgan, hīwan* 'family members.']

hind- ▶ **comb. form** (added to nouns) at the back; posterior: *hindquarters* | *hindbrain.*

hind·brain /'hīnd,brān/ ▶ **n.** the lower part of the brainstem, comprising the cerebellum, pons, and medulla oblongata. Also called RHOMBENCEPHALON.

Hin·den·burg[1] /'hindən,bərg; -,bo͝ork/ former German name (1915–45) of ZABRZE.

Hin·den·burg[2] /'hindənbərg/, Paul Ludwig von Beneckendorff und von (1847–1934), German field marshal and president of the Weimar Republic 1925–34.

Hin·den·burg Line /'hindənbərg/ (in World War I) a German fortified line of defense on the Western Front. Also called SIEGFRIED LINE.

hind·er[1] /'hindər/ ▶ **v.** [trans.] create difficulties for (someone or something), resulting in delay or obstruction. [OE *hindrian* 'injure or damage,' of Gmc. origin; rel. to Ger. *hindern*, also to BEHIND.]

hind·er[2] /'hīndər/ ▶ **adj.** [attrib.] (esp. of a bodily part) rear; hind: *the hinder end of its body.* [ME: perh. from OE *hinderweard* 'backward,' rel. to BEHIND.]

Hin·di /'hindē/ ▶ **n.** a form of Hindustani, an official language of India, and the most widely spoken language of northern India. ▶ **adj.** of or relating to Hindi. [from Urdu *hindī*, from *Hind* 'India.' See INDUS, SINDHI.]

hind·most /'hīnd,mōst/ ▶ **adj.** furthest back.

Hin·doo /'hindo͞o/ ▶ **n. & adj.** archaic spelling of HINDU.

hind·quar·ters /'hīnd,kwôrtərz/ ▶ **plural n.** the hind legs and adjoining parts of a quadruped.

hin·drance /'hindrəns/ ▶ **n.** a thing that provides resistance, delay, or obstruction to something or someone.

hind·sight /'hīnd,sīt/ ▶ **n.** understanding of a situation or event only after it has happened or developed: *with hindsight, I should never have gone.*

Hin·du /'hindo͞o/ ▶ **n.** (pl. **-dus**) a follower of Hinduism. ▶ **adj.** of or relating to Hindus or Hinduism. [Urdu, from Pers. *hindū*, from *Hind* 'India.']

Hin·du·ism /'hindo͞o,izəm/ ▶ **n.** a major religious and cultural tradition of the Indian subcontinent, comprising a diverse family of devotional and ascetic cults and philosophical schools, all sharing a belief in reincarnation and involving the worship of a large pantheon of deities.

Hin·du Kush /'hindo͞o 'ko͞osh/ a mountain range in northern Pakistan and Afghanistan that forms a western continuation of the Himalayas.

Hin·du·stan /,hindo͞o'stan; -'stän/ hist. the Indian subcontinent in general, more specifically that part of India north of the Deccan, esp. the plains of the Ganges and Jumna rivers.

Hin·du·sta·ni /ˌhindo͞oˈstänē/ ▶ **n.** a group of Indic dialects spoken in northwestern India, principally Hindi and Urdu. ■ the Delhi dialect of Hindi, widely used throughout India as a lingua franca. ▶ **adj.** of or relating to the culture of northwestern India.

Hines /hīnz/, Earl Kenneth (1905–83), US pianist and band leader; known as **Fatha Hines**. He originated the "trumpet style" of piano playing.

hinge /hinj/ ▶ **n.** a movable joint or mechanism on which a door, gate, or lid swings as it opens and closes, or that connects linked objects. ■ Biol. a natural joint that performs a similar function, for example that of a bivalve shell. ■ a central point or principle on which everything depends. ▶ **v.** (**hing·ing**) [trans.] (usu. **be hinged**) attach or join with or as if with a hinge. ■ [no obj., with adverbial of direction] (of a door or part of a structure) hang and turn on a hinge. ■ [intrans.] (**hinge on**) depend entirely on: *the future of the industry could hinge on next month's election.* — **hinge·less adj.** [ME *henge*; rel. to HANG.]

hink·y /ˈhiNGkē/ ▶ **adj.** (**hink·i·er, hink·i·est**) informal (of a person) dishonest or suspect: *he knew the guy was hinky.* ■ (of an object) unreliable: *my brakes are a little hinky.* [1950s: of obscure origin.]

hin·ny /ˈhinē/ ▶ **n.** (pl. **-nies**) the offspring of a female donkey and a male horse. [17th C.: via L. from Gk. *hinnos*.]

hint /hint/ ▶ **n.** a slight or indirect indication or suggestion. ■ a small piece of practical information or advice. ■ a very small trace of something: ***a hint of** mockery.* ▶ **v.** [intrans.] suggest or indicate something indirectly or covertly. ■ (**hint at**) (of a thing) be a slight or possible indication of: *the restrained fronts of the houses only hinted at the wealth within.*

– PHRASES **drop a hint** see DROP. **take a** (or **the**) **hint** understand and act on a hint. [17th C.: appar. from obs. *hent* 'grasp, get hold of,' from OE *hentan*, of Gmc. origin; rel. to HUNT.]

hin·ter·land /ˈhintərˌland/ (also **hin·ter·lands**) ▶ **n.** the often uncharted areas beyond a coastal district or a river's banks. ■ an area surrounding a town or port and served by it. ■ the remote areas of a region. ■ fig. an area lying beyond what is visible or known. [19th C.: from Ger., from *hinter* 'behind' + *Land* 'land.']

hip[1] /hip/ ▶ **n. 1** a projection of the pelvis and upper thighbone on each side of the body in human beings and quadrupeds. ■ (**hips**) the circumference of the body at the buttocks. ■ a person's hip joint. **2** the sharp edge of a roof from the ridge to the eaves where two sides meet. [OE *hype*, of Gmc. origin; rel. to Du. *heup* and Ger. *Hüfte*, also to HOP[1].]

hip[2] (also **rose hip**) ▶ **n.** the fruit of a rose. [OE *hēope, hīope*, of West Gmc. origin; rel. to Du. *joop* and Ger. *Hiefe*.]

hip[3] ▶ **adj.** (**hip·per, hip·pest**) informal following the latest fashion, esp. in popular music and clothes. ■ understanding; aware. — **hip·ness n.** [20th C.: prob. of Afr. origin; akin to Wolof *hipi* 'to be aware of what is going on.']

hip[4] ▶ **exclam.** introducing a communal cheer: *hip, hip, hooray!* [18th C.: of unknown origin.]

hip·bone /ˈhipˌbōn/ ▶ **n.** a large bone forming the main part of the pelvis on each side of the body and consisting of the fused ilium, ischium, and pubis. Also called INNOMINATE BONE.

hip boot ▶ **n.** a waterproof boot that reaches the hip.

hip flask ▶ **n.** a small flask for liquor, of a kind intended to be carried in a hip pocket.

hip-hop ▶ **n.** a style of popular music of US black and Hispanic origin, featuring rap with an electronic backing. [1980s: reduplication prob. based on HIP[3].]

hip-hug·gers (also **hip·hug·gers**) ▶ **plural n.** pants hanging from the hips rather than from the waist.

hip joint ▶ **n.** the ball-and-socket joint connecting a leg to the trunk of the body, in which the head of the thigh bone fits into the socket of the ilium.

Hip·par·chus /hiˈpärkəs/ (*c.*170–after 126 BC), Greek astronomer and geographer. He is credited with the invention of trigonometry.

hipped[1] /hipt/ ▶ **adj. 1** [in comb.] (of a person or animal) having hips of a specified kind: *a thin-hipped girl.* **2** (of a roof) having a sharp edge from the ridge to the eaves where two sides meet.

hipped[2] ▶ **adj.** [predic.] (**hipped on**) informal obsessed or infatuated with: *why are you suddenly hipped on discipline?* [1920s.: from HIP[3], or as the past part. of *hip* 'make someone hip (i.e., aware).']

hipped roof ▶ **n.** another term for HIP ROOF.

hip·pie /ˈhipē/ (also **hip·py**) ▶ **n.** (esp. in the 1960s) a person of unconventional appearance, typically having long hair and wearing beads, associated with a subculture involving a rejection of conventional values and the taking of hallucinogenic drugs. ▶ **adj.** of or relating to hippies or the subculture associated with them. — **hip·pie·dom** /-dəm/ **n.** [1950s: from HIP[3] + -IE (sense 1).]

hip·po /ˈhipō/ ▶ **n.** (pl. same or **-pos**) informal term for HIPPOPOTAMUS.

hip·po·cam·pus /ˌhipəˈkampəs/ ▶ **n.** (pl. **-cam·pi** /-ˈkampī; -ˈkampē/) Anat. the elongated ridges on the floor of each lateral ventricle of the brain, thought to be the center of emotion, memory, and the autonomic nervous system. [16th C.: via L. from Gk. *hippokampos*, from *hippos* 'horse' + *kampos* 'sea monster.']

hip pock·et ▶ **n.** a pocket in the back of a pair of pants.

– PHRASES **in someone's hip pocket** completely under someone's control.

hip·po·cras /ˈhipəˌkras/ ▶ **n.** hist. wine flavored with spices. [ME: from OFr. *ipocras* 'Hippocrates' (see HIPPOCRATES), translating med. L. *vinum Hippocraticum* 'Hippocratic wine' (because it was strained through a filter called a *Hippocrates' sleeve*).]

Hip·poc·ra·tes /hiˈpäkrətēz/ (*c.*460–377 BC), Greek physician; traditionally regarded as the father of medicine.

Hip·po·crat·ic oath /ˈhipəˈkratik/ ▶ **n.** an oath stating the obligations and proper conduct of doctors, formerly taken by those beginning medical practice. Parts of the oath are still used in most medical schools. [18th C.: from HIPPOCRATES.]

Hip·po·crene /ˈhipəˌkrēn; ˌhipəˈkrēnē/ ▶ **n.** literary used to refer to poetic or literary inspiration. [17th C.: via L. from Gk. *Hippokrēnē, Hippou krēnē* (from *hippos* 'horse' + *krēnē* 'fountain'), fountain on Mount Helicon sacred to the Muses.]

hip·po·drome /ˈhipəˌdrōm/ ▶ **n. 1** an arena used for equestrian or other sporting events. **2** (in ancient Greece or Rome) a course for chariot or horse races. [16th C. (sense 2): from Fr., via L. from Gk. *hippodromos*, from *hippos* 'horse' + *dromos* 'race, course.']

hip·po·griff /ˈhipəˌgrif/ (also **hip·po·gryph**) ▶ **n.** a mythical creature with the body of a horse and the wings and head of an eagle. [17th C.: from Fr. *hippogriffe*, from Italian *ippogrifo*, from Gk. *hippos* 'horse' + Ital. *grifo* 'griffin.']

Hip·pol·y·tus /hiˈpälətəs/ Gk. Mythol. the son of Theseus, banished and cursed by his father after being falsely accused by Phaedra of rape.

hip·po·pot·a·mus /ˌhipəˈpätəməs/ ▶ **n.** (pl. **-mus·es** or **-mi** /-ˌmī; -ˌmē/) a large thick-skinned semiaquatic African mammal (family Hippopotamidae), with massive jaws and large tusks. Two species: the very large *Hippopotamus amphibius* and the smaller **pygmy hippopotamus** (*Choeropsis liberiensis*). [ME: via L. from Gk. *hippopotamos*, earlier *hippos ho potamios* 'river horse' (from *hippos* 'horse,' *potamos* 'river').]

Hip·po Re·gi·us /ˈhipō ˈrējēəs/ see ANNABA.

hip·py[1] /ˈhipē/ ▶ **n. & adj.** var. of HIPPIE.

hip·py[2] ▶ **adj.** having large hips.

hip roof (also **hipped roof**) ▶ **n.** a roof with the ends inclined, as well as the sides. See illustration at ROOF.

hip·shot /ˈhipˌSHät/ ▶ **adj. & adv.** having a dislocated hip. ■ [as adv.] having a posture with one hip lower than the other.

hip·ster /ˈhipstər/ ▶ **n.** informal a person who follows the latest trends and fashions. — **hip·ster·ism** /-stəˌrizəm/ **n.** [1940s: from HIP[3] + -STER.]

hi·ra·ga·na /ˌhi(ə)rəˈgänə/ ▶ **n.** the more cursive and more widely used form of kana (syllabic writing) used in Japanese, esp. used for function words and inflections. Compare with KATAKANA. [Japanese, 'plain kana.']

hir·cine /ˈhərsīn; -sən/ ▶ **adj.** archaic of or resembling a goat. [17th C.: from L. *hircinus*, from *hircus* 'he-goat.']

hire /hī(ə)r/ ▶ **v.** [trans.] employ (someone) for wages. ■ employ for a short time to do a particular job. ■ (**hire oneself out**) make oneself available for temporary employment. ■ (**hire something out**) grant the temporary use of something for an agreed payment. ▶ **n. 1** the action of hiring someone or something. **2** a recently recruited employee.

– PHRASES **for** (or **on**) **hire** available to be hired. — **hire·a·ble** (also **hir·a·ble**) **adj. hir·er n.** [OE *hȳrian* 'employ,' *hȳr* 'payment,' of West Gmc. origin; rel. to Du. *huren* (v.), *huur* (n.).]

hired girl ▶ **n.** a female domestic servant.

hired hand (also **hired man**) ▶ **n.** a person hired to do short-term manual work.

hire·ling /ˈhī(ə)rliNG/ ▶ **n.** esp. derog. a person employed to undertake menial work, esp. on a casual basis.

hi-res /ˈhī ˈrez/ (also **high-res**) ▶ **adj.** informal (of a display or a photographic or video image) showing a large amount of detail. [20th C.: from *high-resolution*.]

Hi·ro·hi·to /ˌhi(ə)rəˈhētō/ (1901–89), emperor of Japan 1926–89; full name *Michinomiya Hirohito*. He was instrumental in obtaining Japan's agreement to the unconditional surrender that ended World War II. In 1946, the new constitution imposed by the US obliged him to renounce his divinity.

Hi·ro·shi·ma /ˌhi(ə)rəˈSHēmə; hiˈrōSHəmə/ a city in southwestern Japan, on island of Honshu; pop. 1,086,000; the target of the first atom bomb, dropped by US on August 6, 1945. This, with a second attack on Nagasaki three days later, led to Japan's surrender and to the end of World War II.

hir·sute /ˈhərso͞ot; hərˈso͞ot/ ▶ **adj.** hairy: *their hirsute chests.* — **hir·sute·ness n.** [17th C.: from L. *hirsutus*.]

hir·sut·ism /ˈhərso͞oˌtizəm; hərˈso͞o-/ ▶ **n.** Med. abnormal growth of hair on a person's face and body, esp. on a woman.

his /hiz/ ▶ **possessive adj. 1** belonging to or associated with a male person or animal previously mentioned or easily identified: *James sold his business.* ■ belonging to or associated with a person or animal of unspecified sex (in modern use chiefly replaced by "his or her" or "their"): *any child with delayed speech should have his hearing checked.* See usage at HE. **2** (**His**) used in titles: *His Honor | His Lordship.* ▶ **possessive pron.** used to refer to a thing or things belonging to or associated with a male person or animal previously mentioned: *he took my hand in his | some friends **of his**.*

– PHRASES **his and hers** (of matching items) for husband and wife, or men and women: *his and hers towels.* [OE, genitive sing. form of *he, hē* 'he' and *hit* 'it.']

His·pan·ic /hi'spanik/ ▶ **adj.** of or relating to Spain or to Spanish-speaking countries, esp. those of Latin America. ■ of or relating to Spanish-speaking people or their culture, esp. in the US. ▶ **n.** a Spanish-speaking person living in the US, esp. one of Latin American descent. — **His·pan·i·cize** /-i,sīz/ **v.** [from L. *Hispanicus*, from *Hispania* 'Spain.']

His·pan·ic A·mer·i·can ▶ **n.** a US citizen or resident of Hispanic descent. ▶ **adj.** of or relating to Hispanic Americans.

His·pan·io·la /,hispən'yōlə/ an island in the Greater Antilles in the Caribbean Sea, divided into the countries of Haiti and the Dominican Republic.

His·pan·ist /hi'spanist/ (also **His·pa·n·icist** /-əsist/) ▶ **n.** an expert in or student of the language, literature, and civilization of Spanish-speaking countries.

His·pan·o /hi'spanō; -'spänō/ ▶ **n.** (pl. **-pan·os**) a person descended from Spanish settlers in the Southwest before it was annexed to the US. ■ a Hispanic.

Hispano- ▶ **comb. form** Spanish; Spanish and ...: *Hispano-Argentine.* ■ relating to Spain. [from L. *Hispanus* 'Sp.']

His·pan·o·phobe /hi'spanə,fōb/ ▶ **n.** a person who dislikes or fears Spanish-speaking peoples or countries.

his·pid /'hispid/ ▶ **adj.** Bot. Zool. covered with stiff hair or bristles. [17th C.: from L. *hispidus.*]

Hiss /his/, Alger (1904–96), US public official. In 1948 he was accused by journalist Whittaker Chambers (1901–61) of passing State Department documents to a Soviet agent.

hiss /his/ ▶ **v.** [intrans.] make a sharp sibilant sound as of the letter *s.* ■ (of a person) make such a sound as a sign of disapproval or derision. ■ [trans.] express disapproval of (someone) by making such a sound: *he was hissed off the stage.* ■ [reporting verb] whisper something in an urgent or angry way: *he hissed at them to be quiet.* ▶ **n.** a sharp sibilant sound. ■ a sound such as this used as an expression of disapproval or derision. ■ electrical interference at audio frequencies. [ME (as a v.): imitative.]

his·self /hi'self; hiz'self/ ▶ **pron.** nonstandard spelling of HIMSELF, used in representing informal or dialect speech.

his·sy /'hisē/ (also **his·sy fit**) ▶ **n.** an angry outburst or tantrum.

hist. ▶ **abbr.** ■ histology. ■ historian. ■ historical. ■ history.

hist /hist/ ▶ **exclam.** archaic used to attract attention or call for silence. [natural exclamation: first recorded in Engl. in the 16th C.]

hist- ▶ **comb. form** var. of HISTO- shortened before a vowel (as in *histidine*).

his·ta·mine /'histə,mēn; -,min/ ▶ **n.** Biochem. a heterocyclic amine, $C_5H_9N_3$, that is released by cells in response to injury and in allergic and inflammatory reactions, causing contraction of smooth muscle and dilation of capillaries. — **his·ta·min·ic** /,histə'minik/ **adj.** [20th C.: blend of HISTIDINE and AMINE.]

his·ti·dine /'histə,dēn/ ▶ **n.** Biochem. a basic amino acid, $C_6H_9N_3O_2$, that is a constituent of most proteins. It is an essential nutrient in the diet of vertebrates, and is the source from which histamine is derived in the body. [19th C.: from Gk. *histos* 'web, tissue' + -IDE + -INE[4].]

his·ti·o·cyte /'histēə,sīt/ ▶ **n.** Physiol. a stationary phagocytic cell present in connective tissue. [20th C.: from Gk. *histion* (dimin. of *histos* 'tissue, web') + -CYTE.]

histo- (also **hist-** before a vowel) ▶ **comb. form** Biol. relating to organic tissue: *histochemistry* | *histocompatibility.* [from Gk. *histos* 'web, tissue.']

his·to·chem·is·try /,histə'kemэstrē/ ▶ **n.** the branch of science concerned with the identification and distribution of the chemical constituents of tissues by means of stains, indicators, and microscopy. — **his·to·chem·i·cal** /-'kemikəl/ **adj.**

his·to·com·pat·i·bil·i·ty /,histōkəm,patə'bilitē/ ▶ **n.** Med. compatibility between the tissues of different individuals, so that one accepts a graft from the other without having an immune reaction.

his·to·gen·e·sis /,histə'jenəsis/ ▶ **n.** Biol. the differentiation of cells into specialized tissues and organs during growth. — **his·to·ge·net·ic** /,histəjə'netik/ **adj.**

his·to·gram /'histə,gram/ ▶ **n.** Stat. a diagram consisting of rectangles whose area is proportional to the frequency of a variable and whose width is equal to the class interval.

his·tol·o·gy /hi'stäləjē/ ▶ **n.** Biol. the study of the microscopic structure of tissues. — **his·to·log·ic** /,histə'läjik/ **adj. his·to·log·i·cal** /,histə'läjikəl/ **adj. his·tol·o·gist n.**

his·tol·y·sis /hi'stäləsis/ ▶ **n.** Biol. the breaking down of tissues (e.g., during animal metamorphosis). — **his·to·lyt·ic** /,histə'litik/ **adj.**

his·tone /'hi,stōn/ ▶ **n.** Biochem. any of a group of basic proteins found in chromatin. [19th C.: coined in Ger., perh. from Gk. *histanai* 'arrest' or from *histos* 'web, tissue.']

his·to·pa·thol·o·gy /,histōpə'THäləjē/ ▶ **n.** the study of changes in tissues caused by disease. — **his·to·path·o·log·i·cal** /,histō,paTHə'läjikəl/ **adj. his·to·pa·thol·o·gist** /-jist/ **n.**

his·to·plas·mo·sis /,histōplaz'mōsis/ ▶ **n.** Med. infection by a fungus (*Histoplasma capsulatum*) found in the droppings of birds and bats in humid areas. It is not serious if confined to the lungs but can be fatal if spread throughout the body.

his·to·ri·an /hi'stôrēən/ ▶ **n.** an expert in or student of history, esp. that of a particular period, region, or social phenomenon.

his·tor·ic /hi'stôrik; -'stär-/ ▶ **adj.** famous or important in history, or potentially so: ■ archaic of or concerning history; of the past.

his·tor·i·cal /hi'stôrikəl; -'stär-/ ▶ **adj.** of or concerning history; concerning past events. ■ belonging to the past, not the present. ■ (esp. of a novel or movie) set in the past. ■ (of the study of a subject) based on an analysis of its development over a period.

his·tor·i·cal lin·guis·tics ▶ **plural n.** [treated as sing.] the study of the history and development of languages.

his·tor·i·cal·ly /hi'stôrik(ə)lē; -'stär-/ ▶ **adv.** with reference to past events. ■ [sentence adverb] in the past: *historically, government policy has favored urban dwellers.*

his·tor·i·cal ma·te·ri·al·ism ▶ **n.** another term for DIALECTICAL MATERIALISM.

his·tor·i·cism /hi'stôrə,sizəm; -'stär-/ ▶ **n.** **1** the theory that social and cultural phenomena are determined by history. ■ the belief that historical events are governed by laws. **2** the tendency to regard historical development as the most basic aspect of human existence. **3** esp. derog. (in artistic and architectural contexts) excessive regard for past styles. — **his·tor·i·cist n.**

his·to·ric·i·ty /,histə'risitē/ ▶ **n.** historical authenticity.

his·tor·i·cize /his'stôrə,sīz; -'stär-/ ▶ **v.** [trans.] treat or represent as historical. — **his·tor·i·ci·za·tion** /hi,stôrəsə'zāsHən; -,stär-/ **n.**

his·tor·ic pres·ent /'prezənt/ ▶ **n.** Gram. the present tense used instead of the past in vivid narrative.

his·to·ri·og·ra·phy /hi,stôrē'ägrəfē; -,stär-/ ▶ **n.** the study of historical writing. ■ the writing of history. — **his·to·ri·og·ra·pher** /-'ägrəfər/ **n. his·to·ri·o·graph·ic** /-ə'grafik/ **adj. his·to·ri·o·graph·i·cal** /-ə'grafikəl/ **adj.** [16th C.: via med. L. from Gk. *historiographia*, from *historia* 'narrative, history' + *-graphia* 'writing.']

his·to·ry /'hist(ə)rē/ ▶ **n.** (pl. **-ries**) **1** the study of past events, particularly in human affairs. ■ the past considered as a whole. **2** the whole series of past events connected with someone or something: *the history of Aegean painting.* ■ an eventful past. ■ a past characterized by a particular thing: *his family had a history of insanity.* **3** a continuous, typically chronological, record of important or public events or of a particular trend or institution. ■ a historical play.

– PHRASES **be history** be perceived as no longer relevant to the present. ■ informal used to indicate imminent departure, dismissal, or death: *an inch either way and you'd be history.* **go down in history** be remembered or recorded in history. **make history** do something that is remembered in or influences the course of history. [ME (also as a v.): via L. from Gk. *historia* 'finding out, narrative, history,' from *histōr* 'learned, wise man.']

his·tri·on·ic /,histrē'änik/ ▶ **adj.** overly theatrical or melodramatic in character or style. ■ formal of or concerning actors or acting. ▶ **n.** (**histrionics**) exaggerated dramatic behavior designed to attract attention. ■ dramatic performance; theater. — **his·tri·on·i·cal·ly adv.** [17th C.: from late L. *histrionicus*, from L. *histrio(n-)* 'actor.']

hit /hit/ ▶ **v.** (**hit·ting** ; past **hit**) [trans.] **1** bring one's hand or a tool or weapon into contact with (someone or something) quickly and forcefully: *the woman hit the mugger with her umbrella* | [intrans.] *hit out with billy clubs.* ■ accidentally strike (part of one's body) against something, often causing injury. ■ (of a moving object or body) come into contact with (someone or something stationary) quickly and forcefully: *a car hit the barrier.* ■ informal touch or press (part of a machine or other device) in order to operate it. **2** cause harm or distress to: *the area was hit by business closures.* ■ [intrans.] (**hit out**) make a strongly worded criticism or attack: *he hit out at suppliers for hyping their products.* ■ (of a disaster) occur in and cause damage to (an area) suddenly. ■ informal attack and rob or kill: *if they're cops, maybe it's not a good idea to have them hit.* ■ informal be affected by (an unfortunate and unexpected circumstance or event). **3** (of a missile or a person aiming one) strike (a target). ■ informal reach (a particular level, point, or figure): *his career hit rock bottom.* ■ arrive at (a place): *we hit Chicago at dusk.* ■ informal go to (a place): *we hit a diner for coffee.* ■ be suddenly and vividly realized by: [with obj. and clause] *it hit her that I wanted to settle down here.* ■ [intrans.] informal (of a piece of music, film, or play) be successful: *actors are promised a pay increase if a show hits.* ■ [intrans.] take effect: *we waited for the caffeine to hit.* ■ informal give (someone) a dose of a drug or an alcoholic drink. ■ (of the dealer in blackjack) give (a player) a requested additional card. ■ informal (of a product) become available and make an impact on. ■ informal used to express the idea that someone is taking up a pursuit or taking it seriously: *teenagers hitting the books.* ■ (**hit someone for/up for**) informal ask someone for: *she hit her mother for some cash.* **4** propel (a ball) with a bat, racket, stick, etc., to score or attempt to score runs or points in a game. ■ score (runs or points) in this way. ■ Baseball [intrans.] (of a batter) make a base hit. ▶ **n.** **1** an instance of striking or being struck. ■ a verbal attack. ■ informal a murder, typically one planned and carried out by a criminal organization. ■ Baseball short for BASE HIT. **2** an instance of striking the target aimed at. ■ a successful venture, esp. in entertainment. ■ a successful pop record or song. ■ informal a successful and popular person or thing. ■ Comput. an instance of identifying an item of data that matches the requirements of a search. ■ an instance of a particular Web site being accesssed by a user. **3** informal a dose of a psychoactive drug.

– PHRASES **hit-and-miss** done or occurring at random. **hit someone below the belt** behave unfairly, esp. so as to gain an unfair advantage. **hit the bottle** see BOTTLE. **hit the ground running** informal start something and proceed at a fast pace with enthusiasm. **hit the hay** see HAY. **hit home** see HOME. **hit it off** informal be naturally friendly or well suited. **hit the jackpot** see JACKPOT. **hit the mark** be successful in an attempt or accurate in a guess. **hit the nail on the head** find exactly the right answer. **hit-or-miss** as likely to be unsuccessful as successful. **hit the right note** see NOTE. **hit the road** (or **trail**) informal set out on a journey. **hit the roof** see ROOF. **hit the sack** see SACK[1]. **hit the spot** see SPOT. **make a hit** be successful or popular.

– PHRASAL VERBS **hit on** (or **upon**) **1** discover or think of, esp. by chance. **2** informal make sexual advances toward. ▪ attempt to get something, typically money, from someone. — **hit·ter** n. [OE *hittan* (in the sense 'come upon, find'), from ON *hitta* 'come upon, meet with,' of unknown origin.]

hit-and-run (also **hit and run**) ▶ adj. denoting a motor accident in which the vehicle or vessel involved does not stop, or a driver, victim, vehicle, vessel, etc., involved in such an accident. ▪ designating an attack or an attacker using swift action followed by immediate withdrawal. ▪ done or intended for quickness of effect rather than for permanence. ▪ Baseball designating an offensive play in which a base runner, not attempting to steal a base, runs before the pitch is thrown, in an attempt to advance further in case of a hit. — **hit-and-run** (also **hit and run**) n., v.

hitch /hicH/ ▶ v. **1** [with obj., and adverbial of direction] move (something) into a different position with a jerk: *he hitched his pants up*. **2** [intrans.] informal travel by hitchhiking. ▪ [trans.] obtain (a ride) by hitchhiking. **3** [trans.] fasten or tether with a rope. ▪ harness (a draft animal or team): *Thomas hitched the pony to his cart*. ▶ n. **1** a temporary interruption or problem. **2** a knot used for fastening a rope to another rope or something else. ▪ a device for attaching one thing to another, esp. the tow bar of a motor vehicle. **3** informal an act of hitchhiking. **4** informal a period of service: *his 12-year hitch in the navy*.

– PHRASES **get hitched** informal marry. [ME (in the sense 'lift up with a jerk'): of unknown origin.]

Hitch·cock /'hicH,käk/, Sir Alfred Joseph (1899–1980), English director. His movies include *The Thirty-Nine Steps* (1935), *Strangers on a Train* (1951), and *Psycho* (1960).

hitch·er /'hicHər/ ▶ n. a hitchhiker.

hitch·hike /'hicH,hīk/ ▶ v. [intrans.] travel by getting free rides in passing vehicles. ▶ n. a journey made by hitchhiking. — **hitch·hik·er** n.

hi-tech /'hī 'tek/ ▶ adj. var. of HIGH-TECH.

hith·er /'hiT͟Hər/ ▶ adv. archaic literary to or toward this place: *I little knew then that such calamity would summon me hither!* ▶ adj. archaic situated on this side: *on the hither side of the road*.

– PHRASES **hith·er and thith·er** (also **hither and yon**) in various directions, esp. in a disorganized way: [OE *hider*, of Gmc. origin; rel. to HE and HERE.]

hith·er·to /'hiT͟Hər,to͞o; ,hiT͟Hər'to͞o/ ▶ adv. until now or until the point in time under discussion.

hith·er·ward /'hiT͟Hərwərd/ ▶ adv. archaic to or toward this place.

Hit·ler /'hitlər/, Adolf (1889–1945), chancellor of Germany 1933–45; born in Austria. He established the totalitarian Third Reich in 1933. His expansionist foreign policy precipitated World War II, while his fanatical anti-Semitism led to the Holocaust. ▪ [as n.] (**a Hitler**) a person with authoritarian or tyrannical characteristics. — **Hit·ler·i·an** /hit'le(ə)rēən/ adj. **Hit·ler·ite** /-lə,rīt/ n. & adj.

Hit·ler·ism /'hitlə,rizəm/ ▶ n. the political principles or policy of the Nazi Party in Germany 1933–45.

hit list ▶ n. a list of people to be killed for criminal or political reasons. ▪ a list of things to be attacked or opposed.

hit man ▶ n. informal a person who is paid to kill someone, esp. for a criminal or political organization.

hit pa·rade ▶ n. dated a weekly listing of the current best-selling pop records. ▪ any list of popular things: *at the top of the intellectual hit parade among pundits*.

Hit·tite /'hitīt/ (abbr.: **Hitt.**) ▶ n. **1** a member of an ancient people who established an empire in Asia Minor and Syria that flourished from c.1700 to c.1200 BC. ▪ a subject of this empire or one of their descendants, including the members of a Canaanite or Syrian people mentioned in the Bible (11th to 8th century BC). **2** the Anatolian language of the Hittites, the earliest attested Indo-European language. ▶ adj. of or relating to the Hittites, their empire, or their language. [from Heb. *Ḥittīm*, ult. from Hittite *Ḫatti*.]

HIV ▶ abbr. human immunodeficiency virus, a retrovirus that causes AIDS.

hive /hīv/ ▶ n. a beehive. ▪ the bees in a hive. ▪ a thing that has the domed shape of a beehive. ▪ fig. a place in which people are busily occupied. ▶ v. [trans.] place (bees) in a hive. ▪ [intrans.] (of bees) enter a hive.

– PHRASAL VERBS **hive something off** separate something from a larger group or organization. [OE *hȳf*, of Gmc. origin.]

hives /hīvz/ ▶ plural n. [treated as sing. or pl.] another term for URTICARIA. [16th C.: of unknown origin.]

HIV-pos·i·tive (abbr.: **HIV+**) ▶ adj. having had a positive result in a blood test for the AIDS virus HIV.

hi·ya /'hīə/ ▶ exclam. an informal greeting. [1940s: alteration of *how are you?*]

Hiz·bul·lah var. of HEZBOLLAH.

HK ▶ abbr. Hong Kong.

HL ▶ abbr. (in the UK) House of Lords.

hl ▶ abbr. hectoliter(s).

hld. ▶ abbr. hold.

HM ▶ abbr. ▪ (in the UK) Her (or His) Majesty('s): *HM Forces*.

hm ▶ abbr. hectometer(s).

hmm /(h)m/ (also **h'm**) ▶ exclam. & n. var. of HEM[2], HUM[2].

HMO ▶ abbr. health maintenance organization.

Hmong /hmôNG/ ▶ n. (pl. same) **1** a member of a people living traditionally in isolated mountain villages throughout Southeast Asia. **2** the language of this people. ▶ adj. relating to or denoting this people or their language.

HMS ▶ abbr. Her or His Majesty's Ship, used in the names of ships in the British navy: *HMS Ark Royal*.

Ho ▶ symb. the chemical element holmium.

ho[1] /hō/ (also **hoe**) ▶ n. (pl. **hos** or **hoes**) black slang a prostitute. ▪ derog. a woman. [1960s: representing a dial. pronunc. of WHORE.]

ho[2] ▶ exclam. **1** an expression of surprise, admiration, triumph, or derision: *Ho! I'll show you*. ▪ [in comb.] used as the second element of various exclamations: *heave ho*. **2** used to call for attention: *ho there!* ▪ [in comb.] dated, esp. Naut. used to draw attention to something seen: *land ho!* [natural exclamation: first recorded in ME.]

hoa·gie /'hōgē/ ▶ n. (also **hoa·gy**) (pl. **-gies**) another term for SUBMARINE SANDWICH. [of unknown origin.]

hoar /hôr/ archaic literary ▶ adj. grayish white; gray or gray-haired with age. ▶ n. hoarfrost. [OE *hār*, of Gmc. origin; rel. to Ger. *hehr* 'majestic, noble.']

hoard /hôrd/ ▶ n. a store of money or valued objects, typically one that is secret or carefully guarded. ▪ an ancient store of coins or other valuable artifacts. ▪ an amassed store of useful information or facts, retained for future use. ▶ v. [trans.] amass (money or valued objects) and hide or store away. ▪ accumulate a supply of (something) in a time of scarcity. ▪ reserve in the mind for future use. — **hoard·er** n. [OE *hord* (noun), *hordian* (verb), of Gmc. origin; rel. to Ger. *Hort* (n.), *horten* (v.).]

hoard·ing /'hôrdiNG/ ▶ n. **1** a temporary board fence erected around a building site. **2** British term for BILLBOARD. [19th C.: from obs. *hoard* in the same sense (prob. based on OFr. *hourd*; rel. to HURDLE) + -ING[1].]

hoar·frost /'hôr,frôst/ ▶ n. a grayish-white crystalline deposit of frozen water vapor formed in clear still weather on vegetation, fences, etc.

hoar·hound /'hôr,hound/ ▶ n. var. of HOREHOUND.

hoarse /hôrs/ ▶ adj. (of a person's voice) sounding rough and harsh, typically as the result of a sore throat or of shouting. — **hoarse·ly** adv. **hoars·en** v. **hoarse·ness** n. [OE *hās*, of Gmc. origin; rel. to Du. *hees*. The spelling with *r* was influenced by ON.]

hoar·y /'hôrē/ ▶ adj. (**hoar·i·er**, **hoar·i·est**) **1** grayish-white. ▪ (of a person) having gray or white hair; aged. **2** old and trite. — **hoar·i·ly** adv. **hoar·i·ness** n.

hoar·y mar·mot ▶ n. a large stocky grayish-brown marmot (*Marmota caligata*) with a whistling call, found in the mountains of northwestern North America.

ho·at·zin /wät'sēn/ ▶ n. a large tree-dwelling tropical American bird (*Opisthocomus hoazin*) with weak flight. Young hoatzins have hooked claws on their wings, enabling them to climb around among the branches. [17th C.: from Amer. Sp., from Nahuatl *uatzin*, prob. imitative of its call.]

hoax /hōks/ ▶ n. a humorous or malicious deception. ▶ v. [trans.] deceive with a hoax. — **hoax·er** n. [18th C. (as a v.): prob. a contr. of HOCUS.]

hob[1] /häb/ ▶ n. **1** a flat metal shelf at the side or back of a fireplace, having its surface level with the top of the grate and used esp. for heating pans. **2** a machine tool used for cutting gears or screw threads. [16th C.: alt. of HUB.]

hob[2] ▶ n. archaic dialect a sprite or hobgoblin.

– PHRASES **play** (or **raise**) **hob** cause mischief. [ME (in the sense 'country fellow'): nickname for *Rob*, short for *Robin* or *Robert*.]

Ho·ban /'hōbən/, James (1762–1831), US architect; born in Ireland. He designed the White House in Washington, DC 1793–1801.

Ho·bart /'hō,bärt/ the capital and chief port of Tasmania, on the southeastern part of the island; pop. 127,100.

Hobbes /häbz/, Thomas (1588–1679), English philosopher. He believed that human action was motivated by selfish concerns, notably fear of death. — **Hobbes·i·an** /'häbzēən/ adj.

hob·bit /'häbit/ ▶ n. a member of an imaginary race similar to humans, of small size and with hairy feet, in stories by J. R. R. Tolkien. [1937: invented by Tolkien, said to mean 'hole-dweller.']

hob·ble /'häbəl/ ▶ v. **1** [no obj., with adverbial of direction] walk in an awkward way, typically because of pain from an injury. ▪ fig. proceed haltingly in action or speech. **2** [trans.] (often **be hobbled**) tie or strap together (the legs of a horse or other animal) to prevent it from straying. ▪ cause (a person or animal) to limp. ▪ fig. be or cause a problem for: *cotton farmers hobbled by low prices*. ▶ n. **1** [in sing.] an awkward way of walking, typically due to pain from an injury. **2** a rope or strap used for hobbling a horse or other animal. — **hob·bler** /'häb(ə)lər/ n. [ME: prob. of Dutch or Low Ger. origin and rel. to Du. *hobbelen* 'rock from side to side.']

hob·ble·bush /'häbəl,bo͝osH/ ▶ n. a North American viburnum (*Viburnum alnifolium*) that bears clusters of white or pink flowers and purple-black berries.

hob·ble·de·hoy /'häbəldē,hoi/ informal, dated ▶ n. a clumsy or awkward youth. ▶ **adj.** awkward or clumsy: *his hobbledehoy hands.* [16th C.: of unknown origin.]

hob·ble skirt ▶ **n.** a style of skirt so narrow at the hem as to impede walking, popular in the 1910s.

hob·by[1] /ˈhäbē/ ▶ **n.** (pl. **-bies**) **1** an activity done regularly in one's leisure time for pleasure. **2** archaic a small horse or pony. [ME *hobyn, hoby,* from nicknames for the given name *Robin.*]

hob·by[2] ▶ **n.** (pl. **-bies**) a migratory Old World falcon (genus *Falco*) with long narrow wings, catching dragonflies and birds on the wing. [ME: from OFr. *hobet,* dimin. of *hobe* 'falcon.']

hob·by·horse /ˈhäbē,hôrs/ ▶ **n.** **1** a child's toy consisting of a stick with a model of a horse's head at one end. ■ a rocking horse. **2** a preoccupation; a favorite topic.

hob·by·ist /ˈhäbēist/ ▶ **n.** a person who pursues a particular hobby: *a computer hobbyist.*

hob·gob·lin /ˈhäb,gäblən/ ▶ **n.** (in mythology and fairy stories) a mischievous imp or sprite. ■ a fearsome mythical creature. [16th C.: from HOB[2] + GOBLIN.]

hob·nail /ˈhäb,nāl/ ▶ **n.** a short heavy-headed nail used to reinforce the soles of boots. ■ a blunt projection, esp. in cut or molded glassware. ■ glass decorated with such projections. — **hob·nailed adj.** [16th C.: from HOB[1] + NAIL.]

hob·nob /ˈhäb,näb/ ▶ **v.** (**-nobbed, -nob·bing**) [intrans.] informal mix socially, esp. with those of higher social status. [19th C.: from archaic *hob or nob, hob and nob,* used in drinking to a person's health.]

ho·bo /ˈhō,bō/ ▶ **n.** (pl. **-boes** or **-bos**) a homeless person; a tramp. ■ a migrant worker. [19th C.: of unknown origin.]

Ho·bo·ken /ˈhō,bōkən/ a city in northeastern New Jersey, opposite New York City; pop. 33,397.

Hob·son's choice /ˈhäbsənz/ ▶ **n.** a choice of taking what is available or nothing at all. [17th C.: named after Thomas *Hobson* (1554–1631), a livery stable owner in Cambridge, England, who gave the customer the "choice" of the horse nearest the door or none at all.]

Ho Chi Minh /ˈhō ˈCHē ˈmin/, (1890–1969), president of North Vietnam 1954–69; born *Nguyen That Thanh.* He deployed his forces in the guerrilla struggle that became the Vietnam War.

Ho Chi Minh Cit·y a city on the southern coast of Vietnam; pop 3,016,000; as Saigon, it was capital of South Vietnam 1954–75. The name was changed to Ho Chi Minh City in 1975.

Ho Chi Minh Trail a covert system of trails along Vietnam's western frontier, a major supply route for North Vietnamese forces during the Vietnam War.

hock[1] /häk/ ▶ **n.** **1** the joint in a quadruped's hind leg between the knee and the fetlock, the angle of which points backward. **2** a knuckle of meat, esp. of pork or ham. [ME.]

hock[2] ▶ **v.** [trans.] informal term for PAWN[2].
– PHRASES **in hock** having been pawned. ■ in debt. [19th C. (in the phr. *in hock*): from Du. *hok* 'hutch, prison, debt.']

hock[3] ▶ **n.** Brit. a dry white wine from the German Rhineland. [abbrev. of obs. *hockamore,* alt. of Ger. *Hochheimer (Wein)* '(wine) from Hochheim.']

hock·ey /ˈhäkē/ ▶ **n.** **1** short for ICE HOCKEY. **2** short for FIELD HOCKEY. [16th C.: of unknown origin.]

Hock·ney /ˈhäknē/, David (1937–), English painter. Much of his work depicts flat, almost shadowless architecture, lawns, and swimming pools.

ho·cus /ˈhōkəs/ ▶ **v.** (**-cused, -cus·ing** or Brit. **-cussed, -cus·sing**) [trans.] archaic deceive (someone). [17th C.: from an obs. n. *hocus* 'trickery,' from HOCUS-POCUS.]

ho·cus-po·cus /ˈpōkəs/ ▶ **n.** meaningless talk or activity, often designed to draw attention away from and disguise what is actually happening. ■ a form of words often used by a person performing magic tricks. ■ deception; trickery. ▶ **v.** (**-po·cused, -po·cus·ing** or Brit. **-po·cussed, -po·cus·sing**) [intrans.] play tricks. ■ [trans.] play tricks on, deceive. [17th C.: from *hax pax max Deus adimax,* a pseudo-L. phr. used as a magic formula by conjurors.]

hod /häd/ ▶ **n.** a builder's V-shaped open trough on a pole, used for carrying bricks and other building materials. ■ a coal scuttle. [16th C.: var. of north. Engl. dial. *hot* 'a basket for carrying earth,' from OFr. *hotte* 'pannier,' prob. of Gmc. origin.]

Ho·dei·da /hōˈdādə/ the chief port of Yemen, on the Red Sea; pop. 246,000. Arabic name AL-HUDAYDA.

hodge·podge /ˈhäj,päj/ (Brit. **hotch·potch**) ▶ **n.** [in sing.] a confused mixture. [ME: alt. of HOTCHPOTCH.]

Hodg·kin[1] /ˈhäjkin/, Sir Alan Lloyd (1914–98), English physiologist. With Andrew Huxley he demonstrated the role of sodium and potassium ions in the transmission of nerve impulses between cells. Nobel Prize for Physiology or Medicine (1963, shared with John C. Eccles and A. F. Huxley).

Hodg·kin[2], Dorothy Crowfoot (1910–94), British chemist. She developed an X-ray diffraction technique for investigating the structure of crystals. Nobel Prize for Chemistry (1964).

Hodg·kin's dis·ease /ˈhäjkinz/ ▶ **n.** a malignant but often curable disease of lymphatic tissues typically causing painless enlargement of the lymph nodes, liver, and spleen. [19th C.: named after Thomas *Hodgkin* (1798–1866), the English physician who first described it.]

ho·do·scope /ˈhädə,skōp/ ▶ **n.** Physics an instrument for observing the paths of subatomic particles, esp. those arising from cosmic rays. [20th C. (denoting a microscope for examination of light paths in crystals): from Gk. *hodos* 'way' + -SCOPE. The current sense dates from the 1950s.]

Hoe /hō/, Richard March (1812–86), US inventor. In 1846, he developed a successful rotary press.

hoe[1] /hō/ ▶ **n.** a long-handled gardening tool with a thin metal blade, used mainly for weeding and breaking up soil. ▶ **v.** (**hoes, hoed, hoe·ing**) [trans.] use a hoe to dig (earth) or thin out or dig up (plants). — **ho·er n.** [ME: from OFr. *houe,* of Gmc. origin; rel. to Ger. *Haue,* also to HEW.]

hoe[2] ▶ **n.** var. of HO[1].

hoe·cake /ˈhō,kāk/ ▶ **n.** a coarse cake made of cornmeal, originally baked on the blade of a hoe.

hoe·down /ˈhō,doun/ ▶ **n.** a social gathering at which lively folk dancing takes place. ■ a lively folk dance.

Ho·fei variant of HEFEI.

Hof·fa /ˈhäfə/, Jimmy (1913–c.1975), US labor leader; full name *James Riddle Hoffa.* President of the Teamsters union from 1957, he was imprisoned 1967–71 for attempted bribery, fraud, and looting pension funds. He disappeared in 1975 and is thought to have been murdered.

Hoff·mann /ˈhôf,män/, E. T. A. (1776–1822), German writer; full name *Ernst Theodor Amadeus Hoffmann.* His stories provided the inspiration the opera *Tales of Hoffmann* (1881).

Hof·mann /ˈhäfmən/, Hans (1880–1966) US painter; born in Germany. He was an abstract expressionist.

Hof·manns·thal /ˈhôfmən,stäl/, Hugo von (1874–1929), Austrian poet and playwright. He wrote the libretti for many of Richard Strauss's operas.

hog /hôg; häg/ ▶ **n.** **1** a domesticated pig, esp. one over 120 pounds (54 kg) and reared for slaughter. ■ a feral pig. ■ a wild animal of the pig family, for example a warthog. ■ informal a greedy person. **2** informal a large, heavy motorcycle. **3** (also **hogg**) Brit. a young sheep before the first shearing. ▶ **v.** (**hogged, hog·ging**) **1** [trans.] informal keep or use all of (something) for oneself in an unfair or selfish way. **2** (with reference to a ship) bend or become bent convex upward along its length.
– PHRASES **go (the) whole hog** informal do something completely or thoroughly. **live high on** (or **off**) **the hog** informal have a luxurious lifestyle. — **hog·ger n. hog·ger·y n. hog·gish adj. hog·gish·ly adv. hog·like adj.** [OE *hogg, hocg,* perh. of Celtic origin and rel. to Welsh *hwch* and Cornish *hoch* 'pig, sow.']

Ho·gan /ˈhōgən/, Ben (1912–97), US golfer; full name *William Benjamin Hogan.* He won many championship titles during the late 1940s and the early 1950s.

hogan

ho·gan /ˈhō,gän; -gən/ ▶ **n.** a traditional Navajo hut of logs and earth.

Ho·garth /ˈhō,gärTH/, William (1697–1764), English painter and engraver. His engravings include *A Rake's Progress* (1735). — **Ho·garth·i·an** /hōˈgärTHēən/ **adj.**

hog·back /ˈhôg,bak; ˈhäg-/ ▶ **n.** a long hill or mountain ridge with steep sides.

hog deer ▶ **n.** a short-legged heavily built deer (*Cervus porcinus*) having a yellow-brown coat with darker underparts, found in grasslands and paddy fields in Southeast Asia.

hog·fish /ˈhôg,fiSH; ˈhäg-/ ▶ **n.** (pl. same or **-fish·es**) a colorful wrasse (esp. *Lachnolaimus maximus*) found chiefly in the warm waters of the western Atlantic, often acting as a cleaner fish for other species.

hogg /hôg; häg/ ▶ **n.** var. of HOG (sense 3).

hog heav·en ▶ **n.** a state of complete happiness.

Hog·ma·nay /ˈhägmə,nā/ ▶ **n.** (in Scotland) New Year's Eve, and the celebrations that take place at this time. [17th C.: perh. from *hoguinané,* Norman Fr. form of OFr. *aguillanneuf* 'last day of the year, new year's gift.']

hog-nosed bat ▶ **n.** a tiny insectivorous bat (*Craseonycteris thonglongyai*) with a piglike nose and no tail, native to Thailand. It is the smallest known bat.

hog-nosed skunk ▶ **n.** an American skunk (genus *Conepatus*) with a bare elongated snout and a black face, found in rugged terrain.

hog·nose snake /ˈhôg,nōz; ˈhäg-/ (also **hog-nosed snake**) ▶ **n.** a harmless burrowing American snake (genus *Heterodon*) with an upturned snout. When threatened, it inflates itself with air and hisses and may feign death. Also called PUFF ADDER.

hogs·head /ˈhôgz,hed; ˈhägz-/ (abbr.: **hhd**) ▶ **n.** a large cask. ■ a measure of capacity for wine, equal to 63 gallons (238.7 liters). ■ a measure of capacity for beer, equal to 64 gallons (245.5 liters). [ME: from HOG + HEAD.]

hog-tie (also **hog·tie**) ▶ **v.** [trans.] secure by fastening together the hands and feet (of a person) or all four feet (of an animal). ■ fig. impede or hinder greatly.

hog·wash /ˈhôg,wôSH; ˈhäg,wäSH/ ▶ **n.** informal nonsense.

hog-wild (also **hog wild**) ▶ **adj.** informal extremely enthusiastic; out of control.

Ho·hen·stau·fen /ˌhōənˈstoufən; -ˈsʜtou-/ a German dynastic family, some of whom ruled as Holy Roman Emperors between 1138 and 1254.

Ho·hen·zol·lern /ˈhōənˌzälərn/ a German dynastic family from which came the kings of Prussia from 1701 to 1918 and German emperors from 1871 to 1918.

Hoh·hot /ˈhōˈhōt/ (also **Hu·he·hot** /ˈhoo͞ˈhäˈhōt/) the capital of Inner Mongolia, in northeastern China; pop. 1,206,000. Former name (until 1954) **Kweisui**.

ho ho ▶ **exclam.** representing deep, exuberant laughter. ■ used to express triumph, esp. at discovery: *Ho ho! A stranger in our midst!* [16th C.: reduplication of **ho²**.]

ho-hum /ˈhō ˈhəm/ ▶ **exclam.** used to express boredom or resignation. ▶ **adj.** boring: *a ho-hum script.* [1920s: imitative of a yawn.]

hoi pol·loi /ˈhoi pəˌloi/ ▶ **plural n.** (usu. **the hoi polloi**) derog. the masses; the common people: *avoid mixing with the hoi polloi.* [17th C.: Gk., lit. 'the many.']

hoi·sin /ˈhoisin; hoiˈsin/ (also **hoisin sauce**) ▶ **n.** a sweet, spicy, brown sauce made from soybeans, vinegar, sugar, garlic, and various spices, widely used in southern Chinese cooking.

hoist /hoist/ ▶ **v.** [trans.] raise (something) by means of ropes and pulleys. ■ [with obj. and adverbial] raise or haul up: *she hoisted her backpack onto her shoulder.* ▶ **n.** **1** an act of raising or lifting something. ■ fig. an act of increasing something. ■ an apparatus for lifting or raising something. **2** the part of a flag nearest the staff; the vertical dimension of a flag. **3** a group of flags raised as a signal.
– PHRASES **hoist by one's own petard** see **petard**. [15th C.: alt. of dial. *hoise*, prob. from Du. *hijsen* or Low Ger. *hiesen*, but recorded earlier.]

hoi·ty-toi·ty /ˈhoitēˈtoitē/ ▶ **adj.** **1** haughty; snobbish. **2** archaic frolicsome. [17th C.: from obs. *hoit* 'indulge in riotous mirth.']

Ho·kan /ˈhōkən/ ▶ **adj.** relating to or denoting a group of American Indian languages of California and western Mexico, considered as a possible language family and including Yuman and Mojave. ▶ **n.** this hypothetical language family. [from Hokan *hok* 'about two' + **-an**.]

hoke /hōk/ ▶ **v.** [trans.] informal (of an actor) act (a part) in an insincere, sentimental, or melodramatic manner: *just try it straight—don't hoke it up.* [20th C.: back-form. from **hokum**.]

hok·ey /ˈhōkē/ ▶ **adj.** (**hok·i·er, hok·i·est**) informal mawkishly sentimental: *a slightly hokey song.* ■ noticeably contrived: *a hokey country accent.* — **hok·ey·ness** (also **hok·i·ness**) **n.** [1940s: from **hokum** + **-y¹**.]

ho·key-po·key ▶ **n.** informal **1** (**the hokey-pokey**) a circle dance with a synchronized shaking of the limbs in turn, accompanied by a simple song. **2** hocus-pocus; trickery. **3** dated ice cream sold on the street, esp. by Italian street vendors. [19th C.: of unknown origin.]

Hok·kai·do /häˈkīdō/ the northernmost of the four main islands of Japan; pop. 5,644,000; capital, Sapporo.

hok·ku /ˈhōˌkoo͞; ˈhä-/ ▶ **n.** (pl. same) another term for **haiku**. [19th C.: Japanese, lit. 'opening verse' (of a linked sequence of comic verses).]

ho·kum /ˈhōkəm/ ▶ **n.** informal nonsense. ■ trite, sentimental, or unrealistic situations and dialogue in a movie, play, or piece of writing. [20th C.: of unknown origin.]

Ho·ku·sai /ˈhōkəˌsī/, Katsushika (1760–1849), Japanese painter and wood engraver. He represented aspects of everyday Japanese life in his woodcuts.

Hol·arc·tic /hälˈär(k)tik; hōˈl-/ ▶ **adj.** Zool. of, relating to, or denoting a zoogeographical region comprising the Nearctic and Palearctic regions. ■ [as n.] (**the Holarctic**) the Holarctic region. [19th C.: from **holo-** 'whole' + **Arctic**.]

Hol·bein /ˈhōlˌbīn/, Hans (1497–1543), German painter and engraver; known as **Holbein the Younger**. He painted Henry VIII's prospective brides.

hold¹ /hōld/ ▶ **v.** (past **held** /held/) **1** [trans.] grasp, carry, or support with one's arms or hands: *she was holding a suitcase* | [intrans.] *he held onto the back of a chair.* ■ [with obj. and adverbial] keep or sustain in a specified position: *I held the door open for him.* ■ embrace (someone): *Mark pulled her into his arms and held her close.* ■ (**hold something up**) support and prevent from falling. ■ be able to bear (the weight of a person or thing): *I reached up to the nearest branch that seemed likely to hold my weight.* ■ (of a vehicle) maintain close contact with (the road), esp. when driven at speed: *the car holds the corners very well.* ■ (of a ship or an aircraft) continue to follow (a particular course): *the ship is holding a southeasterly course.* **2** [trans.] keep or detain (someone): *the police were holding him on a murder charge.* ■ keep possession of (something), typically in the face of a challenge or attack. *the rebels held the town for many weeks* | [intrans.] *White managed to hold onto his lead.* ■ keep (someone's interest or attention). ■ (of a singer or musician) sustain (a note). ■ stay or cause to stay at a certain value or level: [intrans.] *the savings rate held at 5%.* | [trans.] *he is determined to hold down inflation.* **3** [intrans.] remain secure, intact, or in position without breaking or giving way: *the boat's anchor would not hold.* ■ (of a favorable condition or situation) continue without changing. ■ be or remain valid or available: *I'll have that coffee now, if the offer still holds.* ■ (of an argument or theory) be logical, consistent, or convincing. ■ (**hold to**) refuse to abandon or change (a principle or opinion). ■ [trans.] (**hold someone to**) cause someone to adhere to (a commitment). **4** [trans.] contain or be capable of containing (a specified amount). ■ be able to drink (a reasonable amount of alcohol) without becoming drunk or suffering any ill effects. ■ have or be characterized by: *I don't know what the future holds.* **5** [trans.] have in one's possession. ■ [intrans.] informal be in possession of illegal drugs: *he was holding, and the police hauled him off to jail.* ■ have or occupy (a job or position). ■ have or adhere to (a belief or opinion). ■ [with obj. and complement] consider (someone) to be responsible or liable for a particular situation: *you can't hold yourself responsible for what happened.* ■ (**hold someone/something in**) regard someone or something with (a specified feeling): *the speed limit is held in contempt by many drivers.* ■ [with clause] (of a judge or court) rule; decide. **6** [trans.] keep or reserve for someone. ■ prevent from going ahead or occurring: *hold your fire!* ■ maintain (a telephone connection) until the person telephoned is free to speak: *please hold, and I'll see if he's available* | [intrans.] *will you hold?* ■ informal refrain from adding or using (something, typically an item of food or drink). ■ (**hold it**) informal used as a way of exhorting someone to wait or to stop doing something: *hold it right there, pal!* **7** [trans.] arrange and take part in (a meeting or conversation). ▶ **n.** **1** an act or manner of grasping something; a grip. ■ a particular way of grasping or restraining someone, esp. an opponent in wrestling or judo. ■ a place where one can grip with one's hands or feet while climbing. ■ a way of influencing someone. ■ a degree of power or control. **2** archaic a fortress.
– PHRASES **be left holding the bag** (or **baby**) informal be left with an unwelcome responsibility, typically without warning. **get hold of** grasp (someone or something) physically. ■ grasp (something) intellectually; understand. ■ informal obtain: *if you can't get hold of ripe tomatoes, add some tomato purée.* ■ informal find or manage to contact (someone): *I'll try and get hold of Mark.* **hold court** be the center of attention amid a crowd of one's admirers. **hold someone/something dear** care for or value someone or something greatly. **hold fast** remain tightly secured. ■ continue to believe in or adhere to an idea or principle. **hold the fort** take responsibility for a situation while another person is temporarily absent. **hold one's ground** see **ground¹**. **hold someone's hand** give a person comfort, guidance, or moral support in a difficult situation. **hold hands** (of two or more people) clasp each other by the hand, typically as a sign of affection. **hold someone/something harmless** Law indemnify. **hold one's horses** [usu. as imper.] informal wait a moment. **hold the line** not yield to the pressure of a difficult situation. **hold one's nose** squeeze one's nostrils with one's fingers in order to avoid inhaling an unpleasant smell. **hold one's tongue** [often in imper.] informal remain silent. **hold true** (or **good**) remain true or valid. **hold up one's head** (or **hold one's head high**) see **head**. **hold water** [often with negative] (of a statement, theory, or line of reasoning) appear to be valid, sound, or reasonable. **no holds barred** (in wrestling) with no restrictions on the kinds of holds that are used. ■ fig. used to convey that no rules or restrictions apply in a conflict or dispute. **on hold** waiting to be connected while making a telephone call. ■ temporarily not being dealt with or pursued. **take hold** start to have an effect.
– PHRASAL VERBS **hold something against** allow past actions or circumstances to have a negative influence on one's present attitude toward (someone). **hold back** hesitate to act or speak. **hold someone/something back** prevent or restrict the advance, progress, or development of someone or something. ■ (**hold something back**) refuse or be unwilling to make something known. **hold something down** informal succeed in keeping a job or position for a period of time. **hold forth** talk lengthily, assertively, or tediously about a subject. **hold off** (of bad weather) fail to occur. ■ delay or postpone an action or decision. **hold someone/something off** resist an attacker or challenge. **hold on 1** [often in imper.] wait; stop: *hold on a minute, I'll be right back!* **2** endure or keep going in difficult circumstances. **hold on to** keep. **hold out** resist or survive in dangerous or difficult circumstances. ■ continue to be sufficient: *we can stay here for as long as our supplies hold out.* **hold out for** continue to demand (a particular thing), refusing to accept what has been offered. **hold out on** informal refuse to give something, typically information, to (someone). **hold something over 1** postpone something. **2** use a fact or piece of information to threaten or intimidate (someone). **hold together** (or **hold something together**) remain or cause to remain united. **hold up** remain strong or vigorous. *the dollar held up well against the yen.* **hold someone/something up 1** delay or block the movement or progress of someone or something. **2** rob someone or something using the threat of force or violence. **3** present or expose someone or something as an example or for particular treatment: *they were held up to public ridicule.* **hold with** [with negative] informal approve of: *I don't hold with fighting or violence.* — **hold·a·ble adj.** [OE *haldan, healdan*, of Gmc. origin; rel. to Ger. *halten*.]

hold² ▶ **n.** a large space in the lower part of a ship or aircraft in which cargo is stowed. [16th C.: from obs. *holl*, from OE *hol* (see **hole**).]

hold·all /ˈhōldˌôl/ ▶ **n.** Brit. a large rectangular bag with handles and a shoulder strap, used for carrying clothes and other personal belongings.

hold·back /ˈhōldˌbak/ ▶ **n.** a thing serving to hold something else in place: *a curtain holdback.* ■ a sum of money withheld under certain conditions.

hold but·ton ▶ **n.** a button on a telephone that temporarily interrupts a call so that another call may be taken.

hold·er /ˈhōldər/ ▶ **n.** **1** a device or implement for holding something. **2** a person who holds something: *US passport holders.* ■ the possessor of a trophy, championship, or record.

hold·fast /ˈhōldˌfast/ ▶n. **1** a staple or clamp securing an object to a wall or other surface. **2** Biol. a stalked organ by which an alga or other simple aquatic plant or animal is attached to a substrate.

hold·ing /ˈhōldiNG/ ▶n. **1** an area of land held by lease. ■ the tenure of such land. **2** (**holdings**) stocks, property, and other financial assets in someone's possession. ■ books, periodicals, magazines, and other material in a library. **3** (in certain team sports such as football, basketball, and ice hockey) an illegal move that prevents an opponent from moving freely.

hold·ing com·pa·ny ▶n. a company created to buy and possess the shares of other companies, which it then controls.

hold·ing pat·tern ▶n. the flight path maintained by an aircraft awaiting permission to land. ■ a state or period of no progress or change.

hold·ing tank ▶n. a large container in which liquids are temporarily held.

hold·out /ˈhōldˌout/ ▶n. an act of resisting something or refusing to accept what is offered. ■ a person or organization acting in such a way.

hold·o·ver /ˈhōldˌōvər/ ▶n. a person or thing surviving from an earlier time, esp. someone surviving in office or remaining on a sports team.

hold·up /ˈhōldˌəp/ ▶n. **1** a situation that causes delay, esp. to a journey. **2** a robbery conducted with the use of threats or violence.

hole /hōl/ ▶n. **1** a hollow place in a solid body or surface. ■ an animal's burrow. ■ an aperture passing through something: *he had a hole in his sock.* ■ a cavity or receptacle on a golf course, typically one of eighteen or nine, into which the ball must be hit. ■ a cavity of this type as representing a division of a golf course or of play in golf. ■ Physics a position from which an electron is absent, esp. one regarded as a mobile carrier of positive charge in a semiconductor. **2** informal a small or unpleasant place. ■ informal an awkward situation: *get yourself out of a hole.* ▶v. [trans.] make a hole or holes in.
– PHRASES **blow a hole in** ruin the effectiveness of (something). **in the hole** informal in debt. **make a hole in** use a large amount of: *the holidays can make a big hole in your savings.* **need something like a hole in the head** informal used to emphasize that someone has absolutely no need or desire for something.
– PHRASAL VERBS **hole up** informal hide oneself: *I holed up for two days in a tiny cabin in Pennsylvania.* — **hol·ey** /ˈhōlē/ adj. [OE *hol* (n.), *holian* (v.), of Gmc. origin; Ger. *hohl* 'hollow,' from an Indo-Eur. root meaning 'cover, conceal.']

hole-and-cor·ner ▶adj. attempting to avoid public notice; secret: *a hole-and-corner wedding.*

hole card ▶n. (in stud or other forms of poker) a card that has been dealt face down. ■ fig. a thing that is kept secret until it can be used to one's own advantage.

hole in one ▶n. (pl. **holes in one**) Golf a shot that enters the hole from the tee with no intervening shots.

hole in the heart ▶n. Med. a congenital defect in the heart septum, resulting in inadequate circulation of oxygenated blood (a cause of blue baby syndrome).

hole in the wall ▶n. informal a small dingy place, esp. a bar or restaurant.

hole saw ▶n. a tool for making circular holes, consisting of a metal cylinder with a toothed edge.

Hol·i·day /ˈhäliˌdā/, Billie (1915–59), US singer; born *Eleanora Fagan.* Her autobiography, *Lady Sings the Blues* (1956), was made into a movie in 1972.

hol·i·day /ˈhäliˌdā/ ▶n. a day of festivity or recreation when no work is done. ■ [as adj.] characteristic of a holiday; festive. ■ esp. Brit. (often **holidays**) a vacation. ▶v. [no obj., with adverbial of place] esp. Brit. spend a holiday in a specified place: *he is **holidaying in** Italy.* [OE *hāligdæg* 'holy day.']

hol·i·day·mak·er /ˈhälidāˌmākər/ ▶n. Brit. a person on vacation away from home.

hol·i·day sea·son ▶n. the period of time from Thanksgiving until New Year, including such festivals as Christmas, Hanukkah, and Kwanzaa.

ho·li·er-than-thou ▶adj. characterized by an attitude of moral superiority.

ho·li·ness /ˈhōlēnis/ ▶n. the state of being holy. ■ (**His/Your Holiness**) a title given to the pope, Orthodox patriarchs, and the Dalai Lama, or used in addressing them.

ho·lism /ˈhōlˌizəm/ ▶n. esp. Philos. the theory that parts of a whole are in intimate interconnection, such that they cannot exist or be understood independently of the whole. The opposite of ATOMISM. ■ Med. the treating of the whole person, taking into account mental and social factors, rather than just the physical symptoms of a disease. — **ho·list** adj. & n. [1920s: from HOLO-.]

ho·lis·tic /hōˈlistik/ ▶adj. esp. Philos. characterized by comprehension of the parts of something as intimately interconnected and explicable only by reference to the whole. ■ Med. characterized by the treatment of the whole person, taking into account mental and social factors, rather than just the physical symptoms of a disease. — **ho·lis·ti·cal·ly** /-ik(ə)lē/ adv.

hol·la /ˈhälə/ ▶exclam. archaic used to call attention to something: *"Holla! what storm is this?"* [16th C. (as an order to stop or cease): from Fr. *holà*, from *ho* 'ho!' + *là* 'there.']

Hol·land /ˈhälənd/ another name for the NETHERLANDS.

hol·land /ˈhälənd/ ▶n. a kind of smooth, durable linen fabric, used chiefly for window shades and furniture covering. [ME: from HOLLAND, the name of a former province of the Netherlands where the cloth was made, from Du., earlier *Holtlant* (from *holt* 'wood' + *-lant* 'land').]

hol·lan·daise sauce /ˈhälənˌdāz/ ▶n. a creamy sauce of melted butter, egg yolks, and lemon juice or vinegar, served esp. with fish. [Fr. *hollandaise*, fem. of *hollandais* 'Du.,' from *Hollande* 'Holland.']

Hol·land·er /ˈhäləndər/ ▶n. dated a native of the Netherlands.

Hol·lands /ˈhäləndz/ ▶n. archaic Dutch gin. [from archaic Du. *hollandsch genever* (earlier form of *hollands jenever*) 'Dutch gin.']

hol·ler /ˈhälər/ informal ▶v. [intrans.] (of a person) give a loud shout or cry. ▶n. a loud cry or shout. [17th C. (as a verb): var. of the rare v. *hollo*; rel. to HALLOO.]

Hol·ler·ith /ˈhōləˌriTH/, Herman (1860–1929), US engineer. He invented a tabulating machine using punched cards for computation.

hol·low /ˈhälō/ ▶adj. **1** having a hole or empty space inside. ■ (of a thing) having a depression in its surface; concave: *hollow cheeks.* ■ (of a sound) echoing, as though made in or on an empty container. **2** without significance: *a hollow victory.* ■ insincere: *a hollow promise.* ▶n. a hole or depression in something. ■ a small valley. ▶v. [trans.] form by making a hole.
– PHRASES **beat someone hollow** defeat or surpass someone completely or thoroughly. — **hol·low·ly** adv. **hol·low·ness** n. [OE *holh* 'cave'; obscurely rel. to HOLE.]

hol·low-eyed ▶adj. (of a person) having deeply sunken eyes, typically as a result of illness or tiredness.

hol·low square ▶n. hist. a body of infantry drawn up in a square with a space in the middle.

hol·low·ware /ˈhälōˌwe(ə)r/ ▶n. serving dishes and accessories, esp. of silver, that are hollow or concave. Contrast with FLATWARE.

hol·ly /ˈhälē/ ▶n. a widely distributed shrub (genus *Ilex*, family Aquifoliaceae), typically having prickly dark green leaves, small white flowers, and red berries. There are several deciduous species of holly but the evergreen hollies are more typical and familiar. ■ the branches, foliage, and berries of this plant used as Christmas decorations. [ME *holi*, shortened form of OE *holegn, holen*, of Gmc. origin; rel. to Ger. *Hulst.*]

hol·ly·hock /ˈhälēˌhäk/ ▶n. a tall Eurasian plant (*Alcea rosea*) of the mallow family, widely cultivated for its large showy flowers. [ME: from HOLY + obs. *hock* 'mallow.']

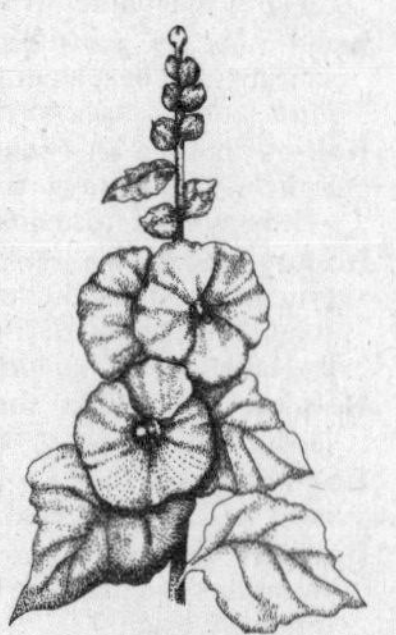
hollyhock

hol·ly oak ▶n. the holm oak or the kermes oak, both of which have tough evergreen leaves that are reminiscent of holly leaves.

Hol·ly·wood /ˈhälēˌwo͝od/ **1** a city in southeastern Florida, on the Atlantic Ocean; pop. 139,357. **2** a district in Los Angeles, the principal center of the US movie industry. ■ the US movie industry and the lifestyles of the people associated with it.

Hol·ly·wood bed ▶n. a bed consisting of a mattress on a box spring supported on short legs, often with an upholstered headboard.

holm /hōm/ (also **holme**) ▶n. Brit. an islet, esp. in a river or near a mainland. ■ a piece of flat ground by a river that is submerged in time of flood. [OE, from ON *holmr.*]

Holmes[1] /hōmz/, Oliver Wendell (1809–94), US physician, poet, and writer; father of Supreme Court justice Oliver Wendell Holmes. His best-known literary works are the humorous essays known as "table talks," which began with *The Autocrat of the Breakfast Table* (1857–58).

Holmes[2], Oliver Wendell (1841–1935), US Supreme Court associate justice 1902–32; the son of physician and writer Oliver Wendell Holmes.

Holmes[3], Sherlock, a private detective in stories by Sir Arthur Conan Doyle. — **Holmes·i·an** /ˈhōmzēən/ adj.

hol·mi·um /ˈhōlmēəm/ ▶n. the chemical element of atomic number 67, a soft silvery-white metal of the lanthanide series. (Symbol: **Ho**) [19th C.: mod. L., from *Holmia*, Stockholm.]

holm oak /hōm/ ▶n. an evergreen southern European oak (*Quercus ilex*) with dark green glossy leaves. [ME: *holm*, alt. of dial. *hollin*, from OE *holen* 'holly.']

hol·o /ˈhälō/ ▶n. (pl. **hol·os**) informal a hologram.

holo- ▶comb. form whole; complete: *holocaust* | *holophytic.* [from Gk. *holos* 'whole.']

ho·lo·blas·tic /ˌhäləˈblastik; ˌhōlə-/ ▶adj. (of an ovum) having cleavage planes that divide the egg into separate blastomeres.

hol·o·caust /ˈhäləˌkôst; ˈhōlə-/ ▶n. **1** destruction or slaughter on a mass scale, esp. caused by fire or nuclear war: *a nuclear holocaust.* ■ (**the Holocaust**) the mass murder of Jews under the German Nazi regime during the period 1941–45. **2** hist. a sacrificial offering that is burned completely on an altar. [ME: from OFr. *holocauste*, via late L. from Gk. *holokauston*, from *holos* 'whole' + *kaustos* 'burned' (from *kaiein* 'burn').]

Hol·o·cene /ˈhäləˌsēn; ˈhōlə-/ ▶adj. Geol. of, relating to, or denoting the present epoch, which is the second epoch in the Quaternary period, after the Pleistocene. The Holocene began about 10,000 years ago, after the retreat of the ice of the last glaciation, and is sometimes regarded as another interglacial period. Also called **Recent.** ■ [as n.] (**the Holocene**) the Holocene epoch or the system of deposits laid down during this time. [19th C.: coined in Fr. from **holo-** 'whole' + Gk. *kainos* 'new.']

hol•o•en•zyme /ˌhälō'enˌzīm; ˌhōlō-/ ▶ **n.** Biochem. a biochemically active compound formed by the combination of an enzyme with a coenzyme.

Hol•o•fer•nes /ˌhälə'fərnēz/ (in the Apocrypha) the Assyrian general of Nebuchadnezzar's forces, who was killed by Judith (Judith 4:1 ff.).

hol•o•gram /'häləˌgram; 'hōlə-/ ▶ **n.** a three-dimensional image formed by the interference of light beams from a laser or other coherent light source. ■ a photograph of an interference pattern that, when suitably illuminated, produces a three-dimensional image.

hol•o•graph /'häləˌgraf; 'hōlə-/ ▶ **n.** a manuscript handwritten by the person named as its author. [17th C.: from Fr. *holographe*, or via late L. from Gk. *holographos*, from *holos* 'whole' + *-graphos* 'written, writing.']

hol•og•ra•phy /hō'lägrəfē/ ▶ **n.** the study or production of holograms. — **hol•o•graph•ic** /ˌhälə'grafik; ˌhōlə-/ **adj.** **hol•o•graph•i•cal•ly** /ˌhälə'grafik(ə)lē; ˌhōlə-/ **adv.**

hol•o•he•dral /ˌhälə'hēdrəl; ˌhōlə-/ ▶ **adj.** Crystallog. having the full number of planes required by the symmetry of a crystal system.

ho•loph•ra•sis /hə'läfrəsis/ ▶ **n.** the expression of a whole phrase in a single word, for example *howdy* for *how do you do.* — **hol•o•phrase** /'häləˌfrāz; 'hōlə-/ **n.** **hol•o•phras•tic** /ˌhälə'frastik; hōlə-/ **adj.**

hol•o•phyt•ic /ˌhälə'fitik; ˌhōlə-/ ▶ **adj.** Biol. (of a plant or protozoan) able to synthesize complex organic compounds by photosynthesis.

hol•o•thu•ri•an /ˌhälə'THo͝orēən; ˌhōlə-/ ▶ **n.** Zool. a sea cucumber. [19th C.: from the mod. L. genus name *Holothuria* (from Gk. *holothourion*, denoting a kind of zoophyte) + **-an.**]

Hol•o•thu•roi•de•a /ˌhäləTHo͝or'oidēə; ˌhōlō-/ Zool. a class of echinoderms that comprises the sea cucumbers. — **hol•o•thu•roid** /-'THo͝oroid/ **n. & adj.**

hol•o•type /'häləˌtīp; 'hōlə-/ ▶ **n.** Bot. & Zool. a single type specimen upon which the description and name of a new species is based. Compare with **syntype.**

hols /hälz/ ▶ **plural n.** Brit., informal holidays. [20th C.: abbrev.]

Hol•stein /'hōlˌstān; -ˌstēn/ ▶ **n.** an animal of a typically black-and-white breed of large dairy cattle.

hol•ster /'hōlstər/ ▶ **n.** a holder for carrying a handgun or other firearm, typically made of leather and worn on a belt or under the arm. ▶ **v.** [trans.] put (a gun) into its holster. [17th C.: corresponding to Du. *holster.*]

holt /hōlt/ ▶ **n.** archaic dialect a wood or wooded hill. [OE, of Gmc. origin; rel. to MDu. *hout* and Ger. *Holz*, from an Indo-Eur. root shared by Gk. *klados* 'twig.']

ho•ly /'hōlē/ ▶ **adj.** (**ho•li•er, ho•li•est**) **1** dedicated or consecrated to God or a religious purpose; sacred: *the Holy Bible | the holy month of Ramadan.* ■ (of a person) devoted to the service of God: *saints and holy men.* ■ morally and spiritually excellent: *I do not lead a holy life.* **2** informal used as an intensifier: *a holy horror.* **3** dated humorous used in exclamations of surprise or dismay: *holy mackerel!* — **ho•li•ly** /'hōləlē/ **adv.** [OE *hālig*, of Gmc. origin; rel. to Du. and Ger. *heilig*, also to **whole.**]

Ho•ly Al•li•ance a loose alliance of European powers pledged to uphold the principles of the Christian religion. It was proclaimed at the Congress of Vienna (1814–15) by the emperors of Austria and Russia and the king of Prussia and was joined by most other European monarchs.

Ho•ly Ark ▶ **n.** see **ark** (sense 2).

ho•ly cit•y ▶ **n.** a city held sacred by the adherents of a religion. ■ (**the Holy City**) Jerusalem. ■ (**the Holy City**) (in Christian tradition) Heaven.

Ho•ly Com•mun•ion ▶ **n.** see **communion** (sense 2).

ho•ly day ▶ **n.** a day on which a religious observance is held.

holy day of obligation ▶ **n.** (in the Roman Catholic Church) a day on which Roman Catholics are required to attend Mass.

Ho•ly Fam•i•ly Jesus as a child with Mary and Joseph, esp. as a subject for a painting.

Ho•ly Fa•ther ▶ **n.** a title of the pope.

ho•ly fool ▶ **n.** a person who appears unintelligent and unsophisticated but who has other redeeming qualities.

Ho•ly Ghost ▶ **n.** another term for **Holy Spirit.**

Ho•ly Grail ▶ **n.** see **Grail.**

Ho•ly Joe ▶ **n.** informal a sanctimonious or pious man. ■ a clergyman. [19th C.: orig. nautical slang.]

Ho•ly Land a region on the eastern shore of the Mediterranean Sea, in what is now Israel and Palestine. ■ a region similarly revered, for example, Arabia in Islam.

Ho•ly League any of various European alliances sponsored by the papacy during the 15th, 16th, and 17th centuries.

Ho•ly Of•fice the ecclesiastical court of the Roman Catholic Church established as the final court of appeal in trials of heresy.

ho•ly of ho•lies /'hōlē əv 'hōlēz/ ▶ **n.** the inner chamber of the sanctuary in the Jewish Temple in Jerusalem, separated by a veil from the outer chamber. ■ a place regarded as most sacred or special.

Hol•yoke /'hōlēˌōk; 'hōlˌyōk/ a city in west central Massachusetts; pop. 43,704.

ho•ly or•ders ▶ **plural n.** the sacrament or rite of ordination as a member of the Christian clergy, esp. in the grades of bishop, priest, or deacon.
– PHRASES **in holy orders** having the status of an ordained member of the clergy. **take holy orders** become an ordained member of the clergy.

ho•ly place ▶ **n.** a place revered as holy, typically one to which religious pilgrimage is made. ■ hist. the outer chamber of the sanctuary in the Jewish Temple in Jerusalem.

Ho•ly Roll•er ▶ **n.** informal, derog. a member of an evangelical Christian group that expresses religious fervor by frenzied excitement or trances.

Ho•ly Ro•man Em•pire the empire set up in western Europe following the coronation of Charlemagne as emperor in the year 800. It was created by the medieval papacy in an attempt to unite Christendom under one rule. At times the territory of the empire was extensive and included Germany, Austria, Switzerland, and parts of Italy and the Netherlands.

Ho•ly Sat•ur•day n. the Saturday preceding Easter Sunday.

Ho•ly Scrip•ture ▶ **n.** the sacred writings of Christianity contained in the Bible.

Ho•ly See the papacy or the papal court; those associated with the pope in the government of the Roman Catholic Church at the Vatican. Also called **See of Rome.**

Ho•ly Sep•ul•cher the place in which the body of Jesus was laid after being taken down from the Cross. ■ the church in Jerusalem erected over the traditional site of this tomb.

Ho•ly Spir•it n. (in Christianity) the third person of the Trinity; God as spiritually active in the world.

ho•ly•stone /'hōlēˌstōn/ esp. hist. ▶ **n.** a piece of soft sandstone used for scouring the decks of ships. ▶ **v.** [trans.] scour (a deck) with a holystone. [19th C.: prob. from **holy** + **stone.** Sailors called the stones "bibles" or "prayer books," perh. because they scrubbed the decks on their knees.]

Ho•ly Thurs•day ▶ **n. 1** (chiefly in the Roman Catholic Church) Maundy Thursday. **2** dated (in the Anglican Church) Ascension Day.

ho•ly war ▶ **n.** a war declared or waged in support of a religious cause.

ho•ly wa•ter ▶ **n.** water blessed by a priest and used in religious ceremonies.

Ho•ly Week ▶ **n.** the week before Easter, starting on Palm Sunday.

Ho•ly Writ ▶ **n.** the Bible. ■ writings or sayings of unchallenged authority.

Ho•ly Year ▶ **n.** (in the Roman Catholic Church) a period of remission from the penal consequences of sin, granted under certain conditions for a year usually at intervals of twenty-five years.

hom•age /'(h)ämij/ ▶ **n.** special honor or respect shown publicly. ■ hist. formal public acknowledgment of feudal allegiance. [ME: OFr., from med. L. *hominaticum*, from L. *homo, homin-* 'man.']

hom•bre /'ämbrā; -brē/ ▶ **n.** informal a man, esp. one of a particular type. [19th C. (orig. denoting a man of Spanish descent): Sp., 'man,' from L. *homo, homin-*.]

hom•burg /'hämbərg/ ▶ **n.** a man's felt hat having a narrow curled brim and a tapered crown with a lengthwise indentation. [19th C.: *Homburg*, a town in Germany.]

homburg

home /hōm/ ▶ **n. 1** the place where one lives permanently, esp. as a member of a family or household. ■ the family or social unit occupying such a place: *he came from a good home.* ■ a house or an apartment considered as a commercial property. ■ a place where something flourishes, is most typically found, or from which it originates: *Piedmont is the home of Italy's finest red wines.* ■ informal a place where an object is kept. **2** an institution for people needing professional care or supervision. **3** Sports the goal or end point. ■ the place where a player is free from attack. ■ Baseball short for **home plate.** ■ a game played or won by a team on their own ground. ▶ **adj.** [attrib.] **1** of or relating to the place where one lives: *your home address.* ■ made, done, or intended for use in the place where one lives: *home cooking.* ■ relating to one's own country and its domestic affairs: *Japanese competitors are selling cars for lower prices in the US than in their home market.* **2** (of a sports team or player) belonging to the country or locality in which a sporting event takes place. ■ played on or connected with a team's own ground: *their first home game of the season.* **3** denoting the administrative center of an organization: *the home office.* ▶ **adv.** to the place where one lives: *what time did he get home last night?* ■ in or at the place where one lives: *I stayed home with the kids.* ■ Baseball to or toward home plate. ■ to the intended or correct position: *he drove the bolt home.* ▶ **v.** [intrans.] **1** (of an animal) return by instinct to its territory after leaving it: *geese homing to their summer nesting grounds.* ■ (of a pigeon bred for long-distance racing) fly back to or arrive at its loft after being released at a distant point. **2** (**home in on**) move or be aimed toward (a target or destination) with great accuracy. ■ focus attention on: *a teaching style that homes in on each pupil.*
– PHRASES **at home** in one's own house. ■ in one's own neighborhood, town, or country: *successful both at home and abroad.* ■ comfortable and at ease in a place or situation: ***make yourself at home.*** ■ confident

or relaxed about doing or using something: *he was quite at home talking about Eisenstein.* ■ (with reference to sports games) at a team's own ground. **bring something home to someone** make someone realize the full significance of something. **close** (or **near**) **to home** (of a remark or topic of discussion) relevant or accurate to the point that one feels uncomfortable or embarrassed. **come home to someone** (of the significance of something) become fully realized by someone. **drive** (or **hammer** or **press** or **ram**) **something home** make something clearly and fully understood by the use of repeated or forcefully direct arguments. **hit** (or **strike**) **home** (of a blow or a missile) reach an intended target. ■ (of words) have the intended, esp. unsettling or painful, effect on their audience. ■ (of the significance or true nature of a situation) become fully realized by someone: *the full impact of life as a celebrity began to hit home.* **home free** having successfully achieved or being within sight of achieving one's objective. **a home away from home** a place where one is as happy, relaxed, or comfortable as in one's own home. **home sweet home** used as an expression of one's pleasure or relief at being in or returning to one's own home. — **home•like** adj. [OE *hām*, of Gmc. origin; rel. to Du. *heem* and Ger. *Heim*.]

home base ▶ n. a place from which operations or activities are carried out; headquarters. ■ the objective toward which players progress in certain games.

home•bod•y /'hōm,bädē/ ▶ n. (pl. **-bod•ies**) informal a person who likes to stay at home, esp. one who is perceived as unadventurous.

home•boy /'hōm,boi/ ▶ n. informal a young acquaintance from one's own town or neighborhood, or from the same social background. ■ (esp. among urban black people) a member of a peer group or gang. ■ a performer of rap music.

home-bred ▶ adj. bred or raised at home. ■ lacking in worldly experience; unsophisticated.

home brew ▶ n. beer or other alcoholic drink brewed at home. ■ [as adj.] informal made at home, rather than in a store or factory. — **home-brewed** adj.

home•buy•er /'hōm,bīər/ ▶ n. a person who buys a house or condominium.

home•com•ing /'hōm,kəmiNG/ ▶ n. an instance of returning home. ■ a high school, college, or university game, dance, or other event to which alumni are invited.

home ec /'hōm 'ek/ ▶ n. informal short for HOME ECONOMICS.

home ec•o•nom•ics ▶ plural n. [often treated as sing.] cooking and other aspects of household management, esp. as taught at school.

home fries (also **home-fried potatoes**) ▶ plural n. fried sliced potatoes.

home front ▶ n. the civilian population and activities of a nation whose armed forces are engaged in war abroad.

home•girl /'hōm,gərl/ ▶ n. a female equivalent of a homeboy.

home•grown /'hōm'grōn/ ▶ adj. grown or produced in one's own garden or country. ■ belonging to one's own particular locality or country.

home key ▶ n. 1 Music the basic key in which a work is written; the tonic key. 2 a key on a computer or typewriter keyboard that acts as the base position for one's fingers in touch-typing.

Ho•mel /hô'm(y)el/ a city in southeastern Belarus; pop. 506,000. Russian name GOMEL.

home•land /'hōm,land/ ▶ n. a person's or a people's native land. ■ an autonomous or semiautonomous state occupied by a particular people. ■ hist. any of ten partially self-governing areas in South Africa designated for particular indigenous African peoples under the former policy of apartheid.

Home•land Se•cu•ri•ty, Of•fice of ▶ n. a US cabinet-level department that coordinates more than 40 federal agencies, including the CIA and Department of Defense, to combat terrorism. It was established by President George W. Bush in 2001.

home•less /'hōmlis/ ▶ adj. (of a person) without a home, and therefore typically living on the streets. — **home•less•ness** n.

home loan ▶ n. a loan advanced to a person to assist in buying a house or condominium.

home•ly /'hōmlē/ ▶ adj. (**home•li•er**, **home•li•est**) 1 (of a person) unattractive in appearance. 2 Brit. (of a place or surroundings) simple but cozy and comfortable, as in one's own home. ■ unsophisticated and unpretentious. — **home•li•ness** n.

home•made /'hō(m)'mād/ ▶ adj. made at home, rather than in a store or factory.

home•mak•er /'hōm,mākər/ ▶ n. a person, esp. a housewife, who manages a home.

home•mak•ing /'hōm,mākiNG/ ▶ n. the creation and management of a home, esp. as a pleasant place in which to live.

home mov•ie ▶ n. a film made at home or without professional equipment or expertise, esp. a movie featuring a family's activities.

ho•me•o•box /'hōmēō,bäks/ ▶ n. Genet. any of a class of closely similar sequences that occur in various genes and are involved in regulating embryonic development in a wide range of species. [1980s: from Gk. *homoios* 'like' + the n. BOX[1]; first discovered in homeotic genes of *Drosophila* fruit flies.]

Home Of•fice the British government department dealing with domestic affairs, including law and order, immigration, and broadcasting, in England and Wales.

ho•me•o•mor•phism /,hōmēə'môrfizəm/ ▶ n. Math. an instance of topological equivalence to another space or figure. — **ho•me•o•mor•phic** /-'môrfik/ adj.

ho•me•o•path /'hōmēə,paTH/ (also **ho•me•op•a•thist** /,hōmē'äpəTHist/, Brit. **ho•moe•o•path**) ▶ n. a person who practices homeopathy. [19th C.: from Ger. *Homöopath* (see HOMEOPATHY).]

ho•me•op•a•thy /,hōmē'äpəTHē/ (Brit. **ho•moe•op•a•thy**) ▶ n. a system for the treatment of disease by minute doses of natural substances that in a healthy person would produce symptoms of disease. Often contrasted with ALLOPATHY. — **ho•me•o•path•ic** /-ə'paTHik/ adj. **ho•me•o•path•i•cal•ly** /-ə'paTHik(ə)lē/ adv. [19th C.: coined in Ger. from Gk. *homoios* 'like' + *patheia* (see -PATHY).]

ho•me•o•sta•sis /,hōmēə'stāsis/ ▶ n. (pl. **-ses** /-sēz/) the tendency toward a relatively stable equilibrium between interdependent elements, esp. as maintained by physiological processes. — **ho•me•o•stat•ic** /-'statik/ adj. [1920s: mod. L., from Gk. *homoios* 'like' + -STASIS.]

ho•me•o•therm /'hōmēə,THərm/ (also **ho•moi•o•therm**) ▶ n. Zool. an organism that maintains its body temperature at a constant level, usually above that of the environment, by its metabolic activity. Often contrasted with POIKILOTHERM; compare with WARM-BLOODED. — **ho•me•o•ther•mal** /,hōmēə'THərməl/ adj. **ho•me•o•ther•mic** /,hōmēə'THərmik/ adj. **ho•me•o•ther•my** n. [19th C.: mod. L., from Gk. *homoios* 'like' + *thermē* 'heat.']

home•own•er /'hōm,ōnər/ ▶ n. a person who owns their own home. — **home•own•er•ship** n.

home page (also **home•page**) ▶ n. Comput. the introductory document of an individual's or organization's Web site. It typically serves as a table of contents to the site's other pages or provides links to other sites.

home plate ▶ n. Baseball the five-sided flat white rubber base next to which the batter stands and over which the pitcher must throw the ball for a strike. A runner must touch home plate after having reached all the other bases to score a run.

home port ▶ n. the port from which a ship originates or in which it is registered.

Ho•mer[1] /'hōmər/ (8th century BC), Greek epic poet. He is traditionally held to be the author of the *Iliad* and the *Odyssey*.

Ho•mer[2], Winslow (1836–1910), US painter. He is noted for his seascapes, such as *Cannon Rock* (1895).

ho•mer /'hōmər/ ▶ n. Baseball a home run. ▶ v. [intrans.] Baseball hit a home run.

home range ▶ n. Zool. an area over which an animal or group of animals regularly travels in search of food or mates.

Ho•mer•ic /hō'merik/ ▶ adj. of or in the style of Homer or the epic poems ascribed to him. ■ of Bronze Age Greece as described in these poems. ■ epic and large-scale.

home•room /'hōm,rōōm; -,rŏŏm/ ▶ n. a classroom in which a group of students assembles daily with the same teacher before dispersing to other classes.

home rule ▶ n. the government of a colony, dependent country, or region by its own citizens.

home run ▶ n. Baseball a fair hit that allows the batter to make a complete circuit of the bases without stopping and score a run.

home•school•ing /'hōm'skōōliNG/ (also **home-school•ing**) ▶ n. the education of children at home by their parents. — **home•school** v. **home•school•er** n.

Home Sec•re•tar•y ▶ n. (in the UK) the Secretary of State in charge of the Home Office.

home shop•ping ▶ n. shopping carried out from one's own home by ordering goods advertised in a catalog or on a television channel, or by using various electronic media.

home•sick /'hōm,sik/ ▶ adj. experiencing a longing for one's home during a period of absence from it. — **home•sick•ness** n.

home•site /'hōm,sīt/ ▶ n. a building plot for a house.

home•spun /'hōm,spən/ ▶ adj. 1 simple and unsophisticated. 2 (of cloth or yarn) made or spun at home. ■ denoting a coarse handwoven fabric similar to tweed. ▶ n. cloth of this type.

home stand ▶ n. a series of consecutive games played at a team's home stadium, field, or court.

home•stead /'hōm,sted/ ▶ n. 1 a house, esp. a farmhouse, and outbuildings. 2 Law a person's or family's residence, which comprises the land, house, and outbuildings, and in most states is exempt from forced sale for collection of debt. 3 hist. (as provided by the federal Homestead Act of 1862) an area of public land in the West (usually 160 acres) granted to any US citizen willing to settle on and farm the land for at least five years. — **home•stead•er** n. [OE *hāmstede* 'a settlement' (see HOME, STEAD).]

Home•stead Act ▶ n. see HOMESTEAD (sense 3)

home•stead•ing /'hōm,stediNG/ ▶ n. life as a settler on a homestead. ■ the granting of homesteads to settlers.

home•stretch /'hōm'strecH/ (also **home stretch**) ▶ n. the concluding straight part of a racecourse. ■ fig. the last part of an activity or campaign.

home stud•y ▶ n. a course of study carried out at home, rather than in a traditional classroom setting.

home•style /'hōm,stīl/ ▶ adj. [attrib.] such as would be made or provided at home; simple and unpretentious. ■ (of a meal in a restaurant) brought to the table in serving dishes from which each plate is served, rather than in individual portions.

home•town /'hōm'toun/ ▶ n. the town where one was born or grew up, or the town of one's present fixed residence.

home truth ▶**n.** (usu. **home truths**) an unpleasant fact about oneself, esp. as pointed out by another person.

home vid·e·o ▶**n.** a film on videotape for viewing at home.

home·ward /'hōmwərd/ ▶**adv.** (also **home·wards**) toward home. ▶**adj.** going or leading toward home.

home·work /'hōm,wərk/ ▶**n.** schoolwork that a student is required to do at home. ■ work or study done in preparation for a certain event or situation. ■ paid work carried out in one's own home, esp. low-paid piecework.

home·work·er /'hōm,wərkər/ ▶**n.** a person who works from home, esp. doing low-paid piecework.

home·wreck·er /'hōm,rekər/ ▶**n.** a person who is blamed for the breakup of a marriage or family, esp. because of his or her affair with one of the partners.

hom·ey[1] /'hōmē/ (also **hom·y**) ▶**adj.** (**hom·i·er, hom·i·est**) (of a place or surroundings) pleasantly comfortable and cozy. — **hom·ey·ness** (also **hom·i·ness**) **n.**

hom·ey[2] ▶**n.** (pl. **hom·eys**) var. of **HOMIE.**

hom·i·cid·al /,hämə'sīdl; ,hōmə-/ ▶**adj.** of, relating to, or tending toward murder: *he had homicidal tendencies.*

hom·i·cide /'hämə,sīd; 'hōmə-/ ▶**n.** the deliberate and unlawful killing of one person by another; murder. ■ (**Homicide**) the police department that deals with such crimes. ■ dated a murderer. [ME: from OFr., from L. *homicidium*, from *homo, homin-* 'man.']

hom·ie /'hōmē/ (also **hom·ey**) ▶**n.** (pl. **hom·ies**) informal a homeboy or homegirl.

hom·i·let·ic /,hämə'letik/ ▶**adj.** of the nature of or characteristic of a homily. ▶**n.** (**homiletics**) the art of preaching or writing sermons. [17th C.: via late L. from Gk. *homilētikos*, from *homilein* 'converse with, consort,' from *homilia* (see **HOMILY**).]

hom·i·ly /'häməlē/ ▶**n.** (pl. **-lies**) a religious discourse that is intended primarily for spiritual edification rather than doctrinal instruction; a sermon. ■ a tedious moralizing discourse. — **hom·i·list n.** [ME: via OFr. from eccles. L. *homilia*, from Gk., 'discourse, conversation,' from *homilos* 'crowd.']

hom·ing /'hōmiNG/ ▶**adj.** relating to an animal's ability to return to a place or territory after traveling a distance away from it. ■ (of a pigeon) trained to fly home from a great distance and bred for long-distance racing. ■ (of a weapon or piece of equipment) fitted with an electronic device that enables it to find and hit a target.

hom·i·nid /'hämə,nid/ ▶**n.** Zool. a primate of a family (Hominidae) that includes humans and their fossil ancestors. [19th C.: from mod. L. *Hominidae* (pl.), from L. *homo, homin-* 'man.']

hom·i·noid /'hämə,noid/ Zool. ▶**n.** a primate of a group (superfamily Hominoidea) that includes humans, their fossil ancestors, and the great apes. ▶**adj.** of or relating to primates of this group; hominid or pongid. [20th C.: from L. *homo, homin-* 'human being' + **-OID.**]

hom·i·ny /'hämənē/ ▶**n.** coarsely ground corn used to make grits. [17th C.: shortened from Virginia Algonquian *uskatahomen.*]

Ho·mo /'hōmō/ the genus of primates of which modern humans (*Homo sapiens*) are the present-day representatives. ■ [with Latin or pseudo-Latin adj.] denoting kinds of modern human, often humorously: *a textbook example of Homo neuroticus.* [L., 'man.']

ho·mo /'hōmō/ derog. ▶**n.** (pl. **-mos**) a homosexual man. ▶**adj.** homosexual.

homo- ▶**comb. form 1** same: *homogametic.* **2** relating to homosexual love: *homoerotic.* [from Gk. *homos* 'same.']

ho·mo·cen·tric[1] /,hōmō'sentrik/ ▶**adj.** having the same center. [17th C.: from Gk. **HOMO-** 'same' + **-CENTRIC**]

ho·mo·cen·tric[2] ▶**adj.** another term for **ANTHROPOCENTRIC.** [20th C.: from L. *homo* 'human being, man' + **-CENTRIC.**]

ho·moe·cious /hō'mēsHəs; hä-/ ▶**adj.** parasitic on a single host throughout life. Compare with **HETEROECIOUS.**

ho·moeo·path ▶**n.** Brit. var. of **HOMEOPATH.**

ho·moe·op·a·thy ▶**n.** Brit. var. of **HOMEOPATHY.**

ho·mo·e·rot·ic /,hōmō-i'rätik/ ▶**adj.** concerning or arousing sexual desire centered on a person of the same sex. — **ho·mo·e·rot·i·cism** /-i,sizəm/ **n.**

ho·mo·ga·met·ic /,hōmōgə'metik/ ▶**adj.** Biol. denoting the sex that has sex chromosomes that do not differ in morphology, resulting in only one kind of gamete, e.g., (in mammals) the female and (in birds) the male.

ho·mog·a·my /hō'mägəmē; hä-/ ▶**n. 1** Biol. inbreeding, esp. as a result of isolation. ■ marriage between people from similar sociological or educational backgrounds. Compare with **HETEROGAMY** (sense 3). **2** Bot. a state in which the flowers of a plant are all of one type (either hermaphrodite or of the same sex). Compare with **HETEROGAMY** (sense 2). **3** Bot. the simultaneous ripening of the stamens and pistils of a flower, ensuring self-pollination. Compare with **DICHOGAMY.** — **ho·mog·a·mous** /-'mägəməs/ **adj.** [19th C.: from **HOMO-** 'same' + Gk. *gamos* 'marriage.']

ho·mog·e·nate /hə'mäjə,nāt; -nət/ ▶**n.** Biol. a suspension of cell fragments and cell constituents obtained when tissue is homogenized.

ho·mo·ge·ne·ous /,hōmə'jēnēəs/ ▶**adj.** of the same kind; alike. ■ consisting of parts all of the same kind. ■ Math. containing terms all of the same degree. — **ho·mo·ge·ne·i·ty** /-jə'nēitē; ,hämə-/ **n.** **ho·mo·ge·ne·ous·ly adv.** **ho·mo·ge·ne·ous·ness n.**

ho·mog·e·nize /hə'mäjə,nīz/ ▶**v.** [trans.] **1** subject (milk) to a process in which the fat droplets are emulsified and the cream does not separate. ■ Biol. prepare a suspension of cell constituents from (tissue) by physical treatment in a liquid. **2** make uniform or similar. — **ho·mog·e·ni·za·tion** /hə,mäjəni'zāsHən/ **n.** **ho·mog·e·niz·er n.**

ho·mog·e·nous /hə'mäjənəs/ ▶**adj. 1** Biol. old-fashioned term for **HOMOLOGOUS. 2** homogeneous. See usage at **HOMOGENEOUS.** [19th C. (in sense 1): from **HOMO-** 'same' + Gk. *genos* 'race, kind' + **-OUS.** Sense 2 (20th C.) is an alt. of *homogeneous*, prob. after *homogenize.*]

ho·mo·graft /'hōmə,graft; 'hämə-/ ▶**n.** a tissue graft from a donor of the same species as the recipient. Compare with **ALLOGRAFT.**

hom·o·graph /'hämə,graf; 'hōmə-/ ▶**n.** each of two or more words spelled the same but not necessarily pronounced the same and having different meanings and origins (e.g., **BOW**[1] and **BOW**[2]). — **hom·o·graph·ic** /,hämə'grafik; ,hōmə-/ **adj.**

ho·moi·o·therm /hō'moiə,THərm/ ▶**n.** var. of **HOMEOTHERM.**

ho·moi·ou·si·an /,hōmoi'ōōsēən/ ▶**n.** hist. in the fourth-century Arian controversy, a person who held that God the Father and God the Son are of like but not identical substance. Compare with **HOMOOUSIAN.** [17th C. (as an adj. in the sense 'of similar but not identical substance'): via eccles. L. from Gk. *homoiousios*, from *homoios* 'like' + *ousia* 'essence, substance.' The n. dates from the mid 18th C.]

ho·mo·log ▶**n.** var. of **HOMOLOGUE.**

ho·mol·o·gate /hō'mälə,gāt; hə-/ ▶**v.** [trans.] formal express agreement with or approval of. — **ho·mol·o·ga·tion** /hō,mälə'gāsHən; hə-/ **n.** [16th C.: from med. L. *homologat-* 'agreed,' from the v. *homologare*, from Gk. *homologein* 'confess.']

ho·mol·o·gize /hō'mälə,jīz; hə-/ ▶**v.** [trans.] formal make or show to have the same relation, relative position, or structure.

ho·mol·o·gous /hō'mäləgəs; hə-/ ▶**adj.** having the same relation, relative position, or structure, in particular: ■ Biol. (of organs) similar in position, structure, and evolutionary origin but not necessarily in function: *a seal's flipper is **homologous with the human arm.*** Often contrasted with **ANALOGOUS.** ■ Biol. (of chromosomes) pairing at meiosis and having the same structural features and pattern of genes. ■ Chem. (of a series of chemical compounds) having the same functional group but differing in composition by a fixed group of atoms. [17th C.: via med. L. from Gk. *homologos* 'agreeing, consistent,' from *homos* 'same' + *logos* 'ratio, proportion.']

ho·mo·logue /'hōmə,lôg; -,läg/ (also **ho·mo·log**) ▶**n.** tech. a homologous thing. [19th C.: from Fr., from Gk. *homologos* (see **HOMOLOGOUS**).]

ho·mol·o·gy /hō'mäləjē; hə-/ ▶**n.** the quality or condition of being homologous.

ho·mo·mor·phism /,hōmə'môr,fizəm/ ▶**n.** Math. a transformation of one set into another that preserves in the second set the relations between elements of the first. — **ho·mo·mor·phic adj.** **ho·mo·mor·phi·cal·ly** /,hōmə'môrfik(ə)lē/ **adv.**

hom·o·nym /'hämə,nim; 'hōmə-/ ▶**n.** each of two words having the same pronunciation but different meanings, origins, or spelling (e.g., **TO, TOO,** and **TWO**); a homophone. ■ each of two or more words having the same spelling but different meanings and origins (e.g., **POLE**[1] and **POLE**[2]); a homograph. ■ Biol. a Latin name that is identical to that of a different organism, the newer of the two names being invalid. — **hom·o·nym·ic** /,hämə'nimik; ,hōmə-/ **adj.** **ho·mon·y·mous** /hō'mänəməs/ **adj.** **ho·mon·y·my** /hō'mänəmē/ **n.** [17th C.: via L. from Gk. *homōnumon*, neut. of *homōnumos* 'having the same name,' from *homos* 'same' + *onoma* 'name.']

ho·mo·ou·si·an /,hōmō'ōōsēən/ ▶**n.** hist. in the fourth-century Arian controversy, a person who held that God the Father and God the Son are of the same substance. Compare with **HOMOIOUSIAN.** [16th C.: from eccles. L. *homousianus*, from *homousius*, from Gk. *homoousios*, from *homos* 'same' + *ousia* 'essence, substance.']

ho·mo·phile /'hōmə,fīl/ ▶**n.** a homosexual man or woman. ■ a person active in supporting the rights of homosexuals. ▶**adj.** of or relating to homosexuals. ■ active in supporting the rights of homosexuals.

ho·mo·pho·bi·a /,hōmə'fōbēə/ ▶**n.** an extreme and irrational aversion to homosexuality and homosexual people. — **ho·mo·phobe** /'hōmə,fōb/ **n.** **ho·mo·pho·bic** /-'fōbik/ **adj.** [1960s: from **HOMOSEXUAL** + **-PHOBIA.**]

ho·mo·phone /'hämə,fōn; 'hōmə-/ ▶**n.** each of two or more words having the same pronunciation but different meanings, origins, or spelling, e.g., **NEW** and **KNEW.**

ho·mo·phon·ic /,hämə'fänik; ,hōmə-/ ▶**adj. 1** Music characterized by the movement of accompanying parts in the same rhythm as the melody. Often contrasted with **POLYPHONIC. 2** another term for **HOMOPHONOUS.** — **ho·mo·phon·i·cal·ly adv.**

ho·moph·o·nous /hō'mäfənəs; hə-/ ▶**adj.** (of a word or words) having the same pronunciation as another or others but different meaning, origin, or spelling. — **ho·moph·o·ny** /-'mäfənē/ **n.**

Ho·mop·ter·a /hō'mäptərə/ Entomol. a group of true bugs (suborder Homoptera, order Hemiptera) comprising those in which the forewings are uniform in texture. Plant bugs such as aphids, whitefly, scale insects, and cicadas belong to this group. Compare with **HETEROPTERA.** ■ [as pl. n.] (**homoptera**) bugs of this group. — **ho·mop·ter·an n. & adj.** **ho·mop·ter·ous** /-tərəs/ **adj.** [mod. L. (pl.), from **HOMO-** 'equal' + Gk. *pteron* 'wing.']

ho•mor•gan•ic /ˌhōmôrˈganik/ ▸ **adj.** denoting sets of speech sounds that are produced using the same vocal organs, e.g., *p*, *b*, and *m*.

Ho•mo sa•pi•ens /ˈhōmō ˈsāpēənz/ the primate species to which modern humans belong; humans regarded as a species. See also **HOMO**. ■ a member of this species. [L., lit. 'wise man.']

ho•mo•sex•u•al /ˌhōməˈsekSHo͞oəl/ ▸ **adj.** (of a person) sexually attracted to people of one's own sex. ■ involving or characterized by sexual attraction between people of the same sex. ▸ **n.** a person who is sexually attracted to people of their own sex. — **ho•mo•sex•u•al•i•ty** /-ˌsekSHo͞oˈalitē/ **n.** **ho•mo•sex•u•al•ly adv.**

ho•mo•trans•plant /ˌhōmōˈtransˌplant/ ▸ **n.** another term for **ALLOGRAFT**.

ho•mo•zy•gote /ˌhōmōˈzīgōt/ ▸ **n.** Genet. an individual having two identical alleles of a particular gene or genes and so breeding true for the corresponding characteristic. Compare with **HETEROZYGOTE**. — **ho•mo•zy•gos•i•ty** /-zīˈgäsitē/ **n.** **ho•mo•zy•gous** /-ˈzīgəs/ **adj.**

Homs /hôms/ (also **Hims** /hims/) a city in western Syria, on the Orontes River; pop. 537,000.

ho•mun•cu•lus /həˈməNGkyələs; hō-/ ▸ **n.** (pl. **-li** /-ˌlī/ or **-les** /-ˌlēz/) a very small human or humanoid creature. ■ hist. a supposed microscopic but fully formed human being from which a fetus was formerly believed to develop. [17th C.: from L., dimin. of *homo, homin-* 'man.']

hom•y ▸ **adj.** var. of **HOMEY**[1].

Hon. ▸ **abbr.** ■ (in official job titles) Honorary: *the Hon. Secretary.* ■ (in titles of some government officials and judges) Honorable: *the Hon. Charles Rothschild.*

hon /hən/ ▸ **n.** informal short for **HONEY** (as a form of address): *It wouldn't interest you, hon.*

Ho•nan /ˈhōˈnan; -ˈnän/ **1** variant of **HENAN**. **2** former name for **LUOYANG**.

hon•cho /ˈhänCHō/ informal ▸ **n.** (pl. **-chos**) a leader or manager; the person in charge: *the company's head honcho in the US.* ▸ **v.** (**-choes, -choed**) [trans.] be in charge of (a project or situation): *the task at hand was to honcho an eighteen-wheeler to St. Louis.* [1940s: from Japanese *hanchō* 'group leader.']

Hon•da /ˈhändə/, Soichiro (1906–92), Japanese industrialist. He began motorcycle manufacture in 1948 and expanded into automobile production during the 1960s.

Honduras

Official name: Republic of Honduras
Location: Central America, bordering the Caribbean Sea on the north, and Nicaragua on the south
Area: 43,200 square miles (111,900 sq km)
Population: 6,283,000
Capital: Tegucigalpa
Languages: Spanish (official), Amerindian languages
Currency: lempira

Hon•du•ras /hänˈd(y)o͝orəs/ a country in Central America. *See box.* — **Hon•du•ran** /-rən/ **adj. & n.**

hone /hōn/ ▸ **v.** [trans.] sharpen with a whetstone. ■ (usu. **be honed**) make sharper or more focused or efficient. ▸ **n.** a whetstone, esp. one used to sharpen razors. ■ the stone of which whetstones are made. [ME: from OE *hān* 'stone,' of Gmc. origin; rel. to ON *hein*.]

Ho•neck•er /ˈhōnəkər/, Erich (1912–94), head of East Germany 1976–89. His repressive regime was marked by a close allegiance to the Soviet Union.

hon•est /ˈänist/ ▸ **adj.** free of deceit and untruthfulness; sincere. ■ morally correct or virtuous: *I did the only right and honest thing.* ■ [attrib.] fairly earned, esp. through hard work: *an honest living.* ■ (of an action) blameless or well intentioned even if unsuccessful or misguided: *an honest mistake.* ■ [attrib.] simple, unpretentious, and unsophisticated: *good honest food.* ▸ **adv.** [sentence adverb] informal used to persuade someone of the truth of something: *you'll like it when you get there, honest.* — PHRASES **to be honest** speaking frankly. [ME: via OFr. from L. *honestus*, from *honos* (see **HONOR**).]

hon•est bro•ker ▸ **n.** an impartial mediator in international, industrial, or other disputes.

hon•est•ly /ˈänistlē/ ▸ **adv.** **1** in a truthful, fair, or honorable way. **2** used to emphasize the sincerity of an opinion, belief, or feeling: *she honestly believed that she was making life easier for Jack.* ■ [sentence adverb] used to emphasize the sincerity or truthfulness of a statement: *honestly, darling, I'm not upset.* ■ [sentence adverb] used to indicate the speaker's disapproval, annoyance, or impatience: *honestly, that man is the absolute limit!*

hon•est-to-God informal ▸ **adj.** [attrib.] genuine; real. ▸ **adv.** genuinely; really: [as exclam.] *"You mean you didn't know?" "Honest to God!"*

hon•est-to-good•ness ▸ **adj.** [attrib.] genuine and straightforward.

hon•es•ty /ˈänistē/ ▸ **n.** **1** the quality of being honest. **2** a European plant (genus *Lunaria*) of the cabbage family, with purple or white flowers and round, flat, translucent seedpods that are used for indoor flower arrangements. Also called **MONEY PLANT**.

hone•wort /ˈhōnˌwərt; -ˌwôrt/ ▸ **n.** a wild plant of the parsley family, esp. *Cryptotaenia canadensis*, a native of North America and eastern Asia. [17th C.: from obs. *hone* 'swelling.']

hon•ey /ˈhənē/ ▸ **n.** (pl. **-eys**) **1** a sweet, sticky, yellowish-brown fluid made by bees and other insects from nectar collected from flowers. ■ this substance used as food, typically as a sweetener. ■ a yellowish-brown or golden color. ■ any sweet substance similar to bees' honey. **2** informal an excellent example of something: *it's one honey of an adaptation.* ■ darling; sweetheart (usually as a form of address). [OE *hunig*, of Gmc. origin; rel. to Du. *honig* and Ger. *Honig*.]

hon•ey ant ▸ **n.** an ant (*Myrmecocystus* and other genera) that stores large amounts of honeydew and nectar in its elastic abdomen. This is then fed to nest mates by regurgitation.

hon•ey badg•er ▸ **n.** another term for **RATEL**.

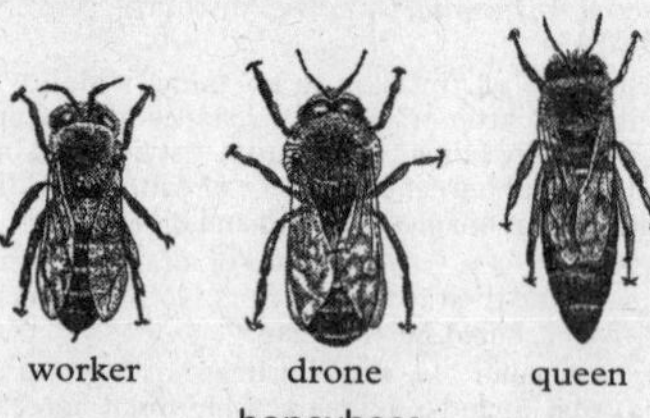

honeybees

hon•ey•bee /ˈhənēˌbē/ ▸ **n.** a stinging winged insect (genus *Apis*, family Apidae), esp. the widespread *A. mellifera*. It collects nectar and pollen, produces wax and honey, and lives in large communities.

hon•ey buck•et ▸ **n.** informal a toilet that does not use water and has to be emptied manually.

hon•ey•bunch /ˈhənēˌbənCH/ (also **hon•ey•bun** /-ˌbən/) ▸ **n.** informal darling (used as a form of address).

hon•ey•comb /ˈhənēˌkōm/ ▸ **n.** **1** a structure of hexagonal cells of wax, made by bees to store honey and eggs. **2** a structure of adjoining cavities or cells: *a honeycomb of caves.* ▸ **v.** [trans.] fill with cavities or tunnels. ■ corrode (something) internally, forming small cavities in it. ■ fig. infiltrate and undermine.

hon•ey•creep•er /ˈhənēˌkrēpər/ ▸ **n.** **1** a tropical American tanager (genera *Cyanerpes* and *Chlorophanes*) with a long curved bill, feeding on nectar and insects. **2** (also **Hawaiian honeycreeper**) a colorful Hawaiian finch with a specialized bill, several kinds of which are now endangered.

hon•ey•dew /ˈhənēˌd(y)o͞o/ ▸ **n.** **1** a sweet, sticky substance excreted by aphids and often deposited on leaves and stems. **2** (also **honeydew melon**) a melon of a variety with smooth pale skin and sweet green flesh.

hon•ey•eat•er /ˈhənēˌētər/ ▸ **n.** an Australasian songbird (family Meliphagidae) with a long brushlike tongue for feeding on nectar.

hon•eyed /ˈhənēd/ (also **hon•ied**) ▸ **adj.** (of food) containing or coated with honey. ■ having a rich sweetness of taste or smell: *as the wine matures, it becomes more honeyed.* ■ fig. (of a person's words or tone of voice) soothing, soft, and intended to please or flatter.

hon•ey fun•gus ▸ **n.** another term for **HONEY MUSHROOM**.

hon•ey•guide /ˈhənēˌgīd/ ▸ **n.** a small bird (*Indicator* and other genera, family Indicatoridae) of the Old World tropics, certain kinds of which lead humans and other mammals, esp. ratels, to bee nests.

hon•ey lo•cust ▸ **n.** a tree (genus *Gleditsia*) of the pea family with long branched thorns. A thornless variety has been cultivated and is typically grown as an ornamental for its fernlike foliage.

hon•ey•moon /ˈhənēˌmo͞on/ ▸ **n.** a vacation spent together by a newly married couple. ■ [often as adj.] fig. an initial period of enthusiasm or goodwill, typically at the start of a new job. ▸ **v.** [no obj., with adverbial of place] spend a honeymoon. — **hon•ey•moon•er n.** [16th C.: from **HONEY** + **MOON**. The original ref. was to affection waning like the moon.]

hon•ey mush•room ▸ **n.** a widespread parasitic fungus (*Armillaria mellea*, family Tricholomataceae) that produces clumps of honey-colored toadstools at the base of trees. Also called **HONEY FUNGUS**.

hon·ey·pot /'hənē,pät/ ▶ n. a container in which honey is kept. ■ fig. a place to which many people are attracted: *its elegant shops make Florence a global honeypot.*

hon·ey·pot ant ▶ n. another term for **HONEY ANT**.

hon·ey·suck·er /'hənē,səkər/ ▶ n. any of a number of long-billed birds that feed on nectar, esp. (in South Africa) a sunbird.

hon·ey·suck·le /'hənē,səkəl/ ▶ n. a widely distributed climbing shrub (genera *Lonicera* and *Diervilla*) with tubular flowers that are typically fragrant and of two colors or shades. [ME *honysoukil*, extension of *honysouke*, from OE *hunigsūce* (see **HONEY, SUCK**).]

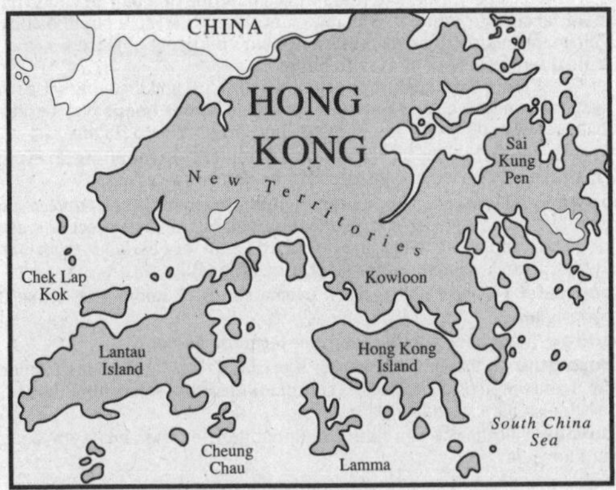

Hong Kong /'häng 'käng; 'hông 'kông/ a former British colony on the southeastern coast of China, returned to China in 1997; pop. 5,900,000; comprising Hong Kong Island, the Kowloon peninsula, and the New Territories (additional areas of the mainland).

Ho·ni·a·ra /,hōnē'ärə/ the capital of the Solomon Islands, on the northwestern coast of Guadalcanal; pop. 35,000.

hon·ied /'hənēd/ ▶ adj. var. of **HONEYED**.

ho·ni soit qui mal y pense /,ônē'swä kē ,mȧl ē 'päns/ ▶ exclam. shame on him who thinks evil of it (the motto of the Order of the Garter). [Fr.]

honk /hängk; hôngk/ ▶ n. the cry of a wild goose. ■ the harsh sound of a car horn. ■ any similar sound. ▶ v. [intrans.] emit such a cry or sound. ■ [trans.] cause (a car horn) to make such a sound. ■ [trans.] express by sounding a car horn: *taxi drivers honking their support.* [19th C.: imitative.]

honk·er /'hängkər; 'hông-/ ▶ n. a person or thing that honks. ■ informal a wild goose.

hon·ky /'hängkē; 'hông-/ ▶ n. (pl. **-kies**) informal a contemptuous term used by black people for a white person or for white people collectively. [1960s: of unknown origin.]

hon·ky-tonk /'hängkē ,tängk; 'hôngkē ,tôngk/ ▶ n. informal **1** a cheap or disreputable bar, club, or dance hall, typically where country music is played. ■ [as adj.] squalid and disreputable. **2** country music, esp. of the 1940s and 1950s. **3** [often as adj.] ragtime piano music. ▶ v. [intrans.] listen to or dance to country music. [19th C.: of unknown origin.]

Hon·o·lu·lu /,hänl'o͞olo͞o/ the capital of Hawaii, on the southeastern coast of Oahu; pop. 371,657.

hon·or /'änər/ (Brit. **hon·our**) ▶ n. **1** high respect; esteem. ■ [in sing.] a person or thing that brings credit. ■ adherence to what is right or to a conventional standard of conduct. **2** a privilege. ■ an exalted position. ■ a thing conferred as a distinction, esp. an official award for bravery or achievement. ■ (**honors**) a special distinction for proficiency in an examination. ■ (**honors**) a class or course of degree studies more specialized than that of the ordinary level. ■ (**His, Your**, etc., **Honor**) a title of respect given to or used in addressing a judge or a mayor. ■ Golf the right of teeing off first, having won the previous hole. **3** dated a woman's chastity or her reputation for this. **4** Bridge an ace, king, queen, or jack. ■ (**honors**) possession in one's hand of at least four of the ace, king, queen, and jack of trumps, or of all four aces in no trumps, for which a bonus is scored. ■ (in whist) an ace, king, queen, or jack of trumps. ▶ v. [trans.] **1** regard with great respect. ■ (often **be honored**) pay public respect to. ■ grace; privilege: *the Princess **honored** the ball with her presence.* ■ (in square dancing) salute (another dancer) with a bow. **2** fulfill (an obligation) or keep (an agreement): *honor the terms of the contract.* ■ accept (a bill) or pay (a check) when due: *the check would not be honored.*
– PHRASES **do the honors** informal perform a social duty or small ceremony for others (often used to describe the serving of food or drink to a guest). **in honor of** as a celebration of or expression of respect for. **on one's honor** under a moral obligation. **on** (or **upon**) **my honor** used as an expression of sincerity. [ME: from OFr. *onor* (n.), *onorer* (v.), from L. *honor*.]

hon·or·a·ble /'änərəbəl/ (Brit. **hon·our·a·ble**) ▶ adj. **1** bringing or worthy of honor: *an honorable course of action.* ■ formal, humorous (of the intentions of a man courting a woman) directed toward marriage. **2** (**Honorable**) used as a title indicating eminence or distinction, given esp. to judges and certain high officials. — **hon·or·a·ble·ness** n. **hon·or·a·bly** adv.

hon·or·a·ble dis·charge ▶ n. discharge from military service with a favorable record.

hon·or·a·ble men·tion ▶ n. a commendation given to a candidate in an examination or competition who is not awarded a prize.

hon·o·rar·i·um /,änə're(ə)rēəm/ ▶ n. (pl. **-rar·i·ums** or **-rar·i·a** /-'re(ə)rēə/) a payment given for professional services that are rendered nominally without charge.

hon·or·ar·y /'änə,rerē/ ▶ adj. conferred as an honor, without the usual requirements or functions. ■ (of a person) holding such a title or position.

hon·o·ree /,änə'rē/ ▶ n. a person who receives an honor.

hon·or guard another term for **GUARD OF HONOR**.

hon·or·if·ic /,änə'rifik/ ▶ adj. given as a mark of respect. ■ (of an office or position) given as a mark of respect, but having few or no duties. ■ denoting a form of address showing high status, politeness, or respect. ▶ n. a title or word implying or expressing high status, politeness, or respect. — **hon·or·if·i·cal·ly** adv.

ho·no·ris cau·sa /ä'nôris 'kôzə; 'kousə/ ▶ adv. (esp. of a degree awarded without examination) as a mark of esteem. [17th C.: L., lit. 'for honor's sake.']

hon·or so·ci·e·ty ▶ n. an organization for high-school or college students of high academic achievement.

hon·ors of war ▶ plural n. privileges granted to a capitulating force, for example that of marching out with colors flying.

hon·or sys·tem ▶ n. [in sing.] a system of payment or examination that relies solely on the honesty of those concerned.

hon·our ▶ n. & v. British spelling of **HONOR**.

hon·our·a·ble ▶ adj. British spelling of **HONORABLE**.

Hon·shu /'hänshoo/ the largest of the four main islands of Japan; pop 99,254,000.

hooch /hoōch/ (also **hootch**) ▶ n. informal alcoholic liquor, esp. inferior or illicit whiskey. [19th C.: abbrev. of *Hoochinoo*, the name of an Alaskan Indian people who made liquor.]

hood[1] /ho͝od/ ▶ n. **1** a covering for the head and neck with an opening for the face, typically forming part of a coat or sweatshirt. ■ a separate garment similar to this worn over a college gown or a surplice to indicate the wearer's degree. **2** a thing resembling a hood in shape or use, in particular: ■ a metal part covering the engine of an automobile. ■ a canopy to protect users of machinery or to remove fumes from it. ■ a hoodlike structure or marking on the head or neck of an animal. ■ a tubular attachment to keep stray light out of a camera lens. ▶ v. [trans.] put a hood on or over. — **hood·less** adj. **hood·like** adj. [OE *hōd*, of West Gmc. origin; rel. to Du. *hoed*, Ger. *Hut* 'hat,' also to **HAT**.]

hood[2] ▶ n. informal a gangster or similar violent criminal; a hoodlum. [1930s: abbrev. of **HOODLUM**.]

hood[3] (also **'hood**) ▶ n. informal a neighborhood, esp. one's own neighborhood. [1970s: shortening of **NEIGHBORHOOD**.]

-hood ▶ suffix forming nouns: **1** denoting a condition or quality: *falsehood* | *womanhood.* **2** denoting a collection or group: *brotherhood.* [OE *-hād*, orig. an independent n. meaning 'person, condition, quality.']

hood·ed /'ho͝odid/ ▶ adj. (of an article of clothing) having a hood. ■ (of a person) wearing a hood. ■ (of eyes) having thick, drooping upper eyelids resembling hoods. ■ (of an animal) having a hoodlike structure or marking on the head or neck.

hood·ed crow ▶ n. a bird (*Corvus corone cornix*) of the northern and eastern European race of the carrion crow, having a gray body with a black head, wings, and tail.

hood·ed seal ▶ n. a true seal (*Cystophora cristata*) with a gray and white blotched coat, found in the Arctic waters of the North Atlantic. The male has a nasal sac that is inflated into a hood during display.

hood·ie /'ho͝odē/ (also **hood·y**) ▶ n. (pl. **-ies**) a hooded sweatshirt, jacket, or other top. ■ informal, chiefly Brit. a person, esp. a youth, wearing a hooded top.

hood·lum /'ho͞odləm; 'ho͝od-/ ▶ n. a person who engages in crime and violence; a hooligan or gangster. [19th C. (orig. US): of unknown origin.]

Hood, Mount a peak in the Cascade Range in northwest Oregon, 11,239 feet (3,426 m).

hoo·doo /'ho͞o,do͞o/ ▶ n. **1** voodoo; witchcraft. ■ a run of bad luck associated with a person or activity. ■ a person or thing that brings or causes bad luck. **2** a column or pinnacle of weathered rock: *a towering sandstone hoodoo.* ▶ v. (**-doos, -dooed**) [trans.] bewitch. ■ bring bad luck to. [19th C. (orig. US): appar. an alt. of **VOODOO**.]

hood·wink /'ho͝od,wingk/ ▶ v. [trans.] deceive or trick (someone). [16th C. (orig. in the sense 'to blindfold'): from the n. **HOOD**[1] + an obs. sense of **WINK** 'close the eyes.']

hoo·ey /'ho͞oē/ ▶ n. informal nonsense. [1920s (orig. US): of unknown origin.]

hoof /ho͝of; ho͞of/ ▶ n. (pl. **hoofs** or **hooves** /ho͝ovz; ho͞ovz/) the horny part of the foot of an ungulate animal, esp. a horse. ▶ v. [trans.] informal (**hoof it**) go on foot. ■ dance.

PRONUNCIATION KEY ə *ago, up*; ər *over, fur*; a *hat*; ā *ate*; ä *car*; e *let*; ē *see*; i *fit*; ī *by*; NG *sing*; ō *go*; ô *law, for*; oi *toy*; o͝o *good*; o͞o *goo*; ou *out*; TH *thin*; T͟H *then*; ZH *vision*

– PHRASES **on the hoof** 1 (of livestock) not yet slaughtered. 2 informal without great thought or preparation. — **hoofed** adj. [OE *hōf*, of Gmc. origin; rel. to Du. *hoef* and Ger. *Huf*.]

hoof-and-mouth dis·ease ▶ n. another term for FOOT-AND-MOUTH DISEASE.

hoof·er /'hōōfər; 'hōōfər/ ▶ n. informal a professional dancer.

Hoo·ghly /'hōōglē/ (also **Hu·gli**) westernmost river in the Ganges delta, in West Bengal, India, flowing for 120 miles (192 km) into the Bay of Bengal.

hoo-ha /'hōō ,hä/ ▶ n. [in sing.] informal a commotion; a fuss: *the book was causing such a hoo-ha.* [1930s: of unknown origin.]

hook /hōōk/ ▶ n. 1 a piece of metal or other material, curved or bent back at an angle, for catching hold of or hanging things on. ■ (also **fish-hook**) a bent piece of metal, typically barbed and baited, for catching fish. ■ a cradle on which a telephone receiver rests. ■ fig. a thing designed to catch people's attention. ■ a chorus or repeated instrumental passage in a piece of music, esp. a pop or rock song, that gives it immediate appeal and makes it easy to remember. 2 a curved cutting instrument, esp. as used for reaping or shearing. 3 a short swinging punch made with the elbow bent, esp. in boxing. ■ Golf a stroke that makes the ball deviate in flight in the direction of the follow-through (from right to left for a right-handed player), typically inadvertently. 4 [usu. in place names] a curved promontory or sand spit. ▶ v. 1 [with obj. and adverbial] attach or fasten with a hook or hooks: *she tried to **hook up** her bra.* ■ [no obj., with adverbial of place] be or become attached with a hook: *a ladder that hooks over the roof ridge.* ■ bend or be bent into the shape of a hook so as to fasten around or to an object: [trans.] *he hooked his thumbs in his belt* | [intrans.] *her legs hooked around mine.* 2 [trans.] catch with a hook. ■ (usu. **be hooked**) informal captivate. 3 [trans.] Golf strike (the ball) or play (a stroke) so that the ball deviates in the direction of the follow-through, typically inadvertently. ■ [intrans.] Boxing punch one's opponent with the elbow bent.

– PHRASES **by hook or by crook** by any possible means. **get** (or **give someone**) **the hook** informal be dismissed (or dismiss someone) from a job. **hook, line, and sinker** used to emphasize that someone has been completely deceived or tricked: *he fell hook, line, and sinker for this year's April Fool joke.* **off the hook** 1 informal no longer in difficulty or trouble. 2 (of a telephone receiver) not on its rest, and so preventing incoming calls. **on the hook for** informal (in a financial context) responsible for. **on one's own hook** informal dated on one's own account; by oneself.

– PHRASAL VERBS **hook up** informal (of two people) meet or form a relationship. **hook someone/something up** (or **hook up**) link or be linked to electronic equipment. — **hook·less** adj. **hook·let** n. **hook·like** adj. [OE *hōc*, of Gmc. origin; rel. to Ger. *Haken* 'hook.']

hookah

hook·ah /'hōōkə; 'hōōkə/ ▶ n. an oriental tobacco pipe with a long, flexible tube that draws the smoke through water contained in a bowl. [18th C.: from Urdu, from Arab. *ḥuḳḳa* 'casket, jar.']

hook and eye

hook and eye ▶ n. a small metal hook and loop used together as a fastener on a garment.

hook-and-lad·der truck ▶ n. a fire engine that carries extension ladders and other firefighting and rescue equipment.

Hooke /hōōk/, Robert (1635–1703), English scientist. He formulated the law of elasticity (Hooke's law) and proposed an undulating theory of light.

hooked /hōōkt/ ▶ adj. 1 having a hook or hooks. ■ curved like a hook. 2 informal captivated; absorbed. ■ addicted. 3 (of a rug or mat) made by pulling yarn through canvas with a hook.

Hook·er /'hōōkər/, Thomas (c. 1586–1647), American clergyman; born in England. He was a founding settler of Hartford, Connecticut.

hook·er[1] /'hōōkər/ ▶ n. informal a prostitute.

hook·er[2] ▶ n. a one-masted sailboat of a kind used esp. in Ireland for fishing. ■ Nautical slang an old boat. [17th C.: from Dutch *hoeker*, from *hoek* 'hook' (used earlier in *hoekboot*, denoting a two-masted Du. fishing vessel).]

hook·er[3] ▶ n. informal a glass or drink of undiluted brandy, whiskey, or other liquor. [19th C.: of unknown origin.]

Hooke's law /hōōks/ Physics a law stating that the strain in a solid is proportional to the applied stress within the elastic limit of that solid.

hook·ey ▶ n. var. of HOOKY.

hook-nosed ▶ adj. having a prominent aquiline nose.

hook shot ▶ n. Basketball a one-handed shot in which a player extends one arm out to the side and over the head toward the basket.

hook·up /'hōōk,əp/ ▶ n. a connection to a public electric, water, or sewer line, or to a similar service. ■ an interconnection of broadcasting equipment for special transmissions.

hook·worm /'hōōk,wərm/ ▶ n. a parasitic nematode (*Ancylostoma*, *Uncinaria*, *Necator*, and other genera, class Phasmida) that inhabits the intestines of humans and other animals. It has hooklike mouthparts with which it attaches itself to the wall of the gut, puncturing the blood vessels and feeding on the blood. ■ a disease caused by an infestation of hookworms, often resulting in severe anemia.

hook·y /'hōōkē/ (also **hook·ey**) ▶ n. (in phrase **play hooky**) informal stay away from school or work without permission or explanation. [19th C. (orig. US): of unknown origin.]

hoo·li·gan /'hōōləgən/ ▶ n. a violent young troublemaker, typically one of a gang. — **hoo·li·gan·ism** /-,nizəm/ n. [19th C.: perh. from *Hooligan*, surname of a family in a music-hall song of the 1890s.]

hoop /hōōp/ ▶ n. a circular band of metal, wood, or similar material, esp. one used for binding the staves of barrels or forming part of a framework. ■ the round metal rim from which a basketball net is suspended. ■ (**hoops**) informal the game of basketball. ■ a large ring used as a toy by being bowled along. ■ a large ring, typically with paper stretched over it, for circus performers to jump through. ■ one of a pair of rings that hold fabric taut while it is being embroidered. ■ hist. a circle of flexible material used for expanding a woman's petticoat or skirt. ▶ v. [trans.] bind or encircle with or as with hoops.

– PHRASES **jump through hoops** perform a difficult and grueling series of tests at someone else's request or command. **shoot hoops** play basketball. — **hooped** adj. [OE *hōp*, of West Gmc. origin; rel. to Du. *hoep*.]

hoop·la /'hōō,plä; 'hōōp,lä/ ▶ n. informal excitement surrounding an event or situation, esp. when considered to be unnecessary fuss.

hoo·poe /'hōō,pō; -,pōō/ ▶ n. a salmon-pink Eurasian bird (*Upupa epops*, family Upupidae) with a long down-curved bill, a large erectile crest, and black and white wings and tail. [17th C.: alt. of obs. *hoop*, from OFr. *huppe*, from L. *upupa*, imitative of the bird's call.]

hoop skirt ▶ n. hist. a skirt worn over a series of hoops that make it spread out.

hoo·ray /hə'rā; hōō-/ ▶ exclam. another term for HURRAH.

hoose·gow /'hōōs,gou/ ▶ n. informal a prison. [20th C.: via Latin Amer. Sp. from Sp. *juzgado* 'tribunal,' from L. *judicatum* 'something judged,' neut. past part. of *judicare*.]

Hoo·sier /'hōōzhər/ ▶ n. a native or inhabitant of Indiana. [19th C.: of unknown origin.]

hoot /hōōt/ ▶ n. a deep or medium-pitched musical sound, often wavering or interrupted, that is the typical call of many kinds of owl. ■ a similar but typically more raucous sound made by a horn, siren, or steam whistle. ■ a shout expressing scorn or disapproval. ■ a short outburst of laughter. ■ (**a hoot**) informal an amusing situation or person. ▶ v. [intrans.] (of an owl) utter a hoot. ■ (of a person) make loud sounds of scorn, disapproval, or merriment. ■ (**hoot something down**) express loud scornful disapproval of something.

– PHRASES **not care** (or **give**) **a hoot** (or **two hoots**) informal not care at all. [ME (in the sense 'make sounds of derision'): perh. imitative.]

hootch /hōōch/ ▶ n. var. of HOOCH.

hoot·en·an·ny /'hōōtn,anē/ ▶ n. (pl. **-nies**) informal an informal gathering with folk music and sometimes dancing. [1920s: of unknown origin.]

hoot·er /'hōōtər/ ▶ n. 1 informal a person's nose. 2 (**hooters**) vulgar slang a woman's breasts.

Hoo·ver[1] /'hōōvər/ a city in north central Alabama; pop. 62,742.

Hoo·ver[2], Herbert Clark (1874–1964), 31st president of the US 1929–33. After serving as secretary of commerce 1921–29, he was elected to the presidency on the Republican ballot. As president, he was faced with the long-term problems of the Depression. Unable to keep his campaign promise of prosperity and to improve his poor record in international affairs, he was defeated for reelection.

Hoo·ver[3], J. Edgar (1895–1972), US director of the FBI 1924–72; full name *John Edgar Hoover*. He reorganized the FBI into an efficient, scientific law-enforcement agency, but came under criticism for the organization's role during the McCarthy era.

Hoo·ver·ville /'hōōvər,vil/ ▶ n. a name for a shantytown built by unemployed and destitute people during the Depression of the early 1930s. [H.C. HOOVER[1].]

hooves /hōōvz; hōōvz/ plural form of HOOF.

hop[1] /häp/ ▶ v. (**hopped, hop·ping**) [no obj., with adverbial of direction] (of a person) move by jumping on one foot. ■ (of a bird or other animal) move by jumping with two or all feet at once. ■ spring or leap a short distance with one jump. ■ [trans.] jump over (something). ■ informal make a quick trip. ■ make a quick change of position, location, or activity. ■ [in comb.] visit a succession of things or places: *regulars liked to table-hop.* ■ [trans.] informal board (a bus, airplane, or other mode of transportation): *she hopped a train in Winnipeg.* ■ [trans.] informal jump onto (a moving vehicle): *veterans looking for work hopped freight trains heading west.* ■ [usu. as n., in comb.] (**-hopping**) (of an aircraft or ferry) pass quickly from one place to another: *two-week island-hopping packages.* ▶ n. 1 a hopping movement. ■ a short journey or distance. 2 an informal dance.

– PHRASES **hop, skip, and (a) jump** 1 old-fashioned term for TRIPLE JUMP. 2 informal a short distance. **hop to it** begin a task quickly; get busy.

– PHRASAL VERBS **hop in** (or **out**) informal get into (or out of) a car. [OE *hoppian*, of Gmc. origin; rel. to German dial. *hopfen* and Ger. *hopsen*.]

hop[2] ▶ n. a twining climbing plant (*Humulus lupulus*, family Cannabaceae) native to north temperate regions, cultivated for its conelike flowers, which are used in brewing beer. ■ (**hops**) the dried conelike flowers of this plant, used in brewing to give a bitter flavor and as a mild sterilant. ▶ v. (**hopped, hop·ping**) 1 [trans.] flavor with hops. 2 (**be hopped up**) informal be stimulated or intoxicated by or as if by a psychoactive drug. — **hop·py** adj. [ME *hoppe*, from Mid. Low Ger. or MDu.]

hope /hōp/ ▶ n. 1 a feeling of expectation and desire for a certain thing to happen. ■ a person or thing that may help or save someone.

■ grounds for believing that something good may happen. **2** archaic a feeling of trust. ▶**v.** [intrans.] want something to happen or be the case: *he's **hoping for** compensation* | [with clause] *I hope that the kids are OK.* ■ [with infin.] intend if possible to do something: *we're hoping to address all these issues.*
– PHRASES **hope against hope** cling to a mere possibility. **hope for the best** hope for a favorable outcome. **in hopes of** with the aim of. **in hopes that** hoping that: *they are screaming in hopes that a police launch will pick us up.* **not a hope** informal no chance at all. — **hop•er n.** [OE *hopa* (n.), *hopian* (v.), of Gmc. origin; rel. to Ger. *hoffen* (v.).]

hope chest ▶**n.** a chest containing household linen and clothing stored by a woman in preparation for her marriage.

hope•ful /ˈhōpfəl/ ▶**adj.** feeling or inspiring optimism about a future event. ▶**n.** a person likely or hoping to succeed. — **hope•ful•ness n.**

hope•ful•ly /ˈhōpfəlē/ ▶**adv.** **1** in a hopeful manner: *he rode on hopefully.* **2** [sentence adverb] it is to be hoped that: *hopefully, it should be finished by next year.*

Ho•peh /ˈhōˈpā/ variant of **Hebei**.

hope•less /ˈhōplis/ ▶**adj.** **1** feeling or causing despair about something. **2** inadequate; incompetent: *I'm hopeless at names.* — **hope•less•ly adv. hope•less•ness n.**

hop•head /ˈhäpˌhed/ ▶**n.** informal a drug addict. [20th C.: from **hop**² + **head**.]

hop horn•beam ▶**n.** see **hornbeam**.

Ho•pi /ˈhōpē/ ▶**n.** (pl. same or **Ho•pis**) **1** a member of a Pueblo Indian people living chiefly in northeastern Arizona. **2** the Uto-Aztecan language of this people. ▶**adj.** of or relating to this people or their language. [the name in Hopi.]

Hop•kins¹ /ˈhäpkinz/ Sir Frederick Gowland (1861–1947), English biochemist. He carried out pioneering work on vitamins. Nobel Prize for Physiology or Medicine (1929, shared with Christiaan Eijkman).

Hop•kins² /ˈhäpkinz/, Gerard Manley (1844–89), English poet. He wrote "The Wreck of the Deutschland."

Hop•kin•son /ˈhäpkinsən/, Francis (1737–91), US patriot. He was a signer of the Declaration of Independence in 1776.

hop•lite /ˈhäpˌlīt/ ▶**n.** a heavily armed foot soldier of ancient Greece. [from Gk. *hoplitēs*, from *hoplon* 'weapon.']

Hop•per¹ /ˈhäpər/, Edward (1882–1967), US painter. His works often depicted isolated figures in bleak scenes from everyday urban life.

Hop•per², Grace Murray (1906–92), US admiral and computer scientist. She served in the US Navy 1943–86 and worked as a computer programmer for the Sperry Rand Corporation 1959–71.

hop•per /ˈhäpər/ ▶**n.** **1** a container for a bulk material such as grain, rock, or trash, typically one that tapers downward and is able to discharge its contents at the bottom. ■ esp. hist. a tapering container, working with a hopping motion, through which grain passed into a mill. ■ (in full **hopper car**) a railroad car able to discharge coal or other bulk material through its floor. ■ a box in which bills are put for consideration by a legislature. **2** a person or thing that hops. ■ informal a person who makes a series of short trips. ■ a hopping insect, esp. a grasshopper.

hop•ping /ˈhäpiNG/ ▶**adj.** informal very active or lively.
– PHRASES **hopping mad** informal extremely angry.

hop•sack /ˈhäpˌsak/ ▶**n.** a coarse fabric of a loose plain weave, used for clothing. ■ a coarse hemp sack used for hops.

hop•scotch /ˈhäpˌskäCH/ ▶**n.** a children's game in which each child by turn hops into and over squares marked on the ground to retrieve a marker thrown into one of these squares. ▶**v.** [intrans.] skip from place to place; move erratically. [19th C.: from **hop**¹ + **scotch**¹.]

hor. ▶**abbr.** ■ horizon. ■ horizontal. ■ horology.

ho•ra /ˈhôrə; ˈhōrə/ (also **ho•rah**) ▶**n.** a Romanian or Israeli dance in which the performers form a ring. [19th C.: from Romanian *horă*, Heb. *hōrāh*.]

Hor•ace /ˈhôrəs; ˈhär-/ (65–68 BC), Roman poet; full name *Quintus Horatius Flaccus*. He is noted for his *Odes*.

ho•ra•ry /ˈhôrərē/ ▶**adj.** archaic of or relating to hours as measurements of time. ■ occurring every hour. [17th C.: from med. L. *horarius*, from L. *hora* 'hour.']

Ho•ra•tian /həˈrāSHən/ ▶**adj.** of or relating to the Roman poet Horace or his work. ■ (of an ode) of several stanzas, each of the same metrical pattern.

horde /hôrd/ ▶**n.** esp. derog. a large group of people. ■ an army or tribe of nomadic warriors: *Tartar hordes.* [16th C.: from Pol. *horda*, from Turk. *ordu* '(royal) camp.']

hore•hound /ˈhôrˌhound/ (also **hoar•hound**) ▶**n.** either of two strong-smelling hairy plants of the mint family: **white horehound** (*Marrubium vulgare*) and **black horehound** (*Ballota nigra*). ■ the bitter aromatic juice of white horehound, used esp. in the treatment of coughs and colds. [OE *hāre hūne*, from *hār* (see **hoar**) + *hūne*, the white horehound.]

Hor•gan /ˈhôrgən/, Paul (1903–95), US writer; full name *Paul George Vincent O'Shaughnessy Horgan*. His works were about the southwestern United States.

ho•ri•zon /həˈrīzən/ ▶**n.** **1** [usu. in sing.] the line at which the earth's surface and the sky appear to meet. ■ (also **apparent** or **visible horizon**) the circular boundary of the part of the earth's surface visible from a particular point, ignoring irregularities and obstructions. ■ (also **celestial horizon**) Astron. a great circle of the celestial sphere, the plane of which passes through the center of the earth and is parallel to that of the apparent horizon of a place. **2** (often **horizons**) the limit of a person's mental perception, experience, or interest. **3** Geol. a layer of soil or rock, or a set of strata, with particular characteristics. ■ Archaeol. a level of an excavated site representing a particular period.
– PHRASES **on the horizon** just imminent or becoming apparent: *trouble could be on the horizon.* [ME: via OFr. from late L. *horizon*, from Gk. *horizōn (kuklos)* 'limiting (circle).']

hor•i•zon•tal /ˌhôrəˈzäntl; ˌhär-/ ▶**adj.** **1** parallel to the plane of the horizon; at right angles to the vertical. ■ (of machinery) having its parts working in a horizontal direction. **2** combining companies engaged in the same stage or type of production: *a horizontal merger.* ■ involving social groups of equal status. **3** of or at the horizon. ▶**n.** a horizontal line, plane, etc. — **hor•i•zon•tal•i•ty** /-zänˈtalitē/ **n. hor•i•zon•tal•ly adv.**

Hork•heim•er /ˈhôrkˌhīmər/, Max (1895–1973), German philosopher and sociologist. He wrote *Critical Theory* (1968).

hor•mone /ˈhôrmōn/ ▶**n.** Physiol. a regulatory substance produced in an organism and transported in tissue fluids such as blood or sap to stimulate specific cells or tissues into action. ■ a synthetic substance with a similar effect. ■ (**hormones**) a person's sex hormones as held to influence behavior or mood. — **hor•mo•nal** /hôrˈmōnl/ **adj.** [20th C.: from Gk. *hormōn*, pres. part. of *horman* 'impel, set in motion.']

Hor•muz, Strait of /hôrˈmo͞oz; -ˈməz/ a strait that links the Persian Gulf with the Gulf of Oman and separates Iran from the Arabian peninsula; it is of strategic and economic importance.

horn /hôrn/ ▶**n.** **1** a hard permanent outgrowth, often curved and pointed, found in pairs on the heads of cattle, sheep, goats, giraffes, etc., and consisting of a core of bone encased in keratinized skin. ■ a woolly keratinized outgrowth, occurring singly or one behind another, on the snout of a rhinoceros. ■ a deer's antler. ■ a horn-shaped projection on the head of another animal, e.g., a snail's tentacle or the tuft of a horned owl. ■ (**horns**) archaic a pair of horns as an emblem of a cuckold. **2** the substance of which horns are composed. ■ a receptacle or instrument made of horn, such as a drinking container or powder flask. **3** a thing resembling or compared to a horn in shape. ■ a sharp promontory or mountain peak. ■ a raised projection on the pommel of a Western saddle. ■ (**the Horn**) Cape Horn. ■ the extremity of the moon or other crescent. **4** a wind instrument, conical in shape or wound into a spiral, originally made from an animal horn (now typically brass) and played by lip vibration. ■ short for **French horn**. **5** an instrument sounding a warning or other signal. ▶**v.** [trans.] (of an animal) butt or gore with the horns.
– PHRASES **blow** (or **toot**) **one's own horn** informal talk boastfully about oneself or one's achievements. **draw** (or **pull**) **in one's horns** become less assertive or ambitious. **on the horn** informal on the telephone. **on the horns of a dilemma** faced with a decision involving equally unfavorable alternatives.
– PHRASAL VERBS **horn in** informal intrude; interfere. — **horn•ist n.** (in sense 4). **horn•less adj. horn•like adj.** [OE, of Gmc. origin; rel. to Du. *hoorn* and Ger. *Horn*, from an Indo-Eur. root shared by L. *cornu* and Gk. *keras*.]

Horn, Cape /hôrn/ the southernmost point of South America, on a Chilean island south of Tierra del Fuego. Also called **the Horn**.

horn•beam /ˈhôrnˌbēm/ ▶**n.** a deciduous tree (genera *Carpinus* and *Ostrya*) of the birch family, with oval serrated leaves and tough winged nuts.

horn•bill /ˈhôrnˌbil/ ▶**n.** a medium to large tropical Old World bird (*Buceros* and other genera, family Bucerotidae), having a very large curved bill that typically has a large horny or bony casque.

horn•blende /ˈhôrnˌblend/ ▶**n.** a dark brown, black, or green mineral of the amphibole group consisting of a hydroxyl alumino-silicate of calcium, magnesium, and iron, occurring in many igneous and metamorphic rocks. [18th C.: from Ger., from *Horn* 'horn' + *blende* (see **blende**).]

horn•book /ˈhôrnˌbo͝ok/ ▶**n.** hist. a teaching aid consisting of a leaf of paper showing the alphabet, and often the ten digits and the Lord's Prayer, mounted on a wooden tablet and protected by a thin plate of horn. ■ Law a one-volume treatise summarizing the law in a specific field.

horned /hôrnd/ ▶**adj.** **1** having a horn or horns. **2** [attrib.] literary crescent-shaped.

regal horned lizard

horned liz•ard ▶**n.** an American lizard (genus *Phrynosoma*, family Iguanidae) that somewhat resembles a toad, with spiny skin and large spines on the head. Its several species include the **Texas horned lizard** (*P. cornutum*) and the **regal horned lizard** (*P. solare*).

horned toad ▶ n. **1** another term for HORNED LIZARD. **2** a large toad with horn-shaped projections of skin over the eyes, in particular a Southeast Asian toad (*Megophrys* and other genera, family Peltobatidae) and a South American toad (*Ceratophrys* and other genera, family Leptodactylidae).

horned vi·per ▶ n. a nocturnal viper (*Cerastes cerastes*) with an upright projection over each eye, native to North Africa and Arabia.

hor·net /ˈhôrnit/ ▶ n. a large stinging wasp (*Vespa* and other genera) that typically nests in hollow trees. Its several species include the **giant hornet** (*V. crabro*) and the **bald-faced** (or **white-faced**) **hornet** (*V. maculata*).
– PHRASES **a hornets' nest** a situation fraught with difficulties or complications. [OE *hyrnet*, of Gmc. origin; rel. to Ger. *Hornisse*.]

bald-faced hornet

Hor·ney /ˈhôr,nī/, Karen Danielsen (1885–1952), US psychoanalyst; born in Germany. She founded the Association for Advancement of Psychoanalysis and the American Institute for Psychoanalysis in 1941.

horn·fels /ˈhôrn,felz/ ▶ n. a dark, fine-grained metamorphic rock consisting largely of quartz, mica, and particular feldspars. [19th C.: from Ger., lit. 'horn rock.']

Horn of Af·ri·ca a peninsula in northeastern Africa that includes Somalia and parts of Ethiopia. Also called SOMALI PENINSULA.

horn of plen·ty ▶ n. a cornucopia.

horn·pipe /ˈhôrn,pīp/ ▶ n. a lively dance associated with sailors, typically performed by one person. ■ a piece of music for such a dance.

horn-rimmed ▶ adj. (of glasses) having rims made of horn or a similar substance.

Horns·by /ˈhôrnzbē/, Rogers (1896–1963), US baseball player. During his career 1915–37, mostly with the St. Louis Cardinals, he won many batting titles and still holds the National League record for career batting average.

horn·swog·gle /ˈhôrn,swägəl/ ▶ v. [trans.] (usu. **be hornswoggled**) informal get the better of (someone) by cheating or deception. [19th C. (orig. US): of unknown origin.]

horn·tail /ˈhôrn,tāl/ ▶ n. a large wasplike sawfly (family Siricidae) that deposits its eggs inside trees and timber.

horn·worm /ˈhôrn,wərm/ ▶ n. the caterpillar of a hawk moth, having a spike or "horn" on its tail.

horn·wort /ˈhôrn,wərt; -,wôrt/ ▶ n. a submerged aquatic plant (genus *Ceratophyllum*, family Ceratophyllaceae) with narrow forked leaves that become translucent and horny as they age.

horn·y /ˈhôrnē/ ▶ adj. (**horn·i·er, horn·i·est**) **1** of or resembling horn. ■ hard and rough. **2** informal feeling or arousing sexual excitement. — **horn·i·ness** n.

hor·o·loge /ˈhôrə,läj/ ▶ n. archaic a timepiece. [ME: from OFr., via L. from Gk. *hōrologion*, from *hōra* 'time' + *-logos* '-telling.']

Hor·o·lo·gi·um /,hôrəˈlōjēəm/ Astron. a faint southern constellation (the Clock), between Hydrus and Eridanus. [L.]

ho·rol·o·gy /həˈräləjē/ (abbr.: **horol.**) ▶ n. the study and measurement of time. ■ the art of making clocks and watches. — **ho·rol·o·ger** /-jər/ n. **hor·o·log·ic** /,hôrəˈläjik/ adj. **hor·o·log·i·cal** /,hôrəˈläjikəl/ adj. **ho·rol·o·gist** n. [19th C.: from Gk. *hōra* 'time' + -LOGY.]

hor·o·scope /ˈhôrə,skōp; ˈhärə-/ ▶ n. Astrol. a forecast of a person's future, typically including a delineation of character and circumstances, based on the relative positions of the stars and planets at the time of that person's birth. ■ a short forecast for people born under a particular sign, esp. as published in a newspaper or magazine. ■ a birth chart. See CHART. — **hor·o·scop·ic** /,hôrəˈskäpik; ,härə-/ adj. **ho·ros·co·py** /həˈräskəpē/ n. [OE: via L. from Gk. *hōroskopos*, from *hōra* 'time' + *skopos* 'observer.']

Hor·o·witz /ˈhôrə,wits; ˈhär-/, Vladimir (1904–89), US pianist; born in Russia. He was best known for his performances of Scarlatti, Liszt, Scriabin, and Prokofiev.

hor·ren·dous /həˈrendəs; hô-/ ▶ adj. extremely unpleasant, horrifying, or terrible: *she suffered horrendous injuries.* — **hor·ren·dous·ly** adv. [17th C.: from L. *horrendus* (gerundive of *horrere* '(of hair) stand on end') + -OUS.]

hor·rent /ˈhôrənt/ ▶ adj. literary **1** (of a person's hair) standing on end. **2** feeling or expressing horror. [17th C.: from L. *horrent-* '(of hair) standing on end,' from the v. *horrere*.]

hor·ri·ble /ˈhôrəbəl; ˈhär-/ ▶ adj. causing or likely to cause horror; shocking. ■ informal very unpleasant. — **hor·ri·ble·ness** n. **hor·ri·bly** adv. [ME: via OFr. from L. *horribilis*, from *horrere* 'tremble, shudder' (see HORRID).]

hor·rid /ˈhôrid; ˈhär-/ ▶ adj. **1** causing horror. ■ informal very unpleasant or disagreeable. **2** literary rough; bristling. — **hor·rid·ly** adv. **hor·rid·ness** n. [16th C.: from L. *horridus*, from *horrere* 'tremble.']

hor·ri·fic /hôˈrifik; hə-/ ▶ adj. causing horror. — **hor·rif·i·cal·ly** adv.

hor·ri·fy /ˈhôrə,fī; ˈhär-/ ▶ v. (**-fies, -fied**) [trans.] (usu. **be horrified**) fill with horror; shock greatly. — **hor·ri·fi·ca·tion** /hô,rifiˈkāshən; hə-/ n. **hor·ri·fied·ly** /-,fī(ə)dlē/ adv. **hor·ri·fy·ing·ly** adv.

hor·rip·i·la·tion /hô,ripəˈlāshən; hə-/ ▶ n. literary the erection of hairs on the skin due to cold, fear, or excitement. — **hor·rip·i·late** /hôˈripə,lāt; hə-/ v. [17th C.: from late L. *horripilatio(n-)*, from L. *horrere* 'stand on end' (see HORRID) + *pilus* 'hair.']

hor·ror /ˈhôrər; ˈhär-/ ▶ n. **1** an intense feeling of fear, shock, or disgust. ■ a thing causing such a feeling. ■ a literary or film genre concerned with arousing such feelings. ■ intense dismay. ■ [as exclam.] (**horrors**) esp. humorous used to express dismay: *horrors, two buttons were missing!* ■ [in sing.] intense dislike. ■ (**the horrors**) an attack of extreme nervousness or anxiety: *the mere thought of it gives me the horrors.* **2** informal a bad or mischievous person, esp. a child. [ME: via OFr. from L. *horror*, from *horrere* 'tremble, shudder' (see HORRID).]

hor·ror-struck (also **hor·ror-strick·en**) ▶ adj. (of a person) briefly paralyzed with horror or shock.

hor·ror va·cui /ˈvakyoo͞,ī/ ▶ n. [in sing.] a fear or dislike of leaving empty spaces, esp. in an artistic composition. [19th C.: mod. L., lit. 'horror of a vacuum.']

hors con·cours /,ôr kônˈko͝or/ ▶ adj. **1** unrivaled; unequaled. **2** formal (of an exhibit or exhibitor) not competing for a prize. [19th C.:Fr., lit. 'out of the competition.']

hors de com·bat /,ôr də kämˈbä/ ▶ adj. out of action due to injury or damage. [18th C.: Fr., lit. 'out of the fight.']

hors d'oeuvre /ôr ˈdərv; ˈdœvrə/ ▶ n. (pl. same or **hors d'oeuvres** pronunc. same or /ˈdərvz/) a small savory dish, typically one served as an appetizer at the beginning of a meal. [18th C.: Fr., lit. 'outside the work.']

horse /hôrs/ ▶ n. **1** a solid-hoofed plant-eating domesticated mammal (*Equus caballus*) with a flowing mane and tail, used for riding, racing, and to carry and pull loads. The **horse family** (Equidae) also includes the asses and zebras. ■ an adult male horse; a stallion or gelding. ■ a wild mammal of the horse family. ■ [treated as sing. or pl.] cavalry: *forty horse and sixty foot.* **2** a frame or structure on which something is mounted or supported, esp. a sawhorse. ■ short for POMMEL HORSE or VAULTING HORSE. **3** informal heroin. **4** informal a unit of horsepower: *the huge 63-horse 701-cc engine.* ▶ v. [trans.] (usu. **be horsed**) provide (a person or vehicle) with a horse or horses.
– PHRASES **don't change horses in midstream** proverb choose a sensible moment to change your mind. **from the horse's mouth** (of information) from the person directly concerned or another authoritative source.
– PHRASAL VERBS **horse around** informal fool around. — **horse·less** adj. **horse·like** adj. [OE *hors*, of Gmc. origin; rel. to Du. *ros* and Ger. *Ross*.]

horse-and-bug·gy ▶ adj. [attrib.] old-fashioned. ■ of a time when horses and buggies were a common mode of transportation.

horse·back /ˈhôrs,bak/ ▶ adj. & adv. mounted on a horse.
– PHRASES **on** (or **by**) **horseback** mounted on a horse.

horse·bean /ˈhôrs,bēn/ (also **horse bean**) ▶ n. another term for BROAD BEAN.

horse chest·nut ▶ n. a deciduous tree (genus *Aesculus*, family Hippocastanaceae) with large leaves of five leaflets, conspicuous sticky winter buds, and upright conical clusters of white, pink, or red flowers. Unrelated to true chestnuts, the horse chestnut bears unpalatable nuts enclosed in fleshy, thorny husks. ■ the fruit or seed of this tree.

horse-drawn ▶ adj. (of a vehicle) pulled by a horse or horses: *a horse-drawn carriage.*

horse·feath·ers /ˈhôrs,fe<u>th</u>ərz/ ▶ exclam. used to express disagreement, disbelief, or frustration.

horse·flesh /ˈhôrs,flesh/ ▶ n. horses considered collectively. ■ the flesh of a horse, esp. when used as food.

horse·fly /ˈhôrs,flī/ ▶ n. (pl. **-flies**) a stoutly built fly (genus *Tabanus*, family Tabanidae), the female of which is a bloodsucker and inflicts painful bites on horses and other mammals.

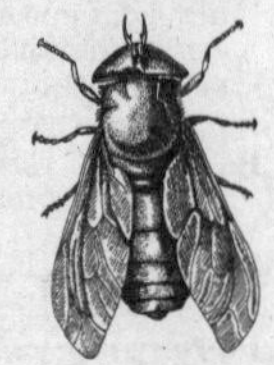
horsefly

Horse Guards ▶ plural n. a mounted brigade from the household troops of the British monarch, used for ceremonial occasions.

horse·hair /ˈhôrs,he(ə)r/ ▶ n. hair from the mane or tail of a horse, typically used in furniture for padding.

horse·hair worm ▶ n. a long slender worm related to the nematodes, the larvae being parasites of arthropods and the adults living in water or damp soil.

Horse·head Neb·u·la /ˈhôrs,hed/ Astron. a dust nebula in the shape of a horse's head, forming a dark silhouette against a bright emission nebula in Orion.

horse·hide /ˈhôrs,hīd/ ▶ n. **1** the skin of a horse. ■ leather made from the skin of a horse. **2** informal a baseball.

horse lat·i·tudes ▶ plural n. a belt of calm air and sea occurring in both the northern and southern hemispheres between the trade winds and the westerlies.

horse·laugh /ˈhôrs,laf/ ▶ n. a loud, coarse laugh.

horse·leech /ˈhôrs,lēch/ ▶ n. a large predatory leech (genus *Haemopis*, family Hirudidae) of freshwater and terrestrial habitats that feeds on carrion and small invertebrates.

horse·less /ˈhôrslis/ ▶ adj. [attrib.] (of a vehicle) not drawn by a horse or horses: *a horseless cabriolet.*

horse·less car·riage ▶ n. archaic or humorous an automobile.

horse mack·er·el ▶ n. a shoaling edible fish (*Trachurus trachurus*) of the jack family.

horse·man /ˈhôrsmən/ ▶ n. (pl. **-men**) a rider on horseback, esp. a skilled one.

horse·man·ship /ˈhôrsmən,ship/ ▶ n. the art or practice of riding on horseback.

horse·mint /'hôrs,mint/ ▶ **n.** a tall coarse kind of mint (genera *Mentha* and *Monarda*).

horse op·er·a ▶ **n.** informal a western movie.

horse pis·tol ▶ **n.** hist. a large pistol carried at the pommel of the saddle by a rider.

horse·play /'hôrs,plā/ ▶ **n.** rough, boisterous play.

horse·play·er /'hôrs,plāər/ ▶ **n.** a person who regularly bets on horse races.

horse·pow·er /'hôrs,pouər/ (abbr.: **hp**) ▶ **n.** (pl. same) a unit of power equal to 550 foot-pounds per second (745.7 watts). ■ the power of an engine measured in terms of this. ■ power; ability to perform strenuous tasks.

horse race ▶ **n. 1** a race between two or more horses ridden by jockeys. **2** a very close contest.

horse rac·ing ▶ **n.** the sport in which horses and their riders take part in races, typically with substantial betting on the outcome.

horse·rad·ish /'hôrs,radisн/ ▶ **n.** a European plant (*Armoracia rusticana*) of the cabbage family, grown for its pungent root. ■ this root, which is scraped or grated as a condiment and often made into a sauce.

horse sense ▶ **n.** informal common sense.

horse·shit /'hôr(s),sнit/ ▶ **n.** vulgar slang **1** horse dung. **2** nonsense.

horse·shoe /'hôr(s),sнo͞o/ ▶ **n.** a shoe for a horse formed of a narrow band of iron in the form of an extended circular arc and secured to the hoof with nails. ■ a shoe of this kind or a representation of one, regarded as bringing good luck. ■ something resembling this in shape: [as adj.] *a horseshoe bend.* ■ (**horseshoes**) [treated as sing.] a game in which horseshoes are thrown at a stake in the ground.

horse·shoe crab ▶ **n.** a large marine arthropod (class Merostomata) with a domed horseshoe-shaped shell, a long tail-spine, and ten legs, little changed since the Devonian period.

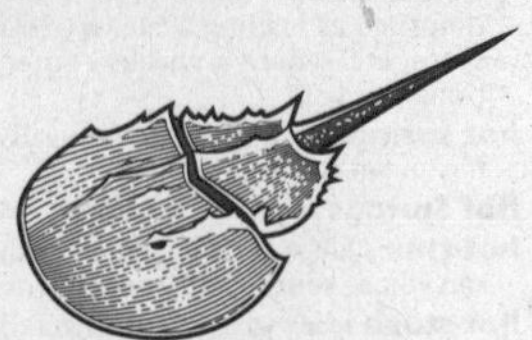
horseshoe crab

Horse·shoe Falls see **NIAGARA FALLS.**

horse's neck ▶ **n.** informal a drink consisting of ginger ale, a twist of lemon peel, and liquor, typically brandy.

horse·tail /'hôrs,tāl/ ▶ **n.** a nonflowering plant (genus *Equisetum*, family Equisetaceae) with a hollow jointed stem that bears whorls of narrow leaves, producing spores in cones at the tips of the shoots.

horse-trad·ing (also **horse trad·ing**) ▶ **n.** the buying and selling of horses. ■ hard and shrewd bargaining, typically in politics. — **horse-trade v. horse-trad·er n.**

horse·whip /'hôrs,(h)wip/ ▶ **n.** a long whip used for driving and controlling horses. ▶ **v.** (**-whipped, -whip·ping**) [trans.] beat with such a whip.

horse·wom·an /'hôrs,wo͝omən/ ▶ **n.** (pl. **-wom·en**) a woman who rides on horseback, esp. a skilled one.

hors·ey /'hôrsē/ (also **hors·y**) ▶ **adj.** (**hors·i·er, hors·i·est**) **1** of or resembling a horse. **2** concerned with or devoted to horses or horse racing. — **hors·i·ly adv. hors·i·ness n.**

horst /hôrst/ ▶ **n.** Geol. a raised elongated block of the earth's crust lying between two faults. [19th C.: from Ger. *Horst* 'heap.']

hort. ▶ **abbr.** ■ horticulture or horticultural.

hor·ta·to·ry /'hôrtə,tôrē/ ▶ **adj.** tending or aiming to exhort. — **hor·ta·tion** /,hôr'tāsнən/ **n. hor·ta·tive** /'hôrtətiv/ **adj.** [16th C.: from L. *hortatorius*, from *hortari* 'exhort.']

hor·ti·cul·ture /'hôrti,kəlcнər/ ▶ **n.** the art or practice of garden cultivation and management. — **hor·ti·cul·tur·al** /,hôrti'kəlcнərəl/ **adj. hor·ti·cul·tur·al·ist** /,hôrti'kəlcнərəlist/ **n. hor·ti·cul·tur·ist** /-,kəlcнərist/ **n.** [17th C.: from L. *hortus* 'garden,' on the pattern of *agriculture*.]

Ho·rus /'hôrəs/ Egyptian Mythol. a god regarded as the protector of the monarchy, and typically represented as a falcon-headed man.

Hos. ▶ **abbr.** Bible Hosea.

ho·san·na /hō'zanə; -'zä-/ (also **ho·san·nah**) ▶ **exclam.** (esp. in biblical, Judaic, and Christian use) used to express adoration, praise, or joy. ▶ **n.** an expression of adoration, praise, or joy. [OE, via late L. from Gk. *hōsanna*, from Rabbinical Heb. *hōša-nā*, abbrev. of biblical *hōšīʿā-nnā* 'save, we pray' (Ps. 118:25).]

hose /hōz/ ▶ **n. 1** a flexible tube conveying water, used esp. for watering plants and in firefighting. **2** [treated as pl.] stockings, socks, and tights (esp. in commercial use): *a chorus girl's fishnet hose.* ■ hist. breeches: *Elizabethan doublet and hose.* ▶ **v.** [trans.] water, spray, or drench with a hose: *he was hosing down the driveway.* [OE *hosa*, of Gmc. origin.]

Ho·se·a /hō'zāə; -'zēə/ a Hebrew minor prophet of the 8th century BC. ■ a book of the Bible containing his prophecies.

ho·sel /'hōzəl/ ▶ **n.** the socket of a golf club head into which the shaft fits. [16th C.: dimin. of **HOSE**, in the dial. sense 'sheathing.']

ho·sier /'hōzнər/ ▶ **n.** a manufacturer or seller of hosiery.

ho·sier·y /'hōzнərē/ ▶ **n.** stockings, socks, and tights collectively.

hosp. ▶ **abbr.** hospital.

hos·pice /'häspis/ ▶ **n.** a home providing care for the sick, esp. the terminally ill. ■ archaic a lodging for travelers, esp. one run by a religious order. [19th C.: from Fr., from L. *hospitium*, from *hospes, hospit-* (see **HOST**[1]).]

hos·pi·ta·ble /hä'spitəbəl; 'häspitəbəl/ ▶ **adj.** friendly and welcoming to strangers or guests. ■ (of an environment) pleasant and favorable for living in. — **hos·pi·ta·bly adv.**

hos·pi·tal /'häspitl/ ▶ **n. 1** an institution providing medical and surgical treatment and nursing care for sick or injured people. ■ a similar institution for the treatment of animals, esp. pets. **2** [usu. in names] Law, Brit. a charitable institution for the education of the young. [ME (sense 2): via OFr. from med. L. *hospitale*, neut. of L. *hospitalis* 'hospitable,' from *hospes, hospit-* (see **HOST**[1]).]

hos·pi·tal cor·ners ▶ **plural n.** overlapping folds used to tuck sheets neatly and securely under the mattress at the corners, in a manner typically used by nurses.

hos·pi·tal·er /'häspitl-ər/ (also **hos·pi·tal·ler**) ▶ **n.** a member of a charitable religious order, originally the Knights Hospitalers.

Hos·pi·ta·let /,äspitl'et; ,ōspētä'let/ (also **Hospitalet de Llobregat**) a suburb of Barcelona in northeastern Spain; pop. 269,000.

hos·pi·tal·i·ty /,häspi'talitē/ ▶ **n.** the friendly and generous reception and entertainment of guests, visitors, or strangers. ▶ **adj.** denoting a suite or room in a hotel where visitors are entertained, typically at a convention. ■ relating to or denoting the business of housing or entertaining visitors.

hos·pi·tal·ize /'häspitl,īz/ ▶ **v.** [trans.] (usu. **be hospitalized**) admit or cause (someone) to be admitted to a hospital for treatment. — **hos·pi·tal·i·za·tion** /,häspitl-i'zāsнən/ **n.**

hos·pi·tal·ler ▶ **n.** British spelling of **HOSPITALER.**

hos·pi·tal ship ▶ **n.** a ship that functions as a hospital, esp. to receive or take home sick or wounded military personnel.

hoss /hôs/ ▶ **n.** nonstandard spelling of **HORSE**, used in representing dialect or informal speech.

host[1] /hōst/ ▶ **n. 1** a person who receives or entertains other people as guests. ■ a person, place, or organization that holds and organizes an event to which others are invited. ■ an area in which particular living things are found: *Australia is host to some of the world's most dangerous animals.* ■ often humorous the landlord or landlady of a pub: *mine host raised his glass of whiskey.* ■ the moderator or emcee of a television or radio program. **2** Biol. an animal or plant on or in which a parasite or commensal organism lives. ■ (also **host cell**) a living cell in which a virus multiplies. ■ a person whose immune system has been invaded by a pathogenic organism. ■ a person or animal that has received transplanted tissue or a transplanted organ. **3** (also **host computer**) a computer that mediates multiple access to databases mounted on it or provides other services to a computer network; a server. ▶ **v.** [trans.] act as host at (an event) or for (a television or radio program). [ME: from OFr. *hoste*, from L. *hospes, hospit-* 'host, guest.']

host[2] ▶ **n.** (**a host of** or **hosts of**) a large number of people or things: *a host of memories rushed into her mind.* ■ archaic an army. ■ literary (in biblical use) the sun, moon, and stars: *the starry host of heaven.* [ME: from OFr. *ost, hoost*, from L. *hostis* 'stranger, enemy' (in med. L. 'army').]

host[3] ▶ **n.** (usu. **the Host**) the bread consecrated in the Eucharist: *the elevation of the Host.* [ME: from OFr. *hoiste*, from L. *hostia* 'victim.']

hos·ta /'hōstə; 'hästə/ ▶ **n.** an eastern Asian plant (genus *Hosta*) of the lily family, widely cultivated for its shade-tolerant foliage. [mod. L., named after Nicolaus T. *Host* (1761–1834), Austrian physician.]

hos·tage /'hästij/ ▶ **n.** a person seized or held as security for the fulfillment of a condition.

– PHRASES **hold** (or **take**) **someone hostage** seize and keep someone as a hostage. **a hostage to fortune** an act, commitment, or remark that is regarded as unwise because it invites trouble or could prove difficult to live up to. [ME: from OFr., based on late L. *obsidatus* 'the state of being a hostage,' from L. *obses, obsid-* 'hostage.']

hos·tel /'hästl/ ▶ **n.** an establishment that provides cheap food and lodging for a specific group of people, such as students, workers, or travelers. ■ short for **YOUTH HOSTEL.** [ME: from OFr., from med. L. *hospitale* (see **HOSPITAL**).]

hos·tel·ry /'hästl-rē/ ▶ **n.** (pl. **-ries**) archaic or humorous an inn. [ME: from OFr. *hostelerie*, from *hostelier* 'innkeeper,' from *hostel* (see **HOSTEL**).]

host·ess /'hōstis/ ▶ **n.** a woman who receives or entertains guests. ■ a woman employed at a restaurant to welcome and seat customers. ■ a woman employed to entertain customers at a nightclub, bar, or dance hall. ■ a stewardess on an aircraft, train, etc. ■ a woman who introduces a television or radio program. ▶ **v.** [trans.] act as a hostess at (an event). ■ [intrans.] act as a hostess.

hos·tile /'hästl; 'hästīl/ ▶ **adj.** unfriendly; antagonistic. ■ of or belonging to a military enemy. ■ [predic.] opposed: *people are very hostile to the idea.* ■ (of a takeover bid) opposed by the company to be bought. — **hos·tile·ly adv.** [16th C.: from Fr., or from L. *hostilis*, from *hostis* 'stranger, enemy.']

hos·tile wit·ness ▶ **n.** Law a witness who is antagonistic to the party calling them and, being unwilling to tell the truth, may have to be cross-examined by the party.

hos·til·i·ty /hä'stilitē/ ▶ **n.** (pl. **-ties**) hostile behavior; unfriendliness or opposition. ■ (**hostilities**) acts of warfare.

hos·tler /ˈ(h)äslər/ (also **os·tler**) ▶ **n.** **1** hist. a man employed to look after the horses of people staying at an inn. **2** a person who is in charge of and services vehicles, esp. railroad engines, when they are not in use. [ME: from OFr. *hostelier* 'innkeeper,' from *hostel* (see HOSTEL).]

hot /hät/ ▶ **adj.** (**hot·ter, hot·test**) **1** having a high degree of heat or a high temperature. ■ feeling or producing an uncomfortable sensation of heat. ■ (of food or drink) prepared by heating and served without cooling. ■ informal (of an electric circuit) at a high voltage; live. ■ informal radioactive. **2** (of food) containing or consisting of pungent spices or peppers that produce a burning sensation when tasted. **3** passionately enthusiastic, eager, or excited. ■ lustful, amorous, or erotic. ■ angry, indignant, or upset. ■ (of music, esp. jazz) strongly rhythmical and excitingly played. **4** involving much activity, debate, or intense feeling: *the environment has become a very hot issue.* ■ (esp. of news) fresh or recent and therefore of great interest. ■ currently popular, fashionable, or in demand: *they know the hottest dance moves.* ■ difficult to deal with; awkward or dangerous: *too hot to handle.* ■ (of a hit or return in ball games) difficult for an opponent to deal with. ■ informal (of goods) stolen and difficult to dispose of because easily identifiable. ■ informal (of a person) wanted by the police. ■ [predic.] (in children's games) very close to finding or guessing something. **5** informal knowledgeable or skillful: *Tony is very hot on local history.* ■ [predic.] [usu. with negative] good; promising: *this is not so hot for business.* ■ [predic.] (**hot on**) informal considering as very important; strict about: *local customs officers are hot on confiscations.*
– PHRASES **get hot** (of an athlete or team) suddenly become effective. **have the hots for** informal be sexually attracted to. **hot and bothered** see BOTHER. **hot and heavy** informal intense; with intensity. **hot on the heels of** following closely. **hot to trot** informal ready and eager to engage in an activity. **hot under the collar** informal angry, resentful, or embarrassed. **in hot pursuit** following closely and eagerly. **in hot water** informal in a situation of difficulty, trouble, or disgrace. **make it** (or **things**) **hot for someone** informal make things unpleasant for someone; persecute. — **hot·ness** n. **hot·tish** adj. [OE *hāt*, of Gmc. origin; rel. to Du. *heet* and Ger. *heiss*.]

hot air ▶ **n.** informal empty talk that is intended to impress: *they dismissed the theory as a load of hot air.*

hot·bed /ˈhät,bed/ ▶ **n.** a bed of earth heated by fermenting manure, for raising or forcing plants. ■ an environment promoting the growth of something, esp. something unwelcome.

hot-blood·ed ▶ **adj.** lustful; passionate.

hot box (also **hot·box**) ▶ **n.** Railroad an overheated axle box or journal box.

hot but·ton ▶ **n.** informal [often as adj.] a topic or issue that is highly charged emotionally or politically.

hotch·pot /ˈhäch,pät/ ▶ **n.** Law the reunion and blending together of properties for the purpose of securing equal division, esp. of the property of an intestate parent. [ME (in the sense 'hodgepodge'): from Anglo-Norman Fr. and OFr. *hochepot*, from *hocher* 'to shake' (prob. of Low Ger. origin) + *pot* 'pot.']

hotch·potch /ˈhäch,päch/ ▶ **n.** Brit. variant of HODGEPODGE. ■ a mutton stew with mixed vegetables. [ME: var. of HOTCHPOT.]

hot cross bun ▶ **n.** a bun marked with a cross and containing dried fruit, traditionally eaten during Lent.

hot dog ▶ **n.** **1** a hot frankfurter served in a long, soft roll and typically topped with various condiments. **2** informal a person who shows off, esp. a skier or surfer who performs stunts or tricks. ▶ **exclam.** informal used to express delight or enthusiastic approval. ▶ **v.** (**hot·dog**) (**-dogged, -dog·ging**) [intrans.] informal perform stunts or tricks; show off. — **hot·dog·ger** n.

ho·tel /hōˈtel/ ▶ **n.** **1** an establishment providing accommodations, meals, and other services for travelers and tourists. **2** a code word representing the letter H, used in radio communication. [18th C.: from Fr. *hôtel*, from OFr. *hostel* (see HOSTEL).]

ho·te·lier /,ôtelˈyā; ,hōtlˈi(ə)r/ ▶ **n.** a person who owns or manages a hotel.

hot flash ▶ **n.** a sudden feeling of feverish heat, typically as a symptom of menopause.

hot·foot /ˈhät,fo͝ot/ ▶ **n.** a practical joke in which a match is inserted into the victim's shoe and then lit. ▶ **v.** (**hotfoot it**) [with adverbial of direction] walk or run quickly and eagerly: *we hotfooted it after him.*

hot·head /ˈhät,hed/ (also **hot-head**) ▶ **n.** a person who is impetuous or who easily becomes angry and violent. — **hot·head·ed** adj. **hot·head·ed·ly** adv. **hot·head·ed·ness** n.

hot·house /ˈhät,hous/ ▶ **n.** a heated building, typically made largely of glass, for rearing plants out of season or in a climate colder than is natural for them. ■ fig. an environment that encourages the rapid growth or development of someone or something, esp. in a stifling or intense way: [as adj.] *the hothouse atmosphere of the college.*

hot key ▶ **n.** Comput. a key or a combination of keys providing quick access to a particular function within a program.

hot·line /ˈhät,līn/ (also **hot line**) ▶ **n.** a direct telephone line set up for a specific purpose, esp. for use in emergencies or for communication between heads of government. ■ a telephone line to a source of information or emergency help.

hot·ly /ˈhätlē/ ▶ **adv.** in a passionate, excited, or angry way. ■ closely and with determination: *a hotly contested tournament.*

hot met·al ▶ **n.** a typesetting technique in which type is newly made each time from molten metal, cast by a composing machine.

hot mon·ey ▶ **n.** capital that is frequently transferred between financial institutions in an attempt to maximize interest or capital gain.

hot pants ▶ **plural n.** tight, brief women's shorts, worn as a fashion garment. ■ informal strong sexual desire.

hot pep·per ▶ **n.** any of several varieties of pungent pepper used dried or chopped as a condiment.

hot plate ▶ **n.** a flat heated surface (or a set of these), typically portable, used for cooking food or keeping it hot.

hot po·ta·to ▶ **n.** informal a controversial issue or situation that is awkward or unpleasant to deal with.

hot press ▶ **n.** a device in which paper or cloth is pressed between glazed boards and hot metal plates in order to produce a smooth or glossy surface. ▶ **v.** (**hot-press**) [trans.] press with such a device.

hot rod ▶ **n.** a motor vehicle that has been specially modified to give it extra power and speed. ▶ **v.** (**hot-rod**) (**-rod·ded, -rod·ding**) **1** [intrans.] drive a hot rod. **2** [trans.] modify (a vehicle or other device) to make it faster or more powerful. — **hot rod·der** (also **hot-rod·der**) **n.**

hot seat ▶ **n.** (**the hot seat**) informal **1** the position of a person who carries full responsibility for something, including facing criticism or being answerable for decisions or actions. **2** the electric chair.

hot shoe ▶ **n.** Photog. a socket on a camera with direct electrical contacts for an attached flashgun or other accessory.

hot·shot /ˈhät,shät/ ▶ **n.** informal an important or exceptionally able person. ■ a show-off; an exhibitionist. ▶ **adj.** aggressive and skillful: *a hotshot broker.*

hot spot ▶ **n.** a small area or region with a relatively hot temperature in comparison to its surroundings. ■ Geol. an area of volcanic activity, esp. where this is isolated. ■ fig. a place of significant activity or danger. ■ Comput. an area on the screen that can be clicked on to start an operation such as loading a file. ■ Comput. a place in a public building, open space, etc. where a wireless Internet signal is available for personal computer use.

hot spring ▶ **n.** a spring of naturally hot water, typically heated by subterranean volcanic activity.

Hot Springs a spa city in central Arkansas; pop. 35,750.

hot·spur /ˈhät,spər/ ▶ **n.** archaic a rash, impetuous person. [ME: lit. 'a person whose spur is hot from rash or constant riding.']

hot-stove ▶ **adj.** [attrib.] denoting a discussion about a favorite sport carried on during the off-season: *hot-stove speculation.*

hot-stove league ▶ **n.** informal sports fans, esp. baseball fans in the off season, who discuss players, teams, and the upcoming season.

hot stuff ▶ **n.** informal used to refer to a person or thing of outstanding quality, interest, or talent. ■ used to refer to a sexually exciting person, movie, book, etc.

hot-swap ▶ **v.** [trans.] informal fit or replace (a computer part) with the power still connected. — **hot-swap·pa·ble adj.**

hot-tem·pered ▶ **adj.** easily angered; quick-tempered.

Hot·ten·tot /ˈhätn,tät/ ▶ **n. & adj.** used to refer to Khoikhoi peoples. [Afrik.]

hot tick·et ▶ **n.** informal a person or thing that is much in demand: *he's the current hot ticket on the hard-core hip-hop block* | [as adj.] *a hot-ticket invitation.*

hot·tie /ˈhätē/ (also **hot·ty**) ▶ **n.** (pl. **-ties**) informal a sexually attractive person. [from *hot* + *-ie* or *-y*.]

hot tub ▶ **n.** a large tub filled with hot aerated water used for recreation or physical therapy.

hot war ▶ **n.** a war with active military hostilities.

hot-wa·ter bot·tle (also **hot-water bag**) ▶ **n.** a flat, oblong container, typically made of rubber, that is filled with hot water and used for warmth.

hot-wire ▶ **v.** [trans.] informal start the engine of (a vehicle) by bypassing the ignition system, typically in order to steal it.

Hou·di·ni /ho͞oˈdēnē/, Harry (1874–1926), US magician; born *Erik Weisz* in Hungary. In the early 1900s, he became known for his ability to escape from all kinds of bonds and containers. ■ [as n.] a person skilled at escaping. ■ an ingenious escape.

houm·mos /ˈho͞oməs/ ▶ **n.** var. of HUMMUS.

hound /hound/ ▶ **n.** a dog of a breed used for hunting, esp. one able to track by scent. ■ any dog. ■ [with adj.] a person who avidly pursues something. ■ informal, dated a despicable or contemptible man. ▶ **v.** [trans.] harass or persecute (someone) relentlessly. ■ pursue relentlessly.
– PHRASES **ride to hounds** see RIDE. [OE *hund*, of Gmc. origin; rel. to Ger. *Hund*, from an Indo-Eur. root shared by Gk. *kuōn, kun-* 'dog.']

hound's-tongue ▶ **n.** a tall plant (*Cynoglossum officinale*) of the borage family that bears long silky hairs, small purplish flowers, and tongue-shaped leaves.

hounds·tooth /ˈhoun(d)z,to͞oth/ ▶ **n.** a large checked pattern with notched corners suggestive of a canine tooth, typically used in cloth for jackets and suits.

houndstooth

hour /ou(ə)r/ ▶ **n.** **1** a period of time equal to a twenty-fourth part of a day and night and divided into 60 minutes: *an extra hour of daylight.* ■ a less definite period of time: *the early morning hours.* ■ the distance traveled in one hour. **2** a point in time: *I wondered if my last hour had come.* ■ a time of day or night: *you can't turn him away at this hour.* ■ a time of day specified as an exact number of hours from midnight or midday: *the clock in the sitting room* ***struck the hour.*** ■ **(hours)** [with preceding numeral] a time so specified on the 24-hour clock: *the first bomb fell at 0051 hours.* ■ the time as formerly reckoned from sunrise: *it was about the ninth hour.* ■ the appropriate time for some specific action: *now that the hour had come, David decided he could not face it.* **3** [usu. with adj.] a period set aside for some purpose or marked by some activity: *leisure hours.* ■ **(hours)** a fixed period of time for an activity, such as work, use of a building, etc.: *shortened working hours.* **4** (usu. **hours**) (in the Western Church) a short service of psalms and prayers to be said at a particular time of day, esp. in religious communities. **5** Astron. 15° of longitude or right ascension (one twenty-fourth part of a circle).

– PHRASES **all hours** any time, esp. outside the time considered usual for something. **keep late hours** get up and go to bed late. **on the hour** at an exact hour, or on each hour, of the day or night. **within the hour** after less than an hour. [ME: from Anglo-Norman Fr. *ure*, via L. from Gk. *hōra* 'season, hour.']

hour·glass /'ou(ə)r,glas/ ▶ **n.** an invertible device with two connected glass bulbs containing sand that takes an hour to pass from the upper to the lower bulb. ■ [as adj.] shaped like such a device: *her hourglass figure.*

hour hand ▶ **n.** the hand on a clock or watch that indicates the hour.

hou·ri /'ho͝orē/ ▶ **n.** (pl. **-ris**) a beautiful young woman, esp. one of the virgin companions of the faithful in the Muslim Paradise. [18th C.: from Fr., from Pers. *ḥūrī*, from Arab. *ḥūr*, pl. of *'aḥwar* 'having eyes with a marked contrast of black and white.']

hour-long (also **hour·long**) ▶ **adj.** [attrib.] lasting for one hour.

hour·ly /'ou(ə)rlē/ ▶ **adj. 1** done or occurring every hour. ■ (with numeral or fraction) occurring at intervals measured in hours: *trains run at half-hourly intervals.* **2** reckoned hour by hour: *standard fees instead of hourly rates.* ▶ **adv. 1** every hour: *sunscreens should be applied hourly.* ■ (with numeral or fraction) at intervals measured in hours: *temperature should be recorded four-hourly.* **2** by the hour: *hourly workers.* **3** frequently; continually: *her curiosity was mounting hourly.*

Hou·sa·ton·ic River /,ho͞osə'tänik/ a river that flows for 130 miles (210 km) from western Massachusetts through Connecticut to Long Island Sound.

house ▶ **n.** /hous/ **1** a building for human habitation, esp. one that is lived in by a family or small group of people. ■ the people living in such a building; a household. ■ (often **House**) a family or family lineage, esp. a noble or royal one; a dynasty. ■ [with adj.] a building in which animals live or in which things are kept: *a reptile house.* **2** a building in which people meet for a particular activity: *a house of prayer.* ■ a business or institution: *a publishing house.* ■ a restaurant or inn: [as adj.] *a bottle of house wine.* ■ a residential hall at a school or college, or its residents. ■ a gambling establishment or its management. ■ a host or proprietor: *help yourself to a drink, compliments of the house!* ■ a theater: *a hundred musicians performed in front of a full house.* ■ an audience in a theater or concert venue: *the house burst into applause.* ■ a religious community that occupies a particular building: *the Cistercian house at Clairvaux.* ■ dated a brothel. ■ Brit., formal a college of a university. **3** a legislative or deliberative assembly. ■ **(the House)** the House of Representatives or (in the UK or Canada) the House of Commons or Lords. **4** (also **house mu·sic**) a style of popular dance music typically using synthesized drum and bass lines, sparse repetitive vocals, and a fast beat. **5** Astrol. any of the twelve divisions of the celestial sphere, based on the positions of the ascendant and midheaven at a given time and place. ■ such a division represented as a sector on an astrological chart, used in allocating elements of character and circumstance to different spheres of human life. ▶ **adj.** /hous/ [attrib.] **1** (of an animal or plant) kept in, frequenting, or infesting buildings. **2** of or relating to resident medical staff at a hospital. **3** of or relating to a business, institution, or society: *a house journal.* ■ (of a band or group) resident or regularly performing in a club or other venue. ▶ **v.** /houz/ [trans.] **1** provide (a person or animal) with shelter or living quarters. **2** provide space for; accommodate. ■ enclose or encase (something). ■ insert or fix (something) in a socket or mortise.

– PHRASES **like a house on fire** (or **afire**) informal vigorously; furiously. ■ excellently: *Ben and my aunt got along like a house on fire.* **house and home** a person's home (used for emphasis). **house of cards** a structure built out of playing cards precariously balanced together. ■ an insubstantial or insecure situation or scheme: *his case was a house of cards until Attorney Jabowski stepped in.* **keep house** do the cooking, cleaning, and other tasks involved in the running of a household. **on the house** (of a drink or meal in a bar or restaurant) at the management's expense; free. **play house** (of a child) play at being a family in their home. **put** (or **set** or **get**) **one's house in order** make necessary reforms. **set up house** make one's home in a specified place. — **house·ful** /-,fo͝ol/ **n.** (pl. **hous·es** /'houziz/) **house·less adj.** [OE *hūs* (noun), *hūsian* (v.), of Gmc. origin; rel. to Ger. *Haus* (n.).]

house ar·rest ▶ **n.** the state of being kept as a prisoner in one's own house, rather than in a prison.

house·boat /'hous,bōt/ ▶ **n.** a boat that is or can be moored for use as a dwelling.

house·bound /'hous,bound/ ▶ **adj.** unable to leave one's house, typically due to illness or old age.

house·boy /'hous,boi/ ▶ **n.** a boy or man employed to undertake domestic duties.

house brand ▶ **n.** a brand name used exclusively by a retailer for a product or line of products typically sold for prices lower than that of comparable items with manufacturer brand names.

house·break /'hous,brāk/ (past. **-broke**; past part. **-brok·en**) ▶ **v.** [trans.] train (a pet) to urinate and defecate outside the house or only in a special place. ■ informal, humorous teach (someone) good manners or neatness.

house·break·ing /'hous,brākiNG/ ▶ **n.** the action of breaking into a building, esp. in daytime, to commit a crime. — **house·break·er** /-,brākər/ **n.**

house·carl /'hous,kärl/ (also **house·carle**) ▶ **n.** hist. a member of the bodyguard of a Danish or English king or noble. [OE *hūscarl*, from ON *húskarl* 'manservant,' (pl.) 'retinue, bodyguard,' from *hús* 'house' + *karl* 'man.']

house·clean·ing /'hous,klēniNG/ ▶ **n. 1** the cleaning of the interior of a dwelling. **2** the removal of unwanted or superfluous items, practices, conditions, or personnel. — **house·clean v. house·clean·er n.**

house·coat /'hous,kōt/ ▶ **n.** a woman's long, loose, lightweight robe for informal wear around the house.

house·dress /'hous,dres/ ▶ **n.** a simple, usually washable, dress suitable for wearing while doing housework.

house finch ▶ **n.** a red-breasted brown finch (*Carpodacus mexicanus*), now common from Canada to Mexico and sometimes regarded as a pest.

house·fly /'hous,flī/ (also **house fly**) ▶ **n.** (pl. **-flies**) a common small fly (*Musca domestica*, family Muscidae) occurring worldwide in and around human habitation. Its eggs are laid in decaying material, and the fly can be a health hazard due to its contamination of food.

house guest (also **house·guest**) ▶ **n.** a guest staying for some days in a private house.

house·hold /'hous,(h)ōld/ ▶ **n.** a house and its occupants regarded as a unit: *the whole household was asleep.* ■ the affairs related to keeping a house: *it is mostly women who run households.*

house·hold·er /'hous,(h)ōldər/ ▶ **n.** a person who owns or rents a house; the head of a household.

house·hold gods ▶ **plural n.** gods presiding over a household, esp. (in Roman History) the lares and penates.

house·hold name (also **house·hold word**) ▶ **n.** a person or thing that is well known by the public.

house·hold troops ▶ **plural n.** troops employed to guard a sovereign.

house-hunt ▶ **v.** [intrans.] seek a house to buy or rent and live in. — **house-hunt·er n. house-hunt·ing n.**

house·hus·band /'hous,həzbənd/ ▶ **n.** a man who lives with a partner and carries out household duties traditionally done by a housewife rather than working outside the home.

house·keep·er /'hous,kēpər/ ▶ **n.** a person, typically a woman, employed to manage a household. — **house·keep v.** (dated).

house·keep·ing /'hous,kēpiNG/ ▶ **n. 1** the management of household affairs. ■ money set aside or given for such a purpose. ■ a department within a hotel or other residential facility that oversees the cleaning of rooms and the provision of necessities such as towels and glassware. **2** operations such as record-keeping or maintenance in an organization or a computer that make work possible but do not directly constitute its performance. ▶ **adj.** (of cabins, cottages, or other rental properties) having basic facilities such as a stove and refrigerator.

house·leek /'hous,lēk/ ▶ **n.** a succulent plant (*Sempervivum* and related genera) of the stonecrop family, with rosettes of fleshy leaves and small pink flowers, and the habit of growing on walls and roofs.

house lights (also **house·lights**) ▶ **plural n.** the lights in the area of a theater where the audience sits.

house·maid /'hous,mād/ ▶ **n.** a female domestic employee, esp. one who cleans reception rooms and bedrooms.

house·maid's knee ▶ **n.** bursitis in the knee, often due to excessive kneeling.

house·man /'housmən/ ▶ **n.** (pl. **-men**) **1** another term for HOUSEBOY. **2** Brit. a hospital intern.

house·mas·ter /'hous,mastər/ ▶ **n.** a teacher, typically male, in charge of a dormitory at a boarding school.

house·mis·tress /'hous,mistris/ ▶ **n.** a female teacher in charge of a dormitory at a boarding school.

house·moth·er /'hous,məT͟Hər/ ▶ **n.** a woman in charge of and living in a boarding school dormitory or children's home.

house mouse ▶ **n.** a grayish-brown mouse (*Mus musculus*) found abundantly as a scavenger in human dwellings.

house mu·sic ▶ **n.** see HOUSE (sense 4).

House of Bur·gess·es ▶ **n.** the lower house of the colonial Virginia legislature.

House of Com·mons (in the UK and Canada) the elected chamber of Parliament.

house of cor·rec·tion ▶ **n.** an institution for the short-term confinement of minor offenders.

house of God ▶ **n.** a place of religious worship, esp. a church.

house of ill fame (also **house of ill repute**) ▶ **n.** archaic or humorous a brothel.

House of Lords (in the UK) the nonelective chamber of Parliament composed of peers and bishops.

House of Rep·re·sent·a·tives the lower house of the US Congress and other legislatures, including most US state governments.

house or·gan ▶ **n.** a periodical published by a company to be read by its employees and other interested parties and dealing mainly with its own activities.

house·par·ent /ˈhous,pe(ə)rənt; -,parənt/ ▶ **n.** a housemother or housefather.

house par·ty ▶ **n.** a party at which the guests stay at a house overnight or for a few days.

house·plant /ˈhous,plant/ (also **house plant**) ▶ **n.** a plant grown indoors.

house-proud ▶ **adj.** attentive to, or preoccupied with, the care and appearance of one's home.

house·room /ˈhous,ro͞om; -,ro͝om/ ▶ **n.** space or accommodations in one's house.

house-sit (also **house·sit**) ▶ **v.** [intrans.] live in and look after a house while its owner is away. — **house-sit·ter n. house-sit·ting n.**

Hous·es of Par·lia·ment (in the UK) the Houses of Lords and Commons regarded together, or the building where they meet (the Palace of Westminster).

house spar·row ▶ **n.** a common brown and gray sparrow (*Passer domesticus*) that nests in the eaves and roofs of houses. Also called **ENGLISH SPARROW.**

house style ▶ **n.** a company's preferred manner of presentation and layout of written material.

house-to-house ▶ **adj. & adv.** performed at or taken to each house in turn.

house·top /ˈhous,täp/ ▶ **n.** the outer surface of the roof of a house.

house-train ▶ **v.** esp. Brit. another term for **HOUSEBREAK.**

house·warm·ing /ˈhous,wôrmiNG/ ▶ **n.** [usu. as adj.] a party celebrating a move to a new home.

house·wife /ˈhous,wīf/ ▶ **n.** (pl. **-wives**) **1** a married woman whose main occupation is caring for her family, managing household affairs, and doing housework. **2** a small case for needles, thread, and other small sewing items. — **house·wife·ly adj. house·wif·er·y n.**

house·work /ˈhous,wərk/ ▶ **n.** regular work done in housekeeping, such as cleaning, shopping, and cooking.

hous·ing[1] /ˈhouziNG/ ▶ **n.** **1** houses and apartments considered collectively. ■ the provision of accommodations. **2** a rigid casing that encloses and protects a piece of moving or delicate equipment. ■ a structure that supports and encloses the bearings at the end of an axle or shaft. **3** a recess or groove cut in one piece of wood to allow another piece to be attached to it. ■ Naut. the part of a mast below the deck.

hous·ing[2] ▶ **n.** archaic a cloth covering put on a horse for protection or ornament. [ME (in the general sense 'covering'): from OFr. *houce*, from med. L. *hultia*, of Gmc. origin.]

hous·ing de·vel·op·ment (Brit. **hous·ing estate**) ▶ **n.** a residential area in which the houses have all been planned and built at the same time.

hous·ing start ▶ **n.** the beginning of construction of a new house. ■ (**housing starts**) the number of new houses begun during a particular period, used as an indicator of economic conditions.

Hous·man /ˈhousmən/, A. E. (1859–1936), English poet; full name *Alfred Edward Housman*. His poems are collected in *A Shropshire Lad* (1896).

Hous·ton[1] /ˈ(h)yo͞ostən/ an inland port in Texas, linked to the Gulf of Mexico by the Houston Ship Canal; pop. 1,953,631; site of the NASA Space Center.

Hous·ton[2], Samuel (1793–1863), US soldier and politician, noted for his part in winning US control of Texas. He was governor of Tennessee 1827–29, president of the Republic of Texas 1836–1838, 1841–44, a US Senator 1846–59, and governor of Texas 1859–61.

hove /hōv/ esp. Naut. past of **HEAVE.**

hov·el /ˈhəvəl; ˈhävəl/ ▶ **n.** a small, squalid, unpleasant, or simply constructed dwelling. ■ archaic an open shed or outbuilding, used for sheltering cattle or storing grain or tools. [ME: of unknown origin.]

hov·er /ˈhəvər/ ▶ **v.** [no obj., with adverbial] remain in one place in the air. ■ remain poised in one place, typically with slight but undirected movement: *her hand hovered over the console.* ■ (of a person) wait or linger close at hand in a tentative or uncertain manner. ■ remain at or near a particular level. ■ remain in a state that is between two specified states or kinds of things: ***hovered between** cynicism and puzzlement.* ▶ **n.** [in sing.] an act of remaining in the air in one place. — **hov·er·er n.** [ME: from archaic *hove* 'hover, linger,' of unknown origin.]

hov·er·craft /ˈhəvər,kraft/ ▶ **n.** (pl. same) a vehicle or craft that travels over land or water on a cushion of air provided by a downward blast.

how[1] /hou/ ▶ **adv.** [usu. interrog. adv.] **1** in what way or manner; by what means: *how does it work?* **2** used to ask about the condition or quality of something: *how was your vacation?* ■ used to ask about someone's physical or mental state: *how are the children?* **3** [with adj. or adv.] used to ask about the extent or degree of something: *how old are you?* ■ used to express a strong feeling such as surprise about the extent of something: *how kind of him!* **4** [relative adv.] the way in which; that: *she told us how she had lived out of a suitcase for a week.* ■ in any way in which; however: *I'll do business how I like.*
– PHRASES **and how!** informal very much so (used to express strong agreement). **here's how!** dated said when drinking to someone's health. **how about 1** used to make a suggestion or offer: *how about a drink?* **2** used when asking for information or an opinion on something: *how about your company?* **the how and why** the methods and reasons for doing something. **how come?** see **COME. how do?** an informal greeting. **how do you do?** a formal greeting. **how many** what number. **how much** what amount or price. **how now?** archaic what is the meaning of this? **how so?** how can you show that that is so? **how's that for ——?** isn't that a remarkable instance of ——? [OE *hū*, of West Gmc. origin; rel. to Du. *hoe*, also to **WHO** and **WHAT.**]

how[2] ▶ **exclam.** a greeting attributed to North American Indians (used in humorous imitation). [19th C.: perh. from Sioux *háo* or Omaha *hou.*]

How·ard[1] /ˈhouərd/, Catherine (*c.*1521–42), fifth wife of Henry VIII.

How·ard[2], John Winston (1939–), prime minister of Australia 1996– .

how·be·it /houˈbē-it/ ▶ **adv.** archaic nevertheless; however: *howbeit, I've no proof of the thing.*

how·dah /ˈhoudə/ ▶ **n.** (in the Indian subcontinent) a seat for riding on the back of an elephant or camel, typically with a canopy and accommodating two or more people. [from Urdu *haudah*, from Arab. *hawdaj* 'litter.']

how-do-you-do /,hou də yə ˈdo͞o/ (also **how-de-do** or **how-d'ye-do**) ▶ **n.** [in sing.] informal an awkward, messy, or annoying situation.

how·dy /ˈhoudē/ ▶ **exclam.** an informal friendly greeting, particularly associated with the western states: *howdy, stranger.* [19th C.: alt. of *how d'ye.*]

Howe[1] /hou/, Elias (1819–67), US inventor. In 1846, he patented the first sewing machine.

Howe[2], Gordie (1928–), Canadian hockey player; full name *Gordon Howe*. A prolific scorer, he played professionally 1945–80.

how·e'er /houˈe(ə)r/ literary ▶ **contr.** however.

how·ev·er /houˈevər/ ▶ **adv.** **1** used to introduce a statement that contrasts with or seems to contradict something that has been said previously: *People tend to put on weight in middle age. However, gaining weight is not inevitable.* **2** [relative adv.] in whatever way; regardless of how: *however you look at it, you can't criticize that.* ■ [with adj. or adv.] to whatever extent: *he was hesitant to take the risk, however small.*

how·itz·er /ˈhouitsər/ ▶ **n.** a short gun for firing shells on high trajectories at low velocities. [17th C.: from Du. *houwitser*, from Ger. *Haubitze*, from Czech *houfnice* 'catapult.']

howitzer

howl /houl/ ▶ **n.** a long, loud, doleful cry uttered by an animal such as a dog or wolf. ■ a loud cry of pain, fear, anger, amusement, or derision. ■ [in sing.] a prolonged wailing noise such as that made by a strong wind: ***the howl of** the gale.* ▶ **v.** [intrans.] make a howling sound. ■ weep and cry out loudly: *a baby started to howl.* ■ [trans.] (**howl someone down**) shout in disapproval in order to prevent a speaker from being heard. [ME *houle* (v.), prob. imitative.]

howl·er /ˈhoulər/ ▶ **n.** **1** informal a stupid or glaring mistake, esp. an amusing one. **2** a person or animal that howls. **3** (also **howler monkey**) a fruit-eating monkey (genus *Alouatta*, family Cebidae) with a prehensile tail and a loud howling call, native to the forests of tropical America.

howl·ing /ˈhouliNG/ ▶ **adj.** [attrib.] **1** producing a long, loud, doleful cry or wailing sound. ■ archaic filled with or characterized by such sounds: *the howling wilderness.* **2** informal extreme; great: *the meal was a howling success.*

How·rah /ˈhourə/ (also **Hao·ra**) a city in eastern India, on the Hooghly River; pop. 947,000.

how·so·ev·er /,housōˈevər/ formal archaic ▶ **adv.** [with adj. or adv.] to whatever extent: *any quantity howsoever small.* ▶ **conj.** in whatever way; regardless of how: *howsoever it came into being, it is good to look at.*

how-to informal ▶ **adj.** [attrib.] providing detailed and practical advice: *read a how-to book.* ▶ **n.** (pl. **-tos**) a book, video, or training session that provides such advice.

Hox·ha /ˈhôjə/, Enver (1908–85), first secretary of the Albanian Communist Party 1954–85. He isolated Albania from Western influences and implemented a program of nationalization and collectivization.

hoy[1] /hoi/ ▶ **exclam.** used to attract someone's attention: *"Hoy! Look!"* [natural exclamation: first recorded in ME.]

hoy[2] ▶ **n.** hist. a small coastal sailing vessel, typically carrying one mast rigged fore-and-aft. [ME: from MDu. *hoei*, of unknown origin.]

hoy·a /ˈhoiə/ ▶ **n.** a climbing or sprawling evergreen shrub (genus *Hoya*, family Asclepiadaceae) with ornamental foliage and waxy flowers, native to Southeast Asia and the Pacific and grown as a greenhouse or indoor plant. [mod. L., named after Thomas *Hoy* (*c.*1750–*c.*1821), Engl. gardener.]

hoy·den /ˈhoidn/ ▶ **n.** dated a boisterous girl. — **hoy·den·ish adj.** [16th C. (denoting a rude or ignorant man): prob. from MDu. *heiden* (see **HEATHEN**).]

Hoyle[1] /hoil/, Sir Fred (1915–2001), English astronomer. He was one of the proponents of the steady state theory of cosmology.

Hoyle[2] ▶ **n.** (in phrase **according to Hoyle**) according to plan or the rules. [20th C.: from the name of Edmond *Hoyle* (1672–1769), English writer on card games.]

h.p. (also **HP**) ▶ **abbr.** ■ high pressure. ■ horsepower.

HPV ▸ abbr. human papilloma virus.

HQ ▸ abbr. headquarters.

HR ▸ abbr. House of Representatives.

Hr. ▸ abbr. Herr.

hr ▸ abbr. hour.

Hra·dec Krá·lo·vé /'(h)rädets 'krälô,ve/ a town in the northern Czech Republic, on the Elbe River; pop. 162,000. German name **Königgrätz**.

HRE ▸ abbr. Holy Roman Empire or Emperor.

H. Res. ▸ abbr. House Resolution.

HRH Brit. ▸ abbr. Her or His Royal Highness (as a title): *HRH Prince Philip.*

hrs ▸ abbr. hours.

HRT ▸ abbr. hormone replacement therapy.

Hr·vat·ska /'KH(ə)rvatskä; 'hərvätskä/ Croatian name for **Croatia**.

Hs ▸ symb. the chemical element hassium.

Hsia-men var. of **Xiamen**.

Hsian var. of **Xian**.

Hsiang var. of **Xiang**.

Hsi·ning var. of **Xining**.

HST ▸ abbr. ■ hypersonic transport. ■ Hubble Space Telescope.

Hsu-chou var. of **Xuzhou**.

HT ▸ abbr. ■ halftime. ■ (electrical) high tension.

HTLV ▸ abbr. **human T cell lymphotropic virus**.

HTML ▸ n. Comput. Hypertext Markup Language, a standardized system for tagging text files to achieve font, color, graphic, and hyperlink effects on World Wide Web pages.

Hts. ▸ abbr. Heights.

HTTP Comput. ▸ abbr. Hypertext Transfer (or Transport) Protocol, the data transfer protocol used on the World Wide Web.

HUAC /'hyo͞o-ak/ ▸ abbr. House Un-American Activities Committee.

Huai·bei /'hwī'bā/ a city in northern Anhui province, in eastern China; pop. 1,308,000.

Huai·nan /'hwī'nän/ a city in east central China, in the province of Anhui; pop. 1,228,000.

Hual·la·ga /wä'yägä/ a river in central Peru, rising in the central Andes and flowing northeast for 700 miles (1,100 km) to the Amazon Basin at Lagunas.

Huam·bo /'wämbō/ a city in the mountains in western Angola; pop. 400,000.

Huang Hai /'hwäNG 'hī/ Chinese name for **Yellow Sea**.

Huang Ho /'hō/ (also **Huang He** /'hə/) Chinese name for **Yellow River**.

hua·ra·che /wə'räCHē/ (also **gua·ra·che**) ▸ n. a leather-thonged sandal, originally worn by Mexican Indians. [19th C.: Mex. Sp.]

huarache

Huas·ca·rán /,wäskə'rän/ an extinct volcano in the Andes of western central Peru, that rises to 22,205 feet (6,768 m); the highest peak in Peru.

hub /həb/ ▸ n. the central part of a wheel, rotating on or with the axle, and from which the spokes radiate. ■ a place or thing that forms the effective center of an activity, region, or network.
– PHRASES **hub-and-spoke** denoting a system of air transportation in which local airports offer flights to a central airport where international or long-distance flights are available. [16th C.: of unknown origin.]

hub·ba hub·ba /'həbə 'həbə/ ▸ exclam. informal used to express approval, excitement, or enthusiasm, esp. with regard to a person's appearance. [1940s: of unknown origin.]

Hub·bard squash /'həbərd/ ▸ n. a winter squash of a variety with a green or yellow rind and yellow flesh.

Hub·ble /'həbəl/, Edwin Powell (1889–1953), US astronomer. He studied galaxies and devised a classification scheme for them.

hub·ble-bub·ble /'həbəl/ ▸ n. a hookah. [17th C.: imitative repetition of **bubble**.]

Hub·ble clas·si·fi·ca·tion Astron. a simple method of describing the shapes of galaxies, using subdivisions of each of four basic types (elliptical, spiral, barred spiral, and irregular).

Hub·ble's con·stant Astron. the ratio of the speed of recession of a galaxy (due to the expansion of the universe) to its distance from the observer.

Hub·ble's law Astron. a law stating that the redshifts in the spectra of distant galaxies (and hence their speeds of recession) are proportional to their distance.

Hub·ble Space Tel·e·scope an orbiting astronomical observatory launched in 1990. The telescope's high-resolution images are far better than can be obtained from the earth's surface.

hub·bub /'həb,əb/ ▸ n. [in sing.] a chaotic din caused by a crowd of people. ■ a busy, noisy situation. [16th C.: perh. of Irish origin; cf. the Irish exclamations *ababú, abú*, used in battle cries.]

hub·by /'həbē/ ▸ n. (pl. **-bies**) informal a husband. [17th C.: familiar abbrev.]

hub·cap /'həb,kap/ ▸ n. a metal or plastic cover for the hub of a motor vehicle's wheel.

Hu·bei /'ho͞o'bā/ (also **Hu·peh**) a province in eastern China; capital, Wuhan.

Hub·li /'ho͝oblē/ (also **Hub·li-Dhar·wad** /där'wäd/, **Hub·li-Dhar·war** /där'wär/) a city in southwestern India; pop. 648,000.

hu·bris /'(h)yo͞obris/ ▸ n. excessive pride or self-confidence. ■ (in Greek tragedy) excessive pride toward or defiance of the gods, leading to nemesis. — **hu·bris·tic** /(h)yo͞o'bristik/ adj. [Gk.]

huck·a·back /'həkə,bak/ ▸ n. a strong linen or cotton fabric with a rough surface, used for toweling. [17th C.: of unknown origin.]

huck·le·ber·ry /'həkəl,berē/ ▸ n. **1** a small, round, edible blue-black berry related to the blueberry. **2** the low-growing North American shrub (genus *Gaylussacia*) of the heath family that bears this fruit. [16th C.: prob. based on dial. *huckle* 'hip, haunch.']

huck·ster /'həkstər/ ▸ n. a person who sells small items, either door-to-door or from a stall or small store. ■ a mercenary person eager to make a profit out of anything. ■ a publicity agent or advertising copywriter, esp. for radio or television. ▸ v. [trans.] promote or sell (something, typically a product of questionable value). ■ [intrans.] bargain; haggle. — **huck·ster·ism** n. [ME (in the sense 'retailer at a stall, hawker'): prob. of Low Ger. origin.]

HUD /həd/ ▸ abbr. ■ (Department of) Housing and Urban Development. ■ head-up display.

Hud·ders·field /'hədərz,fēld/ a town in northern England, formerly in Yorkshire; pop. 149,000.

hud·dle /'hədl/ ▸ v. [no obj., with adverbial] crowd together; nestle closely: *they huddled together for warmth.* ■ curl one's body into a small space: *the watchman huddled under his canvas shelter.* ■ draw together for an informal, private conversation: *selection committee members huddled with attorneys.* ▸ n. a crowded or confused mass of people or things. ■ a brief gathering of players during a game to receive instructions, esp. in football. ■ a small group of people holding an informal, private conversation. [16th C. (in the sense 'conceal'): perh. of Low Ger. origin.]

Hud·son /'hədsən/, Henry (*c.*1565–1611), English explorer. He discovered the North American bay, river, and strait that bear his name.

Hud·son Bay an inland sea in northeastern Canada, connected to the North Atlantic via the Hudson Strait.

Hud·son Riv·er a river that rises in eastern New York and flows south for 350 miles (560 km) to the Atlantic Ocean at New York City.

Hud·son's Bay blan·ket (also **Hud·son Bay blan·ket**) ▸ n. a durable woolen blanket, typically with wide colored stripes. [19th C.: orig. sold by the *Hudson's Bay* Company.]

Hud·son's Bay Com·pa·ny a British colonial trading company set up in 1670 and granted all lands draining into Hudson Bay for purposes of commercial exploitation, principally trade in fur.

Hué /(h)wā/ a city in central Vietnam; pop. 219,000.

hue /(h)yo͞o/ ▸ n. a color or shade: *her face lost its golden hue.* ■ the attribute of a color by virtue of which it is discernible as red, green, etc., and which is dependent on its dominant wavelength, and independent of intensity or lightness. ■ fig. character; aspect: *men of all political hues.* — **hued** adj. [in comb.] *rainbow-hued.* **hue·less** adj. [OE *hīw, hēow*, of Gmc. origin; rel. to Swed. *hy* 'skin, complexion.']

hue and cry ▸ n. a loud clamor or public outcry. ■ hist. a loud cry calling for the pursuit and capture of a criminal, raised by the inhabitants of a hundred in which a robbery had been committed if they were not to become liable for the damages. [ME: from the Anglo-Norman Fr. legal phr. *hu e cri*, lit. 'outcry and cry,' from OFr. *hu* 'outcry' (from *huer* 'to shout').]

hue·vos ran·che·ros /'wāvōs ran'CHerōs; rän-/ ▸ n. a dish of fried or poached eggs served on a tortilla with a spicy tomato sauce. [from Amer. Sp., lit. 'eggs cooked in a ranch style.']

huff /həf/ ▸ v. [intrans.] blow out loudly; puff: *he was huffing under a heavy load.* ■ [trans.] express (one's annoyance or offense): *he huffed out his sudden irritation.*
– PHRASES **huff and puff** breathe heavily with exhaustion. ■ express one's annoyance in an obvious or threatening way. — **huff·ish** adj. [16th C.: imitative of the sound of blowing.]

huff·y /'həfē/ ▸ adj. (**huff·i·er, huff·i·est**) annoyed or irritated and quick to take offense at petty things. — **huff·i·ly** adv. **huff·i·ness** n.

hug /həg/ ▸ v. (**hugged, hug·ging**) [trans.] squeeze (someone) tightly in one's arms, typically to express affection. ■ hold (something) closely or tightly around or against part of one's body. ■ fit tightly around: *a pair of jeans that hugged the contours of his body.* ■ keep close to: *I headed north, hugging the coastline all the way.* ■ (**hug oneself**) congratulate or be pleased with oneself. ■ cherish or cling to (something such as a belief). ▸ n. an act of holding someone tightly in one's arms, typically to express affection. ■ a squeezing grip in wrestling. — **hug·ga·ble** adj. [16th C.: prob. of Scand. origin and rel. to Norw. *hugga* 'comfort, console.']

huge /(h)yo͞oj/ ▸ adj. (**hug·er, hug·est**) extremely large; enormous. — **huge·ness** n. [ME: shortening of OFr. *ahuge*, of unknown origin.]

huge·ly /'(h)yo͞ojlē/ ▸ adv. [often as submodifier] very much; to a great extent: *a hugely expensive house.*

hug·ger-mug·ger /'həgər ,məgər/ ▸ adj. **1** confused; disorderly. **2** secret; clandestine. ▸ n. **1** confusion; muddle. **2** secrecy. [16th C.: prob. rel. to **huddle**.]

PRONUNCIATION KEY ə *ago, up*; ər *over, fur*; a *hat*; ā *ate*; ä *car*; e *let*; ē *see*; i *fit*; ī *by*; NG *sing*; ō *go*; ô *law, for*; oi *toy*; o͝o *good*; o͞o *goo*; ou *out*; TH *thin*; T̲H̲ *then*; ZH *vision*

Hughes[1] /hyo͞oz/, Charles Evans (1862–1948) Chief Justice of the US 1930–41. A Republican, he ran unsuccessfully for the presidency in 1916 and was US secretary of state 1921–25.

Hughes[2], Howard Robard (1905–76), US industrialist, director, and aviator. He made his fortune through the Hughes Tool Company, made his debut as a movie director in 1926, and from 1935 to 1938 broke many world aviation records.

Hughes[3], Langston (1902–67), US writer; full name *James Mercer Langston Hughes.* A leading voice of the Harlem Renaissance, he began a prolific literary career with *The Weary Blues* (1926).

Hughes[4], Ted (1930–98), English poet; full name *Edward James Hughes*; husband of Sylvia Plath. He was Britain's poet laureate 1984–98.

Hug·li var. of HOOGHLY.

Hu·go /'(h)yo͞ogō/ Victor (1802–85), French writer; full name *Victor-Marie Hugo.* He wrote the novel *Les Misérables* (1862).

Hu·gue·not /'hyo͞ogə,nät/ ▶ n. a French Protestant, usually Calvinist, of the 16th–17th centuries. [Fr., alt. of *eiguenot*, from Du. *eedgenot*, from Swiss Ger. *Eidgenoss* 'confederate,' from *Eid* 'oath' + *Genoss* 'associate.']

huh /hə/ ▶ exclam. used to express scorn, anger, disbelief, surprise, or amusement. *"Huh," she snorted, "Over my dead body!"* ■ used in questions to invite agreement or further comment or to express a lack of understanding: *pretty devastating, huh?* [natural utterance: first recorded in Engl. in the 17th C.]

Hu·he·hot /'ho͞ohä,hōt/ variant of HOHHOT.

hui·sa·che /wē'säCHē/ ▶ n. an acacia tree (*Acacia farnesiana*) with violet-scented flowers that yield an essential oil used in perfumery.

hu·la /'ho͞olə/ (also **hu·la-hu·la**) ▶ n. a dance performed by Hawaiian women, characterized by six basic steps, undulating hips, and gestures symbolizing natural phenomena or historical or mythological subjects.

hu·la hoop (also trademark **Hu·la-Hoop**) ▶ n. a large hoop spun around the body by gyrating the hips, for play or exercise.

hulk /həlk/ ▶ n. **1** an old ship stripped of fittings and permanently moored, esp. for use as storage or (formerly) as a prison. ■ any large disused structure. **2** a large or unwieldy boat or other object. ■ a large, clumsy-looking person. ▶ v. [intrans.] appear large or threatening: *cliffs hulking above glacial streams.* ■ move heavily or clumsily: *a single figure hulking across the screen.* [OE *hulc* 'fast ship,' prob. of Mediterranean origin and rel. to Gk. *holkas* 'cargo ship.']

hulk·ing /'həlkiNG/ ▶ adj. informal (of a person or object) large, heavy, or clumsy: *a hulking young man.*

Hull[1] /həl/ a city in northeastern England, situated at the junction of the Hull and Humber rivers; pop. 252,000. Official name KINGSTON-UPON-HULL.

Hull[2], Bobby (1939–), Canadian hockey player; full name *Robert Marvin Hull, Jr.* He played professionally 1957–81.

Hull[3], Cordell (1871–1955), US secretary of state 1933–44. Nobel Peace Prize (1945).

hull[1] /həl/ ▶ n. the main body of a ship or other vessel, including the bottom, sides, and deck but not the masts, superstructure, rigging, engines, and other fittings. ▶ v. [trans.] (usu. **be hulled**) hit and pierce the hull of (a ship) with a shell or other missile. — **hulled** adj. [in comb.] *a wooden-hulled sailboat.* [ME: perh. the same word as HULL[2], or rel. to HOLD[2].]

hull[2] ▶ n. the outer covering of a fruit or seed, esp. the pod of peas and beans, or the husk of grain. ■ the green calyx of a strawberry or raspberry. ▶ v. [trans.] [usu. as adj.] (**hulled**) remove the hulls from (fruit, seeds, or grain). [OE *hulu*, of Gmc. origin; rel. to Ger. *Hülse* 'husk, pod.']

hul·la·ba·loo /'hələbə,lo͞o; ,hələbə'lo͞o/ ▶ n. [in sing.] informal a commotion; a fuss. [18th C.: reduplication of *hallo*, *hullo*, etc.]

hul·lo /hə'lō/ ▶ exclam. var. of HELLO. [first recorded, in this form, in T. Hughes' *Tom Brown's Schooldays* (1857).]

hum[1] /həm/ ▶ v. (**hummed, hum·ming**) [intrans.] make a low, steady continuous sound like that of a bee. ■ sing with closed lips: *humming to himself* | [trans.] *humming a cheerful tune.* ■ (of a place) be filled with a low, steady continuous sound: *the room* ***hummed with*** *an expectant murmur.* ■ informal be in a state of great activity: *the repair shops are humming.* ▶ n. [in sing.] a low, steady, continuous sound. ■ an unwanted low-frequency noise in an amplifier caused by variation of electric current. — **hum·ma·ble** adj. **hum·mer** n. [ME: imitative.]

hum[2] ▶ exclam. used to express hesitation or dissent: *"Ah, hum, Elaine, isn't it?"* [16th C.: imitative or rel. to the v. HUM[1].]

hu·man /'(h)yo͞omən/ ▶ adj. of, relating to, or characteristic of people or human beings. ■ of or characteristic of people as opposed to God or animals or machines, esp. in being susceptible to weaknesses: *the risk of human error.* ■ of or characteristic of people's better qualities, such as kindness or sensitivity: *the human side of politics.* ▶ n. a human being, esp. a person as distinguished from an animal or (in science fiction) an alien. — **hu·man·ness** n. [ME *humaine*, from OFr. *humain(e)*, from L. *humanus*, from *homo* 'man, human being.']

hu·man be·ing ▶ n. a man, woman, or child of the species *Homo sapiens*, distinguished from other animals by superior mental development, power of articulate speech, and upright stance.

hu·man cap·i·tal ▶ n. the skills, knowledge, and experience possessed by an individual or population, viewed in terms of their value or cost to an organization or country.

hu·man chain ▶ n. a line of people formed for passing things quickly from one site to another. ■ a line or circle of people linking hands in a protest or demonstration.

hu·man cho·ri·on·ic go·nad·o·tro·pin /,kôrē'änik ,gō,nadə'trōpin/ (abbr.: **HCG**) ▶ n. a hormone produced in the human placenta that maintains the corpus luteum during pregnancy.

hu·mane /(h)yo͞o'mān/ ▶ adj. **1** having or showing compassion or benevolence. ■ inflicting the minimum of pain. **2** formal (of a branch of learning) intended to have a civilizing or refining effect on people. — **hu·mane·ly** adv. **hu·mane·ness** n. [ME: the earlier form of HUMAN.]

hu·man e·col·o·gy ▶ n. see ECOLOGY.

hu·man en·gi·neer·ing ▶ n. the management of industrial labor, esp. with regard to relationships between people and machines; ergonomics.

Hu·man Ge·nome Pro·ject an international project to map the entire genetic material of a human being.

hu·man in·ter·est ▶ n. the aspect of a story in the media that interests people because it describes the experiences or emotions of individuals.

hu·man·ism /'(h)yo͞omə,nizəm/ ▶ n. an outlook or system of thought attaching prime importance to human rather than divine or supernatural matters. ■ (often **Humanism**) a Renaissance cultural movement that turned away from medieval scholasticism and revived interest in ancient Greek and Roman thought. — **hu·man·ist** n. & adj. **hu·man·is·tic** /,(h)yo͞omə'nistik/ adj. **hu·man·is·ti·cal·ly** /,(h)yo͞omə'nistik(ə)lē/ adv.

hu·man·i·tar·i·an /(h)yo͞o,mani'te(ə)rēən/ ▶ adj. concerned with or seeking to promote human welfare: *groups sending humanitarian aid.* ▶ n. a person who seeks to promote human welfare; a philanthropist. — **hu·man·i·tar·i·an·ism** n.

hu·man·i·ty /(h)yo͞o'manitē/ ▶ n. (pl. **-ties**) **1** the human race; human beings collectively. ■ the fact or condition of being human; human nature. **2** humaneness; benevolence. **3** (**humanities**) learning or literature concerned with human culture, esp. literature, history, art, music, and philosophy.

hu·man·ize /'(h)yo͞omə,nīz/ ▶ v. [trans.] **1** make (something) more humane or civilized. **2** give (something) a human character. — **hu·man·i·za·tion** /,hyo͞oməni'zāSHən/ n.

hu·man·kind /'(h)yo͞omən,kīnd/ ▶ n. human beings considered collectively (used as a neutral alternative to "mankind"): *the origin of humankind.*

hu·man·ly /'(h)yo͞omənlē/ ▶ adv. **1** from a human point of view; in a human manner. ■ by human means; within human ability. **2** esp. archaic with human feeling or kindness.

hu·man na·ture ▶ n. the general psychological characteristics, feelings, and behavioral traits of humankind, regarded as shared by all humans.

hu·man·oid /'(h)yo͞omə,noid/ ▶ adj. having an appearance or character resembling that of a human. ▶ n. (esp. in science fiction) a being resembling a human in its shape.

hu·man re·la·tions ▶ plural n. relations with or between people, particularly the treatment of people in a professional context.

hu·man re·sourc·es ▶ plural n. the personnel of a business or organization, esp. when regarded as a significant asset. ■ the department of a business or organization that deals with the administration, management, and training of personnel.

hu·man right ▶ n. (usu. **human rights**) a right that is believed to belong justifiably to every person.

hu·man shield ▶ n. a person or group of people held near a potential target to deter attack.

hu·man T cell lym·pho·tro·pic vi·rus /,limfō'träpik; -'trōpik/ (abbr.: **HTLV**) ▶ n. any of a group of retroviruses that cause disease by attacking T cells.

Hum·ber /'həmbər/ an estuary in northeastern England, formed at the junction of the Ouse and Trent rivers near Goole and flowing east for 38 miles (60 km) to the North Sea.

hum·ble /'həmbəl/ ▶ adj. (**hum·bler, hum·blest**) **1** having or showing a modest or low estimate of one's own importance. ■ (of an action or thought) offered with or affected by such an estimate of one's own importance. **2** of low social, administrative, or political rank. ■ (of a thing) of modest pretensions or dimensions. ▶ v. [trans.] lower (someone) in dignity or importance: *I knew he had* ***humbled himself*** *to ask for my help.* ■ (usu. **be humbled**) decisively defeat (another team or competitor, typically one that was previously thought to be superior).
– PHRASES **eat humble pie** make a humble apology and accept humiliation. — **hum·ble·ness** n. **hum·bly** adv. [ME: from OFr., from L. *humilis* 'low, lowly,' from *humus* 'ground.']

hum·ble·bee ▶ n. another term for BUMBLEBEE. [ME: prob. from Mid. Low Ger. *hummelbē*, from *hummel* 'to buzz' + *bē* 'bee.']

hum·bug /'həm,bəg/ ▶ n. **1** deceptive or false talk or behavior. ■ a hypocrite. **2** Brit. a hard candy, esp. one flavored with peppermint. ▶ v. (**-bugged, -bug·ging**) [trans.] deceive; trick. — **hum·bug·ger·y** n. [18th C. (in the senses 'hoax, trick' and 'deceiver'): of unknown origin.]

hum·ding·er /'həm'diNGər/ ▶ n. informal a remarkable or outstanding person or thing of its kind. [20th C. (orig. US): of unknown origin.]

hum·drum /'həm,drəm/ ▶ adj. lacking excitement or variety; dull; monotonous. ▶ n. dullness; monotony. [16th C.: prob. a reduplication of HUM[1].]

Hume /hyo͞om/, David (1711–76), Scottish philosopher. He rejected the possibility of certainty in knowledge. — **Hum·e·an** /'hyo͞omēən/ **adj. & n.**

hu·mec·tant /(h)yo͞o'mektənt/ ▶ **adj.** retaining or preserving moisture. ▶ **n.** a substance, esp. a skin lotion or a food additive, used to reduce the loss of moisture. [19th C. (denoting a moistening agent): from L. *humectant-* 'moistening,' from the v. *humectare*, from *humectus* 'moist, wet,' from *humere* 'be moist.']

hu·mer·al /'(h)yo͞omərəl/ ▶ **adj.** [attrib.] of or relating to the humerus of a human or other vertebrate. [16th C.: from Fr., or from late L. *humeralis*, from L. *humerus* (see HUMERUS).]

hu·mer·us /'(h)yo͞omərəs/ ▶ **n.** (pl. **-mer·i** /-mə,rī/) Anat. the bone of the upper arm or forelimb, forming joints at the shoulder and the elbow. [ME: from L., 'shoulder.']

hu·mic /'(h)yo͞omik/ ▶ **adj.** [attrib.] relating to or consisting of humus: *humic acids.*

hu·mid /'(h)yo͞omid/ ▶ **adj.** marked by a relatively high level of water vapor in the atmosphere. — **hu·mid·ly adv.** [ME: from Fr. *humide* or L. *humidus*, from *humere* 'be moist.']

hu·mid·i·fi·er /(h)yo͞o'midə,fī(ə)r/ ▶ **n.** a device for keeping the atmosphere moist in a room.

hu·mid·i·fy /(h)yo͞o'midə,fī/ ▶ **v.** (**-fies, -fied**) [trans.] [often as adj.] (**humidified**) increase the level of moisture in (air): *a regulated flow of humidified air.* — **hu·mid·i·fi·ca·tion** /-,midəfi'kāsHən/ **n.**

hu·mid·i·stat /(h)yo͞o'midi,stat/ ▶ **n.** a machine or device that automatically regulates the humidity of the air in a room or building.

hu·mid·i·ty /(h)yo͞o'miditē/ ▶ **n.** (pl. **-ties**) the state or quality of being humid. ■ a quantity representing the amount of water vapor in the atmosphere or a gas.

hu·mi·dor /'(h)yo͞omi,dôr/ ▶ **n.** an airtight container for keeping cigars or tobacco moist. [20th C.: from HUMID, on the pattern of *cuspidor.*]

hu·mi·fy /'(h)yo͞omə,fī/ ▶ **v.** (**-fies, -fied**) [trans.] convert (plant remains) into humus. — **hu·mi·fi·ca·tion** /,(h)yo͞omifi'kāsHən/ **n.**

hu·mil·i·ate /(h)yo͞o'milē,āt/ ▶ **v.** [trans.] make (someone) feel ashamed and foolish by injuring their dignity and self-respect, esp. publicly. — **hu·mil·i·at·ing·ly** /-,ātiNGlē/ **adv.** **hu·mil·i·a·tion** /-,milē'āsHən/ **n.** **hu·mil·i·a·tor** /-,ātər/ **n.** [16th C.: from late L. *humiliat-* 'made humble,' from the v. *humiliare*, from *humilis* (see HUMBLE).]

hu·mil·i·ty /(h)yo͞o'militē/ ▶ **n.** a modest or low view of one's own importance; humbleness.

hu·mint /'(h)yo͞omint/ ▶ **n.** covert intelligence-gathering by agents or others. [20th C.: from *human intelligence.*]

Hum·mel /'həməl/, Berta (1909–46), German painter and nun; also known as **Sister Maria Innocentia**. She created the sketches upon which M. I. Hummel figurines are based.

hum·ming·bird /'həmiNG,bərd/ ▶ **n.** a small nectar-feeding tropical American bird (family Trochilidae) that is able to hover and fly backward, typically having colorful iridescent plumage. Its numerous species include the **ruby-throated hummingbird** (*Archilochus colubris*) of the eastern US.

hum·ming·bird hawk moth (also **hummingbird moth**) ▶ **n.** a migratory day-flying hawk moth that makes an audible hum while hovering in front of flowers to feed on nectar.

hum·mock /'həmək/ ▶ **n.** a hillock, knoll, or mound. ■ a hump or ridge in an ice field. ■ a piece of forested ground rising above a marsh. — **hum·mock·y adj.** [16th C.: of unknown origin.]

hum·mus /'ho͝oməs; 'həm-/ (also **houm·mos** or **hum·ous**) ▶ **n.** a thick paste or spread made from ground chickpeas and sesame seeds, olive oil, lemon, and garlic, made originally in the Middle East. [from Arab. *ḥummuṣ.*]

hu·mon·gous /(h)yo͞o'məNGgəs; -'mäNG-/ (also **hu·mun·gous**) ▶ **adj.** informal huge; enormous. [1970s: possibly based on HUGE and MONSTROUS.]

hu·mor /'(h)yo͞omər/ (Brit. **hu·mour**) ▶ **n.** **1** the quality of being amusing or comic, esp. as expressed in literature or speech. ■ the ability to perceive or express humor or to appreciate a joke: *she has a great sense of humor.* **2** a mood or state of mind: *the clash hadn't improved his humor.* ■ archaic an inclination or whim. **3** (also **cardinal humor**) hist. each of the four chief fluids of the body (blood, phlegm, yellow bile [choler], and black bile [melancholy]) that were thought to determine a person's physical and mental qualities. ▶ **v.** [trans.] comply with the wishes of (someone) in order to keep them content, however unreasonable such wishes might be.

– PHRASES **out of humor** in a bad mood. — **hu·mor·less adj.** **hu·mor·less·ly adv.** **hu·mor·less·ness n.** [ME (as *humour*): via OFr. from L. *humor* 'moisture,' from *humere* (see HUMID).]

hu·mor·al /'(h)yo͞omərəl/ ▶ **adj.** Med. of or relating to the body fluids, esp. with regard to immune responses involving antibodies in body fluids as distinct from cells (see CELL-MEDIATED). ■ hist. of or relating to the four bodily humors. ■ Med., hist. (of diseases) caused by or attributed to a disordered state of the bodily humors. [ME (in the general sense 'relating to bodily fluids'): from OFr., or from med. L. *humoralis*, from L. *humor* 'moisture' (see HUMOR).]

hu·mor·esque /,(h)yo͞omə'resk/ ▶ **n.** a short, lively piece of music. [19th C.: from Ger. *Humoreske*, from *Humor* 'humor.']

hu·mor·ist /'(h)yo͞omərist/ ▶ **n.** a humorous writer, performer, or artist.

hu·mor·ous /'(h)yo͞omərəs/ ▶ **adj.** causing lighthearted laughter and amusement; comic. ■ having or showing a sense of humor. — **hu·mor·ous·ly adv.** **hu·mor·ous·ness n.**

hu·mour ▶ **n.** British spelling of HUMOR.

hu·mous ▶ **n.** var. of HUMMUS.

hump /həmp/ ▶ **n.** a rounded protuberance found on the back of a camel or other animal or as an abnormality on a person's back. ■ a rounded raised mass of earth or land. ▶ **v.** **1** [with obj. and adverbial of direction] informal lift or carry (a heavy object) with difficulty: *he humped cases up and down the hotel corridor.* ■ [no obj., with adverbial of direction] move heavily and awkwardly: *the elephant seal humping along the ground in waves of blubber.* **2** [trans.] make hump-shaped: *the cat humped himself and purred.* **3** [intrans.] vulgar slang have sexual intercourse. ■ [trans.] have sexual intercourse with (someone).

– PHRASES **over the hump** over the worst or most difficult part of something. — **humped adj.** *a humped back* **hump·less adj.** **hump·y adj.** (**hump·i·er, hump·i·est**). [18th C.: prob. rel. to Low Ger. *humpe* 'hump.']

hump·back /'həmp,bak/ ▶ **n.** **1** (also **humpback whale**) a baleen whale (*Megaptera novaeangliae*) that has a hump (instead of a dorsal fin) and long white flippers. It is noted for its lengthy vocalizations or "songs." **2** (also **humpback salmon**) another term for PINK SALMON. **3** another term for HUNCHBACK. — **hump·backed adj.**

Hum·per·dinck /'həmpər,diNGk/, Engelbert (1854–1921), German composer. He wrote the opera *Hänsel und Gretel* (1893).

humph /həmf/ ▶ **exclam.** used to express slightly scornful doubt or dissatisfaction. [natural utterance: first recorded in Engl. in the 16th C.]

Hum·phrey /'həmfrē/, Hubert Horatio (1911–78) vice president of the US 1965–69. A Democratic presidential candidate in 1968, he served in the US Senate 1949–64, 1971–78.

Hump·ty Dump·ty /'həm(p)tē 'dəm(p)tē/ (also **hump·ty dump·ty**) ▶ **n.** (pl. **Hump·ty Dump·ties**) informal **1** a fat, rotund person. [as adj.] **2** a person or thing that once overthrown cannot be restored. [18th C.: from the egglike nursery-rhyme character *Humpty Dumpty*, who fell off a wall and could not be put together again.]

hu·mun·gous ▶ **adj.** var. of HUMONGOUS.

hu·mus /'(h)yo͞oməs/ ▶ **n.** the organic component of soil, formed by the decomposition of leaves and other plant material by soil microorganisms. [18th C.: from L., lit. 'soil.']

Hum·vee /'həm'vē/ ▶ **n.** trademark a modern military vehicle.

Hun /hən/ ▶ **n.** **1** a member of a warlike Asiatic nomadic people who ravaged Europe in the 4th–5th centuries. ■ a reckless or uncivilized destroyer of something. **2** informal, derog. a German (esp. in military contexts during World War I and World War II). ■ (**the Hun**) Germans collectively. — **Hun·nish adj.** [OE *Hūne, Hūnas* (pl.), from late L. *Hunni*, from Gk. *Hounnoi*, of Middle Iranian origin.]

Hu·nan /'ho͞o'nän/ a province in eastern central China; capital, Changsha.

hunch /hənCH/ ▶ **v.** [trans.] raise (one's shoulders) and bend the top of one's body forward: *he hunched his shoulders* | [intrans.] *he hunched over his glass.* ■ [intrans.] bend one's body into a huddled position: *I hunched up as small as I could.* ▶ **n.** **1** a feeling or guess based on intuition rather than known facts: *acting on a hunch.* **2** a humped position or thing: *the hunch of his back.* [15th C.: of unknown origin. The original meaning was 'push, shove' (n. and v.).]

hunch·back /'hənCH,bak/ ▶ **n.** a back deformed by a sharp forward angle, forming a hump. ■ often offens. a person with such a deformity. — **hunch·backed adj.**

hun·dred /'həndrid/ ▶ **cardinal number** (pl. **-dreds** or (with numeral or quantifying word) **-dred**) (**a/one hundred**) the number equivalent to the product of ten and ten; ten more than ninety; 100: *a hundred yards away* | *there are just a hundred of us here.* (Roman numeral: **c** or **C.**) ■ (**hundreds**) the numbers from 100 to 999: *a large number, probably in the hundreds, were lost.* ■ (**hundreds**) several hundred things or people: *hundreds of dollars.* ■ (usu. **hundreds**) informal an unspecified large number: *hundreds of letters poured in.* ■ (**the —— hundreds**) the years of a specified century: *the early nineteen hundreds.* ■ one hundred years old. ■ one hundred miles per hour. ■ a hundred-dollar bill: ■ (chiefly in spoken English) used to express whole hours in the twenty-four-hour system: *thirteen hundred hours.* ▶ **n.** Brit., hist. a subdivision of a county or shire.

– PHRASES **a** (or **one**) **hundred percent** entirely; completely. ■ [usu. with negative] informal completely fit and healthy: *I wasn't exactly one hundred percent.* ■ informal maximum effort and commitment: *he always gave one hundred percent for the team.* — **hun·dred·fold adj. & adv.** **hun·dredth** /'həndridTH; 'həndritTH/ **ordinal number.** [OE, from *hund* 'hundred' (from an Indo-Eur. root shared with L. *centum* and Gk. *hekaton*) + a second element meaning 'number'.]

Hun·dred Flow·ers a campaign in China 1956–57, when, under the slogan "Let a hundred flowers bloom and a hundred schools of thought contend," citizens were invited to voice their opinions, forcibly ended after fierce criticism of the government.

hun·dred·weight /'həndrid,wāt/ (abbr.: **cwt**) ▶ **n.** (pl. same or **-weights**) a unit of weight equal to one twentieth of a ton, in particular: ■ (also **short hun·dred·weight**) (in the US) equal to 100 lb avoirdupois (about 45.4 kg). ■ (also **metric hundredweight**) (in the metric system) equal to 50 kg. ■ (also **long hundredweight**) (in the UK) equal to 112 lb avoirdupois (about 50.8 kg).

Hun·dred Years War a war between France and England, conventionally dated 1337–1453.

hung /həNG/ past and past participle of HANG. ▶ **adj.** **1** (of a jury) unable to agree on a verdict. **2** [predic.] (**hung up**) informal emotionally confused or disturbed: *people are hung up in all sorts of ways.* ■ (**hung up about/on**) have a psychological or emotional obsession or problem about: *hung up about the way they look.* ■ delayed or detained: *hung up in traffic.*

Hun·gar·i·an /hənɢ'ge(ə)rēən/ ▶ adj. of or relating to Hungary, its people, or their language. ▶ n. **1** a native or national of Hungary. ■ a person of Hungarian descent. **2** an Ugric language, the official language of Hungary, spoken also in Romania. Also called MAGYAR.

Hungary

Official name: Republic of Hungary
Location: central Europe, south of Slovakia, east of Austria, and west of Romania
Area: 35,700 square miles (92,300 sq km)
Population: 10,032,000
Capital: Budapest
Language: Hungarian
Currency: forint

Hun·ga·ry /'hənɢgərē/ a country in central Europe. *See box.* Hungarian name MAGYARORSZÁG.

hun·ger /'hənɢgər/ ▶ n. a feeling of discomfort or weakness caused by lack of food, coupled with the desire to eat. ■ a severe lack of food: *they died from cold and hunger.* ■ a strong desire or craving: *her hunger for knowledge.* ▶ v. [intrans.] (**hunger after/for**) have a strong desire or craving for. [OE *hungor* (n.), *hyngran* (v.), of Gmc. origin; rel. to Du. *honger* and Ger. *Hunger.*]

hun·ger strike ▶ n. a prolonged refusal to eat, carried out as a protest, typically by a prisoner. — **hun·ger strik·er** n.

hung·o·ver /'hənɢ'ōvər/ (also **hung over**) ▶ adj. suffering from a hangover after drinking alcohol.

hun·gry /'hənɢgrē/ ▶ adj. (**-gri·er, -gri·est**) feeling or displaying the need for food. ■ having a strong desire or craving: *he was **hungry for** any kind of excitement* | [in comb.] *power-hungry.* — **hun·gri·ly** adv. **hun·gri·ness** n. [OE *hungrig*, of West Gmc. origin; rel. to Du. *hongerig*, Ger. *hungrig*, also to HUNGER.]

Hun·jiang /'ho͝onɢ'jyänɢ/ a city in Jilin province, in northeastern China; pop. 694,000.

hunk /hənɢk/ ▶ n. **1** a large piece of something, esp. one of food cut or broken off a larger piece. **2** informal a sexually attractive man, esp. a large, strong one. — **hunk·y** adj. (**hunk·i·er, hunk·i·est**). [19th C.: prob. of Du. or Low Ger. origin.]

hunk·er /'hənɢkər/ ▶ v. [intrans.] squat or crouch down low: *he **hunkered down** beside her.* ■ take shelter in a defensive position: ***hunker down** and let it blow over.* ■ fig. apply oneself seriously to a task: *students **hunkered down** for the examinations.* [18th C.: prob. rel. to Du. *huiken* and Ger. *hocken.*]

hunk·y-do·ry /'hənɢkē 'dôrē/ ▶ adj. informal fine; going well: *everything is hunky-dory.* [19th C. (orig. US): *hunky* from Du. *honk* 'home, base' (in games); the origin of *dory* is unknown.]

Hunt[1] /hənt/, Holman (1827–1910), English painter; full name *William Holman Hunt.* He cofounded the Pre-Raphaelite Brotherhood.

Hunt[2], Ward (1810–86), US Supreme Court associate justice 1873–82.

hunt /hənt/ ▶ v. **1** [trans.] pursue and kill (a wild animal) for sport or food: *in the autumn they hunted deer* | [intrans.] *they hunted and fished.* ■ (of an animal) chase and kill (its prey): *mice are hunted by weasels and foxes* | [intrans.] *lionesses hunt in groups.* ■ [intrans.] try to find someone or something by searching carefully: *he **hunted for** a new job.* ■ (**hunt something out/up**) search for something until it is found. ■ [trans.] (of the police) search for (a criminal): *the gang is being hunted by police* | [intrans.] *police are **hunting for** her attacker.* ■ (**hunt someone down**) pursue and capture someone. **2** [intrans.] (of a machine, instrument needle, or system) oscillate around a desired speed, position, or state. ■ (of an automatic transmission in a motor vehicle) keep shifting between gears because of improperly designed shift logic. **3** [intrans.] (**hunt down/up**) (in change-ringing) move the place of a bell in a simple progression. ▶ n. **1** an act of hunting wild animals or game. ■ an association of people who meet regularly to hunt, esp. with hounds. ■ an area where hunting takes place. ■ a search. **2** an oscillating motion around a desired speed, position, or state. [OE *huntian*, of Gmc. origin.]

hunt-and-peck ▶ adj. denoting or using an inexpert form of typing in which only one or two fingers are used: *hunt-and-peck computer users.*

hunt·ed /'həntid/ ▶ adj. being pursued or searched for: *they ran like hunted hares.* ■ appearing worn or harassed as if one is being pursued: *his eyes had a hunted look.*

hunt·er /'hən(t)ər/ ▶ n. a person or animal that hunts: *a deer hunter.* ■ a person searching for something: *a bargain hunter.* ■ a horse of a breed developed for stamina in fox hunting and ability to jump obstacles.

hunt·er-gath·er·er ▶ n. a member of a nomadic people who live chiefly by hunting, fishing, and harvesting wild food.

hunt·er's moon ▶ n. the first full moon after a harvest moon.

hunt·ing /'həntinɢ/ ▶ n. **1** the activity of hunting wild animals or game, esp. for food or sport. **2** (also **plain hunting**) Bell-ringing a simple system of changes in which bells move through the order in a regular progression.

hunt·ing dog ▶ n. a dog of a breed developed for hunting.

hunt·ing ground ▶ n. a place used or suitable for hunting. ■ fig. a place where people can observe or acquire what they want: *the circuit is a favorite hunting ground for talent scouts.*

hunt·ing horn ▶ n. a horn blown to give signals during hunting.

Hun·ting·ton /'həntinɢtən/ **1** a town in northern Long Island in New York that includes Huntington, Cold Spring Harbor, and other villages; pop. 191,474. **2** a city in southwestern West Virginia; pop. 51,475.

Hun·ting·ton Beach a city in southern California, on the Pacific coast; pop. 181,519.

Hun·ting·ton's cho·re·a /'həntinɢtənz kə'rēə/ ▶ n. a hereditary disease marked by degeneration of the brain cells and causing chorea and progressive dementia. [19th C.: named after George *Huntington* (1851–1916), the US neurologist who first described it.]

hunt·ress /'həntris/ ▶ n. a woman who hunts.

hunts·man /'həntsmən/ ▶ n. (pl. **-men**) a person who hunts. ■ a hunt official in charge of hounds.

Hunts·ville /'hənts,vil/ a city in northern Alabama; pop. 158,216.

Hu·on pine /'(h)yo͞o-än/ ▶ n. a tall Tasmanian conifer (*Dacrydium franklinii*, family Podocarpaceae) that has yewlike berries and fragrant red timber. [19th C.: *Huon*, river in Tasmania.]

hup /həp/ ▶ exclam. used as a way of encouraging a marching rhythm: *hup, two, three!*

Hu·peh /'ho͞o'pā/ variant of HUBEI.

hur·dle /'hərdl/ ▶ n. **1** an upright frame, typically one of a series, that athletes in a race must jump over. ■ (**hurdles**) a hurdle race. **2** an obstacle or difficulty. **3** esp. Brit. a portable rectangular frame strengthened with willow branches or wooden bars, used as a temporary fence. ■ a horse race over a series of such frames: *a handicap hurdle.* ■ hist. a frame on which traitors were dragged to execution. ▶ v. [intrans.] [often as n.] (**hurdling**) take part in a race that involves jumping hurdles. ■ [trans.] jump over (a hurdle or other obstacle) while running. [OE *hyrdel* 'temporary fence,' of Gmc. origin; rel. to Du. *horde* and Ger. *Hürde.*]

hur·dler /'hərdlər/ ▶ n. an athlete, dog, or horse that runs in hurdle races.

hur·dy-gur·dy /'hərdē ,gərdē/ ▶ n. (pl. **-dies**) a musical instrument with a droning sound played by turning a handle. ■ informal a barrel organ. [18th C.: prob. imitative of the sound of the instrument.]

hurl /hərl/ ▶ v. [with obj. and adverbial of direction] throw (an object) with great force: *rioters hurled a brick through the windshield of a car.* ■ Baseball informal pitch. ■ push or impel (someone) violently. ■ utter (abuse) vehemently: *they were hurling insults over a back fence.* ■ [intrans.] informal vomit. — **hurl·er** n. [ME: prob. imitative.]

hurl·ing /'hərlinɢ/ ▶ n. an Irish game resembling field hockey.

hurl·y-burl·y /'hərlē 'bərlē/ ▶ n. busy, boisterous activity: *the hurly-burly of school life.* [ME: reduplication based on HURL.]

Hu·ron /'hyo͝o,rän/ ▶ n. (pl. same or **-rons**) **1** a member of a confederation of native North American peoples formerly living in the region east of Lake Huron and now settled mainly in Oklahoma and Quebec. **2** the extinct Iroquoian language of any of these peoples. ▶ adj. of or relating to these peoples or their language. [Fr., lit. 'having hair standing in bristles on the head.']

Hu·ron, Lake /'(h)yo͝orən; '(h)yo͝or,än/ the second largest of the five Great Lakes, on the border between Canada and the US.

hur·rah /ho͞o'rä; hə-/ (also **hoo·ray, hur·ray** /-'rā/) ▶ exclam. used to express joy or approval. ▶ n. an utterance of the word "hurrah." ▶ v. [intrans.] shout "hurrah." [17th C.: alt. of archaic *huzza*; perh. orig. a sailors' cry when hauling.]

Hur·ri·an /'ho͝orēən/ ▶ adj. of, relating to, or denoting an ancient people who inhabited Syria and northern Mesopotamia during the 3rd–2nd millennia BC and were later absorbed by the Hittites and Assyrians. ▶ n. **1** a member of this people. **2** the language of the Hurrians, of unknown affinity.

hur·ri·cane /'həri,kān/ ▶ n. a storm with a violent wind, in particular a tropical cyclone in the Caribbean. ■ a wind of force 12 on the Beaufort scale (equal to or exceeding 64 knots or 74 mph). ■ fig. a violent uproar or outburst. [16th C.: from Sp. *huracán*, prob. from Taino *hurakán* 'god of the storm.']

hur·ri·cane deck ▶ n. a covered deck at or near the top of a ship's superstructure.

hur·ri·cane lamp ▶ n. an oil lamp with a glass chimney, designed to protect the flame even in high winds.

hur·ry /ˈhərē; ˈhə-rē/ ▶ v. (**-ries, -ried**) [intrans.] move or act with haste; rush: *we'd better hurry.* ■ [often in imper.] (**hurry up**) do something more quickly: *hurry up and finish your meal.* ■ [trans.] cause to move or proceed with haste: *she hurried him across the landing.* ■ [trans.] (often **be hurried**) do or finish (something) quickly, typically too quickly: *formalities were hurried over.* ▶ n. great haste. ■ [with negative and in questions] a need for haste; urgency: *there's no hurry to get back.*

– PHRASES **in a hurry** rushed; in a rushed manner: *the city offers fast food if you're in a hurry.* ■ eager to get a thing done quickly: *no one seemed in a hurry for the results.* ■ [usu. with negative] informal easily; readily: *an experience you won't forget in a hurry.* — **hur·ried·ly** /ˈhərēdlē; ˈhəridlē/ adv. **hur·ried·ness** /ˈhərēdnis/ n. [16th C. (as a v.): imitative.]

hur·ry-scur·ry /ˈhərē ˈskərē/ archaic ▶ n. disorderly haste; confused hurrying. ▶ adj. & adv. with hurry and confusion. [18th C.: reduplication of HURRY.]

hur·ry-up ▶ adj. [attrib.] informal showing, involving, or requiring haste or urgency.

hurst /hərst/ ▶ n. a hillock. ■ a sandbank in the sea or a river. ■ [usu. in place names] a wood or wooded rise. [OE *hyrst*, of Gmc. origin; rel. to Ger. *Horst*.]

Hurs·ton /ˈhərstən/, Zora Neale (1901–60), US writer. Her novels reflect her interest in the folklore of the Deep South. She wrote *Seraph on the Suwanee* (1948).

hurt /hərt/ ▶ v. (past and past part. **hurt**) [trans.] cause physical pain or injury to: *Ow! You're hurting me!* | [intrans.] *does acupuncture hurt?* ■ [intrans.] (of a part of the body) suffer pain. ■ cause mental pain or distress to (a person or their feelings). ■ [intrans.] (of a person) feel mental pain or distress: *he was hurting badly.* ■ be detrimental to: *high interest rates are hurting the local economy.* ■ [intrans.] (**hurt for**) informal have a pressing need for: *Frank wasn't hurting for money.* ▶ n. physical injury; harm. ■ mental pain or distress. [ME (orig. in the senses 'to strike' and 'a blow'): from OFr. *hurter* (v.), *hurt* (n.), perh. ult. of Gmc. origin.]

hurt·ful /ˈhərtfəl/ ▶ adj. causing distress to someone's feelings: *his hurtful remarks.* — **hurt·ful·ly** adv. **hurt·ful·ness** n.

hur·tle /ˈhərtl/ ▶ v. [no obj., with adverbial of direction] move at a great speed, typically in a wildly uncontrolled manner: *a runaway car hurtled toward them.* ■ [with obj. and adverbial of direction] cause to move in such a way: *the branch flew off and hurtled us into a ditch.* [ME (in the sense 'strike against, collide with'): frequentative of HURT.]

Hu·sain var. of HUSSEIN[2], HUSSEIN[3].

Hu·sák /ˈhōōsäk/, Gustáv (1913–91), president of Czechoslovakia 1975–89.

hus·band /ˈhəzbənd/ ▶ n. a married man considered in relation to his wife. ▶ v. [trans.] use (resources) economically; conserve. — **hus·band·er** n. (rare). **hus·band·hood** /-ˌhŏŏd/ n. **hus·band·less** adj. **hus·band·ly** adj. [OE (in the senses 'male head of a household' and 'manager, steward'), from ON *húsbóndi* 'master of a house,' from *hús* 'house' + *bóndi* 'occupier and tiller of the soil.']

hus·band·man /ˈhəzbəndmən/ ▶ n. (pl. **-men**) archaic a person who cultivates the land; a farmer. [ME (orig. in north. Engl. use denoting the holder of a *husbandland*, i.e., manorial tenancy): from HUSBAND in the obs. sense 'farmer' + MAN.]

hus·band·ry /ˈhəzbəndrē/ ▶ n. **1** the care, cultivation, and breeding of crops and animals. **2** management and conservation of resources.

hush /həsн/ ▶ v. [trans.] make (someone) be quiet or stop talking. ■ [no obj., often in imper.] be quiet. ■ (**hush something up**) suppress public mention of something. ▶ n. [in sing.] a silence. [16th C.: back-form. from obs. *husht* 'silent, hushed,' from *husht* 'quiet!']

hush·a·by /ˈhəsнəˌbī/ (also **hush·a·bye**) ▶ exclam. archaic used to calm a child.

hushed /həsнt/ ▶ adj. having a calm and still silence. ■ (of a voice or conversation) quiet and serious.

hush-hush ▶ adj. informal (esp. of an official plan or project) highly secret or confidential.

hush mon·ey ▶ n. informal money paid to someone to prevent them from disclosing embarrassing or discreditable information.

hush pup·py ▶ n. cornmeal dough that has been quickly deep-fried.

husk /həsk/ ▶ n. the dry outer covering of some fruits or seeds. ■ a dry or rough outer layer or coating, esp. when empty of its contents. ▶ v. [trans.] remove the husk or husks from. [ME: prob. from Low Ger. *hūske* 'sheath,' lit. 'little house.']

husk·ing bee ▶ n. another term for CORNHUSKING.

husk·y[1] /ˈhəskē/ ▶ adj. (**husk·i·er, husk·i·est**) **1** (of a voice or utterance) sounding low-pitched and slightly hoarse. **2** strong; hefty. — **husk·i·ly** adv. **husk·i·ness** n.

husk·y[2] (also **hus·kie**) ▶ n. (pl. **husk·ies**) a powerful dog of a breed with a thick double coat that is typically gray, used in the Arctic for pulling sleds. [19th C.: abbrev. of obs. *Ehuskemay* or Newfoundland dial. *Huskemaw* 'Eskimo,' prob. from Montagnais (see ESKIMO).]

Huss /həs; hōōs/, John (*c.*1372–1415), Bohemian reformer; Czech name *Jan Hus*. He attacked ecclesiastical abuses, and was excommunicated in 1411. He was later burned at the stake. See also HUSSITE.

hus·sar /həˈzär/ ▶ n. hist. (in the 15th century) a Hungarian light horseman. ■ a soldier in a light cavalry regiment. [from Hungarian *huszár*, from Old Serbian *husar*, from Ital. *corsaro* (see CORSAIR).]

Hus·sein[1] /hŏŏˈsān/, Abdullah ibn, see ABDULLAH IBN HUSSEIN.

Hus·sein[2] (also **Hu·sain**), ibn Talal (1935–99), king of Jordan 1953–99. His moderate policies created problems with Palestinian refugees from Israel within Jordan. In 1994 he signed a treaty that normalized relations with Israel.

Hus·sein[3] (also **Hu·sain**), Saddam (1937–2006), president of Iraq 1979–2003; full name *Saddam bin Hussein at-Takriti*. He maintained a repressive authoritarian government and his presidency included the Iran-Iraq War 1980–88 and Iraq's 1990 invasion of Kuwait. His regime was toppled in March 2003 by US forces, and he was captured in December. On trial 2005–06 for war crimes, crimes against humanity, and genocide, he was sentenced to death and later executed.

Huss·ite /ˈhəsīt/ ▶ n. a member or follower of the religious movement begun by John Huss. ▶ adj. of or relating to the Hussites.

hus·sy /ˈhəsē; ˈhəzē/ ▶ n. (pl. **-sies**) an impudent or immoral girl or woman: *that brazen little hussy!* [ME: contr. of HOUSEWIFE.]

hust·ings /ˈhəstiNGz/ ▶ n. (pl. same) a meeting at which candidates in an election address potential voters. ■ the campaigning associated with an election. [OE *husting* 'council,' from ON *hústhing* 'household assembly held by a leader,' from *hús* 'house' + *thing* 'assembly, parliament.']

hus·tle /ˈhəsəl/ ▶ v. **1** [with obj. and adverbial of direction] force (someone) to move hurriedly or unceremoniously in a specified direction: *they hustled him into the back of a car.* ■ [trans.] push roughly; jostle: *they were hissed and hustled as they went in.* ■ [no obj., with adverbial of direction] hurry; bustle: *he hustled to first base.* **2** [trans.] informal obtain by forceful action or persuasion: *the brothers hustled a record deal.* ■ (**hustle someone into**) coerce or pressure someone into doing or choosing something: *don't be hustled into anything.* ■ sell aggressively: *he hustled his company's oil around the country.* ■ swindle; cheat. **3** [intrans.] informal engage in prostitution. ▶ n. **1** busy movement and activity. ■ energetic effort. **2** informal a fraud or swindle. [17th C. (orig. in the sense 'shake, toss'): from MDu. *hutselen*. Sense 3 dates from the early 20th C.]

hus·tler /ˈhəslər/ ▶ n. informal an aggressively enterprising person; a go-getter. ■ an enterprising and often dishonest person, esp. one trying to sell something. ■ a prostitute.

hut /hət/ ▶ n. a small single-story building of simple or crude construction, serving as a poor, rough, or temporary house or shelter. ▶ v. (**hut·ted, hut·ting**) [trans.] provide with huts. — **hut·like** adj. [16th C. (in the sense 'temporary wooden shelter for troops'): from Fr. *hutte*, from Mid. High Ger. *hütte*.]

hutch /həcн/ ▶ n. **1** a box or cage, typically with a wire mesh front, for keeping rabbits, ferrets, or other small domesticated animals. **2** a storage chest. ■ a cupboard or dresser typically with open shelves above. [ME: from OFr. *huche*, from med. L.]

Hutch·in·son[1] /ˈhəcнinsən/ a city in south central Kansas; pop. 40,787.

Hutch·in·son[2], Anne Marbury (1591–1643) American religious leader; born in England. She was banished from Massachusetts Bay Colony in 1637 for her liberal views on grace and salvation.

hut·ment /ˈhətmənt/ ▶ n. Mil. an encampment of huts.

Hut·ter·ite /ˈhətəˌrīt/ ▶ n. a member of either an Anabaptist Christian sect established in Moravia in the early 16th century, or a North American community holding similar beliefs. ▶ adj. of or relating to Hutterites or their beliefs and practices. [from the name of Jacob *Hutter* (died 1536), a Moravian Anabaptist, + -ITE[1].]

Hu·tu /ˈhōōtōō/ ▶ n. (pl. same or **Hu·tus** or **Ba·hu·tu** /bəˈhōōtōō/) a Bantu-speaking people forming the majority population in Rwanda and Burundi; the long-standing antagonism between the Hutu and Tutsi peoples led to large-scale ethnic violence in 1994. ▶ adj. of or relating to this people. [a local name.]

Hux·ley[1] /ˈhəkslē/, Aldous Leonard (1894–1963), English writer. He wrote *Brave New World* (1932).

Hux·ley[2], Andrew Fielding (1917–), British physiologist; grandson of Thomas Henry Huxley. He worked on the physiology of nerve transmission. Nobel Prize for Physiology or Medicine (1963, shared with John C. Eccles and A. L. Hodgkin).

Hux·ley[3], Thomas Henry (1825–95), English biologist. He was a leading supporter of Darwinism.

Huy·gens /ˈhoigənz/, Christiaan (1629–95), Dutch physicist, mathematician, and astronomer. He explained reflection and refraction.

huz·zah /həˈzä/ (also **huz·za**) archaic ▶ exclam. used to express approval or delight; hurrah. ▶ v. [intrans.] cry "huzzah." [16th C.: perh. used orig. as a sailor's cry when hauling.]

HV (also **h.v.**) ▶ abbr. ■ high velocity. ■ high voltage.

hvy. ▶ abbr. heavy.

HW ▶ abbr. ■ hardwood. ■ high water. ■ hot water (heat).

HWM ▶ abbr. high-water mark.

hwy ▶ abbr. highway.

hy·a·cinth /ˈhīəˌsinTH/ ▶n. **1** a bulbous plant (genus *Hyacinthus*) of the lily family, with straplike leaves and a compact spike of bell-shaped fragrant flowers. ■ a light purplish-blue color typical of some hyacinth flowers. **2** another term for JACINTH. — **hy·a·cin·thine** /ˌhīəˈsinTHin; -THīn/ adj. [16th C. (denoting a gem): from Fr. *hyacinthe*, via L. from Gk. *huakinthos*.]

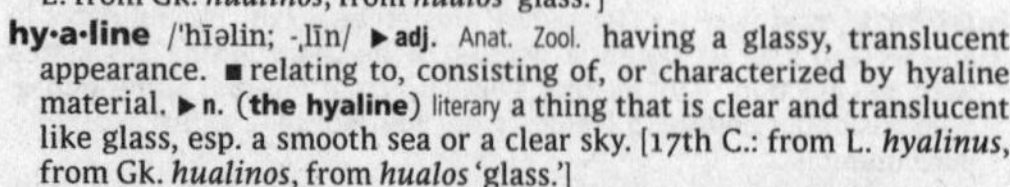
hyacinth

Hy·a·cin·thus /ˌhīəˈsinTHəs/ Gk. Mythol. a beautiful boy whom the god Apollo loved but killed accidentally with a discus. From his blood Apollo caused the hyacinth to spring up.

Hy·a·des /ˈhīədēz/ Astron. an open star cluster in the constellation Taurus, appearing to surround the bright star Aldebaran.

hy·ae·na ▶n. var. of HYENA.

hy·a·lin /ˈhīəlin/ ▶n. Physiol. a clear substance produced esp. by the degeneration of epithelial or connective tissues. [19th C.: via L. from Gk. *hualinos*, from *hualos* 'glass.']

hy·a·line /ˈhīəlin; -ˌlīn/ ▶adj. Anat. Zool. having a glassy, translucent appearance. ■ relating to, consisting of, or characterized by hyaline material. ▶n. **(the hyaline)** literary a thing that is clear and translucent like glass, esp. a smooth sea or a clear sky. [17th C.: from L. *hyalinus*, from Gk. *hualinos*, from *hualos* 'glass.']

hy·a·line car·ti·lage ▶n. a translucent bluish-white type of cartilage present in the joints, the respiratory tract, and the immature skeleton.

hy·a·line mem·brane dis·ease ▶n. a condition in newborn babies in which the lungs are deficient in surfactant, preventing their proper expansion and causing the formation of hyaline material in the lung spaces. Also called RESPIRATORY DISTRESS SYNDROME.

hy·a·lite /ˈhīəˌlīt/ ▶n. a translucent, colorless variety of opal. [18th C.: from Gk. *hualos* 'glass' + -ITE[1].]

hy·a·loid /ˈhīəˌloid/ ▶adj. Anat. glassy; transparent. [19th C.: from Fr. *hyaloïde*, or via late L. from Gk. *hualoeidēs* 'like glass,' from *hualos* 'glass.']

hy·a·loid mem·brane ▶n. a thin transparent membrane enveloping the vitreous humor of the eye.

hy·a·lu·ron·ic ac·id /ˌhīəlo͝oˈränik/ ▶n. Biochem. a viscous fluid carbohydrate present in connective tissue, synovial fluid, and the humors of the eye. — **hy·a·lu·ro·nate** /ˌhīəˈlo͝orəˌnāt/ n. [1930s: *hyaluronic* from a blend of HYALOID and URONIC ACID.]

Hy·an·nis /hīˈanis/ a village in southeastern Massachusetts, on Cape Cod; pop. 14,120.

hy·brid /ˈhīˌbrid/ ▶n. a thing made by combining two different elements; a mixture. ■ Biol. the offspring of two plants or animals of different species or varieties, such as a mule (a hybrid of a donkey and a horse). ■ offens. a person of mixed racial or cultural origin. ■ a word formed from elements taken from different languages, for example *television* (*tele-* from Greek, *vision* from Latin). ▶adj. of mixed character; composed of mixed parts. ■ bred as a hybrid from different species or varieties. — **hy·brid·ism** /ˈhībrəˌdizəm/ n. **hy·brid·i·ty** /hīˈbriditē/ n. [17th C. (as a n.): from L. *hybrida* 'offspring of a tame sow and wild boar.']

hy·brid car ▶n. a car with a gasoline engine and an electric motor, each of which can propel it.

hy·brid·ize /ˈhībriˌdīz/ ▶v. **1** [trans.] crossbreed (individuals of two different species or varieties). ■ [intrans.] (of an animal or plant) breed with an individual of another species or variety. **2** [intrans.] Biochem. form a double-stranded nucleic acid structure from a single-stranded mixture by complementary base pairing. — **hy·brid·iz·a·ble** adj. **hy·brid·i·za·tion** /ˌhībrədiˈzāSHən/ n.

hy·brid vig·or ▶n. another term for HETEROSIS.

hyd. ▶abbr. ■ hydraulics. ■ hydrostatics.

hy·da·thode /ˈhīdəˌTHōd/ ▶n. Bot. a modified pore, esp. on a leaf, that exudes drops of water. [19th C.: from Gk. *hudōr*, *hudat-* 'water' + *hodos* 'way.']

hy·da·tid /ˈhīdətid/ ▶n. Med. a cyst containing watery fluid. ■ such a cyst formed by and containing a tapeworm larva. ■ a tapeworm larva. [17th C.: from mod. L. *hydatis*, from Gk. *hudatis*, *hudatid-* 'watery vesicle,' from *hudōr*, *hudat-* 'water.']

Hyde[1] /hīd/, Edward, see CLARENDON.

Hyde[2], Mr., see JEKYLL.

Hyde Park /hīd/ **1** a town in southeastern New York, on the Hudson River, associated with the family of Franklin D. Roosevelt; pop. 21,320. **2** a park in western central London, England.

Hy·der·a·bad /ˈhīd(ə)rəˌbad; -ˌbäd/ **1** a city in central India, capital of the state of Andhra Pradesh; pop. 3,005,000. **2** a former large state in southern central India. **3** a city in southeastern Pakistan, in the province of Sind; pop. 1,000,000.

hydr- ▶comb. form var. of HYDRO- shortened before a vowel (as in *hydraulic*).

Hy·dra /ˈhīdrə/ **1** Gk. Mythol. a many-headed snake whose heads grew again as they were cut off, killed by Hercules. ■ [as n.] **(hydra)** a thing that is hard to overcome or resist because of its pervasive or enduring quality or its many aspects. **2** Astron. the largest constellation (the Water Snake or Sea Monster), said to represent the beast slain by Hercules. Its few bright stars are close to the celestial equator. Compare with HYDRUS.

hy·dra /ˈhīdrə/ ▶n. a minute freshwater coelenterate (genus *Hydra*, class Hydrozoa) with a stalklike tubular body and a ring of tentacles around the mouth. [via L. from Gk. *hudra* 'water snake' (see HYDRA).]

hy·dran·gea /hīˈdrānjə/ ▶n. a shrub or climbing plant (genus *Hydrangea*, family Hydrangeaceae) with rounded or flattened flowering heads of small white, blue, or blue florets. [mod. L., from Gk. *hudro-* 'water' + *angeion* 'vessel' (from the cup shape of its seed capsule).]

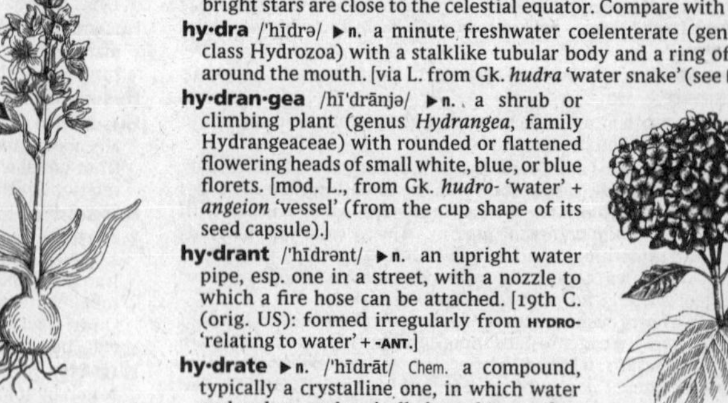
hydrangea

hy·drant /ˈhīdrənt/ ▶n. an upright water pipe, esp. one in a street, with a nozzle to which a fire hose can be attached. [19th C. (orig. US): formed irregularly from HYDRO- 'relating to water' + -ANT.]

hy·drate ▶n. /ˈhīdrāt/ Chem. a compound, typically a crystalline one, in which water molecules are chemically bound to another compound or an element. ▶v. [trans.] cause to absorb water. ■ Chem. combine chemically with water molecules. — **hy·drat·a·ble** adj. **hy·dra·tion** /hīˈdrāSHən/ n. **hy·dra·tor** /-tər/ n. [19th C.: coined in Fr. from Gk. *hudōr* 'water.']

hy·drau·lic /hīˈdrôlik/ ▶adj. **1** denoting, relating to, or operated by a liquid moving in a confined space under pressure: *hydraulic fluid*. **2** of or relating to the science of hydraulics. **3** (of cement) hardening under water. — **hy·drau·li·cal·ly** adv. [17th C.: via L. from Gk. *hudraulikos*, from *hudro-* 'water' + *aulos* 'pipe.']

hy·drau·lic frac·tur·ing ▶n. the forcing open of fissures in subterranean rocks by introducing liquid at high pressure, esp. to extract oil or gas.

hy·drau·lic ram ▶n. an automatic pump in which a large volume of water flows through a valve that it periodically forces shut, the sudden pressure change being used to raise a smaller volume of water to a higher level.

hy·drau·lics /hīˈdrôliks/ ▶plural n. **1** [usu. treated as sing.] the branch of science concerned with the conveyance of liquids through pipes and channels, esp. as a source of mechanical force or control. **2** hydraulic systems, mechanisms, or forces.

hy·dra·zine /ˈhīdrəˌzēn/ ▶n. Chem. a colorless volatile alkaline liquid, N_2H_4, with powerful reducing properties, used in chemical synthesis and rocket fuels. [19th C.: from HYDROGEN + AZO- + -INE[4].]

hy·dric /ˈhīdrik/ ▶adj. Ecol. (of an environment or habitat) containing plenty of moisture; very wet. Compare with MESIC[1] and XERIC. [20th C.: from HYDRO- + -IC.]

hy·dride /ˈhīdrīd/ ▶n. Chem. a binary compound of hydrogen with a metal.

hy·dri·od·ic ac·id /ˌhīdrēˈädik/ ▶n. Chem. a strongly acidic solution of the gas hydrogen iodide, HI, in water.

hy·dro /ˈhīdrō/ ▶n. (pl. **-dros**) **1** a hydroelectric power plant. ■ hydroelectricity. ■ Canadian electricity. **2** Brit. a hotel or clinic originally providing hydropathic treatment. ▶adj. relating to or denoting hydroelectricity.

hydro- (also **hydr-**) ▶comb. form **1** water; relating to water: *hydraulic* | *hydrocolloid*. **2** Chem. combined with hydrogen: *hydrocarbon*. [from Gk. *hudōr* 'water.']

hy·dro·bro·mic ac·id /ˌhīdrəˈbrōmik/ ▶n. Chem. a strongly acidic solution of the gas hydrogen bromide, HBr, in water.

hy·dro·car·bon /ˈhīdrəˌkärbən/ ▶n. Chem. a compound of hydrogen and carbon, such as any of those that are the chief components of petroleum and natural gas.

hy·dro·cele /ˈhīdrəˌsēl/ ▶n. Med. the accumulation of serous fluid in a body sac.

hy·dro·ceph·a·lus /ˌhīdrōˈsefələs/ ▶n. Med. a condition in which fluid accumulates in the brain, typically in young children, enlarging the head and sometimes causing brain damage. — **hy·dro·ce·phal·ic** /ˌhīdrōsəˈfalik/ adj. **hy·dro·ceph·a·ly** /-ˈsefəlē/ n. [17th C.: mod. L., from Gk. *hudrokephalon*, from *hudro-* 'water' + *kephalē* 'head.']

hy·dro·chlo·ric ac·id /ˌhīdrəˈklôrik/ ▶n. Chem. a strongly acidic solution of the gas hydrogen chloride, HCl, in water.

hy·dro·chlo·ride /ˌhīdrəˈklôrīd/ ▶n. Chem. a compound of a particular organic base with hydrochloric acid: [with adj.] *cocaine hydrochloride*.

hy·dro·chlo·ro·fluor·o·car·bon /ˌhīdrōˌklôrōˈflo͝orōˌkärbən/ (abbr.: **HCFC**) ▶n. Chem. any of a class of inert compounds of carbon, hydrogen, chlorine, and fluorine, used in place of chlorofluorocarbons as being less destructive to the ozone layer.

hy·dro·col·loid /ˌhīdrōˈkäloid/ ▶n. a substance that forms a gel in the presence of water, examples of which are used in surgical dressings and in various industrial applications.

hy·dro·cor·ti·sone /ˌhīdrəˈkôrtiˌzōn/ ▶n. Biochem. a steroid hormone produced by the adrenal cortex and used medicinally to treat inflammation resulting from eczema and rheumatism.

hy·dro·cy·an·ic ac·id /ˌhīdrōsīˈanik/ ▶n. Chem. a highly poisonous acidic solution of hydrogen cyanide in water.

hy·dro·dy·nam·ics /ˌhīdrōdīˈnamiks/ ▶plural n. [treated as sing.] the branch of science concerned with forces acting on or exerted by fluids (esp. liquids). — **hy·dro·dy·nam·ic** adj. **hy·dro·dy·nam·i·cal** /-ˈnamikəl/ adj.

hy·dro·dy·nam·i·cist /-'namisist/ n.

hy·dro·e·lec·tric /ˌhīdrōə'lektrik/ ▶ adj. relating to or denoting the generation of electricity using flowing water (typically from a reservoir behind a dam) to drive a turbine that powers a generator. — **hy·dro·e·lec·tric·i·ty** /-ələk'trisitē/ n.

hy·dro·fluor·ic ac·id /ˌhīdrə'flo͝orik/ ▶ n. Chem. an acidic and extremely corrosive solution of the liquid hydrogen fluoride, HF, in water.

hy·dro·fluor·o·car·bon /ˌhīdrō'flo͝orəˌkärbən/ (abbr.: **HFC**) ▶ n. Chem. any of a class of partly chlorinated and fluorinated hydrocarbons, used as an alternative to chlorofluorocarbons.

hy·dro·foil /'hīdrəˌfoil/ ▶ n. a boat whose hull is fitted underneath with vanes (foils) that lift the hull clear of the water to increase the boat's speed. ■ another term for FOIL[4].

hy·dro·gen /'hīdrəjən/ ▶ n. a colorless, odorless, highly flammable gas, the chemical element of atomic number 1. (Symbol: **H**) — **hy·drog·e·nous** /hī'dräjənəs/ adj. [18th C.: coined in Fr. from Gk. *hudro-* 'water' + *-genēs* (see -GEN).]

hy·drog·e·nase /'hīdrəjəˌnās; hī'dräjə-/ ▶ n. [usu. with adj.] Biochem. an enzyme that catalyzes the reduction of a particular substance by hydrogen.

hy·dro·gen·ate /'hīdrəjəˌnāt; hī'dräjənāt/ ▶ v. [trans.] [often as adj.] (**hydrogenated**) charge with or cause to combine with hydrogen. — **hy·dro·gen·a·tion** /ˌhīdrəjə'nāSHən; hīˌdräjə-/ n.

hy·dro·gen bomb ▶ n. an immensely powerful bomb whose destructive power comes from the rapid release of energy during the nuclear fusion of isotopes of hydrogen (deuterium and tritium), using an atom bomb as a trigger.

hy·dro·gen bond ▶ n. Chem. a weak bond between two molecules resulting from an electrostatic attraction between a proton in one molecule and an electronegative atom in the other.

hy·dro·gen cy·a·nide ▶ n. Chem. a highly poisonous gas or volatile liquid, HCN, with an odor of bitter almonds, made by the action of acids on cyanides.

hy·dro·gen per·ox·ide ▶ n. Chem. a colorless, viscous, unstable liquid, H_2O_2, with strong oxidizing properties, commonly used in diluted form in disinfectants and bleaches.

hy·dro·gen sul·fide ▶ n. Chem. a colorless poisonous gas, H_2S, with a smell of rotten eggs, made by the action of acids on sulfides.

hy·drog·ra·phy /hī'drägrəfē/ ▶ n. the science of surveying and charting bodies of water, such as seas, lakes, and rivers. — **hy·drog·ra·pher** /-fər/ n. **hy·dro·graph·ic** /ˌhīdrə'grafik/ adj. **hy·dro·graph·i·cal** /ˌhīdrə'grafikəl/ adj. **hy·dro·graph·i·cal·ly** /ˌhīdrə'grafik(ə)lē/ adv.

hy·droid /'hīˌdroid/ Zool. ▶ n. a coelenterate of an order that includes the hydras.

hy·dro·lase /'hīdrəˌlās; -ˌlāz/ ▶ n. [usu. with adj.] Biochem. an enzyme that catalyzes the hydrolysis of a particular substrate.

hy·drol·o·gy /hī'dräləjē/ ▶ n. the branch of science concerned with the properties of the earth's water, esp. its movement in relation to land. — **hy·dro·log·ic** /ˌhīdrə'läjik/ adj. **hy·dro·log·i·cal** /ˌhīdrə'läjikəl/ adj. **hy·dro·log·i·cal·ly** /ˌhīdrə'läjik(ə)lē/ adv. **hy·drol·o·gist** n.

hy·drol·y·sate /hī'dräləˌsāt/ ▶ n. Chem. a substance produced by hydrolysis.

hy·drol·y·sis /hī'dräləsis/ ▶ n. Chem. the chemical breakdown of a compound due to reaction with water. — **hy·dro·lyt·ic** /ˌhīdrə'litik/ adj.

hy·dro·lyze /'hīdrəˌlīz/ (Brit. **hy·dro·lyse**) ▶ v. [trans.] Chem. break down (a compound) by chemical reaction with water. ■ [intrans.] undergo this process.

hy·dro·man·cy /'hīdrəˌmansē/ ▶ n. divination by means of signs derived from the appearance of water and its movements.

hy·dro·me·chan·ics /ˌhīdrōmə'kaniks/ ▶ plural n. [treated as sing.] the mechanics of liquids; hydrodynamics, esp. in relation to mechanical applications. — **hy·dro·me·chan·i·cal** /-'kanikəl/ adj.

hy·dro·me·du·sa /ˌhīdrōmə'd(y)o͞osə; -zə/ ▶ n. (pl. **-sae** /-sē; -zē/) Zool. the medusoid phase of a hydroid coelenterate.

hy·dro·mel /'hīdrəˌmel/ ▶ n. hist. a drink similar to mead, made with fermented honey and water. [ME: from L., from Gk. *hudromeli*, from *hudro-* 'water' + *meli* 'honey.']

hy·dro·me·te·or /ˌhīdrō'mētēər/ ▶ n. Meteorol. an atmospheric phenomenon or entity involving water or water vapor, such as rain or a cloud.

hy·drom·e·ter /hī'drämitər/ ▶ n. an instrument for measuring the density of liquids. — **hy·dro·met·ric** /ˌhīdrə'metrik/ adj. **hy·drom·e·try** n.

hy·dron·ic /hī'dränik/ ▶ adj. denoting a cooling or heating system in which heat is transported using circulating water.

hy·dro·ni·um i·on /hī'drōnēəm/ ▶ n. Chem. the ion H_3O+, consisting of a protonated water molecule and present in all aqueous acids. [20th C.: *hydronium*, from Ger. (a contr.).]

hy·drop·a·thy /hī'dräpəTHē/ ▶ n. the treatment of illness through the use of water, either internally or through external means such as steam baths. Compare with HYDROTHERAPY. — **hy·dro·path·ic** /ˌhīdrə'paTHik/ adj. **hy·drop·a·thist** n. [19th C.: from HYDRO- 'of water,' on the pattern of *allopathy* and *homeopathy*.]

hy·dro·phil·ic /ˌhīdrə'filik/ ▶ adj. having a tendency to mix with, dissolve in, or be wetted by water. The opposite of HYDROPHOBIC. — **hy·dro·phi·lic·i·ty** /-fə'lisitē/ n.

hy·droph·i·lous /hī'dräfələs/ ▶ adj. Bot. (of a plant) water-pollinated. — **hy·droph·i·ly** /-'dräfəlē/ n.

hy·dro·pho·bi·a /ˌhīdrə'fōbēə/ ▶ n. extreme or irrational fear of water, esp. as a symptom of rabies in humans. ■ rabies, esp. in humans.

hy·dro·pho·bic /ˌhīdrə'fōbik/ ▶ adj. **1** tending to repel or fail to mix with water. The opposite of HYDROPHILIC. **2** of or suffering from hydrophobia. — **hy·dro·pho·bic·i·ty** /-fō'bisitē/ n.

hy·dro·phone /'hīdrəˌfōn/ ▶ n. a microphone that detects sound waves under water.

hy·dro·phyte /'hīdrəˌfīt/ ▶ n. Bot. a plant that grows only in or on water. — **hy·dro·phyt·ic** /ˌhīdrə'fitik/ adj.

hy·dro·plane /'hīdrəˌplān/ ▶ n. **1** a light, fast motorboat designed to skim over the surface of water. **2** a finlike attachment that enables a moving submarine to rise or fall in the water. **3** a seaplane. ▶ v. **1** (of a vehicle) slide uncontrollably on the wet surface of a road. **2** (of a boat) skim over the surface of water with its hull lifted.

hy·dro·pon·ics /ˌhīdrə'päniks/ ▶ plural n. [treated as sing.] the process of growing plants in sand, gravel, or liquid, with added nutrients but without soil. — **hy·dro·pon·ic** adj. **hy·dro·pon·i·cal·ly** adv. [1930s: from HYDRO- 'of water' + Gk. *ponos* 'labor' + -ICS.]

hy·dro·pow·er /'hīdrəˌpouər/ ▶ n. hydroelectric power.

hy·dro·qui·none /ˌhīdrōkwi'nōn; -'kwinōn/ ▶ n. Chem. a crystalline compound, $C_6H_4(OH)_2$, made by the reduction of benzoquinone.

hy·dro·sphere /'hīdrəˌsfi(ə)r/ ▶ n. (usu. **the hydrosphere**) all the waters on the earth's surface, such as lakes and seas, and sometimes including water over the earth's surface, such as clouds.

hy·dro·stat·ic /ˌhīdrə'statik/ ▶ adj. relating to or denoting the equilibrium of liquids and the pressure exerted by liquid at rest. — **hy·dro·stat·i·cal** adj. **hy·dro·stat·i·cal·ly** adv. [17th C.: prob. from Gk. *hudrostatēs* 'hydrostatic balance,' from *hudro-* 'water' + *statikos* (see STATIC).]

hy·dro·stat·ics /ˌhīdrə'statiks/ ▶ plural n. [treated as sing.] the branch of mechanics concerned with the hydrostatic properties of liquids.

hy·dro·ther·a·py /ˌhīdrə'THerəpē/ ▶ n. another term for HYDROPATHY. ■ the use of exercises in a pool as part of treatment for conditions such as arthritis or partial paralysis. — **hy·dro·ther·a·pist** n.

hy·dro·ther·mal /ˌhīdrə'THərməl/ ▶ adj. of, relating to, or denoting the action of heated water in the earth's crust. — **hy·dro·ther·mal·ly** adv.

hy·dro·ther·mal vent ▶ n. an opening in the seafloor out of which heated mineral-rich water flows.

hy·dro·tho·rax /ˌhīdrə'THôˌraks/ ▶ n. the condition of having fluid in the pleural cavity.

hy·drot·ro·pism /hī'drätrəˌpizəm/ ▶ n. Bot. the growth or turning of plant roots toward or away from moisture.

hy·drous /'hīdrəs/ ▶ adj. esp. Chem. Geol. containing water as a constituent: *a hydrous lava flow*. [19th C.: from Gk. *hudro-* 'water' + -OUS.]

hy·drox·ide /hī'dräkˌsīd/ ▶ n. Chem. a compound of a metal with the hydroxide ion OH− (as in many alkalis) or the group −OH.

hydroxy- ▶ comb. form Chem. representing HYDROXYL or HYDROXIDE: *hydroxyapatite*.

hy·drox·y·a·pa·tite /hīˌdräksē'apəˌtīt/ ▶ n. a mineral of the apatite group that is the main inorganic constituent of tooth enamel and bone.

hy·drox·yl /hī'dräksəl/ ▶ n. [as adj.] Chem. of or denoting the radical −OH, present in alcohols and many other organic compounds: *a hydroxyl group*. [19th C.: from a blend of HYDROGEN and OXYGEN, + -YL.]

hy·drox·yl·ate /hī'dräksəˌlāt/ ▶ v. [trans.] [often as adj.] (**hydroxylated**) Chem. introduce a hydroxyl group into (a molecule or compound). — **hy·drox·y·la·tion** /hiˌdräksə'lāSHən/ n.

Hy·dro·zo·a /ˌhīdrə'zōə/ Zool. a class of coelenterates that includes hydras and Portuguese men-of-war. Many of them are colonial, and some kinds have both polypoid and medusoid phases. — **hy·dro·zo·an** n. & adj. [mod. L. (pl.), from HYDRO- 'water' + Gk. *zōion* 'animal.']

Hy·drus /'hīdrəs/ Astron. an inconspicuous southern constellation (the Water Snake), between the star Achernar and the south celestial pole. Compare with HYDRA (sense 2). [L., from Gk. *hudros*.]

hy·e·na /hī'ēnə/ (Brit. **hyaena**) ▶ n. a doglike African mammal (genera *Hyaena* and *Crocuta*, family Hyaenidae) with an erect mane and forelimbs that are longer than the hind limbs. Hyenas are noted as scavengers but most are also effective hunters. See illustration at SPOTTED HYENA. [ME: via L. from Gk. *huaina*, fem. of *hus* 'pig' (prob. because the animal's mane was thought to resemble a hog's bristles).]

hy·giene /'hījēn/ ▶ n. conditions or practices conducive to maintaining health and preventing disease, esp. through cleanliness: *poor standards of food hygiene*. [16th C.: via Fr. from mod. L. *hygieina*, from Gk. *hugieinē (tekhnē)* '(art) of health,' from *hugiēs* 'healthy.']

hy·gi·en·ic /hī'jenik; -jē'en-/ ▶ adj. conducive to maintaining health and preventing disease, esp. by being clean; sanitary: *hygienic conditions*. — **hy·gi·en·i·cal·ly** adv.

hy·gien·ist /hī'jenist; -jē'en-; -'jēnist/ ▶ n. **1** a specialist in the promotion of clean conditions for the preservation of health: *an industrial hygienist*. **2** short for DENTAL HYGIENIST.

hygro- ▶ comb. form relating to moisture: *hygrometer*. [from Gk. *hugros* 'wet.']

hy·grom·e·ter /hī'grämitər/ ▶ n. an instrument for measuring the humidity of the air or a gas. — **hy·gro·met·ric** /ˌhīgrə'metrik/ adj. **hy·grom·e·try** /-trē/ n.

hy·gro·phyte /'hīgrəˌfīt/ ▶ n. Bot. a plant that grows in wet conditions.

hy·gro·scope /ˈhīgrəˌskōp/ ▶n. an instrument that gives an indication of the humidity of the air.

hy·gro·scop·ic /ˌhīgrəˈskäpik/ ▶adj. (of a substance) tending to absorb moisture from the air. —**hy·gro·scop·i·cal·ly** adv.

hy·ing /ˈhī-ING/ present participle of HIE.

Hyk·sos /ˈhiksäs; -sōs/ ▶plural n. a people of mixed Semitic and Asian descent who invaded Egypt and settled in the Nile delta c.1640 BC. They formed the 15th and 16th dynasties of Egypt and ruled a large part of the country until driven out c.1532 BC. [from Gk. *Huksōs*, from Egyptian *heqa khoswe* 'foreign rulers.']

hy·la /ˈhīlə/ ▶n. a tree frog (genus *Hyla*, family Hylidae), typically bright green in color. [mod. L., from Gk. *hulē* 'timber.']

hy·lo·zo·ism /ˌhīləˈzōizəm/ ▶n. Philos. the doctrine that all matter has life. [17th C.: from Greek *hulē* 'matter' + Gk. *zōē* 'life.']

hy·men /ˈhīmən/ ▶n. a membrane that partially closes the opening of the vagina and whose presence is traditionally taken to be a mark of virginity. —**hy·men·al** /ˈhīmənl/ adj. [16th C.: via late L. from Gk. *humēn* 'membrane.']

hy·me·ne·al /ˌhīməˈnēəl/ ▶adj. literary of or concerning marriage. [17th C.: from L. *hymenaeus*, from *Hymen* (from Gk. *Humēn*), the name of the god of marriage, + -AL.]

hy·me·ni·um /hīˈmēnēəm/ ▶n. (pl. **-ni·a** /-nēə/) Bot. (in higher fungi) a surface consisting mainly of spore-bearing structures (asci or basidia). —**hy·me·ni·al** /-nēəl/ adj. [19th C.: from Gk. *humenion*, dimin. of *humēn* 'membrane.']

Hy·me·nop·ter·a /ˌhīməˈnäptərə/ Entomol. a large order of insects that includes the bees, wasps, ants, and sawflies. These insects have four transparent wings and the females often have a sting. ■ [as pl. n.] **(hymenoptera)** insects of this order. —**hy·me·nop·ter·an** n. & adj. **hy·me·nop·ter·ous** /-tərəs/ adj. [mod. L. (pl.), from Gk. *humenopteros* 'membrane-winged,' from *humēn* 'membrane' + *pteron* 'wing.']

Hy·mie /ˈhīmē/ ▶n. informal, offens. a Jewish person. [1980s: colloq. abbrev. of the Jewish male given name *Hyman*.]

hymn /him/ ▶n. a religious song or poem, typically of praise to God or a god. ■ a formal song sung during Christian worship, typically by the whole congregation. ■ a song, text, or other composition praising or celebrating someone or something. ▶v. **1** [trans.] praise or celebrate (something). **2** [intrans.] rare sing hymns. —**hym·nic** /ˈhimnik/ adj. [OE, via L. from Gk. *humnos* 'ode or song in praise of a god or hero.']

hym·nal /ˈhimnəl/ ▶n. a book of hymns. ▶adj. of hymns: *hymnal music*.

hym·na·ry /ˈhimnərē/ ▶n. (pl. **-ries**) another term for HYMNAL.

hym·no·dy /ˈhimnədē/ ▶n. the singing or composition of hymns. —**hym·no·dist** n. [18th C.: via med. L. from Gk. *humnōidia*, from *humnos* 'hymn.']

hym·nol·o·gy /himˈnäləjē/ ▶n. the study or composition of hymns. —**hym·no·log·i·cal** /ˌhimnəˈläjikəl/ adj. **hym·nol·o·gist** n. [17th C.: orig. from Gk. *humnologia* 'hymn-singing,' the early sense until the mid 19th C.]

hy·oid /ˈhīoid/ Anat. Zool. ▶n. (also **hyoid bone**) a U-shaped bone in the neck that supports the tongue. ▶adj. of or relating to this bone or structures associated with it. [19th C.: via Fr. from mod. L. *hyoïdes*, from Gk. *huoeidēs* 'shaped like the letter upsilon (ʊ).']

hy·os·cine /ˈhīəˌsēn/ ▶n. another term for SCOPOLAMINE. [19th C.: from mod. L. *hyoscyamus* (see HYOSCYAMINE) + -INE[4].]

hy·os·cy·a·mine /ˌhīəˈsīəmin; -ˌmēn/ ▶n. Chem. a poisonous compound, $C_{17}H_{23}NO_3$, present in henbane, with similar properties to hyoscine.

hyp. ▶abbr. ■ hypotenuse. ■ hypothesis or hypothetical.

hyp- ▶comb. form var. of HYPO- shortened before a vowel or *h* (as in *hypesthesia*).

hy·pae·thral ▶adj. var. of HYPETHRAL.

hy·pal·la·ge /hīˈpaləjē; hi-/ ▶n. Rhet. a transposition of the natural relations of two elements in a proposition, for example in the sentence "*Melissa shook her doubtful curls.*" [16th C.: via late L. from Gk. *hupallagē*, from *hupo* 'under' + *allassein* 'to exchange.']

hy·pan·thi·um /hiˈpanTHēəm; hī-/ ▶n. (pl. **-thi·a** /-THēə/) Bot. a cuplike or tubular enlargement of the receptacle of a flower, loosely surrounding the gynoecium or united with it.

hype[1] /hīp/ informal ▶n. extravagant or intensive publicity or promotion. ■ a deception carried out for the sake of publicity. ▶v. [trans.] promote or publicize (a product or idea) intensively, often exaggerating its importance or benefits. [1920s: of unknown origin.]

hype[2] informal ▶n. a hypodermic needle or injection. ■ a drug addict. ▶v. [trans.] (usu. **be hyped up**) stimulate or excite (someone): *I was hyped up because I wanted to do well.* [1920s (orig. US): abbrev. of HYPODERMIC.]

hy·per /ˈhīpər/ ▶adj. informal hyperactive or unusually energetic: *eating sugar makes you hyper.*

hyper- ▶prefix **1** over; beyond; above: *hypernym.* ■ exceeding: *hypersonic.* ■ excessively; above normal: *hyperthyroidism.* **2** relating to hypertext: *hyperlink.* [from Gk. *huper* 'over, beyond.']

hy·per·ac·tive /ˌhīpərˈaktiv/ ▶adj. abnormally or extremely active. ■ (of a child) showing constantly active and sometimes disruptive behavior. —**hy·per·ac·tiv·i·ty** /-akˈtivitē/ n.

hy·per·al·ge·si·a /ˌhīpəralˈjēzēə; -ˈjēsēə/ ▶n. Med. abnormally heightened sensitivity to pain. —**hy·per·al·ge·sic** /-ˈjēzik; -ˈjēsik/ adj.

hy·per·al·i·men·ta·tion /ˌhīpərˌaləmənˈtāSHən/ ▶n. Med. artificial supply of nutrients, typically intravenously.

hy·per·bar·ic /ˌhīpərˈbarik/ ▶adj. of or involving a gas at a pressure greater than normal. [1960s: from HYPER- 'above normal' + Gk. *baros* 'heavy.']

hy·per·ba·ton /hīˈpərbəˌtän/ ▶n. Rhet. an inversion of the normal order of words, esp. for the sake of emphasis, as in the sentence "*this I must see.*" [16th C.: via L. from Gk. *huperbaton* 'overstepping' (from *huper* 'over, above' + *bainein* 'go, walk').]

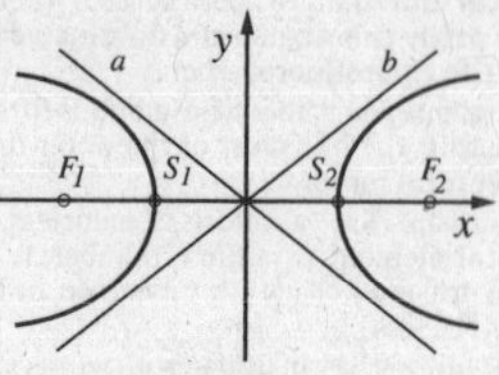

hyperbola

hy·per·bo·la /hīˈpərbələ/ ▶n. (pl. **-bo·las** or **-bo·lae** /-bəlē/) a symmetrical open curve formed by the intersection of a cone with a plane at a smaller angle with its axis than the side of the cone. ■ Math. the pair of such curves formed by the intersection of a plane with two equal cones on opposites of the same vertex. [17th C.: mod. L., from Gk. *huperbolē* 'excess' (from *huper* 'above' + *ballein* 'to throw').]

hy·per·bo·le /hīˈpərbəlē/ ▶n. exaggerated statements or claims not meant to be taken literally. —**hy·per·bol·i·cal** /ˌhīpərˈbälikəl/ adj. **hy·per·bol·i·cal·ly** /ˌhīpərˈbälik(ə)lē/ adv. **hy·per·bo·lism** n. [ME: via L. from Gk. *huperbolē* (see HYPERBOLA).]

hy·per·bol·ic /ˌhīpərˈbälik/ ▶adj. **1** of or relating to a hyperbola. ■ Math. (of a function, e.g., a cosine) having the same relation to a rectangular hyperbola as the unqualified function does to a circle. **2** (of language) exaggerated; hyperbolical.

hy·per·bol·ic pa·rab·o·loid ▶n. Math. a surface whose section parallel to one properly oriented coordinate plane is a hyperbola and whose sections parallel to the other two coordinate planes are parabolas.

hy·per·bo·loid /hīˈpərbəˌloid/ ▶n. a solid or surface having plane sections that are hyperbolas, ellipses, or circles. —**hy·per·bo·loi·dal** /hīˌpərbəˈloidl/ adj.

hy·per·bo·re·an /ˌhīpərˈbôrēən; -bəˈrēən/ literary ▶n. an inhabitant of the extreme north. ■ **(Hyperborean)** Gk. Mythol. a member of a race worshiping Apollo and living in a land of sunshine and plenty beyond the north wind. ▶adj. of or relating to the extreme north. [ME: from late L. *hyperboreanus*, from Gk. *huperboreos*, from *huper* 'beyond' + *boreas* 'north wind.']

hy·per·cho·les·ter·ol·e·mi·a /ˌhīpərkəˌlestərəˈlēmēə/ ▶n. Med. an excess of cholesterol in the bloodstream.

hy·per·cor·rec·tion /ˌhīpərkəˈrekSHən/ ▶n. the erroneous use of a word form or pronunciation based on a false analogy with a correct one, such as *between you and I* for the standard *between you and me*. —**hy·per·cor·rect** adj.

hy·per·crit·i·cal /ˌhīpərˈkritikəl/ ▶adj. excessively and unreasonably critical, esp. of small faults. —**hy·per·crit·i·cal·ly** adv.

hy·per·cube /ˈhīpərˌkyo͞ob/ ▶n. a geometric figure in four or more dimensions that is analogous to a cube in three dimensions.

hy·per·drive /ˈhīpərˌdrīv/ ▶n. (in science fiction) a propulsion system for travel in hyperspace.

hy·per·e·mi·a /ˌhīpəˈrēmēə/ ▶n. Med. an excess of blood in the vessels supplying an organ or other part of the body. —**hy·per·e·mic** /-ˈrēmik/ adj.

hy·per·es·the·sia /ˌhīpərəsˈTHēZHə/ ▶n. Med. excessive physical sensitivity, esp. of the skin. —**hy·per·es·thet·ic** /-ˈTHetik/ adj. [19th C.: from HYPER- 'above normal' + Gk. *aisthēsis* 'sensation.']

hy·per·ex·tend /ˌhīpərikˈstend/ ▶v. [trans.] forcefully extend a limb or joint beyond its normal limits, either in exercise or therapy or so as to cause injury. —**hy·per·ex·ten·sion** /-ˈstenSHən/ n.

hy·per·fo·cal dis·tance /ˌhīpərˈfōkəl/ ▶n. the distance between a camera lens and the closest object that is in focus when the lens is focused at infinity.

hy·per·ga·my /hīˈpərgəmē/ ▶n. the action of marrying a person of a superior caste or class. [19th C.: from HYPER- 'above' + Gk. *gamos* 'marriage.']

hy·per·gly·ce·mi·a /ˌhīpərglīˈsēmēə/ ▶n. Med. an excess of glucose in the bloodstream, often associated with diabetes mellitus. —**hy·per·gly·ce·mic** /-ˈsēmik/ adj. [19th C.: from HYPER- 'above normal' + GLYCO- + -EMIA.]

hy·per·gol·ic /ˌhīpərˈgälik/ ▶adj. (of a rocket propellant) igniting spontaneously on mixing with another substance. [1940s: from Ger. *Hypergol*, prob. from HYPER- 'beyond' + Gk. *ergon* 'work' + -OL.]

hy·per·im·mune /ˌhīpəriˈmyo͞on/ ▶adj. Med. having a high concentration of antibodies produced in reaction to repeated injections of an antigen. —**hy·per·im·mu·ni·za·tion** /-ˌimyəniˈzāSHən/ n. **hy·per·im·mu·nized** /-ˈimyəˌnīzd/ adj.

hy·per·in·fla·tion /hīpərinˈflāSHən/ ▶n. monetary inflation occurring at a very high rate. —**hy·per·in·flat·ed** adj.

Hy·pe·ri·on /hīˈpi(ə)rēən/ Astron. a satellite of Saturn, the sixteenth closest to the planet, discovered in 1848. [named after a Titan of Greek mythology.]

hy·per·ker·a·to·sis /ˌhīpərˌkerəˈtōsis/ ▶ **n.** Med. abnormal thickening of the outer layer of the skin.

hy·per·ki·ne·sis /ˌhīpərkiˈnēsis/ (also **hy·per·ki·ne·sia** /-ˈnēzнə/) ▶ **n.** **1** Med. muscle spasm. **2** Psychiatry a disorder of children marked by hyperactivity and inability to concentrate. [19th C.: from **HYPER-** 'above normal' + Gk. *kinēsis* 'motion.']

hy·per·ki·net·ic /ˌhīpərkəˈnetik/ ▶ **adj.** frenetic; hyperactive. ■ of or affected with hyperkinesis.

hy·per·link /ˈhīpərˌliNGk/ Comput. ▶ **n.** a link from a hypertext file or document to another location or file, typically activated by clicking on a highlighted word or image on the screen. ▶ **v.** [trans.] link (a file) in this way.

hy·per·li·pe·mi·a /ˌhīpərləˈpēmēə/ ▶ **n.** another term for **HYPERLIPIDEMIA**. — **hy·per·li·pe·mic** /-ˈpēmik/ **adj.**

hy·per·lip·i·de·mi·a /ˌhīpərˌlipiˈdēmēə/ ▶ **n.** Med. an abnormally high concentration of fats or lipids in the blood. — **hy·per·lip·i·de·mic** /-ˈdēmik/ **adj.**

hy·per·me·di·a /ˌhīpərˈmēdēə/ ▶ **n.** Comput. an extension to hypertext providing multimedia facilities, such as those handling sound and video.

hy·per·me·tro·pi·a /ˌhīpərməˈtrōpēə/ ▶ **n.** another term for **HYPEROPIA**. — **hy·per·me·tro·pic** /-ˈträpik; -ˈtrō-/ **adj.** [19th C.: from Gk. *hupermetros* 'beyond measure' (from *huper* 'over, above' + *metron* 'measure') + *ōps* 'eye.']

hy·perm·ne·sia /ˌhīpərmˈnēzнə/ ▶ **n.** unusual power or enhancement of memory, typically under abnormal conditions such as trauma, hypnosis, or narcosis.

hy·per·nym /ˈhīpərˌnim/ ▶ **n.** a word with a broad meaning that more specific words fall under; a superordinate. For example, *color* is a hypernym of *red*. Contrasted with **HYPONYM**. [1970s: from **HYPER-** 'beyond,' on the pattern of *hyponym*.]

hy·per·on /ˈhīpəˌrän/ ▶ **n.** Physics an unstable subatomic particle classified as a baryon, heavier than the neutron and proton. [1950s: from **HYPER-** 'beyond, over' + **-ON**.]

hy·per·o·pi·a /ˌhīpəˈrōpēə/ ▶ **n.** farsightedness. — **hy·per·op·ic** /-ˈräpik/ **adj.** [19th C.: from **HYPER-** 'beyond' + Gk. *ōps* 'eye.']

hy·per·par·a·site /ˌhīpərˈparəˌsīt/ ▶ **n.** Biol. a parasite whose host is itself a parasite. — **hy·per·par·a·sit·ic** /-ˌparəˈsitik/ **adj.** **hy·per·par·a·sit·ism** /-sīˌtizəm; -si-/ **n.**

hy·per·par·a·thy·roid·ism /ˌhīpərˌparəˈтнīroiˌdizəm/ ▶ **n.** Med. an abnormally high concentration of parathyroid hormone in the blood, resulting in weakening of the bones through loss of calcium. — **hy·per·par·a·thy·roid adj.**

hy·per·pla·sia /ˌhīpərˈplāzнə/ ▶ **n.** Med. Biol. the enlargement of an organ or tissue caused by an increase in the reproduction rate of its cells, often as an initial stage in the development of cancer. [19th C.: from **HYPER-** 'beyond' + Gk. *plasis* 'formation.']

hy·per·re·al /ˌhīpə(r)ˈrēəl/ ▶ **adj.** **1** exaggerated in comparison to reality. **2** (of artistic representation) extremely realistic in detail. — **hy·per·re·al·ism n. hy·per·re·al·ist adj. hy·per·re·al·is·tic** /ˌhīpə(r)ˌrēəˈlistik/ **adj. hy·per·re·al·i·ty** /-rēˈalitē/ **n.**

hy·per·son·ic /ˌhīpərˈsänik/ ▶ **adj.** **1** relating to speeds of more than five times the speed of sound (Mach 5). **2** relating to sound frequencies above about a thousand million hertz. — **hy·per·son·i·cal·ly adv.**

hy·per·space /ˈhīpərˌspās/ ▶ **n.** space of more than three dimensions. ■ (in science fiction) a notional space-time continuum in which it is possible to travel faster than light. — **hy·per·spa·tial** /ˌhīpərˈspāsнəl/ **adj.**

hy·per·sthene /ˈhīpərˌsтнēn/ ▶ **n.** a greenish rock-forming mineral of the orthopyroxene class, consisting of a magnesium iron silicate. [19th C.: coined in Fr., from **HYPER-** 'exceeding' + Gk. *sthenos* 'strength.']

hy·per·ten·sion /ˌhīpərˈtensнən/ ▶ **n.** Med. abnormally high blood pressure. ■ a state of great psychological stress.

hy·per·ten·sive /ˌhīpərˈtensiv/ ▶ **adj.** exhibiting hypertension. ▶ **n.** Med. a person with high blood pressure.

hy·per·text /ˈhīpərˌtekst/ ▶ **n.** Comput. a software system that links topics on the screen to related information and graphics. ■ a document presented on a computer in this way.

hy·per·ther·mi·a /ˌhīpərˈтнərmēə/ ▶ **n.** Med. the condition of having a body temperature greatly above normal. — **hy·per·ther·mic adj.** [19th C.: from **HYPER-** 'beyond' + Gk. *thermē* 'heat.']

hy·per·thy·roid·ism /ˌhīpərˈтнīroiˌdizəm/ ▶ **n.** Med. overactivity of the thyroid gland, resulting in a rapid heartbeat and an increased rate of metabolism. Also called **THYROTOXICOSIS**. — **hy·per·thy·roid adj. hy·per·thy·roid·ic** /-тнīˈroidik/ **adj.**

hy·per·ton·ic /ˌhīpərˈtänik/ ▶ **adj.** having increased pressure or tone, in particular: ■ Biol. having a higher osmotic pressure than a particular fluid, typically a body fluid or intracellular fluid. ■ Physiol. of or in a state of abnormally high muscle tone. — **hy·per·to·ni·a** /-ˈtōnēə/ **n. hy·per·to·nic·i·ty** /ˌhīpərtəˈnisitē/ **n.**

hy·per·tro·phy /hīˈpərtrəfē/ ▶ **n.** Physiol. the enlargement of an organ or tissue from the increase in size of its cells. ■ excessive growth. ▶ **v.** (**-phies, -phied**) [intrans.] (of a body or an organ) become enlarged due to an increase in cell size. — **hy·per·troph·ic** /ˌhīpərˈträfik; -ˈtrō-/ **adj. hy·per·troph·ied adj.** [19th C.: from **HYPER-** 'beyond, exceeding' + Gk. *-trophia* 'nourishment.']

hy·per·ven·ti·late /ˌhīpərˈventlˌāt/ ▶ **v.** [intrans.] breathe at an abnormally rapid rate, so increasing the rate of loss of carbon dioxide. ■ [trans.] (usu. **be hyperventilated**) cause to breathe in such a way: *the patients were hyperventilated for two minutes.* ■ [as adj.] (**hyperventilated**) fig. inflated or pretentious in style; overblown. — **hy·per·ven·ti·la·tion** /-ˌventlˈāsнən/ **n.**

hyp·es·the·sia /ˌhipəsˈтнēzнə; ˌhīpəs-/ ▶ **n.** a diminished capacity for physical sensation, esp. of the skin. — **hyp·es·thet·ic** /-ˈтнetik/ **adj.** [19th C.: from **HYPO-** 'below' + Gk. *aisthēsis* 'sensation.']

hy·pe·thral /hiˈpēтнrəl; hī-/ (also **hy·pae·thral**) ▶ **adj.** (of a classical building) having no roof; open to the sky. [18th C.: via L. from Gk. *hupaithros* (from *hupo* 'under' + *aithēr* 'air') + **-AL**.]

hy·pha /ˈhīfə/ ▶ **n.** (pl. **-phae** /-fē/) Bot. each of the branching filaments that make up the mycelium of a fungus. — **hy·phal adj.** [19th C.: mod. L., from Gk. *huphē* 'web.']

hy·phen /ˈhīfən/ ▶ **n.** the sign (-) used to join words to indicate that they have a combined meaning or that they are linked in the grammar of a sentence (as in *pick-me-up*, *rock-forming*), to indicate the division of a word at the end of a line, or to indicate a missing or implied element (as in *short-* and *long-term*). ▶ **v.** another term for **HYPHENATE**. [17th C.: via late L. from Gk. *huphen* 'together,' from *hupo* 'under' + *hen* 'one.']

hy·phen·ate /ˈhīfəˌnāt/ ▶ **v.** [trans.] write with a hyphen. ▶ **n.** a person who is active in more than one occupation or sphere: *as a supreme hyphenate, she was the director-producer-star of her new film.* — **hy·phen·a·tion** /ˌhīfəˈnāsнən/ **n.**

hy·phen·at·ed A·mer·i·can ▶ **n.** informal an American citizen with ancestry to another, specified part of the world, such as an African American or an Irish American (so called because terms like *African American* are often written with a hyphen).

hyp·na·gog·ic /ˌhipnəˈgäjik; -ˈgō-/ (also **hyp·no·gog·ic**) ▶ **adj.** Psychol. of or relating to the state immediately before falling asleep. [19th C.: from Fr. *hypnagogique*, from Gk. *hupnos* 'sleep' + *agōgos* 'leading' (from *agein* 'to lead').]

hypno- ▶ **comb. form** relating to sleep: *hypnopedia.* ■ relating to hypnosis: *hypnotherapy.* [from Gk. *hupnos* 'sleep.']

hyp·no·pom·pic /ˌhipnəˈpämpik/ ▶ **adj.** Psychol. of or relating to the state immediately preceding waking up. [20th C.: from Gk. *hupnos* 'sleep' + *pompē* 'sending away' + **-IC**.]

Hyp·nos /ˈhipˌnäs/ Gk. Mythol. the god of sleep, son of Nyx (Night).

hyp·no·sis /hipˈnōsis/ ▶ **n.** the induction of a state of consciousness in which a person apparently loses the power of voluntary action and is highly responsive to suggestion or direction. ■ this state of consciousness. [19th C.: from Gk. *hupnos* 'sleep' + **-OSIS**.]

hyp·no·ther·a·py /ˌhipnōˈтнerəpē/ ▶ **n.** the use of hypnosis as a therapeutic technique. — **hyp·no·ther·a·pist n.**

hyp·not·ic /hipˈnätik/ ▶ **adj.** **1** of, producing, or relating to hypnosis. ■ exerting a compelling, fascinating, or soporific effect. **2** Med. (of a drug) sleep-inducing. ▶ **n.** **1** Med. a sleep-inducing drug. **2** a person under or open to the influence of hypnotism. — **hyp·not·i·cal·ly adv.** [17th C.: from Fr. *hypnotique*, via late L. from Gk. *hupnōtikos* 'narcotic, causing sleep,' from *hupnoun* 'put to sleep,' from *hupnos* 'sleep.']

hyp·no·tism /ˈhipnəˌtizəm/ ▶ **n.** the study or practice of hypnosis. — **hyp·no·tist n.**

hyp·no·tize /ˈhipnəˌtīz/ ▶ **v.** (often **be hypnotized**) [trans.] produce a state of hypnosis in (someone). ■ capture the whole attention of (someone); fascinate. — **hyp·no·tiz·a·ble** /-ˌtīzəbəl; ˌhipnəˈtīzəbəl/ **adj.**

hy·po[1] /ˈhīpō/ ▶ **n.** Photog. the chemical sodium thiosulphate (formerly called hyposulphite) used as a photographic fixer. [19th C.: abbrev. of *hyposulphite*.]

hy·po[2] ▶ **n.** (pl. **-pos**) informal term for **HYPODERMIC**.

hypo- (also **hyp-**) ▶ **prefix** under: *hypodermic.* ■ below normal: *hypoglycemia.* ■ slightly: *hypomanic.* ■ Chem. containing an element with an unusually low valence: *hypochlorous.* [from Gk. *hupo* 'under.']

hy·po·al·ler·gen·ic /ˌhīpōˌalərˈjenik/ ▶ **adj.** (esp. of cosmetics and textiles) relatively unlikely to cause an allergic reaction.

hy·po·blast /ˈhīpəˌblast/ ▶ **n.** Biol. former term for **ENDODERM**.

hy·po·cal·ce·mi·a /ˌhīpōkalˈsēmēə/ (Brit. **hy·po·cal·cae·mi·a**) ▶ **n.** Med. deficiency of calcium in the bloodstream.

hy·po·caust /ˈhīpəˌkôst/ ▶ **n.** a hollow space under the floor of an ancient Roman building, into which hot air was sent for heating a room or bath. [from L. *hypocaustum*, from Gk. *hupokauston* 'place heated from below,' from *hupo* 'under' + *kau-* (base of *kaiein* 'to burn').]

hy·po·cen·ter /ˈhīpəˌsentər/ ▶ **n.** **1** the underground focus of an earthquake. Compare with **EPICENTER**. **2** another term for **GROUND ZERO**.

hy·po·chlo·rous ac·id /ˌhīpəˈklôrəs/ ▶ **n.** Chem. a weak acid, HOCl, with oxidizing properties formed when chlorine dissolves in cold water, used in bleaching and water treatment. — **hy·po·chlo·rite** /-rīt/ **n.** [19th C.: *hypochlorous* from **HYPO-** (denoting an element in a low valency) + **CHLORINE** + **-OUS**.]

hy·po·chon·dri·a /ˌhīpəˈkändrēə/ ▶ **n.** abnormal anxiety about one's health. [ME: via late L. from Gk. *hupokhondria*, denoting the soft body area below the ribs, from *hupo* 'under' + *khondros* 'sternal cartilage.']

hy·po·chon·dri·ac /ˌhīpəˈkändrēˌak/ ▶ **n.** a person who is abnormally anxious about their health. [16th C.: coined in Fr. from Gk. *hupokhondriakos*, from *hupokhondria* (see **HYPOCHONDRIA**).]

hy·po·chon·dri·a·cal /ˌhīpōkənˈdrīəkəl/ ▶ **adj.** of or affected by hypochondria.

hy·po·chon·dri·a·sis /ˌhīpōkən'drīəsis/ ▶n. technical term for HYPOCHONDRIA.

hy·po·co·ris·tic /ˌhīpəkə'ristik/ ▶adj. denoting, or of the nature of, a pet name or diminutive form of a name. ▶n. a hypocoristic name or form. — **hy·poc·o·rism** /hī'päkəˌrizəm; hi-/ n. [19th C.: from Gk. *hupokorisma*, from *hupokorizesthai* 'play the child,' from *hupo* 'under' + *korē* 'child.']

hy·po·cot·yl /'hīpəˌkätl; ˌhīpə'kätl/ ▶n. Bot. the part of the stem of an embryo plant beneath the stalks of the seed leaves, or cotyledons, and directly above the root.

hy·poc·ri·sy /hi'päkrisē/ ▶n. (pl. **-sies**) the practice of claiming to have moral standards or beliefs to which one's own behavior does not conform; pretense. [ME: from OFr. *ypocrisie*, via eccles. L., from Gk. *hupokrisis* 'acting of a theatrical part,' from *hupokrinesthai* 'play a part, pretend,' from *hupo* 'under' + *krinein* 'decide, judge.']

hyp·o·crite /'hipəˌkrit/ ▶n. a person who indulges in hypocrisy. — **hyp·o·crit·i·cal** /ˌhipə'kritikəl/ adj. **hyp·o·crit·i·cal·ly** /ˌhipə'kritik(ə)lē/ adv.

hy·po·cy·cloid /ˌhīpə'sīkloid/ ▶n. Math. the curve traced by a point on the circumference of a circle that is rolling on the interior of another circle. — **hy·po·cy·cloi·dal** /ˌhīpəsī'kloidl/ adj.

hy·po·der·mic /ˌhīpə'dərmik/ ▶adj. [attrib.] Med. of or relating to the region immediately beneath the skin. ■ (of a needle or syringe) used to inject a drug or other substance beneath the skin. ■ (of a drug or other substance or its application) injected beneath the skin. ▶n. a hypodermic syringe or injection. — **hy·po·der·mi·cal·ly** adv.

hy·po·gas·tri·um /ˌhīpə'gastrēəm/ ▶n. (pl. **-tri·a** /-trēə/) Anat. the part of the central abdomen that is situated below the region of the stomach. — **hy·po·gas·tric** adj. [17th C.: mod. L., from Gk. *hupogastrion*, from *hupo* 'under' + *gastēr* 'belly.']

hy·po·ge·al /ˌhīpə'jēəl/ (also **hy·po·ge·an**) ▶adj. Bot. underground; subterranean. Compare with EPIGEAL. ■ (of seed germination) with the seed leaves remaining below the ground. [17th C.: via late L. from Gk. *hupogeios* (from *hupo* 'under' + *gē* 'earth') + -AL.]

hy·po·gene /'hīpəˌjēn/ ▶adj. Geol. producing or occurring under the surface of the earth. — **hy·po·gen·ic** /ˌhīpə'jenik/ adj. [19th C.: from HYPO- 'under' + Gk. *genēs* '-born, of a certain kind.']

hy·po·ge·um /ˌhīpə'jēəm/ ▶n. (pl. **-ge·a** /-'jēə/) an underground chamber. [17th C.: from L., from Gk. *hupogeion*, neut. of *hupogeios* 'underground.']

hy·po·glos·sal nerve /ˌhīpə'gläsəl; -'glô-/ ▶n. Anat. each of the twelfth pair of cranial nerves, supplying the muscles of the tongue. [19th C.: *hypoglossal* from HYPO- 'under' + Gk. *glōssa* 'tongue' + -AL.]

hy·po·gly·ce·mi·a /ˌhīpōglī'sēmēə/ (Brit. **hy·po·gly·cae·mi·a**) ▶n. Med. deficiency of glucose in the bloodstream. — **hy·po·gly·ce·mic** adj. [19th C.: from HYPO- 'below' + GLYCO- + -EMIA.]

hy·po·gon·ad·ism /ˌhīpō'gōnaˌdizəm/ ▶n. Med. reduction or absence of hormone secretion or other physiological activity of the gonads (testes or ovaries). — **hy·po·go·nad·al** /ˌhīpəgō'nadl/ adj. **hy·po·go·nad·ic** /ˌhīpəgō'nadik/ n. & adj.

hy·pog·y·nous /hī'päjənəs/ ▶adj. Bot. (of a plant or flower) having the stamens and other floral parts situated below the carpels (or gynoecium). Compare with EPIGYNOUS, PERIGYNOUS. — **hy·pog·y·ny** /-'päjənē/ n. [19th C.: from mod. L. *hypogynus*, from HYPO- 'below' + *gunē* 'woman' (used to represent 'pistil') + -OUS.]

hy·poid /'hīpoid/ (also **hypoid gear**) ▶n. a bevel wheel with teeth engaging with a spiral pinion mounted at right angles to the wheel's axis, used to connect nonintersecting shafts in vehicle transmissions and other mechanisms. [1920s: perh. a contr. of HYPERBOLOID.]

hy·po·ka·le·mi·a /ˌhīpō¯kā'lēmēə/ ▶n. Med. deficiency of potassium in the bloodstream. — **hy·po·ka·le·mic** /-'lēmik/ adj. [1940s: from HYPO- 'below' + mod. L. *kalium* 'potassium.']

hy·po·lim·ni·on /ˌhīpə'limnēˌän; -nēən/ ▶n. (pl. **-ni·a** /-nēə/) the lower layer of water in a stratified lake, typically cooler than the water above and relatively stagnant. [20th C.: from HYPO- 'below' + Gk. *limnion* (dimin. of *limnē* 'lake').]

hy·po·mag·ne·se·mi·a /ˌhīpəˌmagnə'sēmēə/ ▶n. Med. Vet. Med. deficiency of magnesium in the blood, significant in cattle as the cause of grass tetany. — **hy·po·mag·ne·se·mic** /-'sēmik/ adj.

hy·po·ma·ni·a /ˌhīpə'mānēə/ ▶n. Psychiatry a mild form of mania, marked by elation and hyperactivity. — **hy·po·man·ic** /-'manik/ adj.

hy·po·nym /'hīpəˌnim/ ▶n. a word of more specific meaning than a general or superordinate term applicable to it. For example, *bowl* is a hyponym of *dish*. Contrasted with HYPERNYM. — **hy·pon·y·my** /hī'pänəmē/ n.

hy·po·par·a·thy·roid·ism /ˌhīpōˌparə'THīroiˌdizəm/ ▶n. Med. diminished concentration of parathyroid hormone in the blood, which causes deficiencies of calcium and phosphorus compounds in the blood and results in muscular spasms. — **hy·po·par·a·thy·roid** adj.

hy·poph·y·sis /hī'päfəsis/ ▶n. (pl. **-ses** /-ˌsēz/) Anat. technical term for PITUITARY. — **hy·po·phys·e·al** /ˌhīpə'fizēəl; hīˌpäfə'sēəl/ (also **hy·po·phys·i·al**) adj. [17th C.: mod. L., from Gk. *hupophusis* 'offshoot,' from *hupo* 'under' + *phusis* 'growth.']

hy·po·pi·tu·i·ta·rism /ˌhīpōpi't(y)o͞o-itəˌrizəm/ ▶n. Med. diminished hormone secretion by the pituitary gland, causing dwarfism in children and premature aging in adults. — **hy·po·pi·tu·i·tar·y** /ˌhīpōpə't(y)o͞oiˌterē/ adj.

hy·po·pne·a /hī'päpnēə; hi-/ ▶n. abnormally slow or shallow breathing.

hy·po·sen·si·tiv·i·ty /'hīpōˌsensi'tivitē/ ▶n. a lower than normal sensitivity to stimuli.

hy·po·sen·si·tize /ˌhīpō'sensiˌtīz/ ▶v. reduce the sensitivity or symptomatic reactions to an allergen by frequently injecting small amounts of the allergen; desensitize. — **hy·po·sen·si·ti·za·tion** n. /'hīpōˌsensiti'zāsHən/

hy·po·spray /'hīpōˌsprā/ ▶n. (chiefly in science fiction) a device used to introduce a drug or other substance into the body through the skin without puncturing it.

hy·pos·ta·sis /hī'pästəsis/ ▶n. (pl. **-ses** /-ˌsēz/) **1** Med. the accumulation of fluid or blood in the lower parts of the body or organs under the influence of gravity, as occurs in cases of poor circulation or after death. **2** Philos. an underlying reality or substance, as opposed to attributes or that which lacks substance. ■ Theol. (in Trinitarian doctrine) each of the three persons of the Trinity, as contrasted with the unity of the Godhead. ■ [in sing.] Theol. the single person of Christ, as contrasted with his dual human and divine nature. — **hy·po·stat·ic** /ˌhīpə'statik/ adj. **hy·po·stat·i·cal** adj. [16th C.: via eccles. L. from Gk. *hupostasis* 'sediment,' from *hupo* 'under' + *stasis* 'standing.']

hy·pos·ta·tize /hī'pästəˌtīz/ ▶v. [trans.] formal treat or represent (something abstract) as a concrete reality.

hy·po·sthe·ni·a /ˌhīpäs'THēnēə/ ▶n. an abnormal lack of strength.

hy·po·style /'hīpəˌstīl/ ▶adj. Archit. (of a building) having a roof supported by pillars, typically in several rows. ▶n. a building having such a roof. [19th C.: from Gk. *hupostulos*, from *hupo* 'under' + *stulos* 'column.']

hy·po·tax·is /ˌhīpə'taksis/ ▶n. Gram. the subordination of one clause to another. Contrasted with PARATAXIS. — **hy·po·tac·tic** /ˌhīpə'taktik/ adj. [19th C.: from Gk. *hupotaxis*, from *hupo* 'under' + *taxis* 'arrangement.']

hy·po·ten·sion /ˌhīpə'tensHən/ ▶n. abnormally low blood pressure.

hy·po·ten·sive /ˌhīpō'tensiv/ ▶adj. lowering the blood pressure. ■ relating to or suffering from abnormally low blood pressure.

hy·pot·e·nuse /hī'pätnˌ(y)o͞os/ ▶n. the longest side of a right triangle, opposite the right angle. [16th C.: via L. *hypotenusa* from Gk. *hupoteinousa (grammē)* 'subtending (line),' from the v. *hupoteinein* (from *hupo* 'under' + *teinein* 'stretch').]

hypoth. ▶abbr. ■ hypothesis or hypothetical.

hy·po·thal·a·mus /ˌhīpə'THaləməs/ ▶n. (pl. **-mi** /-ˌmī/) Anat. a region of the forebrain below the thalamus that coordinates both the autonomic nervous system and the activity of the pituitary. — **hy·po·tha·lam·ic** /ˌhīpōˌTHə'lamik/ adj.

hy·poth·e·cate /hi'päTHiˌkāt; hī-/ ▶v. [trans.] pledge (money) by law to a specific purpose. — **hy·poth·e·ca·tion** /hiˌpäTHi'kāsHən; hī-/ n. [17th C.: from med. L. *hypothecat-* 'given as a pledge,' from the v. *hypothecare*, based on Gk. *hupothēkē*.]

hy·po·ther·mal /ˌhīpə'THərməl/ ▶adj. not very hot; tepid. ■ relating to or suffering from hypothermia. ■ Geol. of or relating to mineral deposits formed at relatively high temperature and pressure. — **hy·po·ther·mic** adj.

hy·po·ther·mi·a /ˌhīpə'THərmēə/ ▶n. the condition of having an abnormally low body temperature, typically one that is dangerously low. [19th C.: from HYPO- 'below' + Gk. *thermē* 'heat.']

hy·poth·e·sis /hī'päTHəsis/ ▶n. (pl. **-ses** /-ˌsēz/) a supposition or proposed explanation made on the basis of limited evidence as a starting point for further investigation. ■ Philos. a proposition made as a basis for reasoning, without any assumption of its truth. [16th C.: via late L. from Gk. *hupothesis* 'foundation,' from *hupo* 'under' + *thesis* 'placing.']

hy·poth·e·sis test·ing ▶n. Stat. the theory, methods, and practice of testing a hypothesis by comparing it with the null hypothesis.

hy·poth·e·size /hī'päTHəˌsīz/ ▶v. [trans.] put (something) forward as a hypothesis. — **hy·poth·e·siz·er** n.

hy·po·thet·i·cal /ˌhīpə'THetikəl/ ▶adj. of, based on, or serving as a hypothesis. ■ supposed but not necessarily real or true. ■ Logic denoting or containing a proposition of the logical form *if p then q*. ▶n. (usu. **hypotheticals**) a hypothetical proposition or statement: *Flynn talked in hypotheticals, tossing what-if scenarios to Kernaghan.* — **hy·po·thet·i·cal·ly** adv.

hy·po·thy·roid·ism /ˌhīpō'THīroiˌdizəm/ ▶n. Med. abnormally low activity of the thyroid gland, resulting in retardation of growth and mental development. — **hy·po·thy·roid** n. & adj.

hy·po·ton·ic /ˌhīpə'tänik/ ▶adj. having reduced pressure or tone, in particular: ■ Biol. having a lower osmotic pressure than a particular fluid, typically a body fluid or intracellular fluid. ■ Physiol. of or in a state of abnormally low muscle tone. — **hy·po·to·ni·a** /-'tōnēə/ n. **hy·po·to·nic·i·ty** /ˌhīpōtō'nisitē/ n.

hy·pot·ro·phy /hī'pätrəfē/ ▶n. (pl. **-phies**) a degeneration of an organ or tissue caused by a loss of cells.

hy·po·ven·ti·la·tion /ˌhīpōˌventl'āsHən/ ▶n. Med. breathing at an abnormally slow rate, resulting in an increased amount of carbon dioxide in the blood.

hy·po·vo·le·mi·a /ˌhīpōvə'lēmēə/ ▶n. Med. a decreased volume of circulating blood in the body. — **hy·po·vo·le·mic** /-'lēmik/ adj. [20th C.: from HYPO- 'under' + VOLUME + Gk. *haima* 'blood.']

hy·po·xan·thine /ˌhīpō'zanTHēn/ ▶n. Biochem. a compound, $C_5H_4N_4O$, that occurs in plant tissues and is an intermediate in the metabolism of purines in animals.

hy·pox·e·mi·a /ˌhīpäk'sēmēə/ ▶n. Med. an abnormally low concentration of oxygen in the blood. [19th C.: from HYPO- (denoting an element in a low valency) + OXYGEN + -EMIA.]

hy·pox·i·a /hī'päksēə/ ▶n. Med. deficiency in the amount of oxygen reaching the tissues. — **hy·pox·ic** adj. [1940s: from HYPO- (denoting an element in a low valency) + OXYGEN + -IA[1].]

hypso- ▶ comb. form relating to height or elevation: *hypsometer.* [from Gk. *hupsos* 'height.']

hyp·som·e·ter /hip'sämitər/ ▶ n. a device for calibrating thermometers at the boiling point of water at a known height above sea level or for estimating height above sea level by finding the temperature at which water boils. — **hyp·so·met·ric** /ˌhipsō'metrik/ adj.

Hy·ra·coi·de·a /ˌhīrə'koidēə/ Zool. a small order of mammals that comprises the hyraxes. — **hy·ra·coid** /'hīrəˌkoid/ n. & adj. [mod. L. (pl.), based on Gk. *hurax, hurak-* (see HYRAX).]

hy·ra·co·the·ri·um /ˌhīrəkō'THi(ə)rēəm/ ▶ n. a small forest animal (genus *Hyracotherium*, family Equidae) of the Eocene epoch, with four toes on the front feet and three on the back. It is the earliest fossil ancestor of the horse. Also called EOHIPPUS. [mod. L.: from *hyraco-* (combining form from HYRAX) + Gk. *thērion* 'wild animal.']

hy·rax /'hīraks/ ▶ n. a small herbivorous mammal (family Procaviidae and order Hyracoidea) with a compact body and a very short tail, found in arid country in Africa and Arabia. The nearest relatives to hyraxes are the elephants and other subungulates. [19th C.: mod. L., from Gk. *hurax* 'shrewmouse.']

hy·son /'hīsən/ ▶ n. a type of green China tea. [18th C.: from Chin. *xīchūn*, lit. 'bright spring.']

hys·sop /'hisəp/ ▶ n. **1** a small bushy aromatic plant (*Hyssopus officinalis*) of the mint family, the bitter minty leaves of which are used in cooking and herbal medicine. **2** (in biblical use) a wild shrub of uncertain identity whose twigs were used for sprinkling in ancient Jewish rites of purification. [OE *hysope* (reinforced in ME by OFr. *ysope*), via L. from Gk. *hyssōpos*, of Semitic origin.]

hys·ter·ec·to·my /ˌhistə'rektəmē/ ▶ n. (pl. **-mies**) a surgical operation to remove all or part of the uterus. — **hys·ter·ec·to·mize** /ˌhistə'rektəˌmīz/ v. [19th C.: from Gk. *hustera* 'womb' + -ECTOMY.]

hys·ter·e·sis /ˌhistə'rēsis/ ▶ n. Physics the phenomenon in which the value of a physical property lags behind changes in the effect causing it. [19th C.: from Gk. *husterēsis* 'shortcoming, deficiency,' from *husterein* 'be behind,' from *husteros* 'late.']

hys·te·ri·a /hi'sterēə; -'sti(ə)rēə/ ▶ n. exaggerated or uncontrollable emotion or excitement, esp. among a group of people: *the mass hysteria that characterizes the week before Christmas.* ■ Psychiatry a psychological disorder whose symptoms include conversion of psychological stress into physical symptoms, selective amnesia, shallow volatile emotions, and overdramatic or attention-seeking behavior. [19th C.: from L. *hystericus* (see HYSTERIC).]

hys·ter·ic /hi'sterik/ ▶ n. **1** (**hysterics**) informal a wildly emotional and exaggerated reaction. ■ uncontrollable laughter. **2** a person suffering from hysteria. ▶ adj. another term for HYSTERICAL (sense 2). [17th C.: via L. from Gk. *husterikos* 'of the womb,' from *hustera* 'womb' (hysteria being thought to be specific to women and associated with the womb).]

hys·ter·i·cal /hi'sterikəl/ ▶ adj. **1** deriving from or affected by uncontrolled extreme emotion: *hysterical laughter.* ■ informal extremely funny. **2** Psychiatry relating to, associated with, or suffering from hysteria. — **hys·ter·i·cal·ly** adv.

hys·ter·on prot·er·on /'histəˌrän 'prätəˌrän/ ▶ n. Rhet. a figure of speech in which what should come last is put first, i.e., an inversion of the natural order, for example "*I die! I faint! I fail!*" [16th C.: late L., from Gk. *husteron proteron* 'the latter (put in place of) the former.']

Hy·trel /'hīˌtrel/ ▶ n. trademark a strong, flexible synthetic resin used in shoes, sports equipment, and other manufactured articles.

Hz ▶ abbr. hertz.

Ii

I[1] /ī/ (also **i**) ▶ **n.** (pl. **Is** or **I's**) **1** the ninth letter of the alphabet. ■ denoting the next after H in a set of items, categories, etc. **2** the Roman numeral for one.

I[2] ▶ **pron.** [first person sing.] used by a speaker to refer to himself or herself: *accept me for what I am.* ▶ **n.** (**the I**) Philos. (in metaphysics) the subject or object of self-consciousness; the ego. [OE, of Gmc. origin; rel. to Du. *ik* and Ger. *ich*, from an Indo-Eur. root shared by L. *ego* and Gk. *egō*.]

I[3] ▶ **abbr.** ■ Independent. ■ (preceding a highway number) Interstate. ■ (**I.**) Island(s) or Isle(s) (chiefly on maps). ▶ **symb.** ■ electric current: $V = I/R$. ■ the chemical element iodine.

i ▶ **symb.** (*i*) Math. the imaginary quantity equal to the square root of minus one. Compare with **J**.

-i[1] ▶ **suffix** forming the plural: **1** of nouns adopted from Latin ending in *-us*: *foci* | *timpani.* **2** of nouns adopted from Italian ending in *-e* or *-o*: *dilettanti.*

-i[2] ▶ **suffix** forming adjectives from names of countries or regions in the Near or Middle East: *Azerbaijani* | *Pakistani.* [from Semitic and Indo-Iranian adjectival endings.]

-i- ▶ **suffix** a connecting vowel chiefly forming words ending in *-ana, -ferous, -fic, -form, -fy, -gerous, -vorous.* Compare with **-o-**.

IA ▶ **abbr.** Iowa (in official postal use).

Ia. ▶ **abbr.** Iowa.

-ia[1] /-ēə/ ▶ **suffix 1** forming nouns adopted unchanged from Latin or Greek (such as *mania, militia*), and modern Latin or Greek terms (such as *utopia*). **2** forming names of: ■ Med. states and disorders: *anemia* | *diphtheria.* ■ Bot. Zool. genera and higher groups: *dahlia* | *Latimeria.* **3** forming names of countries: *India.* [representing L. or Gk. endings.]

-ia[2] ▶ **suffix** forming noun plurals: **1** from Greek neuter nouns ending in *-ion* or from those in Latin ending in *-ium* or *-e*: *paraphernalia* | *regalia.* **2** Zool. in the names of classes: *Reptilia.*

IAA Biochem. ▶ **abbr.** indoleacetic acid.

IAAF ▶ **abbr.** International Amateur Athletic Federation.

IABA ▶ **abbr.** International Amateur Boxing Association.

Ia·coc·ca /ˌīəˈkōkə/, Lee (1924–) US industrialist; full name *Lido Anthony Iacocca.* He was president of Ford Motor Company 1970–78 before leading the Chrysler Corporation 1978–92.

IAEA ▶ **abbr.** International Atomic Energy Agency.

-ial /-ēəl/ ▶ **suffix** forming adjectives such as *celestial, primordial.* [from Fr. *-iel* or L. *-ialis.*]

IALC ▶ **abbr.** instrument approach and landing chart.

IAMAW ▶ **abbr.** International Association of Machinists and Aerospace Workers.

i·amb /ˈīam(b)/ ▶ **n.** Pros. a metrical foot consisting of one short (or unstressed) syllable followed by one long (or stressed) syllable.

i·am·bic /īˈambik/ ▶ **adj.** Pros. of or using iambs: *iambic pentameters.* ▶ **n.** a verse using iambs. ■ (**iambics**) verse of this kind. [16th C.: from Fr. *iambique*, via late L. from Gk. *iambikos*, from *iambos* (see **IAMBUS**).]

i·am·bus /īˈambəs/ ▶ **n.** (pl. **-bus·es** or **-bi** /-bī/) Pros. another term for **IAMB.** [16th C.: L., from Gk. *iambos* 'iambus, lampoon,' from *iaptein* 'attack verbally.']

-ian /-ēən/ ▶ **suffix** forming adjectives and nouns such as *antediluvian* and *Christian.* Compare with **-AN.** [from Fr. *-ien* or L. *-ianus.*]

IAP ▶ **abbr.** international airport.

IAS ▶ **abbr.** ■ indicated air speed. ■ Institute for Advanced Studies.

Ia·şi /yäsн/ a city in eastern Romania; pop. 338,000. German name **JASSY.**

-iasis ▶ **suffix** a common form of **-ASIS.**

IATA /īˈätə/ ▶ **abbr.** International Air Transport Association.

iatro- ▶ **comb. form** relating to a physician or to medical treatment: *iatrogenic.* [from Gk. *iatros* 'physician,' from *iasthai* 'heal.']

i·at·ro·gen·ic /īˌatrəˈjenik/ ▶ **adj.** of or relating to illness caused by medical examination or treatment. — **i·at·ro·gen·e·sis** /-ˈjenisis/ **n.**

IAU ▶ **abbr.** ■ International Association of Universities. ■ International Astronomical Union.

ib. ▶ **adv.** short for **IBID.**

I·ba·dan /ēˈbädn/ a city in southwestern Nigeria; pop. 1,295,000.

Iba·gué /ˌēbəˈgā/ a city in west central Colombia, capital of Tolima department; pop. 334,000.

I-beam ▶ **n.** a girder that has the shape of an I when viewed in section.

I·be·ri·a /īˈbi(ə)rēə/ the ancient name of the Iberian peninsula.

I·be·ri·an /īˈbi(ə)rēən/ ▶ **adj.** relating to or denoting Iberia, or the countries of Spain and Portugal. ▶ **n.** **1** a native of Iberia, esp. in ancient times. **2** the extinct Romance language spoken in the Iberian peninsula in late classical times. Also called **Ibero-Romance.** **3** the extinct Celtic language spoken in the Iberian peninsula in ancient times. Also called **CELTIBERIAN.**

I·be·ri·an pen·in·su·la the southwestern peninsula of Europe that contains Spain and Portugal.

Ibero- ▶ **comb. form** Iberian; Iberian and ...: *Ibero-Roman.* ■ relating to Iberia.

i·bex /ˈībeks/ ▶ **n.** (pl. **i·bex·es**) a wild goat (genus *Capra*, esp. *C. ibex*) with long, thick ridged horns that curve back, found in the mountains of the Alps, Pyrenees, central Asia, and Ethiopia. [17th C.: from L.]

IBF ▶ **abbr.** International Boxing Federation.

I·bi·bi·o /ˈibibēō; ibəˈbēō/ ▶ **n.** (pl. same or **-i·os**) **1** a member of a people of southern Nigeria. **2** the Benue-Congo language of this people. ▶ **adj.** of or relating to this people or their language. [the name in Ibibio.]

ibid. /ˈibid/ (also **ib.**) ▶ **adv.** in the same source (used to save space in textual references to a quoted work that has been mentioned in a previous reference). [abbrev. of L. *ibidem* 'in the same place.']

-ibility ▶ **suffix** forming nouns corresponding to adjectives ending in *-ible* (such as *accessibility* corresponding to *accessible*). [from Fr. *-ibilité* or L. *-ibilitas.*]

white ibis

i·bis /ˈībis/ ▶ **n.** (pl. **i·bis·es**) a large wading bird (family Threskiornithidae) with a long down-curved bill, long neck, and long legs. Several genera and species include the **sacred ibis** and **white ibis.** [ME: via L. from Gk.]

I·bi·za /iˈbēтнə; iˈvē-/ the most western of the Balearic Islands, a popular resort. ■ its capital city and port; pop. 25,000. — **I·bi·zan adj. & n.**

I·bi·zan hound /iˈbēzən/ ▶ **n.** a dog of a breed of hound from Ibiza, characterized by large, pointed, pricked ears and white, yellowish-brown, or reddish-brown coloring.

-ible /əbəl; ibəl/ ▶ **suffix** forming adjectives: **1** able to be: *audible* | *defensible.* **2** suitable for being: *reversible* | *edible.* **3** causing: *terrible* | *horrible.* **4** having the quality to: *descendible* | *passible.* [from Fr. *-ible* or L. *-ibilis.*]

-ibly ▶ **suffix** forming adverbs corresponding to adjectives ending in *-ible* (such as *audibly* corresponding to *audible*).

IBM ▶ **abbr.** International Business Machines, a leading US computer manufacturer.

ibn Hus·sein, Abdullah, see **ABDULLAH IBN HUSSEIN.**

Ibn Sa·ud /ˌibən säˈo͞od/ (c.1880–1953) king of Saudi Arabia 1932–53; full name *Abd al-Aziz ibn Abd ar-Rahman ibn Faysal ibn Turki Abd Allah ibn Muhammad Al Saud.* He founded Saudi Arabia 1932.

I·bo /ˈēbō/ (also **Ig·bo**) /ˈigbō/ ▶ **n.** (pl. same or **I·bos**) **1** a member of a people of southeastern Nigeria. **2** the Kwa language of this people. ▶ **adj.** of or relating to this people or their language. [a local name.]

i·bo·ga·ine /iˈbōgəˌēn/ ▶ **n.** a hallucinogenic compound derived from the roots of a West African shrub (*Tabernanthe iboga*) of the dogbane family, sometimes used as a treatment for heroin or cocaine addiction. [from a blend of *iboga* (local name for the compound) and **COCAINE.**]

IBS ▶ **abbr.** irritable bowel syndrome.

Ib·sen /ˈibsən/, Henrik (1828–1906), Norwegian playwright. Notable works: *Peer Gynt* (1867) and *A Doll's House* (1879).

i·bu·pro·fen /ˌībyo͞oˈprōfən/ ▶ **n.** a synthetic compound ($C_{13}H_{18}O_2$) used widely as an analgesic and anti-inflammatory drug. Alternative name:

2-(4-isobutylphenyl) propionic acid. [1960s: from elements of the chemical name.]

IC ▶ abbr. ■ integrated circuit. ■ intensive care. ■ internal combustion: *the IC engine.*

-ic /ik/ ▶ suffix **1** forming adjectives such as *Islamic, terrific.* **2** forming nouns such as *lyric, mechanic.* **3** denoting a particular form or instance of a noun ending in *-ics*: *aesthetic* | *dietetic* | *tactic.* **4** Chem. denoting an element in a higher valence: *ferric* | *sulfuric.* Compare with **-ous.** [from Fr. *-ique*, L. *-icus*, or Gk. *-ikos.*]

-ical /ikəl/ ▶ suffix forming adjectives: **1** corresponding to nouns or adjectives usually ending in *-ic* (such as *comical* corresponding to *comic*). **2** corresponding to nouns ending in *-y* (such as *pathological* corresponding to *pathology*).

-ically /ik(ə)lē/ ▶ suffix forming adverbs corresponding to adjectives ending in *-ic* or *-ical* (such as *tactically* corresponding to *tactical*).

ICANN ▶ abbr. Internet Committee for Assigned Names and Numbers, the nonprofit organization that oversees the use of Internet domains.

Ic·a·rus /ˈikərəs/ Gk. Mythol. the son of Daedalus, who escaped from Crete using wings made by his father but was killed when he flew too near the sun and the wax attaching his wings melted. — **I·car·i·an** /iˈke(ə)rēən; īˈke(ə)r-/ **adj.**

ICBM ▶ abbr. intercontinental ballistic missile.

ICC ▶ abbr. ■ Interstate Commerce Commission. ■ International Chamber of Commerce.

ice /īs/ ▶ n. frozen water, a brittle, transparent crystalline solid. ■ a frozen mixture of fruit juice or flavored water and sugar. ■ informal diamonds. ■ fig. complete absence of friendliness or affection in manner or expression: *ice in his voice.* ■ informal methamphetamine. ▶ v. [trans.] **1** decorate (a cake) with icing. **2** informal clinch (something such as a victory or deal). **3** informal kill. **4** Ice Hockey shoot (the puck) the length of the rink from defensive to offensive territory.
– PHRASES **break the ice** do or say something to relieve tension or get conversation going when people meet for the first time. **on ice** ■ fig. (esp. of a plan or proposal) held in reserve for future consideration: *the recommendation was put on ice.* **on thin ice** in a precarious or risky situation: *you're skating on thin ice.* [OE *īs*, of Gmc. origin; rel. to Du. *ijs* and Ger. *Eis.*]

-ice ▶ suffix forming nouns such as *service, police,* and abstract nouns such as *avarice, justice.* [from OFr. *-ice*, from L. *-itia, -itius, -itium.*]

ice age ▶ n. a glacial episode during a past geological period. See **glacial period.** ■ (**the Ice Age**) the series of glacial episodes during the Pleistocene period.

ice ax (also **ice axe**) ▶ n. an ax used by climbers for cutting footholds in ice, having a head with one pointed and one flattened end, and a spike at the foot.

ice·berg /ˈīs,bərg/ ▶ n. a large floating mass of ice detached from a glacier or ice sheet and carried out to sea.
– PHRASES **the tip of the iceberg** the small, perceptible part of a much larger situation or problem that remains hidden: *the statistics represent just the tip of the iceberg.* [18th C.: from Du. *ijsberg*, from *ijs* 'ice' + *berg* 'hill.']

ice·berg let·tuce ▶ n. a lettuce of a variety having a dense, round head of crisp, pale leaves.

ice·blink /ˈīs,bliNGk/ ▶ n. a bright appearance of the sky caused by reflection from a distant ice sheet.

ice blue ▶ n. a very pale blue color.

ice·boat /ˈīs,bōt/ ▶ n. a light, wind-driven vehicle with sails and runners, used for traveling on ice.

ice·bound /ˈīs,bound/ ▶ adj. completely surrounded or covered by ice.

ice·box /ˈīs,bäks/ ▶ n. a chilled box or cupboard for keeping something cold, esp. food. ■ dated a refrigerator.

ice·break·er /ˈīs,brākər/ ▶ n. a ship designed for breaking a channel through ice. ■ a thing that serves to relieve tension between people, or start a conversation.

ice cap (also **icecap**) ▶ n. a covering of ice over a large area, esp. on the polar region of a planet.

ice-cold ▶ adj. (esp. of a liquid) very cold; as cold as ice. ■ fig. unemotional or dispassionate; unfeeling.

ice cream ▶ n. a soft frozen food made with sweetened and flavored milk fat. [18th C.: alt. of *iced cream.*]

ice cube ▶ n. a small block of ice made in a freezer, esp. for adding to drinks.

iced /īst/ ▶ adj. [attrib.] **1** (of a drink or other liquid) cooled in or mixed with pieces of ice: *iced coffee.* ■ (of a surface or object) covered or coated with ice. **2** (of a cake or cookie) decorated with icing.

iced tea (also **ice tea**) ▶ n. a chilled drink of sweetened tea, typically flavored with lemon.

ice·fall /ˈīs,fôl/ ▶ n. **1** a steep part of a glacier that looks like a frozen waterfall. **2** a fall of loose ice; an avalanche of ice.

ice field ▶ n. a wide flat expanse of floating ice, esp. in polar regions.

ice-fish /ˈīs,fisH/ ▶ v. [intrans.] fish through holes in the ice on a lake or river. ▶ n. (**icefish**) (pl. same or **-fish·es**) **1** another term for **capelin. 2** a scaleless Antarctic fish (*Chaenocephalus aceratus*, family Chaenichthyidae) of pallid appearance with spiny gill covers and a snout shaped like a duck's bill. — **ice fish·ing** n. (in sense 1).

ice floe ▶ n. see **floe.**

ice hock·ey ▶ n. a fast contact sport played on an ice rink between two teams of six skaters, who attempt to drive a small rubber disk (the puck) into the opposing goal with hooked or angled sticks.

ice·house /ˈīs,hous/ (also **ice house** or **ice-house**) ▶ n. a building for storing ice, typically one situated partly or wholly underground.

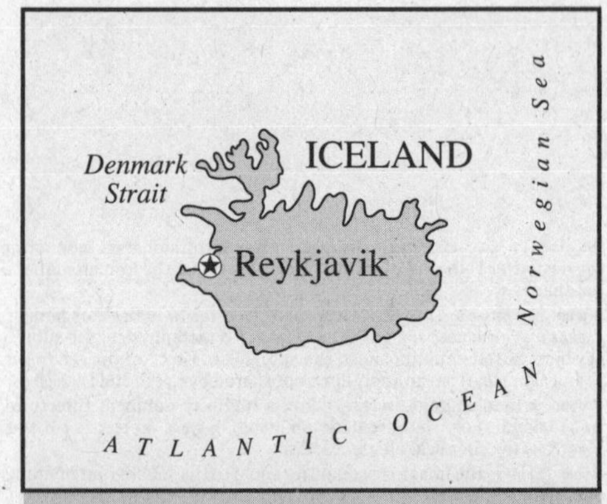

Iceland

Official name: Republic of Iceland
Location: north Atlantic Ocean, just south of the Arctic Circle
Area: 38,700 square miles (100,300 sq km)
Population: 300,000
Capital: Reykjavik
Language: Icelandic
Currency: Icelandic krona

Ice·land /ˈīslənd/ a country in the north Atlantic Ocean. Icelandic name **Island.** *See box.* — **Ice·land·er** n.

Ice·lan·dic /īsˈlandik/ ▶ adj. of or relating to Iceland or its language. ▶ n. the North Germanic language of Iceland, which is very similar to Old Norse.

Ice·land moss (also **Iceland lichen**) ▶ n. a brown, branching lichen (*Cetraria islandica*) with stiff spines along the margins of the fronds, growing in mountain and moorland habitats. It can be boiled to produce an edible jelly.

Ice·land pop·py (also **Ice·lan·dic pop·py**) ▶ n. a tall poppy (*Papaver nudicaule*) that is widely cultivated for its colorful flowers and suitability for cutting, native to arctic and north temperate regions.

Ice·land spar ▶ n. a transparent variety of calcite, showing strong double refraction.

ice·man /ˈīsmən/ ▶ n. (pl. **-men**) a man who sells or delivers ice.

ice milk ▶ n. a sweet frozen food similar to ice cream but containing less butterfat.

ice pack ▶ n. **1** a bag filled with ice and applied to the body to reduce swelling or lower temperature. **2** another term for **pack ice.**

ice pick ▶ n. a sharp, straight, pointed implement with a handle, used to break ice into small pieces for chilling food and drinks.

ice plant ▶ n. either of two succulent plants that are widely cultivated for their flowers: ■ a South African plant (genera *Mesembryanthemum* and *Dorotheanthus*) of the carpetweed family that has leaves covered with glistening fluid-filled hairs that resemble ice crystals. ■ an Asian stonecrop (*Sedum spectabile*) that bears domed heads of tiny pink flowers.

ice sheet ▶ n. a permanent layer of ice covering an extensive tract of land, esp. a polar region.

ice shelf ▶ n. a floating sheet of ice permanently attached to a landmass.

ice skate ▶ n. a boot with a blade attached to the bottom, used for skating on ice. ▶ v. [intrans.] skate on ice as a sport or pastime. — **ice skat·er** n.

figure skate

hockey skate

ice skates

ice skat·ing (also **ice-skat·ing**) ▶ n. skating on ice as a sport or pastime.

ice storm ▶ n. a storm of freezing rain that leaves a coating of ice.

ice tea ▶ n. another term for **iced tea.**

I Ching /ˈē ˈCHiNG; ˈjiNG/ ▶ n. an ancient Chinese manual of divination based on eight symbolic trigrams and sixty-four hexagrams, interpreted in terms of the principles of yin and yang. English name **Book of Changes.**

ich·neu·mon /ikˈn(y)o͞omən/ ▶ n. **1** (also **ichneumon wasp** or **ichneumon fly**) a parasitic wasp (family Ichneumonidae, order Hymenoptera) with long antennae that deposits its eggs in, on, or near the larvae of other insects. **2** another term for EGYPTIAN MONGOOSE. [15th C. (sense 2): via L. from Gk. *ikhneumōn* 'tracker,' from *ikhneuein* 'to track,' from *ikhnos* 'track, footstep.']

ich·nog·ra·phy /ik'nägrəfē/ ▸ **n.** (pl. **-phies**) a ground plan of a building or map of a region. [16th C.: from Fr. *ichnographie*, or via L. from Gk. *ikhnographia*, from *ikhnos* 'track.']

i·chor /'īkôr/ ▸ **n.** Gk. Mythol. the fluid that flows like blood in the veins of the gods. ■ archaic a watery, fetid discharge from a wound. — **i·chor·ous** /'īkərəs/ **adj.** [17th C.: from Gk. *ikhōr*.]

ichthyo- ▸ **comb. form** relating to fish; fishlike: *ichthyosaur.* [from Gk. *ikhthus* 'fish.']

ich·thy·ol·o·gy /,ikTHē'äləjē/ ▸ **n.** the branch of zoology that deals with fishes. — **ich·thy·o·log·i·cal** /-ə'läjikəl/ **adj.** **ich·thy·ol·o·gist** **n.**

ich·thy·oph·a·gous /,ikTHē'äfəgəs/ ▸ **adj.** formal fish-eating.

ich·thy·orn·is /,ikTHē'ôrnis/ ▸ **n.** an extinct, gull-like, fish-eating bird (genus *Ichthyornis*) of the late Cretaceous period, with large toothed jaws. [mod. L., from ICHTHYO- + Gk. *ornis* 'bird.']

ich·thy·o·saur /'ikTHēə,sôr/ (also **ich·thy·o·sau·rus** /,ikTHēə'sôrəs/) ▸ **n.** an extinct marine reptile (order Ichthyosauria) of the Mesozoic era resembling a dolphin, with a long pointed head, four flippers, and a vertical tail. — **ich·thy·o·sau·ri·an** /,ikTHēə'sôrēən/ **adj.** [19th C.: from ICHTHYO- 'fish' + Gk. *sauros* 'lizard.']

ich·thy·o·sis /,ikTHē'ōsis/ ▸ **n.** Med. a congenital skin condition that causes the epidermis to become dry and rough like fish scales. — **ich·thy·ot·ic** /-'ätik/ **adj.**

-ician ▸ **suffix** (forming nouns) denoting a person skilled in or concerned with a field or subject (often corresponding to a noun ending in *-ic* or *-ics*): *politician.* [from Fr. *-icien*.]

i·ci·cle /'īsikəl/ ▸ **n.** a hanging, tapering piece of ice formed by the freezing of dripping water. ■ a thin, shiny strip of plastic or foil hung on a Christmas tree for decoration. [ME: from ICE + dial. *ickle* 'icicle' (from OE *gicel*).]

ic·ing /'īsiNG/ ▸ **n.** **1** a mixture of sugar with liquid or butter, typically flavored and colored, and used as a coating for cakes or cookies. **2** the formation of ice on an aircraft, ship, or other vehicle, or in an engine. **3** Ice Hockey the action of shooting the puck from one's own end of the rink to the other but not into the goal, for which the referee calls a face-off in one's own end.
– PHRASES **the icing** (or **frosting**) **on the cake** an attractive but inessential addition or enhancement: *being a scientist is enjoyable, and winning a Nobel is icing on the cake.*

-icist ▸ **suffix** equivalent to -ICIAN. [based on forms ending in -IC, + -IST.]

-icity ▸ **suffix** forming abstract nouns esp. from adjectives ending in *-ic* (such as *authenticity* from *authentic*). [based on forms ending in -IC, + -ITY.]

ICJ ▸ **abbr.** International Court of Justice.

ick /ik/ ▸ **exclam.** used to express disgust: *oatmeal—ick!* [1940s: prob. imitative.]

-ick ▸ **suffix** archaic var. of -IC.

Ick·es /'ikəs/, Harold LeClair (1874–1952), US secretary of the interior 1933–46.

ick·y /'ikē/ ▸ **adj.** (**ick·i·er, ick·i·est**) informal sticky, esp. unpleasantly so. ■ distastefully sentimental. ■ nasty or repulsive (used as a general term of disapproval): *icky boys with their macho strutting.* [1930s: perh. rel. to SICK[1] or to the child's word *ickle* 'little.']

i·con /'īkän/ ▸ **n.** a painting of Christ or another holy figure, used as an aid to devotion in the Byzantine and other Eastern Churches. ■ a person or thing regarded as a representative symbol of something: *icon of manhood.* ■ Comput. a symbol or graphic representation on a video display terminal of a program, option, or window, esp. one of several for selection. [16th C.: via L. from Gk. *eikōn* 'likeness, image.']

i·con·ic /ī'känik/ ▸ **adj.** of, relating to, or of the nature of an icon: *language is not in general an iconic sign system.* ■ (of a classical Greek statue) depicting a victorious athlete in a conventional style.

icono- ▸ **comb. form** **1** of an image or likeness: *iconology.* **2** relating to icons: *iconoclast.*

i·con·o·clasm /ī'känə,klazəm/ ▸ **n.** **1** the action of attacking or rejecting cherished beliefs and institutions or established values and practices. **2** the rejection or destruction of religious images as heretical; the doctrine of iconoclasts.

i·con·o·clast /ī'känə,klast/ ▸ **n.** **1** a person who attacks cherished beliefs or institutions. **2** a destroyer of images used in religious worship. — **i·con·o·clas·tic** /ī,känə'klastik/ **adj.** **i·con·o·clas·ti·cal·ly** /ī,känə'klastik(ə)lē/ **adv.** [17th C. (sense 2): via med. L. from eccles. Gk. *eikonoklastēs*, from *eikōn* 'likeness' + *klan* 'to break.']

i·co·nog·ra·phy /,īkə'nägrəfē/ ▸ **n.** **1** (pl. **-phies**) the use or study of images or symbols in visual arts. ■ the visual images, symbols, or modes of representation collectively associated with a person, cult, or movement: *the iconography of pop culture.* **2** the illustration of a subject by drawings or figures. ■ a collection of illustrations or portraits. — **i·co·nog·ra·pher** **n.** **i·con·o·graph·ic** /ī,känə'grafik/ **adj.** **i·con·o·graph·i·cal** /ī,känə'grafikəl/ **adj.** [17th C. (denoting a drawing or plan): from Gk. *eikonographia* 'sketch, description,' from *eikōn* 'likeness' + *-graphia* 'writing.']

i·co·nol·o·gy /,īkə'näləjē/ ▸ **n.** the study of visual imagery and its symbolism and interpretation, esp. in social or political terms. ■ symbolism: *the iconology of a work of art.* — **i·con·o·log·i·cal** /ī,känə'läjikəl/ **adj.**

i·co·nos·ta·sis /,īkə'nästəsis/ ▸ **n.** (pl. **-ses** /-,sēz/) a screen bearing icons, separating the sanctuary of many Eastern churches from the nave. [19th C.: from mod. Gk. *eikonostasis*, from *eikōn* 'likeness' + *stasis* 'standing, stopping.']

i·co·sa·he·dron /ī,kōsə'hēdrən; ī,käsə-/ ▸ **n.** (pl. **-drons** or **-dra** /-drə/) a solid figure with twenty plane faces, esp. equilateral triangular ones. — **i·co·sa·he·dral** /-drəl/ **adj.** [16th C.: via late L. from Gk. *eikosaedron*, neut. (used as a n.) of *eikosaedros* 'twenty-faced.']

ICRC ▸ **abbr.** International Committee of the Red Cross.

-ics ▸ **suffix** (forming nouns) denoting arts or sciences, branches of study, or professions: *classics* | *politics.* [from Fr. *-iques*, L. *-ica*, or Gk. *-ika*, pl. forms.]

ic·ter·us /'iktərəs/ ▸ **n.** Med. technical term for JAUNDICE. — **ic·ter·ic** /ik'terik/ **adj.** [18th C.: via Latin from Gk. *ikteros*. The L. term denoted jaundice, also a yellowish-green bird (the sight of which was thought to cure jaundice).]

Ic·ti·nus /ik'tīnəs/ (5th century BC), Greek architect. He helped design the Parthenon.

ic·tus /'iktəs/ ▸ **n.** (pl. same or **ic·tus·es**) **1** Pros. a rhythmical or metrical stress. **2** Med. a stroke or seizure; a fit. [18th C. (denoting the beat of the pulse): from L., lit. 'blow.']

ICU ▸ **abbr.** intensive care unit.

i·cy /'īsē/ ▸ **adj.** (**i·ci·er, i·ci·est**) covered with or consisting of ice. ■ very cold: *an icy wind.* ■ fig. (of a person's tone or manner) very unfriendly; hostile: *her voice was icy.* — **i·ci·ly** **adv.** **i·ci·ness** **n.**

ID ▸ **abbr.** ■ Idaho (in official postal use). ■ identification or identity.

Id ▸ **n.** var. of EID.

I'd /īd/ ▸ **contr.** ■ I would or I should: *I'd like a bath.* ■ I had: *I'd agreed to go.*

id /id/ ▸ **n.** Psychoanal. the part of the mind in which innate instinctive impulses and primary processes are manifest. Compare with EGO and SUPEREGO. [1920s: from L., 'it.']

id. ▸ **abbr.** idem.

-id[1] ▸ **suffix** forming adjectives such as *putrid, torrid.* [from Fr. *-ide*, from L. *-idus*.]

-id[2] ▸ **suffix** **1** forming nouns such as *chrysalid, pyramid.* **2** Biol. forming names of structural constituents: *plastid.* **3** Bot. forming names of plants belonging to a family with a name ending in *-idaceae*: *orchid.* [from or suggested by Fr. *-ide*, via L. *-idis* from Gk. *-is, -id-*.]

-id[3] ▸ **suffix** forming nouns: **1** Zool. denoting an animal belonging to a family with a name ending in *-idae* or to a class with a name ending in *-ida*: *carabid* | *arachnid.* **2** denoting a member of a specified dynasty or family: *Achaemenid* | *Sassanid.* **3** Astron. denoting a meteor in a shower radiating from a specified constellation: *Geminids.*

I·da /'īdə/ **1** a mountain in central Crete, rising to 8,058 feet (2,456 m.). **2** a mountain in northwestern Turkey; 5,797 feet (1,767 m).

I·da·ho /'īdə,hō/ a state in the northwestern US that borders British Columbia, Canada, on the north; pop. 1,293,953; capital, Boise; statehood, July 3, 1890 (43). It was explored by Lewis and Clark in 1805 and was crossed by the Oregon Trail. — **I·da·ho·an** /-,hōən/ **n. & adj.**

Ida·ho Falls a city in southeastern Idaho, on the Snake River; pop. 50,730.

IDE Comput. ▸ **abbr.** Integrated Drive Electronics, a standard for interfacing computers and their peripherals.

-ide ▸ **suffix** Chem. forming nouns: denoting binary compounds of a nonmetallic or more electronegative element or group: *cyanide* | *sodium chloride.* ■ denoting various other compounds: *peptide* | *saccharide.* ■ denoting elements of a series in the periodic table: *lanthanide.* [orig. used in *oxide*.]

i·de·a /ī'dēə/ ▸ **n.** **1** a thought or suggestion as to a possible course of action: *the idea of linking pay to performance.* ■ a concept or mental impression. ■ an opinion or belief: *nineteenth-century ideas.* ■ a feeling that something is probable or possible: *he had an idea that she must feel the same.* **2** (**the idea**) the aim or purpose: *I took a job with the idea of getting some money.* **3** Philos. (in Platonic thought) an eternally existing pattern of which individual things in any class are imperfect copies.
– PHRASES **have no idea** informal not know at all: *she had no idea where she was going.* **not someone's idea of** informal not what someone regards as: *it's not my idea of a happy ending.* **put ideas into someone's head** suggest ambitions or thoughts that a person would not otherwise have had. [ME (sense 3): via L. from Gk. *idea* 'form, pattern,' from the base of *idein* 'to see.']

i·de·al /ī'dē(ə)l/ ▸ **adj.** **1** satisfying one's conception of what is perfect; most suitable: *the pool is ideal for a quick dip.* **2** [attrib.] existing only in the imagination; desirable or perfect but not likely to become a reality: *in an ideal world, we might have made a different decision.* ■ representing an abstract or hypothetical optimum: *mathematical modeling can determine theoretically ideal conditions.* ▸ **n.** a person or thing regarded as perfect: *you're my ideal of a man.* ■ a standard of perfection; a principle to be aimed at: *tolerance and freedom, the liberal ideals.* — **i·de·al·ly** **adv.** [ME: from late L. *idealis*, from L. *idea* (see IDEA).]

i·de·al gas ▶ **n.** Chem. a hypothetical gas whose molecules occupy negligible space and have no interactions, and that consequently obeys the gas laws exactly.

i·de·al·ism /ī'dēə,lizəm/ ▶ **n. 1** the practice of forming or pursuing ideals, esp. unrealistically: *the idealism of youth.* Compare with REALISM. ■ (in art or literature) the representation of things in ideal or idealized form. Often contrasted with REALISM (sense 2). **2** Philos. any of various systems of thought in which the objects of knowledge are held to be in some way dependent on the activity of mind. Often contrasted with REALISM (sense 3). — **i·de·al·ist** **n.** **i·de·al·is·tic** /ī,dēə'listik/ **adj.** **i·de·al·is·ti·cal·ly** /ī,dēə'listik(ə)lē/ **adv.**

i·de·al·i·ty /,īdē'alitē/ ▶ **n.** (pl. **-ties**) formal the state or quality of being ideal.

i·de·al·ize /ī'dēə,līz/ ▶ **v.** [trans.] [often as adj.] (**idealized**) regard or represent as perfect or better than in reality: *idealized accounts of their life together.* — **i·de·al·i·za·tion** /ī,dēəli'zāSHən/ **n.** **i·de·al·iz·er** **n.**

i·de·ate /'īdē,āt/ ▶ **v.** [trans.] [often as adj.] (**ideated**) form an idea of; imagine or conceive.

i·de·a·tion /,īdē'āSHən/ ▶ **n.** Psychol. the formation of ideas or concepts: *paranoid ideation.* — **i·de·a·tion·al** /-SHənl/ **adj.** **i·de·a·tion·al·ly** /-SHənl-ē/ **adv.**

i·dée fixe /,ēdā'fēks/ ▶ **n.** (pl. **i·dées fixes** pronunc. same) an idea or desire that dominates the mind; an obsession. [19th C.:Fr., lit. 'fixed idea.']

i·dem /'īdem; 'ēdem/ ▶ **adv.** used in citations to indicate an author or work that has just been mentioned. [ME: L., 'the same.']

i·dem·po·tent /'īdem,pōtənt/ Math. ▶ **adj.** denoting an element of a set that is unchanged in value when multiplied or otherwise operated on by itself.

i·den·ti·cal /ī'dentikəl/ ▶ **adj.** similar in every detail; exactly alike: *girls in identical outfits.* ■ (of twins) developed from a single fertilized ovum, and therefore of the same sex and usually very similar in appearance. Compare with FRATERNAL (sense 2). — **i·den·ti·cal·ly** **adv.** [16th C.: from med. L. *identicus*, from late L. *identitas* (see IDENTITY).]

i·den·ti·fi·ca·tion /ī,dentəfi'kāSHən/ ▶ **n.** the action or process of identifying someone or something or the fact of being identified: *tagged with a number for identification.* ■ a means of proving a person's identity, esp. in the form of official papers: *I asked to see his identification.* ■ a person's sense of identity with someone or something: ***identification** with storybook characters.* ■ the association or linking of one thing with another: *identification of democracy with anarchy.*

i·den·ti·fi·er /ī'dentə,fīər/ ▶ **n.** a person or thing that identifies something.

i·den·ti·fy /ī'dentə,fī/ ▶ **v.** (**-fies, -fied**) [trans.] **1** (often **be identified**) establish or indicate who or what (someone or something) is: *the judge ordered that the girl not be identified.* ■ recognize or distinguish (esp. something considered worthy of attention): *ensure that their needs are identified.* **2** (**identify someone/something with**) associate (someone) closely with; regard (someone) as having strong links with: *identified with the peace movement.* ■ equate (someone or something) with: *because of my accent, people identified me with a farmer's wife.* ■ [intrans.] (**identify with**) regard oneself as sharing the same characteristics or thinking as someone else: *I liked Fromm and identified with him.* — **i·den·ti·fi·a·ble** /-,fīəbəl/ **adj.** **i·den·ti·fi·a·bly** /-,fīəblē/ **adv.**

i·den·ti·kit /ī'denti,kit/ ▶ **n.** trademark a picture of a person, esp. one sought by the police, reconstructed from typical facial features according to witnesses' descriptions: [as adj.] *an identikit photograph.* [1960s: blend of IDENTITY and KIT[1].]

i·den·ti·ty /ī'dentitē/ ▶ **n.** (pl. **-ties**) **1** the fact of being who or what a person or thing is: *he knows the identity of the bombers.* ■ the characteristics determining this: *a Canadian identity.* **2** a close similarity or affinity: *an identity between the city and the suburbs.* **3** Math. (also **identity operation**) a transformation that leaves an object unchanged. ■ (also **identity element**) an element of a set that, if combined with another element by a specified binary operation, leaves that element unchanged. **4** Math. the equality of two expressions for all values of the quantities expressed by letters, or an equation expressing this, e.g., $(x + 1)2 = x2 + 2x + 1$. [16th C.: from late L. *identitas*, from L. *idem* 'same.']

i·den·ti·ty cri·sis ▶ **n.** Psychiatry a period of uncertainty and confusion in which a person's sense of identity becomes insecure, typically due to a change in their expected aims or role in society.

i·den·ti·ty ma·trix ▶ **n.** Math. a square matrix in which all the elements of the principal diagonal are ones and all other elements are zeros. The effect of multiplying a given matrix by an identity matrix is to leave the given matrix unchanged.

i·den·ti·ty theft ▶ **n.** the fraudulent acquisition and use of a person's private identifying information, usually for financial gain.

id·e·o·gram /'idēə,gram; 'īdēə-/ ▶ **n.** a written character symbolizing the idea of a thing without indicating the sounds used to say it, e.g., numerals and Chinese characters.

id·e·o·graph /'idēə,graf; 'īdēə-/ ▶ **n.** another term for IDEOGRAM. — **id·e·o·graph·ic** /,idēə'grafik; ,īdēə-/ **adj.** **id·e·og·ra·phy** /,idē'ägrəfē; ,īdē-/ **n.**

i·de·o·logue /'īdēə,lôg; -,läg; 'idēə-/ ▶ **n.** an adherent of an ideology, esp. one who is uncompromising and dogmatic: *a Nazi ideologue.* [19th C.: from Fr. *idéologue*; see also IDEOLOGY.]

i·de·ol·o·gy /,īdē'äləjē; ,idē-/ ▶ **n.** (pl. **-gies**) a system of ideas and ideals, esp. one that forms the basis of economic or political policy: *the ideology of republicanism.* ■ the ideas and manner of thinking of a group, social class, or individual: *a critique of bourgeois ideology.* — **i·de·o·log·i·cal** /-ə'läjikəl/ **adj.** **i·de·o·log·i·cal·ly** /-ə'läjik(ə)lē/ **adv.** **i·de·ol·o·gist** **n.** [18th C.: from Fr. *idéologie*, from Gk. *idea* 'form, pattern' + *-logos* (denoting discourse or compilation).]

Chinese character for Earth

Roman numeral three

Wheelchair access sign

Biohazard sign

ideograms

ides /īdz/ ▶ **plural n.** (in the ancient Roman calendar) the 15th day of March, May, July, and October, and the 13th of other months, from which other dates were calculated. Compare with NONES, CALENDS. [OE: from OFr., from L. *idus* (pl.), of unknown origin.]

idio- ▶ **comb. form** distinct; private; personal; own: *idiotype.* [from Gk. *idios* 'own, distinct.']

id·i·o·cy /'idēəsē/ ▶ **n.** (pl. **-cies**) extremely stupid behavior: *the idiocy of decimating rain forests.* [16th C.: from IDIOT.]

id·i·o·lect /'idēə,lekt/ ▶ **n.** the speech habits peculiar to a particular person. [1940s: from IDIO- 'own, personal' + *-lect* as in *dialect.*]

id·i·om /'idēəm/ ▶ **n. 1** a group of words established by usage as having a meaning not deducible from those of the individual words (e.g., *raining cats and dogs*). ■ a form of expression natural to a language, person, or group of people: *he had a feeling for phrase and idiom.* ■ the dialect of a people or part of a country. **2** a characteristic mode of expression in music or art: *a neo-Impressionist idiom.* [16th C.: from Fr. *idiome*, or via late L. from Gk. *idiōma* 'private property, peculiar phraseology,' from *idiousthai* 'make one's own,' from *idios* 'own, private.']

id·i·o·mat·ic /,idēə'matik/ ▶ **adj.** using, containing, or denoting expressions that are natural to a native speaker: *distinctive idiomatic dialogue.* — **id·i·o·mat·i·cal·ly** **adv.**

id·i·op·a·thy /,idē'äpəTHē/ ▶ **n.** (pl. **-thies**) Med. a disease or condition that arises spontaneously or for which the cause is unknown. — **id·i·o·path·ic** /,idēə'paTHik/ **adj.** [17th C.: from mod. L. *idiopathia*, from Gk. *idiopatheia*, from *idios* 'own, private' + *-patheia* 'suffering.']

id·i·o·syn·cra·sy /,idēə'siNGkrəsē/ ▶ **n.** (pl. **-sies**) (usu. **idiosyncrasies**) a mode of behavior or way of thought peculiar to an individual: *one of his idiosyncrasies was always to be first.* ■ a distinctive or peculiar feature or characteristic of a place or thing: *the idiosyncrasies of the prison system.* [17th C.: from Gk. *idiosunkrasia*, from *idios* 'own, private' + *sun* 'with' + *krasis* 'mixture.']

id·i·o·syn·crat·ic /,id,ōōsiNG'kratik/ ▶ **adj.** of or relating to idiosyncrasy; peculiar or individual. — **id·i·o·syn·crat·i·cal·ly** **adv.**

id·i·ot /'idēət/ ▶ **n.** informal a stupid person. ■ Med., archaic a mentally handicapped person. — **id·i·ot·ic** /,idē'ätik/ **adj.** **id·i·ot·i·cal·ly** /,idē'ätik(ə)lē/ **adv.** [ME: via OFr. from L. *idiota* 'ignorant person,' from Gk. *idiōtēs* 'private person, layman, ignorant person,' from *idios* 'own, private.']

id·i·ot box ▶ **n.** informal a television set.

id·i·ot light ▶ **n.** informal a warning light that goes on when a fault occurs in a device, esp. a light on the instrument panel of a motor vehicle.

id·i·ot sa·vant ▶ **n.** (pl. **id·i·ot sa·vants** or **id·i·ots sa·vants** pronunc. same) a person who is considered to be mentally handicapped but displays brilliance in a specific area, esp. one involving memory. [20th C.: Fr., lit. 'learned idiot.']

id·i·o·type /'idēə,tīp/ ▶ **n.** Biol. the set of genetic determinants of an individual. ■ Immunol. a set of antigen-binding sites that characterizes the antibodies produced by a particular clone of antibody-producing cells.

i·dle /'īdl/ ▶ **adj.** (**i·dler, i·dlest**) **1** (esp. of a machine or factory) not active or in use: *assembly lines **standing idle**.* ■ (of a person) not working; unemployed. ■ (of a person) avoiding work; lazy. ■ [attrib.] (of time) characterized by inaction or absence of significant activity: *an idle moment.* ■ (of money) held in cash or in accounts paying no interest. **2** without purpose or effect; pointless: *idle chatter.* ■ (esp. of a threat or boast) without foundation: *idle threats.* ▶ **v.** [intrans.] (of a person) spend time doing nothing; be idle. ■ move aimlessly or lazily. ■ (of an engine) run slowly while disconnected from a load or out of gear. ■ [trans.] cause (an engine) to idle. ■ take out of use or employment: *he will close the newspaper, idling 2,200 workers.*

— **i•dle•ness** n. [OE *īdel* 'empty, useless,' of West Gmc. origin; rel. to Ger. *eitel* 'bare, worthless.']

i•dler /'īdlər/ ▶n. **1** a habitually lazy person. ■ a person who is doing nothing in particular, typically while waiting for something. **2** a pulley that transmits no power but guides or tensions a belt or rope. ■ an idle wheel.

i•dle wheel ▶n. an intermediate wheel between two geared wheels, esp. when its purpose is to allow them to rotate in the same direction.

i•dly /'īdlē/ ▶adv. with no particular purpose, reason, or foundation: *"How was the game?" Katie asked idly.* ■ in an inactive or lazy way: *stand idly by and let him take the blame.*

I•do /'ēdō/ ▶n. an artificial universal language developed from Esperanto. [19th C.: Ido, lit. 'offspring.']

i•do•crase /'īdə,krās; -,krāz; 'idə-/ ▶n. a mineral consisting of a silicate of calcium, magnesium, and aluminum. [19th C.: from Gk. *eidos* 'form' + *krasis* 'mixture.']

i•dol /'īdl/ ▶n. an image or representation of a god used as an object of worship. ■ a person or thing that is greatly admired, loved, or revered: *movie idol Robert Redford.* [ME: from OFr. *idole*, from L. *idolum* 'image,' from Gk. *eidōlon*, from *eidos* 'form, shape.']

i•dol•a•ter /ī'dälətər/ ▶n. a person who worships an idol or idols.

i•dol•a•trous /ī'dälətrəs/ ▶adj. worshiping idols: *the idolatrous peasantry.* ■ treating someone or something as an idol: *America's idolatrous worship of the auto.*

i•dol•a•try /ī'dälətrē/ ▶n. worship of idols. ■ extreme admiration, love, or reverence for something or someone: *idolatry of art.*

i•dol•ize /'īdl,īz/ ▶v. [trans.] admire, revere, or love greatly or excessively: *he idolized his mother.* — **i•dol•i•za•tion** /,īdl-i'zāsHən/ n. **i•dol•iz•er** n.

IDP ▶abbr. ■ integrated data processing. ■ International Driving Permit.

Id ul-A•dha /'id äl 'äTHä/ see **Eid**.

Id ul-Fi•tr /'id äl 'fētər/ see **Eid**.

i•dyll /'īdl/ (also **i•dyl**) ▶n. an extremely happy, peaceful, or picturesque episode or scene, typically an idealized or unsustainable one: *the rural idyll.* ■ a short description in verse or prose of a picturesque scene or incident, esp. in rustic life. [16th C. (in the Latin form): from L. *idyllium*, from Gk. *eidullion*, dimin. of *eidos* 'form, picture.']

i•dyl•lic /ī'dilik/ ▶adj. (esp. of a time or place) like an idyll; extremely happy, peaceful, or picturesque: *an idyllic setting.* — **i•dyl•li•cal•ly** adv.

IE ▶abbr. Indo-European.

i.e. ▶abbr. that is to say (used to add explanatory information or to state something in different words): *a walking boot that is synthetic, i.e., not leather or suede.* [from L. *id est* 'that is.']

-ie ▶suffix var. of -Y[2] (as in *auntie*).

-ier ▶suffix forming personal nouns denoting an occupation or interest: **1** pronounced with stress on the preceding element: *glazier.* [ME: var. of -ER[1].] **2** pronounced with stress on the final element: *brigadier | cashier.* [from Fr. *-ier*, from L. *-arius*.]

if /if/ ▶conj. **1** introducing a conditional clause: ■ on the condition or supposition that; in the event that: *if you have a complaint, write to the director | if you like, I'll put in a word for you.* ■ (with past tense) introducing a hypothetical situation: *if you had stayed, this would never have happened.* **2** despite the possibility that; no matter whether: *if it takes me years, I shall do it.* **3** (often used in indirect questions) whether: *he asked if we would like some coffee.* **4** [with modal] expressing a polite request: *if I could trouble you for your names?* **5** expressing surprise or regret: *well, if it isn't Frank! | if I could just be left alone.* **6** with implied reservation: ■ and perhaps not: *the new leaders have little if any control.* ■ used to admit something as being possible but regarded as relatively insignificant: *so what if he did?* ■ despite being (used before an adjective or adverb to introduce a contrast): *she was honest, if a little brutal.* ▶n. a condition or supposition: *there are so many ifs and buts in the policy.*

– PHRASES **if and when** at a future time (should it arise): *if and when the film gets the green light.* **if not** perhaps even (used to introduce a more extreme term than one first mentioned): *hundreds if not thousands of germs.* **if only 1** even if for no other reason than: *Willy would have to tell George more, if only to keep him from pestering.* **2** used to express a wish, esp. regretfully: *if only I had listened to you.* **if so** if that is the case. [OE *gif*, of Gmc. origin; rel. to Du. *of* and Ger. *ob*.]

I•fe /'ēfā/ a city in southwestern Nigeria; pop. 241,000.

-iferous ▶comb. form common form of -FEROUS.

iff /if/ ▶conj. Logic Math. if and only if. [1950s: arbitrary extension of *if*.]

if•fy /'ifē/ ▶adj. (**if•fi•er, if•fi•est**) informal full of uncertainty; doubtful: *the prospect seems iffy.*

-ific ▶suffix common form of -FIC.

-ification ▶suffix common form of -FICATION.

-iform ▶comb. form common form of -FORM.

IFR ▶abbr. instrument flight rules, used to regulate the flying and navigating of an aircraft using instruments alone.

If•tar /'iftär/ ▶n. the meal eaten by Muslims after sunset during Ramadan.

Ig Biochem. ▶abbr. immunoglobulin.

I.G. ▶abbr. ■ Indo-Germanic. ■ Inspector General.

Ig•bo /'igbō/ ▶n. & adj. see **Ibo**.

ig•loo /'igloo/ ▶n. a dome-shaped Eskimo house, typically built from blocks of solid snow. [19th C.: from Inuit *iglu* 'house.']

Ig•na•tius Loy•o•la, St. /ig'nāsH(ē)əs loi'ōlə/ (1491–1556), Spanish theologian. He founded Society of Jesus (the Jesuit order).

ig•ne•ous /'ignēəs/ ▶adj. Geol. (of rock) having solidified from lava or magma. ■ relating to or involving volcanic processes: *igneous activity.* ■ rare of fire; fiery. [17th C.: from L. *igneus* (from *ignis* 'fire') + -OUS.]

ig•nim•brite /'ignim,brīt/ ▶n. Geol. a volcanic rock formed by the consolidation of material deposited by pyroclastic flows. [1930s: from L. *ignis* 'fire' + *imber, imbr-* 'shower of rain, storm cloud' + -ITE[1].]

ig•nis fat•u•us /'ignəs 'facHooəs/ ▶n. (pl. **ig•nes fat•u•i** /'ignēz 'facHoo,ī/) a phosphorescent light sometimes seen at night over marshy ground, thought to result from the combustion of natural gases. ■ something deceptive or deluding. [16th C.: mod. L., lit. 'foolish fire.']

ig•nite /ig'nīt/ ▶v. catch fire or cause to catch fire. ■ [trans.] fig. arouse (an emotion): *the words ignited new fury in him.* — **ig•nit•a•ble** adj. [17th C.: from L. *ignire* 'set on fire,' from *ignis* 'fire.']

ig•ni•ter /ig'nītər/ ▶n. **1** a device for igniting a fuel mixture in an engine. **2** a device for causing an electric arc.

ig•ni•tion /ig'nisHən/ ▶n. the action of setting something on fire or starting to burn. ■ the process of starting the combustion of fuel in the cylinders of an internal combustion engine. ■ (usu. **the ignition**) the mechanism for bringing this about, typically activated by a key or switch.

ig•no•ble /ig'nōbəl/ ▶adj. (**-no•bler, -no•blest**) **1** not honorable in character or purpose. **2** of humble origin or social status. — **ig•no•bly** adv. [ME (sense 2): from Fr., or from L. *ignobilis*, from *in-* 'not' + *gnobilis*, older form of *nobilis* 'noble.']

ig•no•min•i•ous /,ignə'minēəs/ ▶adj. deserving or causing public disgrace or shame: *ignominious defeat.* — **ig•no•min•i•ous•ly** adv.

ig•no•min•y /'ignə,minē; ig'nämінē/ ▶n. public shame or disgrace: *the ignominy of being imprisoned.* [16th C.: from Fr. *ignominie* or L. *ignominia*, from *in-* 'not' + a var. of *nomen* 'name.']

ig•no•ra•mus /,ignə'rāməs; -'raməs/ ▶n. (pl. **-mus•es**) an ignorant or stupid person. [16th C.: L., lit. 'we do not know' (in legal use 'we take no notice of it').]

ig•no•rance /'ignərəns/ ▶n. lack of knowledge or information: *he acted in ignorance of basic procedures.*

ig•no•rant /'ignərənt/ ▶adj. lacking knowledge or awareness in general; uneducated or unsophisticated. ■ [predic.] lacking knowledge, information, or awareness about something in particular: *ignorant of astronomy.* — **ig•no•rant•ly** adv.

ig•nore /ig'nôr/ ▶v. [trans.] refuse to take notice of or acknowledge; disregard intentionally: *he ignored her question.* ■ fail to consider (something significant): *satellite broadcasting ignores national boundaries.* — **ig•nor•a•ble** adj. **ig•nor•er** n. [15th C. (in the sense 'be ignorant of'): from Fr. *ignorer* or L. *ignorare* 'not know, ignore,' from *in-* 'not' + *gno-*, a base meaning 'know.']

I•gua•çu /,ēgwə'soo/ a river in southern Brazil, rising in southeastern Brazil and flowing west for 800 miles (1,300 km) to the Paraná River.

i•gua•na /i'gwänə/ ▶n. a large, arboreal, tropical American lizard (genus *Iguana*, family Iguanidae), esp. the **green iguana** (*I. iguana*) with a spiny crest along the back and greenish coloration. ■ any iguanid lizard. [16th C.: from Sp., from Arawak *iwana*.]

i•guan•o•don /i'gwänə,dän/ ▶n. a large, partly bipedal, herbivorous dinosaur (genus *Iguanodon*) of the early to mid Cretaceous period, with a broad, stiff tail and the thumb developed into a spike. — **i•guan•o•dont** /-,dänt/ adj. [mod. L., from IGUANA + Gk. *odous, odont-* 'tooth.']

IHS ▶abbr. Jesus. [ME: from late L., representing Gk. ΙΗΣ as an abbrev. of *Iēsous* 'Jesus.']

IJs•sel /'īsəl/ a river in the Netherlands, flowing north 72 miles (115 km) from the Rhine at Arnhem to the IJsselmeer.

IJs•sel•meer /'īsəl,mer/ a shallow lake in the northwestern Netherlands, created in 1932 by damming the old Zuider Zee.

i•kat /'ēkät/ ▶n. fabric made using an Indonesian decorative technique in which warp or weft threads, or both, are tie-dyed before weaving. [1930s: Malay, lit. 'fasten, tie.']

i•ke•ba•na /,ikə'bänə; ,ēke-/ ▶n. the art of Japanese flower arrangement, with formal display according to strict rules. [20th C.: Japanese, lit. 'living flowers,' from *ikeru* 'keep alive' + *hana* 'flower.']

Ikh•na•ton /ik'nätn/ var. of **Akhenaten**.

i•kon ▶n. var. of ICON.

IL ▶abbr. Illinois (in official postal use).

il- ▶prefix var. of IN-[1], IN-[2] assimilated before *l* (as in *illustrate, illogical*).

-il ▶suffix forming adjectives and nouns such as *civil* and *fossil*. [from OFr., from L. *-ilis*.]

ILA ▶abbr. ■ International Law Association. ■ International Longshoremen's Association.

i•lang-i•lang ▶n. var. of YLANG-YLANG.

-ile ▶suffix forming adjectives and nouns such as *agile* and *juvenile*. ■ Stat. forming nouns denoting a value of a variate that divides a population into the indicated number of equal-sized groups, or one of the groups itself: *decile | percentile.* [var. of -IL especially in adoptions from Fr.]

il·e·a /ˈilēə/ plural form of ILEUM.

Île-de-France /ˌēl də ˈfräns/ a region of north central France, incorporating the city of Paris.

il·e·i·tis /ˌilēˈītis/ ▸ n. Med. inflammation of the ileum.

il·e·os·to·my /ˌilēˈästəmē/ ▸ n. (pl. **-mies**) a surgical operation in which a piece of the ileum is diverted to an artificial opening in the abdominal wall. ■ an opening so formed. [19th C.: from ILEUM + Gk. *stoma* 'mouth.']

Iles du Vent /ˌēl dy ˈvän/ French name for WINDWARD ISLANDS (sense 2).

I·le·sha /ēˈlāshə/ a city in southwestern Nigeria; pop. 342,000.

il·e·um /ˈilēəm/ ▸ n. (pl. **il·e·a** /ˈilēə/) Anat. the third portion of the small intestine, between the jejunum and the cecum. — **il·e·ac** /-ˌak/ adj. **il·e·al** /-əl/ adj. [17th C.: from med. L., var. of ILIUM.]

il·e·us /ˈilēəs/ ▸ n. Med. a painful obstruction of the ileum or other part of the intestine. [17th C.: from L., from Gk. *eileos, ilios* 'colic,' appar. from *eilein* 'to roll.']

i·lex /ˈīleks/ ▸ n. **1** another term for HOLM OAK. **2** a tree or shrub of the genus *Ilex* that includes the holly and its relatives. [ME: from L., 'holm oak.']

ILGWU ▸ abbr. International Ladies' Garment Workers' Union.

il·i·a /ˈilēə/ plural form of ILIUM.

il·i·ac /ˈilēˌak/ ▸ adj. of or relating to the ilium or the nearby regions of the lower body: *the iliac artery.* [16th C.: from late L. *iliacus*, from *ilia* 'entrails.']

Il·i·ad /ˈilēəd; -ˌad/ a Greek epic poem ascribed to Homer, telling how Achilles killed Hector at the climax of the Trojan War.

Il·i·um /ˈilēəm/ the Latin name of TROY, the 7th-century BC Greek city.

il·i·um /ˈilēəm/ ▸ n. (pl. **il·i·a** /ˈilēə/) the large broad bone forming the upper part of each half of the pelvis. [16th C.: from L., sing. of *ilia* 'flanks, entrails.']

ilk /ilk/ ▸ n. [in sing.] a type of people or things similar to those already referred to: ***reporters of his ilk.*** [OE *ilca* 'same,' of Gmc. origin; rel. to ALIKE.]

Ill. ▸ abbr. Illinois.

I'll /īl/ ▸ contr. I shall; I will: *I'll arrange it.*

ill /il/ ▸ adj. **1** not in full health; sick: *seriously ill.* **2** [attrib.] poor in quality: *ill judgment.* ■ harmful: *ill effects.* ■ hostile: *I bear you no ill will.* ■ (esp. of fortune) not favorable. ▸ adv. **1** [usu. in comb.] badly, wrongly, or imperfectly: *ill-chosen.* ■ unfavorably or unpropitiously: *something which boded ill.* **2** only with difficulty; hardly: *ill afford the cost.* ▸ n. **1** [as pl. n.] (**the ill**) people who are ill: *the mentally ill.* **2** (usu. **ills**) a problem or misfortune: *the ills of society.* ■ evil; harm: *how could I wish him ill?*
– PHRASES **ill at ease** uncomfortable or embarrassed. **speak** (or **think**) **ill of** say (or think) something critical about. [ME: from ON *illr* 'evil, difficult.']

ill-ad·vised ▸ adj. (of a person) unwise or imprudent.

il·la·tion /iˈlāshən/ ▸ n. archaic the action of inferring or drawing a conclusion. ■ an inference. [16th C.: from L. *illatio(n-)*, from *illat-* 'brought in,' from the v. *inferre* (see INFER).]

il·la·tive /ˈilətiv; iˈlātiv/ ▸ adj. **1** of the nature of or stating an inference. ■ proceeding by inference. **2** Gram. relating to or denoting a case of nouns in some languages used to express motion into something. ▸ n. the illative case, or a word in this case. — **il·la·tive·ly** adv. [16th C.: from L. *illativus*, from *illat-* 'brought in,' from *inferre* (see INFER).]

ill-bred ▸ adj. badly brought up or rude. — **ill breed·ing** n.

ill-con·ceived ▸ adj. not carefully planned or considered: *ill-conceived schemes.*

ill-con·sid·ered ▸ adj. badly thought out: *an ill-considered remark.*

ill-dis·posed ▸ adj. unfriendly or unsympathetic.

il·le·gal /iˈlēgəl/ ▸ adj. contrary to or forbidden by law, esp. criminal law: *illegal drugs.* ▸ n. an illegal immigrant. — **il·le·gal·i·ty** /ˌiliˈgalitē/ n. (pl. **-ties**) **il·le·gal·ly** adv. [17th C.: from Fr. *illégal* or med. L. *illegalis*, from L. *in-* 'not' + *legalis* 'according to the law.']

il·leg·i·ble /iˈlejəbəl/ ▸ adj. not clear enough to be read: *his handwriting is totally illegible.* — **il·leg·i·bil·i·ty** /iˌlejəˈbilitē/ n. **il·leg·i·bly** /-blē/ adv.

il·le·git·i·mate ▸ adj. /ˌiləˈjitəmit/ not authorized by the law; not in accordance with accepted standards or rules: *an illegitimate exercise of power by the military.* ■ (of a child) born of parents not lawfully married to each other. — **il·le·git·i·ma·cy** /-məsē/ n. **il·le·git·i·mate·ly** adv.

ill-fat·ed ▸ adj. destined to fail or have bad luck.

ill-fa·vored ▸ adj. unattractive or offensive.

ill-found·ed ▸ adj. (esp. of an idea or belief) not based on fact or reliable evidence.

ill-got·ten ▸ adj. acquired by illegal or unfair means.

ill hu·mor ▸ n. irritability or bad temper. — **ill-hu·mored** adj.

il·lib·er·al /iˈlib(ə)rəl/ ▸ adj. opposed to liberal principles; restricting freedom of thought or behavior. — **il·lib·er·al·i·ty** /iˌlibəˈralitē/ n. **il·lib·er·al·ly** adv.

il·lic·it /iˈlisit/ ▸ adj. forbidden by law, rules, or custom: *illicit drugs | illicit sex.* — **il·lic·it·ly** adv. **il·lic·it·ness** n. [16th C.: from Fr., or from L. *illicitus*, from *in-* 'not' + *licitus* (see LICIT).]

Il·li·noi·an /ˌiliˈnoi-ən/ ▸ adj. Geol. denoting a Pleistocene glaciation in North America, preceding the Wisconsin. [19th C.: from ILLINOIS.]

Il·li·nois /ˌiləˈnoi; -ˈnoiz/ a state in the eastern central US; pop. 12,419,293; capital, Springfield; statehood, Dec. 3, 1818 (21). Colonized by the French in the 1600s and ceded to Britain in 1763, it was acquired by the US in 1783. — **Il·li·nois·an** /-ˈnoiən; -ˈnoizən/ n. & adj.

Il·li·nois Riv·er a river that rises in northeastern Illinois, and flows southwest for 273 miles (440 km) to the Mississippi River.

il·liq·uid /iˈlikwid/ ▸ adj. (of assets) not easily converted into cash: *illiquid assets.* — **il·li·quid·i·ty** /ˌiliˈkwiditē/ n.

il·lit·er·ate /iˈlitərit/ ▸ adj. unable to read or write. ■ [with submodifier] ignorant in a particular subject or activity: *politically illiterate.* ■ uncultured or poorly educated. ■ (esp. of a piece of writing) showing a lack of education, esp. an inability to read or write well. ▸ n. a person who is unable to read or write.
– PHRASES **functionally illiterate** lacking the literacy necessary for coping with most jobs and many everyday situations. — **il·lit·er·a·cy** /-əsē/ n. **il·lit·er·ate·ly** adv. [ME: from L. *illitteratus*, from *in-* 'not' + *litteratus* (see LITERATE).]

ill-judged ▸ adj. lacking careful consideration; unwise.

ill·ness /ˈilnis/ ▸ n. a disease or period of sickness affecting the body or mind.

il·lo·cu·tion /ˌiləˈkyo͞oshən/ ▸ n. an action performed by saying or writing something, e.g., ordering, warning, or promising. — **il·lo·cu·tion·ar·y** /-ˌnerē/ adj.

il·log·i·cal /iˈläjikəl/ ▸ adj. lacking sense or clear, sound reasoning: *an illogical fear.* — **il·log·i·cal·i·ty** /iˌläjiˈkalitē/ n. (pl. **-ties**) **il·log·i·cal·ly** adv.

ill-starred ▸ adj. destined to fail or have many difficulties; unlucky: *an ill-starred expedition.*

ill tem·per ▸ n. irritability; anger. — **ill-tem·pered** adj.

ill-treat ▸ v. [trans.] act cruelly toward (a person or animal). — **ill-treat·ment** n.

il·lu·mi·nance /iˈlo͞omənəns/ ▸ n. Physics the amount of luminous flux per unit area.

il·lu·mi·nant /iˈlo͞omənənt/ ▸ n. tech. a means of lighting or source of light: *until 1880, oil was the only illuminant in use.* ▸ adj. giving off light. [17th C.: from L. *illuminant-* 'illuminating,' from the v. *illuminare* (see ILLUMINATE).]

il·lu·mi·nate /iˈlo͞oməˌnāt/ ▸ v. [trans.] light up: *illuminated by a single bulb.* ■ [often as adj.] (**illuminated**) decorate (a page or initial letter in a manuscript) with gold, silver, or colored designs. ■ [usu. as adj.] (**illuminating**) fig. help to clarify or explain (a subject or matter): *an illuminating discussion.* ■ enlighten (someone) spiritually or intellectually. — **il·lu·mi·na·tive** /-ˌnātiv; -nətiv/ adj. **il·lu·mi·na·tor** /-ˌnātər/ n. [ME: from L. *illuminat-* 'illuminated,' from the v. *illuminare*, from *in-* 'upon' + *lumen, lumin-* 'light.']

il·lu·mi·na·ti /iˌlo͞oməˈnätē/ ▸ plural n. people claiming to possess special enlightenment or knowledge of something. [16th C.: pl. of Ital. *illuminato* or L. *illuminatus* 'enlightened,' past part. of *illuminare.*]

il·lu·mi·na·tion /iˌlo͞oməˈnāshən/ ▸ n. lighting or light: *higher levels of illumination are needed for reading.* ■ fig. spiritual or intellectual enlightenment. ■ fig. clarification. ■ the art of illuminating a manuscript. ■ an illuminated design in a manuscript. [ME: via OFr. from late L. *illuminatio(n-)*, from the v. *illuminare* (see ILLUMINATE).]

illus. ▸ abbr. ■ illustrated or illustration.

ill-use /ˈil ˈyo͞oz/ ▸ v. [trans.] (usu. **be ill-used**) ill-treat (someone).

il·lu·sion /iˈlo͞ozhən/ ▸ n. a false idea or belief: *he had no illusions about her.* ■ a deceptive appearance or impression: *the illusion of togetherness.* ■ a thing that is or is likely to be wrongly perceived or interpreted by the senses: *Zollner's illusion makes parallel lines seem to diverge.*
– PHRASES **be under the illusion that** believe mistakenly that. **be under no illusion** (or **illusions**) be fully aware of the true state of affairs. — **il·lu·sion·al** /-zhənl/ adj. [ME: via OFr. from L. *illusio(n-)*, from *illudere* 'to mock,' from *in-* 'against' + *ludere* 'play.']

il·lu·sion·ism /iˈlo͞ozhəˌnizəm/ ▸ n. the technique by which artistic representations are made to resemble real objects.

il·lu·sion·ist /iˈlo͞ozhənist/ ▸ n. a person who performs tricks that deceive the eye; a magician.

il·lu·so·ry /iˈlo͞osərē; -zərē/ ▸ adj. based on illusion; not real: *she knew the safety of her room was illusory.* — **il·lu·so·ri·ly** /-rəlē/ adv.

il·lus·trate /ˈiləˌstrāt/ ▸ v. [trans.] provide (a book, newspaper, etc.) with pictures: *illustrated with photographs.* ■ explain or make (something) clear by using examples, charts, pictures, etc.: *the results are illustrated in Figure 7.* ■ serve as an example of: *pieces that illustrate Bach's techniques.* [16th C.: from L. *illustrat-* 'lit up,' from the v. *illustrare*, from *in-* 'upon' + *lustrare* 'illuminate.']

il·lus·tra·tion /ˌiləˈstrāshən/ ▸ n. a picture illustrating a book, newspaper, etc. ■ an example serving to clarify or prove something: *a graphic illustration of the disaster that's waiting to happen.* ■ the action or fact of illustrating something, either pictorially or by exemplification: *by way of illustration, I refer to the following case.*

il·lus·tra·tive /iˈləstrətiv; ˈiləˌstrātiv/ ▸ adj. serving as an example or explanation: *for illustrative purposes only.* — **il·lus·tra·tive·ly** adv.

il·lus·tra·tor /ˈiləˌstrātər/ ▸ n. a person who draws or creates pictures for magazines, books, advertising, etc.

il·lus·tri·ous /iˈləstrēəs/ ▸ adj. well known, respected, and admired for past achievements: *an illustrious career.* — **il·lus·tri·ous·ly** adv. **il·lus·tri·ous·ness** n. [16th C.: from L. *illustris* 'clear, bright.']

il·lu·vi·a·tion /iˌlo͞ovēˈāshən/ ▸ n. Soil Science the introduction of salts or colloids into one soil horizon from another by percolating water.

ill will ▸ n. animosity or bitterness.

Il·lyr·i·a /iˈli(ə)rēə/ an ancient region along the eastern coast of the Adriatic Sea.

Il·lyr·i·an /iˈli(ə)rēən/ ▶ **n.** a native or inhabitant of ancient Illyria. ■ the branch of the Indo-European family of languages possibly represented by modern Albanian. ▶ **adj.** of or relating to the ancient region of Illyria or its language.

il·men·ite /ˈilməˌnīt/ ▶ **n.** a black mineral consisting of iron titanium oxide, of which it is the main ore. [19th C.: named after the *Ilmen* mountains in the Urals + -ITE[1].]

ILO ▶ **abbr.** International Labor Organization.

I·lo·ca·no /ˌēlōˈkänō/ ▶ **n.** (pl. same or **-nos**) **1** a member of a people inhabiting northwestern Luzon in the Philippines. **2** the Austronesian language of this people. ▶ **adj.** of or relating to this people or their language. [Philippine Sp., from *Ilocos*, the name of two provinces in the Philippines.]

I·lo·i·lo /ˌēlōˈēlō/ a port on the southern coast of Panay in the Philippines; pop. 310,000.

I·lo·rin /iˈlôrin/ a city in western Nigeria; pop. 390,000.

ILS ▶ **abbr.** instrument landing system, a system in which an aircraft's instruments interact with ground-based electronics to enable the pilot to land the aircraft safely in poor visibility.

-ily ▶ **suffix** forming adverbs corresponding to adjectives ending in *-y* (such as *happily* corresponding to *happy*). [see -Y[1], -LY[2].]

IM Computing ▶ **abbr.** instant message. ■ instant messaging. ▶ **v.** (**IM's, IM'd, IM'ing**) [trans.] send (someone) a message via an instant-messaging system.

I'm /īm/ ▶ **contr.** I am: *I'm busy.*

im- ▶ **prefix** var. of IN-[1], IN-[2] assimilated before *b, m, p* (as in *imbibe, immure, impart*).

im·age /ˈimij/ ▶ **n.** a representation of the external form of a person or thing in sculpture, painting, etc. ■ a visible impression obtained by a camera, telescope, microscope, or other device, or displayed on a video screen. ■ an optical appearance or counterpart produced by light or other radiation from an object reflected in a mirror or refracted through a lens. ■ a mental representation or idea: *he had an image of Uncle Walter.* ■ a simile or metaphor: *he uses the image of a hole to describe emotional emptiness.* ■ the general impression that a person, organization, or product presents to the public: *an image of youth.* ■ [in sing.] a person or thing that closely resembles another: *he's the image of his father.* ▶ **v.** (usu. **be imaged**) make a visual representation of (something) by scanning it with a detector or electromagnetic beam: *Earth's surface was imaged by the satellite* | [as n.] (**imaging**) *medical imaging.* [ME: from OFr., from L. *imago*; rel. to IMITATE.]

im·age proc·ess·ing ▶ **n.** the analysis and manipulation of a digitized image, esp. in order to improve its quality. — **im·age proc·es·sor n.**

im·ag·er /ˈimijər/ ▶ **n.** an electronic or other device that records images of something: *a thermal imager.*

im·age·ry /ˈimij(ə)rē/ ▶ **n.** visually descriptive or figurative language, esp. in a literary work: *Tennyson uses imagery to create a lyrical emotion.* ■ visual images collectively: *computer-generated imagery.* ■ visual symbolism: *religious imagery.*

im·age·set·ter /ˈimijˌsetər/ ▶ **n.** Comput. a very high-quality type of color printer used to print glossy magazines, newsletters, or other documents.

im·ag·i·na·ble /iˈmaj(ə)nəbəl/ ▶ **adj.** possible to be thought of or believed: *the most spectacular views imaginable.* — **i·mag·i·na·bly** /-blē/ **adv.**

i·ma·gi·nal ▶ **adj. 1** /iˈmaj(ə)nl/ of or relating to an image: *imaginal education methods.* **2** /iˈmāgənl; iˈmä-/ Entomol. of or relating to an adult insect or imago. [19th C.: from L. *imago, imagin-* 'image' + -AL.]

i·ma·gi·nal disk /iˈmāgənəl; iˈmä-/ ▶ **n.** Entomol. a thickening of the epidermis of an insect larva, which, on pupation, develops into a particular organ of the adult insect.

im·ag·i·nar·y /iˈmajəˌnerē/ ▶ **adj. 1** existing only in the imagination: *imaginary conversations.* **2** Math. (of a number or quantity) expressed in terms of the square root of a negative number (usually the square root of −1, represented by *i* or *j*). See also COMPLEX.

im·ag·i·na·tion /iˌmajəˈnāsʜən/ ▶ **n.** the faculty or action of forming new ideas, or images or concepts of external objects not present to the senses: *a vivid imagination.* ■ the ability of the mind to be creative or resourceful. ■ the part of the mind that imagines things: *existed only in my imagination.*

im·ag·i·na·tive /iˈmaj(ə)nətiv/ ▶ **adj.** having or showing creativity or inventiveness. — **i·mag·i·na·tive·ly adv.**

im·ag·ine /iˈmajən/ ▶ **v.** [trans.] **1** form a mental image or concept of. ■ [often as adj.] (**imagined**) believe (something unreal or untrue) to exist or be so: *ill health, real or imagined.* **2** [with clause] suppose or assume: *everyone imagined she would move away.* ■ [as exclam.] just suppose: *imagine! to outwit Heydrich!* [ME: from OFr. *imaginer*, from L. *imaginare* 'form an image of, represent' and *imaginari* 'picture to oneself,' both from *imago, imagin-* 'image.']

im·ag·i·neer /iˌmajəˈni(ə)r/ ▶ **n.** a person who devises and implements a new or highly imaginative concept or technology, in particular one who devises the attractions in Walt Disney theme parks. [1940s: from IMAGINE, on the pattern of *engineer*.]

im·ag·in·ings /iˈmajəninɢz/ ▶ **plural n.** thoughts or fantasies: *this was quite beyond his worst imaginings.*

im·ag·ism /ˈiməˌjizəm/ ▶ **n.** a movement in early 20th-century English and American poetry that sought clarity of expression through the use of precise images. — **im·ag·ist n. im·ag·is·tic** /ˌiməˈjistik/ **adj.**

i·ma·go /iˈmāgō; iˈmä-/ ▶ **n.** (pl. **i·ma·gos, i·ma·goes** or **i·ma·gi·nes** /iˈmāgəˌnēz/) **1** Entomol. the fully developed adult stage of an insect. **2** Psychoanal. an idealized mental image of someone, esp. a parent, that influences a person's behavior. [18th C. (sense 1): mod. L. use of L. *imago* 'image.' Sense 2 dates from the early 20th C.]

i·mam /iˈmäm/ ▶ **n.** the person who leads prayers in a mosque. ■ (**Imam**) a title of various Muslim leaders, esp. of one succeeding Muhammad as leader of Shiite Islam: *Imam Khomeini.* — **i·mam·ate** /-ˌmāt/ **n.** [from Arab. *imām* 'leader,' from *amma* 'lead the way.']

I·ma·ri /iˈmärē/ ▶ **n.** [usu. as adj.] a type of richly decorated Japanese porcelain. [19th C.: the name of a port in Kyushu, Japan.]

IMAX /ˈīˌmaks/ ▶ **n.** trademark a technique of wide-screen cinematography.

im·bal·ance /imˈbaləns/ ▶ **n.** lack of proportion or relation between corresponding things: *imbalance of power.*

im·be·cile /ˈimbəsəl; -ˌsil/ ▶ **n.** informal a stupid person. [16th C.: via Fr. from L. *imbecillus*, lit. 'without a supporting staff,' from *in-* (expressing negation) + *baculum* 'stick, staff.']

im·bed ▶ **v.** var. of EMBED.

im·bibe /imˈbīb/ ▶ **v.** [trans.] formal, often humorous drink (alcohol). ■ fig. absorb or assimilate (ideas or knowledge): *propaganda you imbibed in your youth.* ■ Bot. place (seeds) in water in order to absorb it. — **im·bib·er n.** [ME from L. *imbibere*, from *in-* 'in' + *bibere* 'to drink.']

im·bri·cate /ˈimbriˌkāt/ esp. Zool. Bot. ▶ **v.** [usu. as adj.] (**imbricated**) arrange (scales, sepals, plates, etc.) so that they overlap like roof tiles. ■ [intrans.] [usu. as adj.] (**imbricating**) overlap: *imbricating scales.* ▶ **adj.** (of scales, sepals, plates, etc.) having adjacent edges overlapping. Compare with VALVATE. — **im·bri·ca·tion** /ˌimbriˈkāsʜən/ **n.** [17th C. (in the sense 'shaped like a pantile'): from L. *imbricat-* 'covered with roof tiles,' from the v. *imbricare*, from *imbrex, imbric-* 'roof tile' (from *imber* 'shower of rain').]

im·bro·glio /imˈbrōlyō/ ▶ **n.** (pl. **-glios**) an extremely confused, complicated, or embarrassing situation: *the Watergate imbroglio.* [18th C.: Ital., from *imbrogliare* 'confuse'; rel. to EMBROIL.]

im·bue /imˈbyo͞o/ ▶ **v.** (**-bues, -bued, -bu·ing**) [trans.] (often **be imbued with**) inspire or permeate with a feeling or quality: *imbued with deep piety.* [ME: from Fr. *imbu* 'moistened,' from L. *imbutus*, past part. of *imbuere* 'moisten.']

IMF ▶ **abbr.** International Monetary Fund.

IMHO ▶ **abbr.** in my humble opinion (used esp. in electronic mail).

Im·ho·tep /imˈhōtep/ (*fl.* 27th century BC), Egyptian architect and scholar. It is thought that he designed the step pyramid built at Saqqara.

im·id·az·ole /ˌimiˈdazōl/ ▶ **n.** Chem. a colorless, crystalline, heterocyclic compound, $C_3H_4N_2$, present as a substituent in the amino acid histidine. [19th C.: from IMIDE + AZO- + -OLE.]

im·ide /ˈimīd/ ▶ **n.** Chem. an organic compound containing the group −CONHCO−, related to ammonia by replacement of two hydrogen atoms by acyl groups. [19th C.: from Fr., arbitrary alt. of AMIDE.]

i·mine /iˈmēn; ˈimin/ ▶ **n.** Chem. an organic compound containing the group −C=NH or −C=NR where R is an alkyl or other group. [19th C.: from AMINE, on the pattern of the pair *amide, imide*.]

im·ip·ra·mine /iˈmipräˌmēn/ ▶ **n.** a synthetic compound, $C_{19}H_{24}N_2$, used to treat depression. [1950s: from *imi(ne)* + *pr(opyl)* + AMINE.]

imit. ▶ **abbr.** ■ imitation or imitative.

im·i·tate /ˈimiˌtāt/ ▶ **v.** (often **be imitated**) take or follow as a model: *his style was imitated.* ■ copy (a person's speech or mannerisms), esp. for comic effect: *she imitated my accent.* ■ copy or simulate: *fabric that imitates silk.* — **im·i·ta·ble** /ˈimitəbəl/ **adj. im·i·ta·tor** /-ˌtātər/ **n.** [16th C.: from L. *imitat-* 'copied,' from the v. *imitari*; rel. to *imago* 'image.']

im·i·ta·tion /ˌimiˈtāsʜən/ ▶ **n.** a thing intended to simulate or copy something else: [as adj.] *an imitation diamond.* ■ the action of using someone or something as a model: *a child learns to speak by imitation.* ■ an act of imitating a person's speech or mannerisms, esp. for comic effect.

im·i·ta·tive /ˈimiˌtātiv/ ▶ **adj. 1** copying or following a model or example. ■ following a model or example without any attempt at originality. **2** (of a word) reproducing a sound (e.g., *fizz*) or pronounced in a way that is thought to correspond to the character of the object or action described (e.g., *blob*). — **im·i·ta·tive·ly adv. im·i·ta·tive·ness n.**

im·mac·u·late /iˈmakyəlit/ ▶ **adj.** (esp. of a person or their clothes) perfectly clean, neat, or tidy. ■ free from flaws or mistakes; perfect. ■ Theol. (in the Roman Catholic Church) free from sin. — **im·mac·u·la·cy** /-ləsē/ **n. im·mac·u·late·ly adv. im·mac·u·late·ness n.** [ME: from L. *immaculatus*, from *in-* 'not' + *maculatus* 'stained' (from *macula* 'spot').]

Im·mac·u·late Con·cep·tion ▶ **n.** the doctrine (in the Roman Catholic Church) that God preserved the Virgin Mary from the taint of original sin from the moment she was conceived.

im·ma·nent /ˈimənənt/ ▶ **adj.** existing or operating within; inherent: *the protection of liberties is immanent in constitutional arrangements.* — **im·ma·nence n. im·ma·nen·cy n.** [16th C.: from late L. *immanent-* 'remaining within,' from *in-* 'in' + *manere* 'remain.']

Im·man·u·el var. of EMMANUEL.

PRONUNCIATION KEY ə *ago, up*; ər *over, fur*; a *hat*; ā *ate*; ä *car*; e *let*; ē *see*; i *fit*; ī *by*; NG *sing*; ō *go*; ô *law, for*; oi *toy*; o͝o *good*; o͞o *goo*; ou *out*; TH *thin*; T͟H *then*; ZH *vision*

im·ma·te·ri·al /ˌimə'ti(ə)rēəl/ ▸ **adj.** **1** unimportant under the circumstances; irrelevant: *what the band played was immaterial.* **2** Philos. spiritual, rather than physical. — **im·ma·te·ri·al·ly** **adv.** [ME (sense 2): from late L. *immaterialis*, from *in-* 'not' + *materialis* 'relating to matter.']

im·ma·te·ri·al·ism /ˌimə'ti(ə)rēəˌlizəm/ ▸ **n.** the belief that material things have no objective existence. — **im·ma·te·ri·al·ist** **n.**

im·ma·ture /ˌimə'CHo͝or; -'t(y)o͝or/ ▸ **adj.** not fully developed: *immature fruit.* ■ (of a person or their behavior) having emotional or intellectual development appropriate to someone younger. — **im·ma·ture·ly** **adv.** **im·ma·tu·ri·ty** **n.**

im·meas·ur·a·ble /i'meZHərəbəl/ ▸ **adj.** too large, extensive, or extreme to measure. — **im·meas·ur·a·bil·i·ty** /iˌmeZHərə'bilitē/ **n.** **im·meas·ur·a·bly** /-blē/ **adv.**

im·me·di·a·cy /i'mēdēəsē/ ▸ **n.** the quality of bringing one into direct and instant involvement with something.

im·me·di·ate /i'mēdē-it/ ▸ **adj.** **1** occurring or done at once; instant. ■ relating to or existing at the present time: *his immediate priority.* **2** nearest in time, relationship, or rank: *immediate family.* ■ nearest or next to in space: *immediate vicinity.* ■ (of a relation or action) without an intervening medium or agency; direct: *the immediate cause of death.* — **im·me·di·ate·ness** **n.** [ME: from OFr. *immediat*, or from late L. *immediatus*, from *in-* 'not' + *mediatus* 'intervening,' past part. of *mediare* (see MEDIATE).]

im·me·di·ate·ly /i'mēdē-itlē/ ▸ **adv.** **1** at once; instantly. **2** without any intervening time or space: *sitting immediately behind me.* ■ in direct or very close relation: *the countries immediately affected.*

Im·mel·mann /'iməlmən; -ˌmän/ (also **Immelmann turn**) ▸ **n.** an aerobatic maneuver in which an airplane performs a half loop followed by a half roll, resulting in reversal of direction and increased height. [20th C.: named after Max *Immelmann* (1890–1916), German fighter pilot.]

im·me·mo·ri·al /ˌimə'môrēəl/ ▸ **adj.** originating in the distant past; very old: *an immemorial custom.* — **im·me·mo·ri·al·ly** **adv.** [17th C.: from med. L. *immemorialis*, from *in-* 'not' + *memorialis* 'relating to the memory.']

im·mense /i'mens/ ▸ **adj.** extremely large or great, esp. in scale or degree. — **im·men·si·ty** **n.** [ME: via Fr. from L. *immensus* 'immeasurable,' from *in-* 'not' + *mensus* 'measured.']

im·mense·ly /i'menslē/ ▸ **adv.** to a great extent; extremely: [as submodifier] *immensely popular.*

im·merse /i'mərs/ ▸ **v.** **1** dip or submerge in a liquid. **2** (**immerse oneself** or **be immersed**) fig. involve oneself deeply in a particular interest: *immersed in her work.* [17th C.: from L. *immers-* 'dipped into,' from the v. *immergere*, from *in-* 'in' + *mergere* 'to dip.']

im·mer·sion /i'mərZHən; -SHən/ ▸ **n.** the action of immersing someone or something in a liquid. ■ deep mental involvement: *his total immersion in Marxism.* ■ a method of teaching a foreign language by the exclusive use of that language. ■ baptism by immersing a person in water.

im·mer·sive /i'mərsiv/ ▸ **adj.** (of a computer display or system) generating a three-dimensional image that appears to surround the user.

im·mi·grant /'imigrənt/ ▸ **n.** a person who comes to live permanently in a foreign country. ■ Biol. an animal or plant living or growing in a region to which it has migrated.

im·mi·grate /'imiˌgrāt/ ▸ **v.** [intrans.] come to live permanently in a foreign country. [17th C.: from L. *immigrat-* 'immigrated,' from the v. *immigrare*, from *in-* 'into' + *migrare* 'migrate.']

im·mi·gra·tion /ˌimi'grāSHən/ ▸ **n.** the action of coming to live permanently in a foreign country. ■ (also **Immigration**) a government department dealing with applications from foreign citizens who wish to live in a particular country. ■ the place at an airport or country's border where officials check the documents of people entering.

im·mi·nent /'imənənt/ ▸ **adj.** about to happen: *imminent danger.* — **im·mi·nence** **n.** **im·mi·nent·ly** **adv.** [ME: from L. *imminent-* 'overhanging, impending,' from the v. *imminere*, from *in-* 'upon, toward' + *minere* 'to project.']

im·mis·ci·ble /i'misəbəl/ ▸ **adj.** (of liquids) not forming a homogeneous mixture when added together: ***water is immiscible with suntan oil.*** — **im·mis·ci·bil·i·ty** /-ˌmisə'bilitē/ **n.** **im·mis·ci·bly** /-blē/ **adv.** [17th C.: from late L. *immiscibilis*, from *in-* 'not' + *miscibilis* (see MISCIBLE).]

im·mo·bile /i'mōbəl; -bēl; -bīl/ ▸ **adj.** not moving; motionless. ■ incapable of moving or being moved. — **im·mo·bil·i·ty** /ˌimō'bilitē/ **n.**

im·mo·bi·lize /i'mōbəˌlīz/ ▸ **v.** [trans.] prevent (something or someone) from moving or operating as normal: *immobilize their vehicle.* ■ restrict the movements of (a limb or patient) to allow healing. — **im·mo·bi·li·za·tion** /-ˌmōbəli'zāSHən/ **n.**

im·mod·er·ate /i'mädərit/ ▸ **adj.** not sensible or restrained; excessive. — **im·mod·er·ate·ly** **adv.** **im·mod·er·a·tion** /-ˌmädə'rāSHən/ **n.**

im·mod·est /i'mädist/ ▸ **adj.** lacking humility or decency. — **im·mod·est·ly** **adv.** **im·mod·es·ty** **n.**

im·mo·late /'iməˌlāt/ ▸ **v.** [trans.] kill or offer as a sacrifice, esp. by burning. — **im·mo·la·tion** /ˌimə'lāSHən/ **n.** [16th C.: from L. *immolat-* 'sprinkled with sacrificial meal,' from the v. *immolare*, from *in-* 'upon' + *mola* 'meal.']

im·mor·al /i'môrəl; -'märəl/ ▸ **adj.** not conforming to accepted standards of morality. — **im·mo·ral·i·ty** /ˌimə'ralitē/ **n.** (pl. **-ties**) **im·mor·al·ly** **adv.**

im·mor·tal /i'môrtl/ ▸ **adj.** living forever; never dying or decaying. ■ deserving to be remembered forever: *an immortal classic.* ▸ **n.** an immortal being, esp. a god of ancient Greece or Rome. ■ a person of enduring fame: *one of the immortals of hockey.* ■ (**Immortal**) a member of the French Academy. — **im·mor·tal·i·ty** /ˌimôr'talitē/ **n.** **im·mor·tal·ly** **adv.**

im·mor·tal·ize /i'môrtlˌīz/ ▸ **v.** [trans.] (usu. **be immortalized in**) confer enduring fame upon: *forever immortalized in books.* — **im·mor·tal·i·za·tion** /-ˌmôrtl-i'zāSHən/ **n.**

im·mor·telle /ˌimôr'tel/ ▸ **n.** **1** another term for EVERLASTING (sense 2). **2** a Caribbean tree (genus *Erythrina*) of the pea family, with a spiny trunk and clusters of red, orange, or pinkish flowers. [19th C.: Fr., lit. 'everlasting.']

im·mov·a·ble /i'mo͞ovəbəl/ ▸ **adj.** not able to be moved. ■ (of a person) not yielding to argument or pressure. ■ (esp. of a principle) fixed or unchangeable. ■ Law (of property) consisting of land, buildings, or other permanent items. — **im·mov·a·bil·i·ty** /-ˌmo͞ovə'bilitē/ **n.** **im·mov·a·bly** /-blē/ **adv.**

immun. ▸ **abbr.** ■ immunity or immunization.

im·mune /i'myo͞on/ ▸ **adj.** resistant to a particular infection or toxin owing to the presence of specific antibodies: ***immune to hepatitis.*** ■ protected or exempt, esp. from an obligation or the effects of something: ***immune from legal action.*** ■ [predic.] not affected or influenced by something: ***immune to his charm.*** ■ [attrib.] Biol. of or relating to immunity: *the body's immune system.* [ME: (from L. *immunis* 'exempt from public service,' from *in-* 'not' + *munis* 'ready for service.']

im·mune de·fi·cien·cy ▸ **n.** another term for IMMUNODEFICIENCY.

im·mune re·sponse ▸ **n.** the reaction of the cells and fluids of the body to the presence of a substance that is not recognized as a constituent of the body itself.

im·mu·ni·ty /i'myo͞onitē/ ▸ **n.** (pl. **-ties**) the ability to resist a particular toxin by the action of specific antibodies: ***immunity to typhoid.*** ■ protection or exemption from something, esp. an obligation or penalty: ***immunity from prosecution.*** ■ Law officially granted exemption from legal proceedings. ■ (**immunity to**) lack of susceptibility: *exercises designed to build an immunity to fatigue.*

im·mu·nize /'imyəˌnīz/ ▸ **v.** [trans.] make (a person or animal) immune to infection, typically by inoculation. — **im·mu·ni·za·tion** /ˌimyəni'zāSHən/ **n.**

immuno- ▸ **comb. form** Med. representing IMMUNE, IMMUNITY, or IMMUNOLOGY.

im·mu·no·as·say /ˌimyənō'asā; iˌmyo͞o-/ ▸ **n.** Biochem. a procedure for detecting or measuring specific proteins or other substances through their properties as antigens or antibodies.

im·mu·no·chem·is·try /ˌimyənō'kemistrē; iˌmyo͞o-/ ▸ **n.** the branch of biochemistry concerned with immune responses and systems.

im·mu·no·com·pro·mised /ˌimyənō'kämprəˌmīzd; iˌmyo͞o-/ ▸ **adj.** Med. having an impaired immune system.

im·mu·no·cy·to·chem·is·try /ˌimyənōˌsītō'kemistrē; iˌmyo͞o-/ ▸ **n.** the range of microscopic techniques used in the study of the immune system. — **im·mu·no·cy·to·chem·i·cal** /-'kemikəl/ **adj.**

im·mu·no·de·fi·cien·cy /ˌimyənōdə'fiSHənsē; iˌmyo͞o-/ ▸ **n.** failure of the immune system to protect the body adequately from infection.

im·mu·no·dif·fu·sion /ˌimyənōdi'fyo͞oZHən; iˌmyo͞o-/ ▸ **n.** Biochem. a technique for detecting or measuring antibodies and antigens by their precipitation when diffused together through a gel or other medium.

im·mu·no·e·lec·tro·pho·re·sis /ˌimyənō-iˌlektrōfə'rēsis; i'myo͞o-/ ▸ **n.** Biochem. a technique for the identification of proteins in serum or other fluid by electrophoresis and subsequent immunodiffusion.

im·mu·no·fluo·res·cence /ˌimyənō-flo͝o'resəns; -flô-; iˌmyo͞o-/ ▸ **n.** Biochem. a technique for determining the location of an antigen (or antibody) in tissues by reaction with an antibody (or antigen) labeled with a fluorescent dye. — **im·mu·no·fluo·res·cent** **adj.**

im·mu·no·gen·ic /ˌimyənō'jenik; iˌmyo͞o-/ ▸ **adj.** relating to or denoting substances able to produce an immune response. — **im·mu·no·ge·nic·i·ty** /-jə'nisitē/ **n.**

im·mu·no·glob·u·lin /ˌimyənō'gläbyəlin; iˌmyo͞o-/ ▸ **n.** Biochem. any of a class of proteins present in the serum and cells of the immune system, that function as antibodies.

im·mu·nol·o·gy /ˌimyə'näləjē/ ▸ **n.** the branch of medicine and biology concerned with immunity. — **im·mu·no·log·ic** /ˌimyənə'läjik; iˌmyo͞o-/ **adj.** **im·mu·no·log·i·cal** /ˌimyənə'läjikəl; iˌmyo͞o-/ **adj.** **im·mu·no·log·i·cal·ly** /ˌimyənə'läjik(ə)lē; iˌmyo͞o-/ **adv.** **im·mu·nol·o·gist** **n.**

im·mu·no·sorb·ent /ˌimyənō'sôrbənt; -'zôr-; iˌmyo͞o-/ ▸ **adj.** Biochem. relating to or denoting techniques making use of the absorption of antibodies by insoluble preparations of antigens.

im·mu·no·sup·pres·sion /ˌimyəˌnō-sə'preSHən; iˌmyo͞onō-/ ▸ **n.** Med. the partial or complete suppression of the immune response of an individual, induced to help the survival of an organ after a transplant. — **im·mu·no·sup·pres·sant** /-sə'presənt/ **n.** **im·mu·no·sup·pres·sive** /-sə'presiv/ **adj.**

im·mu·no·ther·a·py /ˌimyənō'THerəpē; iˌmyo͞o-/ ▸ **n.** Med. the prevention or treatment of disease with substances that stimulate the immune response.

im·mure /i'myo͝or/ ▸ **v.** [trans.] (usu. **be immured**) enclose or confine (someone) against their will: *immured in a lunatic asylum.* — **im·mure·ment** **n.** [16th C.: from Fr. *emmurer* or med. L. *immurare*, from *in-* 'in' + *murus* 'wall.']

im·mu·ta·ble /i'myo͞otəbəl/ ▸ **adj.** unchanging over time or unable to be changed: *an immutable fact.* — **im·mu·ta·bil·i·ty** /iˌmyo͞otə'bilitē/ **n.** **im·mu·ta·bly** /-blē/ **adv.** [ME: from L. *immutabilis*, from *in-* 'not' + *mutabilis* (see MUTABLE).]

IMO ▸ **abbr.** International Maritime Organization.

imp /imp/ ▶**n.** a mischievous child. ■ a small, mischievous devil or sprite. [OE *impa, impe* 'young shoot, scion,' *impian* 'to graft,' based on Gk. *emphuein* 'to implant.']

imp. ▶**abbr.** ■ imperative. ■ imperfect. ■ imperial. ■ impersonal. ■ import or imported or importer. ■ important. ■ imprimatur. ■ imprint.

im·pact ▶**n.** /'impakt/ the action of one object coming forcibly into contact with another: *cause injury on impact.* ■ the effect or influence of one person, thing, or action, on another: *our measures had an* ***impact on*** *unemployment.* ▶**v.** /im'pakt/ [intrans.] come into forcible contact with another object. ■ [trans.] come into forcible contact with: *an asteroid impacted the earth.* ■ have a strong effect: *interest rates have* ***impacted on*** *spending* [17th C.: from L. *impact-* 'driven in,' from the v. *impingere* (see IMPINGE).]

im·pact·ed /im'paktid/ ▶**adj. 1** esp. Med. pressed firmly together, in particular: ■ (of a tooth) wedged between another tooth and the jaw. ■ (of a fractured bone) having the parts crushed together. ■ (of feces) lodged in the intestine. **2** strongly affected by something.

im·pac·tion /im'pakshən/ ▶**n.** Med. the condition of being or process of becoming impacted, esp. of feces in the intestine.

im·pac·tor /im'paktər/ ▶**n.** esp. Astron. an object (such as a meteorite) that collides with another body.

im·pair /im'pe(ə)r/ ▶**v.** [trans.] weaken or damage (esp. a human faculty or function): *drug use that impairs job performance.* [ME *enpeire*, from OFr. *empeirier*, based on late L. *pejorare* (from L. *pejor* 'worse').]

im·paired /im'pe(ə)rd/ ▶**adj.** having a disability of a specified kind: [in comb.] *hearing-impaired children.*

im·pair·ment /im'pe(ə)rmənt/ ▶**n.** the state or fact of being impaired, esp. in a specified faculty: *memory impairment.*

im·pal·a /im'palə; -'pälə/ ▶**n.** (pl. same) an antelope (*Aepyceros melampus*) often seen in large herds in open woodland in southern and East Africa. [19th C.: from Zulu *i-mpala.*]

impala

im·pale /im'pāl/ ▶**v.** [trans.] pierce or transfix with a sharp instrument: *his head was impaled on a pike.* — **im·pale·ment n. im·pal·er n.** [16th C.: from Fr. *empaler* or med. L. *impalare*, from L. *in-* 'in' + *palus* 'a stake.']

im·pal·pa·ble /im'palpəbəl/ ▶**adj.** unable to be felt by touch: *an impalpable ghost.* ■ not easily comprehended. — **im·pal·pa·bil·i·ty** /-,palpə'bilitē/ **n. im·pal·pa·bly** /-blē/ **adv.**

im·pan·el /im'panl/ (also **em·pan·el**) ▶**v.** (**-pan·eled, -pan·el·ing** ; Brit. **-pan·elled, -pan·el·ling**) [trans.] enlist or enroll (a jury). ■ enroll (someone) on to a jury. — **im·pan·el·ment n.** [ME: from Anglo-Norman Fr. *empaneller*, from *em-* 'in' + OFr. *panel* 'panel.']

im·part /im'pärt/ ▶**v.** [trans.] make (information) known; communicate: *a duty to* ***impart*** *strong morals to the students.* ■ bestow (a quality): ***impart*** *a high gloss* ***to*** *finished articles.* — **im·par·ta·tion** /,impär'tāshən/ **n.** [ME: from OFr. *impartir*, from L. *impartire*, from *in-* 'in' + *pars, part-* 'part.']

im·par·tial /im'pärshəl/ ▶**adj.** treating all rivals or disputants equally; fair and just. — **im·par·ti·al·i·ty** /-,pärshē'alitē/ **n. im·par·tial·ly adv.**

im·pass·a·ble /im'pasəbəl/ ▶**adj.** impossible to travel along or over. — **im·pass·a·bil·i·ty** /-,pasə'bilitē/ **n. im·pass·a·bly** /-blē/ **adv.**

im·passe /'im,pas; im'pas/ ▶**n.** a situation in which no progress is possible, esp. because of disagreement; a deadlock: *the current political impasse.* [19th C.: from Fr., from *im-* (expressing negation) + the stem of *passer* 'to pass.']

im·pas·sion /im'pashən/ ▶**v.** [trans.] make passionate. [16th C.: from Ital. *impassionare*, from *im-* (expressing intensive force) + *passione* 'passion,' from Christian L. *passio* (see PASSION).]

im·pas·sioned /im'pashənd/ ▶**adj.** filled with or showing great emotion.

im·pas·sive /im'pasiv/ ▶**adj.** not feeling or showing emotion. — **im·pas·sive·ly adv. im·pas·sive·ness n. im·pas·siv·i·ty** /,impə'sivitē/ **n.**

im·pas·to /im'pastō; -'pästō/ ▶**n.** Art the process or technique of laying on paint or pigment thickly so that it stands out from a surface. [18th C.: from Ital., from *impastare*, from *im-* 'upon' + *pasta* 'a paste,' from late L.]

im·pa·tiens /im'pāshənz/ ▶**n.** an East African plant (genus *Impatiens*, family Balsaminaceae) with abundant red, pink, or white flowers, often grown as a houseplant or bedding plant. [18th C.: mod. L., from L., 'impatient.']

im·pa·tient /im'pāshənt/ ▶**adj. 1** having or showing a tendency to be quickly irritated or provoked: ***impatient with*** *any restriction.* ■ [predic.] (**impatient of**) intolerant of: *impatient of bureaucracy.* **2** restlessly eager: ***impatient for*** *change* — **im·pa·tience n. im·pa·tient·ly adv.**

im·peach /im'pēch/ ▶**v.** [trans.] call into question the integrity or validity of (a practice): *a motion to impeach the verdict.* ■ charge (the holder of a public office) with misconduct. — **im·peach·a·ble adj. im·peach·ment n.** [ME: from OFr. *empecher* 'impede,' from late L. *impedicare* 'catch, entangle' (based on *pedica* 'a fetter,' from *pes, ped-* 'foot').]

im·pec·ca·ble /im'pekəbəl/ ▶**adj.** (of behavior, performance, or appearance) in accordance with the highest standards of propriety; faultless. — **im·pec·ca·bil·i·ty** /-,pekə'bilitē/ **n. im·pec·ca·bly** /-blē/ **adv.** [16th C.: from L. *impeccabilis*, from *in-* 'not' + *peccare* 'to sin.']

im·pe·cu·ni·ous /,impə'kyoōnēəs/ ▶**adj.** having little or no money. — **im·pe·cu·ni·os·i·ty** /-,kyoōnē'äsitē/ **n. im·pe·cu·ni·ous·ness n.** [16th C.: from IN-[1] 'not' + obs. *pecunious* 'having money' (from L. *pecunia* 'money').]

im·ped·ance /im'pēdns/ ▶**n.** the effective resistance of an electric circuit or component to alternating current, arising from the combined effects of ohmic resistance and reactance.

im·pede /im'pēd/ ▶**v.** [trans.] delay or prevent (someone or something) by obstructing them; hinder. [16th C.: from L. *impedire* 'shackle the feet of,' based on *pes, ped-* 'foot.']

im·ped·i·ment /im'pedəmənt/ ▶**n.** a hindrance or obstruction in doing something: *an* ***impediment to*** *progress.* ■ (also **speech impediment**) a defect in a person's speech, such as a lisp or stammer.

im·ped·i·men·ta /im,pedə'mentə/ ▶**plural n.** equipment for an activity or expedition, esp. when considered as bulky or an encumbrance.

im·pel /im'pel/ ▶**v.** (**-pelled, -pel·ling**) [trans.] drive, force, or urge (someone) to do something. ■ drive forward; propel: *vital energies impel him in unforeseen directions.* [ME: from L. *impellere*, from *in-* 'toward' + *pellere* 'to drive.']

im·pel·ler /im'pelər/ ▶**n.** the rotating part of a compressor or other machine designed to move a fluid by rotation.

im·pend /im'pend/ ▶**v.** [intrans.] [usu. as adj.] (**impending**) be about to happen: *my impending departure.* ■ (of something bad) loom: *danger of collision impends.* [16th C.: from L. *impendere*, from *in-* 'toward, upon' + *pendere* 'hang.']

im·pen·e·tra·ble /im'penətrəbəl/ ▶**adj. 1** impossible to pass through or enter. ■ impervious to new ideas or influences. **2** impossible to understand: *impenetrable codes.* — **im·pen·e·tra·bil·i·ty** /-,penətrə'bilitē/ **n. im·pen·e·tra·bly adv.** [ME: via Fr. from L. *impenetrabilis*, from *in-* 'not' + *penetrabilis* 'able to be pierced' from *penetrare* (see PENETRATE).]

im·pen·i·tent /im'penitnt/ ▶**adj.** not feeling shame or regret about one's actions or attitudes. — **im·pen·i·tence n. im·pen·i·ten·cy n. im·pen·i·tent·ly adv.**

im·per·a·tive /im'perətiv/ ▶**adj. 1** of vital importance; necessary; crucial. **2** giving an authoritative command; peremptory: *the bell pealed, an imperative call.* ■ Gram. denoting the mood of a verb that expresses a command or exhortation, as in *come here!* ▶**n. 1** an essential or urgent thing: *an economic imperative.* **2** Gram. a verb or phrase in the imperative mood. ■ (**the imperative**) the imperative mood. — **im·per·a·ti·val** /-,perə'tīvəl/ **adj. im·per·a·tive·ly adv. im·per·a·tive·ness n.** [ME: from late L. *imperativus*, from *imperare* 'to command,' from *in-* 'toward' + *parare* 'make ready.']

im·per·cep·ti·ble /,impər'septəbəl/ ▶**adj.** impossible to perceive. — **im·per·cep·ti·bil·i·ty** /-,septə'bilitē/ **n. im·per·cep·ti·bly adv.**

im·per·cep·tive /,impər'septiv/ ▶**adj.** lacking in perception or insight.

im·per·fect /im'pərfikt/ ▶**adj. 1** not perfect; faulty. ■ not fully formed or done; incomplete: *imperfect census records.* **2** Gram. (of a tense) denoting a past action in progress but not completed at the time in question. **3** Music (of a cadence) ending on the dominant chord. **4** Law (of a gift, title, etc.) transferred without all the necessary conditions or requirements being met. ▶**n.** (**the imperfect**) Gram. the imperfect tense. — **im·per·fect·ly adv.** [ME *imparfit, imperfet*, from OFr. *imparfait*, from L. *imperfectus*, from *in-* 'not' + *perfectus* (see PERFECT).]

im·per·fec·tion /,impər'fekshən/ ▶**n.** a fault, blemish, or undesirable feature. ■ the state of being faulty or incomplete.

im·per·fec·tive /,impər'fektiv/ Gram. ▶**adj.** relating to or denoting an aspect of verbs that expresses action without reference to its completion. The opposite of PERFECTIVE. ▶**n.** the imperfective aspect, or an imperfective form of a verb.

im·per·fect rhyme ▶**n.** a rhyme in which there is only a partial matching of sounds (e.g., *love* and *move*). See also PARARHYME.

im·per·fo·rate /im'pərfərit/ ▶**adj.** not perforated, in particular: ■ Anat. Zool. lacking the normal opening. ■ (of a postage stamp or a block or sheet of stamps) lacking perforations, esp. as an error.

im·pe·ri·al /im'pi(ə)rēəl/ ▶**adj. 1** of or relating to an empire: *Britain's imperial era.* ■ of or relating to an emperor: *the imperial family.* ■ majestic; magnificent. **2** of, relating to, or denoting the system of nonmetric weights and measures (the ounce, pound, stone, inch, foot, yard, mile, acre, pint, gallon, etc.) formerly used for all measures in the UK, and still used for some. — **im·pe·ri·al·ly adv.** [ME: via OFr. from L. *imperialis*, from *imperium* 'command, authority, empire.']

im·pe·ri·al·ism /im'pi(ə)rēə,lizəm/ ▶**n.** a policy of extending a country's power and influence through diplomacy or military force. — **im·pe·ri·al·is·tic** /-,pi(ə)rēə'listik/ **adj. im·pe·ri·al·is·ti·cal·ly** /-,pirēə'listik(ə)lē/ **adv.**

im·pe·ri·al·ist /im'pi(ə)rēəlist/ ▶**adj.** of, relating to, supporting, or practicing imperialism. ▶**n.** esp. derog. a person who supports or practices imperialism.

Im·pe·ri·al Val·ley an irrigated section of the Colorado Desert, in southeastern California.

im·per·il /im'perəl/ ▶**v.** (**-per·iled, -per·il·ing** ; Brit. **-per·illed, -per·il·ling**) [trans.] put at risk of being harmed, injured, or destroyed. — **im·per·il·ment n.**

im·pe·ri·ous /im'pi(ə)rēəs/ ▶**adj.** assuming authority without justification;

arrogant; domineering. — **im·pe·ri·ous·ly** adv. **im·pe·ri·ous·ness** n. [16th C.: from L. *imperiosus*, from *imperium*.]

im·per·ish·a·ble /im'perisHəbəl/ ▶ adj. enduring forever: *imperishable truths*. — **im·per·ish·a·bil·i·ty** /-,perisHə'bilitē/ n. **im·per·ish·a·bly** adv.

im·pe·ri·um /im'pi(ə)rēəm/ ▶ n. absolute power or authority. [17th C.: from L., 'command, authority, empire'; rel. to *imperare* 'to command.']

im·per·ma·nent /im'pərmənənt/ ▶ adj. not permanent. — **im·per·ma·nence** n. **im·per·ma·nen·cy** n. **im·per·ma·nent·ly** adv.

im·per·me·a·ble /im'pərmēəbəl/ ▶ adj. not allowing fluid to pass through: *an impermeable membrane*. ■ not liable to be affected by pain or distress; insusceptible or imperturbable: *women who appear impermeable to pain*. — **im·per·me·a·bil·i·ty** /-,pərmēə'bilitē/ n.

im·per·mis·si·ble /,impər'misəbəl/ ▶ adj. not permissible or allowed. — **im·per·mis·si·bil·i·ty** /-,misə'bilitē/ n.

im·per·son·al /im'pərsənl/ ▶ adj. **1** not influenced by, showing, or involving personal feelings. ■ (of a place or organization) large, featureless, and anonymous. ■ not betraying any personal information about the user or subject: *the room was bare and impersonal*. **2** not existing as a person; having no personality: *the impersonal forces of fate*. **3** Gram. (of a verb) used only with a formal subject (in English usually *it*) and expressing an action not attributable to a definite subject (as in *it is snowing*). — **im·per·son·al·i·ty** /-,pərsə'nalitē/ n. **im·per·son·al·ly** adv.

im·per·son·ate /im'pərsə,nāt/ ▶ v. [trans.] pretend to be (another person) as entertainment or in order to deceive someone. — **im·per·son·a·tion** /-,pərsə'nāsHən/ n. **im·per·son·a·tor** /-,nātər/ n. [17th C.: from IN-[2] 'into' + L. *persona* 'person.']

im·per·ti·nent /im'pərtn-ənt/ ▶ adj. **1** not showing proper respect; rude. **2** formal not pertinent to a particular matter; irrelevant. — **im·per·ti·nence** n. **im·per·ti·nent·ly** adv. [ME (sense 2): from OFr., or from late L. *impertinent-* 'not having reference to,' from L. *in-* 'not' + *pertinere* 'pertain.']

im·per·turb·a·ble /,impər'tərbəbəl/ ▶ adj. unable to be upset or excited; calm. — **im·per·turb·a·bil·i·ty** /-tərbə'bilitē/ n. **im·per·turb·a·bly** adv. [ME: from late L. *imperturbabilis*, from *in-* 'not' + *perturbare* (see PERTURB).]

im·per·vi·ous /im'pərvēəs/ ▶ adj. not allowing something to pass through; not penetrable. ■ [predic.] (**impervious to**) unable to be affected by: *impervious to the heat*. — **im·per·vi·ous·ly** adv. **im·per·vi·ous·ness** n. [17th C.: from L. *impervius* (from *in-* 'not' + *pervius* 'pervious') + -OUS.]

im·pe·ti·go /,impi'tīgō; -tē-/ ▶ n. a contagious skin infection caused by streptococcal bacteria, forming pustules and yellow, crusty sores. [ME: from L., from *impetere* 'to assail, attack.']

im·pet·u·ous /im'pecHōōəs/ ▶ adj. acting or done quickly and without thought or care; impulsive. ■ moving forcefully or rapidly: *an impetuous flow of water*. — **im·pet·u·ous·ly** adv. **im·pet·u·ous·ness** n. [ME: from OFr. *impetueux*, from late L. *impetuosus*, from *impetere* 'to assail, attack.']

im·pe·tus /'impitəs/ ▶ n. the force or energy or momentum with which a body moves. ■ the force that makes something happen or happen more quickly: *the crisis provided the* **impetus for** *change*. [17th C.: from L., 'assault, force,' from *impetere* 'assail,' from *in-* 'toward' + *petere* 'seek.']

Imp·hal /'im,pəl/ a city in northeastern India, the capital of the state of Manipur; pop. 157,000.

im·pi /'impē/ ▶ n. (pl. **im·pis**) a body of Zulu warriors. [19th C.: Zulu, lit. 'regiment, armed band.']

im·pi·e·ty /im'pī-itē/ ▶ n. (pl. **-ties**) lack of piety or reverence, esp. for a god.

im·pinge /im'pinj/ ▶ v. (**-ping·ing**) [intrans.] have an effect or impact, esp. a negative one: *the tragedy would* **impinge on** *her life*. ■ advance over an area belonging to someone or something else; encroach: *the site impinges on a greenbelt area*. — **im·pinge·ment** n. [16th C.: from L. *impingere* 'drive something in or at,' from *in-* 'into' + *pangere* 'fix, drive.']

im·pi·ous /'impēəs; im'pī-/ ▶ adj. not showing respect or reverence, esp. for a god. — **im·pi·ous·ly** adv. **im·pi·ous·ness** n.

imp·ish /'impisH/ ▶ adj. inclined to do slightly naughty things for fun; mischievous. — **imp·ish·ly** adv. **imp·ish·ness** n.

im·plac·a·ble /im'plakəbəl/ ▶ adj. unable to be placated. ■ relentless; unstoppable: *implacable advances*. — **im·plac·a·bil·i·ty** /-,plakə'bilitē/ n. **im·plac·a·bly** adv. [ME: from L. *implacabilis*, from *in-* 'not' + *placabilis* (see PLACABLE).]

im·plant /im'plant/ ▶ v. [trans.] insert or fix (tissue or an artificial object) in a person's body, esp. by surgery. ■ (**implant someone/something with**) provide someone or something with (something) by such insertion. ■ [intrans.] (of a fertilized egg) become attached to the wall of the uterus. ■ fig. establish or fix (an idea) in a person's mind. ▶ n. /'im,plant/ a thing implanted in something else, esp. a piece of tissue, prosthetic device, or other object implanted in the body. [ME: from late L. *implantare* 'engraft,' from L. *in-* 'into' + *plantare* 'to plant.']

im·plan·ta·tion /,implan'tāsHən/ ▶ n. the action of implanting or state of being implanted. ■ Zool. Med. (in a mammal) the attachment of the fertilized egg or blastocyst to the wall of the uterus at the start of pregnancy. Also called NIDATION.

im·plau·si·ble /im'plôzəbəl/ ▶ adj. not seeming reasonable or probable; failing to convince; not believable. — **im·plau·si·bil·i·ty** /-,plôzə'bilitē/ n. **im·plau·si·bly** adv.

im·ple·ment ▶ n. /'impləmənt/ a tool, utensil, or other piece of equipment, esp. as used for a particular purpose. ▶ v. /-,ment/ [trans.] put (a decision, plan, agreement, etc.) into effect: *implement the treaty*. — **im·ple·men·ta·tion** /,impləmən'tāsHən/ n. **im·ple·ment·er** (also **im·ple·men·tor** /-,mentər/) n. [ME: partly from med. L. *implementa* (pl.), partly from late L. *implementum* 'filling up,' both from L. *implere* 'fill up,' from *in-* 'in' + *plere* 'fill.']

im·pli·cate /'impli,kāt/ ▶ v. [trans.] **1** show (someone) to be involved in a crime: *police implicated him in more killings*. ■ (**be implicated in**) bear some of the responsibility for (an action or process, esp. a criminal or harmful one): *he is heavily implicated in the bombing*. **2** [with clause] convey (a meaning or intention) indirectly through what one says, rather than stating it explicitly; imply. — **im·pli·ca·tive** /'impli,kātiv; im'plikətiv/ adj. **im·pli·ca·tive·ly** adv. [ME: from L. *implicatus* 'folded in,' past part. of *implicare* (see IMPLY).]

im·pli·ca·tion /,impli'kāsHən/ ▶ n. the conclusion that can be drawn from something, although it is not explicitly stated. ■ a likely consequence of something: *political implications*.

im·plic·it /im'plisit/ ▶ adj. **1** implied though not plainly expressed: *implicit criticism*. ■ [predic.] (**implicit in**) essentially or very closely connected with; always to be found in: *the values implicit in the school ethos*. **2** with no qualification or question; absolute: *an implicit faith*. — **im·plic·it·ly** adv. **im·plic·it·ness** n. [16th C.: from Fr. *implicite* or L. *implicitus*, later form of *implicatus* 'entwined,' past part. of *implicare* (see IMPLY).]

im·plode /im'plōd/ ▶ v. collapse or cause to collapse violently inward. ■ Phonet. [trans.] utter or pronounce (a consonant) with a sharp intake of air. — **im·plo·sion** /im'plōzHən/ n. **im·plo·sive** adj. [19th C.: from IN-[2] 'within' + L. *plodere*, *plaudere* 'to clap,' on the pattern of *explode*.]

im·plore /im'plôr/ ▶ v. [reporting verb] beg someone earnestly or desperately to do something. — **im·plor·ing·ly** adv. [16th C.: from Fr. *implorer* or L. *implorare* 'invoke with tears.']

im·ply /im'plī/ ▶ v. (**-plies, -plied**) [trans.] strongly suggest the truth or existence of (something not expressly stated): [with clause] *the report implies that two million jobs might be lost*. [ME: from OFr. *emplier*, from L. *implicare*, from *in-* 'in' + *plicare* 'to fold.']

im·po·lite /,impə'līt/ ▶ adj. not having or showing good manners; rude. — **im·po·lite·ly** adv. **im·po·lite·ness** n.

im·pol·i·tic /im'päli,tik/ ▶ adj. failing to possess or display prudence; not judicious; unwise. — **im·pol·i·tic·ly** adv.

im·pon·der·a·ble /im'pändərəbəl/ ▶ n. a factor that is difficult or impossible to estimate or assess: *too many imponderables for a prediction*. ▶ adj. difficult or impossible to estimate, assess, or answer: *an imponderable problem*. — **im·pon·der·a·bil·i·ty** /-,pändərə'bilitē/ n. **im·pon·der·a·bly** adv.

im·port ▶ v. /im'pôrt/ [trans.] bring (goods or services) into a country from abroad for sale. ■ introduce (an idea) from a different place or context: *beliefs imported by sailors*. ■ Comput. transfer (data) into a file or document. ▶ n. /'im,pôrt/ **1** (usu. **imports**) a commodity, article, or service brought in from abroad for sale. ■ (**imports**) sales of goods or services brought in from abroad, or the revenue from such sales: *this surplus ought to boost imports*. **2** [in sing.] the meaning or significance of something, esp. when not directly stated: *the import of her message*. ■ great significance; importance: *of world-shaking import*. — **im·port·a·ble** adj. **im·port·er** n. [ME: from L. *importare* 'bring in,' from *in-* 'in' + *portare* 'carry.']

im·por·tance /im'pôrtns/ ▶ n. the state or fact of being of great significance or value: *the importance of democracy*.

im·por·tant /im'pôrtnt/ ▶ adj. of great significance or value; likely to have a profound effect on success, survival, or well-being: *important habitats for wildlife*. ■ (of a person) having high rank or status. ■ (of an artist or artistic work) significantly original and influential. [ME: from med. L. *important-* 'being of consequence,' from the v. *importare* (see IMPORT).]

im·por·tant·ly /im'pôrtnt-lē/ ▶ adv. **1** [sentence adverb] used to emphasize a significant point or matter: *a nondrinking, and, importantly, nonpolitical sportsman*. **2** in a manner designed to draw attention to one's importance.

im·por·tu·nate /im'pôrcHənit/ ▶ adj. persistent, esp. to the point of annoyance or intrusion: *importunate creditors*. — **im·por·tu·nate·ly** adv. **im·por·tu·ni·ty** /,impôr't(y)ōōnitē/ n. (pl. **-ties**).

im·por·tune /,impôr't(y)ōōn; im'pôrcHən/ ▶ v. [trans.] ask (someone) pressingly and persistently for or to do something: *I should importune him with my questions*. [16th C.: from Fr. *importuner* or med. L. *importunari*, from L. *importunus* 'inconvenient,' based on *Portunus*, the god who protects harbors, from *portus* 'harbor.']

im·pose /im'pōz/ ▶ v. **1** [trans.] force (something unwelcome or unfamiliar) to be accepted or put in place: *the decision was theirs and was not imposed on them*. ■ forcibly put (a restriction) in place: *sanctions imposed*. ■ require (a duty, charge, or penalty) to be undertaken or paid. ■ (**impose oneself**) exert firm control over something: *the director* **imposed himself on** *the production*. **2** [intrans.] take advantage of someone by demanding their attention or commitment: *she had* **imposed on** *his kindness*. [15th C.: from Fr. *imposer*, from L. *imponere* 'inflict, deceive' (from *in-* 'in, upon' + *ponere* 'put'), but influenced by *impositus* 'inflicted.']

im·pos·ing /im'pōziNG/ ▶ adj. grand and impressive in appearance: *an imposing house*. — **im·pos·ing·ly** adv.

im·po·si·tion /,impə'zisHən/ ▶ n. **1** the action or process of imposing something or of being imposed: *the imposition of martial law*. **2** a thing that is imposed, in particular: ■ an unfair or resented demand or burden. ■ a tax or duty.

im·pos·si·bil·i·ty /im,päsə'bilitē/ ▶ **n.** (pl. **-ties**) the state or fact of being impossible. ■ an impossible thing or situation.

im·pos·si·ble /im'päsəbəl/ ▶ **adj.** not able to occur, exist, or be done: *an impossible task* | [with infin.] *impossible to keep up.* ■ very difficult to deal with: *an impossible situation.* — **im·pos·si·bly adv.**

im·post¹ /'im,pōst/ ▶ **n.** a tax or similar compulsory payment. ■ Horse Racing the weight carried by a horse as a handicap. [16th C.: from Fr. (earlier form of *impôt*), from med. L. *impostus*, from L. *impositus*, past part. of *imponere* (see IMPOSE).]

im·post² ▶ **n.** Archit. the top course of a pillar that supports an arch. [15th C.: from Ital. *imposta*, fem. past part. of *imporre*, from L. *imponere* (see IMPOSE).]

im·pos·tor /im'pästər/ (also **im·post·er**) ▶ **n.** a person who pretends to be someone else in order to deceive others, esp. for fraudulent gain. [16th C.: from Fr. *imposteur*, from late L. *impostor*, contr. of *impositor*, from L. *imponere* (see IMPOSE).]

im·pos·ture /im'päschər/ ▶ **n.** an instance of pretending to be someone else in order to deceive others. [16th C.: via Fr. from late L. *impostura*, from L. *imposit-* 'imposed upon,' from the v. *imponere* (see IMPOSE).]

im·po·tent /'impətnt/ ▶ **adj.** **1** unable to take effective action; helpless or powerless. **2** (of a man) unable to achieve a sexual erection. — **im·po·tence n. im·po·ten·cy n. im·po·tent·ly adv.** [ME: via OFr. from L. *impotent-* 'powerless,' from *in-* 'not' + *potent-* (see POTENT).]

im·pound /im'pound/ ▶ **v.** [trans.] **1** seize and take legal custody of (something, esp. a vehicle, goods, or documents) because of an infringement of a law or regulation: *vehicles parked here will be impounded.* **2** shut up (domestic animals) in a pound or enclosure. ■ (of a dam) hold back or confine (water). — **im·pound·a·ble adj. im·pound·er n. im·pound·ment n.**

im·pov·er·ish /im'päv(ə)rish/ ▶ **v.** [trans.] make (a person or area) poor: *they impoverish their people* | [as adj.] (**impoverished**) *impoverished farmers.* ■ exhaust the strength, vitality, or natural fertility of: *the soil was impoverished by annual burning.* — **im·pov·er·ish·ment n.** [ME (formerly also as *empoverish*): from OFr. *empoveriss-*, lengthened stem of *empoverir*, based on *povre* 'poor.']

im·prac·ti·ca·ble /im'praktikəbəl/ ▶ **adj.** (of a course of action) impossible in practice to do or carry out: *impracticable to widen the road.* — **im·prac·ti·ca·bil·i·ty** /-,praktikə'bilitē/ **n. im·prac·ti·ca·bly adv.**

im·prac·ti·cal /im'praktikəl/ ▶ **adj.** **1** (of an object or course of action) not adapted for use or action; not sensible or realistic: *impractical high heels* | *his impractical romanticism.* ■ (of a person) not skilled or interested in practical matters. **2** impossible to do; impracticable. — **im·prac·ti·cal·i·ty** /-,prakti'kalitē/ **n. im·prac·ti·cal·ly adv.**

im·pre·ca·tion /,impri'kāshən/ ▶ **n.** formal a spoken curse. — **im·pre·ca·to·ry** /'imprikə,tôrē/ **adj.** [ME: from L. *imprecatio(n-)*, from *imprecari* 'invoke (evil),' from *in-* 'toward' + *precari* 'pray.']

im·pre·cise /,impri'sīs/ ▶ **adj.** lacking exactness and accuracy of expression or detail. — **im·pre·cise·ly adv. im·pre·cise·ness n. im·pre·ci·sion** /-'sizhən/ **n.**

im·preg·na·ble /im'preg,nəbəl/ ▶ **adj.** (of a fortified position) unable to be captured or broken into: *an impregnable wall of solid sandstone* | fig. *impregnable to takeovers.* ■ unable to be defeated or destroyed; unassailable. — **im·preg·na·bil·i·ty** /-,pregnə'bilitē/ **n. im·preg·na·bly adv.** [ME: from OFr. *imprenable*, from *in-* 'not' + *prendre* 'take' (from L. *prehendere*).]

im·preg·nate /im'preg,nāt/ ▶ **v.** [trans.] **1** make (a woman or female animal) pregnant. ■ Biol. fertilize (a female reproductive cell or ovum). **2** (usu. **be impregnated with**) soak or saturate (something) with a substance: *wood impregnated with preservative.* ■ imbue with feelings or qualities: *an atmosphere impregnated with tension.* — **im·preg·na·tion** /,impreg'nāshən/ **n.** [17th C. (in the sense 'fill'): from late L. *impregnat-* 'made pregnant,' from the v. *impregnare.*]

im·pre·sa·ri·o /,imprə'särē,ō; -'se(ə)r-/ ▶ **n.** (pl. **-ri·os**) a person who organizes and often finances concerts, plays, or operas. [18th C.: from Ital., from *impresa* 'undertaking.']

im·press¹ ▶ **v.** /im'pres/ [trans.] **1** make (someone) feel admiration and respect; affect or influence deeply. **2** make a mark or design on (an object) using a stamp or seal; imprint: *she impressed the damp clay with her seal.* ■ (**impress something on**) fig. fix an idea in (someone's mind): *nobody impressed on me the need to save.* ▶ **n.** /'im,pres/ [in sing.] an act of making an impression or mark: *marks made by the impress of his fingers.* ■ a mark made by a seal or stamp. — **im·press·i·ble adj.** [ME: from OFr. *empresser*, from *em-* 'in' + *presser* 'to press.']

im·press² /im'pres/ ▶ **v.** [trans.] hist. force (someone) to serve in an army or navy. ■ commandeer (goods or equipment) for public service. — **im·press·ment n.** [16th C.: from IN-² 'into' + PRESS².]

im·pres·sion /im'preshən/ ▶ **n.** **1** an idea, feeling, or opinion about something or someone, esp. one formed without conscious thought or on the basis of little evidence: *first impressions were positive.* ■ an effect produced on someone: *her courtesy had made a good impression.* ■ a difference made by the action or presence of someone or something: *too dirty for the mop to make much impression.* **2** an imitation of a person or thing, esp. one done to entertain: *an impression of Frank Sinatra.* **3** a mark impressed on a surface by something: *the impression of the tire.* ■ Dentistry a negative copy of the teeth or mouth made by pressing them into a soft substance. **4** the printing of a number of copies of a book, periodical, or picture for issue at one time. ■ [usu. with adj.] a particular printed version of a book or other publication, esp. one reprinted from existing type, plates, or film with no or only minor alteration. Compare with EDITION. ■ a print taken from an engraving.
– PHRASES **under the impression that** believing, mistakenly or on the basis of little evidence, that something is the case. — **im·pres·sion·al** /-shənl/ **adj.** [ME: via OFr. from L. *impressio(n-)*, from *impress-* 'pressed in,' from the v. *imprimere* (see IMPRINT).]

im·pres·sion·a·ble /im'presh(ə)nəbəl/ ▶ **adj.** easily impressed or influenced; susceptible. — **im·pres·sion·a·bil·i·ty** /-presh(ə)nə'bilitē/ **n. im·pres·sion·a·bly adv.**

Im·pres·sion·ism /im'preshə,nizəm/ ▶ **n.** a style or movement in painting originating in France in the 1860s, characterized by a concern with depicting the visual impression of the moment, esp. in terms of the shifting effect of light and color. ■ a literary or artistic style that seeks to capture a feeling or experience rather than to achieve accurate depiction. ■ Music a style of composition (associated esp. with Debussy) which seeks to evoke moods and impressions.

Im·pres·sion·ist /im'preshənist/ ▶ **n.** a painter, writer, or composer who is an exponent of Impressionism. ▶ **adj.** of or relating to Impressionism or its exponents.

im·pres·sion·ist /im'preshənist/ ▶ **n.** an entertainer who impersonates famous people.

im·pres·sion·is·tic /im,preshə'nistik/ ▶ **adj.** **1** based on subjective reactions presented unsystematically. **2** (**Impressionistic**) in the style of Impressionism: *an Impressionistic portrait.* — **im·pres·sion·is·ti·cal·ly adv.**

im·pres·sive /im'presiv/ ▶ **adj.** evoking admiration through size, quality, or skill: grand, imposing, or awesome: *an impressive view.* — **im·pres·sive·ly adv. im·pres·sive·ness n.**

im·prest /'im,prest/ ▶ **n.** a fund used by a business for small items of expenditure, then restored to a fixed amount periodically. ■ a sum of money advanced to a person or business. [16th C.: from the earlier phr. *in prest* 'as a loan,' influenced by Ital. or med. L. *imprestare* 'lend.']

im·pri·ma·tur /,imprə'mätər; -'mātər/ ▶ **n.** an official license by the Roman Catholic Church to print an ecclesiastical or religious book. ■ official approval; sanction. [17th C.: from L., 'let it be printed' from the v. *imprimere* (see IMPRINT).]

im·print ▶ **v.** /im'print/ [trans.] (usu. **be imprinted**) impress or stamp (a mark or outline) on a surface or body: *tire marks were imprinted in the snow.* ■ make an impression or mark on (something): *clothes imprinted with logos.* ■ fig. fix (an idea) firmly in someone's mind: *this ghastly image imprinted on his mind.* ▶ **n.** /'im,print/ **1** a mark made by pressing something on to a softer substance so that its outline is reproduced. ■ fig. a lasting impression or effect: *years in the colonies had left their imprint.* **2** a printer's or publisher's name, address, and other details in a book or other printed item. [ME (orig. as *emprint*): from OFr. *empreinter*, based on L. *imprimere*, from *in-* 'into' + *premere* 'to press.']

im·pris·on /im'prizən/ ▶ **v.** [trans.] (usu. **be imprisoned**) put or keep in prison or a place like a prison. — **im·pris·on·ment n.**

im·prob·a·ble /im'präbəbəl/ ▶ **adj.** not likely to be true or to happen. ■ unexpected and apparently inauthentic: *the characters have improbable names.* — **im·prob·a·bil·i·ty** /-,präbə'bilitē/ **n.** (pl. **-ties**) **im·prob·a·bly adv.**

im·promp·tu /im'prăm(p),t(y)o͞o/ ▶ **adj. & adv.** done without being planned, organized, or rehearsed: [as adj.] *an impromptu press conference.* ▶ **n.** (pl. **-tus**) a short piece of instrumental music, esp. a solo, that is reminiscent of an improvisation. [17th C. (as an adv.): from Fr., from L. *in promptu* 'in readiness,' from *promptus* (see PROMPT).]

im·prop·er /im'präpər/ ▶ **adj.** not in accordance with accepted rules or standards, esp. of morality or honesty. ■ lacking in modesty or decency. — **im·prop·er·ly adv.**

im·prop·er frac·tion ▶ **n.** a fraction in which the numerator is greater than the denominator, such as 5/4.

im·pro·pri·e·ty /,imprə'prī-itē/ ▶ **n.** (pl. **-ties**) a failure to observe standards or show due honesty or modesty; improper language, behavior, or character.

im·prov /'im,präv/ ▶ **n.** informal improvisation, esp. as a theatrical technique.

im·prove /im'pro͞ov/ ▶ **v.** make or become better: [trans.] *efforts to improve relations with China* | [as adj.] (**improved**) *improved rail links* | [intrans.] *his condition improved.* ■ [trans.] develop or increase in mental capacity by education or experience. ■ [intrans.] (**improve on/upon**) achieve or produce something better than: *trying to improve on the old style.* ■ increase the value of (real property) by renovation, construction, landscaping, etc. — **im·prov·a·bil·i·ty** /-,pro͞ovə'bilitē/ **n. im·prov·a·ble adj. im·prov·er n.** [16th C. (as *emprowe* or *improwe*): from Anglo-Norman Fr. *emprower*, based on OFr. *prou* 'profit.']

im·prove·ment /im'pro͞ovmənt/ ▶ **n.** an example or instance of improving or being improved. ■ the action of improving or being improved: *there's still* ***room for improvement.*** ■ a thing that makes something better or is better than something else: *home improvements.*

im·prov·i·dent /im'prävidənt/ ▶ **adj.** not having or showing foresight; spendthrift or thoughtless: *improvident behavior.* — **im·prov·i·dence n. im·prov·i·dent·ly adv.**

im·pro·vise /'imprə,vīz/ ▶ **v.** [trans.] create and perform (music, drama, or verse) spontaneously or without preparation. ■ produce or make (something) from whatever is available: *I improvised a costume for myself.* | [as adj.] **(improvised)** *sleeping on improvised beds.* — **im·prov·i·sa·tion** /im,prävi'zāsHən/ **n.** **im·prov·i·sa·tion·al** /im,prävi'zāsHənl/ **adj.** **im·pro·vis·er n.** [19th C.: from Fr. *improviser* or its source, Ital. *improvvisare,* from *improvviso* 'extempore,' from L. *improvisus* 'unforeseen,' based on *provisus,* past part. of *providere* 'make preparation for.']

im·pru·dent /im'proodnt/ ▶ **adj.** not showing care for the consequences of an action; rash. — **im·pru·dence n.** **im·pru·dent·ly adv.**

im·pu·dent /'impyəd(ə)nt/ ▶ **adj.** not showing due respect for another person; impertinent. — **im·pu·dence n.** **im·pu·dent·ly adv.** [ME (in the sense 'immodest, indelicate'): from L. *impudent-,* from *in-* 'not' + *pudent-* 'ashamed, modest' (from *pudere* 'be ashamed').]

im·pugn /im'pyoon/ ▶ **v.** [trans.] dispute the truth, validity, or honesty of (a statement or motive); challenge; call into question. — **im·pugn·a·ble adj.** **im·pugn·ment n.** [ME: from L. *impugnare* 'assail,' from *in-* 'toward' + *pugnare* 'fight.']

im·pu·is·sant /im'pwisənt; -'pyoo-isənt/ ▶ **adj.** literary unable to take effective action; powerless. — **im·pu·is·sance n.** [17th C.: Fr., from *im-* 'not' + *puissant* 'powerful.']

im·pulse /'im,pəls/ ▶ **n.** **1** a sudden strong urge or desire to act: *an impulse to giggle* | [as adj.] *impulse buying.* ■ the tendency to act in this way: *he was a man of impulse.* **2** a driving or motivating force; an impetus: *an added impulse to this process of renewal.* **3** a pulse of electrical energy; a brief current: *nerve impulses.* **4** Physics a force acting briefly on a body and producing a finite change of momentum. [17th C.: from L. *impuls-* 'driven on,' from the v. *impellere* (see **IMPEL**).]

im·pul·sion /im'pəlsHən/ ▶ **n.** a strong urge to do something; an impulse. ■ the force or motive behind an action or process: *the impulsion of humanitarian considerations.*

im·pul·sive /im'pəlsiv/ ▶ **adj.** acting or done without forethought: *young impulsive teenagers.* — **im·pul·sive·ly adv.** **im·pul·sive·ness n.**

im·pu·ni·ty /im'pyoonitē/ ▶ **n.** exemption from punishment or freedom from the injurious consequences of an action. [16th C.: from L. *impunitas,* from *impunis* 'unpunished,' from *in-* 'not' + *poena* 'penalty' or *punire* 'punish.']

im·pure /im'pyoor/ ▶ **adj.** **1** mixed with foreign matter; adulterated. **2** not proper; unchaste. ■ defiled or contaminated according to ritual prescriptions: *the perception of woman as impure.* — **im·pure·ly adv.** **im·pure·ness n.**

im·pu·ri·ty /im'pyoorite/ ▶ **n.** (pl. **-ties**) the quality or condition of being impure. ■ a thing or constituent that impairs the purity of something: *impurities found in tap water.*

im·pute /im'pyoot/ ▶ **v.** [trans.] represent (something, esp. something undesirable) as being done, caused, or possessed by someone; attribute: *the crimes* **imputed to** *Richard.* ■ Finance assign (a value) to something by inference from the value of the products or processes to which it contributes: [as adj.] **(imputed)** *recovering the initial outlay plus imputed interest.* — **im·put·a·ble adj.** **im·pu·ta·tion** /,impyə'tāsHən/ **n.** [ME: from OFr. *imputer,* from L. *imputare* 'enter in the account,' from *in-* 'in, toward' + *putare* 'reckon.']

IN ▶ **abbr.** Indiana (in official postal use).

In ▶ **symb.** the chemical element indium.

in /in/ ▶ **prep.** **1** expressing the situation of something that is or appears to be enclosed or surrounded by something else: *living in Deep River* | *dressed in their Sunday best* | *soak in water.* ■ expressing motion with the result that something ends up within or surrounded by something else: *don't put dye in the bathtub* | *he got in his car.* **2** expressing a period of time during which an event takes place or a situation remains the case: *they met in 1885.* **3** expressing the length of time before a future event is expected to take place: *I'll see you in fifteen minutes.* **4** (often followed by a noun without a determiner) expressing a state or condition: *in love* | *put my affairs in order* | *in her thirties.* ■ indicating the quality or aspect with respect to which a judgment is made: *no difference in quality.* **5** expressing inclusion or involvement: *I read it in a book.* **6** indicating someone's occupation or profession: *she works in publishing.* **7** indicating the language or medium used: *say it in Polish* | *put it in writing.* ■ indicating the key in which a piece of music is written: *Concerto in E flat.* **8** [with verbal n.] as an integral part of (an activity): *in planning public expenditure it is better to be prudent.* ▶ **adv.** **1** expressing movement with the result that someone or something becomes enclosed or surrounded by something else: *come in* | *bring it in.* **2** expressing the situation of being enclosed or surrounded by something: *we were locked in.* **3** expressing arrival at a destination: *the train got in late.* **4** Baseball (of a pitch) very close to the batter: *he threw a fastball in and up a little.* ▶ **adj.** **1** [predic.] (of a person) present at one's home or office: *we knocked but there was no one in.* **2** informal fashionable: *pastels are in.* **3** [predic.] (of the ball in tennis and similar games) landing within the designated playing area. ▶ **n.** a position of influence: *an in with the nominee.*

– PHRASES **be in for** have good reason to expect (typically something unpleasant): *we're in for a storm.* ■ **(be in for it)** have good reason to expect trouble or retribution. **in and out of** being a frequent visitor to (a house) or frequent inmate of (an institution): *in and out of jail.* **in on** privy to (a secret): *in on the conspiracy.* **in that** for the reason that (used to specify the respect in which a statement is true): *fortunate in that I had friends.* **in with** informal enjoying friendly relations with: *in with the right people.* [OE *in* (preposition), *inn, inne* (adv.); rel. to Du. and Ger. *in* (prep.), from an Indo-Eur. root shared by L. *in* and Gk. *en.*]

in. ▶ **abbr.** inch(es).

in-[1] ▶ **prefix** **1** (added to adjectives) not: *intolerant.* **2** (added to nouns) without; lacking: *inappreciation.* [from L.]

in-[2] ▶ **prefix** in; into; toward; within: *induce* | *influx.* [representing **IN** or the L. prep. *in.*]

-in[1] ▶ **suffix** Chem. forming names of organic compounds, pharmaceutical products, proteins, etc.: *insulin* | *penicillin* | *dioxin.* [alt. of **-INE**[4].]

-in[2] ▶ **comb. form** denoting a gathering of people having a common purpose, typically as a form of protest: *sit-in* | *love-in.*

-ina ▶ **suffix** **1** denoting feminine names and titles: *tsarina.* **2** denoting names of musical instruments: *concertina.* **3** denoting names of plant and animal groups: *globigerina.* [from Ital., Sp., or L.]

in·a·bil·i·ty /,inə'bilitē/ ▶ **n.** [with infin.] the state of being unable to do something: *his inability to accept new ideas.*

in ab·sen·tia /,in əb'sensH(ē)ə/ ▶ **adv.** while not present at the event being referred to: *two foreign suspects will be tried* in absentia. [19th C.: L., lit. 'in absence.']

in·ac·ces·si·ble /,inak'sesəbəl/ ▶ **adj.** not accessible; unable to be reached. — **in·ac·ces·si·bil·i·ty** /-,sesə'bilitē/ **n.** **in·ac·ces·si·bly adv.**

in·ac·cu·ra·cy /in'akyərəsē/ ▶ **n.** (pl. **-cies**) the quality or state of not being accurate. ■ a feature or aspect of something that is not accurate.

in·ac·cu·rate /in'akyərit/ ▶ **adj.** not accurate; not correct. — **in·ac·cu·rate·ly adv.**

in·ac·tion /in'aksHən/ ▶ **n.** lack of action where some is expected or appropriate.

in·ac·ti·vate /in'aktə,vāt/ ▶ **v.** [trans.] make inactive or inoperative: *inactivate the virus.* — **in·ac·ti·va·tion** /-,aktə'vāsHən/ **n.** **in·ac·ti·va·tor** /-,vātər/ **n.**

in·ac·tive /in'aktiv/ ▶ **adj.** not active; not engaging in or involving much physical activity: *the animals become withdrawn and inactive.* ■ not working; inoperative: *the device remains inactive while the computer is started up.* ■ not on active military service or duty. ■ having no chemical or biological effect on something: *the inactive X chromosome.* ■ (of a disease) not exhibiting symptoms. ■ Chem. not rotating the plane of polarization of polarized light. — **in·ac·tive·ly adv.** **in·ac·tiv·i·ty** /,inak'tivitē/ **n.**

in·ad·e·quate /in'adikwit/ ▶ **adj.** not adequate; lacking the quality or quantity required; insufficient for a purpose. ■ (of a person) unable to deal with a situation or with life: ***inadequate to the task.*** — **in·ad·e·qua·cy** /-kwəsē/ **n.** (pl. **-ies**) **in·ad·e·quate·ly adv.**

in·ad·mis·si·ble /,inəd'misəbəl/ ▶ **adj.** (esp. of evidence in court) not allowable; not accepted as valid. — **in·ad·mis·si·bil·i·ty** /-,misə'bilitē/ **n.** **in·ad·mis·si·bly** /-blē/ **adv.**

in·ad·vert·ent /,inəd'vərtnt/ ▶ **adj.** not resulting from or achieved through deliberate planning; unintentional. ■ (of a mistake) made through lack of care; negligent. — **in·ad·vert·ence n.** **in·ad·vert·en·cy n.** **in·ad·vert·ent·ly adv.** [17th C.: from **IN-**[1] 'not' + L. *advertent-* 'turning the mind to' (from the v. *advertere*).]

in·ad·vis·a·ble /,inəd'vīzəbəl/ ▶ **adj.** not advisable; likely to have unfortunate consequences; unwise. — **in·ad·vis·a·bil·i·ty** /-,vīzə'bilitē/ **n.**

in·al·ien·a·ble /in'ālēənəbəl/ ▶ **adj.** unable to be taken away from or given away by the possessor: *inalienable human rights.* — **in·al·ien·a·bil·i·ty** /-,ālēənə'bilitē/ **n.** **in·al·ien·a·bly adv.**

in·al·ter·a·ble /in'ôltərəbəl/ ▶ **adj.** unable to be changed. — **in·al·ter·a·bil·i·ty** /-,ôltərə'bilitē/ **n.** **in·al·ter·a·bly adv.**

in·am·o·ra·ta /in,amə'rätə/ ▶ **n.** a person's female lover.

in·am·o·ra·to /in,amə'rä,tō/ ▶ **n.** (pl. **-tos**) a person's male lover. [16th C.: Ital., lit. 'enamored,' past part. of the v. *inamorare,* based on L. *amor* 'love.']

in-and-out ▶ **adj.** informal involving inward and outward movement, esp. rapid entrance and exit: *a quick in-and-out operation.*

in·ane /i'nān/ ▶ **adj.** silly; stupid; not significant. — **in·ane·ly adv.** **in·ane·ness n.** [16th C.: from L. *inanis* 'empty, vain.']

in·an·i·mate /in'anəmit/ ▶ **adj.** not alive, esp. not in the manner of animals and humans. ■ showing no sign of life; lifeless. — **in·an·i·mate·ly adv.**

in·a·ni·tion /,inə'nisHən/ ▶ **n.** lack of mental or spiritual vigor and enthusiasm. ■ exhaustion caused by lack of nourishment. [ME: from late L. *inanitio(n-),* from L. *inanire* 'make empty,' from *inanis* 'empty, vain.']

in·ap·par·ent /,inə'parənt; -'pe(ə)r-/ ▶ **adj.** Med. causing no noticeable signs or symptoms.

in·ap·pe·tence /in'apətəns/ ▶ **n.** lack of appetite. — **in·ap·pe·tent adj.**

in·ap·pli·ca·ble /in'aplikəbəl; ,inə'plik-/ ▶ **adj.** not relevant or appropriate: *the details are* ***inapplicable to*** *other designs.* — **in·ap·pli·ca·bil·i·ty** /-,aplikə'bilitē/ **n.** **in·ap·pli·ca·bly adv.**

in·ap·po·site /in'apəzit/ ▶ **adj.** not apposite; out of place; inappropriate. — **in·ap·po·site·ly adv.**

in·ap·pre·ci·a·ble /,inə'prēsHəbəl/ ▶ **adj.** too small or insignificant to be valued or perceived. — **in·ap·pre·ci·a·bly adv.**

in·ap·pre·ci·a·tive /,inə'prēsH(ē)ətiv; -sHē,ātiv/ ▶ **adj.** not appreciative. — **in·ap·pre·ci·a·tion** /-,prēsHē'āsHən/ **n.**

in·ap·pro·pri·ate /,inə'prōprē-it/ ▶ **adj.** not suitable or proper in the circumstances: *inappropriate behavior.* — **in·ap·pro·pri·ate·ly adv.** **in·ap·pro·pri·ate·ness n.**

in·apt /in'apt/ ▶ **adj.** not apt; not appropriate or suitable. — **in·ap·ti·tude** /-ti,t(y)ood/ **n.** **in·apt·ly adv.**

in·arch /in'ärcH/ ▶ **v.** [trans.] Horticulture graft (a plant) by connecting a growing branch without separating it from its parent stock.

in·ar·gu·a·ble /in'ärgyōōəbəl/ ▸ **adj.** another term for UNARGUABLE. — **in·ar·gu·a·bly adv.**

in·ar·tic·u·late /,inär'tikyəlit/ ▸ **adj.** unable to speak distinctly or express oneself clearly. ■ not clearly expressed or pronounced: *inarticulate complaints.* ■ having no distinct meaning; unintelligible. — **in·ar·tic·u·la·cy** /-ləsē/ **n. in·ar·tic·u·late·ly adv. in·ar·tic·u·late·ness n.**

in·ar·tis·tic /,inär'tistik/ ▸ **adj.** not artistic; lacking in skill, talent or appreciation of art. — **in·ar·tis·ti·cal·ly adv.**

in·as·much /,inəz'məCH/ ▸ **adv.** (**inasmuch as**) to the extent that; insofar as. ■ considering that; since (used to specify the respect in which a statement is true).

in·at·ten·tive /,inə'tentiv/ ▸ **adj.** not attentive; not mindful. — **in·at·ten·tion n. in·at·ten·tive·ly adv. in·at·ten·tive·ness n.**

in·au·di·ble /in'ôdəbəl/ ▸ **adj.** unable to be heard. — **in·au·di·bil·i·ty** /in,ôdə'bilitē/ **n. in·au·di·bly adv.**

in·au·gu·ral /in'ôg(y)ərəl/ ▸ **adj.** [attrib.] marking the beginning of an institution, activity, or period of office: *his inaugural concert as music director.* ▸ **n.** an inaugural speech, esp. one made by an incoming US president. ■ an inaugural ceremony.

in·au·gu·rate /in'ôg(y)ə,rāt/ ▸ **v.** [trans.] begin or introduce (a system, policy, or period): *inaugurated a new policy of trade.* ■ admit (someone) formally to public office: *he will be inaugurated on January 20.* ■ mark the beginning or first public use of (an organization or project): *the museum was inaugurated on September 12.* — **in·au·gu·ra·tion** /-,ôg(y)ə'rāSHən/ **n. in·au·gu·ra·tor** /-,rātər/ **n.** [16th C.: from L. *inaugurat-* 'interpreted as omens (from the flight of birds),' based on *augurare* 'to augur.']

in·aus·pi·cious /,inô'spiSHəs/ ▸ **adj.** not auspicious; not conducive to success. — **in·aus·pi·cious·ly adv. in·aus·pi·cious·ness n.**

in·au·then·tic /,inô'THentik/ ▸ **n.** not authentic; not in fact what it is said to be. — **in·au·then·ti·cal·ly adv. in·au·then·tic·i·ty** /in,ôTHən'tisitē/ **n.**

in-be·tween informal ▸ **adj.** situated somewhere between two extremes or recognized categories; intermediate: *not unconscious, but in some in-between state.*

in·board /'in,bôrd/ ▸ **adv. & adj.** within a ship, aircraft, or vehicle: [as adv.] *the spray was coming inboard now.* ▸ **n.** a boat's engine housed inside its hull. ■ a boat with such an engine.

in·born /'in'bôrn/ ▸ **adj.** existing from birth: *an inborn defect.* ■ natural to a person or animal: *people think doctors have inborn compassion.*

in·bound /'in,bound/ ▸ **adj. & adv.** traveling toward a particular place, esp. when returning to the original point of departure: [as adj.] *inbound traffic* | [as adv.] *we have three enemy planes inbound on bearing two ninety.*

in·bounds /'in,boundz/ ▸ **adj.** Basketball denoting or relating to a throw that puts the ball into play from out of bounds: *an inbounds pass.*

in-box ▸ **n.** a box on someone's desk for letters addressed to them and other documents that they have to deal with. ■ Computing the window in which a user's received e-mails and similar electronic communications are displayed.

in·bred /'in'bred/ ▸ **adj. 1** produced by inbreeding. **2** existing in a person, animal, or plant from birth; congenital: *inbred disease resistance in crops.*

in·breed /'in'brēd/ ▸ **v.** (past and past part. **-bred**) [intrans.] [often as n.] (**inbreeding**) breed from closely related people or animals, esp. over many generations.

Inc. /iNGk/ ▸ **abbr.** ■ incorporated. ■ (also **inc.**) incomplete.

In·ca /'iNGkə/ ▸ **n. 1** a member of a South American Indian people living in the central Andes before the Spanish conquest. Inca technology and architecture were highly developed. Their descendants, speaking Quechua, still make up about half of Peru's population. **2** the supreme ruler of this people. — **In·can adj.** [16th C.: the name in Quechua, lit. 'lord, royal person.']

in·cal·cu·la·ble /in'kalkyələbəl; iNG-/ ▸ **adj. 1** too great to be calculated or estimated: *incalculable value.* **2** not able to be calculated or estimated. — **in·cal·cu·la·bil·i·ty** /-,kalkyələ'bilitē/ **n. in·cal·cu·la·bly adv.**

in cam·er·a ▸ **adv.** see CAMERA².

in·can·des·cent /,inkən'desənt/ ▸ **adj.** emitting light as a result of being heated. ■ (of an electric light) containing a filament that glows white-hot when heated by a current passed through it. ■ of outstanding quality; brilliant: *an incandescent performance.* — **in·can·desce v. in·can·des·cence n. in·can·des·cent·ly adv.** [18th C.: from Fr., from L. *incandescent-* 'glowing,' from the v. *incandescere*, from *in-* + *candescere* 'become white' (from *candidus* 'white').]

in·can·ta·tion /,inkan'tāSHən/ ▸ **n.** a series of words said as a magic spell or charm. [ME: via OFr. from late L. *incantatio(n-)*, from *incantare* 'chant, bewitch,' from *in-* + *cantare* 'sing.']

in·ca·pa·ble /in'kāpəbəl/ ▸ **adj. 1** [predic.] (**incapable of**) not capable; unable to do or achieve (something). ■ (of a person) too honest or moral to do a certain thing: *incapable of prejudice.* **2** unable to behave rationally or manage one's own affairs: *the pilot may become incapable from the lack of oxygen.* — **in·ca·pa·bil·i·ty** /-,kāpə'bilitē/ **n. in·ca·pa·bly adv.**

in·ca·pac·i·tate /,inkə'pasi,tāt/ ▸ **v.** [trans.] prevent from functioning in a normal way: *incapacitated by a heart attack.* — **in·ca·pac·i·tant** /-'pasitnt/ **n. in·ca·pac·i·ta·tion** /-,pasi'tāSHən/ **n.**

in·ca·pac·i·ty /,inkə'pasitē/ ▸ **n.** (pl. **-ties**) physical or mental inability to do something or to manage one's affairs. ■ legal disqualification: *subject to legal incapacity.*

in·car·cer·ate /in'kärsə,rāt/ ▸ **v.** [trans.] (usu. **be incarcerated**) imprison. — **in·car·cer·a·tion** /-,kärsə'rāSHən/ **n. in·car·cer·a·tor** /-,rātər/ **n.** [16th C.: from med. L. *incarcerat-* 'imprisoned,' from the v. *incarcerare*, from *in-* 'into' + L. *carcer* 'prison.']

in·car·nate ▸ **adj.** /in'kärnit; -nāt/ [often postpositive] (esp. of a deity or spirit) embodied in flesh; in human form: *God incarnate.* ■ [postpositive] represented in the ultimate or most extreme form: *capitalism incarnate.* ▸ **v.** /-nāt/ [trans.] embody or represent (a deity or spirit) in human form. ■ put (an idea or other abstract concept) into concrete form. ■ (of a person) be the living embodiment of (a quality): *the man who incarnates the suffering that has affected every single Mozambican.* [ME: from eccles. L. *incarnat-* 'made flesh,' from the v. *incarnare*, from *in-* 'into' + *caro, carn-* 'flesh.']

in·car·na·tion /,inkär'nāSHən/ ▸ **n. 1** a person who embodies in the flesh a deity, spirit, or abstract quality: *Rama was Vishnu's incarnation on earth.* ■ (**the Incarnation**) (in Christian theology) the embodiment of God the Son in human flesh as Jesus Christ. **2** (with reference to reincarnation) one of a series of lifetimes that a person spends on earth: *in my next incarnation, I'd like to be the Secretary of Fun.*

in·case ▸ **v.** var. of ENCASE.

in·cau·tious /in'kôSHəs/ ▸ **adj.** (of a person or an action) not cautious; heedless of potential problems or risks. — **in·cau·tion n. in·cau·tious·ly adv. in·cau·tious·ness n.**

in·cen·di·ar·y /in'sendē,erē/ ▸ **adj.** (of a device or attack) designed to cause fires: *incendiary grenades.* ▸ **n.** (pl. **-ar·ies**) an incendiary bomb or device. ■ a person who stirs up conflict. [ME: from L. *incendiarius*, from *incendium* 'conflagration,' from *incendere* 'set fire to.']

in·cense¹ ▸ **n.** /'in,sens/ a gum, spice, or other substance that is burned for the sweet smell it produces. ■ the smoke or perfume of such a substance. ▸ **v.** /in'sens/ [trans.] perfume with incense or a similar fragrance: *the aroma of cannabis incensed the air.* [ME (orig. as *encense*): from OFr. *encens* (n.), *encenser* (v.), from eccles. L. *incensum* 'something burned, incense.']

in·cense² /in'sens/ ▸ **v.** [trans.] (usu. **be incensed**) make very angry: *incensed by the accusations.* [ME: from OFr. *incenser*, from L. *incendere* 'set fire to.']

in·cense ce·dar ▸ **n.** a columnar cedar (*Calocedrus decurrens*) with scalelike leaves that smell of turpentine when crushed, found chiefly in California and Oregon.

in·cen·tive /in'sentiv/ ▸ **n.** a thing that motivates or encourages one to do something: *incentive to conserve.* ■ a payment or concession to stimulate greater output or investment: *tax incentives for investing.* [ME: from L. *incentivum* 'something that sets the tune or incites,' from *incantare* 'to chant or charm.']

in·cep·tion /in'sepSHən/ ▸ **n.** [in sing.] the establishment or starting point of something; the beginning. [ME: from L. *inceptio(n-)*, from *incipere* 'begin.']

in·cep·tive /in'septiv/ ▸ **adj.** relating to or marking the beginning of something; initial. ■ Gram. (of a verb) expressing the beginning of an action; inchoative. ▸ **n.** Gram. an inceptive verb.

in·cer·ti·tude /in'sərti,t(y)ōōd/ ▸ **n.** a state of uncertainty or hesitation: *the stresses of policy incertitude.*

in·ces·sant /in'sesənt/ ▸ **adj.** (of something regarded as unpleasant) continuing without pause or interruption: *the incessant beat of the music.* — **in·ces·san·cy n. in·ces·sant·ly adv. in·ces·sant·ness n.** [ME: via OFr. from late L. *incessant-*, from *in-* 'not' + L. *cessant-* 'ceasing' (from the v. *cessare*).]

in·cest /'insest/ ▸ **n.** sexual relations between people classed as being too closely related to marry each other. ■ the crime of having sexual intercourse with a parent, child, sibling, or grandchild. [ME: from L. *incestus*, *incestum* 'unchastity, incest;' from *in-* 'not' + *castus* 'chaste.']

in·ces·tu·ous /in'sesCHōōəs/ ▸ **adj. 1** involving or guilty of incest. **2** (of human relations generally) excessively close and resistant to outside influence. — **in·ces·tu·ous·ly adv. in·ces·tu·ous·ness n.**

inch¹ /inCH/ ▸ **n. 1** a unit of linear measure equal to one twelfth of a foot (2.54 cm): *the toy train is four inches long.* ■ (**inches**) informal a person's height or waist measurement. ■ [often with negative] a very small amount or distance. **2** a unit used to express other quantities, in particular: ■ (as a unit of rainfall) a quantity that would cover a horizontal surface to a depth of one inch. ■ (Symbol: ") (as a unit of atmospheric pressure) an amount that would support a column of mercury one inch high in a barometer (equal to 33.86 millibars). ■ (as a unit of map scale) so many inches representing one mile on the ground: [in comb.] *one-inch maps of Connecticut.* ▸ **v.** [intrans.] move slowly and carefully in a specified direction. ■ [trans.] cause (something) to move in this manner: *he inched the car forward.*

– PHRASES **by inches** very slowly and gradually; bit by bit. **every inch 1** the whole surface, distance, or area: *they know every inch of the country.* **2** entirely; very much so: *every inch the gentleman.* **inch by inch** gradually; bit by bit: *inch by inch he crept along the wall.* [OE *ynce*, from L. *uncia* 'twelfth part,' from *unus* 'one.']

inch² ▸ **n.** [in place names] esp. Scot. a small island or a small area of high land: *Inchkeith.* [ME: from Scot. Gael. *innis*.]

inch·meal /'inCH,mēl/ ▸ **adv.** by inches; little by little. [16th C.: from INCH¹ + *-meal* from OE *mǣlum*, in the sense 'measure, quantity taken at one time.']

PRONUNCIATION KEY ə *ago, up*; ər *over, fur*; a *hat*; ā *ate*; ä *car*; e *let*; ē *see*; i *fit*; ī *by*; NG *sing*; ō *go*; ô *law, for*; oi *toy*; o͝o *good*; ōō *goo*; ou *out*; TH *thin*; T͟H *then*; ZH *vision*

IJ

in·cho·ate ▶ **adj.** /in'kō-it; -āt/ just begun and so not fully formed or developed; rudimentary: *a still inchoate democracy.* — **in·cho·ate·ly** **adv.** **in·cho·ate·ness** **n.** [16th C.: from L. *inchoatus*, past part. of *inchoare*, var. of *incohare* 'begin.']

in·cho·a·tive /in'kō-itiv/ ▶ **adj.** Gram. denoting an aspect of a verb expressing the beginning of an action, typically one occurring of its own accord. Compare with ERGATIVE. ▶ **n.** an inchoative verb.

In·chon /'in'cHän/ a port on the western coast of South Korea, on the Yellow Sea; pop. 1,818,000.

inch·worm /'incH,wərm/ ▶ **n.** a caterpillar of a geometrid moth, which moves forward by arching and straightening its body. Also called LOOPER, MEASURING WORM, or SPANWORM.

in·ci·dence /'insidəns/ ▶ **n.** the occurrence, rate, or frequency of a disease, crime, or something else undesirable: *an increased incidence of cancer.*

in·ci·dent /'insidənt/ ▶ **n.** an event or occurrence: *several amusing incidents.* ■ a violent event, such as a fracas or assault: *one person was stabbed in the incident.* ■ a hostile clash between forces of rival countries. ■ (**incident of**) a case or instance of something happening: *an incident of rudeness.* ■ the occurrence of dangerous or exciting things: *the winter passed without incident.* ▶ **adj.** **1** [predic.] (**incident to**) liable to happen because of; resulting from: *the changes incident to economic development.* ■ Law attaching to: *the costs incident to a suit for foreclosure.* **2** (esp. of light or other radiation) falling on or striking something: *when an ion beam is* ***incident on*** *a surface.* [ME: via OFr. from L. *incident-* 'falling upon, happening to,' from the v. *incidere*, from *in-* 'upon' + *cadere* 'to fall.']

in·ci·den·tal /,insi'dentl/ ▶ **adj.** **1** accompanying but not a major part of something: *incidental expenses.* ■ occurring by chance in connection with something else: *the incidental catch of dolphins in the pursuit of tuna.* **2** [predic.] (**incidental to**) liable to happen as a consequence of (an activity): *risks incidental to a fireman's job.* ▶ **n.** (usu. **incidentals**) an incidental detail, expense, etc.: *meals, taxis, and other incidentals.*

in·ci·den·tal·ly /,insi'dent(ə)lē/ ▶ **adv.** **1** [sentence adverb] used when a person has something more to say, or is about to add a remark unconnected to the current subject; by the way: *incidentally, it was months before the truth was discovered.* **2** in an incidental manner; as a chance occurrence: *the infection was discovered incidentally.*

in·ci·den·tal mu·sic ▶ **n.** music used in a film or play as a background to create or enhance a particular atmosphere.

in·cin·er·ate /in'sinə,rāt/ ▶ **v.** [trans.] (often **be incinerated**) destroy (something, esp. waste material) by burning. — **in·cin·er·a·tion** /-,sinə'rāsHən/ **n.** [15th C.: from med. L. *incinerat-* 'burned to ashes,' from the v. *incinerare*, from *in-* 'into, toward' + *cinis, ciner-* 'ashes.']

in·cin·er·a·tor /in'sinə,rātər/ ▶ **n.** an apparatus for burning waste material, esp. industrial waste, at high temperatures until it is reduced to ash.

in·cip·i·ent /in'sipēənt/ ▶ **adj.** in an initial stage; beginning to happen or develop: *incipient anger.* ■ (of a person) developing into a specified type or role: *incipient lovers.* — **in·cip·i·ence** **n.** **in·cip·i·en·cy** **n.** **in·cip·i·ent·ly** **adv.** [16th C. (as a n. denoting a beginner): from L. *incipient-* 'undertaking, beginning,' from the v. *incipere*, from *in-* 'into, toward' + *capere* 'take.']

in·ci·pit /in'sipit/ ▶ **n.** the opening words of a text, manuscript, early printed book, or chanted liturgical text. [19th C.: L., lit. '(here) begins.']

in·cise /in'sīz/ ▶ **v.** [trans.] (usu. **be incised**) mark (an object or surface) with a cut or a series of cuts. ■ cut (a mark or decoration) into a surface: *figures incised on stones.* ■ cut (skin or flesh) with a surgical instrument: *the wound was incised and drained.* [16th C.: from Fr. *inciser*, from L. *incis-* 'cut into, engraved,' from the v. *incidere*, from *in-* 'into' + *caedere* 'to cut.']

in·ci·sion /in'sizHən/ ▶ **n.** a surgical cut made in skin or flesh. ■ the action or process of cutting into something.

in·ci·sive /in'sīsiv/ ▶ **adj.** (of a person or mental process) intelligently analytical and clear-thinking. ■ (of an account) accurate and sharply focused: *the songs offer incisive pictures of American ways.* — **in·ci·sive·ly** **adv.** **in·ci·sive·ness** **n.**

in·ci·sor /in'sīzər/ ▶ **n.** (also **incisor tooth**) a narrow-edged tooth at the front of the mouth, adapted for cutting.

in·cite /in'sīt/ ▶ **v.** [trans.] encourage or stir up (violent or unlawful behavior). ■ urge or persuade (someone) to act in a violent or unlawful way: *he incited loyal subjects to rebellion.* — **in·ci·ta·tion** /,insī'tāsHən/ **n.** **in·cite·ment** **n.** **in·cit·er** **n.** [15th C.: from Fr. *inciter*, from L. *incitare*, from *in-* 'toward' + *citare* 'rouse.']

in·ci·vil·i·ty /,insi'vilitē/ ▶ **n.** (pl. **-ies**) rude or unsociable speech or behavior; lack of politeness. ■ (often **incivilities**) an impolite or offensive comment.

incl. ▶ **abbr.** ■ including. ■ inclusive.

in·clem·ent /in'klemənt/ ▶ **adj.** (of the weather) unpleasantly cold or wet. — **in·clem·en·cy** **n.** (pl. **-cies**). [17th C.: from Fr. *inclément* or L. *inclement-*, from *in-* 'not' + *clement-* 'clement.']

in·cli·na·tion /,inklə'nāsHən; ,iNGklə-/ ▶ **n.** **1** a person's natural tendency to act or feel in a particular way; a disposition or propensity: *a scientist by inclination.* ■ (**inclination for/to/toward**) an interest in or liking for (something): *an inclination for things with moving parts.* **2** a slope or slant. ■ a bending of the body or head in a bow: *the inclination of his head.* **3** the angle at which a straight line or plane is inclined to another. ■ Astron. the angle between the orbital plane of a planet, comet, etc., and the ecliptic. ■ Astron. the angle between the axis of an astronomical object and a fixed reference angle.

in·cline ▶ **v.** /in'klīn/ **1** (**be inclined to/toward/to do something**) feel willing or favorably disposed toward (an action, belief, or attitude): *inclined to accept.* ■ [with infin.] (esp. as a polite formula) tend toward holding a specified opinion: *inclined to agree.* ■ [intrans.] feel favorably disposed to someone or something: *I incline to his view.* **2** (**be inclined to/to do something**) have a tendency to do something: *inclined to gossip.* ■ [with adverbial] have a specified disposition or talent: *mathematically inclined.* **3** slope, slant, lean or turn away from a given plane or direction, esp. the vertical or horizontal: [as adj.] (**inclined**) *an inclined ramp.* ■ [trans.] bend (one's head) forward and downward. ▶ **n.** /'in,klīn/ an inclined surface or slope, esp. on a road, path, or railway: *the road climbs a long incline.* [ME: from OFr. *encliner*, from L. *inclinare*, from *in-* 'toward' + *clinare* 'to bend.']

in·clined plane ▶ **n.** a plane inclined at an angle to the horizontal. ■ a sloping ramp up which heavy loads can be raised by ropes or chains.

in·cli·nom·e·ter /,inklə'nämitər/ ▶ **n.** a device for measuring the angle of inclination of something, esp. from the horizontal.

in·close ▶ **v.** var. of ENCLOSE.

in·clo·sure ▶ **n.** var. of ENCLOSURE.

in·clude /in'klōōd/ ▶ **v.** [trans.] **1** comprise or contain as part of a whole: *the price includes dinner.* **2** make part of a whole or set: *we have included some hints for beginners in this section.* ■ allow (someone) to share in an activity or privilege: *she's included in the invitation.* [ME (also in the sense 'shut in'): from L. *includere*, from *in-* 'into' + *claudere* 'to shut.']

in·clud·ed /in'klōōdid/ ▶ **adj.** [postpositive] contained as part of a whole being considered: *all of Europe (Russia included).*

in·clud·ing /in'klōōdiNG/ ▶ **prep.** containing as part of the whole being considered: *languages including Welsh.*

in·clu·sion /in'klōōzHən/ ▶ **n.** **1** the action or state of including or of being included within a group or structure: *the inclusion of handicapped students.* ■ a person or thing that is included within a larger group or structure. **2** Biol. Geol. Metallurgy a body or particle recognizably distinct from the substance in which it is embedded. [17th C.: from L. *inclusio(n-)*, from *includere* 'shut in.']

in·clu·sive /in'klōōsiv/ ▶ **adj.** including or covering all the services, facilities, or items normally expected or required: *the price is inclusive.* ■ [predic.] (**inclusive of**) containing (a specified element) as part of a whole: *all prices are inclusive of taxes.* ■ [postpositive] with the inclusion of the extreme limits stated: *between the ages of 55 and 59 inclusive.* ■ not excluding any section of society or any party involved in something: *an inclusive peace process.* ■ (of language) deliberately nonsexist, esp. avoiding the use of masculine pronouns to cover both men and women. — **in·clu·sive·ly** **adv.** **in·clu·sive·ness** **n.**

in·cog·ni·to /,inkäg'nētō; in'kägni,tō/ ▶ **adj. & adv.** (of a person) having one's true identity concealed: [as adv.] *operating incognito.* ▶ **n.** (pl. **-tos**) an assumed or false identity. [17th C.: from Ital., lit. 'unknown,' from L. *incognitus*, from *in-* 'not' + *cognitus* (past part. of *cognoscere* 'know').]

in·cog·ni·zant /in'kägnəzənt/ ▶ **adj.** not cognizant; lacking knowledge or awareness. — **in·cog·ni·zance** **n.**

in·co·her·ent /,inkō'hi(ə)rənt; ,iNG-; -'her-/ ▶ **adj.** (of spoken or written language) expressed in an incomprehensible or confusing way; unclear. ■ (of a person) unable to speak intelligibly. ■ (of an ideology, policy, or system) internally inconsistent; illogical. — **in·co·her·ence** **n.** **in·co·her·en·cy** **n.** (pl. **-cies**) **in·co·her·ent·ly** **adv.**

in·com·bus·ti·ble /,inkəm'bəstəbəl/ ▶ **adj.** (esp. of a building material or component) consisting or made of material that does not burn if exposed to fire. — **in·com·bus·ti·bil·i·ty** /-,bəstə'bilitē/ **n.**

in·come /'in,kəm; 'iNG-/ ▶ **n.** money received, esp. on a regular basis, for work or through investments. [ME: in early use from ON *innkoma*, later from IN + COME.]

in·come tax ▶ **n.** tax levied directly on personal income.

in·com·ing /'in,kəmiNG/ ▶ **adj.** in the process of coming in: *incoming passengers | the incoming tide.* ■ (of a message or communication) being received rather than sent: *an incoming call.* ■ (of an official or administration) having just been elected or appointed to succeed another: *the incoming president.*

in·com·men·su·ra·ble /,inkə'mensərəbəl; -SHər-/ ▶ **adj.** **1** not able to be judged by the same standard as something; having no common standard of measurement: *the two types of science are incommensurable.* **2** Math. (of numbers) in a ratio that cannot be expressed as a ratio of integers. ▶ **n.** (usu. **incommensurables**) an incommensurable quantity. — **in·com·men·su·ra·bil·i·ty** /-,mensərə'bilitē; -SHər-/ **n.** **in·com·men·su·ra·bly** **adv.**

in·com·men·su·rate /,inkə'mensərit; -SHə-/ ▶ **adj.** **1** [predic.] (**incommensurate with**) out of keeping or proportion with: *man's influence on the earth seems incommensurate with his scale.* **2** another term for INCOMMENSURABLE (sense 1). — **in·com·men·su·rate·ly** **adv.**

in·com·mode /,inkə'mōd/ ▶ **v.** [trans.] inconvenience (someone).

in·com·mo·di·ous /,inkə'mōdēəs/ ▶ **adj.** causing inconvenience or discomfort. — **in·com·mo·di·ous·ly** **adv.**

in·com·mu·ni·ca·ble /,inkə'myōōnikəbəl/ ▶ **adj.** not able to be communicated to others: *an incommunicable depression.* — **in·com·mu·ni·ca·bil·i·ty** /-,myōōnikə'bilitē/ **n.** **in·com·mu·ni·ca·bly** **adv.**

in·com·mu·ni·ca·do /,inkə,myōōni'kädō/ ▶ **adj.** not wanting or not able to communicate with other people. [19th C.: from Sp. *incomunicado*, past part. of *incomunicar* 'deprive of communication.']

in·com·mu·ni·ca·tive /ˌinkəˈmyo͞oniˌkətiv/ ▶ **adj.** another term for UNCOMMUNICATIVE. — **in·com·mu·ni·ca·tive·ly adv.**

in·com·mut·a·ble /ˌinkəˈmyo͞otəbəl/ ▶ **adj.** not capable of being changed or exchanged. — **in·com·mut·a·bly adv.**

in·com·pa·ra·ble /inˈkämp(ə)rəbəl/ ▶ **adj.** **1** without an equal in quality or extent; matchless. **2** unable to be compared; totally different in nature or extent: *censorship still exists, but it's incomparable with what it was.* — **in·com·pa·ra·bil·i·ty** /-ˌkämp(ə)rəˈbilitē/ **n.** **in·com·pa·ra·bly adv.**

in·com·pat·i·ble /ˌinkəmˈpatəbəl; ˌiNG-/ ▶ **adj.** (of two things) so opposed in character as to be incapable of existing together. ■ (of two people) unable to live together harmoniously. ■ [predic.] **(incompatible with)** (of one thing or person) not consistent or able to coexist with (another): *long hours are incompatible with family life.* ■ (of equipment, machinery, computer programs, etc.) not capable of being used in combination: *all four camcorders were incompatible with one another.* — **in·com·pat·i·bil·i·ty** /-ˌpatəˈbilitē/ **n.** **in·com·pat·i·bly adv.**

in·com·pe·tent /inˈkämpətənt; iNG-/ ▶ **adj.** not having the necessary skills to do something successfully. ■ Law not qualified to act in a particular capacity: *the patient is deemed legally incompetent.* ▶ **n.** an incompetent person. — **in·com·pe·tence n.** **in·com·pe·ten·cy n.** **in·com·pe·tent·ly adv.**

in·com·plete /ˌinkəmˈplēt; ˌiNG-/ ▶ **adj.** not having all the necessary or appropriate parts. ■ not full or finished. — **in·com·plete·ly adv.** **in·com·plete·ness n.** **in·com·ple·tion n.**

in·com·pre·hen·si·ble /ˌinkämprəˈhensəbəl; inˌkäm-/ ▶ **adj.** not comprehensible; not able to be understood. — **in·com·pre·hen·si·bil·i·ty n.** **in·com·pre·hen·si·bly adv.**

in·com·pre·hen·sion /ˌinkämprəˈhenSHən; inˌkäm-/ ▶ **n.** failure to understand something.

in·com·press·i·ble /ˌinkəmˈpresəbəl/ ▶ **adj.** not able to be compressed. — **in·com·press·i·bil·i·ty** /-ˌpresəˈbilitē/ **n.**

in·com·put·a·ble /ˌinkəmˈpyo͞otəbəl/ ▶ **adj.** rare unable to be computed or calculated.

in·con·ceiv·a·ble /ˌinkənˈsēvəbəl/ ▶ **adj.** not capable of being imagined or grasped mentally; unbelievable: *inconceivable cruelty.* — **in·con·ceiv·a·bil·i·ty** /-ˌsēvəˈbilitē/ **n.** **in·con·ceiv·a·bly adv.**

in·con·clu·sive /ˌinkənˈklo͞osiv; ˌiNG-/ ▶ **adj.** not leading to a firm conclusion; not ending doubt or dispute: *the evidence is inconclusive.* — **in·con·clu·sive·ly adv.** **in·con·clu·sive·ness n.**

in·con·den·sa·ble /ˌinkənˈdensəbəl/ ▶ **adj.** (of a gas or vapor) not able to be condensed.

in·con·gru·ent /inˈkäNGgro͞oənt; ˌinkənˈgro͞o-/ ▶ **adj.** incongruous; incompatible. — **in·con·gru·ence n.** **in·con·gru·ent·ly adv.**

in·con·gru·ous /inˈkäNGgro͞oəs/ ▶ **adj.** not in harmony or keeping with the surroundings or other aspects of something; not in place. — **in·con·gru·i·ty** /ˌinkənˈgro͞o-itē; ˌiNG-; -käNG-/ **n.** (pl. **-ties**) **in·con·gru·ous·ly adv.**

in·con·nu /ˌinkəˈn(y)o͞o; aNkôˈnʏ/ ▶ **n.** **1** an unknown person or thing. **2** (pl. same) an edible predatory freshwater whitefish (*Stenodus leucichthys*) of the salmon family, living close to the Arctic Circle. [19th C.: Fr., lit. 'unknown.']

in·con·sec·u·tive /ˌinkənˈsekyətiv/ ▶ **adj.** not consecutive; not in order or following continuously. — **in·con·sec·u·tive·ly adv.**

in·con·se·quent /inˈkänsəˌkwent; -ˌkwənt/ ▶ **adj.** not connected or following logically; irrelevant. ■ another term for INCONSEQUENTIAL. — **in·con·se·quence n.** **in·con·se·quent·ly adv.** [16th C.: from L. *inconsequent-*, from *in-* 'not' + *consequent-* 'overtaking, following closely' (see CONSEQUENT).]

in·con·se·quen·tial /ˌinkänsəˈkwenCHəl/ ▶ **adj.** not important or significant. — **in·con·se·quen·ti·al·i·ty** /-ˌkwenCHēˈalitē/ **n.** (pl. **-ties**). **in·con·se·quen·tial·ly adv.**

in·con·sid·er·a·ble /ˌinkənˈsidərəbəl/ ▶ **adj.** [usu. with negative] of small size, amount, or extent. ■ unimportant or insignificant.

in·con·sid·er·ate /ˌinkənˈsidərit/ ▶ **adj.** thoughtlessly causing hurt or inconvenience to others. — **in·con·sid·er·ate·ly adv.** **in·con·sid·er·ate·ness n.** **in·con·sid·er·a·tion** /-ˌsidəˈrāSHən/ **n.**

in·con·sist·en·cy /ˌinkənˈsistənsē/ ▶ **n.** (pl. **-cies**) the fact or state of being inconsistent. ■ an inconsistent element or an instance of being inconsistent.

in·con·sist·ent /ˌinkənˈsistənt/ ▶ **adj.** not staying the same throughout; having self-contradictory elements. ■ acting at variance with one's own principles or former conduct: *parents can be inconsistent.* ■ **(inconsistent with)** not compatible or in keeping with. ■ erratic in behavior or action: *too inconsistent to win.* — **in·con·sist·ent·ly adv.**

in·con·sol·a·ble /ˌinkənˈsōləbəl/ ▶ **adj.** (of a person or their grief) not able to be consoled or comforted. — **in·con·sol·a·bil·i·ty** /-ˌsōləˈbilitē/ **n.** **in·con·sol·a·bly adv.**

in·con·spic·u·ous /ˌinkənˈspikyo͞oəs/ ▶ **adj.** not clearly visible or attracting attention; not conspicuous. — **in·con·spic·u·ous·ly adv.** **in·con·spic·u·ous·ness n.**

in·con·stant /inˈkänstənt/ ▶ **adj.** frequently changing; variable or irregular. ■ (of a person or their behavior) not faithful and dependable. — **in·con·stan·cy n.** (pl. **-cies**) **in·con·stant·ly adv.**

in·con·test·a·ble /ˌinkənˈtestəbəl/ ▶ **adj.** not able to be disputed. — **in·con·test·a·bil·i·ty** /-ˌtestəˈbilitē/ **n.** **in·con·test·a·bly adv.**

in·con·ti·nent /inˈkäntənənt; -ˈkäntn-ənt/ ▶ **adj.** **1** having no or insufficient voluntary control over urination or defecation. **2** lacking self-restraint; uncontrolled. — **in·con·ti·nence n.** **in·con·ti·nent·ly adv.** [ME (sense 2): from OFr., or from L. *incontinent-*, from *in-* 'not' + *continent-* 'holding together' (see CONTINENT[2]).]

in·con·tro·vert·i·ble /inˌkäntrəˈvərtəbəl/ ▶ **adj.** not able to be denied or disputed: *incontrovertible proof.* — **in·con·tro·vert·i·bil·i·ty** /-ˌvərtəˈbilitē/ **n.** **in·con·tro·vert·i·bly adv.**

in·con·ven·ience /ˌinkənˈvēn-yəns/ ▶ **n.** trouble or difficulty caused to one's personal requirements or comfort: *the inconvenience of having to change trains.* ■ a cause or instance of such trouble: *the inconveniences of life in a remote city.* ▶ **v.** [trans.] cause such trouble or difficulty to: *traffic would inconvenience residents.*

in·con·ven·ient /ˌinkənˈvēn-yənt/ ▶ **adj.** causing trouble, difficulties, or discomfort. — **in·con·ven·ient·ly adv.**

in·con·vert·i·ble /ˌinkənˈvərtəbəl/ ▶ **adj.** not able to be changed in form, function, or character. ■ (of currency) not able to be converted into another form on demand. — **in·con·vert·i·bil·i·ty** /-ˌvərtəˈbilitē/ **n.** **in·con·vert·i·bly adv.**

in·co·or·di·na·tion /ˌinkōˌôrdnˈāSHən/ ▶ **n.** tech. lack of coordination, esp. the inability to use different parts of the body together smoothly and efficiently.

in·cor·po·rate ▶ **v.** /inˈkôrpəˌrāt/ [trans.] **1** put or take in (something) as part of a whole; include. ■ contain or include (something) as part of a whole. ■ combine (ingredients) into one substance. **2** (often **be incorporated**) constitute (a company, city, or other organization) as a legal corporation. — **in·cor·po·ra·tion** /-ˌkôrpəˈrāSHən/ **n.** **in·cor·po·ra·tor n.** [ME: from late L. *incorporat-* 'embodied,' from the v. *incorporare*, from *in-* 'into' + L. *corporare* 'form into a body' (from *corpus, corpor-* 'body').]

in·cor·po·rat·ed /inˈkôrpəˌrātid/ ▶ **adj.** (of a company or other organization) formed into a legal corporation.

in·cor·po·re·al /ˌinkôrˈpôrēəl/ ▶ **adj.** not composed of matter; having no material existence. ■ Law having no physical existence. — **in·cor·po·re·al·ly adv.** [ME: from L. *incorporeus*, from *in-* 'not' + *corporeus* (from *corpus, corpor-* 'body').]

in·cor·rect /ˌinkəˈrekt/ ▶ **adj.** **1** not correct; not in accordance with fact; wrong. **2** not in accordance with a particular set of standards: *grammatically incorrect.* — **in·cor·rect·ly adv.** **in·cor·rect·ness n.**

in·cor·ri·gi·ble /inˈkôrijəbəl; -ˈkär-/ ▶ **adj.** (of a person or their tendencies) not able to be corrected, improved, or reformed. — **in·cor·ri·gi·bil·i·ty** /-ˌkôrijəˈbilitē; -ˌkär-/ **n.** **in·cor·ri·gi·bly adv.** [ME: from OFr., or from L. *incorrigibilis*, from *in-* 'not' + *corrigibilis* (see CORRIGIBLE).]

in·cor·rupt /ˌinkəˈrəpt/ ▶ **adj.** rare (esp. of a human body) not having undergone decomposition. [ME: from L. *incorruptus*, from *in-* 'not' + *corruptus* 'destroyed, marred' (see CORRUPT).]

in·cor·rupt·i·ble /ˌinkəˈrəptəbəl/ ▶ **adj.** **1** not susceptible to corruption, esp. by bribery. **2** not subject to death or decay; everlasting. — **in·cor·rupt·i·bil·i·ty** /-ˌrəptəˈbilitē/ **n.** **in·cor·rupt·i·bly adv.**

in·crease ▶ **v.** /inˈkrēs/ become or make greater in size, amount, intensity, or degree: [trans.] *increase awareness of social issues* | [as adj.] **(increasing)** *increasing numbers of students.* ▶ **n.** /ˈinˌkrēs/ an instance of growing or making greater: *increase in inflation.* — **in·creas·a·ble adj.** **in·creas·ing·ly adv.** [sentence adverb] *increasingly, attention is paid to health* | [as submodifier] *an increasingly difficult situation.* [ME: from OFr. *encreistre*, from L. *increscere*, from *in-* 'into' + *crescere* 'grow.']

in·cre·ate /ˌinkrēˈāt; inˈkrē-it/ ▶ **adj.** literary not yet created.

in·cred·i·ble /inˈkredəbəl/ ▶ **adj.** **1** impossible to believe: *an incredible tale of triumph.* **2** difficult to believe; extraordinary: *the noise was incredible.* ■ informal amazingly good or beautiful. — **in·cred·i·bil·i·ty** /-ˌkredəˈbilitē/ **n.**

in·cred·i·bly /inˈkredəblē/ ▶ **adv.** **1** [as submodifier] to a great degree; extremely: *incredibly brave.* **2** [sentence adverb] used to introduce a statement that is hard to believe; strangely: *incredibly, he was still alive.*

in·cre·du·li·ty /ˌinkrəˈd(y)o͞olitē/ ▶ **n.** the state of being unwilling or unable to believe something.

in·cred·u·lous /inˈkrejələs/ ▶ **adj.** (of a person or their manner) unwilling or unable to believe something: *an incredulous gasp.* — **in·cred·u·lous·ly adv.**

in·cre·ment /ˈiNGkrəmənt; ˈin-/ ▶ **n.** an increase or addition, esp. one of a series on a fixed scale: *pay can escalate in five-cent increments.* ■ a regular increase in salary on such a scale. ■ Math. a small positive or negative change in a variable quantity or function. — **in·cre·men·tal** /ˌiNGkrəˈmentl; ˌin-/ **adj.** **in·cre·men·tal·ly** /ˌiNGkrəˈmentl-ē; ˌin-/ **adv.** [ME: from L. *incrementum*, from the stem of *increscere* 'grow' (see INCREASE).]

in·cre·men·tal·ism /ˌiNGkrəˈmentlˌizəm; ˌin-/ ▶ **n.** belief in or advocacy of change by degrees; gradualism. — **in·cre·men·tal·ist n. & adj.**

in·crim·i·nate /inˈkriməˌnāt/ ▶ **v.** [trans.] make (someone) appear guilty of a crime or wrongdoing; strongly imply the guilt of (someone): *he refused to answer questions in order not to incriminate himself* | [as adj.] **(incriminating)** *incriminating evidence.* — **in·crim·i·na·tion** /-ˌkriməˈnāSHən/ **n.** **in·crim·i·na·to·ry** /-nəˌtôrē/ **adj.** [18th C.: from late L. *incriminat-* 'accused,' from the v. *incriminare*, from *in-* 'into, toward' + L. *crimen* 'crime.']

in-crowd ▶ **n.** **(the in-crowd)** informal a small group of people perceived by others to be particularly fashionable, informed, or popular.

in·crust ▶ v. var. of ENCRUST.

in·crus·ta·tion ▶ n. var. of ENCRUSTATION.

in·cu·bate /ˈinkyəˌbāt; ˈiNG-/ ▶ v. [trans.] (of a bird) sit on (eggs) in order to keep them warm and bring them to hatching. ■ (esp. in a laboratory) keep (eggs, cells, bacteria, embryos, etc.) at a suitable temperature so that they develop. ■ [intrans.] develop slowly without outward or perceptible signs. [17th C.: from L. *incubat-* 'lain on,' from the v. *incubare*, from *in-* 'upon' + *cubare* 'to lie.']

in·cu·ba·tion /ˌinkyəˈbāsHən; ˌiNG-/ ▶ n. the process of incubating eggs, cells, bacteria, a disease, etc. — **in·cu·ba·tive** /ˈinkyəˌbātiv; ˈiNG-/ adj. **in·cu·ba·to·ry** /inˈkyo͞obəˌtôrē; iNG-/ adj.

in·cu·ba·tion pe·ri·od the period between exposure to an infection and the appearance of the first symptoms.

in·cu·ba·tor /ˈinkyəˌbātər; ˈiNG-/ ▶ n. an enclosed apparatus providing a controlled environment for the care of premature babies. ■ an apparatus used to hatch eggs or grow microorganisms under controlled conditions.

in·cu·bus /ˈiNGkyəbəs; ˈin-/ ▶ n. (pl. **-bi** /-ˌbī/) a male demon believed to have sexual intercourse with sleeping women. ■ fig. a cause of distress or anxiety. [ME: late L. form of L. *incubo* 'nightmare,' from *incubare* 'lie on' (see INCUBATE).]

in·cu·des /inˈkyo͞oˌdēz/ plural form of INCUS.

in·cul·cate /inˈkəlkāt; ˈinkəlˌkāt/ ▶ v. [trans.] instill (an attitude, idea, or habit) by persistent instruction: *the failures of the churches to inculcate a sense of moral responsibility.* ■ teach (someone) an attitude, idea, or habit by such instruction: *they will try to inculcate you with a respect for culture.* — **in·cul·ca·tion** /ˌinkəlˈkāsHən/ n. **in·cul·ca·tor** /-ˌkātər/ n. [16th C.: from L. *inculcat-* 'pressed in,' from the v. *inculcare*, from *in-* 'into' + *calcare* 'to tread' (from *calx*, *calc-* 'heel').]

in·cul·pate /inˈkəlpāt; ˈinkəlˌpāt/ ▶ v. [trans.] accuse or blame; incriminate. — **in·cul·pa·tion** /ˌinkəlˈpāsHən/ n. **in·cul·pa·to·ry** /inˈkəlpəˌtôrē/ adj. [18th C.: from late L. *inculpat-* 'made culpable,' from the v. *inculpare*, from *in-* 'upon, toward' + *culpare* 'to blame' (from *culpa* 'fault').]

in·cul·tu·ra·tion ▶ n. var. of ENCULTURATION.

in·cum·ben·cy /inˈkəmbənsē/ ▶ n. (pl. **-cies**) the holding of an office or the period during which one is held.

in·cum·bent /inˈkəmbənt/ ▶ adj. **1** [predic.] (**incumbent on/upon**) necessary for or resting on (someone) as a duty or responsibility. **2** [attrib.] (of an official or regime) currently holding office: *the incumbent president had been defeated.* ▶ n. the holder of an office or post. [ME (as a n.): from Anglo-Latin *incumbens*, *incumbent-*, from L. *incumbere* 'lie or lean on,' from *in-* 'upon' + a v. rel. to *cubare* 'lie.']

in·cu·na·ble /inˈkyo͞onəbəl/ ▶ n. one book in a collection of incunabula.

in·cu·nab·u·la /ˌinkəˈnab-yələ; ˌiNG-/ ▶ n. (sing. **in·cu·nab·u·lum** /-ləm/ or **in·cu·na·ble** /inˈkyo͞onəbəl/) early printed books, esp. those printed before 1501. [19th C.: L. (neut. pl.), 'swaddling clothes, cradle,' from *in-* 'into' + *cunae* 'cradle.']

in·cur /inˈkər; iNG-/ ▶ v. (**-curred**, **-cur·ring**) [trans.] become subject to (something unwelcome or unpleasant) as a result of one's own behavior or actions: *I will pay any expenses incurred.* [ME: from L. *incurrere*, from *in-* 'toward' + *currere* 'run.']

in·cur·a·ble /inˈkyo͝orəbəl/ ▶ adj. (of a sick person or a disease) not able to be cured. ▶ n. a person who cannot be cured. — **in·cur·a·bil·i·ty** n. **in·cur·a·bly** adv. [as submodifier] *incurably ill patients.*

in·cu·ri·ous /inˈkyo͝orēəs/ ▶ adj. not eager to know something; lacking curiosity. — **in·cu·ri·os·i·ty** /-ˌkyo͝orēˈäsitē/ n. **in·cu·ri·ous·ly** adv. **in·cu·ri·ous·ness** n.

in·cur·rent /inˈkərənt; -ˈkə-rənt/ ▶ adj. esp. Zool. (of a vessel or opening) conveying fluid inward. The opposite of EXCURRENT.

in·cur·sion /inˈkərZHən/ ▶ n. an invasion or attack, esp. a sudden or brief one: *incursions into enemy territory.* — **in·cur·sive** adj. [ME (formerly also as *encursion*): from L. *incursio(n-)*, from the v. *incurrere* (see INCUR).]

in·curve /inˈkərv/ ▶ v. [intrans.] [usu. as adj.] (**incurved**) curve inward: *incurved horns.*

in·cus /ˈiNGkəs/ ▶ n. (pl. **in·cu·des** /inˈkyo͞odēz/) Anat. a small anvil-shaped bone in the middle ear. [17th C.: from L., lit. 'anvil.']

in·cuse /inˈkyo͞oz; -ˈkyo͞os/ ▶ n. an impression hammered or stamped on a coin. [19th C.: from L. *incusus* 'forged with a hammer.']

Ind. ▶ abbr. ■ Independent. ■ India. ■ Indian. ■ Indiana.

in·debt·ed /inˈdetid/ ▶ adj. owing money. ■ owing gratitude for a service or favor: *indebted to her.* — **in·debt·ed·ness** n. [ME *endetted*, from OFr. *endette* 'involved in debt,' past part. of *endetter*. The spelling change in the 16th C. was due to association with med. L. *indebitare* (based on L. *debitum* 'debt').]

in·de·cen·cy /inˈdēsənsē/ ▶ n. (pl. **-cies**) indecent behavior. ■ an indecent act, gesture, or expression.

in·de·cent /inˈdēsənt/ ▶ adj. not conforming with generally accepted standards of behavior or propriety; obscene. ■ not appropriate or fitting. — **in·de·cent·ly** adv.

in·de·cent ex·po·sure ▶ n. the crime of intentionally showing one's sexual organs in public.

in·de·ci·pher·a·ble /ˌindiˈsīfərəbəl/ ▶ adj. not able to be read or understood: *indecipherable scrawls.*

in·de·ci·sion /ˌindiˈsiZHən/ ▶ n. the inability to make a decision quickly.

in·de·ci·sive /ˌindiˈsīsiv/ ▶ adj. **1** not settling an issue: *an indecisive battle.* **2** (of a person) not having or showing the ability to make decisions quickly and effectively. — **in·de·ci·sive·ly** adv. **in·de·ci·sive·ness** n.

in·de·clin·a·ble /ˌindiˈklīnəbəl/ ▶ adj. Gram. (of a noun, pronoun, or adjective in a highly inflected language) having no inflections.

in·de·com·pos·a·ble /ˌindēkəmˈpōzəbəl/ ▶ adj. Math. unable to be expressed as a product of factors or otherwise decomposed into simpler elements.

in·dec·o·rous /inˈdekərəs/ ▶ adj. not decorous; not in keeping with good taste and propriety; improper. — **in·dec·o·rous·ly** adv.

in·de·co·rum /ˌindiˈkôrəm/ ▶ n. failure to conform to good taste, propriety, or etiquette.

in·deed /inˈdēd/ ▶ adv. **1** used to emphasize a statement or response: *"Do you realize this?" "I do indeed."* ■ used to emphasize a description, typically of a quality or condition: *it was a very good buy indeed.* **2** used in a response to express interest, incredulity, or contempt: *Nice boys, indeed—they were going to smash his head in!* [ME: orig. as *in deed*.]

indef. ▶ abbr. indefinite.

in·de·fat·i·ga·ble /ˌindəˈfatigəbəl/ ▶ adj. (of a person or their efforts) persisting tirelessly; untiring. — **in·de·fat·i·ga·bil·i·ty** /-ˌfatigəˈbilitē/ n. **in·de·fat·i·ga·bly** adv. [17th C.: from Fr., or from L. *indefatigabilis*, from *in-* 'not' + *de-* 'away, completely' + *fatigare* 'wear out.']

in·de·fea·si·ble /ˌindəˈfēzəbəl/ ▶ adj. esp. Law Philos. not able to be lost, annulled, or overturned: *an indefeasible right.* — **in·de·fea·si·bil·i·ty** /-ˌfēzəˈbilitē/ n. **in·de·fea·si·bly** adv.

in·de·fen·si·ble /ˌindəˈfensəbəl/ ▶ adj. **1** not justifiable by argument: *the policy was morally indefensible.* **2** not able to be protected against attack. — **in·de·fen·si·bil·i·ty** /-ˌfensəˈbilitē/ n. **in·de·fen·si·bly** adv.

in·de·fin·a·ble /ˌindəˈfīnəbəl/ ▶ adj. not able to be defined or described exactly. — **in·de·fin·a·bly** adv.

in·def·i·nite /inˈdefənit/ ▶ adj. lasting for an unknown length of time: *indefinite detention.* ■ not clearly expressed or defined; vague: *their status remains indefinite.* ■ Gram. (of a word, inflection, or phrase) not determining the person, thing, time, etc., referred to. — **in·def·i·nite·ness** n.

in·def·i·nite ar·ti·cle ▶ n. Gram. a determiner (*a* and *an* in English) that introduces a noun phrase and implies that the thing referred to is nonspecific (as in *she bought me a book*). Compare with DEFINITE ARTICLE.

in·def·i·nite in·te·gral ▶ n. Math. an integral expressed without limits, and so containing an arbitrary constant.

in·def·i·nite·ly /inˈdefənitlē/ ▶ adv. for an unlimited or unspecified period of time. ■ [as submodifier] to an unlimited or unspecified degree or extent: *an indefinitely large number of channels.*

in·def·i·nite pro·noun ▶ n. Gram. a pronoun that does not refer to any person, amount, or thing in particular, e.g., *anything*, *something*, *anyone*, *everyone*.

in·de·his·cent /ˌindiˈhisənt/ ▶ adj. Bot. (of a pod or fruit) not splitting open to release the seeds when ripe. — **in·de·his·cence** n.

in·del·i·ble /inˈdeləbəl/ ▶ adj. (of ink or a pen) making marks that cannot be removed. ■ not able to be forgotten or removed: *his story made an indelible impression on me.* — **in·del·i·bil·i·ty** /-ˌdeləˈbilitē/ n. **in·del·i·bly** adv. [15th C. (as *indeleble*): from Fr., or from L. *indelebilis*, from *in-* 'not' + *delebilis* (from *delere* 'efface, delete').]

in·del·i·cate /inˈdelikit/ ▶ adj. not sensitive, understanding, or tactful. ■ slightly indecent: *an indelicate sense of humor.* — **in·del·i·ca·cy** /-kəsē/ n. (pl. **-cies**). **in·del·i·cate·ly** adv.

in·dem·ni·fy /inˈdemnəˌfī/ ▶ v. (**-fies**, **-fied**) [trans.] compensate (someone) for harm or loss: *insurance carried to indemnify the owner for loss.* ■ secure (someone) against legal responsibility for their actions. — **in·dem·ni·fi·ca·tion** /-ˌdemnəfiˈkāsHən/ n. **in·dem·ni·fi·er** n. [17th C.: from L. *indemnis* 'unhurt, free from loss,' from *in-* + *damnum* 'loss, damage.']

in·dem·ni·ty /inˈdemnitē/ ▶ n. (pl. **-ties**) security or protection against a loss or other financial burden. ■ security against or exemption from legal responsibility for one's actions.

in·dene /ˈinˌdēn/ ▶ n. Chem. a colorless liquid hydrocarbon, C_9H_8, obtained from coal tar and used in making synthetic resins. [19th C.: from INDOLE + -ENE.]

in·dent[1] ▶ v. /inˈdent/ [trans.] **1** start (a line of text) or position (a block of text, table, etc.) further from the margin than the main part of the text. **2** (usu. **be indented**) form deep recesses in (a line or surface): *a coastline indented by many fjords.* ■ make toothlike notches in: *leaves indented at the tip.* ▶ n. /inˈdent; ˈinˌdent/ a space left by indenting a line or block of text. [ME: from Anglo-Norman Fr. *endenter* or med. L. *indentare*, from *en-*, *in-* 'into' + L. *dens*, *dent-* 'tooth.']

in·dent[2] ▶ v. [trans.] make a dent or depression in.

in·den·ta·tion /ˌindenˈtāsHən/ ▶ n. **1** the action of indenting or the state of being indented: *paragraphs are marked by indentation.* **2** a deep recess in a surface or coastline. ■ a toothlike notch.

in·den·ture /inˈdenCHər/ ▶ n. a formal legal agreement, contract, or document, in particular: ■ hist. a deed of contract of which copies were made for the contracting parties with the edges indented for identification. ■ a formal list, certificate, or inventory. ■ an agreement binding an apprentice to a master. ■ hist. a contract by which a person agreed to work for a set period for a landowner in a British colony in exchange for passage to the colony. ■ the fact of being bound to service by such an agreement. ▶ v. [trans.] (usu. **be indentured to**) esp. hist. bind (someone) by an indenture as an apprentice or laborer. — **in·den·ture·ship** n. [ME *endenture*, via Anglo-Norman Fr. from med. L. *indentura*, from *indentatus*, past part. of *indentare* (see INDENT[1]).]

In·de·pend·ence /ˌində'pendəns/ a historic city in northwestern Missouri; pop. 113,288.

In·de·pend·ence Day ▶ n. another term for FOURTH OF JULY.

In·de·pend·ence Hall a building in Philadelphia where the US Declaration of Independence was proclaimed and outside which the Liberty Bell is kept.

in·de·pend·en·cy /ˌində'pendənsē/ ▶ n. (pl. **-cies**) rare an independent or self-governing state.

in·de·pend·ent /ˌində'pendənt/ ▶ adj. **1** free from outside control; not depending on another's authority. ■ (of a country) self-governing. ■ not belonging to or supported by a political party: *the independent candidate.* ■ (of broadcasting, a school, etc.) not supported by public funds. ■ not influenced or affected by others; impartial: *an independent investigation.* **2** not depending on another for livelihood. ■ capable of thinking or acting for oneself: *advice for independent travelers.* ■ (of income or resources) making it unnecessary to earn one's living: *a woman of independent means.* **3** not connected with another or with each other; separate: *two independent witnesses.* ■ not depending on something else for strength or effectiveness; freestanding: *independent columns.* ▶ n. an independent person or body. ■ an independent political candidate, voter, etc. — **in·de·pend·ence** n. **in·de·pend·ent·ly** adv.

in·de·pend·ent var·i·a·ble ▶ n. Math. a variable (often denoted by *x*) whose variation does not depend on that of another.

in-depth ▶ adj. comprehensive and thorough: *in-depth interviews.*

in·de·scrib·a·ble /ˌindi'skrībəbəl/ ▶ adj. too unusual, extreme, or indefinite to be adequately described. — **in·de·scrib·a·bil·i·ty** /-ˌskrībə'bilitē/ n. **in·de·scrib·a·bly** adv.

in·de·struct·i·ble /ˌindi'strəktəbəl/ ▶ adj. not able to be destroyed: *indestructible plastic containers.* — **in·de·struct·i·bil·i·ty** /-ˌstrəktə'bilitē/ n. **in·de·struct·i·bly** adv.

in·de·ter·mi·na·ble /ˌindi'tərmənəbəl/ ▶ adj. not able to be definitely ascertained, calculated, or identified: *a woman of indeterminable age.* — **in·de·ter·mi·na·bly** adv.

in·de·ter·mi·na·cy prin·ci·ple /ˌindi'tərmənəsē/ ▶ n. another term for UNCERTAINTY PRINCIPLE.

in·de·ter·mi·nate /ˌindi'tərmənit/ ▶ adj. not certain, known, or established: *the date of manufacture is indeterminate.* ■ left doubtful; vague. ■ (of a judicial sentence) such that the convicted person's conduct determines the date of release. ■ Math. (of a quantity) having no definite or definable value. ■ Med. (of a condition) from which a diagnosis of the underlying cause cannot be made: *indeterminate colitis.* ■ Bot. (of a plant shoot) not having all the axes terminating in a flower bud and so producing a shoot of indefinite length. — **in·de·ter·mi·na·cy** /-nəsē/ n. **in·de·ter·mi·nate·ly** adv. [17th C.: from late L. *indeterminatus*, from *in-* 'not' + L. *determinatus* 'limited, determined' (see DETERMINATE).]

in·de·ter·min·ism /ˌindi'tərməˌnizəm/ ▶ n. Philos. the doctrine that not all events are wholly determined by antecedent causes. — **in·de·ter·min·ist** n. **in·de·ter·min·is·tic** /-ˌtərmə'nistik/ adj.

in·dex /'indeks/ ▶ n. (pl. **-dex·es** or esp. in technical use **-di·ces** /-dəˌsēz/) **1** an alphabetical list of names, subjects, etc., with references to the places where they occur, typically found at the end of a book. ■ an alphabetical list by title, subject, author, or other category of a collection of books or documents, e.g., in a library. ■ Comput. a set of items each of which specifies one of the records of a file and contains information about its address. **2** an indicator, sign, or measure of something: *index of a teacher's effectiveness.* ■ a figure in a system or scale representing the average value of specified prices, shares, or other items as compared with some reference figure: *the hundred-shares index closed down 9.3.* ■ a pointer on an instrument, showing a quantity, a position on a scale, etc. ■ [with adj.] a number giving the magnitude of a physical property or another measured phenomenon in terms of a standard: *the oral hygiene index was calculated as the sum of the debris and calculus indices.* **3** Math. an exponent or other superscript or subscript number appended to a quantity. **4** Print. a symbol shaped like a pointing hand, typically used to draw attention to a note. ▶ v. [trans.] **1** record (names, subjects, etc.) in an index. ■ provide an index to. **2** link the value of (prices, wages, or other payments) automatically to the value of a price index. — **in·dex·a·ble** adj. **in·dex·er** n. **in·dex·i·ble** adj. [ME: from L. *index, indic-* 'forefinger, informer, sign,' from *in-* 'toward' + a second element rel. to *dicere* 'say' or *dicare* 'make known'; cf. INDICATE.]

in·dex case ▶ n. Med. the first identified case in a group of related cases of a particular disease.

in·dex fin·ger ▶ n. the finger next to the thumb; the forefinger.

In·dex Li·bro·rum Pro·hib·i·to·rum /'inˌdeks lī'brôrəm ˌprōhibə'tôrəm/ an official list of books that Roman Catholics were forbidden to read as contrary to Catholic faith or morals. The first Index was issued in 1557; it was revised at intervals until abolished in 1966. [L., 'index of forbidden books.']

In·di·a /'indēə/ a country in southern Asia. Hindi name BHARAT. *See box.* ■ a code word representing the letter I, used in radio communication.

In·di·a ink ▶ n. deep black ink containing dispersed carbon particles, used esp. in drawing and technical graphics. [17th C.: orig. applied to Chinese and Japanese pigments imported to Europe via India.]

In·di·a·man /'indēəmən/ ▶ n. (pl. **-men**) hist. a ship engaged in trade with India or the East or West Indies. [18th C.: from INDIA + *-man* from MAN-OF-WAR.]

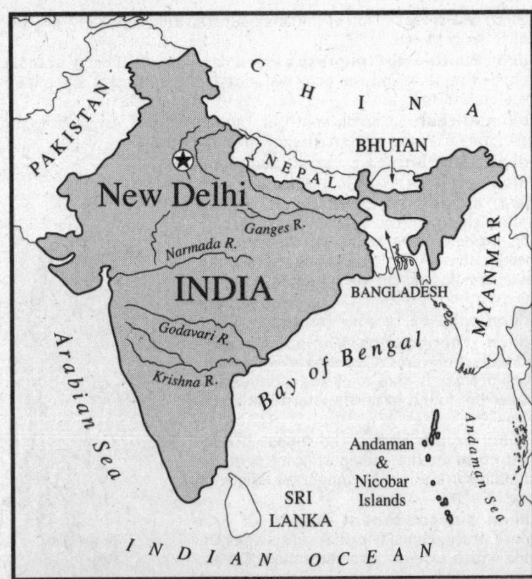

India

Official name: Republic of India
Location: southern Asia, bordered on the west by the Arabian Sea and on the east by the Bay of Bengal
Area: 1,148,300 square miles (2,973,200 sq km)
Population: 1,065,000,000
Capital: New Delhi
Languages: Hindi and English (both official), 14 other official languages according to region
Currency: Indian rupee

In·di·an /'indēən/ ▶ adj. **1** of or relating to the indigenous peoples of America. **2** of or relating to India or to the subcontinent comprising India, Pakistan, and Bangladesh. ▶ n. **1** an American Indian. **2** a native or national of India, or a person of Indian descent. — **In·di·an·i·za·tion** /ˌindēəni'zāsʜən/ n. **In·di·an·ize** v. **In·di·an·ness** n.

– USAGE **Indian**, meaning 'native of America before the arrival of Europeans,' is objected to by many who now favor **Native American**. There are others (including many members of these ethnic groups), however, who see nothing wrong with **Indian** or **American Indian**, which are long-established terms, although the preference where possible is to refer to specific peoples, as **Apache**, **Delaware**, and so on. The terms **Amerind** and **Amerindian**, once proposed as alternatives to **Indian**, are used in linguistics and anthropology, but have never gained widespread use. Newer alternatives, not widely used or established, include **First Nation** (esp. in Canada) and the more generic **aboriginal peoples**. It should be noted that **Indian** is held by many not to include some American groups, for example, Aleuts and Eskimos. A further consideration is that **Indian** also (and in some contexts primarily) refers to inhabitants of India or their descendants, who may be referred to as "Asian Indians" to prevent misunderstanding. See also usage at AMERICAN INDIAN and NATIVE AMERICAN.

In·di·an·a /ˌindē'anə/ a state in the eastern central US; pop. 6,080,485; capital, Indianapolis; statehood, Dec. 11, 1816 (19). It was colonized by the French in the early 1700s and ceded to Britain in 1763. It passed to the US in 1783 by the Treaty of Paris. — **In·di·an·an** n. & adj.

In·di·an·ap·o·lis /ˌindēə'napələs/ the capital of Indiana, in the central part of the state; pop. 781,870.

In·di·an burn ▶ n. informal an act of placing both hands on a person's arm and then twisting it with a wringing motion to produce a burning sensation.

In·di·an club ▶ n. each of a pair of bottle-shaped clubs swung to exercise the arms in gymnastics or to perform juggling tricks.

In·di·an corn ▶ n. any primitive corn with colorful variegated kernels, dried and used for decoration. ■ another term for CORN[1].

In·di·an el·e·phant ▶ n. the elephant of southern Asia (*Elephas maximus*), smaller than the African elephant, with smaller ears and only one lip to the trunk. Also called ASIAN ELEPHANT. See illustration at ELEPHANT.

In·di·an file ▶ n. another term for SINGLE FILE.

In·di·an meal ▶ n. meal ground from corn.

In·di·an Mu·ti·ny a revolt of Indians against British rule, 1857–58. Also called SEPOY MUTINY.

In·di·an Na·tion·al Con·gress a broad-based political party in India, founded in 1885 and the principal party in government since independence in 1947.

In·di·an O·cean an ocean south of India, north of Antarctica, and extending from the eastern coast of Africa to Australia.

In·di·an paint·brush ▸ **n.** see PAINTBRUSH (sense 2).

In·di·an pipe ▸ **n.** a plant (*Monotropa uniflora*) of the wintergreen family, with a yellowish stem that bears a single drooping flower, native to North America and northeastern Asia. It lacks chlorophyll and obtains nourishment via symbiotic fungi in its roots.

Indian pipe

In·di·an poke ▸ **n.** see POKE[3] (sense 2).

In·di·an rhi·noc·er·os ▸ **n.** a large one-horned rhinoceros (*Rhinoceros unicornis*) with prominent skin folds and a prehensile upper lip, found in northeastern India and Nepal.

In·di·an rope-trick ▸ **n.** the supposed feat, performed in the Indian subcontinent, of climbing an upright, unsupported length of rope.

In·di·an sub·con·ti·nent the part of Asia south of the Himalayas that forms a peninsula which extends into the Indian Ocean, now divided among India, Pakistan, and Bangladesh.

In·di·an sum·mer ▸ **n.** a period of unusually dry, warm weather occurring in late autumn. ▪ a period of happiness or success occurring late in life.

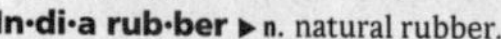

In·di·a rub·ber ▸ **n.** natural rubber.

In·dic /ˈindik/ ▸ **adj.** relating to or denoting the group of Indo-European languages comprising Sanskrit and the modern Indian languages that are its descendants. ▸ **n.** this language group. [via L. from Gk. *Indikos*, from *India* (see INDIA).]

indic. ▸ **abbr.** ▪ indicating. ▪ indicative. ▪ indicator.

in·di·can /ˈindi,kan/ ▸ **n.** Biochem. a potassium salt, $C_8H_6NOSO_2OH$, present in urine, in which it occurs as a product of the metabolism of indole. [19th C.: from L. *indicum* 'indigo.']

in·di·cate /ˈindi,kāt/ [trans.] ▸ **v. 1** point out; show: *dotted lines indicate the margins.* ▪ be a sign or symptom of; strongly imply: *sales indicate a growing market.* ▪ admit to or state briefly: *indicated his willingness.* ▪ (of a gauge or meter) register a reading of (a quantity, dimension, etc.). **2** (usu. **be indicated**) suggest as a desirable or necessary course of action: *the treatment is indicated in depressed patients.* [17th C.: from L. *indicat-* 'pointed out,' from the v. *indicare*, from *in-* 'toward' + *dicare* 'make known.']

in·di·ca·tion /,indiˈkāsʜən/ ▸ **n.** a sign or piece of information that indicates something: *the visit was an **indication of** improvement.* ▪ a reading given by a gauge or meter. ▪ a symptom that suggests certain medical treatment is necessary.

in·dic·a·tive /inˈdikətiv/ ▸ **adj. 1** serving as a sign or indication of something. **2** Gram. denoting a mood of verbs expressing simple statement of a fact. Compare with SUBJUNCTIVE. ▸ **n.** Gram. a verb in the indicative mood. ▪ (**the indicative**) the indicative mood. — **in·dic·a·tive·ly adv.**

in·di·ca·tor /ˈindi,kātər/ ▸ **n. 1** a thing, esp. a trend or fact, that indicates the state or level of something: *an indicator of affluence.* **2** a device providing specific information on the state or condition of something, in particular: ▪ [usu. with adj.] a gauge or meter of a specified kind: *a speed indicator.* **3** Chem. a compound that changes color at a specific pH value or in the presence of a particular substance.

in·di·ces /ˈindi,sēz/ plural form of INDEX.

in·di·ci·a /inˈdisʜ(ē)ə/ ▸ **plural n.** signs, indications, or distinguishing marks: *learned footnotes and other indicia of scholarship.* ▪ markings used on address labels or bulk mail as a substitute for stamps. [17th C.: pl. of L. *indicium*, from *index, indic-* 'informer, sign.']

in·dic·o·lite /inˈdikə,līt/ ▸ **n.** an indigo-blue gem variety of lithium-bearing tourmaline.

in·dict /inˈdīt/ ▸ **v.** [trans.] formally accuse or charge (someone) with a serious crime: ***indicted for** fraud.* — **in·dict·ee** /,indīˈtē/ **n.** **in·dict·er n.** [ME *endite, indite*, from Anglo-Norman Fr. *enditer*, based on L. *indicere* 'proclaim, appoint,' from *in-* 'toward' + *dicere* 'pronounce, utter.']

in·dict·a·ble /inˈdītəbəl/ ▸ **adj.** (of an offense) rendering the person who commits it liable to be charged with a serious crime that warrants a trial by jury. ▪ (of a person) liable to be charged with a crime.

in·dict·ment /inˈdītmənt/ ▸ **n. 1** Law a formal charge or accusation of a serious crime: *an **indictment for** conspiracy.* ▪ the action of indicting or being indicted. **2** a thing that serves to illustrate that a system or situation is bad and deserves to be condemned: *crime figures are an indictment of our society.*

in·die /ˈindē/ informal ▸ **adj.** (of a pop group or record label) not belonging to or affiliated with a major record company. ▪ (of a movie) not produced by a major studio: *she's landed herself the lead in an indie horror movie.* [1920s: abbrev. of INDEPENDENT.]

in·dif·fer·ence /inˈdif(ə)rəns/ ▸ **n.** lack of interest, concern, or sympathy: *his pretended **indifference to** criticism.*

in·dif·fer·ent /inˈdif(ə)rənt/ ▸ **adj. 1** having no particular interest or sympathy; unconcerned: ***indifferent to** foreign affairs | they all seemed indifferent rather than angry.* **2** neither good nor bad; mediocre: *attempts to distinguish between good, bad, and indifferent work.* ▪ not especially good; fairly bad: *he was at best an indifferent driver | a pair of indifferent watercolors.* **3** neutral in respect of some specified physical property. — **in·dif·fer·ent·ly adv.** [ME: via OFr. from L. *indifferent-* 'not making any difference,' from *in-* 'not' + *different-* 'differing' (see DIFFERENT).]

in·dif·fer·ent·ism /inˈdif(ə)rən,tizəm/ ▸ **n.** the belief that differences of religious belief are of no importance. — **in·dif·fer·ent·ist n.**

in·di·gene /ˈindi,jēn/ ▸ **n.** an indigenous person. [16th C.: from Fr. *indigène*, from L. *indigena*, from *indi-* (strengthened form of *in-* 'into') + an element rel. to *gignere* 'beget.']

in·dig·e·nous /inˈdijənəs/ ▸ **adj.** originating or occurring naturally in a particular place; native: *the indigenous peoples of Siberia.* — **in·dig·e·nous·ly adv.** **in·dig·e·nous·ness n.** [17th C.: from L. *indigena* 'a native' (see INDIGENE) + -OUS.]

in·di·gent /ˈindijənt/ ▸ **adj.** poor; needy. ▸ **n.** a needy person. — **in·di·gence n.** [ME: via OFr. from late L. *indigent-* 'lacking,' from the v. *indigere*, from *indi-* (strengthened form of *in-* 'into') + *egere* 'to need.']

in·di·gest·i·ble /,indiˈjestəbəl/ ▸ **adj.** (of food) difficult or impossible to digest. ▪ fig. too complex or awkward to read or understand easily: *an indigestible book.* — **in·di·gest·i·bil·i·ty** /-,jestəˈbilitē/ **n.** **in·di·gest·i·bly adv.**

in·di·ges·tion /,indiˈjescʜən; -dī-/ ▸ **n.** pain or discomfort in the stomach associated with difficulty in digesting food. — **in·di·ges·tive** /-tiv/ **adj.**

In·di·gir·ka /,indəˈgi(ə)rkə/ a river in eastern Siberia in Russia that flows north for 1,112 miles (1,779 km) to the Arctic Ocean.

in·dig·nant /inˈdignənt/ ▸ **adj.** feeling or showing anger or annoyance at what is perceived as unfair treatment. — **in·dig·nant·ly adv.** [16th C.: from L. *indignant-* 'regarding as unworthy,' from the v. *indignari*, from *in-* 'not' + *dignus* 'worthy.']

in·dig·na·tion /,indigˈnāsʜən/ ▸ **n.** anger or annoyance provoked by what is perceived as unfair treatment.

in·dig·ni·ty /inˈdignitē/ ▸ **n.** (pl. **-ties**) treatment or circumstances that cause one to feel shame or to lose one's dignity: *the indignity of needing financial help.*

in·di·go /ˈindi,gō/ ▸ **n.** (pl. **-gos** or **-goes**) **1** a tropical plant (genus *Indigofera*) of the pea family, which was formerly widely cultivated as a source of dark blue dye. **2** the dark blue dye obtained from this plant. ▪ a color between blue and violet in the spectrum. [16th C.: from Port. *índigo*, via L. from Gk. *indikon*, from *indikos* 'Indian (dye).']

in·di·go bunt·ing ▸ **n.** a deep blue bunting (*Passerina cyanea*) of the eastern US.

in·di·go snake ▸ **n.** a large, harmless American snake (*Drymarchon corais*, family Colubridae) that typically has bluish-black skin that may be patterned.

in·dig·o·tin /inˈdigətin; ,indəˈgōtn/ ▸ **n.** Chem. a dark blue crystalline compound, $(C_8H_5NO)_2$, that is the main constituent of the dye indigo. [19th C.: from INDIGO + *-t-* (for ease of pronunc.) + -IN[1].]

In·di·o /ˈindē,ō/ ▸ **n.** (pl. **-os**) a member of any of the indigenous peoples of America or eastern Asia in areas formerly subject to Spain or Portugal. [19th C.: from Sp. and Port., lit. 'Ind.']

in·di·rect /,indəˈrekt/ ▸ **adj. 1** not directly caused by or resulting from something: *an indirect effect.* ▪ not done directly; conducted through intermediaries: *under indirect control.* ▪ (of costs) deriving from overhead charges or subsidiary work. ▪ (of taxation) levied on goods and services rather than income or profits. **2** (of a route) not straight; not following the shortest way. ▪ (of lighting) from a concealed source and diffusely reflected. ▪ Soccer denoting a free kick from which a goal may not be scored directly. — **in·di·rect·ly adv.** **in·di·rect·ness n.**

in·di·rec·tion /,indəˈreksʜən/ ▸ **n.** indirectness or lack of straightforwardness in action or speech.

in·di·rect ob·ject ▸ **n.** Gram. a noun phrase referring to someone or something that is affected by the action of a transitive verb (typically as a recipient), but is not the primary object (e.g., *him* in *give him the book*). Compare with DIRECT OBJECT.

in·di·rect ques·tion ▸ **n.** Gram. a question in reported speech, e.g., *they asked who I was.*

in·di·rect speech ▸ **n.** another term for REPORTED SPEECH.

in·dis·cern·i·ble /,indiˈsərnəbəl/ ▸ **adj.** not discernible; impossible to see or clearly distinguish. — **in·dis·cern·i·bil·i·ty n.** **in·dis·cern·i·bly adv.**

in·dis·ci·pline /inˈdisəplin/ ▸ **n.** lack of discipline.

in·dis·creet /,indiˈskrēt/ ▸ **adj.** having, showing, or proceeding from too great a readiness to reveal things that should remain secret or private: *they have been embarrassed by indiscreet friends.* — **in·dis·creet·ly adv.**

in·dis·cre·tion /,indiˈskresʜən/ ▸ **n.** behavior or speech that is indiscreet or displays a lack of good judgment: *sexual indiscretions.*

in·dis·crim·i·nate /,indiˈskrimənit/ ▸ **adj.** done at random or without careful judgment: *indiscriminate killing.* ▪ (of a person) not using or exercising discrimination. — **in·dis·crim·i·nate·ly adv.** **in·dis·crim·i·nate·ness n.** **in·dis·crim·i·na·tion** /-,skriməˈnāsʜən/ **n.**

in·dis·pen·sa·ble /,indiˈspensəbəl/ ▸ **adj.** absolutely necessary or essential. — **in·dis·pen·sa·bil·i·ty** /-,spensəˈbilitē/ **n.** **in·dis·pen·sa·ble·ness n.** **in·dis·pen·sa·bly adv.**

in·dis·posed /ˌindiˈspōzd/ ▶ **adj.** **1** slightly unwell. **2** averse; unwilling: *indisposed to attend.* — **in·dis·po·si·tion** /ˌindispəˈzisʜən/ **n.** [ME: from **in-**[1] 'not' + **disposed**, or past part. of *indispose* 'make unwell or unwilling.']

in·dis·put·a·ble /ˌindiˈspyo͞otəbəl/ ▶ **adj.** not disputable; unable to be challenged or denied: *an indisputable fact.* — **in·dis·put·a·bil·i·ty** /-ˌspyo͞otəˈbilitē/ **n.** **in·dis·put·a·bly adv.**

in·dis·sol·u·ble /ˌindiˈsälyəbəl/ ▶ **adj.** unable to be destroyed; lasting: *an indissoluble friendship.* — **in·dis·sol·u·bil·i·ty** /-ˌsälyəˈbilitē/ **n.** **in·dis·sol·u·bly adv.**

in·dis·tinct /ˌindiˈstiɴɢkt/ ▶ **adj.** not distinct; not clear or sharply defined. — **in·dis·tinct·ly adv.** **in·dis·tinct·ness n.**

in·dis·tinc·tive /ˌindiˈstiɴɢktiv/ ▶ **adj.** not having a distinctive character or features. — **in·dis·tinc·tive·ly adv.** **in·dis·tinc·tive·ness n.**

in·dis·tin·guish·a·ble /ˌindiˈstiɴɢgwisʜəbəl/ ▶ **adj.** not distinguishable; not able to be identified as different or distinct. — **in·dis·tin·guish·a·bly adv.**

in·di·um /ˈindēəm/ ▶ **n.** the chemical element of atomic number 49, a soft, silvery-white metal occurring naturally in association with zinc and some other metals. (Symbol: **In**) [19th C.: from **indigo**.]

in·di·vid·u·al /ˌindəˈvijo͞oəl/ ▶ **adj.** **1** [attrib.] single; separate: *individual tiny flowers.* **2** of or for a particular person: *individual needs.* ■ designed for use by one person: *individual servings.* ■ characteristic of a particular person or thing: *individual traits.* ■ having a striking or unusual character; original. ▶ **n.** a single human being as distinct from a group, class, or family. ■ a single member of a class. ■ [with adj.] informal a person of a specified kind: *a selfish individual.* ■ a distinctive or original person. [ME: from med. L. *individualis*, from L. *individuus*, from *in-* 'not' + *dividuus* 'divisible,' from *dividere* 'to divide.']

in·di·vid·u·al·ism /ˌindəˈvijo͞oəˌlizəm/ ▶ **n.** the habit or principle of being independent and self-reliant. — **in·di·vid·u·al·ist n. & adj.** **in·di·vid·u·al·is·tic** /-ˌvijo͞oəˈlistik/ **adj.** **in·di·vid·u·al·is·ti·cal·ly** /-ˌvijo͞oəˈlistək(ə)lē/ **adv.**

in·di·vid·u·al·i·ty /ˌindəˌvijo͞oˈalitē/ ▶ **n.** the quality or character of a person or thing that distinguishes them from others of the same kind.

in·di·vid·u·al·ize /ˌindəˈvijo͞oəˌlīz/ ▶ **v.** [trans.] give an individual character to: *have your shirt individualized.* ■ [usu. as adj.] (**individualized**) tailor (something) to suit the individual: *individualized program.* — **in·di·vid·u·al·i·za·tion** /-ˌvijo͞oələˈzāsʜən/ **n.**

in·di·vid·u·al·ly /ˌindəˈvijo͞oəlē/ ▶ **adv.** **1** one by one; singly; separately: *individually wrapped.* ■ in a distinctive manner: *individually crafted.* **2** personally; in an individual capacity: *individually owned.*

in·di·vid·u·ate /ˌindəˈvijo͞oˌāt/ ▶ **v.** [trans.] distinguish from others of the same kind; single out.

in·di·vis·i·ble /ˌindəˈvizəbəl/ ▶ **adj.** not divisible; unable to be divided or separated. ■ (of a number) unable to be divided by another number exactly without leaving a remainder. — **in·di·vis·i·bil·i·ty** /-ˌvizəˈbilitē/ **n.** **in·di·vis·i·bly adv.**

Indo- /ˈindō/ ▶ **comb. form** (used commonly in linguistic and ethnological terms) Indian; Indian and ...: *Indo-Iranian.* ■ relating to India.

In·do-Ar·y·an ▶ **adj.** **1** relating to or denoting an Indo-European people who invaded northwestern India in the 2nd millennium BC. See **Aryan**. **2** another term for **Indic**.

In·do-Chi·na a peninsula in Southeast Asia that consists of Myanmar (Burma), Thailand, Malaya, Laos, Cambodia, and Vietnam. — **In·do-Chi·nese adj. & n.**

in·doc·tri·nate /inˈdäktrəˌnāt/ ▶ **v.** [trans.] teach (a person or group) to accept a set of beliefs uncritically: *broadcasting was a vehicle for indoctrinating the masses.* — **in·doc·tri·na·tion** /-ˌdäktrəˈnāsʜən/ **n.** **in·doc·tri·na·tor** /-ˌnātər/ **n.** [17th C.: from obs. *indoctrine* (v.), from Fr. *endoctriner*, based on *doctrine* 'doctrine.']

In·do-Eu·ro·pe·an ▶ **adj.** of or relating to the family of languages spoken over the greater part of Europe and Asia as far as northern India. ■ another term for **Proto-Indo-European**. ▶ **n.** **1** the ancestral Proto-Indo-European language. ■ the Indo-European family of languages. **2** a speaker of an Indo-European language, esp. Proto-Indo-European.

In·do-Ger·man·ic ▶ **adj. & n.** former term for **Indo-European**.

In·do-I·ra·ni·an ▶ **adj.** relating to or denoting a subfamily of Indo-European languages spoken in northern India and Iran. ▶ **n.** the Indo-Iranian subfamily of languages, divided into the Indic group and the Iranian group. Also called **Aryan**.

in·dole /ˈinˌdōl/ ▶ **n.** Chem. a crystalline organic compound, C_8H_7N, with an unpleasant odor, present in coal tar and in feces. [19th C.: blend of **indigo** and L. *oleum* 'oil.']

in·dole·a·ce·tic ac·id /ˌindōləˈsētik; -ˈsetik/ ▶ **n.** Biochem. a compound, $C_8H_6(CH_3COOH)N$, that is an acetic acid derivative of indole, esp. one found as a natural growth hormone (auxin) in plants.

in·do·lent /ˈindələnt/ ▶ **adj.** **1** wanting to avoid activity or exertion; lazy. **2** Med. (of a disease condition) causing little or no pain. — **in·do·lence n.** **in·do·lent·ly adv.** [17th C.: from late L. *indolent-*, from *in-* 'not' + *dolere* 'suffer or give pain.']

In·do-Ma·lay·sian (also **In·do-Ma·lay·an**) ▶ **adj.** of or relating to both India and Malaya, in particular: ■ denoting an ethnological region comprising Sri Lanka, the Malay Peninsula, and the Malaysian islands. ■ (also **In·do-Ma·le·sian**) Biol. denoting a major biogeographical region comprising the Indian subcontinent, Malesia, and East and Southeast Asia.

in·do·meth·a·cin /ˌindōˈmeтʜəsin/ ▶ **n.** Med. a compound, $C_{19}H_{16}NO_4Cl$, with anti-inflammatory, antipyretic, and analgesic properties, used chiefly to treat rheumatoid arthritis and gout. [1960s: from *indo(le)* + *meth(yl)* + *ac(etic)*. **-in**[1].]

in·dom·i·ta·ble /inˈdämitəbəl/ ▶ **adj.** impossible to subdue or defeat: *indomitable spirit.* — **in·dom·i·ta·bil·i·ty** /-ˌdämitəˈbilitē/ **n.** **in·dom·i·ta·bly adv.** [17th C.: from late L. *indomitabilis*, from *in-* 'not' + L. *domitare* 'to tame.']

Indonesia

Official name: Republic of Indonesia

Location: Southeast Asia, an archipelago between the Indian and Pacific oceans; the largest islands are Bali, Bangka, southern Borneo, Ceram, Flores, western New Guinea (Irian Jaya), Java, Lombok, Madura, Sulawesi, Sumatra, and Timor

Area: 705,400 square miles (1,826,400 sq km)

Population: 238,452,000

Capital: Jakarta

Languages: Bahasa Indonesia (official), Malay, English, Chinese, Javanese, and others

Currency: Indonesian rupiah

In·do·ne·sia /ˌindəˈnēzʜə/ a country in Southeast Asia. Former name (until 1949) **Dutch East Indies**. *See box.*

In·do·ne·sian /ˌindəˈnēzʜən/ ▶ **adj.** of or relating to Indonesia, Indonesians, or their languages. ▶ **n.** **1** a native or national of Indonesia, or a person of Indonesian descent. **2** the group of Austronesian languages, closely related to Malay, that are spoken in Indonesia and neighboring islands. ■ another term for **Bahasa Indonesia**.

in·door /ˈinˌdôr/ ▶ **adj.** [attrib.] situated, conducted, or used within a building or under cover: *indoor sports.*

in·doors /inˈdôrz/ ▶ **adv.** into or within a building: *they went indoors and explored the building.*

In·do-Pa·cif·ic ▶ **adj.** of or relating to the Indian Ocean and the adjacent parts of the Pacific. ■ another term for **Austronesian**. ▶ **n.** the Indo-Pacific seas or ocean.

In·dore /ˈindôr/ a city in central India, in Madhya Pradesh; pop. 1,087,000.

in·dorse ▶ **v.** var. of **endorse**.

in·dorse·ment ▶ **n.** var. of **endorsement**.

in·dox·yl /inˈdäksəl/ ▶ **n.** [as adj.] Chem. of or denoting the radical $-ONC_8H_6$, derived from a hydroxy derivative of indole and present in indigotin.

In·dra /ˈindrə/ Hinduism the warrior king of the heavens, god of war and storm.

in·dri /ˈindrē/ ▶ **n.** (pl. **in·dris** /ˈindrēz/) a large, short-tailed Madagascan lemur (*Indri indri*, family Indriidae) that jumps from tree to tree in an upright position and rarely comes to the ground. [19th C.: from Malagasy *indry!* 'behold!' or *indry izy!* 'there he is!']

in·du·bi·ta·ble /inˈd(y)o͞obitəbəl/ ▶ **adj.** impossible to doubt; unquestionable: *an indubitable truth.* — **in·du·bi·ta·bly adv.**

in·duce /inˈd(y)o͞os/ ▶ **v.** [trans.] **1** succeed in persuading or influencing (someone) to do something. **2** bring about or give rise to: *measures that induced a change.* ■ produce (an electric charge or current or a magnetic state) by induction. **3** Med. bring on (childbirth or abortion) artificially, typically by the use of drugs. ■ bring on childbirth in (a pregnant woman) in this way. ■ bring on the birth of (a baby) in this way. **4** Logic derive by inductive reasoning. — **in·duc·er n.** **in·duc·i·ble adj.** [ME: from L. *inducere* 'lead in,' from *in-* 'into' + *ducere* 'to lead,' or from Fr. *enduire*.]

in·duce·ment /inˈd(y)o͞osmənt/ ▶ **n.** a thing that persuades or influences someone to do something: [with infin.] *no inducement to wait.*

in·duct /inˈdəkt/ ▶ **v.** [trans.] admit (someone) formally to a position or organization. ■ formally introduce (a member of the clergy) into possession of a benefice. ■ enlist (someone) for military service. ■ (**induct someone in/into**) introduce someone to (a difficult or obscure subject): *inducted me into the skills of magic.* — **in·duc·tee** /ˌindəkˈtē/ **n.** [ME: from L. *induct-* 'led into,' from the v. *inducere* (see **induce**).]

in·duc·tance /inˈdəktəns/ ▶ **n.** Physics the property of an electric conductor or circuit that causes an electromotive force to be generated by a change in the current flowing: *an inductance of 40 mH.*

in·duc·tion /in'dəksHən/ ▶ **n.** **1** the action or process of inducting someone to a position or organization: ***induction into the Hall of Fame.*** ■ [usu. as adj.] a formal introduction to a new job or position. ■ enlistment into military service. **2** the process or action of bringing about or giving rise to something. ■ Med. the process of bringing on childbirth or abortion by artificial means, typically by the use of drugs. **3** Logic the inference of a general law from particular instances. Often contrasted with DEDUCTION. ■ (**induction of**) the production of (facts) to prove a general statement. ■ (also **mathematical induction**) Math. a means of proving a theorem by showing that if it is true of any particular case, it is true of the next case in a series, and then showing that it is indeed true in one particular case. **4** Physics the production of an electric or magnetic state by the proximity (without contact) of an electrified or magnetized body. See also MAGNETIC INDUCTION. ■ the production of an electric current in a conductor by varying the magnetic field applied to the conductor. **5** the stage of the working cycle of an internal combustion engine in which the fuel mixture is drawn into the cylinders.

in·duc·tive /in'dəktiv/ ▶ **adj.** **1** characterized by the inference of general laws from particular instances; logical: *inductive reasoning.* **2** of, relating to, or caused by electric or magnetic induction. — **in·duc·tive·ly** adv.

in·duc·tiv·ism /in'dəktə,vizəm/ ▶ **n.** the use of or preference for inductive methods of reasoning, esp. in science. — **in·duc·tiv·ist** n. & adj.

in·duc·tor /in'dəktər/ ▶ **n.** a component in an electric or electronic circuit that possesses inductance.

in·due ▶ **v.** var. of ENDUE.

in·dulge /in'dəlj/ ▶ **v.** [intrans.] (**indulge in**) allow oneself to enjoy the pleasure of: *we indulged in sundaes.* ■ become involved in (an activity, typically one that is undesirable or disapproved of): *indulge in gossip.* ■ [trans.] satisfy or yield freely to (a desire or interest): *indulge a passion for literature.* — **in·dulg·er** n. [17th C.): from L. *indulgere* 'give free rein to.']

in·dul·gence /in'dəljəns/ ▶ **n.** **1** the action or fact of indulging: *indulgence in self-pity.* ■ the state or attitude of being indulgent or tolerant. ■ a thing that is indulged in; a luxury. **2** esp. hist. (in the Roman Catholic Church) a grant by the pope of remission of the temporal punishment in purgatory still due for sins after absolution.

in·dul·gent /in'dəljənt/ ▶ **adj.** having or indicating a readiness or over-readiness to be generous to or lenient with someone: *indulgent parents.* ■ self-indulgent: *a slightly adolescent, indulgent account of a love affair.* — **in·dul·gent·ly** adv.

in·du·rate /'ind(y)ə,rāt/ ▶ **v.** [trans.] [usu. as adj.] (**indurated**) harden: *a bed of indurated clay.* — **in·du·ra·tion** /,ind(y)ə'rāsHən/ n. **in·du·ra·tive** /-,rātiv/ adj. [16th C.: from L. *indurat-* 'made hard,' from the v. *indurare* (based on *durus* 'hard').]

In·dus /'indəs/ a river in southern Asia, about 1,800 miles (2,900 km) long, that flows from Tibet through Kashmir and Pakistan to the Arabian Sea.

indus. ▶ **abbr.** ■ industrial or industry.

in·dus·tri·al /in'dəstrēəl/ ▶ **adj.** of, relating to, or characterized by industry: *an industrial town.* ■ having highly developed industries: *industrial nations.* ■ designed or suitable for use in industry. ▶ **n.** (**industrials**) shares in industrial companies. — **in·dus·tri·al·ly** adv.

in·dus·tri·al es·pi·o·nage ▶ **n.** spying directed toward discovering the secrets of a rival manufacturer or other industrial company.

in·dus·tri·al·ism /in'dəstrēə,lizəm/ ▶ **n.** a social or economic system built on manufacturing industries.

in·dus·tri·al·ist /in'dəstrēəlist/ ▶ **n.** a person involved in the ownership and management of industry.

in·dus·tri·al·ize /in'dəstrēə,līz/ ▶ **v.** [trans.] [often as adj.] (**industrialized**) develop industries in (a country or region) on a wide scale: *the industrialized nations.* ■ [intrans.] (of a country or region) build up a system of industries. — **in·dus·tri·al·i·za·tion** /in,dəstrēəli'zāsHən/ n.

in·dus·tri·al park ▶ **n.** an area of land developed as a site for factories and other industrial businesses.

In·dus·tri·al Rev·o·lu·tion the rapid development of industry in Britain in the late 18th and 19th centuries, brought about by the introduction of machinery.

in·dus·tri·al-strength ▶ **adj.** very strong or powerful: *an industrial-strength cleaner.*

in·dus·tri·al un·ion ▶ **n.** a union whose members all work in various capacities in a single industry.

In·dus·tri·al Work·ers of the World (abbr.: **IWW**) a radical US labor movement, founded in 1905 and dedicated to the overthrow of capitalism. Its popularity declined after World War I, and by 1925 its membership was insignificant. Also called the WOBBLIES.

in·dus·tri·ous /in'dəstrēəs/ ▶ **adj.** diligent and hard-working. — **in·dus·tri·ous·ly** adv.

in·dus·try /'indəstrē/ ▶ **n.** (pl. **-tries**) **1** economic activity concerned with the processing of raw materials and manufacture of goods in factories. ■ [with adj.] a particular form or branch of economic or commercial activity: *the tourist industry.* **2** hard work: *the kitchen became **a hive of industry.*** [ME (sense 2): from Fr. *industrie* or L. *industria* 'diligence.']

in·dwell /in'dwel/ ▶ **v.** (past and past part. **-dwelt**) **1** [trans.] be permanently present in (someone's soul or mind); possess spiritually. **2** [as adj.] (**indwelling**) Med. (of a catheter, needle, etc.) fixed in a person's body for a long period of time. — **in·dwell·er** n.

In·dy /'indē/ ▶ **n.** a form of auto racing in which specially constructed cars are driven around a banked, typically oval circuit. [1950s: after INDIANAPOLIS.]

-ine[1] ▶ **suffix** **1** (forming adjectives) belonging to; resembling in nature: *Alpine* | *canine.* **2** forming adjectives from taxonomic names (such as *bovine* from the genus *Bos*). [from Fr. *-in, -ine,* or from L. *-inus.*]

-ine[2] ▶ **suffix** forming adjectives from the names of minerals, plants, etc.: *crystalline* | *hyacinthine.* [from L. *-inus,* from Gk. *-inos.*]

-ine[3] ▶ **suffix** forming feminine common nouns and proper names such as *heroine, Josephine.* [from Fr., via L. *-ina* from Gk. *-inē,* or from Ger. *-in.*]

-ine[4] ▶ **suffix** **1** forming chiefly abstract nouns and diminutives such as *doctrine, medicine, figurine.* **2** Chem. forming names of alkaloids, halogens, amines, amino acids, and other substances: *cocaine* | *chlorine* | *thymine.* [from Fr., from the L. fem. form *-ina.*]

in·e·bri·ate formal humorous ▶ **v.** /i'nēbrē,āt/ [trans.] [often as adj.] (**inebriated**) make drunk; intoxicate. ▶ **n.** /-brē-it/ a drunkard: *he was marked down as an inebriate.* ▶ **adj.** drunk; intoxicated: *he had been known to get hopelessly inebriate* | *inebriate times by the Bay.* — **in·e·bri·a·tion** /i,nēbrē'āsHən/ n. [ME (as an adj.): from L. *inebriatus,* past part. of *inebriare* 'intoxicate' (based on *ebrius* 'drunk').]

in·ed·i·ble /in'edəbəl/ ▶ **adj.** not fit or suitable for eating. — **in·ed·i·bil·i·ty** /-,edə'bilitē/ n.

in·ed·u·ca·ble /in'ejəkəbəl/ ▶ **adj.** considered incapable of being educated, esp. (formerly) as a result of a mental handicap. — **in·ed·u·ca·bil·i·ty** /-,ejəkə'bilitē/ n.

in·ef·fa·ble /in'efəbəl/ ▶ **adj.** too great or extreme to be expressed or described in words: *ineffable beauty.* ■ too sacred to be uttered. — **in·ef·fa·bil·i·ty** /-efə'bilitē/ n. **in·ef·fa·bly** /-blē/ adv. [ME: from OFr., or from L. *ineffabilis,* from *in-* 'not' + *effabilis* (see EFFABLE).]

in·ef·face·a·ble /,ini'fāsəbəl/ ▶ **adj.** unable to be erased or forgotten. — **in·ef·face·a·bil·i·ty** /-,fāsə'bilitē/ n. **in·ef·face·a·bly** adv.

in·ef·fec·tive /,ini'fektiv/ ▶ **adj.** not effective; not producing the desired effect: *an ineffective president.* — **in·ef·fec·tive·ly** adv. **in·ef·fec·tive·ness** n.

in·ef·fec·tu·al /,ini'fekCHōōəl/ ▶ **adj.** not producing any or the desired effect: *an ineffectual campaign.* ■ (of a person) lacking the ability or qualities to cope with a role or situation: *an ineffectual parent.* — **in·ef·fec·tu·al·i·ty** /-,fekCHōō'alitē/ n. **in·ef·fec·tu·al·ly** adv. **in·ef·fec·tu·al·ness** n.

in·ef·fi·cient /,ini'fisHənt/ ▶ **adj.** not achieving maximum productivity; wasting or failing to make the best use of time or resources. — **in·ef·fi·cien·cy** n. **in·ef·fi·cient·ly** adv.

in·e·gal·i·tar·i·an /,ini,gali'te(ə)rēən/ ▶ **adj.** characterized by or promoting inequality between people.

in·e·las·tic /,ini'lastik/ ▶ **adj.** **1** (of a substance or material) not elastic. ■ Econ. (of demand or supply) insensitive to changes in price or income. **2** Physics (of a collision) involving an overall loss of translational kinetic energy. — **in·e·las·ti·cal·ly** adv. **in·e·las·tic·i·ty** /-la'stisitē/ n.

in·el·e·gant /in'eligənt/ ▶ **adj.** having or showing a lack of physical grace, elegance, or refinement. ■ unappealing through being unnecessarily complicated: *an inelegant piece of legislation.* — **in·el·e·gance** n. **in·el·e·gant·ly** adv.

in·el·i·gi·ble /in'elijəbəl/ ▶ **adj.** not eligible; legally or officially unable to be considered for a position or benefit. — **in·el·i·gi·bil·i·ty** /-,elijə'bilitē/ n. **in·el·i·gi·bly** adv.

in·e·luc·ta·ble /,ini'ləktəbəl/ ▶ **adj.** unable to be resisted or avoided; inescapable: *the ineluctable facts.* — **in·e·luc·ta·bil·i·ty** /-,ləktə'bilitē/ n. **in·e·luc·ta·bly** adv. [17th C.: from L. *ineluctabilis,* from *in-* 'not' + *eluctari* 'struggle out.']

in·ept /i'nept/ ▶ **adj.** having or showing no skill; clumsy. — **in·ept·i·tude** /-ti,t(y)ōōd/ n. **in·ept·ly** adv. **in·ept·ness** n. [16th C. (in the sense 'not apt, unsuitable'): from L. *ineptus,* from *in-* 'not' + *aptus* (see APT).]

in·e·qual·i·ty /,ini'kwälitē/ ▶ **n.** (pl. **-ties**) difference in size, degree, circumstances, etc.; lack of equality. ■ Math. the relation between two expressions that are not equal, employing a sign such as ≠ "not equal to," > "greater than," or < "less than." ■ Math. a symbolic expression of the fact that two quantities are not equal.

in·eq·ui·ta·ble /in'ekwitəbəl/ ▶ **adj.** unfair; unjust. — **in·eq·ui·ta·bly** adv.

in·eq·ui·ty /in'ekwitē/ ▶ **n.** (pl. **-ties**) lack of fairness or justice.

in·e·rad·i·ca·ble /,inə'radikəbəl/ ▶ **adj.** unable to be destroyed or removed: *ineradicable hostility.* — **in·e·rad·i·ca·bly** /-blē/ adv.

in·er·rant /in'erənt/ ▶ **adj.** incapable of being wrong. — **in·er·ran·cy** n. **in·er·ran·tist** n.

in·ert /i'nərt/ ▶ **adj.** lacking the ability or strength to move: *she lay inert in her bed.* ■ lacking vigor: *an inert political system.* ■ chemically inactive. — **in·ert·ly** adv. **in·ert·ness** n. [17th C.: from L. *iners, inert-* 'unskilled,' from *in-* + *ars, art-* 'skill, art.']

in·ert gas ▶ **n.** another term for NOBLE GAS.

in·er·tia /i'nərsHə/ ▶ **n.** **1** a tendency to do nothing or to remain unchanged: *bureaucratic inertia.* **2** Physics a property of matter by which it continues in its existing state of rest or uniform motion in a straight line, unless that state is changed by an external force. See also MOMENT OF INERTIA. ■ [with adj.] resistance to change in some other physical property: *the thermal inertia of the ocean.* [18th C. (sense 2): from L., from *iners, inert-* (see INERT).]

in·er·tial /iˈnərsʜəl/ ▶ **adj.** esp. Physics of, relating to, or arising from inertia. ■ (of navigation or guidance) depending on internal instruments that measure a craft's acceleration and compare the calculated position with stored data. ■ (of a frame of reference) in which bodies continue at rest or in uniform straight motion unless acted on by a force.

in·es·cap·a·ble /ˌiniˈskāpəbəl/ ▶ **adj.** unable to be avoided or denied. — **in·es·cap·a·bil·i·ty** /-iˌskāpəˈbilitē/ **n.** **in·es·cap·a·bly** **adv.**

-iness ▶ **suffix** forming nouns corresponding to adjectives ending in *-y* (such as *clumsiness* corresponding to *clumsy*). [see **-Y**[1], **-NESS**.]

in es·se /in ˈesē; ˈesā/ ▶ **adv.** in actual existence. [16th C.: L., lit. 'in being'(the infinitive used as a n. in an oblique case).]

in·es·sen·tial /ˌiniˈsencʜəl/ ▶ **adj.** not absolutely necessary.

in·es·ti·ma·ble /inˈestəməbəl/ ▶ **adj.** too great to calculate. — **in·es·ti·ma·bly** **adv.** [ME: via OFr. from L. *inaestimabilis*, from *in-* 'not' + *aestimabilis* (see **ESTIMABLE**).]

in·ev·i·ta·ble /inˈevitəbəl/ ▶ **adj.** certain to happen; unavoidable: *war was inevitable.* ■ informal so frequently experienced or seen that it is completely predictable: *the inevitable letter from the bank.* ▶ **n.** (**the inevitable**) a situation that is unavoidable. — **in·ev·i·ta·bil·i·ty** /-ˌevitəˈbilitē/ **n.** **in·ev·i·ta·bly** **adv.** [ME: from L. *inevitabilis*, from *in-* + *evitabilis* 'avoidable' (from *evitare* 'avoid').]

in·ex·act /ˌinigˈzakt/ ▶ **adj.** not exact; not quite accurate or correct. — **in·ex·act·ly** **adv.**

in·ex·cus·a·ble /ˌinikˈskyo͞ozəbəl/ ▶ **adj.** too bad to be justified or tolerated: *Matt's behavior was inexcusable.* — **in·ex·cus·a·bly** **adv.** [ME: from L. *inexcusabilis*, from *in-* 'not' + *excusabilis* 'able to be excused' (see **EXCUSE**).]

in·ex·haust·i·ble /ˌinigˈzôstəbəl/ ▶ **adj.** (of an amount or supply of something) unable to be used up because existing in abundance: *his inexhaustible energy.* — **in·ex·haust·i·bil·i·ty** /-ˌzôstəˈbilitē/ **n.** **in·ex·haust·i·bly** **adv.**

in·ex·o·ra·ble /inˈeksərəbəl/ ▶ **adj.** impossible to stop or prevent: *the inexorable march of technology.* — **in·ex·o·ra·bly** **adv.** [16th C.: from Fr., or from L. *inexorabilis*, from *in-* + *exorabilis* (from *exorare* 'entreat').]

in·ex·pe·di·ent /ˌinikˈspēdēənt/ ▶ **adj.** not practical, suitable, or advisable. — **in·ex·pe·di·en·cy** **n.** **in·ex·pe·di·ence** **n.**

in·ex·pen·sive /ˌinikˈspensiv/ ▶ **adj.** not expensive; not costing a great deal; cheap. — **in·ex·pen·sive·ly** **adv.**

in·ex·pe·ri·ence /ˌinikˈspi(ə)rēəns/ ▶ **n.** lack of experience, knowledge, or skill. — **in·ex·pe·ri·enced** **adj.**

in·ex·pert /inˈekspərt/ ▶ **adj.** having or showing a lack of experience, skill, or knowledge. — **in·ex·pert·ly** **adv.**

in·ex·pli·ca·ble /ˌinekˈsplikəbəl; inˈeksplikəbəl/ ▶ **adj.** unable to be explained or accounted for. — **in·ex·pli·ca·bil·i·ty** /ˈinekˌsplikəˈbilitē/ **n.** **in·ex·pli·ca·bly** **adv.**

in·ex·plic·it /ˌinikˈsplisit/ ▶ **adj.** not explicit; not definitely or clearly expressed or explained. — **in·ex·plic·it·ly** **n.** **in·ex·plic·it·ness** **n.**

in·ex·press·i·ble /ˌinikˈspresəbəl/ ▶ **adj.** (of a feeling) too strong to be described or conveyed in words. — **in·ex·press·i·bly** **adv.**

in·ex·pres·sive /ˌinikˈspresiv/ ▶ **adj.** showing no expression. — **in·ex·pres·sive·ly** /ˌinikˈspresivlē/ **adv.** **in·ex·pres·sive·ness** **n.**

in·ex·ten·si·ble /ˌinikˈstensəbəl/ ▶ **adj.** not extensible; unable to be stretched or drawn out in length.

in ex·ten·so /ˌin ikˈstensō/ ▶ **adv.** in full; at length: *the paper covered their speeches in extenso.* [L., from *in* 'in' + *extensus*, past part. of *extendere* 'stretch out.']

in·ex·tin·guish·a·ble /ˌinikˈstiɴɢɢwisʜəbəl/ ▶ **adj.** unable to be extinguished or quenched: *a small inextinguishable candle* | fig. *inextinguishable good humor.*

in ex·tre·mis /ˌin ekˈstrāmēs; ikˈstrēmis/ ▶ **adv.** in an extremely difficult situation: *in extremis 20 miles out to sea.* ■ at the point of death. [L., from *in* 'in' + *extremis*, ablative pl. of *extremus* 'outermost.']

in·ex·tri·ca·ble /ˌinikˈstrikəbəl; inˈekstri-/ ▶ **adj.** impossible to disentangle or separate. ■ impossible to escape from: *an inextricable situation.* — **in·ex·tri·ca·bil·i·ty** /ˌinikˌstrikəˈbilitē/ **n.** **in·ex·tri·ca·bly** **adv.** [16th C.: from L. *inextricabilis*, from *in-* + *extricare* 'unravel' (see **EXTRICATE**).]

inf. ▶ **abbr.** ■ infantry. ■ inferior. ■ infield or infielder. ■ infinitive. ■ infinity. ■ infirmary. ■ information. ■ after; below. [from L. *infra*]

in·fal·li·bil·i·ty /inˌfaləˈbilitē/ ▶ **n.** the quality of being infallible; the inability to be wrong. ■ (also **papal infallibility**) (in the Roman Catholic Church) the doctrine that the pope is incapable of error in pronouncing dogma.

in·fal·li·ble /inˈfaləbəl/ ▶ **adj.** incapable of making mistakes or being wrong. ■ never failing; always effective: *infallible cures.* ■ (in the Roman Catholic Church) credited with papal infallibility. — **in·fal·li·bly** **adv.** [15th C.: from Fr. *infaillible* or late L. *infallibilis*, from *in-* 'not' + L. *fallere* 'deceive.']

in·fa·mous /ˈinfəməs/ ▶ **adj.** well known for some bad quality or deed. ■ wicked; abominable: *infamous misconduct.* ■ Law, hist. (of a person) deprived of all or some citizens' rights as a consequence of conviction for a serious crime. — **in·fa·mous·ly** **adv.** **in·fa·my** /-mē/ **n.** (pl. **-mies**). [ME: from med. L. *infamosus*, from L. *infamis* (based on *fama* 'fame').]

in·fan·cy /ˈinfənsē/ ▶ **n.** the state or period of early childhood or babyhood. ■ the early stage in the development or growth of something. ■ Law the condition of being a minor.

in·fant /ˈinfənt/ ▶ **n.** a very young child or baby. ■ [as adj.] denoting something in an early stage of its development: *an infant science.* ■ Law a person who has not attained legal majority. [ME: from OFr. *enfant*, from L. *infant-* 'unable to speak,' from *in-* 'not' + *fant-* 'speaking' (from the v. *fari*).]

in·fan·ta /inˈfantə/ ▶ **n.** hist. a daughter of the ruling monarch of Spain or Portugal, esp. the eldest daughter who was not heir to the throne.

in·fan·te /inˈfantā/ ▶ **n.** hist. the second son of the ruling monarch of Spain or Portugal.

in·fan·ti·cide /inˈfantiˌsīd/ ▶ **n.** **1** the crime of killing a child within a year of birth. ■ the practice in some societies of killing unwanted children soon after birth. **2** a person who kills an infant, esp. their own child. — **in·fan·ti·cid·al** /-ˌfantiˈsīdl/ **adj.**

in·fan·tile /ˈinfənˌtīl; ˈinfəntil/ ▶ **adj.** of or occurring among babies or very young children: *infantile colic.* ■ childish; immature: *infantile jokes.* — **in·fan·til·i·ty** /ˌinfənˈtilitē/ **n.** (pl. **-ties**).

in·fan·tile pa·ral·y·sis ▶ **n.** dated poliomyelitis.

in·fan·til·ism /ˈinfəntlˌizəm; inˈfan-/ ▶ **n.** childish behavior. ■ Psychol. the persistence of infantile characteristics or behavior in adult life.

in·fan·til·ize /ˈinfəntlˌīz; inˈfan-/ ▶ **v.** [trans.] treat (someone) as a child or in a way that denies their maturity: *seeing yourself as a victim infantilizes you.* — **in·fan·til·i·za·tion** /ˌinfəntl-iˈzāsʜən; inˌfan-/ **n.**

in·fan·try /ˈinfəntrē/ ▶ **n.** soldiers marching or fighting on foot; foot soldiers collectively. [16th C.: from Fr. *infanterie*, from Ital. *infanteria*, from *infante* 'youth, infantryman,' from L. *infant-* (see **INFANT**).]

in·fan·try·man /ˈinfəntrēmən/ ▶ **n.** (pl. **-men**) a soldier belonging to an infantry unit.

in·farct /ˈinfärkt/ ▶ **n.** Med. a small localized area of dead tissue resulting from failure of blood supply. [19th C.: from mod. L. *infarctus*, from *infarcire* 'stuff into or with,' from *in-* 'into' + L. *farcire* 'to stuff.']

in·farc·tion /inˈfärksʜən/ ▶ **n.** the obstruction of the blood supply to an organ or region of tissue, typically by a thrombus or embolus, causing local death of the tissue.

in·fat·u·ate /inˈfacʜo͞oˌāt/ ▶ **v.** (**be infatuated with**) be inspired with an intense but short-lived passion or admiration for. — **in·fat·u·a·tion** /-ˌfacʜo͞oˈāsʜən/ **n.** [16th C.: from L. *infatuat-* 'made foolish,' from the v. *infatuare*, from *in-* 'into' + *fatuus* 'foolish.']

in·fau·na /inˈfônə/ ▶ **n.** Ecol. the animals living in the sediments of the ocean floor or river or lake beds. Compare with **EPIFAUNA**. — **in·fau·nal** /-ˈfônl/ **adj.**

in·fea·si·ble /inˈfēzəbəl/ ▶ **adj.** not feasible; not possible to do easily or conveniently; impracticable. — **in·fea·si·bil·i·ty** /-ˌfēzəˈbilitē/ **n.**

in·fect /inˈfekt/ ▶ **v.** [trans.] affect (a person, organism, cell, etc.) with a disease-causing organism. ■ contaminate (air, water, etc.) with harmful organisms. ■ Comput. affect with a virus. ■ fig. (of a negative feeling or idea) be communicated to (someone): *the panic in his voice infected her.* — **in·fec·tor** /-ˈfektər/ **n.** [ME: from L. *infect-* 'tainted,' from the v. *inficere*, from *in-* 'into' + *facere* 'put, do.']

in·fec·tion /inˈfeksʜən/ ▶ **n.** the process of infecting or the state of being infected. ■ an infectious disease: *a bacterial infection.* ■ Comput. the presence of a virus in a computer system. [ME: from late L. *infectio(n-)*, from L. *inficere* 'dip in, taint' (see **INFECT**).]

in·fec·tious /inˈfeksʜəs/ ▶ **adj.** (of a disease or disease-causing organism) liable to be transmitted to people, organisms, etc., through the environment. ■ liable to spread infection. ■ likely to spread or influence others in a rapid manner: *infectious enthusiasm.* — **in·fec·tious·ly** **adv.** **in·fec·tious·ness** **n.**

in·fec·tious mon·o·nu·cle·o·sis ▶ **n.** an infectious viral disease characterized by swelling of the lymph glands and prolonged lassitude. Also called **glandular fever.**

in·fec·tive /inˈfektiv/ ▶ **adj.** capable of causing infection. ■ dated infectious. — **in·fec·tive·ness** **n.**

in·fe·cund /inˈfēkənd; -ˈfek-/ ▶ **adj.** Med. Zool. (of a woman or female animal) having low or zero fecundity; unable to bear children or young. — **in·fe·cun·di·ty** /ˌinfiˈkənditē/ **n.** [ME: from L. *infecundus*, from *in-* 'not' + *fecundus* 'fecund.']

in·fe·lic·i·tous /ˌinfəˈlisitəs/ ▶ **adj.** unfortunate; inappropriate. — **in·fe·lic·i·tous·ly** **adv.**

in·fe·lic·i·ty /ˌinfəˈlisitē/ ▶ **n.** (pl. **-ties**) a thing that is inappropriate, esp. a remark or expression: *winced at their infelicities.* ■ archaic unhappiness; misfortune. [ME: from L. *infelicitas*, from *infelix*, *infelic-* 'unhappy,' from *in-* 'not' + *felix* 'happy.']

in·fer /inˈfər/ ▶ **v.** (**-ferred, -fer·ring**) [trans.] deduce or conclude (information) from evidence and reasoning rather than from explicit statements. — **in·fer·a·ble** (also **in·fer·ra·ble**) **adj.** [15th C.: from L. *inferre* 'bring in, bring about' (in med. L. 'deduce'), from *in-* 'into' + *ferre* 'bring.']

in·fer·ence /ˈinf(ə)rəns/ ▶ **n.** a conclusion reached on the basis of evidence and reasoning. ■ the process of reaching such a conclusion: *order, health, and by inference cleanliness.* — **in·fer·en·tial** /ˌinfəˈrencʜəl/ **adj.** **in·fer·en·tial·ly** /ˌinfəˈrencʜəlē/ **adv.**

in·fe·ri·or /inˈfi(ə)rēər/ ▶ **adj.** **1** lower in rank, status, or quality. ■ of low standard or quality. ■ Law (of a court or tribunal) able to have its decisions overturned by a higher court. ■ Econ. denoting goods or services that are in greater demand during a recession than in a boom, e.g., secondhand clothes. **2** esp. Anat. low or lower in position: *the inferior wall* *of the duodenum.* ■ (of a letter, figure, or symbol) written or printed below the line. ■ Bot. (of the ovary of a flower) below the sepals and enclosed in the receptacle. ▶ n. 1 a person lower than another in status or ability. 2 Print. an inferior letter, figure, or symbol. [ME (sense 2): from L., compar. of *inferus* 'low.']

in·fe·ri·or con·junc·tion ▶ n. Astron. a conjunction of an inferior planet with the sun, in which the planet and the earth are on the same side of the sun.

in·fe·ri·or·i·ty /in,fi(ə)rē'ôritē; -'äritē/ ▶ n. the condition of being lower in status or quality than another or others. [16th C.: prob. from med. L. *inferioritas*, from L. *inferior* 'lower.']

in·fe·ri·or·i·ty com·plex ▶ n. an unrealistic feeling of general inadequacy caused by actual or supposed inferiority in one sphere, sometimes marked by aggressive behavior in compensation.

in·fe·ri·or plan·et ▶ n. Astron. either of the two planets Mercury and Venus, whose orbits are closer to the sun than the earth's.

in·fer·nal /in'fərnl/ ▶ adj. 1 of, relating to, or characteristic of hell or the underworld. 2 [attrib.] informal irritating and tiresome (used for emphasis): *an infernal nuisance.* — **in·fer·nal·ly** adv. [ME: from OFr., from Christian Latin *infernalis*, from L. *infernus* 'below, underground,' used by Christians to mean 'hell.']

in·fer·no /in'fərnō/ ▶ n. (pl. **-nos**) 1 a large fire that is dangerously out of control. 2 (usu. **In·fer·no**) hell (with reference to Dante's *Divine Comedy*).

in·fer·tile /in'fərtl/ ▶ adj. (of a person, animal, or plant) not fertile; unable to reproduce. — **in·fer·til·i·ty** /,infər'tilitē/ n.

in·fest /in'fest/ ▶ v. [trans.] (usu. **be infested**) (of insects or other animals) be present (in a place or site) in large numbers, typically so as to cause damage or disease. — **in·fes·ta·tion** /,infe'stāsHən/ n. [ME: from Fr. *infester* or L. *infestare* 'assail,' from *infestus* 'hostile.']

in·fib·u·late /in'fibyə,lāt/ ▶ v. [usu. as adj.] (**infibulated**) perform infibulation on (a girl or woman). [17th C.: from L. *infibulat-* 'fastened with a clasp,' from the v. *infibulare*, from *in-* 'into' + *fibula* 'brooch.']

in·fib·u·la·tion /in,fibyə'lāsHən/ ▶ n. the practice of excising the clitoris and labia of a girl and stitching together the edges of the vulva to prevent sexual intercourse, traditional in some African cultures. Also called **female circumcision**.

in·fi·del /'infədl; -,del/ ▶ n. a person who does not believe in religion or who adheres to a religion other than one's own. ▶ adj. adhering to a religion other than one's own. [15th C.: from Fr. *infidèle* or L. *infidelis*, from *in-* 'not' + *fidelis* 'faithful.']

in·fi·del·i·ty /,infi'delitē/ ▶ n. (pl. **-ties**) 1 the action or state of being unfaithful to a spouse or other sexual partner. 2 unbelief in a particular religion, esp. Christianity.

in·field /'in,fēld/ ▶ n. 1 the inner part of the field of play in various sports, in particular: ■ Baseball the area within and near the four bases. ■ the players stationed in the infield, collectively. 2 the land around or near a farmhouse. ▶ adv. into or toward the inner part of the field of play. — **in·field·er** n. (in sense 1).

in·fight·ing /'in,fītiNG/ ▶ n. conflict or competitiveness within an organization. ■ boxing closer to an opponent than at arm's length. — **in·fight·er** n.

in·fil·trate /'infil,trāt; in'filtrāt/ ▶ v. [trans.] 1 gain access to (an organization, place, etc.) furtively and gradually, esp. in order to acquire secret information. ■ fig. permeate or become a part of (something) in this way: *computing has infiltrated most professions now.* ■ Med. (of a tumor, cells, etc.) spread into or invade (a tissue or organ). 2 (of a liquid) permeate (something) by filtration. ■ introduce (a liquid) into something in this way. — **in·fil·tra·tion** /,infil'trāsHən/ n. **in·fil·tra·tor** /'infil,trātər/ n.

infin. ▶ abbr. infinitive.

in·fi·nite /'infənit/ ▶ adj. 1 limitless or endless in space, extent, or size; impossible to measure or calculate: *an infinite number of stars.* ■ very great in amount or degree: *infinite care.* ■ Math. greater than any assignable quantity or countable number. ■ Math. (of a series) able to be continued indefinitely. 2 Gram. another term for NONFINITE. ▶ n. (**the infinite**) a space or quantity that is infinite. — **in·fi·nite·ly** adv. **in·fi·nite·ness** n. [ME: from L. *infinitus*, from *in-* 'not' + *finitus* 'finished, finite' (see FINITE).]

in·fin·i·tes·i·mal /,infini'tes(ə)məl/ ▶ adj. extremely small. ▶ n. Math. an indefinitely small quantity; a value approaching zero. — **in·fin·i·tes·i·mal·ly** adv.

in·fin·i·tes·i·mal cal·cu·lus ▶ n. see CALCULUS (sense 1).

in·fin·i·tive /in'finitiv/ ▶ n. the basic form of a verb, without an inflection binding it to a particular subject or tense (e.g., *be* in *let him be*). ▶ adj. having or involving such a form. — **in·fin·i·ti·val** /-,fini'tīvəl/ adj. **in·fin·i·ti·val·ly** /-,fini'tīvəlē/ adv. [ME (as an adj.): from L. *infinitivus*, from *infinitus* (see INFINITE). The n. dates from the mid 16th C.]

in·fin·i·tude /in'fini,t(y)o͞od/ ▶ n. the state or quality of being infinite or having no limit.

in·fin·i·ty /in'finitē/ ▶ n. (pl. **-ties**) the state or quality of being infinite. ■ an infinite or very great number or amount. ■ Math. a number greater than any assignable quantity or countable number (symbol ∞). ■ a point in space or time that is or seems infinitely distant.

in·firm /in'fərm/ ▶ adj. not physically or mentally strong, esp. through age or illness. ■ archaic (of a person or their judgment) weak; irresolute. — **in·firm·ly** adv. [ME: from L. *infirmus*, from *in-* 'not' + *firmus* 'firm.']

in·fir·ma·ry /in'fərmərē/ ▶ n. (pl. **-ries**) a place in a large institution for the care of those who are ill. ■ a hospital.

in·fir·mi·ty /in'fərmitē/ ▶ n. (pl. **-ties**) physical or mental weakness: *the infirmities of old age.*

in·fix ▶ v. /in'fiks/ [trans.] 1 implant or insert firmly in something. 2 Gram. insert (a formative element) into the body of a word. ▶ n. /'in,fiks/ Gram. a formative element inserted in a word. — **in·fix·a·tion** /,infik'sāsHən/ n. (in sense 2 of the **verb**).

in fla·gran·te de·lic·to /,in flə'grăntā də'liktō; flə'grantē/ (also informal **in fla·gran·te**) ▶ adv. in the very act of wrongdoing, esp. in an act of sexual misconduct. [18th C.: L., lit. 'in blazing crime.']

in·flame /in'flām/ ▶ v. [trans.] 1 provoke or intensify (strong feelings, esp. anger) in someone. ■ provoke (someone) to strong feelings: *inflamed with jealousy.* ■ make (a situation) worse. 2 (usu. **be inflamed**) cause inflammation in (a part of the body). 3 literary light up with or as if with flames. — **in·flam·er** n.

in·flam·ma·ble /in'flaməbəl/ ▶ adj. easily set on fire. ■ fig. likely to provoke strong feelings: *an inflammable issue.* — **in·flam·ma·bil·i·ty** /-,flamə'bilitē/ n. **in·flam·ma·bly** adv.

in·flam·ma·tion /,inflə'māsHən/ ▶ n. a localized physical condition in which part of the body becomes reddened, swollen, hot, and often painful, esp. as a reaction to injury or infection.

in·flam·ma·to·ry /in'flamə,tôrē/ ▶ adj. 1 relating to or causing inflammation of a part of the body. 2 (esp. of speech or writing) arousing or intended to arouse angry or violent feelings.

in·flat·a·ble /in'flātəbəl/ ▶ adj. capable of being filled with air: *an inflatable mattress.* ▶ n. a plastic or rubber object that must be filled with air before use.

in·flate /in'flāt/ ▶ v. [trans.] 1 fill (a balloon, tire, or other expandable structure) with air or gas so that it becomes distended. ■ [intrans.] become distended in this way. 2 increase (something) by a large or excessive amount: *inflate costs.* ■ [usu. as adj.] (**inflated**) exaggerate: *the numbers have been inflated.* ■ bring about inflation of (a currency) or in (an economy). — **in·flat·ed·ly** adv. **in·fla·tor** /-'flātər/ (also **in·flat·er**) n. [ME: from L. *inflat-* 'blown into,' from the v. *inflare*, from *in-* 'into' + *flare* 'to blow.']

in·fla·tion /in'flāsHən/ ▶ n. 1 the action of inflating something or the condition of being inflated. 2 Econ. a general increase in prices and fall in the purchasing value of money. — **in·fla·tion·ism** n. **in·fla·tion·ist** n. & adj.

in·fla·tion·ar·y /in'flāsHə,nerē/ ▶ adj. of, characterized by, or tending to cause monetary inflation.

in·flect /in'flekt/ ▶ v. [trans.] (often **be inflected**) 1 Gram. change the form of (a word) to express a particular grammatical function or attribute, typically tense, mood, person, number, and gender. ■ [intrans.] (of a word or a language containing such words) undergo such change. 2 vary the intonation or pitch of (the voice), esp. to express mood or feeling. ■ influence or color (music or writing) in tone or style. ■ vary the pitch of (a musical note). 3 tech. bend or deflect (something), esp. inward. — **in·flec·tive** adj. [ME (sense 3): from L. *inflectere*, from *in-* 'into' + *flectere* 'to bend.']

in·flec·tion /in'fleksHən/ (esp. Brit. also **in·flex·ion**) ▶ n. 1 Gram. a change in the form of a word (typically the ending) to express a grammatical function or attribute such as tense, mood, person, number, case, or gender. ■ the process or practice of inflecting words. 2 the modulation of intonation or pitch in the voice. ■ the variation of the pitch of a musical note. 3 esp. Math. a change of curvature from convex to concave at a particular point on a curve. — **in·flec·tion·al** /-sHənl/ adj. **in·flec·tion·al·ly** /-sHənl-ē/ adv. **in·flec·tion·less** adj.

in·flexed /in'flekst/ ▶ adj. tech. bent or curved inward.

in·flex·i·ble /in'fleksəbəl/ ▶ adj. 1 not flexible; unwilling to change or compromise. ■ not able to be changed or adapted to particular circumstances: *inflexible rules.* 2 not able to be bent; stiff: *inflexible armor.* — **in·flex·i·bil·i·ty** /-,fleksə'bilitē/ n. **in·flex·i·bly** adv.

in·flict /in'flikt/ ▶ v. [trans.] cause (something unpleasant or painful) to be suffered by someone or something: *inflict injuries on.* ■ (**inflict something on**) impose something unwelcome on: *he inflicts his beliefs on everyone.* — **in·flict·a·ble** adj. **in·flict·er** n. [16th C.: from L. *inflict-* 'struck against,' from *infligere*, from *in-* 'into' + *fligere* 'to strike.']

in·flic·tion /in'fliksHən/ ▶ n. the action of inflicting something unpleasant or painful on someone or something.

in·flight /'in,flīt/ ▶ adj. occurring or provided during an aircraft flight.

in·flo·res·cence /,inflô'resəns; -flə-/ ▶ n. Bot. the complete flowerhead of a plant including stems, stalks, bracts, and flowers. ■ the arrangement of the flowers on a plant. ■ the process of flowering. [18th C.: from mod. L. *inflorescentia*, from late L. *inflorescere* 'come into flower.']

in·flow /'in,flō/ ▶ n. a large amount of money, people, or water, that moves or is transferred into a place. — **in·flow·ing** n. & adj.

in·flu·ence /'inflo͞oəns/ ▶ n. the capacity to have an effect on the character, development, or behavior of someone or something, or the effect itself: *the influence of television violence.* ■ the power to shape policy or ensure favorable treatment from someone, esp. through status, contacts, or wealth. ■ a person or thing with such a capacity or power: *he's a good influence on her.* ▶ v. [trans.] have an influence on.
– PHRASES **under the influence** informal affected by alcoholic drink; drunk: — **in·flu·ence·a·ble** adj. **in·flu·enc·er** n. [ME: from OFr., or from med. L. *influentia* 'inflow,' from L. *influere*, from *in-* 'into' + *fluere* 'to flow.']

in·flu·ent /'inflo͞oənt/ ▶ adj. flowing in. ▶ n. a stream, esp. a tributary, that flows into another stream or lake. ■ Ecol. a nondominant organism that has a major effect on the balance of a plant or animal community. [ME (as an adj.): from L. *influent-* 'flowing in,' from *influere* (see INFLUENCE). The n. is recorded from the mid 19th C.]

in·flu·en·tial /ˌinflo͞oˈencHəl/ ▶ adj. having great influence on someone or something. — **in·flu·en·tial·ly** adv.

in·flu·en·za /ˌinflo͞oˈenzə/ ▶ n. a contagious viral infection of the respiratory passages causing fever, severe aching, and catarrh. [18th C.: from Ital., lit. 'influence,' from med. L. *influentia* (see INFLUENCE).]

in·flux /ˈinˌfləks/ ▶ n. **1** an arrival or entry of large numbers of people or things. **2** an inflow of water into a river, lake, or the sea. [16th C.: from late L. *influxus*, from *influere* 'flow in' (see INFLUENCE).]

in·fo /ˈinfō/ ▶ n. informal information. [20th C.: abbrev.]

in·fold /inˈfōld/ ▶ v. [trans.] **1** turn or fold inward. **2** dated var. of ENFOLD. — **in·fold·ing** n.

in·fo·mer·cial /ˈinfōˌmərsHəl/ ▶ n. a television program that promotes a product in an informative and supposedly objective way. [1980s: blend of INFORMATION and COMMERCIAL.]

in·form /inˈfôrm/ ▶ v. **1** [reporting verb] give (someone) facts or information; tell: [trans.] *inform her of the situation.* ■ [intrans.] give incriminating information about someone to the police or other authority: *terrorists informed on their comrades.* **2** [trans.] give an essential or formative principle or quality to: *policy is informed by the democratic ideal.* [ME *enforme, informe*, from OFr. *enfourmer*, from L. *informare* 'shape, fashion, describe.']

in·for·mal /inˈfôrməl/ ▶ adj. not formal; having a relaxed, friendly, or unofficial style, manner, or nature: *an informal atmosphere | an informal agreement.* — **in·for·mal·i·ty** /ˌinfôrˈmalitē/ n. **in·for·mal·ly** adv.

in·form·ant /inˈfôrmənt/ ▶ n. a person who gives information to another. ■ another term for INFORMER. ■ a person from whom a linguist or anthropologist obtains information about language or culture.

in·for·mat·ics /ˌinfərˈmatiks/ ▶ plural n. [treated as sing.] Comput. the science of processing data for storage and retrieval; information science. [1960s: from INFORMATION + -ICS, translating Russ. *informatika*.]

in·for·ma·tion /ˌinfərˈmāsHən/ ▶ n. **1** facts provided or learned about something or someone. ■ Law a formal criminal charge lodged with a court or magistrate by a prosecutor without the aid of a grand jury. **2** what is conveyed by a particular arrangement or sequence of things: *genetically transmitted information.* ■ Comput. data as processed, stored, or transmitted by a computer. ■ (in information theory) a mathematical quantity expressing the probability of occurrence of a particular sequence of symbols, impulses, etc., as contrasted with that of alternative sequences. — **in·for·ma·tion·al** /-sHənl/ adj. **in·for·ma·tion·al·ly** /-sHənl-ē/ adv. [ME (also in the sense 'formation of the mind, teaching'), via OFr. from L. *informatio(n-)*, from the v. *informare* (see INFORM).]

in·for·ma·tion re·triev·al ▶ n. Comput. the tracing and recovery of specific information from stored data.

in·for·ma·tion sci·ence ▶ n. Comput. the study of processes for storing and retrieving information, esp. scientific or technical information.

in·for·ma·tion su·per·high·way ▶ n. see SUPERHIGHWAY (sense 2).

in·for·ma·tion the·o·ry ▶ n. the mathematical study of the coding of information in sequences of symbols, impulses, etc., and of the rapid transmission of information, e.g., through computer circuits.

in·for·ma·tive /inˈfôrmətiv/ ▶ adj. providing useful or interesting information. — **in·for·ma·tive·ly** adv.

in·formed /inˈfôrmd/ ▶ adj. having or showing knowledge of a particular subject or situation. ■ (of a decision or judgment) based on an understanding of the facts of the situation. — **in·form·ed·ly** /-m(i)dlē/ adv.

in·form·er /inˈfôrmər/ ▶ n. a person who informs on another person to the police or other authority.

in·fo·tain·ment /ˌinfōˈtānmənt/ ▶ n. broadcast material that is intended both to entertain and to inform. [1980s (orig. US): blend of INFORMATION and ENTERTAINMENT.]

in·fra /ˈinfrə/ ▶ adv. (in a written document) below; further on: *see note, infra.* [19th C.: L., 'below.']

infra- ▶ prefix below: *infrared | infrasonic.*

in·fra·class /ˈinfrəˌklas/ ▶ n. Biol. a taxonomic category that ranks below a subclass.

in·frac·tion /inˈfraksHən/ ▶ n. a violation or infringement of a law, agreement, or set of rules. — **in·frac·tor** /-tər/ n. [ME: from L. *infractio(n-)*, from the v. *infringere* (see INFRINGE).]

in·fra dig ▶ adj. [predic.] informal beneath one; demeaning. [19th C.: abbrev. of L. *infra dignitatem* 'beneath (one's) dignity.']

in·fran·gi·ble /inˈfranjəbəl/ ▶ adj. formal unbreakable; inviolable. — **in·fran·gi·bil·i·ty** /-ˌfranjəˈbilitē/ n. **in·fran·gi·bly** adv. [16th C.: from Fr., or from med. L. *infrangibilis*, from *in-* 'not' + *frangibilis* (see FRANGIBLE).]

in·fra·or·der /ˈinfrəˌôrdər/ ▶ n. Biol. a taxonomic category that ranks below a suborder.

in·fra·red /ˌinfrəˈred/ ▶ adj. (of electromagnetic radiation) having a wavelength just greater than that of the red end of the visible light spectrum but less than that of microwaves. Infrared radiation has a wavelength from about 800 nm to 1 mm. ■ (of equipment or techniques) using or concerned with this radiation. ▶ n. the infrared region of the spectrum; infrared radiation.

in·fra·son·ic /ˌinfrəˈsänik/ ▶ adj. denoting sound waves with a frequency below human audibility.

in·fra·spe·cif·ic /ˌinfrəspəˈsifik/ ▶ adj. Biol. at a taxonomic level below that of species, e.g., subspecies, variety, cultivar, or form.

in·fra·struc·ture /ˈinfrəˌstrəkcHər/ ▶ n. the basic physical and organizational structures and facilities (e.g., buildings, roads, and power supplies) needed for the operation of a society or enterprise. — **in·fra·struc·tur·al** /ˌinfrəˈstrəkcHərəl/ adj.

in·fre·quent /inˈfrēkwənt/ ▶ adj. not occurring often; rare. — **in·fre·quen·cy** n. **in·fre·quent·ly** adv.

in·fringe /inˈfrinj/ ▶ v. [trans.] actively break the terms of (a law, agreement, etc.): *infringe a copyright.* ■ act so as to limit or undermine (something); encroach on: [intrans.] *infringe on his privacy.* — **in·fringe·ment** n. **in·fring·er** n. [16th C.: from L. *infringere*, from *in-* 'into' + *frangere* 'to break.']

in·fun·dib·u·lum /ˌinfənˈdibyələm/ ▶ n. (pl. **-la** /-lə/) Anat. Zool. a funnel-shaped cavity or structure. ■ the hollow stalk that connects the hypothalamus and the posterior pituitary gland. — **in·fun·dib·u·lar** /-lər/ adj. [16th C.: from L., 'funnel,' from *infundere* 'pour in.']

in·fu·ri·ate ▶ v. /inˈfyo͝orēˌāt/ [trans.] make (someone) extremely angry and impatient. — **in·fu·ri·at·ing·ly** adv. [17th C.: from med. L. *infuriat-* 'made angry.']

in·fuse /inˈfyo͞oz/ ▶ v. [trans.] **1** fill; pervade: *her work is infused with an anger.* ■ instill (a quality) in someone or something: *infused good humor into his voice.* ■ Med. allow (a liquid) to flow into a patient's vein, etc. **2** soak (tea, herbs, etc.) in liquid to extract the flavor or healing properties. — **in·fus·er** n. [ME: from L. *infus-* 'poured in,' from the v. *infundere*.]

in·fu·si·ble /inˈfyo͞ozəbəl/ ▶ adj. (of a substance) not able to be melted or fused. — **in·fu·si·bil·i·ty** /inˌfyo͞ozəˈbilitē/ n.

in·fu·sion /inˈfyo͞ozHən/ ▶ n. **1** a drink or extract prepared by soaking the leaves of a plant in liquid. ■ the process of preparing such a drink, remedy, or extract. **2** the introduction of a new element or quality into something: [count noun] *an infusion of talent.* ■ Med. the slow injection of a substance into a vein or tissue.

in·fu·so·ri·a /ˌinfyəˈzôrēə/ ▶ plural n. Zool. single-celled organisms of the former group Infusoria, which consisted mainly of ciliate protozoans, originally found in infusions of decaying organic matter.

-ing[1] /iNG/ ▶ suffix **1** denoting a verbal action, an instance of this, or its result: *fighting | outing | building.* ■ denoting a verbal action relating to an occupation, skill, etc.: *banking | ice skating | welding.* **2** denoting material used for or associated with a process, etc.: *cladding | piping.* ■ denoting something involved in an action or process but with no corresponding verb: *scaffolding.* **3** forming the gerund of verbs (such as *painting* as in *I love painting*). [OE *-ung, -ing*, of Gmc. origin.]

-ing[2] ▶ suffix **1** forming the present participle of verbs: *doing | calling.* ■ forming present participles used as adjectives: *charming.* **2** forming adjectives from nouns: *hulking.* [ME: alt. of earlier *-ende*, later *-inde*.]

-ing[3] ▶ suffix (used esp. in names of coins and fractional parts) a thing belonging to or having the quality of: *farthing | riding.* [OE, of Gmc. origin.]

in·gath·er /ˈinˌgaTHər/ ▶ v. [trans.] formal gather (something) in or together.

Inge /iNG/, William Motter (1913–73) US playwright. He wrote *Come Back, Little Sheba* (1950), *Picnic* (1953) and *Bus Stop* (1955).

in·gem·i·nate /inˈjeməˌnāt/ ▶ v. [trans.] archaic repeat or reiterate (a word or statement), typically for emphasis.

in·gen·ious /inˈjēnyəs/ ▶ adj. (of a person) clever, original, and inventive. ■ (of a machine or idea) cleverly and originally devised and well suited to its purpose. — **in·gen·ious·ly** adv. **in·gen·ious·ness** n. [ME: from Fr. *ingénieux* or L. *ingeniosus*, from *ingenium* 'mind, intellect'; cf. ENGINE.]

in·gé·nue /ˈanjəˌno͞o; ˈänzHə-/ ▶ n. an innocent or unsophisticated young woman. ■ a part of this type in a play. ■ an actress who plays such a part. [Fr., fem. of *ingénu* 'ingenuous,' from L. *ingenuus* (see INGENUOUS).]

in·ge·nu·i·ty /ˌinjəˈn(y)o͞oitē/ ▶ n. the quality of being clever, original, and inventive. [16th C. (also in the senses 'nobility' and 'ingenuousness'): from L. *ingenuitas* 'ingenuousness,' from *ingenuus* 'inborn.' The current meaning arose by confusion of INGENUOUS with INGENIOUS.]

in·gen·u·ous /inˈjenyo͞oəs/ ▶ adj. (of a person or action) innocent and unsuspecting. — **in·gen·u·ous·ly** adv. **in·gen·u·ous·ness** n. [16th C.: from L. *ingenuus*, lit. 'native, inborn.']

in·gest /inˈjest/ ▶ v. [trans.] take (food, drink, or another substance) into the body by swallowing or absorbing it. ■ fig. absorb (information). — **in·ges·tion** /-ˈjescHən/ n. **in·ges·tive** adj. [17th C.: from L. *ingest-* 'brought in,' from the v. *ingerere*, from *in-* 'into' + *gerere* 'carry.']

in·ges·ta /inˈjestə/ ▶ plural n. Med. Zool. substances taken into the body as nourishment; food and drink.

in·gle /ˈiNGgəl/ ▶ n. esp. dialect a domestic fire or fireplace. ■ an inglenook. [16th C. (orig. Scots): perh. from Scot. Gael. *aingeal* 'light, fire,' Irish *aingeal* 'live ember.']

in·gle·nook /ˈiNGgəlˌno͝ok/ ▶ n. a space on either side of a large fireplace.

in·glo·ri·ous /inˈglôrēəs/ ▶ adj. (of an action or situation) causing shame or a loss of honor. ■ not famous or renowned. — **in·glo·ri·ous·ly** adv. **in·glo·ri·ous·ness** n.

in·go·ing /ˈinˌgōiNG/ ▶ adj. [attrib.] going into or toward a particular place.

in·got /ˈiNGgət/ ▶ **n.** a block of steel, gold, silver, or other metal, typically oblong in shape. [ME: perh. from **IN** + OE *goten*, past part. of *geotan* 'pour, cast.']

in·graft ▶ **v.** var. of **ENGRAFT.**

in·grain ▶ **v.** /inˈgrān/ (also **en·grain**) [trans.] firmly fix or establish (a habit, belief, or attitude) in a person. ▶ **adj.** /ˈinˌgrān/ (of a textile) composed of fibers that have been dyed different colors before being woven.

in·grained /inˈgrānd/ ▶ **adj.** (also **en·grained**) **1** (of a habit, belief, or attitude) firmly fixed or established; difficult to change. **2** (of dirt or a stain) deeply embedded and thus difficult to remove.

in·grate /ˈinˌgrāt/ formal literary ▶ **n.** an ungrateful person. ▶ **adj.** ungrateful.

in·gra·ti·ate /inˈgrāsHēˌāt/ ▶ **v.** (**ingratiate oneself**) bring oneself into favor with someone by flattering or trying to please them. — **in·gra·ti·a·tion** /-ˌgrāsHēˈāsHən/ **n.** [17th C.: from L. *in gratiam* 'into favor,' after Ital. *ingratiare*, earlier form of *ingraziare*.]

in·gra·ti·at·ing /inˈgrāsHēˌātiNG/ ▶ **adj.** intended to gain approval or favor: *an ingratiating manner.* — **in·gra·ti·at·ing·ly adv.**

in·grat·i·tude /inˈgratiˌt(y)o͞od/ ▶ **n.** a discreditable lack of gratitude.

in·gre·di·ent /inˈgrēdēənt; iNG-/ ▶ **n.** any of the foods or substances that are combined to make a particular dish or meal. ■ a component part or element of something: *all the ingredients of a mystery.* [ME: from L. *ingredient-* 'entering,' from the v. *ingredi*, from *in-* 'into' + *gradi* 'walk.']

In·gres /ˈaNGgrə/, Jean Auguste Dominique (1780–1867), French painter. Notable works: *Ambassadors of Agamemnon* (1801) and *The Bather* (1808).

in·gress /ˈinˌgres/ ▶ **n.** a place or means of access; an entrance. ■ the action or fact of going in or entering. ■ the capacity or right of entrance. — **in·gres·sion** /-ˈgresHən/ **n.** [ME: from L. *ingressus*, from the v. *ingredi* 'enter.']

in·gres·sive /inˈgresiv/ ▶ **adj. 1** of or relating to ingress; having the quality or character of entering. **2** Phonet. (of a speech sound) made with an intake of air rather than an exhalation. Compare with **EGRESSIVE.**

in·grow·ing /ˈinˌgrōiNG/ ▶ **adj.** growing inward or within something, esp. (of a toenail) growing abnormally so as to press into the flesh.

in·grown /ˈinˌgrōn/ ▶ **adj.** growing or having grown within a thing. ■ (of a toenail) having grown abnormally so as to press into the flesh.

in·growth /ˈinˌgrōTH/ ▶ **n.** a thing that has grown inward or within something. ■ the action of growing inward.

in·gui·nal /ˈiNGgwənəl/ ▶ **adj.** Anat. of the groin. — **in·gui·nal·ly adv.** [ME: from L. *inguinalis*, from *inguen, inguin-* 'groin.']

In·gush /inˈgo͞osH/ ▶ **n.** (pl. same or **-gush·es**) **1** a member of a people living mainly in the central Caucasus, between Chechnya and North Ossetia. **2** the North Caucasian language of this people. ▶ **adj.** of or relating to the Ingush or their language.

in·hab·it /inˈhabit/ ▶ **v.** (**-hab·it·ed, -hab·it·ing**) [trans.] (of a person, animal, or group) live in or occupy (a place or environment): *a bird that inhabits Hawaii.* | [as adj.] (**inhabited**) *an inhabited desert.* — **in·hab·it·a·bil·i·ty** /-ˌhabitəˈbilitē/ **n. in·hab·it·a·ble adj. in·hab·i·ta·tion** /-ˌhabiˈtāsHən/ **n.** [ME *inhabite, enhabite*, from OFr. *enhabiter* or L. *inhabitare*, from *in-* 'in' + *habitare* 'dwell.']

in·hab·it·an·cy /inˈhabitn-sē/ (also **in·hab·it·ance**) ▶ **n.** archaic living in a certain place as an inhabitant, esp. for a specified period so as to acquire certain rights.

in·hab·it·ant /inˈhabitnt/ ▶ **n.** a person or animal that lives in or occupies a place. ■ a person who fulfills the requirements for legal residency.

in·hal·ant /inˈhālənt/ ▶ **n.** a medicine prepared for inhaling. ■ a solvent or other material producing vapor inhaled by drug abusers.

in·ha·la·tion /ˌinhəˈlāsHən/ ▶ **n.** the action of inhaling or breathing in. ■ Med. the inhaling of medicines or anesthetics in the form of a gas or vapor. ■ Med. an inhalant.

in·ha·la·tor /ˈinhəˌlātər/ ▶ **n.** a device assisting someone in inhaling something, esp. oxygen; a respirator or an inhaler.

in·hale /inˈhāl/ ▶ **v.** breathe in (air, gas, smoke, etc.). ■ [trans.] informal eat (food) greedily or rapidly. [18th C.: from L. *inhalare* 'breathe in,' from *in-* 'in' + *halare* 'breathe.']

in·hal·er /inˈhālər/ ▶ **n.** a portable device for administering a drug that is to be inhaled, used for relieving asthma and other bronchial or nasal congestion.

in·har·mon·ic /ˌinhärˈmänik/ ▶ **adj.** esp. Music not harmonic. — **in·har·mo·nic·i·ty** /-məˈnisitē/ **n.**

in·har·mo·ni·ous /ˌinhärˈmōnēəs/ ▶ **adj.** not forming or contributing to a pleasing whole; discordant. — **in·har·mo·ni·ous·ly adv.**

in·here /inˈhi(ə)r/ ▶ **v.** [intrans.] (**inhere in/within**) formal exist essentially or permanently in. ■ Law (of rights, powers, etc.) be vested in a person or group or attached to the ownership of a property.

in·her·ent /inˈhi(ə)rənt; -ˈher-/ ▶ **adj.** existing in something as a permanent, essential, or characteristic attribute: *inherent dangers.* ■ Law vested in (someone) as a right or privilege: *the president's inherent power.* — **in·her·ence n. in·her·ent·ly adv.** [16th C.: from L. *inhaerent-* 'sticking to,' from the v. *inhaerere*, from *in-* 'in, toward' + *haerere* 'to stick.']

in·her·it /inˈherit/ ▶ **v.** (**-her·it·ed, -her·it·ing**) [trans.] receive (money, property, or a title) as an heir at the death of the previous holder. ■ derive (a quality, characteristic, or predisposition) genetically from one's parents or ancestors. ■ receive or be left with (a situation, object, etc.) from a predecessor or former owner: *problems inherited from previous owners.* ■ come into possession of (belongings) from someone else. — **in·her·i·tor** /-ˈheritər/ **n.** [ME *enherite* 'receive as a right,' from OFr. *enheriter*, from late L. *inhereditare* 'appoint as heir.']

in·her·it·a·ble /inˈheritəbəl/ ▶ **adj.** capable of being inherited. — **in·her·it·a·bil·i·ty** /-ˌheritəˈbilitē/ **n.**

in·her·it·ance /inˈheritəns/ ▶ **n.** a thing that is inherited. ■ the action of inheriting: *the inheritance of traits.*

in·her·it·ance tax ▶ **n.** a tax imposed on someone who inherits property or money. Also called **DEATH TAX.**

in·he·sion /inˈhēzHən/ ▶ **n.** formal the action or state of inhering in something. [17th C.: from late L. *inhaesio(n-)*, from L. *inhaerere* 'stick to.']

in·hib·in /inˈhibin/ ▶ **n.** Biochem. a gonadal hormone that inhibits the secretion of follicle-stimulating hormone, under consideration as a potential male contraceptive. [1930s: from L. *inhibere* 'hinder' + **-IN**'.]

in·hib·it /inˈhibit/ ▶ **v.** (**-hib·it·ed, -hib·it·ing**) [trans.] hinder, restrain, or prevent (an action or process). ■ prevent or prohibit someone from doing something. ■ Psychol. voluntarily or involuntarily restrain the direct expression of (an instinctive impulse). ■ make (someone) self-conscious and unable to act in a relaxed and natural way. — **in·hib·i·tive adj. in·hib·i·to·ry** /-ˌtôrē/ **adj.** [ME: from L. *inhibere* 'hinder,' from *in-* 'in' + *habere* 'hold.']

in·hib·it·ed /inˈhibitid/ ▶ **adj.** unable to act in a relaxed and natural way because of self-consciousness or mental restraint.

in·hi·bi·tion /ˌin(h)iˈbisHən/ ▶ **n.** a feeling that makes one self-conscious and unable to act in a relaxed and natural way. ■ Psychol. a voluntary or involuntary restraint on the direct expression of an instinct. ■ the action of inhibiting, restricting, or hindering a process.

in·hib·i·tor /inˈhibitər/ ▶ **n.** a thing that inhibits someone or something. ■ a substance that slows down or prevents a particular chemical reaction or other process.

in·ho·mo·ge·ne·ous /inˌhōməˈjēnēəs; -ˌhämə-/ ▶ **adj.** not uniform in character or content; diverse. ■ Math. consisting of terms that are not all of the same degree or dimensions. — **in·ho·mo·ge·ne·i·ty** /-jəˈnē-itē; -ˈnā-itē/ **n.**

in·hos·pi·ta·ble /ˌinhäˈspitəbəl; inˈhäspi-/ ▶ **adj.** (of an environment) harsh and difficult to live in. ■ (of a person) unfriendly and unwelcoming. — **in·hos·pi·ta·ble·ness n. in·hos·pi·ta·bly adv. in·hos·pi·tal·i·ty** /inˌhäspiˈtalitē; ˌinhäs-/ **n.**

in-house ▶ **adj.** [attrib.] done or existing within an organization: *in-house publication.*

in·hu·man /inˈ(h)yo͞omən/ ▶ **adj. 1** lacking human qualities of compassion and mercy; cruel and barbaric. **2** not human in nature or character. — **in·hu·man·ly adv.**

in·hu·mane /ˌin(h)yo͞oˈmān/ ▶ **adj.** without compassion for misery or suffering; cruel. — **in·hu·mane·ly adv.**

in·hu·man·i·ty /ˌin(h)yo͞oˈmanitē/ ▶ **n.** (pl. **-ties**) extremely cruel and brutal behavior.

in·hume /inˈ(h)yo͞om/ ▶ **v.** [trans.] bury (a body). — **in·hu·ma·tion** /ˌin(h)yo͞oˈmāsHən/ **n.** [17th C.: from L. *inhumare*, from *in-* 'into' + *humus* 'ground.']

in·im·i·cal /iˈnimikəl/ ▶ **adj.** tending to obstruct or harm: *actions inimical to our interests.* ■ unfriendly; hostile. — **in·im·i·cal·ly adv.** [16th C.: from late L. *inimicalis*, from L. *inimicus* (see **ENEMY**).]

in·im·i·ta·ble /iˈnimitəbəl/ ▶ **adj.** so good or unusual as to be impossible to copy; unique. — **in·im·i·ta·bil·i·ty** /iˌnimitəˈbilitē/ **n. in·im·i·ta·bly adv.**

in·i·on /ˈinēən/ ▶ **n.** Anat. the projecting part of the occipital bone at the base of the skull. [19th C.: from Gk., lit. 'nape of the neck.']

in·iq·ui·ty /iˈnikwitē/ ▶ **n.** (pl. **-ties**) immoral or grossly unfair behavior. — **in·iq·ui·tous** /-witəs/ **adj. in·iq·ui·tous·ly** /-witəslē/ **adv.** [ME: from OFr. *iniquite*, from L. *iniquitas*, from *iniquus*, from *in-* 'not' + *aequus* 'equal, just.']

in·i·tial /iˈnisHəl/ ▶ **adj.** [attrib.] existing or occurring at the beginning: *initial impression.* ■ (of a letter) at the beginning of a word. ▶ **n.** (usu. **initials**) the first letter of a name or word, typically a person's name or a word forming part of a phrase: *they carved their initials into the tree.* ▶ **v.** (**-tialed, -tial·ing**; Brit. **-tialled, -tial·ling**) [trans.] mark or sign (a document) with one's initials, esp. in order to authorize or validate it. [16th C.: from L. *initialis*, from *initium* 'beginning,' from *inire* 'go in,' from *in-* 'into' + *ire* 'go.']

in·i·tial·ese /iˌnisHəˈlēz/ ▶ **n.** informal the use of abbreviations formed by using initial letters.

in·i·tial·ism /iˈnisHəˌlizəm/ ▶ **n.** an abbreviation consisting of initial letters pronounced separately (e.g., *CPU*). ■ an acronym.

in·i·tial·ize /iˈnisHəˌlīz/ ▶ **v.** [trans.] Comput. **1** (often **be initialized to**) set to the value or put in the condition appropriate to the start of an operation. **2** format (a computer disk). — **in·i·tial·i·za·tion** /iˌnisHəliˈzāsHən/ **n.**

in·i·tial·ly /iˈnisHəlē/ ▶ **adv.** [usu. sentence adverb] at first: *initially, he thought the new concept was nonsense.*

in·i·tial pub·lic of·fer·ing ▶ **n.** a company's flotation on the stock exchange.

in·i·ti·ate ▶ **v.** /iˈnisHēˌāt/ [trans.] **1** cause (a process or action) to begin: *initiate discussions.* **2** admit (someone) into a secret or obscure society or group, typically with a ritual: *initiate into the sorority.* ■ [as pl. n.] (**the initiated**) fig. a small group of people who share obscure knowledge. ■ (**initiate someone in/into**) introduce someone to a particular activity or skill, esp. a difficult or obscure one. ▶ **n.** /iˈnisHēit/ a person who has been recently initiated into an organization or activity: [as adj.] *initiate Marines.* — **in·i·ti·a·tion** /iˌnisHēˈāsHən/ **n.** **in·i·ti·a·tor n.** **in·i·ti·a·to·ry** /-əˌtôrē/ **adj.** [16th C. (sense 2): from L. *initiat-* 'begun,' from the v. *initiare*, from *initium* 'beginning.']

in·i·ti·a·tive /iˈnisH(ē)ətiv/ ▶ **n.** **1** the ability to assess and initiate things independently. **2** [in sing.] the power or opportunity to act or take charge before others do. **3** an act or strategy intended to resolve a difficulty or improve a situation: *a new initiative against crime.* **4** (**the initiative**) (esp. in some US states and Switzerland) the right of citizens outside the legislature to originate legislation.

– PHRASES **take the initiative** be the first to take action in a particular situation.

in·ject /inˈjekt/ ▶ **v.** [trans.] **1** drive or force (a liquid, esp. a drug or vaccine) into a person or animal's body with a syringe or similar device. ■ administer a drug or medicine to (a person or animal) in this way: *he injected himself with the drug.* ■ introduce (something) into a passage, cavity, or solid material under pressure: *inject the foam.* **2** introduce (a new or different element) into something: *she injected scorn into her tone.* ■ (**inject something with**) imbue something with (a new element): *he injected his voice with confidence.* — **in·ject·a·ble adj. & n.** [16th C.: from L. *inject-* 'thrown in,' from the v. *inicere*, from *in-* 'into' + *jacere* 'throw.']

in·jec·tion /inˈjeksHən/ ▶ **n.** an instance of injecting or being injected. ■ a thing that is injected. ■ the action of injecting. ■ short for **FUEL INJECTION.**

in·jec·tion mold·ing ▶ **n.** the shaping of rubber or plastic articles by injecting heated material into a mold. — **in·jec·tion-mold·ed adj.**

in·jec·tor /inˈjektər/ ▶ **n.** a person or thing that injects something. ■ (also **fuel injector**) (in an internal combustion engine) the nozzle and valve through which fuel is sprayed into a combustion chamber. ■ (in a steam engine) a system of nozzles that uses steam to inject water into a pressurized boiler.

in·ju·di·cious /ˌinjo͞oˈdisHəs/ ▶ **adj.** not judicious; showing poor judgment; unwise. — **in·ju·di·cious·ly adv.** **in·ju·di·cious·ness n.**

in·junc·tion /inˈjənG(k)sHən/ ▶ **n.** an authoritative warning or order. ■ Law a judicial order that restrains a person from effecting legal action, or orders redress to an injured party. — **in·junc·tive** /-ˈjənG(k)tiv/ **adj.** [ME: from late L. *injunctio(n-)*, from L. *injungere* 'enjoin, impose.']

in·jure /ˈinjər/ ▶ **v.** [trans.] do physical harm or damage to (someone). ■ suffer physical harm or damage to (a part of one's body): *he injured his back.* ■ harm or impair (something). ■ archaic do injustice or wrong to (someone). — **in·jur·er n.**

in·ju·ri·ous /inˈjo͝orēəs/ ▶ **adj.** causing or likely to cause damage or harm. ■ (of language) maliciously insulting; libelous. — **in·ju·ri·ous·ly adv.** **in·ju·ri·ous·ness n.**

in·ju·ry /ˈinjərē/ ▶ **n.** (pl. **-ries**) an instance of being injured: *an ankle injury.* ■ the fact of being injured; harm or damage. ■ (**injury to**) offense to: *injury to his feelings.* [ME: from Anglo-Norman Fr. *injurie*, from L. *injuria* 'a wrong,' from *in-* + *jus, jur-* 'right.']

in·jus·tice /inˈjəstis/ ▶ **n.** lack of fairness or justice. ■ an unjust act or occurrence.

– PHRASES **do someone an injustice** judge a person unfairly.

ink /iNGk/ ▶ **n.** a colored fluid used for writing, drawing, printing, or duplicating. ■ informal publicity: *court cases that get lots of ink.* ■ Zool. a black liquid ejected by a cuttlefish, octopus, or squid to confuse a predator. ▶ **v.** [trans.] mark (words or a design) with ink: *the name is inked onto the side.* ■ cover (type or a stamp) with ink before printing: *the raised image is inked.* ■ (**ink something in**) fill in writing or a design with ink. ■ (**ink something out**) obliterate something, esp. writing, with ink. — **ink·er n.** [ME *enke, inke*, from OFr. *enque*, via late L. from Gk. *enkauston*, denoting the purple ink used by Roman emperors for signatures, from *enkaiein* 'burn in.']

ink·ber·ry /ˈiNGkˌberē/ ▶ **n.** (pl. **-ries**) **1** another term for ***LOW GALLBERRY*** (see **GALLBERRY**). **2** another term for **POKEWEED.**

ink·blot test /ˈiNGkˌblät/ ▶ **n.** another term for **RORSCHACH TEST.**

ink·horn /ˈiNGkˌhôrn/ ▶ **n.** hist. a small portable container for ink. ■ [as adj.] denoting pedantic words or expressions used only in academic writing.

ink-jet print·er (also **ink·jet**) ▶ **n.** a printer in which the characters are formed by minute jets of ink.

in·kle /ˈiNGkəl/ ▶ **n.** a kind of linen tape formerly used to make laces, or the linen yarn from which this is manufactured. [16th C.: of unknown origin.]

ink·ling /ˈiNGkliNG/ ▶ **n.** a slight knowledge or suspicion; a hint. [ME: from the rare v. *inkle* 'utter in an undertone,' of unknown origin.]

ink·stand /ˈiNGkˌstand/ ▶ **n.** a stand for one or more ink bottles, typically incorporating a pen tray.

ink·well /ˈiNGkˌwel/ ▶ **n.** a container for ink typically housed in a hole in a desk.

ink·y /ˈiNGkē/ ▶ **adj.** (**ink·i·er, ink·i·est**) **1** as dark as ink. **2** stained with ink. — **ink·i·ness n.**

ink·y cap ▶ **n.** a widely distributed mushroom (genus *Coprinus*, family Coprinaceae) with a tall, narrow cap and slender white stem, turning into a black liquid after the spores are shed. See also **SHAGGY MANE.**

in·laid /ˈinˌlād/ past and past participle of **INLAY.**

in·land /ˈinˌland; -lənd/ ▶ **adj.** situated in the interior of a country rather than on the coast. ▶ **adv.** in or toward the interior of a country. ▶ **n.** (**the inland**) the parts of a country remote from the sea or borders; the interior. — **in·land·er n.**

In·land Sea an almost landlocked arm of the Pacific Ocean that is surrounded by the Japanese islands of Honshu, Shikoku, and Kyushu.

in-law ▶ **n.** a relative by marriage.

in·lay ▶ **v.** /ˌinˈlā/ (past and past part. **-laid**) [trans.] (usu. **be inlaid**) ornament (an object) by embedding pieces of a different material in it, flush with its surface. ■ embed (something) in an object in this way. ■ insert (a page, an illustration, etc.) in a space cut in a larger thicker page. ▶ **n.** /ˈinˌlā/ **1** a design, pattern, or piece of material inlaid in something. ■ a material or substance that is inlaid. ■ inlaid work. ■ the technique of inlaying material. **2** a filling shaped to fit a tooth cavity. — **in·lay·er n.**

in·let /ˈinˌlet; -lit/ ▶ **n.** **1** a small arm of the sea, a lake, or a river. **2** a place or means of entry: *an air inlet.*

in·li·er /ˈinlīər/ ▶ **n.** Geol. an older rock formation isolated among newer rocks.

in-line ▶ **adj.** **1** having parts arranged in a line: *an in-line 6-cylinder engine.* **2** constituting an integral part of a computer program: *the parameters can be set up as in-line code.*

in-line skate ▶ **n.** a roller skate in which the wheels are fixed in a single line under the sole of the boot. — **in-line skat·er n.** **in-line skat·ing n.**

in-line skate

in lo·co pa·ren·tis /in ˌlōkō pəˈrentis/ ▶ **adv. & adj.** (of a teacher or other adult responsible for children) in the place of a parent. [19th C.: L.]

In·man /ˈinmən/, Henry (1801–46), US painter. A leading portraitist, he painted many well-known people of his time.

in·mate /ˈinˌmāt/ ▶ **n.** a person confined to an institution such as a prison or hospital.

in me·di·as res /in ˈmēdēəs ˈres; ˈmādēˌäs/ ▶ **adv.** into the middle of a narrative; without preamble. ■ into the midst of things. [18th C.:L., lit. 'into the middle of things.']

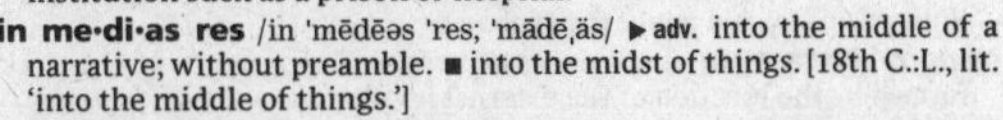

in me·mo·ri·am /ˌin məˈmôrēəm/ ▶ **n.** [often as adj.] an article written in memory of a dead person; an obituary. ▶ **prep.** in memory of (a dead person). [19th C.: L., lit. 'to the memory (of).']

in·most /ˈinˌmōst/ ▶ **adj.** literary innermost.

inn /in/ ▶ **n.** an establishment providing accommodations, food, and drink, esp. for travelers. [OE (in the sense 'dwelling place, lodging'): of Gmc. origin; rel. to **IN.**]

in·nards /ˈinərdz/ ▶ **plural n.** informal entrails. ■ internal workings (of a device or machine).

in·nate /iˈnāt/ ▶ **adj.** inborn; natural. ■ Philos. originating in the mind. — **in·nate·ly adv.** **in·nate·ness n.** [ME: from L. *innatus*, past part. of *innasci*, from *in-* 'into' + *nasci* 'be born.']

in·ner /ˈinər/ ▶ **adj.** [attrib.] **1** situated inside or further in; internal. **2** mental or spiritual: *inner strength.*

in·ner child ▶ **n.** a person's supposed original or true self, esp. when regarded as damaged or concealed by negative childhood experiences.

in·ner cir·cle ▶ **n.** an exclusive group close to the center of power of an organization or movement, regarded as elitist and secretive.

in·ner cit·y ▶ **n.** the area near the center of a city, esp. when associated with social and economic problems.

in·ner ear ▶ **n.** the semicircular canals and cochlea, which form the organs of balance and hearing and are embedded in the temporal bone.

In·ner Mon·go·li·a /mänGˈgōlēə/ an autonomous region in northern China, on the border with Mongolia; capital, Hohhot.

in·ner·most /ˈinərˌmōst/ ▶ **adj.** [attrib.] **1** (of thoughts or feelings) most private and deeply felt. **2** farthest in; closest to the center.

in·ner plan·et ▶ **n.** a planet whose orbit lies within the asteroid belt, i.e., Mercury, Venus, Earth, or Mars.

in·ner prod·uct ▶ **n.** Math. a scalar function of two vectors, equal to the product of their magnitudes and the cosine of the angle between them. Also called **DOT PRODUCT** or **SCALAR PRODUCT.** Compare with **VECTOR PRODUCT.**

in·ner sanc·tum ▶ **n.** the most sacred place in a temple or church. ■ fig. a private or secret place to which few other people are admitted.

in·ner space ▶ **n.** **1** the region between the earth and outer space. ■ the region below the surface of the sea. **2** the part of the mind not normally accessible to consciousness.

in·ner·spring /ˈinərˌspriNG/ ▶ **adj.** (of a mattress) with internal springs.

in·ner tube ▶ **n.** a separate inflatable tube inside a pneumatic tire.

in·ner·vate /iˈnərvāt; ˈinərˌvāt/ ▶ **v.** [trans.] Anat. Zool. supply (an organ or other body part) with nerves. — **in·ner·va·tion** /ˌinərˈvāsHən/ **n.** [19th C.: from **IN-**[2] 'into' + **NERVE** + **-ATE**[3].]

In·ness /ˈinis/, George (1825–94), US painter. His early work was related to the Hudson River School. Later, he painted in a more impressionistic style.

in·ning /ˈiniNG/ ▶ **n.** Baseball a division of a game during which the two teams alternate as offense and defense and during which each team is allowed three outs while batting. ■ a single turn at bat for a team until three outs are made. ■ a similar division of play in other games, such as horseshoes. [OE *innung* 'a putting or getting in,' rel. to IN. The current sense dates from the mid 19th C.]

in·nings /'iniNGz/ ▶ n. (pl. same or informal **in·nings·es** /'iniNGziz/) Cricket each of two or four divisions of a game during which one side has a turn at batting. ■ a player's turn at batting. ■ the score achieved during a player's turn at batting.

inn·keep·er /'in,kēpər/ ▶ n. a person who runs an inn.

in·no·cence /'inəsəns/ ▶ n. the state, quality, or fact of being innocent of a crime or offense. ■ lack of guile or corruption; purity.
– PHRASES **in all innocence** without knowledge of something's significance or possible consequences. [ME: from OFr., from L. *innocentia*, from *innocent-* 'not harming.']

in·no·cent /'inəsənt/ ▶ adj. **1** not guilty of a crime or offense. ■ [predic.] (**innocent of**) without; lacking: *a street innocent of bookshops.* ■ [predic.] (**innocent of**) without experience or knowledge of: *innocent of war's cruelties.* **2** [attrib.] not responsible for or directly involved in an event yet suffering its consequences: *an innocent bystander.* **3** free from moral wrong; not corrupted: *an innocent child.* ■ simple; naive. **4** not intended to cause harm or offense; harmless: *an innocent mistake.* ▶ n. an innocent person, in particular: ■ a pure, guileless, or naive person. ■ a person involved by chance in a situation, esp. a victim of crime or war. — **in·no·cent·ly** adv. [ME: from OFr., or from L. *innocent-* 'not harming,' from *in-* 'not' + *nocere* 'to hurt.']

in·noc·u·ous /i'näkyo͞oəs/ ▶ adj. not harmful or offensive. — **in·noc·u·ous·ly** adv. **in·noc·u·ous·ness** n. [16th C.: from L. *innocuus*, from *in-* 'not' + *nocuus* 'injurious' (see NOCUOUS).]

Inn of Court ▶ n. (in the UK) each of the four legal societies having the exclusive right of admitting people to the English bar. ■ any of the sets of buildings in London occupied by these societies.

in·nom·i·nate /i'nämənit/ ▶ adj. not named or classified.

in·nom·i·nate bone ▶ n. Anat. the bone formed from the fusion of the ilium, ischium, and pubis; the hipbone.

in·nom·i·nate vein ▶ n. Anat. either of two large veins of the neck formed by the junction of the external jugular and subclavian veins.

in·no·vate /'inə,vāt/ ▶ v. [intrans.] make changes in something established, esp. by introducing new methods, ideas, or products. ■ [trans.] introduce something new, esp. a product. — **in·no·va·tor** /-,vātər/ n. **in·no·va·to·ry** /-və,tôrē/ adj. [16th C.: from L. *innovat-* 'renewed, altered,' from the v. *innovare*, from *in-* 'into' + *novare* 'make new' (from *novus* 'new').]

in·no·va·tion /,inə'vāSHən/ ▶ n. the action or process of innovating. ■ a new method, idea, product, etc.: *technological innovations.* — **in·no·va·tion·al** /-SHənl/ adj.

in·no·va·tive /'inə,vātiv/ ▶ adj. (of a product, idea, etc.) featuring new methods; advanced and original. ■ (of a person) introducing new ideas; original and creative in thinking: *an innovative thinker.*

Inn Riv·er /in/ a river in western Europe that rises in eastern Switzerland and flows for 320 miles (508 km) to the Danube at Passau, Germany.

Inns·bruck /'inz,bro͝ok/ a city in western Austria, capital of Tyrol; pop. 115,000.

Inns of Court ▶ plural n. see INN OF COURT.

in·nu·en·do /,inyo͞o'endō/ ▶ n. (pl. **-does** or **-dos**) an allusive or oblique remark or hint, typically a suggestive or disparaging one: *innuendo, gossip, and half-truths.* [16th C.: L., 'by nodding at, by pointing to,' ablative gerund of *innuere*, from *in-* 'toward' + *nuere* 'to nod.']

in·nu·mer·a·ble /i'n(y)o͞omərəbəl/ ▶ adj. too many to be counted (often used hyperbolically). — **in·nu·mer·a·bil·i·ty** /i,n(y)o͞omərə'bilitē/ n. **in·nu·mer·a·bly** adv.

in·nu·mer·ate /i'n(y)o͞omərit/ ▶ adj. without a basic knowledge of mathematics and arithmetic. ▶ n. a person lacking such knowledge. — **in·nu·mer·a·cy** /-rəsē/ n.

in·ob·serv·ance /,inəb'zərvəns/ ▶ n. dated failure to observe or notice.

in·oc·u·lant /i'näkyələnt/ ▶ n. a substance suitable for inoculating.

in·oc·u·late /i'näkyə,lāt/ ▶ v. [trans.] treat (a person or animal) with a vaccine to produce immunity against a disease. Compare with VACCINATE. ■ introduce (an infective agent) into an organism: *it is inoculated into laboratory animals.* ■ introduce (cells or organisms) into a culture medium. — **in·oc·u·la·ble** /-ləbəl/ adj. **in·oc·u·la·tion** /i,näkyə'lāSHən/ n. **in·oc·u·la·tor** /-,lātər/ n. [ME: from L. *inoculat-* 'engrafted,' from the v. *inoculare*, from *in-* 'into' + *oculus* 'eye, bud.']

in·oc·u·lum /i'näkyələm/ ▶ n. (pl. **-la** /-lə/) Med. a substance used for inoculation.

in·o·dor·ous /in'ōdərəs/ ▶ adj. having no smell; odorless.

in·of·fen·sive /,inə'fensiv/ ▶ adj. not objectionable or harmful. — **in·of·fen·sive·ly** adv. **in·of·fen·sive·ness** n.

in·op·er·a·ble /in'äp(ə)rəbəl/ ▶ adj. **1** Med. not able to be suitably operated on: *inoperable cancer.* **2** not able to be operated: *the airfield was inoperable.* **3** impractical; unworkable: *the procedures were inoperable.* — **in·op·er·a·bil·i·ty** /-,äp(ə)rə'bilitē/ n. **in·op·er·a·bly** adv.

in·op·er·a·tive /in'äp(ə)rətiv/ ▶ adj. not working or taking effect: *the telescope is inoperative.*

in·op·por·tune /,inäpər't(y)o͞on/ ▶ adj. not opportune; occurring at an inconvenient time; not appropriate. — **in·op·por·tune·ly** adv.

in·or·di·nate /i'nôrdn-it/ ▶ adj. unusually or disproportionately large; excessive: *an inordinate amount of time.* — **in·or·di·nate·ly** adv. [ME: from L. *inordinatus*, from *in-* 'not' + *ordinatus* 'arranged, set in order.']

in·or·gan·ic /,inôr'ganik/ ▶ adj. not arising from natural growth. ■ Chem. of, relating to, or denoting compounds that are not organic (broadly, compounds not containing carbon). Compare with ORGANIC. ■ without organized physical structure. ■ Ling. not explainable by the normal processes of etymology. — **in·or·gan·i·cal·ly** adv.

in·os·cu·late /in'äskyə,lāt/ ▶ v. [intrans.] formal join by intertwining or fitting closely together. — **in·os·cu·la·tion** /in,äskyə'lāSHən/ n. [17th C.: from IN-[2] 'into' + L. *osculare* 'provide with a mouth or outlet.']

in·o·si·tol /i'nōsi,tôl; -,täl; ī'nō-/ ▶ n. Biochem. a simple carbohydrate, $C_6H_{12}O_6$, that occurs in animal and plant tissue and is a vitamin of the B group.

i·no·trop·ic /,ēnə'träpik; -'trō-; ,īnə-/ ▶ adj. Physiol. modifying the force or speed of contraction of muscles.

in·pa·tient /'in,pāSHənt/ ▶ n. a patient who stays in a hospital while under treatment.

in per·so·nam /,in pər'sōnəm/ ▶ adj. & adv. Law made or availing against or affecting a specific person only; imposing a personal liability. Compare with IN REM. [18th C.: L., lit. 'against a person.']

in-phase ▶ adj. of or relating to electrical signals that are in phase.

in·pour·ing /'in,pôriNG/ ▶ n. the action of pouring something in; an infusion: *inpouring of public money.*

in pro·pri·a per·so·na /,in 'prōprēə pər'sōnə/ ▶ adv. in his or her own person. [17th C.: L.]

in·put /'in,po͝ot/ ▶ n. **1** what is put in, taken in, or operated on by any process or system: *data input.* ■ a contribution of work, information, or material: *input from other members.* ■ energy supplied to a device or system; an electrical signal. ■ the action or process of putting or feeding something in. ■ the information fed into a computer or computer program. **2** Electron. a place where, or a device through which, energy or information enters a system. ▶ v. (**-put·ting** ; past and past part. **-put** or **-put·ted**) [trans.] put (data) into a computer. — **in·put·ter** /-,po͝otər/ n.

in·put/out·put (abbr.: **I/O**) ▶ adj. [attrib.] Electron. of, relating to, or for both input and output.

in·quest /'in,kwest; 'iNG-/ ▶ n. Law a judicial inquiry to ascertain the facts relating to esp. a death.

in·qui·e·tude /in'kwīə,t(y)o͞od/ ▶ n. physical or mental restlessness or disturbance.

in·qui·line /'inkwə,līn; -lin/ ▶ n. Zool. an animal exploiting the living space of another, e.g., an insect that lays its eggs in a gall produced by another. [17th C.: from L. *inquilinus* 'temporary resident,' from *in-* 'into' + *colere* 'dwell.']

in·quire /in'kwī(ə)r; iNG-/ (also esp. Brit. **en·quire**) ▶ v. [reporting verb] ask for information from someone: [with direct speech] ***"How much do you know?" he inquired of me*** | [intrans.] ***he inquired about cottages for sale.*** ■ [intrans.] (**inquire after**) ask about the health and well-being of (someone). ■ [intrans.] (**inquire for**) ask to see or speak to (someone). ■ [intrans.] (**inquire into**) investigate; look into. — **in·quir·er** n. **in·quir·ing·ly** adv. [ME *enquere* (later *inquere*), from OFr. *enquerre*, from a var. of L. *inquirere*, based on *quaerere* 'seek.']

in·quir·ing /in'kwī(ə)riNG; iNG-/ (also esp. Brit. **en·quir·ing**) ▶ adj. showing an interest in learning new things. ■ (of a look or expression) suggesting that information is sought: *an inquiring glance.* — **in·quir·ing·ly** adv.

in·quir·y /in'kwī(ə)rē; 'inkwərē; 'iNG-/ (also esp. Brit. **en·quir·y**) ▶ n. (pl. **-quir·ies**) an act of asking for information. ■ an official investigation.

in·qui·si·tion /,inkwi'ziSHən; ,iNG-/ ▶ n. **1** a period of prolonged and intensive questioning or investigation. ■ hist. a judicial or official inquiry. ■ the verdict or finding of an official inquiry. **2** (**the Inquisition**) an ecclesiastical tribunal established by Pope Gregory IX *c.*1232 for the suppression of heresy, active esp. in northern Italy and southern France and notorious for its use of torture. See also SPANISH INQUISITION. — **in·qui·si·tion·al** /-SHənl/ adj.

in·quis·i·tive /in'kwizitiv; iNG-/ ▶ adj. curious or inquiring: *cats are inquisitive.* — **in·quis·i·tive·ly** adv. **in·quis·i·tive·ness** n.

in·quis·i·tor /in'kwizitər/ ▶ n. a person making an inquiry, esp. one seen to be excessively harsh or searching. ■ hist. an officer of the Inquisition.

in·quis·i·to·ri·al /in,kwizi'tôrēəl/ ▶ adj. of or like an inquisitor. ■ offensively prying. ■ Law (of a trial or legal procedure) in which the judge has an examining or inquiring role. Compare with ACCUSATORIAL, ADVERSARIAL. — **in·quis·i·to·ri·al·ly** adv.

in re /,in 'rā/ ▶ prep. in the legal case of; with regard to. [17th C.:L., 'in the matter of.']

in rem /,in 'rem/ ▶ adj. [often postpositive] Law made or availing against or affecting a thing, and therefore other people generally; imposing a general liability. Compare with IN PERSONAM. [18th C.:L., 'against a thing.']

INRI ▶ abbr. Jesus of Nazareth, King of the Jews (a traditional representation in art of the inscription over Christ's head at the Crucifixion). [from the initials of L. *Iesus Nazarenus Rex Iudaeorum.*]

in·ro /'inrō/ ▶ n. (pl. same or **-ros**) an ornamental box with compartments for items such as seals and medicines, worn suspended from a waist sash as part of traditional Japanese dress. [17th C.: from Japanese *inrō*, from *in* 'seal' + *rō* 'basket.']

in·road /'in,rōd/ ▶ n. **1** [usu. in pl.] progress; an advance: ***make inroads in reducing spending.*** ■ an instance of something being affected, encroached on, or destroyed by something else: ***inroads made into my cash.*** **2** a hostile attack; a raid.

in·rush /'in,rəSH/ ▶ n. [in sing.] the sudden arrival or entry of something. — **in·rush·ing** adj. & n.

INS ▶ abbr. Immigration and Naturalization Service.

in·sa·lu·bri·ous /ˌinsəˈlo͞obrēəs/ ▶ adj. formal (esp. of a climate or locality) not salubrious; unhealthy. — **in·sa·lu·bri·ty** /-britē/ n.

in·sane /inˈsān/ ▶ adj. in a state of mind that prevents normal perception, behavior, or social interaction; seriously mentally ill. ■ (of an action or quality) characterized or caused by madness. ■ in a state of extreme annoyance or distraction: *the buzzing was driving me insane.* ■ (of an action or policy) extremely foolish; irrational or illogical. — **in·sane·ly** adv. [16th C.: from L. *insanus*, from *in-* 'not' + *sanus* 'healthy.']

in·san·i·tar·y /inˈsaniˌterē/ ▶ adj. so dirty or ridden with germs as to be a danger to health.

in·san·i·ty /inˈsanitē/ ▶ n. the state of being seriously mentally ill; madness. ■ extreme foolishness or irrationality.

in·sa·tia·ble /inˈsāsʜəbəl/ ▶ adj. (of an appetite or desire) impossible to satisfy: *an insatiable hunger.* — **in·sa·tia·bil·i·ty** /-ˌsāsʜəˈbilitē/ n. **in·sa·tia·bly** adv. [ME: from OFr. *insaciable* or L. *insatiabilis*, from *in-* 'not' + *satiare* 'fill, satisfy' (see SATIATE).]

in·sa·ti·ate /inˈsāsʜē-it/ ▶ adj. literary never satisfied.

in·scape /ˈinˌskāp/ ▶ n. literary the unique inner nature of a person or object as shown in a work of art, esp. a poem. [19th C. (orig. in the poetic theory of Gerard Manley Hopkins): perh. from IN-[2] 'within' + -SCAPE.]

in·scribe /inˈskrīb/ ▶ v. [trans.] (usu. **be inscribed**) **1** write or carve (words or symbols) on something, esp. as a formal or permanent record. ■ mark (an object) with characters: *inscribed with ten names.* ■ write an informal dedication to someone in or on (a book): *inscribed by the author.* **2** Geom. draw (a figure) within another so that their boundaries touch but do not intersect. Compare with CIRCUMSCRIBE. — **in·scrib·a·ble** adj. **in·scrib·er** n. [ME: from L. *inscribere*, from *in-* 'into' + *scribere* 'write.']

in·scrip·tion /inˈskripsʜən/ ▶ n. words inscribed, as on a monument or in a book. ■ the action of inscribing something. — **in·scrip·tion·al** /-sʜənl/ adj. **in·scrip·tive** /-ˈskriptiv/ adj.

in·scru·ta·ble /inˈskro͞otəbəl/ ▶ adj. impossible to understand or interpret; impenetrable; mysterious. — **in·scru·ta·bil·i·ty** /-ˌskro͞otəˈbilitē/ n. **in·scru·ta·bly** adv. [ME: from eccles. L. *inscrutabilis*, from *in-* 'not' + *scrutari* 'to search' (see SCRUTINY).]

in·seam /ˈinˌsēm/ ▶ n. the seam in a pair of pants from the crotch to the bottom of the leg, or the length of this.

in·sect /ˈinˌsekt/ ▶ n. a small arthropod animal that has six legs and generally one or two pairs of wings. ■ informal any small invertebrate animal, esp. one with several pairs of legs. [17th C.: from L. *(animal) insectum* 'segmented (animal)' (translating Gk. *zōion entomon*), from *insecare* 'cut up or into,' from *in-* 'into' + *secare* 'to cut.']

in·sec·tar·i·um /ˌinsekˈte(ə)rēəm/ (also **in·sec·tar·y** /ˈinsekˌterē; inˈsektə-/) ▶ n. (pl. **in·sec·tar·i·ums** also **in·sec·tar·ies** /ˈinsekˌterēz/) a place where insects are kept, exhibited, and studied.

in·sec·ti·cide /inˈsektiˌsīd/ ▶ n. a substance used for killing insects. — **in·sec·ti·cid·al** /-ˌsektiˈsīdl/ adj.

in·sec·tile /inˈsektl; -ˌtīl/ ▶ adj. resembling or reminiscent of an insect or insects.

in·sec·ti·vore /inˈsektəˌvôr/ ▶ n. an insectivorous animal or plant. ■ Zool. a mammal of the order Insectivora, including the shrews, moles, hedgehogs, tenrecs, and solenodons.

in·sec·tiv·o·rous /ˌinsekˈtivərəs/ ▶ adj. (of an animal) feeding on insects, worms, and other invertebrates. ■ (of a plant such as the Venus flytrap) able to capture and digest insects.

in·se·cure /ˌinsiˈkyo͝or/ ▶ adj. **1** (of a person) not confident or assured; uncertain or anxious. **2** (of a thing) not firm or set; unsafe. ■ (of a job or position) from which removal or expulsion is always possible. ■ not firmly fixed; liable to give way or break: *an insecure bridge.* ■ able to be broken into or illicitly accessed: *insecure windows.* — **in·se·cure·ly** adv. **in·se·cu·ri·ty** n.

in·sel·berg /ˈinsəlˌbərg/ ▶ n. Geol. an isolated hill or mountain rising abruptly from a plain. [20th C.: from Ger., from *Insel* 'island' + *Berg* 'mountain.']

in·sem·i·nate /inˈseməˌnāt/ ▶ v. [trans.] (often **be inseminated**) introduce semen into (a woman or a female animal) by natural or artificial means. — **in·sem·i·na·tion** /-ˌseməˈnāsʜən/ n. **in·sem·i·na·tor** n. [17th C.: from L. *inseminat-* 'sown,' from the v. *inseminare*, from *in-* 'into' + *seminare* 'plant, sow' (from *semen, semin-* 'seed, semen').]

in·sen·sate /inˈsensāt; -sit/ ▶ adj. lacking physical sensation. ■ lacking sympathy or compassion; unfeeling. ■ completely lacking sense or reason. — **in·sen·sate·ly** adv. [15th C.: from L. *insensatus*, from *in-* 'not' + *sensatus* 'having senses' (see SENSATE).]

in·sen·si·ble /inˈsensəbəl/ ▶ adj. **1** [usu. as complement] without one's mental faculties, typically as a result of violence or intoxication; unconscious: *insensible with drink.* ■ (esp. of a body or bodily extremity) numb; without feeling: *the insensible tip of the beak.* **2** [predic.] (**insensible of/to**) unaware of; indifferent to: *insensible of the problem.* ■ without emotion; callous. **3** too small or gradual to be perceived; inappreciable: *insensible degrees.* — **in·sen·si·bil·i·ty** n. **in·sen·si·bly** adv.

in·sen·si·tive /inˈsensitiv/ ▶ adj. showing or feeling no concern for others' feelings. ■ not sensitive to a physical sensation: *insensitive to pain.* — **in·sen·si·tive·ly** adv. **in·sen·si·tive·ness** n. **in·sen·si·tiv·i·ty** /-ˌsensiˈtivitē/ n.

in·sen·ti·ent /inˈsensʜ(ē)ənt/ ▶ adj. incapable of feeling or understanding things; inanimate. — **in·sen·ti·ence** n.

in·sep·a·ra·ble /inˈsep(ə)rəbəl/ ▶ adj. unable to be separated or treated separately. ■ (of one or more people) unwilling to be separated; usually seen together. ■ Gram. (of a prefix) not used as a separate word or (in German) not separated from the base verb when inflected. ▶ n. a person or thing inseparable from another. — **in·sep·a·ra·bil·i·ty** /-ˌsep(ə)rəˈbilitē/ n. **in·sep·a·ra·bly** adv.

in·sert ▶ v. /inˈsərt/ [trans.] place, fit, or thrust (something) into another thing, esp. with care: *inserted the key in the lock.* ■ add (text) to a piece of writing: *insert a clause.* ■ place (a spacecraft or satellite) into an orbit or trajectory. ■ (usu. **be inserted**) Biol. incorporate (a piece of genetic material) into a chromosome. ▶ n. /ˈinˌsərt/ a thing that has been inserted, esp. a loose page or section, typically one carrying an advertisement, in a magazine or other publication. — **in·sert·a·ble** adj. **in·sert·er** n. [15th C.: from L. *insert-* 'put in,' from the v. *inserere*, from *in-* 'into' + *serere* 'to join.']

in·ser·tion /inˈsərsʜən/ ▶ n. **1** the action of inserting something. ■ the placing of a spacecraft or satellite into an orbit or trajectory. **2** a thing that is inserted, in particular: ■ an amendment or addition inserted in a text. ■ each appearance of an advertisement in a newspaper or periodical. **3** Anat. Zool. the manner or place of attachment of an organ. ■ the manner or place of attachment of a muscle to the part that it moves: *muscles and their insertions on the eyeball.*

in-serv·ice ▶ adj. (of training) intended for those actively engaged in the profession or activity concerned.

in·set ▶ n. /ˈinˌset/ a thing that is put in or inserted: *stained-glass insets.* ■ a small picture or map inserted within the border of a larger one. ■ a section of fabric or needlework inserted into the material of a garment. ▶ v. /inˈset/ (**in·set·ting** ; past and past part. **in·set** or **in·set·ted**) (usu. **be inset**) put in (something, esp. a small picture or map) as an inset. — **in·set·ter** n.

in·shal·lah /inˈsʜälə/ ▶ exclam. if Allah wills it. [from Arab. *in š ā Allāh.*]

in·shore /ˈinˈsʜôr/ ▶ adj. at sea but close to the shore. ▶ adv. toward or closer to the shore.

in·side ▶ n. /ˈinˈsīd/ **1** [usu. in sing.] the inner side or surface of a thing. ■ the side of a bend or curve where the edge or surface is shorter. ■ the side of a racetrack nearer to the center, where the lanes are shorter. ■ (in basketball) taking place within the perimeter of the defense: *inside shots.* **2** the inner part; the interior. ■ (usu. **insides**) informal the stomach and bowels. **3** (**the inside**) informal a position affording private information: *my spy on the inside.* ▶ adj. [attrib.] situated on or in, or derived from, the inside: *an inside pocket.* ■ (in some team sports) denoting positions nearer to the center of the field. ■ Baseball (of a pitch) passing between the batter and the strike zone. ▶ prep. & adv. **1** situated within the confines of (something). ■ moving so as to end up within (something): [as prep.] *he reached inside his shirt* | [as adv.] *we walked inside.* ■ [adv.] indoors. ■ within (the body or mind of a person), typically with reference to sensations of self-awareness: *inside my head.* ■ informal in prison: *three years inside.* ■ Baseball (of a pitch) close to the batter. ■ (in basketball, soccer, and other sports) closer to the center of the field than (another player). **2** [prep.] in less than (the period of time specified): *inside 18 months.*

– PHRASES **inside of** informal within: *something inside of me.* ■ in less than (the period of time specified): *inside of a week.*

in·side job ▶ n. informal a crime committed by or with the assistance of a person living or working on the premises where it occurred.

in·side out ▶ adv. with the inner surface turned outward. ▶ adj. in such a condition: *inside-out clothes.*

– PHRASES **know something inside out** know something very thoroughly. **turn something inside out** turn the inner surface of something outward. ■ change something utterly: *turn your life inside out.*

In·side Passage a natural, protected coastal water route stretching from Seattle, Washington to Skagway, Alaska.

in·sid·er /inˈsīdər/ ▶ n. a person within a group or organization, esp. someone privy to information unavailable to others: *political insiders.*

in·sid·er trad·ing ▶ n. the illegal practice of trading on the stock exchange to one's own advantage through having access to confidential information.

in·side track ▶ n. the inner, shorter track of a racecourse. ■ fig. a position of advantage.

in·sid·i·ous /inˈsidēəs/ ▶ adj. proceeding in a gradual, subtle way, but with harmful effects: *the insidious effects of stress.* ■ treacherous; crafty: *an insidious alliance.* — **in·sid·i·ous·ly** adv. **in·sid·i·ous·ness** n. [16th C.: from L. *insidiosus* 'cunning,' from *insidiae* 'an ambush or trick,' from *insidere* 'lie in wait for,' from *in-* 'on' + *sedere* 'sit.']

in·sight /ˈinˌsīt/ ▶ n. the capacity to gain an accurate and deep intuitive understanding of a person or thing. ■ an understanding of this kind: *new insights into the behavior of whales.* — **in·sight·ful** /inˈsītfəl/ adj. **in·sight·ful·ly** /inˈsītfəlē/ adv.

in·sig·ni·a /inˈsignēə/ ▶ n. (pl. same or **-ni·as**) a badge or distinguishing mark of military rank, office, or membership of an organization; an official emblem. [17th C.: from L., pl. of *insigne* 'sign, badge of office,' neut. of *insignis* 'distinguished (as if by a mark),' from *in-* 'toward' + *signum* 'sign.']

in·sig·nif·i·cant /ˌinsigˈnifikənt/ ▶ adj. too small or unimportant to be worth consideration. ■ (of a person) without power or influence.

■ meaningless: *insignificant phrases.* — **in·sig·nif·i·cance** n. **in·sig·nif·i·can·cy** n. **in·sig·nif·i·cant·ly** adv.

in·sin·cere /ˌinsinˈsi(ə)r/ ▶ adj. not expressing genuine feelings: *an insincere smile.* — **in·sin·cere·ly** adv. **in·sin·cer·i·ty** /-ˈseritē/ n. (pl. **-ties**).

in·sin·u·ate /inˈsinyo͞oˌāt/ ▶ v. [trans.] **1** suggest or hint (something negative) in an indirect and unpleasant way. **2** (**insinuate oneself into**) maneuver oneself into (a position of favor or office) by subtle manipulation: *she insinuated herself into management.* — **in·sin·u·at·ing·ly** adv. **in·sin·u·a·tor** /-ˌātər/ n. [16th C.: from L. *insinuat-* 'introduced tortuously,' from the v. *insinuare,* from *in-* 'in' + *sinuare* 'to curve.']

in·sin·u·a·tion /inˌsinyo͞oˈāsʜən/ ▶ n. an unpleasant hint or suggestion of something bad.

in·sip·id /inˈsipid/ ▶ adj. lacking flavor: *insipid coffee.* ■ lacking vigor or interest: *insipid, shallow books.* — **in·si·pid·i·ty** /ˌinsəˈpiditē/ n. **in·sip·id·ly** adv. **in·sip·id·ness** n. [17th C.: from Fr. *insipide* or late L. *insipidus,* from *in-* 'not' + *sapidus* (see **SAPID**).]

in·sist /inˈsist/ ▶ v. [intrans.] demand something forcefully, not accepting refusal. ■ (**insist on**) demand forcefully to have or do something: *she insisted on answers | boots he insisted on wearing.* [16th C. (in the sense 'persist, persevere'): from L. *insistere* 'persist,' from *in-* 'upon' + *sistere* 'stand.']

in·sist·ence /inˈsistəns/ ▶ n. the fact or quality of insisting that something is the case or should be done. — **in·sis·ten·cy** n.

in·sist·ent /inˈsistənt/ ▶ adj. insisting or demanding something; not allowing refusal: *insistent questioning.* ■ regular and repeated, and demanding attention: *a loud and insistent ringing.* — **in·sis·tent·ly** adv.

in si·tu /ˌin ˈsīto͞o; ˈsē-/ ▶ adv. & adj. in its original place; in position: [as adv.] *frescoes have been left in situ.* [18th C.: L.]

in·so·bri·e·ty /ˌinsəˈbrī-itē/ ▶ n. drunkenness.

in·so·far /ˌinsōˈfär/ (also **in so far**) ▶ adv. (**insofar as**) to the extent that.

in·so·la·tion /ˌinsōˈlāsʜən/ ▶ n. tech. exposure to the sun's rays. ■ the amount of solar radiation reaching a given area. [17th C.: from L. *insolatio(n-),* from the v. *insolare,* from *in-* 'toward' + *sol* 'sun.']

in·sole /ˈinˌsōl/ ▶ n. a removable sole worn in a shoe for warmth, as a deodorizer, or to improve the fit. ■ the fixed inner sole of a boot or shoe.

in·so·lent /ˈinsələnt/ ▶ adj. showing a rude or arrogant lack of respect. — **in·so·lence** n. **in·so·lent·ly** adv. [ME: from L. *insolent-* 'immoderate, unaccustomed, arrogant,' from *in-* 'not' + *solent-* 'being accustomed' (from the v. *solere*).]

in·sol·u·ble /inˈsälyəbəl/ ▶ adj. **1** impossible to solve: *insoluble problems.* **2** (of a substance) incapable of being dissolved: *insoluble fibers.* — **in·sol·u·bil·i·ty** /-ˌsälyəˈbilitē/ n. **in·sol·u·bly** adv.

in·solv·a·ble /inˈsälvəbəl/ ▶ adj. rare term for **INSOLUBLE**.

in·sol·vent /inˈsälvənt/ ▶ adj. unable to pay debts: *an insolvent company.* ■ relating to insolvency: *insolvent liquidation.* ▶ n. an insolvent person. — **in·sol·ven·cy** n.

in·som·ni·a /inˈsämnēə/ ▶ n. habitual sleeplessness; inability to sleep. — **in·som·ni·ac** /-nēˌak/ n. & adj. [17th C.: from L., from *insomnis* 'sleepless,' from *in-* + *somnus* 'sleep.']

in·so·much /ˌinsōˈməcʜ/ ▶ adv. **1** (**insomuch that**) to such an extent that. **2** (**insomuch as**) inasmuch as.

in·sou·ci·ance /inˈso͞osēəns; ˌaɴso͞oˈsyäɴs/ ▶ n. casual lack of concern; indifference. — **in·sou·ci·ant** adj. **in·sou·ci·ant·ly** adv. [18th C.: Fr., from *insouciant,* from *in-* 'not' + *souciant* 'worrying.']

in·spect /inˈspekt/ ▶ v. [trans.] look at closely, typically to assess the condition of or to discover any shortcomings: *inspecting my paintwork.* ■ examine (someone or something) to ensure that they reach an official standard: *inspect our documents.* — **in·spec·tion** n. [17th C.: from L. *inspect-* 'looked into, examined,' from the v. *inspicere* (from *in-* 'in' + *specere* 'look at'), or from its frequentative, *inspectare.*]

in·spec·tor /inˈspektər/ ▶ n. **1** an official employed to ensure that official regulations are obeyed, esp. in public services. **2** a police officer ranking below a superintendent or police chief. — **in·spec·to·ri·al** /ˌinspekˈtôrēəl/ adj. **in·spec·tor·ship** n.

in·spec·tor·ate /inˈspektərit/ ▶ n. a body that ensures that the official regulations applying to a particular type of institution or activity are obeyed.

in·spec·tor gen·er·al (abbr.: **IG**) ▶ n. (pl. **in·spec·tors gen·er·al**) an official in charge of inspecting a particular institution or activity. ■ Mil. a staff officer responsible for conducting inspections and investigations.

in·spi·ra·tion /ˌinspəˈrāsʜən/ ▶ n. **1** the process of being mentally stimulated to do or feel something, esp. to do something creative: *flashes of inspiration.* ■ the quality of having been so stimulated, esp. when evident in something: *a moment of inspiration in an otherwise dull display.* ■ a person or thing that stimulates in this way: *an inspiration to everyone.* ■ a sudden brilliant, creative, or timely idea: *I had an inspiration.* **2** the drawing in of breath; inhalation. ■ an act of breathing in; an inhalation.

in·spi·ra·tion·al /ˌinspəˈrāsʜənl/ ▶ adj. providing or showing creative or spiritual inspiration.

in·spir·a·to·ry /inˈspīrəˌtôrē/ ▶ adj. Physiol. relating to the act of breathing in.

in·spire /inˈspī(ə)r/ ▶ v. [trans.] **1** fill (someone) with the urge or ability to do or feel something, esp. to do something creative: *his enthusiasm inspired them.* ■ create (a feeling, esp. a positive one) in a person: *inspire confidence.* ■ (**inspire someone with**) animate someone with (such a feeling): *he inspired his students with his vision.* **2** breathe in (air); inhale. — **in·spir·er** n. **in·spir·ing·ly** adv. [ME *enspire,* from OFr. *inspirer,* from L. *inspirare* 'breathe or blow into,' from *in-* 'into' + *spirare* 'breathe.']

in·spired /inˈspī(ə)rd/ ▶ adj. **1** of extraordinary quality, as if arising from some external creative impulse. ■ (of a person) exhibiting such a creative impulse in the activity specified: *an inspired gardener.* **2** (of air or another substance) that is breathed in. — **in·spir·ed·ly** adv.

in·spir·it /inˈspirit/ ▶ v. (**-spir·it·ed, -spir·it·ing**) [trans.] [usu. as adj.] (**inspiriting**) encourage and enliven (someone). — **in·spir·it·ing·ly** adv.

in·spis·sate /ˈinspiˌsāt; inˈspisāt/ ▶ v. [trans.] [usu. as adj.] (**inspissated**) thicken or congeal. — **in·spis·sa·tion** /ˌinspiˈsāsʜən/ n. [17th C.: from late L. *inspissat-* 'made thick,' from the v. *inspissare.*]

inst. ▶ abbr. ■ dated (in business letters) instant: *your letter of 14 inst.* ■ institute; institution.

in·sta·bil·i·ty /ˌinstəˈbilitē/ ▶ n. (pl. **-ties**) lack of stability; the state of being unstable: *economic instability.* ■ tendency to unpredictable behavior or erratic changes of mood: *mental instability.*

in·stall /inˈstôl/ ▶ v. [trans.] **1** place or fix (equipment or machinery) in position ready for use: *install a new shower.* **2** place (someone) in a new position of authority, esp. with ceremony: *he was installed as music director.* — **in·stall·er** n. [ME (sense 2): from med. L. *installare,* from *in-* 'into' + *stallum* 'place, stall.' Sense 1 dates from the 19th C.]

in·stal·la·tion /ˌinstəˈlāsʜən/ ▶ n. **1** the action or process of installing someone or something, or of being installed. **2** a thing installed, in particular: ■ a large piece of equipment installed for use: *computer installations.* ■ a military or industrial establishment: *nuclear installations.* ■ an art exhibit constructed within a gallery.

in·stall·ment /inˈstôlmənt/ ▶ n. **1** a sum of money due as one of several equal payments for something, spread over an agreed period of time: *paid in installments.* **2** any of several parts of something that are published, broadcast, or made public in sequence at intervals. **3** the process of installing something; installation.

in·stance /ˈinstəns/ ▶ n. **1** an example or single occurrence of something: *an instance of corruption.* ■ a particular case: *in this instance.* **2** Law, rare the institution of a legal suit.

– PHRASES **at the instance of** formal at the request or suggestion of: *at the instance of the police.* **for instance** as an example: *take Canada, for instance.* [ME: via OFr. from L. *instantia* 'presence, urgency,' from *instare* 'be present, press upon,' from *in-* 'upon' + *stare* 'to stand.']

in·stan·cy /ˈinstənsē/ ▶ n. archaic urgency.

in·stant /ˈinstənt/ ▶ adj. **1** happening or coming immediately: *instant dismissal.* ■ (of food) processed to allow quick preparation: *instant coffee.* ■ (of a person) becoming a specified thing immediately or very suddenly: *instant millionaire.* ■ prepared quickly and with little effort: *instant solutions.* ■ producing immediate results: *an instant lottery ticket.* **2** urgent; pressing: *an instant desire to blame.* **3** [postpositive] dated (in business letters) of the current month: *your letter of the 6th instant.* ▶ n. **1** a precise moment of time: *come here this instant!* **2** a very short space of time; a moment: *for an instant.* [ME: via OFr. from L. *instant-* 'being at hand,' from the v. *instare,* from *in-* 'in, at' + *stare* 'to stand.']

in·stan·ta·ne·ous /ˌinstənˈtānēəs/ ▶ adj. **1** occurring or done in an instant or instantly. ■ operating or providing something instantly: *instantaneous communication.* **2** Physics existing or measured at a particular instant: — **in·stan·ta·ne·i·ty** /inˌstantnˈē-itē/ n. **in·stan·ta·ne·ous·ly** adv. **in·stan·ta·ne·ous·ness** n.

in·stan·ter /inˈstantər/ ▶ adv. archaic humorous at once; immediately: *we sealed the bargain instanter.* [17th C.: L.]

in·stan·ti·ate /inˈstancʜēˌāt/ ▶ v. [trans.] represent by an instance; provide an actual example. — **in·stan·ti·a·tion** /-ˌstancʜēˈāsʜən/ n.

in·stant·ly /ˈinstəntlē/ ▶ adv. **1** at once; immediately. **2** archaic urgently or persistently.

in·stant mes·sag·ing (abbr.: **IM**) ▶ n. Computing the exchange of typed messages between computer users in real time via the Internet. — **in·stant mes·sage** n.

in·stant re·play ▶ n. an immediate playback of part of a television broadcast, typically one in slow motion showing an incident in a sports event.

in·star /ˈinˌstär/ ▶ n. Zool. a phase between two periods of molting in the development of an insect larva or other invertebrate animal. [19th C.: from L., lit. 'form, likeness.']

in·state /inˈstāt/ ▶ v. [trans.] (usu. **be instated**) set up in position; install or establish. [17th C. (formerly also as *enstate*): from **EN-**[1], **IN-**[2] 'into' + the n. **STATE**.]

in·stau·ra·tion /ˌinstôˈrāsʜən/ ▶ n. formal the action of restoring or renewing something. — **in·stau·ra·tor** /ˈinstəˌrātər/ n. [17th C.: from L. *instauratio(n-),* from *instaurare* 'renew,' from *in-* 'in, toward' + *staur-* (a stem also found in *restaurare* 'restore').]

in·stead /inˈsted/ ▶ adv. as an alternative or substitute: *she never married, instead remained single.* ■ (**instead of**) as a substitute or alternative to; in place of: *walk instead of drive.*

in·step /ˈinˌstep/ ▶ n. the part of a person's foot between the ball and the ankle. ■ the part of a shoe that fits over or under this part of a foot. ■ a thing shaped like the inner arch of a foot.

in·sti·gate /ˈinstiˌgāt/ ▶ v. [trans.] bring about or initiate (an action or event): *instigating legal proceedings.* ■ (**instigate someone to do something**) incite someone to do something, esp. something bad. — **in·sti·ga·tion** n. **in·sti·ga·tor** /-ˌgātər/ n. [16th C. (in the sense 'urge on'): from L. *instigat-* 'urged, incited,' from the v. *instigare*, from *in-* 'toward' + *stigare* 'prick, incite.']

in·still /in'stil/ ▶v. [trans.] **1** gradually but firmly establish (an idea or attitude, esp. a desirable one) in a person's mind: *instill values.* **2** put (a substance) into something in the form of liquid drops: *instill eye drops.* — **in·stil·la·tion** /ˌinstə'lāsʜən/ n. **in·still·ment** n. [ME (sense 2): from L. *instillare*, from *in-* 'into' + *stillare* 'to drop' (from *stilla* 'a drop').]

in·stinct ▶n. /'instiɴɢkt/ an innate, typically fixed pattern of behavior in animals in response to certain stimuli: *predatory instincts.* ■ a natural or intuitive way of acting or thinking: *rely on your instincts.* ■ a natural propensity or skill of a specified kind: *his instinct for making the most of it.* — **in·stinc·tu·al** /in'stiɴɢkcʜōōəl/ adj. **in·stinc·tu·al·ly** /ins'tiɴɢkcʜōōəlē/ adv. [ME: from L. *instinctus* 'impulse,' from the v. *instinguere*, from *in-* 'toward' + *stinguere* 'to prick.']

in·stinc·tive /in'stiɴɢ(k)tiv/ ▶adj. relating to or prompted by instinct; apparently unconscious or automatic: *an instinctive distaste for conflict.* ■ (of a person) doing or being a specified thing apparently naturally or automatically: *an instinctive writer.* — **in·stinc·tive·ly** adv.

in·sti·tute /'instiˌt(y)ōōt/ ▶n. [usu. in names] **1** a society or organization having a particular object or common factor, esp. a scientific, educational, or social one. **2** (usu. **institutes**) archaic a commentary, treatise, or summary of principles, esp. concerning law. ▶v. [trans.] **1** set in motion or establish (something, esp. a program, system, or inquiry): *the award was instituted in 1900.* ■ begin (legal proceedings) in a court. **2** (often **be instituted**) appoint (someone) to a position, esp. as a cleric. [ME (sense 2 of the **verb**): from Latin *institut-* 'established,' from the v. *instituere*, from *in-* 'in, toward' + *statuere* 'set up.' The n. is from L. *institutum* 'something designed, precept.']

in·sti·tu·tion /ˌinsti't(y)ōōsʜən/ ▶n. **1** a society or organization founded for a religious, educational, social, or similar purpose. ■ an organization providing residential care for people with special needs. ■ an established official organization having an important role in the life of a country, such as a bank, church, or legislature: *the institutions of government.* **2** an established law, practice, or custom: *the institution of marriage.* ■ informal a well-established and familiar person, custom, or object: *he's a national institution.* **3** the action of instituting something.

in·sti·tu·tion·al /ˌinsti't(y)ōōsʜənl/ ▶adj. of, in, or like an institution or institutions: *institutional care.* ■ unappealing or unimaginative; drab: *institutional decor.* ■ (of advertising) intended to create prestige rather than immediate sales. — **in·sti·tu·tion·al·ism** n. **in·sti·tu·tion·al·ly** adv.

in·sti·tu·tion·al·ize /ˌinsti't(y)ōōsʜənlˌīz/ ▶v. [trans.] **1** establish (something, typically a practice or activity) as a convention or norm in an organization or culture: *a system that institutionalizes bad behavior.* **2** (usu. **be institutionalized**) place or keep (someone) in a residential institution. ■ (**institutionalized**) (of a person, esp. a long-term patient or prisoner) made apathetic and dependent after a long period in an institution. — **in·sti·tu·tion·al·i·za·tion** /ˌinstiˌt(y)ōōsʜənl-i'zāsʜən/ n.

instr. ▶abbr. ■ instructor. ■ instrument or instrumental.

in·struct /in'strəkt/ ▶v. **1** [reporting verb] direct or command someone to do something, esp. as an official order: [trans.] *she instructed him to wait.* **2** [trans.] teach (someone) a subject or skill. **3** [trans.] Law give a person direction, information, or authorization, in particular: ■ (of a judge) give information, esp. clarification of legal principles, to (a jury). ■ inform (someone) of a fact or situation. [ME (sense 2): from L. *instruct-* 'constructed, equipped, taught,' from the v. *instruere*, from *in-* 'upon, toward' + *struere* 'pile up.']

in·struc·tion /in'strəksʜən/ ▶n. **1** (often **instructions**) a direction or order: *he issued instructions to the sheriff.* ■ (**instructions**) Law directions to a lawyer or to a jury. ■ Comput. a code or sequence in a computer program that defines an operation and puts it into effect. **2** (**instructions**) detailed information telling how something should be done, operated, or assembled: *follow the instructions.* **3** teaching; education: *personalized instruction.* — **in·struc·tion·al** /-sʜənl/ adj.

in·struc·tive /in'strəktiv/ ▶adj. useful and informative. — **in·struc·tive·ly** adv. **in·struc·tive·ness** n.

in·struc·tor /in'strəktər/ ▶n. a person who teaches something. ■ a college teacher ranking below assistant professor. — **in·struc·tor·ship** n.

in·stru·ment /'instrəmənt/ ▶n. **1** a tool or implement, esp. one for delicate or scientific work. ■ a thing used in pursuing an aim or policy; a means: *an instrument of learning.* **2** a measuring device used to gauge the level, speed, etc., of something, esp. a motor vehicle or aircraft. **3** (also **musical instrument**) an object or device for producing musical sounds. **4** a formal document, esp. a legal one. ▶v. [trans.] equip (something) with measuring instruments. [ME: from OFr., or from L. *instrumentum* 'equipment, implement,' from the v. *instruere* 'construct, equip.']

in·stru·men·tal /ˌinstrə'mentl/ ▶adj. **1** serving as an instrument or means in pursuing an aim or policy: *instrumental in bringing about legislation.* **2** (of music) performed on instruments, not sung. **3** of or relating to an implement or measuring device. **4** Gram. denoting or relating to a case of nouns and pronouns (and words in grammatical agreement with them) indicating a means or instrument. ▶n. **1** a piece of (usually nonclassical) music performed solely by instruments, with no vocals. **2** (**the instrumental**) Gram. the instrumental case. ■ a noun in the instrumental case. — **in·stru·men·tal·ly** adv.

in·stru·ment·tal·ism /ˌinstrə'mentlˌizəm/ ▶n. a pragmatic philosophical approach that regards an activity (such as science, law, or education) chiefly as an instrument or tool for some practical purpose, rather than in more absolute or ideal terms.

in·stru·men·tal·ist /ˌinstrə'mentl-ist/ ▶n. **1** a player of a musical instrument. **2** an adherent of instrumentalism. ▶adj. of or in terms of instrumentalism.

in·stru·men·tal·i·ty /ˌinstrəmən'talitē; -men-/ ▶n. (pl. **-ties**) the fact or quality of serving as an instrument or means to an end.

in·stru·men·ta·tion /ˌinstrəmən'tāsʜən; -men-/ ▶n. **1** the particular instruments used in a piece of music; the manner in which a piece is arranged for instruments. ■ the arrangement or composition of a piece of music for particular musical instruments. **2** measuring instruments regarded collectively. ■ the design, provision, or use of measuring instruments.

in·stru·ment pan·el (also **instrument board**) ▶n. a surface in front of a driver's or pilot's seat, on which the vehicle's or aircraft's instruments are situated.

in·sub·or·di·nate /ˌinsə'bôrdn-it/ ▶adj. defiant of authority; disobedient. — **in·sub·or·di·nate·ly** adv. **in·sub·or·di·na·tion** /-ˌbôrdn'āsʜən/ n.

in·sub·stan·tial /ˌinsəb'stancʜəl/ ▶adj. lacking strength and solidity: *insubstantial evidence.* ■ not solid or real; imaginary. — **in·sub·stan·ti·al·i·ty** /-ˌstancʜē'alitē/ n. **in·sub·stan·tial·ly** adv.

in·suf·fer·a·ble /in'səf(ə)rəbəl/ ▶adj. too extreme to bear; intolerable. ■ having or showing unbearable arrogance or conceit. — **in·suf·fer·a·ble·ness** n. **in·suf·fer·a·bly** adv.

in·suf·fi·cien·cy /ˌinsə'fisʜənsē/ ▶n. the condition of being insufficient. ■ Med. the inability of an organ to perform its normal function: *renal insufficiency.*

in·suf·fi·cient /ˌinsə'fisʜənt/ ▶adj. not enough; inadequate: *insufficient evidence.* — **in·suf·fi·cient·ly** adv. [ME: via OFr. from late L. *insufficient-* 'not sufficing,' from *in-* 'not' + L. *sufficere* (see **SUFFICE**).]

in·suf·flate /'insəˌflāt/ ▶v. [trans.] **1** Med. blow (air, gas, or powder) into a cavity of the body. ■ blow something into (a part of the body) in this way. **2** Theol. blow or breathe on (someone) to symbolize spiritual influence. — **in·suf·fla·tion** /ˌinsə'flāsʜən/ n. **in·suf·fla·tor** n. [17th C.: from late L. *insufflat-* 'blown into,' from *insufflare*, from *in-* 'into' + *sufflare* 'blow.']

in·su·la /'ins(y)ələ/ ▶n. (pl. **-lae** /-ˌlē/) Anat. a region of the brain deep in the cerebral cortex. [19th C.: L., lit. 'island.']

in·su·lant /'ins(y)ələnt/ ▶n. an insulating material.

in·su·lar /'ins(y)ələr/ ▶adj. **1** ignorant of or uninterested in cultures, ideas, or peoples outside one's own experience. ■ lacking contact with other people. **2** of, relating to, or from an island. ■ (of climate) equable because of the influence of the sea. **3** Anat. of or relating to the insula of the brain. — **in·su·lar·i·ty** /ˌins(y)ə'laritē; -'le(ə)r-/ n. **in·su·lar·ly** adv. [16th C. (as a n. denoting an islander): from late L. *insularis*, from *insula* 'island.']

in·su·late /'ins(y)əˌlāt/ ▶v. [trans.] (often **be insulated**) protect (something) by interposing material that prevents the loss of heat or the intrusion of sound. ■ prevent the passage of electricity to or from (something) by covering it in nonconducting material. ■ fig. protect from the unpleasant effects or elements of something: *insulated from outside pressures.* [16th C.: from L. *insula* 'island' + **-ATE**[3].]

in·su·la·tion /ˌins(y)ə'lāsʜən/ ▶n. the action of insulating something or someone. ■ the state of being insulated. ■ material used to insulate something, esp. a building.

in·su·la·tor /'ins(y)əˌlātər/ ▶n. a thing or substance used for insulation, in particular: ■ a substance that does not readily allow the passage of heat or sound. ■ a substance or device that does not readily conduct electricity. ■ a block of material, typically glass or ceramic, enclosing a wire carrying an electric current where it crosses a support.

in·su·lin /'insələn/ ▶n. Biochem. a hormone produced in the pancreas by the islets of Langerhans that regulates the amount of glucose in the blood. The lack of insulin causes a form of diabetes. ■ an animal-derived or synthetic form of this substance used to treat diabetes. [20th C.: from L. *insula* 'island' + **-IN**[1].]

in·su·lin shock ▶n. Med. an acute physiological condition resulting from excess insulin in the blood, involving low blood sugar, weakness, convulsions, and sometimes coma.

in·sult ▶v. /in'səlt/ [trans.] speak to or treat with disrespect or scornful abuse. ▶n. /'inˌsəlt/ **1** a disrespectful or scornfully abusive remark or action. ■ a thing so worthless or contemptible as to be offensive: *the offer is an insult.* **2** Med. an event or occurrence that causes damage to a tissue or organ: *a tissue insult.*

– PHRASES **add insult to injury** act in a way that makes a bad situation worse. — **in·sult·er** n. **in·sult·ing·ly** adv. [16th C. (as a v. in the sense 'exult, act arrogantly'): from L. *insultare* 'jump or trample on.']

in·su·per·a·ble /in'sōōp(ə)rəbəl/ ▶adj. (of a difficulty or obstacle) impossible to overcome. — **in·su·per·a·bil·i·ty** /-ˌsōōp(ə)rə'bilitē/ n. **in·su·per·a·bly** adv. [ME from OFr., or from L. *insuperabilis*, from *in-* 'not' + *superabilis* (from *superare* 'overcome').]

in·sup·port·a·ble /ˌinsə'pôrtəbəl/ ▶adj. unable to be supported or justified. — **in·sup·port·a·bly** /-blē/ adv.

in·sur·ance /in'sʜŏŏrəns/ ▶n. **1** a practice by which a company provides a guarantee of compensation for specified loss, damage, illness, or death in return for payment of a premium. ■ the business of providing such an arrangement. ■ money paid for this: *my insurance has gone up.* ■ money paid out as compensation under such an arrangement: *collect the insurance.* **2** a thing providing protection against a possible eventuality: *snow tires provide* ***insurance against*** *bad weather.* [ME (orig. as *ensurance* in the sense 'ensuring, assurance, a guarantee'): from OFr. *enseurance,* from *enseurer* (see ENSURE).]

in·sure /in'shoor/ ▶v. [trans.] arrange for compensation in the event of damage to or loss of (property), or injury to or the death of (someone), in exchange for regular advance payments to a company: *the car is* ***insured for*** *loss or damage.* ■ provide insurance coverage. ■ (**insure someone against**) fig. secure or protect someone against (a possible contingency): *they insured themselves against violence.* —**in·sur·a·bil·i·ty** /-,shoorə'bilitē/ n. **in·sur·a·ble** adj. [ME (in the sense 'assure someone of something'): alt. of ENSURE.]

in·sured /in'shoord/ ▶adj. covered by insurance. ▶n. (**the insured**) (pl. same) a person or organization covered by insurance.

in·sur·er /in'shoorər/ ▶n. a person or company that underwrites an insurance risk; the party in an insurance contract undertaking to pay compensation.

in·sur·gent /in'sərjənt/ ▶adj. [attrib.] rising in active revolt: *armed insurgent groups.* ■ of or relating to rebels: *insurgent attacks.* ▶n. a rebel or revolutionary. —**in·sur·gence** n. **in·sur·gen·cy** n. . [18th C. (as a n.): via Fr. from L. *insurgent-* 'arising,' from the v. *insurgere,* from *in-* 'into, toward' + *surgere* 'to rise.']

in·sur·mount·a·ble /,insər'mountəbəl/ ▶adj. too great to be overcome: *an insurmountable problem.* —**in·sur·mount·a·bly** adv.

in·sur·rec·tion /,insə'rekshən/ ▶n. a violent uprising against an authority or government: *opposition to the new regime led to armed insurrection.* —**in·sur·rec·tion·ar·y** /-,nerē/ adj. **in·sur·rec·tion·ist** n. & adj. [ME: via OFr. from late L. *insurrectio(n-),* from *insurgere* 'rise up.']

in·sus·cep·ti·ble /,insə'septəbəl/ ▶adj. not susceptible; not likely to be affected: ***insusceptible to*** *treatment.* —**in·sus·cep·ti·bil·i·ty** /-,septə'bilitē/ n.

int. ▶abbr. ■ interior. ■ internal. ■ international.

in·tact /in'takt/ ▶adj. [often as complement] not damaged or impaired in any way; complete. —**in·tact·ness** n.

in·ta·glio /in'talyō; -'täl-/ ▶n. (pl. **-glios**) a design incised or engraved into a material: *a design* ***in intaglio.*** ■ a gem with an incised design. ■ any printing process in which the type or design is etched or engraved, such as photogravure or drypoint. ▶v. (**-glioes, -glioed**) [trans.] [usu. as adj.] (**intaglioed**) engrave or represent by an engraving. [17th C.: Ital., from *intagliare* 'engrave.']

in·take /'in,tāk/ ▶n. an amount of food, air, or other substance taken into the body: *calorie intake.* ■ an act of taking something into the body: *intake of breath.*

in·tan·gi·ble /in'tanjəbəl/ ▶adj. unable to be touched or grasped; not having physical presence: *cyberspace or anything else so intangible.* ■ difficult or impossible to define or understand; vague and abstract. ■ (of an asset) not constituting a physical object, and of a value not precisely measurable: *intangible property like trademarks.* ▶n. (usu. **intangibles**) an intangible thing. —**in·tan·gi·bil·i·ty** /-,tanjə'bilitē/ n. **in·tan·gi·bly** adv.

in·tar·si·a /in'tärsēə/ ▶n. [often as adj.] **1** a method of knitting with a number of colors, in which a separate length or ball of yarn is used for each area of color (as opposed to different yarns being carried at the back of the work). **2** an elaborate form of marquetry using inlays in wood, esp. as practiced in 15th-century Italy. ■ similar inlaid work in stone, metal, or glass. [from Italian *intarsio*; in sense 2 superseding earlier *tarsia* (from Ital., 'marquetry'); the knitting term dates from the mid 19th C.]

in·te·ger /'intijər/ ▶n. **1** a whole number; a number that is not a fraction. **2** a thing complete in itself. [16th C. (as an adj. meaning 'entire, whole'): from L., 'intact, whole,' from *in-* (expressing negation) + the root of *tangere* 'to touch.' Cf. ENTIRE, also with INTEGRAL, INTEGRATE, and INTEGRITY.]

in·te·gral ▶adj. /'intigrəl; in'teg-/ **1** necessary to make complete; essential or fundamental: *integral sections.* ■ [attrib.] included as part of the whole rather than supplied separately: *the unit comes with integral pump and heater.* ■ [attrib.] having or containing all parts that are necessary to be complete: *the only integral recording of the ten Mahler symphonies.* **2** Math. of or denoted by an integer. ■ involving only integers, esp. as coefficients of a function. ▶n. Math. a function of which a given function is the derivative, i.e., which yields that function when differentiated, and which may express the area under the curve of a graph of the function. See also DEFINITE INTEGRAL, INDEFINITE INTEGRAL. ■ a function satisfying a given differential equation. —**in·te·gral·i·ty** /,inti'gralitē/ n. **in·te·gral·ly** adv. [16th C.: from late L. *integralis,* from *integer* 'whole' (see INTEGER). Cf. INTEGRATE and INTEGRITY.]

in·te·gral cal·cu·lus ▶n. a branch of mathematics concerned with the determination, properties, and application of integrals. Compare with DIFFERENTIAL CALCULUS.

in·te·grand /'intigrənd/ ▶n. Math. a function that is to be integrated.

in·te·grant /'intigrənt/ ▶adj. (of parts) making up or contributing to a whole; constituent. ▶n. a component.

in·te·grate ▶v. /'inti,grāt/ [trans.] **1** combine (parts) with another so that they become a whole. **2** bring into equal participation in; give equal consideration to: *integrating children with special needs.* **3** desegregate (a school, neighborhood, etc.), esp. racially. **4** Math. find the integral of. —**in·te·gra·bil·i·ty** /,intigrə'bilitē/ n. **in·te·gra·ble** /-grəbəl/ adj.

in·te·gra·tive /-,grātiv/ adj. [17th C.: from L. *integrat-* 'made whole,' from the v. *integrare,* from *integer* 'whole' (see INTEGER). Cf. INTEGRAL and INTEGRITY.]

in·te·grat·ed /'inti,grātid/ ▶adj. having been integrated, in particular: ■ desegregated, esp. racially: *integrated education* | *the sport was now fully integrated.* ■ with various parts or aspects linked or coordinated: *an integrated public transportation system.*

in·te·grat·ed cir·cuit ▶n. an electronic circuit formed on a small piece of semiconducting material, performing the same function as a larger circuit made from discrete components.

in·te·gra·tion /,inti'grāshən/ ▶n. **1** the action or process of integrating. ■ the intermixing of people or groups previously segregated. **2** Math. the finding of an integral or integrals. **3** Psychol. the coordination of processes in the nervous system, including diverse sensory information and motor impulses. —**in·te·gra·tion·ist** n.

in·te·gra·tor /'inti,grātər/ ▶n. a person or thing that integrates, in particular: ■ (also **system integrator** or **systems integrator**) Comput. a company that markets commercial integrated software and hardware systems. ■ Electron. a computer chip or circuit that performs mathematical integration. ■ an instrument for indicating or registering the total amount or mean value of some physical quality such as area or temperature.

in·teg·ri·ty /in'tegritē/ ▶n. **1** the quality of being honest and having strong moral principles; moral uprightness. **2** the state of being whole and undivided: *territorial integrity.* ■ the condition of being unified, unimpaired, or sound in construction: *structural integrity.* ■ internal consistency or lack of corruption in electronic data. [ME (sense 2): from Fr. *intégrité* or L. *integritas,* from *integer* 'intact' (see INTEGER). Cf. ENTIRETY, INTEGRAL, and INTEGRATE.]

in·teg·u·ment /in'tegyəmənt/ ▶n. a tough outer protective layer, esp. that of an animal or plant. —**in·teg·u·men·tal** /-,tegyə'mentl/ adj. **in·teg·u·men·ta·ry** /-,tegyə'mentərē/ adj. [17th C. (denoting a covering or coating): from L. *integumentum,* from the v. *integere,* from *in-* 'in' + *tegere* 'to cover.']

in·tel·lect /'intl,ekt/ ▶n. the faculty of reasoning and understanding objectively, esp. with regard to abstract or academic matters. ■ the understanding or mental powers of a particular person: *her education, intellect and talent.* [ME: from L. *intellectus* 'understanding,' from *intellegere* 'understand' (see INTELLIGENT).]

in·tel·lec·tion /,intl'ekshən/ ▶n. the action or process of understanding, as opposed to imagination. —**in·tel·lec·tive** adj.

in·tel·lec·tu·al /,intl'ekchooəl/ ▶adj. of or relating to the intellect: *intellectual stimulation.* ■ appealing to or requiring use of the intellect. ■ possessing a highly developed intellect. ▶n. a person possessing a highly developed intellect. —**in·tel·lec·tu·al·i·ty** /,intl,ekchoo'alitē/ n. **in·tel·lec·tu·al·ly** adv.

in·tel·lec·tu·al·ism /,intl'ekchooə,lizəm/ ▶n. the exercise of the intellect at the expense of the emotions. ■ Philos. the theory that knowledge is wholly or mainly derived from pure reason; rationalism. —**in·tel·lec·tu·al·ist** n.

in·tel·lec·tu·al·ize /,intl'ekchooə,līz/ ▶v. [trans.] **1** give an intellectual character to. **2** [intrans.] talk, write, or think intellectually. —**in·tel·lec·tu·al·i·za·tion** /-,ekchooələ'zāshən/ n.

in·tel·lec·tu·al prop·er·ty ▶n. Law a work or invention that is the result of creativity, such as a manuscript or a design, to which one has rights and for which one may apply for a patent, copyright, trademark, etc.

in·tel·li·gence /in'telijəns/ ▶n. **1** the ability to acquire and apply knowledge and skills. **2** the collection of information of military or political value: *military intelligence.* ■ people employed in this, regarded collectively: *French intelligence.* ■ information collected in this way.

in·tel·li·gence quo·tient (abbr.: **IQ**) ▶n. a number representing a person's reasoning ability (measured using problem-solving tests) as compared to the statistical norm or average for their age, taken as 100.

in·tel·li·genc·er /in'telijənsər; -,jen-/ ▶n. archaic a person who gathers intelligence, esp. an informer, spy, or secret agent.

in·tel·li·gence test ▶n. a test designed to measure the ability to think and reason rather than acquired knowledge.

in·tel·li·gent /in'telijənt/ ▶adj. having or showing intelligence, esp. of a high level. ■ (of a device, machine, or building) able to vary its state or action in response to varying situations, varying requirements, and past experience. ■ (esp. of a computer terminal) incorporating a microprocessor and having its own processing capability. —**in·tel·li·gent·ly** adv. [16th C.: from L. *intelligent-* 'understanding,' from the v. *intelligere,* var. of *intellegere* 'understand,' from *inter* 'between' + *legere* 'choose.']

in·tel·li·gent de·sign ▶n. the theory that life, or the universe, cannot have arisen by chance and was designed and created by some intelligent entity.

in·tel·li·gent·si·a /in,teli'jentsēə/ ▶n. (usu. **the intelligentsia**) [treated as sing. or pl.] intellectuals or highly educated people as a group, esp. when regarded as possessing culture and political influence. [20th C.: from Russ. *intelligentsiya,* from Pol. *inteligencja,* from L. *intelligentia* (see INTELLIGENCE).]

in·tel·li·gi·ble /in'telijəbəl/ ▶adj. able to be understood; comprehensible. ■ Philos. able to be understood only by the intellect, not by the senses. —**in·tel·li·gi·bil·i·ty** /-,telijə'bilitē/ n. **in·tel·li·gi·bly** adv.

In·tel·sat /'intel,sat/ an international organization of more than 100 countries, formed in 1964, that owns and operates the worldwide commercial communications satellite system. [from *In(ternational) Tel(ecommunications) Sat(ellite Consortium).*]

in·tem·per·ate /inˈtemp(ə)rit/ ▶ **adj.** having or showing a lack of self-control; immoderate: *intemperate outbursts.* ▪ given to or characterized by excessive indulgence, esp. in alcohol. — **in·tem·per·ance** /-rəns **n. in·tem·per·ate·ly adv. in·tem·per·ate·ness n.**

in·tend /inˈtend/ ▶ **v.** [trans.] **1** have (a course of action) as one's purpose or objective; plan: [with infin.] *we intend to leave.* ▪ plan that (something) function in a particular way: *it was originally intended as an inn.* ▪ plan that speech should have (a particular meaning): *no offense was intended.* **2** design or destine (someone or something) for a particular purpose or end: *intended for human consumption.* ▪ (**be intended for**) be meant or designed for (a particular person or group) to have or use: *intended for children.* — **in·tend·er n.** [ME *entend*, from OFr. *entendre*, from L. *intendere* 'intend, extend, direct,' from *in-* 'toward' + *tendere* 'stretch, tend.']

in·tend·ant /inˈtendənt/ ▶ **n.** esp. hist. a title given to a high-ranking official or administrator, esp. in France, Spain, Portugal, or one of their colonies. — **in·tend·an·cy** /-dənsē/ **n.**

in·tend·ed /inˈtendid/ ▶ **adj.** [attrib.] planned or meant: *the intended victim escaped.* ▶ **n.** (**one's intended**) informal the person one intends to marry; one's fiancé or fiancée. — **in·tend·ed·ly adv.**

in·tend·ment /inˈtendmənt/ ▶ **n.** Law the sense in which the law understands or interprets something, such as the true intention of a piece of legislation.

in·tense /inˈtens/ ▶ **adj.** **1** (of a condition, quality, feeling, etc.) existing in a high degree; forceful or extreme: *this job demands intense concentration.* ▪ (of an action) highly concentrated: *intense competition.* **2** (of a person) feeling, or apt to feel, strong emotion; extremely earnest or serious. — **in·tense·ly adv. in·tense·ness n.** [ME: from OFr., or from L. *intensus* 'stretched tightly, strained,' past part. of *intendere* (see **INTEND**).]

in·ten·si·fi·er /inˈtensəˌfīər/ ▶ **n.** a person or thing that intensifies, in particular: ▪ Photog. a chemical used to intensify a negative. ▪ Gram. an adverb used to give force or emphasis, for example *really* in *my feet are really cold.*

in·ten·si·fy /inˈtensəˌfī/ ▶ **v.** (**-fies, -fied**) **1** become or make more intense: [intrans.] *the dispute intensified.* **2** [trans.] Photog. increase the opacity of (a negative) using a chemical. — **in·ten·si·fi·ca·tion** /-ˌtensəfiˈkāshən/ **n.** [19th C.: coined by Coleridge.]

in·ten·sion /inˈtenshən/ ▶ **n.** **1** Logic the internal content of a concept. Often contrasted with **EXTENSION** (sense 5). **2** archaic resolution or determination. — **in·ten·sion·al** /-shənl/ **adj. in·ten·sion·al·ly** /-shənl-ē/ **adv.**

in·ten·si·ty /inˈtensitē/ ▶ **n.** (pl. **-ties**) **1** the quality of being intense: *the pain grew in intensity.* ▪ an instance or degree of this. **2** esp. Physics the measurable magnitude of a property, such as force, brightness, or a magnetic field.

in·ten·sive /inˈtensiv/ ▶ **adj.** **1** concentrated on a single area or subject or into a short time; very thorough or vigorous: *intensive research.* ▪ (of agriculture) aiming to achieve the highest possible level of production within a limited area, esp. by using chemical and technological aids: *intensive farming.* Often contrasted with **EXTENSIVE** (sense 2). ▪ [usu. in comb.] concentrating on or making much use of a specified thing: *computer-intensive methods.* **2** Gram. (of an adjective, adverb, or particle) expressing intensity; giving force or emphasis. **3** denoting a property that is measured in terms of intensity (e.g., concentration) rather than of extent (e.g., volume), and so is not simply increased by addition of one thing to another. ▶ **n.** Gram. an intensive adjective, adverb, or particle; an intensifier. — **in·ten·sive·ly adv. in·ten·sive·ness n.** [ME (in the sense 'vehement, intense'): from Fr. *intensif, -ive* or med. L. *intensivus*, from *intendere* (see **INTEND**).]

in·ten·sive care ▶ **n.** special medical treatment of a critically ill patient, with constant monitoring. ▪ (in full **intensive care unit**) a hospital ward devoted to such treatment.

in·tent /inˈtent/ ▶ **n.** intention or purpose. ▶ **adj.** **1** [predic.] (**intent on/upon**) resolved or determined to do (something): *intent on achieving efficiency.* ▪ attentively occupied with: *intent on her book.* **2** (esp. of a look) showing earnest and eager attention.
– PHRASES **to** (or **for**) **all intents and purposes** in all important respects. **with intent** Law with the intention of committing a specified crime.
— **in·tent·ly adv. in·tent·ness n.** [ME: from OFr. *entent, entente*, based on L. *intendere* (see **INTEND**).]

in·ten·tion /inˈtenchən/ ▶ **n.** **1** a thing intended; an aim or plan: [with infin.] *both countries have declared their intention to be nuclear-free.* ▪ the action or fact of intending. ▪ (**one's intentions**) a person's aims, esp. a man's, in respect to marriage. **2** Med. the healing process of a wound. See **FIRST INTENTION, SECOND INTENTION.** — **in·ten·tioned adj.** [in comb.] *a well-intentioned remark.* [ME: from OFr. *entencion*, from L. *intentio(n-)* 'stretching, purpose,' from *intendere* (see **INTEND**).]

in·ten·tion·al /inˈtenchənl/ ▶ **adj.** done on purpose; deliberate. — **in·ten·tion·al·ly adv.**

in·ter /inˈtər/ ▶ **v.** (**-terred, -ter·ring**) [trans.] (usu. **be interred**) place (a corpse) in a grave or tomb, typically with funeral rites. [ME: from OFr. *enterrer*, based on L. *in-* 'into' + *terra* 'earth.']

inter- ▶ **prefix** **1** between; among: *interagency* | *interblend.* **2** mutually; reciprocally: *interactive.* [from OFr. *entre-* or L. *inter* 'between, among.']

in·ter·act /ˌintərˈakt/ ▶ **v.** [intrans.] act in such a way as to have an effect on another; act reciprocally: *professional people who interact daily.* — **in·ter·ac·tant** /-ˈaktənt/ **adj. & n.**

in·ter·ac·tion /ˌintərˈakshən/ ▶ **n.** reciprocal action or influence: *interaction between the two countries.* — **in·ter·ac·tion·al** /-shənl/ **adj.**

in·ter·a·gen·cy /ˌintərˈājənsē/ ▶ **adj.** representing or taking place between different government agencies: *an interagency crisis-management team.*

in·ter a·li·a /ˈintər ˈālēə; ˈälēə/ ▶ **adv.** among other things. [17th C.: L.]

in·ter a·li·os /ˈintər ˈālēˌōs; ˈälēˌōs/ ▶ **adv.** among other people. [17th C.: L.]

in·ter·al·lied /ˌintərəˈlīd/ ▶ **adj.** [attrib.] of or relating to two or more states formally cooperating for military purposes.

Inter-American Highway see **PAN-AMERICAN HIGHWAY.**

in·ter·breed /ˌintərˈbrēd/ ▶ **v.** (past and past part. **-bred**) [intrans.] (of an animal) breed with another of a different race or species. ▪ (of an animal) inbreed. ▪ [trans.] cause (an animal) to breed with another of a different race or species to produce a hybrid.

in·ter·ca·lar·y /inˈtərkəˌlerē; ˌintərˈkalərē/ ▶ **adj.** (of a day or a month) inserted in the calendar to harmonize it with the solar year, e.g., February 29 in leap years.

in·ter·ca·late /inˈtərkəˌlāt/ ▶ **v.** [trans.] **1** interpolate (an intercalary period) in a calendar. **2** (usu. **be intercalated**) insert (something) between layers in a crystal lattice, geological formation, or other structure. — **in·ter·ca·la·tion** /-ˌtərkəˈlāshən/ **n.** [17th C.: from L. *intercalat-* 'proclaimed as inserted in the calendar,' from the v. *intercalare*, from *inter-* 'between' + *calare* 'proclaim solemnly.']

in·ter·cede /ˌintərˈsēd/ [intrans.] ▶ **v.** intervene on behalf of another. — **in·ter·ced·er n.** [16th C.: from Fr. *intercéder* or L. *intercedere* 'intervene,' from *inter-* 'between' + *cedere* 'go.']

in·ter·cept ▶ **v.** /ˌintərˈsept/ [trans.] obstruct (someone or something) so as to prevent them from continuing to a destination: *the Coast Guard intercepted their vessel.* ▪ esp. Physics cut off or deflect (light or other electromagnetic radiation). ▪ Math. (of a line or surface) mark or cut off (part of a space, line, or surface). ▪ Football (of a defensive player) catch an opponent's forward pass. ▶ **n.** /ˈintərˌsept/ an act or instance of intercepting something. ▪ Math. the point at which a given line cuts a coordinate axis; the value of the coordinate at that point. — **in·ter·cep·tive adj.** [ME: from L. *intercept-* 'caught between,' from the v. *intercipere*, from *inter-* 'between' + *capere* 'take.']

in·ter·cep·tion /ˌintərˈsepshən/ ▶ **n.** an act or instance of intercepting something, particularly: ▪ Football an act of a defensive player catching an opponent's forward pass. ▪ an act or instance of receiving electronic transmissions before they reach the intended recipient: *clandestine interception of phone calls.*

in·ter·cep·tor /ˌintərˈseptər/ ▶ **n.** a person or thing that stops or catches (someone or something) going from one place to another. ▪ a fast aircraft for repelling hostile aircraft.

in·ter·ces·sion /ˌintərˈseshən/ ▶ **n.** the action of intervening on behalf of another. ▪ the action of saying a prayer on behalf of another person. — **in·ter·ces·sor** /ˈintərˌsesər/ **n. in·ter·ces·so·ry** /-ˈsesərē/ **adj.**

in·ter·change ▶ **v.** /ˌintərˈchānj/ [trans.] (of two or more people) exchange (things) with each other: *we freely interchange information.* ▪ put each of (two things) in the other's place: *the terms are often interchanged.* ▪ [intrans.] (of a thing) be able to be exchanged with another. ▶ **n.** /ˈintərˌchānj/ **1** the action of interchanging things, esp. information: *the interchange of ideas.* ▪ an exchange of words: *a venomous interchange.* **2** a road junction designed on several levels so that traffic streams do not intersect. — **in·ter·change·a·bil·i·ty** /ˌintərˌchānjəˈbilitē/ **n. in·ter·change·a·ble adj. in·ter·change·a·bly adv.**

in·ter·col·le·giate /ˌintərkəˈlēj(ē)it/ ▶ **adj.** existing or conducted between colleges or universities.

in·ter·co·lum·ni·a·tion /ˌintərkəˌləmnēˈāshən/ ▶ **n.** Archit. the distance between two adjacent columns. ▪ the spacing of the columns of a building. — **in·ter·co·lum·nar** /-ˈləmnər/ **adj.**

in·ter·com /ˈintərˌkäm/ ▶ **n.** an electrical device allowing one-way or two-way communication. [World War II: abbrev. of **INTERCOMMUNICATION.**]

in·ter·com·mu·ni·cate /ˌintərkəˈmyo͞oniˌkāt/ ▶ **v.** [intrans.] **1** engage in two-way communication. **2** (of two rooms) have a common connecting door. — **in·ter·com·mu·ni·ca·tion n.**

in·ter·com·mun·ion /ˌintərkəˈmyo͞onyən/ ▶ **n.** participation in Holy Communion or other services by members of different religious denominations.

in·ter·con·nect /ˌintərkəˈnekt/ ▶ **v.** [intrans.] connect with each other. — **in·ter·con·nec·tion** /-ˈnekshən/ **n.**

in·ter·con·ti·nen·tal /ˌintərˌkäntnˈentl/ ▶ **adj.** relating to or traveling between continents. — **in·ter·con·ti·nen·tal·ly adv.**

in·ter·con·vert /ˌintərkənˈvərt/ ▶ **v.** [trans.] (usu. **be interconverted**) cause (two things) to be converted into each other. — **in·ter·con·ver·sion** /-ˈvərzhən/ **n. in·ter·con·vert·i·ble adj.**

in·ter·cool·er /ˌintərˈko͞olər/ ▶ **n.** an apparatus for cooling gas between successive compressions, esp. in a supercharged vehicle engine. — **in·ter·cool v.**

in·ter·cos·tal /ˌintərˈkästəl/ Anat. ▶ **adj.** situated between the ribs: *the fifth left intercostal space.* ▶ **n.** a muscle in this position. — **in·ter·cos·tal·ly adv.**

in·ter·course /ˈintərˌkôrs/ ▶ **n.** communication or dealings between individuals or groups: *everyday social intercourse.* ▪ short for **SEXUAL INTERCOURSE.** [ME: from OFr. *entrecours* 'exchange, commerce,' from L.

intercursus, from *intercurrere* 'intervene,' from *inter-* 'between' + *currere* 'run.']

in·ter·crop ▶ **v.** /ˌintərˈkräp/ (**-cropped, -crop·ping**) [trans.] [often as n.] (**intercropping**) grow (a crop) among plants of a different kind, usually in the space between rows. ▶ **n.** /ˈintərˌkräp/ a crop grown in such a way.

in·ter·cross /ˌintərˈkrôs/ ▶ **v.** [intrans.] (of animals or plants of different breeds or varieties) interbreed. ■ [trans.] cause (animals or plants) to do this. ▶ **n.** an instance of intercrossing of animals or plants. ■ an animal or plant resulting from this.

in·ter·cru·ral /ˌintərˈkro͝orəl/ ▶ **adj.** between the legs.

in·ter·cur·rent /ˌintərˈkərənt; -ˈkə-rənt/ ▶ **adj.** **1** Med. (of a disease) occurring during the progress of another disease. **2** rare (of a time or event) intervening. [17th C.: from L. *intercurrent-* 'intervening,' from the v. *intercurrere*.]

in·ter·cut /ˌintərˈkət/ ▶ **v.** (**-cut·ting**; past and past part. **-cut**) [trans.] alternate (scenes or shots) with contrasting scenes or shots to make one composite scene in a film.

in·ter·de·nom·i·na·tion·al /ˌintərdiˌnäməˈnāsHənl/ ▶ **adj.** of or relating to more than one religious denomination: *an interdenominational Thanksgiving service.* — **in·ter·de·nom·i·na·tion·al·ly** **adv.**

in·ter·den·tal /ˌintərˈdentl/ ▶ **adj.** situated or placed between teeth or the teeth. ■ Phonet. (of a consonant) pronounced by placing the tip of the tongue between the teeth, such as the "th" sounds in the English words "thaw" and "though." ▶ **n.** Phonet. a consonant pronounced in this way. — **in·ter·den·tal·ly** **adv.**

in·ter·de·pend·ent /ˌintərdiˈpendənt/ ▶ **adj.** (of two or more people or things) dependent on each other. — **in·ter·de·pend** **v.** **in·ter·de·pend·ence** **n.** **in·ter·de·pend·en·cy** **n.**

in·ter·dict ▶ **n.** /ˈintərˌdikt/ an authoritative prohibition. ■ (in the Roman Catholic Church) a sentence barring a person, or esp. a place, from ecclesiastical functions and privileges: *a papal interdict.* ▶ **v.** /ˌintərˈdikt/ [trans.] **1** prohibit or forbid (something). ■ (**interdict someone from**) prohibit someone from (doing something). **2** intercept and prevent the movement of (a prohibited commodity or person): *roadblocks established for interdicting drugs.* ■ Mil. impede (an enemy force), esp. by aerial bombing of lines of communication or supply. — **in·ter·dic·tion** /ˌintərˈdiksHən/ **n.** [ME *entredite*, from OFr. *entredit*, from L. *interdictum*, past part. of *interdicere* 'interpose, forbid by decree.']

in·ter·dig·i·tate /ˌintərˈdijiˌtāt/ ▶ **v.** [intrans.] (of two or more things) interlock like the fingers of two clasped hands. [19th C.: from INTER- 'between' + DIGIT + -ATE[3].]

in·ter·dis·ci·pli·nar·y /ˌintərˈdisəpliˌnerē/ ▶ **adj.** of or relating to more than one branch of knowledge.

in·ter·est /ˈint(ə)rist/ ▶ **n.** **1** the state of wanting to know or learn about something or someone: *many people lose interest in history.* ■ (**an interest in**) a feeling of wanting to know or learn about (something): *an interest in art.* ■ the quality of exciting curiosity or holding the attention: *a tale full of interest.* ■ a subject about which one is concerned or enthusiastic: *my interest is poetry.* **2** money paid regularly at a particular rate for the use of money lent, or for delaying the repayment of a debt. **3** the advantage or benefit of a person or group: *conflicting interests | the public interest.* **4** a stake, share, or involvement in an undertaking, esp. a financial one: *he has the controlling interest.* **5** (usu. **interests**) a group or organization having a specified common concern, esp. in politics or business: *national interests in India.* ▶ **v.** [trans.] excite the curiosity or attention of (someone): *I thought this might interest you.* ■ (**interest someone in**) cause someone to undertake or acquire (something): *efforts were made to interest her in a purchase.*
– PHRASES **in the interests** (or **interest**) **of** for the benefit of: *in the interests of security.* **of interest** interesting. **with interest** with interest charged or paid. ■ (of an action) reciprocated with more force or vigor than the original one: *I'll get even, with interest.* [ME: from L. *interesse* 'differ, be important,' from *inter-* 'between' + *esse* 'be.']

in·ter·est·ed /ˈint(ə)ristid; ˈintəˌrestid/ ▶ **adj.** **1** showing curiosity or concern about something or someone; having a feeling of interest: *interested in history.* **2** [attrib.] having an interest or involvement; not impartial or disinterested. — **in·ter·est·ed·ly** **adv.**

in·ter·est-free ▶ **adj.** & **adv.** with no interest charged on borrowed money: [as adj.] *interest-free credit.*

in·ter·est·ing /ˈint(ə)ristiNG; ˈintəˌrestiNG/ ▶ **adj.** arousing curiosity or interest; holding or catching the attention: *an interesting debate.* — **in·ter·est·ing·ly** **adv.**

in·ter·face /ˈintərˌfās/ ▶ **n.** **1** a point where two systems, subjects, organizations, etc., meet and interact. ■ esp. Physics a surface forming a boundary between two portions of matter or space, e.g., between two immiscible liquids. **2** Comput. a device or program enabling a user to communicate with a computer. ■ a device or program for connecting two items of hardware or software so that they can be operated jointly or communicate with each other. ▶ **v.** [intrans.] (**interface with**) **1** interact with (another system, person, organization, etc.). **2** Comput. connect with (another computer or piece of equipment) by an interface.

in·ter·fa·cial /ˌintərˈfāsHəl/ ▶ **adj.** **1** included between two faces of a crystal or other solid. **2** of, relating to, or forming a boundary between two portions of matter or space.

in·ter·fac·ing /ˈintərˌfāsiNG/ ▶ **n.** a moderately stiff material, esp. buckram, typically used between two layers of fabric in collars and facings.

in·ter·faith /ˈintərˈfāTH/ ▶ **adj.** [attrib.] of, relating to, or between different religions or members of different religions.

in·ter·fere /ˌintərˈfi(ə)r/ ▶ **v.** [intrans.] **1** (**interfere with**) prevent (a process or activity) from being carried out properly: *his roommates interfere with his studies.* ■ (of a thing) strike against (something) when working; get in the way of: *the rotors do not interfere with one another.* **2** take part or intervene in an activity without invitation or necessity: *he tried not to interfere in her life.* **3** Physics (of light or other electromagnetic waveforms) act upon each other and produce interference. ■ cause interference to a broadcast radio signal. **4** (of a horse) knock one foot against the fetlock of another leg. — **in·ter·fer·er** **n.** **in·ter·fer·ing·ly** **adv.** [ME: from OFr. *s'entreferir* 'strike each other,' from *entre-* 'between' + *ferir* (from L. *ferire* 'to strike').]

in·ter·fer·ence /ˌintərˈfi(ə)rəns/ ▶ **n.** **1** the action of interfering or the process of being interfered with: *interference in the country's internal affairs.* ■ Football the action of illegally interfering with an opponent's ability to catch a passed or kicked ball. ■ Football the legal blocking of an opponent or opponents to clear a way for the ballcarrier. ■ Baseball any of various forms of hindering a player's ability to make a play, run, hit, etc. ■ (in ice hockey and other sports) the illegal hindering of an opponent not in possession of the puck or ball. **2** Physics the combination of two or more electromagnetic waveforms to form a resultant wave in which the displacement is either reinforced or canceled. ■ the disturbance of received radio signals caused by unwanted signals from other sources, such as broadcasts from other stations.
– PHRASES **run interference** Football move in such a way as to provide legal interference. — **in·ter·fe·ren·tial** /-fəˈrencHəl/ **adj.**

in·ter·fer·om·e·ter /ˌintərfəˈrämitər/ ▶ **n.** Physics an instrument in which wave interference is employed to make precise measurements of length of displacement in terms of the wavelength. — **in·ter·fer·o·met·ric** /-ˌfi(ə)rəˈmetrik/ **adj.** **in·ter·fer·o·met·ri·cal·ly** /-ˌfi(ə)rəˈmetrik(ə)lē/ **adv.** **in·ter·fer·om·e·try** /-trē/ **n.**

in·ter·fer·on /ˌintərˈfi(ə)rˌän/ ▶ **n.** Biochem. a protein released by animal cells, usually in response to the entry of a virus, that has the property of inhibiting virus replication. [1950s: from INTERFERE + -ON.]

in·ter·file /ˌintərˈfīl/ ▶ **v.** [trans.] file (two or more sequences) together. ■ file (one or more items) into an existing sequence.

in·ter·fluve /ˈintərˌflo͞ov/ ▶ **n.** Geol. a region between the valleys of adjacent watercourses, esp. in a dissected upland. — **in·ter·flu·vi·al** /ˌintərˈflo͞ovēəl/ **adj.**

in·ter·fuse /ˌintərˈfyo͞oz/ ▶ **v.** [trans.] literary join or mix (two or more things) together. — **in·ter·fu·sion** /-ˈfyo͞ozHən/ **n.**

in·ter·ga·lac·tic /ˌintərgəˈlaktik/ ▶ **adj.** of, relating to, or situated between two or more galaxies. — **in·ter·ga·lac·ti·cal·ly** **adv.**

in·ter·gla·cial /ˌintərˈglāsHəl/ Geol. ▶ **adj.** of or relating to a period of milder climate between two glacial periods. Compare with INTERSTADIAL. ▶ **n.** an interglacial period.

in·ter·gov·ern·men·tal /ˌintərˌgəvər(n)ˈmentl/ ▶ **adj.** of, relating to, or conducted between two or more governments. — **in·ter·gov·ern·men·tal·ly** **adv.**

in·ter·grade ▶ **v.** /ˌintərˈgrād/ [intrans.] Biol. pass into another form by a series of intervening forms. ▶ **n.** /ˈintərˌgrād/ an intervening form of this kind. — **in·ter·gra·da·tion** /-grāˈdāsHən/ **n.**

in·ter·grow /ˌintərˈgrō/ ▶ **v.** (past **-grew**; past part. **-grown**) [intrans.] [usu. as adj.] (**intergrown**) (chiefly of crystals) grow into each other.

in·ter·growth /ˈintərˌgrōTH/ ▶ **n.** a thing produced by intergrowing, esp. of mineral crystals in rock.

in·ter·im /ˈintərəm/ ▶ **n.** the intervening time: *in the interim I'll keep working.* ▶ **adj.** in or for the intervening period; provisional or temporary: *the interim government.* [16th C. (denoting a temporary or provisional arrangement, orig. for the adjustment of religious differences between the Ger. Protestants and the Roman Catholic Church): from L., 'meanwhile.']

in·te·ri·or /inˈti(ə)rēər/ ▶ **adj.** **1** situated within or inside; relating to the inside; inner: *interior lighting.* ■ [predic.] (**interior to**) esp. tech. situated further in or within: *immediately interior to the epidermis.* ■ drawn, photographed, etc., within a building. **2** [attrib.] remote from the coast or frontier; inland. ■ relating to internal or domestic affairs. **3** existing or taking place in the mind or soul; mental: *an interior monologue.* ▶ **n.** (usu. **the interior**) **1** the inner or indoor part of something, esp. a building; the inside. **2** the inland part of a country or region. ■ the internal affairs of a country: *the Department of the Interior.* — **in·te·ri·or·ize** /-əˌrīz/ **v.** [15th C.: from L., 'inner,' compar. adj. from *inter* 'within.']

in·te·ri·or an·gle ▶ **n.** the angle between adjacent sides of a rectilinear figure.

in·te·ri·or dec·o·ra·tion (also **interior decorating**) ▶ **n.** the decoration of the interior of a building or room, esp. with regard to color combination and artistic effect. — **in·te·ri·or dec·o·ra·tor** **n.**

in·te·ri·or de·sign ▶ **n.** the art or process of designing the interior decoration of a room or building. — **in·te·ri·or de·sign·er** **n.**

in·te·ri·or mon·o·logue ▶ **n.** a piece of writing expressing a character's inner thoughts.

interj. ▶ **abbr.** interjection.

in·ter·ject /ˌintərˈjekt/ ▶ **v.** [trans.] say (something) abruptly, esp. as an aside or interruption: *she interjected a question here and there.* — **in·ter·jec·to·ry** /-ˈjekt(ə)rē/ **adj.** [16th C.: from L. *interject-* 'interposed,' from the v. *interjicere*, from *inter-* 'between' + *jacere* 'to throw.']

in·ter·jec·tion /ˌintərˈjeksHən/ ▶ **n.** an abrupt remark, made esp. as an aside or interruption. ■ an exclamation, esp. as a part of speech, e.g., *ah!* or *dear me!* — **in•ter•jec•tion•al** /-shənl/ **adj.**

in•ter•lace /ˌintərˈlās/ ▶ **v.** [trans.] bind intricately together; interweave. ■ (**interlace something with**) mingle or intersperse something with: *serious discussion interlaced with humor.* ■ [intrans.] (of two or more things) cross each other intricately. — **in•ter•lace•ment n.**

in•ter•lan•guage /ˈintərˌlaNGgwij/ ▶ **n.** a language or form of language having features of two others, typically a pidgin or a version produced by a foreign learner.

in•ter•lard /ˌintərˈlärd/ ▶ **v.** [trans.] (**interlard something with**) intersperse or embellish speech or writing with different material: *reviews interlarded with gossip.* [ME (in the sense 'mix with alternate layers of fat'): from Fr. *entrelarder*, from *entre-* 'between' + *larder* 'to lard.']

in•ter•lay ▶ **v.** /ˌintərˈlā/ (past and past part. **-laid**) [trans.] lay between or among; interpose. ▶ **n.** /ˈintərˌlā/ an inserted layer.

in•ter•leaf /ˈintərˌlēf/ ▶ **n.** (pl. **-leaves**) a typically blank extra page between the leaves of a book.

in•ter•leave /ˌintərˈlēv/ ▶ **v.** [trans.] insert pages, typically blank ones, between the pages of a book.

in•ter•leu•kin /ˈintərˌlo͞okin/ ▶ **n.** Biochem. any of a class of glycoproteins produced by leukocytes for regulating immune responses. [1970s: from INTER- 'occurring between' + LEUKOCYTE + -IN[1].]

in•ter•line[1] /ˌintərˈlīn/ ▶ **v.** [trans.] insert words between the lines of (a document or other text). ■ insert (words) in this way.

in•ter•line[2] ▶ **v.** [trans.] put an extra lining between the ordinary lining and the fabric of (a garment, curtain, etc.), typically to provide extra strength.

in•ter•lin•e•ar /ˌintərˈlinēər/ ▶ **adj.** written or printed between the lines of a text. ■ (of a book) having the same text in different languages printed on alternate lines.

In•ter•lin•gua /ˌintərˈliNGgwə/ ▶ **n.** an artificial international language formed of elements common to the Romance languages, designed primarily for scientific and technical use. [20th C.: from INTER- 'between' + L. *lingua* 'tongue.']

in•ter•lin•gual /ˌintərˈliNGgwəl/ ▶ **adj.** between or relating to two languages: *interlingual dictionaries.*

in•ter•lin•ing /ˈintərˌlīniNG/ ▶ **n.** material used as an extra lining between the ordinary lining and the fabric of a garment, curtain, etc.

in•ter•link /ˌintərˈliNGk/ ▶ **v.** [trans.] join or connect (two or more things) together. — **in•ter•link•age** /-ˈliNGkij/ **n.**

in•ter•lock ▶ **v.** /ˌintərˈläk/ [intrans.] (of two or more things) engage with each other by overlapping or by the fitting together of projections and recesses. ▶ **n.** /ˈintərˌläk/ **1** a device or mechanism for connecting or coordinating the function of different components. **2** (also **interlock fabric**) a fabric knitted with closely interlocking stitches that allow it to stretch, typically used in underwear. — **in•ter•lock•er n.**

in•ter•loc•u•tor /ˌintərˈläkyətər/ ▶ **n.** formal a person who takes part in a dialogue or conversation. — **in•ter•lo•cu•tion** /-ləˈkyo͞oshən/ **n.** [16th C.: mod. L., from L. *interlocut-* 'interrupted (by speech),' from the v. *interloqui*, from *inter-* 'between' + *loqui* 'speak.']

in•ter•loc•u•to•ry /ˌintərˈläkyəˌtôrē/ ▶ **adj.** **1** Law (of a decree or judgment) given provisionally during the course of a legal action. **2** rare of or relating to dialogue or conversation.

in•ter•lop•er /ˈintərˌlōpər; ˌintərˈlōpər/ ▶ **n.** a person who becomes involved in a place or situation where they are not wanted or are considered not to belong. — **in•ter•lope** /ˈintərˌlōp; ˌintərˈlōp/ **v.** [16th C. (denoting an unauthorized trader trespassing on the rights of a trade monopoly): from INTER- 'amid' + *-loper* as in archaic *landloper* 'vagabond' (from MDu. *landlooper*).]

in•ter•lude /ˈintərˌlo͞od/ ▶ **n.** **1** an intervening period of time. ■ a pause between the acts of a play. **2** something performed during a theater intermission. ■ a piece of music played between other pieces or between the verses of a hymn. ■ a temporary amusement or source of entertainment that contrasts with what goes before or after: *a romantic interlude.* [ME: from med. L. *interludium*, from *inter-* 'between' + *ludus* 'play.']

in•ter•mar•riage /ˌintərˈmarij/ ▶ **n.** marriage between people of different races, castes, or religions. ■ marriage between close relations.

in•ter•mar•ry /ˌintərˈmarē/ ▶ **v.** (**-ries, -ried**) [intrans.] (of people belonging to different races, castes, or religions) become connected by marriage. ■ (of close relations) marry each other.

in•ter•me•di•ar•y /ˌintərˈmēdēˌerē/ ▶ **n.** (pl. **-ar•ies**) a person who acts as a link between people in order to try to bring about an agreement or reconciliation; a mediator. ▶ **adj.** intermediate.

in•ter•me•di•ate /ˌintərˈmēdē-it/ ▶ **adj.** coming between two things in time, place, order, character, etc.: *an intermediate stage of development.* ■ having more than a basic knowledge or level of skill but not yet advanced: *intermediate skiers.* ▶ **n.** an intermediate thing. ■ a person at an intermediate level of knowledge or skill. ■ a chemical compound formed by one reaction and then taking part in another, esp. during synthesis. ▶ **v.** [intrans.] act as intermediary; mediate: *middlemen intermediating between buyers and sellers.* — **in•ter•me•di•a•cy** /-əsē/ **n.** **in•ter•me•di•ate•ly adv.** **in•ter•me•di•a•tion** /-ˌmēdēˈāshən/ **n.** **in•ter•me•di•a•tor** /-ˌātər/ **n.** [ME: from med. L. *intermediatus*, from L. *intermedius*, from *inter-* 'between' + *medius* 'middle.']

in•ter•me•di•ate fre•quen•cy ▶ **n.** the frequency to which a radio signal is converted during heterodyne reception.

in•ter•me•di•ate host ▶ **n.** Biol. an organism that supports the immature or nonreproductive forms of a parasite. Compare with DEFINITIVE HOST.

in•ter•ment /inˈtərmənt/ ▶ **n.** the burial of a corpse in a grave or tomb, typically with funeral rites.

in•ter•mez•zo /ˌintərˈmetsō/ ▶ **n.** (pl. **-mez•zi** /-ˈmetsē/ or **-mez•zos**) a short connecting instrumental movement in an opera or other musical work. ■ a similar piece performed independently. ■ a short piece for a solo instrument. ■ a light dramatic, musical, or other performance inserted between the acts of a play. [18th C.: from Ital., from L. *intermedium* 'interval,' neut. of *intermedius* (see INTERMEDIATE).]

in•ter•mi•na•ble /inˈtərmənəbəl/ ▶ **adj.** endless (often used hyperbolically): *interminable meetings.* — **in•ter•mi•na•bil•i•ty** /-ˌtərmənəˈbilitē/ **n.** **in•ter•mi•na•ble•ness n.** **in•ter•mi•na•bly adv.**

in•ter•min•gle /ˌintərˈmiNGgəl/ ▶ **v.** mix or mingle together.

in•ter•mis•sion /ˌintərˈmishən/ ▶ **n.** a pause or break: *the daily work goes on without intermission.* ■ an interval between parts of a play, movie, or concert.

in•ter•mit /ˌintərˈmit/ ▶ **v.** (**-mit•ted, -mit•ting**) [trans.] suspend or discontinue (an action) for a time. ■ [intrans.] (esp. of a fever or pulse) cease or stop for a time. [16th C.: from L. *intermittere*, from *inter-* 'between' + *mittere* 'let go.']

in•ter•mit•tent /ˌintərˈmitnt/ ▶ **adj.** occurring at irregular intervals; not steady: *there were overcast skies, intermittent rain, and heavy mists.* — **in•ter•mit•tence n.** **in•ter•mit•ten•cy n.** **in•ter•mit•tent•ly adv.** [16th C.: from L. *intermittent-* 'ceasing,' from the v. *intermittere* (see INTERMIT).]

in•ter•mix /ˌintərˈmiks/ ▶ **v.** mix together; blend. — **in•ter•mix•a•ble adj.** **in•ter•mix•ture** /-ˈmikschər/ **n.**

in•ter•mod•al /ˌintərˈmōdl/ ▶ **adj.** involving two or more different modes of freight transportation.

in•tern ▶ **n.** /ˈintərn/ a recent medical graduate receiving supervised training in a hospital as an assistant physician. Compare with RESIDENT. ■ a student or trainee who works, sometimes without pay, at an occupation to gain experience. ▶ **v.** /inˈtərn/ **1** [trans.] confine (someone) as a prisoner, esp. for political or military reasons. **2** [intrans.] serve as an intern. — **in•tern•ment n.** (in sense 1 of the verb). **in•tern•ship n.**

in•ter•nal /inˈtərnl/ ▶ **adj.** of or situated on the inside: *internal diameter.* ■ inside the body: *internal bleeding.* ■ existing or occurring within an organization: *she cataloged her views in an internal memo.* ■ relating to affairs and activities within a country rather than with other countries; domestic. ■ experienced in one's mind; inner rather than expressed: *internal fears.* — **in•ter•nal•i•ty** /ˌintərˈnalitē/ **n.** **in•ter•nal•ly adv.** [16th C.: from mod. L. *internalis*, from L. *internus* 'inward, internal.']

in•ter•nal clock ▶ **n.** a person's innate sense of time. ■ another term for BIOLOGICAL CLOCK.

in•ter•nal com•bus•tion en•gine ▶ **n.** an engine that generates motive power by the burning of gasoline, oil, or other fuel with air inside the engine, the hot gases produced being used to drive a piston or do other work as they expand.

in•ter•nal ex•ile ▶ **n.** enforced banishment from a part of one's own country to another, typically remote part.

in•ter•nal•ize /inˈtərnlˌīz/ ▶ **v.** [trans.] **1** Psychol. make (attitudes or behavior) part of one's nature by learning or unconscious assimilation. ■ acquire knowledge of (the rules of a language). **2** Econ. incorporate (costs) as part of a pricing structure, esp. social costs resulting from the manufacture and use of a product. — **in•ter•nal•i•za•tion** /inˌtərnliˈzāshən/ **n.**

in•ter•nal rhyme ▶ **n.** a rhyme involving a word in the middle of a line and another at the end of the line or in the middle of the next.

in•ter•na•tion•al /ˌintərˈnashənl/ ▶ **adj.** existing, occurring, or carried on between two or more nations. ■ agreed on by all or many nations: *international law.* ■ used by people of many nations: *international hotels.* ▶ **n.** (**International**) any of four associations founded (1864–1936) to promote socialist or communist action. ■ a member of any of these. — **in•ter•na•tion•al•i•ty** /-ˌnashəˈnalitē/ **n.** **in•ter•na•tion•al•ly adv.**

in•ter•na•tion•al can•dle ▶ **n.** see CANDLE.

In•ter•na•tion•al Court of Jus•tice a judicial court of the United Nations, formed in 1945, that meets at The Hague.

In•ter•na•tion•al Date Line ▶ **n.** see DATE LINE.

In•ter•na•tio•nale /ˌintərˌnashəˈnal; -ˈnäl/ a revolutionary song composed in France in the late 19th century, adopted by French socialists and subsequently by others.

in•ter•na•tion•al•ism /ˌintərˈnashənlˌizəm/ ▶ **n.** the state or process of being international. ■ the advocacy of cooperation and understanding between nations. — **in•ter•na•tion•al•ist n.**

in•ter•na•tion•al•ize /ˌintərˈnashənlˌīz/ ▶ **v.** [trans.] **1** make (something) international. **2** bring (a place) under the protection or control of two or more nations. — **in•ter•na•tion•al•i•za•tion** /-ˌnashənl-iˈzāshən/ **n.**

In•ter•na•tion•al La•bor Or•gan•i•za•tion (abbr.: **ILO**) an organization established in 1919 whose aim is to encourage lasting peace through social justice, awarded the Nobel Peace Prize in 1969.

in•ter•na•tion•al law ▶ **n.** a body of rules established by custom or treaty and recognized by nations as binding in their relations with one another.

In·ter·na·tion·al Mon·e·tar·y Fund (abbr.: **IMF**) an international organization established in 1945 that aims to promote international trade and monetary cooperation and the stabilization of exchange rates.

In·ter·na·tion·al Or·gan·i·za·tion for Stand·ard·i·za·tion an organization founded in 1946 to standardize measurements for international industrial, commercial, and scientific purposes.

In·ter·na·tion·al Pho·net·ic Al·pha·bet (abbr.: **IPA**) an internationally recognized set of phonetic symbols developed in the late 19th century, based on the principle of strict one-to-one correspondence between sounds and symbols.

In·ter·na·tion·al Style ▶n. a functional style of 20th-century architecture, characterized by the use of steel, glass, reinforced concrete, uninterrupted interior spaces, and geometric forms.

In·ter·na·tion·al Sys·tem of U·nits ▶n. a system of physical units (**SI Units**) based on the meter, kilogram, second, ampere, kelvin, candela, and mole, together with a set of prefixes to indicate multiplication or division by a power of ten. [translating Fr. *Système International d'Unités.*]

in·ter·na·tion·al u·nit ▶n. a unit of activity or potency for vitamins, hormones, or other substances, defined individually for each substance in terms of the activity of a standard quantity or preparation.

in·ter·ne·cine /ˌintərˈnesēn; -ˈnēsēn; -sin/ ▶adj. destructive to both sides in a conflict: *savage internecine warfare.* [17th C.: from L. *internecinus,* based on *inter-* 'among' + *necare* 'to kill.']

in·tern·ee /ˌintərˈnē/ ▶n. a person who is confined as a prisoner, esp. for political or military reasons.

In·ter·net /ˈintərˌnet/ an international computer network providing e-mail and information from computers in educational institutions, government agencies, and industry, accessible to the general public via modem links. [20th C.: from INTER- 'reciprocal, mutual' + NETWORK.]

in·ter·neu·ron /ˌintərˈn(y)o͝orän/ ▶n. Anat. Physiol. a neuron that transmits impulses between other neurons, esp. as part of a reflex arc. — **in·ter·neu·ro·nal** /-ˈn(y)o͝orənl; -n(y)o͝oˈrōnl/ adj. [1930s: from INTERNUNCIAL + NEURON.]

in·tern·ist /inˈtərnist; ˈintər-/ ▶n. Med. a specialist in internal medicine.

in·ter·node /ˈintərˌnōd/ ▶n. a slender part between two nodes or joints. ■ Bot. a part of a plant stem between two of the nodes from which leaves emerge. [17th C.: from L. *internodium,* from *inter-* 'between' + *nodus* 'knot.']

in·ter·nun·cial /ˌintərˈnənsēəl; -SHəl/ ▶adj. [attrib.] Anat. Physiol. (of neurons) forming connections between other neurons in the central nervous system. [19th C.: from L. *internuntius* (from *inter-* 'between' + *nuntius* 'messenger') + -AL.]

in·ter·o·cep·tive /ˌintərōˈseptiv/ ▶adj. Physiol. relating to stimuli produced within an organism, esp. in the gut and other internal organs. Compare with EXTEROCEPTIVE. [20th C.: from INTERIOR + RECEPTIVE.]

in·ter·o·cep·tor /ˌintərōˈseptər/ ▶n. Physiol. a sensory receptor that receives stimuli from within the body, esp. from the gut and other internal organs. Compare with EXTEROCEPTOR.

in·ter·pel·late /ˌintərˈpelāt; inˈtərpəˌlāt/ ▶v. [trans.] (in certain parliamentary systems) interrupt the order of the day by demanding an explanation from (the minister concerned). — **in·ter·pel·la·tion** /ˌintərpəˈlāSHən/ n. **in·ter·pel·la·tor** /-ˌlātər/ n. [16th C.: from L. *interpellat-* 'interrupted (by speech),' from the v. *interpellare,* from *inter-* 'between' + *pellere* 'to drive.']

in·ter·pen·e·trate /ˌintərˈpeniˌtrāt/ ▶v. penetrate or permeate between or within (something else). — **in·ter·pen·e·tra·tion** /-ˌpeniˈtrāSHən/ n. **in·ter·pen·e·tra·tive** /-ˌtrātiv/ adj.

in·ter·per·son·al /ˌintərˈpərsənəl/ ▶adj. [attrib.] of or relating to relationships or communication between people: *interpersonal skills.* — **in·ter·per·son·al·ly** adv.

in·ter·phase /ˈintərˌfāz/ ▶n. Biol. the resting phase between successive mitotic divisions of a cell, or between the first and second divisions of meiosis.

in·ter·plant /ˌintərˈplant/ ▶v. [trans.] (usu. **be interplanted**) plant (a crop or plant) together with another crop or plant.

in·ter·play /ˈintərˌplā/ ▶n. the way in which two or more things have an effect on each other.

in·ter·plead·er /ˌintərˈplēdər/ ▶n. Law a suit pleaded between two parties to determine a matter of claim or right to property held by a third party.

In·ter·pol /ˈintərˌpôl; -ˌpäl/ an organization based in Paris that coordinates investigations made by the police forces of member countries into crimes with an international dimension. [orig. the address for telegrams sent to the International Criminal Police Commission, founded in 1923; from *Inter(national) pol(ice).*]

in·ter·po·late /inˈtərpəˌlāt/ ▶v. [trans.] insert (something) between fixed points. ■ insert (words) in a book or other text, esp. in order to give a false impression as to its date. ■ make such insertions in (a book or text). ■ Math. insert (an intermediate value or term) into a series by estimating or calculating it from surrounding known values. — **in·ter·po·la·tion** /-ˌtərpəˈlāSHən/ n. **in·ter·po·la·tive** /-ˌlātiv/ adj. **in·ter·po·la·tor** n. [17th C.: from L. *interpolat-* 'refurbished, altered,' from the v. *interpolare,* from *inter-* 'between' + *-polare* (rel. to *polire* 'to polish').]

in·ter·pose /ˌintərˈpōz/ ▶v. **1** [trans.] place or insert between one thing and another. **2** [intrans.] intervene between parties. ■ [trans.] say (words) as an interruption. ■ [trans.] exercise or advance (a veto or objection) so as to interfere.

in·ter·po·si·tion /ˌintərpəˈziSHən/ ▶n. the action of interposing someone or something: *the interposition of members into management positions.*

in·ter·pret /inˈtərprit/ ▶v. (**-pret·ed, -pret·ing**) [trans.] **1** explain the meaning of (information, words, or actions): *interpret the evidence.* ■ [intrans.] translate orally the words of another person speaking a different language. ■ perform (a dramatic role or piece of music) in a particular way that conveys one's understanding of the creator's ideas. **2** understand (an action, mood, or way of behaving) as having a particular meaning or significance: *confidence interpreted as brashness.* — **in·ter·pret·a·bil·i·ty** /-ˌtərpritəˈbilitē/ n. **in·ter·pret·a·ble** adj. **in·ter·pre·ta·tive** /-ˌtātiv/ adj. **in·ter·pre·ta·tive·ly** /-ˌtātivlē/ adv. **in·ter·pre·tive** /-ˈtərpritiv/ adj. **in·ter·pre·tive·ly** /-ˈtərpritivlē/ adv. [ME: from OFr. *interpreter* or L. *interpretari* 'explain, translate,' from *interpres, interpret-* 'agent, translator, interpreter.']

in·ter·pre·ta·tion /inˌtərpriˈtāSHən/ ▶n. the action of explaining the meaning of something: *the interpretation of data.* ■ an explanation or way of explaining: *it's open to interpretation.* ■ a stylistic representation of a creative work or dramatic role: *two differing interpretations of the song.* — **in·ter·pre·ta·tion·al** /-SHənl/ adj.

in·ter·pret·er /inˈtərpritər/ ▶n. a person who interprets, esp. one who translates speech orally. ■ Comput. a program that can analyze and execute a program line by line.

in·ter·ra·cial /ˌintərˈrāSHəl/ ▶adj. existing between or involving different races. — **in·ter·ra·cial·ly** adv.

in·ter·reg·num /ˌintərˈregnəm/ ▶n. (pl. **-nums** or **-na** /-nə/) a period when normal government is suspended, esp. between successive reigns or regimes. ■ a lapse or pause in continuity. [16th C.: from L., from *inter-* 'between' + *regnum* 'reign.']

in·ter·re·late /ˌintər-rəˈlāt/ ▶v. relate or connect to one another: [intrans.] *each component interrelates with all the others.* — **in·ter·re·lat·ed·ness** n.

in·ter·re·la·tion·ship /ˌintər-rəˈlāSHənˌSHip/ ▶n. the way in which each of two or more things is related to the other or others. — **in·ter·re·la·tion** n.

interrog. ▶abbr. interrogative.

in·ter·ro·gate /inˈterəˌgāt/ ▶v. [trans.] ask questions of (someone, esp. a suspect or a prisoner) closely, aggressively, or formally. ■ Comput. obtain data from (a database or other computer file, storage device, or terminal). ■ (of an electronic device) transmit a signal to (another device, esp. one on a vehicle) to obtain a response giving information about identity, condition, etc. — **in·ter·ro·ga·tor** /-ˌgātər/ n. [15th C.: from L. *interrogat-* 'questioned,' from the v. *interrogare,* from *inter-* 'between' + *rogare* 'ask.']

in·ter·ro·ga·tion /inˌterəˈgāSHən/ ▶n. the action of interrogating or the process of being interrogated: *criminal interrogations.* — **in·ter·ro·ga·tion·al** /-SHənl/ adj.

in·ter·ro·ga·tion point (also **interrogation mark**) ▶n. another term for QUESTION MARK.

in·ter·rog·a·tive /ˌintəˈrägətiv/ ▶adj. having or conveying the force of a question: *an interrogative stare.* ■ Gram. used in questions: *an interrogative adverb.* Contrasted with AFFIRMATIVE and NEGATIVE. ▶n. a word used in questions, such as *how* or *what.* — **in·ter·rog·a·tive·ly** adv.

in·ter·rog·a·to·ry /ˌintəˈrägəˌtôrē/ ▶adj. conveying the force of a question; questioning. ▶n. (pl. **-ries**) Law a written question that is formally put to one party in a case by another party and that must be answered.

in·ter·rupt /ˌintəˈrəpt/ ▶v. [trans.] **1** stop the continuous progress of (an activity or process): *his education had been interrupted by the war.* ■ stop (someone speaking) by saying or doing something: [with direct speech] *"Hold on," he interrupted.* **2** break the continuity of (a line or surface). — **in·ter·rupt·i·ble** adj. **in·ter·rup·tion** n. **in·ter·rup·tive** adj. [ME: from L. *interrupt-* 'broken, interrupted,' from the v. *interrumpere,* from *inter-* 'between' + *rumpere* 'to break.']

in·ter·rupt·ed /ˌintəˈrəptid/ ▶adj. Bot. (of a compound leaf, inflorescence, or other plant organ) made discontinuous by smaller interposed leaflets or intervals of bare stem.

in·ter·rupt·er /ˌintəˈrəptər/ (also **in·ter·rup·tor**) ▶n. a person or thing that interrupts. ■ a device that automatically breaks an electric circuit if a fault develops.

in·ter se /ˈintər ˈsē; ˈsā/ ▶adv. between or among themselves: *all the shareholders inter se.* [19th C.: L.]

in·ter·sect /ˌintərˈsekt/ ▶v. [trans.] divide (something) by passing or lying across it: *an area intersected only by minor roads.* ■ [intrans.] (of two or more things) pass or lie across each other: *the lines intersect at right angles.* [17th C.: from L. *intersect-* 'cut, intersected,' from the v. *intersecare,* from *inter-* 'between' + *secare* 'to cut.']

in·ter·sec·tion /ˌintərˈsekSHən/ ▶n. a point or line common to lines or surfaces that intersect. ■ a point at which two or more things intersect, esp. roads: *the intersection of Main and Elm.* — **in·ter·sec·tion·al** /-SHənl/ adj.

in·ter·sex /ˈintərˌseks/ ▶n. the abnormal condition of being intermediate between male and female; hermaphroditism. ■ an individual in this condition; a hermaphrodite.

in·ter·sex·u·al /ˌintərˈsekSHo͞oəl/ ▶adj. **1** existing or occurring between the sexes. **2** relating to or having the condition of being intermediate between male and female. — **in·ter·sex·u·al·i·ty** /-ˌsekSHo͞oˈalitē/ n.

in·ter·space ▶ n. /ˈintər,spās/ a space between objects. ▶ v. /,intərˈspās/ [trans.] (usu. **be interspaced**) put or occupy a space between.

in·ter·spe·cif·ic /,intərspiˈsifik/ ▶ adj. Biol. existing or occurring between species. — **in·ter·spe·cif·i·cal·ly** adv.

in·ter·sperse /,intərˈspərs/ ▶ v. [trans.] (often **be interspersed**) scatter among or between other things; place here and there. ■ diversify (a thing or things) with other things at intervals: *debate interspersed with angry exchanges.* — **in·ter·sper·sion** /-ˈspərzHən/ n. [16th C.: from L. *interspers-* 'scattered between,' from *interspergere*, from *inter-* 'between' + *spargere* 'scatter.']

in·ter·sta·di·al /,intərˈstādēəl/ Geol. ▶ adj. of or relating to a minor period of less cold climate during a glacial period. Compare with INTERGLACIAL. ▶ n. an interstadial period. [20th C.: from INTER- 'between' + *stadial* from L. *stadialis*, from *stadium* 'stage.']

in·ter·state ▶ adj. /ˈintər,stāt/ [attrib.] existing or carried on between states: *interstate travel.* ▶ n. (also **interstate highway**) one of a system of expressways covering the 48 contiguous states.

in·ter·stel·lar /,intərˈstelər/ ▶ adj. occurring or situated between stars: *interstellar travel.*

in·ter·stice /inˈtərstis/ ▶ n. (usu. **interstices**) an intervening space, esp. a small or narrow one. [ME: from L. *interstitium*, from *intersistere* 'stand between,' from *inter-* 'between' + *sistere* 'to stand.']

in·ter·sti·tial /,intərˈstisHəl/ ▶ adj. of, forming, or occupying interstices: *the interstitial space.* ■ Ecol. (of minute animals) living in the spaces between individual sand grains in the soil or aquatic sediments: *the interstitial fauna of marine sands.* — **in·ter·sti·tial·ly** adv.

in·ter·sub·jec·tive /,intərsəbˈjektiv/ ▶ adj. Philos. existing between conscious minds; shared by more than one conscious mind. — **in·ter·sub·jec·tive·ly** adv. **in·ter·sub·jec·tiv·i·ty** /-,səbjekˈtivitē/ n.

in·ter·tex·tu·al·i·ty /,intər,teksCHo͞oˈalitē/ ▶ n. the relationship between texts, esp. literary ones. — **in·ter·tex·tu·al** /-ˈteksCHo͞oəl/ adj. **in·ter·tex·tu·al·ly** /-ˈteksCHo͞oəlē/ adv.

in·ter·ti·dal /,intərˈtīdl/ ▶ adj. Ecol. of or denoting the area of a seashore that is covered at high tide and uncovered at low tide.

in·ter·track /ˈintərˈtrak/ ▶ adj. [attrib.] (of betting, esp. on horse races) involving bets placed at racecourses other than the one at which the race betted on is being run.

in·ter·trib·al /,intərˈtrībəl/ ▶ adj. existing or occurring between different tribes. ■ involving members of more than one tribe.

in·ter·trop·i·cal con·ver·gence zone /,intərˈträpikəl/ (abbr.: **ITCZ**) ▶ n. a narrow zone near the equator where northern and southern air masses converge, characterized by low atmospheric pressure.

in·ter·twine /,intərˈtwīn/ ▶ v. twist or twine together. — **in·ter·twine·ment** n.

in·ter·val /ˈintərvəl/ ▶ n. **1** an intervening time or space. **2** a pause; a break in activity. ■ Brit. an intermission in a theatrical or musical performance. **3** a space between two things; a gap. ■ the difference in pitch between two musical sounds.
– PHRASES **at intervals 1** with time between, not continuously. **2** with spaces between. — **in·ter·val·lic** /,intərˈvalik/ adj. [ME: from OFr. *entrevalle*, based on L. *intervallum* 'space between ramparts, interval,' from *inter-* 'between' + *vallum* 'rampart.']

in·ter·val train·ing ▶ n. training in which a runner alternates between running and jogging over set distances. ■ training in which an athlete alternates between two activities, typically requiring different speeds, degrees of effort, etc.

in·ter·vene /,intərˈvēn/ ▶ v. [intrans.] **1** come between so as to prevent or alter a result or course of events. ■ (of an event or circumstance) occur as a delay or obstacle to something being done. ■ interrupt verbally. ■ Law interpose in a lawsuit as a third party. **2** [usu. as adj.] (**intervening**) occur in time between events. ■ be situated between things. — **in·ter·ven·er** n. **in·ter·ven·ient** /-ˈvēnyənt/ adj. **in·ter·ve·nor** /-ˈvēnər/ n. [16th C.: from L. *intervenire*, from *inter-* 'between' + *venire* 'come.']

in·ter·ven·tion /,intərˈvensHən/ ▶ n. the action or process of intervening. ■ interference by a country in another's affairs. ■ action taken to improve a situation, esp. a medical disorder. — **in·ter·ven·tion·al** /-sHənl/ adj.

in·ter·ven·tion·ist /,intərˈvensHənist/ ▶ adj. favoring intervention, esp. by a government in its domestic economy or by one country in the affairs of another. ▶ n. a person who favors intervention of this kind. — **in·ter·ven·tion·ism** n.

in·ter·ver·te·bral disk ▶ n. see DISK (sense 3).

in·ter·view /ˈintər,vyo͞o/ ▶ n. a meeting of people face to face, esp. for consultation. ■ a conversation between a journalist or radio or television host and a person of public interest, used as the basis of a broadcast or publication. ■ an oral examination of an applicant for a job, college admission, etc. ▶ v. [trans.] (often **be interviewed**) hold an interview with (someone). ■ question (someone) to discover their opinions or experience. ■ orally examine (an applicant for a job, college admission, etc.): *he came to be interviewed for a top job* | [intrans.] *I was interviewing all last week.* ■ [no obj., with adverbial] perform (well or badly) at an interview. — **in·ter·view·ee** /,intərvyo͞oˈē/ n. **in·ter·view·er** n. [16th C.: from Fr. *entrevue*, from *voir* 'to see.']

in·ter vi·vos /ˈintər ˈvēvōs; ˈvīvōs/ ▶ adv. & adj. (esp. of a gift as opposed to a legacy) between living people. [L.]

in·ter·vo·cal·ic /,intərvōˈkalik/ ▶ adj. Phonet. occurring between vowels: *in intervocalic position.* — **in·ter·vo·cal·i·cal·ly** adv.

in·ter·war /,intərˈwôr/ ▶ adj. [attrib.] existing in the period between two wars, esp. the two world wars (i.e., between 1918 and 1939).

in·ter·weave /,intərˈwēv/ ▶ v. (past **-wove** ; past part. **-wov·en**) weave or become woven together: [trans.] *the rugs are made by interweaving the warp and weft strands* | [intrans.] *the branches interwove above his head.* ■ [trans.] fig. blend closely.

in·tes·tate /inˈtestāt; -tit/ ▶ adj. [predic.] not having made a will before one dies. ■ [attrib.] of or relating to a person who dies without having made a will. ▶ n. a person who has died without having made a will. — **in·tes·ta·cy** /-təsē/ n. [ME: from L. *intestatus*, from *in-* 'not' + *testatus* 'testified' (see TESTATE).]

in·tes·ti·nal flo·ra /inˈtestənl ˈflôrə/ ▶ plural n. [usu. treated as sing.] the symbiotic bacteria occurring naturally in the intestine.

in·tes·tine /inˈtestən/ (also **in·tes·tines**) ▶ n. (in vertebrates) the lower part of the alimentary canal from the end of the stomach to the anus. See also LARGE INTESTINE, SMALL INTESTINE. ■ (esp. in invertebrates) the whole alimentary canal from the mouth downward. — **in·tes·ti·nal** /-tənl/ adj. [ME: from L. *intestinum*, neut. of *intestinus*, from *intus* 'within.']

in·thrall /inˈTHrôl/ ▶ v. archaic spelling of ENTHRALL.

in·ti /ˈintē/ ▶ n. (pl. same or **in·tis** /ˈintēz/) a former basic monetary unit of Peru, equal to 100 centimos.

in·ti·fa·da /,intəˈfädə/ ▶ n. the Palestinian uprising against Israeli occupation of the West Bank and Gaza Strip, beginning in 1987. [from Arab. *intifāḍa* 'an uprising', from *intifaḍa* 'be shaken.']

in·ti·ma /ˈintəmə/ ▶ n. (pl. **-mae** /-,mē/) Anat. Zool. the innermost coating or membrane of a part or organ, esp. of a vein or artery. — **in·ti·mal** /-məl/ adj. [19th C.: shortening of mod. L. *tunica intima* 'innermost sheath.']

in·ti·ma·cy /ˈintəməsē/ ▶ n. (pl. **-cies**) close familiarity or friendship; closeness. ■ a private cozy atmosphere. ■ an intimate act, esp. sexual intercourse. ■ an intimate remark. ■ [in sing.] closeness of observation or knowledge of a subject: *an intimacy with Swahili literature.*

in·ti·mate[1] /ˈintəmit/ ▶ adj. **1** closely acquainted; familiar, close. ■ (of a place or setting) having or creating an informal friendly atmosphere. ■ [predic.] used euphemistically to indicate that a couple is having a sexual relationship: *having been intimate with her.* ■ involving very close connection. **2** private and personal. ■ used euphemistically to refer to a person's genitals: *touching her in the most intimate places.* **3** (of knowledge) detailed; thorough. ▶ n. a very close friend. — **in·ti·mate·ly** adv. [17th C.: from L. *intimare* 'make familiar,' from *intimus* 'inmost.']

in·ti·mate[2] /ˈintə,māt/ ▶ v. [trans.] imply or hint. ■ state or make known. — **in·ti·ma·tion** /,intəˈmāsHən/ n. [16th C.: from late L. *intimat-* 'made known,' from the v. *intimare* (see INTIMATE[1]).]

in·tim·i·date /inˈtimi,dāt/ ▶ v. frighten or overawe (someone), esp. in order to make them do what one wants. — **in·tim·i·dat·ing·ly** adv. **in·tim·i·da·tion** /-,timiˈdāsHən/ n. **in·tim·i·da·tor** /-,dātər/ n. **in·tim·i·da·to·ry** /-də,tôrē/ adj. [17th C.: from med. L. *intimidat-* 'made timid,' from the v. *intimidare* (based on *timidus* 'timid').]

in·tinc·tion /inˈtiNGksHən/ ▶ n. the action of dipping the bread in the wine at a Eucharist so that a communicant receives both together. [16th C.: from late L. *intinctio(n-)*, from L. *intingere*, from *in-* 'into' + *tingere* 'dip.']

intl. ▶ abbr. international.

in·to /ˈinto͞o/ ▶ prep. **1** expressing movement or action with the result that someone or something becomes enclosed or surrounded by something else: *Sara got into her car.* **2** expressing movement or action with the result that someone or something makes physical contact with something else: *he crashed into a parked car.* **3** indicating a route by which someone or something may arrive at a particular destination: *the narrow road into the village.* **4** indicating the direction toward which someone or something is turned when confronting something else: *with the wind blowing into your face.* **5** indicating an object of attention or interest: *a clearer insight into what is involved.* **6** expressing a change of state: *the fruit can be made into jam.* **7** expressing the result of an action: *they forced the club into a special general meeting.* **8** expressing division: *three into twelve equals four.* **9** informal (of a person) taking a lively and active interest in (something): *he's into surfing.* [OE *intō* (see IN, TO).]

in·tol·er·a·ble /inˈtälərəbəl/ ▶ adj. unable to be endured: *the intolerable pressures of his work.* — **in·tol·er·a·bil·i·ty** /-,tälərəˈbilitē/ n. **in·tol·er·a·ble·ness** n. **in·tol·er·a·bly** adv.

in·tol·er·ant /inˈtälərənt/ ▶ adj. not tolerant of others' views, beliefs, or behavior that differ from one's own. ■ unable to be given (a medicine or other treatment) or to eat (a food) without adverse effects. ■ (of a plant or animal) unable to survive exposure to (physical influence). — **in·tol·er·ance** n. **in·tol·er·ant·ly** adv.

in·to·nate /ˈintə,nāt/ ▶ v. intone. [18th C.: from med. L. *intonat-* 'intoned,' from the v. *intonare* (see INTONE).]

in·to·na·tion /,intəˈnāsHən; -tō-/ ▶ n. **1** the rise and fall of the voice in speaking. ■ the action of intoning or reciting in a singing voice. **2** accuracy of pitch in playing or singing. **3** the opening phrase of a plainsong melody. — **in·to·na·tion·al** /-sHənl/ adj.

PRONUNCIATION KEY ə *ago, up*; ər *over, fur*; a *hat*; ā *ate*; ä *car*; e *let*; ē *see*; i *fit*; ī *by*; NG *sing*; ō *go*; ô *law, for*; oi *toy*; o͝o *good*; o͞o *goo*; ou *out*; TH *thin*; T͟H *then*; ZH *vision*

in·tone /in'tōn/ ▶ **v.** [trans.] say or recite with little rise and fall of the pitch of the voice. — **in·ton·er n.** [15th C.: from med. L. *intonare*, from *in-* 'into' + L. *tonus* 'tone.']

in to·to /,in 'tōtō/ ▶ **adv.** as a whole. [L.]

in·tox·i·cant /in'täksikənt/ ▶ **n.** an intoxicating substance.

in·tox·i·cate /in'täksi,kāt/ ▶ **v.** [trans.] [usu. as adj.] (**intoxicated**) (of alcoholic drink or a drug) cause (someone) to lose control of their faculties or behavior. ■ poison. ■ fig. excite or exhilarate. — **in·tox·i·cat·ing adj. in·tox·i·cat·ing·ly adv. in·tox·i·ca·tion** /-,täksi'kāsHən/ **n.** [ME: from med. L. *intoxicare*, from *in-* 'into' + *toxicare* 'to poison,' from L. *toxicum* (see TOXIC).]

intr. ▶ **abbr.** ■ intransitive. ■ introduce or introduced or introducing or introduction or introductory.

intra- ▶ **prefix** (added to adjectives) on the inside; within: *intramural* | *intrauterine*. [from L. *intra* 'inside.']

in·tra·cel·lu·lar /,intrə'selyələr/ ▶ **adj.** Biol. located or occurring within a cell or cells. — **in·tra·cel·lu·lar·ly adv.**

in·tra·cra·ni·al /,intrə'krānēəl/ ▶ **adj.** within the skull. — **in·tra·cra·ni·al·ly adv.**

in·trac·ta·ble /in'traktəbəl/ ▶ **adj.** hard to control or deal with. ■ (of a person) difficult; stubborn. — **in·trac·ta·bil·i·ty** /-,traktə'bilitē/ **n. in·trac·ta·ble·ness n. in·trac·ta·bly adv.** [15th C.: from L. *intractabilis*, from *in-* 'not' + *tractabilis* (see TRACTABLE).]

in·tra·day /'intrə,dā/ ▶ **adj.** [attrib.] Stock Market occurring within one day.

in·tra·dos /'intrə,däs; -,dōs; in'trā-/ ▶ **n.** (pl. same or **-dos·es**) Archit. the lower or inner curve of an arch. Often contrasted with EXTRADOS. [18th C.: from Fr., from *intra-* 'on the inside' + *dos* 'the back' (from L. *dorsum*).]

in·tra·mo·lec·u·lar /,intrəmə'lekyələr/ ▶ **adj.** existing or taking place within a molecule. — **in·tra·mo·lec·u·lar·ly adv.**

in·tra·mu·ral /,intrə'myŏŏrəl/ ▶ **adj.** situated or done within the walls of a building: *both intramural and churchyard graves.* ■ (esp. of athletics) taking place within a single educational institution. ■ forming part of normal university or college studies. ■ Med. Biol. situated within the wall of a hollow organ or a cell. ■ situated or done within a community. — **in·tra·mu·ral·ly adv.** [19th C.: from INTRA- 'within' + L. *murus* 'wall' + -AL.]

in·tra·mus·cu·lar /,intrə'məskyələr/ ▶ **adj.** situated or taking place within, or administered into, a muscle. — **in·tra·mus·cu·lar·ly adv.**

in·tra·net /'intrə,net/ (also **In·tra·net**) ▶ **n.** Comput. a local or restricted communications network, esp. a private network created using World Wide Web software.

in·tran·si·gent /in'transijənt; -zi-/ ▶ **adj.** unwilling or refusing to change one's views or to agree about something. ▶ **n.** an intransigent person. — **in·tran·si·gence n. in·tran·si·gen·cy n. in·tran·si·gent·ly adv.** [19th C.: from Fr. *intransigeant*, ult. from L. *in-* 'not' + *transigere* 'come to an understanding.']

in·tran·si·tive /in'transitiv; -zi-/ ▶ **adj.** (of a verb or a sense or use of a verb) not taking a direct object, e.g., *look* in *look at the sky*. The opposite of TRANSITIVE. ▶ **n.** an intransitive verb. — **in·tran·si·tive·ly adv. in·tran·si·tiv·i·ty** /-,transi'tivitē; -zi-/ **n.** [17th C.: from late L. *intransitivus* (see TRANSITIVE).]

in·tra·pre·neur /,intrəprə'nər; -'n(y)ŏŏr/ ▶ **n.** a manager within a company who promotes innovative product development and marketing. — **in·tra·pre·neu·ri·al** /-'nərēəl; -'n(y)ŏŏr-/ **adj.** [1970s (orig. US): from INTRA- 'within' + a shortened form of ENTREPRENEUR.]

in·tra·spe·cif·ic /,intrəspə'sifik/ ▶ **adj.** Biol. produced, occurring, or existing within a species or between individuals of a single species: *intraspecific competition.*

in·tra·u·ter·ine /,intrə'yŏŏtərin; -,rīn/ ▶ **adj.** within the uterus.

in·tra·u·ter·ine de·vice (abbr.: **IUD**) ▶ **n.** a contraceptive device fitted inside the uterus and physically preventing the implantation of fertilized ova.

in·tra·ve·nous /,intrə'vēnəs/ (abbr.: **IV**) ▶ **adj.** existing within, or administered into, a vein or veins. — **in·tra·ve·nous·ly adv.**

in·tra·zon·al /,intrə'zōnl/ ▶ **adj.** Soil Science (of a soil) having a well-developed structure different from that expected for its climatic and vegetational zone owing to the overriding influence of relief, parent material, or some other local factor.

in·trench ▶ **v.** var. of ENTRENCH.

in·trep·id /in'trepid/ ▶ **adj.** fearless; adventurous (often used for rhetorical or humorous effect). — **in·tre·pid·i·ty** /,intrə'piditē/ **n. in·trep·id·ly adv. in·trep·id·ness n.** [17th C.: from Fr. *intrépide* or L. *intrepidus*, from *in-* 'not' + *trepidus* 'alarmed.']

in·tri·ca·cy /'intrikəsē/ ▶ **n.** (pl. **-cies**) the quality of being intricate. ■ (**intricacies**) details, esp. of an involved or perplexing subject.

in·tri·cate /'intrikit/ ▶ **adj.** very complicated or detailed. — **in·tri·cate·ly adv.** [ME: from L. *intricat-* 'entangled,' from the v. *intricare*, from *in-* 'into' + *tricae* 'tricks, perplexities.']

in·tri·gant /'intri,gənt; aNtrē'gäN/ (also **in·tri·guant**) ▶ **n.** a person who makes secret plans to do something illicit or detrimental to someone else. [18th C.: var. of Fr. *intriguant*, from *intriguer* 'to intrigue.']

in·trigue ▶ **v.** /in'trēg/ (**-trigues, -trigued, -tri·guing**) **1** [trans.] arouse the curiosity or interest of; fascinate. **2** [intrans.] make secret plans to do something illicit or detrimental to someone. ▶ **n.** /'in,trēg/ **1** the secret planning of something illicit or detrimental to someone. ■ a secret love affair. **2** a mysterious or fascinating quality. — **in·tri·guer n. in·tri·guing·ly adv.**: *the album is intriguingly titled "The Revenge of the Goldfish."* [17th C.: from Fr. *intriguer* 'to tangle, to plot,' via Ital. from L. *intricare* (see INTRICATE).]

in·trin·sic /in'trinzik; -sik/ ▶ **adj.** belonging naturally; essential. ■ (of a muscle) contained wholly within the organ on which it acts. — **in·trin·si·cal·ly adv.** [15th C.: from Fr. *intrinsèque*, from late L. *intrinsecus*, from the earlier adv. *intrinsecus* 'inwardly.']

in·trin·sic fac·tor ▶ **n.** Biochem. a substance secreted by the stomach that enables the body to absorb vitamin B_{12}. It is a glycoprotein.

in·tro /'intrō/ ▶ **n.** (pl. **-tros**) informal an introduction. [19th C.: abbrev.]

intro. ▶ **abbr.** ■ introduce or introduced or introducing or introduction or introductory.

intro- ▶ **prefix** into; inward: *introgression* | *introvert*. [from L. *intro* 'to the inside.']

in·tro·duce /,intrə'd(y)ōōs/ ▶ **v.** [trans.] **1** (often **be introduced**) bring (something, esp. a product, measure, or concept) into use or operation for the first time. ■ (**introduce something to**) bring a subject to the attention of (someone) for the first time. ■ present (a new piece of legislation) for debate in a legislative assembly. ■ bring (a new plant, animal, or disease) to a place and establish it there. **2** make (someone) known by name to another in person, esp. formally. **3** insert or bring into something. **4** occur at the start of; open. ■ (of a person) provide an opening explanation or announcement for (a television program, book, etc.). — **in·tro·duc·er n.** [ME: from L. *introducere*, from *intro-* 'to the inside' + *ducere* 'to lead.']

in·tro·duc·tion /,intrə'dəksHən/ ▶ **n. 1** the bringing of a product, measure, concept, etc., into use or operation for the first time. ■ the action of bringing a new plant, animal, or disease to a place. ■ a thing, such as a product, measure, plant, etc., newly brought in. **2** (often **introductions**) a formal presentation of one person to another, in which each is told the other's name. **3** a thing preliminary to something else. ■ an explanatory section at the beginning of a book, report, etc. ■ a preliminary section in a piece of music, often thematically different from the main section. ■ a book or course of study intended to introduce a subject to a person. ■ [in sing.] a person's first experience of a subject or thing.

in·tro·duc·to·ry /,intrə'dəktərē/ ▶ **adj.** serving as an introduction to a subject or topic; basic or preliminary. ■ intended to persuade someone to purchase something for the first time.

in·tro·gres·sion /,intrə'gresHən/ ▶ **n.** Biol. the transfer of genetic information from one species to another as a result of hybridization between them and repeated backcrossing. — **in·tro·gres·sive** /-'gresiv/ **adj.** [17th C.: from L. *introgredi* 'step in,' from *intro-* 'to the inside' + *gradi* 'proceed, walk,' on the pattern of *egression, ingression.*]

in·tro·it /'intrō-it; -troit/ ▶ **n.** a psalm or antiphon sung or said while the priest approaches the altar for the Eucharist. [ME: via OFr. from L. *introitus*, from *introire* 'enter,' from *intro-* 'to the inside' + *ire* 'go.']

in·tro·jec·tion /,intrə'jeksHən/ ▶ **n.** Psychoanal. the unconscious adoption of the ideas or attitudes of others. — **in·tro·ject** /-'jekt/ **v.** [19th C.: from INTRO- 'into,' on the pattern of *projection.*]

in·tron /'inträn/ ▶ **n.** Biochem. a segment of a DNA or RNA molecule that does not code for proteins and interrupts the sequence of genes. Compare with EXON. — **in·tron·ic** /in'tränik/ **adj.** [1970s: from INTRA- 'within' + -GENIC + -ON.]

in·trorse /'intrôrs/ ▶ **adj.** Bot. Zool. turned inward. The opposite of EXTRORSE. ■ (of anthers) releasing their pollen toward the center of the flower. — **in·trorse·ly adv.** [19th C.: from L. *introrsus*, from *introversus* 'turned inward.']

in·tro·spect /,intrə'spekt/ ▶ **v.** [intrans.] examine one's own thoughts or feelings. [17th C.: from L. *introspect-* 'looked into,' from the v. *introspicere*, or from *introspectare* 'keep looking into.']

in·tro·spec·tion /,intrə'speksHən/ ▶ **n.** the examination or observation of one's own mental and emotional processes: *quiet introspection can be extremely valuable.* — **in·tro·spec·tive** /-'spektiv/ **adj. in·tro·spec·tive·ly** /-'spektivlē/ **adv. in·tro·spec·tive·ness** /-'spektivnis/ **n.**

in·tro·vert ▶ **n.** /'intrə,vərt/ a shy, reticent, and typically self-centered person. ■ Psychol. a person predominantly concerned with their own thoughts and feelings rather than with external things. Compare with EXTROVERT. ▶ **adj.** another term for INTROVERTED. — **in·tro·ver·sion** /-,vərzHən/ **n. in·tro·ver·sive** /-,vərsiv/ **adj.** [17th C.: from mod. L. *introvertere*, from *intro-* 'to the inside' + *vertere* 'to turn.']

in·tro·vert·ed /'intrə,vərtid/ ▶ **adj. 1** of, denoting, or typical of an introvert. ■ (of a community or other group) concerned principally with its own affairs; inward-looking or parochial. **2** Anat. & Zool. (of an organ or other body part) turned or pushed inward on itself.

in·trude /in'trōōd/ ▶ **v. 1** [intrans.] put oneself deliberately into a place or situation where one is unwelcome or uninvited. ■ enter with disruptive or adverse effect. ■ [trans.] introduce into a situation with disruptive or adverse effect. **2** [trans.] Geol. (of igneous rock) be forced into (a preexisting formation). ■ (usu. **be intruded**) force or thrust (igneous rock) into a preexisting formation. [16th C.: from L. *intrudere*, from *in-* 'into' + *trudere* 'to thrust.']

in·trud·er /in'trōōdər/ ▶ **n.** a person who intrudes, esp. into a building with criminal intent.

in·tru·sion /in'trōōzHən/ ▶ **n. 1** the action of intruding. ■ a thing that intrudes. **2** Geol. the action or process of forcing a body of igneous rock between or through existing formations, without reaching the earth's surface. ■ a body of igneous rock that has intruded the surrounding strata.

in·tru·sive /in'trōōsiv/ ▶ **adj. 1** making an unwelcome manifestation with disruptive or adverse effect. ■ (of a person) disturbing another by one's uninvited or unwelcome presence. **2** Phonet. (of a sound) pronounced between words or syllables to facilitate pronunciation, such as an *r* in *saw a movie*, which occurs in the speech of some eastern New Englanders and metropolitan New Yorkers. **3** Geol. of, relating to, or formed by intrusion. — **in·tru·sive·ly** adv. **in·tru·sive·ness** n.

in·trust /in'trəst/ ▶ v. archaic spelling of ENTRUST.

in·tu·bate /'int(y)o͞oˌbāt/ ▶ v. [trans.] Med. insert a tube into (a person or a body part, esp. the trachea for ventilation). — **in·tu·ba·tion** /ˌint(y)o͞o'bāsʜən/ n. [19th C.: from IN-[2] 'into' + L. *tuba* 'tube' + -ATE[3].]

in·tu·it /in't(y)o͞o-it/ ▶ v. [trans.] understand or work out by instinct. — **in·tu·it·a·ble** adj. [18th C.: from L. *intuit-* 'contemplated,' from the v. *intueri*, from *in-* 'upon' + *tueri* 'to look.']

in·tu·i·tion /ˌint(y)o͞o'isʜən/ ▶ n. the ability to understand something immediately, without the need for conscious reasoning. ■ a thing that one knows or considers likely from instinctive feeling rather than conscious reasoning. — **in·tu·i·tion·al** /-'isʜənl/ adj. **in·tu·i·tion·al·ly** /-'isʜənl-ē/ adv.

in·tu·i·tion·ism /ˌint(y)o͞o'isʜəˌnizəm/ (also **in·tu·i·tion·al·ism** /-'isʜənlˌizəm/) ▶ n. Philos. the theory that primary truths and principles (esp. those of ethics and metaphysics) are known directly by intuition. ■ the theory that mathematical knowledge is based on intuition and mental construction, rejecting certain modes of reasoning and the notion of independent mathematical objects. — **in·tu·i·tion·ist** n. & adj.

in·tu·i·tive /in't(y)o͞oitiv/ ▶ adj. using or based on what one feels to be true even without conscious reasoning; instinctive. ■ (chiefly of computer software) easy to use and understand. — **in·tu·i·tive·ly** adv. **in·tu·i·tive·ness** n.

in·tu·mesce /ˌint(y)o͞o'mes/ ▶ v. [intrans.] rare swell up. — **in·tu·mes·cence** /-'mesəns/ n. **in·tu·mes·cent** /ˌint(y)o͞o'mesənt/ adj. [18th C.: from L. *intumescere*, from *in-* 'into' + *tumescere* 'begin to swell' (from *tumere* 'swell').]

in·tus·sus·cep·tion /ˌintəsə'sepsʜən/ ▶ n. **1** Med. the inversion of one portion of the intestine within another. **2** Bot. the growth of a cell wall by the deposition of cellulose. [18th C.: from mod. L. *intussusceptio(n-)*, from L. *intus* 'within' + *susceptio(n-)* (from *suscipere* 'take up').]

in·twine /in'twīn/ ▶ v. archaic spelling of ENTWINE.

In·u·it /'in(y)o͞o-it/ ▶ n. **1** (pl. same or **-its**) a member of an indigenous people of northern Canada and parts of Greenland and Alaska. **2** the family of languages of this people, one of the three branches of the Eskimo-Aleut language family. It is also known, esp. to its speakers, as **Inuktitut**. ▶ adj. of or relating to the Inuit or their language. [Inuit, pl. of *inuk* 'person.']

– USAGE The peoples inhabiting the regions from northwestern Canada to western Greenland speak **Inuit** languages (**Inuit** in Canada, **Greenlandic** in Greenland) and call themselves **Inuit** (not **Eskimo**), and **Inuit** now has official status in Canada. By analogy, **Inuit** is also used in the US, usually in an attempt to be politically correct, as a general synonym for **Eskimo**. This, however, is inaccurate because there are no **Inuit** in Alaska and **Inuit** therefore cannot include people from Alaska (who speak **Inupiaq**, which is closely related to **Inuit**, or **Yupik**, which is also spoken in Siberia). Since neither **Inupiaq** nor **Yupik** is in common US usage, only **Eskimo** includes all of these peoples and their languages. See also usage at ESKIMO.

I·nuk·ti·tut /i'n(y)o͝oktiˌto͞ot/ (also **I·nuk·ti·tuk** /-to͝ok/) ▶ n. the Inuit language spoken in the central and eastern Canadian Arctic. [Inuit, lit. 'the Inuk way,' used as the title of a periodical.]

in·u·lin /'inyəlin/ ▶ n. Biochem. a polysaccharide based on fructose present in the roots of various plants and used medically to test kidney function. [19th C.: from L. *inula* (identified by med. herbalists with elecampane) + -IN[1].]

in·unc·tion /i'nəɴɢ(k)sʜən/ ▶ n. esp. Med. the rubbing of ointment or oil into the skin. [15th C.: from L. *inunctio(n-)*, from *inunguere* 'smear on.']

in·un·date /'inənˌdāt/ ▶ v. [trans.] (usu. **be inundated**) flood. ■ fig. overwhelm (someone) with things or people to be dealt with: *we're inundated with complaints*. — **in·un·da·tion** /ˌinən'dāsʜən/ n. [16th C.: from L. *inundat-* 'flooded,' from the v. *inundare*, from *in-* 'into, upon' + *undare* 'to flow' (from *unda* 'a wave').]

I·nu·pi·aq /i'n(y)o͞opēˌak/ (also **I·nu·pi·at** /-ˌat/, **I·nu·pik** /i'n(y)o͞opik/) ▶ n. (pl. same) **1** a member of a group of the Eskimo people inhabiting northwestern Alaska. **2** the language of this people. ▶ adj. of or relating to this people or their language. [Inupiaq, from *inuk* 'person' + *piaq* 'genuine.']

in·ure /i'n(y)o͝or/ (also **en·ure**) ▶ v. **1** [trans.] (usu. **be inured to**) accustom (someone) to something, esp. something unpleasant. **2** [intrans.] (**enure for/to**) Law come into operation; take effect: *a release given to one of two joint contractors inures to the benefit of both*. — **in·ure·ment** n. [ME *inure*, *enure*, from an Anglo-Norman Fr. phr. meaning 'in use or practice,' from *en* 'in' + OFr. *euvre* 'work' (from L. *opera*).]

in·urn /in'ərn/ ▶ v. [trans.] place or bury (something, esp. ashes after cremation) in an urn. — **in·urn·ment** n.

in u·ter·o /in 'yo͞otərō/ ▶ adv. & adj. in a woman's uterus; before birth. [L.]

in·u·tile /in'yo͞otl; -'yo͞otīl/ ▶ adj. useless; pointless. — **in·u·til·i·ty** /ˌinyo͞o'tilitē/ n. [ME: from OFr., from L. *inutilis*, from *in-* 'not' + *utilis* 'useful.']

inv. ▶ abbr. ■ invent or invented or invention or inventor. ■ inventory. ■ investment. ■ invoice.

in va·cu·o /in 'vakyo͞oˌō/ ▶ adv. in a vacuum. ■ away from or without the normal context or environment. [L.]

in·vade /in'vād/ ▶ v. [trans.] (of an armed force or its commander) enter (a country or region) so as to subjugate or occupy it: *Iraq's intention to invade Kuwait* | [intrans.] *they would invade at dawn*. ■ enter (a place, situation, or sphere of activity) in large numbers, esp. with intrusive effect. ■ (of a parasite or disease) spread into (an organism or bodily part). ■ (of a person or emotion) encroach or intrude on. — **in·vad·er** n. [ME: from L. *invadere*, from *in-* 'into' + *vadere* 'go.']

in·vag·i·nate /in'vajəˌnāt/ ▶ v. (**be invaginated**) esp. Anat. & Biol. be turned inside out or folded back on itself to form a cavity or pouch.

in·vag·i·na·tion /inˌvajə'nāsʜən/ ▶ n. esp. Anat. & Biol. the action or process of being turned inside out or folded back on itself to form a cavity or pouch. ■ a cavity or pouch so formed. [17th C.: from mod. L. *invaginatio(n-)*, based on IN-[2] 'into' + L. *vagina* 'sheath.']

in·va·lid[1] /'invəlid/ ▶ n. a person made weak or disabled by illness or injury. ▶ v. (**-lid·ed**, **-lid·ing**) [trans.] (usu. **be invalided**) remove (someone) from active military service because of injury or illness: *he was invalided out of the infantry*. ■ disable (someone) by injury or illness. — **in·va·lid·ism** n. [17th C.: a special sense of INVALID[2], with a change of pronunciation.]

in·val·id[2] /in'valid/ ▶ adj. not valid, in particular: ■ (esp. of an official document or procedure) not legally recognized and therefore void because contravening a regulation or law. ■ (esp. of an argument, statement, or theory) not true because based on erroneous information or unsound reasoning. ■ (of computer instructions, data, etc.) not conforming to the correct format or specifications. — **in·val·id·ly** adv.

in·val·i·date /in'valiˌdāt/ ▶ v. [trans.] **1** make (an argument, statement, or theory) unsound or erroneous. **2** deprive (an official document or procedure) of legal efficacy because it contravenes a regulation or law. — **in·val·i·da·tion** /-ˌvali'dāsʜən/ n. **in·val·i·da·tor** /-ˌdātər/ n. [17th C.: from med. L. *invalidat-* 'annulled,' from the v. *invalidare* (based on L. *validus* 'strong').]

in·va·lid·i·ty /ˌinvə'liditē/ ▶ n. **1** the fact of not being valid. **2** esp. Brit. the condition of being an invalid.

in·val·u·a·ble /in'valyo͞oəbəl/ ▶ adj. extremely useful; indispensable: *an invaluable source of information*. — **in·val·u·a·ble·ness** n. **in·val·u·a·bly** adv.

In·var /'invär/ ▶ n. trademark an alloy of iron and nickel with a negligible coefficient of expansion, used in the making of clocks and scientific instruments. [20th C.: abbrev. of INVARIABLE.]

in·var·i·a·ble /in've(ə)rēəbəl/ ▶ adj. never changing. ■ (of a noun in an inflected language) having the same form in both the singular and the plural, e.g., *sheep*. ■ Math. (of a quantity) constant. — **in·var·i·a·bil·i·ty** /-ˌve(ə)rēə'bilitē/ n. **in·var·i·a·ble·ness** n.

in·var·i·a·bly /in've(ə)rēəblē/ ▶ adv. in every case or on every occasion; always.

in·var·i·ant /in've(ə)rēənt/ ▶ adj. never changing. ▶ n. Math. a function, quantity, or property that remains unchanged when a specified transformation is applied. — **in·var·i·ance** n.

in·va·sion /in'vāzʜən/ ▶ n. an instance of invading a country or region with an armed force. ■ an incursion by a large number of people or things into a place or sphere of activity: *stadium guards are preparing for another invasion of fans*. ■ an unwelcome intrusion into another's domain. ■ the infestation of a body by harmful organisms.

in·va·sive /in'vāsiv/ ▶ adj. (esp. of plants or a disease) tending to spread prolifically and undesirably or harmfully. ■ (esp. of an action or sensation) tending to intrude on a person's thoughts or privacy. ■ (of medical procedures) involving the introduction of instruments or other objects into the body or body cavities.

in·vec·tive /in'vektiv/ ▶ n. insulting, abusive, or highly critical language. [ME: from OFr. *invectif*, *-ive*, from late L. *invectivus* 'attacking,' from *invehere* (see INVEIGH).]

in·veigh /in'vā/ ▶ v. [intrans.] (**inveigh against**) speak or write about (something) with great hostility. [15th C. (in the sense 'carry in, introduce'; formerly also as *enveigh*): from L. *invehere* 'carry in,' *invehi* 'be carried into, assail,' from *in-* 'into' + *vehere* 'carry.']

in·vei·gle /in'vāgəl/ ▶ v. [with obj. and adverbial] persuade (someone) to do something by means of deception or flattery. ■ (**inveigle oneself** or **one's way into**) gain entrance to (a place) by using such methods. — **in·vei·gle·ment** n. [15th C.: from Anglo-Norman Fr. *envegler*, alt. of OFr. *aveugler* 'to blind,' from *aveugle* 'blind.']

in·vent /in'vent/ ▶ v. [trans.] create or design (something that has not existed before); be the originator of. ■ make up (an idea, name, story, etc.), esp. so as to deceive. [15th C.: from L. *invent-* 'discovered,' from the v. *invenire*, from *in-* 'into' + *venire* 'come.']

in·ven·tion /in'vensʜən/ ▶ n. the action of inventing something, typically a process or device. ■ something, typically a process or device, that has been invented. ■ creative ability. ■ something fabricated or made up. ■ used as a title for a short piece of music: *Bach's two-part Inventions*.

in·ven·tive /in'ventiv/ ▶ adj. (of a person) having the ability to create or design new things or to think originally. ■ (of a product, process, action, etc.) showing creativity or original thought. — **in·ven·tive·ly** adv. **in·ven·tive·ness** n.

in·ven·tor /in'ventər/ ▶ n. a person who invented a particular process or device or who invents things as an occupation.

in·ven·to·ry /'invən,tôrē/ ▶ n. (pl. **-ries**) a complete list of items such as property, goods in stock, or the contents of a building. ■ a quantity of goods held in stock. ■ (in accounting) the entire stock of a business, including materials, components, work in progress, and finished products. ▶ v. (**-ries, -ried**) [trans.] make a complete list of. ■ enter in a list. [ME: from med. L. *inventorium*, lit. 'a list of what is found,' from L. *invenire* 'come upon.']

in·ve·rac·i·ty /,invə'rasitē/ ▶ n. (pl. **-ties**) a lie. ■ untruthfulness.

In·ver·ness¹ /,invər'nes/ a city in Scotland, at the mouth of the Ness River; pop. 41,000.

In·ver·ness² ▶ n. a sleeveless cloak with a removable cape.

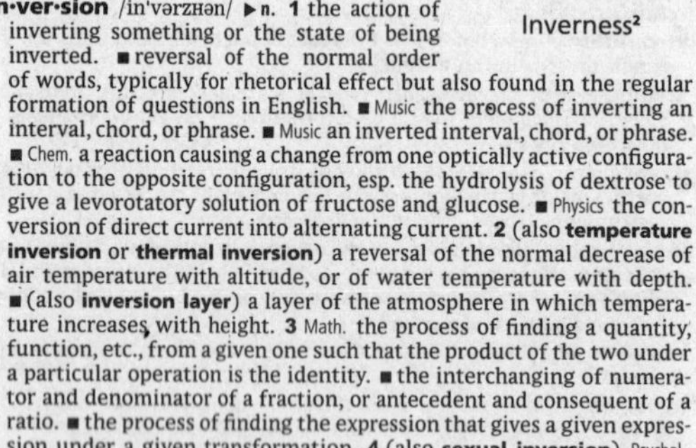
Inverness²

in·verse /'invərs; in'vərs/ ▶ adj. [attrib.] opposite or contrary in position, direction, order, or effect. ■ esp. Math. produced from or related to something else by a process of inversion. ▶ n. [usu. in sing.] something that is the opposite or reverse of something else. ■ Math. a reciprocal quantity, mathematical expression, geometric figure, etc., that is the result of inversion. ■ Math. an element that, when combined with a given element in an operation, produces the identity element for that operation. — **in·verse·ly** adv. [ME: from L. *inversus*, past part. of *invertere* (see INVERT).]

in·verse pro·por·tion (also **inverse ratio**) ▶ n. a relation between two quantities such that one increases in proportion as the other decreases.

in·ver·sion /in'vərzHən/ ▶ n. **1** the action of inverting something or the state of being inverted. ■ reversal of the normal order of words, typically for rhetorical effect but also found in the regular formation of questions in English. ■ Music the process of inverting an interval, chord, or phrase. ■ Music an inverted interval, chord, or phrase. ■ Chem. a reaction causing a change from one optically active configuration to the opposite configuration, esp. the hydrolysis of dextrose to give a levorotatory solution of fructose and glucose. ■ Physics the conversion of direct current into alternating current. **2** (also **temperature inversion** or **thermal inversion**) a reversal of the normal decrease of air temperature with altitude, or of water temperature with depth. ■ (also **inversion layer**) a layer of the atmosphere in which temperature increases with height. **3** Math. the process of finding a quantity, function, etc., from a given one such that the product of the two under a particular operation is the identity. ■ the interchanging of numerator and denominator of a fraction, or antecedent and consequent of a ratio. ■ the process of finding the expression that gives a given expression under a given transformation. **4** (also **sexual inversion**) Psychol., dated the adoption of behavior typical of the opposite sex; homosexuality. — **in·ver·sive** /-'vərsiv/ adj.

in·vert ▶ v. /in'vərt/ [trans.] put upside down or in the opposite position, order, or arrangement. ■ Music modify (a phrase) by reversing the direction of pitch changes. ■ Music alter (an interval or triad) by changing the relative position of the notes in it. ■ esp. Math. subject to inversion; transform into its inverse. ▶ n. /'invərt/ **1** Psychol., dated a person showing sexual inversion; a homosexual. **2** Philately a postage stamp printed with an error such that part of its design is upside down. — **in·vert·i·bil·i·ty** /in,vərtə'bilitē/ n. **in·vert·i·ble** adj. [16th C.: from L. *invertere*, lit. 'turn inside out,' from *in-* 'into' + *vertere* 'to turn.']

in·vert·ase /in'vərtās; 'invər,tās; -,tāz/ ▶ n. Biochem. an enzyme produced by yeast that catalyzes the hydrolysis of sucrose, forming invert sugar. Also called SUCRASE.

in·ver·te·brate /in'vərtəbrit; -,brāt/ ▶ n. an animal lacking a backbone, such as an arthropod, mollusk, annelid, coelenterate, etc. The invertebrates constitute an artificial division of the animal kingdom, comprising 95 percent of animal species and about 30 different phyla. Compare with VERTEBRATE. ▶ adj. of, relating to, or belonging to this division of animals. [19th C. (as a n.): from mod. L. *invertebrata* (pl.) 'the invertebrates' (former taxonomic group), from Fr. *invertébrés*, from *in-* 'without' + L. *vertebra* (see VERTEBRA).]

in·vert·ed com·ma ▶ n. esp. Brit. another term for QUOTATION MARK.

in·vert·er /in'vərtər/ ▶ n. **1** an apparatus that converts direct current into alternating current. **2** Electron. a device that converts either of the two binary digits or signals into the other.

in·vert sug·ar ▶ n. a mixture of glucose and fructose obtained by the hydrolysis of sucrose. [19th C.: *invert* from *inverted*, because of the reversal of optical activity involved in its formation (see the chemical sense of INVERSION.)]

in·vest /in'vest/ ▶ v. **1** [intrans.] expend money with the expectation of achieving a profit or material result by putting it into financial schemes, shares, or property, or by using it to develop a commercial venture: *getting workers to invest in private pension funds* | [trans.] *the company is to invest $12 million in its new manufacturing site.* ■ [trans.] devote (one's time, effort, or energy) to a particular undertaking with the expectation of a worthwhile result. ■ [intrans.] (**invest in**) informal buy (something) whose usefulness will repay the cost. **2** [trans.] (**invest someone/something with**) provide or endow someone or something with (a particular quality or attribute). ■ endow someone with (a rank or office). ■ (**invest something in**) establish a right or power in. **3** [trans.] archaic clothe or cover with a garment. **4** [trans.] archaic surround (a place) in order to besiege or blockade it: *Fort Pulaski was invested and captured.* — **in·vest·a·ble** adj. **in·vest·i·ble** adj. **in·ves·tor** /-'vestər/ n. [16th C.: from Fr. *investir* or L. *investire*, from *in-* 'into, upon' + *vestire* 'clothe.']

in·ves·ti·gate /in'vesti,gāt/ ▶ v. [trans.] carry out a systematic or formal inquiry to discover and examine the facts of (an incident, allegation, etc.) so as to establish the truth. ■ carry out research or study into (a subject, typically one in a scientific or academic field) so as to discover facts or information. ■ make inquiries as to the character, activities, or background of (someone). ■ [intrans.] make a check to find out something. — **in·ves·ti·ga·ble** /in'vestigəbəl/ adj. **in·ves·ti·ga·tor** /-,gātər/ n. **in·ves·ti·ga·to·ry** /-gə,tôrē/ adj. [16th C.: from L. *investigat-* 'traced out,' from the v. *investigare*, from *in-* 'into' + *vestigare* 'track, trace out.']

in·ves·ti·ga·tion /in,vesti'gāsHən/ ▶ n. the action of investigating something or someone; formal or systematic examination or research. ■ a formal inquiry or systematic study. — **in·ves·ti·ga·tion·al** /-sHənl/ adj.

in·ves·ti·ga·tive /in'vesti,gātiv/ ▶ adj. of or concerned with investigating something. ■ (of journalism or a journalist) inquiring intensively into and seeking to expose malpractice, the miscarriage of justice, or other controversial issues.

in·ves·ti·ture /in'vesticHər; -,cHŏŏr/ ▶ n. **1** the action of formally investing a person with honors or rank. ■ a ceremony at which honors or rank are formally conferred on a particular person. **2** the action of clothing or robing. ■ a thing that clothes or covers. [ME: from med. L. *investitura*, from *investire* (see INVEST).]

in·vest·ment /in'ves(t)mənt/ ▶ n. **1** the action or process of investing money for profit or material result. ■ a thing that is worth buying because it may be profitable or useful in the future. ■ an act of devoting time, effort, or energy to a particular undertaking with the expectation of a worthwhile result. **2** archaic the surrounding of a place by a hostile force in order to besiege or blockade it.

in·vest·ment bank ▶ n. a bank that purchases large holdings of newly issued shares and resells them to investors. — **in·vest·ment bank·er** n. **in·vest·ment bank·ing** n.

in·vest·ment trust ▶ n. a limited company whose business is the investment of shareholders' funds, the shares being traded like those of any other public company.

in·vet·er·ate /in'vetərit/ ▶ adj. [attrib.] having a particular habit, activity, or interest that is long-established and unlikely to change. ■ (of a feeling or habit) long-established and unlikely to change. — **in·vet·er·a·cy** /-rəsē/ n. **in·vet·er·ate·ly** adv. [ME: from L. *inveteratus* 'made old,' past part. of *inveterare* (based on *vetus*, *veter-* 'old').]

in·vi·a·ble /in'vīəbəl/ ▶ adj. not viable. — **in·vi·a·bil·i·ty** /-,vīəbilitē/ n.

in·vid·i·ous /in'vidēəs/ ▶ adj. (of an action or situation) likely to arouse or incur resentment or anger in others. ■ (of a comparison or distinction) unfairly discriminating; unjust. — **in·vid·i·ous·ly** adv. **in·vid·i·ous·ness** n. [17th C.: from L. *invidiosus*, from *invidia* (see ENVY).]

in·vig·or·ate /in'vigə,rāt/ ▶ v. [trans.] give strength or energy to. — **in·vig·or·at·ing·ly** adv. **in·vig·or·a·tion** /-,vigə'rāsHən/ n. **in·vig·or·a·tor** /-,rātər/ n. [17th C.: from med. L. *invigorat-* 'made strong,' from the v. *invigorare*, from *in-* 'toward' + L. *vigorare* 'make strong' (from *vigor* 'vigor').]

in·vin·ci·ble /in'vinsəbəl/ ▶ adj. too powerful to be defeated or overcome: *an invincible warrior.* — **in·vin·ci·bil·i·ty** /-,vinsə'bilitē/ n. **in·vin·ci·bly** adv. [ME: via OFr. from L. *invincibilis*, from *in-* 'not' + *vincibilis* (see VINCIBLE).]

in vi·no ve·ri·tas /in 'vēnō 'veri,täs; 'vīnō 'veri,tas/ ▶ exclam. under the influence of alcohol, a person tells the truth. [L., lit. 'truth in wine.']

in·vi·o·la·ble /in'vīələbəl/ ▶ adj. never to be broken, infringed, or dishonored. — **in·vi·o·la·bil·i·ty** /-,vīələ'bilitē/ n. **in·vi·o·la·bly** adv. [ME: from Fr., or from L. *inviolabilis*, from *in-* 'not' + *violabilis* 'able to be violated' (from the v. *violare*).]

in·vi·o·late /in'vīəlit/ ▶ adj. free or safe from injury or violation. — **in·vi·o·la·cy** /-ləsē/ n. **in·vi·o·late·ly** adv. [ME: from L. *inviolatus*, from *in-* 'not' + *violare* 'violate.']

in·vis·i·ble /in'vizəbəl/ ▶ adj. unable to be seen; not visible to the eye. ■ concealed from sight; hidden. ■ fig. (of a person) treated as if unable to be seen; ignored or not taken into consideration. ■ Econ. relating to or denoting earnings from the sale of services or other items not constituting tangible commodities. ▶ n. an invisible thing, person, or being. ■ (**invisibles**) invisible exports and imports. — **in·vis·i·bil·i·ty** /-,vizə'bilitē/ n. **in·vis·i·bly** adv.

in·vis·i·ble ink ▶ n. a type of ink used to produce writing that cannot be seen until the paper is heated or otherwise treated.

in·vi·ta·tion /,invi'tāsHən/ ▶ n. a written or verbal request inviting someone to go somewhere or to do something. ■ the action of inviting someone to go somewhere or to do something. ■ [in sing.] a situation or action that tempts someone to do something or makes a particular outcome likely: *an invitation to disaster.*

in·vi·ta·tion·al /,invi'tāsHənl/ ▶ adj. (esp. of a competition) open only to those invited. ▶ n. a competition of such a type.

in·vi·ta·to·ry /in'vītə,tôrē/ ▶ adj. containing or conveying an invitation. ■ (in the Christian Church) denoting a psalm or versicle acting as an invitation to worshipers, esp. Psalm 95. [ME: from late L. *invitatorius*, from L. *invitare* (see INVITE).]

in·vite ▶ v. /in'vīt/ [trans.] make a polite, formal, or friendly request to (someone) to go somewhere or to do something. ■ make a formal or polite request for (something, esp. an application for a job or opinions on a particular topic) from someone. ■ (of an action or situation) tend to elicit (a particular reaction or response) or to tempt (someone) to do something. ▶ n. /'in,vīt/ informal an invitation. — **in·vi·tee** /,invī'tē/ n. **in·vit·er** /in'vītər/ n. [16th C.: from OFr. *inviter*, or from L. *invitare*.]

in·vit·ing /in'vītiNG/ ▶ adj. offering the promise of an attractive or enjoyable experience. — **in·vit·ing·ly** adv.

in vi·tro /in 'vē,trō/ ▶ adj. & adv. Biol. (of processes or reactions) taking place in a test tube, culture dish, or elsewhere outside a living organism. Compare with IN VIVO. [L., lit. 'in glass.']

in vi·vo /in 'vēvō/ ▶ adv. & adj. Biol. (of processes) taking place in a living organism. Compare with IN VITRO. [L., 'in a living thing.']

in·vo·ca·tion /,invə'kāSHən/ ▶ n. the action of invoking something or someone for assistance or as an authority. ■ the summoning of a deity or the supernatural. ■ an incantation used for this. ■ (in the Christian Church) a form of words such as "In the name of the Father" introducing a prayer, sermon, etc. — **in·voc·a·to·ry** /in'väkə,tôrē/ adj. [ME: via OFr. from L. *invocatio(n-)*, from the v. *invocare* (see INVOKE).]

in·voice /'in,vois/ ▶ n. a list of goods sent or services provided, stating the sum due for these; a bill. ▶ v. [trans.] send an invoice to (someone). ■ send an invoice for (goods or services provided). [16th C.: from Fr. *envoyer* 'send' (see ENVOY).]

in·voke /in'vōk/ ▶ v. [trans.] cite or appeal to (someone or something) as an authority for an action or in support of an argument. ■ call on (a deity or spirit) in prayer, as a witness, or for inspiration. ■ call earnestly for. ■ summon (a spirit) by charms or incantation. ■ give rise to; evoke. ■ Comput. cause (a procedure) to be carried out. — **in·vok·er** n. [15th C.: from Fr. *invoquer*, from L. *invocare*, from *in-* 'upon' + *vocare* 'to call.']

in·vol·a·tile /in'välətl; -,tīl/ ▶ adj. not volatile; unable to be vaporized.

in·vo·lu·cre /'invə,lo͞okər/ (also **in·vo·lu·crum** /-krəm/) ▶ n. Bot. a whorl or rosette of bracts surrounding an inflorescence (esp. a capitulum) or at the base of an umbel. — **in·vo·lu·cral** /,invə'lo͞okrəl/ adj. [16th C.: from Fr., or from L. *involucrum*, from *involvere* 'roll in, envelop' (see INVOLVE).]

in·vol·un·tar·y /in'välən,terē/ ▶ adj. **1** done without conscious control. ■ (esp. of muscles or nerves) concerned in bodily processes that are not under the control of the will. ■ caused unintentionally, esp. through negligence. **2** done against someone's will; compulsory. — **in·vol·un·tar·i·ly** /in,välən'te(ə)rəlē; -'välən,ter-/ adv. **in·vol·un·tar·i·ness** n.

in·vo·lute /'invə,lo͞ot/ ▶ adj. **1** formal involved; intricate. **2** tech. curled spirally. ■ Zool. (of a shell) having the whorls wound closely around the axis. ■ Bot. (of a leaf or the cap of a fungus) rolled inward at the edges. ▶ n. Geom. the locus of a point considered as the end of a taut string being unwound from a given curve in the plane of that curve. Compare with EVOLUTE. ▶ v. [intrans.] become involute; curl up. [17th C.: from L. *involutus*, past part. of *involvere* (see INVOLVE).]

in·vo·lut·ed /'invə,lo͞otid/ ▶ adj. complicated; abstruse.

in·vo·lu·tion /,invə'lo͞oSHən/ ▶ n. **1** Physiol. the shrinkage of an organ in old age or when inactive, e.g., of the uterus after childbirth. **2** Math. a function, transformation, or operator that is equal to its inverse, i.e., which gives the identity when applied to itself. **3** formal the process of involving or complicating, or the state of being involved or complicated. — **in·vo·lu·tion·al** /-SHənl/ adj. **in·vo·lu·tion·ar·y** /-,nerē/ adj. [ME: from L. *involutio(n-)*, from *involvere* (see INVOLVE).]

in·volve /in'välv/ ▶ v. [trans.] (of a situation or event) include (something) as a necessary part or result. ■ cause (a person or group) to experience or participate in an activity or situation. [ME: from L. *involvere*, from *in-* 'into' + *volvere* 'to roll.']

in·volved /in'välvd/ ▶ adj. **1** [predic.] connected or concerned with someone or something, typically on an emotional or personal level. **2** difficult to comprehend; complicated.

in·volve·ment /in'välvmənt/ ▶ n. the fact or condition of being involved with or participating in something. ■ emotional or personal association with someone.

in·vul·ner·a·ble /in'vəlnərəbəl/ ▶ adj. impossible to harm or damage. — **in·vul·ner·a·bil·i·ty** /-,vəlnərə'bilitē/ n. **in·vul·ner·a·bly** adv.

-in-wait·ing ▶ comb. form **1** awaiting a turn, confirmation of a process, etc. ■ about to happen. **2** denoting a position as attendant to a royal personage.

in·ward /'inwərd/ ▶ adj. [attrib.] directed or proceeding toward the inside; coming in from outside. ■ existing within the mind, soul, or spirit, and often not expressed. ▶ adv. (also **in·wards**) toward the inside. ■ into or toward the mind, spirit, or soul. [OE *inweard*, *inneweard*, *innanweard* (see IN, -WARD).]

in·ward·ly /'inwərdlē/ ▶ adv. (of a particular thought, feeling, or action) registered or existing in the mind but not expressed to others. [OE *inweardlīce* (see INWARD, -LY[2]).]

in·ward·ness /'inwərdnis/ ▶ n. preoccupation with one's inner self; concern with spiritual or philosophical matters rather than externalities.

in·wards /'inwərdz/ ▶ adv. variant of INWARD.

in·wrought /in'rôt/ ▶ adj. literary (of a fabric or garment) intricately embroidered with a particular pattern or decoration: *robes inwrought with gold.*

In·yo Moun·tains /'inyō/ a range in east central California.

in-your-face ▶ adj. informal blatantly aggressive or provocative; impossible to ignore or avoid. [1970s: from *in your face*, used as a derisive insult.]

I/O Electron. ▶ abbr. input-output.

I·o /'ī-ō; 'ē-ō/ **1** Gk. Mythol. a priestess of Hera who was loved by Zeus. Trying to protect her from the jealousy of Hera, Zeus turned Io into a heifer. **2** Astron. one of the Galilean moons of Jupiter, the fifth closest satellite to the planet.

IOC ▶ abbr. International Olympic Committee.

iod- ▶ comb. form var. of IODO- shortened before a vowel (as in *iodic*).

i·od·ic ac·id /ī'ädik/ ▶ n. Chem. a crystalline acid, HIO_3, with strong oxidizing properties. — **i·o·date** /'īə,dāt/ n.

i·o·dide /'īə,dīd/ ▶ n. Chem. a compound of iodine with another element or group, esp. a salt of the anion I−.

i·o·din·ate /'īədn,āt/ ▶ v. [trans.] [usu. as adj.] (**iodinated**) Chem. introduce iodine into (a compound). — **i·o·din·a·tion** /,īədn'āSHən/ n.

i·o·dine /'īə,dīn/ ▶ n. the chemical element of atomic number 53, a nonmetallic element of the halogen group, forming black crystals and a violet vapor. As a constituent of thyroid hormones, it is required in small amounts in the body, and deficiency can lead to goiter. (Symbol: **I**) ■ a solution of this in alcohol, used as a mild antiseptic. [19th C.: from Fr. *iode* (from Gk. *iōdēs* 'violet-colored,' from *ion* 'violet' + *-eidēs* 'like') + -INE[4].]

i·o·dism /'īə,dizəm/ ▶ n. Med. iodine poisoning, causing thirst, diarrhea, weakness, and convulsions.

i·o·dize /'īə,dīz/ ▶ v. [trans.] [usu. as adj.] (**iodized**) treat or impregnate with iodine: *iodized salt.* — **i·o·di·za·tion** /,īədi'zāSHən/ n.

iodo- (usu. **iod-** before a vowel) ▶ comb. form Chem. representing IODINE.

i·o·do·form /ī'ōdə,fôrm; ī'ädə-/ ▶ n. a volatile pale yellow sweet-smelling crystalline organic compound of iodine, CHI_3, with antiseptic properties. Also called **triiodomethane**.

i·o·dom·e·try /īə'dämitrē/ ▶ n. Chem. the quantitative analysis of a solution of an oxidizing agent by adding an iodide that reacts to form iodine, which is then titrated. — **i·o·do·met·ric** /,ī-ōdə'metrik/ adj.

I·o moth ▶ n. a large, mainly yellow North American silkworm moth (*Automeris io*, family Saturniidae) with prominent eyespots on the hind wings. [19th C.: after the Gk. priestess IO.]

Ion. ▶ abbr. Ionic.

i·on /'īən; 'īän/ ▶ n. an atom or molecule with a net electric charge due to the loss or gain of one or more electrons. See also CATION, ANION. [19th C.: from Gk., neut. pres. part. of *ienai* 'go.']

-ion ▶ suffix forming nouns denoting verbal action: *communion.* ■ denoting an instance of this: *a rebellion.* ■ denoting a resulting state or product: *oblivion* | *opinion.* [via Fr. from L. *-ion-*.]

I·o·na /ī'ōnə/ a small island in the Inner Hebrides, off the western coast of Mull.

Io·nes·co /yô'neskō; ,ēə'neskō/, Eugène (1912–94), French playwright; born in Romania. A leading exponent of the Theater of the Absurd, he wrote *Rhinoceros* (1959).

i·on ex·change ▶ n. the exchange of ions of the same charge between an insoluble solid and a solution in contact with it, used in water-softening and other purification and separation processes.

I·o·ni·a /ī'ōnēə/ in classical times, the central part of the west coast of Asia Minor.

I·o·ni·an /ī'ōnēən/ ▶ n. a member of an ancient Hellenic people inhabiting Attica, parts of western Asia Minor, and the Aegean Islands in preclassical and classical times. ■ a native or inhabitant of the Ionian Islands. ▶ adj. of or relating to the Ionians, Ionia, or the Ionian Islands.

I·o·ni·an Is·lands a chain of about 40 Greek islands off the western coast of mainland Greece, in the Ionian Sea.

I·o·ni·an Sea the part of the Mediterranean Sea between western Greece and southern Italy.

I·on·ic /ī'änik/ ▶ adj. **1** relating to or denoting a classical order of architecture characterized by a column with scroll shapes (volutes) on either side of the capital. See illustration at CAPITAL[2]. **2** another term for IONIAN. ▶ n. **1** the Ionic order of architecture. **2** the ancient Greek dialect used in Ionia. [16th C.: via L. from Gk. *Iōnikos*, from *Iōnia* (see IONIA).]

i·on·ic /ī'änik/ ▶ adj. of, relating to, or using ions. ■ (of a chemical bond) formed by the electrostatic attraction of oppositely charged ions. Often contrasted with COVALENT. — **i·on·i·cal·ly** adv.

i·on·i·za·tion cham·ber /,īəni'zāSHən/ ▶ n. an instrument for detecting ionizing radiation.

i·on·ize /'īə,nīz/ ▶ v. [trans.] (usu. **be ionized**) convert (an atom, molecule, or substance) into an ion or ions, typically by removing one or more electrons. ■ [intrans.] become converted into an ion or ions in this way. — **i·on·iz·a·ble** adj. **i·on·i·za·tion** /,īəni'zāSHən/ n.

i·on·iz·er /'īə,nīzər/ ▶ n. a device that produces ionization, esp. one used to improve the quality of the air in a room.

i·on·iz·ing ra·di·a·tion ▶ n. radiation consisting of particles, X-rays, or gamma rays with sufficient energy to cause ionization in the medium through which it passes.

i·on·o·phore /ī'änə,fôr/ ▶ n. Biochem. a substance that is able to transport particular ions across a lipid membrane in a cell.

i·on·o·sphere /ī'änə,sfi(ə)r/ ▶ **n.** the layer of the earth's atmosphere that contains a high concentration of ions and free electrons and is able to reflect radio waves. It lies above the mesosphere and extends from about 50 to 600 miles (80 to 1,000 km) (the ionopause) above the earth's surface. ■ a similar region above the surface of another planet. — **i·on·o·spher·ic** /ī,änə'sfi(ə)rik; -'sfer-/ **adj.**

i·on·to·pho·re·sis /ī,äntəfə'rēsis/ ▶ **n.** Med. a technique of introducing ionic medicinal compounds into the body through the skin by applying a local electric current. — **i·on·to·pho·ret·ic** /-'retik/ **adj. i·on·to·pho·ret·i·cal·ly** /-'retik(ə)lē/ **adv.** [20th C.: from ION, on the pattern of *electrophoresis*.]

IOOF ▶ **abbr.** Independent Order of Odd Fellows.

-ior ▶ **suffix** forming adjectives in the comparative degree: *anterior* | *junior* | *senior*. [from L.]

i·o·ta /ī'ōtə/ ▶ **n. 1** the ninth letter of the Greek alphabet (Ι, ι), transliterated as 'i.' **2** [in sing.] [usu. with negative] an extremely small amount: *nothing she said seemed to make an iota of difference.*

IOU ▶ **n.** a signed document acknowledging a debt. [18th C.: representing the pronunc. of *I owe you*.]

-ious ▶ **suffix** (forming adjectives) characterized by; full of: *cautious* | *vivacious*. [from Fr. *-ieux*, from L. *-iosus*.]

I·o·wa /'īəwə/ a state in the northern central US, on the western banks of the Mississippi River; pop. 2,926,324; capital, Des Moines; statehood, Dec. 28, 1846 (29). It was acquired as part of the Louisiana Purchase in 1803. — **I·o·wan adj. & n.**

I·o·wa Cit·y a city in eastern Iowa; pop. 62,220.

IP ▶ **abbr.** Comput. Internet protocol, the method by which information is sent between any two computers on the Internet.

IPA ▶ **abbr.** International Phonetic Alphabet.

IP ad·dress ▶ **n.** Comput. a unique string of numbers separated by periods that identifies each computer attached to the Internet. It also usually has a version containing words separated by periods.

ip·e·cac /'ipikak/ (also **ip·e·cac·u·an·ha** /,ipi,kak(y)o͞o'an(y)ə; ē,pākə-/) ▶ **n. 1** the dried rhizome of a South American shrub, or a drug prepared from this, used as an emetic and expectorant. **2** the shrub (*Cephaelis ipecacuanha*) of the bedstraw family that produces this rhizome, native to Brazil and cultivated elsewhere. ■ used in names of other plants with similar uses, e.g., **American ipecac** (*Gillenia trifoliata*) of the rose family. [17th C.: from Port., from Tupi-Guarani *ipekaaguéne* 'emetic creeper,' from *ipe* 'small' + *kaa* 'leaves' + *guéne* 'vomit.']

Iph·i·ge·ni·a /,ifijə'nīə; -'nēə/ Gk. Mythol. the daughter of Agamemnon, who was obliged to offer her as a sacrifice to Artemis when the Greek fleet was becalmed on its way to the Trojan War.

I·pi·ros Greek name for EPIRUS.

ipm (also **i.p.m.**) ▶ **abbr.** inches per minute.

IPO ▶ **abbr.** initial public offering.

I·poh /'ēpō/ a city in western Malaysia, the capital of the state of Perak; pop. 383,000.

ip·o·moe·a /,ipə'mēə/ ▶ **n.** a plant of the genus *Ipomoea* in the morning glory family. [mod. L., from Gk. *ips* 'worm' + *homoios* 'like.']

i·pro·ni·a·zid /,īprō'nīə,zid/ ▶ **n.** Med. a synthetic compound, $(CH_3)_2CHNHNHCOC_5H_4N$, used as a drug to treat depression. [20th C.: from *i(so)pro(pyl)* + *(iso)niazid*.]

ip·se dix·it /'ipsē 'diksit/ ▶ **n.** a dogmatic and unproven statement. [L., lit. 'he himself said it,' translating Gk. *autos epha*, a phr. used of Pythagoras by his followers.]

ip·si·lat·er·al /,ipsə'latərəl/ ▶ **adj.** belonging to or occurring on the same side of the body. — **ip·si·lat·er·al·ly adv.** [20th C.: formed irregularly from L. *ipse* 'self' + LATERAL.]

ip·sis·si·ma ver·ba /ip'sisəmə 'vərbə/ ▶ **plural n.** the precise words. [L.]

ip·so fac·to /'ipsō 'faktō/ ▶ **adv.** by that very fact or act. [L.]

Ips·wich /'ipswich/ a town in southeastern England, the county town of Suffolk; pop. 116,000.

IQ ▶ **abbr.** intelligence quotient.

i.q. ▶ **abbr.** the same as. [from L. *idem quod*.]

-ique ▶ **suffix** archaic spelling of -IC.

I·qui·tos /ē'kētôs/ a city in northeastern Peru, on the Amazon River; pop. 252,000.

IR ▶ **abbr.** infrared.

Ir ▶ **symb.** the chemical element iridium.

ir- ▶ **prefix** var. of IN-¹, IN-² assimilated before *r* (as in *irrelevant*, *irradiate*).

IRA ▶ **abbr.** ■ /(often 'īrə/) individual retirement account. ■ Irish Republican Army.

I·rá·kli·on /i'räklē,ôn/ Greek name for HERAKLION.

I·ran /i'rän; i'ran; ī'ran/ a country in the Middle East. *See box.*

I·ran-Con·tra af·fair a political scandal of 1987 involving the covert sale by the US of arms to Iran. The proceeds of the arms sales were used by officials to give arms to the anticommunist Contras in Nicaragua, despite congressional prohibition. Also called IRANGATE.

I·ran·gate /i'ran,gāt; i'rän-/ another term for the IRAN-CONTRA AFFAIR.

I·ra·ni·an /i'rānēən; i'rä-/ ▶ **adj.** of or relating to Iran or its people. ■ relating to or denoting the group of Indo-European languages that includes Persian (Farsi), Pashto, Avestan, and Kurdish. ▶ **n.** a native or national of Iran, or a person of Iranian descent.

Iran

Official name: Islamic Republic of Iran
Location: Middle East, east of Iraq, bordered on the south by the Persian Gulf and the Gulf of Oman
Area: 631,800 square miles (1,636,000 sq km)
Population: 69,018,000
Capital: Tehran
Languages: Farsi (Persian) (official), Turkish, Kurdish, Arabic, and others
Currency: Iranian rial

Iraq

Official name: Republic of Iraq
Location: Middle East, west of Iran and east of Syria, with an outlet on the Persian Gulf
Area: 166,900 square miles (432,200 sq km)
Population: 25,374,000
Capital: Baghdad
Languages: Arabic (official), Kurdish, Assyrian, Armenian

I·ran-I·raq War the war of 1980–88 between Iran and Iraq in the general area of the Persian Gulf. It ended inconclusively after great hardship and loss of life on both sides. Also called GULF WAR.

I·raq /i'räk; i'rak; ī'rak/ a country in the Middle East. *See box.*

I·ra·qi /i'räkē; i'rakē/ ▶ **adj.** of or relating to Iraq, its people, or their language. ▶ **n.** (pl. **-qis**) **1** a native or national of Iraq, or a person of Iraqi descent. **2** the form of Arabic spoken in Iraq.

i·ras·ci·ble /i'rasəbəl/ ▶ **adj.** (of a person) easily made angry. ■ characterized by or arising from anger. — **i·ras·ci·bil·i·ty** /i,rasə'bilitē/ **n. i·ras·ci·bly adv.** [ME: via Fr. from late L. *irascibilis*, from L. *irasci* 'grow angry,' from *ira* 'anger.']

i·rate /ī'rāt/ ▶ **adj.** feeling or characterized by great anger. — **i·rate·ly adv. i·rate·ness n.** [19th C.: from L. *iratus*, from *ira* 'anger.']

ire /ī(ə)r/ ▶ **n.** anger. — **ire·ful** /-fəl/ **adj.** [ME: via OFr. from L. *ira*.]

Ire·dell /'ī(ə)r,del/, James (1751–99), US Supreme Court associate justice 1790–99; born in England.

Ire·land /ˈī(ə)rlənd/ an island in the British Isles that lies west of Great Britain, divided between the Republic of Ireland and Northern Ireland.

Ire·land, Republic of a country occupying approximately four fifths of Ireland. Also called IRISH REPUBLIC. *See box.*

i·ren·ic /īˈrenik; īˈrē-/ (also **ei·ren·ic**) ▶ **adj.** formal aiming or aimed at peace. ▶ **n.** (**irenics**) a part of Christian theology concerned with reconciling different denominations and sects. — **i·ren·i·cal adj. i·ren·i·cal·ly adv. i·ren·i·cism n.** [19th C.: from Gk. *eirēnikos,* from *eirēnē* 'peace.']

Ir·gun /irˈgo͞on/ a right-wing Zionist organization founded in 1931, disbanded after the creation of Israel in 1948. [from mod. Heb. *irgūn (ṣĕḇā'ī lĕ'ummī)* '(national military) organization.']

I·ri·an Ja·ya /ˈi(ə)rēˌän ˈjīə/ former name (until 2002) for the Indonesian province of Papua (see PAPUA **sense 2**).

irid. ▶ **abbr.** iridescent.

ir·i·dec·to·my /ˌiriˈdektəmē/ ▶ **n.** (pl. **-mies**) a surgical procedure to remove part of the iris.

ir·i·des·cent /ˌiriˈdesənt/ ▶ **adj.** showing luminous colors that seem to change when seen from different angles. — **ir·i·des·cence n. ir·i·des·cent·ly adv.** [18th C.: from L. *iris, irid-* 'rainbow' + -ESCENT.]

i·rid·i·um /iˈridēəm/ ▶ **n.** the chemical element of atomic number 77, a hard, dense silvery-white metal, a member of the transition series. Iridium-platinum alloys are corrosion-resistant and are used in jewelry and for electrical contacts. (Symbol: **Ir**) [19th C.: mod. L., from L. *iris, irid-* 'rainbow' (so named because it forms compounds of various colors).]

ir·i·dol·o·gy /ˌiriˈdäləjē/ ▶ **n.** (in alternative medicine) diagnosis by examination of the iris of the eye. — **ir·i·dol·o·gist n.** [20th C.: from Gk. *iris, irid-* 'iris' + -LOGY.]

I·ris /ˈīris/ Gk. Mythol. the goddess of the rainbow, who acted as a messenger of the gods.

i·ris /ˈīris/ ▶ **n. 1** a flat, colored, ring-shaped membrane behind the cornea of the eye, with an adjustable circular opening (pupil) in the center. ■ (also **iris diaphragm**) an adjustable diaphragm of thin overlapping plates for regulating the size of a central hole, esp. for the admission of light to a lens. **2** a plant (genus *Iris*) with sword-shaped leaves and showy flowers, typically purple, yellow, or white. Its numerous species include the hybrid **sweet iris** (*I. pallida*). The **iris family** (Iridaceae) also includes the gladioli, crocuses, and freesias. **3** a rainbow or a rainbowlike appearance. ▶ **v.** [no obj., with adverbial of direction] (of an aperture, typically that of a lens) open or close in the manner of an iris or iris diaphragm. [mod. L., via L. from Gk. *iris* 'rainbow, iris.']

iris 2

I·rish /ˈīrisʜ/ ▶ **adj.** of or relating to Ireland, its people, or the Goidelic language traditionally and historically spoken there. ▶ **n. 1** (also **Irish Gaelic**) the Goidelic language that is the first official language of the Republic of Ireland. **2** [as pl. n.] (**the Irish**) the people of Ireland; Irish people collectively.

– PHRASES **get one's Irish up** cause one to become angry. — **I·rish·ness n.** [ME: from OE *Īr-* (stem of *Īras* 'the Irish' and *Īrland* 'Ireland,' obscurely rel. to HIBERNIAN) + -ISH[1].]

I·rish cof·fee ▶ **n.** coffee mixed with a dash of Irish whiskey and served with cream on top.

I·rish elk ▶ **n.** an extinct giant European and North African deer (*Megaloceros giganteus*) of the Pleistocene epoch, with massive antlers up to 10 feet (3 m) across. Also called **giant deer.**

I·rish·man /ˈīrisʜmən/ ▶ **n.** (pl. **-men**) a native or national of Ireland, or a person of Irish descent, esp. a man.

I·rish moss ▶ **n.** another term for CARRAGEEN.

I·rish Re·pub·lic see IRELAND, REPUBLIC OF.

I·rish Re·pub·li·can Ar·my (abbr.: **IRA**) the military arm of Sinn Fein, aiming for union between the Republic of Ireland and Northern Ireland. The IRA was formed during the struggle for independence from Britain in 1916–21; in 1969 it split into Official and Provisional wings. The Provisional IRA stepped up the level of violence against military and civilian targets in Northern Ireland, Britain, and Europe during the next two decades. A ceasefire has been in operation since 1997.

I·rish Sea the sea that separates Ireland from England and Wales.

I·rish set·ter ▶ **n.** a dog of a breed of setter with a long, silky dark red coat and a long feathered tail.

I·rish stew ▶ **n.** a stew made with mutton or other meat, potatoes, and onions.

I·rish ter·ri·er ▶ **n.** a terrier of a rough-haired light reddish-brown breed.

I·rish wolf·hound ▶ **n.** a large, typically grayish hound of a rough-coated breed.

I·rish·wom·an /ˈīrisʜˌwo͝omən/ ▶ **n.** (pl. **-wom·en**) a female native or national of Ireland, or a woman of Irish descent.

i·ri·tis /īˈrītis/ ▶ **n.** Med. inflammation of the iris of the eye. — **i·rit·ic** /īˈritik/ **adj.**

irk /ərk/ ▶ **v.** [trans.] irritate; annoy. [ME: perh. from ON *yrkja* 'to work.']

Ireland, Republic of

Location: western Europe, four fifths of the island of Ireland (one fifth is Northern Ireland), west of Great Britain, bordered on the east by the Irish Sea and on the west by the Atlantic Ocean
Area: 26,600 square miles (68,900 sq km)
Population: 3,523,400
Capital: Dublin
Languages: Irish (official), English
Currency: euro

irk·some /ˈərksəm/ ▶ **adj.** irritating; annoying. — **irk·some·ly adv. irk·some·ness n.**

Ir·kutsk /irˈko͞otsk/ the chief city of Siberia in eastern Russia, on Lake Baikal; pop. 635,000.

i·ron /ˈīərn/ ▶ **n. 1** a strong, hard, magnetic, silvery-gray metal, the chemical element of atomic number 26, a transition element widely distributed as ores such as hematite, magnetite, and siderite, and much used as a material for construction and manufacturing, esp. in the form of steel. (Symbol: **Fe**) ■ compounds of this metal, esp. as a component of the diet. ■ used figuratively as a symbol or type of firmness, strength, or resistance. **2** a tool or implement now or originally made of iron. ■ (**irons**) fetters or handcuffs. ■ informal a handgun. **3** a hand-held implement with a flat steel base that is heated (typically with electricity) to smooth clothes, sheets, etc. **4** a golf club with a metal head (typically with a numeral indicating the degree to which the head is angled in order to loft the ball). ▶ **v.** [trans.] smooth (clothes, sheets, etc.) with an iron.

– PHRASES **have many** (or **other**) **irons in the fire** have many options available or be involved in many activities at the same time. **in irons 1** having the feet or hands fettered. **2** (of a sailing vessel) stalled head to wind and unable to come about or tack either way. **iron hand** (or **fist**) used to refer to firmness or ruthlessness of attitude or behavior. **an iron hand** (or **fist**) **in a velvet glove** firmness or ruthlessness cloaked in outward gentleness.

– PHRASAL VERBS **iron something out** remove creases from clothes, sheets, etc., by ironing. ■ fig. solve or settle difficulties or problems. — **i·ron·er n. i·ron·like adj.** [OE *īren, īsen, īsern,* of Gmc. origin; rel. to Du. *ijzer* and Ger. *Eisen,* and prob. ult. from Celtic.]

I·ron Age 1 a period that followed the Bronze Age, when weapons and tools came to be made of iron, conventionally taken as beginning in Europe in the early 1st millennium BC. **2** (in Greek and Roman mythology) the last and worst age of the world, a time of wickedness and oppression.

i·ron·bark /ˈīərnˌbärk/ ▶ **n.** an Australian eucalyptus tree with thick, solid bark and hard, dense, durable timber.

i·ron·bound /ˈīərnˈbound/ (also **i·ron-bound**) ▶ **adj.** bound with iron. ■ rigorous; inflexible. ■ archaic (of a coast) faced or enclosed with rocks.

I·ron Chan·cel·lor see BISMARCK[2].

i·ron·clad ▶ **adj.** /ˈīərnˌklad/ covered or protected with iron. ■ impossible to contradict, weaken, or change. ▶ **n.** hist. a 19th-century warship with armor plating.

i·ron cur·tain ▶ **n.** a notional barrier that prevents the passage of information or ideas between political entities, in particular: ■ (usu. **the Iron Curtain**) the former Soviet bloc and the West before the decline of communism after the political events in eastern Europe in 1989.

I·ron Duke see WELLINGTON[2].

I·ron Gate a gorge through which a section of the Danube River flows and forms part of the boundary between Romania and Serbia. Romanian name **Porţile de Fier**, Serbo-Croat name **Gvozdena Vrata**.

i·ron gray ▶ n. a dark gray color. ■ a horse of this color.

i·ron horse ▶ n. literary a steam locomotive. ■ **(Iron Horse)** see **Gehrig**.

i·ron·ic /ī'ränik/ ▶ adj. using or characterized by irony. ■ happening in the opposite way to what is expected, thus typically causing wry amusement. — **i·ron·i·cal adj.**

i·ron·i·cal·ly /ī'ränik(ə)lē/ ▶ adv. in an ironic manner. ■ used to denote a paradoxical, unexpected, or coincidental situation.

i·ron·ing /'īərniNG/ ▶ n. the task of ironing clothes, sheets, etc. ■ clothes, sheets, etc., that need to be or have just been ironed.

i·ron·ing board ▶ n. a long, narrow board covered with soft material and having folding legs, on which clothes, sheets, etc., are ironed.

i·ro·nist /'īrənist; 'īərnist/ ▶ n. a person who uses irony. [18th C.: from Gk. *eirōn* 'dissembler' + -ist.]

i·ro·nize /'īrə,nīz; īər'nīz/ ▶ v. [trans.] use ironically.

i·ron lung ▶ n. a rigid case fitted over a patient's body, used for administering prolonged artificial respiration by means of mechanical pumps.

i·ron maid·en ▶ n. (in historical contexts) an instrument of torture consisting of a coffin-shaped box lined with iron spikes.

i·ron man (also **i·ron·man**) ▶ n. (esp. in sporting contexts) an exceptionally strong or robust man. ■ [often as adj.] a multi-event athletic contest demanding stamina, in particular a consecutive triathlon of swimming, cycling, and running.

i·ron·mon·ger /'īərn,məNGgər; -,mäNGgər/ ▶ n. Brit. a person or store selling hardware. — **i·ron·mon·ger·y** /-g(ə)rē/ n. (pl. **-ger·ies**).

i·ron-on ▶ adj. [attrib.] able to be fixed to the surface of a fabric by ironing: *T-shirts with iron-on transfers.*

I·ron·sides /'īərn,sīdz/ **1** a nickname for Oliver Cromwell. **2 (ironsides)** hist. an ironclad.

i·ron·stone /'īərn,stōn/ ▶ n. **1** sedimentary rock containing a substantial proportion of iron compounds. **2** [usu. as adj.] a kind of dense, opaque stoneware.

i·ron·ware /'īərn,we(ə)r/ ▶ n. articles made of iron, typically domestic implements.

i·ron·wood /'īərn,wo͝od/ ▶ n. any of a number of trees that produce very hard timber, in particular a southern African tree of the olive family (*Olea laurifolia*), and the American and Eastern hornbeams.

i·ron·work /'īərn,wərk/ ▶ n. things or parts made of iron.

i·ron·works /'īərn,wərks/ ▶ n. [treated as sing. or pl.] a place where iron is smelted or iron goods are made.

i·ro·ny[1] /'īrənē; 'īərnē/ ▶ n. (pl. **-nies**) the expression of one's meaning by using language that normally signifies the opposite, typically for humorous or emphatic effect. ■ a state of affairs or an event that seems deliberately contrary to what one expects and is often amusing as a result. ■ (also **dra·mat·ic** or **trag·ic i·ro·ny**) a literary technique, originally used in Greek tragedy, by which the full significance of a character's words or actions are clear to the audience or reader although unknown to the character. [16th C.: via L. from Gk. *eirōneia* 'simulated ignorance,' from *eirōn* 'dissembler.']

i·ro·ny[2] /'īərnē/ ▶ adj. of or like iron: *an irony gray color.*

Ir·o·quoi·an /'irə,kwoiən/ ▶ n. a language family of eastern North America, including the languages of the Five Nations, Tuscarora, Huron, Wyandot, and Cherokee. ▶ adj. of or relating to the Iroquois people or the Iroquoian language family.

Ir·o·quois /'irə,kwoi/ ▶ n. (pl. same) **1** a member of a former confederacy of North American Indian peoples originally comprising the Cayuga, Mohawk, Oneida, Onondaga, and Seneca peoples (the **Five Nations**), and later including also the Tuscarora (the **Six Nations**). **2** any of the Iroquoian languages. ▶ adj. of or relating to the Iroquois or their languages. [17th C.: Fr., perh. a term from a Basque-Algonquian pidgin *(h)irokoa* 'killer people', from Basque *(h)ilo* 'kill' + *koa* 'person'.]

ir·ra·di·ance /i'rādēəns/ ▶ n. **1** Physics the flux of radiant energy per unit area (normal to the direction of flow of radiant energy through a medium). **2** literary the fact of shining brightly.

ir·ra·di·ant /i'rādēənt/ ▶ adj. literary shining brightly.

ir·ra·di·ate /i'rādē,āt/ ▶ v. [trans.] **1** (often **be irradiated**) expose to radiation. ■ expose (food) to gamma rays to kill microorganisms. **2** illuminate (something) by or as if by shining light on it. — **ir·ra·di·a·tor** /-,ātər/ n. [16th C.: from L. *irradiat-* 'shone upon,' from the v. *irradiare*, from *in-* 'upon' + *radiare* 'to shine' (from *radius* 'ray').]

ir·ra·di·a·tion /i,rādē'āsHən/ ▶ n. **1** the process or fact of irradiating or being irradiated. **2** Optics the apparent extension of the edges of an illuminated object seen against a dark background.

ir·ra·tion·al /i'rasHənl/ ▶ adj. **1** not logical or reasonable. ■ not endowed with the power of reason. **2** Math. (of a number, quantity, or expression) not expressible as a ratio of two integers, and having an infinite and nonrecurring expansion when expressed as a decimal, e.g., π and the square root of 2. ▶ n. Math. an irrational number. — **ir·ra·tion·al·i·ty** /i,rasHə'nalitē/ n. **ir·ra·tion·al·ize** v. **ir·ra·tion·al·ly** adv.

ir·ra·tion·al·ism /i'rasHənl,izəm/ ▶ n. a system of belief or action that disregards or contradicts rational principles. — **ir·ra·tion·al·ist** n. & adj.

Ir·ra·wad·dy /,irə'wädē/ the principal river of Myanmar, flowing 1,300 miles (2,090 km) to the Bay of Bengal.

ir·re·claim·a·ble /,iri'klāməbəl/ ▶ adj. not able to be reclaimed or reformed. — **ir·re·claim·a·bly** adv.

ir·rec·on·cil·a·ble /i,rekən'sīləbəl; i'rekən,sī-/ ▶ adj. (of ideas, facts, or statements) so different from each other that they are incompatible. ■ (of people) implacably hostile to each other. ▶ n. (usu. **irreconcilables**) any of two or more ideas, facts, or statements that are incompatible. — **ir·rec·on·cil·a·bil·i·ty** /-sīlə'bilitē/ n. **ir·rec·on·cil·a·bly** adv.

ir·re·cov·er·a·ble /,iri'kəvərəbəl/ ▶ adj. not able to be recovered, regained, or remedied. — **ir·re·cov·er·a·bly** adv.

ir·re·cu·sa·ble /,iri'kyo͞ozəbəl/ ▶ adj. rare (of evidence or a statement) not able to be challenged or rejected. [18th C.: via Fr. from late L. *irrecusabilis*, from *in-* 'not' + *recusabilis* 'that should be refused' (from the v. *recusare*).]

ir·re·deem·a·ble /,iri'dēməbəl/ ▶ adj. **1** not able to be saved, improved, or corrected. **2** (of paper currency) for which the issuing authority does not undertake ever to pay coin. — **ir·re·deem·a·bil·i·ty** /-,dēmə'bilitē/ n. **ir·re·deem·a·bly** adv.

ir·re·den·tist /,iri'dentist/ ▶ n. [usu. as adj.] a person advocating the restoration to their country of any territory formerly belonging to it. ■ hist. (in 19th-century Italian politics) an advocate of the return to Italy of all Italian-speaking districts subject to other countries. — **ir·re·den·tism** n. [from Ital. *irredentista*, from *(Italia) irredenta* 'unredeemed (Italy).']

ir·re·duc·i·ble /,iri'd(y)o͞osəbəl/ ▶ adj. not able to be reduced or simplified. ■ not able to be brought to a certain form or condition. — **ir·re·duc·i·bil·i·ty** /-,d(y)o͞osə'bilitē/ n. **ir·re·duc·i·bly** adv.

ir·re·form·a·ble /,irə'fôrməbəl/ ▶ adj. (chiefly of religious dogma) unable to be revised or altered.

ir·ref·ra·ga·ble /i'refrəgəbəl/ ▶ adj. not able to be refuted or disproved; indisputable. — **ir·ref·ra·ga·bly** adv. [16th C.: from late L. *irrefragabilis*, from *in-* 'not' + *refragari* 'oppose.']

ir·ref·u·ta·ble /,irə'fyo͞otəbəl; i'refyə-/ ▶ adj. impossible to deny or disprove. — **ir·ref·u·ta·bil·i·ty** /-,fyo͞otə'bilitē/ n. **ir·ref·u·ta·bly** adv. [17th C.: from late L. *irrefutabilis*, from *in-* 'not' + *refutabilis* (from *refutare* 'repel, rebut').]

irreg. ▶ abbr. irregular or irregularly.

ir·re·gard·less /,iri'gärdlis/ ▶ adj. & adv. informal regardless. [20th C.: prob. a blend of **irrespective** and **regardless**.]

ir·reg·u·lar /i'regyələr/ ▶ adj. **1** not even or balanced in shape or arrangement. ■ occurring at uneven or varying rates or intervals. ■ Bot. (of a flower) having the petals differing in size and shape; zygomorphic. **2** contrary to the rules or to that which is normal or established. ■ [attrib.] (of troops) not belonging to regular or established army units. ■ Gram. (of a verb or other word) having inflections that do not conform to the usual rules. ▶ n. (usu. **irregulars**) **1** a member of an irregular military force. **2** an imperfect piece of merchandise sold at a reduced price. — **ir·reg·u·lar·ly** adv.

ir·reg·u·lar·i·ty /i,regyə'laritē/ ▶ n. (pl. **-ties**) the state or quality of being irregular. ■ mild recurring constipation. ■ (usu. **irregularities**) a thing that is irregular in form or nature.

ir·rel·a·tive /i'relətiv/ ▶ adj. rare unconnected; unrelated. ■ irrelevant. — **ir·rel·a·tive·ly** adv.

ir·rel·e·vant /i'reləvənt/ ▶ adj. not connected with or relevant to something. — **ir·rel·e·vance** n. **ir·rel·e·van·cy** n. (pl. **-cies**) **ir·rel·e·vant·ly** adv.

ir·re·li·gious /,iri'lijəs/ ▶ adj. indifferent or hostile to religion: *an irreligious world.* — **ir·re·li·gion** /-'lijən/ n. **ir·re·li·gious·ly** adv. **ir·re·li·gious·ness** n.

ir·re·me·di·a·ble /,iri'mēdēəbəl/ ▶ adj. impossible to cure or put right. — **ir·re·me·di·a·bly** adv.

ir·re·mis·si·ble /,iri'misəbəl/ ▶ adj. **1** (of a crime) unpardonable. **2** (of an obligation or duty) binding.

ir·re·mov·a·ble /,iri'mo͞ovəbəl/ ▶ adj. incapable of being removed. ■ (of an official) unable to be displaced from office. — **ir·re·mov·a·bil·i·ty** /-,mo͞ovə'bilitē/ n. **ir·re·mov·a·bly** adv.

ir·rep·a·ra·ble /i'rep(ə)rəbəl/ ▶ adj. (of an injury or loss) impossible to rectify or repair. — **ir·rep·a·ra·bil·i·ty** /i,rep(ə)rə'bilitē/ n. **ir·rep·a·ra·bly** adv.

ir·re·place·a·ble /iri'plāsəbəl/ ▶ adj. impossible to replace if lost or damaged. — **ir·re·place·a·bly** adv.

ir·re·press·i·ble /,iri'presəbəl/ ▶ adj. not able to be controlled or restrained. — **ir·re·press·i·bil·i·ty** /-,presə'bilitē/ n. **ir·re·press·i·bly** adv.

ir·re·proach·a·ble /,iri'prōcHəbəl/ ▶ adj. beyond criticism; faultless. — **ir·re·proach·a·bil·i·ty** /-,prōcHə'bilitē/ n. **ir·re·proach·a·bly** adv.

ir·re·sist·i·ble /,iri'zistəbəl/ ▶ adj. too attractive and tempting to be resisted. ■ too powerful or convincing to be resisted. — **ir·re·sist·i·bil·i·ty** /-,zistə'bilitē/ n. **ir·re·sist·i·bly** adv.

ir·res·o·lute /i(r)'rezə,lo͞ot/ ▶ adj. showing or feeling hesitancy; uncertain. — **ir·res·o·lute·ly** adv. **ir·res·o·lute·ness** n. **ir·res·o·lu·tion** /-,rezə'lo͞osHən/ n.

ir·re·solv·a·ble /,iri'zälvəbəl/ ▶ adj. (of a problem or dilemma) impossible to solve or settle.

ir·re·spec·tive /,iri'spektiv/ ▶ adj. [predic.] **(irrespective of)** not taking (something) into account; regardless of. — **ir·re·spec·tive·ly** adv.

ir·re·spon·si·ble /,iri'spänsəbəl/ ▶ adj. (of a person, attitude, or action) not showing a proper sense of responsibility. ▶ n. an irresponsible person. — **ir·re·spon·si·bil·i·ty** /-,spänsə'bilitē/ n. **ir·re·spon·si·bly** adv.

ir·re·spon·sive /ˌiri'spänsiv/ ▶ **adj.** not responsive to someone or something. — **ir·re·spon·sive·ness n.**

ir·re·triev·a·ble /ˌiri'trēvəbəl/ ▶ **adj.** not able to be retrieved or put right. — **ir·re·triev·a·bil·i·ty** /-ˌtrēvə'bilitē/ **n. ir·re·triev·a·bly adv.**

ir·rev·er·ent /i'rev(ə)rənt/ ▶ **adj.** showing a lack of respect for people or things that are generally taken seriously. — **ir·rev·er·ence n. ir·rev·er·en·tial** /iˌrevə'rensнəl/ **adj. ir·rev·er·ent·ly adv.** [ME: from L. *irreverent-* 'not revering,' from *in-* 'not' + *reverent-* 'revering' (see REVERENT).]

ir·re·vers·i·ble /ˌiri'vərsəbəl/ ▶ **adj.** not able to be undone or altered. — **ir·re·vers·i·bil·i·ty** /-ˌvərsə'bilitē/ **n. ir·re·vers·i·bly adv.**

ir·rev·o·ca·ble /ˌi'revəkəbəl/ ▶ **adj.** not able to be changed, reversed, or recovered; final. — **ir·rev·o·ca·bil·i·ty** /iˌrevəkə'bilitē/ **n. ir·rev·o·ca·bly adv.** [ME: from OFr., or from L. *irrevocabilis*, from *in-* 'not' + *revocabilis* 'able to be revoked' (from the v. *revocare*).]

ir·ri·gate /'irigāt/ ▶ **v.** [trans.] supply water to (land or crops) to help growth, typically by means of channels. ■ (of a river or stream) supply (land) with water. ■ Med. apply a continuous flow of water or liquid medication to (an organ or wound). — **ir·ri·ga·ble** /-gəbəl/ **adj. ir·ri·ga·tion** /ˌiri'gāsнən/ **n. ir·ri·ga·tor** /-ˌgātər/ **n.** [17th C.: from L. *irrigat-* 'moistened,' from the v. *irrigare*, from *in-* 'into' + *rigare* 'moisten, wet.']

ir·ri·ta·ble /'iritəbəl/ ▶ **adj.** having or showing a tendency to be easily annoyed or made angry. ■ Med. (of a bodily part or organ) abnormally sensitive. ■ Med. (of a condition) caused by such sensitivity. ■ Biol. (of a living organism) having the property of responding actively to physical stimuli. — **ir·ri·ta·bil·i·ty** /ˌiritə'bilitē/ **n. ir·ri·ta·bly adv.** [17th C.: from L. *irritabilis*, from the v. *irritare* (see IRRITATE).]

ir·ri·ta·ble bow·el syn·drome (abbr.: **IBS**) ▶ **n.** a widespread condition involving recurrent abdominal pain and diarrhea or constipation, often associated with stress, depression, anxiety, or previous intestinal infection.

ir·ri·tant /'iritənt/ ▶ **n.** a substance that causes slight inflammation or other discomfort to the body. ■ fig. a thing that is continually annoying or distracting. ▶ **adj.** causing slight inflammation or other discomfort to the body. — **ir·ri·tan·cy n.**

ir·ri·tate /'iriˌtāt/ ▶ **v.** [trans.] make (someone) annoyed, impatient, or angry. ■ cause inflammation or other discomfort in (a part of the body). ■ Biol. stimulate (an organism, cell, or organ) to produce an active response. — **ir·ri·tat·ed·ly adv. ir·ri·tat·ing·ly adv. ir·ri·ta·tive** /-ˌtātiv/ **adj. ir·ri·ta·tor** /-ˌtātər/ **n.** [16th C. (in the sense 'excite, provoke'): from L. *irritat-* 'irritated,' from the v. *irritare*.]

ir·ri·ta·tion /ˌiri'tāsнən/ ▶ **n.** the state of feeling annoyed, impatient, or angry. ■ a cause of this. ■ the production of inflammation or other discomfort in a bodily part or organ. ■ Biol. the stimulation of an organism, cell, or organ to produce an active response. [ME: from L. *irritatio(n-)*, from the v. *irritare* (see IRRITATE).]

ir·ro·ta·tion·al /irō'tāsнənl/ ▶ **adj.** Physics (esp. of fluid motion) not rotational; having no rotation.

ir·rupt /i'rəpt/ ▶ **v.** [intrans.] enter forcibly or suddenly. ■ (of a bird or other animal) migrate into an area in abnormally large numbers. — **ir·rup·tion n. ir·rup·tive adj.** [19th C.: from L. *irrupt-* 'broken into,' from the v. *irrumpere*, from *in-* 'into' + *rumpere* 'break.']

IRS ▶ **abbr.** Internal Revenue Service.

Ir·tysh /ir'tisн; ər-/ a river in central Asia rising in northern China and flowing west and then northwest for 2,655 miles (4,248 km) to the Ob River in Russia.

Ir·ving¹ /'ərviɴɢ/ a city in northeastern Texas; pop. 191,615.

Ir·ving², John Winslow (1942–) US writer. His works combine tragedy with comedy such as in *The World According to Garp* (1978).

Ir·ving³, Washington (1783–1859), US writer. He wrote *The Sketch Book of Geoffrey Crayon, Gent.* (1819–20), which contains tales such as "Rip Van Winkle" and "The Legend of Sleepy Hollow."

Is. ▶ **abbr.** ■ (also **Isa.**) Bible Isaiah. ■ Island(s). ■ Isle(s).

is /iz/ third person singular present of BE.

I·saac /'īzək/ (in the Bible) a Hebrew patriarch, son of Abraham and Sarah and father of Jacob and Esau.

I·sa·bel·la /ˌizə'belə/ ▶ **n.** another term for FOX GRAPE. ■ a wine made from this grape.

Is·a·bel·la I (1451–1504), queen of Castile 1474–1504 and of Aragon 1479–1504. She and her husband Ferdinand of Aragon instituted the Spanish Inquisition in 1478 and supported the explorations of Christopher Columbus in 1492.

Is·a·bel·la of France (1292–1358), daughter of Philip IV of France and wife of Edward II of England 1308–27.

i·sa·gog·ics /ˌīsə'gäjiks/ ▶ **plural n.** [treated as sing.] introductory study, esp. of the literary and external history of the Bible prior to exegesis. — **i·sa·gog·ic adj.** [19th C.: pl. of *isagogic*, via L. from Gk. *eisagōgikos*, from *eisagōgē* 'introduction,' from *eis* 'into' + *agein* 'to lead.']

I·sa·iah /ī'zāə/ a major Hebrew prophet of Judah in the 8th century BC, who taught the supremacy of the God of Israel. ■ a book of the Bible containing his prophecies and, it is generally thought, those of at least one later prophet.

i·sa·tin /'īsətin/ ▶ **n.** Chem. a red crystalline compound, $C_8H_5NO_2$, used in the manufacture of dyes.

ISBN ▶ **abbr.** international standard book number, a ten- or thirteen-digit number assigned to every book before publication, recording such details as language, provenance, and publisher.

is·che·mi·a /is'kēmēə/ (Brit. **is·chae·mi·a**) ▶ **n.** Med. an inadequate blood supply to an organ or part of the body, esp. the heart muscles. — **is·che·mic** /-mik/ **adj.** [19th C. (denoting the stanching of bleeding): mod. L., from Gk. *iskhaimos* 'stopping blood,' from *iskhein* 'keep back' + *haima* 'blood.']

Is·chi·a /'iskēə/ an island in the Tyrrhenian Sea off the western coast of Italy.

is·chi·um /'iskēəm/ ▶ **n.** (pl. **-chi·a** /-kēə/) the curved bone forming the base of each half of the pelvis. — **is·chi·ad·ic** /ˌiskē'adik/ **adj. is·chi·al** /-kēəl/ **adj.** [17th C.: from L., from Gk. *iskhion* 'hip joint,' later 'ischium.']

ISDN ▶ **abbr.** integrated services digital network.

-ise¹ ▶ **suffix** var. of -IZE.

-ise² ▶ **suffix** forming nouns of quality, state, or function: *expertise* | *franchise* | *merchandise*. [from OFr. *-ise*, from L. *-itia*, *-itium*.]

is·en·trop·ic /ˌīsən'träpik; -'trōpik/ ▶ **adj.** Physics having equal entropy.

I·seult /i'so͞olt; i'zo͞olt/ a princess in medieval legend. According to one account, she was the sister or daughter of the king of Ireland, the wife of King Mark of Cornwall, and loved by Tristram. In another account, she was the daughter of the king of Brittany and wife of Tristram. Also called ISOLDE.

Is·fa·han /ˌisfə'hän/ (also **Es·fa·han** /ˌesfə-/, **Is·pa·han** /ˌispə-/) a city in central Iran; pop. 1,127,000.

-ish¹ /isн/ ▶ **suffix** forming adjectives: **1** (from nouns) having the qualities or characteristics of: *girlish*. ■ of nationality or religious or ethnic group: *Swedish*. **2** (from adjectives) somewhat: *yellowish*. ■ informal denoting an approximate age or time of day: *sixish*. [OE *-isc*, of Gmc. origin; rel. to ON *-iskr*, Ger. and Du. *-isch*, also to Gk. *-iskos* (suffix forming dimin. nouns).]

-ish² ▶ **suffix** forming verbs such as *abolish*, *establish*. [from Fr. *-iss-* (from stems of verbs ending in *-ir*), from L. *-isc-* (suffix forming inceptive verbs); cf. -ISH¹.]

Ish·er·wood /'isнərˌwo͝od/, Christopher William Bradshaw (1904–86), US writer; born in Britain. He wrote *Mr. Norris Changes Trains* (1935).

Ishi·gu·ro /ˌisнi'go͞orō/, Kazuo (1954–), British writer; born in Japan. He wrote *The Remains of the Day* (1989).

Ish·ma·el /'isнmēəl; -mā-/ (in the Bible) a son of Abraham, by his wife Sarah's maid, Hagar. Ishmael is also important in Islamic belief as the traditional ancestor of Muhammad and of the Arab peoples. — **Ish·ma·el·ite** /-əˌlīt/ **n.**

Ish·tar /'isнˌtär/ Near Eastern Mythol. a Babylonian and Assyrian goddess of love and war whose name and functions correspond to those of the Phoenician goddess Astarte.

Is·i·dore of Se·ville, St. /'izəˌdôr/ (*c.*560–636), Spanish archbishop; also called *Isidorus Hispalensis*. He is noted for *Etymologies*, an encyclopedic work.

i·sin·glass /'īzənˌglas; 'īziɴɢ-/ ▶ **n.** a kind of gelatin obtained from fish, esp. sturgeon, and used in making jellies, glue, etc., and for clarifying ale. ■ mica or a similar material in thin transparent sheets. [16th C.: alt. (by association with GLASS) of obs. Du. *huysenblas* 'sturgeon's bladder,' from *huysen* 'sturgeon' + *blas* 'bladder.']

I·sis /'īsis/ Egyptian Mythol. a goddess of fertility, wife of Osiris and mother of Horus. Her worship spread to western Asia, Greece, and Rome, where she was identified with various local goddesses.

Is·ken·de·run /isˌkendə'ro͞on/ a city in southern Turkey; pop. 159,000.

isl. (also **Isl.**) ▶ **abbr.** island or isle.

Is·lam /is'läm; iz-/ ▶ **n.** the religion of the Muslims, a monotheistic faith regarded as revealed through Muhammad as the Prophet of Allah. ■ the Muslim world. — **Is·lam·ic** /-ik/ **adj. Is·lam·i·ci·za·tion** /isˌlämisi'zāsнən; iz-/ **n. Is·lam·i·cize** /is'lämiˌsīz; iz-/ **v. Is·lam·i·za·tion** /isˌlämi'zāsнən; iz-/ **n. Is·lam·ize** /'isləˌmīz; 'iz-/ **v.** [from Arab. *islām* 'submission,' from *aslama* 'submit (to God).']

Is·lam·a·bad /is'läməˌbäd; iz'laməˌbad/ the capital of Pakistan, in the northern part of the country; pop. 201,000.

Is·lam·ic Ji·had /is'lämik ji'had; -'häd; iz-/ (also **Je·had**) a Muslim fundamentalist terrorist group within the Shiite Hezbollah association.

Is·lam·ism /'isləˌmizəm; 'iz-/ ▶ **n.** Islamic militancy or fundamentalism. — **Is·lam·ist** (also **Is·lam·i·cist** /is'läməsist; iz-/) **n. & adj.**

Is·lam·o·pho·bi·a ▶ **n.** extreme or irrational fear of all Islamic persons.

is·land /'īlənd/ ▶ **n.** a piece of land surrounded by water. ■ fig. a thing resembling an island, esp. in being isolated, detached, or surrounded in some way. ■ a freestanding kitchen cupboard unit with a countertop, allowing access from all sides. ■ Anat. a detached portion of tissue or group of cells. Compare with ISLET. ▶ **v.** [trans.] make into or like an island; place or enclose on or as on an island; isolate. [OE *īegland*, from *īeg* 'island' (from a base meaning 'watery, watered') + LAND. The change in the spelling of the first syllable in the 16th C. was due to association with the unrelated word ISLE.]

Is·land /'ēˌslän(t)/ Icelandic name for ICELAND.

is·land·er /'īləndər/ ▶ **n.** a native or inhabitant of an island.

Is·lands of the Bless·ed (in classical mythology) a land, typically located near the place where the sun sets, to which the souls of the good were taken to enjoy a life of eternal bliss.

isle /īl/ ▶**n.** esp. literary an island or peninsula, esp. a small one. [ME *ile*, from OFr., from Latin *insula*. The spelling with *s* (also in 15th-cent. Fr.) is influenced by L.]

is·let /'īlət/ ▶**n. 1** a small island. **2** Anat. a portion of tissue structurally distinct from surrounding tissues. ■ (**islets**) short for ISLETS OF LANGERHANS. [16th C.: from OFr., dimin. of *isle* (see ISLE).]

is·lets of Lang·er·hans /'lanGər,hanz; 'länGər,häns/ (also **is·lands of Lang·er·hans**) ▶**plural n.** groups of pancreatic cells secreting insulin and glucagon. [19th C.: named after Paul *Langerhans* (1847–88), the Ger. anatomist who first described them.]

ism /'izəm/ ▶**n.** informal, esp. derog. a distinctive practice, system, or philosophy, typically a political ideology or an artistic movement. — **ist n.** [17th C.: independent usage of -ISM.]

-ism ▶**suffix** forming nouns: **1** denoting an action or its result: *baptism* | *exorcism.* ■ denoting a state or quality: *barbarism.* **2** denoting a system, principle, or ideological movement: *Anglicanism* | *feminism* | *hedonism.* ■ denoting a basis for prejudice or discrimination: *racism.* **3** denoting a peculiarity in language: *colloquialism* | *Canadianism.* **4** denoting a pathological condition: *alcoholism.* [from Fr. *-isme*, via L. from Gk. *-ismos, -isma.*]

Is·ma·il /,ismä'ēl/ Arabic spelling of ISHMAEL.

Is·ma·il·i /,ismä'ēlē/ ▶**n.** (pl. **-il·is**) a member of a branch of Shiite Muslims that seceded from the main group in the 8th century because of their belief that Ismail, the son of the sixth Shiite imam, should have become the seventh imam.

is·n't /'izənt/ ▶**contr.** is not.

ISO ▶**abbr.** International Organization for Standardization.

iso- ▶**comb. form** equal: *isochron* | *isosceles.* ■ Chem. (chiefly of hydrocarbons) isomeric: *isooctane.* [from Gk. *isos* 'equal.']

i·so·ag·glu·ti·na·tion /,īsō,glōōtn'āsHən/ ▶**n.** Physiol. agglutination of sperms, erythrocytes, or other cells of an individual caused by a substance from another individual of the same species.

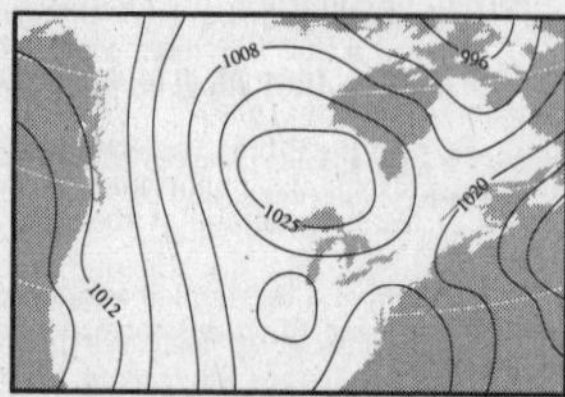

isobar 1

i·so·bar /'īsə,bär/ ▶**n. 1** Meteorol. a line on a map connecting points having the same atmospheric pressure at a given time or on average over a given period. ■ Physics a curve or formula representing a physical system at constant pressure. **2** Physics each of two or more isotopes of different elements, with the same atomic weight. — **i·so·bar·ic** /,īsə'barik; -'bär / **adj.** [19th C.: from Gk. *isobaros* 'of equal weight,' from *isos* 'equal' + *baros* 'weight.']

i·so·bu·tane /,īsə'byōōtān; -byōō'tān/ ▶**n.** Chem. a gaseous hydrocarbon, $CH_3CH(CH_3)_2$, isomeric with butane.

i·so·cheim /'īsə,kīm/ ▶**n.** Meteorol. a line on a map connecting points having the same average temperature in winter. [19th C.: from ISO- 'equal' + Gk. *kheima* 'winter weather.']

i·so·chro·mat·ic /,īsəkrə'matik/ ▶**adj.** of a single color.

i·so·chron /'īsə,krän/ ▶**n.** esp. Geol. a line on a diagram or map connecting points relating to the same time or equal times. [17th C. (as an adj. in the sense 'isochronous'): from Gk. *isokhronos*, from *isos* 'equal' + *khronos* 'time.']

i·soch·ro·nous /ī'säkrənəs/ ▶**adj.** occurring at the same time. ■ occupying equal time. — **i·soch·ro·nous·ly adv.** [18th C. (in the sense 'equal in duration or in frequency'): from mod. L. *isochronus* (from Gk. *isokhronos*, from *isos* 'equal' + *khronos* 'time') + -OUS.]

i·so·cli·nal /,īsə'klīnl/ ▶**adj.** Geol. denoting a fold of strata so acute that the two limbs are parallel. [19th C. (denoting 'equal magnetic inclination'): from ISO- 'equal' + Gk. *klinein* 'to lean, slope' + -AL.]

i·so·cline /'īsə,klīn/ ▶**n.** a line on a diagram or map connecting points of equal gradient or inclination. — **i·so·clin·ic** /,īsə'klinik/ **adj.** [19th C. (denoting an isoclinal line or fold): from Gk. *isoklinēs* 'equally balanced,' from *klinein* 'to lean, slope.']

i·so·clin·ic line /,īsə'klinik/ ▶**n.** a line on a map connecting points where the dip of the earth's magnetic field is the same.

i·so·di·a·met·ric /,īsō,dīə'metrik/ ▶**adj.** esp. Bot. (of a cell, spore, etc.) roughly spherical or polyhedral.

i·so·dy·nam·ic /,īsədī'namik/ ▶**adj.** Geog. indicating or connecting points on the earth's surface at which the intensity of the magnetic force is the same.

i·so·e·lec·tric /,īsō-i'lektrik/ ▶**adj.** having or involving no net electric charge or difference in electrical potential.

i·so·e·lec·tron·ic /,īsō-ilek'tränik; -,ēlek-/ ▶**adj.** Chem. having the same numbers of electrons or the same electronic structure.

i·so·en·zyme /,īsō'enzīm/ ▶**n.** Biochem. another term for ISOZYME.

i·sog·a·my /ī'sägəmē/ ▶**n.** Biol. sexual reproduction by the fusion of similar gametes. Compare with ANISOGAMY. — **i·so·gam·ete** /,īsō'gamēt; īsōgə'mēt/ **n. i·sog·a·mous** /-məs/ **adj.** [19th C.: from ISO- 'equal' + Gk. *-gamia* (from *gamos* 'marriage').]

i·so·gen·ic /,īsə'jenik/ ▶**adj.** Biol. (of organisms) having the same or closely similar genotypes.

i·so·ge·o·therm /,īsə'jēə,THərm/ ▶**n.** Geol. a line or plane on a diagram connecting points representing those in the interior of the earth having the same temperature. — **i·so·ge·o·ther·mal** /-,jēə'THərməl/ **adj.** [19th C.: from ISO- 'equal' + GEO- 'earth' + Gk. *thermē* 'heat.']

i·so·gloss /'īsə,glôs; -,gläs/ ▶**n.** Ling. a line on a dialect map marking the boundary between linguistic features. — **i·so·glos·sal** /,īsə'glôsəl; -'gläsəl/ **adj.** [20th C.: from ISO- 'equal' + Gk. *glōssa* 'tongue, word.']

i·so·gon·ic /,īsə'gänik/ (also **i·sog·o·nal** /ī'sägənl/) ▶**adj.** Geog. indicating or connecting points of the earth's surface at which the magnetic declination is the same. [19th C.: from Gk. *isogōnios* 'equiangular' + -IC.]

i·so·hel /'īsə,hel/ ▶**n.** Meteorol. a line on a map connecting points having the same duration of sunshine. [20th C.: from ISO- 'equal' + Gk. *hēlios* 'sun.']

i·so·hy·et /,īsə'hī-it/ ▶**n.** Meteorol. a line on a map connecting points having the same amount of rainfall in a given period. [19th C.: from ISO- 'equal' + Gk. *huetos* 'rain.']

i·so·late ▶**v.** /'īsə,lāt/ [trans.] cause (a person or place) to be or remain alone or apart from others. ■ identify (something) and examine or deal with it separately. ■ Chem. Biol. obtain or extract (a compound, microorganism, etc.) in a pure form. ■ cut off the electrical or other connection to (something, esp. a part of a supply network). ■ place (a person or animal) in quarantine as a precaution against infectious or contagious disease. ▶**n.** /-lit/ a person or thing that has been or become isolated. ■ Biol. a culture of microorganisms isolated for study. — **i·so·la·ble** /-ləbəl/ **adj. i·so·lat·a·ble adj. i·so·la·tor** /-,lātər/ **n.** [19th C. (as a v.): back-form. from ISOLATED.]

i·so·lat·ed /'īsə,lātid/ ▶**adj.** far away from other places, buildings, or people; remote. ■ having minimal contact or little in common with others. ■ single; exceptional. [18th C.: from Fr. *isolé*, from Ital. *isolato*, from late L. *insulatus* 'made into an island,' from L. *insula* 'island.']

i·so·lat·ing /'īsə,lātiNG/ ▶**adj.** (of a language) tending to have each element as an independent word without inflections.

i·so·la·tion /,īsə'lāsHən/ ▶**n.** the process or fact of isolating or being isolated. ■ an instance of isolating something, esp. a compound or microorganism. ■ [as adj.] denoting a hospital or ward for those with contagious or infectious diseases.

– PHRASES **in isolation** without relation to other people or things; separately. [19th C.: from ISOLATE, partly on the pattern of Fr. *isolation.*]

i·so·la·tion·ism /,īsə'lāsHə,nizəm/ ▶**n.** a policy of remaining apart from the affairs or interests of other groups, esp. the political affairs of other countries. — **i·so·la·tion·ist n.**

I·solde /i'sōld(ə); ē'zôldə/ another name for ISEULT.

i·so·leu·cine /,īsə'lōōsēn; -sin/ ▶**n.** Biochem. a hydrophobic amino acid, $C_2H_5CH(CH_3)CH(NH_2)COOH$, that is a constituent of most proteins. It is an essential nutrient for vertebrates.

i·so·mer /'īsəmər/ ▶**n. 1** Chem. each of two or more compounds with the same formula but a different arrangement of atoms in the molecule and different properties. **2** Physics each of two or more atomic nuclei that have the same atomic number and the same mass number but different energy states. — **i·so·mer·ic** /,īsə'merik/ **adj. i·som·er·ism** /ī'sämə,rizəm/ **n. i·som·er·ize** /ī'sämə,rīz/ **v.** [19th C.: from Gk. *isomerēs* 'sharing equally,' from *isos* 'equal' + *meros* 'a share.']

i·som·er·ase /ī'sämə,rās; -,rāz/ ▶**n.** Biochem. an enzyme that catalyzes the conversion of a specified compound to an isomer.

i·som·er·ous /ī'sämərəs/ ▶**adj.** Biol. having or composed of parts that are similar in number or position. [19th C.: from Gk. *isomerēs* (see ISOMER) + -OUS.]

i·so·met·ric /,īsə'metrik/ ▶**adj. 1** of or having equal dimensions. **2** Physiol. of, relating to, or denoting muscular action in which tension is developed without contraction of the muscle. **3** (in technical or architectural drawing) incorporating a method of showing projection or perspective in which the three principal dimensions are represented by three axes 120° apart. **4** Math. (of a transformation) without change of shape or size. — **i·so·met·ri·cal·ly adv. i·som·e·try** /ī'sämitrē/ **n.** (in sense 4). [19th C.: from Gk. *isometria* 'equality of measure' (from *isos* 'equal' + *-metria* 'measuring') + -IC.]

i·so·met·rics /,īsə'metriks/ ▶**plural n.** a system of physical exercises in which muscles are caused to act against each other or against a fixed object. Also called **isometric exercise**.

i·so·mor·phic /,īsə'môrfik/ (also **i·so·morph·ous** /-fəs/) ▶**adj.** corresponding or similar in form and relations. ■ having the same crystalline form. — **i·so·mor·phism n.**

-ison ▶**suffix** (forming nouns) equivalent to -ATION (as in *comparison, jettison*). [from OFr. *-aison, -eison*, etc., from L. *-atio(n)-*.]

i·so·ni·a·zid /,īsə'nīəzid/ ▶**n.** Med. a synthetic compound, $C_5H_4NCONHNH_2$, used as a bacteriostatic drug, chiefly to treat tuberculosis.

i·so·oc·tane /,īsō'äktān/ ▶**n.** Chem. a liquid hydrocarbon, $(CH_3)_3CCH_2CH(CH_3)CH_3$, present in petroleum. It serves as a standard in the system of octane numbers.

i·so·pach /'īsə,pak/ ▶**n.** Geol. a line on a map or diagram connecting points beneath which a particular stratum or group of strata has the same thickness. [20th C.: from ISO- 'equal' + Gk. *pakhus* 'thick.']

i·so·pleth /'īsə,pleTH/ ▶**n.** a line on a map or diagram connecting points for which a chosen quantity has the same value. [20th C.: from Gk.

isoplēthēs 'equal in quantity,' from *isos* 'equal' + *plēthos* 'multitude, quantity.']

I·sop·o·da /ī'säpədə/ Zool. an order of crustaceans that includes the terrestrial wood lice and several marine and freshwater parasites. They have a flattened segmented body with seven similar pairs of legs. — **i·so·pod** /'īsə,päd/ **n.** [mod. L. (pl.), from Gk. *isos* 'equal' + *pous, pod-* 'foot.']

i·so·prene /'īsə,prēn/ ▶**n.** Chem. a volatile liquid hydrocarbon, $CH_2=C(CH_3)CH=CH_2$, obtained from petroleum, whose molecule forms the basic structural unit of natural and synthetic rubbers.

i·so·pro·pa·nol /,īsə'prōpə,nôl; -,näl/ ▶**n.** Chem. a liquid alcohol, $CH_3CHOHCH_3$, used as a solvent and in the industrial production of acetone.

i·so·pro·pyl /,īsə'prōpəl/ ▶**n.** [as adj.] Chem. of or denoting the alkyl radical $-CH(CH_3)_2$, derived from propane by removal of a hydrogen atom from the middle carbon atom.

i·so·pro·pyl al·co·hol ▶**n.** Chem. another term for **ISOPROPANOL**.

i·so·pro·ter·e·nol /,īsəprō'terə,nôl; -,näl/ ▶**n.** Med. a synthetic derivative of adrenalin, used for the relief of bronchial asthma and pulmonary emphysema. [1950s: from elements of the semisystematic name *N-isopropylarterenol*.]

I·sop·te·ra /ī'säptərə/ Entomol. an order of insects that comprises the termites. — **i·sop·te·ran n. & adj.** [mod. L. (pl.), from Gk. *isos* 'equal' + *pteron* 'wing.']

i·sos·ce·les /ī'säsə,lēz/ ▶**adj.** (of a triangle) having two sides of equal length. [16th C.: via late L. from Gk. *isoskelēs*, from *isos* 'equal' + *skelos* 'leg.']

i·so·seis·mal /,īsə'sīzməl/ ▶**adj.** Geol. relating to or denoting lines on a map connecting places where an earthquake was experienced with equal strength. — **i·so·seis·mic adj.**

i·sos·mot·ic /,īsäz'mätik; -säs-/ ▶**adj.** Biol. having the same osmotic pressure.

i·so·spin /'īsə,spin/ ▶**n.** Physics a vector quantity or quantum number assigned to subatomic particles and atomic nuclei and having values such that similar particles differing only in charge-related properties (independent of the strong interaction between particles) can be treated as different states of a single particle. [1960s: contr. of *isotopic spin, isobaric spin*.]

i·sos·ta·sy /ī'sästəsē/ ▶**n.** Geol. the equilibrium that exists between parts of the earth's crust, which behaves as if it consists of blocks floating on the underlying mantle, rising if material (such as an ice cap) is removed and sinking if material is deposited. — **i·so·stat·ic** /,īsə'statik/ **adj.** [19th C.: from **ISO-** 'equal' + Gk. *stasis* 'station.']

i·so·tac·tic /,īsə'taktik/ ▶**adj.** Chem. (of a polymer) in which all the repeating units have the same stereochemical configuration. [1950s: from **ISO-** 'equal' + Gk. *taktos* 'arranged' + **-IC**.]

i·so·there /'īsə,THi(ə)r/ ▶**n.** Meteorol. a line on a map connecting points having the same average temperature in summer. [19th C.: from Fr. *isothère*, from Gk. *isos* 'equal' + *theros* 'summer.']

i·so·therm /'īsə,THərm/ ▶**n.** a line on a map connecting points having the same temperature at a given time or on average over a given period. ■ Physics a curve on a diagram joining points representing states or conditions of equal temperature. — **i·so·ther·mal** /,īsə'THərməl/ **adj. & n. i·so·ther·mal·ly** /,īsə'THərməlē/ **adv.** [19th C.: from Fr. *isotherme*, from Gk. *isos* 'equal' + *thermē* 'heat.']

i·so·ton·ic /,īsə'tänik/ ▶**adj. 1** Physiol. (of muscle action) taking place with normal contraction. **2** Physiol. denoting or relating to a solution having the same osmotic pressure as some other solution, esp. one in a cell or a body fluid. ■ (of a drink) containing essential salts and minerals in the same concentration as in the body and intended to replace those lost as a result of sweating during vigorous exercise. — **i·so·ton·i·cal·ly adv. i·so·to·nic·i·ty** /-tə'nisitē/ **n.** [19th C. (as a musical term designating a system of tuning, characterized by equal intervals): from Gk. *isotonos*, from *isos* 'equal' + *tonos* 'tone.']

i·so·tope /'īsə,tōp/ ▶**n.** Chem. each of two or more forms of the same element that contain equal numbers of protons but different numbers of neutrons in their nuclei, and hence differ in atomic mass but not in chemical properties; in particular, a radioactive form of an element. — **i·so·top·ic** /,īsə'täpik/ **adj. i·so·top·i·cal·ly** /,īsə'täpik(ə)lē/ **adv. i·sot·o·py** /'īsə,tōpē; ī'sätəpē/ **n.** [1913: coined by F. Soddy, from **ISO-** 'equal' + Gk. *topos* 'place' (because the isotopes occupy the same place in the periodic table of elements).]

i·so·trop·ic /,īsə'träpik; -'trōpik/ ▶**adj.** Physics (of an object or substance) having a physical property that has the same value when measured in different directions. Often contrasted with **ANISOTROPIC**. ■ (of a property or phenomenon) not varying in magnitude according to the direction of measurement. — **i·so·trop·i·cal·ly adv. i·sot·ro·py** /ī'sätrəpē/ **n.** [19th C.: from **ISO-** 'equal' + Gk. *tropos* 'a turn' + **-IC**.]

i·so·zyme /'īsə,zīm/ ▶**n.** Biochem. each of two or more enzymes with identical function but different structure.

ISP ▶**abbr.** Internet service provider.

Is·pa·han var. of **ISFAHAN**.

Is·ra·el[1] /'izrēəl; -rā-/ **1** (also **children of Israel**) the Hebrew nation or people. According to tradition, they are descended from the patriarch Jacob (also named Israel), whose twelve sons became founders of the twelve tribes of ancient Israel. See also **TRIBES OF ISRAEL**. **2** the northern kingdom of the Hebrews (*c.*930–721 BC), formed after the reign of Solomon, whose inhabitants were carried away to captivity in Babylon. See also **JUDAH** (sense 2). [from Heb. *Yiśrā'ēl* 'he that strives with God' (see Gen. 32:28).]

Israel

Official name: State of Israel
Location: Middle East, bordered on the east by Jordan and on the west by the Mediterranean Sea and Egypt
Area: 7,900 square miles (20,300 sq km)
Population: 6,199,000
Capital: Jerusalem (not recognized by the UN; US embassy is in Tel Aviv)
Languages: Hebrew (official), English, Arabic
Currency: new Israeli shekel

Is·ra·el[2] a country in the Middle East. *See box.*

Is·rae·li /iz'rālē/ ▶**adj.** of or relating to the modern country of Israel. ▶**n.** (pl. **-lis**) a native or national of Israel, or a person of Israeli descent.

Is·ra·el·ite /'izrēə,līt/ ▶**n.** a member of the ancient Hebrew nation, esp. in the period from the Exodus to the Babylonian Captivity (*c.*12th to 6th centuries BC). ■ old-fashioned and sometimes offensive term for **JEW**. ▶**adj.** of or relating to the Israelites. [via late L. from Gk. *Israēlitēs*.]

Is·ra·fil /'izrə,fēl/ (in Muslim tradition) the angel of music, who will sound the trumpet on Judgment Day.

Is·sa /ē'sä; i'sä/ ▶**n.** (pl. same or **Is·sas**) a member of a Somali people living in Djibouti. ▶**adj.** of or relating to the Issa. [the name in Somali.]

Is·sa·char /'isə,kär/ (in the Bible) a Hebrew patriarch, son of Jacob and Leah. ■ the tribe of Israel traditionally descended from him.

is·sei /'ē,sā/ ▶**n.** (pl. same) a Japanese immigrant to North America. Compare with **NISEI** and **SANSEI**. [Japanese, lit. 'first generation.']

ISSN ▶**abbr.** international standard serial number, an eight-digit number assigned to many serial publications such as newspapers, magazines, annuals, and series of books.

is·su·ant /'isHōōənt/ ▶**adj.** [predic. or postpositive] Heraldry (of the upper part of an animal) shown rising up or out from another bearing. [17th C.: from **ISSUE** + **-ANT** (on the pattern of Fr. present participles ending in *-ant*).]

is·sue /'isHōō/ ▶**n. 1** an important topic or problem for debate or discussion. ■ (**issues**) personal problems or difficulties. **2** the action of supplying or distributing an item for use, sale, or official purposes. ■ each of a regular series of publications. ■ a number or set of items distributed at one time. **3** formal or Law children of one's own. **4** the action of flowing or coming out. **5** dated a result or outcome of something. ▶**v.** (**is·sues, is·sued, is·su·ing**) **1** [trans.] supply or distribute (something). ■ (**issue someone with**) supply someone with (something). ■ formally send out or make known. ■ put (something) on sale or into general use. **2** [intrans.] (**issue from**) come, go, or flow out from. ■ result or be derived from.

– PHRASES **at issue** under discussion; in dispute. **make an issue of** treat too seriously or as a problem. **take issue with** disagree with; challenge. — **is·su·a·ble adj. is·su·ance** /-əns/ **n. is·sue·less adj. is·su·er n.** [ME (in the sense 'outflowing'): from OFr., based on L. *exitus*, past part. of *exire* 'go out.']

IST ▶**abbr.** insulin shock therapy.

-ist /əst; ist/ ▶**suffix** forming personal nouns and some related adjectives: **1** denoting an adherent of a system of beliefs, principles, etc., expressed by nouns ending in *-ism*: *hedonist* | *Marxist*. See **-ISM** 2. ■ denoting a person who subscribes to a prejudice or practices discrimination: *sexist*. **2** denoting a member of a profession or business activity: *dentist* | *dramatist* | *florist*. ■ denoting a person who uses a thing: *flutist* | *motorist.* ■ denoting a person who does something expressed by a verb ending in *-ize*: *plagiarist.* [from OFr. *-iste*, L. *-ista*, from Gk. *-istēs.*]

Is·tan·bul /'istän,bo͝ol; -tan-; -täm-/ a port in Turkey on the Bosporus that straddles Europe and Asia; pop. 7,309,000. Formerly the Roman city of Constantinople 330–1453, it was built on the site of the ancient Greek city of Byzantium. It was captured by the Ottoman Turks in 1453 and was the capital of Turkey from that time until 1923.

isth. (also **Isth.**) ▶ **abbr.** isthmus.

isth·mi·an /'ismēən/ ▶ **adj.** of or relating to an isthmus. ■ (**Isthmian**) of or relating to the Isthmus of Corinth in southern Greece or the Isthmus of Panama.

isth·mus /'isməs/ ▶ **n.** (pl. **-mus·es**) a narrow strip of land with sea on either side, forming a link between two larger areas of land. ■ (pl. **-mi** /-mī/) Anat. a narrow organ, passage, or piece of tissue connecting two larger parts. [16th C.: via L. from Gk. *isthmos.*]

is·tle /'is(t)lē/ ▶ **n.** var. of IXTLE.

ISV ▶ **abbr.** International Scientific Vocabulary.

it /it/ ▶ **pron.** [third person sing.] **1** used to refer to a thing previously mentioned or easily identified. ■ referring to an animal or child of unspecified sex. ■ referring to a fact or situation previously mentioned, known, or happening. **2** used to identify a person: *it's me* | *it's a boy!* **3** used in the normal subject position in statements about time, distance, or weather: *it's half past five.* **4** used in the normal subject or object position when a more specific subject or object is given later in the sentence: *it is impossible to assess the problem.* **5** [with clause] used to emphasize a following part of a sentence: *it is the child who is the victim.* **6** the situation or circumstances; things in general: *no one can stay here—it's too dangerous now.* **7** exactly what is needed or desired: *I thought she was it.* **8** (usu. **"it"**) informal sex appeal: *he's still got "it."* ■ sexual intercourse. **9** (usu. **"it"**) (in children's games) the player who must do something, typically catch the others.
– PHRASES **at it** see AT[1]. **that's it 1** that is the main point or difficulty. **2** that is enough or the end. **this is it 1** the expected event is about to happen. **2** this is enough or the end. **3** this is the main point or difficulty. [OE *hit*, neut. of HE, of Gmc. origin; rel. to Du. *het.*]

ital. ▶ **abbr.** italic (used as an instruction for a typesetter).

I·tal·ian /i'talyən/ ▶ **adj.** of or relating to Italy, its people, or their language. ▶ **n. 1** a native or national of Italy, or a person of Italian descent. **2** the Romance language of Italy, also one of the official languages of Switzerland. — **I·tal·ian·ize v.** [ME: from Ital. *italiano*, from *Italia* 'Italy.']

I·tal·ian·ate /i'talyə,nāt/ ▶ **adj.** Italian in character or appearance. [16th C.: from Ital. *italianato*, from *Italia* 'Italy.']

I·tal·ian·ism /i'talyə,nizəm/ ▶ **n. 1** an Italian characteristic, expression, or custom. **2** attachment to Italy or Italian ideas or practices.

I·tal·ian pars·ley ▶ **n.** another term for FLAT-LEAFED PARSLEY.

I·tal·ic /i'talik; ī'tal-/ ▶ **adj.** relating to or denoting the branch of Indo-European languages that includes Latin, Oscan, and Umbrian. ▶ **n.** the Italic group of languages. [19th C.: via L. from Gk. *Italikos*, from *Italia* 'Italy.']

i·tal·ic /i'talik; ī'tal-/ ▶ **adj.** Print. of the sloping kind of typeface used esp. for emphasis or distinction and in foreign words. See illustration at TYPE. ■ (of handwriting) modeled on 16th-century Italian handwriting, typically cursive and sloping and with elliptical or pointed letters. ▶ **n.** (also **i·tal·ics**) an italic typeface or letter. [ME (in the general sense 'Italian'): via L. from Gk. *Italikos*, from *Italia* 'Italy.' Senses relating to writing date from the early 17th C.]

i·tal·i·cize /i'tali,sīz; ī'tal-/ ▶ **v.** [trans.] print (text) in italics. — **i·tal·i·ci·za·tion** /i,talisi'zāshən/ **n.**

Italo- ▶ **comb. form** Italian; Italian and ...: *Italophile* | *Italo-Grecian.* ■ relating to Italy.

It·a·ly /'itl-ē/ a country in southern Europe. Italian name ITALIA. *See box.*

ITAR-Tass /'ētär 'täs/ the official news agency of Russia, founded in 1925 in Leningrad as Tass, and renamed in 1992. [from the initials of Russ. *Informatsionnoe telegrafnoe agentstvo Rossii* 'Information Telegraph Agency of Russia,' + TASS.]

itch /ich/ ▶ **n.** [usu. in sing.] an uncomfortable sensation on the skin that causes a desire to scratch. ■ informal a restless or strong desire. ■ [with adj.] a skin disease or condition of which itching is a symptom. ■ (**the itch**) informal scabies. ▶ **v.** [intrans.] be the site of or cause an itch. ■ (of a person) experience an itch. ■ informal feel a restless or strong desire to do something.
– PHRASES **an itchy** (or **itching**) **palm** fig. an avaricious nature. [OE *gycce* (noun), *gyccan* (verb), of West Gmc. origin; rel. to Dutch *jeuk* (n.) and Du. *jeuken*, Ger. *jucken* (v.).]

itch mite ▶ **n.** a parasitic mite (*Sarcoptes scabiei*, family Sarcoptidae) that burrows under the skin, causing scabies in humans and sarcoptic mange in animals.

itch·y /'ichē/ ▶ **adj.** (**itch·i·er**, **itch·i·est**) having or causing an itch: *dry, itchy skin* | *an itchy rash.*
– PHRASES **get** (or **have**) **itchy feet** informal have or develop a strong urge to travel or move from place to place. — **itch·i·ness n.**

it'd /'itid/ ▶ **contr.** ■ it had: *it'd been there for years.* ■ it would: *it'd be great to see you.*

-ite[1] ▶ **suffix 1** forming names denoting natives of a country: *Israelite* | *Samnite.* ■ often derog. denoting followers of a movement, doctrine, etc.: *Luddite* | *Trotskyite.* **2** used in scientific and technical terms: ■ forming names of fossil organisms: *ammonite.* ■ forming names of minerals: *graphite.* ■ forming names of constituent parts of a body or organ: *somite.* ■ forming names of explosives and other commercial products: *vulcanite.* ■ Chem. forming names of salts or esters of acids ending in *-ous*: *sulfite.* [from Fr. *-ite*, via L. *-ita* from Gk. *ites.*]

Italy

Official name: Italian Republic

Location: southern Europe, a peninsula extending into the Mediterranean Sea, south of Austria and Switzerland, including the islands of Sardinia and Sicily

Area: 113,500 square miles (294,000 sq km)

Population: 58,057,000

Capital: Rome

Language: Italian (official), German, French, Slovene

Currency: euro

-ite[2] ▶ **suffix 1** forming adjectives such as *composite, erudite.* **2** forming nouns such as *appetite.* **3** forming verbs such as *unite.* [from L. *-itus*, past part. of verbs ending in *-ere* and *-ire.*]

i·tem /'ītəm/ ▶ **n.** an individual article or unit, esp. one that is part of a list, collection, or set. ■ a piece of news or information. ■ an entry in an account. ▶ **adv.** archaic used to introduce each item in a list: *item two statute books ... item two drums.*
– PHRASES **be an item** informal (of a couple) be involved in an established romantic or sexual relationship. [ME (as an adverb): from L., 'in like manner, also.' The n. sense arose (late 16th C.) from the use of the adv. to introduce each statement in a list.]

i·tem·ize /'ītə,mīz/ ▶ **v.** [trans.] present as a list of individual items. ■ break down (a whole) into its constituent parts. ■ specify (an individual item or items). — **i·tem·i·za·tion** /,ītəmi'zāshən/ **n.** **i·tem·iz·er n.**

it·er·ate /'itə,rāt/ ▶ **v.** [trans.] perform or utter repeatedly. ■ [intrans.] perform mathematical or computational iteration. ▶ **n.** Math. a quantity arrived at by iteration. [16th C.: from L. *iterat-* 'repeated,' from the v. *iterare*, from *iterum* 'again.']

it·er·a·tion /,itə'rāshən/ ▶ **n.** the repetition of a process or utterance. ■ repetition of a mathematical or computational procedure applied to the result of a previous application, typically as a means of obtaining successively closer approximations to the solution of a problem. ■ a new version of a piece of computer hardware or software. [ME: from L. *iteratio(n-)*, from the v. *iterare* (see ITERATE).]

it·er·a·tive /'itə,rātiv; -rətiv/ ▶ **adj.** relating to or involving iteration, esp. mathematical or computational. ■ Ling. denoting a grammatical rule that can be applied repeatedly. ■ Gram. another term for FREQUENTATIVE. — **it·er·a·tive·ly adv.** [15th C.: from Fr. *itératif, -ive*, from L. *iterare* 'to repeat'; the grammar term is from late L. *iterativus.*]

Ith·a·ca /'ithəkə/ an island off the western coast of Greece in the Ionian Sea.

I-Thou ▶ **adj.** [attrib.] (of a personal relationship, esp. one with God) formed by personal encounter.

ith·y·phal·lic /,ithə'falik/ ▶ **adj.** (esp. of a statue of a deity or other carved figure) having an erect penis. [17th C. (as a n. denoting a sexually explicit poem): via late L. from Gk. *ithuphallikos*, from *ithus* 'straight' + *phallos* 'phallus.']

-itic ▶ **suffix** forming adjectives and nouns corresponding to nouns ending in *-ite* (such as *Semitic* corresponding to *Semite*). ■ corresponding to nouns ending in *-itis* (such as *arthritic* corresponding to *arthritis*). ■ from other bases: *syphilitic.* [from Fr. *-itique*, via L. *-iticus* from Gk. *-itikos.*]

i·tin·er·ant /ī'tinərənt; i'tin-/ ▶ **adj.** traveling from place to place. ▶ **n.** a person who travels from place to place. — **i·tin·er·a·cy** /-rəsē/ **n.** **i·tin·er·**

an·cy n. **i·tin·er·ant·ly** adv. [16th C. (used to describe a judge traveling on a circuit): from late L. *itinerant-* 'traveling,' from the v. *itinerari*, from L. *iter, itiner-* 'journey, road.']

i·tin·er·ar·y /ī'tinə,rerē; i'tin-/ ▶ n. (pl. **-ar·ies**) a planned route or journey. ▪ a travel document recording these. [ME: from late L. *itinerarium*, neut. of *itinerarius* 'of a journey or roads,' from L. *iter, itiner-* 'journey, road.']

i·tin·er·ate /ī'tinə,rāt; i'tin-/ ▶ v. [intrans.] (esp. of a church minister or a judge) travel from place to place to perform one's professional duty. — **i·tin·er·a·tion** /ī,tinə'rāsʜən; i,tin-/ n. [17th C.: from late L. *itinerat-* 'traveled,' from the v. *itinerari* (see ITINERANT).]

-ition ▶ suffix (forming nouns) equivalent to -ATION (as in *audition, rendition*). [from Fr., or from L. *-itio(n)-*.]

-itious[1] ▶ suffix forming adjectives corresponding to nouns ending in *-ition* (such as *ambitious* corresponding to *ambition*). [from L. *-itiosus*.]

-itious[2] ▶ suffix (forming adjectives) related to; having the nature of: *fictitious* | *supposititious*. [from late L. *-itius*, alt. of L. *-icius*.]

-itis ▶ suffix forming names of inflammatory diseases: *cystitis* | *hepatitis*. ▪ informal used with reference to a tendency or state of mind that is compared to a disease: *creditcarditis*. [from Gk. fem. form of adjectives ending in *-itēs* (combined with *nosos* 'disease' implied).]

-itive ▶ suffix (forming adjectives) equivalent to -ATIVE (as in *genitive, positive*). [from Fr. *-itif, -itive* or L. *-itivus* (from past participial stems ending in *-it*).]

it'll /'itl/ ▶ contr. it shall; it will.

I·to /'ētō/, Prince Hirobumi (1841–1909), premier of Japan 1885–88, 1892–96, 1898, 1900–01. He was assassinated by a member of the Korean independence movement.

-itous ▶ suffix forming adjectives corresponding to nouns ending in *-ity* (such as *calamitous* corresponding to *calamity*). [from Fr. *-iteux*, from L. *-itosus*.]

its /its/ ▶ possessive adj. belonging to or associated with a thing previously mentioned or easily identified: *turn the camera on its side* | *he chose the area for its atmosphere*. ▪ belonging to or associated with a child or animal of unspecified sex: *a baby in its mother's womb*.

it's /its/ ▶ contr. ▪ it is. ▪ it has.

it·self /it'self/ ▶ pron. [third person sing.] **1** [reflexive] used as the object of a verb or preposition to refer to a thing or animal previously mentioned as the subject of the clause: *his horse hurt itself* | *wisteria was tumbling over itself*. **2** [emphatic] used to emphasize a particular thing or animal mentioned: *the roots are several inches long, though the plant itself is only a foot tall*. ▪ used after a quality to emphasize how nearly perfect an example of that quality someone or something is: *Mrs. Vincent was kindness itself*.
– PHRASES **by itself** see BY ONESELF at BY. **in itself** viewed in its essential qualities; considered separately from other things. [OE (see IT, SELF).]

it·ty-bit·ty /'itē 'bitē/ (also **it·sy-bit·sy** /'itsē 'bitsē/) ▶ adj. informal very small; tiny. [1930s: from a child's form of LITTLE + BITTY.]

-ity ▶ suffix forming nouns denoting quality or condition: *humility* | *probity*. ▪ denoting an instance or degree of this: *a profanity*. [from Fr. *-ité*, from L. *-itas, -itatis*.]

IU ▶ abbr. international unit.

IUCN ▶ abbr. International Union for the Conservation of Nature.

IUD ▶ abbr. intrauterine device.

-ium ▶ suffix **1** forming nouns adopted unchanged from Latin (such as *alluvium*) or based on Latin or Greek words (such as *euphonium*). **2** (also **-um**) forming names of metallic elements: *cadmium* | *magnesium*. **3** denoting a region of the body: *pericardium*. **4** denoting a biological structure: *mycelium*. [mod. L. in senses 2, 3, and 4, via L. from Gk. *-ion*.]

IV ▶ abbr. intravenous(ly). ▶ n. an intravenous drip feed: *they put an IV in me*.

I·van /'īvən/ the name of six rulers of Russia: ▪ Ivan I (*c.*1304–41), grand duke of Muscovy 1328–40. He made Moscow the ecclesiastical capital in 1326. ▪ Ivan II (1326–59), grand duke of Muscovy 1353–59; known as **Ivan the Red**. ▪ Ivan III (1440–1505), grand duke of Muscovy 1462–1505; known as **Ivan the Great**. He defended his territory against a Tartar invasion in 1480. ▪ Ivan IV (1530–84), grand duke of Muscovy 1533–47 and first czar of Russia 1547–84; known as **Ivan the Terrible**. In 1581, Ivan killed his eldest son, Ivan. ▪ Ivan V (1666–96), nominal czar of Russia 1682–96. ▪ Ivan VI (1740–64), infant czar of Russia 1740–41.

I've /īv/ ▶ contr. I have.

-ive /iv/ ▶ suffix (forming adjectives, nouns derived from them) tending to; having the nature of: *active* | *corrosive*. — **-ively** suffix forming corresponding adverbs. **-iveness** suffix forming corresponding nouns. [from Fr. *-if, -ive*, from L. *-ivus*.]

Ives[1] /īvz/, Charles Edward (1874–1954), US composer, noted for his use of polyrhythms, polytonality, quarter-tones, and aleatoric techniques.

Ives[2], James Merritt (1824–1907), US publisher and painter. He partnered with Nathaniel Currier to establish Currier & Ives in 1857.

IVF ▶ abbr. in vitro fertilization.

i·vied /'īvēd/ ▶ adj. covered in ivy: *an ivied church*. ▪ of or relating to Ivy League academic institutions.

i·vo·ry /'īv(ə)rē/ ▶ n. (pl. **-ries**) **1** a hard creamy-white substance composing the main part of the tusks of an elephant, walrus, or narwhal, often (esp. formerly) used to make ornaments and other articles. ▪ an object made of ivory. ▪ (**the ivories**) informal the keys of a piano. ▪ (**ivories**) informal a person's teeth. **2** a creamy-white color. — **i·vo·ried** adj. [ME: from Anglo-Norman Fr. *ivurie*, based on L. *ebur*.]

i·vo·ry black ▶ n. a black carbon pigment made from charred ivory or (now usually) bone, used in drawing and painting.

I·vo·ry Coast See CÔTE D'IVOIRE.

i·vo·ry nut ▶ n. the seed of a tropical American palm (*Phytelephas macrocarpa*), which, when hardened, is a source of vegetable ivory. Also called TAGUA NUT.

i·vo·ry tow·er ▶ n. a state of privileged seclusion from the facts and practicalities of the real world. [20th C.: translating Fr. *tour d'ivoire*, used by the writer Sainte-Beuve (1804–69).]

i·vy /'īvē/ ▶ n. a woody evergreen climbing plant (genus *Hedera*, family Araliaceae), typically having shiny, dark green five-pointed leaves. Several species include the common **English ivy** (*H. helix*), often seen climbing on tree trunks and walls. ▪ used in names of similar climbing plants, e.g., **poison ivy**, **Boston ivy**.

I·vy League ▶ n. a group of long-established eastern colleges and universities having high academic and social prestige. It includes Harvard, Yale, Princeton, Columbia, Dartmouth, Cornell, Brown, and the University of Pennsylvania. — **I·vy Lea·guer** n. [with ref. to the ivy traditionally growing over the walls of these establishments.]

I·wo Ji·ma /,ēwə 'jēmə; ,ēwō/ the largest of the Volcano Islands in the western Pacific Ocean; site of attack and capture of Japanese airbase by US 1944–45; returned to Japan in 1968.

IWW ▶ abbr. Industrial Workers of the World.

ix·i·a /'iksēə/ ▶ n. a South African plant (genus *Ixia*) of the iris family with showy starlike flowers and sword-shaped leaves.

Ix·i·on /ik'sīən; 'iksē,än/ Gk. Mythol. a king who, by Zeus's command, was pinned to a fiery wheel that revolved unceasingly through the underworld, as punishment for his alleged seduction of Hera.

ix·tle /'ikstlē; 'is(t)-/ (also **is·tle**) ▶ n. (in Mexico and Central America) a plant fiber obtained chiefly from the *Agave* species and used for cordage, nets, and carpets. [19th C.: via Amer. Sp. from Nahuatl *ixtli*.]

I·yen·gar /ē'yeɴɢgär/ ▶ n. a type of hatha yoga focusing on the correct alignment of the body, making use of straps, wooden blocks, etc. as aids to achieving the correct postures. [named after the Indian yoga teacher B. K. S. *Iyengar* (1918–), who devised the method.]

Iy·yar /'ēyär; ē'yär/ (also **I·yar**) ▶ n. (in the Jewish calendar) the eighth month of the civil and second of the religious year, usually coinciding with parts of April and May. [from Heb. *'iyyār*.]

iz·ard /'izərd/ ▶ n. (in the Pyrenees) a chamois. [18th C.: from Fr. *isard* or Gascon *isart*, of unknown origin.]

-ize ▶ suffix forming verbs meaning: **1** make or become: *fossilize* | *privatize*. ▪ cause to resemble: *Americanize*. **2** treat in a specified way: *pasteurize*. ▪ treat or cause to combine with a specified substance: *carbonize* | *oxidize*. **3** follow a specified practice: *agonize* | *theorize*. ▪ subject to a practice: *hospitalize*. — **-ization** suffix forming corresponding nouns. **-izer** suffix forming agent nouns. [from Fr. *-iser*, via late L. *-izare* from Gk. verbs ending in *-izein*.]

I·zhevsk /'ēzнefsk/ a city in central Russia; pop. 642,000. Former name (1984–87) USTINOV[1].

Iz·mir /iz'mi(ə)r/ a seaport and naval base in western Turkey; pop. 1,757,000. Former name SMYRNA.

Iz·mit /iz'mit/ a city in northwestern Turkey, on the Gulf of Izmit; pop. 257,000.

J

J[1] /jā/ (also **j**) ▶ **n.** (pl. **Js** or **J's** /jāz/) **1** the tenth letter of the alphabet. ■ denoting the next after I (or H if I is omitted) in a set of items, categories, etc. **2** (**J**) a shape like that of a capital J.

J[2] ▶ **abbr.** ■ jack (used in describing play in card games). ■ Physics joule(s). ■ (in titles) Journal (of): *J. Biol. Chem.* ■ Judge. ■ Justice.

j ▶ **symb.** (*j*) (in electrical engineering and electronics) the imaginary quantity equal to the square root of minus one. Compare with I.

jab /jab/ ▶ **v.** (**jabbed, jab·bing**) [trans.] poke (someone or something) roughly or quickly, esp. with something sharp or pointed. ■ poke someone or something roughly or quickly with (a sharp or pointed object or a part of the body). ▶ **n.** a quick, sharp blow, esp. with the fist. ■ informal a hypodermic injection, esp. a vaccination. ■ a sharp painful sensation or feeling. [19th C. (orig. Scots): from archaic *job* 'prod or stab.']

jab·ber /'jabər/ ▶ **v.** [intrans.] talk rapidly and excitedly but with little sense. ▶ **n.** fast, excited talk that makes little sense. [15th C.: imitative.]

jab·ber·wock·y /'jabər,wäkē/ ▶ **n.** (pl. **-wock·ies**) invented or meaningless language; nonsense. [20th C.: from the title of a nonsense poem in Lewis Carroll's *Through the Looking Glass* (1871).]

jab·i·ru /'jabə,ro͞o/ (also **jabiru stork**) ▶ **n.** a large Central and South American stork (*Jabiru mycteria*) with a black neck, mainly white plumage, and a large black upturned bill. [18th C.: from Tupi-Guarani *jabirú*, from *j* 'that which has' + *abirú* 'swollen' (suggested by the bird's large neck).]

jab·o·ran·di /,jabə'randē/ ▶ **n.** **1** a drug made from the dried leaves of certain South American plants (genus *Pilocarpus*) of the rue family that contain the alkaloid pilocarpine and promote salivation when chewed. **2** any of the plants that yield this drug. [17th C.: from Tupi-Guarani *jaburandi*, lit. 'a person who spits.']

ja·bot /zhaˈbō; ja-/ ▶ **n.** an ornamental frill or ruffle on the front of a shirt or blouse, typically made of lace. [19th C. (denoting a frill on a man's shirt): Fr., orig. 'crop of a bird.']

ja·cal /hä'käl/ ▶ **n.** (pl. **-ca·les** /-'kāläs/) (in Mexico and the southwestern US) a thatched wattle-and-daub hut. [Mex. Sp., from Nahuatl *xacalli*, contr. of *xamitl calli* 'adobe house.']

jac·a·mar /'jakə,mär/ ▶ **n.** an insectivorous bird (family Galbulidae) of tropical American forests, with a long pointed bill, a long tail, and typically iridescent green plumage. [19th C.: from Tupi.]

ja·ca·na /,zhäkə'nä; ,jä-/ (also **ja·ça·na** /,zhäsə'nä; ,jä-/) ▶ **n.** any of several small tropical wading birds (family Jacanidae) with greatly elongated toes and claws that enable it to walk on floating vegetation. Also called **lily-trotter.** [18th C.: from Tupi-Guarani *jasanā*.]

jac·a·ran·da /,jakə'randə/ ▶ **n.** a tropical American tree (genus *Jacaranda*) of the catalpa family that has blue trumpet-shaped flowers, fernlike leaves, and fragrant timber. [18th C.: from Tupi-Guarani *jakara'nda*.]

ja·cinth /'jāsinth; 'jas-/ ▶ **n.** a reddish-orange gem variety of zircon. [ME: from OFr. *iacinte* or med. L. *iacintus*, alt. of L. *hyacinthus* (see HYACINTH).]

jack[1] /jak/ ▶ **n.** **1** a device for lifting heavy objects, esp. one for raising the axle of a motor vehicle off the ground. **2** a playing card bearing a representation of a soldier, page, or knave, normally ranking next below a queen. **3** a socket with two or more pairs of terminals. **4** (also **jack·stone**) a small round pebble or star-shaped piece of metal used in tossing and catching games. ■ (**jacks**) a game played by tossing and catching such pebbles or pieces of metal. **5** in lawn bowling, the small ball at which the players aim. **6** (**Jack**) informal used as a form of address to a man whose name is not known. ■ informal a lumberjack. **7** a small version of a national flag flown at the bow of a vessel in harbor to indicate its nationality. **8** a device for turning a spit. **9** a part of the mechanism in a spinet or harpsichord that connects a key to its corresponding string and causes the string to be plucked when the key is pressed down. **10** a marine fish that is typically laterally compressed with a row of large spiky scales along each side. The **jack family** (Carangidae) includes numerous genera and species and also includes the horse mackerel, pilotfish, and kingfishes. **11** the male of some animals, esp. a merlin or an ass. **12** short for JACKRABBIT. **13** informal short for JACK SHIT.
– PHRASES **jack of all trades (and master of none)** a person who can do many different types of work but who is not necessarily very competent at any of them.
– PHRASAL VERBS **jack someone around** informal cause someone inconvenience or problems, esp. by acting unfairly or indecisively. **jack in** (or **into**) informal log into or connect up (a computer or electronic device). **jack off** vulgar slang masturbate. **jack up** informal inject oneself with a narcotic drug. **jack something up** raise something, esp. a vehicle, with a

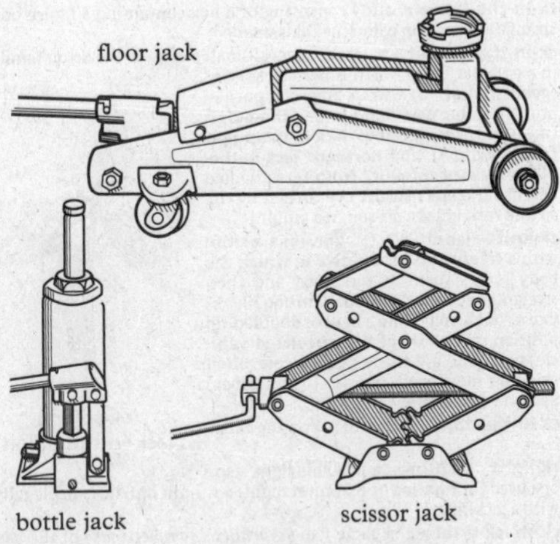

jacks

jack. ■ informal increase something by a considerable amount. [ME: from *Jack*, nickname for the given name *John*. The term was used orig. to denote an ordinary man, hence the 'knave' in cards and 'male animal,' also denoting various devices saving human labor.]

jack[2] ▶ **n.** hist. another term for BLACKJACK (sense 4).

jack[3] ▶ **v.** [trans.] informal take (something) illicitly; steal: *Cynthia and I jacked $50 of jewelry.* ■ rob (someone). [1990s: from *hijack*.]

black-backed jackal

jack·al /'jakəl/ ▶ **n.** a slender, long-legged wild dog (genus *Canis*) that feeds on carrion, game, and fruit and often hunts cooperatively, found in Africa and southern Asia. Four species include the **black-backed jackal** (*C. mesomelas*). [17th C.: from Turk. *çakal*, from Pers. *šagāl*.]

jack·a·napes /'jakə,nāps/ ▶ **n.** **1** dated an impertinent person. **2** archaic a tame monkey. [16th C. (orig. as *Jack Napes*): perh. from a playful name for a tame ape, the initial *n-* by elision of *an ape*.]

jack·ass /'jak,as/ ▶ **n.** **1** a stupid person. **2** a male ass or donkey.

jack bean ▶ **n.** a tropical American climbing plant (genus *Canavalia*, esp. *C. ensiformis*) of the pea family, which yields an edible bean and pod and is widely grown for fodder in tropical countries.

jack·boot /'jak,bo͞ot/ ▶ **n.** a large leather military boot reaching to the knee. ■ [in sing.] used as a symbol of cruel or authoritarian behavior or rule. — **jack·boot·ed** adj.

Jack cheese ▶ **n.** another term for MONTEREY JACK.

jack·daw /'jak,dô/ ▶ **n.** a small, gray-headed Eurasian crow (genus *Corvus*, esp. *C. monedula*) that typically nests in tall buildings and chimneys.

jack·et /'jakit/ ▶ **n.** an outer garment extending either to the waist or the hips, typically having sleeves and a fastening down the front. ■ an outer covering, esp. one placed around a tank or pipe to insulate it. ■ a metal casing for a bullet. ■ the skin of a potato. ■ the dust jacket of a book. ■ a record sleeve. ■ a steel frame fixed to the seabed, forming the support structure of an oil production platform. ▶ v. (**jack·et·ed, jack·et·ing**) [trans.] cover with a jacket. [ME: from OFr. *jaquet*, dimin. of *jaque* (see JACK[2]).]

jack·fish /ˈjak,fisʜ/ ▶ n. (pl. same or **-fish·es**) a pike or sauger, esp. the northern pike.

Jack Frost ▶ n. a personification of frost.

jack·fruit /ˈjak,fro͞ot/ ▶ n. a fast-growing tropical Asian tree (*Artocarpus heterophyllus*) of the mulberry family. ■ the very large edible fruit of this tree, resembling a breadfruit and important as food in the tropics.

jack·ham·mer /ˈjak,hamər/ ▶ n. a portable pneumatic hammer or drill. ▶ v. [trans.] beat or hammer heavily or loudly and repeatedly.

jack-in-the-box ▶ n. a toy consisting of a box containing a figure on a spring that pops up when the lid is opened.

jack-in-the-pul·pit ▶ n. any of several small plants of the arum family, in particular three North American species (genus *Arisaema*) with a green or purple-brown spathe: **woodland jack-in-the-pulpit** (*A. atrorubens*), **swamp jack-in-the-pulpit** (*A. triphyllum*), and **northern jack-in-the-pulpit** (*A. stewardsonii*). [19th C.: so named because the erect spadix overarched by the spathe resembles a person in a pulpit.]

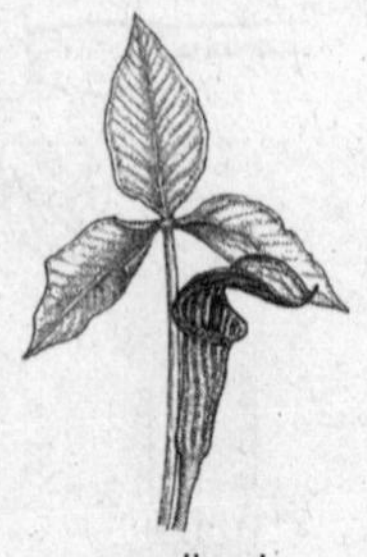
woodland jack-in-the-pulpit

jack·knife /ˈjak,nīf/ ▶ n. (pl. **-knives**) **1** a knife with a folding blade. **2** a dive in which the body is first bent at the waist and then straightened. ▶ v. (**-knifed, -knif·ing**) [trans.] move (one's body) into a bent or doubled-up position. ■ [intrans.] (of an articulated vehicle) bend into a V-shape in an uncontrolled skidding movement. ■ [intrans.] (of a diver) perform a jackknife.

jack·knife clam ▶ n. another term for RAZOR CLAM.

jack·light /ˈjak,līt/ ▶ n. a portable light, esp. one used for hunting or fishing at night. ▶ v. hunt or fish, esp. illegally, with a jacklight.

jack mack·er·el ▶ n. a game fish (*Trachurus symmetricus*) of the jack family, occurring in the eastern Pacific.

jack-o'-lan·tern /ˈjak ə ,lantərn/ ▶ n. a lantern made from a hollowed-out pumpkin in which holes are cut to represent facial features, typically made at Halloween.

jack pine ▶ n. a small, hardy North American pine (*Pinus banksiana*) with very short needles, found chiefly in Canada.

jack·pot /ˈjak,pät/ ▶ n. a large cash prize in a game or lottery, esp. one that accumulates until it is won.
– PHRASES **hit the jackpot** informal **1** win a jackpot. **2** have great or unexpected success, esp. in making a lot of money quickly. [19th C.: from JACK[1] + POT[1].]

black-tailed jackrabbit

jack·rab·bit /ˈjak,rabət/ ▶ n. a hare found in open country in western North America. Several species include the **black-tailed jackrabbit** (*Lepus californicus*). [19th C.: abbrev. of *jackass-rabbit*, because of its long ears.]

Jack Rus·sell /ˈrəsəl/ (also **Jack Russell terrier**) ▶ n. a terrier of a small working breed with short legs. [20th C.: named after John (*Jack*) *Russell* (1795–1883), English clergyman.]

jack screw ▶ n. a screw that can be turned to adjust the position of an object into which it fits. ■ a vehicle jack worked by a screw device. Also called SCREW JACK.

jack shit ▶ n. [usu. with negative] vulgar slang anything at all.

jack·snipe /ˈjak,snīp/ ▶ n. a small dark Eurasian snipe (*Lymnocryptes minima*). ■ any similar wader, e.g., the pectoral sandpiper or the common snipe.

Jack·son[1] /ˈjaksən/ the capital of Mississippi, in the central part of the state; pop. 184,256.

Jack·son[2], Andrew (1767–1845), 7th president of the United States 1829–37; known as **Old Hickory**. A Tennessee Democrat, he served in the US House of Representatives 1796–97 and the US Senate 1797–98, 1823–25. As a general during the War of 1812, he was famed for his defense of New Orleans. As president, he vetoed the renewal of the charter of the Bank of the United States and initiated the spoils system. During his administration, the national debt was paid off and the independence of Texas was recognized.

Jack·son[3], Howell Edmunds (1832–95), US Supreme Court associate justice 1893–95.

Jack·son[4], Rev. Jesse Louis (1941–), US politician, civil rights activist, and clergyman. A Democrat, he sought the presidential nomination in 1984 and 1988, and has traveled extensively to sites of injustice or conflict to intercede for conciliation.

Jack·son[5], Mahalia (1911–72), US gospel singer. Her recordings include "Move Up a Little Higher."

Jack·son[6], Robert Houghwout (1892–1954), US Supreme Court associate justice 1941–54.

Jack·son[7], Thomas Jonathan (1824–63), Confederate general in the American Civil War; known as **Stonewall Jackson**. He commanded the Shenandoah campaign 1861–62.

Jack·son Hole a valley on the Snake River in northwestern Wyoming.

Jack·son·ville /ˈjaksən,vil/ a city and port in northeastern Florida; pop. 735,617.

jack·stay /ˈjak,stā/ ▶ n. Naut. a rope, bar, or batten placed along a ship's yard to bend the head of a square sail to.

jack·stone /ˈjak,stōn/ ▶ n. see JACK[1] (sense 4).

jack·straw /ˈjak,strô/ ▶ n. a game played with a heap of small rods of wood, bone, or plastic, in which players try to remove one at a time without disturbing the others.

Jack the Rip·per an unidentified 19th-century English murderer. The 1888 murders of at least six London prostitutes were attributed to a person calling himself Jack the Ripper.

Ja·cob /ˈjākəb/ (in the Bible) a Hebrew patriarch, the younger of the twin sons of Isaac and Rebecca. His twelve sons became the founders of the twelve tribes of ancient Israel. See also TRIBES OF ISRAEL.

Jac·o·be·an /,jakəˈbēən/ ▶ adj. of or relating to the reign of James I of England. ■ (of furniture) in the style prevalent during the reign of James I, esp. being the color of dark oak. ▶ n. a person who lived during this period. [19th C.: from mod. L. *Jacobaeus* (from eccles. L. *Jacobus* 'James,' from Gk. *Iakōbos* 'Jacob') + -AN.]

Jac·o·bi·an /jəˈkōbēən/ Math. ▶ adj. of or relating to the work of German mathematician K. G. J. Jacobi (1804–51). ▶ n. a determinant whose constituents are the derivatives of a number of functions ($u, v, w, \ldots$) with respect to each of the same number of variables ($x, y, z, \ldots$).

Jac·o·bin /ˈjakəbin/ ▶ n. **1** hist. a member of a democratic club established in Paris in 1789, the most radical and ruthless of the political groups formed in the wake of the French Revolution. ■ an extreme political radical. **2** esp. hist. a Dominican friar. **3** (**jacobin**) a pigeon of a breed with reversed feathers on the back of its neck like a cowl. — **Jac·o·bin·ic** /,jakəˈbinik/ adj. **Jac·o·bin·i·cal** /,jakəˈbinikəl/ adj. **Jac·o·bin·ism** n. [ME (sense 2): from OFr., from med. L. *Jacobinus*, from eccles. L. *Jacobus* 'James.']

Jac·o·bite /ˈjakə,bīt/ ▶ n. a supporter of the deposed James II and his descendants in their claim to the British throne after the Revolution of 1688. — **Jac·o·bit·ism** n. [from L. *Jacobus* 'James' (see JACOBEAN) + -ITE[1].]

Ja·cob's lad·der ▶ n. **1** a plant (*Polemonium vanbruntiae*, family Polemoniaceae) of the northeastern US with loose clusters of purplish-blue flowers and slender pointed leaves, rows of which are said to resemble a ladder. **2** a rope ladder with wooden rungs, esp. for access to a ship up the side.

Ja·cob's staff ▶ n. a rod with a sliding cursor formerly used for measuring distances and heights, esp. in navigation.

jac·o·net /ˈjakə,net/ ▶ n. a lightweight cotton cloth with a smooth and slightly stiff finish. [18th C.: from Hindi *Jagannāth(purī)* (now *Puri*) in India, its place of origin; see also JUGGERNAUT.]

jac·quard /ˈjakärd; jəˈkärd/ ▶ n. an apparatus with perforated cards, fitted to a loom to facilitate the weaving of figured and brocaded fabrics. ■ a fabric made on a loom with such a device, with an intricate variegated pattern. [19th C.: named after Joseph M. *Jacquard* (1787–1834), French weaver and inventor.]

jac·que·rie /zʜäkˈrē/ ▶ n. a communal uprising or revolt. [16th C.: from OFr., lit. 'villeins,' from *Jacques* 'peasant.']

jac·ti·ta·tion /,jaktiˈtāsʜən/ ▶ n. Med. the restless tossing of the body in illness. ■ the twitching of a limb or muscle. [expressive extension of *jactation* 'restless tossing,' from L. *jactare* 'to throw.']

ja·cuz·zi /jəˈko͞ozē/ ▶ n. (pl. **-zis**) (also trademark **Jacuzzi**) a large bath with a system of underwater jets of water to massage the body. [1960s: named after Candido *Jacuzzi* (c.1903–86), Italian-born American inventor.]

jade[1] /jād/ ▶ n. a hard, typically green stone used for ornaments and implements and consisting of the minerals jadeite or nephrite. ■ an ornament made of this. ■ (also **jade green**) a light bluish-green. [16th C.: from Fr. *le jade* (earlier *l'ejade*), from Sp. *piedra de ijada* 'stone of the flank.']

jade[2] ▶ n. archaic **1** a bad-tempered or disreputable woman. **2** an inferior or worn-out horse. [ME: of unknown origin.]

jad·ed /ˈjādid/ ▶ adj. tired, bored, or lacking enthusiasm, typically after having had too much of something. — **jad·ed·ly** adv. **jad·ed·ness** n. [16th C. (in the sense 'disreputable'): from JADE[2].]

jade·ite /ˈjādīt/ ▶ n. a green, blue, or white mineral that is one of the forms of jade. It is a silicate of sodium, aluminum, and iron and belongs to the pyroxene group.

jae·ger /ˈyāgər/ ▶ n. any of the smaller kinds of Arctic-breeding skuas, e.g., the **parasitic jaeger** or Arctic skua (*Stercorarius parasiticus*). [19th C. (applied to any predatory seabird): from Ger. *Jäger* 'hunter.']

Jaf·fa /ˈjäfə; ˈjafə/ a seaport on the Mediterranean coast of Israel, incorporated with Tel Aviv 1950. Hebrew name Yafo; biblical name Joppa.

JAG ▶ abbr. judge advocate general.

Jag /jag/ ▶ n. informal a Jaguar car.

jag[1] /jag/ ▶ n. a sharp projection. ▶ v. (**jagged** /ˈjagd/, **jag·ging**) [trans.] stab, pierce, or prick.

jag[2] ▶ n. informal a bout of unrestrained activity or emotion, esp. drinking, crying, or laughing.

Jag·an·na·tha /ˌjəgəˈnät-hə/ another name for Juggernaut.

jag·ged /ˈjagid/ ▶ adj. with rough, sharp points protruding. — **jag·ged·ly** adv. **jag·ged·ness** n.

jag·gy /ˈjagē/ ▶ adj. (**-gi·er, -gi·est**) jagged. ▶ n. (pl. **-ies**) (usu. **jaggies**) Comput. informal another term for aliasing.

jaguar

jag·uar /ˈjagwär/ ▶ n. a large, heavily built cat (*Panthera onca*) that has a yellowish-brown coat with black spots, found mainly in the dense forests of Central and South America. [17th C.: from Tupi-Guarani *yaguára*.]

ja·gua·run·di /ˌjagwəˈrəndē/ ▶ n. (pl. **-dis**) a small American wildcat (*Felis yagouaroundi*) with a uniform red or gray coat, slender body, and short legs, found from Arizona to Argentina. [19th C.: from Tupi-Guarani, from *yaguára* 'jaguar' + *undi* 'dark.']

jai a·lai /ˈhī (ə)ˌlī/ ▶ n. a game like pelota played with cestas. [Sp., from Basque *jai* 'festival' + *alai* 'merry.']

jail /jāl/ (Brit. also **gaol**) ▶ n. a place for the confinement of people accused or convicted of a crime. ■ confinement in a jail. ▶ v. [trans.] (usu. **be jailed**) put (someone) in jail. [ME: based on L. *cavea* (see cage) via OFr. *jaiole* and Anglo-Norman Fr. *gaole*.]

jail·bait /ˈjālˌbāt/ ▶ n. [treated as sing. or pl.] informal a young woman, or young women collectively, considered in sexual terms but under the age of consent.

jail·bird /ˈjālˌbərd/ ▶ n. informal a person who is or has been in prison, esp. a criminal who has been jailed repeatedly.

jail·break /ˈjālˌbrāk/ ▶ n. an escape from jail.

jail·er /ˈjālər/ (also **jai·lor** or Brit. **gaol·er**) ▶ n. a person in charge of a jail or of the prisoners in it.

jail·house /ˈjālˌhous/ ▶ n. a prison.

Jain /jān/ ▶ n. an adherent of Jainism. ▶ adj. of or relating to Jainism. [via Hindi from Sanskrit *jaina* 'of or concerning a *Jina*' (a great Jain teacher or holy man, lit. 'victor'), from *ji-* 'conquer' or *jyā-* 'overcome.']

Jain·ism /ˈjānizəm/ ▶ n. a nontheistic religion founded in India in the 6th century BC as a reaction against the teachings of orthodox Brahmanism, and still practiced there. The Jain religion teaches salvation by perfection through successive lives, and noninjury to living creatures. — **Jain·ist** n.

Jai·pur /ˈjīpŏŏr/ a city in western India, the capital of Rajasthan; pop. 1,455,000.

Ja·kar·ta /jəˈkärtə/ (also **Dja·kar·ta**) the capital of Indonesia, in northwestern Java; pop. 8,222,500. Former name (until 1949) Batavia.

jake /jāk/ ▶ adj. [predic.] informal all right; satisfactory. [20th C.: of unknown origin.]

jakes /jāks/ ▶ n. a toilet, esp. an outdoor one. [16th C.: perh. from the given name *Jacques*.]

Ja·kob·son /ˈyäkəbsən/, Roman Osipovich (1896–1982), US linguist; born in Russia. His work described universals in phonology.

jal·ap /ˈjäləp; ˈjal-/ ▶ n. a purgative drug obtained chiefly from the tuberous roots of a Mexican climbing plant (*Ipomoea purga*) of the morning glory family.

Ja·la·pa /häˈläpä/ a city in east central Mexico, capital of Veracruz; pop. 288,000. Full name Jalapa Enríquez.

ja·la·pe·ño /ˌhäləˈpānyō; -ˈpē-/ (also **ja·la·pe·ño pep·per**) ▶ n. (pl. **-ños**) a very hot green chili pepper, used esp. in Mexican-style cooking. [1940s (orig. US): from Mex. Sp. *(chile) jalapeño*.]

Ja·lis·co /häˈlēskō/ a state in western central Mexico, on the Pacific coast; capital, Guadalajara.

ja·lop·y /jəˈläpē/ ▶ n. (pl. **-lop·ies**) informal an old car in a dilapidated condition. [1920s (orig. US): of unknown origin.]

jal·ou·sie /ˈjaləˌsē/ ▶ n. a blind or shutter made of a row of angled slats. [18th C.: Fr., lit. 'jealousy,' from Ital. *geloso* 'jealous.']

Jam. ▶ abbr. ■ Jamaica. ■ Bible James.

jam[1] /jam/ ▶ v. (**jammed, jam·ming**) **1** [trans.] squeeze or pack (someone or something) tightly into a specified space. ■ push (something) roughly and forcibly into position or a space. ■ [trans.] crowd onto (a road) so as to block it: *the roads were jammed with traffic.* ■ [trans.] cause (telephone lines) to be continuously busy with a large number of calls. ■ [intrans.] push or crowd into an area or space. **2** become or make unable to move or work due to a part seizing or becoming stuck. ■ [trans.] make (a radio transmission) unintelligible by causing interference. **3** [intrans.] informal improvise with other musicians, esp. in jazz or blues. ▶ n. **1** an instance of a machine or thing seizing or becoming stuck. ■ informal an awkward situation or predicament. ■ short for traffic jam. ■ [often with adj.] Climbing a handhold obtained by stuffing a part of the body such as a hand or foot into a crack in the rock. **2** (also **jam ses·sion**) an informal gathering of musicians improvising together, esp. in jazz or blues.

jam[2] ▶ n. a sweet spread or preserve made from fruit and sugar boiled to a thick consistency. [18th C.: perh. from jam[1].]

Ja·mai·ca /jəˈmākə/ an island country in the Caribbean Sea. *See box.* — **Ja·mai·can** adj. & n.

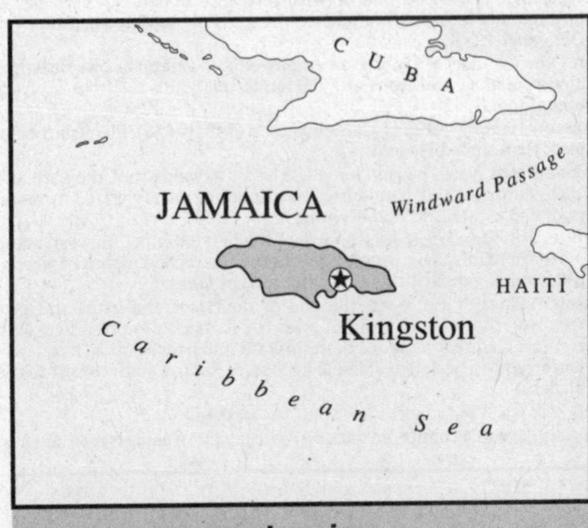

Jamaica

Location: Caribbean Sea, southeast of Cuba
Area: 4,200 square miles (11,000 sq km)
Population: 2,713,000
Capital: Kingston
Languages: English (official), Creole
Currency: Jamaican dollar

Ja·mai·can sat·in·wood ▶ n. see satinwood.

jamb /jam/ ▶ n. a side post or surface of a doorway, window, etc. [ME: from OFr. *jambe* 'leg, vertical support,' based on Gk. *kampē* 'joint.']

jam·ba·lay·a /ˌjəmbəˈlīə/ ▶ n. a Cajun dish of rice with shrimp, chicken, and vegetables. [Louisiana Fr., from Provençal *jambalaia*.]

jam·beau /ˈjambō/ ▶ n. (pl. **-beaux** /-bōz/ or **-beaus**) hist. a piece of armor for the leg. [ME: appar. an Anglo-Norman Fr. deriv. of Fr. *jambe* 'leg.']

Jam·bi /ˈjämbē/ (also **Djambi**) a city in Indonesia, on southern Sumatra; pop. 340,000.

jam·bo·ree /ˌjambəˈrē/ ▶ n. a large celebration or party, typically a lavish and boisterous one. ■ a large rally of Boy Scouts or Girl Scouts. [19th C. (orig. US slang): of unknown origin.]

James[1] /jāmz/, Henry (1843–1916), US novelist and critic, author of *The Portrait of a Lady* (1881) and *The Golden Bowl* (1904).

James[2], Jesse Woodson (1847–82), US outlaw. With brother Frank (1843–1915), he was a member of a gang of train and bank robbers.

James I (1566–1625), son of Mary, Queen of Scots, king of Scotland (as James VI) 1567–1625, and of England and Ireland 1603–25.

James II (1633–1701), son of Charles I, king of England, Ireland, and (as James VII) Scotland 1685–8.

James, St.[1], one of the 12 Apostles; son of Zebedee; brother of John; known as **St. James the Greater**.

James, St.[2], one of the 12 Apostles; known as **St. James the Lesser**.

James, St.[3] leader of the early Christian Church; known as **St. James the Just**. ■ the epistle of the New Testament ascribed to St. James.

James Bay a southern arm of Hudson Bay, between Quebec and Ontario, Canada.

James Riv·er 1 a river that flows from North Dakota through South Dakota into the Missouri River. Also called Dakota River. **2** a river in Virginia that flows into Hampton Roads.

James·town /ˈjāmzˌtoun/ a British settlement on the James River in Virginia, founded in 1607, abandoned when the colonial capital was moved to Williamsburg in 1699.

jam·mer /ˈjamər/ ▶ **n.** a transmitter used for jamming signals.

Jam·mu /ˈjəmo͞o/ a town in northwestern India; pop. 206,000; winter capital of Jammu and Kashmir.

Jam·mu and Kash·mir /ˈkashmi(ə)r; ˈkazh-/ a state in northwestern India, at the western end of the Himalayas, formerly part of Kashmir; capitals, Srinagar (summer), Jammu (winter).

jam-packed ▶ **adj.** informal extremely crowded or full to capacity.

jam ses·sion ▶ **n.** see JAM[1] (sense 2).

Jam·shid /jamˈshid/ a legendary early king of Persia.

Jan. ▶ **abbr.** January.

jane /jān/ ▶ **n.** informal a woman.

– PHRASES **plain Jane** an unattractive girl or woman. [20th C.: from the given name *Jane*.]

jan·gle /ˈjaNGgəl/ ▶ **v.** make or cause to make a ringing metallic sound, typically a discordant one. ■ (with reference to nerves) set or be set on edge. ▶ **n.** [in sing.] a ringing metallic sound. — **jan·gly adj.** [ME: from OFr. *jangler*.]

jan·i·tor /ˈjanitər/ ▶ **n.** a person employed as a caretaker of a building; a custodian. — **jan·i·to·ri·al** /ˌjaniˈtôrēəl/ **adj.** [16th C.: from L., from *janua* 'door.']

Jan·sen /ˈjansən; ˈyänsən/, Cornelius Otto (1585–1638), Flemish theologian. He founded Jansenism.

Jan·sen·ism /ˈjansəˌnizəm/ ▶ **n.** a Christian movement of the 17th and 18th centuries, based on Jansen's writings and characterized by moral rigor and asceticism. — **Jan·sen·ist n.**

Jan·u·ar·y /ˈjanyo͞oˌerē/ ▶ **n.** (pl. **-ar·ies**) the first month of the year, in the northern hemisphere usually considered the second month of winter. [OE, from L. *Januarius (mensis)* '(month) of *Janus*.']

Ja·nus /ˈjānəs/ **1** Rom. Mythol. the god of doorways and gates and protector of the state in time of war. He is usually represented with two faces, so that he looks both forward and backward. ■ [as adj.] two-faced; hypocritical; two-sided. **2** a moon of Saturn, sixth closest to the planet.

Jap /jap/ ▶ **n. & adj.** informal, offens. short for JAPANESE.

Ja·pan /jəˈpan/ a country in eastern Asia. Japanese name NIPPON. *See box.*

Japan

Location: eastern Asia, a chain of islands in the Pacific Ocean roughly parallel with the eastern coast of the Asian mainland
Area: 145,900 square miles (377,800 sq km)
Population: 127,333,000
Capital: Tokyo
Languages: Japanese
Currency: yen

ja·pan /jəˈpan/ ▶ **n.** a hard, dark, enamellike varnish containing asphalt, used to give a black gloss to metal objects. ■ a kind of varnish in which pigments are ground, typically used to imitate lacquer on wood. ■ articles made in a Japanese style, esp. when decorated with lacquer or enamellike varnish. ▶ **v.** (**-panned, -pan·ning**) [trans.] cover (something) with a hard black varnish. [17th C.: from JAPAN.]

Ja·pan, Sea of the sea between Japan and mainland Asia.

Ja·pan Cur·rent another name for KUROSHIO.

Jap·a·nese /ˌjapəˈnēz; -ˈnēs/ ▶ **adj.** of or relating to Japan or its language, culture, or people. ▶ **n.** (pl. same) **1** a native or national of Japan, or a person of Japanese descent. **2** the language of Japan.

Jap·a·nese a·nem·o·ne ▶ **n.** an autumn-flowering anemone (*Anemone hupehensis*) of the buttercup family with large pink or white flowers, cultivated in gardens.

Jap·a·nese bee·tle ▶ **n.** a metallic green and copper chafer (*Popillia japonica*) that is a pest of fruit and foliage as an adult and of grass roots as a larva. It is native to Japan but has spread elsewhere.

Jap·a·nese ce·dar ▶ **n.** see CRYPTOMERIA.

Ja·pan·ese Cur·rent another name for KUROSHIO.

Jap·a·nese knot·weed ▶ **n.** a tall fast-growing Japanese plant (*Reynoutria japonica*) of the dock family, with bamboolike stems and small white flowers. It has been grown as an ornamental but tends to become an aggressive weed. Also called MEXICAN BAMBOO.

Jap·a·nese lan·tern ▶ **n.** another term for CHINESE LANTERN (sense 1).

Jap·a·nese per·sim·mon ▶ **n.** see PERSIMMON.

Jap·a·nese quince ▶ **n.** another term for FLOWERING QUINCE.

Jap·an·i·ma·tion /japˌanəˈmāshən/ ▶ **n.** another term for ANIME. [1980s: blend of JAPAN and ANIMATION.]

jape /jāp/ ▶ **n.** a practical joke. ▶ **v.** [intrans.] say or do something in jest or mockery. — **jap·er·y** /ˈjāp(ə)rē/ **n.** [ME: appar. combining the form of Old Fr. *japer* 'to yelp, yap' with the sense of OFr. *gaber* 'to mock.']

Ja·pheth /ˈjāfeth/ (in the Bible) a son of Noah, traditional ancestor of the peoples living around the Mediterranean.

ja·pon·i·ca /jəˈpänikə/ ▶ **n.** **1** another term for the common camellia. **2** another term for FLOWERING QUINCE. [19th C.: mod. L., fem. of *japonicus* 'Japanese.']

Ja·pu·rá Riv·er /ˌzhäpo͞oˈrä/ (Colombian name **Caquetá**) a river flowing 1,750 miles (2,815 km) from southwestern Colombia to the Amazon in Brazil.

Jaques-Dal·croze /jāk dalˈkrōz/, Émile (1865–1950), Swiss teacher and composer; born in Austria. He developed the eurhythmics method for teaching music and dance.

jar[1] /jär/ ▶ **n.** a wide-mouthed, cylindrical container made of glass or pottery, esp. one used for storing food. ■ the contents of such a container. — **jar·ful** /-ˌfo͝ol/ **n.** (pl. **-fuls**). [16th C.: from Fr. *jarre*, from Arab. *jarra*.]

jar[2] ▶ **v.** (**jarred, jar·ring**) **1** [trans.] send a painful or damaging shock through (something, esp. a part of the body). ■ [intrans.] strike against something with an unpleasant vibration or jolt. **2** [intrans.] have an unpleasant, annoying, or disturbing effect. ■ be incongruous in a striking or shocking way: *the play's symbolism **jarred with** the realism of its setting* | [as adj.] (**jarring**) *the only jarring note was the modern appearance of the customers.* ▶ **n.** a physical shock or jolt.

jar·di·niere /ˌjärdnˈi(ə)r; ˌzhärdnˈye(ə)r/ (also **jar·di·nière**) ▶ **n.** an ornamental pot or stand for the display of growing plants. [19th C.: from Fr. *jardinière*, lit. 'female gardener.']

jar·gon /ˈjärgən/ ▶ **n.** special words or expressions that are used by a particular profession or group and are difficult for others to understand. ■ a form of language regarded as barbarous, debased, or hybrid. — **jar·gon·is·tic** /ˌjärgəˈnistik/ **adj.** **jar·gon·ize** /-ˌnīz/ **v.** [ME (orig. in the sense 'twittering, chattering,' later 'gibberish'): from OFr. *jargoun*, of unknown origin. The main mod. sense dates from the mid 17th C.]

jar·head /ˈjärˌhed/ ▶ **n.** military slang a U.S. Marine.

jarl /yärl/ ▶ **n.** hist. a Norse or Danish chief. [ON, lit. 'man of noble birth;' rel. to EARL.]

Jarls·berg /ˈyärlzˌbərg/ ▶ **n.** trademark a kind of hard yellow Norwegian cheese with many holes and a mild, nutty flavor. [named after the town of *Jarlsberg*, Norway.]

jar·rah /ˈjarə/ ▶ **n.** a eucalyptus tree (*Eucalyptus marginata*) native to western Australia, yielding durable timber. [19th C.: from Nyungar.]

Jar·ry /zhäˈrē/, Alfred (1873–1907), French playwright. He wrote *Ubu Roi* (1896).

Ja·ru·zel·ski /ˌyärəˈzelskē/, Wojciech (1923–), prime minister of Poland 1981–85; head of state 1985–89, and president 1989–90. He supervised Poland's transition to a democracy.

Jar·vik /ˈjärvik/, Robert K. (1946–) US scientist. He patented an artificial heart in 1979.

Jas. ▶ **abbr.** James (in biblical references and generally).

jas·mine /ˈjazmən/ (also **jes·sa·mine** /ˈjesəmin/) ▶ **n.** an Old World shrub or climbing plant (genus *Jasminum*) of the olive family that bears fragrant flowers that are used in perfumery or tea. ■ used in names of other shrubs or climbers with fragrant flowers, e.g., **Cape jasmine, yellow jasmine**. [16th C.: from French *jasmin* and obs. Fr. *jessemin*, from Arab. *yāsamīn*, from Pers. *yāsamīn*.]

Ja·son /ˈjāsən/ Gk. Mythol. the son of the king of Iolcos in Thessaly, and leader of the Argonauts in the quest for the Golden Fleece.

jas·per /ˈjaspər/ ▶ **n.** **1** an opaque reddish-brown variety of chalcedony. **2** a kind of hard fine porcelain invented by Josiah Wedgwood and used for Wedgwood cameos and other delicate work. [ME: from OFr. *jasp(r)e*, from L. *iaspis*, from Gk., of Asian origin.]

Jas·sy /ˈyäsē/ German name for IAŞI.

Jat /jät/ ▶ **n.** a member of a people widely scattered throughout the northwest of the Indian subcontinent. [from Hindi *Jāṭ*.]

ja·to /ˈjātō/ ▶ **n.** (pl. **-tos**) Aeron. (acronym from) jet-assisted takeoff. [World War II (orig. US): acronym.]

jaun·dice /ˈjôndis/ ▶ **n.** a medical condition with yellowing of the skin or whites of the eyes, arising from excess of the pigment bilirubin and typically caused by obstruction of the bile duct, by liver disease, or by excessive breakdown of red blood cells. ■ bitterness, resentment, or envy. — **jaun·diced** adj. [ME *jaunes*, from OFr. *jaunice* 'yellowness,' from *jaune* 'yellow.']

jaunt /jônt/ ▶ n. a short excursion or journey for pleasure. ▶ v. [intrans.] make such an excursion or journey. [16th C.: of unknown origin.]

jaun·ty /'jôntē/ ▶ adj. (-ti·er, -ti·est) having or expressing a lively, cheerful, and self-confident manner. — **jaun·ti·ly** /-tl-ē/ adv. **jaun·ti·ness** n. [17th C. (in the sense 'well-bred, genteel'): from Fr. *gentil* (see GENTLE, GENTEEL).]

Jav. ▶ abbr. Javanese.

Ja·va[1] /'jävə; 'javə/ a large island in the Malay Archipelago that forms part of Indonesia; pop. 112,160,000. — **Ja·van** n. & adj.

Ja·va[2] /'jävə/ ▶ n. trademark a general-purpose computer programming language designed to produce programs that will run on any computer system.

ja·va /'jävə; 'javə/ ▶ n. informal coffee. [19th C.: JAVA[1].]

Ja·va man ▶ n. a fossil hominid (*Homo erectus*) of the middle Pleistocene epoch, whose remains were found in Java in 1891.

Jav·a·nese /,jävə'nēz; -'nēs/ ▶ n. (pl. same) **1** a native or inhabitant of Java, or a person of Javanese descent. **2** the Indonesian language of central Java. ▶ adj. of or relating to Java, its people, or their language.

Ja·va·ri Riv·er /,zʜävä'rē/ (Peruvian name **Yavari**) a river that flows from eastern Peru to the Amazon River.

Ja·va Sea a sea in the Malay Archipelago surrounded by Borneo, Java, and Sumatra.

Ja·va spar·row ▶ n. a waxbill (*Padda oryzivora*) with a large red bill and black-and-white head, native to Java and Bali but popular elsewhere as a pet.

jave·lin /'jav(ə)lin/ ▶ n. a light spear thrown in a competitive sport or as a weapon. ■ **(the javelin)** the athletic event or sport of throwing the javelin. [ME: from OFr. *javeline*, of Celtic origin.]

ja·ve·li·na /,hävə'lēnə/ ▶ n. another term for PECCARY. [19th C.: from Sp. *jabalina*, from the fem. form of *jabalí* 'wild boar,' from Arab. *jabali* 'mountaineer.']

jaw /jô/ ▶ n. each of the upper and lower bony structures in vertebrates forming the framework of the mouth and containing the teeth. ■ the lower movable bone of such a structure or the part of the face containing it. ■ **(jaws)** the mouth with its bones and teeth. ■ **(jaws)** the grasping, biting, or crushing mouthparts of an invertebrate. ■ **(jaws)** used to suggest the notion of being in danger from something such as death or defeat: *victory was snatched* ***from the jaws of defeat***. ■ (usu. **jaws**) the gripping parts of a tool or machine, such as a wrench or vise. ■ **(jaws)** an opening likened to a mouth. ■ informal talk or gossip, esp. when lengthy or tedious. ▶ v. [intrans.] informal talk at length; chatter. — **jawed** adj. [in comb.] *square-jawed young men*. [ME: from OFr. *joe* 'cheek, jaw,' of unknown origin.]

jaw·bone /'jô,bōn/ ▶ n. a bone of the jaw, esp. that of the lower jaw (the mandible), or either half of this. ▶ v. [trans.] attempt to persuade or pressure by the force of one's position of authority.

jaw·break·er /'jô,brākər/ ▶ n. **1** informal a word that is very long or hard to pronounce. **2** a large, hard, spherical candy. **3** a machine with powerful jaws for crushing rock or ore.

Jaws of Life ▶ n. trademark a hydraulic apparatus used to pry apart the wreckage of crashed vehicles in order to free people trapped inside.

Jay /jā/, John (1745–1829), the first Chief Justice of the US 1789–95. With James Madison and Alexander Hamilton, he was the author of the *Federalist Papers* 1787–88. He was responsible for Jay's Treaty 1794–95, which settled outstanding disputes with Britain.

jay /jā/ ▶ n. a bird of the crow family with boldly patterned plumage, typically having blue feathers in the wings or tail. Several genera and numerous species include the crested Eurasian *Garrulus glandarius*, and the common North American blue jay.

Jay·cee /,jā'sē/ ▶ n. a member of a Junior Chamber of Commerce, a civic organization for business and community leaders. [1940s: representing the initials of *Junior Chamber*.]

jay·walk /'jā,wôk/ ▶ v. [intrans.] cross or walk in the street or road unlawfully or without regard for approaching traffic. — **jay·walk·er** n.

jazz /jaz/ ▶ n. a type of music of black American origin characterized by improvisation, syncopation, and usually a regular or forceful rhythm, emerging at the beginning of the 20th century. ■ informal enthusiastic or lively talk, esp. when considered exaggerated or insincere. ▶ v. [intrans.] dated play or dance to jazz music.

– PHRASAL VERBS **jazz something up** make something more lively or cheerful. — **jazz·er** n. [20th C.: of unknown origin.]

Jazz Age the 1920s in the US characterized as a period of carefree hedonism, wealth, freedom, and youthful exuberance, reflected in the novels of writers such as F. Scott Fitzgerald.

jazz·er·cise /'jazər,sīz/ ▶ n. trademark a type of fitness training combining aerobic exercise and dancing to jazz music.

jazz·man /'jazmən; -,man/ ▶ n. (pl. -**men**) a male jazz musician.

jazz·y /'jazē/ ▶ adj. (**jazz·i·er**, **jazz·i·est**) of, resembling, or in the style of jazz. ■ bright, colorful, and showy. — **jazz·i·ly** adv. **jazz·i·ness** n.

JCD ▶ abbr. ■ Doctor of Canon Law. [from mod. L. *Juris Canonici Doctor*.] ■ Doctor of Civil Law. [from L. *Juris Civilis Doctor*.]

JCL ▶ abbr. Comput. job control language.

JCS ▶ abbr. Joint Chiefs of Staff, the chief military advisory body to the president of the United States.

jct. ▶ abbr. junction.

JD ▶ abbr. informal ■ juvenile delinquency. ■ juvenile delinquent.

jeal·ous /'jeləs/ ▶ adj. feeling or showing envy of someone or their achievements and advantages. ■ feeling or showing suspicion of someone's unfaithfulness in a relationship. ■ fiercely protective or vigilant of one's rights or possessions. ■ (of God) demanding faithfulness and exclusive worship. — **jeal·ous·ly** adv. [ME: from OFr. *gelos*, from med. L. *zelosus* (see ZEALOUS).]

jeal·ous·y /'jeləsē/ ▶ n. (pl. -**ous·ies**) the state or feeling of being jealous.

jean /jēn/ ▶ n. heavy twilled cotton cloth, esp. denim. ■ (in commercial use) a pair of jeans. [15th C. (as an adj.): from OFr. *Janne* (now *Gênes*), from med. L. *Janua* 'Genoa.']

jeans /jēnz/ ▶ plural n. hard-wearing trousers made of denim or other cotton fabric, for informal wear. When blue, the typical color of jeans, they are also called BLUE JEANS.

jeb·el /'jebəl/ (also **djeb·el**) ▶ n. (in the Middle East and North Africa) a mountain or hill, or a range of hills. [colloq. Arab. form of *jabal* 'mountain.']

Jed·dah /'jedə/ var. of JIDDAH.

jeep /jēp/ ▶ n. trademark a small, sturdy motor vehicle with four-wheel drive, esp. one used by the military.

jee·pers /'jēpərz/ (also **jee·pers cree·pers**) ▶ exclam. informal used to express surprise or alarm. [1920s: alt. of JESUS.]

jeer /ji(ə)r/ ▶ v. [intrans.] make rude and mocking remarks, typically in a loud voice. ■ [trans.] shout such remarks at (someone). ▶ n. a rude and mocking remark. — **jeer·ing·ly** adv. [16th C.: of unknown origin.]

jeez /jēz/ (also **geez**) ▶ exclam. informal a mild expression used to show surprise or annoyance. [1920s: abbrev. of JESUS.]

Jef·fers /'jefərz/, John Robinson (1887–1962), US poet. Some of his poetry is collected in *Tamar and Other Poems* (1924).

Jef·fer·son /'jefərsən/, Thomas (1743–1826), 3rd president of the US 1801–09. A Democratic Republican from Virginia, he was the principal drafter of the Declaration of Independence 1776. He was the first US secretary of state 1789–93 and the second US vice president 1797–1801. As president, he secured the Louisiana Purchase 1803 and authorized the Lewis and Clark expedition. He founded the University of Virginia in 1819. — **Jef·fer·so·ni·an** /,jefər'sōnēən/ adj. & n.

Jef·fer·son Cit·y the capital of Missouri, in the central part of the state; pop. 39,636.

je·had ▶ n. var. of JIHAD.

Je·hosh·a·phat /jə'häsʜə,fat; -'häs-/ (also **Je·hos·a·phat**) a king of Judah in the mid 9th century BC. ■ [as exclam.] (also **jumping Jehoshaphat**) a mild expletive.

Je·ho·vah /jə'hōvə/ ▶ n. a form of the Hebrew name of God used in some translations of the Bible. [from med. L. *Iehouah*, *Iehoua*, from Heb. *YHWH* or *JHVH*, the consonants of the name of God, with the inclusion of vowels taken from *ădōnāy* 'my lord'; see also YAHWEH.]

Je·ho·vah's Wit·ness ▶ n. a member of a Christian sect (the Watch Tower Bible and Tract Society) founded in the US by Charles Taze Russell (1852–1916).

Je·ho·vist /jə'hōvist/ ▶ n. another name for YAHWIST.

je·june /ji'jo͞on/ ▶ adj. **1** naive, simplistic, and superficial. **2** (of ideas or writings) dry and uninteresting. — **je·june·ly** adv. [17th C.: from L. *jejunus* 'fasting, barren.']

je·ju·num /ji'jo͞onəm/ ▶ n. [in sing.] Anat. the part of the small intestine between the duodenum and ileum. — **je·ju·nal** /'jo͞onl/ adj. [16th C.: from med. L., neut. of *jejunus* 'fasting.']

Jek·yll /'jekəl/, Dr., the central character of Robert Louis Stevenson's story *The Strange Case of Dr. Jekyll and Mr. Hyde* (1886). He discovers a drug that creates a separate personality (appearing in the character of Mr. Hyde) into which Jekyll's evil impulses are channeled.

jell /jel/ ▶ v. [intrans.] (of jelly or a similar substance) set or become firmer. ■ (of a project or idea) take a definite shape; begin to work well. ■ (of people) relate well to one another. [18th C.: back-form. from JELLY.]

jel·la·ba ▶ n. var. of DJELLABA.

jell·o /'jelō/ (also trademark **Jell-O**) ▶ n. a fruit-flavored gelatin dessert made from a commercially prepared powder.

jel·ly /'jelē/ ▶ n. (pl. -**lies**) a sweet, clear, semisolid, somewhat elastic spread or preserve made from fruit juice and sugar boiled to a thick consistency. ■ used figuratively and in similes to refer to sensations of fear or strong emotion. ■ a similar clear preparation made with fruit or other ingredients as a condiment. ■ a gelatinous savory preparation made by boiling meat and bones. ■ any substance of a gelatinous consistency. ■ **(jellies)** jelly shoes. ▶ v. (-**lies**, -**lied**) [trans.] [usu. as adj.] (**jellied**) set (food) as or in a jelly: *jellied cranberry sauce*. — **jel·li·fi·ca·tion** /,jeləfi'kāsʜən/ n. **jel·li·fy** /'jelə,fī/ v. [ME: from OFr. *gelée* 'frost, jelly,' from L. *gelata* 'frozen,' from *gelare* 'freeze,' from *gelu* 'frost.']

jel·ly bean (also **jel·ly·bean**) ▶ n. a bean-shaped candy with a jellylike center and a firm sugar coating.

jel·ly·fish /'jelē,fisʜ/ ▶ n. (pl. same or -**fish·es**) a free-swimming marine coelenterate (classes Scyphozoa and Cubozoa) with a jellylike bell- or saucer-shaped body that is typically transparent and has stinging tentacles around the edge. See illustration at SEA NETTLE.

PRONUNCIATION KEY ə *ago*, *up*; ər *over*, *fur*; a *hat*; ā *ate*; ä *car*; e *let*; ē *see*; i *fit*; ī *by*; NG *sing*; ō *go*; ô *law*, *for*; oi *toy*; o͝o *good*; o͞o *goo*; ou *out*; TH *thin*; T̲H̲ *then*; ZH *vision*

jel·ly roll ▶ **n.** a cylindrical cake with a spiral cross section, made from a flat sponge cake spread with a filling such as jam and rolled up.

jel·ly shoe ▶ **n.** a sandal made from brightly colored or translucent molded plastic.

je ne sais quoi /ˌzʜə nə sā ˈkwä/ ▶ **n.** a quality that cannot be described or named easily. [Fr., lit. 'I do not know what.']

Jen·ner /ˈjenər/, Edward (1749–1823), British physician. He pioneered the use of vaccination against disease.

jen·ny /ˈjenē/ ▶ **n.** (pl. **-nies**) **1** a female donkey or ass. **2** short for **SPINNING JENNY**. [17th C.: nickname for the given name *Janet*.]

jeon /ˈjēän/ ▶ **n.** (pl. same) a monetary unit of South Korea, equal to one hundredth of a won. [Kor.]

jeop·ard·ize /ˈjepərˌdīz/ ▶ **v.** [trans.] put (someone or something) into a situation in which there is a danger of loss, harm, or failure.

jeop·ard·y /ˈjepərdē/ ▶ **n.** danger of loss, harm, or failure. ■ Law danger arising from being on trial for a criminal offense. [ME *iuparti*, from OFr. *ieu parti* '(evenly) divided game.']

Jeph·thah /ˈjefᴛʜə; yifˈtäᴋʜ/ (in the Bible) a judge of Israel.

Jer. ▶ **abbr.** Bible Jeremiah.

rough-legged jerboa

jer·bo·a /jərˈbōə/ ▶ **n.** a desert-dwelling rodent (family Dipodidae) with long hind legs that enable it to perform long jumps, found from North Africa to central Asia. Several genera and species include the **rough-legged** (or **northern three-toed**) **jerboa** (*Dipus sagitta*). [17th C.: mod. L., from Arab. *yarbū'*.]

jer·e·mi·ad /ˌjerəˈmīəd; -ad/ ▶ **n.** a long, mournful complaint or lamentation; a list of woes. [18th C.: from Fr. *jérémiade*, from *Jérémie* 'Jeremiah,' from eccles. L. *Jeremias* (see **JEREMIAH**).]

Jer·e·mi·ah /ˌjerəˈmīə/, (*c.*650–*c.*585 BC) a Hebrew prophet. The biblical Lamentations are ascribed to him. ■ a book of the Bible containing his prophecies. ■ [as n.] (**a Jeremiah**) a person who complains continually or foretells disaster.

Je·rez /hāˈres; -ˈreᴛʜ/ a town in southwestern Spain, in Andalusia; pop. 184,000. Full name **JEREZ DE LA FRONTERA**.

Jer·i·cho /ˈjeriˌkō/ a town in Palestine, on the West Bank, north of the Dead Sea. Occupied by the Israelis since 1967, it was the first area given partial autonomy under the PLO–Israeli peace accord in 1994.

jerk[1] /jərk/ ▶ **n. 1** a quick, sharp, sudden movement. ■ a spasmodic muscular twitch. ■ [in sing.] Weightlifting the raising of a barbell above the head from shoulder level by an abrupt straightening of the arms and legs. **2** informal a contemptibly obnoxious person. ▶ **v.** [trans.] make (something) move with a jerk. ■ [intrans.] move with a jerk. ■ suddenly rouse or jolt (someone). ■ [trans.] Weightlifting raise (a weight) from shoulder level to above the head.

– PHRASAL VERBS **jerk someone around** informal deal with someone dishonestly or unfairly. **jerk off** vulgar slang masturbate. — **jerk·er n.** [16th C. (denoting a stroke with a whip): prob. imitative.]

jerk[2] ▶ **v.** [trans.] [usu. as adj.] (**jerked**) prepare (meat) by marinating it in spices and drying or barbecuing it over a wood fire. ▶ **n.** meat cooked in this way. [18th C.: from L. Amer. Sp. *charquear*, from *charqui*, from Quechua *echarqui* 'dried flesh.']

jer·kin /ˈjərkin/ ▶ **n.** a sleeveless jacket. ■ hist. a man's close-fitting jacket, typically made of leather. [16th C.: of unknown origin.]

jerk·wa·ter /ˈjərkˌwôtər; -ˌwätər/ ▶ **adj.** [attrib.] informal of or associated with small, remote, and insignificant rural settlements: *some jerkwater town.* [19th C.: orig. of a train, from **JERK**[1].]

jerk·y[1] /ˈjərkē/ ▶ **adj.** (**jerk·i·er, jerk·i·est**) **1** characterized by abrupt stops and starts. **2** contemptibly foolish. — **jerk·i·ly adv. jerk·i·ness n.**

jerk·y[2] ▶ **n.** meat that has been cured by being cut into long, thin strips and dried. [19th C.: from Amer. Sp. *charqui*, from Quechua.]

jer·o·bo·am /ˌjerəˈbōəm/ ▶ **n.** a wine bottle with a capacity four times that of an ordinary bottle. [19th C.: named after *Jeroboam*, a king of Israel, "who made Israel to sin" (1 Kings 11:28, 14:16).]

Je·rome, St. /jəˈrōm/ (*c.*342–420), leader of the early Christian Church. He compiled the Vulgate Bible.

jer·ry-built ▶ **adj.** badly or hastily built with materials of poor quality. — **jer·ry-build·er n. jer·ry-build·ing n.** [19th C.: perh. after a firm of builders in Liverpool.]

jer·ry·can /ˈjerēˌkan/ (also **jer·ry can, jer·ri·can**) ▶ **n.** a large, flat-sided metal container for storing or transporting liquids, typically gasoline or water. [World War II: from *Jerry* 'a German' (prob. an alt. of **GERMAN**) + **CAN**[2].]

Jer·sey /ˈjərzē/ the largest of the Channel Islands; pop. 83,000

jer·sey /ˈjərzē/ ▶ **n.** (pl. **-seys**) **1** a knitted garment with long sleeves worn over the upper body. ■ a distinctive shirt worn by a player or competitor in certain sports. ■ a soft, fine knitted fabric. **2** (**Jersey**) an animal of a breed of light brown dairy cattle from Jersey. [16th C.: from **JERSEY**.]

Jer·sey Cit·y a city in northeastern New Jersey, opposite New York City; pop. 240,055.

Je·ru·sa·lem /jəˈro͞os(ə)ləm; -ˈro͞oz-/ a city in east central Israel; pop. 562,000. Holy to Jews, Christians, and Muslims, it was divided between the states of Israel and Jordan from 1947 until 1967 when the Israelis proclaimed it the capital of Israel, although it is not recognized as such by the UN.

Je·ru·sa·lem ar·ti·choke ▶ **n. 1** a knobby edible tuber with white flesh, eaten as a vegetable. **2** the tall North American plant (*Helianthus tuberosus*) of the daisy family, closely related to the sunflower, that produces this tuber. [17th C.: *Jerusalem*, alt. of Ital. *girasole* 'sunflower.']

Je·ru·sa·lem Bi·ble ▶ **n.** a modern English translation of the Bible by mainly Roman Catholic scholars.

Je·ru·sa·lem thorn ▶ **n. 1** a thorny tropical American tree (*Parkinsonia aculeata*) of the pea family, grown as an ornamental. **2** see **CHRIST'S THORN**.

jess /jes/ Falconry ▶ **n.** (usu. **jesses**) a short leather strap that is fastened around each leg of a hawk, usually also having a ring or swivel to which a leash may be attached. ▶ **v.** [trans.] put such straps on (a hawk). [ME: from OFr. *ges*, based on L. *jactus* 'a throw,' from *jacere* 'to throw.']

jes·sa·mine /ˈjesəmin/ ▶ **n.** var. of **JASMINE**.

Jes·se /ˈjesē/ (in the Bible) the father of David, represented as the first in the genealogy of Jesus Christ.

jest /jest/ ▶ **n.** a thing said or done for amusement; a joke. ▶ **v.** [intrans.] speak or act in a joking manner. [ME (orig. 'exploit, heroic deed,' hence 'a narrative of such deeds'): from earlier *gest*, from OFr. *geste*, from L. *gesta* 'actions, exploits.']

jest·er /ˈjestər/ ▶ **n.** hist. a professional joker or "fool" at a medieval court, typically wearing a cap with bells on it and carrying a mock scepter. ■ a person who habitually plays the fool.

Je·su /ˈjāzo͞o; ˈjē-; ˈyā-/ archaic form of **JESUS**. [ME: from OFr.]

Jes·u·it /ˈjezʜo͞oit; ˈjez(y)o͞o-/ ▶ **n.** a member of the Society of Jesus, a Roman Catholic order of priests founded by St. Ignatius Loyola, St. Francis Xavier, and others in 1534, to do missionary work. — **Jes·u·it·i·cal** /ˌjezʜo͞oˈitikəl; ˌjez(y)o͞o-/ **adj. Jes·u·it·i·cal·ly** /ˌjezʜo͞oˈitik(ə)lē; ˌjez(y)o͞o-/ **adv.** [from Fr. *jésuite* or mod. L. *Jesuita*, from Christian L. *Iesus* (see **JESUS**).]

Je·sus /ˈjēzəs/ (also **Jesus Christ** or **Jesus of Nazareth**) the central figure of the Christian religion. Jesus conducted a mission of preaching and healing (with reported miracles) in Palestine in about AD 28–30, which is described in the Gospels. His followers considered him to be the Christ or Messiah and the Son of God, and belief in his resurrection from the dead is the central tenet of Christianity.

jet[1] /jet/ ▶ **n. 1** a rapid stream of liquid or gas forced out of a small opening. ■ a nozzle or narrow opening for sending out such a stream. **2** an aircraft powered by one or more jet engines. ▶ **v.** (**jet·ted, jet·ting**) [intrans.] **1** travel by jet aircraft. **2** spurt out in jets. [16th C. (as a v. meaning 'jut out'): from Fr. *jeter* 'to throw,' based on L. *jactare*, frequentative of *jacere* 'to throw.']

jet[2] ▶ **n.** a hard black semiprecious variety of lignite, capable of being carved and highly polished. ■ a glossy black color. [ME: from OFr. *jaiet*, from L. *Gagates*, from Gk. *gagatēs* 'from *Gagai*,' a town in Asia Minor.]

je·té /zʜəˈtā/ ▶ **n.** Ballet a jump in which a dancer springs from one foot to land on the other with one leg extended outward from the body while in the air. [Fr., past part. of *jeter* 'to throw.']

jet lag ▶ **n.** extreme tiredness and other physical effects felt by a person after a long flight across several time zones. — **jet-lagged adj.**

jet·lin·er /ˈjetˌlīnər/ ▶ **n.** a large jet aircraft carrying passengers. [1940s: blend of **JET**[1] and **AIRLINER**.]

jet-pro·pelled ▶ **adj.** moved by jet propulsion.

jet pro·pul·sion ▶ **n.** propulsion by the backward ejection of a high-speed jet of gas or liquid.

jet·sam /ˈjetsəm/ ▶ **n.** unwanted material or goods that have been thrown overboard from a ship and washed ashore, esp. material that has been discarded to lighten the vessel. Compare with **FLOTSAM**. [16th C. (as *jetson*): contr. of **JETTISON**.]

jet set ▶ **n.** (**the jet set**) informal wealthy and fashionable people who travel widely and frequently for pleasure. — **jet-set·ter n. jet-set·ting adj.**

jet ski ▶ **n.** trademark a small, jet-propelled vehicle that skims across the surface of water and typically is ridden like a a motorcycle. ▶ **v.** (**jet-ski**) [intrans.] [often as n.] (**jet-skiing**) ride on such a vehicle. — **jet-ski·er n.**

jet stream ▶ **n. 1** a narrow, variable band of very strong, predominantly westerly air currents encircling the globe several miles above the earth. **2** a flow of exhaust gasses from a jet engine.

jet·ti·son /ˈjetisən; -zən/ ▶ **v.** [trans.] throw or drop (something) from an aircraft or ship. ■ abandon or discard (someone or something that is no longer wanted). ▶ **n.** the action of jettisoning something. [ME: from OFr. *getaison*, from L. *jactatio(n-)*, from *jactare* 'to throw' (see **JET**[1]).]

jet·ty /ˈjetē/ ▶ **n.** (pl. **-ties**) a landing stage or small pier at which boats can dock or be moored. ■ a breakwater constructed to protect or defend a harbor, stretch of coast, or riverbank. [ME: from OFr. *jetee*, fem. past part. of *jeter* 'to throw' (see JET[1]).]

jet·way /'jet,wā/ ▶ n. (trademark in the UK) a portable bridge put against an aircraft door to allow passengers to embark or disembark.

Jew /jo͞o/ ▶ n. a member of the people and cultural community whose traditional religion is Judaism and who trace their origins through the ancient Hebrew people of Israel to Abraham.
– PHRASES **jew someone down** offens. bargain with someone in a miserly or petty way. [ME: from OFr. *juiu*, via L. from Gk. *Ioudaios*, via Aramaic from Heb. *yĕhūḏī*, from *yĕhūḏāh* 'Judah' (see JUDAH).]

jew·el /'jo͞oəl/ ▶ n. a precious stone, typically a single crystal or a piece of a hard lustrous or translucent mineral, cut into shape with flat facets or smoothed and polished for use as an ornament. ■ (usu. **jewels**) an ornament or piece of jewelry containing such a stone or stones. ■ a hard precious stone used as a bearing in a watch, compass, or other device. ■ a very pleasing or valued person or thing; a very fine example. [ME: from OFr. *joel*, from *jeu* 'game, play,' from L. *jocus* 'jest.']

jew·el box ▶ n. a storage box for a compact disc.

jew·eled /'jo͞oəld/ (Brit. **jew·elled**) ▶ adj. adorned, set with, or made from jewels.

jew·el·er /'jo͞oələr/ (Brit. **jew·el·ler**) ▶ n. a person or company that makes or sells jewels or jewelry.

jew·el·fish /'jo͞oəl,fisн/ ▶ n. (pl. same or **-fish·es**) a scarlet and green tropical freshwater cichlid (*Hemichromis bimaculatus*).

jew·el·ry /'jo͞oəlrē/ (Brit. **jew·el·lery**) ▶ n. personal ornaments, such as necklaces, rings, or bracelets, that are typically made from or contain jewels and precious metal.

jew·el·weed ▶ n. another term for TOUCH-ME-NOT.

Jew·ess /'jo͞o-is/ ▶ n. often offens. a Jewish woman or girl.

Jew·ett /'jo͞oit/, Theodora Sarah Orne (1849–1909), US writer and poet; pen names **A. D. Eliot**, **Alice Eliot**, **Sarah C. Sweet**. Her works include *The King of Folly Island* (1888).

jew·fish /'jo͞o,fisн/ ▶ n. (pl. same or **-fish·es**) a large sporting or food fish of warm coastal waters, esp. *Epinephelus itajara* of the sea bass family, found along the east and west coasts of North America.

Jew·ish /'jo͞o-isн/ ▶ adj. relating to, associated with, or denoting Jews or Judaism. — **Jew·ish·ly** adv. **Jew·ish·ness** n.

Jew·ish cal·en·dar ▶ n. a complex ancient lunar calendar in use among the Jews, consisting of twelve months but having thirteen months in leap years. The years are reckoned from the Creation, which is placed at 3761 BC.

Jew·ish New Year ▶ n. another term for ROSH HASHANAH.

Jew·ry /'jo͞orē/ ▶ n. (pl. **-ries**) **1** Jews collectively. **2** hist. a Jewish quarter in a town or city.

Jew's ear ▶ n. a common fungus (*Auricularia auricula-judae*) with a brown, rubbery, cup-shaped fruiting body, growing on dead or dying trees in both Eurasia and North America. [16th C.: a mistranslation of med. L. *auricula Judae* 'Judas's ear,' from its shape.]

Jew's harp ▶ n. a small, lyre-shaped musical instrument held between the teeth and struck with a finger. It can produce only one note, but harmonics are sounded by the player altering the shape of the mouth cavity.

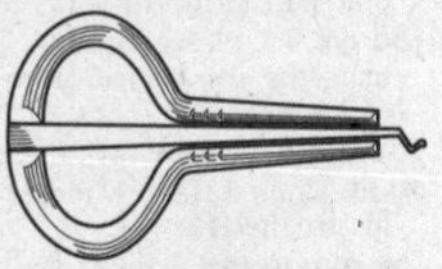

Jew's harp

Je·ze·bel /'jezə,bel; -bəl/ (*fl.*9th century BC), a Phoenician princess, traditionally the great-aunt of Dido and in the Bible the wife of Ahab, king of Israel (1 Kings 16:31, 21:5–15, 2 Kings 9:30–7). ■ [as n.] (**a Jezebel**) a shameless or immoral woman.

jg ▶ abbr. (in the US Navy) junior grade.

Jhe·lum /'jāləm/ a river that rises in the Himalayas and flows through the Vale of Kashmir into Punjab, where it meets the Chenab River.

Jia·mu·si /jē'ä'mo͞o'sē; 'jyä'mʏ'sē/ a city in Heilongjiang province, in northeastern China, on the Sungari River, northeast of Harbin; pop. 493,000.

Jiang Jie Shi /,jäng jē 'sнē/ var. of CHIANG KAI-SHEK.

Jiang·su /jē'äng'so͞o/ (also **Kiang·su**) a province in eastern China; capital, Nanjing.

Jiang·xi /jē'äng'sнē/ (also **Kiang·si**) a province in southeastern China; capital, Nanchang.

jiao /jyou/ ▶ n. (pl. same) a monetary unit of China, equal to one tenth of a yuan. [from Chin. *jiǎo*.]

jib /jib/ ▶ n. **1** Sailing a triangular staysail set forward of the forwardmost mast. **2** the projecting arm of a crane. [17th C.: of unknown origin.]

jib·ba /'jibə/ (also **jib·bah**, **djib·ba**, or **djib·bah**) ▶ n. a long coat worn by Muslim men. [19th C.: Egyptian var. of Arab. *jubba*.]

jibe[1] /jīb/ ▶ n. & v. var. of GIBE.

jibe[2] (Brit. **gybe**) Sailing ▶ v. [intrans.] change course by swinging a fore-and-aft sail across a following wind. ■ [trans.] swing (a sail or boom) across the wind in such a way. ■ (of a sail or boom) swing or be swung across the wind. ▶ n. an act or instance of jibing. [17th C.: from obs. Du. *gijben*.]

jibe[3] ▶ v. [intrans.] informal be in accord; agree. [19th C.: of unknown origin.]

ji·ca·ma /'hikəmə; 'hē-/ ▶ n. the crisp, white-fleshed, edible tuber of a Central American climbing plant (*Pachyrhizus erosus*) of the pea family, cultivated since pre-Columbian times.

Ji·ca·ril·la /,hēkə'rēə; -'rēlyə/ ▶ n. (pl. same or **-las**) **1** (also **Jicarilla Apache**) a member of an Apache people of northern New Mexico. **2** the Athabaskan language of this people. ▶ adj. of or relating to this people or their language. [Mex. Sp.: prob. dimin. of *jícara* 'chocolate-cup.']

Jid·dah /'jidə/ (also **Jid·da**, **Jed·dah**, or **Jed·da** /'jedə/) a seaport on the Red Sea coast of Saudi Arabia; pop. 1,400,000.

jif·fy /'jifē/ (also **jiff**) ▶ n. [in sing.] informal a moment. [18th C.: of unknown origin.]

jig /jig/ ▶ n. **1** a lively dance with leaping movements. ■ a piece of music for such a dance, typically in compound time. **2** a device that holds a piece of work and guides the tools operating on it. **3** Fishing a type of artificial bait that is jerked up and down through the water. ▶ v. (**jigged**, **jig·ging**) **1** [intrans.] dance a jig. ■ [with adverbial] move up and down with a quick jerky motion. **2** [trans.] equip (a factory or workshop) with a jig or jigs. **3** [intrans.] fish with a jig: *he jigged for squid*.
– PHRASES **the jig is up** informal the scheme or deception is revealed or foiled. [16th C.: of unknown origin.]

jig·a·boo /'jigə,bo͞o/ ▶ n. derog. a black person. [20th C.: rel. to slang *jig* (in the same sense); cf. the pair *bug*, *bugaboo*.]

jig·ger[1] /'jigər/ ▶ n. **1** a machine or vehicle with a part that rocks or moves back and forth, e.g., a jigsaw. **2** a person who dances a jig. **3** a small fore-and-aft sail set at the stern of a ship. ■ a small tackle consisting of a double and single block or two single blocks with a rope. **4** a measure or small glass of spirits or wine. **5** used to refer to a thing whose name one does not know or does not wish to mention. ▶ v. [trans.] informal rearrange or tamper with: *jiggering with the controls was a mistake*. [16th C.: from the v. JIG.]

jig·ger[2] ▶ n. var. of CHIGGER.

jig·gle /'jigəl/ ▶ v. [intrans.] move about lightly and quickly from side to side or up and down. ■ [trans.] shake (something) lightly up and down or from side to side. ▶ n. [in sing.] a quick light shake. — **jig·gly** adj. [19th C.: partly an alt. of JOGGLE, reinforced by JIG.]

jig·saw /'jig,sô/ ▶ n. **1** (also **jigsaw puzzle**) a puzzle consisting of a picture printed on cardboard or wood and cut into various pieces of different shapes that have to be fitted together. ■ fig. a puzzle that can only be resolved by assembling various pieces of information. **2** a machine saw with a fine blade enabling it to cut curved lines in a sheet of wood, metal, or plastic.

ji·had /ji'häd/ ▶ n. a holy war undertaken by Muslims against unbelievers. ■ informal a single-minded or obsessive campaign. [from Arab. *jihād*, lit. 'effort.']

ji·had·i /ji'hädē/ (also **je·had·i**) ▶ n. (pl. **-is**) a person involved in a jihad; an Islamic militant. [from Arabic *jihādi*, from *jihād*.]

ji·had·ist /ji'hädist/ ▶ n. a jihadi.

Ji·lin /'jē'lin/ (also **Ki·rin**) a province in northeastern China; capital, Changchun. ■ a city in Jilin province; pop. 2,252,000.

jil·lion /'jilyən/ ▶ cardinal number informal an extremely large number: *they ran jillions of ads*. [1940s: fanciful formation on the pattern of *billion* and *million*.]

jilt /jilt/ ▶ v. [trans.] (often **be jilted**) suddenly reject or abandon (a lover). [17th C. (in the sense 'deceive, trick'): of unknown origin.]

Jim Crow /'jim 'krō/ ▶ n. the former practice of segregating black people in the US. ■ offens. a black person. — **Jim Crow·ism** /'krō,izəm/ n. [19th C.: the name of a black character in a 19th-cent. plantation song.]

jim-dan·dy /'jim 'dandē/ informal ▶ adj. fine, outstanding, or excellent: *it was a jim-dandy birthday party*. ▶ n. an excellent or notable person or thing. [19th C.: from the given name *Jim* (nickname for *James*) + DANDY.]

jim·i·ny /'jimənē/ ▶ exclam. used in phrases as an expression of surprise: *by jiminy, she was right*. [19th C.: alt. of GEMINI.]

Jim·mu /'jēmo͝o/ the legendary first emperor of Japan (660 BC), descendant of the sun goddess Amaterasu and founder of the imperial dynasty.

jim·my /'jimē/ ▶ n. (pl. **-ies**) a short crowbar used by a burglar to force open a window or door. ▶ v. (**-ies**, **-ied**) [trans.] informal force open (a window or door) with a jimmy. [19th C.: pet form of *James* (cf. JACK[1]).]

jim·son weed /'jimsən/ (also **jimp·son weed**) ▶ n. a strong-smelling poisonous datura (*Datura stramonium*) of the nightshade family, with large, trumpet-shaped white flowers and toothed leaves. *See illustration on next page*. [17th C.: orig. *Jamestown weed*, after JAMESTOWN, Virginia.]

Jin /jin/ (also **Chin**) **1** a dynasty that ruled China AD 265–420, commonly divided into **Western Jin** (265–317) and **Eastern Jin** (317–420). **2** a dynasty that ruled Manchuria and northern China AD 1115–1234.

Ji·nan /'jē'nän/ (also **Tsi·nan**) a city in eastern China, the capital of Shandong province; pop. 2,290,000.

jin·gle /'jiNGgəl/ ▶ n. **1** [in sing.] a light ringing sound such as that made by metal objects being shaken together. **2** a short slogan, verse, or tune designed to be easily remembered, esp. as used in advertising. **3** (also **jingle shell**) a bivalve mollusk of the family Anomiidae, with a fragile, slightly translucent shell, the lower valve of which has a hole through which pass byssus threads for anchorage. ▶ v. make or cause to make a light metallic ringing sound. — **jin·gler** n. **jin·gly** adj. [ME: imitative.]

PRONUNCIATION KEY ə *ago, up*; ər *over, fur*; a *hat*; ā *ate*; ä *car*; e *let*; ē *see*; i *fit*; ī *by*; NG *sing*; ō *go*; ô *law, for*; oi *toy*; o͝o *good*; o͞o *goo*; ou *out*; TH *thin*; T͟H *then*; ZH *vision*

jimson weed

jin·go /ˈjiNGgō/ ▶ n. (pl. **-goes**) dated, esp. derog. a vociferous supporter of policy favoring war, esp. in the name of patriotism.
– PHRASES **by jingo!** an exclamation of surprise. —**jin·go·ism** /ˈjiNGgōˌizəm/ n. **jin·go·ist** n. **jin·go·is·tic** /ˌjiNGgōˈistik/ adj. [17th C.: *by jingo* (and the n. sense) come from a late 19th-cent. popular song.]

jink /jiNGk/ ▶ v. [intrans.] change direction suddenly and nimbly, as when dodging a pursuer: *she was too quick for him and jinked away every time.* ▶ n. a sudden quick change of direction.

jinn /jin/ (also **djinn** or **jin·ni** /jiˈnē; ˈjinē/) ▶ n. (pl. same or **jinns**) (in Arabian and Muslim mythology) an intelligent spirit of lower rank than the angels. Compare with GENIE. [from Arab. *jinnī*, pl. *jinn*.]

Jin·nah /ˈjinə/, Muhammad Ali (1876–1948), president of Pakistan 1947–48; born in India. He was a founder of Pakistan.

jin·rik·i·sha /jinˈrikSHô; -SHä/ (also **jin·rick·sha**) ▶ n. another term for RICKSHA. [Japanese, from *jin* 'man' + *riki* 'strength' + *sha* 'vehicle.']

jinx /jiNGks/ ▶ n. a person or thing that brings bad luck. ▶ v. [trans.] (usu. **be jinxed**) bring bad luck to; cast an evil spell on. [20th C.: prob. a var. of *jynx* 'wryneck,' a bird used in witchcraft.]

jird /jərd/ ▶ n. a long-tailed burrowing rodent (genus *Meriones*, family Muridae) related to the gerbils, found in deserts and steppes from North Africa to China. [from Berber *(a)gherda*.]

jism /ˈjizəm/ ▶ n. vulgar slang semen. [19th C.: of unknown origin.]

JIT ▶ abbr. (of manufacturing systems) just-in-time.

jit·ney /ˈjitnē/ ▶ n. (pl. **-neys**) informal a bus or other vehicle carrying passengers for a low fare.

jit·ter /ˈjitər/ informal ▶ n. **1** (**jitters**) feelings of extreme nervousness. **2** slight irregular movement, variation, or unsteadiness, esp. in an electrical signal or electronic device. ▶ v. [intrans.] act nervously. ■ (of a signal or device) suffer from jitter. —**jit·ter·i·ness** n. **jit·ter·y** adj. [1920s: of unknown origin.]

jit·ter·bug /ˈjitərˌbəg/ ▶ n. **1** a fast dance popular in the 1940s, performed chiefly to swing music. ■ dated a person fond of dancing such a dance. **2** informal, dated a nervous person. ▶ v. (**-bugged, -bug·ging**) [intrans.] dance the jitterbug. [1930s (orig. US): from the v. JITTER + BUG.]

jiu-jit·su /ˌjo͞oˈjitso͞o/ ▶ n. var. of JUJITSU.

Ji·va·ro /ˈhēvəˌrō/ ▶ n. (pl. same or **-ros**) **1** a member of an indigenous people of the eastern slopes of the Andes in Ecuador and Peru. **2** any of the group of languages spoken by this people. ▶ adj. of or relating to this people or their languages. [from Sp. *jíbaro*, prob. from the local name *Shuara, Shiwora*.]

jive /jīv/ ▶ n. **1** a lively style of dance popular esp. in the 1940s and 1950s, performed to swing music or rock and roll. ■ swing music. **2** (also **jive talk**) a form of slang associated with black American jazz musicians. ■ informal a thing, esp. talk, that is deceptive or worthless. ▶ v. informal **1** [intrans.] perform the jive or a similar dance to popular music. **2** [trans.] informal taunt or sneer at. ■ [intrans.] talk nonsense. ▶ adj. informal deceitful or worthless. —**jiv·er** n. **jiv·ey** adj. [1920s.]

Jo·a·chim, St. /ˈyōəkim; ˈjō-/ (in Christian tradition) the husband of St. Anne and father of the Virgin Mary.

Joan of Arc, St. /ˌjōn əv ˈärk/ (*c.*1412–31), French heroine; known as **the Maid of Orleans**. She led the French armies against the English in the Hundred Years War. Captured and convicted of heresy, she was burned at the stake.

Job /jōb/ (in the Bible) a prosperous man whose patience and piety were tried by undeserved misfortunes. ■ a book of the Bible telling of Job.

job /jäb/ ▶ n. **1** a paid position of regular employment. **2** a task or piece of work, esp. one that is paid. ■ a responsibility or duty. ■ [in sing.] informal a difficult task. ■ [with adj.] informal a procedure to improve the appearance of something, esp. an operation involving plastic surgery: *she's had a nose job.* ■ [with adj.] informal a thing of a specified nature: *the car was a malevolent-looking job.* ■ informal a crime, esp. a robbery. ■ Comput. an operation or group of operations treated as a single and distinct unit. ▶ v. (**jobbed, job·bing**) **1** [intrans.] [usu. as adj.] (**jobbing**) do casual or occasional work. **2** [trans.] buy and sell (stocks) as a broker-dealer, esp. on a small scale.
– PHRASES **do a job on someone** informal do something that harms or defeats an opponent. [16th C. (sense 2 of the n.): of unknown origin.]

job·ber /ˈjäbər/ ▶ n. **1** a wholesaler. **2** a person who does casual or occasional work.

job·ber·y /ˈjäbərē/ ▶ n. the practice of using a public office or position of trust for one's own gain or advantage.

job con·trol lan·guage ▶ n. Comput. a language enabling the user to define the tasks to be undertaken by the operating system.

job·less /ˈjäblis/ ▶ adj. unemployed. —**job·less·ness** n.

job lot ▶ n. a miscellaneous group of articles, esp. when sold or bought together.

Jobs /jäbz/, Steven Paul (1955–), US entrepreneur. He cofounded the Apple computer company 1976.

Job's com·fort·er /jōbz/ ▶ n. a person who aggravates distress under the guise of giving comfort. [18th C.: alluding to the biblical story (Job 16:2) of JOB.]

Job's tears /ˈjōbz ˈti(ə)rz/ ▶ plural n. a widely cultivated Southeast Asian grass (*Coix lacryma-jobi*) that bears its seeds inside hollow, pear-shaped receptacles, which are gray and shiny and sometimes used as beads.

Jo·burg /ˈjōˌbərg/ a nickname for JOHANNESBURG.

Jo·cas·ta /jōˈkastə/ Gk. Mythol. a Theban woman, wife of Laius and mother and later wife of Oedipus.

jock[1] /jäk/ ▶ n. informal **1** a disc jockey. **2** an enthusiast or participant in a specified activity.

jock[2] ▶ n. informal another term for JOCKSTRAP. ■ an enthusiastic athlete or sports fan, esp. one with few other interests. —**jock·ish** adj.

jock[3] ▶ n. informal a pilot or astronaut. [20th C.: prob. an abbrev. of JOCKEY.]

jock·ey /ˈjäkē/ ▶ n. (pl. **-eys**) a person who rides in horse races, esp. as a profession. ■ an enthusiast or participant in a specified activity. ▶ v. (**-eys, -eyed**) [intrans.] struggle by every available means to gain or achieve something: *jockeying for the top jobs.* ■ [trans.] handle or manipulate (someone or something) in a skillful manner. [16th C.: dimin. of *Jock* 'ordinary man; a rustic,' Scots form of the given name *Jack*.]

jock itch ▶ n. informal a fungal infection of the groin area. [1970s: *jock* from JOCKSTRAP.]

jock·strap /ˈjäkˌstrap/ ▶ n. a support or protection for the male genitals, worn esp. by athletes. [19th C.: from slang *jock* 'genitals' (of unknown origin) + STRAP.]

jo·cose /jōˈkōs/ ▶ adj. formal playful or humorous. —**jo·cose·ly** adv. [17th C.: from L. *jocosus*, from *jocus* (see JOKE).]

joc·u·lar /ˈjäkyələr/ ▶ adj. fond of or characterized by joking; humorous or playful. —**joc·u·lar·i·ty** /ˌjäkyəˈlaritē/ n. **joc·u·lar·ly** adv. [17th C.: from L. *jocularis*, from *joculus*, dimin. of *jocus* (see JOKE).]

joc·und /ˈjäkənd; ˈjō-/ ▶ adj. formal cheerful and lighthearted. —**jo·cun·di·ty** /jōˈkənditē/ n. (pl. **-ties**) **joc·und·ly** adv. [ME: via OFr. from L. *jocundus*, var. (influenced by *jocus* 'joke') of *jucundus* 'pleasant, agreeable,' from *juvare* 'to delight.']

jodh·purs /ˈjädpərz/ ▶ plural n. full-length trousers, worn for horse riding, that are close-fitting below the knee and have reinforced patches on the inside of the leg. [19th C.: named after *Jodhpur*, India.]

joe /jō/ ▶ n. informal **1** coffee. [1940s: of unknown origin.] **2** an ordinary man: *the average joe.* [19th C.: nickname for the given name *Joseph*; cf. JOE BLOW.]

Joe Blow /blō/ ▶ n. informal a name for a hypothetical average man.

Jo·el /jō(ə)l/ a Hebrew minor prophet. ■ a book of the Bible containing his prophecies.

joe-pye weed /jō ˈpī/ (also **joe pye weed**) ▶ n. a tall North American perennial plant (genus *Eupatorium*) of the daisy family that bears clusters of small purple flowers. Several species include **sweet joe-pye weed** (*E. purpureum*) and **spotted joe-pye weed** (*E. maculatum*). [19th C.: of unknown origin.]

Joe Six-pack /ˈsiksˌpak/ ▶ n. a name for a hypothetical ordinary working man.

jo·ey /ˈjō-ē/ ▶ n. (pl. **-eys**) Austral. a young kangaroo, wallaby, or possum. ■ informal a baby or young child. [from Aboriginal *joè*.]

Jof·fre /ˈjôfrə/, Joseph Jacques Césaire (1852–1931), French general. He commanded the French army on the western front during World War I.

jog /jäg/ ▶ v. (**jogged, jog·ging**) **1** [intrans.] run at a steady gentle pace, esp. on a regular basis as a form of physical exercise. ■ (of a horse) move at a slow trot. ■ move in an unsteady way, typically slowly. ■ (**jog along/on**) continue in a steady, uneventful way. **2** [trans.] nudge or knock slightly. ▶ n. **1** a spell of jogging. ■ [in sing.] a gentle running pace. **2** a slight push or nudge. —**jog·ger** n. [ME (in the sense 'stab, pierce'): var. of JAG[1].]

jog·gle /ˈjägəl/ ▶ v. move or cause to move with repeated small bobs or jerks. ▶ n. a bobbing or jerking movement. [16th C.: frequentative of JOG.]

Jog·ja·kar·ta /ˌjägjəˈkärtə/ var. of YOGYAKARTA.

Jo·han·nes·burg /jōˈhänisˌbərg; -ˈhan-/ a city in South Africa, the capital of the province of Gauteng; pop. 1,916,000.

Jo·han·nine /jōˈhanən; -īn/ ▶ adj. relating to the Apostle St. John the Evangelist, or to the Gospel or epistles of John in the New Testament. [19th C.: from the med. L. given name *Johannes* 'John' + -INE[1].]

Jo·han·nis·berg /jōˈhanisbərg/ (also **Johannisberg Riesling**) ▶ n. the chief variety of the Riesling wine grape, originating in Germany and widely grown in California and elsewhere. ■ a white wine made from this grape. [from the name of a castle and village on the Rhine, Germany, where it was orig. produced.]

John[1] /jän/ (1165–1216), king of England 1199–1216; son of Henry II;

known as **John Lackland**. Forced to sign the Magna Carta in 1215, he ignored its provisions and civil war broke out.

John[2] the name of six kings of Portugal: ■ John I (1357–1433), reigned 1385–1433; known as **John the Great**. He won independence for Portugal. ■ John II (1455–95), reigned 1481–95. ■ John III (1502–57), reigned 1521–57. ■ John IV (1604–56), reigned 1640–56; known as **John the Fortunate**. ■ John V (1689–1750), reigned 1706–50. ■ John VI (1767–1826), reigned 1816–26.

john /jän/ ▶ n. informal **1** a toilet. **2** a prostitute's client. [20th C. (sense 2): from the given name *John*.]

John III (1624–96), king of Poland 1674–96; known as **John Sobieski**.

John, St. one of the 12 Apostles; son of Zebedee; brother of James; known as **St. John the Evangelist** or **St. John the Divine**. He is credited with having written the fourth Gospel, Revelation, and three epistles of the New Testament. ■ the fourth Gospel (see GOSPEL sense 2). ■ any of the three epistles of the New Testament attributed to St. John.

John Bar·ley·corn /ˈbärlē,kôrn/ ▶ n. a personification of barley, or of malt liquor.

john·boat /ˈjän,bōt/ ▶ n. a small flat-bottomed boat with square ends, used chiefly on inland waterways.

John Bull ▶ n. a personification of England or the typical Englishman, represented as a stout, red-faced farmer in a top hat and high boots. [18th C.: from the name of a character representing the English nation in a satire, *Law is a Bottomless Pit; or, the History of John Bull* (1712), written by Scottish author John Arbuthnot (1667–1735).]

John Day Riv·er a river flowing across northern Oregon to join the Columbia River.

John Doe /dō/ ▶ n. Law an anonymous party, typically the plaintiff, in a legal action. ■ informal a hypothetical average man.

John Do·ry /ˈdôrē/ ▶ n. (pl. **-ries**) an edible fish (*Zeus faber*, family Zeidae) of the eastern Atlantic and Mediterranean, with a black oval mark on each side.

john·ny /ˈjänē/ ▶ n. (pl. **-nies**) informal a short gown fastened in the back, worn by hospital patients. [17th C.: nickname for the given name *John*.]

john·ny·cake /ˈjänē,kāk/ ▶ n. cornbread typically baked or fried on a griddle. [18th C.: also referred to as *journey cake*, which may be the original form.]

john·ny-come-late·ly ▶ n. informal a newcomer to or late starter at a particular place or sphere of activity.

John·ny-on-the-spot ▶ n. informal, dated a person who is at hand whenever needed.

John·ny Reb ▶ n. another term for REB[2].

John of Gaunt /gônt/ (1340–99), duke of Lancaster; son of Edward III. He was the effective ruler of England during the final years of his father's reign and during the minority of Richard II.

John of the Cross, St. (1542–91), Spanish mystic and poet; born *Juan de Yepis y Alvarez*. He cofounded the Carmelite order in 1568.

John Paul II (1920–2005), pope 1978–2005; born in Poland; born *Karol Jozef Wojtyla*. The first non-Italian pope since 1522, he traveled abroad extensively.

John Q. Pub·lic ▶ n. informal a name for a hypothetical representative member of the general public, or the general public personified.

Johns /jänz/, Jasper, Jr. (1930–), US painter and sculptor, noted for his American flag paintings. He was a key figure in the development of pop art.

John·son[1] /ˈjänsən/, Andrew (1808–75), 17th president of the US 1865–69. As vice president 1865, he succeeded to the presidency upon the assassination of President Lincoln. During his administration, Alaska was purchased from Russia. His lenient policy toward the South after the Civil War and his refusal to cooperate with Congress led him to be the first president to be impeached. He was acquitted by one vote.

John·son[2], Benj. F., see RILEY[2].

John·son[3], Earvin, Jr. (1959–), US basketball player; known as **Magic Johnson**. He played for the Los Angeles Lakers 1979–91.

John·son[4], Jack (1878–1946), US boxer. He was the first black world heavyweight champion 1908–15.

John·son[5], James Weldon (1871–1938), US writer and social activist, noted as a prominent figure in the Harlem Renaissance.

John·son[6], Lyndon Baines (1908–73), 36th president of the US 1963–69; known as **LBJ**. A Texas Democrat, he was a US senator 1949–61 and US vice president 1961–63. He succeeded to the presidency upon the assassination of President Kennedy. His domestic programs, such as those for civil rights, were labeled the Great Society. During his administration, the Vietnam War intensified.

John·son[7], Philip Courtelyou (1906–2005), US architect. His designs include Lincoln Center in New York City.

John·son[8], Samuel (1709–84), British lexicographer and writer; known as **Dr. Johnson**. He is noted particularly for his *Dictionary of the English Language* (1755). — **John·so·ni·an** /jänˈsōnēən/ adj.

John·son[9], Thomas (1732–1819), US Supreme Court associate justice 1791–93.

John·son[10], Walter Perry (1887–1946), US baseball player; known as **the Big Train**. A pitcher, he led the American League in strikeouts for 12 seasons.

John·son[11], William (1771–1834), US Supreme Court associate justice 1804–34.

John·ston /ˈjänstən/, Joseph Eggleston (1807–91), Confederate general in the American Civil War. The highest-ranking US Army officer to resign his commission for the Confederacy, he was defeated by Grant at Vicksburg and surrendered to Sherman in North Carolina two weeks after Lee's surrender at Appomattox Court House.

John·ston Atoll an atoll in the central Pacific Ocean, southwest of Hawaii, controlled by the US.

John the Bap·tist, St., Jewish preacher and prophet; a contemporary of Jesus. In *c.*AD 27 he preached and baptized on the banks of the Jordan River. He was beheaded by Herod Antipas (Matt. 14:1–12).

John the E·van·ge·list, St. (also **John the Divine**) see JOHN, ST.

John the For·tu·nate, John IV of Portugal (see JOHN[2]).

John the Great, John I of Portugal (see JOHN[2]).

Jo·hor /jəˈhôr/ (also **Jo·hore**) a state in Malaysia, at the most southern point of mainland Asia.

joie de vi·vre /,zhwä də ˈvēvrə/ ▶ n. exuberant enjoyment of life. [Fr., lit. 'joy of living.']

join /join/ ▶ v. [trans.] link; connect. ■ become linked or connected to. ■ connect (points) with a line. ■ [intrans.] unite to form one entity or group. ■ become a member or employee of. ■ take part in. ■ [intrans.] (**join up**) become a member of the armed forces. ■ come into the company of: *we were joined by Jessica's sister.* ■ support (someone) in an activity. ▶ n. a place or line where two or more things are connected or fastened together.
– PHRASES **join hands** hold each other's hands. ■ fig. work together.
— **join·a·ble** adj. [ME: from OFr. *joindre*, from L. *jungere* 'to join.']

join·er /ˈjoinər/ ▶ n. **1** a person who constructs the wooden components of a building, such as stairs, doors, and door and window frames. **2** informal a person who readily joins groups or campaigns.

join·er·y /ˈjoinərē/ ▶ n. the wooden components of a building, such as stairs, doors, and door and window frames, viewed collectively.

joint /joint/ ▶ n. **1** a point at which parts of an artificial structure are joined. ■ Geol. a break or fracture in a mass of rock, with no relative displacement of the parts. **2** a structure in the human or animal body at which two parts of the skeleton are fitted together. ■ each of the distinct sections of a body or limb between the places at which they are connected. ■ the part of a stem of a plant from which a leaf or branch grows. ■ a section of a plant stem between such parts; an internode. **3** informal an establishment of a specified kind, esp. one where people meet for eating, drinking, or entertainment. ■ (**the joint**) prison. **4** informal a marijuana cigarette. ▶ adj. [attrib.] shared, held, or made by two or more people or organizations together. ■ shared, held, or made by both houses of a bicameral legislature: *a joint session of Congress.* ■ sharing in a position, achievement, or activity. ■ Law applied or regarded together. Often contrasted with SEVERAL. ▶ v. [trans.] **1** provide or fasten (something) with joints. ■ prepare (a board) for being joined to another by planing its edge. **2** cut (the body of an animal) into joints.
– PHRASES **out of joint** (of a joint of the body) out of position; dislocated. ■ in a state of disorder or disorientation. — **joint·ly** adv. [ME: from OFr., past part. of *joindre* 'to join' (see JOIN).]

Joint Chiefs of Staff ▶ n. the chiefs of staff of the US Army and Air Force, the commandant of the US Marine Corps, and the chief of US Naval Operations.

joint·er /ˈjointər/ ▶ n. a plane used for preparing a wooden edge for fixing or joining to another. ■ a tool used for pointing masonry and brickwork.

joint-stock com·pa·ny ▶ n. Finance a company whose stock is owned jointly by the shareholders.

join·ture /ˈjoinchər/ ▶ n. Law an estate settled on a wife for the period during which she survives her husband, in lien of a dower. [ME: from OFr., from L. *junctura* (see JUNCTURE).]

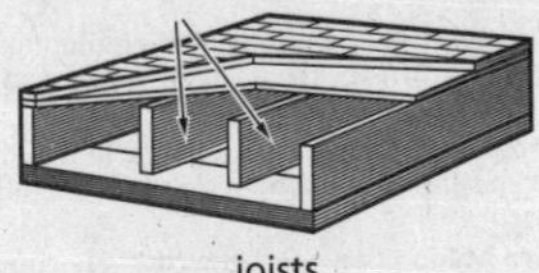

joists

joist /joist/ ▶ n. a length of timber or steel supporting part of the structure of a building, typically arranged in parallel series to support a floor or ceiling. — **joist·ed** adj. [ME *giste*, from OFr., 'beam supporting a bridge,' based on L. *jacere* 'lie down.']

jo·jo·ba /hōˈhōbə/ ▶ n. a leathery-leaved evergreen shrub (*Simmondsia chinensis*) native to the southwestern US, with seeds that produce an oil (**jojoba oil**) widely used in cosmetics [20th C.: from Mex. Sp.]

joke /jōk/ ▶ n. a thing that someone says to cause amusement or laughter, esp. a story with a funny punchline. ■ a trick played on someone for fun. ■ [in sing.] informal a person or thing that is ridiculously inadequate. ▶ v. [intrans.] make jokes; talk humorously or flippantly. ■ [trans.] archaic poke fun at: *he was pretending to joke his daughter.* — **jok·ey** (or **joky**) adj. **jok·i·ly** /-kəlē/ adv. **jok·i·ness** n. **jok·ing·ly** adv. [17th C. (orig. slang): perh. from L. *jocus* 'jest, wordplay.']

jok·er /ˈjōkər/ ▶ n. **1** a person who is fond of joking. ■ informal a foolish or inept person. **2** a playing card, typically bearing the figure of a jester, used in some games as a wild card. **3** a clause unobtrusively inserted in a bill or document and affecting its operation in a way not immediately apparent.

Jo·li·et /ˌjōlēˈet/ a city in northeastern Illinois; pop. 106,221.

Jo·liot /ˈjōlyō/, Jean-Frédéric (1900–58), French physicist. He worked with his wife Irène Joliot-Curie (1897–1956) to discover artificial radioactivity. Nobel Prize for Chemistry (1935, shared with his wife).

Jol·liet /zhôlˈye; zhōlēˈet/, Louis (1645–1700), French-Canadian explorer. With Jacques Marquette, he explored the upper Mississippi River 1673–74.

jol·li·fi·ca·tion /ˌjäləfiˈkāshən/ ▶ n. lively celebration with others; merrymaking.

jol·li·ty /ˈjälitē/ ▶ n. (pl. **-ties**) lively and cheerful activity or celebration. ■ the quality of being cheerful.

jol·ly[1] /ˈjälē/ ▶ adj. (**-li·er, -li·est**) happy and cheerful. ■ informal or dated lively and entertaining. ▶ v. (**-lies, -lied**) [trans.] informal encourage (someone) in a friendly way. ■ (**jolly someone/something up**) make someone or something more lively or cheerful. — **jol·li·ly** /ˈjälәlē/ adv. **jol·li·ness** n. [ME: from OFr. *jolif*, an earlier form of *joli* 'pretty,' perh. from ON *jól* (see YULE).]

jol·ly[2] (also **jol·ly boat**) ▶ n. (pl. **-lies**) a lapstraked ship's boat that is smaller than a cutter, typically hoisted at the stern of the ship. [18th C.: perh. rel. to YAWL.]

Jol·ly Rog·er /ˈjälē ˈräjər/ ▶ n. a pirate's flag with a white skull and crossbones on a black background. [18th C.: of unknown origin.]

Jolly Roger

Jol·son /ˈjōlsən/, Al (1886–1950), US singer; born in Russia; born *Asa Yoelson*. He appeared in the first full-length talking movie, *The Jazz Singer* (1927).

jolt /jōlt/ ▶ v. [trans.] push or shake (someone or something) abruptly and roughly. ■ fig. give a surprise or shock to (someone) in order to make them act or change: *she tried to jolt him out of his depression.* ■ [intrans.] move with sudden lurches. ▶ n. an abrupt rough or violent movement. ■ a surprise or shock, esp. of an unpleasant kind and often manifested physically. — **jolt·y** adj. [16th C.: of unknown origin.]

Jon. ▶ abbr. ■ Bible Jonah. ■ Jonathan.

Jo·nah /ˈjōnə/ (in the Bible) a Hebrew minor prophet. ■ a book of the Bible telling of Jonah.

Jon·a·than[1] /ˈjänәTHәn/ (in the Bible) a son of Saul.

Jon·a·than[2] ▶ n. a cooking apple of a red-skinned variety first grown in the US. [19th C.: named after *Jonathan* Hasbrouk (died 1846), American lawyer.]

Jones[1] /jōnz/, Bobby (1902–71), US golfer; full name *Robert Tyre Jones*. He won 13 major competitions.

Jones[2], Inigo (1573–1652), British architect. He introduced the Palladian style to Britain.

Jones[3], James (1921–77), US writer. His novels include *From Here to Eternity* (1951).

Jones[4], John Paul (1747–92), American naval officer; born *John Paul* in Scotland. He is said to have declared "I have not yet begun to fight!" after victory in a 1779 battle between the Americans and the British.

jones /jōnz/ esp. black slang ▶ n. a fixation on or compulsive desire for someone or something, typically a drug; an addiction. ▶ v. [intrans.] (**jones on/for**) have a fixation on; be addicted to. [1960s: said to come from *Jones* Alley, in Manhattan, associated with drug addicts.]

Jones·es /ˈjōnziz/ (usu. **the Joneses**) ▶ n. a person's neighbors or social equals.
– PHRASES **keep up with the Joneses** try to emulate or not be outdone by one's neighbors. [19th C.: from *Jones*, a commonly found British surname.]

Jones·town /ˈjōnzˌtoun/ a former religious settlement in Guyana, established by Reverend Jim Jones, who led 911 of his followers to a mass suicide in 1978.

Jong /ˈyôNG/, Erica Mann (1942–), US writer. Her novels include *Fear of Flying* (1973), noted for its bold treatment of female sexuality.

jon·gleur /ZHôNˈglər; ˈjäNGglər/ ▶ n. hist. an itinerant minstrel. [Fr., var. of *jougleur* 'juggler,' earlier *jogleor* 'pleasant, smiling,' from L. *joculator* 'joker.']

jon·quil /ˈjänkwəl/ ▶ n. a widely cultivated narcissus (*Narcissus jonquilla*) with clusters of small fragrant yellow flowers and cylindrical leaves, native to southern Europe and northeastern Africa. [17th C.: from Fr. *jonquille*, from Sp. *junquillo*, from L. *juncus* 'rush, reed.']

Jon·son /ˈjänsən/, Ben (1572–1637), British playwright and poet; full name *Benjamin Jonson*. With his play *Every Man in His Humour* (1598), he established his "comedy of humors." — **Jon·so·ni·an** /jänˈsōnēən/ adj.

jook /jo͝ok; jo͞ok/ ▶ n. another term for JUKE JOINT.

Jop·lin /ˈjäplən/, Scott (1868–1917), US pianist and composer. He was the first of the creators of ragtime to write down his compositions.

Jop·pa biblical name for JAFFA.

Jor·daens /ˈyôrˌdäns/, Jacob (1593–1678), Flemish painter. He is noted for his boisterous peasant scenes.

Jor·dan[1] /ˈjôrdən/ **1** a country in the Middle East. Official name HASHEMITE KINGDOM OF JORDAN. *See box.* **2** a river that flows from Syria through the Sea of Galilee into the Dead Sea. — **Jor·da·ni·an** /jôrˈdānēən/ adj. & n.

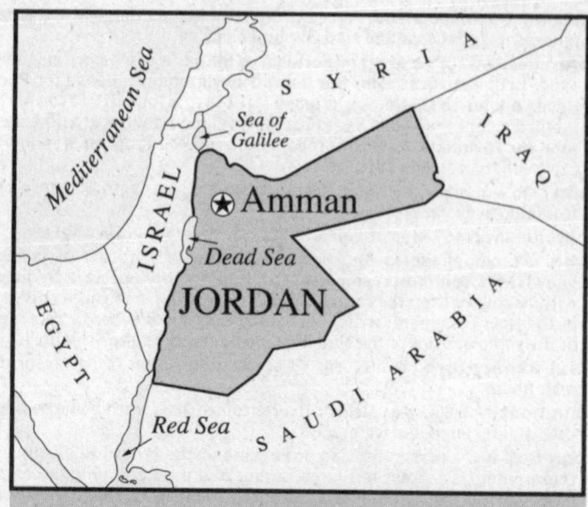

Jordan

Official name: Hashemite Kingdom of Jordan
Location: Middle East, east of the Jordan River
Area: 35,600 square miles (92,300 sq km)
Population: 5,611,000
Capital: Amman
Language: Arabic (official), English
Currency: Jordanian dinar

Jor·dan[2], Barbara Charline (1936–96), US politician. She served in the US House of Representatives 1973–79.

Jor·dan[3], Michael Jeffrey (1963–), US basketball player. During his professional career (1984–98, 2001–03), mostly with the Chicago Bulls, he set numerous records and became the most celebrated individual in basketball.

Jos. ▶ abbr. ■ Joseph. ■ Josiah. ■ Bible Joshua.

Jo·seph[1] /ˈjōzəf; -səf/ (in the Bible) a Hebrew patriarch, son of Jacob and Rachel.

Jo·seph[2] /ˈjōzəf; ˈjosəf/, Chief (c.1840–1904), Nez Percé Indian chief; Indian name **Inmuttooyahlatlat**. He defied government efforts to move his people from Oregon.

Jo·seph, St., husband of the Virgin Mary.

Jo·se·phine /ˈjōzəˌfēn; ˌjōzəˈfēn/ (1763–1814), empress of France 1804–09; full name *Marie Joséphine Rose Tascher de la Pagerie*; wife of Napoleon 1796–1809.

Jo·seph of Ar·i·ma·the·a /ˌarəməˈTHēə/ a member of the council at Jerusalem who, after the Crucifixion, asked Pilate for Jesus' body, which he buried.

Jo·seph·son junc·tion /ˈjōzəfsən; -səf-/ ▶ n. Physics an electrical device in which two superconducting metals are separated by a thin layer of insulator, across which an electric current may flow in the absence of a potential difference. The current may be made to oscillate in proportion to an applied potential difference. [1960s: named after Brian D. *Josephson* (born 1940), British physicist.]

Jo·se·phus /jōˈsēfəs/, Flavius (*c.*37–*c.*100), Jewish historian, general, and Pharisee; born *Joseph ben Matthias*. He was a leader of the Jewish revolt against the Romans in 66.

Josh. ▶ abbr. Bible Joshua.

josh /jäsH/ informal ▶ v. [trans.] tease (someone) in a playful way. ■ [intrans.] engage in joking or playful talk with others. ▶ n. good-natured banter. — **josh·er** n. [19th C. (as a v.): of unknown origin.]

Josh·u·a /ˈjäsHo͞oə/ (*fl.* *c.*13th century BC), Israelite leader who succeeded Moses. ■ the sixth book of the Bible.

Joshua tree

Josh·u·a tree ▶ n. a yucca (*Yucca brevifolia*) that grows as a tree and has clusters of spiky leaves, native to arid regions of southwestern North America.

Josh·u·a Tree National Park a national preserve in southern California, noted for its desert plant and animal life.

joss /jäs/ ▶ **n.** a Chinese religious statue or idol. [18th C.: from Javanese *dejos*, from obs. Port. *deos*, from L. *deus* 'god.']

joss house ▶ **n.** a Chinese temple.

joss stick ▶ **n.** a thin stick consisting of a substance that burns slowly and with a fragrant smell, used as incense.

jos·tle /'jäsəl/ ▶ **v.** [trans.] push, elbow, or bump against (someone) roughly, typically in a crowd. ■ [intrans.] **(jostle for)** struggle or compete forcefully for. ▶ **n.** the action of jostling. [ME *justle*, from *just*, an earlier form of JOUST.]

jot /jät/ ▶ **v.** **(jot·ted, jot·ting)** [trans.] write (something) quickly: *when you've found the answers, jot them down.* ▶ **n.** [usu. with negative] a very small amount: *you didn't care a jot.* [15th C.: via L. from Gk. *iōta* (see IOTA).]

jo·ta /'hōtə/ ▶ **n.** a folk dance from northern Spain, danced in couples in fast triple time.

jot·ting /'jätiNG/ ▶ **n.** (usu. **jottings**) a brief note.

Jo·tun /'yôto͝on/ ▶ **n.** Scand. Mythol. a member of the race of giants, enemies of the gods. [from ON *jǫtunn*, rel. to OE *eoten*, of Gmc. origin.]

jou·al /zHo͞o'al; -'äl/ ▶ **n.** a nonstandard form of popular Canadian French, influenced by English vocabulary and grammar. [Canad. Fr. dial., from Fr. *cheval* 'horse.']

Joule /jo͞ol/, James Prescott (1818–89), British physicist. He established that all forms of energy are basically the same and interchangeable—the first law of thermodynamics.

joule /jo͞ol; joul/ (abbr.: **J**) ▶ **n.** the SI unit of work or energy, equal to the work done by a force of one newton when its point of application moves one meter in the direction of action of the force, equivalent to one 3600th of a watt-hour. [19th C.: named after J. P. JOULE.]

jounce /jouns/ ▶ **v.** jolt or bounce. [ME: prob. symbolic; cf. BOUNCE.]

jour. ▶ **abbr.** ■ journal. ■ journeyman.

jour·nal /'jərnl/ ▶ **n.** **1** a newspaper or magazine that deals with a particular subject or professional activity. **2** a daily record of news and events of a personal nature; a diary. ■ (in bookkeeping) a daily record of business transactions with a statement of the accounts to which each is to be debited and credited. **3** Mech. the part of a shaft or axle that rests on bearings. [ME: from OFr. *jurnal*, from late L. *diurnalis* (see DIURNAL).]

jour·nal box ▶ **n.** Mech. a box that houses a journal and its bearing.

jour·nal·ese /,jərnl'ēz/ ▶ **n.** informal a hackneyed style of writing supposedly characteristic of newspapers and magazines.

jour·nal·ism /'jərnl,izəm/ ▶ **n.** the activity or profession of writing for newspapers or magazines or of broadcasting news on radio or television. ■ the product of such activity.

jour·nal·ist /'jərnl-ist/ ▶ **n.** a person who writes for newspapers or magazines or prepares news to be broadcast on radio or television. — **jour·nal·is·tic** /,jərnl'istik/ **adj.** **jour·nal·is·ti·cal·ly** /,jərnl'istik(ə)lē/ **adv.**

jour·nal·ize /'jərnl,īz/ ▶ **v.** [trans.] dated enter (notes or information) in a journal or account book.

jour·ney /'jərnē/ ▶ **n.** (pl. **-neys**) an act of traveling from one place to another. ▶ **v.** **(-neys, -neyed)** [intrans.] travel somewhere. — **jour·ney·er n.** [ME: from OFr. *jornee* 'day,' based on L. *diurnum* 'daily portion,' from *diurnus* (see DIURNAL).]

jour·ney·man /'jərnēmən/ ▶ **n.** (pl. **-men**) a trained worker who is employed by someone else. ■ a worker or sports player who is reliable but not outstanding.

joust /joust/ ▶ **v.** [intrans.] [often as n.] **(jousting)** hist. (of a medieval knight) engage in a sports contest in which two opponents on horseback fight with lances. ■ fig. compete closely for superiority. ▶ **n.** a medieval sports contest in which two opponents on horseback fought with lances. — **joust·er n.** [ME: from OFr. *jouster* 'bring together,' based on L. *juxta* 'near.']

Jove /jōv/ another name for JUPITER.

– PHRASES **by Jove** dated an exclamation indicating surprise or used for emphasis. [from Latin *Jov-*, stem of Old L. *Jovis*.]

jo·vi·al /'jōvēəl/ ▶ **adj.** cheerful and friendly. — **jo·vi·al·i·ty** /,jōvē'alitē/ **n.** **jo·vi·al·ly adv.** [16th C.: from Fr., from late L. *jovialis* 'of Jupiter' (see JOVE).]

Jo·vi·an /'jōvēən/ ▶ **adj.** **1** (in Roman mythology) of or like the god Jove (or Jupiter). **2** of or relating to the planet Jupiter or the class of giant planets to which Jupiter belongs.

jowl /joul/ ▶ **n.** (often **jowls**) the lower part of a person's or animal's cheek, esp. when it is fleshy or drooping. ■ the cheek of a pig used as meat. ■ the loose fleshy part of the neck of certain animals, such as the dewlap of cattle or the wattle of birds. — **jowled adj.** [in comb.] *ruddy-jowled.* **jowl·y adj.** [OE *ceole* (related to Ger. *Kehle* 'throat, gullet'), partly merged with OE *ceafl* 'jaw' (rel. to Du. *kevels* 'cheekbones').]

joy /joi/ ▶ **n.** a feeling of great pleasure and happiness. ■ a thing that causes joy. [ME: from OFr. *joie*, based on L. *gaudium*, from *gaudere* 'rejoice.']

Joyce /jois/, James Augustine Aloysius (1882–1941), Irish writer. His novel *Ulysses* (1922) revolutionized the structure of the modern novel and developed the stream-of-consciousness technique. — **Joyc·e·an** /'joisēən/ **adj. & n.**

joy·ful /'joifəl/ ▶ **adj.** feeling, expressing, or causing great pleasure and happiness. — **joy·ful·ly adv.** **joy·ful·ness n.**

joy·ous /'joiəs/ ▶ **adj.** esp. literary full of happiness and joy. — **joy·ous·ly adv.** **joy·ous·ness n.**

joy·pad /'joi,pad/ ▶ **n.** an input device for a computer games console which uses buttons to control the motion of an image on the screen. [20th C.: blend of JOYSTICK and KEYPAD.]

joy·ride /'joi,rīd/ ▶ **n.** informal a fast and dangerous ride, esp. one taken in a stolen vehicle: *kids stealing cars for a Saturday night joyride.* ▶ **v.** go for a joyride. — **joy·rid·er** /-,rīdər/ **n.** **joy·rid·ing n.**

joy·stick /'joi,stik/ ▶ **n.** informal the control column of an aircraft. ■ a lever that can be moved in several directions to control the movement of an image on a computer or similar display screen.

JP ▶ **abbr.** Justice of the Peace.

JPEG /'jā,peg/ ▶ **n.** Comput. a format for compressing images. [1990s: abbrev. of *Joint Photographic Experts Group*.]

Jr. ▶ **abbr.** junior (in names): *John Smith, Jr.*

JSD ▶ **abbr.** Doctor of the Science of Law (Doctor of Juristic Science).

Juan Car·los /'(h)wän 'kärlōs/ (1938–), king of Spain 1975– ; full name *Juan Carlos Victor María de Borbón y Borbón*; grandson of Alfonso XIII. His reign has seen Spain's increasing liberalization.

Juan de Fu·ca Strait /'(h)wän də 'fyo͞okə/ a strait between northwestern Washington and Vancouver Island, British Columbia.

Juan Fer·nan·dez Is·lands /'(h)wän fər'nandəs/ a group of three almost uninhabited islands in the Pacific Ocean, 400 miles (640 km) west of Chile.

Juá·rez /(h)wä'rez; '(h)wärəs/, Benito Pablo (1806–72), president of Mexico 1861–64, 1867–72.

Ju·ba /'jo͞obə/ the capital of the southern region of Sudan; pop. 100,000.

ju·ba /'jo͞obə/ ▶ **n.** a dance originating among plantation slaves in the southern US, featuring rhythmic handclapping and slapping of the thighs. [19th C.: of unknown origin.]

Jub·ba /'jo͞obə/ a river in East Africa that rises in central Ethiopia and flows south through Somalia to the Indian Ocean.

ju·bi·lant /'jo͞obələnt/ ▶ **adj.** feeling or expressing great happiness and triumph. — **ju·bi·lance n.** **ju·bi·lant·ly adv.** [17th C.: from L. *jubilant-* 'calling, hallooing,' from the v. *jubilare*.]

Ju·bi·la·te /,jo͞obə'lātē; ,yo͞obə'lätā/ ▶ **n.** [in sing.] Psalm 100 (99 in the Vulgate), esp. as used as a canticle in the Anglican service of matins. ■ a musical setting of this. [L., 'shout for joy!,' imper. of *jubilare*.]

ju·bi·la·tion /,jo͞obə'lāsHən/ ▶ **n.** a feeling of great happiness and triumph.

ju·bi·lee /'jo͞obə,lē; ,jo͞obə'lē/ ▶ **n.** a special anniversary of an event, esp. one celebrating twenty-five or fifty years of a reign or activity. ■ Judaism (in Jewish history) a year of emancipation and restoration, celebrated every fifty years. ■ (in full **Jubilee Year**) a period of remission from the penal consequences of sin, granted by the Roman Catholic Church under certain conditions for a year, usually at intervals of twenty-five years. ▶ **adj.** [postpositive] (of desserts) flambé. [ME: from OFr. *jubile*, based on Heb. *yōḇēl*, orig. 'ram's-horn trumpet.']

Jud. ▶ **abbr.** Bible ■ Judges. ■ Judith.

Ju·dae·a /jo͞o'dēə; -'dāə/ the southern part of ancient Palestine. — **Ju·dae·an adj.**

Judaeo- ▶ **comb. form** esp. Brit. alternate spelling of JUDEO-.

Ju·dah /'jo͞odə/ **1** (in the Bible) a Hebrew patriarch, the fourth son of Jacob and Leah. ■ the tribe of Israel traditionally descended from him, the most powerful of the twelve tribes of Israel. **2** the southern part of ancient Palestine, occupied by the tribe of Judah. Later known as JUDAEA.

Ju·da·ic /jo͞o'dāik/ ▶ **adj.** of or relating to Judaism or the ancient Jews. [17th C.: from L. *Judaicus*, from Gk. *Ioudaïkos*, from *Ioudaios* (see JEW).]

Ju·da·ism /'jo͞odē,izəm; -dā-/ ▶ **n.** the monotheistic religion of the Jews, based on the laws revealed to Moses and recorded in the Torah (supplemented by the rabbinical Talmud). ■ the Jews collectively.

Ju·da·ize /'jo͞odē,īz; -dā-/ ▶ **v.** [trans.] make Jewish; convert to Judaism. ■ [intrans.] follow Jewish customs or religious rites. — **Ju·da·i·za·tion** /,jo͞odē-i'zāsHən; -dā-/ **n.** **Ju·da·iz·er n.**

Ju·das[1] /'jo͞odəs/ one of the 12 Apostles; full name *Judas Iscariot*. He betrayed Jesus to the Jewish authorities in return for thirty pieces of silver. ■ [as n.] (usu. **a Judas**) a person who betrays a friend or comrade.

Ju·das[2] see JUDE, ST.

ju·das /'jo͞odəs/ (also **judas hole**) ▶ **n.** a peephole in a door. [19th C.: from *Judas* Iscariot.]

Ju·das kiss ▶ **n.** an act of betrayal, esp. one disguised as a gesture of friendship.

Ju·das Mac·ca·bae·us /,makə'bēəs/ (died *c.*161 BC), Jewish leader. The leader of a Jewish revolt in Judaea against Antiochus IV Epiphanes, he recovered Jerusalem and rededicated the Temple.

Ju·das tree ▶ **n.** a Mediterranean tree (*Cercis siliquastrum*) of the pea family, with purple flowers that typically appear before the rounded leaves. [17th C.: from the belief that Judas Iscariot hanged himself on this kind of tree.]

jud·der /'jədər/ ▶ **v.** [intrans.] esp. Brit. (esp. of something mechanical) shake and vibrate rapidly and with force. ▶ **n.** an instance of rapid and forceful shaking and vibration. — **jud·der·y** adj. [1930s: imitative; cf. SHUDDER.]

Jude, St. /jōōd/, one of the 12 Apostles; supposedly the brother of James; also known as **Judas.** ■ the last epistle of the New Testament, ascribed to St. Jude.

Judeo- (also esp. Brit. **Judaeo-**) ▶ comb. form Jewish; Jewish and ...: *Judeo-Christian.* ■ relating to Judaea. [from L. *Judaeus* 'Jewish.']

Ju·dez·mo /jōō'dezmō/ ▶ n. another term for LADINO.

Judg. ▶ abbr. Bible Judges.

judge /jəj/ ▶ n. a public official appointed to decide cases in a court of law. ■ a person who decides the results of a competition. ■ an official at a sports contest who watches for infractions of the rules. ■ a person able or qualified to give an opinion on something. ■ a leader having temporary authority in ancient Israel in the period between Joshua and the kings. See also JUDGES. ▶ v. [trans.] form an opinion or conclusion about. ■ decide (a case) in a court of law. ■ [trans. and complement] give a verdict on (someone) in a court of law. ■ decide the results of (a competition). — **judge·ship** n. [ME: from OFr. *juge* (n.), *juger* (v.), from L. *judex, judic-*, from *jus* 'law' + *dicere* 'to say.']

judge ad·vo·cate ▶ n. Law a lawyer who advises a court-martial on points of law and sums up the case.

judge ad·vo·cate gen·er·al ▶ n. an officer in supreme control of the courts-martial of one of the armed forces.

judge-made ▶ adj. Law constituted by judicial decisions rather than explicit legislation.

judge·ment ▶ n. var. of JUDGMENT.

judge·men·tal ▶ adj. var. of JUDGMENTAL.

Judg·es /'jəjiz/ the seventh book of the Bible, describing the conquest of Canaan under the leaders called "judges" in an account that is parallel to that of the Book of Joshua.

judg·ment /'jəjmənt/ (also **judge·ment**) ▶ n. **1** the ability to make considered decisions or come to sensible conclusions. ■ an opinion or conclusion. ■ a decision of a law court or judge. ■ a monetary or other obligation awarded by a court. ■ the document recording this obligation. ■ short for LAST JUDGMENT. **2** formal humorous a misfortune or calamity viewed as a divine punishment.

judg·men·tal /jəj'mentl/ (also **judge·men·tal**) ▶ adj. of or concerning the use of judgment. ■ having or displaying an excessively critical point of view. — **judg·men·tal·ly** adv.

Judg·ment Day ▶ n. the time of the Last Judgment; the end of the world.

ju·di·ca·ture /'jōōdikə,CHŏŏr; -,kāCHər/ ▶ n. the administration of justice. ■ (**the judicature**) judges collectively; the judiciary. — **ju·di·ca·to·ry** /-kə,tôrē/ adj. [16th C.: from med. L. *judicatura*, from L. *judicare* 'to judge.']

ju·di·cial /jōō'disHəl/ ▶ adj. of, by, or appropriate to a court or judge. — **ju·di·cial·ly** adv. [ME: from L. *judicialis*, from *judicium* 'judgment,' from *judex* (see JUDGE).]

ju·di·cial re·view ▶ n. (in the US) review by the Supreme Court of the constitutional validity of a legislative act.

ju·di·ci·ar·y /jōō'disHē,erē; -'disHərē/ ▶ n. (pl. **-ar·ies**) (usu. **the judiciary**) the judicial authorities of a country; judges collectively.

ju·di·cious /jōō'disHəs/ ▶ adj. having, showing, or done with good judgment or sense. — **ju·di·cious·ly** adv. **ju·di·cious·ness** n.

Ju·dith /'jōōdəTH/ (in the Apocrypha) a rich Israelite widow who saved the town of Bethulia from Nebuchadnezzar's army. ■ a book of the Apocrypha recounting the story of Judith.

ju·do /'jōōdō/ ▶ n. a sport of unarmed combat derived from jujitsu and intended to train the body and mind. [19th C.: Japanese, from *jū* 'gentle' + *dō* 'way.']

ju·do·ka /'jōōdō,kä; ,jōōdō'kä/ ▶ n. a person who practices or is an expert in judo. [Japanese, from JUDO + *-ka* 'person, profession.']

Ju·dy /'jōōdē/ ▶ n. (pl. **-dies**) the wife of Punch in the Punch and Judy show. [19th C.: nickname for the given name *Judith.*]

jug /jəg/ ▶ n. **1** a large container for liquids, with a narrow mouth and typically a stopper or cap. ■ the contents of such a container. **2** (**the jug**) informal prison. **3** (**jugs**) vulgar slang a woman's breasts. ▶ v. (**jugged, jug·ging**) [trans.] **1** [usu. as adj.] (**jugged**) stew or boil (a hare or rabbit) in a covered container. **2** informal prosecute and imprison (someone). — **jug·ful** /-,fōōl/ n. (pl. **-fuls**). [16th C.: perh. from *Jug*, nickname for the given names *Joan, Joanna*, and *Jenny.*]

ju·gal /'jōōgəl/ ▶ adj. **1** Anat. of or relating to the zygoma (the bony arch of the cheek). **2** Entomol. of or relating to the jugum of an insect's forewing. [16th C.: from L. *jugalis*, from *jugum* 'yoke.']

jug band ▶ n. a group of jazz, blues, or folk musicians using simple or improvised instruments such as jugs and washboards.

Jug·ger·naut /'jəgər,nôt/ Hinduism the form of Krishna worshiped in Puri, Orissa, where in the annual festival his image is dragged through the streets on a heavy chariot. Also called JAGANNATHA. [via Hindi from Sanskrit *Jagannātha* 'Lord of the world.']

jug·ger·naut /'jəgər,nôt/ ▶ n. a huge, powerful, and overwhelming force or institution. [19th C.: extension of JUGGERNAUT.]

jug·gle /'jəgəl/ ▶ v. [trans.] continuously toss into the air and catch (a number of objects) so as to keep at least one in the air while handling the others, typically for the entertainment of others. ■ cope with by adroitly balancing. ■ misrepresent (something) so as to deceive or cheat someone. ▶ n. [in sing.] an act of juggling. — **jug·gler** /'jəg(ə)lər/ n. **jug·gler·y** /'jəglərē/ n. [ME: back-form. from *juggler*, or from OFr. *jogler*, from L. *joculari* 'to jest,' from *joculus*, dimin. of *jocus* 'jest.']

jug·u·lar /'jəgyələr/ ▶ adj. **1** of the neck or throat. **2** Zool. (of fish's pelvic fins) located in front of the pectoral fins. ▶ n. short for JUGULAR VEIN.
– PHRASES **go for the jugular** be aggressive or unrestrained in making an attack. [16th C.: from late L. *jugularis*, from L. *jugulum* 'collarbone, throat,' dimin. of *jugum* 'yoke.']

jug·u·lar vein ▶ n. any of several large veins in the neck, carrying blood from the head and face.

Ju·gur·tha /jōō'gərTHə/ (died 104 BC), joint king of Numidia c.118–104. — **Ju·gur·thine** /-'gərTHən/ adj.

juice /jōōs/ ▶ n. the liquid obtained from or present in fruit or vegetables. ■ a drink made from such a liquid. ■ (**juices**) fluid secreted by the body, esp. in the stomach to help digest food. ■ (**juices**) the liquid that comes from meat or other food when cooked. ■ informal electrical energy. ■ informal gasoline. ■ informal alcoholic drink. ■ (**juices**) a person's vitality or creative faculties. ▶ v. [trans.] **1** extract the juice from (fruit or vegetables). **2** (**juice something up**) informal liven something up. **3** [as adj.] (**juiced**) informal drunk. [ME: via OFr. from L. *jus* 'broth, vegetable juice.']

juic·er /'jōōsər/ ▶ n. **1** an appliance for extracting juice from fruit and vegetables. **2** informal a person who drinks alcoholic beverages excessively.

juic·y /'jōōsē/ ▶ adj. (**juic·i·er, juic·i·est**) (of food) full of juice; succulent. ■ informal interestingly scandalous. ■ informal temptingly appealing. — **juic·i·ly** /-səlē/ adv. **juic·i·ness** n.

Juil·li·ard /'jōōlē,ärd/, Augustus D. (1840–1919), US merchant. He founded the Juilliard Musical Foundation in 1920. It became the Juilliard School of Music in 1926.

ju·jit·su /,jōō'jitsōō/ (also **jiu·jit·su** or **ju·jut·su** /,jōō'jət-/) ▶ n. a Japanese system of unarmed combat and physical training. Compare with JUDO. [Japanese *jūjutsu*, from *jū* 'gentle' + *jutsu* 'skill.']

ju·ju[1] /'jōō,jōō/ ▶ n. a style of music popular among the Yoruba in Nigeria and characterized by the use of guitars and variable-pitch drums. [perh. from Yoruba *jo jo* 'dance.']

ju·ju[2] ▶ n. a charm or fetish, esp. of a type used by some West African peoples. ■ supernatural power attributed to such a charm or fetish. [17th C.: of West African origin; compare Bantu *njiu* 'danger.']

ju·jube /'jōō,jōōb/ ▶ n. **1** the edible berrylike fruit of a Eurasian plant, formerly taken as a cough cure. ■ (**also**) a jujube-flavored lozenge or gumdrop. **2** (also **jujube bush**) the shrub or small tree (*Ziziphus jujuba*) of the buckthorn family that produces this fruit. [from Fr., or from med. L. *jujuba*, based on Gk. *zizuphos.*]

juke·box /'jōōk,bäks/ ▶ n. a machine that automatically plays a selected musical recording when a coin is inserted. ■ Comput. a device that stores several computer disks in such a way that data can be read from any of them. [1930s: of West African origin; compare Wolof *dzug* 'to misbehave.']

juke joint ▶ n. a bar featuring music on a jukebox and typically having an area for dancing.

Jul. ▶ abbr. July.

ju·lep /'jōōləp/ ▶ n. a sweet flavored drink made from a sugar syrup, sometimes containing alcohol or medication. ■ short for MINT JULEP. [ME: from OFr., from med. L. *julapium*, via Arab. from Pers. *gulāb*, from *gul* 'rose' + *āb* 'water.']

Jul·ian[1] /'jōōlyən; -lēən/ ▶ adj. of or associated with Julius Caesar.

Jul·ian[2] (c.AD 331–363), Roman emperor 360–363; full name *Flavius Claudius Julianus*; nephew of Constantine; known as **the Apostate**.

Ju·lian Alps an Alpine range in western Slovenia and northeastern Italy.

Jul·ian cal·en·dar ▶ n. a calendar introduced by the authority of Julius Caesar in 46 BC, in which the year consisted of 365 days, every fourth year having 366 days. It was superseded by the Gregorian calendar though it is still used by some Orthodox Churches. Dates in the Julian calendar are sometimes designated "Old Style."

Jul·ian of Nor·wich (c.1342–c.1413), English mystic. She described her visions in *Revelations of Divine Love* (c.1393).

ju·li·enne /,jōōlē'en/ ▶ n. a portion of food cut into short, thin strips. ▶ v. [trans.] cut (food) into short, thin strips. [18th C.: Fr., from the male given names *Jules* or *Julien.*]

Ju·li·et /,jōōlē'et; 'jōōlyət/ ▶ n. a code word representing the letter J, used in radio communication.

Ju·li·et cap ▶ n. a type of women's small ornamental cap, typically made of lace or net and often worn by brides. [20th C.: after the heroine of Shakespeare's *Romeo and Juliet.*]

Jul·ius Cae·sar /'jōōlyəs/ see CAESAR[2].

Ju·ly /jōō'lī/ ▶ n. (pl. **Ju·lys**) the seventh month of the year, in the northern hemisphere usually considered the second month of summer. [ME: from L. *Julius (mensis)* '(month) of July,' named after Julius Caesar.]

ju·mar /'jōōmər; -,mär/ Climbing ▶ n. a clamp that is attached to a fixed rope and automatically tightens when weight is applied and relaxes when it is removed. ▶ v. (**-mared, -mar·ing**) [intrans.] climb with the aid of such a clamp. [1960s: orig. in Swiss use, of unknown origin.]

jum·bie /'jəmbē/ ▶ n. W. Indian a spirit of a dead person, typically an evil one. [from Kikongo *zumbi* 'fetish.']

jum·ble /'jəmbəl/ ▶ n. an untidy collection or pile of things. ▶ v. [trans.] mix up in a confused or untidy way. [16th C.: prob. symbolic.]

jum·bo /'jəmbō/ informal ▶ n. (pl. **-bos**) a very large person or thing. ■ (also **jum·bo jet**) a very large airliner (originally and specifically a Boeing

747). ▶ **adj.** [attrib.] very large. [19th C.: prob. the second element of MUMBO-JUMBO.]

Jum·na /ˈjəmnə/ a river in northern India that rises in the Himalayas and flows through Delhi, before joining the Ganges River below Allahabad. Hindi name YAMUNA.

jump /jəmp/ ▶ **v. 1** [intrans.] push oneself off a surface and into the air by using the muscles in one's legs and feet. ■ [trans.] pass over (an obstacle or barrier) in such a way. ■ [with adverbial] (of an athlete or horse) perform in a competition involving such action: *his horse jumped well and won by five lengths.* ■ (esp. of prices or figures) rise suddenly and by a large amount. ■ informal (of a place) be full of lively activity. ■ [trans.] get on or off (a train or other vehicle) quickly, typically illegally or dangerously. **2** [intrans.] (of a person) move suddenly and quickly in a specified way. ■ (of a person) make a sudden involuntary movement in reaction to something that causes surprise or shock. ■ pass quickly or abruptly from one idea, subject, or state to another. ■ [trans.] omit or skip over (part of something) and pass on to a further point or stage. ■ (of a machine or device) move or jerk suddenly and abruptly. ■ (of a person) make a sudden, impulsive rush to do something. ■ [trans.] (in checkers) capture (an opponent's piece) by jumping over it. ■ Bridge make a bid that is higher than necessary, in order to signal a strong hand. ■ [trans.] informal attack (someone) suddenly and unexpectedly. ■ vulgar slang have sexual intercourse with (someone). **3** [trans.] informal start (a vehicle) using jumper cables. ▶ **n. 1** an act of jumping from a surface by pushing upward with one's legs and feet. ■ an obstacle to be jumped, esp. by a horse and rider in an equestrian competition. ■ an act of descending from an aircraft by parachute. ■ a sudden dramatic rise in amount, price, or value. ■ a large or sudden transition or change. ■ (in checkers) the act of capturing an opponent's piece by jumping over it. ■ Bridge a bid that is higher than necessary, signaling strength. **2** a sudden involuntary movement caused by shock or surprise. ■ (**the jumps**) informal extreme nervousness or anxiety.

– PHRASES **get** (or **have**) **the jump on someone** informal get (or have) an advantage over someone as a result of one's prompt action. **jump bail** see BAIL[1]. **jump someone's bones** vulgar slang have sexual intercourse with someone. **jump down someone's throat** informal respond to what someone has said in a sudden and angrily critical way. **jump the gun** see GUN. **jump on the bandwagon** see BANDWAGON. **jump out of one's skin** informal be extremely startled. **jump the track** (of a train) become derailed. **jump ship** (of a sailor) leave the ship on which one is serving without having obtained permission to do so: *he jumped ship in Cape Town* | fig. *the producers jumped ship after the show's debut.* **jump through hoops** go through an elaborate or complicated procedure in order to achieve an objective. **jump** (or **leap**) **to conclusions** (or **the conclusion**) form an opinion hastily, before one has learned or considered all the facts.

– PHRASAL VERBS **jump at** accept (an opportunity or offer) eagerly. **jump off** (of a military campaign) begin. **jump on** informal attack or take hold of (someone) suddenly. ■ criticize (someone) suddenly and severely. ■ seize on (something) eagerly; give sudden (typically critical) attention to. **jump out** have a strong visual or mental impact; be very striking. [16th C.: prob. imitative.]

jump ball ▶ **n.** Basketball a ball put in play by the referee, who throws it up between two opposing players.

jump blues ▶ **n.** a style of popular music combining elements of swing and blues.

jump cut ▶ **n.** (in film or television) an abrupt transition from one scene to another. ▶ **v.** (**jump-cut**) [intrans.] make such a transition.

jump·er[1] /ˈjəmpər/ ▶ **n. 1** a collarless sleeveless dress, typically worn over a blouse. **2** hist. a loose outer jacket worn by sailors. [19th C.: prob. from dial. *jump* 'short coat,' perh. from Scots *jupe* 'a loose jacket or tunic,' via OFr. from Arab. *jubba*.]

jump·er[2] ▶ **n. 1** a person or animal that jumps. **2** (also **jumper wire**) a short wire used to complete an electric circuit or bypass a break in a circuit. **3** Basketball another term for JUMP SHOT. **4** Naut. a rope made fast to keep a yard or mast from jumping. **5** a heavy chisel-ended steel bar for drilling blast holes.

jump·er ca·ble ▶ **n.** each of a pair of electric cables with clips at each end, used for starting a vehicle by connecting its dead battery to the battery of another vehicle.

jump·ing bean ▶ **n.** the seed from certain plants of the spurge family (esp. *Sebastiana pavoniana*) that jumps as a result of the movement of a moth larva that is developing inside it.

jump·ing gene ▶ **n.** informal term for TRANSPOSON.

jump·ing jack ▶ **n. 1** a calisthenic jump done from a standing position with legs together and arms at the sides to a position with the legs apart and the arms over the head. **2** a toy figure of a man, with movable limbs.

jump·ing Je·hosh·a·phat ▶ exclam. see JEHOSHAPHAT.

jump·ing mouse ▶ **n.** a mouselike rodent (family Zapodidae) that has long back feet and typically moves in short hops, found in North America and China.

jump·ing-off place (also **jump·ing-off point**) ▶ **n.** the point from which something is begun.

jump·ing spi·der ▶ **n.** a small spider (family Salticidae) that does not build a web, but hunts prey by stalking and pouncing on it.

jump jet ▶ **n.** a jet aircraft that can take off and land vertically, without need of a runway.

jump-off ▶ **n.** a deciding round in a show-jumping competition.

jump ring ▶ **n.** a wire ring made by bringing the two ends together without soldering or welding.

jump rope (also **jump·rope**) ▶ **n.** a length of rope used for jumping by swinging it over the head and under the feet.

jump seat ▶ **n.** an extra seat, esp. in a car or taxicab, that folds back when not in use.

jump shot ▶ **n.** Basketball a shot made while jumping. — **jump shoot·er n.**

jump-start ▶ **v.** [trans.] start (a car with a dead battery) with jumper cables or by a sudden release of the clutch while it is being pushed. ■ fig. give an added impetus to (something that is proceeding slowly or is at a standstill). ▶ **n.** an act of starting a car in such a way. ■ fig. an added impetus.

jump·suit /ˈjəm(p),so͞ot/ ▶ **n.** a garment incorporating trousers and a sleeved top in one piece.

jump·y /ˈjəmpē/ ▶ **adj.** (**jump·i·er, jump·i·est**) informal (of a person) anxious and uneasy. ■ characterized by abrupt stops and starts or an irregular course. — **jump·i·ly** /-pəlē/ **adv. jump·i·ness n.**

Jun. ▶ **abbr.** ■ June. ■ Junior (in names): *John Smith, Jun.*

jun /CHən/ ▶ **n.** (pl. same) a monetary unit of North Korea, equal to one hundredth of a won.

junc. (also **Junc.**) ▶ **abbr.** Junction.

jun·co /ˈjəNGkō/ ▶ **n.** (pl. **-cos**) a North American songbird (genus *Junco*) related to the buntings, with mainly gray and brown plumage. See also SNOWBIRD. [18th C.: from Sp., from L. *juncus* 'rush, reed.']

junc·tion /ˈjəNGkSHən/ ▶ **n. 1** a point where two or more things are joined. ■ a place where two or more roads or railroad lines meet. **2** Electron. a region of transition in a semiconductor between a part where conduction is mainly by electrons and a part where it is mainly by holes. **3** the action or fact of joining or being joined. — **junc·tion·al** /-SHənl/ **adj.** [18th C. (sense 3): from L. *junctio(n-)*, from *jungere* 'to join.']

junc·ture /ˈjəNGkCHər/ ▶ **n.** a particular point in events or time. ■ a place where things join. ■ Phonet. the set of features in speech that enable a hearer to detect a word or phrase boundary, e.g., distinguishing *I scream* from *ice cream*.

June /jo͞on/ ▶ **n.** the sixth month of the year, in the northern hemisphere usually considered the first month of summer. [ME: from OFr. *juin*, from L. *Junius (mensis)* '(month) of June,' var. of *Junonius* 'sacred to Juno.']

Ju·neau /ˈjo͞onō/ the capital of Alaska, a seaport on the Pacific Ocean, in the southern part of the state; pop. 30,711.

june·ber·ry /ˈjo͞on,berē/ (also **June·ber·ry**) ▶ **n.** (pl. **-ries**) a North American shrub (genus *Amelanchier*) of the rose family, some kinds of which are grown for their showy white flowers. Also called **serviceberry**. ■ the black edible berry of this plant.

June bug (also **June beetle**) ▶ **n.** a large brown scarab beetle (genus *Phyllophaga*) that appears in late spring and early summer. Several species include the **northern June bug** (*P. fusca*). Also called MAY BEETLE.

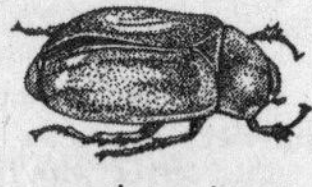
northern June bug

Jung /yo͝oNG/, Carl Gustav (1875–1961), Swiss psychologist. He originated the concept of introvert and extrovert personality. — **Jung·i·an** /ˈyo͝oNGgēən/ **adj. & n.**

jun·gle /ˈjəNGgəl/ ▶ **n. 1** an area of land overgrown with dense forest and tangled vegetation, typically in the tropics. ■ a wild tangled mass of vegetation or other things. ■ a situation or place of bewildering complexity or brutal competitiveness. ■ (also **hobo jungle**) informal a hobo camp. **2** (also **jungle music**) a style of dance music incorporating elements of ragga, hip-hop, and hard core and consisting almost exclusively of very fast electronic drum tracks and slower synthesized bass lines, originating in Britain in the early 1990s. Compare with DRUM AND BASS.

– PHRASES **the law of the jungle** the principle that those who are strong and apply ruthless self-interest will be most successful. — **jun·gled adj. jun·gly adj.** [18th C.: via Hindi from Sanskrit *jāṅgala* 'rough and arid (terrain).']

jun·gle cat ▶ **n.** a small wildcat (*Felis chaus*) that has a yellowish or grayish coat with dark markings on the legs and tail, found in small numbers from Egypt to Southeast Asia.

jun·gle fe·ver ▶ **n.** a severe form of malaria.

jun·gle fowl ▶ **n.** (pl. same) a southern Asian game bird (genus *Gallus*, family Phasianidae) related to the domestic fowl. Four species include the **red jungle fowl** (*G. gallus*), the ancestor of the domestic fowl.

jun·gle gym ▶ **n.** a structure of joined bars or logs for children to climb on.

jun·glist ▶ **n.** a performer or enthusiast of jungle music. ▶ **adj.** of or relating to jungle music.

jun·ior /ˈjo͞onyər/ ▶ **adj. 1** of, for, or denoting young or younger people: *junior tennis.* ■ of or for students in the third year of a course lasting four years in college or high school. ■ (often **Junior**) [postpositive] [in names] denoting the younger of two who have the same name in a family, esp. a son as distinct from his father. **2** low or lower in rank or status. ▶ **n. 1** a person who is a specified number of years younger than someone else. ■ a student in the third year of college or high school. ■ (in sports) a young competitor, typically under sixteen or eighteen.

■ informal used as a nickname or form of address for one's son. **2** a person with low rank or status compared with others. **3** a size of clothing for young teenagers or slender women. — **jun·ior·i·ty** /jo͞on'yôritē; -'yär-/ **n.** [ME: from L., compar. of *juvenis* 'young.']

jun·ior col·lege ▶ **n.** a college offering courses for two years beyond high school, as a complete training or in preparation for completion at a four-year college.

jun·ior high school ▶ **n.** another term for MIDDLE SCHOOL.

jun·ior light·weight ▶ **n.** a weight in professional boxing of 125 to 130 pounds (57.1 to 59 kg). ■ a professional boxer of this weight.

jun·ior mid·dle·weight ▶ **n.** a weight in professional boxing of 146 to 154 pounds (66.7 to 69.8 kg). ■ a professional boxer of this weight.

jun·ior wel·ter·weight ▶ **n.** a weight in professional boxing of 135 to 140 pounds (61.2 to 63.5 kg). ■ a professional boxer of this weight.

ju·ni·per /'jo͞onəpər/ ▶ **n.** an evergreen shrub or tree (genus *Juniperus*) of the cypress family that bears aromatic berrylike cones, widely distributed throughout Eurasia and North America. Many species include the **common juniper** (*J. communis*), used for flavoring gin. [ME: from L. *juniperus*.]

junk[1] /jəNGk/ ▶ **n. 1** informal old or discarded articles that are considered useless or of little value. ■ worthless writing, talk, or ideas. ■ Finance junk bonds. **2** informal heroin. ▶ **v.** [trans.] informal discard or abandon unceremoniously. [ME: of unknown origin.]

junk[2]

junk[2] ▶ **n.** a flat-bottomed sailing vessel typical in China and the East Indies, with a prominent stem, a high stern, and lugsails. [16th C.: from obs. Fr. *juncque* or Port. *junco*, from Malay *jong*, reinforced by Du. *jonk*.]

junk bond ▶ **n.** a high-yield, high-risk security, typically issued by a company seeking to raise capital quickly in order to finance a takeover.

Jun·ker /'yo͝oNGkər/ ▶ **n.** hist. a German nobleman or aristocrat, esp. a member of the Prussian aristocracy. [Ger., earlier *Junkher*, from Mid. High Ger. *junc* 'young' + *herre* 'lord.']

jun·ket /'jəNGkit/ ▶ **n. 1** a dish of sweetened and flavored curds of milk, often served with fruit. **2** informal an extravagant trip or celebration, in particular one enjoyed by a government official at public expense. ▶ **v.** (**-ket·ed, -ket·ing**) [intrans.] [often as n.] (**junketing**) informal attend or go on such a trip or celebration. — **jun·ke·teer** /,jəNGki'ti(ə)r/ **n.** [ME: from OFr. *jonquette* 'rush basket,' from *jonc* 'rush,' from L. *juncus*.]

junk food ▶ **n.** food that has low nutritional value, typically produced in the form of packaged snacks needing little or no preparation.

junk·ie /'jəNGkē/ (also **junk·y**) ▶ **n.** informal a drug addict. ■ [with adj.] a person with a compulsive habit or obsessive dependency on something.

junk mail ▶ **n.** informal unsolicited advertising or promotional material received through the mail and e-mail.

junk·y /'jəNGkē/ informal ▶ **adj.** useless or of little value. ▶ **n.** (pl. **junk·ies**) var. of JUNKIE.

junk·yard /'jəNGk,yärd/ ▶ **n.** a place where scrap is collected before being discarded, reused, or recycled.

Ju·no /'jo͞o,nō/ **1** Rom. Mythol. the most important goddess of the Roman state, wife of Jupiter. Greek equivalent HERA. **2** Astron. asteroid 3, discovered in 1804 (diameter 244 km).

Ju·no·esque /,jo͞onō'esk/ ▶ **adj.** (of a woman) imposingly tall and shapely.

Junr ▶ **abbr.** Junior (in names).

jun·ta /'ho͝ontə; 'jəntə/ ▶ **n. 1** a military or political group that rules a country after taking power by force. **2** hist. a deliberative or administrative council in Spain or Portugal. [17th C. (sense 2): from Sp. and Port., from L. *juncta*, fem. past part. of *jungere* 'to join.']

Ju·pi·ter /'jo͞opitər/ **1** Rom. Mythol. the chief god of the Roman state religion, originally a sky god associated with thunder and lightning. His wife was Juno. Also called JOVE. Greek equivalent ZEUS. **2** Astron. the largest planet in the solar system, a gas giant that is the fifth in order from the sun and one of the brightest objects in the night sky.

Ju·ra[1] /'jo͝orə; ZHY'rä/ a system of mountain ranges on the border of France and Switzerland. It has given its name to the Jurassic period, when most of its rocks were laid down.

Ju·ra[2] an island of the Inner Hebrides, north of Islay and south of Mull.

Ju·ras·sic /jə'rasik/ ▶ **adj.** Geol. of, relating to, or denoting the second period of the Mesozoic era, between the Triassic and Cretaceous periods. ■ [as n.] (**the Jurassic**) the Jurassic period or the system of rocks deposited during it. It lasted from about 208 million to 146 million years ago. Large reptiles, including the largest known dinosaurs, were dominant, and the first birds appeared. [19th C.: from Fr. *jurassique*; named after the *Jura* Mountains (see JURA[1]).]

ju·rid·i·cal /jo͞o'ridikəl/ ▶ **adj.** Law of or relating to judicial proceedings and the administration of the law. — **ju·rid·i·cal·ly adv.** [16th C.: from L. *juridicus* (from *jus, jur-* 'law' + *dicere* 'say') + -AL.]

ju·ris·dic·tion /,jo͝oris'dikSHən/ ▶ **n.** the official power to make legal decisions and judgments. ■ the extent of this power. ■ a system of law courts; a judicature. ■ the territory or sphere of activity over which the legal authority of a court or other institution extends. — **ju·ris·dic·tion·al** /-SHənl/ **adj.** [ME: from OFr. *juredicion*, from L. *jurisdictio(n-)*, from *jus, jur-* 'law' + *dictio* 'saying' (from *dicere* 'say').]

ju·ris·pru·dence /,jo͝oris'pro͞odns/ ▶ **n.** the theory or philosophy of law. ■ a legal system. — **ju·ris·pru·dent adj. & n. ju·ris·pru·den·tial** /-pro͞o'denCHəl/ **adj.** [17th C.: from late L. *jurisprudentia*, from L. *jus, jur-* 'law' + *prudentia* 'knowledge.']

ju·rist /'jo͝orist/ ▶ **n.** an expert in or writer on law. ■ a lawyer or a judge. — **ju·ris·tic** /jo͝o'ristik/ **adj.** [15th C. (in the sense 'lawyer'): from Fr. *juriste*, med. L. *jurista*, from *jus, jur-* 'law.']

ju·ror /'jo͝orər; -ôr/ ▶ **n.** a member of a jury. [ME: from OFr. *jureor*, from L. *jurator*, from *jurare* 'swear,' from *jus, jur-* 'law.']

Ju·ruá Riv·er /,ZHo͞oro͞o'ä/ a river that flows from eastern Peru through Brazil to the Amazon River.

ju·ry[1] /'jo͝orē/ ▶ **n.** (pl. **-ries**) a body of people (typically twelve in number) sworn to give a verdict in a legal case on the basis of evidence submitted to them in court. ■ a body of people selected to judge a competition. ▶ **v.** (**-ries, -ried**) [trans.] (usu. **be juried**) judge (an art or craft exhibition or exhibit). [ME: from OFr. *juree* 'oath, inquiry,' from L. *jurata*, fem. past part. of *jurare* 'swear' (see JUROR).]

ju·ry[2] ▶ **adj.** [attrib.] Naut. (of a mast or other fitting) improvised or temporary. [19th C.: *jury-mast* 'temporary mast.']

ju·ry-rigged ▶ **adj.** (of a ship) having temporary makeshift rigging. ■ makeshift; improvised. — **ju·ry-rig v.** [18th C.: *jury* perh. based on OFr. *ajurie* 'aid.']

jus /ZHo͞o(s); jo͞os/ ▶ **n.** (esp. in French cuisine) a sauce.

jus·sive /'jəsiv/ ▶ **adj.** Gram. (of a form of a verb) expressing a command. [19th C.: from L. *juss-* 'commanded' (from the v. *jubere*) + -IVE.]

just /jəst/ ▶ **adj.** based on or behaving according to what is morally right and fair: *a just society.* ■ (of treatment) deserved or appropriate in the circumstances. ■ (of an opinion or appraisal) well founded; justifiable. ▶ **adv. 1** exactly. ■ exactly or almost exactly at this or that moment: *we were just finishing breakfast.* **2** very recently; in the immediate past. **3** barely; by a little: *I got here just after nine.* **4** simply; only; no more than. ■ really; absolutely (used for emphasis): *they're just great.* ■ [with modal] possibly (used to indicate a slight chance of something happening or being true).
– PHRASES **just about** informal almost exactly; nearly. **just as well** a good or fortunate thing: *it was just as well I didn't know.* **just in case** as a precaution. **just a minute, moment, second, etc.** used to ask someone to wait or pause for a short time. ■ used to interrupt someone, esp. in protest or disagreement. **just now 1** at this moment. **2** a little time ago. **just the same** nevertheless. **just so** arranged or done very neatly and carefully. — **just·ly adv. just·ness n.** [ME: via OFr. from L. *justus*, from *jus* 'law, right.']

jus·tice /'jəstis/ ▶ **n. 1** just behavior or treatment. ■ the quality of being fair and reasonable. ■ the administration of the law or authority in maintaining this. ■ (**Justice**) the personification of justice, usually a blindfolded woman holding scales and a sword. **2** a judge or magistrate, in particular a judge of the supreme court of a country or state.
– PHRASES **bring someone to justice** arrest someone for a crime and ensure that they are tried in court. **do oneself justice** perform as well as one is able to. **do someone/something justice** do, treat, or represent with due fairness or appreciation. **rough justice** see ROUGH. — **jus·tice·ship n.** (in sense 2). [OE *iustise* 'administration of the law,' via OFr. from L. *justitia*, from *justus* (see JUST).]

jus·tice of the peace ▶ **n.** a magistrate appointed to hear minor cases, perform marriages, grant licenses, etc., in a town, county, or other local district.

jus·ti·fi·a·ble /'jəstə,fīəbəl; ,jəstə'fī-/ ▶ **adj.** able to be shown to be right or reasonable; defensible. — **jus·ti·fi·a·bil·i·ty** /,jəstə,fīə'bilitē/ **n. jus·ti·fi·a·ble·ness n. jus·ti·fi·a·bly adv.**

jus·ti·fied /'jəstə,fīd/ ▶ **adj. 1** having, done for, or marked by a good or legitimate reason: *the doctors were justified in treating her.* **2** Theol. declared or made righteous in the sight of God. **3** Print. having been adjusted so that the print fills a space evenly or forms a straight line at one or both margins: [in comb.] *the output is left-justified.*

jus·ti·fy /'jəstə,fī/ ▶ **v.** (**-fies, -fied**) [trans.] **1** show or prove to be right or reasonable. ■ be a good reason for. **2** Theol. declare or make righteous in the sight of God. **3** Print. adjust (a line of type or piece of text) so that the print fills a space evenly or forms a straight edge at one or both margins. — **jus·ti·fi·ca·tion** /,jəstəfi'kāSHən/ **n. jus·tif·i·ca·to·ry** /jə'stifəkə,tôrē; ,jəstəfi'kātôrē/ **adj. jus·ti·fi·er n.** [ME: from OFr. *justifier*, from Christian Latin *justificare* 'do justice to,' from L. *justus* (see JUST).]

Jus·tin, St. /'jəstən/ (*c.*100–165), Christian philosopher; known as **St. Justin the Martyr.** He is remembered for his *Apologia* (*c.*150).

Jus·tin·i·an /jə'stinēən/ (483–565), Byzantine emperor 527–565; Latin name *Flavius Petrus Sabbatius Justinianus.* He codified Roman law 529.

just-in-time ▶ **adj.** [attrib.] denoting a manufacturing system in which materials or components are delivered immediately before they are required in order to minimize inventory costs.

jut /jət/ ▶ v. (**jut·ted, jut·ting**) [intrans.] extend out, over, or beyond the main body or line of something. ■ [trans.] cause (something, such as one's chin) to protrude. ▶ n. a point that sticks out. [16th C.: var. of JET[1].]

Jute /jo͞ot/ ▶ n. a member of a Germanic people that may have come from Jutland and joined the Angles and Saxons in invading Britain in the 5th century, settling in a region including Kent and the Isle of Wight. [OE *Eotas, Iotas*.]

jute /jo͞ot/ ▶ n. **1** rough fiber made from the stems of a tropical Old World plant, used for making twine, rope, matting, etc. **2** the herbaceous plant (genus *Corchorus*) of the linden family that is cultivated for this fiber, in particular *C. capsularis* of China and *C. olitorius* of India. ■ used in names of other plants that yield fiber, e.g., **Chinese jute**. [18th C.: from Bengali *jhuṭo*.]

Jut·land /ˈjətlənd/ a peninsula in northwestern Europe that includes the mainland of Denmark as well as the northern German state of Schleswig-Holstein. Danish name JYLLAND.

Jut·land, Bat·tle of a major naval battle in World War I, fought between the British Grand Fleet and the German High Seas Fleet in the North Sea west of Jutland on May 31, 1916.

juv. ▶ abbr. juvenile.

Ju·ve·nal /ˈjo͞ovənl/ (*c.*60–*c.*140), Roman satirist; Latin name *Decimus Junius Juvenalis*. His satires attacked the vices and follies of Roman society.

ju·ve·nile /ˈjo͞ovə,nīl; -vənl/ ▶ adj. of, for, or relating to young people. ■ childish; immature. ■ of or denoting a theatrical or film role representing a young person. ■ of or relating to young birds or other animals. ▶ n. a young person. ■ Law a person below the age at which ordinary criminal prosecution is possible (18 in most countries). ■ a young bird or other animal. — **ju·ve·nil·i·ty** /,jo͞ovəˈnilitē/ n. [17th C.: from L. *juvenilis*, from *juvenis* 'young, a young person.']

ju·ve·nile court ▶ n. a court of law responsible for the trial or legal supervision of children under a specified age (18 in most countries).

ju·ve·nile de·lin·quen·cy ▶ n. the habitual committing of criminal acts or offenses by a young person, esp. one below the age at which ordinary criminal prosecution is possible. — **ju·ve·nile de·lin·quent** n.

ju·ve·nil·i·a /,jo͞ovəˈnilēə/ ▶ plural n. works produced by an author or artist while still young. [17th C.: from L., neut. pl. of *juvenilis* (see JUVENILE).]

Ju·ven·tud, Isla de la /ˈēslä dä lä ,ho͞ovänˈto͞od/ (English name **Isle of Youth**; formerly **Isle of Pines**) an island off southwestern Cuba, in the Caribbean Sea; pop. 71,000. Renamed in 1978, it has many facilities dedicated to youth.

ju·vie /ˈjo͞ovē/ ▶ n. (pl. **-vies**) informal a juvenile delinquent.

jux·ta·pose /ˈjəkstə,pōz; ,jəkstəˈpōz/ ▶ v. [trans.] place or deal with close together for contrasting effect: *black-and-white photos were juxtaposed with color images.* — **jux·ta·po·si·tion** /,jəkstəpəˈzisHən/ n. **jux·ta·po·si·tion·al** /,jəkstəpəˈzisHənl/ adj. [19th C.: from French *juxtaposer*, from L. *juxta* 'next' + Fr. *poser* 'to place.']

JV ▶ abbr. junior varsity.

Jyl·land /ˈyo͞o,län/ Danish name for JUTLAND.

Kk

K[1] /kā/ (also **k**) ▶ **n.** (pl. **Ks** or **K's**) the eleventh letter of the alphabet. ■ denoting the next after J in a set of items, categories, etc.

K[2] ▶ **abbr.** ■ kelvin(s). ■ Comput. kilobyte(s). ■ kilometer(s). ■ kindergarten. ■ king (used esp. in describing play in card games). ■ knit (as an instruction in knitting patterns). ■ Köchel (catalog of Mozart's works). ■ informal thousand (used chiefly in expressing salaries or other sums of money). [from KILO- 'thousand.'] ■ Baseball strikeout. ▶ **symb.** the chemical element potassium. [from mod. L. *kalium*.]

k ▶ **abbr.** ■ karat. ■ [in comb.] (in units of measurement) kilo-: *a distance of 700 kpc.* ■ kopeck(s). ▶ **symb.** a constant in a formula or equation. ■ Chem. Boltzmann's constant.

K2 the highest mountain in the Karakoram range, between Pakistan and China. The second highest peak in the world, it rises to 28,250 feet (8,611 m). Formerly known as Mount Godwin-Austen. Also called DAPSANG.

Kaa·ba /'käbə/ (also **Caa·ba**) a square stone building in the center of the Great Mosque at Mecca, the site most holy to Muslims and toward which they must face when praying.

Ka·ba·le·ga Falls /,käbə'lāgə/ a waterfall on the lower Victoria Nile River near Lake Albert, Uganda. Former name MURCHISON FALLS.

Kab·ar·di·no-Bal·kar·i·a /,kabər'dēnō,bôl'karēə/ an autonomous republic in southwestern Russia, on the border with Georgia; pop. 768,000; capital, Nalchik. Also called KABARDA-BALKAR REPUBLIC.

Kab·ba·lah /'kabələ; kə'bä-/ (also **Kab·ba·la, Ca·ba·la, Cab·ba·la,** or **Qa·ba·lah**) ▶ **n.** the ancient Jewish tradition of mystical interpretation of the Bible, first transmitted orally and using esoteric methods (including ciphers). — **Kab·ba·lism** /'kabə,lizəm/ **n.** **Kab·ba·list n.** **Kab·ba·lis·tic** /,kabə'listik/ **adj.** [from med. L. *cabala, cabbala*, from Rabbinical Heb. *qabbālāh* 'tradition,' from *qibbēl* 'receive, accept.']

Ka·bi·la /kə'bēlə/, Laurent (1937–2001), president of the Democratic Republic of the Congo (formerly Zaire) 1997–2001; assassinated in January 2001.

Ka·bi·nett /,kabi'net/ ▶ **n.** a wine of German origin or style of superior or reserve quality. [from Ger. *Kabinettwein*, lit. 'chamber wine.']

ka·bloo·ey (also **ka·bloo·ie**) /kə'bloo͞ē/ ▶ **adj.** informal destroyed or ruined. ▶ **exclam.** used to convey that something has happened in an abrupt way.

ka·bob ▶ **n.** var. of KEBAB.

ka·boo·dle ▶ **n.** var. of CABOODLE.

ka·boom /kə'bo͞om/ ▶ **exclam.** used to represent the sound of a loud explosion.

ka·bu·ki /kə'bo͝okē/ ▶ **n.** a form of traditional Japanese drama with highly stylized song, mime, and dance, now performed only by male actors, using exaggerated gestures and body movements. [Japanese, orig. as a v. meaning 'act dissolutely.']

Ka·bul /'käbəl; kə'bo͞ol/ the capital of Afghanistan, situated in the northeast; pop. 700,000.

Ka·bwe /'käbwā/ a town in central Zambia, site of a cave that has yielded human fossils associated with the Upper Pleistocene period; pop. 167,000. Former name (1904–65) BROKEN HILL.

Ka·byle /kə'bīl/ ▶ **n.** **1** a member of a Berber people inhabiting northern Algeria. **2** the Berber dialect of this people. ▶ **adj.** of or relating to this people or their language. [prob. from Arab. *ḳabā'il*, pl. of *ḳabīla* 'tribe.']

Ka·chin /kə'CHin/ ▶ **n.** **1** a member of an indigenous people living in northern Myanmar (Burma) and adjacent parts of China and India. **2** the Tibeto-Burman language of this people. ▶ **adj.** of or relating to this people or their language. [19th C.: Burmese.]

ka·chi·na /kə'CHēnə/ (also **kat·si·na** /kət'sēnə/) ▶ **n.** (pl. **-nas**) a deified ancestral spirit in the mythology of Pueblo Indians. ■ (also **ka·ch·ina danc·er**) a person who represents such a spirit in ceremonial dances. ■ (also **ka·chi·na doll**) a small carved figure representing such a spirit. [from Hopi *kacina* 'supernatural,' of Keres origin.]

Ká·dár /'kä,där/, János (1912–89), first secretary of the Hungarian Socialist Workers' Party 1956–88 and prime minister of Hungary 1956–58, 1961–65. He consistently supported the Soviet Union.

Kad·dish /'kädisH/ ▶ **n.** an ancient Jewish prayer sequence regularly recited in the synagogue service, including thanksgiving and praise and concluding with a prayer for universal peace. ■ a form of this prayer sequence recited for the dead. [from Aramaic *qaddīš* 'holy.']

ka·di ▶ **n.** (pl. **ka·dis**) var. of CADI.

Ka·di·köy /kä'dikœi; -koi/ Turkish name for CHALCEDON.

Kae·song /'kā'sôNG/ a city in southern North Korea; pop. 346,000.

kaf·fee·klatsch /'käfē,kläCH; -,klaCH; 'kôfē-/ ▶ **n.** an informal social gathering at which coffee is served. ■ talking or gossip at such gatherings. [Ger., from *Kaffee* 'coffee' + *Klatsch* 'gossip.']

Kaf·fir /'kafər/ ▶ **n.** offens., esp. S. African an insulting and contemptuous term for a black African. [from Arab. *kāfir* 'infidel,' from *kafara* 'not believe.']

kaf·fir lime /'kafər/ ▶ **n.** a citrus tree of southeast Asia with green fruit and aromatic leaves that are used in Thai and Indonesian cooking.

kaf·fi·yeh /kə'fē(y)ə/ (also **kef·fi·yeh**) ▶ **n.** a Bedouin Arab's kerchief worn as a headdress. [19th C.: from Arab. *keffiyya, kūfiyya*.]

Kaf·ir /'kafər/ ▶ **n.** a member of a people of the Hindu Kush mountains of northeastern Afghanistan. — **Kaf·i·ri** /'kafərē; kə'fi(ə)rē/ **adj.** & **n.** [from Arab. *kāfir* (see KAFFIR).]

kaf·ir /'kafər/ ▶ **n.** a person who is not a Muslim (used chiefly by Muslims). [from Arab. *kāfir* 'infidel, unbeliever.' Cf. KAFFIR.]

Kaf·ka /'käfkə/, Franz (1883–1924), Czech writer. His novels include *The Metamorphosis* (1917).

kaffiyeh

Kaf·ka·esque /,käfkə'esk/ ▶ **adj.** characteristic or reminiscent of the oppressive or nightmarish qualities of Franz Kafka's fictional world.

kaf·tan /'kaftən; -,tan/ (also **caf·tan**) ▶ **n.** a man's long belted tunic, worn in countries of the Near East. ■ a woman's long loose dress. ■ a loose shirt or top. [16th C.: from Turk., from Pers. *ḳaftān*.]

Ka·go·shi·ma /,kägə'SHēmə; kä'gōSHēmə/ a city in Japan, on the southern coast of Kyushu island; pop. 537,000.

Ka·ha·na·mo·ku /kə,hänə'mōko͞o/, Duke Paoa (1890–68), US swimmer and surfer. The developer of the flutter kick, he won Olympic gold medals 1912, 1920.

Kah·lo /'kälō/, Frida (1907–54), Mexican painter; wife of Diego Rivera. Noted for colorful surrealism and female themes, her works include *Mi nana y yo* (1937).

Kah·lú·a /kə'lo͞oə/ ▶ **n.** trademark a coffee-flavored liqueur.

Ka·ho·o·la·we /kä,hō-ō'läwā/ an island in Hawaii, southwest of Maui, formerly used as a military range.

ka·hu·na /kə'ho͞onə/ ▶ **n.** (in Hawaii) a wise man or shaman. ■ informal an important person; the person in charge. ■ informal (in surfing) a very large wave.

Kai·bab Plateau /'kī,bab/ a highland region in northwestern Arizona that adjoins southern Utah.

Kai·feng /'kī'feNG/ a city in eastern China, in Henan province; pop. 693,100.

kai·nic ac·id /'kīnik/ ▶ **n.** Med. an organic acid, $C_{10}H_{15}NO_4$, extracted from a red alga, used to kill intestinal worms. [20th C.: from Japanese *kainin-sō*, name of the alga *Digenea simplex* from which it is extracted.]

Kai·pa·ro·wits Plateau /kī'pärō-its/ a highland region in south central Utah.

Kair·ouan /ker'wän/ a city in northeastern Tunisia; pop. 72,250. It is a Muslim holy city.

kai·ser /'kīzər/ ▶ **n.** **1** hist. the German emperor, the emperor of Austria, or the head of the Holy Roman Empire. **2** (also **kaiser roll**) a round, soft bread roll with a crisp crust. [ME *cayser*, from ON *keisari*, based on L. *Caesar* (see CAESAR[2]); later from Ger. *Kaiser*.]

Kai·ser Wil·helm, Wilhelm II of Germany (see WILHELM II).

kai·zen /'kīzən/ ▶ **n.** a Japanese business philosophy of continuous improvement of working practices, personal efficiency, etc. [Japanese, lit. 'improvement.']

ka·ka /'käkə/ ▶ **n.** a large New Zealand parrot (*Nestor meridionalis*) with olive-brown and dull green upper parts and reddish underparts. [18th C.: from Maori.]

ka·ka·po /'käkə,pō/ ▶ **n.** (pl. **-pos**) a large, flightless, nocturnal New Zealand parrot (*Strigops habroptilus*) with greenish plumage, now endangered. Also called OWL PARROT. [19th C.: Maori, 'night kaka.']

ka·ki /'käkē/ ▶ **n.** the Japanese persimmon.

Ka·laal·lit Nu·naat /kä'lätlēt no͞o'nät; -'lälēt/ Inuit name for GREENLAND.

ka·la-a·zar /,kälə ə'zär/ ▶ **n.** a form of the disease leishmaniasis caused by the protozoan *Leishmania donovani* and marked by emaciation, anemia, fever, and enlargement of the liver and spleen. [19th C.: from Assamese, from *kālā* 'black' + *āzār* 'disease.']

Ka·la·ha·ri Des·ert /ˌkälə'härē/ a high, vast, arid plateau in southern Africa, comprising most of Botswana with parts in Namibia and South Africa.

Ka·lam /kə'läm/, Abdul (1931–), president of India 2002–; full name *Avul Pakir Jainulabdeen Abdul Kalam.*

Kal·a·ma·zoo /ˌkaləmə'zo͞o/ a city in southwestern Michigan; pop. 77,145.

kal·an·cho·e /ˌkalən'kō-ē; kə'laNGkō-ē/ ▶**n.** a tropical succulent plant (genus *Kalanchoe*) of the stonecrop family, with clusters of tubular flowers, sometimes producing miniature plants along the edges of the leaves and grown as an indoor or greenhouse plant. [19th C.: mod. L., from Fr., based on Chin. *gālāncài.*]

Ka·lash·ni·kov /kə'läsHnəˌkôf; -ˌkôv/ ▶**n.** a type of rifle or submachine gun made in Russia, esp. the AK-47 assault rifle. [1970s: named after Mikhail T. *Kalashnikov* (1919–), the Russ. designer of the weapons.]

kale /kāl/ ▶**n. 1** a hardy cabbage of a variety that produces erect stems with large leaves and no compact head. See also CURLY KALE. **2** informal, dated money. [ME: north. Engl. form of COLE.]

ka·lei·do·scope /kə'līdəˌskōp/ ▶**n.** a toy consisting of a tube containing mirrors and pieces of colored glass or paper, whose reflections produce changing patterns that are visible through an eyehole when the tube is rotated. ■ [in sing.] a constantly changing pattern or sequence of objects or elements. — **ka·lei·do·scop·ic** /-ˌlīdə'skäpik/ **adj.** **ka·lei·do·scop·i·cal·ly** /-ˌlīdə'skäpik(ə)lē/ **adv.** [19th C.: from Gk. *kalos* 'beautiful' + *eidos* 'form' + -SCOPE.]

kal·ends ▶ **plural n.** var. of CALENDS.

Kal·gan /'kälˈgän; 'kal'gan/ Mongolian name for ZHANGJIAKOU.

Ka·li /'kälē/ Hinduism the most terrifying goddess, wife of Shiva. She is typically depicted as black, naked, old, and hideous. [from Sanskrit *Kālī* 'black.']

Ka·li·man·tan /ˌkälē'mänˌtän/ a region of Indonesia on the southern part of the island of Borneo.

ka·lim·ba /kə'limbə/ ▶**n.** a type of African thumb piano. [1950s: a local word; rel. to MARIMBA.]

Ka·li·nin[1] /kə'lēnən; kəl'yēnyēn/ former name (1931–91) of TVER.

Ka·li·nin[2] /kə'lēnin/, Mikhail Ivanovich (1875–1946), head of state of the Soviet Union 1919–46.

Ka·li·nin·grad /kə'lēninˌgrät; kəl'yēnyēn-/ **1** a port on the Baltic coast of eastern Europe, capital of the Russian region of Kaliningrad; pop. 406,000. **2** a region of Russia, an enclave situated on the Baltic coast of eastern Europe; capital, Kaliningrad.

Kal·mar Sound /'kälmär/ a narrow strait between the mainland of southeastern Sweden and the island of Öland in the Baltic Sea.

Kal·mar, Un·ion of the treaty that unified the crowns of Denmark, Sweden, and Norway in 1397, dissolved in 1523.

kal·mi·a /'kalmēə/ ▶**n.** a North American evergreen shrub (genus *Kalmia*) of the heath family, bearing large clusters of pink, white, or red flowers, grown as an ornamental. [mod. L., after Pehr *Kalm* (1716–79), Swedish botanist.]

Kal·muck /'kalˌmək; kal'mək/ (also **Kal·myk**) ▶**n.** (pl. same or **-mucks** also **-myks** /-miks/) **1** a member of a mainly Buddhist people of Mongolian origin living chiefly in Kalmykia. **2** the Altaic language of this people. ▶**adj.** of or relating to this people or their language. [from Russ. *kalmyk.*]

Kal·myk·ia /kal'mikēə/ an autonomous republic in southwestern Russia, on the Caspian Sea; pop. 325,000; capital, Elista. Official name REPUBLIC OF KALMYKIA-KHALMG TANGCH.

ka·long /'kälôNG; -läNG/ ▶**n.** a flying fox (genus *Pteropus*) found in Southeast Asia and Indonesia. [19th C.: Javanese.]

kal·so·mine ▶**n. & v.** var. of CALCIMINE.

Kal·yan /kəl'yän/ a city on the west coast of India, in the state of Maharashtra; pop. 1,014,000.

Ka·ma /'kämə/ Hinduism the god of love, typically represented as a youth with a bow of sugar cane, a bowstring of bees, and arrows of flowers.

kam·a·cite /'kaməˌsīt/ ▶**n.** an alloy of iron and nickel occurring in some meteorites. [19th C.: from Gk. *kamax, kamak-* 'vine pole.']

Ka·ma Riv·er /'kämə/ a river in Russia that flows from the Ural Mountains to the Volga River near Kazan.

Ka·ma Su·tra /'kämə 'so͞otrə/ an ancient Sanskrit treatise on the art of love and sexual technique.

Kam·ba /'kämbə/ ▶**n.** (pl. same, **Kam·bas,** or **Wa·kam·ba** /wä'kämbə/) **1** a member of a people of central Kenya, ethnically related to the Kikuyu. **2** the Bantu language of this people. ▶**adj.** of or relating to this people or their language. [a local name.]

Kam·chat·ka /käm'cHätkə/ a peninsula on the northeastern coast of Siberia in Russia; chief port, Petropavlovsk.

kame /kām/ ▶**n.** Geol. a steep-sided mound of sand and gravel deposited by a melting ice sheet. [18th C.: Scots form of COMB.]

Ka·me·ha·me·ha I /kəˌmäə'mäə/ (*c.*1758–1819), king of the Hawaiian islands 1795–1819; known as *Kamehameha the Great.* He united all the islands.

Ka·men·sko·ye /'käminskəyə/ former name (until 1936) for DNIPRODZERZHINSK.

Ka·mer·lingh On·nes /'kämərliNG 'ônəs/, Heike (1853–1926), Dutch physicist. He liquefied helium and discovered superconductivity. Nobel Prize for Physics (1913).

ka·mi /'kämē/ ▶**n.** (pl. same) a divine being in the Shinto religion.

ka·mi·ka·ze /ˌkämi'käzē/ ▶**n.** (in World War II) a Japanese aircraft loaded with explosives and making a deliberate suicidal crash on an enemy target. ■ the pilot of such an aircraft. ▶**adj.** [attrib.] of or relating to such an attack or pilot. ■ reckless or potentially self-destructive. [Japanese, from *kami* 'divinity' + *kaze* 'wind.']

Ka·mi·la·roi /'kämēˌläroi/ ▶**n.** (pl. same) **1** a member of a group of Australian Aboriginal peoples of northeastern New South Wales. **2** the language of these peoples, now extinct. ▶**adj.** of or relating to the Kamilaroi or their language. [the name in Kamilaroi.]

Kam·pa·la /käm'pälə/ the capital of Uganda, on the northern shores of Lake Victoria; pop. 773,000.

kam·pong /'kämpôNG; -päNG/ ▶**n.** a Malaysian enclosure or village.

Kam·pu·che·a /ˌkämpə'cHēə/ former name (1976–89) for CAMBODIA. — **Kam·pu·che·an n. & adj.**

Kan. ▶**abbr.** Kansas.

ka·na /'känə/ ▶**n.** the system of syllabic writing used for Japanese, having two forms, hiragana and katakana. Compare with KANJI.

ka·nak·a /kə'näkə/ ▶**n.** a native of Hawaii. [Hawaiian, lit. 'man.']

Ka·na·rese /ˌkänə'rēz; -'rēs/ ▶**n.** (pl. same) **1** a member of a people living mainly in Kanara, a district in southwestern India. **2** another term for KANNADA. ▶**adj.** of or relating to Kanara, its people, or their language.

Kan·chen·jun·ga /ˌkənCHən'jəNGgə; -'jo͝oNGgə/ (also **Kang·chen·jun·ga** or **Kin·chin·jun·ga**) a mountain in the Himalayas, on the border between Nepal and Sikkim. The third highest peak in the world, it rises to 28,209 feet (8,598 m).

Kan·da·har /ˌkəndə'här; 'kəndəˌhär/ a city in southern Afghanistan, the capital 1773–78; pop. 225,500.

Kan·din·sky /kən'dinskē/, Wassily (1866–1944), Russian painter, noted as a pioneer in abstract art.

Kan·dy /'kandē/ a city in Sri Lanka, site of the Dalada Maligava, a sacred Buddhist shrine; pop. 104,000. — **Kan·dy·an** /-dēən/ **adj.**

kan·ga·roo /ˌkaNGgə'ro͞o/ ▶**n.** a large plant-eating macropod (genus *Macropus,* family Macropodidae) with a long powerful tail and strongly developed hind limbs that enable it to travel by leaping, found only in Australia and New Guinea. [18th C.: from an Aboriginal language.]

kan·ga·roo care ▶**n.** a method of caring for premature babies in which the infants are held skin-to-skin with a parent, usually the mother, for as many hours as possible every day.

kan·ga·roo court ▶**n.** an unofficial court held by a group of people in order to try someone regarded, esp. without good evidence, as guilty of a crime or misdemeanor.

kan·ga·roo paw ▶**n.** an Australian plant (genera *Anigozanthos* and *Macropidia,* family Haemodoraceae) that has long straplike leaves and tubular flowers with woolly outer surfaces.

kan·ga·roo rat ▶**n.** a seed-eating hopping rodent (genus *Dipodomys,* family Heteromyidae) with long hind legs, found from Canada to Mexico.

Kang·chen·jun·ga /ˌkäNGCHən'jo͝oNGgə/ var. of KANCHENJUNGA.

kan·ji /'känjē/ ▶**n.** a system of Japanese writing using Chinese characters. Compare with KANA. [Japanese, from *kan* 'Chinese' + *ji* 'character.']

Kan·na·da /'känədə/ ▶**n.** a Dravidian language related to Telugu and using a similar script. It is spoken by about 24 million people, mainly in Kanara and Karnataka in southwestern India. Also called KANARESE. ▶**adj.** of or relating to this language. [the name in Kannada.]

Kan·pur /'känˌpo͝or/ (also **Cawn·pore**) a city in Uttar Pradesh, in northern India; pop. 2,100,000.

Kans. ▶**abbr.** Kansas.

Kan·sa /'kanzə; -sə/ ▶**n.** a North American people of eastern Kansas. ■ the language of this people. Also called KAW.

Kan·sas /'kanzəs/ a state in the central US; pop. 2,688,418; capital, Topeka; statehood, Jan. 29, 1861 (34). It was acquired by the US as part of the Louisiana Purchase in 1803. — **Kan·san** /-zən/ **adj. & n.**

Kan·sas Cit·y each of two adjacent cities at the junction of the Missouri and Kansas rivers; one in northeastern Kansas, pop. 146,866; the other in northwestern Missouri, pop. 441,545.

Kan·su /'kanˌso͞o; 'gän'so͞o/ variant of GANSU.

Kant /känt/, Immanuel (1724–1804), German philosopher. In the *Critique of Pure Reason* (1781) he argued that any affirmation or denial regarding the ultimate nature of reality ("noumenon") makes no sense. — **Kant·i·an** /'käntēən/ **adj. & n.** **Kant·i·an·ism** /-ˌnizəm/ **n.**

Kao·hsiung /'gousHē'o͝oNG; -'sHo͝oNG/ the chief port of Taiwan, on the southwestern coast; pop. 1,390,000.

kao·li·ang /ˌkoulē'aNG/ ▶**n.** sorghum of a variety (*Sorghum bicolor* var. *nervosum*) grown in China and used to make dough and alcoholic drinks. [20th C.: from Chin. *gāoliang,* from *gāo* 'high' + *liáng* 'fine grain.']

ka·o·lin /'kāəlin/ ▶**n.** a fine soft white clay, used for making porcelain and china, as a filler in paper and textiles, and in medicinal absorbents. Also called CHINA CLAY. — **ka·o·lin·ize** /-ˌnīz/ **v.** [18th C.: from Fr., from Chin. *gāolǐ ng,* a mountain in Jiangxi province.]

ka·o·lin·ite /'kāələˌnīt/ ▶**n.** a white or gray clay mineral that is the chief constituent of kaolin.

ka·on /'kāˌän/ ▶**n.** Physics a meson having a mass several times that of a pion. [1950s: from *ka* representing the letter *K* (as a symbol for the particle) + -ON.]

ka·pell·meis·ter /kə'pelˌmīstər/ ▶**n.** the leader or conductor of an orchestra or choir. ■ hist. a leader of a chamber ensemble or orchestra attached to a German court. [19th C.: Ger., from *Kapelle* 'court orchestra' (from med. L. *capella* 'chapel') + *Meister* 'master.']

ka·pok /ˈkāˌpäk/ ▶**n.** a fine, fibrous cottonlike substance that grows around the seeds of the ceiba tree, used as stuffing for cushions, soft toys, etc. ■ (also **kapok tree**) another term for CEIBA. [18th C.: from Malay *kapuk*.]

Ka·po·si's sar·co·ma /kəˈpōsēz särˈkōmə; ˈkapəˌsēz; ˈkäpōˌshēz/ ▶**n.** Med. a form of cancer involving multiple tumors of the lymph nodes or skin, occurring chiefly in people with depressed immune systems, e.g., as a result of AIDS. [19th C.: named after Moritz K. *Kaposi* (1837–1902), Hungarian dermatologist.]

kap·pa /ˈkapə/ ▶**n.** the tenth letter of the Greek alphabet (Κ, κ), transliterated in the traditional Latin style as 'c' (as in *Socrates* or *cyan*) or in the modern style as 'k' (as in *kyanite* and in the etymologies of this dictionary). ■ [as adj.] Biochem. denoting one of the two types of light polypeptide chain present in all immunoglobulin molecules (the other being lambda).

ka·pu /ˈkäpō/ ▶**n.** (in Hawaiian traditional culture and religion) a set of rules and prohibitions for everyday life.

ka·put /kəˈpo͝ot; kä-/ ▶**adj.** [predic.] informal broken and useless; no longer working or effective. [19th C.: from Ger. *kaputt*, from Fr. *(être) capot* '(be) without tricks in a card game.']

kar·a·bi·ner ▶**n.** var. of CARABINER.

Ka·ra·chai /ˌkarəˈchī/ ▶**n.** **1** a member of an indigenous people living in Karachai-Cherkessia. **2** (also **Karachai-Balkar**) the Turkic language of this people. ▶**adj.** of or relating to this people or their language.

Ka·ra·chai-Cher·kes·sia /ˌkarəˈchī chirˈkesēə/ an autonomous republic in the northern Caucasus, in southwestern Russia; pop. 436,000; capital, Cherkessk. Official name KARACHAI-CHERKESS REPUBLIC.

Ka·ra·chi /kəˈrächē/ a major city and port in Pakistan, capital of Sind province; pop. 6,700,000.

Ka·ra-Kal·pak /ˌkärə kälˈpäk; karə kalˈpak; kəˈrä kəlˈpäk/ ▶**n.** **1** a member of an indigenous people living in the Kara-Kalpak Autonomous Republic of Russia, south of the Aral Sea. **2** the Turkic language of this people. ▶**adj.** of or relating to this people or their language.

Ka·ra·ko·ram /ˌkarəˈkôrəm/ a mountain system in central Asia extending 300 miles (480 km) southeast from Afghanistan to Kashmir and forming part of the borders of India and Pakistan with China; highest peak, K2.

kar·a·kul /ˈkarəkəl/ (also **car·a·cul**) ▶**n.** a sheep of an Asian breed with a dark, curled fleece when young. ■ cloth or fur made from or resembling the fleece of such a sheep. [19th C.: from Russ., from the name of an oasis in Uzbekistan.]

Ka·ra Kum /ˌkarə ˈko͞om; ˌkärə/ a desert in central Asia that covers much of Turkmenistan. Russian name KARAKUMY.

kar·a·o·ke /ˌkarēˈōkē/ ▶**n.** a form of entertainment, offered typically by bars and clubs, in which people take turns singing popular songs into a microphone over prerecorded backing tracks. [1970s: from Japanese, lit. 'empty orchestra.']

Ka·ra Sea /ˈkarə; ˈkärə/ an arm of the Arctic Ocean off the northern coast of Russia.

kar·at /ˈkarət/ (esp. Brit. also **car·at**) ▶**n.** a measure of the purity of gold, pure gold being 24 karats.

ka·ra·te /kəˈrätē/ ▶**n.** an Asian system of unarmed combat using the hands and feet to deliver and block blows, widely practiced as a sport. [Japanese, from *kara* 'empty' + *te* 'hand.']

Ka·re·lia /kəˈrēlēə/ a region of northeastern Europe on the border between Russia and Finland. —**Ka·re·li·an** adj. & n.

Ka·ren /kəˈren/ ▶**n.** (pl. same or **-rens**) **1** a member of an indigenous people of eastern Myanmar (Burma) and western Thailand. **2** the language of this people, probably Sino-Tibetan. ▶**adj.** of or relating to this people or their language. [from Burmese *ka-reng* 'wild unclean man.']

Ka·ren State a state in southeastern Myanmar (Burma), on the border with Thailand; capital, Pa-an.

Ka·ri·ba, Lake /kəˈrēbə/ a large man-made lake on the Zambia–Zimbabwe border in central Africa.

Ka·ri·ba Dam a concrete arch dam on the Zambezi River on the Zambia-Zimbabwe border, 240 miles (385 km) downstream from Victoria Falls.

Karl XII var. of CHARLES XII.

Karl-Marx-Stadt /kärl ˈmärks ˌshtät/ former name (1953–90) for CHEMNITZ.

kar·ma /ˈkärmə/ ▶**n.** (in Hinduism and Buddhism) the sum of a person's actions in this and previous states of existence, viewed as deciding their fate in future existences. ■ informal destiny or fate, following as effect from cause. —**kar·mic** /-mik/ **adj.** **kar·mi·cal·ly** /-mik(ə)lē/ **adv.** [from Sanskrit *karman* 'action, effect, fate.']

Kar·nak /ˈkärˌnak/ a village in Egypt on the Nile, site of ancient Thebes.

Kar·na·ta·ka /kärˈnätəkə/ a state in southwestern India; capital, Bangalore. Former name (until 1973) MYSORE.

Kar·oo /kəˈro͞o/ (also **Kar·roo**) an elevated semidesert plateau in South Africa. ■ [as n.] (**a karoo**) S. African a tract of semidesert land.

kar·ri /ˈkarē/ ▶**n.** (pl. **-ris**) a tall Australian eucalyptus (*Eucalyptus diversicolor*) with hard red wood. [19th C.: from Nyungar.]

karst /kärst/ ▶**n.** Geol. landscape underlain by limestone that has been eroded by dissolution, producing ridges, towers, fissures, sinkholes, and other characteristic landforms. —**kars·tic** /ˈkärstik/ **adj.** [19th C.: from Ger. *der Karst*, the name of a limestone region in Slovenia.]

kart /kärt/ ▶**n.** a small unsprung racing vehicle typically having four wheels and consisting of a tubular frame with a rear-mounted engine. —**kart·ing** **n.** [20th C.: shortening of GO-KART.]

Kart·ve·lian /kärtˈvēlēən/ ▶**adj.** & **n.** another term for SOUTH CAUCASIAN (see CAUCASIAN sense 3). [from Georgian *Kartvelebi* 'Georgians' + -IAN.]

karyo- ▶**comb. form** Biol. denoting the nucleus of a cell: *karyokinesis* | *karyotype*. [from Gk. *karuon* 'kernel.']

kar·y·o·ki·ne·sis /ˌkarēōkəˈnēsis/ ▶**n.** Biol. division of a cell nucleus during mitosis.

kar·y·o·type /ˈkarēəˌtīp/ ▶**n.** Biol. & Med. the number and visual appearance of the chromosomes in the cell nuclei of an organism or species. —**kar·y·o·typ·ic** /ˌkarēəˈtipik/ **adj.**

kar·y·o·typ·ing /ˈkarēəˌtīping/ ▶**n.** Biol. & Med. the determination of a karyotype, e.g., to detect chromosomal abnormalities.

Ka·sai Riv·er /käˈsī/ (also **Cassai**) a river flowing from central Angola through the Democratic Republic of the Congo (formerly Zaire) into the Congo River.

kas·bah /ˈkäzbä/ ▶**n.** var. of CASBAH.

ka·sha /ˈkäshə/ ▶**n.** a soft food made from cooked buckwheat or similar grain. ■ uncooked buckwheat groats. [Russ.]

Kash·mir /ˈkashˌmi(ə)r; ˈkazh-/ a region on the northern border of India and in northeastern Pakistan. Formerly a state of India, it has been fought over by India and Pakistan since partition in 1947. The northwestern part is controlled by Pakistan, most of it forming the state of Azad Kashmir, while the remainder is incorporated into the Indian state of Jammu and Kashmir.

Kash·mir goat ▶**n.** a goat of a Himalayan breed, yielding fine, soft wool that is used to make cashmere.

Kash·mir·i /ˌkashˈmi(ə)rē; ˌkazh-/ ▶**adj.** of or relating to Kashmir, its people, or their language. ▶**n.** **1** a native or inhabitant of Kashmir. **2** the Dardic language of Kashmir, written in both Devanagari and Arabic script.

kash·ruth /ˈkäshrəth; -ro͞ot; käshˈro͞ot/ (also **kash·rut**) ▶**n.** the body of Jewish religious laws concerning the suitability of food, the use of ritual objects, etc. ■ the observance of these laws. [Heb., lit. 'legitimacy (in religion)'; see also KOSHER.]

kat·a·bat·ic /ˌkatəˈbatik/ ▶**adj.** Meteorol. (of a wind) caused by local downward motion of cool air. [19th C.: from Gk. *katabatikos*, from *katabainein* 'go down.']

Ka·tah·din, Mount /kəˈtädn/ a peak in north central Maine, 5,267 feet (1,606 m), site of the northern end of the Appalachian Trail.

ka·ta·ka·na /ˌkätəˈkänə/ ▶**n.** the more angular form of kana (syllabic writing) used in Japanese, primarily for words of foreign origin. Compare with HIRAGANA. [18th C.: Japanese, lit. 'side kana.']

ka·ta·na /kəˈtänə/ ▶**n.** a long, single-edged sword used by Japanese samurai. [17th C.: Japanese.]

Ka·tan·ga /kəˈtänggə; -ˈtanggə/ a copper-mining region of the Democratic Republic of the Congo (Zaire); capital, Lubumbashi. It was known as Shaba 1972–97.

Kat·ang·ese /ˌkatängˈgēz; -ˈgēs; -ang-/ ▶**n.** (pl. same) a native or inhabitant of Shaba (before 1972 called Katanga). ▶**adj.** of or relating to the Katangese.

ka·tha·re·vou·sa /ˌkäthäˈrevo͞osä/ ▶**n.** a heavily archaized form of modern Greek used in traditional literary writing, as opposed to the form that is spoken and used in everyday writing (called demotic). [20th C.: mod. Gk., lit. 'purifying.']

Ka·thi·a·war /ˌkätēəˈwär/ a peninsula on the western coast of India, in the state of Gujarat.

Kath·man·du /ˌkätmänˈdo͞o; ˌkatˌman-/ the capital of Nepal, in the east central part of the country; pop. 419,000.

Kat·mai Na·tion·al Park /ˈkatˌmī/ a national preserve in southwestern Alaska, noted for its volcanic activity and wildlife.

kat·si·na /kəˈchēnə; kətˈsēnə/ ▶**n.** (pl. **-nam** /-nəm/ or **-nas**) variant of KACHINA.

Kat·te·gat /ˈkätəˌgät; ˈkatəˌgat/ a strait, 140 miles (225 km) long, between Sweden and Denmark.

ka·ty·did /ˈkātēˌdid/ ▶**n.** a large, typically green, North American grasshopper (*Microcentrum* and other genera, family Tettigoniidae), the males of which make a sound that resembles the name.

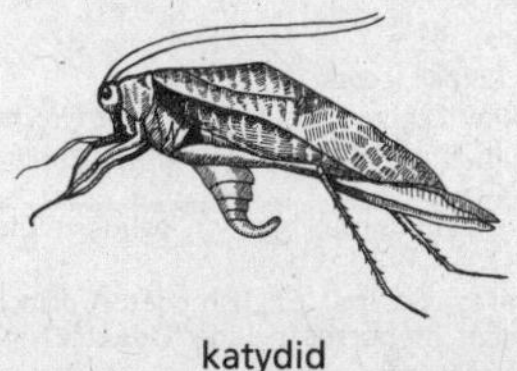

katydid

PRONUNCIATION KEY ə *ago, up*; ər *over, fur*; a *hat*; ā *ate*; ä *car*; e *let*; ē *see*; i *fit*; ī *by*; NG *sing*; ō *go*; ô *law, for*; oi *toy*; o͝o *good*; o͞o *goo*; ou *out*; TH *thin*; TH *then*; ZH *vision*

katz·en·jam·mer /'katsən,jamər/ ▶ **n.** informal, dated confusion; uproar. ■ a hangover; a severe headache resulting from a hangover. [19th C.: from Ger. *Katzen* (combining form of *Katze* 'cat') + *Jammer* 'distress.']

Kau·ai /'kou,ī/ an island in Hawaii, separated from Oahu by the Kauai Channel; chief town, Lihue.

Kauf·man /'kôfmən/, George Simon (1889–1961), US playwright. He collaborated with George Gershwin to write *Of Thee I Sing* (1931) and with Moss Hart to write *The Man Who Came to Dinner* (1939).

Ka·un·da /kə'o͞ondə/, Kenneth David (1924–), president of Zambia 1964–91.

kau·ri /'kourē/ ▶ **n.** (pl. **-ris**) (also **kau·ri pine**) a tall coniferous forest tree (genus *Agathis*) of the monkey puzzle family that produces valuable timber and dammar resin. It grows in warm countries from Malaysia to New Zealand. [19th C.: from Maori.]

ka·va /'kävə/ (also **ka·va-ka·va**) ▶ **n.** **1** a narcotic sedative drink made in Polynesia from the crushed roots of a plant of the pepper family. **2** the Polynesian shrub (*Piper methysticum*) from which this root is obtained. [18th C.: from Tongan.]

Ka·ver·i var. of CAUVERY.

Kaw /käw/ ▶ **n.** another name for KANSA.

Ka·wa·ba·ta /,käwə'bätə/, Yasunari (1899–1972), Japanese writer. His novels include *The Sound of the Mountain* (1949–54). Nobel Prize for Literature (1968).

Ka·wa·sa·ki /,käwə'säkē; ,kouə-/ a city in eastern Japan, on the island of Honshu; pop. 1,174,000.

Ka·wa·sa·ki dis·ease ▶ **n.** a disease of unknown cause, occurring primarily in young children and giving rise to a rash, glandular swelling, and sometimes damage to the heart. [1960s: named after Tomisaku *Kawasaki*, Japanese physician.]

kayak

kay·ak /'kī,ak/ ▶ **n.** a canoe of a type used originally by the Eskimo, made of a light frame with a watertight covering having a small opening in the top to sit in. ▶ **v.** (**kay·aked, kay·ak·ing**) [intrans.] [usu. as n.] (**kayaking**) travel in or use a kayak. — **kay·ak·er n.** [18th C.: from Inuit *qayaq*.]

Kay·an /'kīən/ ▶ **n.** (pl. same or **-ans**) **1** a member of an indigenous people of Sarawak and Borneo. **2** the Indonesian language of this people. ▶ **adj.** of or relating to this people or their language. [the name in Kayan.]

kay·o /'kā'ō/ Boxing, informal ▶ **n.** (pl. **kay·os**) a knockout. ▶ **v.** (**kay·oes, kay·oed**) [trans.] knock (someone) out. [1920s: representing the pronunc. of *KO*.]

ka·za·choc /kəzä'CHôk/ ▶ **n.** a Slavic dance with a fast and typically quickening tempo, featuring a step in which a squatting dancer kicks out each leg alternately to the front. [20th C.: Russ., dimin. of *kazak* 'Cossack.']

Ka·zakh /kə'zäk/ ▶ **n.** **1** a member of a people living chiefly in Kazakhstan. Traditionally nomadic, Kazakhs are predominantly Sunni Muslims. **2** the Turkic language of this people. ▶ **adj.** of or relating to this people or their language. [Russ., from Turkic; see COSSACK.]

Ka·zakh·stan /kəzäk'stän; -zak'stan/ a republic in central Asia. *See box.*

Ka·zan¹ /kə'zän(yə)/ a port in western Russia, on the Volga River, capital of the autonomous republic of Tatarstan; pop. 1,103,000.

Ka·zan² /kə'zan/, Elia (1909–2003), US director; born in Turkey; born *Elia Kazanjoglous*. In 1947, he cofounded the Actors' Studio.

ka·zil·lion /kə'zilyən/ ▶ **cardinal number** informal another term for GAZILLION.

ka·zoo /kə'zo͞o/ ▶ **n.** a small, simple musical instrument consisting of a hollow pipe with a hole in it, over which is a thin covering that vibrates and produces a buzzing sound when the player sings or hums into the pipe. [19th C.: appar. imitative of the sound produced.]

KB ▶ **abbr.** (also **Kb**) kilobyte(s).

kb Biochem. ▶ **abbr.** kilobase(s).

Kbps ▶ **abbr.** kilobits per second.

kbyte /'kā,bīt/ ▶ **abbr.** kilobyte(s).

KC ▶ **abbr.** Kansas City.

kc ▶ **abbr.** kilocycle(s).

kcal ▶ **abbr.** kilocalorie(s).

kcl ▶ **abbr.** kilocalorie.

kc/s ▶ **abbr.** kilocycles per second.

ke·a /kēə/ ▶ **n.** a New Zealand mountain parrot (*Nestor notabilis*) with a long, narrow bill and mainly olive-green plumage. [19th C.: Maori, imitative of its call.]

Kea·ting /'kētiNG/, Paul John (1944–), prime minister of Australia 1991–96.

Keats /kēts/, John (1795–1821), English poet. A principal figure of the romantic movement, his poems include "Ode to a Nightingale" (1818). — **Keats·i·an** /'kētsēən/ **adj.**

ke·bab /kə'bäb/ (also **ka·bob**) ▶ **n.** a dish of pieces of meat roasted or grilled on a skewer or spit. ■ [usu. with adj.] a dish of any kind of food cooked in pieces in this way: *swordfish kebabs.* [17th C.: from Arab. *kabāb*, partly via Urdu, Pers., and Turk.]

Kazakhstan

Official name: Republic of Kazakhstan
Location: central Asia, south of Russia, extending east from the Caspian Sea to the Altai Mountains and China
Area: 1,049,400 square miles (2,717,300 sq km)
Population: 15,143,000
Capital: Astana
Languages: Kazakh, Russian (both official)
Currency: tenge

Ke·ble /'kēbəl/, John (1792–1866), English clergyman. He cofounded the Oxford Movement 1833.

kedge /kej/ ▶ **v.** [trans.] move (a ship or boat) by hauling in a hawser attached to a small anchor dropped at some distance. ■ [intrans.] (of a ship or boat) move in such a way. ▶ **n.** (also **kedge anchor**) a small anchor used for such a purpose. [15th C.: perh. a specific use of dial. *cadge* 'bind, tie.']

ked·ger·ee /'kejə,rē/ ▶ **n.** **1** an Indian dish consisting chiefly of rice, lentils, onions, and eggs. **2** a European dish consisting chiefly of fish, rice, and hard-boiled eggs. [from Hindi *khichṛī*, from Sanskrit *khiccā*, a dish of rice and sesame.]

keel¹ /kēl/ ▶ **n.** the longitudinal structure along the centerline at the bottom of a vessel's hull, on which the rest of the hull is built, in some vessels extended downward as a blade or ridge to increase stability. ■ Zool. a ridge along the breastbone of many birds to which the flight muscles are attached; the carina. ■ literary a ship. ▶ **v.** [intrans.] (**keel over**) (of a boat or ship) turn over on its side; capsize. ■ informal (of a person or thing) fall over; collapse. — **keeled adj.** [in comb.] *a deep-keeled yacht.* [ME: from ON *kjǫlr*, of Gmc. origin.]

keel² ▶ **n.** Brit. a flat-bottomed freight boat; a keelboat. [ME: from Mid. Low Ger. *kēl*, MDu. *kiel* 'ship, boat.']

keel·boat /'kēl,bōt/ ▶ **n.** **1** a yacht built with a permanent keel rather than a centerboard. **2** a large, flat freight boat used on rivers.

keel·haul /'kēl,hôl/ ▶ **v.** [trans.] hist. punish (someone) by dragging them through the water under the keel of a ship, either across the width or from bow to stern. ■ often humorous punish or reprimand severely. [17th C.: from Du. *kielhalen*.]

Kee·ling Is·lands /'kēliNG/ another name for COCOS ISLANDS.

keel·son /'kēlsən/ (also **kel·son**) ▶ **n.** a centerline structure running the length of a ship and fastening the transverse members of the floor to the keel below. [ME *kelswayn*, rel. to Low Ger. *kielswin*, from *kiel* 'keel of a ship' + *swin* 'swine.']

Kee·lung /'kē'lo͝oNG/ see CHILUNG, Taiwan.

keen¹ /kēn/ ▶ **adj.** **1** having or showing eagerness or enthusiasm. ■ [predic.] (**keen on**) interested in or attracted by (someone or something). **2** sharp or penetrating, in particular: ■ (of a sense) highly developed. ■ (of mental faculties) quick to understand or function. ■ (of the air or wind) extremely cold; biting. ■ (of the edge or point of a blade) sharp. ■ literary (of a smell, light, or sound) penetrating; clear. **3** [predic.] informal & dated excellent. — **keen·ly adv. keen·ness n.** [OE *cēne* 'wise, clever,' of Gmc. origin; rel. to Ger. *kühn* 'bold, brave.']

keen² ▶ **v.** [intrans.] wail in grief for a dead person; sing a keen. ■ [usu. as n.] (**keening**) make an eerie wailing sound. ▶ **n.** an Irish funeral song accompanied by wailing in lamentation for the dead. — **keen·er n.** [19th C.: from Irish *caoinim* 'I wail.']

keep /kēp/ ▶ **v.** (past **kept** /kept/) [trans.] **1** have or retain possession of: *my father would keep the best for himself.* ■ retain or reserve for use in the future. ■ put or store in a regular place. ■ retain one's place in or on (a seat or saddle, the ground, etc.) against opposition or difficulty. ■ delay or detain; cause to be late: *I won't keep you.* **2** continue or cause to continue in a specified condition, position, course, etc. ■ [intrans.] continue doing or do repeatedly or habitually: *he keeps going on about the* *murder.* ■ [intrans.] (of a perishable commodity) remain in good condition. ■ [trans.] make (someone) do something for a period of time: *I have kept her waiting.* **3** provide for the sustenance of (someone). ■ provide (someone) with a regular supply of a commodity: *the money should keep him in cigarettes for a week.* ■ own and look after (an animal) for pleasure or profit. ■ own and manage (a shop or business). ■ guard; protect: *his only thought was to keep the boy from harm.* ■ support (someone, esp. a woman) financially in return for sexual favors: [as adj.] *a kept woman.* **4** honor or fulfill (a commitment or undertaking). ■ observe (a religious occasion) in the prescribed manner: *keep the Sabbath.* ■ pay due regard to (a law or custom). **5** make written entries in (a diary) on a regular basis. ■ write down as (a record). ▶**n. 1** food, clothes, and other essentials for living: *working overtime to earn his keep.* ■ the cost of such items. **2** the strongest or central tower of a castle, acting as a final refuge.

– PHRASES **for keeps** informal permanently; indefinitely.

– PHRASAL VERBS **keep someone after** make a pupil stay at school after normal hours as a punishment. **keep at** (or **keep someone at**) persist (or force someone to persist) with. **keep away** (or **keep someone away**) stay away (or make someone stay away). **keep back** (or **keep someone/something back**) remain (or cause someone or something to remain) at a distance. **keep someone back** make a student repeat a year at school because of poor grades. **keep something back** retain or withhold something. ■ decline to disclose something. ■ prevent tears from flowing. **keep down** stay hidden by crouching or lying down. **keep someone down** hold someone in subjection. **keep something down 1** cause something to remain at a low level. **2** retain food or drink in one's stomach without vomiting. **keep from** (or **keep someone from**) avoid (or cause someone to avoid) doing something. **keep something from 1** cause something to remain a secret from (someone). **2** cause something to stay out of. **keep someone in** confine someone indoors or in a particular place. **keep something in** restrain oneself from expressing a feeling. **keep off 1** avoid encroaching on or touching. ■ avoid consuming or smoking. ■ avoid (a subject). **2** (of bad weather) fail to occur. **keep someone/something off** prevent someone or something from encroaching on or touching. **keep on** continue to do something. **keep on about** speak about (something) repeatedly. **keep someone/something on** continue to use or employ someone or something. **keep out** (or **keep someone/something out**) remain (or cause someone or something to remain) outside. **keep to** avoid leaving (a path, road, or place). ■ adhere to (a schedule). ■ observe (a promise). ■ confine or restrict oneself to. **keep up** move or progress at the same rate as someone or something else. ■ meet a commitment to pay or do something regularly. **keep up with** learn about or be aware of (current events or developments). ■ continue to be in contact with (someone). **keep someone up** prevent someone from going to bed or to sleep. **keep something up** maintain or preserve something in the existing state; continue a course of action. ■ keep something in an efficient or proper state. ■ make something remain at a high level. [OE *cēpan* 'seize, take in,' also 'care for, attend to,' of unknown origin.]

keep·er /ˈkēpər/ ▶**n. 1** a person who manages or looks after something or someone, in particular: ■ a guard at a prison or a museum. ■ short for ZOOKEEPER. ■ short for GAMEKEEPER. ■ short for GOALKEEPER. ■ a person who is regarded as being in charge of someone else. **2** [with adj.] a food or drink that remains in a specified condition if stored: *hazelnuts are good keepers.* **3** informal a thing worth keeping. ■ a fish large enough to be kept when caught. **4** an object that keeps another in place, or protects something more fragile or valuable, in particular: ■ a ring worn to keep a more valuable one on the finger. ■ a bar of soft iron placed across the poles of a horseshoe magnet to maintain its strength. **5** Football a play in which the quarterback runs with the ball instead of handing it off or passing it. — **keep·er·ship n.**

keep·ing /ˈkēpiNG/ ▶**n.** the action of owning, maintaining, or protecting something.

– PHRASES **in** (or **out of**) **keeping with** in (or out of) harmony or conformity with.

keep·sake /ˈkēpˌsāk/ ▶**n.** a small item kept in memory of the person who gave it or originally owned it.

keeshond

kees·hond /ˈkāsˌhänd; -ˌhônt/ ▶**n.** a dog of a Dutch breed with long thick gray hair resembling a large Pomeranian. [1920s: Du., from *Kees* (nickname for the given name *Cornelius*) + *hond* 'dog.']

kees·ter ▶**n.** var. of KEISTER.

kef /kef/ (also **kif**) ▶**n.** a substance, esp. cannabis, smoked to produce a drowsy state. [19th C.: from Arab. *kayf* 'enjoyment, well-being.']

kef·fi·yeh ▶**n.** var. of KAFFIYEH.

Kef·la·vik /ˈkefləˌvēk; ˈkyeblə-/ a fishing port in southwestern Iceland; pop. 8,000. Iceland's international airport is located nearby.

keg /keg/ ▶**n. 1** a small barrel, esp. one of less than 30 gallons or (in the UK) 10 gallons. **2** a unit of weight equal to 100 lb (45 kg), used for nails. [17th C.: var. of Scots and US dial. *cag*, from ON *kaggi*.]

Ke·gel ex·er·cise /ˈkēgəl; ˈkeg-/ ▶**n.** an exercise to strengthen the pelvic floor muscles, used to treat urinary incontinence, or to prepare for or recover from childbirth. [from California physician Dr. Arnold *Kegel*.]

keg·ger /ˈkegər/ ▶**n.** informal (also **keg party**) a party at which beer is served, typically from kegs. ■ a keg of beer.

kei·ret·su /kāˈretso͞o/ ▶**n.** (pl. same) (in Japan) a conglomeration of businesses linked together by cross-shareholdings to form a robust corporate structure. [Japanese, from *kei* 'systems' + *retsu* 'tier.']

keis·ter /ˈkēstər/ (also **kees·ter**) ▶**n. 1** informal a person's buttocks. **2** dated a suitcase, bag, or box. [19th C. (in the sense 'suitcase, bag'): of unknown origin.]

Kel·ler /ˈkelər/, Helen Adams (1880–1968), US writer and social reformer. Blind and deaf from an early age, she learned how to read, type, and speak with the help of tutor Anne Sullivan (1866–1936).

Kel·logg Pact /ˈkelôg; -äg/ (also **Kellogg–Briand Pact**) a treaty renouncing war as an instrument of national policy, signed in Paris in 1928 by representatives of fifteen nations. It grew out of a proposal made by the French premier Aristide Briand (1862–1932) to Frank B. Kellogg (1856–1937), US secretary of state.

Kel·ly[1] /ˈkelē/, Emmett Lee (1898–1979), US entertainer. He played Weary Willie, the mournful clown.

Kel·ly[2], Grace Patricia (1928–82), US actress; also called (from 1956) **Princess Grace of Monaco**. She retired from movies in 1956 to marry Prince Rainier III of Monaco.

ke·loid /ˈkēˌloid/ ▶**n.** Med. an area of irregular fibrous tissue formed at the site of a scar or injury. [19th C.: via Fr. from Gk. *khēlē* 'crab's claw' + -OID.]

kelp /kelp/ ▶**n.** a large brown seaweed (family Laminariaceae) used as a source of various salts. Some kinds form underwater "forests" that support large populations of animals. ■ the calcined ashes of seaweed. [ME: of unknown origin.]

kelp·fish /ˈkelpˌfisH/ ▶**n.** (pl. same or **-fish·es**) any of a number of fish that live among kelp or other marine algae, in particular a small fish of the Pacific coast of North America (*Gibbonsia* and other genera, family Clinidae), and an Australian fish (family Chironemidae) that lives among seagrass and algae.

kel·pie /ˈkelpē/ ▶**n. 1** a water spirit of Scottish folklore, typically taking the form of a horse, reputed to delight in the drowning of travelers. **2** a sheepdog of an Australian breed with a smooth coat, originally bred from a Scottish collie. [17th C.: perh. from Scot. Gael. *cailpeach, colpach* 'bullock, colt.']

Kel·vin /ˈkelvən/, William Thomson, 1st Baron (1824–1907), British physicist. He introduced the absolute scale of temperature and restated the second law of thermodynamics.

kel·vin /ˈkelvən/ (abbr.: **K**) ▶**n.** the SI base unit of thermodynamic temperature, equal in magnitude to the degree Celsius. [19th C.: named after Lord KELVIN.]

Kel·vin scale ▶**n.** a scale of temperature with absolute zero as zero, and the triple point of water as exactly 273.16 degrees.

Ke·mal Pa·sha /keˈmäl ˈpäsHə; kəˈmäl/ see ATATÜRK.

Ke·me·ro·vo /ˈkyemirəvə; -əˌvō/ a city in south central Russia, to the east of Novosibirsk; pop. 521,000.

kemp /kemp/ ▶**n.** a coarse hair or fiber in wool. — **kemp·y adj.** [ME: from ON *kampr* 'beard, whisker.']

Kem·pis /ˈkempəs/, Thomas à, see THOMAS À KEMPIS.

kempt /kem(p)t/ ▶**adj.** esp. Brit. (of a person or a place) maintained in a neat and clean condition; well cared for. [OE *cemd-*, past part. of *cemban* 'to comb,' of Gmc. origin; rel. to COMB.]

ken /ken/ ▶**n.** [in sing.] one's range of knowledge or sight. ▶**v.** (**ken·ning**; past and past part. **kenned** or **kent** /kent/) [trans.] Scot. & N. English know. ■ recognize; identify. [OE *cennan* 'tell, make known,' from an Indo-Eur. root shared by CAN[1] and KNOW.]

ke·naf /kəˈnaf/ ▶**n.** a tropical plant (*Hibiscus cannabinus*) of the mallow family that yields a jutelike fiber. ■ the brown fiber of this plant, used to make paper, ropes, and coarse cloth. [19th C.: from Pers., var. of *kanab* 'hemp.']

Ke·nai Peninsula /ˈkēˌnī/ a region in southern Alaska, in the Gulf of Alaska, south of Anchorage.

Ken·dal Green /ˈkendl/ ▶**n.** a kind of rough green woolen cloth. ■ the green color of this cloth.

Ken·dall /ˈkendl/, Edward Calvin (1886–1972), US biochemist. He isolated crystalline thyroxine from the thyroid and discovered cortisone. Nobel Prize for Physiology or Medicine (1950, shared with Philip S. Hench 1896–1965 and Tadeus Reichstein 1897–1996).

ken·do /ˈkenˌdō/ ▶**n.** a Japanese form of fencing with two-handed bamboo swords, originally developed as a safe form of sword training for samurai. — **ken·do·ist** /-dōist/ **n.** [Japanese, from *ken* 'sword' + *dō* 'way.']

Ke·neal·ly /kə'nēlē/, Thomas Michael (1935–), Australian writer. His works include *Schindler's Ark* (1982).

Ken·nan /'kenən/, George Frost (1904–2005), US diplomat. He was ambassador to the Soviet Union 1952 and to Yugoslavia 1961–63.

Ken·ne·bec Riv·er /'kenə,bek/ a river that flows through west central Maine to the Atlantic Ocean.

Ken·ne·dy[1] /'kenidē/ a US political family, prominent in the Democratic Party. Joseph Patrick (1888–1969), ambassador to England 1938–40, made his fortune in banking, the stock market, shipbuilding, and movies. His son John Fitzgerald (1917–63), known as **Jack** or **JFK**, was the 35th president of the US 1961–63. He served as a US representative from Massachusetts 1947–53 and a US senator 1953–60 before being the youngest person elected to the presidency. As president, he successfully demanded the withdrawal of Soviet missiles from Cuba during the Cuban Missile Crisis. He was assassinated in Dallas, Texas. JFK's brother Robert Francis (1925–68), known as **Bobby**, was US attorney general 1961–64. A champion of the civil rights movement, he served as a US senator from New York 1965–68 and was assassinated during his presidential campaign in 1968. Their brother Edward Moore (1932–), known as **Ted**, has served as a US senator from Massachusetts 1962– .

Ken·ne·dy[2], Anthony McLeod (1935–), US Supreme Court associate justice 1988– .

Ken·ne·dy[3], William (1928–), US writer. His novels include *Ironweed* (1983).

Ken·ne·dy, Cape former name (1963–73) for **Canaveral, Cape**.

ken·nel /'kenl/ ▶ **n.** a small shelter for a dog or cat. ■ a boarding or breeding establishment for dogs or cats. ■ fig. a small or sordid dwelling. ▶ **v.** (**-neled, -nel·ing**; esp. Brit. **-nelled, -nel·ling**) [trans.] put (a dog or cat) in a kennel. [ME: from an Old North. Fr. var. of OFr. *chenil*, from L. *canis* 'dog.']

Ken·neth I /'kenɪᴛʜ/ (died 858), king of Scotland *c.*844–858; known as **Kenneth MacAlpin**. He is traditionally viewed as the founder of the kingdom of Scotland.

ken·ning /'kenɪɴɢ/ ▶ **n.** a compound expression in Old English and Old Norse poetry with metaphorical meaning, e.g., *oar-steed* = ship. [19th C.: from ON, from *kenna* 'know, perceive'; rel. to **ken**.]

ke·no /'kēnō/ ▶ **n.** a game of chance similar to lotto, based on the drawing of numbers that must correspond with selected numbers on cards. [19th C.: from Fr. *kine*, denoting a set of five winning lottery numbers.]

ke·no·sis /kə'nōsis/ ▶ **n.** (in Christian theology) the renunciation of the divine nature, at least in part, by Christ in the Incarnation. — **ke·not·ic** /-'nätik/ **adj.** [19th C.: from Gk. *kenōsis* 'an emptying,' from *kenoun* 'to empty,' from *kenos* 'empty.']

Ken·sing·ton /'kenzɪɴɢtən/ a fashionable residential district in central London, England.

Kent /kent/ a county on the southeastern coast of England. — **Kent·ish adj.**

kent /kent/ ▶ **v.** past and past participle of **ken**.

ken·te /'kentə; -tē/ ▶ **n.** a brightly colored, banded material made in Ghana. ■ a long garment made from this material, worn loosely around the shoulders and waist. [20th C.: from Twi, 'cloth.']

Ken·ton /'kentn/, Stan (1912–79), US bandleader, composer, and arranger; born *Stanley Newcomb*. He is associated with the big-band jazz style of the 1950s.

Ken·tuck·y /kən'təkē/ a state in the southeastern US; pop. 4,041,769; capital, Frankfort; statehood, June 1, 1792 (15). Ceded by the French to the British in 1763 and then to the US in 1783 by the Treaty of Paris, it was explored by Daniel Boone. — **Ken·tuck·i·an** /-ēən/ **adj.**

Ken·tuck·y Der·by ▶ **n.** an annual horse race for three-year-olds at Louisville, Kentucky. First held in 1875, it is the oldest horse race in the US. It is the first race of horse racing's Triple Crown.

Ken·ya /'kenyə; 'kēnyə/ a country in East Africa. *See box.* — **Ken·yan adj. & n.**

Ken·ya, Mount a mountain in central Kenya, south of the equator.

Ken·yat·ta /ken'yätə/, Jomo (*c.*1891–1978), prime minister 1963 and president 1964–78 of Kenya.

kep·i /'kāpē; 'kepē/ ▶ **n.** (pl. **kep·is**) a French military cap with a flat top and horizontal bill. [19th C.: from Fr. *képi*, from Swiss Ger. *Käppi*, dimin. of *Kappe* 'cap.']

Kep·ler /'keplər/, Johannes (1571–1630), German astronomer. He discovered the laws of orbital motion. — **Kep·ler·i·an** /kep'li(ə)rēən/ **adj.**

Kep·ler's laws three theorems describing orbital motion. The first law states that planets move in elliptical orbits with the sun at one focus. The second states that the radius vector of a planet sweeps out equal areas in equal times. The third law relates the distances of the planets from the sun to their orbital periods.

kept /kept/ past and past participle of **keep**.

Ke·ra·la /'kerələ/ a state on the southwestern coast of India; capital, Trivandrum. — **Ke·ra·lite** /-,līt/ **adj. & n.**

kerat- ▶ **comb. form** var. of **kerato-** shortened before a vowel (as in *keratectomy*).

ker·a·tec·to·my /,kerə'tektəmē/ ▶ **n.** surgical removal of a section or layer of the cornea, usually performed using a laser to correct myopia.

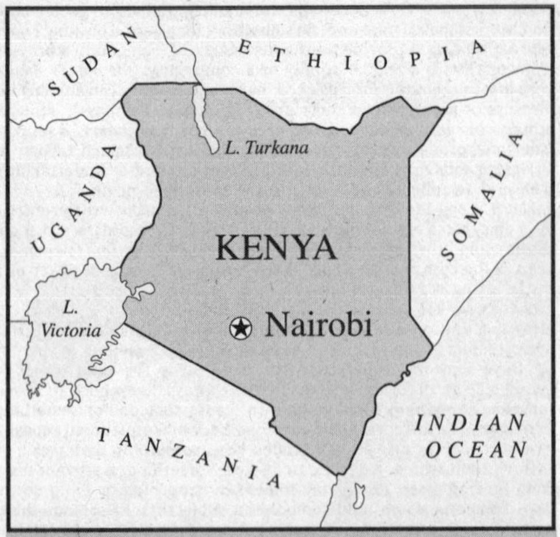

Kenya

Official name: Republic of Kenya
Location: East Africa, on the Indian Ocean
Area: 225,000 square miles (582,700 sq km)
Population: 32,021,000
Capital: Nairobi
Languages: English, Kiswahili (both official), numerous indigenous languages
Currency: Kenyan shilling

ker·a·tin /'kerətin/ ▶ **n.** a fibrous protein forming the main structural constituent of hair, feathers, hoofs, claws, horns, etc. — **ke·rat·i·nous** /kə'ratn-əs/ **adj.** [19th C.: from Gk. *keras*, *kerat-* 'horn' + **-in**[1].]

ker·a·tin·ize /'keratn,īz/ ▶ **v.** Biol. change or become changed into a form containing keratin. — **ker·a·tin·i·za·tion** /,keratn-i'zāsʜən/ **n.**

ker·a·tin·o·cyte /kə'ratn-ə,sīt/ ▶ **n.** Biol. an epidermal cell that produces keratin.

ker·a·ti·tis /,kerə'tītis/ ▶ **n.** Med. inflammation of the cornea of the eye.

kerato- ▶ **comb. form** (also **kerat-**) **1** relating to keratin or horny tissue. **2** relating to the cornea. [from Gk. *keras*, *kerat-* 'horn.']

ker·a·to·plas·ty /'kerətə,plastē/ ▶ **n.** surgery carried out on the cornea, esp. corneal transplantation.

ker·a·tose /'kerə,tōs/ ▶ **adj.** Zool. (of certain sponges) composed of a horny substance.

ker·a·to·sis /,kerə'tōsis/ ▶ **n.** (pl. **-ses** /-sēz/) Med. a horny growth, esp. on the skin.

ker·a·tot·o·my /,kerə'tätəmē/ ▶ **n.** a surgical operation involving cutting into the cornea of the eye. The most common form is **radial keratotomy**, performed to correct myopia.

kerb /kərb/ ▶ **n.** British spelling of **curb**.

ker·chief /'kərcʜəf; -,cʜēf/ ▶ **n.** a piece of fabric used to cover the head, or worn tied around the neck. ■ a handkerchief. — **ker·chiefed adj.** [ME *kerchef*, from OFr. *cuevrechief*, from *couvrir* 'to cover' + *chief* 'head.']

Ke·res /'kā,rās/ ▶ **n.** (pl. same) **1** a member of a Pueblo Indian people of New Mexico. **2** the language of this people, of unknown affinity. ▶ **adj.** of or relating to this people or their language. — **Ker·e·san** /'kerisən/ **adj.** [from Amer. Sp. *Queres*, from Amer. Ind.]

kerf /kərf/ ▶ **n.** a slit made by cutting, esp. with a saw. — **kerfed adj.** [OE *cyrf* 'cutting, a cut,' of West Gmc. origin; rel. to **carve**.]

ker·fuf·fle /kər'fəfəl/ ▶ **n.** [in sing.] informal, esp. Brit. a commotion or fuss. [19th C.: perh. from Scots *curfuffle* (prob. from Scot. Gael. *car* 'twist, bend' + imitative Scots *fuffle* 'to disorder').]

Ker·gue·len Is·lands /'kərgələn; ,kərgə'len/ a group of islands in the southern Indian Ocean, part of the French Southern and Antarctic Territories. The only settlement is a scientific base.

Kér·ki·ra /'kerki(ə)rə/ modern Greek name for **Corfu**.

Ker·mad·ec Is·lands /kər'madik/ a group of uninhabited islands in the western South Pacific Ocean, administered by New Zealand.

ker·mes /'kermēz/ ▶ **n.** **1** a red dye used, esp. formerly, for coloring fabrics and manuscripts. ■ the dried bodies of a female scale insect, which are crushed to yield this dye. **2** (**oak kermes**) the scale insect (*Kermes ilicis*, family Eriococcidae) that is used for this dye, forming berrylike galls on the kermes oak. [16th C.: from Fr. *kermès*, from Arab. *ḳirmiz*.]

ker·mes oak ▶ **n.** a very small evergreen Mediterranean oak (*Quercus coccifera*). It has prickly hollylike leaves and was formerly prized as a host plant for the insect kermes.

Kern /kərn/, Jerome David (1885–1945), US composer. A major influence in the development of the musical, he wrote *Showboat* (1927).

kern /kərn/ Print. ▶ v. [trans.] [usu. as n.] (**kerning**) adjust the spacing between (letters or characters) in a piece of text to be printed. ■ make (letters) overlap. [17th C.: perh. from Fr. *carne* 'corner,' from L. *cardo, cardin-* 'hinge.']

ker·nel /'kərnl/ ▶ n. a softer, usually edible part of a nut, seed, or fruit stone contained within its hard shell. ■ the seed and hard husk of a cereal, esp. wheat. ■ [in sing.] the central or most important part of something. ■ the most basic level or core of an operating system of a computer, responsible for resource allocation, file management, and security. [OE *cyrnel*, dimin. of CORN[1].]

ker·o·gen /'kerəjən/ ▶ n. a complex fossilized organic material, found in oil shale and other sedimentary rock. [20th C.: from Gk. *kēros* 'wax' + -GEN.]

ker·o·sene /'kerə,sēn; 'kar-; ,kerə'sēn; ,kar-/ (also esp. Brit. **ker·o·sine**) ▶ n. a light fuel oil obtained by distilling petroleum, used esp. in jet engines and domestic heaters and lamps and as a cleaning solvent. [19th C.: from Gk. *kēros* 'wax.']

Ker·ou·ac /'kero͞o,ak/, Jack (1922–69), US writer and poet; born *Jean-Louis Lebris de Kérouac*. A leading figure of the beat generation, he is best known for his semiautobiographical novel *On the Road* (1957).

ker·ri·a /'kerēə/ ▶ n. an eastern Asian shrub (*Kerria japonica*) of the rose family, cultivated for its yellow flowers. [19th C.: after William *Ker(r)* (died 1814), English botanical collector.]

Ker·ry /'kerē/ a county of the Republic of Ireland, on the southwestern coast in the province of Munster; county town, Tralee.

Ker·ry blue (also **Kerry blue terrier**) ▶ n. a terrier of a breed with a silky blue-gray coat.

ker·sey /'kərzē/ ▶ n. a kind of coarse, ribbed cloth with a short nap, woven from short-stapled wool. [ME: prob. from *Kersey*, England.]

ker·sey·mere /'kərzē,mi(ə)r/ ▶ n. a fine twilled woolen cloth. [18th C.: alt. of *cassimere*, var. of CASHMERE.]

Ke·sey /'kēzē/, Ken Elton (1935–2001), US writer. His novels include *One Flew Over the Cuckoo's Nest* (1962).

kes·trel /'kestrəl/ ▶ n. a small falcon (genus *Falco*) that hovers with rapidly beating wings while searching for prey on the ground. Several species include the **common kestrel** (*F. tinnunculus*) of Eurasia and Africa, and the **American kestrel** (*F. sparverius*). [ME *castrel*, var. of OFr. *crecerelle*, perh. imitative of its call.]

ke·ta·mine /'ketə,mēn; -min/ ▶ n. a synthetic compound, $C_{13}H_{16}NOCl$, used as an anesthetic and analgesic drug and also (illicitly) as a hallucinogen. [20th C.: blend of KETONE and AMINE.]

ketch /kecн/ ▶ n. a two-masted, fore-and-aft-rigged sailboat with a mizzenmast stepped forward of the rudder and smaller than the foremast. [17th C.: later form of obs. *catch*, prob. from CATCH.]

ketch·up /'kecнəp/ (also **cat·sup** pronunc. same or /'kacнəp; 'katsəp/) ▶ n. a spicy sauce made chiefly from tomatoes and vinegar, used as a condiment. [17th C.: perh. from Chin. (Cantonese dial.) *k'ē chap* 'tomato juice.']

ke·tene /'kē,tēn/ ▶ n. Chem. a pungent colorless reactive gas, $CH_2{=}C{=}O$, used as an intermediate in chemical synthesis. ■ any substituted derivative of this. [20th C.: from KETONE + -ENE.]

ke·to ac·id /'kētō/ ▶ n. Chem. a compound whose molecule contains both a carboxyl group (–COOH) and a ketone group (–CO–).

ke·tone /'kē,tōn/ ▶ n. Chem. an organic compound containing a carbonyl group =C=O bonded to two alkyl groups, made by oxidizing secondary alcohols. The simplest such compound is acetone. — **ke·ton·ic** /kē'tänik/ adj. [19th C.: from Ger. *Keton*, alt. of *Aketon* 'acetone.']

ke·tone bod·y ▶ n. Biochem. any of three related compounds (acetone, acetoacetic acid, beta-hydroxybutyric acid) produced during the metabolism of fats.

ke·to·ne·mi·a /,kētə'nēmēə/ (Brit. **ke·to·nae·mi·a**) ▶ n. Med. the presence of an abnormally high concentration of ketone bodies in the blood.

ke·to·nu·ri·a /,kētō'n(y)o͝orēə/ ▶ n. Med. the excretion of abnormally large amounts of ketone bodies in the urine, characteristic of diabetes mellitus, starvation, or other medical conditions.

ke·to·sis /kē'tōsis/ ▶ n. Med. a condition characterized by raised levels of ketone bodies in the body, associated with abnormal fat metabolism and diabetes mellitus. — **ke·tot·ic** /-'tätik/ adj.

Ket River /'ket/ a river in Russia that flows west from Krasnoyarsk into the Ob River at Kolpashevo.

Ket·ter·ing /'ketəriнg/, Charles Franklin (1876–1958), US engineer. He developed the electric starter for automobiles 1912 and worked to define the octane rating of fuels.

ket·tle /'ketl/ ▶ n. a vessel, usually made of metal and with a handle, used for boiling liquids or cooking foods; a pot. ■ a teakettle.

– PHRASES **a different kettle of fish** informal a completely different type of person or thing from the one previously mentioned. **the pot calling the kettle black** see POT[1]. **a fine** (or **pretty**) **kettle of fish** informal an awkward state of affairs. — **ket·tle·ful** /-,fo͝ol/ n. (pl. **-fuls**). [OE *cetel, cietel*, of Gmc. origin, based on L. *catillus*, dimin. of *catinus* 'deep container.']

kettledrum

ket·tle·drum /'ketl,drəm/ ▶ n. a large drum shaped like a bowl, with a tension-adjustable membrane (for pitch) stretched across. Also collectively called TIMPANI. — **ket·tle·drum·mer** n.

ket·tle hole ▶ n. Geol. a hollow, typically filled by a lake, resulting from the melting of a mass of ice trapped in glacial deposits.

keV ▶ abbr. kiloelectronvolt(s).

Kev·lar /'kevlär/ ▶ n. trademark a synthetic fiber of high tensile strength used esp. as a reinforcing agent in the manufacture of tires and other rubber products and protective gear such as helmets and vests.

Kew Gar·dens /kyo͞o/ the Royal Botanic Gardens at Kew, in Richmond, London.

kew·pie /'kyo͞opē/ (also **kew·pie doll**) ▶ n. trademark a type of doll characterized by a large head, big eyes, chubby cheeks, and a curl on top of its head.

Key /kē/, Francis Scott (1779–1843), US lawyer and poet. A witness to US defense of Fort McHenry in Baltimore in 1814, he wrote the poem "Defence of Fort M'Henry." The poem was later set to music, renamed "The Star-Spangled Banner," and, in 1931, adopted as the US national anthem.

key[1] /kē/ ▶ n. (pl. **keys**) **1** a small piece of shaped metal, with incisions cut to fit the wards of a particular lock, that is inserted into a lock and turned to open or close it. ■ a similar implement for operating a switch in the form of a lock, esp. one operating the ignition of a motor vehicle. ■ short for KEY CARD. ■ an instrument for grasping and turning a screw, peg, or nut, esp. one for winding a clock or turning a valve. ■ a pin, bolt, or wedge inserted between other pieces, or fitting into a hole or space designed for it, so as to lock parts together. **2** one of several buttons on a panel for operating a typewriter, word processor, or computer terminal. ■ a lever depressed by the finger in playing an instrument such as the organ, piano, flute, or concertina. ■ a lever operating a mechanical device for making or breaking an electric circuit, for example, in telegraphy. **3** a thing that provides a means of gaining access to or understanding something. ■ an explanatory list of symbols used in a map, table, etc. ■ a set of answers to exercises or problems. ■ a word or system for solving a cipher or code. ■ the first move in the solution of a chess problem. ■ Comput. a field in a record that is used to identify that record uniquely. **4** Music a group of notes based on a particular note and comprising a scale, regarded as forming the tonal basis of a piece or passage of music: *the key of E minor.* ■ the tone or pitch of someone's voice. ■ fig. the prevailing tone or tenor of a piece of writing, situation, etc. ■ the prevailing range of tones or intensities in a painting. **5** the dry winged fruit of an ash, maple, or sycamore maple, typically growing in bunches; a samara. **6** Basketball the keyhole-shaped area marked on the court near each basket, comprising the free-throw circle and the foul line. ▶ adj. of paramount or crucial importance. ▶ v. (**keys, keyed** /kēd/) [trans.] **1** enter or operate on (data) by means of a computer keyboard: *she keyed in a series of commands.* **2** [trans.] (usu. **be keyed**) fasten (something) in position with a pin, wedge, or bolt. ■ (**key something to**) make something fit in with or be linked to. ■ (**key someone/something into/in with**) cause someone or something to be in harmony with. **3** [trans.] vandalize a car by scraping the paint from it with a key.

– PHRASAL VERBS **key someone up** (usu. **be keyed up**) make someone nervous, tense, or excited, esp. before an important event. — **keyed** adj. **key·er** n. [OE *cǣg, cǣge*, of unknown origin.]

key[2] ▶ n. a low-lying island or reef, esp. in the Caribbean. Compare with CAY. [17th C.: from Sp. *cayo* 'shoal, reef,' influenced by QUAY.]

key·board /'kē,bôrd/ ▶ n. **1** a panel of keys that operate a computer or typewriter. **2** a set of keys on a piano or similar musical instrument. ■ an electronic musical instrument with keys arranged as on a piano. ▶ v. [trans.] enter (data) by means of a keyboard. — **key·board·er** n. **key·board·ist** n. (sense 2).

key card (also **card key**) ▶ n. a small plastic card that can be used instead of a door key, bearing magnetically encoded data that can be read and processed by an electronic device.

key grip ▶ n. the person in a film crew who is in charge of the camera equipment.

key·hole /'kē,hōl/ ▶ n. a hole in a lock into which the key is inserted. ■ a circle cut out of a garment as a decorative effect, typically at the front or back neckline of a dress.

key·hole saw ▶ n. a saw with a long, narrow blade for cutting small holes such as keyholes.

Key Lar·go /'kē 'lärgō/ a resort island off the southern coast of Florida.

Key lime ▶ n. a small yellowish lime with a sharp flavor. [named after the Florida *Keys*.]

Keynes /kānz/, John Maynard, 1st Baron (1883–1946), English economist. He laid the foundations of modern macroeconomics. — **Keynes·i·an** /'kānzēən/ adj. & n. **Keynes·i·an·ism** /'kānzēə,nizəm/ n.

key·note /'kē,nōt/ ▶ n. **1** a prevailing tone or central theme, typically one set or introduced at the start of a conference. **2** Music the note on which a key is based. — **key·not·er** n.

key·pad /'kē,pad/ ▶ n. a miniature keyboard or set of buttons for operating a portable electronic device, telephone, or other equipment.

key·punch /'kē,pəncн/ ▶ n. a device for transferring data by means of punching holes or notches on a series of cards or paper tape. ▶ v. [trans.]

put into the form of punched cards or paper tape by means of such a device. — **key·punch·er** n.

key ring ▶ n. a metal ring onto which keys may be threaded in order to keep them together.

key sig·na·ture ▶ n. Music any of several combinations of sharps or flats after the clef at the beginning of each stave indicating the key of a composition.

key·stone /'kē,stōn/ ▶ n. a central stone at the summit of an arch, locking the whole together. ■ [usu. in sing.] the central principle or part of a policy, system, etc., on which all else depends.

keystone

key·stroke /'kē,strōk/ ▶ n. a single depression of a key on a keyboard, esp. as a measure of work.

key·way /'kē,wā/ ▶ n. a slot cut in a part of a machine or an electrical connector to ensure correct orientation with another part that is fitted with a key. ■ a keyhole for a flat key.

Key West a city in southern Florida, on Key West Island, the southernmost city in the continental US; pop. 25,478.

key·word /'kē,wərd/ ▶ n. a word or concept of great significance. ■ a word that acts as the key to a cipher or code. ■ an informative word used in an information retrieval system to indicate the content of a document. ■ a significant word mentioned in an index.

kg ▶ abbr. ■ keg(s). ■ kilogram(s).

KGB the state security police (1954–91) of the former USSR. [Russ., abbrev. of *Komitet gosudarstvennoĭ bezopasnosti* 'Committee of State Security.']

Kgs ▶ abbr. Bible Kings.

Kha·ba·rovsk /kHə'bärəfsk/ an administrative territory on the eastern coast of Siberia in Russia. ■ its capital, a city on the Amur River; pop. 608,000.

Kha·kas·sia /kHə'käsyə/ an autonomous republic in south central Russia; pop. 569,000; capital, Abakan.

khak·i /'kakē/ ▶ n. (pl. **khak·is**) a textile fabric of a dull brownish-yellow color, in particular a strong cotton fabric used in military clothing. ■ a dull brownish-yellow color. ■ (**khakis**) clothing, esp. pants, of this fabric and color. [19th C.: from Urdu *ḵākī* 'dust-colored,' from *ḵāk* 'dust,' from Pers.]

Khal·kha /'kalkə/ ▶ n. 1 a member of a section of the Mongolian people, constituting the bulk of the population of Mongolia. 2 the language of these people, a demotic form of Mongolian adopted as the official language of Mongolia. ▶ adj. of or relating to this people or their language. [of unknown origin.]

Khal·sa /'kälsə/ ▶ n. the body or company of fully initiated Sikhs, to which devout orthodox Sikhs are ritually admitted at puberty. [via Urdu from Pers., from the fem. form of Arab. *ḵāliṣ* 'pure, belonging to.']

Kha·ma /'kämə/, Sir Seretse (1921–80), president of Botswana 1966–80.

Kham·bhat, Gulf of /'kəmbət/ (also **Gulf of Khambat**) another name for CAMBAY, GULF OF.

kham·sin /käm'sēn/ ▶ n. an oppressive, hot southerly or southeasterly wind blowing in Egypt in spring. [17th C.: from Arab. *ḵamsīn*, from *ḵamsūn* 'fifty.']

khan[1] /kän/ ▶ n. a title given to rulers and officials in central Asia, Afghanistan, and certain other Muslim countries. ■ any of the successors of Genghis Khan, supreme rulers of the Turkish, Tartar, and Mongol peoples and emperors of China in the Middle Ages. — **khan·ate** /'känāt/ n. [ME: from OFr. *chan*, med. L. *canus*, *caanus*, from Turkic *ḵān* 'lord, prince.']

khan[2] ▶ n. (in the Middle East) an inn for travelers, built around a central courtyard. [from Pers. *ḵān*.]

Kharg Is·land /kärg; kHärg/ a small island at the head of the Persian Gulf, site of Iran's principal deep-water oil terminal.

Khar·kiv /'kHärkif; 'kär,kôf/ a city in northeastern Ukraine; pop. 1,618,000. Russian name KHARKOV.

Khar·toum /kär'to͞om/ the capital of Sudan, situated at the junction of the Blue Nile and the White Nile rivers; pop. 925,000. It was the capital of the Anglo-Egyptian government of Sudan until 1956, when it became capital of the independent Republic of Sudan.

khat /kät/ ▶ n. 1 the leaves of an Arabian shrub, which are chewed (or drunk as an infusion) as a stimulant. 2 the shrub (*Catha edulis*, family Celastraceae) that produces these leaves, often cultivated. [19th C.: from Arab. *ḵāt*.]

Kha·zar /kə'zär/ ▶ n. a member of a Turkic people who occupied a large part of southern Russia from the 6th to the 11th centuries and who converted to Judaism in the 8th century. ▶ adj. of or relating to the Khazars. [of unknown origin.]

Khe·dive /kə'dēv/ ▶ n. the title of the viceroy of Egypt under Turkish rule (1867–1914). — **Khe·div·al** /-'dēvəl/ adj. **Khe·div·i·al** /-'dēvēəl/ adj. [via Fr. from Ottoman Turk. *ḵediv*, from Pers. *ḵadiw* 'prince' (var. of *ḵudaiw* 'minor god,' from *ḵudā* 'god').]

Khe Sanh /'kā'sän/ a village in the northwest hills of the former South Vietnam, site of one of the costliest battles of the Vietnam War.

Khi·os /'kHē,ôs; 'kē-/ Greek name for CHIOS.

Khi·tai /'kē'tī/ variant of CATHAY.

Khmer /kə'me(ə)r/ ▶ n. 1 an ancient kingdom in Southeast Asia that reached the peak of its power in the 11th century. 2 a native or inhabitant of the ancient Khmer kingdom. 3 a native or inhabitant of Cambodia. 4 the Mon-Khmer language that is the official language of Cambodia. Also called CAMBODIAN. ▶ adj. of, relating to, or denoting the Khmers or their language. [the name in Khmer.]

Khmer Re·pub·lic former official name (1970–75) for CAMBODIA.

Khmer Rouge /'ro͞ozH/ a communist guerrilla organization that opposed the Cambodian government in the 1960s and waged a civil war from 1970, taking power in 1975. [from KHMER + Fr. *rouge* 'red.']

Khoi·khoi /'koi,koi/ (also **Khoi-khoin** /-,koi-in/, **Khoi**) ▶ n. (pl. same) a member of a group of indigenous peoples of South Africa and Namibia, traditionally nomadic hunter-gatherers. ▶ adj. of or relating to this people or their languages. [Nama, lit. 'men of men.']

Khoi·san /'koi,sän/ ▶ n. 1 [usu. treated as pl.] a collective term for the Khoikhoi (Hottentot) and San (Bushmen) peoples of southern Africa. 2 a language family of southern Africa, including the languages of the Khoikhoi and San, notable for the use of clicks as consonants. ▶ adj. of or relating to these languages or their speakers. [blend of KHOIKHOI and SAN.]

Kho·mei·ni /kō'mānē; kHō-; ,kHōmā'nē/, Ruhollah (1900–89), Iranian Shiite Muslim leader; known as **Ayatollah Khomeini**. He returned from exile in 1979 to lead an Islamic revolution that overthrew the shah.

Khon·su /'kHän,so͞o/ Egyptian Mythol. a moon god worshiped esp. at Thebes, a member of a triad as the divine son of Amun and Mut.

Khor·ram·shahr /,kHôrəm'sHähər; ,kôr-/ an oil port on the Shatt al-Arab waterway in western Iran, almost totally destroyed during the Iran–Iraq War.

khoum /ko͞om; ko͝om/ ▶ n. a monetary unit of Mauritania, equal to one fifth of an ouguiya. [from Arab. *ḵums* 'one fifth.']

Khru·shchev /'kro͞osH,cHev; -,cHôf; kHro͞osH'cHyôf/, Nikita Sergeevich (1894–1971), premier of the Soviet Union 1958–64. He came close to war with the US over the Cuban Missile Crisis in 1962 and also clashed with China. — **Khru·shchev·i·an** /kro͞osH'cHevēən/ adj.

Khu·fu /'ko͞o,fo͞o/ see CHEOPS.

Khun·jer·ab Pass /'ko͝onjə,räb/ a pass through the Himalayas, on the Karakoram highway at a height of 16,088 feet (4,900 m), that links China and Pakistan.

Khy·ber Pass /'kībər/ a pass in the Hindu Kush, on the border between Pakistan and Afghanistan, at a height of 3,520 feet (1,067 m).

kHz ▶ abbr. kilohertz.

ki ▶ n. var. of QI.

KIA (also **K.I.A.**) ▶ abbr. killed in action.

ki·ang /kē'äNG/ ▶ n. a wild ass (*Equus hemionus kiang*) with a thick furry coat, native to the Tibetan plateau. [19th C.: from Tibetan *kyang*.]

Kiang·si /'kyaNG'sē; 'gyäNG-/ variant of JIANGXI.

Kiang·su /'kyaNG'so͞o; 'gyäNG-/ variant of JIANGSU.

kib·ble /'kibəl/ ▶ v. [trans.] [usu. as adj.] (**kibbled**) grind or chop (beans, grain, etc.) coarsely. ▶ n. ground meal shaped into pellets, esp. for pet food. [18th C.: of unknown origin.]

kib·butz /ki'bo͝ots/ ▶ n. (pl. **kib·but·zim** /ki,bo͝ot'sēm/) a communal settlement in Israel, typically a farm. [1930s: from mod. Heb. *qibbūṣ* 'gathering.']

kib·butz·nik /ki'bo͝otsnik/ ▶ n. a member of a kibbutz.

kibe /kīb/ ▶ n. an ulcerated chilblain, esp. one on the heel. [ME: of unknown origin.]

kib·itz /'kibits/ ▶ v. [intrans.] informal look on and offer unwelcome advice, esp. at a card game. ■ speak informally; chat. — **kib·itz·er** n. [1920s: Yiddish, from colloq. German, from Ger. *Kiebitz* 'interfering onlooker' (lit. 'lapwing').]

kib·lah ▶ n. var. of QIBLA.

ki·bosh /kə'bäsH; 'kī,bäsH/ ▶ n. (in phrase **put the kibosh on**) informal put an end to; dispose of decisively. [19th C.: of unknown origin.]

kick /kik/ ▶ v. 1 [trans.] strike or propel forcibly with the foot. ■ [intrans.] strike out or flail with the foot or feet. ■ (**kick oneself**) be annoyed with oneself for doing something foolish or missing an opportunity. ■ (in football, rugby, etc.) score (a goal) by a kick. ■ [intrans.] (of a gun) recoil when fired. 2 [trans.] informal succeed in giving up (a habit or addiction). ▶ n. 1 a blow or forceful thrust with the foot. ■ (in sports) an instance of striking the ball with the foot. ■ the recoil of a gun when discharged. ■ a sudden forceful jolt. 2 [in sing.] informal the sharp stimulant effect of something, esp. alcohol. ■ a thrill of pleasurable, often reckless excitement: *turning to crime just for kicks*. ■ [with adj.] a specified temporary interest or enthusiasm: *the jogging kick*.

– PHRASES **kick (some) ass** (or **butt**) vulgar slang act in a forceful or aggressive manner. **kick someone's ass** (or **butt**) vulgar slang beat, dominate, or defeat someone. **kick the bucket** informal die. **a kick in the pants** (or **up the backside**) informal an unwelcome surprise that prompts or forces fresh effort. **a kick in the teeth** informal a grave setback or disappointment. **kick someone in the teeth** informal cause someone a grave setback or disappointment. **kick someone when they are down** cause further misfortune to someone who is already in a difficult situation. **kick up a fuss** (or **a stink**) informal object loudly or publicly to something. **kick up one's heels** see HEEL[1].

– PHRASAL VERBS **kick around** (or **about**) (of a thing) lie unwanted or unexploited. ■ (of a person) drift idly from place to place. **kick someone around** (or **about**) treat someone roughly or without respect. **kick something around** (or **about**) discuss an idea casually or idly. **kick back** informal be at leisure; relax. **kick in** (esp. of a device or drug) become activated; come into effect. **kick something in** informal contribute something, esp. money. **kick off** (of a football game, soccer game, etc.) be started or resumed after a score by a player kicking the ball from a designated spot. ■ (of a team or player) begin or resume a game in this way. ■ informal (of an event) begin. **kick something off 1** remove something, esp. shoes, by striking out vigorously with the foot or feet. **2** informal begin something. **kick someone out** informal expel or dismiss someone. [ME: of unknown origin.]

Kick·a·poo /ˈkikəˌpo͞o/ ▶ **n.** (pl. same or **-poos**) **1** a member of an American Indian people formerly living in Wisconsin, and now in Kansas, Oklahoma, and north central Mexico. **2** the Algonquian language of this people. ▶ **adj.** of or relating to this people or their language. [from Kickapoo *kiikaapoa.*]

kick-ass ▶ **adj.** [attrib.] informal forceful, vigorous, and aggressive.

kick·back /ˈkikˌbak/ ▶ **n. 1** a sudden forceful recoil. **2** informal a payment made to someone who has facilitated a transaction or appointment, esp. illicitly.

kick·ball /ˈkikˌbôl/ ▶ **n.** an informal game combining elements of baseball and soccer, in which an inflated ball is thrown to a person who kicks it and proceeds to run the bases.

kick·box·ing (also **kick·box·ing**) ▶ **n.** a form of martial art that combines boxing with elements of karate, in particular kicking with bare feet. — **kick·box·er n.**

kick·er /ˈkikər/ ▶ **n. 1** a person or animal that kicks. ■ the player in a team who scores by kicking or who kicks to gain positional advantage. **2** informal an unexpected and often unpleasant discovery or turn of events. ■ an extra clause in a contract. **3** informal a small outboard motor.

kick·ing /ˈkikiNG/ ▶ **n.** the action of striking or propelling someone or something with the foot. ■ a punishment or assault in which the victim is kicked repeatedly.

kick·off /ˈkikˌôf/ ▶ **n.** the start or resumption of a football game, in which a player kicks the ball from the center of the field. ■ informal a start of an event or activity.

kick plate ▶ **n.** a metal plate at the base of a door or panel to protect it from damage or wear.

kick pleat ▶ **n.** an inverted pleat in a narrow skirt to allow freedom of movement.

kick pleat

kick·stand /ˈkikˌstand/ ▶ **n.** a metal rod attached to a bicycle or motorcycle, lying horizontally when not in use, that may be kicked into a vertical position to support the vehicle when it is stationary.

kick-start ▶ **v.** [trans.] start (an engine on a motorcycle) with a downward thrust of a pedal. ■ fig. provide the initial impetus to: *they need to kick-start the economy.* ▶ **n.** (also **kick start** or **kick starter**) a device to start an engine by the downward thrust of a pedal, as in older motorcycles. ■ an act of starting an engine in this way. ■ fig. an impetus given to get something started or restarted.

kick turn ▶ **n.** Skiing a turn carried out while stationary by lifting first one and then the other ski through 180°. ■ (in skateboarding) a turn performed with the front wheels lifted off the ground. — **kick-turn v.**

kick·y /ˈkikē/ ▶ **adj.** informal exciting or fashionable.

kid[1] /kid/ ▶ **n. 1** informal a child or young person. ■ used as an informal form of address. **2** a young goat. ■ leather made from a young goat's skin. ▶ **v.** (**kid·ded, kid·ding**) [intrans.] (of a goat) give birth.

– PHRASES **kids'** (also **kid**) **stuff** informal a thing regarded as childishly simple or naive. [ME (sense 2): from ON *kith*, of Gmc. origin; rel. to Ger. *Kitze.*]

kid[2] ▶ **v.** (**kid·ded, kid·ding**) [trans.] informal deceive (someone) in a playful or teasing way. ■ [trans.] deceive or fool (someone). — **kid·der n. kid·ding·ly adv.** [19th C.: perh. from KID[1].]

Kidd /kid/, William (1645–1701), Scottish pirate; known as **Captain Kidd**. In 1699, he went to Boston in the hope of obtaining a pardon, but was arrested and later hanged in London.

kid·die /ˈkidē/ (also **kid·dy**) ▶ **n.** (pl. **-dies**) informal a young child.

kid·do /ˈkidō/ ▶ **n.** (pl. **-dos** or **-does**) informal used as a friendly or slightly condescending form of address.

kid·dush /ˈkidəsh; kēˈdo͞osh/ ▶ **n.** [in sing.] a ceremony of prayer and blessing over wine, performed by the head of a Jewish household at the meal ushering in the Sabbath (on a Friday night) or a holy day, or at the lunch preceding it. [18th C.: from Heb. *qiddūš* 'sanctification.']

kid gloves ▶ **plural n.** gloves made of fine kid leather. ■ (also **kid-glove**) [as adj.] used in reference to careful and delicate treatment of a person or situation.

kid·nap /ˈkidˌnap/ ▶ **v.** (**-napped, -nap·ping**; also **-naped, -nap·ing**) [trans.] take (someone) away illegally by force, typically to obtain a ransom. ▶ **n.** the action of kidnapping someone. — **kid·nap·per n.** [17th C.: back-form. from *kidnapper*, from KID[1] + slang *nap* 'nab, seize.']

kid·ney /ˈkidnē/ ▶ **n.** (pl. **-neys**) each of a pair of organs in the abdominal cavity of mammals, birds, and reptiles, excreting urine. ■ the kidney of a sheep, ox, or pig as food. ■ temperament, nature, or kind: *I hoped that he would not prove of similar kidney.* [ME: of obscure origin.]

kid·ney bean ▶ **n.** a kidney-shaped bean, esp. a dark red variety of the common bean plant *Phaseolus vulgaris.*

kid·ney di·al·y·sis ▶ **n.** see DIALYSIS.

kid·ney stone ▶ **n.** a hard mass formed in the kidneys, typically consisting of insoluble calcium compounds.

kid·ney tu·bule ▶ **n.** Anat. each of the tubules conveying urine from the glomeruli to the renal pelvis in the vertebrate kidney.

kid·skin /ˈkidˌskin/ ▶ **n.** another term for KID[1] (sense 2).

kid·vid /ˈkidˌvid/ ▶ **n.** informal children's television or video entertainment. ■ a children's program or videotape. [20th C.: from *kids' video.*]

Kiel /kēl/ a port in northern Germany, capital of Schleswig-Holstein, on the Kiel Canal; pop. 247,000.

kiel·ba·sa /kilˈbäsə; kēl-/ ▶ **n.** a type of highly seasoned Polish sausage, typically containing garlic. [Pol., lit. 'sausage.']

Kiel Ca·nal a man-made waterway, in northwestern Germany, 61 miles (98 km) long, that connects the North Sea with the Baltic Sea.

Kiel·ce /ˈkyeltsə/ a city in southern Poland; pop. 214,000.

Kier·ke·gaard /ˈki(ə)rkiˌgärd; -ˌgôr/, Søren Aabye (1813–55), Danish philosopher. He was a founder of existentialism. — **Kier·ke·gaard·i·an** /ˌki(ə)rkiˈgärdēən/ **adj.**

kie·sel·guhr /ˈkēzelgər/ ▶ **n.** a form of diatomaceous earth used in various manufacturing and laboratory processes, chiefly as a filter, filler, or insulator. [19th C.: from Ger., from *Kiesel* 'gravel' + dial. *Guhr* (lit. 'yeast') used to denote a loose earthy deposit, found in the cavities of rocks.]

Ki·ev /ˈkēˌ(y)ef; -ˌ(y)ev/ the capital of Ukraine, a city and port on the Dnieper River; pop. 2,616,000.

kif /kif/ ▶ **n. & adj.** var. of KEF.

Ki·ga·li /kiˈgälē/ the capital of Rwanda, in the central part of the country; pop. 234,000.

kike /kīk/ ▶ **n.** informal offens. a Jewish person. [20th C.: of unknown origin.]

Ki·klá·dhes /kiˈkläT͟His/ Greek name for CYCLADES.

Ki·kon·go /kēˈkäNGgō/ ▶ **n.** either of two similar Bantu languages spoken in the Congo, the Republic of Congo, and adjacent areas. ▶ **adj.** of or relating to this language. [the name in Kikongo.]

Ki·ku·yu /kiˈko͞oyo͞o/ ▶ **n.** (pl. same or **-yus**) **1** a member of the largest ethnic group in Kenya. **2** the Bantu language of this people. **3** (**ki·ku·yu, ki·ku·yu grass**) a creeping perennial grass (*Pennisetum clandestinum*) native to Kenya and cultivated elsewhere as a lawn and fodder grass. ▶ **adj.** of or relating to the Kikuyu people or their language. [a local name.]

Ki·lau·ea /ˌkiləˈwāə; ˌkēˌlouˈäə/ an active volcano on Mauna Loa, Hawaii; rising 4,090 feet (1,247 m).

Kil·dare /kilˈde(ə)r/ a county in the Republic of Ireland, in the province of Leinster; county town, Naas.

kil·der·kin /ˈkildərkin/ ▶ **n.** a cask for liquids or other substances, holding 16 or 18 gallons. ■ this amount as a unit of measurement. [ME: from MDu. *kinderkin*, var. of *kinerkijn*, dimin. of *kintal* (see QUINTAL).]

ki·lim /kēˈlēm; ˈkiləm/ ▶ **n.** a flat-woven carpet or rug made in Turkey, Kurdistan, and neighboring areas. [19th C.: via Turk. from Pers. *gelīm.*]

Kil·i·man·ja·ro, Mount /ˌkiləmənˈjärō/ an extinct volcano in northern Tanzania; highest peak, Kibo, (19,340 feet; 5,895 m), is the highest in Africa.

Kil·ken·ny /kilˈkenē/ a county of the Republic of Ireland, in the southeast, in the province of Leinster. ■ its county town; pop. 9,000.

kill[1] /kil/ ▶ **v.** [trans.] **1** cause the death of (a person, animal, or other living thing). ■ put an end to or cause the failure or defeat of (something). ■ stop (a computer program or process). ■ informal switch off (a light or engine). ■ informal delete (a line, paragraph, or file) from a document or computer. ■ (in soccer or other ball games) make (the ball) stop. ■ (in tennis and similar games) hit (the ball) so forcefully that it cannot be returned. ■ neutralize or subdue (an effect or quality). ■ informal consume the entire contents of (a bottle containing an alcoholic drink). **2** informal overwhelm (someone) with an emotion. ■ (**kill oneself**) overexert oneself. ■ used hyperbolically to indicate that someone is extremely angry with another person. ■ cause pain or anguish to. **3** pass (time, or a specified amount of it), typically while waiting for a particular event. ▶ **n.** [usu. in sing.] an act of killing, esp. of one animal by another. ■ an animal or animals killed, either by a hunter or by another animal. ■ informal an act of destroying or disabling an enemy aircraft, submarine, tank, etc. ■ (in tennis and similar games) a very forceful shot that cannot be returned.

– PHRASAL VERBS **kill someone/something off** get rid of or destroy completely, esp. in large numbers. ■ (of a writer) bring about the "death" of a fictional character. [ME: prob. of Gmc. origin and rel. to QUELL.]

kill[2] ▶ **n.** [in place names] esp. New York State a stream, creek, or tributary: *Kill Van Kull.* [17th C.: from Du. *kil*, from MDu. *kille* 'riverbed, channel.']

Kil·lar·ney /kilˈärnē/ a town in southwestern Republic of Ireland, in County Kerry; pop. 7,000.

killdeer

kill·deer /ˈkilˌdi(ə)r/ (also **killdeer plover**) ▶n. a widespread American plover (*Charadrius vociferus*) with a plaintive call that resembles its name. [18th C.: imitative of its call.]

kill·er /ˈkilər/ ▶n. a person, animal, or thing that kills. ■ informal a formidable or excellent person or thing. ■ a hilarious joke.

kill·er bee ▶n. informal an Africanized honeybee. See AFRICANIZE (sense 2).

kill·er cell ▶n. Physiol. a white blood cell (a type of lymphocyte) that destroys infected or cancerous cells.

kill·er in·stinct ▶n. a ruthless determination to succeed or win.

kill·er whale ▶n. another term for ORCA.

kil·lick /ˈkilik/ ▶n. a heavy stone used by small craft as an anchor. ■ any anchor, esp. a small one. [17th C.: of unknown origin.]

kil·li·fish /ˈkilēˌfisн/ ▶n. (pl. same or **-fish·es**) a small carplike fish (families Fundulidae and Cyprinodontidae) of fresh, brackish, or salt water, typically brightly colored. [19th C.: appar. from KILL² and FISH¹.]

kill·ing /ˈkiliNG/ ▶n. an act of causing death, esp. deliberately. ▶adj. causing death: [in comb.] *weed-killing.* ■ informal exhausting; unbearable. ■ dated overwhelmingly funny.
– PHRASES **make a killing** have a great financial success. — **kill·ing·ly** adv.

kill·ing field ▶n. (usu. **killing fields**) a place where a heavy loss of life has occurred, typically as the result of massacre or genocide during a time of warfare or violent civil unrest.

kill·joy /ˈkilˌjoi/ ▶n. a person who deliberately spoils the enjoyment of others through resentful or overly sober behavior.

kill zone (also **kill·ing zone**) ▶n. **1** the area of a military engagement with a high concentration of fatalities. **2** the area of the human body where entry of a projectile would kill, esp. as indicated on a target for shooting practice.

Kil·mer /ˈkilmər/, Joyce (1888–1918), US poet; full name *Alfred Joyce Kilmer.* Some of his poetry is collected in *Trees and Other Poems* (1914).

kiln /kiln; kil/ ▶n. a furnace or oven for burning, baking, or drying, esp. one for calcining lime or firing pottery. ▶v. [trans.] burn, bake, or dry in a kiln. [OE *cylene,* from L. *culina* 'kitchen, cooking stove.']

kiln-dry ▶v. [trans.] [usu. as n.] (**kiln-drying**) dry (a material such as wood or sand) in a kiln.

ki·lo /ˈkēlō/ ▶n. (pl. **ki·los**) **1** a kilogram. **2** rare a kilometer. **3** a code word representing the letter K, used in radio communication. [19th C.: from Fr., abbrev. of *kilogramme, kilomètre.*]

kilo- ▶comb. form (used commonly in units of measurement) denoting a factor of 1,000: *kiloliter.* [via Fr. from Gk. *khilioi* 'thousand.']

kil·o·base /ˈkiləˌbās/ (abbr.: **kb**) ▶n. Biochem. (in expressing the lengths of nucleic acid molecules) 1,000 bases.

kil·o·bit /ˈkiləˌbit/ ▶n. a unit of computer memory or data equal to 1,024 (2^{10}) bits.

kil·o·byte /ˈkiləˌbīt/ (abbr.: **Kb** or **KB**) ▶n. Comput. a unit of memory or data equal to 1,024 (2^{10}) bytes.

kil·o·cal·o·rie /ˈkiləˌkalərē/ ▶n. a unit of energy of 1,000 calories (equal to 1 large calorie).

kil·o·cy·cle /ˈkiləˌsīkəl/ (abbr.: **kc**) ▶n. a former measure of frequency, equivalent to 1 kilohertz.

kil·o·gram /ˈkiləˌgram/ (Brit. also **kil·o·gramme**) ▶n. the SI unit of mass, equivalent to the international standard kept at Sèvres near Paris (approximately 2.205 lb).

kil·o·hertz /ˈkiləˌhərts/ (abbr.: **kHz**) ▶n. a measure of frequency equivalent to 1,000 cycles per second.

kil·o·li·ter /ˈkiləˌlētər/ (Brit. **kil·o·li·tre**) (abbr.: **kl**) ▶n. 1,000 liters.

kil·o·me·ter /kiˈlämitər; ˈkiləˌmētər/ (Brit. **kil·o·me·tre**) (abbr.: **km**) ▶n. a metric unit of measurement equal to 1,000 meters (approximately 0.62 miles). — **kil·o·met·ric** /ˌkiləˈmetrik/ adj.

kil·o·ton /ˈkiləˌtən/ ▶n. a unit of explosive power equivalent to 1,000 tons of TNT.

kil·o·volt /ˈkiləˌvōlt/ (abbr.: **kV**) ▶n. 1,000 volts.

kil·o·watt /ˈkiləˌwät/ (abbr.: **kW**) ▶n. a measure of 1,000 watts of electrical power.

kil·o·watt-hour (abbr.: **kWh**) ▶n. a measure of electrical energy equivalent to a power consumption of 1,000 watts for 1 hour.

Kil·roy /ˈkilˌroi/ a mythical person, popularized by American servicemen in World War II, who left such inscriptions as "Kilroy was here" on walls all over the world. [perh. from James J. *Kilroy* of Halifax, Massachusetts, a shipyard employee.]

kilt

kilt /kilt/ ▶n. a knee-length skirt of pleated tartan cloth, traditionally worn by men as part of Scottish Highland dress and now also worn by women and girls. ▶v. [trans.] gather (a garment or material) in vertical pleats. — **kilt·ed** adj. [ME: of Scand. origin; cf. Dan. *kilte (op)* 'tuck (up).']

kil·ter /ˈkiltər/ ▶n. (in phrase **out of kilter**) out of harmony or balance. [17th C.: of unknown origin.]

kilt·ie /ˈkiltē/ (also **kilt·y**) ▶n. a casual or sports shoe with a fringed tongue that covers the lacing. ■ the tongue of such a shoe.

kim·ber·lite /ˈkimbərˌlīt/ ▶n. Geol. a rare, blue-tinged, coarse-grained intrusive igneous rock sometimes containing diamonds, found esp. in South Africa and Siberia. Also called BLUE GROUND. [19th C.: from *Kimberley,* South Africa + -ITE¹.]

Kim·bun·du /kimˈbo͝ondo͞o/ see MBUNDU.

kim·chi /ˈkimCHē/ (also **kim·chee**) ▶n. spicy pickled cabbage, the national dish of Korea.

Kim Dae Jung /ˈkim ˌdī ˈjo͝oNG/ (1925–), president of South Korea 1997–2003. He worked to reunify North and South Korea. Nobel Peace Prize (2000).

Kim Il Sung /ˌkim ˌil ˈso͝oNG; ˈsəNG/ (1912–94), president of North Korea 1972–94; born *Kim Song Ju.* He precipitated the Korean War 1950–53. He was succeeded by his son Kim Jong Il /ˈjôNG ˈil/ (1942–).

ki·mo·no /kəˈmōnō; -nə/ ▶n. (pl. **-nos**) a long, loose robe with wide sleeves and tied with a sash, originally worn as a formal garment in Japan and now also used elsewhere as a robe. — **ki·mo·noed** /-nōd; -nəd/ adj. [17th C.: Japanese, from *ki* 'wearing' + *mono* 'thing.']

kimono

Ki-moon, Ban, see BAN KI-MOON.

kin /kin/ ▶n. [treated as pl.] one's family and relations. ■ a natural class, group, or division of people, animals, plants, etc., with shared attributes or ancestry. ▶adj. [predic.] related. See also AKIN. [OE *cynn,* rel. to Gk. *genos* and L. *genus* 'race.']

-kin ▶suffix forming diminutive nouns such as *bumpkin.* [from MDu. *-kijn, -ken,* Mid. Low Ger. *-kin.*]

ki·na /ˈkēnə/ ▶n. (pl. same) the basic monetary unit of Papua New Guinea, equal to 100 toea.

Ki·na·ba·lu, Mount /ˌkinəbəˈlo͞o/ a mountain in eastern Malaysia, on the northern coast of Borneo; the highest peak in Borneo at 13,431 feet (4,094 m).

kin·aes·the·sia ▶n. British spelling of KINESTHESIA.

ki·nase /ˈkīˌnās; ˈkinās/ ▶n. [usu. with adj.] Biochem. an enzyme that catalyzes the transfer of a phosphate group from ATP to a specified molecule. [20th C.: from Gk. *kinein* 'to move' + -ASE.]

Kin·chin·jun·ga /ˌkinCHənˈjo͝oNGgə/ variant of KANCHENJUNGA.

kind¹ /kīnd/ ▶n. a group of people or things having similar characteristics: *all kinds of music.* ■ character; nature.
– PHRASES **in kind** in the same way; with something similar: *they would respond in kind.* ■ (of payment) in goods or services as opposed to money. **kind of** informal rather; to some extent (often expressing vagueness or used as a meaningless filler): *it got kind of cozy.* [OE *cynd(e), gecynd(e),* of Gmc. origin; rel. to KIN.]

kind² ▶adj. having or showing a friendly, generous, and considerate nature: *a kind woman.* ■ [predic.] used in a polite request: *would you be kind enough to repeat what you said?* ■ [predic.] (**kind to**) (of a consumer product) gentle on (a part of the body): *rollers that are kind to hair.* [OE *gecynde* 'natural, native.']

kind·a /ˈkīndə/ informal ▶contr. kind of. [20th C. (orig. US).]

kin·der·gar·ten /ˈkindərˌgärtn; -ˌgärdn/ ▶n. a school or class that prepares children for first grade. A child in kindergarten is typically 5 or 6 years old. — **kin·der·gar·ten·er** /-ˌgärtnər; -ˌgärd-/ (also **kin·der·gart·ner**) n. [19th C.: from Ger., lit. 'children's garden.']

kind·heart·ed /ˈkīndˈhärtid/ ▶adj. having a kind and sympathetic nature. — **kind·heart·ed·ly** adv. **kind·heart·ed·ness** n.

kin·dle /ˈkindl/ ▶v. [trans.] light or set on fire. ■ arouse or inspire (an emotion or feeling). ■ [intrans.] (of an emotion) be aroused. [ME: based on ON *kynda.*]

kin·dling /ˈkindliNG/ ▶n. **1** easily combustible small sticks or twigs used for starting a fire. **2** (in neurology) a process by which a seizure or other brain event is both initiated and its recurrence made more likely.

kind·ly /ˈkīn(d)lē/ ▶adv. in a kind manner. ■ please (used in a polite request or demand, often ironically): *will you kindly sign the enclosed letter.* ▶adj. (**-li·er, -li·est**) kind; warmhearted; gentle. — **kind·li·ness** n.

kind·ness /ˈkīn(d)nis/ ▶n. the quality of being friendly, generous, and considerate. ■ a kind act.

kin·dred /ˈkindrid/ ▶n. [treated as pl.] one's family and relations. ■ relationship by blood. ▶adj. [attrib.] similar in kind; related. [ME: from KIN + *-red* (from OE *rǣden* 'condition'), with insertion of *-d-.*]

kin·dred spir·it ▶n. a person whose interests or attitudes are similar to one's own.

kin·e·mat·ics /ˌkinəˈmatiks/ ▶plural n. [usu. treated as sing.] the branch of mechanics concerned with the motion of objects without reference to the forces that cause the motion. Compare with DYNAMICS. ■ [usu. treated as pl.] the features or properties of motion in an object, regarded in such a way. — **kin·e·mat·ic** adj. **kin·e·mat·i·cal·ly** /-ˈmatik(ə)lē/ adv. [19th C.: from Gk. *kinēma, kinēmat-* 'motion' (from *kinein* 'to move') + -ICS.]

kin·e·scope /ˈkinəˌskōp/ ▶n. a television picture tube. ■ a film recording of a television broadcast. [20th C.: orig. a proprietary name.]

ki·ne·sics /kə'nēsiks; -ziks/ ▶ **plural n.** [usu. treated as sing.] the study of the way in which certain body movements and gestures serve as a form of nonverbal communication. ■ [usu. treated as pl.] certain body movements and gestures regarded in such a way. [1950s: from Gk. *kinēsis* 'motion' (from *kinein* 'to move') + -ICS.]

ki·ne·si·ol·o·gy /kə,nēsē'äləjē; -zē-/ ▶ **n.** the study of the mechanics of body movements. — **ki·ne·si·o·log·i·cal** /-sēə'läjikəl; -zēə-/ **adj.** **ki·ne·si·ol·o·gist n.**

ki·ne·sis /kə'nēsis/ ▶ **n.** (pl. **-ses** /-,sēz/) movement; motion. ■ Biol. an undirected movement of a cell, organism, or part in response to an external stimulus. Compare with TAXIS. [17th C.: from Gk. *kinēsis* 'movement,' from *kinein* 'to move.']

kin·es·the·sia /,kinəs'THēZHə/ (Brit. **kin·aes·the·sia**) ▶ **n.** awareness of the position and movement of the parts of the body by means of sensory organs (proprioceptors) in the muscles and joints. — **kin·es·thet·ic** /-'THetik/ **adj.** [19th C.: from Gk. *kinein* 'to move' + *aisthēsis* 'sensation.']

ki·net·ic /kə'netik/ ▶ **adj.** of, relating to, or resulting from motion. ■ (of a work of art) depending on movement for its effect. — **ki·net·i·cal·ly adv.** [19th C.: from Gk. *kinētikos*, from *kinein* 'to move.']

ki·net·ic art ▶ **n.** a form of art that depends on movement for its effect.

ki·net·ic en·er·gy ▶ **n.** Physics energy that a body possesses by virtue of being in motion. Compare with POTENTIAL ENERGY.

ki·net·ics /kə'netiks/ ▶ **plural n.** [usu. treated as sing.] the branch of chemistry or biochemistry concerned with measuring and studying the rates of reactions. ■ [usu. treated as pl.] the rates of chemical or biochemical reaction. ■ Physics the study of forces acting on mechanisms.

ki·net·ic the·o·ry ▶ **n.** the body of theory that explains the physical properties of matter in terms of the motions of its constituent particles.

kineto- ▶ **comb. form** relating to movement. [from Gk. *kinētos* 'movable.']

ki·ne·to·chore /kə'netə,kôr; -'nētə-/ ▶ **n.** another term for CENTROMERE. [20th C.: from KINETO- 'of movement' + Gk. *khōros* 'place.']

ki·ne·to·plast /kə'netə,plast; -'nētə-/ ▶ **n.** Biol. a mass of mitochondrial DNA lying close to the nucleus in some flagellate protozoa.

ki·ne·to·some /kə'netə,sōm; -'nētə-; kī-/ ▶ **n.** another term for BASAL BODY.

kin·folk /'kin,fōk/ (also **kins·folk** /'kinz-/ or **kin·folks**) ▶ **plural n.** (in anthropological or formal use) a person's blood relations, regarded collectively. ■ a group of people related by blood.

King[1] /kiNG/, B. B. (1925–), US blues singer and guitarist; born *Riley B. King*. His style of guitar playing was imitated by rock musicians.

King[2], Martin Luther, Jr. (1929–68), US minister and civil rights leader. A noted orator, he opposed discrimination against blacks by organizing nonviolent resistance and peaceful mass demonstrations. He was assassinated in Memphis, Tennessee. Nobel Peace Prize (1964).

King[3], Stephen Edwin (1947–), US writer; pen name **Richard Bachman**. He is known for his stories of horror and suspense, such as *Carrie* (1974) and *The Shining* (1977).

King[4], William Lyon Mackenzie (1874–1950), prime minister of Canada 1921–26, 1926–30, 1935–48.

king /kiNG/ ▶ **n.** **1** the male ruler of an independent state, esp. one who inherits the position by right of birth. ■ a person or thing regarded as the finest or most important in its sphere or group. ■ [attrib.] used in names of animals and plants that are particularly large, e.g., **king cobra**. **2** the most important chess piece, of which each player has one, which the opponent has to checkmate in order to win. The king can move in any direction, including diagonally, to any adjacent square that is not attacked by an opponent's piece or pawn. ■ a piece in the game of checkers with extra capacity for moving, made by crowning an ordinary piece that has reached the opponent's baseline. ■ a playing card bearing a representation of a king, normally ranking next below an ace. — **king·hood n.** **king·li·ness n.** **king·ly adj.** **king·ship n.** [OE *cyning*, *cyng*, of Gmc. origin; rel. to Du. *koning* and Ger. *König*, also to KIN.]

king·bird /'kiNG,bərd/ ▶ **n.** a large American tyrant flycatcher (genus *Tyrannus*, several species), typically with a gray head and back and yellowish or white underparts.

king bo·lete ▶ **n.** another term for CEP.

King Charles span·iel ▶ **n.** a spaniel of a small breed, typically with a white, black, and tan coat.

king co·bra ▶ **n.** a cobra (*Ophiophagus hannah*), native to the Indian subcontinent, the largest of all venomous snakes. Also called HAMADRYAD.

king crab ▶ **n.** **1** another term for HORSESHOE CRAB. **2** an edible crab (genus *Paralithodes*, family Lithodidae) of the North Pacific, resembling a spider crab.

king·dom /'kiNGdəm/ ▶ **n.** **1** a country, state, or territory ruled by a king or queen. ■ a realm associated with or regarded as being under the control of a particular person or thing. **2** the spiritual reign or authority of God. ■ the rule of God or Christ in a future age. ■ heaven as the abode of God and of the faithful after death. **3** each of the three traditional divisions (animal, vegetable, and mineral) in which natural objects have conventionally been classified. ■ Biol. the highest category in taxonomic classification.
– PHRASES **till** (or **to**) **kingdom come** informal forever. **to kingdom come** informal into the next world.

king·fish /'kiNG,fiSH/ ▶ **n.** (pl. same or **-fish·es**) **1** any of a number of large sporting fish, many of which are edible: ■ a fish of the jack family, including the **yellowtail kingfish** (*Seriola grandis*) of the South Pacific. ■ a fish of the drum family, including the **northern kingfish** (*Menticirrhus saxatilis*) of the east coast of North America. ■ a western Atlantic fish of the mackerel family (*Scomberomorus cavalla*). **2** informal a person regarded as an authority figure; an influential leader or boss.

king·fish·er /'kiNG,fiSHər/ ▶ **n.** an often brightly colored bird (family Alcedinidae) with a long sharp beak, typically diving for fish from a perch. Many of the tropical kinds live in forests and feed on insects and lizards. Its many genera and numerous species include the **belted kingfisher** (*Ceryle alcyon*), found throughout North America.

belted kingfisher

King James Bi·ble (also **King James Version**) ▶ **n.** an English translation of the Bible made in 1611 at the order of King James I and still widely used. Also called AUTHORIZED VERSION, chiefly in the UK.

king·let /'kiNGlit/ ▶ **n.** **1** esp. derog. a minor king. **2** a very small greenish bird (genus *Regulus*, family Sylviidae) with a bright orange or yellow crown.

king·mak·er /'kiNG,mākər/ ▶ **n.** a person who brings leaders to power through the exercise of political influence.

king of beasts ▶ **n.** esp. literary the lion (used in reference to the animal's perceived grandeur).

King of Kings ▶ **n.** used as a name or form of address for God. ■ (in the Christian Church) used as a name or form of address for Jesus Christ. ■ a title assumed by certain kings who rule over lesser kings.

king pen·guin ▶ **n.** a large penguin (*Aptenodytes patagonica*) native to Antarctic islands as well as the Falklands and other subantarctic islands.

King Phil·ip's War (1675–77) the first large-scale military action in the American colonies, pitting various Indian tribes against New England colonists and their Indian allies.

king·pin /'kiNG,pin/ ▶ **n.** a main or large bolt in a central position. ■ a vertical bolt used as a pivot. ■ a person or thing that is essential to the success of an organization or operation.

king post ▶ **n.** an upright post in the center of a roof truss, extending from the tie beam to the apex of the truss.

Kings /kiNGz/ the name of two books of the Bible, recording the history of Israel from the accession of Solomon to the destruction of the Temple in 586 BC.

Kings Can·yon Na·tion·al Park a national park in the Sierra Nevada, in south central California, north of Sequoia National Park. Established in 1940, it preserves groves of ancient sequoia trees, including some of the largest in the world.

king's e·vil ▶ **n.** (usu. **the king's evil**) hist. scrofula, formerly held to be curable by the royal touch.

king-sized (also **king-size**) ▶ **adj.** (esp. of a commercial product) of a larger size than the standard; very large.

king snake ▶ **n.** a large, smooth-scaled North American constrictor (genus *Lampropeltis*, family Colubridae) that typically has shiny dark brown or black skin with lighter markings.

Kings·ton /'kiNGstən/ **1** the capital and chief port of Jamaica; pop. 538,000. **2** a port in southeastern Canada, on Lake Ontario, at the head of the St. Lawrence River; pop. 56,597.

Kings·ton-up·on-Hull official name for HULL[1].

Kings·town /'kiNGz,toun/ the capital and chief port of St. Vincent and the Grenadines in the Caribbean; pop. 26,220.

ki·nin /'kīnin/ ▶ **n.** **1** Biochem. any of a group of substances formed in body tissue in response to injury. **2** Bot. a compound that promotes cell division and inhibits aging in plants. Also called CYTOKININ. [1950s: from Gk. *kinein* 'to move' + -IN[1].]

kink /kiNGk/ ▶ **n.** a sharp twist or curve in something that is otherwise straight. ■ fig. a flaw or obstacle in a plan, operation, etc. ■ a stiffness in the neck, back, etc.; crick. ■ fig. a quirk of character or behavior. ▶ **v.** form or cause to form a sharp twist or curve. [17th C.: from Mid. Low Ger. *kinke*, prob. from Du. *kinken* 'to kink.']

kin·ka·jou /'kiNGkə,jōō/ ▶ **n.** an arboreal nocturnal fruit-eating mammal (*Potos flavus*) of the raccoon family, with a prehensile tail and a long tongue, found in the tropical forests of Central and South America. [18th C.: from Fr. *quincajou*, alt. of CARCAJOU.]

kink·y /'kiNGkē/ ▶ **adj.** (**kink·i·er**, **kink·i·est**) **1** informal, involving or given to unusual sexual behavior. ■ (of clothing) sexually provocative in an unusual way. **2** having kinks or twists. — **kink·i·ly** /-kilē/ **adv.** **kink·i·ness n.**

Kin·ner·et, Lake /kē'neret/ another name for Sea of Galilee (see **Galilee, Sea of**).

kin·ni·kin·nick /,kiniki'nik/ (also **kin·ni·kin·nic** or **kin·ni·kin·nik**) ▶ **n.** a smoking mixture used by North American Indians as a substitute for tobacco or for mixing with it. ■ the bearberry. [18th C.: from a Delaware (Unami) word meaning 'mixture.']

ki·no /'kēnō/ ▶ **n.** a gum obtained from certain tropical trees (genera *Pterocarpus* and *Butea*) of the pea family, used locally as an astringent in medicine and in tanning. [18th C.: West Afr.]

Kin·o·rhyn·cha /,kinə'riNGkə; ,kē-/ Zool. a small phylum of minute marine invertebrates that have a spiny body and burrow in sand or mud. — **kin·o·rhynch** /'kinə,riNGk; 'kē-/ **n.** [mod. L. (pl.), from Gk. *kinein* 'set in motion' + *rhunkos* 'snout.']

-kins ▶ **suffix** equivalent to **-kin**, often expressing endearment.

Kin·sey /'kinzē/, Alfred Charles (1894–1956), US zoologist. He carried out pioneering studies on sexual behavior.

kins·folk /'kinz,fōk/ ▶ **plural n.** another term for **kinfolk**.

Kin·sha·sa /kin'SHäsə/ the capital of the Democratic Republic of the Congo, a port on the Congo River, in the southwestern part of the country; pop. 3,804,000.

kin·ship /'kin,SHip/ ▶ **n.** blood relationship. ■ a sharing of characteristics or origins.

kins·man /'kinzmən/ ▶ **n.** (pl. **-men**) (in anthropological or formal use) one of a person's blood relations, esp. a male.

kins·wom·an /'kinz,wŏŏmən/ ▶ **n.** (pl. **-wom·en**) (in anthropological or formal use) one of a person's female blood relations.

ki·osk /'kē,äsk/ ▶ **n.** a small open-fronted hut or cubicle from which newspapers, refreshments, tickets, etc., are sold. [17th C. (in the sense 'pavilion'): from Fr. *kiosque*, from Turk. *köşk* 'pavilion,' from Pers. *kuš*.]

Ki·o·wa /'kīəwə/ ▶ **n.** (pl. same or **-was**) **1** a member of an American Indian people of the southern plains of the US, now living mainly in Oklahoma. **2** the language of this people, related to the Tanoan group. **3** (in full **Kiowa Apache**) an Athabaskan (Apache) language of western Oklahoma and neighboring areas. ▶ **adj.** of or relating to this people or these languages. [from Amer. Sp. *Caygua*, perh. from Caddoan *kā'hiwa'* 'Kiowa.']

kip[1] /kip/ ▶ **n.** (pl. same or **kips**) the basic monetary unit of Laos, equal to 100 ats. [Thai.]

kip[2] ▶ **n.** a unit of weight equal to 1,000 lb (453.6 kg).

Kip·ling /'kipliNG/, Rudyard (1865–1936), British writer and poet; born in India; full name *Joseph Rudyard Kipling*. He wrote *The Jungle Book* (1894) and *Just So Stories* (1902). Nobel Prize for Literature (1907). — **Kip·ling·esque** /,kipliNG'esk/ **adj.**

kip·pa /kē'pä/ (also **kip·pah**) ▶ **n.** another term for **yarmulke** [20th C.: from mod. Heb. *kippāh*.]

kip·per /'kipər/ ▶ **n.** **1** a kippered fish, esp. a herring. **2** a male salmon in the spawning season. ▶ **v.** [trans.] [usu. as adj.] (**kippered**) cure (a herring or other fish) by splitting it open and salting and drying it in the open air or in smoke. [OE *cypera* (sense 2), of Gmc. origin; rel. to Old Saxon *kupiro*, perh. also to **copper[1]**.]

Kir /ki(ə)r/ (also **kir**) ▶ **n.** trademark a drink made from dry white wine and crème de cassis. [1960s: named after Canon Félix *Kir* (1876–1968), a mayor of Dijon, France.]

Kirch·hoff /'ki(ə)r,KHôf/, Gustav Robert (1824–87), German physicist. He was a pioneer in spectroscopy.

Kir·ghiz /ki(ə)r'gēz/ (also **Kyr·gyz**) ▶ **n.** (pl. same) **1** a member of an indigenous people of central Asia, living chiefly in Kyrgyzstan. **2** the Turkic language of this people. ▶ **adj.** of or relating to this people or their language. [the name in Kirghiz.]

Kir·ghi·zia /ki(ə)r'gēZHə; -'gēzēə/ former name for **Kyrgyzstan**.

Ki·ri·ba·ti /'ki(ə)rə,bas/ a country in the southwestern Pacific Ocean that includes the Gilbert, Line, and Phoenix Islands, as well as Banaba (Ocean Island); pop. 100,700,000; capital, Bairiki (on Tarawa).

Ki·rin /'kē'rin/ variant of **Jilin**.

Ki·riti·mati /kə'rismәs; 'kris-/ one of the Line Islands of Kiribati, the largest atoll in the Pacific; pop. 3,000. It was discovered by Captain James Cook on Christmas Eve 1777. Former name (until 1981) **Christmas Island**.

kirk /kərk/ ▶ **n.** Scot. & N. English a church. [ME: from ON *kirkja*, from OE *cirice* (see **church**).]

Kirk·pat·rick /,kərk'patrik/, Jeane Jordan (1926–2006), US public official. She served as US ambassador to the United Nations 1981–85.

Kir·li·an pho·tog·ra·phy /'ki(ə)rlēən/ ▶ **n.** a technique for recording photographic images of corona discharges and hence, supposedly, the auras of living creatures. [20th C.: from the name of Semyon D. and Valentina K. *Kirlian*, Russian electricians.]

kirsch /ki(ə)rSH/ (also **kirsch·wa·sser** /-,väsər/) ▶ **n.** brandy distilled from the fermented juice of cherries. [Ger., abbrev. of *Kirschenwasser*, from *Kirsche* 'cherry' + *Wasser* 'water.']

kir·tle /'kərtl/ ▶ **n.** archaic a woman's gown or outer petticoat. ■ a man's tunic or coat. [OE *cyrtel*, of Gmc. origin, prob. based on L. *curtus* 'short.']

Ki·shi·nev /'kisHə,nef; -,nev/ Russian name for **Chişinău**.

Ki·shi·nyov /'kisHə,nef; -,nev; kyisHə'nyôf/ Russian name for **Chişinău**.

kish·ke /'kisHkə/ ▶ **n.** a beef intestine stuffed with a seasoned filling. ■ (usu. **kishkes**) informal a person's guts. [20th C.: Yiddish, from Pol. *kiszka* or Ukrainian *kishka*.]

kis·ka·dee /'kiskə,dē/ ▶ **n.** a large tyrant flycatcher, esp. the **greater kiskadee** (*Pitangus sulphuratus*), found mainly in tropical America and noted for aggressive behavior [19th C.: imitative of its call.]

Kis·ka Is·land /'kiskə/ an island in the Aleutian Islands, in southwestern Alaska.

Kis·lev /'kisləv; kēs'lev/ (also **Kislew**) ▶ **n.** (in the Jewish calendar) the third month of the civil and ninth of the religious year, usually coinciding with parts of November and December. [from Heb. *kislēw*.]

kis·met /'kizmit; -,met/ ▶ **n.** destiny; fate. [19th C.: from Turk., from Arab. *ḳismat* 'division, portion, lot,' from *ḳasama* 'to divide.']

kiss /kis/ ▶ **v.** [trans.] touch with the lips as a sign of love, sexual desire, reverence, or greeting. ■ Billiards (of a ball) lightly touch (another ball) in passing. ▶ **n.** **1** a touch with the lips in kissing. ■ Billiards a slight touch of a ball against another ball. ■ used to express affection at the end of a letter (conventionally represented by the letter X). **2** a small cake or cookie, typically a meringue. ■ a small candy, esp. one made of chocolate.

– PHRASES **kiss and make up** become reconciled. **kiss of death** an action or event that causes certain failure for an enterprise. **kiss of life** mouth-to-mouth resuscitation. ■ fig. an action or event that revives a failing enterprise.

– PHRASAL VERBS **kiss someone/something off** informal dismiss someone rudely; end a relationship abruptly. **kiss up to** informal behave sycophantically or obsequiously toward (someone) in order to obtain something. — **kiss·a·ble adj.** [OE *cyssan* (v.), of Gmc. origin; rel. to Du. *kussen* and Ger. *küssen*.]

kiss-and-tell ▶ **adj.** revealing private or confidential information.

kiss-ass ▶ **adj.** vulgar slang having or showing an obsequious or sycophantic eagerness to please. ▶ **n.** a person who behaves in such a way.

kiss·er /'kisər/ ▶ **n.** **1** [usu. with adj.] a person who kisses someone. **2** informal a person's mouth.

kiss·ing bug ▶ **n.** a bloodsucking North American assassin bug that can inflict a painful bite on humans and often attacks the face.

kiss·ing cous·in ▶ **n.** a relative known well enough to be given a kiss in greeting.

kiss·ing dis·ease ▶ **n.** informal a disease transmitted by contact with infected saliva, esp. infectious mononucleosis.

Kis·sin·ger /'kisənjər/, Henry Alfred (1923–), US statesman and diplomat; born in Germany. He was secretary of state 1973–77. In 1973, he helped negotiate the withdrawal of US troops from South Vietnam. His many trips to foster Middle East negotiations led to the term "shuttle diplomacy." Nobel Peace Prize (1973).

kiss-off ▶ **n.** informal a rude or abrupt dismissal, esp. from a job or romantic relationship.

kiss·y /'kisē/ ▶ **adj.** informal characterized by or given to kissing; amorous.

kiss·y-face ▶ **n.** informal a puckering of the lips as if to kiss someone.

– PHRASES **play kissy-face** (or **kissy-kissy**) engage in kissing or petting, esp. in public. ■ behave in an excessively friendly way in order to gain favor.

kist /kist/ ▶ **n.** var. of **cist**.

Ki·swa·hi·li /,kiswä'hēlē/ ▶ **n.** another term for **Swahili** (sense 1). [from the Bantu prefix *ki-* (used in names of languages) + **Swahili**.]

kit[1] /kit/ ▶ **n.** a set of articles or equipment needed for a specific purpose. ■ a set of all the parts needed to assemble something. [ME: from MDu. *kitte* 'wooden vessel.']

kit[2] ▶ **n.** the young of certain animals, such as the beaver, fox, ferret, and mink. ■ informal term for **kitten**.

Ki·ta·kyu·shu /,kētä'kyōōsHōō/ a port in southern Japan, on Kyushu island; pop. 1,026,000.

kitch·en /'kicHən/ ▶ **n.** **1** a room or area where food is prepared and cooked. ■ a set of fixtures, cabinets, and appliances that are sold together and installed in such a room or area. ■ cuisine. **2** informal the percussion section of an orchestra. **3** [as adj.] (of a language) in an uneducated or domestic form: *kitchen Swahili*. [OE *cycene*, of West Gmc. origin; based on L. *coquere* 'to cook.']

kitch·en cab·i·net ▶ **n.** a group of unofficial advisers to the holder of an elected office who are considered to be unduly influential.

kitch·en·ette /,kicHə'net/ ▶ **n.** a small kitchen or part of a room equipped as a kitchen.

kitch·en gar·den ▶ **n.** a garden or area where vegetables, fruit, or herbs are grown for domestic use.

kitch·en mid·den ▶ **n.** a prehistoric refuse heap that marks an ancient settlement, chiefly containing bones, shells, and stone implements.

kitch·en po·lice (abbr.: **KP**) ▶ **n.** [usu. treated as pl.] military slang enlisted personnel detailed to help the cook. ■ the assigned duty of these personnel.

kitch·en-sink ▶ **adj.** [attrib.] (in art forms) characterized by great realism in the depiction of drab or sordid subjects: *a kitchen-sink drama*.

kitch·en·ware /'kicHən,we(ə)r/ ▶ **n.** the utensils used in a kitchen.

kite /kīt/ ▶ **n.** **1** a toy consisting of a light frame with thin material stretched over it, flown in the wind at the end of a long string. ■ Sailing, informal a spinnaker or other high, light sail. **2** a medium to large long-winged bird of prey (family Accipitridae) that typically has a forked tail and frequently soars on updrafts of air. Several genera and many species include the **American swallow-tailed kite** (*Elanoides forficatus*). **3** informal a fraudulent check, bill, or receipt. ■ an illicit or surreptitious letter or note. **4** Geom. a quadrilateral figure having two

pairs of equal adjacent sides, symmetrical only about its diagonals. ▶ **v.** **1** [intrans.] [usu. as n.] (**kiting**) fly a kite. **2** [trans.] informal write or use (a check, bill, or receipt) fraudulently.
– PHRASES (**as**) **high as a kite** informal intoxicated with drugs or alcohol. [OE *cȳta*; prob. of imitative origin and rel. to Ger. *Kauz* 'screech owl.']

kite 2

kite·fly·ing ▶ **n.** the action of flying a kite on a string. ■ the action of trying something out to test public opinion. ■ informal the fraudulent writing or using of a check, bill, or receipt.

kit fox ▶ **n.** a small nocturnal fox (*Vulpes macrotis*) with a yellowish-gray back and large, close-set ears, found in the deserts and plains of the southwestern US. [19th C.: *kit* prob. from KIT[2] (because of its small size).]

kith /kiTH/ ▶ **n.** (in phrase **kith and kin** or **kith or kin**) one's friends, acquaintances, and relations. [OE *cȳth*, of Gmc. origin; rel. to COUTH.]

kith·a·ra /'kiTHərə/ ▶ **n.** var. of CITHARA.

kitsch /kiCH/ ▶ **n.** art, objects, or design considered to be in poor taste because of excessive garishness or sentimentality, but appreciated in an ironic way. — **kitsch·i·ness n. kitsch·y adj.** [1920s: Ger.]

kit·ten /'kitn/ ▶ **n.** a young cat. ■ the young of several other animals, such as the rabbit and beaver. ▶ **v.** [intrans.] (of a cat or certain other animals) give birth.
– PHRASES **have kittens** informal be extremely nervous or upset. [ME *kitoun, ketoun*, from an Anglo-Norman Fr. var. of OFr. *chitoun*, dimin. of *chat* 'cat.']

kit·ten·ish /'kitn-iSH/ ▶ **adj.** playful, lively, or flirtatious. — **kit·ten·ish·ly adv. kit·ten·ish·ness n.**

kit·ti·wake /'kitē,wāk/ ▶ **n.** a small gull (genus *Rissa*, family Laridae) that nests in colonies on sea cliffs. Two species include the black-legged *Rissa tridactyla* of the North Atlantic and North Pacific. [17th C. (orig. Scots): imitative of its call.]

kit·ty[1] /'kitē/ ▶ **n.** (pl. **-ties**) a fund of money for communal use, made up of contributions from a group of people. ■ a pool of money in some gambling card games. [19th C. (denoting a jail): of unknown origin.]

kit·ty[2] ▶ **n.** (pl. **-ties**) a pet name or a child's name for a kitten or cat.

kit·ty-cor·ner ▶ **adj. & adv.** another term for CATER-CORNERED.

Kit·ty Hawk /'kitē ,hôk/ a town on the Atlantic coast of North Carolina, site where the Wright brothers made the first powered airplane flight 1903.

ki·va /'kēvə/ ▶ **n.** a chamber, built wholly or partly underground, used by male Pueblo Indians for religious rites. [19th C.: from Hopi *kíva*.]

Ki·vu, Lake /'kēvo͞o/ a lake in central Africa, on the Democratic Republic of the Congo–Rwanda border.

Ki·wa·nis /kə'wänis/ (in full **Kiwanis Club**) ▶ **n.** a North American society of business and professional people. — **Ki·wa·ni·an** /-nēən/ **n. & adj.**

ki·wi /'kēwē/ ▶ **n.** (pl. **ki·wis**) **1** a flightless New Zealand bird (genus *Apteryx*, family Apterygidae) with hairlike feathers, having a long down-curved bill with sensitive nostrils at the tip. **2** (**Kiwi**) informal a New Zealander, esp. a soldier or member of a national sports team. [19th C.: from Maori.]

ki·wi fruit (also **ki·wi·fruit**) ▶ **n.** (pl. same) a fruit with a thin hairy skin, green flesh, and black seeds, obtained from the eastern Asian climbing plant *Actinidia chinensis* (family Actinidiaceae). Also called CHINESE GOOSEBERRY.

Ki·zil Ir·mak /ki'zil ir'mäk/ (ancient name **Halys**) the longest river in Turkey, flowing 715 miles (1,150 km) through central Anatolia to the Black Sea.

KJV ▶ **abbr.** King James Version.

KKK ▶ **abbr.** Ku Klux Klan.

kl ▶ **abbr.** kiloliter(s).

Klai·pe·da /'klīpədə/ a city and port in Lithuania, on the Baltic Sea; pop. 206,000. Former name MEMEL.

Klam·ath /'klaməTH/ ▶ **n.** (pl. same or **Klam·aths**) **1** a member of an American Indian people of southern Oregon and northern California. **2** the Penutian language of this people. ▶ **adj.** of or relating to this people or their language. [from the Chinook name *łámał* 'those of the river.']

Klam·ath Moun·tains a range in southwestern Oregon and northern California, through which the **Klamath River** flows to the Pacific Ocean.

Klan /klan/ ▶ **n.** the Ku Klux Klan or a large organization within it. — **Klans·man** /'klanzmən/ **n.** (pl. **-men**). **Klans·wom·an** /'klanz,wo͝omən/ **n.** (pl. **-wom·en**).

klatch /kläCH; klaCH/ (also **klatsch**) ▶ **n.** a social gathering, esp. for coffee and conversation. [20th C.: from Ger. *Klatsch* 'gossip.']

klax·on /'klaksən/ ▶ **n.** trademark an electric horn or a similar loud warning device.

kleb·si·el·la /,klebzē'elə; ,klepsē-/ ▶ **n.** a bacterium (genus *Klebsiella*) that causes respiratory, urinary, and wound infections. [mod. L., after E. *Klebs* (1834–1913).]

Klee /klā/, Paul (1879–1940), Swiss painter who lived in Germany from 1906 and taught at the Bauhaus 1920–33.

Kleen·ex /'klē,neks/ ▶ **n.** (pl. same or **Kleen·ex·es**) trademark an absorbent disposable paper tissue.

Klein[1] /klīn/, Calvin Richard (1942–), US fashion designer.

Klein[2], Melanie (1882–1960), Austrian psychoanalyst. She specialized in the psychoanalysis of small children.

Klein bot·tle ▶ **n.** Math. a closed surface with only one side, formed by passing one end of a tube through the side of the tube and joining it to the other end. [1940s.: named after Felix *Klein* (1849–1925), the German mathematician who first described it.]

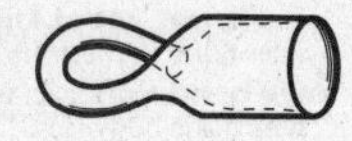

Klein bottle

Klem·per·er /'klempərər/, Otto (1885–1973), US conductor; born in Germany. He conducted the Los Angeles Symphony Orchestra 1933–39.

klep·to·ma·ni·a /,kleptə'mānēə; -'mānyə/ ▶ **n.** a recurrent urge to steal, typically without regard for need or profit. — **klep·to·ma·ni·ac** /-'mānē,ak/ **n. & adj.** [19th C.: from Gk. *kleptēs* 'thief' + -MANIA.]

Klerk, F. W. de, see DE KLERK.

klez·mer /'klezmər/ ▶ **n.** (pl. **klez·mo·rim** /klez'môrim; ,klezmə,rēm/) (also **klezmer music**) traditional eastern European Jewish music. ■ a musician who plays this kind of music. [20th C.: Yiddish, contr. of Heb. *kĕlē zemer* 'musical instruments.']

klick /klik/ (also **click**) ▶ **n.** informal a kilometer.

klieg /klēg/ (usu. **klieg light**) ▶ **n.** a powerful electric lamp used in filming. [1920s: named after the American brothers, Anton T. *Kliegl* (1872–1927) and John H. *Kliegl* (1869–1959), who invented it.]

Klimt /klimt/, Gustav (1862–1918), Austrian painter. He is known for his decorative paintings and portraits of women.

Kline·fel·ter's syn·drome /'klīn,feltərz/ ▶ **n.** Med. a syndrome affecting males in which the cells have an extra X chromosome, characterized by a tall thin physique, small infertile testes, and enlarged breasts. [20th C.: named after Harry F. *Klinefelter* (born 1912), Amer. physician.]

klip·spring·er /'klip,spriNGər/ ▶ **n.** a small, agile, rock-dwelling antelope (*Oreotragus oreotragus*) with a yellowish-gray coat, native to southern Africa. [18th C.: from Afrik., *klip* 'rock' + *springer* 'jumper.']

Klon·dike /'klän,dīk/ a tributary of the Yukon River, in northwestern Canada, that rises in the Ogilvie Mountains and flows west for 100 miles (160 km) to the Yukon at Dawson. ■ [as n.] fig. a source of valuable material. ■ [as n.] a form of the card game patience or solitaire.

kludge /klo͞oj/ (also **kluge**) informal ▶ **n.** an ill-assorted collection of parts assembled to fulfill a particular purpose. ■ Comput. a machine, system, or program that has been badly put together. ▶ **v.** [trans.] use ill-assorted parts to make (something). [1960s: invented word.]

klutz /kləts/ ▶ **n.** informal a clumsy, awkward, or foolish person. — **klutz·i·ness n. klutz·y adj.** [1960s: from Yiddish *klots* 'wooden block.']

km ▶ **abbr.** kilometer(s).

K-me·son ▶ **n.** another term for KAON. [1950s: from *K* (for KAON) + MESON.]

kmph ▶ **abbr.** kilometers per hour.

kmps ▶ **abbr.** kilometers per second.

kn ▶ **abbr.** knot(s).

knack /nak/ ▶ **n.** [in sing.] an acquired or natural skill at performing a task: *she got the **knack** of it in the end.* ■ a tendency to do something. [ME: prob. rel. to obs. *knack* 'sharp blow or sound,' of imitative origin.]

knack·wurst /'näk,wərst/ (also **knock·wurst**) ▶ **n.** a type of short, fat, highly seasoned German sausage. [20th C.: from Ger. *Knackwurst*, from *knacken* 'make a cracking noise' + *Wurst* 'sausage.']

knai·del /'k(ə)nādl/ (also **knei·del**) ▶ **n.** (pl. **knai·dlach** /'k(ə)nād,läKH/) (usu. **knaidels**) a type of dumpling eaten esp. in Jewish households during Passover. [from Yiddish *kneydel*.]

knap /nap/ ▶ **v.** (**knapped, knap·ping**) [trans.] Archit. & Archaeol. shape (a piece of stone, typically flint) by striking it so as to make stone tools or weapons or to give a flat-faced stone for building walls. — **knap·per n.** [ME: imitative.]

knap·sack /'nap,sak/ ▶ **n.** a bag with shoulder straps, carried on the back, and typically made of canvas or other weatherproof material. [17th C.: from Mid. Low Ger., from Du. *knapzack*, prob. from Ger. *knappen* 'to bite' + *zak* 'sack.']

knap·weed /'nap,wēd/ ▶ **n.** a tough-stemmed plant (genus *Centaurea*) of the daisy family that typically has purple thistlelike flowerheads, found in grassland and on roadsides. Several species include the **black knapweed** (*C. nigra*) (also called HARDHEADS).

knave /nāv/ ▶ **n.** archaic a dishonest or unscrupulous man. ■ another term for JACK[1] in cards. — **knav·er·y** /-vərē/ **n.** (pl. **-er·ies**). **knav·ish adj.**

knav·ish·ly adv. **knav·ish·ness** n. [OE *cnafa* 'boy, servant,' of West Gmc. origin; rel. to Ger. *Knabe* 'boy.']

knawel /nôl/ ▶ n. a low-growing inconspicuous plant (genus *Scleranthus*) of the pink family, growing in temperate regions of the northern hemisphere. [16th C.: from Ger. *Knauel, Knäuel* 'knotgrass.']

knead /nēd/ ▶ v. [trans.] work (moistened flour or clay) into dough or paste with the hands. ■ make (bread or pottery) by such a process. ■ massage or squeeze with the hands. — **knead·a·ble** adj. **knead·er** n. [OE *cnedan*, of Gmc. origin; rel. to Du. *kneden* and Ger. *kneten*.]

knee /nē/ ▶ n. the joint between the thigh and the lower leg in humans. ■ the corresponding or analogous joint in other animals. ■ the upper surface of someone's thigh when sitting; a person's lap. ■ the part of a garment covering the knee. ■ an angled piece of wood or metal frame used to connect and support the beams and timbers of a wooden vessel; a triangular plate serving the same purpose in a modern vessel. ▶ v. (**knees, kneed, knee·ing**) [trans.] hit (someone) with one's knee: *she kneed him in the groin.* [OE *cnēow, cnēo*; rel. to Ger. *Knie*, L. *genu*.]

knee bend ▶ n. an act of bending the knee, esp. as a physical exercise in which the body is raised and lowered without the use of the hands.

knee·board /ˈnē,bôrd/ ▶ n. a short board for surfing or waterskiing in a kneeling position. — **knee·board·er** n. **knee·board·ing** n.

knee·cap /ˈnē,kap/ ▶ n. the convex bone in front of the knee joint; the patella. ▶ v. (**-capped, -cap·ping**) [trans.] shoot (someone) in the knee or leg as a form of punishment.

knee-deep ▶ adj. immersed up to the knees. ■ having more than one needs or wants of something. ■ so deep as to reach the knees. ▶ adv. so as to be immersed up to the knees: *I plodded knee-deep through the mud.*

knee-high ▶ adj. & adv. so high as to reach the knees. ▶ n. (usu. **knee-highs**) a nylon stocking with an elasticized top that reaches to a person's knee.

knee·hole /ˈnē,hōl/ ▶ n. a space for the knees, esp. one under a desk.

knee-jerk ▶ n. a sudden involuntary reflex kick caused by a blow on the tendon just below the knee. ▶ adj. [attrib.] (of a response) automatic and unthinking: *a knee-jerk reaction.* ■ (of a person) responding in this way.

kneel /nēl/ ▶ v. (past and past part. **knelt** /nelt/ also **kneeled**) [intrans.] (of a person) be in or assume a position in which the body is supported by a knee or the knees, typically as a sign of reverence or submission. [OE *cnēowlian*, from *cnēow* (see KNEE).]

kneel·er /ˈnēlər/ ▶ n. a person who kneels, esp. in prayer. ■ a cushion or bench for kneeling on.

knee-slap·per ▶ n. informal an uproariously funny joke. — **knee-slap·ping** adj.

knei·del /k(ə)ˈnādl/ ▶ n. (pl. **knei·dlach** /ˈk(ə)nād,läkh/) var. of KNAIDEL.

knell /nel/ literary ▶ n. the sound of a bell, esp. when rung solemnly for a death or funeral. ■ fig. used with reference to an announcement, event, or sound that is regarded as a solemn warning of the end of something. ▶ v. [intrans.] (of a bell) ring solemnly, esp. for a death or funeral. ■ [trans.] proclaim (something) by or as if by a knell. [OE *cnyll* (noun), *cnyllan* (verb), of West Gmc. origin; rel. to Du. *knal* (n.), *knallen* (v.) 'bang, pop, crack.']

knelt /nelt/ past and past participle of KNEEL.

Knes·set /k(ə)ˈneset/ the parliament of modern Israel.

knew /n(y)o͞o/ past of KNOW.

knick·er·bock·er /ˈnikər,bäkər/ ▶ n. **1** (**knickerbockers**) see KNICKERS. **2** (**Knickerbocker**) a New Yorker. ■ a descendant of the original Dutch settlers in New York. — **knick·er·bock·ered** adj. [19th C.: named after Diedrich *Knickerbocker*, pretended author of W. Irving's *History of New York* (1809).]

knick·ers /ˈnikərz/ ▶ plural n. (also **knick·er·bock·ers**) loose-fitting trousers gathered at the knee or calf. [19th C.: abbrev. of *knickerbockers*.]

knickers

knick·knack /ˈnik,nak/ (also **nick-nack**) ▶ n. (usu. **knickknacks**) small worthless objects, esp. household ornaments. — **knick·knack·er·y** /-,nakərē/ n. [16th C. (in the sense 'a petty trick'): reduplication of KNACK.]

knife /nīf/ ▶ n. (pl. **knives** /nīvz/) a cutting instrument composed of a blade and a handle into which it is fixed, either rigidly or with a joint. ■ an instrument such as this used as a weapon. ■ a cutting blade forming part of a machine. ▶ v. [trans.] stab (someone) with a knife. ■ [intrans.] cut like a knife.
– PHRASES **go** (or **be**) **under the knife** informal have surgery. **twist** (or **turn**) **the knife** (**in the wound**) deliberately make someone's sufferings worse. [OE *cnīf*, from ON *knífr*, of Gmc. origin.]

knife edge ▶ n. the edge of a knife. ■ [as adj.] (of creases or pleats in a garment) very fine. ■ [in sing.] a tense or uncertain situation, esp. one finely balanced between success and failure. ■ a steel wedge on which a pendulum or other device oscillates or is balanced. ■ a narrow, sharp ridge; an arête.

knife pleat ▶ n. a sharp, narrow pleat on a skirt made in one direction and typically overlapping another.

knife·point /ˈnīf,point/ ▶ n. the pointed end of a knife.

knight /nīt/ ▶ n. **1** (in the Middle Ages) a man who served his sovereign or lord as a mounted soldier in armor. ■ (in the Middle Ages) a man raised by a sovereign to honorable military rank after service as a page and squire. **2** (in the UK) a man awarded a nonhereditary title by the sovereign in recognition of merit or service and entitled to use the honorific "Sir" in front of his name. **3** a chess piece, typically with its top shaped like a horse's head, that moves by jumping to the opposite corner of a rectangle two squares by three. ▶ v. [trans.] (usu. **be knighted**) invest (someone) with the title of knight.

knife pleats

– PHRASES **knight in shining armor** (or **knight on a white charger**) an idealized or chivalrous man who comes to the rescue of a woman in a difficult situation. — **knight·li·ness** n. **knight·ly** adj. & (literary) adv. [OE *cniht* 'boy, youth, servant,' of West Gmc. origin; rel. to Ger. *Knecht*.]

knight-er·rant (also **knight er·rant**) ▶ n. (pl. **knights-er·rant**) a medieval knight wandering in search of chivalrous adventures. — **knight-er·rant·ry** n.

knight·hood /ˈnīt,ho͝od/ ▶ n. the title, rank, or status of a knight.

Knights·bridge /ˈnīts,brij/ a district in the West End of London, noted for its fashionable shops.

knish /k(ə)ˈnish/ ▶ n. a dumpling of dough that is stuffed with a filling and baked or fried. [Yiddish, from Russ. *knish, knysh*, denoting a kind of bun or dumpling.]

knit /nit/ ▶ v. (**knit·ting**; past and past part. **knit·ted** or (esp. in sense 2) **knit**) **1** [trans.] make (a garment, blanket, etc.) by interlocking loops of wool or other yarn with knitting needles or on a machine. ■ make (a stitch or row of stitches) in such a way. ■ knit with a knit stitch. **2** [intrans.] become united. ■ (of parts of a broken bone) become joined during healing. ■ [trans.] cause to unite or combine. **3** [trans.] tighten (one's brow or eyebrows) in a frown of concentration, disapproval, or anxiety. ■ [intrans.] (of someone's brow or eyebrows) tighten in such a frown. ▶ adj. denoting or relating to a knitting stitch made by putting the needle through the front of the stitch from left to right. Compare with PURL[1]. ▶ n. a knitted fabric. ■ a garment made of such fabric. — **knit·ter** n. [OE *cnyttan*; rel. to Ger. dial. *knütten*, also to KNOT[1].]

knit·bone /ˈnit,bōn/ ▶ n. another term for COMFREY.

knit·ting /ˈniting/ ▶ n. the craft or action of knitting. ■ material that is in the process of being knitted.

knit·ting nee·dle ▶ n. a long, thin, pointed rod used as part of a pair for knitting by hand.

knit·wear /ˈnit,we(ə)r/ ▶ n. knitted garments.

knives /nīvz/ plural form of KNIFE.

knob /näb/ ▶ n. a rounded lump or ball, esp. at the end or on the surface of something. ■ a handle on a door or drawer shaped like a ball. ■ a rounded button for adjusting or controlling a machine. ■ a prominent round hill. ■ vulgar slang a penis. — **knobbed** adj. **knob·by** adj. [ME: from Mid. Low Ger. *knobbe* 'knot, knob, bud.']

knob·bly /ˈnäblē/ ▶ adj. (**-bli·er, -bli·est**) having lumps that give a misshapen appearance: *knobbly knees | knobbly potatoes.*

knock /näk/ ▶ v. **1** [intrans.] strike a surface noisily to attract attention, esp. when waiting to be let in through a door. ■ strike or thump together or against something. ■ (of a motor or other engine) make a regular thumping or rattling noise because of improper ignition. **2** [trans.] collide with (someone or something), giving them a hard blow. ■ [trans.] force to move or fall with a deliberate or accidental blow or collision. ■ injure or damage by striking. ■ make (a hole or a dent) in something by striking it forcefully. ■ informal talk disparagingly about; criticize. ▶ n. **1** a sudden short sound caused by a blow, esp. on a door to attract attention or gain entry. ■ a continual thumping or rattling sound made by an engine because of improper ignition. **2** a blow or collision. ■ an injury caused by a blow or collision. ■ a discouraging experience; a setback. ■ informal a critical comment.
– PHRASES **knock someone's block off** informal hit someone very hard in anger. **knock the bottom out of** see BOTTOM. **knock someone dead** informal greatly impress someone. **knock someone for a loop** see LOOP. **knock someone into the middle of next week** informal hit someone very hard. **knock someone** (or **something**) **into shape** see SHAPE. **knock it off** informal used to tell someone to stop doing something that one finds annoying or foolish. **knock on wood** see WOOD. **knock someone's socks off** see SOCK. **the school of hard knocks** painful or difficult experiences that are seen to be useful in teaching someone about life.
– PHRASAL VERBS **knock around** (or **about**) informal travel without a specific purpose. ■ happen to be present. **knock someone/something about** (or **around**) injure or damage by rough treatment. **knock something back** informal consume a drink quickly and entirely. **knock someone down** (of a person or vehicle) strike or collide with someone so as to cause them to fall to the ground. **knock something down 1** demolish a building. ■ take machinery or furniture to pieces for transportation. **2** (at an auction) confirm the sale of an article to a bidder by a knock with a hammer. ■ informal reduce the price of an article. **3** informal earn a specified sum as a wage. **knock off** informal stop work. **knock someone off** informal kill someone. **knock something off 1** informal produce a piece of work quickly and easily, esp. to order. **2** informal deduct an amount from a total. **3** another way of saying KNOCK SOMETHING OVER. ■ informal make an illegal copy of a product. **knock someone out** make a person unconscious, typically with a blow to the head. ■ knock down (a boxer) for a count of ten, thereby winning the contest. ■ (**knock one-

self out) informal work so hard that one is exhausted. ■ informal astonish or greatly impress someone. **knock something out 1** destroy a machine or damage it so that it stops working. ■ destroy or disable enemy installations or equipment. **2** informal produce work at a steady fast rate. **3** empty a tobacco pipe by tapping it against a surface. **knock someone over** another way of saying KNOCK SOMEONE DOWN. **knock something over** informal rob a store or similar establishment. **knock something together** assemble something in a hasty and makeshift way. **knock someone up** vulgar slang make a woman pregnant. [OE *cnocian*, of imitative origin.]

knock·a·bout /ˈnäkəˌbout/ ▶ **adj. 1** denoting a rough, slapstick comic performance. **2** (of clothes) suitable for rough use. ▶ **n. 1** a rough, slapstick comic performance. **2** a tramp or vagrant. **3** a small yacht or dinghy.

knock·down /ˈnäkˌdoun/ (also **knock-down**) ▶ **adj.** [attrib.] **1** informal (of a price) very low. **2** capable of knocking down or overwhelming someone or something. ■ (of furniture) easily dismantled and reassembled. ▶ **n.** Boxing an act of knocking an opponent down. ■ (also **knockdown pitch**) Baseball a pitch aimed so close to the body that the batter must drop to the ground to avoid being hit. ■ Sailing an instance of a vessel being knocked on its side by the force of the wind.

knock-down-drag-out ▶ **n.** informal a free-for-all fight.

knock·er /ˈnäkər/ ▶ **n. 1** short for DOOR KNOCKER. **2** informal a person who continually finds fault. **3** (**knockers**) vulgar slang a woman's breasts.

knock knees ▶ **plural n.** a condition in which the legs curve inward so that the feet are apart when the knees are touching. — **knock-kneed adj.**

knock·off /ˈnäkˌôf/ (also **knock-off**) ▶ **n.** informal a copy or imitation, esp. of an expensive or designer product.

knock·out /ˈnäkˌout/ ▶ **n.** an act of knocking someone out, esp. in boxing. ■ informal an extremely attractive or impressive person or thing.

knock·out drops ▶ **plural n.** a drug in liquid form added to a drink to cause unconsciousness.

knock·wurst /ˈnäkˌwərst/ ▶ **n.** var. of KNACKWURST.

knoll /nōl/ ▶ **n.** a small hill or mound. [OE *cnoll* 'hilltop,' of Gmc. origin; rel. to Ger. *Knolle* 'clod, lump, tuber' and Du. *knol* 'tuber, turnip.']

Knos·sos /ˈnäsəs/ the ancient city of Minoan Crete, the remains of which are situated on the northern coast of Crete, occupied from Neolithic times until *c.*1200 BC.

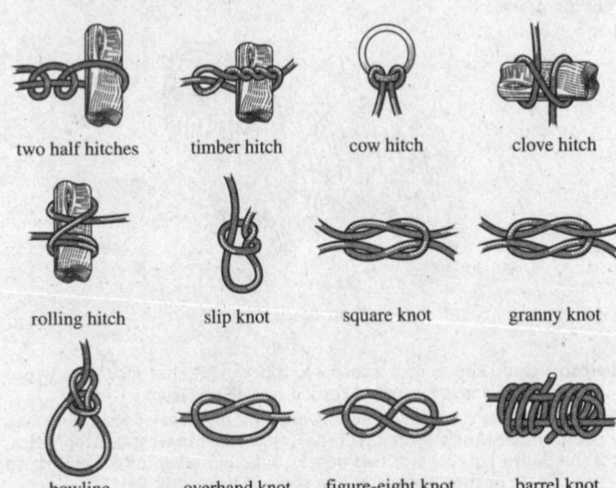

knots

knot¹ /nät/ ▶ **n. 1** a fastening made by tying a piece of string, rope, or something similar. ■ a particular method of tying a knot. ■ a tangled mass in something such as hair. ■ a complex and intractable problem. ■ a tied or folded ribbon, worn as an ornament. **2** a knob, protuberance, or node in a stem, branch, or root. ■ a hard mass formed in a tree trunk at the intersection with a branch, resulting in a round cross-grained piece in timber when cut through. ■ a hard lump of tissue in an animal or human body. ■ a tense constricted feeling in the body. ■ a small tightly packed group of people. **3** a unit of speed equivalent to one nautical mile per hour, used esp. of ships, aircraft, and winds. ■ esp. hist. a length marked by knots on a log line, as a measure of speed. ▶ **v.** (**knot·ted, knot·ting**) [trans.] **1** fasten with a knot. ■ make (a carpet or other decorative item) with knots. ■ make (something, esp. hair) tangled. **2** cause (a muscle) to become tense and hard. ■ [intrans.] (of the stomach) tighten as a result of nervousness or tension.
– PHRASES **tie someone (up) in knots** informal make someone completely confused. **tie the knot** informal get married. — **knot·ter n.** [OE *cnotta*, of West Gmc. origin; rel. to Du. *knot*.]

knot² ▶ **n.** (pl. same or **knots**) a small, relatively short-billed sandpiper (genus *Calidris*) with a reddish-brown or blackish breast in the breeding season. Two species include the **red knot** (*C. canutus*), which breeds in the Arctic and winters in the southern hemisphere. [ME: of unknown origin.]

knot·grass /ˈnätˌgras/ ▶ **n.** a common Eurasian plant (genus *Polygonum*) of the dock family, with jointed creeping stems and small pink flowers. It is a serious weed in some areas. ■ any of a number of other plants, esp. grasses, with jointed stems.

knot·hole /ˈnätˌhōl/ ▶ **n.** a hole in a piece of timber where a knot has fallen out, or in a tree trunk where a branch has decayed.

knot·ting /ˈnätiNG/ ▶ **n.** the action or craft of tying knots in yarn or string to make carpets or other decorative items. ■ the knots tied in a carpet or other item.

knot·ty /ˈnätē/ ▶ **adj.** (**knot·ti·er, knot·ti·est**) full of knots. ■ (of a problem or matter) extremely difficult or intricate. — **knot·ti·ly** /ˈnätəlē/ **adv. knot·ti·ness n.**

knot·weed /ˈnätˌwēd/ ▶ **n.** a plant (*Polygonum* and other genera) of the dock family that typically has sheaths where the leaves join the stems. It is often an invasive weed. ■ knotgrass.

knout /nout/ ▶ **n.** (in imperial Russia) a whip used to inflict punishment, often causing death. ▶ **v.** [trans.] flog (someone) with such a whip. [17th C.: via Fr. from Russ. *knut*, from ON *knútr*; rel. to KNOT¹.]

know /nō/ ▶ **v.** (past **knew** /n(y)o͞o/; past part. **known** /nōn/) **1** [with clause] be aware of through observation, inquiry, or information. ■ [trans.] have knowledge or information concerning. ■ be absolutely certain or sure about something. **2** [trans.] have developed a relationship with (someone) through meeting and spending time with them; be familiar or friendly with. ■ have a good command of (a subject or language). ■ recognize (someone or something): *she knew the voice.* ■ be familiar or acquainted with (something). ■ have personal experience of (an emotion or situation): *he had known better times.* ■ (usu. **be known as**) regard or perceive as having a specified characteristic. ■ (usu. **be known as**) give (someone or something) a particular name or title. ■ (**know someone/something from**) be able to distinguish one person or thing from (another).
– PHRASES **be in the know** be aware of something known only to a few people. **don't I know it!** informal used as an expression of rueful assent or agreement. **God** (or **goodness** or **heaven**) **knows 1** used to emphasize that one does not know something: *God knows what else they might find.* **2** used to emphasize the truth of a statement: *God knows, we deserve it.* **know better than** be wise or polite enough to avoid doing a particular thing. **know the ropes** have experience of the appropriate procedures. **not know from nothing** informal be totally ignorant, either generally or concerning something in particular. **not know what to do with oneself** be at a loss as to know what to do, typically through boredom, embarrassment, or anxiety. **what does —— know?** informal used to indicate that someone knows nothing about the subject in question: *what does he know about football, anyway?* **what do you know** (**about that**)? informal used as an expression of surprise. **wouldn't you like to know?** informal used to express the speaker's firm intention not to reveal something in spite of a questioner's curiosity. **you know** informal used to imply that what is being referred to is known to or understood by the listener. ■ used as a gap-filler in conversation. **you know something** (or **what**)? informal used to indicate that one is going to say something interesting or surprising. **you never know** informal you can never be certain; it's impossible to predict. — **know·a·ble adj. know·er n.** [OE *cnāwan* 'recognize, identify'; from an Indo-Eur. root shared by L. *(g)noscere*, Gk. *gignōskein*.]

know-how ▶ **n.** practical knowledge or skill; expertise.

know·ing /ˈnōiNG/ ▶ **adj.** showing or suggesting that one has knowledge or awareness that is secret or known to only a few people. ■ esp. derog. experienced or shrewd, esp. excessively or prematurely so. ■ done in full awareness or consciousness. ▶ **n.** the state of being aware or informed. — **know·ing·ly adv. know·ing·ness n.**

know-it-all ▶ **n.** informal a person who behaves as if they know everything.

knowl·edge /ˈnälij/ ▶ **n. 1** information and skills acquired through experience or education; the theoretical or practical understanding of a subject. ■ what is known in a particular field or in total; facts and information. ■ Philos. true, justified belief; certain understanding, as opposed to opinion. **2** awareness or familiarity gained by experience of a fact or situation: *the program had been developed without his knowledge.* [ME: based on OE *cnāwan* (see KNOW).]

knowl·edge·a·ble /ˈnälijəbəl/ (also **knowl·edg·a·ble**) ▶ **adj.** intelligent and well informed. — **know·ledge·a·bil·i·ty** /ˌnälijəˈbilitē/ **n. know·ledge·a·bly adv.**

known /nōn/ past participle of KNOW. ▶ **adj.** recognized, familiar, or within the scope of knowledge. ■ [attrib.] publicly acknowledged to be. ■ Math. (of a quantity or variable) having a value that can be stated.

know-noth·ing ▶ **n. 1** an ignorant person. **2** (**Know-Nothing**) hist. a member of a political party in the US, prominent from 1853 to 1856, that was antagonistic toward Roman Catholics and recent immigrants and whose members preserved its secrecy by denying its existence. — **know-no·thing·ism n.**

Knox¹ /näks/, Henry (1750–1806), American military officer. He served in the American Revolution and became the first US secretary of war 1785–94.

Knox², John (*c.*1505–72), Scottish Protestant reformer. He played an important part in the establishment of the Church of Scotland.

Knox·ville /ˈnäksˌvil; -vəl/ a city in eastern Tennessee, on the Tennessee River; pop. 173,890.

Knt. ▶ abbr. Knight.

knuck·le /ˈnəkəl/ ▶ n. a part of a finger at a joint where the bone is near the surface, esp. where the finger joins the hand. ■ a projection of the carpal or tarsal joint of a quadruped. ■ a cut of meat consisting of such a projection together with the adjoining parts. ▶ v. [trans.] rub or press (something, esp. the eyes) with the knuckles.
– PHRASAL VERBS **knuckle down 1** apply oneself seriously to a task. **2** (also **knuckle under**) give in; submit. — **knuck·ly** adj. [ME *knokel* (orig. denoting the rounded shape when a joint such as the elbow or knee is bent), from Mid. Low Ger., MDu. *knökel*, dimin. of *knoke* 'bone.']

knuck·le·ball /ˈnəkəlˌbôl/ (also **knuck·ler**) ▶ n. Baseball a slow pitch that has virtually no spin and moves erratically, typically made by releasing the ball from between the thumb and the knuckles of the first joints of the index and middle finger. — **knuck·le·ball·er** n.

knuck·le·bone /ˈnəkəlˌbōn/ ▶ n. a bone forming or corresponding to a knuckle. ■ a knuckle of meat.

knuck·le·head /ˈnəkəlˌhed/ ▶ n. informal a stupid person.

knuck·le joint ▶ n. a joint connecting two parts of a mechanism, in which a projection in one fits into a recess in the other.

knuck·le sand·wich ▶ n. informal a punch in the mouth.

knurl /nərl/ ▶ n. a small projecting knob or ridge, esp. in a series around the edge of something. — **knurled** adj. [17th C.: prob. from *knur* 'concretion,' rel. to Mid. Low Ger. *knorre* 'protuberance.']

Knut /kəˈno͞ot/ var. of CANUTE.

KO /ˌkāˈō/ Boxing ▶ n. a knockout in a boxing match. See also KAYO. ▶ v. (**KO's, KO'd, KO'ing**) [trans.] knock (an opponent) out in a boxing match. [1920s: abbrev.]

ko·a /ˈkōə/ ▶ n. a large Hawaiian forest tree (*Acacia koa*) of the pea family that yields dark red timber. [19th C.: Hawaiian.]

ko·a·la /kōˈälə/ ▶ n. an arboreal Australian marsupial (*Phascolarctos cinereus*, family Phascolarctidae) with thick gray fur that feeds on eucalyptus leaves. [19th C.: from Dharuk.]

ko·an /ˈkōˌän/ ▶ n. a paradoxical anecdote or riddle, used in Zen Buddhism to demonstrate the inadequacy of logical reasoning and to provoke enlightenment. [Japanese, lit. 'matter for public thought,' from Chin. *gōngàn* 'official business.']

kob /käb; kōb/ ▶ n. (pl. same) an antelope (*Kobus kob*) with a reddish coat and lyre-shaped horns, found on the savannas of southern Africa. [18th C.: from Wolof *kooba*.]

Ko·be /ˈkōbā; -bē/ a port in central Japan, on the island of Honshu; pop. 1,477,000.

Kø·ben·havn /ˌkœbənˈhoun/ Danish name for COPENHAGEN.

ko·bo /ˈkōbō/ ▶ n. (pl. same) a monetary unit of Nigeria, equal to one hundredth of a naira. [corruption of COPPER[1].]

ko·bold /ˈkōˌbôld/ ▶ n. Germanic Mythol. **1** a familiar spirit that haunts houses; a brownie. **2** a gnome that haunts mines and other underground areas. [from Ger. *Kobold*.]

Koch /kôKH/, Robert (1843–1910), German bacteriologist. He identified the organisms that cause anthrax, tuberculosis, and cholera. Nobel Prize for Physiology or Medicine (1905).

Kö·chel num·ber /ˈkərsHəl; -kəl; ˈkœKHəl/ ▶ n. Music a number given to each of Mozart's compositions in the catalog of his works compiled by Austrian scientist Ludwig von Köchel (1800–77) and his successors.

ko·chi·a /ˈkōkēə/ ▶ n. a shrubby Eurasian plant (*Bassia scoparia*) of the goosefoot family, grown for its decorative foliage, which turns deep fiery red in the autumn. Also called BURNING BUSH, SUMMER CYPRESS. [19th C.: after Wilhelm D. J. *Koch* (1771–1849), German botanist.]

Ko·dá·ly /kōˈdī(yə); ˈkōdī/, Zoltán (1882–1967), Hungarian composer. He collected and published Hungarian folk songs.

Ko·di·ak bear /ˈkōdēˌak/ ▶ n. an animal (*Ursus arctos middendorffi*) of a large race of the North American brown bear or grizzly, found on islands to the south of Alaska. [19th C.: after *Kodiak* Island, Alaska.]

Ko·di·ak Is·land an island in the Gulf of Alaska, in southwestern Alaska.

ko·el /ˈkōəl/ ▶ n. an Asian and Australasian cuckoo (genus *Eudynamys*) with a call that resembles its name, the male typically having all-black plumage. [19th C.: from Hindi *koēl*, from Sanskrit *kokila*.]

K of C ▶ abbr. Knights of Columbus.

Koh-i-noor /ˈkō ə ˌno͝or/ a famous Indian diamond that has a history going back to the 14th century.

Kohl /kōl/, Helmut (1930–), chancellor of the Federal Republic of Germany 1982–90, and of Germany 1990–98. He showed a strong commitment to NATO and to closer ties within the EU.

kohl /kōl/ ▶ n. a black powder, usually antimony sulfide or lead sulfide, used as eye makeup esp. in Eastern countries. [18th C.: from Arab. *kuḥl*.]

kohl·ra·bi /kōlˈräbē/ ▶ n. (pl. **-bies**) a cabbage of a variety with an edible turniplike swollen stem. [19th C.: via Ger. from Ital. *cavolo rapa*, from med. L. *caulorapa*, from L. *caulis* + *rapum*, *rapa* 'turnip.']

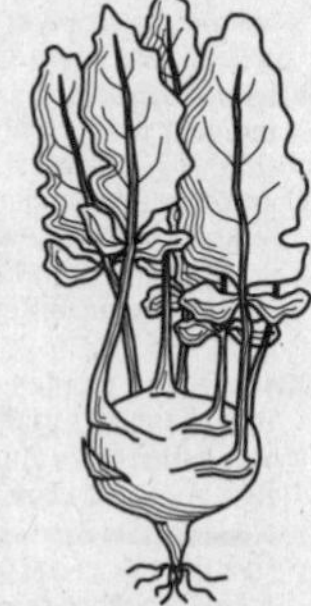
kohlrabi

koi /koi/ (also **koi carp**) ▶ n. (pl. same) a common carp of a large ornamental variety, originally bred in Japan. [18th C.: from Japanese, 'carp.']

koi·ne /koiˈnā; ˈkoinā/ ▶ n. the common language of the Greeks from the close of the classical period to the Byzantine era. ■ a common language shared by various peoples; a lingua franca. [19th C.: from Gk. *koinē (dialektos)* 'common (language).']

ko·kan·ee /kōˈkanē/ ▶ n. (pl. same or **-ees**) a sockeye salmon of a dwarf variety that lives in landlocked lakes in western North America. [19th C.: from Interior Salish.]

ko·la /ˈkōlə/ ▶ n. var. of COLA (sense 2).

Ko·la Pen·in·su·la /ˈkōlə/ a peninsula on the northwestern coast of Russia that separates the White Sea from the Barents Sea.

ko·lin·sky /kəˈlinskē/ ▶ n. (pl. **-skies**) a dark brown weasel (*Mustela sibirica*) with a bushy tail, found from Siberia to Japan. Also called **Siberian weasel**. [19th C.: from *Kola*, Russia, + *-insky*.]

Kol·ka·ta /kōlˈkätə/ official name (from 2000) for CALCUTTA.

Kol·khis /ˈkôlkēs/ Greek name for COLCHIS.

kol·khoz /kəlˈkôz; -ˈKHôz/ ▶ n. (pl. same or **-khoz·es** or **-kho·zy** /-ˈKHôzē/) a collective farm in the former USSR. [1920s: Russ., from *kol(lektivnoe) khoz(yaĭstvo)* 'collective farm.']

Köln /kœln/ German name for COLOGNE.

Kol Ni·dre /kōl ˈnidrā; ˈnidrə; ˌkôl nēˈdrā/ ▶ n. an Aramaic prayer annulling vows made before God, sung by Jews on the eve of Yom Kippur. [from Aramaic *kol nidrē* 'all the vows.']

Ko·ly·ma /kəˈlēmə/ a river in eastern Siberia, flowing north to the Arctic Ocean.

Ko·man·dor·ski Is·lands /ˌkəmənˈdôrskyē/ an island group in extreme eastern Russia, off the eastern Kamchatka Peninsula.

Ko·ma·ti Riv·er /kəˈmätē/ (also **Rio Incomati**) a river flowing from the Drakensberg Range in South Africa to the Indian Ocean north of Maputo.

Ko·mi /ˈkōmē/ an autonomous republic in northwestern Russia; pop. 1,265,000.

Ko·mo·do /kəˈmōdō/ a small island in Indonesia, in the Lesser Sunda Islands.

Ko·mo·do drag·on ▶ n. a monitor lizard (*Varanus komodoensis*) occurring only on Komodo and neighboring Indonesian islands; the largest living lizard.

Komondor

Ko·mon·dor /ˈkōmənˌdôr; ˈkäm-/ ▶ n. a powerful sheepdog of a white breed with a dense matted or corded coat. [Hungarian.]

Kon·go /ˈkäNGgō/ ▶ n. (pl. same or **-gos**) **1** a member of an indigenous people inhabiting the region of the Congo River in west central Africa. **2** the Bantu language of this people; Kikongo. ▶ adj. of or relating to this people or their language. [the name in Kikongo.]

kon·go·ni /käNGˈgōnē/ ▶ n. (pl. same) a hartebeest (*Alcelaphus buselaphus cokii*), in particular one of a pale yellowish-brown race found in Kenya and Tanzania. [20th C.: from Kiswahili.]

Kö·nig·grätz /ˈkœnikHˌgrets/ German name for HRADEC KRÁLOVÉ.

Kö·nigs·berg /ˈkœniKHsˌberk/ German name for KALININGRAD.

Kon·ka·ni /ˈkôNGkəˌnē; ˈkäNG-/ ▶ n. an Indic language that is the main language of Goa and adjacent parts of Maharashtra. Also called GOANESE (see GOA). ▶ adj. of or relating to this language. [from Marathi and Hindi *koṅkaṇī*, from Sanskrit *koṅkaṇa* 'Konkan' (a coastal region of western India).]

Kon-Ti·ki /kän ˈtēkē/ the raft made of balsa logs in which Thor Heyerdahl sailed from the western coast of Peru to the islands of Polynesia in 1947.

kook /ko͞ok/ ▶ n. informal a crazy or eccentric person. [1960s: prob. from CUCKOO.]

kook·a·bur·ra /ˈko͝okəˌbərə/ ▶ n. a very large Australasian kingfisher (genus *Dacelo*) that feeds on terrestrial prey such as reptiles and birds. Two species: the **blue-winged kookaburra** (*D. leachii*) and the loud, cackling **laughing kookaburra** (*D. gigas*, or *D. novaeguineae*). [19th C.: from Wiradhuri *gugubarra*.]

kook·y /ˈko͞okē/ ▶ adj. (**kook·i·er, kook·i·est**) informal strange or eccentric. — **kook·i·ly** /-kəlē/ adv. **kook·i·ness** n.

Koon·ing, Willem de, see DE KOONING.

laughing kookaburra

Koop /ko͝op/, C. Everett (1916–), US physician; full name *Charles Everett Koop*. As the US surgeon general 1982–89, he campaigned vigorously against the tobacco industry.

Koo·te·nai Riv·er /'ko͞otn-,ā/ a river flowing from southeastern British Columbia into Montana and Idaho and then back into British Columbia, where it joins the Columbia River. Canadian name **Kootenay**.

ko·pek /'kōpek/ (also **co·peck** or **ko·peck**) ▶ **n.** a monetary unit of Russia and some other countries of the former USSR, equal to one hundredth of a ruble. [from Russ. *kopeĭka*, dimin. of *kop'ë* 'lance.']

Ko·ran /kə'rän; kô-; 'kōrän/ (also **Qu·r'an** or **Qu·ran**) ▶ **n.** the Islamic sacred book, believed to be the word of God as dictated to Muhammad by the archangel Gabriel and written down in Arabic. — **Ko·ran·ic** /-'ränik/ **adj.** [from Arab. *ḳur'ān* 'recitation,' from *ḳara'a* 'read, recite.']

Kor·da /'kôrdə/, Sir Alexander (1893–1956), British movie producer and director; born in Hungary; born *Sándor Kellner*. He produced *The Third Man* (1949).

ko·re /'kôrē; 'kōrā/ ▶ **n.** (pl. **ko·rai** /'kôrī/) an archaic Greek statue of a young woman, standing and clothed in long loose robes. [from Gk. *korē* 'maiden.']

Ko·re·a /kə'rēə/ a region in eastern Asia that forms a peninsula between the Sea of Japan and the Yellow Sea, now divided into the countries of North Korea and South Korea.

Ko·re·a, Dem·o·crat·ic Peo·ple's Re·pub·lic of official name for NORTH KOREA.

Ko·re–a, Re·pub·lic of official name for SOUTH KOREA.

Ko·re·an /kə'rēən; kô-/ ▶ **adj.** of or relating to North or South Korea or its people or language. ▶ **n.** **1** a native or national of North or South Korea, or a person of Korean descent. **2** the language of Korea.

Ko·re·an War the war of 1950–53 between North and South Korea.

Kó·rin·thos /'kōrin,THôs/ Greek name for CORINTH.

Kor·sa·koff's syn·drome /'kôrsə,kôfs/ (also **Korsakoff's psychosis**) ▶ **n.** Psychiatry a mental illness, typically the result of chronic alcoholism, characterized by disorientation and a tendency to invent explanations to cover a loss of memory of recent events. [20th C.: named after Sergei S. *Korsakoff* (1854–1900), Russian psychiatrist.]

ko·ru·na /'kôrənə/ ▶ **n.** the basic monetary unit of the Czech Republic and Slovakia, equal to 100 haleru. [Czech, lit. 'crown.']

Kos·ci·us·ko /,käskē'əskō; ,käse-; kôsH'CHo͞oSHkō/, Thaddeus (1746–1817), Polish soldier and patriot; Polish name *Tadeusz Andrzej Bonawentura Kościuszko*. He fought for the Americans during the American Revolution.

Kos·ci·us·ko, Mount /,käzē'əskō/ a mountain in southeastern New South Wales, the highest mountain in Australia at 7,234 feet (2,228 m).

ko·sher /'kōsHər/ ▶ **adj.** (of food, or premises in which food is sold, cooked, or eaten) satisfying the requirements of Jewish law. ■ (of a person) observing Jewish food laws. ■ fig. genuine and legitimate. [19th C.: from Heb. *kāšēr* 'proper.']

Ko·sin·ski /kə'zinskē/, Jerzy Nikodem (1933–91), US writer; born in Poland. His works include *Being There* (1971) and *Blind Date* (1977).

Ko·so·vo /'kôsə,vō; 'käs-/ an autonomous province of Serbia, bordering on Albania; capital, Priština.

Ko·sy·gin /kə'sēgin; -gyin/, Aleksei Nikolaevich (1904–80), premier of the Soviet Union 1964–80. He devoted most of his attention to internal economic affairs.

ko·to /'kōtō/ ▶ **n.** (pl. **-tos**) a Japanese zither about six feet long, with thirteen silk strings passed over small movable bridges.

kou·miss /'ko͞o'mis; 'ko͞omis/ (also **ku·miss** or **ku·mis**) ▶ **n.** a drink made from fermented mare's milk, used also as a medicine by Asian nomads. [16th C.: based on Tartar *kumiz*.]

kou·ros /'ko͞oräs/ ▶ **n.** (pl. **kou·roi** /'ko͞oroi/) an archaic Greek statue of a young man, standing and often naked. [Gk., Ionic form of *koros* 'boy.']

Kow·loon /'kou'lo͞on/ a peninsula on the southeastern coast of China that forms part of Hong Kong.

kow·tow /'kou'tou/ ▶ **v.** [intrans.] hist. kneel and touch the ground with the forehead in worship or submission as part of Chinese custom. ■ fig. act in an excessively subservient manner. [19th C.: from Chin. *kētóu*, from *kē* 'knock' + *tóu* 'head.']

Ko·zhi·kode /'kōzHi,kōd/ another name for CALICUT.

KP ▶ **abbr.** kitchen police.

kph ▶ **abbr.** kilometers per hour.

Kr ▶ **symb.** the chemical element krypton.

kr. ▶ **abbr.** ■ krona. ■ krone.

Kra, Isthmus of /krä/ the narrowest part of the Malay Peninsula, forming part of southern Thailand.

kraal /kräl/ S. African ▶ **n.** a traditional African village of huts, typically enclosed by a fence. ■ another term for HOMESTEAD (sense 3). ■ an enclosure for cattle or sheep. [Du., from Port. *curral* (see CORRAL).]

kraft /kraft/ (also **kraft paper**) ▶ **n.** a kind of strong, smooth brown wrapping paper. [20th C.: from Swed., lit. 'strength.']

krait /krīt/ ▶ **n.** a highly venomous Asian snake (genus *Bungarus*) of the cobra family. Several species include the black and yellow **banded krait** (*B. fasciatus*). See also SEA KRAIT. [19th C.: from Hindi *karait*.]

Kra·ka·toa /,krakə'tōə; ,kräk-/ a small volcanic island in Indonesia that lies between Java and Sumatra.

kra·ken /'kräkən/ ▶ **n.** an enormous mythical sea monster said to appear off the coast of Norway.

Kra·ków /'krä,ko͞of/ Polish name for CRACOW.

Kras·no·dar /,kräsnə'där/ an administrative territory in the northern Caucasus Mountains, on the Black Sea, in southern Russia. ■ its capital, on the lower Kuban River; pop. 627,000.

Kras·no·yarsk /,kräsnə'yärsk/ an administrative territory in south central Russia. ■ its capital, on the Yenisei River; pop. 922,000.

kraut /krout/ ▶ **n.** informal sauerkraut. ■ (also **Kraut**) informal, offens. a German.

Krebs cy·cle /krebz/ ▶ **n.** Biochem. the sequence of reactions by which most living cells generate energy during the process of aerobic respiration. [1940s: named after Sir Hans A. *Krebs* (1900–81), German-born British biochemist.]

Kreis·ler /'krīslər/, Fritz (1875–1962), US violinist and composer; born in Austria.

krem·lin /'kremlin/ ▶ **n.** a citadel within a Russian town. ■ (**the Kremlin**) the citadel in Moscow. ■ the Russian or (formerly) USSR government housed within this citadel. [17th C.: via Fr. from Russ. *kreml'* 'citadel.']

Krem·lin·ol·o·gy /,kremlə'näləjē/ ▶ **n.** the study and analysis of Soviet or Russian policies. — **Krem·lin·ol·o·gist n.**

krep·lach /'krepläKH/ ▶ **plural n.** (in Jewish cooking) triangular noodles filled with chopped meat or cheese and served with soup. [from Yiddish *kreplekh*, pl. of *krepel*, from Ger. dial. *Kräppel* 'fritter.']

Kriem·hild /'krēmhilt/ (in the Nibelungenlied) a Burgundian princess, wife of Siegfried and later of Etzel (Attila the Hun), whom she marries in order to be revenged on her brothers for Siegfried's murder.

krill /kril/ ▶ **n.** (pl. same) a small shrimplike planktonic crustacean (*Meganyctiphanes norvegica*, class Malacostraca) of the open seas. It is eaten by a number of larger animals, notably the baleen whales. [20th C.: from Norw. *kril* 'young fry of fish.']

Krin·gle /'kriNGgəl/, Kris (or Kriss). Another name for SANTA CLAUS.

Kri·o /'krēō/ ▶ **n.** an English-based Creole language of Sierra Leone. ▶ **adj.** of or relating to this language. [prob. an alt. of CREOLE.]

kris /krēs/ (also archaic **creese**) ▶ **n.** a Malay or Indonesian dagger with a wavy blade. [16th C.: based on Malay *keris*.]

Krish·na /'krisHnə/ Hinduism one of the most popular gods, the eighth and most important avatar or incarnation of Vishnu.

Krish·na Riv·er a river that rises in southern India and flows generally east to the Bay of Bengal.

Kris·ti·an·i·a var. of CHRISTIANIA.

Krí·ti /'krētē/ Greek name for CRETE.

Kri·voi Rog /kri'voi 'rōg; 'rôk/ Russian name for KRYVYY RIH.

Kroc /kräk/, Raymond Albert (1902–84), US entrepreneur. He founded McDonald's restaurants in 1955.

kro·na /'krōnə/ ▶ **n.** **1** (pl. **-nor** /-nôr/) the basic monetary unit of Sweden, equal to 100 öre. [Swed., 'crown.'] **2** (pl. **-nur** /-nər/) the basic monetary unit of Iceland, equal to 100 aurar. [from ON *króna* 'crown.']

kro·ne /'krōnə/ ▶ **n.** (pl. **-ner** /-nər/) the basic monetary unit of Denmark and Norway, equal to 100 øre. [Dan. and Norw., lit. 'crown.']

Kro·nos var. of CRONUS.

Kron·stadt /'krän,stät/ German name for BRAŞOV.

kroon /kro͞on/ ▶ **n.** (pl. **kroons** or **kroo·ni** /'kro͞onē/) the basic monetary unit of Estonia, equal to 100 senti. [Estonian, lit. 'crown'; cf. KRONA, KRONE.]

Kru /kro͞o/ ▶ **n.** (pl. same) **1** a member of a seafaring people of the coast of Liberia and Ivory Coast. **2** the Niger–Congo language of this people. ▶ **adj.** of or relating to the Kru or their language. [from a West African language.]

Kru Coast a section of the coast of Liberia to the northwest of Cape Palmas.

Kru·ger /'kro͞ogər; 'krYər/, Stephanus Johannes Paulus (1825–1904), South African soldier and president of Transvaal 1883–99.

Kru·ger·rand /'kro͞ogə,rand/ (also **kru·ger·rand** or **Kru·ger**) ▶ **n.** a South African gold coin with a portrait of President Kruger on the obverse.

krumm·holz /'kro͝omhōlts/ ▶ **n.** stunted windblown trees growing near the tree line on mountains. [20th C.: from Ger., lit. 'crooked wood.']

krumm·horn /'kro͝om,hôrn/ (also **crum·horn**) ▶ **n.** a medieval wind instrument with an enclosed double reed and an upward-curving end, producing an even, nasal sound. [from Ger., from *krumm* 'crooked' + *Horn* 'horn.']

Krupp /krəp; kro͞op/, Alfred (1812–87), German industrialist. His company was a major arms producer for Germany from the 1840s until 1945.

kryp·ton /'krip,tän/ ▶ **n.** the chemical element of atomic number 36, a member of the noble gas series. (Symbol: **Kr**) [19th C.: from Gk. *krupton*, neut. of *kruptos* 'hidden.']

Kry·vyy Rih /kri'vi 'rikH/ a city in southern Ukraine, an iron-ore mining region; pop. 717,000. Russian name KRIVOI ROG.

KS ▶ **abbr.** ■ Kansas (in official postal use). ■ Kaposi's sarcoma.

Kshat·ri·ya /k(ə)'sʜätrēə/ ▶ **n.** a member of the second of the four great Hindu castes, the military caste. [18th C.: from Sanskrit *kṣatriya*, from *kṣhatra* 'rule, authority.']

Kt ▶ **abbr.** Knight.

kt. ▶ **abbr.** ■ karat(s). ■ kiloton(s). ■ knot(s).

K/T bound·a·ry short for CRETACEOUS–TERTIARY BOUNDARY. [20th C.: *K/T*, from the symbols for *Cretaceous* and *Tertiary*.]

Ku ▶ **symb.** the chemical element kurchatovium.

Kua·la Lum·pur /ˌkwälə 'lo͝om,po͝or; lo͝om'po͝or/ the capital of Malaysia, in the southwestern part of the Malay Peninsula; pop. 1,145,000.

Kua·la Treng·ga·nu /ˌkwälə trenɢ'gäno͞o/ (also **Kua·la Te·reng·ga·nu** /ˌterenɢ-/) a city in Malaysia, on the east coast of the Malay Peninsula; pop. 229,000.

Ku·blai Khan /'ko͞oblə 'kän; 'ko͞oblī/ (1216–94), Mongol emperor of China; grandson of Genghis Khan. He led the conquest of China and founded the Yuan dynasty.

Ku·brick /'ko͞obrik/, Stanley (1928–99), US director. His movies include *A Clockwork Orange* (1971) and *Full Metal Jacket* (1987).

ku·chen /'ko͞okən; -ᴋʜən/ ▶ **n.** (pl. same) a cake, esp. one eaten with coffee. [from Ger. *Kuchen*.]

Ku·ching /'ko͞ocʜiɴɢ/ a port in Malaysia, near the northwestern coast of Borneo; pop. 148,000.

ku·dos /'k(y)o͞o,dōs; -,dōz; -,däs/ ▶ **n.** praise and honor received for an achievement. [18th C.: Gk.]

ku·du /'ko͞odo͞o/ ▶ **n.** (pl. same or **ku·dus**) an African antelope (genus *Tragelaphus*) that has a grayish or brownish coat with white vertical stripes, and a short bushy tail. The male has long spirally curved horns. Several species include the **greater kudu** (*T. strepsiceros*) and the **lesser kudu** (*T. imberbis*). [18th C.: from Afrik. *koedoe*, from Xhosa *i-qudu*.]

kud·zu /'ko͞odzo͞o/ (also **kud·zu vine**) ▶ **n.** a quick-growing eastern Asian climbing plant (*Pueraria lobata*) of the pea family, with reddish-purple flowers, used as a fodder crop and for erosion control. [19th C.: from Japanese *kuzu*.]

Ku·fic /'k(y)o͞ofik/ ▶ **n.** an early angular form of the Arabic alphabet found chiefly in decorative inscriptions. ▶ **adj.** of or in this type of script. [18th C.: from *Kufa*, Iraq.]

ku·gel /'ko͞ogəl; 'ko͞o-/ ▶ **n.** (in Jewish cooking) a kind of sweet or savory pudding of noodles or potatoes. [Yiddish, lit. 'ball.']

Kui·by·shev /'kwēbə,sʜef/ former name (1935–91) of SAMARA.

Ku Klux Klan /'ko͞o ˌkləks 'klan/ (abbr.: **KKK**) an extremist right-wing secret society in the US, founded in the southern states after the Civil War to oppose social change and black emancipation by violence and terrorism. — **Ku Klux·er n. Ku Klux Klans·man** /'klanzmən/ **n.** (pl. **-men**).

kuk·ri /'ko͝okrē/ ▶ **n.** (pl. **kuk·ris**) a curved knife broadening toward the point, used by Gurkhas. [19th C.: from Nepalese *khukuri*.]

ku·lak /ko͞o'lak; -'läk/ ▶ **n.** hist. a peasant in Russia wealthy enough to own a farm and hire labor. [Russ., lit. 'fist, tightfisted person,' from Turkic *ḳol* 'hand.']

Kul·tur /ko͝ol'to͝or/ ▶ **n.** German civilization and culture (sometimes used derogatorily to suggest elements of racism, authoritarianism, or militarism). [Ger., from L. *cultura* or Fr. *culture* (see CULTURE).]

Kul·tur·kampf /ko͝ol'to͝or,käm(p)f/ a conflict from 1872 to 1887 between the German government (headed by Bismarck) and the papacy for the control of schools and Church appointments. [Ger., from KULTUR + *Kampf* 'struggle.']

Kum var. of QOM.

Ku·ma·si /ko͞o'mäsē; -'masē/ a city in southern Ghana, capital of the Ashanti region; pop. 376,250.

Kumbh Me·la /'ko͝om mə'lä/ ▶ **n.** a Hindu festival and assembly, held once every twelve years at four locations in India, at which pilgrims bathe in the waters of the Ganges and Jumna rivers for the purification of sin. [from Sanskrit, lit. 'pitcher festival,' from *kumbh* 'pitcher' + *melā* 'assembly.']

ku·mis (also **ku·miss**) ▶ **n.** var. of KOUMISS.

kum·kum /'ko͝om,ko͝om/ ▶ **n.** a red powder used ceremonially and cosmetically, esp. by Hindu women to make a small distinctive mark on the forehead. [20th C.: from Sanskrit *kuṅkuma* 'saffron.']

kum·quat /'kəm,kwät/ (also **cumquat**) ▶ **n. 1** an orangelike fruit with an edible sweet rind and acid pulp. **2** the eastern Asian shrub or small tree (genus *Fortunella*) of the rue family that yields this fruit and that hybridizes with citrus trees. [17th C.: from Chin. (Cantonese dial.) *kam kwat* 'little orange.']

ku·na /'ko͞onə/ ▶ **n.** (pl. **-ne** /-nā/) the basic monetary unit of Croatia, equal to 100 lipa.

kun·da·li·ni /ˌko͝ondl'ēnē/ ▶ **n.** (in yoga) latent female energy believed to lie coiled at the base of the spine. ■ (also **kundalini yoga**) a system of meditation directed toward the release of such energy. [Sanskrit, lit. 'snake.']

Kun·de·ra /'ko͝ondərə; ˌkən'derə/, Milan (1929–), Czech writer. His novels include *The Unbearable Lightness of Being* (1984).

Kung /ko͝oɴɢ/ ▶ **n. 1** (pl. same) a member of a San (Bushman) people of the Kalahari Desert in southern Africa. **2** the Khoisan language of this people. ▶ **adj.** of or relating to the Kung or their language. [Khoikhoi *!Kung*, lit. 'people.']

kung fu /'kəɴɢ 'fo͞o; 'ko͝oɴɢ/ ▶ **n.** a primarily unarmed Chinese martial art resembling karate. [from Chin. *gōngfú*, from *gōng* 'merit' + *fú* 'master.']

K'ung Fu-tzu /'ko͝oɴɢ 'fo͞o 'dzə/ see CONFUCIUS.

Ku·nitz /'ko͞onits/, Stanley Jasspon (1905–2006), US poet. He was US poet laureate 1974–76 (before "laureate" was part of the title) and 2000–01.

Kun·lun Shan /'ko͞on'lo͞on 'sʜän/ a range of mountains in western China, extending east from the Pamir Mountains.

Kun·ming /'ko͞on'miɴɢ/ a city in southwestern China, capital of Yunnan province; pop. 1,612,000.

kunz·ite /'ko͝ont,sīt/ ▶ **n.** a lilac-colored gem variety of spodumene that fluoresces or changes color when irradiated. [20th C.: from the name of George F. *Kunz* (1856–1932), American gemologist, + -ITE¹.]

Kuo·min·tang /'kwō'min'taɴɢ; -'täɴɢ; 'gwô-/ (also **Guo·min·dang** /'gwō'min'däɴɢ/) a nationalist party founded in China under Sun Yat-sen in 1912, and led by Chiang Kai-shek from 1925.

Ku·ra Riv·er /kə'rä; 'ko͝orə/ a river flowing from northeastern Turkey through Georgia and Azerbaijan to the Caspian Sea.

Kurd /kərd/ ▶ **n.** a member of a mainly pastoral Islamic people living in Kurdistan. [the name in Kurdish.]

Kurd·ish /'kərdisʜ/ ▶ **adj.** of or relating to the Kurds or their language. ▶ **n.** the Iranian language of the Kurds.

Kur·di·stan /ˌkərdə'stän; ˌko͝or-; -'stan/ a region including parts of eastern Turkey, northern Iraq, western Iran, eastern Syria, Armenia, and Azerbaijan, traditional home of the Kurdish people.

kur·gan /ko͝or'gän; -'gan/ ▶ **n.** Archaeol. a prehistoric burial mound or barrow of a type found in southern Russia and Ukraine. ■ (**Kurgan**) a member of the ancient people who built such burial mounds. ▶ **adj.** of or relating to the ancient Kurgans. [Russ., of Turkic origin; cf. Turk. *kurgan* 'castle.']

Ku·rile Is·lands /'k(y)o͝or,ēl; k(y)o͝o'rēl/ (also **Ku·ril Is·lands** or **the Ku·rils**) a chain of 56 islands belonging to Russia between the Sea of Okhotsk and the North Pacific Ocean, from the Kamchatka peninsula to the Japanese island of Hokkaido.

Ku·ro·sa·wa /ˌko͝orə'säwə/, Akira (1910–98), Japanese director. His movies include *Rashomon* (1950).

Ku·ro·shi·o /ˌko͝orō'sʜē-ō/ a warm current in the Pacific Ocean that flows northeast past Japan and toward Alaska. Also called JAPANESE CURRENT, JAPAN CURRENT.

kur·ra·jong /'kərə,jôɴɢ; -jäɴɢ/ (also **cur·ra·jong**) ▶ **n.** an Australian tree or shrub (esp. *Brachychiton populneus*, family Sterculiaceae) that produces useful tough fiber. [19th C.: from Dharuk *garrajung* 'fiber fishing line.']

Kursk /ko͝orsk/ a city in southwestern Russia; pop. 430,000.

kur·ta /'kərtə/ ▶ **n.** a loose collarless shirt worn by people from the Indian subcontinent. [from Urdu and Pers. *kurtah*.]

kur·to·sis /kər'tōsis/ ▶ **n.** Stat. the sharpness of the peak of a frequency-distribution curve. [20th C.: from Gk. *kurtōsis* 'a bulging,' from *kurtos* 'bulging, convex.']

ku·rus /kə'ro͞osʜ/ ▶ **n.** (pl. same) a monetary unit of Turkey, equal to one hundredth of a Turkish lira. [from Turk. *kuruş*.]

Ku·shan /'ko͞o,sʜän/ ▶ **n.** (pl. same or **-shans**) a member of an Iranian dynasty that invaded the Indian subcontinent and established a powerful empire in the northwest between the 1st and 3rd centuries AD. ▶ **adj.** of or relating to this people or their dynasty. [from Prakrit *kuṣāṇa* (adj.), from Iranian.]

Ku·ta·i·si /ˌko͞otä'ēsē/ a city in central Georgia; pop. 236,000; one of the oldest cities in Transcaucasia.

Kutch, Gulf of /kəcʜ/ an inlet of the Arabian Sea on the west coast of India.

Kutch, Rann of /'kəcʜ, 'rän əv/ a vast salt marsh, on the shores of the Arabian Sea between southeastern Pakistan and the state of Gujarat in northwestern India.

Ku·te·nai /'ko͞otn,ā/ (also **Ku·te·nay**) ▶ **n.** (pl. same or **-nais**) **1** a member of an American Indian people of the Rocky Mountains in British Columbia, Idaho, and Montana. **2** the language of this people, of unknown affinity. ▶ **adj.** of or relating to the Kutenai or their language. [from Blackfoot *Kotonáai-*.]

Ku·wait /kə'wāt/ a country in the Middle East. *See box on next page.* — **Ku·wai·ti** /-'wātē/ **adj. & n.**

Ku·wait Cit·y a port on the Persian Gulf, the capital city of Kuwait; pop. 150,000.

Kuz·nets Ba·sin /kəz'nyets/ (also **Kuz·netsk** /-'nyetsk/) a region in southern Russia, between Tomsk and Novokuznetsk, rich in iron and coal deposits. Also called KUZBASS.

kV ▶ **abbr.** kilovolt(s).

kvass /k(ə)'väs; kfäs/ ▶ **n.** (esp. in Russia) a fermented drink, low in alcohol, made from rye flour or bread with malt. [from Russ. *kvas*.]

kvell /k(ə)vel/ ▶ **v.** [intrans.] informal feel happy and proud. [1960s: from Yiddish *kveln*, from Mid. High Ger., lit. 'well up.']

kvetch /k(ə)vecʜ; kfecʜ/ informal ▶ **n.** a person who complains a great deal. ■ a complaint. ▶ **v.** [intrans.] complain. [1960s: from Yiddish *kvetsh* (n.), *kvetshn* (v.), from Mid. High Ger. *quetschen*, lit. 'crush.']

kW ▶ **abbr.** kilowatt(s).

Kwa /kwä/ ▶ **n.** a major branch of the Niger–Congo family of languages, spoken from the Ivory Coast to Nigeria and including Ibo and Yoruba. ▶ **adj.** of or relating to this group of languages. [the name in Kwa.]

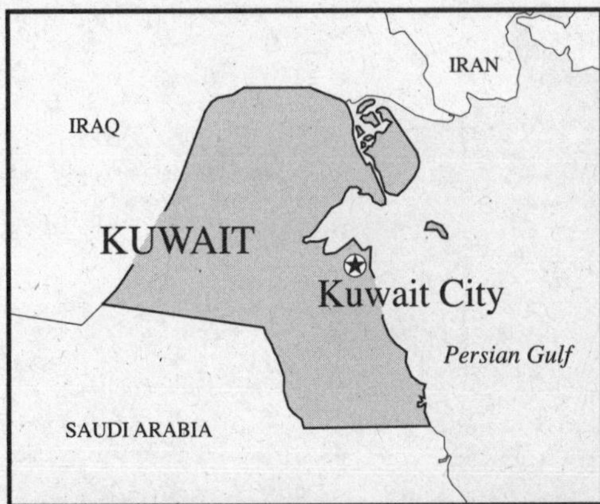

Kuwait

Official name: State of Kuwait
Location: Middle East, on the northwestern coast of the Persian Gulf, south of Iraq
Area: 6,900 square miles (17,800 sq km)
Population: 2,257,000
Capital: Kuwait
Languages: Arabic (official), English
Currency: Kuwait dinar

Kyrgyzstan

Official name: Kyrgyz Republic
Location: central Asia, on the northwestern border of China
Area: 76,700 square miles (198,500 sq km)
Population: 5,081,000
Capital: Bishkek
Languages: Kirghiz and Russian (both official)
Currency: Kyrgyzstani som

kwa·cha /ˈkwächə/ ▶ **n.** the basic monetary unit of Zambia and Malawi, equal to 100 ngwee in Zambia and 100 tambala in Malawi. [from Chibemba (a Bantu language of Zambia) *kwacha* 'dawn.']

Kwa·ja·lein /ˈkwäjələn; -ˌlān/ the largest atoll in the Marshall Islands, in the west central Pacific Ocean.

Kwa·ki·u·tl /ˌkwäkēˈo͞otl/ ▶ **n.** (pl. same or **-u·tls**) **1** a member of an American Indian people of the northwestern Pacific coast, living mainly on Vancouver Island. **2** the Wakashan language of this people. ▶ **adj.** of or relating to the Kwakiutl or their language. [the name in Kwakiutl.]

Kwang·chow /ˈkwängˈchō; ˈgwängˈjō/ variant of GUANGZHOU.

Kwang·ju /ˈgwôngˈjo͞o/ a city in southwestern South Korea; pop. 1,145,000.

Kwang·si Chuang /ˈkwängˌsē ˈchwäng; ˈgwängˌsē/ variant of GUANGXI ZHUANG.

Kwang·tung /ˈkwängˈto͝ong; ˈgwängˈdo͝ong/ variant of GUANGDONG.

kwan·za /ˈkwänzə/ ▶ **n.** (pl. same or **-zas**) the basic monetary unit of Angola, equal to 100 lwei. [perh. from a Swahili word meaning 'first.']

Kwan·zaa /ˈkwänzə/ ▶ **n.** a secular festival observed by many African Americans from December 26 to January 1 as a celebration of their cultural heritage and traditional values. [from Kiswahili *matunda ya kwanza*, lit. 'first fruits (of the harvest),' from *kwanza* 'first.']

kwash·i·or·kor /ˌkwäshēˈôrkôr; -kər/ ▶ **n.** a form of malnutrition caused by protein deficiency in the diet, typically affecting young children in the tropics. [1930s: a local word in Ghana.]

Kwa·Zu·lu-Na·tal /kwäˈzo͞olo͞o näˈtäl/ a province of eastern South Africa, on the Indian Ocean; capital, Pietermaritzburg. See also NATAL.

Kwei·chow /ˈkwāˈchou; -ˈchō; ˈgwāˈjō/ variant of GUIZHOU.

Kwei·lin /ˈkwāˈlin; ˈgwā-/ variant of GUILIN.

Kwei·sui /ˈkwāˈswā; ˈgwā-/ former name (until 1954) of HOHHOT.

Kwei·yang /ˈkwāˈyäng; ˈgwā-/ variant of GUIYANG.

kWh ▶ **abbr.** kilowatt-hour(s).

kW-hr ▶ **abbr.** kilowatt-hour.

KY ▶ **abbr.** Kentucky (in official postal use).

Ky. ▶ **abbr.** Kentucky.

ky·a·nite /ˈkīəˌnīt/ (also **cy·a·nite** /ˈsīə-/) ▶ **n.** a blue or green crystalline mineral consisting of aluminum silicate, used in heat-resistant ceramics. — **ky·a·nit·ic** /ˌkīəˈnitik/ **adj.** [18th C.: from Gk. *kuanos, kuaneos* 'dark blue' + -ITE[1].]

kyat /kēˈ(y)ät; kyät; chät/ ▶ **n.** (pl. same or **kyats**) the basic monetary unit of Myanmar (Burma), equal to 100 pyas.

Kyd /kid/, Thomas (1558–94), English playwright. His anonymously published *The Spanish Tragedy* (1592) was popular on the Elizabethan stage.

ky·lix /ˈkīliks; ˈkiliks/ ▶ **n.** (pl. **ky·li·kes** /ˈkīliˌkēz; kili-/ or **ky·lix·es**) an ancient Greek cup with a shallow bowl and a tall stem. [from Gk. *kulix*.]

ky·mo·graph /ˈkīməˌgraf/ ▶ **n.** an instrument for recording variations in pressure, e.g., in sound waves or in blood within blood vessels, by the trace of a stylus on a rotating cylinder. — **ky·mo·graph·ic** /ˌkīməˈgrafik/ **adj.** [19th C.: from Gk. *kuma* 'wave' + -GRAPH.]

Kyo·to /kēˈōtō/ a city in central Japan, on the island of Honshu; pop. 1,461,000.

ky·pho·sis /kīˈfōsis/ ▶ **n.** Med. excessive outward curvature of the spine, causing hunching of the back. Compare with LORDOSIS. — **ky·phot·ic** /-ˈfätik/ **adj.** [19th C.: from Gk. *kuphōsis*, from *kuphos* 'bent, hunchbacked.']

Kyr·gyz /kirˈgiz/ ▶ **n. & adj.** var. of KIRGHIZ.

Kyr·gyz·stan /ˌki(ə)rgiˈstän; -ˈstan; ˌkər-/ a country in central Asia. Also called KYRGYZ REPUBLIC and (formerly) KIRGHIZIA. *See box.*

Kyr·i·e /ˈki(ə)rēˌā/ (also **Kyr·i·e e·le·i·son** /iˈlā-iˌsän; -sən/) ▶ **n.** a short repeated invocation (in Greek or in translation) used in many Christian liturgies, esp. at the beginning of the Eucharist or as a response in a litany. [from Gk. *Kurie eleēson* 'Lord, have mercy.']

Kyu·shu /kēˈo͞oshoo͞/ the most southerly of the four main islands of Japan, constituting an administrative region; pop. 13,296,000; capital, Fukuoka.

Ky·zyl /kəˈzil/ a city in south central Russia, capital of the republic of Tuva; pop. 88,000.

Ky·zyl Kum /kəˈzil ˈko͞om/ a desert region in central Asia, southeast of the Aral Sea, covering part of Uzbekistan and southern Kazakhstan.

L

L[1] /el/ (also **l**) ▶ **n.** (pl. **Ls** or **L's**) **1** the twelfth letter of the alphabet. ■ denoting the next after K in a set of items, categories, etc. **2** (**L**) a shape like that of a capital L: [in comb.] *a four-story L-shaped building.* **3** the Roman numeral for 50.

L[2] ▶ **abbr.** ■ (in tables of sports results) games lost. ■ Chem. levorotatory: *L-tryptophan.* ■ (**L.**) Lake, Loch, or Lough (chiefly on maps): *L. Ontario.* ■ large (as a clothes size). ■ Latin. ■ Liberal. ■ (**L.**) Linnaeus (as the source of names of animal and plant species). ■ lire. ▶ **symb.** ■ Chem. Avogadro's number. ■ Physics inductance.

l ▶ **abbr.** ■ (giving position or direction) left: *l to r.* ■ (chiefly in horse racing) length(s): *distances 5 l, 3 l.* ■ (**l.**) (in textual references) line. ■ Chem. liquid. ■ liter(s). ▶ **symb.** (in mathematical formulas) length.

£ ▶ **abbr.** (preceding a numeral) pound or pounds (of money). [L. *libra* 'pound, balance.']

LA ▶ **abbr.** ■ Library Association. ■ Los Angeles. ■ Louisiana (in official postal use).

La ▶ **abbr.** ■ (**La.**) Louisiana. ▶ **symb.** ■ the chemical element lanthanum.

la /lä/ (Brit. also **lah**) ▶ **n.** Music (in solmization) the sixth note of a major scale. ■ the note A in the fixed-do system. [ME: from L. *labii.*]

laa·ger /'lägər/ S. African ▶ **n.** hist. a camp or encampment formed by a circle of wagons. ■ fig. an entrenched position or viewpoint that is defended against opponents: *an educational laager.* ▶ **v.** [trans.] hist. form (vehicles) into a laager. ■ [intrans.] make camp. [South Afr. Dutch, from Du. *leger, lager* 'camp.']

Laa·youne var. of LA'YOUN.

Lab /lab/ ▶ **abbr.** a Labrador dog.

lab /lab/ ▶ **n.** informal a laboratory: *a science lab.*

la Bar·ca, Pe·dro Cal·de·rón de see CALDERÓN DE LA BARCA.

lab·a·rum /'labərəm/ ▶ **n.** rare a banner or flag bearing symbolic motifs. [17th C.: from late L., of unknown origin.]

lab·da·num /'labdənəm/ (also **la·da·num** /'lādn-əm; 'ladnəm/) ▶ **n.** a gum resin obtained from the twigs of a southern European rockrose (esp. *Cistus ladanifer*) used in perfumery and for fumigation. [16th C.: via L. from Gk. *ladanon, lēdanon,* from *lēdon* 'mastic.']

lab·e·fac·tion /,labə'fakSHən/ ▶ **n.** archaic deterioration or downfall. [17th C.: from L. *labefactio(n-),* from *labefacere* 'weaken,' from *labi* 'to fall' + *facere* 'make.']

la·bel /'lābəl/ ▶ **n. 1** a small piece of paper, fabric, plastic, or similar material attached to an object and giving information about it. ■ a piece of fabric sewn inside a garment and bearing the brand name, size, or instructions for care. ■ the piece of paper in the center of a phonograph record giving the artist and title. ■ a company that produces recorded music: *independent labels.* ■ the name or trademark of a fashion company. ■ a classifying phrase or name applied to a person or thing, esp. one that is inaccurate or restrictive. ■ (in a dictionary entry) a word or words used to specify the subject area, register, or geographical origin of the word being defined. ■ Comput. a string of characters used to refer to a particular instruction in a program. ■ Biol. & Chem. a radioactive isotope, fluorescent dye, or enzyme used to make something identifiable for study. **2** Heraldry a narrow horizontal strip, typically with three downward projections, that is superimposed on a coat of arms by an eldest son during the life of his father. ▶ **v.** (**la·beled, la·bel·ing**; Brit. **la·belled, la·bel·ling**) [trans.] attach a label to (something). ■ assign to a category, esp. inaccurately or restrictively. ■ give a name to (something). ■ Biol. & Chem. make (a substance, molecule, or cell) identifiable or traceable by replacing an atom with one of a distinctive radioactive isotope, or by attaching a fluorescent dye, enzyme, or other molecule. — **la·bel·er n.** [ME (denoting a narrow strip or band): from OFr., 'ribbon,' prob. of Gmc. origin and rel. to LAP[1].]

la·bel·lum /lə'beləm/ ▶ **n.** (pl. **-bel·la** /-'belə/) **1** Entomol. each of a pair of lobes at the tip of the proboscis in some insects. **2** Bot. a central petal at the base of an orchid flower, typically larger than the other petals and of a different shape. [19th C.: from L., dimin. of *labrum* 'lip.']

la·bi·a /'lābēə/ ▶ **plural n. 1** Anat. the inner and outer folds of the vulva, at either side of the vagina. **2** plural form of LABIUM.

la·bi·al /'lābēəl/ ▶ **adj. 1** esp. Anat. of or relating to the lips. ■ Dentistry (of the surface of a tooth) adjacent to the lips. ■ Zool. of, resembling, or serving as a lip, liplike part, or labium. **2** Phonet. (of a consonant) requiring complete or partial closure of the lips (e.g., *p, b, f, v, m, w*), or (of a vowel) requiring rounded lips (e.g., *oo* in *moon*). ▶ **n.** Phonet. a labial sound. — **la·bi·al·ize** /-,līz/ **v.** (in sense 2). **la·bi·al·ly adv.** [16th C.: from med. L. *labialis,* from L. *labium* 'lip.']

la·bi·a ma·jo·ra /mə'jôrə/ ▶ **plural n.** Anat. the larger outer folds of the vulva.

la·bi·a mi·no·ra /mə'nôrə/ ▶ **plural n.** Anat. the smaller inner folds of the vulva.

la·bi·ate /'lābē-it; -,āt/ ▶ **n.** Bot. a plant of the mint family (Labiatae) with a distinctive two-lobed flower. ▶ **adj. 1** Bot. of, relating to, or denoting plants of the mint family. **2** Bot. & Zool. resembling or possessing a lip or labium. [18th C.: from mod. L. *labiatus,* from *labium* 'lip.']

la·bile /'lā,bīl; -bəl/ ▶ **adj.** tech. liable to change; easily altered. ■ of or characterized by emotions that are easily aroused or freely expressed, and that tend to alter quickly and spontaneously; emotionally unstable. ■ Chem. easily broken down or displaced. — **la·bil·i·ty** /lā'bilətē; lə-/ **n.** [ME (in the sense 'liable to err or sin'): from late L. *labilis,* from *labi* 'to fall.']

labio- /'lābēō/ ▶ **comb. form** of or relating to the lips. [from L. *labium* 'lip.']

la·bi·o·den·tal /,lābēō'dentl/ ▶ **adj.** Phonet. (of a sound) made with the lips and teeth, for example *f* and *v.* ▶ **n.** Phonet. a labiodental sound.

la·bi·o·ve·lar /,lābēō'vēlər/ ▶ **adj.** Phonet. (of a sound) made with the lips and soft palate, for example *w.* ▶ **n.** Phonet. a labiovelar sound.

la·bi·um /'lābēəm/ ▶ **n.** (pl. **-bi·a** /-bēə/) **1** Entomol. a fused mouthpart that forms the floor of the mouth of an insect. ■ Anat. a lip or liplike structure, esp. any of the four folds of skin on either side of the vulva. **2** Bot. the lower lip of the flower of a plant of the mint family. [16th C.: from L., 'lip.']

la·bor /'lābər/ (Brit. **la·bour**) ▶ **n. 1** work, esp. hard physical work: *manual labor.* ■ workers, esp. manual workers, considered collectively. ■ such workers considered as a social class or political force. ■ (**Labor**) a department of government concerned with a nation's workforce. **2** the process of childbirth, esp. the period from the start of uterine contractions to delivery. **3** (**Labour**) [treated as sing. or pl.] (in the UK or Canada) the Labour Party. ▶ **v.** [intrans.] work hard; make great effort. ■ work at an unskilled manual occupation. ■ have difficulty in doing something despite working hard. ■ (of an engine) work noisily and with difficulty: *the engine was laboring.* ■ [with adverbial of direction] move or proceed with trouble or difficulty. ■ (of a ship) roll or pitch heavily.

– PHRASES **a labor of Hercules** see HERCULES. **a labor of love** a task done for pleasure, not reward. **labor the point** explain or discuss something at excessive or unnecessary length.

– PHRASAL VERBS **labor under 1** carry (a heavy load or object) with difficulty. **2** be deceived or misled by (a mistaken belief). [ME *labo(u)r,* from OFr. *labour* (n.), *labourer* (v.), both from L. *labor* 'toil, trouble.']

lab·o·ra·to·ry /'labrə,tôrē/ ▶ **n.** (pl. **-ries**) a room or building equipped for scientific research, or teaching, or for the manufacture of drugs or chemicals. ■ [as adj.] (of an animal) bred for or used in experiments in laboratories: *studies on laboratory rats.* [17th C.: from med. L. *laboratorium,* from L. *laborare* 'to labor.']

la·bor camp ▶ **n.** a prison camp in which a regime of hard labor is enforced.

La·bor Day ▶ **n.** a public holiday or day of festivities held in honor of working people, in the US and Canada on the first Monday in September, in many other countries on May 1.

la·bored /'lābərd/ (Brit. **la·boured**) ▶ **adj.** done with great effort and difficulty: *his breathing was labored.* ■ (esp. of humor or a performance) not spontaneous.

la·bor·er /'lāb(ə)rər/ (Brit. **la·bour·er**) ▶ **n.** a person doing unskilled manual work for wages: *a farm laborer.*

la·bor force ▶ **n.** all the members of a particular organization or population who are able to work.

la·bor-in·ten·sive ▶ **adj.** (of a form of work) needing a large workforce or a large amount of work in relation to output: *the labor-intensive task of lexicography.*

la·bo·ri·ous /lə'bôrēəs/ ▶ **adj.** (esp. of a task, process, or journey) requiring considerable effort and time. ■ (esp. of speech or writing style) showing obvious signs of effort and lacking in fluency. — **la·bo·ri·ous·ly adv. la·bo·ri·ous·ness n.**

la·bor mar·ket ▶ **n.** the supply of available workers with reference to the demand for them.

la·bor pain ▶ **n.** [usu. in pl.] a recurrent pain felt by a woman during childbirth. Also called BIRTH PANG.

la·bor par·ty ▶ **n.** a left-of-center political party formed to represent the interests of ordinary working people.

la·bor-sav·ing ▶ **adj.** [attrib.] (of an appliance) designed to reduce the work needed to complete a task.

la·bor un·ion ▶ n. an organized association of workers, often in a trade or profession, formed to protect and further their rights and interests.

la·bour, etc. ▶ n. British spelling of LABOR, etc.

La·bour Par·ty ▶ n. a major left-of-center British party that since World War II has been in power 1945–51, 1964–70, 1974–79, and since 1997.

la·bra /ˈlābrə; ˈlabrə/ plural form of LABRUM.

Lab·ra·dor[1] /ˈlabrəˌdôr/ a coastal region of eastern Canada that forms the mainland part of the province of Newfoundland.

Lab·ra·dor[2] (also **Labrador retriever**) ▶ n. a retriever that predominantly has a black or yellow coat, widely used as a gun dog or as a guide for a blind person. [20th C.: named after the LABRADOR PENINSULA, where the breed was developed.]

Labrador retriever

Lab·ra·dor Cur·rent a cold ocean current that flows south from the Arctic Ocean along the northeastern coast of North America.

lab·ra·dor·ite /ˈlabrədôˌrīt/ ▶ n. a mineral of the plagioclase feldspar group, found in many igneous rocks. [19th C.: from LABRADOR PENINSULA, where it was found, + -ITE[1].]

Lab·ra·dor Pen·in·su·la a peninsula in eastern Canada, between Hudson Bay, the Atlantic Ocean, and the Gulf of St. Lawrence. Also called LABRADOR-UNGAVA.

Lab·ra·dor Sea a section of the Atlantic Ocean between Labrador and southern Greenland.

la·bret /ˈlābret; -brit/ ▶ n. an object such as a small piece of shell, bone, or stone inserted into the lip as an ornament in some cultures. [19th C.: dimin. of LABRUM.]

la·brum /ˈlābrəm; ˈlabrəm/ ▶ n. (pl. **la·bra** /ˈlābrə; ˈlabrə/) Zool. a structure corresponding to a lip, esp. the upper border of the mouthparts of a crustacean or insect. — **la·bral** /ˈlābrəl/ adj. [18th C.: from L., lit. 'lip'; rel. to LABIUM.]

la·bru·sca /ləˈbrəskə/ ▶ n. another term for FOX GRAPE: [as adj.] *labrusca grapes.* ■ a wine made from this grape. [from L. *labrusca*, denoting a wild vine.]

La·bu·an /ləˈbo͞oən/ a Malaysian island off the northern coast of Borneo; pop. 26,000.

la·bur·num /ləˈbərnəm/ ▶ n. a small European tree (genus *Laburnum*) of the pea family, with poisonous seeds preceded by hanging clusters of yellow flowers. The hard timber is sometimes used as an ebony substitute.

lab·y·rinth /ˈlab(ə)ˌrinTH/ ▶ n. **1** a complicated irregular network of passages or paths in which it is difficult to find one's way; a maze. ■ fig. an intricate and confusing arrangement. **2** Anat. a complex structure in the inner ear that contains the organs of hearing and balance. It consists of the **bony labyrinth** and the **membranous labyrinth**. ■ Zool. an organ of intricate structure, in particular the accessory respiratory organs of certain fishes. — **lab·y·rin·thi·an** /ˌlabəˈrinTHēən/ adj. **lab·y·rin·thine** /ˌlabəˈrinˌTHēn; -ˈrinTHin; -ˈrinˌTHīn/ adj. [ME: from Fr. *labyrinthe* or L. *labyrinthus*, from Gk. *laburinthos*.]

labyrinth 1

lab·y·rinth fish ▶ n. a freshwater fish (Belontiidae and related families) with poorly developed gills and a labyrinthine accessory breathing organ.

lab·y·rin·thi·tis /ˌlabərənˈTHītis/ ▶ n. Med. inflammation of the labyrinth or inner ear.

lac[1] /lak/ ▶ n. a resinous substance secreted as a protective covering by the lac insect, used to make shellac. [ME: from med. L. *lac, lac(c)a*, from Port. *laca*, based on Hindi *lākh* or Pers. *lāk*.]

lac[2] ▶ adj. [attrib.] Biol. denoting the ability of normal strains of the bacterium *E. coli* to metabolize lactose, or the genetic factors involved in this ability. [1940s: abbrev. of LACTOSE.]

lac[3] ▶ n. var. of LAKH.

Lac·ca·dive Is·lands /ˈlakəˌdīv/ a group of islands in the Arabian Sea, part of the Indian territory of Lakshadweep.

lac·co·lith /ˈlakəˌliTH/ ▶ n. Geol. a mass of igneous rock, typically lens-shaped, that has been intruded between rock strata causing uplift in the shape of a dome. [19th C.: from Gk. *lakkos* 'reservoir' + -LITH.]

lace /lās/ ▶ n. **1** a fine open fabric, typically one of cotton or silk, made by looping, twisting, or knitting thread in patterns. ■ braid used for trimming, esp. on military uniforms. **2** (usu. **laces**) a cord or leather strip passed through eyelets or hooks on opposite sides of a shoe or garment and then pulled tight and fastened. ▶ v. [trans.] **1** fasten or tighten by tying laces. ■ (**lace someone into**) fasten someone into (a garment) by tightening the laces. ■ compress the waist of (someone) with a laced corset. ■ [intrans.] (of a garment or shoe) be fastened by means of laces. **2** [trans.] entwine or tangle (things, esp. fingers) together: *he laced his fingers together.* **3** (often **be laced with**) add an ingredient, esp. alcohol, to enhance its flavor or strength. ■ streak with color or something contrasting. **4** hit (something, esp. a baseball) hard: *lace a double.*

– PHRASAL VERBS **lace into** informal assail or tackle (something). [ME: from OFr. *laz, las* (n.), *lacier* (v.), based on L. *laqueus* 'noose.']

lace-cur·tain ▶ adj. informal, often offens. having social pretensions; genteel: *lace-curtain Boston lawyers.*

lace·mak·ing /ˈlāsˌmākiNG/ ▶ n. the activity of making lace. — **lace·mak·er** n.

lace pil·low ▶ n. a cushion placed on the lap to provide support in lacemaking.

lac·er·ate /ˈlasəˌrāt/ ▶ v. [trans.] tear or deeply cut (something, esp. flesh or skin). ■ fig. (of feelings or emotions) wound or injure. — **lac·er·a·tion** /ˌlasəˈrāSHən/ n. [ME: from L. *lacerat-* 'mangled,' from the v. *lacerare*, from *lacer* 'mangled, torn.']

la·cer·tid /ləˈsərtid/ ▶ n. Zool. a lizard of a large family (Lacertidae). [19th C.: from mod. L. *Lacertidae* (pl.), from L. *lacerta* 'lizard.']

Lac·er·til·i·a /ˌlasərˈtilēə; -ˈtilyə/ Zool. a group of reptiles (order Squamata) that comprises the lizards. Also called SAURIA. — **lac·er·til·i·an** /-ˈtilēən; -ˈtilyən/ n. & adj. [mod. L. (pl.), from L. *lacerta* 'lizard.']

lace-up ▶ adj. (of a shoe or garment) fastened with laces.

lace·wing /ˈlāsˌwiNG/ ▶ n. a slender, delicate insect (order Neuroptera) with large clear membranous wings. Both the adults and larvae are typically predators of aphids. Its several families include Chrysopidae (the **green lacewings**).

lace·work /ˈlāsˌwərk/ ▶ n. lace fabric and other items made of lace viewed collectively. ■ the process of making lace.

lach·es /ˈlaCHiz/ ▶ n. Law unreasonable delay in making an assertion or claim. [ME: from OFr. *laschesse*, from *lasche* 'loose, lax,' based on L. *laxus*.]

Lach·e·sis /ˈlakəsis/ Gk. Mythol. one of the Fates.

Lach·lan /ˈläklən/ a river rising in New South Wales in Australia and flowing about 920 miles (1,472 km) to the Murrumbidgee River near the border with Victoria.

lach·ry·mal /ˈlakrəməl/ (also **lac·ri·mal** or **lac·ry·mal**) ▶ adj. **1** formal literary related to weeping or tears. **2** (usu. **lacrimal**) Physiol. & Anat. concerned with the secretion of tears: *lacrimal cells.* ▶ n. (usu. **lacrimal** or **lacrimal bone**) Anat. a small bone forming part of the eye socket. [ME (sense 2 of the adj.): from med. L. *lachrymalis*, from L. *lacrima* 'tear.']

lach·ry·ma·tor /ˈlakrəˌmātər/ (also **lac·ri·ma·tor**) ▶ n. esp. Med. a substance that irritates the eyes and causes tears to flow.

lach·ry·ma·to·ry /ˈlakrəməˌtôrē/ (also **lac·ri·ma·to·ry**) ▶ adj. tech. literary relating to, tending to cause, or containing tears: *a lachrymatory secretion.* [17th C.: from L. *lacrima*.]

lach·ry·mose /ˈlakrəˌmōs; -ˌmōz/ ▶ adj. formal literary tearful or given to weeping. ■ inducing tears; sad: *a lachrymose children's classic.* — **lach·ry·mose·ly** adv. **lach·ry·mos·i·ty** /ˌlakrəˈmäsətē/ n. [17th C.: from L. *lacrimosus*, from *lacrima* 'tear.']

lac·ing /ˈlāsiNG/ ▶ n. **1** a laced fastening. ■ lace trimming, esp. on a uniform. **2** a dash of liquor added to a drink.

la·cin·i·ate /ləˈsinēˌāt; -ē-it/ (also **la·cin·i·at·ed** /-ˌātid/) ▶ adj. Bot. & Zool. divided into deep narrow irregular segments. [18th C.: from L. *lacinia* 'fringe, hem, flap of a garment' + -ATE[2].]

lac in·sect ▶ n. an Asian scale insect (*Laccifer lacca*, family Lacciferidae) that lives on trees and produces secretions that are used in the production of shellac.

lack /lak/ ▶ n. the state of being without or not having enough of something: *for lack of evidence.* ▶ v. [trans.] be without or deficient in: *he lacks imagination.* [ME: corresponding to Mid. Low Ger. *lak* 'deficiency.']

lack·a·dai·si·cal /ˌlakəˈdāzikəl/ ▶ adj. lacking enthusiasm and determination; carelessly lazy. — **lack·a·dai·si·cal·ly** adv. [18th C. (also in the sense 'feebly sentimental'): from the archaic interjection *lackaday*, *lackadaisy* + -ICAL.]

lack·a·day /ˈlakəˌdā/ ▶ exclam. archaic an expression of surprise, regret, or grief. [17th C.: shortening of *alack-a-day*.]

lack·ey /ˈlakē/ ▶ n. (pl. **-eys**) a servant. ■ derog. a person who is obsequiously willing to obey or serve another person or group of people. ▶ v. (also **lac·quey**) (**-eys, -eyed**) [trans.] archaic behave servilely to; wait upon as a lackey. [16th C.: from Fr. *laquais*, perh. from Catalan *alacay*, from Arab. *al-ḳā'id* 'the chief.']

lack·ing /ˈlakiNG/ ▶ adj. [predic.] not available. ■ (of a quality) missing or absent. ■ deficient or inadequate.

lack·lus·ter /ˈlakˌləstər/ (Brit. **lack·lus·tre**) ▶ adj. lacking in vitality, force, or conviction; uninspired. ■ (of the hair or the eyes) not shining; dull.

Lac Lé·man /ˌläk leˈmäɴ/ French name for Lake Geneva (see **GENEVA, LAKE**).

La·co·nia /ləˈkōnēə; -ˈkōnyə/ (also **La·ko·ni·a**) a modern department and an ancient region of Greece, in the southeastern Peloponnese. — **La·co·ni·an adj. & n.**

la·con·ic /ləˈkänik/ ▸ **adj.** (of a person, speech, or style of writing) using very few words. — **la·con·i·cal·ly** /-(ə)lē/ **adv.** **la·con·i·cism** /ləˈkänəˌsizəm/ **n.** **lac·o·nism** /ˈlakəˌnizəm/ **n.** [16th C. (in the sense 'Laconian'): via L. from Gk. *Lakōnikos*, from *Lakōn* 'Laconia, Sparta,' the Spartans being known for their terse speech.]

La Co·ru·ña /ˌlä kəˈrōōnyə/ Spanish name for **CORUNNA**.

lac·quer /ˈlakər/ ▸ **n. 1** a liquid made of shellac dissolved in alcohol, or of synthetic substances, that dries to form a hard protective coating for wood, metal, etc. **2** the sap of the lacquer tree used to varnish wood or other materials. ■ decorative wood objects coated with lacquer. ▸ **v.** [trans.] [often as adj.] (**lacquered**) coat with lacquer. — **lac·quer·er n.** [16th C. (denoting lac): from obs. Fr. *lacre* 'sealing wax,' from Port. *laca* (see **LAC[1]**).]

lac·quer tree ▸ **n.** an eastern Asian tree (*Rhus verniciflua*) of the cashew family, with white sap that turns dark on exposure to air, producing a hard-wearing varnish traditionally used in lacquerware.

lac·quer·ware /ˈlakərˌwe(ə)r/ ▸ **n.** articles that have a decorative lacquer coating, viewed collectively.

lac·quey ▸ **n. & v.** archaic spelling of **LACKEY**.

lac·ri·mal ▸ **adj. & n.** var. of **LACHRYMAL**.

lac·ri·ma·tor ▸ **n.** var. of **LACHRYMATOR**.

lac·ri·ma·to·ry ▸ **adj.** var. of **LACHRYMATORY**.

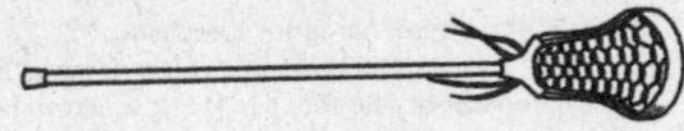

lacrosse stick

la·crosse /ləˈkrôs; -ˈkräs/ ▸ **n.** a team game, originally played by North American Indians, in which the ball is thrown, caught, and carried with a netted stick. [19th C.: from Fr. *(le jeu de) la crosse* '(the game of) the hooked stick.' Cf. **CROSSE**.]

lac·ry·mal ▸ **adj. & n.** var. of **LACHRYMAL**.

lac·tam /ˈlakˌtam/ ▸ **n.** Chem. an organic compound containing an amide group –NHCO– as part of a ring. [19th C.: blend of **LACTONE** and **AMIDE**.]

lac·tase /ˈlakˌtās; -tāz/ ▸ **n.** Biochem. an enzyme that catalyzes the hydrolysis of lactose to glucose and galactose.

lac·tate[1] /ˈlakˌtāt/ ▸ **v.** [intrans.] (of a female mammal) secrete milk. [19th C.: back-form. from **LACTATION**.]

lac·tate[2] ▸ **n.** Chem. a salt or ester of lactic acid.

lac·ta·tion /lakˈtāsʜən/ ▸ **n.** the secretion of milk by the mammary glands. ■ the suckling of young. — **lac·ta·tion·al** /-ˈtāsʜənl/ **adj.** [17th C.: from L. *lactatio(n-)*, from *lactare* 'suckle,' from *lac, lact-* 'milk.']

lac·te·al /ˈlaktēəl/ ▸ **adj.** of milk. ■ Anat. (of a vessel) conveying chyle or other milky fluid. ▸ **plural n.** (**lacteals**) Anat. the lymphatic vessels of the small intestine that absorb digested fats. [17th C.: from L. *lacteus* (from *lac, lact-* 'milk') + **-AL**.]

lac·tes·cent /lakˈtesənt/ ▸ **adj.** milky in appearance. ■ Bot. yielding a milky latex. [17th C.: from L. *lactescent-* 'being milky,' from the v. *lactere*, from *lac, lact-* 'milk.']

lac·tic /ˈlaktik/ ▸ **adj.** of or relating to milk. [18th C.: from L. *lac, lact-* 'milk' + **-IC**.]

lac·tic ac·id ▸ **n.** Biochem. a colorless syrupy organic acid, $CH_3CH(OH)COOH$, formed in sour milk, and produced in the muscle tissues during strenuous exercise.

lac·tif·er·ous /lakˈtif(ə)rəs/ ▸ **adj.** esp. Anat. forming or conveying milk or milky fluid: *lactiferous ducts.* [17th C.: from L. *lac, lact-* 'milk' + **-FEROUS**.]

lacto- ▸ **comb. form 1** of or relating to milk: *lactometer.* **2** from or relating to lactic acid or lactose: *lactobacillus.* [from L. *lac, lact-* 'milk.']

lac·to·ba·cil·lus /ˌlaktōbəˈsiləs/ ▸ **n.** (pl. **-cil·li** /-ˈsiˌlī; -ˈsiˌlē/) Biol. a rod-shaped, nonmotile Gram-positive bacterium (genus *Lactobacillus*) that produces lactic acid from the fermentation of carbohydrates.

lac·to·fer·rin /ˌlaktōˈferin; -tə-/ ▸ **n.** Biochem. a milk protein with bactericidal and iron-binding properties.

lac·to·gen·ic /ˌlaktəˈjenik/ ▸ **adj.** Physiol. (of a hormone or other substance) inducing milk secretion.

lac·tom·e·ter /lakˈtämətər/ ▸ **n.** an instrument for measuring the density of milk.

lac·tone /ˈlakˌtōn/ ▸ **n.** Chem. an organic compound containing an ester group –OCO– as part of a ring.

lac·to·pro·tein /ˌlaktōˈprōˌtēn/ ▸ **n.** the protein component of milk.

lac·tose /ˈlakˌtōs; -ˌtōz/ ▸ **n.** Chem. a sugar present in milk. It is a disaccharide containing glucose and galactose units.

la·cu·na /ləˈk(y)ōōnə/ ▸ **n.** (pl. **-nae** /-nī; -nē/ or **-nas**) an unfilled space or interval; a gap. ■ a missing portion in a book or manuscript. ■ Anat. a cavity or depression, esp. in bone. — **la·cu·nal** /ləˈk(y)ōōnl/ **adj.** **lac·u·nar·y** /ˈlakyəˌnerē; ləˈk(y)ōōnərē/ **adj.** **la·cu·nate** /-ˌnāt; -nit; ˈlakyəˌnāt/ **adj.** **la·cu·nose** /ˈlakyəˌnōs; -ˌnōz/ **adj.** [17th C.: from L., 'pool,' from *lacus* 'lake.']

la·cu·nar[1] /ləˈk(y)ōōnər/ ▸ **adj.** of or relating to a lacuna.

la·cu·nar[2] ▸ **n.** a vault or ceiling of recessed panels. ■ a panel in such a vault or ceiling.

la·cus·trine /ləˈkəstrin/ ▸ **adj.** tech. literary of, relating to, or associated with lakes: *fluvial and lacustrine deposits.* [19th C.: from Latin *lacus* 'lake' (the stem *lacustr-* influenced by L. *palustris* 'marshy') + **-INE[1]**.]

lac·y /ˈlāsē/ ▸ **adj.** (**lac·i·er, lac·i·est**) made of, resembling, or trimmed with lace: *a lacy petticoat.* — **lac·i·ly** /-səlē/ **adv.** **lac·i·ness n.**

lad /lad/ ▸ **n.** informal a boy or young man (often as a form of address). [ME: of unknown origin.]

La·dakh /ləˈdäk/ a region in northwestern India, Pakistan, and China that contains the Ladakh and Karakoram mountain ranges.

lad·a·num /ˈladn-əm; ˈladnəm/ ▸ **n.** var. of **LABDANUM**.

lad·der /ˈladər/ ▸ **n.** a structure consisting of a series of bars or steps between two lengths of wood, metal, or rope, used for climbing up or down something. ■ fig. a series of ascending stages by which someone or something may advance or progress. [OE *hlǣd(d)er*, of West Gmc. origin; rel. to Du. *leer* and Ger. *Leiter*.]

lad·der-back (also **ladder-back chair**) ▸ **n.** an upright chair with a back resembling a ladder.

lad·der stitch ▸ **n.** a stitch in embroidery consisting of transverse bars.

lad·die /ˈladē/ ▸ **n.** informal, esp. Scot. a boy or young man (often as a form of address): *he's just a wee laddie.*

lade /lād/ ▸ **v.** (past part. **lad·en** /ˈlādn/) [trans.] archaic load (a ship or other vessel). ■ ship (goods) as cargo. ■ [intrans.] (of a ship) take on cargo. [OE *hladan*, of West Gmc. origin; rel. to Ger. *laden* 'to load.']

lad·en /ˈlādn/ ▸ **adj.** heavily loaded or weighed down. [16th C.: past part. of **LADE**.]

la-di-da /ˌlä dē ˈdä/ (also **lah-di-dah** or **la-de-da**) informal ▸ **adj.** pretentious or snobbish, esp. in manner or speech: *do I really sound like a la-di-da society lawyer?* ▸ **exclam.** expressing derision at someone's pretentious manner or speech. [19th C.: imitative of an affected manner of speech.]

la·dies /ˈlādēz/ plural form of **LADY**.

la·dies' man (also **la·dy's man**) ▸ **n.** [in sing.] informal a man who enjoys flirting with women.

la·dies' room ▸ **n.** a restroom for women in a public or institutional building.

la·dies' tress·es (also **lady's tresses**) ▸ **plural n.** [usu. treated as sing.] a short orchid (genera *Spiranthes* and *Goodyera*) with small white flowers arranged in a single or double spiral, growing chiefly in north temperate regions.

La·din /ləˈdēn/ ▸ **n.** the Rhaeto-Romanic dialect of the Engadine in Switzerland. [19th C.: from L. *Latinus* (see **LATIN**).]

lad·ing /ˈlādiɴɢ/ ▸ **n.** archaic the action or process of loading a ship or other vessel with cargo. ■ a cargo.

La·di·no /ləˈdēnō/ ▸ **n.** (pl. **-nos**) **1** the language of some Sephardic Jews, esp. formerly in Mediterranean countries. Also called **JUDEZMO**. **2** a mestizo or Spanish-speaking white person in Central America. [Sp., from L. *Latinus* (see **LATIN**).]

la·di·no /ləˈdīnō; -ˈdēnō/ ▸ **n.** (pl. **-nos**) a white clover native to Italy and cultivated for fodder in North America.

Lad·is·laus I /ˈlädisˌlôs/ (*c.* 1040–95), king of Hungary 1077–95; canonized as **St. Ladislaus**.

Lad·is·laus II (*c.* 1351–1434), king of Poland 1386–1434; Polish name **Władysław**.

la·dle /ˈlādl/ ▸ **n.** a large long-handled spoon with a cup-shaped bowl, used for serving soup, stew, or sauce. ■ a vessel for transporting molten metal in a foundry. ▸ **v.** [trans.] serve (soup, stew, or sauce) with a ladle: *she ladled out onion soup.* ■ transfer (liquid) from one receptacle to another. — **la·dle·ful** /-ˌfōōl/ **n.** (pl. **-fuls**). **la·dler n.** [OE *hlædel*, from *hladan* (see **LADE**).]

Lad·o·ga, Lake /ˈlädəgə; ˈlad-/ a lake in northwestern Russia, the largest lake in Europe with an area of 6,837 square miles (17,700 sq km).

la·dy /ˈlādē/ ▸ **n.** (pl. **-dies**) **1** a woman (used as a polite or old-fashioned form of reference). **2** a woman of superior social position, esp. one of noble birth: *lords and ladies.* ■ a courteous, decorous, or genteel woman. ■ (also **la·dy friend**) (in the UK) a title used by peeresses, female relatives of peers, the wives and widows of knights, etc. ■ a woman at the head of a household. **3** (**one's lady**) dated a man's wife. ■ (also **lady friend**) a woman with whom a man is romantically or sexually involved.
– PHRASES **it isn't over till the fat lady sings** used to convey that there is still time for a situation to change. [by association with the final aria in tragic opera.] **Lady Bountiful** a woman who engages in ostentatious acts of charity, more to impress others than out of a sense of concern for those in need. [19th C.: from the name of a character in Farquhar's *The Beaux' Stratagem* (1707).] **Lady Luck** chance personified as a controlling power in human affairs. — **la·dy·hood n.** [OE *hlǣfdīge*, from *hlāf* 'loaf' + a Gmc. base meaning 'knead,' rel. to **DOUGH**; cf. **LORD**.]

convergent ladybug

la·dy·bug /ˈlādēˌbəg/ ▸ **n.** a small beetle (family Coccinellidae), typically red or yellow with black spots. Both the adults and larvae are important predators of aphids. Several genera and species, including the familiar **convergent ladybug** (*Hippodamia convergens*).

La·dy chap·el ▶ n. a chapel in a church or cathedral dedicated to the Virgin Mary.

la·dy·fin·ger /'lādē,fiNGgər/ ▶ n. a small finger-shaped sponge cake.

la·dy·fish /'lādē,fisH/ ▶ n. (pl. same or **-fish·es**) any of a number of marine fishes of warm coastal waters. ■ the tenpounder. ■ a bonefish.

la·dy-in-wait·ing ▶ n. (pl. **la·dies-in-wait·ing**) a woman who attends a queen or princess.

la·dy·kill·er /'lādē,kilər/ ▶ n. informal an attractive, charming man who habitually seduces women.

la·dy·like /'lādē,līk/ ▶ adj. behaving or dressing in a way considered appropriate for or typical of a well-bred, decorous woman or girl. ■ (of an activity or occupation) considered suitable for such a woman or girl. — **la·dy·like·ness** n.

la·dy of the night ▶ n. euphemistic a prostitute.

la·dy·ship /'lādē,sHip/ ▶ n. (**Her/Your Ladyship**) a respectful form of address to a woman who has a title. ■ ironic a form of reference or address to a woman thought to be acting pretentiously or snobbishly.

la·dy's man ▶ n. var. of LADIES' MAN.

la·dy's-slip·per (also **la·dy's slip·per**) ▶ n. an orchid (genus *Cypripedium*) of north temperate regions, the flower of which has a lip that is a conspicuous slipper-shaped pouch. Its several species include the large-pouched **showy lady's-slipper** (*C. reginae*), with bicolored (white and rose) flowers.

la·dy's tress·es ▶ n. var. of LADIES' TRESSES.

La·e·trile /'lāə,tril; -trəl/ ▶ n. trademark a compound extracted from amygdalin, formerly used controversially to treat cancer.

La Farge /lə 'färzH; 'färj/, John (1835–1910) US painter. Noted for his stained glass panels, he invented opaline glass.

La·fa·yette[1] /,läfē'et/ a city in southern Louisiana; pop. 110,257.

La·fa·yette[2] /,läfē'et; ,lafī-; ,lä-/ (also **La Fay·ette**), Marie Joseph Paul Yves Roch Gilbert du Motier, Marquis de (1757–1834), French soldier. He fought with the colonists in the American Revolution.

Laf·fer curve /'lafər/ ▶ n. Econ. a theory about the relationship between economic activity and rate of taxation. [1970s: named after Arthur *Laffer* (born 1942), American economist.]

La Fol·lette /lə 'fälit/, Robert Marion, Sr. (1855–1925) US politician. A US senator 1906–25, he was a Progressive Party presidential candidate in 1924.

La Fon·taine /lä fän'tān; fôn'ten/, Jean de (1621–95), French poet. He is chiefly known for *Fables* (1668–94).

lag[1] /lag/ ▶ v. (**lagged, lag·ging**) [intrans.] **1** fall behind in movement, progress, or development; not keep pace with another or others. **2** [intrans.] Billiards determine the order of play by striking the cue ball from balk to rebound off the top cushion, first stroke going to the player whose ball comes to rest nearer the bottom cushion. ▶ n. **1** (also **time lag**) a period of time between one event or phenomenon and another. **2** Physics a retardation in an electric current or movement. — **lag·ger** n. [16th C.: rel. to the dial. adj. *lag* 'last,' perh. alt. of LAST[1].]

lag[2] ▶ v. (**lagged, lag·ging**) [trans.] (usu. **be lagged**) enclose or cover (a boiler, pipes, etc.) with material that provides heat insulation. ▶ n. the nonheat-conducting cover of a boiler, etc.; lagging. ■ a piece of this. — **lag·ger** n. [19th C.: from earlier *lag* 'piece of insulating cover.']

lag·an /'lagən/ ▶ n. archaic (in legal contexts) goods or wreckage lying on the bed of the sea. [16th C.: from OFr., perh. of Scand. origin and rel. to LAY[1].]

lag bolt ▶ n. another term for LAG SCREW.

Lag b'O·mer /'läg bə'ōmər; 'bōmər/ ▶ n. a Jewish festival held on the 33rd day of the Omer (the period between Passover and Pentecost), traditionally regarded as celebrating the end of a plague in the 2nd century. [from Heb. *lāg* (pronunc. of the letters L (*lamed*) and G (*gimel*) symbolizing 33) + *bā* 'in the' + *ōmer* (see OMER).]

la·ger /'lägər/ ▶ n. a kind of beer, effervescent and light in color and body. [19th C.: from Ger. *Lagerbier* 'beer brewed for keeping,' from *Lager* 'storehouse.'.]

La·ger·löf /'lägər,ləv; -,lœf/, Selma Ottiliana Lovisa (1858–1940), Swedish writer. She wrote *Gösta Berlings Saga* (1891). Nobel Prize for Literature (1909).

lag·gard /'lagərd/ ▶ n. a person who makes slow progress and falls behind others: *I have no time for laggards.* ▶ adj. slower than desired or expected. — **lag·gard·ly** adj. & adv. **lag·gard·ness** n. [18th C. (as an adj.): from LAG[1].]

lagged /lagd/ ▶ adj. Econ. showing a delayed effect.

lag·ging /'lagiNG/ ▶ n. material providing heat insulation for a boiler, pipes, etc. [19th C.: from LAG[2].]

La Gio·con·da /,lä jō'kôndə; jō'kändə/ another name for **MONA LISA**.

la·gniappe /,lan'yap; 'lan,yap/ ▶ n. something given as a bonus or extra gift. [Louisiana Fr., from Sp. *la ñapa*.]

Lag·o·mor·pha /,lagə'môrfə/ Zool. an order of mammals that comprises the hares, rabbits, and pikas. — **lag·o·morph** /'lagə,môrf/ n. & adj. [mod. L. (pl.), from Gk. *lagōs* 'hare' + *morphē* 'form.']

la·goon /lə'gōōn/ ▶ n. a stretch of salt water separated from the sea by a low sandbank or coral reef. ■ the enclosed water of an atoll. ■ a small freshwater lake near a larger lake or river. ■ an artificial pool for the treatment of effluent or to accommodate an overspill from surface drains during heavy rain. — **la·goon·al** /-'gōōnl/ adj. [17th C.: from Ital. and Sp. *laguna*, from L. *lacuna* (see LACUNA).]

La·gos /'lä,gōs; 'lā,gäs; 'lägəs/ a chief city in Nigeria, on the Gulf of Guinea; pop. 13,050,000.

La Grande Riv·er /lə 'gräNd; 'grand/ a river that flows across central Quebec to Hudson Bay.

La·grange /lə'grānj/, Joseph Louis, Comte de (1736–1813), French mathematician; born in Italy. He worked on mechanics and its application to the description of planetary and lunar motion.

La·gran·gi·an point /lə'granjēən; -'grän-/ ▶ n. one of five points in the plane of orbit of one body around another (e.g., the moon around the earth) at which a small third body can remain stationary.

lag screw ▶ n. a heavy wood screw with a square or hexagonal head. Also called COACH SCREW, LAG BOLT. ▶ v. [trans.] (**lag-screw**) fasten with a lag screw.

La Guar·di·a /lə 'gwärdēə/, Fiorello Henry (1882–1947) US politician; nickname the **Little Flower**. He was mayor of New York City 1933–45.

La Ha·ba·na /,lä ä'bänä/ Spanish name for **HAVANA**[1].

la·har /'lä,här/ ▶ n. Geol. a destructive mudflow on the slopes of a volcano. [1920s: from Javanese.]

lah-di-dah ▶ n. & exclam. var. of LA-DI-DA.

Lahn·da /'ländə/ ▶ n. an Indic language of the western Punjab and adjacent areas of Pakistan, sometimes classified as a dialect of Punjabi. ▶ adj. of or relating to this language. [20th C.: from Punjabi *lahandā*, lit. 'western.']

La·hore /lə'hôr/ the capital of Punjab province and second largest city in Pakistan; pop. 6,350,000.

Lai·bach /'lī,bäk; -,bäKH/ German name for **LJUBLJANA**.

la·ic /'lāik/ formal ▶ adj. nonclerical; lay. ▶ n. a layperson; a noncleric. — **la·i·cal** /-ikəl/ adj. **la·i·cal·ly** /-ik(ə)lē/ adv. [16th C.: from late L. *laicus* (see LAY[2]).]

la·i·cize /'lāə,sīz/ ▶ v. [trans.] formal withdraw clerical character, control, or status from (someone or something); secularize. — **la·i·cism** /-,sizəm/ n. **la·i·ci·za·tion** /,lāəsə'zāsHən/ n.

laid /lād/ past and past participle of LAY[1].

laid-back ▶ adj. informal relaxed and easygoing.

laid pa·per ▶ n. paper that has a finely ribbed appearance. Compare with WOVE PAPER.

lain /lān/ past participle of LIE[1].

Laing /laNG/, R. D. (1927–89), Scottish psychiatrist; full name *Ronald David Laing*. He was known for his controversial views on schizophrenia.

lair /le(ə)r/ ▶ n. a wild animal's resting place, esp. one that is well hidden. ■ a secret or private place. [OE *leger* 'resting place, bed,' of Gmc. origin; rel. to Ger. *Lager* 'storehouse,' also to LIE[1].]

laird /le(ə)rd/ ▶ n. (in Scotland) a person who owns a large estate. — **laird·ship** n. [ME: Scots form of LORD.]

lais·sez-faire /,lesā 'fe(ə)r; ,lezā/ ▶ n. a policy of leaving things to take their own course, without interfering. ■ Econ. abstention by governments from interfering in the workings of the free market. — **lais·sez-faire·ism** /'fe(ə)r,izəm/ n. [Fr., lit. 'allow to do.']

lais·sez-pas·ser /,lesāpa'sā; ,lezā/ ▶ n. a document allowing the holder to pass; a permit. [Fr., lit. 'allow to pass.']

la·i·ty /'lāətē/ ▶ n. [usu. treated as pl.] (**the laity**) lay people, as distinct from the clergy. ■ ordinary people, as distinct from professionals. [ME: from LAY[2] + -ITY.]

La·ius /'lāəs/ Gk. Mythol. a king of Thebes.

La Jol·la /lə'hoiə/ a resort section of northern San Diego in California.

lake[1] /lāk/ ▶ n. a large body of water surrounded by land: *boys were swimming in the lake.* ■ a pool of liquid. [OE (denoting a pond or pool), from OFr. *lac*, from L. *lacus* 'basin, pool, lake.']

lake[2] ▶ n. [often with adj.] an insoluble pigment made from a soluble organic dye and an insoluble mordant. ■ a purplish-red pigment of this kind, originally one made with lac, used in dyes, inks, and paints. [17th C.: var. of LAC[1].]

lake·bed /'lāk,bed/ ▶ n. the floor or bottom of a lake.

Lake Charles /cHärlz/ a city in southwestern Louisiana; pop. 71,757.

Lake Dis·trict a region of lakes and mountains in northwestern England.

lake dwell·ing ▶ n. a prehistoric hut built on piles driven into the bed or shore of a lake. — **lake dwell·er** n.

lake·front /'lāk,frənt/ ▶ n. the land along a lake edge. ▶ adj. located along the edge of a lake.

Lake·hurst /'lākhərst/ a borough in east central New Jersey, associated with the 1937 crash of the dirigible *Hindenburg*.

Lake·land ter·ri·er ▶ n. a terrier of a small stocky breed originating in the Lake District of England.

Lake Plac·id /'plasid/ a village in the Adirondacks, in northeastern New York, site of the Winter Olympics in 1932 and 1980; pop. 2,638.

lak·er /'lākər/ ▶ n. informal **1** a lake trout. **2** a ship constructed for carrying cargo on the Great Lakes.

lake·side /'lāk,sīd/ ▶ n. the land adjacent to a lake.

lake trout ▶ n. any of a number of fishes of the salmon family that live in large lakes and are highly prized as a game fish and as food, in particular the North American char *Salvelinus namaycush*.

North American lake trout

Lake·wood /'lāk,wo͝od/ **1** a city in southwestern California; pop. 73,557. **2** a city in north central Colorado; pop. 144,126.

lakh /läk; lak/ (also **lac**) ▶ **n.** Indian a hundred thousand. [via Hindi from Sanskrit *lakṣa*.]

La·ko·ni·a var. of LACONIA.

La·ko·ta /lə'kōtə/ ▶ **n.** (pl. same or **-tas**) **1** a member of an American Indian people of western South Dakota. Also called *TETON SIOUX* (see TETON). **2** the Siouan language of this people. ▶ **adj.** of or relating to this people or their language. [the name in Lakota, rel. to the word DAKOTA[1].]

Lak·shad·weep /lək'sHäd,wēp/ a territory of India that consists of the Laccadive, Minicoy, and Amindivi Islands; pop. 51,680.

Laksh·mi /'ləksHmē/ Hinduism the goddess of prosperity, consort of Vishnu.

la-la land /'lä ,lä/ ▶ **n.** informal Los Angeles or Hollywood, esp. with regard to the lifestyle and attitudes of those living there or associated with it. ■ a fanciful state or dreamworld. [*la-la*, reduplication of LA (i.e., Los Angeles).]

la·la·pa·loo·za ▶ **n.** var. of LOLLAPALOOZA.

La Le·che League /lə 'lā,CHā/ ▶ **n.** an international nonprofit breastfeeding advocacy group.

La·lique /lä'lēk/, René (1860–1945), French jeweler, known for his brooches, combs, and decorative glassware.

Lal·lans /'lalənz/ ▶ **n.** a distinctive Scottish literary form of English, based on standard older Scots. ▶ **adj.** of, in, or relating to this language. [18th C.: Scots var. of *Lowlands*.]

lal·ly·gag ▶ **v.** var. of LOLLYGAG.

Lam. ▶ **abbr.** Bible Lamentations.

lam[1] /lam/ ▶ **v.** (**lammed, lam·ming**) [trans.] informal hit (someone) hard. ■ [intrans.] (**lam into**) attack. [16th C.: perh. of Scand. origin and rel. to Norw. and Dan. *lamme* 'paralyze.']

lam[2] informal ▶ **n.** (in phrase **on the lam**) in flight, esp. from the police. ▶ **v.** (**lammed, lam·ming**) [intrans.] escape; flee. [19th C.: from LAM[1].]

la·ma /'lämə/ ▶ **n.** **1** an honorific title applied to a spiritual leader in Tibetan Buddhism: *the Dalai Lama*. **2** a Tibetan or Mongolian Buddhist monk. [17th C.: from Tibetan *bla-ma*, lit. 'superior one.']

La·ma·ism /'lämə,izəm/ ▶ **n.** the system of doctrine maintained by lamas; Tibetan Buddhism. — **La·ma·ist n. & adj. La·ma·is·tic** /,lämə'istik/ **adj.**

La·mar /lə'mär/ a family of US jurists. Lucius Quintus Cincinnatus (1825–93) was a US Supreme Court associate justice 1888–93. A Mississippi Democrat, he was a US representative 1857–60, 1873–77, a US senator 1877–85, and US secretary of the interior 1885–88. His cousin Joseph Rucker (1857–1916) was a US Supreme Court associate justice 1911–16.

La·marck /lə'märk/, Jean Baptiste de (1744–1829), French naturalist. He advocated organic evolution. — **La·marck·i·an** /lə'märkēən/ **n. & adj. La·marck·ism** /lə'mär,kizəm/ **n.**

La·mar·tine /lämär'tēn/, Alphonse Marie Louis de (1790–1869), French poet. Some of his poetry is collected in *Méditations* (1820).

la·ma·ser·y /'lämə,serē/ ▶ **n.** (pl. **-ser·ies**) a monastery of lamas.

La·maze /lə'mäz/ ▶ **adj.** [attrib.] relating to a drug-free method of childbirth. [1950s: from the name of Fernand *Lamaze* (1891–1957), French physician.]

Lamb[1] /lam/, Charles (1775–1834), English writer and critic; pen name **Elia**. He wrote *Essays of Elia* (1823).

Lamb[2], Wally (1950–) US writer. His works include *I Know This Much Is True* (1998).

lamb /lam/ ▶ **n.** a young sheep. ■ the flesh of such young sheep as food. ■ fig. used as the epitome of meekness, gentleness, or innocence. ■ used to describe or address someone regarded with affection or pity, esp. a young child. ■ (**the Lamb**) short for LAMB OF GOD. ▶ **v.** [intrans.] (of a ewe) give birth to lambs. ■ [trans.] tend (ewes) at lambing time.
– PHRASES **like a lamb to the slaughter** as a helpless victim. — **lamb·er n. lamb·like adj.** [OE, of Gmc. origin; rel. to Du. *lam* and Ger. *Lamm*.]

lam·ba·da /lam'bädə/ ▶ **n.** a fast, erotic Brazilian dance that couples perform with stomachs touching. [1980s: Port., lit. 'a beating,' from *lambar* 'to beat.']

lam·baste /lam'bāst; -'bast/ (also **lam·bast** /-'bast/) ▶ **v.** [trans.] criticize (someone or something) harshly. [17th C.: from LAM[1] + BASTE[3].]

lamb·da /'lamdə/ ▶ **n.** the eleventh letter of the Greek alphabet (Λ, λ), transliterated as 'l.' ■ Biol. a type of bacteriophage virus used in genetic research: [as adj.] *lambda phage*. ■ Anat. the point at the back of the skull where the parietal bones and the occipital bone meet. ■ [as adj.] Biochem. denoting a type of light polypeptide chain present in all immunoglobulin molecules. ▶ **symb.** ■ (λ) wavelength. ■ (λ) Astron. celestial longitude.

lamb·doid /'lam,doid/ ▶ **adj.** resembling the Greek letter lambda in form. ■ Anat. denoting the suture near the back of the skull connecting the parietal bones with the occipital. — **lamb·doi·dal** /lam'doidl/ **adj.**

lam·bent /'lambənt/ ▶ **adj.** literary (of light or fire) glowing, gleaming, or flickering with a soft radiance. ■ (of wit, humor, etc.) lightly brilliant. — **lam·ben·cy** /-bənsē/ **n. lam·bent·ly adv.** [17th C.: from L. *lambent-* 'licking,' from the v. *lambere*.]

lam·bert /'lambərt/ ▶ **n.** a former unit of luminance, equal to the emission or reflection of one lumen per square centimeter. [20th C.: named after Johann H. *Lambert* (1728–77), German physicist.]

Lam·beth /'lambəTH/ a borough of inner London, England; pop. 220,000.

Lam·beth Pal·ace the residence of the Archbishop of Canterbury since 1197, in London, England.

lamb·ing /'lamiNG/ ▶ **n.** the birth of lambs on a farm.

lamb·kin /'lamkin/ ▶ **n.** a small or young lamb. ■ used as a term of endearment for a young child.

Lamb of God ▶ **n.** a title of Jesus (see John 1:29). Compare with AGNUS DEI.

lam·bre·quin /'lambərkin; -brə-/ ▶ **n.** **1** a short piece of decorative drapery. **2** a piece of cloth covering the back of a medieval knight's helmet. [18th C. (sense 2): from Fr., from the Du. dimin. of *lamper* 'veil.']

Lam·bru·sco /lam'bro͞oskō; -'bro͞os-/ ▶ **n.** a variety of wine grape grown in northern Italy. ■ a sparkling red wine made from this grape. [Ital., lit. 'grape of the wild vine.']

lamb's ears ▶ **plural n.** [usu. treated as sing.] a widely cultivated Asian plant (*Stachys byzantina*) of the mint family that has gray-green woolly leaves.

lamb·skin /'lam,skin/ ▶ **n.** prepared skin from a lamb, either with the wool on or as leather.

lamb's let·tuce ▶ **n.** another term for CORN SALAD.

lamb's-quar·ters ▶ **n.** a herbaceous plant (Chenopodiaceae) of the goosefoot family, with mealy, edible leaves, often considered to be a weed.

lamb's tongue ▶ **n.** another term for LAMB'S EARS.

lambs·wool /'lamz,wo͝ol/ ▶ **n.** wool from a young sheep.

lame /lām/ ▶ **adj.** **1** (of a person or animal) unable to walk normally because of an injury or illness affecting the leg or foot: *his horse went lame*. ■ (of a leg or foot) affected in this way. **2** (of an explanation or excuse) unconvincingly feeble. ■ (of something intended to be entertaining) uninspiring and dull. ■ (of a person) naive or inept, esp. socially. ■ (of verse or metrical feet) halting; metrically defective. ▶ **v.** [trans.] make (a person or animal) lame. — **lame·ly adv. lame·ness n.** [OE *lama*, of Gmc. origin, rel. to Du. *lam* and Ger. *lahm*.]

la·mé /la'mā; lä-/ ▶ **n.** fabric with interwoven gold or silver threads. ▶ **adj.** (of fabric or a garment) having such threads. [1920s: Fr., from L. *lamina* (see LAMINA).]

lame·brain /'lām,brān/ ▶ **n.** informal a stupid person. — **lame·brained adj.**

lame duck ▶ **n.** an official (esp. the president) in the final period of office, after the election of a successor. ■ an ineffectual or unsuccessful person or thing.

la·mel·la /lə'melə/ ▶ **n.** (pl. **-mel·lae** /-'melē; -'melī/) a thin layer, membrane, scale, or platelike tissue or part, esp. in bone tissue. ■ Bot. a membranous fold in a chloroplast. — **la·mel·lar** /-'melər/ **adj. la·mel·late** /'lamələt; lə'melit; 'lamə,lāt/ **adj. la·mel·li·form** /-'melə,fôrm/ **adj. la·mel·lose** /-,lōs; -,lōz/ **adj.** [17th C.: from L., dimin. of *lamina* 'thin plate.']

la·mel·li·branch /lə'melə,braNGk/ ▶ **n.** another term for BIVALVE. [19th C.: from mod. L. *Lamellibranchia*, from L. *lamella* + Gk. *brankhia* 'gills.']

la·mel·li·corn /lə'melə,kôrn/ ▶ **n.** former term for SCARABAEOID. [19th C.: from mod. L. *Lamellicornia*, from L. *lamella* + *cornu* 'horn.']

la·mel·li·po·di·um /lə,melə'pōdēəm/ ▶ **n.** (pl. **-di·a** /-dēə/) Zool. a flattened extension of a cell, by which it moves over or adheres to a surface. — **la·mel·li·po·di·al** /-dēəl/ **adj.** [1970s: from LAMELLA.]

la·ment /lə'ment/ ▶ **n.** a passionate expression of grief. ■ a song, piece of music, or poem expressing such emotions. ■ an expression of regret or disappointment; a complaint. ▶ **v.** [trans.] mourn (a person's loss or death). ■ [intrans.] (**lament for/over**) express one's grief passionately about. ■ [reporting verb] express regret or disappointment over something considered unsatisfactory, unreasonable, or unfair. — **lam·en·ta·tion** /,lamən'tāSHən/ **n. la·ment·er n.** [ME (as a v.): from Fr. *lamenter* or L. *lamentari*, from *lamenta* (pl.) 'weeping, wailing.']

lam·en·ta·ble /'laməntəbəl; lə'mentəbəl/ ▶ **adj.** **1** (of circumstances or conditions) deplorably bad or unsatisfactory: *the squalid facilities were lamentable*. ■ (of an action or attitude) unfortunate; regrettable. **2** archaic full of or expressing sorrow or grief. — **la·men·ta·bly adv.** [as submodifier] *she was lamentably ignorant*.

Lam·en·ta·tions /,lamən'tāSHənz/ (in full **the Lamentations of Jeremiah**) a book of the Bible about the desolation of Judah after Jerusalem's fall in 586 BC.

la·ment·ed /lə'mentid/ ▶ **adj.** (often **the late lamented**) a conventional way of describing someone who has died or something that has been lost or that has ceased to exist: *the much lamented Leonard Bernstein*.

la·mi·a /'lāmēə/ ▶ **n.** (pl. **-mi·as** or **-mi·ae** /-mē,ē/) a mythical monster, with the body of a woman or with the head and breasts of a woman and the body of a snake, said to prey on human beings. [via L. from Gk.]

lam·i·na /'lamənə/ ▶ **n.** (pl. **-nae** /-,nē; -,nī/) tech. a thin layer, plate, or scale of sedimentary rock, organic tissue, or other material. — **lam·i·nose** /-,nōs; -,nōz/ **adj.** [17th C.: from L.]

PRONUNCIATION KEY ə *ago, up*; ər *over, fur*; a *hat*; ā *ate*; ä *car*; e *let*; ē *see*; i *fit*; ī *by*; NG *sing*; ō *go*; ô *law, for*; oi *toy*; o͝o *good*; o͞o *goo*; ou *out*; TH *thin*; T͟H *then*; ZH *vision*

lam·i·nar /'lamənər/ ▶**adj.** **1** consisting of laminae. **2** Physics (of a flow) taking place along constant streamlines; not turbulent.

lam·i·nate ▶**v.** /'lamə,nāt/ [trans.] [often as adj.] (**laminated**) overlay (a flat surface, esp. paper) with a layer of plastic or some other protective material. ■ manufacture by placing layer on layer. ■ split into layers or leaves. ■ beat or roll (metal) into thin plates. ▶**n.** /-nit; -,nāt/ a laminated structure or material. ▶**adj.** /-nit; -,nāt/ in the form of a lamina or laminae. — **lam·i·na·ble** /-nəbəl/ **adj.** **lam·i·na·tion** /,lamə'nāsʜən/ **n.** **lam·i·na·tor** /-,nātər/ **n.**

lam·i·nec·to·my /,lamə'nektəmē/ ▶**n.** (pl. **-mies**) a surgical operation to remove the back of a vertebrae.

lam·i·nin /'lamənin/ ▶**n.** Biochem. a fibrous protein present in the basal lamina of the epithelia.

lam·i·ni·tis /,lamə'nītis/ ▶**n.** inflammation of sensitive layers of tissue (laminae) inside the hoof in horses and other animals. It is particularly prevalent in ponies.

Lam·mas /'laməs/ (also **Lammas Day**) ▶**n.** the first day of August, formerly observed in Britain as a harvest festival, during which bread was blessed. [OE *hlāfmæsse* (see LOAF[1], MASS.]

lam·mer·gei·er /'lamər,gīər/ (also **lam·mer·gey·er**) ▶**n.** a large Old World vulture (*Gypaetus barbatus*) of mountainous country, with a wingspan of 10 feet (3 m) and bristly tufts above and below its bill. Also called BEARDED VULTURE. [19th C.: from Ger. *Lämmergeier*, from *Lämmer* (pl. of *Lamm* 'lamb') + *Geier* 'vulture.']

lamp /lamp/ ▶**n.** a device for giving light, either one consisting of an electric bulb, together with its holder and shade or cover, or one burning gas or a liquid fuel. ■ an electrical device producing ultraviolet, infrared, or other radiation, used for therapeutic purposes. — **lamp·less adj.** [ME: via OFr. from late L. *lampada*, from L. *lampas*, *lampad-* 'torch,' from Gk.]

lam·pas[1] /'lampəs/ (also **lam·pers** /-pərz/) ▶**n.** a condition of horses, in which there is swelling of the fleshy lining of the roof of the mouth behind the front teeth. [16th C.: from French, prob. via Fr. dial. from the Gmc. base of the v. LAP[3].]

lam·pas[2] ▶**n.** a patterned drapery and upholstery fabric similar to brocade, made of silk, cotton, or rayon. [19th C.: from Fr. *lampas, lampasse*, of unknown origin.]

lamp·black /'lamp,blak/ ▶**n.** a black pigment made from soot.

lamp chim·ney ▶**n.** a glass cylinder encircling the wick of an oil lamp to provide a draft for the flame.

lamp·light /'lamp,līt/ ▶**n.** the light cast from a lamp. — **lamp·lit** /-,lit/ **adj.**

lamp·light·er /'lamp,lītər/ ▶**n.** hist. a person employed to light street gaslights by hand.

lam·poon /lam'po͞on/ ▶**v.** [trans.] publicly criticize (someone or something) by using ridicule or sarcasm. ▶**n.** a speech or text criticizing someone or something in this way: *does this sound like a lampoon of student life?* — **lam·poon·er n.** **lam·poon·ist n.** [17th C.: from Fr. *lampon*, perh. based on *lamper* 'gulp down.']

lamp·post /'lam(p),pōst/ ▶**n.** a tall pole with a light at the top; a street light.

lam·prey /'lamprē/ ▶**n.** (pl. **-preys**) an eellike aquatic jawless vertebrate (family Petromyzonidae) that has a sucker mouth with horny teeth and a rasping tongue. The adult is often parasitic, attaching itself to other fish and sucking their blood. [ME: from OFr. *lampreie*, from med. L. *lampreda*, prob. from L. *lambere* 'to lick' + *petra* 'stone.']

lamp·shade /'lamp,sʜād/ ▶**n.** a cover for a lamp, used to soften or direct its light.

lamp shell (also **lamp·shell**) ▶**n.** a marine invertebrate (phylum Brachiopoda) that superficially resembles a bivalve mollusk but has two or more arms of ciliated tentacles (lophophores) that are extended for filter feeding. Also called BRACHIOPOD.

LAN /lan/ ▶**abbr.** local area network.

La·na·i /lə'näē; lə'nī/ an island in Hawaii, west of Maui.

la·na·i /lə'näē; lə'nī/ ▶**n.** (pl. **-na·is**) a porch or veranda. [Hawaiian.]

Lan·cas·ter /'lanɢ,kastər; -kəstər/ **1** a city in northwestern England, the county town of Lancashire; pop. 44,000. **2** a city in southwestern California; pop. 118,718.

Lan·cas·ter, House of the English royal house descended from John of Gaunt, Duke of Lancaster, that ruled from 1399 to 1461.

Lan·cas·tri·an /lanɢ'kastrēən/ ▶**n.** **1** a native of Lancashire or Lancaster in England. **2** hist. a follower of the British House of Lancaster. ▶**adj.** of or relating to Lancashire or Lancaster, or the House of Lancaster.

lance /lans/ ▶**n.** hist. a long weapon for thrusting, used by a horseman in charging. ■ a similar weapon used in hunting fish or whales. ■ another term for LANCER (sense 1). ■ [usu. with adj.] a metal pipe supplying a jet of oxygen to a furnace or to a hot flame for cutting. ■ a rigid tube at the end of a hose for pumping or spraying liquid. ▶**v.** [trans.] Med. prick or cut open with a lancet or other sharp instrument. ■ pierce with or as if with a lance. ■ [intrans.] move suddenly and quickly. [ME: from OFr. *lance* (noun), *lancier* (v.), from L. *lancea* (n.).]

lance cor·po·ral ▶**n.** an enlisted person in the US Marine Corps, above private first class and below corporal. [18th C.: on the analogy of obs. *lancepesade*, based on Ital. *lancia spezzata* 'broken lance.']

lance·let /'lanslit/ ▶**n.** a small elongated marine invertebrate (subphylum Cephalochordata, phylum Chordata) that resembles a fish but lacks jaws and obvious sense organs. Lancelets possess a notochord and are among the most primitive chordates.

Lan·ce·lot /'lansə,lät; 'län-; -s(ə)lət/ (also **Laun·ce·lot**) (in Arthurian legend) one of Arthur's knights, lover of Queen Guinevere and father of Galahad.

lan·ce·o·late /'lansēəlit; -,lāt/ ▶**adj.** tech. shaped like the head of a lance; of a narrow oval shape tapering to a point at each end: *the leaves are lanceolate.* See illustration at LEAF. [18th C.: from late L. *lanceolatus*, from L. *lanceola*, dimin. of *lancea* 'a lance.']

lanc·er /'lansər/ ▶**n.** **1** hist. a soldier of a cavalry regiment armed with lances. **2** (**lancers**) [treated as sing.] a quadrille for eight or sixteen pairs. [16th C.: from Fr. *lancier*, from *lance* 'a lance.']

lan·cet /'lansit/ ▶**n.** **1** a small, broad, two-edged surgical knife or blade with a sharp point. **2** a lancet arch or window. ■ [as adj.] shaped like a lancet arch: *a lancet clock.* — **lan·cet·ed adj.** [ME (also denoting a small lance): from OFr. *lancette*, dimin. of *lance* 'a lance.']

lan·cet arch ▶**n.** an arch with an acutely pointed head.

lan·cet win·dow ▶**n.** a high and narrow window with an acutely pointed head.

lance·wood /'lans,wo͝od/ ▶**n.** any of a number of hardwood trees with tough elastic timber, in particular a Caribbean tree (*Oxandra lanceolata* of the custard apple family. ■ the timber of any of these trees, used esp. where flexibility is required, such as in carriage shafts and fishing rods.

Lan·chow /'län'jō; 'län'cʜou/ variant of LANZHOU.

Land /land/, Edwin (1909–91) US inventor. He introduced the first Polaroid Land camera in 1947.

land /land/ ▶**n.** **1** the part of the earth's surface that is not covered by water, as opposed to the sea or the air. ■ [as adj.] living or traveling on land rather than in water or the air. ■ an expanse of land; an area of ground, esp. in terms of its ownership or use. ■ (**the land**) ground or soil used as a basis for agriculture. ■ property in the form of land. **2** a country: *America, the land of political equality.* ■ fig. a realm or domain: *a fantasy land.* **3** the space between the rifling grooves in a gun. ▶**v.** **1** [trans.] put ashore: *the lifeboat landed the survivors.* ■ [intrans.] go ashore; disembark. ■ unload (goods) from a ship. ■ bring (a fish) to land, esp. with a net or hook. ■ informal succeed in obtaining or achieving (something desirable), esp. in the face of strong competition: *she landed the role.* **2** [intrans.] come down through the air to the ground. ■ [trans.] bring (an aircraft or spacecraft) to the ground or the surface of water, esp. in a controlled way. ■ reach the ground after falling or jumping. ■ [with adverbial of place] (of an object) come to rest after falling or being thrown. ■ informal (of something unpleasant or unexpected) arrive suddenly. **3** [trans.] (**land someone in**) informal cause someone to be in (a difficult or unwelcome situation). **4** [trans.] informal inflict (a blow) on someone.

– PHRASES **how the land lies** the state of affairs. **in the land of the living** humorous alive or awake. **land on one's feet** have good luck or success. **live off the land** live on whatever food one can obtain by hunting, gathering, or subsistence farming.

– PHRASAL VERBS **land up** reach a place or destination; end up. [OE, of Gmc. origin; rel. to Du. *land* and Ger. *Land*.]

Lan·dau /'lan,dou; lən'dou/, Lev Davidovich (1908–68), Soviet physicist. He was noted for his work on liquid helium. Nobel Prize for Physics (1962).

lan·dau /'lan,dou/ ▶**n.** a horse-drawn four-wheeled enclosed carriage with a removable front cover and a back cover that can be raised and lowered. [18th C.: after *Landau*, near Karlsruhe in Germany, where it was first made.]

lan·dau·let /,landô'let/ ▶**n.** a small landau. ■ esp. hist. a car with a folding hood over the rear seat.

land bank ▶**n.** **1** a bank whose main function is to provide loans for land purchase, esp. by farmers. **2** a large body of land held by a public or private organization for future development or disposal.

land breeze ▶**n.** a breeze blowing toward the sea from the land. Compare with SEA BREEZE.

land bridge ▶**n.** a connection between two landmasses, esp. a prehistoric one that allowed humans and animals to colonize new territory.

land crab ▶**n.** a crab (*Cardisoma* and other genera, family Gecarcinidae) that lives in burrows inland and migrates in large numbers to the sea to breed.

land·ed /'landid/ ▶**adj.** [attrib.] owning much land. ■ consisting of, including, or relating to such land.

land·er /'landər/ ▶**n.** a spacecraft designed to land on a planet or moon. Compare with ORBITER.

land·fall /'land,fôl/ ▶**n.** **1** an arrival on land. ■ the contact of a hurricane with a landmass. **2** a collapse of a mass of land.

land·fill /'lan(d),fil/ ▶**n.** the disposal of refuse and other waste material by burying it and covering it over with soil. ■ waste material used to reclaim ground in this way. ■ an area filled in by this process.

land·form /'lan(d),fôrm/ ▶**n.** a natural feature of the earth's surface.

land-grab·ber ▶**n.** a person who seizes and possesses land in an unfair or illegal manner. — **land-grab n.** **land-grab·bing n.**

land grant ▶**n.** a grant of public land.

land·grave /'lan(d),grāv/ ▶**n.** hist. a count having jurisdiction over a territory. ■ the title of certain German princes. [ME: from Mid. Low Ger., from *land* 'land' + *grave* 'count' (used as a title).]

land·hold·er /'land,hōldər/ ▶**n.** a person who owns land.

land·ing /'landiɴɢ/ ▶**n.** **1** an instance of coming or bringing something to land, from the air or water. ■ the action or process of doing this.

■ (also **landing place**) a place where people and goods can be landed from a boat or ship. **2** a level area at the top of a staircase or between one flight of stairs and another.

land·ing craft ▶ n. a boat specially designed for putting troops and military equipment ashore on a beach.

land·ing gear ▶ n. the undercarriage of an aircraft on which it rests while not in the air.

land·ing net ▶ n. a net for landing a large fish that has been hooked.

land·ing pad ▶ n. a small area designed for helicopters to land on and take off from.

land·ing stage ▶ n. a platform, typically a floating one, onto which passengers from a boat or ship disembark or cargo is unloaded.

land·ing strip ▶ n. an airstrip.

land·la·dy /'lan(d),lādē/ ▶ n. (pl. **-dies**) a woman who rents land, a building, or an apartment to a tenant. ■ a woman who owns or runs a boardinghouse, inn, or similar establishment.

land·less /'lan(d)lis/ ▶ adj. owning no land. — **land·less·ness** n.

land·locked /'lan(d),läkt/ ▶ adj. almost or entirely surrounded by land; having no coastline or seaport. ■ (of a lake) enclosed by land and having no navigable route to the sea. ■ (of a fish, esp. a North American salmon) cut off from the sea in the past and now confined to fresh water.

land·lord /'lan(d),lôrd/ ▶ n. a person who rents land, a building, or an apartment to a tenant. ■ a person who owns or runs a boardinghouse, inn, or similar establishment.

land·lord·ism /'lan(d)lôr,dizəm/ ▶ n. the system whereby land (or property) is owned by landlords to whom tenants pay a fixed rent.

land·lub·ber /'lan(d),ləbər/ ▶ n. informal a person unfamiliar with the sea or sailing.

land·mark /'lan(d),märk/ ▶ n. **1** an object or feature of a landscape or town that enables someone to establish their location. **2** an event, discovery, or change marking an important stage or turning point in something: *the birth of a child is an important landmark in the lives of all concerned.*

land·mass /'lan(d),mas/ (also **land mass**) ▶ n. a continent or other large body of land.

land mine ▶ n. an explosive mine laid on or just under the surface of the ground.

land of·fice ▶ n. a government office recording dealings in public land.
– PHRASES **do a land-office business** informal do a lot of successful business: *the open-air air show did a land-office business.*

land·own·er /'land,ōnər/ ▶ n. a person who owns land. — **land·own·er·ship** n. **land·own·ing** adj. & n.

land re·form ▶ n. the statutory division of agricultural land and its reallocation to landless people.

Land·sat /'lan(d),sat/ a series of artificial satellites that monitor the earth's resources by photographing the surface at different wavelengths.

land·scape /'lan(d),skāp/ ▶ n. **1** all the visible features of an area of countryside or land, often considered in terms of their aesthetic appeal. ■ a picture representing an area of countryside. ■ fig. the distinctive features of a particular situation or intellectual activity. **2** [as adj.] (of a page, book, or illustration, or the manner in which it is set or printed) wider than it is high. Compare with PORTRAIT (sense 2). ▶ v. [trans.] (usu. **be landscaped**) improve the aesthetic appearance of (a piece of land) by changing its contours, adding ornamental features and plantings. — **land·scap·er** n. **land·scap·ist** /-,skāpist/ n. [16th C.: from MDu. *lantscap*, from *land* 'land' + *scap* (equivalent of **-SHIP**).]

land·scape ar·chi·tec·ture ▶ n. the art and practice of designing the outdoor environment. — **land·scape ar·chi·tect** n.

land scrip ▶ n. see SCRIP[1] (sense 2).

Land's End a cape in Cornwall that is England's westernmost point.

land·slide /'lan(d),slīd/ ▶ n. **1** the sliding down of a mass of earth or rock from a mountain or cliff. **2** an overwhelming majority of votes for one party in an election: *winning the election **by a landslide**.*

Lands·mål /'länts,môl/ ▶ n. another term for NYNORSK. [Norw., lit. 'language of the land.']

lands·man /'lan(d)zmən/ ▶ n. (pl. **-men**) a person unfamiliar with the sea or sailing.

Land·stei·ner /'lan(d),stīnər; 'länt,SHtīnər/, Karl (1868–1943), US physician; born in Austria. In 1930, he devised the ABO system of classifying blood. Nobel Prize for Physiology or Medicine (1930).

land·ward /'lan(d)wərd/ ▶ adv. (also **land·wards** /-wərdz/) toward land: *the ship turned landward.* ▶ adj. facing toward land as opposed to sea.

lane /lān/ ▶ n. **1** a narrow road, esp. in a rural area. ■ [in place names] a street in an urban area: *Park Lane.* ■ Astron. a dark streak or band that shows up against a bright background. **2** a division of a road marked off with painted lines and intended to separate single lines of traffic according to speed or direction: *the car moved into the outside lane.* ■ each of a number of parallel strips of track or water for runners, rowers, or swimmers in a race. ■ a path or course prescribed for or regularly followed by ships or aircraft. ■ (in basketball) a 12-foot-wide area extending from the free-throw line to below the basket. ■ (in bowling) a long narrow strip of floor down which the ball is bowled. ■ Biochem. each of a number of notional parallel strips in the gel of an electrophoresis plate, occupied by a single sample. [OE, rel. to Du. *laan*; of unknown ultimate origin.]

lang. ▶ abbr. language.

Lange /laNG/, Dorothea (1895–1965) US photographer. She was noted for her documentary photographs of the Great Depression.

Lang·land /'laNGlənd/, William (*c.*1330–*c.*1400), English poet. He wrote *Piers Plowman* (*c.*1367–70).

lang·lauf /'läNG,louf/ ▶ n. cross-country skiing. [1920s: from Ger., lit. 'long run.']

Lang·ley /'laNG(g)lē/, Samuel Pierpoint (1834–1906), US astronomer and aviation pioneer. He invented the bolometer (1879–81) and contributed to aircraft design.

Lang·muir /'laNG,myŏŏr/, Irving (1881–1957), US chemist and physicist. His principal work was in surface chemistry, esp. applied to catalysis.

lan·gouste /läNG'gōōst/ ▶ n. a spiny lobster, esp. in French cuisine; crawfish. [Fr., from Old Provençal *lagosta*, based on L. *locusta* 'locust, crustacean.']

lan·gous·tine /'laNGgə,stēn/ ▶ n. a large, commercially important prawn (*Nephrops norvegicus*). [Fr., from *langouste* (see LANGOUSTE).]

lang syne /,laNG 'zīn; 'sīn/ Scot., archaic ▶ adv. in the distant past; long ago: *we talked of races run lang syne.* ▶ n. times gone by; the old days, esp. in the phrase, "auld lang syne." [16th C.: from *lang*, Scots var. of LONG[1] + SYNE.]

Lang·ton /'laNGtən/, Stephen (*c.* 1150–1228), archbishop of Canterbury 1207–15, 1218–28.

Lang·try /'laNGtrē/, Lillie (1853–1929), British actress; born *Emilie Charlotte le Breton.*

lan·guage /'laNGgwij/ ▶ n. **1** the method of human communication, either spoken or written, consisting of the use of words in a structured and conventional way. ■ any nonverbal method of expression or communication: *a language of gesture and facial expression.* **2** the system of communication used by a particular community or country. ■ Comput. a system of symbols and rules for writing programs or algorithms. **3** the manner or style of a piece of writing or speech. ■ the phraseology and vocabulary of a certain profession, domain, or group of people: *legal language.* ■ (usu. as **bad/strong language**) coarse, crude, or offensive language.
– PHRASES **speak the same language** understand one another as a result of shared opinions or values. [ME: from OFr. *langage*, based on L. *lingua* 'tongue.']

lan·guage ar·e·a ▶ n. **1** Physiol. the area of the cerebral cortex thought to be particularly involved in the processing of language. **2** a region where a particular language is spoken.

lan·guage arts ▶ n. the study of grammar, composition, spelling, and (sometimes) public speaking.

lan·guage en·gi·neer·ing ▶ n. any of a variety of computing procedures that use tools such as machine-readable dictionaries and sentence parsers in order to process natural languages for industrial applications such as speech recognition and speech synthesis.

lan·guage lab·o·ra·to·ry (also **language lab**) ▶ n. a room equipped with audio and visual equipment for learning a foreign language.

langue /läNG(g)/ ▶ n. (pl. same) Ling. a language viewed as an abstract system used by a speech community, in contrast to the actual linguistic behavior of individuals. Contrasted with PAROLE. [1920s: Fr., from L. *lingua* 'language, tongue.']

langued /laNGd/ ▶ adj. Heraldry having the tongue of a specified tincture. [ME: from Fr. *langué* 'tongued' + **-ED**[2].]

langue d'oc /,läNG(gə) 'dôk/ ▶ n. the form of medieval French spoken south of the Loire, forming the basis of modern Provençal. Compare with OCCITAN. [from OFr. *langue* 'language,' *d'* (from *de* 'of'), and *oc* (from L. *hoc*) 'yes.']

langue d'oïl /,läNG(gə) 'doi(l)/ ▶ n. the form of medieval French spoken north of the Loire, forming the basis of modern French. [from OFr. *langue* 'language,' *d'* (from *de* 'of'), and *oïl* (from L. *hoc ille*) 'yes.']

lan·guid /'laNGgwid/ ▶ adj. **1** (of a person, manner, or gesture) displaying or having a disinclination for physical exertion or effort; slow and relaxed. ■ (of an occasion or period of time) lazy and peaceful. **2** weak or faint from illness or fatigue. — **lan·guid·ly** adv. **lan·guid·ness** n. [16th C. (sense 2): from Fr. *languide* or L. *languidus*, from *languere* (see LANGUISH).]

lan·guish /'laNGgwisH/ ▶ v. [intrans.] **1** (of a person or other living thing) lose or lack vitality; grow weak. ■ fail to make progress or be successful. ■ archaic pine with love or grief: *she still languished after Richard.* **2** be forced to remain in an unpleasant place or situation. — **lan·guish·er** n. **lan·guish·ing·ly** adv. [ME: from OFr. *languiss-*, lengthened stem of *languir* 'languish,' from a var. of L. *languere*, rel. to *laxus* 'loose, lax.']

lan·guor /'laNG(g)ər/ ▶ n. **1** the state or feeling, often pleasant, of tiredness or inertia. **2** an oppressive stillness of the air. — **lan·guor·ous** /-g(ə)rəs; 'laNGərəs/ adj. **lan·guor·ous·ly** /-g(ə)rəslē; 'laNGərəslē/ adv. [ME: via OFr. from L., from *languere* (see LANGUISH)]

lan·gur /läNG'gŏŏr/ ▶ n. a long-tailed arboreal Asian monkey (*Presbytis* and other genera, family Cercopithecidae) with a characteristic loud call. [19th C.: via Hindi from Sanskrit *lāṅgūla*.]

lank /laNGk/ ▶ adj. (of hair) long, limp, and straight. ■ (of a person) lanky. — **lank·ly** adv. **lank·ness** n. [OE *hlanc* 'thin, not filled out,' of Gmc. origin; rel. to Ger. *lenken* 'to bend, turn.']

lank·y /'laNGkē/ ▶ adj. (**lank·i·er**, **lank·i·est**) (of a person) ungracefully thin and tall. — **lank·i·ly** /-kəlē/ adv. **lank·i·ness** n.

lan·ner /'lanər/ (also **lanner falcon**) ▶ n. a falcon (*Falco biarmicus*) with a dark brown back and buff cap, found in southeastern Europe, the Middle East, and Africa. [ME: from OFr. *lanier*, perh. from *lanier* 'wool merchant.']

lan·o·lin /'lanl-in/ ▶ n. a fatty substance found naturally on sheep's wool. [19th C.: coined in Ger. from L. *lana* 'wool' + *oleum* 'oil' + -IN[1].]

Lan·sing /'lansiNG/ the capital of Michigan, in the southern part of the state; pop. 119,128.

lan·ta·na /lan'tanə; -'tänə/ ▶ n. a tropical evergreen shrub (genus *Lantana*) of the verbena family, several kinds of which are cultivated as ornamentals.

lan·tern /'lantərn/ ▶ n. **1** a lamp with a transparent case protecting the flame or electric bulb and a handle by which it can be carried or hung. ■ the light chamber at the top of a lighthouse. ■ short for MAGIC LANTERN. **2** a structure on the top of a dome or a room, with the sides glazed or open, to admit light. [ME: from OFr. *lanterne*, from L. *lanterna*, from Gk. *lamptēr* 'torch, lamp,' from *lampein* 'to shine.']

lan·tern fish ▶ n. (pl. same or **fishes**) a deep-sea fish (family Myctophidae) that has organs on its body that emit light, seen chiefly when it rises to the surface at night.

lan·tern jaw ▶ n. a long, thin jaw and prominent chin. — **lan·tern-jawed** adj.

lan·tern slide ▶ n. hist. a mounted photographic transparency for projection by a magic lantern.

lan·tha·nide /'lanTHə,nīd/ ▶ n. Chem. any of the series of fifteen metallic elements from lanthanum to lutetium in the periodic table. See also RARE EARTH. [1920s: from LANTHANUM + -IDE.]

lan·tha·num /'lanTHənəm/ ▶ n. the chemical element of atomic number 57, a silvery-white rare earth metal. (Symbol: **La**) [19th C.: from Gk. *lanthanein* 'escape notice.']

la·nu·go /lə'n(y)ōōgō/ ▶ n. fine, soft hair, esp. that which covers the body and limbs of a human fetus or newborn. [17th C.: from L., 'down,' from *lana* 'wool.']

lan·yard /'lanyərd/ ▶ n. a rope used to adjust the tension in the rigging of a sailing vessel. ■ a cord passed around the neck, shoulder, or wrist for holding a knife, whistle, or similar object. ■ a cord attached to a breech mechanism for firing a gun. [ME *lanyer*, 'a short length of rope,' from OFr. *laniere*.]

Lan·zhou /'län'jō/ (also **Lan·chow**) a city in northern China, capital of Gansu province; pop. 1,480,000.

Lao /lou/ ▶ n. (pl. same or **Laos** /louz/) **1** a member of an indigenous people of Laos and northeastern Thailand. **2** the Thai language of this people. Also called LAOTIAN. ▶ adj. of or relating to the Lao or their language. [the name in Lao.]

La·oc·o·on /lā'äkō,än/ Gk. Mythol. a Trojan priest who, with his two sons, was crushed to death by two great sea serpents.

La·od·i·ce·an /lā,ädə'sēən/ archaic ▶ adj. lukewarm or halfhearted, esp. with respect to religion or politics. ▶ n. a person with such an attitude. [17th C.: from L. *Laodicea* in Asia Minor, with ref. to the early Christians there (Rev. 3:16), + -AN.]

lao·gai /,lou'gī/ ▶ n. (**the laogai**) (in China) a system of labor camps, mainly for political dissidents. [Chin., 'reform through labor.']

Laois /lāsH; lēsH/ (also **Laoighis, Leix**) a county of the Republic of Ireland, in the province of Leinster.

Laos /'lä-ōs; lous; 'lā,äs/ a country in Southeast Asia. *See box.* — **La·o·tian** /lā'ōsHən/ adj. & n.

Lao-tzu /'lä-ō 'tsōō; 'dzə/ (also **Lao·ze** /-'tsä; -'dzä/) (*fl.* 6th century BC), Chinese philosopher. He is traditionally regarded as the founder of Taoism.

lap[1] /lap/ ▶ n. (usu. **one's lap**) the flat area between the waist and knees of a seated person.

– PHRASES **fall** (or **drop**) **into someone's lap** (of something pleasant or desirable) come someone's way without any effort having been made. **in someone's lap** as someone's responsibility. **in the lap of luxury** in conditions of great comfort and wealth. — **lap·ful** /-,fōōl/ n. (pl. **-fuls**). [OE *læppa*, of Gmc. origin.]

lap[2] ▶ n. **1** one circuit of a track or racetrack. ■ a stage in a swim consisting of two lengths of a pool. ■ a section of a journey or other undertaking. **2** an overlapping or projecting part. ■ the amount by which one thing overlaps or covers a part of another. ■ Metallurgy a defect formed in rolling when a projecting part is accidentally folded over and pressed against the surface of the metal. ■ (in a steam engine) the distance by which the valve overlaps the steam port (or the exhaust port). **3** a single turn of rope, thread, or cable around a reel. ■ a layer or sheet into which cotton or wool is formed during its manufacture. **4** (in a lapping machine) a rotating disk with a coating of fine abrasive for polishing. ▶ v. (**lapped, lap·ping**) [trans.] **1** overtake (a competitor in a race) to become one or more laps ahead. ■ [intrans.] (of a competitor or vehicle in a race) complete a lap, esp. in a specified time. **2** (**lap someone/something in**) literary enfold or swathe a person or thing, esp. a part of the body, in (something soft). **3** [intrans.] project beyond or overlap something. **4** polish with a lapping machine. [ME: from LAP[1].]

lap[3] ▶ v. (**lapped, lap·ping**) [trans.] **1** (of an animal) take up (liquid) with the tongue in order to drink. ■ (**lap something up**) accept something eagerly and with obvious pleasure: *she's lapping up the attention.* **2** (of water) wash against (something) with a gentle rippling sound: *the waves lapped the shore.* ▶ n. [in sing.] the action of water washing gently against something: *the lap of the waves against the shore.* — **lap·per** n. [OE *lapian*, of Gmc. origin; rel. to Mid. Low Ger. and MDu. *lapen*.]

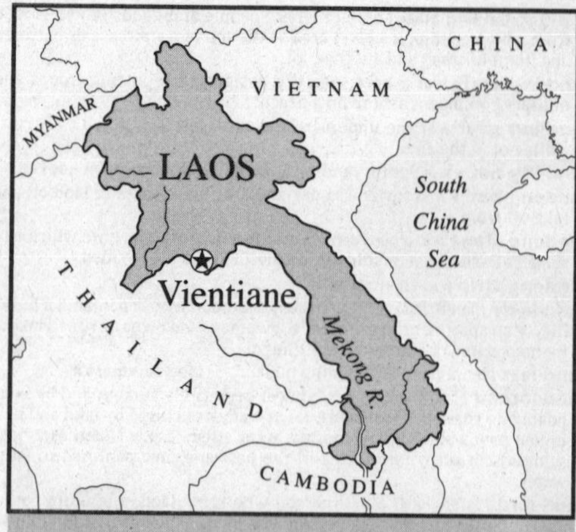

Laos

Official name: Lao People's Democratic Republic
Location: Southeast Asia, west of Vietnam and east of Thailand
Area: 91,500 square miles (236,800 sq km)
Population: 6,068,000
Capital: Vientiane
Languages: Lao (official), French, English, and others
Currency: kip

lap·a·ros·co·py /,lapə'räskəpē/ ▶ n. (pl. **-pies**) a surgical procedure in which a fiber-optic instrument is inserted through the abdominal wall to view the organs in the abdomen or to permit a surgical procedure. — **lap·a·ro·scope** /'lap(ə)rə,skōp/ n. **lap·a·ro·scop·ic** /,lap(ə)rə'skäpik/ adj. **lap·a·ro·scop·i·cal·ly** adv. [19th C.: from Gk. *lapara* 'flank' + -SCOPY.]

lap·a·rot·o·my /,lapə'rätəmē/ ▶ n. (pl. **-mies**) a surgical incision into the abdominal cavity, for diagnosis or in preparation for major surgery. [19th C.: from Gk. *lapara* 'flank' + -TOMY.]

La Paz /lä 'päz; 'päs/ the capital of Bolivia, in the northwestern part of the country; pop. 713,400.

lap belt ▶ n. a seat belt worn across the lap.

lap dance ▶ n. an erotic dance or striptease performed close to, or sitting on the lap of, a paying customer. — **lap danc·er** n. **lap danc·ing** n.

lap dis·solve ▶ n. a fade-out of a scene in a movie that overlaps with a fade-in of a new scene, so that one appears to dissolve into the other.

lap·dog /'lap,dôg; -,däg/ (also **lap dog**) ▶ n. a small dog kept as a pet. ■ fig. a person or organization that is influenced or controlled by another.

la·pel /lə'pel/ ▶ n. the part on each side of a coat or jacket immediately below the collar that is folded back. — **la·pelled** adj. [in comb.] *a narrow-lapelled suit.* [17th C.: dimin. of LAP[1].]

lap·i·dar·y /'lapə,derē/ ▶ adj. (of language) engraved on or suitable for engraving on stone. ■ of or relating to stone and gems and the work involved in engraving, cutting, or polishing. ▶ n. (pl. **-dar·ies**) a person who cuts, polishes, or engraves gems. ■ the art of cutting, polishing, or engraving gems. [ME (as a n.): from L. *lapidarius*, from *lapis, lapid-* 'stone.']

la·pil·li /lə'pilī/ ▶ plural n. Geol. rock fragments ejected from a volcano. [18th C.: via Ital. from L., pl. of *lapillus*, dimin. of *lapis* 'stone.']

lap·is laz·u·li /'lapis 'lazyə,lī; 'lazHə,lī; 'lazyəlē/ (also **lap·is**) ▶ n. a bright blue metamorphic rock consisting largely of lazurite. ■ a bright blue pigment formerly made by crushing this. ■ the color ultramarine. [ME: from L. *lapis* 'stone' and med. L. *lazuli*, genitive of *lazulum*, from Pers. *lāžward* 'lapis lazuli.' Cf. AZURE.]

Lap·ith /'lapiTH/ ▶ n. Gk. Mythol. a Thessalian who fought and defeated the centaurs. [via L. from Gk. *Lapithai* (pl.).]

lap joint ▶ n. a joint made with two pieces of metal, timber, etc., by halving the thickness of each member at the joint and fitting them together.

La·place /lä'pläs/, Pierre Simon, Marquis de (1749–1827), French mathematician and physicist. He analyzed planetary and lunar motion.

Lap·land /'lap,land; -lənd/ a region in northern Europe that consists of the northern parts of Norway, Sweden, Finland, and the Kola Peninsula of Russia. — **Lap·land·er** n.

La Pla·ta /lə 'plätə; lä 'plätä/ a city in eastern Argentina; pop. 640,000.

Lapp /lap/ ▶ n. **1** a member of an indigenous people of far northern Scandinavia. **2** the Finno-Ugric language of this people. ▶ adj. of or relating to the Lapps or their language. [Swed., perh. rel. to Mid. High Ger. *lappe* 'simpleton.']

lap·pet /'lapit/ ▶ n. a small flap or fold, in particular: ■ a fold or hanging piece of flesh in some animals. ■ a loose or overlapping part of a garment. — **lap·pet·ed** adj. [ME: dimin. of LAP[1].]

Lap·pish /'lapisн/ ▶ **adj.** of or relating to the Lapps (Sami) or their language. ▶ **n.** the Lapp language.

lap pool ▶ **n.** a swimming pool specially designed or designated for swimming laps.

lap robe ▶ **n.** a thick blanket or pelt used for warming the lap and legs while traveling or sitting outdoors.

lap·sang sou·chong /'lap,sang 'so͞o,CHäNG; 'läp,säNG; 'so͞o,SHäNG/ ▶ **n.** a variety of souchong tea. [19th C.: from an invented first element + SOUCHONG.]

lapse /laps/ ▶ **n.** **1** a temporary failure of concentration, memory, or judgment: *a lapse of concentration.* ■ a weak or careless decline from previously high standards: *tracing his lapse into petty crime.* ■ Law the termination of a right or privilege through disuse or failure to follow appropriate procedures. **2** an interval or passage of time. ▶ **v.** [intrans.] **1** (of a right, privilege, or agreement) become invalid because it is not used or renewed; expire. ■ (of a state or activity) fail to be maintained; end. ■ (of an adherent to a particular religion or doctrine) cease to follow the rules and practices of that religion or doctrine: [as adj.] **(lapsed)** *a lapsed Catholic.* **2** **(lapse into)** pass gradually into (an inferior state or condition): *the country has lapsed into chaos.* ■ revert to (a previous or more familiar style of speaking or behavior): *the girls lapsed into French.* [ME: from L. *lapsus*, from *labi* 'to glide, slip, or fall.']

lapse rate ▶ **n.** the rate at which air temperature falls with increasing altitude.

lap·strake /'lap,strāk/ ▶ **n.** a clinker-built boat. ▶ **adj.** (also **lap·straked**) clinker-built.

lap·sus ca·la·mi /'lapsəs 'kalə,mī; -,mē/ ▶ **n.** (pl. same) formal a slip of the pen. [L.]

lap·sus lin·guae /'läpsəs 'liNG,gwī; -,gwē/ ▶ **n.** (pl. same) formal a slip of the tongue. [L.]

Lap·tev Sea /'lap,tev; -,tef/ a part of the Arctic Ocean that lies to the north of Russia.

lap·top /'lap,täp/ (also **laptop computer**) ▶ **n.** a portable microcomputer, suitable for use while traveling.

lap-weld ▶ **v.** [trans.] weld with the edges overlapping. ▶ **n.** **(lap weld)** a weld made in this way.

lap·wing /'lap,wiNG/ ▶ **n.** a large plover (genus *Vanellus*), typically having a black and white head and underparts and a loud call. [OE *hlēapewince*, from *hlēapan* 'to leap' and a base meaning 'move from side to side.']

lar·board /'lär,bôrd; -bərd/ ▶ **n.** Naut. archaic term for PORT[3]. [ME *ladebord* (see LADE, BOARD.]

lar·ce·ny /'lärsənē/ ▶ **n.** (pl. **-nies**) theft of personal property. See also GRAND LARCENY, PETTY LARCENY. — **lar·ce·nist n. lar·ce·nous** /-nəs/ **adj.** [15th C.: from OFr. *larcin*, from L. *latrocinium*, from *latro(n-)* 'robber,' earlier 'mercenary soldier,' from Gk. *latreus.*]

larch /lärCH/ ▶ **n.** a coniferous tree (genus *Larix*) of the pine family with bunches of deciduous bright green needles, found in cool regions of the northern hemisphere. It is grown for its tough timber and its resin (which yields turpentine). [16th C.: from Mid. High Ger. *larche*, based on L. *larix.*]

lard /lärd/ ▶ **n.** fat from the abdomen of a pig that is rendered and clarified for use in cooking. ■ informal excess human fat. — **lard·y adj.** [ME (also denoting fat bacon or pork): from OFr., 'bacon,' from L. *lardum, laridum*, rel. to Gk. *larinos* 'fat.']

lard·er /'lärdər/ ▶ **n.** a room or large cupboard for storing food.

lar·der bee·tle ▶ **n.** a brownish scavenging beetle (*Dermestes lardarius*, family Dermestidae) that is a pest of stored products, esp. meat.

Lard·ner /'lärdnər/, Ring (1885–1933), US writer and sports journalist, full name *Ringgold Wilmer Lardner*. His baseball fiction featured the gullible character Jack Keefe.

lar·don /'lärdn/ (also **lar·doon** /lär'do͞on/) ▶ **n.** a chunk or cube of bacon used to smear or cover meat. [ME: from Fr., from *lard* 'bacon' (see LARD).]

La·re·do /lə'rādō/ a city in southern Texas; pop. 176,576.

lar·es /'lā,rēz; 'le(ə)rēz/ ▶ **plural n.** gods of the household worshiped in ancient Rome. See also PENATES.
– PHRASES **lares and penates** the home. [L.]

large /lärj/ ▶ **adj.** **1** of considerable or relatively great size, extent, or capacity. ■ of greater size than the ordinary, esp. with reference to a size of clothing or to the size of a packaged commodity. ■ pursuing an occupation or commercial activity on a significant scale: *many large investors.* **2** of wide range or scope: *a larger view of the situation.*
– PHRASES **at large** **1** (esp. of a criminal or dangerous animal) at liberty; escaped or not yet captured. **2** as a whole; in general: *a loss of community values in society at large.* **3** (also **at-large**) in a general way; without particularizing: *editor at large.* **4** dated at length; in great detail: *writing at large on the policies.* **in large measure** (or **part**) to a great extent. — **large·ness n. larg·ish** /-jisн/ **adj.** (usu. in sense 1). [ME: via OFr. from L. *larga*, fem. of *largus* 'copious.']

large cal·o·rie ▶ **n.** see CALORIE.

large-heart·ed ▶ **adj.** sympathetic and generous.

large in·tes·tine ▶ **n.** Anat. the cecum, colon, and rectum collectively.

large·ly /'lärjlē/ ▶ **adv.** [sentence adverb] to a great extent; on the whole; mostly.

large-mind·ed ▶ **adj.** open to and tolerant of other people's ideas; liberal.

large·mouth /'lärj,mouTH/ ▶ **n.** the largemouth bass (see BLACK BASS).

large-scale ▶ **adj.** **1** involving large numbers or area. **2** (of a map or model) made to a scale large enough to show certain features in detail.

lar·gesse /lär'jes; 'lärjis/ (also **lar·gess**) ▶ **n.** generosity in bestowing money or gifts upon others. ■ money or gifts given generously. [ME: from OFr., from L. *largus* 'copious.']

lar·ghet·to /lär'getō/ Music ▶ **adv. & adj.** (esp. as a direction) in a fairly slow tempo. ▶ **n.** (pl. **-tos**) a passage or movement marked to be performed in this way. [Ital., dimin. of *largo* 'broad.']

lar·go /'lärgō/ Music ▶ **adv. & adj.** (esp. as a direction) in a slow tempo and dignified in style. ▶ **n.** (often **Largo**) (pl. **-gos**) a passage, movement, or composition marked to be performed in this way. [Ital., from L. *largus* 'copious, abundant.']

lark[1] /lärk/ ▶ **n.** a small ground-dwelling songbird (family Alaudidae), typically with brown streaky plumage, a crest, and elongated hind claws, and with a song that is delivered in flight. [OE *lāferce, lǣwerce*; rel. to Ger. *Lerche.*]

lark[2] informal ▶ **n.** something done for fun. ▶ **v.** [intrans.] enjoy oneself by behaving in a playful and mischievous way: *he jumped the fence to go larking.* — **lark·ish adj. lark·y adj.** [19th C.: perh. from dial. *lake* 'play,' from ON *leika.*]

lark·spur /'lärk,spər/ ▶ **n.** an annual Mediterranean plant (genus *Consolida*, formerly *Delphinium*) of the buttercup family that bears spikes of spurred flowers. It is closely related to the delphiniums.

larn /lärn/ ▶ **v.** dialect form of LEARN.

La·rousse /lə'ro͞os; lä-/, Pierre (1817–75), French lexicographer and encyclopedist. He edited the *Grand dictionnaire universel du XIXe siècle* (1866–76).

lar·ri·kin /'larikin/ ▶ **n.** Austral. a boisterous, often badly behaved young man. ■ a person who disregards convention; a maverick. [19th C.: from Engl. dial., perh. from the given name *Larry* (nickname for *Lawrence*) + -KIN.]

lar·rup /'larəp/ ▶ **v.** (**-ruped, -rup·ing**) [trans.] informal thrash or whip (someone). [19th C. (orig. dial.): perh. rel. to LATHER or LEATHER.]

lar·va /'lärvə/ ▶ **n.** (pl. **-vae** /-vē; -,vī/) the immature form of an insect. Compare with NYMPH (sense 2). ■ an immature form of other animals that undergo some metamorphosis, e.g., a tadpole. — **lar·val** /-vəl/ **adj. lar·vi·cide** /-,sīd/ **n.** [17th C.: from L., 'ghost, mask.']

la·ryn·ge·al /lə'rinj(ē)əl; ,larən'jēəl/ ▶ **adj.** of or relating to the larynx: *the laryngeal artery.* ■ Phonet. (of a speech sound) made in the larynx with the vocal cords partly closed and partly vibrating (producing, in English, the so-called "creaky voice" sound): *laryngeal consonants.* ▶ **n.** Phonet. a laryngeal sound. [18th C.: from mod. L. *laryngeus* 'relating to the larynx' + -AL.]

la·ryn·ges /lə'rin,jēz/ plural form of LARYNX.

lar·yn·gi·tis /,larən'jītis/ ▶ **n.** inflammation of the larynx, typically resulting in huskiness or loss of the voice, harsh breathing, and a painful cough. — **lar·yn·git·ic** /-'jitik/ **adj.**

lar·yn·gol·o·gy /,laraNG'gäləjē/ ▶ **n.** the branch of medicine that deals with the larynx and its diseases. — **lar·yn·gol·o·gist** /-jist/ **n.**

la·ryn·go·scope /lə'riNGgə,skōp; -'rinjə-/ ▶ **n.** an instrument for examining the larynx. — **lar·yn·gos·co·py** /,larən'gäskəpē; ,larəNG-/ **n.**

lar·yn·got·o·my /,larən'gätəmē; ,larəNG-/ ▶ **n.** surgical incision into the larynx, typically to provide an air passage when breathing is obstructed.

lar·ynx /'lariNGks/ ▶ **n.** (pl. **la·ryn·ges** /lə'rin,jēz/ or **lar·ynx·es**) Anat. the hollow muscular organ forming an air passage to the lungs and holding the vocal cords in humans and other mammals; the voice box. [16th C.: mod. L., from Gk. *larunx.*]

la·sa·gna /lə'zänyə/ (also **la·sa·gne**) ▶ **n.** pasta in the form of wide strips. ■ a baked Italian dish consisting of this and layered with meat or vegetables, cheese, and tomato sauce. [Ital., pl. of *lasagna*, based on L. *lasanum* 'chamber pot.']

La Salle /lə 'sal; lä 'säl/, René-Robert Cavelier, Sieur de (1643–87), French explorer. He sailed from Canada to the Gulf of Mexico in 1682, naming the Mississippi basin Louisiana in honor of Louis XIV.

La Sca·la /lä 'skälə/ an opera house in Milan built 1776–78.

las·car /'laskər/ ▶ **n.** dated a sailor from India or Southeast Asia. [17th C.: from Port. *lascari*, from Urdu and Pers. *laškarī* 'soldier,' from *laškar* 'army.']

Las·caux /läs'kō; las-/ the site of a cave in the Dordogne, France, containing Paleolithic wall paintings.

las·civ·i·ous /lə'sivēəs/ ▶ **adj.** (of a person, manner, or gesture) feeling or revealing an overt and often offensive sexual desire: *he gave her a lascivious wink.* — **las·civ·i·ous·ly adv. las·civ·i·ous·ness n.** [ME: from late L. *lasciviosus*, from L. *lascivia* 'lustfulness,' from *lascivus* 'lustful, wanton.']

Las Cru·ces /läs 'kro͞osəs/ a city in southern New Mexico; pop. 74,267.

lase /lāz/ ▶ **v.** [intrans.] (of a substance, esp. a gas or crystal) undergo the physical processes employed in a laser; function as or in a laser. [1960s: back-form. from LASER.]

la·ser /'lāzər/ ▶ **n.** a device that generates an intense beam of coherent monochromatic light (or other electromagnetic radiation) by stimulated emission of photons from excited atoms or molecules. [1960s: acronym from *light amplification by stimulated emission of radiation*, on the pattern of *maser*.]

la·ser·disc /ˈlāzərˌdisk/ (also **la·ser disc**) ▶n. a disk that resembles a compact disc and functions in a similar manner; an optical disc.

la·ser gun ▶n. a hand-held device with a laser beam. ■ (in science fiction) a weapon using a laser beam.

la·ser point·er ▶n. a pen-shaped pointer that contains an intense beam of light.

la·ser print·er ▶n. a printer linked to a computer producing printed material by using a laser to form a pattern of electrostatically charged dots on a light-sensitive drum, which attract toner (or dry ink powder).

lash /lasH/ ▶v. [trans.] **1** strike (someone) with a whip or stick: *they lashed him repeatedly about the head.* ■ beat forcefully against (something). **2** [trans.] (of an animal) move (a part of the body, esp. the tail) quickly and violently. ■ [intrans.] (of a part of the body) move in this way. **3** [trans.] fasten (something) securely with a cord or rope: *the hatch was securely lashed down.* ▶n. **1** a sharp blow or stroke with a whip or rope, typically given as a form of punishment. ■ the flexible leather part of a whip, used for administering such blows. ■ (**the lash**) punishment in the form of a beating with a whip or rope. **2** (usu. **lashes**) an eyelash.
– PHRASAL VERBS **lash out** hit or kick out at someone or something.
— **lashed** adj. [in comb.] *long-lashed eyes.* **lash·er** n. [ME: prob. imitative.]

lash·ing /ˈlasHiNG/ ▶n. **1** an act or instance of whipping: *I threatened to give him a good lashing!* **2** (usu. **lashings**) a cord used to fasten something.

lash·ings /ˈlasHiNGz/ ▶plural n. Brit., informal a copious amount of something, esp. food or drink.

lash-up ▶n. esp. Brit. a makeshift, improvised structure or arrangement.

LASIK /ˈlāzik/ ▶n. eye surgery to correct vision in which a laser reshapes the inner cornea. [from L(aser) A(ssisted) I(n-)S(itu) K(eratomileusis).]

Las Pal·mas /läs ˈpälməs/ the capital of the Canary Islands, on Gran Canaria; pop. 372,000. Full name **Las Palmas de Gran Canaria.**

La Spe·zia /lä ˈspetsēə/ a city in northwestern Italy; pop. 103,000.

lass /las/ ▶n. esp. Scot. & N. English a girl or young woman: *he married a lass from Yorkshire.* [ME: based on ON *laskura* (fem. adj.) 'unmarried.']

Las·sa fe·ver /ˈläsə; ˈlasə/ ▶n. an acute and often fatal viral disease, occurring chiefly in West Africa. [1970s: named after the village of *Lassa*, in northwestern Nigeria, where it was first reported.]

las·sie /ˈlasē/ ▶n. esp. Scot. & N. English another term for **lass.**

las·si·tude /ˈlasəˌt(y)o͞od/ ▶n. a state of physical or mental weariness; lack of energy. [ME: from Fr., from L. *lassitudo*, from *lassus* 'tired.']

las·so /ˈlasō; ˈlaso͞o; laˈso͞o/ ▶n. (pl. **-sos** or **-soes**) a rope with a noose at one end, used esp. in North America for catching cattle or horses. ▶v. (**-soes, -soed**) [trans.] catch (an animal) with a lasso. — **las·so·er** n. [18th C.: representing a Spanish American pronunc. of Sp. *lazo*, based on L. *laqueus* 'noose.' Cf. **lace.**]

last[1] /last/ ▶adj. [attrib.] **1** coming after all others in time or order; final: *they caught the last bus.* ■ met with or encountered after any others. ■ the lowest in importance or rank: *last place.* ■ (**the last**) the least likely or suitable: *the last thing she needed was a husband.* **2** most recent in time; latest: *last year.* ■ immediately preceding in order; previous in a sequence. ■ most recently mentioned or enumerated. **3** only remaining: *it's our last hope.* **4** single; individual: *every last crumb.* ▶adv. **1** on the last occasion before the present; previously: *he looked much older than when I'd last seen him.* **2** [in comb.] after all others in order or sequence. **3** (esp. in enumerating points) finally; in conclusion. ▶n. (pl. same) the last person or thing; the one occurring, mentioned, or acting after all others. ■ (**the last of**) what remains: *the last of the wine.* ■ [in sing.] last position in a race, contest, or ranking. ■ (**the last**) the end or last moment, esp. death: *to the last.* ■ (**the last**) the last mention or sight of someone or something.
– PHRASES **at last** (or **at long last**) after much delay. **as a last resort** see **resort. last but not least** last in order of mention or occurrence but just as important. **last call** (in a bar) an expression used to inform customers that closing time is approaching and that any further drinks should be purchased immediately. **last ditch** used to denote a final, often desperate, act to achieve something in the face of difficulty. **one's** (or **the**) **last gasp** see **gasp. the last straw** see **straw. on one's last legs** see **leg.** [OE *latost* (adv.) 'after all others in a series,' of Gmc. origin; rel. to Du. *laatst, lest* and Ger. *letzt*, also to **late.**]

last[2] ▶v. [intrans.] **1** [with adverbial] (of a process, activity, or state of things) continue for a specified period of time: *the guitar solo lasted for twenty minutes.* **2** continue to function well or to be in good condition for a considerable or specified length of time. ■ (of a person) manage to continue in a job or course of action: *how long does he think he'll last as manager?* ■ survive or endure. ■ [trans.] (of provisions or resources) be adequate or sufficient for (someone), esp. for a specified length of time. [OE *lǣstan*, of Gmc. origin, rel. to Ger. *leisten* 'afford, yield,' also to **last**[3].]

last[3] ▶n. a shoemaker's model for shaping or repairing a shoe or boot. [OE *lǣste*, of Gmc. origin, from a base meaning 'follow'; rel. to Du. *leest* and Ger. *Leisten*.]

last-born ▶adj. last in order of birth; youngest. ▶n. a youngest or last-born child.

last hur·rah ▶n. a final act, performance, or effort.

last·ing /ˈlastiNG/ ▶adj. enduring or able to endure over a long period of time: *they left a lasting impression.* — **last·ing·ly** adv. **last·ing·ness** n.

Last Judg·ment ▶n. the judgment of humankind expected in some religious traditions to take place at the end of the world.

last·ly /ˈlastlē/ ▶adv. in the last place: *lastly, I thank my parents.*

last min·ute (also **last moment**) ▶n. the latest possible time before an event: [as adj.] *a last-minute change.*

last name ▶n. one's surname.

last rites ▶plural n. (in the Christian Church) rites administered to a person who is about to die.

Last Sup·per the supper eaten by Jesus and his disciples on the night before the Crucifixion, commemorated by Christians in the Eucharist. ■ an artistic representation based on this event.

last word ▶n. **1** a final or definitive pronouncement on or decision about a subject. **2** the finest or most modern, fashionable, or advanced example of something: *the last word in luxury.*

Las Ve·gas /läs ˈvāgəs/ a city in southern Nevada; pop. 478,434.

lat /lat; lät/ ▶n. (pl. **la·ti** /ˈlätē/ or **lats**) the basic monetary unit of Latvia, equal to 100 santims. [from the first syllable of *Latvija* 'Latvia.']

lat. ▶abbr. latitude: *between 40° and 50° S. lat.*

Lat·a·ki·a /ˌlatəˈkēə/ a city in western Syria; pop. 293,000.

latch /lacH/ ▶n. a metal bar with a catch and lever used for fastening a door or gate. ■ a spring lock for an outer door that catches when the door is closed and can only be opened from the outside with a key. ■ Electron. a circuit that retains whatever output state results from a momentary input signal until reset by another signal. ■ the part of a knitting machine needle that closes or opens to hold or release the wool. ▶v. [trans.] fasten (a door or gate) with a latch. ■ [intrans.] Electron. (of a device) become fixed in a particular state.
– PHRASAL VERBS **latch onto** informal attach oneself to (someone) as a constant and usually unwelcome companion. ■ take up (an idea or trend) enthusiastically. ■ (of a substance) cohere with. [OE *læccan* 'take hold of, grasp (physically or mentally),' of Gmc. origin.]

latch·et /ˈlacHit/ ▶n. archaic a narrow thong or lace for fastening a shoe or sandal. [ME: from OFr. *lachet*, var. of *lacet*, from *laz* 'lace.']

latch·key /ˈlacHˌkē/ ▶n. (pl. **-keys**) a key of an outer door of a house.

latch·key child (also informal **latch·key kid**) ▶n. a child who is at home without adult supervision for some part of the day, esp. after school.

late /lāt/ ▶adj. **1** doing something or taking place after the expected, proper, or usual time: *his late arrival.* **2** belonging or taking place near the end of a particular time or period: *they won the game with a late goal.* ■ [attrib.] denoting the advanced stage of a period: *the late 1960s.* ■ far on into the day or night. ■ originating at a point well into an artistic period or artist's life: *his late landscapes.* ■ flowering or ripening toward the end of the season. **3** (**the/one's late**) (of a specified person) no longer alive: *her late husband's grave.* ■ no longer having the specified status; former. **4** (**latest**) of recent date: *the latest news.* ▶adv. **1** after the expected, proper, or usual time. **2** toward the end of a period: *it happened late in 1984.* ■ at or until a time far into the day or night. ■ (**later**) at a time in the near future; afterward: *I'll see you later.* ▶n. (**the latest**) the most recent news or fashion.
– PHRASES **at the latest** no later than the time specified. **late in the game** (or **day**) at a late stage in proceedings, esp. too late to be useful. **of late** recently. — **late·ness** n. [OE *læt* (adj.), *late* (adv.); rel. to Ger. *lass*, L. *lassus* 'weary,' **let**[1], and **let**[2].]

late·com·er /ˈlātˌkəmər/ ▶n. a person who arrives late.

la·teen /ləˈtēn; la-/ ▶n. (also **lateen sail**) a triangular sail on a long yard at an angle of 45° to the mast. ■ a ship rigged with such a sail. [16th C.: from Fr. *(voile) Latine* 'Latin (sail).']

lateen

late-gla·cial (also **late gla·cial**) ▶adj. Geol. of or relating to the later stages of the final glaciation, from about 15,000 to 10,000 years ago. Compare with **postglacial.**

late Lat·in ▶n. Latin of about AD 200–600.

late·ly /ˈlātlē/ ▶adv. recently; not long ago.

late-mod·el ▶adj. (esp. of a car) recently made.

la·ten·cy /ˈlātn-sē/ ▶n. another term for **latent period.**

La Tène /lə ˈten/ ▶n. [usu. as adj.] Archaeol. the second cultural phase of the European Iron Age, following the Halstatt period (*c.*480 BC) and lasting until the coming of the Romans. [19th C.: named after a district in Switzerland.]

la·tent /ˈlātnt/ ▶adj. (of a quality or state) existing but not yet developed or manifest; hidden; concealed. ■ Biol. (of a bud, resting stage, etc.) lying dormant or hidden until circumstances are suitable for development or manifestation. ■ (of a disease) in which the usual symptoms are not yet manifest. ■ (of a microorganism, esp. a virus) present in the body without causing disease, but capable of doing so at a later stage or when transmitted to another body. — **la·tent·ly** adv. [ME: from L. *latent-* 'being hidden,' from the v. *latere*.]

la·tent heat ▶ n. Physics the heat required to convert a solid into a liquid or vapor, or a liquid into a vapor, without change of temperature.

la·tent pe·ri·od ▶ n. **1** Med. (also **la·ten·cy pe·ri·od**) the period between infection with a virus or other microorganism and the onset of symptoms. **2** Physiol. (also **la·ten·cy**) the delay between the receipt of a stimulus by a sensory nerve and the response to it.

lat·er /'lātər/ ▶ adj. & adv. comparative of LATE. ▶ exclam. informal goodbye for the present; see you later.

-later ▶ comb. form denoting a person who worships a specified thing: *idolater*. [from Gk. *-latrēs* 'worshiper.']

lat·er·al /'lat(ə)rəl/ ▶ adj. of, at, toward, or from the side or sides: *the plant gets water through lateral roots*. ■ Anat. & Zool. situated on one side or other of the body or of an organ, esp. in the region furthest from the median plane. The opposite of MEDIAL. ■ Med. (of a disease or condition) affecting the side or sides of the body, or confined to one side of the body. ■ Physics acting or placed at right angles to the line of motion or of strain. ■ Phonet. (of a consonant, esp. *l*, or its articulation) formed by or involving partial closure of the air passage by the tongue, so that air flows on one or both sides of the contact point. ▶ n. **1** a side part of something, esp. a shoot or branch growing out from the side of a stem. **2** Phonet. a lateral consonant. **3** Football (also **lateral pass**) a pass thrown either sideways or backward from the position of the passer. ▶ v. [trans.] throw (a football) sideways or backward. ■ [intrans.] throw a lateral. — **lat·er·al·ly** adv. [ME: from L. *lateralis*, from *latus, later-* 'side.']

lat·er·al bud ▶ n. another term for AXILLARY BUD.

lat·er·al·ize /'latərə,līz; 'latrə-/ ▶ v. (**be lateralized**) (of the brain) show dominance of one side in controlling particular activities or functions. ■ [with adverbial] (of an organ, function, or activity) be largely under the control of one side of the brain. ■ [with adverbial] Med. (of a lesion or pathological process) be diagnosed as localized to one side of the brain. — **lat·er·al·i·za·tion** /,latərəli'zāshən; ,latrə-; -,lī'zā/ n.

lat·er·al line ▶ n. Zool. a visible line along the side of a fish consisting of a series of sense organs.

lat·er·al ven·tri·cle ▶ n. Anat. each of the first and second ventricles in the center of each cerebral hemisphere of the brain.

Lat·er·an /'latərən/ the site in Rome containing the cathedral church of Rome and the Lateran Palace.

Lat·er·an Coun·cil any of five general councils of the Western Church held in the Lateran Palace in 1123, 1139, 1179, 1215, and 1512–17.

Lat·er·an Trea·ty a concordat signed in 1929 in the Lateran Palace between the kingdom of Italy (represented by Mussolini) and the Holy See (represented by Pope Pius XI), which recognized Vatican City as fully sovereign and independent.

lat·er·ite /'latə,rīt/ ▶ n. a reddish claylike material, hard when dry, forming a topsoil in some tropical or subtropical regions and sometimes used for building. ■ Geol. a claylike soil horizon rich in iron and aluminum oxides, formed by weathering of igneous rocks in moist warm climates. — **lat·er·it·ic** /,latə'ritik/ adj. [19th C.: from L. *later* 'brick' + -ITE[1].]

la·tex /'lā,teks/ ▶ n. (pl. **la·tex·es** or **lat·i·ces** /'latə,sēz/) a milky fluid found in many plants. The latex of the rubber tree is the chief source of natural rubber. ■ a synthetic product resembling this. [17th C.: from L., 'liquid, fluid.']

lath /laTH/ ▶ n. (pl. **laths** /laTHz; laTHs/) a thin flat strip of wood, esp. used to form a foundation for wall plaster or roof tiles. ■ laths collectively as a building material, esp. as a foundation for supporting plaster. ▶ v. [trans.] cover (a wall or ceiling) with laths. [OE *lætt*, of Gmc. origin; rel. to Du. *lat* and Ger. *Latte*, also to LATTICE.]

lathe /lāTH/ ▶ n. a machine for shaping wood, metal, or other material by means of a rotating drive that turns the worked-on piece against changeable cutting tools. ▶ v. [trans.] shape with a lathe. [ME: prob. from Old Dan. *lad* 'structure, frame.']

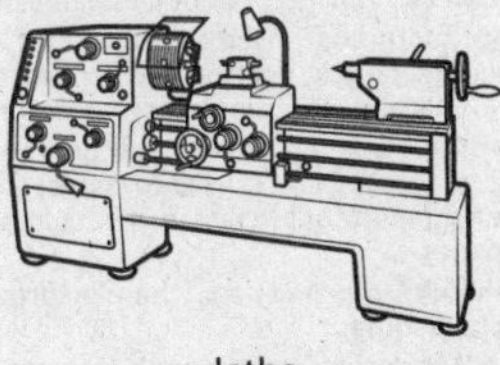

lathe

lath·er /'laTHər/ ▶ n. a frothy white mass of bubbles produced by soap or a similar cleansing substance when mixed with water. ■ heavy sweat visible on a horse's coat as a white foam. ■ (**a lather**) informal a state of agitation or nervous excitement: *Larry was worked into a lather and shouted at the mayor*. ▶ v. [trans.] **1** cause (soap) to form a frothy white mass of bubbles when mixed with water. ■ [intrans.] (of soap or a similar cleansing substance) form a frothy white mass of bubbles in such a way. ■ rub soap onto (a part of the body) until a lather is produced. ■ cause (a horse) to become covered with sweat. **2** informal thrash (someone). — **lath·er·y** adj. [OE *læthor* (denoting washing soda or its froth), *lēthran* (v.); rel. to ON *lauthr* (n.), Gk. *loutron* 'bath.']

lath·y·rism /'laTHə,rizəm/ ▶ n. a tropical disease marked by tremors, muscular weakness, and paraplegia, esp. prevalent in the Indian subcontinent. [19th C.: from mod. L. *Lathyrus*.]

lat·i·ces /'latə,sēz/ plural form of LATEX.

la·tic·i·fer /lā'tisəfər/ ▶ n. Bot. a cell, tissue, or vessel that contains or conducts latex. — **lat·i·cif·er·ous** /,latə'sif(ə)rəs/ adj. [19th C.: from L. *latex, latic-* 'fluid' + *-fer* 'bearing.']

lat·i·fun·di·um /,latə'fəndēəm/ ▶ n. (pl. **-di·a** /-dēə/) a large landed estate or ranch in ancient Rome or more recently in Spain or Latin America, typically worked by slaves. [17th C.: from L., from *latus* 'broad' + *fundus* 'landed estate,' partly via Sp.]

Lat·in /'latn/ ▶ n. **1** the language of ancient Rome and its empire. **2** a native or inhabitant of a country whose language developed from Latin, esp. a Latin American. ■ music of a kind originating in Latin America. ▶ adj. of, relating to, or in the Latin language. ■ of or relating to the countries or peoples using languages, esp. Spanish, that developed from Latin. ■ of, relating to, or characteristic of Latin American music or dance. ■ of or relating to the Western or Roman Catholic Church (as historically using Latin for its rites). ■ hist. of or relating to ancient Latium or its inhabitants. — **Lat·in·ism** n. **Lat·in·ist** n. [from L. *Latinus* 'of Latium' (see LATIUM).]

La·ti·na /lə'tēnə; la-/ ▶ n. a female Latin American inhabitant of the US. ▶ adj. of or relating to these inhabitants. [L. Amer. Sp., fem. of *Latino* (see LATINO).]

Lat·in A·mer·i·ca the parts of the American continent (Mexico, Central and South America, and many of the Caribbean islands) where Spanish, Portuguese, or French is the national language. — **Lat·in A·mer·i·can** n. & adj.

Lat·in·ate /'latn,āt/ ▶ adj. (of language) having the character of Latin: *Latinate suffixes*.

Lat·in Church the Christian Church that originated in the Western Roman Empire, giving allegiance to the pope of Rome, and historically using Latin for the liturgy; the Roman Catholic Church.

Lat·in cross ▶ n. a plain cross in which the vertical part below the horizontal is longer than the other three parts. See illustration at CROSS.

La·tin·i·ty /lə'tinətə; la-/ ▶ n. the use of Latin style or words of Latin origin.

Lat·in·ize /'latn,īz/ ▶ v. [trans.] **1** give a Latin or Latinate form to (a word). **2** make (a people or culture) conform to the ideas and customs of the ancient Romans, the Latin peoples, or the Latin Church. — **Lat·in·i·za·tion** /,latn-ə'zāsHən/ n. **Lat·in·iz·er** n.

La·ti·no /lə'tēnō; la-/ ▶ n. (pl. **-nos**) a Latin American inhabitant of the US. ▶ adj. of or relating to these inhabitants. [Latin Amer. Sp., prob. a special use of Sp. *latino* (see LATIN).]

Lat·in square ▶ n. an arrangement of letters or symbols that each occur *n* times, in a square array of n^2 compartments so that no letter appears twice in the same row or column. ■ such an arrangement used as the basis of experimental procedures in which it is desired to allow for two sources of variability while investigating a third.

lat·ish /'lātisH/ ▶ adj. & adv. fairly late.

la·tis·si·mus /lə'tisəməs/ (also **la·tis·si·mus dor·si** /'dôrsī/) ▶ n. (pl. **-mi** /-,mī; -,mē/) Anat. either of a pair of large, roughly triangular muscles covering the lower part of the back. [17th C.: mod. L., from *musculus latissimus dorsi*, lit. 'broadest muscle of the back.']

lat·i·tude /'latə,t(y)o͞od/ ▶ n. **1** the angular distance of a place north or south of the earth's equator, usually expressed in degrees and minutes. ■ (**latitudes**) regions, esp. with reference to their temperature and distance from the equator. ■ Astron. see CELESTIAL LATITUDE. **2** freedom of action or thought: *the media has a lot of latitude*. — **lat·i·tu·di·nal** /,latə't(y)o͞odn-əl/ adj. **lat·i·tu·di·nal·ly** /,latə't(y)o͞odn-əlē/ adv. [ME: from L. *latitudo* 'breadth,' from *latus* 'broad.']

latitude 1

lat·i·tu·di·nar·i·an /,latə,t(y)o͞odn'erēən/ ▶ adj. allowing latitude in religion; showing no preference among varying creeds and forms of worship. ▶n. a person with a latitudinarian attitude. —**lat·i·tu·di·nar·i·an·ism** n.

La·ti·um /ˈlāsʜ(ē)əm/ an ancient region in west central Italy, dominated by Rome by the end of the 4th century BC.

lat·ke /ˈlätkə/ ▶n. (in Jewish cooking) a pancake, esp. one made with grated potato. [Yiddish.]

La·to·na /ləˈtōnə/ Rom. Mythol. Roman name for LETO.

la·trine /ləˈtrēn/ ▶n. a toilet, esp. a communal one in a camp or barracks. [ME: via Fr. from L. *latrina*, contr. of *lavatrina*, from *lavare* 'to wash.']

La·trobe /ləˈtrōb/, Benjamin Henry (1764–1820), US architect; born in England. He designed the south wing of the US Capitol in Washington, DC.

-latry ▶comb. form denoting worship of a specified thing: *idolatry*. [from Gk. *-latreia* 'worship.']

lat·te /ˈlä,tā/ ▶n. short for CAFFÈ LATTE.

lat·ten /ˈlatn/ ▶n. hist. an alloy of copper and zinc resembling brass and hammered into thin sheets. [ME: from OFr. *laton*, of unknown origin.]

lat·ter /ˈlatər/ ▶adj. [attrib.] **1** situated or occurring nearer to the end of something than to the beginning. ■ belonging to the final stages of something. ■ recent. **2** (**the latter**) denoting the second or second mentioned of two people or things. [OE *lætra* 'slower,' compar. of *læt* (see LATE).]

lat·ter-day ▶adj. [attrib.] modern or contemporary.

Lat·ter-Day Saints (abbr.: **LDS**) ▶plural n. the Mormons' name for themselves.

lat·ter·ly /ˈlatərlē/ ▶adv. recently. ■ in the later stages of a period of time.

lat·tice /ˈlatis/ ▶n. a structure consisting of strips of wood or metal crossed and fastened together with square or diamond-shaped spaces left between. ■ an interlaced structure or pattern resembling this. ■ Physics a regular repeated three-dimensional arrangement of atoms, ions, or molecules in a metal or other crystalline solid. [ME: from OFr. *lattis*, from *latte* 'lath,' of Gmc. origin.]

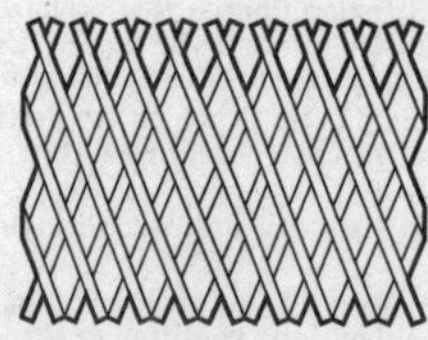

lattice

lat·ticed /ˈlatist/ ▶adj. decorated with a lattice.

lat·tice win·dow ▶n. a window with small panes set in diagonally crossing strips of lead.

lat·tice·work /ˈlatis,wərk/ ▶n. interlacing strips of wood, metal, or other material forming a lattice.

lat·ti·ci·nio /,latiˈcʜēnyō/ (also **lat·ti·ci·no** /-ˈcʜēnō/) ▶n. an opaque white glass used in threads to decorate clear Venetian glass. [Ital., lit. 'dairy produce,' from med. L. *lacticinium*.]

Lat·via /ˈlatvēə/ a country in eastern Europe. *See box.*

Latvia

Official name: Republic of Latvia
Location: eastern Europe, on the eastern shore of the Baltic Sea, between Estonia and Lithuania
Area: 24,900 square miles (64,600 sq km)
Population: 2,306,000
Capital: Riga
Languages: Latvian (official), Lithuanian, Russian
Currency: lat

Lat·vi·an /ˈlatvēən/ ▶adj. of or relating to Latvia, its people, or its language. ▶n. **1** a native or citizen of Latvia, or a person of Latvian descent. **2** the Baltic language of Latvia.

lau·an /ˈlo͞o-än/ ▶n. another term for PHILIPPINE MAHOGANY.

Laud /lôd/, William (1573–1645), archbishop of Canterbury 1633–45.

laud /lôd/ ▶v. [trans.] formal praise highly, esp. in a public context. [ME: from L. *laudare*, from *laus*, *laud-* 'praise.']

laud·a·ble /ˈlôdəbəl/ ▶adj. (of an action, idea, or goal) deserving praise and commendation. —**laud·a·bil·i·ty** /,lôdəˈbilətē/ n. **laud·a·bly** adv.

lau·da·num /ˈlôdn-əm; ˈlôdnəm/ ▶n. an alcoholic solution prepared from opium and containing morphine, formerly used as a painkiller. [16th C.: mod. L.; perh. a var. of L. *ladanum* (see LABDANUM).]

laud·a·to·ry /ˈlôdə,tôrē/ ▶adj. (of speech or writing) expressing praise and commendation.

lauds /lôdz/ ▶n. a service of morning prayer in the Divine Office of the Western Christian Church, traditionally said or chanted at daybreak. [ME: from L. imper. *laudate!* 'praise ye!']

laugh /laf/ ▶v. [intrans.] make the spontaneous sounds and movements of the face and body that are the instinctive expressions of lively amusement and sometimes also of contempt or derision. ■ (**laugh at**) ridicule; scorn. ■ (**laugh something off**) dismiss something embarrassing, unfortunate, or potentially serious by treating it in a lighthearted way or making a joke of it. ▶n. **1** an act of laughing. **2** (**a laugh**) informal a thing that causes laughter or derision: *that's a laugh, the idea of you cooking a meal!* ■ a person who is good fun or amusing company: *he's a good laugh.* ■ a source of fun or amusement.

– PHRASES **be laughing all the way to the bank** informal be making a great deal of money very easily. **have the last laugh** be finally vindicated, thus confounding earlier skepticism. **laugh one's head off** laugh heartily or uncontrollably. **laugh in someone's face** show open contempt for someone by laughing rudely at them in their presence. **the laugh is on me** (or **you**, **him**, etc.) the tables are turned and now the other person is the one who appears ridiculous. **a laugh a minute** very funny. **laugh out of the other side of one's mouth** be discomfited after feeling satisfaction or confidence about something. **laugh oneself silly** (or **sick**) laugh uncontrollably or for a long time. **laugh up one's sleeve** be secretly or inwardly amused. **no laughing matter** something serious that should not be joked about. [OE *hlæhhan*, *hliehhan*, of Gmc. origin; rel. to Du. and Ger. *lachen*, also to LAUGHTER.]

laugh·a·ble /ˈlafəbəl/ ▶adj. so ludicrous as to be amusing. —**laugh·a·bly** adv.

laugh·er /ˈlafər/ ▶n. **1** a person who laughs. **2** informal a sports contest or competition that is so easily won by one team or competitor, it seems absurd.

laugh·ing gas ▶n. nontechnical term for NITROUS OXIDE.

laugh·ing hy·e·na ▶n. another term for SPOTTED HYENA.

laugh·ing jack·ass ▶n. Austral. the laughing kookaburra. See KOOKABURRA.

laugh·ing·ly /ˈlafiNGlē/ ▶adv. with amused ridicule or ludicrous inappropriateness. ■ in an amused way; with laughter.

laugh·ing·stock /ˈlafiNG,stäk/ ▶n. [in sing.] a person subjected to general mockery or ridicule.

laugh·ter /ˈlaftər/ ▶n. the action or sound of laughing. [OE *hleahtor*, of Gmc. origin; rel. to Ger. *Gelächter*, also to LAUGH.]

launce /lôns; läns/ ▶n. another term for SAND EEL. [17th C.: early var. of LANCE (because of its shape).]

Laun·ce·lot /ˈlônsə,lät; ˈlän-; -lət/ var. of LANCELOT.

launch[1] /lôncʜ; läncʜ/ ▶v. [trans.] **1** set (a boat) in motion by pushing it or allowing it to roll into the water. ■ set (a newly built ship or boat) afloat for the first time, typically as part of an official ceremony. ■ send (a missile, satellite, or spacecraft) on its course or into orbit. ■ [trans.] hurl (something) forcefully. ■ [with adverbial of direction] (**launch oneself**) (of a person) make a sudden energetic movement. ■ utter (criticism or a threat) vehemently. **2** start or set in motion (an activity or enterprise). ■ introduce (a new product or publication) to the public for the first time. ▶n. an act or an instance of launching something. ■ an occasion at which a new product or publication is introduced to the public.

– PHRASAL VERBS **launch into** begin (something) energetically and enthusiastically. **launch out** make a start on a new enterprise. [ME: from Anglo-Norman Fr. *launcher*, var. of OFr. *lancier* (see LANCE).]

launch[2] ▶n. a large motorboat, used esp. for short trips. Also called MOTOR LAUNCH. ■ hist. the largest boat carried on a man-of-war. [17th C.: from Sp. *lancha* 'pinnace,' perh. from Malay *lancharan*.]

launch·er /ˈlôncʜər; ˈlän-/ ▶n. a structure that holds a rocket or missile during launching. ■ a rocket that is used to convey a satellite or spacecraft into orbit. ■ a catapult for aircraft. ■ an attachment to a rifle muzzle for firing grenades.

launch pad (also **launch·ing pad**) ▶n. the platform area on which a rocket stands for launching.

launch ve·hi·cle ▶n. a rocket-powered vehicle used to send artificial satellites or spacecraft into space.

laun·der /ˈlôndər; ˈlän-/ ▶v. [trans.] wash and iron (clothes or linens). ■ conceal the origins of (money obtained illegally) by transfers to foreign banks or legitimate businesses. ■ alter (information) to make it more acceptable. ▶n. a trough for holding or conveying water, esp. (in mining) one used for washing ore. ■ a channel for conveying molten metal from a furnace or container to a ladle or mold. —**laun·der·er** n. [ME: contr. of *lavender*, from OFr. *lavandier*, based on L. *lavanda* 'things to be washed,' from *lavare* 'to wash.']

laun·dress /'lôndrəs; 'län-/ ▶ n. a woman who is employed to launder clothes and linens.

Laun·dro·mat /'lôndrə,mat; 'län-/ (also **laun·dro·mat**) ▶ n. trademark an establishment with coin-operated washing machines and dryers for public use.

laun·dry /,lôndrē; 'län-/ ▶ n. (pl. **-dries**) **1** clothes and linens that need to be washed or that have been washed. ■ the action or process of washing such items. **2** a room in a house, hotel, or institution where clothes and linens can be washed and ironed. ■ a business that washes and irons clothes and linens commercially. [16th C.: contr. of ME *lavendry*, from OFr. *lavanderie*, from *lavandier* 'person who washes linen' (see LAUNDER).]

laun·dry list ▶ n. a long or exhaustive list.

laun·dry·man /'lôndrēmən; 'län-/ ▶ n. (pl. **-men**) a man who is employed to launder clothes and linens.

Laur·a·sia /lô'rāzHə/ a vast area believed to have existed in the northern hemisphere, comprising the present North America, Greenland, Europe, and most of Asia north of the Himalayas.

lau·re·ate /'lôrē-it; 'lär-/ ▶ n. a person who is honored with an award for outstanding achievement. ■ short for POET LAUREATE. ▶ adj. literary wreathed with laurel as a mark of honor. ■ (of a crown or wreath) consisting of laurel. — **lau·re·ate·ship** n. [ME (as an adj.): from L. *laureatus*, from *laurea* 'laurel wreath,' from *laurus* 'laurel.']

lau·rel /'lôrəl; 'lär-/ ▶ n. **1** any of a number of shrubs and other plants with dark green glossy leaves, in particular the mountain laurel and the bay tree. **2** an aromatic evergreen shrub (family Lauraceae) related to the bay tree, several kinds of which form forests in tropical and warm countries. **3** (usu. **laurels**) the foliage of the bay tree woven into a wreath or crown and worn on the head as an emblem of victory or mark of honor in classical times. ■ fig. honor: *she has rightly won laurels for her first novel.* ▶ v. (**-reled, -rel·ing**; Brit. **-relled, -rel·ling**) [trans.] adorn with or as if with a laurel.

– PHRASES **look to one's laurels** be careful not to lose one's superior position to a rival. **rest on one's laurels** be so satisfied with what one has already achieved that one makes no further effort. [ME *lorer*, from OFr. *lorier*, from Provençal *laurier*, from earlier *laur*, from L. *laurus*.]

Lau·ren·tian Pla·teau /lô'rensHən/ another name for CANADIAN SHIELD.

Lau·ri·er /'lôrē,ā; lôr'yā/, Sir Wilfrid (1841–1919), prime minister of Canada 1896–1911.

Lau·sanne /lō'zän/ a town in southwestern Switzerland, on the north shore of Lake Geneva; pop. 123,000.

Lau·sit·zer Neis·se /'louzitsər 'nīsə/ German name for NEISSE (sense 1).

lav /lav/ ▶ n. informal a lavatory.

la·va /'lävə; 'lavə/ ▶ n. hot molten or semifluid rock erupted from a volcano or fissure, or solid rock resulting from cooling of this. [18th C.: from Ital. (Neapolitan dial.), from *lavare* 'to wash,' from L.]

la·va·bo /lə'väbō; -'vābō/ ▶ n. (pl. **-boes**) (in the Roman Catholic Church) a towel or basin used for the ritual washing of the celebrant's hands at the offertory of the Mass. ■ ritual washing of this type. ■ dated a washbasin. [18th C.: from L., 'I will wash.']

la·va dome ▶ n. a mound of viscous lava that has been extruded from a volcanic vent.

la·va flow ▶ n. a mass of flowing or solidified lava.

la·vage /lə'väzH; 'lavij/ ▶ n. Med. washing out of a body cavity with water or a medicated solution. [18th C.: from Fr., from *laver* 'to wash.']

la·va lamp ▶ n. a transparent electric lamp containing a viscous liquid in which a brightly colored waxy substance is suspended, rising and falling in irregular and constantly changing shapes.

lav·a·to·ry /'lavə,tôrē/ ▶ n. (pl. **-ries**) a room or compartment with a toilet and washbasin; a bathroom. ■ a sink or washbasin in a bathroom. [ME: from late L. *lavatorium* 'place for washing,' from L. *lavare* 'to wash.']

lave /lāv/ ▶ v. [trans.] literary wash. ■ (of water) wash against or over (something). — **la·va·tion** /lə'vāsHən/ n. [OE *lafian*, from L. *lavare* 'to wash.']

lav·en·der /'lavəndər/ ▶ n. **1** a small aromatic evergreen shrub (genus *Lavandula*) of the mint family, with narrow leaves and bluish-purple flowers. ■ the flowers and stalks of such a shrub dried and used to give a pleasant smell to clothes and bed linens. ■ (also **lavender oil**) a scented oil distilled from lavender flowers. ■ used in names of similar plants, e.g., **sea lavender**. ■ informal used in reference to effeminacy or homosexuality: *he has a touch of lavender.* ■ dated used in reference to refinement or gentility: [as adj.] *lavender charm.* **2** a pale blue color with a trace of mauve. ▶ v. [trans.] perfume with lavender. [ME: from Anglo-Norman Fr. *lavendre*, based on med. L. *lavandula*.]

La·ver /'lāvər/, Rod (1938–), Australian tennis player; full name *Rodney George Laver*. In 1962 and 1969, he won the four major singles championships (British, American, French, and Australian).

la·ver[1] /'lāvər; 'lävər/ (also **purple laver**) ▶ n. an edible seaweed (*Porphyra umbilicaulis*, division Rhodophyta) with thin sheetlike fronds of a reddish-purple and green color that becomes black when dry. [OE, from L.]

la·ver[2] /'lāvər/ ▶ n. archaic literary a basin or similar container used for washing oneself. ■ (in biblical use) a large brass bowl for the ritual ablutions of Jewish priests. [ME: from OFr. *laveoir*, from late L. *lavatorium* 'place for washing' (see LAVATORY).]

lav·ish /'lavisH/ ▶ adj. sumptuously rich and elaborate. ■ (of a person) very generous or extravagant. ▶ v. [trans.] (**lavish something on**) bestow something in generous or extravagant quantities upon. ■ (**lavish something with**) cover something thickly or liberally with. — **lav·ish·ly** adv. **lav·ish·ness** n. [ME (as a n. denoting profusion): from OFr. *lavasse* 'deluge of rain,' from *laver* 'to wash,' from L. *lavare*.]

La·voi·sier /lə'vwäzyā; lävwä'zyā/, Antoine Laurent (1743–94), French scientist. He is regarded as the father of modern chemistry.

law /lô/ ▶ n. **1** (often **the law**) the system of rules that a particular country or community recognizes as regulating the actions of its members and may enforce by the imposition of penalties. ■ an individual rule as part of such a system. ■ such systems as a subject of study or as the basis of the legal profession. Compare with JURISPRUDENCE. ■ a thing regarded as having the binding force or effect of a formal system of rules. ■ (**the law**) informal the police. ■ statutory law and the common law. Compare with EQUITY. ■ a rule defining correct procedure or behavior in a sport. **2** a statement of fact, deduced from observation, to the effect that a particular natural or scientific phenomenon always occurs if certain conditions are present. ■ a generalization based on a fact or event perceived to be recurrent: *the first law of corporate life is that dead wood floats.* **3** the body of divine commandments as expressed in the Bible or other religious texts. ■ (**the Law**) the Pentateuch as distinct from the other parts of the Hebrew Bible (the Prophets and the Writings). ■ (also **the Law of Moses**) the precepts of the Pentateuch. Compare with TORAH.

– PHRASES **at** (or **in**) **law** according to or concerned with the laws of a country: *an attorney-at-law.* **be a law unto oneself** behave in a manner that is not conventional or predictable. **law and order** a situation characterized by respect for and obedience to the rules of a society. **the law of the jungle** see JUNGLE. **lay down the law** issue instructions to other people in an authoritative or dogmatic way. **take the law into one's own hands** punish someone for an offense according to one's own ideas of justice, esp. in an illegal or violent way. **there's no law against it** informal used in spoken English to assert that one is doing nothing wrong, esp. in response to an actual or implied criticism. [OE *lagu*, from ON *lag* 'something laid down or fixed,' of Gmc. origin and rel. to LAY[1].]

law-a·bid·ing ▶ adj. obedient to the laws of society. — **law-a·bid·ing·ness** n.

law·break·er /'lô,brākər/ ▶ n. a person who violates the law. — **law·break·ing** /-,brākiNG/ n. & adj.

law clerk ▶ n. an assistant to an experienced attorney.

law court ▶ n. a court of law.

law·ful /'lôfəl/ ▶ adj. conforming to, permitted by, or recognized by law or rules. ■ dated (of a child) born within a lawful marriage. — **law·ful·ly** adv. **law·ful·ness** n.

law·giv·er /'lô,givər/ ▶ n. a person who draws up and enacts laws.

law·less /'lôləs/ ▶ adj. not governed by or obedient to laws; characterized by a lack of civic order. — **law·less·ly** adv. **law·less·ness** n.

law·mak·er /'lô,mākər/ ▶ n. a legislator. — **law·mak·ing** /-,mākiNG/ adj. & n.

law·man /'lô,mən; -man/ ▶ n. (pl. **-men**) a law-enforcement officer, esp. a sheriff.

lawn[1] /lôn/ ▶ n. an area of short, regularly mown grass in a yard, garden, or park. — **lawned** adj. [16th C.: alt. of dial. *laund* 'glade, pasture,' from OFr. *launde* 'wooded district, heath,' of Celtic origin.]

lawn[2] ▶ n. a fine linen or cotton fabric. — **lawn·y** adj. [ME: prob. from *Laon*, France.]

lawn bowl·ing (Brit. **bowls**) ▶ n. a game played with heavy wooden balls, the object of which is to propel one's ball as close as possible to a previously bowled small ball (the jack) without touching it.

lawn mow·er ▶ n. a machine for cutting the grass on a lawn.

lawn ten·nis ▶ n. dated or formal the standard form of tennis, played with a soft ball on an open court. Compare with COURT TENNIS.

law of av·er·ag·es ▶ n. the supposed principle that future events are likely to balance any past deviation from a presumed average.

law of mass ac·tion n. Chem. the principle that the rate of a chemical reaction is proportional to the masses of the reacting substances.

law of na·ture ▶ n. **1** another term for NATURAL LAW. **2** informal a regularly occurring or apparently inevitable phenomenon observable in human society.

law of suc·ces·sion ▶ n. the law regulating the inheritance of property. ■ the law regulating the appointment of a new monarch or head of state.

Law·rence[1] /'lôrəns; 'lär-/ a city in northeastern Kansas, home to the University of Kansas, the scene of fierce fighting before and during the Civil War; pop. 80,098.

Law·rence[2], D. H. (1885–1930), English writer; full name *David Herbert Lawrence*. He wrote *Lady Chatterley's Lover* (1928) and *Sons and Lovers* (1913).

Law·rence[3], Ernest Orlando (1901–58), US physicist. He developed the first circular particle accelerator, later called cyclotron. Nobel Prize for Physics (1939).

Law·rence[4], Jacob (1917–2000), US painter. His *Migration* (1941–42), a series of 60 murals, depicts the migration of blacks northward in hopes of finding employment.

Law·rence[5], T. E. (1888–1935), British soldier; full name *Thomas Edward*

Lawrence; known as **Lawrence of Arabia**. From 1916 on, he helped to organize the Arab revolt against the Turks in the Middle East.

Law•rence, St. (died 258), Roman martyr; Latin name *Laurentius*. According to tradition, when Lawrence offered the poor people of Rome as the treasure of the Church to the prefect of Rome, he was roasted to death on a gridiron.

law•ren•ci•um /lôˈrensēəm/ ▶ **n.** the chemical element of atomic number 103, a radioactive metal of the actinide series. (Symbol: **Lr**) [1960s: mod. L., named after E. O. *Lawrence* (see LAWRENCE[3]).]

laws of war ▶ **plural n.** international rules and conventions that limit belligerents' action.

Law•son cy•press /ˈlôsən/ ▶ **n.** another term for PORT ORFORD CEDAR. [19th C.: named after Peter *Lawson* (died 1820) and his son Charles (1794–1873), the Scottish nurserymen who first cultivated it.]

law•suit /ˈlô,so͞ot/ ▶ **n.** a claim or dispute brought to a court of law for adjudication.

Law•ton /ˈlôtn/ a city in southwestern Oklahoma; pop. 92,757.

law•yer /ˈloi-ər; ˈlôyər/ ▶ **n.** a person who practices or studies law; an attorney or a counselor. ▶ **v.** [intrans.] practice law; work as a lawyer: [as n.] (**lawyering**) *lawyering is a craft.* ■ [trans.] (of a lawyer) work on the legal aspects of (a contract, lawsuit, etc.). — **law•yer•ly adj.**

law•yer•ing /ˈloi-əriNG; ˈlôyər-/ ▶ **n.** the work of practicing law.

lax /laks/ ▶ **adj. 1** not sufficiently strict or severe. ■ careless. **2** (of the limbs or muscles) relaxed. ■ (of the bowels) loose. ■ Phonet. (of a speech sound, esp. a vowel) pronounced with the vocal muscles relaxed. The opposite of TENSE[1]. — **lax•i•ty** /ˈlaksətē/ **n. lax•ly adv. lax•ness n.** [ME: from L. *laxus*.]

lax•a•tive /ˈlaksətiv/ ▶ **adj.** (chiefly of a drug or medicine) tending to stimulate or facilitate evacuation of the bowels. ▶ **n.** a medicine that has such an effect. [ME: via OFr. *laxatif, -ive* or late L. *laxativus*, from L. *laxare* 'loosen' (from *laxus* 'loose').]

lay[1] /lā/ ▶ **v.** (past **laid** /lād/) **1** [trans.] put down, esp. gently or carefully. ■ [trans.] prevent (something) from rising off the ground. **2** [trans.] put down and set in position for use. ■ set cutlery, crockery, and mats on (a table) in preparation for a meal. ■ (often **be laid with**) cover (a surface) with objects or a substance: *the floor was laid with tiles.* ■ make ready (a trap) for someone. ■ put the material for (a fire) in place and arrange it. ■ work out (an idea or suggestion) in detail ready for use or presentation. ■ (**lay something before**) present information or suggestions to be considered and acted upon by (someone). ■ Naut. follow (a specified course). ■ [trans.] stake (an amount of money) in a wager. **3** [trans.] used with an abstract noun so that the phrase formed has the same meaning as the verb related to the noun used, e.g., 'lay the blame on' means 'to blame': *she laid great stress on little courtesies.* ■ (**lay something on**) require (someone) to endure or deal with a responsibility or difficulty. **4** [trans.] (of a female bird, insect, reptile, or amphibian) produce (an egg) from inside the body. **5** [trans.] vulgar slang have sexual intercourse with. ■ [intrans.] (**get laid**) have sexual intercourse. ▶ **n. 1** [in sing.] the general appearance of an area: *the lay of the countryside.* ■ the position or direction in which something lies: *roll the carpet against the lay of the nap.* ■ the direction or amount of twist in rope strands. **2** vulgar slang an act of sexual intercourse. ■ [with adj.] a person with a particular ability or availability as a sexual partner. **3** the laying of eggs or the period during which they are laid.

– PHRASES **lay something at someone's door** see DOOR. **lay claim to something** assert that one has a right to something. ■ assert that one possesses a skill or quality: *she has never laid claim to medical knowledge.* **lay down the law** see LAW. **lay eyes on** see EYE. **lay hands on 1** find and take possession of. **2** place one's hands on or over, esp. in confirmation, ordination, or spiritual healing. **lay** (or **put**) **one's hands on** find and acquire: *every book I could lay my hands on.* **lay hold of** (or **on**) catch at with one's hands. ■ gain possession of. **lay it on the line** see LINE[1]. **the lay of the land** the way in which the features or characteristics of an area present themselves. ■ fig. the current situation or state of affairs. **lay someone low** (of an illness) reduce someone to inactivity. ■ bring to an end the high position or good fortune formerly enjoyed by someone. **lay something on the table** see TABLE. **lay something on thick** (or **with a trowel**) informal grossly exaggerate or overemphasize something. **lay someone open to** expose someone to the risk of (something). **lay over** break one's journey. **lay siege to** see SIEGE. **lay store by** see STORE. **lay someone/something to rest** bury a body in a grave. ■ soothe and dispel fear, anxiety, grief, or a similar unpleasant emotion. **lay something (to) waste** see WASTE.

– PHRASAL VERBS **lay something aside** put something to one side. ■ keep business to deal with later. ■ reserve money for the future or for a particular cause. ■ give up a practice or attitude. **lay something down 1** put something that one has been holding on the ground or another surface. ■ give up the use or enjoyment of something: *they laid down their arms.* ■ sacrifice one's life in a noble cause. **2** formulate and enforce or insist on a rule or principle: *stringent criteria have been laid down.* **3** set something in position for use on the ground or a surface. ■ establish something in or on the ground. ■ begin to construct a ship or railroad. ■ (usu. **be laid down**) build up a deposit of a substance: *these cells lay down new bone tissue.* **4** store wine in a cellar. **5** pay or wager money. **lay something in/up** build up a stock of something in case of need. **lay into** informal attack violently with words or blows. **lay off** informal give up. ■ [usu. in imper.] used to advise someone to stop doing something. **lay someone off** discharge a worker, esp. temporarily because of a shortage of work. **lay someone out 1** prepare someone for burial after death. **2** informal knock someone unconscious. **lay something out** spread something out to its full extent, esp. so that it can be seen.

lay[2] ▶ **adj.** [attrib.] **1** not of the clergy: *a lay preacher.* **2** not having professional qualifications or expert knowledge. [ME: from OFr. *lai*, via late L. from Gk. *laïkos*, from *laos* 'people.' Cf. LAIC.]

lay[3] ▶ **n.** a short lyric or narrative poem that is sung. ■ literary a song. [ME: from OFr. *lai*.]

lay[4] past of LIE[1].

lay•a•bout /ˈlāə,bout/ ▶ **n.** derog. a person who habitually does little or no work.

lay•a•way /ˈlāə,wā/ ▶ **n.** (also **layaway plan**) a system of paying a deposit to secure an item for later purchase.

lay broth•er ▶ **n.** a man who has taken the vows of a religious order but is not ordained or obliged to take part in the full cycle of liturgy.

lay•er /ˈlāər/ ▶ **n. 1** a sheet, quantity, or thickness of material, typically one of several, covering a surface. ■ a level of seniority in the hierarchy of an organization: *a managerial layer.* **2** [in comb.] a person or thing that lays something. ■ a hen that lays eggs. **3** a shoot fastened down to take root while attached to the parent plant. ▶ **v.** [trans.] [often as adj.] (**layered**) **1** arrange in a layer or layers: *the current trend for layered clothes.* ■ cut (hair) in overlapping layers. **2** propagate (a plant) as a layer: *a layered shoot.* [ME (denoting a mason): from LAY[1] + -ER[1].]

lay•er cake ▶ **n.** a cake of two or more layers with icing or another filling between them.

lay•er•ing /ˈlāəriNG/ ▶ **n. 1** the action of arranging something in layers. ■ Geol. the presence or formation of layers in sedimentary or igneous rock. **2** the method or activity of propagating a plant by producing layers.

lay•ette /lāˈet/ ▶ **n.** a set of clothing for a newborn child. [19th C.: from Fr., dimin. of OFr. *laie* 'drawer,' from MDu. *laege*.]

lay fig•ure ▶ **n.** a dummy or jointed manikin of a human body used by artists when a live model is not available. [18th C.: from obsolete *layman*, from Du. *leeman*, from obs. *led*, earlier form of *lid* 'joint.']

lay figure

lay•man /ˈlāmən/ ▶ **n.** (pl. **-men**) **1** a nonordained member of a church. **2** a person without professional or specialized knowledge in a particular subject.

lay•off /ˈlā,ôf; -,äf/ ▶ **n. 1** a discharge, esp. temporary, of a worker or workers. ■ a period when this is in force. **2** a period during which someone does not take part in a customary sport or other activity.

La'youn /läˈyo͞on/ (also **Laa•youne**) the capital of Western Sahara; pop. 97,000. Arabic name EL AAIÚN.

lay•out /ˈlā,out/ ▶ **n.** the way in which the parts of something are arranged or laid out. ■ the way in which text or pictures are set out on a page. ■ the process of setting out material on a page or in a work. ■ a thing arranged in a particular way.

lay•o•ver /ˈlā,ōvər/ ▶ **n.** a period of rest or waiting before a further stage in a journey.

lay•per•son /ˈlā,pərsən/ ▶ **n.** (pl. **lay•peo•ple**) a nonordained member of a church. ■ a person without professional or specialized knowledge in a particular subject.

lay read•er ▶ **n.** (in the Anglican Church) a layperson licensed to preach and to conduct some religious services, but not licensed to celebrate the Eucharist.

lay sis•ter ▶ **n.** a woman who has taken the vows of a religious order but is not ordained or obliged to take part in the full cycle of liturgy.

lay•up /ˈlāəp/ ▶ **n. 1** Basketball a one-handed shot made from near the basket. **2** (also **lay-up**) the state or action of something, esp. a ship, being laid up.

lay•wom•an /ˈlā,wo͝omən/ ▶ **n.** (pl. **-wom•en**) a nonordained female member of a church.

laz•ar /ˈlazər; ˈlāzər/ ▶ **n.** archaic a poor and diseased person, esp. one afflicted with leprosy. [ME: from med. L. *lazarus*, with biblical allusion to *Lazarus*, the name of a beggar covered in sores (Luke 16:20).]

laz•a•rette /,lazəˈret/ (also **laz•a•ret**) ▶ **n. 1** a small compartment below the deck in the after end of a vessel. **2** a lazaretto. [17th C.: from Fr. *lazaret*, from Ital. *lazaretto* (see LAZARETTO).]

laz•a•ret•to /,lazəˈretō/ ▶ **n.** (pl. **-tos**) esp. hist. an isolation hospital for people with infectious diseases. ■ a building (or ship) used for quarantine. ■ a military or prison hospital. [16th C.: from Ital., dimin. of *lazzaro* 'beggar,' from med. L. *lazarus* (see LAZAR).]

Laz•a•rus /ˈlazərəs/, Emma (1849–87) US poet. She wrote "The New Colossus" (1883), which is carved on the pedestal of the Statue of Liberty.

laze /lāz/ ▶ **v.** [intrans.] spend time in a lazy manner. ■ [trans.] (**laze something away**) pass time in such a way: *we watched movies and basically lazed the day away.* ▶ **n.** [in sing.] a spell of acting in such a way. [16th C.: back-form. from LAZY.]

laz•u•li /ˈlaz(y)ə,lī; ˈlazHə-; -lē/ ▶ **n.** short for LAPIS LAZULI.

laz•u•lite /ˈlazyo͞o,līt; ˈlazə-/ ▶ **n.** an azure-blue mineral, $(FeMg)A_{12}P_2O_8(OH)_2$, with a glasslike luster.

laz•u•rite /ˈlaz(y)ə,rīt; ˈlazHə-/ ▶ **n.** a bright blue mineral that is the main constituent of lapis lazuli.

la·zy /ˈlāzē/ ▶ **adj.** (**la·zi·er, la·zi·est**) **1** unwilling to work or use energy: *he was too lazy to cook.* ■ characterized by lack of effort or activity. ■ showing a lack of effort or care. ■ (of a river) slow-moving. **2** (of a livestock brand) placed on its side rather than upright: *an E with a lazy E.* — **la·zi·ly** /-zəlē/ **adv.** **la·zi·ness n.** [16th C.: perh. rel. to Low Ger. *lasich* 'languid, idle.']

la·zy·bones /ˈlāzēˌbōnz/ ▶ **n.** (pl. same) informal a lazy person (often as a form of address).

la·zy dai·sy stitch ▶ **n.** an embroidery stitch in the form of a flower petal. See illustration at EMBROIDERY.

la·zy eye ▶ **n.** an eye with poor vision.

la·zy Su·san /ˈsōōzən/ ▶ **n.** a revolving stand or tray on a table, used esp. for holding condiments.

la·zy tongs ▶ **n.** a set of extending tongs for grasping objects at a distance, with several connected pairs of levers pivoted like scissors.

lb. ▶ **abbr.** pound(s) (in weight). [from L. *libra*.]

LBO ▶ **abbr.** leveraged buyout.

LC ▶ **abbr.** ■ landing craft. ■ Library of Congress.

L/C (also **l.c.**) ▶ **abbr.** letter of credit.

l.c. ▶ **abbr.** ■ in the passage cited. [from L. *loco citato*.] ■ letter of credit. ■ lowercase.

LCD ▶ **abbr.** ■ Electron. & Comput. liquid crystal display. ■ Math. lowest (or least) common denominator.

LCL ▶ **abbr.** less-than-carload lot.

LCM Math. ▶ **abbr.** lowest (or least) common multiple.

LCpl ▶ **abbr.** lance corporal.

LCS ▶ **abbr.** ■ landing craft support. ■ liquid crystal shutter.

LCT ▶ **abbr.** ■ land conservation trust. ■ landing craft, tank. ■ local civil time.

LD ▶ **abbr.** ■ learning disabled. ■ lethal dose (of a toxic compound, drug, or pathogen). It is usually written with a following numeral indicating the percentage of a group of animals or cultured cells or microorganisms killed by such a dose, typically standardized at 50 percent (**LD_{50}**).

Ld. ▶ **abbr.** Lord: *Ld. Lothian.*

ld. ▶ **abbr.** ■ lead. ■ load.

LDC ▶ **abbr.** less-developed country.

LDL Biochem. ▶ **abbr.** low-density lipoprotein.

L-do·pa /ˈel ˈdōpə/ ▶ **n.** Biochem. the levorotatory form of dopa, used to treat Parkinson's disease. Also called LEVODOPA.

LDS ▶ **abbr.** Latter-Day Saints.

LE ▶ **abbr.** language engineering.

-le¹ ▶ **suffix** **1** forming names of appliances or instruments: *bridle* | *thimble.* **2** forming names of animals and plants: *beetle.* [OE, of Gmc. origin.]

-le² (also **-el**) ▶ **suffix** forming nouns having or originally having a diminutive sense: *mantle* | *battle* | *castle.* [ME *-el, -elle,* partly from OE and partly from OFr. (based on L. forms).]

-le³ ▶ **suffix** (forming adjectives from an original verb) apt to; liable to: *brittle* | *nimble.* [ME: from earlier *-el,* of Gmc. origin.]

-le⁴ ▶ **suffix** forming verbs, chiefly those expressing repeated action or movement (as in *babble, dazzle*), or having diminutive sense (as in *nestle*). [OE *-lian,* of Gmc. origin.]

lea /lē/ ▶ **n.** literary an open area of grassy or arable land: *the lowing herd winds slowly o'er the lea.* [OE *lēa(h)*; rel. to Old High Ger. *loh* 'grove,' L. *lucus* 'grove.']

lea. ▶ **abbr.** league.

leach /lēcн/ ▶ **v.** [trans.] make (a soluble chemical or mineral) drain away from soil, ash, or similar material by the action of percolating liquid, esp. rainwater. ■ [intrans.] (of a soluble chemical or mineral) drain away from soil in this way. ■ [trans.] subject (soil) to this process. [OE *leccan* 'to water,' of West Gmc. origin.]

leach·ate /ˈlēˌcнāt/ ▶ **n.** tech. water that has percolated through a solid and leached out some of the constituents.

lead¹ /lēd/ ▶ **v.** (past and past part. **led** /led/) [trans.] **1** cause (a person or animal) to go with one by holding them by the hand, a halter, a rope, etc., while moving forward: *she emerged leading a bay horse.* ■ [trans.] show (someone or something) the way to a destination by going in front of or beside them. ■ [intrans.] be a route or means of access to a particular place or in a particular direction. ■ [intrans.] (**lead to**) culminate in (a particular event). ■ (**lead something through**) cause a liquid or easily moving matter to pass through (a channel). **2** be in charge or command of: *led by the Chief of Staff.* ■ organize and direct. ■ set (a process) in motion. ■ be the principal player of (a group of musicians). ■ [intrans.] (**lead with**) assign the most important position to (a particular news item). **3** be superior to (competitors or colleagues). ■ have the first place in (a competition); be ahead of (competitors). ■ [intrans.] have the advantage in a race or game. **4** have or experience (a particular way of life): *she leads a sheltered life.* **5** initiate (action in a game or contest), in particular: ■ (in card games) play (the first card) in a trick or round of play. ■ [intrans.] (**lead with**) Boxing make an attack with (a particular punch or fist). ■ [intrans.] Baseball (of a base runner) advance one or more steps from the base one occupies while the pitcher has the ball. ▶ **n.** **1** the initiative in an action; an example for others to follow. ■ a clue to be followed in the resolution of a problem: *detectives are following new leads.* ■ (in card games) an act or right of playing first in a trick or round of play. ■ the card played first in a trick or round. **2** (**the lead**) first place. ■ an amount by which a competitor is ahead of the others. ■ Baseball an advance of one or more steps taken by a base runner from the base they occupy while the pitcher has the ball. **3** the chief part in a play or film. ■ the person playing the chief part: *a romantic lead.* ■ [usu. as adj.] the chief performer or instrument of a specified type. ■ [often as adj.] the item of news given the greatest prom-inence in a newspaper or magazine. **4** esp. Brit. a dog's leash. **5** a wire that conveys electric current from a source to an appliance, or that connects two points of a circuit. **6** the distance advanced by a screw in one turn. **7** a channel, in particular an artificial watercourse leading to a mill.

– PHRASES **lead someone astray** cause someone to act or think foolishly or wrongly. **lead someone by the nose** informal control someone totally, esp. by deceiving them. **lead from the front** take an active role in what one is urging and directing others to do. **lead someone up** (or **down**) **the garden path** informal give someone misleading clues or signals. **lead the way** see WAY. **lead with one's chin** informal (of a boxer) leave one's chin unprotected. ■ fig. behave or speak incautiously.

– PHRASAL VERBS **lead off** **1** start. ■ Baseball bat first in a game or inning. **2** (of a door, room, or path) provide access away from a central space. **lead someone on** mislead or deceive someone, esp. into believing that one is in love with or attracted to them. **lead up to** immediately precede. ■ result in. [OE *lǣdan,* of Gmc. origin; rel. to Du. *leiden* and Ger. *leiten,* also to LOAD and LODE.]

lead² /led/ ▶ **n.** **1** a heavy, bluish-gray, soft, ductile metal, the chemical element of atomic number 82. (Symbol: **Pb**) **2** an item or implement made of lead, in particular: ■ Naut. a lead casting suspended on a line to determine the depth of water. ■ bullets. **3** graphite used as the part of a pencil that makes a mark. **4** Print. a blank space between lines of print. [orig. with ref. to the metal strip used to create this space.]

– PHRASES **get the lead out** informal move or work more quickly. [OE *lēad,* of West Gmc. origin; rel. to Du. *lood* 'lead' and Ger. *Lot* 'plummet, solder.']

lead ar·ti·cle /lēd/ ▶ **n.** the principal article in a newspaper or magazine.

lead bal·loon /led/ ▶ **n.** (in phrase **go over like a lead balloon**) (of something said or written) be poorly received.

lead crys·tal /led/ ▶ **n.** another term for LEAD GLASS.

lead·ed /ˈledid/ ▶ **adj.** **1** (of windowpanes or a roof) framed, covered, or weighted with lead. **2** (of gasoline) containing tetraethyl lead: *leaded fuel.* **3** (of type) having the lines separated by leads.

lead·en /ˈledn/ ▶ **adj.** dull, heavy, or slow. ■ of the color of lead; dull gray. — **lead·en·ly adv.**

lead·er /ˈlēdər/ ▶ **n.** **1** the person who leads or commands a group, organization, or country. ■ a person followed by others. ■ an organization or company that is the most advanced or successful in a particular area. ■ the horse placed at the front in a team or pair. **2** the principal player in a music group. ■ a conductor of a band or small musical group. **3** a short strip of nonfunctioning material at each end of a reel of film or recording tape for connection to the spool. ■ a length of filament attached to the end of a fishing line to carry the hook or fly. **4** a shoot of a plant at the apex of a stem or main branch. **5** (**leaders**) Print. a series of dots or dashes across the page to guide the eye, esp. in tabulated material.

lead·er board ▶ **n.** a scoreboard showing the names and current scores of the leading competitors, esp. in a golf tournament.

lead·er·ship /ˈlēdərˌsнip/ ▶ **n.** the action of leading a group of people or an organization. ■ the state or position of being a leader. ■ [treated as sing. or pl.] the leaders of an organization, country, etc. ■ the ability to lead skillfully.

lead foot /led/ ▶ **n.** [in sing.] informal used to refer to someone's habit or practice of driving too quickly.

lead-foot·ed /led/ ▶ **adj.** informal **1** slow; clumsy. **2** tending to drive too quickly.

lead glass /led/ ▶ **n.** glass containing a substantial proportion of lead oxide. Also called LEAD CRYSTAL.

lead-in /ˈlēd ˌin/ ▶ **n.** **1** an introduction or preamble that allows one to move smoothly on to the next part. **2** a wire leading in from outside, esp. from an antenna.

lead·ing¹ /ˈlēdiNG/ ▶ **adj.** [attrib.] most important: *leading politicians.*

lead·ing² /ˈlediNG/ ▶ **n.** the amount of blank space between lines of print.

lead·ing ec·o·nom·ic in·di·ca·tor ▶ **n.** a variable that reflects current economic conditions and can suggest future trends in the nation's economy.

lead·ing edge /ˈlēdiNG/ ▶ **n.** the front edge of something, in particular: ■ Aeron. the foremost edge of an airfoil, esp. a wing or propeller blade. ■ Electron. the part of a pulse in which the amplitude increases. ■ the forefront or vanguard, esp. of technological development.

lead·ing la·dy /ˈlēdiNG/ ▶ **n.** the actress playing the principal female part.

lead·ing light /ˈlēdiNG/ ▶ **n.** a person who is prominent or influential in a particular field or organization.

lead·ing man /ˈlēdiNG/ ▶ **n.** the actor playing the principal male part.

lead·ing note /ˈlēdiNG/ ▶n. Music another term for SUBTONIC.

lead·ing ques·tion /ˈlēdiNG/ ▶n. a question that prompts or encourages the desired answer.

lead·ing tone /ˈlēdiNG/ ▶n. Music another term for SUBTONIC.

lead-off /ˈlēd/ ▶adj. (of an action) beginning a series or a process: *the album's lead-off track.* ■ (**lead·off**) Baseball denoting the first batter in a lineup or of an inning.

lead poi·son·ing /led/ ▶n. poisoning from the absorption of lead into the body. Also called PLUMBISM.

lead shot /led/ ▶n. another term for SHOT[1] (sense 3).

lead tet·ra·eth·yl /led/ ▶n. Chem. another term for TETRAETHYL LEAD.

lead time /lēd/ ▶n. the time between the initiation and completion of a production process.

lead-up /lēd/ ▶n. [in sing.] an event, point, or sequence that leads up to something else.

Lead·ville /ˈled,vil/ a historic mining city in central Colorado, the highest US city at 10,190 feet (3,108 m); pop. 2,821.

lead·wort /ˈled,wərt; -,wôrt/ ▶n. another term for PLUMBAGO (sense 2).

leaf /lēf/ ▶n. (pl. **leaves** /lēvz/) **1** a flattened structure of a higher plant, typically green and bladelike, that is attached to a stem directly or via a stalk. Compare with COMPOUND LEAF, LEAFLET. ■ any of a number of similar plant structures, e.g., bracts, sepals, and petals. ■ foliage regarded collectively. ■ the state of having leaves. ■ the leaves of tobacco or tea. **2** a thing that resembles a leaf in being flat and thin, typically something that is one of two or more similar items forming a set or stack. ■ a single thickness of paper, esp. in a book with each side forming a page. ■ [with adj.] gold, silver, or other metal in the form of very thin foil. ■ the hinged part or flap of a door, shutter, or table. ■ an extra section inserted to extend a table. ■ the inner or outer part of a cavity wall or double-glazed window. ■ any of the stacked metal strips that form a leaf spring. ▶v. [intrans.] **1** (of a plant, esp. a deciduous one in spring) put out new leaves. **2** (**leaf through**) turn over (the pages of a book or the papers in a pile), reading them quickly or casually.
– PHRASES **shake** (or **tremble**) **like a leaf** (of a person) tremble greatly, esp. from fear. **take a leaf out of someone's book** see BOOK. **turn over a new leaf** see TURN. — **leaf·age** /ˈlēfij/ n. [OE *lēaf*, of Gmc. origin; rel. to Du. *loof* and Ger. *Laub.*]

lobed

toothed

clasping

ovate

lanceolate

basal

alternate

opposite

pinnate

palmate

leaves

leaf bee·tle ▶n. a small beetle (family Chrysomelidae) that feeds chiefly on leaves and typically has bright metallic coloring. Some kinds are serious crop pests.

leaf curl ▶n. a plant condition distinguished by the presence of curling leaves.

leafed /ˈlēft/ ▶adj. another term for LEAVED.

leaf fat ▶n. dense fat occurring in layers around the kidneys of some animals, esp. pigs.

leaf·hop·per /ˈlēf,häpər/ ▶n. a small plant bug (family Cicadellidae, suborder Homoptera) that is typically brightly colored and leaps when disturbed. It can be a serious crop pest.

leaf in·sect ▶n. a large, slow-moving tropical insect (*Phyllium* and other genera, family Phylliidae) related to the stick insects, with a flattened body that is leaflike in shape and color.

leaf·let /ˈlēflit/ ▶n. **1** a printed sheet of paper, sometimes folded, containing information or advertising. **2** Bot. each of the leaflike structures that together make up a compound leaf. ■ (in general use) a young leaf.

leaf lit·ter ▶n. see LITTER (sense 3).

leaf min·er ▶n. a small fly, moth, beetle, or sawfly whose larvae burrow between the two surfaces of a leaf.

leaf mold (also **leaf·mold**) ▶n. **1** soil consisting chiefly of decayed leaves. **2** a disease of plants in which mold develops on the leaves, caused by the fungus *Fulvia fulva.*

leaf-nosed bat ▶n. a bat (families Hipposideridae and Phyllostomatidae) with a leaflike appendage on the snout.

leaf spot ▶n. [usu. with adj.] any of a large number of fungal, bacterial, or viral plant diseases that cause leaves to develop discolored spots.

leaf spring ▶n. a spring made of a number of strips of metal curved slightly upward and clamped together one above the other.

leaf·stalk /ˈlēf,stôk/ ▶n. a petiole.

leaf·y /ˈlēfē/ ▶adj. (**leaf·i·er, leaf·i·est**) (of a plant) having many leaves. ■ having or characterized by much foliage because of an abundance of trees or bushes. ■ (of a plant) producing or grown for its broad-bladed leaves. ■ resembling a leaf or leaves. — **leaf·i·ness** n.

league[1] /lēg/ ▶n. **1** a collection of people, countries, or groups that combine for a particular purpose. ■ an agreement to combine in this way. **2** a group of sports clubs that play each other over a period for a championship. ■ the contest for the championship of such a league. **3** a class or category of quality or excellence. ▶v. (**leagues, leagued, lea·guing**) [intrans.] join in a league or alliance.
– PHRASES **in league** conspiring with another or others. [ME: via Fr. from Ital. *lega*, from *legare* 'to bind,' from L. *ligare*.]

league[2] ▶n. a former measure of distance by land, usually about three miles. [ME: from late L. *leuga, leuca*, late Gk. *leugē*, or from Provençal *lega* (mod. Fr. *lieue*).]

League of Na·tions an association of countries established in 1919 by the Treaty of Versailles to promote international cooperation and achieve international peace and security. It was replaced by the United Nations in 1945.

lea·guer /ˈlēgər/ ▶n. [with adj.] a member of a particular league, esp. a sports player: *a minor leaguer.*

leak /lēk/ ▶v. [intrans.] (of a container or covering) accidentally lose or admit contents, esp. liquid or gas, through a hole or crack. ■ [with adverbial of direction] (of liquid, gas, etc.) pass in or out through a hole or crack in such a way. ■ fig. (of secret information) become known. ■ [trans.] intentionally disclose (secret information). ▶n. a hole in a container or covering through which contents, esp. liquid or gas, may accidentally pass. ■ the action of leaking in such a way: *a gas leak.* ■ a similar escape of electric charge or current. ■ an intentional disclosure of secret information.
– PHRASES **take a leak** informal urinate. — **leak·er** n. [ME: prob. of Low Ger. or Du. origin and rel. to LACK.]

leak·age /ˈlēkij/ ▶n. the accidental admission or escape of a fluid or gas through a hole or crack. ■ Physics the gradual escape of an electric charge or current, or magnetic flux. ■ deliberate disclosure of confidential information.

Lea·key /ˈlēkē/ a family of Kenyan archaeologists and anthropologists. Louis Seymour Bazett (1903–72), born in Kenya, pioneered the investigation of human origins in East Africa. He began excavations at Olduvai Gorge. His wife Mary Douglas (1913–96), born in England, discovered *Homo habilis* and *Homo erectus* at Olduvai in 1960. Their son Richard Erskine (1944–) directed the Kenya Wildlife Service 1989–94.

leak·proof /ˈlēk,pro͞of/ ▶adj. designed or constructed to prevent leakage.

leak·y /ˈlēkē/ ▶adj. (**leak·i·er, leak·i·est**) having a leak or leaks: *a leaky roof.* — **leak·i·ness** n.

lean[1] /lēn/ ▶v. (past and past part. **leaned** /lēnd/ or esp. Brit. **leant** /lent/) [intrans.] be in or move into a sloping position: *he leaned back in his chair.* ■ (**lean against/on**) incline from the perpendicular and rest for support on or against (something). ■ [trans.] (**lean something against/on**) cause something to rest on or against. ▶n. a deviation from the perpendicular; an inclination.
– PHRASAL VERBS **lean on 1** rely on or derive support from. **2** put pressure on (someone) to act in a certain way. **lean to/towards** incline or be partial to (a view or position): *I now lean toward sabotage as the cause.* [OE *hleonian, hlinian*; rel. to Ger. *lehnen*, L. *inclinare.*]

lean[2] ▶adj. **1** (of a person or animal) thin, esp. healthily so; having no superfluous fat. ■ (of meat) containing little fat. ■ (of an industry or company) efficient and with no waste. **2** (of an activity or a period of time) offering little reward, substance, or nourishment; meager. **3** (of a vaporized fuel mixture) having a high proportion of air: *lean air-to-fuel ratios.* ▶n. the lean part of meat. — **lean·ly** adv. **lean·ness** n. [OE *hlǣne*, of Gmc. origin.]

Le·an·der /lēˈandər/ Gk. Mythol. a young man, the lover of the priestess Hero.

lean·ing /ˈlēniNG/ ▶n. (often **leanings**) a tendency or partiality of a particular kind.

lean-to ▶n. (pl. **-tos**) a building sharing one wall with a larger building, with a roof leaning against that wall. ■ a temporary shelter, either supported or freestanding.

leap /lēp/ ▶v. (past or past part. **leaped** /lēpt/ or **leapt** /lept/) [intrans.] jump or spring a long way, to a great height, or with great force. ■ move quickly and suddenly. ■ [trans.] jump across or over. ■ make a sudden rush to do something; act eagerly and suddenly: *leap into action.* ■ (**leap at**) accept (an opportunity) eagerly. ■ (of a price or figure) increase dramatically. ■ (**leap out**) (esp. of writing) be conspicuous; stand out. ▶n. a forceful jump or quick movement. ■ a dramatic increase in price, amount, etc. ■ a sudden, abrupt change or transition. ■ [in place names] a thing to be leaped over or from: *Lover's Leap.*
– PHRASES **a leap in the dark** a daring step or enterprise whose consequences are unpredictable. **by** (or **in**) **leaps and bounds** with startlingly rapid progress. **leap to the eye** (or **to mind**) be immediately

apparent. — **leap·er** n. [OE *hlēapan* (verb), *hlȳp* (n.); rel. to Ger. *laufen* (v.) 'run,' also to LOPE.]

leap day ▶ n. the intercalary day in a leap year; February 29.

leap·frog /ˈlēp,frôg; -,fräg/ ▶ n. a game in which players in turn vault over others who are bending down. ▶ v. (**-frogged**, **-frog·ging**) [intrans.] perform such a vault. ■ [intrans.] (of a person or group) surpass or overtake another to move into a leading or dominant position: *she leapfrogged into a sales position.* ■ [trans.] pass over (a stage or obstacle).

leap sec·ond ▶ n. a second that is occasionally inserted into the atomic scale of reckoning time in order to bring it into line with solar time.

leap year ▶ n. a year, occurring once every four years, that has 366 days including February 29 as an intercalary day.

Lear[1] /li(ə)r/ a legendary early king of Britain, the central figure in Shakespeare's tragedy *King Lear*.

Lear[2], Edward (1812–88), English humorist and illustrator. He wrote *A Book of Nonsense* (1845) and *Laughable Lyrics* (1877).

learn /lərn/ ▶ v. (past **learned** /lərnd/ or esp. Brit. **learnt** /lərnt/) [trans.] gain or acquire knowledge of or skill in (something) by study, experience, or being taught. ■ commit to memory. ■ become aware of (something) by information or from observation.
– PHRASES **learn one's lesson** see LESSON. — **learn·a·bil·i·ty** /,lərnəˈbilətē/ n. **learn·a·ble** adj. **learn·er** n. [OE *leornian* 'learn' (in ME also 'teach'), of West Gmc. origin; rel. to Ger. *lernen*, also to LORE[1].]

learn·ed /ˈlərnid/ ▶ adj. (of a person) having much knowledge acquired by study. ■ showing, requiring, or characterized by learning; scholarly: *an article in a learned journal.* — **learn·ed·ly** /-nidlē/ adv. **learn·ed·ness** /-nidnis/ n.

learn·fare /ˈlərn,fe(ə)r/ ▶ n. a public assistance program in which attendance at school, college, or a training program is necessary to receive benefits.

learn·ing /ˈlərniNG/ ▶ n. the acquisition of knowledge or skills through experience, practice, or study, or by being taught. ■ knowledge acquired in this way.

learn·ing curve ▶ n. the rate of a person's progress in gaining experience or new skills.

learn·ing dis·a·bil·i·ty ▶ n. a condition giving rise to difficulties in acquiring knowledge and skills to the normal level expected of those of the same age. — **learn·ing-dis·a·bled** adj.
– USAGE The phrase **learning disability** became prominent in the 1980s. It is broad in scope, covering general conditions such as Down syndrome as well as more specific cognitive or neurological conditions such as dyslexia and attention deficit disorder. In emphasizing the difficulty experienced rather than any perceived 'deficiency,' it is considered less discriminatory and more positive than other terms such as **mentally handicapped**, and is now the standard accepted term in official contexts. See also usage at HANDICAPPED.

lease /lēs/ ▶ n. a contract by which one party conveys land, property, services, etc., to another for a specified time, usually in return for a periodic payment. ▶ v. [trans.] grant (property) on lease; let. ■ take (property) on lease; rent.
– PHRASES **a new lease on life** a substantially improved chance to lead a happy or successful life. — **leas·a·ble** adj. [ME: from OFr. *lais, leis*, from *lesser, laissier* 'let, leave,' from L. *laxare* 'make loose,' from *laxus* 'loose, lax.']

lease·back /ˈlēs,bak/ ▶ n. [often as adj.] the leasing of a property back to the vendor.

lease·hold /ˈlēs,hōld/ ▶ n. the holding of property by lease. Often contrasted with FREEHOLD. ■ a property held by lease. — **lease·hold·er** n.

leash /lēSH/ ▶ n. a strap or cord for restraining and guiding a dog or other domestic animal. ■ Falconry a thong or string attached to the jesses of a hawk, used for tying it to a perch. ■ fig. a restraint. ▶ v. [trans.] put a leash on (a dog). ■ fig. restrain. [ME: from OFr. *lesse, laisse*, from *laissier* (see LEASE).]

least /lēst/ ▶ adj. & pron. (usu. **the least**) smallest in amount, extent, or significance. ▶ adj. used in names of very small animals and plants, e.g., **least shrew**. ▶ adv. to the smallest extent or degree.
– PHRASES **at least 1** not less than; at the minimum. **2** if nothing else (used to add a positive comment about a generally negative situation). **3** anyway (used to modify something just stated): *they seldom complained — officially at least.* **at the least** (or **very least**) **1** (used after amounts) not less than; at the minimum. **2** taking the most pessimistic or unfavorable view. **not in the least** not in the smallest degree; not at all. **to say the least** used as an understatement (implying the reality is more extreme, usually worse). [OE *lǣst, lǣsest*, of Gmc. origin; rel. to LESS.]

least com·mon de·nom·i·na·tor ▶ n. another term for LOWEST COMMON DENOMINATOR.

least com·mon mul·ti·ple ▶ n. another term for LOWEST COMMON MULTIPLE.

least sig·nif·i·cant bit (abbr.: **LSB**) ▶ n. Comput. the bit of the lowest numerical value in a binary number.

least squares ▶ n. a method of estimating a quantity or fitting a graph to data so as to minimize the sum of the squares of the differences between the observed values and the estimated values.

least·ways /ˈlēst,wāz/ (also **least·wise** /-,wīz/) ▶ adv. dialect informal at least.

leath·er /ˈleT͟Hər/ ▶ n. **1** a material made from the skin of an animal by tanning or a similar process. **2** a thing made of leather, in particular: ■ a piece of leather as a polishing cloth. ■ (**leathers**) leather clothes, esp. those worn by a motorcyclist. ▶ adj. informal of, relating to, or catering to people who wear leather clothing and accessories as a sign of rough masculinity, esp. homosexuals who practice sadomasochistic sex. ▶ v. [trans.] **1** [usu. as adj.] (**leathered**) cover with leather. **2** beat or thrash (someone): *he leathered me black and blue* | [as n.] (**leathering**) *go, before you get a leathering.* [OE *lether*; rel. to Ger. *Leder*, Irish *leathar*.]

leath·er·back /ˈleT͟Hər,bak/ (also **leatherback turtle**) ▶ n. a very large black turtle (*Dermochelys coriacea*, family Dermochelyidae) with a thick leathery shell, living chiefly in tropical seas.

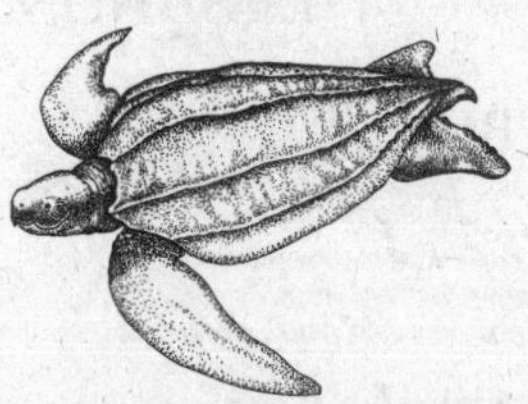

leatherback

leath·er carp ▶ n. a carp of a variety that lacks scales.

leath·er·ette /,leT͟Həˈret/ ▶ n. imitation leather.

leath·ern /ˈleT͟Hərn/ ▶ adj. [attrib.] archaic made of leather.

leath·er·neck /ˈleT͟Hər,nek/ ▶ n. informal a US marine.

leath·er·wood /ˈleT͟Hər,wo͝od/ ▶ n. **1** see TITI[2]. **2** a North American shrub (*Dirca palustris*, family Thymelaeaceae) with yellow flowers and very short leafstalks. Its tough, pliant bark was formerly used by American Indians for making baskets, fishing lines, and bowstrings.

leath·er·y /ˈleT͟H(ə)rē/ ▶ adj. having a tough, hard texture like leather. — **leath·er·i·ness** n.

leave[1] /lēv/ ▶ v. (past and past part. **left** /left/) **1** [trans.] go away from. ■ depart from permanently. ■ cease attending (a school or college) or working for (an organization). **2** [trans.] allow to remain. ■ (**be left**) remain to be used or dealt with. ■ [trans.] go away from a place without taking (someone or something). ■ abandon (a spouse or partner). ■ have as (a surviving relative) after one's death. ■ bequeath. **3** [trans.] cause (someone or something) to be in a particular state or position. ■ [trans.] let (someone) do or deal with something without offering help or assistance. ■ [trans.] cause to remain as a trace or record. ■ [trans.] deposit or entrust to be kept, collected, or attended to. ■ [trans.] (**leave something to**) entrust a decision, choice, or action to (someone else, esp. someone considered better qualified). ▶ n. (in pool, billiards, snooker, croquet, and other games) the position of the balls after a shot.
– PHRASES **be left at the post** be beaten from the start of a race or competition. **be left for dead** be abandoned as being almost dead or certain to die. **be left to oneself** be allowed to do what one wants. ■ be in the position of being alone or solitary. **leave someone/something alone** see ALONE. **leave someone be** informal refrain from disturbing or interfering with someone. **leave someone cold** fail to interest someone. **leave hold of** cease holding. **leave it at that** abstain from further comment or action. **leave much** (or **a lot**) **to be desired** be highly unsatisfactory.
– PHRASAL VERBS **leave off** discontinue (an activity). ■ come to an end. **leave something off** omit to put on. **leave someone/something out** fail to include. — **leav·er** n. [OE *lǣfan* 'bequeath,' also 'allow to remain, leave in place,' of Gmc. origin; rel. to Ger. *bleiben* 'remain.']

leave[2] ▶ n. **1** (also **leave of absence**) time when one has permission to be absent from work or from duty in the armed forces: *Joe was home on leave.* **2** [often with infin.] permission: *he is seeking leave.*
– PHRASES **by** (or **with**) **your leave** with your permission. **take one's leave** formal say goodbye. **take leave of one's senses** see SENSE. [OE *lēaf* 'permission,' of West Gmc. origin; rel. to LIEF and LOVE.]

leave[3] ▶ v. put forth leaves.

leaved /lēvd/ (also **leafed**) ▶ adj. [in comb.] having a leaf or leaves of a particular kind or number.

leav·en /ˈlevən/ ▶ n. a substance, typically yeast, that is added to dough to make it ferment and rise. ■ dough that is reserved from an earlier batch in order to start a later one fermenting. ■ fig. a pervasive influence that modifies something or transforms it for the better. ▶ v. [trans.] **1** [usu. as adj.] (**leavened**) cause (dough or bread) to ferment and rise by adding leaven. **2** permeate and modify or transform (something) for the better: *the proceedings should be leavened by humor* | [as n.] (**leavening**) *militia volunteers with a leavening of regular soldiers.* [ME: from OFr. *levain*, based on L. *levamen* 'relief' (lit. 'means of raising'), from *levare* 'to lift.']

leave of ab·sence ▶ n. see LEAVE[2] (sense 1).

leaves /lēvz/ plural form of LEAF.

leave-tak·ing ▶ n. an act of saying goodbye.

leav·ings /ˈlēviNGz/ ▶ plural n. things that have been left as worthless.

Leb·a·non /ˈlebəˌnän; -ˌnən/ a country in the Middle East. *See box.* — **Leb·a·nese** /ˌlebəˈnēz; -ˈnēs/ **adj. & n.**

Lebanon

Official name: Republic of Lebanon
Location: Middle East, with a western coastline on the Mediterranean Sea
Area: 4,000 square miles (10,400 sq km)
Population: 3,777,000
Capital: Beirut
Languages: Arabic (official), French, English, Armenian
Currency: Lebanese pound

Leb·a·non Moun·tains a range of mountains in Lebanon that runs parallel to the Mediterranean coast.

Le·bens·raum /ˈlābənsˌroum; -bənz-/ ▶ **n.** the territory believed needed for a nation's natural development. [Ger., lit. 'living space.']

Le·brun /ləˈbrœN/, Charles (1619–90), French painter and designer.

Le Car·ré /lə käˈrā/, John (1931–), English writer; pen name of *David John Moore Cornwell.* His spy novels featuring British agent George Smiley include *Tinker, Tailor, Soldier, Spy* (1974).

lech /lecH/ informal, derog. ▶ **n.** a lecher. ■ a lecherous urge or desire. ▶ **v.** [intrans.] act in a lecherous or lustful manner. [18th C.: back-form. from LECHER.]

lech·er /ˈlecHər/ ▶ **n.** a lecherous man. [ME: from OFr. *lichiere, lecheor,* from *lechier* 'live in debauchery or gluttony,' ult. of West Gmc. origin and rel. to LICK.]

lech·er·ous /ˈlecH(ə)rəs/ ▶ **adj.** having or showing excessive or offensive sexual desire. — **lech·er·ous·ly adv. lech·er·ous·ness n.**

lech·er·y /ˈlecH(ə)rē/ ▶ **n.** excessive or offensive sexual desire; lustfulness.

lech·u·guil·la /ˌlecHəˈgēə/ ▶ **n.** a succulent desert plant (*Agave lechuguilla*) of Mexico, with pointed basal leaves and a tall flower spike. It is a principal source of ixtle.

le·chwe /ˈlecHwē; -ˌwā/ ▶ **n.** (pl. same) a rough-coated grazing antelope (genus *Kobus*) with pointed hooves and long horns, found in swampy grassland in southern Africa and Sudan. [19th C.: from Setswana.]

lec·i·thin /ˈlesəTHin/ ▶ **n.** Biochem. a substance widely distributed in animal tissues, egg yolk, and some higher plants, consisting of phospholipids linked to choline. [19th C.: from Gk. *lekithos* 'egg yolk' + -IN[1].]

lec·i·thin·ase /ˈlesəTHiˌnās; -ˌnāz/ ▶ **n.** Biochem. another term for PHOSPHOLIPASE.

Le Cor·bu·sier /lə ˌkôrbəˈzyā; -byˈzyā/ (1887–1965), French architect and city planner; born in Switzerland; born *Charles Édouard Jeanneret.* He was a pioneer of the international style.

lect. ▶ **abbr.** lecture.

lec·tern /ˈlektərn/ ▶ **n.** a tall stand with a sloping top to hold a book or notes, and from which someone, typically a preacher or lecturer, can read while standing up. [ME: from OFr. *letrun,* from med. L. *lectrum,* from *legere* 'to read.']

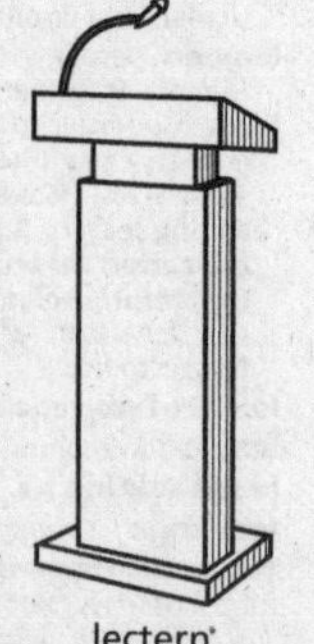
lectern

lec·tin /ˈlektin/ ▶ **n.** Biochem. any of a class of proteins that bind specifically to certain sugars and so cause agglutination of particular cell types. [1950s: from L. *lect-* 'chosen' (from the v. *legere*) + -IN[1].]

lec·tion·ar·y /ˈleksHəˌnerē/ ▶ **n.** (pl. **-ar·ies**) a list or book of portions of the Bible appointed to be read at a church service. [18th C.: from med. L. *lectionarium,* from L. *lect-* 'chosen, read,' from *legere.*]

lec·tor /ˈlektər; -ˌtôr/ ▶ **n. 1** a reader, esp. someone

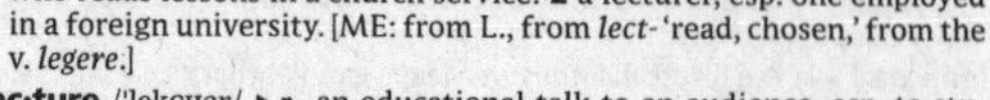
who reads lessons in a church service. **2** a lecturer, esp. one employed in a foreign university. [ME: from L., from *lect-* 'read, chosen,' from the v. *legere.*]

lec·ture /ˈlekcHər/ ▶ **n.** an educational talk to an audience, esp. to students in a university or college. ■ a long, serious speech, esp. one given as a reprimand. ▶ **v.** [intrans.] deliver an educational lecture or lectures. ■ [trans.] give a lecture to (a class or other audience). ■ [trans.] talk seriously or reprovingly to (someone). [ME: from OFr., or from med. L. *lectura,* from L. *lect-* 'read, chosen,' from *legere.*]

lec·tur·er /ˈlekcHərər/ ▶ **n.** a person who gives lectures, esp. as an occupation at a university or college.

lec·ture·ship /ˈlekcHərˌsHip/ ▶ **n.** a post as a lecturer.

LED ▶ **abbr.** light-emitting diode, a semiconductor diode that glows when a voltage is applied.

led /led/ past and past participle of LEAD[1].

Le·da /ˈlēdə/ Gk. Mythol. the wife of Tyndareus, king of Sparta. She was loved by Zeus, who visited her in the form of a swan; among her children were the Dioscuri, Helen, and Clytemnestra.

Led·bet·ter /ˈledˌbetər/, Huddie (1885–1949), US blues singer and composer; known as **Leadbelly**.

le·der·ho·sen /ˈlādərˌhōzən/ ▶ **plural n.** leather shorts with H-shaped suspenders, traditionally worn by men in Alpine regions such as Bavaria. [from Ger., from *Leder* 'leather' + *Hosen* 'trousers.']

ledge /lej/ ▶ **n. 1** a narrow horizontal surface projecting from a wall, cliff, or other surface. **2** an underwater ridge. **3** Mining a stratum of metal- or ore-bearing rock; a vein of quartz or other mineral. [ME: perh. from an early form of LAY[1].]

ledg·er /ˈlejər/ ▶ **n. 1** a book or other collection of financial accounts of a particular type. **2** a flat stone slab covering a grave. **3** a horizontal scaffolding pole, parallel to the face of the building. [ME *legger, ligger,* prob. from vars. of LAY[1] and LIE[1].]

ledg·er line (also **leg·er line**) ▶ **n.** Music a short line added for notes above or below the range of a staff.

Lee[1] /lē/, Ann (1736–84), American religious leader; born in England; known as **Mother Ann**. In Watervliet, New York, she founded the first American Shaker colony 1774.

Lee[2], Francis Lightfoot (1734–97), American statesman. A delegate to the Continental Congress 1775–79, he signed the Declaration of Independence 1776.

Lee[3], Gypsy Rose (1914–70), US entertainer; born *Rose Louise Hovick.* In the 1930s, she became famous on Broadway for her sophisticated striptease act.

Lee[4], Harper (1926–), US writer; full name *Nelle Harper Lee.* She wrote *To Kill a Mockingbird* (1960).

Lee[5], Henry (1756–1818), US soldier and politician; known as **Light-Horse Harry**; father of Robert E. Lee. He was governor of Virginia 1792–95 and a member of the US House of Representatives 1799–1801.

Lee[6], Robert E. (1807–70), Confederate general in the American Civil War; full name *Robert Edward Lee.* His invasion of the North was repulsed at the Battle of Gettysburg (1863), and he surrendered to Grant at Appomattox Court House in 1865.

lee /lē/ ▶ **n.** shelter from wind or weather given by a neighboring object, esp. nearby land. ■ (also **lee side**) the sheltered side; the side away from the wind. Contrasted with WEATHER. [OE *hlēo, hlēow* 'shelter,' of Gmc. origin; prob. rel. to *luke-* in LUKEWARM.]

lee·board /ˈlēˌbôrd/ ▶ **n.** a plate or board fixed to the side of a flat-bottomed boat and let down into the water to reduce drift to the leeward side.

leech[1] /lēcH/ ▶ **n. 1** an aquatic or terrestrial annelid (class Hirudinea) with suckers at both ends. Many species are bloodsucking parasites, esp. of vertebrates, and others are predators. **2** a person who extorts profit from or sponges on others. ▶ **v.** [intrans.] habitually exploit or rely on: *he's leeching off the abilities of others.* [OE *lǣce, lȳce*; rel. to MDu. *lake, lieke.*]

leech[2] ▶ **n.** Sailing the after or leeward edge of a fore-and-aft sail, the leeward edge of a spinnaker, or a vertical edge of a square sail. [15th C.: prob. of Scand. origin and rel. to Swed. *lik,* denoting a rope.]

Leeds /lēdz/ a city in northern England; pop. 674,000.

leek /lēk/ ▶ **n.** a plant (*Allium porrum*) of the lily family, closely related to the onion, with flat overlapping leaves forming an elongated cylindrical bulb that together with the leaf bases is eaten as a vegetable. [OE *lēac,* of Gmc. origin; rel. to Du. *look* and Ger. *Lauch.*]

leer /li(ə)r/ ▶ **v.** [intrans.] look or gaze in an unpleasant, malicious, or lascivious way. ▶ **n.** an unpleasant, malicious, or lascivious look. — **leer·ing·ly adv.** [16th C.: perh. from obs. *leer* 'cheek,' from OE *hlēor.*]

leer·y /ˈli(ə)rē/ ▶ **adj.** (**leer·i·er, leer·i·est**) cautious or wary due to realistic suspicions: *a city leery of gang violence.* — **leer·i·ness n.**

lees /lēz/ ▶ **plural n.** the sediment of wine in the barrel. ■ fig. dregs; refuse: *the lees of the underworld.* [ME: plural of obs. *lee* in the same sense, from OFr. *lie,* from med. L. *liae* (pl.), of Gaulish origin.]

lee shore ▶ **n.** a shore lying on the leeward side of a ship (and onto which a ship could be blown).

leet /lēt/ ▶ **n.** hist. (in England) a yearly or half-yearly court of record that the lords of certain manors held. ■ the jurisdiction of such a court. [ME: from Anglo-Norman Fr. *lete* or Anglo-L. *leta,* of unknown origin.]

Lee·u·wen·hoek /ˈlāvənˌho͝ok; ˈlāyən-/, Antoni van (1632–1723), Dutch naturalist. He developed a microscope lens for scientific purposes.

lee·ward /ˈlēwərd; ˈlo͞oərd/ ▶ **adj. & adv.** on or toward the side sheltered from the wind or toward which the wind is blowing; downwind. Contrasted with WINDWARD. ▶ **n.** the side sheltered or away from the wind.

Lee·ward Is·lands /ˈlēwərd/ a group of islands in the Caribbean Sea that constitutes the northern part of the Lesser Antilles, including Guadeloupe, Antigua, St. Kitts, and Montserrat.

lee·way /ˈlē,wā/ ▶ **n.** **1** the amount of freedom to move or act that is available. ■ margin of safety: *there is little leeway.* **2** the sideways drift of a ship or an aircraft to leeward of the desired course: *the leeway is only about 2°.*

left[1] /left/ ▶ **adj.** **1** on, toward, or relating to the side of a human body or of a thing that is to the west when the person or thing is facing north: *her left eye.* ■ denoting the side of something that is in an analogous position: *the left edge of the text.* ■ on this side from the point of view of a spectator. **2** (often **Left**) of or relating to a person or group favoring liberal, socialist, or radical views: *Left politics.* ▶ **adv.** on or to the left side: *turn left here | keep left.* ▶ **n.** **1** (**the left**) the left-hand part, side, or direction. ■ (in soccer or a similar sport) the left-hand half of the field when facing the opponents' goal. ■ (**left**) Baseball short for LEFT FIELD. ■ the left wing of an army. **2** (often **the Left**) [treated as sing. or pl.] a group or party favoring liberal, socialist, or radical views. ■ the section of a party or group holding such views more strongly: *he is on the left of the party.* **3** a thing on the left-hand side or done with the left hand, in particular: ■ a left turn. ■ a road, entrance, etc., on the left. ■ a person's left fist, esp. a boxer's. ■ a blow given with this.
– PHRASES **have two left feet** be clumsy or awkward. **left, right, and center** (also **left and right** or **right and left**) on all sides. — **left·ish** **adj.** [OE *lyft, left* 'weak,' of West Gmc. origin.]

left[2] past and past participle of LEAVE[1].

Left Bank a district of Paris, France, on the left bank of the Seine River.

left brain /ˈleft ,brān/ ▶ **n.** the left-hand side of the human brain, which is believed to be associated with linear and analytical thought.

left face ▶ **exclam.** (**left face!**) (in military contexts) a command to turn 90 degrees to the left.

left field ▶ **n.** Baseball the part of the outfield to the left of center field from the perspective of home plate. ■ the position of the defensive player stationed in left field. ■ fig. a position or direction that is surprising or unconventional. ■ fig. a position of ignorance, error, or confusion. — **left field·er** **n.**

left hand ▶ **n.** the hand of a person's left side. ■ the region on the left side of a person or thing. ▶ **adj.** [attrib.] on or toward the left side of a person or thing: *his left-hand pocket.* ■ done with or using the left hand.

left-hand·ed ▶ **adj.** **1** (of a person) using the left hand more naturally than the right: *a left-handed batter.* ■ (of a tool or item of equipment) made to be used with the left hand: *left-handed golf clubs.* ■ made or performed with the left hand: *my left-handed scrawl.* **2** turning to the left; toward the left, in particular: ■ (of a screw) advanced by turning counterclockwise. ■ Biol. (of a spiral shell or helix) sinistral. **3** perverse: *we take a left-handed pleasure in our errors.* ■ (esp. of a compliment) ambiguous. ▶ **adv.** with the left hand. — **left-hand·ed·ly** **adv.** **left-hand·ed·ness** **n.**

left-hand·er ▶ **n.** a left-handed person. ■ a blow struck with a person's left hand.

left·ie ▶ **n.** var. of LEFTY.

left·ist /ˈleftist/ ▶ **n.** a person who supports the political views or policies of the left. ▶ **adj.** supportive of the political views or policies of the left: *leftist radicals.* — **left·ism** /ˈleftizəm/ **n.**

left-lean·ing ▶ **adj.** sympathetic to or tending toward the left in politics: *a left-leaning professor.*

left·o·ver /ˈleft,ōvər/ ▶ **n.** (usu. **leftovers**) something, esp. food, remaining after the rest has been used. ▶ **adj.** [attrib.] remaining; surplus: *yesterday's leftover bread.*

left turn ▶ **n.** a turn that brings a person's front to face the way their left side did before.

left·ward /ˈleftwərd/ ▶ **adv.** (also **left·wards** /-wərdz/) toward the left. ▶ **adj.** going toward or facing the left.

left wing ▶ **n.** (**the left wing**) **1** the liberal, socialist, or radical section of a political party or system. **2** the left side of a team on the field in soccer, rugby, and field hockey: *his usual position on the left wing.* ■ the left side of an army: *the Allied left wing.* ▶ **adj.** liberal, socialist, or radical: *left-wing activists.* — **left-wing·er** **n.**

left·y /ˈleftē/ (also **left·ie**) ▶ **n.** (pl. **left·ies**) informal **1** a left-handed person. **2** a leftist.

leg /leg/ ▶ **n.** **1** each of the limbs on which a person or animal walks and stands: *Adams broke his leg.* ■ a leg of an animal or bird as food: *a roast leg of lamb.* ■ a part of a garment covering a leg or part of a leg: *his trouser leg.* **2** each of the supports of a chair, table, or other piece of furniture: *table legs.* ■ a long, thin support or prop: *the house was set on legs.* **3** a section or stage of a journey or process. ■ Sailing a run made on a single tack. ■ (in soccer and other sports) each of two games constituting a round of a competition. ■ a section of a relay or other race done in stages. ■ a single game in a darts match. **4** a branch of a forked object. ▶ **v.** (**legged** /ˈlegd/, **leg·ging**) [trans.] (**leg it**) informal travel by foot; walk. ■ run away: *he legged it after someone shouted at him.*
– PHRASES **feel** (or **find**) **one's legs** become able to stand or walk. **leg up** help to mount a horse or high object: *give me a leg up over the wall.* ■ help to improve one's position: *the council is to provide a financial leg up for the club.* **not have a leg to stand on** have no facts or sound reasons to support one's argument or justify one's actions. **on one's last legs** near the end of life, usefulness, or existence: *the foundry business was on its last legs.* — **leg·ged** /ˈlegid/ **adj.** [in comb.] *a four-legged animal.* **leg·ger** **n.** [in comb.] *a three-legger.* [ME: from ON *leggr* of Gmc. origin.]

leg. ▶ **abbr.** ■ legal. ■ legate. ■ Music legato. ■ legend. ■ legislation or legislative or legislature.

leg·a·cy /ˈlegəsē/ ▶ **n.** (pl. **-cies**) an amount of money or property left to someone in a will. ■ a thing handed down by a predecessor. ▶ **adj.** Comput. denoting software or hardware that has been superseded but is difficult to replace because of its wide use. [ME: from OFr. *legacie*, from med. L. *legatia* 'legateship,' from *legatus* 'person delegated' (see LEGATE).]

le·gal /ˈlēgəl/ ▶ **adj.** **1** [attrib.] of, based on, or concerned with the law: *the American legal system.* ■ appointed or required by the law: *a legal requirement.* ■ of or relating to theological legalism. ■ Law recognized by common or statutory law, as distinct from equity. ■ (of paper) measuring 8 ½ by 14 inches. **2** permitted by law: *he claimed that it had all been legal.* — **le·gal·ly** **adv.** [ME: from Fr., or from L. *legalis*, from *lex, leg-* 'law.']

le·gal age ▶ **n.** the age at which a person takes on the rights and responsibilities of an adult.

le·gal aid ▶ **n.** payment from public funds allowed, in cases of need, to pay for legal advice or proceedings.

le·gal ea·gle (also **le·gal bea·gle**) ▶ **n.** informal a lawyer, esp. one who is keen and astute.

le·gal·ese /,lēgəˈlēz; -ˈlēs/ ▶ **n.** informal, derog. the formal and technical language of legal documents.

le·gal hol·i·day ▶ **n.** a public holiday established by law.

le·gal·ism /ˈlēgə,lizəm/ ▶ **n.** excessive adherence to law or formula. ■ Theol. dependence on moral law rather than on personal religious faith. — **le·gal·ist** **n. & adj.** **le·gal·is·tic** /,lēgəˈlistik/ **adj.** **le·gal·is·ti·cal·ly** /,lēgəˈlistik(ə)lē/ **adv.**

le·gal·i·ty /ləˈgalətē/ ▶ **n.** (pl. **-ties**) the quality or state of being in accordance with the law. ■ (**legalities**) obligations imposed by law.

le·gal·ize /ˈlēgə,līz/ ▶ **v.** [trans.] make (something that was previously illegal) permissible by law. — **le·gal·i·za·tion** /-,lēgələˈzāsʜən; -,līˈzā-/ **n.**

le·gal pad ▶ **n.** a ruled writing tablet that measures 8 ½ by 14 inches. ■ a ruled pad of paper.

le·gal per·son ▶ **n.** Law an individual, company, or other entity that has legal rights and is subject to obligations.

le·gal sep·a·ra·tion ▶ **n.** **1** an arrangement by which a husband and wife remain married but live apart, following a court order. **2** an arrangement by which a child lives apart from a natural parent and with the other natural parent or a foster parent, following a court order.

le·gal-size ▶ **adj.** (of paper) measuring 8 ½ by 14 inches. ■ designed to hold paper of this size.

le·gal ten·der ▶ **n.** coins or banknotes that must be accepted if offered in payment of a debt.

leg·ate /ˈlegit/ ▶ **n.** **1** a member of the clergy, esp. a cardinal, representing the pope. ■ archaic an ambassador or messenger. **2** a general or governor of an ancient Roman province, or their deputy: *the Roman legate of Syria.* — **leg·ate·ship** **n.** **leg·a·tine** /ˈlegə,tēn; -,tīn/ **adj.** [OE, from OFr. *legat*, from L. *legatus*, past part. of *legare* 'depute, delegate, bequeath.']

leg·a·tee /,legəˈtē/ ▶ **n.** a person who receives a legacy.

le·ga·tion /liˈgāsʜən/ ▶ **n.** **1** a diplomatic minister, esp. one below the rank of ambassador, and their staff. ■ the official residence of a diplomatic minister. **2** archaic the position or office of legate; a legateship. ■ the sending of a legate on a mission. [ME (denoting the sending of a papal legate; also the mission itself): from L. *legatio(n-)*, from *legare* 'depute, delegate, bequeath.']

le·ga·to /liˈgätō/ ▶ **adv. & adj.** Music in a smooth, flowing manner, without breaks. Compare with STACCATO. ▶ **n.** performance in this manner. [Ital., lit. 'bound.']

le·ga·tor /liˈgātər/ ▶ **n.** rare a testator, esp. one who leaves a legacy.

leg·end /ˈlejənd/ ▶ **n.** **1** a traditional story sometimes popularly regarded as historical but unauthenticated. **2** an extremely famous or notorious person. **3** an inscription, esp. on a coin or medal. ■ a caption. ■ the wording on a map or diagram explaining the symbols used: *see legend to Fig. 1.* **4** hist. the story of a saint's life. ▶ **adj.** [predic.] very well known: *his speed was legend.* [ME (sense 4): from OFr. *legende*, from med. L. *legenda* 'things to be read,' from L. *legere* 'read.']

leg·end·ar·y /ˈlejən,derē/ ▶ **adj.** **1** of, described in, or based on legends. **2** remarkable enough to be famous; very well known. — **leg·end·ar·i·ly** /-,derəlē; ,lejənˈde(ə)r-/ **adv.**

Lé·ger /lāˈzʜā/, Fernand (1881–1955), French painter. He painted the *Contrast of Forms* series (1913).

leg·er·de·main /,lejərdəˈmān; ˈlejərdə,mān/ ▶ **n.** skillful use of one's hands when performing tricks. ■ deception; trickery. [ME: from Fr. *léger de main* 'dexterous,' lit. 'light of hand.']

leg·er line /ˈlejər/ ▶ **n.** Music var. of LEDGER LINE. [19th C.: *leger*, var. of LEDGER.]

leg·gings /ˈlegiNGz/ ▸**plural n.** tight-fitting stretch pants. ■ protective coverings for the legs.

leg·gy /ˈlegē/ ▸**adj.** (**-gi·er**, **-gi·est**) **1** (of a woman) having attractively long legs: *a leggy redhead.* ■ long-legged: *a leggy type of collie.* **2** (of a plant) having a long and straggly stem. — **leg·gi·ness** **n.**

Le·gha·ri /legˈhärē/, Farooq Ahmed (1940–), president of Pakistan 1993–97.

leg·hold trap /ˈleg,hōld/ ▸**n.** a trap with a mechanism that catches and holds an animal by one of its legs.

Leg·horn /ˈleg,hôrn/ another name for **Livorno**.

leg·horn /ˈleg,hôrn; ˈlegərn/ ▸**n.** **1** fine plaited straw. ■ (also **leghorn hat**) a hat made of this. **2** (**Leg·horn** /ˈlegərn; -,hôrn/) a chicken of a small hardy breed. [18th C.: from Ital. *Leghorno* (now **Livorno**).]

leg·i·ble /ˈlejəbəl/ ▸**adj.** (of handwriting or print) clear enough to read: *the original typescript is scarcely legible.* — **leg·i·bil·i·ty** /,lejəˈbilətē/ **n.** **leg·i·bly** **adv.** [ME: from late L. *legibilis*, from *legere* 'to read.']

le·gion /ˈlējən/ ▸**n.** **1** a unit of 3,000–6,000 men in the ancient Roman army. ■ (**the Legion**) the Foreign Legion. ■ (**the Legion**) any of the national associations of former servicemen and servicewomen instituted after World War I, such as the American Legion. **2** (**a legion/legions of**) a vast host; multitude. ▸**adj.** [predic.] great in number: *her fans are legion.* [ME: via OFr. from L. *legion-*, from *legere* 'choose, levy.']

le·gion·ar·y /ˈlējə,nerē/ ▸**n.** (pl. **-ar·ies**) a soldier in a Roman legion. ▸**adj.** [attrib.] of an ancient Roman legion.

le·gion·naire /,lējəˈner/ ▸**n.** a member of a legion, esp. of a Roman legion or the French Foreign Legion. [19th C.: from Fr. *légionnaire*, from *légion* 'legion,' from L. *legio* (see **legion**).]

le·gion·naires' dis·ease ▸**n.** a form of pneumonia caused by the bacterium *Legionella pneumophila*, first identified after an outbreak at an American Legion meeting in 1976.

Le·gion of Hon·or a French order of distinction founded in 1802.

Le·gion of Mer·it (abbr.: **LM**) a US military decoration, ranking between the Silver Star and the Distinguished Flying Cross.

legis. ▸**abbr.** legislation or legislative or legislature.

leg·is·late /ˈlejə,slāt/ ▸**v.** [intrans.] make or enact laws. ■ [trans.] cover, affect, or create by making laws. [18th C.: back-form. from **legislator**.]

leg·is·la·tion /,lejəˈslāsHən/ ▸**n.** laws.

leg·is·la·tive /ˈlejə,slātiv/ ▸**adj.** having the power to make laws: *the country's supreme legislative body.* ■ of or relating to laws or the making of them: *legislative proposals.* Often contrasted with **executive**. ■ of or relating to a legislature: *legislative elections.* — **leg·is·la·tive·ly** **adv.**

leg·is·la·tor /ˈlejə,slātər/ ▸**n.** a person who makes laws. [15th C.: from L. *legis lator*, lit. 'proposer of a law,' from *lex* 'law' and *lator* 'proposer, mover,' from *latus*, past part. of *ferre* 'bring.']

leg·is·la·ture /ˈlejə,slāCHər/ ▸**n.** the legislative body of a country or state.

le·git /liˈjit/ ▸**adj.** informal legitimate; legal; conforming to the rules. ■ (of a person) not engaging in illegal activity or attempting to deceive; honest.

le·git·i·mate ▸**adj.** /liˈjitəmit/ conforming to the law or to rules: *his claims to legitimate authority.* ■ able to be defended with logic or justification. ■ (of a child) born of parents lawfully married to each other. ■ (of a sovereign) having a title based on strict hereditary right. ■ constituting or relating to serious drama as distinct from musical comedy, revue, etc.: *the legitimate theater.* ▸**v.** /-,māt/ [trans.] justify or make lawful. — **le·git·i·ma·cy** /-məsē/ **n.** **le·git·i·mate·ly** /-mitlē/ **adv.** **le·git·i·ma·tize** /-mə,tīz/ **v.** [ME: from med. L. *legitimatus* 'made legal,' from the v. *legitimare*, from L. *legitimus* 'lawful,' from *lex, leg-* 'law.']

le·git·i·mize /liˈjitə,mīz/ ▸**v.** [trans.] make legitimate. — **le·git·i·mi·za·tion** /li,jitəməˈzāsHən/ **n.**

leg·man /ˈleg,man/ ▸**n.** (pl. **-men**) a reporter whose job it is to gather information about news stories. ■ a person employed to do simple tasks such as running errands or collecting outside information.

leg-of-mut·ton sleeve ▸**n.** a sleeve that is full on the upper arm but close-fitting on or near the wrist.

leg-of-mutton sleeve

leg rest ▸**n.** a support for a seated person's leg.

leg·room /ˈleg,ro͞om; -,ro͝om/ ▸**n.** space where a seated person can put their legs.

leg·ume /ˈleg,yo͞om; ləˈgyo͞om/ ▸**n.** a leguminous plant. ■ a seed, pod, or other edible part of a leguminous plant used as food. ■ Bot. the long seedpod of a leguminous plant. [17th C.: from Fr. *légume*, from L. *legumen*, from *legere* 'to pick.']

le·gu·mi·nous /liˈgyo͞omənəs/ ▸**adj.** Bot. of, relating to, or denoting plants of the pea family (Leguminosae), with seeds in pods. Compare with **papilionaceous**.

leg·work /ˈleg,wərk/ ▸**n.** work that involves much traveling to collect information.

Le·hár /ˈlā,här/, Franz (Ferencz) (1870–1948), Hungarian composer, chiefly known for his operettas.

Le Ha·vre /lə ˈhäv(rə)/ a city in northern France at the mouth of the Seine River; pop. 197,000.

Le·high Riv·er /ˈlē,hī/ a river that flows through eastern Pennsylvania to the Delaware River.

lei[1] /lā/ ▸**n.** a Polynesian garland of flowers. [Hawaiian.]

lei[2] plural form of **leu**.

Leib·niz /ˈlīb,nits; ˈlīp-/, Gottfried Wilhelm (1646–1716), German rationalist philosopher and mathematician. He devised a method of calculus. — **Leib·niz·i·an** /lībˈnitsēən/ **adj. & n.**

Lei·bo·vitz /ˈlēbə,vits/, Annie (1950–), US photographer. As chief photographer of *Rolling Stone* magazine 1973–83, she photographed many celebrities.

Leices·ter[1] /ˈlestər/ a city in central England; pop. 271,000.

Leices·ter[2] ▸**n.** **1** (also **Red Leicester**) a kind of mild, firm cheese, typically orange-colored. **2** (also **Border Leicester**) a sheep of a breed often crossed with other breeds for the meat industry. **3** (also **Blue-faced Leicester**) a sheep of a breed similar to the Border Leicester, but with finer wool and a darker face.

Leices·ter·shire /ˈlestərsHər; -,sHi(ə)r/ a county in central England; county town, Leicester.

Lei·den /ˈlīdn; ˈlādn/ (also **Ley·den**) a city in the western Netherlands; pop. 111,950.

Leif Er·ics·son /,lēf ˈeriksən/ see **Ericsson**[2].

Leigh /lē/, Vivien (1913–67), British actress; born in India; born *Vivian Mary Hartley*. Her movies include *Gone with the Wind* (1939) and *A Streetcar Named Desire* (1951).

Lein·ster /ˈlenstər/ a province of the Republic of Ireland, in the southeastern part of the country.

Leip·zig /ˈlīpsig; -sik/ a city in east central Germany; pop. 503,000.

leish·man·i·a /lēsHˈmānēə; -ˈmanēə/ ▸**n.** (pl. same or **-ma·ni·as** or **-m·an·iae** /-ˈmānē-ē; -ˈman-; -ē,ī/) a single-celled parasitic protozoan (genus *Leishmania*, phylum Kinetoplastida) that spends part of its life cycle in the gut of a sandfly and part in the blood and other tissues of a vertebrate. [mod. L., from the name of William B. *Leishman* (1856–1926), British pathologist.]

leish·man·i·a·sis /,lēsHməˈnīəsəs/ ▸**n.** a tropical and subtropical disease caused by leishmania and transmitted by the bite of sandflies.

leis·ter /ˈlēstər/ ▸**n.** a spear used for catching salmon. ▸**v.** [trans.] spear (a fish) with a leister. [16th C.: from ON *ljóstr*, from *ljósta* 'to strike.']

lei·sure /ˈlēzHər; ˈlezHər/ ▸**n.** free time. ■ use of free time for enjoyment. ■ (**leisure for/to do something**) opportunity afforded by free time to do something.

– PHRASES **at leisure** **1** not occupied; free. **2** in an unhurried manner. **at one's leisure** at one's ease or convenience. **lady** (or **man** or **gentleman**) **of leisure** a woman or man of independent means or whose time is free from obligations to others. **leisure class** a social class that is independently wealthy or has much leisure. [ME: from OFr. *leisir*, based on L. *licere* 'be allowed.']

lei·sured /ˈlēzHərd; ˈlezHərd/ ▸**adj.** having ample leisure, esp. through being rich: *the leisured classes.* ■ leisurely: *a new, more leisured lifestyle.*

lei·sure·ly /ˈlēzHərlē; ˈlezHər-/ ▸**adj.** acting or done at leisure; unhurried or relaxed. ▸**adv.** without hurry: *couples strolled leisurely along.* — **lei·sure·li·ness** **n.**

lei·sure suit ▸**n.** a man's casual suit, consisting of pants and a matching shirtlike jacket, often in pastel colors.

lei·sure·wear /ˈlēzHər,we(ə)r; ˈlezHər-/ ▸**n.** casual clothes.

leit·mo·tif /ˈlītmō,tēf/ (also **leit·mo·tiv**) ▸**n.** a recurrent theme throughout a musical or literary composition. [19th C.: from Ger. *Leitmotiv*, from *leit-* 'leading' (from *leiten* 'to lead') + *Motiv* 'motive.']

Lei·trim /ˈlētrəm/ a county of the Republic of Ireland, in the province of Connacht.

Leix var. of **Laois**.

lek[1] /lek/ ▸**n.** the basic monetary unit of Albania, equal to 100 qintars.

lek[2] ▸**n.** a patch of ground used for communal display in the breeding season by the males of certain birds and mammals, esp. black grouse. ▸**v.** [intrans.] [usu. as adj.] (**lekking**) take part in such a display: *antelopes mate in lekking grounds.* [19th C.: perh. from Swed. *leka* 'to play.']

LEM /lem/ ▸**abbr.** lunar excursion module.

lem·an /ˈlemən/ ▸**n.** (pl. **lem·ans**) archaic a lover. ■ an illicit lover, esp. a mistress. [ME *lēofman*, from *lēof* (see **lief**) + **man**.]

Le Mans /lə mäN/ a city in northwestern France; pop. 148,000.

Lem·berg /ˈlembərg; -bərk/ German name for **Lviv**.

lem·ma[1] /ˈlemə/ ▸**n.** (pl. **lem·mas** or **lem·ma·ta** /ˈlemətə/) **1** a subsidiary or intermediate theorem in an argument or proof. **2** a heading indicating the subject of a literary composition, an annotation, or a dictionary entry. [16th C.: via L. from Gk. *lēmma* 'something assumed'; derived from *lambanein* 'take.']

lem·ma[2] ▸**n.** (pl. **lem·mas** or **lem·ma·ta** /ˈlemətə/) Bot. the lower bract of a grass floret. Compare with **palea**. [18th C. (denoting the husk or shell of a fruit): from Gk., from *lepein* 'to peel.']

lem·ma·tize /ˈlemə,tīz/ ▸**v.** [trans.] sort so as to group together inflected or variant forms of the same word. — **lem·ma·ti·za·tion** /,lemətəˈzāsHən/ **n.**

lem·me /ˈlemē/ informal ▸**contr.** let me: *lemme ask.*

lem·ming /ˈlemiNG/ ▸**n.** a small, short-tailed, thickset rodent (*Lemmus*, *Dicrostonyx*, and other genera, family Muridae) found in the Arctic tundra. The **Norway lemming** (*L. lemmus*) is noted for its fluctuating populations and periodic mass migrations. ■ a person who unthinkingly joins a mass movement, esp. a headlong rush to destruction. [18th C.: from Norw. and Dan.; rel. to ON *lómundr*.]

Lem·nitz·er /ˈlem,nitsər/, Lyman Louis (1899–1988), US general. He commanded UN forces in Korea 1955–57 and was supreme allied commander in Europe 1962–69.

Lem·nos /ˈlemnäs; -nōs; -nəs/ a Greek island in the northern Aegean Sea. Greek name **LÍMNOS**.

lem·on /ˈlemən/ ▶ **n.** **1** a yellow, oval citrus fruit with thick skin and fragrant, acidic juice. ■ a drink made from or flavored with lemon juice: *a port and lemon* | [as adj.] *lemon tea.* **2** (also **lemon tree**) the evergreen citrus tree (*Citrus limon*) that produces this fruit, widely cultivated in warm climates. **3** a pale yellow color. **4** informal a person or thing, esp. an automobile, regarded as unsatisfactory, disappointing, or feeble. — **lem·on·y** adj. [ME: via OFr. *limon* from Arab. *līmūn*.]

lem·on·ade /ˌleməˈnād; ˈleməˌnād/ ▶ **n.** a drink made from lemon juice and sweetened water.

lem·on balm ▶ **n.** see **BALM** (sense 3).

LeMond /lə ˈmôn(d)/, Greg (1971–), US cyclist. In 1986, he became the first American to win the Tour de France bicycle race, which he also won in 1989 and 1990.

lem·on·grass (also **lem·on grass**) ▶ **n.** a fragrant tropical grass (*Cymbopogon citratus*) that yields an oil that smells lemony. It is widely used in Asian cooking and in perfumery and medicine.

lem·on sole ▶ **n.** a common European flatfish (*Microstomus kitt*) of the plaice family. It is an important food fish. [19th C.: *lemon* from Fr. *limande*, of unknown origin.]

lem·on ver·be·na ▶ **n.** a South American shrub (*Aloysia triphylla*) of the verbena family, with lemon-scented leaves that are used as flavoring and to make tea.

lem·pi·ra /lemˈpi(ə)rə/ ▶ **n.** the basic monetary unit of Honduras, equal to 100 centavos. [named after *Lempira*, a 16th-cent. Indian chieftain.]

le·mur /ˈlēmər/ ▶ **n.** an arboreal primate (Lemuridae and other families) with a pointed snout and typically a long tail, found only in Madagascar. See illustration at **RING-TAILED LEMUR**. [18th C.: mod. L., from L. *lemures* (pl.) 'spirits of the dead' (from its specterlike face).]

lem·u·res /ˈleməˌrās; ˈlemyəˌrēz/ ▶ **plural n.** the family spirits of the dead in ancient Rome.

Le·na /ˈlānə; ˈlē-/ a river in Siberia, Russia, that rises near Lake Baikal and flows to the Laptev Sea.

Len·a·pe ▶ **n.** see **LENNI LENAPE**.

lend /lend/ ▶ **v.** (past and past part. **lent** /lent/) [with two objs.] **1** grant to (someone) the use of (something) on the understanding that it shall be returned. ■ allow (a person or organization) the use of (a sum of money) under an agreement to pay it back later, typically with interest: *no one would lend him the money.* **2** contribute or add (something, esp. a quality) to. **3** (**lend oneself to**) accommodate or adapt oneself to. ■ (**lend itself to**) (of a thing) be suitable for.
– PHRASES **lend an ear** (or **one's ears**) listen sympathetically or attentively. **lend a hand** (or **a helping hand**) see ***GIVE A HAND*** at **HAND**. **lend one's name to** allow oneself to be publicly associated with. — **lend·a·ble** adj. [OE *lǣnan*, of Gmc. origin; rel. to Du. *lenen*, also to **LOAN**.]

lend·er /ˈlendər/ ▶ **n.** an organization or person that lends money: *a mortgage lender.*

lend·ing li·brar·y ▶ **n.** a public library from which books may be borrowed.

Len·dl /ˈlendl/, Ivan (1960–), US tennis player; born in Czechoslovakia. During 1984–90, he won eight Grand Slam singles titles.

Lend-Lease hist. an arrangement made in 1941 whereby the US supplied military equipment and armaments to the UK and its allies, originally as a loan in return for the use of British-owned military bases.

L'Enfant /länˈfän/, Pierre Charles (1754–1825), US architect; born in France. In 1791, he designed the city of Washington, DC.

length /leNG(k)TH; lenth/ ▶ **n.** **1** the measurement or extent of something from end to end; the greater of the two or three dimensions of a body. ■ the amount of time occupied by something. ■ the quality of being long. ■ the full distance that a thing extends for. ■ the extent of a garment in a vertical direction when worn. ■ Pros. & Phonet. the metrical quantity or duration of a vowel or syllable. **2** the extent of something, esp. as a unit of measurement: ■ the length of a swimming pool as a measure of the distance swum. ■ the length of a horse, boat, etc., as a measure of the lead in a race. ■ (**one's length**) the full extent of one's body. **3** a stretch or piece of something. **4** the extreme to which a course of action is taken.
– PHRASES **at length** **1** in detail; fully. **2** after a long time. **the length and breadth of** the whole extent of. [OE *lengthu*, of Gmc. origin; rel. to Du. *lengte*, also to **LONG**[1].]

-length ▶ **comb. form** reaching up to or down to the place specified: *knee-length.* ■ of the size, duration, or extent specified: *full-length.*

length·en /ˈleNG(k)THən; ˈlen-/ ▶ **v.** make longer. ■ [trans.] Pros. & Phonet. make (a vowel or syllable) long.

length·ways /ˈleNG(k)THˌwāz; ˈlenTH-/ ▶ **adv.** lengthwise.

length·wise /ˈleNG(k)THˌwīz; ˈlenTH-/ ▶ **adv.** in a direction parallel with a thing's length. ▶ **adj.** [attrib.] lying or moving lengthwise.

length·y /ˈleNG(k)THē; ˈlen-/ ▶ **adj.** (**length·i·er**, **length·i·est**) (esp. in reference to time) of considerable or unusual length, esp. so as to be tedious: *lengthy delays.* — **length·i·ly** /-THəlē/ **adv.** **length·i·ness** **n.**

le·ni·ent /ˈlēnēənt; ˈlēnyənt/ ▶ **adj.** **1** (of punishment or a person in authority) permissive, merciful, or tolerant. **2** archaic emollient. — **le·ni·ence** **n.** **le·ni·en·cy** **n.** **le·ni·ent·ly** **adv.** [17th C. (sense 2): from L. *lenient-* 'soothing,' from the v. *lenire*, from *lenis* 'mild, gentle.']

Le·nin /ˈlenən; ˈlyenyin/, Vladimir Ilich (1870–1924), premier of the Soviet Union 1918–24; born *Vladimir Ilich Ulyanov*. In 1917 he established Bolshevik control after the overthrow of the czar.

Len·in·grad /ˈlenənˌgrad/ former name (1924–91) for **ST. PETERSBURG**.

Le·nin·ism /ˈlenəˌnizəm/ ▶ **n.** Marxism as interpreted and applied by Lenin. — **Le·nin·ist** **n.** & **adj.** **Le·nin·ite** /-ˌnīt/ **n.** & **adj.**

le·nis /ˈlēnis; ˈlā-/ Phonet. ▶ **adj.** (of a consonant, in particular a voiced consonant) weakly articulated. ▶ **n.** (pl. **-nes** /-nēz/) a consonant of this type. — **le·ni·tion** /liˈnisHən/ **n.** [20th C.: from L., 'mild, gentle.']

le·ni·tion /liˈnisHən/ ▶ **n.** the process or result of weakened articulation of a consonant. [20th C.: from L. *lenis* 'soft' + **-ITION**, suggested by Ger. *Lenierung*.]

len·i·tive /ˈlenətiv/ Med., archaic ▶ **adj.** (of a medicine) laxative. ▶ **n.** a medicine of this type. [ME: from med. L. *lenitivus*, from *lenit-* 'softened,' from the v. *lenire*.]

len·i·ty /ˈlenətē/ ▶ **n.** literary kindness; gentleness. [ME: from OFr. *lenite*.]

Len·ni Len·a·pe /ˈlenē ˈlenəpē; ləˈnäpē/ ▶ **n.** **1** a group of North American Indian peoples who formerly occupied the Delaware and Hudson River valleys, now in Oklahoma, Kansas, Wisconsin, and Ontario. ■ a member of one of the Delaware peoples. **2** the Eastern Algonquian language spoken by any of the Delaware peoples.

le·no /ˈlēnō/ ▶ **n.** (pl. **-nos**) an openwork fabric with the warp threads twisted in pairs before weaving. [18th C.: from Fr. *linon*, from *lin* 'flax,' from L. *linum*. Cf. **LINEN**.]

lens /lenz/ ▶ **n.** a piece of glass or other transparent substance with curved sides for concentrating or dispersing light rays. ■ the light-gathering device of a camera. ■ Physics a device that focuses or otherwise modifies the direction of movement of light, sound, electrons, etc. ■ Anat. short for **CRYSTALLINE LENS**. ■ short for **CONTACT LENS**. — **lensed** **adj.** **lens·less** **adj.** [17th C.: from L., 'lentil.']

lens hood ▶ **n.** a tube or ring attached to the front of a camera lens to prevent the entry of light.

Lent /lent/ ▶ **n.** the period of 40 weekdays that in the Christian Church is devoted to fasting, abstinence, and penitence. In the Western Church it starts on Ash Wednesday. [ME: abbrev. of **LENTEN**.]

lent /lent/ past and past participle of **LEND**.

-lent ▶ **suffix** (forming adjectives) full of; characterized by: *pestilent* | *violent.* Compare with **-ULENT**.

len·tan·do /lenˈtändō/ ▶ **adv.** & **adj.** Music (as a direction) slowing gradually.

Lent·en /ˈlent(ə)n/ ▶ **adj.** [attrib.] of or appropriate to Lent. [OE *lencten* 'spring, Lent,' of Gmc. origin, rel. to **LONG**[1].]

len·tic /ˈlentik/ ▶ **adj.** Ecol. (of organisms or habitats) situated in still, fresh water. Compare with **LOTIC**. [20th C.: from L. *lentus* 'calm, slow' + **-IC**.]

len·ti·cel /ˈlentəˌsel/ ▶ **n.** Bot. one of many raised pores in the stem of a woody plant that allow gas exchange between the atmosphere and plant tissues. [19th C.: from mod. L. *lenticella*, dimin. of L. *lens, lent-* 'lentil.']

len·tic·u·lar /lenˈtikyələr/ ▶ **adj.** **1** shaped like a lentil. **2** of or relating to the lens of the eye. [ME: from L. *lenticularis*, from *lenticula*, dimin. of *lens, lent-* 'lentil.']

len·ti·form nu·cle·us /ˈlentəˌfôrm/ ▶ **n.** Anat. the lower of the two gray nuclei of the corpus striatum. [18th C.: *lentiform* from L. *lens, lent-* 'lentil' + **-IFORM**.]

len·ti·go /lenˈtīgō; -ˈtē-/ ▶ **n.** (pl. **-tig·i·nes** /-ˈtijəˌnēz/) a condition marked by small brown patches on the skin, typically in elderly people. [ME (denoting a freckle or pimple): from L., from *lens, lent-* 'lentil.']

len·til /ˈlent(ə)l/ ▶ **n.** **1** a high-protein pulse that is dried and then soaked and cooked before eating. **2** the plant (*Lens culinaris*) that yields this pulse, native to the Mediterranean and Africa. [ME: from OFr. *lentille*, from L. *lenticula*, dimin. of *lens, lent-* 'lentil.']

len·tis·si·mo /lenˈtisiˌmō; -ˈtēsē-/ ▶ **adj.** & **adv.** Music (as a direction) at a very slow tempo.

len·ti·vi·rus /ˈlentəˌvīrəs/ ▶ **n.** Med. any of a group of retroviruses producing illnesses characterized by a delay in the onset of symptoms after infection. [1970s: from L. *lentus* 'slow' + **VIRUS**.]

len·to /ˈlentō/ ▶ **adv.** & **adj.** Music (esp. as a direction) slow or slowly. ▶ **n.** (pl. **-tos**) a passage to be performed this way. [Ital.]

Le·o[1] /ˈlēō/ the name of 13 popes, notably: ■ Leo I (died 461), pope 440–461; known as **Leo the Great**; canonized as **St. Leo I.** ■ Leo X (1475–1521), pope 1513–21; born *Giovanni de' Medici*.

Le·o[2] **1** Astron. a large constellation (the Lion), said to represent the lion slain by Hercules. **2** Astrol. the fifth sign of the zodiac, which the sun enters about July 23. ■ (**a Leo**) (pl. **Le·os**) a person born under this sign. — **Le·on·i·an** /lēˈōnēən/ **n.** & **adj.** (in sense 2).

Le·o III (*c.*680–741), Byzantine emperor 717–741. In 726, he banned icons and other religious images.

Le·o Mi·nor Astron. a small northern constellation (the Little Lion), immediately north of Leo.

Le·ón /lāˈōn/ **1** a city in central Mexico; pop. 872,000. **2** a city in western Nicaragua; pop. 159,000.

Leon·ard, Sugar Ray (1956–), US boxer; full name *Ray Charles Leonard*.

He won world championship titles in four different weight divisions.

Le·o·nar·do da Vin·ci /ˌlēə'närdō də 'vinchē; ˌlā-/ (1452–1519), Italian painter, scientist, and engineer. His paintings include *The Last Supper* (1498) and the *Mona Lisa* (1504–05). He devoted himself to a wide range of other subjects, from anatomy and biology to mechanics and hydraulics.

Le·on·berg·er /'lēənˌbərgər/ ▶**n.** a large dog that is a cross between a St. Bernard and a Newfoundland. [20th C.: named after a town in southwestern Germany.]

le·one /lē'ōn/ ▶**n.** the basic monetary unit of Sierra Leone, equal to 100 cents.

Le·o·nids /'lēənidz/ Astron. an annual meteor shower that reaches a peak about November 17. [19th C.: from L. *leo, leon-* (see LEO[2]) + -ID[3].]

Le·o·nine ▶**adj. 1** of or relating to one of the popes named Leo. **2** Pros. (of medieval Latin verse) in hexameter or elegiac meter with internal rhyme. ■ (of English verse) with internal rhyme. ▶**plural n.** (**Leonines**) Pros. verse of this type. [ME: from the name *Leo*, from L. *leo* 'lion.']

le·o·nine /'lēəˌnīn/ ▶**adj.** of or resembling a lion. [ME: from OFr., or from L. *leoninus*, from *leo, leon-* 'lion.']

Le·on·ti·ef /lē'(y)ônˌtyef/, Wassily (1906–99), US economist; born in Russia. He wrote *The Structure of the American Economy, 1919–29* (1941). Nobel Prize for Economics (1973).

leop·ard /'lepərd/ ▶**n.** a large, solitary cat (*Panthera pardus*) that has a yellowish-brown or brown coat with black spots and usually hunts at night, widespread in the forests of Africa and southern Asia. Also called PANTHER. ■ Heraldry the spotted leopard as a heraldic device; also, a lion passant guardant as in the arms of England. ■ [as adj.] spotted like a leopard.

– PHRASES **a leopard can't change his spots** proverb people can't change their basic nature. [ME: via OFr. from late L. *leopardus*, from late Gk. *leopardos*.]

leop·ard·ess /'lepərdis/ ▶**n.** a female leopard.

leop·ard frog ▶**n.** a common greenish-brown North American true frog (*Rana pipiens*) that has dark leopardlike spots with a pale border.

leop·ard seal ▶**n.** a large, gray Antarctic true seal (*Hydrurga leptonyx*) that has leopardlike spots and preys on penguins and other seals.

leop·ard-skin ▶**adj.** (of a garment) made of a fabric resembling the spotted skin of a leopard.

Le·o·pold I /'lēəˌpōld/ (1790–1865), the king of Belgium 1831–65.

Leé·o·pold·ville /'lēəˌpōldˌvil; 'lā-/ former name (until 1966) of KINSHASA.

le·o·tard /'lēəˌtärd/ ▶**n.** a close-fitting one-piece garment, made of a stretchy fabric, which covers a person's body from the shoulders to the top of the thighs and typically the arms. ■ (**leotards**) close-fitting leggings or tights. [20th C.: named after Jules *Léotard* (1839–70), French trapeze artist.]

Le·o the Great Pope Leo I (see LEO[1]).

Le·pan·to, Bat·tle of /lə'päntō; -'pan-/ a naval battle in 1571 at the entrance to the Gulf of Corinth, in which European forces defeated a large Turkish fleet.

Le·pan·to, Gulf of another name for the Gulf of Corinth (see CORINTH, GULF OF).

Lep·cha /'lepchə/ ▶**n. 1** a member of a people living mainly in parts of India, Bhutan, and Nepal. **2** the Tibeto-Burman language of this people. ▶**adj.** of or relating to the Lepchas or their language. [from Nepali *lāpche*.]

lep·er /'lepər/ ▶**n.** a person suffering from leprosy. ■ a person who is avoided or rejected by others for moral or social reasons: *she was a social leper.* [ME: based on Gk. *lepra*, fem. of *lepros* 'scaly,' from *lepos, lepis* 'scale.']

le·pid·o·lite /li'pidlˌīt/ ▶**n.** a mineral of the mica group containing lithium, typically gray or lilac in color. [18th C.: from Gk. *lepis, lepid-* 'scale' + -LITE.]

Lep·i·dop·ter·a /ˌlepə'däptərə/ Entomol. an order of insects that comprises the butterflies and moths. ■ (**lepidoptera**) [as pl. n.] insects of this order. — **lep·i·dop·ter·an** adj. & n. **lep·i·dop·ter·ous** /-tərəs/ adj. [mod. L. (pl.), from Gk. *lepis, lepid-* 'scale' + *pteron* 'wing.']

lep·i·dop·ter·ist /ˌlepə'däptərist/ ▶**n.** a person who studies or collects butterflies and moths.

Lep·i·dus /'lepidəs/, Marcus Aemilius (died c.13 BC), Roman politician.

Le·pon·tic /lə'päntik/ ▶**n.** an ancient Celtic language once spoken in Switzerland and northern Italy.

lep·o·rine /'lepəˌrīn; -rin/ ▶**adj.** of or resembling a hare. [17th C.: from L. *leporinus*, from *lepus, lepor-* 'hare.']

lep·re·chaun /'leprəˌkän; -ˌkôn/ ▶**n.** (in Irish folklore) a small, mischievous sprite. [17th C.: from Irish *leipreachán*, based on Old Irish *luchorpán*, from *lu* 'small' + *corp* 'body.']

le·prom·a·tous /li'prämətəs; -'prōmə-/ ▶**adj.** Med. relating to or denoting the more severe of the two principal forms of leprosy. Compare with TUBERCULOID.

lep·ro·sar·i·um /ˌleprə'se(ə)rēəm/ ▶**n.** a leper hospital. [19th C.: from late L. *leprosus* 'leprous' + -ARIUM.]

lep·ro·sy /'leprəsē/ ▶**n.** a contagious disease caused by the bacterium *Mycobacterium leprae* that affects the skin, mucous membranes, and nerves, causing discoloration and lumps on the skin and, in severe cases, disfigurement and deformities. Leprosy is now mainly confined to tropical Africa and Asia. Also called HANSEN'S DISEASE. [16th C.: from LEPROUS + -Y[3].]

lep·rous /'leprəs/ ▶**adj. 1** suffering from leprosy. ■ relating to or resembling leprosy: *leprous growths.* **2** covered with scales; scaly. [ME: via OFr. from late L. *leprosus*, from L. *lepra* 'scaly', from Gk. (see LEPER).]

lep·tin /'leptin/ ▶**n.** Biochem. a protein produced by fatty body tissue and believed to regulate fat storage. [1990s: from Gk. *leptos* 'fine, thin' + -IN[1].]

lepto- ▶**comb. form** small; narrow: *leptocephalic.* [from Gk. *leptos* 'fine, thin, delicate.']

lep·to·kur·tic /ˌleptə'kərtik/ ▶**adj.** Stat. (of a frequency distribution or its graphical representation) having greater kurtosis than the normal distribution. Compare with PLATYKURTIC, MESOKURTIC. — **lep·to·kur·to·sis** /-tōˌkər'tōsis/ n. [20th C.: from LEPTO- 'narrow' + Gk. *kurtos* 'bulging' + -IC.]

lep·ton[1] /'lepˌtän/ ▶**n.** (pl. **-ta** /-tə/) a monetary unit of Greece until the introduction of the euro, worth one hundredth of a drachma (used only in calculations). [from Gk. *lepton*, neut. of *leptos* 'small.']

lep·ton[2] ▶**n.** Physics a subatomic particle, such as an electron, muon, or neutrino, that does not take part in the strong interaction. — **lep·ton·ic** /lep'tänik/ adj. [1940s: from Gk. *leptos* 'small' + -ON.]

lep·to·spi·ro·sis /ˌleptəˌspī'rōsis/ ▶**n.** an infectious bacterial disease that occurs in rodents, dogs, and other mammals and can be transmitted to humans. The bacterium is a spirochete of the genus *Leptospira.* [1920s: from LEPTO- 'narrow' + Gk. *speira* 'coil' + -OSIS.]

lep·to·tene /'leptəˌtēn/ ▶**n.** Biol. the first stage of the prophase of meiosis. [20th C.: from LEPTO- 'narrow, fine' + Gk. *tainia* 'band, ribbon.']

Lep·us /'lepəs; 'lēpəs/ Astron. a small constellation (the Hare) at the foot of Orion.

Ler·ner /'lərnər/, Alan Jay (1918–86), US lyricist and playwright. His musicals written with composer Frederick Loewe include *My Fair Lady* (1956).

Ler·wick /'lərwik/ the capital of the Shetland Islands, on the island of Mainland; pop. 7,220.

les /lez/ (also **lez**) ▶**n.** informal, usu. offens. a lesbian.

Les·bi·an /'lezbēən/ ▶**adj.** from or relating to Lesbos.

les·bi·an /'lezbēən/ ▶**n.** a homosexual woman. ▶**adj.** of or relating to homosexual women. — **les·bi·an·ism** n. [19th C.: via L. from Gk. *Lesbios*, from LESBOS, home of Sappho, who expressed affection for women in her poetry, + -IAN.]

les·bo /'lezbō/ ▶**n.** (pl. **-bos**) usu. offens. a lesbian.

Les·bos /'lezˌbäs; 'lezbəs/ a Greek island in the eastern Aegean Sea. Greek name LÉSVOS.

lèse-maj·es·té /ˌlez ˌmäjə'stā; 'majəstē; ˌlēz/ ▶**n.** the insulting of a monarch or other ruler; treason. [ME: from Fr. *lèse-majesté*, from L. *laesa majestas* 'injured sovereignty.']

le·sion /'lēzʜən/ ▶**n.** esp. Med. a region in an organ or tissue that has suffered damage. [ME: via OFr. from L. *laesio(n-)*, from *laedere* 'injure.']

Le·so·tho /lə'sōōtōō; lə'sōtō/ a country in southeastern Africa. *See box.*

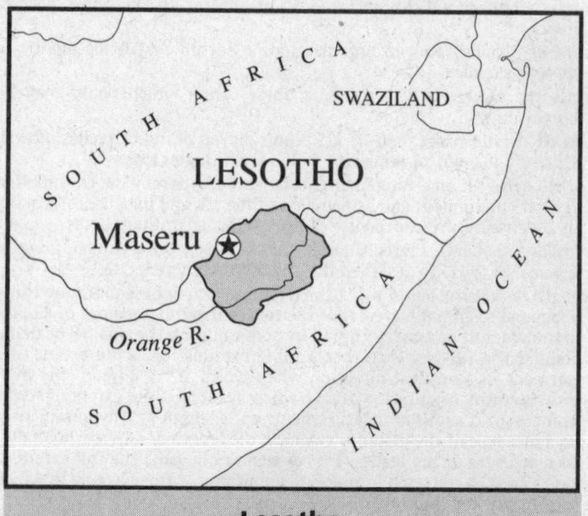

Lesotho

Official name: Kingdom of Lesotho

Location: southeastern Africa, landlocked within South Africa

Area: 11,700 square miles (30,400 sq km)

Population: 1,816,000

Capital: Maseru

Languages: English (official), Sesotho (southern Sotho), Zulu, Xhosa

Currency: loti, South African rand

less /les/ ▶**adj. & pron.** a smaller amount of; not as much. ■ fewer in number. ▶**adj.** archaic of lower rank or importance: *James the Less.* ▶**adv.** to a smaller extent; not so much. ■ (**less than**) far from; certainly not. ▶**prep.** minus: *$900,000 less tax.*

– PHRASES **in less than no time** informal very quickly or soon. **less and**

less at a continually decreasing rate. **much** (or **still**) **less** used to introduce something as being even less likely or suitable than something else already mentioned. **no less** used to suggest, often ironically, that something is surprising or impressive: *fillet steak and champagne, no less.* ■ (**no less than**) used to emphasize a surprisingly large amount. [OE *lǣssa*; rel. to Old Frisian *lēssa*, Gk. *loisthos* 'last.']

-less /ləs; lis/ ▶ **suffix** forming adjectives and adverbs: **1** (from nouns) not having; without; free from. **2** (from verbs) not affected by or not carrying out the action of the verb: *fathomless* | *tireless.* — **-lessly suffix** forming corresponding adverbs. **-lessness suffix** forming corresponding nouns. [OE *-lēas*, from *lēas* 'devoid of.']

less-de·vel·op·ed coun·try ▶ **n.** a nonindustrialized or Third World country.

les·see /le'sē/ ▶ **n.** a person who holds the lease of a property; a tenant. — **les·see·ship n.** [15th C.: from OFr. *lesse*, past part. of *lesser* 'to let, leave,' + -EE.]

less·en /'lesən/ ▶ **v.** make or become less; diminish.

Les·seps /'lesəps; lə'seps/, Ferdinand Marie, Vicomte de (1805–94), French diplomat. From 1854, while in the consular service in Egypt, he devoted himself to the Suez Canal project.

less·er /'lesər/ ▶ **adj.** [attrib.] not so great or important as the other or the rest: *he was convicted of a lesser charge.* ■ lower in terms of rank or quality: *the lesser aristocracy.*

– PHRASES **the lesser evil** (or **the lesser of two evils**) the less harmful or unpleasant of two bad choices or possibilities. [ME: a double compar., from LESS + -ER[2].]

Less·er An·til·les see ANTILLES.

less·er cel·an·dine ▶ **n.** see CELANDINE.

less·er-known ▶ **adj.** not as well or widely known as others of the same kind.

less·er pan·da ▶ **n.** another term for RED PANDA.

Less·er Sun·da Is·lands see SUNDA ISLANDS.

Les·sing /'lesiNG/, Doris May (1919–), British writer. Her novels include a science-fiction quintet, *Canopus in Argus: Archives* (1979–83).

Les Six /lā 'sēs/ (also **the Six**) a group of six Parisian composers (Louis Durey 1888–1979, Arthur Honegger 1892–1955, Darius Milhaud 1892–1974, Germaine Tailleferre 1892–1983, Georges Auric 1899–1983, and Francis Poulenc 1899–1963) formed after World War I, whose music represents a reaction against romanticism and Impressionism. [Fr., lit. 'the Six.']

les·son /'lesən/ ▶ **n. 1** an amount of teaching given at one time; a period of learning or teaching. ■ a thing learned or to be learned by a student. ■ a thing learned by experience. ■ an occurrence, example, or punishment that warns or encourages: *let that be a lesson to you!* **2** a Bible passage read aloud during a church service. ▶ **v.** [trans.] archaic instruct or teach (someone). ■ admonish or rebuke (someone).

– PHRASES **learn one's lesson** acquire a greater understanding through experience. **teach someone a lesson** punish or hurt someone as a deterrent. [ME: from OFr. *leçon*, from L. *lectio*.]

les·sor /'les,ôr; le'sôr/ ▶ **n.** a person who leases or lets a property to another; a landlord. [ME: from Anglo-Norman Fr., from OFr. *lesser* 'let, leave.']

lest /lest/ ▶ **conj.** formal with the intention of preventing (something undesirable); to avoid the risk of. ■ (after a clause indicating fear) because of the possibility of something undesirable happening; in case. [OE *thȳ lǣs the* 'whereby less that,' later *the lǣste*.]

Lés·vos /'lez,vôs/ Greek name for LESBOS.

let[1] /let/ ▶ **v.** (**let·ting**; past **let**) [trans.] **1** not prevent or forbid; allow: *my boss let me leave early.* ■ [with obj. and adverbial of direction] allow to pass in a particular direction: *could you let the dog out?* **2** [with obj. and infin.] used in the imperative to formulate various expressions: ■ (**let us** or **let's**) used as a polite way of making or responding to a suggestion, giving an instruction, or introducing a remark: *let's have a drink.* ■ (**let me** or **let us**) used to make a polite offer of help: *let me carry that.* ■ used to express one's strong desire for something to happen or be the case: *please let him be all right.* ■ used as a way of expressing defiance or challenge. ■ used to express an assumption upon which a theory or calculation is to be based: *let A and B stand for X and Y.* **3** esp. Brit allow someone to have the use of (a room or property) in return for regular payments; rent.

– PHRASES **let alone** used to indicate that something is far less likely, possible, or suitable than something else already mentioned: *he was incapable of leading a bowling team, let alone a country.* **let someone/something alone** see ALONE. **let someone/something be** stop disturbing or interfering with. **let someone down gently** seek to give someone bad news in a way that avoids causing them too much distress or humiliation. **let something drop** (or **fall**) casually reveal a piece of information. **let fly** attack, either physically or verbally: *the troops let fly with loaded shells.* **let oneself go 1** act in an unrestrained or uninhibited way. **2** become careless or untidy in one's habits or appearance. **let someone/something go 1** allow someone or something to escape or go free. ■ dismiss an employee. **2** (also **let go** or **let go of**) relinquish one's grip on someone or something. **let someone have it** informal attack someone physically or verbally. **let it drop** (or **rest**) say or do no more about a matter or problem. **let it go** (or **pass**) choose not to react to an action or remark. **let someone know** inform someone. **let me see** (or **think**) used when one is pausing, trying to remember something, or considering one's next words. **let me tell you** used to emphasize a statement. **let off steam** see STEAM. **let rip** see RIP[1]. **let's face it** (or **let's be honest**) informal used to convey that one must be realistic about an unwelcome fact or situation. **let slip** see SLIP[1]. **let's pretend** a game or set of circumstances in which one behaves as though a fictional or unreal situation were a real one. **let's say** (or **let us say**) used as a way of introducing a hypothetical or possible situation: *so let's say we leave on Friday morning.*

– PHRASAL VERBS **let someone down** fail to support or help someone as they had hoped or expected. ■ (**let someone/something down**) have a detrimental effect on the overall quality or success of someone or something. **let something down 1** lower something slowly or in stages. **2** lower the hem. **let oneself in for** informal involve oneself in (something likely to be difficult or unpleasant). **let someone in on/into** allow someone to know or share (something secret or confidential). **let someone off 1** punish someone lightly or not at all for a misdemeanor or offense. **2** excuse someone from a task or obligation. **let something off** cause a gun, firework, or bomb to fire or explode. **let on** informal **1** reveal or divulge information to someone: *she knows a lot more than she lets on.* **2** pretend: [with clause] *they all let on that they didn't hear me.* **let out** (of lessons at school, a meeting, or an entertainment) finish, so that those attending are able to leave. **let someone out** release someone from obligation or suspicion: *they're looking for motives—that lets me out.* **let something out 1** utter a sound or cry. **2** make a garment looser or larger, typically by adjusting a seam. **3** reveal a piece of information. **let up** informal (of something undesirable) become less intense or severe. ■ relax one's efforts. ■ (**let up on**) informal treat or deal with in a more lenient manner: *she didn't let up on Cunningham.* [OE *lǣtan* 'leave behind, leave out,'; rel. to Ger. *lassen*, also to LATE.]

let[2] ▶ **n.** (in racket sports) a play that is nullified and has to be played again, esp. a when a served ball touches the top of the net.

– PHRASES **play a let** (in tennis, squash, etc.) play a point again because the ball or one of the players has been obstructed. [OE *lettan* 'hinder,' of Gmc. origin; rel. to Du. *letten*, also to LATE.]

-let ▶ **suffix 1** (forming nouns) denoting a smaller or lesser kind: *booklet* | *starlet.* **2** denoting articles of ornament or dress: *anklet.* [orig. corresponding to Fr. *-ette* added to nouns ending in *-el*.]

let·down /'let,doun/ ▶ **n. 1** a disappointment. ■ a decrease in size, volume, force: *letdowns in sales.* **2** the release of milk in a nursing mother or lactating animal. **3** Aeron. the descent of an aircraft or spacecraft before landing.

le·thal /'lēTHəl/ ▶ **adj.** sufficient to cause death. ■ harmful or destructive. — **le·thal·i·ty** /lē'THalətē/ **n. le·thal·ly adv.** [16th C.: from L. *lethalis*, from *lethum*, a var. of *letum* 'death.']

le·thal gene ▶ **n.** a gene that is capable of causing the death of an organism. Also called **lethal factor**, **lethal mutation**.

le·thal in·jec·tion ▶ **n.** an injection administered for the purposes of euthanasia or as capital punishment.

le·thar·gic /lə'THärjik/ ▶ **adj.** affected by lethargy; sluggish and apathetic: *I felt tired and a little lethargic.* — **le·thar·gi·cal·ly adv.**

leth·ar·gy /'leTHərjē/ ▶ **n.** a lack of energy; sleepiness. [ME: via OFr. from late L. *lethargia*, from Gk. *lēthargia*, from *lēthargos* 'forgetful,' from the base of *lanthanesthai* 'forget.']

Le·the /'lēTHē; li'THē-/ Gk. Mythol. a river in Hades. — **Le·the·an** /'lēTHēən/ **adj.**

Le·to /'lētō/ Gk. Mythol. mother (by Zeus) of Artemis and Apollo. Roman name LATONA.

let's /lets/ ▶ **contr.** let us.

let·ter /'letər/ ▶ **n. 1** a character representing one or more of the sounds used in speech; any of the symbols of an alphabet. ■ a school or college initial as a mark of proficiency, esp. in sports: *I earned a varsity letter in tennis.* **2** a written, typed, or printed communication, esp. one sent in an envelope by mail or messenger. ■ (**letters**) a legal or formal document of this kind. **3** the precise terms of a statement or requirement; the strict verbal interpretation. **4** (**letters**) literature. ■ archaic scholarly knowledge; erudition. **5** Print. a style of typeface. ▶ **v. 1** [trans.] inscribe letters or writing on. ■ classify with letters: *he lettered the paragraphs.* **2** [intrans.] informal be given a school or college initial as a mark of proficiency in sports.

– PHRASES **to the letter** adhering to every detail. [ME: from OFr. *lettre*, from L. *litera*, *littera* 'letter of the alphabet,' (pl.) 'epistle, literature, culture.']

let·ter bomb ▶ **n.** an explosive device hidden in a small package.

let·ter·box /'letər,bäks/ ▶ **n.** esp. Brit. a mailbox. ■ [usu. as adj.] a format for presenting wide-screen films on a standard television screen in which the image is displayed across the middle of the screen, leaving horizontal black bands above and below. ▶ **v.** [trans.] record (a wide-screen film) onto video in letterbox format.

let·ter car·ri·er ▶ **n.** a mail carrier.

let·tered /'letərd/ ▶ **adj.** dated formally educated.

let·ter·head /'letər,hed/ ▶ **n.** a printed heading on stationery stating a name and address. ■ a sheet of paper with such a heading.

let·ter·ing /'letəriNG/ ▶ **n.** the inscription of letters. ■ the letters inscribed on something.

let·ter·man /'letər,man; -mən/ ▶ **n.** a high school or college student who has earned a letter in an interscholastic or intercollegiate activity, esp. a sport.

let·ter mis·sive (also **let·ters mis·sive**) ▶ **n.** a letter from a superior to a group or an individual conveying a command, recommendation, permission, or an invitation.

let·ter of cred·it ▶ **n.** a letter issued by a bank to another bank (typically in a different country) to serve as a guarantee for payments made to a specified person.

let·ter of in·tent ▶ **n.** a document containing a declaration of the intentions of the writer.

let·ter·per·fect ▶ **adj.** (of an actor or speaker) knowing by heart the words for one's part or speech. ■ accurate to the smallest verbal detail.

let·ter·press /ˈletər,pres/ ▶ **n.** printing from a hard, raised image under pressure, using viscous ink.

let·ter-qual·i·ty ▶ **adj.** (of a computer printer) print of a quality suitable for business letters. ■ (of a document) printed to such a standard.

let·ter·set /ˈletər,set/ ▶ **n.** a printing method in which ink goes from a raised surface to a blanket wrapped around a cylinder and from that to paper. [1960s: blend of LETTERPRESS and OFFSET.]

let·ters mis·sive ▶ **n.** variant of LETTER MISSIVE.

let·ters of ad·min·is·tra·tion ▶ **plural n.** Law authority to administer the estate of someone who has died without making a will.

let·ters pat·ent /ˈpatnt/ ▶ **plural n.** an open document issued by a monarch or government conferring a patent or other right. [ME: from med. L. *litterae patentes*, lit. 'letters lying open.']

let·ters tes·ta·men·ta·ry ▶ **plural n.** Law a document from a court or public official authorizing the executor to carry out the will of a deceased person.

let·tuce /ˈletis/ ▶ **n.** **1** a cultivated plant (*Lactuca sativa*) of the daisy family, with edible leaves that are a usual ingredient of salads. Many varieties of lettuce have been developed with a range of form, texture, and color. ■ used in names of other plants with edible green leaves, e.g., **lamb's lettuce**, **sea lettuce**. **2** informal paper money; greenbacks. [ME: from OFr. *letues*, *laitues*, pl. of *laitue*, from L. *lactuca*, from *lac*, *lact-* 'milk' (because of its milky juice).]

let·up /ˈlet,əp/ ▶ **n.** [in sing.] informal a pause or reduction in the intensity of something.

Letz·e·burg·esch /ˈletse,bo͝orgəsh/ (also **Letz·e·buerg·esch**) ▶ **n. & adj.** another term for LUXEMBURGISH. [from a local name for LUXEMBOURG + *-esch* (equivalent of -ISH[1]).]

le·u /ˈlā(y)o͞o/ ▶ **n.** (pl. **lei** /lā/) the basic monetary unit of Romania, equal to 100 bani. [Romanian, lit. 'lion.']

leu·cine /ˈlo͞o,sēn; -sin/ ▶ **n.** Biochem. a hydrophobic amino acid, $(CH_3)_2CHCH_2CH(NH_2)COOH$, that is a constituent of most proteins. It is an essential nutrient in the diet of vertebrates. [19th C.: coined in Fr. from Gk. *leukos* 'white' + -INE[4].]

leu·cite /ˈlo͞o,sīt/ ▶ **n.** a gray or white potassium aluminosilicate, typically found in alkali volcanic rocks. — **leu·cit·ic adj.** /lo͞oˈsitik/

leuco- ▶ **comb. form** esp. Brit. var. of LEUKO-.

leu·co·der·ma (also **leu·ko·der·ma**) ▶ **n.** another term for VITILIGO.

leu·con /ˈlo͞o,kän/ ▶ **n.** Zool. a sponge of the most complex structure, composed of a mass of flagellated chambers and water canals. Compare with ASCON and SYCON. — **leu·co·noid** /-kə,noid/ **adj.**

leu·co·plast /ˈlo͞okə,plast/ ▶ **n.** Bot. a colorless organelle found in plant cells, used to store starch or oil.

leu·ke·mi·a /lo͞oˈkēmēə/ (Brit. **leu·kae·m·ia**) ▶ **n.** a malignant progressive disease in which the bone marrow and other blood-forming organs produce increased numbers of immature or abnormal leukocytes, suppressing the production of normal blood cells. — **leu·ke·mic** /-ˈkēmik/ **adj.** [19th C.: coined in Ger. from Gk. *leukos* 'white' + *haima* 'blood.']

leuko- (also esp. Brit. **leuco-**) ▶ **comb. form** **1** white. [from Gk. *leukos* 'white.'] **2** representing LEUKOCYTE.

leu·ko·cyte /ˈlo͞okə,sīt/ (Brit. also **leu·co·cyte**) ▶ **n.** Physiol. a colorless cell that circulates in the blood and body fluids and is involved in counteracting foreign substances and disease; a white (blood) cell. — **leu·ko·cyt·ic** /,lo͞okəˈsitik/ **adj.**

leu·ko·cy·to·sis /,lo͞okəsīˈtōsis; -kō-/ (Brit. also **leu·co·cy·to·sis**) ▶ **n.** Med. an increase in the number of white cells in the blood, esp. during an infection. — **leu·ko·cy·tot·ic** /-ˈtätik/ **adj.**

leu·ko·der·ma (also **leu·co·der·ma**) /,lo͞okəˈdərmə/ ▶ **n.** another term for VITILIGO.

leu·ko·ma /lo͞oˈkōmə/ ▶ **n.** Med. a white opacity in the cornea of the eye. [18th C.: mod. L., from Gk. *leukōma*.]

leu·ko·pe·ni·a /,lo͞okəˈpēnēə/ (Brit. also **leu·co·pe·ni·a**) ▶ **n.** Med. a reduction in the number of white cells in the blood, typical of various diseases. — **leu·ko·pe·nic** /-nik/ **adj.** [19th C.: from Gk. *leukos* 'white' + *penia* 'poverty.']

leu·ko·pla·ki·a /,lo͞okəˈplākēə/ ▶ **n.** (also **leu·co·pla·ki·a**) a mucous membrane disorder characterized by white patches, esp. on the cheek, tongue, vulva, or penis. Also called **leukoplasia**.

leu·kor·rhe·a /,lo͞okəˈrēə/ (also **leu·cor·rhe·a**, Brit. **leu·cor·rhoe·a**) ▶ **n.** a whitish or yellowish discharge of mucus from the vagina.

leu·kot·o·my /lo͞oˈkätəmē/ ▶ **n.** (pl. **-mies**) the surgical cutting of white nerve fibers within the brain, esp. prefrontal lobotomy, formerly used to treat mental illness.

leu·ko·tri·ene /,lo͞okəˈtrī,ēn/ ▶ **n.** Biochem. any of a group of biologically active compounds, originally isolated from leukocytes. They are metabolites of arachidonic acid, containing three conjugated double bonds.

Lev. ▶ **abbr.** Bible Leviticus.

lev /lev; lef/ ▶ **n.** (pl. **lev·a** /ˈlevə/) the basic monetary unit of Bulgaria, equal to 100 stotinki. [Bulgarian, var. of *lăv* 'lion.']

Le·val·lois /lə,valˈwä; -ˈval,wä/ ▶ **n.** [usu. as adj.] Archaeol. a flint-working technique associated with the Mousterian culture of the Neanderthals. — **Le·val·loi·si·an** /,levəˈloizēən; lə,valˈwäzēən/ **adj.** [20th C.: named after a suburb of northern Paris.]

le·va·mi·sole /ləˈvamə,sōl/ ▶ **n.** Med. a synthetic compound, $C_{11}H_{12}N_2S$, used as an anthelmintic drug (esp. in animals) and in cancer chemotherapy. [1960s: from LEVO- + *(tetra)misole*, the name of an anthelmintic drug.]

Le·vant /ləˈvant; ləˈvänt/ archaic the eastern part of the Mediterranean.

le·vant·er /ləˈvantər/ ▶ **n.** a strong easterly wind in the Mediterranean region.

Le·vant mo·roc·co /ləˈvant/ (also **Le·vant**) ▶ **n.** high-grade, large-grained morocco leather.

Le·vant worm·seed ▶ **n.** see WORMSEED.

le·va·tor /ləˈvātər/ (also **levator muscle**) ▶ **n.** Anat. a muscle whose contraction causes the raising of a part of the body. [17th C.: from L., lit. 'a person who lifts,' from *levare* 'raise, lift.']

lev·ee[1] /ˈlevē/ ▶ **n.** an embankment built to prevent the overflow of a river. ■ a ridge of sediment deposited naturally alongside a river by overflowing water. ■ a landing place; a quay. ■ a ridge of earth surrounding a field to be irrigated. [18th C. (orig. US): from Fr. *levée*, fem. past part. of *lever* 'to lift.']

lev·ee[2] ▶ **n.** a reception, in particular: ■ a formal reception of visitors or guests. ■ hist. an afternoon assembly for men held by the British monarch or their representative. [17th C.: from Fr. *levé*, var. of *lever* 'rising,' from the v. *lever*.]

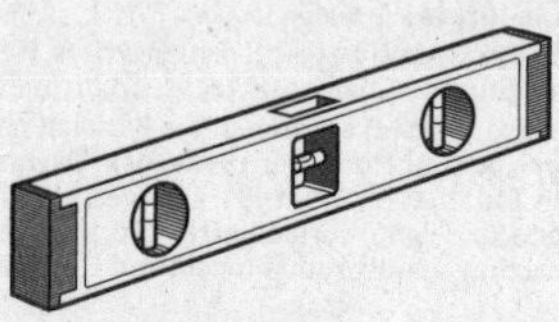

level 3

lev·el /ˈlevəl/ ▶ **n.** **1** a position on a real or imaginary scale of amount, quantity, extent, or quality. ■ a social, moral, or intellectual standard. ■ a position in a real or notional hierarchy. **2** a height or distance from the ground or another stated or understood base. **3** an instrument giving a line parallel to the plane of the horizon, for testing whether things are horizontal. ■ Surveying an instrument for giving a horizontal line of sight. **4** a flat tract of land. ▶ **adj.** **1** having a flat and even surface. ■ horizontal. ■ at the same height as someone or something else. ■ having the same relative position; not in front of or behind. ■ (of a quantity of a dry substance) with the contents not rising above the brim of the measure. ■ unchanged; not having risen or fallen. **2** calm and steady. ▶ **v.** (**-eled**, **-el·ing**; also esp. Brit. **-elled**, **-el·ling**) **1** [trans.] give a flat and even surface to. ■ Surveying ascertain differences in the height of (land). ■ demolish (a building or town). **2** [intrans.] (**level off/out**) begin to fly horizontally after climbing or diving. ■ (of a path, road, or incline) cease to slope upward or downward. ■ cease to fall or rise in number, amount, or quantity: *inflation has leveled out.* **3** [trans.] aim (a weapon). ■ direct (a criticism or accusation): *accusations of corruption had been leveled against him.* **4** [intrans.] (**level with**) informal be frank or honest with (someone).

– PHRASES **do one's level best** do one's utmost; make all possible efforts. **find its (own) level** (of a liquid) reach the same height in containers which are interconnected. ■ reach a stable level, value, or position without interference. **find one's (own) level** (of a person) reach a position that seems appropriate and natural in relation to one's associates. **a level playing field** a situation in which everyone has a fair and equal chance. **on the level** informal honest; truthful. **on a level with** in the same horizontal plane as. ■ equal with. — **lev·el·ly adv.** (in sense 2 of the adjective). **lev·el·ness n.** [ME: from OFr. *livel*, based on L. *libella*, dimin. of *libra* 'scales, balance.']

lev·el·er /ˈlev(ə)lər/ (Brit. **lev·el·ler**) ▶ **n.** **1** a person who advocates the abolition of social distinctions. ■ (**Leveller**) an extreme radical dissenter in the English Civil War (1642–49). **2** a person or thing that levels something.

lev·el·head·ed /ˈlevəlˈhedid/ ▶ **adj.** calm and sensible. — **lev·el·head·ed·ly adv.** **lev·el·head·ed·ness n.**

lev·eling rod ▶ **n.** a graduated pole with a movable marker, held upright and used with a surveying instrument to measure differences in elevation. Also called **leveling pole**, **leveling staff**.

lev·er /ˈlevər; ˈlēvər/ ▶ **n.** a rigid bar resting on a pivot, used to help move a heavy or firmly fixed load with one end when pressure is applied to the other. *See illustration on next page.* ■ a projecting arm or handle that is moved to operate a mechanism. ■ fig. a means of exerting pressure on someone to act in a particular way. ▶ **v.** [trans.] lift or move with a lever. ■ move (someone or something) with a concerted physical effort: *she levered herself up.* ■ [intrans.] use a lever: *the men levered at it with crowbars.* [ME: from OFr. *levier*, *leveor*, from *lever* 'to lift.']

lever

lev·er·age /ˈlev(ə)rij; ˈlēv(ə)rij/ ▸ **n.** **1** the exertion of force by means of a lever or an object used in the manner of a lever. ▪ mechanical advantage gained in this way. ▪ fig. the power to influence a person or situation to achieve a particular outcome. **2** Finance the ratio of a company's loan capital (debt) to the value of its common stock (equity). ▸ **v.** [trans.] [usu. as adj.] (**leveraged**) use borrowed capital for (an investment), expecting the profits made to be greater than the interest payable.

lev·er·aged buy·out ▸ **n.** the purchase of a controlling share in a company by its management.

lev·er·et /ˈlev(ə)rit/ ▸ **n.** a young hare in its first year. [ME: from Anglo-Norman Fr., dimin. of *levre*, from L. *lepus, lepor-* 'hare.']

Le·vi[1] /ˈlē,vī/ (in the Bible) a Hebrew patriarch, third son of Jacob and Leah. ▪ the tribe of Israel traditionally descended from him.

Le·vi[2] /ˈlevē/, Primo (1919–87), Italian writer. He wrote about his experiences as a survivor of Auschwitz.

le·vi·a·than /ləˈvīəᴛʜən/ ▸ **n.** (in biblical use) a sea monster, identified in different passages with the whale and the crocodile, and with the Devil. ▪ a very large aquatic creature, esp. a whale. ▪ a thing that is very large or powerful, esp. a ship. ▪ an autocratic monarch or state. [via late L. from Heb. *liwyāṯān*.]

lev·i·gate /ˈlevə,gāt/ ▸ **v.** [trans.] reduce (a substance) to a fine powder or smooth paste. — **lev·i·ga·tion** /,levəˈgāsʜən/ **n.** [16th C.: from L. *levigat-* 'made smooth, polished,' from the v. *levigare*, from *levis* 'smooth.']

lev·in /ˈlevin/ ▸ **n.** archaic lightning; thunderbolts. [ME: prob. of Scand. origin.]

lev·i·rate /ˈlevərit; -,rāt/ ▸ **n.** (usu. **the levirate**) a custom of the ancient Hebrews and other peoples by which a man had to marry his brother's widow. [18th C.: from L. *levir* 'brother-in-law' + **-ATE**[1].]

Le·vi's /ˈlē,vīz/ ▸ **plural n.** trademark a type of denim jeans.

Lé·vi-Strauss /ˈlāvē ˈstrous/, Claude (1908–), French social anthropologist. He regarded language as an essential common denominator underlying cultural phenomena.

lev·i·tate /ˈlevə,tāt/ ▸ **v.** [intrans.] rise and hover in the air, esp. by means of supernatural or magical power. ▪ [trans.] cause (something) to rise and hover in such a way. — **lev·i·ta·tion** /,levəˈtāsʜən/ **n.** **lev·i·ta·tor** /-,tātər/ **n.** [17th C.: from L. *levis* 'light,' on the pattern of *gravitate*.]

Le·vite /ˈlē,vīt/ ▸ **n.** a member of the Hebrew tribe of Levi. [ME: from late L. *levita*, from Gk. *leuitēs*, from Heb. *Lēwī* 'Levi.']

Le·vit·i·cal /ləˈvitikəl/ ▸ **adj.** **1** of or relating to the Levites or the tribe of Levi. **2** Judaism (of rules concerning codes of conduct, temple rituals, etc.) derived from the biblical Book of Leviticus.

Le·vit·i·cus /ləˈvitikəs/ the third book of the Bible.

Lev·it·town /ˈlevət,toun/ a village in central Long Island in New York, noted for its "cookie-cutter" houses, developed after World War II; pop. 53,067.

lev·i·ty /ˈlevətē/ ▸ **n.** humor or frivolity, esp. the treatment of a serious matter with humor or in a manner lacking due respect. [16th C.: from L. *levitas*, from *levis* 'light.']

levo- (also esp. Brit. **laevo-**) ▸ **comb. form** on or to the left. [from L. *laevus* 'left.']

le·vo·do·pa /,levəˈdōpə; ,lēvə/ (also **le·vo·do·pa·mine** /-ˈdōpəmēn/) ▸ **n.** another term for **L-DOPA**.

le·vo·nor·ges·trel /,lēvənôrˈjestrəl/ ▸ **n.** Biochem. a synthetic steroid hormone used for contraception. [1970s: from **LEVO-** + *norgestrel*, a synthetic steroid hormone.]

le·vo·ro·ta·to·ry /,lēvəˈrōtə,tôrē/ (Brit. **lae·vo·ro·ta·to·ry**) ▸ **adj.** Chem. (of a compound) having the property of rotating the plane of a polarized light ray to the left, i.e., counterclockwise facing the oncoming radiation. The opposite of **DEXTROROTATORY**. — **le·vo·ro·ta·tion** /-rōˈtāsʜən/ **n.**

lev·u·lose /ˈlevyə,lōs; -,lōz/ (Brit. **laev·u·lose**) ▸ **n.** Chem. another term for **FRUCTOSE**.

le·vy /ˈlevē/ ▸ **v.** (**-vies, -vied**) [trans.] **1** (often **be levied**) impose (a tax, fee, or fine). ▪ impose a tax, fee, or fine on. ▪ [intrans.] (**levy on/upon**) seize (property) to satisfy a legal judgment. **2** archaic enlist (someone) for military service. ▪ begin to wage (war). ▸ **n.** (pl. **-vies**) **1** an act of levying a tax, fee, or fine. ▪ a tax so raised. ▪ an item or set of items of property seized to satisfy a legal judgment. **2** hist. an act of enlisting troops. ▪ (usu. **levies**) a body of enlisted troops. — **lev·i·a·ble adj.** [ME (as a n.): from OFr. *levee*, fem. past part. of *lever* 'raise,' from L. *levare*, from *levis* 'light.']

lewd /lo͞od/ ▸ **adj.** crude and offensive in a sexual way. — **lewd·ly adv.** **lewd·ness n.** [OE *lǣwede* 'belonging to the laity.']

Lew·is[1] /ˈlo͞o-is/, Cecil Day, see **DAY LEWIS**.

Lew·is[2], C. S. (1898–1963), British writer; full name *Clive Staples Lewis*. His fantasy septology *The Chronicles of Narnia* includes *The Lion, the Witch, and the Wardrobe* (1950).

Lew·is[3], Carl (1961–), US track and field athlete; full name *Frederick Carleton Lewis*. During 1984–96, he won nine Olympic gold medals.

Lew·is[4], John Llewellyn (1880–1969), US labor leader. He was president of the Congress of Industrial Organizations (CIO) 1935–40.

Lew·is[5], Meriwether (1774–1809), US explorer. Together with William Clark, he led an expedition to explore the Louisiana Purchase (1804–06).

Lew·is[6], Sinclair (1885–1951), US writer; full name *Harry Sinclair Lewis*. He wrote *Main Street* (1920). Nobel Prize for Literature (1930).

lew·is /ˈlo͞o-is/ ▸ **n.** a steel device for gripping heavy blocks of stone or concrete for lifting, consisting of three pieces arranged to form a dovetail, the outside pieces being fixed in a dovetail mortise by the insertion of the middle piece. [ME: prob. from OFr. *lous*, pl. of *lou(p)* 'wolf,' the name of a kind of siege engine.]

Lew·is ac·id ▸ **n.** Chem. a compound or ionic species that can accept an electron pair from a donor compound. [1940s: named after Gilbert N. *Lewis* (1875–1946), US chemist.]

Lew·is base ▸ **n.** Chem. a compound or ionic species that can donate an electron pair to an acceptor compound. [1960s: named after G. N. *Lewis* (see **LEWIS ACID**).]

lew·is·ite /ˈlo͞oə,sīt/ ▸ **n.** a dark, oily liquid, $ClCH{=}CHAsCl_2$, producing an irritant gas that causes blisters, developed for use in chemical warfare. [1920s: named after Winford L. *Lewis* (1878–1943), US chemist.]

lex /leks/ ▸ **n.** (pl. **le·ges** /ˈlējēz; ˈleges/) law. [L.]

lex. ▸ **abbr.** ▪ lexical. ▪ lexicon.

Lex·an /ˈlek,san/ ▸ **n.** trademark a transparent plastic (polycarbonate) of high impact strength, used for cockpit canopies, bulletproof screens, etc. [1950s: an invented name.]

lex·eme /ˈlek,sēm/ ▸ **n.** Ling. a basic lexical unit of a language, consisting of one word or several words, considered as an abstract unit, and applied to a family of words related by form or meaning. [1940s: from **LEXICON** + **-EME**.]

lex·i·cal /ˈleksikəl/ ▸ **adj.** of or relating to the words or vocabulary of a language. ▪ relating to or of the nature of a lexicon or dictionary. — **lex·i·cal·ly adv.** [19th C.: from Gk. *lexikos* 'of words' (from *lexis* 'word') + **-AL**.]

lex·i·cal mean·ing ▸ **n.** the meaning of a word considered in isolation from the sentence containing it and regardless of its grammatical context, e.g., of *love* in or as represented by *loves, loved, loving*, etc.

lex·i·cog·ra·pher /,leksəˈkägrəfər/ ▸ **n.** a person who compiles dictionaries.

lex·i·cog·ra·phy /,leksəˈkägrəfē/ ▸ **n.** the practice of compiling dictionaries. — **lex·i·co·graph·ic** /-kəˈgrafik/ **adj.** **lex·i·co·graph·i·cal** /-kəˈgrafikəl/ **adj.** **lex·i·co·graph·i·cal·ly** /-kəˈgrafik(ə)lē/ **adv.**

lex·i·col·o·gy /,leksəˈkäləjē/ ▸ **n.** the study of the form, meaning, and use of words. — **lex·i·co·log·i·cal** /-kəˈläjikəl/ **adj.** **lex·i·co·log·i·cal·ly** /-kəˈläjik(ə)lē/ **adv.**

lex·i·con /ˈleksi,kän; -kən/ ▸ **n.** (pl. **-cons** or **-ca** /-kə/) **1** the vocabulary of a person, language, or branch of knowledge. ▪ a dictionary, esp. of Greek, Hebrew, Syriac, or Arabic: *a Greek–Latin lexicon*. **2** Ling. the complete set of meaningful units in a language. [17th C.: mod. L., from Gk. *lexikon (biblion)* '(book) of words,' from *lexis* 'word,' from *legein* 'speak.']

lex·i·gram /ˈleksi,gram/ ▸ **n.** a symbol representing a word, esp. one used in learning a language.

Lex·ing·ton /ˈleksɪɴɢtən/ **1** a city in central Kentucky; pop. 260,512. **2** a town in northeastern Massachusetts; pop. 28,970. In 1775, it was the scene of the first battle in the American Revolution.

lex·is /ˈleksis/ ▸ **n.** the stock of words in a language. ▪ the level of language consisting of vocabulary, as opposed to grammar or syntax. [1950s: from Gk., 'word' (see **LEXICON**).]

lex lo·ci /ˈleks ˈlōsī; -,sē; -,kē; -,kī/ ▸ **n.** Law the law of the country in which a transaction is performed. [L., 'law of the place.']

lex ta·li·o·nis /ˈleks ,tälēˈōnis; ,talē-/ ▸ **n.** the law of retaliation. [L., from *lex* 'law' and *talio(n-)* 'retaliation' (from *talis* 'such').]

Ley·den /ˈlīdn/ var. of **LEIDEN**.

Ley·den jar ▸ **n.** a capacitor consisting of a glass jar with layers of metal foil outside and inside. [18th C.: named after *Leyden* (see **LEIDEN**), where it was invented (1745).]

Ley·te /ˈlā,tē; -,tā/ an island in the central Philippines; pop. 1,362,050.

Ley·te Gulf /ˈlātē; ˈlātā/ an inlet of the Philippine Sea, in the eastern Philippines, between Leyte and Samar.

lez ▸ **n.** var. of **LES**.

lez·zy /ˈlezē/ ▸ **n.** (pl. **-zies**) informal, usu. offens. a lesbian.

LF ▸ **abbr.** low frequency.

lg. ▸ **abbr.** ▪ large. ▪ long.

lge. ▸ **abbr.** large.

LH Biochem. ▸ **abbr.** luteinizing hormone.

l.h. ▸ **abbr.** left hand.

Lha·sa /ˈläsə/ the capital of Tibet, in the northern Himalayas; pop. 140,000.

Lha·sa ap·so /ˈläsə ˈäpsō; ˈlasə ˈapsō/ ▸ **n.** (pl. **ap·sos**) a dog of a small, long-coated breed, typically gold or gray and white, originating at Lhasa. *See illustration on next page.* [20th C.: from **LHASA** + Tibetan *a-sob*.]

LHRH ▸ **abbr.** luteinizing hormone-releasing hormone.

Lhasa apso

LI ▶ abbr. ■ Long Island.

Li ▶ symb. the chemical element lithium.

li /lē/ ▶ n. (pl. same) a Chinese unit of distance, equal to about 0.4 miles (0.6 km).

li·a·bil·i·ty /ˌlīəˈbilətē/ ▶ n. (pl. **-ties**) **1** the state of being responsible for something, esp. by law. ■ (usu. **liabilities**) a thing for which someone is responsible, esp. a debt or financial obligation. **2** [usu. in sing.] a person or thing whose behavior is likely to cause embarrassment or put one at a disadvantage.

li·a·ble /ˈlī(ə)bəl/ ▶ adj. [predic.] **1** responsible by law. **2** [with infin.] likely to do or to be something. ■ (**liable to**) likely to experience (something undesirable). [ME: perh. from Anglo-Norman French, from Fr. *lier* 'to bind,' from L. *ligare*.]

li·aise /lēˈāze/ [intrans.] establish a working relationship, typically in order to cooperate on a matter of mutual concern.

li·ai·son /ˈlēəˌzän; lēˈā-/ ▶ n. **1** communication or cooperation that facilitates a close working relationship between people or organizations. ■ a person who acts as a link to assist communication or cooperation between groups of people. ■ a sexual relationship, esp. one that is secret and involves unfaithfulness to a partner. **2** the binding or thickening agent of a sauce. **3** Phonet. (in French and other languages) the sounding of a consonant that is normally silent at the end of a word because the next word begins with a vowel. [17th C. (as a culinary term): from Fr., from *lier* 'to bind.']

li·ai·son of·fi·cer ▶ n. a person who is employed to form a working relationship between two organizations.

li·a·na /lēˈänə; -ˈanə/ (also **li·a·ne** /-ˈän; -ˈan/) ▶ n. a woody climbing plant that hangs from trees. ■ the free-hanging stem of such a plant. [18th C.: from Fr. *liane* 'clematis, liana,' of unknown origin.]

Liao[1] /lēˈou/ a river in northeastern China that flows to the Gulf of Liaodong.

Liao[2] /liˈou/ a dynasty that ruled much of Manchuria and part of northeastern China AD 947–1125.

Liao·dong Pen·in·su·la /lēˈouˈdōōNG/ a peninsula in northeastern China.

Liao·ning /lēˈouˈniNG/ a province in northeastern China; capital, Shenyang.

li·ar /ˈlīər/ ▶ n. a person who tells lies. [OE *lēogere* (see LIE², -AR⁴).]

Li·ard Riv·er /ˈlēˌärd; lēˈärd/ a river flowing from the Yukon Territory to the Mackenzie River.

Li·as /ˈlīəs/ ▶ n. (**the Lias**) Geol. the earliest epoch of the Jurassic period, as much as 208 million years ago. ■ the system of rocks deposited during this epoch. — **li·as·sic** /līˈasik/ adj. [ME (denoting blue lias): from OFr. *liais* 'hard limestone,' prob. from *lie* (see LEES).]

Lib. ▶ abbr. Liberal.

lib /lib/ ▶ n. informal (in the names of political movements) liberation.

li·ba·tion /līˈbāSHən/ ▶ n. a drink poured out as an offering to a deity. ■ the pouring out of such a drink-offering. ■ humorous a drink. [ME: from L. *libatio(n-)*, from *libare* 'pour as an offering.']

lib·ber /ˈlibər/ ▶ n. [usu. with adj.] informal a member or advocate of a movement calling for the liberation of people or animals: *a women's libber.*

li·bel /ˈlībəl/ ▶ n. **1** Law a published false statement that is damaging to a person's reputation; a written defamation. Compare with SLANDER. ■ the action or crime of publishing such a statement. ■ a false and malicious statement about a person. ■ a thing or circumstance that brings undeserved discredit on a person by misrepresentation. **2** (in admiralty and ecclesiastical law) a plaintiff's written declaration. ▶ v. (**-beled, -bel·ing**; Brit. **-belled, -bel·ling**) [trans.] **1** Law defame (someone) by publishing a libel. ■ make a false and malicious statement about. **2** (in admiralty and ecclesiastical law) bring a suit against. — **li·bel·er** n. [ME: via OFr. from L. *libellus*, dimin. of *liber* 'book.']

li·bel·ous /ˈlībələs/ (Brit. **li·bel·lous**) ▶ adj. containing or constituting a libel. — **li·bel·ous·ly** adv.

lib·er·al /ˈlib(ə)rəl/ ▶ adj. **1** open to new behavior or opinions and willing to discard traditional values. ■ favorable to or respectful of individual rights and freedoms: *liberal citizenship laws.* ■ (in a political context) favoring maximum individual liberty in political and social reform. ■ (**Liberal**) of or characteristic of Liberals or a Liberal Party. ■ (**Liberal**) (in the UK) of or relating to the Liberal Democrat Party. ■ Theol. regarding many traditional beliefs as dispensable, invalidated by modern thought, or liable to change. **2** [attrib.] (of education) concerned mainly with broadening a person's general knowledge and experience, rather than with technical or professional training. **3** (esp. of an interpretation of a law) broadly construed or understood; not strictly literal or exact. **4** given, used, or occurring in generous amounts. ■ (of a person) giving generously. ▶ n. a person of liberal views. ■ (**Liberal**) a supporter or member of a Liberal Party. — **lib·er·al·ism** n. **lib·er·al·ist** n. **lib·er·al·is·tic** /ˌlib(ə)rəˈlistik/ adj. **lib·er·al·ly** adv. **lib·er·al·ness** n. [ME: via OFr. from L. *liberalis*, from *liber* 'free (man).']

lib·er·al arts ▶ plural n. academic subjects such as literature, philosophy, mathematics, and the sciences as distinct from professional and technical subjects. ■ hist. the medieval trivium and quadrivium.

lib·er·al·i·ty /ˌlibəˈralətē/ ▶ n. **1** the quality of giving or spending freely. **2** the quality of being open to new ideas and free from prejudice.

lib·er·al·ize /ˈlib(ə)rəˌlīz/ ▶ v. [trans.] remove or loosen restrictions on (something, typically an economic or political system). — **lib·er·al·i·za·tion** /ˌlib(ə)rələˈzāSHən; -ˌlīˈzā-/ n. **lib·er·al·iz·er** n.

Lib·er·al Par·ty ▶ n. a political party of liberal policies in Britain. The name was discontinued in 1988 and the party is now known as the Liberal Democrats.

lib·er·ate /ˈlibəˌrāt/ ▶ v. [trans.] (often **be liberated**) set (someone) free. ■ free (a country, city, or people) from enemy occupation. ■ release (someone) from a state or situation that limits freedom of thought or behavior. ■ free (someone) from rigid social conventions, esp. those concerned with accepted sexual roles. ■ informal steal (something). ■ Chem. & Physics release (gas, energy, etc.) as a result of chemical reaction or physical decomposition. — **lib·er·a·tion** /ˌlibəˈrāSHən/ n. **lib·er·a·tion·ist** /ˌlibəˈrāSHənist/ n. **lib·er·a·tor** /-ˌrātər/ n. [16th C.: from L. *liberat-* 'freed,' from the v. *liberare*, from *liber* 'free.']

lib·er·at·ed /ˈlibəˌrātid/ ▶ adj. **1** (of a person) showing freedom from social conventions or traditional ideas. **2** (of a place or people) freed from enemy occupation.

lib·er·a·tion the·ol·o·gy ▶ n. a movement in Christian theology that emphasizes liberation from social, political, and economic oppression as an anticipation of ultimate salvation.

Lib·er·a·tion Ti·gers of Tam·il Ee·lam /ˈtaməl ˈēˌlam/ another name for TAMIL TIGERS.

Li·be·ri·a /līˈbi(ə)rēə/ a country in West Africa. *See box.* — **Li·be·ri·an** adj. & n.

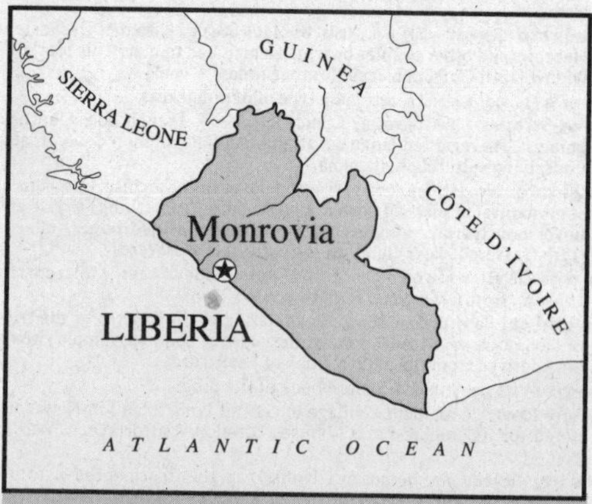

Liberia

Official name: Republic of Liberia
Location: West Africa, on the Atlantic coast
Area: 43,000 square miles (111,400 sq km)
Population: 3,390,000
Capital: Monrovia
Languages: English (official), some 20 local languages
Currency: Liberian dollar

lib·er·tar·i·an /ˌlibərˈte(ə)rēən/ ▶ n. **1** an adherent of libertarianism. ■ a person who advocates civil liberty. **2** Philos. a person who believes in free will.

lib·er·tar·i·an·ism /ˌlibərˈte(ə)rēəˌnizəm/ ▶ n. an extreme laissez-faire political philosophy advocating only minimal state intervention in the lives of citizens.

lib·er·tine /ˈlibərˌtēn/ ▶ n. **1** a person, esp. a man, who behaves without moral principles. **2** a person who rejects accepted opinions in matters of religion; a freethinker. ▶ adj. **1** characterized by a disregard of morality. **2** freethinking in matters of religion. — **lib·er·tin·age** /-ˌtēnij/ n. **lib·er·tin·ism** n. [ME: from L. *libertinus* 'freedman,' from *liber* 'free.']

lib·er·ty /ˈlibərtē/ ▶ n. (pl. **-ties**) **1** the state of being free within society from oppressive restrictions imposed by authority on one's way of life. ■ (usu. **liberties**) an instance of this; a right or privilege, esp. a statutory one. ■ the state of not being imprisoned or enslaved. ■ (**Liberty**) the personification of liberty as a female figure. **2** the power or scope to act as one pleases. ■ Philos. a person's freedom from control. ■ Naut. shore leave granted to a sailor.

– PHRASES **at liberty 1** not imprisoned. **2** allowed or entitled to do something. **take liberties 1** behave in an unduly familiar manner toward a person. **2** treat something freely, without strict faithfulness to the facts or to an original. **take the liberty** venture to do something without first asking permission. [ME: from OFr. *liberte*, from L. *libertas*, from *liber* 'free.']

Lib·er·ty Bell ▶ n. a bell in Philadelphia first rung on July 8, 1776, to celebrate the first public reading of the Declaration of Independence.

lib·er·ty cap ▶ n. a soft conical cap given to Roman slaves on their emancipation and often used as a republican symbol in more recent times, esp. during the French Revolution.

Lib·er·ty Is·land an island in New York Bay, site (since 1885) of the Statue of Liberty.

Lib·er·ty, Statue of see STATUE OF LIBERTY.

li·bid·i·nous /lə'bidn-əs/ ▶ adj. showing excessive sexual drive; lustful. — **li·bid·i·nous·ly** adv. **li·bid·i·nous·ness** n. [ME: from L. *libidinosus*, from *libido* 'desire, lust.']

li·bi·do /lə'bēdō/ ▶ n. (pl. **-dos**) sexual desire. ■ Psychoanal. the energy of the sexual drive as a component of the life instinct. — **li·bid·i·nal** /-'bidn-əl/ adj. **li·bid·i·nal·ly** /-'bidn-əlē/ adv. [20th C.: from L., 'desire, lust.']

Li Bo /'lē 'bō; 'bô/ variant of **LI PO**.

Li·bra /'lēbrə; 'lī-/ **1** Astron. a small constellation (the Scales or Balance), said to represent justice. **2** Astrol. the seventh sign of the zodiac, which the sun enters about September 23. ■ (**a Libra**) a person born when the sun is in this sign. — **Li·bran** n. & adj. (in sense 2).

li·bra /'lēbrə; 'lī-/ ▶ n. (pl. **-brae** /-ˌbrī; -ˌbrē/) (in ancient Rome) a unit of weight, equal to 12 ounces (0.34 kg). [L., 'pound, balance.']

li·brar·i·an /lī'bre(ə)rēən/ ▶ n. a person who administers or assists in a library. — **li·brar·i·an·ship** /-ˌSHip/ n.

li·brar·y /'līˌbrerē; -brərē/ ▶ n. (pl. **-brar·ies**) a building or room containing collections of books, periodicals, and sometimes films and recorded music for people to read, borrow, or refer to. ■ a collection of books and periodicals held in such a building or room. ■ a collection of films, recorded music, genetic material, etc., organized systematically and kept for research or borrowing. ■ a room in a private house where books are kept. ■ (also **software library**) Comput. a collection of programs and software packages made generally available. [ME: via OFr. from L. *libraria* 'bookshop,' fem. (used as a n.) of *librarius* 'relating to books,' from *liber, libr-* 'book.']

Li·brar·y of Con·gress the US national library, in Washington, DC.

li·brar·y sci·ence ▶ n. the study of collecting, preserving, and cataloging books and other documents in libraries.

li·bra·tion /lī'brāSHən/ ▶ n. Astron. an apparent or real oscillation of the moon, by which often not visible parts near the edge of the disc come into view. — **li·brate** /'līˌbrāt/ v. [17th C.: from L. *libratio(n-)*, from the v. *librare*, from *libra* 'a balance.']

li·bret·to /lə'bretō/ ▶ n. (pl. **-bret·ti** /-'bretē/ or **-bret·tos**) the text of an opera or other long vocal work. — **li·bret·tist** /-'bretist/ n. [18th C.: from Ital., dimin. of *libro* 'book,' from L. *liber*.]

Li·bre·ville /'lēbrəˌvil/ the capital of Gabon, a port on the Atlantic coast; pop. 419,596.

Lib·ri·um /'librēəm/ ▶ n. trademark for **CHLORDIAZEPOXIDE**.

Lib·ya /'libēə/ a country in North Africa. *See box.* ■ ancient northern Africa that lies west of Egypt. — **Lib·y·an** adj. & n.

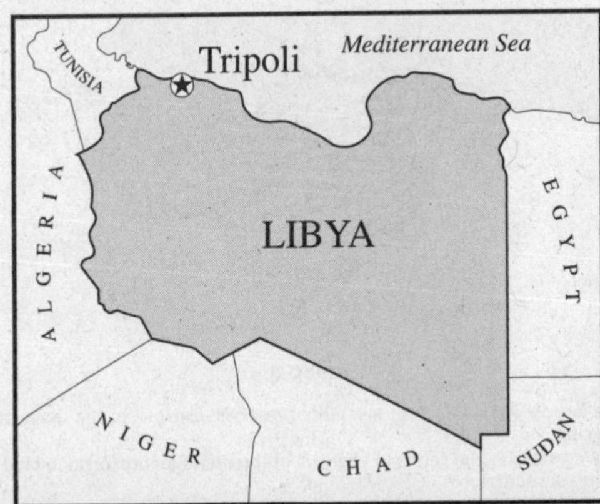

Libya

Official name: Socialist People's Libyan Arab Jamahiriya
Location: North Africa, in the Sahara Desert, with a northern coastline on the Mediterranean Sea
Area: 679,500 square miles (1,759,500 sq km)
Population: 5,631,000
Capital: Tripoli
Languages: Arabic (official), Italian, English
Currency: Libyan dinar

Lib·yan Desert the northeastern Sahara Desert.

lice /līs/ plural form of **LOUSE**.

li·cense /'līsəns/ ▶ n. (Brit. **li·cence**) a permit from an authority to own or use something, do a particular thing, or carry on a trade (esp. in alcoholic beverages). ■ formal or official permission to do something. ■ a writer's or artist's freedom to deviate from fact or from conventions such as grammar, meter, or perspective, for effect. ■ freedom to behave as one wishes, esp. in a way that results in excessive or unacceptable behavior. ■ (**a license to do something**) a reason or excuse to do something wrong or excessive. ▶ v. (Brit. also **li·cence**) [trans.] (often **be licensed**) grant a license to permit the use of something or to allow an activity to take place. ■ authorize the use, performance, or release of (something). — **li·cens·a·ble** adj. **li·cens·er** n. **li·cen·sor** /-sər; ˌlīsən'sôr/ n. [ME: via OFr. from L. *licentia* 'freedom, licentiousness,' from *licere* 'be lawful or permitted.']

li·censed /'līsənst/ ▶ adj. having an official license.

li·cen·see /ˌlīsən'sē/ ▶ n. the holder of a license.

li·cense plate ▶ n. a sign affixed to a vehicle indicating that the vehicle has been registered.

li·cen·ti·ate /lī'sensH(ē)it/ ▶ n. the holder of a certificate of competence to practice a certain profession. ■ (in certain universities, esp. in Europe) a degree between that of bachelor and master or doctor. ■ the holder of such a degree. — **li·cen·ti·ate·ship** n.

li·cen·tious /lī'sensHəs/ ▶ adj. promiscuous and unprincipled in sexual matters. — **li·cen·tious·ly** adv. **li·cen·tious·ness** n. [ME: from L. *licentiosus*, from *licentia* 'freedom.']

li·chee ▶ n. var. of **LITCHI**.

li·chen /'līkən/ ▶ n. **1** a simple plant consisting of a fungus, usually of the subdivision Ascomycotina, that grows symbiotically with algae, forming a low crustlike or branching growth on rocks, walls, and trees. **2** [usu. with adj.] a skin disease in which small round hard lesions occur close together. — **li·chened** adj. (in sense 1). **li·chen·ol·o·gy** /ˌlīkə'näləjē/ n. (in sense 1). **li·chen·ous** /-nəs/ adj. (in sense 2). [17th C.: via L. from Gk. *leikhēn*.]

licht /likHt/ ▶ n., adj. & v. Scottish variant of **LIGHT**[1], **LIGHT**[2].

Lich·ten·stein /'liktənˌstēn/, Roy (1923–97), US painter and sculptor. A leading exponent of pop art, he became known for paintings inspired by comic strips.

-licious ▶ comb. form forming adjectives denoting someone or something delightful or very attractive: *bootylicious*. [1950s: from **DELICIOUS**.]

lic·it /'lisit/ ▶ adj. not forbidden; lawful. — **lic·it·ly** adv. [15th C.: from L. *licitus* 'allowed,' from the v. *licere*.]

lick /lik/ ▶ v. [trans.] **1** pass the tongue over (something), typically in order to taste, moisten, or clean it. ■ [intrans.] fig. (of a flame, wave, or breeze) move lightly and quickly like a tongue. **2** informal defeat (someone) comprehensively. ■ thrash. ▶ n. **1** an act of licking something with the tongue. ■ fig. a movement of flame, water, etc., resembling this. **2** informal a small amount or quick application of something, esp. paint. **3** informal a smart blow.
– PHRASES **at a lick** informal at a fast pace; with considerable speed. **a lick and a promise** informal a hasty performance of a task, esp. of cleaning something. **lick someone's boots** (or vulgar slang **ass**) be excessively obsequious toward someone, esp. to gain favor from them. **lick someone/something into shape** see **SHAPE**. **lick one's lips** (or **chops**) look forward to something with eager anticipation. **lick one's wounds** retire to recover one's strength or confidence after a defeat or humiliating experience. — **lick·er** n. [usu. in comb.]. [OE *liccian*; rel. to Ger. *lecken*, L. *lingere*.]

lick·er·ish /'lik(ə)risH/ ▶ adj. lecherous. — **lick·er·ish·ly** adv. [15th C.: alt. of obs. *lickerous*, based on OFr. *lecheros* (see **LECHEROUS**).]

lick·e·ty-split /'likətē 'split/ ▶ adv. informal as quickly as possible; immediately. [19th C.: from a fanciful extension of **LICK** + the v. **SPLIT**.]

lick·ing /'likiNG/ ▶ n. informal a severe defeat or beating.

lick·spit·tle /'likˌspitl/ ▶ n. a person who behaves obsequiously to those in power.

lic·o·rice /'lik(ə)risH; -ris/ (Brit. **liq·uo·rice**) ▶ n. **1** a sweet, chewy, aromatic black substance made by evaporation from the juice of a root. ■ a candy flavored with such a substance. **2** the widely distributed plant (genus *Glycyrrhiza*) of the pea family from which this product is obtained. [ME: from OFr. *licoresse*, from late L. *liquiritia*, from Gk. *glukurrhiza*, from *glukus* 'sweet' + *rhiza* 'root.']

lic·tor /'liktər/ ▶ n. (in ancient Rome) an officer attending the consul or other magistrate. [L., perh. rel. to *ligare* 'to bind.']

lid /lid/ ▶ n. a removable or hinged cover for a container. ■ (usu. **lids**) an eyelid. ■ Bot. the operculum of a moss capsule. ■ informal a hat.
– PHRASES **blow** (or **take**) **the lid off** informal reveal unwelcome secrets about. **keep a** (or **the**) **lid on** informal keep (an emotion or process) from going out of control. ■ keep secret. **put a** (or **the**) **lid on** informal put a stop to or be the culmination of. — **lid·ded** adj. [OE *hlid*, of Gmc. origin, from a base meaning 'cover'; rel. to Du. *lid*.]

li·dar /'līdär/ ▶ n. a detection system that works on the principle of radar, but uses light from a laser. [1960s: blend of **LIGHT**[1] and **RADAR**.]

Li·do /'lēdō/ an island reef off the coast of northeastern Italy.

li·do /'lēdō/ ▶ n. (pl. **li·dos**) a public, open-air swimming pool or bathing beach. [17th C.: from Ital. *Lido*,a bathing beach near Venice.]

li·do·caine /ˈlīdəˌkān/ ▶ **n.** Med. a synthetic compound, $C_{14}H_{22}N_2O$, used as a local anesthetic, e.g., for dental surgery, and in treating abnormal heart rhythms.

Lie /lē/, Trygve Halvdan (1896–1968), Norwegian politician; first secretary-general of the UN 1946–53.

lie[1] /lī/ ▶ **v.** (**ly·ing** /ˈlī-ing/; past **lay** /lā/; past part. **lain** /lān/) [intrans.] **1** (of a person or animal) be in or assume a horizontal or resting position. ■ (of a thing) rest flat on a surface. ■ (of a dead person) be buried in a particular place. **2** be, remain, or be kept in a specified state. ■ (of something abstract) reside or be found. **3** (of a place) be situated in a specified position or direction. ■ (of a scene) extend from the observer's viewpoint in a specified direction: *America lies before you.* **4** Law (of an action, charge, or claim) be admissible or sustainable. ▶ **n.** (usu. **the lie**) the way, direction, or position in which something lies.

– PHRASES **let something lie** take no action regarding a controversial or problematic matter. **lie in state** (of the corpse of a person of national importance) be laid in a public place of honor before burial. **lie in wait** conceal oneself, waiting to surprise, attack, or catch someone. **lie low** (esp. of a criminal) keep out of sight; avoid detection or attention. **take something lying down** [usu. with negative] accept an insult, setback, rebuke, etc., without reacting or protesting.

– PHRASAL VERBS **lie ahead** be going to happen; be in store. **lie around/about** (of an object) be left carelessly out of place. ■ (of a person) pass the time lazily or aimlessly. **lie behind** be the real, often hidden, reason for. **lie off** Naut. (of a ship) stand some distance from shore or from another ship. **lie to** Naut. (of a ship) come almost to a stop with its head toward the wind. **lie with** (of a responsibility or problem) be attributable to (someone): *responsibility lies with the president.* [OE *licgan*; rel. to Ger. *liegen* 'to lie,' Gk. *lektron*, L. *lectus* 'bed.']

lie[2] ▶ **n.** an intentionally false statement. ■ used with reference to a situation involving deception or founded on a mistaken impression. ▶ **v.** (**lies, lied, ly·ing** /ˈlī-ing/) [intrans.] tell a lie or lies. ■ (**lie one's way into/out of**) get oneself into or out of a situation by lying. ■ (of a thing) present a false impression; be deceptive.

– PHRASES **lie through one's teeth** informal tell an outright lie without remorse. [OE *lyge* (n.), *lēogan* (v.), of Gmc. origin; rel. to Du. *liegen* and Ger. *lügen*.]

Lieb·frau·milch /ˈlēbˌfrouˌmilch; -ˌmilk; -ˌmilkh; ˈlēp-/ ▶ **n.** a light white wine from the Rhine region. [Ger., from *lieb* 'dear' + *Frau* 'lady' (the Virgin Mary, patroness of the convent where it was first made) + *Milch* 'milk.']

Liech·ten·stein /ˈliktənˌstīn; -ˌshtīn/ a country in central Europe, in the Alps between Switzerland and Austria; pop. 33,400; capital, Vaduz. — **Liech·ten·stein·er** n.

lied /lēd; lēt/ ▶ **n.** (pl. **lie·der** /ˈlēdər/) a type of German song, typically for solo voice with piano accompaniment. [from Ger. *Lied*.]

lie de·tec·tor ▶ **n.** an instrument for determining whether a person is telling the truth by testing for physiological changes. Compare with POLYGRAPH.

lief /lēf/ ▶ **adv.** (**as lief**) archaic as happily; as gladly. [OE *lēof* 'dear, pleasant,' of Gmc. origin: rel. to LEAVE[2] and LOVE.]

Liège /lēˈezh/ a province of eastern Belgium. Flemish name **Luik.** ■ its capital city, situated at the junction of the Meuse and Ourthe rivers; pop. 207,496.

liege /lēj; lēzh/ hist. ▶ **adj.** [attrib.] relating to the relationship between a feudal superior and a vassal. ▶ **n.** (also **liege lord**) a feudal superior or sovereign. ■ a vassal or subject. [ME: via OFr. *lige, liege* from med. L. *laeticus*, prob. of Gmc. origin.]

liege·man /ˈlējˌman; -mən/ ▶ **n.** (pl. **-men**) hist. a vassal.

lien /ˈlē(ə)n/ ▶ **n.** Law a right to keep property belonging to another person until a debt is paid. [16th C.: from Fr., via OFr. *loien* from L. *ligamen* 'bond,' from *ligare* 'to bind.']

li·erne /lēˈərn/ ▶ **n.** [usu. as adj.] Archit. (in vaulting) a short rib connecting the bosses and intersections of the principal ribs: *a fine lierne vault.* [ME: from French, perh. a transferred use of dial. *lierne* (standard Fr. *liane*) 'clematis.']

lieu /lo͞o/ ▶ **n.** (in phrase **in lieu**) instead. [ME: via Fr. from L. *locus* 'place.']

Lieut. ▶ **abbr.** lieutenant.

lieu·ten·ant /lo͞oˈtenənt/ ▶ **n.** a deputy. ■ see FIRST LIEUTENANT, SECOND LIEUTENANT. ■ a commissioned officer in the US Navy or Coast Guard ranking above lieutenant junior grade and below lieutenant commander. ■ a police or fire department officer next in rank below captain. — **lieu·ten·an·cy** /-ˈtenənsē/ n. (pl. **-cies**). [ME: from OFr. (see LIEU, TENANT).]

lieu·ten·ant colo·nel ▶ **n.** a commissioned officer in the US Army, Air Force, or Marine Corps ranking above major and below colonel.

lieu·ten·ant com·man·der ▶ **n.** a commissioned officer in the US Navy or Coast Guard ranking above lieutenant and below commander.

lieu·ten·ant gen·er·al ▶ **n.** a commissioned officer in the US Army, Air Force, or Marine Corps ranking above major general and below general.

lieu·ten·ant gov·er·nor ▶ **n.** the executive officer of a state who is next in rank to a governor. — **lieu·ten·ant gov·er·nor·ship** n.

lieu·ten·ant jun·ior grade ▶ **n.** a commissioned officer in the US Navy or Coast Guard ranking above ensign and below lieutenant.

life /līf/ ▶ **n.** (pl. **lives** /līvz/) **1** the condition that distinguishes animals and plants from inorganic matter, including the capacity for growth, reproduction, functional activity, and continual change preceding death. ■ living things and their activity: *some sort of life existed on Mars.* ■ the state of being alive as a human being. ■ [with adj.] a particular type or aspect of people's existence: *school life.* ■ vitality, vigor, or energy: *she was full of life.* **2** the existence of an individual human being or animal: *a disaster that claimed the lives of 266 Americans.* ■ [often with adj.] a way of living: *his father decided to start a new life in California.* ■ a biography: *a life of Shelley.* ■ either of the two states of a person's existence separated by death (as in Christianity and other religions): *too much happiness in this life could reduce the chances of salvation in the next.* ■ any of a number of successive existences in which a soul is held to be reincarnated (as in Hinduism and other religions). ■ a chance to live after narrowly escaping death. **3** (usu. **one's life**) the period between the birth and death of a living thing, esp. a human being: *lived all her life in the country.* ■ the period during which something inanimate or abstract continues to exist, function, or be valid: *underlay helps to prolong the life of a carpet.* ■ informal a sentence of imprisonment for life. **4** (in art) the depiction of a subject from a real model, rather than from an artist's imagination: *the pose and clothing were sketched from life.* See also STILL LIFE.

– PHRASES **bring** (or **come**) **to life** regain or cause to regain consciousness or return as if from death. ■ (with reference to a fictional character or inanimate object) cause or seem to be alive or real: *all the puppets came to life again.* ■ make or become active, lively, or interesting: *with the return of the fishermen, the village comes to life.* **for dear** (or **one's**) **life** as if or in order to escape death: *I clung to the tree for dear life.* **for the life of me** informal however hard I try; even if my life depended on it: *I can't for the life of me understand what it is you see in that place.* **frighten the life out of** terrify. **get a life** [often in imper.] informal start living a fuller or more interesting existence. **give one's life for** die for. **life and limb** see LIMB[1]. **the life of the party** a vivacious and sociable person. **life in the fast lane** informal an exciting and eventful lifestyle, esp. one bringing wealth and success. **lose one's life** be killed. **a matter of life and death** a matter of vital importance. **not on your life** informal said to emphasize one's refusal to comply with a request. **see life** gain a wide experience of the world, esp. its more pleasurable aspects. **take one's life in one's hands** risk being killed. **take someone's** (or **one's own**) **life** kill someone (or oneself). **that's life** an expression of one's acceptance of a situation, however difficult. **this is the life** an expression of contentment with one's present circumstances. **to the life** exactly like the original: *there he was, Nathan to the life, sitting at a table.* **to save one's life** even if one's life were to depend on it: *she couldn't stop crying now to save her life.* [OE *līf*, of Gmc. origin; rel. to Du. *lijf*, Ger. *Leib* 'body,' also to LIVE[1].]

life-and-death ▶ **adj.** deciding whether someone lives or dies; vitally important: *life-and-death decisions.*

life·belt /ˈlīfˌbelt/ ▶ **n.** a life preserver in the shape of a belt.

life·blood /ˈlīfˌbləd/ ▶ **n.** the blood, as being necessary to life. ■ fig. the indispensable factor or influence that gives something its strength and vitality.

life·boat /ˈlīfˌbōt/ ▶ **n.** a specially constructed boat launched from land to rescue people in distress at sea. ■ a small boat kept on a ship for use in emergency. — **life·boat·man** /-mən/ **n.** (pl. **-men**).

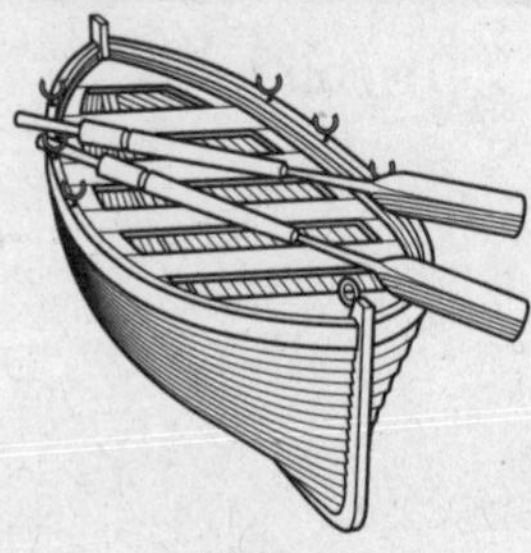

lifeboat

life·bu·oy /ˈlīfˌbo͞o-ē; -ˌboi/ ▶ **n.** a life preserver, esp. one in the shape of a ring.

life cy·cle ▶ **n.** the series of changes in the life of an organism, including reproduction.

life ex·pec·tan·cy ▶ **n.** the average period that a person may expect to live.

life force ▶ **n.** the force or influence that gives something its vitality or strength: *the life force of the symphony.* ■ the spirit or energy that animates living creatures; the soul.

life form ▶ **n.** any living thing.

life-giv·ing ▶ **adj.** sustaining or revitalizing life.

life·guard /ˈlīfˌgärd/ ▶ **n.** an expert swimmer employed to rescue bathers who get into difficulty at a beach or swimming pool. ▶ **v.** [intrans.] work as a lifeguard.

life his·to·ry ▶ **n.** the series of changes undergone by an organism during its lifetime. ■ the story of a person's life, esp. when told at tedious length.

life in·stinct ▶ n. Psychoanal. an innate desire for self-preservation. Compare with DEATH INSTINCT.

life in·sur·ance ▶ n. insurance that pays out a sum of money either on the death of the insured person or after a set period.

life in·ter·est ▶ n. Law a right to property that a person holds for life but cannot dispose of further.

life jack·et ▶ n. a sleeveless buoyant or inflatable jacket for keeping a person afloat in water.

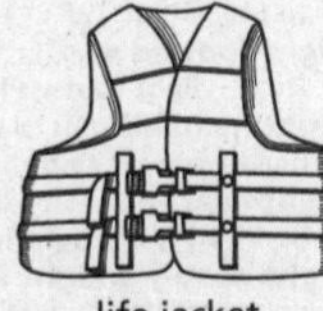
life jacket

life·less /ˈlīflis/ ▶ adj. dead or apparently dead. ■ lacking vigor, vitality, or excitement: *my hair always seems to look lifeless.* ■ devoid of living things. — **life·less·ly** adv. **life·less·ness** n.

life·like /ˈlīfˌlīk/ ▶ adj. very similar to the person or thing represented: *the artist had etched a lifelike horse.* — **life·like·ness** n.

life·line /ˈlīfˌlīn/ ▶ n. **1** a rope or line used for life-saving, typically one thrown to rescue someone in water or one used by sailors to secure themselves to a boat. ■ a line used by a diver for sending signals to the surface. ■ fig. a thing that is essential for the continued existence of someone or something or that provides a solution to a problem: *fertility treatment can seem like a lifeline to childless couples.* **2** (in palmistry) a line on the palm of a person's hand, regarded as indicating how long they will live.

life list ▶ n. Ornithol. a list of all the kinds of birds observed by a person during his or her life.

life·long /ˈlīfˌlôNG; -ˌläNG/ ▶ adj. lasting or remaining in a particular state throughout a person's life.

life peer ▶ n. (in the UK) a peer whose title cannot be inherited. — **life peer·age** n.

life peer·ess ▶ n. a woman holding a life peerage.

life pre·serv·er ▶ n. **1** a device made of buoyant or inflatable material, such as a life jacket or lifebelt, to keep someone afloat in water. **2** Brit. a short club with a heavily weighted end, used as a weapon; a blackjack.

lif·er /ˈlīfər/ ▶ n. **1** informal a person serving a life sentence in prison. **2** a person who spends their life in a particular career, esp. in one of the armed forces.

life raft ▶ n. a raft, typically inflatable, for use in an emergency at sea.

life·sav·er /ˈlīfˌsāvər/ ▶ n. informal a thing that saves one from serious difficulty: *a microwave oven could be a lifesaver this Christmas.*

life sci·enc·es ▶ plural n. the sciences concerned with the study of living organisms, including biology, botany, zoology, microbiology, physiology, and biochemistry. Often contrasted with PHYSICAL SCIENCES. — **life sci·en·tist** n.

life sen·tence ▶ n. a punishment for a felon of imprisonment for life.

life-size (also **life-sized**) ▶ adj. of the same size as the person or thing represented.

life span (also **life·span**) ▶ n. the length of time for which a person or animal lives or a thing functions.

life·style /ˈlīfˌstīl/ ▶ n. the way in which a person or group lives: *the benefits of a healthy lifestyle.*

life·style drug ▶ n. a drug used to improve the quality of one's life rather than alleviating pain or curing disease.

life sup·port ▶ n. Med. maintenance of the vital functions of a critically ill or comatose person or a person undergoing surgery: [as adj.] *a life-support machine.* ■ informal equipment in a hospital used for this.

life ta·ble ▶ n. Zool. a table of statistics relating to life expectancy and mortality for a population of animals divided into cohorts of given age.

life·time /ˈlīfˌtīm/ ▶ n. the duration of a person's life. ■ the duration of a thing's existence or usefulness: *a plan to extend the lifetime of satellites.* ■ informal used to express the view that a period is very long: *five weeks was a lifetime.*

– PHRASES **of a lifetime** (of a chance or experience) such as does not occur more than once in a person's life: *she had rejected the opportunity of a lifetime.*

life·work /ˈlīfwərk/ ▶ n. the entire or principal work, labor, or task of a person's lifetime.

LIFO /ˈlīfō/ ▶ abbr. last in, first out (chiefly with reference to methods of stock valuation and data storage). Compare with **FIFO**.

lift /lift/ ▶ v. **1** [trans.] raise to a higher position or level: *he lifted his trophy over his head.* ■ move (one's eyes or face) to face upward: *he lifted his eyes for an instant.* ■ increase the volume or pitch of (one's voice). ■ increase (a price or amount): *higher than expected oil prices lifted Oklahoma's revenue.* ■ transport by air: *a helicopter lifted 11 crew members to safety.* ■ hit or kick (a ball) high into the air. ■ [intrans.] move upward; be raised: *their voices lifted in wails and cries.* ■ [intrans.] (of a cloud, fog, etc.) move upward or away. ■ perform cosmetic surgery on (esp. the face or breasts) to reduce sagging. **2** pick up and move to a different position: *he lifted her down from the pony's back.* ■ fig. enable (someone or something) to escape from a particular state of mind or situation: *two billion barrels of oil could* **lift** *this nation* **out of** *poverty.* **3** [trans.] raise (a person's spirits or confidence); encourage or cheer: *inspiring talks lifted our spirits.* ■ [intrans.] (of a person's mood) become happier. **4** [trans.] formally remove or end (a legal restriction, decision, or ban): *the European Community lifted its oil embargo against South Africa.* **5** [trans.] informal steal (something, esp. something minor). ■ use (a person's work or ideas) without permission or acknowledgment; plagiarize. ▶ n. **1** something that is used for lifting, in particular: ■ British term for ELEVATOR. ■ a device incorporating a moving cable for carrying people, typically skiers, up or down a mountain. ■ a built-up heel or device worn in a boot or shoe to make the wearer appear taller. **2** an act of lifting: *a particularly heavy lift.* ■ a rise in price or amount: *a 10 percent lift in profits.* ■ an increase in volume or pitch of a person's speaking voice. ■ informal an instance of stealing or plagiarizing something. ■ upward force that counteracts the force of gravity, produced by changing the direction and speed of a moving stream of air: *it had separate engines to provide lift and generate forward speed.* ■ the maximum weight that an aircraft can raise. **3** a free ride in another person's vehicle. **4** [in sing.] a feeling of encouragement or increased cheerfulness: *winning has given everyone a lift.*

– PHRASES **lift a finger** (or **hand**) [usu. with negative] make the slightest effort to do something: *he never once lifted a finger to get Jimmy released from prison.*

– PHRASAL VERBS **lift off** (of an aircraft, spacecraft, or rocket) rise from the ground or a launch pad, esp. vertically. — **lift·a·ble** adj. **lift·er** n. [ME: from ON *lypta*, of Gmc. origin; rel. to LOFT.]

lift·off /ˈliftˌôf; -ˌäf/ ▶ n. takeoff, esp. the vertical takeoff of a spacecraft, rocket, or helicopter.

lift pump ▶ n. a simple pump consisting of a piston moving in a cylinder, both parts incorporating a valve.

lig·a·ment /ˈligəmənt/ ▶ n. Anat. a short band of tough, flexible, fibrous connective tissue that connects two bones or cartilages or holds together a joint. ■ a membranous fold that supports an organ and keeps it in position. ■ any similar connecting or binding structure. — **lig·a·men·tal** /ˌligəˈmentl/ adj. **lig·a·men·ta·ry** /ˌligəˈment(ə)rē/ adj. **lig·a·men·tous** /ˌligəˈmentəs/ adj. [ME: from L. *ligamentum* 'bond,' from *ligare* 'to bind.']

li·gand /ˈligənd; ˈlī-/ ▶ n. Chem. an ion or molecule attached to a metal atom by coordinate bonding. ■ Biochem. a molecule that binds to another (usually larger) molecule. [1950s: from L. *ligandus* 'that can be tied,' gerundive of *ligare* 'to bind.']

li·gase /ˈlīˌgās; -ˌgāz/ ▶ n. Biochem. an enzyme that brings about ligation of DNA or another substance. [1960s: from L. *ligare* 'to bind' + -ASE.]

li·gate /ˈlīˌgāt/ ▶ v. [trans.] (usu. **be ligated**) Surg. tie up or otherwise close off (an artery or vessel). [16th C.: from L. *ligat-* 'tied,' from the v. *ligare.*]

li·ga·tion /līˈgāSHən/ ▶ n. **1** the surgical procedure of closing off a blood vessel or other duct or tube in the body by means of a ligature or clip. **2** Biochem. the joining of two DNA strands or other molecules by a phosphate ester linkage.

li·ga·ture /ˈligəCHər; -ˌCHŏŏr/ ▶ n. **1** a thing used for tying or binding something tightly. ■ a cord or thread used in surgery. **2** Music a slur or tie. **3** Print. a character consisting of two or more joined letters, e.g., *æ*, *fl*. ■ a stroke that joins adjacent letters in writing or printing. ▶ v. [trans.] bind or connect with a ligature.

li·ger /ˈlīgər/ ▶ n. the hybrid offspring of a male lion and a tigress. Compare with TIGON. [1930s: blend of LION and TIGER.]

light[1] /līt/ ▶ n. **1** the natural agent that stimulates sight and makes things visible; electromagnetic radiation from about 390 to 740 nm in wavelength. ■ a source of illumination, esp. an electric lamp. ■ (**lights**) decorative illuminations: *Christmas lights.* ■ a traffic light. ■ [in sing.] an expression in someone's eyes indicating a particular emotion or mood: *a shrewd light entered his eyes.* ■ the amount or quality of light in a place: *the plant requires good light.* **2** understanding of a problem or mystery; enlightenment. ■ spiritual illumination by divine truth. ■ (**lights**) a person's opinions, standards, and abilities: *leaving the police to do the job* **according to their lights.** **3** an area of something that is brighter or paler than its surroundings: *sunshine will brighten the natural lights in your hair.* **4** a device used to produce a flame or spark. **5** a window or opening in a wall to let light in. ■ any of the perpendicular divisions of a mullioned window. ■ any of the panes of glass forming the roof or side of a greenhouse or the top of a cold frame. **6** a person notable or eminent in a particular sphere of activity or place. ▶ v. (past and past part. **lit** /lit/ or **light·ed**) [trans.] **1** provide with light or lighting; illuminate: *the room was lighted by a number of small lamps.* ■ switch on (an electric light). ■ [intrans.] (**light up**) become illuminated: *the sign to fasten seat belts lit up.* **2** make (something) start burning; ignite: *Allen gathered sticks and lit a fire.* ■ [intrans.] begin to burn; be ignited: *the gas wouldn't light properly.* ■ (**light something up**) ignite a cigarette, cigar, or pipe and begin to smoke it: *she lit up a cigarette* | [intrans.] *workers who light up in prohibited areas face dismissal.* ▶ adj. **1** having a considerable or sufficient amount of natural light; not dark: *the bedrooms are light and airy.* **2** (of a color) pale.

– PHRASES **bring** (or **come**) **to light** make (or become) widely known or evident. **go out like a light** informal fall asleep or lose consciousness suddenly. **in a —— light** in the way specified: *the audit portrayed the company in a very favorable light.* **in** (**the**) **light of** taking (something) into consideration: *the exorbitant prices are explainable in the light of the facts.* **light a fire under someone** see FIRE. **light the fuse** see FUSE[2]. **the light of day** daylight. ■ general public attention: *bringing old family secrets into the light of day.* **the light of someone's life** a much loved person. **lights out** bedtime in a school dormitory, military

barracks, or other institution, when lights should be switched off. ■ a bell, bugle call, or other signal announcing this. **see the light** understand or realize something after prolonged thought or doubt. ■ undergo religious conversion. **see the light of day** be born. ■ fig. come into existence; be made public, visible, or available: *this software first saw the light of day back in 1993.* **shed** (or **throw** or **cast**) **light on** help to explain (something) by providing further information about it.
– PHRASAL VERBS **light up** (or **light something up**) suddenly become or cause to be animated with liveliness or joy: *his eyes lit up and he smiled.* — **light·ish** adj. **light·less** adj. **light·ness** n. [OE *lēoht, līht* (n. and adj.), *līhtan* (v.), of Gmc. origin.]

light[2] ▶ adj. **1** of little weight; easy to lift: *they are very light and portable.* ■ deficient in weight, esp. by a specified amount: *the sack of potatoes is 5 pounds light.* ■ not strongly or heavily built or constructed; small of its kind: *light armor.* ■ carrying or suitable for small loads: *light commercial vehicles.* ■ carrying only light armaments: *light infantry.* ■ (of a vehicle, ship, or aircraft) traveling unladen or with less than a full load. ■ (of food or a meal) small in quantity and easy to digest. ■ (of a foodstuff) low in fat, cholesterol, sugar, or other rich ingredients: *stick to a light diet.* ■ (of drink) not heavy on the stomach or strongly alcoholic: *a glass of light wine.* ■ (of food, esp. pastry or sponge cake) fluffy or well aerated during cooking. ■ (of soil) friable, porous, and workable. ■ (of an isotope) having not more than the usual mass; (of a compound) containing such an isotope. **2** relatively low in density, amount, or intensity: *trading was light for most of the day.* ■ (of sleep or a sleeper) easily disturbed. ■ easily borne or done: *a relatively light sentence | light housework.* **3** gentle or delicate: *she planted a light kiss on his cheek.* ■ (of a building) having an appearance suggestive of lightness: *the building is lofty and light in its tall nave and choir.* ■ (of type) having thin strokes; not bold. **4** (of entertainment) requiring little mental effort; not profound or serious: *light reading.* ■ not serious or solemn: *his tone was light.* ■ free from worry or unhappiness; cheerful: *a light heart.* **5** archaic (of a woman) unchaste; promiscuous.
– PHRASES **be light on** be rather short of: *light on hard news.* **be light on one's feet** be quick or nimble. **a** (or **someone's**) **light touch** the ability to deal with something delicately, tactfully, or in an understated way: *a novel that handles its tricky subject with a light touch.* **make light of** treat as unimportant. **make light work of** accomplish (a task) quickly and easily. **travel light** travel with a minimum load or minimum luggage. — **light·ish** adj. **light·ly** adv. **light·ness** n. [OE *lēocht, līht*; rel. to Ger. *leicht* and LUNG.]

light[3] ▶ v. (past and past part. **lit** /lit/ or **light·ed**) [intrans.] **1** (**light on/upon**) come upon or discover by chance: *he lit on a possible solution.* **2** archaic descend: *from the horse he lit down.* ■ (**light on**) fall and settle or land on (a surface): *a feather just lighted on the ground.*
– PHRASAL VERBS **light into** informal criticize severely; attack: *he lit into him for his indiscretion.* **light out** informal depart hurriedly. [OE *līhtan*, from LIGHT[2].]

light air ▶ n. a wind of force 1 on the Beaufort scale (1–3 knots or 1–3.5 mph).

light box ▶ n. a flat box with a side of translucent glass or plastic and containing an electric light, so as to provide an evenly lighted flat surface or even illumination, such as in an art or photography studio.

light breeze ▶ n. a wind of force 2 on the Beaufort scale (4–6 knots or 4.5-7 mph).

light bulb (also **light·bulb**) ▶ n. a glass bulb inserted into a lamp or other socket that provides light by passing an electric current through a pocket of inert gas.

light chain ▶ n. Biochem. a protein subunit that, as one of a pair, forms part of the main antigen-binding region of an immunoglobulin molecule.

light curve ▶ n. Astron. a graph showing the variation in the light received over a period of time from a variable star or other varying celestial object.

light-emit·ting di·ode ▶ n. see LED.

light·en[1] /ˈlītn/ ▶ v. make or become lighter in weight, pressure, or severity: [trans.] *efforts to lighten regulations* | [intrans.] *the strain had lightened.* ■ make or become more cheerful or less serious: [trans.] *her joke lightened the atmosphere* | [intrans.] *his spirits lightened a little.*

light·en[2] ▶ v. **1** make or become lighter or brighter: [intrans.] *the sky began to lighten in the east* | [trans.] *she had lightened her hair.* ■ [trans.] archaic enlighten spiritually. **2** [intrans.] (**it lightens, it is lightening,** etc.) rare emit flashes of lightning; flash with lightning: *it thundered and lightened.*

light·en·ing /ˈlītn-iNG; ˈlītniNG/ ▶ n. a drop in the level of the uterus during the last weeks of pregnancy as the head of the fetus engages in the pelvis.

light·er[1] /ˈlītər/ ▶ n. a device that produces a small flame, typically used to light cigarettes.

light·er[2] ▶ n. a barge or other unpowered boat used to transfer cargo to and from ships in harbor. ▶ v. [trans.] transport (goods) in a lighter. — **light·er·man** /-mən/ n. (pl. **-men**). [ME: from LIGHT[2] (in the sense 'unload'), or from Mid. Low Ger. *luchter*.]

light·er·age /ˈlītərij/ ▶ n. the transfer of cargo by means of a lighter, or the charge levied for such transfer.

light·er-than-air ▶ adj. [attrib.] relating to or denoting a balloon or other aircraft weighing less than the air it displaces, and so flying as a result of its own buoyancy.

light·face /ˈlītˌfās/ ▶ n. typeface or font characterized by light, thin lines.

light·fast /ˈlītˌfast/ ▶ adj. (of a dye or pigment) not prone to discolor when exposed to light. — **light·fast·ness** n.

light-fin·gered ▶ adj. **1** prone to steal. **2** having or showing delicate skill with the hands.

light fly·weight ▶ n. the lowest weight in amateur boxing, ranging up to 106 pounds (48 kg). ■ an amateur boxer of this weight.

light-foot·ed ▶ adj. fast, nimble, or stealthy on one's feet: *a light-footed leap.* — **light-foot·ed·ly** adv.

light·head·ed /ˈlītˌhedid/ ▶ adj. dizzy and slightly faint. — **light·head·ed·ly** adv. **light·head·ed·ness** n.

light·heart·ed /ˈlītˌhärtid/ ▶ adj. cheerful and carefree. — **light·heart·ed·ly** adv. **light·heart·ed·ness** n.

light heav·y·weight ▶ n. a weight in boxing and other sports intermediate between middleweight and heavyweight. In the amateur boxing scale it ranges from 165 to 178 pounds (75 to 81 kg). ■ a boxer or other competitor of this weight.

Light-Horse Har·ry see LEE[5].

light·house /ˈlītˌhous/ ▶ n. a tower or other structure containing a beacon light to warn or guide ships at sea.

lighthouse

light in·dus·try ▶ n. the manufacture of small or light articles.

light·ing /ˈlītiNG/ ▶ n. equipment in a home, workplace, studio, theater, or street for producing light. ■ the arrangement or effect of lights: *the lighting was very flat.*

light me·ter ▶ n. an instrument for measuring the intensity of light, used chiefly to show the correct exposure when taking a photograph. Also called EXPOSURE METER.

light·ning /ˈlītniNG/ ▶ n. the occurrence of a natural electrical discharge of very short duration and high voltage between a cloud and the ground or within a cloud, accompanied by a bright flash and typically also thunder. ▶ v. [intrans.] (of the sky) emit a flash or discharge of this kind: *what's a person supposed to do when it starts to lightning?* ▶ adj. [attrib.] very quick. [ME: special use of *lightening* (verbal n. from LIGHTEN[2]).]

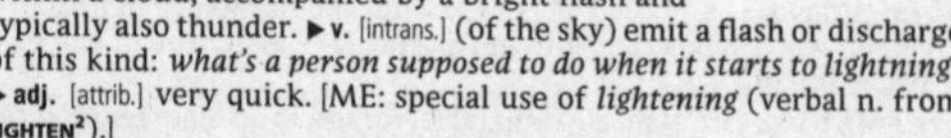

light·ning bug ▶ n. another term for FIREFLY.

light·ning rod ▶ n. a metal rod or wire fixed to an exposed part of a building or other tall structure to divert lightning harmlessly into the ground. ■ fig. a person or thing that attracts a lot of criticism, esp. in order to divert attention from other issues or another person.

light op·er·a ▶ n. another term for OPERETTA.

light pen ▶ n. **1** Comput. a hand-held, penlike photosensitive device held to the display screen of a computer terminal for passing information to the computer. **2** a hand-held, light-emitting device used for reading bar codes.

light pol·lu·tion ▶ n. brightening of the night sky that inhibits the observation of stars and planets, caused by street lights and other man-made sources.

light·proof /ˈlītˌpro͞of/ ▶ adj. able to block out light completely.

light re·ac·tion ▶ n. **1** the reaction of something, esp. the iris of the eye, to different intensities of light. **2** (**the light reaction**) Biochem. the reaction that occurs as the first phase of photosynthesis, in which energy in the form of light is absorbed and converted to chemical energy in the form of ATP.

lights /līts/ ▶ plural n. the lungs of sheep or pigs used as food, esp. for pets. [ME: use of LIGHT[2] as a n.]

light-sen·si·tive ▶ adj. (of a surface or substance) changing physically or chemically when exposed to light. ■ Biol. (of a cell, organ, or tissue) able to detect the presence or intensity of light.

light·ship /ˈlītˌSHip/ ▶ n. a moored or anchored vessel with a beacon light to warn or guide ships at sea.

light show ▶ n. a spectacle of colored lights that move and change, esp. at a pop concert.

light·some /ˈlītsəm/ ▶ adj. esp. literary **1** merry and carefree. **2** gracefully nimble: *lightsome, high-flying dancers.* — **light·some·ly** adv. **light·some·ness** n.

light ta·ble ▶ n. a horizontal or tilted surface of translucent glass or plastic with a light behind it, used as a light box for viewing transparencies or negatives.

light trap ▶ n. **1** Zool. an illuminated trap for attracting and catching nocturnal animals, esp. flying insects. **2** Photog. a device for excluding light from a darkroom without preventing entry into it.

light wa·ter ▶ n. **1** water containing the normal proportion (or less) of deuterium oxide, i.e., about 0.02 percent, esp. to distinguish it from heavy water. **2** foam formed by water and a fluorocarbon surfactant, which floats on flammable liquids lighter than water and is used in firefighting.

light·weight /ˈlītˌwāt/ ▶ n. **1** a weight in boxing and other sports intermediate between featherweight and welterweight. In the amateur boxing scale it ranges from 125 to 132 pounds (57 to 60 kg). ■ a boxer or other competitor of this weight. **2** a person or thing that is lightly built or constructed. ■ a person of little importance or influence, esp. in a particular sphere: *he was regarded as a political lightweight.* ▶ **adj. 1** of thin material or build and weighing less than average: *a lightweight gray suit.* **2** containing little serious matter: *the newspaper is lightweight and trivial.*

light well ▶ **n.** an open area or vertical shaft in the center of a building, typically roofed with glass, bringing natural light to the lower floors or basement.

light·wood /ˈlīt,wŏŏd/ ▶ **n.** firewood that burns easily and with a bright flame, esp. dry, resinous pine.

light year ▶ **n.** Astron. a unit of astronomical distance equivalent to the distance that light travels in one year, which is 9.4607×10^{12} km (nearly 6 trillion miles). ■ **(light years)** informal a long distance or great amount.

lig·ne·ous /ˈlignēəs/ ▶ **adj.** made, consisting of, or resembling wood; woody. [17th C.: from L. *ligneus* 'relating to wood' + **-ous.**]

ligni- ▶ **comb. form** relating to wood: *lignify.* [from L. *lignum* 'wood.']

lig·ni·fy /ˈlignə,fī/ ▶ **v.** **(-fies, -fied)** [trans.] [usu. as adj.] **(lignified)** Bot. make rigid and woody by the deposition of lignin in cell walls. — **lig·ni·fi·ca·tion** /,lignəfəˈkāsʜən/ **n.**

lig·nin /ˈlignin/ ▶ **n.** Bot. a complex organic polymer deposited in the cell walls of many plants, making them rigid and woody.

lig·nite /ˈlig,nīt/ ▶ **n.** a soft brownish coal showing traces of plant structure, intermediate between bituminous coal and peat. — **lig·nit·ic** /ligˈnitik/ **adj.**

lig·no·cel·lu·lose /,lignōˈselyə,lōs; -,lōz/ ▶ **n.** Bot. a complex of lignin and cellulose present in the cell walls of woody plants.

lig·num vi·tae /ˈlignəm ˈvī,tē; ˈvē,tī/ ▶ **n.** another term for **GUAIACUM.** [L., 'wood of life.']

lig·ro·in /ˈligrō-in/ ▶ **n.** Chem. a volatile hydrocarbon mixture obtained from petroleum and used as a solvent. [19th C.: of unknown origin.]

lig·u·la /ˈligyələ/ ▶ **n.** (pl. **-lae** /-,lē; -,lī/) Entomol. the strap-shaped terminal part of an insect's labium, typically lobed. — **lig·u·lar adj.** [18th C.: from L., 'strap.']

lig·u·late /ˈligyə,lāt; -lit/ ▶ **adj.** esp. Bot. strap-shaped, such as the ray florets of plants of the daisy family. ■ (of a plant) having ray florets or ligules.

lig·ule /ˈlig,yŏŏl/ ▶ **n.** Bot. a narrow strap-shaped part of a plant, esp., in most grasses and sedges, a membranous scale on the inner side of the leaf sheath at its junction with the blade. [19th C.: from L. *ligula* 'strap.']

Li·gu·ri·a /liˈg(y)ŏŏrēə/ a coastal region of northwestern Italy that extends along the Mediterranean from Tuscany to France; capital, Genoa. — **Li·gu·ri·an adj. & n.**

Li·gu·ri·an Sea /liˈg(y)ŏŏrēən/ a part of the northern Mediterranean Sea, between Corsica and Italy.

lik·a·ble /ˈlīkəbəl/ (also **like·a·ble**) ▶ **adj.** (esp. of a person) pleasant, friendly, and easy to like. — **lik·a·bil·i·ty** /,līkəˈbilətē/ **n. lik·a·ble·ness n. lik·a·bly adv.**

like[1] /līk/ ▶ **prep. 1** having the same characteristics or qualities as; similar to: *they were like brothers.* ■ in the manner of; in the same way or to the same degree as: *he was screaming like a banshee.* ■ in a way appropriate to: *students were being treated like children.* ■ such as one might expect from; characteristic of: *just like you to put a damper on people's enjoyment.* ■ used in questions to ask about the characteristics or nature of someone or something: *What is it like to be a tuna fisherman?* **2** used to draw attention to the nature of an action or event: *why are you talking about me like that?* **3** such as; for example: *the cautionary vision of works like* Animal Farm. ▶ **conj.** informal **1** in the same way that; as: *people who change countries like they change clothes.* **2** as though; as if: *I felt like I'd been kicked by a camel.* ▶ **n.** used with reference to a person or thing of the same kind as another: *the quotations could be arranged to put like with like.* ■ **(the like)** a thing or things of the same kind (often used to express surprise or for emphasis): *did you ever hear the like?* ▶ **adj.** [attrib.] (of a person or thing) having similar qualities or characteristics to another person or thing: *I responded in like manner.* ■ [predic.] (of a portrait or other image) having a faithful resemblance to the original: *"Who painted the dog's picture? It's very like."* ▶ **adv. 1** informal used in speech as a meaningless filler or to signify the speaker's uncertainty about an expression just used: *there was this funny smell—sort of dusty like.* **2** **(like as/to)** archaic in the manner of: *like as a ship with dreadful storm long tossed.*

– PHRASES **and the like** and similar things; et cetera. **like anything** informal to a great degree. **(as) like as not** probably. **like ——, like ——** as —— is, so is ——: *like father, like son.* **like so** informal in this manner. **the likes of** informal used of someone or something regarded as a type: *she didn't want to associate with the likes of me.* **more like** informal nearer to (a specified number or description) than one previously given: *he believes the figure should be more like $10 million.* ■ **(more like it)** nearer to what is required or expected; more satisfactory. **of (a) like mind** (of a person) sharing the same opinions or tastes. [ME: from ON *líkr*; rel. to **ALIKE.**]

like[2] ▶ **v.** [trans.] **1** find agreeable, enjoyable, or satisfactory: *I like all Angela Carter's stories.* **2** wish for; want: *would you like a cup of coffee?* | [intrans.] *we would like for you to work for us.* ■ choose to have (something); prefer: *how do you like your coffee?* ■ [in questions] feel about or regard (something): *how would you like it if it happened to you?* ▶ **n.** **(likes)** the things one likes or prefers.

– PHRASES **if you like 1** if it suits or pleases you. **2** used when expressing something in a new or unusual way: *it's a whole new branch of chemistry, a new science if you like.* **like it or not** informal used to indicate that someone has no choice in a matter: *you're celebrating with us, like it or not.* **not like the look** (or **sound**) **of** find worrying or alarming: *I don't like the look of that head injury.* [OE *līcian* 'be pleasing,' of Gmc. origin; rel. to Du. *lijken.*]

-like ▶ **comb. form** (added to nouns) similar to; characteristic of: *pealike* | *crustlike.*

like·a·ble ▶ **adj.** var. of **LIKABLE.**

like·li·hood /ˈlīklē,hŏŏd/ ▶ **n.** the state or fact of something's being likely; probability.

– PHRASES **in all likelihood** very probably.

like·ly /ˈlīklē/ ▶ **adj.** **(like·li·er, like·li·est) 1** such as well might happen or be true; probable. **2** apparently suitable; promising: *a likely-looking spot.* ■ appearing to have vigor or ability: *likely lads.* ▶ **adv.** probably: *we will most likely go to a bar.*

– PHRASES **a likely story** used to express disbelief in an account or excuse. — **like·li·ness n.** [ME: from ON *líkligr*, from *líkr* (see **LIKE**[1]).]

like-mind·ed ▶ **adj.** having similar tastes or opinions. — **like-mind·ed·ness n.**

lik·en /ˈlīkən/ ▶ **v.** [trans.] **(liken someone/something to)** point out the resemblance of someone or something to: *they likened the reigning emperor to a god.*

like·ness /ˈlīknis/ ▶ **n.** the fact or quality of being alike; resemblance: *her likeness to him was astonishing.* ■ the semblance, guise, or outward appearance of: *humans are described as being made in God's likeness.* ■ a portrait or representation: *the only known likeness of Dorothy as a young woman.* [OE *gelīknes* (see **ALIKE, -NESS**).]

like·wise /ˈlīk,wīz/ ▶ **adv. 1** in the same way; also: *the dream of young people is to grow old, and it is likewise the dream of their parents to relive youth.* **2** in a like manner; similarly: *I stuck out my tongue and Frankie did likewise.* [ME: from the phr. *in like wise.*]

lik·ing /ˈlīkɪɴɢ/ ▶ **n.** [in sing.] a feeling of regard or fondness: *Mrs. Parsons had a liking for gin and tonic.*

– PHRASES **to one's liking** to one's taste; pleasing: *his coffee was just to his liking.*

Li·kud /liˈkŏŏd; -ˈkōōd/ a coalition of right-wing Israeli political parties, formed in 1973.

li·ku·ta /liˈkōōtə/ ▶ **n.** (pl. **ma·ku·ta** /məˈkōōtə/) a monetary unit of the Democratic Republic of the Congo (formerly Zaire), equal to one hundredth of a zaire.

li·lac /ˈlī,läk; -,lak; -lək/ ▶ **n.** a widely cultivated Eurasian shrub or small tree (genus *Syringa*) of the olive family, that has fragrant violet, pink, or white blossoms. ■ a pale pinkish-violet color. [17th C.: from obs. Fr., via Sp. and Arab. from Pers. *līlak*, var. of *nīlak* 'bluish,' from *nīl* 'blue.']

li·lan·ge·ni /,lilänGˈgenē/ ▶ **n.** (pl. **e·ma·lan·ge·ni** /,emaläNGˈgenē/) the basic monetary unit of Swaziland, equal to 100 cents. [from the Bantu prefix *li-* (used to denote a sing.) + *-langeni* 'member of a royal family.']

lil·i·a·ceous /,liléˈāsʜəs/ ▶ **adj.** Bot. of, relating to, or denoting plants of the lily family (Liliaceae). [18th C.: from mod. L. *Liliaceae* (pl.), based on L. *lilium* 'lily,' + **-ous.**]

Lil·ith /ˈliliтн/ a female demon of Jewish folklore, who tries to kill newborn children. In the Talmud she is the first wife of Adam, dispossessed by Eve.

Li·li·u·o·ka·la·ni /lī,lēōō,ōkəˈlänē/ (1838–1917) queen of Hawaii; also known as **Lydia Paki Liliuokalani.** The last reigning queen of the Hawaiian Islands 1891–93, she fought for the independence of Hawaii.

Lille /lēl/ a city in northern France; pop. 178,000.

Lil·le·ham·mer /ˈlilə,hämər/ a town in southern Norway, site of the 1994 Winter Olympics; pop. 23,000.

Lil·li·pu·tian /,liləˈpyōōsʜən/ ▶ **adj.** trivial or very small. ▶ **n.** a trivial or very small person or thing. [18th C.: from the imaginary country of *Lilliput* in Swift's *Gulliver's Travels.*]

Li·lon·gwe /liˈlôɴɢwā/ the capital of Malawi, founded in 1975; pop. 234,000.

lilt /lilt/ ▶ **n.** a characteristic rising and falling of the voice when speaking; a pleasant gentle accent: *he spoke with a faint Irish lilt.* ■ a pleasant, gently swinging rhythm in a song or tune. ▶ **v.** [intrans.] [often as adj.] **(lilting)** speak, sing, or sound with a lilt: *a lilting Welsh accent.* [ME *lulte.*]

lil·y /ˈlilē/ ▶ **n. 1** a widely cultivated bulbous plant (genus *Lilium*) with large trumpet-shaped, typically fragrant, flowers on a tall, slender stem. ■ short for **WATER LILY.** ■ used in names of other plants with similar flowers or leaves, e.g., **arum lily. 2** a heraldic fleur-de-lis. — **lil·ied** /ˈlilēd/ **adj.** [OE *lilie*, from L. *lilium*, from Gk. *leirion.*]

lil·y-liv·ered ▶ **adj.** weak and cowardly.

lil·y of the val·ley ▶ **n.** a widely cultivated European plant (*Convallaria majalis*) of the lily family, with broad leaves and arching stems of fragrant, bell-shaped white flowers.

lily of the valley

lil·y pad ▶ n. a round, floating leaf of a water lily.

lil·y-white ▶ adj. pure or ideally white. ■ without fault or corruption; totally innocent or immaculate. ■ consisting only of white people and excluding nonwhite people: *lily-white suburbs.*

Li·ma /'lēmə/ the capital of Peru; pop. 5,706,000. It was founded in 1535 by Francisco Pizarro. ■ a code word representing the letter L, used in radio communication.

li·ma bean /'līmə/ ▶ n. 1 an edible flat whitish bean. See also BUTTER BEAN. 2 the tropical American plant (*Phaseolus lunatus*, or *P. limensis*) that yields this bean. [18th C.: from LIMA.]

limb[1] /lim/ ▶ n. an arm or leg of a person or four-legged animal, or a bird's wing. ■ a large branch of a tree. ■ a projecting landform such as a spur of a mountain range, or each of two or more such projections as in a forked peninsula or archipelago. ■ a projecting section of a building. ■ a branch of a cross. ■ each half of an archery bow.
– PHRASES **life and limb** life and all bodily faculties. **out on a limb** in a dangerous or uncompromising position; vulnerable. — **limbed** adj. [in comb.] *long-limbed.* [OE *lim*, of Gmc. origin.]

limb[2] ▶ n. 1 Astron. the edge of the disk of a celestial object, esp. the sun or moon. 2 Bot. the blade or broad part of a leaf or petal. ■ the spreading upper part of a tube-shaped flower. 3 the graduated arc of a quadrant or other scientific instrument, used for measuring angles. [ME: from Fr. *limbe* or L. *limbus* 'hem, border.']

Lim·ba /'limbə/ ▶ n. (pl. same or **Lim·bas**) 1 a member of a people of Sierra Leone and Guinea. 2 the Niger-Congo language of this people. ▶ adj. of or relating to the Limbas or their language. [the name in Limba.]

lim·ber[1] /'limbər/ ▶ adj. (of a person or body part) lithe; supple. ■ (of a thing) flexible. ▶ v. [intrans.] warm up in preparation for exercise or activity, esp. sports: *the acrobats were limbering up for the big show.* ■ [trans.] make (oneself or a body part) supple: *I limbered my fingers with a few practice bars.* — **lim·ber·ness** n. [16th C. (as an adj.): perh. from LIMBER[2].]

lim·ber[2] ▶ n. the detachable front part of a gun carriage, consisting of two wheels and an axle, a pole, and a frame holding one or more ammunition boxes. ▶ v. [trans.] attach a limber to (a gun). [ME *lymour*, appar. rel. to med. L. *limonarius*, from *limo, limon-* 'shaft.']

lim·bi /'lim,bī; -,bē/ plural form of LIMBUS.

lim·bic sys·tem /'limbik/ ▶ n. a complex system of nerves and networks in the brain that controls the basic emotions and drives. [19th C.: *limbic* from Fr. *limbique*, from L. *limbus* 'edge.']

lim·bo[1] /'limbō/ ▶ n. 1 (also **Limbo**) (in some Christian beliefs) the abode of the souls of unbaptized infants, and of the just who died before Christ's coming. 2 an uncertain period of awaiting a decision or resolution; an intermediate state or condition. ■ a state of neglect or oblivion. [ME: from the med. L. phr. *in limbo*, from *limbus* 'hem, border, limbo.']

lim·bo[2] ▶ n. (pl. **-bos**) a West Indian dance in which the dancer bends backward to pass under a horizontal bar that is progressively lowered to a position just above the ground. ▶ v. [intrans.] dance in such a way. [1950s: from LIMBER[1].]

Lim·burg·er /'lim,bərgər/ ▶ n. a soft white cheese with a characteristic strong smell, originally made in Limburg, a former duchy of Lorraine.

lim·bus /'limbəs/ ▶ n. (pl. **-bi** /-,bī; -,bē/) Anat. the border or margin of a structure, esp. the junction of the cornea and sclera in the eye. [ME: from L., 'edge, border.']

lime[1] /līm/ ▶ n. (also **quick·lime**) a white caustic alkaline substance consisting of calcium oxide, obtained by heating limestone. ■ (also **slaked lime**) a white alkaline substance consisting of calcium hydroxide, made by adding water to quicklime. ■ (in general use) any of a number of calcium compounds, esp. calcium hydroxide, used as an additive to soil or water. ■ archaic birdlime. ▶ v. [trans.] 1 treat (soil or water) with lime to reduce acidity and improve fertility or oxygen levels. ■ [often as adj.] (**limed**) give (wood) a bleached appearance by treating it with lime: *limed oak furniture.* 2 archaic catch (a bird) with birdlime. — **lim·y** /'līmē/ adj. (**lim·i·er, lim·i·est**). [OE *līm*, of Gmc. origin; rel. to Du. *lijm*, Ger. *Leim*, also to LOAM.]

lime[2] ▶ n. 1 a rounded citrus fruit similar to a lemon but greener, smaller, and with a distinctive acid flavor. 2 (also **lime tree**) the evergreen citrus tree (*Citrus aurantifolia*) that produces this fruit, widely cultivated in warm climates. 3 a bright light green color like that of a lime. [17th C.: from Fr., from mod. Provençal *limo*, Sp. *lima*, from Arab. *līma*; cf. LEMON.]

lime[3] (also **lime tree**) ▶ n. another term for LINDEN, esp. the European linden. [17th C.: alt. of obs. *line*, from OE *lind* (see LINDEN).]

lime·ade /,līm'ād; 'līm,ād/ ▶ n. a drink made from lime juice and water sweetened with sugar.

lime-burn·er ▶ n. hist. a person whose job was burning limestone in order to obtain lime.

lime·kiln /'līm,kil(n)/ ▶ n. a kiln in which limestone is burned or calcined to produce quicklime.

lime·light /'līm,līt/ ▶ n. intense white light obtained by heating a cylinder of lime in an oxyhydrogen flame, formerly used in theaters. ■ (**the limelight**) the focus of public attention.

li·men /'līmən/ ▶ n. (pl. **li·mens** or **lim·i·na** /'limənə/) Psychol. a threshold below which a stimulus is not perceived or is not distinguished from another. [17th C.: from L., 'threshold.']

Lim·er·ick /'lim(ə)rik/ a county in the Republic of Ireland, in the western part of the province of Munster. ■ its county town, on the Shannon River; pop. 52,000.

lim·er·ick /'lim(ə)rik/ ▶ n. a humorous, frequently bawdy, verse of three long and two short lines rhyming *aabba*, popularized by Edward Lear. [19th C.: said to be from the chorus "Will you come up to Limerick?"]

lime·stone /'līm,stōn/ ▶ n. a hard sedimentary rock, composed mainly of calcium carbonate or dolomite, used as building material and in the making of cement.

lime sul·fur ▶ n. an insecticide and fungicide containing calcium polysulfides, made by boiling lime and sulfur in water.

lime·wa·ter /'līm,wôtər; -,wätər/ ▶ n. Chem. a solution of calcium hydroxide in water, which is alkaline and turns milky in the presence of carbon dioxide.

Lim·ey /'līmē/ ▶ n. (pl. **-eys**) esp. derog. a British person. [19th C.: from LIME[2].]

lim·i·na /'limənə/ plural form of LIMEN.

lim·i·nal /'limənl/ ▶ adj. tech. 1 of or relating to a transitional or initial stage of a process. 2 occupying a position at, or on both sides of, a boundary or threshold. — **lim·i·nal·i·ty** /,limə'nalətē/ n. [19th C.: from L. *limen, limin-* 'threshold' + -AL.]

lim·it /'limit/ ▶ n. 1 a point or level beyond which something does not or may not extend or pass. ■ (often **limits**) the terminal point or boundary of an area or movement: *the city limits.* ■ the furthest extent of one's physical or mental endurance: *Mary Ann tried everyone's patience to the limit.* 2 a restriction on the size or amount of something permissible or possible: *an age limit.* ■ a speed limit: *a 30 mph limit.* ■ (in card games) an agreed maximum stake or bet. ■ (also **legal limit**) the maximum concentration of alcohol in the blood that the law allows in the driver of a motor vehicle. 3 Math. a point or value that a sequence, function, or sum of a series can be made to approach progressively, until it is as close to the point or value as desired. ▶ v. (**lim·it·ed, lim·it·ing**) [trans.] set or serve as a limit to: *try to limit the amount you drink.*
– PHRASES **be the limit** informal be intolerably troublesome or irritating. **off limits** out of bounds. **within limits** moderately; up to a point. — **lim·i·ta·tive** /'limə,tātiv/ adj. [ME: from L. *limes, limit-* 'boundary, frontier.']

lim·i·tar·y /'limə,terē/ ▶ adj. rare of, relating to, or subject to restriction.

lim·i·ta·tion /,limə'tāsHən/ ▶ n. 1 (often **limitations**) a limiting rule or circumstance; a restriction. ■ a condition of limited ability; a defect or failing. ■ the action of limiting something: *the limitation of local authorities' powers.* 2 (also **limitation period**) Law a legally specified period beyond which an action may be defeated or a property right is not to continue. See also STATUTE OF LIMITATIONS.

lim·it·ed /'limitid/ ▶ adj. restricted in size, amount, or extent; few, small, or short: *a limited number of places are available.* ■ (of a monarchy or government) exercised under limitations of power prescribed by a constitution. ■ (of a person) not great in ability or talents. ■ (of a train or other vehicle of public transportation) making few intermediate stops; express. ■ (**Limited**) Brit. denoting a company whose owners are legally responsible for its debts only to the extent of the amount of capital they invested (used after a company name): *Times Newspapers Limited.* — **lim·it·ed·ness** n.

lim·it·ed ed·i·tion ▶ n. an edition of a book, or reproduction of a print or object, limited to a specific number of copies.

lim·it·ed part·ner ▶ n. a partner in a company or venture whose liability toward its debts is legally limited to the extent of his or her investment. — **lim·it·ed part·ner·ship** n.

lim·it·ed war ▶ n. a war in which the weapons, the territory, or the objectives are restricted in some way, in particular in the use of nuclear weapons.

lim·it·er /'limitər/ ▶ n. a person or thing that limits something, in particular: ■ Electron. a circuit whose output is restricted to a certain range of values irrespective of the size of the input. Also called CLIPPER.

lim·it·less /'limitlis/ ▶ adj. without end, limit, or boundary: *our resources are not limitless.* — **lim·it·less·ly** adv. **lim·it·less·ness** n.

lim·it point ▶ n. Math. a point for which every neighborhood contains at least one point belonging to a given set.

limn /lim/ ▶ v. [trans.] literary depict or describe in painting or words. ■ suffuse or highlight (something) with a bright color or light. [ME (in the sense 'illuminate a manuscript'): alt. of obs. *lumine* 'illuminate,' via OFr. *luminer* from L. *luminare* 'make light.']

lim·ner /'lim(n)ər/ ▶ n. esp. hist. a painter, esp. of portraits or miniatures.

lim·nol·o·gy /lim'näləjē/ ▶ n. the study of the biological, chemical, and physical features of lakes and other bodies of fresh water. — **lim·no·log·i·cal** /,limnə'läjikəl/ adj. **lim·nol·o·gist** n. [19th C.: from Gk. *limnē* 'lake' + -LOGY.]

Lím·nos /'lim,nôs/ Greek name for LEMNOS.

lim·o /'limō/ ▶ n. (pl. **lim·os**) short for LIMOUSINE.

Li·moges /lē'mōzH/ a city in west central France; pop. 136,000. It is noted for the production of porcelain.

lim·o·nene /'limə,nēn/ ▶ n. Chem. a colorless liquid hydrocarbon, $C_{10}H_{16}$, with a lemonlike scent, present in lemon oil, orange oil, and similar essential oils.

li·mo·nite /'līmə,nīt/ ▶ n. an amorphous brownish secondary mineral consisting of a mixture of hydrous ferric oxides, important as an iron ore. — **li·mo·nit·ic** /,līmə'nitik/ adj. [19th C.: from Ger. *Limonit*, prob. from Gk. *leimōn* 'meadow.']

lim·ou·sine /ˈlimə,zēn; ˌliməˈzēn/ ▶ **n.** a large, luxurious automobile, esp. one driven by a chauffeur who is separated from the passengers by a partition. ▪ a passenger vehicle carrying people to and from an airport. [20th C.: from Fr., fem. adj. meaning 'of Limousin,' orig. denoting a caped cloak worn in *Limousin*.]

lim·ou·sine lib·er·al ▶ **n.** derog. a wealthy liberal.

limp[1] /limp/ ▶ **v.** [intrans.] walk with difficulty, typically because of a damaged or stiff leg or foot. ▪ [with adverbial of direction] (of a damaged ship, aircraft, or vehicle) proceed with difficulty: *the damaged aircraft limped back to Sicily.* ▶ **n.** a tendency to limp; a gait impeded by injury or stiffness. [ME (in the sense 'fall short of'): rel. to obs. *limphalt* 'lame,' and prob. of Gmc. origin.]

limp[2] ▶ **adj.** lacking internal strength or structure; not stiff or firm: *the flags hung limp and still.* ▪ having or denoting a book cover that is not stiffened with board. ▪ without energy or will: *a limp handshake.* — **limp·ly adv. limp·ness n.**

lim·pet /ˈlimpit/ ▶ **n.** a marine mollusk (Patellidae, Fissurellidae, and other families) with a shallow conical shell and a broad muscular foot, noted for the way it clings tightly to rocks. [OE *lempedu*, from med. L. *lampreda* 'limpet, lamprey.']

lim·pet mine ▶ **n.** a mine designed to be attached magnetically to a ship's hull and set to explode after a certain time.

lim·pid /ˈlimpid/ ▶ **adj.** (of a liquid) free of anything that darkens; completely clear. ▪ (of a person's eyes) unclouded; clear. ▪ (esp. of writing or music) clear and accessible or melodious. — **lim·pid·i·ty** /limˈpidətē/ **n. lim·pid·ly adv.** [ME: from L. *limpidus*; perh. rel. to LYMPH.]

limp·kin /ˈlim(p)kin/ ▶ **n.** a wading marsh bird (*Aramus guarauna*, family Aramidae) related to the rails, with long legs and a long bill, found in the southeastern US and tropical America. [19th C.: from LIMP[1].]

Lim·po·po /limˈpōpō/ a river in southeastern Africa. Rising near Johannesburg, it flows 1,100 miles (1,770 km) north and east to meet the Indian Ocean.

limp-wrist·ed ▶ **adj.** informal, derog. (of a man, esp. a homosexual) effeminate.

lim·u·lus /ˈlimyələs/ ▶ **n.** (pl. **-li** /-ˌlī; -ˌlē/) an arthropod of a genus (*Limulus*) that comprises the North American horseshoe crab and its extinct relatives. [mod. L., from L. *limulus* 'somewhat oblique,' from *limus* 'oblique.']

Lin /lin/, Maya (1959–), US architect. She designed the Vietnam Veterans Memorial in Washington, DC, 1982.

lin. ▶ **abbr.** ▪ lineal or linear. ▪ liniment.

lin·ac /ˈlin,ak/ ▶ **n.** short for LINEAR ACCELERATOR.

lin·age /ˈlīnij/ ▶ **n.** the number of lines in printed or written matter, esp. when used to calculate payment.

linch·pin /ˈlinCH,pin/ (also **lynch·pin**) ▶ **n. 1** a pin passed through the end of an axle to keep a wheel in position. **2** a person or thing vital to an enterprise or organization. [ME: from OE *lynis* (in the sense 'linchpin') + PIN.]

Lin·coln[1] /ˈliNGkən/ the capital of Nebraska, in the southeastern part of the state; pop. 225,581.

Lin·coln[2], Abraham (1809–65), 16th president of the US 1861–65. A Republican, his election to the presidency on an anti-slavery platform helped to precipitate the Civil War. He was assassinated shortly after the war ended and before he could fulfill his campaign promise to reconcile the North and the South. — **Lin·coln·esque** /ˌliNGkəˈnesk/ **adj.**

Lin·coln·shire /ˈliNGkənSHər; -ˌSHi(ə)r/ a county on the eastern coast of England; county town, Lincoln.

Lin·coln's Inn one of the Inns of Court in London.

Lind /ˈlind/, Jenny (1820–87), Swedish singer; born *Johanna Maria Lind Goldschmidt*; known as "the Swedish nightingale."

lin·dane /ˈlin,dān/ ▶ **n.** a synthetic organochlorine insecticide, $C_6H_{12}Cl_6$, now generally restricted in use due to its toxicity and persistence in the environment. [1940s: named after Teunis van der *Linden*, 20th-cent. Dutch chemist.]

Lind·bergh[1] /ˈlin(d),bərg/, Anne Morrow (1906–2001), US writer; wife of Charles Lindbergh. She wrote *Gift from the Sea* (1955).

Lind·bergh[2], Charles Augustus, Jr. (1902–74), US aviator; known as Lucky Lindy and the Lone Eagle. In 1927, he made the first solo transatlantic flight in a single-engined monoplane, *Spirit of St. Louis*.

lin·den /ˈlindən/ ▶ **n.** a deciduous tree (genus *Tilia*, family Tiliaceae) with heart-shaped leaves and fragrant yellowish blossoms, native to north temperate regions. [OE: from *lind* 'lime tree.']

Lind·say /ˈlinzē/, Vachel (1879–1931), US poet; full name *Nicholas Vachel Lindsay*. His works are collected in volumes such as *General Booth Enters into Heaven and Other Poems* (1913).

line[1] /līn/ ▶ **n. 1** a long, narrow mark or band: *I can't draw a straight line.* ▪ Math. a straight or curved continuous extent of length without breadth. ▪ a positioning or movement of a thing or things that creates or appears to follow such a line: *the ball rose in a straight line.* ▪ a furrow or wrinkle in the skin of the face or hands. ▪ a contour or outline considered as a feature of design or composition: *crisp architectural lines.* ▪ (on a map or graph) a curve connecting all points having a specified common property. ▪ a line marking the starting or finishing point in a race. ▪ a line marked on a field or court that relates to the rules of a game or sport. ▪ Football the line of scrimmage. ▪ (**the Line**) the equator. ▪ a notional limit or boundary: *the issue of peace cut across class lines.* ▪ each of the very narrow horizontal sections forming a television picture. ▪ (**the line**) the level of the base of most letters, such as *h* and *x*, in printing and writing. ▪ [as adj.] Print. & Comput. denoting an illustration or graphic consisting of lines and solid areas, with no gradation of tone: *line art.* ▪ each of (usually five) horizontal lines forming a staff in musical notation. ▪ a sequence of notes or tones forming an instrumental or vocal melody: *a powerful melodic line.* ▪ a dose of a powdered narcotic or hallucinatory drug, esp. cocaine or heroin, laid out in a line. **2** a length of cord, rope, wire, or other material serving a particular purpose: *a telephone line.* ▪ one of a vessel's mooring ropes. ▪ a telephone connection: *she had a crank **on the line**.* ▪ a railroad track. ▪ a branch or route of a railroad system. ▪ a company that provides ships, aircraft, or buses on particular routes on a regular basis: *a major shipping line.* **3** a horizontal row of written or printed words. ▪ a part of a poem forming one such row: *each stanza has eight lines.* ▪ (**lines**) the words of an actor's part in a play or film. ▪ a particularly noteworthy written or spoken sentence: *his speech ended with a line about the failure of justice.* **4** a row of people or things: *a line of acolytes proceeded down the aisle.* ▪ a row or sequence of people or vehicles awaiting their turn to be attended to or to proceed. ▪ a connected series of people following one another in time (used esp. of several generations of a family): *we follow the history of a family through the male line.* ▪ (in football, hockey, etc.) a set of players in the forwardmost positions for offense or defense. ▪ Football one of the positions on the line of scrimmage. ▪ a series of related things: *the bill is the latest in a long line of measures to protect society from criminals.* ▪ a range of commercial goods: *the company intends to hire more people and expand its product line.* ▪ the point spread for sports events on which bets may be made. **5** an area or branch of activity: *the stresses unique to their **line of work**.* ▪ a direction, course, or channel: *lines of communication.* ▪ (**lines**) a manner of doing or thinking about something: *the superintendent was thinking **along the same lines**.* ▪ an agreed-upon approach; a policy: *the official line is that there were no chemical attacks on allied troops.* ▪ informal a false or exaggerated account or story: *he feeds me a line about this operation.* **6** a connected series of military fieldworks or defenses facing an enemy force: *raids behind enemy lines.* ▪ an arrangement of soldiers or ships in a column or line formation; a line of battle. ▶ **v.** [trans.] **1** stand or be positioned at intervals along: *a processional route lined by people waving flags.* **2** [usu. as adj.] (**lined**) mark or cover with lines: *a thin woman with a lined face.* **3** Baseball hit a line drive.

– PHRASES **all** (**the way**) **down** (or **along**) **the line** at every point or stage: *the mistakes were caused by lack of care all down the line.* **along** (or **down**) **the line** at a further, later, or unspecified point: *I knew that somewhere down the line there would be an inquest.* **bring someone/something into line** cause someone or something to conform. **the end of the line** the point at which further effort is unproductive or one can go no further. **in line 1** under control: *that threat **kept a lot of people in line**.* **2** in a row waiting to proceed: *I always peer at other people's shopping carts as we **stand in line**.* **in line for** likely to receive: *she might be in line for a cabinet post.* **in the line of duty** while one is working (used mainly of police officers, firefighters, or soldiers). **in** (or **out of**) **line with** in (or not in) alignment or accordance with: *remuneration is in line with comparable international organizations.* **lay** (or **put**) **it on the line** speak frankly.

line[2] ▶ **v.** [trans.] cover the inside surface of (a container or garment) with a layer of different material. ▪ form a layer on the inside surface of (an area); cover as if with a lining: *hundreds of telegrams lined the walls.*

– PHRASES **line one's pockets** make money, esp. by dishonest means. [ME: from obs. *line* 'flax.']

lin·e·age /ˈlinē-ij/ ▶ **n. 1** lineal descent from an ancestor; ancestry or pedigree. **2** Biol. a sequence of species each of which is considered to have evolved from its predecessor: *the chimpanzee and gorilla lineages.*

lin·e·al /ˈlinēəl/ ▶ **adj. 1** in a direct line of descent or ancestry: *a lineal descendant.* **2** of, relating to, or consisting of lines; linear. — **lin·e·al·ly adv.** [ME: via OFr. from late L. *linealis*, from *linea* 'a line' (see LINE[1]).]

lin·e·a·ment /ˈlin(ē)əmənt/ ▶ **n. 1** (usu. **lineaments**) literary a distinctive feature or characteristic, esp. of the face. **2** Geol. a linear feature on the earth's surface, such as a fault. [ME: from L. *lineamentum*, from *lineare* 'make straight,' from *linea* 'a line' (see LINE[1]).]

lin·e·ar /ˈlinēər/ ▶ **adj. 1** arranged in or extending along a straight or nearly straight line: *linear arrangements.* ▪ consisting of or predominantly formed using lines or outlines: *simple linear designs.* ▪ involving one dimension only: *linear elasticity.* ▪ Math. able to be represented by a straight line on a graph; involving or exhibiting directly proportional change in two related quantities: *linear functions.* **2** progressing from one stage to another in a single series of steps; sequential: *a linear narrative.* — **lin·e·ar·i·ty** /ˌlinēˈaritē/ **n. lin·e·ar·ly adv.**

Lin·e·ar A /ˌlinēər/ a still largely unintelligible form of writing on tablets discovered in Crete between 1894 and 1901, dating from *c.*1700 to 1450 BC.

lin·e·ar ac·cel·er·a·tor ▶ **n.** Physics an accelerator in which particles travel in straight lines, not in closed orbits.

Lin·e·ar B a form of Bronze Age writing discovered on tablets in Crete, dating from *c.*1400 to 1200 BC. It was derived from Linear A and represents a form of Mycenaean Greek.

lin·e·ar e·qua·tion ▶ **n.** an equation between two variables that gives a straight line when plotted on a graph.

lin·e·ar·ize /ˈlinēəˌrīz/ ▶ v. [trans.] tech. make linear; represent in or transform into a linear form. — **lin·e·ar·i·za·tion** /ˌlinēərəˈzāSHən/ n. **lin·e·ar·iz·er** n.

lin·e·ar mo·tor ▶ n. an electric induction motor that produces straight-line motion by means of a linear stator and rotor placed in parallel. It has been used to drive streetcars and monorails.

lin·e·ar per·spec·tive ▶ n. a type of perspective used by artists in which the relative size, shape, and position of objects are determined by drawn or imagined lines converging at a point on the horizon.

lin·e·ar pro·gram·ming ▶ n. a mathematical technique for maximizing or minimizing a linear function of several variables, such as output or cost.

lin·e·a·tion /ˌlinēˈāSHən/ ▶ n. the action or process of drawing lines or marking with lines. ■ a line or linear marking; an arrangement or group of lines: *magnetic lineations.* ■ a contour or outline. ■ the division of text into lines: *the punctuation and lineation are reproduced accurately.*

line·back·er /ˈlīnˌbakər/ ▶ n. Football a defensive player normally positioned behind the line of scrimmage, but in front of the safeties.

line breed·ing ▶ n. the selective breeding of animals for a desired feature by mating them within a closely related line.

line cut ▶ n. a photoengraving from a drawing consisting of solid blacks and whites, without gradations of color.

line danc·ing ▶ n. a type of country and western dancing in which dancers line up in a row without partners and follow a choreographed pattern of steps to music. — **line dance** n. **line-dance** v. **line danc·er** n.

line draw·ing ▶ n. a drawing done using only narrow lines, the variation of which, in width and density, produces such effects as tone and shading.

line drive ▶ n. Baseball a powerfully hit ball that travels in the air and relatively close to and parallel with the ground.

line en·grav·ing ▶ n. the art or technique of engraving by lines incised on the plate, as distinguished from etching and mezzotint. ■ an engraving executed in this manner. — **line-en·graved** adj. **line en·grav·er** n.

line feed ▶ n. the action of advancing paper in a printing machine by the space of one line. ■ Comput. the analogous movement of text on a VDT screen.

line in·te·gral ▶ n. Math. the integral, taken along a line, of any function that has a continuously varying value along that line.

Line Is·lands a group of 11 islands in the central Pacific Ocean south of Hawaii. Eight of the islands form part of Kiribati; the remaining three are uninhabited dependencies of the US.

line i·tem ▶ n. an entry that appears on a separate line in a bookkeeping ledger or a fiscal budget. ■ a single item in a legislative appropriations bill.

line-i·tem ve·to ▶ n. (also **i·tem ve·to**) the power of a president, governor, or other elected executive to reject individual provisions of a bill.

line·man /ˈlīnmən/ ▶ n. (pl. **-men**) **1** a person employed in laying and maintaining railroad track. ■ a person employed for the repair and maintenance of telephone or electricity power lines. **2** Football a player normally positioned on the line of scrimmage.

lin·en /ˈlinin/ ▶ n. cloth woven from flax. ■ garments or other household articles such as sheets made, or originally made, of linen. [OE *līnen* (as an adj. in the sense 'made of flax'), of West Gmc. origin; rel. to Du. *linnen*, Ger. *Leinen*, also to obs. *line* 'flax.']

line of bat·tle ▶ n. a disposition of troops for action in battle.

line of scrim·mage ▶ n. Football the imaginary line separating the teams at the beginning of a play.

line print·er ▶ n. a machine that prints output from a computer a line at a time rather than character by character.

lin·er¹ /ˈlīnər/ ▶ n. **1** (also **ocean liner**) a large luxurious passenger ship of a type formerly used on a regular line. **2** a fine paintbrush used for painting thin lines and for outlining. ■ a cosmetic used for outlining or accentuating a facial feature, or a brush or pencil for applying this. **3** informal another term for LINE DRIVE.

lin·er² ▶ n. a lining in an appliance, device, garment, or container, esp. a removable one.

-liner ▶ comb. form informal denoting a text of a specified (usually small) number of lines such as an advertisement or a spoken passage: *two-liner.*

lin·er note ▶ n. (usu. **liner notes**) the text printed on a paper insert issued as part of the packaging of a compact disc or on the sleeve of a phonograph record.

line score ▶ n. a summary of the scoring in a game displayed in a horizontal table, esp. an inning-by-inning record of the runs, hits, and errors in a baseball game.

lines·man /ˈlīnzmən/ ▶ n. (pl. **-men**) (in games played on a field or court) an official who assists the referee or umpire from the sideline, esp. in deciding on whether the ball is out of play.

line squall ▶ n. Meteorol. a violent local storm occurring as one of a number along a cold front.

line-up /ˈlīnˌəp/ ▶ n. **1** a group of people or things brought together in a particular context, esp. the members of a sports team or a group of musicians or other entertainers. ■ the schedule of television programs for a particular period. **2** a group of people including a suspect for a crime assembled for the purpose of having an eyewitness identify the suspect from among them. ■ a line or linelike arrangement of people or things.

line work ▶ n. **1** drawings or designs carried out with a pen or pencil. **2** work on lines, esp. as a lineman or a production-line worker.

ling¹ /liNG/ ▶ n. any of a number of long-bodied edible marine fishes, in particular a large, commercially important eastern Atlantic fish (genus *Molva*) of the cod family. [ME *lenge*, prob. from MDu.; rel. to LONG¹.]

ling² ▶ n. the common heather of Eurasia. [ME: from ON *lyng*, of unknown origin.]

ling. ▶ abbr. linguistics.

-ling ▶ suffix **1** forming nouns from nouns, adjectives, and verbs (such as *hireling, youngling*). **2** forming nouns from adjectives and adverbs (such as *darling, sibling, underling*). **3** forming diminutive words: *gosling* | *sapling.* ■ often with depreciatory reference: *princeling.* [OE; sense 3 from ON.]

Lin·ga·la /liNGˈgälə/ ▶ n. a Bantu language used by over 8 million people as a lingua franca in northern parts of Congo and the Democratic Republic of the Congo (formerly Zaire). [a local name.]

lin·gam /ˈliNGgəm/ (also **lin·ga** /-gə/) ▶ n. Hinduism a symbol of divine generative energy, esp. a phallus or phallic object worshiped as a symbol of Shiva. Compare with YONI. [from Sanskrit *liṅga* 'mark.']

ling·cod /ˈliNGˌkäd/ ▶ n. (pl. same) a large slender greenling (*Ophiodon elongatus*) that has large teeth and is greenish-brown with golden spots. It lives along the Pacific coast of North America.

lin·ger /ˈliNGgər/ ▶ v. [intrans.] stay in a place longer than necessary, typically because of a reluctance to leave: *she lingered in the yard, enjoying the warm sunshine.* ■ (**linger over**) spend a long time over (something): *she lingered over her meal.* ■ be slow to disappear or die: *the tradition seems to linger on.* — **lin·ger·er** n. [ME: frequentative of obs. *leng* 'prolong,' of Gmc. origin; rel. to LONG¹.]

lin·ge·rie /ˌlänZHəˈrā; -jə-/ ▶ n. women's underwear and nightclothes. [19th C.: from Fr., from *linge* 'linen.']

lin·ger·ing /ˈliNGg(ə)riNG/ ▶ adj. [attrib.] lasting for a long time or slow to end. — **lin·ger·ing·ly** adv.

lin·go /ˈliNGgō/ ▶ n. (pl. **-gos** or **-goes**) informal, often humorous or derog. a foreign language or local dialect. ■ the vocabulary or jargon of a particular subject or group of people: *fat, known in medical lingo as adipose tissue.* [17th C.: prob. via Port. *lingoa* from L. *lingua* 'tongue.']

ling·on·ber·ry /ˈliNGənˌberē/ ▶ n. (pl. **-ries**) another term for the mountain cranberry, esp. in Scandinavia. [1950s: from Swed. *lingon* 'mountain cranberry' + BERRY.]

lin·gua fran·ca /ˈliNGgwə ˈfraNGkə/ ▶ n. (pl. **lin·gua fran·cas**) a language that is adopted as a common language between speakers whose native languages are different. ■ hist. a mixture of Italian with French, Greek, Arabic, and Spanish, formerly used in the Levant. [17th C.: from Ital., lit. 'Frankish tongue.']

lin·gual /ˈliNGgwəl/ ▶ adj. tech. **1** of or relating to the tongue. ■ Phonet. (of a sound) formed by the tongue. **2** of or relating to speech or language: *his demonstrations of lingual dexterity.* ▶ n. Phonet. a lingual sound. — **lin·gual·ly** adv. [17th C.: from med. L. *lingualis*, from L. *lingua* 'tongue, language.']

lin·gui·ne /liNGˈgwēnē/ (also **lin·gui·ni**) ▶ n. pasta in the form of narrow ribbons. [Ital., pl. of *linguina*, dimin. of *lingua* 'tongue.']

lin·guist /ˈliNGgwist/ ▶ n. **1** a person skilled in foreign languages. **2** a person who studies linguistics. [16th C.: from L. *lingua* 'language' + -IST.]

lin·guis·tic /liNGˈgwistik/ ▶ adj. of or relating to language or linguistics. — **lin·guis·ti·cal·ly** /-tik(ə)lē/ adv.

lin·guis·tics /liNGˈgwistiks/ ▶ plural n. [treated as sing.] the scientific study of language and its structure, including the study of morphology, syntax, phonetics, and semantics. — **lin·guis·ti·cian** /ˌliNGgwəˈstiSHən/ n.

lin·gu·late /ˈliNGgyəˌlāt/ ▶ adj. Bot. & Zool. tongue-shaped. [19th C.: from L. *lingulatus*, based on *lingua* 'tongue,' from *lingere* 'to lick.']

lin·i·ment /ˈlinəmənt/ ▶ n. a liquid or lotion, esp. one made with oil, for rubbing on the body to relieve pain. [ME: from late L. *linimentum*, from L. *linire* 'to smear.']

lin·ing /ˈlīniNG/ ▶ n. a layer of different material covering the inside surface of something: *a lining of fireproof insulation.*

link¹ /liNGk/ ▶ n. **1** a relationship between two things or situations, esp. where one thing affects the other. ■ a social or professional connection between people or organizations. ■ something that enables communication between people: *sign language interpreters represent a vital link between the deaf and hearing communities.* ■ a means of contact by radio, telephone, or computer between two points: *a satellite link with Tokyo.* ■ a means of travel or transport between two places: *a rail link.* ■ Comput. a code or instruction that connects one part of a program or an element in a list to another. **2** a ring or loop in a chain. ■ a unit of measurement of length equal to one hundredth of a surveying chain (7.92 inches). ■ a piece in a chain of sausages. ▶ v. make, form, or suggest a connection with or between: [trans.] *rumors that linked his name with Judith* | [intrans.] *she was linked up with an artistic group.* ■ connect or join physically: [trans.] *a network of routes linking towns and villages* | [intrans.] *three different groups, each linking with the other.* ■ [trans.] clasp; intertwine: *once outside he linked arms with her.* — **link·er** n. [ME: from ON *hlekkr*, of Gmc. origin; rel. to Ger. *Gelenk* 'joint.']

link² ▶ n. hist. a torch of pitch and tow for lighting the way in dark streets. [16th C.: perh. from med. L. *li(n)chinus* 'wick,' from Gk. *lukhnos* 'light.']

linked list ▶ n. Comput. an ordered set of data elements, each containing a link to its successor (and sometimes its predecessor).

link·ing verb /ˈliNGkiNG/ ▶ n. Gram. another term for COPULA.

Lin·kö·ping /'lin,CHŌŌPING; -,CHœ-/ a town in southeastern Sweden; pop. 122,000.

links /liNGks/ ▶ **plural n.** (also **golf links**) [treated as sing. or pl.] a golf course. [OE *hlinc* 'rising ground,' perh. rel. to LEAN[1].]

links·land /'liNGksland/ ▶ **n.** Scot. level or undulating sandy ground covered by coarse grass and near the sea.

link·up /'liNGk,əp/ (also **link-up**) ▶ **n.** an instance of two or more people or things connecting or joining. ■ a connection enabling two or more people or machines to communicate with each other: *a live satellite linkup.*

link·work /'liNGk,wərk/ ▶ **n.** something made of links, as a chain. ■ a kind of gearing that transmits motion by a series of links rather than by wheels or bands.

linn /lin/ ▶ **n.** Scot., archaic a waterfall. ■ the pool below a waterfall. ■ a steep precipice. [16th C.: from Scot. Gael. *linne*, Irish *linn*, rel. to Welsh *llyn* 'lake.']

Lin·nae·us /li'nēəs/, Carolus (1707–78), Swedish botanist; Latinized name of *Carl von Linné*. He founded modern systematic botany and zoology. — **Lin·nae·an** /-'nēən; -'nā-/ (also **Lin·ne·an**) **adj. & n.**

lin·net /'linit/ ▶ **n.** a mainly brown and gray finch (genus *Acanthis*) with a reddish breast and forehead. [16th C.: from OFr. *linette*, from *lin* 'flax.']

li·no /'līnō/ ▶ **n.** (pl. **-nos**) esp. Brit. informal term for LINOLEUM.

li·no·cut /'līnō,kət/ ▶ **n.** a design or form carved in relief on a block of linoleum. ■ a print made from such a block. — **li·no·cut·ting n.**

lin·o·le·ic ac·id /,linə'lēik; -'lā-; lə'nōlēik/ ▶ **n.** Chem. a polyunsaturated fatty acid, $C_{17}H_{31}COOH$, present as a glyceride in linseed oil and other oils and essential in the human diet. — **li·no·le·ate** /lə'nōlē,āt/ **n.** [19th C.: from L. *linum* 'flax' + OLEIC ACID.]

lin·o·le·nic ac·id /,linə'lēnik; -'lenik/ ▶ **n.** Chem. a polyunsaturated fatty acid, $C_{17}H_{29}COOH$ (with one more double bond than linoleic acid), present as a glyceride in linseed and other oils and essential in the human diet. — **lin·o·le·nate** /-'lē,nāt; -'len,āt/ **n.** [19th C.: from Ger. *Linolensaüre*, from *Linolsaüre* 'linoleic acid,' with the insertion of *-en-* (from -ENE).]

li·no·le·um /lə'nōlēəm/ ▶ **n.** a material consisting of a canvas backing coated with linseed oil and powdered cork, used esp. as a floor covering. — **li·no·le·umed adj.** [19th C.: from L. *linum* 'flax' + *oleum* 'oil.']

Lin·o·type /'līnə,tīp/ ▶ **n.** Print., trademark a composing machine producing lines of words as single strips of metal, formerly used for newspapers.

lin·sang /'lin,SANG/ ▶ **n.** a small secretive mammal (genera *Prionodon* and *Poiana*) of the civet family, with a spotted or banded coat and a long tail, found in the forests of Southeast Asia and West Africa. [19th C.: via Javanese from Malay.]

lin·seed /'lin,sēd/ ▶ **n.** the seeds of the flax plant. Also called FLAXSEED. ■ the flax plant, esp. when grown for linseed oil. [OE *līnsǣd*, from *līn* 'flax' + *sǣd* 'seed.']

lin·seed oil ▶ **n.** a pale yellow oil extracted from linseed, used esp. in paint and varnish.

lin·sey-wool·sey /'linzē'wo͝olzē/ ▶ **n.** a strong, coarse fabric with a linen or cotton warp and a woolen weft. [15th C.: from *linsey*, a coarse linen fabric (prob. from *Lindsey*, England) + WOOL + *-sey*.]

lin·stock /'lin,stäk/ ▶ **n.** hist. a long pole used to hold a match for firing a cannon. [16th C.: from earlier *lintstock*, from Du. *lontstok*, from *lont* 'match' + *stok* 'stick.']

lint /lint/ ▶ **n.** short, fine fibers that separate from the surface of cloth or yarn. ■ a fabric, originally of linen, with a raised nap on one side, used for dressing wounds. ■ the fibrous material of a cotton boll. — **lint·y adj.** [ME *lynnet* 'flax prepared for spinning,' perh. from OFr. *linette* 'linseed,' from *lin* 'flax.']

lin·tel /'lintl/ ▶ **n.** a horizontal support of timber, stone, concrete, or steel across the top of a door or window. — **lin·teled** (Brit. **lin·telled**) **adj.** [ME: from OFr., based on late L. *liminare*, from L. *limen* 'threshold.']

lint·er /'lintər/ ▶ **n.** a machine for removing the short fibers from cotton seeds after ginning. ■ (**linters**) fibers of this kind.

Lin·ux /'linəks/ ▶ **n.** Trademark an open-source version of the UNIX operating system.

lin·y /'līnē/ ▶ **adj.** (**lin·i·er, lin·i·est**) informal marked with lines; wrinkled.

Linz /lin(t)s/ a city in northern Austria; pop. 203,000.

lion

li·on /'līən/ ▶ **n.** a large tawny-colored cat (*Panthera leo*) that lives in prides, found in Africa and northwestern India. The male has a flowing shaggy mane and takes little part in hunting, which is done cooperatively by the females. ■ (**the Lion**) the zodiacal sign or constellation Leo. ■ fig. a brave or strong person. ■ an influential or celebrated person: *a literary lion.* ■ (**Lion**) a member of a Lions Club.
– PHRASES **throw someone to the lions** cause someone to be in an extremely dangerous or unpleasant situation. [ME: from Anglo-Norman Fr. *liun*, from L. *leo, leon-*, from Gk. *leōn, leont-*.]

li·on·ess /'līənəs/ ▶ **n.** a female lion.

li·on·heart·ed /'līən,härtid/ ▶ **adj.** brave and determined.

li·on·ize /'līə,nīz/ ▶ **v.** [trans.] give a lot of public attention and approval to (someone); treat as a celebrity. — **li·on·i·za·tion** /,līənə'zāSHən/ **n.** **li·on·iz·er n.**

Li·ons Club ▶ **n.** a worldwide charitable society devoted to social and international service, taking its membership primarily from business and professional groups.

lion's share ▶ **n.** the biggest or greatest part: *William was appointed editor, which meant that he did the lion's share of the work.*

li·on tam·a·rin ▶ **n.** a rare tamarin (genus *Leontopithecus*) with a golden or black and golden coat and an erect mane, found only in Brazil. Four species include the **golden lion tamarin** (*L. rosalia*).

lip /lip/ ▶ **n. 1** either of the two fleshy parts that form the upper and lower edges of the opening of the mouth. ■ (**lips**) used to refer to a person's speech or to current topics of conversation: *downsizing is on everyone's lips at the moment.* ■ another term for LABIUM. ■ another term for LABELLUM. **2** the edge of a hollow container or an opening: *drawing her finger around the lip of the cup.* ■ a rounded, raised, or extended piece along an edge. **3** informal impudent talk: *don't give me any of your lip!* ▶ **v.** (**lipped, lip·ping**) [trans.] (of water) lap against: *beaches lipped by the surf rimming the Pacific.* ■ Golf hit the rim of (a hole) but fail to go in.
– PHRASES **bite one's lip** repress an emotion; stifle laughter or a retort. **curl one's lip** raise a corner of one's upper lip to show contempt; sneer. **lick** (or **smack**) **one's lips** look forward to something with relish; show one's satisfaction. **my** (or **his**, etc.) **lips are sealed** see SEAL[1]. **pass one's lips** be eaten, drunk, or spoken. **pay lip service to** express approval of or support for (something) without taking any significant action. — **lip·like** /-,līk/ **adj. lipped adj.** [in comb.] *her pale-lipped mouth.* [OE *lippa*, of Gmc. origin; rel. to Du. *lip* and Ger. *Lippe*, from an Indo-Eur. root shared by L. *labia, labra* 'lips.']

li·pa /'lē,pä; -pə/ ▶ **n.** (pl. same or **li·pas**) a monetary unit of Croatia, equal to one hundredth of a kuna.

Lip·a·ri Is·lands /'lipərē/ seven volcanic islands in the Tyrrhenian Sea, off the northeastern coast of Sicily, in Italian possession. Formerly known as the Aeolian Islands.

li·pase /'lip,ās; 'lī,pās/ ▶ **n.** Biochem. a pancreatic enzyme that catalyzes the breakdown of fats to fatty acids and glycerol or other alcohols. [19th C.: from Gk. *lipos* 'fat' + -ASE.]

lip balm ▶ **n.** a preparation, typically in stick form, to prevent or relieve chapped lips.

Lip·chitz /'lipSHits/, Jacques (1891–1973), French sculptor; born in Lithuania; born *Chaim Jacob Lipchitz*. He explored the interpenetration of solids and voids in his "transparent" sculptures of the 1920s.

lip·ec·to·my /li'pektəmē; lī-/ ▶ **n.** the surgical removal of fatty tissue, esp. from the abdomen in obese persons.

Li·petsk /'lē,pitsk/ a city in southwestern Russia; pop. 455,000.

lip·gloss /'lip,gläs; -,glôs/ (also **lip gloss**) ▶ **n.** a cosmetic applied to the lips to provide a glossy finish, often tinted.

lip·id /'lipid/ ▶ **n.** Chem. any of a class of organic compounds that are fatty acids or their derivatives and are insoluble in water but soluble in organic solvents. They include many natural oils, waxes, and steroids. [20th C.: from Fr. *lipide*, based on Gk. *lipos* 'fat.']

Lip·iz·za·ner /'lipə,zänər; ,lipə'tsänər/ (also **Lip·pi·za·ner**) ▶ **n.** a horse of a fine white breed used esp. in displays of dressage. [20th C.: from Ger., from *Lippiza*, near Trieste.]

lip·lin·er /'lip,līnər/ ▶ **n.** a cosmetic applied to the outline of the lips, mainly to prevent the unwanted spreading of lipstick or lipgloss.

Li Po /'lē 'pō; 'bō/ (also **Li Bo** /'lē 'bō/ or **Li T'ai Po** /'lē 'tī 'bō/) (AD 701–62), Chinese poet.

lipo- ▶ **comb. form** relating to fat or other lipids: *liposuction* | *lipoprotein.* [from Gk. *lipos* 'fat.']

lip·o·gen·e·sis /,lipō'jenəsis; ,lī-/ ▶ **n.** Physiol. the metabolic formation of fat. — **li·po·gen·ic** /-'jenik/ **adj.**

lip·o·gram /'lipə,gram; 'lī-/ ▶ **n.** a composition from which the writer systematically omits a certain letter or certain letters of the alphabet. — **lip·o·gram·mat·ic** /,lipōgrə'matik; ,lī-/ **adj.** [18th C.: back-form. from Gk. *lipogrammatos* 'lacking a letter,' from *lip-* (stem of *leipein* 'to leave (out)') + *gramma* 'letter.']

lip·oid /'lip,oid; 'lī,poid/ ▶ **adj.** (also **lip·oid·al**) Biochem. relating to or resembling fat. ▶ **n.** a fatlike substance; a lipid. [19th C.: from Gk. *lipos* 'fat' + -OID.]

li·pol·y·sis /li'päləsis; lī-/ ▶ **n.** Physiol. the breakdown of fats and other lipids by hydrolysis to release fatty acids. — **li·po·lyt·ic** /,lipə'litik; ,lī-/ **adj.**

li·po·ma /li'pōmə/ ▶ **n.** (pl. **-mas** or **-ma·ta** /-mətə/) Med. a benign tumor of fatty tissue. — **li·pom·a·tous** /-mətəs/ **adj.**

lip·o·phil·ic /,lipə'filik; ,lī-/ ▶ **adj.** Biochem. tending to combine with or dissolve in lipids or fats.

lip·o·pol·y·sac·cha·ride /'lipō,pälē'sakə,rīd; 'lī-/ ▶ **n.** Biochem. a complex molecule containing both lipid and polysaccharide parts.

lip·o·pro·tein /ˌlipəˈprōˌtēn; ˌlī-/ ▶ **n.** Biochem. any of a group of soluble proteins that combine with and transport fat or other lipids in the blood plasma.

lip·o·some /ˈlipəˌsōm; ˈlī-/ ▶ **n.** Biochem. a minute spherical sac of phospholipid molecules enclosing a water droplet, esp. as formed artificially to carry drugs or other substances into the tissues.

lip·o·suc·tion /ˈlipōˌsəksHən; ˈlī-/ ▶ **n.** a technique in cosmetic surgery for removing excess fat from under the skin by suction.

lip·o·tro·pin /ˌlipəˈtrōpin; ˌlīpə-/ (also **lip·o·tro·phin** /-ˈtrōfən/) ▶ **n.** Biochem. a hormone secreted by the anterior pituitary gland. It promotes the release of fat reserves from the liver into the bloodstream.

Lip·pes loop /ˈlipēz/ ▶ **n.** a type of intrauterine contraceptive device made of inert plastic in a double S-shape, which can be inserted for long periods. [1960s: named after Jack *Lippes* (1924–), US obstetrician.]

Lip·pi·zan·er /ˈlipəˌzänər; ˌlipəˈtsänər/ ▶ **n.** var. of **LIPIZZANER.**

Lipp·mann[1] /ˈlipmən/, Gabriel Jonas (1845–1921), French physicist. He produced the first fully orthochromatic color photograph in 1893.

Lipp·mann[2], Walter (1899–1974), US journalist. He was a founder of the *New Republic* and a columnist for the *New York Herald Tribune* 1931–67.

lip·py /ˈlipē/ informal ▶ **adj.** (**-pi·er, -pi·est**) **1** insolent; impertinent. **2** having prominent lips.

lip-read /-ˌrēd/ (also **lip·read**) ▶ **v.** [intrans.] (of a deaf person) understand speech from observing a speaker's lip movements. — **lip-read·er n.**

lip·stick /ˈlipˌstik/ ▶ **n.** colored cosmetic applied to the lips from a small solid stick.

lip-sync /-ˌsiNGk/ (also **lip-synch**) ▶ **v.** [trans.] (of an actor or singer) move the lips silently in synchronization with (a recorded soundtrack). ▶ **n.** the action of using such a technique. — **lip-sync·er n.**

Lip·ton /ˈliptən/, Sir Thomas Johnstone (1850–1931), Scottish merchant and yachtsman. He invented the tea bag. Noted for his yachts, he entered five of them in the America's Cup races.

liq. ▶ **abbr.** ■ liquid. ■ liquor. ■ (in prescriptions) solution. [from L. *liquor*]

li·quate /ˈlīˌkwāt; ˈlikˌwāt/ ▶ **v.** [trans.] Metallurgy separate or purify (a metal) by melting it. — **li·qua·tion** /līˈkwāsHən; li-/ **n.** [19th C.: from L. *liquat-* 'made liquid,' from the v. *liquare*; rel. to **LIQUOR.**]

liq·ue·fied pet·ro·le·um gas (abbr.: **LPG**) ▶ **n.** a mixture of light gaseous hydrocarbons (ethane, propane, butane, etc.) made liquid by pressure and used as fuel.

liq·ue·fy /ˈlikwəˌfī/ (also **liq·ui·fy**) ▶ **v.** (**-fies, -fied**) make or become liquid. ■ convert (solid food) into a liquid or purée, typically by using a blender. — **liq·ue·fac·tion** /ˌlikwəˈfaksHən/ **n. liq·ue·fac·tive** /ˌlikwəˈfaktiv/ **adj. liq·ue·fi·a·ble** /ˌlikwəˈfīəbəl/ **adj. liq·ue·fi·er n.** [ME: from Fr. *liquéfier*, from L. *liquefacere* 'make liquid,' from *liquere* 'be liquid.']

li·ques·cent /liˈkwesənt/ ▶ **adj.** literary becoming or apt to become liquid. — **li·ques·cence n.**

li·queur /liˈkər; -ˈk(y)o͝or/ ▶ **n.** a strong, sweet flavored alcoholic liquor, usually drunk after a meal. [18th C.: from Fr., 'liquor.']

liq·uid /ˈlikwid/ ▶ **adj.** **1** having a consistency like that of water or oil, i.e., flowing freely but of constant volume. ■ having the translucence of water; clear: *liquid dark eyes.* ■ [attrib.] denoting a substance normally a gas that has been liquefied by cold or pressure: *liquid oxygen.* ■ not fixed or stable; fluid. **2** (of a sound) clear, pure, and flowing; harmonious: *the liquid song of the birds.* **3** Phonet. (of a consonant) produced by allowing the airstream to flow over the sides of the tongue, typically *l* and *r*, and able to be prolonged like a vowel. **4** (of assets) held in cash or easily converted into cash. ▶ **n.** **1** a liquid substance: *drink plenty of liquids.* **2** Phonet. a liquid consonant. — **liq·uid·ly adv. liq·uid·ness n.** [ME: from L. *liquidus*, from *liquere* 'be liquid.']

liq·uid·am·bar /ˌlikwidˈambər/ ▶ **n.** a deciduous North American and Asian tree (genus *Liquidambar*, family Hamamelidaceae) with maple-like leaves and bright autumn colors, yielding aromatic resinous balsam. ■ liquid balsam obtained chiefly from the Asian liquidambar tree, used medicinally and in perfume. Also called **STORAX.** [16th C.: mod. L., appar. formed irregularly from L. *liquidus* 'liquid' + med. L. *ambar* 'amber.']

liq·ui·date /ˈlikwəˌdāt/ ▶ **v.** [trans.] **1** wind up the affairs of (a company or firm) by ascertaining liabilities and apportioning assets. ■ [intrans.] (of a company) undergo such a process. ■ convert (assets) into cash. ■ pay off (a debt). **2** eliminate, typically by violent means; kill. — **liq·ui·da·tion** /ˌlikwəˈdāsHən/ **n.**

liq·ui·da·tor /ˈlikwəˌdātər/ ▶ **n.** a person appointed to wind up the affairs of a company or firm.

liq·uid crys·tal ▶ **n.** a substance that flows like a liquid but has some degree of ordering in the arrangement of its molecules.

liq·uid crys·tal dis·play (abbr.: **LCD**) ▶ **n.** an electronic visual display in which the application of an electric current to a liquid crystal layer makes it opaque.

liq·uid·i·ty /liˈkwidətē/ ▶ **n.** Finance the availability of liquid assets to a market or company. ■ liquid assets; cash.

liq·uid·ize /ˈlikwəˌdīz/ ▶ **v.** [trans.] Brit. another term for **LIQUEFY.** — **liq·uid·iz·er n.**

liq·uid lunch ▶ **n.** informal, humorous a drinking session at lunchtime taking the place of a meal.

liq·uid meas·ure ▶ **n.** a unit for measuring the volume of liquids.

liq·ui·fy /ˈlikwəˌfī/ ▶ **v.** var. of **LIQUEFY.**

liq·uor /ˈlikər/ ▶ **n.** **1** alcoholic drink, esp. distilled spirits. **2** a liquid produced or used in a process of some kind, in particular: ■ water used in brewing. ■ liquid in which something has been steeped or cooked. ■ liquid that drains from food during cooking. ■ the liquid from which a substance has been crystallized or extracted.
– PHRASAL VERBS **liquor up** (or **liquor someone up**) informal get (or make someone) drunk. [ME: from OFr. *lic(o)ur*, from L. *liquor*; rel. to *liquere* 'be fluid.']

liq·uo·rice /ˈlik(ə)risH; -ris/ ▶ **n.** British spelling of **LICORICE.**

liq·uor·ish /ˈlik(ə)risH/ ▶ **adj.** archaic form of **LICKERISH.** — **liq·uor·ish·ness n.**

li·ra /ˈli(ə)rə/ ▶ **n.** (pl. **li·re** /ˈli(ə)rā; ˈli(ə)rə/) **1** the former basic monetary unit of Italy (until the introduction of the euro), notionally equal to 100 centesimos. **2** the basic monetary unit of Turkey, equal to 100 kurus. [Ital., from Provençal *liura*, from L. *libra* 'pound.']

lir·i·pipe /ˈli(ə)rəˌpīp/ ▶ **n.** a long tail hanging from the back of a hood, esp. in medieval or academic dress. [17th C.: from med. L. *liripipium* 'tippet of a hood, cord,' of unknown origin.]

Lis·bon /ˈlizbən/ the capital of Portugal, on the Atlantic coast; pop. 678,000. Portuguese name **LISBOA.**

li·sen·te /liˈsentē/ plural form of **SENTE.**

-lish ▶ **suffix** forming nouns denoting a blend of a particular language with English, as used by native speakers of the first language: *Spanglish.*

lisle /līl/ (also **lisle thread**) ▶ **n.** a fine, smooth cotton thread used esp. for hosiery. [16th C.: from *Lisle*, former spelling of **LILLE.**]

Lisp /lisp/ (also **LISP**) ▶ **n.** a high-level computer programming language devised for list processing. [1950s: from *lis(t) p(rocessor).*]

lisp /lisp/ ▶ **n.** a speech defect in which *s* is pronounced like *th* in *thick* and *z* is pronounced like *th* in *this.* ▶ **v.** [intrans.] speak with a lisp. — **lisp·er n. lisp·ing·ly adv.** [OE *wlispian* (recorded in *āwlyspian*), from *wlisp* (adj.) 'lisping,' of imitative origin; cf. Du. *lispen* and Ger. *lispeln.*]

lis pen·dens /ˈlis ˈpenˌdenz/ ▶ **n.** Law a pending legal action. ■ a formal notice of this. [L.]

lis·some /ˈlisəm/ (also esp. Brit. **lis·som**) ▶ **adj.** (of a person or their body) thin, supple, and graceful. — **lis·some·ness n.** [18th C.: contr., from **LITHE** + **-SOME[1]**.]

list[1] /list/ ▶ **n.** **1** a number of connected items or names written or printed consecutively, typically one below the other: *consult the list of drugs on page 326.* ■ a set of items considered as being in the same category or having a particular order of priority: *tourism is at the top of the list of potential job creators.* ■ Comput. a formal structure analogous to a list by which items of data can be stored or processed in a definite order. **2** (**lists**) hist. barriers enclosing an area for a jousting tournament. ■ the scene of a contest or combat. **3** a selvage of a piece of fabric. ▶ **v.** [trans.] make a list of: *I have listed four reasons below.* ■ (often **be listed**) include or enter in a list: *93 men were still listed as missing.* ■ [intrans.] (**list at/for**) be on a list of products at (a specified price): *the bottom-of-the-line Mercedes lists for $52,050.*
– PHRASES **enter the lists** issue or accept a challenge. — **list·a·ble adj.** [OE *liste* 'border,' from Gmc. Senses 1, 2 via (Old) Fr.]

list[2] ▶ **v.** [intrans.] (of a ship) lean to one side, typically because of a leak or unbalanced cargo. Compare with **HEEL[2]**. ▶ **n.** an instance of a ship leaning over in such a way. [17th C.: of unknown origin.]

list[3] archaic ▶ **v.** [intrans.] want; like: [with clause] *let them think what they list.* ▶ **n.** desire; inclination: *I have little list to write.* [OE *lystan* (v.), of Gmc. origin, from a base meaning 'pleasure.']

list·box /ˈlis(t)ˌbäks/ ▶ **n.** Comput. a box on the screen that contains a list of options, only one of which can be selected.

list·ed /ˈlistid/ ▶ **adj.** **1** admitted for trading on a stock exchange: *listed securities.* **2** represented in a telephone directory.

lis·tel /ˈlistəl/ ▶ **n.** Archit. a narrow strip with a flat surface running between moldings. Also called **FILLET.** [16th C.: from Ital. *listello*, dimin. of *lista* 'strip, band.']

lis·ten /ˈlisən/ ▶ **v.** [intrans.] give one's attention to a sound: *sit and listen to the radio.* ■ take notice of and act on what someone says; respond to advice or a request: *I told her over and over, but she wouldn't listen.* ■ make an effort to hear something; be alert and ready to hear something: *they* **listened for** *sounds from the room.* ■ [in imper.] used to urge someone to pay attention to what one is going to say: *listen, I've got an idea.* ▶ **n.** [in sing.] an act of listening to something.
– PHRASAL VERBS **listen in** listen to a private conversation, often secretly. ■ use a radio receiving set to listen to a broadcast or conversation. [OE *hlysnan* 'pay attention to,' of Gmc. origin.]

lis·ten·a·ble /ˈlisənəbəl/ ▶ **adj.** easy or pleasant to listen to. — **lis·ten·a·bil·i·ty** /ˌlis(ə)nəˈbilitē/ **n.**

lis·ten·er /ˈlis(ə)nər/ ▶ **n.** a person who listens, esp. someone who does so in an attentive manner. ■ a person listening to a radio station or program.

lis·ten·ing post ▶ **n.** a station for intercepting electronic communications. ■ a position from which to listen or gather information. ■ a point near an enemy's lines for detecting movements by sound.

Lis·ter /ˈlistər/, Joseph, 1st Baron (1827–1912), English surgeon. He invented antiseptic techniques in surgery.

list·er /ˈlistər/ ▶ **n.** a plow with a double moldboard. [19th C.: from **LIST[1]**.]

lis·te·ri·a /liˈsti(ə)rēə/ ▶ **n.** a type of bacterium (*Listeria monocytogenes*) that infects humans and other warm-blooded animals through contaminated food. ■ informal food poisoning or other disease caused by infection with listeria; listeriosis. [1940s: mod. L., named after Joseph *Lister* (1827–1912), English surgeon.]

lis·te·ri·o·sis /li,sti(ə)rē'ōsis/ ▶ **n.** disease caused by infection with listeria.

list·ing /'listiNG/ ▶ **n. 1** a list or catalog. ■ the drawing up of a list. ■ an entry in a list or register. **2** a selvage of a piece of fabric.

list·less /'lis(t)lis/ ▶ **adj.** (of a person or their manner) lacking energy or enthusiasm: *bouts of listless depression.* — **list·less·ly** adv. **list·less·ness** n. [ME: from obs. *list* 'appetite, desire' + -LESS.]

Lis·ton /'listən/, Sonny (1932–70), US boxer; born *Charles Liston.* He was world heavyweight champion 1962–64.

list price ▶ **n.** the price of an article as shown in a list issued by the manufacturer.

list proc·ess·ing ▶ **n.** Comput. the manipulation of data organized as lists.

LISTSERV /'lis(t),sərv/ ▶ **n.** trademark an electronic mailing list of people who wish to receive specified information from the Internet. ■ (also **listserv**) any similar application.

Liszt /list/, Franz (1811–86), Hungarian composer and pianist, a key figure in the romantic movement. His 12 symphonic poems 1848–58 created a new musical form. — **Liszt·i·an** /'listēən/ adj. & n.

lit[1] /lit/ past and past participle of LIGHT[1], LIGHT[3].

lit[2] ▶ **adj.** Informal drunk.

lit. ▶ **abbr.** ■ liter or liters. ■ literal or literally. ■ literary or literature.

Li T'ai Po /'lē 'tī 'bō; 'pō/ variant of LI PO.

lit·a·ny /'litn-ē/ ▶ **n.** (pl. **-nies**) a series of petitions for use in church services, usually recited by the clergy and responded to in a recurring formula by the people. ■ a tedious recital or repetitive series. [ME: from OFr. *letanie*, via eccles. L. from Gk. *litaneia* 'prayer,' from *litē* 'supplication.']

li·tas /'lē,täs/ ▶ **n.** (pl. same) the basic monetary unit of Lithuania, equal to 100 centas.

LitB ▶ **abbr.** Bachelor of Letters or Bachelor of Literature. [from L., *Lit(t)erārum Baccalaureus.*]

li·tchi /'lēCHē/ (also **ly·chee** or **li·chee**) ▶ **n. 1** a small rounded fruit with sweet white scented flesh, a large central stone, and a thin rough skin. Also called **litchi nut** when dried. **2** the Chinese tree (*Nephelium litchi*, or *Litchi chinensis*) of the soapberry family that bears this fruit. [16th C.: from Chin. *lìzhī.*]

lit crit /'lit ,krit/ ▶ **abbr.** literary criticism.

LitD ▶ **abbr.** Doctor of Letters or Doctor of Literature. [from mod. L., *Lit(t)erārum Doctor.*]

lite /līt/ ▶ **adj.** of or relating to low-fat or low-sugar versions of manufactured food or drink products: *lite beer.* ■ informal lacking in substance; superficial. ▶ **n. 1** beer with relatively few calories. **2** informal used as a simplified spelling of LIGHT[1], esp. commercially. [1950s: a deliberate respelling of LIGHT[1], LIGHT[2].]

-lite ▶ **suffix** forming names of rocks, minerals, and fossils: *rhyolite* | *zeolite.* [from Fr., from Gk. *lithos* 'stone.']

li·ter /'lētər/ (Brit. **li·tre**) (abbr.: **l**) ▶ **n.** a metric unit of capacity, formerly defined as the volume of 1 kilogram of water under standard conditions, now equal to 1,000 cubic centimeters (about 1.75 pints). [18th C.: from Fr. *litre*, alt. of *litron*, via med. L. from Gk. *litra*, a Sicilian monetary unit.]

lit·er·a·cy /'lit(ə)rəsē/ ▶ **n.** the ability to read and write. ■ competence or knowledge in a specified area: *wine literacy can't be taught in three hours.* [19th C.: from LITERATE, on the pattern of *illiteracy.*]

lit·er·al /'lit(ə)rəl/ ▶ **adj. 1** taking words in their usual or most basic sense without metaphor or allegory: *dreadful in its literal sense, full of dread.* ■ free from exaggeration or distortion: *you shouldn't take this as a literal record of events.* ■ informal absolute: *fifteen years of literal hell.* **2** (of a translation) representing the exact words of the original text. ■ (of a visual representation) exactly copied; realistic. **3** (also **literal-minded**) (of a person or performance) lacking imagination; prosaic. **4** of, in, or expressed by a letter or the letters of the alphabet: *literal mnemonics.* ▶ **n.** Print., Brit. a misprint of a letter. — **lit·er·al·i·ty** /,litə'ralətē/ n. **lit·er·al·ize** /-,līz/ v. **lit·er·al·ness** n. [ME: from OFr., or from late L. *litteralis*, from L. *littera* (see LETTER).]

lit·er·al·ism /'lit(ə)rə,lizəm/ ▶ **n.** the interpretation of words in their basic sense, without allowing for metaphor or exaggeration: *biblical literalism.* ■ literal or nonidealistic representation in literature or art. — **lit·er·al·ist** n. **lit·er·al·is·tic** /,lit(ə)rə'listik/ adj.

lit·er·al·ly /'lit(ə)rəlē/ ▶ **adv.** in a literal manner or sense; exactly: *the driver took it literally when asked to go straight over the traffic circle.* ■ informal used to acknowledge that something is not literally true but is used for emphasis or to express strong feeling: *I have received literally thousands of letters.*

lit·er·ar·y /'litə,rerē/ ▶ **adj. 1** [attrib.] concerning the writing, study, or content of literature, esp. of the kind valued for quality of form. ■ concerned with literature as a profession: *it was signed by such literary figures as Maya Angelou.* **2** (of language) associated with formal writing; having a marked style intended to create a particular emotional effect. — **lit·er·ar·i·ly** /,litə're(ə)rəlē/ adv. **lit·er·ar·i·ness** n. [17th C.: from L. *litterarius*, from *littera* (see LETTER).]

lit·er·ar·y a·gent ▶ **n.** a professional agent who acts on behalf of an author in dealing with publishers and others involved in promoting the author's work.

lit·er·ar·y crit·i·cism ▶ **n.** the art or practice of judging and commenting on the qualities and character of literary works. — **lit·er·ar·y crit·ic** n.

lit·er·ar·y ex·ec·u·tor ▶ **n.** a person entrusted with a dead writer's papers.

lit·er·ate /'litərit/ ▶ **adj.** (of a person) able to read and write. ■ having or showing education or knowledge, typically in a specified area: *people who are politically literate.* ▶ **n.** a literate person. — **lit·er·ate·ly** adv. [ME: from L. *litteratus*, from *littera* (see LETTER).]

lit·e·ra·ti /,litə'rätē; -'rā-/ ▶ **plural n.** well-educated people who are interested in literature. [17th C.: from L., pl. of *literatus* 'acquainted with letters,' from *littera* (see LETTER).]

lit·e·ra·tim /,litə'rätim/ ▶ **adv.** formal (of the copying of a text) letter by letter. [from med. L.]

lit·er·a·ture /'lit(ə)rəCHər; -,CHŏŏr; -,t(y)ŏŏr/ ▶ **n. 1** written works, esp. those considered of superior or lasting artistic merit: *a great work of literature.* ■ books and writings published on a particular subject: *the literature on environmental epidemiology.* ■ the writings of a country or period: *early French literature.* ■ advertising leaflets or similar printed matter. **2** the production or profession of writing.

-lith ▶ **suffix** denoting types of stone: *laccolith.* [from Gk. *lithos* 'stone.']

lith·arge /'liTH,ärj; li'THärj/ ▶ **n.** lead monoxide, PbO, esp. a red form used as a pigment and in glass and ceramics. [ME: from OFr. *litarge*, via L. from Gk. *litharguros*, from *lithos* 'stone' + *arguros* 'silver.']

lithe /līTH/ (also **lithe·some**) ▶ **adj.** (esp. of a person's body) thin, supple, and graceful. — **lithe·ly** adv. **lithe·ness** n. [OE *līthe* 'gentle, meek,' also 'mellow,' of Gmc. origin; rel. to Ger. *lind* 'soft, gentle.']

lith·i·a /'liTHēə/ ▶ **n.** Chem. lithium oxide, Li_2O, a white alkaline solid. [19th C.: mod. L., alt. of earlier *lithion*, from Gk., neut. of *litheios*, from *lithos* 'stone.']

li·thi·a·sis /li'THīəsis/ ▶ **n.** Med. the formation of stony concretions (calculi) in the body. [17th C.: from med. L., based on Gk. *lithos* 'stone.']

lith·ic /'liTHik/ ▶ **adj.** esp. Archaeol. & Geol. of the nature of or relating to stone. ■ Med., dated relating to calculi. [18th C.: from Gk. *lithikos*, from *lithos* 'stone.']

lith·i·fy /'liTHə,fī/ ▶ **v.** (**-fies, -fied**) [trans.] esp. Geol. transform (a sediment or other material) into stone. — **lith·i·fi·ca·tion** /,liTHəfi'kāSHən/ n. [19th C.: from Gk. *lithos* 'stone' + -FY.]

lith·i·um /'liTHēəm/ ▶ **n.** the chemical element of atomic number 3, a soft silver-white metal. It is the lightest of the alkali metals. (Symbol: **Li**) ■ lithium carbonate or another lithium salt, used as a mood-stabilizing drug. [19th C.: from LITHIA + -IUM.]

lith·o /'liTHō/ informal ▶ **n.** (pl. **-os**) short for LITHOGRAPHY or LITHOGRAPH. ▶ **adj.** short for LITHOGRAPHIC. ▶ **v.** (**-oes, -oed**) short for LITHOGRAPH.

litho- ▶ **comb. form 1** of or relating to stone: *lithosol.* **2** relating to a calculus: *lithotomy.* [from Gk. *lithos* 'stone.']

lith·o·graph /'liTHə,graf/ ▶ **n.** a lithographic print. ▶ **v.** [trans.] print by lithography: [as adj.] (**lithographed**) *a set of lithographed drawings.*

li·thog·ra·phy /li'THägrəfē/ ▶ **n.** the process of printing from a flat surface treated so as to repel the ink except where it is required for printing. ■ Electron. an analogous method for making printed circuits. — **li·thog·ra·pher** /-fər/ n. **lith·o·graph·ic** /li'THägrəfē/ adj. **lith·o·graph·i·cal·ly** /-ik(ə)lē/ adv.

li·thol·o·gy /li'THäləjē/ ▶ **n.** the study of the general physical characteristics of rocks. Compare with PETROLOGY. ■ the general physical characteristics of rocks in a particular area: *the lithology of South Dakota.* — **lith·o·log·ic** /,liTHə'läjik/ adj. **lith·o·log·i·cal** /,liTHə'läjikəl/ adj. **lith·o·log·i·cal·ly** /,liTHə'läjik(ə)lē/ adv.

lith·o·phyte /'liTHə,fīt/ ▶ **n. 1** Bot. a plant that grows on bare rock or stone. **2** Zool. a polyp with a calcareous skeleton; a stony coral. — **lith·o·phyt·ic** /,liTHə'fitik/ adj.

lith·o·pone /'liTHə,pōn/ ▶ **n.** a white pigment made from zinc sulfide and barium sulfate. [19th C.: from LITHO- 'stone, crystals' + Gk. *ponos* '(thing) produced by work.']

lith·o·sphere /'liTHə,sfi(ə)r/ ▶ **n.** Geol. the crust and upper mantle of the earth. — **lith·o·spher·ic** /,liTHə'sferik; -'sfi(ə)r-/ adj.

li·thot·o·my /li'THätəmē/ ▶ **n.** surgical removal of a stone from the bladder, kidney, or urinary tract. — **li·thot·o·mist** n.

lith·o·trip·sy /'liTHə,tripsē/ ▶ **n.** Surg. a treatment, typically using ultrasound shock waves, by which a kidney stone or other calculus is broken into small particles that can be passed out by the body. — **lith·o·trip·ter** /-,triptər/ n. **lith·o·trip·tic** /,liTHə'triptik/ adj. [19th C.: from LITHO- 'of stone' + Gk. *tripsis* 'rubbing,' from *tribein* 'to rub.']

li·thot·ri·ty /li'THätrətē/ ▶ **n.** Surg. a surgical procedure involving the mechanical breaking down of gallstones or other calculi. [19th C.: from LITHO- 'of stone' + L. *tritor* 'thing that rubs' + -Y[3].]

Lith·u·a·ni·a /,liTHōō'ānēə; -nyə/ a country in eastern Europe. *See box on next page.*

Lith·u·a·ni·an /,liTHōō'ānēən/ ▶ **adj.** of or relating to Lithuania or its people or language. ▶ **n. 1** a native or citizen of Lithuania, or a person of Lithuanian descent. **2** the Baltic language of Lithuania.

lit·i·gant /'litəgənt/ ▶ **n.** a person involved in a lawsuit. ▶ **adj.** archaic involved in a lawsuit: *the parties litigant.*

Lithuania

Official name: Republic of Lithuania
Location: eastern Europe, on the southeastern shore of the Baltic Sea
Area: 25,200 square miles (65,200 sq km)
Population: 3,765,000
Capital: Vilnius
Languages: Lithuanian (official), Polish, Russian
Currency: litas

lit·i·gate /'litə,gāt/ ▶v. [intrans.] go to law; be a party to a lawsuit. ■ [trans.] take (a claim or a dispute) to a court of law. — **lit·i·ga·tion** /,litə'gāsHən/ n. **lit·i·ga·tive** /'litə,gātiv/ adj. **lit·i·ga·tor** /-,gātər/ n. [17th C.: from L. *litigat-* 'disputed in a lawsuit,' from the v. *litigare*, from *lis, lit-* 'lawsuit.']

li·ti·gious /lə'tijəs/ ▶adj. concerned with lawsuits or litigation. ■ unreasonably prone to go to law to settle disputes. ■ suitable to become the subject of a lawsuit. — **li·ti·gious·ly** adv. **li·ti·gious·ness** n.

lit·mus /'litməs/ ▶n. a dye obtained from certain lichens that is red under acid conditions and blue under alkaline conditions. [ME: from ON *lit-mosi*, from *litr* 'dye' + *mosi* 'moss.']

lit·mus pa·per ▶n. paper stained with litmus, used to indicate the acidity or alkalinity of a substance.

lit·mus test ▶n. Chem. a test for acidity or alkalinity using litmus. ■ fig. a decisively indicative test: *opposition to the nomination became a litmus test for candidates.*

li·to·tes /'lītə,tēz; 'lit-; lī'tōtēz/ ▶n. Rhet. ironical understatement in which an affirmative is expressed by the negative of its contrary (e.g., *you won't be sorry*, meaning *you'll be glad*). [16th C.: via late L. from Gk. *litotēs*, from *litos* 'plain, meager.']

li·tre ▶n. British spelling of LITER.

LittB ▶abbr. Bachelor of Letters, Bachelor of Literature. [from L. *Lit(t)erārum Baccalaureus.*]

LittD ▶abbr. Doctor of Letters. [from L. *Lit(t)erarum Doctor.*]

litter 4

lit·ter /'litər/ ▶n. **1** trash, such as paper, cans, and bottles, that is left lying in an open or public place. ■ [in sing.] an untidy collection of things lying about: *a litter of sleeping bags on the floor.* **2** a number of young animals born to an animal at one time: *a litter of five kittens.* **3** material forming a surface-covering layer, in particular: ■ (also **cat litter**) granular absorbent material lining a tray where a cat can urinate and defecate when indoors. ■ straw or other plant matter used as bedding for animals. ■ (also **leaf litter**) decomposing leaves and other debris on top of the soil, esp. in forests. **4** hist. a vehicle containing a bed or seat enclosed by curtains and carried on men's shoulders or by animals. ■ a stretcher for transporting the sick and wounded. ▶v. [trans.] **1** make (a place) untidy with rubbish or a large number of objects left lying about: *newspapers littered the floor.* ■ (usu. **be littered**) leave (rubbish or a number of objects) lying untidily in a place. ■ (usu. **be littered with**) fig. fill (a text, history, etc.) with examples of something unpleasant: *news pages littered with gloom.* **2** archaic provide (a horse or other animal) with litter as bedding. — **lit·ter·er** n. [ME: from OFr. *litiere*, from med. L. *lectaria*, from L. *lectus* 'bed.']

lit·té·ra·teur /,litərə'tər/ ▶n. a person who is interested in and knowledgeable about literature. [19th C.: Fr.]

lit·ter box ▶n. a box or tray containing granular absorbent material into which a cat can urinate or defecate.

lit·ter·bug /'litər,bəg/ ▶n. informal a person who carelessly drops litter in a public place.

lit·ter·mate /'litər,māt/ ▶n. one member of a pair or group of animals born in the same litter.

lit·tle /'litl/ ▶adj. small in size, amount, or degree (often used to convey an appealing diminutiveness or express an affectionate or condescending attitude): *the plants will grow into little bushes* | *a little puppy dog.* ■ (of a person) young or younger: *my little brother.* ■ [attrib.] denoting something, esp. a place, that is named after a similar larger one: *New York's Little Italy.* ■ [attrib.] used in names of animals and plants that are smaller than related kinds, e.g., **little grebe**. ■ [attrib.] of short distance or duration: *stay for a little while.* ■ [attrib.] relatively unimportant; trivial (often used ironically): *we have a little problem.* ▶adj. & pron. **1** (**a little**) a small amount of: [as adj.] *we got a little help from my sister* | [as pron.] *you only see **a little of** what he can do.* ■ [pron.] a short time or distance: *after a little, the rain stopped.* **2** used to emphasize how small an amount is: [as adj.] *I have little doubt of their identity* | [as pron.] *he ate and drank very little.* ▶adv. (**less** /les/, **least** /lēst/) **1** (**a little**) to a small extent: *he reminded me a little of my parents.* **2** (used for emphasis) only to a small extent; not much or often: *he was little known in this country.* ■ hardly or not at all: ***little did he know** what wheels he was putting into motion.*

– PHRASES **in little** archaic on a small scale; in miniature. **little by little** by degrees; gradually. **make little of** treat as unimportant. **no little** considerable: *a factor of no little importance.* **not a little** a great deal (of); much: *not a little consternation was caused.* ■ very: *it was not a little puzzling.* **quite a little** a fairly large amount of: *some spoke quite a little English.* ■ a considerable: *it turned out to be quite a little bonanza.* — **lit·tle·ness** n. [OE *ly̆tel*, of Gmc. origin; rel. to Du. *luttel*, Ger. dial. *lützel*.]

Lit·tle Ar·a·rat see ARARAT, MOUNT.

Lit·tle Bear the constellation Ursa Minor.

Lit·tle Big·horn, Bat·tle of a battle in which General George Custer and his forces were defeated by Sioux and Cheyenne warriors (June 25, 1876), popularly known as Custer's Last Stand. It took place in the valley of the Little Bighorn River in Montana.

Lit·tle Cor·po·ral a nickname for Napoleon.

Little Dip·per /'litl 'dipər/ ▶n. the seven bright stars of the constellation Ursa Minor.

lit·tle fin·ger ▶n. the smallest finger, at the outer end of the hand, farthest from the thumb.

– PHRASES **twist** (or **wrap** or **wind**) **someone around one's little finger** have the ability to make someone do whatever one wants.

Lit·tle Flow·er see LA GUARDIA.

lit·tle grebe ▶n. a small, puffy-looking Old World grebe (genus *Tachybaptus*) with a short neck and bill and a trilling call.

lit·tle hours ▶plural n. (in the Roman Catholic Church) the offices of prime, terce, sext, and none.

Lit·tle Ice Age ▶n. a comparatively cold period occurring between major glacial periods, in particular one such period that reached its peak during the 17th century.

Lit·tle League ▶n. youth baseball or softball under the auspices of an organization founded in 1939, for children up to age 12. — **Little Leaguer** n.

Lit·tle Lord Faunt·le·roy see FAUNTLEROY.

Lit·tle Mac see MCCLELLAN.

lit·tle man ▶n. a person who conducts business or life on a small or ordinary scale; an average person. ■ dated used as a form of address to a young boy.

Lit·tle Mis·sou·ri Riv·er a river that flows for 560 miles (900 km) from Wyoming to the Missouri River.

lit·tle peo·ple ▶plural n. **1** the ordinary people in a country, organization, etc., who do not have much power. **2** people of small physical stature; midgets. ■ small supernatural creatures such as fairies and leprechauns.

Lit·tle Rock the capital of Arkansas, located in the central part of the state; pop. 183,133.

Lit·tle Rus·sian ▶n. & adj. former term for UKRAINIAN.

Lit·tle St. Ber·nard Pass see ST. BERNARD PASS.

lit·tle the·a·ter ▶n. a small independent theater used for experimental or avant-garde drama, or for community, noncommercial productions.

Lit·tle Ti·bet another name for BALTISTAN.

lit·tle toe ▶n. the smallest toe, on the outer side of the foot.

Lit·tle·ton /'litl-tən/ a city in north central Colorado, scene of a shooting at Columbine High School in April 1999; pop. 40,340.

Lit·tle Tur·tle (c.1752–1812), Miami Indian chief. He led raids on settlers in the Northwest Territory.

lit·to·ral /'litərəl/ ▶adj. of, relating to, or situated on the shore of the sea or a lake: *the littoral states of the Indian Ocean.* ■ Ecol. of, relating to, or denoting the zone of the seashore between high- and low-water marks, or the zone near a lake shore with rooted vegetation. ▶ n. a region lying along a shore. ■ Ecol. the littoral zone. [17th C.: from L. *littoralis*, from *litus, litor-* 'shore.']

Lit·tré /lē'trä/, Émile (1801–81), French lexicographer and philosopher. He was the author of the major *Dictionnaire de la langue française* (1863–77).

li·tur·gi·cal /li'tərjikəl/ ▶ adj. of or related to liturgy or public worship. — **li·tur·gi·cal·ly** adv.

li·tur·gics /li'tərjiks/ ▶ plural n. [treated as sing.] the study of liturgies.

li·tur·gi·ol·o·gy /li,tərjē'äləjē/ ▶ n. another term for LITURGICS. — **li·tur·gi·o·log·i·cal** /-jēə'läjikəl/ adj. **li·tur·gi·ol·o·gist** n.

lit·ur·gy /'litərjē/ ▶ n. (pl. **-gies**) a form or formulary according to which public religious worship, esp. Christian worship, is conducted. ■ a religious service conducted according to such a form or formulary. ■ **(the Liturgy)** the Eucharistic service of the Eastern Orthodox Church. — **lit·ur·gist** /'litərjəst/ n. [16th C.: via Fr. or late L. from Gk. *leitourgia* 'public service, worship of the gods,' from *leitourgos* 'minister,' from *lēitos* 'public' + *-ergos* 'working.']

Liu·zhou /li'yōō'jō/ (also **Liu·chow** pronunc. same) a city in southern China; pop. 740,000.

liv·a·ble /'livəbəl/ (also **live·a·ble**) ▶ adj. worth living: *fatherhood makes life more livable.* ■ (of an environment or climate) fit to live in: *one of the most livable cities in the world.* — **liv·a·bil·i·ty** /,livə'bilətē/ n.

live[1] /liv/ ▶ v. **1** [intrans.] remain alive: *the doctors said she had only six months to live.* ■ [with adverbial] be alive at a specified time: *he lived four centuries ago.* ■ [with adverbial] spend one's life in a particular way or under particular circumstances: *living in fear in the wake of the shootings.* ■ [trans.] lead (one's life) in a particular way: *he was living a life of luxury in Australia.* ■ supply oneself with the means of subsistence: *they **live by** hunting.* ■ survive in someone's mind; be remembered: *only the name **lived on**.* ■ have an exciting or fulfilling life: *he couldn't wait to get out of school and really start living.* **2** [intrans.] make one's home in a particular place or with a particular person: *they lived with his grandparents.*

– PHRASES **as I live and breathe** used, esp. in spoken English, to express one's surprise at coming across someone or something. **be living on borrowed time** see BORROW. **live and breathe something** be extremely interested in or enthusiastic about a particular subject or activity and so devote a great deal of one's time to it. **live by one's wits** see WIT[1]. **live dangerously** do something risky, esp. on a habitual basis. **live for the moment** see MOMENT. **live in sin** see SIN[1]. **live it up** informal spend one's time in an extremely enjoyable way, typically by spending a great deal of money or engaging in an exciting social life. **live off** (or **on**) **the fat of the land** see FAT. **live off the land** see LAND. **live out of a suitcase** live or stay somewhere on a temporary basis and with only a limited selection of one's belongings. **live one's own life** follow one's own plans and principles independent of others. **live to fight another day** survive a particular experience or ordeal. **live to regret something** come to wish that one had not done something: *those who put work before their family life often live to regret it.* **live to tell the tale** survive a dangerous experience and be able to tell others about it. **live with oneself** be able to retain one's self-respect as a consequence of one's actions: *taking money from children—how can you live with yourself?* **long live ——!** said to express loyalty or support for a specified person or thing: *long live the Queen!* **where one lives** informal at, to, or in the right, vital, or most vulnerable spot: *it gets me where I live.*

– PHRASAL VERBS **live something down** succeed in making others forget something embarrassing that has happened. **live for** regard as the purpose or most important aspect of one's life: *Tony lived for his painting.* **live in** (of an employee or student) reside at the place where one works or studies. **live off** (or **on**) depend on (someone or something) as a source of income or support. ■ have (a particular amount of money) with which to buy food and other necessities. ■ subsist on (a particular type of food). ■ (of a person) eat, or seem to eat, only (a particular type of food): *she used to live on bacon and tomato sandwiches.* **live something out 1** do in reality that which one has thought or dreamed about: *your wedding day is the one time that you can live out your most romantic fantasies.* **2** spend the rest of one's life in a particular place or particular circumstances: *he lived out his days as a happy family man.* **live through** survive (an unpleasant experience or period): *both men lived through the Depression.* **live together** (esp. of a couple not married to each other) share a home and have a sexual relationship. **live up to** fulfill (expectations or an undertaking). **live with 1** share a home and have a sexual relationship with (someone to whom one is not married). **2** accept or tolerate (something unpleasant). [OE *libban, lifian*, of Gmc. origin; rel. to Du. *leven* and Ger. *leben*, also to LIFE and LEAVE[1].]

live[2] /līv/ ▶ adj. **1** [attrib.] not dead or inanimate; living: *live animals | the number of live births and deaths.* ■ (of a vaccine) containing viruses or bacteria that are living but of a mild or attenuated strain. ■ (of yogurt) containing the living microorganisms by which it is formed. **2** (of a musical performance) given in concert, not on a recording: *there is traditional live music played most nights.* ■ (of a broadcast) transmitted at the time of occurrence, not from a recording: *live coverage of the match.* ■ (of a musical recording) made during a concert, not in a studio: *a live album.* **3** (of a wire or device) connected to a source of electric current. ■ of, containing, or using undetonated explosive: *live ammunition.* ■ (of coals) burning; glowing. ■ (of a match) unused. ■ (of a wheel or axle in machinery) moving or imparting motion. ■ (of a ball in a game) in play, esp. in contrast to being foul or out of bounds. **4** (of a question or subject) of current or continuing interest and importance: *the future organization of Europe has become a live issue.* ▶ adv. as or at an actual event or performance: *the match will be televised live.*

– PHRASES **go live** Comput. (of a system) become operational. [16th C.: shortening of ALIVE.]

live·a·ble /'livəbəl/ ▶ adj. var. of LIVABLE.

live·bear·er /'līv,be(ə)rər/ ▶ n. a small, chiefly freshwater, carplike American fish (family Poeciliidae) that has internal fertilization and gives birth to live young. Many livebearers, including the guppy, swordtail, mollies, and gambusias, are popular in aquariums.

live·bear·ing /'līv,be(ə)riNG/ ▶ adj. (of an animal) bearing live young rather than laying eggs; viviparous or ovoviviparous.

lived-in /'livd ,in/ ▶ adj. (of a room or building) showing comforting signs of wear and habitation.

live-in /'liv ,in/ ▶ adj. [attrib.] (of a domestic employee) resident in an employer's house: *a live-in housekeeper.* ■ living with another in a sexual relationship: *a live-in lover.* ■ residential: *a live-in treatment program.* ▶ n. informal a person who shares another's living accommodations as a sexual partner or as an employee.

live·li·hood /'līvlē,hōōd/ ▶ n. a means of securing the necessities of life. [OE *līflād* 'way of life,' from *līf* 'life' + *lād* 'course' (see LODE).]

live load /līv/ ▶ n. the weight of people or goods in a building or vehicle. Often contrasted with DEAD LOAD.

live·long /'liv,lôNG; -,läNG/ ▶ adj. [attrib.] literary (of a period of time) entire: *all this livelong day.* [ME *leve longe* 'dear long' (see LIEF, LONG[1]).]

live·ly /'līvlē/ ▶ adj. (**live·li·er, live·li·est**) full of life and energy; active and outgoing: *a lively team of reporters.* ■ (of a place or atmosphere) full of activity and excitement: *Barcelona's many lively bars.* ■ intellectually stimulating or perceptive: *a lively discussion.* ■ (of a vessel) buoyant and responsive in a sea. — **live·li·ly** /-ləlē/ adv. **live·li·ness** n. [OE *līflic* 'living, animate' (see LIFE, -LY[1]).]

liv·en /'līvən/ ▶ v. make or become more lively or interesting: [trans.] ***liven up** bland foods with mustard* | [intrans.] *the game didn't **liven up** until the second half.*

live oak /līv/ ▶ n. a large, spreading oak (*Quercus virginiana*) of the southern US that has leathery, elliptical evergreen leaves. Live oaks typically support a large quantity of Spanish moss and other epiphytes.

liv·er[1] /'livər/ ▶ n. a large lobed glandular organ in the abdomen of vertebrates, involved in processing digestive products, neutralizing toxins, and other metabolic processes. ■ a similar organ in other animals. ■ the flesh of an animal's liver as food: *slices of calf's liver* | [as adj.] *liver pâté.* ■ (also **liver color**) a dark reddish brown. [OE *lifer*, of Gmc. origin; rel. to Ger. *Leber*, Du. *lever*.]

liv·er[2] ▶ n. [with adj.] a person who lives in a specified way: *a clean liver* | *high livers.*

liv·er fluke ▶ n. a fluke that has a complex life cycle and is of medical and veterinary importance. The adult lives within the liver tissues of a vertebrate, and the larva within one or more secondary hosts such as a snail or fish.

liv·er·ish /'liv(ə)riSH/ ▶ adj. slightly ill, as though having a disordered liver. ■ unhappy and bad-tempered. ■ resembling liver in color: *a liverish red.* — **liv·er·ish·ly** adv. **liv·er·ish·ness** n.

Liv·er·more /'livər,môr/ a city in north central California; pop. 56,741.

Liv·er·pool[1] /'livər,pōōl/ a city in northwestern England; pop. 448,000.

Liv·er·pool[2], Robert Banks Jenkinson, 2nd Earl of (1770–1828), prime minister of Britain 1812–27.

Liv·er·pud·li·an /,livər'pədlēən/ ▶ n. a native of Liverpool. ■ the dialect or accent of people from Liverpool. ▶ adj. of or relating to Liverpool. [19th C.: humorous formation from LIVERPOOL[1] + PUDDLE.]

liv·er spot ▶ n. a small brown spot on the skin, esp. as caused by a skin condition such as lentigo. — **liv·er-spot·ted** adj.

liv·er·wort /'livər,wərt; -,wôrt/ ▶ n. a small flowerless green plant (class Hepaticae) with leaflike stems or lobed leaves, occurring in moist habitats. Liverworts lack true roots and reproduce by means of spores released from capsules.

liv·er·wurst /'livər,wərst/ ▶ n. a seasoned meat paste in the form of a sausage containing cooked liver, or a mixture of liver and pork. [19th C.: partial translation of Ger. *Leberwurst* 'liver sausage.']

liv·er·y[1] /'liv(ə)rē/ ▶ n. (pl. **-er·ies**) **1** special uniform worn by a servant or official. ■ a special design and color scheme used on the vehicles, aircraft, or products of a particular company. **2** short for LIVERY STABLE. **3** (in the UK) the members of a livery company collectively.

– PHRASES **at livery** (of a horse) kept for the owner and fed and cared for at a fixed charge. — **liv·er·ied** /'liv(ə)rēd/ adj. (in sense 1). [ME: from OFr. *livree* 'delivered,' fem. past part. of *livrer*, from L. *liberare* 'liberate' (in med. L. 'hand over').]

liv·er·y[2] ▶ adj. resembling liver in color or consistency. ■ informal liverish: *port always makes you livery.*

liv·er·y com·pa·ny ▶ n. (in the UK) any of a number of companies of the City of London descended from the medieval trade guilds. They are now largely social and charitable organizations.

PRONUNCIATION KEY ə *ago, up*; ər *over, fur*; a *hat*; ā *ate*; ä *car*; e *let*; ē *see*; i *fit*; ī *by*; NG *sing*; ō *go*; ô *law, for*; oi *toy*; ŏŏ *good*; ōō *goo*; ou *out*; TH *thin*; T͟H *then*; ZH *vision*

liv·er·y·man /'liv(ə)rēmən/ ▶ **n.** (pl. **-men**) **1** an owner of or attendant in a livery stable. **2** (in the UK) a member of a livery company.

liv·er·y sta·ble (also **livery yard**) ▶ **n.** a stable where horses are kept at livery or let out for hire.

lives /līvz/ plural form of LIFE.

live·stock /'līv,stäk/ ▶ **n.** farm animals regarded as an asset: *markets for the trading of livestock.*

live·ware /'līv,we(ə)r/ ▶ **n.** informal working personnel, esp. computer personnel, as distinct from the inanimate or abstract things they work with.

live wire /līv/ ▶ **n.** informal an energetic and unpredictable person.

liv·id /'livid/ ▶ **adj. 1** informal furiously angry. **2** (of a color or the skin) having a dark inflamed tinge: *his face went livid, then purple.* ■ of a bluish leaden color: *livid bruises.* —**li·vid·i·ty** /lə'vidətē/ **n. liv·id·ly adv. liv·id·ness n.** [ME: from Fr. *livide* or L. *lividus*, from *livere* 'be bluish.']

liv·ing /'liviNG/ ▶ **n. 1** [usu. in sing.] an income sufficient to live on or the means of earning it. ■ Brit. (in church use) a position as a vicar or rector with an income or property. **2** [with adj.] the pursuit of a lifestyle of the specified type: *the benefits of country living.* ▶ **adj.** alive: *living creatures* | [as pl. n.] **(the living)** *flowers were for the living.* ■ [attrib.] (of a place) used for living rather than working in: *the living quarters of the ship.* ■ (of a language) still spoken and used. ■ [attrib.] literary (of water) perennially flowing: *streams of living water.*

liv·ing death ▶ **n.** [in sing.] a life of hopeless and unbroken misery.

liv·ing rock ▶ **n.** rock that is not detached but still forms part of the earth: *a chamber cut out of the living rock.*

liv·ing room ▶ **n.** a room in a house for general and informal everyday use.

Liv·ing·ston /'liviNGstən/, Henry Brockholst (1757–1823) US Supreme Court associate justice 1806–23.

liv·ing stone ▶ **n.** a small succulent southern African plant (genus *Lithops*) of the carpetweed family that resembles a pebble in appearance. It consists of two fleshy cushionlike leaves divided by a slit through which a daisylike flower emerges.

liv·ing wage ▶ **n.** [in sing.] a wage that is high enough to maintain a normal standard of living.

liv·ing will ▶ **n.** a written statement detailing a person's desires regarding their medical treatment in circumstances in which they are no longer able to express informed consent, esp. an advance directive.

Li·vo·nia /li'vōnēə; -yə/ **1** a region on the eastern coast of the Baltic Sea that comprises most of present-day Latvia and Estonia. German name LIVLAND. **2** a city in southeastern Michigan; pop. 100,545. —**Li·vo·ni·an adj. & n.**

Li·vor·no /lē'vôrnō/ a city in northwestern Italy on the Ligurian Sea; pop. 171,265. Also called LEGHORN.

Liv·y /'livē/ (59 BC–AD 17), Roman historian; Latin name *Titus Livius.* His history of Rome filled 142 books, of which 35 survive.

lix·iv·i·ate /lik'sivē,āt/ ▶ **v.** [trans.] Chem., archaic separate (a substance) into soluble and insoluble constituents by the percolation of liquid. —**lix·iv·i·a·tion** /-,sivē'āSHən/ **n.** [17th C.: from mod. L. *lixiviat-* 'impregnated with lye,' from the v. *lixiviare*, from *lixivius* 'made into lye,' from *lix* 'lye.']

Liz·ard /'lizərd/ a promontory in southwestern England. Its tip is the southernmost point Britain's mainland.

liz·ard /'lizərd/ ▶ **n.** a reptile (suborder Lacertilia or Sauria, order Squamata) that typically has a long body and tail, four legs, movable eyelids, and a rough, scaly, or spiny skin. [ME: from OFr. *lesard(e)*, from L. *lacertus.*]

liz·ard·fish /'lizərd,fiSH/ ▶ **n.** (pl. same or **-fish·es**) a fish (esp. *Trachinocephalus myops*, family Synodontidae) of lizardlike appearance with a broad bony head, pointed snout, and heavy shiny scales. It lives in warm shallow seas, where it often rests on the bottom propped up on its pelvic fins.

Lju·blja·na /lē,ōōblē'änə; lē'ōōblēə,nä/ the capital of Slovenia; pop. 267,000. German name LAIBACH.

Lk. ▶ **abbr.** Bible the Gospel of Luke.

ll. ▶ **abbr.** (in textual references) lines.

'll ▶ **contr.** shall; will: *I'll get the food on.*

lla·ma /'lämə/ ▶ **n.** a domesticated pack animal (*Lama glama*) of the camel family found in the Andes, valued for its soft woolly fleece. ■ the wool of the llama. ■ cloth made from such wool. [17th C.: from Sp., prob. from Quechua.]

lla·no /'länō; 'yä-/ ▶ **n.** (pl. **-nos**) (in South America) a treeless grassy plain. [Sp., from L. *planum* 'plain.']

LLB ▶ **abbr.** Bachelor of Laws. [from L. *legum baccalaureus.*]

LLD ▶ **abbr.** Doctor of Laws. [from L. *legum doctor.*]

Llew·e·lyn /lōō'(w)elən/ (died 1282), prince of Gwynedd in North Wales; also known as **Llywelyn ap Gruffydd**. Proclaiming himself prince of all Wales in 1258, he was recognized by Henry III in 1265.

LLM ▶ **abbr.** Master of Laws. [from L. *legum magister.*]

Llo·sa, Mario Vargas, see VARGAS LLOSA.

Lloyd George, David, 1st Earl Lloyd George of Dwyfor (1863–1945), prime minister of Britain 1916–22. His coalition government was threatened by economic problems and trouble in Ireland.

Lloyd's /loidz/ an incorporated society of insurance underwriters in London, made up of private syndicates. Founded in 1871, Lloyd's originally dealt only in marine insurance. ■ short for LLOYD'S REGISTER. [named after the coffeehouse of Edward *Lloyd* (*fl.* 1688–1726).]

Lloyd's Reg·is·ter (in full **Lloyd's Register of Shipping**) a classified list of merchant ships over a certain tonnage giving their seaworthiness classification and published annually in London. ■ the corporation that produces this list.

Lloyd Web·ber /'webər/, Sir Andrew, Baron Lloyd-Webber of Sydmonton (1948–), English composer. His collaborations with lyricist Sir Tim Rice include the stage musicals *Cats* (1981) and *The Phantom of the Opera* (1986).

Lly·wel·yn ap Gruff·ydd /(h)lōō'elin äp 'grifiTH/ see LLEWELYN.

LM ▶ **abbr.** ■ long meter. ■ lunar module.

lm ▶ **abbr.** lumen(s).

ln Math. ▶ **abbr.** natural logarithm. [from mod. L. *logarithmus naturalis.*]

LNG ▶ **abbr.** liquefied natural gas.

lo /lō/ ▶ **exclam.** archaic used to draw attention to an interesting or amazing event.

– PHRASES **lo and behold** used to present a new scene, situation, or turn of events, often with the suggestion that though surprising, it could in fact have been predicted. [natural exclamation: first recorded as *lā* in OE.]

loach /lōCH/ ▶ **n.** a small elongated bottom-dwelling freshwater fish (families Cobitidae and Homalopteridae, or Balitoridae) with several barbels near the mouth, found in Eurasia and northwestern Africa. [ME: from OFr. *loche*, of unknown origin.]

load /lōd/ ▶ **n. 1** a heavy or bulky thing that is being carried or is about to be carried. ■ the total number or amount that can be carried in something, esp. a vehicle of a specified type: *a trailer **load of** appliances.* ■ the material carried along by a stream, glacier, ocean current, etc. ■ an amount of items washed or to be washed in a washing machine or dishwasher at one time. **2** a weight or source of pressure borne by someone or something: *the increased **load on** the heart.* ■ the amount of work to be done by a person or machine: *Arthur has a light teaching load.* ■ a burden of responsibility, worry, or grief: *difficult to service their heavy load of debt.* ■ a commission charged on the purchase of mutual funds. **3 (a load of)** informal a lot of: *she was talking **a load of** garbage.* ■ **(a load/loads)** informal plenty: ***loads of** money.* **4** the amount of power supplied by a source; the resistance of moving parts to be overcome by a motor. ■ the amount of electricity supplied by a generating system at any given time. ■ Electron. an impedance or circuit that receives or develops the output of a transistor or other device. ▶ **v.** [trans.] **1** put a load or large amount of something on or in (a vehicle, ship, container, etc.): ***load up** the canoes.* ■ [trans.] (often **be loaded**) place (a load or large quantity of something) on or in a vehicle, ship, container, etc.: *the stolen property was **loaded into** a taxi.* ■ [intrans.] (of a ship or vehicle) take on a load: *the ship was still loading.* **2** make (someone or something) carry or hold a large or excessive amount of heavy things: ***loaded down with** full bags.* ■ **(load someone/something with)** fig. supply someone or something in overwhelming abundance or to excess with. ■ **(load someone with)** fig. burden someone with (worries, responsibilities, etc.). **3** insert (something) into a device so that it will operate: *load the cassette into the camcorder.* ■ charge (a firearm) with ammunition. ■ Comput. transfer (a program or data) into memory, or into the central processor from storage. ■ Comput. transfer programs into (a computer memory or processor). **4** add an extra charge to (an insurance premium) in the case of a poorer risk.

– PHRASES **get a load of** informal used to draw attention to someone or something: *get a load of what we've just done.* **get** (or **have**) **a load on** informal become (or be) drunk. **load the bases** Baseball fill all three bases with runners. **load the dice against/in favor of someone** put someone at a disadvantage or advantage. **take a** (or **the**) **load off one's feet** sit or lie down. **take a load off someone's mind** bring someone relief from anxiety.

– PHRASAL VERBS **load up on** consume a substantial amount of (food or beverage): *we were loading up on beer and raw oysters.* [OE *lād* 'way, journey, conveyance,' of Gmc. origin; rel. to Ger. *Leite*, also to LEAD[1].]

load dis·place·ment ▶ **n.** the weight of water displaced by a ship when laden.

load·ed /'lōdid/ ▶ **adj. 1** carrying or bearing a load, esp. a large one: *a heavily loaded freight train.* ■ (of a firearm) charged with ammunition. ■ [predic.] **(loaded with)** containing in abundance or to excess: *your average chocolate bar is loaded with fat.* ■ [predic.] informal having a lot of money; wealthy: *she doesn't really have to work—they're loaded.* ■ [predic.] informal having had too much alcohol; drunk: *man, did I get loaded after I left his house.* ■ informal (of a car) equipped with many optional extras; deluxe. **2** weighted or biased toward a particular outcome: *a trick like the one with the loaded dice.* ■ (of a word, statement, or question) charged with an underlying meaning or implication.

– PHRASES **loaded for bear** see BEAR[2].

load·er /'lōdər/ ▶ **n. 1** a machine or person that loads something. ■ an attendant who loads guns at a shoot. **2** [in comb.] a gun, machine, or truck that is loaded in a specified way: *a front-loader.*

load fac·tor ▶ **n.** the ratio of the average or actual amount of some quantity and the maximum possible or permissible. ■ the ratio between the lift and the weight of an aircraft.

load·ing /'lōdiNG/ ▶ **n. 1** the application of a mechanical load or force to something. ■ the amount of electric current or power delivered to a device. ■ the maximum electric current or power taken by an appliance. ■ the provision of extra electrical inductance to improve the properties of a transmission wire or antenna. **2** the application of an extra amount of something to balance some other factor. ■ an increase in an insurance premium due to a factor increasing the risk involved. ■ another term for LOAD (sense 2). ▶ **adj.** [in comb.] (of a gun, machine, or truck) loaded in a specified way: *a front-loading dishwasher.*

load·ing coil ▶ **n.** a coil used to provide additional inductance in an electric circuit.

load·ing dock ▶ **n.** see DOCK[1].

load line ▶ **n.** another term for PLIMSOLL LINE.

load·mas·ter /ˈlōd,mastər/ ▶ **n.** the member of an aircraft's crew responsible for the cargo.

load·stone ▶ **n.** archaic spelling of LODESTONE.

loaf[1] /lōf/ ▶ **n.** (pl. **loaves** /lōvz/) a quantity of bread that is shaped and baked in one piece and usually sliced before being eaten. ■ [usu. with adj.] a quantity of other food formed into a particular shape, and often sliced into portions. [OE *hlāf*, of Gmc. origin; rel. to Ger. *Laib*.]

loaf[2] ▶ **v.** [intrans.] idle one's time away, typically by aimless wandering or loitering. [19th C.: prob. a back-form. from LOAFER.]

loaf·er /ˈlōfər/ ▶ **n.** **1** a person who idles time away. **2** trademark a leather shoe shaped like a moccasin, with a low flat heel. [19th C.: perh. from Ger. *Landläufer* 'tramp,' from *Land* 'land' + *laufen* (dial. *lofen*) 'to run.']

loafer 2

loam /lōm/ ▶ **n.** a fertile soil of clay and sand containing humus. ■ Geol. a soil with roughly equal proportions of sand, silt, and clay. ■ a paste of clay and water with sand, chopped straw, etc., used in making bricks and plastering walls. — **loam·i·ness n. loamy adj.** [OE *lām* 'clay,' of West Gmc. origin: rel. to Du. *leem* and Ger. *Lehm*, also to LIME[1].]

loan /lōn/ ▶ **n.** a thing that is borrowed, esp. a sum of money that is expected to be paid back with interest. ■ an act of lending something to someone: *she offered to buy him dinner in return for the loan of the car.* ▶ **v.** [trans.] (often **be loaned**) borrow (a sum of money or item of property): *the word processor was loaned to us by the theater.*

– PHRASES **on loan** (of a thing) being borrowed: *the painting is at present on loan to the gallery.* ■ (of a worker or sports player) released to another organization or team, typically for an agreed fixed period. — **loan·a·ble adj. loan·ee** /,lōˈnē/ **n. loan·er n.** [ME: from ON *lán*, of Gmc. origin; rel. to LEND.]

loan shark ▶ **n.** informal, often derog. a moneylender who charges extremely high rates of interest. — **loan·shark·ing** /ˈlōn,SHärkiNG/ **n.**

loan trans·la·tion ▶ **n.** an expression adopted by one language from another in a more or less literally translated form. Also called CALQUE.

loan·word /ˈlōn,wərd/ ▶ **n.** a word adopted from a foreign language with little or no modification.

loath /lōTH; lōT͟H/ (also **loth**) ▶ **adj.** [predic., with infin.] reluctant; unwilling: *I was loath to leave.* [OE *lāth* 'hostile, spiteful,' of Gmc. origin; rel. to Du. *leed*, Ger. *Leid* 'sorrow.']

loathe /lōT͟H/ ▶ **v.** [trans.] feel intense dislike or disgust for. — **loath·er n.** [OE *lāthian*, of Gmc. origin; rel. to LOATH.]

loath·some /ˈlōTHsəm; ˈlōT͟H-/ ▶ **adj.** causing hatred or disgust; repulsive: *this loathsome little swine.* — **loath·some·ly adv. loath·some·ness n.** [ME: from archaic *loath* 'disgust, loathing' + -SOME[1].]

loaves /lōvz/ plural form of LOAF[1].

lob /läb/ ▶ **v.** (**lobbed, lob·bing**) [trans.] throw or hit (a ball or missile) in a high arc: *he lobbed the ball over their heads.* ■ [trans.] (in tennis) hit the ball over (an opponent) in such a way. ▶ **n.** (chiefly in tennis) a ball hit in a high arc over an opponent. [16th C.: from the archaic n. *lob* 'lout,' 'pendulous object,' prob. from Low Ger. or Du.]

Lo·ba·chev·sky /,lōbəˈCHefskē; ləbəˈCHyefskyē/, Nikolai Ivanovich (1792–1856), Russian mathematician. He was a discoverer of non-Euclidean geometry.

lo·bar /ˈlō,bär; -bər/ ▶ **adj.** [attrib.] esp. Anat. & Med. of or affecting a lobe.

lo·bate /ˈlō,bāt/ ▶ **adj.** Biol. having a lobe or lobes. — **lo·ba·tion** /lōˈbāSHən/ **n.**

lob·by /ˈläbē/ ▶ **n.** (pl. **-bies**) **1** a room providing a space out of which other rooms or corridors lead, typically one near the entrance of a public building. **2** a group of people seeking to influence politicians or public officials on a particular issue: *the anti-abortion lobby.* ■ [in sing.] an organized attempt by members of the public to influence politicians or public officials: *a recent lobby of Congress by retirees.* ▶ **v.** (**-bies, -bied**) [trans.] seek to influence (a politician or public official) on an issue: *booksellers lobbied their representatives* | [intrans.] *a group lobbying for better rail services.* — **lob·by·ist** /-ist/ **n.** [16th C.: from med. L. *lobia, lobium* 'covered walk, portico.']

lobe /lōb/ ▶ **n.** a roundish and flattish part of something, typically each of two or more such parts divided by a fissure, and often projecting or hanging. ■ each of the parts of the cerebrum of the brain. — **lobed adj. lobe·less adj.** [ME: via late L. from Gk. *lobos* 'lobe, pod.']

lo·bec·to·my /lōˈbektəmē/ ▶ **n.** (pl. **-mies**) surgical removal of a lobe of an organ.

lobe-finned fish (also **lobe·fin**) ▶ **n.** a fish of a largely extinct group (subclass Crossopterygia, Actinistia, or Coelacanthimorpha) having fleshy lobed fins, including the probable ancestors of the amphibians. The only living representative is the coelacanth. Compare with RAY-FINNED FISH.

lo·bel·ia /lōˈbēlēə; -ˈbēlyə/ ▶ **n.** a chiefly tropical or subtropical plant (genus *Lobelia*) of the bellflower family, in particular an annual widely grown as a bedding plant. Some kinds are aquatic, and some grow as thick-trunked shrubs or trees on African mountains. [mod. L., named after Matthias de *Lobel* (1538–1616), Flemish botanist to James I.]

lob·lol·ly /ˈläb,lälē/ ▶ **n.** (pl. **-lies**) **1** (also **loblolly pine**) a pine tree (*Pinus taeda*) of the southern US that has very long slender needles and is an important source of timber. **2** (also **loblolly bay**) a small evergreen tree (*Gordonia lasianthus*) of the tea family, with baylike leaves and white camellialike flowers, native to the southeastern US. **3** a miry patch of ground; a mudhole. **4** Cooking, dated a thick mush or gruel.

lo·bo /ˈlōbō/ ▶ **n.** (pl. **-bos**) (in the southwestern US and Mexico) a timber wolf. [19th C.: from Sp., from L. *lupus* 'wolf.']

lo·bot·o·mize /ləˈbätə,mīz/ ▶ **v.** [trans.] (often **be lobotomized**) Surg. perform a lobotomy on. ■ informal reduce the mental or emotional capacity or ability to function of: *couples were lobotomized by the birth of their children.* — **lo·bot·o·mi·za·tion** /-,bätəməˈzāshən/ **n.**

lo·bot·o·my /ləˈbätəmē/ ▶ **n.** (pl. **-mies**) a surgical operation involving incision into the prefrontal lobe of the brain, formerly used to treat mental illness.

lob·scouse /ˈläb,skous/ ▶ **n.** a stew formerly eaten by sailors, consisting of meat, vegetables, and hardtack. [18th C.: cf. Ger. *Lapskaus*.]

lob·ster /ˈläbstər/ ▶ **n.** a large marine crustacean (*Homarus* and other genera, class Malacostraca) with stalked eyes and the first of its five pairs of limbs modified as pincers. Several species include the **American lobster** (*H. americanus*). ■ the flesh of this animal as food. ■ any of various similar crustaceans, esp. certain crayfish whose claws are eaten as food. ▶ **v.** [intrans.] catch lobsters. [OE *lopustre*, alt. of L. *locusta* 'crustacean, locust.']

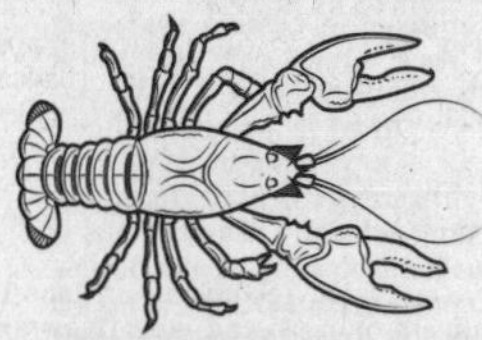

American lobster

lob·ster·man /ˈläbstərmən/ ▶ **n.** a person whose occupation is trapping lobsters.

lob·ster pot (also **lobster trap**) ▶ **n.** a cratelike or basketlike trap in which lobsters are caught.

lob·ster ther·mi·dor /ˈTHərmə,dôr/ ▶ **n.** a dish of lobster cooked in a cream sauce, returned to its shell, sprinkled with cheese, and browned under the grill. [*thermidor* from *Thermidor,* eleventh month of the French revolutionary calendar.]

lob·ule /ˈläb,yo͞ol/ ▶ **n.** esp. Anat. a small lobe. — **lob·u·lar** /-yələr/ **adj. lob·u·late** /-yə,lāt/ **adj. lob·u·lat·ed** /-yə,lātid/ **adj.**

lob·worm /ˈläb,wərm/ ▶ **n.** another term for LUGWORM.

lo·cal /ˈlōkəl/ ▶ **adj.** belonging or relating to a particular area or neighborhood, typically exclusively so: *researching local history.* ■ denoting a telephone call made to a nearby place and charged at a relatively low rate. ■ denoting a train or bus serving a particular district, with frequent stops. ■ (in technical use) relating to a particular region or part, or to each of any number of these: *a local infection.* ■ Comput. denoting a variable or other entity that is only available for use in one part of a program. ■ Comput. denoting a device that can be accessed without the use of a network. Compare with REMOTE. ▶ **n.** a local person or thing, in particular: ■ an inhabitant of a particular area or neighborhood. ■ Brit., informal a pub convenient to a person's home: *a pint in the local.* ■ a local train or bus service. ■ a local branch of an organization, esp. a labor union. ■ short for LOCAL ANESTHESIA. ■ Stock Exchange slang a floor trader who trades on their own account, rather than on behalf of other investors. — **lo·cal·ly adv. lo·cal·ness n.** [ME: from late L. *localis*, from L. *locus* 'place.']

lo·cal an·es·the·sia ▶ **n.** anesthesia that affects a restricted area of the body. Compare with GENERAL ANESTHESIA.

lo·cal ar·e·a net·work (abbr.: **LAN**) ▶ **n.** a computer network that links devices within a building or group of adjacent buildings.

lo·cal bus ▶ **n.** Comput. a high-speed data connection directly linking peripheral devices to the processor and memory, allowing activities that require high data transmission rates such as video display.

lo·cal col·or ▶ **n.** the customs, manner of speech, dress, or other typical features of a place or period that contribute to its particular character.

lo·cale /lōˈkal/ ▶ **n.** a place where something happens or is set, or that has events associated with it. [18th C.: from Fr. *local* (n.).]

lo·cal gov·ern·ment ▶ **n.** the administration of a particular town, county or district, with representatives elected by those who live there.

Lo·cal Group Astron. the cluster of galaxies of which the Milky Way is a member.

lo·cal·ism /ˈlōkəˌlizəm/ ▶ n. preference for a locality, particularly to one's own area or region. ■ derog. the limitation of ideas and interests resulting from this. ■ a characteristic of a particular locality, such as a local idiom or custom. — **lo·cal·ist** n. & adj.

lo·cal·i·ty /lōˈkalətē/ ▶ n. (pl. **-ties**) the position or site of something. ■ an area or neighborhood, esp. as regarded as a place occupied by certain people or as the scene of particular activities: *a working-class locality.*

lo·cal·ize /ˈlōkəˌlīz/ ▶ v. [trans.] [often as adj.] (**localized**) restrict (something) to a particular place: *symptoms include localized pain and numbness.* ■ make (something) local in character: *localized news service.* ■ assign (something) to a particular place: *most vertebrates localize sounds by orienting movements.* — **lo·cal·iz·a·ble** adj. **lo·cal·i·za·tion** /ˌlōkələˈzāsʜən/ n.

lo·cal op·tion ▶ n. a choice available to a local administration to accept or reject national legislation (e.g., concerning the sale of alcoholic liquor).

lo·cal time ▶ n. time as reckoned in a particular region or time zone. ■ time at a particular place as measured from the sun's transit over the meridian at that place, defined as noon.

Lo·car·no /lōˈkärnō/ a town in southern Switzerland, a popular resort; pop. 14,000.

lo·cate /ˈlōˌkāt; lōˈkāt/ ▶ v. [trans.] discover the exact place or position of: *engineers working to locate the fault.* ■ [trans.] (usu. **be located**) situate in a particular place: *these apartments are centrally located.* ■ [trans.] place within a particular context: *they locate their policies in terms of wealth creation.* ■ [intrans.] establish oneself or one's business in a specified place: *his marketing strategy has been to locate in small towns.* — **lo·cat·a·ble** /-ˌkātəbəl; lōˈkāt-/ adj. [16th C.: from L. *locat-* 'placed,' from the v. *locare,* from *locus* 'place.']

lo·ca·tion /lōˈkāsʜən/ ▶ n. a particular place or position. ■ an actual place or natural setting in which a film or broadcast is made, as distinct from a simulation in a studio: *the movie was filmed **on location**.* ■ the action or process of placing someone or something in a particular position: *the location of new housing beyond the existing built-up areas.* ■ a position or address in computer memory. — **lo·ca·tion·al** /-sʜənl; -sʜənəl/ adj.

loc·a·tive /ˈläkətiv/ Gram. ▶ adj. relating to or denoting a case in some languages of nouns, pronouns, and adjectives, expressing location. ▶ n. (**the locative**) the locative case. ■ a word in the locative case.

lo·ca·tor /ˈlōˌkātər; lōˈkā-/ ▶ n. a device or system for locating something, typically by means of radio signals.

loc. cit. ▶ abbr. in the passage already cited. [from L. *loco citato.*]

loch /läk; läkʜ/ ▶ n. Scot. a lake. ■ (also **sea loch**) an arm of the sea, esp. when narrow or partially landlocked. [ME: from Scot. Gael.]

lo·chi·a /ˈlōkēə; ˈläk-/ ▶ n. Med. the normal discharge from the uterus after childbirth. — **lo·chi·al** adj. [17th C.: mod. L., from Gk. *lokhia,* neut. pl. (used as a n.) of *lokhios* 'of childbirth.']

Loch Ness /ˌläk ˈnes; ˌläkʜ/ a deep lake in northwestern Scotland.

Loch Ness mon·ster a large creature alleged to live in the deep waters of Loch Ness. Reports of its existence date from the 6th century.

lo·ci /ˈlōˌsī; -ˌsē; -ˌkē; -ˌkī/ plural form of **locus**.

lock[1] /läk/ ▶ n. **1** a mechanism for keeping a door, lid, etc., fastened, typically operated by a particular key or combination: *the key turned firmly in the lock.* ■ a similar device used to prevent the operation or movement of a vehicle or other machine: *a bicycle lock.* ■ (in wrestling and martial arts) a hold that prevents an opponent from moving a limb. ■ [in sing.] archaic a number of interlocked or jammed items: *a street closed by a lock of carriages.* **2** a short confined section of a canal or other waterway in which the water level can be changed by the use of gates and sluices, used for raising and lowering vessels between two gates. ■ an airlock. **3** (**a lock**) informal a person or thing that is certain to succeed; a certainty. **4** archaic a mechanism for exploding the charge of a gun. ▶ v. **1** [trans.] fasten or secure (something) with a lock: *she closed and locked her desk.* ■ (**lock something up**) shut and secure something, esp. a building, by fastening its doors with locks: *the diplomatic personnel locked up their building and walked off* | [intrans.] *you could lock up for me when you leave.* ■ [trans.] enclose or shut in by locking or fastening a door, lid, etc.: *the prisoners are locked up overnight.* ■ (**lock someone up/away**) imprison someone. ■ (**lock something up/away**) invest money in something so that it is not easily accessible: *vast sums of money locked up in pension funds.* ■ (**lock someone down**) confine prisoners to their cells. ■ [intrans.] (of a door, window, box, etc.) become or be able to be secured through activation of a lock: *the door will automatically lock behind you.* **2** make or become rigidly fixed or immovable: [trans.] *he locked his hands behind her neck* | [intrans.] *their gaze locked for several long moments.* ■ [trans.] (**lock someone/something in**) engage or entangle in (an embrace or struggle). ■ [trans.] trap or fix firmly or irrevocably: *this may tend to lock in many traders with their present holdings.* ■ [trans.] (**lock someone/something into**) cause to become caught or involved in: *they were now locked into the system.* ■ [trans.] (of land, hills, ice, etc.) enclose; surround: *the vessel was **locked in** ice.* **3** [intrans.] [with adverbial of direction] go through a lock on a canal: *we locked through at Moore Haven.*

– PHRASES **have a lock on** informal have an unbreakable hold on or total control over. **lock horns** engage in conflict. **lock, stock, and barrel** including everything; completely.

– PHRASAL VERBS **lock onto** locate (a target) by radar or similar means and then track. **lock someone out 1** keep someone out of a room or building by locking the door. **2** (of an employer) subject employees to a lockout. **lock someone out of** exclude someone from: *those now locked out of the job market.* — **lock·a·ble** adj. **lock·less** adj. [OE *loc,* of Gmc. origin; rel. to Ger. *Loch* 'hole.']

lock[2] ▶ n. a piece of a person's hair that coils or hangs together: *she pushed back **a lock of hair**.* ■ (**locks**) esp. literary a person's hair. ■ a tuft of wool or cotton. ■ (**locks**) short for **dreadlocks**. — **locked** adj. [in comb.] *his curly-locked comrades.* [OE *locc,* of Gmc. origin; rel. to Du. *lok,* Ger. *Locke,* possibly also to **lock**[1].]

lock·age /ˈläkij/ ▶ n. the construction or use of locks on waterways. ■ the amount of rise and fall of water levels resulting from the use of locks. ■ money paid as a toll for the use of a lock.

lock·box /ˈläk ˌbäks/ ▶ n. **1** a box that locks, usually for storing money or valuables. **2** a service provided by a bank, whereby the bank receives, processes, and deposits all of a company's receivables.

lock·down /ˈläkˌdoun/ ▶ n. the confining of prisoners to their cells, typically during a riot.

Locke /läk/, John (1632–1704), English philosopher. He founded empiricism and political liberalism. — **Lock·e·an** /ˈläkēən/ adj.

lock·er /ˈläkər/ ▶ n. **1** a small lockable closet or compartment, typically as one of a number placed together for public or general use, e.g., in schools, gymnasiums, or train stations. ■ a chest or compartment on a ship or boat for clothes, stores, equipment, or ammunition. **2** a device that locks something.

Lock·er·bie /ˈläkərbē/ a town in southwestern Scotland; pop. 4,000. In 1988, a US airliner, destroyed by a terrorist bomb, crashed on the town.

lock·er room ▶ n. a room containing lockers for personal belongings, esp. in schools or gymnasiums. ▶ adj. [attrib.] characteristic of or suited to a men's locker room, esp. as being coarse or ribald.

lock·et /ˈläkit/ ▶ n. **1** a small ornamental case, typically made of gold or silver, worn around a person's neck on a chain and used to hold things of sentimental value, such as a photograph or lock of hair. **2** a metal plate or band on a scabbard. [ME: from OFr. *locquet,* dimin. of *loc* 'latch, lock,' of Gmc. origin; rel. to **lock**[1].]

lock-in ▶ n. the act or fact of locking in a person or thing. an arrangement according to which a person or company is obliged to negotiate or trade only with a specific company. ■ a protest demonstration in which a group locks itself within an office, building, or factory.

lock·jaw /ˈläkˌjô/ ▶ n. nontechnical term for **trismus**.

lock·nut /ˈläkˌnət/ ▶ n. a nut screwed down on another to keep it tight. ■ a nut designed so that, once tightened, it cannot be accidentally loosened.

lock·out /ˈläkˌout/ ▶ n. the exclusion of employees by their employer from their place of work until certain terms are agreed to.

lock·set /ˈläkˌset/ ▶ n. a complete locking system, including knobs, plates, and a locking mechanism.

lock·smith /ˈläkˌsmiᴛʜ/ ▶ n. a person who makes and repairs locks.

lock·step /ˈläkˌstep/ ▶ n. a way of marching with each person as close as possible to the one in front: *the trio marched **in lockstep**.* ■ fig. close adherence to and emulation of another's actions: *they raised prices in lockstep with those of foreign competitors.*

lock·stitch ▶ n. a stitch made by a sewing machine by firmly linking together two threads or stitches.

lock·up /ˈläkˌəp/ ▶ n. **1** a jail, esp. a temporary one. **2** the locking up of premises for the night. **3** the action of becoming fixed or immovable: *anti-lock braking helps prevent wheel lockup.* **4** an investment in assets that cannot readily be realized or sold on in the short term.

Lock·yer /ˈläkyər/, Sir Joseph Norman (1836–1920), English astronomer. He discovered helium.

lo·co ▶ adj. informal crazy. [19th C.: from Sp., 'insane.']

lo·co·mo·tion /ˌlōkəˈmōsʜən/ ▶ n. movement or the ability to move from one place to another. [17th C.: from L. *loco,* ablative of *locus* 'place' + *motio* (see **motion**).]

lo·co·mo·tive /ˌlōkəˈmōtiv/ ▶ n. a powered rail vehicle used for pulling trains: *a diesel locomotive.* ▶ adj. [attrib.] of, relating to, or effecting locomotion: *locomotive power.*

lo·co·mo·tor /ˌlōkəˈmōtər/ ▶ adj. [attrib.] esp. Biol. of or relating to locomotion: *locomotor organs.* [19th C.: from **locomotion** + **motor**.]

lo·co·mo·tor a·tax·i·a ▶ n. another term for **tabes dorsalis**.

lo·co·mo·to·ry /ˌlōkəˈmōtərē/ ▶ adj. esp. Zool. relating to or having the power of locomotion: *locomotory cilia.*

lo·co·weed /ˈlōkōˌwēd/ ▶ n. **1** a widely distributed plant (genera *Astragalus* and *Oxytropis*) of the pea family that, if eaten by livestock, can cause a brain disorder, the symptoms of which include unpredictable behavior and loss of coordination. **2** informal cannabis.

loc·ule /ˈläkˌyo͞ol/ ▶ n. esp. Bot. each of a number of small separate cavities, esp. in an ovary. — **loc·u·lar** /-yələr/ adj. [19th C.: via Fr. from L. *loculus.*]

loc·u·lus /ˈläkyələs/ ▶ n. (pl. **-li** /-ˌlī; -ˌlē/) another term for **locule**. [19th C.: from L., 'compartment,' dimin. of *locus* 'place.']

lo·cum te·nens /ˈlōkəm ˈtenənz; ˈtēˌnenz/ ▶ n. (pl. **lo·cum te·nen·tes** /təˈnentēz/) esp. Brit. a person who stands in temporarily for someone else of the same profession, esp. a cleric or doctor. — **lo·cum te·nen·cy** /ˈtenənsē; ˈtēnən-/ n. [17th C.: from med. L., lit. 'one holding a place' (see **locus, tenant**).]

lo·cus /ˈlōkəs/ ▸ **n.** (pl. **lo·ci** /ˈlōˌsī; -ˌsē; -ˌkē; -ˌkī/) **1** tech. a particular position, point, or place. ■ the effective or perceived location of something abstract: *the real locus of power is the informal council.* ■ Genet. the position of a gene or mutation on a chromosome. **2** Math. a curve or other figure formed by all the points satisfying a particular equation of the relation between coordinates, or by a point, line, or surface moving according to mathematically defined conditions. [18th C.: from L., 'place.']

lo·cus clas·si·cus /ˈlōkəs ˈklasikəs/ ▸ **n.** (pl. **lo·ci clas·si·ci** /ˈlōˌsī ˈklasəˌsī; ˈlōˌsē ˈklasəˌsē; ˈlōˌkē ˈklasiˌkē; ˈlōˌkī ˈklasiˌkī/) a passage considered to be the best known or most authoritative on a particular subject. [L., 'classical place.']

lo·cust /ˈlōkəst/ ▸ **n.** **1** a large and mainly tropical grasshopper, esp. the **migratory locust** (*Locusta migratoria*), with strong powers of flight. It is usually solitary, but from time to time there is a population explosion, and it migrates in vast swarms that cause extensive damage to crops. ■ (also **seventeen-year locust**) the periodical cicada. **2** (also **locust bean**) the large edible pod of some plants of the pea family, in particular the carob bean, which is said to resemble a locust. **3** (also **locust tree**) any of a number of pod-bearing trees of the pea family, in particular the carob tree and the black locust. [ME: via OFr. *locuste* from L. *locusta* 'locust, crustacean.']

lo·cu·tion /lōˈkyo͞oshən/ ▸ **n.** a word or phrase, esp. with regard to style or idiom. ■ a person's style of speech: *his impeccable locution.* — **lo·cu·tion·ar·y** /-shəˌnerē/ **adj.** [ME: from OFr., or from L. *locutio(n-)*, from *loqui* 'speak.']

lode /lōd/ ▸ **n.** a vein of metal ore in the earth. ■ [in sing.] fig. a rich source of something. [OE *lād* 'way, course,' var. of LOAD.]

lo·den /ˈlōdn/ ▸ **n.** a thick waterproof woolen cloth. ■ the dark green color in which such cloth is often made. [20th C.: from Ger. *Loden.*]

lode·star /ˈlōdˌstär/ ▸ **n.** a star that is used to guide the course of a ship, esp. Polaris. ■ fig. a person or thing that serves as a guide.

lode·stone /ˈlōdˌstōn/ ▸ **n.** a piece of magnetite or other naturally magnetized mineral, able to be used as a magnet. ■ a mineral of this kind; magnetite. ■ fig. a thing that is the focus of attention or attraction.

Lodge /läj/, a family of US politicians. Henry Cabot (1850–1924) was a US senator 1893–1924 and opposed accepting the peace treaty that ended World War I. His grandson Henry Cabot (1902–85) served as ambassador to South Vietnam 1963–64, 1965–67.

lodge /läj/ ▸ **n.** **1** a small house at the gates of a park or in the grounds of a large house, typically occupied by a gatekeeper, gardener, or other employee. ■ a small country house occupied in season for sports such as hunting, shooting, fishing, and skiing. ■ [in names] a large house or hotel: *Cumberland Lodge.* ■ an American Indian hut. ■ a beaver's den. **2** a branch or meeting place of an organization such as the Freemasons. ■ the membership of such an organization. ▸ **v.** **1** [trans.] present (a complaint, appeal, claim, etc.) formally to the proper authorities: *he lodged an appeal.* ■ (**lodge something in/with**) leave money or a valuable item in (a place) or with (someone) for safekeeping. **2** [with adverbial of place] make or become firmly fixed or embedded in a particular place: [trans.] *a bullet lodged near his spine* | [intrans.] fig. *the image had lodged in her mind.* **3** [intrans.] stay or sleep in another person's house, paying money for one's accommodations: *the man who lodged in the room next door.* ■ provide (someone) with a place to sleep or stay in return for payment. **4** [trans.] (of wind or rain) flatten (a standing crop). ■ [intrans.] (of a crop) be flattened in such a way. [ME *loge*, via OFr. *loge* 'arbor, hut' from med. L. *laubia, lobia* (see LOBBY), of Gmc. origin; rel. to Ger. *Laube* 'arbor.']

lodge·pole pine /ˈläjˌpōl/ ▸ **n.** a straight-trunked pine tree (*Pinus contorta* var. *latifolia*) that grows in the mountains of western North America, widely grown for timber and traditionally used by some American Indians in the construction of lodges.

lodg·er /ˈläjər/ ▸ **n.** a roomer.

lodg·ing /ˈläjiNG/ ▸ **n.** a place in which someone lives or stays temporarily: *a fee for board and lodging.* ■ (**lodgings**) a room or rooms rented out to someone, usually in the same residence as the owner.

lodg·ing house ▸ **n.** a rooming house.

lodg·ment /ˈläjmənt/ (also **lodge·ment**) ▸ **n.** **1** esp. literary a place in which a person or thing is located, deposited, or lodged. **2** the depositing of money in a particular bank, account, etc. **3** Mil. a temporary defensive work made on a captured part of an enemy's fortifications.

Lo·di /ˈlōˌdī/ a city in north central California; pop. 51,874.

lod·i·cule /ˈlädəˌkyo͞ol/ ▸ **n.** Bot. a small green or white scale below the ovary of a grass flower. [19th C.: from L. *lodicula*, dimin. of *lodix* 'coverlet.']

Łódź /lädz; lo͞oj/ a city in central Poland, southwest of Warsaw; pop. 842,000.

lo·ess /les; ləs; ˈlōˌes/ ▸ **n.** Geol. a loosely compacted yellowish-gray deposit of windblown sediment of which extensive deposits occur, e.g., in eastern China and the American Midwest. — **lo·ess·i·al** /ˈlesēəl; ˈləs-; lōˈes-/ **adj.** **lo·ess·ic** /ˈlesik; ˈləs-; lōˈes-/ **adj.** [19th C.: from German *Löss*, from Swiss Ger. *lösch* 'loose.']

Loewe /lō/, Frederick (1901–88) US composer; born in Austria. He wrote the scores for *My Fair Lady* (1956) and *Camelot* (1960).

Loe·wi /ˈlō-ē/, Otto (1873–1961), US pharmacologist and physiologist; born in Germany. He showed that acetylcholine is produced at the junction of a parasympathetic nerve and a muscle. Nobel Prize for Physiology or Medicine (1936, shared with Sir Henry Dale).

lo-fi /ˈlō ˈfī/ (also **low-fi**) ▸ **adj.** of or employing sound reproduction of a lower quality than hi-fi: *defiantly lo-fi recording techniques.* ■ (of popular music) recorded and produced with basic equipment and thus having a raw and unsophisticated sound. ▸ **n.** sound reproduction or music of such a kind. [1950s: from an alt. of LOW[1] + *-fi* on the pattern of *hi-fi.*]

Lo·fo·ten Is·lands /ˈlōˌfōtn/ an island group off the northwestern coast of Norway.

loft /lôft; läft/ ▸ **n.** **1** a room or space directly under the roof of a house or other building, which may be used for accommodations or storage. ■ a room or space over a stable or barn, used esp. for storing hay and straw. ■ a gallery in a church or hall: *a choir loft.* ■ short for ORGAN LOFT. ■ a large, open area over a shop, warehouse, or factory, sometimes converted into living space. **2** Golf upward inclination given to the ball in a stroke. ■ backward slope of the head of a club, designed to give upward inclination to the ball. **3** the thickness of insulating matter in an object such as a sleeping bag or a padded coat. ▸ **v.** [trans.] kick, hit, or throw (a ball or missile) high up: *he lofted the ball over the infield.* ■ [trans.] [usu. as adj.] (**lofted**) give backward slope to the head of (a golf club). [OE, from ON *lopt* 'air, sky, upper room,' of Gmc. origin; rel. to Du. *lucht* and Ger. *Luft.*]

loft·y /ˈlôftē; ˈläf-/ ▸ **adj.** (**loft·i·er, loft·i·est**) **1** of imposing height. ■ of a noble or exalted nature: *lofty ideals.* ■ proud, aloof, or self-important: *lofty disdain.* **2** (of wool and other textiles) thick and resilient. — **loft·i·ly** /-təlē/ **adv.** **loft·i·ness** **n.**

log[1] /lôg; läg/ ▸ **n.** **1** a part of the trunk or a large branch of a tree that has fallen or been cut off. **2** (also **log·book**) an official record of events during the voyage of a ship or aircraft: *a ship's log.* ■ a regular or systematic record of incidents or observations: *keep a detailed log of your activities.* **3** an apparatus for determining the speed of a ship, originally consisting of a float attached to a knotted line wound on a reel, the distance run out in a certain time being used as an estimate of the vessel's speed. ▸ **v.** (**logged, log·ging**) [trans.] **1** enter (an incident or fact) in the log of a ship or aircraft or in another systematic record: *the red book where we log our calls.* ■ (of a ship or aircraft) achieve (a certain distance or speed): *she had logged more than 12,000 miles since she had been launched.* ■ (of an aircraft pilot) attain (a certain amount of flying time). **2** cut down (an area of forest) in order to exploit the timber commercially.

– PHRASAL VERBS **log in** (or **on**) go through the procedures to begin use of a computer system. **log off** (or **out**) go through the procedures to conclude use of a computer system.

log[2] ▸ **n.** short for LOGARITHM: [as adj.] *log tables.*

-log ▸ **comb. form** var. of -LOGUE.

Lo·gan, Mount /ˈlōgən/ a mountain in southwestern Yukon Territory, Canada. Rising to 19,850 feet (6,054 m), it is the highest peak in Canada.

lo·gan·ber·ry /ˈlōgənˌberē/ ▸ **n.** **1** an edible dull-red soft fruit, considered to be a hybrid of a raspberry and an American dewberry. **2** the scrambling blackberrylike plant (*Rubus loganobaccus*) of the rose family that bears this fruit. [19th C.: from the name of John H. *Logan* (1841–1928), American horticulturalist, + BERRY.]

log·a·rithm /ˈlôgəˌri*TH*əm; ˈlägə-/ (abbr.: **log**) ▸ **n.** a quantity representing the power to which a fixed number (the base) must be raised to produce a given number. The base of a **common logarithm** is 10, and that of a **natural logarithm** is the number *e* (2.71828...). [17th C.: from mod. L. *logarithmus*, from Gk. *logos* 'reckoning, ratio' + *arithmos* 'number.']

log·a·rith·mic /ˌlôgəˈri*TH*mik; ˌlägə-/ ▸ **adj.** of, relating to, or expressed in terms of logarithms. ■ (of a scale) constructed so that successive points along an axis, or graduations that are an equal distance apart, represent values that are in an equal ratio. ■ (of a curve) forming a straight line when plotted on a logarithmic scale; exponential. — **log·a·rith·mi·cal·ly** /-mik(ə)lē/ **adv.**

log·book /ˈlôgˌbo͝ok; ˈläg-/ ▸ **n.** another term for LOG[1] (sense 2).

loge /lōzh/ ▸ **n.** a private box or enclosure in a theater. ■ the front section of the first balcony in a theater. ■ a similar section in an arena or stadium. [18th C.: from Fr.]

-loger ▸ **comb. form** equivalent to -LOGIST.

log·ger /ˈlôgər; ˈlägər/ ▸ **n.** **1** a person who fells trees for timber; a lumberjack. **2** a device for making a systematic recording of events, observations, or measurements.

log·ger·head /ˈlôgərˌhed; ˈlägər-/ ▸ **n.** **1** (also **loggerhead turtle**) a reddish-brown turtle (*Caretta caretta*, family Cheloniidae) with a very large head, occurring chiefly in warm seas. *See illustration on next page.* **2** (also **loggerhead shrike**) a widespread North American shrike (*Lanius ludovicianus*), having mainly gray plumage with a black eyestripe, wings, and tail. **3** archaic a foolish person.

– PHRASES **at loggerheads** in stubborn dispute or disagreement: *council was at loggerheads with the government.* [16th C. (sense 3): from dial. *logger* 'block of wood for hobbling a horse' + HEAD.]

log·gia /ˈlōj(ē)ə; ˈlô-/ ▸ **n.** a gallery or room with one or more open sides, esp. one that forms part of a house and has one side open to the garden. ■ an open-sided extension to a house. [18th C.: from Ital., 'lodge.']

loggerhead turtle

log·ging /ˈlôgiNG; ˈlägiNG/ ▶ **n.** the activity or business of felling trees and cutting and preparing the timber.

lo·gi·a /ˈlōgēə; -jēə/ plural form of LOGION.

log·ic /ˈläjik/ ▶ **n. 1** reasoning conducted or assessed according to strict principles of validity: *experience is a better guide to this than deductive logic.* ■ a particular system or codification of the principles of proof and inference: *Aristotelian logic.* ■ the systematic use of symbolic and mathematical techniques to determine the forms of valid deductive argument. ■ the quality of being justifiable by reason: *there's no logic in telling her not to hit people when that's what you're doing.* ■ (**logic of**) the course of action or line of reasoning suggested or made necessary by: *if the logic of capital is allowed to determine events.* **2** a system or set of principles underlying the arrangements of elements in a computer or electronic device so as to perform a specified task. ■ logical operations collectively. — **lo·gi·cian** /ləˈjisHən; lō-/ **n.** [ME: via OFr. *logique* and late L. *logica* from Gk. *logikē (tekhnē)* '(art) of reason,' from *logos* 'word, reason.']

-logic ▶ **comb. form** equivalent to -LOGICAL (as in *pharmacologic*). [from Gk. *-logikos.*]

log·i·cal /ˈläjikəl/ ▶ **adj.** of or according to the rules of logic or formal argument: *a logical impossibility.* ■ characterized by clear, sound reasoning. ■ (of an action, development, decision, etc.) natural or sensible given the circumstances: *it is a logical progression from the job before.* ■ capable of clear rational thinking: *her logical mind.* — **log·i·cal·i·ty** /ˌläjəˈkalətē/ **n. log·i·cal·ly adv.**

-logical ▶ **comb. form** in adjectives corresponding chiefly to nouns ending in *-logy.*

log·i·cal em·pir·i·cism ▶ **n.** see LOGICAL POSITIVISM.

log·i·cal form ▶ **n.** Logic the abstract form in which an argument or proposition may be expressed in logical terms, as distinct from its particular content.

log·i·cal ne·ces·si·ty ▶ **n.** that state of things that obliges something to be as it is because no alternative is logically possible. ■ a thing that logically must be so.

log·i·cal op·er·a·tion ▶ **n.** an operation of the kind used in logic, e.g., conjunction or negation. ■ Comput. an operation that acts on binary numbers to produce a result according to the laws of Boolean logic (e.g., the AND, OR, and NOT functions).

log·i·cal pos·i·tiv·ism ▶ **n.** a form of positivism, developed by members of the Vienna Circle, that considers that the only meaningful philosophical problems are those that can be solved by logical analysis. Also called LOGICAL EMPIRICISM.

log·ic bomb ▶ **n.** Comput. a set of instructions secretly incorporated into a program so that if a particular condition is satisfied they will be carried out, usually with harmful effects.

log·in /ˈlôg,in; ˈläg-/ (also **log·on**) ▶ **n.** an act of logging in to a computer system.

lo·gi·on /ˈlōgē,än; -jē-/ ▶ **n.** (pl. **-gi·a** /-gēə; -jēə/) a saying attributed to Christ, esp. one not recorded in the canonical Gospels. [19th C.: from Gk., 'oracle,' from *logos* 'word.']

-logist ▶ **comb. form** indicating a person skilled or involved in a branch of study denoted by a noun ending in *-logy* (such as *biologist* corresponding to *biology*).

lo·gis·tic /ləˈjistik; lō-/ ▶ **adj.** of or relating to logistics. — **lo·gis·ti·cal** /-tikəl/ **adj. lo·gis·ti·cal·ly** /-tik(ə)lē/ **adv.**

lo·gis·tics /ləˈjistiks; lō-/ ▶ **plural n.** [treated as sing. or pl.] the detailed coordination of a complex operation involving many people, facilities, or supplies. ■ Mil. the organization of moving, housing, and supplying troops and equipment. ■ the commercial activity of transporting goods to customers. [19th C.: from Fr. *logistique,* from *loger* 'lodge.']

log·jam /ˈlôg,jam; ˈläg-/ ▶ **n.** a crowded mass of logs blocking a river. ■ a situation that seems irresolvable: *the president can* **break the logjam** *over this issue.* ■ a backlog: *keeping a diary may ease the logjam of work considerably.*

log·nor·mal ▶ **adj.** Stat. of or denoting a set of data in which the logarithm of the variate is distributed according to a normal distribution. — **log·nor·mal·i·ty n. log·nor·mal·ly adv.**

LOGO ▶ **n.** Comput. a high-level programming language used to teach computer programming to children. [from Gk. *logos* 'word,' spelled as if an acronym.]

lo·go /ˈlōgō/ ▶ **n.** (pl. **-gos**) a symbol or other small design adopted by an organization to identify its products, uniform, vehicles, etc.: *the Olympic logo.* [1930s: abbrev. of LOGOGRAM or LOGOTYPE.]

log·off /ˈlôg,ôf; -äf; ˈläg-/ ▶ **n.** another term for LOGOUT.

log·o·gram /ˈlôgə,gram; ˈlägə-/ ▶ **n.** a sign or character representing a word or phrase, such as those used in shorthand and some writing systems. [19th C.: from Gk. *logos* 'word' + -GRAM[1].]

log·o·graph /ˈlôgə,graf; ˈlägə-/ ▶ **n.** another term for LOGOGRAM. — **log·o·graph·ic** /ˌlôgəˈgrafik; ˌlägə-/ **adj.**

log·o·griph /ˈlôgə,grif; ˈlägə-/ ▶ **n.** a puzzle involving anagrams. [16th C.: from Gk. *logos* 'word' + *griphos* 'fishing basket, riddle.']

lo·gom·a·chy /lōˈgäməkē/ ▶ **n.** (pl. **-chies**) rare an argument about words. [16th C.: from Gk. *logomakhia,* from *logos* 'word' + *-makhia* 'fighting.']

log·on /ˈlôg,ôn; ˈläg,än/ ▶ **n.** another term for LOGIN.

log·o·phile /ˈlôgə,fīl; ˈlägə-/ ▶ **n.** a lover of words.

log·or·rhe·a /ˌlôgəˈrēə; ˌlägə-/ (Brit. **log·or·rhoe·a**) ▶ **n.** a tendency to extreme loquacity. — **log·or·rhe·ic** /-ˈrēik/ **adj.** [20th C.: from Gk. *logos* 'word' + *rhoia* 'flow.']

Lo·gos /ˈlō,gōs; -,gäs/ ▶ **n.** Christian Theol. the Word of God, made incarnate in Jesus Christ. ■ (in Jungian psychology) the principle of reason and judgment, associated with the animus. Often contrasted with EROS. [Gk., 'word, reason.']

lo·go·type /ˈlôgə,tīp; ˈlägə-/ ▶ **n.** Print. a single piece of type that prints a word or group of separate letters. ■ a single piece of type that prints a logo or emblem. ■ a logo. [19th C.: from Gk. *logos* 'word' + TYPE.]

log·out /ˈlôg,out; ˈläg-/ (also **log·off**) ▶ **n.** an act of logging out of a computer system.

log·roll·ing /ˈlôg,rōliNG; ˈläg-/ ▶ **n. 1** informal the practice of exchanging favors, esp. in politics by reciprocal voting for each other's proposed legislation. [from the phr. *you roll my log and I'll roll yours.*] **2** a sport in which two contestants stand on a floating log and try to knock each other off by spinning it. — **log·roll·er** /-lər/ **n.**

Lo·gro·ño /ləˈgrōnyō/ a town in northern Spain; pop. 127,000.

-logue (also **-log**) ▶ **comb. form 1** denoting discourse of a specified type: *dialogue.* **2** denoting compilation: *catalogue.* **3** equivalent to -LOGIST. [from Fr. *-logue,* from Gk. *-logos, -logon.*]

log·wood /ˈlôg,wŏŏd; ˈläg-/ ▶ **n.** a spiny Caribbean tree (*Haematoxylon campechianum*) of the pea family, the dark heartwood of which yields hematoxylin and other dyes.

lo·gy /ˈlōgē/ ▶ **adj.** (**lo·gi·er, lo·gi·est**) dull and heavy in motion or thought; sluggish. [19th C.: of uncert. origin; cf. Du. *log* 'heavy, dull.']

-logy ▶ **comb. form 1** (usu. as **-ology**) denoting a subject of study or interest: *psychology.* **2** denoting a characteristic of speech or language: *eulogy.* ■ denoting a type of discourse: *trilogy.* [from Fr. *-logie* or med. L. *-logia,* from Gk.]

Lo·hen·grin /ˈlōən,grin/ (in medieval French and German romances) the son of Perceval (Parsifal) and a knight of the Holy Grail.

lo·i·a·sis /lōˈīəsis/ ▶ **n.** a tropical African disease caused by infestation with eye worms that cause transient subcutaneous swellings. [20th C.: mod. L., from *loa* (a local Angolan word for the parasite) + -IASIS.]

loin /loin/ ▶ **n.** (usu. **loins**) the part of the body on both sides of the spine between the lowest (false) ribs and the hipbones. ■ (**loins**) esp. literary the region of the sexual organs, esp. when regarded as the source of erotic or procreative power. ■ (**loin**) a joint of meat that includes the vertebrae of the loins: ***loin of pork.*** [ME: from OFr. *loigne,* based on L. *lumbus.*]

loin·cloth /ˈloin,klôTH; -,kläTH/ ▶ **n.** a single piece of cloth wrapped round the hips, typically worn by men in some hot countries as their only garment.

Loire /lwär/ a river in west central France. The country's longest river, it rises in the Massif Central and flows 630 miles (1,015 km) north and west to the Atlantic Ocean at the town of Saint-Nazaire.

loi·ter /ˈloitər/ ▶ **v.** [intrans.] stand or wait around idly or without apparent purpose. ■ [with adverbial of direction] travel indolently and with frequent pauses: *they loitered along in the sunshine, stopping at the least excuse.* — **loi·ter·er n.** [ME: perh. from MDu. *loteren* 'wag around.']

Lo·ki /ˈlōkē/ Scand. Mythol. a mischievous and sometimes evil god.

Lo·li·ta /lōˈlētə/ ▶ **n.** a sexually precocious young girl. [from the novel *Lolita* (1958) by Vladimir Nabokov.]

loll /läl/ ▶ **v.** [intrans.] sit, lie, or stand in a lazy, relaxed way: *the two girls lolled in their chairs.* ■ hang loosely; droop: *he slumped against a tree trunk, his head lolling back.* ■ [trans.] stick out (one's tongue) so that it hangs loosely out of the mouth. [ME: prob. symbolic of dangling.]

lol·la·pa·loo·za /ˌläləpəˈlōōzə/ (also **la·la·pa·loo·za** or **lol·la·pa·loo·sa**) ▶ **n.** informal a person or thing that is particularly impressive or attractive. [19th C.: of fanciful formation.]

Lol·lard /ˈlälərd/ ▶ **n.** a follower of John Wyclif. — **Lol·lard·ism n. Lol·lard·y n.** [from a Du. word meaning 'mumbler,' based on *lollen* 'to mumble.']

lol·li·pop /ˈlälē,päp/ ▶ **n.** a flat, rounded candy on the end of a stick. [18th C.: perh. from dial. *lolly* 'tongue' + POP[1].]

lol·lop /ˈläləp/ ▶ **v.** (**-loped, -lop·ing**) [intrans.] move in an ungainly way in a series of clumsy paces or bounds: *the bear lolloped along the path.* [18th C.: prob. from LOLL, associated with TROLLOP.]

lol·ly·gag /ˈlälē,gag/ (also **lal·ly·gag**) ▶ **v.** (**-gagged, -gag·ging**) [intrans.] informal spend time aimlessly; idle: *lollygagging in the sun.* ■ [with adverbial of direction] dawdle: *we're just lollygagging along.* [19th C.: of unknown origin.]

Lomb /läm/, Henry (1828–1908) US optician; born in Germany. He cofounded Bausch & Lomb Optical Company in 1853.

Lom·bard /ˈläm,bärd; -bərd/ ▶ **n. 1** a member of a Germanic people who invaded Italy in the 6th century. **2** a native of Lombardy in northern Italy. **3** the Italian dialect of Lombardy. ▶ **adj.** of or relating to Lombardy, or to the Lombards or their language. — **Lom·bar·dic** /lämˈbärdik/ **adj.**

(in sense 1). [from Ital. *lombardo*, representing late L. *Langobardus*, of Gmc. origin, from the base of LONG[1] + the ethnic name *Bardi*.]

Lom·bar·di /läm'bärdē; ˌləm-/, Vincent Thomas (1913–70) US football coach. He coached the Green Bay Packers 1959–67.

Lom·bar·do /läm'bärdō; ˌləm-/, Guy (1902–77) US band leader; born in Canada; full name *Gaetano Alberto Lombardo*. New Year's Eve broadcasts of his band's music from New York City's Waldorf Astoria hotel became a national tradition.

Lom·bar·dy /'läm,bärdē; -bərdē/ a region of central northern Italy; capital, Milan. Italian name **LOMBARDIA**.

Lom·bard·y pop·lar ▶ **n.** a black poplar of a variety (*Populus nigra* var. *italica*) that has a distinctive tall, slender columnar form.

Lom·bok /'läm,bäk/ a volcanic island of the Lesser Sunda group in Indonesia; pop. 2,500,000; chief town, Mataram.

Lo·mé /lō'mā/ the capital of Togo; pop. 450,000.

lo·ment /'lōmənt; -ˌment/ (also **lo·men·tum** /lō'mentəm/) ▶ **n.** Bot. the pod of some leguminous plants, breaking up when mature into one-seeded joints. [19th C.: from L., 'bean meal,' from *lavare* 'to wash.']

Lon·don[1] /'ləndən/ **1** the capital of the United Kingdom, in southeastern England on the Thames River; pop. 6,377,000. **2** a city in southeastern Ontario, Canada; pop. 303,165. — **Lon·don·er n.**

Lon·don[2], Jack (1876-1916), US writer; pen name of *John Griffith Chaney*. He wrote *The Call of the Wild* (1903) and *White Fang* (1906).

Lon·don broil ▶ **n.** a grilled steak served cut diagonally in thin slices.

Lon·don·der·ry /'ləndən,derē; ˌləndən'derē/ one of the Six Counties of Northern Ireland. ■ its chief town; pop. 63,000.

lone /lōn/ ▶ **adj.** [attrib.] having no companions; solitary or single: *I approached a lone drinker across the bar.* ■ lacking the support of others; isolated: *I am by no means a lone voice.* ■ literary (of a place) unfrequented and remote: *houses in lone rural settings.* [ME: shortening of **ALONE**.]

lone hand ▶ **n.** (in euchre or quadrille) a hand played against the rest, or a player playing such a hand.

lone·ly /'lōnlē/ ▶ **adj.** (**-li·er**, **-li·est**) sad because one has no friends or company. ■ without companions; solitary: *passing long lonely hours looking onto the street.* ■ (of a place) unfrequented and remote: *a lonely stretch of country lane.* — **lone·li·ness n.**

lone·ly heart ▶ **n.** [usu. as adj.] a person looking for a lover or friend by advertising in a newspaper: *a lonely hearts column.* — **lone·ly-heart·ed adj.**

lon·er /'lōnər/ ▶ **n.** a person who prefers not to associate with others.

lone·some /'lōnsəm/ ▶ **adj.** solitary or lonely: *she felt lonesome and out of things.* ■ remote and unfrequented: *a lonesome, unfriendly place.*
– PHRASES **by one's lonesome** informal all alone. — **lone·some·ness n.**

lone wolf ▶ **n.** a person who prefers to act alone.

Long[1] /lôNG; läNG/, Huey Pierce (1893–1935) US politician; known as the **Kingfish**. He was governor of Louisiana 1928–31 and a US senator 1932–35.

Long[2], Stephen Harriman (1784–1864) US Army officer and explorer. He explored the upper Mississippi in 1817 and the Rocky Mountain region in 1820.

long[1] /lôNG; läNG/ ▶ **adj.** (**long·er** /'lôNGgər; 'läNG-/, **long·est** /lôNGgist; 'läNG-/) **1** measuring a great distance from end to end: *a long corridor.* ■ (after a measurement and in questions) measuring a specified distance from end to end: *a boat 150 feet long.* ■ (of a journey) covering a great distance: *a long walk.* ■ (of a garment or sleeves on a garment) covering the whole of a person's legs or arms. ■ of elongated shape: *shaped like a torpedo, long and thin.* ■ (of a ball in sports) traveling a great distance, or further than expected or intended: *he threw a long ball to the catcher.* ■ informal (of a person) tall. **2** lasting or taking a great amount of time: *a long and distinguished career.* ■ (after a noun of duration and in questions) lasting or taking a specified amount of time: *the debates will be 90 minutes long.* ■ [attrib.] seeming to last more time than is the case; lengthy or tedious: *serving long hours on the committee.* ■ (of a person's memory) retaining things for a great amount of time. **3** relatively great in extent: *write a long report.* ■ (after a noun of extent and in questions) having a specified extent: *the statement was three pages long.* **4** Phonet. (of a vowel) categorized as long with regard to quality and length (e.g., in standard American English, the vowel in *food* is long, as distinct from the short vowel in *good*). ■ Pros. (of a vowel or syllable) having the greater of the two recognized durations. **5** (of odds or a chance) reflecting or representing a low level of probability: *winning against long odds.* **6** Finance (of shares, bonds, or other assets) bought in advance, with the expectation of a rise in price. ■ (of a broker or their position in the market) buying or based on long stocks. ■ (of a security) maturing at a distant date. **7** [predic.] (**long on**) informal well-supplied with: *long on ideas but short on cash.* ▶ **n.** **1** a long interval or period: *see you **before long**.* **2** a long sound such as a long signal in Morse code or a long vowel or syllable: *two longs and a short.* **3** (**longs**) Finance long-dated securities, esp. gilt-edged securities. ■ assets held in a long position. ▶ **adv.** (**longer**; **longest**) **1** for a long time: *we hadn't known them long | an experience they will long remember.* ■ in questions about a period of time: ***how long** have you been working?* ■ at a time distant from a specified event or point of time: *it was abandoned long ago.* ■ [comparative with negative] after an implied point of time: *he could not wait any longer.* ■ (after a noun of duration) throughout a specified period of time: *it rained all day long.* **2** (with reference to the ball in sports) at, to, or over a great distance, or further than expected or intended: *the quarterback dropped back and threw the ball long.* ■ beyond the point aimed at; too far.
– PHRASES **as** (or **so**) **long as 1** during the whole time that: *they have been there as long as anyone can remember.* **2** provided that: *as long as you fed him, he would be cooperative.* **in the long run** over or after a long period of time; eventually. **the long and the short of it** all that can or need be said. **long in the tooth** rather old. **not by a long shot** by no means. **take the long view** think beyond the current situation; plan for the future. — **long·ish adj.** [OE *lang, long* (adj.), *lange, longe* (adv.), of Gmc. origin; rel. to Du. and Ger. *lang*.]

long[2] ▶ **v.** [intrans.] have a strong wish or desire: *she **longed for** a little more excitement.* [OE *langian*, of Gmc. origin; rel. to Ger. *langen* 'reach, extend.']

long. ▶ **abbr.** longitude.

-long ▶ **comb. form** (added to nouns) for the duration of: *lifelong.*

lon·gan /'lôNGgən; 'läNG-/ ▶ **n.** an edible juicy fruit from a plant (*Dimocarpus longan*) of the soapberry family, related to the litchi and cultivated in Southeast Asia. [18th C.: from Chin. *lóngyaˇn*, lit. 'dragon's eye.']

Long Beach a city in southwestern California, south of Los Angeles; pop. 461,522.

long·board /'lôNG,bôrd; 'läNG-/ ▶ **n.** a type of long surfboard.

long·boat /'lôNG,bōt; 'läNG-/ ▶ **n.** a large boat that may be launched from a sailing ship.

long·bow /'lôNG,bō; 'läNG-/ ▶ **n.** a large bow drawn by hand and shooting a long feathered arrow.

long·case clock (also **long-case clock**) ▶ **n.** another term for **GRANDFATHER CLOCK**.

long-day ▶ **adj.** [attrib.] (of a plant) needing a long period of light each day to initiate flowering.

long 'dis·tance ▶ **adj.** (usu. **long-dis·tance**) traveling or operating between distant places. ▶ **adv.** between distant places: *traveling long distance.* ▶ **n.** [often as adj.] Track & Field a race distance of 6 miles or 10,000 meters (6 miles 376 yds), or longer.

long di·vi·sion ▶ **n.** arithmetical division in which the divisor has two or more figures, and a series of steps is written down as successive groups of digits of the dividend are divided by the divisor.

long doz·en ▶ **n.** (**a long dozen**) thirteen.

long-drawn (often **long-drawn-out**) ▶ **adj.** continuing for a long time, esp. for longer than is necessary.

longe /lənj/ (also **lunge**) ▶ **n.** a long rein on which a horse is held and made to move in a circle around its trainer. ▶ **v.** (**longe·ing**) [trans.] exercise (a horse or rider) on a longe. [18th C.: Fr., from *allonge* 'lengthening out.']

lon·ge·ron /'länjərən; -ˌrän/ ▶ **n.** a longitudinal structural component of an aircraft's fuselage. [20th C.: from Fr., lit. 'girder.']

lon·gev·i·ty /lôn'jevətē; län-/ ▶ **n.** long life. ■ long duration of service: *her longevity in office now appeared as a handicap to the party.* [17th C.: from late L. *longaevitas*, from L. *longus* 'long' + *aevum* 'age.']

long face ▶ **n.** an unhappy or disappointed expression. — **long-faced adj.**

Long·fel·low /'lôNG,felō; läNG-/, Henry Wadsworth (1807–82), US poet. His narrative poems include *Evangeline* (1847), *The Song of Hiawatha* (1855), and *Paul Revere's Ride* (1861).

long·hair /'lôNG,he(ə)r; 'läNG-/ ▶ **n.** **1** a person with long hair or characteristics associated with it, such as a hippie or intellectual. ■ a devotee of classical music. **2** a cat of a long-haired breed.

long·hand /'lôNG,hand; 'läNG-/ ▶ **n.** ordinary handwriting (as opposed to shorthand, typing, or printing).

long haul ▶ **n.** a long distance (in reference to the transport of freight or passengers): [as adj.] *a long-haul flight.* ■ a prolonged and difficult effort or task: *getting the proposal passed is likely to be a long haul.*
– PHRASES **over the long haul** over an extended period of time.

long-head·ed ▶ **adj.** **1** having a long head; dolichocephalic. **2** dated having or showing foresight and good judgment. — **long-head·ed·ness n.**

long·horn /'lôNG,hôrn; 'läNG-/ ▶ **n.** **1** an animal of a breed of cattle with long horns. **2** (also **longhorn beetle**) an elongated beetle (family Cerambycidae) with long antennae, the larva of which typically bores in wood and can be a pest of timber.

long-horned grass·hop·per ▶ **n.** an insect (family Tettigoniidae) related to the grasshoppers, with very long antennae and a mainly carnivorous diet.

long·house /'lôNG,hous; 'läNG-/ ▶ **n.** a type of dwelling housing a family and animals under one roof. ■ hist. the traditional dwelling of the Iroquois and other North American Indians.

long hun·dred·weight ▶ **n.** see **HUNDREDWEIGHT**.

lon·gi·corn /'länjə,kôrn/ ▶ **n.** former term for **LONGHORN** (sense 2). [19th C.: from mod. L. *longicornis*, from L. *longus* 'long' + *cornu* 'horn.']

long·ing /'lôNGiNG; 'läNG-/ ▶ **n.** a yearning desire. ▶ **adj.** [attrib.] having or showing such desire: *her longing eyes.* — **long·ing·ly adv.**

Long Is·land an island in eastern New York. Its western tip comprises the New York boroughs of Brooklyn and Queens.

lon·gi·tude /'länji,t(y)o͞od; 'lôn-/ ▶ **n.** the angular distance of a place east or west of the meridian at Greenwich, England, or west of the standard meridian of a celestial object, usually expressed in degrees and minutes:

at a longitude of 2° W | *lines of longitude.* ■ Astron. see CELESTIAL LONGITUDE. [ME: from L. *longitudo*, from *longus* 'long.']

longitude

lon·gi·tu·di·nal /ˌlänjəˈt(y)o͞odn-əl; -ˈt(y)o͞odnəl; ˌlôn-/ ▶ adj. **1** running lengthwise rather than across: *longitudinal stripes.* ■ (of research or data) involving information about an individual or group gathered over a long period. **2** of or relating to longitude; measured from east to west: *longitudinal positions.* — **lon·gi·tu·di·nal·ly** adv.

lon·gi·tu·di·nal wave ▶ n. Physics a wave vibrating in the direction of propagation.

long johns ▶ plural n. informal underwear with closely fitted legs that extend to the wearer's ankles, often with a long-sleeved top.

long jump ▶ n. (**the long jump**) an athletic event in which competitors jump as far as possible along the ground in one leap. — **long jump·er** n.

long·leaf pine /ˈlôngˌlēf; ˈläng-/ ▶ n. a large pine tree (*Pinus palustris*) of the southeastern US with very long needles and cones. It was formerly an important source of turpentine.

long·line /ˈlôngˌlīn; ˈläng-/ ▶ n. a deep-sea fishing line.

long·lin·er /ˈlôngˌlīnər; ˈläng-/ ▶ n. a fishing vessel or fisherman that uses longlines.

long-lived /livd/ ▶ adj. living or lasting a long time.

long-lost ▶ adj. [attrib.] lost or absent for a long time.

Long March the epic withdrawal of the Chinese communists, led by Mao Zedong, from southeastern to northwestern China in 1934–35, over a distance of 6,000 miles (9,600 km).

long me·ter (abbr.: **LM**) ▶ n. (also **long measure**) a metrical pattern for hymns in which the stanzas have four lines with eight syllables each.

Long·mont /ˈlôngˌmänt; ˈläng-/ a city in northern Colorado; pop. 71,093.

long·neck /ˈlôngˌnek; ˈläng-/ ▶ n. informal a beer bottle with a long, narrow neck: *he smashed the bottom of his longneck on the bar.* ■ a bottle of beer: *drinking a cold longneck.*

Long Par·lia·ment the English Parliament that sat from 1640 until dismissed by Cromwell in 1653. It was restored briefly in 1659 and dissolved in 1660.

long pig ▶ n. a translation of a term formerly used in some Pacific Islands for human flesh as food.

long-play·ing ▶ adj. (of a phonograph record) designed to be played at 33⅓ revolutions per minute.

long-range ▶ adj. **1** (esp. of vehicles or missiles) able to be used or be effective over long distances. **2** relating to a period of time that extends far into the future: *long-range forecasts.*

long-run·ning ▶ adj. continuing for a long time.

long s ▶ n. an obsolete form of lower-case s, written or printed as ſ. It was generally abandoned in English-language printing shortly before 1800.

long·ship /ˈlôngˌship; ˈläng-/ ▶ n. a long, narrow warship, powered by both oar and sail, used by the Vikings and other northern European peoples.

longship

long·shore /ˈlôngˌshôr; ˈläng-/ ▶ adj. [attrib.] existing on, frequenting, or moving along the seashore: *longshore currents.* [19th C.: from *along shore.*]

long·shore·man /ˌlôngˈshôrmən; ˌläng-/ ▶ n. (pl. **-men**) a person employed in a port to load and unload ships.

long shot ▶ n. a venture or guess that has only the slightest chance of succeeding or being accurate: *it's a long shot, but well worth trying.* ■ Film a shot including objects at a distance: *using a dummy in long shot.*

– PHRASES **(not) by a long shot** informal (not) by far or at all.

long-sight·ed /ˈlôngˌsītid; ˈläng-/ ▶ adj. British term for FARSIGHTED. — **long·sight·ed·ly** adv. **long·sight·ed·ness** n.

long·spur /ˈlôngˌspər; ˈläng-/ ▶ n. a mainly Canadian songbird (genus *Calcarius*) of the bunting family, with brownish plumage and a boldly marked head in the male.

long-stand·ing (also **long·stand·ing**) ▶ adj. having existed or continued for a long time.

Long·street /ˈlôngˌstrēt; ˈläng-/, James (1821–1904) Confederate general in the American Civil War. He surrendered with Robert E. Lee at Appomattox Court House.

long-suf·fer·ing ▶ adj. having or showing patience in spite of troubles: *his long-suffering wife.* — **long-suf·fer·ing·ly** adv.

long suit ▶ n. (in bridge or whist) a holding of several cards of one suit in a hand, typically 5 or more out of the 13. ■ [usu. with negative] an outstanding personal quality or achievement: *tact was not his long suit.*

long-term ▶ adj. occurring over or relating to a long period of time: *the long-term unemployed.*

long·time /ˈlôngˌtīm; ˈläng-/ (also **long-time**) ▶ adj. [attrib.] (esp. of a person) having had a specified role or identity for a long time: *his longtime friend and colleague.*

long tom ▶ n. informal, hist. **1** a large cannon with a long range. **2** a trough for washing gold-bearing deposits.

long ton ▶ n. see TON[1].

lon·gueur /lôngˈgər; läng-/ ▶ n. a tedious passage in a book or other work. ■ tedious periods of time: *the last act is sometimes marred by longueur.* [Fr., lit. 'length.']

Long·view /ˈlôngˌvyo͞o; ˈläng-/ a city in eastern Texas; pop. 70,311.

long waist ▶ n. a low waist on a dress or a person's body. — **long-waist·ed** adj.

long wave ▶ n. a radio wave of a wavelength above one kilometer (and a frequency below 300 kHz). ■ broadcasting using radio waves of 1 to 10 km wavelength: *listening to news radio* ***on long wave.***

long-wind·ed /ˈwindid/ ▶ adj. (of speech or writing) continuing at length and in a tedious way. ■ archaic capable of doing something for a long time without needing a rest. — **long-wind·ed·ly** adv. **long-wind·ed·ness** n.

long·wise /ˈlôngˌwīz; ˈläng-/ (also **long·ways** /-ˌwāz/) ▶ adv. lengthwise.

loo[1] /lo͞o/ ▶ n. Brit., informal a toilet. [1940s: perh. from *Waterloo*, a trade name for iron cisterns.]

loo[2] ▶ n. a former gambling card game in which a player who fails to win a trick must pay a sum to a pool. [17th C.: abbrev. of obs. *lanterloo*, from Fr. *lanturlu*, a meaningless song refrain.]

loo·ey /ˈlo͞o-ē/ (also **loo·ie**) ▶ n. (pl. **loo·eys** or **loo·ies**) military slang short for LIEUTENANT.

loo·fah /ˈlo͞ofə/ (also **loo·fa, luf·fa**) ▶ n. **1** a coarse, fibrous cylindrical object used like a bath sponge for washing. It consists of the dried fibrous matter of the fluid-transport system of a marrowlike fruit. **2** the tropical Old World climbing plant (*Luffa cylindrica*) of the gourd family that produces these fruits, which are also edible. [19th C.: from Egyptian Arab. *lūfa*, denoting the plant.]

look /lo͝ok/ ▶ v. [intrans.] **1** [intrans.] direct one's gaze toward someone or something or in a specified direction: *people were* ***looking at*** *him.* ■ (of a building or room) have a view or outlook in a specified direction: *the principal rooms* ***look out over*** *Nahant Bay.* ■ (**look through**) ignore (someone) by pretending not to see them: *he glanced up but looked right through me.* ■ (**look something over**) inspect something quickly with a view to establishing its merits: *they looked over a property on Ryer Avenue.* ■ (**look through**) peruse (a book or other written material). ■ (**look round/around**) move around (a place or building) in order to view whatever it might contain that is of interest: *he spent the morning and afternoon looking around Cambridge.* ■ (**look at/on**) think of or regard in a specified way: *I look at tennis differently from some coaches.* ■ (**look at**) examine (a matter, esp. a problem) and consider what action to take: *a committee is looking at the financing of PBS.* ■ (**look into**) investigate. ■ (**look for**) attempt to find. ■ [with clause] ascertain with a quick glance: *people finishing work don't* ***look where*** *they're going.* **2** [with complement or adverbial] have the appearance or give the impression of being: *her father looked unhappy.* ■ (**look like**) informal show a likelihood of: [with clause] *it doesn't look like you'll be moving to Brooklyn.* ■ (**look oneself**) appear one's normal, healthy self: *he just didn't look himself at all.* **3** (**look to**) rely on to do or provide something: *she will look to you for help.* ■ [with infin.] hope or expect to do something: *universities are looking to expand their intakes.* ■ [with clause] archaic take care; make sure: *Look ye obey the masters of the craft.* ▶ n. **1** an act of directing one's gaze in order to see someone or something: *let me get a closer look.* ■ an expression of a feeling or thought by such an act: *Brenton gave me a funny look.* ■ a scrutiny or examination: *the government should be* ***taking a look at*** *the amount of grant the council receives.* **2** the appearance of someone or something, esp. as expressing a particular quality: *the bedraggled look of the village.* ■ (**looks**) a person's facial appearance considered aesthetically. ■ a style or fashion: *Italian designers unveiled their latest look.* ▶ exclam. (also **look here!**) used to call attention to what one is going to say: *"Look, this is ridiculous."*

– PHRASES **look one's age** appear to be as old as one really is. **look alive** see LIVELY. **look daggers at** see DAGGER. **look down one's nose at** another way of saying *LOOK DOWN ON*. **look for trouble** see TROUBLE. **look someone in the eye** (or **face**) look directly at someone without showing embarrassment, fear, or shame. **look lively** see LIVELY. **look the other way** deliberately ignore wrongdoing by others. **look sharp** be quick. **look small** see SMALL. **look to the future** consider and plan for what is in the future, rather than worrying about the past or present. **look someone up and down** scrutinize someone carefully.

– PHRASAL VERBS **look after** take care of. **look back 1** think of the past. **2** [with negative] suffer a setback or interrupted progress: *she launched her own company in 1981 and has never looked back.* **look down on** regard (someone) with a feeling of superiority. **look forward to** await eagerly. **look in** make a short visit or call: *I will look in on you tomorrow.* **look on** watch without getting involved. **look out** [usu. in imper.] be vigilant and take notice. **look up** (of a situation) improve: *things seemed to be looking up at last.* **look someone up** informal make social contact with someone. **look something up** search for and find a piece of information in a reference book. **look up to** have a great deal of respect for (someone). [OE *lōcian* (v.), of West Gmc. origin; rel. to Ger. dial. *lugen*.]

look-a·like (also **look·a·like**) ▶ **n.** a person or thing that closely resembles another, esp. a famous, person: *an Elvis Presley look-alike.*

look-and-say (also **look-say**) ▶ **n.** [as adj.] denoting a method of teaching reading based on the visual recognition of words rather than the association of sounds and letters. Compare with **PHONIC**.

look·er /'lo͝okər/ ▶ **n. 1** a person who looks: *the percentage of lookers who actually buy is pretty low.* **2** [with adj.] a person with a specified appearance: *a tough looker is not necessarily a tough fighter.* ■ informal a very attractive person, esp. a woman.

look·er-on ▶ **n.** (pl. **look·ers-on**) a spectator.

look-in ▶ **n. 1** an informal and brief visit. **2** Football a short pass pattern in which the receiver runs diagonally toward the center of the field.

look·ing glass ▶ **n.** a mirror. ■ [as adj.] being or involving the opposite of what is normal or expected: *looking-glass logic.*

look·it /'lo͝okit/ informal ▶ **v.** [trans.] look at: *Hey, lookit that!* ▶ **exclam.** used to draw attention to what one is about to say: *lookit, Pete, this is serious.*

look·out /'lo͝ok,out/ ▶ **n.** a place from which to keep watch or view landscape. ■ a person stationed to keep watch for danger or trouble. ■ archaic a view over a landscape. ■ (**one's lookout**) informal a person's own concern: *everyone's life is his own lookout.* ■ informal, esp. Brit. a consequence; outcome.

– PHRASES **be on the lookout** (or **keep a lookout**) **for** be alert to: *he told them to be on the lookout for dangerous gas.* ■ keep searching for (something wanted): *we kept a sharp lookout for animals.*

Look·out Moun·tain /'lo͝ok,out/ an Appalachian ridge, site near Chattanooga of a November 1863 Civil War battle.

look-see ▶ **n.** informal a brief look or inspection: *we are just about to take a little look-see around the hotel.*

look·up /'lo͝ok,əp/ ▶ **n.** Comput. systematic electronic information retrieval, or a facility for doing this.

look·y /'lo͝okē/ (also **look·ie**) ▶ **exclam.** informal used to draw attention to what one is about to say: *Looky there! You've gone and broken it.*

loom[1] /lo͞om/ ▶ **n.** an apparatus for making fabric by weaving yarn or thread. [OE *gelōma* 'tool.']

loom[1]

loom[2] ▶ **v.** appear as a shadowy form, esp. one that is large or threatening: *vehicles loomed out of the darkness.* ■ (of an event regarded as ominous or threatening) seem about to happen: *there is a crisis looming.* ▶ **n.** [in sing.] a vague and often exaggerated first appearance of an object seen in darkness or fog, esp. at sea: *the loom of the land.* [16th C.: prob. from Low Ger. or Du.; cf. East Frisian *lōmen* 'move slowly.']

loon[1] /lo͞on/ ▶ **n.** informal a silly or foolish person. [19th C.: from **LOON**[2].]

loon[2] ▶ **n.** a large diving waterbird (genus *Gavia*, family Gaviidae) with a straight pointed bill and short legs set far back under the body. Five species include the **common loon** (*G. immer*) of Canada and Eurasia. [17th C.: prob. by alt. of Shetland dial. *loom*, denoting esp. a guillemot or a diver, from ON.]

loon[2]

loon·ie /'lo͞onē/ ▶ **n.** (pl. **-ies**) Canadian, informal a Canadian one-dollar coin, introduced in 1987.

loon·y /'lo͞onē/ informal ▶ **n.** (pl. **loon·ies**) a crazy or silly person; a lunatic. ▶ **adj.** (**loon·i·er**, **loon·i·est**) crazy or silly: *loony drivers.* — **loon·i·ness n.** [19th C.: abbrev. of **LUNATIC**.]

loon·y bin ▶ **n.** informal, offens. a home or hospital for the mentally ill.

loop /lo͞op/ ▶ **n. 1** a shape produced by a curve that bends around and crosses itself. ■ a length of thread, rope, or similar material, doubled or crossing itself, typically used as a fastening or handle. ■ a curved stroke forming part of a letter (e.g., *b*, *p*). ■ (also **loop-the-loop**) a maneuver in which an aircraft describes a vertical circle in the air. ■ Skating a maneuver describing a curve that crosses itself, made on a single edge. ■ (**the Loop**) informal name for the commercial district in downtown Chicago. **2** a structure, series, or process the end of which is connected to the beginning. ■ an endless strip of tape or film allowing continuous repetition. ■ a complete circuit for an electric current. ■ Comput. a programmed sequence of instructions that is repeated until or while a particular condition is satisfied. ▶ **v.** [trans.] form (something) into a loop or loops; encircle: *she looped her arms around his neck.* ■ [intrans.] follow a course that forms a loop or loops: *the canal loops for two miles through the city.* ■ put into or execute a loop of tape, film, or computing instructions. ■ (also **loop the loop**) circle an aircraft vertically in the air.

– PHRASES **in** (or **out of**) **the loop** informal aware (or unaware) of information known to only a privileged few. **throw** (or **knock**) **someone for a loop** informal surprise or astonish someone; catch someone off guard. [ME: of unknown origin; cf. Scot. Gael. *lùb* 'loop, bend.']

loop·er /'lo͞opər/ ▶ **n. 1** another term for **INCHWORM**. **2** Baseball a blooper.

loop·hole /'lo͞op,(h)ōl/ ▶ **n. 1** an ambiguity or inadequacy in the law or a set of rules. **2** archaic an arrow slit in a wall. ▶ **v.** [trans.] make arrow slits in (a wall or building). [16th C. (denoting an arrow slit): from obs. *loop* 'embrasure' + **HOLE**.]

loop of Hen·le /'henlē/ ▶ **n.** Anat. the part of a kidney tubule that forms a long loop in the medulla of the kidney, from which water and salts are resorbed into the blood. [19th C.: named after Friedrich G. J. *Henle* (1809–85), Ger. anatomist.]

loop stitch ▶ **n.** a method of sewing or knitting in which each stitch incorporates a free loop of thread for ornament or to give a thick pile. — **loop-stitched adj. loop stitch·ing n.**

loop·y /'lo͞opē/ ▶ **adj.** (**loop·i·er**, **loop·i·est**) **1** informal crazy or silly. **2** having many loops. — **loop·i·ness n.**

loose /lo͞os/ ▶ **adj. 1** not firmly or tightly fixed in place; detached or able to be detached: *a loose tooth.* ■ not held or tied together; not packaged or placed in a container: *wear your hair loose.* ■ (of a person or animal) free from confinement; not bound or tethered: *the tethered horses* **broke loose**. ■ not strict or exact: *a loose interpretation.* ■ not close or compact in structure: *a loose weave* | fig. *a loose federation of industrial groups.* ■ typical of diarrhea: *loose bowel movements.* **2** (of a garment) not fitting tightly or closely. **3** relaxed; physically slack: *an easy, loose stride* | [in comb.] *a loose-limbed walk.* ■ careless and indiscreet in what is said: *there is too much loose talk about the situation.* ■ dated promiscuous; immoral: *a loose woman.* ■ (of the ball in a game) in play but not in any player's possession. ▶ **v.** [trans.] set free; release: *the hounds have been loosed.* ■ untie; unfasten: *the ropes were loosed.* ■ relax (one's grip): *he loosed his grip suddenly.*

– PHRASES **hang** (or **stay**) **loose** informal be relaxed; refrain from taking anything too seriously. **on the loose** having escaped from confinement: *a serial killer is on the loose.* — **loose·ly adv. loose·ness n.** [ME *loos* 'free from bonds,' from ON *lauss*, of Gmc. origin; rel. to Du. and Ger. *los*.]

loose can·non ▶ **n.** an unpredictable or uncontrolled person who is likely to cause unintentional damage.

loose con·struc·tion ▶ **n.** Law a broad interpretation of a statute or document by a court. — **loose con·struc·tion·ist n.**

loose end ▶ **n.** a detail not yet settled or explained.

– PHRASES **be at loose ends** have nothing specific to do.

loose-joint·ed ▶ **adj.** having or characterized by easy, free movement; limber. ■ having loose joints. ■ loosely built, badly put together.

loose-knit ▶ **adj.** knitted with large loose stitches. ■ connected in a tenuous or ill-defined way; not closely linked: *a loose-knit grouping of independent states.*

loose-leaf (also **loose·leaf**) ▶ **adj. 1** (of a notebook or folder) having each sheet of paper separate and removable. **2** (of lettuce) having leaves that overlap each other loosely rather than forming a compact head.

loos·en /'lo͞osən/ ▶ **v.** [trans.] make (something tied, fastened, or fixed in place) less tight or firm. ■ make more lax: *his main mistake was to loosen monetary policy.* ■ relax (one's grip or muscles): *he loosened his hold so she could pull free.* ■ [intrans.] become relaxed or less tight: *the stiffness in his shoulders had loosened.* ■ make (a connection or relationship) less strong: *he wanted to loosen union links.* ■ (with reference to the bowels) make or become relaxed before excretion: [intrans.] *his bowels loosened in terror.*

– PHRASES **loosen someone's tongue** make someone talk freely.

– PHRASAL VERBS **loosen up** warm up in preparation for an activity: *arrive early to loosen up and hit some practice shots.* ■ make or become relaxed: *they taught me to have fun at work and loosen up.* — **loos·en·er n.**

loose·strife /'lo͞o(s),strīf/ ▶ **n.** any of various tall plants that bear upright spikes of flowers, in particular **purple loosestrife** (*Lythrum salicaria*, family Lythraceae) and the yellow-flowered **garden loosestrife** (*Lysimachia vulgaris*) of the primrose family. [16th C.: from LOOSE + STRIFE, taking the Gk. name *lusimakheion* (actually from *Lusimakhos*, the name of its discoverer) to be directly from *luein* 'undo' + *makhē* 'battle.']

loos·ey-goos·ey /'lo͞osē 'go͞osē/ ▶ **adj.** informal not tense; relaxed and comfortable.

loot /lo͞ot/ ▶ **n.** goods, esp. private property, taken from an enemy in war. ■ stolen money or valuables. ■ informal money; wealth: *he left his wife plenty of loot.* ▶ **v.** [trans.] steal goods from (a place), typically during a war or riot: *rioters were looting shops.* ■ steal (goods) in such circumstances: *tons of food aid awaiting distribution had been looted.* — **loot·er** **n.** [19th C. (as a v.): from Hindi *lūṭ*, from Sanskrit *luṇṭh-* 'rob.']

lop[1] /läp/ ▶ **v.** **(lopped, lop·ping)** [trans.] cut off (a branch, limb, etc.) from the main body of a tree. ■ informal remove (something unnecessary or burdensome): *it lops an hour off commuting time.* ■ remove branches from (a tree). ▶ **n.** branches and twigs lopped off trees. [ME (as a n. denoting branches and twigs of trees).]

lop[2] ▶ **v.** **(lopped, lop·ping)** [intrans.] hang loosely or limply; droop: *a stomach that lopped over his belt.* ■ move in a loping or slouching way: *he lopped toward the plane.* [16th C.: prob. symbolic of limpness; cf. LOB.]

lope /lōp/ ▶ **v.** run or move with a long bounding stride: *the dog was loping along by his side.* ▶ **n.** [in sing.] a long bounding stride: *they set off at a fast lope.* [ME: var. of Scots *loup*, from ON *hlaupa* 'leap.']

lop-eared ▶ **adj.** (of an animal) having ears that droop down by the sides of the head: *a lop-eared mule.*

lopho- ▶ **comb. form** Zool. crested: *lophophore.* [from Gk. *lophos* 'crest.']

lo·phoph·o·rate /lə'fäfə,rāt; ,lōfə'fôr,āt/ Zool. ▶ **adj.** of or relating to small aquatic invertebrates belonging to a group of phyla characterized by the possession of lophophores. ▶ **n.** a lophophorate animal.

loph·o·phore /'läfə,fôr; 'lōfə-/ ▶ **n.** Zool. a horseshoe-shaped structure bearing ciliated tentacles around the mouth in certain small marine invertebrates.

Lop Nor /'lôp 'no͝or/ (also **Lop Nur**) a dried-up salt lake in northwestern China, used for nuclear testing.

lop·pers /'läpərz/ ▶ **plural n.** a cutting tool, esp. for pruning trees: *a good pair of loppers.*

lop·sid·ed /'läp,sīdid/ ▶ **adj.** with one side lower or smaller than the other: *a lopsided grin.* — **lop·sid·ed·ly** **adv.** **lop·sid·ed·ness** **n.**

loq. ▶ **abbr.** Latin loquitur.

lo·qua·cious /lō'kwāsHəs/ ▶ **adj.** talkative. — **lo·qua·cious·ly** **adv.** **lo·qua·cious·ness** **n.** **lo·quac·i·ty** /'kwasətē/ **n.** [17th C.: from L. *loquax, loquac-* (from *loqui* 'talk') + -IOUS.]

lo·quat /'lō,kwät/ ▶ **n.** **1** a small yellow egg-shaped acidic fruit. **2** the evergreen eastern Asian tree (*Eriobotrya japonica*) of the rose family that bears this fruit. [19th C.: from Chin. dial. *luh kwat* 'rush orange.']

lo·qui·tur /'läkwitər; 'lōkwi-/ (abbr.: **loq.**) ▶ **v.** (he or she) speaks (with the speaker's name following, as a stage direction or to inform the reader). [L., from *loqui* 'talk, speak.']

Lo·rain /lô'rān/ a city in north central Ohio; pop. 68,652.

lo·ran /'lôr,an/ (also **Lo·ran**) ▶ **n.** a system of long-distance navigation in which position is determined from the intervals between signal pulses received from widely spaced radio transmitters. [1940s: from *lo(ng-)ra(nge) n(avigation).*]

lor·az·e·pam /lô'razə,pam; -'räzə-/ ▶ **n.** Med. a drug of the benzodiazepine group, used esp. to treat anxiety. [1960s: from *(ch)lor(o-)* + *-azepam.*]

Lor·ca /'lôrkə/, Federico García (1898–1936), Spanish poet and playwright. His works include *Gypsy Ballads* (1928) and *The House of Bernarda Alba* (1936).

lord /lôrd/ ▶ **n.** (in the UK) a man of noble rank or high office; a peer. ■ **(Lord)** (in the UK) a title given formally to a baron, and less formally to a marquess, earl, or viscount (prefixed to a family or territorial name): *Lord Derby.* ■ **(the Lords)** (in the UK) the House of Lords, or its members collectively. ■ **(Lord)** (in the UK) a courtesy title given to a younger son of a duke or marquess (prefixed to a Christian name): *Lord John Russell.* ■ (in the UK) in compound titles of other people of authority: *Lord High Executioner.* ■ hist. a feudal superior, esp. the proprietor of a manor house. ■ a master or ruler: *our lord the king.* ■ **(Lord)** a name for God or Christ: *give thanks to the Lord.* ■ Astrol., dated the ruling planet of a sign, house, or chart. ▶ **exclam.** **(Lord)** used in exclamations expressing surprise or worry, or for emphasis: *Lord, I'm cold!* ▶ **v.** **1** [trans.] archaic confer the title of Lord upon. **2** **(lord it over)** act in a superior and domineering manner toward (someone).
– PHRASES **live like a lord** live sumptuously. **lord of the manor** the owner of a manor house (formerly the master of a feudal manor). **the Lord's Day** Sunday. **the Lord's Prayer** the prayer taught by Jesus to his disciples, beginning "Our Father." **the Lord's Supper** the Eucharist; Holy Communion (esp. in Protestant use). — **lord·less** **adj.** **lord·like** **adj.** [OE *hlāford*, from *hlāfweard* 'bread-keeper,' from a Gmc. base (see LOAF[1], WARD). Cf. LADY.]

Lord Chan·cel·lor (also **Lord High Chancellor**) ▶ **n.** (in the UK) the highest officer of the Crown, who presides in the House of Lords.

Lord Faunt·le·roy see FAUNTLEROY.

lord·ling /'lôrdliNG/ ▶ **n.** archaic, esp. derog. a minor lord.

lord·ly /'lôrdlē/ ▶ **adj.** **(lord·li·er, lord·li·est)** of, characteristic of, or suitable for a lord: *putting on lordly airs.* — **lord·li·ness** **n.**

lord may·or ▶ **n.** the title of the mayor in London and some other large British cities.

lor·do·sis /lôr'dōsis/ ▶ **n.** Med. excessive inward curvature of the spine. Compare with KYPHOSIS. ■ a posture assumed by some female mammals during mating, in which the back is arched downward. — **lor·dot·ic** /-'dätik/ **adj.** [18th C.: mod. L., from Gk. *lordōsis*, from *lordos* 'bent backward.']

Lord Pro·tec·tor ▶ **n.** see PROTECTOR (sense 3).

lord·ship /'lôrd,SHip/ ▶ **n.** **1** supreme power or rule: *his lordship over the other gods.* ■ archaic the authority or state of being a lord. ■ hist. a piece of land or territory belonging to or under the jurisdiction of a lord. **2** **(His/Your, etc., Lordship)** in the UK, a respectful form of reference or address to a judge, a bishop, or a man with a title: *if Your Lordship pleases.*

Lords spir·it·u·al ▶ **plural n.** the bishops in the House of Lords.

Lords tem·po·ral ▶ **plural n.** the members of the House of Lords other than the bishops.

Lord·y /'lôrdē/ ▶ **exclam.** informal used to express surprise or dismay: *Lordy! Whatever happened?*

lore[1] /lôr/ ▶ **n.** a body of traditions and knowledge on a subject or held by a particular group, typically passed from person to person by word of mouth: *the jinns of Arabian lore* | *baseball lore.* [OE *lār* 'instruction,' of Gmc. origin: rel. to Du. *leer*, Ger. *Lehre*, also to LEARN.]

lore[2] ▶ **n.** Zool. the surface on each side of a bird's head between the eye and the upper base of the beak, or between the eye and nostril in snakes. [19th C.: from L. *lorum* 'strap.']

Lorelei /'lôrə,lī/ a rock on the bank of the Rhine, held by legend to be the home of a siren whose song lures boatmen to destruction. ■ the siren said to live on this rock.

Lo·rentz /'lôrənts/, Hendrik Antoon (1853–1928), Dutch physicist. He realized that electrons and cathode rays were the same thing. Nobel Prize for Physics (1902, shared with Pieter Zeeman 1865–1943).

Lo·rentz trans·for·ma·tion ▶ **n.** Physics the set of equations that, in Einstein's special theory of relativity, relate the space and time coordinates of one frame of reference to those of another.

Lo·renz /'lôrənz; -rents/, Konrad Zacharias (1903–89), Austrian zoologist. He pioneered the science of ethology. Nobel Prize for Physiology or Medicine (1973), shared with Karl von Frisch and Nikolaas Tinbergen.

Lo·renz curve ▶ **n.** Econ. a graph on which the cumulative percentage of total national income is plotted against the cumulative percentage of the corresponding population. The extent to which the curve sags below a straight diagonal line indicates the degree of inequality of distribution. [20th C.: named after Max O. *Lorenz* (born 1876), the Amer. statistician who devised the curve.]

Lo·ren·zo de' Me·di·ci /lə'renzō də 'mediCHē; lô'rentsō/ (1449–92), Italian statesman and scholar. He was noted as a patron of the arts.

lo-res /'lō 'rez/ ▶ **adj.** var. of LOW-RES.

lor·gnette /lôrn'yet/ (also **lor·gnettes**) ▶ **n.** a pair of glasses or opera glasses held by a long handle at one side. [19th C.: from Fr., from *lorgner* 'to squint.']

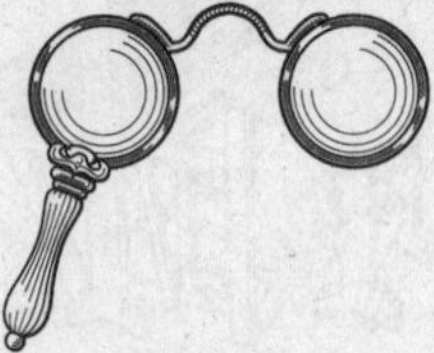

lorgnette

lo·ri·ca /lə'rīkə/ ▶ **n.** (pl. **-cae** /-,kē; -,sē/ or **-cas**) **1** hist. a Roman corselet or cuirass of leather. **2** Zool. the rigid case or shell of some rotifers and protozoans. [L., 'breastplate.']

lor·i·cate /'lôrə,kāt; -kit; 'lär-/ ▶ **adj.** Zool. (of an animal) having a protective covering of plates or scales. ■ having a lorica.

lor·i·keet /'lôrə,kēt; 'lär-/ ▶ **n.** a small bird (*Charmosyna* and other genera) of the lory family, found chiefly in New Guinea. [18th C.: dimin. of LORY, on the pattern of *parakeet.*]

lo·ris /'lôris/ ▶ **n.** (pl. **-ris·es**) a small, slow-moving nocturnal primate (family Lorisidae) with a short or absent tail, living in dense vegetation in South Asia. Its two genera are *Loris* **(slender loris)** and *Nycticebus* **(slow loris)**. [18th C.: from Fr., perh. from obs. Du. *loeris* 'clown.']

lorn /lôrn/ ▶ **adj.** literary lonely and abandoned; forlorn. [ME: past part. of obs. *lese* from OE *lēosan* 'lose.']

Lor·rain, Claude see CLAUDE LORRAINE.

Lor·raine /lə'rān; lô'ren/ a region in northeastern France.

Lor·raine cross ▶ **n.** a cross with one vertical and two horizontal bars. It was the symbol of Joan of Arc, and in World War II it was adopted by the Free French forces of General de Gaulle.

lor·ry /'lôrē; 'lärē/ ▶ **n.** (pl. **-ries**) Brit. a large, heavy motor vehicle for transporting goods or troops; a truck. [19th C.: perh. from the given name *Laurie.*]

lo·ry /'lôrē/ ▶ **n.** (pl. **-ries**) a small Australasian and Southeast Asian parrot (family Loridae, or Psittacidae) with a brush-tipped tongue for feeding on nectar and pollen, having mainly green plumage with patches of bright color. [17th C.: from Malay *lūrī*.]

LOS ▶ **abbr.** ■ law of the sea. ■ length of stay. ■ line of scrimmage. ■ line of sight. ■ loss of signal.

Los Al·a·mos /lôs 'alə,mōs; läs/ a town in northern New Mexico, a nuclear research center; pop. 11,455.

Los An·ge·le·no /lôs ,anjə'lēnō; läs/ ▶ **n.** variant of ANGELENO.

Los An·ge·les /lôs 'anjələs; läs; -,lēz/ a city in southern California; pop. 3,694,820.

lose /lo͞oz/ ▶ **v.** (past and past part. **lost**) [trans.] **1** be deprived of or cease to have or retain (something): *I've lost my appetite.* ■ cause (someone) to fail to gain or retain (something): *you lost me my appointment at the university.* ■ be deprived of (a close relative or friend) through their death or as a result of the breaking off of a relationship: *she lost her husband in the fire.* ■ (of a pregnant woman) miscarry (a baby) or suffer the death of (a baby) during childbirth. ■ (**be lost**) be destroyed or killed, esp. through accident or as a result of military action: *a fishing disaster in which 19 local men were lost.* ■ decrease in (body weight); undergo a reduction of (a specified amount of weight). ■ waste or fail to take advantage of (time or an opportunity). ■ (of a watch or clock) become slow by (a specified amount of time): *this clock will neither gain nor lose a second.* ■ (**lose it**) informal lose control of one's temper or emotions: *I completely lost it—I was screaming at them.* **2** become unable to find (something or someone): *I've lost the car keys.* ■ cease or become unable to follow (the right route): *we lost the path.* ■ evade or shake off (a pursuer): *he came after me, but I easily lost him.* ■ informal get rid of (an undesirable person or thing): *lose that creep!* ■ informal cause (someone) to be unable to follow an argument or explanation: *Tim, you've lost me there.* ■ (**lose oneself in**/**be lost in**) be or become deeply absorbed in (something): *lost in thought.* **3** fail to win (a game or contest): *the Bears lost the final game of the series* | [intrans.] *they lost by one vote.* ■ [with two objs.] cause (someone) to fail to win (a game or contest): *that shot lost him the championship.* **4** earn less (money) than one is spending or has spent: *the paper is losing $500,000 a month* | [intrans.] *he lost heavily on box-office flops.*

– PHRASES **lose face** come to be less highly respected. **lose heart** become discouraged. **lose one's heart to** see HEART. **lose one's mind** (or **one's marbles**) informal go insane. **lose sleep** [usu. with negative] worry about something: *no one is losing any sleep over what he thinks of us.* **lose one's** (or **the**) **way** become lost; fail to reach one's destination. ■ fig. no longer have a clear idea of one's purpose or motivation in an activity or business: *the company has lost its way and should pull out of general insurance.*

– PHRASAL VERBS **lose out** be deprived of an opportunity to do or obtain something; be disadvantaged: *youngsters who were* ***losing out*** *on regular schooling.* ■ be beaten in competition or replaced by: *they were disappointed at losing out to Chicago in the playoffs.* [OE *losian* 'perish, destroy,' also 'become unable to find,' from *los* 'loss.']

lo·sel /'lōzəl/ archaic dialect ▶ **n.** a worthless person. ▶ **adj.** good-for-nothing; worthless. [ME: appar. from *los-*, stem of obs. *lese* 'lose,' + -EL.]

los·er /'lo͞ozər/ ▶ **n.** a person or thing that loses or has lost something, esp. a game or contest. ■ [with adj.] a person who accepts defeat with good or bad grace, as specified: *they should concede that and be good losers.* ■ a person or thing that is put at a disadvantage by a particular situation or course of action: *children are the losers when politicians keep fiddling around with education.* ■ informal a person who fails frequently or is generally unsuccessful in life.

los·ing bat·tle ▶ **n.** [in sing.] a struggle that seems certain to end in failure.

los·ing·est /'lo͞oziNGist/ ▶ **adj.** informal losing more often than others of its kind; least successful.

loss /lôs; läs/ ▶ **n.** the fact or process of losing something or someone: *avoiding loss of time.* ■ the state or feeling of grief when deprived of someone or something of value: *a terrible sense of loss.* ■ the detriment or disadvantage resulting from losing: *his fall from power was no loss to the world.* ■ [in sing.] a person or thing that is badly missed when lost: *he will be a great loss to many people.* ■ Physics a reduction of power within or among circuits, measured as a ratio of power input to power output.

– PHRASES **at a loss 1** puzzled or uncertain what to think, say, or do. **2** making less money than is spent buying, operating, or producing something: *a railroad running at a loss.* [OE *los* 'destruction,' of Gmc. origin; rel. to LOOSE.]

loss-lead·er ▶ **n.** a product sold at a loss to attract customers.

loss·less /'lôsləs; 'läs-/ ▶ **adj.** having or involving no dissipation of electrical or electromagnetic energy. ■ Comput. of or relating to data compression without loss of information.

loss ra·tio ▶ **n.** the ratio of the claims paid by an insurer to the premiums earned, usually for a one-year period.

loss·y /'lôsē; 'läsē/ ▶ **adj.** having or involving the dissipation of electrical or electromagnetic energy. ■ Comput. of or relating to data compression in which unnecessary information is discarded.

lost /lôst; läst/ past and past participle of LOSE. ▶ **adj. 1** unable to find one's way; not knowing one's whereabouts: *they got lost in the fog.* ■ unable to be found: *he turned up with my lost golf clubs.* ■ [predic.] (of a person) very confused or insecure or in great difficulties: *I'd be lost without her.* **2** denoting something that has been taken away or cannot be recovered: *lost youth!* ■ (of time or an opportunity) not used advantageously; wasted. ■ having perished or been destroyed: *a memorial to the lost crewmen.* **3** (of a game or contest) in which a defeat has been sustained: *the lost election of 1994.*

– PHRASES **be lost for words** be so surprised, confused, or upset that one cannot think what to say. **be lost on** fail to influence or be noticed or appreciated by (someone): *the significance of his remarks was not lost on Scott.* **get lost** [often in imper.] informal go away (used as an expression of anger or impatience). **give someone up for lost** stop expecting that a missing person will be found alive. **make up for lost time** do something faster or more often in order to compensate for not having done it quickly or often enough before.

lost-and-found ▶ **n.** a place where lost items are kept to await reclaiming by their owners.

lost cause ▶ **n.** a person or thing that can no longer hope to succeed or be changed for the better. ■ (**the Lost Cause**) the Confederacy and its defeat in the Civil War.

lost gen·er·a·tion ▶ **n.** the generation reaching maturity during and just after World War I, a high proportion of whose men were killed during those years. ■ an unfulfilled generation coming to maturity during a period of instability.

Lost Tribes (also **Ten Lost Tribes of Israel**) the ten tribes of Israel taken to captivity in Assyria *c.*720 BC (2 Kings 17:6).

lost wax ▶ **n.** a method of bronze casting using a clay core and a wax coating placed in a mold. The wax is melted and drained out, and bronze poured into the space left, producing a hollow bronze figure when the core is discarded.

Lot[1] /lät/ a river in southern France that flows 300 miles (480 km) west to meet the Garonne River.

Lot[2] (in the Bible) the nephew of Abraham, who escaped the destruction of Sodom. His wife, who looked back, became a pillar of salt.

lot /lät/ ▶ **pron.** (**a lot** or **lots**) informal a large number or amount; a great deal: *there are* ***a lot of*** *actors in the cast* | *we had* ***lots of*** *fun.* ■ (**the lot** or **the whole lot**) the whole number or quantity that is involved or implied: *you might as well take the whole lot.* ▶ **adv.** (**a lot** or **lots**) informal a great deal; much: *my life is a lot better now.* ▶ **n. 1** [treated as sing. or pl.] informal a particular group, collection, or set of people or things: *it's just one lot of rich people stealing from another.* ■ esp. Brit. a group or a person of a particular kind (generally used in a derogatory or dismissive way): *an inefficient lot, our town council* | *you lot think you're clever, don't you?* **2** an article or set of articles for sale at an auction: *nineteen lots failed to sell.* **3** one of a set of objects such as straws, stones, or pieces of paper that are randomly selected as part of a decision-making process: *they* ***drew lots*** *to determine the order in which they asked questions.* ■ the making of a decision by such random selection. ■ [in sing.] the choice resulting from such a process. **4** [in sing.] a person's luck or condition in life, particularly as determined by fate or destiny: *plans to improve the lot of the disadvantaged.* **5** a plot of land assigned for sale or for a particular use. ■ short for PARKING LOT. ■ an area of land near a television or movie studio where outside filming may be done. ■ the area at a car dealership where cars for sale are kept. ▶ **v.** (**lot·ted**, **lot·ting**) [trans.] divide (items) into lots for sale at an auction: *the contents have already been lotted up, and the auction takes place on Monday.*

– PHRASES **all over the lot** informal in a state of confusion or disorganization. **fall to someone's lot** become someone's task or responsibility. **throw in one's lot with** decide to ally oneself closely with and share the fate of (a person or group). [OE *hlot* (n.), of Gmc. origin; rel. to Ger. *Los.*]

lo·ta /'lōtə/ ▶ **n.** Indian a round water pot, typically of polished brass. [from Hindi *loṭā*.]

lo-tech ▶ **adj.** & **n.** var. of LOW-TECH.

loth ▶ **adj.** var. of LOATH.

Lo·thar·i·o /lō'THe(ə)rē,ō; -'THär-/ ▶ **n.** (pl. **-i·os**) a man who behaves selfishly and irresponsibly in his sexual relationships with women. [from a character in Rowe's *Fair Penitent* (1703).]

lo·ti /'lōtē/ ▶ **n.** (pl. **ma·lo·ti** /mə'lōtē/) the basic monetary unit of Lesotho, equal to 100 lisente.

lo·tic /'lōtik/ ▶ **adj.** Ecol. (of organisms or habitats) inhabiting or situated in rapidly moving fresh water. Compare with LENTIC. [20th C.: from L. *lotus* 'washing' + -IC.]

lo·tion /'lōSHən/ ▶ **n.** a thick, smooth liquid preparation applied to the skin for medicinal or cosmetic purposes. [ME: from OFr., or from L. *lotio(n-)*, from *lot-* 'washed,' from the v. *lavare*.]

lot·ta /'lätə/ informal (also **lot·sa** /'lätsə/) ▶ **contr.** lots of (representing nonstandard use): *I saw a lotta courage out there.*

lot·ter·y /'lätərē/ ▶ **n.** (pl. **-ter·ies**) a means of raising money by selling numbered tickets and giving prizes to the holders of numbers drawn at random. ■ [in sing.] a process or thing whose success or outcome is governed by chance: *the lottery of life.* [16th C.: prob. from Du. *loterij*, from *lot* 'lot.']

lot·to /'lätō/ ▶ **n.** a lottery game similar to bingo. [18th C.: from Ital.]

lo·tus /'lōtəs/ ▶ **n. 1** any of a number of large water lilies, in particular: ■ (also **sacred lotus**) a water lily (*Nelumbo nucifera*, family Nelumbonaceae) of Asia and northern Australia, typically with dark pink or white-and-pink flowers. ■ (also **American lotus**) a yellow-flowered North American water lily (*Nelumbo lutea*, family Nelumbonaceae) with bowl-shaped leaves. ■ (also **Egyptian lotus**) a water lily (the white-flowered *Nymphaea lotus* and the blue-flowered *N. caerulea*, family Nymphaeaceae) regarded as sacred in ancient Egypt. **2** (in Greek mythology) a legendary plant whose fruit induces a dreamy forgetfulness and an unwillingness to depart. ■ the flower of the sacred lotus as a symbol in Asian art and religion. ■ short for LOTUS POSITION. [15th C.: via L. from Gk. *lōtos*, of Semitic origin.]

lo·tus-eat·er ▶ n. a person who spends time indulging in pleasure and luxury rather than dealing with practical concerns. — **lo·tus-eat·ing** adj. [19th C.: from the people in Homer's *Odyssey* who lived on the fruit of the lotus.]

lo·tus·land /ˈlōtəs,land/ ▶ n. a place or state concerned solely with, or providing, idle pleasure and luxury: *a lush lotusland where you can shed your inhibitions.*

lo·tus po·si·tion ▶ n. a cross-legged position for meditation, with the feet resting on the thighs.

louche /lo͞osн/ ▶ adj. disreputable or sordid in a rakish or appealing way: *the louche world of the theater.* [19th C.: from Fr., lit. 'squinting.']

loud /loud/ ▶ adj. producing or capable of producing much noise; easily audible. ■ strong or emphatic in expression: *there were loud protests from the lumber barons.* ■ vulgarly obtrusive; flashy: *a man in a loud checked suit.* ■ (of smell or flavor) powerful or offensive. ▶ adv. with a great deal of volume: *they shouted as loud as they could.*
– PHRASES **out loud** aloud; audibly. — **loud·en** /ˈloudn/ v. **loud·ly** adv. **loud·ness** n. [OE *hlūd*; rel. to Ger. *laut*, from an Indo-Eur. root shared by Gk. *kluein* 'hear.']

loud-hail·er (also **loud·hail·er**) ▶ n. esp. Brit. another term for BULLHORN

loud·mouth /ˈloud,mouтн/ ▶ n. informal a person who tends to talk too much in an offensive or tactless way. — **loud·mouthed** /ˈloud,mouтнd; -,mouтнt/ (also **loud-mouthed**) adj.

loud·speak·er /ˈloud,spēkər/ ▶ n. an apparatus that converts electrical impulses into sound, typically as part of a public address system or stereo equipment.

Lou Gehr·ig's dis·ease /,lo͞o ˈgerigz/ ▶ n. another term for AMYOTROPHIC LATERAL SCLEROSIS. [1940s: named after H. L. GEHRIG, who died from it.]

lough ▶ n. Anglo-Irish spelling of LOCH. [ME: from Irish *loch*.]

Lou·is[1] /ˈlo͞o-ē; lwē/ the name of 18 kings of France: ■ Louis I (778–840), king of the West Franks and Holy Roman Emperor 814–40; son of Charlemagne. ■ Louis II (846–879), reigned 877–879. ■ Louis III (863–882), reigned 879–882; son of Louis II. ■ Louis IV (921–954), reigned 936–954. ■ Louis V (967–987), reigned 979–987. ■ Louis VI (1081–1137), reigned 1108–37. ■ Louis VII (1120–80), reigned 1137–80. ■ Louis VIII (1187–1226), reigned 1223–26. ■ Louis IX (1214–70), reigned 1226–70; son of Louis VIII; canonized as **St. Louis**. ■ Louis X (1289–1316), reigned 1314–16. ■ Louis XI (1423–83), reigned 1461–83; son of Charles VII. ■ Louis XII (1462–1515), reigned 1498–1515. ■ Louis XIII (1601–43), reigned 1610–43; son of Henry IV of France. ■ Louis XIV (1638–1715), reigned 1643–1715; son of Louis XIII; known as **the Sun King**. ■ Louis XV (1710–74), reigned 1715–74; great-grandson and successor of Louis XIV. ■ Louis XVI (1754–93), reigned 1774–92; grandson and successor of Louis XV. ■ Louis XVII (1785–95), son of Louis XVI; titular king who died in prison during the revolution. ■ Louis XVIII (1755–1824), reigned 1814–24; brother of Louis XVI.

Lou·is[2] /ˈlo͞o-is/, Joe (1914–81), US boxer; born *Joseph Louis Barrow*; known as the **Brown Bomber**. He was heavyweight champion of the world 1937–49.

lou·is /ˈlo͞o-ē/ (also **louis d'or** /dôr/) ▶ n. (pl. same) a gold coin issued in France between 1640 and 1793. ■ another term for NAPOLEON (sense 2). [from *Louis*, the name of many kings of France.]

Lou·is I /ˈlo͞o-is; ˈlo͞o-ē/ (1326–82), king of Hungary 1342–82 and of Poland 1370–82; known as **Louis the Great**.

Lou·is, St., Louis IX of France (see LOUIS[1]).

Lou·i·si·an·a /lo͞o,ēzēˈanə/ a state in the southern US, on the Gulf of Mexico; pop. 4,468,976; capital, Baton Rouge; statehood, Apr. 30, 1812 (18). It was sold by the French to the US as part of the Louisiana Purchase in 1803. — **Lou·i·si·an·an** (also **Lou·i·si·an·i·an** /-nēən/) adj. & n.

Lou·i·si·an·a French ▶ n. French as spoken in Louisiana, esp. by the descendants of the original French settlers; Cajun.

Lou·i·si·an·a Pur·chase the territory sold by France to the US in 1803, comprising the western part of the Mississippi valley.

Lou·is Phi·lippe /ˈlo͞o-ē fēˈlēp/ (1773–1850), king of France 1830–48. After the restoration of the Bourbons, he was made king, replacing Charles X.

Lou·is the Great, Louis I of Hungary (see LOUIS I).

Lou·is·ville /ˈlo͞oē,vil; ˈlo͞owəvəl/ a city in northern Kentucky, site of the Kentucky Derby; pop. 256,231.

lounge /lounj/ ▶ v. [intrans.] lie, sit, or stand in a relaxed or lazy way: *students were lounging about reading papers.* ▶ n. **1** a public room, as in a hotel, theater, or club, in which to sit and relax. ■ a spacious area in an airport with seats for waiting passengers. ■ short for COCKTAIL LOUNGE. **2** a couch or sofa, esp. a backless one having a headrest at one end. ■ esp. Brit. another term for CHAISE LONGUE.

lounge·core /ˈlounj,kôr/ ▶ n. songs from the 1960s and 1970s, including easy listening music, orchestral versions of rock songs, and television or movie theme songs.

lounge liz·ard ▶ n. informal an idle person, usually a man, who spends time in lounges and nightclubs.

loung·er /ˈlounjər/ ▶ n. a person spending time lazily or in a relaxed way.

lounge·wear /ˈlounj,we(ə)r/ ▶ n. clothing suitable for leisure activities.

loupe /lo͞op/ ▶ n. a small magnifying glass used by jewelers and watchmakers. [19th C.: from Fr.]

lour ▶ v. & n. var. of LOWER[3].

Lourdes /lo͝ord(z)/ a town in southwestern France, the site where Marie Bernarde Soubirous (St. Bernadette) claimed to have had a series of visions of the Virgin Mary.

Lou·ren·ço Mar·ques /ləˈrensō ,märˈkes/ former name, until 1976, of MAPUTO.

louse /lous/ ▶ n. **1** (pl. **lice** /līs/) a small, wingless, parasitic insect that lives on the skin of mammals and birds. ■ (**sucking louse**) an insect with piercing mouthparts, found only on mammals (order Anoplura, or Siphunculata). See illustration at BODY LOUSE. ■ (**biting louse**) an insect with a large head and jaws, found chiefly on birds (order Mallophaga). **2** (pl. **lous·es**) informal a contemptible or unpleasant person. ▶ v. /lous; louz/ [trans.] **1** (**louse something up**) informal spoil or ruin something. **2** archaic remove lice from. [OE *lūs*, (pl.) *lȳs*, of Gmc. origin; rel. to Du. *luis*, Ger. *Laus*.]

louse fly ▶ n. a flattened bloodsucking fly (family Hippoboscidae) that may have reduced or absent wings and typically spends much of its life on one individual of the host species.

louse·wort /ˈlous,wərt; -,wôrt/ ▶ n. a partially parasitic herbaceous plant (genus *Pedicularis*) of the figwort family, typically favoring damp habitats and formerly reputed to harbor lice.

lous·y /ˈlouzē/ ▶ adj. (**lous·i·er**, **lous·i·est**) **1** informal very poor or bad; disgusting: *lousy weather.* ■ [predic.] ill; in poor physical condition: *she felt lousy.* **2** infested with lice. ■ [predic.] (**lousy with**) informal teeming with (something regarded as bad or undesirable): *the town is lousy with tourists.* — **lous·i·ly** adv. **lous·i·ness** n.

lout /lout/ ▶ n. an uncouth or aggressive man or boy: *drunken louts.* — **lout·ish** adj. **lout·ish·ly** adv. **lout·ish·ness** n. [16th C.: perh. from archaic *lout* 'to bow down,' of Gmc. origin.]

Louth /louтн; louтн/ a county of the Republic of Ireland; county town, Dundalk.

lou·ver /ˈlo͞ovər/ (also **lou·vre**) ▶ n. **1** each of a set of angled slats or flat strips fixed or hung at regular intervals in a door, shutter, or screen to allow air or light to pass through. **2** a domed structure on a roof, with side openings for ventilation. — **lou·vered** adj. [ME (sense 2): from OFr. *lover, lovier* 'skylight,' prob. of Gmc. origin and rel. to LODGE.]

Louvre /ˈlo͞ov(rə)/ the principal museum and art gallery of France, in Paris.

lov·a·ble /ˈləvəbəl/ (also **love·a·ble**) ▶ adj. inspiring or deserving love or affection. — **lov·a·bil·i·ty** /,ləvəˈbilətē/ n. **lov·a·ble·ness** n. **lov·a·bly** adv.

lov·age /ˈləvij/ ▶ n. a large, edible, white-flowered plant (esp. *Levisticum officinale*) of the parsley family. [ME *loveache*, alt. of OFr. *luvesche, levesche*, via late L. *levisticum* from L. *ligusticum*, neut. of *ligusticus* 'Ligurian.']

lov·at /ˈləvət/ ▶ n. a muted green color used esp. in tweed and woolen garments. [20th C.: from *Lovat*, a place name in Highland Scotland.]

love /ləv/ ▶ n. **1** an intense feeling of deep affection: *their love for their country.* ■ a deep romantic or sexual attachment to someone: *it was love at first sight.* ■ (**Love**) a personified figure of love, often represented as Cupid. ■ a great interest and pleasure in something: *his love for football.* ■ affectionate greetings conveyed to someone on one's behalf. ■ a formula for ending an affectionate letter: *take care, lots of love, Judy.* **2** a person or thing that one loves: *she was the love of his life.* ■ Brit., informal a friendly form of address: *it's all right, love.* ■ (**a love**) Brit., informal used to express affectionate approval for someone: *don't fret, there's a love.* **3** (in tennis, squash, and some other sports) a score of zero; nil. ▶ v. [trans.] feel a deep romantic or sexual attachment to (someone): *do you love me?* ■ like very much; find pleasure in: *I'd love a cup of tea* | [as adj., in comb.] (**-loving**) *a fun-loving girl.*
– PHRASES **for love** for pleasure, not profit: *he played for the love of the game.* **make love 1** have sexual intercourse. **2** (**make love to**) dated pay amorous attention to (someone). **not for love or money** informal not for any inducement or in any circumstances. — **love·less** adj. **love·less·ly** adv. **love·less·ness** n. **love·wor·thy** adj. [OE *lufu*, from an Indo-Eur. root shared by L. *libido* 'desire,' also by LEAVE[2] and LIEF.]

love·a·ble /ˈləvəbəl/ ▶ adj. var. of LOVABLE.

love af·fair ▶ n. a romantic or sexual relationship between two people, esp. one that is outside marriage. ■ an intense enthusiasm or liking for something: *the great American love affair with the automobile.*

love ap·ple ▶ n. an old-fashioned term for a tomato.

love beads ▶ n. a necklace of small beads, esp. as worn by hippies in the 1960s as a symbol of peace and goodwill.

love·bird /ˈləv,bərd/ ▶ n. **1** a very small African and Madagascan parrot (genus *Agapornis*) with mainly green plumage and typically a red or black face, noted for the affectionate behavior of mated birds. **2** (**lovebirds**) informal an openly affectionate couple.

love bite ▶ n. a temporary red mark on a person's skin caused by a lover biting or sucking it as a sexual act; a hickey.

Love Canal /ləv/ a section of Niagara Falls in New York that was evacuated after 1970s exposure that chemical wastes were buried here.

love child ▶ n. a child born to parents who are not married to each other.

love feast ▶ n. hist. a feast in token of fellowship among early Christians; an agape. ■ a religious service or gathering imitating this.

love game ▶ n. (in tennis and similar sports) a game in which the loser makes no score.

love han·dles ▶ plural n. informal deposits of excess fat at a person's waistline.

love-hate ▶ adj. [attrib.] (of a relationship) characterized by ambivalent feelings of love and hate.

love-in ▶ n. informal, dated a gathering at which people express feelings of friendship and physical attraction, associated with the hippies of the 1960s.

love-in-a-mist ▶ n. a Mediterranean plant (*Nigella damascena*) of the buttercup family that bears blue flowers surrounded by delicate threadlike green bracts, giving a hazy appearance to the flowers.

love-in-i·dle·ness ▶ n. another term for HEARTSEASE.

love in·ter·est ▶ n. a theme or subsidiary plot in a story or film in which the main element is the affection of lovers. ■ an actor whose role is chiefly concerned with this.

Love·lace /ˈləvlās/, Richard (1618–57), English poet. A Royalist, he was imprisoned in 1642, when he probably wrote "To Althea, from Prison."

Love·land /ˈləvlənd/ a city in north central Colorado; pop. 50,608.

love-lies-bleed·ing ▶ n. a South American plant (*Amaranthus caudatus*) of the amaranth family, with long, drooping tassels of crimson flowers. Cultivated today as an ornamental, it was formerly an important cereal-type crop in the Andes.

love life ▶ n. the area of a person's life concerning their relationships with lovers.

Love·lock /ˈləvläk; -lək/, James (Ephraim) (1919–), English scientist. He is noted for the Gaia hypothesis.

love·lock /ˈləvˌläk/ ▶ n. archaic a curl of hair worn on the temple or forehead.

love·lorn /ˈləvˌlôrn/ ▶ adj. unhappy because of unrequited love.

love·ly /ˈləvlē/ ▶ adj. (**-li·er, -li·est**) exquisitely beautiful. ■ informal very pleasant or enjoyable; delightful. ▶ n. (pl. **-lies**) informal a glamorous woman or girl. — **love·li·ly** adv. **love·li·ness** n.

love·mak·ing /ˈləvˌmākiNG/ ▶ n. sexual activity between lovers, esp. sexual intercourse. ■ archaic courtship.

love match ▶ n. a marriage based on mutual love rather than social or financial considerations.

love nest ▶ n. informal a place where two lovers spend time together, esp. in secret.

lov·er /ˈləvər/ ▶ n. a person having a sexual or romantic relationship with someone, esp. outside marriage. ■ a person who likes or enjoys something specified: *he was a great lover of cats* | *music lovers.* — **lov·er·less** adj.

love seat ▶ n. a small sofa for two people. ■ a small sofa for two people, designed in an S-shape so that the couple can face each other

love·sick /ˈləvˌsik/ ▶ adj. in love, or missing the person one loves, so much that one is unable to act normally. — **love·sick·ness** n.

love·some /ˈləvsəm/ ▶ adj. literary lovely or lovable.

love·y-dove·y /ˈləvē ˈdəvē/ ▶ adj. informal very affectionate or romantic, esp. excessively so.

lov·ing /ˈləviNG/ ▶ adj. feeling or showing love or great care. ▶ n. the demonstration of love or great care. — **lov·ing·ly** adv. **lov·ing·ness** n.

lov·ing cup ▶ n. a large two-handled cup, passed around at banquets for each guest to drink from in turn.

lov·ing·kind·ness /ˌləviNGˈkīn(d)nis/ ▶ n. tenderness and consideration toward others.

Low /lō/, Juliette Gordon (1860–1927), founder of the Girl Scouts of America in 1912.

low[1] /lō/ ▶ adj. **1** of less than average height from top to bottom or to the top from the ground: *a low table.* ■ situated not far above the ground, the horizon, or sea level: *the sun was low in the sky.* ■ located at or near the bottom of something: *low back pain.* ■ Baseball (of a pitched ball) below the strike zone. ■ (of a river or lake) below the usual water level; shallow. ■ (of latitude) near the equator. ■ (of women's clothing) cut so as to reveal the neck and the upper part of the breasts. ■ Phonet. (of a vowel) pronounced with the tongue held low in the mouth; open. ■ (of a sound or note) deep: *his low, husky voice.* **2** below average in amount, extent, or intensity; small: *shops with low levels of service* | *cook over low heat.* ■ (of a substance or food) containing smaller quantities than usual of a specified ingredient: *vegetables are* ***low in*** *calories* | [in comb.] *low-fat spreads.* ■ (of a supply) small or reduced in quantity: *food was* ***running low.*** ■ having a small or reduced quantity of a supply: *they were* ***low on*** *fuel.* ■ (of a sound) not loud: *they were told to keep the volume very low.* **3** ranking below other people or things in importance or class: *jobs with low status.* ■ (of art or culture) considered to be inferior in quality and refinement: *the dual traditions of high and low art.* ■ less good than is expected or desired; inferior: *the standard of living is low.* ■ unscrupulous or dishonest: *low tricks.* ■ (of an opinion) unfavorable. **4** [predic.] depressed or lacking in energy: *I was feeling low.* ▶ n. a low point, level or figure: *his popularity ratings are at an all-time low.* ■ a particularly bad or difficult moment: *the highs and lows of an actor's life.* ■ informal a state of depression or low spirits. ■ an area of low atmospheric pressure; a depression. ▶ adv. **1** in or into a low position or state: *she pressed on, bent low to protect her face.* **2** quietly: *we were talking low so we wouldn't wake Dean.* ■ at or to a low pitch: *the sopranos have to sing rather low.*
– PHRASES **the lowest of the low** the people regarded as the most immoral or socially inferior of all. — **low·ness** n. [ME: from ON *lágr*, of Gmc. origin; rel. to Du. *laag*, also to LIE[1].]

low[2] ▶ v. [intrans.] (of a cow) make a characteristic deep sound: [as n.] (**lowing**) *the lowing of cattle.* ▶ n. a sound made by cattle; a moo. [OE *hlōwan*, of Gmc. origin; rel. to Du. *loeien*.]

low·ball /ˈlōˌbôl/ ▶ adj. informal (of an estimate, bid, etc.) deceptively or unrealistically low. ▶ v. [trans.] offer a deceptively or unrealistically low estimate, bid, etc. — **low·ball·ing** n.

low beam ▶ n. an automobile headlight providing short-range illumination.

low blow ▶ n. Boxing an illegal blow that strikes below an opponent's waist. ■ fig. an unfair or unsportsmanlike comment.

low-born ▶ adj. born to a family that has a low social status.

low·boy /ˈlōˌboi/ ▶ n. a low chest or table with drawers and short legs. Compare with HIGHBOY.

low·bred /ˈlōˈbred/ ▶ adj. characterized by coarse behavior or vulgar breeding.

low·brow /ˈlōˌbrou/ ▶ adj. not highly intellectual or cultured: *lowbrow tabloids.* ▶ n. a person of such a type.

Low Church ▶ adj. of or adhering to a tradition within the Anglican Church that gives relatively little emphasis to ritual, sacraments, and the authority of the clergy. Compare with HIGH CHURCH, BROAD CHURCH. ▶ n. [treated as sing. or pl.] the principles or adherents of this tradition. — **Low Church·man** n. (pl. **-men**).

low-class ▶ adj. of a low or inferior standard, quality, or social class: *low-class places of amusement.*

low com·e·dy ▶ n. comedy in which the subject and the treatment border on farce.

Low Coun·tries the region of northwestern Europe that includes the Netherlands, Belgium, and Luxembourg.

low-den·si·ty lip·o·pro·tein (abbr.: **LDL**) ▶ n. the form of lipoprotein in which cholesterol is transported in the blood.

low·down /ˈlōˌdoun/ informal ▶ adj. mean and unfair: *dirty lowdown tricks.* ▶ n. (**the lowdown**) the true facts or relevant information about something: *get the lowdown on the sit-in.*

Low·ell[1] /ˈlōəl/ a city in northeastern Massachusetts; pop. 105,167.

Low·ell[2], Amy Lawrence (1874–1925), US poet. Her works include *A Critical Fable* (1922).

Low·ell[3], James Russell (1819–91), US poet and critic. His works include the *Biglow Papers* (1848, 1867).

Low·ell[4], Percival (1855–1916), US astronomer; brother of Amy Lowell. He inferred the existence of a ninth planet beyond Neptune.

Low·ell[5], Robert Traill Spence (1917–77), US poet. His poetry is notable for its intense confessional nature and for its complex imagery.

low-end ▶ adj. denoting the cheaper products of a range, esp. of audio or computer equipment.

low·er[1] /ˈlōər/ ▶ adj. **1** comparative of LOW[1]. **2** less high: *the lower levels of the building.* ■ (of an animal or plant) showing relatively primitive or simple characteristics. ■ (often **Lower**) Geol. & Archaeol. denoting an older (and hence usually deeper) part of a stratigraphic division or archaeological deposit or the period in which it was formed or deposited: *Lower Cretaceous* | *Lower Paleolithic.* **3** [in place names] situated on less high land or to the south or toward the sea: *the Lower East Side.* ▶ adv. in or into a lower position: *the sun sank lower.* — **low·er·most** adj.

low·er[2] /ˈlōər/ ▶ v. [trans.] move (someone or something) in a downward direction: *the coffin was lowered into the ground.* ■ reduce the height, pitch, or elevation of: *she lowered her voice to a whisper.* ■ make or become less in amount, extent, or value: [trans.] *traffic speeds must be lowered* | [intrans.] *temperatures lowered.* ■ direct (one's eyes) downward. ■ (**lower oneself**) behave in a way that is perceived as unworthy or debased.
– PHRASES **lower the boom on** informal treat (someone) severely. ■ put a stop to (an activity).

low·er[3] /ˈlou(ə)r/ (also **lour**) ▶ v. [intrans.] look angry or sullen; frown: *the lofty statue lowers at patients in the infirmary.* ■ (of the sky, weather, or landscape) look dark and threatening: [as adj.] (**lowering**) *lowering clouds.* ▶ n. a scowl. ■ a dark and gloomy appearance of the sky, weather or landscape. — **low·er·ing·ly** adv. [ME: of unknown origin.]

Low·er Cal·i·for·nia another name for BAJA CALIFORNIA.

Low·er Can·a·da the mainly French-speaking region of Canada in what is now southern Quebec.

low·er·case /ˈlōərˌkās/ (also **low·er case**) ▶ n. small letters as opposed to capital letters (uppercase). [referring orig. to the lower of two cases of type positioned on an angled stand for use by a compositor (see UPPERCASE).]

low·er cham·ber /ˈlōər/ ▶ n. another term for LOWER HOUSE.

low·er class /ˈlōər/ ▶ n. [treated as sing. or pl.] the social group that has the lowest status; the working class. ▶ adj. of, relating to, or characteristic of people belonging to such a group: *a lower-class area.*

low·er court /ˈlōər/ ▶ n. Law a court whose decisions may be overruled by another court on appeal.

low·er crit·i·cism /ˈlōər/ ▶ n. dated another term for TEXTUAL CRITICISM (esp. as applied to the Bible, in contrast to HIGHER CRITICISM).

low·er deck /ˈlōər/ ▶ **n.** the deck of a ship situated immediately above the hold.

Low·er East Side a district of southeastern Manhattan in New York City.

Low·er Forty-eight States a term for the 48 contiguous US states, excluding Alaska and Hawaii.

low·er house /ˈlōər/ ▶ **n.** the larger and typically more representative of two sections of a bicameral legislature or parliament. ■ **(the Lower House)** (in the UK) the House of Commons.

low·er or·ders /ˈlōər/ ▶ **plural n.** dated the lower classes of society.

low·er re·gions /ˈlōər/ ▶ **plural n.** archaic hell or the underworld.

Low·er Sax·o·ny a state of northwestern Germany; capital, Hanover. German name NIEDERSACHSEN.

low·est com·mon de·nom·i·na·tor ▶ **n.** Math. the lowest common multiple of the denominators of several fractions. ■ fig. the broadest or most widely applicable requirement or circumstance. ■ derog. the level of the least discriminating audience or consumer group.

low·est com·mon mul·ti·ple (abbr.: **LCM**) ▶ **n.** Math. the lowest quantity that is a multiple of two or more given quantities (e.g., 12 is the lowest common multiple of 2, 3, and 4).

low-fi ▶ **adj.** var. of LO-FI.

low fre·quen·cy ▶ **n.** (in radio) 30–300 kilohertz.

low gear ▶ **n.** a gear that causes a wheeled vehicle to move slowly, because of a low ratio between the speed of the wheels and that of the mechanism driving them.

Low Ger·man ▶ **n.** a vernacular language spoken in much of northern Germany, closely related to Dutch. Also called PLATTDEUTSCH.

low-grade ▶ **adj.** of low quality or strength: *low-grade steel.* ■ at a low level in a salary or employment structure: *low-grade clerical jobs.* ■ (of a medical condition) of a less serious kind; minor: *a low-grade malignancy.*

low-im·pact ▶ **adj.** [attrib.] **1** denoting exercises, typically aerobics, designed to put little or no harmful stress on the body. **2** (of an activity, industry, or product) affecting or altering the environment as little as possible.

low-key ▶ **adj.** not elaborate, showy, or intensive; modest or restrained: *a very quiet, low-key affair.* ■ Art & Photog. having a predominance of dark or muted tones. ▶ **v.** [trans.] behave or speak with restraint: [as adj.] *a simple, low-keyed style.*

low·land /ˈlōlənd; -ˌland/ ▶ **n.** (also **lowlands**) low-lying country. ■ **(the Lowlands)** the region of Scotland lying south and east of the Highlands. — **low·land·er** (also **Low·land·er**) **n.**

Low Lat·in ▶ **n.** medieval and later forms of Latin.

low-lev·el ▶ **adj.** situated or occurring relatively near or below ground level: *low-level flying was banned.* ■ of or showing a small degree of some measurable quantity, for example radioactivity: *the dumping of low-level waste.* ■ of relatively little importance, scope, or prominence: *beyond low-level jobs.* ■ Comput. of or relating to programming languages or operations that are relatively close to machine code in form.

low·life /ˈlōˌlīf/ (also **low life**) ▶ **n.** people or activities characterized as being disreputable and often criminal. ■ informal a person of such a kind. — **low·lif·er n.**

low·light /ˈlōˌlīt/ ▶ **n.** informal a particularly disappointing or dull event or feature.

low·ly /ˈlōlē/ ▶ **adj.** (**low·li·er, low·li·est**) low in status or importance; humble. ■ (of an organism) primitive or simple. ▶ **adv.** to a low degree; in a low manner: *lowly paid workers.* — **low·li·ly adv. low·li·ness n.**

low-ly·ing ▶ **adj.** at low altitude above sea level.

Low Mass ▶ **n.** (in the Roman Catholic Church) formerly, a Mass recited, not sung, by the celebrant.

low-mind·ed ▶ **adj.** vulgar or sordid in mind or character. — **low-mind·ed·ness n.**

low-necked ▶ **adj.** (of a dress or garment) cut so as to leave the neck and shoulders exposed.

low-pitched ▶ **adj. 1** (of a sound or voice) deep or relatively quiet. **2** (of a roof) having only a slight slope.

low pro·file ▶ **n.** [in sing.] a position of avoiding or not attracting much attention or publicity: *he's not the sort to **keep a low profile**.* ▶ **adj.** avoiding attention or publicity: *a low-profile campaign.*

low re·lief ▶ **n.** Sculpture another term for BAS-RELIEF (see RELIEF sense 4).

low-res /ˈlōˈrez/ ▶ **adj.** informal (of a display or an image) showing a small amount of detail. [20th C.: from *low-resolution.*]

low-res·o·lu·tion ▶ **adj.** Comput. of or relating to a visual output device, such as a CRT or a printer, whose images are not sharply defined. ■ of or relating to an image that lacks sharp focus or fine detail.

low·rid·er /ˈlōˌrīdər/ ▶ **n.** a customized vehicle with hydraulic jacks that allow the chassis to be lowered nearly to the road. — **low·rid·ing n.**

low-rise ▶ **adj. 1** (of a building) having few stories: *low-rise apartment blocks.* **2** (of pants) cut so as to fit low on the hips rather than on the waist. ▶ **n.** a building having few stories.

low road ▶ **n.** informal a behavior or approach that is unscrupulous or immoral.

low spir·its ▶ **plural n.** a feeling of sadness and despondency: *he was in low spirits.* — **low-spir·it·ed adj. low-spir·it·ed·ness n.**

Low Sun·day ▶ **n.** the Sunday after Easter.

low-tech /ˈlōˈtek/ (also **lo-tech**) ▶ **adj.** involved in, employing, or requiring only low technology: *low-tech solar heating systems.* ▶ **n.** (**low tech**) short for LOW TECHNOLOGY.

low tech·nol·o·gy ▶ **n.** relatively unsophisticated technological development or equipment.

low ten·sion (also **low voltage**) ▶ **n.** an electrical potential not large enough to cause injury or damage if diverted.

low tide ▶ **n.** the state of the tide when at its lowest level: *islets visible at low tide.*

low wa·ter ▶ **n.** another term for LOW TIDE. ■ water in a stream or river at its lowest point.

low-wa·ter mark ▶ **n.** the level reached by the sea at low tide, or by a lake or river during a drought or dry season. ■ a minimum recorded level or value: *the market was approaching its low-water mark.*

low-yield ▶ **adj.** producing little; giving a low return: *low-yield investment.* ■ (of a nuclear weapon) having a relatively low explosive force.

lox[1] /läks/ (also **LOX**) ▶ **n.** (acronym from) liquid oxygen. [20th C.: acronym from *liquid oxygen explosive.*]

lox[2] ▶ **n.** smoked salmon. [1940s: from Yiddish *laks.*]

lox·o·drome /ˈläksəˌdrōm/ ▶ **n.** another term for RHUMB (sense 1).

loy·al /ˈloiəl/ ▶ **adj.** giving or showing firm and constant support or allegiance to a person or institution: *he remained **loyal to** the government.* — **loy·al·ly adv.** [16th C.: from Fr., via OFr. *loial* from L. *legalis* (see LEGAL).]

loy·al·ist /ˈloiəlist/ ▶ **n.** a person who remains loyal to the established ruler or government, esp. in the face of a revolt. ■ **(Loyalist)** a colonist of the American revolutionary period who supported the British cause; a Tory. ■ **(Loyalist)** a supporter of union between Great Britain and Northern Ireland. ■ **(Loyalist)** a supporter of the republic and opposer of Franco's revolt in the Spanish Civil War. — **loy·al·ism n.**

loy·al·ty /ˈloiəltē/ ▶ **n.** (pl. **-ties**) the quality of being loyal to someone or something. ■ (often **loyalties**) a strong feeling of support or allegiance: *fights with in-laws cause **divided loyalties**.*

Loy·al·ty Is·lands islands in the southwestern Pacific Ocean that form part of New Caledonia; pop. 18,000.

loz·enge /ˈläzənj/ ▶ **n.** a rhombus or diamond shape. ■ a small medicinal tablet, originally of this shape, taken for sore throats and dissolved in the mouth: *throat lozenges.* [ME: from OFr. *losenge*, prob. derived from the base of Sp. *losa* 'slab.']

LP ▶ **abbr.** ■ long-playing (phonograph record): *two LP records | a collection of LPs.* ■ low pressure.

l.p. ▶ **abbr.** low pressure.

LPG ▶ **abbr.** liquefied petroleum gas.

LPGA ▶ **abbr.** Ladies' Professional Golf Association.

LPM (also **lpm**) ▶ **abbr.** lines per minute.

LPN ▶ **abbr.** Licensed Practical Nurse. See PRACTICAL NURSE.

LR ▶ **abbr.** ■ living room. ■ lower right. ■ low rate.

L/R ▶ **abbr.** left/right.

Lr ▶ **symb.** the chemical element lawrencium.

LRV ▶ **abbr.** lunar roving vehicle.

LSAT ▶ **abbr.** Law School Admission Test.

LSB Comput. ▶ **abbr.** least significant bit.

LSD ▶ **abbr.** lysergic acid diethylamide, a synthetic crystalline compound, $C_{20}H_{26}N_2O$, that is a potent hallucinogenic drug.

LSI ▶ **abbr.** large-scale integration.

Lt. ▶ **abbr.** ■ lieutenant. ■ (also **lt**) light.

lt. ▶ **abbr.** light.

l.t. ▶ **abbr.** ■ Football left tackle. ■ local time. ■ long ton.

Lt. Col. (also **LTC**) ▶ **abbr.** Lieutenant Colonel.

Lt. Comdr. (also **Lt. Com.**) ▶ **abbr.** Lieutenant Commander.

Ltd. Brit. ▶ **abbr.** (after a company name) Limited.

Lt. Gen. (also **LTG**) ▶ **abbr.** Lieutenant General.

Lt. Gov. ▶ **abbr.** Lieutenant Governor.

LTJG ▶ **abbr.** Lieutenant Junior Grade.

LTP ▶ **abbr.** long-term potentiation. See POTENTIATION.

Lu ▶ **symb.** the chemical element lutetium.

Lu·a·la·ba /ˌlo͞oəˈläbə/ a river in central Africa that rises in the Democratic Republic of the Congo (formerly Zaire) and flows north to help form the Congo River.

Lu·an·da /lo͞oˈändə/ the capital of Angola, a port on the Atlantic coast; pop. 2,250,000.

lu·au /ˈlo͞oˌou/ ▶ **n.** (pl. same or **lu·aus**) a Hawaiian party or feast, esp. one accompanied by entertainment. [from Hawaiian *lu'au.*]

Lu·ba /ˈlo͞obə/ ▶ **n.** (pl. same or **Lu·bas**) **1** a member of a people living mainly in southeastern Democratic Republic of the Congo (formerly Zaire). **2** the Bantu language of this people. Also called CHILUBA. ▶ **adj.** of or relating to the Luba or their language. [a local name.]

Lu·ba·vitch·er /ˈlo͞obəˌviCHər; lo͞oˈbäviCHər/ ▶ **n.** a member of a Hasidic community founded in the 1700s by Rabbi Shneour Zalman.

lub·ber /ˈləbər/ ▶ **n. 1** archaic dialect a big, clumsy person. **2** short for LANDLUBBER. — **lub·ber·like adj. lub·ber·ly adj. & adv.** [ME: perh. via OFr. *lobeor* 'swindler, parasite' from *lober* 'deceive.']

lub·ber's line (also **lub·ber line**) ▶ **n.** a line marked on the compass in a ship or aircraft, showing the direction straight ahead.

Lub·bock /ˈləbək/ a city in northwestern Texas; pop. 199,564.

lube /lo͞ob/ informal ▶ **n.** a lubricant. ■ lubrication: [as adj.] *a lube job.* ▶ **v.** [trans.] lubricate (something).

Lü·beck /ˈlo͞oˌbek; ˈlʏ-/ a city in northern Germany, on the Baltic coast in Schleswig-Holstein; pop. 211,000.

lu·bri·cant /ˈlo͞obrəkənt/ ▶ **n.** a substance, such as oil or grease, used for minimizing friction, esp. in an engine or component. ▶ **adj.** lubricating.

lu·bri·cate /ˈlo͞obrəˌkāt/ ▶ **v.** [trans.] apply a substance such as oil or grease to (an engine or component) to minimize friction and allow smooth movement: *remove the nut and lubricate the thread.* ■ make (something) slippery or smooth by applying an oily substance. ■ fig. make (a process) run smoothly: *the availability of credit lubricated the channels of trade.* ■ fig. make someone convivial, esp. with alcohol. — **lu·bri·ca·tion** /ˌlo͞obrəˈkāSHən/ **n.** **lu·bri·ca·tor** /-ˌkātər/ **n.** [17th C.: from L. *lubricat-* 'made slippery,' from the v. *lubricare*, from *lubricus* 'slippery.']

lu·bri·cious /lo͞oˈbriSHəs/ (also **lu·bri·cous** /ˈlo͞obrikəs/) ▶ **adj.** **1** offensively displaying or intended to arouse sexual desire. **2** smooth and slippery with oil or a similar substance. — **lu·bri·cious·ly adv. lu·bric·i·ty** /-ˈbrisitē/ **n.** [16th C.: from L. *lubricus* 'slippery' + -IOUS.]

Lucan[1] /ˈlo͞okən/ (AD 39–65), Roman poet; born in Spain; Latin name *Marcus Annaeus Lucanus.* His major work *Pharsalia* deals with the civil war between Julius Caesar and Pompey.

Lu·can[2] ▶ **adj.** of or relating to St. Luke. [from eccles. L. *Lucas* 'Luke.']

Lu·cas /ˈlo͞okəs/, George (1944–), US director, producer, and screenwriter. He wrote, directed, and produced the *Star Wars* series of movies (1977–2005) and wrote and produced the "Indiana Jones" series (1981–89).

Luce[1] /lo͞os/ a family of US literary figures. Henry Robinson (1898–1967), a publisher and editor born in China of US parents, cofounded the magazines *Time* 1924, *Fortune* 1929, *Life* 1936, *House and Home* 1952, and *Sports Illustrated* 1954. His wife, Clare Boothe (1903–97), wrote the plays *The Women* (1936) and *Kiss the Boys Goodbye* (1938). She was ambassador to Italy 1953–57.

luce /lo͞os/ ▶ **n.** (pl. same) a pike (fish), esp. when full-grown. [ME: via OFr. *lus, luis* from late L. *lucius.*]

lu·cent /ˈlo͞osənt/ ▶ **adj.** literary glowing with or giving off light. — **lu·cen·cy n.** [ME: from L. *lucent-* 'shining,' from the v. *lucere* (see LUCID).]

Lu·cerne /lo͞oˈsərn/ a resort on Lake Lucerne, in central Switzerland; pop. 59,000.

lu·cerne /lo͞oˈsərn/ ▶ **n.** esp. Brit. another term for ALFALFA. [17th C.: from Fr. *luzerne*, from mod. Provençal *luzerno* 'glowworm' (with ref. to its shiny seeds).]

Lu·cerne, Lake a lake in central Switzerland. Also called **FOUR CANTONS, LAKE OF THE**; German name **VIERWALDSTÄTTERSEE.**

lu·cid /ˈlo͞osid/ ▶ **adj.** **1** expressed clearly; easy to understand: *a clear and lucid style.* ■ showing ability to think clearly, esp. in the intervals between periods of confusion or insanity: *he has a few lucid moments every now and then.* **2** literary bright or luminous: *birds dipped their wings in the lucid flow of air.* — **lu·cid·i·ty** /lo͞oˈsiditē/ **n.** **lu·cid·ly adv. lu·cid·ness n.** [16th C. (sense 2): from L. *lucidus* (perh. via Fr. *lucide* or Ital. *lucido*), from *lucere* 'shine,' from *lux, luc-* 'light.']

Lu·ci·fer /ˈlo͞osəfər/ ▶ **n.** **1** another name for SATAN. [by association with the 'son of the morning' (Isa. 14:12), believed by Christian interpreters to be a ref. to Satan.] **2** literary the planet Venus when it rises in the morning. **3** (**lucifer**) archaic a match struck by rubbing it on a rough surface.

Lu·cite /ˈlo͞oˌsīt/ (also **lu·cite**) ▶ **n.** trademark a solid transparent plastic made of polymethyl methacrylate.

luck /lək/ ▶ **n.** success or failure apparently brought by chance rather than through one's own actions. ■ chance considered as a force that causes good or bad things to happen: *luck was with me.* ■ something regarded as bringing about or portending good or bad things: *Fridays are bad luck.* ▶ **v.** [intrans.] (**luck into/onto**) informal chance to find or acquire: *he lucked into a disc-jockey job.* ■ (**luck out**) achieve success or advantage by good luck: *I lucked out and found a wonderful woman.*
– PHRASES **as luck would have it** used to indicate the fortuitousness of a situation. **tough luck** informal used to express a lack of sympathy: *tough luck if they complain.* **be in** (or **out of**) **luck** be fortunate (or unfortunate). **for luck** to bring good fortune. **the luck of the draw** the outcome of chance rather than something one can control. **no such luck** informal used to express disappointment that something has not happened or is unlikely to happen. **try one's luck** do something that involves risk or luck, hoping to succeed. **worse luck** Brit. informal used to express regret about something: *I have to go to secretarial school, worse luck.* [ME (as a v.): perh. from Middle Low Ger. or MDu. *lucken*; n. from Mid. Low Ger. *lucke.*]

luck·i·ly /ˈləkəlē/ ▶ **adv.** [sentence adverb] it is fortunate that: *luckily they didn't recognize me.*

luck·less /ˈləkləs/ ▶ **adj.** having bad luck; unfortunate. — **luck·less·ly adv. luck·less·ness n.**

Luck·now /ˈləkˌnou/ a city in northern India, capital of Uttar Pradesh; pop. 1,592,000.

luck·y /ˈləkē/ ▶ **adj.** (**luck·i·er, luck·i·est**) having, bringing, or resulting from good luck: *a lucky escape.*
– PHRASES **you, he,** etc., **should be so lucky** used to imply in an ironic or resigned way that someone's wishes or expectations are unlikely to be fulfilled: *"Moving in?" "You should be so lucky."* **lucky devil** (or **lucky you, her,** etc.) used to express envy at someone else's good fortune. — **luck·i·ness n.**

luck·y dip ▶ **n.** British term for GRAB BAG.

lu·cra·tive /ˈlo͞okrətiv/ ▶ **adj.** producing a great deal of profit. — **lu·cra·tive·ly adv. lu·cra·tive·ness n.** [ME: from L. *lucrativus*, from *lucrat-* 'gained,' from the v. *lucrari*, from *lucrum* (see LUCRE).]

lu·cre /ˈlo͞okər/ ▶ **n.** money, esp. when regarded as sordid or distasteful or gained in a dishonorable way. [ME: from Fr. *lucre* or L. *lucrum.*]

Lu·cre·tius /lo͞oˈkrēSHəs/ (*c.*94–*c.*55 BC), Roman poet and philosopher; full name *Titus Lucretius Carus.* He wrote *On the Nature of Things.*

lu·cu·brate /ˈlo͞ok(y)əˌbrāt/ ▶ **v.** [intrans.] archaic discourse learnedly in writing. — **lu·cu·bra·tor** /-ˌbrātər/ **n.** [17th C.: from L. *lucubrat-* '(having) worked by lamplight,' from the v. *lucubrare.*]

lu·cu·bra·tion /ˌlo͞ok(y)əˈbrāSHən/ ▶ **n.** formal study; meditation. ■ (usu. **lucubrations**) a piece of writing, typically a pedantic or overelaborate one.

Lu·cul·lan /lo͞oˈkələn/ ▶ **adj.** (esp. of food) extremely luxurious: *Lucullan feasts.* [19th C.: from Licinius *Lucullus*, Roman general of the 1st cent. BC.]

Lu·cy /ˈlo͞osē/ the nickname of a female skeleton of a fossil hominid (*Australopithecus afarensis*) found in Ethiopia in 1974, about 3.2 million years old. This species may be the ancestor of all subsequent *Australopithecus* and *Homo* species.

Lu·da /ˈlo͞oˈdä/ a port in northeastern China, at the southeastern tip of the Liaodong Peninsula; pop. 1,630,000. It consists of the cities of Lushun and Dalian.

Lud·dite /ˈlədˌīt/ ▶ **n.** a member of any of the bands of English workers who destroyed machinery, esp. in cotton and woolen mills, that they believed was threatening their jobs (1811–16). ■ a person opposed to increased industrialization or new technology. — **Lud·dism n. Lud·dit·ism** /-ītˌizəm/ **n.** [perh. named after Ned *Lud*, a participant in the destruction of machinery, + -ITE[1].]

Lu·dhi·a·na /ˌlo͞odēˈänə/ a city in northwestern India; pop. 1,012,000.

lu·dic /ˈlo͞odik/ ▶ **adj.** formal showing spontaneous and undirected playfulness. [1940s: from Fr. *ludique*, from L. *ludere* 'to play,' from *ludus* 'sport.']

lu·di·crous /ˈlo͞odəkrəs/ ▶ **adj.** so foolish, unreasonable, or out of place as to be amusing. — **lu·di·crous·ly adv.** [as submodifier] *a ludicrously inadequate army.* **lu·di·crous·ness n.** [17th C.: from L. *ludicrus* (prob. from *ludicrum* 'stage play') + -OUS.]

Lud·lum /ˈlədləm/, Robert (1927–2001) US writer; pen names **Jonathan Ryder, Michael Shepherd.** His novels include *The Bourne Identity* (1980) and *The Prometheus Deception* (2000).

Lud·wig /ˈlədwig; ˈlo͞od-; ˈlo͞otviKH/ the name of three kings of Bavaria: ■ Ludwig I (1786–1868), reigned 1825–48. ■ Ludwig II (1845–86), reigned 1864–86. ■ Ludwig III (1845–1921), reigned 1913–18.

Lud·wigs·ha·fen /ˌlo͞odviksˈhäfən/ a port in west central Germany; pop. 165,000.

lu·es /ˈlo͞oˌēz/ (also **lu·es ve·ne·re·a** /vəˈni(ə)rēə/) ▶ **n.** dated a serious infectious disease, particularly syphilis. — **lu·et·ic** /lo͞oˈetik/ **adj.** [17th C.: from L. *lues* (*venerea*), lit. '(venereal) plague.']

luff /ləf/ esp. Sailing ▶ **n.** the edge of a fore-and-aft sail next to the mast or stay. ▶ **v.** [trans.] **1** steer (a sailing vessel) nearer the wind to the point at which the sails just begin to shake: *I came aft and luffed her for the open sea.* ■ obstruct (an opponent in yacht racing) by sailing closer to the wind. **2** raise or lower (the jib of a crane or derrick). [ME: from OFr. *lof*, prob. from Low Ger.]

luf·fa /ˈləfə; ˈlo͞ofə/ ▶ **n.** var. of LOOFAH.

Luft·waf·fe /ˈlo͞oftˌwäfə; -ˌväfə/ the German air force. [Ger., from *Luft* 'air' + *Waffe* 'weapon.']

lug[1] /ləg/ ▶ **v.** (**lugged, lug·ging**) carry or drag (a heavy or bulky object) with great effort: *she began to lug her suitcase down the stairs.* ■ fig. be encumbered with: *he had lugged his poor wife around for so long.* ▶ **n.** a box or crate used for transporting fruit. [ME: prob. of Scand. origin: cf. Swed. *lugga* 'pull a person's hair' (from *lugg* 'forelock').]

lug[2] ▶ **n.** **1** a projection on an object by which it may be carried or fixed in place. **2** informal an uncouth, aggressive man. **3** (usu. **lugs**) Scot. or informal a person's ear. [15th C. (denoting the earflap of a hat): prob. of Scand. origin: cf. Swed. *lugg* 'forelock, nap of cloth.']

lug[3] ▶ **n.** short for LUGWORM.

lug[4] ▶ **n.** short for LUGSAIL.

Lu·gan·da /lo͞oˈgändə; -ˈgan-/ ▶ **n.** the Bantu language of the Baganda people, widely used in Uganda. ▶ **adj.** of or relating to this language.

Lu·ga·no /lo͞oˈgänō/ a town in southern Switzerland, on Lake Lugano; pop. 26,000.

Lug·du·num /ləgˈdo͞onəm/ Roman name for LYONS.

luge /lo͞oZH/ ▶ **n.** a light toboggan for one or two people, ridden in a sitting or supine position. ■ a sport in which competitors make a timed descent of a course riding such toboggans. ▶ **v.** [intrans.] ride on a luge. [19th C. (as a v.): from Swiss Fr.]

Lu·ger /ˈlo͞ogər/ ▶ **n.** trademark a type of German automatic pistol. [20th C.: named after George *Luger* (1849–1923), Ger. firearms expert.]

lug·gage /ˈləgij/ ▶ **n.** suitcases or other bags in which to pack personal belongings for traveling. [16th C.: from LUG[1] + -AGE.]

lug·ger /ˈləgər/ ▶ **n.** a small sailing ship with two or three masts and a lugsail on each. [18th C.: from LUGSAIL + -ER[1].]

lug nut ▶ n. a large rounded nut that fits over a heavy bolt, used esp. to attach the wheel of a vehicle to its axle.

lug·sail /ˈləgsəl; -ˌsāl/ ▶ n. an asymmetrical four-sided sail that is hoisted on a steeply inclined yard. [17th C.: prob. from LUG[2] + the n. SAIL.]

lu·gu·bri·ous /ləˈg(y)o͞obrēəs/ ▶ adj. looking or sounding sad and dismal. — **lu·gu·bri·ous·ly** adv. **lu·gu·bri·ous·ness** n. [17th C.: from L. *lugubris* (from *lugere* 'mourn') + -OUS.]

lug·worm /ˈləgˌwərm/ ▶ n. a bristle worm (genus *Arenicola*) that lives in muddy sand. It is widely used as bait for fishing. [19th C.: from earlier *lug* 'lugworm' (of unknown origin) + WORM.]

Luik /loik/ Flemish name for LIÈGE.

Luke, St. /lo͝ok/ an evangelist, closely associated with St. Paul and traditionally the author of the third Gospel and the Acts of the Apostles. ■ the third Gospel (see GOSPEL sense 2).

luke·warm /ˈlo͝okˈwôrm/ ▶ adj. (of liquid or food) only moderately warm; tepid: *lukewarm coffee.* ■ (of a person, attitude, or action) unenthusiastic. — **luke·warm·ly** adv. **luke·warm·ness** n. [ME: from dialect *luke* (prob. from dial. *lew* 'lukewarm' and rel. to LEE) + WARM.]

lull /ləl/ ▶ v. [trans.] calm or send to sleep, typically with soothing sounds or movements: *the rhythm of the boat lulled her to sleep.* ■ cause (someone) to feel deceptively secure or confident: *the rarity of earthquakes there has lulled people into a false sense of security.* ■ allay (a person's doubts, fears, or suspicions), typically by deception. ■ [intrans.] (of noise or a storm) abate or fall quiet: *conversation lulled for an hour.* ▶ n. a temporary interval of quiet or lack of activity.
– PHRASES **the lull before the storm** see STORM. [ME: imitative.]

lull·a·by /ˈlələˌbī/ ▶ n. (pl. **-bies**) a quiet, gentle song sung to put a child to sleep. ▶ v. (**-bies, -bied**) [trans.] rare sing to (someone) to get them to go to sleep: *she lullabied us, she fed us.* [16th C.: from LULL + *bye-bye*, a sound used as a refrain in lullabies.]

Lul·ly /ˈlo͞olē; lyˈlē/, Jean-Baptiste (1632–87), French composer; born in Italy; Italian name *Giovanni Battista Lulli.* His operas include *Alceste* (1674) and *Armide* (1686).

lu·lu /ˈlo͞oˌlo͞o/ ▶ n. informal an outstanding example of a particular type of person or thing: *as far as nightmares went, this one was a lulu.* [19th C.: perh. from *Lulu*, nickname for the given name *Louise.*]

lum·ba·go /ˌləmˈbāgō/ ▶ n. pain in the muscles and joints of the lower back. [17th C.: from L., from *lumbus* 'loin.']

lum·bar /ˈləmbər; -ˌbär/ ▶ adj. [attrib.] relating to the lower part of the back: *backache in the lumbar region.* [17th C.: from med. L. *lumbaris*, from L. *lumbus* 'loin.']

lum·ber[1] /ˈləmbər/ ▶ v. [intrans.] move in a slow, heavy, awkward way: *a truck filled his mirror and lumbered past.* [ME *lomere*, perh. symbolic of clumsy movement.]

lum·ber[2] ▶ n. **1** timber sawn into rough planks or otherwise partly prepared. **2** esp. Brit. household items that are no longer useful and inconveniently take up storage space: [as adj.] *a lumber room.* ▶ v. **1** [intrans.] [usu. as n.] (**lumbering**) cut and prepare forest timber for transport and sale. **2** [trans.] (usu. **be lumbered with**) Brit., informal burden (someone) with an unwanted responsibility or task. [16th C.: perh. from LUMBER[1].]

lum·ber·er /ˈləmbərər/ ▶ n. a person engaged in the lumber trade, esp. a lumberjack.

lum·ber·jack /ˈləmbərˌjak/ (also **lumberman**) ▶ n. (a person who fells trees, cuts them into logs, or transports them to a sawmill.

lum·ber·jack·et /ˈləmbərˌjakit/ ▶ n. a warm, thick jacket, typically in a bright color with a check pattern, of the kind worn by lumberjacks.

lum·ber·yard /ˈləmbərˌyärd/ ▶ n. a place that sells lumber and other building materials, usu. outdoors.

lu·men[1] /ˈlo͞omən/ (abbr.: **lm**) ▶ n. Physics the SI unit of luminous flux, equal to the amount of light emitted per second in a unit solid angle of one steradian from a uniform source of one candela. [19th C.: from L., 'light.']

lu·men[2] ▶ n. (pl. **-mi·na** /-mənə/) Anat. the central cavity of a tubular or other hollow structure in an organism or cell. — **lu·mi·nal** /-mənl/ adj. [19th C.: from L., 'opening.']

Lu·mière /ˌlo͞omēˈe(ə)r; lymˈyer/, French inventors. Brothers *Auguste Marie Louis Nicholas* (1862–1954) and *Louis Jean* (1864–1948), patented their "Cinématographe," which combined a movie camera and projector.

lu·mi·naire /ˌlo͞oməˈne(ə)r/ ▶ n. a complete electric light unit (used esp. in technical contexts). [20th C.: from Fr.]

lu·mi·nance /ˈlo͞omənəns/ ▶ n. Physics the intensity of light emitted from a surface per unit area in a given direction. [19th C.: from L. *luminant-* 'illuminating' (from the v. *luminare*) + -ANCE.]

lu·mi·nar·i·a /ˌlo͞oməˈne(ə)rēə/ ▶ n. **1** a Christmas lantern consisting of a votive candle set in a small paper bag weighted with sand and typically placed with others outdoors as a holiday decoration. Also called FAROLITO. **2** (in New Mexico) a Christmas Eve bonfire.

lu·mi·nar·y /ˈlo͞oməˌnerē/ ▶ n. (pl. **-nar·ies**) **1** a person who inspires or influences others, esp. one prominent in a particular sphere. **2** an artificial light. ■ literary a natural light-giving body, esp. the sun or moon. [ME: from OFr. *luminarie* or late L. *luminarium*, from L. *lumen, lumin-* 'light.']

lu·mi·nesce /ˌlo͞oməˈnes/ ▶ v. [intrans.] emit light by luminescence. [19th C.: back-form. from LUMINESCENCE.]

lu·mi·nes·cence /ˌlo͞oməˈnesəns/ ▶ n. the emission of light by a substance that has not been heated, as in fluorescence and phosphorescence. — **lu·mi·nes·cent** adj.

lu·mi·nif·er·ous /ˌlo͞oməˈnif(ə)rəs/ ▶ adj. esp. archaic producing or transmitting light.

lu·mi·nos·i·ty /ˌlo͞oməˈnäsətē/ ▶ n. (pl. **-ties**) luminous quality: *acrylic colors retain freshness and luminosity.* ■ Astron. the intrinsic brightness of a celestial object (as distinct from its apparent brightness diminished by distance). ■ Physics the rate of emission of radiation, visible or otherwise.

lu·mi·nous /ˈlo͞omənəs/ ▶ adj. bright or shining, esp. in the dark. ■ (of a person's complexion or eyes) glowing with health, vigor, or a particular emotion: *her eyes were luminous with joy.* ■ (of a color) very bright; harsh to the eye: *he wore luminous green socks.* — **lu·mi·nous·ly** adv. **lu·mi·nous·ness** n. [ME: from OFr. *lumineux* or L. *luminosus*, from *lumen, lumin-* 'light.']

lum·mox /ˈləməks/ ▶ n. informal a clumsy, stupid person: *watch it, you great lummox!* [19th C.: of unknown origin.]

lump[1] /ləmp/ ▶ n. a compact mass of a substance, esp. one without a definite or regular shape. ■ a swelling under the skin, esp. one caused by injury or disease. ■ informal a heavy, ungainly, or slow-witted person: *I wouldn't stand a chance against a big lump like you.* ■ a small cube of sugar. ▶ v. **1** [trans.] put in an indiscriminate mass or group; treat as alike without regard for particulars: *Hong Kong and Bangkok tend to **be lumped together** in holiday brochures.* ■ [intrans.] (in taxonomy) classify plants or animals in relatively inclusive groups, disregarding minor variations. **2** [intrans.] (**lump along**) proceed heavily or awkwardly: *I came lumping along behind him.* **3** [intrans.] concentrate or assemble together in an irregular mass: *we're lumped in a limo, bound for Los Angeles.*
– PHRASES **a lump in the throat** a feeling of tightness or dryness in the throat caused by strong emotion, esp. sadness. **take** (or **get**) **one's lumps** informal suffer punishment; be attacked or defeated. [ME: perh. from a Gmc. base meaning 'shapeless piece'; cf. Dan. *lump* 'lump.']

lump[2] ▶ v. (**lump it**) informal accept or tolerate a disagreeable situation: *you can like it or lump it but I've got to work.* [16th C.: symbolic.]

lump·ec·to·my /ˌləmˈpektəmē/ ▶ n. (pl. **-mies**) a surgical operation in which a lump is removed from the breast.

lum·pen /ˈləmpən; ˈlo͝om-/ ▶ adj. (in Marxist contexts) uninterested in revolutionary advancement: *the lumpen public is enveloped in a culture of dependency.* ■ boorish and stupid: *lumpen, uninhibited, denim-clad youth.* ▶ plural n. (**the lumpen**) the lumpenproletariat. [20th C.: back-form. from LUMPENPROLETARIAT.]

lum·pen·pro·le·tar·i·at /ˈləmpənˌprōləˈte(ə)rēət; ˈlo͝om-/ ▶ n. [treated as sing. or pl.] (esp. in Marxist terminology) the unorganized and unpolitical lower orders of society who are not interested in revolutionary advancement. [20th C.: from Ger., from *Lumpen* 'rag, rogue.']

lump·er /ˈləmpər/ ▶ n. **1** a laborer who unloads cargo. **2** a person (esp. a taxonomist) who attaches more importance to similarities than to differences in classification. Contrasted with SPLITTER.

lump·fish /ˈləmpˌfish/ ▶ n. (pl. same or **-fish·es**) a North Atlantic lumpsucker (*Cyclopterus lumpus*), the roe of which is used as a substitute for caviar. [17th C.: from Mid. Low Ger. *lumpen*, MDu. *lompe* + FISH[1].]

lump·ish /ˈləmpish/ ▶ adj. roughly or clumsily formed or shaped: *large lumpish hands.* ■ (of a person) stupid and lethargic. — **lump·ish·ly** adv. **lump·ish·ness** n.

lump·suck·er /ˈləmpˌsəkər/ ▶ n. a globular fish (family Cyclopteridae) of cooler northern waters, typically having a ventral sucker and spiny fins.

lump sum ▶ n. a single payment made at a particular time, as opposed to a number of smaller payments or installments.

lump·y /ˈləmpē/ ▶ adj. (**lump·i·er, lump·i·est**) full of or covered with lumps. ■ Naut. (of water) formed by the wind into small waves: *a large lumpy sea.* — **lump·i·ly** adv. **lump·i·ness** n.

lump·y jaw ▶ n. infection of the jaw with actinomycete bacteria, common in cattle.

lu·na·cy /ˈlo͞onəsē/ ▶ n. (pl. **-cies**) the state of being a lunatic; insanity (not in technical use): *it has been suggested that originality demands a degree of lunacy.*

lu·na moth /ˈlo͞onə/ ▶ n. a very large North American moth (*Actias luna*, family Saturniidae) that has pale green wings with long tails and transparent eyespots bearing crescent-shaped markings. [19th C.: *luna* from L. *luna* 'moon' (from its markings).]

luna moth

lu·nar /ˈlo͞onər/ ▶ **adj.** of, determined by, relating to, or resembling the moon: *a lunar landscape.* [ME: from L. *lunaris*, from *luna* 'moon.']

lu·nar caus·tic ▶ **n.** Chem., archaic silver nitrate, esp. fused in the form of a stick. [19th C.: *lunar* in the sense 'containing silver.']

lu·nar day ▶ **n.** the interval of time between two successive crossings of the earth's meridian by the moon (roughly 24 hours and 50 minutes).

lu·nar dis·tance ▶ **n.** the angular distance of the moon from the sun, a planet, or a star, used in finding longitude at sea.

lu·nar e·clipse ▶ **n.** an eclipse in which the moon appears darkened as it passes into the earth's shadow.

Lu·nar·i·an /lo͞oˈne(ə)rēən/ ▶ **n.** (in science fiction) an imagined inhabitant of the moon.

lu·nar mod·ule (abbr.: **LM**) ▶ **n.** a small craft used for traveling between the moon's surface and an orbiting spacecraft (formerly known as **lunar excursion module** or **LEM**).

lu·nar month ▶ **n.** a month measured between successive new moons (roughly 29½ days). ■ (in general use) a period of four weeks.

lu·nar rov·ing ve·hi·cle (abbr.: **LRV**) (also **lu·nar rov·er**) ▶ **n.** a vehicle designed for use by astronauts on the moon's surface, used on the last three missions of the Apollo project. Also called **MOON BUGGY**.

lu·nar year ▶ **n.** a period of twelve lunar months (approximately 354 days).

lu·nate /ˈlo͞oˌnāt/ ▶ **adj.** crescent-shaped. [18th C.: from L. *lunatus*, from *luna* 'moon.']

lu·na·tic /ˈlo͞onəˌtik/ ▶ **n.** a mentally ill person (not in technical use). ■ an extremely foolish or eccentric person: *this lunatic just accelerated out of the side of the road.* ▶ **adj.** [attrib.] mentally ill (not in technical use). ■ extremely foolish, eccentric, or absurd. [ME: from OFr. *lunatique*, from late L. *lunaticus*, from L. *luna* 'moon.']

lu·na·tic fringe ▶ **n.** an extreme or eccentric minority within society or a group.

lu·na·tion /lo͞oˈnāSHən/ ▶ **n.** Astron. another term for **LUNAR MONTH**. [ME: from med. L. *lunatio(n-)*, from L. *luna* 'moon.']

lunch /lənCH/ ▶ **n.** a meal eaten in the middle of the day, typically one that is lighter or less formal than an evening meal. ▶ **v.** [intrans.] eat lunch: *he was lunching with a client.* ■ [trans.] take (someone) out for lunch: *public relations people lunch their clients there.*
– PHRASES **do lunch** informal meet for lunch. **out to lunch** informal unaware of or inattentive to present conditions. — **lunch·er n.** [19th C.: abbrev. of **LUNCHEON**.]

lunch·box /ˈlənCHˌbäks/ ▶ **n.** (also **lunch bucket** or **lunch pail**) a container in which to carry a packed meal. ■ a portable computer slightly larger than a laptop.

lunch·eon /ˈlənCHən/ ▶ **n.** a formal lunch or a formal word for lunch. [16th C. (in the sense 'thick piece, hunk'): possibly an extension of obs. *lunch* 'thick piece, hunk,' from Sp. *lonja* 'slice.']

lunch·eon·ette /ˌlənCHəˈnet/ ▶ **n.** a small, informal restaurant serving light lunches.

lunch·meat /ˈlənCHˌmēt/ (also **lunch·eon meat**) ▶ **n.** meat sold in slices for sandwiches; cold cuts.

lunch·pail ▶ **adj.** lunchbox.

lunch·room /ˈlənCHˌro͞om; -ˌro͝om/ ▶ **n.** a room or establishment in which lunch is served or in which it may be eaten; a school or office cafeteria.

lunch·time /ˈlənCHˌtīm/ ▶ **n.** the time in the middle of day when lunch is eaten.

Lun·da /ˈlo͞ondə; ˈlo͝on-/ ▶ **n.** (pl. same or **Ba·lun·da** /bəˈlo͞ondə; -ˈlo͝on-/ or **Lun·das**) **1** a member of any of several peoples living mainly in northern Zambia and adjoining parts of the Democratic Republic of the Congo (formerly Zaire) and Angola. **2** any of several Bantu languages of these peoples. ▶ **adj.** of, relating to, or denoting this people or their language. [a local name.]

lune /lo͞on/ ▶ **n.** a crescent-shaped figure formed on a sphere or plane by two arcs intersecting at two points. [18th C.: from Fr., from L. *luna* 'moon.']

lu·nette /lo͞oˈnet/ ▶ **n.** something crescent-shaped, in particular: ■ an arched aperture or window, esp. one in a domed ceiling. ■ a crescent-shaped or semicircular alcove containing something such as a painting or statue. ■ a fortification with two faces forming a projecting angle, and two flanks. [16th C. (denoting a semicircular horseshoe): from Fr., dimin. of *lune* 'moon,' from L. *luna*.]

lung /ləNG/ ▶ **n.** (in vertebrates other than fish) each of the pair of organs situated within the rib cage, consisting of elastic sacs with branching passages into which air is drawn, so that oxygen can pass into the blood and carbon dioxide be removed. — **lunged** /ləNGd/ **adj.** [in comb.] *strong-lunged* **lung·ful n.** (pl. **-fuls**) [OE *lungen*, from an Indo-Eur. root shared by **LIGHT²**.]

lunge¹ /lənj/ ▶ **n.** a sudden forward thrust of the body, typically with an arm outstretched to attack someone or seize something. ■ the basic attacking move in fencing, in which the leading foot is thrust forward with the knee bent while the back leg remains straightened. ■ an exercise or gymnastic movement resembling the lunge of a fencer. ▶ **v.** (**lung·ing** or **lunge·ing**) [intrans.] make a lunge: *the guests lunged at the food.* ■ [trans.] make a sudden forward thrust with: *Billy lunged his spear at the fish.* [18th C.: from earlier *allonge*, from Fr. *allonger* 'lengthen.']

lunge² ▶ **n.** variant of **LONGE**.

lung·fish /ˈləNGˌfiSH/ ▶ **n.** (pl. same or **-fish·es**) an elongated freshwater fish (families Ceratodontidae, Lepidosirenidae, and Protopteridae) with one or two sacs that function as lungs, enabling it to breathe air. It can estivate in mud for long periods to survive drought.

lun·gi /ˈlo͞oNGgē/ ▶ **n.** (pl. **lun·gis**) a length of cotton cloth worn as a loincloth in India or as a skirt in Myanmar (Burma). [Urdu.]

lung·wort /ˈləNGˌwərt; -ˌwôrt/ ▶ **n.** a bristly herbaceous plant (genus *Pulmonaria*) of the borage family, typically having white-spotted leaves and pink flowers that turn blue as they age.

lu·ni·so·lar /ˌlo͞oniˈsōlər/ ▶ **adj.** of or concerning the combined motions or effects of the sun and moon. [17th C.: from L. *luna* 'moon' + **SOLAR**.]

lu·ni·tid·al /ˌlo͞oniˈtīdl/ ▶ **adj.** denoting the interval between the time at which the moon crosses a meridian and the time of high tide at that meridian.

lunk /ləNGk/ ▶ **n.** short for **LUNKHEAD**.

lun·ker /ˈləNGkər/ ▶ **n.** informal an exceptionally large specimen of something, esp. (among anglers) a fish. [20th C.: of unknown origin.]

lunk·head /ˈləNGkˌhed/ ▶ **n.** informal a slow-witted person. — **lunk·head·ed adj.** [19th C.: prob. from an alt. of **LUMP¹** + **HEAD**.]

Lunt /lənt/, Alfred, see **FONTANNE**.

lu·nu·la /ˈlo͞onyələ/ ▶ **n.** (pl. **-lae** /-ˌlē; -ˌlī/) a crescent-shaped object or mark, in particular: ■ the white area at the base of a fingernail. ■ Print. one of a pair of parentheses. — **lu·nu·lar** /-lər/ **adj.** **lu·nu·late** /-ˌlāt; -lit/ **adj.** [16th C.: from L., dimin. of *luna* 'moon.']

lu·nule /ˈlo͞onˌyo͞ol/ ▶ **n.** a crescent-shaped or oval part or marking. [16th C.: from L.]

Lu·o /ˈlo͞oˌō/ ▶ **n.** (pl. same or **Lu·os**) **1** a member of an East African people of Kenya and the upper Nile valley. **2** the Nilotic language of this people. ▶ **adj.** of or relating to the Luo or their language. [the name in Luo.]

Luo·yang /ˈlo͞oˈyäNG/ a city in east central China, in Henan province, on the Luo River; pop. 1,160,000. Former name **HONAN**.

Lu·per·ca·li·a /ˌlo͞opərˈkālēə; -ˈkālyə/ (also in sing. **Lu·per·cal** /ˈlo͞opərˌkal/) ▶ **plural n.** [usu. treated as sing.] an ancient Roman festival of purification and fertility, held annually on February 15. — **Lu·per·ca·li·an adj.** [L., neut. pl. of *lupercalis* 'relating to *Lupercus*,' Roman equivalent of the Gk. god Pan.]

lu·pine¹ /ˈlo͞opin/ ▶ **n.** a plant (genus *Lupinus*) of the pea family, with deeply divided leaves and tall, colorful, tapering spikes of flowers. [ME: from L. *lupinus*.]

lu·pine² /ˈlo͞oˌpīn/ ▶ **adj.** of, like, or relating to a wolf or wolves. ■ fierce or ravenous as a wolf. [17th C.: from L. *lupinus*, from *lupus* 'wolf.']

lu·pu·lin /ˈlo͞opyəlin/ ▶ **n.** a bitter, yellowish powder found on glandular hairs beneath the scales of the flowers of the female hop plant. [19th C.: from the mod. L. use of L. *lupulus*.]

Lu·pus /ˈlo͞opəs/ Astron. a southern constellation (the Wolf), lying partly in the Milky Way between Scorpius and Centaurus.

lu·pus /ˈlo͞opəs/ ▶ **n.** any of various ulcerous skin diseases, esp. lupus vulgaris or lupus erythematosus. — **lu·poid** /-ˌpoid/ **adj.** **lu·pous** /-pəs/ **adj.** [16th C.: from L., 'wolf.']

lu·pus er·y·the·ma·to·sus /ˌerəˌTHēməˈtōsəs/ ▶ **n.** an inflammatory autoimmune disease causing scaly red patches on the skin, esp. on the face, and sometimes affecting connective tissue in the internal organs. [from **LUPUS** + mod. L. *erythematosus*, from Gk. *eruthēma* 'reddening.']

lu·pus vul·ga·ris /ˌvəlˈge(ə)ris/ ▶ **n.** tuberculosis of the skin, characterized by dark red patches. [1940s: from **LUPUS** + L. *vulgaris* 'common.']

lurch¹ /lərCH/ ▶ **n.** [usu. in sing.] an abrupt uncontrolled movement, esp. an unsteady tilt or roll. ▶ **v.** [intrans.] make an abrupt, unsteady, uncontrolled movement or series of movements; stagger: *the car lurched forward.*

lurch² ▶ **n.** (in phrase **leave someone in the lurch**) leave an associate or friend abruptly and without assistance or support in a difficult situation. [16th C.: from Fr. *lourche*, a game.]

lurch·er /ˈlərCHər/ ▶ **n.** **1** Brit. a crossbred dog, typically one crossed with a greyhound, originally used for hunting and by poachers for catching rabbits. **2** archaic a prowler, swindler, or petty thief. [16th C. (sense 2): from obs. *lurch* 'remain in a place furtively,' var. of **LURK**.]

lur·dan /ˈlərdn/ (also **lur·dane**) archaic ▶ **n.** an idle or incompetent person. ▶ **adj.** lazy; good-for-nothing. [ME: from OFr. *lourdin*, from *lourd* 'heavy,' *lort* 'foolish,' from L. *luridus* 'lurid.']

lure /lo͝or/ ▶ **v.** [trans.] tempt (a person or an animal) to do something or to go somewhere, esp. by offering some form of reward: *the child was lured into a car.* ▶ **n.** something that tempts or is used to tempt a person or animal to do something. ■ the strongly attractive quality of a person or thing: *the lure of the exotic East.* ■ a type of bait used in fishing or hunting. ■ Falconry a bunch of feathers with a weighted object attached to a long string, to recall a hawk. [ME: from OFr. *luere*, of Gmc. origin; prob. rel. to Ger. *Luder* 'bait.']

Lur·ex /ˈlo͝orˌeks/ (also **lur·ex**) ▶ **n.** trademark a type of yarn or fabric that incorporates metallic thread.

lu·rid /ˈlo͝orid/ ▶ **adj.** very vivid in color, esp. so as to create an unpleasantly harsh or unnatural effect: *lurid food colorings.* ■ (of a description) presented in vividly shocking or sensational terms, esp. giving explicit details of crimes or sexual matters: *the lurid details of the massacre.* — **lu·rid·ly adv.** **lu·rid·ness n.** [17th C.: from L. *luridus*; rel. to *luror* 'wan or yellow color.']

lurk /lərk/ ▸ **v.** [intrans.] (of a person or animal) be or remain hidden so as to wait in ambush for someone or something: *a killer lurked in the darkness.* ▪ (of an unpleasant quality) be present in a latent or barely discernible state, although still presenting a threat: *fear lurks beneath the surface.* ▪ [intrans.] read communications on an electronic network without making one's presence known. — **lurk·er** n. [ME: perh. from LOUR + the frequentative suffix *-k* (as in *talk*).]

Lur·ton /'lərtn/, Horace Harmon (1844–1914) US Supreme Court associate justice 1909–14.

Lu·sa·ka /lo͞o'säkə/ the capital of Zambia; pop. 982,000.

Lu·sa·tian /lo͞o'sāsHən/ ▸ **adj. & n.** another term for SORBIAN.

lus·cious /'ləsHəs/ ▸ **adj.** having a pleasingly rich, sweet taste: *a luscious and fragrant dessert wine.* ▪ richly verdant or opulent. ▪ (of a woman) very sexually attractive. — **lus·cious·ly** adv. **lus·cious·ness** n. [ME: perh. an alt. of obs. *licious*, shortened form of DELICIOUS.]

lush[1] /ləsH/ ▸ **adj.** (of vegetation) growing luxuriantly. ▪ opulent and luxurious: *a hall of gleaming marble, as lush as a Byzantine church.* ▪ (of color or music) very rich and providing great sensory pleasure: *lush orchestrations.* ▪ (of a woman) very sexually attractive. — **lush·ly** adv. **lush·ness** n. [ME: perh. an alt. of obs. *lash* 'soft, lax,' from OFr. *lasche* 'lax,' by association with LUSCIOUS.]

lush[2] informal ▸ **n.** a heavy drinker, esp. a habitual one. ▸ **v.** [trans.] dated make (someone) drunk: *Mr. Hobart got so **lushed up** he was spilling drinks down his shirt.* [18th C.: perh. a humorous use of LUSH[1].]

Lu·shun /'lo͞o'sHo͞on; 'lʏ-/ a port on the Liaodong Peninsula in northeastern China, now part of the urban complex of Luda. Formerly Port Arthur.

Lu·si·ta·ni·a[1] /ˌlo͞osə'tānēə; -nyə/ an ancient Roman province on the Iberian peninsula. — **Lu·si·ta·ni·an** adj. & n.

Lu·si·ta·ni·a[2] a Cunard liner that was sunk by a German submarine in the Atlantic in May 1915.

lust /ləst/ ▸ **n.** very strong sexual desire. ▪ [in sing.] a passionate desire for something: *a **lust for** power.* ▪ (usu. **lusts**) esp. Theol. a sensual appetite regarded as sinful: *lusts of the flesh.* ▸ **v.** [intrans.] have a very strong sexual desire for someone: *he really **lusted after** me in those days.* ▪ feel a strong desire for something: *pregnant women **lusting for** pickles and ice cream.* — **lust·ful** adj. **lust·ful·ly** adv. **lust·ful·ness** n. [OE: of Gmc. origin; rel. to Ger. *Lust*.]

lus·ter[1] /'ləstər/ (Brit. **lus·tre**) ▸ **n.** **1** a gentle sheen or soft glow, esp. that of a partly reflective surface. ▪ fig. glory or distinction: *a celebrity player to **add luster to** the lineup.* ▪ the manner in which the surface of a mineral reflects light. **2** a substance imparting or having a shine or glow, in particular: ▪ a thin coating containing unoxidized metal that gives an iridescent glaze to ceramics. ▪ ceramics with such a glaze; lusterware. ▪ a type of finish on a photographic print, less reflective than a glossy finish. ▪ a fabric or yarn with a sheen or gloss. ▪ Brit. a glossy dress material of cotton and wool. **3** a prismatic glass pendant on a chandelier or other ornament. ▪ a cut-glass chandelier or candelabra. — **lus·ter·less** adj. [16th C.: from Fr. *lustre*, from Ital. *lustro*, from the v. *lustrare*, from L. *lustrare* 'illuminate.']

lus·ter[2] (Brit. **lus·tre**) ▸ **n.** another term for LUSTRUM.

lus·tered /'ləstərd/ ▸ **adj.** (esp. of ceramics) having an iridescent surface; shining.

lus·ter·ware /'ləstərˌwe(ə)r/ (Brit. **lus·tre·ware**) ▸ **n.** ceramic articles with an iridescent metallic glaze.

lus·tra /'ləstrə/ plural form of LUSTRUM.

lus·tral /'ləstrəl/ ▸ **adj.** relating to or used in ceremonial purification. [16th C.: from L. *lustralis*, from *lustrum* (see LUSTRUM).]

lus·trate /'ləsˌtrāt/ ▸ **v.** [trans.] rare purify by ritual action: *a soul lustrated in the baptismal waters.* — **lus·tra·tion** /ˌləs'trāsHən/ n. [17th C.: from L. *lustrat-* 'purified by lustral rites,' from the v. *lustrare*, from *lustrum* (see LUSTRUM).]

lus·tre /'ləstər/ ▸ **n.** British spelling of LUSTER[1], LUSTER[2].

lus·tre·ware /'ləstərˌwe(ə)r/ ▸ **n.** British spelling of LUSTERWARE.

lust·ring /'ləstriNG/ ▸ **n.** var. of LUTESTRING.

lus·trous /'ləstrəs/ ▸ **adj.** having luster; shining. — **lus·trous·ly** adv. **lus·trous·ness** n.

lus·trum /'ləstrəm/ ▸ **n.** (pl. **-tra** /-trə/ or **-trums**) esp. literary hist. a period of five years. [16th C.: from L., orig. denoting a purificatory sacrifice after a quinquennial census.]

lust·y /'ləstē/ ▸ **adj.** (**lust·i·er**, **lust·i·est**) healthy and strong; full of vigor: *lusty singing.* — **lust·i·ly** adv. **lust·i·ness** n.

lu·sus na·tu·rae /'lo͞osəs nə't(y)o͝orˌē; -'t(y)o͝orˌī/ ▸ **n.** (pl. same or **lu·sus·es na·tu·rae**) rare a freak of nature. [L., 'a sport of nature.']

lu·ta·nist ▸ **n.** var. of LUTENIST.

lute[1] /lo͞ot/ ▸ **n.** a plucked stringed instrument with a long neck bearing frets and a rounded body with a flat front that is shaped like a halved egg. [ME: from OFr. *lut*, *leut*, prob. via Provençal from Arab. *al-'ūd*.]

lute[2] ▸ **n.** (also **lut·ing**) liquid clay or cement used to seal a joint, coat a crucible, or protect a graft. ▸ **v.** [trans.] seal, join, or coat with lute. [ME: from OFr. *lut* or med. L. *lutum*, a special use of L. *lutum* 'potter's clay.']

lu·te·al /'lo͞otēəl/ ▸ **adj.** Anat. of or relating to the corpus luteum.

lu·te·fisk /'lo͞otəˌfisk/ ▸ **n.** a Scandinavian dish consisting of dried cod soaked in lye and then boiled.

lu·te·in /'lo͞otēən; 'lo͞oˌtēn/ ▸ **n.** Biochem. a deep yellow pigment of the xanthophyll class, found in the leaves of plants, in egg yolk, and in the corpus luteum. [19th C.: from L. *luteum* 'yolk of egg' (neut. of *luteus* 'yellow') + -IN[1].]

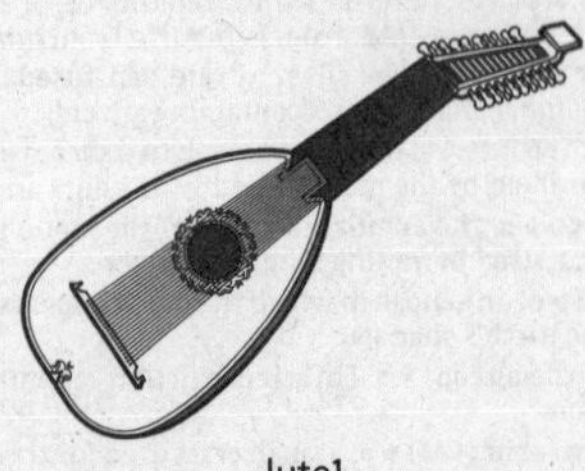

lute[1]

lu·te·in·iz·ing hor·mone /'lo͞otēəˌnīziNG; 'lo͞otnˌīziNG/ ▸ **n.** Biochem. a hormone secreted by the anterior pituitary gland that stimulates ovulation in females and the synthesis of androgen in males.

lu·te·nist /'lo͞otn-ist/ (also **lu·ta·nist**) ▸ **n.** a lute player. [17th C.: from med. L. *lutanista*, from *lutana* 'lute.']

luteo- ▸ **comb. form 1** orange-colored: *luteofulvous.* **2** relating to the corpus luteum: *luteotrophic.* [from L. *luteus* (or neut. *luteum*) 'yellow.']

lu·te·o·trop·ic hor·mone /ˌlo͞otēə'trōpik; -'träpik/ (also **lu·te·o·troph·ic hormone** /-'träfik; -'trō-/) ▸ **n.** another term for PROLACTIN.

lute·string /'lo͞otˌstriNG/ (also **lus·trine** /'ləstrēn/ or **lus·tring** /'ləstriNG/) ▸ **n.** hist. a glossy silk fabric, or a satin-weave fabric resembling it. [17th C.: from Fr. *lustrine* or from Ital. *lustrino*, from *lustro* 'luster.']

Lu·te·tia /lo͞o'tēsH(ē)ə/ Roman name for PARIS[1].

lu·te·ti·um /lo͞o'tēsH(ē)əm/ ▸ **n.** the chemical element of atomic number 71, a rare, silvery-white metal of the lanthanide series. (Symbol: **Lu**) [20th C.: from Fr. *lutécium*, from L. *Lutetia*, the ancient name of Paris, the home of its discoverer.]

Lu·ther /'lo͞oTHər/, Martin (1483–1546), German theologian. The principal figure of the German Reformation, he preached justification by faith and railed against the sale of indulgences and papal authority.

Lu·ther·an /'lo͞oTH(ə)rən/ ▸ **n.** a follower of Martin Luther. ▪ a member of the Lutheran Church. ▸ **adj.** of or characterized by the theology of Martin Luther. ▪ of or relating to the Lutheran Church. — **Lu·ther·an·ism** n. **Lu·ther·an·ize** v.

Lu·ther·an Church the Protestant Church founded on the teachings of Luther.

lu·thern /'lo͞oTHərn/ ▸ **n.** old-fashioned term for DORMER. [17th C.: perh. an alt. of earlier *lucarne* 'skylight,' from OFr.]

lu·thi·er /'lo͞otēər/ ▸ **n.** a maker of stringed instruments such as violins or guitars. [19th C.: from Fr., from *luth* 'lute.']

Lu·thu·li /lo͞o'to͞olē/ (also **Lu·tu·li**), Albert John (*c.*1898–1967), South African political leader. He was president of the African National Congress 1952–60. Nobel Peace Prize (1960).

lut·ing /'lo͞otiNG/ ▸ **n.** see LUTE[2].

lut·ist /'lo͞otist/ ▸ **n.** a lute player. ▪ a maker of lutes; a luthier.

Lut·yens /'lətyənz/, Sir Edwin Landseer (1869–1944), English architect. He is particularly known for his open garden-city layout in New Delhi in 1912 and for the Cenotaph in London (1919–21).

lutz /ləts; lo͝ots/ (also **Lutz**) ▸ **n.** Figure Skating a jump with a backward takeoff from the backward outside edge of one skate to the backward outside edge of the other, with one or more full turns in the air. [1930s: prob. from the name of Gustave *Lussi* (born 1898), who invented it.]

luv /ləv/ ▸ **n. & v.** nonstandard spelling of LOVE (representing informal or dialect use).

Lu·va·le /lo͞o'välā/ ▸ **n.** (pl. same) **1** a member of a people living mainly in eastern Angola and western Democratic Republic of the Congo (formerly Zaire). **2** the Bantu language of this people. ▸ **adj.** of or relating to this people or their language.

Lu·wi·an /'lo͞o-ēən/ (also **Lu·vi·an** /-vēən/) ▸ **n.** an Anatolian language of the 2nd millennium BC. It is recorded in both cuneiform and hieroglyphic scripts. [from *Luwia*, part of Asia Minor, + -AN.]

lux /ləks/ (abbr.: **lx**) ▸ **n.** (pl. same) the SI unit of illuminance, equal to one lumen per square meter. [19th C.: from L., 'light.']

lux·ate /'ləkˌsāt/ ▸ **v.** [trans.] Med. dislocate. — **lux·a·tion** /ˌlək'sāsHən/ n. [17th C.: from L. *luxat-* 'dislocated,' from the v. *luxare*, from *luxus* 'out of joint.']

luxe /ləks; lo͝oks/ ▸ **n.** luxury: [as adj.] *the luxe life.* [16th C.: from Fr., from L. *luxus* 'abundance.']

Lux·em·bourg /'ləksəmˌbərg; 'lo͝oksəmˌbo͝ork/ a country in western Europe, between Belgium and Germany and north of France; pop. 462,000; capital, Luxembourg. ▪ the capital of the Grand Duchy of Luxembourg; pop. 76,000. — **Lux·em·bourg·er** n.

Lux·em·burg·ish /'ləksəmˌbərgisH; 'lo͝oksəmˌbo͝or-/ ▸ **n.** the local language of Luxembourg, a form of German with a strong admixture of French. Also called LETZEBURGESCH.

Lux·or /'ləkˌsôr; 'lo͝ok-/ a city in eastern Egypt, the site of ancient Thebes; pop. 142,000. Arabic name EL UQSUR.

lux·u·ri·ant /ˌləg'zHo͝orēənt; ˌlək'sHo͝or-/ ▸ **adj.** (of vegetation) rich and profuse in growth; lush: *forests of dark, luxuriant foliage* | fig. *luxuriant prose.* ▪ (of hair) thick and healthy. — **lux·u·ri·ance** n. **lux·u·ri·ant·ly** adv.

lux·u·ri·ate /,ləg'zHŏŏrē,āt; ,lək'sHŏŏr-/ ▶ **v.** [intrans.] (often **luxuriate in**) enjoy oneself in a luxurious way; take self-indulgent delight: *she was luxuriating in a long bath.*

lux·u·ri·ous /,ləg'zHŏŏrēəs; ,lək'sHŏŏr-/ ▶ **adj.** extremely comfortable, elegant, or enjoyable, esp. in a way that involves great expense: *the bedrooms have luxurious marble bathrooms.* ■ giving self-indulgent or sensuous pleasure: *a luxurious wallow in a scented bath.* — **lux·u·ri·ous·ly adv. lux·u·ri·ous·ness n.**

lux·u·ry /'ləksH(ə)rē; 'ləgzH(ə)-/ ▶ **n.** (pl. **-ries**) the state of great comfort and extravagant living. ■ an inessential, desirable item that is expensive or difficult to obtain: *he considers bananas a luxury.* ▶ **adj.** [attrib.] luxurious or of the nature of a luxury: *a luxury yacht | luxury goods.* [ME: from OFr. *luxurie, luxure*, from L. *luxuria*, from *luxus* 'excess.']

Lu·zon /lŏŏ'zän/ the largest and most northern island in the Philippines.

lv. ▶ **abbr.** ■ leave or leaves.

Lviv /lə'vēf/ a city in western Ukraine; pop. 798,000. Russian name **Lvov**; Polish name **Lwów**; German name **Lemberg**.

LVN ▶ **abbr.** licensed vocational nurse.

lwei /lə'wā/ ▶ **n.** (pl. same) a monetary unit of Angola, equal to one hundredth of a kwanza.

LWM ▶ **abbr.** low-water mark.

Lwów /lə'vôf; -'vôv/ Polish name for **Lviv**.

LWV ▶ **abbr.** League of Women Voters.

lx Physics ▶ **abbr.** lux.

LXX ▶ **symb.** Septuagint. [special use of the Roman numeral for 70.]

-ly[1] /lē/ ▶ **suffix** forming adjectives meaning: **1** having the qualities of: *brotherly | rascally.* **2** recurring at intervals of: *hourly | quarterly.* [OE *-lic*, of Gmc. origin; rel. to **like**[1].]

-ly[2] ▶ **suffix** forming adverbs from adjectives, chiefly denoting manner or degree: *greatly | happily.* [OE *-līce*, of Gmc. origin.]

Lyall·pur /'līl,pŏŏr/ former name (until 1979) for **Faisalabad**.

ly·ase /'lī,ās; -,āz/ ▶ **n.** Biochem. an enzyme that catalyzes the joining of specified molecules or groups by a double bond.

ly·can·thrope /'līkən,THrōp/ ▶ **n.** a werewolf. [17th C.: from mod. L. *lycanthropus*, from Gk. *lukanthrōpos* 'wolf man' (see **lycanthropy**).]

ly·can·thro·py /lī'kanTHrəpē/ ▶ **n.** the supernatural transformation of a person into a wolf, as recounted in folk tales. ■ archaic a form of madness involving the delusion of being an animal, usually a wolf, with correspondingly altered behavior. — **ly·can·throp·ic** /,līkən'THräpik/ **adj.** [16th C. (as a supposed form of madness): from mod. L. *lycanthropia*, from Gk. *lukanthrōpia*, from *lukos* 'wolf' + *anthrōpos* 'human being, man.']

ly·cée /lē'sā/ ▶ **n.** (pl. pronounced same) a secondary school in France that is funded by the government. [Fr., from L. *lyceum* (see **Lyceum**).]

Ly·ce·um /lī'sēəm/ the garden at Athens in which Aristotle taught philosophy. ■ [as n.] (**the Lyceum**) Aristotelian philosophy and its followers. ■ [as n.] (**a lyceum**) archaic a literary institution, lecture hall, or teaching place. [via L. from Gk. *Lukeion*, neut. of *Lukeios*, epithet of Apollo.]

ly·chee /'lēchē/ ▶ **n.** var. of **litchi**.

lych·gate /'licH,gāt/ (also **lich·gate**) ▶ **n.** a roofed gateway to a churchyard, formerly used at burials for sheltering a coffin until the clergyman's arrival. [15th C.: from OE *līc* 'body' + **gate**.]

lych·nis /'liknis/ ▶ **n.** a plant of a genus (*Lychnis*) that includes the campions and a number of other, esp. ornamental, flowers of the pink family. [mod. L., via L. from Gk. *lukhnis*, denoting a red flower, from *lukhnos* 'lamp.']

Ly·cia /'lisH(ē)ə/ an ancient region in southwestern Asia Minor, between Caria and Pamphylia.

Ly·ci·an /'lisH(ē)ən/ ▶ **n.** **1** a native or inhabitant of ancient Lycia. **2** the Anatolian language of the Lycians.

ly·co·pene /'līkə,pēn/ ▶ **n.** Biochem. a red carotenoid pigment present in many fruits, such as the tomato. [1930s: from the var. *lycopin* (from mod. L. *Lycopersicon* + **-ene**.]

ly·co·pod /'līkə,päd/ ▶ **n.** Bot. a club moss (class Lycopsida), esp. a lycopodium. Giant lycopods the size of trees were common in the Carboniferous period. [19th C.: Anglicized form of **lycopodium**.]

ly·co·po·di·um /,līkə'pōdēəm/ ▶ **n.** a plant of a genus (*Lycopodium*) that includes the common club mosses. ■ (usu. **lycopodium powder** or **lycopodium seed**) a flammable powder consisting of club moss spores, formerly used as an absorbent in surgery and in making fireworks. [mod. L., from Gk. *lukos* 'wolf' + *pous, pod-* 'foot.']

Ly·cop·si·da /lī'käpsədə/ Bot. a class of pteridophyte plants that comprises the club mosses and their extinct relatives. — **ly·cop·sid** /-sid/ **n. & adj.** [mod. L. (pl.), from Gk. *lukos* 'wolf' + *opsis* 'appearance.']

Ly·cra /'līkrə/ ▶ **n.** trademark an elastic polyurethane fiber or fabric used esp. for close-fitting sports clothing.

lydd·ite /'lid,īt/ ▶ **n.** esp. hist. a high explosive containing picric acid, used during World War I. [19th C.: named after *Lydd*, England.]

Lyd·i·a /'lidēə/ an ancient region of western Asia Minor.

Lyd·i·an /'lidēən/ ▶ **n.** **1** a native or inhabitant of Lydia. **2** the Anatolian language of the Lydians. ▶ **adj.** of or relating to the Lydians or their language.

lye /lī/ ▶ **n.** a strongly alkaline solution, esp. of potassium hydroxide, used for washing or cleansing. [OE *lēag*, of Gmc. origin: rel. to Du. *loog*, Ger. *Lauge*, also to **lather**.]

ly·ing[1] /'lī-iNG/ present participle of **lie**[1].

ly·ing[2] present participle of **lie**[2]. ▶ **adj.** [attrib.] not telling the truth: *he's a lying, cheating, snake in the grass.* — **ly·ing·ly adv.**

ly·ing-in ▶ **n.** archaic seclusion before and after childbirth; confinement.

Ly·ly /'lilē/, John (*c.*1554–1606), English writer and playwright. His prose romance *Euphues* was written in a style that became known as *euphuism*.

Lyme dis·ease /līm/ ▶ **n.** an inflammatory disease characterized at first by a rash, headache, fever, and chills, and later by possible arthritis and neurological and cardiac disorders. It is caused by the spirochete *Borrelia burgdorferi*, which is transmitted by ticks. [1970s: named after *Lyme*, Connecticut.]

lymph /limf/ ▶ **n.** **1** Physiol. a colorless fluid containing white blood cells, which bathes the tissues and drains through the lymphatic system into the bloodstream. ■ fluid exuding from a sore or inflamed tissue. **2** literary pure water. — **lymph·ous** /-fəs/ **adj.** [16th C. (sense 2): from Fr. *lymphe* or L. *lympha, limpa* 'water.']

lymph- ▶ **comb. form** var. of **lympho-** shortened before a vowel, as in *lymphangiography*.

lym·phad·e·ni·tis /,lim,fadn'ītis/ ▶ **n.** Med. inflammation of the lymph nodes.

lym·phad·e·nop·a·thy /,lim,fadn'äpəTHē/ ▶ **n.** Med. a disease affecting the lymph nodes.

lym·phan·gi·og·ra·phy /,lim,fanjē'ägrəfē/ ▶ **n.** Med. X-ray examination of the vessels of the lymphatic system after injection of a substance opaque to X-rays. — **lym·phan·gi·o·gram** /lim'fanjēə,gram/ **n. lym·phan·gi·o·graph·ic** /-jēə'grafik/ **adj.**

lym·phan·gi·tis /,lim,fan'jītis/ ▶ **n.** Med. inflammation of the walls of the lymphatic vessels.

lym·phat·ic /lim'fatik/ ▶ **adj.** **1** [attrib.] Physiol. of or relating to lymph or its secretion. **2** archaic (of a person) pale, flabby, or sluggish. ▶ **n.** Anat. a vein-like vessel conveying lymph in the body. [17th C.: from L. *lymphaticus* 'mad,' from Gk. *numpholēptos* 'seized by nymphs.']

lym·phat·ic sys·tem ▶ **n.** the network of vessels through which lymph drains from the tissues into the blood.

lymph gland ▶ **n.** less technical term for **lymph node**.

lymph node ▶ **n.** Physiol. each of a number of small swellings in the lymphatic system where lymph is filtered and lymphocytes are formed.

lympho- (also **lymph-** before a vowel) ▶ **comb. form** representing **lymph**: *lymphocyte.*

lym·pho·blast /'limfə,blast/ ▶ **n.** Med. an abnormal cell resembling a large lymphocyte, produced in large numbers in a form of leukemia. — **lym·pho·blas·tic** /,limfə'blastik/ **adj.**

lym·pho·cyte /'limfə,sīt/ ▶ **n.** Physiol. a form of small leukocyte (white blood cell) with a single round nucleus, occurring esp. in the lymphatic system. — **lym·pho·cyt·ic** /,limfə'sitik/ **adj.**

lym·phog·ra·phy /lim'fägrəfē/ ▶ **n.** short for **lymphangiography**.

lym·phoid /'lim,foid/ ▶ **adj.** Anat. & Med. of, relating to, or denoting the tissue responsible for producing lymphocytes and antibodies.

lym·pho·kine /'limfə,kīn/ ▶ **n.** Physiol. a substance produced by lymphocytes, such as interferon, that acts upon other cells of the immune system, e.g., by activating macrophages. [1960s: from **lympho-** + Gk. *kinein* 'to move.']

lym·pho·ma /lim'fōmə/ ▶ **n.** (pl. **-mas** or **-ma·ta** /-mətə/) Med. cancer of the lymph nodes.

lym·pho·re·tic·u·lar /,limfō-ri'tikyələr/ ▶ **adj.** another term for **reticuloendothelial**.

lym·pho·tox·in /,limfə'täksin/ ▶ **n.** Immunol. a lymphokine that causes the destruction of certain cells, esp. tumor cells.

lynch /lincH/ ▶ **v.** [trans.] (of a mob) kill (someone), esp. by hanging, for an alleged offense with or without a legal trial. — **lynch·er n.** [19th C.: named after Capt. William *Lynch*, head of a self-constituted judicial tribunal in Virginia *c.*1780.]

Lynch·burg /'lincH,bərg/ a city in west central Virginia; pop. 65,269.

lynch mob ▶ **n.** a band of people intent on lynching someone.

lynch·pin /'lincH,pin/ ▶ **n.** var. of **linchpin**.

Lynn /lin/ a city in northeastern Massachusetts; pop. 89,050.

Lynx /liNGks/ Astron. an inconspicuous northern constellation (the Lynx), between Ursa Major and Gemini.

lynx /liNGks/ ▶ **n.** a wild cat (genus *Lynx*) with yellowish-brown fur, a short tail, and tufted ears, found chiefly in the northern latitudes of North America and Eurasia. Two species include the **Eurasian lynx** (L. lynx) and the **Canadian lynx** (L. canadensis or L. lynx). *See illustration on next page.* ■ (**African lynx**) see **caracal**. [ME: via L. from Gk. *lunx*.]

lynx-eyed ▶ **adj.** keen-sighted.

Lyon /'līən/, Mary Mason (1797–1849), US educator. She founded Mount Holyoke Female Seminary (later Mount Holyoke College).

ly·on·naise /,līə'nāz/ ▶ **adj.** (of food, esp. sliced potatoes) cooked with onions or a wine and onion sauce. [Fr., 'characteristic of the city of Lyons.']

Ly·ons /lē'ôN; 'līənz/ a city in southeastern France; pop. 422,000. French name **Lyon**.

PRONUNCIATION KEY ə *ago, up*; ər *over, fur*; a *hat*; ā *ate*; ä *car*; e *let*; ē *see*; i *fit*; ī *by*; NG *sing*; ō *go*; ô *law, for*; oi *toy*; ŏŏ *good*; ōō *goo*; ou *out*; TH *thin*; T͟H *then*; ZH *vision*

Eurasian lynx

ly·o·phil·ic /ˌlīəˈfilik/ ▶adj. Chem. (of a colloid) readily dispersed by a solvent and not easily precipitated. [20th C.: from Gk. *luein* 'loosen, dissolve' + *philos* 'loving.']

ly·oph·i·lize /līˈäfəˌlīz/ ▶v. [trans.] tech. freeze-dry (a substance). —**ly·oph·i·li·za·tion** /-ˌäfələˈzāshən; -ˌlīˈzā-/ n.

ly·o·pho·bic /ˌlīəˈfōbik/ ▶adj. Chem. (of a colloid) not lyophilic.

lyr. ▶abbr. lyric.

Ly·ra /ˈlīrə/ Astron. a small northern constellation (the Lyre), said to represent the lyre invented by Hermes. It contains the bright star Vega.

lyre /lī(ə)r/ ▶n. a stringed instrument like a small U-shaped harp with strings fixed to a crossbar, used esp. in ancient Greece. [ME: via OFr. *lire* and L. *lyra* from Gk. *lura*.]

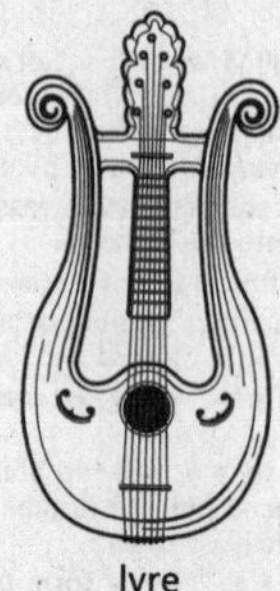
lyre

lyre·bird /ˈlī(ə)rˌbərd/ ▶n. a large Australian songbird (genus *Menura*, family Menuridae), the male of which has a long, lyre-shaped tail and is noted for his remarkable song and display.

lyr·ic /ˈlirik/ ▶adj. **1** (of poetry) expressing the writer's emotions, usually briefly and in stanzas. ■ (of a poet) writing in this manner. **2** (of a singing voice) using a light register: *a lyric soprano with a light, clear timbre.* ▶n. (usu. **lyrics**) **1** a lyric poem or verse. ■ lyric poetry as a literary genre. **2** the words of a song. [16th C.: from Fr. *lyrique* or L. *lyricus*, from Gk. *lurikos*, from *lura* 'lyre.']

lyr·i·cal /ˈlirikəl/ ▶adj. **1** (of literature, art, or music) expressing the writer's emotions in an imaginative and beautiful way: *the poet's combination of lyrical and descriptive power.* ■ (of poetry or a poet) lyric: *Wordsworth's Lyrical Ballads.* **2** of or relating to the words of a popular song. —**lyr·i·cal·ly** adv.

lyr·i·cism /ˈlirəˌsizəm/ ▶n. an artist's expression of emotion in an imaginative and beautiful way; the quality of being lyrical.

lyr·i·cist /ˈlirəsist/ ▶n. a person who writes the words to a popular song or musical.

lyr·i·cize /ˈlirəˌsīz/ ▶v. [intrans.] Music write or sing lyrics. ■ to write in a lyric style. ■ [trans.] to treat in a lyric style or put into lyric form.

lyr·ist /ˈlī(ə)rist; ˈlirist/ ▶n. **1** a person who plays the lyre. **2** a lyric poet.

Ly·san·der /līˈsandər/ (died 395 BC) Spartan general. He captured Athens in 404, bringing the Peloponnesian War to an end.

ly·sate /ˈlīˌsāt/ ▶n. Biol. a preparation containing the products of lysis of cells.

lyse /līs; līz/ ▶v. Biol. undergo or cause to undergo lysis. [20th C.: back-form. from LYSIS.]

Ly·sen·ko /līˈsenkō; liˈsyenkə/, Trofim Denisovich (1898–1976), Soviet biologist and geneticist. He was an adherent of Lamarck's theory of evolution by the inheritance of acquired characteristics. —**Ly·sen·ko·ism** /-kōˌizəm/ n. **Ly·sen·ko·ist** /-kōˌist/ adj, n.

ly·ser·gic ac·id /līˈsərjik; li-/ ▶n. Chem. a crystalline compound, $C_{16}H_{16}N_2O_2$, prepared from natural ergot alkaloids or synthetically, from which the drug LSD can be made. [1930s: *lysergic* from *(hydro)lys(is) + erg(ot)* + -IC.]

ly·sin /ˈlīsin/ ▶n. Biol. an antibody or other substance able to cause lysis of cells (esp. bacteria).

ly·sine /ˈlīˌsēn/ ▶n. Biochem. a basic amino acid, $NH_2(CH_2)_4CH(NH_2)COOH$, that is a constituent of most proteins. It is an essential nutrient in the diet of vertebrates. [19th C.: from Ger. *Lysin*, based on LYSIS.]

ly·sis /ˈlīsis/ ▶n. **1** Biol. the disintegration of a cell by rupture of the cell wall or membrane. **2** the gradual decline of disease symptoms. [19th C.: from L., from Gk. *lusis* 'loosening,' from *luein* 'loosen.']

-lysis ▶comb. form denoting disintegration or decomposition: ■ in nouns specifying an agent: *hydrolysis.* ■ in nouns specifying a reactant: *hemolysis.* ■ in nouns specifying the nature of the process: *autolysis.* [via L. from Gk. *lusis* 'loosening.']

Ly·sol /ˈlīˌsôl; -ˌsäl/ ▶n. trademark a disinfectant consisting of a mixture of cresols and soft soap.

ly·so·some /ˈlīsəˌsōm/ ▶n. Biol. an organelle in the cytoplasm of eukaryotic cells containing degradative enzymes enclosed in a membrane. —**ly·so·so·mal** /ˌlīsəˈsōməl/ adj.

ly·so·zyme /ˈlīsəˌzīm/ ▶n. Biochem. an enzyme that catalyzes the destruction of the cell walls of certain bacteria, occurring notably in tears and egg white. [20th C.: from LYSIS + a shortened form of ENZYME.]

lyt·ic /ˈlitik/ ▶adj. Biol. of, relating to, or causing lysis. —**lyt·i·cal·ly** adv.

-lytic ▶comb. form in adjectives corresponding to nouns ending in *-lysis*. [from Gk. *-lutikos* 'able to loosen.']

Lyt·ton /ˈlitn/, 1st Baron (1803–73), British writer; born *Edward George Earle Bulwer-Lytton.* His historical romances include *The Last Days of Pompeii* (1834).

LZ ▶abbr. landing zone.

Mm

M¹ /em/ (also **m**) ▶ **n.** (pl. **Ms** or **M's**) **1** the thirteenth letter of the alphabet. See also **EM.** ▪ denoting the next after L in a set of items, categories, etc. **2** (**M**) a shape like that of a capital M. **3** the Roman numeral for 1,000. [from L. *mille*.]

M² ▶ **abbr.** ▪ Majesty. ▪ male. ▪ Manitoba. ▪ Marquis. ▪ Music measure. ▪ medicine. ▪ medium (as a clothes size). ▪ [in comb.] (in units of measurement) mega-: *8 Mbytes of memory.* ▪ meridian. ▪ Chem. (with reference to solutions) molar. ▪ Monday. ▪ Monsieur: *M Chirac.*

m ▶ **abbr.** ▪ mare. ▪ (in Germany) mark; marks. ▪ married: *m twice; two d.* ▪ masculine. ▪ Physics mass. ▪ (*m*-) [in comb.] Chem. meta-: *m-xylene.* ▪ meter(s). ▪ mile(s). ▪ [in comb.] (in units of measurement) milli-: *100 mA.* ▪ million(s): *$5 m.* ▪ minute(s). ▪ modification of. ▪ month. ▪ moon. ▪ morning. ▶ **symb.** Physics mass: $E = mc^2$.

'm¹ /m/ informal ▶ **abbr.** am: *I'm a doctor.*

'm² ▶ **n.** informal madam: *yes'm.*

M-1 ▶ **n.** a.30-caliber semiautomatic clip-fed rifle capable of firing eight rounds before reloading, the standard rifle used by US troops in World War II and the Korean War.

M-16 ▶ **n.** a lightweight, fully automatic assault rifle that shoots small-caliber bullets at an extremely high velocity, used by US troops after 1966.

MA ▶ **abbr.** ▪ Massachusetts (in official postal use). ▪ Master of Arts: *David Jones, MA.* ▪ Military Academy.

Ma /mä/, Yo-Yo (1955–), US cellist; born in France. He debuted at New York City's Carnegie Hall at age nine.

ma /mä/ ▶ **n.** informal one's mother. [19th C.: abbrev. of **MAMA.**]

ma'am /mam/ ▶ **n.** a term of respectful or polite address used for a woman: *excuse me, ma'am.* [17th C.: contr. of **MADAM.**]

maar /mär/ ▶ **n.** Geol. a broad, shallow crater, typically filled by a lake, formed by a volcanic explosion. [19th C.: from Ger., orig. a kind of crater lake in the Eifel district.]

Maas /mäs/ Dutch name for **MEUSE.**

Maa·sai ▶ **n. & adj.** var. of **MASAI.**

Maas·tricht /'mäs,trikt; -,trikht/ a city in the Netherlands on the Meuse River near the Belgian and German borders; pop. 117,000.

Ma·at /mät/ Egyptian Mythol. the goddess of truth, justice, and cosmic order, daughter of Ra.

Ma Bell ▶ **n.** informal a nickname for the American Telephone and Telegraph Corporation.

Mac /mak/ ▶ **n.** informal a form of address for a man whose name is unknown to the speaker. [17th C.: from *Mac-*, a patronymic prefix in many Scots and Irish surnames.]

ma·ca·bre /mə'käbrə; -'käb/ ▶ **adj.** disturbing and horrifying because of involvement with or depiction of death and injury: *a macabre series of murders.* [19th C.: from Fr. *macabre*, from *Danse Macabre* 'dance of death,' from OFr., perh. from *Macabé* 'a Maccabee,' with ref. to a miracle play depicting the slaughter of the Maccabees.]

mac·ad·am /mə'kadəm/ ▶ **n.** broken stone, bound with tar or bitumen, used for surfacing roads. ▪ a stretch of road with such a surface. — **mac·ad·amed adj. mac·ad·am·ize v.** [19th C.: after John L. *McAdam* (1756–1836).]

mac·a·da·mi·a /,makə'dāmēə/ ▶ **n.** an Australian tree (genus *Macadamia*, family Proteaceae) with glossy evergreen leaves and globular edible nuts. Several species include *M. integrifolia* and *M. tetraphylla*, cultivated for their nuts. ▪ (also **macadamia nut**) the edible nut of this tree. [mod. L., after John *Macadam* (1827–65), Australian chemist.]

Mac·Al·pin /mə'kalpən/, Kenneth, see **KENNETH I.**

Ma·cao /mə'kou/ a Special Administrative Region (SAR) of China, on the southeastern coast opposite Hong Kong, comprising the Macao peninsula and the islands of Taipa and Cologne; pop. 467,000; capital, Macao City. In 1999 Macao passed to China, as agreed in 1987. Portuguese name **MACAU.** — **Mac·a·nese** /,makə'nēz; -'nēs/ **adj. & n.**

Ma·ca·pá /,mäkə'pä/ a town in northern Brazil; pop. 167,000.

ma·caque /mə'käk; -'kak/ (also **macaque monkey**) ▶ **n.** a medium-sized Old World monkey (genus *Macaca*, family Cercopithecidae) that has a long face and cheek pouches for holding food. [17th C.: via Fr. and Port.; based on Bantu *ma* (denoting a pl.) + *kaku* 'monkey.']

Ma·ca·re·na /,mäkə'rānə/ ▶ **n.** a dance performed with hand and body language, including exaggerated hip motion, to 16 beats of music.

Mac·a·ro·ne·sia /,makərə'nēzhə/ Bot. a phytogeographical region comprising the Azores, Madeira, Canary Islands, and Cape Verde Islands. — **Mac·a·ro·ne·sian** /-'nēzhēən/ **adj.** [from Gk. *makarōn nēsoi* 'islands of the Blessed.']

mac·a·ro·ni /,makə'rōnē/ ▶ **n.** (pl. **-nies**) **1** a variety of pasta formed in narrow tubes. **2** an 18th-century British dandy affecting Continental fashions. [16th C.: from Ital. *maccaroni* (now usually spelled *maccheroni*), pl. of *maccarone*, from late Gk. *makaria* 'food made from barley.']

mac·a·ron·ic /,makə'ränik/ ▶ **adj.** denoting language, esp. burlesque verse, containing words or inflections introduced from another language. ▶ **n.** (usu. **macaronics**) macaronic verse, esp. that which mixes the vernacular with Latin. [17th C.: from mod. L. *macaronicus*, from obs. Ital. *macaronico*.]

mac·a·ro·ni pen·guin ▶ **n.** a penguin (*Eudyptes chrysolophus*) with an orange crest, breeding on islands in the Antarctic. [19th C.: because the crest was thought to resemble the hairstyle of dandies known as *macaronies* (see **MACARONI**).]

mac·a·roon /,makə'ro͞on/ ▶ **n.** a cookie made with egg white, sugar, and ground almonds or coconut.

Mac·Ar·thur /mə'kärthər/, Douglas (1880–1964), US general. Commander of US (later Allied) forces in the southwestern Pacific during World War II, he accepted Japan's surrender in 1945 and administered the ensuing Allied occupation. He was in charge of UN forces in Korea 1950–51.

Ma·cas·sar /mə'kasər/ ▶ **n.** **1** (also **Macassar oil**) a kind of oil formerly used, esp. by men, to make the hair shine and lie flat. **2** var. of **MAKASSAR.**

Ma·cau /mə'kou/ Portuguese name for **MACAO.**

Ma·cau·lay /mə'kôlē/, Thomas Babington, 1st Baron (1800–59), English historian. His works include *History of England* (1849–61).

ma·caw /mə'kô/ ▶ **n.** a large long-tailed parrot (*Ara* and related genera) with brightly colored plumage, native to Central and South America. [17th C.: from Port. *macao*, of unknown origin.]

Mac·beth /mək'beth, mak-/ (*c.*1005–57), king of Scotland 1040–57; protagonist of a tragedy by Shakespeare. He came to the throne after killing his cousin Duncan I in battle.

Macc. ▶ **abbr.** Maccabees (Apocrypha) (in biblical references).

Mac·ca·bae·us, Judas, see **JUDAS MACCABAEUS.**

Mac·ca·bees /'makə,bēz/ ▶ **plural n.** hist. the members or followers of the family of Judas Maccabaeus. ▪ (in full **the Books of the Maccabees**) four books of Jewish history and theology. — **Mac·ca·be·an** /,makə'bēən/ **adj.** [ME: from L. *Maccabaeus*, an epithet applied to Judas, perh. from Heb. *maqqeḇet* 'hammer' (by association with the religious revolt led by Judas).]

Mac·don·ald¹ /mək'dänəld/, Sir John Alexander (1815–91), prime minister of Canada 1867–73, 1878–91; born in Scotland. He played a leading role in the confederation of the Canadian provinces.

Mac·Don·ald², James Ramsay (1866–1937), prime minister of Britain 1924, 1929–35.

Mac·Don·nel Rang·es /mək'dänl/ a series of mountain ranges in Northern Territory, Australia.

Mace /mās/ ▶ **n.** trademark an irritant chemical used in an aerosol to disable attackers. ▶ **v.** (also **mace**) [trans.] spray (someone) with Mace.

mace¹ /mās/ ▶ **n.** **1** hist. a heavy club, typically having a metal head and spikes. **2** a ceremonial staff of office. [ME: from OFr. *masse* 'large hammer.']

mace² ▶ **n.** the reddish fleshy outer covering of the nutmeg, dried as a spice.

mac·é·doine /,mäsə'dwän/ ▶ **n.** a mixture of vegetables or fruit cut into small pieces and served as a salad. ▪ fig. a medley or jumble. [Fr., lit. 'Macedonia,' from the mixture of peoples in the Macedonian Empire of Alexander the Great.]

Mac·e·do·ni·a /,masə'dōnēə; -nyə/ **1** (also **Mac·e·don** /'masədən; -,dän/) an ancient country in southeastern Europe, north of Greece. **2** a region in northeastern Greece; capital, Thessaloníki. **3** a republic in the Balkans. *See box on next page.*

Mac·e·do·ni·an /,masə'dōnēən/ ▶ **n.** **1** a native or inhabitant of the Former Yugoslav Republic of Macedonia. **2** a native of ancient Macedonia. ▪ a native or inhabitant of the region of Macedonia in modern Greece. **3** the South Slavic language of the republic of Macedonia and adjacent parts of Bulgaria. **4** the language of ancient Macedonia. ▶ **adj.** of or relating to Macedonia or Macedonian.

Macedonia

Official name: Republic of Macedonia
Location: southeastern Europe, bordered by Serbia, Montenegro, Bulgaria, Albania, and Greece
Area: 9,800 square miles (25,300 sq km)
Population: 2,038,000
Capital: Skopje
Languages: Macedonian (official), Albanian, Turkish, Serbo-Croatian
Currency: Macedonian denar

Mac·e·do·ni·an Wars a series of four wars between Rome and Macedonia in the 3rd and 2nd centuries BC.

Ma·ceió /ˌmäsäˈō/ a city in eastern Brazil; pop. 700,000.

mac·er·ate /ˈmasəˌrāt/ ▶ **v.** [trans.] soften or break up (something, esp. food) by soaking in a liquid. ■ [intrans.] become softened or broken up by soaking. — **mac·er·a·tion** /ˌmasəˈrāsʜən/ **n.** **mac·er·a·tor** /-ˌrātər/ **n.** [16th C.: from L. *macerat-* 'made soft, soaked,' from *macerare*.]

Mach¹ /mäk; mäкн/, Ernst (1838–1916), Austrian physicist. He did important work on aerodynamics.

Mach² /mäk/ (also **Mach number**) ▶ **n.** the ratio of the speed of a body to the speed of sound. It is often used with a numeral (as **Mach 1, Mach 2,** etc.) to indicate the speed of sound, twice the speed of sound, etc.

mache /mäsʜ/ (also **mâche**) ▶ **n.** another term for CORN SALAD.

mach·er /ˈmäкнər/ ▶ **n.** informal a person who gets things done. ■ derog. an overbearing person. [1930s: from Yiddish *makher*, from Mid. High Ger. *macher* 'doer, active person.']

ma·chet·e /məˈsʜetē/ ▶ **n.** a broad, heavy knife used as an implement or weapon. [16th C.: from Sp., from *macho* 'hammer.']

Mach·i·a·vel·li /ˌmäkēəˈvelē; ˌmak-/, Niccolò di Bernardo dei (1469–1527), Italian statesman and political philosopher. In *The Prince* (1532), he advises rulers that the effective use of power may necessitate unethical methods.

Mach·i·a·vel·li·an /ˌmakēəˈvelēən; ˌmäk-/ ▶ **adj.** **1** cunning, scheming, and unscrupulous, esp. in politics or in advancing one's career. **2** of or relating to Niccolò Machiavelli. ▶ **n.** a person who schemes in such a way. — **Mach·i·a·vel·li·an·ism n.**

ma·chin·a·ble /məˈsʜēnəbəl/ ▶ **adj.** (of a material) able to be worked by a machine tool. — **ma·chin·a·bil·i·ty** /məˌsʜēnəˈbilətē/ **n.**

mach·i·nate /ˈmakəˌnāt; ˈmasʜə-/ ▶ **v.** [intrans.] engage in plots and intrigues; scheme. — **mach·i·na·tion** /ˌmakəˈnāsʜən; ˌmasʜə-/ **n.** **mach·i·na·tor** /-ˌnātər/ **n.** [16th C.: from L. *machinat-* 'contrived,' from *machinari*, from *machina*.]

ma·chine /məˈsʜēn/ ▶ **n.** an apparatus using or applying mechanical power to perform a particular task. ■ [usu. with adj.] a coin-operated dispenser: *a candy machine*. ■ tech. any device that transmits a force or directs its application. ■ fig. an efficient and well-organized group of powerful people: *a powerful political machine*. ▶ **v.** [trans.] (esp. in manufacturing) make or operate on with a machine: [as adj.] (**machined**) *a decoratively machined brass rod*. [16th C.: from Fr., via L. from Doric Greek *makhana* (cognate with Attic Gk. *mēkhanē*, from *mēkhos* 'contrivance').]

ma·chine code (also **machine language**) ▶ **n.** a computer programming language consisting of binary or hexadecimal instructions.

ma·chine gun ▶ **n.** an automatic gun that fires bullets in rapid succession for as long as the trigger is pressed.

ma·chine-read·a·ble ▶ **adj.** (of data or text) in a form that a computer can process.

ma·chin·er·y /məˈsʜēn(ə)rē/ ▶ **n.** machines collectively: *farm machinery*. ■ the components of a machine. ■ the organization or structure of something: *the machinery of democracy*. ■ the means devised or available to do something: *with the grievance machinery in place*.

ma·chine screw ▶ **n.** a fastening device similar to a bolt that can be turned with a screwdriver. See illustration at SCREW.

ma·chine tool ▶ **n.** a nonportable power tool, such as a lathe, used for cutting or shaping metal, wood, etc. — **ma·chine-tooled adj.**

ma·chin·ist /məˈsʜēnist/ ▶ **n.** a person who operates a machine, esp. a machine tool. ■ a person who makes or repairs machinery.

ma·chis·mo /məˈcʜēzmō; -ˈkēz-/ ▶ **n.** strong or aggressive masculine pride. [1940s: Mex. Sp., from *macho* 'male' (see MACHO).]

ma·cho /ˈmäcʜō/ ▶ **adj.** showing aggressive pride in one's masculinity: *the big macho tough guy*. ▶ **n.** (pl. **-chos**) a man who is aggressively proud of his masculinity. ■ machismo. [1920s: Mex. Sp., 'masc. or vigorous,' from L. *masculus*.]

Ma·chu Pic·chu /ˌmäcʜo͞o ˈpi(k)cʜo͞o/ a fortified Inca town, high on a steep-sided ridge in the Andes Mountains in Peru.

Mc·In·tosh /ˈmakənˌtäsʜ/ (also **McIntosh red**) ▶ **n.** a dessert apple of a variety native to North America. [19th C.: after John *McIntosh* (1777–1845 or 1846), on whose farm the apple was discovered.]

mac·in·tosh ▶ **n.** var. of MACKINTOSH.

Mac·ken·zie¹ /məˈkenzē/, Sir Alexander (1764–1820), Scottish explorer. He discovered the Mackenzie River in Canada in 1789 and is the first person known to have crossed Canada from Atlantic to Pacific.

Mac·ken·zie², William Lyon (1795–1861), Canadian politician born in Scotland, an advocate for political reform in Canada.

Mac·ken·zie Riv·er /məˈkenzē/ a river that flows northwest for 1,060 miles (1,700 km) from Great Slave Lake in Canada to the Arctic Ocean.

mack·er·el /ˈmak(ə)rəl/ ▶ **n.** (pl. same or **-er·els**) a migratory surface-dwelling predatory fish. The **mackerel family** (Scombridae) includes many species, in particular the **North Atlantic mackerel** (*S. scombrus*), commercially important as a food fish. [ME: from OFr. *maquerel*, of unknown origin.]

mack·er·el sky ▶ **n.** a sky dappled with rows of typically cirrocumulus clouds, like the pattern on a mackerel's back.

Mack·i·nac, Straits of /ˈmakəˌnô/ a passage between lakes Huron and Michigan, crossed since 1957 by the Mackinac Bridge.

mack·i·naw /ˈmakəˌnô/ (also **mackinaw coat** or **jacket**) ▶ **n.** a short coat or jacket made of a thick, heavy woolen cloth, typically with a plaid design. [19th C.: after *Mackinaw* City, Michigan.]

mack·in·tosh /ˈmakənˌtäsʜ/ (also **mac·in·tosh**) ▶ **n.** esp. Brit. a full-length waterproof coat. ■ [usu. as adj.] cloth waterproofed with rubber. [19th C.: after Charles *Macintosh* (1766–1843), Scot. inventor.]

mack·le /ˈmakəl/ ▶ **n.** a blurred impression in printing. [16th C.: from Fr. *macule*, from L. *macula* 'stain.']

ma·cle /ˈmakəl/ ▶ **n.** a diamond or other crystal that is twinned. [19th C.: from Fr., from Anglo-L. *mascula* 'mesh.']

Mac·lean /məˈklēn/, Alistair (1922–87), Scottish writer. His novels include *The Guns of Navarone* (1957).

Mac·Leish /məˈklēsʜ/, Archibald (1892–1982), US poet. His works include *Conquistador* (1932), *Collected Poems* (1952), and *J.B.* (1958).

Mac·leod /məˈkloud/, John James Rickard (1876–1935), Scottish physiologist. He directed the research that led to the discovery of insulin. Nobel Prize for Physiology or Medicine (1923, shared with F.G. Banting).

Mac·mil·lan /məkˈmilən/, Maurice Harold, 1st Earl of Stockton (1894–1986), prime minister of Britain 1957–63. During his term, the Test Ban Treaty (1963) with the US and the Soviet Union was signed.

Ma·con /ˈmākən/ a city in central Georgia; pop. 97,255.

Mac·quar·ie Riv·er /məˈkwôrē; -ˈkwärē/ a river in New South Wales, Australia, that rises on the Great Dividing Range and flows northwest for 600 miles (960 km) to the Darling River.

mac·ra·mé /ˈmakrəˌmā/ ▶ **n.** the art of knotting cord or string in patterns to make decorative articles. ■ [usu. as adj.] fabric or articles made in this way. [19th C.: Fr., from Turk. *makrama* 'tablecloth or towel,' from Arab. *miḳrama* 'bedspread.']

mac·ro /ˈmakrō/ ▶ **n.** (pl. **-ros**) **1** (also **macro instruction**) Comput. a single instruction that expands automatically into a set of instructions. **2** Photog. short for MACRO LENS. ▶ **adj.** **1** large-scale; overall: *the analysis of social events at the macro level*. Often contrasted with MICRO. **2** Photog. relating to or used in macrophotography.

macro- ▶ **comb. form** **1** long; over a long period: *macroevolution*. **2** large; large-scale: *macromolecule* | *macronutrient*. ■ (used in medical terms) large compared with the norm: *macrocephaly*. [from Gk. *makros* 'long, large.']

mac·ro·bi·ot·ic /ˌmakrōbīˈätik/ ▶ **adj.** relating to a diet of whole pure prepared foods, based on the Taoist principles of yin and yang. ▶ **plural n.** (**macrobiotics**) [treated as sing.] the use or theory of such a diet.

mac·ro·ce·phal·ic /ˌmakrōsəˈfalik/ (also **mac·ro·ceph·a·lous** /-ˈsefələs/) ▶ **adj.** Anat. having an unusually large head. — **mac·ro·ceph·a·ly** /-ˈsefəlē/ **n.**

mac·ro·cosm /ˈmakrəˌkäzəm/ (also **mac·ro·cos·mos** /-ˌkäzməs; -mōs/) ▶ **n.** the universe; the cosmos. ■ the whole of a complex structure, esp. as represented or epitomized in a small part of itself (a microcosm). — **mac·ro·cos·mic** /ˌmakrəˈkäzmik/ **adj.** **mac·ro·cos·mi·cal·ly adv.**

mac·ro·cy·clic /ˌmakrōˈsiklik; -ˈsīklik/ ▶ **adj.** Chem. of, relating to, or denoting a ring composed of a relatively large number of atoms. — **mac·ro·cy·cle** /ˈmakrōˌsīkəl/ **n.**

mac·ro·ec·o·nom·ics /ˈmakrōˌekəˈnämiks; -ˌēkə-/ ▶ **plural n.** [treated as sing.] the part of economics concerned with large-scale or general economic factors, such as interest rates and national productivity. — **mac·ro·ec·o·nom·ic** adj. **mac·ro·e·con·o·mist** /-iˈkänəmist/ n.

mac·ro·e·con·o·my /ˈmakrō-iˈkänəmē/ ▶ n. a large-scale economic system.

mac·ro·ev·o·lu·tion /ˌmakrō-evəˈlo͞osʜən; -ˌēvə-/ ▶ n. Biol. major evolutionary change. — **mac·ro·ev·o·lu·tion·ar·y** adj.

mac·ro·gam·ete /ˌmakrōgəˈmēt; -ˈgamˌēt/ ▶ n. Biol. (esp. in protozoans) the larger of a pair of conjugating gametes, usually regarded as female.

mac·ro lens ▶ n. Photog. a lens suitable for taking photographs unusually close to the subject.

mac·ro·lep·i·dop·ter·a /ˈmakrōˌlepəˈdäptərə/ ▶ plural n. Entomol. the butterflies and larger moths.

mac·ro·mol·e·cule /ˌmakrōˈmäləˌkyo͞ol/ ▶ n. Chem. a molecule containing a very large number of atoms. — **mac·ro·mo·lec·u·lar** /-məˈlekyələr/ adj.

ma·cron /ˈmāˌkrän; ˈmak-; ˈmākrən/ ▶ n. a written or printed mark (¯) used to indicate a long or stressed vowel in some languages. [19th C.: from Gk. *makron*, neut. of *makros* 'long.']

mac·ro·nu·tri·ent /ˌmakrōˈno͞otrēənt/ ▶ n. Biol. a substance required in relatively large amounts by living organisms, in particular: ■ a type of food required in large amounts in the human diet. ■ a chemical element required in large amounts for plant growth.

mac·ro·phage /ˈmakrəˌfāj/ ▶ n. Physiol. a large phagocytic cell found in stationary form in the tissues or as a mobile white blood cell, esp. at sites of infection.

mac·ro·pho·tog·ra·phy /ˌmakrōfəˈtägrəfē/ ▶ n. photography producing photographs of small items larger than life size.

mac·ro·phyte /ˈmakrəˌfīt/ ▶ n. Bot. a plant, esp. an aquatic plant, large enough to be seen by the naked eye.

mac·ro·pod /ˈmakrəˌpäd/ ▶ n. Zool. a plant-eating marsupial mammal (*Macropus* and other genera) of an Australasian family (Macropodidae) that comprises the kangaroos and wallabies. [19th C.: from mod. L. *Macropodidae* (pl.), from MACRO- 'large' + Gk. *pous*, *pod-* 'foot.']

mac·ro·scop·ic /ˌmakrəˈskäpik/ ▶ adj. visible to the naked eye; not microscopic. ■ of or relating to large-scale or general analysis. — **mac·ro·scop·i·cal·ly** adv.

mac·ro·struc·ture /ˈmakrōˌstrəkcʜər/ ▶ n. the large-scale or overall structure of something, e.g., an organism, a mechanical construction, or a written text. ■ a large-scale structure. — **mac·ro·struc·tur·al** /ˌmakrōˈstrəkcʜərəl/ adj.

ma·cru·ran /məˈkro͝orən/ ▶ adj. Zool. of, relating to, or denoting those decapod crustaceans (such as lobsters and crayfish) that have a relatively long abdomen. — **ma·cru·rous** /-ˈkro͝orəs/ adj. [19th C. (as a n.): from mod. L. *Macrura* (former suborder name), from Gk. *makros* 'long' + *oura* 'tail,' + -AN.]

mac·u·la /ˈmakyələ/ ▶ n. (pl. **-lae** /-ˌlē; -ˌlī/) a distinct spot, such as a discolored spot on the skin. Also called MACULE. ■ (also **mac·u·la lu·te·a**) /ˈlo͞otēə/ (pl. **mac·u·lae lu·te·ae** /ˈlo͞otēˌē; -tēˌī/) Anat. an oval yellowish area surrounding the fovea near the center of the retina in the eye. It is the region of greatest visual acuity. — **mac·u·lar** /ˈmakyələr/ adj.

mac·u·late /ˈmakyəˌlāt/ literary ▶ adj. spotted or stained. ▶ v. [trans.] mark with a spot or spots; stain. — **mac·u·la·tion** /ˌmakyəˈlāsʜən/ n.

mac·ule /ˈmakˌyo͞ol/ ▶ n. another term for MACULA. [15th C.: from Fr., or from L. *macula* 'spot.']

ma·cum·ba /məˈko͝ombə/ ▶ n. a black religious cult practiced in Brazil, using sorcery, ritual dance, and fetishes. [Port.]

MAD ▶ abbr. mutual assured destruction.

mad /mad/ ▶ adj. (**mad·der**, **mad·dest**) mentally ill; insane: *he felt as if he were going mad.* ■ (of a person, conduct, or an idea) extremely foolish or ill-advised: *he had some mad idea.* ■ in a frenzied mental or physical state: *mad with anxiety.* ■ informal enthusiastic about someone or something: *mad about bikes.* ■ informal very angry: *mad at each other.* ■ (of a dog) rabid.
– PHRASES **like mad** informal with great intensity, energy, or enthusiasm: *I ran like mad.* **(as) mad as a hatter** informal completely crazy. [with ref. to Lewis Carroll's character in *Alice's Adventures in Wonderland* (1865), from the effects of the use of mercurous nitrate in the manufacture of felt hats.] [OE *gemǣd(e)d* 'maddened,' participial form rel. to *gemād* 'mad,' of Gmc. origin.]

Mad·a·gas·car /ˌmadəˈgaskər/ an island country off the eastern coast of Africa. *See box.* — **Mad·a·gas·can** /-ˈgaskən/ adj. & n.

mad·am /ˈmadəm/ ▶ n. used to address or refer to a woman in a polite or respectful way. ■ (**Madam**) used to address a woman at the start of a formal or business letter: *Dear Madam, ...* ■ (**Madam**) used before a title to address or refer to a female holder of that position: *Madam President.* ■ a woman who runs a brothel. [ME: from OFr. *ma dame* 'my lady.']

Mad·ame /məˈdäm; -ˈdam/ ▶ n. (pl. **Mes·dames** /māˈdäm; -ˈdam/) a title or form of address used of or to a French-speaking woman: *Madame Bovary.*

Mad An·tho·ny /ˈantʜənē/ see WAYNE[2].

mad·cap /ˈmadˌkap/ ▶ adj. amusingly eccentric. ■ crazy or reckless: *a madcap scheme.*

mad cow dis·ease ▶ n. informal bovine spongiform encephalopathy. See **BSE**.

MADD /mad/ ▶ abbr. Mothers Against Drunk Driving.

mad·den /ˈmadn/ ▶ v. [trans.] make (someone) extremely irritated or annoyed. ■ [often as adj.] (**maddened**) drive (someone) insane.

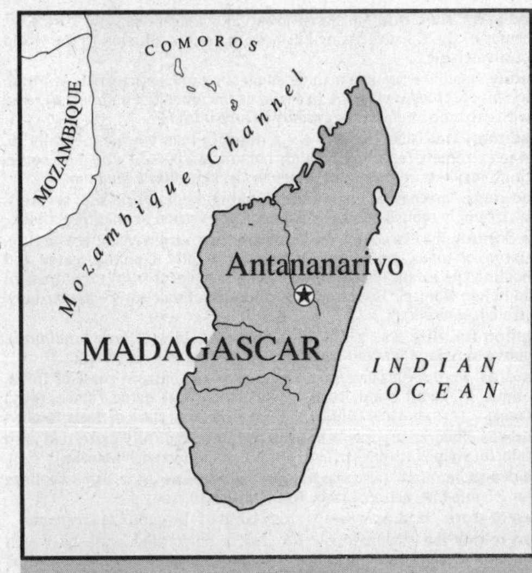

Madagascar

Official name: Republic of Madagascar
Location: Indian Ocean, off the eastern coast of Africa
Area: 226,700 square miles (587,000 sq km)
Population: 17,501,000
Capital: Antananarivo
Languages: Malagasy, French (both official)
Currency: Malagasy franc

mad·den·ing /ˈmadniɴɢ; ˈmadn-iɴɢ/ ▶ adj. extremely annoying; infuriating: *his maddening stories.* — **mad·den·ing·ly** adv.

mad·der /ˈmadər/ ▶ n. a scrambling or prostrate Eurasian plant (genera *Rubia* and *Sherardia*) of the bedstraw family, with whorls of four to six leaves, in particular *R. tinctorum* of southern Europe and western Asia, formerly cultivated for its root, which yields a red dye. ■ a red dye or pigment obtained from the root of this plant, or a synthetic dye resembling it. [OE *mædere*, of Gmc. origin; obscurely rel. to Du. *mede*, in the same sense.]

mad·ding /ˈmadiɴɢ/ ▶ adj. literary **1** acting madly; frenzied. **2** maddening.
– PHRASES **far from the madding crowd** secluded or removed from public notice. [in allusion to use in Gray's *Elegy*, also to the title of one of Thomas Hardy's novels.]

made /mād/ past and past participle of MAKE. ▶ adj. [usu. in comb.] made or formed in a particular place or by a particular process: *a handmade dress.*

Ma·dei·ra[1] /məˈdi(ə)rə; məˈde(ə)rə/ **1** an island in the Atlantic Ocean off the northwestern coast of Africa, the largest of the Madeiras, a group of islands that constitutes an autonomous region of Portugal; pop. 270,000; capital, Funchal. **2** a river in northwestern Brazil that rises on the Bolivian border and flows about 900 miles (1,450 km) to the Amazon River east of Manaus. — **Ma·dei·ran** adj. & n.

Ma·dei·ra[2] /məˈdirə; məˈderə/ (also **Madeira wine**) ▶ n. a fortified white wine from the island of Madeira.

mad·e·leine /ˈmadl-ən; ˌmadl-ˈān/ ▶ n. a small rich cake, typically baked in a shell-shaped mold. [French, prob. after *Madeleine* Paulmier, 19th-cent. Fr. pastry cook.]

Mad·e·moi·selle /ˌmad(ə)m(w)əˈzel; mamˈzel/ ▶ n. (pl. **Mes·de·moi·selles** /ˌmād(ə)m(w)əˈzel(z)/) a title or form of address used of or to an unmarried French-speaking woman. ■ (**mademoiselle**) a young Frenchwoman. [Fr., from *ma* 'my' + *demoiselle* 'damsel.']

made to or·der ▶ adj. specially made according to a customer's specifications. ■ fig. ideally suited to certain requirements.

made-up ▶ adj. **1** wearing makeup. **2** invented; not true: *a made-up story.*

mad·house /ˈmadˌhous/ ▶ n. hist. a mental institution. ■ informal a psychiatric hospital. ■ [in sing.] a scene of extreme confusion or uproar.

Ma·dhya Pra·desh /ˈmədyə prəˈdesʜ/ a large state in central India, formed in 1956; capital, Bhopal.

Mad·i·son[1] /ˈmadəsən/ the capital of Wisconsin, in the central part of the state; pop. 208,054.

Mad·i·son[2], James (1751–1836), 4th president of the US 1809–17. A principal framer of the US Constitution 1787, he proposed the Bill of Rights 1791. As president, he led the US successfully through the War of 1812.

Mad·i·son Av·e·nue /ˌmadəsən ˈavən(y)o͞o/ a street in New York City, center of the US advertising business. ■ used in allusion to the world of advertising.

mad·ly /ˈmadlē/ ▶ **adv.** in a manner suggesting or characteristic of insanity: *his eyes bulged madly.* ■ in a wild or uncontrolled manner. ■ informal with extreme intensity: ***he's madly in love with her.***

mad·man /ˈmadˌman; -mən/ ▶ **n.** (pl. **-men**) a man who is mentally ill. ■ an extremely foolish or reckless person. ■ a person who does something very fast, intensely, or violently: *working like a madman.*

mad·ness /ˈmadnəs/ ▶ **n.** the state of being mentally ill, esp. severely. ■ extremely foolish behavior. ■ a state of frenzied or chaotic activity.

Ma·don·na /məˈdänə/ ▶ **n.** (**the Madonna**) the Virgin Mary. ■ a picture, statue, or medallion of the Madonna, typically depicted seated and holding the infant Jesus. [16th C. (as a respectful form of address to an Italian woman): Ital., from *ma* (old form of *mia* 'my') + *donna* 'lady' (from L. *domina*).]

ma·don·na lil·y ▶ **n.** a tall white-flowered lily (*Lilium candidum*), native to Asia Minor and traditionally associated with purity.

Ma·dras /məˈdras; məˈdräs/ **1** a port city on the eastern coast of India, capital of Tamil Nadu; pop. 3,795,000. Official name (since 1995) **Chenai**. **2** former name (until 1968) of the Indian state of **Tamil Nadu**.

mad·ras /ˈmadrəs; məˈdras/ ▶ **n.** a cotton fabric, typically patterned with colorful stripes or checks. [19th C.: by association with **Madras**.]

ma·dra·sa /məˈdrasə/ (also **ma·dra·sah** or **me·dre·se** /-ˈdresə/) ▶ **n.** a college for Islamic instruction. [Arab., from *darasa* 'to study.']

mad·re·pore /ˈmadrəˌpôr/ ▶ **n.** a stony coral of the genus *Madrepora.*

mad·re·por·ite /ˈmadrəˌpôˌrīt/ ▶ **n.** Zool. a perforated plate by which the entry of seawater into the vascular system of an echinoderm is controlled.

Ma·drid /məˈdrid/ the capital of Spain, in the center of the country, pop. 2,985,000.

mad·ri·gal /ˈmadrigəl/ ▶ **n.** a part-song for several voices, typically arranged in elaborate counterpoint and without instrumental accompaniment. — **mad·ri·gal·i·an** /ˌmadriˈgālēən/ **adj.** **mad·ri·gal·ist n.** [from Ital. *madrigale,* from *matricalis* 'maternal or primitive,' from *matrix* 'womb.']

mad·ri·lene /ˌmadrəˈlān; -ˈlen/ ▶ **n.** a clear soup, usually served cold. [from Fr. *(consommé à la) madrilène,* lit. 'soup in the Madrid style.']

ma·dro·ne /məˈdrōnə/ (also **ma·dro·ño** /-ˈdrōnyō/) ▶ **n.** an evergreen tree (genus *Arbutus*) of the heath family with white flowers, red berries, and glossy leaves, native to western North America. [19th C.: from Sp.]

mad·tom /ˈmadˌtäm/ ▶ **n.** a small North American freshwater catfish (genus *Noturus*) that has a venom gland at the base of the pectoral fin spines which can inflict a painful wound.

Ma·du·ra /məˈdo͝orə/ an island of Indonesia, off the northeastern coast of Java.

Ma·du·rai /ˌmädəˈrī/ a city in Tamil Nadu in southern India; pop. 952,000.

Mad·u·rese /ˌmadyəˈrēz; -ˈrēs/ ▶ **n.** (pl. same) **1** a native or inhabitant of the island of Madura in Indonesia. **2** an Indonesian language spoken in Madura. ▶ **adj.** of or relating to the inhabitants of Madura or their language.

mad·wom·an /ˈmadˌwo͝omən/ ▶ **n.** (pl. **-wom·en**) a woman who is mentally ill. ■ a woman who does something very fast, intensely, or violently.

MAE ▶ **abbr.** Master of Aeronautical Engineering. ■ Master of Art Education. ■ Master of Arts in Education.

M.A.Ed. ▶ **abbr.** Master of Arts in Education.

mael·strom /ˈmālˌsträm; -strəm/ ▶ **n.** a powerful whirlpool in the sea or a river. ■ fig. a scene or state of confused and violent movement or upheaval. [17th C.: from early mod. Du., from *maalen* 'grind, whirl' + *stroom* 'stream.']

mae·nad /ˈmēˌnad/ ▶ **n.** (in ancient Greece) a female follower of Bacchus, traditionally associated with divine possession and frenzied rites. — **mae·nad·ic** /mēˈnadik/ **adj.** [16th C.: via L. from Gk. *Mainas, Mainad-,* from *mainesthai* 'to rave.']

ma·es·to·so /mīˈstōsō; ˌmīe-; -ˈstōzō/ Music ▶ **adv. & adj.** (esp. as a direction) in a majestic manner. ▶ **n.** (pl. **-sos**) a movement or passage marked to be performed in this way. [based on L. *majestas* 'majesty.']

maes·tro /ˈmīstrō/ ▶ **n.** (pl. **maes·tri** /ˈmīstrē/ or **maes·tros**) a distinguished musician, esp. a conductor of classical music. ■ a great or distinguished figure in any sphere. [18th C.: Ital., 'master,' from L. *magister.*]

Mae·ter·linck /ˈmetərˌlingk/, Count Maurice (1862–1949), Belgian poet and playwright. He was a leading figure in the symbolist movement. Nobel Prize for Literature (1911).

Mae West /ˈmā ˈwest/ ▶ **n.** informal, dated an inflatable life jacket, issued to pilots during World War II. [1940s: after US movie actress *Mae West* (1892–1980), noted for her large bust.]

Ma·fe·teng /ˈmafˌteng/ a town in western Lesotho; pop. 206,000.

Ma·fi·a /ˈmäfēə/ ▶ **n.** (**the Mafia**) [treated as sing. or pl.] an organized international body of criminals, operating originally in Sicily and now esp. in Italy and the US. ■ (usu. **mafia**) any similar group using extortion and other criminal methods. [Ital. (Sicilian dial.), orig. in the sense 'bragging.']

Ma·fi·o·so /ˌmäfēˈōsō; -zō/ (also **ma·fi·o·so**) ▶ **n.** (pl. **-si** /-sē; -zē/) a member of the Mafia.

mag /mag/ ▶ **n.** informal **1** a magazine (periodical). **2** a magazine (of ammunition). **3** magnesium or magnesium alloy. **4** a magneto.

Ma·ga·di, Lake /məˈgädē/ a salt lake in the Great Rift Valley, in southern Kenya.

mag·a·zine /ˌmagəˈzēn; ˈmagəˌzēn/ ▶ **n.** **1** a periodical publication containing articles and illustrations, typically covering a particular subject. ■ a regular television or radio program comprising a variety of topical news or entertainment items. **2** a chamber for holding a supply of cartridges to be fed automatically to the breech of a gun. ■ a similar device feeding a camera, compact disc player, etc. **3** a store for military arms, ammunition, and explosives. [16th C.: from Fr. *magasin,* from Ital. *magazzino,* from Arab. *makzin, makzan* 'storehouse.']

Mag·da·le·na /ˌmagdəˈlānə; ˌmäg-/ a river that rises in the Andes in Colombia and flows north about 1,000 miles (1,600 km) to the Caribbean Sea.

mag·da·lene /ˈmagdaˌlēn; -ˌlin/ (also **mag·da·len**) ▶ **n.** (**the Magdalene**) St. Mary Magdalene. ■ archaic a reformed prostitute.

Mag·da·le·ni·an /ˌmagdəˈlēnēən/ ▶ **adj.** Archaeol. denoting the final Paleolithic culture in Europe, about 17,000–11,500 years ago, characterized by bone and horn tools and highly developed cave art. [19th C.: from Fr. *Magdalénien* 'from La Madeleine,' a site in the Dordogne, France.]

Mag·de·burg /ˈmagdəbərg; ˈmägdəˌbo͝ork/ a city in Germany, the capital of Saxony-Anhalt, on the Elbe River; pop. 290,000.

mage /māj/ ▶ **n.** archaic literary a magician or learned person. [ME: Anglicized form of L. *magus* (see **magus**).]

Ma·gel·lan[1] /məˈjelən/ an American space probe launched in 1989 to map the surface of Venus, using radar to penetrate the dense cloud cover. The probe was deliberately burned up in Venus's atmosphere in 1994.

Ma·gel·lan[2], Ferdinand (c.1480–1521), Portuguese explorer; Portuguese name *Ferna-o Magalha-es.* In 1519, he sailed from Spain and reached the Philippines in 1521, where he was killed in a skirmish.

Ma·gel·lan, Strait of a passage that separates Tierra del Fuego from mainland South America. It connects the Atlantic and Pacific oceans.

Mag·el·lan·ic Clouds /ˌmajeˈlanik/ Astron. two diffuse luminous patches in the southern sky, now known to be small irregular galaxies that are the closest to our own.

Ma·gen Da·vid /mäˈgen däˈvēd; ˈmôgən ˈdôvid/ ▶ **n.** another name for **Star of David**. [20th C.: Heb., 'shield of David,' with ref. to David, King of Israel.]

ma·gen·ta /məˈjentə/ ▶ **n.** a light purplish red that is one of the primary subtractive colors. ■ the dye fuchsin. [19th C.: after *Magenta,* Italy, where the dye was discovered.]

Mag·gio·re, Lake /mäˈjôrā/ a lake in northern Italy and southern Switzerland.

mag·got /ˈmagət/ ▶ **n.** a soft-bodied legless larva, esp. that of a fly found in decaying matter. — **mag·got·y adj.**

Ma·ghrib /ˈməgrəb/ (also **Ma·ghreb**) a region of north and northwestern Africa between the Atlantic Ocean and Egypt. Compare with **Barbary**.

Ma·gi /ˈmāˌjī/ (**the Magi**) (in the Bible) the "wise men" from the East who brought gifts to the infant Jesus. [see **magus**.]

ma·gi /ˈmāˌjī/ plural form of **magus**.

ma·gi·an /ˈmāj(ē)ən; ˈmāˌjīən/ (also **Ma·gi·an**) ▶ **adj.** of or relating to the magi of ancient Persia. ■ of or relating to the Magi who brought gifts to the infant Jesus. ▶ **n.** a magus or Magus.

mag·ic /ˈmajik/ ▶ **n.** the power of apparently influencing the course of events by using mysterious or supernatural forces. ■ mysterious tricks, such as making things disappear and reappear, performed as entertainment. ■ a quality that makes something seem removed from everyday life, esp. in a way that gives delight: *the magic of the theater.* ▶ **adj.** used in magic or working by magic; having or apparently having supernatural powers: *a magic wand.* ■ [attrib.] very effective in producing results, esp. desired ones: *confidence is the magic ingredient.* [ME: from OFr. *magique,* from L. *magicus* (adj.), late L. *magica* (n.), from Gk. *magikē (tekhnē)* '(art of) a magus.']

mag·i·cal /ˈmajikəl/ ▶ **adj.** **1** relating to or using magic. ■ resembling, produced or working as if by magic. **2** beautiful or delightful in such a way as to seem removed from everyday life: *a magical evening.* — **mag·i·cal·ly adv.**

mag·ic bul·let ▶ **n.** informal a medicine or other remedy, esp. an undiscovered or hypothetical one, with wonderful or highly specific properties.

mag·ic eye ▶ **n.** **1** informal a photoelectric cell or similar electrical device used for identification, detection, or measurement. **2** a small cathode-ray tube that displays a pattern that enables a radio to be accurately tuned.

ma·gi·cian /məˈjishən/ ▶ **n.** a person with magical powers. ■ a person who performs magic tricks for entertainment. ■ informal a person with exceptional skill in a particular area.

mag·ic lan·tern ▶ **n.** hist. a simple form of image projector used for showing photographic slides.

Mag·ic Mark·er ▶ **n.** trademark an indelible felt-tip marker, esp. one with a wide tip.

mag·ic mush·room ▶ **n.** informal any toadstool of the genus *Psilocybe,* family Strophariaceae, with hallucinogenic properties. Several species include *P. mexicana,* traditionally consumed by American Indians in Mexico.

mag·ic re·al·ism (also **mag·i·cal re·al·ism**) ▶**n.** a literary or artistic genre in which realistic narrative or technique are combined with surreal elements of dream or fantasy.

mag·ic square ▶**n.** a square that is divided into smaller squares, each containing a number, such that the figures in each vertical, horizontal, and diagonal row add up to the same value.

8	18	16
22	14	6
12	10	20

magic square

Ma·gi·not Line /ˈmazʜə,nō; ˈmaj-/ a line of defensive fortifications constructed by the French along their eastern border during the 1930s, but outflanked by German forces in 1940. [after André *Maginot* (1877–1932), a Fr. minister of war.]

mag·is·te·ri·al /,majəˈsti(ə)rēəl/ ▶**adj. 1** having or showing great authority: *a magisterial pronouncement.* ■ domineering; dictatorial. **2** relating to or conducted by a magistrate. — **mag·is·te·ri·al·ly** **adv.** [17th C.: from med. L. *magisterialis*, from late L. *magisterius*, from L. *magister* 'master.']

mag·is·tra·cy /ˈmajəstrəsē/ ▶**n.** (pl. **-cies**) the office or authority of a magistrate. ■ (**the magistracy**) magistrates collectively.

mag·is·trate /ˈmajə,strāt/ ▶**n.** a civil officer or lay judge who administers the law, esp. one who conducts a court that deals with minor offenses. — **mag·is·tra·ture** /-,strāCHər; -strə,CHŏŏ(ə)r/ **n.**

mag·lev /ˈmag,lev/ ▶**n.** [usu. as adj.] a transportation system in which trains glide above a track, supported by magnetic repulsion and propelled by a linear motor. [20th C.: from *mag(netic) lev(itation).*]

mag·ma /ˈmagmə/ ▶**n.** hot fluid or semifluid material below or within the earth's crust from which lava and other igneous rock is formed by cooling. — **mag·mat·ic** /magˈmatik/ **adj.** [ME: via L. from Gk. *magma* (from *massein* 'knead').]

mag·ma·tism /ˈmagmə,tizəm/ ▶**n.** Geol. the motion or activity of magma.

Mag·na Car·ta /,magnə ˈkärtə/ a charter of liberty and political rights obtained from King John of England by his rebellious barons at Runnymede in 1215. [from med. L., 'great charter.']

mag·na cum lau·de /,magnə kŏŏm ˈloudə; ,kəm ˈlôdə/ ▶**adv. & adj.** with great distinction (with reference to college degrees and diplomas). [L., lit. 'with great praise.']

mag·nan·i·mous /magˈnanəməs/ ▶**adj.** very generous or forgiving, esp. toward a rival or someone less powerful than oneself. — **mag·na·nim·i·ty** /,magnəˈnimətē/ **n.** **mag·nan·i·mous·ly** **adv.** [16th C.: from L. *magnanimus* (from *magnus* 'great' + *animus* 'soul') + **-ous.**]

mag·nate /ˈmag,nāt; ˈmagnət/ ▶**n.** a wealthy and influential person, esp. in business: *a media magnate.* [ME: from late L. *magnas, magnat-* 'great man,' from L. *magnus* 'great.']

mag·ne·sia /magˈnēzʜə; -ˈnēsʜə/ ▶**n.** Chem. magnesium oxide, MgO. ■ hydrated magnesium carbonate used as an antacid and laxative. [ME: via med. L. from Gk. *Magnēsia*, denoting a mineral from Magnesia in Asia Minor.]

mag·ne·site /ˈmagnə,sīt/ ▶**n.** a whitish mineral consisting of magnesium carbonate, used as a heat-resistant lining in some furnaces.

mag·ne·si·um /magˈnēzēəm; -zʜəm/ ▶**n.** the chemical element of atomic number 12, a silver-white metal used to make strong lightweight alloys, esp. for the aerospace industry, and also used in flashbulbs and pyrotechnics. (Symbol: **Mg**)

mag·ne·si·um flare (also **magnesium light**) ▶**n.** a brilliant white flare containing metallic magnesium wire or ribbon.

mag·net /ˈmagnət/ ▶**n.** a piece of iron (or an ore, alloy, or other material) that has its component atoms so ordered that it exhibits properties of magnetism. ■ archaic term for **LODESTONE.** ■ fig. a person or thing that has a powerful attraction: *a magnet for trouble.* [ME: from L. *magnes, magnet-*, from Gk. *magnēs lithos* 'lodestone,' prob. influenced by Anglo-Norman Fr. *magnete.*]

mag·net·ic /magˈnetik/ ▶**adj. 1** having the properties of a magnet; exhibiting magnetism. ■ capable of being attracted by or acquiring the properties of a magnet: *steel is magnetic.* ■ (of a bearing in navigation) measured relative to magnetic north. **2** very attractive or alluring: *a magnetic personality.* — **mag·net·i·cal·ly** **adv.**

mag·net·ic disk ▶**n.** see **DISK** (sense 1).

mag·net·ic e·qua·tor ▶**n.** the irregular imaginary line, passing around the earth near the equator, on which a magnetic needle has no dip (see **DIP** sense 4).

mag·net·ic field ▶**n.** a region around a magnetic material or a moving electric charge within which the force of magnetism acts.

mag·net·ic in·duc·tion ▶**n. 1** magnetic flux or flux density. **2** the process by which an object or material is magnetized by an external magnetic field.

mag·net·ic mine ▶**n.** a mine detonated by the proximity of a magnetized body such as a ship or tank.

mag·net·ic mo·ment ▶**n.** Physics the property of a magnet that interacts with an applied field to give a mechanical moment.

mag·net·ic nee·dle ▶**n.** a piece of magnetized steel used as an indicator on the dial of a compass and in magnetic and electrical apparatus.

mag·net·ic north ▶**n.** the direction in which the north end of a compass needle or other freely suspended magnet will point in response to the earth's magnetic field.

mag·net·ic pole ▶**n.** each of the points near the extremities of the axis of rotation of the earth where a magnetic needle dips vertically. ■ each of the two points of a magnet to and from which the lines of magnetic force are directed.

mag·net·ic res·o·nance im·ag·ing (abbr.: **MRI**) ▶**n.** a form of medical imaging that measures the response of the atomic nuclei of body tissues to high-frequency radio waves when placed in a strong magnetic field, and that produces images of the internal organs.

mag·net·ic storm ▶**n.** a disturbance of the magnetic field of the earth (or other celestial body).

mag·net·ic tape ▶**n.** tape used in recording sound, pictures, or computer data.

mag·net·ic var·i·a·tion ▶**n.** see **VARIATION** (sense 1).

mag·net·ism /ˈmagnə,tizəm/ ▶**n.** a physical phenomenon produced by the motion of electric charge, resulting in attractive and repulsive forces between objects. ■ the property of being magnetic. ■ fig. the ability to attract and charm people.

mag·net·ite /ˈmagnə,tīt/ ▶**n.** a gray-black magnetic mineral that consists of an oxide of iron and is an important form of iron ore.

mag·net·ize /ˈmagnə,tīz/ ▶**v.** [trans.] give magnetic properties to; make magnetic. ■ fig. attract strongly as if by a magnet. — **mag·net·iz·a·ble** **adj.** **mag·net·i·za·tion** /,magnətəˈzāsʜən/ **n.** **mag·net·iz·er** **n.**

mag·ne·to /magˈnētō/ ▶**n.** (pl. **-tos**) a small electric generator containing a permanent magnet and used to provide high-voltage pulses. [19th C.: abbrev. of **MAGNETO-ELECTRIC.**]

magneto- ▶**comb. form** relating to a magnet or magnetism: *magneto-electric.*

mag·ne·to-e·lec·tric ▶**adj.** relating to the electric currents generated in a material by its motion in a magnetic field. ■ (of an electric generator) using permanent magnets. — **mag·ne·to-e·lec·tric·i·ty** **n.**

mag·ne·to·graph /magˈnētə,graf/ ▶**n.** an instrument for recording measurements of magnetic forces.

mag·ne·tom·e·ter /,magnəˈtämətər/ ▶**n.** an instrument used for measuring magnetic forces, esp. the earth's magnetism. — **mag·ne·tom·e·try** /-ətrē/ **n.**

mag·ne·to·mo·tive force /mag,nētōˈmōtiv/ ▶**n.** Physics a quantity representing the line integral of the magnetic intensity around a closed line (e.g., the sum of the magnetizing forces along a circuit).

mag·ne·ton /ˈmagnə,tän/ ▶**n.** a unit of magnetic moment in atomic and nuclear physics.

mag·ne·to-op·ti·cal ▶**adj.** of, relating to, or employing both optical and magnetic phenomena or technology.

mag·ne·to·re·sist·ance /mag,nētəriˈzistəns/ ▶**n.** Physics the dependence of the electrical resistance of a body on an external magnetic field. — **mag·ne·to·re·sist·ive** /mag,nētəriˈzistiv/ **adj.**

mag·ne·to·sphere /magˈnētə,sfi(ə)r/ ▶**n.** the region surrounding the earth or another astronomical body in which its magnetic field is the predominant effective magnetic field. — **mag·ne·to·spher·ic** /,mag,nētəˈsfi(ə)rik/ **adj.**

mag·ne·tron /ˈmagnə,trän/ ▶**n.** an electron tube for amplifying or generating microwaves, with the flow of electrons controlled by an external magnetic field. [20th C.: from **MAGNETIC** + *-tron* from **ELECTRON.**]

mag·net school ▶**n.** a public school offering special instruction unavailable elsewhere, designed to attract a diverse student body.

Mag·nif·i·cat /magˈnifi,kät; mänˈyifi-/ ▶**n.** a canticle used in Christian liturgy, the text being the hymn of the Virgin Mary (Luke 1:46–55). [ME: L., lit. 'magnifies' (from the opening words, which translate as 'my soul magnifies the Lord').]

mag·ni·fi·ca·tion /,magnəfiˈkāsʜən/ ▶**n.** the act of magnifying something or the state of being magnified. ■ the degree to which something is or can be magnified. ■ the magnifying power of an instrument: *a magnification of about 100.* ■ a magnified reproduction of something.

mag·nif·i·cence /magˈnifəsəns/ ▶**n.** the quality of being magnificent.

mag·nif·i·cent /magˈnifəsənt/ ▶**adj. 1** impressively beautiful, elaborate, or extravagant; striking. **2** very good; excellent. — **mag·nif·i·cent·ly** **adv.** [ME: via OFr. from L. *magnificent-* 'making great, serving to magnify,' based on *magnus* 'great.']

mag·nif·i·co /magˈnifi,kō/ ▶**n.** (pl. **-coes**) informal an eminent, powerful, or illustrious person.

mag·ni·fy /ˈmagnə,fī/ ▶**v.** (**-fies, -fied**) [trans.] **1** make (something) appear larger than it is, esp. with a lens or microscope. ■ [intrans.] be capable of increasing the size or apparent size of something. ■ increase the volume of (a sound). ■ intensify: *the risk is magnified.* ■ exaggerate the importance or effect of. **2** archaic extol; glorify. — **mag·ni·fi·er** /-,fīər/ **n.**

[ME: from OFr. *magnifier* or L. *magnificare*, based on L. *magnus* 'great.' Sense 1 dates from the mid 17th C.]

mag·ni·fy·ing glass ▶ n. a lens that produces an enlarged image, typically set in a frame with a handle.

mag·nil·o·quent /mag'niləkwənt/ ▶ adj. using high-flown or bombastic language. — **mag·nil·o·quence** n. **mag·nil·o·quent·ly** adv. [17th C.: from L. *magniloquus* (from *magnus* 'great' + *-loquus* '-speaking') + -ENT.]

Mag·ni·to·gorsk /məg,nētə'gôrsk/ a city in southern Russia, on the Ural River; pop. 443,000.

mag·ni·tude /'magnə,t(y)o͞od/ ▶ n. **1** the great size or extent of something: *the magnitude of the task.* ■ great importance: *events of tragic magnitude.* **2** size: *less than average magnitude.* ■ a numerical quantity or value: *the magnitudes of all the variables.* **3** the degree of brightness of a star. See also APPARENT MAGNITUDE, ABSOLUTE MAGNITUDE. ■ the class into which a star falls by virtue of its brightness. ■ a difference of one on a scale of brightness, treated as a unit of measurement.
– PHRASES **of the first magnitude** see FIRST. [ME: from L. *magnitudo*, from *magnus* 'great.']

mag·no·lia /mag'nōlyə/ ▶ n. a tree or shrub (genus *Magnolia*, family Magnoliaceae) with typically creamy-pink, waxy flowers, widely grown as ornamentals. Numerous species include *M. campbellii*, native to the Himalayas. [mod. L., after Pierre *Magnol* (1638–1715), Fr. botanist.]

magnolia

mag·num /'magnəm/ ▶ n. (pl. **-nums**) a thing of a type that is larger than normal, in particular: ■ a wine bottle of twice the standard size, normally 1½ liters. ■ (often **Magnum**) [often as adj.] trademark a gun designed to fire cartridges that are more powerful than its caliber would suggest. [18th C.: from L., *magnus* 'great.']

mag·num o·pus /'magnəm 'ōpəs/ ▶ n. (pl. **mag·num o·pus·es** or **mag·na o·pe·ra** /'magnə 'ōpərə; 'äpərə/) an important work of art, music, or literature, esp. the most important achievement of an artist or writer. [18th C.: from L., 'great work.']

Ma·gog /mə'gäg/ see GOG AND MAGOG.

mag·pie /'mag,pī/ ▶ n. **1** a long-tailed crow with boldly marked plumage and a raucous voice. Five genera and several species include the black-and-white **black-billed magpie** (*Pica pica*) of Eurasia and North America. **2** used in similes or comparisons to refer to a person who collects things, esp. things of little value, or a person who chatters idly. [16th C.: from *Magot* (ME nickname for given name *Marguerite*) + PIE[2].]

black-billed magpie

M.Agr. ▶ abbr. Master of Agriculture.

Ma·gritte /mə'grēt; ma-/, René François Ghislain (1898–1967), Belgian painter. His works are startling or amusing juxtapositions of the ordinary, the strange, and the erotic.

mag·uey /mə'gā/ ▶ n. an agave plant, esp. one yielding pulque. [16th C.: via Sp. from Taino.]

ma·gus /'māgəs/ ▶ n. (pl. **ma·gi** /'mā,jī/) a member of a priestly caste of ancient Persia. See also MAGI. ■ a sorcerer. [ME: via L. and Gk. from Old Pers. *maguš*.]

mag wheel /mag/ ▶ n. a motor-vehicle wheel made from lightweight magnesium steel.

Mag·yar /'mag,yär/ ▶ n. **1** a member of a people who originated in the Urals and migrated westward to settle in what is now Hungary in the 9th century AD. **2** the Uralic language of this people; Hungarian. ▶ adj. of or relating to this people or language. [the name in Hungarian.]

Ma·gyar·or·szág /'mädyär,ôr,säg/ Hungarian name for HUNGARY.

Ma·ha·bha·ra·ta /,mähə'bärətə/ one of the two great Sanskrit epics of the Hindus, existing in its present form since *c.*AD 400. [Sanskrit, lit. 'great Bharata,' i.e., the great epic of the Bharata dynasty.]

ma·hant /mə'hənt/ ▶ n. Hinduism a chief priest of a temple or the head of a monastery.

ma·ha·ra·ja /,mähə'räjə; -'räzhə/ (also **ma·ha·ra·jah**) ▶ n. hist. an Indian prince. [from Hindi *mahārājā*, from Sanskrit *mahā* 'great' + *rājan* 'raja.']

ma·ha·ra·ni /,mähə'ränē/ (also **ma·ha·ra·nee**) ▶ n. a maharaja's wife or widow. [from Hindi *mahārānī*, from Sanskrit *mahā* 'great' + *rājñī* 'ranee.']

Ma·ha·rash·tra /,mä(h)ə'räshtrə/ a large state in western India; capital, Bombay. — **Ma·ha·rash·tri·an** /-trēən/ adj. & n.

Ma·ha·ri·shi /,mähə'rēshē; mə'härəshē/ ▶ n. a great Hindu sage or spiritual leader. [alt. of Sanskrit *maharṣi*, from *mahā* 'great' + *ṛṣi* 'rishi.']

ma·hat·ma /mə'hätmə; -'hatmə/ ▶ n. (in the Indian subcontinent) a person regarded with reverence or loving respect; a holy person or sage. ■ (**the Mahatma**) Mahatma Gandhi. ■ (in some forms of theosophy) a person in India or Tibet said to have supernatural powers. [from Sanskrit *mahātman*, from *mahā* 'great' + *ātman* 'soul.']

Ma·ha·we·li /,mähə'wālē/ a major river in Sri Lanka, flowing north for 206 miles (330 km) to the Bay of Bengal.

Ma·ha·ya·na /,mähə'yänə/ (also **Mahayana Buddhism**) ▶ n. one of the two major traditions of Buddhism, now practiced in a variety of forms esp. in China, Tibet, Japan, and Korea. [from Sanskrit, from *mahā* 'great' + *yāna* 'vehicle.']

Mah·di /'mädē/ ▶ n. (pl. **Mah·dis**) (in popular Muslim belief) a spiritual and temporal leader who will rule before the end of the world and restore religion and justice. — **Mah·dism** /'mä,dizəm/ n. **Mah·dist** /'mädist/ n. & adj. [from Arab. *(al-)mahdī* 'he who is guided in the right way.']

Mah·fouz /mä'fo͞oz/, Naguib (1911–2006), Egyptian novelist, noted for his Cairo Trilogy (1956–57). Nobel Prize for Literature (1988).

Ma·hi·can /mə'hēkən/ (also **Mo·hi·can**) ▶ n. **1** a member of an American Indian people formerly inhabiting the Upper Hudson Valley in New York. Compare with MOHEGAN. **2** the Algonquian language of this people. ▶ adj. of or relating to the Mahicans or their language. [the name in Mahican, meaning 'people of the estuary'.]

Ma·hi·lyow /məgil'yôf/ a city in eastern Belarus; pop. 363,000. Russian name MOGILYOV.

ma·hi·ma·hi /,mähē'mähē/ ▶ n. an edible marine fish (genus *Coryphaena*, family Coryphaenidae) of warm seas, with silver and bright blue or green coloration when alive. Also called **dolphinfish** or **dorado**. [1940s: from Hawaiian.]

mah-jongg /mä 'zhäng; -zhông/ (also **mah-jong** or **mah·jongg** or **mah·jong**) ▶ n. a Chinese game played usually by four people with 136 or 144 rectangular pieces called tiles, the object being to collect winning sets of these. [20th C.: from Chin. dial. *ma-tsiang*, lit. 'sparrows.']

Mah·ler /'mälər/, Gustav (1860–1911), Austrian composer. His works link romanticism and the experimentalism of Schoenberg.

mahl·stick /'môl,stik/ (also **maul·stick**) ▶ n. a light stick with a padded leather ball at one end, held against work by a painter or signwriter to support and steady the brush hand. [17th C.: from Du. *maalstok*, from *malen* 'to paint' + *stok* 'stick.']

ma·hog·a·ny /mə'hägənē/ ▶ n. **1** hard reddish-brown timber from a tropical tree, used for high-quality furniture. ■ a rich reddish-brown color like that of mahogany wood. **2** the tropical American tree (genus *Swietenia*, family Meliaceae) that produces this timber, widely harvested from the wild. ■ used in names of trees that yield similar timber, e.g., **Philippine mahogany**.

Ma·hon /mə'hōn; mä'ōn/ (also **Port Mahon**) the capital of Minorca, on the southeastern coast; pop. 22,000. Spanish name **Mahón**.

ma·ho·ni·a /mə'hōnēə/ ▶ n. an evergreen shrub (genus *Mahonia*) of the barberry family, native to eastern Asia and North and Central America. [after Bernard Mc*Mahon* (*c.*1775–1816), Amer. botanist.]

ma·hout /mə'hout/ ▶ n. (in the Indian subcontinent and Southeast Asia) a person who works with, rides, and tends an elephant.

Mah·rat·ta /mə'rätə/ ▶ n. var. of MARATHA.

Mah·rat·ti /mə'rätē/ ▶ n. var. of MARATHI.

ma·hua /'mähwä; -ho͞oə/ (also **ma·hwa**) ▶ n. an Indian tree (*Madhuca latifolia*) of the sapodilla family that has edible flowers and oil-rich seeds. ■ an alcoholic drink produced from the flowers of this tree. [17th C.: via Hindi from Sanskrit *madhūka*, from *madhu* 'sweet.']

Ma·ia[1] /'mīə/ Gk. Mythol. the daughter of Atlas and mother of Hermes.

Ma·ia[2] Rom. Mythol. a goddess associated with Vulcan and also (by confusion with MAIA[1]) with Mercury (Hermes). The month of May is named after her.

maid /mād/ ▶ n. a female domestic servant. ■ archaic literary a girl or young woman, esp. an unmarried one. ■ archaic literary a virgin. [ME: abbrev. of MAIDEN.]

maid·en /'mādn/ ▶ n. archaic literary a girl or young woman, esp. an unmarried one. ■ a virgin. ▶ adj. [attrib.] **1** (of a woman, esp. an older one) unmarried: *a maiden aunt.* ■ (of a female animal) unmated: *the top-priced maiden heifer.* **2** being or involving the first attempt or act of its kind: *the ship's maiden voyage.* ■ denoting a horse that has never won a race, or a race intended for such horses. ■ (of a tree or other fruiting plant) in its first year of growth. — **maid·en·hood** n. **maid·en·ish** adj. **maid·en·like** adj. **maid·en·ly** adj. [OE *mægden*, rel. to Ger. *Mädchen*, dimin. of *Magd* 'maid.']

maid·en·hair /'mādn,he(ə)r/ (also **maidenhair fern**) ▶ n. a chiefly tropical fern (genus *Adiantum*, family Adiantaceae) of delicate appearance, having slender-stalked fronds and often grown as a houseplant.

maid·en·hair tree ▶ n. the ginkgo, whose leaves resemble those of the maidenhair fern.

maid·en·head /'mādn,hed/ ▶ n. virginity. ■ dated the hymen.

maid·en name ▶ n. the surname that a married woman used from birth, prior to changing it at marriage.

maid of hon·or ▶ n. an unmarried woman acting as principal bridesmaid at a wedding. ■ an unmarried woman, typically of noble birth, attending a queen or princess.

maid·serv·ant /'mād,sərvənt/ ▶ n. dated a female domestic servant.

Mai·kop /mī'käp/ a city in southwestern Russia, capital of the republic of Adygea; pop. 120,000.

mail¹ /māl/ ▶ n. letters and packages conveyed by the postal system. ■ (also **the mails**) the postal system: *you can order by mail | the check is in the mail* | [as adj.] *a mail truck.* ■ [in sing.] a single delivery or collection of mail: *it came in the mail today.* ■ Comput. electronic mail. ▶ v. [trans.] send (a letter or package) using the postal system: *please mail the postcard.* ■ Comput. send (someone) electronic mail. — **mail·a·ble** adj. [ME: from OFr. *male* 'wallet,' of West Gmc. origin.]

mail² ▶ n. hist. flexible armor made of metal rings or plates. ■ the protective shell or scales of certain animals. ▶ v. [trans.] clothe or cover with mail. [ME: from OFr. *maille*, from L. *macula* 'spot, mesh.']

mail·bag /'māl,bag/ ▶ n. a large sack or bag for carrying mail.

mail bomb ▶ n. **1** another term for LETTER BOMB. **2** an overwhelmingly large quantity of e-mail messages sent to one e-mail address. ▶ v. (**mail-bomb**) [trans.] send an overwhelmingly large quantity of e-mail messages to (someone).

mail·box /'māl,bäks/ ▶ n. a public box with a slot into which mail is placed for collection by the post office. ■ a private box into which mail is delivered, esp. one at the entrance to a person's property. ■ a computer file in which e-mail messages are stored.

mail call ▶ n. Mil. the distribution of mail to soldiers.

mail car·ri·er ▶ n. a person who is employed to deliver and collect letters and parcels.

Mail·er /'mālər/, Norman (1923–), US writer. His works include the nonfictional *The Armies of the Night* (1968) and the novel *Harlot's Ghost* (1991).

mail·er /'mālər/ ▶ n. the sender of a letter or package by mail. ■ a person employed to dispatch newspapers or periodicals by mail. ■ a free advertising pamphlet, brochure, or catalog sent out by mail. ■ a container used for conveying items by mail, e.g., a padded envelope.

mail·ing /'māliNG/ ▶ n. something sent by mail, esp. a piece of mass advertising.

mail·ing list ▶ n. a list of the names and addresses of people to whom material such as advertising matter, information, or a magazine may be mailed.

mail·lot /mī'ō/ ▶ n. (pl. same) **1** a pair of tights worn for dancing or gymnastics. ■ a woman's tight-fitting one-piece swimsuit. **2** a jersey or top, esp. one worn in sports such as cycling. [Fr.]

mail·man /'māl,man/ ▶ n. (pl. **-men**) a person who is employed to deliver and collect letters and parcels.

mail merge ▶ n. Comput. the automatic addition of names and addresses from a database to letters and envelopes in order to facilitate sending mail, esp. advertising, to many addresses.

mail or·der ▶ n. the selling of goods to customers by mail, generally involving selection from a catalog: *available by mail order only.*

maim /mām/ ▶ v. [trans.] wound or injure (someone) so that part of the body is permanently damaged.

Mai·mon·i·des /mī'mänidēz/ (1135–1204), Jewish philosopher and scholar; born in Spain; born *Moses ben Maimon*. He wrote *Guide for the Perplexed* (1190).

Main /mīn/ a river in southwestern Germany that rises in northern Bavaria and flows west for 310 miles (500 km) to the Rhine River at Mainz.

main /mān/ ▶ adj. [attrib.] chief in size or importance: *a main road | the main problem.* ■ denoting the center of a network, from which other parts branch out: *the main office.* ▶ n. **1** a principal pipe carrying water or gas to buildings, or taking sewage from them: [with adj.] *a gas main.* **2** (**the main**) archaic literary the high seas; the open ocean. **3** Naut. short for MAINSAIL or MAINMAST. [ME: from OE *mægen* 'physical force,' reinforced by ON *meginn, megn* 'strong, powerful,' both from a Gmc. base meaning 'have power.']

main clause ▶ n. Gram. a clause that can form a complete sentence standing alone, having a subject and a predicate. Contrasted with SUBORDINATE CLAUSE.

main course ▶ n. **1** the most substantial course of a meal. **2** the mainsail of a square-rigged sailing ship.

main drag ▶ n. (usu. **the main drag**) informal the main street of a town.

Maine /mān/ a state in the northeastern US, one of the six New England states, on the Atlantic coast, on the US-Canada border; pop. 1,274,923; capital, Augusta; statehood, Mar. 15, 1820 (23). Visited by John Cabot in 1498 and colonized by England in the 1600s and 1700s, it was annexed to Massachusetts from 1652 until 1820. — **Main·er** n.

Maine coon (also **Maine coon cat**) ▶ n. a large, powerful domestic cat of a long-haired breed, native to America. [1970s: so named because of partial resemblance to the raccoon.]

Maine Coon

main·frame /'mān,frām/ ▶ n. **1** a large high-speed computer, esp. one supporting numerous workstations or peripherals. **2** the central processing unit and primary memory of a computer.

Main·land /'mānlənd; -,land/ **1** the largest island in the Orkney Islands. **2** the largest island in the Shetland Islands.

main·land /'mān,land; -lənd/ ▶ n. a large continuous extent of land that includes the greater part of a country or territory, as opposed to offshore islands and detached territories. — **main·land·er** n.

main line ▶ n. a chief railroad line: [as adj.] *a main-line station.* ■ a principal route, course, or connection: *the main line of evolution.* ■ a chief road or street. ■ informal a principal vein as a site for a drug injection. ▶ v. (**main·line**) [trans.] informal inject (a drug) intravenously. — **main·lin·er** n.

main·ly /'mānlē/ ▶ adv. more than anything else: *he is mainly concerned with fiction.* ■ for the most part: *the west will be mainly dry.*

main·mast /'mān,mast/ ▶ n. the principal mast of a sailing ship.

main·sail /'mānsəl; -,sāl/ ▶ n. the principal sail of a ship, esp. the lowest sail on the mainmast. ■ the sail set on the after side of the mainmast in a fore-and-aft-rigged vessel.

main·sheet /'mān,SHēt/ ▶ n. a sheet used for controlling the mainsail of a sailing vessel.

main·spring /'mān,spriNG/ ▶ n. the principal spring in a watch, clock, or other mechanism. ■ fig. something that plays a principal part in motivating or maintaining a movement, process, or activity: *the mainspring of anticommunism.*

main·stay /'mān,stā/ ▶ n. a stay that extends from the maintop to the foot of the foremast of a sailing ship. ■ fig. a thing on which something else is based or depends: *whitefish are the mainstay of the local industry.*

main·stream /'mān,strēm/ ▶ n. (**the mainstream**) the ideas, attitudes, or activities that are regarded as normal or conventional; the dominant trend in opinion, fashion, or the arts. ▶ adj. belonging to or characteristic of the mainstream: *mainstream politics.* ■ (of a school or class) for students without special needs. ▶ v. [trans.] (often **be mainstreamed**) bring (something) into the mainstream. ■ place (a student with special needs) into a mainstream class or school.

main·tain /mān'tān/ ▶ v. [trans.] **1** cause or enable (a condition or state of affairs) to continue: *maintain close links between industry and schools.* ■ keep (something) at the same level or rate: *prices will have to be maintained.* ■ keep (a building, machine, or road) in good condition or in working order by checking or repairing it regularly. ■ hold (a position) in the face of attack or competition: *maintain a competitive market position.* **2** provide with necessities for life or existence: *the costs of maintaining a child.* ■ keep (a military unit) supplied with equipment and other requirements. **3** [reporting verb] state something strongly to be the case; assert: [trans.] *he maintained his innocence.* — **main·tain·a·bil·i·ty** /,mān,tānə'bilətē/ n. **main·tain·a·ble** adj. [ME: from OFr. *maintenir*, from L. *manu tenere* 'hold in the hand.']

main·tain·er /mān'tānər/ ▶ n. a person or thing that maintains something, in particular computer software.

main·te·nance /'mānt(ə)nəns; 'mántn-əns/ ▶ n. **1** the process of maintaining or preserving someone or something, or the state of being maintained: *the maintenance of democratic government.* ■ the process of keeping something in good condition: *car maintenance* | [as adj.] *essential maintenance work.* **2** the provision of financial support for a person's living expenses, or the support so provided. ■ alimony or child support.

Main·te·non /,mant(ə)'nôN/, Françoise d'Aubigné, Marquise de (1635–1719), mistress and later second wife of the French king Louis XIV.

main·top /'mān,täp/ ▶ n. a platform around the head of the lower section of a sailing ship's mainmast.

main·top·mast ▶ n. the second section of a sailing ship's mainmast.

main verb ▶ n. Gram. **1** the verb in a main clause. **2** the head of a verb phrase, for example *eat* in *might have been going to eat it.*

Mainz /mīn(t)s/ a city in western Germany, capital of Rhineland-Palatinate; pop. 183,000.

ma·iol·i·ca /mī'äləkə/ ▶ n. fine earthenware with colored decoration on an opaque white tin glaze, originating in Italy during the Renaissance. [16th C.: Ital., from *Maiolica* 'Majorca.']

mai·son·ette /,māzə'net/ ▶ n. a set of rooms for living in, typically on two stories of a larger building and with its own entrance from outside. [18th C.: from Fr. *maisonnette*, dimin. of *maison* 'house.']

mai tai /'mī ,tī/ ▶ n. a cocktail based on light rum, curaçao, and fruit juices. [Polynesian.]

Mai·thi·li /'mītilē/ ▶ n. a Bihari language spoken in northern Bihar, elsewhere in India, and in Nepal. [Sanskrit (as an adj.), from *Mithilā*, a place in northern Bihar.]

maî·tre d'hô·tel /,mātrədō'tel; ,metrə/ (also **mai·tre d'** /,mātrə'dē; ,mātər/) ▶ n. (pl. **maî·tres d'hô·tel** pronunc. same; also **maître d's**) the person in a restaurant who oversees the waitpersons and busboys, and who typically handles reservations. ■ the manager of a hotel. [16th C.: Fr., lit. 'master of (the) house.']

maize /māz/ ▶ n. technical or chiefly British term for CORN¹. [16th C.: from Sp. *maíz*, from Taino *mahiz.*]

PRONUNCIATION KEY ə *ago, up*; ər *over, fur*; a *hat*; ā *ate*; ä *car*; e *let*; ē *see*; i *fit*; ī *by*; NG *sing*; ō *go*; ô *law, for*; oi *toy*; o͝o *good*; o͞o *goo*; ou *out*; TH *thin*; T͟H *then*; ZH *vision*

Maj. ▶ abbr. Major.

ma·jes·tic /məˈjestik/ ▶ adj. having or showing impressive beauty or dignity. — **ma·jes·ti·cal·ly** adv.

maj·es·ty /ˈmajəstē/ ▶ n. (pl. **-ties**) **1** impressive stateliness, dignity, or beauty: *the majesty of the Rockies.* **2** royal power: *the majesty of the royal household.* ■ (**His, Your,** etc., **Majesty**) a title given to a sovereign or a sovereign's wife or widow: *Her Majesty the Queen.* [ME: from OFr. *majeste*, from L. *majestas*, from a var. of *majus*, *major-* (see MAJOR).]

Maj. Gen. ▶ abbr. Major General.

maj·lis /ˈmajlis; majˈlis/ ▶ n. the parliament of various North African and Middle Eastern countries, esp. Iran. [Arab., lit. 'assembly.']

ma·jol·i·ca /məˈjälikə/ ▶ n. a kind of earthenware made in imitation of Italian maiolica, esp. in England during the 19th century. [var. of MAIOLICA.]

Ma·jor /ˈmājər/, Sir John (1943–), prime minister of Britain; 1990–97.

ma·jor /ˈmājər/ ▶ adj. **1** [attrib.] important, serious, or significant: *the use of drugs is a major problem.* ■ greater or more important; main: *he got the major share.* ■ (of a surgical operation) serious or life-threatening: *major surgery.* **2** Music (of a scale) having an interval of a semitone between the third and fourth degrees and the seventh and eighth degrees. Contrasted with MINOR. ■ (of an interval) equivalent to that between the tonic and another note of a major scale, and greater by a semitone than the corresponding minor interval. ■ [postpositive] (of a key) based on a major scale, tending to produce a bright or joyful effect: *Prelude in G Major.* ■ (of a triad) having a major third as the bottom interval. **3** of full legal age. **4** Logic (of a term) occurring as the predicate in the conclusion of a categorical syllogism. ■ (of a premise) containing the major term in a categorical syllogism. ▶ n. **1** an army officer of high rank, in particular (in the US Army, Air Force, and Marine Corps) an officer ranking above captain and below lieutenant colonel. [Shortening of SERGEANT MAJOR, formerly a high rank.] **2** Music a major key, interval, or scale. **3** a student's principal subject or course of study. ■ [often with adj.] a student specializing in a specified subject: *a math major.* **4** a major world organization, company, or competition. ■ (**the majors**) the major leagues. **5** a person of full legal age. ▶ v. [intrans.] (**major in**) specialize in (a particular subject) at a college or university: *she'll major in English.* [ME: from L., compar. of *magnus* 'great'; perh. influenced by Fr. *majeur*.]

Ma·jor·ca /məˈjôrkə; mäˈyôrkə/ the largest of the Balearic Islands; pop. 614,000; capital, Palma. Spanish name MALLORCA. — **Ma·jor·can** adj. & n.

ma·jor-do·mo /ˌmājər ˈdōmō/ ▶ n. (pl. **-do·mos**) the chief steward of a large household. [16th C.: via Sp. and Ital. from med. L. *major domus* 'highest official of the household.']

ma·jor·ette /ˌmājəˈret/ ▶ n. short for DRUM MAJORETTE.

ma·jor gen·er·al ▶ n. (pl. **ma·jor gen·er·als**) an officer in the US Army, Air Force, and Marine Corps ranking above brigadier general and below lieutenant general. [17th C.: shortening of *sergeant major general.*]

ma·jor·i·ty /məˈjôrətē; -ˈjär-/ ▶ n. (pl. **-ties**) **1** the greater number: *in the majority of cases* | [as adj.] *a majority decision.* ■ the number by which votes for one candidate in an election are more than those for all other candidates combined. ■ a party or group receiving the greater number of votes. **2** the age when a person is legally considered a full adult, in most contexts either 18 or 21. **3** the rank or office of a major.
– PHRASES **be in the majority** belong to or constitute the larger group or number. [16th C. (denoting superiority): from Fr. *majorité*, from med. L. *majoritas*, from L. *major* (see MAJOR).]

ma·jor·i·ty lead·er ▶ n. the head of the majority party in a legislative body, esp. the US Senate or House of Representatives.

ma·jor·i·ty rule ▶ n. the principle that the greater number should exercise greater power.

ma·jor league ▶ n. a professional baseball league of the highest level, in the US either the American League or the National League. ■ the highest-level professional league or leagues in another sport. ■ fig. the highest attainable level in any endeavor or activity: [as adj.] *major-league corporations.* — **ma·jor-lea·guer** n.

ma·jor·ly /ˈmājərlē/ ▶ adv. [as submodifier] informal very; extremely: *I'm majorly depressed.*

ma·jor med·i·cal ▶ n. insurance designed to cover medical expenses due to severe or prolonged illness.

ma·jor suit ▶ n. Bridge spades or hearts. [20th C.: so named because of their higher scoring value.]

ma·jus·cule /ˈmajəsˌkyo͞ol/ ▶ n. large lettering, either capital or uncial, in which all the letters are usually the same height. ■ a large letter. — **ma·jus·cu·lar** /məˈjəskyələr/ adj. [18th C.: from Fr., from L. *majuscula (littera)* 'somewhat greater (letter).']

Ma·kar·i·os III /məˈkarēəs; -ˌōs; mäˈkärēˌôs/ (1913–77), president of Cyprus 1960–77; born *Mikhail Christodolou Mouskos.* He reorganized the movement for enosis (union of Cyprus with Greece).

Ma·kas·sar /məˈkasər/ (also **Ma·cas·sar** or **Ma·kas·ar**) a city in Indonesia, on southwest Sulawesi; pop. 944,300. Former name (1971-1999) UJUNG PANDANG.

Ma·kas·sar Strait /məˈkasər/ a stretch of water that separates the islands of Borneo and Sulawesi.

make /māk/ ▶ v. (past **made**) [trans.] **1** form (something) by putting parts together or combining substances; construct; create: *she made a dress* | *baseball bats are made of ash.* ■ (**make something into**) alter something so that it forms or constitutes (something else): *milk can be made into cheese.* ■ compose, prepare, or draw up: *she made her will* | *make a list.* ■ prepare (a dish, drink, or meal) for consumption: *she was making lunch.* ■ arrange bedclothes tidily on (a bed) ready for use: *make your bed.* **2** cause (something) to exist or come about; bring about: *the drips had made a pool on the floor.* ■ [with obj. and complement or infin.] cause to become or seem: *decorative features make brickwork more interesting.* ■ carry out, perform, or produce (a specified action, movement, or sound): *make a mistake.* ■ communicate or express (an idea, request, or requirement): ***make demands on** people* | *make him an offer.* ■ undertake or agree to (an aim or purpose): *make a promise.* ■ [with obj. and complement] appoint or designate (someone) to a position: *he was made a colonel.* ■ [with obj. and complement] represent or cause to appear in a specified way: *the sale price makes it an excellent value.* ■ cause or ensure the success or advancement of: *the film that made his reputation.* **3** [with obj. and infin.] compel (someone) to do something: *she made me drink it.* **4** constitute; amount to: *they made an unusual duo.* ■ serve as or become through development or adaptation: *this fern makes a good houseplant.* ■ agree or decide on (a specified arrangement), typically one concerning a time or place: *let's **make it** 7:30.* **5** gain or earn (money or profit): *he made a lot of money.* **6** arrive at (a place) within a specified time or in time for (a train or other transport): *we can make the shuttle.* ■ (**make it**) succeed in something; become successful. ■ achieve a place in: *they **made it** to the semifinals.* ■ achieve the rank of: *make captain.* **7** [no obj., with adverbial of direction] go or prepare to go in a particular direction: *he **made toward** the car.* ■ [with infin.] act as if one is about to perform an action: *she **made as if to** leave.* **8** informal to have sexual intercourse with. **9** (in bridge, whist, and similar games) win (a trick). ■ win a trick with (a card). ■ win the number of tricks that fulfills (a contract). ■ shuffle (a pack of cards) for dealing. ▶ n. **1** the manufacturer or trade name of a particular product: *the make, model, and year of his car.* ■ the structure or composition of something. **2** the making of electrical contact.
– PHRASES **be made of money** informal be very rich. **have (got) it made** informal be in a position where success is certain. **make a day** (or **night**) **of it** devote a whole day (or night) to an activity, esp. an enjoyable one. **make someone's day** make an otherwise ordinary or dull day pleasingly memorable for someone. **make do** manage with the limited or inadequate means available. **make like** informal pretend to be; imitate: *make like a tree and leave!* **make or break** be the factor that decides whether (something) will succeed or fail. **make sail** Sailing spread a sail or sails. **make time** find an occasion when time is available to do something. **make up one's mind** make a decision; decide. **make way 1** allow room for someone or something else. **2** esp. Naut. make progress; travel. **on the make** informal intent on gain, typically in an unscrupulous way. ■ looking for a sexual partner. **put the make on** informal make sexual advances to (someone).
– PHRASAL VERBS **make for 1** move or head toward (a place): *I made for the life raft.* ■ approach (someone) to attack them. **2** tend to result in or be received as (a particular thing): *job descriptions never make for exciting reading.* **3** (**be made for**) be eminently suited for (a particular function): *a man made for action.* ■ form an ideal partnership; be ideally suited: *we were **made for each other**.* **make something of** give or ascribe a specified amount of attention or importance to: *he makes **little** of his experiences.* ■ understand or derive advantage from: *they stared but could **make nothing of** it.* ■ [with negative or in questions] conclude to be the meaning or character of: *he wasn't sure what to make of Debra.* **make off** leave hurriedly, esp. in order to avoid duty or punishment: *they made off without paying.* **make off with** carry (something) away illicitly. **make out** informal **1** make progress; fare: *how are you making out?* **2** informal engage in kissing or caressing. **make someone/something out 1** manage with some difficulty to see or hear something: *it was difficult to make out the shape.* **2** [with infin. or clause] assert; represent: *I'm not as bad as I'm **made out to be**.* **3** draw up or write out a list or document, esp. an official one: *advice about making out a will.* **make something over** completely transform or remodel something, esp. a person's hairstyle, makeup, or clothes. **make up** be reconciled after a quarrel. **make someone up** apply cosmetics to oneself or another. **make something up 1** (also **make up for**) serve or act to compensate for something lost, missed, or deficient: *I'll make up the time tomorrow.* ■ (**make it up to**) compensate someone for negligent or unfair treatment. **2** (**make up**) (of parts) compose or constitute (a whole): *women make up 56 percent of the student body.* **3** put together or prepare something from parts or ingredients: *make up the mortar.* ■ prepare a bed for use with fresh sheets, etc. **4** concoct or invent a story, lie, or plan: *making up tall tales.* — **mak·a·ble** (also **make·a·ble**) adj. [OE *macian*, of West Gmc. origin, from a base meaning 'fitting'; rel. to MATCH[1].]

make-be·lieve ▶ n. the action of pretending or imagining, typically that things are better than they really are. ▶ adj. imitating something real; pretend. ▶ v. [intrans.] pretend; imagine.

make-do ▶ adj. [attrib.] makeshift, ad hoc, or temporary: *his make-do clothes and borrowed tie.*

make·o·ver /ˈmākˌōvər/ ▶ n. a complete transformation or remodeling of something, esp. a person's hairstyle, makeup, or clothes.

mak·er /ˈmākər/ ▶ n. **1** [usu. in comb.] a person or thing that makes or produces something: *a cabinetmaker.* **2** (**our, the,** etc., **Maker**) God; the Creator.
– PHRASES **meet one's Maker** esp. humorous die.

make·shift /ˈmākˌsʜift/ ▶ adj. serving as a temporary substitute; sufficient for the time being. ▶ n. a temporary substitute or device.

make·up /ˈmākˌəp/ (also **make-up**) ▶ n. **1** cosmetics such as lipstick or powder applied to the face. **2** the composition or constitution of something: *the makeup of ocean sediments.* ■ the combination of qualities that form a person's temperament: *a nastiness was in his makeup.* **3** Print. the arrangement of type, illustrations, etc., on a printed page: *page makeup.* **4** a supplementary test or assignment given to a student who missed or failed the original one: [as adj.] *a makeup exam.*

make·weight /'māk,wāt/ ▶ **n.** something put on a scale to make up the required weight. ■ an extra person or thing needed to complete something; a filler: *use it for makeweight in meatloaf.* ■ an unimportant point added to make an argument seem stronger: *a suggestion thrown in as a makeweight.*

make-work ▶ **adj.** denoting an activity that serves mainly to keep someone busy and is of little value in itself. ▶ **n.** work or activity of this kind.

Ma·khach·ka·la /mə,käcʜkə'lä/ a city in southwestern Russia, on the Caspian Sea, capital of Dagestan; pop. 327,000. Former name (until 1922) **Port Petrovsk.**

mak·ing /'mākiɴɢ/ ▶ **n. 1** the process of making or producing something: *the making of videos* | [in comb.] *glassmaking.* **2** (**makings**) informal money made; earnings or profit. **3** (**makings**) essential qualities or ingredients needed for something: *the makings of a champion.*

– PHRASES **in the making** in the process of developing or being made: *history in the making.* **of one's (own) making** (of a difficulty) caused by oneself.

Mak·kah /'mak(k)ə; -kä/ Arabic name for **Mecca.**

ma·ko /'mākō; 'mäkō/ (also **ma·ko shark**) ▶ **n.** (pl. **-kos**) a large fast-moving oceanic shark (genus *Isurus,* family Lamnidae) with a deep blue back and white underparts. [19th C.: from Maori.]

Ma·kon·de /mə'kändā/ ▶ **n.** (pl. same or **-des**) **1** a member of a people inhabiting southern Tanzania and northeastern Mozambique. **2** the Bantu language of this people. ▶ **adj.** of or relating to this people or their language. [the name in Makonde.]

Ma·kua /'makōōə/ ▶ **n.** (pl. same or **-ku·as**) **1** a member of a people inhabiting the border regions of Mozambique, Malawi, and Tanzania. **2** the Bantu language of this people. [a local name.]

ma·ku·ta /mə'kōōtə/ plural form of **likuta.**

Mal. ▶ **abbr.** Bible Malachi.

mal- ▶ **comb. form 1** in an unpleasant degree: *malodorous.* **2** in a faulty manner: *malfunction.* ■ in an improper manner: *malpractice.* ■ in an inadequate manner: *malnourishment.* **3** not: *maladroit.* [from Fr. *mal,* from L. *male* 'badly.']

Mal·a·bar Coast /'malə,bär/ the southern part of the western coast of India.

Ma·la·bo /mə'läbō/ the capital of Equatorial Guinea; pop. 10,000.

mal·ab·sorp·tion /,maləb'sôrpsʜən; -'zôrp-/ ▶ **n.** imperfect absorption of food by the small intestine.

Ma·lac·ca var. of **Melaka.**

ma·lac·ca /mə'lakə/ ▶ **n.** brown cane that is widely used for walking sticks and umbrella handles. The cane is obtained from the stem of a Malaysian climbing palm (*Calamus scipionum*). [19th C.: from the place name **Malacca.**]

Ma·lac·ca, Strait of /mə'läkə; -'lakə/ the channel between the Malay Peninsula and the Indonesian island of Sumatra.

Mal·a·chi /'malə,kī/ a book of the Bible belonging to a period before Ezra and Nehemiah. [from Heb. *mal'āḵī,* lit. 'my messenger.']

mal·a·chite /'malə,kīt/ ▶ **n.** a bright green mineral consisting of copper hydroxyl carbonate. [ME: from OFr. *melochite,* via L. from Gk. *molokhitis,* from *molokhē,* var. of *malakhē* 'mallow.']

malaco- ▶ **comb. form** soft: *malacostracan.* [from Gk. *malakos* 'soft.']

mal·a·col·o·gy /,malə'käləjē/ ▶ **n.** the branch of zoology that deals with mollusks. Compare with **conchology.** — **mal·a·co·log·i·cal** /-kə'läjikəl/ **adj.** **mal·a·col·o·gist n.**

Mal·a·cos·tra·ca /,malə'kästrəkə/ Zool. a large class of crustaceans that includes crabs, shrimps, lobsters, isopods, and amphipods. — **mal·a·cos·tra·can** /-kən/ **adj. & n.** [mod. L. (pl.), from **malaco-** 'soft' + Gk. *ostrakon* 'shell.']

mal·a·dap·tive /,malə'daptiv/ ▶ **adj.** tech. not providing adequate or appropriate adjustment to the environment or situation. — **mal·ad·ap·ta·tion** /-,adap'tāsʜən; -,ad,ap-/ **n.** **mal·a·dap·ted** /-'daptəd/ **adj.**

mal·ad·just·ed /,malə'jəstid/ ▶ **adj.** failing or unable to cope with the demands of a normal social environment: *maladjusted behavior.* — **mal·ad·just·ment n.**

mal·ad·min·is·ter /,maləd'ministər/ ▶ **v.** [trans.] formal manage or administer inefficiently, badly, or dishonestly. — **mal·ad·min·is·tra·tion** /-,minə'strāsʜən/ **n.**

mal·a·droit /,malə'droit/ ▶ **adj.** ineffective or bungling; clumsy. — **mal·a·droit·ly adv.** **mal·a·droit·ness n.** [17th C.: Fr.]

mal·a·dy /'malədē/ ▶ **n.** (pl. **-dies**) a disease or ailment. [ME: from OFr. *maladie,* from *malade* 'sick,' based on L. *male* 'ill' + *habitus* 'having (as a condition).']

ma·la fi·de /,malə 'fīdē; fīdə/ ▶ **adj. & adv.** esp. Law in bad faith; with intent to deceive: [as adj.] *a mala fide abuse of position.* [L.]

Ma·la·ga /'maləgə; 'mälə,gä/ a seaport on the Andalusian coast of southern Spain; pop. 525,000. Spanish name **Málaga.**

Mal·a·gas·y /,malə'gasē/ ▶ **n.** (pl. same or **-gas·ies**) **1** a native or national of Madagascar. **2** the Austronesian language of Madagascar. ▶ **adj.** of or relating to Madagascar or its people or language. [var. of **Madagascar.**]

Mal·a·gas·y Re·pub·lic former name (1960–75) for **Madagascar.**

ma·la·gue·ña /,mälə'g(w)ānyə; ,mal-/ ▶ **n.** a Spanish dance similar to the fandango.

ma·laise /mə'lāz; -'lez/ ▶ **n.** a general feeling of discomfort, illness, or uneasiness whose exact cause is difficult to identify. [18th C.: from Fr., from OFr. *mal* 'bad' (from L. *malus*) + *aise* 'ease.']

Mal·a·mud /'maləməd/, Bernard (1914–86), US writer. His works include *Dubin's Lives* (1979).

mal·a·mute /'malə,myōōt/ (also **mal·e·mute**) ▶ **n.** see **Alaskan malamute.**

ma·lan·ga /mə'laɴɢgə/ ▶ **n.** see **yautia.**

mal·a·prop /'malə,präp/ (also **mal·a·prop·ism**) ▶ **n.** the mistaken use of a word in place of a similar-sounding one, often with unintentionally amusing effect, as in, for example, "dance a *flamingo*" (instead of *flamenco*). [19th C.: from the character Mrs. *Malaprop* in Sheridan's play *The Rivals* (1775) + **-ism.**]

mal·ap·ro·pos /,mal,aprə'pō/ formal ▶ **adv.** inopportunely; inappropriately. ▶ **adj.** inopportune; inappropriate. ▶ **n.** (pl. same) something inappropriately said or done. [17th C.: from Fr. *mal à propos,* from *mal* 'ill' + *à* 'to' + *propos* 'purpose.']

ma·lar /'mālər/ ▶ **adj.** Anat. & Med. of or relating to the cheek: *a slight malar flush.* ▶ **n.** (also **malar bone**) another term for **zygomatic bone.** [18th C.: from mod. L. *malaris,* from L. *mala* 'jaw.']

Mä·lar·en /'mä,lär,ən/ a lake in southeastern Sweden.

ma·lar·i·a /mə'le(ə)rēə/ ▶ **n.** an intermittent and remittent fever caused by a protozoan parasite that invades the red blood cells. The parasite belongs to the genus *Plasmodium* (phylum Sporozoa) and is transmitted by female mosquitoes of the genus *Anopheles.* — **ma·lar·i·al** /-ēəl/ **adj.** **ma·lar·i·an** /-ēən/ **adj.** **ma·lar·i·ous** /-ēəs/ **adj.** [18th C.: from Ital., from *mal'aria,* contracted form of *mala aria* 'bad air,' orig. denoting the unwholesome air from marshes, to which the disease was formerly attributed.]

ma·lar·key /mə'lärkē/ ▶ **n.** informal meaningless talk; nonsense. [1920s: of unknown origin.]

mal·a·thi·on /,malə'ᴛʜī,än/ ▶ **n.** a synthetic organophosphorus compound that is used as an insecticide.

Ma·la·wi /mə'läwē/ a country in southern central Africa. *See box.* — **Ma·la·wi·an** /-wēən/ **adj. & n.**

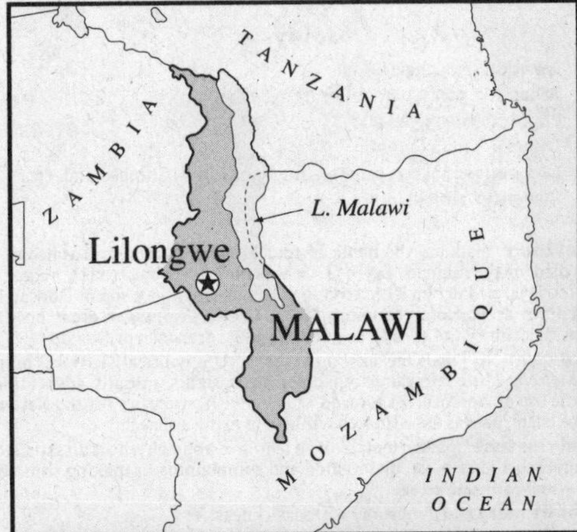

Malawi

Official name: Republic of Malawi
Location: southern central Africa, in the Great Rift Valley, on the western shore of Lake Malawi
Area: 45,800 square miles (118,480 sq km)
Population: 11,906,000
Capital: Lilongwe
Languages: English, Chichewa (both official)
Currency: Malawian kwacha

Ma·la·wi, Lake another name for Lake Nyasa (see **Nyasa, Lake**).

Ma·lay /mə'lā; 'mā,lā/ ▶ **n. 1** a member of a people inhabiting Malaysia and Indonesia. ■ a person of Malay descent. **2** the Austronesian language of the Malays. ▶ **adj.** of or relating to this people or language.

Ma·la·ya /mə'lāə/ a former country in Southeast Asia that consists of the southern part of the Malay Peninsula and some adjacent islands and that now forms the western part of the federation of Malaysia and is known as West Malaysia.

PRONUNCIATION KEY ə *ago, up;* ər *over, fur;* a *hat;* ā *ate;* ä *car;* e *let;* ē *see;* i *fit;* ī *by;* ɴɢ *sing;* ō *go;* ô *law, for;* oi *toy;* ŏŏ *good;* ōō *goo;* ou *out;* ᴛʜ *thin;* ᴛʜ *then;* ᴢʜ *vision*

Mal·a·ya·lam /mälē'äləm/ ▶n. the Dravidian language of the Indian state of Kerala, closely related to Tamil. ▶adj. of or relating to this language or its speakers. [19th C.: from Malayalam, from *mala* (Tamil *malai*) 'mountain' + *āl* 'man.']

Ma·lay·an /mə'lāən/ ▶n. another term for MALAY. ▶adj. of or relating to Malays, the Malay language, or Malaya (now part of Malaysia).

Ma·lay Ar·chi·pel·a·go a large group of islands, including Sumatra, Java, Borneo, the Philippines, and New Guinea, that lie between Southeast Asia and Australia.

Malayo- ▶comb. form Malay; Malay and ...: *Malayo-Polynesian.*

Ma·lay·o-Pol·y·ne·sian /mə'lāō ˌpälə'nēzʜən/ ▶n. another term for AUSTRONESIAN.

Ma·lay Pen·in·su·la a peninsula in Southeast Asia that separates the Indian Ocean from the South China Sea. It extends approximately 700 miles (1,100 km) south from the Isthmus of Kra and comprises the southern part of Thailand and all of Malaya (West Malaysia).

Ma·lay·sia /mə'lāzʜə/ a country in Southeast Asia. *See box.* — **Ma·lay·sian** adj. & n.

Malaysia

Location: Southeast Asia
Area: 127,300 square miles (329,800 sq km)
Population: 23,522,000
Capital: Kuala Lumpur
Languages: Malay (official), English, Tamil, Chinese dialects
Currency: ringgit

Mal·colm /'malkəm/ the name of four kings of Scotland: ■ Malcolm I (died 954), reigned 943–954. ■ Malcolm II (c.954–1034), reigned 1005–34. ■ Malcolm III (c.1031–93), reigned 1058–93; son of Duncan I; known as **Malcolm Canmore** (from Gaelic *Ceann-mor* great head). ■ Malcolm IV (1141–65), reigned 1153–65; grandson of David I.

Mal·colm X /'malkəm 'eks/ (1925–65), US political activist; born *Malcolm Little.* He campaigned for black rights, initially advocating the use of violence. An avowed Muslim with animosity for the Nation of Islam, he was assassinated while delivering a speech.

mal·con·tent /ˌmalkən'tent; 'malkənˌtent/ ▶n. a person who is dissatisfied and rebellious. ▶adj. dissatisfied and complaining or making trouble. — **mal·con·tent·ed** adj.

mal de mer /ˌmal də 'me(ə)r/ ▶n. seasickness. [Fr.]

mal·de·vel·op·ment /ˌmaldi'veləpmənt/ ▶n. esp. Med. & Biol. faulty or imperfect development.

mal·dis·tri·bu·tion /ˌmalˌdistrə'byo͞osʜən/ ▶n. uneven distribution of something, esp. when disadvantageous or unfair. — **mal·dis·trib·ut·ed** /ˌmaldə'stribyətəd/ adj.

Mal·dives /'môlˌdēvz; -ˌdīvz; 'mäl-/ (also **Mal·dive Is·lands**) an island country in the Indian Ocean. *See box.* — **Mal·div·i·an** /môl'divēən; mäl-/ adj. & n.

Ma·le /'mälā/ the capital of the Maldives; pop. 55,000.

male /māl/ ▶adj. of or denoting the sex that produces small, typically motile gametes, esp. spermatozoa, with which a female may be fertilized or inseminated to produce offspring: *male children.* ■ relating to or characteristic of men or male animals; masculine. ■ (of a plant or flower) bearing stamens but lacking functional pistils. ■ (of parts of machinery, fittings, etc.) designed to enter, fill, or fit inside a corresponding female part. ▶n. a male person, plant, or animal. — **male·ness** n. [ME: from OFr. *masle*, from L. *masculus*, from *mas* 'a male.']

mal·e·dic·tion /ˌmalə'diksʜən/ ▶n. a magical word or phrase uttered with the intention of bringing about evil or destruction; a curse. — **mal·e·dic·tive** /-'diktiv/ adj. **mal·e·dic·to·ry** /-'diktərē/ adj. [ME: from L. *maledictio(n-)*, from *maledicere* 'speak evil of.']

mal·e·fac·tor /'maləˌfaktər/ ▶n. formal a person who commits a crime or some other wrong. — **mal·e·fac·tion** /ˌmalə'faksʜən/ n. [ME: from L., from *malefact-* 'done wrong,' from the v. *malefacere*, from *male* 'ill' + *facere* 'do.']

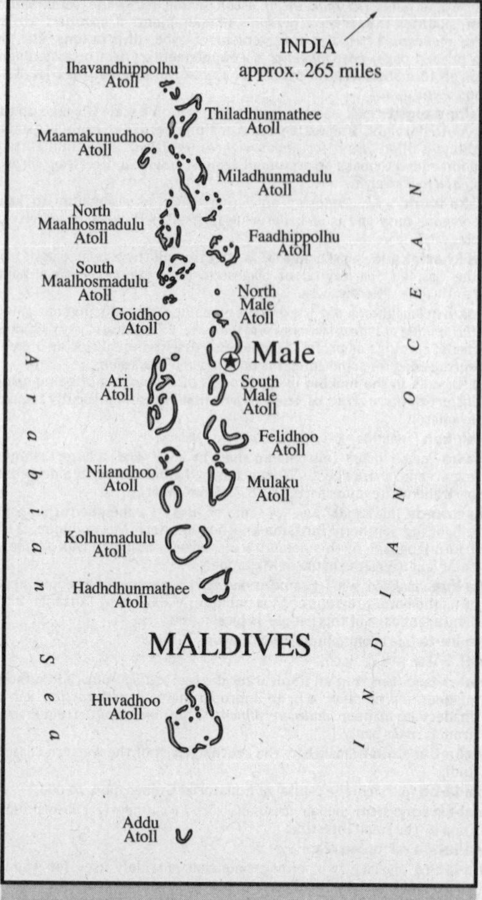

Maldives

Official name: Republic of Maldives
Location: Indian Ocean, southwest of India and Sri Lanka, a chain of coral islands
Area: 120 square miles (300 sq km)
Population: 339,000
Capital: Male
Languages: Maldivian (official), English
Currency: rufiyaa

male fern ▶n. a fern (genus *Dryopteris*, family Dryopteridaceae) with brown scales on the stalks of the fronds, found in wooded areas of the northeastern US, but much more common in Eurasia.

ma·lef·ic /mə'lefik/ ▶adj. literary causing or capable of causing harm or destruction, esp. by supernatural means. — **ma·lef·i·cence** /-'lefəsəns/ n. **ma·lef·i·cent** /-'lefəsənt/ adj. [17th C.: from L. *maleficus*, from *male* 'ill' + *-ficus* 'doing.']

ma·le·ic ac·id /mə'lēik; -'lā-/ ▶n. Chem. a crystalline acid, HOOCCH=CHCOOH, made by distilling malic acid and used in making synthetic resins.

male men·o·pause ▶n. a stage in a middle-aged man's life supposedly corresponding to the menopause of a woman, associated with the loss of sexual potency and a crisis of confidence and identity.

mal·e·mute /'maləˌmyo͞ot/ ▶n. var. of MALAMUTE.

Ma·len·kov /'mälənˌkôf; məlyin'kôf/, Georgi Maksimilianovich (1902–88), prime minister of the Soviet Union 1953–55.

Ma·le·vich /məl'yāvicʜ/, Kazimir Severinovich (1878–1935), Russian painter and designer. He used basic geometric shapes and restricted color.

ma·lev·o·lent /mə'levələnt/ ▶adj. having or showing a wish to do evil to others. — **ma·lev·o·lence** n. **ma·lev·o·lent·ly** adv. [16th C.: from L. *malevolent-* 'wishing evil,' from *male* 'ill' + *volent-* 'wishing.']

mal·fea·sance /mal'fēzəns/ ▶n. Law wrongdoing, esp. by a public official. — **mal·fea·sant** /-'fēzənt/ n. & adj. [17th C.: from Anglo-Norman Fr. *malfaisance*, from *mal-* 'evil' + OFr. *faisance* 'activity.' Cf. MISFEASANCE.]

mal·for·ma·tion /ˌmalfôr'māsʜən; -fər-/ ▶n. a deformity; an abnormally formed part of the body. ■ the condition of being abnormal in shape or form. — **mal·formed** /mal'fôrmd/ **adj.**

mal·func·tion /mal'fəNGkSHən/ ▶ **v.** [intrans.] (of a piece of equipment or machinery) fail to function normally or satisfactorily. ▶ **n.** a failure to function in a normal or satisfactory manner: *a computer malfunction.*

Ma·li /'mälē/ a country in West Africa. Former name (until 1958) **French Sudan.** *See box.* — **Ma·li·an** /-ēən/ **adj. & n.**

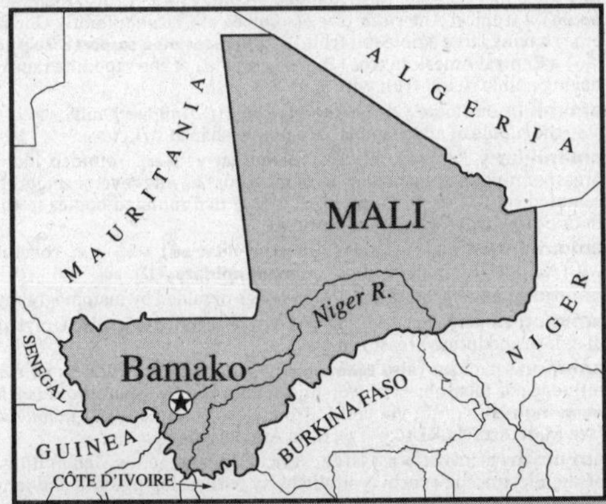

Mali

Official name: Republic of Mali
Location: West Africa, south of Algeria, in the Sahel except for desert in the north
Area: 478,900 square miles (1,240,000 sq km)
Population: 11,900,000
Capital: Bamako
Languages: French (official), Bambara, numerous African languages
Currency: CFA franc

Mal·i·bu /'malə,bo͞o/ a resort on the Pacific coast of southern California.

mal·ic ac·id /'malik/ ▶ **n.** Chem. a crystalline acid, HOOCCH$_2$CH(OH)COOH, present in unripe apples and other fruits. — **mal·ate** /'mal,āt; 'mā,lāt/ **n.** [18th C.: *malic* from Fr. *malique*, from L. *malum* 'apple.']

mal·ice /'maləs/ ▶ **n.** the intention or desire to do evil; ill will. ■ Law wrongful intention, esp. as increasing the guilt of certain offenses. [ME: via OFr. from L. *malitia*, from *malus* 'bad.']

mal·ice a·fore·thought ▶ **n.** Law the intention to kill or harm, which is held to distinguish unlawful killing from murder.

ma·li·cious /mə'lisHəs/ ▶ **adj.** characterized by malice; intending or intended to do harm: *malicious rumors.* — **ma·li·cious·ly adv. ma·li·cious·ness n.**

ma·li·cious mis·chief ▶ **n.** Law the willful destruction of another person's property for vicious, wanton, or mischievous purposes.

ma·lign /mə'līn/ ▶ **adj.** evil in nature or effect: malevolent: *a malign influence.* ▶ **v.** [trans.] speak about (someone) in a spitefully critical manner. — **ma·lign·er n. ma·lig·ni·ty** /-'lignətē/ **n. ma·lign·ly adv.** [ME: via OFr. *maligne*, based on L. *malignus* 'tending to evil,' from *malus* 'bad.']

ma·lig·nan·cy /mə'lignənsē/ ▶ **n.** (pl. **-cies**) **1** the state or presence of a malignant tumor; cancer. ■ a cancerous growth. **2** the quality of being malign or malevolent.

ma·lig·nant /mə'lignənt/ ▶ **adj. 1** (of a disease) very virulent or infectious. ■ (of a tumor) tending to invade normal tissue or to recur after removal; cancerous. Contrasted with **benign. 2** malevolent. — **ma·lig·nant·ly adv.** [16th C.: from late L. *malignant-* 'contriving maliciously,' used in its early sense to describe those sympathetic to the royalist cause during the Engl. Civil War (1642–49).]

ma·lin·ger /mə'liNGgər/ ▶ **v.** [intrans.] exaggerate or feign illness in order to escape duty or work. — **ma·lin·ger·er n.**

Ma·lin·ke /mə'liNGkā/ ▶ **n.** (pl. same or **-kes**) **1** a member of a people living mainly in Senegal, Mali, and Côte d'Ivoire. **2** the Mande language of this people. ▶ **adj.** of or relating to the Malinke or their language. [the name in Malinke.]

Ma·li·now·ski /,malə'nôfskē; -'näf-; ,mäl-/, Bronisław Kaspar (1884–1942), Polish anthropologist. He initiated the "participant observation" approach to anthropology.

mall /môl/ ▶ **n. 1** (also **shopping mall**) a large building or series of connected buildings containing a variety of retail stores. **2** a sheltered walk or promenade. ■ (also **pedestrian mall**) a section of a street, typically in the downtown area of a city, from which vehicular traffic is excluded. [17th C.: Sense 1 dates from the 1960s. Sense 2 derives from *The Mall*, a tree-bordered walk in St. James's Park, London, so named because it was the site of a pall-mall alley.]

mal·lard /'malərd/ ▶ **n.** (pl. same or **-lards**) the most common duck (*Anas platyrhynchos*) of the northern hemisphere and the ancestor of most domestic ducks, the male having a dark green head and white collar. [ME: from OFr. 'wild drake,' from *masle* 'male.']

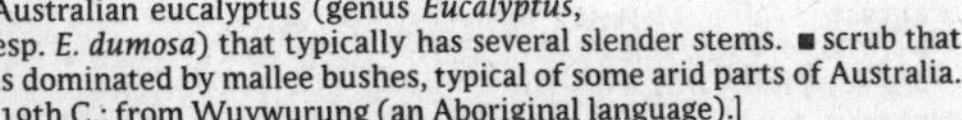
mallard

mal·le·a·ble /'malyəbəl; 'malēə-/ ▶ **adj.** (of a metal or other material) able to be hammered or pressed permanently out of shape without breaking or cracking. ■ fig. easily influenced; pliable. — **mal·le·a·bil·i·ty** /,malyə'bilitē; ,malēə-/ **n. mal·le·a·bly adv.** [ME: via OFr. from med. L. *malleabilis*, from L. *malleus* 'a hammer.']

mal·lee /'malē/ ▶ **n.** a low-growing bushy Australian eucalyptus (genus *Eucalyptus*, esp. *E. dumosa*) that typically has several slender stems. ■ scrub that is dominated by mallee bushes, typical of some arid parts of Australia. [19th C.: from Wuywurung (an Aboriginal language).]

mal·le·o·lus /mə'lēələs/ ▶ **n.** (pl. **-li** /-,lī; -,lē/) Anat. a bony projection with a shape likened to a hammer head, esp. on either side of the ankle. — **mal·le·o·lar** /mə'lēələr/ **adj.** [17th C.: from L., dimin. of *malleus* 'hammer.']

mal·let /'malət/ ▶ **n.** a hammer with a large wooden head, used esp. for hitting a chisel. ■ a long-handled wooden stick with a head like a hammer, used for hitting a croquet or polo ball. ■ Music a wooden or plastic stick with a rounded head, used to play certain percussion instruments. [ME: from OFr. *maillet*, from *mail* 'hammer,' from L. *malleus*.]

mal·le·us /'malēəs/ ▶ **n.** (pl. **mal·le·i** /'malē,ī; -ē,ē/) Anat. a small bone in the middle ear that transmits vibrations of the eardrum to the incus.

mall·ing /'môliNG/ ▶ **n. 1** the development of shopping malls. **2** the activity of passing time in a shopping mall.

Mal·loph·a·ga /mə'läfəgə/ Entomol. an order of insects that comprises the biting lice. See also **Phthiraptera.** — **mal·loph·a·gan** /-gən/ **n. & adj.** [mod. L. (pl.), from Gk. *mallos* 'lock of wool' + *-phagos* 'eating.']

Mal·lor·ca /mä'yôrkə/ Spanish name for **Majorca.**

mal·low /'malō/ ▶ **n.** a herbaceous plant (genus *Malva*) with pink or purple flowers and disk-shaped fruit. The **mallow family** (Malvaceae) also includes the hollyhocks, hibiscus, and abutilon. See also **marsh mallow, rose mallow.** [OE *meal(u)we*, from L. *malva*; rel. to Gk. *malakhē*; cf. **mauve.**]

malm /mä(l)m/ ▶ **n.** a soft, crumbly, chalky rock, or the fertile loamy soil produced as it weathers. ■ (also **malm brick**) a fine-quality brick made originally from malm, marl, or a similar chalky clay. [OE *mealm-*, of Gmc. origin; rel. to **meal**[2].]

Malmö /'mäl,mo͞o; -,mœ/ a port city in southwestern Sweden; pop. 234,000.

malm·sey /'mä(l)mzē/ ▶ **n.** a fortified Madeira wine of the sweetest type.

mal·nour·ished /mal'nərisHt; -'nə-risHt/ ▶ **adj.** suffering from malnutrition. — **mal·nourish·ment** /-'nərisHmənt/ **n.**

mal·nu·tri·tion /,malno͞o'trisHən/ ▶ **n.** lack of proper nutrition.

mal·oc·clu·sion /,malə'klo͞ozHən/ ▶ **n.** Dentistry imperfect positioning of the teeth when the jaws are closed.

mal·o·dor /mal'ōdər/ ▶ **n.** a very unpleasant smell.

mal·o·dor·ous /mal'ōdərəs/ ▶ **adj.** smelling very unpleasant.

ma·lo·lac·tic /,malə'laktik; ,mālə-/ ▶ **adj.** of or denoting bacterial fermentation that converts malic acid to lactic acid, esp. as a secondary process used to reduce the acidity of some wines.

ma·lo·nic ac·id /mə'lōnik; -'län-/ ▶ **n.** Chem. a crystalline acid (HOOCCH$_2$COOH) obtained by the oxidation of malic acid. — **mal·o·nate** /'malə,nāt; 'mā-/ **n.**

Mal·o·ry /'malərē/, Sir Thomas (d.1471), English writer. He wrote *Le Morte d'Arthur* (1483).

ma·lo·ti /mə'lōtē; -'lo͞otē/ plural form of **loti.**

mal·per·for·mance /,malpər'fôrməns/ ▶ **n.** faulty or inadequate performance of a task.

Mal·pi·ghi /mal'pigē; mäl-/, Marcello (*c.*1628–94), Italian microscopist. He demonstrated the pathway of blood from arteries to veins.

Mal·pigh·i·an lay·er /,mal'pigēən; -'pēgē-/ ▶ **n.** Zool. & Anat. a layer in the epidermis in which skin cells are continually formed by division.

Mal·pigh·i·an tu·bule ▶ **n.** Zool. a tubular excretory organ in insects and some other arthropods.

mal·prac·tice /mal'praktəs/ ▶ **n.** improper, illegal, or negligent professional activity or treatment, esp. by a medical practitioner, lawyer, or public official.

Mal·raux /mal'rō; mäl-/, André (1901–76), French writer and art critic. His novels include *Man's Fate* (1931).

malt /môlt/ ▶ **n.** barley or other grain that has been steeped, germinated, and dried, used esp. for brewing or distilling and vinegar-making. ■ short for **malted milk.** ▶ **v.** [trans.] convert (grain) into malt: [as n.] **(malting)** *barley grown for malting.* ■ [intrans.] (of a seed) become malt when germination is checked by drought. — **malt·i·ness n. malt·y adj.** [OE *m(e)alt*, of Gmc. origin; rel. to **melt.**]

Mal·ta /'môltə/ an island country in the central Mediterranean Sea, south of Sicily; pop. 398,000; capital, Valletta.

malt·ase /'môl,tās; -,tāz/ ▶ **n.** Biochem. an enzyme, present in saliva and pancreatic juice, that catalyzes the breakdown of maltose and similar sugars to form glucose.

malt·ed /môltid/ ▶ **adj.** mixed with malt or a malt extract. ■ [as n.] malted milk.

malt·ed milk ▶ **n.** a drink combining milk, a malt preparation, and ice cream or flavoring. ■ the powdered mixture from which this drink is made.

Mal·tese[1] /môl'tēz/ ▶ **n.** (pl. same) **1** a native or national of Malta or a person of Maltese descent. **2** the national language of Malta, a Semitic language derived from Arabic. ▶ **adj.** of or relating to Malta, its people, or their language.

Mal·tese[2] (also **Maltese terrier**) ▶ **n.** a dog of a very small long-haired breed, typically with white hair.

Maltese[2]

Mal·tese cross ▶ **n.** **1** a cross with arms of equal length that broaden from the center and have their ends indented in a shallow V-shape. See illustration at CROSS. **2** a plant of the pink family (*Lychnis chalcedonica*), with scarlet petals arranged in the shape of a Maltese cross. [so named because the cross was formerly worn by the Knights of Malta, a religious order.]

Mal·thus /'malTHəs; 'môl-/, Thomas Robert (1766–1834), English economist and clergyman. He wrote *Essay on Population* (1798). — **Mal·thu·sian** /mal'TH(y)o͞oZHən; môl-/ **adj. & n. Mal·thu·sian·ism** /mal'TH(y)o͞oZHə,nizəm; môl-/ **n.**

malt liq·uor ▶ **n.** alcoholic liquor made from malt by fermentation rather than distillation; beer with a relatively high alcohol content.

mal·to·dex·trin /,môltō'dekstrən/ ▶ **n.** dextrin containing maltose, used as a food additive.

malt·ose /'môl,tōs; -,tōz/ ▶ **n.** Chem. a sugar, $C_{12}H_{22}O_{11}$, produced by the breakdown of starch, e.g., by enzymes found in malt and saliva.

mal·treat /mal'trēt/ ▶ **v.** [trans.] (often **be maltreated**) treat (a person or animal) cruelly or with violence. — **mal·treat·er n. mal·treat·ment n.** [18th C.: from Fr. *maltraiter*.]

malt whis·key ▶ **n.** whiskey made only from malted barley and not blended with grain whiskey.

Ma·lu·ku Indonesian name for MOLUCCA ISLANDS.

Mal·va·si·a /mal'vāZHə/ ▶ **n.** a variety of grape used to make white and red wines, esp. in Italy. [Ital. form of the place name *Monemvasia*, in the Peloponnese (see MALMSEY).]

mal·ver·sa·tion /,malvər'sāSHən/ ▶ **n.** formal corrupt behavior in a position of trust, esp. in public office. [16th C.: from Fr., from *malverser*, from L. *male* 'badly' + *versari* 'behave.']

Mal·vi·nas, Islas /môl'vēnəs/ the name by which the Falkland Islands are known in Argentina.

mal·ware /'mal,we(ə)r/ ▶ **n.** Comput. software that is intended to damage or disable computers and computer systems [blend of MALICIOUS and SOFTWARE.]

ma·ma /'mämə/ (also **mam·ma**) ▶ **n.** **1** one's mother (esp. as a child's term): [as name] *come and meet Mama.* **2** informal a mature woman: *a tough mama.* [16th C.: imitative of a child's first syllables *ma, ma*.]

ma·ma-san /'mämə ,sän/ ▶ **n.** (in Japan and the Far East) a woman in a position of authority, esp. one in charge of a geisha house or bar. [Japanese, from *mama* 'mother' + *san*, an honorific title used as a mark of politeness.]

ma·ma's boy ▶ **n.** a boy or man who is excessively influenced by or attached to his mother.

mam·ba /'mämbə/ ▶ **n.** a large, agile, highly venomous African snake (genus *Dendroaspis*, family Elapidae). See also BLACK MAMBA. [19th C.: from Zulu *imamba*.]

mam·bo /'mämbō/ ▶ **n.** (pl. **-bos**) **1** a Latin American dance similar in rhythm to the rumba. **2** a voodoo priestess. ▶ **v.** (**-boes, -boed**) [intrans.] dance the mambo. [1940s: from Amer. Sp., prob. from Haitian Creole, from Yoruba, lit. 'to talk.']

mam·ee /mäm'ē/ ▶ **n.** var. of MAMMEE.

Mam·e·luke /'mamə,lo͞ok/ ▶ **n.** a member of a regime that formerly ruled parts of the Middle East.

Mam·et /'mamit/, David Alan (1947–), US playwright and screenwriter. His plays include *Glengarry Glen Ross* (1984).

ma·mey /mäm'ē/ ▶ **n.** var. of MAMMEE.

ma·mil·la /mam'ilə/ ▶ **n.** var. of MAMMILLA.

mam·ma[1] ▶ **n.** var. of MAMA.

mam·ma[2] /'mamə/ ▶ **n.** (pl. **mam·mae** /'mamē; 'mam,ī/) a milk-secreting organ of female mammals (in humans, the breast). ■ a corresponding nonsecretory structure in male mammals. — **mam·mi·form** /'mamə,fôrm/ **adj.** [OE, from L., 'breast.']

mam·mal /'maməl/ ▶ **n.** a warm-blooded vertebrate animal of a class that is distinguished by the possession of hair or fur, the secretion of milk by females, and (typically) the birth of live young. — **mam·ma·li·an** /mə'mālēən/ **adj.** [19th C.: Anglicized form of mod. L. *mammalia*, neut. pl. of L. *mammalis*, from *mamma* 'breast.']

mam·ma·lif·er·ous /,mamə'lifərəs/ ▶ **adj.** Geol. containing mammalian fossil remains.

mam·mal·o·gy /mə'maləjē/ ▶ **n.** the branch of zoology concerned with mammals. — **mam·mal·o·gist n.**

mam·ma·ry /'mamərē/ ▶ **adj.** [attrib.] denoting or relating to the human female breasts or the milk-secreting organs of other mammals. ▶ **n.** (pl. **-ries**) informal a breast.

mam·ma·ry gland ▶ **n.** the milk-producing gland of women or other female mammals.

mam·mee /mä'mā; -'mē/ (also **ma·mee, ma·mey**) ▶ **n.** **1** (also **mammee apple**) a tropical American tree (*Mammea americana*, family Guttiferae) having large edible red fruit. **2** (also **mam·mee sa·po·te** /sə'pōtē; -tā/) a Central American tree (*Pouteria sapota*) of the sapodilla family, having edible russet fruit with spicy red flesh.

mam·mil·la /mə'milə/ (also **ma·mil·la**) ▶ **n.** (pl. **-mil·lae** /-'milē; -'mil,ī/) Anat. the nipple of any mammal. ■ a nipple-shaped structure.

mam·mil·lar·y /'mamə,lerē/ (also **mam·il·lar·y**) ▶ **adj.** rounded like a breast or nipple, in particular: ■ (of minerals) having several smoothly rounded convex surfaces. ■ Anat. denoting two rounded bodies in the floor of the hypothalamus in the brain.

mam·mil·lat·ed /'mamə,lātid/ (also **mam·il·lat·ed**) ▶ **adj.** tech. covered with rounded mounds or lumps. — **mam·mil·late** /-,lāt/ **adj.**

mam·mo·gram /'mamə,gram/ ▶ **n.** an image obtained by mammography.

mam·mog·ra·phy /ma'mägrəfē/ ▶ **n.** Med. a technique using X-rays to diagnose and locate breast tumors.

mam·mon /'mamən/ (also **Mam·mon**) ▶ **n.** wealth regarded as an evil influence or false object of worship and devotion. — **mam·mon·ism n. mam·mon·ist n.** [ME: via late L. from New Testament Gk. *mamōnas* (see Matt. 6:24, Luke 16:9–13), from Aramaic *māmōn* 'riches.']

mam·moth /'maməTH/ ▶ **n.** a large extinct elephant (genus *Mammuthus*) of the Pleistocene epoch, typically hairy with a sloping back and long curved tusks. ▶ **adj.** huge: *a mammoth corporation.* [18th C.: from Russ. *mamo(n)t*, prob. of Siberian origin.]

Mam·moth Cave Na·tion·al Park a national park in west central Kentucky, site of the largest known cave system in the world.

mam·my /'mamē/ ▶ **n.** (pl. **-mies**) informal one's mother (esp. as a child's word). ■ offens. (formerly in the southern US) a black nursemaid or nanny in charge of white children.

Mam'·selle /mam'zel/ ▶ **n.** short for MADEMOISELLE.

Man. ▶ **abbr.** ■ Manitoba. ■ Manila.

man /man/ ▶ **n.** (pl. **men**) **1** an adult human male. ■ a male worker or employee: *more than 700 men were laid off.* ■ a male member of a sports team. ■ (**men**) ordinary members of the armed forces as distinct from the officers: *a platoon of forty men.* ■ a husband, boyfriend, or lover: *man and wife.* ■ [with adj.] a male person associated with a particular place, activity, or occupation: *a Harvard man.* ■ a male pursued or sought by another, esp. in connection with a crime: *they'll find their man.* ■ dated a manservant or valet: *get me a cocktail, my man.* **2** a human being of either sex; a person. ■ (also **Man**) [in sing.] human beings in general; the human race: *the ravages of man.* ■ [in sing.] an individual; one: *a man could buy a lot with a million dollars.* ■ a person with the qualities often associated with males such as bravery, spirit, or toughness: *she was more of a man than any of them.* ■ [in sing.] [with adj.] a type of prehistoric human named after the place where the remains were found: *Cro-Magnon man.* **3** (usu. **the Man**) informal a group or person in a position of authority over others, such as the police. ■ black slang white people collectively regarded as the controlling group in society. **4** a figure or token used in playing a board game. ▶ **v.** (**manned, man·ning**) [trans.] (often **be manned**) provide (something, esp. a place or machine) with the personnel to run, operate, or defend it: *man the pumps.* ▶ **exclam.** informal used, irrespective of the sex of the person addressed, to express surprise, admiration, delight, etc., or for emphasis: *man, what a show!*

– PHRASES **as —— as the next man** as —— as the average person: *as ambitious as the next man.* **be someone's man** be the person perfectly suited to a particular requirement or task: *for perming services, David's your man.* **be man enough for** (or **to do**) be brave enough to do: *who's man enough for the job?* **every man for himself** proverb everyone should (or does) look after their own interests rather than considering those of others. **man about town** a fashionable male socialite. **the man in the moon** the imagined likeness of a face seen on the surface of a full moon. ■ fig. used, esp. in comparisons, to refer to someone regarded as out of touch with real life: *a kid with no more idea of what to do than the man in the moon.* **the man in** (or **on**) **the street** an ordinary person, often with regard to their opinions, or as distinct from an expert. **man of action** see ACTION. **man of the cloth** a clergyman. **man of God** a clergyman. ■ a holy man or saint. **man of honor** a man who adheres to what is right or to a high standard of conduct. **man of the house** the male head of a household. **man of letters** a male scholar or author. **man of the moment** a man of importance at a particular time. **man of the world** see WORLD. **man's best friend** an affectionate or approving way of referring to the dog. **a man's man** a man whose personality is such that he is as popular and at ease, or more so, with other men than with women. **man to man** (or **man-to-man**) **1** in a direct and frank way between two men; openly and honestly. **2** denoting a defensive tactic in a sport such as football or basketball in which each player is responsible for defending against one opponent. **men in white coats** humorous psychiatrists or psychiatric workers (used to imply that someone is mad or mentally unbalanced). **separate** (or **sort out**) **the men from the boys** informal show or prove which people in a group are truly competent, brave, or mature. — **man·less adj.** [OE *man(n)*, (pl.)

menn (n.), *mannian* (v.), of Gmc. origin; rel. to Du. *man*, Ger. *Mann*, and Sanskrit *manu* 'mankind.']

-man ▶ **comb. form** in nouns denoting: ■ a male of a specified nationality or origin: *Frenchman* | *Yorkshireman.* ■ a man belonging to a distinct specified group: *layman.* ■ a person, esp. a male, having a specified occupation or role: *exciseman* | *chairman* | *oarsman.* ■ a ship of a specified kind: *merchantman.*

Man, Isle of /man/ an island in the Irish Sea off the northwest coast of England; a British crown possession; pop. 70,000; capital, Douglas.

man·a·cle /'manikəl/ ▶ **n.** (usu. **manacles**) a metal band, chain, or shackle for fastening someone's hands or ankles. ▶ **v.** [trans.] (usu. **be manacled**) fetter (a person or a part of the body) with manacles. [ME: from OFr. *manicle* 'handcuff,' from L. *manicula*, dimin. of *manus* 'hand.']

man·age /'manij/ ▶ **v. 1** [trans.] be in charge of (a company, establishment, or undertaking); administer; run. ■ administer and regulate (resources under one's control): *we manage our cash well.* ■ have the position of supervising (staff) at work. ■ be the manager of (a sports team or a performer). ■ maintain control or influence over (a person or animal): *she manages horses better than anyone I know.* ■ (often **be managed**) control the use or exploitation of (land): *the forest is managed to achieve maximum growth.* **2** [intrans.] succeed in surviving or in attaining one's aims, esp. against heavy odds; cope: *Christine* **managed on** *five hours' sleep a night.* ■ [trans.] succeed in doing, achieving, or producing (something, esp. something difficult): *Sue managed a brave smile.* ■ [trans.] succeed in dealing with or withstanding (something): *more stress than we could manage.* [16th C.: from Ital. *maneggiare*, based on L. *manus* 'hand.']

man·age·a·ble /'manijəbəl/ ▶ **adj.** able to be managed, controlled, or accomplished without great difficulty. — **man·age·a·bil·i·ty** /,manijə'bilətē/ **n.** **man·age·a·ble·ness n. man·age·a·bly adv.**

man·aged care ▶ **n.** a system of health care in which patients agree to visit only certain doctors and hospitals, and in which the cost of treatment is monitored.

man·aged fund ▶ **n.** an investment fund run on behalf of an investor by an agent.

man·age·ment /'manijmənt/ ▶ **n.** the process of dealing with or controlling things or people: *the management of deer.* ■ the responsibility for and control of a company or similar organization: *the management of a newspaper.* ■ [treated as sing. or pl.] the people in charge of running a company or organization, regarded collectively: *management has not been cooperative.* ■ Med. & Psychiatry the treatment or control of diseases, injuries, or disorders, or the care of patients who suffer from them: *the management of cancer.*

man·age·ment in·for·ma·tion sys·tem (abbr. **MIS**) ▶ **n.** a computerized information-processing system designed to support the activities of company or organizational management.

man·ag·er /'manijər/ ▶ **n.** a person responsible for controlling or administering all or part of a company or similar organization: *the sales manager.* ■ a person who controls the activities, business dealings, and other aspects of the career of an entertainer, athlete, group of musicians, etc. ■ a person in charge of the activities, tactics, and training of a sports team. ■ [with adj.] Comput. a program or system that controls or organizes a peripheral device or process: *a file manager.* — **man·ag·er·ship n.**

man·a·ge·ri·al /,manə'ji(ə)rēəl/ ▶ **adj.** relating to management or managers, esp. of a company or similar organization: *managerial skills.* — **man·a·ge·ri·al·ly adv.**

man·a·ge·ri·al·ism /,manə'ji(ə)rēə,lizəm/ ▶ **n.** belief in or reliance on the use of professional managers in administering or planning an activity. — **man·a·ge·ri·al·ist n. & adj.**

man·ag·ing /'manijiNG/ ▶ **adj.** [attrib.] having executive or supervisory control or authority: *we have faith in our managing editor.*

Ma·na·gua /mə'nägwə/ the capital of Nicaragua; pop 682,000. It was almost completely destroyed by a 1972 earthquake.

man·a·kin /'manə,kin/ ▶ **n.** a small tropical American bird (family Pipridae, several genera and species) with a large head and small bill, the male of which is typically brightly colored. Compare with **MANNIKIN.**

Ma·na·ma /mə'nämə/ the capital of Bahrain, in the eastern part of the country; pop. 140,400.

ma·ña·na /mən'yänə/ ▶ **adv.** in the indefinite future: *the exhibition will be ready mañana.* [Sp., lit. 'tomorrow.']

Ma·nas·seh /mə'nasə/ (in the Bible) a Hebrew patriarch; the elder son of Joseph. ■ the tribe of Israel traditionally descended from him.

ma·nat /'man,at/ ▶ **n.** (pl. same) the basic monetary unit of Azerbaijan and Turkmenistan, equal to 100 gopik in Azerbaijan and 100 tenge in Turkmenistan.

man-at-arms ▶ **n.** (pl. **men-at-arms**) archaic a soldier, esp. one heavily armed and mounted on horseback.

man·a·tee /'manə,tē/ ▶ **n.** an aquatic mammal (family Trichechidae, genus *Trichechus*) with a rounded tail flipper, living in shallow coastal waters of the tropical Atlantic. Three species, all of which are endangered, include the **West Indian manatee** (*T. manatus*).

Ma·naus /mä'nous/ a city in northwestern Brazil; pop. 1,012,000.

Man·che·go /man'CHāgō/ ▶ **n.** a Spanish cheese traditionally made with sheep's milk. [Sp., from *La Mancha*, the region of Spain where the cheese originates.]

Man·ches·ter[1] /'man,CHestər; 'manCHi-/ **1** a city in northwestern England; pop. 397,000. **2** a city in southern New Hampshire; pop. 107,006.

West Indian manatee

Man·ches·ter[2], William (1922–2004), US historian and biographer. He wrote *The Death of a President* (1967).

Man·ches·ter ter·ri·er ▶ **n.** a small terrier of a breed with a short black-and-tan coat.

man·chi·neel /,manCHə'nēl/ ▶ **n.** a Caribbean tree (*Hippomane mancinella*) of the spurge family that has acrid applelike fruit and poisonous milky sap.

Man·chu /'man,CHōō; man'CHōō/ ▶ **n.** (pl. same or **-chus**) **1** a member of a people originally living in Manchuria who formed the last imperial dynasty of China (1644–1912). **2** the Tungusic language of the Manchus. ▶ **adj.** of or relating to the Manchu people or their language. [the name in Manchu, lit. 'pure.']

Man·chu·ri·a /man'CHŏŏrēə/ a mountainous region that forms the northeastern portion of China.

-mancy ▶ **comb. form** divination by a specified means: *geomancy.* — **-mantic comb. form** in corresponding adjectives. [from OFr. *-mancie*, via late L. *-mantia* from Gk. *manteia* 'divination.']

man·da·la /'mandələ; 'mən-/ ▶ **n.** a geometric figure representing the universe in Hindu and Buddhist symbolism. ■ Psychoanal. such a symbol in a dream, representing the dreamer's search for completeness. — **man·da·lic** /man'dalik; ,mən-/ **adj.** [from Sanskrit *maṇḍala* 'disk.']

Man·da·lay /,mandl'ā/ a port city on the Irrawaddy River in central Myanmar (Burma); pop. 533,000.

man·da·mus /man'dāməs/ ▶ **n.** Law a judicial writ issued as a command to an inferior court or ordering a person to perform a public or statutory duty: *a writ of mandamus.* [16th C.: from L., lit. 'we command.']

Man·dan /'mandən; -,dan/ ▶ **n.** (pl. same or **-dans**) **1** a member of an American Indian people formerly living on the Missouri River in North Dakota. **2** the Siouan language of this people. ▶ **adj.** of or relating to this people or their language. [from Canad. Fr. *Mandane*, prob. from Dakota Sioux *mawáta-na.*]

man·da·rin[1] /'mandərən/ ▶ **n. 1** (**Mandarin**) the standard literary and official form of Chinese based on the Beijing dialect, spoken by over 730 million people: [as adj.] *Mandarin Chinese.* **2** an official in any of the nine top grades of the former imperial Chinese civil service. ■ [as adj.] (esp. of clothing) characteristic or supposedly characteristic of such officials. ■ an ornament consisting of a nodding figure in traditional Chinese dress, typically made of porcelain. ■ porcelain decorated with Chinese figures dressed as mandarins. ■ a powerful official or senior bureaucrat, esp. one perceived as reactionary and secretive: *a civil service mandarin.* [16th C. (denoting a Chin. official): from Port. *mandarim*, via Malay from Hindi *mantrī* 'counselor.']

man·da·rin[2] /-də,rēn/ (also **man·da·rine** /-də,rēn/, **man·da·rin or·ange**) ▶ **n. 1** a small flattish citrus fruit (*Citrus reticulata*) with a loose skin, esp. a variety with yellow-orange skin. Compare with **TANGERINE. 2** the citrus tree that yields this fruit. [18th C.: from Fr. *mandarine*; perh. rel. to **MANDARIN**[1], the color of the fruit being likened to the official's yellow robes.]

man·da·rin col·lar ▶ **n.** a small, close-fitting upright collar.

man·da·rin duck ▶ **n.** a small tree-nesting eastern Asian duck (*Aix galericulata*), the male of which has showy plumage with an orange ruff and orange saillike feathers on each side of the body.

mandarin collar

man·date /'man,dāt/ ▶ **n. 1** an official order or commission to do something: *a federal mandate.* ■ Law a commission by which a party is entrusted to perform a service, esp. without payment and with indemnity against loss by that party. ■ Law an order from an appellate court to a lower court to take a specific action. ■ a written authority enabling someone to carry out transactions on another's bank account. **2** the authority to carry out a policy or course of action, given by the electorate to a party that is victorious in an election. ▶ **v.** [trans.] give (someone) authority to act in a certain way: *other colleges have mandated coed fraternities.* ■ require (something) to be done; make mandatory: *the government began mandating better car safety.* [16th C.: from L. *mandatum* 'something commanded,' from *mandare*, from *manus* 'hand' + *dare* 'give.']

man·da·to·ry /ˈmandəˌtôrē/ ▶ **adj.** required by law or rules; compulsory: *wearing helmets is mandatory.* ■ of or conveying a command: *he did not want the guidelines to be mandatory.* — **man·da·to·ri·ly** /-ˌtôrəlē/ **adv.** [15th C.: from late L. *mandatorius,* from L. *mandatum* 'something commanded.']

Man·de /ˈmänˌdā; mänˈdā/ ▶ **n.** (pl. same or **-des**) **1** a member of any of a large group of peoples of West Africa. **2** any of the Niger–Congo languages or dialects spoken by these peoples. ▶ **adj.** of or relating to these peoples or the Mande group of languages. [the name in Mande.]

Man·de·la /manˈdelə/, Nelson Rolihlahla (1918–), president of South Africa 1994–99. He was the country's first democratically elected president. Nobel Peace Prize (1993, shared with F. W. de Klerk).

Man·del·brot /ˈmandlˌbrät; -ˌbrō; ˌmändelˈbrô/, Benoit (1924–), French mathematician; born in Poland. He was a pioneer of fractal geometry.

Man·del·brot set ▶ **n.** Math. a particular set of complex numbers that has a highly convoluted fractal boundary when plotted.

man·di·ble /ˈmandəbəl/ ▶ **n.** Anat. & Zool. the jaw or a jawbone, esp. the lower jawbone. ■ either of the upper and lower parts of a bird's beak. ■ either half of the crushing organ in an arthropod's mouthparts. — **man·dib·u·lar** /manˈdibyələr/ **adj.** **man·dib·u·late** /manˈdibyəˌlāt/ **adj.** [ME: from OFr., or from late L. *mandibula,* from *mandere* 'to chew.']

Man·ding /ˈmandiNG/ (also **Man·din·go** /manˈdiNGgō/) ▶ **n. & adj.** another term for **MANDE**.

Man·din·ka /manˈdiNGkə/ ▶ **n.** (pl. same or **-kas**) **1** a member of a people living mainly in Senegal, Gambia, and Sierra Leone. **2** the Mande language of this people. ▶ **adj.** of or relating to the Mandinkas or their language. [the name in Mandinka.]

man·do·la /manˈdōlə/ ▶ **n.** a large tenor or bass mandolin, used in ensembles and folk groups. ■ (also **man·do·ra** /-ˈdôrə/) hist. an early stringed instrument of the mandolin or cittern type. [18th C.: from Ital.]

mandolin 1

man·do·lin /ˌmandlˈin; ˈmandl-in/ ▶ **n.** **1** a musical instrument resembling a lute, having paired metal strings plucked with a plectrum. It is played with a characteristic tremolo on long sustained notes. **2** var. of **MANDOLINE**. — **man·do·lin·ist** /-ˈlinist/ **n.** [18th C.: from Fr. *mandoline,* from Ital. *mandolino,* dimin. of *mandola* (see **MANDOLA**).]

mandoline

man·do·line /ˌmandlˈin; ˈmandl-in/ (also **man·do·lin**) ▶ **n.** a kitchen utensil consisting of a flat frame with adjustable cutting blades for slicing vegetables.

man·dor·la /manˈdôrlə/ (also **Man·dor·la**) ▶ **n.** a pointed oval figure used as an architectural feature and as an aureole enclosing figures such as Christ or the Virgin Mary in medieval art. Also called **VESICA PISCIS**. [19th C.: from Ital., lit. 'almond.']

man·drag·o·ra /manˈdragərə/ ▶ **n.** literary the mandrake, esp. when used as a narcotic. [OE, via med. L. from L. and Gk. *mandragoras.*]

man·drake /ˈmanˌdrāk/ ▶ **n.** **1** a Mediterranean plant (*Mandragora officinarum*) of the nightshade family, with white or purple flowers and yellow berries. It has a forked root that supposedly resembles the human form and was formerly used in medicine and magic. **2** another term for **MAYAPPLE**. [ME *mandrag(g)e,* from MDu. *mandrag(r)e,* from med. L. *mandragora;* associated with **MAN** (because of the shape of its root) + *drake* in the OE sense 'dragon.']

man·drel /ˈmandrəl/ ▶ **n.** **1** a shaft or spindle in a lathe to which work is fixed while being turned. **2** a cylindrical rod around which metal or other material is forged or shaped.

man·drill /ˈmandrəl/ ▶ **n.** a large West African baboon (*Mandrillus sphinx*) with a brightly colored red and blue face, the male having a blue rump. [18th C.: prob. from **MAN** + **DRILL**[3].]

mandrill

mane /mān/ ▶ **n.** a growth of long hair on the neck of a horse, lion, or other animal. ■ a person's long or thick hair. — **maned** **adj.** [in comb.] *a black-maned lion.* **mane·less** **adj.**

man-eat·er ▶ **n.** an animal that has a propensity for killing and eating humans. — **man-eat·ing** **adj.**

man·eb /ˈmanˌeb/ ▶ **n.** a white compound, $C_4H_6N_2S_4Mn$, used as a fungicidal powder on vegetables and fruit.

maned wolf ▶ **n.** a large, endangered wild dog (*Chrysocyon brachyurus*) that has a reddish coat and large erect ears, native to the grasslands of South America.

ma·nège /maˈnezH; mə-/ ▶ **n.** an arena or enclosed area in which horses and riders are trained. ■ the movements of a trained horse. ■ horsemanship. [17th C.: Fr., from Ital. (see **MANAGE**).]

ma·nes /ˈmänˌās; ˈmāˌnēz/ ▶ **plural n.** (in Roman mythology) the deified souls of dead ancestors. [L.]

Ma·net /mäˈnā/, Édouard (1832–83), French painter. He adopted a realist approach that greatly influenced the Impressionists.

ma·neu·ver /məˈnoōvər/ (Brit. **ma·noeu·vre**) ▶ **n.** **1** a movement or series of moves requiring skill and care: *jumps and other daring maneuvers.* ■ a carefully planned scheme or action, esp. one involving deception: *shady financial maneuvers.* ■ the fact or process of taking such action. **2** (**maneuvers**) a large-scale military exercise of troops, warships, and other forces: *a Russian vessel on maneuvers.* ▶ **v.** (**-vered, -ver·ing**) **1** perform or cause to perform a movement or series of moves requiring skill and care: [intrans.] *the truck was unable to maneuver comfortably.* **2** [trans.] carefully guide or manipulate (someone or something) in order to achieve an end: *maneuvering him into betrayal.* ■ [intrans.] carefully manipulate a situation to achieve an end: [as n.] (**maneuvering**) *political maneuvering.* — **ma·neu·ver·er** **n.** [18th C.: from Fr. *manœuvre* (n.), *manœuvrer* (v.), from med. L. *manuoperare,* from L. *manus* 'hand' + *operari* 'to work.']

ma·neu·ver·a·ble /məˈnoōvərəbəl/ (Brit. **ma·noeu·vra·ble**) ▶ **adj.** (esp. of a craft or vessel) able to be maneuvered easily while in motion. — **ma·neu·ver·a·bil·i·ty** /məˌnoōvərəˈbilətē/ **n.**

man Fri·day ▶ **n.** a male helper or follower. [from *Friday,* the name of a character in Defoe's novel *Robinson Crusoe* (1719).]

man·ful /ˈmanfəl/ ▶ **adj.** resolute or brave, esp. in the face of adversity. — **man·ful·ly** **adv.** **man·ful·ness** **n.**

man·ga /ˈmaNGˌgä/ ▶ **n.** a Japanese genre of cartoons, comic books, and animated films, typically having a science-fiction or fantasy theme and sometimes including violent or sexually explicit material. Compare with **ANIME**. [Japanese, from *man* 'indiscriminate' + *ga* 'picture.']

man·ga·bey /ˈmaNGgəˌbā/ ▶ **n.** a medium-sized long-tailed monkey (genus *Cercocebus,* family Cercopithecidae) native to the forests of western and central Africa. [18th C.: by erroneous association with *Mangabey,* a region of Madagascar.]

man·ga·nate /ˈmaNGgəˌnāt/ ▶ **n.** Chem. a salt in which the anion contains both manganese and oxygen, esp. one of the anion MnO_4 II.

man·ga·nese /ˈmaNGgəˌnēz; -ˌnēs/ ▶ **n.** the chemical element of atomic number 25, a hard gray metal that is an component of special steels and magnetic alloys. (Symbol: **Mn**) ■ the black dioxide of this as an industrial raw material or additive, esp. in glassmaking. [17th C.: via Fr. from Ital. *manganese,* unexplained alt. of med. L. *magnesia* (see **MAGNESIA**).]

man·gan·ic /manˈganik; maNG-/ ▶ **adj.** Chem. of manganese with a valence of three. Compare with **MANGANOUS**.

man·ga·nite /ˈmaNGgəˌnīt/ ▶ **n.** a mineral consisting of manganese oxyhydroxide, typically occurring as steel-gray or black prisms.

man·ga·nous /ˈmaNGgənəs/ ▶ **adj.** Chem. of manganese with a valence of two. Compare with **MANGANIC**.

mange /mānj/ ▶ **n.** a skin disease of mammals caused by parasitic mites that causes severe itching, hair loss, and the formation of scabs and lesions. [ME: from OFr. *mangeue,* from *mangier* 'eat,' from L. *manducare* 'to chew.']

man·gel /ˈmaNGgəl/ (also **man·gel-wur·zel**) ▶ **n.** a beet of a variety (*Beta vulgaris* subsp. *crassa*) with a large root, cultivated as feed for livestock. [19th C.: from Ger. *Mangoldwurzel,* from *Mangold* 'beet' + *Wurzel* 'root.']

man·ger /ˈmānjər/ ▶ **n.** a long open box or trough for horses or cattle to eat from. [ME: from OFr. *mangeure,* based on L. *manducat-* 'chewed.']

man·gey /ˈmānjē/ ▶ **adj.** var. of **MANGY**.

man·gle[1] /ˈmaNGgəl/ ▶ **v.** [trans.] severely mutilate, disfigure, or damage by cutting, tearing, or crushing: *mangled beyond recognition* | fig. *mangling Bach on the piano.* — **man·gler** **n.** [ME: from Anglo-Norman Fr. *mahangler,* appar. a frequentative of *mahaignier* 'maim.']

man·gle[2] ▶ **n.** a large machine that uses heated rollers to iron sheets or other fabrics. ▶ **v.** [trans.] press or squeeze with a mangle. [17th C.: from Du. *mangel,* from *mangelen* 'to mangle,' from med. L. *mango, manga,* from Gk. *manganon* 'axis, engine.']

man·go /ˈmaNGgō/ ▶ **n.** (pl. **-goes** or **-gos**) **1** a fleshy yellowish-red tropical fruit that is eaten ripe or used green for pickles or chutneys. **2** (also **man·go tree**) the evergreen Indian tree (*Mangifera indica*) of the cashew family that bears this fruit, widely cultivated in the tropics. **3** a tropical American hummingbird (genus *Anthracothorax*) that typically has green plumage with purple feathers on the wings, tail, or head. [16th C.: from Port. *manga,* from a Dravidian language.]

man·gold /ˈmaNGgōld/ ▶ **n.** another term for **MANGEL**.

man·go·nel /ˈmaNGgəˌnel/ ▶ **n.** hist. a military device for throwing stones and other missiles. [ME: from OFr. *mangonel(le),* from med. L. *manganellus,* dimin. of late L. *manganum,* from Gk. *manganon* 'axis of a pulley.']

man·go·steen /ˈmaNGgəˌstēn/ ▶ **n.** **1** a tropical fruit with sweet juicy white segments of flesh inside a thick rind. **2** the slow-growing Malaysian tree (*Garcinia mangostana,* family Guttiferae) that bears this fruit. [16th C.: from Malay *manggustan,* dial. var. of *manggis.*]

man·grove /ˈmanˌgrōv; ˈmaNG-/ ▶ **n.** a tree or shrub (families Rhizophoraceae and Verbenaceae or Avicenniaceae) that grows in muddy, chiefly tropical coastal swamps, typically having numerous tangled roots above ground that form dense thickets. ■ (also **mangrove swamp**) a tidal swamp that is dominated by mangroves and associated vegetation. [17th C.: prob. from Port. *mangue,* Sp. *mangle,* from Taino.]

man·gy /ˈmānjē/ (also **man·gey**) ▶ **adj.** (**-gi·er, -gi·est**) having mange. ■ in poor condition; shabby. — **man·gi·ness n.**

man·han·dle /ˈman,handl/ ▶ **v.** [trans.] move (a heavy object) by hand with great effort: *Joe manhandled the desk down the stairs.* ■ informal handle (someone) roughly by dragging or pushing.

Man·hat·tan /manˈhatn; mən-/ an island near the mouth of the Hudson River that forms a borough of New York City.

man·hat·tan /manˈhatn; mən-/ (also **Man·hat·tan**) ▶ **n.** a cocktail made of whiskey and vermouth, sometimes with a dash of bitters.

Man·hat·tan clam chow·der ▶ **n.** a chowder made with clams, vegetables, salt pork, and seasonings in a tomato-based broth.

Man·hat·tan Pro·ject the code name for the American project set up in 1942 to develop an atom bomb. The project culminated in 1945 with the detonation of the first nuclear weapon in New Mexico.

man·hole /ˈman,hōl/ ▶ **n.** a small covered opening in a floor, pavement, or other surface to allow a person to enter, esp. an opening in a city street leading to a sewer.

man·hood /ˈman,ho͝od/ ▶ **n.** the state or period of being a man rather than a child. ■ men, esp. those of a country, regarded collectively. ■ qualities traditionally associated with men, such as courage, strength, and sexual potency: *we drank to prove our manhood.* ■ (**one's manhood**) informal used euphemistically to refer to a man's genitals.

man·hunt /ˈman,hənt/ ▶ **n.** an organized search for a person, esp. a criminal.

ma·ni·a /ˈmānēə/ ▶ **n.** mental illness marked by periods of great excitement, euphoria, delusions, and overactivity. ■ an excessive enthusiasm or desire; an obsession: *our mania for details.* [ME: via late L. from Gk., lit. 'madness,' from *mainesthai* 'be mad.']

-mania ▶ **comb. form** Psychol. denoting a specified type of mental abnormality or obsession: *kleptomania.* ■ denoting extreme enthusiasm or admiration: *Beatlemania.* — **-maniac comb. form** in corresponding nouns.

ma·ni·ac /ˈmānē,ak/ ▶ **n.** informal a person exhibiting extreme symptoms of wild behavior, esp. when violent and dangerous: *a homicidal maniac.* ■ [with adj.] an obsessive enthusiast: *a gambling maniac.* — **ma·ni·a·cal** /məˈnīəkəl/ **adj. ma·ni·a·cal·ly** /məˈnīək(ə)lē/ **adv.**

man·ic /ˈmanik/ ▶ **adj.** showing wild and apparently deranged excitement and energy: *manic enthusiasm.* ■ frenetically busy; frantic: *the pace is manic as we near our deadline.* ■ Psychiatry relating to or affected by mania.

man·ic de·pres·sion ▶ **n.** another term, esp. formerly, for BIPOLAR DISORDER. — **man·ic-de·pres·sive adj. & n.**

Man·i·chae·an /,manəˈkēən/ (also **Man·i·che·an**) ▶ **adj.** esp. hist. of or relating to Manichaeism. ■ of or characterized by dualistic contrast or conflict between opposites. ▶ **n.** an adherent of Manichaeism. — **Man·i·chae·an·ism** /-ˈkēə,nizəm/ **n.**

Man·i·chae·ism /ˈmanə,kēizəm/ (also **Man·i·che·ism**) ▶ **n.** a dualistic religious system with Christian, Gnostic, and pagan elements, founded in Persia in the 3rd century by Manes (*c.*216–*c.*276). [17th C.: from late L. *Manichaeus* (from the name *Manes*: see above) + -ISM.]

ma·ni·cot·ti /,manəˈkätē/ ▶ **n.** pasta in the shape of large tubes. ■ [treated as sing.] an Italian dish consisting of these stuffed with cheese and served with tomato sauce. [Ital., pl. of *manicotto* 'muff.']

man·i·cure /ˈmani,kyo͝or/ ▶ **n.** a cosmetic treatment of the hands involving cutting, shaping, and often painting the nails. ▶ **v.** [trans.] give a manicure to. ■ [usu. as adj.] (**manicured**) trim neatly: *manicured lawns.* [19th C.: from Fr., from L. *manus* 'hand' + *cura* 'care.']

man·i·cur·ist /ˈmani,kyo͝orist/ ▶ **n.** a person who performs manicures professionally.

man·i·fest¹ /ˈmanə,fest/ ▶ **adj.** clear or obvious to the eye or mind: *the system's manifest failings.* ▶ **v.** [trans.] display or show (a quality or feeling) by one's acts or appearance; demonstrate: *manifest signs of depression.* ■ (often **be manifested in**) be evidence of; prove: *bad industrial relations are often manifested in strikes.* ■ [intrans.] (of an ailment) become apparent through the appearance of symptoms: *a disorder that manifests in middle age.* — **man·i·fest·ly adv.**

man·i·fest² ▶ **n.** a document giving the details of a ship and its cargo, passengers, and crew for the use of customs officers. ■ a list of passengers or cargo in an aircraft. ■ a list of the cars forming a freight train. ▶ **v.** [trans.] record in such a manifest: *every passenger is manifested at the point of departure.* [16th C.: from Ital. *manifesto* (see MANIFESTO).]

man·i·fes·ta·tion /,manəfəˈstāsʜən; -,fesˈtāsʜən/ ▶ **n.** an event, action, or object that clearly shows or embodies something, esp. a theory or an abstract idea: *manifestations of global warming.* ■ the action or fact of showing something in such a way: *the manifestation of anxiety.* ■ a symptom or sign of an ailment: *a characteristic manifestation of Lyme disease.* ■ a version, materialization, or incarnation of something or someone. [ME: from late L. *manifestatio(n-)*, from *manifestare* 'make public.']

Man·i·fest Des·ti·ny ▶ **n.** the 19th-century doctrine or belief that the expansion of the United States throughout the American continents was both justified and inevitable.

man·i·fes·to /,manəˈfestō/ ▶ **n.** (pl. **-tos**) a public declaration of policy and aims, esp. one issued before an election by a political party or candidate. [17th C.: from Ital., from *manifestare*, from L., 'make public,' from *manifestus* 'obvious.']

man·i·fold /ˈmanə,fōld/ ▶ **adj.** formal literary many and various: *the implications were manifold* | *the manifold divisions that have wrought such damage.* ■ having many different forms or elements. ▶ **n.** **1** [often with adj.] a pipe or chamber branching into several openings: *the pipeline manifold.* ■ (in an internal combustion engine) the part conveying air and fuel from the carburetor to the cylinders or leading from the cylinders to the exhaust pipe: *the exhaust manifold.* **2** tech. something with many different parts or forms, in particular: ■ Math. a collection of points forming a certain kind of set, such as those of a topologically closed surface or an analog of this in three or more dimensions. ■ (in Kantian philosophy) the sum of the particulars furnished by sense before they have been unified by the synthesis of the understanding. — **man·i·fold·ly adv. man·i·fold·ness n.** [OE *manigfeald*; current n. senses date from the mid 19th C.]

man·i·kin /ˈmanikən/ (also **man·ni·kin**) ▶ **n.** **1** a person who is very small, esp. one not otherwise abnormal or deformed. **2** a jointed model of the human body, used in anatomy or as an artist's lay figure. [16th C.: from Du. *manneken*, dimin. of *man* 'man.']

Ma·nil·a¹ /məˈnilə/ the capital and chief port of the Philippines, on the island of Luzon; pop. 1,599,000.

Ma·nil·a² (also **Ma·nil·la**) ▶ **n.** **1** (also **Manila hemp**) the strong fiber of a Philippine plant, used for rope, matting, paper, etc. See also ABACA. ■ (also **Manila paper**) strong brown paper, originally made from Manila hemp. **2** [often as adj.] a cigar or cheroot made in Manila. [17th C. (as an adj. meaning 'from Manila'): from MANILA¹.]

man·i·oc /ˈmanē,äk/ ▶ **n.** another term for CASSAVA. [16th C.: from Fr., from Tupi *manioca*.]

man·i·ple /ˈmanəpəl/ ▶ **n.** **1** a subdivision of a Roman legion, containing either 120 or 60 men. **2** (in church use) a vestment formerly worn by a priest celebrating the Eucharist, consisting of a strip hanging from the left arm. — **ma·nip·u·lar** /məˈnipyələr/ **adj.** (in sense 1). [ME (sense 2): from OFr. *maniple*, from L. *manipulus* 'handful, troop,' from *manus* 'hand' + the base of *plere* 'fill.']

ma·nip·u·late /məˈnipyə,lāt/ ▶ **v.** [trans.] **1** handle or control (a tool, mechanism, etc.), typically in a skillful manner: *he manipulated the dials.* ■ alter, edit, or move (text or data) on a computer. ■ examine or treat (a part of the body) by feeling or moving it with the hand: *manipulate the ligaments of the spine.* **2** control or influence (a person or situation) cleverly, unfairly, or unscrupulously. ■ alter (data) or present (statistics) so as to mislead. — **ma·nip·u·la·bil·i·ty** /-,nipyələˈbilətē/ **n.** **ma·nip·u·la·ble** /-ləbəl/ **adj. ma·nip·u·lat·a·ble** /-,lātəbəl/ **adj. ma·nip·u·la·tion** /mə,nipyəˈlāsʜən/ **n. ma·nip·u·la·tor** /-,lātər/ **n. ma·nip·u·la·to·ry** /-lə,tôrē/ **adj.** [19th C.: back-form. from earlier *manipulation*, from L. *manipulus* 'handful.']

ma·nip·u·la·tive /məˈnipyələtiv; -,lātiv/ ▶ **adj.** **1** characterized by unscrupulous control of a situation or person: *she was sly, selfish, and manipulative.* **2** of or relating to manipulation of an object or part of the body: *a manipulative skill.* — **ma·nip·u·la·tive·ly adv. ma·nip·u·la·tive·ness n.**

Ma·ni·pur /ˈmanə,po͝or; ,mənəˈpo͝or/ a small state in eastern India, east of Assam, on the border with Myanmar (Burma); capital, Imphal.

Man·i·pu·ri /,manəˈpo͝orē/ ▶ **n.** (pl. same or **-ris**) **1** a native or inhabitant of Manipur. **2** the official language of Manipur, belonging to the Tibeto-Burman family. ▶ **adj.** of or relating to the people of Manipur or their language.

Manit. ▶ **abbr.** Manitoba.

Man·i·to·ba /,manəˈtōbə/ a province in central Canada, with a coastline on Hudson Bay; pop. 1,092,942; capital, Winnipeg. — **Man·i·to·ban adj. & n.**

man·i·tou /ˈmani,to͞o/ ▶ **n.** (among certain Algonquian Indians) a good or evil spirit as an object of reverence.

Man·i·tou·lin Is·land /,maniˈto͞olən/ an island in southern Canada, in the province of Ontario, in northern Lake Huron; 1,068 square miles (2,766 sq km).

Man·ka·to /manˈkātō/ a city in south central Minnesota; pop. 31,477.

Man·kil·ler /ˈman,kilər/, Wilma Pearl (1945–), Cherokee Nation tribal leader 1985–95 and historian. A women's rights activist, she wrote *Mankiller: A Chief and Her People* (1993).

man·kind /,manˈkīnd; ˈman,kīnd/ ▶ **n.** human beings considered collectively; the human race:

Man·ley /ˈmanlē/, Michael Norman (1923–97), prime minister of Jamaica 1972–80, 1989–92.

man·like /ˈman,līk/ ▶ **adj.** **1** resembling a human being: *a manlike creature.* **2** (of a woman) having an appearance or qualities associated with men.

man·ly /ˈmanlē/ ▶ **adj.** (**-li·er, -li·est**) having or denoting those good qualities traditionally associated with men, such as courage and strength. ■ (of an activity) befitting a man, esp. in a traditional sense: *the manly art of knife-throwing.* — **man·li·ness n.**

man-made ▶ **adj.** made or caused by human beings (as opposed to occurring naturally); artificial: *a man-made lake.*

Mann¹ /man/, Horace (1796–1859), US education reformer and politician, considered the father of public education.

Mann² /män; man/, Thomas (1875–1955), German writer. His works include *Death in Venice* (1912) and *Dr. Faustus* (1947). Nobel Prize for Literature (1929).

man·na /ˈmanə/ ▶ **n.** (in the Bible) the substance miraculously supplied as food to the Israelites in the wilderness (Exod. 16). ■ an unexpected or gratuitous benefit: *the cakes were **manna from heaven**.* ■ a sweet secretion from the manna ash or a similar plant, used as a source of mannitol. [OE, via late L. and Gk. from Aramaic *mannā*, from Heb. *mān*, corresponding to Arab. *mann*.]

man·na ash ▶ **n.** an ash tree (*Fraxinus ornus*) that bears fragrant white flowers and exudes a sweet edible gum (manna) from its branches when they are damaged, native to southern Europe and southwestern Asia.

Man·nar, Gulf of an inlet of the Indian Ocean that lies between Sri Lanka and southern India.

manned /mand/ ▶ **adj.** (esp. of an aircraft or spacecraft) having a human crew: *a manned mission to Mars.*

man·ne·quin /ˈmanikən/ ▶ **n.** a dummy used to display clothes in a store window. ■ esp. hist. a young woman or man employed to show clothes to customers. [18th C.: from Fr. (see MANIKIN).]

man·ner /ˈmanər/ ▶ **n.** **1** a way in which a thing is done or happens: *taking notes in an unobtrusive manner.* ■ a style in literature or art: *a dramatic poem **in the manner of** Goethe.* ■ Gram. a semantic category of adverbs and adverbials that answer the question "how?": *an adverb of manner.* ■ (**manner of**) esp. literary a kind or sort: *what manner of man is he?* **2** a person's outward bearing or way of behaving toward others: *a shy and diffident manner.* **3** (**manners**) polite or well-bred social behavior: *didn't your mother teach you any manners?* ■ social behavior or habits: *Tim apologized for his son's bad manners.*
– PHRASES **all manner of** many different kinds of: *all manner of evil things.* **by no** (or **any**) **manner of means** see MEANS. **in a manner of speaking** in some sense; so to speak. **to the manner born** naturally at ease in a specified job or situation. [with allusion to Shakespeare's *Hamlet* I. iv. 17.] ■ destined by birth to follow a custom or way of life.
— **man·ner·less adj.** [ME: from OFr. *maniere*, based on L. *manuarius* 'of the hand,' from *manus* 'hand.']

man·nered /ˈmanərd/ ▶ **adj.** **1** [in comb.] behaving in a specified way: *pleasant-mannered.* **2** (of a writer, artist, or artistic style) marked by idiosyncratic mannerisms; artificial, stilted, and overelaborate in delivery: *inane dialogue and mannered acting.*

man·ner·ism /ˈmanəˌrizəm/ ▶ **n.** **1** a habitual gesture or way of speaking or behaving; an idiosyncrasy. ■ Psychiatry a gesture or expression that becomes abnormal through exaggeration or repetition. **2** excessive or self-conscious use of a distinctive style in art, literature, or music. **3** (**Mannerism**) a style of 16th-century Italian art, characterized by unusual effects of scale, lighting, and perspective, and the use of intense colors. — **man·ner·ist n. & adj. man·ner·is·tic** /ˌmanəˈristik/ **adj.**

man·ner·ly /ˈmanərlē/ ▶ **adj.** well-mannered; polite. — **man·ner·li·ness n.**

Mann·heim /ˈmanˌhīm; ˈmän-/ a city in southwestern Germany; pop. 315,000.

man·ni·kin /ˈmanikən/ ▶ **n.** **1** a small waxbill (genus *Lonchura*, many species) of the Old World tropics, typically having brown, black, and white plumage. Compare with MANAKIN. **2** var. of MANIKIN.

man·nish /ˈmanisн/ ▶ **adj.** often derog. (of a woman) having characteristics that are associated with men and can be considered unbecoming in a woman. — **man·nish·ly adv. man·nish·ness n.**

man·ni·tol /ˈmanəˌtôl; -ˌtäl/ ▶ **n.** Chem. a colorless sweet-tasting crystalline compound, $CH_2OH(CHOH)_4CH_2OH$, that is found in many plants and is used in various foods and medical products.

man·nose /ˈmanˌōs; -ˌōz/ ▶ **n.** Chem. a sugar of the hexose class that occurs as a component of many natural polysaccharides.

Ma·no /ˈmänō/ a river rising in northwestern Liberia and flowing southwest to the Atlantic Ocean.

ma·no a ma·no /ˌmänō ä ˈmänō/ (also **ma·no-a-ma·no**) informal ▶ **adj.** (of combat or competition) hand-to-hand. ▶ **adv.** in the manner of hand-to-hand combat or a duel: *they want to settle this mano a mano.* ▶ **n.** (pl. **-nos**) an intense fight or contest between two adversaries; a duel. [Sp., 'hand-to-hand.']

ma·noeu·vre ▶ **n. & v.** British spelling of MANEUVER.

man-of-war (also **man-o'-war**) ▶ **n.** (pl. **men-of-war** also **men-o'-war**) hist. an armed sailing ship. ■ (also **man-o'-war bird**) another term for FRIGATE BIRD. ■ short for PORTUGUESE MAN-OF-WAR.

man-of-war fish ▶ **n.** a fish of tropical oceans (*Nomeus gronovii*, family Nomeidae) that is often found among the tentacles of the Portuguese man-of-war.

ma·nom·e·ter /məˈnämətər/ ▶ **n.** an instrument for measuring the pressure acting on a column of fluid. — **man·o·met·ric** /ˌmanəˈmetrik/ **adj. man·o·met·ri·cal·ly** /ˌmanəˈmetrik(ə)lē/ **adv. ma·nom·e·try n.** [18th C.: from Fr. *manomètre*, from Gk. *manos* 'thin' + *-mètre* '(instrument) measuring.']

ma non trop·po /ˌmä ˌnôn ˈtrôpō/ ▶ **adv.** see TROPPO[1].

man·or /ˈmanər/ ▶ **n.** (also **manor house**) a large country house with lands. ■ esp. hist. (esp. in England and Wales) a unit of land, originally a feudal lordship, consisting of a lord's demesne and lands rented to tenants. ■ hist. (in North America) an estate or district leased to tenants, esp. one granted by royal charter in a British colony or by the Dutch governors of what is now New York. — **ma·no·ri·al** /məˈnôrēəl/ **adj.** [ME: from Anglo-Norman Fr. *maner* 'dwelling,' from L. *manere* 'remain.']

man·pow·er /ˈmanˌpouər/ ▶ **n.** the number of people working or available for work: *limited manpower.*

man·qué /mänGˈkā/ ▶ **adj.** [postpositive] having failed to become what one might have been; unfulfilled. [18th C.: Fr., past part. of *manquer* 'to lack.']

Man Ray see RAY[2].

Mans, Le /lə ˈmäN/ see LE MANS.

man·sard /ˈmanˌsärd; -sərd/ ▶ **n.** (also **mansard roof**) a roof that has four sloping sides, each of which becomes steeper halfway down. See illustration at ROOF. [18th C.: from Fr. *mansarde*, named after the French architect François *Mansart* (1598–1666).]

manse /mans/ ▶ **n.** the house occupied by a minister of a Presbyterian church. ■ a large stately house; a mansion. [15th C. (denoting the principal house of an estate): from med. L. *mansus* 'house, dwelling,' from *manere* 'remain.']

man·serv·ant /ˈmanˌsərvənt/ ▶ **n.** (pl. **men·ser·vants** /ˈmenˌsərvənts/) a male servant.

Mans·field /ˈmanzfēld/, Katherine (1888–1923), New Zealand writer; pen name of *Kathleen Mansfield Beauchamp Murry*. Her short stories are collected in volumes such as *In a German Pension* (1911).

-manship ▶ **suffix** (forming nouns) denoting skill in a subject or activity: *marksmanship.*

man·sion /ˈmansHən/ ▶ **n.** a large, impressive house. ■ a manor house (see MANOR). [ME: via OFr. from L. *mansio(n-)* 'place where someone stays,' from *manere* 'remain.']

man-sized (also **man-size**) ▶ **adj.** of the size of a human being: *man-sized plants.* ■ large enough to occupy, suit, or satisfy a man: *a man-sized breakfast.* ■ formidable: *a man-sized job.*

man·slaugh·ter /ˈmanˌslôtər/ ▶ **n.** the crime of killing a human being without malice aforethought, or otherwise in circumstances not amounting to murder.

Man·son /ˈmansən/, Charles (1934–), US cult leader; born *Charles Milles Maddox*. In 1969, its members carried out a series of murders, for which he was sentenced to life imprisonment.

man·ta /ˈmantə/ ▶ **n.** **1** (also **manta ray**) a devil ray (*Manta birostris*, family Mobulidae) that occurs in all tropical seas and may reach very great size. **2** a rough-textured cotton fabric made and used in Spanish America. ■ a shawl made of this fabric. [17th C.: from L. Amer. Sp., lit. 'large blanket.']

man·teau /manˈtō/ ▶ **n.** (pl. **-teaus** or **-teaux** /-ˈtōz/) hist. a loose gown or cloak worn by women. [17th C.: from Fr.; cf. MANTUA.]

Man·te·gna /mänˈtānyə/, Andrea (1431–1506), Italian painter and engraver, noted for his frescoes.

man·tel /ˈmantl/ (also **man·tle**) ▶ **n.** a mantelpiece or mantelshelf. [16th C.: specialized use of MANTLE[1].]

man·te·let /ˈmantlət; ˈmantl-ət/ (also **mant·let**) ▶ **n.** **1** hist. a woman's short, loose cloak or shawl. **2** a bulletproof screen for a soldier. [ME: from OFr. *mantelet*, dimin. of *mantel* 'mantle.']

man·tel·piece /ˈmantlˌpēs/ (also **man·tle·piece**) ▶ **n.** a structure of wood, marble, or stone above and around a fireplace. ■ a mantelshelf.

man·tel·shelf /ˈmantlˌsHelf/ (also **man·tle·shelf**) ▶ **n.** a shelf above a fireplace. ■ Climbing a projecting shelf or ledge of rock. ■ Climbing a move for climbing on such a ledge from below by pressing down on it with the hands to raise the upper body, enabling a foot or knee to reach the ledge. ▶ **v.** [intrans.] Climbing perform a mantelshelf move.

man·tic /ˈmantik/ ▶ **adj.** formal of or relating to divination or prophecy. [19th C.: from Gk. *mantikos*, from *mantis* 'prophet.']

man·ti·core /ˈmantiˌkôr/ ▶ **n.** a mythical beast typically depicted as having the body of a lion, the face of a man, and the sting of a scorpion. [ME: from OFr., via L. from Gk. *mantikhōras*, corrupt reading in Aristotle for *martikhoras*, from an Old Pers. word meaning 'man-eater.']

mantilla

man·tid /ˈmantid/ ▶ **n.** another term for MANTIS.

man·til·la /manˈtē(y)ə; -ˈtilə/ ▶ **n.** a lace or silk scarf worn by women over the hair and shoulders, esp. in Spain. [Sp., dimin. of *manta* 'mantle.']

man·tis /ˈmantis/ (also **pray·ing man·tis**) ▶ **n.** (pl. same or **-tis·es**) a predatory insect (suborder Mantodea) related to the cockroach, with large spiky forelegs folded like hands in prayer. Mantidae and other families, and many species include *Mantis religiosa*, introduced to America from southern Europe. [17th C.: mod. L., from Gk., lit. 'prophet.']

mantis

man·tis·sa /manˈtisə/ ▶ **n.** **1** Math. the part of a logarithm that follows the decimal point. **2** Comput. the part of a floating-point number that represents the significant digits of that number, and that is multiplied by the base raised to the exponent to give the actual value of the number. [17th C.: from L., lit. 'makeweight,' perh. from Etruscan.]

man·tis shrimp ▶ **n.** a predatory marine crustacean (order Stomatopoda, many species) with a pair of large spined front legs that resemble those of a mantis and are used for capturing prey.

Man·tle /ˈmantl/, Mickey Charles(1931–95), US baseball player. An outfielder for the New York Yankees 1951–69, he played in 12 World Series, setting several series records.

man·tle¹ /ˈmantl/ ▶n. **1** a loose sleeveless cloak or shawl, worn esp. by women. ■fig. a covering of a specified sort: *a thick mantle of snow.* ■(also **gas mantle**) a fragile mesh cover fixed around a gas jet or kerosene wick, etc., to give an incandescent light when heated. ■Ornithol. a bird's back, scapulars, and wing coverts, esp. when of a distinctive color. ■Zool. an outer or enclosing layer of tissue, esp. (in mollusks, cirripedes, and brachiopods) a fold of skin enclosing the viscera and secreting the substance that produces the shell. **2** an important role or responsibility that passes from one person to another: *the second son has now assumed his father's mantle.* [with allusion to the passing of Elijah's cloak (mantle) to Elisha (2 Kings 2:13).] **3** Geol. the region of the earth's interior between the crust and the core. ■the corresponding part of another planetary body: *the lunar mantle.* ▶v. **1** [trans.] literary clothe in or as if in a mantle; cloak or envelop: *heavy mists mantled the forest.* ■[intrans.] (of the face) glow with a blush: *she stared intently, her face mantling with emotion.* **2** [intrans.] (of a bird of prey) spread the wings and tail, esp. so as to cover captured prey. [OE *mentel*, from L. *mantellum* 'cloak'; reinforced in ME by OFr. *mantel*.]

man·tle² ▶n. var. of MANTEL.

man·tle·piece ▶n. var. of MANTELPIECE.

man·tle plume ▶n. see PLUME.

man·tle·shelf ▶n. var. of MANTELSHELF.

mant·let /ˈmantlet/ ▶n. var. of MANTELET.

man·tra /ˈmantrə; ˈmän-/ ▶n. (originally in Hinduism and Buddhism) a word or sound repeated to aid concentration in meditation. ■a statement that is frequently repeated; a characteristic formula or refrain: *the mantra "practice, practice, practice" has never been so applicable.* —**man·tric** adj. [18th C.: Sanskrit, lit. 'instrument of thought,' from *man* 'think.']

man·tu·a /ˈmantoo͞ə/ ▶n. a woman's loose gown of a kind fashionable during the 17th and 18th centuries. [alt. of Fr. *manteau*.]

Man·u /ˈmäno͞o; ˈmano͞o/ the archetypal first man of Hindu mythology, survivor of the great flood and father of the human race.

man·u·al /ˈmanyə(wə)l/ ▶adj. of or done with the hands: *manual hauling of boats.* ■(of a machine or device) worked by hand, not automatically or electronically: *a manual typewriter.* ■[attrib.] using or working with the hands: *a manual laborer.* ▶n. **1** a book of instructions, esp. for operating a machine or learning a subject; a handbook: *a computer manual.* **2** a thing operated or done by hand rather than automatically or electronically, in particular: ■an organ keyboard played with the hands. ■a vehicle with a manual transmission. —**man·u·al·ly** adv. [ME: from OFr. *manuel*, from L. *manualis*, from *manus* 'hand.']

man·u·al al·pha·bet ▶n. a set of sign-language symbols used in fingerspelling, in which different finger configurations correspond to letters of the alphabet.

man·u·al trans·mis·sion ▶n. an automotive transmission consisting of interlocking gear wheels and a lever that enables the driver to shift gears manually.

ma·nu·bri·um /məˈno͞obrēəm/ ▶n. (pl. **-bri·a** /-brēə/ or **-bri·ums**) Anat. & Zool. a handle-shaped projection or part, in particular: ■the broad upper part of the sternum of mammals, with which the clavicles and first ribs articulate. ■the tube that bears the mouth of a coelenterate. —**ma·nu·bri·al** /-brēəl/ adj. [17th C.: from L., 'haft.']

man·u·code /ˈmanyə,kōd/ ▶n. a bird of paradise (genus *Manucodia*, five species) of which the male and female have similar blue-black plumage and breed as stable pairs. [19th C.: from Fr., from mod. L. *manucodiata*, from Malay *manuk dewata* 'bird of the gods.']

man·u·fac·ture /,manyəˈfakCHər/ ▶n. the making of articles on a large scale using machinery: *the manufacture of autos.* ■[with adj.] a specified branch of industry: *the porcelain manufacture.* ■the production of a natural substance by a living thing: *the manufacture of protein.* ■(**manufactures**) manufactured goods or articles. ▶v. [trans.] **1** make (something) on a large scale using machinery: *they manufacture paint* | [as adj.] (**manufacturing**) *a manufacturing company.* ■(of a living thing) produce (a substance) naturally. ■make or produce (something abstract) in a merely mechanical way: [as adj.] (**manufactured**) *manufactured love songs.* **2** invent or fabricate (evidence or a story): *the tabloids that manufacture epochal discoveries.* —**man·u·fac·tur·a·bil·i·ty** /-,fakCHərəˈbilətē/ n. **man·u·fac·tur·a·ble** adj. **man·u·fac·tur·er** n. [16th C.: from Fr. (re-formed by association with L. *manu factum* 'made by hand'), from Ital. *manifattura*. Sense 1 dates from the early 17th C.]

man·u·mit /,manyəˈmit/ ▶v. (**-mit·ted, -mit·ting**) [trans.] hist. release from slavery; set free. —**man·u·mis·sion** /-ˈmisHən/ n. **man·u·mit·ter** n. [ME: from L. *manumittere*, lit. 'send forth from the hand,' from *manus* 'hand' + *mittere* 'send.']

ma·nure /məˈn(y)o͝or/ ▶n. animal dung used for fertilizing land. ■any compost or artificial fertilizer. ▶v. [trans.] (often **be manured**) apply manure to (land). [ME: from Anglo-Norman Fr. *mainoverer*, OFr. *manouvrer* (see MANEUVER).]

ma·nus /ˈmānəs; ˈmänəs/ ▶n. (pl. same) esp. Zool. the terminal segment of a forelimb, corresponding to the hand and wrist in humans. [19th C.: from L., 'hand.']

man·u·script /ˈmanyə,skript/ ▶n. a book, document, or piece of music written by hand rather than typed or printed. ■an author's text that has not yet been published: *we are preparing the final manuscript.* [16th C.: from med. L. *manuscriptus*, from *manu* 'by hand' + *scriptus* 'written.']

man·u·script pa·per ▶n. paper printed with staves for writing music on.

Manx /maNGks/ ▶adj. of or relating to the Isle of Man. ▶n. **1** the now extinct Goidelic language formerly spoken in the Isle of Man. **2** (**the Manx**) the Manx people collectively. —**Manx·man** n. (pl. **-men**). **Manx·wom·an** n. (pl. **-wom·en**). [from ON, from Old Irish *Manu* 'Isle of Man' + *-skr* (equivalent of -ISH¹).]

Manx cat ▶n. a cat of a breed having no tail or an extremely short one.

Manx shear·wa·ter ▶n. a shearwater (*Puffinus puffinus*) that nests on remote islands in the northeastern Atlantic, Mediterranean, and Hawaiian waters.

man·y /ˈmenē/ ▶adj. & pron. (**more, most**) a large number of: [as adj.] *many people agreed with her* | [as pron.] *the solution to many of our problems.* ▶n. [as pl. n.] (**the many**) the majority of people: *TV for the many.*

– PHRASES **as many** the same number of: *for the third time in as many months.* **a good** (or **great**) **many** a large number. **have one too many** informal become slightly drunk. **how many** used to ask what a particular quantity is: *how many books did you sell?* **many's the ——** used to indicate that something happens often: *many's the night we've been wakened by that racket.* [OE *manig*, of Gmc. origin; rel. to Du. *menig* and Ger. *manch*.]

man·y·fold /ˈmenē,fōld/ ▶adv. by many times: *the problems would be multiplied manyfold.* ▶adj. involving multiplication by many times: *the manyfold increase in staffing levels.*

man·za·nil·la /,manzəˈnē(y)ə/ ▶n. a pale, very dry Spanish sherry. [Sp., lit. 'chamomile' (because the flavor is said to be reminiscent of that of chamomile).]

man·za·ni·ta /,manzəˈnētə/ ▶n. an evergreen dwarf shrub (genus *Arctostaphylos*, several species) of the heath family, native to California. [19th C.: from Sp., dimin. of *manzana* 'apple.']

MAO Biochem. ▶abbr. monoamine oxidase.

Mao /mou/ ▶n. [as adj.] denoting a jacket or suit of a plain style with a mandarin collar, associated with communist China. [1960s: after MAO ZEDONG.]

Mao·ism /ˈmou,izəm/ ▶n. the communist doctrines of Mao Zedong, stressing permanent revolution, the importance of the peasantry, small-scale industry, and agricultural collectivization. —**Mao·ist** n. & adj.

Ma·o·ri /ˈmourē; ˈmäōrē/ ▶n. (pl. same or **-ris**) **1** a member of the aboriginal people of New Zealand. **2** the Polynesian language of this people. ▶adj. of or relating to the Maoris or their language. [the name in Maori.]

Mao Ze·dong /ˈmou ,zəˈdôNG/ (also **Mao Tse-tung** /,tsə ˈto͝oNG; ,dzə ˈdo͝oNG/) (1893–1976), Chinese communist leader; chairman of the Communist Party of the Chinese People's Republic 1949–76 and head of state 1949–59. He defeated both the occupying Japanese and rival Kuomintang nationalist forces to create the People's Republic of China in 1949.

MAP ▶abbr. modified American plan (see AMERICAN PLAN).

map /map/ ▶n. a diagrammatic representation of an area of land or sea showing physical features, cities, roads, etc.: *a street map.* ■a two-dimensional representation of the positions of stars or other astronomical objects. ■a diagram or collection of data showing the spatial arrangement or distribution of something over an area: *an electron density map.* ■Biol. a representation of the sequence of genes on a chromosome or of bases in a DNA or RNA molecule. ■Math. another term for MAPPING. ▶v. (**mapped, map·ping**) [trans.] represent (an area) on a map; make a map of. ■record in detail the spatial distribution of (something): *the project to map the human genome.* ■[trans.] associate (a group of elements or qualities) with an equivalent group, according to a particular formula or model: *the transformational rules map deep structures into surface structures.* ■Math. associate each element of (a set) with an element of another set. ■[intrans.] be associated or linked to something: *the subprocesses of language will map onto individual brain areas.*

– PHRASES **off the map** (of a place) very distant or remote. **put something on the map** bring something to prominence: *the exhibition put Cubism on the map.*

– PHRASAL VERBS **map something out** plan a route or course of action in detail: *I mapped out a route.* —**map·less** adj. **map·pa·ble** adj. **map·per** n. [16th C.: from med. L. *mappa mundi*, lit. 'sheet of the world,' from L. *mappa* 'sheet, napkin' + *mundi* 'of the world.']

ma·ple /ˈmāpəl/ ▶n. a tree (genus *Acer*, family Aceraceae) with lobed leaves, winged fruits, and colorful autumn foliage, grown as an ornamental or for its timber or syrupy sap. Its many species include the North American **sugar maple** (*A. saccharum*), which yields the sap from which maple sugar and maple syrup are made. ■the flavor of maple syrup or maple sugar. [OE *mapel* (as the first element of *mapeltrēow*, *mapulder* 'maple tree'); used as an independent word from ME onward.]

ma·ple sug·ar ▶n. sugar produced by evaporating the sap of certain maples, esp. the sugar maple.

ma·ple syr·up ▶n. syrup produced from the sap of certain maples, esp. the sugar maple.

map·mak·er /ˈmap,mākər/ ▶n. a cartographer. —**map·mak·ing** n.

Map·pa Mun·di /,mapə ˈmo͝ondē/ a famous 13th-century map of the world, now in Hereford cathedral, England. [from med. L., lit. 'sheet of the world.']

map·ping /ˈmapiNG/ ▶n. Math. & Ling. an operation that associates each element of a given set (the domain) with one or more elements of a second set (the range).

map pro·jec·tion ▶n. see PROJECTION (sense 6).

map tur·tle ▶n. a small North American freshwater turtle (genus *Graptemys*, family Emydidae, several species) with bold patterns on the shell and head.

Ma·pu·che /məˈpōōCHē/ ▶n. (pl. same or **-ches**) **1** a member of an American Indian people of central Chile and adjacent parts of Argentina, noted for their resistance to colonial Spanish and later Chilean domination. **2** the Araucanian language of this people. ▶adj. relating to or denoting this people or their language. [the name in Mapuche, from *mapu* 'land' + *che* 'people.']

Ma·pu·to /məˈpōōtō/ the capital of Mozambique, in the southern part of the country; pop. 1,098,000. Former name (until 1976) LOURENÇO MARQUES.

ma·quette /maˈket/ ▶n. a sculptor's small preliminary model or sketch. [20th C.: from Fr., from Ital. *machietta*, dimin. of *macchia* 'spot.']

ma·qui·la /məˈkēlə/ ▶n. another term for MAQUILADORA.

ma·qui·la·do·ra /ˌmakiləˈdôrə/ ▶n. a factory in Mexico run by a foreign company and exporting its products to the country of that company. [Mex. Sp., from *maquilar* 'assemble.']

ma·quil·lage /ˌmäkē(y)äZH/ ▶n. makeup; cosmetics. [Fr., from *maquiller* 'to make up,' from OFr. *masquiller* 'to stain.']

ma·quis /mäˈkē/ ▶n. (pl. same) **1** (**the Maquis**) the French resistance movement during the German occupation (1940–45). ■ a member of this movement. **2** dense scrub vegetation consisting of hardy evergreen shrubs and small trees, characteristic of coastal regions in the Mediterranean. [19th C. (sense 2): from Fr., 'brushwood,' from Corsican Ital. *macchia*.]

ma·qui·sard /ˌmäkēˈzär/ ▶n. a member of the Maquis.

Mar. ▶abbr. March.

mar /mär/ ▶v. (**marred**, **mar·ring**) [trans.] impair the appearance of; disfigure. ■ impair the quality of; spoil: *violence marred their celebration.* [OE *merran* 'hinder, damage,' prob. rel. to Du. *marren* 'loiter.']

mar·a·bou /ˈmarəˌbōō/ ▶n. (also **marabou stork**) **1** a large African stork (*Leptoptilos crumeniferus*) with a massive bill and large neck pouch. ■ down from the marabou used for trimming clothing or on fishing lures. **2** raw silk that can be dyed without being separated from the gum. [19th C.: from Fr., from Arab. *murābiṭ* 'holy man,' the stork being regarded as holy.]

Ma·ra·cai·bo /ˌmarəˈkībō/ a city and port in northwestern Venezuela; pop. 1,401,000.

Ma·ra·cai·bo, Lake a lake in northwestern Venezuela, linked to the Gulf of Venezuela and the Caribbean Sea.

ma·rac·as /məˈräkəz/ ▶plural n. a pair of hollow clublike gourd or gourd-shaped containers filled with beans, pebbles, or similar objects, shaken as a percussion instrument. [17th C.: from Port. *maracá*, from Tupi.]

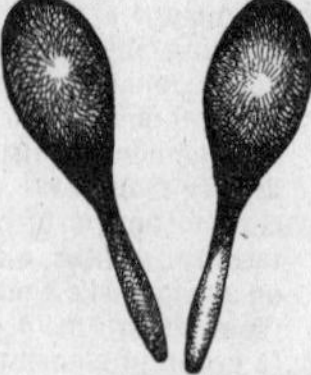

maracas

Ma·ra·ñón /ˌmäräˈnyōn/ a river in northern Peru that forms a principal headwater of the Amazon River.

mar·a·schi·no /ˌmarəˈSHēˌnō;-ˈskē-/ ▶n. (pl. **-nos**) a strong, sweet liqueur made from a variety of small bitter cherries. ■ a maraschino cherry. [Ital., from *marasca* (the name of the cherry), from *amaro* 'bitter,' from L. *amarus*.]

mar·a·schi·no cher·ry ▶n. a cherry preserved in maraschino or maraschino-flavored syrup.

ma·ras·mus /məˈrazməs/ ▶n. Med. severe undernourishment causing an infant's or child's weight to be significantly low for their age (e.g., below 60 percent of normal). — **ma·ras·mic** adj. [17th C.: mod. L., from Gk. *marasmos* 'withering,' from *marainein* 'wither.']

Ma·rat /mäˈrä/, Jean Paul (1743–93), French revolutionary. A critic of the moderate Girondists, he was instrumental in their fall from power in 1793.

Ma·ra·tha /məˈrätə/ (also **Mah·rat·ta**) ▶n. a member of the princely and military castes of the former Hindu kingdom of Maharashtra in central India. [via Hindi from Sanskrit *Mahārāṣṭra* 'great kingdom.']

Ma·ra·thi /məˈrätē/ (also **Mah·rat·ti**) ▶n. the Indic language of the Marathas.

mar·a·thon /ˈmarəˌTHän/ ▶n. a long-distance running race, strictly one of 26 miles and 385 yards (42.195 km). ■ [usu. with adj.] a long-lasting or difficult task or operation of a specified kind. ■ [as adj.] of great duration or distance; very long: *marathon workdays.* — **mar·a·thon·er** n. [19th C.: from *Marathōn* in Greece, from the tradition that a messenger ran from Marathon to Athens (22 miles) with the news of victory over the Persians in 490 BC.]

ma·raud /məˈrôd/ ▶v. [intrans.] [often as adj.] (**marauding**) roam in search of things to steal or people to attack: *marauding gangs of looters.* ■ [trans.] raid and plunder (a place). — **ma·raud·er** n. [17th C.: from Fr. *marauder*, from *maraud* 'rogue.']

Mar·a·vich /ˈmarəˌviCH/, Pete (1947–88), US basketball player; full name *Peter Press Maravich*; known as **Pistol Pete**. His 44.2 points per game is an NCAA record.

Mar·bel·la /märˈbāə/ a resort town in southern Spain; pop. 81,000.

mar·ble /ˈmärbəl/ ▶n. **1** a hard crystalline metamorphic form of limestone, typically white with mottlings or streaks of color. ■ used in similes and comparisons with reference to the smoothness, hardness, or color of marble: *skin as white as marble.* **2** a small ball of colored glass or similar material used as a toy. ■ (**marbles**) [treated as sing.] a game in which such balls are rolled along the ground. **3** (**one's marbles**) informal one's mental faculties: *she's lost her marbles.* ▶v. [trans.] stain or streak (something) so that it looks like variegated marble: *stone walls marbled with moss.* — **mar·bler** n. **mar·bly** /-blē; -bəlē/ adj. [ME: via OFr. (var. of *marbre*) from L. *marmor*, from Gk. *marmaros* 'shining stone,' associated with *marmairein* 'to shine.']

mar·ble cake ▶n. a cake with a streaked appearance, made of light and dark (esp. chocolate) batter.

mar·bled /ˈmärbəld/ ▶adj. having a streaked and patterned appearance like that of variegated marble. ■ (of meat) streaked with alternating layers or swirls of lean and fat.

mar·ble·ize /ˈmärbəˌlīz/ ▶v. [trans.] give a marblelike variegated finish to (an object or material): [as adj.] (**marbleized**) *an old dictionary with a marbleized cover.*

mar·bling /ˈmärbəliNG/ ▶n. coloring or marking that resembles variegated marble. ■ streaks of fat in lean meat.

marc /märk/ ▶n. the refuse of grapes or other fruit that has been pressed for winemaking. ■ an alcoholic spirit distilled from this. [17th C.: from Fr., from *marcher* in the early sense 'to tread or trample.']

mar·ca·site /ˈmärkəˌsīt/ ▶n. a semiprecious stone consisting of pyrite. ■ a piece of polished steel or a similar metal cut as a gem. [ME: from med. L. *marcasita*, from Arab. *marḳašīṯa*, from Pers.]

mar·ca·to /märˈkäˌtō/ ▶adv. & adj. Music (esp. as a direction) played with emphasis. [Ital., 'marked, accented,' of Gmc. origin.]

Mar·ceau /märˈsō/, Marcel (1923–), French mime artist; born *Marcel Mangel*. He is known for appearing as the white-faced Bip.

mar·cel /märˈsel/ dated ▶n. (also **mar·cel wave**) a deep artificial wave in the hair. ▶v. (**-celled**, **-cel·ling**) [trans.] give such a wave to (hair). [19th C.: after *Marcel* Grateau (1852–1936), Parisian hairdresser.]

mar·ces·cent /märˈsesənt/ ▶adj. Bot. (of leaves or fronds) withering but remaining attached to the stem. — **mar·ces·cence** n. [18th C.: from L. *marcescent-* 'beginning to wither,' from *marcere* 'wither.']

March /märCH/ ▶n. the third month of the year, in the northern hemisphere usually considered the first month of spring. [ME: from an OFr. dial. var. of *marz*, from L. *Martius (mensis)* '(month) of Mars.']

march[1] /märCH/ ▶v. [intrans.] walk in a military manner with a regular measured tread. ■ walk or proceed quickly and with determination: *without a word she marched from the room.* ■ [intrans.] force (someone) to walk somewhere quickly: *she marched him out the door.* ■ walk along public roads in an organized procession to protest about something: *protesters marched through major cities.* ■ fig. (of something abstract) proceed or advance inexorably: *time marches on.* ▶n. [usu. in sing.] an act or instance of marching: *it's more than a day's march away.* ■ a piece of music composed to accompany marching or with a rhythmic character suggestive of marching: *a funeral march.* ■ a procession as a protest or demonstration: *a protest march.* ■ fig. the progress or continuity of something abstract that is considered to be moving inexorably onward: *the march of history.*

– PHRASES **march to (the beat of) a different drummer** informal consciously adopt a different approach or attitude from the majority of people; be unconventional. [ME: from Fr. *marcher* 'to walk' (earlier 'to trample'), of uncert. origin.]

march[2] ▶n. (usu. **Marches**) a frontier or border area between two countries or territories, esp. between England and Wales or (formerly) England and Scotland: *the Welsh Marches.* ■ (**the Marches**) a region of east central Italy, between the Apennines and the Adriatic Sea; capital, Ancona. Italian name MARCHE. [ME: from OFr. *marche* (n.), *marchir* (v.), of Gmc. origin; rel. to MARK[1].]

march·er /ˈmärCHər/ ▶n. a person who marches, esp. one taking part in a protest march.

mar·che·sa /märˈkāzə/ ▶n. (pl. **-che·se** /-ˈkāzā/) an Italian marchioness. [Ital., fem. of MARCHESE.]

mar·che·se /märˈkāzā/ ▶n. (pl. **-che·si** /-ˈkāzē/) an Italian marquis. [Ital.]

March hare ▶n. informal a hare in the breeding season, noted for its leaping, boxing, and chasing in circles.

– PHRASES **(as) mad as a March hare** (of a person) completely mad or irrational; crazy.

march·ing or·ders ▶plural n. instructions from a superior officer for troops to depart. ■ informal a dismissal or sending off: *the ref gave me my marching orders.*

mar·chion·ess /ˈmärSH(ə)nəs/ ▶n. the wife or widow of a marquess. ■ a woman holding the rank of marquess in her own right. [16th C.: from med. L. *marchionissa*, fem. of *marchio(n-)* 'ruler of a border territory.']

March Mad·ness ▶n. informal the time of the annual NCAA college basketball tournament, generally throughout the month of March.

Mar·ci·a·no /ˌmärsēˈänō; -ˈänō/, Rocky (1923–69), US boxer; born *Rocco Francis Marchegiano*. He was world heavyweight champion 1952–56.

Mar·co·ni /märˈkōnē/, Guglielmo (1874–1937), Italian engineer. In 1912 he produced a continuously oscillating wave, essential for the transmission of sound. Nobel Prize for Physics (1909, shared with Carl Braun).

Mar·co Po·lo /ˈmärkōˈpōlō/ (*c.*1254–*c.*1324), Italian traveler. His account of his travels to China 1271–75 spurred the European quest for the riches of the East.

Mar·cos /ˈmär,kōs/, Ferdinand Edralin (1917–89), president of the Philippines 1965–86. Amid charges of corruption, he was forced into exile after a government takeover in 1986 led by Corazon Aquino.

Mar·cus Au·re·li·us /ˈmärkəs ôˈrēlēəs; ôˈrēlyəs/ see AURELIUS.

Mar·cu·se /märˈko͞ozə/, Herbert (1898–1979), US philosopher, born in Germany. He argued in *Soviet Marxism* (1958) that revolutionary change can come only from alienated elites such as students.

Mar del Pla·ta /,mär dəl ˈplätə/ a port city in eastern Argentina; pop. 520,000.

Mar·di Gras /ˈmärdē,grä/ ▶ **n.** a carnival held in some countries on Shrove Tuesday, most famously in New Orleans. [Fr., lit. 'fat Tuesday,' alluding to the last day of feasting before the fast and penitence of Lent.]

Mare, Walter de la, see DE LA MARE.

mare[1] /me(ə)r/ ▶ **n.** the female of a horse or other equine animal. [OE *mearh* 'horse,' *mere* 'mare,' from a Gmc. base.]

ma·re[2] /ˈmärā/ ▶ **n.** (pl. **ma·ri·a** /ˈmärēə/) Astron. a large, level basalt plain on the surface of the moon, appearing dark by contrast with highland areas: [in names] *Mare Imbrium.* [19th C.: special use of L. *mare* 'sea'; these areas were once thought to be seas.]

Ma·rek's dis·ease /ˈmariks; ˈmär-/ ▶ **n.** an infectious disease of poultry caused by a herpesvirus that attacks nerves and causes paralysis or initiates widespread tumor formation. [1960s: named after Josef *Marek* (died 1952), Hungarian veterinary surgeon.]

ma·rem·ma /məˈremə/ ▶ **n.** (pl. **-rem·me** /-ˈremē/) (esp. in Italy) an area of low, marshy land near a seashore. [19th C.: Ital., from L. *maritima*, fem. of *maritimus* (see MARITIME).]

Ma·ren·go /məˈreNGgō/ ▶ **adj.** [postpositive] (of chicken or veal) sautéed in oil, served with a tomato sauce, and traditionally garnished with eggs and crayfish. [after Marengo, Italy, where the dish is said to have been served to Napoleon after defeating the Austrian army in 1800.]

mare's nest ▶ **n.** **1** a complex and difficult situation; a muddle: *your desk is usually a mare's nest.* **2** an illusory discovery: *the mare's nest of perfect safety.* [16th C.: formerly in the phr. *to have found* (or *spied*) *a mare's nest* (i.e., something that does not exist), used in the sense 'to have discovered something amazing.']

mare's tail ▶ **n.** **1** a widely distributed water plant (*Hippuris vulgaris*, family Haloragaceae) with whorls of narrow leaves around a tall stout stem. **2** (**mare's tails**) long straight streaks of cirrus cloud.

Mar·fan's syn·drome /ˈmärfənz; märˈfänz/ (also **Mar·fan syn·drome**) ▶ **n.** Med. a hereditary disorder of connective tissue, resulting in abnormally long digits and frequently in optical and cardiovascular defects. [1930s: named after Antonin B. J. *Marfan* (1858–1942), Fr. pediatrician.]

mar·ga·rine /ˈmärjərən/ ▶ **n.** a butter substitute made from vegetable oils or animal fats. [19th C.: from Fr., from Gk. *margaron* 'pearl' (because of the luster of the crystals of margaric acid) + -INE[4].]

Mar·ga·ri·ta /,märgəˈrētə/ an island in the Caribbean Sea, off the coast of Venezuela.

mar·ga·ri·ta /,märgəˈrētə/ ▶ **n.** a cocktail made with tequila and citrus fruit juice. [from the Sp. given name equivalent to *Margaret*.]

mar·gate /ˈmärgit; -,gāt/ ▶ **n.** a deep-bodied grunt (two species, esp. *Haemulon album*) that typically occurs in small groups in warm waters of the western Atlantic and is an important food fish. [18th C.: of unknown origin.]

mar·gay /ˈmär,gā; märˈgā/ ▶ **n.** a small South American wild cat (*Felis wiedii*) with large eyes and a yellowish coat with black spots and stripes. [18th C.: via Fr. from Tupi *marakaya*.]

marge /märj/ ▶ **n.** literary a margin or edge. [16th C.: from Fr., from L. *margo* 'margin.']

mar·gin /ˈmärjən/ ▶ **n.** **1** the edge or border of something: *the eastern margin of the Atlantic* | fig. *the margins of society.* ■ the blank border on each side of the print on a page. ■ a line ruled on paper to mark off a margin. **2** an amount by which a thing is won or falls short: *they won by a 17-point margin.* ■ an amount of something included so as to be sure of success or safety: *no margin for error.* ■ the lower limit of possibility, success, etc.: *the margins of acceptability.* ■ a profit margin. ■ Finance a sum deposited with a broker to cover the risk of loss on a transaction; security. ▶ **v.** (**-gined, -gin·ing**) [trans.] **1** provide with an edge or border: *its leaves are margined with yellow.* **2** deposit an amount of money with a broker as security for (an account or transaction): [as adj.] (**margined**) *a margined transaction.*

– PHRASES **margin of error** an amount (usually small) that is allowed for in case of miscalculation or change of circumstances. — **mar·gined** **adj.** [in comb.] *a wide-margined volume.* [ME: from L. *margo, margin-* 'edge.']

mar·gin·al /ˈmärjənl/ ▶ **adj.** of, relating to, or situated at the edge or margin of something. ■ of secondary or minor importance; not central: *it made only a marginal difference.* ■ (of a decision or distinction) very narrow: *a marginal offside decision.* ■ of or written in the margin of a page. ■ of or relating to water adjacent to the land's edge or coast: *marginal aquatics.* ■ (chiefly of costs or benefits) relating to or resulting from small or unit changes. ■ (of taxation) relating to increases in income. ▶ **n.** a plant that grows in water adjacent to the edge of land. — **mar·gin·al·i·ty** /,märjəˈnalətē/ **n.**

mar·gi·na·li·a /,märjəˈnālēə/ ▶ **plural n.** marginal notes.

mar·gin·al·ize /ˈmärjənə,līz/ ▶ **v.** [trans.] treat (a person, group, or concept) as insignificant or peripheral: *they marginalize those who disagree* | [as adj.] (**marginalized**) *marginalized groups.* — **mar·gin·al·i·za·tion** /,märjənələˈzāSHən/ **n.**

mar·gin·al·ly /ˈmärjənəlē/ ▶ **adv.** to only a limited extent; slightly: *inflation dropped marginally* | [as submodifier] *marginally worse.*

mar·gin·ate Biol. ▶ **v.** /ˈmärjə,nāt/ [trans.] provide with a margin or border; form a border to. ▶ **adj.** /-nit; ,nāt/ having a distinct margin or border. — **mar·gin·a·tion** /,märjəˈnāSHən/ **n.**

mar·gin call ▶ **n.** Finance a demand by a broker that an investor deposit further cash or securities to cover possible losses.

mar·grave /ˈmär,grāv/ ▶ **n.** hist. the hereditary title of some princes of the Holy Roman Empire. — **mar·gra·vate** /ˈmärgrə,vāt/ **n.** [16th C., from MDu. *markgrave* 'count of a border territory.']

Mar·gre·the II /märˈgrātə/ (1940–), queen of Denmark 1972– .

mar·gue·rite /,märg(y)əˈrēt/ ▶ **n.** another term for OXEYE DAISY.

Ma·ri /ˈmärē/ an ancient city on the western bank of the Euphrates River in Syria.

ma·ri·a /ˈmärēə/ plural form of MARE[2].

ma·ri·a·chi /,märēˈächē/ ▶ **n.** (pl. **-chis**) [as adj.] denoting a type of traditional Mexican folk music, typically performed by a small group of strolling musicians dressed in native costume. ■ a musician in such a group. [from Mex. Sp. *mariache, mariachi* 'street singer.']

Ma·ri·a de' Me·di·ci /mäˈrēä de ˈmedēCHē/ see MARIE DE MÉDICIS.

Mar·i·an /ˈme(ə)rēən/ ▶ **adj.** **1** of or relating to the Virgin Mary. **2** of or relating to Queen Mary I of England.

Ma·ri·an·a Is·lands /,me(ə)rēˈanə; ,marēˈänə/ (also **the Ma·ri·an·as**) a group of islands in the western Pacific comprising Guam and the Northern Marianas. In 1978 the Northern Marianas became self-governing.

Ma·ri·a The·re·sa /məˈrēə təˈrāsə; -zə/ (1717–80), queen of Hungary and Bohemia 1740–80. Her accession triggered the War of the Austrian Succession.

Ma·ri Au·ton·o·mous Re·pub·lic another name for MARI EL.

mar·i·cul·ture /ˈmari,kəlCHər/ ▶ **n.** the cultivation of fish or other marine life for food. [20th C.: from *mare, mari-* 'sea' + CULTURE.]

Ma·rie An·toi·nette /məˈrē ,ant(w)əˈnet; ,äNtwäˈnet/ (1755–93), queen of France 1774–93; wife of Louis XVI; daughter of Maria Theresa. Her extravagant lifestyle led to widespread unpopularity.

Ma·rie Byrd Land /məˈrē bərd/ a region of Antarctica between Ellsworth Land and the Ross Sea.

Ma·rie de Mé·di·cis /mäˈrē də mādēˈsēs/ (1573–1642), queen of France 1610–17; Italian name *Maria de' Medici*. She ruled as regent during the minority of her son Louis XIII.

Ma·ri El /ˈmärē ˈel/ an autonomous republic in European Russia; pop. 754,000; capital, Yoshkar-Ola. Also called MARI AUTONOMOUS REPUBLIC.

Mar·i·et·ta /,marēˈetə/ a city in northwestern Georgia; pop. 58,748.

mar·i·gold /ˈmari,gōld/ ▶ **n.** a plant of the daisy family, typically with yellow, orange, or copper-brown flowers, widely cultivated as an ornamental. Several genera include *Tagetes* (the **French** and **African marigolds**) and *Calendula* (the **common** (or **pot**) **marigold**). ■ used in names of other plants with yellow flowers, e.g., **marsh marigold**. [ME: from the given name *Mary* + dial. *gold*.]

ma·ri·jua·na /,marəˈ(h)wänə/ (also **ma·ri·hua·na**) ▶ **n.** cannabis, esp. as smoked in cigarettes. [19th C.: from L. Amer. Sp.]

ma·rim·ba /məˈrimbə/ ▶ **n.** a deep-toned xylophone of African origin. [18th C.: from Kimbundu, perh. via Port.]

ma·ri·na /məˈrēnə/ ▶ **n.** a specially designed harbor with moorings for pleasure craft and small boats. [19th C.: from Ital. or Sp., fem. of *marino*, from L. *marinus* (see MARINE).]

mar·i·nade /,marəˈnād/ ▶ **n.** a sauce made of oil, vinegar, spices, herbs, etc., in which meat, fish, or other food is soaked before cooking to flavor or soften it. ▶ **v.** /also ˈmarə,nād/ another term for MARINATE. [17th C.: from Fr., from Sp. *marinada*, via *marinar* 'pickle in brine.']

ma·ri·na·ra /,marəˈnarə; ,märəˈnärə/ ▶ **n.** [usu. as adj.] (in Italian cooking) a sauce made from tomatoes, onions, and herbs, served esp. with pasta. [from the Ital. phr. *alla marinara* 'sailor-style.']

mar·i·nate /ˈmarə,nāt/ ▶ **v.** [trans.] soak (meat, fish, or other food) in a marinade. ■ [intrans.] (of food) undergo such a process. — **mar·i·na·tion** /,marəˈnāSHən/ **n.** [17th C.: from Ital. *marinare* 'pickle in brine,' or from Fr. *mariner* (from *marine* 'brine').]

ma·rine /məˈrēn/ ▶ **adj.** of, found in, or produced by the sea: *marine plants* | *marine biology.* ■ of or relating to shipping or naval matters: *marine insurance.* ▶ **n.** a member of a body of troops trained to serve on land or at sea, esp. a member of the US Marine Corps. [ME (as a n. in the sense 'seashore'): from OFr. *marin, marine*, from L. *marinus*, from *mare* 'sea.']

Ma·rine Corps /məˈrēn kô(ə)rz/ a branch of the US armed services (part of the US Navy), founded in 1775 and trained to operate on land and at sea.

ma·rine i·gua·na ▶ **n.** a large iguana (*Amblyrhynchus cristatus*) with webbed feet that swims strongly and feeds on marine algae, native to the Galapagos Islands.

Ma·rine One ▶ **n.** the helicopter used by the president of the United States.

Mar·i·ner /ˈmarənər/ a series of American space probes launched in 1962–77 to investigate the planets Venus, Mars, and Mercury.

mar·i·ner /ˈmarənər/ ▶ n. a sailor.

Ma·ri·net·ti /ˌmarəˈnetē; ˌmär-/, Filippo Tommaso (1876–1944), Italian poet and playwright. He issued a manifesto in 1909 that exalted technology, glorified war, and demanded revolution in the arts.

Mar·i·on, Francis (c. 1732–95), American Revolution military officer; known as the **Swamp Fox**. His evasion and ambush strategies against the British were precursors of modern guerilla warfare.

mar·i·on·ette /ˌmarēəˈnet/ ▶ n. a puppet worked from above by strings attached to its limbs. [17th C.: from Fr. *marionnette*, from *Marion*, dimin. of the given name *Marie*.]

marionette

mar·i·po·sa lil·y /ˌmarəˈpōsə; -ˈpōzə/ (also **mariposa tulip**) ▶ n. a plant (genus *Calochortus*) of the lily family, with brightly colored cup-shaped flowers, native to Mexico and the western US. Closely related to the SEGO. [19th C.: *mariposa* from Sp., 'butterfly.']

Mar·is /ˈmaris/, Roger Eugene (1934–85), US baseball player. An outfielder for the New York Yankees, he hit 61 home runs in 1961, breaking Babe Ruth's season record.

Mar·ist /ˈme(ə)rəst; ˈmar-/ ▶ n. **1** (also **Marist Father**) a member of the Society of Mary, a Roman Catholic missionary and teaching congregation. **2** (also **Marist Brother**) a member of the Little Brothers of Mary, a Roman Catholic teaching congregation. [19th C.: from Fr. *Mariste*, from the given name *Marie*, equivalent of *Mary*.]

mar·i·tal /ˈmaritl/ ▶ adj. of or relating to marriage or the relations between husband and wife. — **mar·i·tal·ly** adv. [16th C.: from L. *maritalis*, from *maritus* 'husband.']

mar·i·time /ˈmari,tīm/ ▶ adj. connected with the sea, esp. in relation to seafaring commercial or military activity: *maritime law.* ■ living or found in or near the sea: *maritime mammals.* ■ bordering on the sea. ■ denoting a climate that is moist and temperate owing to the influence of the sea. [16th C.: from L. *maritimus*, from *mare* 'sea.']

Mar·i·time Prov·inc·es (also **the Mar·i·times**) the Canadian provinces of New Brunswick, Nova Scotia, and Prince Edward Island. Compare with ATLANTIC PROVINCES.

Ma·ri·tsa /məˈrētsə/ a river in southern Europe that rises in Bulgaria and flows 300 miles (480 km) south to the Aegean Sea. Its ancient name is the Hebros or Hebrus. Turkish name MERIÇ; Greek name ÉVROS.

Ma·ri·u·pol /ˌmärēˈoopəl/ a port in southern Ukraine; pop. 517,000. Former name (1948–89) ZHDANOV.

Mar·i·us /ˈme(ə)rēəs; ˈmar-/, Gaius (*c.*157–86 BC), Roman general and politician. Elected consul in 107 BC, he defeated Jugurtha and invading Germanic tribes.

mar·jo·ram /ˈmärjərəm/ ▶ n. (also **sweet marjoram**) a southern European plant (*Origanum majorana*) of the mint family, used as a culinary herb. ■ (also **wild marjoram**) another term for OREGANO. [ME: from OFr. *majorane*, from med. L. *majorana*, of unknown ultimate origin.]

mark¹ /märk/ ▶ n. **1** a small area on a surface having a different color from its surroundings, typically one caused by accident or damage: *scratch marks.* ■ a spot, area, or feature on a person's or animal's body by which they may be identified or recognized: *no distinguishing marks.* **2** a line, figure, or symbol made as an indication or record of something. ■ a written symbol made on a document in place of a signature. ■ a level or stage that is considered significant: *the two million mark.* ■ a sign or indication of a quality or feeling: *a mark of respect.* ■ a characteristic property or feature: *the mark of a civilized society.* ■ a competitor's starting point in a race. ■ Naut. a piece of material or a knot used to indicate a depth on a sounding line. ■ Telecom. one of two possible states of a signal in certain systems. The opposite of SPACE. **3** a point awarded for a correct answer or for proficiency in an examination or competition. ■ a figure or letter representing the total of such points and signifying a person's score: *the highest mark was 98.* ■ (esp. in track and field) a time or distance achieved by a competitor, esp. one which represents a record or personal best. **4** (followed by a numeral) a particular model or type of a vehicle, machine, or device: *a Mark 10 Jaguar.* **5** a target: *the bullet missed its mark.* ■ informal a person who is easily deceived or taken advantage of: *they figure I'm an easy mark.* ▶ v. [trans.] **1** make (a visible impression or stain) on: *be careful not to mark it.* ■ [intrans.] become stained: *a surface that doesn't mark or tear.* **2** write a word or symbol on (an object), typically for identification: *she marked her possessions with her name.* ■ write (a word or figure) on an object: ***mark** the date **down** here.* ■ (**mark something off**) put a line by or through something written or printed to indicate that it has passed or been dealt with. **3** show the position of: *the river marks the border.* ■ separate or delineate (a particular section or area of something): ***mark out** the sunny part of the garden.* ■ (of a particular quality or feature) separate or distinguish (someone or something) from other people or things: *his sword **marked** him **out** as an officer.* ■ (**mark someone out for**) select or destine someone for (a particular role or condition). ■ (**mark someone down as**) judge someone to be (a particular type or class of person): *marked him down as a liberal.* ■ acknowledge, honor, or celebrate (an important event or occasion) with a particular action: *a party to mark their anniversary.* ■ be an indication of (a significant occasion, stage, or development): *mark a new phase in the campaign.* ■ (usu. **be marked**) characterize as having a particular quality or feature: *marked by hysteria.* **4** (of a teacher or examiner) assess the standard of (a piece of written work) by assigning points for proficiency or correct answers: *mark term papers.* **5** (of a player in a team game) stay close to (a particular opponent) in order to prevent them getting or passing the ball.

– PHRASES **be quick** (or **slow**) **off the mark** be fast (or slow) in responding to a situation or understanding something. **get off the mark** get started. **leave** (or **make**) **its** (or **one's** or **a**) **mark** have a lasting or significant effect. **make one's mark** attain recognition or distinction. **mark time** (of troops) march on the spot without moving forward. ■ fig. pass one's time in routine activities until a more favorable or interesting opportunity presents itself. **near** (or **close**) **to the mark** almost accurate: **off** (or **wide of**) **the mark** incorrect or inaccurate. **on the mark** correct; accurate. **on your marks** used to instruct competitors in a race to prepare themselves in the correct starting position: *on your marks, get set, go!*

– PHRASAL VERBS **mark something down** (of a retailer) reduce the indicated price of an item. **mark something up 1** (of a retailer) add a certain amount to the cost of goods to cover overhead and profit. **2** annotate or correct text for printing, keying, or typesetting. [OE *mearc, gemerce* (n.), *mearcian* (v.), of Gmc. origin; from an Indo-Eur. root shared by L. *margo* 'margin.']

mark² ▶ n. the basic monetary unit of Germany (until the introduction of the euro), equal to 100 pfennig; a Deutschmark. [OE *marc*, from ON *mǫrk*; prob. rel. to MARK¹.]

Mark, St. /märk/ one of the twelve Apostles. Companion of St. Peter and St. Paul, he is the traditional author of the second Gospel. ■ the second Gospel, the earliest in date (see GOSPEL sense 2).

Mark An·to·ny see ANTONY.

mark·down /ˈmärk,doun/ ▶ n. a reduction in price.

marked /märkt/ ▶ adj. **1** having a visible mark: *plants with beautifully marked leaves.* ■ (of playing cards) having distinctive marks on their backs to assist cheating. ■ Ling. (of words or forms) distinguished by a particular feature: *the word "drake" is semantically marked as masculine* **2** clearly noticeable; evident: *a marked increase.* — **mark·ed·ly** /ˈmärkidlē/ adv. (in sense 2). **mark·ed·ness** /ˈmärkidnis/ n.

marked man ▶ n. a person who is singled out for special treatment, esp. to be harmed or killed.

mark·er /ˈmärkər/ ▶ n. **1** an object used to indicate a position, place, or route: *a granite marker at the boundary.* ■ a thing serving as a standard of comparison or as an indication of what may be expected. ■ a radio beacon used to guide the pilot of an aircraft. ■ informal a promissory note; an IOU. **2** a felt-tip pen with a broad tip. **3** (chiefly in soccer) a player who is assigned to mark a particular opponent.

mar·ket /ˈmärkit/ ▶ n. **1** a regular gathering of people for the purchase and sale of provisions, livestock, and other commodities. ■ an open space or covered building where vendors convene to sell their goods. **2** an area or arena in which commercial dealings are conducted: *the labor market.* ■ a demand for a particular commodity or service: ***a market** for ornamental daggers.* ■ the state of trade at a particular time or in a particular context: *the bottom's fallen out of the market.* ■ the free market; the operation of supply and demand. ■ a stock market. ▶ v. (**-ket·ed, -ket·ing**) [trans.] advertise or promote (something): *the product was marketed as "aspirin."* ■ offer for sale: *market their wares.* ■ [intrans.] buy or sell provisions in a market: [as n.] (**marketing**) *he liked to do their marketing.*

– PHRASES **be in the market for** wish to buy. **make a market** Finance take part in active dealing in particular shares or other assets. **on the market** available for sale. — **mar·ket·er** n. [ME, via Anglo-Norman Fr. from L. *mercatus*, from *mercari* 'buy' (see also MERCHANT).]

mar·ket·a·ble /ˈmärkitəbəl/ ▶ adj. able or fit to be sold or marketed: *the fish are perfectly marketable.* ■ in demand: *marketable skills.* — **mar·ket·a·bil·i·ty** /ˌmärkitəˈbilətē/ n.

mar·ket·eer /ˌmärkəˈti(ə)r/ ▶ n. a person who sells goods or services in a market: *a consumer-goods marketeer.* ■ [with adj.] a person who works in or advocates a particular type of market: *free-marketeers.*

mar·ket forc·es ▶ plural n. the economic factors affecting the price, demand, and availability of a commodity.

mar·ket·ing /ˈmärkitiNG/ ▶ n. the action or business of promoting and selling products or services.

mar·ket·i·za·tion /ˌmärkitəˈzāSHən/ ▶ n. the exposure of an industry or service to market forces. ■ the conversion of a national economy from a planned to a market economy. — **marketize** /ˈmärki,tīz/ v.

mar·ket mak·er (also **mar·ket-mak·er**) ▶ n. a dealer in securities or other assets who undertakes to buy or sell at specified prices at all times.

mar·ket·place /ˈmärkət,plās/ ▶ n. an open space where a market is or was formerly held in a town. ■ the arena of competitive or commercial dealings; the world of trade: *the global marketplace.*

mar·ket price ▶ n. the price of a commodity when sold in a given market.

mar·ket share ▶ n. the portion of a market controlled by a particular company or product.

mar·ket val·ue ▶ n. the amount for which something can be sold on a given market. Often contrasted with BOOK VALUE.

mark·ing /ˈmärkiNG/ ▶ n. (usu. **markings**) an identification mark, esp.

a mark or pattern of marks on an animal's fur, feathers, or skin. ■ Music a word or symbol on a score indicating the correct tempo, dynamic, etc.

mark·ka /ˈmär(k),kä/ ▶ **n.** (pl. **-kaa** /-kä/) the basic monetary unit of Finland (until the introduction of the euro), equal to 100 penniä. [Finn.]

Mar·ko·va /märˈkōvə/, Dame Alicia (1910–2004), British prima ballerina; born *Lilian Alice Marks*.

marks·man /ˈmärksmən/ ▶ **n.** (pl. **-men**) a person skilled in shooting, esp. with a pistol or rifle. — **marks·man·ship n.**

marks·wom·an /ˈmärks,wŏŏmən/ ▶ **n.** (pl. **-wom·en**) a woman skilled in shooting, esp. with a pistol or rifle.

mark-to-mar·ket ▶ **adj.** Finance denoting a system of valuing assets by the most recent market price.

mark·up /ˈmär,kəp/ ▶ **n. 1** the amount added to the cost price of goods to cover overhead and profit. **2** the process or result of correcting text in preparation for printing. ■ the process of making the final changes in a legislative bill: *the acid rain bill is in markup.* **3** Comput. a set of tags assigned to elements of a text to indicate their relation to the rest of the text.

marl[1] /märl/ ▶ **n.** an unconsolidated sedimentary rock or soil consisting of clay and lime, formerly used as fertilizer. ▶ **v.** [trans.] (often **be marled**) apply marl to. — **marl·y adj.** [ME: from OFr. *marle*, from med. L. *margila*, from L. *marga*, of Celtic origin.]

marl[2] ▶ **v.** Naut. fasten with marline or other light rope; wind marline around (a rope), securing it with a half hitch at each turn.

Marl·bor·ough /ˈmärl,bərō; -,bərə/, John Churchill, 1st Duke of (1650–1722), British general. He was victorious over the French armies at Blenheim in 1704.

mar·lin /ˈmärlən/ ▶ **n.** a large edible billfish (genera *Makaira* and *Tetrapterus*) of warm seas. Several species include the **striped marlin** (*T. audax*). [20th C.: from MARLINSPIKE (with ref. to its pointed snout).]

striped marlin

mar·line /ˈmärlən/ ▶ **n.** Naut. light two-stranded rope. [ME: from Mid. Low Ger. *marling*, with the ending influenced by LINE[1].]

mar·lin·spike /ˈmärlən,spīk/ (also **mar·line·spike**) ▶ **n.** a pointed metal tool used by sailors to separate strands of rope or wire, esp. in splicing. [17th C. (orig. as *marling spike*): from *marling*, pres. part. of *marl* 'fasten with marline' (from Du. *marlen* 'keep binding') + SPIKE[1].]

Mar·lowe /ˈmärlō/, Christopher (1564–93), English playwright and poet. His works include *Doctor Faustus* (c.1590).

mar·ma·lade /ˈmärmə,lād/ ▶ **n.** a preserve made from citrus fruit, esp. bitter oranges, prepared like jam. [15th C.: from Port. *marmelada* 'quince jam,' from *marmelo* 'quince,' based on Gk. *melimēlon* (from *meli* 'honey' + *mēlon* 'apple').]

Mar·ma·ra, Sea of /ˈmärmərə/ a small sea in northwestern Turkey, separating European Turkey from Asian Turkey.

mar·mite /ˈmär,mīt/ ▶ **n.** an earthenware cooking container. [19th C.: Fr., from OFr. *marmite* 'hypocritical,' with ref. to the hidden contents of the lidded pot, from *marmotter* 'to mutter' + *mite* 'cat.']

mar·mo·re·al /märˈmôrēəl/ ▶ **adj.** literary made of or likened to marble. — **mar·mo·re·al·ly adv.** [18th C.: from L. *marmoreus* (from *marmor* 'marble') + -AL.]

mar·mo·set /ˈmärmə,set; -,zet/ ▶ **n.** a small Central and South American monkey (genera *Callithrix* and *Cebuella*, family Callitrichidae) with a silky coat and a long nonprehensile tail. [ME): from OFr. *marmouset* 'grotesque image,' of unknown ultimate origin.]

mar·mot /ˈmärmət/ ▶ **n.** a heavily built, gregarious, burrowing rodent (genus *Marmota*) of the squirrel family, typically living in mountainous regions of Eurasia and North America. [17th C.: from Fr. *marmotte*, prob. via Romansh *murmont* from late L. *mus montanus* 'mountain mouse.']

Marne /märn/ a river in east central France that rises north of Dijon and flows 328 miles (525 km) north and then west to join the Seine River near Paris.

Mar·o·nite /ˈme(ə)rə,nīt/ ▶ **n.** a member of a Christian sect of Syrian origin that is in communion with the Roman Catholic Church and living chiefly in Lebanon. ▶ **adj.** [attrib.] of or relating to the Maronites. [16th C.: from med. L. *Maronita*, from the name of John *Maro*, a 7th-cent. Syrian religious leader.]

Ma·roon /məˈrōōn/ ▶ **n.** a member of a group of black people living in the mountains and forests of Suriname and the West Indies, descended from escaped slaves. [17th C.: from Fr. *marron* 'feral,' from Sp. *cimarrón* 'wild,' (as a n.) 'escaped slave'; cf. SEMINOLE.]

ma·roon[1] /məˈrōōn/ ▶ **adj.** of a brownish-crimson color. ▶ **n.** a brownish-crimson color. [17th C. (in the sense 'chestnut'): from Fr. *marron* 'chestnut,' via Ital. from med. Gk. *maraon*.]

ma·roon[2] ▶ **v.** [trans.] (often **be marooned**) leave (someone) trapped and isolated in an inaccessible place, esp. an island: *he was marooned by pirates.* [18th C.: from MAROON, orig. in the form *marooned* 'lost in the wilds.']

Mar·quand /,märˈkwänd/, John Phillips (1893–1960), US writer. He created the character Mr. Moto, a Japanese detective featured in several of his novels. Other works include *The Late George Apley* (1937).

marque /märk/ ▶ **n.** a make of car, as distinct from a specific model. [20th C.: from Fr., back-form. from *marquer* 'to brand.']

mar·quee /märˈkē/ ▶ **n.** a rooflike projection over the entrance to a theater, hotel, or other building. ■ [as adj.] leading; preeminent: *a marquee player.* [17th C.: from MARQUISE, taken as pl. and assimilated to -EE.]

Mar·que·san /märˈkāzən/ ▶ **n. 1** a native or inhabitant of the Marquesas Islands, esp. a member of the aboriginal Polynesian inhabitants. **2** the Polynesian language of this people. ▶ **adj.** of or relating to the Marquesans or their language.

Mar·que·sas Is·lands /ˈmärkēsəz/ a group of volcanic islands in the South Pacific Ocean that forms part of French Polynesia; pop. 8,000.

mar·quess /ˈmärkwəs/ ▶ **n.** a British nobleman ranking above an earl and below a duke. Compare with MARQUIS. [16th C.: var. of MARQUIS.]

mar·que·try /ˈmärkətrē/ (also **mar·que·terie** or **mar·que·tery**) ▶ **n.** inlaid work made from small pieces of variously colored wood or other materials. [16th C.: from Fr. *marqueterie*, from *marqueter* 'to variegate.']

Mar·quette[1] /märˈket/ a city in the Upper Peninsula in Michigan; pop. 21,977.

Mar·quette[2], Jacques (1637–75), French Jesuit missionary and explorer. He explored the Wisconsin, Mississippi, and Illinois rivers, and attempted to Christianize the American Indians.

Már·quez, Gabriel García, see GARCÍA MÁRQUEZ.

mar·quis /märˈkē; ˈmärkwəs/ ▶ **n.** (in some European countries) a nobleman ranking above a count and below a duke. Compare with MARQUESS. ■ another term for MARQUESS. — **mar·quis·ate n.** [ME: from Old Fr. *marchis*, reinforced by OFr. *marquis*, both from the base of MARCH[2].]

Mar·quis de Sade /märˈkē də ˈsäd/ see SADE.

mar·quise /märˈkēz/ ▶ **n. 1** the wife or widow of a marquis. Compare with MARCHIONESS. ■ a woman holding the rank of marquis. **2** a ring set with a pointed oval gem or cluster of gems.

mar·qui·sette /,märk(w)əˈzet/ ▶ **n.** a fine light cotton, rayon, or silk gauze fabric, chiefly used for curtains. [20th C.: from Fr., dimin. of MARQUISE.]

Mar·ra·kesh /,marəˈkesʜ; ˈmarə,kesʜ; məˈrä-/ (also **Mar·ra·kech**) a city in western Morocco; pop. 602,000.

Mar·ra·no /məˈränō/ ▶ **n.** (pl. **-nos**) (in medieval Spain) a Christianized Jew or Moor, esp. one who merely professed conversion in order to avoid persecution. [Sp., of unknown origin.]

mar·riage /ˈmarij/ ▶ **n. 1** the formal union of a man and a woman, typically recognized by law, by which they become husband and wife. ■ a relationship between married people or the period for which it lasts. ■ fig. a combination or mixture of two or more elements. **2** (in pinochle and other card games) a combination of a king and queen of the same suit.

– PHRASES **by marriage** as a result of a marriage. **in marriage** as husband or wife: *he asked my father for my hand in marriage.* **marriage of convenience** a marriage concluded to achieve a practical purpose.

mar·riage·a·ble /ˈmarijəbəl/ ▶ **adj.** fit, suitable, or attractive for marriage, esp. in being of the right age. — **mar·riage·a·bil·i·ty** /,marijəˈbilitē/ **n.**

mar·ried /ˈmarēd/ ▶ **adj.** (of two people) united in marriage. ■ (of one person) having a husband or wife. ■ of or relating to marriage. ■ fig. closely combined or linked. ▶ **n.** (usu. **marrieds**) a married person.

mar·ron gla·cé /maˈrôɴ gläˈsā/ ▶ **n.** (pl. **mar·rons gla·cés** pronunc. same) a chestnut preserved in and coated with sugar. [Fr., 'iced chestnut.']

mar·row /ˈmarō/ ▶ **n. 1** (also **bone marrow**) a soft fatty substance in the cavities of bones, in which blood cells are produced (often taken as typifying strength and vitality). **2** (also **vegetable marrow**) Brit. a white-fleshed green-skinned gourd, eaten as a vegetable.

– PHRASES **to the marrow** to one's innermost being. — **mar·row·y adj.** [OE *mearg*, *mærg*, denoting the plant that produces vegetable marrow; rel. to Ger. *Mark*.]

mar·row·bone /ˈmarō,bōn/ ▶ **n.** a bone containing edible marrow. ■ (**marrowbones**) dated, humorous the knees.

mar·row·fat pea /ˈmarō,fat/ ▶ **n.** a pea of a large variety that is processed and sold in cans.

mar·ry[1] /ˈmarē/ ▶ **v.** (**-ries, -ried**) [trans.] **1** join in marriage: *I was married in church.* ■ take (someone) as one's wife or husband in marriage. ■ [intrans.] enter into marriage. ■ [intrans.] (**marry into**) become a member of (a family) by marriage. ■ (of a parent or guardian) give (a son or daughter) in marriage, esp. for reasons of expediency. **2** cause to meet or fit together; combine. ■ [intrans.] meet or blend with something: *most Chardonnays don't marry well with salmon.* ■ Naut. splice (ropes) without increasing their girth. [ME: from OFr. *marier*, from L. *maritare*, from *maritus*, lit. 'married,' (as a n.) 'husband.']

mar·ry[2] ▶ **exclam.** archaic expressing surprise, indignation, or emphatic assertion. [ME: var. of MARY[1].]

mar·ry·ing /ˈmarē-iɴɢ/ ▶ **adj.** [attrib.] likely or inclined to marry: *I'm not the marrying kind.*

Mars /märz/ **1** Rom. Mythol. the god of war and the most important Roman god after Jupiter. The month of March is named after him. Greek equivalent ARES. **2** Astron. a small, reddish planet that is the fourth in order from the sun and is periodically visible to the naked eye. It orbits between earth and Jupiter at an average distance of 141.6 million miles (228 million km) from the sun, has an equatorial diameter of 4,208 miles (6,787 km), and has two small satellites, Phobos and Deimos.

Mar·sa·la /mär'sälə/ ▶**n.** a dark, sweet, fortified dessert wine that resembles sherry, produced in Sicily. ▶**adj.** [postpositive] cooked or flavored with Marsala. [named after *Marsala*, a town in Sicily where it was orig. made.]

Mar·seil·laise /,märse'yez/ the national anthem of France, written by Rouget de Lisle in 1792. [Fr., fem. of *Marseillais* 'of Marseilles.']

Mar·seilles /mär'sā/ a city in southern France; pop. 807,725. French name **Marseille.**

marsh /märsн/ ▶**n.** an area of low-lying land that is flooded in wet seasons or at high tide, and typically remains waterlogged at all times. —**marsh·i·ness** /'märsнēnis/ **n. marsh·y adj.** [OE *mer(i)sc* (perh. influenced by late L. *mariscus* 'marsh'), of West Gmc. origin.]

mar·shal /'märsнəl/ ▶**n.** **1** an officer of the highest rank in the armed forces of some countries, including France. ■ esp. hist. a high-ranking officer of state. **2** a federal or municipal law officer. ■ the head of a police department. ■ the head of a fire department. **3** an official responsible for supervising public events, esp. sports events or parades. ▶**v.** (**-shaled, -shal·ing**; esp. Brit. **-shalled, -shal·ling**) [trans.] **1** arrange or assemble (a group of people, esp. soldiers) in order. ■ [trans.] guide or usher (someone) ceremoniously. **2** Heraldry combine (coats of arms), typically to indicate marriage, descent, or the bearing of office. —**mar·shal·er n. mar·shal·ship n.** [ME: from OFr. *mareschal* 'blacksmith, commander,' from late L. *mariscalcus*, from Gmc. elements meaning 'horse' (cf. **mare**[1]) and 'servant.']

Mar·shall[1] /'märsнəl/, George C. (1880–1959), US general and statesman; full name *George Catlett Marshall*. A career army officer, he served as chief of staff 1939–45 during World War II. As secretary of state 1947–49, he initiated the Marshall Plan. Nobel Peace Prize (1953).

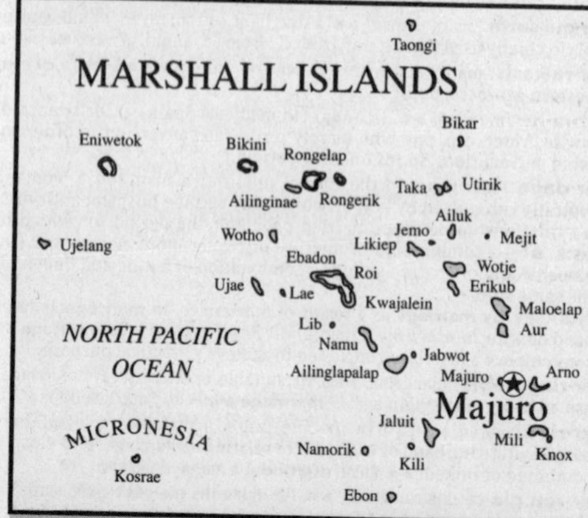

Marshall Islands

Official name: Republic of the Marshall Islands
Location: northwestern Pacific Ocean
Area: 70 square miles (180 sq km)
Population: 57,700
Capital: Majuro
Languages: English (official), local Austronesian languages, Japanese
Currency: US dollar

Mar·shall[2], John (1755–1835), Chief Justice of the US 1801–35. He is considered the father of the American system of constitutional law, esp. of the doctrine of judicial review.

Mar·shall[3], Thurgood (1908–93), US Supreme Court associate justice 1967–91. The first black justice, he was appointed to the Court by President Lyndon Johnson.

Mar·shall·ese /,märsнə'lēz; -'lēs/ ▶**n.** (pl. same) **1** a native or inhabitant of the Marshall Islands. **2** the Micronesian language of the Marshall Islands. ▶**adj.** of or relating to the Marshall Islands, their inhabitants, or their language.

Mar·shall Is·lands (also **the Mar·shalls**) a country that consists of two chains of islands in the northwestern Pacific Ocean. *See box.*

Mar·shall Plan a program of financial aid and other initiatives, sponsored by the US, designed to boost the economies of western European countries after World War II.

marsh gas ▶**n.** methane, esp. as generated by decaying matter in marshes. Also called **swamp gas.**

marsh hawk ▶**n.** another term for **northern harrier.**

marsh·land /'märsн,land/ ▶**n.** (also **marshlands**) land consisting of marshes.

marsh·mal·low /'märsн,melō; -,malō/ ▶**n.** a spongy confection made from a soft mixture of sugar, albumen, and gelatin.

marsh mal·low ▶**n.** a tall pink-flowered mallow (*Althaea officinalis*) that typically grows in brackish marshes. The roots were formerly used to make marshmallow, and it is sometimes cultivated for use in medicine.

marsh mar·i·gold ▶**n.** a plant (*Caltha palustris*) of the buttercup family that has large yellow flowers and grows in damp ground and shallow water, native to northern temperate regions. Also called **cowslip.**

marsh tread·er /märsн 'tredər/ ▶**n.** another term for **water measurer.**

Mars Path·find·er see **Pathfinder.**

Mars·ton Moor, Bat·tle of /'märstən/ a battle of the English Civil War, fought in 1644 on Marston Moor near York, in which the Royalists were defeated.

marsh marigold

mar·su·pi·al /mär'sōōpēəl/ Zool. ▶**n.** a mammal of an order (Marsupialia) whose members are born incompletely developed and are typically carried and suckled in a pouch on the mother's belly. Marsupials are found mainly in Australia and New Guinea, although three families, including the opossums, live in America. ▶**adj.** of or relating to this order. [17th C.: (see **marsupium**).]

mar·su·pi·um /mär'sōōpēəm/ ▶**n.** (pl. **-pi·a** /-pēə/) Zool. a pouch that protects eggs, offspring, or reproductive structures. [17th C.: via L. from Gk. *marsupion*, dimin. of *marsipos* 'purse.']

mart /märt/ ▶**n.** [usu. with adj.] a trade center or market: *Atlanta's downtown apparel marts.* [ME: from MDu. *mart*, var. of *marct* 'market.']

Mar·ta·ban, Gulf of /,märtə'bän; -'ban/ an inlet of the Andaman Sea, a part of the Indian Ocean.

Mar·tel /mär'tel/, Charles, see **Charles Martel.**

Mar·tel·lo /mär'telō/ (also **Mar·tel·lo tow·er**) ▶**n.** (pl. **-los**) any of numerous small circular forts that were erected for defense purposes along the southeast coasts of England during the Napoleonic Wars. [alt. of Cape *Mortella* in Corsica, where such a tower proved difficult for the English to capture in 1794.]

mar·ten /'märtn/ ▶**n.** a chiefly arboreal mammal (genus *Martes*) of the weasel family found in Eurasia and North America, hunted for its fur in many northern countries. [ME: from OFr. *(peau) martrine* 'marten (fur),' from *martre*, of West Gmc. origin.]

mar·tens·ite /'märtn,sīt/ ▶**n.** Metallurgy a hard and very brittle solid solution of carbon in iron that is the main constituent of hardened steel. —**mar·ten·sit·ic** /,märtn'sitik/ **adj.** [19th C.: named after Adolf *Martens* (1850–1914), Ger. metallurgist, + **-ite**[1].]

Mar·tial /'märsнəl/ (c.40–c.AD 104), Roman poet, born in Spain; Latin name *Marcus Valerius Martialis*. He wrote 15 books of epigrams.

mar·tial /'märsнəl/ ▶**adj.** of or appropriate to war; warlike: *martial bravery.* —**mar·tial·ly adv.** [ME: from OFr., or from L. *martialis*, from *Mars, Mart-* (see **Mars**).]

mar·tial arts ▶**plural n.** various sports or skills, mainly of Japanese origin, that originated as forms of self-defense or attack, such as judo, karate, and kendo. —**mar·tial art·ist n.**

mar·tial law ▶**n.** military government involving the suspension of ordinary law.

Mar·tian /'märsнən/ ▶**adj.** of or relating to the planet Mars or its supposed inhabitants. ▶**n.** a hypothetical or fictional inhabitant of Mars.

Martin /'märtn/, Paul Edgar Philippe (1938–), prime minister of Canada 2003–2006.

mar·tin /'märtn/ ▶**n.** a swift-flying, insectivorous songbird of the swallow family, typically having a less strongly forked tail than a swallow. [ME: probably a shortening of obs. *martinet*, from Fr., prob. from the name of St. *Martin* of Tours, celebrated at **Martinmas.**]

Mar·tin, St. (died 397), French priest; bishop of Tours from 371. He is a patron saint of France.

mar·ti·net /,märtn'et/ ▶**n.** a strict disciplinarian, esp. in the armed forces. —**mar·ti·net·ish** (also **mar·ti·net·tish**) **adj.** [17th C.: named after Jean *Martinet*, 17th-cent. Fr. drillmaster.]

Mar·ti·nez /mär'tēnez/ a city in north central California; pop. 31,808.

mar·tin·gale /'märtn,gāl/ ▶**n.** **1** a strap, or set of straps, attached at one end to the noseband (**standing martingale**) or reins (**running martingale**) of a horse and at the other end to the girth. See illustration at **harness.** **2** a gambling system of continually doubling the stakes in the hope of an eventual win. [16th C.: from Fr., ult. from Occitan *martegal* 'inhabitant of Martigues (in Provence).']

mar·ti·ni /mär'tēnē/ ▶**n.** a cocktail made from gin and dry vermouth. [named after *Martini* and Rossi, an Ital. firm selling vermouth.]

Mar·ti·nique /,märtn'ēk/ a French island in the Caribbean's Lesser Antilles group; pop. 360,000; capital, Fort-de-France. —**Mar·ti·niq·uan** /-'ēkən/ **n. & adj.**

Mar·tin·mas /'märtnməs/ ▶**n.** St. Martin's Day, November 11.

mar·tyr /'märtər/ ▶**n.** a person who is killed because of their religious or other beliefs. ■ a person who displays or exaggerates their discomfort or distress in order to obtain sympathy or admiration. ■ **(martyr to)**

a constant sufferer from (an ailment): *I'm a martyr to migraines!* ▶ v. [trans.] (usu. **be martyred**) kill (someone) because of their beliefs: *she was martyred for her faith.* ■ cause great pain or distress to. — **mar·tyr·i·za·tion** /ˌmärtərəˈzāSHən/ n. **mar·tyr·ize** /ˈmärtəˌrīz/ v. [OE *martir*, via eccles. L. from Gk. *martur* 'witness.']

mar·tyr·dom /ˈmärtərdəm/ ▶ n. the death or suffering of a martyr. ■ a display of feigned or exaggerated suffering. [OE *martyrdōm* (see MARTYR, -DOM).]

mar·tyred /ˈmärtərd/ ▶ adj. (of a person) having been martyred. ■ (of an attitude or manner) showing feigned or exaggerated suffering to obtain sympathy or admiration.

mar·tyr·ol·o·gy /ˌmärtəˈräləjē/ ▶ n. (pl. **-gies**) the branch of history or literature that deals with the lives of martyrs. ■ a list or register of martyrs. — **mar·tyr·o·log·i·cal** /-rəˈläjikəl/ adj. **mar·tyr·ol·o·gist** n.

mar·tyr·y /ˈmärtərē/ ▶ n. (pl. **-tyr·ies**) a shrine or church erected in honor of a martyr.

mar·vel /ˈmärvəl/ ▶ v. (**-veled, -vel·ing**; esp. Brit. **-velled, -vel·ling**) [intrans.] be filled with wonder or astonishment: *she marveled at Jeffrey's composure.* ▶ n. a wonderful or astonishing person or thing. — **mar·vel·er** n. [ME: from OFr. *merveille*, from L. *mirabilis* 'wonderful,' from *mirari* 'wonder at.']

Mar·vell /ˈmärvəl/, Andrew (1621–78), English poet. He wrote "To His Coy Mistress."

mar·vel·ous /ˈmärv(ə)ləs/ (Brit. **mar·vel·lous**) ▶ adj. causing great wonder; extraordinary. ■ extremely good or pleasing; splendid. — **mar·vel·ous·ly** adv. **mar·vel·ous·ness** n.

marv·y /ˈmärvē/ ▶ adj. informal wonderful; marvelous.

Marx /märks/, Karl Heinrich (1818–83), German political philosopher and economist. The founder of modern communism with Friedrich Engels, he collaborated with him in the writing of the *Communist Manifesto* (1848) and enlarged it into a series of books, most notably the three-volume *Das Kapital*.

Marx·ism /ˈmärkˌsizəm/ ▶ n. the political and economic theories of Karl Marx and Friedrich Engels, later developed as the basis for communism. — **Marx·i·an** adj. **Marx·ist** n. & adj.

Marx·ism–Le·nin·ism ▶ n. the doctrines of Marx as interpreted and put into effect by Lenin in the Soviet Union and (at first) by Mao Zedong in China. — **Marx·ist–Le·nin·ist** n. & adj.

Mar·y[1] /ˈme(ə)rē/, mother of Jesus; known as **the (Blessed) Virgin Mary**, or **St. Mary**, or **Our Lady**. According to the Gospels, she was a virgin betrothed to Joseph and conceived Jesus by the power of the Holy Spirit. She has been venerated by Roman Catholic and Orthodox Churches from earliest Christian times

Mar·y[2] the name of two queens of England: ■ Mary I (1516–58), reigned 1553–58; daughter of Henry VIII; known as **Mary Tudor** or **Bloody Mary**. ■ Mary II (1662–94), reigned 1689–94; daughter of James II.

Mar·y, Queen of Scots (1542–87), queen of Scotland 1542–67; daughter of James V; known as **Mary Stuart**. A devout Catholic, she was unable to control her Protestant lords and fled to England in 1567.

Mar·y Ce·leste /səˈlest/ (also **Ma·rie Ce·leste**) an American brig found adrift in the North Atlantic in December 1872 in perfect condition but abandoned.

Mar·y·land /ˈmerələnd/ a state in the eastern US that surrounds Chesapeake Bay, on the Atlantic coast; pop. 5,296,486; capital, Annapolis; statehood, Apr. 28, 1788 (7). Colonized by England in the 1600s, it was one of the original thirteen states. — **Mar·y·land·er** /-ˌlandər/ n.

Mar·y Mag·da·lene, St. /ˈmagdəˌlēn; -lən/ (also **Magdalen** /-lən/) (in the New Testament) a follower of Jesus, who cured her of evil spirits.

Mar·y Stu·art /ˈst(y)o͞oərt/ see MARY, QUEEN OF SCOTS.

Mar·y Tu·dor /ˈt(y)o͞odər/ Mary I of England (see MARY[2]).

mar·zi·pan /ˈmärzəˌpan/ ▶ n. a yellowish paste of ground almonds, sugar, and egg whites, often colored and used to make small cakes or confections or as an icing for larger cakes. Also called ALMOND PASTE. ■ a confection or cake made of or based on marzipan. [15th C. (as *marchpane*): from Ital. *marzapane*.]

Ma·sa·da /məˈsädə/ the site of the ruins of a palace and fortification built by Herod the Great on the southwestern shore of the Dead Sea 1st century BC.

Ma·sai /ˈmäˌsī; mäˈsī/ (also **Maa·sai**) ▶ n. (pl. same or **-sais**) **1** a member of a pastoral people living in Tanzania and Kenya. **2** the Nilotic language of the Masai. ▶ adj. of or relating to the Masai or their language.

ma·sa·la /məˈsälə/ ▶ n. any of a number of spice mixtures ground into a paste or powder for use in Indian cooking. ■ a dish flavored with this: *chicken masala.* [from Urdu *maṣālaḥ* based on Arab. *maṣāliḥ* 'ingredients, materials.']

Ma·san /ˈmäˌsän/ a city in southeastern South Korea; pop. 497,000.

Ma·sa·ryk /ˈmäsəˌrik/, Tomáš Garrigue (1850–1937), president of Czechoslovakia 1918–35.

Mas·ba·te /mäsˈbätē/ an island in the central Philippines; pop. 599,000.

masc. ▶ abbr. masculine.

Mas·ca·gni /məˈskänē; mäˈskänyē/, Pietro (1863–1945), Italian composer. He is noted for the opera *Cavalleria Rusticana* (1890).

mas·car·a /maˈskarə/ ▶ n. a cosmetic for darkening and thickening the eyelashes. — **mas·car·aed** adj. [19th C.: from Ital., lit. 'mask,' from Arab. *maskara* 'buffoon.']

Mas·ca·rene Is·lands /ˌmaskəˈrēn/ (also **the Mas·ca·renes**) a group of three islands—Réunion, Mauritius, and Rodrigues—in the western Indian Ocean.

mas·car·po·ne /ˌmäskärˈpōn(e)/ ▶ n. a soft, mild Italian cream cheese.

mas·cot /ˈmasˌkät; -kət/ ▶ n. a person or thing that is supposed to bring good luck or that is used to symbolize a particular event or organization. [19th C.: from Fr. *mascotte*, from Provençal *mascotto*, from *masco* 'witch.']

mas·cu·line /ˈmaskyələn/ ▶ adj. **1** having qualities or appearance traditionally associated with men, esp. strength and aggressiveness. ■ of or relating to men; male. **2** Gram. of or denoting a gender of nouns and adjectives, conventionally regarded as male. **3** Music (of a cadence) occurring on a metrically strong beat. ▶ n. (**the masculine**) the male sex or gender. ■ Gram. a masculine word or form. — **mas·cu·line·ly** adv. **mas·cu·lin·i·ty** /ˌmaskyəˈlinitē/ n. [ME: via OFr. from L. *masculinus*, from *masculus* 'male.']

mas·cu·line rhyme ▶ n. Pros. a rhyme of final stressed syllables (e.g., *blow/flow, confess/redress*). Compare with FEMININE RHYME.

mas·cu·lin·ist /ˈmaskyələˌnist/ (also **mas·cu·list**) ▶ adj. characterized by or denoting attitudes or values held to be typical of men. ■ of or relating to the advocacy of the rights or needs of men. ▶ n. an advocate of the rights or needs of men.

mas·cu·lin·ize /ˈmaskyələˌnīz/ ▶ v. [trans.] induce male physiological characteristics in. ■ cause to appear or seem masculine. — **mas·cu·lin·i·za·tion** /ˌmaskyələnəˈzāSHən/ n.

Mase·field /ˈmāsˌfēld/, John Edward (1878–1967), English poet and writer, appointed England's poet laureate in 1930.

ma·ser /ˈmāzər/ ▶ n. a device using the stimulated emission of radiation by excited atoms to amplify or generate coherent monochromatic electromagnetic radiation in the microwave range. [1950s: acronym from *microwave amplification by the stimulated emission of radiation*.]

Ma·se·ru /ˈmäzəˌro͞o; ˈmaz-/ the capital of Lesotho, in the western part of the country; pop. 367,000.

MASH /mash/ ▶ abbr. mobile army surgical hospital.

mash /masH/ ▶ n. a uniform mass made by crushing a substance into a soft pulp, sometimes with the addition of liquid. ■ bran mixed with hot water given as a warm food to horses or other animals. ■ (in brewing) a mixture of powdered malt and hot water, which is stood until the sugars dissolve to form the wort. ▶ v. [trans.] **1** reduce (a food or other substance) to a uniform mass by crushing it. ■ crush or smash (something) to a pulp. ■ [trans.] informal press forcefully on (something): *the worst thing you can do is mash the brake pedal.* **2** (in brewing) mix (powdered malt) with hot water to form wort. [OE *māsc* (used as a brewing term), of West Gmc. origin; perh. ult. rel. to MIX.]

mash·er /ˈmasHər/ ▶ n. **1** a utensil for mashing food. **2** informal a man who makes unwelcome sexual advances, often in public places and typically to women he does not know.

Mash·had /məˈsHäd/ (also **Me·shed** /məˈsHed/) a city in northeastern Iran; pop. 1,463,000.

mash·ie /ˈmasHē/ ▶ n. Golf, dated an iron used for lofting or for medium distances.

mash note ▶ n. informal a letter that expresses infatuation with or gushing appreciation of someone.

Ma·sho·na /məˈsHōnə; -ˈsHänə/ ▶ n. the Shona people collectively. ▶ adj. of or relating to the Shona people. [the name in Shona.]

Ma·sho·na·land /məˈsHōnəˌland; -ˈsHänə-/ an area of northern Zimbabwe, occupied by the Shona people.

mash-up ▶ n. a mixture or fusion of disparate elements, esp. a musical track comprising the vocals of one recording placed over the instrumental backing of another.

mas·jid /ˈməsjid; ˈmas-/ ▶ n. Arabic word for a mosque.

mask /mask/ ▶ n. **1** a covering for all or part of the face, in particular: ■ a covering worn as a disguise, or to amuse or terrify other people. ■ a covering made of fiber or gauze and fitting over the nose and mouth to protect against dust or air pollutants, or made of sterile gauze and worn to prevent infection. ■ a protective covering fitting over the whole face, worn in fencing, ice hockey, and other sports. ■ a respirator used to filter inhaled air or to supply gas for inhalation. ■ (also **masque**) a cosmetic preparation spread over the face and left for some time to cleanse and improve the skin. ■ Entomol. the enlarged lower lip of a dragonfly larva. **2** a likeness of a person's face in clay or wax, esp. one made by taking a mold from the face. ■ a person's face regarded as having set into a particular expression: *a mask of rage.* ■ a hollow model of a human head worn by ancient Greek and Roman actors. ■ the face or head of an animal, esp. of a fox, as a hunting trophy. **3** fig. a disguise or pretense. **4** Photog. a piece of something, such as a card, used to cover a part of an image that is not required when exposing a print. ■ Electron. a patterned metal film used in the manufacture of microcircuits to allow selective modification of the underlying material. ▶ v. [trans.] cover (the face) with a mask. ■ conceal (something) from view. ■ disguise or hide (a sensation or quality). ■ cover (an object or surface) to protect it from a process, esp. painting. — **masked** adj. [16th C.: from Fr. *masque*, from Ital. *maschera, mascara*.]

masked ball ▶ n. a ball at which participants wear masks to conceal their faces.

mask·er /ˈmaskər/ ▶ n. **1** a thing that masks or conceals something else. **2** a person taking part in a masquerade or masked ball.

mask·ing tape ▶ n. adhesive tape used in painting to cover areas on which paint is not wanted.

mas·ki·nonge /ˈmaskəˌnänj/ ▶ n. another term for MUSKELLUNGE.

Mas·low /ˈmazlō/, Abraham Harold (1908–70), US psychologist. He explained human motivation with a hierarchy of needs.

mas·och·ism /ˈmasəˌkizəm; ˈmaz-/ ▶ n. the tendency to derive pleasure, esp. sexual gratification, from one's own pain or humiliation. ■ (in general use) the enjoyment of what appears to be painful or tiresome. — **mas·och·ist** n. **mas·och·is·tic** /ˌmasəˈkistik; ˌmaz-/ adj. **mas·och·is·ti·cal·ly** /ˌmasəˈkistik(ə)lē; ˌmaz-/ adv. [19th C.: named after Leopold von Sacher-*Masoch* (1835–95), the Austrian novelist who described it, + -ISM.]

ma·son /ˈmāsən/ ▶ n. **1** a builder and worker in stone. **2** (**Mason**) a Freemason. ▶ v. [trans.] build from or strengthen with stone. ■ cut, hew, or dress (stone). [ME: from OFr. *masson*, prob. of Gmc. origin.]

ma·son bee ▶ n. a solitary bee (*Osmia* and other genera, family Apidae) that nests in cavities within which it constructs cells of sand and other particles glued together with saliva.

Ma·son Cit·y /ˈmāsən/ a city in north central Iowa; pop. 29,172.

Ma·son–Dix·on line /ˈdiksən/ (also **Ma·son-Dix·on Line**) ▶ n. (in the US) the boundary between Maryland and Pennsylvania, taken as the northern limit of the slave-owning states before the abolition of slavery. [named after Charles *Mason* and Jeremiah *Dixon*, the 18th-cent. Engl. astronomers who surveyed it in 1763–67.]

Ma·son·ic /məˈsänik/ ▶ adj. of or relating to Freemasons: *a Masonic lodge.*

Ma·son·ite /ˈmāsəˌnīt/ ▶ n. trademark a type of hardboard. [1920s: from the name of the *Mason* Fibre Co., Laurel, Mississippi, + -ITE¹.]

ma·son jar (also **Ma·son jar**) ▶ n. a wide-mouthed glass jar with an airtight screw top. [19th C.: named after John L. *Mason* (died 1902), US inventor.]

ma·son·ry /ˈmāsənrē/ ▶ n. **1** stonework. ■ the work of a mason. **2** (**Masonry**) Freemasonry.

ma·son wasp ▶ n. a solitary wasp (family Eumenidae) that nests in a cavity or in a hole in the ground, sealing the nest with mud or similar material.

Ma·so·rah /məˈsôrə/ (also **Mas·so·rah**) ▶ n. (**the Masorah**) the collection of information and comment on the text of the Hebrew Bible by the Masoretes. ■ the Masoretic text of the Bible. [from Heb. *māsōrāh*, based on *ʾāsar* 'to bind.']

Mas·o·rete /ˈmasəˌrēt/ (also **Mas·so·rete**) ▶ n. any of the Jewish scholars of the 6th–10th centuries AD who contributed to the establishment of a recognized text of the Hebrew Bible. — **Mas·o·ret·ic** /ˌmasəˈretik/ adj. [from Heb. *māsōreṯ*; rel. to *māsōrāh* (see MASORAH).]

masque /mask/ ▶ n. **1** a form of amateur dramatic entertainment, popular among the nobility in 16th- and 17th-century England, which consisted of dancing and acting performed by masked players. ■ a masked ball. **2** var. of MASK (sense 1). — **mas·quer** n. [16th C.: prob. from *masker*, from Ital. *mascar* 'person wearing a mask.']

mas·quer·ade /ˌmaskəˈrād/ ▶ n. a false show or pretense. ■ the wearing of disguise. ■ a masked ball. ▶ v. [intrans.] pretend to be someone one is not: *a journalist **masquerading as** a man in distress.* ■ be disguised or passed off as something else: *the idle gossip that **masquerades as** news.* — **mas·quer·ad·er** n. [16th C.: from Fr. *mascarade*, from Ital. *maschera*, from *maschera* 'mask.']

Mass /mas/ ▶ n. the Christian Eucharist or Holy Communion, esp. in the Roman Catholic Church. ■ a celebration of this. ■ a musical setting of parts of the liturgy used in the Mass. [OE *mæsse*, from L. *missa* 'dismissed,' from *mittere*, perh. from the last words of the service, *Ite, missa est* 'Go, it is the dismissal.']

Mass. ▶ abbr. Massachusetts.

mass /mas/ ▶ n. **1** a coherent, typically large body of matter with no definite shape. ■ a large number of people or objects crowded together. ■ a large amount of material. ■ (**masses**) informal a large quantity or amount of something: *we get **masses of** homework.* ■ any of the main portions in a painting or drawing that each have some unity in color, lighting, or some other quality. **2** (**the mass of**) the majority of. ■ (**the masses**) the ordinary people. **3** Physics the quantity of matter that a body contains, as measured by its acceleration under a given force or by the force exerted on it by a gravitational field. ■ (in general use) weight. ▶ adj. [attrib.] relating to, done by, or affecting large numbers of people or things. ▶ v. assemble or cause to assemble into a mass or as one body: [trans.] *both countries began massing troops in the region* | [intrans.] *clouds massed on the horizon.*
– PHRASES **be a mass of** be completely covered with. **in the mass** as a whole. — **mass·less** adj. [ME: from OFr. *masse*, from L. *massa*, from Gk. *maza* 'barley cake'; perh. rel. to *massein* 'knead.']

Mas·sa·chu·sett /ˌmasəˈCHōosit/ (**Mas·sa·chu·set**) ▶ n. **1** (pl. same or **-setts**) a member of an extinct North American Indian people, formerly found in eastern Massachusetts. **2** the Algonquian language of this people.

Mas·sa·chu·setts /ˌmasəˈCHōosits/ a state in the northeastern US, one of the six New England states; pop. 6,349,097; capital, Boston; statehood, Feb. 6, 1788 (6). Settled by the Pilgrims in 1620, it was a center of resistance to the British before becoming one of the original thirteen states.

Mas·sa·chu·setts Bay an inlet of the Atlantic Ocean between Cape Cod and Cape Ann.

mas·sa·cre /ˈmasikər/ ▶ n. an indiscriminate and brutal slaughter of people: *the attack was described as a cold-blooded massacre* | *she says he is an accomplice to massacre.* ■ informal a heavy defeat of a sports team or contestant. ▶ v. [trans.] deliberately and violently kill (a large number of people). ■ informal inflict a heavy defeat on (a sports team or contestant). [16th C.: from Fr., of unknown origin.]

mas·sage /məˈsäZH; -ˈsäj/ ▶ n. the rubbing and kneading of muscles and joints of the body with the hands, esp. to relieve tension or pain. ▶ v. [trans.] **1** rub and knead (a person or part of the body) with the hands. ■ (**massage something in/into/onto**) rub a substance into (the skin or hair). ■ flatter (someone's ego). **2** manipulate (figures) to give a more acceptable result. — **mas·sag·er** n. [19th C.: from Fr., from *masser* 'knead,' prob. from Port. *amassar* 'knead,' from *massa* 'dough.']

mas·sage par·lor ▶ n. an establishment providing massages. ■ such an establishment that is actually a front for prostitution.

mas·sa·sau·ga /ˌmasəˈsôgə/ ▶ n. a small North American rattlesnake (*Sistrurus catenatus*) of variable color that favors damp habitats. [19th C.: formed irregularly from MISSISSAUGA.]

Mas·sa·soit /ˌmasəˈsoit/ (c.1580–1661), Wampanoag Indian chief; father of King Philip. He signed a peace treaty with the Pilgrims at Plymouth in 1621.

mass de·fect ▶ n. Physics the difference between the mass of an isotope and its mass number.

mas·sé /maˈsā/ ▶ n. [usu. as adj.] Billiards a stroke made with an inclined cue, imparting swerve to the ball.

mass en·er·gy ▶ n. Physics mass and energy regarded as interconvertible manifestations of the same phenomenon, according to the laws of relativity. ■ the mass of a body regarded relativistically as energy.

mas·se·ter /məˈsētər; ma-/ (also **masseter muscle**) ▶ n. Anat. a muscle that runs through the rear part of the cheek from the temporal bone to the lower jaw. [16th C.: from Gk. *masētēr*, from *masasthai* 'to chew.']

mas·seur /maˈsər; mə-/ ▶ n. a person, esp. a man, who provides massages professionally.

mas·seuse /maˈsōos; mə-; maˈsœz/ ▶ n. a female masseur.

mas·sif /maˈsēf/ ▶ n. a compact group of mountains. [16th C.: Fr. adj. meaning 'massive,' used as a n.]

Mas·sif Cen·tral /mäˈsēf/ a mountainous plateau in south central France.

Mas·sine /mäˈsēn/, Léonide Fédorovitch (1895–1979), French choreographer, born in Russia; born *Leonid Fyodorovich Myasin.* He choreographed the movie *The Red Shoes* (1948).

mas·sive /ˈmasiv/ ▶ adj. **1** large and heavy or solid. **2** exceptionally large: *massive crowds are expected.* ■ very intense or severe: *a massive heart attack.* ■ informal particularly successful or influential. **3** Geol. (of rocks or beds) having no discernible form or structure. ■ (of a mineral) not visibly crystalline. — **mas·sive·ly** adv. **mas·sive·ness** n. [ME: from Fr. *massive*, based on L. *massa* (see MASS).]

mass mar·ket ▶ n. the market for goods that are produced in large quantities. ▶ v. (**mass-mar·ket**) [trans.] market (a product) on a large scale.

mass me·di·a ▶ plural n. (usu. **the mass media**) [treated as sing. or pl.] the media.

mass noun ▶ n. Gram. **1** a noun denoting something that cannot be counted (e.g., a substance or quality), usually a noun that lacks a plural in ordinary usage and is not used with the indefinite article, e.g., *luggage, china, happiness.* Contrasted with COUNT NOUN. **2** a noun denoting something that normally cannot be counted but that may be countable when it refers to different units or types, e.g., *coffee, bread.*

mass num·ber ▶ n. Physics the total number of protons and neutrons in a nucleus.

Mas·son /məˈsän; mäˈsôN/, André (1896–1987), French painter and graphic artist. He pioneered "automatic" drawing, which expresses images emerging from the unconscious.

Mas·so·rah /məˈsôrə/ ▶ n. var. of MASORAH.

Mas·so·rete /ˈmasəˌrēt/ ▶ n. var. of MASORETE.

mass-pro·duce /prəˈdōos/ ▶ v. [trans.] produce large quantities of (a standardized article) by an automated mechanical process. — **mass-pro·duc·er** n. **mass pro·duc·tion** n.

mass spec·tro·graph ▶ n. a mass spectrometer in which the particles are detected photographically.

mass spec·trom·e·ter ▶ n. an apparatus for separating isotopes, molecules, and molecular fragments according to mass.

mass spec·trum ▶ n. a distribution of ions shown by the use of a mass spectrograph or mass spectrometer.

mass trans·it ▶ n. public transportation.

mass·y /ˈmasē/ ▶ adj. literary archaic consisting of a large mass; bulky; massive: *a round massy table.*

mast¹ /mast/ ▶ n. **1** a tall upright post, spar, or other structure on a ship or boat, in sailing

mast¹ 1

vessels generally carrying a sail or sails. ■ a similar structure on land, esp. a flagpole or a television or radio transmitter. **2** (in full **captain's mast**) (in the US Navy) a session of court presided over by the captain of a ship, esp. to hear cases of minor offenses. — **mast·ed** adj. [OE *mæst*, of West Gmc. origin; rel. to Du. *mast* and Ger. *Mast*.]

mast² ▶ n. the fruit of beech, oak, chestnut, and other forest trees, esp. as food for pigs and wild animals. [OE *mæst*, of West Gmc. origin; prob. rel. to MEAT.]

mas·ta·ba /'mastəbə/ (also **mas·ta·bah**) ▶ n. Archaeol. an ancient Egyptian tomb, rectangular in shape with sloping sides and a flat roof, consisting of an underground burial chamber with rooms above it in which to store offerings.

mast cell ▶ n. a cell filled with basophil granules, found in connective tissue and releasing histamine during inflammatory and allergic reactions. [19th C.: *mast* from Ger. *Mast* 'fattening, feeding.']

mas·tec·to·my /ma'stektəmē/ ▶ n. (pl. **-mies**) a surgical operation to remove a breast. [1920s: from Gk. *mastos* 'breast' + -ECTOMY.]

mas·ter¹ /'mastər/ ▶ n. **1** esp. hist. a man who has people working for him, esp. servants or slaves. ■ a person who has dominance or control of something. ■ a machine or device directly controlling another: [as adj.] *a master cylinder.* Compare with SLAVE. ■ dated a male head of a household. ■ the owner of a dog, horse, or other domesticated animal. **2** a skilled practitioner of a particular art or activity. ■ a great artist, esp. one belonging to the accepted canon. ■ a very strong chess or bridge player, esp. one who has qualified for the title at international tournaments. See also GRAND MASTER. ■ (**Masters**) [treated as sing.] (in some sports) a class for competitors over the usual age for the highest level of competition. **3** a person who holds a second or further degree from a university or other academic institution (only in titles and set expressions). **4** a man in charge of an organization or group, in particular: ■ esp. Brit. a male schoolteacher, esp. at a public or prep school. ■ the head of a college or school. ■ the captain of a merchant ship. **5** used as a title prefixed to the name of a boy not old enough to be called "Mr.": *Master James Williams.* **6** an original movie, recording, or document from which copies can be made: [as adj.] *the master tape.* ▶ adj. [attrib.] **1** having or showing very great skill or proficiency. ■ denoting a person skilled in a particular trade and able to teach others. **2** main; principal: *the master bedroom.* ▶ v. [trans.] **1** acquire complete knowledge or skill in (an accomplishment, technique, or art). **2** gain control of; overcome: *to master one's fears.* **3** make a master copy of (a movie or record). — **mas·ter·dom** n. **mas·ter·hood** n. **mas·ter·less** adj. **mas·ter·ship** n. [OE *mæg(i)ster*, from L. *magister*.]

mas·ter² ▶ n. [in comb.] a ship or boat with a specified number of masts: *a three-master.*

mas·ter-at-arms ▶ n. (pl. **mas·ters-at-arms** /'mastərz ət 'ärmz/) a naval petty officer appointed to carry out or supervise police duties on board a ship.

mas·ter chief pet·ty of·fi·cer ▶ n. a noncommissioned officer in the US Navy or Coast Guard ranking above senior chief petty officer.

mas·ter class (also **mas·ter·class**) ▶ n. a class, esp. in music, given by an expert to highly talented students.

mas·ter·ful /'mastərfəl/ ▶ adj. **1** powerful and able to control others: *behind the lace and ruffles was a masterful woman.* **2** performed or performing very skillfully: *a masterful assessment of the difficulties.* — **mas·ter·ful·ly** adv. **mas·ter·ful·ness** n.

mas·ter gun·ner·y ser·geant ▶ n. a noncommissioned officer in the US Marine Corps ranking above master sergeant and below sergeant major.

mas·ter key ▶ n. a key that opens several locks, each of which also has its own key: *the custodian has the master key to all the classrooms.*

mas·ter·ly /'mastərlē/ ▶ adj. performed or performing in a very skillful and accomplished way: *his masterly account of rural France.*

mas·ter ma·son ▶ n. **1** a skilled mason, esp. one who employs other workers. **2** a fully qualified Freemason.

mas·ter·mind /'mastər,mīnd/ ▶ n. a person with an outstanding intellect. ■ someone who plans and directs an ingenious and complex scheme or enterprise. ▶ v. [trans.] plan and direct (an ingenious and complex scheme or enterprise).

mas·ter of cer·e·mo·nies ▶ n. a person in charge of procedure at a state or public occasion. ■ a person who introduces speakers, players, or entertainers.

mas·ter·piece /'mastər,pēs/ ▶ n. a work of outstanding artistry, skill, or workmanship. ■ an artist's or craftsman's best piece of work.

mas·ter plan ▶ n. a comprehensive or far-reaching plan of action.

Mas·ters /'mastərz/, Edgar Lee (1869–1950), US poet. His verse is collected in such works as *Spoon River Anthology* (1915).

mas·ter ser·geant ▶ n. a noncommissioned officer in the US armed forces of high rank, in particular (in the Army) an NCO above sergeant first class and below sergeant major, (in the Air Force) an NCO above technical sergeant and below senior master sergeant, or (in the Marine Corps) an NCO above gunnery sergeant and below master gunnery sergeant.

mas·ter·sing·er /'mastər,siNGər/ ▶ n. another term for MEISTERSINGER.

Mas·ters Tour·na·ment /'mastərz/ a prestigious US golf competition, held in Augusta, Georgia, in which golfers (chiefly professionals) compete only by invitation on the basis of their past achievements.

mas·ter stroke ▶ n. an outstandingly skillful and opportune act; a very clever move.

mas·ter·work /'mastər,wərk/ ▶ n. a masterpiece.

mas·ter·y /'mast(ə)rē/ ▶ n. **1** comprehensive knowledge or skill in a subject or accomplishment. ■ the action or process of mastering a subject or accomplishment. **2** control or superiority over someone or something. [ME: from OFr. *maistrie*, from *maistre* 'master.']

mast·head /'mast,hed/ ▶ n. **1** the highest part of a ship's mast or of the lower section of a mast. **2** the title of a newspaper or magazine at the head of the front or editorial page. ■ the listed details in a newspaper or magazine referring to ownership, advertising rates, etc.

mas·tic /'mastik/ ▶ n. **1** an aromatic gum or resin exuded from the bark of a Mediterranean tree, used in making varnish and chewing gum and as a flavoring. **2** (also **mastic tree**) the bushy evergreen Mediterranean tree (*Pistacia lentiscus*) of the cashew family that yields mastic and has aromatic leaves and fruit, closely related to the pistachio. **3** a puttylike waterproof filler and sealant used in building. [ME: via OFr. and L. from Gk. *mastikhē* (perh. from *mastikhan* 'masticate').]

mas·ti·cate /'masti,kāt/ ▶ v. [trans.] chew (food). — **mas·ti·ca·tion** /,masti'kāsHən/ n. **mas·ti·ca·tor** /-,kātər/ n. **mas·ti·ca·to·ry** /'mastikə,tôrē/ adj. [17th C.: from late L. *masticat-* 'chewed,' from the v. *masticare*, from Gk. *mastikhan* 'gnash the teeth' (rel. to *masasthai* 'to chew').]

mas·tiff /'mastif/ ▶ n. a dog of a large, strong breed with drooping ears and a smooth coat. [ME: obscurely representing OFr. *mastin*, based on L. *mansuetus* 'tame.']

mastiff

Mas·ti·goph·o·ra /,masti'gäfərə/ Zool. a group of single-celled animals (subphylum or superclass Mastigophora) that includes the protozoal flagellates, which are now generally divided among several phyla of the kingdom Protista. — **mas·ti·goph·o·ran** /-'gäf(ə)rən/ n. & adj. [mod. L. (pl.), from Gk. *mastigophoros*, from *mastix, mastig-* 'whip' + *-phoros* 'bearing.']

mas·ti·tis /ma'stītis/ ▶ n. inflammation of the mammary gland in the breast or udder. [19th C.: from Gk. *mastos* 'breast' + -ITIS.]

mas·to·don /'mastə,dän/ ▶ n. a large, extinct, elephantlike mammal (Mammutidae and other families, many species) of the Miocene to Pleistocene epochs, having teeth of a relatively primitive form and number. [19th C.: mod. L., from Gk. *mastos* 'breast' + *odous, odont-* 'tooth' (with ref. to nipple-shaped tubercles on the crowns of its molar teeth).]

mas·toid /'mas,toid/ ▶ adj. Anat. of or relating to the mastoid process. ▶ n. Anat. the mastoid process. ■ (**mastoids**) [treated as sing.] informal mastoiditis. [18th C.: via Fr. and mod. L. from Gk. *mastoeidēs* 'breast-shaped,' from *mastos* 'breast.']

mas·toid·i·tis /,mas,toid'ītis/ ▶ n. Med. inflammation of the mastoid process.

mas·toid proc·ess ▶ n. a conical prominence of the temporal bone behind the ear, to which neck muscles are attached, and which has air spaces linked to the middle ear.

mas·tur·bate /'mastər,bāt/ ▶ v. [intrans.] stimulate one's own genitals for sexual pleasure. ■ [trans.] stimulate the genitals of (someone) to give them sexual pleasure. — **mas·tur·ba·tion** /,mastər'bāsHən/ n. **mas·tur·ba·tor** /-,bātər/ n. **mas·tur·ba·to·ry** /-bə,tôrē/ adj. [19th C.: from L. *masturbat-* 'masturbated,' from *masturbari*, of unknown origin.]

Ma·su·ri·a /mə'so͝orēə/ a low-lying forested lakeland region in northeastern Poland. Also called MASURIAN LAKES.

mat¹ /mat/ ▶ n. **1** a piece of protective material placed on a floor, in particular: ■ a piece of coarse material placed on a floor for people to wipe their feet on. ■ a piece of resilient material for landing on in gymnastics, wrestling, or similar sports. ■ a small rug. ■ a piece of coarse material for lying on. **2** a small piece of cork, card, or similar material placed on a table or other surface to protect it from heat or moisture. **3** a thick, untidy layer of something hairy or woolly. ▶ v. (**mat·ted, mat·ting**) [trans.] tangle (something, esp. hair) in a thick mass: *sweat matted his hair.* ■ [intrans.] become tangled.
– PHRASES **go to the mat** informal vigorously engage in an argument or dispute, typically on behalf of a particular person or cause. **on the mat** informal being reprimanded by someone in authority. [OE *m(e)att(e)*; rel. to Ger. *Matte*, from late L. *matta*, from Phoenician.]

mat² ▶ n. short for MATRIX (sense 2).

mat³ ▶ n. var. of MATTE¹.

Mat·a·be·le /,matə'bēlē/ ▶ n. the Ndebele people collectively, particularly those of Zimbabwe. [from Sotho *matebele*, sing. *letebele*, the name given to this people.]

mat·a·dor /'matə,dôr/ ▶ n. a bullfighter whose task is to kill the bull. [Sp., lit. 'killer,' from *matar* 'to kill.']

Mat·a·gor·da Bay /,matə'gôrdə/ an inlet of the Gulf of Mexico in southeastern Texas, at the mouth of the Colorado River.

Ma·ta Ha·ri /'mätə 'härē; 'matə 'harē/ (1876–1917), Dutch dancer and secret agent; born *Margaretha Geertruida Zelle.* She probably worked for both French and German intelligence services. ■ [as n.] (**a Mata Hari**) a beautiful and seductive female spy. [from Malay *mata* 'eye' and *hari* 'day,' as a compound meaning 'sun.']

Mat·a·nus·ka Val·ley /ˌmatəˈno͞oskə/ a region in south central Alaska, northeast of Anchorage.

match[1] /mach/ ▶ **n.** **1** a contest in which people or teams compete against each other in a particular sport. **2** a person or thing able to contend with another as an equal in quality or strength. **3** a person or thing that resembles or corresponds to another. ■ a pair that corresponds or is very similar. ■ the fact or appearance of corresponding. **4** a person viewed in regard to their eligibility for marriage, esp. as regards class or wealth. ■ a marriage. ▶ **v.** [trans.] **1** correspond or cause to correspond in some essential respect; make or be harmonious: [trans.] *she matched her steps to his* | [intrans.] *the jacket and pants do not match.* ■ [trans.] team (someone or something) with someone or something else appropriate or harmonious: *they matched suitably qualified applicants with institutions.* **2** be equal to (something) in quality or strength: *his anger matched her own.* ■ succeed in reaching or equaling (a standard or quality): *he tried to match her nonchalance.* ■ equalize (two coupled electrical impedances) so as to bring about the maximum transfer of power. **3** place (a person or group) in contest or competition with another: [as adj., with submodifier] (**matched**) *evenly matched teams.*

– PHRASES **make a match** form a partnership, esp. by getting married. **meet one's match** encounter one's equal in strength or ability. **to match** corresponding in some essential respect with something previously mentioned or chosen: *a new coat and a hat to match.*

– PHRASAL VERBS **match up to** be as good as or equal to. — **match·a·ble** adj. [OE *gemæcca* 'mate, companion,' of West Gmc. origin; rel. to the base of MAKE.]

match[2] ▶ **n.** a short, thin piece of wood or cardboard used to light a fire, being tipped with a composition that ignites when rubbed against a rough surface. ■ hist. a piece of wick or cord designed to burn at a uniform rate.

– PHRASES **put a match to** set fire to. [ME (in the sense 'wick of a candle'): from OFr. *meche*, perh. from L. *myxa* 'spout of a lamp,' later 'lamp wick.']

match·board /ˈmachˌbôrd/ ▶ **n.** any of a set of interlocking boards joined together by a tongue cut along the edge of one board and fitting into a groove along along the edge of another. Also called **matched board.**

match·book /ˈmachˌbo͝ok/ ▶ **n.** a small cardboard folder of matches with a striking surface on one side.

match·box /ˈmachˌbäks/ ▶ **n.** a small box in which matches are sold. ■ [usu. as adj.] something very small, esp. a house, apartment, or room: *a matchbox apartment.*

match·less /ˈmachləs/ ▶ **adj.** unable to be equaled; incomparable: *the Parthenon has a matchless beauty.* — **match·less·ly** adv.

match·lock /ˈmachˌläk/ ▶ **n.** hist. a type of gun with a lock in which a piece of wick or cord is placed for igniting the powder. ■ a lock of this kind.

match·mak·er /ˈmachˌmākər/ ▶ **n.** a person who arranges relationships and marriages between others. ■ fig. a person or company that brings parties together for commercial purposes. — **match·mak·ing** n.

match point ▶ **n.** (in tennis and other sports) a point that, if won by one contestant will also win the match.

match·stick /ˈmachˌstik/ ▶ **n.** the stem of a match, esp. a wooden one. ■ something likened to a match in being long and thin.

matchup /ˈmachəp/ (also **match-up**) ▶ **n.** a contest between athletes or sports teams. ■ Basketball another term for a man-to-man defense. See *MAN-TO-MAN* at MAN.

match·wood /ˈmachˌwo͝od/ ▶ **n.** very small pieces or splinters of wood: *shattered into matchwood.* ■ light wood suitable for making matches.

mate[1] /māt/ ▶ **n.** **1** each of a pair of birds or other animals. ■ informal a person's husband, wife, or other sexual partner. ■ one of a matched pair: *a sock without its mate.* **2** [in comb.] a fellow member or joint occupant of a specified thing. **3** an assistant or deputy, in particular: ■ an assistant to a skilled worker. ■ a deck officer on a merchant ship subordinate to the master. See also FIRST MATE. ▶ **v.** **1** [intrans.] (of animals or birds) come together for breeding; copulate: *successful males may mate with many females.* ■ [trans.] bring (animals or birds) together for breeding. ■ join in marriage or sexual partnership. **2** [trans.] join or connect mechanically: *a four-cylinder engine mated to a five-speed gearbox.* ■ [intrans.] be connected or joined. — **mate·less** adj. [ME: from Mid. Low Ger. *māt(e)* 'comrade,' of West Gmc. origin.]

mate[2] ▶ **n. & v.** Chess short for CHECKMATE. [ME: from Anglo-Norman Fr. *mat* (from *eschec mat* 'checkmate').]

ma·té /ˈmäˌtā/ (also **yer·ba ma·té**) ▶ **n.** **1** (also **maté tea**) a bitter, caffeine-rich infusion of the leaves of a South American shrub. ■ the leaves of this shrub. **2** the South American shrub (*Ilex paraguariensis*) of the holly family that produces these leaves. [18th C.: from Sp. *mate*, from Quechua *mati*.]

mate·lot /ˌmatlˈō; matˈlō/ ▶ **n.** Brit., informal a sailor. [19th C.: from Fr., from MDu. *mattenoot* 'bed companion,' because sailors had to share hammocks.]

mat·e·lote /ˌmatlˈōt; matˈlōt/ ▶ **n.** a dish of fish in a sauce of wine and onions. [Fr., from *à la matelote*, lit. 'mariner-style,' from *matelot* 'sailor' (see MATELOT).]

ma·ter do·lo·ro·sa /ˈmätər ˌdōləˈrōsə; ˈmätər; ˌdäl-/ the Virgin Mary sorrowing for the death of Christ, esp. as a representation in art. [from med. L., 'sorrowful mother.']

ma·ter·fa·mil·i·as /ˌmātərfəˈmilēəs; ˌmätər-/ ▶ **n.** (pl. **ma·tres·fa·mil·i·as** /ˌmäˌtrās-; ˌmätərz-/) the female head of a family or household. Compare with PATERFAMILIAS. [L., from *mater* 'mother' + *familias*, old genitive form of *familia* 'family.']

ma·te·ri·al /məˈti(ə)rēəl/ ▶ **n.** **1** the matter from which a thing is or can be made. ■ (usu. **materials**) things needed for an activity: *cleaning materials.* ■ [with adj.] a person of a specified quality or suitability. **2** facts, information, or ideas for use in creating a book or other work: *good material for sermons.* ■ items, esp. songs or jokes, comprising a performer's act. **3** cloth or fabric. ▶ **adj.** **1** [attrib.] denoting or consisting of physical objects rather than the mind or spirit. ■ concerned with physical needs or desires. ■ concerned with the matter of reasoning, not its form: *political conflict lacks mathematical or material certitude.* **2** important; essential; relevant. ■ esp. Law (of evidence or a fact) significant, influential, or relevant, esp. to the extent of determining a cause or affecting a judgment: *information that could be material to a murder inquiry.* [ME: from late L. *materialis*, from L. *materia* 'matter.']

ma·te·ri·al cause ▶ **n.** Philos. (in Aristotelian thought) the matter or substance that constitutes a thing.

ma·te·ri·al·ism /məˈti(ə)rēəˌlizəm/ ▶ **n.** **1** a tendency to consider material possessions and physical comfort as more important than spiritual values. **2** Philos. the doctrine that nothing exists except matter and its movements and modifications. ■ the doctrine that consciousness and will are wholly due to material agency. See also DIALECTICAL MATERIALISM. — **ma·te·ri·al·ist** n. & adj. **ma·te·ri·al·is·tic** /məˌti(ə)rēəˈlistik/ adj. **ma·te·ri·al·is·ti·cal·ly** /-tik(ə)lē/ adv.

ma·te·ri·al·i·ty /məˌti(ə)rēˈalitē/ ▶ **n.** (pl. **-ties**) the quality or character of being material. ■ esp. Law the quality of being relevant or significant.

ma·te·ri·al·ize /məˈti(ə)rēəˌlīz/ ▶ **v.** [intrans.] **1** (of a ghost, spirit, or similar entity) appear in bodily form. ■ [trans.] cause to appear in bodily or physical form. ■ [trans.] rare represent or express in material form. **2** become actual fact; happen. ■ appear or be present. — **ma·te·ri·al·i·za·tion** /məˌti(ə)rēələˈzāshən/ n.

ma·te·ri·al·ly /məˈti(ə)rēəlē/ ▶ **adv.** **1** substantially; considerably: *materially different.* **2** in terms of wealth or material possessions: *a materially and culturally rich area.*

ma·te·ria med·i·ca /məˈti(ə)rēə ˈmedikə/ ▶ **n.** the body of remedial substances used in the practice of medicine. ■ the study of the origin and properties of these substances. [17th C.: mod. L., translation of Gk. *hulē iatrikē* 'healing material.']

ma·te·ri·el /məˌti(ə)rēˈel/ (also **ma·té·ri·el**) ▶ **n.** military materials and equipment. [19th C.: from Fr. *matériel*, adj. (used as a n.).]

ma·ter·nal /məˈtərnl/ ▶ **adj.** of or relating to a mother, esp. during pregnancy or shortly after childbirth. ■ [attrib.] related through the mother's side of the family: *my maternal grandfather.* ■ denoting feelings associated with or typical of a mother; motherly. — **ma·ter·nal·ism** n. **ma·ter·nal·ist** adj. **ma·ter·nal·is·tic** /məˌtərnlˈistik/ adj. **ma·ter·nal·ly** adv. [15th C.: from Fr. *maternel*, from L. *maternus*, from *mater* 'mother.']

ma·ter·ni·ty /məˈtərnətē/ ▶ **n.** motherhood. ■ [usu. as adj.] the period during pregnancy and shortly after childbirth. ■ a maternity ward in a hospital. [17th C.: from Fr. *maternité*, from L. *maternus*, from *mater* 'mother.']

mate·y /ˈmātē/ Brit., informal ▶ **n.** used as a familiar and sometimes hostile form of address, esp. to a stranger. ▶ **adj.** (**mat·i·er, mat·i·est**) familiar and friendly; sociable.

math /math/ ▶ **n.** informal mathematics. [19th C.: abbrev.]

math·e·mat·i·cal /ˌmath(ə)ˈmatikəl/ (also **math·e·mat·ic**) ▶ **adj.** of or relating to mathematics. ■ (of a proof or analysis) rigorously precise. — **math·e·mat·i·cal·ly** /-ik(ə)lē/ adv.

math·e·mat·i·cal in·duc·tion ▶ **n.** see INDUCTION (sense 3).

math·e·mat·i·cal log·ic ▶ **n.** the part of mathematics concerned with the study of formal languages, formal reasoning, the nature of mathematical proof, provability of mathematical statements, computability, and other aspects of the foundations of mathematics.

math·e·ma·ti·cian /ˌmath(ə)məˈtishən/ ▶ **n.** an expert in or student of mathematics.

math·e·mat·ics /math(ə)ˈmatiks/ ▶ **plural n.** [usu. treated as sing.] the abstract science of number, quantity, and space. ■ [often treated as pl.] the mathematical aspects of something: *the mathematics of general relativity.* [16th C.: pl. of obs. *mathematic* 'mathematics,' from OFr. *mathematique*, from L. *(ars) mathematica* 'mathematical (art),' from Gk. *mathēmatikē (tekhnē)*, from the base of *manthanein* 'learn.']

math·e·ma·tize /ˈmath(ə)məˌtīz/ ▶ **v.** [trans.] regard or treat (a subject or problem) in mathematical terms. — **math·e·ma·ti·za·tion** /ˌmath(ə)mətəˈzāshən/ n.

Math·er /ˈmaTHər/, a family of American ministers. Increase (1639–1723) was president of Harvard College 1685–1701. His son Cotton (1663–1728), noted for his political writings, is thought to have influenced the events that led to the Salem witch trials in 1692.

Math·ew·son /ˈmaTHyo͞osən/, Christy (1880–1925), US baseball player; full name *Christopher Mathewson*. A pitcher for the New York Giants 1900–16, four times he won 30 or more games in a season.

Ma·thi·as /məˈTHīəs/, Bob (1930–2006), US track and field athlete and politician; full name *Robert Bruce Mathias*. He won two Olympic gold medals (1948, 1952), the first as the youngest Olympic decathlon winner. A California Republican, he served in the US House of Representatives 1967–75.

maths /maTHs/ ▶**plural n.** [treated as sing.] Brit., informal mathematics: [as adj.] *her mother was a maths teacher.* [20th C.: abbrev.]

Ma·til·da /mə'tildə/ (1102–67), English princess; daughter of Henry I; mother of Henry II; known as **the Empress Maud**. Henry's only legitimate child, she was named his heir, but her cousin Stephen seized the throne on Henry's death in 1135.

mat·in·al /'matn-l/ ▶**adj.** rare relating to or taking place in the morning. [19th C.: from Fr., from *matin* 'morning.']

mat·i·nee /,matn'ā/ (also **mat·i·née**) ▶**n.** a performance in a theater or a showing of a movie that takes place in the daytime. [19th C.: from Fr. *matinée*, lit. 'morning.']

mat·i·nee i·dol ▶**n.** informal, dated a handsome actor admired chiefly by women.

mat·ins /'matnz/ (Brit. also **mat·tins**) ▶**n.** a service of morning prayer, esp. in the Anglican Church. ■ a service forming part of the traditional Divine Office of the Western Christian Church. ■ (also **matin**) literary the morning song of birds. [ME: from OFr. *matines*, pl. of *matin* 'morning,' from L. *matutinum*, neut. of *matutinus* 'early in the morning.']

Ma·tisse /mə'tēs; mä-/, Henri Emile Benoît (1869–1954), French painter and sculptor. His use of nonnaturalistic color led him to be considered a leader among the fauvists.

Ma·to Gros·so /,mätə 'grōsōō/ a high plateau region in southwestern Brazil.

ma·tri·arch /'mātrē,ärk/ ▶**n.** a woman who is the head of a family or tribe. ■ an older woman who is powerful within a family or organization. — **ma·tri·ar·chal** /,mātrē'ärkəl/ **adj.**

ma·tri·ar·chate /'mātrē,är,kāt; -,ärkət/ ▶**n.** a matriarchal form of social organization, esp. in a tribal society.

ma·tri·ar·chy /'mātrē,ärkē/ ▶**n.** (pl. **-chies**) a system of society or government ruled by a woman or women. ■ a form of social organization in which descent and relationship are reckoned through the female line. ■ the state of being an older, powerful woman in a family or group.

ma·tri·ces /'mātrə,sēz/ plural form of MATRIX.

mat·ri·cide /'matrə,sīd; 'mā-/ ▶**n.** the killing of one's mother. ■ a person who kills their mother. — **mat·ri·cid·al** /,matrə'sīdl; ,mā-/ **adj.**

ma·tric·u·late /mə'trikyə,lāt/ ▶**v.** [intrans.] be enrolled at a college or university. ■ [trans.] admit (a student) to membership of a college or university. ▶**n.** a person who has been matriculated. — **ma·tric·u·la·tion** /mə,trikyə'lāsHən/ **n.** [16th C.: from med. L. *matriculat-* 'enrolled,' from the v. *matriculare*, from late L. *matricula* 'register,' dimin. of L. *matrix*.]

mat·ri·fo·cal /'matri,fōkəl; 'mā-/ ▶**adj.** (of a society, culture, etc.) based on the mother as the head of the family or household. [1950s: from L. *mater, matr-* 'mother' + FOCAL.]

mat·ri·lin·e·al /,matrə'linēəl; ,mā-/ ▶**adj.** of or based on kinship with the mother or the female line. — **mat·ri·lin·e·al·ly adv.** [20th C.: from L. *mater, matr-* 'mother' + LINEAL.]

mat·ri·lo·cal /,matrə'lōkəl; 'mā-/ ▶**adj.** of or denoting a custom in marriage whereby the husband goes to live with the wife's community. — **mat·ri·lo·cal·i·ty** /-lō'kalətē/ **n.** [20th C.: from L. *mater, matr-* 'mother' + LOCAL.]

mat·ri·mo·ni·al /,matrə'mōnēəl/ ▶**adj.** of or relating to marriage or married people: *matrimonial bonds.* — **mat·ri·mo·ni·al·ly adv.**

mat·ri·mo·ny /'matrə,mōnē/ ▶**n.** the state or ceremony of being married; marriage. [ME: via OFr. from L. *matrimonium*, based on *mater, matr-* 'mother.']

ma·trix /'mātriks/ ▶**n.** (pl. **-tri·ces** /'mātrisēz/ or **-trix·es**) **1** an environment or material in which something develops. ■ a mass of fine-grained rock in which gems, crystals, or fossils are embedded. ■ Biol. the substance between cells or in which structures are embedded. ■ fine material: *matrix of gravel paths.* **2** a mold in which something, such as printing type or a phonograph record, is cast or shaped. **3** Math. a rectangular array of quantities or expressions in rows and columns that is treated as a single entity and manipulated according to particular rules. ■ an organizational structure in which two or more lines of command, responsibility, or communication may run through the same individual. [ME: from L., 'breeding female,' later 'womb,' from *mater, matr-* 'mother.']

ma·tron /'mātrən/ ▶**n.** **1** a woman in charge of domestic and medical arrangements at a boarding school or other establishment. ■ a female prison officer. **2** a married woman, esp. a dignified and sober middle-aged one. — **ma·tron·hood n.** [ME: from OFr. *matrone*, from L. *matrona*, from *mater, matr-* 'mother.']

ma·tron·ly /'mātrənlē/ ▶**adj.** like or characteristic of a matron, esp. in being dignified and staid and typically associated with having a large or plump build.

ma·tron of hon·or ▶**n.** a married woman attending the bride at a wedding.

mat·ro·nym·ic /,matrə'nimik/ (also **met·ro·nym·ic** /,me-/) ▶**n.** a name derived from the name of a mother or female ancestor. ▶**adj.** (of a name) so derived. [18th C.: from L. *mater, matr-* 'mother,' on the pattern of *patronymic*.]

Ma·tsu·ya·ma /,mätsə'yämə/ a city in Japan, on the island of Shikoku; pop. 443,000.

Matt. ▶**abbr.** Bible Matthew.

matt ▶**adj., n., & v.** var. of MATTE¹.

matte¹ /mat/ (also **matt** or **mat**) ▶**adj.** (of a color, paint, or surface) dull and flat, without a shine: *matte black.* ▶**n.** **1** a matte color, paint, or finish. **2** a sheet of cardboard placed on the back of a picture, either as a mount or to form a border around the picture. ▶**v.** (**mat·ted, mat·ting**) [trans.] (often **be matted**) give a matte appearance to (something). [17th C.: from Fr. *mat*.]

matte² ▶**n.** an impure product of the smelting of sulfide ores, esp. those of copper or nickel. [19th C.: from Fr. 'dull, matte,' used as a n.]

matte³ ▶**n.** a mask used to obscure part of an image in a film and allow another image to be substituted. [19th C.: from Fr., perh. from *mat* (see MATTE¹).]

mat·ted /'matid/ ▶**adj.** **1** (esp. of hair or fur) tangled into a thick mass: *a cardigan of matted gray wool.* **2** covered or furnished with mats: *the matted floor.*

mat·ter /'matər/ ▶**n.** **1** physical substance in general, as distinct from mind and spirit; (in physics) that which occupies space and possesses rest mass, esp. as distinct from energy. ■ a substance or material: *organic matter.* ■ a substance in or discharged from the body: *fecal matter.* ■ written or printed material: *reading matter.* **2** an affair or situation under consideration; a topic. ■ Law something that is to be tried or proved in court; a case. ■ (**matters**) the present situation or state of affairs. ■ (**a matter for/of**) something that evokes a specified feeling: *it's a matter of indifference to me.* ■ (**a matter for**) something that is the concern of a specified person or agency. **3** [usu. with negative or in questions] (**the matter**) the reason for distress or a problem: *what's the matter?* **4** the substance or content of a text as distinct from its manner or form. ■ Print. the body of a printed work. ■ Logic the particular content of a proposition, as distinct from its form. ▶**v.** [intrans.] [usu. with negative or in questions] be of importance; have significance: *what did it matter to them?* ■ (of a person) be important or influential.
– PHRASES **for that matter** used to indicate that a subject or category, though mentioned second, is as relevant or important as the first. **in the matter of** as regards. **it is only a matter of time** there will not be long to wait. **a matter of 1** no more than (a specified period of time). **2** a thing that involves or depends on: *it's a matter of working out how to get something done.* **a matter of course** the natural or expected thing. **a matter of form** a point of correct procedure. **a matter of record** see RECORD. **no matter 1** [with clause] regardless of: *no matter what the government calls them, they are cuts.* **2** it is of no importance. **to make matters worse** with the result that a bad situation is made worse. [ME: via OFr. from L. *materia* 'timber, substance,' also 'subject of discourse.']

Mat·ter·horn /'matər,hôrn/ a mountain in the Alps that is 14,688 feet (4,477 m) high. French name MONT CERVIN; Italian name MONTE CERVINO.

mat·ter of fact ▶**n.** something that belongs to the sphere of fact as distinct from opinion or conjecture. ■ Law the part of a judicial inquiry concerned with the truth of alleged facts. Often contrasted with MATTER OF LAW. ▶**adj.** (**matter-of-fact**) unemotional and practical. ■ concerned only with factual content rather than style or expression.
– PHRASES **as a matter of fact** in reality (used esp. to correct a falsehood or misunderstanding). — **mat·ter-of-fact·ly adv. mat·ter-of-fact·ness n.**

mat·ter of law ▶**n.** Law the part of a judicial inquiry concerned with the interpretation of the law. Often contrasted with MATTER OF FACT.

Mat·thew, St. /'maTHyōō/ one of the 12 Apostles; a tax collector; traditional author of the first Gospel. ■ the first Gospel, written after AD 70 and based largely on that of St. Mark.

Mat·thew Par·is (*c.*1199–1259), English chronicler. He wrote *Chronica Majora*, a history of the world.

Mat·thews /'maTHyōōz/, Stanley (1824–89), US Supreme Court associate justice 1881–89.

Mat·thi·as, St. /mə'THīəs/ an Apostle. He replaced Judas.

Mat·thies·sen /'maTH(y)əsən/, Peter (1927–), US writer and naturalist. His nonfiction, usually based on his travels, includes *The Snow Leopard* (1978).

mat·ting /'matiNG/ ▶**n.** **1** material used for mats, esp. coarse fabric woven from a natural fiber: *rush matting.* **2** the process of becoming matted.

mat·tins /'matnz/ ▶**n.** var. of MATINS.

mat·tock /'matək/ ▶**n.** an agricultural tool shaped like a pickax, with an adze and a chisel edge as the ends of the head. [OE *mattuc*, of uncert. origin.]

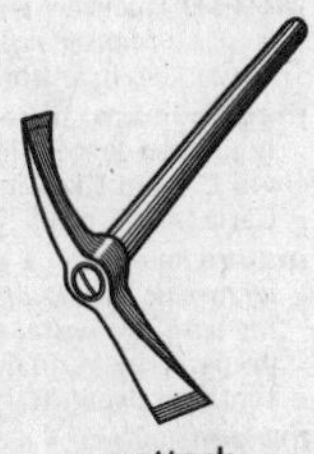
mattock

mat·tress /'matrəs/ ▶**n.** a fabric case filled with deformable or resilient material, used for sleeping on. ■ Engin. a flat structure of brushwood, concrete, etc., used as strengthening or support. [ME: via OFr. and Ital. from Arab. *maṭraḥ* 'carpet or cushion,' from *ṭaraḥa* 'to throw.']

mat·u·rate /'macHə,rāt/ ▶**v.** [intrans.] Med. (of a boil, abscess, etc.) form pus.

mat·u·ra·tion /,macHə'rāsHən/ ▶**n.** the action or process of maturing: *sexual maturation.* ■ (of wine or other fermented drink) the process of becoming ready for drinking. ■ the ripening of fruit. ■ Med. the development of functional ova or sperm cells. ■ the formation of pus in a boil, abscess, etc. — **mat·u·ra·tion·al** /-'rāsHənl/ **adj.** **ma·tur·a·tive** /'macHə,rātiv/ **adj.**

ma·ture /mə'cHŏŏr; -'t(y)ŏŏr/ ▶ **adj.** (**-tur·er, -tur·est**) **1** fully developed physically; full-grown. ■ having reached an advanced stage of mental or emotional development characteristic of an adult. ■ (of thought or planning) careful and thorough. ■ used euphemistically to describe someone as being middle-aged or old. ■ (of a style) fully developed. ■ (of a plant or planted area) complete in natural development. ■ (of certain foodstuffs or drinks) ready for consumption. **2** denoting an economy, industry, or market that has developed to a point where substantial expansion and investment no longer take place. **3** (of a bill) due for payment. ▶ **v.** [intrans.] **1** (of a person or animal) become physically mature. ■ develop fully. ■ (of a person) reach an advanced stage of mental or emotional development: *men mature as they grow older.* ■ (with reference to certain foodstuffs or drinks) become or cause to become ready for consumption. **2** (of an insurance policy, security, etc.) reach the end of its term and hence become payable. — **ma·ture·ly adv.** [ME: from L. *maturus* 'timely, ripe'; perh. rel. to MATINS.]

ma·tu·ri·ty /mə'cHŏŏritē; mə't(y)ŏŏr-/ ▶ **n.** the state, fact, or period of being mature. ■ the time when an insurance policy, security, etc., matures. [ME: from L. *maturitas*, from *maturus* (see MATURE).]

ma·tu·ti·nal /mə't(y)ōōtn-əl/ ▶ **adj.** formal of or occurring in the morning. [16th C.: from late L. *matutinalis*, from L. *matutinus* 'early.']

mat·zo /'mätsə/ (also **mat·zoh** or **mat·zah**) ▶ **n.** (pl. **-zos** or **-zoth** /-,sōt; -,sōs/) a crisp biscuit of unleavened bread, traditionally eaten by Jews during Passover. [Yiddish, from Heb. *maṣṣāh*.]

mat·zo ball ▶ **n.** a small dumpling made of seasoned matzo meal bound together with egg and chicken fat.

maud·lin /'môdlin/ ▶ **adj.** self-pityingly or tearfully sentimental, often through drunkenness. [ME: from OFr. *Madeleine*, from eccles. L. *Magdalena* (see MAGDALENE). The sense derives from allusion to pictures of Mary Magdalene weeping.]

Maugham /môm/, William Somerset (1874–1965), British writer; born in France. His novels include *Of Human Bondage* (1915).

Mau·i /'mouē/ one of the Hawaiian islands.

maul /môl/ ▶ **v.** [trans.] (of an animal) wound (a person or animal) by scratching and tearing. ■ treat (someone or something) roughly. ▶ **n.** a tool with a heavy head and a handle, used for tasks such as ramming, crushing, and driving wedges. — **maul·er n.** [ME: from OFr. *mail*, from L. *malleus* 'hammer.']

Mau Mau /'mou ,mou/ an African secret society that in the 1950s used violence and terror to try to expel European settlers and end British rule in Kenya. ■ **(mau-mau)** [as v.] [trans.] informal terrorize or threaten (someone). [Kikuyu.]

Mau·na Ke·a /,mounə 'kāə; ,mônə/ an extinct volcano on the island of Hawaii, in the central Pacific.

Mau·na Lo·a /'lōə; ,mônə/ an active volcano on the island of Hawaii.

maun·der /'môndər/ ▶ **v.** [intrans.] talk in a rambling manner. ■ move or act in a dreamy or idle manner. [17th C.: perh. from obs. *maunder* 'to beg.']

Maun·dy Thurs·day /'môndē/ ▶ **n.** the Thursday before Easter, observed in the Christian Church as a commemoration of the Last Supper.

Mau·pas·sant /,mōpä'sän/, Guy de (1850–93), French writer; full name *Henri René Albert Guy de Maupassant*. His novels include *Une Vie* (1883).

Mau·re·ta·ni·a /,môri'tānēə; -'tānyə/ an ancient region of North Africa. — **Mau·re·ta·ni·an adj. & n.**

Mau·riac /,môr'yäk/, François (1885–1970), French writer and playwright. His works include the novel *Thérèse Desqueyroux* (1927) and the play *Asmodée* (1938). Nobel Prize for Literature (1952).

Mau·ri·ta·ni·a /,môri'tānēə; -'tānyə/ a country in West Africa. *See box.* — **Mau·ri·ta·ni·an adj. & n.**

Mau·ri·tius /mô'risHəs/ an island country in the Indian Ocean. *See box.* — **Mau·ri·tian** /-'risHən/ **adj. & n.**

Mau·ry /'môrē/, Matthew Fontaine (1806–73), US oceanographer. He conducted the first systematic survey of oceanic winds and currents.

Mau·ser /'mouzər/ ▶ **n.** trademark a make of firearm, esp. a repeating rifle: [as adj.] *a Mauser rifle.* [19th C.: named after Paul von *Mauser* (1838–1914), Ger. inventor.]

mau·so·le·um /,môzə'lēəm; ,môsə-/ ▶ **n.** (pl. **-le·a** /-'lēə/ or **-le·ums**) a building, esp. a large and stately one, housing a tomb or tombs. [15th C.: via L. from Gk. *Mausōleion*, from *Mausōlos*, the name of a king of Caria (4th C. BC).]

mauve /mōv; môv/ ▶ **adj.** of a pale purple color. ▶ **n. 1** a pale purple color: *a few pale streaks of mauve were all that remained of the sunset | glowing with soft pastel mauves and pinks.* **2** hist. a pale purple aniline dye prepared by William H. Perkin (1838–1907) in 1856. It was the first synthetic dyestuff. [19th C.: from Fr., lit. 'mallow,' from L. *malva*.]

ma·ven /'māvən/ ▶ **n.** [often with adj.] informal an expert or connoisseur: *fashion mavens.* [1960s: Yiddish.]

mav·er·ick /'mav(ə)rik/ ▶ **n. 1** an unorthodox or independent-minded person. ■ a person who refuses to conform to a particular party or group. **2** an unbranded calf or yearling. ▶ **adj.** unorthodox. [19th C.: from the name of Samuel A. *Maverick* (1803–70), a Texas engineer and rancher who did not brand his cattle.]

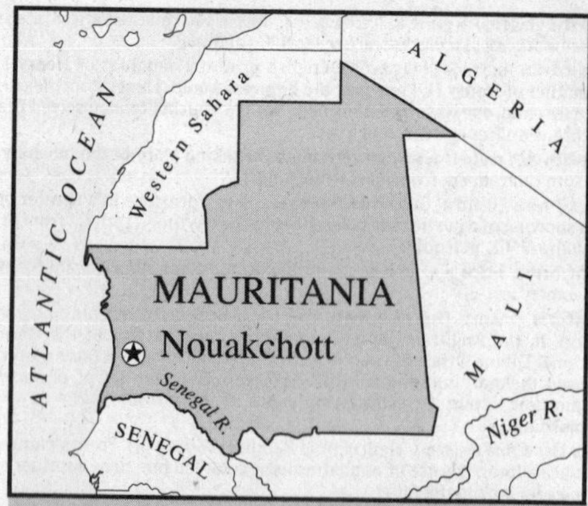

Mauritania

Official name: Islamic Republic of Mauritania
Location: West Africa, with a coastline on the Atlantic Ocean
Area: 398,100 square miles (1,030,700 sq km)
Population: 2,900,000
Capital: Nouakchott
Languages: Arabic and Wolof (both official), French
Currency: ouguiya

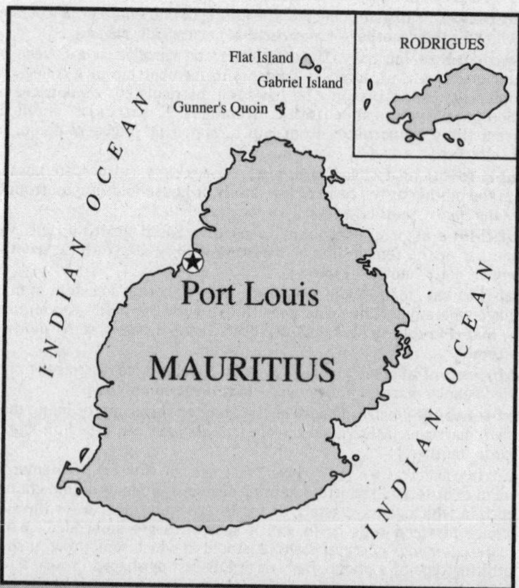

Mauritius

Official name: Republic of Mauritius
Location: Indian Ocean, east of Madagascar
Area: 720 square miles (1,900 sq km)
Population: 1,220,000
Capital: Port Louis
Languages: English (official), Creole, French, Hindi, Urdu, Hakka
Currency: Mauritian rupee

ma·vis /'māvis/ ▶ **n.** literary a song thrush. [ME: from OFr. *mauvis*, of unknown origin.]

maw /mô/ ▶ **n.** the jaws or throat of a voracious animal. ■ informal the mouth or gullet of a greedy person. [OE *maga*; of Gmc. origin; rel. to Ger. *Magen* 'stomach.']

mawk·ish /'môkisH/ ▶ **adj.** sentimental in a feeble or sickly way: *a mawkish poem.* ■ archaic dialect having a faint sickly flavor: *the mawkish smell of warm beer.* — **mawk·ish·ly adv.** **mawk·ish·ness n.** [17th C.: from obs. *mawk* 'maggot,' from ON *mathkr*.]

Max /maks/, Peter (1937–), US pop artist; born in Germany; born *Peter*

Finkelstein. Noted since the 1960s for combining serious art with commercial outlets, he was part of the psychedelic genre he called "up art."

max /maks/ ▶ abbr. maximum. ▶ n. informal a maximum amount or setting. ▶ adv. informal at the most. ▶ v. informal reach or cause to reach the limit of capacity or ability.

max·i /'maksē/ ▶ n. (pl. **max·is**) a thing that is very large of its kind, in particular: ■ a MAXISKIRT or MAXICOAT. ■ (also **max·i·yacht** or **max·i·boat**) a racing yacht of between approximately 15 to 20 meters in length.

max·il·la /mak'silə/ ▶ n. (pl. **max·il·lae** /mak'silē; -'sil,ī/) Anat. & Zool. the jaw or jawbone, specifically the upper jaw in most vertebrates. ■ (in many arthropods) each of a pair of mouthparts used in chewing. [ME: from L., 'jaw.']

max·il·lar·y /'maksə,lerē/ ▶ adj. Anat. & Zool. of or attached to a jaw or jawbone, esp. the upper jaw. ■ of or relating to the maxillae of an arthropod.

max·il·li·ped /mak'silə,ped/ ▶ n. Zool. (in crustaceans) an appendage modified for feeding, situated in pairs behind the maxillae. [19th C.: from MAXILLA + L. *pes, ped-* 'foot.']

max·il·lo·fa·cial /mak,silō'fāshəl; maksəlō-/ ▶ n. Anat. of or relating to the jaws and face.

max·im /'maksim/ ▶ n. a short, pithy statement expressing a general truth or rule of conduct. [ME: from Fr. *maxime*, from med. L. *(propositio) maxima* 'most important (proposition).']

max·i·ma /'maksəmə/ plural form of MAXIMUM.

max·i·mal /'maksəməl/ ▶ adj. of or constituting a maximum; the highest or greatest possible. — **max·i·mal·ly** adv.

max·i·mal·ist /'maksəməlist/ ▶ n. (esp. in politics) a person who holds extreme views and is not prepared to compromise. ▶ adj. of or denoting an extreme opinion. — **max·i·mal·ism** n.

max·i·mand /'maksə,mand/ ▶ n. esp. Econ. a quantity or thing that is to be maximized. [1950s: from MAXIMIZE + -AND.]

Max·im gun /'maksim/ ▶ n. the first fully automatic water-cooled machine gun, designed in Britain in 1884 and used esp. in World War I. [named after Sir Hiram S. *Maxim* (1840–1916), American-born British inventor.]

Max·i·mil·ian /,maksə'milyən/ (1832–67), Austrian emperor of Mexico 1864–67; full name *Ferdinand Maximilian Joseph*, brother of Franz Josef. He was executed after a popular uprising led by Mexico's president Benito Juárez.

max·i·min /'maksə,min; -sē-/ ▶ n. Math. the largest of a series of minima. Compare with MINIMAX. ■ [as adj.] denoting a method or strategy in game theory that maximizes the smallest gain that can be relied on by a participant in a game or other situation of conflict. [1950s: blend of MAXIMUM and MINIMUM.]

max·i·mize /'maksə,mīz/ ▶ v. [trans.] make as large or great as possible. ■ make the best use of. — **max·i·mi·za·tion** /,maksəmə'zāshən/ n. **max·i·miz·er** n.

max·i·mum /'maksəməm/ ▶ adj. [attrib.] as great, high, or intense as possible or permitted. ■ denoting the greatest or highest point or amount attained. ▶ n. (pl. **-ma** /-mə/ or **-mums**) the greatest or highest amount possible or attained. ■ a maximum permitted prison sentence for an offense. ▶ adv. at the most. [17th C.: from L. *maximus*, superlative of *magnus* 'great.']

max·i·mum sus·tain·a·ble yield (abbr.: **MSY**) ▶ n. (esp. in forestry and fisheries) the maximum level at which a natural resource can be routinely exploited without long-term depletion.

Max·well /'maks,wel; -wəl/, James Clerk (1831–79), Scottish physicist. He identified the electromagnetic nature of light and postulated the existence of other electromagnetic radiation.

max·well /'maks,wel; -wəl/ (abbr.: **Mx**) ▶ n. Physics a unit of magnetic flux in the centimeter-gram-second system, equal to that induced through one square centimeter by a perpendicular magnetic field of one gauss. [20th C.: named after J. C. *Maxwell* (see MAXWELL).]

Max·well's e·qua·tions Physics a set of four linear partial differential equations that summarize the classical properties of the electromagnetic field. [20th C.: named after J. C. *Maxwell* (see MAXWELL).]

May /mā/ ▶ n. the fifth month of the year, in the northern hemisphere usually considered the last month of spring. ■ (usu. **one's May**) literary one's bloom or prime. [OE, from OFr. *mai*, from L. *Maius* 'the goddess *Maia*.']

may[1] /mā/ ▶ modal verb (3rd sing. pres. **may**; past **might**) **1** expressing possibility. ■ used when admitting that something is so before making another, more important point. **2** expressing permission. **3** expressing a wish or hope.

– PHRASES **be that as it may** despite that; nevertheless. **may as well** another way of saying MIGHT AS WELL (see MIGHT[1]). [OE *mæg*, of Gmc. origin; rel. to Ger. *mögen*, also to MAIN and MIGHT[2].]

may[2] ▶ n. the hawthorn or its blossom. [ME: from MAY.]

Ma·ya /'mīə/ ▶ n. (pl. same or **Ma·yas**) **1** a member of a an American Indian people of Yucatán and adjacent areas. Mayan civilization developed over southern Mexico, Guatemala, and Belize from the 2nd millennium BC, reaching its peak c.AD 300–c. 900. **2** the Mayan language of this people. ▶ adj. of or relating to this people or their language. [the name in Maya.]

ma·ya /'mīə; 'mäyə/ ▶ n. Hinduism the supernatural power wielded by gods and demons to produce illusions. ■ Hinduism the power by which the universe becomes manifest. ■ Hinduism & Buddhism the illusion or appearance of the phenomenal world. [from Sanskrit *māyā*, from *mā* 'create.']

Ma·ya·kov·sky /,mäyə'kôfskē; -skyē/, Vladimir Vladimirovich (1893–1930), Soviet poet and playwright. He was a fervent futurist.

Ma·yan /'mīən/ ▶ n. a large family of American Indian languages spoken in Central America. ▶ adj. **1** denoting, relating to, or belonging to this family of languages. **2** relating to or denoting the Maya people.

may·ap·ple /'mā,apəl/ (also **May ap·ple**) ▶ n. an American herbaceous plant (*Podophyllum peltatum*) of the barberry family with large, deeply divided leaves. It bears a yellow, egg-shaped edible fruit in May and is used medicinally. Also called MANDRAKE.

may·be /'mābē/ ▶ adv. perhaps; possibly. ▶ n. a mere possibility or probability.

May bee·tle ▶ n. another term for JUNE BUG.

May Day ▶ n. May 1, celebrated in many countries as a traditional springtime festival or as an international day honoring workers.

May·day /'mā,dā/ (also **may·day**) ▶ exclam. an international radio distress signal used by ships and aircraft. ▶ n. a distress signal using the word "Mayday": *we sent out a Mayday* | [as adj.] *a Mayday call*. [1920s: representing a pronunc. of Fr. *m'aider*, from *venez m'aider* 'come and help me.']

May·er /'māər/, Louis Burt (1885–1957), US movie executive, born in Russia; born *Eliezer Mayer*. In 1924, with Samuel Goldwyn, he formed MGM.

may·est /'mā-ist; māst/ archaic second person singular present of MAY[1].

May·fair /'mā,fe(ə)r/ a district in London.

May·flow·er /'mā,flouər/ the ship in which the Pilgrims sailed from England to America in 1620.

may·flow·er /'mā,flouər/ ▶ n. a name given to several plants that bloom in May, esp. certain hepaticas and anemones and the trailing arbutus.

may·fly /'mā,flī/ ▶ n. (pl. **-flies**) a short-lived, slender insect (order Ephemeroptera) with delicate, transparent wings and two or three long filaments on the tail. It lives close to water, where the chiefly herbivorous aquatic larvae develop.

may·hap /'mā,hap/ ▶ adv. archaic perhaps; possibly.

may·hem /'mā,hem/ ▶ n. violent or damaging disorder; chaos. ■ Law, & esp. hist. the crime of maliciously injuring or maiming someone, originally so as to render the victim defenseless. [16th C.: from OFr. *mayhem* (see MAIM).]

may·ing /'mā-iNG/ (also **May·ing**) ▶ n. archaic celebration of May Day.

may·n't /'mā(ə)nt/ rare ▶ contr. may not.

Ma·yo[1] /'mā-ō/ a county in the Republic of Ireland.

Ma·yo[2] a family of US physicians. William Worrall (1819–1911), born in England, helped found St. Mary's Hospital in Rochester, Minnesota, in 1899. His sons William James (1861–1939) and Charles Horace (1865–1939), both surgeons, developed the Mayo Clinic as a part of the hospital.

may·o /'mā-ō/ ▶ n. informal short for MAYONNAISE.

may·on·naise /'māə,nāz; ,māə'nāz/ ▶ n. a thick, creamy dressing consisting of egg yolks beaten with oil and vinegar and seasoned. [Fr., prob. from *mahonnais* 'of or from Port *Mahon*,' the capital of Minorca.]

may·or /'māər/ ▶ n. the elected head of a city, town, or other municipality. ■ the titular head of a municipality that is administered by a city manager. — **may·or·al** /mā'ôrəl; 'māərəl/ adj. **may·or·ship** n. [ME: from OFr. *maire*, from the L. adj. *major* 'greater.']

may·or·al·ty /'māərəltē/ ▶ n. (pl. **-ties**) the office of mayor. ■ a mayor's period of office.

may·or·ess /'māərəs/ ▶ n. **1** the wife of a mayor. **2** a woman holding the office of mayor.

Ma·yotte /mä'yôt/ an island in the Indian Ocean, an overseas territory of France; pop. 94,000; capital, Mamoutzu.

may·pole /'mā,pōl/ (also **May·pole**) ▶ n. a pole painted and decorated with flowers, around which people traditionally dance on May Day.

may·pop /'mā,päp/ ▶ n. the yellow edible fruit of a passionflower (*Passiflora incarnata*), grown chiefly in the southern US.

May queen ▶ n. a girl or young woman chosen to be crowned in traditional celebrations of May Day.

Mayr /'māər/, Ernst Walter (1904), US zoologist; born in Germany. He took a neo-Darwinian approach to evolution.

Mays /māz/, Willie Howard, Jr. (1931–), US baseball player; known as the **Say Hey Kid**. The preeminent center fielder for much of his career (1951–73), he was the first player with both 500 home runs and 3,000 hits to his name.

mayst /māst/ archaic second person singular present of MAY[1].

may·weed /'mā,wēd/ ▶ n. a plant of the daisy family that typically grows as a weed of fields and waste ground, in particular **stinking mayweed** (*Anthemis cotula*). [16th C.: from *maythe(n)*, an earlier name for this plant + WEED.]

Ma·zar-e-Sha·rif /mə'zär ē shə'rēf/ a city in northern Afghanistan; pop. 131,000.

Maz·a·rin /'mäzərin; mäzä'ran/, Jules (1602–61), French statesman and clergyman; born in Italy; Italian name *Giulio Mazzarino*. He became a cardinal in 1641 and chief minister of France in 1642.

Ma·za·tlán /ˌmäsətˈlän/ a city in Mexico, in the state of Sinaloa; pop. 314,000.

Maz·da·ism /ˈmäzdəˌizəm; maz-/ ▶ **n.** another term for **ZOROASTRIANISM.** — **Maz·da·ist n. & adj.** [19th C.: from Avestan *mazdā* (short for **AHURA MAZDA**) + **-ISM.**]

maze /māz/ ▶ **n.** a network of paths and hedges designed as a puzzle through which one has to find a way. ■ a complex network of paths or passages: *a maze of corridors.* ■ a confusing mass of information. ▶ **v.** (**be mazed**) archaic or dialect be dazed and confused. [ME (denoting delirium or delusion): prob. from the base of **AMAZE**, of which the v. is a shortening.]

ma·zel tov /ˈmäzəl ˌtôv; ˌtôf/ ▶ **exclam.** a Jewish phrase expressing congratulations or wishing someone good luck. [from mod. Heb. *mazzāl ṭōḇ*, lit. 'good star.']

ma·zer /ˈmāzər/ ▶ **n.** hist. a hardwood drinking bowl. [ME: from OFr. *masere*, of Gmc. origin.]

ma·zu·ma /məˈzo͞omə/ ▶ **n.** informal money; cash. [20th C.: Yiddish, from Heb. *mĕzummān*, from *zimmēn* 'prepare.']

ma·zur·ka /məˈzərkə; -ˈzo͝or-/ ▶ **n.** a lively Polish dance in triple time. [19th C.: via Ger. from Pol. *mazurka*, denoting a woman of the province Mazovia.]

ma·zy /ˈmāzē/ ▶ **adj.** (**ma·zi·er, ma·zi·est**) like a maze; labyrinthine: *the museum's mazy treasure house.*

maz·zard /ˈmazərd/ ▶ **n.** (in full **mazzard cherry**) a cherry tree (*Prunus avium*) native to both Eurasia and North America, commercially important for both its fruit and wood. Also called **SWEET CHERRY.**

Maz·zi·ni /məˈzēnē; mädˈzēnē/, Giuseppe (1805–72), Italian patriot. He founded the Young Italy movement 1831 and was a leader of the Risorgimento.

MB ▶ **abbr.** ■ Bachelor of Medicine. ■ Manitoba (in official postal use). ■ (also **Mb**) Comput. megabyte.

MBA ▶ **abbr.** Master of Business Administration.

Mba·ba·ne /(əm)bäˈbänä/ the capital of Swaziland, in the northwestern part of the country; pop. 38,300.

mba·qan·ga /(əm)bəˈkäNGgə/ ▶ **n.** a rhythmical popular music style of southern Africa.

mbi·ra /(ə)mˈbi(ə)rə/ ▶ **n.** (esp. in southern Africa) another term for **THUMB PIANO.** [19th C.: from Shona, prob. an alt. of *rimba* 'a note.']

Mbun·du /(ə)mˈbo͝ondo͞o/ ▶ **n.** (pl. same) **1** a member of either of two peoples of western Angola (sometimes distinguished as **Mbundu** and **Ovimbundu**). **2** either of the Bantu languages of these peoples, often distinguished as **Umbundu** (related to Herero) and **Kimbundu** (related to Kikongo). ▶ **adj.** of or relating to these peoples or their languages.

Mbu·ti /(ə)mˈbo͞otē/ ▶ **n.** (pl. same or **Mbu·tis**) a member of a pygmy people of western Uganda and adjacent areas of the Democratic Republic of the Congo (formerly Zaire). ▶ **adj.** of or relating to this people. [the name in local languages.]

Mbyte ▶ **abbr.** megabyte(s).

MC ▶ **abbr.** ■ Master of Ceremonies. ■ (in the US) Member of Congress. ■ (in the UK) Military Cross. ■ music cassette.

Mc ▶ **abbr.** megacycle(s), a unit of frequency equal to one million cycles.

Mc·Al·len /miˈkalən/ a city in southern Texas; pop. 84,021.

MCAT ▶ **abbr.** Medical College Admissions Test.

Mc·Car·thy[1] /məˈkärTHē/, Joseph Raymond (1909–57), US politician. A US senator from Wisconsin 1947–57, he was the instigator of widespread investigations into alleged communist infiltration in US public life.

Mc·Car·thy[2], Mary Therese (1912–89), US writer. Her novels include *The Group* (1963).

Mc·Car·thy·ism /məˈkärTHēˌizəm/ ▶ **n.** a campaign against alleged communists in the US government and other institutions carried out under Senator Joseph McCarthy in the period 1950–54.

Mc·Clel·lan /məˈklelən/, George Brinton (1826–85), Union general in the American Civil War; known as **Little Mac**. Although the victor at Antietam 1862, he was removed from command due to a lack of military aggressiveness.

Mc·Clin·tock /məˈklinˌtäk/, Barbara (1902–92), US geneticist. Nobel Prize for Physiology or Medicine (1983).

Mc·Cor·mick /məˈkôrmək/, Cyrus Hall (1809–84), US inventor and industrialist. His patented reaper (1834) was the basis of his machinery company.

Mc·Court /məˈkôrt/, Frank (1930–), US writer; full name *Francis McCourt*. He wrote the memoirs *Angela's Ashes* (1996) and *Teacher Man* (2006).

Mc·Coy /məˈkoi/ ▶ **n.** (in phrase **the real McCoy**) informal the real thing; the genuine article.

Mc·Cul·lers /məˈkələrz/, Carson (1917–67), US writer; born *Lula Carson Smith*. Her novels include *The Member of the Wedding* (1946).

Mc·Cul·lough /məˈkələ(k)/, Colleen (1937–), Australian writer. Her novels include *The Thorn Birds* (1977).

Mc·En·roe /ˈmakənˌrō/, John Patrick, Jr. (1959–), US tennis player. He won 77 singles titles during 1978–91.

mcf (also **MCF** or **Mcf**) ▶ **abbr.** one thousand cubic feet.

mcg ▶ **abbr.** microgram.

Mc·Gov·ern /məˈgəvərn/, George Stanley (1922–), US politician. A Democrat from South Dakota, he was a member of the US House of Representatives 1957–61 and the US Senate 1963–81.

Mc·Guf·fey /məˈgəfē/, William Holmes (1800–73), US educator, known for his *McGuffey Readers*.

mCi ▶ **abbr.** millicurie(s), a quantity of a radioactive substance having one thousandth of a curie of radioactivity: *15 mCi of the radionuclide.*

Mc·Ken·na /məˈkenə/, Joseph (1843–1926), US Supreme Court associate justice 1898–1925.

Mc·Kin·ley[1] /məˈkinlē/, John (1780–1852), US Supreme Court associate justice 1837–52.

Mc·Kin·ley[2], William (1843–1901), 25th president of the US 1897–1901. A Republican, he favored big business and waged the Spanish–American War of 1898, which resulted in the acquisition of Puerto Rico, Cuba, and the Philippines, as well as the annexation of Hawaii, and brought the US to the forefront of world power. He was assassinated by an anarchist while in Buffalo, New York.

Mc·Kin·ley, Mount a mountain in south central Alaska. Rising to 20,110 feet (6,194 m), it is the highest mountain in North America. Also called **DENALI.**

MCL ▶ **abbr.** ■ Master of Civil Law. ■ Master of Comparative Law.

Mc·Lean /məˈklēn/, John (1785–1861), US Supreme Court associate justice 1829–61.

Mc·Lu·han /məˈklo͞oən/, Marshall (1911–80), Canadian writer and philosopher; full name *Herbert Marshall McLuhan*. He argued that it is the characteristics of a particular medium rather than the information it disseminates that influence and control society.

Mc·Na·mar·a /ˈmaknəˌmarə/, Robert Strange (1916–), US businessman and public official. He was US secretary of defense 1961–68 (during the Vietnam War) and president of the World Bank 1968–81.

MCP informal ▶ **abbr.** male chauvinist pig.

Mc·Phee /məkˈfē/, John Angus (1931–), US journalist. He wrote for the *New Yorker* magazine from 1964 and also wrote nonfiction works such as *Basin and Range* (1981).

MCPO ▶ **abbr.** master chief petty officer.

Mc·Rey·nolds /məkˈrenl(d)z/, James Clark (1862–1946), US Supreme Court associate justice 1914–41.

Mc/s ▶ **abbr.** megacycles per second, a unit of frequency equal to one million cycles per second.

MD ▶ **abbr.** ■ Doctor of Medicine. ■ Brit. Managing Director. ■ Maryland (in official postal use). ■ musical director.

Md ▶ **symb.** the chemical element mendelevium.

Md. ▶ **abbr.** Maryland.

M.Div. ▶ **abbr.** Master of Divinity.

MDMA ▶ **abbr.** methylenedioxymethamphetamine, the drug Ecstasy.

mdse. ▶ **abbr.** merchandise.

MDT ▶ **abbr.** Mountain Daylight Time (see **MOUNTAIN TIME**).

ME ▶ **abbr.** ■ Maine (in official postal use). ■ medical examiner. ■ Middle English. ■ myalgic encephalomyelitis.

Me ▶ **abbr.** ■ Maine. ■ Maître (title of a French advocate).

me /mē/ ▶ **pron.** [first person sing.] **1** used by a speaker to refer to himself or herself as the object of a verb or preposition: *wait for me!* Compare with **I[2]**. ■ used after the verb "to be" and after "than" or "as". ■ informal to or for myself: *I've got me a job.* **2** informal used in exclamations: *dear me!* | *silly me!* [OE *mē*, accusative and dative of **I[2]**, of Gmc. origin; rel. to Du. *mij*, Ger. *mir* (dative), from an Indo-Eur. root shared by L. *me*, Gk. *(e)me*, and Sanskrit *mā*.]

me·a cul·pa /ˌmāə ˈko͝olpə; -pä/ ▶ **n.** an acknowledgment of one's fault or error. [L., 'by my fault.']

Mead /mēd/, Margaret (1901–78), US anthropologist. Her studies of primitive cultures include *Coming of Age in Samoa* (1928).

mead[1] /mēd/ ▶ **n.** esp. hist. an alcoholic drink of fermented honey and water. [OE *me(o)du*, of Gmc. origin; rel. to Ger. *Met* 'mead,' Gk. *methu* 'wine.']

mead[2] ▶ **n.** literary a meadow. [OE *mǣd*, of Gmc. origin; rel. to **MOW[1]**.]

Meade /mēd/, George Gordon (1815–72), Union general in the American Civil War; born in Spain. Commander of the Army of the Potomac 1863–65, he was victorious at Gettysburg in 1863.

Mead, Lake /mēd/ a reservoir in southeast Nevada, created 1933 by the Hoover Dam on the Colorado River.

mead·ow /ˈmedō/ ▶ **n.** a piece of grassland. ■ a piece of low ground near a river. — **mead·ow·y adj.** [OE *mǣdwe*, oblique case of *mǣd* (see **MEAD[2]**), from the Gmc. base of **MOW[2]**.]

mead·ow fes·cue ▶ **n.** a tall Eurasian fescue (*Festuca pratensis*) that is grown in North America as a pasture and hay grass.

mead·ow·land /ˈmedōˌland; ˈmedə-/ ▶ **n.** (also **meadowlands**) land used for the cultivation of grass, esp. for hay.

mead·ow·lark /ˈmedōˌlärk; ˈmedə-/ ▶ **n.** a ground-dwelling songbird (genus *Sturnella*) of the American blackbird family, with a brown streaky back and typically yellow and black underparts.

eastern meadowlark

mead·ow mush·room ▶ **n.** another term for **CHAMPIGNON.**

mead·ow rue ▶ **n.** a widely distributed plant (genus *Thalictrum*) of the buttercup family that typically has divided leaves and heads of small fluffy flowers or delicate drooping flowers.

mead·ow saf·fron ▶ n. a poisonous autumn crocus (*Colchicum autumnale*) that produces its flowers, usually lilac, in the autumn while leafless. Native to Europe and North Africa, it is a source of the drug colchicine.

mead·ow·sweet /'medō,swēt; 'medə-/ ▶ n. a tall plant of the rose family with clusters of sweet-smelling flowers, in particular *Spiraeae latifola*, with white or pale pink flowers, and *Filipendula ulmaria*, with creamy white flowers.

mea·ger /'mēgər/ (Brit. **mea·gre**) ▶ adj. lacking in quantity or quality: *their meager earnings.* ■ (of a person or animal) lean; thin. — **mea·ger·ly** adv. **mea·ger·ness** n. [ME (in the sense 'lean'): from OFr. *maigre*, from L. *macer*.]

meal[1] /mēl/ ▶ n. any of the regular occasions in a day when a reasonably large amount of food is eaten. ■ the food eaten on such an occasion.
– PHRASES **meals on wheels** meals delivered to some elderly people or to invalids. [OE *mǣl* (also in the sense 'measure,' 'fixed time'), of Gmc. origin.]

meal[2] ▶ n. the edible part of any grain or pulse ground to powder, such as cornmeal. ■ any powdery substance made by grinding. [OE *melu*, *meolo*, rel. to Ger. *Mehl*.]

meal·ie /'mēlē/ ▶ n. (usu. **mealies**) esp. S. African corn, esp. sweet corn. [19th C.: from Afrik. *mielie*, from Port. *milho* 'corn, millet' from L. *milium*.]

meal tick·et ▶ n. a person or thing that is used as a source of regular income.

meal·time /'mēl,tīm/ ▶ n. the time when a meal is eaten.

meal·worm /'mēl,wərm/ ▶ n. the larva of a darkling beetle (genus *Tenebrio*), which is widely fed to captive birds and other insectivorous animals.

meal·y /'mēlē/ ▶ adj. (**meal·i·er**, **meal·i·est**) of, like, or containing meal: *a mealy flavor.* ■ pale. ■ (of part of a plant or fungus) covered with granules resembling meal. — **meal·i·ness** n.

meal·y·bug /'mēlē,bəg/ (also **meal·y bug**) ▶ n. a small, sap-sucking scale insect (*Pseudococcus* and other genera, family Pseudococcidae) that is coated with a white, powdery wax that resembles meal. It forms large colonies and can be a serious pest, esp. in greenhouses.

meal·y-mouthed /'mēlē 'mouT͟Hd; -,mouTHt/ (also **meal·y·mouthed**) ▶ adj. afraid to speak frankly.

mean[1] /mēn/ ▶ v. (past and past part. **meant**) [trans.] **1** intend to indicate or refer to (a particular thing or notion); signify: *I don't know what you mean.* ■ (of a word) have (something) as its signification in the same language or its equivalent in another language: *its name means "painted rock" in Cherokee.* ■ genuinely intend to convey or express (something). ■ (**mean something to**) be of some specified importance to (someone), esp. as a source of benefit or object of affection. **2** intend (something) to occur or be the case. ■ (**be meant to do something**) be supposed or intended to do something. ■ (often **be meant for**) designed for a particular purpose. ■ (**mean something by**) have as a motive or excuse in explanation. **3** have as a consequence or result. ■ necessarily or usually entail or involve.
– PHRASES **I mean** used to clarify or correct a statement or to introduce a justification or explanation. **mean business** be in earnest. **mean to say** [usu. in questions] really admit or intend to say: *do you mean to say you quit?* **mean well** have good intentions, but not always the ability to carry them out. [OE *mænan*; rel. to Du. *meenen* and Ger. *meinen*.]

mean[2] ▶ adj. **1** unwilling to give or share things, esp. money; not generous: *she felt mean not giving a tip.* **2** unkind, spiteful, or unfair: *she is mean to my brother.* ■ vicious or aggressive in behavior. **3** (esp. of a place) poor in quality and appearance. ■ (of a person's mental capacity) inferior; poor. **4** informal excellent; very skillful or effective: *a mean cook*
– PHRASES **no mean ——** denoting something very good of its kind: *it was no mean feat.* — **mean·ly** adv. **mean·ness** n. [ME, shortening of OE *gemǣne*, of Gmc. origin, from an Indo-Eur. root shared by L. *communis* 'common.']

mean[3] ▶ n. **1** the quotient of the sum of several quantities and their number; an average. See also ARITHMETIC MEAN, GEOMETRIC MEAN. **2** a condition, quality, or course of action equally removed from two opposite extremes. ▶ adj. [attrib.] **1** (of a quantity) average. **2** equally far from two extremes. [ME: from OFr. *meien*, from L. *medianus* 'middle' (see MEDIAN).]

me·an·der /mē'andər/ ▶ v. [no obj., with adverbial of direction] (of a river or road) follow a winding course. ■ (of a person) wander at random. ■ [intrans.] (of a speaker or text) proceed aimlessly or with little purpose. ▶ n. (usu. **meanders**) a winding curve or bend of a river or road: *the river flows in sweeping meanders.* ■ [in sing.] a circuitous journey, esp. an aimless one. ■ an ornamental pattern of winding or interlocking lines, e.g., in a mosaic. [16th C. (as a n.): from L. *maeander*, from Gk. *Maiandros*, the name of a river (see MENDERES).]

mean free path ▶ n. Physics the average distance traveled by a gas molecule or other particle between collisions with other particles.

mean·ie /'mēnē/ (also **mean·y**) ▶ n. (pl. **mean·ies**) informal a mean or small-minded person.

mean·ing /'mēniNG/ ▶ n. what is meant by something. ■ implied or explicit significance: *a look full of meaning.* ■ important or worthwhile quality; purpose. ▶ adj. [attrib.] intended to communicate something that is not directly expressed: *she gave Gabriel a meaning look.* — **mean·ing·ly** adv. [ME: verbal n. from MEAN[1].]

mean·ing·ful /'mēniNGfəl/ ▶ adj. having meaning. ■ having a serious, important, or useful quality or purpose. ■ communicating something that is not directly expressed. ■ Logic having a recognizable function in a logical language or other sign system. — **mean·ing·ful·ly** adv. **mean·ing·ful·ness** n.

mean·ing·less /'mēniNGlis/ ▶ adj. having no meaning or significance. ■ having no purpose or reason. — **mean·ing·less·ly** adv. **mean·ing·less·ness** n.

means /mēnz/ ▶ plural n. **1** [usu. treated as sing.] (often **means of something** or **means to do something**) an action or system by which a result is brought about. **2** money; financial resources. ■ resources; capability: *every country in the world has the means to make ethanol.* ■ wealth: *a man of means.*
– PHRASES **beyond** (or **within**) **one's means** beyond (or within) one's budget or income. **by all means** of course; certainly (granting a permission). **by any means** (or **by any manner of means**) (following a negative) in any way; at all. **by means of** with the help of. **by no means** (or **by no manner of means**) not at all; certainly not. **a means to an end** a thing that is not valued or important in itself but is useful in achieving an aim. [ME: pl. of MEAN[3].]

mean sea lev·el ▶ n. the sea level halfway between the mean levels of high and low water.

means of production ▶ n. (esp. in a political context) the facilities and resources for producing goods: *in this society, the means of production are communally owned.*

mean so·lar day ▶ n. Astron. the time between successive passages of the mean sun across the meridian.

mean so·lar time ▶ n. Astron. time as calculated by the motion of the mean sun. The time shown by an ordinary clock corresponds to mean solar time. Compare with APPARENT SOLAR TIME.

mean-spir·it·ed ▶ adj. unkind and ungenerous; unwilling to help others.

means test ▶ n. an official investigation into someone's financial circumstances. ▶ v. (**means-test**) [trans.] [usu. as adj.] (**means-tested**) make (a payment, etc.) conditional on a means test. ■ subject (someone) to a means test.

mean sun ▶ n. an imaginary sun conceived as moving through the sky throughout the year at a constant speed equal to the mean rate of the real sun, used in calculating mean solar time.

meant /ment/ past and past participle of MEAN[1].

mean·time /'mēn,tīm/ ▶ adv. (also **in the meantime**) meanwhile: *in the meantime, I'll make some inquiries.* [ME (as a n.): from MEAN[3] + TIME.]

mean time ▶ n. another term for MEAN SOLAR TIME. See also GREENWICH MEAN TIME.

mean·while /'mēn,(h)wīl/ ▶ adv. (also **in the meanwhile**) in the intervening period of time. ■ at the same time: *meanwhile, make a white sauce.* [ME: from MEAN[3] + WHILE.]

Mea·ny /'mēnē/, George (1894–1980), US labor leader. He was president of the AFL-CIO 1955–79.

mean·y /'mēnē/ ▶ n. var. of MEANIE.

meas. ▶ abbr. ■ measurable; measured; measurement.

mea·sles /'mēzəlz/ ▶ plural n. (often **the measles**) [treated as sing.] an infectious viral disease causing fever and a red rash on the skin. ■ a disease of pigs and other animals caused by the encysted larvae of the human tapeworm. [ME *maseles*, prob. from MDu. *masel* 'pustule.']

mea·sly /'mēzlē/ ▶ adj. (**mea·sli·er**, **mea·sli·est**) informal contemptibly small or few: *three measly votes.* [16th C.: from MEASLES + -Y[1].]

meas·ur·a·ble /'meZH(ə)rəbəl/ ▶ adj. that can be measured. ■ large enough to be measured; noticeable; definite. — **meas·ur·a·bil·i·ty** /,meZH(ə)rə'bilətē/ n. **meas·ur·a·bly** adv.

meas·ure /'meZHər/ ▶ v. [trans.] **1** ascertain the size, amount, or degree of (something) by using an instrument or device marked in standard units or by comparing it with an object of known size. ■ be of (a specified size or degree). ■ ascertain the size and proportions of (someone) in order to make or provide clothes for them. ■ (**measure something out**) take an exact quantity or fixed amount of something. ■ estimate or assess the extent, quality, value, or effect of (something). ■ (**measure someone/something against**) judge someone or something by comparison with (a certain standard). ■ [intrans.] (**measure up**) reach the required or expected standard; fulfill expectations. ■ scrutinize (someone) keenly in order to form an assessment of them. **2** consider (one's words or actions) carefully. ▶ n. **1** a plan or course of action taken to achieve a particular purpose: *cost-cutting measures.* ■ a legislative bill: *the Senate passed the measure.* **2** a standard unit used to express the size, amount, or degree of something: *tables of weights and measures.* ■ a system or scale of such units: *imperial measure.* ■ a container of standard capacity used for taking fixed amounts of a substance. ■ a particular amount of something. ■ a standard official amount of an alcoholic drink as served in a licensed establishment. ■ a graduated rod or tape used for ascertaining the size of something. ■ Print. the width of a full line of type or print, typically expressed in picas. ■ Math. a quantity contained in another an exact number of times; a divisor. **3** a certain quantity or degree of something. ■ an indication or means of assessing the degree, extent, or quality of something. **4** the rhythm

of a piece of poetry or a piece of music. ■ a particular metrical unit or group: *measures of two or three syllables.* ■ any of the sections, typically of equal time value, into which a musical composition is divided, shown on a score by vertical lines across the staff. **5** (**measures**) [with adj.] a group of rock strata.
– PHRASES **beyond measure** to a very great extent. **for good measure** in addition to what has already been done, said, or given. [ME: from OFr. *mesure*, from L. *mensura*, from *mens-* 'measured,' from the v. *metiri*.]

meas·ured /ˈmezHərd/ ▶ **adj.** having a slow, regular rhythm: *he walks with confident, measured steps.* ■ (of speech or writing) carefully considered; deliberate and restrained: *his measured prose.* — **meas·ured·ly adv.**

meas·ure·less /ˈmezHərlis/ ▶ **adj.** having no bounds or limits; unlimited: *Otto had measureless charm.*

meas·ure·ment /ˈmezHərmənt/ ▶ **n.** the action of measuring something: *accurate measurement is essential.* ■ the size, length, or amount of something, as established by measuring. ■ a system of measuring.

meas·ur·ing cup /ˈmezH(ə)riNG/ ▶ **n.** a cup marked in graded amounts, used for measuring ingredients.

meas·ur·ing tape ▶ **n.** another term for TAPE MEASURE.

meas·ur·ing worm ▶ **n.** another term for INCHWORM.

meat /mēt/ ▶ **n.** the flesh of an animal as food. ■ the flesh of a person's body: *put some meat on your bones!* ■ the edible part of fruits or nuts. ■ (**the meat of**) the essence or chief part of something.
– PHRASES **meat and potatoes** ordinary but fundamental things; basic ingredients. **one man's meat is another man's poison** proverb things liked or enjoyed by one person may be distasteful to another. — **meat·less adj.** [OE *mete* 'food' or 'article of food' (as in *sweetmeat*), of Gmc. origin.]

meat·ball /ˈmēt,bôl/ ▶ **n.** a ball of minced or chopped meat, usually beef, with added seasonings. ■ informal a dull, stupid, or foolish person.

meat grind·er ▶ **n.** fig. a destructive process: *trench warfare was the meat grinder that every soldier dreaded.*

Meath /mēTH; mēTH/ a county in the eastern part of the Republic of Ireland; county town, Navan.

meat·head /ˈmēt,hed/ ▶ **n.** informal, offens. a stupid person.

meat·hook /ˈmēt,ho͝ok/ ▶ **n.** a sharp metal hook of a kind used to hang meat carcasses. ■ (**meathooks**) informal a person's hands or arms.

meat loaf (also **meat·loaf**) ▶ **n.** minced or chopped meat, usually beef, with added seasonings, molded into the shape of a loaf and baked.

meat mar·ket ▶ **n.** informal a meeting place such as a bar or nightclub for people seeking sexual encounters.

me·a·tus /mēˈātəs/ ▶ **n.** (pl. same or **-tus·es**) Anat. an opening leading to the interior of the body. ■ (also **ex·ter·nal au·di·to·ry me·a·tus**) the passage leading into the ear. [ME: from L., 'passage,' from *meare* 'to flow, run.']

meat·y /ˈmētē/ ▶ **adj.** (**meat·i·er, meat·i·est**) consisting of or full of meat: *a meaty flavor.* ■ fleshy; brawny. ■ full of substance; satisfying. — **meat·i·ly adv. meat·i·ness n.**

Mec·ca /ˈmekə/ a city in western Saudi Arabia, considered by Muslims to be the holiest city of Islam; pop. 618,000. It is the birthplace in AD 570 of the prophet Muhammad. Arabic name MAKKAH. ■ [as n.] (**a Mecca**) a place that attracts people of a particular group or with a particular interest. — **Mec·can adj. & n.**

mech /mek/ ▶ **n.** informal a mechanic.

me·chan·ic /məˈkanik/ ▶ **n.** a person who repairs and maintains machinery: *a car mechanic.* [ME: via OFr. or L. from Gk. *mēkhanikos*, from *mēkhanē* (see MACHINE).]

me·chan·i·cal /məˈkanikəl/ ▶ **adj.** **1** working or produced by machines or machinery: *a mechanical device.* ■ of or relating to machines or machinery. **2** (of a person or action) not having or showing thought or spontaneity; automatic. **3** relating to physical forces or motion; physical. ■ (of a theory) explaining phenomena in terms only of physical processes. ■ of or relating to mechanics as a science. ▶ **n.** **1** (**mechanicals**) the working parts of a machine. **2** Print. a completed assembly of artwork and copy. — **me·chan·i·cal·ly adv. me·chan·i·cal·ness n.**

me·chan·i·cal ad·van·tage ▶ **n.** the ratio of the force produced by a machine to the force applied to it, used in assessing the performance of a machine.

me·chan·i·cal draw·ing ▶ **n.** a scale drawing of a mechanical or architectural structure done with precision instruments. ■ the action or process of making such drawings.

me·chan·i·cal en·gi·neer·ing ▶ **n.** the branch of engineering dealing with machines. — **me·chan·i·cal en·gi·neer n.**

me·chan·i·cal pen·cil ▶ **n.** a pencil with a thin replaceable lead that may be extended by twisting the outer casing as the point is worn away.

mech·a·ni·cian /,mekəˈnisHən/ ▶ **n.** a person skilled in the design or construction of machinery.

me·chan·ics /məˈkaniks/ ▶ **plural n.** **1** [treated as sing.] the branch of applied mathematics dealing with motion and forces producing motion. ■ machinery as a subject; engineering. **2** the machinery or working parts of something. ■ the way in which something is done or operated; the practicalities or details of something.

mech·an·ism /ˈmekə,nizəm/ ▶ **n.** **1** a system of parts working together in a machine; a piece of machinery. **2** a natural or established process by which something takes place or is brought about. ■ a contrivance in the plot of a literary work. [17th C.: from mod. L. *mechanismus*, from Gk. *mēkhanē* (see MACHINE).]

mech·a·nist /ˈmekənist/ ▶ **n.** **1** Philos. a person who believes in the doctrine of mechanism. **2** a person skilled in the construction of machinery.

mech·a·nis·tic /,mekəˈnistik/ ▶ **adj.** of or relating to theories that explain phenomena in purely physical or deterministic terms. ■ determined by physical processes alone. — **mech·a·nis·ti·cal·ly adv.**

mech·a·nize /ˈmekə,nīz/ ▶ **v.** [trans.] (often **be mechanized**) introduce machines or automatic devices into. ■ equip (a military force) with modern weapons and vehicles. ■ give a mechanical character to: *public virtue cannot be mechanized or formulated.* — **mech·a·ni·za·tion** /,mekənəˈzāsHən/ **n. mech·a·niz·er n.**

mech·a·no·re·cep·tor /,mekə,nōriˈseptər/ ▶ **n.** Zool. a sense organ or cell that responds to mechanical stimuli such as touch or sound. — **mech·a·no·re·cep·tive** /-ˈseptiv/ **adj.**

Mech·lin /ˈmeklin/ (also **Mech·lin lace**) ▶ **n.** lace made in the Belgian city of Mechelen (formerly Mechlin).

Meck·len·burg-West Pom·er·a·ni·a /ˈmeklən,bərg; ,päməˈrānēə/ a state in northeastern Germany; capital, Schwerin.

MEcon ▶ **abbr.** Master of Economics.

me·co·ni·um /miˈkōnēəm/ ▶ **n.** Med. the dark green substance forming the first feces of a newborn infant. [18th C.: from L., lit. 'poppy juice,' from Gk. *mēkōnion*, from *mēkōn* 'poppy.']

Me·cop·ter·a /miˈkäptərə/ Entomol. an order of insects that comprises the scorpionflies. — **me·cop·ter·an n. & adj.** [mod. L. (pl.), from Gk. *mēkos* 'length' + *pteron* 'wing.']

MEd ▶ **abbr.** Master of Education.

med. ▶ **abbr.** ■ informal medical: *med. school.* ■ medium.

mé·dail·lon /,mädīˈyōN/ ▶ **n.** (pl. same) a small flat round or oval cut of meat or fish. [Fr., lit. 'medallion.']

med·al /ˈmedl/ ▶ **n.** a metal disk with an inscription or design, made to commemorate an event or as an award. ▶ **v.** (**med·aled, med·al·ing**; also esp. Brit. **med·alled, med·al·ling**) [intrans.] earn a medal, esp. in an athletic contest. — **me·dal·lic** /məˈdalik/ **adj.** [16th C.: from Fr. *médaille*, from Ital. *medaglia*, from med. L. *medalia* 'half a denarius,' from L. *medialis* 'medial.']

med·al·ist /ˈmedl-ist/ (Brit. **med·al·list**) ▶ **n.** **1** an athlete or other person awarded a medal. **2** the lowest scorer in a qualifying round of a golf tournament. **3** an engraver or designer of medals.

me·dal·lion /məˈdalyən/ ▶ **n.** a piece of jewelry in the shape of a medal, typically worn as a pendant. ■ an oval or circular painting, panel, or design used for decoration. ■ another term for MÉDAILLON. [17th C.: from Fr. *médaillon*, from Ital. *medaglione*, augmentative of *medaglia* (see MEDAL).]

Med·al of Hon·or (also **Congressional Medal of Honor**) ▶ **n.** the highest US military decoration, awarded by Congress to a member of the armed forces for gallantry and bravery in combat.

Me·dan /mäˈdän/ a city in Indonesia, in northeastern Sumatra; pop. 1,730,000.

Med·a·war /ˈmedəwər/, Sir Peter (Brian) (1915–87), English immunologist. He showed that the rejection of tissue grafts was the result of an immune mechanism. Nobel Prize for Physiology or Medicine (1960).

med·dle /ˈmedl/ ▶ **v.** [intrans.] interfere in or busy oneself unduly with something that is not one's concern. ■ (**meddle with**) touch or handle (something) without permission: *don't meddle with my things.* — **med·dler** /ˈmedlər; ˈmedl-ər/ **n.** [ME (in the sense 'mingle, mix'): from OFr. *medler*, var. of *mesler*, based on L. *miscere* 'to mix.']

med·dle·some /ˈmedlsəm/ ▶ **adj.** interfering. — **med·dle·some·ly adv. med·dle·some·ness n.**

Mede /mēd/ ▶ **n.** a member of an Iranian people who inhabited ancient Media. [from L. *Medi*, Gk. *Mēdoi*, pl. forms.]

Me·de·a /miˈdēə/ Gk. Mythol. a sorceress, daughter of Aeetes king of Colchis, who helped Jason to obtain the Golden Fleece and married him.

Me·del·lín /ˈmedə,yēn; ,medəˈyēn/ a city in eastern Colombia; pop. 1,581,000. It is considered the hub of the Colombian drug trade.

med·e·vac /ˈmedi,vak/ (also **med·i·vac**) ▶ **n.** the evacuation of military or other casualties to the hospital in a helicopter or airplane. ▶ **v.** (**-vacked, -vack·ing**) [with obj. and adverbial of direction] transport to the hospital in this way. [1960s: blend of MEDICAL and EVACUATION.]

med·fly /ˈmed,flī/ ▶ **n.** (pl. **-flies**) another term for MEDITERRANEAN FRUIT FLY.

Med. Gr. ▶ **abbr.** Medieval Greek.

Me·di·a /ˈmēdēə/ an ancient region of Asia, southwest of the Caspian Sea. — **Me·di·an adj.**

me·di·a[1] /ˈmēdēə/ ▶ **n.** **1** plural form of MEDIUM. **2** (usu. **the media**) [treated as sing. or pl.] the main means of mass communication regarded collectively: [as adj.] *the campaign won media attention.*

me·di·a[2] ▶ **n.** (pl. **-di·ae** /-dē,ē; -dē,ī/) **1** Anat. an intermediate layer, esp. in the wall of a blood vessel. **2** Phonet. a voiced unaspirated stop; (in Greek) a voiced stop. [19th C.: from L., fem. of *medius* 'middle.'] [19th C.: shortening of mod. L. *tunica* (or *membrana*) *media* 'middle sheath (or layer).']

me·di·a·cy /ˈmēdēəsē/ ▶ **n.** the quality of being mediate.

me·di·ae·val ▶ **adj.** var. of MEDIEVAL.

me·di·a e·vent ▶ **n.** an event intended primarily to attract publicity: *a staged media event.*

me•di•a•gen•ic /ˌmēdēəˈjenik/ ▶**adj.** tending to convey a favorable impression when reported by the media, esp. by television.

me•di•al /ˈmēdēəl/ ▶**adj.** tech. situated in the middle, in particular: ■ Anat. & Zool. situated near the median plane of the body or the midline of an organ. The opposite of LATERAL. ■ Phonet. (of a speech sound) in the middle of a word. ■ Phonet. (esp. of a vowel) pronounced in the middle of the mouth; central. — **me•di•al•ly** adv. [16th C.: from late L. *medialis*, from L. *medius* 'middle.']

me•di•an /ˈmēdēən/ ▶**adj.** [attrib.] **1** denoting or relating to a value or quantity lying at the midpoint of a frequency distribution of observed values or quantities, such that there is an equal probability of falling above or below it: *the median duration was four months.* ■ denoting the middle term of a series arranged in order of magnitude, or (if there is no middle term) the average of the middle two terms. **2** tech., esp. Anat. situated in the middle. ▶**n.** **1** the median value of a range of values. **2** (also **median strip**) the strip of land between the lanes of opposing traffic on a divided highway. **3** Geom. a straight line drawn from any vertex of a triangle to the middle of the opposite side. — **me•di•an•ly** adv. [ME (denoting a median vein or nerve): from med. L. *medianus*, from *medius* 'middle, middle of.']

me•di•ant /ˈmēdēənt/ ▶**n.** Music the third note of the diatonic scale of any key. [18th C.: from Fr. *médiante*, from Ital. *mediante* 'coming between,' pres. part. of obs. *mediare* 'come between,' from late L. *mediare* 'be in the middle of.']

me•di•as•ti•num /ˌmēdēəˈstīnəm/ ▶**n.** (pl. **-as•ti•na** /-əˈstīnə/) Anat. a membranous partition between two body cavities or two parts of an organ. — **me•di•as•ti•nal** /-ˈstīnl/ adj. [ME: neut. of med. L. *mediastinus* 'medial,' based on L. *medius* 'middle.']

me•di•a stud•ies ▶**plural n.** [usu. treated as sing.] the study of the mass media, esp. as an academic subject.

me•di•ate ▶**v.** /ˈmēdēˌāt/ **1** [intrans.] intervene between people in a dispute in order to bring about an agreement or reconciliation. ■ [trans.] intervene in (a dispute) to bring about an agreement. ■ [trans.] bring about (an agreement or solution) by intervening in a dispute. **2** [trans.] tech. bring about (a result such as a physiological effect). ■ be a means of conveying: *this important ministry of mediating the power of the word.* ■ form a connecting link between: *structures that mediate gender divisions.* — **me•di•a•tion** /ˌmēdēˈāsʜən/ n. **me•di•a•tor** /ˈmēdēˌātər/ n. **me•di•a•to•ry** /ˈmēdēəˌtôrē/ adj. [ME (as an adj. in the sense 'interposed'): from late L. *mediatus* 'placed in the middle,' past part. of the v. *mediare*, from L. *medius* 'middle.']

med•ic[1] /ˈmedik/ ▶**n.** informal a medical practitioner. ■ Mil. a medical corpsman who dispenses first aid at combat sites. [17th C.: from L. *medicus* 'physician,' from *mederi* 'heal.']

med•ic[2] ▶**n.** var. of MEDICK.

Med•i•caid /ˈmediˌkād/ (in the US) a federal system of health insurance for those requiring financial assistance.

med•i•cal /ˈmedikəl/ ▶**adj.** of or relating to the science of medicine, or to the treatment of illness and injuries. ■ of or relating to conditions requiring medical but not surgical treatment: *a medical ward.* — **med•i•cal•ly** adv.

med•i•cal•ize /ˈmedikəˌlīz/ ▶**v.** [trans.] view (something) in medical terms; treat as a medical problem. — **med•i•cal•i•za•tion** /ˌmedikələˈzāsʜən/ n.

med•i•cal ju•ris•pru•dence ▶**n.** the branch of law relating to medicine. ■ forensic medicine.

med•i•cal prac•ti•tion•er ▶**n.** a physician or surgeon.

me•dic•a•ment /məˈdikəmənt; ˈmedikəˌment/ ▶**n.** a substance used for medical treatment. [ME: via Fr. from L. *medicamentum*, from *medicari* (see MEDICATE).]

Med•i•care /ˈmediˌke(ə)r/ (in the US) a federal system of health insurance for people over 65 years of age and for certain younger people with disabilities.

med•i•cate /ˈmediˌkāt/ ▶**v.** [trans.] (often **be medicated**) administer medicine or a drug to (someone). ■ treat (a condition) using medicine or a drug. ■ add a medicinal substance to (a dressing or product). — **med•i•ca•tive** /-ˌkātiv/ adj.

med•i•ca•tion /ˌmedəˈkāsʜən/ ▶**n.** a substance used for medical treatment, esp. a medicine or drug. ■ treatment using drugs.

Med•i•ce•an /ˌmediˈcʜēən/ ▶**adj.** of or relating to the Medici family.

Med•i•ci /ˈmedicʜē/ (also **de' Med•i•ci** /də/) an Italian family of bankers and merchants. Cosimo and Lorenzo de' Medici were patrons of the arts in Florence; the family also provided four popes (including Leo X) and two queens of France (Catherine de' Medici and Marie de Médicis).

me•dic•i•nal /məˈdisənl/ ▶**adj.** (of a substance or plant) having healing properties: *medicinal herbs.* ■ relating to or involving medicines or drugs. ▶**n.** a medicinal substance. — **me•dic•i•nal•ly** adv.

med•i•cine /ˈmedisən/ ▶**n.** **1** the science or practice of the diagnosis, treatment, and prevention of disease (in technical use often taken to exclude surgery). **2** a compound or preparation used for the treatment or prevention of disease, esp. a drug or drugs. ■ such substances collectively: *food and medicine.* **3** (among North American Indians and some other peoples) a spell, charm, or fetish believed to have healing, protective, or other power.

– PHRASES **give someone a dose** (or **taste**) **of their own medicine** give someone the same bad treatment that they have given to others. **take one's medicine** submit to something disagreeable. [ME: via OFr. from L. *medicina*, from *medicus* 'physician.']

med•i•cine ball ▶**n.** a large, heavy solid ball thrown and caught for exercise.

Med•i•cine Bow Moun•tains /ˈmedisin bō/ a range of the Rocky Mountains in Colorado and Wyoming.

Med•i•cine Hat a commercial and industrial city in southeastern Alberta in Canada, on the South Saskatchewan River; pop. 43,625.

med•i•cine man ▶**n.** (among North American Indians and some other peoples) a person believed to have healing powers and of seeing the future; a shaman.

Mé•di•cis, Marie de, see MARIE DE MÉDICIS.

med•ick /ˈmedik/ ▶**n.** a plant (genus *Medicago*) of the pea family related to alfalfa. Some kinds are grown for fodder or green manure and some kinds are troublesome weeds. Its several species include the prostrate **black medick** (*M. lupulina*). [ME: from L. *medica*, from Gk. *Mēdikē (poa)* 'Median (grass).']

med•i•co /ˈmediˌkō/ ▶**n.** (pl. **-cos**) informal a medical practitioner or student. [17th C.: via Ital. from L. *medicus* 'physician.']

medico- ▶**comb. form** relating to the field of medicine: *medico-social.* [from L. *medicus* 'physician.']

me•di•e•val /ˌmed(ē)ˈēvəl; ˌmē-; ˌmid-/ (also **me•di•ae•val**) ▶**adj.** of or relating to the Middle Ages. ■ informal, derog. very old-fashioned or primitive. — **me•di•e•val•ism** n. **me•di•e•val•ist** n. **me•di•e•val•ize** v. **me•di•e•val•ly** adv. [19th C.: from mod. L. *medium aevum* 'middle age' + -AL.]

me•di•e•val Lat•in ▶**n.** Latin of about AD 600–1500.

Me•di•na /məˈdīnə/ a city in western Saudi Arabia; pop. 500,000. It is Muhammad's burial place. Arabic name AL MADINAH.

me•di•na /məˈdēnə/ ▶**n.** the old Arab or non-European quarter of a North African town. [Arab., lit. 'town.']

me•di•o•cre /ˌmēdēˈōkər/ ▶**adj.** of only moderate quality; not very good: *a mediocre actor.* — **me•di•o•cre•ly** adv. [16th C.: from Fr. *médiocre*, from L. *mediocris*, from *medius* 'middle' + *ocris* 'rugged mountain.']

me•di•oc•ri•ty /ˌmēdēˈäkrətē/ ▶**n.** (pl. **-ties**) the quality or state of being mediocre. ■ a person of mediocre ability.

med•i•tate /ˈmedəˌtāt/ ▶**v.** [intrans.] think deeply or focus for a time for spiritual purposes or to relax. ■ (**meditate on/upon**) think deeply or carefully about (something). ■ [trans.] plan mentally; consider. — **med•i•ta•tor** /-ˌtātər/ n. [16th C.: from L. *meditat-* 'contemplated,' from the v. *meditari*, from a base meaning 'measure'; rel. to METE[1].]

med•i•ta•tion /ˌmedəˈtāsʜən/ ▶**n.** the action or practice of meditating: *a life of meditation.* ■ a written or spoken discourse expressing considered thoughts on a subject: *his letters are meditations.*

med•i•ta•tive /ˈmedəˌtātiv/ ▶**adj.** of, involving, or absorbed in meditation or considered thought. — **med•i•ta•tive•ly** adv. **med•i•ta•tive•ness** n.

Med•i•ter•ra•ne•an /ˌmedətəˈrānēən/ ▶**adj.** of or characteristic of the Mediterranean Sea, the countries bordering it, or their inhabitants. ■ (of a person's complexion) relatively dark. ▶**n.** **1** the Mediterranean Sea or the countries bordering it. **2** a native of a country on the Mediterranean.

Med•i•ter•ra•ne•an cli•mate ▶**n.** a climate distinguished by warm, wet winters under prevailing westerly winds and calm, hot, dry summers.

Med•i•ter•ra•ne•an fruit fly ▶**n.** a fruit fly (*Ceratitis capitata*, family Tephritidae) whose larvae can be a serious pest of citrus and other fruits. Also called MEDFLY.

Med•i•ter•ra•ne•an Sea an almost landlocked sea between southern Europe, the northern coast of Africa, and southwestern Asia.

me•di•um /ˈmēdēəm/ ▶**n.** (pl. **-di•a** /-dēə/ or **-di•ums**) **1** an agency or means of doing something. ■ a means by which something is communicated or expressed. **2** the intervening substance through which impressions are conveyed to the senses or a force acts on objects at a distance. ■ the substance in which an organism lives or is cultured: *grow bacteria in a nutrient-rich medium.* **3** a particular form of storage material for digitized information, such as magnetic tape or discs. **4** a liquid (e.g., oil or water) with which pigments are mixed to make paint. ■ the material or form used by an artist, composer, or writer: *oil paint is the most popular medium for glazing.* **5** (pl. **-di•ums**) a person claiming to be in contact with the spirits of the dead. **6** the middle quality or state between two extremes; a reasonable balance: *a happy medium.* ▶**adj.** about halfway between two extremes of size or another quality; average: *medium-length hair.* ■ (of cooked meat) between rare and well-done. — **me•di•um•ism** n. (in sense 4). **me•di•um•is•tic** /ˌmēdēəˈmistik/ adj. (in sense 4). **me•di•um•ship** n. (in sense 4). [16th C.: from L., lit. 'middle,' neut. of *medius*.]

me•di•um fre•quen•cy ▶**n.** a radio frequency between 300 kilohertz and 3 megahertz.

me•di•um-range ▶**adj.** (of an aircraft or missile) able to travel or operate over a medium distance.

med•i•vac ▶**n.** & **v.** var. of MEDEVAC.

med•lar /ˈmedlər/ ▶**n.** a small, bushy tree (*Mespilus germanica*) of the rose family that bears small, brown, applelike fruits. ■ the fruit of this tree, which is edible only after it has begun to decay. [ME: from OFr. *medler*, from *medle* 'medlar fruit,' from L. *mespila*, from Gk. *mespilē*, *mespilon*.]

Med. Lat. ▶ abbr. Medieval Latin.

med·ley /ˈmedlē/ ▶ n. (pl. **-leys**) a varied mixture of people or things; a miscellany. ■ a collection of songs or other musical items performed as a continuous piece. ■ a swimming race in which contestants swim sections in different strokes, either individually or in relay teams. [ME: from OFr. *medlee*, var. of *meslee* 'melee,' based on med. L. *misculare* 'to mix.']

Mé·doc /mäˈdôk; -ˈdäk/ ▶ n. (pl. same) a red wine produced in the Médoc area in southwestern France.

me·dre·se /məˈdresə/ ▶ n. var. of MADRASA.

me·dul·la /məˈdələ/ ▶ n. Anat. the inner region of an organ or tissue, esp. when it is distinguishable from the outer region or cortex. ■ short for MEDULLA OBLONGATA. ■ Bot. the soft internal tissue or pith of a plant. — **med·ul·lar·y** /mədələrē; ˈmejəlerē/ adj. [ME (in the sense 'bone marrow'): from L., 'pith or marrow.']

me·dul·la ob·long·a·ta /ˌäbˌlôNGˈgätə/ ▶ n. the continuation of the spinal cord within the skull, containing control centers for the heart and lungs. [17th C.: mod. L., lit. 'elongated medulla.']

Me·du·sa /məˈd(y)o͞osə; -zə/ Gk. Mythol. the only mortal Gorgon, whom Perseus killed.

me·du·sa /məˈdo͞osə; -zə/ ▶ n. (pl. **-sae** /-sē; -sī; -zē; -zī/ or **-sas**) Zool. a free-swimming sexual form of a coelenterate such as a jellyfish, typically having an umbrella-shaped body with stinging tentacles around the edge. Compare with POLYP. ■ a jellyfish. [18th C.: MEDUSA.]

me·du·soid /məˈdo͞oˌsoid; -ˌzoid/ Zool. ▶ adj. of, relating to, or resembling a medusa or jellyfish. ■ of, relating to, or denoting the medusa phase in the life cycle of a coelenterate. Compare with POLYPOID (sense 1). ▶ n. a medusa or jellyfish. ■ a medusoid reproductive bud.

meek /mēk/ ▶ adj. quiet, gentle, and easily imposed on; submissive: *the meek compliance of our politicians.* — **meek·ly** adv. **meek·ness** n. [ME *me(o)c*, from ON *mjúkr* 'soft, gentle.']

meer·kat /ˈmi(ə)rˌkat/ ▶ n. a small southern African mongoose (*Suricata* and other genera), esp. the suricate. See illustration at SURICATE. [18th C.: from South Afr. Dutch, from Du., 'long-tailed monkey,' appar. from *meer* 'sea' + *kat* 'cat.']

meer·schaum /ˈmi(ə)rˌSHôm; -SHəm/ ▶ n. a claylike material consisting of hydrated magnesium silicate. ■ (also **meerschaum pipe**) a tobacco pipe with the bowl made from this. [18th C.: from Ger., lit. 'sea-foam,' from *Meer* 'sea' + *Schaum* 'foam.']

meet /mēt/ ▶ v. (past and past part. **met**) [trans.] **1** come into the presence or company of (someone) by chance or arrangement: [intrans.] *we met for lunch.* ■ make the acquaintance of (someone) for the first time. ■ [intrans.] (of a group of people) assemble for a particular purpose. ■ [intrans.] (**meet with**) have a meeting with (someone). ■ go to a place and wait there for (a person or their means of transport) to arrive. ■ play or oppose in a contest: *the US will meet Brazil.* ■ touch; join. ■ encounter or be faced with (a particular fate, situation, attitude, or reaction). ■ (**meet something with**) have (a particular reaction) to. ■ [intrans.] (**meet with**) receive (a particular reaction): *it doesn't meet with your approval.* **2** fulfill or satisfy (a need, requirement, or condition). ■ deal with or respond to (a problem or challenge) satisfactorily. ■ pay (a financial claim or obligation). ▶ n. an organized event at which a number of races or other sporting contests are held: *a swim meet.*

– PHRASES **meet someone's eye** (or **eyes**) be visible. **meet someone's eye** (or **eyes** or **gaze**) look directly at someone. **meet someone halfway** compromise. **meet one's Maker** see MAKER. **meet one's match** see MATCH[1]. **there's more to someone/something than meets the eye** a person or situation is more complex or interesting than they appear. [OE *mētan* 'come upon, come across,' of Gmc. origin; rel. to Du. *moeten*, 'meet.']

meet·ing /ˈmētiNG/ ▶ n. **1** an assembly of people for discussion or entertainment. ■ a gathering of people, esp. Quakers, for worship. **2** a coming together of two or more people, by chance or arrangement: *he intrigued her on their first meeting.*

– PHRASES **a meeting of (the) minds** an understanding or agreement between people.

meet·ing·house /ˈmētiNGˌhous/ (also **meet·ing house**) ▶ n. a Quaker place of worship.

meg /meg/ ▶ n. (pl. same or **megs**) short for MEGABYTE.

meg·a /ˈmegə/ informal ▶ adj. very large; huge: *a mega city.* ■ of great significance or importance. ▶ adv. [as submodifier] extremely: *they are mega rich.* [1980s: independent usage of MEGA-.]

mega- ▶ comb. form **1** very large: *megalith.* **2** (in units of measurement) denoting a factor of one million (10^6): *megahertz* | *megadeath.* **3** Comput. denoting a factor of 2^{20}. [from Gk. *megas* 'great.']

meg·a·bit /ˈmegəˌbit/ ▶ n. Comput. a unit of data size or (when expressed per second) network speed, equal to one million or (strictly) 1,048,576 bits.

meg·a·buck /ˈmegəˌbək/ ▶ n. (usu. **megabucks**) informal a million dollars. ■ a huge sum of money: [as adj.] *megabuck salaries.*

meg·a·byte /ˈmegəˌbīt/ (abbr.: **Mb** or **MB**) ▶ n. Comput. a unit of information equal to 2^{20} bytes or, loosely, one million bytes.

Meg·a·chi·rop·ter·a /ˌmegəˌkīˈräptərə/ Zool. a division of bats that comprises the fruit bats and flying foxes. — **meg·a·chi·rop·ter·an** /-tərən/ n. & adj.

meg·a·death /ˈmegəˌdeTH/ ▶ n. a unit used in quantifying the casualties of nuclear war, equal to the deaths of one million people.

meg·a·dose /ˈmegəˌdōs/ ▶ n. a dose many times larger than the usual, esp. of a vitamin or drug.

Me·gae·ra /məˈji(ə)rə/ Gk. Mythol. one of the Furies.

meg·a·flop[1] /ˈmegəˌfläp/ ▶ n. Comput. a unit of computing speed equal to one million floating-point operations per second. [1970s: back-form. from *megaflops* (see MEGA-, -FLOP).]

meg·a·flop[2] ▶ n. informal a complete failure.

meg·a·ga·mete /ˌmegəˈgamˌēt; ˌmegəgəˈmēt/ ▶ n. another term for MACROGAMETE.

meg·a·hertz /ˈmegəˌhərts/ (abbr.: **MHz**) ▶ n. (pl. same) one million hertz, esp. as a measure of radiotransmission frequencies or computer clock speed.

meg·a·lith /ˈmegəˌliTH/ ▶ n. Archaeol. a large stone that forms a prehistoric monument. [19th C.: back-form. from MEGALITHIC.]

meg·a·lith·ic /ˌmegəˈliTHik/ ▶ adj. Archaeol. of, relating to, or denoting prehistoric monuments made of or containing megaliths. ■ (often **Megalithic**) of, relating to, or denoting prehistoric cultures characterized by the erection of megalithic monuments. ■ fig. massive. [19th C.: from MEGA- 'large' + Gk. *lithos* 'stone' + -IC.]

megalo- ▶ comb. form abnormally large or great. [from Gk. *megas, megal-* 'great.']

meg·a·lo·blast /ˈmegələˌblast/ ▶ n. Med. a large, abnormally developed red blood cell typical of certain forms of anemia, associated with a deficiency of folic acid or of vitamin B_{12}. — **meg·a·lo·blas·tic** /ˌmegəlōˈblastik/ adj.

meg·a·lo·ma·ni·a /ˌmegəlōˈmānēə/ ▶ n. obsession with the exercise of power. ■ delusion about one's own power or importance. — **meg·a·lo·man·ic** /-ˈmanik/ adj.

meg·a·lop·o·lis /ˌmegəˈläpələs/ ▶ n. a very large, heavily populated city or urban complex. [19th C.: from MEGALO- 'great' + Gk. *polis* 'city.']

meg·a·lo·saur /ˌmegələˈsôr/ (also **meg·a·lo·sau·rus** /-ˈsôrəs/) ▶ n. a large carnivorous bipedal dinosaur (genus *Megalosaurus*, suborder Theropoda, order Saurischia) of the mid Jurassic period, whose remains have been found only in England and France. It was the first dinosaur to be described and named (1824). — **meg·a·lo·sau·ri·an** /-ˈsôrēən/ adj. [mod. L., from MEGALO- 'great' + Gk. *sauros* 'lizard.']

meg·a·mouth /ˈmegəˌmouTH/ (also **megamouth shark**) ▶ n. a shark (*Megachasma pelagios*, family Megachasmidae) with a very large wide mouth and tiny teeth, first captured in 1976 off the Hawaiian Islands.

Meg·an's Law /ˈmegənz; ˈmā-/ ▶ n. a law from 1995 that requires authorities to notify communities of the whereabouts of convicted sex offenders. [*Megan* Kauka, a girl murdered by a convicted sex offender.]

meg·a·phone /ˈmegəˌfōn/ ▶ n. a large funnel-shaped device for amplifying and directing the voice. ▶ v. [trans.] utter through, or as if through, a megaphone. — **meg·a·phon·ic** /ˌmegəˈfänik/ adj.

meg·a·pix·el /ˈmegəˌpiksəl/ ▶ n. Comput. a unit of graphic resolution equivalent to 2^{20} or (strictly) 1,048,576 pixels.

meg·a·pode /ˈmegəˌpōd/ ▶ n. a large ground-dwelling Australasian and Southeast Asian bird (family Megapodiidae) that builds a large mound of debris to incubate its eggs by the heat of decomposition. Also called MOUND BUILDER. [19th C.: from mod. L. *Megapodius* (genus name), from MEGA- 'large' + Gk. *pous, pod-* 'foot.']

meg·a·spore /ˈmegəˌspôr/ ▶ n. Bot. the larger of the two kinds of spores produced by some ferns. Compare with MICROSPORE.

meg·a·star /ˈmegəˌstär/ ▶ n. informal a very famous person, esp. in the world of entertainment. — **meg·a·star·dom** /ˌmegəˈstärdəm/ n.

meg·a·ton /ˈmegəˌtən/ (abbr.: **MT**) ▶ n. a unit of explosive power chiefly used for nuclear weapons, equivalent to one million tons of TNT. — **meg·a·ton·nage** /ˌmegəˈtənij/ n.

meg·a·volt /ˈmegəˌvōlt/ (abbr.: **MV**) ▶ n. a unit of electromotive force equal to one million volts.

meg·a·watt /ˈmegəˌwät/ (abbr.: **MW**) ▶ n. a unit of power equal to one million watts.

me gen·er·a·tion ▶ n. a generation of people that are concerned chiefly with themselves.

Me·gha·la·ya /ˌmāgəˈlāə/ a small state in northeastern India.

Me·gid·do /miˈgidō/ an ancient city in northwestern Palestine, southeast of Haifa in present-day Israel.

Me·gil·lah /məˈgilə/ one of five books of the Hebrew scriptures (the Song of Solomon, Ruth, Lamentations, Ecclesiastes, and Esther). ■ [as n.] (**the whole megillah**) informal something in its entirety. [from Heb. *mĕgillāh*, lit. 'scroll.']

me·gilp /məˈgilp/ ▶ n. a mixture of mastic resin and linseed oil added to oil paints. [18th C.: of unknown origin.]

meg·ohm /ˈmegˌōm/ ▶ n. a unit of electrical resistance equal to one million ohms. [19th C.: from MEGA-.]

me·grim /ˈmēgrim/ ▶ n. archaic **1** (**megrims**) depression; low spirits. **2** a whim or fancy. **3** old-fashioned term for MIGRAINE. [ME: var. of MIGRAINE.]

Meh·ta /ˈmātä/, Zubin (1936–), US conductor; born in India. He has conducted several symphony orchestras, including the Los Angeles Philharmonic 1962–78 and the New York Philharmonic 1978–91.

Mei·ji /ˈmājē/ ▶ n. [usu. as adj.] the period when Japan was ruled by the emperor Meiji Tenno, marked by the modernization and westernization of the country.

Mei·ji Ten·no /ˈmāˈjē ˈtenˌō/ (1852–1912), emperor of Japan 1868–1912; born *Mutsuhito.* He encouraged Japan's rapid modernization and political reform.

mei·o·sis /mīˈōsəs/ ▶ n. (pl. **-ses** /-sēz/) **1** Biol. a type of cell division that results in two daughter cells each with half the chromosome number of the parent cell. Compare with MITOSIS. 2 another term for LITOTES. —**mei·ot·ic** /mī'ätik/ adj. **mei·ot·i·cal·ly** /-ik(ə)lē/ adv. [16th C.: mod. L., from Gk. *meiōsis*, from *meioun* 'lessen,' from *meiōn* 'less.']

Me·ir /mā'i(ə)r/, Golda (1898–1978), prime minister of Israel 1969–74; born in Ukraine; born *Goldie Mabovich*.

Meis·sen /'mīsən/ ▶n. a fine hard-paste porcelain from Meissen since 1710. Often called DRESDEN CHINA (see DRESDEN[2]). [named after the city of *Meissen* in eastern Germany.]

-meister ▶comb. form denoting a person regarded as skilled or prominent in a specified area of activity. [from Ger. *Meister* 'master.']

Mei·ster·sing·er /'mīstər,siNGər/ ▶n. (pl. same) a member of one of the guilds of German lyric poets and musicians that flourished 12th–17th century. [Ger., from *Meister* 'master' + *Singer* 'singer.']

Meit·ner /'mītnər/, Lise (1878–1968), Swedish physicist; born in Austria. She discovered the element protactinium with Otto Hahn in 1917.

meit·ner·i·um /mīt'ni(ə)rēəm/ ▶n. the chemical element of atomic number 109, a very unstable element made by high-energy atomic collisions. (Symbol: **Mt**) [mod. L., from the name of L. MEITNER.]

Me·kong /'mā'kôNG; -'mē-/ a river in Southeast Asia that rises in Tibet and flows to the South China Sea.

me·lae·na ▶n. British spelling of MELENA.

Me·la·ka /mə'läkə/ (also **Ma·lac·ca**) a state of Malaysia, on the southwestern coast of the Malay Peninsula. ■ its capital and chief port; pop. 88,000.

mel·a·mine /'melə,mēn/ ▶n. 1 Chem. a white crystalline compound, $(CNH_2)_3N_3$, made by heating cyanamide and used in making plastics. 2 (also **melamine resin**) a plastic used chiefly for laminated coatings, made by copolymerizing this compound with formaldehyde. [19th C.: from Ger. *melam* (an arbitrary formation) + AMINE.]

mel·an·cho·li·a /,melən'kōlēə/ ▶n. deep sadness or gloom; melancholy. ■ dated a mental condition marked by persistent depression and ill-founded fears. —**mel·an·cho·li·ac** /-'kōlē-ak/ n. & adj. [ME (denoting black bile): from late L. (see MELANCHOLY).]

mel·an·chol·y /'melən,kälē/ ▶n. a deep, pensive, and long-lasting sadness. ■ another term for MELANCHOLIA (as a mental condition). ■ hist. another term for BLACK BILE. ▶adj. sad, gloomy, or depressed. ■ causing or expressing sadness; depressing. —**mel·an·chol·ic** /,melən'kälik/ adj. **mel·an·chol·i·cal·ly** /,melən'käläk(ə)lē/ adv. [ME: from OFr. *melancolie*, via late L. from Gk. *melankholia*, from *melas, melan-* 'black' + *kholē* 'bile.']

Me·lanch·thon /mə'laNGkTHən; mā'länKHtôn/, Philipp (1497–1560), German reformer; born *Philipp Schwarzerd*. He was mainly responsible for the Augsburg Confession in 1530.

Mel·a·ne·sia /,melə'nēZHə/ a region in the western Pacific Ocean, including the Bismarck Archipelago, the Solomon Islands, Vanuatu, New Caledonia, and Fiji.

Mel·a·ne·sian /,melə'nēZHən/ ▶adj. of or relating to Melanesia, its peoples, or their languages. ▶n. 1 a native or inhabitant of Melanesia. 2 any of the languages of Melanesia, mostly Austronesian languages related to Malay but also Neo-Melanesian (or Tok Pisin), an English-based pidgin.

mé·lange /mā'länj/ (also **me·lange**) ▶n. a mixture; a medley: *a mélange of tender vegetables and herbs*. [from Fr. *mélange*, from *mêler* 'to mix.']

mel·a·nin /'melənin/ ▶n. a dark brown to black pigment occurring in the hair, skin, and iris of the eye in people and animals. [19th C.: from Gk. *melas, melan-* 'black' + -IN[1].]

mel·a·nism /'melə,nizəm/ ▶n. esp. Zool. unusual darkening of body tissues caused by excessive production of melanin. —**me·lan·ic** /mə'lanik/ adj. **mel·a·nis·tic** /,melə'nistik/ adj.

mel·a·nite /'melə,nīt/ ▶n. a velvet-black variety of andradite (garnet). [19th C.: from Gk. *melas, melan-* 'black' + -ITE[1].]

me·lan·o·cyte /'melənə,sīt; mə'lanō-/ ▶n. Physiol. a mature melanin-forming cell, typically in the skin.

mel·a·noid /'melə,noid/ ▶adj. 1 resembling melanin. 2 resembling melanosis.

mel·a·no·ma /,melə'nōmə/ ▶n. (pl. **-no·mas** or **-no·ma·ta** /-'nōmətə/) Med. a tumor of melanin-forming cells, typically a malignant tumor associated with skin cancer. [19th C.: from Gk. *melas, melan-* 'black' + -OMA.]

mel·a·no·sis /,melə'nōsəs/ ▶n. Med. a condition of abnormal or excessive production of melanin. —**mel·a·not·ic** /-'nätik/ adj.

mel·a·to·nin /,melə'tōnin/ ▶n. Biochem. a hormone secreted by the pineal gland that inhibits melanin formation and may regulate the reproductive cycle. [1950s: from Gk. *melas* 'black' + *(sero)tonin*.]

Mel·ba /'melbə/, Dame Nellie (1861–1931), Australian opera singer; born *Helen Porter Mitchell*.

Mel·ba toast ▶n. very thin crisp toast.

Mel·bourne[1] /'melbərn/ a city in southeastern Australia; pop. 2,762,000.

Mel·bourne[2], William Lamb, 2nd Viscount (1779–1848), prime minister of Britain 1834, 1835–41.

Mel·chi·or[1] /'melkē,ôr/ one of the three Magi, represented as a king of Nubia.

Mel·chi·or[2], Lauritz Lebrecht Hommel (1890–1973), US opera singer; born in Denmark. A tenor, he sang with the Metropolitan Opera 1926–50.

Mel·chiz·e·dek /mel'kizə,dek/ (in the Bible) a priest and king of Salem (identified with Jerusalem).

meld[1] /meld/ ▶v. blend; combine. ▶n. a thing formed by merging or blending: *a meld of many contributions*. [1930s: perh. a blend of MELT and WELD[1].]

meld[2] ▶v. [trans.] (in rummy, canasta, and other card games) lay down or declare (a combination of cards) in order to score points: *a player has melded four kings*. ▶n. a completed set or run of cards in any of these games. [19th C. (orig. US): from Ger. *melden* 'announce.']

me·lee /'mā,lā; mā'lā/ (also **mê·lée**) ▶n. a confused fight, skirmish, or scuffle. ■ a confused mass of people. [17th C.: from Fr. *mêlée*, from an OFr. var. of *meslee* (see MEDLEY).]

me·le·na /mə'lēnə/ (Brit. **me·lae·na**) ▶n. Med. dark sticky feces containing partly digested blood. ■ the production of such feces, following internal bleeding or the swallowing of blood. [19th C.: mod. L., from Gk. *melaina*, fem. of *melas* 'black.']

mel·ic /'melik/ ▶adj. (of a poem, esp. an ancient Greek lyric) meant to be sung. [17th C.: via L. from Gk. *melikos*, from *melos* 'song.']

Me·lil·la /mə'lēə/ a Spanish enclave on the Mediterranean coast of Morocco; pop. 57,000. With Ceuta, it forms a community of Spain.

mel·i·lot /'melə,lät/ ▶n. a widespread fragrant herbaceous plant (genus *Melilotus*) of the pea family, sometimes grown as forage or green manure. Also called SWEET CLOVER. [ME: from OFr., via L. from Gk. *melilōtos* 'honey lotus.']

mel·io·rate /'mēlēə,rāt/ ▶v. formal another term for AMELIORATE. —**mel·io·ra·tion** /,mēlēə'rāSHən/ n. **mel·io·ra·tive** /-,rātiv/ adj. [16th C.: from late L. *meliorat-* 'improved,' from the v. *meliorare*, based on *melior* 'better.']

mel·io·rism /'mēlēə,rizəm/ ▶n. Philos. the belief that the world can be made better by human effort. —**mel·io·rist** n. & adj. **mel·io·ris·tic** /,mēlēə'ristik/ adj.

me·lis·ma /mə'lizmə/ ▶n. (pl. **-mas** or **-ma·ta** /-mətə/) Music a group of notes sung to one syllable of text. —**mel·is·mat·ic** /,meliz'matik/ adj. [19th C.: from Gk., lit. 'melody.']

mel·lif·er·ous /mə'lifərəs/ ▶adj. yielding or producing honey. [17th C.: from L. *mellifer* (from *mel* 'honey' + *-fer* 'bearing') + -OUS.]

mel·lif·lu·ent /mə'liflōōənt/ ▶adj. another term for MELLIFLUOUS. —**mel·lif·lu·ence** /-lōōəns/ n.

mel·lif·lu·ous /mə'liflōōəs/ ▶adj. (of a voice or words) sweet or musical; pleasant to hear. —**mel·lif·lu·ous·ly** adv. **mel·lif·lu·ous·ness** n. [15th C.: from late L. *mellifluus* (from *mel* 'honey' + *fluere* 'to flow') + -OUS.]

Mel·lon /'melən/, a family of US philanthropists. **Andrew William** (1855–1937) was US Secretary of the Treasury 1921–32 and donated his art collection to establish the National Gallery of Art in Washington, DC, in 1941. His son **Paul** (1907–99) continued his work.

mel·lo·phone /'melə,fōn/ ▶n. a brass instrument similar to the orchestral French horn. [1920s: from MELLOW + -PHONE.]

mel·lo·tron /'melə,trän/ ▶n. an electronic keyboard instrument in which each key controls the playback of a single prerecorded musical sound. [1960s: from MELLOW + *-tron*, element of ELECTRONIC.]

mel·low /'melō/ ▶adj. 1 (esp. of sound, taste, and color) pleasantly smooth or soft; free from harshness. ■ archaic (of fruit) ripe, soft, sweet, and juicy. ■ (of wine) well-matured and smooth. 2 (of a person's character) softened or matured by age or experience: *a more mellow personality*. ■ relaxed and good-humored: *Jean was feeling mellow*. ■ informal relaxed and cheerful through being slightly drunk: *everybody got very mellow and slept well*. 3 (of earth) rich and loamy. ▶v. make or become mellow. —**mel·low·ly** adv. **mel·low·ness** n. [ME: perh. from attributive use of OE *melu, melw-* (see MEAL[2]).]

me·lo·de·on /mə'lōdēən/ (also **me·lo·di·on**) ▶n. 1 a small accordion of German origin, played esp. by folk musicians. [19th C.: prob. from MELODY, on the pattern of *accordion*.] 2 a small organ popular in the 19th century, similar to the harmonium. [alt. of earlier *melodium*.]

me·lod·ic /mə'lädik/ ▶adj. of or having melody. ■ pleasant-sounding; melodious: *his voice was melodic*. —**me·lod·i·cal·ly** adv.

me·lod·i·ca /mə'lädikə/ ▶n. a wind instrument with a small keyboard controlling a row of reeds, and a mouthpiece at one end. [1960s: from MELODY, on the pattern of *harmonica*.]

me·lo·di·ous /mə'lōdēəs/ ▶adj. of, producing, or having a pleasant tune; tuneful: *melodious chant of monks*. ■ pleasant-sounding: *a melodious voice*. —**me·lo·di·ous·ly** adv. **me·lo·di·ous·ness** n.

mel·o·dist /'melədist/ ▶n. a composer of melodies. ■ a singer.

mel·o·dize /'melə,dīz/ ▶v. [intrans.] rare make or play music.

mel·o·dra·ma /'melə,drämə/ ▶n. 1 a sensational dramatic piece with exaggerated characters and exciting events intended to appeal to the emotions. ■ the genre of drama of this type. ■ language, behavior, or events that resemble drama of this kind. 2 hist. a play interspersed with songs and orchestral music accompanying the action. —**mel·o·dram·a·tist** /,melə'drämətist/ n. **mel·o·dram·a·tize** /,melə'drämə,tīz/ v. [19th C.: from Fr. *mélodrame*, from Gk. *melos* 'music' + Fr. *drame* 'drama.']

mel·o·dra·mat·ic /,melədrə'matik/ ▶adj. of or relating to melodrama. ■ characteristic of melodrama, esp. in being exaggerated, sensationalized, or overemotional. —**mel·o·dra·mat·i·cal·ly** adv.

mel·o·dra·mat·ics /,melədrə'matiks/ ▶plural n. melodramatic behavior, action, or writing.

mel·o·dy /ˈmelədē/ ▶**n.** (pl. **-dies**) a sequence of single notes that is musically satisfying. ■ such sequences of notes collectively. ■ the principal part in harmonized music. [ME: from OFr. *melodie*, via late L. from Gk. *melōidia*, from *melos* 'song.']

mel·on /ˈmelən/ ▶**n.** **1** the large round fruit of a plant of the gourd family, with sweet pulpy flesh and many seeds. ■ the edible flesh of such fruit: *a slice of melon.* **2** the Old World plant (*Cucumis melo* subsp. *melo*) that yields this fruit. **3** Zool. a mass of waxy material in the head of dolphins and other toothed whales, thought to focus acoustic signals. [ME: via OFr. from late L. *melo, melon-*, contr. of L. *melopepo*, from Gk. *mēlopepōn*, from *mēlon* 'apple' + *pepōn* 'gourd.']

Me·los /ˈmē,läs; ˈmelōs/ a Greek island in the Aegean Sea. Greek name **Mílos.**

Mel·pom·e·ne /melˈpämənē/ Greek & Rom. Mythol. the Muse of tragedy.

melt /melt/ ▶**v.** [intrans.] **1** become liquefied by heat. ■ [trans.] change (something) to a liquid condition by heating it. ■ [trans.] (**melt something down**) melt something, esp. a metal article, so that the material it is made of can be used again. ■ dissolve in liquid. **2** become more tender or loving. ■ [trans.] make (someone) more tender or loving. **3** [no obj., with adverbial] leave or disappear unobtrusively: *the figure melted into thin air.* ■ (of a feeling or state) disappear. ■ (**melt into**) change or merge imperceptibly into (another form or state). ▶**n.** an act of melting: *the spring melt.* ■ metal or other material in a melted condition. ■ an amount melted at any one time. ■ [with adj.] a sandwich, hamburger, or other dish containing or topped with melted cheese: *a tuna melt.*
– PHRASES **melt in the** (or **your**) **mouth** (of food) be light or tender and need little or no chewing. — **melt·a·ble adj. melt·er n. melt·ing·ly adv.** [OE *meltan, mieltan*; rel. to ON *melta* 'to malt, digest,' L. *mollis* 'soft.']

melt·down /ˈmelt,doun/ ▶**n.** an accident in a nuclear reactor in which the fuel overheats and melts the reactor core or shielding. ■ fig. a disastrous event, esp. a rapid fall in share prices: *the 1987 stock market meltdown.*

melt·ing point ▶**n.** the temperature at which a given solid will melt.

melt·ing pot ▶**n.** a pot in which metals or other materials are melted and mixed. ■ fig. a place where different peoples, styles, theories, etc., are mixed together.

mel·ton /ˈmeltən/ ▶**n.** heavy woolen cloth with a close-cut nap, used for overcoats and jackets. [19th C.: *Melton* Mowbray, England.]

melt·wa·ter /ˈmelt,wôtər; -,wätər/ ▶**n.** (also **melt·wa·ters**) water formed by the melting of snow and ice.

Mel·ville /ˈmelvəl; -,vil/, Herman (1819–91), US writer. His novels include *Moby Dick* (1851).

mem. ▶**abbr.** ■ member. ■ memoir. ■ memorandum. ■ memorial.

mem·ber /ˈmembər/ ▶**n.** **1** an individual belonging to a group such as a society or team: *a drama club member.* ■ an animal or plant belonging to a taxonomic group: *a member of the lily family.* ■ (also **Member**) a person formally elected to take part in the proceedings of certain organizations: *Member of Parliament.* ■ a part or branch of a political body: [as adj.] *member countries of the Central African Customs Union.* **2** a constituent piece of a complex structure. ■ a part of a sentence, equation, group of figures, mathematical set, etc. **3** archaic a part or organ of the body, esp. a limb. ■ (also **male member**) the penis. ■ Bot. any part of a plant viewed with regard to its form and position, rather than to its function. — **mem·bered adj.** [in comb.] (esp. Chem.) *a six-membered oxygen-containing ring.* [ME: via OFr. from L. *membrum* 'limb.']

mem·ber·ship /ˈmembər,SHip/ ▶**n.** the fact of being a member of a group: [as adj.] *a membership card.* ■ [in sing.] the number or body of members in a group.

mem·brane /ˈmem,brān/ ▶**n.** Anat. & Zool. a pliable sheetlike structure acting as a boundary, lining, or partition in an organism. ■ a thin pliable sheet or skin of various kinds: *a membrane to prevent water seepage.* ■ Biol. a microscopic double layer of lipids and proteins that bounds cells and organelles and forms structures within cells. — **mem·bra·na·ceous** /,membrəˈnāSHəs/ **adj. mem·bra·ne·ous** /memˈbrānēəs/ **adj. mem·bra·nous** /ˈmembrənəs; memˈbrānəs/ **adj.** [ME: from L. *membrana*, from *membrum* 'limb.']

mem·bra·nous lab·y·rinth /ˈmembrənəs; memˈbrānəs/ ▶**n.** see **labyrinth.**

meme /mēm/ ▶**n.** Biol. an element of a culture or behavior that may be passed from one individual to another by nongenetic means, esp. imitation. — **me·met·ic** /mēˈmetik; mə-/ **adj.** [1970s: from Gk. *mimēma* 'that which is imitated,' on the pattern of *gene.*]

Me·mel /ˈmāməl/ **1** German name for **Klaipeda. 2** the Neman River in its lower course (see **Neman**).

me·men·to /məˈmen,tō/ ▶**n.** (pl. **-tos** or **-toes**) an object kept as a reminder or souvenir of a person or event. [ME (denoting a prayer of commemoration): from L., lit. 'remember!,' imper. of *meminisse.*]

me·men·to mo·ri /məˈmen,tō ˈmôrē/ ▶**n.** (pl. same) an object serving as a warning or reminder of death. [L., lit. 'remember (that you have) to die.']

mem·o /ˈmemō/ ▶**n.** (pl. **mem·os**) informal a written message, esp. in business; a memorandum.

mem·oir /ˈmem,wär; -,wôr/ ▶**n.** **1** a historical account or biography written from personal knowledge. ■ (**memoirs**) an autobiography or a written account of one's memory of certain events or people. **2** an essay on a learned subject. — **mem·oir·ist n.** [15th C. (denoting a memorandum or record): from Fr. *mémoire* (masc.), a special use of *mémoire* (fem.) 'memory.']

mem·o·ra·bil·i·a /,mem(ə)rəˈbilēə/ ▶**plural n.** objects kept or collected because of their historical interest: *World Series memorabilia.* [18th C.: from L., neut. pl. of *memorabilis* 'memorable.']

mem·o·ra·ble /ˈmem(ə)rəbəl/ ▶**adj.** worth remembering or easily remembered. — **mem·o·ra·bil·i·ty** /,mem(ə)rəˈbilətē/ **n. mem·o·ra·bly adv.** [15th C.: from L. *memorabilis*, from *memorare* 'bring to mind,' from *memor* 'mindful.']

mem·o·ran·dum /,meməˈrandəm/ ▶**n.** (pl. **-da** /-də/ or **-dums**) a note or record made for future use. ■ a written message, esp. in business or diplomacy. ■ Law a document recording the terms of a contract or other legal details. [ME: from L., lit. 'something to be brought to mind,' gerundive of *memorare.*]

me·mo·ri·al /məˈmôrēəl/ ▶**n.** **1** something, esp. a structure, that reminds people of a person or event. ■ [as adj.] intended to commemorate someone or something: *a memorial service in the dead man's honor.* **2** esp. hist. a statement of facts, esp. as the basis of a petition: *the council sent a strongly worded memorial.* ■ a record or chronicle. ■ an informal diplomatic paper. [ME: from late L. *memoriale* 'record, memory, monument,' from L. *memorialis* 'serving as a reminder,' from *memoria* 'memory.']

Me·mo·ri·al Day ▶**n.** a day, the last Monday in May, on which those who died in active military service are remembered. Also called (esp. formerly) **Decoration Day.** ■ (also **Confederate Memorial Day**) (in the Southern states) any of various days (esp. the fourth Monday in April) for similar remembrances.

me·mo·ri·al·ist /məˈmôrēəlist/ ▶**n.** a person who gives a memorial address or writes a memorial. ■ a writer of biographical or historical memorials; a memoirist.

me·mo·ri·al·ize /məˈmôrēə,līz/ ▶**v.** [trans.] preserve the memory of; commemorate. — **me·mo·ri·al·i·za·tion** /mə,môrēələˈzāSHən/ **n. me·mo·ri·al·iz·er n.**

mem·o·rize /ˈmemə,rīz/ ▶**v.** [trans.] commit to memory; learn by heart: *he memorized thousands of verses.* — **mem·o·riz·a·ble** /-,rīzəbəl/ **adj. mem·o·ri·za·tion** /,memərəˈzāSHən/ **n. mem·o·riz·er n.**

mem·o·ry /ˈmem(ə)rē/ ▶**n.** (pl. **-ries**) **1** a person's power to remember things: *I've a great* **memory for** *faces.* ■ the power of the mind to remember things: *the brain regions responsible for memory.* ■ the mind regarded as a store of things remembered. ■ the capacity of a substance to return to a previous state or condition after having been altered or deformed. **2** something remembered from the past; a recollection. ■ the remembering or recollection of a dead person, esp. one who was popular or respected. ■ the length of time over which people continue to remember a person or event: *the worst slump in recent memory.* **3** the part of a computer in which data or program instructions can be stored for retrieval.
– PHRASES **from memory** without reading or referring to notes. **in memory of** intended to remind people of, esp. to honor a dead person. **take a trip** (or **walk**) **down memory lane** deliberately recall pleasant or sentimental memories. [ME: from OFr. *memorie*, from L. *memoria*, from *memor* 'mindful, remembering.']

mem·o·ry board ▶**n.** Comput. a board containing memory chips that can be connected to a computer.

mem·o·ry trace ▶**n.** a hypothetical permanent change in the nervous system brought about by memorizing something; an engram.

Mem·phis /ˈmemfəs/ **1** an ancient city in Egypt, about 10 miles (15 km) south of Cairo. **2** a city in southwestern Tennessee; pop. 650,100.

mem·sa·hib /ˈmem,sä(h)ib; -,säb/ ▶**n.** Indian, dated a married white or upper-class woman (often used as a respectful form of address by nonwhites). [from *mem* (representing an Ind. pronunc. of **ma'am**) + **sahib.**]

men /men/ plural form of **man.**

men·ace /ˈmenəs/ ▶**n.** a person or thing that is likely to cause harm; a threat or danger: *the menace of drugs.* ■ a threatening quality, tone, or atmosphere. ■ often humorous a person or thing that causes trouble or annoyance. ▶**v.** [trans.] (often **be menaced**) threaten, esp. in a malignant or hostile manner. — **men·ac·er n. men·ac·ing adj. men·ac·ing·ly adv.** [ME: via OFr. from late L. *minacia*, from L. *minax, minac-* 'threatening,' from *minae* 'threats.']

men·a·di·one /,menəˈdī,ōn/ ▶**n.** Med. a synthetic yellow compound, $C_{11}H_8O_2$, related to menaquinone, used to treat hemorrhage. Also called **vitamin** K_3. [1940s: from *me(thyl)* + *na(phthalene)* + *-dione.*]

mé·nage /māˈnäZH; mə-/ ▶**n.** the members of a household: *crisis had recently unsettled the Clelland ménage.* ■ the management of a household. [ME: from OFr. *menage*, from *mainer* 'to stay,' based on L. *manere* 'remain.']

mé·nage à trois /māˈnäZH ä ˈt(r)wä; mə-/ ▶**n.** (pl. **mé·nages à trois** pronunc. same) an arrangement in which three people share a sexual relationship. [Fr., 'household of three.']

me·nag·er·ie /məˈnajərē; -ˈnaZH-/ ▶**n.** a collection of wild animals kept in captivity for exhibition. ■ fig. a strange or diverse collection. [17th C.: from Fr. *ménagerie*, from *ménage* (see **ménage**).]

Me·nan·der /məˈnandər/ (*c.*342–292 BC), Greek playwright. His comic plays deal with domestic situations and capture colloquial speech patterns.

men·a·qui·none /,menəˈkwin,ōn; -ˈkwī,nōn/ ▶**n.** Biochem. one of the K vitamins, a compound produced by bacteria in the large intestine and essential for the blood-clotting process. It is an isoprenoid derivative of menadione. Also called **vitamin** K_2. [1940s: from the chemical name *me(thyl)-na(phtho)quinone.*]

men·ar·che /'men,ärkē/ ▶ **n.** the first menstrual period. — **men·ar·che·al** /men'ärkēəl/ or **men·ar·chi·al adj.** [19th C.: mod. L., from Gk. *mēn* 'month' + *arkhē* 'beginning.']

Men·ci·us /'mencHēəs/ (*c.*371–*c.*289 BC), Chinese philosopher; Latinized name of *Meng-tzu* or *Mengzi* ("Meng the Master"). He helped to develop Confucianism. ■ one of the Four Books of Confucianism.

Menck·en /'meNGkən/, H. L. (1880–1956), US journalist and critic; full name *Henry Louis Mencken.* In *The American Language* (1919), he argued for the study of American English in its own right.

mend /mend/ ▶ **v.** [trans.] repair (something that is broken or damaged): *workmen were mending faulty cabling.* ■ [intrans.] return to health; heal. ■ improve (an unpleasant situation, esp. a disagreement). ▶ **n.** a repair in a material.
– PHRASES **mend (one's) fences** make peace with a person. **mend one's ways** improve one's habits or behavior. **on the mend** improving in health or condition; recovering. — **mend·a·ble adj. mend·er n.** [ME: shortening of AMEND.]

men·da·cious /men'dāsHəs/ ▶ **adj.** not telling the truth; lying: *mendacious propaganda.* — **men·da·cious·ly adv. men·da·cious·ness n.** [17th C.: from L. *mendax, mendac-* 'lying' (rel. to *mendum* 'fault') + -IOUS.]

men·dac·i·ty /men'dasitē/ ▶ **n.** untruthfulness. [17th C.: from eccles. L. *mendacitas,* from *mendax, mendac-* 'lying' (see MENDACIOUS).]

Men·de /'mendē/ ▶ **n.** (pl. same or **Men·des**) **1** a member of a people inhabiting Sierra Leone in West Africa. **2** the Mende language of this people. ▶ **adj.** relating to or denoting this people or their language. [the name in Mende.]

Men·del /'mendl/, Gregor Johann (1822–84), Moravian monk. He is called the father of genetics. From systematically breeding peas, he demonstrated the transmission of characteristics by genes.

Men·de·le·ev /,mendə'lāəf; myindi'leyef/, Dmitri Ivanovich (1834–1907), Russian chemist. He developed the periodic table.

men·de·le·vi·um /,mendə'lēvēəm; -'lā-/ ▶ **n.** the chemical element of atomic number 101, a radioactive metal of the actinide series. It was first made in 1955 by bombarding einsteinium with helium ions. (Symbol: **Md**) [mod. L., from the name of D. MENDELEEV.]

Men·de·li·an /men'dēlēən/ ▶ **adj.** Biol. of or relating to Mendel's theory of heredity: *Mendelian genetics.* ▶ **n.** a person who accepts or advocates Mendel's theory.

Men·dels·sohn /'mendl-sən/, Felix (1809–47), German composer and pianist; full name *Jakob Ludwig Felix Mendelssohn-Bartholdy.* His works include *Fingal's Cave* (1830–32) and *Elijah* (1846).

Men·de·res /,mendə'res/ a river in southwestern Turkey that flows to the Aegean Sea.

men·di·cant /'mendikənt/ ▶ **adj.** given to begging. ■ of or denoting one of the religious orders that originally relied solely on alms: *a mendicant friar.* ▶ **n.** a beggar. ■ a member of a mendicant order. — **men·di·can·cy** /-kənsē/ **n.** [ME: from L. *mendicant-* 'begging,' from the v. *mendicare,* from *mendicus* 'beggar,' from *mendum* 'fault.']

men·dic·i·ty /men'disitē/ ▶ **n.** the condition or activities of a beggar.

mend·ing /'mendiNG/ ▶ **n.** things to be repaired by sewing or darning: *a muddle of books and mending.*

Men·do·za[1] /men'dōzə/ a city in western Argentina, located in the foothills of the Andes; pop. 122,000.

Men·do·za[2], Antonio de (*c.*1490–1552), Spanish colonial administrator. He was the first viceroy of New Spain 1535–50.

Men·e·la·us /,menə'lāəs/ Gk. Mythol. king of Sparta, husband of Helen and brother of Agamemnon.

Me·nes /'mēnēz/, Egyptian pharaoh; reigned *c.*3100 BC. He founded the first dynasty that ruled Egypt.

men·folk /'men,fōk/ (also **men·folks**) ▶ **plural n.** a group of men considered collectively, esp. the men of a particular family or community.

Meng-tzu /'meNG 'tsōō; 'dzə/ (also **Meng·zi** /-'zē/) Chinese name for MENCIUS.

men·ha·den /men'hādn; mən-/ ▶ **n.** a large deep-bodied fish (genus *Brevoortia*) of the herring family that occurs along the east coast of North America. The oil-rich flesh is used to make fish meal and fertilizer. [18th C.: from Algonquian.]

men·hir /'men,hi(ə)r/ ▶ **n.** Archaeol. a tall upright stone of a kind erected in prehistoric times in western Europe. [19th C.: from Breton *men* 'stone' + *hir* 'long.']

me·ni·al /'mēnēəl/ ▶ **adj.** (of work) not requiring much skill and lacking prestige: *menial factory jobs.* ■ [attrib.] dated (of a servant) domestic. ▶ **n.** a person with a menial job. ■ dated a domestic servant. — **me·ni·al·ly adv.** [ME (in the sense 'domestic'): from OFr., from *mesnee* 'household.']

Mé·nière's dis·ease /mān'ye(ə)rz/ (also **Ménière's syndrome**) ▶ **n.** a disease of the ear that causes progressive deafness and attacks of tinnitus and vertigo. [19th C.: named after Prosper *Ménière* (1799–1862), Fr. physician.]

me·nin·ges /mə'ninjēz/ ▶ **plural n.** (sing. **me·ninx** /'mēniNGks; 'meniNGks/) Anat. the three membranes (dura mater, arachnoid, and pia mater) that line the skull and vertebral canal and enclose the brain and spinal cord. — **me·nin·ge·al** /mə'ninjēəl/ **adj.** [mod. L., from Gk. *mēninx, mēning-* 'membrane.']

me·nin·gi·o·ma /mə,ninjē'ōmə/ ▶ **n.** (pl. **-mas** or **-ma·ta** /-'ōmətə/) Med. a tumor, usually benign, in the brain.

men·in·gi·tis /,menən'jītis/ ▶ **n.** inflammation of the meninges caused by viral or bacterial infection. — **men·in·git·ic** /-'jitik/ **adj.**

me·nin·go·coc·cus /mə,niNGgō'käkəs/ ▶ **n.** (pl. **-coc·ci** /-'käksī; -'käksē/) a bacterium (*Neisseria meningitidis*) involved in some forms of meningitis and cerebrospinal infection. — **me·nin·go·coc·cal** /-'käkəl/ **adj.**

me·ninx /'mēniNGks; 'men-/ singular form of MENINGES.

me·nis·cus /mə'niskəs/ ▶ **n.** (pl. **-ci** /-kē; -kī/ or **-cus·es**) Physics the curved upper surface of a liquid in a tube. ■ Optics [usu. as adj.] a lens that is convex on one side and concave on the other. ■ Anat. a thin fibrous cartilage between the surfaces of some joints. [17th C.: mod. L., from Gk. *mēniskos* 'crescent,' dimin. of *mēnē* 'moon.']

Men·lo Park a community in central New Jersey, the site of the laboratory of Thomas Edison.

Men·nin·ger /'menənjər/, Karl Augustus (1893–1990), US psychiatrist. He cofounded the Menninger Clinic in 1920.

Men·non·ite /'menə,nīt/ ▶ **n.** (chiefly in the US and Canada) a member of a Protestant sect originating in Friesland in the 16th century. — **Men·no·nit·ism n.** [*Menno* Simons (1496–1561).]

me·no /'menō/ ▶ **adv.** Music (in directions) less. [Ital.]

meno- ▶ **comb. form** relating to menstruation: *menopause.* [from Gk. *mēn* 'month.']

me·nol·o·gy /mə'näləjē/ ▶ **n.** (pl. **-gies**) an ecclesiastical calendar of the months, esp. a calendar of the Greek Orthodox Church containing biographies of the saints. [17th C.: via mod. L. from eccles. Gk. *mēnologion,* from *mēn* 'month' + *logos* 'account.']

Me·nom·i·nee /mə'nämənē/ (also **Me·nom·i·ni**) ▶ **n.** (pl. same or **-nees** or **-nis**) **1** a member of an American Indian people of northeastern Wisconsin. **2** the Algonquian language of this people. ▶ **adj.** relating to or denoting this people or their language. [from Ojibwa *manōminī,* lit. 'wild-rice person.']

men·o·pause /'menə,pôz/ ▶ **n.** the ceasing of menstruation. ■ the period in a woman's life (typically between 45 and 50 years of age) when this occurs. — **men·o·pau·sal** /,menə'pôzəl/ **adj.**

me·nor·ah /mə'nôrə/ ▶ **n.** (**the Menorah**) a sacred candelabrum with seven branches used in the Temple in Jerusalem, originally that made by the craftsman Bezalel and placed in the sanctuary of the Tabernacle (Exod. 37: 17–24). ■ a candelabrum used in Jewish worship. [Heb.]

menorah

men·or·rha·gi·a /,menə'rāj(ē)ə/ ▶ **n.** Med. abnormally heavy bleeding at menstruation. [18th C.: mod. L., from MENO- 'of menstruation' + *-rrhag-,* stem of Gk. *rhēgnunai* 'to burst.']

men·or·rhe·a /,menə'rēə/ (also esp. Brit. **men·or·rhoe·a**) ▶ **n.** Med. the flow of blood at menstruation. [19th C.: back-form. from AMENORRHEA.]

Me·not·ti /mə'nätē/, Gian Carlo (1911–), US composer; born in Italy. He wrote the opera *Amahl and the Night Visitors* (1951).

Men·sa[1] /'mensə/ Astron. a small, faint southern constellation (the Table or Table Mountain). It contains part of the Large Magellanic Cloud.

Men·sa[2] /'mensə/ an international organization for people with very high scores in IQ tests.

mensch /mencH/ ▶ **n.** (pl. **mensch·en** /'mencHən/ or **mensch·es**) informal a person of integrity and honor. [1930s: Yiddish *mensh,* from Ger. *Mensch,* lit. 'person.']

men·ses /'men,sēz/ ▶ **plural n.** blood and other matter discharged from the uterus at menstruation. ■ [treated as sing.] the time of menstruation. [16th C.: from L., pl. of *mensis* 'month.']

Men·she·vik /'mencHə,vik/ ▶ **n.** (pl. **Men·she·viks** /'mencHə,viks/ or **Men·she·vi·ki** /,mencHə'vikē/) hist. a member of the non-Leninist wing of the Russian Social Democratic Workers' Party. ▶ **adj.** of, relating to, or characteristic of Mensheviks. — **Men·she·vism n. Men·she·vist n.** [from Russ. *Men'shevik* 'a member of the minority,' from *men'she* 'less.']

men's move·ment ▶ **n.** a movement aimed at liberating men from traditional roles in society.

mens re·a /menz 'rēə/ ▶ **n.** Law the intention or knowledge of wrongdoing that constitutes part of a crime, as opposed to the action or conduct of the accused. [19th C.: L., 'guilty mind.']

men·stru·al /'menstr(ōō)əl/ ▶ **adj.** of or relating to the menses or menstruation: *menstrual blood.*

men·stru·al cy·cle ▶ **n.** the process of ovulation and menstruation in women and other female primates.

men·stru·al per·i·od ▶ **n.** see PERIOD (sense 4).

men·stru·ate /'menstrōō,āt; 'men,strāt/ ▶ **v.** [intrans.] (of a woman) discharge blood and other material from the lining of the uterus as part of the menstrual cycle. [17th C.: from late L. *menstruat-* 'menstruated,' from the v. *menstruare,* from L. *menstrua* 'menses.']

men·stru·a·tion /,menstrōō'āsHən; men'strā-/ ▶ **n.** the process in a woman of menstruating monthly from puberty until menopause, except during pregnancy.

men·stru·um /'menstr(ōō)əm/ ▶ **n.** (pl. **-stru·a** /-str(ōō)ə/) **1** menses.

2 (pl. also **-stru·ums**) archaic a solvent. [ME (sense 1): from L., neut. of *menstruus* 'monthly,' from *mensis* 'month.']

men·sur·a·ble /ˈmenchərəbəl; ˈmensər-/ ▶ **adj.** able to be measured; having fixed limits. ■ Music another term for MENSURAL. — **men·sur·a·bil·i·ty** /ˌmenchərəˈbilətē; ˌmensər-/ **n.**

men·su·ral /ˈmenchərəl; ˈmensərəl/ ▶ **adj.** of or involving measuring: *mensural investigations.* ■ Music involving notes of definite duration and usually a regular meter. [16th C.: from L. *mensuralis,* from *mensura* 'measure.']

men·su·ra·tion /ˌmenchəˈrāshən; ˌmensə-/ ▶ **n.** measuring. ■ Math. the measuring of geometric magnitudes, lengths, areas, and volumes.

-ment /mənt/ ▶ **suffix 1** forming nouns expressing the means or result of an action: *treatment.* **2** forming nouns from adjectives (such as *merriment* from *merry*). [from Fr., or from L. *-mentum.*]

men·tal /ˈmentl/ ▶ **adj. 1** of or relating to the mind. ■ carried out by or taking place in the mind. **2** of, relating to, or suffering from disorders or illnesses of the mind: *a mental hospital.* ■ [predic.] informal insane; crazy: *they go mental.* — **men·tal·ly adv.** [ME: from late L. *mentalis,* from L. *mens, ment-* 'mind.']

men·tal age ▶ **n.** a person's mental ability expressed as the age at which an average person's is the same.

men·tal·ism /ˈmentlˌizəm/ ▶ **n.** Philos. the theory that physical and psychological phenomena are ultimately explicable only in terms of a creative and interpretative mind. — **men·tal·ist n. & adj. men·tal·is·tic** /ˌmentlˈistik/ **adj.**

men·tal·i·ty /menˈtalitē/ ▶ **n.** (pl. **-ties**) **1** the characteristic attitude of mind or way of thinking of a person or group: *the yuppie mentality of the eighties.* **2** the capacity for intelligent thought.

men·tal·ly hand·i·capped ▶ **adj.** (of a person) having very limited intellectual functions.

men·tal res·er·va·tion ▶ **n.** a qualification tacitly added; an unexpressed doubt or criticism.

men·ta·tion /menˈtāshən/ ▶ **n.** tech. mental activity. [19th C.: from L. *mens, ment-* 'mind' + -ATION.]

men·thol /ˈmenˌthôl; -ˌthäl/ ▶ **n.** a crystalline compound, $C_{10}H_{19}OH$, with a cooling minty taste and odor, found in peppermint and other natural oils. It is used as a flavoring and in decongestants and analgesics. [19th C.: from Ger., from L. *mentha* 'mint' + -OL.]

men·tho·lat·ed /ˈmenthəˌlātid/ ▶ **adj.** treated with or containing menthol: *mentholated shaving creams.*

men·tion /ˈmenchən/ ▶ **v.** [trans.] refer to something briefly and without going into detail. ■ [trans.] (often **be mentioned**) make a reference to (someone) as being noteworthy. ▶ **n.** a reference to someone or something. ■ a formal acknowledgment of something outstanding or noteworthy. See also HONORABLE MENTION.

– PHRASES **don't mention it** a polite expression used to indicate that an apology or thanks is not necessary. **mention someone in one's will** leave a legacy to someone. **not to mention** used to introduce an additional fact or point that reinforces the point being made. — **men·tion·a·ble adj.** [ME: via OFr. from L. *mentio(n-).*]

men·to /ˈmentō/ ▶ **n.** (pl. **-tos**) a style of Jamaican folk music based on a dance rhythm in duple time. [20th C.: of unknown origin.]

men·tor /ˈmenˌtôr; -tər/ ▶ **n.** an adviser. ■ a person in a company, college, or school who trains and counsels new employees or students. ▶ **v.** [trans.] to advise or train (someone). — **men·tor·ship n.** [18th C.: via Fr. and L. from Gk. *Mentōr,* the adviser in Homer's *Odyssey.*]

men·u /ˈmenyoo/ ▶ **n.** (pl. **men·us**) a list of dishes available in a restaurant: fig. *politics and sport are on the menu tonight.* ■ the food available or to be served in a restaurant or at a meal: *a dinner-party menu.* ■ Comput. a list of commands or options, esp. one displayed on screen. [19th C.: from Fr., 'detailed list' (n. use of *menu* 'small, detailed'), from L. *minutus* 'very small.']

men·u bar ▶ **n.** Comput. a horizontal bar, typically located at the top of the screen below the title bar, containing drop-down menus.

men·u-driv·en ▶ **adj.** (of a program or computer) used by making selections from menus.

Men·u·hin /ˈmenyooin/, Sir Yehudi (1916–99), British violinist; born in the US. In 1962, he founded a school of music in Surrey, England.

Men·zies /ˈmenzēz/, Sir Robert Gordon (1894–1978), prime minister of Australia 1939–41, 1949–66.

me·ow /mēˈou/ (also **mi·aow**) ▶ **n.** the characteristic crying sound of a cat. ▶ **v.** [intrans.] (of a cat) make such a sound. [17th C.: imitative.]

me·per·i·dine /məˈperəˌdēn; -ˌdin/ ▶ **n.** Med. a synthetic compound used as a painkilling drug. [1940s: blend of METHYL and PIPERIDINE.]

Meph·i·stoph·e·les /ˌmefəˈstäfəlēz/ (also **Me·phis·to** /məˈfistō/) ▶ **n.** an evil spirit to whom Faust sold his soul. — **Meph·is·to·phe·le·an** /məˌfistəˈfēlēən; ˌmefəstə-/ (also **Meph·is·to·phe·li·an**) **adj.**

me·phit·ic /məˈfitik/ ▶ **adj.** (esp. of a gas or vapor) foul-smelling; noxious. [17th C.: from late L. *mephiticus,* from *mephitis* 'noxious exhalation.']

me·phi·tis /məˈfītis/ ▶ **n.** a noxious gas emanating from something, esp. from the earth. ■ a foul or poisonous stench. [18th C.: from L.]

me·pro·ba·mate /məˈprōbəˌmāt; ˌmeprōˈbamˌāt/ ▶ **n.** a bitter-tasting addictive carbamate, $CH_3CH_2CH_2C(CH_2OCONH_2)_2CH_3$, used, esp. formerly, as a mild tranquilizer. [20th C.: from *me(thyl)* + *pro(pyl)* + *(car)bamate.*]

mer. ▶ **abbr.** ■ meridian.

-mer ▶ **comb. form** denoting polymers and related kinds of molecule: *elastomer.* [from Gk. *meros* 'part.']

mer·bro·min /mərˈbrōmən/ ▶ **n.** a greenish iridescent crystalline compound that dissolves in water to give a red solution used as an antiseptic. It is a fluorescein derivative containing bromine and mercury. [1940s: from MERCURIC + BROMO- + -IN¹.]

mer·ca·do /mərˈkädō/ ▶ **n.** (pl. **-dos**) (in Spanish-speaking regions) a market. [Sp., from L. *mercatus* 'market.']

Mer·cal·li scale /mərˈkalē/ a twelve-point scale for expressing the local intensity of an earthquake. [1920s: named after Giuseppe *Mercalli* (1850–1914), Ital. geologist.]

mer·can·tile /ˈmərkənˌtēl; -ˌtīl/ ▶ **adj.** of or relating to trade or commerce; commercial. ■ of or relating to mercantilism. ▶ **n.** dated a general store: *we walked to the local mercantile.* [17th C.: from Fr., from Ital., from *mercante* 'merchant.']

mer·can·til·ism /ˈmərkəntiˌlizəm; -ˌtē-; -ˌtī-/ ▶ **n.** belief in the benefits of profitable trading; commercialism. ■ esp. hist. the economic theory that trade generates wealth and is stimulated by the accumulation of profitable balances, which a government should encourage by means of protectionism. — **mer·can·til·ist n. & adj. mer·can·til·is·tic** /ˌmərkəntiˈlistik; -ˌtē-; -ˌtī-/ **adj.**

Mer·ca·tor /mərˈkātər/, Gerardus (1512–94), Flemish cartographer; Latinized name of *Gerhard Kremer.* He invented a system of map projection.

Mer·ca·tor pro·jec·tion /mərˈkātər/ (also **Mer·ca·tor's pro·jec·tion**) ▶ **n.** a projection of a map of the world onto a cylinder in such a way that all the parallels of latitude have the same length as the equator, used esp. for marine charts and certain climatological maps.

mer·ce·nar·y /ˈmərsəˌnerē/ ▶ **adj.** derog. (of a person or their behavior) primarily concerned with making money at the expense of ethics. ▶ **n.** (pl. **-nar·ies**) a professional soldier hired to serve in a foreign army. ■ a person primarily concerned with material reward at the expense of ethics. — **mer·ce·nar·i·ness n.** [ME (as a n.): from L. *mercenarius* 'hireling,' from *merces, merced-* 'reward.']

mer·cer·ize /ˈmərsəˌrīz/ ▶ **v.** [trans.] [often as adj.] (**mercerized**) treat (cotton fabric or thread) under tension with caustic alkali to increase its strength and give it a shiny, silky appearance. [19th C.: John *Mercer* (1791–1866), said to have invented the process, + -IZE.]

mer·chan·dise ▶ **n.** /ˈmərchənˌdīz; -ˌdīs/ goods to be bought and sold. ▶ **v.** /ˈmərchənˌdīz/ (also **mer·chan·dize**) [trans.] promote the sale of (goods), esp. by their presentation in retail outlets. ■ advertise or publicize (an idea or person): *they are merchandising "niceness" to children.* — **mer·chan·dis·a·ble** /-ˌdīzəbəl/ **adj. mer·chan·dis·er** /-ˌdīzər/ **n.** [ME: from OFr. *marchandise,* from *marchand* 'merchant.']

mer·chan·dis·ing /ˈmərchənˌdīziNG/ ▶ **n.** the activity of promoting the sale of goods.

mer·chant /ˈmərchənt/ ▶ **n. 1** a person or company involved in wholesale trade, esp. one dealing with foreign countries or supplying merchandise to a particular trade: *the area's leading timber merchant | a tea merchant.* ■ a retail trader; a store owner. ■ (esp. in historical contexts) a person involved in trade or commerce. **2** [usu. with adj.] informal, esp. derog. a person with a partiality or aptitude for a particular activity or viewpoint: *a merchant of death.* ▶ **adj.** [attrib.] of or relating to merchants, trade, or commerce: *the growth of the merchant classes.* ■ (of ships, sailors, or shipping activity) involved with commerce rather than military activity. [ME: from OFr. *marchant,* based on L. *mercari* 'to trade,' from *merx, merc-* 'merchandise.']

mer·chant·a·ble /ˈmərchəntəbəl/ ▶ **adj.** suitable for purchase or sale; marketable: *of merchantable quality.*

mer·chant·man /ˈmərchəntmən/ ▶ **n.** (pl. **-men**) a ship used in commerce; a vessel of the merchant marine.

mer·chant ma·rine ▶ **n.** (often **the merchant marine**) a country's shipping that is involved in commerce and trade, as opposed to military activity.

Mer·ci·a /ˈmərsh(ē)ə/ a former kingdom in central England. — **Mer·ci·an adj. & n.**

mer·ci·ful /ˈmərsifəl/ ▶ **adj.** showing or exercising mercy: *the will of a merciful God that all should be saved.* ■ (of an event) coming as a mercy; bringing someone relief from something unpleasant. — **mer·ci·ful·ness n.**

mer·ci·ful·ly /ˈmərsif(ə)lē/ ▶ **adv. 1** in a merciful way. **2** to one's great relief; fortunately.

mer·ci·less /ˈmərsiləs/ ▶ **adj.** showing no mercy or pity. — **mer·ci·less·ly adv. mer·ci·less·ness n.**

mer·cu·ri·al /mərˌkyoorēəl/ ▶ **adj. 1** (of a person) subject to sudden or unpredictable changes. ■ (of a person) sprightly; lively. **2** of or containing the element mercury. **3** (**Mercurial**) of the planet Mercury. ▶ **n.** (usu. **mercurials**) a drug or other compound containing mercury. — **mer·cu·ri·al·i·ty** /-ˌkyoorēˈalitē/ **n. mer·cu·ri·al·ly adv.**

mer·cu·ric /mərˌkyoorik/ ▶ **adj.** Chem. of mercury with a valence of two; of mercury(II). Compare with MERCUROUS.

mer·cu·ric chlo·ride ▶ **n.** a toxic white crystalline compound, $HgCl_2$, used as a fungicide and antiseptic.

Mer·cu·ro·chrome /mə(r)ˈkyoorəˌkrōm/ (also **mer·cu·ro·chrome**) ▶ **n.** trademark for MERBROMIN.

mer·cu·rous /ˈmərkyərəs/ ▶ **adj.** Chem. of mercury with a valence of one; of mercury(I). Compare with MERCURIC.

mer·cur·ous chlor·ide ▶ **n.** another term for CALOMEL.

Mer·cu·ry /ˈmərkyərē/ **1** Rom. Mythol. the Roman god of eloquence, skill, trading, and thieving; the herald and messenger of the gods. **2** Astron. a small planet that is the closest to the sun in the solar system, sometimes visible to the naked eye. **3** a series of US space missions, 1958–1963, that achieved the first US manned spaceflights. — **Mer·cu·ri·an** /mərˈkyo͝orēən/ **adj.**

mer·cu·ry[1] /ˈmərkyərē/ ▶ **n.** the chemical element of atomic number 80, a heavy silvery-white metal that is liquid at ordinary temperatures. (Symbol: **Hg**) Also called QUICKSILVER. ■ the column of such metal in a thermometer or barometer, or its height as indicating atmospheric temperature or pressure: *the mercury rises, the skies steam, and the nights swelter.* ■ hist. this metal or one of its compounds used medicinally, esp. to treat syphilis. [ME: from L. *Mercurius* (see sense 1 of MERCURY).]

mer·cu·ry[2] ▶ **n.** a plant (genera *Mercurialis* and *Acalypha*) of the spurge family, in particular the **three-seeded mercury** (*A. virginica*) of North America. [16th C.: from L. *mercurialis* 'of the god Mercury.']

mer·cu·ry switch ▶ **n.** an electric switch in which the circuit is made by mercury flowing into a gap when the device tilts.

mer·cu·ry va·por lamp (also **mer·cu·ry-va·por lamp**) ▶ **n.** a lamp in which light is produced by an electrical discharge through mercury vapor.

mer·cy /ˈmərsē/ ▶ **n.** (pl. **-cies**) compassion or forgiveness shown toward someone whom it is within one's power to punish or harm: *the boy was begging for mercy.* ■ an event to be grateful for, esp. because its occurrence prevents something unpleasant or provides relief from suffering: *his death was in a way a mercy.* ■ [as adj.] (esp. of a journey or mission) performed out of a compassionate desire to relieve suffering.

– PHRASES **at the mercy of** completely in the power or under the control of. **have mercy on** show compassion or forgiveness to. **throw oneself on someone's mercy** intentionally place oneself in someone's hands in the expectation that they will behave mercifully toward one. [ME: from OFr. *merci* 'pity' or 'thanks,' from L. *merces, merced-* 'reward.']

mer·cy kill·ing ▶ **n.** the killing of a patient suffering from an incurable and painful disease, typically by the administration of large doses of painkilling drugs. See also EUTHANASIA. ■ the killing of an animal that is suffering from an incurable and painful disease or from extreme, life-threatening injuries.

merde /me(ə)rd/ ▶ **exclam.** a French word for "shit."

mere[1] /mi(ə)r/ ▶ **adj.** [attrib.] that is solely or no more or no better than what is specified: *it happened a mere decade ago.* ■ (**the merest**) the smallest or slightest. [ME: from L. *merus* 'undiluted.']

mere[2] ▶ **n.** esp. literary a lake, pond, or arm of the sea. [OE, of Gmc. origin; rel. to Ger. *Meer* 'sea.']

mere·ly /ˈmi(ə)rlē/ ▶ **adv.** just; only.

me·ren·gue /məˈreNGgā/ ▶ **n.** a Caribbean style of dance music chiefly associated with Dominica and Haiti. ■ a style of dancing associated with such music.

mer·e·tri·cious /merəˈtrisHəs/ ▶ **adj.** apparently attractive but having in reality no value or integrity: *meretricious souvenirs for the tourist trade.* — **mer·e·tri·cious·ly adv. mer·e·tri·cious·ness n.** [17th C.: from L. *meretricius* (adj. from *meretrix, meretric-* 'prostitute,' from *mereri* 'be hired') + **-ous**.]

mer·gan·ser /mərˈgansər/ ▶ **n.** a fish-eating diving duck with a long, thin serrated and hooked bill. [17th C.: mod. L., from L. *mergus* 'diver' (from *mergere* 'to dive') + *anser* 'goose.']

merge /mərj/ ▶ **v.** combine or cause to combine to form a single entity, esp. a commercial organization. ■ [intrans.] blend or fade gradually into something else so as to become indistinguishable from it. ■ [trans.] cause to blend or fade into something else in such a way. [17th C.: from L. *mergere* 'to dip, plunge.']

merg·er /ˈmərjər/ ▶ **n.** a combination of two things, esp. companies, into one. [18th C.: from Anglo-Norman Fr. *merger* (v. used as a n.): see MERGE.]

mer·guez /mərˈgez/ (also **merguez sausage**) ▶ **n.** (pl. same) a spicy beef and lamb sausage colored with red peppers, originally made in parts of North Africa. [Fr., from Arabic *mirkās, mirqās*.]

Me·riç /məˈrēCH/ Turkish name for MARITSA.

Mé·ri·da /ˈmeridə; ˈmārē,dä/ a city in southeastern Mexico, capital of the state of Yucatán; pop. 557,000.

me·rid·i·an /məˈridēən/ ▶ **n.** **1** a circle of constant longitude passing through a given place on the earth's surface and the terrestrial poles. ■ (also **celestial meridian**) Astron. a circle passing through the celestial poles and the zenith of a given place on the earth's surface. **2** (in acupuncture and Chinese medicine) each of a set of pathways in the body along which vital energy is said to flow. ▶ **adj.** [attrib.] relating to or situated at a meridian. ■ literary of noon. ■ literary of the period of greatest splendor, vigor, etc. [ME: from OFr. *meridien*, from L. *meridianum* 'noon,' from *medius* 'middle' + *dies* 'day.']

me·rid·i·o·nal /məˈridēənəl/ ▶ **adj.** **1** of or in the south; southern: *the meridional leg of the journey.* ■ relating to or characteristic of the inhabitants of southern Europe, esp. the south of France. **2** of or relating to a meridian. ■ Meteorol. (chiefly of winds and air flow) aligned with lines of longitude. ▶ **n.** a native or inhabitant of the south, esp. the south of France. [ME: via OFr. from late L. *meridionalis*, formed irregularly from L. *meridies* 'midday, south.']

me·ringue /məˈraNG/ ▶ **n.** a sweet food made from a mixture of beaten egg whites and sugar, baked until crisp, typically used as a topping for desserts, esp. pies. [from Fr., of unknown origin.]

me·ri·no /məˈrēnō/ ▶ **n.** (pl. **-nos**) (also **me·ri·no sheep**) a sheep of a breed with long, fine wool. ■ a soft woolen or wool-and-cotton material resembling cashmere, originally of merino wool. ■ a fine woolen yarn. [18th C.: from Sp., of unknown origin.]

mer·i·stem /ˈmerə,stem/ ▶ **n.** Bot. a region of plant tissue consisting of actively dividing cells forming new tissue. — **mer·i·ste·mat·ic** /merəstəˈmatik/ **adj.** [19th C.: from Gk. *meristos* 'divisible,' from *merizein* 'divide into parts,' from *meros* 'part.']

mer·it /ˈmerit/ ▶ **n.** the quality of being particularly good or worthy, esp. so as to deserve praise or reward. ■ a feature or fact that deserves praise or reward. ■ (**merits**) esp. Law the intrinsic rights and wrongs of a case, outside of any other considerations. ■ (**merits**) Theol. good deeds regarded as entitling someone to a future reward from God. ▶ **v.** (**mer·it·ed, mer·it·ing**) [trans.] deserve or be worthy of (something, esp. reward, punishment, or attention).

– PHRASES **judge** (or **consider**) **something on its merits** assess something solely with regard to its intrinsic quality rather than other external factors. [ME: via OFr. from L. *meritum* 'due reward,' from *mereri* 'earn, deserve.']

mer·i·toc·ra·cy /,meriˈtäkrəsē/ ▶ **n.** (pl. **-cies**) government or the holding of power by people selected on the basis of their ability. ■ a society governed by such people. ■ a ruling or influential class of educated or skilled people. — **mer·i·to·crat·ic** /,meritəˈkratik/ **adj.**

mer·i·to·ri·ous /ˈmeri,tôrēəs/ ▶ **adj.** deserving reward or praise: *a medal for meritorious conduct.* ■ Law (of an action or claim) likely to succeed on the merits of the case. — **mer·i·to·ri·ous·ly adv. mer·i·to·ri·ous·ness n.** [ME: from late L. *meritorius* (from *merit-* 'earned,' from the v. *mereri*).]

Mer·lin /ˈmərlən/ (in Arthurian legend) a magician who aided and supported King Arthur.

mer·lin ▶ **n.** a small dark falcon (*Falco columbarius*) that hunts small birds, found throughout most of Eurasia and much of North America. [ME: from Anglo-Norman Fr. *merilun*, from OFr. *esmerillon*, augmentative of *esmeril*, of Gmc. origin; rel. to Ger. *Schmerl*.]

mer·lon /ˈmərlən/ ▶ **n.** the solid part of an embattled parapet between two embrasures. [18th C.: from Fr., from Ital. *merlone*, from *merlo* 'battlement.']

Mer·lot /mərˈlō/ (also **mer·lot**) ▶ **n.** a variety of black wine grape originally from France's Bordeaux region. ■ a red wine made from this grape.

mer·maid /ˈmər,mād/ ▶ **n.** a fictitious or mythical half-human sea creature with the head and trunk of a woman and the tail of a fish. [ME: from MERE[2].]

mer·man /ˈmər,man; -mən/ ▶ **n.** (pl. **-men**) the male equivalent of a mermaid.

mero- ▶ **comb. form** partly; partial: *meronym.* Often contrasted with HOMO-. [from Gk. *meros* 'part.']

Mer·oe /ˈmerō,ē/ an ancient city on the Nile River, in present-day Sudan. It was the capital of the ancient kingdom of Cush. — **Mer·o·it·ic** /,merōˈitik/ **adj. & n.**

mer·o·nym /ˈmerə,nim/ ▶ **n.** Ling. a term that denotes part of something but which is used to refer to the whole of it. — **meronymy** /məˈränəmē/ **n.** [from Gk. *meros* 'part' + *onuma* 'name.']

-merous ▶ **comb. form** Biol. having a specified number of parts: *pentamerous.* [on the pattern of words such as *(di)merous* (see also **-MER**).]

Mer·o·vin·gi·an /,merəˈvinj(ē)ən/ ▶ **adj.** of or relating to the Frankish dynasty reigning in Gaul *c.*500–750. ▶ **n.** a member of this dynasty. [from Fr. *mérovingien*, from med. L. *Merovingi* 'descendants of Merovich' (5th-cent. Frankish leader).]

mer·ri·ly /ˈmerəlē/ ▶ **adv.** **1** in a cheerful way. ■ in a brisk and lively way: *a fire burned merrily.* **2** without consideration of future implications.

Mer·ri·mack Riv·er /ˈmerə,mak/ a river that flows through New Hampshire and Massachusetts.

mer·ri·ment /ˈmerēmənt/ ▶ **n.** gaiety and fun.

mer·ry /ˈmerē/ ▶ **adj.** (**mer·ri·er, mer·ri·est**) cheerful and lively: *the streets were dense with merry throngs of students.* ■ (of an occasion or season) characterized by festivity and rejoicing: *he wished me a merry Christmas.*

– PHRASES **go on one's merry way** informal carry on with a course of action regardless of the consequences. **make merry** enjoy oneself with others. **the more the merrier** the more people or things there are, the better or more enjoyable a situation will be. — **mer·ri·ness n.** [OE *myrige* 'pleasing, delightful,' of Gmc. origin; rel. to MIRTH.]

mer·ry-go-round ▶ **n.** a revolving machine with model horses or other animals on which people ride for amusement. ■ a large revolving device for children to ride on. ■ fig. a continuous cycle of activities or events, esp. when perceived as having no purpose or producing no result.

mer·ry·mak·ing /ˈmerē,mākiNG/ ▶ **n.** the process of enjoying oneself with others. — **mer·ry·mak·er n.**

Mer·senne num·ber /mərˈsen/ **n.** Math. a number of the form $2p-1$, where *p* is a prime number. Such a number which is itself prime is also called a **Mersenne prime.** [19th C.: named after Marin *Mersenne* (1588–1648), Fr. mathematician.]

Mer·sey /ˈmərzē/ a river in northwestern England that flows to the Irish Sea.

Mer·ton /ˈmərtn/, Thomas James (1915–68), US Trappist monk and writer; born in France. His works include *The Seven Storey Mountain* (1948).

Me·sa /ˈmāsə/ a city in south central Arizona, east of Phoenix; pop. 396,375.

me·sa /ˈmāsə/ ▶ **n.** an isolated flat-topped hill with steep sides, found in landscapes with horizontal strata. [18th C.: Sp., lit. 'table,' from L. *mensa*.]

Me·sa·bi Range /məˈsäbē/ low hills in northeastern Minnesota, site of a large iron source.

mé·sal·li·ance /ˌmāzəˈlīəns; ˌmā,zalˈyäns/ ▶ **n.** a marriage with a person of a lower social position. [Fr., from *més-* 'wrong, misdirected' + *alliance* (see ALLIANCE).]

Me·sa Ver·de /ˈmāsə ˈvərdē/ a high plateau in southern Colorado, home to prehistoric Pueblo Indian dwellings.

mes·cal /meˈskal; mə-/ ▶ **n. 1** an intoxicating liquor distilled from the sap of an agave. Compare with TEQUILA, PULQUE. **2** another term for PEYOTE. [18th C.: from Sp. *mezcal*, from Nahuatl *mexcalli*.]

mes·cal but·tons ▶ **plural n.** another term for PEYOTE BUTTONS.

Mes·ca·le·ro /ˌmeskəˈle(ə)rō/ ▶ **n.** (pl. same or **-ros**) **1** a member of an American Indian people of New Mexico. **2** the Athabaskan (Apache) language of this people. ▶ **adj.** of or relating to this people or their language. [Sp., lit. 'people of the mescal.']

mes·ca·line /ˈmeskəlin; -ˌlēn/ ▶ **n.** a hallucinogenic and intoxicating compound, $(CH_3O)_3C_6H_2CH_2CH_2NH_2$, present in mescal buttons from the peyote cactus.

mes·clun /ˈmesklən/ (also **mesclun salad**) ▶ **n.** a salad made from lettuces with other edible leaves such as dandelion greens, and radicchio. [Provençal, lit. 'mixture,' from *mesclar* 'mix thoroughly.']

Mes·dames /māˈdäm/ ▶ **plural n. 1** plural form of MADAME. **2** formal used as a title to refer to more than one woman simultaneously: *Mesdames Carter, Roseby, and Barrington.*

Mes·de·moi·selles /ˈmādəm(w)əˌzel; ˈmādˌmwäˌzel/ plural form of MADEMOISELLE.

me·sem·bry·an·the·mum /məˌzembrēˈanᴛʜəməm/ ▶ **n.** a fleshy succulent plant (*Mesembryanthemum*, *Carpobrotus*, and other genera) of the carpetweed family, often with showy flowers. [mod. L., based on Gk. *mesēmbria* 'noon' + *anthemon* 'flower.']

mes·en·ceph·a·lon /ˌmezenˈsefəˌlän; ˌmes-; -lən/ ▶ **n.** Anat. another term for MIDBRAIN. — **mes·en·ce·phal·ic** /-ˌensəˈfalik/ **adj.** [19th C.: from Gk. *mesos* 'middle' + ENCEPHALON.]

mes·en·chyme /ˈmezənˌkīm; ˈmes-/ ▶ **n.** Embryol. a loosely organized, mainly mesodermal embryonic tissue that develops into connective and skeletal tissues, including blood and lymph. — **mes·en·chy·mal** /ˌmezenˈkīməl; ˌmes-/ **adj.** [19th C.: from Gk. *mesos* 'middle' + *enkhuma* 'infusion.']

mes·en·ter·on /məˈzentəˌrän; məˈsent-/ ▶ **n.** Zool. the middle section of the intestine. — **mes·en·ter·on·ic** /-ˌzentəˈränik; -ˌsent-/ **adj.** [19th C.: from Gk. *mesos* 'middle' + *enteron* 'intestine.']

mes·en·ter·y /ˈmezənˌterē; ˈmes-/ ▶ **n.** (pl. **-ter·ies**) Anat. a fold of the peritoneum that attaches the stomach and other organs to the posterior wall of the abdomen. — **mes·en·ter·ic** /ˌmezənˈterik; ˌmes-/ **adj.** [ME: via med. L. from Gk. *mesenterion*, from *mesos* 'middle' + *enteron* 'intestine.']

mesh /mesʜ/ ▶ **n. 1** material made of a network of wire or thread: *mesh for fishing nets.* ■ the spacing of the strands of such material. **2** an interlaced structure. ■ [in sing.] fig. used with reference to a complex or constricting situation. ■ Comput. a set of finite elements used to represent a geometric object for modeling or analysis. ■ Comput. a computer network in which each computer or processor is connected to a number of others, esp. as an n-dimensional lattice. ▶ **v. 1** [intrans.] (of the teeth of a gearwheel) lock together or be engaged with another gearwheel. ■ make or become entangled or entwined. ■ fig. be or bring into harmony. **2** [trans.] represent a geometric object as a set of finite elements for computational analysis or modeling.
– PHRASES **in mesh** (of the teeth of gearwheels) engaged. — **meshed adj. mesh·y adj.** [ME: prob. from an unrecorded OE word rel. to (and perh. reinforced in ME by) MDu. *maesche*, of Gmc. origin.]

Me·shed variant of MASHHAD.

me·shu·ga /məˈsʜo͝ogə/ (also **me·shug·ga** or **me·shu·gah**) ▶ **adj.** informal (of a person) mad; idiotic. [19th C.: from Yiddish *meshuge*, from Heb.]

me·shu·gaas /məsʜo͝oˈgäs/ ▶ **n.** informal mad or idiotic ideas or behavior. [20th C.: Yiddish, n. from MESHUGA.]

me·shug·ga·na /məˈsʜo͝ogənə/ (also **me·shug·ge·ner** or **me·shu·ge·nah**) ▶ **n.** informal a mad or idiotic person. [20th C.: var. of MESHUGA.]

me·si·al /ˈmezēəl/ ▶ **adj.** Anat. of, in, or directed toward the middle line of a body. — **me·si·al·ly adv.** [19th C.: formed irregularly from Gk. *mesos* 'middle' + -IAL.]

mes·ic[1] /ˈmezik; ˈmē-/ ▶ **adj.** Ecol. (of an environment or habitat) containing a moderate amount of moisture. Compare with HYDRIC and XERIC. [1920s: from Gk. *mesos* 'middle' + -IC.]

mes·ic[2] ▶ **adj.** Physics of or relating to a meson.

mes·mer·ic /mezˈmerik/ ▶ **adj.** causing a person to become completely transfixed and unaware of anything else around them. — **mes·mer·i·cal·ly adv.**

mes·mer·ism /ˈmezməˌrizəm/ ▶ **n.** hist. the therapeutic system of hypnosis devised by Austrian physician of Franz Anton Mesmer (1734–1815). ■ (in general use) hypnotism. — **mes·mer·ist n.**

mes·mer·ize /ˈmezməˌrīz/ ▶ **v.** [trans.] (often **be mesmerized**) hold the attention of (someone) to the exclusion of all else: *she was mesmerized* | [as adj.] (**mesmerizing**) *a mesmerizing stare.* — **mes·mer·i·za·tion** /ˌmezmərəˈzāsʜən/ **n. mes·mer·iz·er n. mes·mer·iz·ing·ly adv.**

mesne /mēn/ ▶ **adj.** Law intermediate. [ME (as adv. and n.): from legal French, var. of Anglo-Norman Fr. *meen* 'middle' (see MEAN[3]).]

mesne prof·its ▶ **plural n.** Law the profits of an estate received by a tenant in wrongful possession and recoverable by the landlord.

meso- ▶ **comb. form** middle; intermediate: *mesomorph.* [from Gk. *mesos* 'middle.']

Mes·o-A·mer·i·ca /ˈmezō; ˈmesō/ the central region of America, from central Mexico to Nicaragua. — **Mes·o-A·mer·i·can adj. & n.**

mes·o·blast /ˈmezəˌblast; ˈmē-/ ▶ **n.** Embryol. the mesoderm of an embryo in its earliest stages. — **mes·o·blas·tic** /ˌmezəˈblastik; ˌmē-/ **adj.**

mes·o·carp /ˈmezəˌkärp; ˈmē-/ ▶ **n.** Bot. the middle layer of the pericarp of a fruit, between the endocarp and the exocarp.

mes·o·ce·phal·ic /ˈmezəsəˈfalik; ˌmē-/ ▶ **adj.** Anat. having a head of medium proportions. — **mes·o·ceph·al·y** /-ˈsefəlē/ **n.**

mes·o·derm /ˈmezəˌdərm; ˈmē-/ ▶ **n.** Embryol. the middle layer of an embryo in early development. — **mes·o·der·mal** /ˌmezəˈdəməl; mē-/ **adj. mes·o·der·mic** /-ˈdərmik/ **adj.** [19th C.: from MESO- 'middle' + Gk. *derma* 'skin.']

mes·o·gas·tri·um /ˌmezəˈgastrēəm; ˌmē-/ ▶ **n.** (pl. **-tri·a** /-trēə/) Anat. the middle region of the abdomen. — **mes·o·gas·tric** /-trik/ **adj.** [19th C.: mod. L., from MESO- 'middle' + Gk. *gastēr, gastr-* 'stomach.']

mes·o·kur·tic /ˌmezəˈkərtik; ˌmē-/ ▶ **adj.** Stat. (of a frequency distribution or its graphical representation) having the same kurtosis as the normal distribution. Compare with LEPTOKURTIC, PLATYKURTIC. — **mes·o·kur·to·sis** /ˌmezəkərˈtōsis; ˌmē-/ **n.** [20th C.: from MESO- 'middle' + Gk. *kurtos* 'bulging' + -IC.]

Mes·o·lith·ic /ˌmezəˈliᴛʜik; ˌmē-/ ▶ **adj.** Archaeol. of, relating to, or denoting the middle part of the Stone Age, between the Paleolithic and Neolithic. ■ [as n.] (**the Mesolithic**) the Mesolithic period. Also called MIDDLE STONE AGE. [19th C.: from MESO- 'middle' + Gk. *lithos* 'stone' + -IC.]

mes·o·morph /ˈmezəˌmôrf; ˈmē-/ ▶ **n.** Physiol. a person with a compact and muscular body build. Compare with ECTOMORPH and ENDOMORPH. — **mes·o·mor·phic** /ˌmezəˈmôrfik; ˌmē-/ **adj.** [1920s: *meso-* from *mesodermal*.]

me·son /ˈmezˌän; ˈmāˌzän; ˈmēˌzän/ ▶ **n.** Physics a subatomic particle that is intermediate in mass between an electron and a proton. — **me·son·ic** /meˈzänik; mā-; mē-/ **adj.** [1930s: from MESO- 'intermediate' + -ON.]

mes·o·pause /ˈmezəˌpôz; ˈmē-/ ▶ **n.** the boundary in the earth's atmosphere at which the temperature stops decreasing with increasing height and begins to increase.

mes·o·phyll /ˈmezəˌfil; ˈmē-/ ▶ **n.** Bot. the inner tissue (parenchyma) of a leaf. — **mes·o·phyl·lic** /ˌmezəˈfilik; ˌmē-/ **adj. mes·o·phyl·lous** /ˌmezəˈfiləs; ˌmē-/ **adj.** [19th C.: from MESO- 'middle' + Gk. *phullon* 'leaf.']

mes·o·phyte /ˈmezəˌfīt; ˈmē-/ ▶ **n.** Bot. a plant needing only a moderate amount of water. — **mes·o·phyt·ic** /ˌmezəˈfitik; ˌmē-/ **adj.**

Mes·o·po·ta·mi·a /ˌmesəpəˈtāmēə/ an ancient region of southwestern Asia in present-day Iraq. — **Mes·o·po·ta·mi·an adj. & n.**

mes·o·saur /ˈmezəˌsôr; ˈmē-/ (also **mes·o·sau·rus** /ˌmezəˈsôrəs/) ▶ **n.** an extinct small aquatic reptile (genus *Mesosaurus*, order Mesosauria) of the early Permian period, with an elongated body, flattened tail, and a long narrow snout with numerous needlelike teeth. — **mes·o·sau·ri·an adj.** [1950s: mod. L., from Gk. *mesos* 'middle' + *sauros* 'lizard.']

mes·o·sphere /ˈmezəˌsfi(ə)r; ˈmē-/ ▶ **n.** the region of the earth's atmosphere above the stratosphere and below the thermosphere. — **mes·o·spher·ic** /ˌmezəˈsfi(ə)rik; ˌmē-/ **adj.**

mes·o·the·li·o·ma /ˈmezəˌᴛʜēlēˈōmə; ˌmē-/ ▶ **n.** (pl. **-mas** or **-ma·ta**) Med. a cancer of mesothelial tissue, associated esp. with exposure to asbestos.

mes·o·the·li·um /ˌmezəˈᴛʜēlēəm; ˌmē-/ ▶ **n.** (pl. **-the·li·a** /-ˈᴛʜēlēə/) Anat. the epithelium that lines the pleurae, peritoneum, and pericardium. ■ Embryol. the surface layer of the embryonic mesoderm, from which this is derived. — **mes·o·the·li·al** /-ˈᴛʜēlēəl/ **adj.** [19th C.: from MESO- 'middle' + a shortened form of EPITHELIUM.]

mes·o·tho·rax /ˌmezəˈᴛʜôrˌaks/ ▶ **n.** (pl. **-thor·ax·es** or **-tho·ra·ces** /-ˈᴛʜôrəˌsēz/) Entomol. the middle segment of the thorax of an insect, bearing the forewings or elytra. — **mes·o·tho·rac·ic** /-ᴛʜəˈrasik/ **adj.**

mes·o·zo·an /ˌmezəˈzōən; ˌmē-/ ▶ **n.** Zool. a minute worm (phyla Orthonectida and Rhombozoa) that is an internal parasite of marine invertebrates. It lacks any internal organs other than reproductive cells, and dissolved nutrients are absorbed directly from the host's tissues. [20th C.: from mod. L. *Mesozoa* (from *mesos* 'intermediate' + *zōion* 'animal') + -AN.]

Mes·o·zo·ic /ˈmezəˈzōik; ˌmē-/ ▶ **adj.** Geol. of, relating to, or denoting the era between the Paleozoic and Cenozoic eras, comprising the Triassic, Jurassic, and Cretaceous periods. ■ [as n.] (**the Mesozoic**) the Mesozoic era or the system of rocks deposited during it. [19th C.: from MESO- + Gk. *zōion* 'animal.']

Mes·quite /məˈskēt/ a city in northeastern Texas; pop. 101,484.

mes·quite /me'skēt/ ▶n. a spiny tree or shrub (genus *Prosopis*) of the pea family, native to arid regions of southwestern US and Mexico. It yields useful timber, tanbark, medicinal products, and edible pods. [18th C.: from Mex. Sp. *mezquite*.]

mes·quite bean ▶n. an edible pod from the mesquite.

mess /mes/ ▶n. [usu. in sing.] **1** a dirty or untidy state of things or of a place: *she made a mess of the kitchen.* ■ a thing or collection of things causing such a state. ■ a person who is dirty or untidy. ■ a portion of semisolid or pulpy food, esp. one that looks unappetizing. ■ [with adj.] used euphemistically to refer to the excrement of a domestic animal. ■ fig. a situation or state of affairs that is confused or full of difficulties. ■ fig. a person whose life or affairs are confused or troubled. **2** a building or room in which members of the armed forces take their meals; mess hall: *the sergeants' mess.* ■ a meal taken there. ▶v. [trans.] make untidy or dirty. ■ [intrans.] (of a domestic animal) defecate. ■ make dirty by defecating: *he feared he would mess the bed.*
– PHRASES **mess with someone's head** informal cause someone to feel frustrated, anxious, confused, or upset.
– PHRASAL VERBS **mess around/about** behave in a silly or playful way, esp. so as to cause irritation. ■ spend time doing something in a pleasantly desultory way, with no definite purpose or serious intent: *messing about in boats.* **mess around/about with** interfere with. ■ informal engage in a sexual relationship with. **mess up** informal mishandle a situation. **mess someone up** informal cause someone emotional or psychological problems. ■ inflict violence or injury on someone: *the wreck messed him up.* **mess something up** informal cause something to be spoiled by inept handling: *mess up an entire day's work.* **mess with** informal meddle or interfere with so as to spoil or cause trouble: *stop messing with things.* [ME: from OFr. *mes* 'portion of food,' from late L. *missum* 'something put on the table,' past part. of *mittere* 'send, put.']

mes·sage /'mesij/ ▶n. a verbal, written, or recorded communication sent to or left for a recipient who cannot be contacted directly. ■ an official or formal communication, esp. a speech delivered by a head of state to a legislative assembly or the public. ■ an item of electronic mail. ■ an electronic communication generated automatically by a computer program and displayed on a VDT: *an error message.* ■ a significant point or central theme: *get the message about home security across.* ■ a divinely inspired communication from a prophet or preacher. ■ a television or radio commercial.
– PHRASES **get the message** informal infer an implication from a remark or action. **send a message** make a significant statement, either implicitly or by one's actions: *the elections sent a message to political quarters.* [ME: from OFr., based on L. *missus*, past part. of *mittere* 'send.']

mes·sag·ing /'mesijiNG/ ▶n. the sending and processing of electronic mail by computer.

Mes·sei·gneurs /,māsān'yər(z)/ plural form of MONSEIGNEUR.

mes·sen·ger /'mesənjər/ ▶n. **1** a person who carries a message or is employed to carry messages. ■ Biochem. a substance that conveys information or a stimulus within the body. **2** Naut. (also **messenger line**) an endless rope, cable, or chain used with a capstan to haul an anchor cable or to drive a powered winch. ■ a light line used to haul or support a larger cable. ▶v. [trans.] send (a document or package) by messenger: *have it messengered to me?*
– PHRASES **shoot** (or **kill**) **the messenger** treat the bearer of bad news as if they were to blame for it. [ME: from Old North. Fr. *messanger*, var. of OFr. *messager*, from L. *missus* (see MESSAGE).]

mes·sen·ger RNA (abbr.: **mRNA**) ▶n. the form of RNA in which genetic information transcribed from DNA as a sequence of bases is transferred to a ribosome.

mess hall ▶n. a room or building where groups of people, esp. soldiers, eat together.

Mes·siaen /mes'yäN/, Olivier Eugène Prosper Charles (1908–92), French composer. His music was influenced by his Roman Catholic faith.

mes·si·ah /mə'sīə/ ▶n. **1** (**the Messiah**) the promised deliverer of the Jewish nation prophesied in the Hebrew Bible. ■ Jesus, regarded by Christians as the Messiah of the Hebrew prophecies and the savior of humankind. **2** a leader or savior of a particular group or cause. — **mes·si·ah·ship** n. [OE *Messias*: via late L. and Gk. from Heb. *māšîaḥ* 'anointed.']

mes·si·an·ic /,mesē'anik/ ▶adj. (also **Messianic**) of or relating to the Messiah: *the messianic role of Jesus.* ■ inspired by hope or belief in a messiah. ■ fervent or passionate: *an admirable messianic zeal.* — **mes·si·a·nism** /'mesēə,nizəm; mə'sīə-/ n. [19th C.: from Fr. *messianique*, from *Messie* (see MESSIAH).]

Mes·sier /'mesē,ā; mes'yā/, Charles (1730–1817), French astronomer. He discovered a number of nebulae, galaxies, and star clusters.

Mes·sieurs /məs'yœ(r)(z); mās-; me'syœ/ plural form of MONSIEUR.

Mes·si·na /mə'sēnə/ a city in northeastern Sicily; pop. 274,850.

Mes·si·na, Strait of a channel that separates the island of Sicily from the "toe" of Italy.

mess jacket ▶n. a short jacket worn by a military officer on formal occasions. ■ a similar jacket worn as part of a waiter's or bellhop's uniform.

mess kit ▶n. a set of cooking and eating utensils, as used esp. by soldiers, scouts, or campers.

mess·mate /'mes,māt/ ▶n. a person with whom one takes meals, esp. in the armed forces.

Messrs. ▶plural n. dated or esp. Brit. used as a title to refer formally to more than one man simultaneously, or in names of companies: *Messrs. Sotheby.* [18th C.: abbrev. of MESSIEURS.]

mes·suage /'meswij/ ▶n. Law a dwelling house with outbuildings and land assigned to its use. [ME: from Anglo-Norman Fr., based on L. *manere* 'dwell.']

mess·y /'mesē/ ▶adj. (**mess·i·er, mess·i·est**) **1** untidy or dirty: *his messy hair.* ■ generating or involving mess or untidiness. **2** (of a situation) confused and difficult to deal with. — **mess·i·ly** adv. **mess·i·ness** n.

mes·ti·za /mə'stēzə/ ▶n. (in Latin America) a woman of mixed race. [Sp., fem. of *mestizo* (see MESTIZO).]

mes·ti·zo /me'stēzō/ ▶n. (pl. **-zos**) (in Latin America) a man of mixed race. [Sp., 'mixed,' based on L. *mixtus*.]

met /met/ past and past participle of MEET.

met. ▶abbr. ■ metaphor. ■ metaphysics. ■ meteorology. ■ metropolitan.

met- ▶comb. form var. of META- shortened before a vowel or *h* (as in *metonym*).

meta- (also **met-** before a vowel or h) ▶comb. form **1** denoting a change of position or condition: *metamorphosis* | *metathesis.* **2** denoting position behind, after, or beyond: *metacarpus.* **3** denoting something of a higher or second-order kind: *metalanguage* | *metonym.* **4** Chem. denoting substitution at two carbon atoms separated by one other in a benzene ring, e.g., in 1,3 positions: *metadichlorobenzene.* Compare with ORTHO- and PARA-[1]. **5** Chem. denoting a compound formed by dehydration: *metaphosphoric acid.* [from Gk. *meta* 'with, across, or after.']

met·a·bol·ic path·way /'metə'bälik/ ▶n. see PATHWAY.

me·tab·o·lism /mə'tabə,lizəm/ ▶n. the chemical processes that occur within a living organism in order to maintain life. — **met·a·bol·ic** /'metə'bälik/ adj. **met·a·bol·i·cal·ly** /,metə'bälik(ə)lē/ adv. [19th C.: from Gk. *metabolē* 'change' (from *metaballein* 'to change') + -ISM.]

me·tab·o·lite /mə'tabə,līt/ ▶n. Biochem. a substance formed in or necessary for metabolism.

me·tab·o·lize /mə'tabə,līz/ ▶v. [trans.] (of a body or organ) process (a substance) by metabolism. ■ [intrans.] (of a substance) undergo metabolism. — **me·tab·o·liz·a·ble** adj. **me·tab·o·liz·er** n.

met·a·car·pal /'metə,kärpəl/ ▶n. any of the hand bones. ■ any of the equivalent bones in an animal's forelimb. ▶adj. of or relating to these bones.

met·a·car·pus /'metə,kärpəs/ ▶n. (pl. **-pi** /-pē; -,pī/) the five hand bones between the wrist and fingers. ■ this part of the hand. ■ the equivalent group of bones in an animal's forelimb. [ME: mod. L., alt. of Gk. *metakarpion*.]

met·a·cen·ter /'metə,sentər/ (Brit. **met·a·cen·tre**) ▶n. the point of intersection between a vertical line through the center of buoyancy of a floating body such as a ship and a vertical line through the new center of buoyancy when the body is tilted, which must be above the center of gravity to ensure stability. — **met·a·cen·tric** /,metə'sentrik/ adj.

met·a·chro·ma·sia /,metəkrō'māzH(ē)ə/ (also **met·a·chro·ma·sy** /-'krōməsē/) ▶n. Biol. the property of certain biological materials of staining a different color from that of the stain used. — **met·a·chro·mat·ic** /-krō'matik/ adj. [20th C.: mod. L., from META- (expressing change) + Gk. *khrōma* 'color.']

Met·a·com·et /,metə'kämit/ see PHILIP[4].

met·a·da·ta /'metə,datə; -,dātə/ ▶n. a set of data that describes and gives information about other data.

met·a·fic·tion /'metə,fiksHən/ ▶n. fiction in which the author self-consciously alludes to the artificiality or literariness of a work by parodying or departing from novelistic conventions (esp. naturalism) and traditional narrative techniques. — **met·a·fic·tion·al** /,metə'fiksHənl/ adj.

met·age /'metij/ ▶n. the official weighing of loads of coal, grain, or other material. ■ the duty paid for this. [16th C.: from METE[1] + -AGE.]

met·a·gen·e·sis /,metə'jenəsis/ ▶n. Biol. the alternation of sexual and asexual generations.

Met·air·ie /'metərē/ a city in southeastern Louisiana; pop. 149,428.

met·al /'metl/ ▶n. **1** a solid material that is typically hard, shiny, malleable, fusible, and ductile, with good electrical and thermal conductivity. ■ Heraldry gold and silver (as tinctures in blazoning). **2** molten glass before it is blown or cast. **3** heavy metal or similar rock music. ▶v. (**met·aled, met·al·ing**; esp. Brit. **met·alled, met·al·ling**) [trans.] [usu. as adj.] (**metaled**) make out of metal. [ME: from OFr. *metal* or L. *metallum*, from Gk. *metallon* 'mine, quarry, or metal.']

metal. (also **metall.**) ▶abbr. ■ metallurgical or metallurgy.

met·a·lan·guage /'metə,laNG(g)wij/ ▶n. a form of language used to describe another language. Compare with OBJECT LANGUAGE. ■ Logic a system of propositions about propositions.

met·al de·tec·tor ▶n. an electronic device that gives a signal when it is close to metal.

met·al·head /'metl,hed/ ▶n. informal another term for HEADBANGER.

met·a·lin·guis·tics /,metə,liNG'gwistiks/ ▶plural n. [treated as sing.] the branch of linguistics that deals with metalanguages. — **met·a·lin·guis·tic** adj.

met·al·ize /'metl,īz/ (also **met·al·lize**) ▶v. [trans.] coat with a thin layer of metal. — **met·al·i·za·tion** /,metlə'zāsHən/ n.

metall. ▶abbr. var. of METAL.

me·tal·lic /mə'talik/ ▶ **adj.** resembling metal or metals. ■ (of sound) resembling that produced by metal objects striking each other; sharp and ringing. ■ (of a person's voice); emanating or as if emanating via an electronic medium. ■ having the sheen of metal. ▶ **n.** a paint, fiber, fabric, or color with a metallic sheen. — **me·tal·li·cal·ly adv.**

met·al·lif·er·ous /,metl'ifərəs/ ▶ **adj.** (chiefly of deposits of minerals) containing or producing metal. [17th C.: from L. *metallifer* 'metal-bearing' + **-ous**.]

met·al·log·ra·phy /,metl'ägrəfē/ ▶ **n.** the descriptive science of the structure and properties of metals. — **met·al·log·ra·pher n. me·tal·lo·graph·ic** /'metl-ə'grafik/ **adj. me·tal·lo·graph·i·cal** /,metl-ə'grafikəl/ **adj. me·tal·lo·graph·i·cal·ly** /,metl-ə'grafik(ə)lē/ **adv.**

met·al·loid /'metl,oid/ ▶ **n.** Chem. an element (e.g., germanium or silicon) whose properties are intermediate between those of metals and solid nonmetals. They are electrical semiconductors.

met·al·lur·gy /'metl,ərjē/ ▶ **n.** the branch of science that deals with the properties of metals. — **met·al·lur·gic** /,metl'ərjik/ **adj. met·al·lur·gi·cal** /,metl'ərjikəl/ **adj. met·al·lur·gi·cal·ly** /,metl'ərjik(ə)lē/ **adv. met·al·lur·gist n.** [18th C.: from Gk. *metallon* 'metal' + *-ourgia* 'working.']

met·al·work /'metl,wərk/ ▶ **n.** the art of making things out of metal. ■ metal objects collectively. ■ the metal part of a construction: *cracks in the metalwork.* — **met·al·work·er n. met·al·work·ing n.**

met·a·math·e·mat·ics /,metə,maTH(ə)'matiks/ ▶ **plural n.** [usu. treated as sing.] the study of the structure and formal properties of mathematics. — **met·a·math·e·mat·i·cal** /-'matikəl/ **adj. met·a·math·e·mat·i·cal·ly** /-'matik(ə)lē/ **adv. met·a·math·e·ma·ti·cian** /-mə'tisHən/ **n.**

met·a·mere /'metəmi(ə)r/ ▶ **n.** Zool. another term for **somite**. [19th C.: from **meta-** 'together with' + Gk. *meros* 'part.']

met·a·mer·ic /,metə'merik/ ▶ **adj. 1** Zool. of, relating to, or consisting of several similar segments or somites. **2** Chem., dated having the same proportional composition and molecular weight, but different functional groups and chemical properties; isomeric. — **met·a·mer** /'metəmər/ **n. met·a·mer·i·cal·ly** /,metə'merik(ə)lē/ **adv. me·tam·er·ism** /mə'tamə,rizəm/ **n.**

met·a·mor·phic /'metə'môrfik/ ▶ **adj. 1** Geol. denoting rock that has undergone transformation by heat, pressure, or other natural agencies. ■ of or relating to such rocks or metamorphism. **2** of or marked by metamorphosis. [19th C.: from **meta-** (denoting a change of condition) + Gk. *morphē* 'form' + **-ic**.]

met·a·mor·phism /'metə'môr,fizəm/ ▶ **n.** Geol. alteration of the composition or structure of a rock.

met·a·mor·phose /,metə'môr,fōz; -,fōs/ ▶ **v.** [intrans.] (of an insect or amphibian) undergo metamorphosis. ■ change completely in form or nature. ■ [trans.] cause (something) to change completely. ■ [trans.] Geol. subject (rock) to metamorphism. [16th C.: from Fr. *métamorphoser*, from *métamorphose* (see **metamorphosis**).]

met·a·mor·pho·sis /,metə'môrfəsəs/ ▶ **n.** (pl. **-pho·ses** /-fə,sēz/) Zool. (in an insect or amphibian) the process of transformation from an immature form to an adult form in two or more distinct stages. ■ a change of the form or nature of a thing or person into a completely different one, by natural or supernatural means: *his metamorphosis from presidential candidate to talk-show host.* [ME: via L. from Gk. *metamorphōsis*, from *metamorphoun* 'transform, change shape.']

met·a·phase /'metə,fāz/ ▶ **n.** Biol. the second stage of cell division during which the chromosomes become attached to the spindle fibers.

met·a·phor /'metə,fôr; -fər/ ▶ **n.** a figure of speech in which a word or phrase is applied to an object or action to which it is not literally applicable: *I had fallen through a trapdoor of depression.* | *her poetry depends on suggestion and metaphor.* ■ a thing regarded as representative or symbolic of something else, esp. something abstract. — **met·a·phor·ic** /,metə'fôrik; -'fär-/ **adj. met·a·phor·i·cal** /,metə'fôrikəl; -'fär-/ **adj. met·a·phor·i·cal·ly** /,metə'fôrik(ə)lē/ **adv.** [15th C.: from Fr. *métaphore*, via L. from Gk. *metaphora*, from *metapherein* 'to transfer.']

met·a·phos·phor·ic ac·id /,metə,fäs'fôrik; -'fär-/ ▶ **n.** Chem. a glassy deliquescent solid, $(HPO_3)_n$, obtained by heating phosphoric acid. — **met·a·phos·phate** /-'fäs,fāt/ **n.**

met·a·phrase /'metə,frāz/ ▶ **n.** a literal, word-for-word translation, as opposed to a paraphrase. ▶ **v.** [trans.] alter the phrasing or language of.

met·a·phys·ic /,metə'fizik/ ▶ **n.** a system of metaphysics.

met·a·phys·i·cal /,metə'fizikəl/ ▶ **adj. 1** of or relating to metaphysics: *metaphysical question.* ■ based on abstract reasoning. ■ transcending physical matter or the laws of nature. **2** of or characteristic of the metaphysical poets. ▶ **n.** (**the Metaphysicals**) the metaphysical poets. — **met·a·phys·i·cal·ly adv.**

met·a·phys·i·cal po·ets a group of 17th-century poets whose work is characterized by the use of complex and elaborate images or conceits.

met·a·phys·ics /,metə'fiziks/ ▶ **plural n.** [usu. treated as sing.] the branch of philosophy that deals with the first principles of things, including abstract concepts such as being, knowing, cause, identity, time, and space. ■ abstract theory or talk with no basis in reality. — **met·a·phy·si·cian** /-fə'zisHən/ **n.** [16th C.: representing med. L. *metaphysica* (neut. pl.), based on Gk. *ta meta ta phusika* 'the things after the Physics,' referring to the sequence of Aristotle's works.]

met·a·pla·sia /,metə'plāzH(ē)ə/ ▶ **n.** Physiol. abnormal change in the nature of a tissue. — **met·a·plas·tic** /-'plastik/ **adj.** [19th C.: mod. L., from Ger. *Metaplase*, based on Gk. *metaplassein* 'mold into a new form.']

met·a·psy·chol·o·gy /'metə,sī'käləjē/ ▶ **n.** speculation concerning mental processes and the mind–body relationship, beyond what can be studied. — **met·a·psy·cho·log·i·cal** /-,sīkə'läjikəl/ **adj.**

Me·ta Riv·er /'mātə/ a river that flows from central Colombia to the Orinoco River.

met·a·se·quoi·a /,metəsi'kwoiə/ ▶ **n.** another term for **dawn redwood**.

met·a·so·ma·tism /,metə'sōmə,tizəm/ ▶ **n.** Geol. change in the composition of a rock as a result of the introduction or removal of chemical constituents. — **met·a·so·mat·ic** /-sə'matik/ **adj. met·a·so·ma·tize** /-'sōmə,tīz/ **v.** [19th C.: from **meta-** (expressing change) + Gk. *sōma, somat-* 'body' + **-ism**.]

met·a·sta·ble /'metə,stābəl; ,metə'stābəl/ ▶ **adj.** Physics (of a state of equilibrium) stable, provided it is subjected to no more than small disturbances. ■ (of a substance or particle) theoretically unstable, but so long-lived as to be stable for practical purposes. — **met·a·sta·bil·i·ty** /-stə'bilətē/ **n.**

me·tas·ta·sis /mə'tastəsəs/ ▶ **n.** (pl. **-ses** /-,sēz/) Med. the development of secondary malignant growths at a distance from the primary site. — **met·a·stat·ic** /,metə'statik/ **adj.** [16th C.: from Gk., lit. 'removal or change,' from *methistanai* 'to change.']

me·tas·ta·size /mə'tastə,sīz/ ▶ **v.** [intrans.] Med. (of a cancer) spread to other sites in the body by metastasis. ■ (of a condition or circumstance) spread or grow.

met·a·tar·sal /,metə'tärsəl/ ▶ **n.** any of the bones of the foot (metatarsus). ■ any of the equivalent bones in an animal's hind limb.

met·a·tar·sus /,metə'tärsəs/ ▶ **n.** (pl. **-si** /-sē; -,sī/) foot bones between the ankle and the toes. ■ this part of the foot. ■ the equivalent group of bones in an animal's hind limb. [ME: mod. L. (see **meta-**, **tarsus**).]

me·ta·te /mə'tätā/ (also **metate stone**) ▶ **n.** (in Central America) a flat or slightly hollowed oblong stone on which materials such as grain and cocoa are ground. [from Amer. Sp., from Nahuatl *métatl*.]

Met·a·the·ri·a /,metə'THi(ə)rēə/ Zool. a group of mammals (infraclass Metatheria, subclass Theria) that comprises the marsupials. Compare with **Eutheria**. — **met·a·the·ri·an n. & adj.** [mod. L. (plural), from **meta-** (expressing change) + Gk. *thēria*, pl. of *thērion* 'wild animal.']

me·tath·e·sis /mə'taTHəsəs/ ▶ **n.** (pl. **-ses** /-,sēz/) **1** Gram. the transposition of sounds or letters in a word. **2** (also **me·tath·e·sis re·ac·tion**) Chem. a reaction in which two compounds exchange ions. — **met·a·thet·ic** /,metə'THetik/ **adj. met·a·thet·i·cal** /,metə'THetikəl/ **adj.** [16th C.: from Gk., from *metatithenai* 'transpose, change the position of.']

met·a·tho·rax /,metə'THôr,aks/ ▶ **n.** (pl. **-tho·rax·es** or **-tho·ra·ces** /-'THôrə,sēz/) Entomol. the posterior segment of the thorax of an insect, bearing the hind wings. — **met·a·tho·rac·ic** /-THə'rasik/ **adj.**

Met·a·zo·a /,metə'zōə/ Zool. a major division (subkingdom Metazoa) of the animal kingdom that comprises all animals other than protozoans and sponges. They are multicellular animals with differentiated tissues. ■ [as pl. n.] (**metazoa**) animals of this division. — **met·a·zo·an** /-'zōən/ **n. & adj.** [mod. L. (plural), from **meta-** (expressing change) + *zōia* (pl. of *zōion* 'animal').]

mete[1] /mēt/ ▶ **v.** [trans.] (**mete something out**) dispense or allot (justice or a punishment). ■ (in biblical use) measure out. [OE *metan* 'measure'; rel. Ger. *messen* 'to measure,' L. *meditari* 'meditate.']

mete[2] ▶ **n.** (usu. **metes and bounds**) esp. hist. a boundary or boundary stone. [ME: from OFr., from L. *meta* 'boundary, goal.']

me·tem·psy·cho·sis /,metəm,sī'kōsəs; mə,temsi'kōsəs/ ▶ **n.** (pl. **-ses** /-sēz/) the supposed transmigration at death of the soul of a human being or animal into a new body. — **me·tem·psy·chot·ic** /-'kätik/ **adj. me·tem·psy·chot·i·cal·ly** /-'kätik(ə)lē/ **adv. me·tem·psy·cho·sist** /-'kōsist/ **n.** [16th C.: via late L. from Gk. *metempsukhōsis*, from *meta-* (expressing change) + *en* 'in' + *psukhē* 'soul.']

me·te·or /'mētēər; -ē,ôr/ ▶ **n.** a small body of matter from outer space that enters the earth's atmosphere, appearing as a streak of light. [16th C.: from mod. L. *meteorum*, from Gk. *meteōron*, neut. of *meteōros* 'lofty.']

meteor. ▶ **abbr.** ■ meteorological or meteorology.

me·te·or·ic /,mētē'ôrik; -'är-/ ▶ **adj. 1** of or relating to meteors or meteorites: *meteoric iron.* ■ fig. (of the development of something, esp. a person's career) very rapid: *her meteoric rise.* **2** esp. Geol. relating to or denoting water derived from the atmosphere by precipitation or condensation. — **me·te·or·i·cal·ly adv.**

me·te·or·ite /'mētēə,rīt/ ▶ **n.** a meteor that survives its passage through the earth's atmosphere such that part of it strikes the ground. — **me·te·or·it·ic** /',mētēə'ritik/ **adj.**

me·te·or·o·graph /,mētē'ôrə,graf; -'är-/ ▶ **n.** archaic an apparatus that records several meteorological phenomena at the same time.

me·te·or·oid /'mētēə,roid/ ▶ **n.** Astron. a small body moving in the solar system that would become a meteor if it entered the earth's atmosphere. — **me·te·o·roid·al** /,mētēə'roidl/ **adj.**

me·te·or·ol·o·gy /,mētēə'räləjē/ ▶ **n.** the branch of science concerned with the processes and phenomena of the atmosphere, esp. as a means of forecasting the weather. ■ the climate and weather of a region. — **me·te·or·o·log·i·cal** /-rə'läjikəl/ **adj. me·te·or·o·log·i·cal·ly** /-rə'läjik(ə)lē/ **adv. me·te·or·ol·o·gist** /-'räləjist/ **n.**

me·te·or show·er ▶ **n.** Astron. a number of meteors that appear to radiate from one point in the sky at a particular date each year.

me·ter[1] /'mētər/ (Brit. **me·tre**) ▶ **n.** the fundamental unit of length in the metric system, equal to 100 centimeters or approximately 39.37 inches. — **me·ter·age** /-ij/ **n.** [18th C.: from Fr. *mètre*, from Gk. *metron* 'measure.']

me·ter[2] (Brit. **me·tre**) ▶ **n.** the rhythm of a piece of poetry, determined by the number and length of feet in a line. [OE, from L. *metrum*, from Gk. *metron* 'measure.']

me·ter[3] ▶ **n.** a device that measures and records the quantity, degree, or rate of something. ■ Philately an imprint of specified value produced under government permit for the prepayment of postage. ▶ **v.** [trans.] [often as adj.] (**metered**) measure by a meter. [ME: from METE[1].]

-meter ▶ **comb. form 1** in names of measuring instruments: *thermometer*. **2** Pros. in nouns denoting lines of poetry with a specified number of feet or measures: *hexameter*. [from Gk. *metron* 'measure.']

me·ter-kil·o·gram-sec·ond (abbr.: **mks**) ▶ **adj.** denoting a system of measure using the meter, kilogram, and second as the basic units of length, mass, and time.

meth /meTH/ ▶ **n.** informal **1** (also **crystal meth**) the drug methamphetamine. **2** short for METHADONE.

meth·a·cryl·ic ac·id /ˌmeTHəˈkrilik/ ▶ **n.** Chem. a colorless, low-melting solid, $CH_2=C(CH_3)COOH$, that polymerizes when distilled and is used in the manufacture of synthetic resins. — **meth·ac·ry·late** /meTHˈakrəˌlāt/ **n.**

meth·a·done /ˈmeTHəˌdōn/ ▶ **n.** a synthetic analgesic drug that is used as a substitute to treat morphine and heroin addiction. [1940s: from its chemical name, *(6-di)meth(yl)a(mino-4,4-)d(iphenyl-3-heptan)one*.]

meth·am·phet·a·mine /ˌmeTHamˈfetəˌmēn; -min/ ▶ **n.** a synthetic drug, $C_6H_5CH_2CH(CH_3)NH(CH_3)$, with more rapid and lasting effects than amphetamine, used illegally as a stimulant and as a prescription drug to treat narcolepsy and maintain blood pressure.

meth·a·nal /ˈmeTHəˌnal/ ▶ **n.** systematic chemical name for FORMALDEHYDE. [19th C.: blend of METHANE and ALDEHYDE.]

meth·ane /ˈmeTHˌān/ ▶ **n.** Chem. a colorless, odorless flammable gas, CH_4, that is the main constituent of natural gas. It is the simplest member of the alkane series of hydrocarbons. [19th C.: from METHYL + -ANE[2].]

meth·an·o·gen /ˈmeTHənəjən/ ▶ **n.** Biol. a methane-producing bacterium. — **meth·an·o·gen·ic** /ˌmeTHənəˈjenik/ **adj.**

meth·a·no·ic ac·id /ˌmeTHəˈnōik/ ▶ **n.** systematic chemical name for FORMIC ACID. — **methanoate** /məˈTHanōˌāt/ **n.** [19th C.: *methanoic*, from METHANE + *-oic*.]

meth·a·nol /ˈmeTHəˌnôl; -ˌnōl/ ▶ **n.** Chem. a toxic, colorless, volatile flammable liquid alcohol, CH_3OH, originally made by distillation from wood and now chiefly by oxidizing methane. Also called METHYL ALCOHOL. [19th C.: from METHANE + -OL.]

meth·e·drine /ˈmeTHəˌdrēn; -drin/ (also **Meth·e·drine**) ▶ **n.** trademark another term for METHAMPHETAMINE. [1930s: blend of METHYL and BENZEDRINE.]

me·theg·lin /məˈTHeglən/ ▶ **n.** hist. a spiced or medicated variety of mead. [16th C.: from Welsh *meddyglyn*, from *meddyg* 'medicinal' (from L. *medicus*) + *llyn* 'liquor.']

met·he·mo·glo·bin /metˈhēməˌglōbən/ (Brit. **met·hae·mo·glo·bin**) ▶ **n.** Biochem. a stable oxidized form of hemoglobin that is unable to release oxygen to the tissues.

meth·i·cil·lin /ˌmeTHəˈsilən/ ▶ **n.** Med. a semisynthetic form of penicillin. [1960s: from *meth(yl)* and *(pen)icillin*.]

me·thinks /miˈTHiNGks/ ▶ **v.** (past **me·thought** /miˈTHôt/) [intrans.] archaic humorous it seems to me. [OE *mē thyncth*, from *mē* 'to me' + *thyncth* 'it seems' (from *thyncan* 'seem,' rel. to, but distinct from, THINK).]

me·thi·o·nine /məˈTHīəˌnēn/ ▶ **n.** Biochem. a sulfur-containing amino acid, $CH_3S(CH_2)_2CH(NH_2)COOH$, that is a constituent of most proteins. It is an essential nutrient in the diet of vertebrates. [1920s: from METHYL + Gk. *theion* 'sulfur.']

meth·od /ˈmeTHəd/ ▶ **n.** (often **method for/of**) a particular procedure for accomplishing or approaching something, esp. a systematic or established one. ■ orderliness of thought or behavior; systematic planning or action: *combination of knowledge and method*. ■ (often **Method**) short for METHOD ACTING.

– PHRASES **there is method in one's madness** there is a sensible foundation for what appears to be foolish or strange behavior. [ME: via L. from Gk. *methodos* 'pursuit of knowledge,' from *meta-* + *hodos* 'way.']

meth·od act·ing ▶ **n.** a technique of acting in which an actor aspires to complete emotional identification with a part. — **meth·od ac·tor n.**

me·thod·i·cal /məˈTHädikəl/ ▶ **adj.** done according to a systematic or established form of procedure. ■ (of a person) orderly in thought or behavior. — **me·thod·ic adj. me·thod·i·cal·ly adv.**

Meth·od·ist /ˈmeTHədist/ ▶ **n.** a member of a Christian Protestant denomination. ▶ **adj.** of or relating to Methodists or Methodism. — **Meth·od·ism n. Meth·od·is·tic** /ˌmeTHəˈdistik/ **adj.**

meth·od·ize /ˈmeTHəˌdīz/ ▶ **v.** [trans.] rare arrange in an orderly or systematic manner. — **meth·od·iz·er n.**

meth·od·ol·o·gy /ˌmeTHəˈdäləjē/ ▶ **n.** (pl. **-gies**) a system of methods used in a particular area of study. — **meth·od·o·log·i·cal** /-ədəˈläjikəl/ **adj. meth·od·o·log·i·cal·ly** /-ədəˈläjik(ə)lē/ **adv. meth·od·ol·o·gist** /-əˈdäləjist/ **n.**

meth·o·trex·ate /ˌmeTHəˈtrekˌsāt/ ▶ **n.** Med. a synthetic compound, $C_{20}H_{22}N_8O_5$, that interferes with cell growth and is used to treat leukemia and other forms of cancer. [1950s: from *meth-* + elements of unknown origin.]

me·thought /miˈTHôt/ past of METHINKS.

Me·thu·se·lah /məˈTH(y)o͞oz(ə)lə/ (in the Bible) the grandfather of Noah. ■ used to refer to a very old person: *I'm feeling older than Methuselah*.

me·thu·se·lah ▶ **n.** a wine bottle of eight times the standard size. [1930s: from METHUSELAH.]

meth·yl /ˈmeTHəl/ ▶ **n.** [as adj.] Chem. of or denoting the alkyl radical $-CH_3$, derived from methane. [19th C.: from Ger. *Methyl* or Fr. *méthyle*, back-formations from Ger. *Methylen* and Fr. *méthylène* (see METHYLENE).]

meth·yl al·co·hol ▶ **n.** another term for METHANOL.

meth·yl·ate /ˈmeTHəˌlāt/ ▶ **v.** [trans.] [often as adj.] (**methylated**) mix or impregnate with methanol or methylated spirit. ■ Chem. introduce a methyl group into (a molecule or compound). — **meth·yl·a·tion** /ˌmeTHəˈlāSHən/ **n.**

meth·yl·at·ed spir·it (also **meth·yl·at·ed spir·its**) ▶ **n.** alcohol for general use that has been made unfit for drinking by the addition of about 10 percent methanol and typically also some pyridine and a violet dye.

meth·yl·ben·zene /ˌmeTHəlˈbenˌzēn/ ▶ **n.** systematic chemical name for TOLUENE.

meth·yl·ene /ˈmeTHəˌlēn/ ▶ **n.** [as adj.] Chem. the divalent radical or group $-CH_2-$, derived from methane by loss of two hydrogen atoms: *methylene chloride*. [19th C.: from Fr. *méthylène* (formed irregularly from Gk. *methu* 'wine' + *hulē* 'wood') + -ENE.]

meth·yl·phen·i·date /ˌmeTHəlˈfenəˌdāt/ ▶ **n.** Med. a synthetic drug that stimulates the sympathetic and central nervous systems and is used to improve mental activity in attention deficit disorder.

me·tic·u·lous /məˈtikyələs/ ▶ **adj.** showing great attention to detail; very careful and precise. — **me·tic·u·lous·ly adv. me·tic·u·lous·ness n.** [16th C.: from L. *meticulosus*, from *metus* 'fear.']

mé·tier /meˈtyā; ˈmeˌtyā/ ▶ **n.** a trade or occupation. ■ an occupation or activity that one is good at. ■ an outstanding or advantageous characteristic. [18th C.: Fr., based on L. *ministerium* 'service.']

Mé·tis /māˈtēs/ (also **Me·tis**) ▶ **n.** (pl. same) (esp. in western Canada) a person of mixed American Indian and Euro-American ancestry. ▶ **adj.** denoting or relating to such people. [from Fr., from late L. *mixticius*, from L. *mixtus* 'mixed' (see also MESTIZO).]

Me·tol /ˈmeˌtôl; -ˌtōl/ ▶ **n.** trademark a soluble white compound, $CH_3NHC_6H_4OH$, used as a photographic developer. [19th C.: from Ger., arbitrarily named by the inventor.]

Me·ton·ic cy·cle /meˈtänik/ ▶ **n.** a period of 19 years (235 lunar months), after which the new and full moons return to the same days of the year. [named after *Metōn*, an Athenian astronomer of the 5th C. BC.]

met·o·nym /ˈmetəˌnim/ ▶ **n.** a word, name, or expression used as a substitute for something else with which it is closely associated. For example, *Washington* is a metonym for the US federal government. [19th C.: back-form. from METONYMY.]

me·ton·y·my /məˈtänəmē/ ▶ **n.** (pl. **-mies**) the substitution of the name of an attribute or adjunct for that of the thing meant, for example *suit* for *business executive*. — **met·o·nym·ic** /ˌmetəˈnimik/ **adj. met·o·nym·i·cal** /ˌmetəˈnimikəl/ **adj. met·o·nym·i·cal·ly** /ˌmetəˈnimik(ə)lē/ **adv.** [16th C.: via L. from Gk. *metōnumia*, lit. 'change of name.']

met·o·pe /ˈmetəpē/ ▶ **n.** Archit. a square space between triglyphs in a Doric frieze. [16th C.: via L. from Gk. *metopē*, from *meta* 'between' + *opē* 'hole for a beam-end.']

me·tre ▶ **n.** British spelling of METER[1], METER[2].

met·ric[1] /ˈmetrik/ ▶ **adj. 1** of or based on the meter as a unit of length; relating to the metric system. ■ using the metric system. **2** Math. & Physics relating to or denoting a metric. ▶ **n. 1** tech. a system or standard of measurement. ■ (**metrics**) a method of measuring something, or the figures or statistics obtained from this. **2** informal metric units, or the metric system.

met·ric[2] ▶ **adj.** relating to or composed in a poetic meter. ▶ **n.** (**metrics**) [treated as sing.] the meter of a poem.

-metric ▶ **comb. form** in adjectives corresponding to nouns ending in *-meter* (such as *geometric* corresponding to *geometer* and *geometry*). — **-metrically comb. form** in corresponding adverbs. [from Fr. *-métrique*, from L.]

met·ri·cal /ˈmetrikəl/ ▶ **adj. 1** of, relating to, or composed in poetic meter: ***metrical translations of the Psalms***. **2** of or involving measurement. — **met·ri·cal·ly adv.**

-metrical ▶ **comb. form** equivalent to -METRIC.

met·ri·cate /ˈmetriˌkāt/ ▶ **v.** [trans.] change or adapt to a metric system of measurement. — **met·ri·ca·tion** /ˌmetriˈkāSHən/ **n.**

met·ric hun·dred·weight ▶ **n.** see HUNDREDWEIGHT.

met·ric mile ▶ **n.** a distance or race of 1,500 meters.

met·rics /ˈmetriks/ ▶ **n.** [treated as sing. or pl.] the use or study of poetic meters; prosody.

-met·rics ▶ **comb. form** denoting the science of measuring as applied to a specific field of study: *econometrics*.

met·ric sys·tem ▶ **n.** the decimal measuring system based on the meter, liter, and gram as units of length, capacity, and weight or mass.

met·ric ton (also **tonne**) ▶ **n.** a unit of weight equal to 1,000 kilograms (2,205 lb).

me·tri·tis /miˈtrītəs/ ▶ **n.** Med. inflammation of the uterus. [19th C.: from Gk. *mētra* 'womb' + -ITIS.]

met·ro /ˈmetrō/ ▶ **n.** (pl. **-ros**) (also **Metro**) a subway system in a city, esp. Paris. ▶ **adj.** [attrib.] metropolitan: *the Detroit metro area.* [20th C.: from Fr. *métro,* abbrev. of *métropolitain* (from *Chemin de Fer Métropolitain* 'Metropolitan Railroad').]

me·trol·o·gy /məˈträləjē/ ▶ **n.** the scientific study of measurement. — **met·ro·log·i·cal** /ˌmetrəˈläjikəl/ **adj.** **me·trol·o·gist** **n.** [19th C.: from Gk. *metron* 'measure' + -LOGY.]

met·ro·ni·da·zole /ˌmetrəˈnīdəˌzōl/ ▶ **n.** Med. a synthetic drug, $C_6H_9N_3O_3$, used to treat trichomoniasis and some similar infections. [20th C.: from *me(thyl)* + *(ni)tro-* + *(im)idazole.*]

met·ro·nome /ˈmetrəˌnōm/ ▶ **n.** a device used by musicians that marks time at a selected rate. — **met·ro·nom·ic** /ˌmetrəˈnämik/ **adj.** **met·ro·nom·i·cal·ly** /ˌmetrəˈnämik(ə)lē/ **adv.** [19th C.: from Gk. *metron* 'measure' + *nomos* 'law.']

metronome

me·tro·nym·ic /ˌmetrəˈnimik/ ▶ **adj. & n.** var. of MATRONYMIC.

met·ro·plex /ˈmetrəˌpleks/ ▶ **n.** a very large metropolitan area, esp. an aggregation of two or more cities. [1960s: blend of METROPOLITAN and COMPLEX.]

me·trop·o·lis /məˈträp(ə)ləs/ ▶ **n.** the capital or chief city of a country or region. ■ a very large and densely populated city. [ME: via late L. from Gk. *mētropolis* 'mother state,' from *mētēr, mētr-* 'mother' + *polis* 'city.']

met·ro·pol·i·tan /ˌmetrəˈpälitn/ ▶ **adj.** **1** of, relating to, or denoting a metropolis, often inclusive of its surrounding areas: *the Boston metropolitan area.* **2** of, relating to, or denoting the parent state of a colony or dependency: *metropolitan Spain.* **3** Christian Church of, relating to, or denoting a metropolitan or his see: *a metropolitan bishop.* ▶ **n.** **1** Christian Church a bishop having authority over the bishops of a province. **2** an inhabitant of a metropolis. — **met·ro·pol·i·tan·ate** /-ˈpälitnˌāt/ **n.** (in sense 1 of the **noun**). **met·ro·pol·i·tan·ism** /-ˌpälətnˌizəm/ **n.** **metropolitical** /-pəˈlitikəl/ **adj.** (in sense 1 of the **noun**). [ME (in the eccles. sense): from late L. *metropolitanus,* from Gk. *mētropolitēs* 'citizen of a mother state,' from *mētropolis* (see METROPOLIS).]

me·tror·rha·gi·a /ˌmētrəˈrāj(ē)ə; ˌmetrə-/ ▶ **n.** abnormal bleeding from the uterus. [19th C.: mod. L., from Gk. *mētra* 'womb' + *-rrhag-,* stem of *rhēgnunai* 'to burst.']

met·ro·sex·u·al /ˌmetrōˈsekSHo͞oəl/ ▶ **n.** a heterosexual urban man whose lifestyle, concern for personal appearance, and spending habits are likened to those considered typical of a fashionable male homosexual. — **met·ro·sex·u·al·i·ty** /-ˌsekSHo͞oˈalitē/ **n.** [1990s: blend of METROPOLITAN and HETEROSEXUAL.]

-metry ▶ **comb. form** in nouns denoting procedures and systems corresponding to names of instruments ending in *-meter* (such as *calorimetry* and *calorimeter*). [from Gk. *-metria,* from *-metrēs* 'measurer.']

Met·ter·nich /ˈmetərˌnik; -ˌniKH/, Klemens Wenzel Nepomuk Lothar, Prince of Metternich-Winneburg-Beilstein (1773–1859), foreign minister of Austria 1809–48.

met·tle /ˈmetl/ ▶ **n.** a person's ability to cope well with difficulties or to face a demanding situation in a spirited and resilient way: *the team showed their true mettle.*

– PHRASES **be on one's mettle** be ready or forced to prove one's ability to cope well with a demanding situation. **put someone on their mettle** (of a demanding situation) test someone's ability to face difficulties. — **met·tle·some** **adj.** [16th C.: from METAL.]

meu·nière /mœnˈyer/ ▶ **adj.** [usu. postpositive] (esp. of fish) cooked or served in lightly browned butter. [from Fr. *(à la) meunière* '(in the manner of) a miller's wife.']

Meur·sault /mərˈsō; mœr-/ ▶ **n.** (pl. same) a burgundy wine, typically white. [named after a commune in the Côte d'Or region of France.]

Meuse /myo͞oz; mo͞oz; mœz/ a river that rises in France and flows to the North Sea. Flemish and Dutch name MAAS.

MeV ▶ **abbr.** mega-electron volt(s).

mew[1] /myo͞o/ ▶ **v.** [intrans.] (of a cat or some kinds of bird) make a characteristic high-pitched crying noise. ▶ **n.** the high-pitched crying noise made by a cat or bird. [ME: imitative.]

mew[2] Falconry ▶ **n.** (usu. **mews**) a cage or building for trained hawks, esp. while they are molting. ▶ **v.** **1** [intrans.] (esp. of a trained hawk) molt. **2** [trans.] confine (a trained hawk) to a cage or building at the time of molting. [ME: from OFr. *mue,* from *muer* 'to molt,' from L. *mutare* 'to change.']

mewl /myo͞ol/ ▶ **v.** [intrans.] [often as adj.] (**mewling**) (esp. of a baby) cry feebly or querulously; whimper. ■ (of a cat or bird) mew: *the mewling cry of a hawk.* [ME: imitative.]

mews /myo͞oz/ ▶ **n.** (pl. same) esp. Brit. a row or street of houses or apartments that have been converted from stables or built to look like former stables. ■ a group of stables, typically with rooms above, built around a yard or along an alley. [ME: pl. of MEW[2].]

Mex /meks/ ▶ **adj. & n.** informal Mexican.

Mex·i·cal·i /ˌmeksəˈkalē/ a city in northwestern Mexico; pop. 602,000.

Mex·i·can bam·boo ▶ **n.** another term for JAPANESE KNOTWEED.

Mex·i·can hair·less ▶ **n.** a small dog of a breed lacking hair except for tufts on the head and tail.

Mex·i·ca·no /ˌmeksiˈkänō; ˌmāhē-/ ▶ **n. & adj.** informal **1** the Nahuatl language. **2** a person of Mexican descent. [Sp.]

Mex·i·co /ˈmeksiˌkō; ˈmāhēkō/ a country in southwestern North America. *See box on next page.* ■ a state in central Mexico, west of Mexico City. — **Mex·i·can** /ˈmeksəkən/ **adj. & n.**

Mex·i·co, Gulf of a large extension of the western Atlantic Ocean. It is bounded in a sweeping curve by the US, Mexico, and Cuba.

Mex·i·co Cit·y the capital of Mexico, in the south central part of the city; pop. 13,636,000.

Mey·er·beer /ˈmāərˌbi(ə)r; ˈmīərˌbe(ə)r/, Giacomo (1791–1864), German composer; born *Jakob Liebmann Beer.* He was a leading exponent of French grand opera.

Mey·er·hof /ˈmīərˌhôf/, Otto Fritz (1884–1951), US biochemist; born in Germany. He clarified the process by which glucose is broken down to provide energy. Nobel Prize for Physiology or Medicine (1922, shared with Archibald Hill 1886–1977).

me·ze·re·on /məˈzi(ə)rēən/ (also **me·ze·re·um** /-əm/) ▶ **n.** a Eurasian shrub (*Daphne mezereum,* family Thymelaeaceae) with fragrant purplish-red flowers and poisonous red berries. [15th C.: from med. L., from Arab. *māzaryūn.*]

me·zu·zah /məˈzo͞ozə/ (also **me·zu·za**) ▶ **n.** (pl. **me·zu·zahs** or **me·zu·zas** or **me·zu·zot** or **me·zu·zoth** /məˈzo͞ozōt/) a parchment inscribed with religious texts and attached in a case to the doorpost of a Jewish house as a sign of faith. [17th C.: from Heb. *mĕzûzāh* 'doorpost.']

mez·za·nine /ˈmezəˌnēn; ˌmezəˈnēn/ ▶ **n.** a low story between two others in a building, typically between the ground and first floors. ■ the lowest balcony of a theater, stadium, etc., or the front rows of the balcony. [18th C.: from Fr., from Ital. *mezzanino,* dimin. of *mezzano* 'middle,' from L. *medianus* 'median.']

mez·za vo·ce /ˌmetsä ˈvōCHā; ˌmedzä/ Music ▶ **adv. & adj.** (esp. as a direction) using part of singer's vocal power. ▶ **n.** singing performed in this way. [Ital., lit. 'half voice.']

mez·zo /ˈmetsō; ˈmedzō/ ▶ **n.** (pl. **-zos**) (also **mez·zo-so·pra·no**) a female singer with a voice pitched between soprano and contralto. ■ a singing voice of this type, or a part written for one. ▶ **adv.** half, moderately. [18th C.: Ital., from L. *medius* 'middle.']

mez·zo for·te /ˌmetsō ˈfôrtā; ˌmedzō/ Music ▶ **adv. & adj.** (esp. as a direction) moderately loud. ▶ **n.** a moderately high volume of sound.

Mez·zo·gior·no /ˌmetsōˈjôrnō/ southern Italy.

mez·zo pi·a·no /ˌmetsō ˈpyänō; ˌmedzō/ Music ▶ **adv. & adj.** (esp. as a direction) moderately soft. ▶ **n.** a moderately low volume of sound.

mez·zo·tint /ˈmetsōˌtint; ˈmedzō-/ ▶ **n.** a print made from an engraved copper or steel plate on which the surface has been partially roughened, for shading, and partially scraped smooth, giving light areas. ■ the process of making pictures in this way. ▶ **v.** [trans.] engrave (a picture) in mezzotint. — **mez·zo·tint·er** **n.** [from Ital. *mezzotinto,* from *mezzo* 'half' + *tinto* 'tint.']

MF ▶ **abbr.** medium frequency.

mf ▶ **abbr.** mezzo forte.

MFA ▶ **abbr.** Master of Fine Arts.

mfd. ▶ **abbr.** ■ manufactured. ■ microfarad.

mfg. ▶ **abbr.** manufacturing.

MFP ▶ **abbr.** Physics mean free path.

mfr. ▶ **abbr.** ■ manufacture. ■ (pl. **mfrs.**) manufacturer.

Mg ▶ **symb.** the chemical element magnesium.

mg ▶ **abbr.** milligram(s): *100 mg paracetamol.*

MGM Metro-Goldwyn-Mayer, a movie company formed in 1924.

mgmt. ▶ **abbr.** management.

Mgr. ▶ **abbr.** ■ (**mgr**) manager. ■ Monseigneur. ■ Monsignor.

mgt. ▶ **abbr.** management.

MH ▶ **abbr.** Medal of Honor.

mh (also **mH**) ▶ **abbr.** millihenry or millihenries.

MHC ▶ **abbr.** major histocompatibility complex.

MHL ▶ **abbr.** Master of Hebrew Literature.

mho /mō/ ▶ **n.** (pl. **mhos**) the reciprocal of an ohm, a former unit of electrical conductance. [19th C.: the word OHM reversed.]

MHR ▶ **abbr.** (in the US and Australia) Member of the House of Representatives.

MHz ▶ **abbr.** megahertz.

MI ▶ **abbr.** ■ Michigan (in official postal use). ■ Brit., hist. Military Intelligence: *MI5.*

mi /mē/ ▶ **n.** Music (in solmization) the third note of a major scale. ■ the note E in the fixed-do system. [ME *mi,* representing the first syllable of *mira.*]

mi. ▶ **abbr.** mile(s): *10 km/6 mi.*

MI5 (in the UK) the governmental agency responsible for dealing with internal security and counter-intelligence on British territory.

MI6 (in the UK) the governmental agency responsible for dealing with matters of internal security and counter-intelligence overseas.

MIA ▶ **abbr.** missing in action.

Mi·am·i[1] /mīˈamē/ a city in southeastern Florida; pop. 362,470.

Mi·am·i[2] ▶ **n.** (pl. same or **Mi·am·is**) **1** a member of an American Indian people formerly living mainly in Illinois, Indiana, and Wisconsin and more recently inhabiting areas of Ohio, Kansas, and Oklahoma. **2** the dialect of Illinois of this people. ▶ **adj.** of or relating to this people or their language. [Fr., from Illinois (an Algonquian language).]

Mexico

Official name: United Mexican States
Location: southwestern North America, with extensive coastlines on the Gulf of Mexico and the Pacific Ocean, bordered by the US on the north
Area: 761,800 square miles (1,972,600 sq km)
Population: 104,959,000
Capital: Mexico City
Languages: Spanish (official), various Mayan, Nahuatl, and other indigenous languages
Currency: Mexican peso

Mi·ami Beach a city in southeastern Florida across Biscayne Bay from Miami; pop. 92,639.

Mi·ao /mē'ou/ ▸ **n.** (pl. same) & **adj.** another term for HMONG. [from Chin. *Miáo*, lit. 'tribes.']

mi·aow ▸ **n.** & **v.** var. of MEOW.

mi·as·ma /mī'azmə; mē-/ ▸ **n.** (pl. **-mas** or **-ma·ta** /-mətə/) literary a highly unpleasant or unhealthy smell or vapor: ***a miasma of stale alcohol.*** ■ fig. an oppressive or unpleasant atmosphere that surrounds or emanates from something. — **mi·as·mal adj. mi·as·mat·ic** /,mīəz'matik/ **adj. mi·as·mic** /-mik/ **adj. miasmically** /mik(ə)lē/ **adv.** [17th C.: from Gk., 'defilement,' from *miainein* 'pollute.']

Mic. ▸ **abbr.** Bible Micah.

mi·ca /'mīkə/ ▸ **n.** a shiny silicate mineral with a layered structure, found as minute scales in granite and other rocks, or as crystals. — **mi·ca·ceous** /mī'kāsнəs/ **adj.** [18th C.: from L., 'crumb.']

Mi·cah /'mīkə/ (in the Bible) a Hebrew minor prophet. ■ a book of the Bible bearing his name.

mice /mīs/ plural form of MOUSE.

mi·celle /mī'sel/ ▸ **n.** Chem. an aggregate of molecules in a colloidal solution, such as those in detergents. — **mi·cel·lar** /mī'selər/ **adj.** [19th C.: coined as a dimin. of L. *mica* 'crumb.']

Mich. ▸ **abbr.** Michigan.

Mich·ael·mas /'mikəlməs/ ▸ **n.** the feast of St. Michael, September 29. [OE *Sanct Michaeles mæsse* 'Saint Michael's Mass,' referring to the Archangel.]

Mi·chel·an·ge·lo /,mikəl'anjəl,ō; ,mīkəl-; ,mēkel'änjelō/ (1475–1564), Italian sculptor, painter, architect, and poet; full name *Michelangelo Buonarroti*. A leading figure of the High Renaissance, he is noted for his sculpture of the *Pietà* (c.1497–1500) and for decorating the ceiling of the Sistine Chapel in Rome (1508–12).

Mi·chel·son /'mīkəlsən/, Albert Abraham (1852–1931), US physicist. He worked in experimental physics. Nobel Prize for Physics (1907).

Miche·ner /'micн(ə)nər/, James Albert (1907–97), US writer. His *Tales of the South Pacific* (1947) was made into the Broadway musical *South Pacific* (1949).

Mich·i·gan /'misнigən/ a state in the northern US, bordered on the west, north, and east by lakes Michigan, Superior, Huron, and Erie; pop. 9,938,444; capital, Lansing; statehood, Jan. 26, 1837 (26). It was acquired from Britain by the US in 1783.

Mich·i·gan·der /,misнi'gandər/ ▸ **n.** a native or inhabitant of Michigan.

Mich·i·gan, Lake one of the five Great Lakes, the only one to lie wholly within the US.

Mi·cho·a·cán /,mēcнō-ə'kän/ a state in western Mexico.

Mick /mik/ ▸ **n.** informal, offens. an Irishman. [19th C.: nickname for the given name *Michael*.]

mick·ey /'mikē/ ▸ **n.** (also **Mickey**) short for MICKEY FINN: ***I bet some guy slipped me a mickey.*** [1950s: of unknown origin.]

Mick·ey Finn /'mikē 'fin/ ▸ **n.** informal a surreptitiously drugged drink to make someone drunk. ■ the substance used to adulterate such a drink. [1920s: of unknown origin; sometimes said to be the name of a notorious Chicago saloonkeeper (c.1896–1906).]

Mick·ey Mouse /'mikē 'mous/ a Walt Disney cartoon character who first appeared as Mortimer Mouse in 1927, becoming Mickey in 1928. ■ [as adj.] (also **mickey mouse**) informal trivial or of inferior quality.

mick·le /'mikəl/ (also **muck·le** /'məkəl/) archaic Scot. N. English ▸ **n.** a large amount. ▸ **adj.** very large. ▸ **adj.** & **pron.** much; a large amount. [OE *micel* 'great, numerous, much,' of Gmc. origin; from an Indo-Eur. root shared by Gk. *megas*, *megal-*.]

Mic·mac /'mik,mak/ (also **Mi'k·maq**) ▶ n. (pl. same or **-macs**) **1** a member of an American Indian people inhabiting the Maritime Provinces of Canada. **2** the Algonquian language of this people. ▶ adj. of or relating to this people or their language. [via Fr. from the Micmac self-designation *mīkəmaw*.]

mi·cro /'mīkrō/ ▶ n. (pl. **-cros**) **1** short for MICROCOMPUTER. **2** short for MICROPROCESSOR. ▶ adj. [attrib.] extremely small. ■ small-scale. Often contrasted with MACRO. [19th C.: from MICRO-.]

micro- ▶ comb. form **1** small: *microcar*. ■ of reduced or restricted size: *microprocessor*. **2** (used commonly in units of measurement) denoting a factor of one millionth (10^{-6}): *microfarad*. [from Gk. *mikros* 'small.']

mi·cro·a·nal·y·sis /,mīkrōə'naləsəs/ ▶ n. the analysis of chemical compounds using a small sample. — **mi·cro·an·a·lyt·ic** /-,anl'itik/ adj. **mi·cro·an·a·lyt·i·cal** /-,anl'itikəl/ adj.

mi·cro·bal·ance /,mīkrō'baləns/ ▶ n. a balance for weighing masses of a fraction of a gram.

mi·crobe /'mī,krōb/ ▶ n. a microorganism, esp. a bacterium causing disease or fermentation. — **mi·cro·bi·al** /mī'krōbēəl/ adj. **mi·cro·bic** /mī'krōbik/ adj. [19th C.: from Fr., from Gk. *mikros* 'small' + *bios* 'life.']

mi·cro·bi·ol·o·gy /,mīkrō,bī'äləjē/ ▶ n. the branch of science that deals with microorganisms. — **mi·cro·bi·o·log·ic** /-,bīə'läjik/ adj. **mi·cro·bi·o·log·i·cal** /-,bīə'läjikəl/ adj. **mi·cro·bi·o·log·i·cal·ly** /-,bīə'läjik(ə)lē/ adv. **mi·cro·bi·ol·o·gist** n.

mi·cro·brew /'mīkrō,brōō/ ▶ n. a type of beer produced in a microbrewery. ▶ v. [trans.] (usu. **be microbrewed**) produce (beer) in a microbrewery. — **mi·cro·brew·er** n.

mi·cro·brew·er·y /'mīkrō,brōō(ə)rē/ ▶ n. (pl. **-er·ies**) a brewery, typically producing specialty beers.

mi·cro·burst /'mīkrō,bərst/ ▶ n. a sudden, powerful, localized air current, esp. a downdraft.

mi·cro·cap·sule /,mīkrō'kapsəl; -sōōl/ ▶ n. a small capsule used to contain drugs, dyes, or other substances and render them temporarily inactive.

mi·cro·car /'mīkrō,kär/ ▶ n. a small, efficient car.

mi·cro·cel·lu·lar /,mīkrō'selyələr/ ▶ adj. containing or made up of minute cells.

mi·cro·ceph·a·ly /,mīkrō'sefəlē/ ▶ n. Med. abnormal smallness of the head. — **mi·cro·ce·phal·ic** /-sə'falik/ adj. & n. **mi·cro·ceph·a·lous** /-'sefələs/ adj.

mi·cro·chem·is·try /,mīkrō'kemistrē/ ▶ n. the branch of chemistry concerned with the reactions and properties of substances in minute quantities.

mi·cro·chip /'mīkrō,CHip/ ▶ n. a tiny wafer of semiconducting material used to make an integrated circuit.

Mi·cro·chi·rop·ter·a /,mīkrō-kə'räptərə/ Zool. a major division of bats that comprises all but the fruit bats. — **mi·cro·chi·rop·ter·an** n. & adj. [mod. L. (pl.), from MICRO- 'small' + Gk. *kheir* 'hand' + *pteron* 'wing.']

mi·cro·cir·cuit /'mīkrō,sərkət/ ▶ n. a minute electric circuit, esp. an integrated circuit. — **mi·cro·cir·cuit·ry** /,mīkrō'sərkətrē/ n.

mi·cro·cir·cu·la·tion /,mīkrō,sərkyə'lāSHən/ ▶ n. circulation of the blood in the smallest blood vessels. — **mi·cro·cir·cu·la·to·ry** /-'sərkyələ,tôrē/ adj.

mi·cro·cli·mate /'mīkrō,klīmət/ ▶ n. the climate of a very small or restricted area. — **mi·cro·cli·mat·ic** /,mīkrō,klī'matik/ adj. **mi·cro·cli·mat·i·cal·ly** /,mīkrō,klī'matik(ə)lē/ adv.

mi·cro·cline /'mīkrō,klīn/ ▶ n. a green, pink, or brown crystalline mineral of potassium-rich feldspar. [19th C.: from Ger. *Microklin*, from Gk. *mikros* 'small' + *klinein* 'to lean.']

mi·cro·coc·cus /,mīkrō'käkəs/ ▶ n. (pl. **-coc·ci** /-'käk,(s)ī; -'käk(s)ē/) a spherical bacterium (family Micrococcaceae, esp. genera *Micrococcus* and *Staphylococcus*) that is typically found on dead or decaying organic matter. Nonpathogenic forms are found on human and animal skin. — **mi·cro·coc·cal** adj.

mi·cro·com·pu·ter /'mīkrō-kəm,pyōōtər/ ▶ n. a small computer that contains a microprocessor.

mi·cro·cop·y /'mīkrō,käpē/ ▶ n. (pl. **-cop·ies**) a copy of printed matter that has been reduced in size. ▶ v. (**-cop·ies, -cop·ied**) [trans.] make a microcopy of.

mi·cro·cosm /'mīkrə,käzəm/ (also **mi·cro·cos·mos** /,mīkrə'käzməs; -mōs/) ▶ n. a community, place, or situation regarded as encapsulating in miniature the characteristic features of something much larger: *Berlin is a microcosm of Germany, in unity as in division.* ■ humankind regarded as the epitome of the universe.
– PHRASES **in microcosm** in miniature. — **mi·cro·cos·mic** /,mīkrə'käzmik/ adj. **mi·cro·cos·mi·cal·ly** adv. [ME: from OFr. *microcosme* or med. L. *microcosmus*, from Gk. *mikros kosmos* 'little world.']

mi·cro·cos·mic salt ▶ n. Chem. a white crystalline salt, $HNaNH_4PO_4.4H_2O$, originally obtained from human urine.

mi·cro·cred·it /'mīkrō,kredit/ ▶ n. the lending of small amounts of money at low interest to new businesses in the developing world.

mi·cro·crys·tal·line /,mīkrō'krisl-in; -,īn; -,ēn/ ▶ adj. (of a material) formed of microscopic crystals.

mi·cro·cyte /'mīkrə,sīt/ ▶ n. Med. an unusually small red blood cell, associated with certain anemias. — **mi·cro·cyt·ic** /,mīkrə'sitik/ adj.

mi·cro·der·ma·bra·sion /,mīkrō,dərmə'brāZHən/ ▶ n. a cosmetic treatment intended to make the skin appear younger and healthier, in which the face is sprayed with exfoliant crystals to remove dead epidermal cells.

mi·cro·dot /'mīkrə,dät/ ▶ n. a microphotograph that is only about 0.04 inch (1 mm) across. ■ [usu. as adj.] denoting a pattern of very small dots.

mi·cro·ec·o·nom·ics /,mīkrō,ekə'nämiks; -,ēkə-/ ▶ plural n. [treated as sing.] the part of economics about single factors and the effects of individual decisions. — **mi·cro·ec·o·nom·ic** adj.

mi·cro·e·lec·tron·ics /,mīkrō-i,lek'träniks/ ▶ plural n. [usu. treated as sing.] the design, manufacture, and use of microchips and microcircuits. — **mi·cro·e·lec·tron·ic** adj.

mi·cro·en·vi·ron·ment /,mīkrō-in'vīrə(n)mənt; -'vī(ə)r(n)mənt/ ▶ n. Biol. the immediate small-scale environment of an organism or a part of an organism. — **mi·cro·en·vi·ron·men·tal** /-,vīrə(n)'mentl; -,vī(ə)r(n)-/ adj.

mi·cro·ev·o·lu·tion /,mīkrō-evə'lōōSHən; -,ēvə-/ ▶ n. Biol. evolutionary change over a short period. — **mi·cro·ev·o·lu·tion·ar·y** /-'lōōSHə,nerē/ adj.

mi·cro·far·ad /'mīkrō,farəd; -ad/ ▶ n. one millionth of a farad. Symbol µF.

mi·cro·fau·na /,mīkrō'fônə; -'fänə/ ▶ n. (pl. **-fau·nas** or **-fau·nae** /-'fônē; -'fänē/) Biol. microscopic animals. ■ Ecol. the animals of a microhabitat. — **mi·cro·fau·nal** adj.

mi·cro·fi·ber /'mīkrō,fībər/ ▶ n. a fine synthetic yarn.

mi·cro·fiche /'mīkrə,fēSH/ ▶ n. (pl. same or **-fich·es**) a flat piece of film containing microphotographs of the pages of a newspaper, catalog, or other document. ▶ v. [trans.] make a microfiche of.

mi·cro·film /'mīkrə,film/ ▶ n. film containing microphotographs, esp. of a newspaper. ▶ v. [trans.] make a microfilm of.

mi·cro·flo·ra /,mīkrō'flôrə/ ▶ n. (pl. **-flo·ras** or **-flo·rae** /-'flôrē/) Biol. microscopic plants. ■ Ecol. the plants of a microhabitat. — **mi·cro·flo·ral** adj.

mi·cro·form /'mīkrə,fôrm/ ▶ n. microphotographic reproduction on film or paper.

mi·cro·fos·sil /'mīkrō,fäsəl/ ▶ n. a fossil or fossil fragment that can be seen only with a microscope.

mi·cro·gam·ete /,mīkrō'gam,ēt; -gə'mēt/ ▶ n. Biol. (esp. in protozoans) the smaller of a pair of conjugating gametes, usually regarded as male.

mi·cro·gram /'mīkrə,gram/ ▶ n. one millionth of a gram. (Symbol: µg)

mi·cro·graph /'mīkrə,graf/ ▶ n. a photograph taken by means of a microscope. — **mi·cro·graph·ic** /,mīkrə'grafik/ adj. **mi·cro·graph·ics** /,mīkrə'grafiks/ n. **mi·crog·ra·phy** /mī'krägrəfē/ n.

mi·cro·grav·i·ty /,mīkrō'gravətē/ ▶ n. very weak gravity, as in an orbiting spacecraft.

mi·cro·groove /'mīkrə,grōōv/ ▶ n. the very narrow groove on a long-playing phonograph record.

mi·cro·hab·i·tat /,mīkrō'habə,tat/ ▶ n. Ecol. a small habitat that differs in character from some surrounding more extensive habitat.

mi·cro·lep·i·dop·ter·a /,mīkrō,lepə'däptərə/ ▶ plural n. Entomol. the numerous small moths.

mi·cro·li·ter /,mīkrō'lētər/ (Brit. also **mi·cro·li·tre**) ▶ n. one millionth of a liter. Symbol µl.

mi·cro·lith /'mīkrə,liTH/ ▶ n. Archaeol. a minute shaped flint, typically part of a tool such as a spear. — **mi·cro·lith·ic** /,mikrə'liTHik/ adj.

mi·cro·man·age /,mīkrō'manij/ ▶ v. [trans.] control every part, however small, of (an activity). — **mi·cro·man·age·ment** /'manijmənt/ n. **mi·cro·man·ag·er** n.

mi·cro·me·te·or·oid /,mīkrō'mētēə,roid/ ▶ n. a microscopic particle in space that will not burn up if it enters the earth's atmosphere.

mi·cro·me·te·or·ol·o·gy /,mīkrō,mētēə'räləjē/ ▶ n. the branch of meteorology concerned with small areas and with small-scale meteorological phenomena. — **mi·cro·me·te·or·o·log·i·cal** /-,mētēərə'läjikəl/ adj.

mi·crom·e·ter[1] /mī'krämətər/ (also **micrometer caliper**) ▶ n. a gauge that measures small distances or thicknesses. — **mi·crom·e·try** /-ətrē/ n.

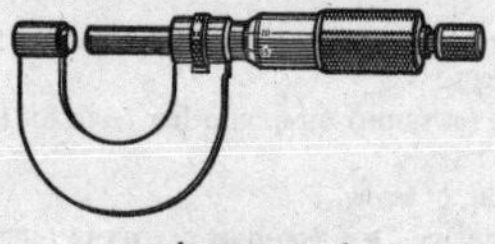

micrometer[1]

mi·cro·me·ter[2] /'mīkrō,mētər/ (abbr.: µm) ▶ n. one millionth of a meter.

mi·cron /'mī,krän/ ▶ n. a unit of length equal to one millionth of a meter. [19th C.: from Gk. *mikron*, neut. of *mikros* 'small.']

Mi·cro·ne·sia /,mīkrə'nēZHə/ **1** a region of the western Pacific Ocean that includes the Mariana, Caroline, and Marshall island groups and Kiribati. **2** a group of associated island states in the western Pacific Ocean. *See box on next page.*

Mi·cro·ne·sian /,mīkrə'nēZHən/ ▶ adj. of or relating to Micronesia, its people, or their languages. ▶ n. **1** a native of Micronesia. **2** the Austronesian languages spoken in Micronesia.

mi·cron·ize /'mīkrə,nīz/ ▶ v. [trans.] break (a substance) into very fine particles. — **mi·cron·i·za·tion** /,mīkrənə'zāSHən/ n. **mi·cron·iz·er** n.

mi·cro·nu·tri·ent /,mīkrō'n(y)ōōtrēənt/ ▶ n. a chemical element or substance required in trace amounts for the normal growth and development of organisms.

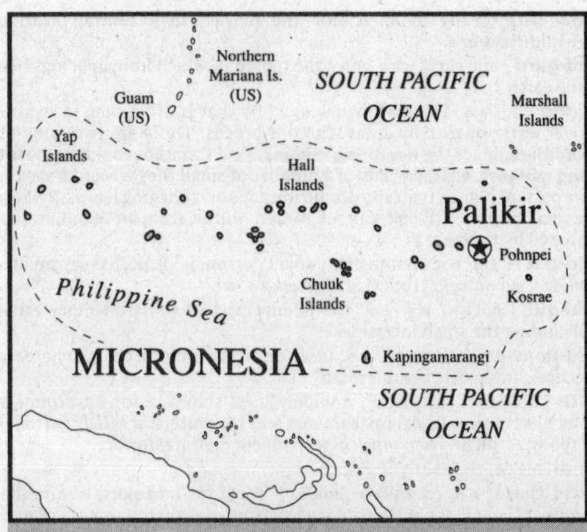

Micronesia

Official name: Federated States of Micronesia
Location: western Pacific Ocean, north of the equator, including the 600 islands of the Caroline Islands
Area: 270 square miles (700 sq km)
Population: 108,000
Capital: Palikir
Languages: English (official), Austronesian languages
Currency: US dollar

mi·cro·or·gan·ism /ˌmīkrōˈôrgəˌnizəm/ ▶ **n.** a microscopic organism, esp. a bacterium, virus, or fungus.

mi·cro·pay·ment /ˈmīkrəˌpāmənt/ ▶ **n.** a very small payment made each time a user accesses a service, esp. on the Internet.

mi·cro·phone /ˈmīkrəˌfōn/ ▶ **n.** an instrument for converting sound waves into electrical energy variations, which may then be amplified. — **mi·cro·phon·ic** /ˌmīkrəˈfänik/ **adj.**

mi·cro·pho·to·graph /ˌmīkrəˈfōtəˌgraf/ ▶ **n.** a photograph reduced to a very small size. ■ another term for PHOTOMICROGRAPH. — **mi·cro·pho·to·graph·ic** /-ˌfōtəˈgrafik/ **adj.** **mi·cro·pho·tog·ra·phy** /-fəˈtägrəfē/ **n.**

mi·cro·phys·ics /ˌmīkrōˈfiziks/ ▶ **plural n.** [treated as sing.] the branch of physics that deals with bodies and phenomena on a microscopic or smaller scale. — **mi·cro·phys·i·cal** /-ˈfizikəl/ **adj.**

mi·cro·print /ˈmīkrəˌprint/ ▶ **n.** printed text reduced by microphotography. — **mi·cro·print·ing n.**

mi·cro·proc·es·sor /ˌmīkrəˈpräsesər; -ˈprōsesər/ ▶ **n.** an integrated circuit that contains all the functions of a central processing unit of a computer. — **mi·cro·proc·ess·ing n.**

mi·cro·pro·gram /ˈmīkrəˌprōgrəm; -gram/ ▶ **n.** a microinstruction program that controls a computer's central processing unit or peripheral controller. ▶ **v.** [trans.] use microprogramming with (a computer); bring about by means of a microprogram. — **mi·cro·pro·gram·ma·ble adj.** **mi·cro·pro·gram·mer n.**

mi·cro·pro·gram·ming /ˈmīkrəˌprōgrəmiNG; ˈmīkrəˌprōgramiNG/ ▶ **n.** the technique of making machine instructions generate sequences of microinstructions in accordance with a microprogram.

mi·crop·si·a /mīˈkräpsēə/ ▶ **n.** a condition of the eyes in which objects appear smaller than normal. [19th C.: from MICRO- 'small' + Gk. *-opsia* 'seeing.']

mi·cro·pyle /ˈmīkrəˌpīl/ ▶ **n.** Bot. a small opening in the surface of an ovule, through which the pollen tube penetrates, often visible as a small pore in the ripe seed. ■ a small opening in the egg of a fish, insect, etc., through which spermatozoa can enter. — **mi·cro·py·lar** /ˌmīkrəˈpīlər/ **adj.** [19th C.: from MICRO- 'small' + Gk. *pulē* 'gate.']

mi·cro·scope /ˈmīkrəˌskōp/ ▶ **n.** an optical instrument used for viewing very small objects, typically magnified several hundred times.
– PHRASES **under the microscope** under critical examination.

mi·cro·scope slide ▶ **n.** see SLIDE (sense 3).

mi·cro·scop·ic /ˌmīkrəˈskäpik/ ▶ **adj.** **1** so small as to be visible only with a microscope: *microscopic algae.* ■ informal extremely small. ■ concerned with minute detail. **2** of or relating to a microscope. — **mi·cro·scop·i·cal adj.** (in sense 2). **mi·cro·scop·i·cal·ly adv.**

Mi·cro·sco·pi·um /ˌmīkrəˈskoˉpēəm/ Astron. a small and inconspicuous southern constellation (the Microscope), between Piscis Austrinus and Sagittarius.

mi·cro·sec·ond /ˈmīkroˉˌsekənd/ (abbr.: μs) ▶ **n.** one millionth of a second.

mi·cro·seism /ˈmīkroˉˌsīzəm/ ▶ **n.** Geol. a very small earthquake, less than 2 on the Richter scale. — **mi·cro·seis·mic** /ˌmīkroˉˈsīzmik/ **adj.**

mi·cro·some /ˈmīkrəˌsoˉm/ ▶ **n.** Biol. a fragment of endoplasmic reticulum and attached ribosomes obtained by the centrifugation of homogenized cells. — **mi·cro·so·mal** /ˌmīkrəˈsoˉməl/ **adj.**

mi·cro·sphere /ˈmīkrəˌsfi(ə)r/ ▶ **n.** a microscopic hollow sphere, esp. of a protein or synthetic polymer.

mi·cro·spo·ran·gi·um /ˌmīkrōspəˈranj(ē)əm/ ▶ **n.** (pl. **-gi·a** /-j(ē)ə/) Bot. a sporangium containing microspores.

mi·cro·spore /ˈmīkrəˌspôr/ ▶ **n.** Bot. the smaller of the two kinds of spore produced by some ferns. See also MEGASPORE.

mi·cro·struc·ture /ˌmīkrəˈstrəkCHər/ ▶ **n.** the fine structure that can be made visible with a microscope.

mi·cro·tome /ˈmīkrəˌtōm/ ▶ **n.** esp. Biol. an instrument for cutting extremely thin sections of material for examination under a microscope.

mi·cro·tone /ˈmīkrəˌtōn/ ▶ **n.** Music an interval smaller than a semitone. — **mi·cro·ton·al** /ˌmīkrəˈtōnl/ **adj.** **mi·cro·to·nal·i·ty** /ˌmīkrətōˈnalətē/ **n.** **mi·cro·ton·al·ly** /ˌmīkrəˈtōnl-ē/ **adv.**

mi·cro·tu·bule /ˌmīkrəˈt(y)o͞obyo͞ol/ ▶ **n.** Biol. a microscopic tubular structure present in numbers in the cytoplasm of cells, sometimes aggregating to form more complex structures.

mi·cro·vil·lus /ˌmīkrōˈviləs/ ▶ **n.** (pl. **-vil·li** /-ˈvilˌī; -ˈvilē/) Biol. each of a large number of minute projections from the surface of some cells. — **mi·cro·vil·lar** /-ˈvilər/ **adj.** **mi·cro·vil·lous** /-ˈviləs/ **adj.**

mi·cro·wave /ˈmīkrəˌwāv/ ▶ **n.** an electromagnetic wave with a wavelength in the range 0.001–0.3 m. Microwaves are used in radar, in communications, and for heating. ■ short for MICROWAVE OVEN. ▶ **v.** [trans.] cook (food) in a microwave oven. — **mi·cro·wave·a·ble** (also **mi·cro·wav·a·ble**) **adj.**

mi·cro·wave back·ground ▶ **n.** Astron. weak uniform microwave radiation that is detectable in nearly every direction of the sky.

mi·cro·wave ov·en ▶ **n.** an oven that uses microwaves to cook or heat food.

mic·tu·rate /ˈmikCHəˌrāt/ ▶ **v.** [intrans.] formal urinate. — **mic·tu·ri·tion** /ˌmikCHəˈrisHən/ **n.** [19th C.: back-form. from *micturition*, from L. *micturit-* 'urinated,' from the v. *micturire*.]

mid[1] /mid/ ▶ **adj.** [attrib.] of or in the middle part. ■ Phonet. (of a vowel) pronounced with the tongue neither high nor low: *a mid-central vowel.* [OE *midd*, rel. to Old High Ger. *mitti*, L. *medius*.]

mid[2] ▶ **prep.** literary in the middle of. [Shortening of AMID.]

mid- ▶ **comb. form** denoting the middle of: *mid-sentence.* ■ in the middle; medium; half: *midway.*

mid·air /ˈmidˈe(ə)r/ (also **mid-air**) ▶ **n.** a part or section of the air above ground level or above another surface: *he caught Murray's keys in midair.*

Mi·das /ˈmīdəs/ Gk. Mythol. a king of Phrygia, who, according to one story, had the power to turn what he touched into gold.
– PHRASES **the Midas touch** the ability to make money out of anything one undertakes.

mid-At·lan·tic ▶ **adj.** **1** situated or occurring in the middle of the Atlantic Ocean: *the mid-Atlantic fault line.* ■ having characteristics of both Britain and America, or designed to appeal to the people of both countries. **2** of or relating to states on the middle Atlantic coast of the US, including New York, Pennsylvannia, New Jersey, West Virginia, Delaware, and Maryland.

Mid-At·lan·tic Ridge a submarine ridge system that extends the length of the Atlantic Ocean.

mid·brain /ˈmidˌbrān/ ▶ **n.** Anat. a small central part of the brainstem. Also called MESENCEPHALON.

mid·day /ˈmidˈdā/ ▶ **n.** the middle of the day; noon.

mid·den /ˈmidn/ ▶ **n.** a dunghill or refuse heap. ■ short for KITCHEN MIDDEN. [ME *myddyng*, of Scand. origin; cf. Dan. *mødding* 'dunghill.']

mid·dle /ˈmidl/ ▶ **adj.** [attrib.] **1** at an equal distance from the extremities of something; central. ■ (of a member of a group, series, or sequence) so placed as to have the same number of members on each side: *in her middle forties.* ■ intermediate in rank, quality, or ability: *at the middle level.* ■ (of a language) of the period between the old and modern forms. **2** Gram. denoting a voice of verbs in some languages, such as Greek, that expresses reciprocal or reflexive action. ■ denoting a transitive or intransitive verb in English with a passive sense, e.g., *cuts* in *this meat cuts well.* ▶ **n.** **1** [usu. in sing.] the point or position at an equal distance from the sides, edges, or ends of something. ■ the point at or around the center of a process or activity, period of time, etc.: *in the middle of December.* ■ informal a person's waist or waist and stomach. **2** Gram. the form or voice of a verb expressing reflexive or reciprocal action, or a passive sense for a transitive or intransitive verb. **3** short for MIDDLE TERM.
– PHRASES **down the middle** divided or dividing something equally into two parts. **in the middle of** engaged in or in the process of doing something. ■ involved in something. **the middle of nowhere** informal a place that is remote and isolated. **steer** (or **take**) **a middle course** adopt a policy that avoids extremes. [OE *middel*, of West Gmc. origin; rel. to Du. *middel* and Ger. *Mittel*, also to MID[1].]

mid·dle age ▶ **n.** the period between early adulthood and old age, usually considered to be from 45 to 65. — **mid·dle-aged** (also **mid·dle-age**) **adj.**

Mid·dle Ag·es ▶ **plural n.** the period of European history from the fall of the Roman Empire in the West (5th century) to the fall of Constantinople (1453), or, more narrowly, from *c.*1100 to 1453.

mid·dle-age spread ▶ n. the fat that may accumulate around one's abdomen and buttocks during middle age.
Mid·dle A·mer·i·ca ▶ n. **1** the middle class in the US. ■ the Midwest of the US. **2** the North American region that includes Mexico and Central America, and often the West Indies. — **Mid·dle A·mer·i·can** n. **Mid·dle-A·mer·i·can** adj.
mid·dle·brow /ˈmidlˈbrou/ informal, esp. derog. ▶ adj. (of art or literature or a system of thought) demanding or involving only a moderate degree of intellectual application. ▶ n. a person who is capable of or enjoys only a moderate degree of intellectual effort.
mid·dle C ▶ n. Music the C near the middle of the piano keyboard, written on the first ledger line below the treble staff or the first ledger line above the bass staff.
mid·dle class ▶ n. [treated as sing. or pl.] the social group between the upper and working classes. ▶ adj. of, relating to, or characteristic of this group. — **mid·dle-class·ness** n.
mid·dle dis·tance ▶ n. **1** (**the middle distance**) the part of a real or painted landscape between the foreground and the background. **2** [usu. as adj.] Track & Field a race distance of between 800 and 5,000 meters: *middle-distance runners.*
Mid·dle Dutch ▶ n. the Dutch language from c.1100 to 1500.
mid·dle ear ▶ n. the air-filled central cavity of the ear, behind the eardrum.
Mid·dle East an area of southwestern Asia and northern Africa that stretches from the Mediterranean Sea to Pakistan and includes the Arabian peninsula. — **Mid·dle East·ern** adj.
mid·dle eight (also **mid·dle-eight**) ▶ n. a short section (typically of eight bars) in the middle of a conventionally structured popular song.
Mid·dle Eng·lish ▶ n. the English language from c.1150 to c.1470.
mid·dle fin·ger ▶ n. the finger between the forefinger and the ring finger.
mid·dle game ▶ n. the phase of a chess game after the opening, when all or most of the pieces and pawns remain on the board.
mid·dle ground ▶ n. (usu. **the middle ground**) **1** an area of compromise or possible agreement between two extreme positions, esp. political ones. **2** the middle distance of a painting or photograph.
Mid·dle High Ger·man ▶ n. the language of southern Germany from c.1200 to 1500.
Mid·dle King·dom 1 a period of ancient Egyptian history (c.2040–1640 BC, 11th–14th dynasty). **2** hist. China or its eighteen inner provinces.
Mid·dle Low Ger·man ▶ n. the Low German language (spoken in northern Germany) from c.1200 to 1500.
mid·dle·man /ˈmidlˌman/ ▶ n. (pl. **-men**) a person who buys goods from producers and sells them to retailers or consumers. ■ a person who arranges business or political deals between other people.
mid·dle man·age·ment ▶ n. the level in an organization just below that of senior administrators. ■ the managers at this level regarded collectively. — **mid·dle man·ag·er** n.
mid·dle name ▶ n. a person's name after the first name and before the surname. ■ a quality for which a person is notable: *optimism is my middle name.*
mid·dle-of-the-road ▶ adj. moderate. ■ (of music) tuneful but bland and unadventurous. — **mid·dle-of-the-road·er** n.
mid·dle pas·sage ▶ n. hist. the journey taken by slave ships from West Africa to the West Indies.
Mid·dle Per·sian ▶ n. the Persian language from c.300 BC to AD 800. See also PAHLAVI[2].
mid·dle school ▶ n. a school between elementary and high school, typically sixth, seventh, and eighth grades.
mid·dle-sized ▶ adj. of medium size.
Mid·dle Stone Age the Mesolithic period.
mid·dle term ▶ n. Logic the term common to both premises of a syllogism.
Mid·dle·ton /ˈmidltən/, Thomas (c.1570–1627), English playwright. His works include *Women Beware Women* (1620–27).
mid·dle watch ▶ n. the period from midnight to 4 a.m. on board a ship.
mid·dle way ▶ n. **1** a policy or course of action that avoids extremes. **2** (**the Middle Way**) the eightfold path of Buddhism between indulgence and asceticism.
mid·dle·weight /ˈmidlˌwāt/ ▶ n. a weight in boxing and other sports intermediate between welterweight and light heavyweight. ■ a boxer or other competitor of this weight.
Middle West another term for MIDWEST. — **Mid·dle Wes·tern·er** n.
mid·dling /ˈmidliNG; ˈmidlin/ ▶ adj. moderate or average in size, amount, or rank. ■ neither very good nor very bad: *he had had a fair to middling season.* ■ [predic.] informal (of a person) in reasonably good but not perfect health. ▶ n. (**middlings**) bulk goods of medium grade. ▶ adv. [as submodifier] informal, dated fairly or moderately. — **mid·dling·ly** adv. [ME (orig. Scots): prob. from MID- + the adverbial suffix *-ling.*]
mid·dy /ˈmidē/ ▶ n. (pl. **-dies**) **1** informal a midshipman. **2** (also **mid·dy blouse**) esp. hist. a loose blouse with a square back collar, resembling that worn by a sailor.
Mid·east /ˈmidˈēst/ US term for MIDDLE EAST.
mid-en·gine (also **mid-en·gined**) ▶ adj. (of a car) having the engine located between the front and rear axles.
mid·field /ˈmidˌfēld; midˈfēld/ ▶ n. (in football, soccer, etc.) the central part of the field. ■ Soccer the players in a central position. — **mid·field·er** n.
Mid·gard /ˈmidˌgärd/ Scand. Mythol. the region in which human beings live; the earth.
midge /mij/ ▶ n. **1** a small two-winged fly that is often seen in swarms near water or marshy areas where it breeds. There are two families: Chironomidae (the **nonbiting midges**), and Ceratopogonidae (the **biting midges**). ■ [with adj.] any of a number of small flies whose larvae can be pests of plants, typically producing galls or damaging leaves. **2** informal a small person. [OE *mycg(e)*; rel. to Ger. *Mücke*, from an Indo-Eur. root shared by L. *musca.*]
mid·get /ˈmijit/ ▶ n. an unusually small person. ▶ adj. [attrib.] very small: *a midget submarine.* [19th C.: from MIDGE + -ET[1].]
mid·gut /ˈmidˌgət/ ▶ n. Zool. the middle part of the alimentary canal, including the small intestine.
mid·heav·en /ˈmidˌhevən/ ▶ n. Astrol. (on an astrological chart) where the ecliptic intersects the meridian.
MIDI /ˈmidē/ ▶ n. [usu. as adj.] a widely used standard for interconnecting electronic musical instruments and computers: *a MIDI controller.* [1980s: acronym from *musical instrument digital interface.*]
Mi·di /mēˈdē/ the south of France.
mid·i /ˈmidē/ ▶ n. (pl. **mid·is** /ˈmidēz/) short for **midiskirt**, a skirt that ends at the middle of the calf. [1960s: from MID[1], on the pattern of *maxi* and *mini.*]
mid·i·nette /ˌmidnˈet; ˌmēdēˈnet/ ▶ n. a seamstress or assistant in a Parisian fashion house. [Fr., from *midi* 'midday' + *dînette* 'light dinner.']
Mi·di-Py·ré·nées /mēˈdē ˌpirəˈnā/ a region in southern France, centered on Toulouse.
mid·i·ron /ˈmidˌī(ə)rn/ ▶ n. Golf an iron with a medium degree of loft, such as a four-, five-, or six-iron.
mid·land /ˈmidlənd; -ˌland/ ▶ n. the middle part of a country. ■ (**the Midlands**) a region of central England. ▶ adj. of or in the middle part of a country. — **mid·land·er** n.
mid·life /ˈmidˈlīf/ (also **mid-life**) ▶ n. the central period of a person's life, generally from about 45 to 55.
mid·life cri·sis ▶ n. an emotional crisis of identity and self-confidence that can occur in early middle age.
mid·line /ˈmidˌlīn/ ▶ n. [often as adj.] a median line or plane of bilateral symmetry, esp. that of the body.
mid·most /ˈmidˌmōst/ ▶ adj. & adv. literary in the very middle or nearest the middle.
mid·night /ˈmidˌnīt/ ▶ n. twelve o'clock at night. ■ [often as adj.] the middle period of the night: *the midnight hours.*
mid·night blue ▶ n. a very dark blue.
mid·night sun ▶ n. the sun when seen at midnight during summer in the Arctic or Antarctic Circle.
mid·o·cean ridge /midˈōSHən/ (also **mid-o·cean ridge**) ▶ n. Geol. a long, seismically active submarine ridge system situated in the middle of an ocean basin.
mid·point /ˈmidˌpoint/ ▶ n. the exact middle point. ■ a point somewhere in the middle.
mid·range /ˈmidˈrānj/ (also **mid-range**) ▶ n. **1** Stat. the arithmetic mean of the largest and the smallest values in a sample or other group. **2** the middle part of the range of audible frequencies. ▶ adj. (of a product) in the middle of a range of products with regard to size, quality, or price.
Mid·rash /ˈmidˌräSH/ (also **mid·rash**) ▶ n. (pl. **Mid·ra·shim** /midˈräSHim/) an ancient commentary on part of the Hebrew scriptures. — **Mid·rash·ic** /midˈräSHik/ adj. [from Heb. *miḏrāš* 'commentary,' from *dāraš* 'expound.']
mid·rib /ˈmidˌrib/ ▶ n. a large strengthened vein along the midline of a leaf.
mid·riff /ˈmidˌrif/ ▶ n. the region of the front of the body between the chest and the waist. ■ Anat., dated the diaphragm. [OE *midhrif*, from MID[1] + *hrif* 'belly.']
mid·sec·tion /ˈmidˌsekSHən/ ▶ n. the middle part. ■ the midriff.
mid·ship /ˈmidˌSHip/ ▶ n. [usu. as adj.] the middle part of a ship or boat: *its powerful midship section.*
mid·ship·man /ˈmidˌSHipmən; midˈSHip-/ ▶ n. (pl. **-men**) **1** a naval cadet in the US Navy. **2** an American toadfish (genus *Porichthys*) with dorsal and anal fins that run most of the length of the body and rows of light organs on the underside.
mid·ships /ˈmidˌSHips/ ▶ adv. & adj. another term for AMIDSHIPS.
mid·sole /ˈmidˌsōl/ ▶ n. a layer of material between the inner and outer soles of a shoe, for absorbing shock.
midst /midst/ ▶ prep. archaic literary in the middle of.
– PHRASES **in the midst of** in the middle of. **in our** (or **your**, **their**, etc.) **midst** among us (or you or them). [ME: from *in middes* 'in the middle.']
mid·stream /ˈmidˈstrēm/ ▶ n. the middle of a stream.
– PHRASES **in midstream** ■ fig. (of an interrupted activity) partway through its course.
mid·sum·mer /ˈmidˈsəmər/ ▶ n. [often as adj.] the middle part of summer: *the midsummer heat.* ■ another term for SUMMER SOLSTICE.
Mid·sum·mer Day (also **Mid·sum·mer's Day**) ▶ n. (in England, Wales, and Ireland) June 24, originally coinciding with the summer solstice.

mid·term /'mid,tərm/ ▶ **n.** the middle of a period of office, an academic term, or a pregnancy. ■ an exam in the middle of an academic term.

mid·town /'mid,toun/ ▶ **n.** [usu. as adj.] the central part of a city between the downtown and uptown areas.

mid-Vic·to·ri·an ▶ **adj.** of or relating to the middle of the Victorian era.

mid·wa·ter /'mid,wôtər; -,wätər/ ▶ **n.** the part of a body of water near neither the bottom nor the surface.

mid·way /'mid,wā; -'wā/ ▶ **adv. & adj.** in or toward the middle of something. ■ having some of the characteristics of one thing and some of another. ▶ **n.** an area of sideshows, games of chance or skill, or other amusements at a fair or exhibition.

Mid·way Is·lands two small islands, in the central Pacific Ocean, in the western part of the Hawaiian chain. They are a US territory and were the scene of a decisive World War II battle in 1942.

mid·week /'mid,wēk/ ▶ **n.** the middle of the week. ▶ **adj. & adv.** in the middle of the week.

Mid·west /'mid'west/ the region of northern states of the US from Ohio west to the Rocky Mountains. Formerly called **Far West**. — **Mid·west·ern** /,mid'westərn/ **adj.**

mid·wife /'mid,wīf/ ▶ **n.** (pl. **-wives**) a person (typically a woman) trained to assist women in childbirth. ■ fig. a person or thing that helps to bring something into being or assists its development. ▶ **v.** [trans.] assist (a woman) during childbirth. ■ fig. bring into being. — **mid·wife·ry** /mid'wīf(ə)rē; -'wīf(ə)rē/ **n.** [ME: prob. from the obs. prep. *mid* 'with' + **wife**.]

mid·win·ter /'mid'wintər/ ▶ **n.** the middle of winter. ■ another term for **winter solstice**.

mien /mēn/ ▶ **n.** literary a person's look or manner, indicating their character or mood. [16th C.: prob. from Fr. *mine* 'expression.']

Mies van der Ro·he /'mēz van dər 'rōə; 'mēs vän/, Ludwig (1886–1969), German architect. He designed the Seagram Building in New York 1954–58 and was noted for his tubular steel furniture. — **Mies·i·an** /'mēzēən/ **adj.**

mi·fep·ri·stone /,mifə'pris,tōn/ ▶ **n.** Med. a synthetic steroid that inhibits the action of progesterone. Also called **RU-486** (trademark). [1980s: prob. from Du. *mifepriston*, from *mife-* (representing *aminophenol*) + *-pr-* (representing *propyl*) + *-ist-* (representing **estradiol**) + **-one**.]

miff /mif/ ▶ **v.** [trans.] (usu. **be miffed**) informal annoy. ▶ **n.** archaic a petty quarrel or fit of pique. [17th C.: perh. imitative.]

MiG /mig/ (also **Mig** or **MIG**) ▶ **n.** a type of Russian fighter aircraft. [1940s: from the initial letters of the surnames of A. I. Mikoyan and M. I. Gurevich, linked by Russ. *i* 'and.']

might[1] /mīt/ ▶ **modal verb** (3rd sing. pres. **might**) **1** past of **may**[1], used esp.: ■ in reported speech, expressing possibility or permission. ■ expressing a possibility based on a condition not fulfilled. ■ expressing annoyance about something that someone has not done: *you might have told me!* ■ expressing purpose: *he avoided them so that he might work.* **2** used in questions and requests: ■ tentatively asking permission: *might I ask one question?* ■ asking for information, esp. condescendingly: *and who might you be?* **3** expressing possibility: *this might be true.* ■ making a suggestion: *you might try pain relievers.*

– PHRASES **might as well** used to make an unenthusiastic suggestion. **might have known** (or **guessed**) used to express one's lack of surprise about something.

might[2] ▶ **n.** great and impressive power or strength.

– PHRASES **with all one's might** using all one's power or strength. **with might and main** with all one's strength or power. [OE *miht*, *mieht*, of Gmc. origin; rel. to **may**[1].]

might-have-been ▶ **n.** informal a past possibility.

might·n't /'mītnt/ ▶ **contr.** might not.

might·y /'mītē/ ▶ **adj.** (**might·i·er**, **might·i·est**) possessing great and impressive power or strength. ■ (of an action) performed with or requiring great strength: *a mighty heave.* ■ informal very large. ▶ **adv.** [as submodifier] informal extremely: *this is mighty early.* — **might·i·ly adv. might·i·ness n.**

mig·ma·tite /'migmə,tīt/ ▶ **n.** Geol. a rock composed of two intermingled but distinguishable components. [20th C.: from Gk. *migma*, *migmat-* 'mixture' + **-ite**[1].]

mi·gnon·ette /,minyə'net/ ▶ **n.** a herbaceous plant (genus *Reseda*, family Resedaceae) with spikes of small fragrant greenish flowers. [18th C.: from Fr. *mignonnette*, dimin. of *mignon* 'small and sweet.']

mi·graine /'mī,grān/ (also **migraine headache**) ▶ **n.** a recurrent throbbing headache that typically affects one side of the head and is often accompanied by nausea and disturbed vision. — **mi·grain·ous** /-,grānəs/ **adj.** [ME: from Fr., via late L. from Gk. *hēmikrania*, from *hēmi-* 'half' + *kranion* 'skull.']

mi·grant /'mīgrənt/ ▶ **n.** an animal that migrates. ■ (also **migrant worker**) a worker who moves from place to place to do seasonal work. ▶ **adj.** [attrib.] tending to migrate or having migrated.

mi·grate /'mī,grāt/ ▶ **v.** [intrans.] (of an animal, typically a bird or fish) move from one region to another. ■ (of a person) move from one area or country to settle in another. ■ move from one specific part of something to another. ■ Comput. change from using one system to another. ■ [trans.] Comput. transfer (programs or hardware) from one system to another. — **mi·gra·tion** /mī'grāsHən/ **n. mi·gra·tion·al** /mī'grāsHənl/ **adj. mi·gra·tor** /-,grātər/ **n. mi·gra·to·ry** /'mīgrə,tôrē/ **adj.** [17th C.: from L. *migrat-* 'moved, shifted,' from the v. *migrare*.]

mih·rab /'mi(ə)rəb/ ▶ **n.** a niche in the wall of a mosque, at the point nearest to Mecca. [from Arab. *miḥrāb* 'place for prayer.']

mi·ka·do /mi'kädō/ ▶ **n.** hist. a title given to the emperor of Japan. [Japanese, from *mi* 'august' + *kado* 'gate.']

mike[1] /mīk/ ▶ **n.** a code word representing the letter M, used in radio communication.

mike[2] informal ▶ **n.** a microphone. ▶ **v.** [trans.] place a microphone close to (someone or something) or in (a place).

Mi'k·maq /'mik,mak/ ▶ **n. & adj.** var. of **Micmac**.

Mí·ko·nos /'mēkə,nôs/ Greek name for **Mykonos**.

mil[1] /mil/ informal ▶ **abbr.** ■ millimeters. ■ milliliters. ■ (used in sums of money) millions.

mil[2] ▶ **n.** one thousandth of an inch. [17th C.: from L. *millesimum* 'thousandth,' from *mille* 'thousand.']

mil. ▶ **abbr.** ■ military. ■ militia.

mi·la·dy /mə'lādē; mī-/ ▶ **n.** (pl. **-dies**) hist. humorous used to address or refer to an English noblewoman: *yes, milady | that it was against the law would not worry milady in the least.* [18th C.: via Fr. from Engl. *my lady*; cf. **milord**.]

mil·age ▶ **n.** var. of **mileage**.

Mi·lan /mə'län; mə'lan/ a city in northwestern Italy; pop. 1,432,000. Italian name **Milano**. — **Mil·a·nese** /,milə'nēz; -'nēs/ **adj. & n.**

milch /milk; milcH/ ▶ **adj.** denoting a cow or other domestic mammal giving or kept for milk. [ME: from OE *-milce*, only in *thrimilce* 'May,' from the Gmc. base of **milk**.]

mild /mīld/ ▶ **adj.** gentle and not easily provoked. ■ (of a rule or punishment) of only moderate severity. ■ not keenly felt or seriously intended. ■ (of an illness or pain) not serious or dangerous. ■ (of weather) moderately warm, esp. less cold than expected. ■ (of a medicine or cosmetic) acting gently and without causing harm. ■ (of food, drink, or tobacco) not sharp or strong in flavor. — **mild·ish adj. mild·ness n.** [OE *milde*; rel. to Ger. *mild*, from an Indo-Eur. root shared by L. *mollis*.]

mil·dew /'mil,d(y)o͞o/ ▶ **n.** a whitish coating of minute fungal hyphae, growing on plants or damp organic material. ▶ **v.** affect or be affected with mildew. — **mil·dew·y adj.** [OE *mildēaw* 'honeydew,' of Gmc. origin. The first element is rel. to L. *mel* and Gk. *meli* 'honey.']

mild·ly /'mīldlē/ ▶ **adv.** in a mild manner. ■ not seriously or dangerously. ■ [as submodifier] to a slight extent.

– PHRASES **to put it mildly** (or **putting it mildly**) used to imply that the reality is more extreme, usually worse.

mild-man·nered ▶ **adj.** (of a person) gentle and not given to extremes of emotion.

mile /mīl/ ▶ **n.** (also **statute mile**) a unit of linear measure equal to 5,280 feet, or 1,760 yards (approximately 1.609 km). ■ hist. (also **Roman mile**) a Roman measure of 1,000 paces (approximately 1,620 yards). ■ (usu. **miles**) informal a very long way or a very great amount. ▶ **adv.** [as submodifier] (**miles**) informal by a great amount or a long way: *the second tape is miles better.*

– PHRASES **be miles away** informal be lost in thought and consequently unaware of what is happening around one. **go the extra mile** be especially assiduous in one's attempt to achieve something. **a mile a minute** informal very quickly. **miles from anywhere** informal in a very isolated place. **see** (or **tell** or **spot**) **something a mile off** informal recognize something very easily. [OE *mīl*, based on L. *mil(l)ia*, pl. of *mille* 'thousand.']

mile·age /'mīlij/ (also **mil·age**) ▶ **n. 1** [usu. in sing.] a number of miles traveled or covered. ■ [usu. as adj.] traveling expenses paid according to the number of miles traveled. **2** informal the contribution made by something to one's aims or interests: *he made sure he got mileage out of the mix-up.* ■ the likely potential of someone or something: *he still has a lot of mileage and is well worth supporting.*

mile·post /'mīl,pōst/ ▶ **n.** a marker to indicate distance. ■ another term for **milestone**. ■ a post one mile from the finishing post of a race.

mil·er /'mīlər/ ▶ **n.** informal a person or horse trained specially to run a mile. — **mil·ing** /'mīliNG/ **n.**

mi·les glo·ri·o·sus /'mē,lās ,glôrē'ōsəs/ ▶ **n.** (pl. **mi·li·tes glo·ri·o·si** /'mēlə,tās ,glôrē'ōsē/) (in literature) a boastful soldier as a stock figure. [L., from the title of a comedy by Plautus.]

Mi·le·sian /mə'lēzHən; mī-/ ▶ **n.** a native or inhabitant of ancient Miletus. ▶ **adj.** of or relating to Miletus or its inhabitants. [16th C.: via L.]

mile·stone /'mīl,stōn/ ▶ **n.** a stone set up beside a road to mark the distance in miles to a particular place. ■ fig. an action or event marking a significant change or stage in development.

Mi·le·tus /mī'lētəs; mə-/ an ancient city of the Ionian Greeks in southwestern Asia Minor.

mil·foil /'mil,foil/ ▶ **n. 1** the common Eurasian yarrow. See illustration at **yarrow**. **2** (also **water milfoil**) a widely distributed and highly invasive aquatic plant (genus *Myriophyllum*, family Haloragaceae) with whorls of fine submerged leaves and wind-pollinated flowers. [ME: via OFr. from L. *millefolium*, from *mille* 'thousand' + *folium* 'leaf.']

mil·i·a /'milēə/ plural form of **milium**.

mil·i·ar·i·a /,milē'e(ə)rēə/ ▶ **n.** medical term for **prickly heat**. [19th C.: mod. L., from L. *miliarius* (see **miliary**).]

PRONUNCIATION KEY ə *ago, up*; ər *over, fur*; a *hat*; ā *ate*; ä *car*; e *let*; ē *see*; i *fit*; ī *by*; NG *sing*; ō *go*; ô *law, for*; oi *toy*; o͝o *good*; o͞o *goo*; ou *out*; TH *thin*; T̲H̲ *then*; ZH *vision*

mil·i·ar·y /ˈmilēˌerē/ ▶ **adj.** (of a disease) accompanied by a rash with lesions resembling millet seed. [17th C.: from L. *miliarius*, from *milium* 'millet.']

mi·lieu /milˈyoo͞; mēlˈyœ/ ▶ **n.** (pl. **mi·lieux** pronunc. same, or **mi·lieus**) a person's social environment: *a military milieu.* [19th C.: Fr., from *mi* 'mid' + *lieu* 'place.']

mil·i·tant /ˈmilətənt/ ▶ **adj.** combative and aggressive in support of a political or social cause: *militant Islamic fundamentalists.* ▶ **n.** a person who is active in this way. — **mil·i·tan·cy n. mil·i·tant·ly adv.**

mil·i·tar·i·a /ˌmiliˈte(ə)rēə/ ▶ **plural n.** military articles of historical interest. [1960s: from MILITARY + -IA².]

mil·i·ta·rism /ˈmilətəˌrizəm/ ▶ **n.** esp. derog. the belief that a country should maintain a strong military capability and be prepared to use it aggressively to defend or promote national interests. — **mil·i·ta·rist n. & adj. mil·i·ta·ris·tic** /ˌmilətəˈristik/ **adj.**

mil·i·ta·rize /ˈmilətəˌrīz/ ▶ **v.** [trans.] [often as adj.] (**militarized**) give (something, esp. an organization) a military character or style: *militarized police forces.* ■ equip or supply with military resources. — **mil·i·ta·ri·za·tion** /ˌmilətərəˈzāsHən/ **n.**

mil·i·tar·y /ˈmiləˌterē/ ▶ **adj.** of, relating to, or characteristic of soldiers or armed forces: *both leaders condemned the buildup of military activity.* ▶ **n.** (**the military**) the armed forces of a country. — **mil·i·tar·i·ly** /ˌmiləˈte(ə)rəlē/ **adv.** [ME: from Fr. *militaire* or L. *militaris*, from *miles, milit-* 'soldier.']

mil·i·tar·y at·ta·ché ▶ **n.** an army officer serving with an embassy or as an observer to a foreign army.

mil·i·tar·y-in·dus·tri·al com·plex ▶ **n.** a country's military establishment and those industries producing arms or other military materials.

mil·i·tar·y law ▶ **n.** the law governing the armed forces.

mil·i·tar·y po·lice ▶ **n.** [treated as pl.] the corps responsible for police and disciplinary duties in an army. — **mil·i·tar·y po·lice·man n. mil·i·tar·y po·lice·wom·an n.**

mil·i·ta·ry sci·ence ▶ **n.** the study of the causes and tactical principles of warfare.

mil·i·tar·y trib·une ▶ **n.** see TRIBUNE¹.

mil·i·tate /ˈmiləˌtāt/ ▶ **v.** [intrans.] (**militate against**) (of a fact or circumstance) be a powerful or conclusive factor in preventing. [16th C.: from L. *militat-* 'served as a soldier,' from the v. *militare*, from *miles, milit-* 'soldier.']

mi·li·tes glo·ri·o·si /ˈmēləˌtās ˌglôrēˈōsē/ plural form of MILES GLORIOSUS.

mi·li·tia /məˈlisHə/ ▶ **n.** a military force of civilians to supplement a regular army in an emergency. ■ a military force that engages in rebel activities. [16th C.: from L., 'military service,' from *miles, milit-* 'soldier.']

mil·i·um /ˈmilēəm/ ▶ **n.** (pl. **mil·i·a** /ˈmilēə/) Med. a small, hard, pale keratinous nodule formed on the skin, typically by a blocked sebaceous gland. [19th C.: from L., 'millet.']

milk /milk/ ▶ **n.** an opaque white fluid secreted by female mammals for the nourishment of their young. ■ the milk of cows (or occasionally goats or ewes) as food for humans. ■ the white juice of certain plants. ■ a creamy liquid with a particular ingredient or use. ▶ **v.** [trans.] draw milk from. ■ [intrans.] (of an animal, esp. a cow) produce or yield milk. ■ extract sap, venom, or other substances from. ■ fig. exploit or defraud (someone), typically by taking regular small amounts of money over a period of time. ■ fig. get all possible advantage from (a situation): *the newspapers were milking the story.* ■ fig. elicit a favorable reaction from (an audience) and prolong it for as long as possible.
– PHRASES **it's no use crying over spilt** (or **spilled**) **milk** proverb there is no point in regretting something that has already happened and cannot be changed or reversed. **milk and honey** prosperity and abundance. **milk of human kindness** care and compassion for others. [OE *milc, milcian*; rel. to Ger. *Milch*, from an Indo-Eur. root shared by L. *mulgere*.]

milk-and-wa·ter ▶ **adj.** [attrib.] lacking the will or ability.

milk choc·o·late ▶ **n.** solid chocolate made with milk.

milk·er /ˈmilkər/ ▶ **n.** **1** a cow or other animal that is kept for milk, esp. one of a specified productivity. **2** a person or contrivance that milks cows.

milk fe·ver ▶ **n.** **1** a calcium deficiency in female cows, goats, etc., that have just produced young. **2** a fever in women caused by infection after childbirth.

milk·fish /ˈmilkˌfisH/ ▶ **n.** (pl. same or **-fish·es**) a large silvery fish (*Chanos chanos*, family Chanidae) of the Indo-Pacific region, farmed for food in Southeast Asia and the Philippines.

milk glass ▶ **n.** semitranslucent whitened glass. Also called OPALINE.

milk leg ▶ **n.** painful swelling of the leg after giving birth, caused by thrombophlebitis in the femoral vein.

milk·maid /ˈmilkˌmād/ ▶ **n.** esp. archaic a girl or woman who milks cows or does other work in a dairy.

milk·man /ˈmilkmən; -ˌman/ ▶ **n.** (pl. **-men**) a person who delivers and sells milk.

milk of mag·ne·sia ▶ **n.** a white suspension of hydrated magnesium carbonate in water, an antacid or laxative.

Milk Riv·er a river that flows through northwestern Montana and southern Alberta, into the Missouri River.

milk run ▶ **n.** a routine, uneventful journey.

milk shake (also **milk·shake**) ▶ **n.** a cold drink of milk, flavoring, and typically ice cream, whisked until it is frothy.

milk sick·ness ▶ **n.** a condition of cattle and sheep in the western US, caused by eating white snakeroot, which contains a toxic alcohol.

milk snake ▶ **n.** a harmless North American constrictor (genus *Lampropeltis*, family Colubridae) that is typically strongly marked with red and black on yellow or white. It was formerly supposed to suck milk from sleeping cows.

milk·sop /ˈmilkˌsäp/ ▶ **n.** an ineffective, indecisive person.

milk sug·ar ▶ **n.** another term for LACTOSE.

milk this·tle ▶ **n.** a European thistle (*Silybum marianum*) with a solitary purple flower and glossy marbled leaves, naturalized in North America and used in herbal medicine. ■ another term for SOW THISTLE.

milk tooth ▶ **n.** any of a set of early, temporary (deciduous) teeth in children or young mammals that fall out as the permanent teeth erupt.

milk vetch (also **milk-vetch**) ▶ **n.** a plant (genus *Astragalus*) of the pea family found throughout the temperate zone of the northern hemisphere, grown in several regions as a fodder plant.

milk·weed /ˈmilkˌwēd/ ▶ **n.** **1** a herbaceous American plant (genus *Asclepias*, family Asclepiadaceae) with milky sap. Some kinds attract butterflies, some yield a variety of useful products, and some are grown as ornamentals. **2** (also **milkweed butterfly**) another term for MONARCH (sense 2).

common milkweed

milk-white ▶ **adj.** of the opaque white color of milk.

milk·wort /ˈmilkˌwərt; -ˌwôrt/ ▶ **n.** a small plant (genus *Polygala*, family Polygalaceae) that was formerly believed to increase the milk yield of cows and nursing mothers. Its tiny flowers, which may be white, pink, yellow-orange, blue, or greenish, usually appear in cloverlike heads.

milk·y /ˈmilkē/ ▶ **adj.** (**milk·i·er, milk·i·est**) **1** containing or mixed with a large amount of milk. ■ (of a cow) producing a lot of milk. ■ resembling milk, esp. in color. ■ (of something that is usually clear) cloudy. **2** informal, dated weak and compliant. — **milk·i·ly adv. milk·i·ness n.**

Milk·y Way a faint band of light crossing the night sky, made up of vast numbers of faint stars forming the bulk of the galaxy of which our solar system is a part.

Mill /mil/, John Stuart (1806–73), English philosopher and economist. In *On Liberty* (1859) he argued the importance of individuality. — **Mill·i·an** /ˈmilēən/ **adj.**

mill¹ /mil/ ▶ **n.** **1** a building equipped with machinery for grinding grain into flour. ■ a piece of machinery of this type. ■ a domestic device for grinding a solid substance to powder or pulp. ■ a building fitted with machinery for a manufacturing process. ■ a piece of manufacturing machinery. ■ a place that processes things or people in a mechanical way: *a diploma mill.* **2** informal an engine. **3** informal, dated a boxing match or a fistfight. ▶ **v.** **1** [trans.] grind or crush (something) in a mill. ■ cut or shape (metal) with a rotating tool: [as adj.] (**milling**) *lathes and milling machines.* ■ [usu. as adj.] (**milled**) produce regular ribbed markings on the edge of (a coin). **2** [intrans.] (**mill about/around**) (of people or animals) move around in a confused mass. **3** [trans.] thicken (wool or another animal fiber) by fulling it.
– PHRASES **go** (or **put someone**) **through the mill** undergo (or cause to undergo) an unpleasant experience. — **mill·a·ble adj.** [OE *mylen*, based on late L. *molinum*, from L. *mola* 'grindstone, mill,' from *molere* 'to grind.']

mill² ▶ **n.** a monetary unit used only in calculations, worth one thousandth of a dollar. [18th C.: from L. *millesimum* 'thousandth part'; cf. CENT.]

Mil·lais /məˈlā/, Sir John Everett (1829–96), English painter. He produced lavish portraits and landscapes.

Mil·lay /məˈlā/, Edna St. Vincent (1892–1950), US poet and writer. Much of her poetry is collected in *Collected Lyrics* (1943).

mill·board /ˈmilˌbôrd/ ▶ **n.** stiff gray pasteboard, used for the covers of books.

mill·dam /ˈmilˌdam/ ▶ **n.** a dam built across a stream to raise the level of the water so that it will turn the wheel of a water mill.

mil·le·fi·o·ri /ˌmiləfēˈôrē/ ▶ **n.** a kind of ornamental glass in which a number of glass rods of different sizes and colors are fused together and cut into sections that form various patterns. [19th C.: from Ital. *millefiore*, lit. 'a thousand flowers.']

mille·fleurs /mēlˈflər; -ˈflo͝or/ ▶ **n.** a pattern of flowers and leaves used in decorative items. [19th C.: Fr., lit. 'a thousand flowers.']

mil·le·nar·i·an /ˌmiləˈne(ə)rēən/ ▶ **adj.** relating to or believing in Christian millenarianism. ■ fig. believing in the imminence or inevitability of a golden age of peace, justice, and prosperity. ■ denoting a religious or political group seeking solutions to present crises through rapid and radical transformation of politics and society. ▶ **n.** a person who believes in the millennium doctrine. — **mil·le·nar·i·an·ism n. mil·le·nar·i·an·ist n. & adj.**

mil·le·nar·y /ˈmiləˌnerē/ ▶ **n.** (pl. **-nar·ies**) a period of a thousand years. Compare with MILLENNIUM. ■ a thousandth anniversary. ▶ **adj.** consisting of a thousand people, years, etc. [16th C.: from late L. *millenarius* 'containing a thousand,' based on L. *mille* 'thousand.']

mil·len·ni·um /məˈlenēəm/ ▶ **n.** (pl. **-len·ni·a** /-ˈlenēə/ or **-len·ni·ums**) a period of a thousand years, esp. when calculated from the traditional date of Christ's birth. ■ an anniversary of a thousand years. *the millennium of the Russian Orthodox Church.* ■ **(the millennium)** the point at which one period of a thousand years ends and another begins. ■ **(the millennium)** Christian Theol. the prophesied thousand-year reign of Christ at the end of the age (Rev. 20:1–5). ■ **(the millennium)** fig. a utopian period of good government, great happiness, and prosperity. — **mil·len·ni·al** /-ēəl/ **adj.** [17th C.: mod. L., from L. *mille* 'thousand,' on the pattern of *biennium*.]

mil·le·pede /'milə,pēd/ ▶ **n.** var. of MILLIPEDE.

mil·le·pore /'milə,pôr/ ▶ **n.** Zool. a fire coral. [18th C.: from Fr. *millépore* or mod. L. *millepora*, from L. *mille* 'thousand' + *porus* 'pore.']

Mill·er[1] /'milər/, Arthur Asher (1915–2005), US playwright. His plays include *Death of a Salesman* (1949) and the *The Crucible* (1953), which used the Salem witch trials of 1692 as an allegory for McCarthyism.

Mill·er[2], Glenn (1904–44), US bandleader. From 1938, he led his celebrated big band, with which he recorded his theme song "Moonlight Serenade."

Mill·er[3], Henry Valentine (1891–1980), US writer. His novels *Tropic of Cancer* (1934) and *Tropic of Capricorn* (1939) were banned in the US until the 1960s.

Miller[4], Samuel Freeman (1816–90), US Supreme Court associate justice 1862–90.

mill·er /'milər/ ▶ **n.** a person who owns or works in a grain mill.

mill·er·ite /'milə,rīt/ ▶ **n.** a mineral consisting of nickel sulfide and typically occurring as slender needle-shaped bronze crystals. [19th C.: named after William H. *Miller* (1801–80), Engl. scientist, + -ITE[1].]

mill·er's thumb ▶ **n.** a small European freshwater fish (*Cottus gobio*) of the sculpin family, having a broad flattened head and most active at night. Also called BULLHEAD.

mil·les·i·mal /mə'lesəməl/ ▶ **adj.** consisting of thousandth parts; thousandth. ▶ **n.** a thousandth part. — **mil·les·i·mal·ly adv.** [18th C.: from L. *millesimus* (from *mille* 'thousand') + -AL.]

Mil·let /mē'ye; -'lā/, Jean François (1814–75), French painter.

mil·let /'milit/ ▶ **n.** a fast-growing cereal plant that is widely grown in warm countries and regions with poor soils. Its several species include **common millet** (*Panicum miliaceum*), of temperate regions.

Mil·lett /'milit/, Kate (1934–), US feminist; full name *Katherine Millett*. She advocated a radical feminism in *Sexual Politics* (1970).

milli- ▶ **comb. form** (used commonly in units of measurement) a thousand, chiefly denoting a factor of one thousandth: *milligram* | *millipede.* [from L. *mille* 'thousand.']

mil·li·amp /'milē,amp/ ▶ **n.** short for MILLIAMPERE.

mil·li·am·pere /,milē'am,pi(ə)r/ ▶ **n.** one thousandth of an ampere, a measure for small electric currents.

mil·liard /'mil,yärd; -yərd/ ▶ **n.** Brit. one thousand million (a term now largely superseded by billion). [18th C.: Fr., from *mille* 'thousand.']

mil·li·bar /'milə,bär/ ▶ **n.** one thousandth of a bar, the cgs unit of atmospheric pressure equivalent to 100 pascals.

mil·li·gram /'milə,gram/ (Brit. also **mil·li·gramme**) (abbr.: **mg**) ▶ **n.** one thousandth of a gram.

Mil·li·kan /'milikən/, Robert Andrews (1868–1953), US physicist. He worked with electrons. Nobel Prize for Physics (1923).

mil·li·li·ter /'milə,lētər/ (Brit. **mil·li·li·tre**) (abbr.: **ml**) ▶ **n.** one thousandth of a liter (0.002 pint).

mil·li·me·ter /'milə,mētər/ (Brit. **mil·li·me·tre**) (abbr.: **mm**) ▶ **n.** one thousandth of a meter (0.039 in.).

mil·li·ner /'milənər/ ▶ **n.** a person who makes or sells women's hats. [ME: from MILAN.]

mil·li·ner·y /'milə,nerē/ ▶ **n.** (pl. **-ner·ies**) women's hats. ■ the trade or business of a milliner.

mil·lion /'milyən/ ▶ **cardinal number** (pl. **-lions** or (with numeral or quantifying word) same) **(a/one million)** the number equivalent to the product of a thousand and a thousand; 1,000,000 or 10^6: *a million people.* ■ **(millions)** the numbers from a million to a billion. ■ **(millions)** several million things or people. *millions of TV viewers.* ■ informal an unspecified but very large number or amount of something. ■ **(the millions)** the bulk of the population: *movies for the millions.* ■ a million dollars.
– PHRASES **look** (or **feel**) **(like) a million dollars** informal (of a person) look or feel extremely good. — **mil·lion·fold adj. & adv. mil·lionth** /-yənTH/ **ordinal number.** [ME: from OFr., prob. from Ital. *milione*, from *mille* 'thousand' + the augmentative suffix *-one*.]

mil·lion·aire /,milyə'ne(ə)r; 'milyə,ne(ə)r/ ▶ **n.** a person whose assets are worth one million dollars or more. [19th C.: from Fr. *millionnaire*, from *million* (see MILLION).]

mil·lion·air·ess /,milyə'ne(ə)rəs/ ▶ **n.** a female millionaire.

mil·li·pede /'milə,pēd/ (also **mil·le·pede**) ▶ **n.** a myriapod invertebrate (class Diplopoda) with an elongated body composed of many segments, most of which bear two pairs of legs. [17th C.: from L. *millepeda* 'wood louse,' from *mille* 'thousand' + *pes, ped-* 'foot.']

mil·li·sec·ond /'milə,sekənd/ ▶ **n.** one thousandth of a second.

mil·li·volt /'milə,vōlt/ ▶ **n.** one thousandth of a volt.

mil·li·watt /"mili,wät/ (abbr.: **mW**) ▶ **n.** a unit of power equal to one thousandth of a watt.

mill·pond /'mil,pänd/ (also **mill pond**) ▶ **n.** the pool that is created by a milldam.

mill·race /'mil,rās/ ▶ **n.** the channel carrying the swift current of water that drives a mill wheel.

mill·stone /'mil,stōn/ ▶ **n.** each of two circular stones used for grinding grain. ■ fig. a heavy and inescapable responsibility.

mill·stream /'mil,strēm/ ▶ **n.** the water in a millrace. ■ another term for MILLRACE.

mill wheel ▶ **n.** a wheel used to drive a water mill.

mill·work·er /'mil,wərkər/ ▶ **n.** a worker in a mill or factory.

mill·wright /'mil,rīt/ ▶ **n.** a person who designs or builds mills or who maintains mill machinery.

Milne /miln/, A. A. (1882–1956), English writer and poet; full name *Alan Alexander Milne*. He created the character Winnie the Pooh for his son Christopher Robin (1920–96).

mi·lo /'mīlō/ ▶ **n.** a drought-resistant variety of sorghum. [19th C.: from Sesotho *maili*.]

mi·lord /mə'lôrd; mī-/ ▶ **n.** hist. humorous used to address or refer to an English nobleman: *the previous occupant had been evicted to make way for the English milord and his lady.* [17th C.: via Fr. from Engl. *my lord*; cf. MILADY.]

Mí·los /'mē,läs; -,lôs/ Greek name for MELOS.

Mi·losz /'mēlôsH/, Czeslaw (1911–2004), US poet and writer; born in Lithuania. His novels include *The Seizure of Power* (1953).

milque·toast /'milk,tōst/ (also **Milque·toast**) ▶ **n.** a person who is timid or submissive. [1930s: from the name of a cartoon character, Caspar *Milquetoast*, created by H. T. Webster in 1924.]

milt /milt/ ▶ **n.** the semen of a male fish. ■ a sperm-filled reproductive gland of a male fish. [OE *milte* 'spleen,' of Gmc. origin; perh. rel. to MELT.]

Mil·ton /'miltn/, John (1608–74), English poet. His three major works, *Paradise Lost* (1667; revised, 1674), *Paradise Regained* (1671), and *Samson Agonistes* (1671) show his mastery of blank verse. — **Mil·to·ni·an** /mil'tōnēən/ **adj. Mil·ton·ic** /mil'tänik/ **adj.**

Mil·wau·kee /mil'wôkē/ a city in southeastern Wisconsin; pop. 596,974.

Mi·mas /'mīməs; 'mē-/ Astron. a satellite of Saturn, the seventh closest to the planet.

mime /mīm/ ▶ **n.** **1** the theatrical technique of suggesting action, character, or emotion without words, using only gesture, expression, and movement. ■ a theatrical performance or part of a performance using such a technique. ■ an action or set of actions intended to convey the idea of another action or an idea or feeling. *he performed a brief mime of someone fencing.* ■ a practitioner of mime or a performer in a mime. **2** (in ancient Greece and Rome) a simple farcical drama including mimicry. ▶ **v.** [trans.] use gesture and movement without words in the acting of (a play or role). ■ convey an impression of (an idea or feeling) by gesture and movement, without using words; mimic. — **mim·er n.** [17th C. (also in the sense 'mimic or jester'): from L. *mimus*, from Gk. *mimos*.]

mim·e·o /'mimē,ō/ ▶ **n.** short for MIMEOGRAPH.

mim·e·o·graph /'mimēə,graf/ ▶ **n.** a duplicating machine that produces copies from a stencil. ■ a copy produced on such a machine. ▶ **v.** [trans.] make a copy of (a document) with such a machine. [19th C.: formed irregularly from Gk. *mimeomai* 'I imitate' + -GRAPH.]

mi·me·sis /mə'mēsis; mī-/ ▶ **n.** formal tech. imitation, in particular: ■ representation or imitation of the real world in art and literature. ■ the deliberate imitation of the behavior of one group of people by another as a factor in social change. ■ Zool. another term for MIMICRY. [16th C.: from Gk. *mimēsis*, from *mimeisthai* 'to imitate.']

mi·met·ic /mə'metik/ ▶ **adj.** formal tech. relating to, constituting, or habitually practicing mimesis. — **mi·met·i·cal·ly adv.** [17th C.: from Gk. *mimētikos* 'imitation,' from *mimeisthai* 'to imitate.']

mim·e·tite /'mimə,tīt; 'mī-/ ▶ **n.** a mineral consisting of a chloride and arsenate of lead, typically found as a crust or needlelike crystals in lead deposits. [19th C.: from Gk. *mimētēs* 'imitator' + -ITE[1].]

mim·ic /'mimik/ ▶ **v.** **(mim·icked, mim·ick·ing)** [trans.] imitate (someone or their actions or words), typically in order to entertain or ridicule. ■ (of an animal or plant) resemble or imitate (another animal or plant), esp. to deter predators or for camouflage. ■ (of a drug) replicate the physiological effects of (another substance). ■ (of a disease) exhibit symptoms that bear a deceptive resemblance to those of (another disease). ▶ **n.** a person skilled in imitating the voice, mannerisms, or movements of others in an entertaining way. ■ an animal or plant that exhibits mimicry. ▶ **adj.** [attrib.] imitative of something, esp. for amusement. — **mim·ick·er n.** [16th C. (as n. and adj.): via L. from Gk. *mimikos*, from *mimos* 'mime.']

mim·ic·ry /'mimәkrē/ ▶ **n.** (pl. **-ries**) the action or art of imitating someone or something, typically in order to entertain or ridicule: *gently teasing mimicry.* ■ Biol. the close external resemblance of an animal or plant (or part of one) to another. See also BATESIAN MIMICRY, MÜLLERIAN MIMICRY.

mi·mo·sa /mi'mōsə; -zə; mī-/ ▶ **n.** **1** an Australian acacia tree (*Acacia dealbata*) with delicate fernlike leaves and yellow flowers that are used by florists. **2** a pea-family plant of a genus (*Mimosa*) that includes the sensitive plant. **3** a drink of champagne and orange juice. [mod. L., appar. from L. *mimus* 'mime' + *-osa*.]

min. ▶ abbr. ■ minim (fluid measure). ■ minimum. ■ minute(s).

mi·na·cious /mə'nāsHəs/ ▶ adj. rare menacing; threatening. [17th C.: from L. *minax, minac-* 'threatening' (from *minari* 'threaten') + **-ous**.]

Min·a·ma·ta dis·ease /,mēnə'mätə/ ▶ n. chronic poisoning by alkyl mercury compounds from industrial waste. [1950s: named after *Minamata*, a town in Japan.]

min·a·ret /,minə'ret/ ▶ n. a tall slender tower, typically part of a mosque, with a balcony from which a muezzin calls Muslims to prayer. —**min·a·ret·ed** adj. [17th C.: from Fr., or from Sp. *minarete*, Ital. *minaretto*, via Turk. from Arab. *manār(a)* 'lighthouse, minaret,' based on *nār* 'fire or light.']

minaret

min·a·to·ry /'minə,tôrē; 'mī-/ ▶ adj. formal expressing or conveying a threat: *minatory finger-wagging.* [16th C.: from late L. *minatorius*, from *minat-* 'threatened,' from the v. *minari.*]

min·au·dière /,mēnō'dyer/ ▶ n. a small, decorative handbag without handles or a strap. [Fr., lit. 'coquettish woman,' from *minauder* 'simper.']

min·bar /'min,bär/ (also **mim·bar** /'mim-/) ▶ n. steps used as a platform by a preacher in a mosque. [from Arab. *minbar.*]

mince /mins/ ▶ v. [trans.] **1** [often as adj.] (**minced**) cut up or grind (food, esp. meat) into very small pieces, typically in a machine with revolving blades. **2** [no obj., with adverbial of direction] walk with an affected fastidiousness, typically with short quick steps. ▶ n. something minced, esp. mincemeat. ■ a quantity of something minced: *a mince of garlic.*
– PHRASES **not mince words** (or **one's words**) speak candidly and directly, esp. when criticizing someone or something. —**minc·er** n. **minc·ing·ly** adv. (in sense 2). [ME: from OFr. *mincier*, based on L. *minutia* 'smallness.']

mince·meat /'mins,mēt/ ▶ n. **1** a mixture of currants, raisins, sugar, apples, candied citrus peel, spices, and suet, typically baked in a pie. **2** minced meat.
– PHRASES **make mincemeat of someone** informal defeat someone decisively or easily.

mince pie ▶ n. a small, round pie or tart containing sweet mincemeat, typically eaten at Christmas.

Minch /minCH/ (**the Minch**) a channel in the Atlantic Ocean, between the mainland of Scotland and the Outer Hebrides.

mind /mīnd/ ▶ n. **1** the element of a person that enables them to be aware of the world and their experiences, to think, and to feel; the faculty of consciousness and thought: *as the thoughts ran through his mind, he came to a conclusion.* ■ a person's mental processes contrasted with physical action: *I wrote a letter in my mind.* **2** a person's intellect. ■ the state of normal mental functioning in a person. ■ a person's memory: *the company's name slips my mind.* ■ a person identified with their intellectual faculties: *one of the greatest minds of his time.* **3** a person's attention. ■ the will or determination to achieve something. ▶ v. [trans.] **1** [often with negative] be distressed, annoyed, or worried by: *I don't mind the rain.* ■ have an objection to. ■ [with negative or in questions] (**mind doing something**) be reluctant to do something (often used in polite requests): *I don't mind admitting I was worried.* ■ (**would not mind something**) informal used to express one's strong enthusiasm for something. **2** regard as important and worthy of attention. ■ [intrans.] feel concern. ■ [with clause, in imper.] dated used to urge someone to remember or take care to bring about something: *mind you look after the children.* ■ [no obj., in imper.] (also **mind you**) used to introduce a qualification to a previous statement: *we've got some decorations up—not a lot, mind you.* ■ [no obj., in imper.] informal used to make a command more insistent or to draw attention to a statement: *be early to bed tonight, mind.* ■ be obedient to. **3** take care of temporarily. ■ [in imper.] used to warn someone to avoid injury or damage from a hazard: *mind your head on that cupboard!* ■ [in imper.] be careful about the quality or nature of: *mind your manners!* **4** [with infin.] (**be minded**) esp. formal be inclined or disposed to do a particular thing: *he was minded to reject the application.*
– PHRASES **be of two minds** be unable to decide between alternatives. **be of one** (or **a different**) **mind** share the same (or hold a different) opinion. **bear** (or **keep**) **in mind** remember and take into account. **close one's mind to** refuse to consider or acknowledge. **come** (or **spring**) **to mind** (of a thought or idea) occur to someone. **don't mind if I do** informal used to accept an invitation. **give someone a piece of one's mind** tell someone what one thinks of them, esp. in anger. **have a** (or **a good** or **half a**) **mind to do something** be very much inclined to do something. **have someone or something in mind** be thinking of. ■ intend: *I had it in mind to ask you to work for me.* **have a mind of one's own** be capable of independent opinion or action. ■ (of an inanimate object) seem capable of thought and intention, esp. by behaving contrary to the will of the person using it. **in one's mind's eye** in one's imagination or mental view. **mind over matter** the use of willpower to overcome physical problems. **mind one's own business** refrain from prying or interfering. **mind one's Ps & Qs** be careful to behave well and avoid giving offense. **mind the store** informal have charge of something temporarily. **never mind 1** used to urge someone not to feel anxiety or distress. ■ used to suggest that a problem or objection is not important. **2** (also **never you mind**) used in refusing to answer a question: *never mind where I'm going.* **3** used to indicate that what has been said of one thing applies even more to another. **not pay someone any mind** not pay someone any attention. **on someone's mind** preoccupying someone, esp. in a disquieting way. **an open mind** the readiness to consider something without prejudice. **open one's mind to** be receptive to. **out of one's mind** having lost control of one's mental faculties. ■ informal suffering from a particular condition to a very high degree: *she was bored out of her mind.* **put someone in mind of** resemble and so cause someone to think of or remember. **put** (or **set**) **one's mind to** direct all one's attention to (achieving something). **put someone/something out of one's mind** deliberately forget someone or something. **to my mind** in my opinion.

mind-al·ter·ing ▶ adj. (of a hallucinogenic drug) producing mood changes or giving a sense of heightened awareness.

Min·da·na·o /,mində'nä,ō; -'nou/ an island in southeastern Philippines; chief town Davao.

mind-bend·ing ▶ adj. informal (chiefly of a hallucinogenic drug) influencing or altering one's state of mind. —**mind-bend·er** n. **mind-bend·ing·ly** adv.

mind-blow·ing ▶ adj. informal overwhelmingly impressive: *for a kid, Chicago was really mind-blowing.* ■ (of a drug) inducing hallucinations. —**mind-blow·ing·ly** adv.

mind-bog·gling ▶ adj. informal overwhelming; startling. —**mind-bog·gling·ly** adv.

mind·ed /'mīndid/ ▶ adj. [in comb. or with submodifier] inclined to think in a particular way: *liberal-minded.* ■ [in comb.] interested in or enthusiastic about.

mind-ex·pand·ing ▶ adj. (esp. of a hallucinogenic drug) giving a sense of heightened awareness.

mind·ful /'mīndfəl/ ▶ adj. [predic.] conscious or aware of. —**mind·ful·ly** adv. **mind·ful·ness** n.

mind game ▶ n. a series of deliberate actions or responses planned for psychological effect on another.

mind·less /'mīndlis/ ▶ adj. (of a person) acting without concern for the consequences. ■ (esp. of harmful or evil behavior) done for no particular reason. ■ [predic.] (**mindless of**) not thinking of or concerned about. ■ (of an activity) so simple or repetitive as to be performed automatically without thought or skill. —**mind·less·ly** adv. **mind·less·ness** n.

mind-numb·ing ▶ adj. so extreme or intense as to prevent normal thought: *hours of mind-numbing testimony.* —**mind-numb·ing·ly** adv.

Min·do·ro /min'dôrō/ an island in the Philippines.

mind read·er (also **mind-read·er** or **mind·read·er**) ▶ n. a person who can supposedly discern what another person is thinking. —**mind-read** v. **mind-read·ing** n.

mind-set (also **mind·set**) ▶ n. [usu. in sing.] the established set of attitudes held by someone.

mine[1] /mīn/ ▶ possessive pron. used to refer to a thing or things belonging to or associated with the speaker. [OE *mīn*, of Gmc. origin.]

mine[2] ▶ n. **1** an excavation in the earth for extracting coal or other minerals: *a copper mine.* ■ [in sing.] an abundant source of something. **2** a type of bomb placed on or just below the surface of the ground or in the water that detonates when disturbed. ▶ v. [trans.] (often **be mined**) **1** obtain (coal or other minerals) from a mine. ■ dig in (the earth) for coal or other minerals. ■ dig or burrow in (the earth). ■ fig. delve into (an abundant source) to extract something of value, esp. information or skill. **2** lay explosive mines on or just below the surface of (the ground or water): *the area was heavily mined.* ■ destroy by means of an explosive mine. —**mine·a·ble** (also **min·a·ble**) adj. [ME: from OFr. *mine* (n.), *miner* (v.), perh. of Celtic origin; cf. Welsh *mwyn* 'ore,' earlier 'mine.']

mine·field /'mīn,fēld/ (also **mine field**) ▶ n. an area planted with explosive mines. ■ fig. a situation presenting unseen hazards.

mine·lay·er /'mīn,lāər/ ▶ n. a warship, aircraft, or land vehicle from which explosive mines are laid. —**mine·lay·ing** n.

min·er /'mīnər/ ▶ n. **1** a person who works in a mine. ■ a device used to mine ores, etc. ■ hist. a person who digs tunnels in order to destroy an enemy position with explosives. **2** an Australian bird (genus *Manorina*) of the honeyeater family, having a loud call and typically nesting colonially. **3** a small South American bird (genus *Geositta*) of the ovenbird family that excavates a long burrow for breeding. **4** short for LEAF MINER.

min·er·al /'min(ə)rəl/ ▶ n. **1** a solid inorganic substance of natural occurrence. ■ a substance obtained by mining. ■ an inorganic substance needed by the human body for good health. **2** (**minerals**) Brit. (in commercial use) effervescent soft drinks. ▶ adj. of or denoting a mineral. [ME: from med. L. *minerale*, neut. (used as a n.) of *mineralis*, from *minera* 'ore.']

min·er·al·ize /'min(ə)rə,līz/ ▶ v. [trans.] convert (organic matter) wholly or partly into a mineral or inorganic material or structure. ■ change (a metal) into an ore. ■ impregnate (water or another liquid) with a mineral substance. —**min·er·al·i·za·tion** /,min(ə)rələ'zāsHən/ n.

min·er·al·o·cor·ti·coid /,min(ə)rə,lō'kôrti,koid/ ▶ n. Biochem. a corticosteroid, such as aldosterone, that is involved with maintaining the salt balance in the body.

min·er·al·o·gy /,minə'räləjē; -'ral-/ ▶ n. the scientific study of minerals. —**min·er·al·og·i·cal** /,min(ə)rə'läjikəl/ adj. **min·er·al·og·i·cal·ly** /,min(ə)rə'läjik(ə)lē/ adv. **min·er·al·o·gist** n.

min·er·al oil ▶ n. a distillation product of petroleum, esp. one used as a lubricant, moisturizer, or laxative.

min·er·al spir·its ▶ n. a volatile liquid distilled from petroleum, used as a paint thinner and solvent.

min·er·al wa·ter ▶ n. water found in nature with some dissolved salts present. ■ esp. Brit. an artificial imitation of this.

min·er·al wool ▶ n. a substance resembling matted wool and made from inorganic mineral material, used chiefly for packing or insulation.

Mi·ner·va /mə'nərvə/ Rom. Mythol. the goddess of handicrafts, identified with the Greek goddess Athena.

mine shaft (also **mine·shaft**) ▶ n. a deep narrow vertical hole, or sometimes a horizontal tunnel, that gives access to a mine.

min·e·stro·ne /,minə'strōnē/ ▶ n. a thick soup containing vegetables and pasta. [Ital.]

mine·sweep·er /'mīn,swēpər/ ▶ n. a warship equipped for detecting and removing explosive mines. — **mine·sweep·ing** n.

Ming /miNG/ ▶ n. the dynasty ruling China 1368–1644. ■ [usu. as adj.] Chinese porcelain made during the rule of the Ming dynasty. [Chin., lit. 'clear or bright.']

min·gle /'miNGgəl/ ▶ v. mix or cause to mix together. [trans.] *an expression that mingled compassion and bewilderment.* ■ [intrans.] move freely around a place or at a social function, associating with others. [ME: frequentative of obs. *meng* 'mix or blend' (rel. to AMONG).]

Min·gus /'miNGgəs/, Charles (1922–79), US bassist and composer. A leading figure of the 1940s jazz scene, he experimented with atonality.

min·gy /'minjē/ ▶ adj. (**-gi·er**, **-gi·est**) informal mean and stingy: *you've been mingy with the sunscreen.* ■ unexpectedly or undesirably small. — **ming·i·ly** adv. [20th C.: perh. a blend of MEAN[2] and STINGY.]

Mi·nho /'mēnyōō/ Portuguese name for MIÑO.

min·i /'minē/ ▶ adj. [attrib.] denoting a miniature version of something: *a bouquet of mini carnations.* ▶ n. (pl. **min·is**) **1** short for MINISKIRT. **2** short for MINICOMPUTER.

mini- ▶ comb. form very small; miniature.

min·i·a·ture /'min(ē)əCHər; -,CHŏŏr/ ▶ adj. [attrib.] (esp. of a replica of something) of a much smaller size than normal; very small: *children dressed as miniature adults.* ▶ n. a thing that is much smaller than normal. ■ a plant or animal that is a smaller version of an existing variety or breed. ■ a very small and highly detailed portrait or other painting. ■ a picture or decorated letter in an illuminated manuscript. ▶ v. [trans.] rare represent on a smaller scale; reduce to miniature dimensions.

– PHRASES **in miniature** on a small scale, but otherwise a replica: *a place that is Greece in miniature.* [18th C.: from Ital. *miniatura*, via med. L. from L. *miniare* 'rubricate, illuminate,' from *minium* 'red lead, vermilion.']

min·i·a·ture golf ▶ n. an informal version of golf played on a series of short constructed obstacle courses.

min·i·a·tur·ist /'min(ē)ə,CHŏŏrist; -CHərist/ ▶ n. a painter of miniatures or an illuminator of manuscripts.

min·i·a·tur·ize /'min(ē)əCHə,rīz/ ▶ v. [trans.] [usu. as adj.] (**miniaturized**) make on a smaller scale. — **min·i·a·tur·i·za·tion** /,min(ē)əCHərə'zāSHən/ n.

min·i·bar /'minē,bär/ ▶ n. a refrigerator in a hotel room containing a selection of refreshments for sale.

min·i·bus /'minē,bəs/ ▶ n. a small bus.

min·i·cam /'minē,kam/ ▶ n. a hand-held video camera.

min·i·com·pu·ter /'minēkəm,pyōōtər/ ▶ n. a computer of medium power, between a microcomputer and a mainframe.

Min·i·coy Is·lands /'minə,koi/ islands in the Indian Ocean, part of the Indian Union Territory of Lakshadweep.

min·i·dress /'minē,dres/ ▶ n. a very short dress.

min·im /'minim/ ▶ n. **1** one sixtieth of a fluid dram, about one drop of liquid. **2** Calligraphy a short vertical stroke, as in the letters *i*, *m*. [ME: from L. *minima*, from *minimus* 'smallest.']

min·i·ma /'minəmə/ plural form of MINIMUM.

min·i·mal /'minəməl/ ▶ adj. **1** of a minimum amount, quantity, or degree; negligible. **2** Art characterized by the use of simple or primary forms or structures, esp. geometric or massive ones. ■ Music characterized by the repetition and gradual alteration of short phrases. **3** Ling. (of a pair of forms) distinguished by only one feature. — **min·i·mal·ly** adv. [17th C.: from L. *minimus* 'smallest' + -AL.]

min·i·mal·ism /'minəmə,lizəm/ ▶ n. **1** a 1950s trend in art that used simple, typically massive, forms. **2** an avant-garde movement in music characterized by the repetition of very short phrases that change gradually, producing a hypnotic effect.

min·i·mal·ist /'minəməlist/ ▶ n. **1** a person advocating minor or moderate reform in politics. **2** a person who advocates or practices minimalism in art or music. ▶ adj. **1** advocating moderate political policies. **2** of or relating to minimalism in art or music.

min·i·max /'minē,maks/ ▶ n. Math. the lowest of a set of maximum values. Compare with MAXIMIN. ■ [as adj.] denoting a method or strategy in game theory that minimizes the greatest risk to a participant in a game or other situation of conflict. ■ [as adj.] denoting the theory that in a game with two players, a player's smallest possible maximum loss is equal to the same player's greatest possible minimum gain. [1940s: blend of MINIMUM and MAXIMUM.]

min·i·mize /'minə,mīz/ ▶ v. [trans.] reduce (something) to the smallest possible amount or degree. ■ represent or estimate at less than the true value or importance: *they may minimize, or even overlook, it.* — **min·i·mi·za·tion** /,minəmə'zāSHən/ n. **min·i·miz·er** n.

min·i·mum /'minəməm/ ▶ n. (pl. **-ma** /-mə/ or **-mums**) [usu. in sing.] the least or smallest amount or quantity possible, attainable, or required. ■ the lowest or smallest amount of a varying quantity (e.g., temperature) allowed, attained, or recorded. ■ Math. a point at which a continuously varying quantity ceases to decrease and begins to increase; the value of a quantity at such a point. ■ Math. the smallest element in a set. ▶ adj. [attrib.] smallest or lowest: *the minimum amount of effort.*

– PHRASES **at a** (or **the**) **minimum** at the very least. [17th C.: from L., neut. of *minimus* 'least.']

min·i·mum wage ▶ n. the lowest wage permitted by law or by a special agreement.

min·ing /'mīniNG/ ▶ n. the process or industry of obtaining coal or other minerals from a mine.

min·ion /'minyən/ ▶ n. a follower or underling of a powerful person, esp. a servile or unimportant one. [15th C.: from Fr. *mignon*, *mignonne*.]

min·is·cule ▶ adj. nonstandard spelling of MINUSCULE.

min·i·se·ries /'minē,si(ə)rēz/ ▶ n. (pl. same) a television drama shown in a number of episodes.

min·i·skirt /'minē,skərt/ ▶ n. a very short skirt.

min·is·ter /'minəstər/ ▶ n. **1** (also **minister of religion**) a member of the clergy, esp. in Protestant churches. ■ (also **minister general**) the superior of some religious orders. **2** (in certain countries) a head of a government department: *Britain's defense minister.* ■ a diplomatic agent representing a state or sovereign in a foreign country. **3** archaic a person or thing used to achieve or convey something: *the Angels are ministers of the Divine Will.* ▶ v. [intrans.] **1** (**minister to**) attend to the needs of. **2** act as a minister of religion. ■ [trans.] administer (a sacrament). — **min·is·ter·ship** n. [ME: from OFr. *ministre*, from L. *minister* 'servant,' from *minus* 'less.']

min·is·te·ri·al /,minə'sti(ə)rēəl/ ▶ adj. **1** of or relating to a minister of religion. **2** of or relating to a government minister or ministers. — **min·is·te·ri·al·ly** adv.

min·is·tra·tion /,minə'strāSHən/ ▶ n. (usu. **ministrations**) esp. formal humorous the provision of assistance. ■ the services of a minister of religion. ■ the action of administering the sacrament. — **min·is·trant** /'minəstrənt/ n.

min·i·stroke /'minē,strōk/ ▶ n. a temporary blockage of the blood supply to the brain, leaving no noticeable effects. Also called TRANSIENT ISCHEMIC ATTACK.

min·is·try /'minəstrē/ ▶ n. (pl. **-tries**) **1** [usu. in sing.] the work or vocation of a minister of religion. ■ the period of tenure of a minister of religion. ■ the spiritual work or service of any Christian or a group of Christians, esp. evangelism. **2** (in certain countries) a government department headed by a minister of state. **3** (in certain countries) a period of government under one prime minister: *Gladstone's first ministry.*

min·i·van /'minē,van/ ▶ n. a small van, typically one fitted with seats in the back for passengers.

min·i·ver /'minəvər/ ▶ n. plain white fur used for lining or trimming clothes. [ME: from OFr. *menu vair* 'little vair,' from *menu* 'little' + *vair* 'squirrel fur.']

mink /miNGk/ ▶ n. (pl. same or **minks**) a small, semiaquatic, stoatlike carnivore (genus *Mustela*) of the weasel family, native to North America and Eurasia. The **American mink** (*M. vison*) is widely farmed for its fur. ■ the thick brown fur of the mink. ■ a coat made of this. [ME (denoting the animal's fur): from Swed.]

minke /'miNGkē/ (also **minke whale**) ▶ n. a small rorqual whale (*Balaenoptera acutorostrata*) with a dark gray back, white underparts, and pale markings on the fins and behind the head. [1930s: prob. from *Meincke*, the name of a Norw. whaler.]

Minn. ▶ abbr. Minnesota.

Min·ne·ap·o·lis /,minē'apəlis/ a city in southeastern Minnesota; pop. 382,618.

min·ne·o·la /,minē'ōlə/ ▶ n. a deep reddish tangelo. [20th C.: named after a town in Florida.]

min·ne·sing·er /'minə,siNGər; -,ziNGər/ ▶ n. a German lyric poet and singer of the 12th–14th centuries. [19th C.: from Ger. *Minnesinger* 'love-singer.']

Min·ne·so·ta /,minə'sōtə/ a state in north central US, on the Canadian border; pop. 4,919,479; capital, St. Paul; statehood, May 11, 1858 (32). Part of it was ceded to Britain by the French in 1763 and then acquired by the US in 1783. The remainder formed part of the Louisiana Purchase in 1803. — **Min·ne·so·tan** n. & adj.

Min·ne·so·ta Mul·ti·pha·sic Per·son·al·i·ty In·ven·to·ry (abbr.: **MMPI**) ▶ n. a test of true-false questions, used as a diagnostic tool by psychologists.

Min·ne·so·ta Riv·er a river that flows through Minnesota to join the Mississippi River.

min·now /'minō/ ▶ n. a small freshwater Eurasian cyprinoid fish (*Phoxinus phoxinus*, family Cyprinidae) that typically forms large shoals. ■ any fish of the **minnow family** (Cyprinidae), the largest family of fishes, which includes carps, shiners, spinefins, squawfishes, chubs, daces, and stonerollers. ■ used in names of similar small freshwater fishes, e.g., **topminnow**. ■ a person or organization of relatively small size, power, or influence. [ME: prob. rel. to Ger. *Münne*.]

Mi·ño /'mēnyō/ a river that flows through Spain and Portugal to the Atlantic Ocean. Portuguese name **Minho**.

Mi·no·an /mə'nōən; mī-/ ▶ **adj.** of, relating to, or denoting a Bronze Age civilization centered on Crete (*c.*3000–1050 BC), its people, or its language. ▶ **n. 1** an inhabitant of Minoan Crete or member of the Minoan people. **2** the language or scripts associated with the Minoans. [named after the legendary Cretan king **Minos**, to whom a palace excavated at Knossos was attributed.]

mi·nor /'mīnər/ ▶ **adj. 1** lesser in importance, seriousness, or significance. ■ (of a surgical operation) comparatively simple. **2** Music (of a scale) having intervals of a semitone between the second and third degrees, and (usually) the fifth and sixth, and the seventh and eighth. Contrasted with **major**. ■ (of an interval) characteristic of a minor scale and less by a semitone than the equivalent major interval. Compare with **diminished**. ■ [usu. postpositive] (of a key or mode) based on a minor scale, tending to produce a sad or pensive effect: *Concerto in A minor.* **3** Logic (of a term) occurring as the subject of the conclusion of a categorical syllogism. ■ (of a premise) containing the minor term in a categorical syllogism. ▶ **n. 1** a person under the age of full legal responsibility. **2** Music a minor key, interval, or scale. ■ **(Minor)** Bell-ringing a system of change-ringing using six bells. **3** (**the minors**) the minor leagues in a particular professional sport, esp. baseball. **4** a college student's subsidiary area of concentration. **5** Logic a minor term or premise.
– PHRASAL VERBS **minor in** study or qualify in as a subsidiary subject. [ME: from L., 'smaller, less'; rel. to *minuere* 'lessen.']

mi·nor ax·is ▶ **n.** Geom. the shorter axis of an ellipse that is perpendicular to its major axis.

Mi·nor·ca /mə'nôrkə/ one of the Balearic Islands of Spain, in the western Mediterranean Sea; pop. 59,000; capital, Mahón. — **Mi·nor·can adj. & n.**

Mi·nor·ite /'mīnə,rīt/ a Franciscan friar, or Friar Minor.

mi·nor·i·ty /mə'nôrətē; -'när; mī-/ ▶ **n.** (pl. **-ties**) **1** the smaller number or part, esp. a number that is less than half the whole number. ■ the number of votes cast for or by the smaller party in a legislative assembly. ■ a relatively small group of people, esp. one commonly discriminated against in a community, society, or nation, differing from others in race, religion, language, or political persuasion. **2** the state or period of being under the age of full legal responsibility.
– PHRASES **be** (or **find oneself**) **in a minority of one** often humorous be the sole person to be in favor of or against something. **in the minority** belonging to or constituting the smaller group or number. [15th C. (denoting the state of being a minor): from Fr. *minorité* or med. L. *minoritas*, from L. *minor* 'smaller' (see **minor**).]

mi·nor league ▶ **n.** a league below the level of the major league in a professional sport, esp. baseball. ■ [as adj.] fig. of lesser power or significance. — **mi·nor-lea·guer n.**

mi·nor or·ders ▶ **plural n.** esp. hist. the formal grades of Catholic or Orthodox clergy below the rank of deacon (most now discontinued).

mi·nor proph·et ▶ **n.** any of the twelve prophets after whom the shorter prophetic books of the Bible, from Hosea to Malachi, are named.

mi·nor tran·quil·iz·er ▶ **n.** a tranquilizer of the kind used to treat anxiety states; an anxiolytic.

Mi·nos /'mī,näs; -nôs/ Gk. Mythol. a legendary king of Crete, son of Zeus and Europa.

Min·o·taur /'minə,tôr; 'mī-/ Gk. Mythol. a creature who was half man and half bull.

min·ox·i·dil /mə'näksə,dil/ ▶ **n.** Med. a synthetic drug that is used as a vasodilator in the treatment of hypertension, and also to promote hair growth. [1970s: from **amino** + **oxide** + *-dil* (perh. representing **dilate**).]

Minsk /minsk/ the capital of Belarus, in the central part of the country; pop. 1,613,000.

min·ster /'minstər/ ▶ **n.** a large or important church. *York Minster.* [OE *mynster*, via eccles. L. from Gk. *monastērion* (see **monastery**).]

min·strel /'minstrəl/ ▶ **n.** a medieval singer or musician, esp. one who sang or recited poetry. ■ a member of a band of entertainers with blackened faces who perform songs and music ostensibly of black American origin. [ME: from OFr. *menestral* 'entertainer, servant,' via Provençal from late L. *ministerialis* 'servant' (see **ministerial**).]

min·strel show ▶ **n.** a popular stage entertainment featuring songs, dances, and comedy, usually performed by white actors in blackface.

mint[1] /mint/ ▶ **n. 1** an aromatic plant with two-lobed flowers (genus *Mentha*) native to temperate regions of the Old World, several kinds of which are used as culinary herbs. **2** a mint-flavored candy. — **mint·y adj.** (**mint·i·er, mint·i·est**). [OE *minte*, of West Gmc. origin; rel. to Ger. *Minze*, ult. via L. from Gk. *minthē*.]

mint[2] ▶ **n.** a place where money is coined. ■ **(a mint)** informal a vast sum of money. ▶ **adj.** (of an object) in pristine condition; as new. ▶ **v.** [trans.] (often **be minted**) make (a coin) by stamping metal. ■ [usu. as adj., with submodifier] (**minted**) produce for the first time: *an example of newly minted technology.*
– PHRASES **in mint condition** (of an object) new or as if new. — **mint·er n.** [OE *mynet* 'coin,' of West Gmc. origin; from L. *moneta* 'money.']

mint·age /'mintij/ ▶ **n.** the minting of coins. ■ the number of copies issued of a particular coin.

mint·ed /'mintid/ ▶ **adj.** flavored or seasoned with mint.

mint ju·lep ▶ **n.** a drink consisting of bourbon, crushed ice, sugar, and fresh mint.

Min·ton /'mintn/, Sherman (1890–1965), US Supreme Court associate justice 1949–56.

min·u·end /'minyoo͞,end/ ▶ **n.** Math. a quantity or number from which another is to be subtracted. [18th C.: from L. *minuendus*, gerundive of *minuere* 'diminish.']

min·u·et /,minyoo͞'et/ ▶ **n.** a slow, stately ballroom dance for two in triple time. ■ music in triple time in the style of such a dance. ▶ **v.** (**-et·ed, -et·ing**) [intrans.] dance a minuet. [17th C.: from Fr. *menuet*, 'fine, delicate,' dimin. (used as a n.) of *menu* 'small.']

Min·u·it /'minyoo͞it/, Peter (1580–1638), Dutch colonial administrator. The director general of New Netherland 1626–31, he purchased Manhattan Island from the Algonquin Indians in 1626 for 60 guilders ($24).

mi·nus /'mīnəs/ ▶ **prep. 1** with the subtraction of. ■ informal lacking; deprived of. **2** (of temperature) below zero: *minus 10° Fahrenheit.* ▶ **adj. 1** (before a number) below zero; negative. **2** (after a grade) slightly worse than: *a B minus.* **3** having a negative electric charge. ▶ **n. 1** short for **minus sign**. ■ a mathematical operation of subtraction. **2** a disadvantage: *for every plus there can be a minus.* [15th C.: from L., neut. of *minor* 'less.']

mi·nus·cule /'minə,skyo͞ol; mi'nəs,kyo͞ol/ ▶ **adj. 1** extremely small; tiny: *a minuscule fragment of DNA.* ■ informal so small as to be negligible or insufficient. **2** of or in lowercase letters, as distinct from capitals or uncials. ■ of or in a small cursive script of the Roman alphabet, developed in the 7th century AD. ▶ **n.** minuscule script. ■ a small or lowercase letter. — **mi·nus·cu·lar** /mə'nəskyələr/ **adj.** [18th C.: from Fr., from L. *minuscula (littera)* 'somewhat smaller (letter).']

mi·nus sign ▶ **n.** the symbol –, indicating subtraction or a negative value.

mi·nute[1] /'minit/ ▶ **n. 1** a period of time equal to sixty seconds or a sixtieth of an hour. ■ the distance covered in this length of time by someone driving or walking: *just ten minutes from the center.* ■ informal a very short time. ■ an instant or a point of time. **2** (also **arc minute** or **minute of arc**) a sixtieth of a degree of angular measurement (symbol: ′).
– PHRASES **any minute** (or **at any minute**) very soon. **by the minute** (esp. of the progress of a change) very rapidly. **just** (or **wait**) **a minute 1** used as a request to delay an action, departure, or decision for a short time, usually to allow the speaker to do something. **2** as a prelude to a challenge, query, or objection: *just a minute—where do you think you're going?* **the minute** (or **the minute that**) as soon as. **not for a minute** not at all. *don't think for a minute that our pricing has affected our quality standards.* **this minute** (or **this very minute**) informal at once; immediately. [ME: via OFr. from late L. *minuta*, fem. (used as a n.) of *minutus* 'made small.']

mi·nute[2] /mī'n(y)o͞ot; mi-/ ▶ **adj.** (**-nut·est**) extremely small: *a minute fraction of an inch.* ■ so small as to verge on insignificance. ■ (of an inquiry or investigation, or an account of one) taking the smallest points into consideration; precise and meticulous. — **mi·nute·ly adv. mi·nute·ness n.** [ME: from L. *minutus* 'lessened,' past part. of *minuere*.]

mi·nute[3] /'minit/ ▶ **n.** (**minutes**) a summarized record of the proceedings at a meeting. ■ an official memorandum authorizing or recommending a course of action. ▶ **v.** [trans.] record or note (the proceedings of a meeting or a specified item among such proceedings). [ME: from Fr. *minute*, from the notion of a rough copy in "small writing" (L. *scriptura minuta*).]

mi·nute gun ▶ **n.** a gun fired at intervals of a minute.

min·ute hand ▶ **n.** the hand on a watch or clock that indicates minutes.

min·ute·man /'minət,man/ ▶ **n.** (pl. **-men**) hist. (in the period preceding and during the American Revolution) an American militiamen who volunteered to be ready for service at a minute's notice. ■ **(Minuteman)** a type of three-stage intercontinental ballistic missile.

mi·nu·ti·ae /mə'n(y)o͞oshē,ē; -shē,ī/ (also **mi·nu·ti·a** /-shē,ə; -shə/) ▶ **plural n.** trivial details of something. [18th C.: L., 'trifles,' from *minutia* 'smallness,' from *minutus* (see **minute**[2]).]

minx /mingks/ ▶ **n.** humorous derog. an impudent, cunning, or boldly flirtatious girl or young woman: *you saucy little minx!* — **minx·ish adj.** [16th C. (denoting a pet dog): of unknown origin.]

min·yan /'minyən/ ▶ **n.** (pl. **min·ya·nim** /,minyə'nēm/) a quorum of ten men over the age of 13 required for traditional Jewish public worship. ■ a meeting of Jews for public worship. [18th C.: from Heb. *minyān*, lit. 'reckoning.']

Mi·o·cene /'mīə,sēn/ ▶ **adj.** Geol. of, relating to, or denoting the fourth epoch of the Tertiary period. ■ [as n.] (**the Miocene**) the Miocene epoch or the system of rocks deposited during it. [19th C.: formed irregularly from Gk. *meiōn* 'less' + *kainos* 'new.']

mi·o·sis /mī'ōsis/ (also **my·o·sis**) ▶ **n.** excessive constriction of the pupil of the eye. — **mi·ot·ic** /mī'ätik/ **adj.** [19th C.: from Gk. *muein* 'shut the eyes' + **-osis**.]

MIPS /mips/ ▶ **n.** a unit of computing speed equivalent to a million instructions per second. [1970s: acronym.]

Mique·lon /mē'klôn/ see **St. Pierre and Miquelon**.

Mir /'mi(ə)r/ a Soviet space station, launched in 1986.

Mi·ra /'mīrə/ Astron. a star in the constellation Cetus.

Mi·ra·beau /,mi(ə)rə'bō/, Honoré Gabriel Riqueti, Comte de (1749–91),

French revolutionary. He pressed for a form of constitutional monarchy.

mir·a·belle /'mirə,bel/ ▶ **n.** a sweet yellow plumlike fruit that is a variety of the greengage. ■ the tree that bears such fruit. ■ a liqueur distilled from such fruit. [18th C.: from Fr.]

mi·ra·bi·le dic·tu /mə'räbə,lā 'diktōō; mə'rabəlē/ ▶ **adv.** wonderful to relate. [L.]

mi·ra·cid·i·um /,mīrə'sidēəm/ ▶ **n.** (pl. **-cid·i·a** /-sidēə/) Zool. a free-swimming ciliated larval stage in which a parasitic fluke passes from egg to first host. [19th C.: from Gk. *meirakidion*, dimin. of *meirakion* 'boy, stripling.']

mir·a·cle /'mirikəl/ ▶ **n.** a surprising and welcome event that is not explicable by natural or scientific laws and is considered to be divine. ■ a highly improbable or extraordinary event, development, or accomplishment. ■ an amazing product or achievement. [ME: via OFr. from L. *miraculum* 'object of wonder,' from *mirari* 'to wonder,' from *mirus* 'wonderful.']

mir·a·cle play ▶ **n.** a mystery play.

mi·rac·u·lous /mə'rakyələs/ ▶ **adj.** occurring through divine or supernatural intervention. ■ highly improbable and extraordinary and bringing very welcome consequences: *our miraculous escape.* — **mi·rac·u·lous·ly adv. mi·rac·u·lous·ness n.** [ME: from Fr. *miraculeux* or med. L. *miraculosus*, from L. *miraculum* (see MIRACLE).]

mir·a·dor /'mirə,dôr; ,mirə'dôr/ ▶ **n.** a turret or tower attached to a building and providing an extensive view. [17th C.: from Sp., from *mirar* 'to look.']

mi·rage /mə'räzн/ ▶ **n.** an optical illusion caused by atmospheric conditions. ■ something that appears real or possible but is not. [19th C.: from Fr., from *se mirer* 'be reflected,' from L. *mirare* 'look at.']

Mi·ran·da[1] /mə'randə/ Astron. a satellite of Uranus, the eleventh closest to the planet, with a diameter of 301 miles (485 km).

Mi·ran·da[2] /mə'randə/ ▶ **adj.** Law denoting or relating to the duty of the police to inform a person taken into custody of their right to legal counsel and the right to remain silent under questioning. [20th C.: from *Miranda* v. Arizona (1966).]

mire /mī(ə)r/ ▶ **n.** a stretch of swampy or boggy ground. ■ soft and slushy mud or dirt. ■ fig. a situation or state of difficulty, distress, or embarrassment from which it is hard to extricate oneself. ■ Ecol. a wetland area or ecosystem based on peat. ▶ **v.** [trans.] (usu. **be mired**) cause to be stuck in mud. ■ cover or spatter with mud. ■ (**mire someone/something in**) fig. involve in (difficulties). [ME: from ON *mýrr*, of Gmc. origin; rel. to MOSS.]

mi·rex /'mī,reks/ ▶ **n.** a synthetic insecticide of the organochlorine type used chiefly against ants. [1960s: of unknown origin.]

mir·li·ton /'mərlə,tän/ ▶ **n.** a musical instrument with a nasal tone produced by a vibrating membrane, typically a toy instrument resembling a kazoo. [19th C.: from Fr., 'reed pipe,' of imitative origin.]

Mi·ró /mi'rō/, Joan (1893–1983), Spanish painter. He was a prominent figure of surrealism.

mir·ror /'mirər/ ▶ **n.** a reflective surface, glass coated with a metal amalgam, that reflects a clear image. ■ fig. something regarded as accurately representing something else. ■ (also **mirror site**) Comput. a site on a network that stores some or all of the contents from another site. ▶ **v.** [trans.] (of a reflective surface) show a reflection of. ■ fig. correspond to. ■ Comput. keep a copy of the contents of (a network site) at another site. ■ [usu. as n.] (**mirroring**) Comput. store copies of data on (two or more hard disks) as a method of protecting it. — **mir·rored adj.** [ME: from OFr. *mirour*, based on L. *mirare* 'look at.']

mir·ror carp ▶ **n.** a common carp of an ornamental variety that has a row of platelike scales along each side.

mir·ror fin·ish ▶ **n.** a reflective finish on metal.

mir·ror im·age ▶ **n.** an image or object that is identical in form to another, but with the structure reversed. ■ a person or thing that closely resembles another.

mir·ror sym·me·try ▶ **n.** symmetry about a plane, like that between an object and its reflection.

mir·ror writ·ing ▶ **n.** reversed writing resembling ordinary writing reflected in a mirror.

mirth /mərтн/ ▶ **n.** amusement, esp. as expressed in laughter: *his six-foot frame shook with mirth.* — **mirth·ful adj. mirth·ful·ly adv.** [OE *myrgth*, of Gmc. origin; rel. to MERRY.]

mirth·less /'mərтнləs/ ▶ **adj.** (of a smile or laugh) lacking real amusement and typically expressing irony. — **mirth·less·ly adv. mirth·less·ness n.**

MIRV /mərv/ ▶ **n.** a type of intercontinental nuclear missile carrying several independent warheads. [1960s: acronym from *Multiple Independently targeted Re-entry Vehicle*.]

mir·y /'mī(ə)rē/ ▶ **adj.** very muddy or boggy.

MIS Comput. ▶ **abbr.** management information system.

mis-[1] ▶ **prefix** (added to verbs and their derivatives) wrongly: *misapply.* ■ badly: *mismanage.* ■ unsuitably: *misname.* [OE, of Gmc. origin.]

mis-[2] ▶ **prefix** occurring in a few words adopted from French expressing a sense with negative force: *misadventure* | *mischief.* [from OFr. *mes-* (based on L. *minus*), assimilated to MIS-[1].]

mis·ad·ven·ture /,misəd'vencнər/ ▶ **n.** an unfortunate incident; a mishap: *an expensive misadventure.*

mis·al·li·ance /,misə'līəns/ ▶ **n.** an unsuitable, unhappy, or unworkable alliance or marriage.

mis·an·dry /mis'andrē/ ▶ **n.** the hatred of men by women: *her feminism is just poorly disguised misandry.* [1940s: from Gk. *miso-* 'hating' + *anēr, andr-* 'man,' on the pattern of *misogyny*.]

mis·an·thrope /'misən,тнrōp; 'miz/ (also **mis·an·thro·pist** /mis'anтнrəpist/) ▶ **n.** a person who dislikes humankind and avoids human society. — **mis·an·throp·ic** /,misən'тнräpik/ **adj. mis·an·throp·i·cal** /,misən'тнräpikəl/ **adj. mis·an·throp·i·cal·ly** /,misən'тнräpik(ə)lē/ **adv.** [16th C.: from Gk. *misanthrōpos*, from *misein* 'to hate' + *anthrōpos* 'man.']

mis·an·thro·py /mis'anтнrəpē/ ▶ **n.** a dislike of humankind.

mis·ap·pre·hend /,mis,apri'hend/ ▶ **v.** misunderstand (words, a person, a situation, etc.).

mis·ap·pre·hen·sion /,mis,apri'hensнən/ ▶ **n.** a mistaken belief about or interpretation of something. — **mis·ap·pre·hen·sive** /-'hensiv/ **adj.**

mis·ap·pro·pri·ate /,misə'prōprē,āt/ ▶ **v.** [trans.] (of a person) dishonestly or unfairly take (something, esp. money, belonging to another) for one's own use. — **mis·ap·pro·pri·a·tion** /-,prōprē'āsнən/ **n.**

mis·be·got·ten /,misbə'gätn/ ▶ **adj.** badly conceived, designed, or planned: *a misbegotten journey.* ■ contemptible (used as a term of abuse).

mis·be·have /,misbi'hāv/ ▶ **v.** [intrans.] (of a person, esp. a child) fail to conduct oneself in a way that is acceptable to others; behave badly. ■ (of a machine) fail to function correctly. — **mis·be·hav·ior** /-'hāvyər/ **n.**

mis·be·lief /,misbə'lēf/ ▶ **n.** a wrong or false belief or opinion. ■ less common term for DISBELIEF. — **mis·be·liev·er** /-bəlēvər; -bē-/ **n.**

misc. ▶ **abbr.** miscellaneous.

mis·cal·cu·late /mis'kalkyə,lāt/ ▶ **v.** [trans.] calculate (an amount, distance, or measurement) wrongly. ■ assess (a situation) wrongly. — **mis·cal·cu·la·tion** /,mis,kalkyə'lāsнən/ **n.**

mis·call /mis'kôl/ ▶ **v.** [with obj. and complement] call (something) by a wrong or inappropriate name.

mis·car·riage /mis'karij; 'mis,karij/ ▶ **n. 1** the expulsion of a fetus from the womb before it is able to survive independently, esp. spontaneously or as the result of accident: *his wife had a miscarriage.* **2** an unsuccessful outcome of something planned: *the miscarriage of the project.*

mis·car·riage of jus·tice ▶ **n.** a failure of a court or judicial system to attain the ends of justice, esp. one that results in the conviction of an innocent person.

mis·car·ry /mis'karē; 'mis,karē/ ▶ **v.** (**-ries, -ried**) [intrans.] **1** (of a pregnant woman) have a miscarriage. **2** (of something planned) fail to attain an intended or expected outcome. ■ dated (of a letter) fail to reach its intended destination.

mis·cast /mis'kast/ ▶ **v.** (past and past part. **-cast**) [trans.] (usu. **be miscast**) allot an unsuitable role to (a particular actor): *he is badly miscast in the romantic lead.* ■ allot the roles in (a play, movie, television show, etc.) to unsuitable actors.

mis·ceg·e·na·tion /mi,sejə'nāsнən; ,misəjə-/ ▶ **n.** the interbreeding of people of different racial types. [19th C.: formed irregularly from L. *miscere* 'to mix' + *genus* 'race' + -ATION.]

mis·cel·la·ne·a /,misə'lānēə/ ▶ **plural n.** miscellaneous items that have been collected together. [16th C.: from L., neut. pl. of *miscellaneus* (see MISCELLANEOUS).]

mis·cel·la·ne·ous /,misə'lānēəs/ ▶ **adj.** (of items or people gathered or considered together) of various types or from different sources. ■ (of a collection or group) composed of members or elements of different kinds: *a miscellaneous collection.* — **mis·cel·la·ne·ous·ly adv. mis·cel·la·ne·ous·ness n.** [17th C.: from L. *miscellaneus* (from *miscellus* 'mixed,' from *miscere* 'to mix') + -OUS.]

mis·cel·la·ny /'misə,lānē/ ▶ **n.** (pl. **-nies**) a group or collection of different items; a mixture. ■ a book containing writings by different authors.

mis·chance /mis'cнans/ ▶ **n.** bad luck. ■ an unlucky occurrence. [ME: from OFr. *mescheance*, from the v. *mescheoir*, from *mes-* 'adversely' + *cheoir* 'befall.']

mis·chief /'miscнif/ ▶ **n.** playful misbehavior or troublemaking, esp. in children: *get into mischief.* ■ playfulness that is intended to tease, mock, or create trouble. ■ harm or trouble caused by someone or something. [ME (denoting misfortune or distress): from OFr. *meschief*, from the v. *meschever*, from *mes-* 'adversely' + *chever* 'come to an end' (from *chef* 'head').]

mis·chief-mak·er ▶ **n.** a person who deliberately creates trouble for others. — **mis·chief-mak·ing n.**

mis·chie·vous /'miscнivəs/ ▶ **adj.** (of a person, animal, or their behavior) causing or showing a fondness for causing trouble in a playful way: *two mischievous kittens.* ■ (of an action or thing) causing or intended to cause harm or trouble. *a mischievous allegation for which there is not a shred of evidence.* — **mis·chie·vous·ly adv. mis·chie·vous·ness n.** [ME: from Anglo-Norman Fr. *meschevous*, from OFr. *meschever* 'come to an unfortunate end' (see MISCHIEF).]

misch met·al /misн/ ▶ **n.** an alloy of cerium, lanthanum, and other rare earth metals. [1920s: from Ger. *Mischmetall*, from *mischen* 'to mix' + *Metall* 'metal.']

mis·ci·ble /'misəbəl/ ▶ **adj.** (of liquids) forming a homogeneous mixture when added together. — **mis·ci·bil·i·ty** /,misə'bilətē/ **n.** [16th C.: from med. L. *miscibilis*, from L. *miscere* 'to mix.']

mis·con·ceive /ˌmiskən'sēv/ ▶v. [trans.] fail to understand correctly: *professors misconceived her essays.* ■ (usu. **be misconceived**) judge or plan badly, typically on the basis of faulty understanding. — **mis·con·ceiv·er** n.

mis·con·cep·tion /ˌmiskən'sepSHən/ ▶n. a view or opinion that is incorrect because based on faulty thinking or understanding.

mis·con·duct ▶n. /mis'känˌdəkt/ **1** unacceptable or improper behavior: *professional misconduct.* ■ Ice Hockey a penalty for unsportsmanlike conduct. **2** mismanagement, esp. culpable neglect of duties. ▶v. /ˌmiskən'dəkt/ **1** (**misconduct oneself**) behave in an improper or unprofessional manner. **2** [trans.] mismanage (duties or a project).

mis·con·strue /ˌmiskən'stro͞o/ ▶v. (**-strues, -strued, -stru·ing**) [trans.] interpret (something, esp. a person's words or actions) wrongly. — **mis·con·struc·tion** /-'strəkSHən/ n.

mis·count /mis'kount/ ▶v. [trans.] count incorrectly. ▶n. /'misˌkount/ an incorrect reckoning of the total number of something: *a miscount necessitates a recount.*

mis·cre·ant /'miskrēənt/ ▶n. a person who behaves badly or in a way that breaks the law. ▶adj. (of a person) behaving badly or breaking a law. [ME: from OFr. *mescreant*, pres. part. of *mescreire* 'disbelieve,' from *mes-* 'mis-' + *creire* 'believe' (from L. *credere*).]

mis·cue[1] /mis'kyo͞o/ ▶n. (in billiards) a shot in which the player fails to strike the ball properly with the cue. ■ (in other sports) a faulty strike, kick, or catch. ■ fig. a miscalculated action; a mistake. ▶v. (**-cues, -cued, -cu·ing** or **-cue·ing**) [trans.] (in billiards and other games) fail to strike (the ball or a shot) properly.

mis·cue[2] ▶n. Ling. an error in reading, esp. one caused by failure to respond to a cue in the text. ▶v. [intrans.] (of a performer, esp. an actor on stage) miss one's cue, or answer to another's cue. ■ [trans.] give (a performer) the wrong cue.

mis·deal /mis'dēl/ ▶v. (past and past part. **-dealt**) [intrans.] make a mistake when dealing cards. ▶n. a hand dealt wrongly.

mis·deed /mis'dēd/ ▶n. a wicked or illegal act.

mis·de·mean·ant /ˌmisdə'mēnənt/ ▶n. formal a person convicted of a misdemeanor or guilty of misconduct.

mis·de·mean·or /'misdiˌmēnər/ (Brit. **mis·de·mean·our**) ▶n. a minor wrongdoing. ■ Law a nonindictable offense.

mis·di·ag·nose /mis'dīəgˌnōs; -ˌnōz/ ▶v. [trans.] make an incorrect diagnosis of (a particular illness). — **mis·di·ag·no·sis** /ˌmisˌdīəg'nōsəs/ n.

mis·di·rect /ˌmisdə'rekt; -dī-/ ▶v. [trans.] (often **be misdirected**) send (someone or something) to the wrong place or in the wrong direction. ■ aim (something) in the wrong direction. ■ (of a judge) instruct wrongly. ■ use or apply (something) wrongly or inappropriately. — **mis·di·rec·tion** /-'rekSHən/ n.

mis·doubt /mis'dout/ ▶v. [trans.] esp. archaic have doubts about the truth, reality, or existence of. ■ fear or be suspicious about.

mis·ed·u·cate /mis'ejəˌkāt/ ▶v. [trans.] educate, teach, or inform wrongly. — **mis·ed·u·ca·tion** /ˌmisˌejə'kāSHən/ n. **mis·ed·u·ca·tive** /-'ejəˌkātiv/ adj.

mise en scène /ˌmēz ˌäN 'sen/ ▶n. [usu. in sing.] the arrangement of scenery and stage properties in a play. ■ the setting or surroundings of an event or action. [Fr., lit. 'putting on stage.']

mi·ser /'mīzər/ ▶n. a person who hoards wealth and spends as little money as possible. [15th C. (as an adj. in the sense 'miserly'): from L., 'wretched.']

mis·er·a·ble /'miz(ə)rəbəl/ ▶adj. **1** (of a person) wretchedly unhappy or uncomfortable. ■ (of a situation or environment) causing someone to feel wretchedly unhappy or uncomfortable. *horribly wet and miserable conditions.* ■ (of a person) habitually morose. **2** pitiably small or inadequate: *a miserable $10,000 a year.* ■ [attrib.] contemptible (used as a term of abuse or for emphasis): *you miserable old creep!* — **mis·er·a·ble·ness** n. **mis·er·a·bly** adv. [ME: from Fr. *misérable*, from L. *miserabilis* 'pitiable,' from *miserari* 'to pity,' from *miser* 'wretched.']

mis·e·re·re /ˌmizə're(ə)rē; -'ri(ə)rē/ ▶n. (also **Miserere**) a psalm in which mercy is sought, or the music for it. ■ any prayer or cry for mercy. [ME: from L., 'have mercy!,' imper. of *misereri*, from *miser* 'wretched.']

mis·er·i·cord /mə'zeriˌkôrd/ ▶n. **1** a ledge projecting from the underside of a hinged seat in a choir stall that, when the seat is turned up, gives support to someone standing. **2** hist. an apartment in a monastery in which some relaxations of the monastic rule are permitted. **3** hist. a small dagger used to deliver a death stroke. [ME (denoting pity): from OFr. *misericorde*, from L. *misericordia*, from *misericors* 'compassionate,' from the stem of *misereri* 'to pity' + *cor, cord-* 'heart.']

mi·ser·ly /'mīzərlē/ ▶adj. of, relating to, or characteristic of a miser. ■ (of a quantity) pitiably small or inadequate. — **mi·ser·li·ness** n.

mis·er·y /'miz(ə)rē/ ▶n. (pl. **-er·ies**) a state or feeling of great distress or discomfort of mind or body. ■ (usu. **miseries**) a cause or source of great distress.

– PHRASES **make someone's life a misery** (or **make life a misery for someone**) cause someone severe distress by continued unpleasantness or harassment. **put someone/something out of their misery** end the suffering of a person or animal in pain by killing them. ■ informal release someone from suspense or anxiety by telling them something they are anxious to know.

mis·fea·sance /mis'fēzəns/ ▶n. Law a transgression. [17th C.: from OFr. *mesfaisance*, from *mesfaire*, from *mes-* 'wrongly' + *faire* 'do' (from L. *facere*). Cf. MALFEASANCE.]

mis·file /mis'fīl/ ▶v. [trans.] file wrongly.

mis·fire /mis'fī(ə)r/ ▶v. [intrans.] (of a gun or missile) fail to discharge or fire properly. ■ (of an internal combustion engine) undergo failure of the fuel to ignite correctly or at all. ■ (esp. of a plan) fail to produce the intended result. ■ (of a nerve cell) fail to transmit an electrical impulse at an appropriate moment. ▶n. /'misˌfī(ə)r/ a failure of a gun or missile to fire correctly or of fuel in an internal combustion engine to ignite.

mis·fit /'misˌfit/ ▶n. a person whose behavior or attitude sets them apart from others.

mis·for·tune /mis'fôrCHən/ ▶n. bad luck. ■ an unfortunate condition or event.

mis·give /mis'giv/ ▶v. (past **-gave**; past part. **-giv·en**) [trans.] literary (of a person's mind or heart) fill (that person) with doubt, apprehension, or foreboding: *my heart misgave me.*

mis·giv·ing /mis'giviNG/ ▶n. (usu. **misgivings**) a feeling of doubt or apprehension about the outcome or consequences of something.

mis·guide /mis'gīd/ ▶v. [trans.] rare mislead. — **mis·guid·ance** /-gīdns/ n.

mis·guid·ed /mis'gīdid/ ▶adj. having or showing faulty judgment or reasoning: *misguided attempts.* — **mis·guid·ed·ly** adv. **mis·guid·ed·ness** n.

mis·han·dle /mis'handəl/ ▶v. [trans.] **1** manage or deal with (something) wrongly or ineffectively. **2** manipulate roughly or carelessly.

mis·hap /'misˌhap/ ▶n. an unlucky accident.

Mi·shi·ma /mi'SHēmə; 'mēSHēˌmä/, Yukio (1925–70), Japanese writer; pen name of *Hiraoka Kimitake.* His works include the *The Sea of Fertility* (1965–70).

mis·hit /ˌmis'hit/ ▶v. (**-hit·ting**; past and past part. **-hit**) [trans.] hit or kick (a ball) wrongly. ▶n. an instance of hitting or kicking a ball in such a way.

mish·mash /'miSHˌmaSH; -ˌmäSH/ ▶n. [in sing.] a confused mixture: *a mishmash of outmoded ideas.* [15th C.: reduplication of MASH.]

Mish·nah /'miSHnə/ ▶n. (**the Mishnah**) an authoritative collection of exegetical material embodying the oral tradition of Jewish law and forming the first part of the Talmud. — **Mish·na·ic** /miSH'nāik/ adj. [from Heb. *mišnāh* '(teaching by) repetition.']

mi·shu·gas /ˌmiSHo͝o'gäs/ ▶n. var. of MESHUGAAS.

mis·in·form /ˌmisin'fôrm/ ▶v. [trans.] (often **be misinformed**) give false or inaccurate information.

mis·in·for·ma·tion /ˌmisinfər'māSHən/ ▶n. false or inaccurate information, esp. in order to deceive.

mis·in·ter·pret /ˌmisin'tərprət/ ▶v. (**-pret·ed, -pret·ing**) [trans.] interpret wrongly. — **mis·in·ter·pre·ta·tion** /-inˌtərprə'tāSHən/ n. **mis·in·ter·pret·er** n.

mis·judge /ˌmis'jəj/ ▶v. [trans.] form a wrong opinion or conclusion about: *we misjudged the size of the surf.* ■ make an incorrect estimation or assessment of. — **mis·judg·ment** (also **mis·judge·ment**) n.

mis·key /mis'kē/ ▶v. (**-keys, -keyed**) [trans.] key (a word) into a computer or other machine incorrectly.

Mis·ki·to /mə'skētō/ (also **Mos·qui·to**) ▶n. (pl. same or **-tos**) **1** a member of an American Indian people of the Atlantic coast of Nicaragua and Honduras. **2** the language of this people. ▶adj. of or relating to the Miskito or their language. [the name in Miskito.]

mis·lay /mis'lā/ ▶v. (past and past part. **-laid**) [trans.] unintentionally put (an object) where it cannot readily be found and so lose it temporarily: *I seem to have mislaid my car keys.*

mis·lead /mis'lēd/ ▶v. (past and past part. **-led**) [trans.] cause (someone) to have a wrong idea or impression about someone or something: *the government misled the public about the road's environmental impact.* — **mis·lead·er** n.

mis·lead·ing /mis'lēdiNG/ ▶adj. giving the wrong idea or impression: *your article contains a number of misleading statements.* — **mis·lead·ing·ly** adv. **mis·lead·ing·ness** n.

mis·like /mis'līk/ archaic ▶v. [trans.] consider to be unpleasant, dislike: *the pony snorted, misliking the smell of blood.* ▶n. distaste; dislike.

mis·mat·ed /ˌmis'mātid/ ▶adj. badly matched or not matching.

mis·no·mer /mis'nōmər/ ▶n. a wrong or inaccurate name or designation: *"king crab" is a misnomer.* ■ a wrong or inaccurate use of a name or term. [ME: from Anglo-Norman Fr., from the OFr. v. *mesnommer*, from *mes-* 'wrongly' + *nommer* 'to name' (based on L. *nomen* 'name').]

mi·sog·a·my /mə'sägəmē/ ▶n. rare the hatred of marriage. — **mi·sog·a·mist** n. [17th C.: from Gk. *misos* 'hatred' + *gamos* 'marriage.']

mi·sog·y·nist /mə'säjənist/ ▶n. a woman hater. ▶adj. reflecting or inspired by a hatred of women. — **mi·sog·y·nis·tic** /məˌsäjə'nistik/ adj.

mi·sog·y·ny /mə'säjənē/ ▶n. the hatred of women by men: *struggling against thinly disguised misogyny.* — **mi·sog·y·nous** /-nəs/ adj. [17th C.: from Gk. *misos* 'hatred' + *gunē* 'woman.']

mis·place /mis'plās/ ▶v. [trans.] (usu. **be misplaced**) put in the wrong place and lose temporarily; mislay. — **mis·place·ment** n.

mis·placed /mis'plāst/ ▶adj. **1** incorrectly positioned. ■ not appropriate or correct in the circumstances: *misplaced priorities.* ■ (of an emotion) directed unwisely or to an inappropriate object. *he began to wonder if his sympathy were misplaced.* **2** [attrib.] temporarily lost: *her misplaced keys.*

mis·placed mod·i·fi·er ▶n. Gram. a phrase or clause placed awkwardly in a sentence so that it appears to modify or refer to an unintended word. See also DANGLING PARTICIPLE.

mis·play ▶v. [trans.] /mis'plā/ play (a ball or card) wrongly, badly, or in contravention of the rules. ▶n. /'misˌplā/ an instance of playing a ball or card in such a way.

mis·print ▶n. /ˈmisˌprint/ an error in printed text. *Galway might be a misprint for Galloway.* ▶v. /ˌmisˈprint/ [trans.] print (something) incorrectly.

mis·pri·sion[1] /misˈprizhən/ (also **misprision of treason** or **felony**) ▶n. Law, esp. hist. the deliberate concealment of one's knowledge of a treasonable act or a felony. [ME: from OFr. *mesprision* 'error,' from *mesprendre*, from *mes-* 'wrongly' + *prendre* 'to take.']

mis·pri·sion[2] ▶n. rare erroneous judgment, esp. of the value or identity of something. [16th C.: from MISPRIZE, influenced by MISPRISION[1].]

mis·prize /misˈprīz/ ▶v. [trans.] rare fail to appreciate the value of (something); undervalue. [15th C.: from OFr. *mesprisier*, from *mes-* 'wrongly' + *prisier* 'estimate the value of.']

mis·quote /misˈkwōt/ ▶v. [trans.] quote (a person or a piece of written or spoken text) inaccurately. ▶n. a passage or remark quoted inaccurately. — **mis·quo·ta·tion** /ˌmiskwōˈtāshən/ n.

mis·read /misˈrēd/ ▶v. (past and past part. **-read** /-ˈred/) [trans.] read (a piece of text) wrongly. ■ judge or interpret (a situation or a person's manner or behavior) incorrectly.

mis·rep·re·sent /ˌmisˌrepriˈzent/ ▶v. [trans.] give a false or misleading account of the nature of. — **mis·rep·re·sen·ta·tion** /-ˌzenˈtāshən; -zən-/ n. **mis·rep·re·sen·ta·tive** /-ˈzentətiv/ adj.

mis·rule /misˈrool/ ▶n. the unfair or inefficient conduct of the affairs of a country or state. ■ the disruption of peace; disorder. ▶v. [trans.] govern (a country or state) badly.

Miss. ▶abbr. Mississippi.

miss[1] /mis/ ▶v. [trans.] **1** fail to hit, reach, or come into contact with (something aimed at): *missed its target.* | [intrans.] *he was given two free throws, but missed both times.* ■ pass by without touching; chance not to hit: *shrapnel missed him by inches.* ■ fail to catch (something thrown or dropped): *Mandy missed the catch, and flung the ball back crossly.* ■ be too late to catch (a passenger vehicle, etc.). ■ fail to notice, hear, or understand. ■ fail to attend, participate in, or watch (something one is expected to do or habitually does). ■ fail to see or have a meeting with (someone): *you've just missed him.* ■ not be able to experience or fail to take advantage of (an opportunity or chance): *it was just too good an opportunity to miss* | *don't miss the chance.* ■ not be able or fortunate enough to experience or be involved in: *they're going to miss all the fun* | *having just bought your magazine for the first time, I now realize what I have been missing.* ■ avoid; escape: *miss the crowds.* ■ fail to include (someone or something); omit. ■ (of a woman) fail to have (a monthly period). ■ [intrans.] (of an engine or motor vehicle) undergo failure of ignition in one or more cylinders: *the motor began missing and investigation found a cracked cylinder head.* **2** notice the loss or absence of: *he won't miss the money.* ■ feel regret or sadness at no longer being able to enjoy the presence of. ■ feel regret or sadness at no longer being able to go to, do, or have: *what they miss most are bread and sausages.* ▶n. a failure to hit, catch, or reach something. ■ a failure, esp. an unsuccessful movie, television show, recording, etc.: *a hit or a miss.*
– PHRASES **miss a beat 1** (of the heart) temporarily fail or appear to fail to beat. **2** [usu. with negative] informal hesitate or falter, esp. in demanding circumstances or when making a transition from one activity to another. **miss the boat** (or **bus**) informal be too slow to take advantage of an opportunity. **a miss is as good as a mile** proverb the fact of failure or escape is not affected by the narrowness of the margin. **not miss a trick** informal never fail to take advantage of a situation. — **miss·a·ble** adj. [OE *missan*, of Gmc. origin; rel. to Du. and Ger. *missen*.]

miss[2] ▶n. **1** (**Miss**) a title prefixed to the name of an unmarried woman or girl or to a married woman retaining her maiden name. ■ used in the title of the winner in a beauty contest. *Miss World.* ■ used as a polite form of address to a young woman or to a waitress, etc. **2** (**misses**) a range of sizes, 8 to 20, in women's clothing. [17th C.: abbrev. of MISTRESS.]

mis·sal /ˈmisəl/ ▶n. a book containing the texts used in the Roman Catholic Mass throughout the year. [ME: from med. L. *missale*, neut. of eccles. L. *missalis* 'relating to the Mass,' from *missa* 'Mass.']

mis·sel thrush ▶n. var. of MISTLE THRUSH.

mis·sile /ˈmisəl/ ▶n. an object that is forcibly propelled at a target, by hand or mechanically. ■ a self-propelled or remote-controlled weapon that carries a conventional or nuclear explosive. [17th C.: from L. *missile*, neut. (used as a n.) of *missilis*, from *miss-* 'sent,' from the v. *mittere*.]

mis·sile·ry /ˈmisəlrē/ ▶n. **1** the study of missiles. **2** missiles collectively.

miss·ing /ˈmisiNG/ ▶adj. (of a thing) not able to be found because it is not in its expected place. ■ not present or included when expected or supposed to be. ■ (of a person) absent from a place, esp. home, and of unknown whereabouts: *her son was missing.* ■ (of a person) not yet traced or confirmed as alive, but not known to be dead, after an accident or during wartime: *missing in action.*

miss·ing link ▶n. a thing that is needed to complete a series, provide continuity, or gain complete knowledge. ■ a hypothetical fossil form intermediate between two living forms, esp. between humans and apes.

mis·si·ol·o·gy /ˌmisēˈäləjē/ ▶n. the study of religious (typically Christian) missions. — **mis·sio·log·i·cal** /ˌmisēəˈläjikəl/ adj. [1930s: formed irregularly from MISSION + -LOGY.]

mis·sion /ˈmishən/ ▶n. an important assignment carried out for political, religious, or commercial purposes, typically involving travel. ■ [treated as sing. or pl.] a group of people taking part in such an assignment. ■ [in sing.] an organization or institution involved in a long-term assignment in a foreign country. ■ the vocation or calling of a religious organization, esp. a Christian one, to go out into the world and spread its faith. ■ a strongly felt aim, ambition, or calling. ■ an expedition into space. ■ an operation carried out by military aircraft at a time of conflict. [16th C.: from L. *missio(n-)*, from *mittere* 'send.']

mis·sion·ar·y /ˈmishəˌnerē/ ▶n. (pl. **-ar·ies**) a person sent on a religious mission, esp. one sent to promote Christianity in a foreign country. ▶adj. of, relating to, or characteristic of a missionary or a religious mission: *missionary work.* | *they have lost the missionary zeal they once had.*

mis·sion·ar·y po·si·tion ▶n. informal a position for sexual intercourse in which a couple lies face to face with the woman underneath the man.

Mis·sion·ary Ridge /ˈmishəˌnerē/ a historic site in Tennessee, site of an 1863 Civil War battle.

mis·sion state·ment ▶n. a summary of the aims and values of a company, organization, or individual.

mis·sis ▶n. var. of MISSUS.

Mis·sis·sau·ga /ˌmisəˈsôgə/ a town in southern Ontario, Canada; pop. 463,388.

Mis·sis·sip·pi /ˌmisəˈsipē/ **1** a river in the US that rises in Minnesota and flows south to a delta on the Gulf of Mexico in Louisiana. With its chief tributary, the Missouri River, it is 3,710 miles (5,970 km) long. **2** a state in the southern US, on the Gulf of Mexico, bounded on the west by the lower Mississippi River; pop. 2,844,658; capital, Jackson; statehood, Dec. 10, 1817 (20). It was ceded to Britain by the French in 1763 and to the US in 1783.

Mis·sis·sip·pi·an /ˌmisiˈsipēən/ ▶adj. **1** of or relating to the state of Mississippi. **2** Geol. of, relating to, or denoting the early part of the Carboniferous period in North America from about 363 to 323 million years ago, following the Devonian and preceding the Pennsylvanian. ■ Archaeol. of, relating to, or denoting a settled culture of the southeastern US, to about AD 800–1300. ▶n. **1** a native or inhabitant of Mississippi. **2** (**the Mississippian**) Geol. the Mississippian period or the system of rocks deposited during it. ■ Archaeol. the Mississippian culture or period.

Mis·sis·sip·pi mud pie ▶n. a type of rich, mousselike chocolate cake or pie.

mis·sive /ˈmisiv/ ▶n. a letter, esp. a long or official one. [ME (as an adj.): from med. L. *missivus*, from L. *mittere* 'send.']

Mis·sou·la /məˈzoolə/ a city in western Montana; pop. 57,053.

Mis·sou·ri /məˈzoorē; -ˈzoorə/ **1** a river in the US, one of the main tributaries of the Mississippi River. It rises in Montana and flows 2,315 miles (3,736 km) to meet the Mississippi River. **2** a state in the central part of the US, bounded on the east by the Mississippi River; pop. 5,595,211; capital, Jefferson City; statehood, Aug. 10, 1821 (24). It was part of the Louisiana Purchase in 1803 and admitted as a state as part of the Missouri Compromise. — **Mis·sour·i·an** /-ēən/ n. & adj.

miss·peak /misˈspēk/ ▶v. (past **-spoke**; past part. **-spok·en**) [intrans.] express oneself insufficiently clearly or accurately.

mis·spend /misˈspend/ ▶v. (past and past part. **-spent**) [trans.] [usu. as adj.] (**misspent**) spend (one's time or money) foolishly, wrongly, or wastefully.

mis·state /misˈstāt/ ▶v. [trans.] make wrong or inaccurate statements about. — **mis·state·ment** n.

mis·step /misˈstep; ˈmisˌstep/ ▶n. a clumsy or badly judged step: *one misstep could be fatal.* ■ a mistake or blunder.

mis·sus /ˈmisəz; -əs/ (also **mis·sis**) ▶n. [in sing.] informal humorous a man's wife: *I promised the missus I'd be home.* ■ informal used as a form of address to a woman whose name is not known: *sit down, missus.* [18th C.: alt. of MISTRESS.]

miss·y /ˈmisē/ ▶n. (pl. **miss·ies**) used as an affectionate or disparaging form of address to a young girl. ■ of or relating to the misses range of garment sizes.

mist /mist/ ▶n. a cloud of tiny water droplets suspended in the atmosphere at or near the earth's surface. ■ [in sing.] a condensed vapor settling in fine droplets on a surface. ■ [in sing.] a haze or film over the eyes, esp. caused by tears, and resulting in blurred vision. ■ used in reference to something that blurs one's perceptions or memory: *the mists of time.* ▶v. cover or become covered with mist. ■ [intrans.] (of a person's eyes) become covered with a film of tears causing blurred vision. *her eyes misted at this heroic image.* ■ [trans.] spray (something, esp. a plant) with a fine cloud of water droplets. [OE, of Gmc. origin.]

mis·take /məˈstāk/ ▶n. an action or judgment that is misguided or wrong: *coming here was a mistake.* ■ something that is not correct; an inaccuracy. *a couple of spelling mistakes.* ▶v. (past **-took**; past part. **-tak·en**) [trans.] be wrong about. ■ (**mistake someone/something for**) wrongly identify someone or something as.
– PHRASES **by mistake** accidentally; in error. **make no mistake (about it)** informal do not be deceived into thinking otherwise. **there is no mistaking someone or something** it is impossible not to recognize someone or something. — **mis·tak·a·ble** adj. **mis·tak·a·bly** adv. [ME (as a v.): from ON *mistaka* 'take in error.']

mis·tak·en /məˈstākən/ ▶adj. [predic.] wrong in one's opinion or judgment. ■ [attrib.] (esp. of a belief) based on or resulting from a misunderstanding or faulty judgment: *an unfortunate case of mistaken identity.* — **mis·tak·en·ly** adv. **mis·tak·en·ness** n.

mis·ter[1] /ˈmistər/ ▶ **n.** var. of **Mr.**, often used humorously or with offensive emphasis. ■ informal used as a form of address to a man whose name is not known. ■ dialect a woman's husband. [16th C.: weakened form of **master**[1].]

mis·ter[2] ▶ **n.** a device, such as a bottle, with a nozzle for spraying a mist of water, esp. on houseplants.

mis·time /misˈtīm/ ▶ **v.** [trans.] choose a bad or inappropriate moment to do or say (something).

mis·tle thrush /ˈmisəl ˌTHrəsh/ (also **mis·sel thrush**) ▶ **n.** a large Eurasian thrush (*Turdus viscivorus*) with a spotted breast and harsh rattling call, with a fondness for mistletoe berries. [17th C.: *mistle* from OE *mistel* (see **mistletoe**).]

mis·tle·toe /ˈmisəlˌtō/ ▶ **n.** a leathery-leaved parasitic plant that grows on apple, oak, and other broadleaf trees and bears white glutinous berries in winter. Its several species include the Eurasian *Viscum album* (family Viscaceae) and the American *Phoradendron serotinum* (family Loranthaceae). [OE *misteltān*, from *mistel* 'mistletoe' (of Gmc. origin, rel. to Du. *mistel* and Ger. *Mistel*) + *tān* 'twig.']

American mistletoe

mis·took /məˈstŏŏk/ past of **mistake**.

mis·tral /ˈmistrəl; miˈsträl/ ▶ **n.** a strong, cold northwesterly wind that blows through the Rhône valley and southern France into the Mediterranean. [17th C.: Fr., from Provençal, from L. *magistralis (ventus)*, lit. 'master wind.']

mis·treat /misˈtrēt/ ▶ **v.** [trans.] treat (a person or animal) badly, cruelly, or unfairly. — **mis·treat·ment n.**

mis·tress /ˈmistris/ ▶ **n. 1** a woman in a position of authority or control: *mistress of the situation* | fig. *Britain was, in 1914, undisputed mistress of the seas.* ■ a woman who is skilled in a particular subject or activity: *a mistress of the sound bite.* ■ the female owner of a dog, cat, or other domesticated animal. ■ archaic a female head of a household. ■ (esp. formerly) a female employer of domestic staff. **2** a woman having an extramarital sexual relationship, esp. with a married man. ■ archaic literary a woman loved and courted by a man. **3** (**Mistress**) archaic dialect used as a title prefixed to the name of a married woman; Mrs. [ME: from OFr. *maistresse*, from *maistre* 'master.']

mis·tri·al /ˈmisˌtrī(ə)l/ ▶ **n.** a trial rendered invalid through an error in the proceedings. ■ an inconclusive trial.

mis·trust /misˈtrəst/ ▶ **v.** [trans.] be suspicious of. ▶ **n.** lack of trust: suspicion: *mistrust of government.*

mis·trust·ful /ˌmisˈtrəstfəl/ ▶ **adj.** lacking in trust; suspicious: *he had been unduly mistrustful of her.* — **mis·trust·ful·ly adv. mis·trust·ful·ness n.**

mist·y /ˈmistē/ ▶ **adj.** (**mist·i·er**, **mist·i·est**) full of, covered with, or accompanied by mist. ■ (of a person's eyes) full of tears so as to blur the vision. ■ indistinct or dim in outline. ■ (of a color) not bright; soft. — **mist·i·ly adv. mist·i·ness n.**

mis·type /misˈtīp/ ▶ **v.** [trans.] **1** make a mistake in typing (a word or letter). **2** assign to an incorrect category.

mis·un·der·stand /ˌmisˌəndərˈstand/ ▶ **v.** (past and past part. **-stood**) [trans.] fail to interpret or understand (something) correctly. ■ fail to interpret or understand the words or actions of (someone) correctly.

mis·un·der·stand·ing /ˌmisˌəndərˈstandiNG/ ▶ **n.** a failure to understand something correctly. ■ a disagreement or quarrel.

mis·use ▶ **v.** /misˈyo͞oz; ˈmisˌyo͞oz/ [trans.] use (something) in the wrong way or for the wrong purpose. ■ treat (someone or something) badly or unfairly. ▶ **n.** /ˌmisˈyo͞os; ˈmisˌyo͞os/ the wrong or improper use of something: *their misuse can have dire consequences.* — **mis·us·er** /-ˈyo͞ozər/ **n.**

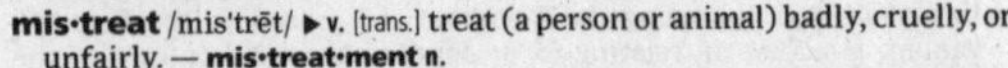

MIT ▶ **abbr.** Massachusetts Institute of Technology.

Mitch·ell[1] /ˈmicHəl/, Billy (1879–1936), US army officer; full name *William Mitchell*; born in France. He preached the importance of air power in warfare and was the defendant in a controversial court-martial.

Mitch·ell[2], Margaret (1900–49), US writer. She wrote *Gone with the Wind* (1936).

Mitchell[3], Maria (1818–89), US astronomer. She was the first woman elected to the American Academy of Arts and Sciences (1848).

mite[1] /mīt/ ▶ **n.** a minute arachnid (order or subclass Acari) that has four pairs of legs when adult, related to the ticks. Many kinds live in the soil and a number are parasitic on plants or animals. [OE *mīte*, of Gmc. origin.]

mite[2] ▶ **n. 1** a small child or animal, esp. when regarded as an object of sympathy: *the poor little mite.* **2** a very small amount: *a mite of discipline.* ■ hist. a small coin, in particular a small Flemish copper coin of low face value. See also **widow's mite**. ▶ **adv.** (**a mite**) informal a little; slightly: *a mite awkward.* [ME: from MDu. *mīte*; prob. from the same Gmc. word as **mite**[1].]

miter 1

mi·ter /ˈmītər/ (Brit. **mi·tre**) ▶ **n. 1** a tall headdress worn by bishops and senior abbots as a symbol of office, tapering to a point at front and back with a deep cleft between. ■ hist. a headdress worn by a Jewish high priest. ■ hist. a headband worn by women in ancient Greece. **2** (also **miter joint**) a joint made between two pieces of wood or other material at an angle of 90°, such that the line of junction bisects this angle. ■ a diagonal seam of two pieces of fabric that meet at a corner joining. **3** (also **miter shell**) a mollusk (*Mitra* and other genera, family Mitridae) of warm seas that has a sharply pointed shell with a narrow aperture, supposedly resembling a bishop's miter. ▶ **v.** [trans.] join by means of a miter. [ME: from OFr., via L. from Gk. *mitra* 'belt or turban.']

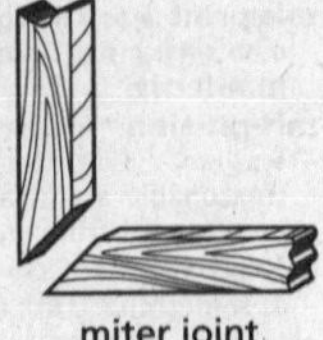

miter joint

mi·ter box ▶ **n.** a guide to enable a saw to cut miter joints.

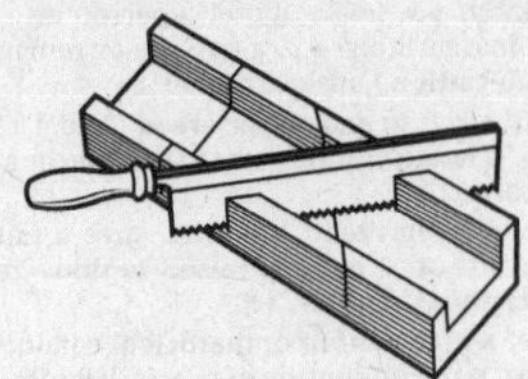

miter box

mi·tered /ˈmītərd/ ▶ **adj. 1** joined with a miter joint or seam: *complete the sides with mitered corners.* **2** bearing, wearing, or entitled to wear a miter.

Mit·ford /ˈmitfərd/, English writers. Nancy Freeman (1904–73) wrote *Love in a Cold Climate* (1949). Her sister Jessica Lucy (1917–96) wrote *The American Way of Death* (1963).

Mith·ra·ism /ˈmiTHrəˌizəm/ ▶ **n.** the cult of the god Mithras, popular in the first three centuries AD. — **Mith·ra·ic** /miˈTHrā-ik/ **adj. Mith·ra·ist** /miˈTHrā-ist/ **n.**

Mith·ras /ˈmiTHˌräs/ Mythol. a god of light, truth, and honor, the central figure of the cult of Mithraism but probably of Persian origin.

Mith·ri·da·tes VI /ˌmiTHrəˈdātēz/ (also **Mith·ra·da·tes VI**) (*c.*132–63 BC), king of Pontus 120–163; known as **Mithridates the Great**.

mith·ri·da·tize /ˌmiTHrəˈdātīz/ ▶ **v.** [trans.] rare render immune against a poison by administering gradually increasing doses of the poison. [19th C.: **Mithridates VI**).]

mit·i·gate /ˈmitəˌgāt/ ▶ **v.** [trans.] make less severe, serious, or painful: *he wanted to mitigate misery in the world.* ■ lessen the gravity of (an offense or mistake). — **mit·i·ga·ble adj. mit·i·ga·tor n. mit·i·ga·to·ry** /-gəˌtôrē/ **adj.** [ME: from L. *mitigat-* 'softened, alleviated,' from the v. *mitigare*, from *mitis* 'mild.']

mit·i·ga·tion /ˌmitəˈgāsHən/ ▶ **n.** the action of reducing the severity, seriousness, or painfulness of something.

– PHRASES **in mitigation** so as to make something, esp. a crime, appear less serious and thus be punished more leniently.

mi·to·chon·dri·on /ˌmītəˈkändrēən/ ▶ **n.** (pl. **-dri·a** /-drēə/) Biol. an organelle found in large numbers in most cells, in which the biochemical processes of respiration and energy production occur. — **mi·to·chon·dri·al** /-drēəl/ **adj.** [20th C.: mod. L., from Gk. *mitos* 'thread' + *khondrion* (dimin. of *khondros* 'granule').]

mi·to·gen /ˈmītəjən/ ▶ **n.** Physiol. a substance that induces or stimulates mitosis. — **mi·to·gen·ic** /ˌmītəˈjenik/ **adj.** [1960s: from **mitosis** + **-gen**.]

mi·to·sis /mīˈtōsəs/ ▶ **n.** (pl. **-ses** /-sēz/) Biol. a type of cell division that results in two daughter cells each the same as the parent nucleus, typical of ordinary tissue growth. Compare with **meiosis**. — **mi·tot·ic** /mīˈtätik/ **adj.** [19th C.: mod. L., from Gk. *mitos* 'thread.']

mi·tral /ˈmītrəl/ ▶ **adj.** relating to the mitral valve. [17th C.: from mod. L. *mitralis*, from L. *mitra* 'belt or turban.']

mi·tral valve ▶ **n.** Anat. the valve between the left atrium and the left ventricle of the heart.

mi·tre ▶ **n. & v.** British spelling of **miter**.

mitt /mit/ ▶ **n.** (usu. **mitts**) a mitten: *oven mitts.* ■ Baseball a mittenlike glove, worn by the catcher and first baseman. ■ a glove leaving the fingers and thumb-tip exposed. ■ informal a person's hand.

– PHRASES **keep one's mitts off** informal keep one's hands away from; not touch. [18th C.: abbrev. of **mitten**.]

Mit·tel·land Ca·nal /ˈmitlˌländ/ a canal in northwestern Germany, part of an inland waterway network linking the Rhine and Elbe rivers.

mit·ten /ˈmitn/ ▶ **n.** (usu. **mittens**) a glove with two sections, one for the thumb and one for all four fingers. — **mit·tened adj.** [ME: from OFr. *mitaine*, perhaps from *mite*, pet name for a cat.]

Mit·ter·rand /ˈmitəränd(d); mētˈräN/, François Maurice Marie (1916–96), president of France 1981–95.

Mit·ty /ˈmitē/ see **Walter Mitty**.

mitz·vah /ˈmitsvə/ ▶ **n.** (pl. **mitz·voth** /ˈmitsˌvōt; -ˌvōs/) Judaism a precept or commandment. ■ a good deed done from religious duty. [17th C.: from Heb. *miṣwāh* 'commandment.']

mix /miks/ ▶ **v.** [trans.] combine or put together to form one substance or mass. ■ [intrans.] [often with negative] (of different substances) be able to be combined in this way: *oil and water don't mix.* ■ make or prepare by combining various ingredients. ■ (esp. in sound recording) combine (two or more signals or soundtracks) into one. ■ produce (a sound signal or recording) by combining a number of separate signals or recorded soundtracks. ■ juxtapose or put together to form a whole whose constituent parts are still distinct: *mix an offhand sense of humor with a sharp insight.* ■ [intrans.] (of a person) associate with others socially. ▶ **n.** [usu. in sing.] two or more different qualities, things, or people placed, combined, or considered together. ■ a group of people of different types within a particular society or community. ■ [often with adj.] a commercially prepared mixture of ingredients for making a particular type of food or a product such as concrete: *cake mixes.* ■ the proportion of different people or other constituents that make up a mixture. ■ [often with adj.] a version of a recording in which the component tracks are mixed in a different way from the original. ■ an image or sound produced by the combination of two separate images or sounds.

– PHRASES **be** (or **get**) **mixed up in** be (or become) involved in (something regarded as dubious or dishonest). **be** (or **get**) **mixed up with** be (or become) associated with (someone unsuitable or unreliable). **mix and match** select and combine different but complementary items, such as clothing or pieces of equipment, to form a coordinated set. **mix one's drinks** drink different kinds of alcohol in close succession.

– PHRASAL VERBS **mix something up** spoil the order or arrangement of a collection of things. ■ (**mix someone/something up**) confuse someone or something with another person or thing: *I'd gotten her mixed up with her sister.* — **mix·a·ble** adj. [ME: back-form. from MIXED (taken as a past part.).]

Mix·co /'mēsнkō/ a city in south central Guatemala; pop. 413,000.

mixed /mikst/ ▶ **adj.** consisting of different qualities or elements: *a varied, mixed diet.* ■ (of an assessment of, reaction to, or feeling about something) containing a mixture of both favorable and negative elements. *mixed reviews.* ■ composed of different varieties of the same thing: *mixed greens.* ■ involving or showing a mixture of races or social classes. ■ (esp. of an educational establishment or a sports team or competition) of or for members of both sexes. [ME *mixt*: from OFr. *mixte*, from L. *mixtus*, past part. of *miscere* 'to mix.']

mixed bag ▶ **n.** [in sing.] a diverse assortment of things or people.

mixed bless·ing ▶ **n.** a situation or thing that has disadvantages as well as advantages.

mixed com·pa·ny ▶ **n.** a group of people consisting of members of both sexes.

mixed dou·bles ▶ **plural n.** [treated as sing.] (esp. in tennis and badminton) a game or competition involving teams, each consisting of a man and a woman.

mixed drink ▶ **n.** an alcoholic drink consisting of liquor combined with fruit juice or other ingredients.

mixed e·con·o·my ▶ **n.** an economic system combining private and public enterprise.

mixed grill ▶ **n.** a dish consisting of various items of grilled food.

mixed mar·riage ▶ **n.** a marriage between people of different races or religions.

mixed me·di·a ▶ **n.** the use of a variety of media. ▶ **adj.** (**mixed-me·di·a**) another term for MULTIMEDIA.

mixed met·a·phor ▶ **n.** a combination of two or more incompatible metaphors.

mixed num·ber ▶ **n.** a number consisting of an integer and a proper fraction.

mixed-up ▶ **adj.** informal (of a person) suffering from psychological or emotional problems.

mix·er /'miksər/ ▶ **n.** **1** [often with adj.] a machine or device for mixing things, esp. an electrical appliance for mixing foods: *a food mixer.* **2** [with adj.] a person considered in terms of their ability to mix socially with others. **3** a social gathering where people meet others. **4** a soft drink that can be mixed with alcohol. **5** (in sound recording and cinematography) a device for merging input signals to produce a combined output in the form of sound or pictures. ■ [often with adj.] a person who operates such a device: *a sound mixer.*

Mix·mas·ter /'miks,mastər/ ▶ **n.** trademark a type of electric food processor. ■ (also **mixmaster**) informal a sound-recording engineer or disc jockey who mixes music.

mix·ol·o·gist /mik'säləjist/ ▶ **n.** informal a person who is skilled at mixing cocktails and other drinks. — **mix·ol·o·gy** /-əjē/ **n.**

mixt ▶ **v.** archaic past and past participle of MIX.

Mix·tec /'mēstek/ ▶ **n.** (pl. same or **-tecs**) **1** a member of an American Indian people of southern Mexico. **2** the Otomanguean language of this people. ▶ **adj.** of or relating to the Mixtec or their language. [Sp., from Nahuatl *mixtecah* 'person from a cloudy place.']

mix·ture /'miksснər/ ▶ **n.** a substance made by mixing other substances together. ■ the process of mixing or being mixed. ■ (**a mixture of**) a combination of different qualities, things, or emotions in which the component elements are individually distinct. ■ a person regarded as a combination of qualities and attributes: *he was a curious mixture.* ■ Chem. the product of the random distribution of one substance through another without any chemical reaction, as distinct from a compound. ■ the charge of gas or vapor mixed with air that is admitted to the cylinder of an internal combustion engine, esp. as regards the ratio of fuel to air. ■ (also **mixture stop**) an organ stop in which each key sounds a group of small pipes of different pitches, giving a very bright tone. [ME: from Fr. *mixture* or L. *mixtura* (see MIXED).]

mix-up (also **mixup**) ▶ **n.** informal a confusion of one thing with another, or a misunderstanding or mistake that results in confusion: *there's been a mix-up over the tickets.* ■ a combination of different things, esp. one whose effect is inharmonious: *a mix-up of furniture styles.*

Mi·zo /'mēzō/ ▶ **n.** (pl. same or **-zos**) **1** a member of a people inhabiting Mizoram. **2** the Tibeto-Burman language of this people. Also called **Lushai.** ▶ **adj.** of or relating to this people or their language. [the name in Mizo, lit. 'highlander,' from *mi-* 'person' + *zo* 'hill.']

Mi·zo·ram /mə'zôrəm/ a state in northeastern India; capital, Aizawl.

miz·zen /'mizən/ (also **miz·en**) ▶ **n.** **1** (also **miz·zen·mast**) the mast aft of a ship's mainmast. **2** (also **miz·zen·sail**) the lowest sail on a mizzenmast. [ME: from Ital. *mezzana* 'mizzensail,' fem. (used as a n.) of *mezzano* 'middle,' from L. *medianus* (see MEDIAN).]

miz·zle /'mizəl/ esp. dialect ▶ **n.** light rain; drizzle. ▶ **v.** [intrans.] (**it mizzles, it is mizzling,** etc.) rain lightly. — **miz·zly** adj. [ME: prob. a frequentative from the base of MIST; compare Du. dial. *miezelen.*]

Mk ▶ **abbr.** ■ the German mark. ■ the Gospel of Mark (in biblical references).

mk. ▶ **abbr.** ■ (pl. **mks.**) MARK². ■ markka.

mks ▶ **abbr.** meter-kilogram-second.

mksA (also **MKSA** or **mksa**) ▶ **abbr.** meter-kilogram-second-ampere.

mkt. ▶ **abbr.** market.

mktg. ▶ **abbr.** marketing.

ml ▶ **abbr.** ■ mile(s). ■ milliliter(s).

MLA ▶ **abbr.** ■ Member of the Legislative Assembly. ■ Modern Language Association (of America).

MLB ▶ **abbr.** major league baseball.

MLC ▶ **abbr.** Member of the Legislative Council.

MLD ▶ **abbr.** ■ minimum lethal dose. ■ moderate learning difficulties: [as adj.] *a school for MLD pupils.*

MLF ▶ **abbr.** multilateral nuclear force.

MLitt ▶ **abbr.** Master of Letters: *Susan Williams, M Litt.* [from L. *Magister Litterarum.*]

Mlle (pl. **Mlles**) ▶ **abbr.** Mademoiselle.

MLS ▶ **abbr.** Master of Library Science.

MLW ▶ **abbr.** (of the tide) mean low water.

MM ▶ **abbr.** Messieurs.

mm ▶ **abbr.** millimeter(s).

Mme (pl. **Mmes**) ▶ **abbr.** Madame.

m.m.f. ▶ **abbr.** magnetomotive force.

MMPI ▶ **abbr.** Minnesota Multiphasic Personality Inventory.

MMR ▶ **abbr.** measles, mumps, and rubella, a vaccination given to small children.

MMus ▶ **abbr.** Master of Music.

MN ▶ **abbr.** ■ Minnesota (in official postal use).

Mn ▶ **symb.** the chemical element manganese.

MNA ▶ **abbr.** (in Canada) Member of the National Assembly (of Quebec).

mne·mon·ic /nə'mänik/ ▶ **n.** a device such as a pattern of letters, ideas, or associations that assists in remembering something. ▶ **adj.** aiding or designed to aid the memory. ■ of or relating to the power of memory. — **mne·mon·i·cal·ly** adv. [18th C. (as an adj.): via med. L. from Gk. *mnēmonikos*, from *mnēmōn* 'mindful.']

mne·mon·ics /nə'mäniks/ ▶ **plural n.** [usu. treated as sing.] the study and development of systems for improving and assisting the memory.

Mne·mos·y·ne /nə'mäsənē; -'mäz-/ Gk. Mythol. the Greek goddess of memory, and the mother of the Muses by Zeus.

mngr. ▶ **abbr.** manager.

MO ▶ **abbr.** ■ Comput. (of a disk or disk drive) magneto-optical. ■ Missouri (in official postal use). ■ modus operandi. ■ money order.

Mo ▶ **symb.** the chemical element molybdenum.

mo. ▶ **abbr.** month.

-mo ▶ **suffix** forming nouns denoting a book size by the number of leaves into which a sheet of paper has been folded: *twelvemo.* [from the final syllable of L. ordinal numbers such as *duodecimo* (masc. ablative sing.).]

mo·a /'mōə/ ▶ **n.** a large, extinct, flightless bird (family Dinornithidae) resembling the emu, formerly found in New Zealand. Of its several species, *Dinornis maximus* was the tallest known bird, with a height of about 10 feet (3 m). [19th C.: from Maori.]

Mo·ab /'mō,ab/ the ancient kingdom of the Moabites, east of the Dead Sea.

Mo·ab·ite /'mōə,bīt/ ▶ **n.** a member of a Semitic people living in Moab in biblical times, traditionally descended from Lot. ▶ **adj.** of or relating to Moab or its people.

moan /mōn/ ▶ **n.** a long, low sound made by a person expressing physical or mental suffering or sexual pleasure. ■ a sound resembling this, esp. one made by the wind. ■ informal a complaint that is perceived as trivial and not taken seriously by others. ▶ **v.** [intrans.] make a long, low sound expressing physical or mental suffering or sexual pleasure. ■ (of a thing) make a sound resembling this: *the foghorn moaned at intervals.* ■ [reporting verb] informal complain or grumble, typically about something trivial. ■ literary lament. — **moan·er** n. **moan·ful** adj. [ME: of unknown origin.]

moat /mōt/ ▶n. a deep, wide ditch surrounding a castle, fort, or town, typically filled with water and intended as a defense against attack. ▶v. [trans.] [often as adj.] (**moated**) surround (a place) with a moat. [ME: from OFr. *mote* 'mound.']

mob /mäb/ ▶n. a large crowd of people, esp. one that is disorderly and intent on causing trouble or violence. ■ (usu. **the Mob**) the Mafia or a similar criminal organization. ■ (**the mob**) the ordinary people. ▶v. (**mobbed, mob·bing**) [trans.] (often **be mobbed**) crowd around (someone) in an unruly and excitable way in order to admire or attack them. ■ (of a group of birds or mammals) surround and attack (a predator or other source of threat) in order to drive it off. ■ crowd into (a building or place). — **mob·ber** n. [17th C.: abbrev. of archaic *mobile*, short for L. *mobile vulgus* 'excitable crowd.']

mob·cap /'mäb,kap/ ▶n. a large soft hat covering all of the hair and typically having a decorative frill, worn indoors by women in the 18th and early 19th centuries. [18th C.: *mob*, var. of obs. *mab* 'slut.']

Mo·bile /mō'bēl; 'mō,bēl/ a city on the coast of southern Alabama; pop. 198,915.

mo·bile ▶adj. /'mōbəl; -,bēl; -,bīl/ able to move or be moved freely or easily. ■ (of the face or its features) indicating feelings with fluid and expressive movements. ■ (of a store, library, or other service) accommodated in a vehicle so as to travel around and serve various places. ■ (of a military or police unit) equipped and prepared to move quickly to any place it is needed. ■ able or willing to move easily or freely between occupations, places of residence, or social classes. ▶n. /'mō,bēl/ a decorative structure that is suspended so as to turn freely in the air. [15th C.: via Fr. from L. *mobilis*, from *movere* 'to move.']

mo·bile home ▶n. a large house trailer that is parked in one particular place and used as a permanent living accommodation.

mo·bile phone (also **mobile telephone**) ▶n. another term for CELLULAR PHONE.

mo·bil·i·ty /mō'bilətē/ ▶n. the ability to move or be moved freely and easily. ■ the ability to move between different levels in society or employment.

mo·bi·lize /'mōbə,līz/ ▶v. [trans.] **1** (of a country or its government) prepare and organize (troops) for active service. ■ organize and encourage (people) to act in a concerted way in order to bring about a particular political objective. ■ bring (resources) into use in order to achieve a particular goal. **2** make (something) movable or capable of movement. ■ make (a substance) able to be transported by or as a liquid. — **mo·bi·liz·a·ble** adj. **mo·bi·li·za·tion** /,mōbələ'zāsHən/ n. **mo·bi·liz·er** n.

Mö·bi·us strip /'mōbēəs/ ▶n. a surface with one continuous side formed by joining the ends of a rectangular strip after twisting one end through 180°. [20th C.: named after August F. *Möbius* (1790–1868), Ger. mathematician.]

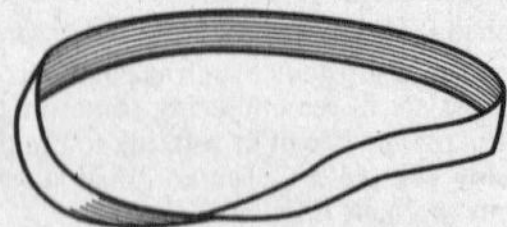
Möbius strip

mo·blog /'mō,blôg; -,bläg/ ▶n. a weblog that consists of pictures and other content posted from a cellphone. — **mob·log·ger** n. **mob·log·ging** n. [21st C.: blend of MOBILE and WEBLOG.]

mob·oc·ra·cy /mäb'äkrəsē/ ▶n. (pl. **-cies**) rule or domination by the masses.

mob rule ▶n. control of a political situation by those outside the conventional or lawful realm, typically involving violence and intimidation.

mob·ster /'mäbstər/ ▶n. informal a member of a group of violent criminals; a gangster.

Mo·bu·tu /mō'bŏŏtŏŏ/, Sese Seko (1930–97), president of Zaire 1965–97; born *Joseph-Désiré Mobutu*.

Mobutu Se·se Se·ko, Lake Zairean name for Lake Albert (see ALBERT, LAKE).

moc /mäk/ ▶n. informal short for MOCCASIN.

moc·ca·sin /'mäkəsən/ ▶n. **1** a soft leather slipper or shoe, without a separate heel, having the sole turned up on all sides and sewn to the upper in a simple gathered seam, in a style originating among North American Indians. **2** a venomous American pit viper (genus *Agkistrodon*). Its several species include the **water moccasin** (see COTTONMOUTH) and the **highland moccasin** (see COPPERHEAD). [17th C.: from Virginia Algonquian *mockasin*.]

moc·ca·sin flow·er ▶n. another term for *PINK LADY'S-SLIPPER* (see LADY'S-SLIPPER).

mo·cha /'mōkə/ ▶n. **1** a fine-quality coffee. ■ a drink or flavoring made with or in imitation of this, typically with chocolate added. ■ a dark brown color. **2** a soft kind of leather made from sheepskin. [18th C.: named after *Mocha*, a port on the Red Sea, from where the coffee and leather were first shipped.]

Mo·che /'mōcHā/ ▶n. Archaeol. a pre-Inca culture that flourished on the coast of Peru in the 1st to 7th centuries AD. [from the name of an archaeological site on the northwest coast of Peru.]

mock /mäk/ ▶v. [trans.] tease or laugh at in a scornful or contemptuous manner. ■ make (something) seem laughably unreal or impossible. ■ mimic (someone or something) scornfully or contemptuously. ▶adj. [attrib.] not authentic or real, but without the intention to deceive. ■ (of an examination, battle, etc.) arranged for training or practice, or performed as a demonstration. ▶n. dated an object of derision. — **mock·a·ble** adj. **mock·er** n. **mock·ing·ly** adv. [ME: from OFr. *mocquer* 'deride.']

mock·er·y /'mäk(ə)rē/ ▶n. (pl. **-er·ies**) derision; ridicule. ■ [in sing.] an absurd misrepresentation or imitation of something.
– PHRASES **make a mockery of** make (something) seem foolish or absurd.

mock-he·ro·ic ▶adj. (of a literary work or its style) imitating the style of heroic literature in order to satirize an unheroic subject. ▶n. (often as **mock heroics**) a burlesque imitation of the heroic character or literary style.

mock·ing·bird /'mäkiNG,bərd/ ▶n. a long-tailed thrushlike songbird (*Mimus* and other genera) with grayish plumage, found mainly in tropical America and noted for mimicking the calls of other birds.

northern mockingbird

mock moon ▶n. informal term for PARASELENE.

mock or·ange ▶n. a bushy shrub (genus *Philadelphus*) of the hydrangea family of north temperate regions that is cultivated for its strongly scented white flowers whose perfume resembles orange blossom.

mock sun ▶n. informal term for PARHELION.

mock-up (also **mock·up**) ▶n. a model or replica of a machine or structure, used for instructional or experimental purposes. ■ an arrangement of text and pictures to be printed.

mod[1] /mäd/ ▶adj. informal modern.

mod[2] ▶prep. Math. another term for MODULO.

mod. ▶abbr. ■ moderate. ■ Music moderato. ■ modern.

mod·al /'mōdl/ ▶adj. **1** of or relating to mode or form as opposed to substance. **2** Gram. of or denoting the mood of a verb. ■ relating to a modal verb. **3** Stat. of or relating to a mode; occurring most frequently in a sample or population. **4** Music of or denoting music using melodies or harmonies based on modes other than the ordinary major and minor scales. **5** Logic (of a proposition) in which the predicate is affirmed of the subject with some qualification, or which involves the affirmation of possibility, impossibility, necessity, or contingency. ▶n. Gram. a modal word or construction. — **mod·al·ly** adv.

mod·al·ism /'mōdl,izəm/ ▶n. **1** Theol. the doctrine that the persons of the Trinity represent only three modes or aspects of the divine revelation, not distinct and coexisting persons in the divine nature. **2** Music the use of modal melodies and harmonies. — **mod·al·ist** n. & adj.

mo·dal·i·ty /mō'dalitē/ ▶n. (pl. **-ties**) **1** modal quality. **2** a particular mode in which something exists or is experienced or expressed. ■ a particular method or procedure. ■ a particular form of sensory perception.

mod·al verb ▶n. Gram. an auxiliary verb that expresses necessity or possibility. English modal verbs include *must, shall, will, should, would, can, could, may*, and *might*. See also AUXILIARY VERB.

mode /mōd/ ▶n. **1** a way or manner in which something occurs or is experienced, expressed, or done. ■ an option allowing a change in the method of operation of a device, esp. a camera: *a camcorder in automatic mode*. ■ Comput. a way of operating or using a system. ■ Physics any of the distinct kinds or patterns of vibration of an oscillating system. ■ Logic the character of a modal proposition (whether necessary, contingent, possible, or impossible). ■ Logic Gram. another term for MOOD[2]. **2** a fashion or style in clothes, art, literature, etc. **3** Stat. the value that occurs most frequently in a given set of data. **4** Music a set of musical notes forming a scale and from which melodies and harmonies are constructed. **5** (in full **mode beige**) a drab or light gray color. [ME: from L. *modus* 'measure,' from an Indo-Eur. root shared by METE[1].]

mod·el /'mädl/ ▶n. **1** a three-dimensional representation of a person or thing or of a proposed structure, typically on a smaller scale than the original. ■ (in sculpture) a figure or object made in clay or wax, to be reproduced in another more durable material. **2** a system or thing used as an example to follow or imitate. ■ a simplified description, esp. a mathematical one, of a system or process, to assist calculations and predictions. ■ (**model of**) a person or thing regarded as an excellent example of a specified quality. ■ (**model for**) an actual person or place on which a specified fictional character or location is based. **3** a person, typically a woman, employed to display clothes by wearing them. ■ a person employed to pose for an artist, photographer, or sculptor. **4** a particular design or version of a product. ▶v. (**-eled, -el·ing**; Brit. **-elled, -el·ling**) [trans.] **1** fashion or shape (a three-dimensional figure or object) in a malleable material such as clay or wax. ■ (in drawing or painting) represent so as to appear three-dimensional. ■ (**model something on/after**) use (esp. a system or procedure) as an example to follow or imitate. ■ (**model oneself on**) take (someone admired or respected) as an example to copy. ■ devise a representation, esp. a mathematical one, of (a phenomenon or system). **2** display (clothes) by wearing them. ■ [intrans.] work as a model by displaying clothes or posing for an artist, photographer, or sculptor. — **mod·el·er** /'mädl-ər/ n. [16th C. (denoting a set of plans of a building): from Fr. *modelle*, from Ital. *modello*, from an alt. of L. *modulus* (see MODULUS).]

mod·el home ▸ **n.** a house in a newly built development that is furnished and decorated to be shown to prospective buyers.

mod·el·ing /ˈmädl-iNG/ (Brit. **mod·el·ling**) ▸ **n.** **1** the work of a fashion model. **2** the art or activity of making three-dimensional models. ■ [often with adj.] the devising or use of abstract or mathematical models.

mo·dem /ˈmōdəm; ˈmō,dem/ ▸ **n.** a combined device for modulation and demodulation, for example, between the digital data of a computer and the analog signal of a telephone line. ▸ **v.** [trans.] send (data) by modem. [20th C.: blend of *modulator* and *demodulator*.]

mod·er·ate ▸ **adj.** /ˈmäd(ə)rət/ average in amount, intensity, quality, or degree. ■ (of a person, party, or policy); not radical or excessively right- or left-wing. ▸ **n.** a person who holds moderate views, esp. in politics. ▸ **v.** /ˈmädə,rāt/ **1** make or become less extreme, intense, rigorous, or violent. **2** [trans.] (in academic and ecclesiastical contexts) preside over (a deliberative body) or at (a debate). **3** [trans.] Physics retard (neutrons) with a moderator. — **mod·er·at·ism n.** [ME: from L. *moderat-* 'reduced, controlled,' from the v. *moderare*; rel. to MODEST.]

mod·er·ate breeze ▸ **n.** a wind of force 4 on the Beaufort scale (13–18 miles per hour, or 11–16 knots).

mod·er·ate gale ▸ **n.** a wind of force 7 on the Beaufort scale (32–38 miles per hour, or 28–33 knots).

mod·er·ate·ly /ˈmäd(ə)rətlē/ ▸ **adv.** [as submodifier] to a certain extent; quite; fairly. ■ in a moderate manner. ■ within reasonable limits.

mod·er·a·tion /,mädəˈrāsHən/ ▸ **n.** **1** the avoidance of excess or extremes, esp. in one's behavior or political opinions. ■ the action of making something less extreme, intense, or violent. **2** Physics the retardation of neutrons by a moderator.
– PHRASES **in moderation** within reasonable limits; not to excess.

mod·e·ra·to /,mädəˈrätō/ Music ▸ **adv. & adj.** (esp. as a direction after a tempo marking) at a moderate pace. ▸ **n.** (pl. **-tos**) a passage marked to be performed in such a way. [Ital., lit. 'moderate.']

mod·er·a·tor /ˈmädə,rātər/ ▸ **n.** **1** an arbitrator or mediator. ■ a presiding officer, esp. a chairman of a debate. ■ a Presbyterian minister presiding over an ecclesiastical body. **2** Physics a substance used in a nuclear reactor to retard neutrons. — **mod·er·a·tor·ship n.**

mod·ern /ˈmädərn/ ▸ **adj.** of or relating to the present or recent times as opposed to the remote past. ■ characterized by or using the most up-to-date techniques, ideas, or equipment. ■ [attrib.] denoting the form of a language that is currently used, as opposed to any earlier form. ■ [attrib.] denoting a current or recent style or trend in art, architecture, or other cultural activity marked by a significant departure from traditional styles and values. ▸ **n.** (usu. **moderns**) a person who advocates or practices a departure from traditional styles or values. — **mo·der·ni·ty** /mäˈdərnitē; mə-; -ˈder-/ **n.** **mod·ern·ly adv.** **mod·ern·ness n.** [ME: from late L. *modernus*, from L. *modo* 'just now.']

mod·ern dance ▸ **n.** a free, expressive style of dancing started in the early 20th century as a reaction to classical ballet. In recent years it has included elements not usually associated with dance, such as speech and film.

mo·derne /mäˈdern; mə-/ ▸ **adj.** of or relating to a popularization of the art deco style marked by bright colors and geometric shapes. ■ often derog. denoting an ultramodern style. [20th C.: Fr., 'mod.']

mod·ern Eng·lish ▸ **n.** the English language as it has been since about 1500.

mod·ern his·to·ry ▸ **n.** history up to the present day, from some arbitrary point taken to represent the end of the Middle Ages.

mod·ern·ism /ˈmädər,nizəm/ ▸ **n.** modern character or quality of thought, expression, or technique. ■ a style or movement in the arts that aims to break with classical and traditional forms. ■ a movement toward modifying traditional beliefs in accordance with modern ideas, esp. in the Roman Catholic Church in the late 19th and early 20th centuries.

mod·ern·ist /ˈmädərnist/ ▸ **n.** a believer in or supporter of modernism, esp. in the arts. ▸ **adj.** of or associated with modernism, esp. in the arts. — **mod·ern·is·tic** /,mädərˈnistik/ **adj.**

mod·ern·ize /ˈmädər,nīz/ ▸ **v.** [trans.] adapt (something) to modern needs or habits, typically by installing modern equipment or adopting modern ideas or methods. — **mod·ern·i·za·tion** /,mädərnəˈzāsHən/ **n.** **mod·ern·iz·er n.**

mod·ern jazz ▸ **n.** jazz as developed in the 1940s and 1950s, esp. bebop and the related music that followed it.

mod·ern lan·guages ▸ **plural n.** European languages (esp. French and German) as a subject of study, as contrasted with classical Latin and Greek.

mod·ern Lat·in ▸ **n.** Latin as developed since 1500, used esp. in scientific terminology.

mod·ern pen·tath·lon ▸ **n.** see PENTATHLON.

mod·est /ˈmädəst/ ▸ **adj.** **1** unassuming or moderate in the estimation of one's abilities or achievements. **2** (of an amount, rate, or level of something) relatively moderate, limited, or small. ■ (of a place in which one lives, eats, or stays) not excessively large, elaborate, or expensive. **3** (of a woman) dressing or behaving so as to avoid impropriety or indecency, esp. to avoid attracting sexual attention. ■ (of clothing) not revealing or emphasizing the figure. — **mod·est·ly adv.** [16th C.: from Fr. *modeste*, from L. *modestus* 'keeping due measure,' rel. to *modus* 'measure.']

Mo·des·to /məˈdestō/ a city in north central California; pop. 164,730.

mod·es·ty /ˈmädəstē/ ▸ **n.** the quality or state of being unassuming or moderate in the estimation of one's abilities. ■ the quality of being relatively moderate, limited, or small in amount, rate, or level. ■ behavior, manner, or appearance intended to avoid impropriety or indecency.

mod·i·cum /ˈmädikəm; ˈmōd-/ ▸ **n.** [in sing.] a small quantity of a particular thing, esp. something considered desirable or valuable: *his statement had more than a modicum of truth.* [15th C.: from L., neut. of *modicus* 'moderate,' from *modus* 'measure.']

mod·i·fi·ca·tion /,mädəfəˈkāsHən/ ▸ **n.** the action of modifying something. ■ a change made.

mod·i·fi·er /ˈmädə,fīər/ ▸ **n.** a person or thing that makes partial or minor changes to something. ■ Gram. a word, esp. an adjective or noun used attributively, that restricts or adds to the sense of a head noun (e.g., *good* and *family* in *a good family house*). ■ Genet. a gene that modifies the phenotypic expression of a gene at another locus.

mod·i·fy /ˈmädə,fī/ ▸ **v.** (**-fies, -fied**) [trans.] make partial or minor changes to (something), typically so as to improve it or to make it less extreme. ■ Biol. transform (a structure) from its original anatomical form during development or evolution. ■ Gram. (esp. of an adjective) restrict or add to the sense of (a noun). ■ Phonet. pronounce (a speech sound) in a way that is different from the norm for that sound. — **mod·i·fi·a·ble adj.** **mod·i·fi·ca·to·ry** /ˈmädəfəkə,tôrē; ,mädəˈfikə,tôrē/ **adj.** [ME: from OFr. *modifier*, from L. *modificare*, from *modus* (see MODE).]

Mo·di·glia·ni /,mōdēlˈyänē/, Amedeo (1884–1920), Italian painter and sculptor. His portraits and nudes are noted for their elongated forms.

mo·dil·lion /mōˈdilyən/ ▸ **n.** Archit. a projecting bracket under the corona of a cornice in the Corinthian and other orders. [16th C.: from Fr. *modillon*, from Ital. *modiglione*, based on L. *mutulus*.]

mo·di·o·lus /məˈdīələs/ ▸ **n.** (pl. **-li** /-,lī; -,lē/) Anat. the conical central axis of the cochlea of the ear. [19th C.: from L., lit. 'nave of a wheel.']

mod·ish /ˈmōdisH/ ▸ **adj.** often derog. conforming to or following what is currently popular and fashionable. — **mod·ish·ly adv.** **mod·ish·ness n.**

mo·diste /mōˈdēst/ ▸ **n.** dated a fashionable milliner or dressmaker. [19th C.: Fr., from *mode* 'fashion.']

mod·u·lar /ˈmäjələr/ ▸ **adj.** employing or involving a module or modules in design or construction. ■ Math. of or relating to a modulus. — **mod·u·lar·i·ty** /,mäjəˈle(ə)ritē/ **n.**

mod·u·late /ˈmäjə,lāt/ ▸ **v.** [trans.] exert a modifying or controlling influence on: *the state attempts to modulate private business's cash flow.* ■ vary the strength, tone, or pitch of (one's voice). ■ alter the amplitude or frequency of (an electromagnetic wave or other oscillation) in accordance with the variations of a second signal, typically one of a lower frequency. ■ [intrans.] Music change from one key to another. ■ [intrans.] (**modulate into**) change from one form or condition into (another). — **mod·u·la·tion** /,mäjəˈlāsHən/ **n.** **mod·u·la·tor** /-,lātər/ **n.**

mod·ule /ˈmäjōōl/ ▸ **n.** each of a set of standardized parts or independent units that can be used to construct a more complex structure, such as an item of furniture or a building. ■ [usu. with adj.] an independent self-contained unit of a spacecraft. ■ Comput. any of a number of distinct but interrelated units from which a program may be built up or into which a complex activity may be analyzed. [16th C.: from Fr., or from L. *modulus* (see MODULUS).]

mod·u·lo /ˈmäjə,lō/ ▸ **prep.** Math. (in number theory) with respect to or using a modulus of a specified number. Two numbers are congruent modulo a given number if they give the same remainder when divided by that number: *19 and 64 are congruent modulo 5.* ■ [as adj.] using moduli: *modulo operations.* [19th C.: from L., ablative of *modulus* (see MODULUS).]

mod·u·lus /ˈmäjələs/ Math. ▸ **n.** (pl. **-li** /-,lī; -,lē/) **1** another term for ABSOLUTE VALUE. ■ the positive square root of the sum of the squares of the real and imaginary parts of a complex number. **2** a constant factor or ratio. ■ a constant indicating the relation between a physical effect and the force producing it. **3** a number used as a divisor for considering numbers in sets, numbers being considered congruent when giving the same remainder when divided by a particular modulus. [16th C.: from L., 'measure,' dimin. of *modus*.]

mo·dus op·e·ran·di /ˈmōdəs ,äpəˈrandē; -,dī/ ▸ **n.** (pl. **mo·di op·e·ran·di** /ˈmōdē; ˈmōdī/) [usu. in sing.] a particular way or method of doing something, esp. one that is characteristic or well-established: *buy systems using our usual modus operandi—with cash.* ■ the way something operates or works. [L., lit. 'way of operating.']

mo·dus vi·ven·di /ˈmōdəs vəˈvendē; -,dī/ ▸ **n.** (pl. **mo·di vi·ven·di** /ˈmōdē; ˈmōdī/) [usu. in sing.] an arrangement or agreement allowing conflicting parties to coexist peacefully, either indefinitely or until a final settlement is reached. ■ a way of living. [L., lit. 'way of living.']

mo·fo /ˈmō,fō/ ▸ **n.** vulgar slang short for MOTHERFUCKER.

Mo·ga·di·shu /,môgəˈdisHōō; ,mägə-; -ˈdēsHōō/ the capital of Somalia, on the Indian Ocean; pop. 377,000. Also called MUQDISHO; Italian name MOGADISCIO.

Mo·gi·lyov /,məgilˈyôf/ (also **Mo·gi·lev**) Russian name for MAHILYOW.

Mo·gul /ˈmōgəl/ (also **Mo·ghul** or **Mu·ghal**) ▸ **n.** a member of the Muslim dynasty of Mongol origin founded by the successors of Tamerlane, which ruled much of India from the 16th to the 19th century. ■ (often **the Great Mogul**) hist. the Mogul emperor of Delhi. [from Pers. *muġul* 'Mongol.']

mo·gul[1] /ˈmōgəl/ ▸ **n.** informal an important or powerful person, esp. in the motion picture or media industry. [17th C.: figurative use of MOGUL.]

mo•gul² ▶ **n.** a bump on a ski slope formed by the repeated turns of skiers over the same path. [1960s: prob. from southern Ger. dial. *Mugel, Mugl.*]

mo•hair /ˈmō,he(ə)r/ ▶ **n.** the long, silky hair of the angora goat. ■ a yarn or fabric made from this, typically mixed with wool. [16th C.: from Arab. *mukayyar* 'cloth made of goat's hair' (lit. 'choice, select').]

Mo•ham•med ▶ **n.** var. of MUHAMMAD¹.

Mo•ham•me•dan ▶ **n. & adj.** var. of MUHAMMADAN.

Mo•ham•me•rah /məˈhämərə/ former name (until 1924) for KHORRAMSHAHR.

Mo•ha•ve Des•ert var. of MOJAVE DESERT.

Mo•hawk /ˈmō,hôk/ ▶ **n.** (pl. same or **-hawks**) **1** a member of an American Indian people, one of the Five Nations, originally inhabiting parts of eastern New York. **2** the Iroquoian language of this people. **3** a hairstyle with the head shaved except for a strip of hair from the middle of the forehead to the back of the neck, typically stiffened to stand erect or in spikes. [erroneously associated with the Mohawk people] **4** Figure Skating a step from either edge of the skate to the same edge on the other foot in the opposite direction. ▶ **adj.** of or relating to the Mohawks or their language. [from Narragansett *mohowawog*, lit. 'man-eaters.']

Mo•hawk Riv•er a river that flows across central New York to join the Hudson River above Albany.

Mo•he•gan /mōˈhēgən/ (also **Mo•hi•can** /-ˈhēkən/) ▶ **n. 1** a member of an American Indian people formerly inhabiting eastern Connecticut. Compare with MAHICAN. **2** the Algonquian language of this people, closely related to Pequot. ▶ **adj.** of or relating to the Mohegans or their language. [from Mohegan, lit. 'people of the tidal waters.']

mo•hel /moil; ˈmō(h)el/ ▶ **n.** a person who performs the Jewish rite of circumcision. [17th C.: from Heb. *mōhēl*.]

Mo•hen•jo-Da•ro /mōˈhenjō ˈdärō/ an ancient city of the civilization of the Indus valley (*c.*2600–1700 BC), now a major archaeological site in Pakistan.

Mo•hi•can /mōˈhēkən/ ▶ **adj. & n.** old-fashioned var. of MAHICAN or MOHEGAN.

Mo•ho /ˈmō,hō/ ▶ **n.** Geol. short for MOHOROVIČIĆ DISCONTINUITY.

Mo•ho•ro•vi•čić dis•con•ti•nu•i•ty /,mōhəˈrōvi,CHiCH/ ▶ **n.** Geol. the boundary surface between the earth's crust and the mantle, lying at a depth of about 6–7 miles (10–12 km) under the ocean bed and about 24–30 miles (40–50 km) under the continents. [1930s: named after Andrija *Mohorovičić* (1857–1936), Yugoslav seismologist.]

Mohs' scale /mōz; mōs; ˈmōsəz/ ▶ **n.** a scale of hardness used in classifying minerals. It runs from 1 to 10 using a series of reference minerals, and a position on the scale depends on the ability to scratch minerals ranked lower. [19th C.: named after Friedrich *Mohs* (1773–1839), Ger. mineralogist.]

moi /mwä/ ▶ **exclam.** (usu. **moi?**) humorous me? (used esp. when accused of something that one knows one is guilty of). [Fr., 'me.']

moi•e•ty /ˈmoiətē/ ▶ **n.** (pl. **-ties**) formal tech. each of two parts into which a thing is or can be divided. ■ Anthropol. each of two social or ritual groups into which a people is divided, esp. among Australian Aboriginals and some American Indians. ■ a part or portion, esp. a lesser share. ■ Chem. a distinct part of a large molecule. [ME: from OFr. *moite*, from L. *medietas* 'middle,' from *medius* 'mid, middle.']

moil /moil/ ▶ **v.** [intrans.] work hard. ■ [with adverbial] move around in confusion or agitation. ▶ **n.** hard work; drudgery. ■ turmoil; confusion: *the moil of his intimate thoughts.* [ME: from OFr. *moillier* 'paddle in mud, moisten,' based on L. *mollis* 'soft.']

Moi•rai /ˈmoi,rī/ Gk. Mythol. the Fates.

moire /môˈrā; mwä; mwär/ (also **moi•ré** /mwäˈrā; mô-/) ▶ **n.** silk fabric that has been subjected to heat and pressure rollers after weaving to give it a rippled appearance. ▶ **adj.** (of silk) having a rippled, lustrous finish. ■ denoting or showing a pattern of irregular wavy lines like that of such silk, produced by the superposition at a slight angle of two sets of closely spaced lines. [17th C.: Fr. *moire* 'mohair' (the original fabric); the var. *moiré* 'given a watered appearance' (past part. of *moirer*, from *moire*).]

Mois•san /mwäˈsäN/, Ferdinand Frédéric Henri (1852–1907), French chemist. In 1892, he invented the electric-arc furnace that bears his name. Nobel Prize for Chemistry (1906).

moist /moist/ ▶ **adj.** slightly wet; damp or humid. ■ (of the eyes) wet with tears. ■ (of a climate) rainy. ■ Med. marked by a fluid discharge. — **moist•ly adv. moist•ness n.** [ME: from OFr. *moiste*, based on L. *mucidus* 'moldy.']

mois•ten /ˈmoisən/ ▶ **v.** [trans.] wet slightly. ■ [intrans.] (of the eyes) fill with tears.

mois•ture /ˈmoisCHər/ ▶ **n.** water or other liquid diffused in a small quantity as vapor, within a solid, or condensed on a surface. — **mois•ture•less adj.**

mois•tur•ize /ˈmoisCHə,rīz/ ▶ **v.** [trans.] make (something, esp. the skin) less dry.

mois•tur•iz•er /ˈmoisCHə,rīzər/ ▶ **n.** a lotion or cream used to prevent dryness in the skin.

Mo•ja•ve Des•ert /mōˈhävē/ (also **Mo•ha•ve**) a desert in southern California.

mo•jo /ˈmōjō/ ▶ **n.** (pl. **-jos**) a magic charm, talisman, or spell. ■ magic power. [20th C.: prob. of Afr. origin.]

mol /mōl/ Chem. ▶ **abbr.** MOLE⁴.

mo•la /ˈmōlə/ ▶ **n.** (pl. same or **mo•las**) another term for SUNFISH (sense 1). [16th C.: from L., lit. 'millstone,' with ref. to the shape.]

mo•lal /ˈmōləl/ ▶ **adj.** Chem. (of a solution) containing one mole of solute per kilogram of solvent. — **molality** /mōˈlalitē/ **n.**

mo•lar¹ /ˈmōlər/ ▶ **n.** a grinding tooth at the back of a mammal's mouth. [ME: from L. *molaris*, from *mola* 'millstone.']

mo•lar² ▶ **adj.** of or relating to mass; acting on or by means of large masses or units. [19th C.: from L. *moles* 'mass' + -AR¹.]

mo•lar³ ▶ **adj.** Chem. of or relating to one mole of a substance. ■ (of a solution) containing one mole of solute per liter of solvent. — **mo•lar•i•ty** /mōˈle(ə)ritē/ **n.**

mo•las•ses /məˈlasəz/ ▶ **n.** thick, dark brown, uncrystallized juice obtained from raw sugar during the refining process. ■ a paler, sweeter version of this used as a table syrup and in baking. [16th C.: from Port. *melaço*, from late L. *mellacium* 'must,' based on *mel* 'honey.']

mold¹ /mōld/ (Brit. **mould**) ▶ **n.** a hollow container used to give shape to molten or hot liquid material (such as wax or metal) when it cools and hardens. ■ something made in this way, esp. a gelatin dessert or a mousse. ■ [in sing.] fig. a distinctive and typical style, form, or character: *the latest policy is still stuck in the old mold.* ■ a frame or template for producing moldings. ▶ **v.** [trans.] form (an object with a particular shape) out of easily manipulated material. ■ give a shape to (a malleable substance). ■ influence the formation or development of: *helping to mold US policy.* ■ shape (clothing) to fit a particular part of the body. ■ [often as adj.] (**molded**) shape (a column, ceiling, or other part of a building) to a particular design, esp. a decorative molding: *a corridor with a molded cornice.*

— PHRASES **break the mold** put an end to a restrictive pattern of events or behavior by doing things in a markedly different way. — **mold•a•ble adj. mold•er n.** [ME: appar. from OFr. *modle*, from L. *modulus* (see MODULUS).]

mold² (Brit. **mould**) ▶ **n.** a furry growth of minute fungal hyphae (subdivision Deuteromycotina, or Ascomycotina) occurring typically in moist conditions, esp. on food or other organic matter. [ME: prob. from obs. *mould*, past part. of *moul* 'grow moldy,' of Scand. origin.]

mold³ (Brit. **mould**) ▶ **n.** soft loose earth. See also LEAF MOLD. ■ the upper soil of cultivated land, esp. when rich in organic matter. [OE *molde*, from a Gmc. base meaning 'pulverize or grind.']

Mol•dau /ˈmôl,dou/ German name for VLTAVA.

Mol•da•vi•a /mälˈdāvēə; môl-; -vyə/ **1** a former principality of southeastern Europe. In 1861, Moldavia united with Wallachia to form Romania. **2** another name for MOLDOVA.

Mol•da•vi•an /mälˈdāvēən; mô-/ ▶ **n. 1** a native or national of Moldavia. **2** the Romanian language as spoken and written (in the Cyrillic alphabet) in Moldavia. ▶ **adj.** of or relating to Moldavia, its inhabitants, or their language.

mold•board /ˈmōld,bôrd/ ▶ **n.** a curved metal blade in a plow that turns the earth over: [as adj.] *moldboard plows.* ■ a similar device on the front of a snowplow or bulldozer, used for pushing snow or loose earth.

mold•er /ˈmōldər/ (Brit. **mould•er**) ▶ **v.** [intrans.] [often as adj.] (**moldering**) slowly decay or disintegrate, esp. because of neglect: *the smell of moldering books.* [16th C.: perh. from MOLD³.]

mold•ing /ˈmōldiNG/ (Brit. **mould•ing**) ▶ **n.** an ornamentally shaped outline as an architectural feature, esp. in a cornice. ■ material such as wood, plastic, or stone shaped for use as a decorative or architectural feature.

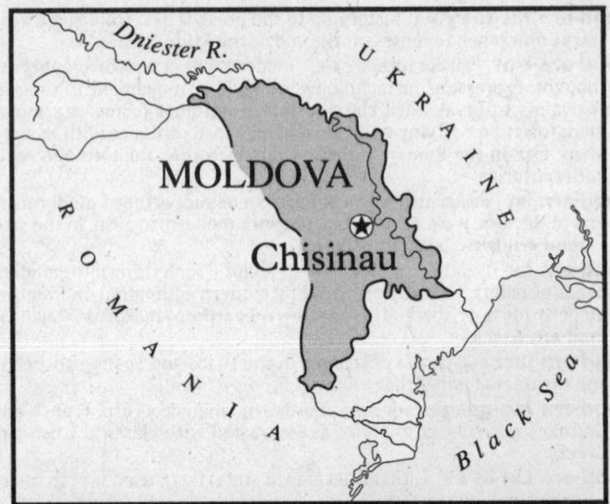

Moldova

Official name: Republic of Moldova
Location: southeastern Europe, between Romania and Ukraine
Area: 13,100 square miles (33,800 sq km)
Population: 4,384,000
Capital: Chisinau
Languages: Moldovan (official), Russian
Currency: Moldovan leu

Mol·do·va /məl'dōvə/ a landlocked country in southeastern Europe. *See box.* — **Mol·do·van adj. & n.**

mold·y /'mōldē/ (Brit. **mould·y**) ▶ **adj.** (**mold·i·er, mold·i·est**) covered with a fungal growth that causes decay, due to age or damp conditions. ■ tediously old-fashioned. — **mold·i·ness n.**

mole[1] /mōl/ ▶ **n.** **1** a small burrowing insectivorous mammal (family Talpidae) with dark velvety fur, a long muzzle, and very small eyes. Its several species include the **eastern mole** (*Scalopus aquaticus*) of North America. **2** a spy who achieves over a long period an important position within the security defenses of a country. ■ someone within an organization who anonymously betrays confidential information. [ME: from the Gmc. base of MDu. and Mid. Low Ger. *mol*.]

mole[1]

mole[2] /mōl/ ▶ **n.** a small, often slightly raised blemish on the skin made dark by a high concentration of melanin. [OE *māl* 'discolored spot,' of Gmc. origin.]

mole[3] /mōl/ ▶ **n.** a large solid structure on a shore serving as a pier, breakwater, or causeway. ■ a harbor formed or protected by such a structure. [16th C.: from Fr. *môle*, from L. *moles* 'mass.']

mole[4] /mōl/ ▶ **n.** Chem. the SI unit of amount of substance, equal to the quantity containing as many elementary units as there are atoms in 0.012 kg of carbon-12. [20th C.: from Ger. *Mol*, from *Molekul*, from L. (see MOLECULE).]

mole[5] /mōl/ ▶ **n.** Med. an abnormal mass of tissue in the uterus. [ME: from Fr. *môle*, from L. *mola* in the sense 'false conception.']

mo·le[6] /'mōlā/ ▶ **n.** a highly spiced Mexican sauce made chiefly from chili peppers and chocolate, served with meat. [Mex. Sp., from Nahuatl *molli* 'sauce, stew.']

mole crick·et ▶ **n.** a large burrowing nocturnal insect (family Gryllotalpidae) with broad forelegs, the female of which lays her eggs in an underground nest and guards the young.

mo·lec·u·lar /mə'lekyələr/ ▶ **adj.** of, relating to, or consisting of molecules. — **mo·lec·u·lar·i·ty** /mə,lekyə'laritē/ **n.** **mo·lec·u·lar·ly adv.**

mo·lec·u·lar bi·ol·o·gy ▶ **n.** the branch of biology that studies the structure and function of the macromolecules (e.g., proteins and nucleic acids) essential to life.

mo·lec·u·lar weight ▶ **n.** Chem. the ratio of the average mass of one molecule of an element or compound to one twelfth of the mass of an atom of carbon-12.

mol·e·cule /'mälə,kyōōl/ ▶ **n.** Chem. a group of atoms bonded together, representing the smallest fundamental unit of a chemical compound that can take part in a chemical reaction. [18th C.: from Fr. *molécule*, from mod. L. *molecula*, dimin. of L. *moles* 'mass.']

mole·hill /'mōl,hil/ ▶ **n.** a small mound of earth thrown up by a mole burrowing near the surface.
– PHRASES **make a mountain out of a molehill** exaggerate the importance of something trivial.

mole rat ▶ **n.** a herbivorous, short-legged, ratlike rodent (families Bathyergidae and Muridae) that typically lives permanently underground, with long incisors that protrude from the mouth and are used in digging.

mole sal·a·man·der ▶ **n.** a stocky, broad-headed North American salamander (*Ambystoma* and genera, family Ambystomatidae) that spends much of its life underground.

mole·skin /'mōl,skin/ ▶ **n.** **1** the skin of a mole used as fur. **2** a thick, strong cotton fabric with a shaved pile surface. ■ (**moleskins**) clothes, esp. trousers, made of such a fabric. ■ a soft fabric with adhesive backing used as a foot bandage.

mo·lest /mə'lest/ ▶ **v.** [trans.] pester or harass (someone), typically in an aggressive or persistent manner. ■ assault or abuse (a person, esp. a woman or child) sexually. — **mo·les·ta·tion** /,mōlə'stāshən/ **n.** **mo·lest·er n.** [ME: from L. *molestare* 'annoy,' from *molestus* 'troublesome.']

Mo·lière /mōl'ye(ə)r; mōl'yer/ (1622–73), French playwright; pen name of *Jean-Baptiste Poquelin*. He wrote more than 20 comic plays about contemporary France.

Mo·line /mō'lēn/ a city in northwestern Illinois; pop. 43,202.

moll /mäl/ ▶ **n.** informal **1** (also **gun moll**) a gangster's female companion. **2** a prostitute. [17th C.: nickname for the given name *Mary*.]

mol·li·fy /'mälə,fī/ ▶ **v.** (**-fies, -fied**) [trans.] appease the anger or anxiety of (someone). ■ rare reduce the severity of (something); soften. — **mol·li·fi·ca·tion** /,mäləfə'kāshən/ **n.** **mol·li·fi·er n.** [ME: from L. *mollificare*, from *mollis* 'soft.']

mol·lusk /'mäləsk/ (esp. Brit. also **mollusc**) ▶ **n.** an invertebrate of a large phylum (Mollusca) that includes snails, slugs, mussels, and octopuses. They have a soft, unsegmented body and live in aquatic or damp habitats, and most kinds have an external calcareous shell. — **mol·lus·kan** /mə'ləs,kən/ (or **mol·lus·can**) **adj.** [18th C.: from mod. L. *mollusca*, neut. pl. of L. *molluscus*, from *mollis* 'soft.']

Moll·wei·de pro·jec·tion /'môl,vidə; -,wīdə/ ▶ **n.** a projection of a map of the world onto an ellipse, with lines of latitude represented by straight lines (spaced more closely toward the poles) and meridians represented by equally spaced elliptical curves. This projection distorts shape but preserves relative area. [20th C.: named after Karl B. *Mollweide* (died 1825), Ger. mathematician and astronomer.]

mol·ly /'mälē/ (also **mol·lie**) ▶ **n.** a small, livebearing freshwater fish (genus *Poecilia*, family Poeciliidae) that is popular in aquariums and has been bred in many colors, esp. black. [1930s: from mod. L. *Mollienisia* (former genus name), from the name of Count *Mollien* (1758–1850), Fr. statesman.]

mol·ly·cod·dle /'mälē,kädl/ ▶ **v.** [trans.] treat (someone) very indulgently or protectively. ▶ **n.** an effeminate or ineffectual man or boy; a milksop. [19th C.: from *molly* 'girl or prostitute' (see MOLL) + CODDLE.]

Mo·loch /'mälək; 'mō,läk/ a Canaanite idol to whom children were sacrificed. ■ [as n.] (**a Moloch**) a tyrannical object of sacrifices. [via late L. from Gk. *Molokh*, from Heb. *mōlek*.]

mo·loch /'mälək; 'mō,läk/ ▶ **n.** a harmless spiny lizard (*Moloch horridus*, family Agamidae) of grotesque appearance that feeds chiefly on ants and is found in arid inland Australia.

Mo·lo·kai /,mälə'kī; ,mō-/ an island in Hawaii.

Mo·lo·tov[1] /'mälə,tôf; -,täf; 'mōlə-/ former name (1940–57) for PERM.

Mo·lo·tov[2], Vyacheslav Mikhailovich (1890–1986), Soviet diplomat; born *Vyacheslav Mikhailovich Skryabin*. He negotiated the nonaggression pact with Nazi Germany in 1939 and after 1945 represented the Soviet Union at the UN.

Mo·lo·tov cock·tail ▶ **n.** a crude incendiary device typically consisting of a bottle filled with flammable liquid and with a means of ignition. The production of similar grenades was organized by Vyacheslav Molotov during World War II.

molt /mōlt/ (Brit. **moult**) ▶ **v.** [intrans.] (of an animal) shed old feathers, hair, or skin, or an old shell, to make way for a new growth. ■ (of hair or feathers) fall out to make way for new growth. ▶ **n.** a loss of plumage, skin, or hair, esp. as a regular feature of an animal's life cycle. [ME *moute*, from an OE v. based on L. *mutare* 'to change.']

mol·ten /'mōltn/ ▶ **adj.** (esp. of materials with a high melting point, such as metal and glass) liquefied by heat. [ME: archaic past part. of MELT.]

mol·to /'mōl,tō; 'môl-/ ▶ **adv.** Music (in directions) very. [Ital., from L. *multus* 'much.']

Mo·luc·ca Is·lands /mə'ləkə/ islands in Indonesia, between Sulawesi and New Guinea; capital, Ambon. Indonesian name MALUKU. — **Mo·luc·can n. & adj.**

mol. wt. ▶ **abbr.** molecular weight.

mol·y[1] /'mōlē/ ▶ **n.** (pl. **mol·ies**) **1** a southern European plant (*Allium moly*) of the lily family, related to the onions, with small yellow flowers. **2** a mythical herb with white flowers and black roots, endowed with magic properties. [16th C. (sense 2): via L. from Gk. *mōlu*.]

moly[2] ▶ **n.** short for MOLYBDENUM. See also CHROME-MOLY.

mo·lyb·date /mə'lib,dāt/ ▶ **n.** Chem. a salt in which the anion contains both molybdenum and oxygen, esp. one of the anion $MoO_4 2-$. [18th C.: from *molybdic (acid)*, a parent acid of molybdates, + -ATE[1].]

mo·lyb·de·nite /mə'libdə,nīt/ ▶ **n.** a blue-gray mineral, typically occurring as hexagonal crystals.

mo·lyb·de·num /mə'libdənəm/ ▶ **n.** the chemical element of atomic number 42, a brittle silver-gray metal of the transition series, used in some alloy steels. (Symbol: **Mo**) [19th C.: mod. L., from Gk. *molubdaina* 'plummet,' from *molubdos* 'lead.']

mom /mäm/ ▶ **n.** informal one's mother. [19th C.: abbrev. of MOMMA.]

mom-and-pop ▶ **adj.** informal denoting a small store or business of a type often run by a married couple.

Mom·ba·sa /mäm'bäsə/ a city in southeastern Kenya; pop. 465,000.

mo·ment /'mōmənt/ ▶ **n.** **1** a very brief period of time. ■ an exact point in time. ■ an appropriate time for doing something; an opportunity. ■ a particular stage in something's development or in a course of events. **2** formal importance: *the issues were of little moment.* **3** Physics a turning effect produced by a force acting at a distance on an object. ■ the magnitude of such an effect, expressed as the product of the force and the distance from its line of action to a given point. **4** Stat. a quantity that expresses the average or expected value of the first, second, third, or fourth power of the deviation of each component of a frequency distribution from some given value, typically mean or zero.
– PHRASES **have one's** (or **its**) **moments** have short periods that are better or more impressive than others. **in a moment** **1** very soon: *I'll be back in a moment.* **2** instantly: *the fugitive was captured in a moment.* **live for the moment** live or act without worrying about the future. **the moment —— ** as soon as ——: *the heavens opened the moment we left the house.* **moment of truth** a time when a person or thing is tested, a decision has to be made, or a crisis has to be faced. **not a moment too**

soon almost too late. **not for a** (or **one**) **moment** not at all; never. **of the moment** currently popular, famous, or important: *the buzzword of the moment.* **one moment** (or **just a moment**) a request for someone to wait for a short period of time, esp. to allow the speaker to do or say something. [ME: from L. *momentum* (see MOMENTUM).]

mo·men·ta /mō'mentə; mə-/ plural form of MOMENTUM.

mo·men·tar·i·ly /,mōmən'te(ə)rəlē/ ▶ **adv.** **1** for a very short time. **2** at any moment; very soon.

mo·men·tar·y /'mōmən,terē/ ▶ **adj.** lasting for a very short time; brief. — **mo·men·tar·i·ness** n.

mo·ment of in·er·tia ▶ **n.** Physics a quantity expressing a body's tendency to resist angular acceleration. It is the sum of the products of the mass of each particle in the body with the square of its distance from the axis of rotation.

mo·men·tous /mō'mentəs; mə'-/ ▶ **adj.** (of a decision, event, or change) of great importance or significance, esp. in its bearing on the future. — **mo·men·tous·ly** adv. **mo·men·tous·ness** n.

mo·men·tum /mō'mentəm; mə-/ ▶ **n.** (pl. **-ta** /-tə/ or **-tums**) **1** Physics the quantity of motion of a moving body, measured as a product of its mass and velocity. **2** the impetus gained by a moving object. ■ the impetus and driving force gained by the development of a process or course of events. [17th C.: from L., from *movimentum*, from *movere* 'to move.']

mom·ism /'mäm,izəm/ ▶ **n.** informal excessive attachment to or domination by one's mother.

mom·ma ▶ **n.** var. of MAMA.

mom·my /'mämē/ ▶ **n.** (pl. **-mies**) informal one's mother (chiefly as a child's term). [20th C.: from MOMMA + -Y².]

Mon /mōn/ ▶ **n.** (pl. same or **Mons**) **1** a member of a people now inhabiting parts of southeastern Myanmar (Burma) and western Thailand but having their ancient capital at Pegu in southern Myanmar. **2** the language of this people, related to Khmer (Cambodian). ▶ **adj.** of or relating to this people or their language. See also MON-KHMER. [the name in Mon.]

Mon. ▶ **abbr.** Monday.

mon- ▶ **comb. form** var. of MONO- shortened before a vowel (as in *monamine*).

Mon·a·co /'mänəkō/ a principality that forms an enclave within French territory. *See box.*

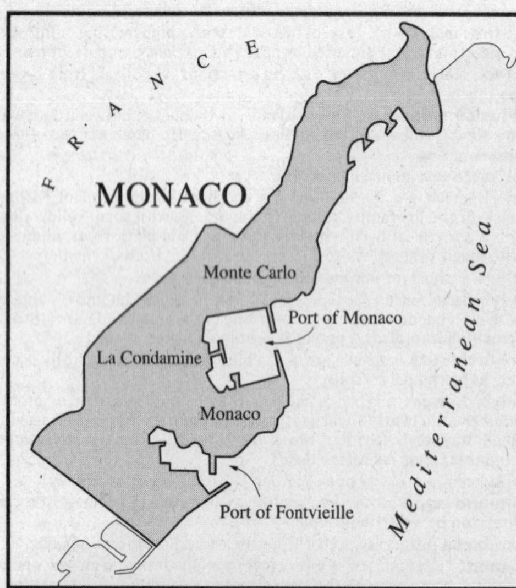

Monaco

Official name: Principality of Monaco
Location: southwestern Europe, on the Mediterranean coast
Area: three quarters of a square mile (1.95 sq km)
Population: 32,000
Capital: Monaco
Languages: French (official), English, Italian, Monegasque
Currency: euro

mon·ad /'mō,nad/ ▶ **n.** tech. a single unit; the number one. ■ Philos. (in the philosophy of Leibniz) an indivisible and hence ultimately simple entity, such as an atom or a person. ■ Biol., dated a single-celled organism, esp. a flagellate protozoan, or a single cell. — **mo·nad·ic** /mō'nadik; mə-/ adj. **mon·ad·ism** n. (Philos.). [17th C.: via late L. from Gk. *monas, monad-* 'unit,' from *monos* 'alone.']

mon·a·del·phous /,mänə'delfəs/ ▶ **adj.** Bot. (of stamens) united by their filaments so as to form one group. [19th C.: from Gk. *monos* 'one' + *adelphos* 'brother' + -OUS.]

mo·nad·nock /mə'nad,näk/ ▶ **n.** an isolated hill or erosion-resistant rock rising above a peneplain. [19th C.: named after Mount *Monadnock* in New Hampshire.]

Mon·a·ghan /'mänə,han; -hən/ a county of the Republic of Ireland. ■ its county town; pop. 5,750.

Mo·na Li·sa /'mōnə 'lēsə; 'lēzə/ a painting of a slightly smiling woman (now in the Louvre in Paris) executed 1503–06 by Leonardo da Vinci. Also called LA GIOCONDA.

mon·amine /'mänə,mēn/ ▶ **n.** var. of MONOAMINE.

mo·nan·dry /'män,andrē; mə'nan/ ▶ **n.** **1** the custom of having only one husband at a time. **2** Bot. the state of having a single stamen. — **mo·nan·drous** /mə'nandrəs/ adj. [19th C.: from MONO- 'single,' on the pattern of words such as *polyandry*.]

mon·arch /'mänərk; 'män,ärk/ ▶ **n.** **1** a sovereign head of state, esp. a king, queen, or emperor. **2** (also **monarch butterfly**) a large migratory orange and black butterfly (*Danaus plexippus*, family Nymphalidae) that occurs mainly in North America. The caterpillar feeds on milkweed, using the toxins in the plant to render both itself and the adult unpalatable to predators. — **mo·nar·chal** /mə'närkəl/ adj. (in sense 1). **mo·nar·chi·al** /mə'närkēəl/ adj. (in sense 1). **mo·nar·chic** /mə'närkik/ adj. (in sense 1). **mo·nar·chi·cal** /mə'närkikəl/ adj. (in sense 1). **mo·nar·chi·cal·ly** /mə'närkik(ə)lē/ adv. (in sense 1). [ME: from late L. *monarcha*, from Gk. *monarkhēs*, from *monos* 'alone' + *arkhein* 'to rule.']

monarch butterfly

Mo·nar·chi·an /mə'närkēən; mä-/ ▶ **n.** a Christian heretic of the 2nd or 3rd century who denied the doctrine of the Trinity. ▶ **adj.** of or relating to the Monarchians or their beliefs.

mon·ar·chism /'mänər,kizəm; 'män,är-/ ▶ **n.** support for the principle of having monarchs. — **mon·ar·chist** n. & adj.

mon·ar·chy /'mänərkē; 'män,är-/ ▶ **n.** (pl. **-chies**) a form of government with a monarch at the head. ■ a state that has a monarch. ■ (**the monarchy**) the monarch and royal family of a country.

mon·as·ter·y /'mänə,sterē/ ▶ **n.** (pl. **-ter·ies**) a community of persons, esp. monks or nuns, living under religious vows. ■ the place of residence occupied by such persons. [ME: via ecclesiastical L. from eccles. Gk. *monastērion*, from *monazein* 'live alone,' from *monos* 'alone.']

mo·nas·tic /mə'nastik/ ▶ **adj.** of or relating to monks, nuns, or others living under religious vows, or the buildings in which they live. ■ resembling or suggestive of monks or their way of life, esp. in being austere, solitary, or celibate. ▶ **n.** a monk or other follower of a monastic rule. — **mo·nas·ti·cal·ly** adv. **mo·nas·ti·cism** /-tə,sizəm/ n.

mon·a·tom·ic /,mänə'tämik/ (also **mon·o·a·tom·ic** /,monō-ə'tämik/) ▶ **adj.** Chem. consisting of one atom. ■ monovalent.

mon·au·ral /,män'ôrəl/ ▶ **adj.** of or involving one ear. ■ another term for MONOPHONIC (sense 1). — **mon·au·ral·ly** adv.

mon·a·zite /'mänə,zīt/ ▶ **n.** a brown crystalline mineral consisting of a phosphate of cerium, lanthanum, other rare earth elements, and thorium. [19th C.: from Ger. *Monazit*, from Gk. *monazein* 'live alone.']

Mön·chen·glad·bach /,mŏŏnkən'gläd,bäk; ,mœnkʜən'glät,bäkʜ/ a city in northwestern Germany; pop. 263,000.

Monck /məngk/, George, 1st Duke of Albemarle (1608–70), English general. He negotiated the return of Charles II in 1660.

Mon·day /'məndā; -dē/ ▶ **n.** the day of the week before Tuesday and following Sunday. ▶ **adv.** on Monday: *I'll call you Monday.* ■ (**Mondays**) on Mondays; each Monday. [OE *Mōnandæg* 'day of the moon.']

Mon·day morn·ing quar·ter·back ▶ **n.** informal a person who passes judgment on and criticizes something after the event. — **Mon·day morn·ing quar·ter·back·ing** n.

mon·do /'mändō/ ▶ **adv. & adj.** informal used in reference to something very striking or remarkable of its kind. [from Ital. *Mondo Cane*, lit. 'dog's world,' the title of a film (1961) depicting bizarre behavior.]

Mon·dri·an /'môndrē,än/, Piet (1872–1944), Dutch painter; born *Pieter Cornelis Mondriaan.* He was a cofounder of the De Stijl movement and the originator of neo-plasticism.

Mon·é·gasque /,mänə'gäsk; -'gask/ ▶ **n.** a native or national of Monaco. ▶ **adj.** of or relating to Monaco or its inhabitants. [Fr.]

Mo·nel /mō'nel/ (also **Monel metal**) ▶ **n.** trademark a nickel-copper alloy with high tensile strength and resistance to corrosion. [20th C.: named after Ambrose *Monell* (died 1921), US businessman.]

Mo·net /mō'nā/, Claude (1840–1926), French painter. A founding member of the Impressionists, he produced the *Haystacks* series (1890–91) and *Rouen Cathedral* (1892–95).

mon·e·ta·rism /'mänitə,rizəm; 'mən-/ ▶ **n.** the theory or practice of controlling the supply of money as the chief method of stabilizing the economy. — **mon·e·ta·rist** n. & adj.

mon·e·tar·y /ˈmänəˌterē; ˈmən-/ ▶ adj. of or relating to money or currency. — **mon·e·tar·i·ly** /-ˌte(ə)rəlē/ adv. [19th C.: from Fr. *monétaire* or late L. *monetarius*, from L. *moneta* 'money.']

mon·e·tize /ˈmänəˌtīz; ˈmən-/ ▶ v. [trans.] convert into or express in the form of currency. ■ [usu. as adj.] (**monetized**) adapt (a society) to the use of money. — **mon·e·ti·za·tion** /ˌmänətəˈzāshən; ˌmänəˌtīˈzāshən/ n.

mon·ey /ˈmənē/ ▶ n. a current medium of exchange in the form of coins and banknotes; coins and banknotes collectively. ■ (**moneys** or **monies**) formal sums of money. ■ the assets, property, and resources owned by someone or something; wealth. ■ financial gain. ■ payment for work; wages. ■ a wealthy person or group.

– PHRASES **be in the money** informal have or win a lot of money. **for my money** in my opinion or judgment. **money talks** proverb wealth gives power and influence to those who possess it. **one's money's worth** good value for one's money. **on the money** accurate; correct. **put money on 1** place a bet on. **2** used to express one's confidence in the truth or success of something. **put one's money where one's mouth is** informal take action to support one's statements or opinions. **throw one's money around** spend one's money extravagantly or carelessly. **throw money at something** try to solve a problem by recklessly spending money on it, without due consideration of what is required. [ME: from OFr. *moneie*, from L. *moneta* 'mint, money,' orig. a title of the goddess Juno.]

mon·ey·bags /ˈmənēˌbagz/ ▶ plural n. [usu. treated as sing.] informal a wealthy person.

mon·ey·chang·er (also **mon·ey-chang·er**) ▶ n. a person whose business is the exchanging of one currency for another. — **mon·ey·chang·ing** (or **mon·ey-chang·ing** or **mon·ey chang·ing**) n.

mon·eyed /ˈmənēd/ ▶ adj. having much money; affluent. ■ characterized by affluence.

mon·ey·er /ˈmənēər/ ▶ n. archaic a person who mints money.

mon·ey-grub·bing ▶ adj. informal overeager to make money; grasping. — **mon·ey-grub·ber** /-ˌgrəbər/ n.

mon·ey·lend·er /ˈmənēˌlendər/ (also **mon·ey-lend·er**) ▶ n. a person whose business is lending money to others who pay interest. — **mon·ey·lend·ing** (or **mon·ey-lend·ing**) n. & adj.

mon·ey·mak·er /ˈmənēˌmākər/ (also **mon·ey-mak·er**) ▶ n. a person or thing that earns a lot of money. — **mon·ey·mak·ing** (or **mon·ey-mak·ing**) n. & adj.

mon·ey mar·ket ▶ n. the trade in short-term loans between banks and other financial institutions.

mon·ey of ac·count ▶ n. a denomination of money used in reckoning, but not issued as actual coins or paper money.

mon·ey or·der ▶ n. a printed order for payment of a specified sum, issued by a bank or post office.

mon·ey plant ▶ n. another term for HONESTY sense 2.

mon·ey tree ▶ n. a source of easily obtained or unlimited money. ■ a real or artificial tree to which people attach paper money, esp. as a gift or donation.

mon·ey·wort /ˈmənēˌwərt; -ˌwôrt/ ▶ n. a trailing evergreen plant (*Lysimachia nummularia*) of the primrose family, with round glossy leaves and yellow flowers, growing in damp places and by water.

-monger ▶ comb. form denoting a dealer or trader in a specified commodity: *fishmonger*. ■ a person who promotes a specified activity, situation, or feeling, esp. one that is undesirable or discreditable: *rumormonger* | *warmonger*. [OE *mangere*, from *mangian* 'to traffic,' of Gmc. origin, based on L. *mango* 'dealer.']

mon·go /ˈmänggō/ ▶ n. (pl. same or **-gos**) a monetary unit of Mongolia, equal to one hundredth of a tugrik. [from Mongolian *möngö* 'silver.']

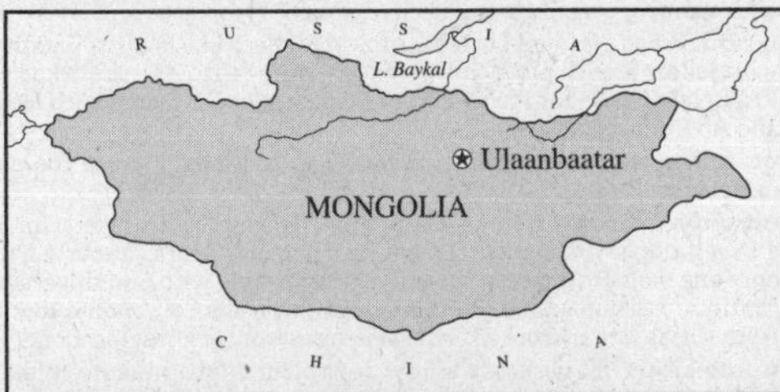

Mongolia

Official name: State of Mongolia

Location: eastern Asia, bordered by Siberia in Russia on the north and by China on the south; includes the Gobi Desert

Area: 604,400 square miles (1,565,000 sq km)

Population: 2,750,000

Capital: Ulaanbaatar

Languages: Khalkha Mongol (official), Turkic, Russian

Currency: tugrik

Mon·gol /ˈmänggəl/ ▶ adj. **1** of or relating to the people of Mongolia or their language. **2** (**mongol**) offens. suffering from Down syndrome. ▶ n. **1** a native or national of Mongolia; a Mongolian. **2** the language of this people; Mongolian. **3** (**mongol**) offens. a person suffering from Down syndrome. [Mongolian, perh. from *mong* 'brave.']

Mon·go·li·a /mängˈgōlēə/ a country in eastern Asia. *See box.*

Mon·go·li·an /mänˈgōlēən; mäng-/ ▶ adj. of or relating to Mongolia, its people, or their language. ▶ n. **1** a native or national of Mongolia. **2** the Altaic language of Mongolia, written in an unusual vertical cursive script; related forms are spoken in northern China.

mon·gol·ism /ˈmänggəˌlizəm/ ▶ n. offens. another term for DOWN SYNDROME.

Mon·gol·oid /ˈmänggəˌloid/ ▶ adj. **1** of or relating to the broad division of humankind including the indigenous peoples of eastern Asia, Southeast Asia, and the Arctic region of North America. **2** (**mongoloid**) offens. affected with Down syndrome. ▶ n. **1** a person of a Mongoloid physical type. **2** offens. a person with Down syndrome.

banded mongoose

mon·goose /ˈmänˌgōōs; ˈmäng-/ ▶ n. (pl. **-goos·es**) a small carnivorous mammal (*Herpestes*, *Mungos*, and other genera) of the civet family, with a long body and tail and a grizzled or banded coat, native to Africa and Asia. Its many species include the **banded mongoose** (*M. mungo*). [17th C.: from Marathi *mangūs*.]

mon·grel /ˈmänggrəl; ˈməng-/ ▶ n. a dog of no definable type or breed. ■ any other animal resulting from the crossing of different breeds or types. ■ offens. a person of mixed descent. — **mon·grel·ism** /-grəˌlizəm/ n. [ME: of Gmc. origin, appar. from a base meaning 'mix,' and rel. to MINGLE and AMONG.]

mon·grel·ize /ˈmänggrəˌlīz; ˈməng-/ ▶ v. [trans.] cause to become mixed in race, composition, or character: [as adj.] (**mongrelized**) *a patois of mongrelized French*. — **mon·grel·i·za·tion** /ˌmänggrələˈzāshən; ˌməng-/ n.

'mongst /ˈməngst/ ▶ prep. literary short for *AMONGST* (see AMONG).

mon·ic /ˈmänik/ ▶ adj. Math. (of a polynomial) having the coefficient of the term of highest degree equal to one.

mon·ies /ˈmənēz/ plural form of MONEY, as used in financial contexts.

mon·i·ker /ˈmänikər/ (also **mon·ick·er**) ▶ n. informal a name. — **mon·i·kered** adj. [19th C.: of unknown origin.]

mo·nil·i·a /məˈnilēə/ ▶ n. (pl. usu. same or **-nil·i·ae** /-ˈnilēˌē; -ēˌī/) former term for CANDIDA. [mod. L., from L. *monile* 'necklace.']

mo·nil·i·form /məˈniləˌfôrm/ ▶ adj. Zool. & Bot. resembling a string of beads. [19th C.: from mod. L. *moniliformis*, from L. *monile* 'necklace' + -IFORM.]

mon·ism /ˈmänˌizəm; ˈmōˌnizəm/ ▶ n. Philos. & Theol. a theory or doctrine that denies the existence of a distinction or duality in some sphere, such as that between matter and mind, or God and the world. ■ the doctrine that only one supreme being exists. Compare with PLURALISM. — **mon·ist** n. & adj. **mo·nis·tic** /mänˈistik; mōˈnistik/ adj. [19th C.: from mod. L. *monismus*, from Gk. *monos* 'single.']

mo·ni·tion /məˈnishən/ ▶ n. rare a warning of impending danger. ■ a formal notice from a bishop or ecclesiastical court admonishing a person not to do something specified. [ME: via OFr. from L. *monitio(n-)*, from *monere* 'warn.']

mon·i·tor /ˈmänətər/ ▶ n. **1** an instrument or device used for observing, checking, or keeping a continuous record of a process or quantity: *a heart monitor*. ■ a person operating such an instrument or device. ■ a person who observes a process or activity to check that it is carried out fairly or correctly, esp. in an official capacity. ■ a person who listens to and reports on foreign radio broadcasts and signals. ■ a jointed nozzle from which water streams in any desired direction, used in firefighting and hydraulic mining. ■ a raised section of roof running down the center of a railroad car, building, etc., providing light or ventilation; a clerestory. **2** a student with disciplinary or other special duties during school hours: *show the hall monitor your pass*. **3** a television receiver used in a studio to select or verify the picture being broadcast from a particular camera. ■ a television that displays an image generated by a computer. ■ a loudspeaker, esp. one used by performers on stage to hear themselves or in the studio to hear what has been recorded. **4** (also **monitor lizard**) a large tropical Old World lizard (genus *Varanus*, family Varanidae) with a long neck, narrow head, forked tongue, strong claws, and a short body. Monitors were formerly believed to give warning of crocodiles. **5** hist. a shallow-draft armored warship mounting one or two heavy guns for bombardment. ▶ **v.** [trans.] observe and check the progress or quality of (something) over a period of time; keep under systematic review: *equipment was installed to monitor air quality.* ■ maintain regular surveillance over: *it was easy for the enemy to monitor his movements.* ■ listen to and report on (a foreign radio broadcast or a telephone conversation). ■ check or regulate the technical quality of (a radio transmission or television signal). — **mon·i·to·ri·al** /ˌmänəˈtôrēəl/ **adj.** **mon·i·tor·ship** **n.** [16th C.: from L., from *monit-* 'warned,' from the v. *monere.*]

mon·i·to·ry /ˈmänəˌtôrē/ ▶ **adj.** rare giving or serving as a warning. ▶ **n.** (pl. **-ries**) (in church use) a letter of admonition from the pope or a bishop.

Monk /məNGk/, Thelonious Sphere (1917–82), US pianist and composer. He was a founder of the bebop style in the early 1940s.

monk /məNGk/ ▶ **n.** a member of a religious community of men typically living under vows of poverty, chastity, and obedience. — **monk·ish** **adj.** **monk·ish·ly** **adv.** **monk·ish·ness** **n.** [OE *munuc*, based on Gk. *monakhos* 'solitary,' from *monos* 'alone.']

monk·er·y /ˈməNGkərē/ ▶ **n.** derog. monasticism. ■ a monastery.

mon·key /ˈməNGkē/ ▶ **n.** (pl. **-keys**) **1** a small to medium-sized primate that typically has a long tail, most kinds of which live in trees in tropical countries. The **New World monkeys** (families Cebidae and Callitrichidae, or Callithricidae) have prehensile tails; the **Old World monkeys** (family Cercopithecidae) do not. ■ (in general use) any primate. ■ a mischievous person, esp. a child: *you little monkey!* ■ fig. a person who is dominated or controlled by another (with reference to the monkey traditionally kept by an organ grinder). **2** a pile-driving machine consisting of a heavy hammer or ram working vertically in a groove. ▶ **v.** (**-keys, -keyed**) [intrans.] (**monkey around/about**) behave in a silly or playful way. ■ (**monkey with**) tamper with. ■ [trans.] archaic ape; mimic.

– PHRASES **make a monkey of** (or **out of**) **someone** humiliate someone by making them appear ridiculous. **a monkey on one's back** informal a burdensome problem. ■ a dependence on drugs. [16th C.: of unknown origin, perh. from Low Ger.]

mon·key bars ▶ **plural n.** a piece of playground equipment consisting of a horizontally mounted overhead ladder, from which children may swing.

mon·key bread ▶ **n.** the baobab tree or its fruit.

mon·key busi·ness ▶ **n.** informal mischievous or deceitful behavior.

mon·key flow·er ▶ **n.** a plant (genus *Mimulus*) of the figwort family, having yellow or red tubular, often spotted flowers and growing in boggy ground.

mon·key jack·et ▶ **n.** a short, close-fitting jacket worn by sailors or waiters or by officers in their mess.

mon·key puz·zle (also **monkey puzzle tree**) ▶ **n.** an ornamental evergreen coniferous tree (*Araucaria araucana*, family Araucariaceae), native to Chile, with branches covered in spirals of tough, spiny, leaflike scales.

mon·key·shines /ˈməNGkēˌSHīnz/ ▶ **plural n.** informal mischievous behavior.

mon·key suit ▶ **n.** informal a man's evening dress or formal suit.

mon·key wrench ▶ **n.** an adjustable wrench with large jaws that has its adjusting screw contained in the handle. ▶ **v.** (**mon·key·wrench**) [trans.] informal sabotage (something), esp. as a form of protest.

– PHRASES **a monkey wrench in the works** (or **schedule**, **plan**, etc.) a person or thing that prevents the successful implementation of a plan. — **mon·key·wrench·er** **n.**

monk·fish /ˈməNGkˌfiSH/ ▶ **n.** (pl. same or **-fish·es**) a bottom-dwelling anglerfish (*Lophius piscatorius*, family Lophiidae) of European waters. ■ another term for GOOSEFISH, esp. when referring to the fish as food.

Mon-Khmer /ˈmōn kəˈme(ə)r; kme(ə)r/ ▶ **n.** a family of languages spoken throughout Southeast Asia, of which the most important are Mon and Khmer. They are distantly related to Munda, with which they form the Austro-Asiatic phylum. ▶ **adj.** relating to or denoting this group of languages.

monks·hood /ˈməNGksˌho͝od/ ▶ **n.** an aconite with blue or purple flowers. The upper sepal of the flower covers the topmost petals, giving a hoodlike appearance.

Mon·mouth /ˈmänməTH/, James Scott, Duke of (1649–85), English pretender to the throne of England.

mon·o /ˈmänō/ ▶ **adj.** **1** monophonic. **2** monochrome. ▶ **n.** (pl. **-os**) **1** a monophonic recording. ■ monophonic reproduction. **2** a monochrome picture. ■ monochrome reproduction. **3** short for INFECTIOUS MONONUCLEOSIS. **4** short for MONOFILAMENT.

mono- (also **mon-** before a vowel) ▶ **comb. form** **1** one; alone; single: *monorail.* ■ with an extreme, singular character to the point of dominance or exclusion: *monopoly.* **2** Chem. (forming names of compounds) containing one atom or group of a specified kind: *monoamine.* [from Gk. *monos* 'alone.']

mon·o·a·mine /ˌmänōəˈmēn; ˌmänōˈamēn/ (also **mon·a·mine** /ˈmänəˌmēn/) ▶ **n.** Chem. a compound having a single amine group in its molecule, esp. one that is a neurotransmitter (e.g., serotonin, norepinephrine).

mon·o·a·mine ox·i·dase (abbr.: **MAO**) ▶ **n.** Biochem. an enzyme (present in most tissues) that catalyzes the oxidation and inactivation of monoamine neurotransmitters.

mon·o·a·mine ox·i·dase in·hib·i·tor ▶ **n.** Med. any of a group of antidepressant drugs that inhibit the activity of monoamine oxidase (so allowing accumulation of serotonin and norepinephrine in the brain).

mon·o·a·tom·ic ▶ **n.** var. of MONATOMIC.

mon·o·car·pic /ˌmänōˈkärpik/ (also **mon·o·car·pous** /-pəs/) ▶ **adj.** Bot. (of a plant) flowering only once and then dying. [19th C.: from MONO- 'single' + Gk. *karpos* 'fruit' + -IC.]

mon·o·caus·al /ˌmänōˈkôzəl/ ▶ **adj.** in terms of a sole cause.

Mo·noc·er·os /məˈnäsərəs/ Astron. an inconspicuous constellation (the Unicorn), lying on the celestial equator in the Milky Way between Canis Major and Canis Minor.

mon·o·cha·si·um /ˌmänōˈkaZH(ē)əm/ ▶ **n.** (pl. **-si·a** /-ZH(ē)ə/) Bot. a cyme in which each flowering branch gives rise to one lateral branch, so that the inflorescence is helicoid or asymmetrical. [19th C.: mod. L., from MONO- 'one' + Gk. *khasis* 'separation.']

mon·o·chord /ˈmänəˌkôrd/ ▶ **n.** Music an instrument with a single string and a movable bridge, used esp. to determine intervals.

mon·o·chro·mat·ic /ˌmänəkrōˈmatik/ ▶ **adj.** containing or using only one color. ■ Physics (of light or other radiation) of a single wavelength or frequency. ■ lacking in variety; monotonous. — **mon·o·chro·mat·i·cal·ly** **adv.**

mon·o·chro·ma·tism /ˌmänəˈkrōməˌtizəm/ ▶ **n.** complete color-blindness in which all colors appear as shades of one color.

mon·o·chrome /ˈmänəˌkrōm/ ▶ **n.** a photograph or picture developed or executed in black and white or in varying tones of only one color. ■ representation or reproduction in black and white or in varying tones of only one color. ▶ **adj.** (of a photograph or picture, or a television screen) consisting of or displaying images in black and white or in varying tones of only one color. — **mon·o·chro·mic** /ˌmänəˈkrōmik/ **adj.** [17th C.: based on Gk. *monokhrōmatos* 'of a single color.']

mon·o·cle /ˈmänikəl/ ▶ **n.** a single eyeglass, kept in position by the muscles around the eye. — **mon·o·cled** /-kəld/ **adj.** [19th C.: from Fr., from late L. *monoculus* 'one-eyed.']

mon·o·cline /ˈmänəˌklīn/ ▶ **n.** Geol. a bend in rock strata that are otherwise uniformly dipping or horizontal. — **mon·o·cli·nal** /ˌmänəˈklīnl/ **adj.** [19th C.: from MONO- 'single' + Gk. *klinein* 'to lean.']

mon·o·clin·ic /ˌmänəˈklinik/ ▶ **adj.** of or denoting a crystal system or three-dimensional geometric arrangement having three unequal axes of which one is at right angles to the other two.

mon·o·clo·nal /ˌmänəˈklōnl/ ▶ **adj.** Biol. forming a clone derived asexually from a single individual or cell.

mon·o·coque /ˈmänəˌkōk; -ˌkäk/ ▶ **n.** an aircraft or vehicle structure in which the chassis is integral with the body. [20th C.: from Fr., from *mono-* 'single' + *coque* 'shell.']

mon·o·cot /ˈmänəˌkät/ ▶ **n.** Bot. short for MONOCOTYLEDON.

mon·o·cot·y·le·don /ˌmänəˌkätlˈēdn/ ▶ **n.** Bot. a flowering plant (class Monocotyledoneae or Liliopsida) with an embryo that bears a single cotyledon (seed leaf). Compare with DICOTYLEDON. — **mon·o·cot·y·le·don·ous** /-ˈēdn-əs/ **adj.**

mo·noc·ra·cy /məˈnäkrəsē; mä-/ ▶ **n.** (pl. **-cies**) a system of government by only one person. — **mon·o·crat** /ˈmänəˌkrat/ **n.** **mon·o·crat·ic** /ˌmänəˈkratik/ **adj.**

mo·noc·u·lar /məˈnäkyələr; mä-/ ▶ **adj.** with, for, or in one eye. ▶ **n.** an optical instrument for viewing distant objects with one eye, like one half of a pair of binoculars. — **mo·noc·u·lar·ly** **adv.**

mon·o·cul·ture /ˈmänəˌkəlCHər/ ▶ **n.** the cultivation of a single crop in a given area. — **mon·o·cul·tur·al** /ˌmänəˈkəlCHərəl/ **adj.**

mon·o·cy·cle /ˈmänəˌsīkəl/ ▶ **n.** another term for UNICYCLE.

mon·o·cy·clic /ˌmänōˈsīklik; -ˈsik-/ ▶ **adj.** **1** Chem. having one ring of atoms in its molecule. **2** Bot. (of a set of floral parts such as sepals or stamens) forming a single whorl. **3** of or relating to a single cycle of activity.

mon·o·cyte /ˈmänəˌsīt/ ▶ **n.** Physiol. a large phagocytic white blood cell with a simple oval nucleus and clear, grayish cytoplasm.

Mo·nod /môˈnō/, Jacques Lucien (1910–76), French biochemist. Together with fellow French biochemist François Jacob (1920–), he worked on RNA. Nobel Prize for Physiology or Medicine (1965, shared with Jacob and André Lwoff 1902–94).

mon·o·dra·ma /ˈmänəˌdrämə; -ˌdramə/ ▶ **n.** a dramatic piece for one performer.

mon·o·dy /ˈmänədē/ ▶ **n.** (pl. **-dies**) **1** an ode sung by a single actor in a Greek tragedy. **2** a poem lamenting a person's death. **3** music with only one melodic line, esp. an early Baroque style with one singer and continuo accompaniment. — **mo·nod·ic** /məˈnädik/ **adj.** **mon·o·dist** **n.** [17th C.: via late L. from Gk. *monōdia*, from *monōdos* 'singing alone.']

mo·noe·cious /məˈnēSHəs/ ▶ **adj.** Biol. (of a plant or invertebrate animal) having both the male and female reproductive organs in the same individual; hermaphrodite. Compare with DIOECIOUS. — **mo·noe·cy** /ˈmänˌēsē; ˈmō-/ **n.** [18th C.: from mod. L. *Monoecia*, from Gk. *monos* 'single' + *oikos* 'house.']

mon·o·fil·a·ment /ˌmänəˈfiləmənt/ (also **mon·o·fil** /ˈmänəˌfil/) ▶ **n.** a single strand of man-made fiber. ■ a type of fishing line using such a strand.

mo·nog·a·my /məˈnägəmē/ ▶ **n.** the practice or state of being married to one person at a time. ■ the practice or state of having a sexual relationship with only one partner. ■ Zool. the habit of having only one mate at a time. — **mo·nog·a·mist** **n.** **mo·nog·a·mous** /-məs/ **adj.** **mo·nog·a·mous·ly** /-məslē/ **adv.** [17th C.: from Fr. *monogamie*, via eccles. L. from Gk. *monogamia*, from *monos* 'single' + *gamos* 'marriage.']

mon·o·gen·e·sis /ˌmänəˈjenəsəs/ ▶**n.** the theory that humans are all descended from a single pair of ancestors. Also called MONOGENY. ■ Ling. the hypothetical origination of language or of a surname from a single source at a particular place and time. — **mon·o·ge·net·ic** /-jəˈnetik/ **adj.**

mon·o·gen·ic /ˌmänəˈjenik/ ▶**adj.** Genet. involving or controlled by a single gene. — **mon·o·gen·i·cal·ly** **adv.**

mo·nog·e·ny /məˈnäjənē/ ▶**n.** another term for MONOGENESIS. — **mo·nog·e·nism** **n.** **mo·nog·e·nist** **n.**

mon·o·glot /ˈmänəˌglät/ ▶**adj.** using or speaking only one language. ▶**n.** a person who speaks only one language. [19th C.: from Gk. *monoglōttos*, from *monos* 'single' + *glōtta* 'tongue.']

mon·o·gram /ˈmänəˌgram/ ▶**n.** a motif of two or more letters, typically a person's initials, usually interwoven or otherwise combined in a decorative design, used as a logo or to identify a personal possession. ▶**v.** [trans.] decorate with a monogram. — **mon·o·gram·mat·ic** /ˌmänəgrəˈmatik/ **adj.**

mon·o·graph /ˈmänəˌgraf/ ▶**n.** a detailed written study of a single specialized subject or an aspect of it. ▶**v.** [trans.] write a monograph on; treat in a monograph. — **mo·nog·ra·pher** /məˈnägrəfər/ **n.** **mo·nog·ra·phist** /məˈnägrəfist/ **n.**

mon·o·graph·ic /ˌmänəˈgrafik/ ▶**adj.** of or relating to a monograph. ■ (of an art gallery or exhibition) showing the works of a single artist.

mo·nog·y·nous /məˈnäjənəs/ ▶**adj.** Bot. having only one pistil.

mo·nog·y·ny /məˈnäjənē/ ▶**n.** the custom of having only one wife at a time. ■ Entomol. the condition of having a single egg-laying queen in a colony of social insects. [19th C.: from MONO- 'one' + Gk. *gunē* 'woman, wife.']

mon·o·hull /ˈmänōˌhəl/ ▶**n.** a boat with only one hull, as opposed to a catamaran or multihull.

mon·o·hy·drate /ˌmänōˈhīˌdrāt/ ▶**n.** Chem. a hydrate containing one mole of water per mole of the compound.

mon·o·hy·dric /ˌmänōˈhīdrik/ ▶**adj.** Chem. (of an alcohol) containing one hydroxyl group.

mon·o·lay·er /ˈmänəˌlāər/ ▶**n.** Chem. a layer one molecule thick. ■ Biol. & Med. a cell culture in a layer one cell thick.

mon·o·lin·gual /ˌmänəˈliNGg(yə)wəl/ ▶**adj.** (of a person or society) speaking only one language. ■ (of a text, conversation, etc.) written or conducted in only one language. ▶**n.** a person who speaks only one language. — **mon·o·lin·gual·ism** **n.**

mon·o·lith /ˈmänl-iTH/ ▶**n. 1** a large single upright block of stone, esp. one shaped into or serving as a pillar or monument. ■ a very large and characterless building. ■ a large block of concrete sunk in water, e.g., in the building of a dock. **2** a large and impersonal political, corporate, or social structure regarded as intractably indivisible and uniform. [19th C.: from Gk. *monolithos*, from *monos* 'single' + *lithos* 'stone.']

mon·o·lith·ic /ˌmänəˈliTHik/ ▶**adj. 1** formed of a single large block of stone. ■ (of a building) very large and characterless. **2** (of an organization or system) large, powerful, and intractably indivisible and uniform. **3** Electron. (of a solid-state circuit) composed of active and passive components formed in a single chip.

mon·o·logue /ˈmänlˌôg; -ˌäg/ ▶**n.** a long speech by one actor in a play or movie, or as part of a theatrical or broadcast program. ■ the form or style of such speeches. ■ a long and typically tedious speech by one person during a conversation. — **mon·o·log·ic** /ˌmänlˈäjik/ **adj.** **mon·o·log·i·cal** /ˌmänlˈäjikəl/ **adj.** **mon·o·log·ist** /məˈnäləjist/ (also **-logu·ist**) **n.** **mon·o·log·ize** /məˈnäləˌjīz/ **v.** [17th C.: from Gk. *monologos* 'speaking alone.']

mon·o·ma·ni·a /ˌmänəˈmānēə/ ▶**n.** exaggerated enthusiasm for or preoccupation with one thing. — **mon·o·ma·ni·ac** /-ˈmānēˌak/ **n. & adj.** **mon·o·ma·ni·a·cal** /-məˈnīəkəl/ **adj.**

mon·o·mer /ˈmänəmər/ ▶**n.** Chem. a molecule that can be bonded to other identical molecules to form a polymer. — **mon·o·mer·ic** /ˌmänəˈmerik/ **adj.**

mon·o·me·tal·lic /ˌmänōməˈtalik/ ▶**adj.** consisting of one metal only. ■ of, involving, or using a standard of currency based on one metal. — **mon·o·met·al·lism** /-ˈmetlˌizəm/ **n.** **mon·o·met·al·list** /-ˈmetl-ist/ **n. & adj.**

mo·no·mi·al /məˈnōmēəl; mä-/ Math. ▶**adj.** (of an algebraic expression) consisting of one term. ▶**n.** an algebraic expression of this type. [18th C.: from MONO- 'one,' on the pattern of *binomial*.]

mon·o·mo·lec·u·lar /ˌmänōməˈlekyələr/ ▶**adj.** Chem. (of a layer) one molecule thick. ■ consisting of or involving one molecule.

mon·o·mor·phic /ˌmänəˈmôrfik/ ▶**adj.** esp. Biol. having or existing in only one form, in particular: ■ (of a species or population) showing little or no variation in morphology or phenotype. ■ (of an animal species) having sexes that are similar in size and appearance. — **mon·o·mor·phism** **n.** **mon·o·mor·phous** /-fəs/ **adj.** [19th C.: from MONO- 'single' + Gk. *morphē* 'form.']

Mo·non·ga·he·la Riv·er /məˌnäNGgəˈhēlə/ a river that flows from West Virginia to Pennsylvania to join the Allegheny River to form the Ohio River.

mon·o·nu·cle·ar /ˌmänōˈn(y)o͞oklēər/ ▶**adj.** Biol. (of a cell) having one nucleus.

mon·o·nu·cle·o·sis /ˌmänəˌn(y)o͞oklēˈōsəs/ ▶**n.** Med. an abnormally high proportion of monocytes in the blood. ■ short for INFECTIOUS MONONUCLEOSIS.

mo·noph·a·gous /məˈnäfəgəs/ ▶**adj.** Zool. (of an animal) eating only one kind of food.

mon·o·phon·ic /ˌmänəˈfänik/ ▶**adj. 1** Music consisting of a single musical line, without accompaniment. **2** (of sound reproduction) using only one channel of transmission. Compare with STEREOPHONIC. — **mon·o·phon·i·cal·ly** **adv.** **mo·noph·o·ny** /məˈnäfənē/ **n.**

mon·oph·thong /ˈmänə(f)ˌTHôNG/ ▶**n.** Phonet. a vowel that has a single perceived auditory quality. Contrasted with DIPHTHONG, TRIPHTHONG. — **mon·oph·thon·gal** /ˌmänə(f)ˈTHôNG(g)əl/ **adj.** [17th C.: from Gk. *monophthongos*, from *monos* 'single' + *phthongos* 'sound.']

mon·o·phy·let·ic /ˌmänōfīˈletik/ ▶**adj.** Biol. (of a group of organisms) descended from a common evolutionary ancestor or ancestral group, esp. one not shared with any other group.

Mo·noph·y·site /məˈnäfəˌsīt/ ▶**n.** Christian Theol. a person who holds that in the person of Christ there is only one nature (wholly divine or only subordinately human), not two. — **Mo·noph·y·sit·ism** /-ˌsītˌizəm/ **n.** [17th C.: via ecclesiastical L. from eccles. Gk. *monophusitēs*, from *monos* 'single' + *phusis* 'nature.']

mon·o·plane /ˈmänəˌplān/ ▶**n.** an airplane with one pair of wings. Often contrasted with BIPLANE, TRIPLANE.

mon·o·ple·gi·a /ˌmänōˈplēj(ē)ə/ ▶**n.** paralysis restricted to one limb or region of the body. Compare with PARAPLEGIA. — **mon·o·ple·gic** /-ˈplējik/ **adj.**

mon·o·ploid /ˈmänəˌploid/ ▶**adj.** less common term for HAPLOID.

mon·o·pod /ˈmänəˌpäd/ ▶**n.** a one-legged support for a camera or fishing rod. [19th C.: via L. from Gk. *monopodion*, from *monos* 'single' + *pous, pod-* 'foot.']

mon·o·po·di·um /ˌmänəˈpōdēəm/ ▶**n.** (pl. **-po·di·a** /-ˈpōdēə/) Bot. a single continuous growth axis that extends at its apex and produces successive lateral shoots. Compare with SYMPODIUM. — **mon·o·po·di·al** /-dēəl/ **adj.**

mon·o·pole /ˈmänəˌpōl/ ▶**n. 1** Physics a single electric charge or magnetic pole, esp. a hypothetical isolated magnetic pole. **2** a radio antenna or pylon consisting of a single pole or rod.

mo·nop·o·list /məˈnäpəlist/ ▶**n.** a person or business that has a monopoly. — **mo·nop·o·lis·tic** /məˌnäpəˈlistik/ **adj.** **mo·nop·o·lis·ti·cal·ly** /məˌnäpəˈlistik(ə)lē/ **adv.**

mo·nop·o·lize /məˈnäpəˌlīz/ ▶**v.** [trans.] (of an organization or group) obtain exclusive possession or control of (a trade, commodity, or service). ■ have or take the greatest share of. ■ get or keep exclusively to oneself. — **mo·nop·o·li·za·tion** /məˌnäpələˈzāSHən/ **n.** **mo·nop·o·liz·er** **n.**

mo·nop·o·ly /məˈnäpəlē/ ▶**n.** (pl. **-lies**) **1** the exclusive possession or control of the supply or trade in a commodity or service. ■ [usu. with negative] the exclusive possession, control, or exercise of something: ***men don't have a monopoly on unrequited love.*** ■ a company or group having exclusive control over a commodity or service. ■ a commodity or service controlled in this way. **2** (**Monopoly**) trademark a board game in which players engage in simulated property and financial dealings using imitation money. [16th C.: via L. from Gk. *monopōlion*, from *monos* 'single' + *pōlein* 'sell.']

mon·o·pro·pel·lant /ˌmänōprəˈpelənt/ ▶**n.** a substance used as rocket fuel without an additional oxidizing agent. ▶**adj.** using such a substance.

mo·nop·so·ny /məˈnäpsənē/ ▶**n.** (pl. **-nies**) Econ. a market situation in which there is only one buyer. [1930s: from MONO- 'one' + Gk. *opsōnein* 'buy provisions' + -Y[3].]

mon·o·rail /ˈmänəˌrāl/ ▶**n.** a railroad in which the track consists of a single rail, typically elevated, with the trains suspended from it or balancing on it.

mon·o·sac·cha·ride /ˌmänəˈsakəˌrīd/ ▶**n.** Chem. any of the class of sugars (e.g., glucose) that cannot be hydrolyzed to give a simpler sugar.

mon·o·ski /ˈmänəˌskē/ ▶**n.** a single broad ski attached to both feet. — **mon·o·ski·er** /-ˌskēər/ **n.** **mon·o·ski·ing** /-ˌskē-iNG/ **n.**

mon·o·so·di·um glu·ta·mate /ˌmänəˌsōdēəm ˈglo͞otəˌmāt/ (abbr.: **MSG**) ▶**n.** a compound, $HOOC(CH_2)_2(NH_2)COONa$, that occurs naturally as a breakdown product of proteins and is used as a flavor enhancer in food (although itself tasteless).

mon·o·some /ˈmänəˌsōm/ ▶**n.** Biol. an unpaired (usually X) chromosome in a diploid chromosome complement.

mon·o·so·my /ˈmänəˌsōmē/ ▶**n.** Biol. the condition of having a diploid chromosome complement in which one (usually the X) chromosome lacks its homologous partner. — **mon·o·so·mic** /ˌmänəˈsōmik/ **adj.**

mon·o·spe·cif·ic /ˌmänōspəˈsifik/ ▶**adj.** Biol. relating to or consisting of only one species. ■ (of an antibody) specific to one antigen.

mon·o·syl·lab·ic /ˌmänəsəˈlabik/ ▶**adj.** (of a word or utterance) consisting of one syllable. ■ (of a person) using brief words to signify reluctance to engage in conversation. — **mon·o·syl·lab·i·cal·ly** **adv.**

mon·o·syl·la·ble /ˌmänəˈsiləbəl; ˈmänəˌsil-/ ▶**n.** a word consisting of only one syllable. ■ (**monosyllables**) brief words, signifying reluctance to engage in conversation: ***if she spoke at all it was in monosyllables.***

mon·o·syn·ap·tic /ˌmänōsəˈnaptik/ ▶**adj.** Physiol. (of a reflex pathway) involving a single synapse.

mon·o·the·ism /ˈmänəˌTHēˌizəm/ ▶**n.** the doctrine or belief that there is only one God. — **mon·o·the·ist** **n. & adj.** **mon·o·the·is·tic** /ˌmänəTHēˈistik/ **adj.** **mon·o·the·is·ti·cal·ly** /ˌmänəTHēˈistik(ə)lē/ **adv.**

Mo·noth·e·lite /mə'näTHə,līt/ (also **Mo·noth·e·lete** /-,lēt/) ▶ **n.** Christian Theol. an adherent of the doctrine that Jesus had only one will, proposed in the 7th century to reconcile Monophysite and orthodox parties in the Byzantine Empire but condemned as heresy. [ME: via ecclesiastical L. from eccles. Gk. *monotheletēs*, from *monos* 'single' + *thelētēs* 'one that wills'(from *thelein* 'to will').]

mon·o·tone /'mänə,tōn/ ▶ **n.** [usu. in sing.] a continuing sound, esp. of someone's voice, that is unchanging in pitch and without intonation. ▶ **adj.** (of a voice or other sound) unchanging in pitch; without intonation or expressiveness. ■ fig. without vividness or variety; dull. ■ of a single color. [17th C.: from mod. L. *monotonus*, from late Gk. *monotonos*.]

mon·o·ton·ic /,mänə'tänik/ ▶ **adj.** **1** Math. (of a function or quantity) varying in such a way that it either never decreases or never increases. **2** speaking or uttered with an unchanging pitch or tone. — **mon·o·ton·i·cal·ly** adv. **mo·no·ton·ic·i·ty** /,mänətn'isətē/ n.

mo·not·o·nous /mə'nätn-əs/ ▶ **adj.** dull, tedious, and repetitious; lacking in variety and interest. ■ (of a sound or utterance) lacking in variation in tone or pitch. — **mo·not·o·nous·ly** adv.

mo·not·o·ny /mə'nätn-ē/ ▶ **n.** lack of variety and interest; tedious repetition and routine. ■ sameness of pitch or tone in a sound or utterance.

mon·o·treme /'mänə,trēm/ ▶ **n.** Zool. a primitive mammal (order Monotremata, subclass Prototheria) that lays large yolky eggs and has a common opening for the urogenital and digestive systems. Monotremes are now restricted to Australia and New Guinea, and comprise the platypus and the echidnas. [19th C.: from MONO- 'single' + Gk. *trēma* 'hole.']

mon·o·type /'mänə,tīp/ ▶ **n.** **1** (**Monotype**) [usu. as adj.] Print., trademark a typesetting machine, now little used, that casts type in metal, one character at a time. **2** a single print taken from a design created in oil paint or printing ink on glass or metal. **3** Biol. a monotypic genus or other taxon.

mon·o·typ·ic /,mänə'tipik/ ▶ **adj.** esp. Biol. having only one type or representative, esp. (of a genus) containing only one species.

mon·o·un·sat·u·rat·ed /,mänō,ən'sacHə,rātid/ ▶ **adj.** Chem. (of an organic compound, esp. a fat) saturated except for one multiple bond.

mon·o·va·lent /,mänə'vālənt/ ▶ **adj.** Chem. having a valence of one.

mon·ox·ide /mə'näk,sīd/ ▶ **n.** Chem. an oxide containing one atom of oxygen in its molecule or empirical formula.

mon·o·zy·got·ic /,mänō,zī'gätik/ (also **mon·o·zy·gous** /,mänə'zīgəs/) ▶ **adj.** (of twins) derived from a single ovum, and so identical. — **mon·o·zy·gos·i·ty** n.

Mon·roe /mən'rō/, James (1758–1831), 5th president of the US 1817–25. In 1803, as minister to France, he negotiated and ratified the Louisiana Purchase. During his presidency, the Adams-Onis Treaty 1819, which allowed the US to acquire Florida from Spain, was negotiated. A Democrat Republican, he originated the Monroe Doctrine.

Mon·roe Doc·trine a US policy, originated by President James Monroe in 1823, that any intervention by external powers in the politics of the Americas is a potentially hostile act against the US.

Mon·ro·vi·a /mən'rōvēə/ the capital of Liberia; pop. 500,000. It was founded for resettled US slaves.

mons /mänz/ ▶ **n.** short for MONS PUBIS.

Mon·sei·gneur /,mônsān'yər/ ▶ **n.** (pl. **Mes·sei·gneurs** /,māsān'yər(z)/) a title or form of address used of or to a French-speaking prince, cardinal, archbishop, or bishop. [Fr., from *mon* 'my' + *seigneur* 'lord.']

Mon·sieur /mə'syœ(r); mə'syər/ ▶ **n.** (pl. **Mes·sieurs** /mə'syœ(r)(z); mā-; mə'syər(z)/) a title or form of address used of or to a French-speaking man, corresponding to *Mr.* or *sir*. [Fr., from *mon* 'my' + *sieur* 'lord.']

Mon·si·gnor /män'sēnyər; mən-/ ▶ **n.** (pl. **Mon·si·gno·ri** /,mänsēn'yôrē/) the title of various senior Roman Catholic positions, such as a prelate or an officer of the papal court. [Ital.]

mon·soon /män'so͞on; 'män,so͞on/ ▶ **n.** a seasonal prevailing wind in the region of the Indian subcontinent and Southeast Asia, blowing from the southwest between May and September and bringing rain (the **wet monsoon**), or from the northeast between October and April (the **dry monsoon**). ■ the rainy season accompanying the wet monsoon. — **mon·soon·al** /män'so͞onl/ adj. [16th C.: from Port. *monção*, from Arab. *mawsim* 'season,' from *wasama* 'to mark, brand.']

mons pu·bis /'mänz 'pyo͞obis/ ▶ **n.** (pl. **mon·tes p·ubis** /'mäntēz/) the rounded mass of fatty tissue lying over the joint of the pubic bones, in women typically more prominent and also called the **mons veneris**. [19th C.: L., 'mount of the pubes.']

mon·ster /'mänstər/ ▶ **n.** an imaginary creature that is typically large, ugly, and frightening. ■ an inhumanly cruel or wicked person. ■ often humorous a person, typically a child, who is rude or badly behaved. ■ a thing or animal that is excessively or dauntingly large. ■ a congenitally malformed or mutant animal or plant. ▶ **adj.** [attrib.] informal of an extraordinary and daunting size or extent. [ME: from OFr. *monstre*, from L. *monstrum* 'portent or monster,' from *monere* 'warn.']

mon·ster·a /'mänstərə/ ▶ **n.** a large tropical American climbing plant (genus *Monstera*) of the arum family that typically has divided or perforated leaves and corky aerial roots. Several kinds are cultivated as indoor plants when young. [mod. L., perh. from L. *monstrum* 'monster.']

mon·ster truck ▶ **n.** an extremely large pickup truck, typically with oversized tires. They are often raced across rough terrain or featured in exhibitions in which they drive over and demolish smaller automobiles.

mon·strance /'mänstrəns/ ▶ **n.** (in the Roman Catholic Church) an open or transparent receptacle in which the consecrated Host is exposed for veneration. [ME: from med. L. *monstrantia*, from L. *monstrare* 'to show.']

mon·stros·i·ty /män'sträsətē/ ▶ **n.** (pl. **-ties**) **1** something, esp. a building, that is very large and is considered unsightly. ■ something that is outrageously or offensively wrong. ■ a grossly malformed animal, plant, or person. **2** the state or fact of being monstrous.

mon·strous /'mänstrəs/ ▶ **adj.** having the ugly or frightening appearance of a monster. ■ (of a person or an action) inhumanly or outrageously evil or wrong. ■ extremely and dauntingly large. — **mon·strous·ly** adv. **mon·strous·ness** n.

mons ve·ne·ris /'mänz 'venərəs/ ▶ **n.** (pl. **mon·tes ve·ne·ris** /'mäntēz/) (in women) the mons pubis. [17th C.: L., 'mount of Venus.']

Mont. ▶ **abbr.** Montana.

mon·tage /män'täzH; mōn-; mōN-/ ▶ **n.** the process or technique of selecting, editing, and piecing together separate sections of film to form a continuous whole. ■ a sequence of film resulting from this. ■ the technique of producing a new composite whole from fragments of pictures, text, or music. [20th C.: Fr., from *monter* 'to mount.']

Mon·ta·gnais /,mäntən'yā/ ▶ **n.** (pl. same) **1** a member of an American Indian people living in a vast area of Canada from north of the Gulf of St. Lawrence to the southern shores of Hudson Bay. **2** the Algonquian language of this people, closely related to Cree. ▶ **adj.** of or relating to this people or their language. [from Fr., lit. 'of the mountains.']

Mon·ta·gnard /,mäntən'yärd/ ▶ **n. & adj.** former term for HMONG. [Fr., from *montagne* 'mountain.']

Mon·taigne /män'tān; môn'tenyə/, Michel Eyquem de (1533–92), French writer. He is regarded as the originator of the modern essay.

Mon·tan·a[1] /män'tanə/ a state in the western US, on the Canadian border, east of the Rocky Mountains; pop. 902,195; capital, Helena; statehood, Nov. 8, 1889 (41). It was acquired from France as part of the Louisiana Purchase in 1803. — **Mon·tan·an** adj. & n.

Mon·tan·a[2], Joe (1956–), US football player; full name *Joseph Clifford Montana, Jr.* He quarterbacked for the San Francisco 49ers and Kansas City Chiefs 1979–94.

mon·tane /män'tān; 'män,tān/ ▶ **adj.** [attrib.] of or inhabiting mountainous country. [19th C.: from L. *montanus*, from *mons, mont-* 'mountain.']

Mont Blanc /,môN 'bläNGk/ the highest mountain in the Alps, rising 15,771 feet (4,807 m).

Mont·calm /,mänt'käm/, Louis Joseph de Montcalm-Gozon, Marquis de (1712–59), French general. He defended Quebec, Canada, against the British, but was defeated and fatally wounded in the battle on the Plains of Abraham.

Mont Cer·vin /,môN sər'ven/ French name for MATTERHORN.

mon·te /'mäntē/ ▶ **n.** **1** short for THREE-CARD MONTE. **2** a Spanish game of chance, played with forty-five cards. [19th C.: Sp., lit. 'mountain,' also 'heap.']

Mon·te Al·bán /'môntā äl'bän/ an ancient city, now in ruins, in Oaxaca, southern Mexico.

Mon·te Car·lo /,mäntē 'kärlō/ a gambling resort in Monaco that forms one of the four communes of the principality; pop. 12,000.

Mon·te Car·lo meth·od ▶ **n.** Stat. a technique in which a large quantity of randomly generated numbers is studied using a probabilistic model to find an approximate solution to a numerical problem that would be difficult to solve by other methods.

Mon·te Cas·si·no /,mäntā kə'sēnō/ a hill in central Italy, the site of the principal monastery of the Benedictines, founded by St. Benedict *c.*529.

Mon·te Cer·vi·no /,mōntā cHər'vēnō/ Italian name for MATTERHORN.

Mon·te·go Bay /mən'tēgō/ a city on the northern coast of Jamaica; pop. 82,000.

Mon·te·ne·gro /,mäntə'negrō/ a mountainous, landlocked republic in the Balkans; pop. 632,000; capital, Podgorica. — **Mon·te·ne·grin** /-'negrən/ adj. & n.

Mon·te·rey cy·press ▶ **n.** a cypress tree (*Cupressus macrocarpa*) with a large spreading crown of horizontal branches and leaves that smell of lemon when crushed, native to a small area of California and widely planted in temperate climates.

Mon·te·rey Jack (also **Monterey cheese** or **Jack cheese**) ▶ **n.** a kind of cheese resembling cheddar. [from the name of *Monterey* County, California, where it was first made; the origin of *Jack* is unknown.]

Mon·ter·rey /,mäntə'rā/ a city in northeastern Mexico; pop. 2,522,000.

Mon·tes·quieu /,mänti'skyo͞o; mônte'skyœ/, Charles Louis de Secondat, Baron de La Brède et de (1689–1755), French philosopher. He wrote *L'Esprit des lois* (1748), a comparative study of political systems.

Mon·tes·so·ri[1] /,mäntə'sôrē/, Maria (1870–1952), Italian educator. She advocated a child-centered approach to education.

Mon·tes·so·ri[2] ▶ **n.** [usu. as adj.] a system of education for young children that seeks to develop natural interests and activities rather than use formal teaching methods.

Mon·te·ver·di /,mäntə'verdē; ,mônte-/, Claudio (1567–1643), Italian composer. He wrote the opera *Orfeo* (1607).

Mon·te·vi·de·o /,mäntəvi'dāō/ the capital of Uruguay, on the Plate River; pop. 1,360,000.

Mon·te·zu·ma II /,mänti'zo͞omə/ (1466–1520), Aztec emperor 1502–20. He was the last ruler of the Aztec empire in Mexico.

Mon·te·zu·ma's re·venge ▶ **n.** informal diarrhea suffered by travelers, esp. visitors to Mexico.

Mont·fort /ˈmäntfərt; môNˈfôr/, Simon de (*c.*1165–1218), French soldier. From 1209, he led the Albigensian Crusade in southern France.

Mont·gom·er·y[1] /məntˈgəm(ə)rē/ the capital of Alabama, in the central part of the state; pop. 201,568.

Mont·gom·er·y[2], Bernard Law, 1st Viscount Montgomery of Alamein (1887–1976), British field marshal; nicknamed **Monty**. He commanded the Allied ground forces in the invasion of Normandy in 1944 and accepted the German surrender on May 7, 1945.

Mont·gom·er·y[3], L. M. (1874–1942), Canadian writer; full name *Lucy Maud Montgomery*. She wrote *Anne of Green Gables* (1908).

month /mənTH/ ▶ **n.** (also **calendar month**) each of the twelve named periods into which a year is divided. ▪ a period of time between the same dates in successive calendar months. ▪ a period of 28 days or four weeks. ▪ a lunar month.
– PHRASES **a month of Sundays** informal a very long, seemingly endless period of time. [OE *mōnath*, of Gmc. origin; rel. to Ger. *Monat*, MOON.]

month·ly /ˈmənTHlē/ ▶ **adj.** [attrib.] done, produced, or occurring once a month. ▶ **adv.** once a month; every month; from month to month. ▶ **n.** (pl. **-lies**) **1** a magazine that is published once a month. **2** (**monthlies**) informal a menstrual period.

Mon·ti·cel·lo /ˌmäntəˈselō/ a historic estate southeast of Charlottesville, in central Virginia, the home of Thomas Jefferson.

mon·ti·cule /ˈmäntiˌkyo͞ol/ ▶ **n.** a small hill. ▪ a small mound caused by a volcanic eruption. [18th C.: from Fr., from late L. *monticulus*, dimin. of *mons, mont-* 'mountain.']

Mont·mar·tre /môNˈmärtrə/ a district in northern Paris, on a hill above the Seine River.

mont·mo·ril·lon·ite /ˌmäntməˈriləˌnīt/ ▶ **n.** an aluminum-rich clay mineral of the smectite group, containing sodium and magnesium. [19th C.: from *Montmorillon*, the name of a town in France, + -ITE[1].]

Mont·par·nasse /ˌmôNpärˈnäs/ a district of Paris, on the left bank of the Seine River.

Mont·pe·lier /mäntˈpēlyər/ the capital of Vermont, in the north central part of the state; pop. 8,035.

Mont·pel·lier /ˌmôNpelˈyā/ a city in southern France, near the Mediterranean coast; pop. 211,000.

Mon·tra·chet /ˌmōNträˈSHe/ ▶ **n.** a white wine produced in the Montrachet region of France.

Mont·re·al /ˌmäntrēˈôl/ a city on the St. Lawrence River in Quebec, southeastern Canada; pop. 1,016,376. Much of its population is French-speaking. French name **MONTRÉAL.**

Mont St. Mi·chel /ˈmôN saN mēˈSHel,/ a rocky islet off the coast of Normandy in northwestern France.

Mont·ser·rat /ˌmäntsəˈrät/ an island in the Caribbean, one of the Leeward Islands; pop. 12,000. — **Mont·ser·ra·ti·an** /-ˈrätēən/ **adj. & n.**.

mon·ty /ˈmäntē/ ▶ **n.** (in phrase **the full monty**) Brit., informal the full amount expected, desired, or possible: *they'll do the full monty for a few thousand each.* [perh. from *the full Montague Burton*, 'Sunday-best three-piece suit' (from the name of a tailor.)]

mon·u·ment /ˈmänyəmənt/ ▶ **n.** a statue, building, or other structure erected to commemorate a famous or notable person or event. ▪ a statue or other structure placed by or over a grave in memory of the dead. ▪ a building, structure, or site that is of historical importance or interest. ▪ fig. an outstanding, enduring, and memorable example of something. ▪ a marker, typically of concrete or stone, placed at the boundary of a piece of property. [ME: from L. *monumentum*, from *monere* 'remind.']

mon·u·men·tal /ˌmänyəˈmentl/ ▶ **adj.** great in importance, extent, or size. ▪ (of a work of art) great in ambition and scope. ▪ of or serving as a monument. — **mon·u·men·tal·ism n. mon·u·men·tal·i·ty** /ˌmänyəˌmenˈtalətē/ **n. mon·u·men·tal·ly adv.**

mon·u·men·tal·ize /ˌmänyəˈmentlˌīz/ ▶ **v.** [trans.] make a permanent record of (something) by or as if by creating a monument: *a culture that too eagerly monumentalizes what it values.*

-mony ▶ **suffix** forming nouns often denoting an action, state, or quality: *ceremony* | *harmony.* [from L. *-monia, -monium*.]

mon·zo·nite /ˈmänzəˌnīt/ ▶ **n.** Geol. a granular igneous rock with a composition intermediate between syenite and diorite, containing approximately equal amounts of orthoclase and plagioclase. — **mon·zo·nit·ic** /ˌmänzəˈnitik/ **adj.** [19th C.: named after Mount *Monzoni* in the Tyrol, Italy, + -ITE[1].]

moo /mo͞o/ ▶ **v.** (**moos, mooed**) [intrans.] make the characteristic deep vocal sound of a cow. ▶ **n.** (pl. **moos**) a sound of this kind. [16th C.: imitative.]

mooch /mo͞oCH/ ▶ **v.** informal **1** [trans.] ask for or obtain (something) without paying for it. **2** [intrans.] (**mooch around/about**) loiter in a bored or listless manner. ▶ **n.** (also **mooch·er**) a beggar or scrounger. [ME: prob. from Anglo-Norman Fr. *muscher* 'hide, skulk.']

moo-cow ▶ **n.** a child's name for a cow.

mood[1] /mo͞od/ ▶ **n.** a temporary state of mind or feeling. ▪ an angry, irritable, or sullen state of mind. ▪ the atmosphere or pervading tone of something, esp. a work of art. ▶ **adj.** [attrib.] (esp. of music) inducing or suggestive of a particular feeling or state of mind. [OE *mōd*, of Gmc. origin; rel. to Ger. *Mut*.]

mood[2] ▶ **n. 1** Gram. a category of verb use, typically expressing fact (indicative mood), command (imperative mood), question (interrogative mood), wish (optative mood), or conditionality (subjunctive mood). ▪ a form or set of forms of a verb in an inflected language such as French, Latin, or Greek, serving to indicate whether it expresses fact, command, wish, or conditionality. **2** Logic any of the valid forms into which each of the figures of a categorical syllogism may occur. [16th C.: var. of **MODE**, influenced by **MOOD**[1].]

mood-al·ter·ing ▶ **adj.** (of a drug) capable of inducing changes of mood.

Moo·dy /ˈmo͞odē/, William Henry (1853–1917), US Supreme Court associate justice 1906–10.

mood·y /ˈmo͞odē/ ▶ **adj.** (**mood·i·er, mood·i·est**) (of a person) given to unpredictable changes of mood, esp. sudden bouts of gloominess or sullenness. ▪ giving an impression of melancholy or mystery. — **mood·i·ly adv. mood·i·ness n.**

moo goo gai pan /ˈmo͞o ˈgo͞o ˈgī ˈpan/ ▶ **n.** a Cantonese dish consisting of chicken sautéed with mushrooms, vegetables, and spices. [from Chin., lit. 'mushroom chicken slice.']

moo·la /ˈmo͞oˌlä/ (also **moo·lah**) ▶ **n.** informal money. [1930s: origin unknown.]

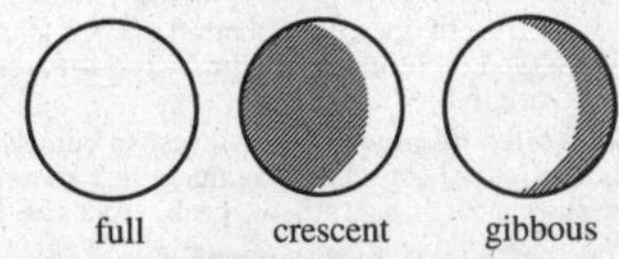

phases of the moon

moon /mo͞on/ ▶ **n.** (also **Moon**) the natural satellite of the earth, visible (chiefly at night) by reflected light from the sun. ▪ a natural satellite of any planet. ▪ (**the moon**) fig. anything that one could desire. ▪ a month, esp. a lunar month. ▶ **v. 1** [intrans.] behave or move in a listless and aimless manner. ▪ act in a dreamily infatuated manner. **2** [trans.] informal expose one's buttocks to someone in order to insult or amuse them.
– PHRASES **over the moon** informal extremely happy; delighted. — **moon·less adj. moon·like adj.** [OE *mōna*, of Gmc. origin; rel. to Du. *maan* and Ger. *Mond*, also to **MONTH**.]

moon·beam /ˈmo͞onˌbēm/ ▶ **n.** a ray of moonlight.

moon blind·ness ▶ **n.** (in horses) a recurrent inflammatory eye disease, causing intermittent blindness. — **moon-blind adj.**

moon bug·gy ▶ **n.** informal term for **LUNAR ROVING VEHICLE.**

moon·calf /ˈmo͞onˌkaf/ ▶ **n.** (pl. **-calves**) a foolish person.

moon child ▶ **n.** a person born under the astrological sign of Cancer.

moon dog (also **moon·dog**) ▶ **n.** informal term for **PARASELENE.**

moon-faced ▶ **adj.** having a round face.

moon·fish /ˈmo͞onˌfiSH/ ▶ **n.** (pl. same or **-fish·es**) a deep-bodied laterally compressed marine fish, in particular: ▪ a silvery fish of the jack family, including *Selene setapinnis* of the Atlantic. ▪ an opah.

moon·flow·er /ˈmo͞onˌflouər/ ▶ **n.** a tropical American climbing plant (*Ipomoea alba*) of the morning glory family, with large, sweet-smelling white flowers that open at dusk and close at midday.

moon gate (also **moon·gate**) ▶ **n.** (in China) a circular gateway in a wall.

Moon·ie /ˈmo͞onē/ ▶ **n.** informal, often derog. a member of the Unification Church. [1970s: from the name of its founder, Sun Myung *Moon*.]

moon·let /ˈmo͞onlət/ ▶ **n.** a small moon. ▪ an artificial satellite.

moon·light /ˈmo͞onˌlīt/ ▶ **n.** the light of the moon. ▶ **adj.** [attrib.] illuminated or happening by the light of the moon. ▶ **v.** (past and past part. **-light·ed**) [intrans.] informal have a second job in addition to one's regular employment. — **moon·light·er n.**

moon·lit /ˈmo͞onˌlit/ ▶ **adj.** lit by the moon.

moon·quake /ˈmo͞onˌkwāk/ ▶ **n.** a tremor of the moon's surface.

moon·rise /ˈmo͞onˌrīz/ ▶ **n.** [in sing.] the rising of the moon above the horizon. ▪ the time of this.

moon·roof /ˈmo͞onˌro͞of; -ˌro͝of/ ▶ **n.** a transparent section of the roof of an automobile, typically tinted and able to be opened.

moon·scape /ˈmo͞onˌskāp/ ▶ **n.** a landscape having features characteristic of the surface of the moon, esp. in being rocky and barren. ▪ the landscape of the moon.

moon·seed /ˈmo͞onˌsēd/ ▶ **n.** a North American climbing plant (genus *Menispermum*, family Menispermaceae) with crescent-shaped seeds.

moon·set /ˈmo͞onˌset/ ▶ **n.** [in sing.] the setting of the moon below the horizon. ▪ the time of this: *we left before moonset in the morning.*

moon-shaped ▶ **adj. 1** crescent-shaped. **2** round.

moon·shine /ˈmo͞onˌSHīn/ ▶ **n. 1** informal illicitly distilled or smuggled liquor. **2** foolish talk or ideas: *whatever I said, it was moonshine.* **3** another term for **MOONLIGHT.** — **moon·shin·er n.**

moon shot (also **moon·shot**) ▶ **n.** the launching of a spacecraft to the moon. ▪ fig. a difficult or expensive task, the outcome of which is expected to have great significance.

moon·stone /ˈmo͞onˌstōn/ ▶ **n.** a pearly white semiprecious stone consisting of alkali feldspar.

PRONUNCIATION KEY ə *ago, up*; ər *over, fur*; a *hat*; ā *ate*; ä *car*; e *let*; ē *see*; i *fit*; ī *by*; NG *sing*; ō *go*; ô *law, for*; oi *toy*; o͝o *good*; o͞o *goo*; ou *out*; TH *thin*; T͟H *then*; ZH *vision*

moon·struck /'mo͞on,strək/ ▶ **adj.** unable to think or act normally, esp. because of being in love.

moon·walk /'mo͞on,wôk/ ▶ **n.** **1** an act of walking on the surface of the moon. **2** a dance step with a gliding motion, appearing as a forward step but in fact moving the dancer backward, resembling the characteristic weightless movement of walking on the moon. ▶ **v.** [intrans.] **1** walk on the surface of the moon. **2** dance a moonwalk. — **moon·walk·er n.**

moon·wort /'mo͞on,wərt; -,wôrt/ ▶ **n.** a widely distributed fern (genus *Botrychium*, family Ophioglossaceae) with a single small frond of fan-shaped lobes and a separate spike bearing the spore-producing organs, growing typically in grassy uplands and old meadows.

moon·y /'mo͞onē/ ▶ **adj.** (**moon·i·er, moon·i·est**) **1** dreamy and unaware of one's surroundings, for example because one is in love. **2** of or like the moon.

Moor /mo͝or/ ▶ **n.** a member of a northwestern African Muslim people of mixed Berber and Arab descent. In the 8th century they conquered the Iberian peninsula, but were finally driven out of their last stronghold in Granada at the end of the 15th century. — **Moor·ish adj.** [from OFr. *More*, via L. from Gk. *Mauros* 'inhabitant of Mauretania.']

moor[1] /mo͝or/ ▶ **n.** a tract of open uncultivated upland; a heath. ■ a tract of such land preserved for hunting. ■ a fen. — **moor·ish adj. moor·y adj.** [OE *mōr*, of Gmc. origin.]

moor[2] ▶ **v.** [trans.] (often **be moored**) make fast (a vessel) to the shore or to an anchor. ■ [intrans.] (of a boat) be made fast somewhere in this way. — **moor·age** /'mo͝orij/ **n.** [15th C.: prob. from the Gmc. base of Du. *meren*.]

moor·cock /'mo͝or,käk/ ▶ **n.** Brit. a male red grouse.

Moore[1] /mo͝or/, Alfred (1755–1810), US Supreme Court associate justice 1799–1804.

Moore[2], Clement Clarke (1779–1863), US writer. The poem "A Visit from St. Nicholas" (1922) is attributed to him.

Moore[3], Henry Spencer (1898–1986), English sculptor. His work is characterized by semiabstract reclining forms, large upright figures, and family groups, which he intended to be viewed in the open air.

Moore[4], Marianne Craig (1887–1972), US poet. Her work is collected in *The Complete Poems of Marianne Moore* (1967).

Moore[5], Thomas (1779–1852), Irish poet. He wrote patriotic and nostalgic songs set to Irish tunes.

moor·fowl /'mo͝or,foul/ ▶ **n.** (pl. same) Brit. another term for RED GROUSE.

moor·hen /'mo͝or,hen/ ▶ **n.** **1** a small aquatic rail with mainly blackish plumage, esp. the common gallinule (*Gallinula chloropus*), with a red and yellow bill. **2** Brit. a female red grouse.

moor·ing /'mo͝oriNG/ ▶ **n.** (often **moorings**) a place where a boat or ship is moored. ■ the ropes, chains, or anchors by or to which a boat, ship, or buoy is moored. ■ fig. the ideas, beliefs, or habits to which one is accustomed and from which one gains security or stability.

moor·land /'mo͝orlənd; -,land/ ▶ **n.** (also **moorlands**) an extensive area of moor.

moose /mo͞os/ ▶ **n.** (pl. same) a large deer (*Alces alces*) with palmate antlers, a sloping back, and a growth of skin hanging from the neck. It is native to northern Eurasia and northern North America. Called ELK in Britain. [17th C.: from an Eastern Algonquian language; compare Narragansett *moòs*.]

moose

Moose·head Lake /'mo͞os,hed/ the largest lake in Maine, in the west central part of the state.

moose pas·ture ▶ **n.** Canadian land of no value.

moo shu pork /'mo͞o 'SHo͞o/ ▶ **n.** a Chinese dish consisting of shredded pork with vegetables and seasonings, rolled in thin pancakes.

moot /mo͞ot/ ▶ **adj.** subject to debate, dispute, or uncertainty, and typically not admitting of a final decision. ■ having no practical significance, typically because the subject is too uncertain to allow a decision. ▶ **v.** [trans.] (usu. **be mooted**) raise (a question or topic) for discussion; suggest (an idea or possibility). [OE *mōt* 'assembly or meeting,' of Gmc. origin.]

moot court ▶ **n.** a mock court at which law students argue imaginary cases for practice.

mop /mäp/ ▶ **n.** an implement consisting of a sponge or a bundle of thick loose strings attached to a handle, used for wiping floors or other surfaces. ■ a thick mass of disordered hair. ■ [in sing.] an act of wiping something clean, esp. a floor. ▶ **v.** (**mopped, mop·ping**) [trans.] clean or soak up liquid by wiping. ■ [trans.] wipe (something) away from a surface. ■ wipe sweat or tears from (one's face or eyes).
– PHRASAL VERBS **mop up** informal finish a task. **mop something up** informal put an end to or dispose of something. — **mop·py adj.** [15th C.: perh. ult. rel. to L. *mappa* 'napkin.']

mop·board /'mäp,bôrd/ ▶ **n.** another term for BASEBOARD.

mope /mōp/ ▶ **v.** [intrans.] be dejected and apathetic. ■ (**mope around/about**) wander around listlessly and aimlessly because of unhappiness or boredom. ▶ **n.** a person given to prolonged spells of low spirits. ■ (**mopes**) dated low spirits; depression. — **mop·er n. mop·ey** (also **mop·y**) **adj. mop·i·ly** /'mōpəlē/ **adv. mop·i·ness** /'mōpēnis/ **n. mop·ish adj.** [16th C.: perh. of Scand. origin; cf. Swed. dial. *mopa* 'to sulk.']

mo·ped /'mō,ped/ ▶ **n.** a low-power, lightweight motorized bicycle. [1950s: from Swed., from *(trampcykel med) mo(tor och) ped(aler)* 'pedal cycle with motor and pedals.']

mop·er·y /'mōpərē/ ▶ **n.** **1** informal the action of committing a minor or petty offense such as loitering. **2** feelings of apathy and dejection.

mop·pet /'mäpət/ ▶ **n.** informal a small endearingly sweet child. [17th C.: from obs. *moppe* 'baby or rag doll' + -ET[1].]

MOR ▶ **abbr.** (of music) middle-of-the-road.

mor /môr/ ▶ **n.** Soil Science humus formed under acid conditions. [1930s: from Dan.]

mo·raine /mə'rān/ ▶ **n.** Geol. a mass of rocks and sediment deposited by a glacier, typically as ridges at its edges or extremity. — **mo·rain·al** /-'rānl/ **adj. mo·rain·ic** /-'rānik/ **adj.** [18th C.: from Fr., from Ital. dialect *morena*, from Fr. dial. *morre* 'snout'; rel. to MORION[1].]

mor·al /'môrəl; 'mär-/ ▶ **adj.** concerned with the principles of right and wrong behavior and the goodness or badness of human character. ■ concerned with or adhering to the code of interpersonal behavior that is considered right or acceptable in a particular society. ■ holding or manifesting high principles for proper conduct. ■ derived from or based on ethical principles or a sense of these. ■ [attrib.] examining the nature of ethics and the foundations of good and bad character and conduct. ▶ **n.** **1** a lesson, esp. one concerning what is right or prudent, that can be derived from a story, a piece of information, or an experience. **2** (**morals**) a person's standards of behavior or beliefs concerning what is and is not acceptable for them to do. ■ standards of behavior that are considered good or acceptable. [ME: from L. *moralis*, from *mos, mor-* 'custom,' (pl.) *mores* 'morals.']

mo·rale /mə'ral/ ▶ **n.** the confidence, enthusiasm, and discipline of a person or group at a particular time. [18th C.: from Fr. *moral*.]

mor·al haz·ard ▶ **n.** Econ. lack of incentive to guard against risk where one is protected from its consequences, e.g., by insurance.

mor·al·ism /'môrə,lizəm; 'mär-/ ▶ **n.** the practice of moralizing, esp. showing a tendency to make judgments about others' morality.

mor·al·ist /'môrəlist; 'mär-/ ▶ **n.** a person who teaches or promotes morality. ■ a person given to moralizing. ■ a person who behaves in a morally commendable way. — **mor·al·is·tic** /,môrə'listik; ,mär-/ **adj. mor·al·is·ti·cal·ly** /,môrə'listik(ə)lē; ,mär-/ **adv.**

mo·ral·i·ty /mə'ralətē; mô-/ ▶ **n.** (pl. **-ties**) principles concerning the distinction between right and wrong or good and bad behavior. ■ behavior as it is affected by the observation of these principles. ■ a particular system of values and principles of conduct, esp. one held by a specified person or society. ■ the extent to which an action is right or wrong. ■ behavior or qualities judged to be good.

mo·ral·i·ty play ▶ **n.** a kind of drama with personified abstract qualities as the main characters and presenting a lesson about good conduct and character, popular in the 15th and early 16th centuries.

mor·al·ize /'môrə,līz; 'mär-/ ▶ **v.** [intrans.] [often as n.] (**moralizing**) comment on issues of right and wrong, typically with an unfounded air of superiority. ■ [trans.] interpret or explain as giving lessons on good and bad character and conduct. ■ [trans.] reform the character and conduct of. — **mor·al·i·za·tion** /,môrələ'zāSHən; ,mär-/ **n. mor·al·iz·er n. mor·al·iz·ing·ly adv.**

mor·al law ▶ **n.** (in some systems of ethics) an absolute principle defining the criteria of right action (whether conceived as a divine ordinance or a truth of reason).

mor·al·ly /'môrəlē; 'mär-/ ▶ **adv.** **1** in relation to standards of good and bad character or conduct. ■ in a way that conforms to standards of good behavior. **2** [usu. as submodifier] on the basis of strong though not irresistible evidence or probability, esp. regarding a person's character: *I am morally certain that he is incapable of deliberately harming anyone.*

Mor·al Ma·jor·i·ty ▶ **n.** a political action group formed in the 1970s to further a conservative and religious agenda, including the allowance of prayer in schools and strict laws against abortion. ■ (**moral majority**) [treated as pl.] the majority of people, regarded as favoring firm moral standards.

mor·al phi·los·o·phy ▶ **n.** the branch of philosophy concerned with ethics.

Mor·ar, Loch /'môrər, läk/ a lake in western Scotland. At 1,017 feet (310 m), it is Scotland's deepest lake.

mo·rass /mə'ras; mô-/ ▶ **n.** an area of muddy or boggy ground. ■ fig. a complicated or confused situation. [15th C.: from MDu. *marasch*, from OFr. *marais* 'marsh,' from med. L. *mariscus*.]

mor·a·to·ri·um /,môrə'tôrēəm; ,mär-/ ▶ **n.** (pl. **-to·ri·ums** or **-to·ri·a** /-'tôrēə/) a temporary prohibition of an activity. ■ Law a legal authorization to debtors to postpone payment. ■ Law the period of this postponement. [19th C.: from late L. *moratorius* 'delaying,' from L. *morat-* 'delayed,' from the v. *morari*, from *mora* 'delay.']

Mo·ra·vi·a /mə'rāvēə/ a region of the Czech Republic, located between Bohemia on the west and the Carpathians on the east; chief town, Brno.

Mo·ra·vi·an /mə'rāvēən/ ▶n. a native of Moravia. ■ a member of a Protestant Church founded in Saxony by emigrants from Moravia holding views derived from the Hussites and accepting the Bible as the only source of faith. ▶adj. of or relating to Moravia or its people. ■ of or relating to the Moravian Church.

mo·ray /'môr,ā; mə'rā/ (also **moray eel**) ▶n. a mainly nocturnal eellike predatory fish (family Muraenidae) of warm seas that typically hides in crevices with just the head protruding. [17th C.: from Port. *moréia*, via L. from Gk. *muraina*.]

Mor·ay Firth a deep inlet of the North Sea on the northeastern coast of Scotland.

mor·bid /'môrbəd/ ▶adj. **1** characterized by or appealing to an abnormal and unhealthy interest in disturbing and unpleasant subjects, esp. death and disease. **2** Med. of the nature of or indicative of disease. — **mor·bid·i·ty** /môr'bidətē/ n. **mor·bid·ly** adv. **mor·bid·ness** n. [17th C. (in the medical sense): from L. *morbidus*, from *morbus* 'disease.']

mor·bil·li /môr'bil,ī/ ▶plural n. technical term for MEASLES. [16th C.: L., pl. of *morbillus* 'pustule,' from *morbus* 'disease.']

mor·bil·li·vi·rus /môr'bilə,vīrəs/ ▶n. Med. any of a group of paramyxoviruses that cause measles, rinderpest, and canine distemper.

mor·ceau /môr'sō/ ▶n. (pl. **-ceaux** /-'sō(z)/) a short literary or musical composition. [18th C.: Fr., lit. 'morsel, piece.']

mor·da·cious /môr'dāshəs/ ▶adj. formal **1** denoting or using biting sarcasm or invective. **2** (of a person or animal) given to biting. [17th C.: from L. *mordax*, *mordac-* 'biting' + -IOUS.]

mor·dant /'môrdnt/ ▶adj. (esp. of humor) having or showing a sharp or critical quality; biting. ▶n. a substance, typically an inorganic oxide, that combines with a dye or stain and thereby fixes it in a material. ■ an adhesive compound for fixing gold leaf. ■ a corrosive liquid used to etch the lines on a printing plate. ▶v. [trans.] impregnate or treat (a fabric) with a mordant. — **mor·dan·cy** /-dnsē/ n. **mor·dant·ly** adv. [15th C.: from Fr., pres. part. of *mordre* 'to bite,' from L. *mordere*.]

mor·dent /'môrdnt/ ▶n. Music an ornament consisting of one rapid alternation of a written note with the note immediately below or above it in the scale (sometimes further distinguished as **lower mordent** and **upper mordent**). The term **inverted mordent** usually refers to the **upper mordent**. [19th C.: via Ger. from Ital. *mordente*, pres. part. of *mordere* 'to bite.']

Mor·dred /'môrdrəd/ (in Arthurian legend) the nephew of King Arthur who abducted Guinevere and raised a rebellion against Arthur.

Mord·vin·i·a /môrd'vinēə/ an autonomous republic in Russia, southeast of Nizhni Novgorod; pop. 964,000; capital, Saransk.

More /môr/, Sir Thomas (1478–1535), English scholar; canonized as **St. Thomas More**. His *Utopia* (1516), which described an ideal city-state, established him as a leading humanist of the Renaissance.

more /môr/ ▶adj. & pron. comparative of MANY, MUCH. a greater or additional amount or degree: [as adj.] *I poured myself more coffee* | [as pron.] *tell me more.* ▶adv. **1** comparative of MUCH. forming the comparative of adjectives and adverbs, esp. those of more than one syllable: *for them, enthusiasm is more important than talent.* **2** to a greater extent: *I like chicken more than turkey.* ■ (**more than**) extremely (used before an adjective conveying a positive feeling or attitude): *she is more than happy to oblige.* **3** again: *repeat once more.* **4** moreover: *he was rich, and more, he was handsome.*
– PHRASES **more like it** see LIKE[1]. **more or less** speaking imprecisely; to a certain extent: *they are more or less a waste of time.* ■ approximately: *more or less symmetrical.* **no more 1** nothing further. **2** no further: *you must have some soup, but no more wine.* **3** (**be no more**) exist no longer. **4** never again: *mention his name no more to me.* **5** neither. [OE *māra*, of Gmc. origin; rel. to Du. *meer* and Ger. *mehr*.]

mo·rel /mə'rel; mô-/ ▶n. a widely distributed edible fungus (genus *Morchella*, family Morchellaceae) that has a brown oval or pointed fruiting body with an irregular honeycombed surface bearing the spores. [17th C.: from Fr. *morille*, from Du. *morilje*; rel. to Ger. *Morchel* 'fungus.']

Mo·re·li·a /mə'rālyə/ a city in central Mexico, capital of the state of Michoacán; pop. 490,000.

mo·rel·lo /mə'relō/ ▶n. (pl. **-los**) a dark cherry of a sour kind used in cooking. [17th C.: from Ital. *morello* 'blackish,' from med. L. *morellus*, dimin. of L. *Maurus* 'Moor.']

Mo·re·los /mə'rāləs/ a state in central Mexico, west of Mexico City; capital, Cuernavaca.

Mo·re·no Val·ley /mə'rānō/ a city in southwestern California; pop. 118,779.

more·o·ver /môr'ōvər/ ▶adv. as a further matter; besides: *moreover, glass is electrically insulating.*

mo·res /'môr,āz/ ▶plural n. the essential or characteristic customs and conventions of a community: *an offense against social mores.* [19th C.: from L., pl. of *mos*, *mor-* 'custom.']

Mo·resque /mə'resk/ ▶adj. (of art or architecture) Moorish in style or design. [ME: from Fr., from Ital. *moresco*, from *Moro* 'Moor.']

Mor·gan[1] /'môrgən/, J. P. (1837–1913), US financier, philanthropist, and art collector; full name *John Pierpont Morgan*. He created General Electric in 1892 and the US Steel Corporation in 1901. He left his art collection to New York City's Museum of Modern Art.

Mor·gan[2], Thomas Hunt (1866–1945), US zoologist. He was a pioneer in the study of genetics. Nobel Prize for Physiology or Medicine (1933).

Mor·gan[3] ▶n. a horse of a light thickset breed developed in New England. [19th C.: named after Justin *Morgan* (1747–98), US teacher and owner of the original sire of the breed.]

mor·ga·nat·ic /,môrgə'natik/ ▶adj. of or denoting a marriage in which neither the spouse of lower rank nor any children have any claim to the possessions or title of the spouse of higher rank. — **mor·ga·nat·i·cal·ly** adv. [18th C.: from mod. L. *morganaticus*, from med. L. *matrimonium ad morganaticam* 'marriage with a morning gift.']

mor·gan·ite /'môrgə,nīt/ ▶n. a pink transparent variety of beryl, used as a gemstone. [20th C.: from the name of J. P. *Morgan* (see MORGAN[1]) + -ITE[1].]

Mor·gan le Fay /'môrgən lə 'fā/ (in Arthurian legend) an enchantress, sister of King Arthur.

mor·gen /'môrgən/ ▶n. a measure of land, in particular: ■ (in the Netherlands, South Africa, and parts of the US) a measure of land equal to about 0.8 hectare or two acres. ■ (in Norway, Denmark, and Germany) a measure of land now equal to about 0.3 hectare or two thirds of an acre. [17th C.: from Du., or from Ger. *Morgen* 'morning.']

morgue /môrg/ ▶n. **1** a place where bodies are kept, esp. to be identified or claimed. ■ used metaphorically to refer to a place that is quiet, gloomy, or cold. **2** informal in a newspaper office, a collection of old cuttings, photographs, and information. [19th C.: from Fr., orig. the name of a building in Paris.]

mor·i·bund /'môrə,bənd; 'mär-/ ▶adj. (of a person) at the point of death. ■ (of a thing) in terminal decline; lacking vitality or vigor. — **mor·i·bun·di·ty** /,môrə'bəndətē; ,mär-/ n. [18th C.: from L. *moribundus*, from *mori* 'to die.']

mo·ri·on[1] /'môrēən/ ▶n. a kind of helmet without beaver or visor, worn by soldiers in the 16th and 17th centuries. [Fr., from Sp. *morrión*, from *morro* 'round object.']

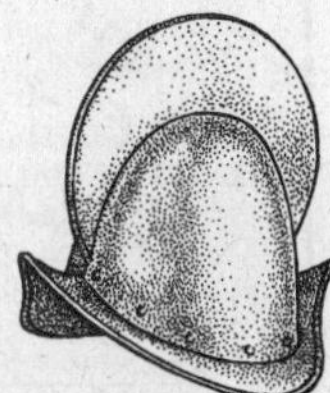
morion[1]

mo·ri·on[2] ▶n. a brown or black variety of quartz. [18th C.: from Fr., from L. *morion*, a misreading (in Pliny) for *mormorion*.]

Mo·ris·co /mə'riskō/ ▶n. (pl. **-cos** or **-coes**) hist. a Moor in Spain, esp. one who had accepted Christian baptism. [Sp., from *Moro* 'Moor.']

Mor·i·son /'môrəsən; 'mär-/, Samuel Eliot (1887–1976), US historian and naval officer. He wrote *The Oxford History of the United States* (1927).

Mo·ri·sot /môrē'sō; -'zō/, Berthe Marie Pauline (1841–95), French painter. Her works depicted women and children and waterside scenes.

Mor·ley /'môrlē/, Edward Williams (1838–1923), US chemist. In 1887, he collaborated with Albert Michelson in an experiment to determine the speed of light.

Mor·mon /'môrmən/ ▶n. a member of the Church of Jesus Christ of Latter-Day Saints, a religion founded in the US in 1830 by Joseph Smith, Jr. ▶adj. of or relating to the Church of Jesus Christ of Latter-Day Saints: *the leader of a Mormon congregation.* — **Mor·mon·ism** n. [the name of a prophet to whom Smith attributed *The Book of Mormon*.]

morn /môrn/ ▶n. literary term for MORNING. [OE *morgen*, of Gmc. origin.]

mor·nay /môr'nā/ (also **Mor·nay**) ▶adj. denoting or served in a cheese-flavored white sauce: *mornay sauce* | [postpositive] *cauliflower mornay.* [named after *Mornay*, the Fr. cook and son of Joseph Voiron, chef and inventor of the sauce.]

morn·ing /'môrniNG/ ▶n. the period of time between midnight and noon, esp. from sunrise to noon. ■ this time on a particular day, characterized by a specified type of activity or particular weather conditions. ■ sunrise. ▶adv. (**mornings**) informal every morning. ▶exclam. informal short for GOOD MORNING.
– PHRASES **morning, noon, and night** all the time. [ME: from MORN, on the pattern of *evening*.]

morn·ing af·ter ▶n. informal a morning on which a person has a hangover. ■ a hangover. ■ an unpleasant aftermath of imprudent behavior.

morn·ing-af·ter pill ▶n. a contraceptive pill that is effective within about thirty-six hours after intercourse.

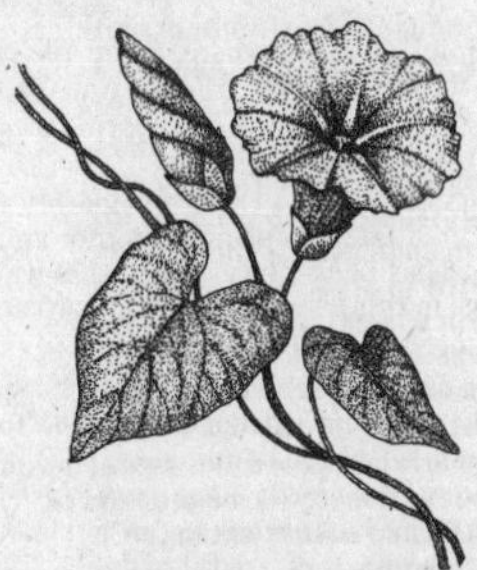
common morning glory

morn·ing glo·ry ▶n. a climbing plant (genus *Ipomoea*, family Convolvulaceae) often cultivated for its showy trumpet-shaped flowers, which typically open in the early morning and wither by midday. Its several species include the **common morning glory** (*I. purpurea*).

morn·ing prayer ▶n. (usu. **morning prayers**) a formal act of worship held in the morning, esp. regularly or by a group assembled for this purpose. ■ [in sing.] (in the Anglican Church) the service of matins.

morn·ing sick·ness ▶n. nausea in pregnancy, typically occurring in the first few months. Despite its name, the nausea can affect pregnant women at any time of day.

morn·ing star ▶n. **1** (**the morning star**) a bright planet, esp. Venus, when visible in the east before sunrise. **2** hist. a club with a heavy spiked head, sometimes attached to the handle by a chain.

Mo·ro /ˈmôrō/ ▶n. (pl. **-ros**) a Muslim inhabitant of the Philippines. [Sp., lit. 'Moor.']

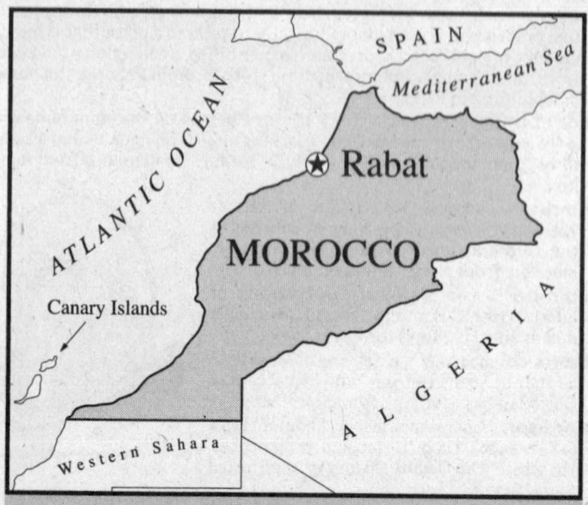

Morocco

Official name: Kingdom of Morocco
Location: northwestern Africa, with coastlines on the Mediterranean Sea and Atlantic Ocean
Area: 172,500 square miles (446,600 sq km)
Population: 32,209,000
Capital: Rabat
Languages: Arabic (official), Berber dialects, French
Currency: Moroccan dirham

Mo·roc·co /məˈräkō/ a country in northwestern Africa. *See box.* — **Mo·roc·can** /-ˈräkən/ adj. & n.

mo·roc·co /məˈräkō/ ▶n. (pl. **-cos**) fine flexible leather made (originally in Morocco) from goatskin tanned with sumac, used esp. for book covers and shoes.

Mo·rón /məˈrōn/ a city in eastern Argentina; pop. 642,000.

mo·ron /ˈmôr,än/ ▶n. informal a stupid person. — **mo·ron·ic** /məˈränik; mô-/ adj. **mo·ron·i·cal·ly** /məˈränik(ə)lē; mô-/ adv. [20th C.: from Gk. *mōron*, neut. of *mōros* 'foolish.']

Mo·ro·ni /məˈrōnē; mô-/ the capital of Comoros, on the island of Grande Comore; pop. 22,000.

mo·rose /məˈrōs; mô-/ ▶adj. sullen and ill-tempered. — **mo·rose·ly** adv. **mo·rose·ness** n. [16th C.: from L. *morosus* 'peevish,' from *mos, mor-* 'manner.']

morph[1] /môrf/ ▶n. an actual linguistic form: *the present participle in English is always the morph "-ing."* [1940s: from Gk. *morphē* 'form.']

morph[2] ▶n. Biol. each of several variant forms of an animal or plant. [1950s: from Gk. *morphē* 'form.']

morph[3] ▶v. change or cause to change smoothly from one image to another by small gradual steps using computer animation techniques. ▶n. an image that has been processed in this way. ■ an instance of changing an image in this way. [1990s: element from METAMORPHOSIS.]

morph. ▶abbr. ■ morphological or morphology.

-morph ▶comb. form denoting something having a specified form or character: *endomorph | polymorph.* [from Gk. *morphē* 'form.']

mor·phal·lax·is /,môrfəˈlaksəs/ ▶n. Zool. regeneration by the transformation of existing body tissues. — **mor·phal·lac·tic** /-ˈlaktik/ adj. [19th C.: from Gk. *morphē* 'form' + *allaxis* 'exchange.']

mor·pheme /ˈmôr,fēm/ ▶n. Ling. a meaningful morphological unit of a language that cannot be further divided (e.g., *in, come, -ing,* forming *incoming*). ■ a morphological element considered with respect to its functional relations in a linguistic system. — **mor·phe·mic** /môrˈfēmik/ adj. **mor·phe·mi·cal·ly** /môrˈfēmik(ə)lē/ adv. [19th C.: from Fr. *morphème*, from Gk. *morphē* 'form.']

mor·phe·mics /môrˈfēmiks/ ▶plural n. [treated as sing.] Ling. the study of word structure in terms of minimal meaningful units.

Mor·phe·us /ˈmôrfēəs; ˈmôr,f(y)o͞os/ Rom. Mythol. the son of Somnus (god of sleep), the god of dreams and, in later writings, also god of sleep.

mor·phi·a /ˈmôrfēə/ ▶n. old-fashioned term for MORPHINE.

mor·phine /ˈmôr,fēn/ ▶n. an analgesic and narcotic drug, $C_{17}H_{19}NO_3$, obtained from opium and used medicinally to relieve pain. [19th C.: from Ger. *Morphin*, from MORPHEUS).]

mor·phin·ism /ˈmôrfə,nizəm/ ▶n. Med. dependence on or addiction to morphine.

mor·pho·gen /ˈmôrfəjən/ ▶n. Biol. a chemical agent able to cause or determine morphogenesis.

mor·pho·gen·e·sis /,môrfəˈjenəsəs/ ▶n. **1** Biol. the origin and development of morphological characteristics. **2** Geol. the formation of landforms or other structures. — **mor·pho·ge·net·ic** /-jəˈnetik/ adj. **mor·pho·gen·ic** /-ˈjenik/ adj. [19th C.: mod. L., from Gk. *morphē* 'form' + GENESIS.]

mor·phol·o·gy /môrˈfäləjē/ ▶n. (pl. **-gies**) the study of the forms of things, in particular: ■ Biol. the branch of biology that deals with the form of living organisms, and with relationships between their structures. ■ Ling. the study of word forms. — **mor·pho·log·ic** /,môrfəˈläjik/ adj. **mor·pho·log·i·cal** /,môrfəˈläjikəl/ adj. **mor·pho·log·i·cal·ly** /,môrfəˈläjik(ə)lē/ adv. **mor·phol·o·gist** /-jist/ n. [19th C.: from Gk. *morphē* 'form' + -LOGY.]

mor·pho·met·rics /,môrfəˈmetriks/ ▶plural n. [usu. treated as sing.] esp. Biol. morphometry, esp. of living organisms.

mor·phom·e·try /môrˈfämətrē/ ▶n. the process of measuring the external shape and dimensions of landforms, living organisms, or other objects. — **mor·pho·met·ric** /,môrfəˈmetrik/ adj. **mor·pho·met·ri·cal·ly** /,môrfəˈmetrik(ə)lē/ adv.

Morris[1] /ˈmôris; ˈmär-/, Desmond John (1928–), British zoologist and writer. He wrote *The Naked Ape* (1967).

Morris[2], Gouverneur (1752–1816), US politician. An active proponent of American independence, he represented New York as a member of the Continental Congress 1777–79, at the Constitutional Convention 1787, and in the US Senate 1800–03.

Morris[3], Robert (1734–1806), US politician and financier. He represented Pennsylvania at the Continental Congress 1775–78 and signed the Declaration of Independence in 1776.

Mor·ris[4], William (1834–96), English craftsman. He was a leading figure in the Arts and Crafts Movement.

Mor·ris chair ▶n. a type of armchair with open padded arms and an adjustable back. [19th C.: named after William *Morris* (see MORRIS[4]).]

Mor·ri·son /ˈmôrisən; ˈmär-/, Toni (1931–), US writer; born *Chloe Anthony Wofford*. Her novels, such as *Beloved* (1987), depict the black American experience. Nobel Prize for Literature (1993).

mor·row /ˈmôrō; ˈmärō/ ▶n. (**the morrow**) archaic literary the following day. ■ the time following an event. ■ the near future. [ME *morwe*, from OE *morgen* (see MORN).]

Morse code /môrs/ ▶n. an alphabet or code in which letters are represented by combinations of long and short signals of light or sound. ▶v. [trans.] signal (something) using Morse code. [19th C.: named after Samuel F. B. *Morse* (1791–1872), US inventor.]

mor·sel /ˈmôrsəl/ ▶n. a small piece or amount of food; a mouthful. ■ a small piece or amount. [ME: from OFr., dimin. of *mors* 'a bite,' from L. *mors-* 'bitten,' from the v. *mordere*.]

mor·ta·del·la /,môrtəˈdelə/ ▶n. a type of light pink, smooth-textured Italian sausage containing pieces of fat, typically served in slices. [Ital. dimin., formed irregularly from L. *murtatum* '(sausage) seasoned with myrtle berries.']

mor·tal /ˈmôrtl/ ▶adj. **1** (of a living human being, often in contrast to a divine being) subject to death. ■ informal conceivable or imaginable. **2** [attrib.] causing or liable to cause death; fatal. ■ (of a battle) fought to the death: *screams of men in mortal combat.* ■ (of an enemy or a state of hostility) admitting or allowing no reconciliation until death. ■ Christian Theol. denoting a grave sin that is regarded as depriving the soul of divine grace. Often contrasted with VENIAL. ■ (of a feeling, esp. fear) very intense. ■ informal very great. ■ informal, dated long and tedious. ▶n. a human being subject to death, often contrasted with a divine being. ■ humorous a person contrasted with others regarded as being of higher status or ability. [ME: from OFr., or from L. *mortalis*, from *mors, mort-* 'death.']

mor·tal·i·ty /môrˈtalətē/ ▶n. (pl. **-ties**) **1** the state of being subject to death. **2** death, esp. on a large scale. ■ (also **mortality rate**) the number of deaths in a given area or period, or from a particular cause.

mor·tal·ly /ˈmôrtl-ē/ ▶adv. in such a manner as to cause death. ■ very intensely or seriously.

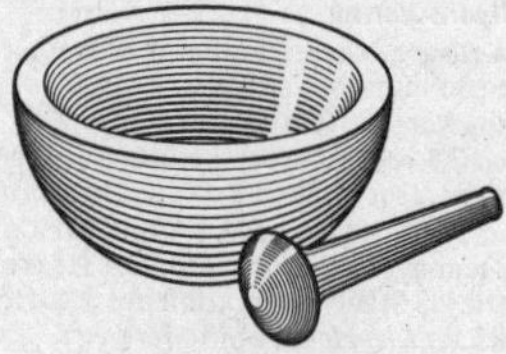

mortar and pestle

mor·tar[1] /ˈmôrtər/ ▶n. **1** a cup-shaped receptacle made of hard material, in which ingredients are crushed or ground, used esp. in cooking or pharmacy. **2** a short, smoothbore gun for firing shells (technically called bombs) at high angles. ■ a similar device used for firing a lifeline or firework. ▶ v. [trans.] attack or bombard with shells fired from a mortar. [OE, from OFr. *mortier*, from L. *mortarium*.]

mor·tar[2] ▶ n. a mixture of lime with cement, sand, and water, used in building to bond bricks or stones. ▶ v. [trans.] fix or join using mortar. — **mor·tar·less** adj. **mor·tar·y** adj. [ME: from OFr. *mortier*, from L. *mortarium* (see MORTAR[1]).]

mortar[1] 2

mor·tar·board /ˈmôrtər,bôrd/ ▶ n. **1** an academic cap with a stiff, flat, square top and a tassel. **2** a small square board with a handle on the underside, used by bricklayers for holding mortar.

mortarboard

mort·gage /ˈmôrgij/ ▶ n. the charging of real (or personal) property by a debtor to a creditor as security for a debt (esp. one incurred by the purchase of the property), on the condition that it shall be returned on payment of the debt within a certain period. ■ a deed effecting such a transaction. ■ a loan obtained through the conveyance of property as security. ▶ v. [trans.] (often **be mortgaged**) convey (a property) to a creditor as security on a loan. ■ fig. expose to future risk or constraint for the sake of immediate advantage. — **mort·gage·a·ble** adj. [ME: from OFr., lit. 'dead pledge,' from *mort* (from L. *mortuus* 'dead') + *gage* 'pledge.']

mort·ga·gee /,môrgəˈjē/ ▶ n. the lender in a mortgage, typically a bank.

mort·gage rate ▶ n. the rate of interest charged by a mortgage lender.

mort·ga·gor /,môrgiˈjôr; ˈmôrgijər/ ▶ n. the borrower in a mortgage, typically a homeowner.

mor·tice /ˈmôrtəs/ ▶ n. & v. var. of MORTISE.

mor·ti·cian /môrˈtisнən/ ▶ n. an undertaker. [19th C.: from L. *mors, mort-* 'death' + -ICIAN.]

mor·ti·fy /ˈmôrtə,fī/ ▶ v. (-fies, -fied) [trans.] **1** (often **be mortified**) cause (someone) to feel embarrassed, ashamed, or humiliated: [trans.] *she was mortified to see wrinkles* | [as adj.] (**mortifying**) *she refused to accept this mortifying disgrace.* **2** subdue (the body or its needs and desires) by self-denial or discipline: *return to heaven by mortifying the flesh.* — **mor·ti·fi·ca·tion** /,môrtəfəˈkāsнən/ n. **mor·ti·fy·ing·ly** adv. [ME: from OFr. *mortifier*, from eccles. L. *mortificare* 'kill, subdue,' from *mors, mort-* 'death.']

mor·tise /ˈmôrtis/ (also **mor·tice**) ▶ n. a hole or recess cut into a part, designed to receive a corresponding projection (a tenon) on another part so as to join or lock the parts together. See illustration at DOVETAIL. ▶ v. [trans.] join securely by using a mortise and tenon. ■ [trans.] [often as adj.] (**mortised**) cut a mortise in or through. — **mor·tis·er** n. [ME: from OFr. *mortaise*.]

mort·main /ˈmôrt,mān/ ▶ n. Law the status of lands or tenements held inalienably by an ecclesiastical or other corporation. [ME: from OFr. *mortemain*, from med. L. *mortua manus* 'dead hand.']

Mor·ton[1] /ˈmôrtn/, Jelly Roll (1885–1941), US jazz pianist, composer, and bandleader; born *Ferdinand Joseph La Menthe Morton*. He was a principal link between ragtime and New Orleans jazz.

Mor·ton[2], John (*c.*1420–1500), archbishop of Canterbury 1486–1500.

mor·tu·ar·y /ˈmôrcнo͞o,erē/ ▶ n. (pl. **-ar·ies**) a funeral home or morgue. ▶ adj. [attrib.] of or relating to burial or tombs. [ME: from L. *mortuarius*, from *mortuus* 'dead.']

mor·u·la /ˈmôrələ; ˈmär-/ ▶ n. (pl. **-lae** /-lē/) Embryol. a solid ball of cells resulting from division of a fertilized ovum, and from which a blastula is formed. [19th C.: mod. L., dimin. of L. *morum* 'mulberry.']

MOS ▶ abbr. Electron. metal oxide semiconductor.

mos. ▶ abbr. months.

Mo·sa·ic /mōˈzā-ik/ ▶ adj. of or associated with Moses. [17th C.: from Fr. *mosaïque* or mod. L. *Mosaicus*.]

mo·sa·ic /mōˈzā-ik/ ▶ n. **1** a picture or pattern produced by arranging together small colored pieces of hard material, such as stone, tile, or glass. ■ decorative work of this kind. ■ a colorful and variegated pattern. ■ a combination of diverse elements forming a more or less coherent whole. ■ an arrangement of photosensitive elements in a television camera. **2** Biol. an individual (esp. an animal) composed of cells of two genetically different types. **3** (also **mosaic disease**) a viral disease that results in leaf variegation in tobacco, corn, sugar cane, and other plants. ▶ v. (**-sa·icked, -sa·ick·ing**) [trans.] decorate with a mosaic: [as adj.] (**mosaicked**) *the mosaicked swimming pool.* ■ combine (distinct or disparate elements) to form a picture or pattern. — **mo·sa·i·cist** /mōˈzāəsist/ n. [ME: from Fr. *mosaïque*, based on L. *musi(v)um* decoration with small square stones, perh. ult. from Gk. *mousa* 'a muse.']

mo·sa·ic gold ▶ n. an imitation gold pigment consisting of tin disulfide.

mo·sa·i·cism /mōˈzāə,sizəm/ ▶ n. Biol. the property or state of being composed of cells of two genetically different types.

Mo·sa·ic Law ▶ n. another term for THE LAW OF MOSES (see LAW sense 3).

mos·ca·to /masˈkätō/ ▶ n. a sweet Italian dessert wine. [Ital.; rel. to MUSCAT.]

Mos·cow /ˈmäs,kou; -kō/ the capital of Russia, located at the center of European Russia, on the Moskva River; pop. 9,000,000. Russian name MOSKVA.

Mo·sel /mōˈzel/ (also **Mo·selle**) a river of western Europe that rises in northeastern France and flows northeast to meet the Rhine River at Koblenz, Germany.

Mo·selle /mōˈzel/ (also **Mo·sel**) ▶ n. a light medium-dry white wine produced in the valley of the Moselle River (see MOSEL).

Mo·ses[1] /ˈmōzis; -zəz/ (*fl.* *c.*14th–13th centuries BC), Hebrew prophet and lawgiver; brother of Aaron. He was inspired by God on Mount Sinai to write down the Ten Commandments on tablets of stone.

Mo·ses[2], Grandma (1860–1961), US painter; full name *Anna Mary Robertson Moses*. She took up painting as a hobby when widowed in 1927 and produced more than a thousand paintings in a primitive style.

Mo·ses[3], Edwin Corley (1955–), US track and field athlete. He won Olympic gold medals for the 400-meter hurdles in 1976 and 1984.

Mo·ses of Her Peo·ple see TUBMAN.

mo·sey /ˈmōzē/ informal ▶ v. (**-seys, -seyed**) [intrans.] walk or move in a leisurely manner. [19th C.: of unknown origin.]

MOSFET /ˈmäs,fet/ ▶ n. Electron. a field-effect transistor that has a thin layer of silicon oxide between the gate and the channel. [1960s: acronym from *metal oxide semiconductor field-effect transistor*.]

mosh /mäsн/ ▶ v. [intrans.] dance to rock music in a violent manner involving jumping up and down and deliberately colliding with other dancers. [1980s: perh. from MASH or MUSH[1].]

mo·shav /mōˈsнäv/ ▶ n. (pl. **mo·sha·vim** /,mōsнəˈvēm/) in Israel, a cooperative community of farmers. [from Heb. *mōšāḇ*, lit. 'dwelling.']

mosh pit ▶ n. an area where moshing occurs, esp. in front of the stage at a rock concert.

Mos·kva /ˈmäskvä; ˈməsk-/ Russian name for MOSCOW.

Mos·lem /ˈmäzləm; ˈmäs-/ ▶ n. & adj. var. of MUSLIM.
– USAGE See usage at MUSLIM.

Mo·so·tho /məˈso͞oto͞o/ singular form of BASOTHO.

mosque /mäsk/ ▶ n. a Muslim place of worship. [ME: from Fr. *mosquée*, via Ital. and Sp. from Egyptian Arab. *masgid*.]

Mos·qui·to ▶ n. (pl. **-tos**) & adj. var. of MISKITO.

mos·qui·to /məˈskētō/ ▶ n. (pl. **-toes** or **-tos**) a slender long-legged fly (*Culex, Anopheles*, and other genera, family Culicidae) with aquatic larvae. The bite of the bloodsucking female can transmit a number of serious diseases including malaria and encephalitis.— **mos·qui·to·ey**/məˈskētəwē/ adj. [16th C.: from Sp. and Port., dimin. of *mosca*, from L. *musca* 'fly.']

Anopheles mosquito

Mos·qui·to Coast /məˈskētōˈkōst/ a strip of swamp, lagoon, and tropical forest along the coasts of Nicaragua and Honduras.

mos·qui·to coil ▶ n. a spiral typically made from a dried paste of pyrethrum powder, which when lit burns slowly to produce a mosquito-repellent smoke.

mos·qui·to·fish /məˈskētō,fisн/ (also **mos·qui·to fish**) ▶ n. a small livebearing fish (genus *Gambusia*, family Poecilidae) found chiefly in vegetated ponds and lakes and brackish waters of the US and northern Mexico, esp. *G. affinis*, widely introduced for mosquito control.

mos·qui·to hawk ▶ n. **1** a nighthawk. **2** a dragonfly.

mos·qui·to net·ting (also **mos·qui·to net**) ▶ n. a fine net hung across a door or window or around a bed to keep mosquitoes away.

moss /môs/ ▶ n. a small flowerless green plant (class Musci, division Bryophyta) that lacks true roots, growing in low carpets or rounded cushions in damp habitats and reproducing by means of spores released from stalked capsules. ■ used in names of algae, lichens, and higher plants resembling moss, e.g., **Spanish moss**. ▶ v. [usu. as adj.] (**mossed**) cover with moss. [OE *mos* 'bog or moss,' of Gmc. origin; rel. to Du. *mos* and Ger. *Moos*.]

Mos·sad /mäˈsäd; mə-/ **1** the Supreme Institution for Intelligence and Special Assignments, the principal secret intelligence service of the state of Israel, founded in 1951. **2** the Institution for the Second Immigration, an earlier organization formed in 1938 for the purpose of bringing Jews from Europe to Palestine. [from Heb. *mōsāḏ* 'institution.']

moss ag·ate ▶ n. agate with mosslike dendritic inclusions.

moss an·i·mal ▶ n. a sedentary colonial aquatic animal (phylum Bryozoa) found chiefly in the sea, either encrusting rocks, seaweeds, or other surfaces, or forming stalked fronds. Each minute zooid filter-feeds by means of a crown of ciliated tentacles (lophophore).

moss·back /ˈmôs,bak/ ▶ n. informal an old-fashioned or extremely conservative person. — **moss·backed** adj.

Möss·bau·er ef·fect /ˈməs,bouər/ ▶ n. Chem. an effect in which certain atomic nuclei bound in a crystal emit gamma rays of sharply defined frequency, which can be used as a probe of energy levels in other nuclei. [1960s: named after Rudolf L. *Mössbauer* (1929–), Ger. physicist.]

moss-grown ▶ adj. overgrown with moss. ■ fig. old; antiquated.

Mos·si /ˈmäsē/ ▶ n. (pl. same or **Mos·sis**) a member of a people of Burkina Faso in West Africa. ▶ adj. of or relating to this people.

moss·y /ˈmôsē/ ▶ adj. (**moss·i·er, moss·i·est**) covered in or resembling moss. ■ informal old-fashioned or extremely conservative. — **moss·i·ness** n.

moss·y·cup oak /ˈmôsē,kəp/ ▶ n. another term for BUR OAK.

most /mōst/ ▶ adj. & pron. superlative of MANY, MUCH. greatest in amount or degree: [as adj.] *they've had the most success* | [as pron.] *they had the most to lose.* ■ the majority of; nearly all of. ▶ adv. superlative of MUCH. **1** to the greatest extent: *the things he most enjoyed.* ■ forming the superlative of adjectives and adverbs, esp. those of more than one syllable: *the most important event of my life.* **2** extremely; very: *it was most kind of you.* **3** informal almost.
– PHRASES **at (the) most** not more than. **be the most** informal be the best of all; be the ultimate. **for the most part** in most cases; usually. **make the most of** use to the best advantage. ■ represent at its best: *make the most of your features.* [OE *māst*, of Gmc. origin; rel. to Du. *meest* and Ger. *meist.*]

-most ▶ suffix forming superlative adjectives and adverbs from prepositions and other words indicating relative position: *innermost* | *uppermost.* [OE *-mest*, assimilated to MOST.]

Mo·star /ˈmōstär/ a city in southern Bosnia and Herzegovina, southwest of Sarajevo; pop. 126,000.

most·est /ˈmōstəst/ ▶ pron. humorous most.

most fa·vored na·tion ▶ n. a country that has been granted the most favorable trading terms afforded by another country.

Most High (**the Most High**) God.

most·ly /ˈmōstlē/ ▶ adv. as regards the greater part or number. ■ usually.

Most Rev·er·end ▶ n. the title of an Anglican archbishop or an Irish Roman Catholic bishop.

most sig·nif·i·cant bit (abbr.: **MSB**) ▶ n. Comput. the bit in a binary number that is of the greatest numerical value.

Mo·sul /məˈso͞ol; ˈmō,so͞ol/ a city in northern Iraq, on the Tigris River; pop. 571,000.

mot /mō/ ▶ n. (pl. **mots** /mō(z)/) short for BON MOT.

mote /mōt/ ▶ n. a tiny piece of a substance. [OE *mot*, rel. to Du. *mot* 'dust, sawdust.']

mo·tel /mōˈtel/ ▶ n. a roadside hotel designed primarily for motorists, typically having the rooms arranged in low blocks with parking directly outside. [1920s: blend of MOTOR and HOTEL.]

mo·tet /mōˈtet/ ▶ n. a short piece of sacred choral music, typically polyphonic and unaccompanied. [ME: from OFr., dimin. of *mot* 'word.']

moth /môTH/ ▶ n. (pl. **moths** /môT͟HZ; môTHS/) a chiefly nocturnal insect related to the butterflies. It lacks the clubbed antennae of butterflies and typically has a stout body, drab coloration, and wings that fold flat when resting. ■ informal short for CLOTHES MOTH.
– PHRASES **like a moth to the flame** with an irresistible attraction to someone or something. [OE *moththe*, of Gmc. origin; rel. to Du. *mot* and Ger. *Motte.*]

moth·ball /ˈmôTH,bôl/ ▶ n. (usu. **mothballs**) a small pellet of a pungent substance, typically naphthalene, put among stored clothes to repel moths. ▶ v. [trans.] store (clothes) among or in mothballs. ■ stop using (a ship, a piece of equipment, or a building) but keep it in good condition so that it can readily be used again. ■ cancel or postpone work on (a plan or project).
– PHRASES **in mothballs** unused but kept in good condition for future use.

moth-eat·en /ˈmôTH ,ētn/ ▶ adj. damaged or destroyed by moths. ■ old-fashioned and no longer appropriate or useful.

moth·er /ˈməT͟Hər/ ▶ n. **1** a woman in relation to a child or children to whom she has given birth. ■ a person who provides the care and affection normally associated with a female parent. ■ a female animal in relation to its offspring: [as adj.] *a mother penguin.* ■ (**Mother, Mother Superior**, or **Reverend Mother**) (esp. as a title or form of address) the head of a female religious community. ■ [as adj.] denoting an institution or organization from which more recently founded institutions of the same type derive: *the mother church.* ■ fig. something that is the origin or of stimulus for something else. ■ informal an extreme example or very large specimen of something: *I got stuck in the mother of all traffic jams.* **2** vulgar slang short for MOTHERFUCKER. ▶ v. [trans.] **1** [often as n.] (**mothering**) bring up (a child) with care and affection: *the art of mothering.* ■ look after kindly and protectively, sometimes excessively so: *she felt mothered by her older sister.* **2** dated give birth to. — **moth·er·hood** n. [OE *mōdor*; rel. toGer. *Mutter*, L. *mater* and Gk. *mētēr.*]

Moth·er Ann see LEE[1].

moth·er·board /ˈməT͟Hər,bôrd/ ▶ n. Comput. a printed circuit board containing the principal components of a microcomputer or other device, with connectors into which other circuit boards can be slotted.

Moth·er Car·ey's chick·en /ˈke(ə)rēz/ ▶ n. old-fashioned term for STORM PETREL. [18th C.: of unknown origin.]

moth·er coun·try ▶ n. (often **the mother country**) a country in relation to its colonies.

Moth·er Earth ▶ n. the earth considered as the source of all its living beings and inanimate things.

moth·er fig·ure ▶ n. a woman who is regarded as a source of nurture and support.

moth·er·fuck·er /ˈməT͟Hər,fəkər/ ▶ n. vulgar slang a despicable or very unpleasant person or thing. — **moth·er·fuck·ing** adj.

moth·er god·dess ▶ n. a mother-figure deity, a central figure of many early nature cults in which maintenance of fertility was of prime religious importance. Examples of such goddesses include Isis, Astarte, Cybele, and Demeter. Also called GREAT MOTHER.

Moth·er Goose ▶ n. the fictitious creator of a collection of nursery rhymes that was first published in London in the 1760s.

moth·er hen ▶ n. a hen with chicks. ■ a person who sees to the needs of others, esp. in a fussy or interfering way.

moth·er·house /ˈməT͟Hər,hous/ ▶ n. the founding house of a religious order.

Moth·er Hub·bard /ˈhəbərd/ ▶ n. a long, loose-fitting, shapeless woman's dress or undergarment. ■ a kind of cloak.

moth·er-in-law ▶ n. (pl. **moth·ers-in-law**) the mother of one's husband or wife.

moth·er·land /ˈməT͟Hər,land/ ▶ n. (often **the motherland**) one's native country.

moth·er lode ▶ n. Mining a principal vein of an ore or mineral. ■ fig. a rich source of something.

moth·er·ly /ˈməT͟Hərlē/ ▶ adj. of, resembling, or characteristic of a mother, esp. in being caring, protective, and kind. — **moth·er·li·ness** n.

moth·er·na·ked ▶ adj. [predic.] wearing no clothes at all.

Moth·er Na·ture nature personified as a creative and controlling force.

Moth·er of God Christian Church a name given to the Virgin Mary (as mother of the divine Christ).

moth·er-of-pearl ▶ n. a smooth shining iridescent substance forming the inner layer of the shell of some mollusks, esp. oysters and abalones, used in ornamentation.

Moth·er's Day ▶ n. a day of the year (in the US, the second Sunday in May) on which mothers are particularly honored.

moth·er's help·er ▶ n. a person who helps a mother, mainly by looking after her children.

moth·er ship ▶ n. a large spacecraft or ship from which smaller craft are launched or maintained.

moth·er's milk ▶ n. the milk of a particular child's own mother. ■ fig. something providing sustenance or regarded by a person as entirely appropriate to them. ■ informal alcoholic liquor.

moth·er's son ▶ n. informal a man.

Moth·er Su·pe·ri·or (also **mother superior**) ▶ n. the head of a female religious community.

Moth·er Te·re·sa /təˈrēsə; təˈrāsə; təˈrēzə; təˈrāzə/ see TERESA, MOTHER.

moth·er-to-be ▶ n. (pl. **moth·ers-to-be**) a woman who is expecting a baby.

moth·er tongue ▶ n. the language that a person has grown up speaking from early childhood.

Moth·er·well /ˈməT͟Hər,wel/, Robert (1915–91), US painter. He was a founder and leading exponent of the New York school of abstract expressionism.

moth·er wit ▶ n. natural ability to cope with everyday matters; common sense.

moth·er·wort /ˈməT͟Hər,wərt; -,wôrt/ ▶ n. a tall strong-smelling plant (*Leonurus cardiaca*) of the mint family, with purplish-pink lipped flowers clustering close to the axils. It is used in herbal medicine, esp. in the treatment of gynecological disorders.

moth·proof /ˈmôTH,pro͞of/ ▶ adj. (of clothes or fabrics) treated with a substance that repels moths. ▶ v. [trans.] treat with a substance that repels moths.

moth·y /ˈmôTHē/ ▶ adj. (**moth·i·er, moth·i·est**) infested with or damaged by moths.

mo·tif /mōˈtēf/ ▶ n. a decorative design or pattern. ■ a distinctive feature or dominant idea in an artistic or literary composition. ■ Music a short succession of notes producing a single impression; a brief melodic or rhythmic formula out of which longer passages are developed. ■ an ornament of lace, braid, etc., sewn separately on a garment. ■ Biochem. a distinctive sequence on a protein or DNA, having a three-dimensional structure that allows binding interactions to occur. [19th C.: from Fr.]

mo·tile /ˈmōtl; ˈmō,tīl/ ▶ adj. **1** Zool. & Bot. (of cells, gametes, and single-celled organisms) capable of motion. **2** Psychol. of, relating to, or characterized by responses that involve muscular rather than audiovisual sensations. — **mo·til·i·ty** /mōˈtilətē/ n. [19th C.: from L. *motus* 'motion,' on the pattern of *mobile.*]

mo·tion /ˈmōSHən/ ▶ n. **1** the action or process of moving or being moved. ■ a gesture. ■ a piece of moving mechanism. **2** a formal

proposal put to a legislature or committee. ■ Law an application for a rule or order of court. **3** Music the movement of a melodic line between successive pitches. ▶ **v.** [trans.] direct or command (someone) with a movement of the hand or head.
– PHRASES **go through the motions** do something perfunctorily, without any enthusiasm or commitment. ■ simulate an action. **set in motion** start something moving or working. ■ start or trigger a process or series of events. — **mo·tion·al** /-SHənl/ **adj.** [ME: via OFr. from L. *motio(n-)*, from *movere* 'to move.']

mo·tion pic·ture ▶ **n.** another term for MOVIE.

mo·tion sick·ness ▶ **n.** nausea caused by motion, esp. by traveling in a vehicle.

mo·ti·vate /'mōtə,vāt/ ▶ **v.** [trans.] provide (someone) with a motive for doing something. ■ stimulate (someone's) interest in or enthusiasm for doing something. — **mo·ti·va·tor** /-,vātər/ **n.**

mo·ti·va·tion /,mōtə'vāSHən/ ▶ **n.** the reason or reasons one has for acting or behaving in a particular way. ■ the general desire or willingness of someone to do something. — **mo·ti·va·tion·al** /-SHənl/ **adj.** **mo·ti·va·tion·al·ly** /-SHənl-ē/ **adv.**

mo·ti·va·tion re·search ▶ **n.** the psychological or sociological investigation of motives, esp. those influencing the decisions of consumers.

mo·tive /'mōtiv/ ▶ **n.** **1** a reason for doing something, esp. one that is hidden or not obvious. **2** (in art, literature, or music) a motif. ▶ **adj.** [attrib.] **1** producing physical or mechanical motion. **2** causing or being the reason for something. [ME: from OFr. *motif*, from late L. *motivus*, from *movere* 'to move.']

mo·tive pow·er ▶ **n.** the energy (in the form of steam, electricity, etc.) used to drive machinery. ■ the locomotive engines of a railroad system collectively.

mo·ti·vic /'mōtəvik/ ▶ **adj.** Music of or relating to a motif or motifs.

mot juste /,mō 'ZHYst/ ▶ **n.** (pl. **mots justes** pronunc. same) the exact, appropriate word.

mot·ley /'mätlē/ ▶ **adj.** (**mot·li·er**, **mot·li·est**) incongruously varied in appearance or character; disparate: ***a motley crew** of discontents and zealots.* ▶ **n.** **1** [usu. in sing.] an incongruous mixture: ***a motley of** interacting interest groups.* **2** hist. the particolored costume of a jester: *life-size mannequins **in full motley**.* [ME: of unknown origin.]

mot·mot /'mät,mät/ ▶ **n.** a tree-dwelling tropical American bird (family Momotidae) with colorful plumage, typically having two long racket-like tail feathers. [19th C.: from L. Amer. Sp., of imitative origin.]

mo·to·cross /'mōtō,krôs; -,kräs/ ▶ **n.** cross-country racing on motorcycles. — **mo·to·cross·er** **n.** [20th C.: abbrev. of MOTOR + CROSS.]

mo·to·neu·ron /,mōtə'n(y)o͝or,än/ ▶ **n.** another term for MOTOR NEURON.

mo·tor /'mōtər/ ▶ **n.** a machine, esp. one powered by electricity or internal combustion, that supplies motive power for a vehicle or for some other device with moving parts. ■ a source of power, energy, or motive force. ▶ **adj.** [attrib.] **1** giving, imparting, or producing motion or action. ■ Physiol. relating to muscular movement or the nerves activating it. **2** esp. Brit. driven by a motor. ■ of or relating to motor vehicles. ▶ **v.** [intrans.] informal travel in a motor vehicle, typically a car or a boat. ■ informal run or move as fast as possible. [ME: from L., lit. 'mover,' from *movere* 'to move.']

mo·tor ar·e·a ▶ **n.** Anat. a part of the central nervous system concerned with muscular action, esp. the motor cortex.

mo·tor·bike /'mōtər,bīk/ ▶ **n.** a lightweight motorcycle. ■ a motorized bicycle.

mo·tor·boat /'mōtər,bōt/ ▶ **n.** a boat powered by a motor, esp. a recreational boat.

mo·tor·bus /'mōtər,bəs/ ▶ **n.** old-fashioned term for BUS (sense 1).

mo·tor·cade /'mōtər,kād/ ▶ **n.** a procession of motor vehicles, typically carrying and escorting a prominent person. [20th C.: from MOTOR, on the pattern of *cavalcade*.]

mo·tor·car /'mōtər,kär/ ▶ **n.** **1** dated or Brit. an automobile. **2** a self-propelled railroad vehicle used to carry railroad workers.

mo·tor coach ▶ **n.** another term for COACH[1] (sense 3).

mo·tor cor·tex ▶ **n.** Anat. the part of the cerebral cortex in the brain where the nerve impulses originate that initiate voluntary muscular activity.

mo·tor·cy·cle /'mōtər,sīkəl/ ▶ **n.** a two-wheeled vehicle that is powered by a motor and has no pedals. — **mo·tor·cy·cling** /-,sīk(ə)liNG/ **n.** **mo·tor·cy·clist** /-,sīk(ə)list/ **n.**

motorcycle

mo·tor drive ▶ **n.** a mechanical system that includes an electric motor and drives a machine. ■ a battery-driven motor in a camera used to wind the film rapidly between exposures.

mo·tor home ▶ **n.** a motor vehicle equipped like a trailer for living in, with kitchen facilities, beds, etc.

mo·tor inn (also **motor hotel** or **motor lodge**) ▶ **n.** a motel.

mo·tor·ist /'mōtərist/ ▶ **n.** the driver of an automobile.

mo·tor·ize /'mōtə,rīz/ ▶ **v.** [trans.] [usu. as adj.] (**motorized**) equip (a vehicle or device) with a motor to operate or propel it. ■ equip (troops) with motor transportation. — **mo·tor·i·za·tion** /,mōtərə'zāSHən/ **n.**

mo·tor launch ▶ **n.** see LAUNCH[2].

mo·tor·man /'mōtər,mən/ ▶ **n.** (pl. **-men**) the driver of an electric vehicle, esp. a streetcar or subway train.

mo·tor·mouth /'mōtər,mouTH/ (also **mo·tor-mouth**) ▶ **n.** informal a person who talks quickly and incessantly. — **mo·tor·mouthed** /-,mouT͟Hd; -,mouTHt/ (or **mo·tor-mouthed**) **adj.**

mo·tor nerve ▶ **n.** a nerve carrying impulses from the brain or spinal cord to a muscle or gland.

mo·tor neu·ron ▶ **n.** a nerve cell forming part of a pathway along which impulses pass from the brain or spinal cord to a muscle or gland.

mo·tor·sail·er /'mōtər,sālər/ ▶ **n.** a boat equipped with both sails and an engine.

mo·tor scoot·er ▶ **n.** see SCOOTER.

mo·tor ve·hi·cle ▶ **n.** a road vehicle powered by an internal combustion engine; an automobile.

mo·tor·way /'mōtər,wā/ ▶ **n.** Brit. an expressway. ■ informal a wide, fast, easy ski run.

Mo·town /'mō,toun/ ▶ **n.** **1** (also trademark **Tamla Motown**) music released on or reminiscent of the US record label Tamla Motown. The first black-owned record company in the US, Tamla Motown was founded in Detroit in 1959 by Berry Gordy, and was important in popularizing soul music. **2** informal name for DETROIT.

Mott /mät/, Lucretia Coffin (1793–1880), US social activist. She fought for abolition, women's rights, and religious freedom.

motte /mät/ ▶ **n.** **1** (also **mott**) a stand of trees, esp. in the southwestern US; a grove. **2** hist. a mound forming the site of a castle or camp. [19th C.: from Fr., 'mound,' from OFr. *mote* (see MOAT).]

mot·tle /'mätl/ ▶ **v.** [trans.] (usu. **be mottled**) mark with spots or smears of color. ▶ **n.** an irregular arrangement of spots or patches of color. ■ (also **mottling**) a spot or patch forming part of such an arrangement. [18th C.: prob. a back-form. from MOTLEY.]

mot·to /'mätō/ ▶ **n.** (pl. **-toes** or **-tos**) a short sentence or phrase chosen as encapsulating the beliefs or ideals guiding an individual, family, or institution. ■ Music a phrase that recurs throughout a musical work and has some symbolic significance. [16th C.: from Ital., 'word.']

mo·tu pro·pri·o /'mōto͞o 'prōprē,ō/ ▶ **n.** (pl. **mo·tu pro·pri·os**) an edict issued by the pope personally to the Roman Catholic Church or to a part of it. [L., lit. 'of one's own volition.']

moue /mo͞o/ ▶ **n.** a pouting expression used to convey annoyance or distaste. [19th C.: Fr., earlier having the sense 'lip.']

mouf·lon /'mo͞of,lôN/ (also **mouf·flon**) ▶ **n.** a small wild sheep (*Ovis orientalis*) with chestnut-brown wool, found in mountainous country from Iran to Asia Minor. It is the ancestor of the domestic sheep. [18th C.: from Fr., from Ital. *muflone*.]

mouil·lé /mo͞o'yā/ ▶ **adj.** Phonet. (of a consonant) palatalized. [Fr., 'wetted.']

mou·jik /mo͞o'ZHēk; -'ZHik/ ▶ **n.** var. of MUZHIK.

mould /mōld/ ▶ **n. & v.** British spelling of MOLD[1], MOLD[2], and MOLD[3].

mou·lin /mo͞o'lan/ ▶ **n.** a vertical or nearly vertical shaft in a glacier, formed by surface water percolating through a crack in the ice. [19th C.: Fr., lit. 'mill.']

Mou·lin Rouge /mo͞o'lan 'ro͞oZH/ a cabaret in Montmartre, Paris, a favorite resort of poets and artists around the end of the 19th century. Toulouse-Lautrec immortalized its dancers in his posters.

Moul·mein /,mo͞ol'mān; ,mōl'mīn/ a city in southeastern Myanmar (Burma); pop. 220,000.

moult /mōlt/ ▶ **v. & n.** British spelling of MOLT.

mound[1] /mound/ ▶ **n.** a rounded mass projecting above a surface. ■ a raised mass of earth, stones, or other compacted material, sometimes created artificially for purposes of defense or burial. ■ a small hill. ■ (**a mound of/mounds of**) a large pile or quantity of something. ■ Baseball (in full **pitcher's mound**) the elevated area from which the pitcher delivers the ball. ▶ **v.** [trans.] heap up into a rounded pile.
– PHRASES **take the mound** Baseball (of a pitcher) have a turn at pitching. [16th C.: of obscure origin.]

mound[2] ▶ **n.** archaic a ball representing the earth, used as part of royal regalia, e.g., on top of a crown, typically of gold and surmounted by a cross. [ME (denoting the world): from OFr. *monde*, from L. *mundus* 'world.']

mound build·er ▶ **n.** another term for MEGAPODE.

mounds·man /'moun(d)zmən/ ▶ **n.** (pl. **-men**) Baseball a pitcher.

mount[1] /mount/ ▶ **v.** [trans.] **1** climb (stairs, a hill, or other rising surface). ■ climb or move up on to (a raised surface). ■ get up on (an animal or bicycle) in order to ride it. ■ (often **be mounted**) set (someone) on horseback; provide with a horse. ■ (of a male mammal or bird) get on (a female) for the purpose of copulation. ■ [intrans.] (of the blood or its color) rise into the cheeks. **2** organize and initiate (a campaign or other significant course of action). ■ establish; set up. ■ produce (a play, exhibition, or other artistic event); present for public view or display. **3** [intrans.] grow larger or more numerous. ■ (of a feeling) become stronger or more intense: *tensions mounted.* **4** [trans.] place or fix (an object) on an elevated support. ■ fix (an object) in position. ■ [trans.] place (a gun) on a fixed mounting. ■ [trans.] set in or attach to a backing or setting. ■ [trans.] fix (an object for viewing) on a microscope slide. ■ [trans.] Comput. make (a disk or disk drive) available for use. ▶ **n. 1** a backing or setting on which a photograph, gem, or work of art is set for display. ■ a glass microscope slide for securing a specimen to be viewed. ■ Philately a clear plastic or paper sleeve used to display a postage stamp. **2** a support for a gun, camera, or similar piece of equipment. **3** a horse being ridden or that is available for riding. ■ an opportunity to ride a horse, esp. as a jockey. — **mount·a·ble adj. mount·er n.** [ME: from OFr. *munter*, based on L. *mons, mont-* 'mountain.']

mount² ▶ **n.** a mountain or hill (archaic except in place names): *Mount Everest.* ■ any of several fleshy prominences on the palm of the hand regarded in palmistry as signifying the degree of influence of a particular planet: *mount of Mars.* [OE *munt*, from L. *mons, mont-* 'mountain.']

moun·tain /ˈmountn/ ▶ **n.** a large natural elevation of the earth's surface rising abruptly from the surrounding level; a large steep hill. ■ **(mountains)** a region where there are many such features, characterized by remoteness and inaccessibility. ■ **(a mountain/mountains of)** a large pile or quantity of something. ■ [usu. with adj.] a large surplus stock of a commodity.

– PHRASES **make a mountain out of a molehill** see MOLEHILL. **move mountains 1** achieve spectacular and apparently impossible results. **2** make every possible effort. [ME: from OFr. *montaigne*, based on L. *mons, mont-* 'mountain.']

moun·tain ash ▶ **n. 1** a small deciduous tree (genus *Sorbus*) of the rose family, with compound leaves, white flowers, and red berries. Also called ROWAN. **2** Austral. a eucalyptus tree that is widely used for timber.

moun·tain av·ens ▶ **n.** a creeping arctic-alpine plant (*Dryas octopetala*) of the rose family, with white flowers and glossy leaves.

moun·tain bike ▶ **n.** a bicycle with a light sturdy frame, broad deep-treaded tires, and multiple gears, originally designed for riding on mountainous terrain. — **moun·tain bik·er n. moun·tain bik·ing n.**

moun·tain chain ▶ **n.** a connected series of mountains.

moun·tain cran·ber·ry ▶ **n.** (pl. **-ries**) a low-growing evergreen dwarf shrub (*Vaccinium vitis-idaea*) of the heath family that bears dark red berries and grows in upland habitats in the north. ■ the edible acid berry of this plant, used as a cranberry substitute.

moun·tain dew ▶ **n.** informal illicitly distilled liquor, esp. whiskey or rum; moonshine.

moun·tain dul·ci·mer ▶ **n.** see DULCIMER.

moun·tain·eer /ˌmountnˈi(ə)r/ ▶ **n.** a person who takes part in mountaineering. ■ rare a person living in a mountainous area.

moun·tain·eer·ing /ˌmountnˈi(ə)riNG/ ▶ **n.** the sport or activity of climbing mountains.

moun·tain goat ▶ **n. 1** (also **Rocky Mountain goat**) a goat-antelope (*Oreamnos americanus*) with shaggy white hair and backward curving horns, living in the Rocky Mountains. **2** any goat that lives on mountains, proverbial for agility.

mountain goat

moun·tain lau·rel ▶ **n.** a North American kalmia (*Kalmia latifolia*) that bears clusters of white or pink flowers.

moun·tain li·on ▶ **n.** another term for COUGAR.

moun·tain·ous /ˈmountn-əs/ ▶ **adj.** (of a region) having many mountains. ■ huge.

moun·tain range ▶ **n.** a line of mountains connected by high ground.

moun·tain sheep ▶ **n.** another term for BIGHORN. ■ any sheep that lives on mountains.

moun·tain sick·ness ▶ **n.** another term for ALTITUDE SICKNESS.

moun·tain·side /ˈmountn,sīd/ ▶ **n.** the sloping surface of a mountain.

Moun·tain States US states that contain part of the Rocky Mountains—New Mexico, Colorado, Wyoming, Utah, Idaho, and Montana.

Moun·tain time the standard time in a zone including parts of the US and Canada in or near the Rocky Mountains, specifically: ■ **(Mountain Standard Time** abbrev.: **MST)** standard time based on the mean solar time at the meridian 105° W., seven hours behind GMT. ■ **(Mountain Daylight Time** abbrev.: **MDT)** Mountain time during daylight saving time, eight hours behind GMT.

Mount·bat·ten /ˌmountˈbatn/, Louis Francis Albert Victor Nicholas, 1st Earl Mountbatten of Burma (1900–79), British military officer and administrator. He was the first governor general of India 1947–48.

Mount Des·ert Is·land an island in the Atlantic Ocean, in southeastern Maine.

moun·te·bank /ˈmounti,baNGk/ ▶ **n.** a person who deceives others, esp. in order to trick them out of their money; a charlatan. ■ hist. a person who sold patent medicines in public places. — **moun·te·bank·er·y** /-,baNGkərē/ **n.** [16th C.: from Ital. *montambanco*, from the imper. phr. *monta in banco!* 'climb on the bench!']

mount·ed /ˈmountid/ ▶ **adj.** [attrib.] riding an animal, typically a horse, esp. for military or other duty.

Moun·tie /ˈmountē/ ▶ **n.** informal a member of the Royal Canadian Mounted Police.

mount·ing /ˈmountiNG/ ▶ **n. 1** a backing, setting, or support for something. **2** the action of mounting something.

Mount of Ol·ives the highest point in the range of hills to the east of Jerusalem. It is a holy place for both Judaism and Christianity.

Mount Ver·non /ˈvərnən/ an estate in northeastern Virginia, overlooking the Potomac River. It was the home of George Washington 1747–99.

mourn /môrn/ ▶ **v.** [trans.] feel or show deep sorrow or regret for (someone or their death), typically by following conventions such as the wearing of black clothes. ■ feel regret or sadness about (the loss or disappearance of something). [OE *murnan*, of Gmc. origin.]

mourn·er /ˈmôrnər/ ▶ **n.** a person who attends a funeral as a relative or friend of the dead person. ■ esp. hist. a person hired to attend a funeral.

mourn·ful /ˈmôrnfəl/ ▶ **adj.** feeling or expressing sadness, regret, or grief. ■ suggestive of or inducing sadness, regret, or unhappiness. — **mourn·ful·ly adv. mourn·ful·ness n.**

mourn·ing /ˈmôrniNG/ ▶ **n.** the expression of deep sorrow for someone who has died, typically involving following certain conventions such as wearing black clothes. ■ black clothes worn as an expression of grief when someone dies.

mourn·ing band ▶ **n.** a strip of black material that is worn around a person's sleeve as a mark of respect for someone who has recently died.

mourn·ing cloak ▶ **n.** a migratory butterfly (*Nymphalis antiopa*, family Nymphalidae) with deep purple yellow-bordered wings.

mourning cloak

mourn·ing dove ▶ **n.** a North and Central American dove (*Zenaida macroura*) with a long tail, a gray-brown back, and a plaintive call.

mourn·ing ring ▶ **n.** hist. a ring worn to remind the wearer of someone who has died.

mouse ▶ **n.** /mous/ (pl. **mice** /mīs/) **1** a small rodent (family Muridae) that typically has a pointed snout, relatively large ears and eyes, and a long tail. Certain species may belong to the families Heteromyidae, Zapodidae, and Muscardinidae. ■ (in general use) any similar small mammal, such as a shrew or vole. ■ a shy, timid, and quiet person. **2** (pl. also **mous·es**) Comput. a small hand-held device that is dragged across a flat surface to move the cursor on a computer screen, typically having buttons that are pressed to control computer functions. **3** informal a lump or bruise, esp. one on or near the eye. ▶ **v.** /mouz/ [intrans.] **1** (of a cat or an owl) hunt for or catch mice. ■ prowl around as if searching. **2** Comput., informal use a mouse to move a cursor on a computer screen: *mouse your way over to the window and click on it.* [OE *mūs*, (pl.) *mȳs*; rel. to Ger. *Maus*, L. and Gk. *mus*.]

mouse·bird /ˈmous,bərd/ ▶ **n.** a small gregarious African bird (genera *Colius* and *Urocolius*, family Coliidae) with mainly drab plumage, a crest, and a long tail.

mouse deer ▶ **n.** another term for CHEVROTAIN.

mouse-ear chickweed ▶ **n.** see CHICKWEED.

mouse pad (also **mouse·pad**) ▶ **n.** a small piece of rigid or slightly resilient material on which a computer mouse is moved.

mouse po·ta·to ▶ **n.** informal a person who spends large amounts of time operating a computer. [1990s: on the pattern of *couch potato*.]

mous·er /ˈmousər; -zər/ ▶ **n.** an animal that catches mice, esp. a cat.

mouse·trap /ˈmous,trap/ ▶ **n.** a trap for catching and usually killing mice, esp. one with a spring bar that snaps down onto the mouse when it touches bait attached to the mechanism. ▶ **v.** **(-trapped, -trap·ping)** [trans.] informal induce (someone) to do something by means of a trick.

mous·ey ▶ **adj.** var. of MOUSY.

mous·sa·ka /mo͞oˈsäkə; ˌmo͞osəˈkä/ ▶ **n.** a Greek dish made of minced lamb, eggplant, and tomatoes, with cheese on top. [from Turk. *musakka*, based on Arab.]

mousse /mo͞os/ ▶ **n.** a sweet or savory dish made as a smooth light mass with whipped cream and beaten egg white, flavored with chocolate, fish, etc., and typically served chilled. ■ a soft, light, or aerated gel such as a soap preparation. ■ a frothy preparation that is applied to the hair, enabling it to be styled more easily. ▶ v. [trans.] style (hair) using mousse. [19th C.: from Fr., 'moss or froth.']

mousse·line /ˌmo͞osəˈlēn; -ˈslēn/ ▶ n. **1** a fine, semiopaque fabric similar to muslin, typically made of silk, wool, or cotton. **2** a soft, light mousse. **3** (also **sauce mousseline**) hollandaise sauce that has been made frothy with whipped cream or egg white, served mainly with fish or asparagus. [17th C.: from Fr. (see MUSLIN).]

mous·seux /mo͞oˈsœ/ ▶ adj. (of wine) sparkling. ▶ n. (pl. same) sparkling wine. [from Fr., from *mousse* 'froth.']

mous·tache ▶ n. var. of MUSTACHE.

Mous·te·ri·an /mo͞oˈsti(ə)rēən/ ▶ adj. Archaeol. of, relating to, or denoting the main culture of the Middle Paleolithic period in Europe, between the Acheulian and Aurignacian periods (chiefly 80,000–35,000 years ago), and associated with Neanderthal peoples. ■ [as n.] (**the Mousterian**) the Mousterian culture or period. [19th C.: from Fr. *moustiérien*, from *Le Moustier*, a cave in southwestern France where objects from this culture were found.]

mous·y /ˈmousē; -zē/ (also **mous·ey**) ▶ adj. (**mous·i·er, mous·i·est**) of or like a mouse. ■ (of hair) of a dull light brown color. ■ (of a person) nervous, shy, or timid; lacking in presence or charisma. — **mous·i·ness** n.

mouth ▶ n. /mouTH/ (pl. **mouths** /mou<u>TH</u>z; mouTHs/) **1** the opening in the lower part of the human face, surrounded by the lips, through which food is taken in and from which speech and other sounds are emitted. ■ the cavity behind this, containing the teeth and tongue. ■ the corresponding opening through which an animal takes in food (at the front of the head in vertebrates and many other creatures), or the cavity behind this. ■ [usu. with adj.] a horse's readiness to feel and obey the pressure of the bit in its mouth. ■ the character or quality of a wine as judged by its feel or flavor in the mouth (rather than its aroma). ■ informal talkativeness; impudence. **2** an opening or entrance to a structure that is hollow, concave, or almost completely enclosed. ■ the opening for filling or emptying something used as a container. ■ the muzzle of a gun. ■ the opening or entrance to a harbor or bay. ■ the place where a river enters the sea. ▶ v. /mou<u>TH</u>; mouTH/ [trans.] **1** say (something dull or unoriginal), esp. in a pompous or affected way. ■ utter very clearly and distinctly. ■ move the lips as if saying (something) or in a grimace. **2** take in or touch with the mouth. ■ train the mouth of (a horse) so that it responds to a bit.

– PHRASES **be all mouth** informal tend to talk boastfully without any intention of acting on one's words. **open one's mouth** informal say something. **watch one's mouth** informal be careful about what one says.

– PHRASAL VERBS **mouth off** informal talk in an unpleasantly loud and boastful or opinionated way. ■ (**mouth off at**) loudly criticize or abuse. — **mouthed** /mou<u>TH</u>d; mouTHt/ adj. [in comb.] *wide-mouthed.* **mouth·er** /ˈmou<u>TH</u>ər/ n. [OE *mūth*; rel. to Ger. *Mund*, L. *mentum* 'chin.']

mouth·brood·er /ˈmouTHˌbro͞odər/ ▶ n. a freshwater cichlid (*Sarotherodon* and other genera) that protects its eggs (and in some cases its young) by carrying them in its mouth.

mouth·ful /ˈmouTHˌfo͝ol/ ▶ n. (pl. **-fuls**) **1** a quantity of food or drink that fills or can be put into the mouth. **2** a long or complicated word or phrase that is difficult to say.

– PHRASES **give someone a mouthful** informal talk to or shout at someone in an angry, abusive, or severely critical way. **say a mouthful** informal say something noteworthy.

mouth·guard /ˈmouTHˌgärd/ ▶ n. a plastic shield held in the mouth by an athlete to protect the teeth and gums.

mouth or·gan ▶ n. another term for HARMONICA.

mouth·part /ˈmouTHˌpärt/ ▶ n. (usu. **mouthparts**) Zool. any of the appendages, typically found in pairs, surrounding the mouth of an insect or other arthropod and adapted for feeding.

mouth·piece /ˈmouTHˌpēs/ ▶ n. **1** a thing designed to be put in or against the mouth. ■ a part of a musical instrument placed between or against the lips. ■ the part of a telephone for speaking into. ■ the part of a tobacco pipe placed between the lips. ■ a mouthguard. **2** esp. derog. a person or organization that speaks on behalf of another person or organization. ■ informal a lawyer.

mouth-to-mouth ▶ adj. denoting a method of artificial respiration in which a person breathes into an unconscious patient's lungs through the mouth. ▶ n. respiration of this kind.

mouth·wash /ˈmouTHˌwôsH; -ˌwäsH/ ▶ n. a liquid used for rinsing the mouth or gargling with, typically containing an antiseptic.

mouth·wa·ter·ing /ˈmouTHˌwôtəriNG; -ˌwôtəriNG/ ▶ adj. smelling, looking, or sounding delicious. ■ highly attractive or tempting.

mouth·y /ˈmou<u>TH</u>ē; ˈmouTHē/ ▶ adj. (**mouth·i·er, mouth·i·est**) informal inclined to talk a lot, esp. in an impudent way.

mou·ton /ˈmo͞oˌtän; mo͞oˈtän/ ▶ n. sheepskin cut and dyed to resemble beaver fur or sealskin. [20th C.: from Fr., lit. 'sheep.']

mov·a·ble /ˈmo͞ovəbəl/ (also **move·a·ble**) ▶ adj. **1** capable of being moved. ■ (of a feast or festival) variable in date from year to year. See also MOVABLE FEAST. **2** Law (of property) of the nature of a chattel, as distinct from land or buildings. ▶ n. (usu. **movables**) property or possessions not including land or buildings. ■ an article of furniture that may be removed from a house, as distinct from a fixture. — **mov·a·bil·i·ty** /ˌmo͞ovəˈbilətē/ n. **mov·a·bly** adv.

mov·a·ble-do /ˈmo͞ovəbəl ˈdō/ (Brit. **mov·a·ble-doh**) ▶ adj. [attrib.] Music denoting a system of solmization (such as tonic sol-fa) in which do is the keynote of any major scale. Compare with FIXED-DO.

mov·a·ble feast ▶ n. a religious feast day that does not occur on the same calendar date each year, e.g., Easter.

mov·ant /ˈmo͞ovənt/ ▶ n. Law a person who applies to or petitions a court or judge for a ruling in his or her favor. [19th C.: from MOVE + -ANT.]

move /mo͞ov/ ▶ v. **1** [intrans.] go in a specified direction or manner; change position. ■ [trans.] change the place or position of. ■ change one's place of residence or work. ■ [trans.] change the date or time of (an event). ■ (of a player) change the position of a piece in a board game. **2** change or cause to change from one state, opinion, sphere, or activity to another. ■ [trans.] influence or prompt (someone) to do something. ■ [intrans.] take action. ■ [trans.] (usu. **be moved**) provoke a strong feeling, esp. of sorrow or sympathy, in: *he was moved to tears by a get-well message.* **3** [intrans.] make progress; develop in a particular manner or direction. ■ [intrans.] informal depart; start off. ■ [in imper.] (**move it**) informal used to urge or command someone to hurry up. ■ [intrans.] informal go quickly. ■ [intrans.] (of merchandise) be sold. ■ [trans.] sell (merchandise). **4** [intrans.] (**move in/within**) spend one's time or be socially active in (a particular sphere) or among (a particular group of people): *they moved in different circles of friends.* **5** [trans.] propose for discussion and resolution at a meeting or legislative assembly. ■ make a formal request or application to (a court or assembly) for something. **6** [trans.] empty (one's bowels). ■ [intrans.] (of the bowels) be emptied. ▶ n. a change of place or position. ■ a change of house or business premises. ■ a change of job, career, or business direction. ■ a change of state or opinion. ■ an action that initiates or advances a process or plan. ■ a maneuver in a sport or game. ■ a change of position of a piece in a board game. ■ a player's turn to make such a change.

– PHRASES **get a move on** [often in imper.] informal hurry up. **get moving** [often in imper.] informal make a prompt start (on a journey or an undertaking). **make a move** take action. ■ Brit. set off; leave somewhere: *I think I'd better be making a move.* **make a move on** (or **put the moves on**) informal make a proposition to (someone), esp. of a sexual nature. **move the goalposts** see GOALPOST. **move heaven and earth** see HEAVEN. **move mountains** see MOUNTAIN. **move with the times** keep abreast of current thinking or developments. **not move a muscle** see MUSCLE. **on the move** in the process of moving from one place or job to another. ■ making progress.

– PHRASAL VERBS **move along** [often in imper.] change to a new position, esp. to avoid causing an obstruction. **move aside** see MOVE OVER below. **move in 1** take possession of a new house or business premises. ■ (**move in with**) start to share accommodations with (an existing resident). **2** intervene, esp. so as to take control of a situation. **move in on** approach, esp. so as to take action. ■ become involved with so as to take control of or put pressure on. **move on** (or **move someone on**) go or cause to leave somewhere, esp. because one is causing an obstruction. ■ (**move on**) progress. **move out** (or **move someone out**) leave or cause to leave one's place of residence or work. **move over** (or **aside**) adjust one's position to make room for someone else. ■ relinquish a job or leading position, typically because of being superseded by someone or something more competent or important. **move up** adjust one's position, either to be nearer or make room for someone else. [ME: from OFr. *moveir*, from L. *movere*.]

move·a·ble /ˈmo͞ovəbəl/ ▶ adj. & n. var. of MOVABLE.

move·ment /ˈmo͞ovmənt/ ▶ n. **1** an act of changing physical location or position or of having this changed. ■ an arrival or departure of an aircraft. ■ (also **bowel movement**) an act of defecation. ■ (**movements**) the activities and whereabouts of someone, esp. during a particular period of time. ■ the general activity or bustle of people or things in a particular place. ■ the quality of suggesting motion in a work of art. ■ the progressive development of a poem or story. ■ a change or development in something. **2** [often with adj.] a group of people working together to advance their shared political, social, or artistic ideas. ■ [usu. in sing.] a campaign undertaken by such a group: *a movement to declare war on poverty.* ■ a change in policy or general attitudes seen as positive. **3** Music a principal division of a longer musical work, self-sufficient in terms of key, tempo, and structure. **4** the moving parts of a mechanism, esp. a clock or watch.

mov·er /ˈmo͞ovər/ ▶ n. **1** a person or thing in motion, esp. an animal. ■ a person whose job is to remove and transport furniture from one building, esp. a house, to another. **2** a person who makes a formal proposal at a meeting or in an assembly. ■ a person who instigates or organizes something.

– PHRASES **mover and shaker** a powerful person who initiates events and influences people. [from *movers and shakers*, a phr. from O'Shaughnessy's *Music & Moonlight* (1874).]

mov·ie /ˈmo͞ovē/ ▶ n. a story or event recorded by a camera as a set of moving images and shown in a theater or on television; a motion picture. ■ (**the movies**) a movie theater. ■ motion pictures generally or the motion-picture industry.

mov·ie·go·er /ˈmo͞ovēˌgōər/ ▶ n. a person who goes to the movies, esp. regularly. — **mov·ie·go·ing** n. & adj.

mov·ie·mak·er /ˈmo͞ovēˌmākər/ ▶ n. a person who makes motion pictures; filmmaker. — **mov·ie·mak·ing** n.

mov·ing /ˈmo͞oviNG/ ▶ adj. **1** [often with submodifier] in motion: *a fast-moving river.* **2** producing strong emotion, esp. sadness or sympathy. **3** relating to the process of changing one's residence. **4** [attrib.] involving a moving vehicle. — **mov·ing·ly** adv. (in sense 2).

PRONUNCIATION KEY ə *ago, up*; ər *over, fur*; a *hat*; ā *ate*; ä *car*; e *let*; ē *see*; i *fit*; ī *by*; NG *sing*; ō *go*; ô *law, for*; oi *toy*; o͝o *good*; o͞o *goo*; ou *out*; TH *thin*; <u>TH</u> *then*; ZH *vision*

mov·ing pic·ture ▶ n. dated a movie.

mov·ing side·walk (Brit. **moving pavement**) ▶ n. a mechanism resembling a conveyor belt for pedestrians in a place such as an airport.

mov·ing stair·way ▶ n. another term for ESCALATOR.

mov·i·ol·a /ˌmōōvēˈōlə/ (also **Mov·i·o·la** or **mov·ie·o·la**) ▶ n. trademark a device that reproduces the picture and sound of a movie on a small scale, to allow checking and editing.

mow[1] /mō/ ▶ v. (past part. **mowed** or **mown** /mōn/) [trans.] cut down (an area of grass) with a machine. ■ esp. hist. cut down (grass or a cereal crop) with a scythe or a sickle.
– PHRASAL VERBS **mow someone down** kill someone with a fusillade of bullets or other missiles. ■ recklessly knock someone down with a car or other vehicle. — **mow·er** n. [OE *māwan*; rel. to Ger. *mähen* 'mow,' MEAD[2].]

mow[2] /mou/ ▶ n. [often with adj.] a stack of hay, grain, or other similar crop: *the hay mow.* ■ a place in a barn where such a stack is put. [OE *mūga*; cf. Norw. *muga* 'heap.']

mow·ing /ˈmō-iNG/ ▶ n. the action of mowing. ■ (**mowings**) loose pieces of grass resulting from mowing. ■ a field of grass grown for hay.

mox·a /ˈmäksə/ ▶ n. a downy substance obtained from the dried leaves of an Asian composite plant (*Crossostephium artemisioides*). It is burned on or near the skin in Eastern medicine as a counterirritant. [17th C.: from Japanese *mogusa*, from *moe kusa* 'burning herb.']

mox·i·bus·tion /ˌmäksəˈbəsCHən/ ▶ n. (in Eastern medicine) the burning of moxa on or near a person's skin as a counterirritant.

mox·ie /ˈmäksē/ ▶ n. informal force of character, determination, or nerve. [20th C.: from *Moxie*, the proprietary name of a soft drink.]

Moy·ga·shel /ˈmoigəSHəl/ ▶ n. trademark a type of Irish linen.

Moy·ni·han /ˈmoi-nəˌhan/, Daniel Patrick (1927–2003), US politician. A Democrat from New York, he was a US senator 1977–2001.

Mo·zam·bique /ˌmōzamˈbēk/ a country on the eastern coast of southern Africa. *See box.* — **Mo·zam·bi·can** /-ˈbēkən/ adj. & n.

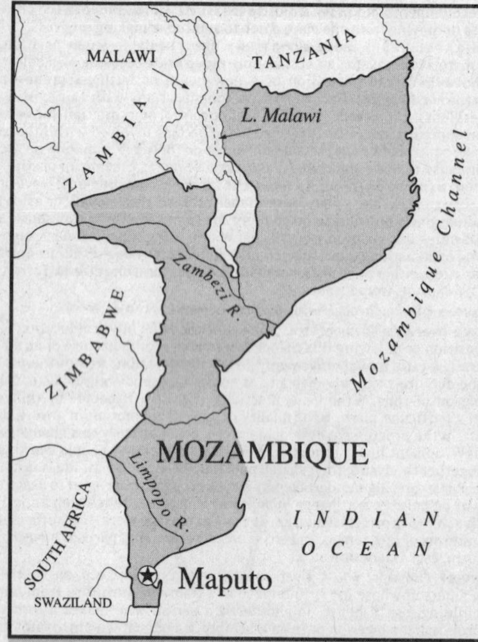

Mozambique

Official name: Republic of Mozambique
Location: southern Africa, on the eastern coast
Area: 309,600 square miles (801,600 sq km)
Population: 18,811,000
Capital: Maputo
Languages: Portuguese (official), Bantu languages
Currency: metical

Mo·zam·bique Chan·nel an arm of the Indian Ocean that separates mainland Africa from Madagascar.

Moz·ar·a·bic /mōˈzarəbik/ ▶ adj. hist. of or relating to the Christian inhabitants of Spain under the Muslim Moorish kings. — **Moz·ar·ab** n. [17th C.: from Sp. *mozárabe* (from Arab. *musta rib*, lit. 'making oneself an Arab') + -IC.]

Mo·zart /ˈmōtˌsärt/, Wolfgang Amadeus (1756–91), Austrian composer; full name *Johann Chrysostom Wolfgang Amadeus Mozart*. He wrote many symphonies, piano concertos, and string quartets, as well as operas. — **Mo·zar·ti·an** /mōtˈsärtēən/ adj. & n.

mo·zo /ˈmōsō; -zō/ ▶ n. (pl. **-zos**) (in Spanish-speaking regions) a male servant or attendant. [Sp., lit. 'boy.']

moz·za·rel·la /ˌmätsəˈrelə/ ▶ n. a mild, semisoft white Italian cheese, often used in Italian cooking as a melted topping, esp. on pizzas. [Ital., dimin. of *mozza*, denoting a kind of cheese, from *mozzare* 'cut off.']

moz·zet·ta /mōtˈsetə; mōˈzetə/ (also **mo·zet·ta**) ▶ n. (pl. **-zet·tas** or **-zet·te** /-ˈsetā; -ˈzetā/) a short cape with a hood, worn by the pope, cardinals, and some other ecclesiastics in the Roman Catholic Church. [18th C.: Ital., shortened form of *almozzetta*, from med. L. *almucia* 'amice.']

MP ▶ abbr. ■ Member of Parliament. ■ military police. ■ military policeman.

mp ▶ abbr. mezzo piano.

m.p. ▶ abbr. melting point.

MPA ▶ abbr. ■ Master of Public Administration. ■ Master of Public Accounting.

MPC ▶ abbr. multimedia personal computer.

MPD ▶ abbr. multiple personality disorder.

MPE ▶ abbr. Master of Public Education.

MPEG ▶ n. Comput. an international standard for encoding and compressing video images. [20th C.: from *Motion Pictures Experts Group.*]

mpg ▶ abbr. miles per gallon (a measurement of a vehicle's rate of fuel consumption).

MPH ▶ abbr. Master of Public Health.

mph ▶ abbr. miles per hour.

MPhil ▶ abbr. Master of Philosophy.

MPLA the Popular Movement for the Liberation of Angola, a Marxist organization founded in the 1950s that emerged as the ruling party in Angola after independence from Portugal in 1975. Once in power, the MPLA fought UNITA and other rival groups for many years.

MP3 ▶ n. a means of compressing a sound sequence into a very small file, used as a way of downloading audio files from the Internet. [1990s: from **MPEG** + *Audio Layer-3*.]

MPV ▶ abbr. multipurpose vehicle, a large vanlike car.

Mr. /ˈmistər/ ▶ n. a title used before a surname or full name to address or refer to a man without a higher or honorific or professional title. [ME: orig. an abbrev. of MASTER[1].] ■ used before the name of an office to address a man who holds it: *yes, Mr. President.* ■ humorous used before an invented surname to imply that someone has a particular characteristic: *Mr. Big-Shot.* ■ (often as **Mister**) used in the armed forces to address a senior warrant officer, officer cadet, or junior naval officer.

MRBM ▶ abbr. medium-range ballistic missile.

Mr. Clean ▶ n. trademark a brand of household cleaner. ■ informal a man, esp. a public figure, who has an impeccable image, record, or reputation. Sometimes used with **Miss, Mrs.,** or **Ms.** when referring to a woman.

MRE ▶ abbr. meal ready to eat (a precooked and prepackaged meal used by military personnel).

MRI ▶ abbr. magnetic resonance imaging.

mri·dan·gam /mriˈdäNGgəm/ ▶ n. a barrel-shaped double-headed drum with one head larger than the other, used in southern Indian music. [19th C.: Tamil alt. of Sanskrit *mṛdaṅga*.]

mRNA Biol. ▶ abbr. messenger RNA.

Mr. Right ▶ n. informal the ideal future husband.

Mrs. /ˈmisəz; ˈmiz-; -əs/ ▶ n. a title used before a surname or full name to address or refer to a married woman, or a woman who has been married, without a higher or honorific or professional title. [17th C.: abbrev. of MISTRESS.]

Mrs. Grun·dy /ˈgrəndē/ ▶ n. (pl. **Mrs. Grun·dys**) a person with conventional standards of propriety. [19th C.: a person mentioned in T. Morton's comedy *Speed the Plough* (1798), often in the phrase "What will Mrs. Grundy say?"]

MS ▶ abbr. ■ (also **ms**) manuscript. ■ Master of Surgery. ■ Master of Science. ■ Mississippi (in official postal use). ■ multiple sclerosis. ■ motor ship.

Ms. /miz/ ▶ n. a title used before the surname or full name of any woman regardless of her marital status (a neutral alternative to **Mrs.** or **Miss**). ■ humorous used before an invented surname to imply that someone has a particular characteristic: *Ms. Do-Right.* [1950s: combination of MRS. and MISS[2].]

MSB ▶ abbr. most significant bit.

MSc ▶ abbr. Master of Science.

MS-DOS /ˌemˌesˈdäs; dôs/ Comput., trademark ▶ abbr. Microsoft disk operating system.

msec. ▶ abbr. millisecond or milliseconds.

Mses. ▶ abbr. plural form of **Ms.**

MSG ▶ abbr. monosodium glutamate.

Msgr ▶ abbr. ■ Monseigneur. ■ Monsignor.

MSgt (also **MSGT**) ▶ abbr. master sergeant.

MS in LS ▶ abbr. Master of Science in Library Science.

MSN ▶ abbr. Master of Science in Nursing.

MSS (also **mss**) ▶ abbr. manuscripts.

MST ▶ abbr. Mountain Standard Time (see MOUNTAIN TIME).

MSW ▶ abbr. ■ Master of Social Welfare. ■ Master of Social Work.

MSY ▶ abbr. maximum sustainable yield.

MT ▶ **abbr.** ■ machine translation. ■ megaton. ■ (also **m.t.**) metric ton. ■ Montana (in official postal use).

Mt ▶ **abbr.** ■ the Gospel of Matthew (in biblical references). ■ [in place names] (also **Mt.**) Mount: *Mt. Everest.* ▶ **symb.** the chemical element meitnerium.

MTB ▶ **abbr.** mountain bike.

MTBF ▶ **abbr.** mean time between failures, a measure of the reliability of a device or system.

mtg. ▶ **abbr.** ■ meeting. ■ mortgage.

mtge. ▶ **abbr.** mortgage.

mtn. ▶ **abbr.** mountain.

mts. (also **Mts.**) ▶ **abbr.** mountains.

MTV trademark a cable and satellite television channel that broadcasts popular music and promotional music videos. [20th C.: abbrev. of *music television*.]

mu /m(y)o͞o/ ▶ **n.** the twelfth letter of the Greek alphabet (Μ, μ), transliterated as 'm.' ■ [as adj.] Physics relating to muons: *mu particle.* ▶ **symb.** ■ (μ) micron. ■ (μ) [in comb.] "micro-" in symbols for units: *the recommended daily amount is 750μg.* ■ (μ) permeability.

Mu·ba·rak /mo͝o'bärək/, Muhammad Hosni Said (1928–), president of Egypt 1981– . He has worked to establish closer links among Egypt and other Arab nations.

much /məCH/ ▶ **adj. & pron.** (**more** /môr/, **most**) [often with negative or in questions] a large amount: [as adj.] *I did not get much sleep* | [as pron.] *he does not eat much.* ■ [as pron.] [with negative] used to refer disparagingly to someone or something as being a poor specimen: *I'm not much of a gardener.* ▶ **adv.** to a great extent; a great deal: *did it hurt much?* ■ [usu. with negative or in questions] for a large part of one's time; often: *I'm not there much.*
– PHRASES **as much** the same: *I am sure she would do as much for me.* **a bit much** informal somewhat excessive or unreasonable: *expecting you to work seven days a week is a bit much.* **how much** used to ask what a particular amount or cost is. **make much of** give or ascribe a significant amount of attention or importance to. **(as) much as** even though: *much as I had enjoyed my adventure, it was good to be back.* **much less** see LESS. **so much the better** (or **worse**) that is even better (or worse): *if you can make it short, so much the better.* **this much** the fact about to be stated: *I know this much, you would defy the world to get what you wanted.* **too much** an intolerable, impossible, or exhausting situation or experience: *the effort proved too much for her.* — **much·ly adv.** (humorous). [ME: shortened from *muchel*, from OE *micel* (see MICKLE).]

mu·cha·cha /mo͞o'CHäCHə/ ▶ **n.** (in Spanish-speaking regions) a young woman.

mu·cha·cho /mo͞o'CHäCHō/ ▶ **n.** (pl. **-chos**) (in Spanish-speaking regions) a young man.

much·ness /'məCHnəs/ ▶ **n.** [in sing.] greatness in quantity or degree: *this romantic muchness can be overlooked in a story that has a good deal to say.*

mu·cho /'mo͞oCHō/ informal, humorous ▶ **adj.** much or many. ▶ **adv.** [usu. as submodifier] very. [Sp.]

mu·ci·lage /'myo͞os(ə)lij/ ▶ **n.** a viscous secretion or bodily fluid. ■ a polysaccharide substance extracted as a viscous or gelatinous solution from plant roots, seeds, etc., and used in medicines and adhesives. ■ an adhesive solution; gum, glue. — **mu·ci·lag·i·nous** /ˌmyo͞osə'lajənəs/ **adj.** [ME: via Fr. from late L. *mucilago* 'musty juice,' from L. *mucus* (see MUCUS).]

mu·cin /'myo͞osən/ ▶ **n.** Biochem. a glycoprotein constituent of mucus. [19th C.: from MUCUS + -IN[1].]

mu·ci·nous /'myo͞osənəs/ ▶ **adj.** of, relating to, or covered with mucus.

muck /mək/ ▶ **n.** dirt, rubbish, or waste matter. ■ farmyard manure, widely used as fertilizer. ■ informal something regarded as worthless, sordid, or corrupt. ▶ **v.** [trans.] **1** (**muck up**) informal mishandle (a job or situation); spoil (something). **2** (**muck out**) esp. Brit. remove (manure and other dirt) from a horse's stable or other animal's dwelling. **3** rare spread manure on (land).
– PHRASES **make a muck of** esp. Brit., informal handle incompetently.
– PHRASAL VERBS **muck about/around** esp. Brit., informal behave in a silly or aimless way, esp. by wasting time when serious activity is expected: *he spent his summers mucking about in boats.* ■ (**muck about/around with**) spoil (something) by interfering with it. [ME *muk*, prob. of Scand. origin: cf. ON *myki* 'dung.']

muck·er /'məkər/ ▶ **n. 1** informal or dated a rough or coarse person. [19th C.: prob. from Ger. *Mucker* 'sulky person.'] **2** a person who removes dirt and waste, esp. from stables.

muck·et·y-muck /'məkətē ˌmək/ (also **muck·y-muck** /'məkē ˌmək/ or **muck-a-muck** /'mək ə ˌmək/) ▶ **n.** informal a person of great importance or self-importance. [19th C.: from Chinook Jargon, shortening of HIGH MUCK-A-MUCK.]

muck·le /'məkəl/ ▶ **n., adj. & pron.** var. of MICKLE.

muck·rak·ing /'məkˌrākiNG/ ▶ **n.** the action of searching out and publicizing scandalous information about famous people in an underhanded way. — **muck·rake v. muck·rak·er n.**

muck·y /'məkē/ ▶ **adj.** (**muck·i·er, muck·i·est**) covered with or consisting of dirt or filth. — **muck·i·ness n.**

muco- /'myo͞okō/ ▶ **comb. form** Biochem. representing MUCUS.

mu·coid /'myo͞oˌkoid/ ▶ **adj.** of, involving, resembling, or of the nature of mucus. ▶ **n.** a substance resembling mucin, esp. a proteoglycan.

mu·co·sa /myo͞o'kōzə/ ▶ **n.** (pl. **-sae** /-zē; -ˌzī/) a mucous membrane. — **mu·co·sal adj.** [19th C.: mod. L., fem. of *mucosus*, from *mucus*.]

mu·cous /'myo͞okəs/ ▶ **adj.** relating to, producing, covered with, or of the nature of mucus. — **mu·cos·i·ty** /ˌmyo͞o'käsətē/ **n.**

mu·cous mem·brane ▶ **n.** an epithelial tissue that secretes mucus and that lines many body cavities and tubular organs including the gut and respiratory passages.

mu·cro /'myo͞okrō/ ▶ **n.** Bot. & Zool. a short sharp point at the end of a part or organ. [17th C.: from L., 'sharp point.']

mu·cro·nate /'myo͞okrəˌnāt/ ▶ **adj.** Bot. & Zool. ending abruptly in a short sharp point or mucro. [18th C.: from L. *mucronatus*, from *mucro, mucron-* 'point.']

mu·cus /'myo͞okəs/ ▶ **n.** a slimy substance, typically not miscible with water, secreted by mucous membranes and glands for lubrication, protection, etc. ■ a gummy substance found in plants; mucilage. [17th C.: from L.]

MUD /məd/ ▶ **n.** a computer-based text or virtual reality game that several players play at the same time, interacting with each other as well as with characters controlled by the computer. [20th C.: from *multiuser dungeon* or *multiuser dimension*.]

mud /məd/ ▶ **n.** soft, sticky matter resulting from the mixing of earth and water. ■ fig. information or allegations regarded as damaging, typically concerned with corruption.
– PHRASES **as clear as mud** informal not at all easy to understand. **drag someone through the mud** slander or denigrate someone publicly. **here's mud in your eye!** esp. Brit., informal used to express friendly feelings toward one's companions before drinking. **one's name is mud** informal one is in disgrace or unpopular. [ME: prob. from Mid. Low Ger. *mudde*.]

mud·bank /'mədˌbaNGk/ ▶ **n.** a bank of mud on the bed of a river or the bottom of the sea.

mud bath ▶ **n.** a bath in the mud of mineral springs, taken esp. for therapeutic purposes, such as to relieve rheumatic ailments, or as part of a beauty treatment. ■ a muddy place.

mud·bug /'mədˌbəg/ ▶ **n.** informal a freshwater crayfish.

mud daub·er ▶ **n.** a solitary wasp (family Sphecidae) that builds a mud nest typically consisting of a series of tubelike cells on an exposed surface.

blue mud dauber

mud·dle /'mədl/ ▶ **v.** [trans.] bring into a disordered or confusing state: *they were **muddling up** the cards.* ■ confuse (a person or their thoughts). ■ [intrans.] busy oneself in a confused and ineffective way. ■ mix (a drink) or stir (an ingredient) into a drink. ▶ **n.** [usu. in sing.] an untidy and disorganized state or collection. ■ a mistake arising from or resulting in confusion.
– PHRASAL VERBS **muddle through** cope more or less satisfactorily despite lack of expertise, planning, or equipment. **muddle something up** confuse two or more things with each other. — **mud·dling·ly** /'mədliNGlē; 'mədl-iNGlē/ **adv. mud·dly** /'mədlē; 'mədl-ē/ **adj.** [ME (in the sense 'wallow in mud'): perh. from MDu. *moddelen*, frequentative of *modden* 'dabble in mud'; cf. MUD.]

mud·dled /'mədld/ ▶ **adj.** in a state of bewildered or bewildering confusion or disorder.

mud·dle-head·ed (also **mud·dle·head·ed**) ▶ **adj.** mentally disorganized or confused. — **mud·dle-head·ed·ness** (or **mud·dle·head·ed·ness**) **n.**

mud·dler /'mədlər; 'mədl-ər/ ▶ **n. 1** a person who creates muddles, esp. because of a disorganized method of thinking or working. **2** (also **muddler minnow**) a type of fly used in trout fishing. **3** a stick used to stir mixed drinks.

mud·dy /'mədē/ ▶ **adj.** (**-di·er, -di·est**) covered in or full of mud. ■ (of a liquid) discolored and made cloudy by mud. ■ (of a color) dull and dirty-looking. ■ (of a sound, esp. in music) not clearly defined. ■ confused, vague, or illogical. ▶ **v.** (**-dies, -died**) [trans.] cause to become covered in or full of mud. ■ make (something) hard to perceive or understand.
– PHRASES **muddy the waters** make an issue or a situation more confusing by introducing complications. — **mud·di·ly adv. mud·di·ness n.**

mud·fish /'mədˌfiSH/ ▶ **n.** (pl. same or **-fish·es**) any of a number of fish that are able to survive long periods of drought by burrowing in the mud, in particular the bowfin.

mud flap (also **mud·flap**) ▶ **n.** a flap that hangs behind the wheel of a vehicle and is designed to prevent water, mud, and stones thrown up from the road from hitting the bodywork of the vehicle or any following vehicles.

mud·flat /'mədˌflat/ (also **mud flat**) ▶ **n.** (usu. **mudflats**) a stretch of muddy land left uncovered at low tide.

mud·flow /'mədˌflō/ ▶ **n.** a fluid or hardened stream or avalanche of mud.

mud·guard /ˈmədˌgärd/ ▶ **n.** a curved strip or cover over a wheel of a vehicle, esp. a bicycle or motorcycle, designed to protect the vehicle and rider from water and dirt thrown up from the road.

mud·pack /ˈmədˌpak/ ▶ **n.** a paste of fuller's earth or a similar substance, applied thickly to the face to improve the condition of the skin.

mud pie (also **mud·pie**) ▶ **n.** **1** mud made into a pie shape by a child. **2** short for MISSISSIPPI MUD PIE. ■ any of a variety of similar desserts, typically with a chocolate cookie crust, an ice cream filling and a chocolate sauce topping.

mud·pup·py ▶ **n.** a large aquatic salamander (*Necturus maculosus*, family Proteidae) of the eastern US, reaching sexual maturity while retaining an immature body form with feathery external gills.

mu·dra /məˈdrä/ ▶ **n.** a symbolic hand gesture used in Hindu and Buddhist ceremonies and statuary, and in Indian dance. ■ a movement or pose in yoga. [from Sanskrit *mudrā* 'sign or token.']

mud·skip·per /ˈmədˌskipər/ ▶ **n.** a goby (*Periopthalmodon* and related genera) with its eyes on raised bumps on top of the head, found in mangrove swamps from East Africa to Australia. It moves around on land with great agility, often basking on mud or mangrove roots.

mud·slide /ˈmədˌslīd/ ▶ **n.** a mass of mud and other earthy material that is falling or has fallen down a hillside or other slope.

mud·sling·ing /ˈmədˌsliNGiNG/ (also **mud-sling·ing**) ▶ **n.** informal the use of insults and accusations, esp. unjust ones, with the aim of damaging the reputation of an opponent. —**mud·sling** (also **mud-sling**) **v.** **mud·sling·er** (also **mud-sling·er**) **n.**

mud·stone /ˈmədˌstōn/ ▶ **n.** a dark sedimentary rock formed from consolidated mud and lacking the laminations of shale.

mud tur·tle ▶ **n.** any of a number of drab-colored freshwater turtles that often crawl onto mudbanks, in particular an American turtle (genus *Kinosternon*, family Kinosternidae) with scent glands that produce an unpleasant odor.

Muen·ster /ˈmənstər; ˈmo͝on-/ (also **muen·ster**, **Mun·ster**, or **mun·ster**) ▶ **n.** a mild, semisoft cheese made from whole milk. [for *Munster*, a town in the Alsace region of France.]

mues·li /ˈmyo͞ozlē; ˈmyo͞os-/ ▶ **n.** (pl. **mues·lis**) a mixture of cereals (esp. rolled oats), dried fruit, and nuts, typically eaten with milk at breakfast. [Swiss Ger.]

mu·ez·zin /m(y)o͞oˈezən; ˈmo͞oəzən/ ▶ **n.** a man who calls Muslims to prayer from the minaret of a mosque. [16th C.: dial. var. of Arab. *mu'addin*, active part. of *'addana* 'proclaim.']

muff[1] /məf/ ▶ **n.** **1** a tube made of fur or other warm material into which the hands are placed for warmth. ■ a warm or protective covering for other parts of the body. **2** vulgar slang a woman's genitals. [16th C.: from Du. *mof*, MDu. *muffel*, from med. L. *muff(u)la*, of unknown ultimate origin.]

muff[2] informal ▶ **v.** [trans.] handle (a situation, task, or opportunity) clumsily or badly. ■ fail to catch or receive (a ball) or to hit (a shot or a target). ■ speak (lines from a theatrical part) badly. ▶ **n.** a mistake or failure, esp. a failure to catch or receive a ball cleanly. [19th C.: of unknown origin.]

muf·fin /ˈməfən/ ▶ **n.** a small domed cake or quick bread made from batter or dough: *blueberry muffins*. ■ short for ENGLISH MUFFIN. [18th C.: of unknown origin.]

muf·fle /ˈməfəl/ ▶ **v.** [trans.] (often **be muffled**) wrap or cover for warmth. ■ cover or wrap up (a source of sound) to reduce its loudness. ■ make (a sound) quieter or less distinct. ■ restrain or conceal (someone) with wrappings. ▶ **n.** [usu. as adj.] a receptacle in a furnace or kiln in which things can be heated without contact with combustion products. [ME: perh. based onOFr. *moufle* 'thick glove.']

muf·fler /ˈməf(ə)lər/ ▶ **n.** **1** a scarf or wrap worn around the neck and face for warmth. **2** a part of a motor vehicle's exhaust system, serving to muffle the sound of the vehicle. ■ a device used to deaden the sound of a drum, bell, piano, or other instrument.

muf·ti[1] /ˈməftē/ ▶ **n.** (pl. **muf·tis**) a Muslim legal expert who is empowered to give rulings on religious matters. [16th C.: from Arab. *muftī*, active part. of *'aftā* 'decide a point of law.']

muf·ti[2] ▶ **n.** plain clothes worn by a person who wears a uniform for their job, such as a soldier or police officer. [19th C.: perh. humorously from MUFTI[1].]

mug[1] /məg/ ▶ **n.** **1** a large cup, typically cylindrical and with a handle and used without a saucer. ■ the contents of such a cup. **2** informal a person's face. **3** informal a hoodlum or thug. ▶ **v.** (**mugged**, **mug·ging**) informal **1** [trans.] (often **be mugged**) attack and rob (someone) in a public place. ■ dated fight or hit (someone). **2** [intrans.] make faces, esp. silly or exaggerated ones, before an audience or a camera: *he mugged for the camera*. —**mug·ful** **n.** (pl. **-fuls**). [16th C.: prob. of Scand. origin; cf. Swed. *mugg* 'pitcher.']

mug[2] ▶ **v.** (**mugged**, **mug·ging**) [trans.] (**mug something up**) Brit., informal learn or revise a subject as much as possible in a short time; cram: *I'm constantly having to mug up things ahead of teaching them* | [intrans.] *we had mugged up on all things Venetian before the start of the course.* [19th C.: of unknown origin.]

Mu·ga·be /mo͞oˈgäbē/, Robert Gabriel (1924–) president of Zimbabwe 1987– .

Mu·gan·da /mo͞oˈgändə/ ▶ **n.** singular form of BAGANDA.

mug·ger[1] /ˈməgər/ ▶ **n.** a person who attacks and robs another in a public place.

mug·ger[2] ▶ **n.** a large short-snouted Indian crocodile (*Crocodylus palustris*), venerated by many Hindus. [19th C.: from Hindi *magar*.]

mug·gy /ˈməgē/ ▶ **adj.** (**-gi·er**, **-gi·est**) (of the weather) unpleasantly warm and humid. —**mug·gi·ness** **n.** [18th C.: from dial. *mug* 'mist, drizzle,' from ON *mugga*.]

Mu·ghal /ˈmo͞ogəl/ var. of MOGUL.

mug shot (also **mug·shot**) ▶ **n.** informal a photograph of a person's face made for an official purpose, esp. police records. ■ humorous any photograph of a person's face.

mug·wump /ˈməgˌwəmp/ ▶ **n.** a person who remains aloof or independent, esp. from party politics. ■ a Republican who in 1884 refused to support James G. Blaine, the Republican nominee for president. [19th C.: from Algonquian *mugquomp* 'great chief.']

Mu·ha·mad /mo͝oˈhäməd; məˈhäməd/, Mahathir (1925–), prime minister of Malaysia 1981–2003.

Mu·ham·mad[1] /mo͝oˈhäməd; -ˈhäm-; mə-/ (also **Mo·ham·med**) (*c.*570–632), Arab prophet and founder of Islam. In *c.*610, in Mecca, he received the first of a series of revelations that, as the Koran, became the doctrinal and legislative basis of Islam.

Mu·ham·mad[2], Elijah (1897–1975), US activist; born Elijah Poole. Leader of the Black Muslim movement 1934–75, he advocated black separatism.

Mu·ham·mad Ah·mad /ˈaməd; ˈäm-/ see MAHDI.

Mu·ham·mad A·li[1] /mo͝oˈhäməd äˈlē; -ˈham-; mə-/ (1769–1849), viceroy of Egypt 1805–49. He modernized Egypt's infrastructure.

Mu·ham·mad A·li[2] see ALI[2].

Mu·ham·mad·an /mo͝oˈhämədən; ˈham-; mə-/ (also **Mo·ham·med·an**) ▶ **n. & adj.** archaic term for MUSLIM (not favored by Muslims). —**Mu·ham·mad·an·ism** **n.**

– USAGE See usage at MUSLIM.

Mu·har·ram /mo͝oˈhärəm/ ▶ **n.** the first month of the year in the Islamic calendar. ■ an annual celebration in this month commemorating the death of Husayn, grandson of Muhammad, and his retinue. [from Arab. *muḥarram* 'inviolable.']

Mühl·hau·sen /ˈmyo͞olˌhoizən; ˈmʏl-/ German name for MULHOUSE.

mu·ja·hi·deen /ˌmo͞ojəhiˈdēn/ (also **mu·ja·he·din**, **mu·ja·hi·din**, or **mu·ja·hed·din**) ▶ **plural n.** guerrilla fighters in Islamic countries, esp. those who are Islamic fundamentalists. [from Pers. and Arab. *mujāhidīn*, colloq. pl. of *mujāhid*, denoting a person who fights a jihad.]

Mu·ji·bur Rah·man /ˈmo͞ojiˌbo͝or ˈräKHmən; ˈräKHˌmän/ (1920–75), first prime minister of independent Bangladesh 1972–75 and president 1975; known as **Sheikh Mujib**. After failing to establish parliamentary democracy, he assumed dictatorial powers in 1975.

Muk·den /ˈmo͝okdən/ former name for SHENYANG.

mukh·tar /mo͝okˈtär/ ▶ **n.** (in Turkey and some Arab countries) the head of local government of a town or village. [from Arab. *muktār*, passive part. of *iktāra* 'choose.']

muk·luk /ˈməkˌlək/ ▶ **n.** a high, soft boot that is worn in the American Arctic and is traditionally made from sealskin. [19th C.: from Yupik *maklak* 'bearded seal.']

muk·tuk /ˈməkˌtək/ ▶ **n.** the skin and blubber of a whale, typically the narwhal or the beluga, used as food by the Inuit. [from Inuit *maktak*.]

mu·lat·to /m(y)o͝oˈlätō; -ˈlatō/ dated ▶ **n.** (pl. **-toes** or **-tos**) a person of mixed white and black ancestry, esp. a person with one white and one black parent. ▶ **adj.** relating to or denoting a mulatto or mulattoes. [16th C.: from Sp. *mulato*, from Arab. *muwallad* 'person of mixed race.']

mul·ber·ry /ˈməlˌberē/ ▶ **n.** **1** (also **mulberry tree** or **bush**) a small deciduous tree (genus *Morus*, family Moraceae) with broad leaves, native to the Far East and long cultivated elsewhere. ■ the dark red or white loganberrylike fruit of this tree. **2** a dark red or purple color. [OE *mōrberie*, from L. *morum* + BERRY.]

mulch /məlCH/ ▶ **n.** a material (such as decaying leaves, bark, or compost) spread around or over a plant to enrich or insulate the soil. ■ an application of such a material. ■ a formless mass or pulp. ▶ **v.** [intrans.] apply a mulch. ■ [trans.] treat or cover with mulch. [17th C.: prob. from dial. *mulch* 'soft' used as a n., from OE *melsc*, *mylsc*.]

mulct /məlkt/ formal ▶ **v.** [trans.] extract money from (someone) by fine or taxation: *no government dared propose to mulct the taxpayer for such a purpose.* ■ (**mulct someone of**) deprive (someone) of (money or possessions) by fraudulent means. ▶ **n.** a fine or compulsory payment. [15th C.: from L. *mulctare*, *multare*, from *mulcta* 'a fine.']

Mul·doon /məlˈdo͞on/, Sir Robert David (1921–92), New Zealand statesman; prime minister 1975–84. His premiership was marked by domestic measures to tackle low economic growth and high inflation.

mule[1] /myo͞ol/ ▶ **n.** **1** the offspring of a donkey and a horse (strictly, a male donkey and a female horse), typically sterile and used as a beast of burden. Compare with HINNY. ■ a person compared to a mule, esp. in being stubborn or obstinate. ■ informal a courier for illegal drugs. ■ a small tractor or locomotive, typically one that is electrically powered. **2** a hybrid plant or animal, esp. a sterile one. ■ any of several standard crossbred varieties of sheep. **3** (also **spinning mule**) a kind of spinning machine producing yarn on spindles, invented by Samuel Crompton (1753–1827) in 1779. **4** a coin with the obverse and reverse of designs not originally intended to be used together. [OE *mūl*, prob. of Gmc. origin, from L. *mulus*, *mula*.]

mule[2] ▶**n.** a slipper or light shoe without a back. [16th C.: from Fr., 'slipper.']

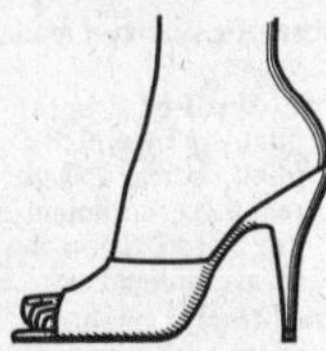

mule[2]

mule deer ▶**n.** a western North American deer (*Odocoileus hemionus*) with large ears. The mule deer of the Rocky Mountains has a black tipped tail; the subspecies of the northwest Pacific coast (the blacktail deer) has a tail with a blackish upper side.

mule ears ▶**plural n.** [usu. treated as sing.] a sunflowerlike composite plant (genus *Wyethia*) of the western US, with large oval leaves. Its several species include the yellow-flowered **gray mule ears** (*W. helenioides*), with gray-haired leaves and very large bracts, and the white-flowered **white mule ears** (*W. helianthoides*).

gray mule ears

mu·le·ta /myo͞oˈlätə/ ▶**n.** a small red cape fixed to a stick, employed by a matador to guide the bull during a bullfight. [Sp.]

mu·le·teer /ˌmyo͞oləˈti(ə)r/ ▶**n.** a person who drives mules. [16th C.: from Fr. *muletier*, from *mulet*, dimin. of OFr. *mul* 'mule.']

mul·ey[1] /ˈmyo͞olē/ ▶**adj.** (of cattle) hornless. ▶**n.** informal a cow, esp. a hornless one. [16th C.: perh. from Irish *maol* or Welsh *moel*, lit. 'bald.']

mul·ey[2] (also **mul·ie**) ▶**n.** (pl. **mul·eys** or **mul·ies**) informal a mule deer.

Mül·heim /ˈmyo͞olˌhīm; ˈmYl-/ a city in western Germany; pop. 177,000. Full name **Mülheim an der Ruhr**.

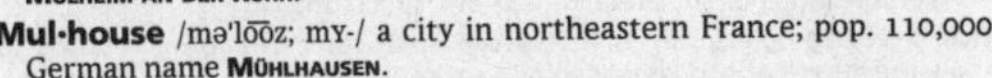

Mul·house /məˈlo͞oz; mY-/ a city in northeastern France; pop. 110,000. German name **Mühlhausen**.

mu·li·eb·ri·ty /ˌmyo͞olēˈebrətē/ ▶**n.** literary womanly qualities; womanhood. [16th C.: from late L. *muliebritas*, from L. *mulier* 'woman.']

mul·ish /ˈmyo͞olisн/ ▶**adj.** resembling or likened to a mule in being stubborn: *Belinda's face took on a mulish expression.* —**mul·ish·ly adv. mul·ish·ness n.**

Mull /məl/ a large island of the Inner Hebrides.

mull[1] /məl/ ▶**v.** [trans.] think about (a fact, proposal, or request) deeply and at length: *she began to **mull over** the various possibilities.* [19th C.: of uncert. origin.]

mull[2] ▶**v.** [trans.] [usu. as adj.] (**mulled**) warm (a beverage, esp. wine, beer, or cider) and add spices and sweetening to it. [17th C.: of unknown origin.]

mull[3] ▶**n.** Soil Science humus formed under nonacid conditions. [1920s: from Dan. *muld* 'soil.']

mull[4] ▶**n.** thin, soft, plain muslin, used in bookbinding for joining the spine of a book to its cover. [17th C.: abbrev., from Hindi *malmal*.]

mul·lah /ˈmələ; ˈmo͝olə; ˈmo͞olə/ (also **mul·la**) ▶**n.** a Muslim learned in Islamic theology and sacred law. [17th C.: from Pers., Turk., and Urdu *mullā*, from Arab. *mawlā*.]

mul·lein /ˈmələn/ ▶**n.** a herbaceous Eurasian plant (genus *Verbascum*) of the figwort family, with woolly leaves and tall spikes of yellow flowers. Its several species include the widespread **common** (or **great**) **mullein** (*V. thapsus*). [ME: from OFr. *moleine*, of Celtic origin; cf. Welsh *melyn* 'yellow.']

Mul·ler /ˈmələr; ˈmyo͞o-/, Hermann Joseph (1890–1967), US geneticist. He discovered that X-rays induce mutations in the genetic material of the fruit fly. Nobel Prize for Physiology or Medicine (1946).

Mül·ler[1] /ˈm(y)o͞olər/, Johannes Peter (1801–58), German anatomist and zoologist. He was a pioneer of comparative and microscopical methods in biology.

Mül·ler[2], Paul Hermann (1899–1965), Swiss chemist. He synthesized DDT 1939 and patented it as an insecticide. Nobel Prize for Physiology or Medicine (1948).

mull·er /ˈmələr/ ▶**n.** a stone or other heavy weight used for grinding artists' pigments or other material on a slab. [ME: perh. from Anglo-Norman Fr. *moldre* 'to grind.']

common mullein

Mül·ler·i·an mim·ic·ry /myo͞oˈli(ə)rēən; milˈi(ə)r-/ ▶**n.** Zool. a form of mimicry in which two or more noxious animals develop similar appearances as a shared protective device, the theory being that if a predator learns to avoid one of the noxious species, it will avoid the mimic species as well. Compare with **Batesian mimicry**. [19th C.: named after Johann F. T. *Müller* (1821–97), Ger. zoologist.]

mul·let[1] /ˈmələt/ ▶**n.** a chiefly marine fish (families Mullidae and Mugilidae) that is widely caught for food. [ME: from OFr. *mulet*, dimin. of L. *mullus* 'red mullet,' from Gk. *mullos*.]

mul·let[2] ▶**n.** Heraldry a star with five (or more) straight-edged points or rays, as a charge or a mark of cadency for a third son. [ME: from OFr. *molette* 'rowel,' dimin. of *meule* 'millstone,' from L. *mola* 'grindstone.']

mul·li·gan /ˈməligən/ ▶**n.** informal **1** (also **mulligan stew**) a stew made from odds and ends of food. **2** (in informal golf) an extra stroke allowed after a poor shot, not counted on the scorecard. [20th C.: appar. from the surname *Mulligan*.]

mul·li·ga·taw·ny /ˌməligəˈtônē; -ˈtänē/ (also **mulligatawny soup**) ▶**n.** a spicy meat soup originally made in India. [from Tamil *miḷaku-taṇṇi* 'pepper-water.']

mul·lion /ˈməlyən/ ▶**n.** a vertical bar between the panes of glass in a window. Compare with **transom**. —**mul·lioned adj.** [16th C.: prob. an alt. form of *monial*, based on OFr. *moien*, *meien* 'middle' (see **mean**[3].)]

mullion

Mul·ro·ney /məlˈrōnē; -ˈro͞o-/, Brian (1939–), prime minister of Canada 1984–93; full name *Martin Brian Mulroney*.

Mul·tan /mo͞olˈtän/ a commercial city in Punjab province, in east central Pakistan; pop. 980,000.

mul·tan·gu·lar /ˌməlˈtaNGgyələr/ ▶**adj.** rare (of a polygon) having many angles. [17th C.: from med. L. *multangularis*.]

multi- ▶**comb. form** more than one; many, esp. variegated: *multicolor* | *multicultural*. [from L. *multus* 'much, many.']

mul·ti·ac·cess /ˌməltēˈakˌses; ˌməltī-/ ▶**adj.** (of a computer system) allowing the simultaneous connection of a number of terminals.

mul·ti·a·gen·cy /ˌməltēˈājənsē; ˌməltī-/ ▶**adj.** involving cooperation among several organizations, esp. in crime prevention, social welfare programs, or research.

mul·ti·cast /ˈməltiˌkast; ˌməltiˈkast/ ▶**v.** (past and past part. **-cast**) [trans.] send (data) across a computer network to several users at the same time. ▶**n.** a set of data sent across a computer network to many users at the same time.

mul·ti·cul·tur·al /ˌməltēˈkəlcн(ə)rəl; ˌməltī-/ ▶**adj.** of, relating to, or constituting several cultural or ethnic groups within a society. —**mul·ti·cul·tur·al·ism n. mul·ti·cul·tur·al·ist** /-list/ **n. & adj. mul·ti·cul·tur·al·ly adv.**

mul·ti·dis·ci·pli·nar·y /ˌməltiˈdisəpliˈnerē; ˌməltī-/ ▶**adj.** combining or involving several academic disciplines or professional specializations in an approach to a topic or problem.

mul·ti·fac·to·ri·al /ˌməltiˌfakˈtôrēəl; ˌməltī-/ ▶**adj.** involving or dependent on a number of factors or causes.

mul·ti·far·i·ous /ˌməlt(ə)ˈfe(ə)rēəs/ ▶**adj.** many and of various types. ■ having many varied parts or aspects. —**mul·ti·far·i·ous·ly adv. mul·ti·far·i·ous·ness n.** [16th C.: from L. *multifarius* + **-ous**.]

mul·ti·fid /ˈməltiˌfid; ˈməltə-; ˈməltī-/ ▶**adj.** Bot. & Zool. divided into several or many parts by deep clefts or notches. [18th C.: from L. *multifidus*, from *multus* 'much, many' + *-fid* from *fidus* 'cleft, split.']

mul·ti·fil·a·ment /ˌməltiˈfiləmənt; ˌməltī-/ ▶**adj.** denoting a cord or yarn composed of a number of strands or filaments wound together.

mul·ti·flo·ra /ˈməltiˌflôrə/ (also **multiflora rose**) ▶**n.** an eastern Asian shrubby or climbing rose (*Rosa multiflora*) that bears clusters of small single pink or white flowers. [19th C.: from late L., fem. of *multiflorus* 'multiflorous.']

mul·ti·fold /ˈməltiˌfōld/ ▶**adj.** manifold.

mul·ti·form /ˈməltiˌfôrm/ ▶**adj.** existing in many forms or kinds. —**mul·ti·for·mi·ty** /-ˈfôrmətē/ **n.**

mul·ti·grade /ˈməltiˌgrād; ˈməltə-; ˈməltī-/ ▶**n.** **1** an engine oil meeting the requirements of several standard grades. **2** (**Multigrade**) trademark a kind of photographic paper made with two emulsions of different sensitivities, from which prints with different levels of contrast can be made using color filters.

mul·ti·grav·i·da /ˌməltiˈgravədə/ ▶**n.** (pl. **-grav·id·ae** /-ˈgravəˌdē; -ˌdī/) Med. & Zool. a woman (or female animal) who is or has been pregnant for at least a second time. [19th C.: from **multi-** 'many,' on the pattern of *primigravida*.]

mul·ti·hull /ˈməltiˌhəl; ˈməltī-/ ▶**n.** a boat with two or more hulls, esp. three.

mul·ti·lat·er·al /ˌməltiˈlatərəl/ ▶**adj.** agreed upon or participated in by three or more parties, esp. the governments of different countries. ■ having members or contributors from several groups, esp. several different countries. —**mul·ti·lat·er·al·ism n. mul·ti·lat·er·al·ist** /-list/ **adj. & n. mul·ti·lat·er·al·ly adv.**

mul·ti·me·di·a /ˈməltiˈmēdēə; ˈməltī-/ ▶**adj.** (of art, education, etc.) using more than one medium of expression or communication. ▶**n.** an extension of hypertext allowing the provision of audio and video material cross-referenced to a computer text.

mul·tim·e·ter /ˈməltiˌmētər; ˌməlˈtimətər/ ▶**n.** an instrument designed to measure electric current, voltage, and usually resistance, typically over several ranges of value.

mul·ti·mil·lion /ˈməltiˈmilyən; ˈməltī-/ ▶**adj.** [attrib.] costing or involving several million units of a currency: [in comb.] *a multimillion-dollar campaign.*

PRONUNCIATION KEY ə *ago, up*; ər *over, fur*; a *hat*; ā *ate*; ä *car*; e *let*; ē *see*; i *fit*; ī *by*; NG *sing*; ō *go*; ô *law, for*; oi *toy*; o͝o *good*; o͞o *goo*; ou *out*; TH *thin*; T͟H *then*; ZH *vision*

mul·ti·mil·lion·aire /ˌməltiˌmilyəˈne(ə)r; ˌməltī-/ ▶ **n.** a person with assets worth several million dollars.

mul·ti·mod·al /ˈməltiˌmōd; ˈməltī-/ (also **mul·ti·mode**) ▶ **adj.** characterized by several different modes of activity or occurrence. ■ Stat. (of a frequency curve or distribution) having several modes or maxima. ■ Stat. (of a property) occurring with such a distribution.

mul·ti·na·tion·al /ˌməltiˈnashənl; ˌməltī-/ ▶ **adj.** including or involving several countries or individuals of several nationalities. ■ (of a business organization) operating in several countries. ▶ **n.** a company operating in several countries. — **mul·ti·na·tion·al·ly adv.**

mul·ti·no·mi·al /ˌməltiˈnōmēəl; ˌməltī-/ ▶ **adj. & n.** Math., rare another term for POLYNOMIAL.

mul·ti·pack /ˈməltiˌpak; ˈməltī-/ ▶ **n.** a package containing a number of similar or identical products sold at a discount compared to the price when bought separately.

mul·tip·a·ra /məlˈtipərə/ ▶ **n.** (pl. **-rae** /-ˌrē; -ˌrī/) Med. & Zool. a woman (or female animal) who has had more than one pregnancy resulting in viable offspring. [19th C.: mod. L., fem. of *multiparus* 'multiparous.']

mul·tip·a·rous /məlˈtipərəs/ ▶ **adj.** Med. (of a woman) having borne more than one child. ■ esp. Zool. producing more than one young at a birth.

mul·ti·par·tite /ˌməltiˈpärˌtīt/ ▶ **adj.** having several or many parts or divisions. ■ Biol. (of a virus) existing as two or more separate but incomplete particles. ■ another term for MULTIPARTY.

mul·ti·par·ty /ˈməltiˈpärtē; ˈməltī-/ ▶ **adj.** of or involving several political parties: *multiparty elections.*

mul·ti·phase /ˈməltēˌfāz/ ▶ **adj.** in, of, or relating to more than one phase. ■ (of an electrical device or circuit) polyphase.

mul·ti·play /ˈməltiˌplā; ˈməltī-/ ▶ **adj.** denoting a compact disc player that can be stacked with a number of discs before needing to be reloaded.

mul·ti·play·er /ˈməltiˌplāər; ˈməltī-/ ▶ **n.** a multimedia computer and home entertainment system that integrates a number of conventional and interactive audio and video functions with those of a personal computer. ▶ **adj.** denoting a computer game designed for or involving several players.

mul·ti·ple /ˈməltəpəl/ ▶ **adj.** having or involving several parts, elements, or members. ■ numerous and often varied. ■ (of a disease, injury, or disability) complex in its nature or effects, or affecting several parts of the body. ■ of or designating electrical circuits arranged in parallel. ■ of or designating an electrical circuit that has several points at which connection can occur. ▶ **n. 1** a number that can be divided by another number without a remainder: *15, 20, or any multiple of five.* **2** an arrangement of terminals that allows connection with an electrical circuit at any one of several points. [17th C.: from Fr., from late L. *multiplus*, alt. of L. *multiplex* (see MULTIPLEX).]

mul·ti·ple-choice ▶ **adj.** (of a question on a test) accompanied by several possible answers from which the candidate must try to choose the correct one.

mul·ti·ple fruit ▶ **n.** Bot. a fruit formed from carpels derived from several flowers, such as a pineapple.

mul·ti·ple per·son·al·i·ty ▶ **n.** [often as adj.] Psychol. a rare dissociative disorder in which two or more personalities with distinct memories and behavior patterns apparently exist in one individual: *multiple-personality disorder.*

mul·ti·ple scle·ro·sis ▶ **n.** a chronic, typically progressive disease involving damage to the sheaths of nerve cells in the brain and spinal cord, whose symptoms may include numbness, impairment of speech and of muscular coordination, blurred vision, and fatigue.

mul·ti·ple star ▶ **n.** a group of stars very close together as seen from the earth, esp. one whose members are in fact close together and rotate around a common center.

mul·ti·plet /ˈməltəplit/ ▶ **n.** Physics a group of closely associated things, esp. closely spaced spectral lines or atomic energy levels, or subatomic particles differing only in a single property (e.g., charge or strangeness). [1920s: from MULTIPLE.]

mul·ti·plex /ˈməltiˌpleks/ ▶ **adj.** consisting of many elements in a complex relationship. ■ involving simultaneous transmission of several messages along a single channel of communication. ■ (of a movie theater) having several separate screens within one building. ▶ **n. 1** a system or signal involving simultaneous transmission of several messages along a single channel of communication. **2** a movie theater with several separate screens. ▶ **v.** [trans.] incorporate into a multiplex signal or system. — **mul·ti·plex·er** (also **mul·ti·plex·or**) **n.** [ME in the mathematical sense 'multiple': from L.]

mul·ti·pli·a·ble /ˈməltəˌplīəbəl; ˈməltē-/ (also **mul·ti·plic·a·ble** /ˌməltəˈplikəbəl; ˌməltē-/) ▶ **adj.** able to be multiplied.

mul·ti·pli·cand /ˌməltəpliˈkand/ ▶ **n.** a quantity that is to be multiplied by another (the multiplier). [16th C.: from med. L. *multiplicandus* 'to be multiplied,' gerundive of L. *multiplicare* (see MULTIPLY¹).]

mul·ti·pli·ca·tion /ˌməltəpliˈkāshən/ ▶ **n.** the process or skill of multiplying. ■ Math. the process of combining matrices, vectors, or other quantities under specific rules to obtain their product.

mul·ti·pli·ca·tion sign ▶ **n.** a sign, esp. ×, used to indicate that one quantity is to be multiplied by another, as in $2\times3=6$.

mul·ti·pli·ca·tion ta·ble ▶ **n.** a table of the products of two factors, esp. the integers 1 to 12.

mul·ti·pli·ca·tive /ˌməltəˈplikətiv; ˈməltəpləˌkātiv/ ▶ **adj.** subject to or of the nature of multiplication.

mul·ti·plic·i·ty /ˌməltəˈplisətē/ ▶ **n.** (pl. **-ties**) a large number. ■ a large variety.

mul·ti·pli·er /ˈməltəˌplīər/ ▶ **n.** a person or thing that multiplies. ■ a quantity by which a given number (the multiplicand) is to be multiplied. ■ Econ. a factor by which an increment of income exceeds the resulting increment of savings or investment. ■ a device for increasing by repetition the intensity of an electric current, force, etc., to a measurable level.

mul·ti·ply¹ /ˈməltəˌplī/ ▶ **v.** (**-plies, -plied**) [trans.] obtain from (a number) another that contains the first number a specified number of times. ■ increase or cause to increase greatly in number or quantity. ■ [intrans.] (of an animal or other organism) increase in number by reproducing. ■ propagate (plants). [ME: from OFr. *multiplier*, from L. *multiplicare*.]

mul·ti·ply² /ˈməltəplē/ ▶ **adv.** [often as submodifier] in several different ways or respects: *multiply injured patients.*

mul·ti·po·lar /ˌməltiˈpōlər; ˌməltī-/ ▶ **adj. 1** having many poles or extremities. **2** polarized in several ways or directions. — **mul·ti·po·lar·i·ty** /-pōˈlaritē; -pə-/ **n. mul·ti·pole** /ˈməltiˌpōl; ˈməltī-/ **n.**

mul·ti·proc·ess·ing /ˌməltiˈpräsesiNG; ˌməltī-; -ˈpräsəsiNG/ (also **mul·ti·pro·gram·ming**) ▶ **n.** Comput. the running of two or more programs or sequences of instructions simultaneously by a computer with more than one central processor.

mul·ti·proc·es·sor /ˌməltiˈpräsesər; -ˈpräsəsər/ ▶ **n.** a computer with more than one central processor.

mul·ti·role /ˈməltiˌrōl; ˈməltī-/ ▶ **adj.** [attrib.] (chiefly of an aircraft) capable of performing several roles.

mul·ti·ses·sion /ˈməltiˌseshən; ˈməltī-/ ▶ **adj.** Comput. denoting a format for recording digital information onto a CD-ROM disc over two or more separate sessions.

mul·ti·spec·tral /ˌməltiˈspektrəl; ˌməltī-/ ▶ **adj.** operating in or involving several regions of the electromagnetic spectrum.

mul·ti·stage /ˈməltiˈstāj; ˌməltī-/ ▶ **adj.** [attrib.] consisting of or relating to several stages or processes. ■ (of a rocket) having at least two sections, each of which contains its own motor and is jettisoned as its fuel runs out. ■ (of a pump, turbine, or similar device) having more than one rotor.

mul·ti·sto·ry /ˈməltiˌstôrē; ˈməltī-/ (also **mul·ti·sto·ried**) ▶ **adj.** [attrib.] (of a building) having several stories.

mul·ti·task·ing /ˌməltiˈtaskiNG; ˌməltī-/ ▶ **n.** Comput. the simultaneous execution of more than one program or task by a single computer processor. — **mul·ti·task** /ˈməltiˌtask; ˈməltī-/ **v.**

mul·ti·thread·ing /ˈməltiˈTHrediNG; ˈməltī-/ ▶ **n.** Comput. a technique by which a single set of code can be used by several processors at different stages of execution. — **mul·ti·thread·ed** /-ˈTHredəd/ **adj.**

mul·ti·track /ˈməltiˌtrak; ˈməltī-/ ▶ **adj.** relating to or made by the mixing of several separately recorded tracks of sound: *a digital multitrack recorder.* ▶ **n.** a recording made from the mixing of several separately recorded tracks. ▶ **v.** [trans.] record using multitrack recording: [as adj.] (**multitracked**) *multitracked vocals.*

mul·ti·tude /ˈməltəˌt(y)o͞od/ ▶ **n.** a large number. ■ (**the multitudes**) large numbers of people. ■ (**the multitude**) a large gathering of people. ■ (**the multitude**) the mass of ordinary people without power or influence.

– PHRASES **cover a multitude of sins** see COVER. [ME: via OFr. from L. *multitudo*, from *multus* 'many.']

mul·ti·tu·di·nous /ˌməltəˈt(y)o͞odn-əs/ ▶ **adj.** very numerous. ■ consisting of or containing many individuals or elements. ■ literary (of a body of water) vast. — **mul·ti·tu·di·nous·ly adv. mul·ti·tu·di·nous·ness n.**

mul·ti·us·er /ˈməltēˈyo͞ozər; ˈməltī-/ ▶ **adj.** [attrib.] (of a computer system) able to be used by a number of people simultaneously. ■ denoting a computer game in which several players interact simultaneously using the Internet or other communications.

mul·ti·va·lent /ˌməltiˈvālənt; ˌməltī-/ ▶ **adj. 1** having or susceptible to many applications, interpretations, meanings, or values. **2** Med. (of an antigen or antibody) having several sites at which attachment to an antibody or antigen can occur. Compare with POLYVALENT. **3** Chem. another term for POLYVALENT. — **mul·ti·va·lence n.**

mul·ti·valve /ˌməltiˈvalv; ˌməltī-/ ▶ **adj.** [attrib.] **1** Zool. (of a shell, etc.) having several valves. **2** (of an internal combustion engine) having more than two valves per cylinder, typically four (two inlet and two exhaust). ▶ **n.** a multivalve shell, or an animal having such a shell, as a chiton.

mul·ti·var·i·ate /ˌməltiˈve(ə)rēət; ˌməltī-/ ▶ **adj.** Stat. involving two or more variable quantities.

mul·ti·ven·dor /məltiˈvendər/ ▶ **adj.** [attrib.] denoting or relating to computer hardware or software products or network services from more than one supplier.

mul·ti·verse /ˈməltiˌvərs/ ▶ **n.** an infinite realm of being or potential being of which the universe is regarded as a part or instance.

mul·ti·ver·si·ty /ˌməltiˈvərsətē/ ▶ **n.** (pl. **-ties**) a large university with many different departments. [20th C.: from MULTI- + a shortened form of UNIVERSITY.]

mul·ti·vi·bra·tor /ˌməltiˈvīˌbrātər/ ▶ **n.** Electron. a device consisting of two amplifying transistors or valves, each with its output connected to the input of the other, producing an oscillatory signal.

mul·ti·vi·ta·min /ˌməltiˈvītəmən/ ▶ **adj.** [attrib.] containing a combination of vitamins. ▶ **n.** a pill containing a combination of vitamins.

mul·ti·way /ˈməltiˌwā; ˈməltī-/ ▶ **adj.** having several paths, routes, or channels.

mul·tum in par·vo /ˈmo͝oltəm in ˈpärvō; -ˈpärwō/ ▶ **n.** a great deal in a small space. [L., lit. 'much in little.']

mul·ture /ˈməlCHər/ ▶ **n.** hist. a toll of grain or flour due to a miller in return for grinding grain. ■ the right to collect this. [ME: from OFr. *moulture*, from med. L. *molitura*, from *molit-* 'ground,' from the v. *molere*.]

mum[1] /məm/ ▶ **adj.** silent.
– PHRASES **mum's the word** informal (as a request or warning) say nothing; don't reveal a secret. [ME: imitative of a sound made with closed lips.]

mum[2] ▶ **v.** **(mummed, mum·ming)** [intrans.] act in a traditional masked mime or a mummers' play. [ME: cf. MUM[1] and Mid. Low Ger. *mummen*.]

mum[3] ▶ **n.** informal a cultivated chrysanthemum.

mum[4] ▶ **n.** British term for MOM. [17th C.: abbrev. of MUMMY[2].]

Mum·bai /ˈməm,bī/ official name (from 1995) for BOMBAY.

mum·ble /ˈməmbəl/ ▶ **v.** **1** [reporting verb] say something indistinctly and quietly, making it difficult for others to hear. **2** [trans.] bite or chew with toothless gums or eat without making much use of the teeth. ▶ **n.** [usu. in sing.] a quiet and indistinct utterance. — **mum·bler** /ˈməmb(ə)lər/ **n.** **mum·bling·ly** /ˈməmb(ə)liNGlē/ **adv.** [ME: frequentative of MUM[1].]

mum·ble·ty-peg /ˈməmbəltē,peg/ (also **mum·ble·ty·peg**) ▶ **n.** a game in which each player in turn throws a knife or pointed stick from a series of positions, continuing until it fails to stick in the ground. [17th C.: also *mumble the peg*, from *mumble* 'bite as if with toothless gums,' from the requirement of the game that an unsuccessful player withdraw a peg from the ground using the mouth.]

mum·bo-jum·bo /ˈməmbō ˈjəmbō/ (also **mum·bo· jum·bo**) ▶ **n.** informal language or ritual causing or intended to cause confusion or bewilderment. [18th C.: perh. of Afr. origin; compare *Mama Dyumbo*, a spirit worshiped by the Mande.]

mu me·son /myo͞o/ ▶ **n.** another term for MUON.

Mum·ford /ˈməmfərd/, Lewis (1895–1990), US social philosopher. He wrote *The Renewal of Life* in four volumes (1934–51) and *The Myth of the Machine* (1967).

mum·mer /ˈməmər/ ▶ **n.** an actor in a traditional masked mime, esp. of a type associated with Christmas and popular in England in the 18th and early 19th centuries. ■ a pantomimist. [ME: from OFr. *momeur*, from *momer* 'act in a mime'; perh. of Gmc. origin.]

mum·mer·y /ˈməmərē/ ▶ **n.** (pl. **-mer·ies**) a performance by mummers. ■ ridiculous ceremonial, esp. of a religious nature.

mum·mi·fy /ˈməmə,fī/ ▶ **v.** **(-fies, -fied)** [trans.] [usu. as adj.] **(mummified)** (esp. in ancient Egypt) preserve (a body) by embalming it and wrapping it in cloth. See also MUMMY[1]. ■ shrivel or dry up (a body or a thing), thus preserving it. — **mum·mi·fi·ca·tion** /,məməfiˈkāSHən/ **n.**

mum·my[1] /ˈməmē/ ▶ **n.** (pl. **-mies**) **1** (esp. in ancient Egypt) a body of a human being or animal that has been ceremonially preserved by removal of the internal organs, treatment with natron and resin, and wrapping in bandages. **2** a well-preserved, desiccated body. [ME: from Fr. *momie*, from med. L. *mumia* and Arab. *mūmiyā* 'embalmed body,' perh. from Pers. *mūm* 'wax.']

mum·my[2] ▶ **n.** (pl. **-mies**) British term for MOMMY. [18th C.: perh. an alt. of earlier MAMMY.]

mump·ish /ˈməmpiSH/ ▶ **adj.** informal, dated sullen or sulky. [18th C.: from obs. *mump* 'grimace, have a miserable expression' + -ISH[1].]

mumps /məmps/ ▶ **plural n.** [treated as sing.] a contagious and infectious viral disease causing swelling of the parotid salivary glands in the face, and a risk of sterility in adult males. [16th C.: from obs. *mump* 'grimace, have a miserable expression.']

mump·si·mus /ˈməmpsiməs/ ▶ **n.** (pl. **-mus·es**) a traditional custom or notion adhered to although shown to be unreasonable. ■ a person who obstinately adheres to such a custom or notion. [16th C.: erroneously for L. *sumpsimus* 'we have taken.']

Munch /məNGk; mo͝oNGk/, Edvard (1863–1944), Norwegian painter. His works expressed feelings about life and death.

munch /mənCH/ ▶ **v.** [trans.] eat (something) with a continuous and often audible action of the jaws: *he munched a chicken wing* | [intrans.] *popcorn to munch on while watching the movie*. — **munch·er** **n.** [ME: imitative; cf. CRUNCH.]

Mun·chau·sen, Ba·ron /ˈmo͞on,CHouzən; ˈmən-/ the hero of a book of fantastic travelers' tales (1785) written in English by a German, Rudolph Erich Raspe. The original Baron Munchausen is said to have lived 1720–97, to have served in the Russian army against the Turks, and to have related tales of his prowess.

Mun·chau·sen's syn·drome ▶ **n.** Psychiatry a mental disorder in which a person repeatedly feigns severe illness so as to obtain hospital treatment. ■ **(Munchausen's syndrome by proxy)** a mental disorder in which a person seeks attention by inducing or feigning illness in another person, typically a child.

Mün·chen /ˈminCHən; ˈmYnKHən/ German name for MUNICH.

munch·ie /ˈmənCHē/ ▶ **n.** (pl. **munch·ies**) (usu. **munchies**) informal a snack or small item of food. ■ **(the munchies)** a sudden strong desire for food.

munch·kin /ˈmənCHkin/ ▶ **n.** informal a child. [from the *Munchkins*, depicted as a race of small childlike creatures, in L. Frank Baum's *The Wonderful Wizard of Oz* (1900).]

Mun·cie /ˈmənsē/ a city in east central Indiana; pop. 67,430.

Mun·da /ˈmo͝ondə/ ▶ **n.** (pl. same or **-das**) **1** a member of a group of indigenous peoples living scattered in a region from east central India to Nepal and Bangladesh. **2** a family of languages spoken by these peoples, distantly related to the Mon-Khmer family, with which they are sometimes classified as Austro-Asiatic. ■ any language of this family. ▶ **adj.** relating to or denoting the Munda or their languages. [the name in Munda.]

mun·dane /,mənˈdān/ ▶ **adj.** **1** lacking interest or excitement; dull. **2** of this earthly world rather than a heavenly or spiritual one. ■ of, relating to, or denoting the branch of astrology that deals with political, social, economic, and geophysical events and processes. — **mun·dane·ly** **adv.** **mun·dane·ness** **n.** **mun·dan·i·ty** /-ˈdānətē/ **n.** (pl. **-ties**). [ME: from OFr. *mondain*, from late L. *mundanus*, from L. *mundus* 'world.']

mung /məNG/ (also **mung bean**) ▶ **n.** **1** a small round green bean. **2** the tropical Old World plant (*Vigna radiata*, or *Phaseolus aureus*) that yields these beans, commonly grown as a source of bean sprouts. [19th C.: from Hindi *mūng*.]

mu·ni /ˈmyo͞onē/ ▶ **n.** (pl. **mu·nis**) short for MUNICIPAL BOND.

Mu·nich /ˈmyo͞onik; -niKH/ a city in southeastern Germany; pop. 1,229,000. German name MÜNCHEN.

Mu·nich Pact (also **Munich Agreement**) an agreement between Britain, France, Germany, and Italy, signed at Munich on September 29, 1938, under which the Sudetenland was ceded to Nazi Germany, often cited as an example of misjudged or dishonorable appeasement.

mu·nic·i·pal /myo͞oˈnisəpəl; myə-/ ▶ **adj.** of or relating to a city or town or its governing body. — **mu·nic·i·pal·ly** **adv.** [16th C.: from L. *municipalis*, from *municipium* 'free city,' from *municeps*, *municip-* 'citizen with privileges,' from *munia* 'civic offices' + *capere* 'take.']

mu·nic·i·pal bond ▶ **n.** a security issued by or on behalf of a local authority.

mu·nic·i·pal·i·ty /myo͞o,nisəˈpalətē; myə-/ ▶ **n.** (pl. **-ties**) a city or town that has corporate status and local government. ■ the governing body of such an area.

mu·nic·i·pal·ize /myo͞oˈnisəpə,līz; myə-/ ▶ **v.** [trans.] bring under the control or ownership of the authorities of a city or town. — **mu·nic·i·pal·i·za·tion** /-,nisəpələˈzāSHən/ **n.**

mu·nif·i·cent /myo͞oˈnifəsənt; myə-/ ▶ **adj.** (of a gift or sum of money) larger or more generous than is usual or necessary. ■ (of a person) very generous. — **mu·nif·i·cence** **n.** **mu·nif·i·cent·ly** **adv.** [16th C.: from L. *munificent-*, stem of *munificentior*, compar. of *munificus* 'bountiful,' from *munus* 'gift.']

mu·ni·ment /ˈmyo͞onəmənt/ ▶ **n.** (usu. **muniments**) a document or record, esp. one kept in an archive. [ME: via OFr. from L. *munimentum* 'defense' (in med. L. 'title deed'), from *munire* 'fortify.']

mu·ni·tion /myo͞oˈniSHən; myə-/ ▶ **plural n.** **(munitions)** military weapons, ammunition, equipment, and stores. ▶ **v.** [trans.] supply with munitions. — **mu·ni·tion·er** **n.** (rare). [ME: from Fr., from L. *munitio(n-)* 'fortification,' from *munire* 'fortify or secure.']

Mun·ro[1] /mənˈrō/, Alice (1931–), Canadian writer; born *Alice Ann Laidlaw*. Many of her short stories are collected in *Dance of the Happy Shades* (1968) and *The View from Castle Rock* (2006).

Mun·ro[2], H. H., see SAKI.

Mun·si /ˈmo͝onsē/ ▶ **n.** see DELAWARE[2] (sense 2). [the name in Munsi.]

Mun·ster /ˈmənstər/ a province of the Republic of Ireland, in the southwestern part of the country.

Mün·ster /ˈminstər; ˈmYn-/ a city in northwestern Germany; pop. 250,000.

mun·tin /ˈməntn/ ▶ **n.** a bar or rigid supporting strip between adjacent panes of glass. — **mun·tined** /ˈməntnd/ **adj.** [17th C.: var. of obs. *montant* (from Fr., lit. 'rising').]

munt·jac /ˈmənt,jak/ ▶ **n.** a small Southeast Asian deer (genus *Muntiacus*), the male of which has tusks, small antlers, and a doglike bark. [18th C.: from Sundanese *minchek*.]

mu·on /ˈmyo͞o,än/ ▶ **n.** Physics an unstable subatomic particle of the same class as an electron (a lepton), but with a mass around 200 times greater. Muons make up much of the cosmic radiation reaching the earth's surface. — **mu·on·ic** /myo͞oˈänik/ **adj.** [1950s: contr. of MU MESON; the particle, however, is no longer regarded as a meson.]

Muq·di·sho /mo͝okˈdiSHō/ another name for MOGADISHU.

mu·ral /ˈmyo͝orəl/ ▶ **n.** a painting or other work of art executed directly on a wall. ▶ **adj.** [attrib.] of, like, or relating to a wall. ■ Med. of, relating to, or occurring in the wall of a body cavity or blood vessel. — **mu·ral·ist** /-list/ **n.** [ME: from Fr., from L. *muralis*, from *murus* 'wall.']

Mu·ra·no glass /myo͞oˈränō/ ▶ **n.** another term for VENETIAN GLASS.

Mu·rat /m(y)o͞oˈrä(t); mYˈrä/, Joachim (*c.*1767–1815), king of Naples 1808–15. He was a cavalry commander in Napoleon's Italian campaign 1800.

Mur·chi·son Falls /ˈmərCHəsən/ former name for KABALEGA FALLS.

Mur·cia /ˈmərSH(ē)ə; ˈmo͝orsēə/ an autonomous region in southeastern Spain. ■ its capital city; pop. 329,000.

mur·der /ˈmərdər/ ▶ **n.** the unlawful premeditated killing of one human being by another. ■ informal a very difficult or unpleasant task or experience. ■ informal something causing great discomfort to a part of the body. ▶ **v.** [trans.] kill (someone) unlawfully and with premeditation. ■ informal punish severely or be very angry with. ■ informal conclusively defeat (an opponent) in a game or sport. ■ spoil by lack of skill or knowledge.

– PHRASES **get away with murder** informal succeed in doing whatever one chooses without being punished or suffering any disadvantage. **murder one** (or **two**) informal first-degree (or second-degree) murder. **murder will out** murder cannot remain undetected. **scream** (or **yell**) **bloody murder** informal scream loudly due to pain or fright; make an extravagant and noisy protest. — **mur·der·er** n. **mur·der·ess** /'mərdərəs/ n. [OE *morthor*; rel. to Ger. *Mord*, Sanskrit *mará* 'death' and L. *mors*.]

mur·der·ous /'mərdərəs/ ▶ **adj.** capable of or intending to murder; dangerously violent. ■ (of an action, event, or plan) involving murder or extreme violence. ■ informal extremely arduous or unpleasant. ■ informal (of a person or their expression) extremely angry. — **mur·der·ous·ly** adv. **mur·der·ous·ness** n.

Mur·doch /'mərdäk; -dək/, Dame Iris (1919–99), British writer, born in Ireland; full name *Jean Iris Murdoch*. Her novels include *The Sea, The Sea* (1978).

mu·rex /'myo͝or,eks/ ▶ **n.** (pl. **-ri·ces** /-rə,sēz/ or **-rex·es**) a predatory tropical marine mollusk (genus *Murex*, family Muricidae), the shell of which bears spines and forms a long narrow canal extending downward from the aperture. [16th C.: from L.; perh. rel. to Gk. *muax* 'sea mussel.']

mu·ri·at·ic ac·id /,myo͝orē'atik/ ▶ **n.** archaic term for **HYDROCHLORIC ACID**. — **mu·ri·ate** /'myo͝orē,āt/ n. [17th C.: *muriatic* from L. *muriaticus*, from *muria* 'brine.']

mu·ri·cate /'myo͝ori,kāt; -kit/ (also **mu·ri·cat·ed**) ▶ **adj.** Bot. & Zool. studded with short rough points. [17th C.: from L. *muricatus* 'shaped like a murex.']

mu·rid[1] /'myo͝orid/ ▶ **n.** Zool. a rodent of a very large family (Muridae) that includes most kinds of rats, mice, and voles. [20th C.: from mod. L. *Muridae* (pl.), based on L. *mus, mur-* 'mouse.']

mu·rid[2] ▶ **n.** a follower of a Muslim holy man, esp. a Sufi disciple. ■ (**Murid**) a member of any of several Muslim movements, esp. one that advocated rebellion against the Russians in the Caucasus in the late 19th century. [from Arab. *murīd*, lit. 'he who desires.']

Mu·ril·lo /m(y)o͞o'rilō; mo͞o'rēlyō/, Bartolomé Esteban (*c.*1618–82), Spanish painter. He is noted for his genre scenes of urchins and peasants.

mu·rine /'myo͝or,īn/ ▶ **adj.** Zool. of, relating to, or affecting mice or related rodents of the family Muridae. [17th C.: from L. *murinus*, from *mus, mur-* 'mouse.']

murk /mərk/ ▶ **n.** darkness or thick mist that makes it difficult to see. [OE *mirce*, of Gmc. origin.]

murk·y /'mərkē/ ▶ **adj.** (**murk·i·er, murk·i·est**) dark and gloomy, esp. due to thick mist. ■ (of liquid) dark and dirty; not clear. ■ not fully explained or understood, esp. with concealed dishonesty or immorality. — **murk·i·ly** adv. **murk·i·ness** n.

Mur·mansk /mo͝or'mansk; -'mänsk/ a city in northwestern Russia; pop. 472,000.

mur·mur /'mərmər/ ▶ **n.** a soft, indistinct sound made by a person or group of people speaking quietly or at a distance. ■ a softly spoken or almost inaudible utterance. ■ the quiet or subdued expression of a particular feeling by a group of people. ■ a rumor. ■ a low continuous sound. ■ Med. a recurring sound heard in the heart through a stethoscope that is usually a sign of disease or damage. ■ informal a condition in which the heart produces or is apt to produce such a sound. ▶ **v.** [reporting verb] say something in a low, soft, or indistinct voice. ■ [intrans.] make a low continuous sound. ■ say something cautiously and discreetly. — **mur·mur·er** n. **mur·mur·ous** /-mərəs/ adj. [ME: from OFr. *murmure*, from L. *murmur* 'a murmur.']

mur·mur·ing /'mərməriNG/ ▶ **n.** a soft, low, or indistinct sound produced by a person or group of people speaking quietly or at a distance. ■ (usu. **murmurings**) a subdued or private expression of discontent or dissatisfaction. ■ (usu. **murmurings**) an insinuation. ■ a low continuous sound. — **mur·mur·ing·ly** adv.

Murphy[1] /'mərfē/, Audie (1924–71), US soldier and actor. The most decorated combat soldier of World War II, he later appeared in war adventure movies.

Murphy[2], Frank (1890–1949), US Supreme Court associate justice 1940–49.

mur·phy /'mərfē/ ▶ **n.** (pl. **-phies**) informal a potato. [19th C.: from *Murphy*, an Irish surname.]

Mur·phy's Law /'mərfēz/ a supposed law of nature, expressed in various humorous popular sayings, to the effect that anything that can go wrong will go wrong.

mur·rain /'mərən/ ▶ **n.** an infectious disease, esp. babesiosis, affecting cattle or other animals. [ME: from OFr. *morine*, based on L. *mori* 'to die.']

Mur·ray[1], Gilbert (1866–1957), British classical scholar; born in Australia; full name *George Gilbert Aimé Murray*. His translations of Greek dramatists revived interest in Greek drama.

Mur·ray[2], Sir James Augustus Henry (1837–1915), Scottish lexicographer. He was chief editor of the *Oxford English Dictionary* (1879–1915).

Mur·ray Riv·er a river in Australia that flows for 1,610 miles (2,590 km) to empty into the Indian Ocean southeast of Adelaide.

murre /mər/ ▶ **n.** a white-breasted North American auk (genus *Uria*). [16th C.: of unknown origin.]

murre·let /'mərlit/ ▶ **n.** a small North Pacific auk (genera *Brachyramphus* and *Synthliboramphus*), typically having a gray back and white underparts.

mur·rey /'mərē/ ▶ **n.** archaic a deep purple-red cloth. ■ the deep purple-red color of a mulberry. ■ Heraldry another term for **SANGUINE**. [ME: via OFr. from med. L. *moratus*, from *morum* 'mulberry.']

Mur·row /'mərō; 'mə-rō/, Edward R. (1908–65), US journalist; born *Egbert Roscoe Murrow*. He broadcast from bomb-ridden London during World War II, ending each program with "Good night, and good luck."

Mur·rum·bidg·ee /,mərəm'bijē/ a river in southeastern Australia, in New South Wales, a major tributary of the Murray River.

mur·ther /'mərTHər/ ▶ **n. & v.** archaic spelling of **MURDER**.

mus. ▶ **abbr.** ■ museum. ■ music or musical or musician.

MusB (also **Mus Bac**) ▶ **abbr.** Bachelor of Music. [from L. *Musicae Baccalaureus*.]

Mus·ca /'məskə/ Astron. a small southern constellation (the Fly), lying in the Milky Way between the Southern Cross and the south celestial pole.

mus·ca·del /,məskə'del/ ▶ **n.** var. of **MUSCATEL**.

Mus·ca·det /,məskə'dā; mYskə'de/ ▶ **n.** a dry white wine from the part of the Loire region in France nearest the west coast. [Fr., from *muscade* 'nutmeg,' from *musc* 'musk.']

mus·ca·dine /'məskə,dīn/ ▶ **n.** any of a group of species and varieties of wine grape (genus *Vitis*, section Muscadinia) native to Mexico and the southeastern US, typically having thick skins and a musky flavor. [prob. an alt. of **MUSCATEL**.]

mus·cae vol·i·tan·tes /'məskē ,välə'tan,tēz/ ▶ **plural n.** Med. dark specks appearing to float before the eyes, generally caused by particles in the vitreous humor of the eye. [18th C.: L., lit. 'flying flies.']

mus·ca·rine /'məskə,rēn/ ▶ **n.** Chem. a poisonous compound ($C_9H_{21}NO_3$) present in certain fungi, including the fly agaric. [19th C.: based on L. *musca* 'fly.']

Mus·cat /'məs,kät/ the capital of Oman, in the northeastern part of the country; pop. 41,000.

mus·cat /'məs,kat; -kət/ ▶ **n.** [often as adj.] a variety of white, red, or black grape with a musky scent, grown in warm climates for wine or raisins or as table grapes. ■ a wine made from a muscat grape, esp. a sweet or fortified white wine. [Fr., from Provençal, from *musc* 'musk.']

Mus·cat and O·man former name (until 1970) for **OMAN**.

mus·ca·tel /,məskə'tel/ (also **mus·ca·del** /-'del/) ▶ **n.** a muscat grape, esp. as grown for drying to make raisins. ■ a raisin made from such a grape. ■ a wine made from such a grape. [via OFr. from Provençal, dimin. of *muscat* (see **MUSCAT**).]

mu·schel·kalk /'mo͞osHəl,kälk/ ▶ **n.** Geol. a limestone or chalk deposit from the Middle Triassic in Europe, esp. in Germany. [19th C.: from Ger., lit. 'mussel chalk.']

mus·cid /'məsid/ ▶ **n.** Entomol. an insect of the housefly family (Muscidae). [19th C.: from mod. L. *Muscidae* (pl.), from L. *musca* 'fly.']

mus·cle /'məsəl/ ▶ **n.** **1** a band or bundle of fibrous tissue in a human or animal body that has the ability to contract, producing movement in or maintaining the position of parts of the body. ■ such a band or bundle of tissue when well developed or prominently visible under the skin. **2** physical power; strength. ■ informal a person or persons exhibiting such power or strength. ■ power or influence, esp. in a commercial or political context. ▶ **v.** [trans.] informal move (an object) in a particular direction by using one's physical strength. ■ informal coerce by violence or by economic or political pressure.

– PHRASES **flex one's muscles** give a show of strength or power. **not move a muscle** be completely motionless.

– PHRASAL VERBS **muscle in/into** informal force one's way into (something), typically in order to gain an advantage. — **mus·cled** /'məsəld/ adj. [in comb.] *hard-muscled.* **mus·cle·less** adj. [ME: from Fr., from L. *musculus*, dimin. of *mus* 'mouse.']

mus·cle-bound ▶ **adj.** having well-developed or overdeveloped muscles.

mus·cle·man /'məsəl,man/ ▶ **n.** (pl. **-men**) a large, strong man, esp. one employed to protect someone or to intimidate people.

mus·cle tone ▶ **n.** see **TONE** (sense 6).

mus·cly /'məs(ə)lē/ ▶ **adj.** muscular.

mus·co·va·do /,məskə'vädō; -'vādō/ (also **muscovado sugar**) ▶ **n.** unrefined sugar made from the juice of sugar cane by evaporating it and draining off the molasses. [17th C.: from Port. *mascabado (açúcar)* '(sugar) of the lowest quality.']

Mus·co·vite /'məskə,vīt/ ▶ **n.** a native or citizen of Moscow. ■ archaic a Russian. ▶ **adj.** of or relating to Moscow. ■ archaic of or relating to Russia. [from mod. L. *Muscovita*, from *Muscovia* (see **MUSCOVY**).]

mus·co·vite /'məskə,vīt/ ▶ **n.** a silver-gray form of mica occurring in many igneous and metamorphic rocks. [19th C.: from obs. *Muscovy glass* (in the same sense) + **-ITE**[1].]

Mus·co·vy /'məskəvē/ a medieval principality in west central Russia that was centered around Moscow and formed the nucleus of modern Russia. ■ archaic name for Russia.

Mus·co·vy duck /'məskəvē; -,kōvē/ ▶ **n.** a large tropical American tree-nesting duck (*Cairina moschata*), having glossy greenish-black plumage in the wild but bred in a variety of colors as a domestic bird.

mus·cu·lar /'məskyələr/ ▶ **adj.** of or affecting the muscles. ■ having well-developed muscles. ■ fig. vigorously robust. — **mus·cu·lar·i·ty** /,məskyə'le(ə)ritē/ n. **mus·cu·lar·ly** adv.

mus·cu·lar dys·tro·phy ▶ **n.** a hereditary condition marked by progressive weakening and wasting of the muscles.

common morel
Morchella esculenta

false morel
Gyromitra esculenta

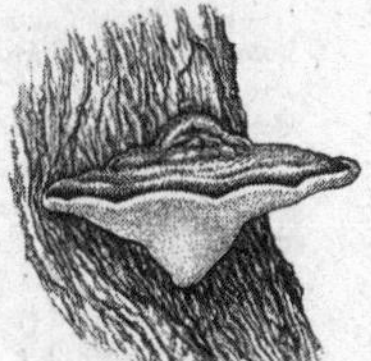
artist's fungus
Ganoderma applanatum

turkey tail
Coriolus versicolor

destroying angel
Amanita muscaria

honey mushroom
Armillaria mellea

common chanterelle
Cantharellus cibarius

golden coral
Ramaria largentii

king bolete
Boletus edulis

fly agaric
Amanita muscaria

puffball
Lycoperdon perlatum

earthstar
Geastrum saccatum

mushrooms and related fungi

mus·cu·la·ture /'məskyələCHər; -,CHŏŏr/ ▶ n. the system or arrangement of muscles in a body, a part of the body, or an organ.

mus·cu·lo·skel·e·tal /,məskyəlō'skelətl/ ▶ adj. relating to or denoting the musculature and skeleton together.

MusD (also **Mus Doc**) ▶ abbr. Doctor of Music. [from L. *Musicae Doctor*.]

Muse /myōōz/ ▶ n. (in Greek and Roman mythology) each of nine goddesses, the daughters of Zeus and Mnemosyne, who preside over the arts and sciences. ■ (**muse**) a woman, or a force personified as a woman, who is the source of inspiration for a creative artist. [ME: from OFr., or from L. *musa*, from Gk. *mousa*.]

muse /myōōz/ ▶ v. [intrans.] be absorbed in thought. ■ [with direct speech] say to oneself in a thoughtful manner. ■ (**muse on**) gaze thoughtfully at. ▶ n. dated an instance or period of reflection. — **mus·ing·ly** adv. [ME: from OFr. *muser* 'meditate, waste time,' perh. from med. L. *musum* 'muzzle.']

muse·og·ra·phy /,myōōzē'ägrəfē/ ▶ n. another term for MUSEOLOGY. — **museographic** /,myōōzēə'grafik/ adj. **museographical** /,myōōzēə'grafikəl/ adj.

mu·se·ol·o·gy /,myōōzē'äləjē/ ▶ n. the science or practice of organizing, arranging, and managing museums. — **mu·se·o·log·i·cal** /-zēə'läjikəl/ adj. **mu·se·ol·o·gist** n.

mu·sette /myōō'zet/ ▶ n. **1** a kind of small bagpipe played with bellows, common in the French court in the 17th–18th centuries and in later folk music. ■ a tune or piece of music imitating the sound of this, typically with a drone. ■ a dance to such a tune, esp. in the 18th-century French court. ■ a small simple variety of oboe, used chiefly in 19th-century France. **2** (also **musette bag**) a small knapsack. [ME: from OFr., dimin. of *muse* 'bagpipe.']

mu·se·um /myōō'zēəm/ ▶ n. a building in which objects of historical, scientific, artistic, or cultural interest are stored and exhibited. [17th C.: via L. from Gk. *mouseion* 'seat of the Muses,' based on *mousa* 'muse.']

mu·se·um piece ▶ n. an object that is worthy of display in a museum. ■ a person or object regarded as old-fashioned, irrelevant, or useless.

Mu·se·ve·ni /,mŏŏsə'vānē/, Yoweri Kaguta (1944–), president of Uganda 1986– .

mush[1] /məSH/ ▶ n. **1** a soft, wet, pulpy mass. ■ fig. feeble or cloying sentimentality. **2** thick porridge, esp. made of cornmeal. ▶ v. [trans.] [usu. as adj.] (**mushed**) reduce (a substance) to a soft, wet, pulpy mass. [17th C. (sense 2): appar. a var. of MASH.]

mush[2] ▶ v. [intrans.] go on a journey across snow with a dogsled. ■ [trans.] urge on (the dogs) during such a journey. ▶ exclam. a command urging on dogs during such a journey. ▶ n. a journey across snow with a dogsled. [19th C.: prob. an alt. of Fr. *marchez!* or *marchons!*, imperatives of *marcher* 'to advance.']

Mu·shar·raf /mōō'SHärəf/, Pervez (1943–); president of Pakistan 1999– .

mush·er /'məSHər/ ▶ n. the driver of a dogsled.

Mu·shin /'mōōSHin/ a city in southwestern Nigeria; pop. 294,000.

mush·rat /'məSH,rat/ ▶ n. another term for MUSKRAT.

mush·room /'məSH,rōōm; -,rŏŏm/ ▶ n. a fungal growth that typically takes the form of a domed cap on a stalk, often with gills on the underside of the cap. ■ a thing resembling a mushroom in shape. ■ a pale pinkish-brown color. ■ fig. a person or thing that appears or develops suddenly or is ephemeral. ▶ v. [intrans.] **1** increase, spread, or develop rapidly. **2** (of the smoke, fire, or flames produced by an explosion) spread into the air in a shape resembling that of a mushroom. ■ (of a bullet) expand and flatten on reaching its target. **3** [usu. as n.] (**mushrooming**) (of a person) gather mushrooms. — **mush·room·y** adj. [ME: from OFr. *mousseron*, from late L. *mussirio(n-)*.]

mush·room an·chor ▶ n. an anchor whose shape resembles that of a mushroom. See illustration at ANCHOR.

mush·room cloud ▶ n. a mushroom-shaped cloud of dust and debris formed after a nuclear explosion.

mush·y /'məSHē/ ▶ adj. (**mush·i·er, mush·i·est**) soft and pulpy. ■ (of a motor vehicle's brakes) lacking firmness; spongy. ■ fig. excessively sentimental. — **mush·i·ly** adv. **mush·i·ness** n.

Mu·si·al /'myōōzēəl/, Stanley Frank (1920–), US baseball player; known as **Stan the Man**. An outfielder and first baseman for the St. Louis Cardinals 1941–63, he led the National League in batting seven times.

mu·sic /'myōōzik/ ▶ n. **1** the art or science of combining vocal or instrumental sounds (or both) to produce beauty of form, harmony, and expression of emotion. ■ the vocal or instrumental sound produced in this way. ■ a sound perceived as pleasingly harmonious. **2** the written or printed signs representing such sound. ■ the score or scores of a musical composition or compositions.

– PHRASES **face the music** see FACE. **music of the spheres** see SPHERE. **music to one's ears** something that is pleasant or gratifying to hear or discover. [ME: from OFr. *musique*, via L. from Gk. *mousikē (tekhnē)* '(art) of the Muses,' from *mousa* 'muse.']

mu·si·ca fic·ta /'myōōzikə 'fiktə/ ▶ n. Music (in early contrapuntal music) the introduction by a performer of sharps, flats, or other accidentals to avoid unacceptable intervals. [19th C.: L., lit. 'feigned music.']

mu·si·cal /'myōōzikəl/ ▶ adj. **1** of or relating to music. ■ set to or accompanied by music. ■ fond of or skilled in music. **2** having a pleasant sound; melodious; tuneful. ▶ n. a play or movie in which singing and dancing play an essential part. Musicals developed from light opera in the early 20th century. — **mu·si·cal·ly** adv.

mu·si·cal chairs ▶ n. a party game in which players compete for a decreasing number of chairs, the losers in successive rounds being those unable to find a chair to sit on when the accompanying music is abruptly stopped. ■ a series of changes or exchanges of position, esp. in a political or commercial organization.

mu·si·cal com·e·dy ▶ n. a light play or movie with songs, dialogue, and dancing, connected by a plot.

mu·si·cale /,myōōzi'kal/ ▶ n. a musical gathering or concert, typically small and informal. [19th C.: Fr., from *soirée musicale* 'evening of music.']

mu·si·cal glass·es ▶ plural n. a series of drinking glasses or bowls filled with varying amounts of water and played as a musical instrument by rubbing the rims with the fingers. See also GLASS HARMONICA.

mu·si·cal in·stru·ment ▶ n. see INSTRUMENT (sense 3).

mu·si·cal·i·ty /,myōōzi'kalətē/ ▶ n. tastefulness and accomplishment in music. ■ the quality of being melodious and tuneful. ■ awareness of music and rhythm, esp. in dance.

mu·si·cal·ize /'myōōzikə,līz/ ▶ v. [trans.] set (a text or play) to music.

mu·si·cal saw ▶ n. a saw used as a musical instrument, typically held between the knees and played with a bow like a cello, the note varying with the degree of bending of the blade.

mu·sic box ▶ n. a small box that plays a tune, typically when the lid is opened. A traditional music box contains a cylinder, turned by clockwork, with projecting teeth that pluck a row of tuned metal strips as it revolves.

mu·sic dra·ma ▸ n. an opera whose structure is governed by considerations of dramatic effectiveness, rather than by the convention of having a series of formal arias.

mu·sic hall ▸ n. a theater where musical events are staged. ■ a form of variety entertainment popular in Britain from c.1850, consisting of singing, dancing, comedy, acrobatics, and novelty acts.

mu·si·cian /myōō'zisʜən/ ▸ n. a person who is talented or skilled in music. ■ a person who plays a musical instrument, esp. professionally. — **mu·si·cian·ly** adj. **mu·si·cian·ship** n.

mu·si·col·o·gy /ˌmyōōzi'käləjē/ ▸ n. the study of music as an academic subject, as distinct from training in performance or composition; scholarly research into music. — **mu·si·co·log·i·cal** /-kə'läjikəl/ adj. **mu·si·col·o·gist** n.

mu·sic stand ▸ n. a rack or light frame on which written or printed music is supported.

mu·sic vid·e·o ▸ n. a videotaped performance of a recorded popular song, usually accompanied by dancing and visual images interpreting the lyrics. Typically three to five minutes long, music videos typically feature quick cuts, computer graphics, and fanciful or erotic imagery.

mu·sique con·crète /m(y)ōō'zēk kōɴ'kret/ ▸ n. music constructed by mixing recorded sounds, first developed by experimental composers in the 1940s. [Fr., lit. 'concrete music.']

musk /məsk/ ▸ n. **1** a strong-smelling reddish-brown substance that is secreted by the male musk deer for scent-marking and is an important ingredient in perfumery. ■ a similar secretion of another animal, such as a civet. **2** (also **musk plant** or **musk flower**) a plant (genus *Mimulus*) of the figwort family that was formerly cultivated for its musky perfume. [ME: from late L. *muscus*, from Pers. *mušk*, perh. from Sanskrit *muṣka* 'scrotum' (because of the similarity in shape of a musk deer's musk bag).]

musk deer ▸ n. a small solitary deerlike eastern Asian mammal (genus *Moschus*, family Moschidae) without antlers, the male having long protruding upper canine teeth. Musk is produced in a sac on the abdomen of the male.

musk duck ▸ n. an Australian stiff-tailed duck (*Biziura lobata*) with dark gray plumage and a musky smell, the male having a large black lobe of skin hanging below the bill.

mus·keg /'məsˌkeg/ ▸ n. a North American swamp or bog consisting of a mixture of water and partly dead vegetation, frequently covered by a layer of sphagnum or other mosses. [19th C.: from Cree.]

mus·kel·lunge /'məskəˌlənj/ ▸ n. a large pike (*Esox masquinongy*) that occurs only in the Great Lakes region. [18th C.: from Canad. Fr. *maskinongé*, from Ojibwa *māskinōs ̆ē*.]

mus·ket /'məskit/ ▸ n. hist. an infantryman's light gun with a long barrel, typically smooth-bored, muzzleloading, and fired from the shoulder. [16th C.: from Fr. *mousquet*, from Ital. *moschetto* 'crossbow bolt,' from *mosca* 'a fly.']

mus·ket·eer /ˌməskə'ti(ə)r/ ▸ n. hist. a soldier armed with a musket.

mus·ket·ry /'məskətrē/ ▸ n. musket fire. ■ soldiers armed with muskets. ■ the art or technique of handling a musket.

Mus·kie /'məskē/, Edmund Sixtus (1914–96), US secretary of state 1980–81. A Maine Democrat, he was a US senator 1959–80.

musk·mel·on /'məskˌmelən/ ▸ n. an edible melon of a type that has a raised network of markings on the skin. Its many varieties include those with orange, yellow, green, or white juicy flesh.

Mus·ko·ge·an /mə'skōgēən/ ▸ n. a family of American Indian languages spoken in southeastern North America, including Chikasaw, Choctaw, Creek, and Seminole. ▸ adj. of or relating to this language family. [from MUSKOGEE + -AN.]

Mus·ko·gee /ˌməs'kōgē/ ▸ n. (pl. same or **-gees**) **1** a member of an American Indian people of the southeastern US, who led the Creek Indian confederacy. **2** the Muskogean language of this people. ▸ adj. of or relating to the Muskogees or their language. [from Creek *ma:skó:ki*.]

musk·ox /'məskˌäks/ (also **musk ox**) ▸ n. (pl. **-ox·en**) a large heavily built goat-antelope (*Ovibos moschatus*) with a thick shaggy coat and large curved horns, native to the tundra of North America and Greenland.

musk·rat /'məskˌrat/ ▸ n. a large semiaquatic North American rodent (*Ondatra zibethicus*, family Muridae) with a musky smell, valued for its fur. ■ the fur of the muskrat.

musk rose ▸ n. a rambling rose (*Rosa moschata*) with large white musk-scented flowers.

musk tur·tle ▸ n. a small drab-colored American freshwater turtle (genus *Sternotherus*, family Kinosternidae) that has scent glands that produce an unpleasant musky odor when the turtle is disturbed.

musk·y /'məskē/ ▸ adj. (**musk·i·er**, **musk·i·est**) of or having a smell or taste of musk, or suggestive of musk. — **musk·i·ness** n.

Mus·lim /'məzləm; 'mōōz-/ (also **Mos·lem** /'mäzləm; 'mäs-/) ▸ n. a follower of the religion of Islam. ▸ adj. of or relating to the Muslims or their religion. [17th C.: from Arab., active part. of *'aslama* (see ISLAM).]

– USAGE **Muslim** is the preferred term for 'follower of Islam,' although **Moslem** is also widely used. The archaic term **Muhammadan** (or **Mohammedan**) should be avoided.

Mus·lim Broth·er·hood an Islamic religious and political organization dedicated to the establishment of a nation based on Islamic principles. Founded in Egypt in 1928, it has become a radical underground force in Egypt and other Sunni countries, promoting strict moral discipline and opposing Western influence, often by violence.

mus·lin /'məzlən/ ▸ n. lightweight cotton cloth in a plain weave. — **mus·lined** /'məzlənd/ adj. [17th C.: from Fr. *mousseline*, from Ital. *mussolina*, from *Mussolo* 'Mosul' (the name of the place of manufacture in Iraq).]

Mus.M. ▸ abbr. Master of Music. [from mod. L. *Mūsicae Magister*.]

mus·quash /'məsˌkwäsʜ; 'məsˌkwôsʜ/ ▸ n. archaic term for MUSKRAT. [17th C.: from Abnaki *mòskwas*.]

muss /məs/ informal ▸ v. [trans.] make (someone's hair or clothes) untidy or messy. ▸ n. [usu. in sing.] a state of disorder. — **muss·y** /'məsē/ adj. (dated). [19th C.:a var. of MESS.]

mus·sel /'məsəl/ ▸ n. any of a number of bivalve mollusks with a brown or purplish-black shell, in particular: ■ a marine bivalve (family Mytilidae) that uses byssus threads to anchor to a firm surface, including the **edible mussel** (*Mytilus edulis*). ■ a freshwater bivalve (family Unionidae) that typically lies on the bed of a river, some species forming small pearls. [OE *mus(c)le*, based on late L. *muscula*, from L. *musculus* (see MUSCLE).]

Mus·so·li·ni /ˌmōōsə'lēnē/, Benito Amilcare Andrea (1883–1945), prime minister of Italy 1922–43; known as **Il Duce** ("the leader"). He founded the Italian Fascist Party in 1919 and entered World War II on Germany's side in 1940.

Mus·sorg·sky /mə'sôrgskē; -'zôrg-/ (also **Mous·sorg·sky**), Modest Petrovich (1839–81), Russian composer. He wrote the opera *Boris Godunov* (1874).

Mus·sul·man /'məsəlmən/ ▸ n. (pl. **-mans** or **-men**) & adj. archaic term for MUSLIM. [16th C.: from Pers. *musulmān* (orig. an adj.), from *muslim* (see MUSLIM).]

must[1] /məst/ ▸ modal verb (past **had to** or in reported speech **must**) **1** be obliged to; should (expressing necessity): *you must show your ID card.* ■ expressing insistence: *you must try some of this fish.* ■ used in ironic questions expressing irritation: *must you look so utterly suburban?* **2** expressing an opinion about something that is logically very likely: *you must be tired.* ▸ n. informal something that should not be overlooked or missed: *this video is a must for parents.*

– PHRASES **I must say** see SAY. **must needs do something** see NEEDS. [OE *mōste*, past tense of *mōt* 'may,' of Gmc. origin; rel. to Ger. *müssen*.]

must[2] ▸ n. grape juice before or during fermentation. [OE, from L. *mustum*, neut. (used as a n.) of *mustus* 'new.']

must[3] ▸ n. mustiness, dampness, or mold. [17th C.: back-form. from MUSTY.]

must[4] (also **musth**) ▸ n. the frenzied state of certain male animals, esp. elephants or camels, that is associated with the rutting season. ▸ adj. (of a male elephant or camel) in such a state. [19th C.: via Urdu from Pers. *mast* 'intoxicated.']

mus·tache /'məsˌtasʜ; mə'stasʜ/ (also **mous·tache**) ▸ n. a strip of hair left to grow above the upper lip. ■ (**mustaches**) a long mustache. ■ a similar growth, or a marking that resembles it, around the mouth of some animals. — **mus·tached** adj. [16th C.: from Fr., from Ital. *mostaccio*, from Gk. *mustax*, *mustak-*.]

mus·ta·chios /mə'stasʜēˌōz/ ▸ plural n. a long or elaborate mustache. — **mus·ta·chioed** /-ˌōd/ adj. [16th C.: from Sp. *mostacho* (sing.), from Ital. *mostaccio* (see MUSTACHE).]

mus·tang /'məsˌtaɴɢ/ ▸ n. an American feral horse, typically small and lightly built. [19th C.: from a blend of Sp. *mestengo* and *mostrenco*, both meaning 'wild or masterless cattle.']

mus·tard /'məstərd/ ▸ n. **1** a pungent-tasting yellow or brown paste made from the crushed seeds of certain plants, typically eaten with meat or used as a cooking ingredient. **2** the yellow-flowered Eurasian plant (genera *Brassica* and *Sinapis*) of the cabbage family whose seeds are used to make this paste. **3** a dark yellow color.

– PHRASES **cut the mustard** see CUT. — **mus·tard·y** adj. [ME: from OFr. *moustarde*, from L. *mustum* 'must' (the condiment being orig. prepared with 'must').]

mus·tard gas ▸ n. a colorless oily liquid ($(ClCH_2CH_2)_2S$) whose vapor is a powerful irritant and vesicant, used in chemical weapons.

mus·tard greens ▸ plural n. the leaves of the mustard plant used in salads.

mus·tard plas·ter ▸ n. a poultice made with mustard.

mus·te·lid /'məstəlid/ ▸ n. Zool. a mammal of the weasel family (Mustelidae), distinguished by having a long body, short legs, and musky scent glands under the tail. [20th C.: from mod. L. *Mustelidae* (pl.), from L. *mustela* 'weasel.']

mus·ter /'məstər/ ▸ v. [trans.] **1** assemble (troops), esp. for inspection or in preparation for battle. ■ [intrans.] (of troops) come together in this way. ■ [intrans.] (of a group of people) gather together. **2** collect or assemble (a number or amount). ■ summon up (a particular feeling, attitude, or response). ▸ n. a formal gathering of troops, esp. for inspection, display, or exercise. ■ short for MUSTER ROLL.

– PHRASES **pass muster** be accepted as adequate or satisfactory: *a treaty that might pass muster with the voters.*

– PHRASAL VERBS **muster someone in** (or **out**) enroll someone into (or discharge someone from) military service. [ME: from OFr. *moustrer* (v.), *moustre* (n.), from L. *monstrare* 'to show.']

mus·ter roll ▸ n. an official list of officers and men in a military unit or ship's crew.

musth /məst/ ▸ n. var. of MUST[4].

must·n't /'məsənt/ ▸ contr. must not.

must-read /rēd/ ▸ n. informal a piece of writing that should or must be read.

must-see ▶ **n.** informal something that should or must be seen, esp. a remarkable sight or entertainment.

mus·ty /ˈməstē/ ▶ **adj.** (**mus·ti·er, mus·ti·est**) having a stale, moldy, or damp smell. ■ having a stale taste. ■ fig. lacking originality or interest. — **mus·ti·ly adv. mus·ti·ness n.** [16th C.: perh. an alt. of *moisty* 'moist,' influenced by MUST[2].]

Mut /mo͞ot/ Egyptian Mythol. a goddess who was the wife of Amun and mother of Khonsu.

mu·ta·ble /ˈmyo͞otəbəl/ ▶ **adj.** liable to change. ■ literary inconstant in one's affections. — **mu·ta·bil·i·ty** /ˌmyo͞otəˈbilətē/ **n.** [ME: from L. *mutabilis*, from *mutare* 'to change.']

mu·ta·gen /ˈmyo͞otəjən/ ▶ **n.** an agent, such as radiation or a chemical substance, that causes genetic mutation. — **mu·ta·gen·e·sis** /ˌmyo͞otəˈjenəsəs/ **n. mu·ta·gen·ic** /ˌmyo͞otəˈjenik/ **adj.** [1940s: from MUTATION + -GEN.]

mu·ta·gen·ize /ˈmyo͞otəjəˌnīz/ ▶ **v.** [trans.] [usu. as adj.] (**mutagenized**) Biol. treat (a cell, organism, etc.) with mutagenic agents.

mu·tant /ˈmyo͞otnt/ ▶ **adj.** resulting from or showing the effect of mutation: *a mutant gene.* ▶ **n.** a mutant form. [20th C.: from L. *mutant-* 'changing,' from the v. *mutare*.]

mu·tate /ˈmyo͞oˌtāt/ ▶ **v.** change or cause to change in form or nature. ■ Biol. (with reference to a cell, DNA molecule, etc.) undergo or cause to undergo change in a gene or genes. — **mu·ta·tor** /-ˌtātər/ **n.** [19th C.: back-form. from MUTATION.]

mu·ta·tion /myo͞oˈtāsнən/ ▶ **n. 1** the action or process of mutating. **2** the changing of the structure of a gene, resulting in a variant form that may be transmitted to subsequent generations, caused by the alteration of single base units in DNA, or the deletion, insertion, or rearrangement of larger sections of genes or chromosomes. ■ a distinct form resulting from such a change. **3** Ling. regular change of a sound when it occurs adjacent to another, in particular: ■ (in Germanic languages) the process by which the quality of a vowel was altered in certain phonetic contexts; umlaut. ■ (in Celtic languages) change of an initial consonant in a word caused (historically) by the preceding word. See also LENITION. — **mu·ta·tion·al** /-sнənl/ **adj. mu·ta·tion·al·ly** /-sнənl-ē/ **adv. mu·ta·tive** /ˈmyo͞otətiv/ **adj.** [ME: from L. *mutatio(n-)*, from *mutare* 'to change.']

mu·ta·tis mu·tan·dis /m(y)o͞oˈtätəs m(y)o͞oˈtändəs; -ˈtātəs; -ˈtandəs/ ▶ **adv.** (used when comparing two or more cases or situations) making necessary alterations while not affecting the main point at issue: *what is true of undergraduate teaching in England is equally true, mutatis mutandis, of American graduate schools.* [L., lit. 'things being changed that have to be changed.']

mutch·kin /ˈməcнkin/ ▶ **n.** a Scottish unit of capacity equal to a little less than a pint, or roughly three quarters of an imperial pint (0.43 liters). [ME: from early mod. Du. *mudsekin*, dimin. of *mud* 'hectoliter.']

mute /myo͞ot/ ▶ **adj. 1** refraining from speech or temporarily speechless. ■ not expressed in speech. ■ characterized by an absence of sound; quiet. ■ dated (of a person) without the power of speech. **2** (of a letter) not pronounced. ▶ **n. 1** dated a person without the power of speech. ■ hist. (in some Asian countries) a servant who was deprived of the power of speech. ■ hist. an actor in a dumbshow. ■ hist. a professional attendant or mourner at a funeral. **2** a device that softens the sound (and typically alters the tone) of a musical instrument, in particular: ■ a clamp placed over the bridge of a stringed instrument to deaden the resonance without affecting the vibration of the strings. ■ a pad or cone placed in the opening of a brass or other wind instrument. **3** a device on a television, telephone, or other appliance that temporarily turns off the sound. ▶ **v.** [trans.] **1** (often **be muted**) deaden, muffle, or soften the sound of. ■ muffle the sound of (a musical instrument), esp. by the use of a mute. ■ fig. reduce the strength or intensity of. **2** activate the mute on a television, telephone, or other appliance. — **mute·ly adv. mute·ness n.** [ME: from OFr. *muet*, dimin. of *mu*, from L. *mutus*.]

mut·ed /ˈmyo͞otid/ ▶ **adj.** (of a sound or voice) quiet and soft. ■ (of a musical instrument) having a muffled sound as a result of being fitted with a mute. ■ fig. not expressed strongly or openly. ■ (of color or lighting) not bright; subdued.

mute swan ▶ **n.** the most common Eurasian swan (*Cygnus olor*), having white plumage and an orange-red bill with a black knob at the base. Introduced to the northeastern US, its range is expanding along the Atlantic coast and the Great Lakes region.

mute swan

muth·a /ˈməтнə/ ▶ **n.** var. of MOTHER (esp. sense 2).

mu·ti·late /ˈmyo͞otlˌāt/ ▶ **v.** [trans.] (usu. **be mutilated**) inflict a violent and disfiguring injury on. ■ inflict serious damage on. — **mu·ti·la·tion** /ˌmyo͞otlˈāsнən/ **n. mu·ti·la·tor** /-ˌātər/ **n.** [16th C.: from L. *mutilat-* 'maimed,' from the v. *mutilare*, from *mutilus* 'maimed.']

mu·ti·neer /ˌmyo͞otnˈi(ə)r/ ▶ **n.** a person, esp. a soldier or sailor, who rebels or refuses to obey the orders of a person in authority.

mu·ti·nous /ˈmyo͞otn-əs/ ▶ **adj.** (of a soldier or sailor) refusing to obey the orders of a person in authority. ■ willful or disobedient. — **mu·ti·nous·ly adv.**

mu·ti·ny /ˈmyo͞otn-ē/ ▶ **n.** (pl. **-nies**) an open rebellion against the proper authorities, esp. by soldiers or sailors against their officers. ▶ **v.** (**-nies, -nied**) [intrans.] refuse to obey the orders of a person in authority. [16th C.: from obs. *mutine* 'rebellion,' from Fr. *mutin* 'mutineer,' based on L. *movere* 'to move.']

mut·ism /ˈmyo͞otˌizəm/ ▶ **n.** inability to speak, typically as a result of congenital deafness or brain damage. ■ (in full **elective mutism**) unwillingness or refusal to speak, arising from psychological causes such as depression or trauma.

mu·ton /ˈmyo͞oˌtän; ˈmyo͞otn/ ▶ **n.** Biol. the smallest element of genetic material capable of undergoing a distinct mutation, usually identified as a single pair of nucleotides.

Mu·tsu·hi·to /ˌmo͞otso͞oˈhētō/ see MEIJI TENNO.

mutt /mət/ ▶ **n.** informal **1** a dog, esp. a mongrel. **2** humorous, derog. a person regarded as stupid or incompetent. [19th C.: abbrev. of MUTTONHEAD.]

mut·ter /ˈmətər/ ▶ **v.** [reporting verb] say something in a low or barely audible voice, esp. in dissatisfaction or irritation. ■ [intrans.] speak privately or unofficially about someone or something; spread rumors. ▶ **n.** a barely audible utterance, esp. a dissatisfied or irritated one. — **mut·ter·er n. mut·ter·ing·ly adv.** [ME: imitative; cf. Ger. dial. *muttern*.]

mut·ton /ˈmətn/ ▶ **n.** the flesh of sheep, esp. mature sheep, used as food. — **mut·ton·y adj.** [ME: from OFr. *moton*, from med. L. *multo(n-)*, prob. of Celtic origin; cf. Scot. Gael. *mult*.]

mut·ton·chops /ˈmətnˌcнäps/ (also **mut·ton·chop whis·kers**) ▶ **n.** the whiskers on a man's cheek when shaped like a meat chop, narrow at the top and broad and rounded at the bottom.

muttonchops

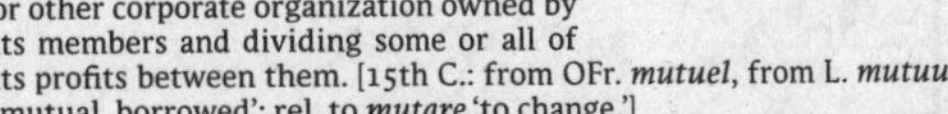

mut·ton·head /ˈmətnˌhed/ ▶ **n.** informal, dated a dull or stupid person (often used as a general term of abuse). — **mut·ton·head·ed adj.**

mu·tu·al /ˈmyo͞ocнo͞oəl/ ▶ **adj. 1** (of a feeling or action) experienced or done by each of two or more parties toward the other or others. ■ (of two or more people) having the same specified relationship to each other. **2** held in common by two or more parties: *we were introduced by a mutual friend.* ■ denoting an insurance company or other corporate organization owned by its members and dividing some or all of its profits between them. [15th C.: from OFr. *mutuel*, from L. *mutuus* 'mutual, borrowed'; rel. to *mutare* 'to change.']

mu·tu·al fund ▶ **n.** an investment program funded by shareholders that trades in diversified holdings and is professionally managed.

mu·tu·al·ism /ˈmyo͞ocнo͞oəˌlizəm/ ▶ **n.** the doctrine that mutual dependence is necessary to social well-being. ■ Biol. symbiosis that is beneficial to both organisms involved. — **mu·tu·al·ist n. & adj. mu·tu·al·is·tic** /ˌmyo͞ocнo͞oəˈlistik/ **adj. mu·tu·al·is·ti·cal·ly** /ˌmyo͞ocнo͞oəˈlistik(ə)lē/ **adv.**

mu·tu·al·i·ty /ˌmyo͞ocнo͞oˈalitē/ ▶ **n.** mutual character, quality, or activity.

mu·tu·al·ize /ˈmyo͞ocнo͞oəˌlīz/ ▶ **v.** [trans.] organize (a company or business) on mutual principles. ■ divide (something, esp. insurance losses) between involved parties.

mu·tu·al·ly /ˈmyo͞ocнo͞oəlē/ ▶ **adv.** with mutual action; in a mutual relationship.

mu·tu·el /ˈmyo͞ocнo͞oəl/ ▶ **n.** (in betting) a pari-mutuel. [20th C.: shortening of PARI-MUTUEL.]

muu·muu /ˈmo͞oˌmo͞o/ ▶ **n.** a woman's loose, brightly colored dress, esp. one traditionally worn in Hawaii. [20th C.: from Hawaiian *mu'u mu'u*, lit. 'cut off.']

mux /məks/ ▶ **n.** a multiplexer. ▶ **v.** short for MULTIPLEX.

Mu·zak /ˈmyo͞oˌzak/ ▶ **n.** trademark recorded light background music played through speakers in public places.

mu·zhik /mo͞oˈzнēk; -ˈzнik/ (also **mou·jik**) ▶ **n.** hist. a Russian peasant.

Muz·tag /mo͞osˈtäg/ a mountain in western China, in the Kunlun Shan range. It rises to 25,338 feet (7,723 m).

muz·zle /ˈməzəl/ ▶ **n. 1** the projecting part of the face, including the nose and mouth, of an animal such as a dog or horse. ■ a guard, typically made of straps or wire, fitted over this part of an animal's face to stop it from biting or feeding. ■ informal the part of a person's face including the nose, mouth, and chin. ■ fig. any restraint on free speech. **2** the open end of the barrel of a firearm. ▶ **v.** [trans.] put a muzzle on (an animal). ■ fig. prevent (a person or an institution, esp. the press) from expressing their opinions freely. [ME: from OFr. *musel*, dimin. of med. L. *musum*, of unknown ultimate origin.]

muz·zle·load·er /ˈməzəlˌlōdər/ (also **muz·zle-load·er**) ▶ **n.** hist. a gun that is loaded through its muzzle. — **muz·zle·load·ing** (also **muz·zle-load·ing**) **adj.**

muz·zle ve·loc·i·ty ▸ **n.** the velocity with which a bullet or shell leaves the muzzle of a gun.

muz·zy /ˈməzē/ ▸ **adj.** (**muz·zi·er, muz·zi·est**) **1** unable to think clearly; confused. ■ not thought out clearly; vague. **2** (of a person's eyes or a visual image) blurred. ■ (of a sound) indistinct. — **muz·zi·ly adv. muz·zi·ness n.** [18th C.: of unknown origin.]

MV ▸ **abbr.** ■ megavolt(s). ■ motor vessel. ■ muzzle velocity.

MVP ▸ **abbr.** most valuable player (an award given in various sports to the best player on a team or in a league).

MW ▸ **abbr.** ■ megawatt(s).

mW ▸ **abbr.** milliwatt(s).

MX ▸ **abbr.** missile experimental (a US intercontinental ten-warhead ballistic missile).

Mx ▸ **abbr.** maxwell(s).

my /mī/ ▸ **possessive adj.** **1** belonging to or associated with the speaker: *my name is John* | *my friend.* ■ informal used with a name to refer to a member of the speaker's family. ■ used with forms of address in affectionate, sympathetic, humorous, or patronizing contexts: *my poor baby.* **2** used in various expressions of surprise: *my goodness!* | *oh my!* [ME *mi*, reduced from *min*, from OE *mīn* (see MINE[1]).]

m.y. ▸ **abbr.** million years.

my- ▸ **comb. form** var. of MYO- shortened before a vowel (as in *myalgia*).

my·al·gi·a /mīˈalj(ē)ə/ ▸ **n.** pain in a muscle or group of muscles. — **my·al·gic** /-jik/ **adj.**

my·al·gic en·ceph·a·li·tis ▸ **n.** clinical term for chronic fatigue syndrome.

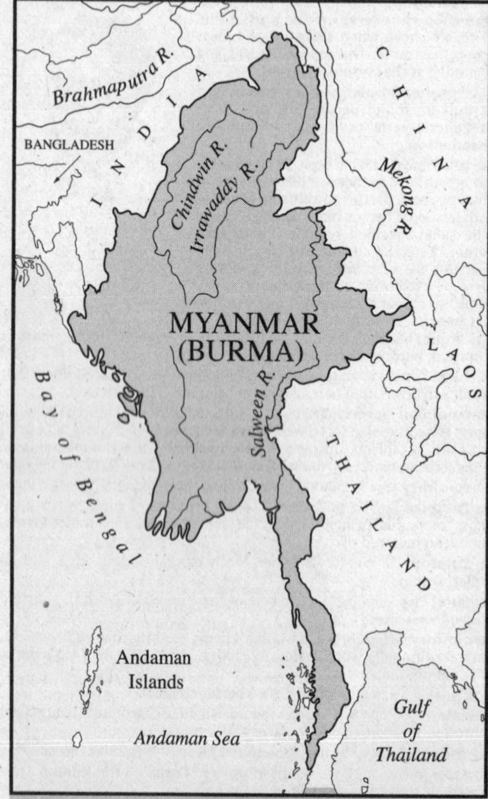

Myanmar

Official name: Union of Myanmar (also called Burma)
Location: Southeast Asia, on the Bay of Bengal
Area: 262,000 square miles (678,500 sq km)
Population: 42,528,000
Capital: Naypyidaw (formerly Rangoon)
Languages: Burmese (official), local languages
Currency: kyat

My·an·mar /myänˈmär; ˌmī,änˈmär/ a country in Southeast Asia. *See box.*

my·as·the·ni·a /ˌmīəsˈTHēnēə/ ▸ **n.** a condition causing abnormal weakness of certain muscles. ■ (in full **myasthenia gravis** /ˈgravis/) a rare chronic autoimmune disease marked by muscular weakness without atrophy, and caused by a defect in the action of acetylcholine at neuromuscular junctions.

my·ce·li·um /mīˈsēlēəm/ ▸ **n.** (pl. **-li·a** /-lēə/) Bot. the vegetative part of a fungus, consisting of a network of fine white filaments (hyphae). — **my·ce·li·al** /-lēəl/ **adj.** [19th C.: mod. L., from Gk. *mukēs* 'fungus,' on the pattern of *epithelium.*]

My·ce·nae /mīˈsēnē/ an ancient city in Greece, near the coast in the northeastern Peloponnese, the center of Mycenaean civilization.

My·ce·nae·an /mīˈsēnēən/ (also **My·ce·ne·an**) Archaeol. ▸ **adj.** of, relating to, or denoting a late Bronze Age civilization in Greece represented by finds at Mycenae and other ancient cities of Peloponnesus. ▸ **n.** an inhabitant of Mycenae or member of the Mycenaean people.

my·ce·to·ma /ˌmīsəˈtōmə/ ▸ **n.** Med. chronic inflammation of the tissues caused by infection with a fungus or with certain bacteria. [19th C.: mod. L., from Gk. *mukēs, mukēt-* 'fungus' + -OMA.]

-mycin ▸ **comb. form** in names of antibiotic compounds derived from fungi: *streptomycin.* [based on MYCO-.]

myco- ▸ **comb. form** relating to fungi: *mycoprotein.* [formed irregularly from Gk. *mukēs* 'fungus, mushroom.']

my·co·bac·te·ri·um /ˌmīkōbakˈti(ə)rēəm/ ▸ **n.** (pl. **-te·ri·a** /-ˈti(ə)rēə/) a bacterium (genus *Mycobacterium*, family Mycobacteriaceae) of a group that includes the causative agents of leprosy and tuberculosis. — **my·co·bac·te·ri·al** /-ˈti(ə)rēəl/ **adj.**

my·col·o·gy /mīˈkäləjē/ ▸ **n.** the scientific study of fungi. — **my·co·log·i·cal** /ˌmīkəˈläjikəl/ **adj. my·co·log·i·cal·ly** /ˌmīkəˈläjik(ə)lē/ **adv. my·col·o·gist n.**

my·co·plas·ma /ˌmīkōˈplazmə/ ▸ **n.** (pl. **-mas** or **-ma·ta** /-mətə/) any of a group of small typically parasitic bacteria (class Mollicutes, order Mycoplasmatales) that lack cell walls and sometimes cause diseases.

my·co·plas·ma pneu·mo·nia ▸ **n.** technical term for WALKING PNEUMONIA.

my·cor·rhi·za /ˌmīkəˈrīzə/ ▸ **n.** (pl. **-rhi·zae** /-ˈrīzē/) Bot. a fungus that grows in association with the roots of a plant in a symbiotic or mildly pathogenic relationship. — **my·cor·rhi·zal adj.** [19th C.: mod. L., from MYCO- 'of fungi' + Gk. *rhiza* 'root.']

my·co·sis /mīˈkōsəs/ ▸ **n.** (pl. **-ses** /-sēz/) a disease caused by infection with a fungus, such as ringworm or thrush. — **my·cot·ic** /-ˈkätik/ **adj.**

my·co·tox·in /ˌmīkəˈtäksən/ ▸ **n.** any toxic substance produced by a fungus.

my·co·troph·ic /ˌmīkəˈträfik/ ▸ **adj.** Bot. (of a plant) living in association with a mycorrhiza or another fungus that appears to improve the uptake of nutrients. — **my·cot·ro·phy** /mīˈkätrəfē/ **n.**

my·dri·a·sis /məˈdrīəsəs/ ▸ **n.** Med. dilation of the pupil of the eye. [19th C.: via L. from Gk. *mudriasis.*]

my·e·lin /ˈmīələn/ ▸ **n.** Anat. & Physiol. a mixture of proteins and phospholipids forming a whitish insulating sheath around many nerve fibers, increasing the speed at which impulses are conducted. — **my·e·li·nat·ed** /-lə,nātəd/ **adj. my·e·li·na·tion** /ˌmīələˈnāSHən/ **n.** [19th C.: from Gk. *muelos* 'marrow' + -IN[1].]

my·e·li·tis /ˌmīəˈlītəs/ ▸ **n.** Med. inflammation of the spinal cord. [19th C.: mod. L., from Gk. *muelos* 'marrow' + -ITIS.]

my·e·loid /ˈmīə,loid/ ▸ **adj.** **1** of or relating to bone marrow. ■ (of leukemia) characterized by the proliferation of cells originating in the bone marrow. **2** of or relating to the spinal cord. [19th C.: from Gk. *muelos* 'marrow' + -OID.]

my·e·lo·ma /ˌmīəˈlōmə/ ▸ **n.** (pl. **-mas** or **-ma·ta** /-mətə/) Med. a malignant tumor of the bone marrow. [19th C.: mod. L., from Gk. *muelos* 'marrow' + -OMA.]

my·e·lop·a·thy /ˌmīəˈläpəTHē/ ▸ **n.** Med. disease of the spinal cord.

my·en·ter·ic /ˌmīenˈterik/ ▸ **adj.** Anat. relating to or denoting a plexus of nerves of the sympathetic and parasympathetic systems situated between and supplying the two layers of muscle in the small intestine.

Myk·o·nos /ˈmēkə,nôs; ˈmikə,näs/ a Greek island in the Aegean Sea, one of the Cyclades. Greek name **Míkonos.**

My Lai /ˈmēˈlī/ a village in central Vietnam, south of Quang Ngai, site of a 1968 massacre of Vietnamese civilians by US troops during the Vietnam War.

My·lar /ˈmī,lär/ ▸ **n.** trademark a form of polyester resin used to make heat-resistant plastic films and sheets.

my·lo·nite /ˈmīlə,nīt; ˈmil-/ ▸ **n.** Geol. a fine-grained metamorphic rock, typically banded, resulting from the grinding or crushing of other rocks. [19th C.: from Gk. *mulōn* 'mill' + -ITE[1].]

my·nah /ˈmīnə/ (also **my·na** or **my·nah bird**) ▸ **n.** an Asian and Australasian starling that typically has dark plumage, gregarious behavior, and a loud call; in particular the **hill mynah** (*Gracula religiosa*), which is popular as a pet bird. [18th C.: from Hindi *mainā.*]

hill mynah

myo- (also **my-** before a vowel) ▸ **comb. form** of muscle; relating to muscles: *myocardium* | *myometrium.* [from Gk. *mus, mu-* 'mouse or muscle.']

my·o·car·di·al in·farc·tion /ˌmīəˈkärdēəl/ ▸ **n.** another term for HEART ATTACK.

my·o·car·di·tis /ˌmīə,kärˈdītəs/ ▸ **n.** Med. inflammation of the heart muscle.

my·o·car·di·um /ˌmīəˈkärdēəm/ ▶n. Anat. the muscular tissue of the heart. — **my·o·car·di·al** /-dēəl/ adj. [19th C.: mod. L., from MYO- 'muscle' + Gk. *kardia* 'heart.']

my·oc·lo·nus /mīˈäklənəs/ ▶n. Med. spasmodic jerky contraction of groups of muscles. — **my·o·clon·ic** /ˌmīəˈklänik/ adj.

my·o·fi·bril /ˌmīōˈfībrəl; -ˈfib-/ ▶n. any of the elongated contractile threads found in striated muscle cells.

my·o·gen·ic /ˌmīəˈjenik/ ▶adj. Physiol. originating in muscle tissue (rather than from nerve impulses).

my·o·glo·bin /ˌmīəˈglōbən; ˈmīəˌglōbən/ ▶n. Biochem. a red protein containing heme that carries and stores oxygen in muscle cells. It is structurally similar to a subunit of hemoglobin.

my·ol·o·gy /mīˈäləjē/ ▶n. the study of the structure, arrangement, and action of muscles. — **my·o·log·i·cal** /ˌmīəˈläjikəl/ adj. **my·ol·o·gist** /-jist/ n.

my·o·mere /ˈmīəˌmi(ə)r/ ▶n. see MYOTOME.

my·o·me·tri·um /ˌmīəˈmētrēəm/ ▶n. Anat. the smooth muscle tissue of the uterus. [20th C.: mod. L., from MYO- 'muscle' + Gk. *mētra* 'womb.']

my·op·a·thy /mīˈäpəᴛʜē/ ▶n. (pl. **-thies**) Med. a disease of muscle tissue. — **my·o·path·ic** /ˌmīəˈpaᴛʜik/ adj.

my·ope /ˈmīˌōp/ ▶n. a nearsighted person. [18th C.: from Fr., via late L. from Gk. *muōps*, from *muein* 'to shut' + *ōps* 'eye.']

my·o·pi·a /mīˈōpēə/ ▶n. nearsightedness. ■ lack of imagination, foresight, or intellectual insight. — **my·op·ic** /mīˈäpik/ adj. **my·op·i·cal·ly** /mīˈäpik(ə)lē/ adv. [18th C.: mod. L., from late Greek *muōpia*, from Gk. *muōps* (see MYOPE).]

my·o·sin /ˈmīəsən/ ▶n. Biochem. a fibrous protein that forms (together with actin) the contractile filaments of muscle cells and is also involved in motion in other types of cell.

my·o·sis /mīˈōsəs/ ▶n. var. of MIOSIS.

my·o·si·tis /mīōˈsītəs/ ▶n. Med. inflammation and degeneration of muscle tissue. [19th C.: formed irregularly from Gk. *mus, mu-* 'muscle' + -ITIS.]

my·o·so·tis /ˌmīəˈsōtəs/ ▶n. a borage-family plant of a genus (*Myosotis*) that includes the forget-me-nots. [mod. L., from Gk. *muosōtis*, from *mus, mu-* 'mouse' + *ous, ōt-* 'ear.']

my·o·tome /ˈmīəˌtōm/ ▶n. Embryol. the dorsal part of each somite in a vertebrate embryo, giving rise to the skeletal musculature. Compare with DERMATOME, SCLEROTOME. ■ each of the muscle blocks along either side of the spine in vertebrates (esp. fish and amphibians). Also called MYOMERE.

my·o·to·ni·a /ˌmīəˈtōnēə/ ▶n. inability to relax voluntary muscle after vigorous effort. — **my·o·ton·ic** /-ˈtänik/ adj. [19th C.: from MYO- + Gk. *tonos* 'tone.']

my·o·ton·ic dys·tro·phy ▶n. Med. a form of muscular dystrophy accompanied by myotonia.

Myr·dal /ˈmi(ə)rˌdäl/ Swedish Nobelists. Gunnar (1898–1987), economist and sociologist; full name *Karl Gunnar Myrdal*. Nobel Prize for Economics (1974, shared with Friedrich Hayek). His wife, Alva Reimer (1902–86), a politician and social activist, wrote *The Game of Disarmament* (1976). Nobel Peace Prize (1982, shared with Alfonso Garcia Robles (1911–91)).

myr·i·ad /ˈmirēəd/ literary ▶n. **1** a countless or extremely great number. **2** (chiefly in classical history) a unit of ten thousand. ▶adj. countless or extremely great in number. ■ having countless or very many elements or aspects. [16th C. (sense 2 of the n.): via late L. from Gk. *murias, muriad-*, from *murioi* '10,000.']

myr·i·a·pod /ˈmirēəˌpäd/ ▶n. Zool. an arthropod of a group (classes Chilopoda, Diplopoda, Pauropoda, and Symphyla) that includes the centipedes, millipedes, and related animals. Myriapods have elongated bodies with numerous leg-bearing segments. ▶adj. (also **myriapodous**) of or belonging to the myriapods. [19th C.: from mod. L. *Myriapoda*, from Gk. *murias* (see MYRIAD) + *pous, pod-* 'foot.']

myr·in·got·o·my /ˌmirənˈgätəmē/ ▶n. surgical incision into the eardrum, to relieve pressure or drain fluid. [19th C.: from mod. L. *myringa* 'eardrum' + -TOMY.]

myr·me·col·o·gy /ˌmərməˈkäləjē/ ▶n. the branch of entomology that deals with ants. — **myr·me·co·log·i·cal** /-kəˈläjikəl/ adj. **myr·me·col·o·gist** n. [19th C.: from Gk. *murmēx, murmēk-* 'ant' + -LOGY.]

myr·me·co·phile /ˈmərmikōˌfīl/ ▶n. Biol. an invertebrate or plant that has a symbiotic relationship with ants, such as being tended and protected by ants or living inside an ants' nest. — **myr·me·coph·i·lous** /ˌmərməˈkäfələs/ adj. **myr·me·coph·i·ly** /ˌmərməˈkäfəlē/ n.

Myr·mi·don /ˈmərməˌdän; -mədən/ ▶n. a member of a warlike Thessalian people led by Achilles at the siege of Troy. ■ (usu. **myrmidon**) a hired ruffian or unscrupulous subordinate. [ME: from L. *Myrmidones* (pl.), from Gk. *Murmidones*.]

my·rob·a·lan /mīˈräbələn; mə-/ ▶n. **1** (also **myrobalan plum**) a shrub or small tree (*Prunus cerasifera*) of the rose family, with white flowers and small red and yellow edible fruit. Native to southwestern Asia, it is used as stock for commercial varieties of plum. ■ the fruit of this tree. **2** a tropical tree (genus *Terminalia*, family Combretaceae) of a characteristic pagoda shape that yields a number of useful items including dye, timber, and medicinal products. ■ (also **myrobalan nut**) the fruit of this tree, used esp. for tanning leather. [ME: from Fr. *myrobolan* or L. *myrobalanum*, from Gk. *murobalanos*, from *muron* 'unguent' + *balanos* 'acorn.']

myrrh[1] /mər/ ▶n. a fragrant gum resin obtained from certain trees (genus *Commiphora*, family Burseraceae) and used, esp. in the Near East, in perfumery, medicines, and incense. — **myrrh·y** adj. [OE *myrra, myrre*, via L. from Gk. *murra*, of Semitic origin; cf. Arab. *murr* 'bitter.']

myrrh[2] ▶n. another term for CICELY. [16th C.: from L. *myrris*, from Gk. *murris*.]

myr·tle /ˈmərtl/ ▶n. **1** an evergreen shrub (*Myrtus communis*) that has glossy aromatic foliage and white flowers followed by purple-black oval berries. The **myrtle family** (Myrtaceae) also includes several aromatic plants (clove, allspice) and many characteristic Australian plants (eucalyptus trees, bottlebrushes). **2** the lesser periwinkle (*Vinca minor*). [ME: from med. L. *myrtilla, myrtillus*, dimin. of L. *myrta, myrtus*, from Gk. *murtos*.]

my·self /mīˈself; mə-/ ▶pron. [first person sing.] **1** [reflexive] used by a speaker to refer to himself or herself as the object of a verb or preposition when he or she is the subject of the clause: *I hurt myself* | *I strolled around, muttering to myself.* **2** [emphatic] I or me personally (used to emphasize the speaker): *I wrote it myself.* **3** poetic/literary term for I[2].
– PHRASES **(not) be myself** see *BE ONESELF, NOT BE ONESELF* at BE. **by myself** see *BY ONESELF* at BY.

My·sia /ˈmisʜēə/ an ancient region in northwestern Asia Minor, on the Mediterranean coast south of the Sea of Marmara. — **My·si·an** adj. & n.

my·sid /ˈmīsid/ ▶n. Zool. a crustacean of an order (Mysidacea) that comprises the opossum shrimps. [20th C.: from mod. L. *Mysis* (genus name) + -ID[3].]

My·sore /mīˈsôr/ **1** a city in southern India; pop. 480,000. **2** former name (until 1973) for KARNATAKA.

mys·ta·gogue /ˈmistəˌgäg/ ▶n. a teacher or propounder of mystical doctrines. — **mys·ta·go·gy** /-ˌgōjē/ n. [16th C.: from Fr., or via L. from Gk. *mustagōgos*, from *mustēs* 'initiated person' + *agōgos* 'leading.']

mys·te·ri·ous /məˈsti(ə)rēəs/ ▶adj. **1** difficult or impossible to understand, explain, or identify. ■ (of a location) having an atmosphere of strangeness or secrecy. **2** (of a person) deliberately enigmatic. — **mys·te·ri·ous·ly** adv. **mys·te·ri·ous·ness** n.

mys·ter·y[1] /ˈmist(ə)rē/ ▶n. (pl. **-ter·ies**) **1** something that is difficult or impossible to understand or explain. ■ the condition or quality of being secret, strange, or difficult to explain. ■ a person or thing whose identity or nature is puzzling or unknown. **2** a novel, play, or movie dealing with a puzzling crime, esp. a murder. **3** (**mysteries**) the secret rites of Greek and Roman pagan religion, or of any ancient or tribal religion, to which only initiates are admitted. ■ the practices, skills, or lore peculiar to a particular trade or activity and regarded as baffling to those without specialized knowledge. ■ the Christian Eucharist. **4** esp. Christian Theol. a religious belief based on divine revelation, esp. one regarded as beyond human understanding. ■ an incident in the life of Jesus or of a saint as a focus of devotion in the Roman Catholic Church, esp. each of those commemorated during recitation of successive decades of the rosary. [ME: from OFr. *mistere* or L. *mysterium*, from Gk. *mustērion*; rel. to MYSTIC.]

mys·ter·y[2] ▶n. (pl. **-ter·ies**) archaic a handicraft or trade. [ME: from med. L. *misterium*, contr. of *ministerium* 'ministry,' by association with *mysterium* (see MYSTERY[1]).]

mys·ter·y play ▶n. a popular medieval play based on biblical stories or the lives of the saints. Also called MIRACLE PLAY.

mys·tic /ˈmistik/ ▶n. a person who seeks by contemplation and self-surrender to obtain unity with or absorption into the Deity or the absolute, or who believes in the spiritual apprehension of truths that are beyond the intellect. ▶adj. another term for MYSTICAL. [ME: from OFr. *mystique*, or via L. from Gk. *mustikos*, from *mustēs* 'initiated person,' from *muein* 'close the eyes or lips,' also 'initiate.']

mys·ti·cal /ˈmistikəl/ ▶adj. **1** of or relating to mystics or religious mysticism. ■ spiritually allegorical or symbolic; transcending human understanding. ■ of or relating to ancient religious mysteries or other occult or esoteric rites. ■ of hidden or esoteric meaning. **2** inspiring a sense of spiritual mystery, awe, and fascination. ■ concerned with the soul or the spirit, rather than with material things. — **mys·ti·cal·ly** adv.

Mys·ti·ce·ti /ˌmistəˈsēˌtī/ Zool. a division of the whales that comprises the baleen whales. — **mys·ti·cete** /ˈmistəˌsēt/ n. & adj. [mod. L., from Gk. *mustikētos* representing *ho mus to kētos* 'the mouse, the whale so called.']

mys·ti·cism /ˈmistəˌsizəm/ ▶n. **1** belief that union with or absorption into the Deity or the absolute, or the spiritual apprehension of knowledge inaccessible to the intellect, may be attained through contemplation and self-surrender. **2** belief characterized by self-delusion or dreamy confusion of thought, esp. when based on the assumption of occult qualities or mysterious agencies.

mys·ti·fy /ˈmistəˌfī/ ▶v. (**-fies, -fied**) [trans.] utterly bewilder or perplex (someone). ■ dated take advantage of the credulity of; hoax. ■ make obscure or mysterious. — **mys·ti·fi·ca·tion** /ˌmistəfiˈkāsʜən/ n. **mys·ti·fi·er** n. **mys·ti·fy·ing·ly** adv. [19th C.: from Fr. *mystifier*, formed irregularly from *mystique* 'mystic' or from *mystère* 'mystery.']

mys·tique /misˈtēk/ ▶n. a fascinating aura of mystery, awe, and power surrounding someone or something. ■ an air of secrecy surrounding a particular activity or subject that makes it impressive or baffling to those without specialized knowledge. [19th C.: from Fr., from OFr. (see MYSTIC).]

myth /miTH/ ▶n. **1** a traditional story, esp. one concerning the early history of a people or explaining some natural or social phenomenon, and typically involving supernatural beings or events. ■ such stories collectively. **2** a widely held but false belief or idea. ■ a misrepresentation of the truth. ■ a fictitious or imaginary person or thing. ■ an exaggerated or idealized conception of a person or thing. [19th C.: from mod. L. *mythus*, via late L. from Gk. *muthos*.]

myth·ic /'miTHik/ ▶adj. of, relating to, or resembling myth. ■ exaggerated or idealized. ■ fictitious.

myth·i·cal /'miTHikəl/ ▶adj. occurring in or characteristic of myths or folk tales. ■ idealized, esp. with reference to the past. ■ fictitious. — **myth·i·cal·ly** adv.

myth·i·cize /'miTHə,sīz/ ▶v. [trans.] turn into myth; interpret mythically. — **myth·i·cism** n. **myth·i·cist** n.

mytho- ▶comb. form of or relating to myth: *mythography*. [from Gk. *muthos*, or from MYTH.]

my·thog·ra·pher /mə'THägrəfər/ ▶n. a writer or collector of myths.

my·thog·ra·phy /mə'THägrəfē/ ▶n. **1** the representation of myths, esp. in the plastic arts. **2** the creation or collection of myths.

my·thol·o·gize /mə'THäləjīz/ ▶v. [trans.] convert into myth or mythology; make the subject of a myth. — **my·thol·o·giz·er** n.

my·thol·o·gy /mə'THäləjē/ ▶n. (pl. **-gies**) **1** a collection of myths, esp. one belonging to a particular religious or cultural tradition. ■ a set of stories or beliefs about a particular person, institution, or situation, esp. when exaggerated or fictitious. **2** the study of myths. — **my·thol·o·ger** /-jər/ n. **myth·o·log·ic** /,miTHə'läjik/ adj. **myth·o·log·i·cal** /,miTHə'läjikəl/ adj. **myth·o·log·i·cal·ly** /,miTHə'läjik(ə)lē/ adv. **my·thol·o·gist** n.

myth·o·ma·ni·a /,miTHə'mānēə/ ▶n. an abnormal or pathological tendency to exaggerate or tell lies. — **myth·o·ma·ni·ac** /-'mānē,ak/ n. & adj.

myth·o·poe·ia /,miTHə'pēə/ ▶n. the making of a myth or myths. — **myth·o·poe·ic** /-'pēik/ adj. [1950s: from Gk. *muthopoiia*, from *muthos* 'myth' + *poiein* 'make.']

myth·o·po·et·ic /,miTHəpō'etik/ ▶adj. of or relating to the making of a myth or myths. ■ relating to or denoting a movement for men that uses activities such as storytelling and poetry reading as a means of self-understanding.

myth·os /'miTHōs; -äs/ ▶n. (pl. **myth·oi** /'miTHoi/) esp. tech. a myth or mythology. ■ (in literature) a traditional or recurrent narrative theme or plot structure. ■ a set of beliefs or assumptions about something. [18th C.: from Gk.]

myx·e·de·ma /,miksə'dēmə/ (Brit. **myx·oe·de·ma**) ▶n. Med. swelling of the skin and underlying tissues giving a waxy consistency, typical of patients with underactive thyroid glands. ■ the more general condition associated with hypothyroidism, including weight gain, mental dullness, and sensitivity to cold.

myxo- (also **myx-**) ▶comb. form relating to mucus: *myxodoema* | *myxovirus*. [from Gk. *muxa* 'slime, mucus.']

myx·o·ma /mik'sōmə/ ▶n. (pl. **-mas** or **-ma·ta** /-mətə/) Med. a benign tumor of connective tissue containing mucous or gelatinous material. — **myx·om·a·tous** /-mətəs/ adj.

myx·o·ma·to·sis /mik,sōmə'tōsəs/ ▶n. a highly infectious and usually fatal viral disease of rabbits, causing swelling of the mucous membranes and inflammation and discharge around the eyes.

myx·o·my·cete /,miksə'mī,sēt/ ▶n. Biol. a slime mold (division Myxomycota), esp. an acellular one whose vegetative stage is a multinucleate plasmodium. [19th C.: from mod. L. *Myxomycetes*, from MYXO- 'slime' + Gk. *mukētes* 'fungi.']

myx·o·vi·rus /'miksə,vīrəs/ ▶n. any of a group of RNA viruses, including the influenza virus.

Nn

N¹ /en/ (also **n**) ▶ **n.** (pl. **Ns** or **N's**) the fourteenth letter of the alphabet. See also EN. ■ denoting the next after M in a set of items, categories, etc.

N² ▶ **abbr.** ■ (used in recording moves in chess) knight: *17.Na4?* ■ Nationalist. ■ (on a gear lever) neutral. ■ (chiefly in place names) New: *N Zealand.* ■ Physics newton(s). ■ Noon. ■ Chem. (with reference to solutions) normal: *the pH was adjusted to 7.0 with 1 N HCl.* ■ Norse. ■ North or Northern: *78° N | N Ireland.* ■ Finance note. ■ nuclear: *the N bomb.* ▶ **symb.** the chemical element nitrogen.

n ▶ **abbr.** ■ name. ■ [in comb.] (in units of measurement) nano- (10^{-9}): *the plates were coated with 500 ng of protein in sodium carbonate buffer.* ■ born. ■ nephew. ■ net. ■ Gram. neuter. ■ new. ■ nominative. ■ noon. ■ (*n*-) [in comb.] Chem. normal (denoting straight-chain hydrocarbons): n-*hexane.* ■ north or northern. ■ note (used in a book's index to refer to a footnote): *450n.* ■ Finance note. ■ Gram. noun. ■ number. ▶ **symb.** an unspecified or variable number: *at the limit where n equals infinity.* See also NTH.

'n' /ən/ ▶ **contr.** and (conventionally used in informal contexts to coordinate two closely connected elements): *rock 'n' roll.*

-n¹ ▶ **suffix** var. of -EN².

-n² ▶ **suffix** var. of -EN³.

NA ▶ **abbr.** ■ North America. ■ not applicable.

Na ▶ **symb.** the chemical element sodium. [from mod. L. *natrium.*]

n/a ▶ **abbr.** ■ not applicable. ■ not available.

NAACP /'en dəbəl ā sē 'pē/ ▶ **abbr.** National Association for the Advancement of Colored People.

naan ▶ **n.** var. of NAN.

NAB ▶ **abbr.** ■ National Association of Broadcasters. ■ New American Bible.

nab /nab/ ▶ **v.** (**nabbed, nab·bing**) [trans.] informal catch (someone) doing something wrong: *Olympic drug tests nabbed another athlete yesterday.* ■ take or grab (something): *Dan nabbed the seat next to mine.* ■ steal: *the raider nabbed $215.* [17th C. of unknown origin.]

Nab·a·tae·an /ˌnabə'tēən/ (also **Nab·a·te·an**) ▶ **n.** **1** a member of an ancient Arabian people who formed an independent kingdom with its capital at Petra (now in Jordan). **2** the Aramaic dialect of this people. ▶ **adj.** of or relating to the Nabataeans or their language. [from L. *Nabat(h)aeus*, Gk. *Nabat(h)aios.*]

nabe /nāb/ ▶ **n.** informal a neighborhood. ■ a local movie theater. ■ a neighbor.

Nab·lus /'näbləs; 'na-/ a town in the West Bank; pop. 120,000.

na·bob /'nābäb/ ▶ **n.** hist. a Muslim official or governor under the Mogul empire. ■ a person of conspicuous wealth or high status. ■ chiefly hist. a person who returned from India to Europe with a fortune. [from Port. *nababo* or Sp. *nabab*, from Urdu; see also NAWAB.]

Na·bo·kov /'näbəˌkôf; nə'bôˌkôf/, Vladimir Vladimirovich (1899–1977), US writer; born in Russia. His novels include *Lolita* (1958).

na·celle /nə'sel/ ▶ **n.** a streamlined housing or tank for something on the outside of an aircraft or motor vehicle. ■ the outer casing of an aircraft engine. ■ esp. hist. the car of an airship. [20th C.: from Fr., from late L. *navicella*, dimin. of L. *navis* 'ship.']

nach·es /'näkнəs/ (also **nach·as** pronunc. same) ▶ **n.** pride or gratification, esp. at the achievements of one's children. ■ congratulations. [20th C.: from Yiddish *nakhes*, from Heb. *naḥat* 'contentment.']

na·cho /'näcнō/ ▶ **n.** (pl. **-chos**) a small crisp piece of a tortilla, typically topped with melted cheese and spices. [perh. from Mex. Sp. *Nacho*, nickname for *Ignacio*, given name of a chef.]

na·cre /'nākər/ ▶ **n.** mother-of-pearl. — **na·cre·ous** /-krēəs/ **adj.** [16th C.: from Fr., of unknown origin.]

NACU ▶ **abbr.** National Association of Colleges and Universities.

NAD Biochem. ▶ **abbr.** nicotinamide adenine dinucleotide, a coenzyme important in many biological oxidation reactions.

na·da /'nädə/ ▶ **pron.** informal nothing. [Sp.]

Na-De·ne /ˌnä dā'nā; nä 'dānē/ ▶ **adj.** denoting or belonging to a phylum of North American Indian languages including the Athabaskan family, Tlingit, and Haida. ▶ **n.** this language group. [20th C.: from Tlingit *naa* 'tribe' (rel. to Haida *náa* 'dwell') + North Athabaskan *dene* 'tribe.']

Na·der /'nādər/, Ralph (1934–), US consumer-rights advocate. He prompted legislation concerning car design, radiation hazards, food packaging, and insecticides.

NADH ▶ **abbr.** nicotinamide adenine dinucleotide.

na·dir /'nādər; 'nādi(ə)r/ ▶ **n.** [in sing.] the lowest point in the fortunes of a person or organization. ■ Astron. the point on the celestial sphere directly below an observer. The opposite of ZENITH. [ME (in the astronomical sense): via Fr. from Arab. *naẓīr (as-samt)* 'opposite (to the zenith).']

NADP ▶ **abbr.** nicotinamide adenine dinucleotide phosphate.

NADPH ▶ **abbr.** nicotinamide adenine dinucleotide phosphate (reduced).

nae /nā/ ▶ **adj., exclam., adv., & n.** Scottish form of NO. ▶ **adv. & n.** Scottish form of NOT.

naff¹ /naf/ ▶ **v.** [no obj., usu. in imper.] (**naff off**) Brit., informal go away: *she told press photographers to naff off.* [1950s: euphemism for FUCK.]

naff² ▶ **adj.** Brit., informal lacking taste or style. — **naff·ness** **n.** [1960s: of unknown origin.]

NAFTA /'naftə/ (also **Nafta**) ▶ **abbr.** North American Free Trade Agreement.

nag¹ /nag/ ▶ **v.** (**nagged, nag·ging**) [trans.] annoy or irritate (a person) with persistent faultfinding or continuous urging: *she constantly nags her daughter **about** getting married* | [intrans.] *he's always **nagging at** her for staying out late.* ■ [often as adj.] (**nagging**) be persistently painful, troublesome, or worrying to: *a nagging pain in his chest* | [intrans.] *something nagged at the back of his mind.* ▶ **n.** a person who nags someone. ■ a persistent feeling of anxiety. — **nag·ger** **n.** **nag·ging·ly** **adv.** **nag·gy** **adj.** [19th C.: perh. of Scand. or Low Ger. origin; cf. Norw. *nagga* 'gnaw, irritate.']

nag² ▶ **n.** informal, often derog. a horse, esp. one that is old or in poor health. ■ archaic a horse suitable for riding as opposed to a draft animal. [ME: of unknown origin.]

Na·ga /'nägə/ ▶ **n.** **1** a member of a group of peoples living in or near the Naga Hills of Myanmar (Burma) and northeastern India. **2** any of the Tibeto-Burman languages of these peoples with about 340,000 speakers altogether. ▶ **adj.** of or relating to the Nagas or their language. [perh. from Sanskrit *nagna* 'naked' or *naga* 'mountain.']

na·ga·na /nə'gänə/ ▶ **n.** a disease of cattle, antelope, and other livestock in southern Africa, characterized by fever, lethargy, and edema, and caused by trypanosome parasites transmitted by the tsetse fly. [19th C.: from Zulu *nakane.*]

Na·ga·no /nä'gänō/ a city in central Japan, on central Honshu Island, site of the 1998 Winter Olympics; pop. 347,000.

Na·ga·sa·ki /ˌnägə'säkē/ a city in southwestern Japan, on western Kyushu island; pop. 445,000. On August 9, 1945, it became the target of the second atom bomb dropped by the US.

Na·gor·no-Ka·ra·bakh /nə'gôrnō ˌkarə'bäk; -'bäкн/ a region of Azerbaijan in the southern foothills of the Caucasus; pop. 192,000; capital, Xankändi.

Na·go·ya /nə'goiə; 'nägōyä/ a city in central Japan, on the southern coast of Honshu, capital of Chubu region; pop. 2,155,000.

Nag·pur /'nägˌpŏŏr/ a city in central India; pop. 1,622,000.

nag·ware /'nagˌwe(ə)r/ ▶ **n.** informal computer software that is free for a trial period and thereafter frequently reminds the user to pay for it.

Nagy /näj; 'nädyə/, Imre (1896–1958), prime minister of Hungary 1953–55, 1956.

Nah. ▶ **abbr.** Bible Nahum.

nah /nä/ ▶ **exclam.** var. of NO, used to answer a question: *"Want a lift?" "Nah, that's okay."*

Na·ha /'nähä/ a city in southern Japan, capital of Okinawa island; pop. 305,000.

Na·hua·tl /'näˌwätl/ ▶ **n.** (pl. same) **1** a member of a group of peoples native to southern Mexico and Central America, including the Aztecs. **2** the Uto-Aztecan language of these peoples, with more than 1 million speakers. ▶ **adj.** of or relating to these peoples or their language. [via Sp. from Nahuatl *náhuatl* 'what pleases the ear'.]

Na·hum /'nāhəm/ (in the Bible) a Hebrew minor prophet. ■ a book of the Bible containing his prophecy of the fall of Nineveh (early 7th century BC).

NAIA ▶ **abbr.** National Association of Intercollegiate Athletics.

nai·ad /'nāad; -əd; nī-/ ▶ **n.** (pl. **-ads** or **-ades** /-əˌdēz/) **1** (also **Naiad**) (in classical mythology) a water nymph said to inhabit a river, spring, or waterfall. **2** the aquatic larva or nymph of a dragonfly, mayfly, or stonefly. **3** a submerged aquatic plant (genus *Najas*, family Najadaceae) with narrow leaves and minute flowers. [via L. from Gk. *Naias, Naiad-*, from *naein* 'to flow.']

na•if /nī'ēf/ (also **na•ïf**) ▶ **adj.** naive or ingenuous. ▶ **n.** a naive or ingenuous person. [from Fr. *naïf.*]

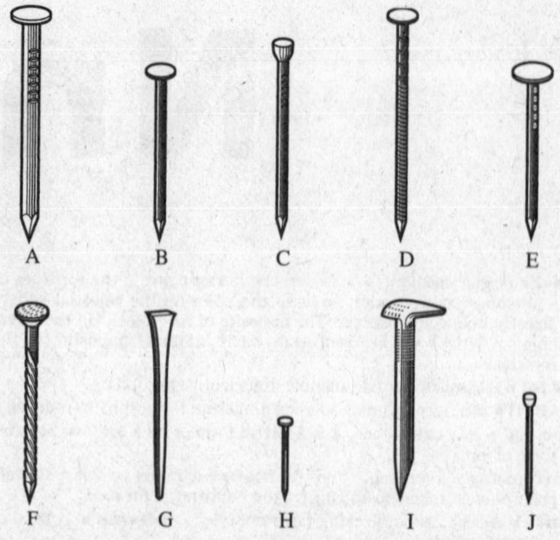

A common nail
B box nail
C finish *or* finishing nail
D ring *or* anchor nail
E roofing nail
F screw nail
G cut *or* flooring nail
H wire nail
I wrought nail
J brad

nails

nail /nāl/ ▶ **n. 1** a small metal spike with a broadened flat head, driven typically into wood with a hammer to join things together or to serve as a peg or hook. **2** a horny covering on the upper surface of the tip of the finger and toe in humans and other primates: *she began to bite her nails* | [as adj.] *a pair of nail clippers.* ■ an animal's claw. ■ a hard growth on the upper mandible of some soft-billed birds. **3** hist. a medieval unit of measurement of length for cloth, equal to 2¼ inches. ▶ **v.** [trans.] **1** [with obj. and adverbial of place] fasten to a surface or to something else with a nail or nails: *nail the edge framing to the wall.* **2** informal expose (someone) as deceitful or criminal; catch or arrest: *have you nailed the killer?* ■ expose (a lie or other instance of deception). **3** Football, informal tackle the quarterback or ballcarrier esp. at or behind the line of scrimmage. ■ Baseball (of a fielder) put (a runner) out by throwing to a base. ■ (of a player) defeat or outwit (an opponent). ■ (of a player) secure (esp. a victory) conclusively: *there's no doubt I had chances to nail it in the last set.* **4** vulgar slang (of a man) have sexual intercourse with (someone).
– PHRASES **fight tooth and nail** see TOOTH. **hard as nails** (of a person) very tough; completely callous or unfeeling: *I can fight for whatever I want and I'm hard as nails.* **a nail in the coffin** an action or event likely to have a detrimental effect on a situation, enterprise, or person.
– PHRASAL VERBS **nail someone down** elicit a firm promise or commitment from someone. **nail something down 1** fasten something securely with nails: *the floorboards aren't nailed down* | fig. *a society where everybody was stealing everything that wasn't nailed down.* **2** identify something precisely. **3** secure something, esp. an agreement. **nail something up 1** fasten something, esp. a door or window, with nails so that it cannot be opened: *the outer door had been nailed up from the outside.* **2** fasten something to a vertical surface with a nail or nails: *the teacher was nailing up the lists.* — **nailed adj.** [in comb.] *dirty-nailed fingers.* **nail•less adj.** [OE *nægel* (n.), *næglan* (v.), of Gmc. origin; rel. to Du. *nagel* and Ger. *Nagel*, from an Indo-Eur. root shared by L. *unguis* and Gk. *onux.*]

nail bed ▶ **n.** the formative layer of cells underlying the fingernail or toenail.

nail-bit•er (also **nail bit•er**) ▶ **n.** a situation causing great anxiety or tension: *a nail-biter of a victory.* — **nail-bit•ing adj.**

nail brush ▶ **n.** a small brush designed for cleaning the fingernails and toenails.

nail file ▶ **n.** a strip of roughened metal or an emery board used for smoothing and shaping the fingernails and toenails.

nail•head /'nāl,hed/ ▶ **n.** the rounded head of a nail. ■ an ornament like the head of a nail, used chiefly in architecture and on clothing.

nail pol•ish ▶ **n.** varnish applied to the fingernails or toenails to color them or make them shiny.

nail set (also **nail punch**) ▶ **n.** a tool hit with a hammer to sink the head of a nail below a surface.

nail wrap ▶ **n.** a type of beauty treatment, in which a nail strengthener, usu. containing fibers, is either brushed on or applied with adhesive.

nain•sook /'nān,so͝ok/ ▶ **n.** a fine, soft cotton fabric, originally from the Indian subcontinent. [18th C.: from Hindi *nainsukh*, from *nain* 'eye' + *sukh* 'pleasure.']

Nai•paul /'nīpôl; nī'pôl/, V. S. (1932–), Trinidadian writer; full name *Sir Vidiadhar Surajprasad Naipaul.* His novels include *A House for Mr. Biswas* (1961) and *Magic Seeds* (2004). Nobel Prize for Literature (2001).

nai•ra /'nīrə/ ▶ **n.** the basic monetary unit of Nigeria, equal to 100 kobo. [contr. of NIGERIA.]

Nai•ro•bi /nī'rōbē/ the capital of Kenya, in the southwestern part of the country; pop. 1,346,000.

Nai•smith /'nā,smiᴛʜ/, James A. (1861–1939), Canadian teacher. He invented the game of basketball in 1891, in Springfield, Massachusetts.

na•ive /nī'ēv/ (also **na•ïve**) ▶ **adj.** (of a person or action) showing a lack of experience, wisdom, or judgment: *the rather naive young man had been totally misled.* ■ (of a person) natural and unaffected; innocent: *Andy had a sweet, naive look when he smiled.* ■ of or denoting art produced in a straightforward style that rejects sophisticated techniques and has a bold directness resembling a child's work. — **na•ive•ly adv. na•ive•ness n.** [17th C.: from Fr. *naïve*, fem. of *naïf*, from L. *nativus* 'native, natural.']

na•ive•té /,nī,ēv(ə)'tā; nī'ēv(ə),tā/ (also **na•ïve•té**, Brit. **na•ive•ty**) ▶ **n.** lack of experience, wisdom, or judgment. ■ innocence or unsophistication. [17th C.: from Fr. *naïveté*, from *naïf*, *-ive* (see NAIVE).]

Na•jaf /'näjəf/ (also **An Na•jaf** /än 'näjəf/) a city in southern Iraq, on the Euphrates River; pop. 243,000.

na•ked /'nākid/ ▶ **adj.** (of a person or part of the body) without clothes. ■ (of an object) without the usual covering or protection: *a naked bulb* | *each man was carrying a naked sword.* ■ (of a tree, plant, or animal) without leaves, hairs, scales, shell, etc. ■ (of rock) not covered by soil: *he slipped on the naked rock.* ■ fig. exposed to harm; unprotected or vulnerable: *I felt naked and exposed as I crossed the deserted square.* ■ [attrib.] (of something such as feelings or behavior) undisguised; blatant: *naked fear made him tremble* | *naked, unprovoked aggression.* — **na•ked•ly adv. na•ked•ness n.** [OE *nacod*, of Gmc. origin; rel. to Du. *naakt* and Ger. *nackt*, from an Indo-Eur. root shared by L. *nudus* and Sanskrit *nagna.*]

na•ked eye ▶ **n.** (usu. **the naked eye**) unassisted vision, without a telescope, microscope, or other device: *through his telescope Galileo observed myriads of stars invisible to the naked eye.*

Na•khi•che•van /,näkicʜə'vän/ Russian name for NAXÇIVAN.

Nal•chik /'nälcʜik/ a city in the Caucasus, in southwestern Russia, capital of the republic of Kabardino-Balkaria; pop. 237,000.

nal•ox•one /nə'läksōn/ ▶ **n.** Med. a synthetic drug, similar to morphine, that blocks opiate receptors in the nervous system. [1960s: contr. of *N-allylnoroxymorphone.*]

nal•trex•one /nal'treksōn/ ▶ **n.** Med. a synthetic drug, similar to morphine, that blocks opiate receptors in the nervous system and is used chiefly in the treatment of heroin addiction. [1970s: from *N-al(lylnoroxymorph)one* (see NALOXONE) + *-trex-.*]

NAM ▶ **abbr.** National Association of Manufacturers.

Nam /näm; nam/ (also **'Nam**) informal name for VIETNAM in the context of the Vietnam War.

Na•ma /'nämä/ ▶ **n.** (pl. same or **Na•mas**) **1** a member of one of the Khoikhoi peoples of South Africa and southwestern Namibia. **2** the Khoisan language of this people, the only language of the Khoikhoi with a substantial number of speakers (more than 100,000). ▶ **adj.** of or relating to this people or their language. [the name in Nama.]

Na•ma•qua•land /nə'mäkwə,land/ a region of southwestern Africa, the homeland of the Nama people.

Na•math /'nāməᴛʜ/, Joe (1943–), US football player. He quarterbacked for the New York Jets 1965–76.

nam•by-pam•by /'nambē 'pambē/ derog. ▶ **adj.** lacking energy, strength, or courage: *these weren't namby-pamby fights, but brutal affairs where heads hit the sidewalk.* ▶ **n.** (pl. **-bies**) a feeble or effeminate person. [18th C.: after *Ambrose* Philips (died 1749), Engl. writer whose pastorals were ridiculed.]

name /nām/ ▶ **n. 1** a word or set of words by which a person, animal, place, or thing is known, addressed, or referred to. ■ someone or something regarded as existing merely as a word and lacking substance or reality: *simply a name in a gossip column.* **2** a famous person. ■ [in sing.] a reputation, esp. a good one: *a school with a name for excellence.* ▶ **v.** [trans.] give a name to: *hundreds of diseases with were isolated and named* | [with obj. and complement] *she named the child Edward.* ■ identify by name; give the correct name for: *the dead man has been **named as** John Mackintosh.* ■ give a particular title or epithet to: *she was named "Artist of the Decade."* ■ appoint (someone) to a particular position or task: *he was named to head a joint UN–OAS diplomatic effort.* ■ mention or cite by name: *the sea is as crystal clear as any spot in the Caribbean you might care to name.* ■ specify (an amount, time, or place) as something desired, suggested, or decided on: *he showed them the picture and named a price.* ▶ **adj.** [attrib.] (of a person or commercial product) having a name that is widely known: ***name brands** geared to niche markets.*

– PHRASES **by name** using the name of someone or something: *ask for the street by name.* **by the name of** called: *a woman by the name of Smith.* **call someone names** insult someone verbally. **give one's name to** invent, discover, found, or be closely associated with something that then becomes known by one's name: *Lou Gehrig gave his name to the disease that claimed his life.* **something has someone's name on it** a person is destined or particularly suited to receive or experience a specified thing: *he feared the next bullet would have his name on it.* **have to one's name** [often with negative] have in one's possession: *I had hardly a penny to my name.* **in all but name** existing in a particular state but not formally recognized as such: *these new punks are hippies in all but name.* **in someone's name 1** formally registered as belonging to or reserved for someone. **2** on behalf of someone. **in the name of** bearing or using the name of a specified person or organization: *a driver's license in the name of William Sanders.* ■ for the sake of: *he withdrew his candidacy in the name of party unity.* ■ by the authority of: *crimes committed in the name of religion.* **in name only** by description but not in reality: *a college in name only.* **make a name for oneself** become well known. **name the day** arrange a date for a specific occasion, esp. a wedding. **one's name is mud** see MUD. **name names** mention specific names, esp. of people involved in something wrong or illegal. **the name of the game** informal the main purpose or most important aspect of a situation. **put down** (or **enter**) **one's** (or **someone's**) **name** apply to enter an educational institution, course, competition, etc.: *I **put my name down for** the course.* **put a name to** remember or report what someone or something is called: *viewers were asked if they could put a name to the voice of the kidnapper.* **take someone's name in vain** see VAIN. **to name** (**but**) **a few** giving only these as examples, even though more could be cited. **under the name ——** using a name that is not one's real name, esp. for professional purposes: *that mad doctor who, under the name Céline, produced some of the greatest fiction in Western literature.* ■ (of a product, company, or organization) sold, doing business as, or known by a particular name: *a synthetic version is sold in the US **under the name of** Actigall.* **what's in a name?** names are arbitrary labels. **you name it** informal whatever you can think of (used to express the extent or variety of something): *easy-to-assemble kits of trains, cars, trucks, ships ... you name it.*

– PHRASAL VERBS **name someone/something after** (also **for**) call someone or something by the same name as: *Nathaniel **was named after** his maternal grandfather.* — **name•a•ble** adj. **nam•er** n. [OE *nama, noma* (n.), *(ge)namian* (v.), of Gmc. origin; rel. to Du. *naam* and Ger. *Name*, from a root shared by L. *nomen* and Gk. *onoma*.]

name-call•ing ▶ n. abusive language or insults. — **name-call•er** n.

name day ▶ n. the feast day of a saint after whom a person is named.

name-drop•ping ▶ n. the practice of casually mentioning the names of famous people one knows or claims to know in order to impress others. — **name-drop** v. **name-drop•per** n.

name•less /ˈnāmlis/ ▶ adj. **1** having no name or no known name: *some pictures were taken by a nameless photographer | the clinic was situated in a little nameless square off James Street.* ■ deliberately not identified; anonymous: *in this crowd he was nameless and faceless as a hunted man could wish to be.* ■ archaic (of a child) illegitimate. **2** (esp. of an emotion) not easy to describe; indefinable. ■ too loathsome or horrific to be described. — **name•less•ly** adv. **name•less•ness** n.

name•ly /ˈnāmlē/ ▶ adv. that is to say; to be specific.

Na•men /ˈnämən/ Flemish name for NAMUR.

name•plate /ˈnām,plāt/ ▶ n. a plate or sign displaying the name of someone, such as the person working in a building or the builder of a ship. ■ a brand of a product, esp. a maker of automobiles.

name•sake /ˈnām,sāk/ ▶ n. a person or thing that has the same name as another: *because she was my namesake, Elizabeth received many Christmas presents from me.* [17th C.: from *for the name's sake*.]

name•tape /ˈnām,tāp/ ▶ n. a piece of cloth tape bearing the name of a person, fixed to a garment of theirs to identify it.

Na•mib Des•ert /ˈnämib/ a desert in southwestern Africa. It extends for 1,200 miles (1,900 km) along the Atlantic coast from the Curoca River in southwestern Angola through Namibia to the border between Namibia and South Africa.

Na•mib•i•a /nəˈmibēə/ a country in southwestern Africa. *See box.*— **Na•mib•i•an** adj. & n.

Na•mur /nəˈmo͝or/ a province in central Belgium. It was the scene of the last German offensive in the Ardennes in 1945. Flemish name NAMEN. ■ the capital of this province, at the junction of the Meuse and Sambre rivers; pop. 103,000.

nan /nän/ (also **naan**) ▶ n. (in Indian cooking) a type of leavened bread, typically of teardrop shape and traditionally cooked in a clay oven. [from Urdu and Pers. *nān*.]

nan•a /ˈnanə/ ▶ n. informal one's grandmother. [19th C.: child's pronunc. of *nanny* or *gran*.]

Na•nak /ˈnänək/ (1469–1539), Indian religious leader; known as **Guru Nanak**. In 1499 he underwent a religious experience and became a wandering preacher. Not seeking to create a new religion, he founded Sikhism.

nance /nans/ ▶ n. another term for NANCY.

Nan•chang /ˈnänˈCHÄNG/ a city in southeastern China, capital of Jiangxi province; pop. 1,330,000.

Nan•cy /näNˈsē/ a city in northeastern France, chief town of Lorraine; pop. 102,000.

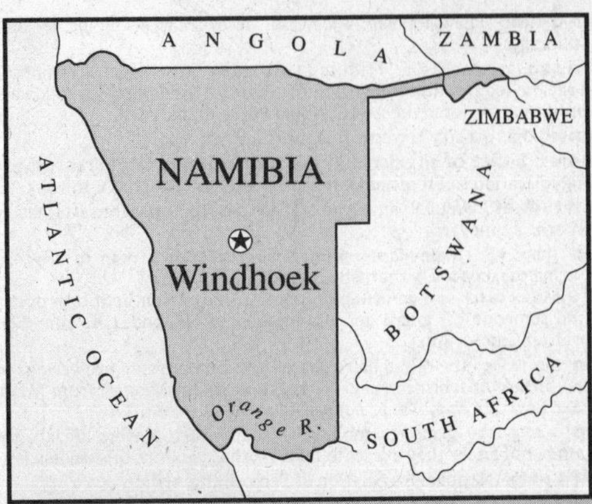

Namibia

Official name: Republic of Namibia
Location: southwestern Africa, largely desert, with a coastline on the Atlantic Ocean
Area: 318,800 square miles (825,400 sq km)
Population: 1,834,000
Capital: Windhoek
Languages: English (official), Afrikaans, German, various Bantu and Khoisan languages
Currency: Namibian dollar, South African rand

nan•cy /ˈnansē/ derog. esp. Brit. ▶ n. (pl. **-cies**) (also **nancy boy**) an effeminate or homosexual man. ▶ adj. effeminate. [20th C.: nickname for the given name *Ann*.]

nan•di•na /nanˈdēnə/ ▶ n. an evergreen eastern Asian shrub (*Nandina domestica*) of the barberry family that resembles bamboo and is cultivated for its foliage, which turns red or bronze in autumn.

Nan•ga Par•bat /,nəNGgə ˈpərbət/ a mountain in northern Pakistan, in the western Himalayas. It is 26,660 feet (8,126 m) high.

Nan•jing /ˈnänˈjiNG/ (also **Nan•king** /ˈnanˈkiNG/) a city in eastern China, on the Yangtze River, capital of Jiangsu province; pop. 3,682,000.

nan•keen /nanˈkēn/ ▶ n. a yellowish cotton cloth. ■ (**nankeens**) hist. pants made of this cloth. ■ the characteristic yellowish-buff color of this cloth. ▶ adj. of this color. [18th C.: *Nanking* (see NANJING).]

Nan•ning /ˈnäˈniNG/ the capital of Guangxi Zhuang, an autonomous region in southern China; pop. 1,070,000.

nan•no•fos•sil /,nanəˈfäsəl/ (also **nan•o•fos•sil**) ▶ n. the fossil of a minute planktonic organism, esp. a calcareous unicellular alga. [1960s: *nanno-* from *nannoplankton* (var. of NANOPLANKTON) + FOSSIL.]

nan•ny /ˈnanē/ ▶ n. (pl. **-nies**) **1** a person, typically a woman, employed to care for a child in its own home: *she works and leaves her daughters with a nanny* | [as name] *Nanny came to pick me up in a taxi.* ■ fig. a person or institution regarded as interfering and overprotective. **2** (in full **nanny goat**) a female goat. ▶ v. (**-nies, -nied**) [trans.] [usu. as n.] (**nannying**) be overprotective toward: *his well-intentioned nannying.* [18th C.: nickname for the given name *Ann*.]

na•no /ˈnanō/ ▶ n. informal short for NANOTECHNOLOGY: [in comb.] *nanoscientists are talking about shrinking supercomputers to the size of a hardback book.*

nano- ▶ comb. form denoting a factor of 10^{-9} (used commonly in units of measurement): *nanosecond.* ■ denoting a very small item: *nanoplankton.* [via L. from Gk. *nanos* 'dwarf.']

nan•o•bot /ˈnanə,bät/ ▶ n. a very small self-propelled machine, esp. one that has some degree of autonomy and can reproduce.

nan•o•me•ter /ˈnanə,mētər/ (Brit. **nan•o•me•tre**) (abbr.: **nm**) ▶ n. one billionth of a meter.

nan•o•plank•ton /,nanəˈplaNGktən/ ▶ n. Biol. very small unicellular plankton, at the limits of resolution of light microscopy. [20th C.: from Ger., from Gk. *nanos* 'dwarf' + PLANKTON.]

nan•o•scale /ˈnanə,skāl, ˈnā-/ ▶ adj. of a size measurable in nanometers or microns.

nan•o•scop•ic /,nanəˈskäpik; ,nā-/ ▶ adj. another term for NANOSCALE. ■ extremely small.

nan•o•sec•ond /ˈnanə,sekənd/ (abbr.: **ns**) ▶ n. one billionth of a second.

nan•o•tech•nol•o•gy /,nanə,tekˈnäləjē; ,nanō-/ ▶ n. the branch of technology that deals with dimensions and tolerances of less than 100 nanometers, esp. the manipulation of individual atoms and molecules. — **nan•o•tech•no•log•i•cal** /,teknəˈläjikəl/ adj. **nan•o•tech•nol•o•gist** n.

nan·o·tube /ˈnanəˌt(y)o͞ob/ ▶**n.** Chem. a cylindrical molecule of a fullerene.

Nan·sen /ˈnansən; ˈnän-/, Fridtjof (1861–1930), Norwegian explorer. In 1888, he led the first expedition to cross the Greenland ice fields and until 1893 explored the Arctic. Nobel Peace Prize, 1922.

Nantes /nänt/ a city in western France; pop. 252,000.

Nantes, E·dict of an edict of 1598 signed by Henry IV of France granting toleration to Protestants. It was revoked by Louis XIV in 1685.

Nan·tuck·et /nanˈtəkit/ an island off the coast of Massachusetts, east of Martha's Vineyard.

nap[1] /nap/ ▶**v.** (**napped, nap·ping**) [intrans.] sleep lightly or briefly, esp. during the day. ▶**n.** a short sleep, esp. during the day.
– PHRASES **catch someone napping** informal (of a person, action, or event) find someone off guard and unprepared to respond. [OE *hnappian*, prob. of Gmc. origin.]

nap[2] ▶**n.** [in sing.] the raised hairs, threads, or similar small projections on the surface of fabric or suede. — **nap·less adj.** [ME *noppe*, from MDu., Mid. Low Ger. *noppe* 'nap,' *noppen* 'trim the nap from.']

nap[3] ▶**n.** a card game resembling whist in which players declare the number of tricks they expect to take. [19th C.: abbrev. of NAPOLEON.]

NAPA ▶**abbr.** National Association of Performing Artists.

Na·pa /ˈnapə/ a commercial city in north central California, hub of the winemaking Napa Valley; pop. 61,842.

na·pa ▶**n.** var. of NAPPA.

na·pa cab·bage /ˈnapə; ˈnä-/ ▶**n.** a cabbagelike Chinese plant whose long, white leaves are used in salads and cooking. [*napa*, of unknown origin.]

na·palm /ˈnāˌpä(l)m/ ▶**n.** a highly flammable sticky jelly used in incendiary bombs and flamethrowers, consisting of gasoline thickened with special soaps. ■ the thickening agent used in this, made from the aluminum salts of palmitic and other fatty acids. ▶**v.** [trans.] attack with bombs containing napalm. [1940s: from *na(phthenic)* and *palm(itic acid)*.]

nape /nāp/ ▶**n.** (also **nape of the neck**) the back of a person's neck: *her hair was coiled demurely at the nape of her neck.* [ME: of unknown origin.]

Na·per·ville /ˈnāpərˌvil/ a city in northeastern Illinois; pop. 128,358.

na·per·y /ˈnāpərē/ ▶**n.** household linen, esp. tablecloths and napkins. [ME: from OFr. *naperie*, from *nape* 'tablecloth.']

Naph·ta·li /ˈnaftəˌlī/ (in the Bible) a Hebrew patriarch, second son of Jacob and Bilhah. ■ the tribe of Israel traditionally descended from him.

naph·tha /ˈnafᴛʜə; ˈnap-/ ▶**n.** Chem. a flammable oil containing various hydrocarbons, obtained by the dry distillation of organic substances such as coal. [ME *napte*, from L. *naphtha*, from Gk., of Asian origin.]

naph·tha·lene /ˈnafᴛʜəˌlēn; ˈnap-/ ▶**n.** Chem. a volatile white crystalline compound, $C_{10}H_8$, produced by the distillation of coal tar, used in mothballs and as a raw material for chemical manufacture. — **naph·thal·ic** /nafˈᴛʜalik; nap-/ **adj.**

naph·thene /ˈnafᴛʜēn; nap-/ ▶**n.** Chem. any of a group of cyclic aliphatic hydrocarbons (e.g., cyclohexane) obtained from petroleum. — **naph·the·nic** /nafˈᴛʜēnik; nap-; -ᴛʜenik/ **adj.**

naph·thol /ˈnafᴛʜôl; ˈnap-; -ᴛʜäl/ ▶**n.** Chem. a crystalline solid, $C_{10}H_7OH$, derived from naphthalene, used to make antiseptics and dyes.

Na·pi·er /ˈnāpēər; nəˈpi(ə)r/, John (1550–1617), Scottish mathematician. He invented the logarithm.

Na·pier·i·an log·a·rithm /nāˈpi(ə)rēən; nə-/ ▶**n.** another term for NATURAL LOGARITHM. [19th C.: named after J. *Napier* (see NAPIER).]

nap·kin /ˈnapkin/ ▶**n.** **1** (also **table napkin**) a square piece of cloth or paper used at a meal to wipe the fingers or lips and to protect garments. **2** another term for SANITARY NAPKIN. **3** Brit., dated a baby's diaper. [ME: from OFr. *nappe* 'tablecloth' (from L. *mappa*: see MAP) + -KIN.]

nap·kin ring ▶**n.** a ring used to hold (and distinguish) a person's table napkin when not in use.

Na·ples /ˈnāpəlz/ a city on the western coast of Italy, capital of Campania region; pop. 1,206,000. Italian name NAPOLI.

Na·ples yel·low ▶**n.** a pale yellow pigment containing lead and antimony oxides. ■ the pale yellow color of this pigment, now commonly produced using cadmium, zinc, or iron-based substitutes. [18th C.: NAPLES.]

Na·po·le·on /nəˈpōlēən; -yən/ the name of three rulers of France: ■ Napoleon I (1769–1821), emperor 1804–14 and 1815; full name *Napoleon Bonaparte*; known as **Napoleon**. In 1799, he joined a conspiracy that overthrew the Directory, becoming the supreme ruler of France. He was exiled to the island of Elba in 1814. He returned to power in 1815, but was defeated at Waterloo and exiled to the island of St. Helena. ■ Napoleon II (1811–1832), son of Napoleon I and Empress Marie-Louise; full name *Napoleon François Charles Joseph Bonaparte*. ■ Napoleon III (1808–73), emperor 1852–70; full name *Charles Louis Napoleon Bonaparte*; known as **Louis-Napoleon**. A nephew of Napoleon I, Napoleon III was elected president of the Second Republic in 1848 and staged a coup in 1851.

na·po·le·on /nəˈpōlēən; -yən/ ▶**n.** **1** a flaky rectangular pastry with a sweet filling. **2** hist. a gold twenty-franc French coin minted during the reign of Napoleon I.

Na·po·le·on·ic Wars /nəˌpōlēˈänik/ a series of campaigns (1800–15) of French armies under Napoleon against Austria, Russia, Great Britain, Portugal, Prussia, and other European powers. They ended with Napoleon's defeat at the Battle of Waterloo.

Na·po·li /ˈnäpəlē/ Italian name for NAPLES.

nap·pa /ˈnapə/ (also **nap·a**) ▶**n.** a soft leather made by a special tawing process from the skin of sheep or goats. [19th C.: from *Napa*, the name of a valley in California.]

nappe /nap/ ▶**n.** Geol. a sheet of rock that has moved sideways over neighboring strata as a result of an overthrust or folding. [19th C.: from Fr. *nappe* 'tablecloth.']

nap·py[1] /ˈnapē/ ▶**n.** (pl. **-pies**) Brit. a baby's diaper. [20th C.: abbrev. of NAPKIN.]

nap·py[2] ▶**adj.** informal (of a black person's hair) frizzy. [15th C. (in the sense 'shaggy'): from MDu. *noppigh*, Mid. Low Ger. *noppich*, from *noppe* (see NAP[2]).]

na·prox·en /nəˈpräksən/ ▶**n.** Med. a synthetic compound, $C_{14}H_{14}O_3$, used as an anti-inflammatory drug, esp. in the treatment of headache and arthritis. [1970s: from *na(phthyl)* + *pr(opionic)* + *ox(y-)*, + *-en*.]

Na·ra·yan /nəˈrīən/, R. K. (1906–2001), Indian writer; full name *Rasipuram Krishnaswamy Narayan*. Many of his novels are set in Malgudi, an imaginary town.

Na·ra·ya·nan /nəˈrīənən/, K. R. (1920–2005), president of India 1997–2002; full name *Kocheril Raman Narayanan*.

narc /närk/ (also **nark**) ▶**n.** informal a federal agent or police officer who enforces the laws regarding illicit sale or use of drugs and narcotics. [1960s: abbrev. of NARCOTIC.]

nar·cis·sism /ˈnärsəˌsizəm/ ▶**n.** excessive or erotic interest in oneself and one's physical appearance. ■ Psychol. extreme selfishness, with a grandiose view of one's own talents and a craving for admiration. ■ Psychoanal. self-centeredness arising from failure to distinguish the self from external objects. — **nar·cis·sist** /ˈnärsəsəst/ **n.** **nar·cis·sis·tic** /ˌnärsəˈsistik/ **adj.** **nar·cis·sis·ti·cal·ly** /ˌnärsəˈsistik(ə)lē/ **adv.** [19th C.: via L. from the Gk. name *Narkissos* (see NARCISSUS) + -ISM.]

Nar·cis·sus /närˈsisəs/ Gk. Mythol. a beautiful youth who rejected the nymph Echo and fell in love with his own reflection in a pool. He pined away and was changed into the flower that bears his name.

nar·cis·sus /närˈsisəs/ ▶**n.** (pl. same, **-cis·si** /-ˈsisī; -sē/, or **-cissuses**) a bulbous Eurasian plant of the lily family. Its genus (*Narcissus*) includes the daffodil, esp. one with flowers that have white or pale outer petals and a shallow orange or yellow cup in the center. [via L. from Gk. *narkissos*, perh. from *narkē* 'numbness,' with ref. to its narcotic effects.]

nar·co /ˈnärkō/ ▶**n.** (pl. **-cos**) informal short for NARCOTIC. ■ a dealer in drugs. ■ a narcotics officer.

narco- ▶**comb. form** relating to a state of insensibility: *narcolepsy*. ■ relating to narcotic drugs or their use: *narcoterrorism*. [from Gk. *narkē* 'numbness.']

nar·co·lep·sy /ˈnärkəˌlepsē/ ▶**n.** Med. a condition characterized by an extreme tendency to fall asleep whenever in relaxing surroundings. — **nar·co·lep·tic** /ˌnärkəˈleptik/ **adj. & n.** [19th C.: from Gk. *narkē* 'numbness,' on the pattern of *epilepsy*.]

nar·co·sis /närˈkōsis/ ▶**n.** Med. a state of stupor, drowsiness, or unconsciousness produced by drugs. See also NITROGEN NARCOSIS. [17th C.: from Gk. *narkōsis*, from *narkoun* 'make numb.']

nar·co·ter·ror·ism /ˌnärkōˈterəˌrizəm/ ▶**n.** terrorism associated with trade in illicit drugs. — **nar·co·ter·ror·ist n.**

nar·cot·ic /närˈkätik/ ▶**n.** a drug or other substance affecting mood or behavior and sold for nonmedical purposes, esp. an illegal one: *cultivation of a plant used to make a popular local narcotic.* ■ (often **narcotics**) any illegal drug: *he and a friend were busted for possession of narcotics.* ■ Med. a drug that relieves pain and induces drowsiness, stupor, or insensibility. ▶**adj.** relating to or denoting narcotics or their effects or use: *illicit traffic in narcotic drugs.* — **nar·cot·i·cal·ly adv.** **nar·co·tism** /ˈnärkəˌtizəm/ **n.** [ME: from OFr. *narcotique*, via med. L. from Gk. *narkōtikos*, from *narkoun* 'make numb.']

nar·co·tize /ˈnärkəˌtīz/ ▶**v.** [trans.] stupefy with or as if with a drug. ■ make (something) have a soporific or narcotic effect. — **nar·co·ti·za·tion** /ˌnärkətiˈzāsʜən/ **n.**

nard /närd/ ▶**n.** the Himalayan spikenard. [OE, via L. from Gk. *nardos*; rel. to Sanskrit *nalada*, *narada*.]

nar·es /ˈne(ə)rēz/ ▶**plural n.** (sing. **nar·is** /ˈne(ə)ris/) Anat. Zool. the nostrils. — **nar·i·al** /-ēəl/ **adj.** [17th C.: pl. of L. *naris* 'nostril, nose.']

nar·ghi·le /ˈnärgəlē/ (also **nar·gi·leh**) ▶**n.** an oriental tobacco pipe with a long tube that draws the smoke through water; a hookah. [18th C.: from Pers. *nārgīl* 'coconut, hookah,' from Sanskrit *nārikela* 'coconut.']

nar·is /ˈne(ə)ris/ singular form of NARES.

nark /närk/ informal ▶**n.** **1** var. of NARC. **2** esp. Brit. a police informer. [19th C.: from Romany *nāk* 'nose.']

Nar·ma·da /nərˈmədə/ a river that rises in central India and flows west to the Gulf of Cambay.

Nar·ra·gan·sett /ˌnarəˈgansit/ (also **Nar·ra·gan·set**) ▶**n.** (pl. same or **-setts**) **1** a member of an American Indian people originally of Rhode Island. **2** the Algonquian language of this people. [the name in Narragansett, lit. 'people of the promontory.']

Nar·ra·gan·sett Bay /ˌnarəˈgansit; ˌner-/ an inlet of the Atlantic Ocean in eastern Rhode Island.

nar·rate /ˈnarˌāt/ ▶**v.** [trans.] (often **be narrated**) give a spoken or written account of: *the voyages, festivities, and intrigues are narrated with* *unflagging gusto* | *the tough-but-sensitive former bouncer narrates much of the story.* ■ provide a spoken commentary to accompany (a movie, broadcast, piece of music, etc.): *the series is narrated by Richard Baker.* — **nar·rat·a·ble** adj. **nar·ra·tion** /na'rāsʜən/ n. [17th C.: from L. *narrat-* 'related, told,' from the v. *narrare* (from *gnarus* 'knowing').]

nar·ra·tive /'narətiv/ ▶n. a spoken or written account of connected events; a story: *a bare **narrative of the details**.* ■ the narrated part or parts of a literary work, as distinct from dialogue. ■ the practice or art of narration: *traditions of oral narrative.* ▶adj. in the form of or concerned with narration. — **nar·ra·tive·ly** adv.

nar·ra·tol·o·gy /,narə'täləjē/ ▶n. the branch of literary criticism that deals with the structure and function of narrative themes, conventions, and symbols. — **nar·ra·to·log·i·cal** /,narətl'äjikəl/ adj. **nar·ra·tol·o·gist** n.

nar·ra·tor /'narātər/ ▶n. a person who narrates something, esp. the events of a novel or narrative poem: *his poetic efforts are mocked by **the narrator of** the story.* | [with adj.] *a first-person narrator.* ■ a person who delivers a commentary accompanying a movie, broadcast, piece of music, etc. — **nar·ra·to·ri·al** /,narə'tôrēəl/ adj.

nar·row /'narō/ ▶adj. (**-row·er, -row·est**) **1** (esp. of something that is longer or higher than it is wide) of small width; lacking breadth: *a man with a narrow, turned-down mouth* | *the path became narrower and more overgrown.* **2** limited in extent, amount, or scope; restricted: *different measures of money supply—some narrow, some broad.* ■ (of a person's attitude or beliefs) limited in range and lacking willingness or ability to appreciate alternative views: *their narrow commitment to materialistic principles overlooked moral considerations.* ■ precise or strict in meaning: *some of the narrower definitions of democracy.* ■ (of a phonetic transcription) showing fine details of accent. ■ Phonet. denoting a vowel pronounced with the root of the tongue drawn back so as to narrow the pharynx. **3** (esp. of a victory, defeat, or escape) with only a small margin; barely achieved: *the home team just hung on for a narrow victory.* | *the resolution was passed by the narrowest of majorities* | *thanking her lucky stars for a narrow escape.* ▶v. **1** become or make less wide: [intrans.] *the road narrowed and crossed an old bridge* | [trans.] *the embankment was built to narrow the river.* ■ [intrans.] (of a person's eyes) almost close so as to focus on something or someone, or to indicate anger, suspicion, or other emotion: *Jake's eyes had **narrowed to pinpoints**.* ■ [trans.] (of a person) cause (one's eyes) to do this: *she narrowed her eyes at him suspiciously.* **2** become or make more limited or restricted in extent or scope: [intrans.] *their trade surplus **narrowed to** $70 million in January* | [trans.] *New England had narrowed Denver's lead from 13 points to 4.* ▶n. (**narrows**) a narrow channel connecting two larger areas of water.

– PHRASES **narrow circumstances** poverty.

– PHRASAL VERBS **narrow something down** reduce the number of possibilities or options of something: *it should now be possible to narrow down your choice.* — **nar·row·ish** adj. **nar·row·ness** n. [OE *nearu*, of Gmc. origin; rel. to Du. *naar* 'dismal, unpleasant.']

nar·row·cast /'narō,kast/ ▶v. (past and past part. **-cast** or **-cast·ed**) [intrans.] transmit a television program, esp. by cable, to a comparatively small audience defined by special interest or geographical location. ▶n. transmission or dissemination in this way. — **nar·row·cast·er** n. [1930s: back-form. from *narrowcasting*, on the pattern of *broadcasting*.]

nar·row gauge ▶n. a railroad gauge that is narrower than the standard gauge of 56.5 inches (143.5 cm).

nar·row·ly /'narōlē/ ▶adv. **1** by only a small margin; barely: *narrowly avoiding the numerous potholes* | *he narrowly defeated Anderson to win a 12th term in office.* **2** closely or carefully: *he was looking at her narrowly.* **3** in a limited or restricted way: *narrowly defined tasks.*

nar·row-mind·ed ▶adj. not willing to listen to or tolerate other people's views; prejudiced: *it would be narrow-minded not to welcome these developments* | *narrow-minded provincialism.* — **nar·row-mind·ed·ly** adv. **nar·row-mind·ed·ness** n.

Nar·rows /'narōz/ (**the Narrows**) a strait that connects upper and lower New York Bay.

nar·thex /'närtʜeks/ ▶n. an antechamber or porch at the western entrance of early Christian churches, separated off by a railing and used by catechumens, penitents, etc. ■ an antechamber or large porch in a modern church. [17th C.: via L. from Gk. *narthēx*.]

nar·whal /'närwəl/ ▶n. a small Arctic whale (*Monodon monoceros*, family Monodontidae), the male of which has a long spirally twisted tusk developed from one of its teeth. [17th C.: from Du. *narwal*, Dan. *narhval*, ON *nár* 'corpse,' with ref. to its skin color.]

nar·y /'ne(ə)rē/ ▶adj. informal or dialect form of NOT: *nary a murmur or complaint.* [18th C.: from the phr. *ne'er a*.]

NASA /'nasə/ ▶abbr. National Aeronautics and Space Administration.

na·sal /'nāzəl/ ▶adj. **1** of, for, or relating to the nose: *the nasal passages* | *nasal congestion* | *a nasal spray.* **2** (of a speech sound) pronounced by the voice resonating in the nose, e.g., *m, n, ng.* Compare with ORAL (sense 2). ■ (of the voice or speech) produced or characterized by resonating in the nose as well as the mouth. ▶n. **1** a nasal speech sound. **2** hist. a nosepiece on a helmet. — **na·sal·i·ty** /nā'zalitē/ n. **na·sal·ly** adv. [ME (sense 2 of the **n.**): from med. L. *nasalis*, from L. *nasus* 'nose.']

na·sal·ize /'nāzə,līz/ ▶v. [trans.] pronounce or utter (a speech sound) with the breath resonating in the nose: [as adj.] (**nasalized**) *a nasalized vowel.* — **na·sal·i·za·tion** /,nāzəli'zāsʜən/ n.

NASCAR /'nas,kär/ ▶abbr. National Association for Stock Car Auto Racing.

nas·cent /'nāsənt; 'nasənt/ ▶adj. (esp. of a process or organization) just coming into existence and beginning to display signs of future potential; not yet fully developed: *maintaining the momentum of the nascent economic recovery.* ■ Chem. (chiefly of hydrogen) freshly generated in a reactive form. — **nas·cence** n. **nas·cen·cy** n. [17th C.: from L. *nascent-* 'being born,' from the v. *nasci*.]

NASDAQ /'nazdak/ ▶abbr. National Association of Securities Dealers Automated Quotations, a computerized system for trading in securities.

Nase·by, Bat·tle of /'nāzbē/ a major battle of the English Civil War, which took place in 1645 near the village of Naseby in Northamptonshire. The Royalist army was defeated by Oliver Cromwell. Following this defeat Charles I's cause collapsed completely.

Nash /nasʜ/, Ogden (1902–71), US poet; full name *Frederic Ogden Nash*. His light verse consisted of puns, epigrams, and other verbal eccentricities.

Nashe /nasʜ/, Thomas (1567–1601), English writer and playwright. His novels include *The Unfortunate Traveller* (1594).

Nash·ua /'nasʜōōə/ a city in southern New Hampshire; pop. 86,605.

Nash·ville /'nasʜ,vil; -vəl/ the capital of Tennessee, in the north central part of the state; pop. 569,891.

naso- ▶comb. form relating to the nose: *nasogastric.* [from L. *nasus* 'nose.']

na·so·gas·tric /,nāzō'gastrik/ ▶adj. reaching or supplying the stomach via the nose.

na·so·phar·ynx /,nāzō'fariɴgks/ ▶n. Anat. the upper part of the pharynx, connecting with the nasal cavity above the soft palate. — **na·so·pha·ryn·ge·al** /-fə'rinj(ē)əl; -,farin'jēəl/ adj.

Nas·sau[1] /'na,sô/ **1** a former duchy of western Germany from which the House of Orange arose. **2** the capital of the Bahamas; on the island of New Providence; pop. 172,000.

Nas·sau[2] ▶n. Golf an eighteen-hole match in which the players bet on the first nine holes, the second nine holes, and the entire round.

Nas·ser /'nasər; 'nä-/, Gamal Abdel (1918–70), president of Egypt 1956–70. His nationalization of the Suez Canal brought war with Britain, France, and Israel in 1956; he also waged two unsuccessful wars against Israel 1956, 1967.

Nas·ser, Lake a lake in southeastern Egypt created by building two dams on the Nile River at Aswan.

Nast /nast/, Thomas (1840–1902), US political cartoonist; born in Germany. He created the Republican elephant and the Democratic donkey symbols as well as the US image of Santa Claus.

nas·tic /'nastik/ ▶adj. Bot. (of the movement of plant parts) caused by an external stimulus but unaffected in direction by it. [20th C.: from Gk. *nastos* 'squeezed together' (from *nassein* 'to press') + -IC.]

nas·tur·tium /nə'stərsʜəm; nə-/ ▶n. a South American trailing plant (*Tropaeolum majus*, family Tropaeolaceae) with round leaves and bright orange, yellow, or red flowers that is widely grown as an ornamental. [OE, from L., appar. from *naris* 'nose' + *torquere* 'to twist.']

nas·ty /'nastē/ ▶adj. (**-ti·er, -ti·est**) **1** highly unpleasant, esp. to the senses; physically nauseating. ■ (of the weather) unpleasantly cold or wet. ■ repugnant to the mind; morally bad: *her stories are very nasty, full of murder and violence.* **2** (of a person or animal) behaving in an unpleasant or spiteful way. ■ annoying or unwelcome: *life has a nasty habit of repeating itself.* **3** physically or mentally damaging or harmful: *a nasty, vicious-looking hatchet.* ■ (of an injury, illness, or accident) having caused harm; severe: *a nasty bang on the head.* ▶n. (pl. **-ties**) (often **nasties**) informal an unpleasant or harmful person or thing. — **nas·ti·ly** adv. **nas·ti·ness** n. [ME: of unknown origin.]

nas·ty·gram ▶n. Comput. an offensive or threatening electronic communication.

nat. ▶abbr. ■ national. ■ nationalist. ■ native. ■ natural.

Na·tal /nə'täl/ **1** a province on the eastern coast of South Africa that was renamed KwaZulu-Natal in 1994. **2** a port on the Atlantic coast of northeastern Brazil; pop. 606,000.

na·tal[1] /'nātl/ ▶adj. of or relating to the place or time of one's birth. [ME: from L. *natalis*, from *nat-* 'born,' from the v. *nasci*.]

na·tal[2] ▶adj. Anat. of or relating to the buttocks: *the natal cleft.* [19th C.: from NATES + -AL.]

na·tal·i·ty /nā'talitē; nə-/ ▶n. the ratio of the number of births to the size of the population; birth rate.

na·tant /'nātnt/ ▶adj. formal, rare swimming or floating. [18th C.: from L. *natant-* 'swimming,' from the v. *natare*.]

na·ta·tion /nā'tāsʜən; na-/ ▶n. tech. literary swimming. — **na·ta·to·ri·al** /,nātə'tôrēəl; ,nat-/ adj. **na·ta·to·ry** /'nātə,tôrē; 'nat-/ adj.

na·ta·to·ri·um /,nātə'tôrēəm; ,na-/ ▶n. a swimming pool, esp. one that is indoors. [19th C.: late L., from L. *natare* 'to swim.']

natch /nacʜ/ ▶adv. informal term for NATURALLY.

NATE ▶abbr. National Association of Teachers of English.

na·tes /'nā,tēz/ ▶plural n. Anat. the buttocks. [17th C.: L., pl. of *natis* 'buttock, rump.']

nathe·less /'nātʜlis; 'na-/ (also **nath·less**) ▶adv. archaic nevertheless. [OE.]

PRONUNCIATION KEY ə *ago, up*; ər *over, fur*; a *hat*; ā *ate*; ä *car*; e *let*; ē *see*; i *fit*; ī *by*; ɴɢ *sing*; ō *go*; ô *law, for*; oi *toy*; ŏŏ *good*; ōō *goo*; ou *out*; ᴛʜ *thin*; T͟H *then*; ᴢʜ *vision*

Na·tion /ˈnāsʜən/, Carrie Amelia Moore (1846–1911), US social activist. Her prohibitionist activism was characterized by scenes of hatchet-wielding saloon smashing, primarily in Kansas.

na·tion /ˈnāsʜən/ ▶ n. a large aggregate of people united by common descent, history, culture, or language, inhabiting a particular country or territory. ■ a North American Indian people or confederation of peoples. — **na·tion·hood** n. [ME: via OFr. from L. *natio(n-)*, from *nat-* 'born,' from the v. *nasci*.]

na·tion·al /ˈnasʜənəl/ ▶ adj. of or relating to a nation; common to or characteristic of a whole nation. ■ owned, controlled, or financially supported by the federal government: *a national art library.* ▶ n. **1** a citizen of a particular country, typically entitled to hold that country's passport: *a German national.* **2** (usu. **nationals**) a nationwide competition or tournament: *she finished 16th at the nationals that year.* — **na·tion·al·ly** adv. [16th C.: from Fr., from L. *natio(n-)* 'birth, race of people' (see NATION).]

na·tion·al an·them ▶ n. see ANTHEM (sense 1).

Na·tion·al As·sem·bly ▶ n. an elected legislature in various countries. ■ hist. the elected legislature in France during the first part of the French Revolution, 1789–91.

Na·tion·al As·so·ci·a·tion for the Ad·vance·ment of Col·ored Peo·ple (abbr.: **NAACP**) a US civil rights organization set up in 1909 to oppose racial segregation and discrimination by nonviolent means.

na·tion·al bank ▶ n. another term for CENTRAL BANK. ■ a commercial bank chartered under the federal government and belonging to the Federal Reserve System.

na·tion·al con·ven·tion ▶ n. a convention of a major political party, esp. one that nominates a candidate for the presidency.

na·tion·al debt ▶ n. the total amount of money that a country's government has borrowed, by various means.

Na·tion·al Foot·ball League (abbr.: **NFL**) ▶ n. the major professional football league in the US, consisting of the National and American football conferences and totaling 31 teams.

na·tion·al for·est ▶ n. a large expanse of forest owned and maintained by the federal government.

Na·tion·al Guard ▶ n. the primary reserve military force, partly maintained by the states but also available for federal use. ■ the primary military force of some other countries. — **Na·tion·al Guards·man** n.

na·tion·al in·come ▶ n. the total amount of money earned within a country.

na·tion·al·ism /ˈnasʜənəˌlizəm/ ▶ n. patriotic feeling, principles, or efforts. ■ an extreme form of this, esp. marked by a feeling of superiority over other countries. ■ advocacy of political independence for a particular country.

na·tion·al·ist /ˈnasʜənəlist/ ▶ n. a person who advocates political independence for a country. ■ a person with strong patriotic feelings, esp. one who believes in the superiority of their country over others. ▶ adj. of or relating to nationalists or nationalism. — **na·tion·al·is·tic** /ˌnasʜənəˈlistik/ adj. **na·tion·al·is·ti·cal·ly** /ˌnasʜənəˈlistik(ə)lē/ adv.

na·tion·al·i·ty /ˌnasʜəˈnalitē/ ▶ n. (pl. **-ties**) **1** the status of belonging to a particular nation. ■ distinctive national or ethnic character: *the change of a name does not discard nationality.* ■ patriotic sentiment; nationalism. **2** an ethnic group forming a part of one or more political nations.

na·tion·al·ize /ˈnasʜənəˌlīz/ ▶ v. [trans.] **1** transfer (a major branch of industry or commerce) from private to state ownership or control. **2** make distinctively national; give a national character to. **3** [usu. as adj.] (**nationalized**) naturalize (a foreigner). — **na·tion·al·i·za·tion** /ˌnasʜənəliˈzāsʜən/ n. **na·tion·al·iz·er** n.

Na·tion·al League ▶ n. one of the two major leagues in American professional baseball.

na·tion·al mon·u·ment ▶ n. a historic site or geographical area set aside by a national government and maintained for public use.

na·tion·al park ▶ n. a scenic or historically important area of countryside protected by the federal government for the enjoyment of the general public or the preservation of wildlife.

Na·tio·nal Ri·fle As·so·ci·a·tion (abbr.: **NRA**) ▶ n. a national organization founded in 1871 that promotes the legal use of guns and gun safety in the US and defends a US citizen's constitutional right to own and bear arms.

na·tion·al sea·shore ▶ n. an expanse of sea coast protected and maintained by the federal government for the study of wildlife and for public recreational use.

Na·tion·al Se·cu·ri·ty A·gen·cy (abbr.: **NSA**) a body established after World War II to gather intelligence, deal with coded communications from around the world, and safeguard US transmissions.

Na·tion·al Se·cu·ri·ty Coun·cil (abbr.: **NSC**) a body created in the US by Congress after World War II to advise the president on issues relating to national security in domestic, foreign, and military policy.

Na·tion·al So·cial·ism ▶ n. hist. the political doctrine of the Nazi Party of Germany. See NAZI. — **Na·tion·al So·cial·ist** n.

Na·tion of Is·lam an exclusively black Islamic sect proposing a separate black nation, founded in Detroit *c.*1930. It came to prominence under the influence of Malcolm X.

na·tion-state ▶ n. a sovereign state whose citizens or subjects are relatively homogeneous in factors such as language or common descent.

na·tion·wide /ˈnāsʜənˈwīd/ ▶ adj. extending or reaching throughout the whole nation. ▶ adv. throughout a whole nation.

na·tive /ˈnātiv/ ▶ n. a person born in a specified place or associated with a place by birth, whether subsequently resident there or not. ■ a local inhabitant. ■ dated, often offens. one of the original inhabitants of a country, esp. a nonwhite as regarded by European colonists or travelers. ■ an animal or plant indigenous to a place. ▶ adj. **1** associated with the country, region, or circumstances of a person's birth. ■ of the indigenous inhabitants of a place. **2** (of a plant or animal) of indigenous origin or growth. **3** (of a quality) belonging to a person's character from birth rather than acquired; innate: *a jealousy and rage **native to** him.* ■ Comput. designed for or built into a given system. **4** (of a metal or other mineral) found in a pure or uncombined state.

– PHRASES **go native** humorous derog. abandon one's own culture, customs, or way of life and adopt those of the country or region one is living in. — **na·tive·ly** adv. **na·tive·ness** n. [ME: from L. *nativus*, from *nat-* 'born,' from the v. *nasci*.]

Na·tive A·mer·i·can ▶ n. a member of any of the indigenous peoples of the Americas. ▶ adj. of or relating to these peoples.

– USAGE **Native American** is now an accepted term in many contexts. The term **American Indian** is also used widely and acceptably. See also usage at AMERICAN INDIAN.

na·tive speak·er ▶ n. a person who has spoken the language in question from earliest childhood.

na·tiv·ism /ˈnātiˌvizəm/ ▶ n. **1** the policy of protecting the interests of native-born or established inhabitants against those of immigrants. **2** a return to or emphasis on traditional or local customs, in opposition to outside influences. **3** the theory or doctrine that concepts, mental capacities, and mental structures are innate rather than acquired or learned. — **na·tiv·ist** n. & adj. **na·tiv·is·tic** /ˌnātiˈvistik/ adj.

na·tiv·i·ty /nəˈtivitē; nā-/ ▶ n. (pl. **-ties**) the occasion of a person's birth. ■ (usu. **the Nativity**) the birth of Jesus Christ. ■ a picture, carving, or model representing Jesus Christ's birth. ■ a nativity play. ■ the Christian festival of Christ's birth; Christmas. ■ Astrol., dated a horoscope relating to the time of birth; a birth chart. [ME: from OFr. *nativite*, from late L. *nativitas*, from L. *nativus* 'arisen by birth' (see NATIVE).]

natl. ▶ abbr. national.

NATO /ˈnātō/ ▶ abbr. North Atlantic Treaty Organization.

na·tri·u·re·sis /ˌnātrəyo͝oˈrēsis/ ▶ n. Physiol. excretion of sodium in the urine. — **na·tri·u·ret·ic** /-ˈretik/ adj. [1950s: from NATRON + Gk. *ourēsis* 'urination.']

na·tron /ˈnāträn; -trən/ ▶ n. a mineral salt found in dried lake beds, consisting of hydrated sodium carbonate. [17th C.: from Fr., from Sp. *natrón*, via Arab. from Gk. *nitron* (see NITER).]

nat·ter /ˈnatər/ informal ▶ v. [intrans.] talk casually, esp. about unimportant matters; chatter. ▶ n. [in sing.] a casual and leisurely conversation. — **nat·ter·er** n. [19th C. (in the dial. sense 'grumble, fret'): imitative.]

nat·ter·jack /ˈnatərˌjak/ (also **natterjack toad**) ▶ n. a small European toad (*Bufo calamita*, family Bufonidae) that runs in short bursts and has a bright yellow stripe down its back. [18th C.: perh. from NATTER (because of its loud croak) + JACK[1].]

nat·ty /ˈnatē/ ▶ adj. (**-ti·er**, **-ti·est**) informal (esp. of a person or an article of clothing) smart and fashionable: *a natty blue blazer and designer jeans.* — **nat·ti·ly** adv. **nat·ti·ness** n. [18th C. (orig. slang): perh. rel. to NEAT[1].]

Na·tu·fi·an /nəˈto͞ofēən/ ▶ adj. Archaeol. of, relating to, or denoting a late Mesolithic culture of the Middle East, dated to about 12,500–10,000 years ago. It provides evidence for the first settled villages. ■ [as n.] (**the Natufian**) the Natufian culture or period. [1930s: from Wadi *an-Natuf*, the type-site (a cave northwest of Jerusalem), + -IAN.]

nat·u·ral /ˈnacʜərəl/ ▶ adj. **1** existing in or caused by nature; not made or caused by humankind. ■ (of fabric) having a color characteristic of the unbleached and undyed state; off-white. **2** of or in agreement with the character or makeup of, or circumstances surrounding, someone or something: *sharks have no natural enemies.* ■ [attrib.] (of a person) born with a particular skill, quality, or ability. ■ (of a skill, quality, or ability) coming instinctively to a person; innate. ■ (of a person or their behavior) relaxed and unaffected. ■ occurring as a matter of course and without debate; inevitable: *Ken was a natural choice for coach.* ■ [attrib.] (of law or justice) based on innate moral sense; instinctively felt to be right and fair. See also NATURAL LAW. ■ Bridge (of a bid) straightforwardly reflecting one's holding of cards. Often contrasted with CONVENTIONAL or ARTIFICIAL. **3** [attrib.] (of a parent or child) related by blood. ■ esp. archaic illegitimate. **4** Music (of a note) not sharped or flatted: [postpositive, in comb.] *the bassoon plays G-natural instead of A-flat.* ■ of or relating to the notes and intervals of the harmonic series. **5** Christian Theol. relating to earthly or unredeemed human or physical nature as distinct from the spiritual or supernatural realm. ▶ n. **1** a person regarded as having an innate gift or talent for a particular task or activity. ■ a thing that is particularly suited for something. **2** Music a sign (♮) denoting a natural note when a previous sign or the key signature would otherwise demand a sharp or a flat. ■ a natural note. ■ any of the longer keys on a keyboard instrument that are normally white. **3** a creamy beige color. **4** a hand of cards, throw of dice, or other result that wins immediately, in particular: ■ a hand of two cards making 21 in the first deal in blackjack and similar games. ■ a first throw of 7 or 11 at craps. **5** Fishing an insect or other small creature used as bait, rather than an artificial imitation. **6** archaic, offens. a person mentally handicapped from birth. ▶ adv. informal dialect naturally: *keep walking—just act natural.* — **nat·u·ral·ness** n. [ME: from OFr., from L. *naturalis*, from *natura* 'birth, nature, quality' (see NATURE).]

nat·u·ral-born ▶ **adj.** having a specified innate characteristic or ability: *Glen was a natural-born sailor.*

nat·u·ral food ▶ **n.** food that has undergone a minimum of processing or treatment with preservatives.

nat·u·ral fre·quen·cy ▶ **n.** Physics the frequency at which a system oscillates when not subjected to a continuous or repeated external force.

nat·u·ral gas ▶ **n.** flammable gas, consisting largely of methane and other hydrocarbons, occurring naturally underground and used as fuel.

nat·u·ral his·to·ry ▶ **n.** the scientific study of animals or plants, presented in popular rather than academic form. — **nat·u·ral his·to·ri·an n.**

nat·u·ral·ism /ˈnacHərəˌlizəm/ ▶ **n.** **1** (in art and literature) a style and theory of representation based on the accurate depiction of detail. Naturalism rejected the idealization of experience and adopted an objective and often uncompromisingly realistic approach to art. **2** a philosophical viewpoint according to which everything arises from natural properties and causes, and supernatural or spiritual explanations are excluded or discounted. ■ another term for NATURAL RELIGION.

nat·u·ral·ist /ˈnacHərəlist/ ▶ **n.** **1** an expert in or student of natural history. **2** a person who practices naturalism in art or literature. ■ a person who adopts philosophical naturalism. ▶ **adj.** another term for NATURALISTIC.

nat·u·ral·is·tic /ˌnacHərəˈlistik/ ▶ **adj.** **1** derived from real life or nature, or imitating it very closely. **2** based on the theory of naturalism in art or literature. ■ of or according to the philosophy of naturalism: *phenomena once considered supernatural have yielded to naturalistic explanation.* — **nat·u·ral·is·ti·cal·ly adv.**

nat·ur·al·ize /ˈnacHərəˌlīz/ ▶ **v.** [trans.] **1** (often **be/become naturalized**) admit (a foreigner) to the citizenship of a country: *he was born in a foreign country and had never been naturalized.* ■ [intrans.] (of a foreigner) be admitted to the citizenship of a country: *the opportunity to naturalize as American.* ■ alter (an adopted foreign word) so that it conforms more closely to the phonology or orthography of the adopting language. **2** [usu. as adj.] (**naturalized**) Biol. establish (a plant or animal) so that it lives wild in a region where it is not indigenous: *native and naturalized species.* ■ establish (a cultivated plant) in a natural situation: *this species of crocus **naturalizes itself** very easily.* ■ [intrans.] (of a cultivated plant) become established in a natural situation: *these perennials should be planted where they can naturalize.* **3** regard as or cause to appear natural: *although women do more child care than men, feminists should beware of naturalizing that fact.* ■ explain (a phenomenon) in a naturalistic way. — **na·t·ura·l·iz·ation** /ˌnacHərələˈzāsHən/ **n.**

nat·u·ral kill·er cell ▶ **n.** Med. a lymphocyte able to bind to certain tumor cells and virus-infected cells without the stimulation of antigens, and kill them.

nat·u·ral lan·guage ▶ **n.** a language that has developed naturally in use (as contrasted with an artificial language or computer code).

nat·u·ral law ▶ **n.** **1** a body of unchanging moral principles regarded as a basis for all human conduct. **2** an observable law relating to natural phenomena. ■ such laws collectively.

nat·u·ral life ▶ **n.** the expected span of a person's life or a thing's existence under normal circumstances.

nat·u·ral log·a·rithm (abbr.: **ln** or **loge**) ▶ **n.** Math. a logarithm to the base *e* (2.71828...).

nat·u·ral·ly /ˈnacH(ə)zrəlē/ ▶ **adv.** **1** in a natural manner, in particular: ■ in a normal manner; without distortion or exaggeration: *act naturally.* ■ as a natural result: *one leads naturally into the other.* ■ without special help or intervention: *naturally curly hair.* **2** as may be expected; of course.

nat·u·ral num·bers ▶ **plural n.** the positive integers (whole numbers) 1, 2, 3, etc., and sometimes zero as well.

nat·u·ral phi·los·o·phy ▶ **n.** archaic natural science, esp. physical science. — **nat·u·ral phi·los·o·pher n.**

nat·u·ral re·li·gion ▶ **n.** religion, esp. deism, based on reason rather than divine revelation.

nat·u·ral re·sources ▶ **plural n.** materials or substances such as minerals, forests, water, and fertile land that occur in nature and can be used for economic gain.

nat·u·ral sci·ence ▶ **n.** (usu. **natural sciences**) a branch of science that deals with the physical world, e.g., physics, chemistry, geology, and biology. ■ the branch of knowledge that deals with the study of the physical world. — **nat·u·ral sci·en·tist n.**

nat·u·ral se·lec·tion ▶ **n.** Biol. the process whereby organisms better adapted to their environment tend to survive and produce more offspring. The theory of its action was first fully expounded by Charles Darwin and is now believed to be the main process that brings about evolution. Compare with SURVIVAL OF THE FITTEST (see SURVIVAL).

nat·u·ral the·ol·o·gy ▶ **n.** theology or knowledge of God based on observed facts and experience apart from divine revelation.

nat·u·ral vir·tue ▶ **n.** any of the traditional chief moral virtues, esp. the cardinal virtues.

na·ture /ˈnācHər/ ▶ **n.** **1** the phenomena of the physical world collectively, including plants, animals, the landscape, and other features and products of the earth, as opposed to humans or human creations. ■ the physical force regarded as causing and regulating these phenomena: *it is impossible to change the laws of nature.* See also MOTHER NATURE. ■ the countryside, esp. when picturesque. ■ archaic a living thing's vital functions or needs. **2** [in sing.] the basic or inherent features of something, esp. when seen as characteristic of it: *there are a lot of other documents **of that nature**.* ■ the innate or essential qualities or character of a person or animal: *I'm not violent **by nature**.* See also HUMAN NATURE. ■ inborn or hereditary characteristics as an influence on or determinant of personality. Often contrasted with NURTURE. ■ [with adj.] archaic a person of a specified character: *Emerson was so much more luminous a nature.*
– PHRASES **against nature** unnatural or immoral. **someone's better nature** the good side of a person's character. **call of nature** used euphemistically to refer to a need to urinate or defecate. **from nature** (in art) using natural scenes or objects as models. **get** (or **go**) **back to nature** return to the type of life that existed before the development of complex industrial societies. **in the nature of** similar in type to or having the characteristics of: *the promise was in the nature of a check that bounced.* **in the nature of things 1** inevitable. **2** inevitably. **in a state of nature 1** in an uncivilized or uncultivated state. **2** totally naked. **the nature of the beast** informal the inherent or essential quality or character of something, which cannot be changed. [ME: from OFr., from L. *natura* 'birth, nature, quality,' from *nat-* 'born,' from the v. *nasci*.]

na·tured /ˈnācHərd/ ▶ **adj.** [in comb.] having a nature or disposition of a specified kind: *a good-natured man.*

na·ture re·serve (also **nature preserve**) ▶ **n.** a tract of land managed so as to preserve its flora, fauna, and physical features.

na·ture stud·y ▶ **n.** the practical study of plants, animals, and natural phenomena, esp. as a school subject.

na·tur·ism /ˈnācHəˌrizəm/ ▶ **n.** **1** the practice of wearing no clothes in a vacation camp or for other leisure activities; nudism. **2** the worship of nature or natural objects. — **na·tur·ist n. & adj.**

na·tur·op·a·thy /ˌnācHəˈräpəTHē; ˌnacH-/ ▶ **n.** a system of alternative medicine based on the theory that diseases can be treated or prevented without drugs by techniques such as diet and exercise. — **na·tur·o·path** /ˈnācHərəˌpaTH; ˈnacH-/ **n.** **na·tur·o·path·ic** /ˌnācHərəˈpaTHik; ˌnacH-/ **adj.**

Nau·ga·hyde /ˈnôgəˌhīd/ ▶ **n.** (trademark) an artificial material designed to resemble leather, made from fabric coated with rubber or vinyl resin. [20th C.: from *Nauga(tuck)*, town in Connecticut + *-hyde* (alt. of HIDE²).]

naught /nôt/ ▶ **n.** the digit 0; zero. ▶ **pron.** archaic nothing: *he's naught but a worthless fool.* ▶ **adj.** archaic or literary worthless; useless.
– PHRASES **bring to naught** archaic ruin; foil. **come to naught** be ruined or foiled: *his hopes of becoming commissioner have come to naught.* **set at naught** archaic disregard; despise: *your efforts are set at naught by those beneath you.* [OE *nāwiht*, *-wuht*, from *nā* 'no' + *wiht* 'thing' (see WIGHT).]

naugh·ty /ˈnôtē/ ▶ **adj.** (**-ti·er, -ti·est**) **1** (esp. of children) disobedient; badly behaved. **2** informal mildly rude or indecent, typically because related to sex. **3** archaic wicked. — **naugh·ti·ly adv.** **naugh·ti·ness n.** [ME: from NAUGHT + -Y¹.]

nau·pli·us /ˈnôplēəs/ ▶ **n.** (pl. **-pli·i** /-plēˌī/) Zool. the first larval stage of many crustaceans, having an unsegmented body and a single eye. [19th C.: perh. from L., a kind of shellfish.]

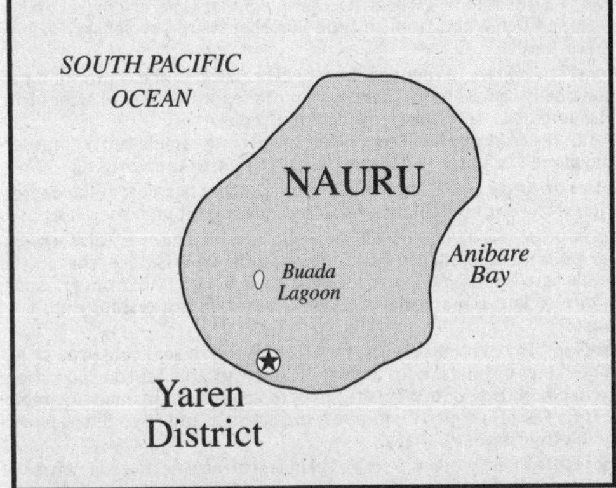

Nauru

Official name: Republic of Nauru
Location: southwestern Pacific Ocean, near the equator
Area: 8 square miles (21 sq km)
Population: 12,800
Capital: no official capital; government is in Yaren District
Languages: Nauruan (official), English
Currency: Australian dollar

Na·u·ru /nä'ōōrōō/ an island country in the southwestern Pacific Ocean. *See box on previous page.* — **Na·u·ru·an** /-rōōwən/ **adj. & n.**

nau·se·a /'nôzēə; -zhə/ ▶ **n.** a feeling of sickness with an inclination to vomit. ■ loathing; revulsion. [ME: via L. from Gk. *nausia*, from *naus* 'ship.']

nau·se·ate /'nôzē,āt; -zhē,āt/ ▶ **v.** [trans.] make (someone) feel sick; affect with nausea. | [as adj.] (**nauseating**) *the stench became nauseating.* ■ fill (someone) with revulsion; disgust: *I was nauseated by the vicious comment.* — **nau·se·at·ing·ly adv.**

nau·seous /'nôshəs; -zhəs; -ēəs/ ▶ **adj.** 1 affected with nausea; inclined to vomit. 2 causing nausea; offensive to the taste or smell. ■ disgusting, repellent, or offensive. — **nau·seous·ly adv. nau·seous·ness n.**

naut. ▶ **abbr.** nautical.

nautch /nôch/ ▶ **n.** (in the Indian subcontinent) a traditional dance performed by professional dancing girls. [from Hindi *nāc*, from Prakrit *nachcha*, from Sanskrit *nṛtya* 'dancing.']

nau·ti·cal /'nôtikəl/ ▶ **adj.** of or concerning sailors or navigation; maritime: *nautical charts.* — **nau·ti·cal·ly adv.** [16th C.: from Fr. *nautique*, or via L. from Gk. *nautikos*, from *nautēs* 'sailor,' from *naus* 'ship.']

nau·ti·cal mile ▶ **n.** a unit used in measuring distances at sea, equal to approximately 2,025 yards (1,852 m). Compare with SEA MILE.

nau·ti·loid /'nôtl,oid/ ▶ **n.** Zool. a mollusk of a group of mainly extinct marine mollusks (subclass Nautiloidea, class Cephalopoda) that includes the pearly nautilus.

nau·ti·lus /'nôtl-əs/ ▶ **n.** (pl. **nau·ti·lus·es** or **nau·ti·li** /'nôtl-ī/) 1 a cephalopod (genus *Nautilus*, subclass Nautiloidea) with a light external spiral shell and numerous short tentacles around the mouth; species include the common **chambered nautilus** (*Nautilus pompilius*) of the Indo-Pacific. 2 (also **paper nautilus**) another term for ARGONAUT. [mod. L., from L., from Gk. *nautilos*, lit. 'sailor.']

chambered nautilus

NAV ▶ **abbr.** net asset value.

nav /nav/ ▶ **n.** informal short for NAVIGATION. ■ short for NAVIGATOR.

Nav·a·jo /'navə,hō; 'nä-/ (also **Nav·a·ho**) ▶ **n.** (pl. same or **-jos**) 1 a member of an American Indian people of New Mexico and Arizona. 2 the Athabaskan language of this people. ▶ **adj.** of or relating to this people or their language. [from Sp. *(Apaches de) Navajó* '(Apaches from) Navajo,' from Tewa *navahu:* 'fields adjoining an arroyo.']

na·val /'nāvəl/ ▶ **adj.** of, in, or relating to a navy or navies: *a naval officer* | *naval operations.* [ME: from L. *navalis*, from *navis* 'ship.']

na·val ar·chi·tec·ture ▶ **n.** the designing of ships. — **na·val ar·chi·tect n.**

na·val stores ▶ **plural n.** articles or materials used in shipping.

na·va·rin /'navərin/ ▶ **n.** a stew of lamb or mutton with vegetables. [Fr.]

Na·varre /nə'vär/ an autonomous region of northern Spain; capital, Pamplona. Spanish name NAVARRA.

nave[1] /nāv/ ▶ **n.** the central part of a church building, intended to accommodate most of the congregation. [17th C.: from L. *navis* 'ship.']

nave[2] ▶ **n.** the hub of a wheel. [OE *nafu, nafa*, of Gmc. origin; rel. to Du. *naaf* and Ger. *Nabe*, from an Indo-Eur. root shared by Sanskrit *nābhis* 'nave, navel.']

na·vel /'nāvəl/ ▶ **n.** a rounded, knotty depression in the center of a person's belly caused by the detachment of the umbilical cord after birth; the umbilicus. ■ fig. the central point of a place.

– PHRASES **contemplate one's navel** spend time complacently considering oneself or one's own interests. [OE *nafela*, of Gmc. origin.]

na·vel or·ange ▶ **n.** a large, seedless orange that has a navellike depression at the top, containing a small secondary fruit underneath it.

na·vic·u·lar /nə'vikyələr/ ▶ **adj.** esp. archaic boat-shaped. ▶ **n.** (also **navicular bone**) a boat-shaped bone in the ankle or wrist, esp. that in the ankle between the talus and the cuneiform bones. [ME: from Fr. *naviculaire* or late L. *navicularis*, from L. *navicula* 'little ship,' dimin. of *navis*.]

nav·i·ga·ble /'navigəbəl/ ▶ **adj.** 1 (of a waterway or sea) able to be sailed on by ships or boats. ■ (of a track or road) suitable for transportation; passable. ■ (esp. of a Web site) easy to get around in; maneuverable. 2 (of a vessel) properly equipped, maintained, and operated. — **nav·i·ga·bil·i·ty** /,navəgə'bilitē/ **n.**

nav·i·gate /'navi,gāt/ ▶ **v.** 1 [intrans.] plan and direct the route or course of a ship, aircraft, or other form of transportation, esp. by using instruments or maps. ■ [no obj., with adverbial of direction] travel on a desired course after planning a route: *he taught them how to navigate across the oceans.* ■ (of an animal or bird) find its way, esp. over a long distance. ■ (of a passenger in a vehicle) assist the driver by reading the map and planning a route: *we'll go in my car—you can navigate.* ■ (of a ship or boat) sail; proceed: [with adverbial of direction] *we sailed out, navigating around larger grounded icebergs.* 2 [trans.] sail or travel over (a stretch of water or terrain), esp. carefully or with difficulty: *ships had been lost while navigating the narrows.* ■ guide (a vessel or vehicle) over a specified route or terrain: *she navigated the car through the traffic.* ■ make one's way with difficulty over (a route or terrain): *the drivers navigated a twisting and muddy course.* ■ Computing move from one page, section, Web site, etc., to another: *use any browser to navigate the Web site* | [intrans.] *it is extremely easy to navigate through the screens.* [16th C.: from L. *navigat-* 'sailed,' from the v. *navigare*, from *navis* 'ship' + *agere* 'drive.']

nav·i·ga·tion /,navi'gāshən/ ▶ **n.** 1 the process or activity of accurately ascertaining one's position and planning and following a route. 2 the passage of ships: *bridges to span rivers without hindering navigation.* — **nav·i·ga·tion·al** /-nəl/ **adj.**

nav·i·ga·tor /'navi,gātər/ ▶ **n.** a person who directs the route or course of a ship or aircraft, esp. by using instruments and maps. ■ an instrument that assists in directing the course of a vessel or aircraft. ■ Comput. a browser program for retrieving data on the World Wide Web or another information system. ■ hist. a person who explores by sea.

Nav·ra·ti·lo·va /,navrətə'lōvə; ,näv-/, Martina (1956–), US tennis player; born in Czechoslovakia. During 1975–2006, she won 59 Grand Slam titles. Her career titles for singles and doubles each set a record over all players (men or women).

NAVSTAR ▶ **abbr.** Navigation Satellite Timing and Ranging.

nav·vy /'navē/ ▶ **n.** (pl. **-vies**) Brit., dated a laborer employed in the excavation and construction of a road, railroad, or canal. [19th C.: abbrev. of NAVIGATOR.]

na·vy /'nāvē/ ▶ **n.** (pl. **-vies**) 1 (often **the navy** or **the Navy**) the branch of a nation's armed services that conducts military operations at sea. ■ the ships of a navy. ■ literary a fleet of ships. 2 (also **navy blue**) a dark blue color. [ME: from OFr. *navie* 'ship, fleet,' from pop. L. *navia* 'ship,' from L. *navis* 'ship.']

na·vy bean ▶ **n.** a small white type of kidney bean.

Na·vy Cross ▶ **n.** a decoration bestowed by the US Navy upon individuals who have shown exceptional heroism, esp. in enemy combat.

na·vy yard ▶ **n.** a shipyard for the construction, repair, and equipping of naval vessels.

naw /nô/ ▶ **exclam.** informal. var. of NO, used to answer a question: *"Want some toast?" "Naw."*

na·wab /nə'wäb/ ▶ **n.** Indian, hist. a native governor during the time of the Mogul empire. ■ a Muslim nobleman or person of high status. [from Urdu *nawwāb*, var. of Arab. *nuwwāb*, pl. of *nā'ib* 'deputy.']

Nax·çi·van /,nəkēchi'vän/ an Azerbaijani autonomous republic that is located on the borders of Turkey and northern Iran and is separated from the rest of Azerbaijan by a narrow strip of Armenia; pop. 300,000. Russian name NAKHICHEVAN. ■ the capital city of this republic; pop. 51,000.

Nax·os /'näk,sôs; 'naksəs/ a Greek island in the southern Aegean Sea, the largest of the Cyclades.

nay /nā/ ▶ **adv.** 1 or rather; and more than that (used to emphasize a more appropriate word than one just used): *it is difficult, nay, impossible, to understand* | *it will take months, nay years.* 2 archaic dialect no: *nay, I must not think thus.* ▶ **n.** a negative answer: *the cabinet sits to give the final yea or nay to policies.* [ME (sense 2): from ON *nei*, from *ne* 'not' + *ei* 'ever' (cf. AYE[2]).]

Na·ya·rit /näyä'rēt/ a state in western Mexico; capital, Tepic.

nay·say /'nā,sā/ ▶ **v.** (past and past part. **-said**) [trans.] say no to; deny or oppose. — **nay·say·er n.**

Naz·a·rene /'nazə,rēn/ ▶ **n.** a native or inhabitant of Nazareth. ■ (**the Nazarene**) Jesus Christ. ■ (chiefly in Jewish or Muslim use) a Christian. ■ a member of an early sect or faction of Jewish Christians who observed much of the Jewish law. ■ a member of the Church of the Nazarene, a Christian Protestant denomination. ▶ **adj.** of or relating to Nazareth or Nazarenes.

Naz·a·reth /'naz(ə)rəth/ a town in lower Galilee, in present-day northern Israel; pop. 39,000. It is mentioned in the Gospels as the home of Mary and Joseph, and is associated with the childhood of Jesus Christ.

Na·zi /'nätsē/ ▶ **n.** (pl. **Na·zis**) hist. a member of the National Socialist German Workers' Party. ■ a member of an organization with similar ideology. ■ derog. a person who holds and acts brutally in accordance with extreme racist or authoritarian views. ▶ **adj.** of or concerning the Nazis or Nazism. — **Na·zi·dom n. Na·zi·fy** /'nätsi,fī/ **v.** (**-fies, -fied**). **Na·zi·ism n. Na·zism** /'nät,sizəm/ **n.** [Ger., from *Nationalsozialist* 'national socialist.']

Na·zi sa·lute ▶ **n.** a gesture or salute in which the right arm is straightened and inclined upward, with the hand open and palm down.

NB ▶ **abbr.** ■ nota bene; take special note (used to precede a written note). [L.]

Nb ▶ **symb.** the chemical element niobium.

NBA ▶ **abbr.** ■ National Basketball Association. ■ National Boxing Association.

NBC ▶ **abbr.** ■ National Broadcasting Company. ■ (of weapons or warfare) nuclear, biological, and chemical.

NbE ▶ **abbr.** north by east.

NbW ▶ **abbr.** north by west.

NC ▶ **abbr.** ■ network computer. ■ North Carolina (in official postal use).

NC-17 ▶ **symb.** no one 17 and under admitted, a rating in the Voluntary Movie Rating System forbidding admission to children 17 years old and under. [representing *no children (under) 17.*]

NCAA ▶ **abbr.** National Collegiate Athletic Association.

NCO ▶ **abbr.** noncommissioned officer.

NCTE ▶ **abbr.** National Council of Teachers of English.

NCTM ▶ **abbr.** National Council of Teachers of Mathematics.

ND ▶ **abbr.** North Dakota (in official postal use).

Nd ▶ symb. the chemical element neodymium.

n.d. ▶ abbr. no date (used esp. in bibliographies).

-nd ▶ suffix var. of -AND, -END.

N.Dak. ▶ abbr. North Dakota.

NDEA ▶ abbr. National Defense Education Act.

Nde·be·le /ˌ(ə)ndəˈbelā; -ˈbēlē/ ▶ n. (pl. same or **-les**) **1** a member of a Bantu people of Zimbabwe and northeastern South Africa. See also MATABELE. **2** the Nguni language of this people. ▶ adj. of or relating to this people or their language. [the name in the Nguni languages.]

N'Dja·me·na /ənjəˈmā/ the capital of Chad, in the southwestern part of the country; pop. 531,000. Former name (1900–73) FORT LAMY.

NE ▶ abbr. ■ Nebraska (in official postal use). ■ New England. ■ northeast or northeastern.

Ne ▶ symb. the chemical element neon.

né /nā/ ▶ adj. originally called; born (used before the name by which a man was originally known): *Al Kelly, né Kabish.* [1930s: Fr., lit. 'born,' masc. past part. of *naître*; cf. NÉE.]

NEA ▶ abbr. ■ National Education Association. ■ National Endowment for the Arts. ■ Nuclear Energy Agency.

Ne·an·der·thal /nēˈandərˌTHôl; -ˌtäl/ ▶ n. (also **Neanderthal man**) an extinct species of human (*Homo neanderthalensis*) that was widely distributed in Ice-Age Europe between *c.*120,000 and 35,000 years ago, with a receding forehead and prominent brow ridges. ■ fig. an uncivilized, unintelligent, or uncouth person, esp. a man. ▶ adj. of or relating to this extinct human species. ■ fig. (esp. of a man) uncivilized, unintelligent, or uncouth. [19th C.: from *Neanderthal*, region in Germany.]

neap /nēp/ ▶ n. (usu. **neap tide**) a tide just after the first or third quarters of the moon when there is the least difference between high and low water. [ME, orig. an adj. from OE *nēp*, first element of *nēpflōd* 'neap flood,' of unknown origin.]

Ne·a·pol·i·tan /ˌnēəˈpälitn/ ▶ n. a native or citizen of Naples. ▶ adj. of or relating to Naples. [from L. *Neapolitanus*, from L. *Neapolis* 'Naples,' from Gk. *neos* 'new' + *polis* 'city.']

Ne·a·pol·i·tan ice cream ▶ n. ice cream made in layers of different colors, typically including chocolate, vanilla, and strawberry.

near /ni(ə)r/ ▶ adv. **1** at or to a short distance away; nearby: *a bomb exploding somewhere near* | [comparative] *she took a step nearer.* **2** a short time away in the future: *the time for his retirement was near.* **3** [as submodifier] almost: *a near perfect fit.* **4** archaic dialect almost: *I near fell out of the chair.* ▶ prep. (also **near to**) **1** at or to a short distance away from (a place): *the parking lot near the sawmill* | [superlative] *the table nearest the door.* **2** a short period of time from: *near the end of the war* | [comparative] *details will be given nearer the date.* **3** close to (a state); verging on: *she was near death.* ■ (used before an amount) a small amount below (something); approaching: *temperatures near 2 million degrees K.* **4** similar to: *a shape near to the original.* ▶ adj. **1** located a short distance away: *a big house **in the near distance*** | [superlative] *fifteen miles from the nearest town.* **2** only a short time ahead: *the conflict can be resolved **in the near future**.* **3** similar: [superlative] *walking in these shoes is **the nearest thing to** floating on air.* ■ [attrib.] close to being (the thing mentioned): *a near disaster.* ■ [attrib.] having a close family connection: *the loss of a child or other near relative.* **4** [attrib.] located on the side of a vehicle that is normally closest to the curb: *the near right-hand end window of the trailer.* Compare with OFF (sense 3). **5** archaic (of a person) stingy; miserly. ▶ v. [trans.] come near to (someone or something); approach: *soon the cab would be nearing State Street* | [intrans.] *lunchtime neared.*

– PHRASES **near at hand** within easy reach. ■ about to happen or come about. **near enough** sufficiently close to being the case for all practical purposes: *maybe not quite the equal of her groundbreaking debut, but near enough.* **one's nearest and dearest** one's close friends and relatives. **so near and yet so far** a rueful comment on someone's narrow failure to achieve an aim. — **near·ish** adj. **near·ness** n. [ME: from ON *nær* 'nearer,' compar. of *ná*.]

near·by ▶ adj. /ˈni(ə)rˌbī/ close at hand; not far away. ▶ adv. (Brit. also **near by**) close by; very near.

Ne·arc·tic /nēˈär(k)tik/ ▶ adj. Zool. of, relating to, or denoting a zoogeographical region comprising Greenland and North America as far south as northern Mexico. Compare with HOLARCTIC. ■ [as n.] (**the Nearctic**) the Nearctic region. [19th C.: from NEO- 'new' + ARCTIC.]

near-death ex·pe·ri·ence ▶ n. an unusual experience taking place on the brink of death and recounted by a person after recovery, typically an out-of-body experience or a vision of a tunnel of light.

Near East (**the Near East**) a term generally applied to the countries of southwestern Asia between the Mediterranean Sea and India (including the Middle East). — **Near East·ern** adj.

near gale ▶ n. another term for MODERATE GALE.

Near Is·lands an island group in southwestern Alaska at the western end of the Aleutian Islands.

near·ly /ˈni(ə)rlē/ ▶ adv. **1** very close to; almost: *David was nearly asleep* **2** closely: *in the absence of anyone more nearly related, I had been designated next of kin.*

– PHRASES **not nearly** nothing like; far from.

near miss ▶ n. **1** a narrowly avoided collision, esp. between two aircraft. ■ something narrowly avoided; a lucky escape. **2** a bomb or shot that just misses its target. ■ something almost achieved.

near rhyme ▶ n. rhyming in which the words sound the same but do not rhyme perfectly. Also called OFF RHYME.

near·sight·ed /ˈni(ə)rˌsītid/ ▶ adj. unable to see things clearly unless they are relatively close to the eyes, owing to the focusing of rays of light by the eye at a point in front of the retina; myopic. — **near·sight·ed·ly** adv. **near·sight·ed·ness** n.

near-term ▶ adj. short-term.

neat[1] /nēt/ ▶ adj. **1** (of a place or thing) arranged in an orderly, tidy way. ■ (of a person) habitually tidy, well groomed, or well organized. ■ having a pleasing shape or appearance; well formed or regular. ■ informal very good or pleasant; excellent: *I've been taking lessons in tracking from this really neat Indian guide.* **2** done with or demonstrating skill or efficiency. ■ tending to disregard specifics for the sake of convenience; slick or facile: *this neat division does not take into account a host of associated factors.* **3** (of liquid, esp. liquor) not diluted or mixed with anything else: *he drank neat Scotch.* — **neat·ly** adv. **neat·ness** n. [15th C.: from Fr. *net*, from L. *nitidus* 'shining,' from *nitere* 'to shine'; rel. to NET[2].]

neat[2] ▶ n. archaic a bovine animal. ■ cattle. [OE, of Gmc. origin; rel. to Du. *noot*.]

neat·en /ˈnētn/ ▶ v. [trans.] make neat; arrange in an orderly, tidy way: *she made an attempt to neaten her hair.*

'neath /nēTH/ (also **neath**) ▶ prep. esp. literary beneath: *'neath the trees.*

neat's-foot oil ▶ n. oil obtained by boiling the feet of cattle, used to dress leather.

NEB ▶ abbr. ■ New English Bible.

Neb. ▶ abbr. Nebraska.

neb /neb/ ▶ n. Scot. N. English a projecting part of something, in particular: ■ a nose or snout. ■ a bird's beak or bill. ■ the brim of a cap. [OE *nebb*, of Gmc. origin; rel. to Du. *neb(be)*; cf. NIB.]

Neb·bi·o·lo /ˌnebēˈōlō/ ▶ n. a variety of black wine grape grown in Piedmont in northern Italy. ■ a red wine made from this. [Ital., from *nebbia* 'mist.']

neb·bish /ˈnebisH/ ▶ n. informal a person, esp. a man, who is pitifully ineffectual, timid, or submissive. — **neb·bish·y** adj. [19th C.: from Yiddish *nebekh* 'poor thing.']

NEbE ▶ abbr. northeast by east.

NEbN ▶ abbr. northeast by north.

Nebr. ▶ abbr. Nebraska.

Ne·bras·ka /nəˈbraskə/ a state in the central US, west of the Missouri River; pop. 1,711,263; capital, Lincoln; statehood, Mar. 1, 1867 (37). It was acquired as part of the Louisiana Purchase in 1803. — **Ne·bras·kan** adj. & n.

Neb·u·chad·nez·zar /ˌneb(y)əkə(d)ˈnezər/ ▶ n. a very large wine bottle, equivalent in capacity to about twenty regular bottles. [20th C.: from *Nebuchadnezzar* (see NEBUCHADNEZZAR II).]

Neb·u·chad·nez·zar II (*c.*630–562 BC), king of Babylon 605–562 BC. In 586 BC, he captured and destroyed Jerusalem and deported many Israelites during the Babylonian Captivity.

neb·u·la /ˈnebyələ/ ▶ n. (pl. **-lae** /-lē/ or **-las**) **1** Astron. a cloud of gas and dust in outer space, visible in the night sky either as an indistinct bright patch or as a dark silhouette against other luminous matter. ■ (in general use) any indistinct bright area in the night sky, e.g., a distant galaxy. **2** Med. a clouded spot on the cornea causing defective vision. [17th C. (as a medical term): from L., lit. 'mist.']

neb·u·lar /ˈnebyələr/ ▶ adj. of, relating to, or denoting a nebula or nebulae: *a vast nebular cloud.*

neb·u·lar hy·poth·e·sis (also **nebular theory**) ▶ n. the theory that the solar and stellar systems were developed from a primeval nebula.

neb·u·liz·er /ˈnebyəˌlīzər/ ▶ n. a device for producing a fine spray of liquid, used for example for inhaling a medicinal drug. — **neb·u·lize** v. [19th C.: from L. *nebula* 'mist' + *-izer* (see -IZE).]

neb·u·lous /ˈnebyələs/ ▶ adj. in the form of a cloud or haze; hazy. ■ (of an idea) unclear, vague, or ill-defined. ■ another term for NEBULAR. — **neb·u·los·i·ty** /ˌnebyəˈläsitē/ adv. **neb·u·lous·ly** adv. **neb·u·lous·ness** n. [ME: from Fr. *nébuleux* or L. *nebulosus*, from *nebula* 'mist.']

nec·es·sar·i·an /ˌnesəˈse(ə)rēən/ ▶ n. & adj. Philos. another term for *DETERMINIST* (see DETERMINISM). — **nec·es·sar·i·an·ism** n.

nec·es·sar·i·ly /ˌnesəˈse(ə)rəlē/ ▶ adv. as a necessary result; inevitably.

– PHRASES **not necessarily** (as a response) what has been said or suggested may not be true or unavoidable.

nec·es·sar·y /ˈnesəˌserē/ ▶ adj. **1** required to be done, achieved, or present; essential. **2** determined, existing, or happening by natural laws or predestination; inevitable: *a necessary consequence.* ■ Philos. (of a concept, statement, judgment, etc.) inevitably resulting from or produced by the nature of things, so that the contrary is impossible. ■ Philos. (of an agent) having no independent volition. ▶ n. (usu. **necessaries**) (also **necessaries of life**) the basic requirements of life, such as food and warmth. ■ small items required for a journey or purpose.

– PHRASES **a necessary evil** something that is undesirable but must be accepted. [ME: from L. *necessarius*, from *necesse* 'needful.']

ne·ces·si·tar·i·an /nəˌsesəˈte(ə)rēən/ ▶ n. & adj. Philos. another term for *DETERMINIST* (see DETERMINISM). — **ne·ces·si·tar·i·an·ism** /-ˌnizəm/ n.

ne·ces·si·tate /nə'sesə,tāt/ ▶**v.** [trans.] make (something) necessary as a result: *the arthritis necessitated a hip replacement.* ■ [with obj. and pres. part.] force or compel (someone) to do something: *the late arrival had necessitated her getting out of bed.*

ne·ces·si·tous /nə'sesitəs/ ▶**adj.** (of a person) lacking the necessities of life; needy.

ne·ces·si·ty /nə'sesətē/ ▶**n.** (pl. **-ties**) **1** the fact of being required or indispensable: *the* ***necessity for*** *law and order.* ■ unavoidability: *the* ***necessity of*** *growing old.* ■ a state of things or circumstances enforcing a certain course: *created more by necessity than design.* **2** an indispensable thing. **3** Philos. the principle according to which something must be so, by virtue either of logic or of natural law. ■ a condition that cannot be otherwise, or a statement asserting this.
– PHRASES **of necessity** unavoidably. [ME: from OFr. *necessite*, from L. *necessitas*, from *necesse* 'needful.']

neck /nek/ ▶**n.** **1** the part of a person's or animal's body connecting the head to the rest of the body. ■ the part of a shirt, dress, or other garment that is around or close to the neck. ■ meat from an animal's neck. ■ fig. a person's neck regarded as bearing a burden of responsibility or guilt for something: *he'll be stuck with a loan* ***around his neck.*** **2** a narrow part of something, resembling a neck in shape or position: ■ the part of a bottle or other container near the mouth. ■ a narrow piece of terrain or sea, such as an isthmus, channel, or pass. ■ Anat. a narrow part near one end of an organ such as the uterus. ■ the part of a violin, guitar, or other similar instrument that bears the fingerboard. ■ Archit. another term for **NECKING**. ■ (often **volcanic neck**) Geol. a column of solidified lava or igneous rock formed in a volcanic vent, esp. when exposed by erosion. ■ Bot. a narrow supporting part in a plant, esp. the terminal part of the fruiting body in a fern, bryophyte, or fungus. **3** the length of a horse's head and neck as a measure of its lead in a race. ▶**v.** **1** [intrans.] informal (of two people) kiss and caress amorously. **2** [intrans.] form a narrowed part at a particular point when subjected to tension: *the nylon filament* ***necks down*** *to a fraction of its original diameter.*
– PHRASES **break one's neck 1** dislocate or seriously damage a vertebra or the spinal cord in one's neck. **2** (**break one's neck to do something**) informal exert oneself to the utmost to achieve something. **get** (or **catch**) **it in the neck** informal be severely criticized or punished. **neck and neck** even in a race, competition, or comparison. **neck of the woods** informal a particular area or locality. — **necked adj.** [in comb.] *an open-necked shirt.* **neck·er n. neck·less adj.** [OE *hnecca* 'back of the neck,' of Gmc. origin; rel. to Du. *nek* 'neck' and Ger. *Nacken* 'nape.']

Neck·ar /'nekər/ a river in western Germany that meets the Rhine River at Mannheim.

neck·band /'nek,band/ ▶**n.** a strip of material around the neck of a garment.

neck·cloth /'nek,klôTH/ ▶**n.** a cravat.

Neck·er /'nekər; ne'ker/, Jacques (1732–1804), French financier; born in Switzerland.

neck·er·chief /'nekər,CHif; -,CHēf/ ▶**n.** a square of cloth worn around the neck.

Neck·er cube ▶**n.** a line drawing of a transparent cube in which the lines of opposite sides are drawn parallel, so that the perspective is ambiguous and the orientation of the cube appears to alternate. [20th C.: after L. A. *Necker* (1786–1861), Swiss naturalist.]

Necker cube

neck·ing /'nekiNG/ ▶**n.** **1** the action of two people kissing and caressing each other amorously. **2** Archit. a short, plain, concave section between the capital and the shaft of a Doric or Tuscan column.

neck·lace /'neklis/ ▶**n.** **1** an ornamental chain or string of beads, jewels, or links worn around the neck. **2** (chiefly in South Africa) a tire doused or filled with gasoline, placed around a victim's neck, and set on fire. ▶**v.** [trans.] (chiefly in South Africa) kill (someone) with a tire necklace.

neck·let /'neklit/ ▶**n.** a fairly close-fitting and typically rigid ornament worn around the neck.

neck·line /'nek,līn/ ▶**n.** the edge of a woman's garment at or below the neck, referring to its height or shape.

neck·tie /'nek,tī/ ▶**n.** another term for **TIE** (sense 2).

neck·tie par·ty ▶**n.** informal a lynching or hanging.

neck·wear /'nek,we(ə)r/ ▶**n.** items worn around the neck, such as ties or scarves, collectively.

necro- ▶**comb. form** relating to a corpse or death: *necromancy.* [from Gk. *nekros* 'corpse.']

nec·ro·bi·o·sis /,nekrōbī'ōsis/ ▶**n.** Med. gradual degeneration and death of cells in the body tissues. — **nec·ro·bi·ot·ic** /-,bī'ätik/ **adj.**

ne·crol·o·gy /ne'kräləjē/ ▶**n.** (pl. **-gies**) formal **1** an obituary notice. **2** a list of deaths. — **ne·cro·log·i·cal** /,nekrə'läjikəl/ **adj. ne·crol·o·gist** /ne'kräləjist/

nec·ro·man·cy /'nekrə,mansē/ ▶**n.** the supposed practice of communicating with the dead, esp. in order to predict the future. ■ witchcraft, sorcery, or black magic in general. — **nec·ro·man·cer** /-sər/ **n. nec·ro·man·tic** /,nekrə'mantik/ **adj.** [ME *nigromancie*, via OFr. from med. L. *nigromantia*, from late L. *necromantia*, from Gk. (see **NECRO-**, **-MANCY**).]

nec·ro·phil·i·a /,nekrə'filēə/ ▶**n.** a morbid and esp. erotic attraction toward corpses. ■ sexual intercourse with a corpse. — **nec·ro·phile** /'nekrə,fīl/ **n. nec·ro·phil·i·ac** /-'filē,ak/ **n. nec·ro·phil·ic** /-'filik/ **adj. ne·croph·i·lism** /ne'kräfə,lizəm/ **n. ne·croph·i·list** /ne'kräfəlist/ **n.**

nec·ro·pho·bi·a /,nekrə'fōbēə/ ▶**n.** extreme or irrational fear of death or dead bodies.

ne·crop·o·lis /ne'kräpəlis/ ▶**n.** a cemetery, esp. a large one belonging to an ancient city. [19th C.: from Gk., from *nekros* 'dead person' + *polis* 'city.']

nec·rop·sy /'nekräpsē/ ▶**n.** (pl. **-sies**) another term for **AUTOPSY**.

ne·cro·sis /ne'krōsis/ ▶**n.** Med. the death of most or all of the cells in an organ or tissue due to disease, injury, or failure of the blood supply. — **ne·crot·ic** /-'krätik/ **adj.**

nec·ro·tiz·ing /'nekrə,tīziNG/ ▶**adj.** [attrib.] causing or accompanied by necrosis. — **nec·ro·tized adj.**

nec·tar /'nektər/ ▶**n.** **1** a sugary fluid secreted by plants, esp. within flowers to encourage pollination by insects and collected by bees to make honey. **2** (in Greek and Roman mythology) the drink of the gods. ■ a delicious drink. ■ a thick fruit juice. — **nec·tar·e·an** /nek'te(ə)rēən/ **adj. nec·tar·e·ous** /nek'te(ə)rēəs/ **adj. nec·tar·ous** /-əs/ **adj.** [16th C. (sense 2): via L. from Gk. *nektar*.]

nec·tar·if·er·ous /,nektə'rifərəs/ ▶**adj.** Bot. (of a flower) producing nectar.

nec·tar·ine /,nektə'rēn/ ▶**n.** a peach of a variety with smooth, thin, brightly colored skin and rich firm flesh. ■ the tree bearing this fruit.

nec·ta·ry /'nektərē/ ▶**n.** (pl. **-ries**) Bot. a nectar-secreting glandular organ in a flower (floral) or on a leaf or stem (extrafloral).

Ne·der·land /'nādər,länt/ Dutch name for **NETHERLANDS**.

née /nā/ ▶**adj.** originally called; born (used esp. in adding a woman's maiden name after her married name): *Mary Toogood, née Johnson.* [18th C.: Fr., lit. 'born,' fem. past part. of *naître*.]

need /nēd/ ▶**v.** [trans.] **1** require (something) because it is essential or very important: *I need help now.* ■ (**not need something**) not want to be subjected to something: *I don't need your sarcasm.* **2** [as modal verb] [with negative or in questions] expressing necessity or obligation: *need I say more?* **3** [intrans.] archaic be necessary: *lest you, even more than needs, embitter our parting.* ▶**n.** **1** circumstances in which something is necessary, or that require some course of action; necessity: *the* ***need for*** *food.* **2** (often **needs**) a thing wanted or required: *day-to-day needs.* **3** the state of lacking basic necessities such as food or money: *a family whose need was pressing.* ■ the state of requiring help or support: *our* ***hour of need.***
– PHRASES **at need** archaic when needed; in an emergency. **had need** archaic ought to: *you had need hire men to chip it all over artistically.* **have need of** formal need. **if need be** if necessary. **in need** requiring help. **in need of** requiring or needing (something). [OE *nēodian* (v.), *nēod*, *nēd* (n.), of Gmc. origin; rel. to Du. *nood* and Ger. *Not* 'danger.']

need·ful /'nēdfəl/ ▶**adj. 1** formal necessary; requisite. **2** needy. — **need·ful·ly adv. need·ful·ness n.**

nee·dle /'nēdl/ ▶**n.** **1** a very fine slender piece of polished metal with a point at one end and a hole or eye for thread at the other, used in sewing. **2** something resembling a sewing needle in use, shape, or appearance, esp.: ■ such an instrument used in crafts such as crochet, knitting, and lacemaking. ■ the pointed hollow end of a hypodermic syringe. ■ a very fine metal spike used in acupuncture. ■ a thin, typically metal pointer on a dial, compass, or other instrument. ■ an etching tool. ■ the sharp, stiff, slender leaf of a fir or pine tree. ■ a pointed rock or peak. ■ a stylus used to play phonograph records. ■ an obelisk: *Cleopatra's Needle.* ■ a steel pin that explodes the cartridge of a breech-loading gun. ▶**v.** [trans.] **1** prick or pierce (something) with or as if with a needle: *dust needled his eyes.* **2** informal provoke or annoy (someone), esp. by continual criticism or questioning.
– PHRASES **give someone the needle** informal provoke or annoy someone. — **nee·dler** /'nēdl-ər; -lər/ **n.** [OE *nǣdl*, of Gmc. origin; rel. to Du. *naald* and Ger. *Nadel*, from an Indo-Eur. root shared by L. *nere* 'to spin' and Gk. *nēma* 'thread.']

nee·dle·craft /'nēdl,kraft/ ▶**n.** needlework.

nee·dle·fish /'nēdl,fiSH/ ▶**n.** (pl. same or **-fish·es**) another term for **GARFISH**.

nee·dle·lace /'nēdl,lās/ ▶**n.** another term for **NEEDLEPOINT** (sense 2).

nee·dle·point /'nēdl,point/ ▶**n.** **1** embroidery worked over canvas, typically in a diagonal stitch covering the entire surface of the fabric. **2** (also **needlepoint lace**) lace made by hand using a needle rather than bobbins. ▶**v.** [trans.] embroider in needlepoint.

need·less /'nēdlis/ ▶**adj.** (of something bad) unnecessary; avoidable: *I deplore needless waste.*
– PHRASES **needless to say** of course. — **need·less·ly adv. need·less·ness n.**

nee·dle valve ▶**n.** a valve closed by a thin tapering part.

nee·dle·wom·an /'nēdl,wo͝omən/ ▶**n.** (pl. **-wom·en**) a woman who has sewing skills or sews for a living.

nee·dle·work /'nēdl,wərk/ ▶**n.** the art or practice of sewing or embroidery. ■ sewn or embroidered items collectively. — **nee·dle·work·er n.**

need·n't /'nēdnt/ ▶**contr.** need not.

needs /nēdz/ ▶**adv.** (in phrase **must needs** (or **needs must**) **do something**) archaic cannot avoid or help doing something: *they must needs depart.* [OE *nēdes* (see **NEED**, **-S**[3]).]

need·y /'nēdē/ ▶**adj.** (**need·i·er**, **need·i·est**) (of a person) lacking the necessities of life; very poor. ■ (of circumstances) characterized by poverty: *those from needy backgrounds.* — **need·i·ness** n.

neem /nēm/ ▶ n. a tropical Old World tree (*Azadirachta indica,* family Meliaceae) that yields mahoganylike timber, oil, medicinal products, and insecticide. [19th C.: via Hindi from Sanskrit *nimba.*]

neep /nēp/ ▶ n. Scot. N. English a turnip. [OE *nǣp,* from L. *napus.*]

ne'er /ne(ə)r/ literary dialect ▶ contr. never.

ne'er-do-well /'ne(ə)r do͞o ˌwel/ ▶ n. a person who is lazy and irresponsible. ▶ adj. [attrib.] lazy and irresponsible.

ne·far·i·ous /ni'fe(ə)rēəs/ ▶ adj. (of an action or activity) wicked or criminal: *the nefarious activities of the organized-crime syndicates.* — **ne·far·i·ous·ly** adv. **ne·far·i·ous·ness** n. [17th C.: from L. *nefarius,* from *nefas, nefar-* 'wrong' (from *ne-* 'not' + *fas* 'divine law') + **-ous.**]

Nef·er·ti·ti /ˌnefər'tētē/ (also **Nof·re·te·te** /ˌnäfri'tētē/) (*fl.* 14th century BC), queen of Egypt. She is best known from the painted limestone bust of her, now in Berlin (*c.*1350).

neg /neg/ ▶ n. informal a photographic negative.

neg. ▶ abbr. negative: *HIV neg.*

nega- ▶ comb. form denoting the negative counterpart of a unit of measurement, in particular a unit of energy saved as a result of conservation measures. [abbrev. of **negative.**]

ne·gate /nə'gāt/ ▶ v. [trans.] **1** nullify; make ineffective: *alcohol negates the effects of the drug.* **2** Logic Gram. make (a clause, sentence, or proposition) negative in meaning. **3** deny the existence of (something): *negating the political nature of education.* [17th C. (in senses 1 and 3): from L. *negat-* 'denied,' from the v. *negare.*]

ne·ga·tion /nə'gāsʜən/ ▶ n. **1** the contradiction or denial of something: *there should be confirmation—or negation—of the findings.* ■ Gram. denial of the truth of a clause or sentence, typically involving the use of a negative word (e.g., *not, no*) or a word or affix with negative force (e.g., *nothing, non-*). ■ Logic a proposition whose assertion specifically denies the truth of another proposition: *the negation of A is, briefly, "not A."* ■ Math. inversion. **2** the absence or opposite of something actual or positive: *evil is not merely the negation of goodness.* — **neg·a·to·ry** /'negəˌtôrē/ adj.

neg·a·tive /'negətiv/ ▶ adj. **1** consisting in or characterized by the absence rather than the presence of distinguishing features. ■ (of a statement or decision) expressing or implying denial, disagreement, or refusal: *a negative answer.* ■ (of the results of a test or experiment) indicating that a certain substance is not present or a certain condition does not exist: *so far all the patients have tested negative for TB.* ■ [in comb.] (of a person or their blood) not having a specified substance or condition: *HIV-negative.* ■ (of a person, attitude, or situation) not optimistic; harmful or unwelcome: *not all the news is negative.* ■ informal denoting a lack of something: *they were described as having negative vulnerability to water entry.* ■ Gram. Logic (of a word, clause, or proposition) expressing denial, negation, or refutation. Contrasted with **affirmative** and **interrogative. 2** (of a quantity) less than zero; to be subtracted from others or from zero. ■ denoting a direction of decrease or reversal: *negative interest rates | negative growth in 1992.* **3** of, containing, producing, or denoting the kind of electric charge carried by electrons. **4** (of a photographic image) showing light and shade or colors reversed from those of the original. **5** Astrol. relating to or denoting any of the earth or water signs, considered passive in nature. ▶ n. **1** a word or statement that expresses denial, disagreement, or refusal: *she replied in the negative.* ■ (often **the negative**) a bad, unwelcome, or unpleasant quality, characteristic, or aspect of a situation or person: *confidence will not be instilled by harping on the negative.* ■ Gram. a word, affix, or phrase expressing negation. ■ Logic another term for **negation. 2** a photographic image made on film or specially prepared glass that shows the light and shade or color values reversed from the original, and from which positive prints can be made. **3** a result of a test or experiment indicating that a certain substance is not present or a certain condition does not exist. **4** the part of an electric circuit that is at a lower electrical potential than another part designated as having zero electrical potential. **5** a number less than zero. ▶ exclam. no (usually used in a military context): *"Any snags, Captain?" "Negative, she's running like clockwork."* ▶ v. [trans.] **1** reject; refuse to accept; veto: *the bill was negatived by 130 votes to 129.* ■ disprove; contradict: *the insurer's main arguments were negatived by Lawrence.* **2** render ineffective; neutralize: *should criminal law allow consent to negative what would otherwise be a crime?* — **neg·a·tive·ly** adv. **neg·a·tive·ness** n. **neg·a·tiv·i·ty** /ˌnegə'tivitē/ n.

neg·a·tive feed·back ▶ n. esp. Biol. the diminution or counteraction of an effect by its own influence on the process giving rise to it, as when a high level of a particular hormone in the blood may inhibit further secretion of that hormone. ■ Electron. the return of part of an output signal to the input, which is out of phase with it, so that amplifier gain is reduced and the output is improved.

neg·a·tive in·come tax ▶ n. money credited as allowances to a taxed income, and paid as a benefit when it exceeds debited tax.

neg·a·tive pole ▶ n. the south-seeking pole of a magnet. ■ a cathode.

neg·a·tive sign ▶ n. another term for **minus sign.**

neg·a·tiv·ism /'negətivˌizəm/ ▶ n. the practice of being or tendency to be negative or skeptical in attitude while failing to offer positive suggestions or views. — **neg·a·tiv·ist** n. & adj. **neg·a·tiv·is·tic** /ˌnegətiv'istik/ adj.

ne·ga·tor /nə'gātər/ ▶ n. Gram. a word expressing negation, esp. (in English) the word *not.*

Neg·ev /'negev/ (**the Negev**) an arid region that forms most of southern Israel on the Egyptian border. Many Israeli communities have been established here.

ne·glect /ni'glekt/ ▶ v. [trans.] fail to care for properly: *the old churchyard has been sadly neglected* | [as adj.] (**neglected**) *some severely neglected children.* ■ not pay proper attention to; disregard: *you neglect our advice at your peril.* ■ [with infin.] fail to do something: *he neglected to write to her.* ▶ n. the state or fact of being uncared for: *animals dying through disease or neglect.* ■ the action of not taking proper care of someone or something: *she was accused of child neglect.* ■ failure to do something: *neglect of duty.* — **ne·glect·ful** adj. **ne·glect·ful·ly** adv. **ne·glect·ful·ness** n. [16th C.: from L. *neglect-* 'disregarded,' from the v. *neglegere,* from *neg-* 'not' + *legere* 'choose, pick up.']

neg·li·gee /'negləˌzʜā/ ▶ n. a woman's light dressing gown, typically made of a filmy, soft fabric. [18th C.: from Fr., lit. 'given little thought,' fem. past part. of *négliger* 'to neglect.']

neg·li·gence /'negləjəns/ ▶ n. failure to take proper care in doing something: *some of these accidents are due to negligence.* ■ Law failure to use reasonable care, resulting in damage or injury to another.

neg·li·gent /'negləjənt/ ▶ adj. failing to take proper care in doing something: *directors have been negligent in the performance of their duties.* — **neg·li·gent·ly** adv. [ME: from OFr., or from L. *negligent-, negligere* (var. of *neglegere* 'disregard, slight': see **neglect**).]

neg·li·gi·ble /'neglijəbəl/ ▶ adj. so small or unimportant as to be not worth considering; insignificant: *sound could at last be recorded with incredible ease and at negligible cost.* — **neg·li·gi·bil·i·ty** /ˌnegləjə'bilitē/ n. **neg·li·gi·bly** adv.

ne·go·ti·a·ble /nə'gōsʜəbəl/ ▶ adj. open to discussion or modification: *the price was not negotiable.* ■ (of a document) able to be transferred or assigned to the legal ownership of another person, who thus becomes entitled to any benefit to which the previous owner was entitled. ■ (of an obstacle or pathway) able to be traversed; passable: *such walkways must be accessible and negotiable for all users.* — **ne·go·ti·a·bil·i·ty** /nəˌgōsʜə'bilitē/ n.

ne·go·ti·ate /nə'gōsʜēˌāt/ ▶ v. **1** [intrans.] try to reach an agreement or compromise by discussion with others: *his government's willingness to negotiate.* ■ [trans.] obtain or bring about by negotiating: *he negotiated a contract with the sellers.* **2** [trans.] find a way over or through (an obstacle or difficult path): *there was a puddle to be negotiated.* **3** [trans.] transfer (a check, bill, or other document) to the legal ownership of another person, who thus becomes entitled to any benefit. ■ convert (a check) into cash or notes. — **ne·go·ti·ant** /-sʜ(ē)ənt/ n. (archaic). **ne·go·ti·a·tor** n. [17th C.: from L. *negotiat-* 'done in the course of business,' from the v. *negotiari,* from *negotium* 'business,' from *neg-* 'not' + *otium* 'leisure.']

ne·go·ti·a·tion /nəˌgōsʜē'āsʜən/ ▶ n. (also **negotiations**) discussion aimed at reaching an agreement: *a worldwide ban is currently under negotiation | negotiations between unions and employers.* ■ the action or process of negotiating: *negotiation of the deals.* ■ the action or process of transferring ownership of a document.

Ne·gress /'nēgris/ ▶ n. dated a woman or girl of black African origin. See usage at **Negro.** [18th C.: from Fr. *négresse,* fem. of *nègre* 'Negro.']

Ne·gril·lo /nə'grilō/ ▶ n. (pl. **-los**) a member of a black people of short stature native to central and southern Africa. [Sp., dimin. of *negro* 'black' (see **Negro**).]

Ne·gri·to /nə'grētō/ ▶ n. (pl. **-tos**) a member of a black people of short stature native to the Austronesian region. [Sp., dimin. of *negro* 'black' (see **Negro**).]

ne·gri·tude /'negriˌt(y)o͞od; 'nē-/ (also **Ne·gri·tude**) ▶ n. the quality or fact of being of black African origin. ■ the affirmation or consciousness of the value of black or African culture, heritage, and identity. [1950s: from Fr. *négritude* 'blackness.']

Ne·gro /'nēgrō/ ▶ n. (pl. **-groes**) a member of a dark-skinned group of peoples originally native to Africa south of the Sahara. ▶ adj. of or relating to such people. [via Sp. and Port. from L. *niger, nigr-* 'black.']

– USAGE The word **Negro** was adopted from Spanish and Portuguese and first recorded from the mid 16th century. It remained the standard term throughout the 17th–19th centuries and was used by such prominent black American campaigners as W.E.B. DuBois and Booker T. Washington in the early 20th century. Since the Black Power movement of the 1960s, however, when the term **black** was favored as the term to express racial pride, **Negro** has dropped out of favor and now seems out of date or even offensive in both US and British English. See also usage at **black.**

Ne·groid /'nēgroid/ ▶ adj. of or relating to the division of humankind represented by the indigenous peoples of central and southern Africa.

Ne·gro Leagues ▶ n. associations of professional baseball teams made up of African-American players, esp. active from the 1920s through the 1940s.

Ne·gro·pho·bi·a /ˌnēgrə'fōbēə/ ▶ n. intense or irrational dislike or fear of black people. — **Ne·gro·phobe** /'nēgrəˌfōb/ n.

Ne·gros /'nāgrōs/ the fourth largest of the Philippine islands; pop. 3,182,000; chief city, Bacolod.

Ne·gro spir·it·u·al ▶ n. see **spiritual.**

Ne·gus /ˈnēgəs/ ▶ **n.** hist. a ruler, or the supreme ruler, of Ethiopia. [from Amharic *n'gus* 'king.']

ne·gus /ˈnēgəs/ ▶ **n.** hist. a hot drink of port, sugar, lemon, and spices. [named after Colonel Francis *Negus* (died 1732), who created it.]

Neh. ▶ **abbr.** Bible Nehemiah.

Ne·he·mi·ah /ˌnēəˈmīə/ (5th century BC) a Hebrew leader who supervised the rebuilding of the walls of Jerusalem (*c.*444) and introduced religious reforms (*c.*432). ■ a book of the Bible telling of this rebuilding and of the reforms.

Neh·ru /ˈnāˌro͞o; ˈne(ə)rˌo͞o/, Jawaharlal (1889–1964), prime minister of India 1947–64; known as **Pandit Nehru**; father of Indira Gandhi.

neigh /nā/ ▶ **n.** a characteristic high-pitched sound uttered by a horse. ▶ **v.** [intrans.] (of a horse) make such a sound; utter a neigh. ■ (of a person) make a similar sound: *they neighed dutifully at jokes they did not understand.* [OE *hnǣgan* (v.), of imitative origin; cf. Du. dial. *neijen.*]

neigh·bor /ˈnābər/ (Brit. **neigh·bour**) ▶ **n.** a person living near or next door to the speaker or person referred to. ■ a person or place in relation to others near or next to it: *I chatted with my neighbor on the flight to New York.* ■ any person in need of one's help or kindness (after biblical use): *love thy neighbor as thyself.* ▶ **v.** [trans.] (of a place or thing) be situated next to or very near (another): *the square neighbors the old quarter of the town.* — **neigh·bor·less adj.** [OE *nēahgebūr*, from *nēah* 'nigh, near' + *gebūr* 'inhabitant, peasant, farmer' (cf. BOOR).]

neigh·bor·hood /ˈnābərˌho͝od/ (Brit. **neigh·bour·hood**) ▶ **n.** a district, esp. one forming a community within a town or city. ■ the people of such a district. ■ neighborly feeling or conduct. ■ the area surrounding a particular place, person, or object: *he was reluctant to leave the neighborhood of Butte.* ■ Math. the set of points whose distance from a given point is less than some value.
– PHRASES **in the neighborhood of** approximately.

neigh·bor·hood watch ▶ **n.** a program of systematic local vigilance by residents of a neighborhood to discourage crime, esp. burglary.

neigh·bor·ly /ˈnābərlē/ (Brit. **neigh·bour·ly**) ▶ **adj.** characteristic of a good neighbor, esp. helpful,or kind. — **neigh·bor·li·ness n.**

Neis·se /ˈnīsə/ **1** a river in central Europe that rises in northern Czech Republic and flows to the Oder River northeast of Cottbus. German name LAUSITZER NEISSE; Polish name NYSA. **2** a river in southern Poland that flows to the Oder River. German name GLATZER NEISSE.

nei·ther /ˈnēT͟Hər; ˈnī-/ ▶ **adj. & pron.** not the one nor the other of two people or things; not either: [as adj.] *neither side of the brain is dominant over the other* | [as pron.] *neither of us believes it.* ▶ **adv. 1** used before the first of two (or more) alternatives specified (the others being introduced by "nor") to indicate that they are each untrue or each do not happen: *neither a liberal nor a conservative.* **2** used to introduce a further negative statement: *he didn't remember, and neither did I.*
– PHRASES **neither here nor there** see HERE. [ME: alt. (by association with EITHER) of OE *nawther*, contr. of *nāhwæther* (from *nā* 'no' + *hwæther* 'whether').]

Nejd /nejd/ an arid plateau region in central Saudi Arabia.

nek·ton /ˈnektən; -tän/ ▶ **n.** Zool. aquatic animals that are able to swim and move independently of water currents. Often contrasted with PLANKTON. — **nek·ton·ic** /nekˈtänik/ **adj.** [19th C.: via Ger. from Gk. *nēkton*, neut. of *nēktos* 'swimming,' from *nēkhein* 'to swim.']

Nel·son[1] /ˈnelsən/, Horatio, Viscount Nelson, Duke of Bronte (1758–1805), British admiral. He became a national hero as a result of his victories at sea in the Napoleonic Wars, esp. at the Battle of Trafalgar, in which he was mortally wounded.

Nelson[2], Samuel (1792–1873), US Supreme Court associate justice 1845–72.

nel·son /ˈnelsən/ ▶ **n.** a wrestling hold in which one arm is passed under the opponent's arm from behind and the hand is applied to the neck (**half nelson**), or both arms and hands are applied (**full nelson**). [19th C.: appar. from the surname *Nelson.*]

Nel·son River a river in Manitoba, Canada, that flows to Hudson Bay.

ne·lum·bo /nəˈləmbō/ ▶ **n.** (pl. **-bos**) a lotus with huge leaves and solitary large flowers that grow on stalks that can extend 6 feet (2 m) above the surface of the water. Two species: **American lotus** and **sacred lotus** (see LOTUS). [mod. L., from Sinhalese *neḷumba.*]

Ne·man /ˈnemən/ a river in eastern Europe that flows from Belarus to the Baltic Sea. Its lower course is called the Memel. Belorusian name NYOMAN.

ne·mat·ic /niˈmatik/ ▶ **adj.** relating to or denoting a state of a liquid crystal in which the molecules are oriented in parallel but not well-defined planes. Compare with SMECTIC. ▶ **n.** a nematic substance. [20th C.: from Gk. *nēma, nēmat-* 'thread' + -IC.]

nemato- (also **nemat-** before a vowel) ▶ **comb. form** denoting something threadlike in shape: *nematocyst.* ■ relating to Nematoda. [from Gk. *nēma, nēmat-* 'thread.']

nem·a·to·cyst /ˈnemətəˌsist; niˈmatə-/ ▶ **n.** Zool. a specialized cell in the tentacles of a jellyfish or other coelenterate, containing a barbed or venomous coiled thread that can be projected in self-defense or to capture prey.

Nem·a·to·da /ˌnēməˈtōdə/ Zool. a large phylum of worms with slender, unsegmented, cylindrical bodies, including the roundworms and threadworms. — **nem·a·tode** /ˈnēməˌtōd/ **n.** [mod. L. (pl.), from Gk. *nēma, nēmat-* 'thread.']

nem·a·tol·o·gy /ˌneməˈtäləjē/ ▶ **n.** the scientific study of nematodes. — **nem·a·tol·o·gist n.**

Nem·bu·tal /ˈnembyəˌtäl/ ▶ **n.** (trademark) the drug pentobarbital sodium.

nem. con. ▶ **abbr.** nemine contradicente, with no one dissenting; unanimously. [L.]

Ne·mer·te·a /niˈmərtēə/ Zool. a small phylum that comprises the ribbon worms. — **ne·mer·te·an adj. & n. ne·mer·tine** /ˈnemərˌtēn/ **adj. & n.** [mod. L. (pl.), from Gk. *Nēmertēs*, a sea nymph.]

Nem·e·sis /ˈneməsis/ Gk. Mythol. a goddess usually portrayed as the agent of divine punishment for wrongdoing or presumption (hubris).

nem·e·sis /ˈneməsis/ ▶ **n.** (pl. **-ses** /-ˌsēz/) (usu. **one's nemesis**) the inescapable or implacable agent of someone's or something's downfall. ■ a downfall caused by such an agent: *one risks nemesis by uttering such words.* ■ (often **Nemesis**) retributive justice. [16th C.: Gk., lit. 'retribution,' from *nemein* 'give what is due.']

ne·ne /ˈnānā/ (also **ne-ne**) ▶ **n.** (pl. same or **ne·nes**) another term for HAWAIIAN GOOSE. [20th C.: from Hawaiian.]

Nen·ets /ˈnenets/ ▶ **n.** (pl. same or **Nen·tsy** /ˈnentsē/ or **Nen·tsi** /ˈnentsē/) **1** a member of a nomadic people of Siberia, whose main occupation is reindeer herding. **2** the Samoyedic language of this people, with about 27,000 speakers. [the name in Russ.]

neo- ▶ **comb. form 1** new: *neonate.* **2** a new or revived form of: *neoconservative.* [from Gk. *neos* 'new.']

ne·o·clas·si·cal /ˌnēōˈklasikəl/ (also **ne·o·clas·sic** /-ˈklasik/) ▶ **adj.** of or relating to neoclassicism.

ne·o·clas·si·cism /ˌnēōˈklasiˌsizəm/ ▶ **n.** the revival of a classical style or treatment in art, literature, architecture, or music. — **ne·o·clas·si·cist n. & adj.**

ne·o·co·lo·ni·al·ism /ˌnēōkəˈlōnēəˌlizəm/ ▶ **n.** the use of economic, political, and cultural pressures to influence other countries, esp. former dependencies. — **ne·o·co·lo·ni·al adj. ne·o·co·lo·ni·al·ist n. & adj.**

ne·o·con /ˌnēōˈkän/ ▶ **adj.** neoconservative, esp. in advocating democratic capitalism. ▶ **n.** a neoconservative.

ne·o·con·serv·a·tive /ˌnēōkənˈsərvətiv/ ▶ **adj.** of or relating to an approach to politics, literary criticism, theology, or history that represents a return to a modified form of a traditional viewpoint, in contrast to more radical or liberal schools of thought. ▶ **n.** a person with neoconservative views. — **ne·o·con·serv·a·tism n.**

ne·o·cor·tex /ˌnēōˈkôrteks/ ▶ **n.** (pl. **-cor·ti·ces** /-ˈkôrtiˌsēz/) Anat. a part of the cerebral cortex concerned with sight and hearing in mammals, regarded as the most recently evolved part of the cortex. — **ne·o·cor·ti·cal** /-ˈkôrtikəl/ **adj.**

ne·o-Dar·win·i·an /ˌnēōdärˈwinēən/ ▶ **adj.** Biol. of or relating to the modern version of Darwin's theory of evolution by natural selection, incorporating the findings of genetics. — **ne·o-Dar·win·ism** /ˈdärwiˌnizəm/ **n. ne·o-Dar·win·ist** /ˈdärwinist/ **n.**

ne·o·dym·i·um /ˌnēōˈdimēəm/ ▶ **n.** the chemical element of atomic number 60, a silvery-white metal of the lanthanide series, used in coloring glass and ceramics. (Symbol: **Nd**) [19th C.: from NEO- 'new' + a shortened form of DIDYMIUM.]

ne·o·fas·cist /ˌnēōˈfaSHist/ (also **ne·o-Fas·cist**) ▶ **n.** a member of an organization similar to the Italian Fascist movement of the early 20th century. ▶ **adj.** of or relating to neofascists or neofascism. — **ne·o·fas·cism n.**

Ne·o·gae·a /ˌnēəˈjēə/ (also **Ne·o·ge·a**) Zool. a zoogeographical area comprising the Neotropical region. — **Ne·o·gae·an adj.** [mod. L., from Gk. *neos* 'new' + *gaia* 'earth.']

Ne·o·gene /ˈnēəjēn/ ▶ **adj.** Geol. of, relating to, or denoting the later division of the Tertiary period, comprising the Miocene and Pliocene epochs. ■ [as n.] (**the Neogene**) the Neogene subperiod or the system of rocks deposited during it. [19th C.: from NEO- 'new' + Gk. *-genēs* 'born, of a specified kind' (see -GEN).]

ne·o·Im·pres·sion·ism (also **Ne·o-Im·pres·sion·ism**) ▶ **n.** a late 19th-century movement in French painting that sought to improve on Impressionism through a systematic approach to form and color, particularly using pointillist technique. The movement's leading figures included Georges Seurat, Paul Signac, and Camille Pissarro. — **ne·o·Im·pres·sion·ist adj. & n.**

Ne·o-Lat·in ▶ **n.** another term for MODERN LATIN.

ne·o·lib·er·al /ˌnēōˈlibərəl/ ▶ **adj.** relating to or denoting a modified form of liberalism tending to favor free-market capitalism. ▶ **n.** a person holding such views. — **ne·o·lib·er·al·ism n.**

ne·o·lith /ˈnēəˌliTH/ ▶ **n.** a stone implement used during the Neolithic Period.

Ne·o·lith·ic /ˌnēəˈliTHik/ ▶ **adj.** Archaeol. of, relating to, or denoting the later part of the Stone Age, when ground or polished stone implements prevailed. ■ [as n.] (**the Neolithic**) the Neolithic period. Also called NEW STONE AGE. [19th C.: from NEO- 'new' + Gk. *lithos* 'stone' + -IC.]

ne·ol·o·gism /nēˈäləˌjizəm/ ▶ **n.** a newly coined word or expression. ■ the coining or use of new words. — **ne·ol·o·gist n. ne·ol·o·gize** /-ˌjīz/ **v.** [19th C.: from Fr. *néologisme.*]

ne·o·my·cin /ˌnēōˈmīsin/ ▶ **n.** Med. an antibiotic related to streptomycin, obtained from the bacterium *Streptomyces fradiae* and active against a wide variety of bacterial infections.

ne·on /ˈnēän/ ▶ **n.** the chemical element of atomic number 10, an inert gaseous element of the noble gas group, used in fluorescent lamps and advertising signs. (Symbol: **Ne**) ■ fluorescent lighting or signs. ■ a small lamp containing neon. ■ short for NEON TETRA. ■ a very bright or fluorescent color. [19th C.: from Gk., lit. 'something new,' neut. of the adj. *neos*.]

ne·o·na·tal /ˌnēō'nātl/ ▶ **adj.** of or relating to newborn children (or mammals). — **ne·o·na·tol·o·gist** /-nā'tälәjist/ **n.** **ne·o·na·tol·o·gy** /-nā'tälәjē/ **n.**

ne·o·nate /'nēәˌnāt/ ▶ **n.** a newborn child or mammal. ■ Med. an infant less than four weeks old. [1930s: from mod. L. *neonatus*, from Gk. *neos* 'new' + L. *nat-* 'born' (from the v. *nasci*).]

ne·o-Na·zi ▶ **n.** (pl. **ne·o-Na·zis**) a member of an organization similar to the German Nazi Party. ■ a person of extreme racist or nationalist views. ▶ **adj.** of or relating to neo-Nazis or neo-Nazism. — **ne·o-Na·zism** **n.**

ne·on tet·ra ▶ **n.** a small Amazonian characin (*Paracheirodon innesi*) with a shining blue-green stripe along each side and a red band near the tail, popular in aquariums.

ne·o·pa·gan·ism /ˌnēō'pāgiˌnizәm; -gә-/ ▶ **n.** a modern religious movement that seeks to incorporate beliefs or ritual practices from outside world religions, esp. from pre-Christian Europe. — **ne·o·pa·gan** **n. & adj.**

ne·o·phyte /'nēәˌfīt/ ▶ **n.** a person who is new to a subject, skill, or belief. ■ a new convert to a religion. ■ a novice in a religious order, or a newly ordained priest. [ME: via eccles. L. from Gk. *neophutos*, from *neos* 'new' + *phuton* 'plant.']

ne·o·pla·sia /ˌnēō'plāzʜә/ ▶ **n.** Med. the formation or presence of a new, abnormal growth of tissue.

ne·o·plasm /'nēәˌplazәm/ ▶ **n.** a new and abnormal growth of tissue in some part of the body, esp. as a characteristic of cancer. [19th C.: from NEO- 'new' + Gk. *plasma* 'formation' (see PLASMA).]

ne·o·plas·tic¹ /ˌnēә'plastik/ ▶ **adj.** Med. of or relating to a neoplasm or neoplasia.

ne·o·plas·tic² ▶ **adj.** Art of or relating to neoplasticism.

ne·o·plas·ti·cism /ˌnēō'plastiˌsizәm/ ▶ **n.** a style of abstract painting developed by Piet Mondrian, using only vertical and horizontal lines and rectangular shapes in black, white, gray, and primary colors.

Ne·o·pla·to·nism /ˌnēō'plātnˌizәm/ a philosophical and religious system developed by the followers of Plotinus in the 3rd century AD, combining Platonic and other ancient Greek thought with oriental mysticism. — **Ne·o·pla·ton·ic** /-plә'tänik/ **adj.** **Ne·o·pla·to·nist** **n.**

ne·o·prene /'nēәˌprēn/ ▶ **n.** a synthetic polymer resembling rubber, resistant to oil, heat, and weathering. [1930s: from NEO- 'new' + *prene* (perh. from PROPYL + -ENE).]

ne·o·re·al·ism (also **ne·o·re·al·ism**) ▶ **n.** a movement or school in art or philosophy representing a modified form of realism. ■ a naturalistic movement in Italian literature and cinema that emerged in the 1940s. — **ne·o·re·al·ist** **n. & adj.**

Ne·o·sho Riv·er /nē'ōsʜō; -sʜә/ (also **Grand River**) a river that flows from central Kansas to the Arkansas River.

ne·ot·e·ny /nē'ätn-ē/ ▶ **n.** Zool. the retention of juvenile features in the adult animal. Also called PEDOMORPHOSIS. ■ the sexual maturity of an animal while it is still in a mainly larval state, as in the axolotl. Also called PEDOGENESIS. — **ne·o·te·nic** /ˌnēō'tenik; -'tēnik/ **adj.** **ne·o·te·nous** /nē'ätn-әs/ **adj.** [19th C.: coined in Ger. as *Neotenie*, from Gk. *neos* 'new' + *teinein* 'extend.']

ne·o·ter·ic /ˌnēә'terik/ ▶ **adj.** recent; new; modern. ▶ **n.** a modern person; a person who advocates new ideas. [16th C.: via late L. from Gk. *neōterikos*, from *neōteros* 'newer,' compar. of *neos*.]

Ne·o·trop·i·cal /ˌnēō'träpikәl/ (also **ne·o·trop·i·cal**) ▶ **adj.** Zool. of, relating to, or denoting a zoogeographical region comprising Central and South America, including the tropical southern part of Mexico and the Caribbean. Compare with NEOGAEA. ■ Bot. relating to or denoting a phytogeographical kingdom comprising Central and South America excluding southern Chile and Argentina. — **Ne·o·trop·ics** /-piks/ **plural n.**

Ne·pal /nә'pôl; -'päl/ a mountainous landlocked country in southern Asia. *See box.* — **Nep·a·lese** /ˌnepә'lēz; -'lēs/ **adj. & n.**

Ne·pal·i /nә'pôlē; -'pälē/ ▶ **n.** (pl. same or **-pal·is**) a native or national of Nepal. ■ the Indic language that is the official language of Nepal, with about 8 million speakers altogether ▶ **adj.** of or relating to Nepal or its language or people.

ne·pen·thes /nә'penᴛʜēz/ ▶ **n.** **1** (also **ne·pen·the**) /-ᴛʜē/ literary a drug described in the *Odyssey* as banishing grief or trouble from a person's mind. ■ any drug or potion bringing welcome forgetfulness. **2** an Old World pitcher plant (genus *Nepenthes*, family Nepenthaceae). [via L. from Gk. *nēpenthēs* 'dispelling pain,' from *nē-* 'not' + *penthos* 'grief.']

neph·e·line /'nefәlin/ ▶ **n.** a colorless, greenish, or brownish mineral consisting of an aluminosilicate of sodium (often with potassium) and occurring as crystals and grains in igneous rocks. [19th C.: from Fr. *néphéline*, from Gk. *nephelē* 'cloud.']

neph·e·lin·ite /'nefәlәˌnīt/ ▶ **n.** Geol. a fine-grained basaltic rock containing nepheline in place of plagioclase feldspar.

neph·e·lom·e·ter /ˌnefә'lämitәr/ ▶ **n.** an instrument for measuring the size and concentration of particles suspended in a liquid or gas, esp. by means of the light they scatter.

neph·ew /'nefyo͞o/ ▶ **n.** a son of one's brother or sister, or of one's brother-in-law or sister-in-law. [ME: from OFr. *neveu*, from L. *nepos* 'grandson, nephew,' from an Indo-Eur. root shared by Du. *neef* and Ger. *Neffe*.]

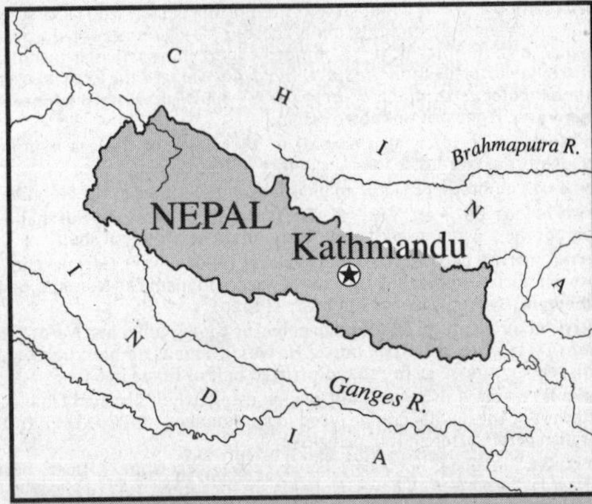

Nepal

Official name: Kingdom of Nepal
Location: southern Asia, in the Himalayas (including Mount Everest), north of India
Area: 54,400 square miles (140,800 sq km)
Population: 27,000,000
Capital: Kathmandu
Languages: Nepali (official), English
Currency: Nepalese rupee

ne·phol·o·gy /nә'fälәjē/ ▶ **n.** the study of clouds. [19th C.: from Gk. *nephos* 'cloud' + -LOGY.]

nephr- ▶ **comb. form** var. of NEPHRO- shortened before a vowel (as in *nephrectomy*).

ne·phrec·to·my /nә'frektәmē/ ▶ **n.** (pl. **-mies**) surgical removal of one or both of the kidneys.

ne·phrid·i·um /nә'fridēәm/ ▶ **n.** (pl. **-phrid·i·a** /-'fridēә/) Zool. (in many invertebrate animals) a tubule open to the exterior that acts as an organ of excretion or osmoregulation. — **ne·phrid·i·al** /-ēәl/ **adj.** [19th C.: mod. L.]

neph·rite /'nefrīt/ ▶ **n.** a hard pale green or white mineral that is one of the forms of jade. It is a silicate of calcium and magnesium. [18th C.: from Ger. *Nephrit*, from Gk. *nephros* 'kidney' (with ref. to its supposed efficacy in treating kidney disease).]

ne·phrit·ic /nә'fritik/ ▶ **adj.** of or in the kidneys; renal. ■ of or relating to nephritis.

ne·phri·tis /nә'frītis/ ▶ **n.** Med. inflammation of the kidneys. Also called BRIGHT'S DISEASE.

nephro- (also **nephr-** before a vowel) ▶ **comb. form** of a kidney; relating to the kidneys: *nephrotoxic*. [from Gk. *nephros* 'kidney.']

ne·phrol·o·gy /nә'frälәjē/ ▶ **n.** the branch of medicine that deals with the kidneys. — **neph·ro·log·i·cal** /ˌnefrә'läjikәl/ **adj.** **ne·phrol·o·gist** **n.**

neph·ron /'nefrän/ ▶ **n.** Anat. each of the functional units in the kidney, consisting of a glomerulus and its associated tubule. [1930s: via Ger. from Gk. *nephros* 'kidney.']

ne·phro·sis /nә'frōsis/ ▶ **n.** kidney disease, esp. when characterized by edema and the loss of protein from the plasma into the urine due to increased glomerular permeability (also called **nephrotic syndrome**). — **ne·phrot·ic** /nә'frätik/ **adj.**

ne plus ul·tra /'nē ˌplәs 'әltrә; 'nā ˌplo͝os 'o͝oltrә/ ▶ **n.** the perfect or most extreme example of its kind; the ultimate. [L., lit. 'not further beyond.']

nep·o·tism /'nepәˌtizәm/ ▶ **n.** the practice among those with power or influence of favoring relatives or friends, esp. by giving them jobs. — **nep·o·tist** **n.** **nep·o·tis·tic** /ˌnepә'tistik/ **adj.** [17th C.: from Fr. *népotisme*, from Ital. *nepotismo*, from *nipote* 'nephew.']

Nep·tune /'nept(y)o͞on/ **1** Rom. Mythol. the god of water and of the sea. Greek equivalent POSEIDON. **2** Astron. a distant planet of the solar system, eighth in order from the sun, discovered in 1846.

Nep·tu·ni·an /nep't(y)o͞onēәn/ ▶ **adj.** **1** of or relating to the Roman sea god Neptune or to the sea. **2** of or relating to the planet Neptune.

nep·tu·ni·um /nep't(y)o͞onēәm/ ▶ **n.** the chemical element of atomic number 93, a radioactive metal of the actinide series. It was discovered as a product of the bombardment of uranium with neutrons, and occurs only in trace amounts in nature. (Symbol: **Np**) [19th C.: from NEPTUNE, on the pattern of *uranium*.]

nerd /nərd/ ▶ **n.** informal a foolish or contemptible person who lacks social skills or is boringly studious: *one of those nerds who never asked a girl to dance.* ■ an intelligent, single-minded expert in a particular technical discipline or profession: *he single-handedly changed the Zero image of the computer nerd into one of savvy Hero.* — **nerd·ish adj. nerd·ish·ness n. nerd·y adj.** [1950s: of unknown origin.]

Ne·re·id /'ni(ə)rēid/ **1** (also **nereid**) Gk. Mythol. any of the sea nymphs, daughters of Nereus. **2** Astron. a satellite of Neptune.

Ne·re·us /'ni(ə)rēəs/ Gk. Mythol. an old sea god, the father of the Nereids.

ne·rit·ic /nə'ritik/ ▶ **adj.** Biol. Geol. of, relating to, or denoting the shallow part of the sea near a coast and overlying the continental shelf.

Nernst /nərnst; nernst/, Hermann Walther (1864–1941), German chemist. He discovered the third law of thermodynamics (**Nernst's heat theorem**). Nobel Prize for Chemistry (1920).

Ne·ro /'ni(ə)rō/ (AD 37–68), Roman emperor 54–68; full name *Nero Claudius Caesar Augustus Germanicus.* He was infamous for his cruelty, and his reign witnessed a fire that destroyed half of Rome in 64.

ner·o·li /'nerəlē/ (also **neroli oil**) ▶ **n.** an essential oil distilled from the flowers of the Seville orange, used in perfumery. [17th C.: via Fr. from Italian *neroli,* after an Ital. princess.]

Ne·ru·da /nə'ro͞odə; ne'ro͞odä/, Pablo (1904–73), Chilean poet; born *Ricardo Eliezer Neftalí Reyes.* Nobel Prize for Literature (1971).

ner·va·tion /,nər'vāshən/ ▶ **n.** Bot. the arrangement of nerves in a leaf.

nerve /nərv/ ▶ **n.** **1** (in the body) a whitish fiber or bundle of fibers that transmits impulses of sensation to the brain or spinal cord, and impulses from these to the muscles and organs. **2** (**nerves**) a person's mental state, in particular the extent to which they are agitated or worried: *an amazing journey that tested her nerves to the full.* ■ nervousness or anxiety: *his first-night nerves soon disappeared.* **3** (often **one's nerve**) a person's steadiness, courage, and sense of purpose when facing a demanding situation: *the army was beginning to* ***lose its nerve*** | *I got up* ***the nerve*** *to ask Miss Kinnian to have dinner with me.* ■ informal impudence or audacity: *he* ***had the nerve*** *to insult my cooking.* **4** Bot. a prominent unbranched rib in a leaf, esp. in the midrib of the leaf of a moss. ▶ **v.** (**nerve oneself**) brace oneself mentally to face a demanding situation: *she nerved herself to enter the room.* | *he nerved himself for a final effort.*

– PHRASES **a bundle of nerves** informal someone who is extremely timid or tense. **get on someone's nerves** informal irritate or annoy someone. **strain every nerve** make every possible effort. [from the earlier sense of *nerve* as 'tendon, sinew.'] **touch** (or **hit** or **strike**) **a nerve** (or **a raw nerve**) provoke a reaction by referring to a sensitive topic. **war of nerves** a struggle in which opponents try to wear each other down by psychological means. — **nerved adj.** [usu. in comb.]. [ME: from L. *nervus*; rel. to Gk. *neuron* 'nerve' (see NEURON).]

nerve block ▶ **n.** Med. the production of insensibility in a part of the body by injecting an anesthetic close to the nerves that supply it.

nerve cell ▶ **n.** a neuron.

nerve cen·ter ▶ **n.** a group of closely connected nerve cells that perform a particular function in the body; a ganglion. ■ the control center of an organization or operation.

nerve cord ▶ **n.** Zool. the major cord of nerve fibers running the length of an animal's body, esp. a ventral cord in invertebrates that connects segmental nerve ganglia.

nerve fi·ber ▶ **n.** the axon of a neuron. A nerve is formed of a bundle of many such fibers, with their sheaths.

nerve gas ▶ **n.** a poisonous vapor that rapidly disables or kills by disrupting the transmission of nerve impulses.

nerve im·pulse ▶ **n.** a signal transmitted along a nerve fiber. It consists of a wave of electrical depolarization that reverses the potential difference across the nerve cell membranes.

nerve·less /'nərvlis/ ▶ **adj.** **1** inert; lacking vigor or feeling: *the knife dropped from Grant's nerveless fingers.* ■ (of literary or artistic style) diffuse or insipid. **2** confident; not nervous: *with nerveless panache.* **3** Anat. Biol. lacking nerves or nervures. — **nerve·less·ly adv. nerve·less·ness n.**

nerve net ▶ **n.** Zool. (in invertebrates such as coelenterates) a diffuse network of neurons that conducts impulses in all directions from a point of stimulus.

nerve-rack·ing (also **nerve-wrack·ing**) ▶ **adj.** causing stress or anxiety: *his driving test was a nerve-racking ordeal.*

nerve trunk ▶ **n.** Anat. the main stem of a nerve.

nerv·ine /'nərvēn/ ▶ **adj.** (of a medicine) used to calm the nerves. ▶ **n.** a medicine of this kind.

nerv·ous /'nərvəs/ ▶ **adj.** **1** easily agitated or alarmed; tending to be anxious; highly strung: *a sensitive, nervous person* | *these quick, nervous birds.* ■ anxious or apprehensive: *staying in the house on her own made her nervous* | *I was nervous about my new job.* ■ (of a feeling or reaction) resulting from anxiety or anticipation. **2** relating to or affecting the nerves: *a nervous disorder.* — **nerv·ous·ly adv. nerv·ous·ness n.**

nerv·ous break·down ▶ **n.** a period of mental illness resulting from severe depression, stress, or anxiety.

nerv·ous sys·tem ▶ **n.** the network of nerve cells and fibers that transmits nerve impulses between parts of the body. See also AUTONOMIC NERVOUS SYSTEM, CENTRAL NERVOUS SYSTEM, PERIPHERAL NERVOUS SYSTEM.

nerv·ous wreck ▶ **n.** informal a person suffering from stress or emotional exhaustion: *by the end of the day I was a nervous wreck.*

ner·vure /'nərvyo͝or/ ▶ **n.** Entomol. each of the hollow veins that form the framework of an insect's wing. ■ Bot. the principal vein of a leaf. [19th C.: from Fr., from *nerf* 'nerve.']

nerv·y /'nərvē/ ▶ **adj.** (**nerv·i·er, nerv·i·est**) **1** informal bold or impudent: *it was kind of nervy for Billy to be telling him how to play.* **2** esp. Brit. easily agitated or alarmed; nervous. ■ characterized or produced by apprehension or uncertainty. **3** archaic literary sinewy or strong. — **nerv·i·ly** /'nərvəlē/ **adv. nerv·i·ness n.**

Nes·bit /'nezbit/, Edith (1858–1924), English writer. Her children's books include *The Railway Children* (1906).

nes·cient /'nesh(ē)ənt/ ▶ **adj.** literary lacking knowledge; ignorant: *I ventured into the new Korean restaurant with some equally nescient companions.* — **nesc·ience n.** [ME: from L. *nescient-* 'not knowing,' from the v. *nescire,* from *ne-* 'not' + *scire* 'know.']

ness /nes/ ▶ **n.** [usu. in place names] a headland or promontory: *Orford Ness.* [OE *næs,* rel. to *nasu* 'nose.']

-ness /nəs; nis/ forming nouns chiefly from adjectives: ▶ **suffix** **1** denoting a state or condition: *liveliness* | *sadness.* ■ an instance of this: *a kindness.* **2** something in a certain state: *wilderness.* [OE *-nes, -ness,* of Gmc. origin.]

Nes·sie /'nesē/ informal name for LOCH NESS MONSTER.

Ness, Loch see LOCH NESS.

nest /nest/ ▶ **n.** **1** a structure or place made or chosen by a bird for laying eggs and sheltering its young. ■ a place where an animal or insect breeds or shelters: *an ants' nest.* ■ a person's snug or secluded retreat or shelter. ■ a bowl-shaped object likened to a bird's nest: *arrange in nests of lettuce leaves.* ■ a place filled with or frequented by undesirable people or things: ***a nest of*** *spies.* **2** a set of similar objects of graduated sizes, made so that each smaller one fits into the next in size for storage: ***a nest of*** *tables.* ▶ **v.** **1** [intrans.] (of a bird or other animal) use or build a nest: *the owls often nest in barns* | [as adj.] (**nesting**) *do not disturb nesting birds.* **2** [trans.] (often **be nested**) fit (an object or objects) inside a larger one: *the town is nested inside a large crater on the flanks of a volcano.* ■ [intrans.] (of a set of objects) fit inside one another: *Russian dolls that nest inside one another.* ■ (esp. in computing and linguistics) place (an object or element) in a hierarchical arrangement, typically in a subordinate position | [as adj.] (**nested**) *organisms classified in a series of nested sets* | *a nested relative clause.* — **nest·ful n.** (pl. **-fuls**). **nest·like adj.** [OE *nest,* of Gmc. origin; rel. to L. *nidus,* from the Indo-Eur. bases of NETHER (meaning 'down') and SIT.]

nest egg ▶ **n.** **1** a sum of money saved for the future. **2** a real or artificial egg left in a nest to induce hens to lay eggs there.

nest·er /'nestər/ ▶ **n.** **1** [usu. with adj.] a bird that nests in a specified manner or place: *hole-nesters.* **2** a squatter who occupies rangeland in the US West.

nes·tle /'nesəl/ ▶ **v.** [no obj., with adverbial of place] settle or lie comfortably within or against something: *the baby deer nestled in her arms* | [trans.] *she nestled her head against his shoulder.* ■ (of a place) lie or be situated in a half-hidden or obscured position: *picturesque villages nestle in the wooded hills.* [OE *nestlian,* from NEST.]

nest·ling /'nes(t)ling/ ▶ **n.** a bird that is too young to leave its nest.

Nes·tor /'nestər/ Gk. Mythol. a king of Pylos in Peloponnesus, who in old age led his subjects to the Trojan War. His wisdom and eloquence were proverbial.

Nes·to·ri·an·ism /nes'tôrēə,nizəm/ ▶ **n.** Theol. the doctrine that there were two separate persons, one human and one divine, in the incarnate Christ. It is named after Nestorius, patriarch of Constantinople (428–31). — **Nes·to·ri·an adj. & n.**

net[1] /net/ ▶ **n.** **1** a length of open-meshed material made of twine, cord, rope, or something similar, used typically for catching fish or other animals. ■ a piece of such material supported by a frame at the end of a handle, used typically for catching fish or insects. ■ a length of such material supported on a frame and forming part of the goal in various games such as soccer and hockey. ■ a length of such material supported on a cord between two posts to divide the playing area in various games such as tennis, badminton, and volleyball. ■ the total amount of fish caught in one session or expedition: *he finished with a heavy mixed net of fish* | *good nets of roach, chub, and perch.* ■ a safety net: *he felt like a tightrope-walker without a net.* ■ a hairnet. **2** a fine fabric with a very open weave: [as adj.] *net curtains.* **3** fig. a system or procedure for catching or entrapping someone; a trap. ■ a system or procedure for selecting or recruiting someone: *he spread his net far and wide in his search for success.* **4** a network, in particular: ■ a communications or broadcasting network, esp. of maritime radio: *the radio net was brought to life with a Mayday.* ■ a network of interconnected computers: *a computer news net.* ■ (**the Net**) the Internet. ▶ **v.** (**net·ted, net·ting**) [trans.] **1** catch or land (a fish or other animal) with a net. ■ fish with nets in (a river): *he has netted the creeks and found them clogged with fish.* ■ fig. acquire or obtain as if with a net: *customs officials have netted large caches of drugs.* **2** (in sports) hit or kick (a ball or puck) into the net; score (a goal). **3** cover with a net: *we fenced off a rabbit-proof area for vegetables and netted the top.* — **net·ful n.** (pl. **-fuls**). **net·like adj.** [OE *net, nett,* of Gmc. origin; rel. to Du. *net* and Ger. *Netz.*]

net[2] ▶ **adj.** **1** (of an amount, value, or price) remaining after a deduction, such as tax or a discount, has been made: *net earnings per share rose.* Often contrasted with GROSS (sense 2). ■ (of a price) to be paid in full; not reducible. ■ (of a weight) excluding that of the packaging or container. ■ (of a score in golf) adjusted to take account of a player's handicap. **2** (of an effect or result) final or overall. ▶ **v.** (**net·ted, net·ting**) [trans.] acquire or obtain (a sum of money) as clear profit: *they netted a huge profit.* ■ [with two objs.] return (profit or income) for (someone): *the land netted a turnover of $800,000.* ■ get; obtain: *the Bills netted 5,276 yards of offense.* [ME: from Fr. *net* 'neat'; see NEAT¹.]

Net·an·ya·hu /ˌnetänˈyähoo/, Benjamin (1949–), prime minister of Israel 1996–99.

net as·set val·ue ▶ **n.** the value of a mutual fund that is reached by deducting the fund's liabilities from the market value of all of its shares and then dividing by the number of issued shares.

neth·er /ˈneT͟Hər/ ▶ **adj.** lower in position: *the ballast is suspended from its nether end.* — **neth·er·most** adj. [OE *nithera, neothera,* of Gmc. origin; rel. to Ger. *nieder,* from an Indo-Eur. root meaning 'down.']

Netherlands

Official name: Kingdom of the Netherlands
Location: western Europe, on the North Sea
Area: 16,000 square miles (41,500 sq km)
Population: 16,318,000
Capital: Amsterdam; The Hague is the seat of government
Language: Dutch
Currency: euro

Neth·er·lands /ˈneT͟Hərlən(d)z/ a country in western Europe. *See box.* — **Neth·er·land·er** /-ˌlandər/ **n.** **Neth·er·land·ish** /-ˌlandisH/ **adj.**

Neth·er·lands An·til·les two widely separated groups of Dutch islands in the Caribbean Sea, in the Lesser Antilles; capital, Willemstad, on Curaçao; pop. 189,000. The southernmost group, off the north coast of Venezuela, consists of the islands of Bonaire and Curaçao. The northern group comprises the islands of St. Eustatius, St. Martin, and Saba.

neth·er re·gions ▶ **plural n.** (**the nether regions**) the lowest or furthest parts of a place, esp. with allusion to hell or the underworld. ■ (**one's nether regions**) used euphemistically to refer to a person's genitals and buttocks.

neth·er·world /ˈneT͟Hərˌwərld/ ▶ **n.** (**the netherworld**) the underworld of the dead; hell. ■ a hidden underworld or ill-defined area: *the narcotic netherworld in America.*

net·i·quette /ˈnetəkit; -ˌket/ ▶ **n.** the correct or acceptable way of communicating on the Internet. [1990s: blend of NET¹ and ETIQUETTE.]

net·i·zen /ˈnetəzən/ ▶ **n.** a user of the Internet, esp. a habitual or avid one. [1990s: blend of NET¹ (sense 4) and CITIZEN.]

net na·tion·al prod·uct (abbr.: **NNP**) ▶ **n.** the total value of goods produced and services provided in a country during one year, after depreciation of capital goods has been allowed for.

net pres·ent val·ue ▶ **n.** see PRESENT VALUE.

net prof·it ▶ **n.** the profit after expenses not included in the calculation of gross profit have been paid.

ne·tsu·ke /ˈnets(ə)kē/ ▶ **n.** (pl. same or **-kes** /-kēz/) a carved buttonlike ornament, esp. of ivory or wood, formerly worn in Japan to suspend articles from the sash of a kimono.

net·ter /ˈnetər/ ▶ **n.** **1** a fisherman who uses nets to catch fish. ■ [usu. in comb.] someone who uses a net of a specified type: *drift-netters.* **2** (also **Netter**) a person who uses the Internet.

net·ting /ˈnetiNG/ ▶ **n.** open-meshed material made by knotting together twine, wire, rope, or thread.

net·tle /ˈnetl/ ▶ **n.** a herbaceous plant (genus *Urtica,* family Urticaceae) that has jagged leaves covered with stinging hairs. Its several species include the Eurasian **stinging nettle** (*U. dioica*). ■ used in names of other plants of a similar appearance or properties, e.g., **dead-nettle.** ▶ **v.** [trans.] irritate or annoy (someone): *I was nettled by her tone.* [OE *netle, netele,* of Gmc. origin; rel. to Ger. *Nessel.*]

net·tle·rash /ˈnetlˌrasH/ ▶ **n.** another term for URTICARIA (from its resemblance to the sting of a nettle).

net·tle·some /ˈnetlsəm/ ▶ **adj.** causing annoyance or difficulty: *complicated and nettlesome regional disputes.*

net ton ▶ **n.** another term for TON¹ (sense 1).

net·work /ˈnetˌwərk/ ▶ **n.** **1** an arrangement of intersecting horizontal and vertical lines. ■ a complex system of roads, railroads, or other transportation routes. **2** a group or system of interconnected people or things: *a trade network.* ■ a group of people who exchange information, contacts, and experience for professional or social purposes: *a support network.* ■ a group of broadcasting stations that connect for the simultaneous broadcast of a program: *the introduction of a second TV network* | [as adj.] *network television.* ■ a number of interconnected computers, machines, or operations: *specialized computers that manage multiple outside connections to a network* | *a local cellular phone network.* ■ a system of connected electrical conductors. ▶ **v.** [trans.] connect as or operate with a network: *the stock exchanges are resourceful in networking these deals.* ■ link (machines, esp. computers) to operate interactively: [as adj.] (**networked**) *networked workstations.* ■ [intrans.] [often as n.] (**networking**) interact with other people to exchange information and develop contacts, esp. to further one's career: *the skills of networking and negotiation.* — **net·work·a·ble** adj.

net·work·er /ˈnetˌwərkər/ ▶ **n.** **1** Comput. a person who operates from home or from an external office via a computer network. **2** a person who interacts or exchanges information with others working in a similar field, esp. to further their career.

Neu·châ·tel, Lake /ˌnoosHäˈtel; nœ-/ a lake in western Switzerland.

Neuf·châ·tel /ˌnoosHəˈtel; ˌnœsHä-/ ▶ **n.** a creamy white cheese made from whole or partly skimmed milk in Neufchâtel, France.

Neu·mann /ˈn(y)oomən; ˈnoimän/, John von (1903–57), US mathematician; born in Hungary. He pioneered the design and operation of electronic computers.

neume /n(y)oom/ ▶ **n.** Music (in plainsong) a note or group of notes to be sung to a single syllable. ■ a sign indicating this. [ME: from OFr. *neume,* from med. L. *neu(p)ma,* from Gk. *pneuma* 'breath.']

neur. ▶ **abbr.** ■ neurological or neurology.

neu·ral /ˈn(y)oorəl/ ▶ **adj.** of or relating to a nerve or the nervous system. — **neu·ral·ly** adv. [19th C.: from Gk. *neuron.*]

neu·ral arch ▶ **n.** Anat. the curved rear (dorsal) section of a vertebra, enclosing the canal through which the spinal cord passes.

neu·ral·gia /n(y)ooˈraljə/ ▶ **n.** intense, typically intermittent pain along the course of a nerve, esp. in the head or face. — **neu·ral·gic** /-jik/ **adj.**

neu·ral net·work (also **neu·ral net**) ▶ **n.** a computer system modeled on the human brain and nervous system.

neu·ral tube ▶ **n.** Zool. Med. (in an embryo) a hollow structure from which the brain and spinal cord form.

neu·ra·min·i·dase /ˌn(y)ooraˈminəˌdās/ ▶ **n.** Biochem. an enzyme, present in many pathogenic or symbiotic microorganisms, that catalyzes the breakdown of glycosides containing neuraminic acid.

neur·as·the·ni·a /ˌn(y)oorəsˈTHēnēə/ ▶ **n.** an ill-defined medical condition characterized by lassitude, fatigue, headache, and irritability, associated chiefly with emotional disturbance. — **neur·as·then·ic** /-ˈTHenik/ **adj. & n.**

neu·rec·to·my /n(y)ooˈrektəmē/ ▶ **n.** Med. surgical removal of all or part of a nerve.

neu·ri·lem·ma /ˌn(y)ooraˈlemə/ ▶ **n.** (pl. **-lem·mas** or **-lem·ma·ta** /-li ˈmätə/) Anat. the thin sheath around a nerve axon (including myelin where this is present). — **neu·ri·lem·mal** adj.

neu·ri·tis /n(y)ooˈrītis/ ▶ **n.** Med. inflammation of a peripheral nerve or nerves, usually causing pain and loss of function. ■ (in general use) neuropathy. — **neu·rit·ic** /-ˈritik/ **adj.**

neuro- ▶ **comb. form** relating to nerves or the nervous system: *neuroanatomy* | *neurohormone.* [from Gk. *neuron* 'nerve, sinew, tendon.']

neu·ro·a·nat·o·my /ˌn(y)oorōəˈnatəmē/ ▶ **n.** the anatomy of the nervous system. — **neu·ro·an·a·tom·i·cal** /-ˌanəˈtämikəl/ **adj.** **neu·ro·a·nat·o·mist** n.

neu·ro·bi·ol·o·gy /ˌn(y)oorōbīˈäləjē/ ▶ **n.** the biology of the nervous system. — **neu·ro·bi·o·log·i·cal** /-bīəˈläjikəl/ **adj.** **neu·ro·bi·ol·o·gist** n.

neu·ro·blast /ˈn(y)oorəˌblast/ ▶ **n.** Embryol. an embryonic cell from which nerve fibers originate.

neu·ro·blas·to·ma /ˌn(y)oorōblaˈstōmə/ ▶ **n.** Med. a malignant tumor composed of neuroblasts, most commonly in the adrenal gland.

neu·ro·en·do·crine /ˌn(y)oorōˈendəkrin/ ▶ **adj.** Physiol. relating to or involving both nervous stimulation and endocrine secretion. — **neu·ro·en·do·cri·nol·o·gy** /-ˌendōkrəˈnäləjē/ **n.**

neu·ro·fi·bril /ˌn(y)oorəˈfībrəl; -ˈfib-/ ▶ **n.** Anat. a fibril in the cytoplasm of a nerve cell, visible by light microscopy. — **neu·ro·fi·bril·lar·y** /-ˈfibrəˌlerē/ **adj.**

neu·ro·fi·bro·ma /ˌn(y)oorōfīˈbrōmə/ ▶ **n.** (pl. **-mas** or **-ma·ta** /-mətə/) Med. a tumor formed on a nerve cell sheath, frequently symptomless but occasionally malignant.

neu·ro·fi·bro·ma·to·sis /ˌn(y)o͝orōˌfībrəməˈtōsis/ ▶ **n.** Med. a disease in which neurofibromas form throughout the body.

neu·ro·gen·ic /ˌn(y)o͝orəˈjenik/ ▶ **adj.** Physiol. caused by, controlled by, or arising in the nervous system.

neu·rog·li·a /n(y)o͝oˈräglēə/ ▶ **n.** another term for GLIA. [19th C.: from NEURO- 'of nerves' + Gk. *glia* 'glue.']

neu·ro·hor·mone /ˌn(y)o͝orōˈhôrˌmōn/ ▶ **n.** Physiol. a hormone (such as vasopressin or norepinephrine) produced by nerve cells and secreted into the circulation. — **neu·ro·hor·mo·nal** /-hôrˈmōnəl/ **adj.**

neu·ro·hy·poph·y·sis /ˌn(y)o͝orōhīˈpäfəsis/ ▶ **n.** (pl. **-ses** /-ˌsēz/) Anat. the posterior lobe of the hypophysis, which stores and releases oxytocin and vasopressin produced in the hypothalamus. — **neu·ro·hy·po·phys·e·al** /-ˌpäfəˈsēəl/ **adj.**

neu·ro·lep·tic /ˌn(y)o͝orəˈleptik/ Med. ▶ **adj.** (chiefly of a drug) tending to reduce nervous tension by depressing nerve functions. ▶ **n.** a drug of this kind; a major tranquilizer. [20th C.: from NEURO- 'relating to nerves,' on the pattern of *psycholeptic*.]

neu·rol·o·gy /n(y)o͝oˈräləjē/ ▶ **n.** the branch of medicine that deals with the anatomy, functions, and organic disorders of nerves and the nervous system. — **neu·rolog·i·cal** /-rəˈläjikəl/ **adj.** **neu·ro·log·i·cal·ly** /-rəˈläjik(ə)lē/ **adv.** **neu·rol·o·gist** **n.**

neu·ro·ma /n(y)o͝oˈrōmə/ ▶ **n.** (pl. **-mas** or **-ma·ta** /-mətə/) another term for NEUROFIBROMA.

neu·ro·mast /ˈn(y)o͝orəˌmast/ ▶ **n.** Zool. a sensory organ of fishes and larval or aquatic amphibians, typically forming part of the lateral line system. [20th C.: from NEURO- 'of nerves' + Gk. *mastos* 'breast.']

neu·ro·mus·cu·lar /ˌn(y)o͝orōˈməskyələr/ ▶ **adj.** of or relating to nerves and muscles.

neu·ron /ˈn(y)o͝orän/ (esp. Brit. also **neu·rone** /-rōn/) ▶ **n.** a specialized cell transmitting nerve impulses; a nerve cell. — **neu·ron·al** /ˈn(y)o͝orənl; n(y)o͝oˈrōnl/ **adj.** **neu·ron·ic** /n(y)o͝oˈränik/ **adj.** [19th C.: from Gk. *neuron*, 'sinew, tendon.']

neu·ro·path /ˈn(y)o͝orəˌpaTH/ ▶ **n.** dated a person affected by nervous disease.

neu·ro·pa·thol·o·gy /ˌn(y)o͝orōpəˈTHäləjē/ ▶ **n.** the branch of medicine concerned with diseases of the nervous system. — **neu·ro·path·o·log·i·cal** /-ˌpaTHəˈläjikəl/ **adj.** **neu·ro·pa·thol·o·gist** **n.**

neu·rop·a·thy /n(y)o͝oˈräpəTHē/ ▶ **n.** Med. disease or dysfunction of one or more peripheral nerves. — **neu·ro·path·ic** /ˌn(y)o͝orəˈpaTHik/ **adj.**

neu·ro·pep·tide /ˌn(y)o͝orōˈpeptīd/ ▶ **n.** Biochem. any of a group of compounds that act as neurotransmitters and are short-chain polypeptides.

neu·ro·phar·ma·col·o·gy /ˌn(y)o͝orōˌfärməˈkäləjē/ ▶ **n.** the branch of pharmacology that deals with the action of drugs on the nervous system. — **neu·ro·phar·ma·co·log·ic** /-kəˈläjik/ **adj.** **neu·ro·phar·ma·co·log·i·cal** /-kəˈläjikəl/ **adj.** **neu·ro·phar·ma·col·o·gist** **n.**

neu·ro·phys·i·ol·o·gy /ˌn(y)o͝orōˌfizēˈäləjē/ ▶ **n.** the physiology of the nervous system. — **neu·ro·phys·i·o·log·i·cal** /-ˌfizēəˈläjikəl/ **adj.** **neu·ro·phys·i·ol·o·gist** **n.**

neu·ro·psy·chi·a·try /ˌn(y)o͝orōsəˈkīətrē; -sīˈkī-/ ▶ **n.** psychiatry relating mental or emotional disturbance to disordered brain function. — **neu·ro·psy·chi·at·ric** /-ˌsīkēˈatrik/ **adj.** **neu·ro·psy·chi·a·trist** **n.**

neu·ro·psy·chol·o·gy /ˌn(y)o͝orōsīˈkäləjē/ ▶ **n.** the study of the relationship between behavior, emotion, and cognition on the one hand, and brain function on the other. — **neu·ro·psy·cho·log·i·cal** /-ˌsīkəˈläjikəl/ **adj.** **neu·ro·psy·chol·o·gist** **n.**

Neu·rop·ter·a /n(y)o͝oˈräptərə/ Entomol. an order of predatory flying insects that includes the lacewings, snake flies, and ant lions. They have four finely veined membranous wings. ■ **(neuroptera)** [as pl. n.] insects of this order. — **neu·rop·ter·an** **n.** & **adj.** **neu·rop·ter·ous** /-rəs/ **adj.** [mod. L. (pl.), from NEURO- in the sense 'veined' + Gk. *pteron* 'wing.']

neu·ro·sci·ence /ˌn(y)o͝orōˈsīəns/ ▶ **n.** any of the sciences, such as neurochemistry, that deal with the structure or function of the nervous system and brain. ■ such sciences collectively. — **neu·ro·sci·en·tist** /-ˈsīəntist/ **n.**

neu·ro·sis /n(y)o͝oˈrōsis/ ▶ **n.** (pl. **-ses** /-ˌsēz/) Med. a relatively mild mental illness that is not caused by organic disease, involving symptoms of stress (depression, anxiety) but not a loss of touch with reality. Compare with PSYCHOSIS. ■ (in nontechnical use) excessive and irrational anxiety or obsession: *apprehension over mounting debt has created a collective neurosis in the business world.*

neu·ro·sur·ger·y /ˌn(y)o͝orōˈsərjərē/ ▶ **n.** surgery performed on the nervous system, esp. the brain and spinal cord. — **neu·ro·sur·geon** /ˈn(y)ərōˌsərjən/ **n.** **neu·ro·sur·gi·cal** /-jikəl/ **adj.**

neu·ro·syph·i·lis /ˌn(y)o͝orōˈsifəlis/ ▶ **n.** syphilis that involves the central nervous system. — **neu·ro·syph·i·lit·ic** /-sifəˈlitik/ **adj.** & **n.**

neu·rot·ic /n(y)o͝oˈrätik/ ▶ **adj.** Med. suffering from, caused by, or relating to neurosis. ■ abnormally sensitive, obsessive, or tense and anxious: *Alex was too jumpy, too neurotic* | *everyone was neurotic about burglars* | *a neurotic obsession with neat handwriting.* ▶ **n.** a neurotic person. — **neu·rot·i·cal·ly** **adv.** **neu·rot·i·cism** /-ˈrätəˌsizəm/ **n.**

neu·rot·o·my /n(y)o͝oˈrätəmē/ ▶ **n.** the surgical cutting of a nerve to produce sensory loss and relief of pain or to suppress involuntary movements.

neu·ro·tox·in /ˈn(y)o͝orōˌtäksin/ ▶ **n.** a poison that acts on the nervous system. — **neu·ro·tox·ic** /ˌn(y)o͝orōˈtäksik/ **adj.** **neu·ro·tox·ic·i·ty** /ˌn(y)o͝orōtäkˈsisitē/ **n.** **neu·ro·tox·i·col·o·gy** /ˌn(y)o͝orōˌtäksiˈkäləjē/ **n.**

neu·ro·trans·mit·ter /ˌn(y)o͝orōˈtranzmitər/ ▶ **n.** Physiol. a chemical substance that is released at the end of a nerve fiber by the arrival of a nerve impulse and causes the transfer of the impulse to another nerve fiber, a muscle fiber, or some other structure. — **neu·ro·trans·mis·sion** /-ˌtranzˈmisHən/ **n.**

neu·ro·trop·ic /ˌn(y)o͝orəˈträpik; -ˈtrō-/ ▶ **adj.** Med. (of a virus, toxin, or chemical) tending to attack or affect the nervous system preferentially. — **neu·rot·ro·pism** /n(y)o͝oˈrätrəˌpizəm/ **n.**

neus·ton /ˈn(y)o͞ostän/ ▶ **n.** Biol. small aquatic organisms inhabiting the surface layer or moving on the surface film of water. — **neus·ton·ic** /n(y)o͞oˈstänik/ **adj.** [20th C.: via Ger. from Gk., neut. of *neustos* 'swimming.']

neut. ▶ **abbr.** ■ neuter. ■ neutral.

neu·ter /ˈn(y)o͞otər/ ▶ **adj.** **1** of or denoting a gender of nouns in some languages, typically contrasting with masculine and feminine or common. **2** (of an animal) lacking developed sexual organs, or having had them removed. ■ (of a plant or flower) having neither functional pistils nor functional stamens. ■ (of a person) apparently having no sexual characteristics; asexual. ▶ **n.** **1** Gram. a neuter word. ■ **(the neuter)** the neuter gender. **2** a nonfertile caste of social insect, esp. a worker bee or ant. ■ a castrated or spayed domestic animal. ■ a person who appears to lack sexual characteristics. ▶ **v.** [trans.] castrate or spay (a domestic animal): [as adj.] **(neutered)** *a neutered tomcat.* ■ render ineffective; deprive of vigor or force: *disarmament negotiations that will neuter their military power.* [ME: via OFr. from L. *neut.* 'neither,' from *ne-* 'not' + *uter* 'either.']

neu·tral /ˈn(y)o͞otrəl/ ▶ **adj.** **1** not helping or supporting either of two opposing sides, esp. countries at war; impartial. ■ belonging to an impartial party, country, or group: *on neutral ground.* ■ unbiased; disinterested. **2** having no strongly marked or positive characteristics or features: *the tone was neutral, devoid of sentiment.* | ■ Chem. neither acid nor alkaline; having a pH of about 7. ■ electrically neither positive nor negative. ▶ **n.** **1** an impartial and uninvolved country or person. ■ an unbiased person. **2** a neutral color or shade, esp. light gray or beige. **3** a disengaged position of gears in which the engine is disconnected from the driven parts. **4** an electrically neutral point, terminal, conductor, or wire. — **neu·tral·i·ty** /n(y)o͞oˈtralitē/ **n.** **neu·tral·ly** **adv.** [ME (as a n.): from L. *neutralis* 'of neuter gender,' from *neuter* (see NEUT.).]

neu·tral cor·ner ▶ **n.** Boxing either of the two corners of a boxing ring not used by the boxers and their handlers between rounds.

neu·tral den·si·ty fil·ter ▶ **n.** a photographic or optical filter that absorbs light of all wavelengths to the same extent, causing dimming but no change in color.

neu·tral·ism /ˈn(y)o͞otrəˌlizəm/ ▶ **n.** a policy of political neutrality. — **neu·tral·ist** **n.**

neu·tral·ize /ˈn(y)o͞otrəˌlīz/ ▶ **v.** [trans.] render (something) ineffective or harmless by applying an opposite force or effect: *impatience at his frailty began to neutralize her fear.* ■ make (an acidic or alkaline substance) chemically neutral. ■ disarm (a bomb or similar weapon). ■ a euphemistic way of saying kill or destroy, esp. in a covert or military operation. — **neu·tral·i·za·tion** /ˌn(y)o͞otrəliˈzāsHən/ **n.** **neu·tral·iz·er** **n.**

neu·tral zone ▶ **n.** **1** the central area of a hockey rink, lying between the two blue lines. **2** Football (before the start of a play) the imaginary zone running sideline to sideline from the front to the back point of the football.

neu·tri·no /n(y)o͞oˈtrēnō/ ▶ **n.** (pl. **-nos**) a neutral subatomic particle with a mass close to zero and half-integral spin, rarely reacting with normal matter. [20th C.: from Ital., dimin. of *neutro* 'neutral.']

neu·tron /ˈn(y)o͞oträn/ ▶ **n.** a subatomic particle of about the same mass as a proton but without an electric charge, present in all atomic nuclei except those of ordinary hydrogen. [20th C.: from NEUTRAL + -ON.]

neu·tron bomb ▶ **n.** a nuclear weapon that produces large numbers of neutrons rather than heat or blast like conventional nuclear weapons.

neu·tron star ▶ **n.** Astron. a celestial object of very small radius (typically 18 miles/30 km) and very high density, composed predominantly of closely packed neutrons and believed to be formed by the gravitational collapse of a star.

neu·tro·phil /ˈn(y)o͞otrəfil/ ▶ **n.** Physiol. a neutrophilic white blood cell.

neu·tro·phil·ic /ˌn(y)o͞otrəˈfilik/ ▶ **adj.** Physiol. (of a cell or its contents) readily stained only by neutral dyes. [19th C.: from NEUTRAL + *-philic* (see -PHILIA).]

Nev. ▶ **abbr.** Nevada.

Ne·va /ˈnēvə; ˈnā-/ a river in northwestern Russia that flows to the Gulf of Finland.

Ne·va·da /nəˈvadə; -ˈvädə/ a state in the western US, almost totally in the Great Basin area; pop. 1,998,257; capital, Carson City; statehood, Oct. 31, 1864 (36). It was acquired from Mexico in 1848. — **Ne·vad·an** **adj.** & **n.**

né·vé /nāˈvā/ ▶ **n.** another term for FIRN. [19th C.: from Swiss Fr., lit. 'glacier,' based on L. *nix*, *niv-* 'snow.']

nev·er /ˈnevər/ ▶ **adv.** **1** at no time in the past or future; on no occasion; not ever: *I will never ever forget it.* **2** not at all: *he never turned up.*
– PHRASES **never fear** see FEAR. **never mind** see MIND. **never say die** see DIE[1]. **well I never!** informal expressing great surprise or indignation. [OE *nǣfre*, from *ne* 'not' + *ǣfre* 'ever.']

nev·er-end·ing ▶**adj.** (esp. of something unpleasant) having or seeming to have no end.

nev·er·more /ˌnevərˈmôr/ ▶**adv.** literary at no future time; never again: *I order you gone, nevermore to return.*

nev·er-nev·er land ▶**n.** an imaginary utopian place or situation.

nev·er·the·less /ˌnevərT͟Həˈles/ ▶**adv.** in spite of that; notwithstanding; all the same: *statements which, although literally true, are nevertheless misleading.*

Ne·vis /ˈnēvəs/ a Leeward Island that is part of St. Kitts and Nevis. — **Nevisian** /ˌnevəˈsēən/ **n. & adj.**

ne·vus /ˈnēvəs/ ▶**n.** (pl. **-vi** /-ˌvī/) a birthmark or a mole on the skin, esp. a birthmark in the form of a raised red patch. [19th C.: from L.]

new /n(y)o͞o/ ▶**adj. 1** not existing before; made, introduced, or discovered recently or now for the first time: *new crop varieties* | [as n.] (**the new**) *a fascinating mix of the old and the new.* ■ in original condition; not worn or used. ■ not previously used or owned: *a secondhand bus cost a fraction of a new one.* ■ of recent origin or arrival. ■ (of food or drink) freshly or recently produced. ■ (of vegetables) dug or harvested early in the season. **2** already existing but seen, experienced, or acquired recently or now for the first time: *her new bike.* ■ [predic.] (**new to**) unfamiliar or strange to (someone). ■ [predic.] (**new to/at**) (of a person) inexperienced at or unaccustomed to doing (something): *I'm quite new to gardening.* ■ different from a recent previous one: *I have a new assistant.* ■ in addition to another or others already existing: *recruiting new pilots overseas.* ■ [in place names] discovered or founded later than and named after: *New York.* **3** just beginning and regarded as better than what went before: *starting a new life.* ■ (of a person) reinvigorated or restored: *a bottle of pills would make him a new man.* ■ (**the new**) renewed or reformed: *the new South Africa.* ■ superseding another or others of the same kind, and advanced in method or theory. ■ reviving another or others of the same kind: *the New Bohemians.* ■ recently affected or produced by social change: *the new rich.* ▶**adv.** [usu. in comb.] newly; recently: *new-mown hay.*
– PHRASES **a new one** informal an account, idea, or joke not previously encountered by someone. **what's new? 1** (said on greeting someone) what's going on? how are you? **2** (also **what else is new?**) that is the usual situation: *she and I squabbled—so what's new?* — **new·ish adj. new·ness n.** [OE *nīwe, nēowe*; rel. to Ger. *neu*, from an Indo-Eur. root shared by L. *novus*, Gk. *neos* 'new.']

New Age ▶**n.** a broad movement characterized by alternative approaches to traditional Western culture, with an interest in spirituality, mysticism, holism, and environmentalism: [as adj.] *the New Age movement.* — **New Ag·er n. New Agey adj.**

New Age mus·ic ▶**n.** a style of chiefly instrumental music characterized by light melodic harmonies, improvisation, and sounds reproduced from the natural world, intended to promote serenity.

New Am·ster·dam former name for the city of **New York**.

New·ark /ˈn(y)o͞oˌərk/ an industrial city in northeastern New Jersey; pop. 273,546.

New Bed·ford a city in southeastern Massachusetts; pop. 93,768.

new·bie /ˈn(y)o͞obē/ ▶**n.** (pl. **-bies**) an inexperienced newcomer, esp. in computing.

new·born /ˈn(y)o͞oˌbôrn/ ▶**adj.** (of a child or animal) recently or just born. ▶**n.** a recently born child or animal.

New Brit·ain 1 a mountainous island in the South Pacific Ocean, part of Papua New Guinea; pop. 312,000; capital, Rabaul. **2** a city in central Connecticut; pop. 71,538.

New Bruns·wick a province in southeastern Canada; pop. 726,900; capital, Fredericton.

New Cal·e·do·ni·a /ˌkaləˈdōnēə/ an island in the South Pacific; pop. 178,000; capital, Nouméa. Since 1946 it has formed, with its dependencies, a French overseas territory. French name **Nouvelle-Calédonie**. — **New Cal·e·do·ni·an n. & adj.**

New·cas·tle /ˈn(y)o͞oˌkasəl/ **1** a city in northeastern England; pop. 263,000. Full name **Newcastle-upon-Tyne**. **2** a town in west central England; pop. 117,000. Full name **Newcastle-under-Lyme**. **3** a city in southeastern Australia; pop. 262,000.

New·cas·tle dis·ease ▶**n.** an acute infectious viral fever affecting birds, esp. poultry. [1920s: so named because it was first recorded near Newcastle-upon-Tyne, England, in 1927.]

New·com·en /n(y)o͞oˈkəmən/, Thomas (1663–1729), English engineer. He developed the first practical steam engine.

new·com·er /ˈn(y)o͞oˌkəmər/ ▶**n.** a person or thing that has recently arrived in a place or joined a group. ■ a novice in a particular activity or situation.

New Crit·i·cism an influential movement in literary criticism in the mid 20th century that stressed the importance of focusing on the text itself rather than being concerned with external biographical or social considerations.

New Deal the economic measures introduced by President Franklin D. Roosevelt in 1933 to counteract the effects of the Great Depression. — **New Deal·er n.**

New Del·hi see **Delhi**.

new e·con·o·my ▶**n.** new industries, such as biotechnology or the Internet, that are characterized by cutting-edge technology and high growth.

new·el /ˈn(y)o͞oəl/ ▶**n.** the central supporting pillar of a spiral or winding staircase. ■ (also **newel post**) a post at the head or foot of a flight of stairs, supporting a handrail. [ME: from OFr. *nouel* 'knob,' from med. L. *nodellus*, dimin. of L. *nodus* 'knot.']

newel post

New Eng·land an area on the northeastern coast of the US that consists of Maine, New Hampshire, Vermont, Massachusetts, Rhode Island, and Connecticut. — **New Eng·land·er n.**

New Eng·land clam chow·der ▶**n.** a thick chowder made with clams, onions, potatoes, salt pork, and milk.

New Eng·lish Bi·ble (abbr.: **NEB**) ▶**n.** a modern English translation of the Bible, published in the UK in 1961–70.

new·fan·gled /ˈn(y)o͞oˈfaNGgəld; -ˌfaNG-/ (also **new-fan·gled**) ▶**adj.** derog. different from what one is used to; objectionably new. [ME: from *newfangle* 'liking what is new,' from the adv. **new** + a second element rel. to an OE word meaning 'to take.']

new-fash·ioned ▶**adj.** of a new type or style; up to date.

New·fie /ˈn(y)o͞ofē/ informal ▶**n.** (pl. **-fies**) a Newfoundlander. ▶**adj.** coming from or associated with Newfoundland.

new·found /ˈn(y)o͞oˌfound/ (Brit. **new-found**) ▶**adj.** recently found or discovered.

New·found·land¹ /ˈn(y)o͞ofən(d)lənd; -ˌland; n(y)o͞oˈfound-/ a large island off the eastern coast of Canada, at the mouth of the St. Lawrence River. — **New·found·land·er n.**

Newfoundland²

New·found·land² (in full **Newfoundland dog**) ▶**n.** a dog of a very large breed with a thick, coarse coat.

New·found·land and Lab·ra·dor a province of Canada that consists of the island of Newfoundland and the Labrador coast of eastern Canada; pop. 568,474; capital, St. John's.

New·gate /ˈn(y)o͞oˌgāt/ a former London prison whose unsanitary conditions were notorious.

New Geor·gia a volcanic island group in the west central Solomon Islands, northwest of Guadalcanal. ■ the largest of these islands.

New Guin·ea an island in the western South Pacific Ocean. The world's second largest island, it is divided into two parts; half is part of Irian Jaya, an Indonesian province; half forms part of Papua New Guinea. — **New Guin·e·an** /ˈginēən/ **n. & adj.**

New Hamp·shire /ˈhampsHər/ a state in the northeastern US, with a short border on the Atlantic coast, one of the six New England states; pop. 1,235,786; capital, Concord; statehood, June 21, 1788 (9). It was the first colony to declare independence from Britain in 1776 and then became one of the original thirteen states.

New Ha·ven /ˌn(y)o͞o ˈhāvən/ a city in south central Connecticut; pop. 123,626.

New Heb·ri·des former name (until 1980) for **Vanuatu**.

Ne Win /ˌne ˈwin/ (1911–2002), president of Burma (now Myanmar) 1974–81; born *Shu Maung.*

New In·ter·na·tion·al Ver·sion (abbr.: **NIV**) ▶**n.** a modern English translation of the Bible published in 1973–78.

New Ire·land an island in the South Pacific Ocean, part of Papua New Guinea, that lies north of New Britain; pop. 87,000; capital, Kavieng.

New Jer·sey a state in the northeastern US, on the Atlantic coast; pop. 8,414,350; capital, Trenton; statehood, Dec. 18, 1787 (3). Colonized by Dutch settlers and ceded to Britain in 1664, it became one of the original thirteen states. — **New Jer·sey·an** /-zēən/ **n. & adj.**

New Je·ru·sa·lem Theol. the abode of the blessed in heaven (with reference to Rev. 21:2). ■ [as n.] (**a New Jerusalem**) an ideal place or situation.

New Je·ru·sa·lem Church a Christian sect instituted by followers of Emanuel Swedenborg.

New Lat·in ▶**n.** another term for **Modern Latin**.

new·ly /ˈn(y)o͞olē/ ▶**adv. 1** recently. **2** again; afresh. ■ in a new or different manner.

new·ly·wed /ˈn(y)o͞olēˌwed/ ▶**n.** (usu. **newlyweds**) a recently married person.

New·man, John Henry (1801–90), English clergyman and theologian. A founder of the Oxford Movement, he turned to Roman Catholicism in 1845.

New·mar·ket /ˈn(y)o͞o,märkət/ ▶ n. (also **Newmarket coat**) a close-fitting overcoat of a style originally worn for riding.

new math ▶ n. a system of teaching mathematics to younger children, with emphasis on investigation and discovery and on set theory.

New Mex·i·co a state in the southwestern US, on the border with Mexico; pop. 1,819,046; capital, Santa Fe; statehood, Jan. 6, 1912 (47). It was obtained from Mexico in 1845 (annexation of Texas), in 1848 (Treaty of Guadalupe Hidalgo that ended the Mexican-American War), and in 1853 (Gadsden Purchase). — **New Mex·i·can** /-kən/ adj. & n.

new mon·ey ▶ n. a fortune recently acquired; funds recently raised.

new moon ▶ n. the phase of the moon when it is in conjunction with the sun and invisible from earth, or shortly thereafter when it appears as a slender crescent. ■ the time when this occurs.

New Or·le·ans /ˈôrl(ē)ənz; ôrˈlēnz/ a city in southeastern Louisiana; pop. 484,674.

New·port /ˈn(y)o͞o,pôrt/ a city in southern Wales, on the Bristol Channel; pop. 130,000. Welsh name CASNEWYDD.

New·port News a city in southeastern Virginia, on the Hampton Roads estuary; pop. 180,150.

New Prov·i·dence an island in the central Bahamas; pop. 172,000.

New Re·vised Stand·ard Ver·sion (abbr.: **NRSV**) ▶ n. a modern English translation of the Bible, based on the Revised Standard Version and published in 1990.

New Ro·chelle /rəˈsʜel; rō-/ a city in southeastern New York, northeast of New York City; pop. 72,182.

news /n(y)o͞oz/ ▶ n. newly received or noteworthy information, esp. about recent or important events. ■ (**the news**) a broadcast or published report of news. ■ (**news to**) informal information not previously known to (someone). ■ a person or thing considered interesting enough to be reported in the news: *Chanel became the hottest news in fashion.*
– PHRASES **make news** become a story in the news. **no news is good news** proverb without information to the contrary one can assume that all is well. [ME: pl. of NEW.]

news a·gen·cy ▶ n. an organization that collects news items and distributes them to newspapers or broadcasters.

news·a·gent /ˈn(y)o͞oz,ājənt/ ▶ n. Brit. a person or a shop selling newspapers and magazines.

news·boy /ˈn(y)o͞oz,boi/ ▶ n. a boy who sells or delivers newspapers.

news brief ▶ n. a brief item of print or broadcast news.

news bul·le·tin ▶ n. Brit. a short radio or television broadcast of news reports.

news·cast /ˈn(y)o͞oz,kast/ ▶ n. a radio or television broadcast of news reports.

news·cast·er /ˈn(y)o͞oz,kastər/ ▶ n. a person who reads broadcast news stories.

news con·fer·ence ▶ n. a press conference.

news desk ▶ n. the department of a broadcasting organization or newspaper responsible for collecting and reporting the news.

news·feed /ˈn(y)o͞oz,fēd/ ▶ n. **1** a service by which news is provided on a regular or continuous basis for onward distribution or broadcasting. ■ an item of information so provided. **2** a system by which data is transferred or exchanged between central computers to provide newsgroup access to networked users.

news flash ▶ n. an item of important news broadcast separately, often interrupting other programs.

news-gath·er·ing (also **news gath·er·ing**) ▶ n. the process of researching news items, esp. those for broadcast or publication. — **news·gath·er·er** /-(ə)rər/ n.

news·group /ˈn(y)o͞oz,gro͞op/ ▶ n. a group of Internet users who exchange e-mail messages on a topic of mutual interest.

news·hound /ˈn(y)o͞oz,hound/ ▶ n. informal a newspaper reporter.

news·ie /ˈn(y)o͞ozē/ ▶ n. (also **news·y**) (pl. **-ies**) informal a reporter. ■ informal a person who sells or delivers newspapers.

news·let·ter /ˈn(y)o͞oz,letər/ ▶ n. a bulletin issued periodically to the members of a society, business, or organization.

news·mag·a·zine /ˈn(y)o͞oz,magə,zēn/ ▶ n. a periodical that reports and comments on current events. ■ a regularly scheduled television news program consisting of short segments on a variety of subjects and featuring a varied format combining interviews, commentary, and entertainment.

news·man /ˈn(y)o͞oz,man/ ▶ n. (pl. **-men**) a reporter or journalist.

news·mon·ger /ˈn(y)o͞oz,mänggər/ ▶ n. a gossip.

New South Wales a state of southeastern Australia; pop. 5,827,000; capital, Sydney.

New Spain a former Spanish viceroyalty in Central and North America from 1535 to 1821 that was centered around present-day Mexico City. It included all the land under Spanish control north of the Isthmus of Panama and parts of the southern US, as well as the Spanish possessions in the Caribbean and the Philippines.

news·pa·per /ˈn(y)o͞oz,pāpər/ ▶ n. a printed publication consisting of folded unstapled sheets and containing news, feature articles, advertisements, and correspondence. ■ the organization responsible for producing a particular newspaper. ■ another term for NEWSPRINT.

news·pa·per·man /ˈn(y)o͞oz,pāpər,man; -mən/ ▶ n. (pl. **-men**) a male newspaper journalist.

news·pa·per·wom·an /ˈn(y)o͞oz,pāpər,wo͝omən/ ▶ n. (pl. **-wom·en**) a female newspaper journalist.

new·speak /ˈn(y)o͞o,spēk/ ▶ n. ambiguous euphemistic language used chiefly in political propaganda. [1949: the name of an artificial official language in George Orwell's *Nineteen Eighty-Four*.]

news·peo·ple /ˈn(y)o͞oz,pēpəl/ ▶ plural n. professional reporters or journalists.

news·print /ˈn(y)o͞oz,print/ ▶ n. cheap, low-quality, absorbent printing paper made from coarse wood pulp and used chiefly for newspapers.

news·read·er /ˈn(y)o͞oz,rēdər/ ▶ n. **1** Comput. a computer program for reading e-mail messages posted to newsgroups. **2** Brit. a newscaster.

news·reel /ˈn(y)o͞oz,rēl/ ▶ n. a short film of news and current affairs, formerly made for showing as part of the program in a movie theater.

news·room /ˈn(y)o͞oz,ro͞om; -,ro͝om/ ▶ n. the area in a newspaper or broadcasting office where news is written and edited.

news-sheet ▶ n. a simple form of newspaper; a newsletter.

news·stand /ˈn(y)o͞oz,stand/ ▶ n. a stand or stall for the sale of newspapers.

New Stone Age the Neolithic period.

New Style (abbr.: **NS**) ▶ n. the method of calculating dates using the Gregorian calendar.

new-style ▶ adj. [attrib.] having a new style; different from and usually better than a previous version.

news·week·ly /ˈn(y)o͞oz,wēklē/ (pl. **-lies**) ▶ n. a newspaper or newsmagazine published on a weekly basis.

news wire ▶ n. an electronically transmitted service providing up-to-the-minute news stories, financial market updates, and other information.

news·wor·thy /ˈn(y)o͞oz,wərᴛʜē/ ▶ adj. noteworthy as news; topical. — **news·wor·thi·ness** n.

news·y ▶ adj. (**news·i·er, news·i·est**) informal full of news, esp. of a personal kind: *short, newsy letters.* ▶ n. var. of NEWSIE.

newt /n(y)o͞ot/ ▶ n. a small, slender-bodied amphibian (*Notophthalmus, Taricha*, and other genera, family Salamandridae) with lungs and a well-developed tail, typically spending its adult life on land and returning to water to breed. [ME: from *an ewt* (*ewt* from OE *efeta*: see EFT), interpreted (by wrong division) as *a newt*.]

rough-skinned newt

New Ter·ri·to·ries a part of Hong Kong on the southern coast of mainland China. It includes the islands of Lantau, Tsing Yi, and Lamma.

New Tes·ta·ment ▶ n. the second part of the Christian Bible, written originally in Greek and recording the life and teachings of Jesus and his earliest followers. It includes the four Gospels, the Acts of the Apostles, twenty-one epistles by St. Paul and others, and the book of Revelation.

New·ton, Sir Isaac (1642–1727), English mathematician and physicist. In *Principia Mathematica* (1687), he gave a mathematical description of the laws of mechanics and gravitation and applied these to planetary motion.

new·ton /ˈn(y)o͞otn/ (abbr.: **N**) ▶ n. Physics the SI unit of force. It is equal to the force that would give a mass of one kilogram an acceleration of one meter per second per second, and is equivalent to 100,000 dynes. [20th C.: named after Sir Isaac NEWTON.]

New·ton's laws of mo·tion Physics three fundamental laws of classical physics. The first states that a body continues in a state of rest or uniform motion in a straight line unless it is acted on by an external force. The second states that the rate of change of momentum of a moving body is proportional to the force acting to produce the change. The third states that if one body exerts a force on another, there is an equal and opposite force (or reaction) exerted by the second body on the first.

new town ▶ n. a planned urban center created in an undeveloped or rural area, esp. with government sponsorship.

new wave ▶ n. **1** another term for NOUVELLE VAGUE. **2** a style of rock music popular in the 1970s and 1980s, deriving from punk but generally more pop in sound and less aggressive in performance.

New World North and South America regarded collectively in relation to Europe, esp. after the early voyages of European explorers.

new year ▶ n. the calendar year just begun or about to begin. ■ the first few days or weeks of a year. ■ (usu. **New Year**) the period immediately before and after December 31.
– PHRASES **New Year's** informal New Year's Eve or New Year's Day. **ring in** (or **out**) **the new year** see RING[2].

New Year's Day n. the first day of the year; in the modern Western calendar, January 1.

New Year's Eve n. the last day of the year; in the modern Western calendar, December 31. ■ the evening of this day, typically marked with a celebration.

New·yor·i·can /n(y)o͞oˈyôrikən/ ▶ n. another term for NUYORICAN.

New York 1 a state in the northeastern US, on the Canadian border and

Lake Ontario in the northwest, as well as on the Atlantic coast in the southeast; pop. 18,976,457; capital, Albany; statehood, July 26, 1788 (11). Originally settled by the Dutch, it was surrendered to the British in 1664. New York was one of the original thirteen states. **2** a major city in southeastern New York, at the mouth of the Hudson River; pop. 7,322,564. It consists of five boroughs: Manhattan, Brooklyn, the Bronx, Queens, and Staten Island. Terrorist attacks on the World Trade Center on September 11, 2001, toppled its two towers and destroyed surrounding buildings. Former name (until 1664) NEW AMSTERDAM. — **New York·er** n.

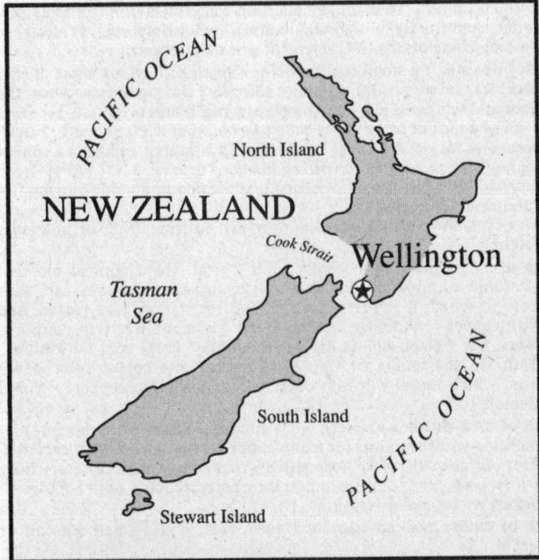

New Zealand

Location: South Pacific Ocean about 1,200 miles (1900 km) east of Australia
Area: 103,800 square miles (268,700 sq km)
Population: 3,990,000
Capital: Wellington
Languages: English (official), Maori
Currency: New Zealand dollar

New Zea·land /ˈzēlənd/ an island country in the South Pacific Ocean. *See box.* — **New Zea·land·er** n.

NEX ▶ abbr. Navy exchange.

next /nekst/ ▶ adj. **1** (of a time or season) coming immediately after the time of writing or speaking: *next week's parade.* ■ (of a day of the week) nearest (or the nearest but one) after the present: *not this Wednesday, next Wednesday.* ■ (of an event or occasion) occurring directly in time after the present or most recent one, without anything of the same kind intervening: *the next election.* **2** coming immediately after the present one in order or space: *the woman in the next room* | *the next chapter* | *who's next?* ■ coming immediately after the present one in rank: *building materials were next in importance.* ▶ adv. on the first or soonest occasion after the present; immediately afterward: *wondering what would happen next* | *next, I heard the sound of voices.* ■ [with superlative] following in the specified order: *Joe was the next oldest after Martin.* ▶ n. the next person or thing: *the week **after next.*** ▶ prep. archaic next to: *he plodded along next him.*
– PHRASES **next in line** immediately below the present holder of a position in order of succession: *he is **next in line to** the throne.* **next to 1** in or into a position immediately to one side of; beside: *we sat next to each other.* **2** following in order or importance: *next to buying a whole new wardrobe, nothing lifts the spirits quite like a new hairdo!* **3** almost: *Charles knew **next to nothing** about farming.* **4** in comparison with: *next to her I felt like a fraud.* **the next world** (according to some religious beliefs) the place where one goes after death. **what next** an expression of surprise or amazement. [OE *nēhsta* 'nearest,' superlative of *nēah* 'nigh.']

next best ▶ adj. [attrib.] second in order of preference; to be preferred if one's first choice is not available.

next door ▶ adv. in or to the next house or room. ▶ adj. (**next-door**) living or situated next door. ▶ n. the building, room, or people next door.
– PHRASES **the boy** (or **girl**) **next door** a person or type of person perceived as familiar, approachable, and dependable, typically in the context of a romantic partnership. **next door to** in the next house or room to: *the Old Executive Office Building next door to the White House.* ■ nearly; almost; near to: *it is next door to impossible.*

next of kin ▶ n. [treated as sing. or pl.] a person's closest living relative or relatives.

nex·us /ˈneksəs/ ▶ n. (pl. same or **-us·es**) a connection or series of connections linking two or more things. ■ a connected group or series: *a nexus of ideas.* ■ the central and most important point or place. [17th C.: from L., 'a binding together,' from *nex-* 'bound,' from the v. *nectere.*]

Nez Per·cé /ˌnez ˈpərz; pərˈsā/ ▶ n. (pl. same or **Nez Per·cés**) **1** a member of an American Indian people of central Idaho, northeastern Oregon, and southeastern Washington. **2** the Penutian language of this people. ▶ adj. of or relating to this people or their language. [Fr., lit. 'pierced nose.']

NF ▶ abbr. ■ Newfoundland (in official postal use).

n/f (also **N/F**) ▶ abbr. no funds.

NFC ▶ abbr. ■ National Finance Center. ■ National Football Conference.

NFL ▶ abbr. National Football League.

NG ▶ abbr. ■ National Guard. ■ natural gas. ■ newsgroup. ■ no good. ■ Football nose guard.

ng ▶ abbr. nanogram.

Nga·li·e·ma, Mount /əNGˌgäleˈämə/ Zairean name for Mount Stanley (see STANLEY, MOUNT).

NGF ▶ abbr. ■ National Golf Foundation. ■ nerve growth factor.

NGO ▶ abbr. nongovernmental organization.

NGU ▶ abbr. nongonococcal urethritis.

ngul·trum /əNGˈgəltrəm/ ▶ n. (pl. same) the basic monetary unit of Bhutan, equal to 100 chetrum.

Ngu·ni /əNGˈgo͞onē/ ▶ n. (pl. same) **1** a member of a group of peoples living mainly in southern Africa. **2** the group of closely related Bantu languages, including Ndebele, Swazi, Xhosa, and Zulu. ▶ adj. of or relating to these peoples or their languages. [from Zulu.]

ngwee /əNGˈgwē/ ▶ n. (pl. same) a monetary unit of Zambia, equal to one hundredth of a kwacha.

NH ▶ abbr. New Hampshire (in official postal use).

NHL ▶ abbr. National Hockey League.

Ni ▶ symb. the chemical element nickel.

ni·a·cin /ˈnīəsin/ ▶ n. another term for NICOTINIC ACID.

Ni·ag·a·ra Falls /nīˈag(ə)rə/ waterfalls on the Niagara River that consist of two principal parts separated by Goat Island: the Horseshoe Falls adjoin the western (Canadian) bank and fall 158 feet (47 m); the American Falls adjoin the eastern (US) bank and fall 167 feet (50 m). ■ a city in New York; pop. 55,593. ■ a city in Canada, in southern Ontario; pop. 75,399.

Ni·ag·a·ra Riv·er a river in North America that flows between Lake Erie and Lake Ontario and forms part of the border between Canada and the US.

Nia·mey /nēˈämā/ the capital of Niger, a port on the Niger River; pop. 410,000.

nib /nib/ ▶ n. the pointed end part of a pen, which distributes the ink on the writing surface: *a fine gold-plated nib.* ■ a pointed or projecting part of an object: *slide the tile into place until the nibs hook on.* [16th C. (in the sense 'beak, nose'): prob. from MDu. *nib* or Mid. Low Ger. *nibbe*, var. of *nebbe* 'beak' (see NEB).]

nib·ble /ˈnibəl/ ▶ v. take small bites out of: [trans.] *he sat nibbling a cookie* | [intrans.] *she **nibbled at** her food.* ■ [intrans.] eat in small amounts, esp. between meals: *I put on weight because I was constantly nibbling.* ■ gently bite at (a part of the body), esp. amorously or nervously: [trans.] *Tamar nibbled her bottom lip* | [intrans.] *he **nibbled at** her earlobe.* ■ fig. gradually erode or eat away: [intrans.] *inflation was **nibbling away at** spending power.* ■ [intrans.] fig. show cautious interest in a project or proposal: *there's a New York agent nibbling.* ▶ n. [in sing.] **1** an instance of nibbling something: *coming back for another little nibble* | *I'm distracted by a nibble on my line.* ■ a small piece of food bitten off: *I took a nibble from one of the sandwiches.* ■ an expression of cautious interest in a project or proposal: *now and then she gets a nibble, but no one will commit to an interview.* **2** Comput. a unit of memory equal to half a byte; four bits. — **nib·bler** /ˈnib(ə)lər/ n. [15th C.: prob. of Low Ger. or Du. origin; cf. Low Ger. *nibbeln* 'gnaw.']

Ni·be·lung /ˈnēbəˌlo͝oNG/ ▶ n. (pl. **-lungs** or **-lung·en** /-ˌlo͝oNGgen/) Germanic Mythol. **1** a member of a race of dwarfs, owners of a hoard of gold and magic treasures, who were ruled by a king called Nibelung. **2** (in the Nibelungenlied) a supporter of Siegfried or one of the Burgundians who stole the hoard from him. [from Old High Ger.]

Ni·be·lung·en·lied /ˌnēbəˈlo͝oNGgənˌlēd/ a 13th-century German poem, embodying a story found in the (Poetic) Edda, telling of the life and death of Siegfried, a prince of the Netherlands. [Ger., from NIBELUNG + *Lied* 'song.']

nib·lick /ˈniblik/ ▶ n. Golf, dated an iron with a heavy, lofted head, such as a nine-iron, used esp. for playing out of bunkers. [19th C.: of unknown origin.]

nibs /nibz/ ▶ n. (**his nibs**) informal a mock title used to refer to a self-important man, esp. one in authority. [19th C.: of unknown origin.]

NIC ▶ abbr. ■ newly industrialized country.

ni·Cad /ˈnīˌkad/ (also trademark **Ni·cad**) ▶ n. [usu. as adj.] a battery or cell with a nickel anode, a cadmium cathode, and a potassium hydroxide electrolyte. They are used chiefly as a rechargeable power source for portable equipment. [1950s: blend of NICKEL and CADMIUM.]

PRONUNCIATION KEY ə *ago, up*; ər *over, fur*; a *hat*; ā *ate*; ä *car*; e *let*; ē *see*; i *fit*; ī *by*; NG *sing*; ō *go*; ô *law, for*; oi *toy*; o͝o *good*; o͞o *goo*; ou *out*; TH *thin*; T͟H *then*; ZH *vision*

Ni·cae·a /nī'sēə/ an ancient city in Asia Minor, on the site of modern Iznik in Turkey, which was important in Roman and Byzantine times. See also **Nicene Creed**.

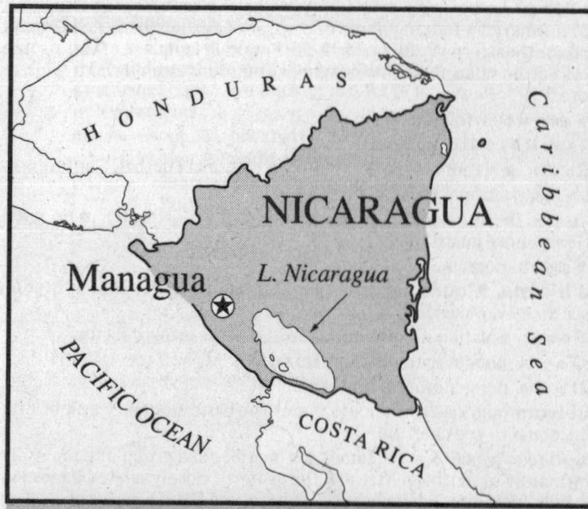

Nicaragua

Official name: Republic of Nicaragua
Location: Central America, with a coastline on both the Atlantic and the Pacific Oceans
Area: 50,000 square miles (129,500 sq km)
Population: 5,359,000
Capital: Managua
Language: Spanish (official)
Currency: cordoba

Nic·a·ra·gua /nikə'rägwə/ a country, the largest, in Central America. *See box.* — **Nic·a·ra·guan** adj. & n.

Nic·a·ra·gua, Lake a lake in western Nicaragua.

Nice /nēs/ a city in southeastern France; pop. 346,000.

nice /nīs/ ▶ adj. **1** pleasant; agreeable; satisfactory: *we had a nice time.* ■ (of a person) pleasant in manner; good-natured; kind: *he's a really nice guy.* **2** fine or subtle: *a nice distinction.* ■ requiring careful thought or attention: *a nice point.* **3** archaic fastidious; scrupulous.
– PHRASES **make nice** (or **nice-nice**) informal be pleasant or polite to someone, typically in a hypocritical way. **nice and ——** satisfactorily or adequately in terms of the quality described: *it's nice and warm in here.* **nice one** informal expressing approval or commendation. ■ used sarcastically to comment on an inept act. **nice to meet you** a polite formula used on being introduced to someone. **nice work** informal expressing approval of a task well done. — **nice·ness** n. [ME (in the sense 'stupid'): from OFr., from L. *nescius* 'ignorant,' from *nescire* 'not know.']

nice·ly /'nīslē/ ▶ adv. in a pleasant, agreeable, or attractive manner: *nicely dressed in flowered cotton.* ■ politely: *say goodbye nicely to Miss Nicandra.* ■ satisfactorily; perfectly well: *we're doing very nicely now* | *the point is nicely illustrated by the following case.*

Ni·cene Creed /'nīsēn; nī'sēn/ a formal statement of Christian belief widely used in Christian liturgies, adopted at the first Council of Nicaea in 325.

ni·ce·ty /'nīsitē/ ▶ n. (pl. **-ties**) (usu. **niceties**) a fine detail or distinction, esp. one regarded as intricate and fussy: *legal niceties are wasted on him* | *she was never interested in the niceties of Greek and Latin.* ■ accuracy or precision: *she prided herself on her nicety of pronunciation.* ■ a minor aspect of polite social behavior; a detail of etiquette: *we were brought up to observe the niceties.*
– PHRASES **to a nicety** precisely. [ME: from OFr. *nicete*, based on L. *nescius* (see **nice**).]

niche /nicн/ ▶ n. a shallow recess, esp. one in a wall to display a statue or other ornament: *each niche holding a shepherdess in Dresden china.* ■ (**one's niche**) a comfortable or suitable position in life or employment: *he is now a partner at a leading law firm and feels he has found his niche.* ■ a specialized but profitable corner of the market: *it has found a niche in the staff recruitment market* | [as adj.] *important new niche markets.* ■ Ecol. a position or role taken by a particular kind of organism within its community. Such a position may be occupied by different organisms in different localities, e.g., antelopes in Africa and kangaroos in Australia. ▶ v. [trans.] place or position (something) in a niche: *these elements were niched within the shadowy reaches* | [as adj.] (**niched**) *decorated with niched statues* | fig. *a distinct and highly niched product.* [17th C.: from Fr., lit. 'recess,' from *nicher* 'make a nest,' based on L. *nidus* 'nest.']

Ni·chi·ren /'nicнərən/ (also **Nichiren Buddhism**) ▶ n. a Japanese Buddhist sect founded by the religious teacher Nichiren (1222–82) with the Lotus Sutra as its central scripture. See also **Soka Gakkai**.

Nich·o·las /'nik(ə)ləs/ the name of two tsars of Russia: ■ Nicholas I (1796–1855), reigned 1825–55, brother of Alexander I. ■ Nicholas II (1868–1918), reigned 1894–1917, son of Alexander III. He was forced to abdicate after the Russian Revolution in 1917 and was shot along with his family a year later.

Nich·o·las, St. (4th century), Christian clergyman. The cult of Santa Claus (a corruption of his name) comes from the Dutch custom of giving gifts to children on his feast day, December 6.

Nich·ol·son /'nikəlsən/, Ben (1894–1982), English painter; full name *Benjamin Lauder Nicholson.* He was a pioneer of British abstract art.

ni·chrome /'nī,krōm/ (also **Ni·chrome**) ▶ n. trademark an alloy of nickel with chromium (10 to 20 percent) and sometimes iron (up to 25 percent), used chiefly in high-temperature applications such as electrical heating elements. [20th C.: blend of **nickel** and **chrome**.]

nick /nik/ ▶ n. **1** a small cut or notch: *a small nick on his wrist.* **2** (**the nick**) Brit., informal prison. ■ a police station. **3** the junction between the floor and side walls in a court for playing real tennis or squash. ▶ v. [trans.] **1** make a nick or nicks in: *he had nicked himself while shaving.* **2** (**nick someone for**) informal cheat someone of (something, typically a sum of money): *he nicked me for fifteen hundred dollars.* **3** Brit., informal steal: *he'd had his car nicked by joyriders.* ■ arrest or apprehend (someone): *I got nicked for burglary.*
– PHRASES **in the nick of time** only just in time. [ME: of unknown origin.]

nick·el /'nikəl/ ▶ n. **1** a silvery-white metal, the chemical element of atomic number 28. The chief use of nickel is in alloys, esp. with iron, to which it imparts strength and resistance to corrosion, and with copper for coinage. (Symbol: **Ni**) **2** informal a five-cent coin; five cents. ▶ v. (**-eled, -el·ing**; Brit. **-elled, -el·ling**) [trans.] coat with nickel. [18th C.: shortening of Ger. *Kupfernickel*, the copper-colored ore from which nickel was first obtained, from *Kupfer* 'copper' + *Nickel* 'demon.']

nick·el-and-dime ▶ v. [trans.] put a financial strain on (someone) by charging small amounts for many minor services: *we don't nickel-and-dime our customers like some vendors that charge extra for every little utility.* ▶ adj. [attrib.] of little importance; petty: *the only games this weekend are nickel-and-dime stuff.*

nick·el brass ▶ n. an alloy of copper, zinc, and a small amount of nickel.

nick·el·o·de·on /,nikə'lōdēən/ ▶ n. **1** informal, dated a jukebox, originally one operated by the insertion of a nickel coin. **2** hist. a movie theater with an admission fee of one nickel. [20th C.: from **nickel** in the sense 'five-cent coin' + a shortened form of **melodeon**.]

nick·el steel ▶ n. a type of stainless steel containing chromium and nickel.

nick·er[1] /'nikər/ ▶ v. [intrans.] (of a horse) give a soft, low whinny. ▶ n. a sound of this kind. [16th C.: imitative.]

nick·er[2] ▶ n. (pl. same) Brit., informal a pound sterling. [20th C.: of unknown origin.]

Nick·laus /'nikləs/, Jack William (1940–), US golfer. He won more than 80 tournaments during his professional career.

nick·nack /'nik,nak/ (also **nick-nack**) ▶ n. var. of **knickknack**.

nick·name /'nik,nām/ ▶ n. a familiar or humorous name given to a person or thing instead of or as well as the real name. ▶ v. [with obj. and complement] give a nickname to; call by a nickname. [ME: from *an eke-name* (*eke* meaning 'addition': see **eke**[2]), misinterpreted, by wrong division, as *a neke name*.]

Nic·o·bar·ese /,nikəbä'rēz; -'rēs/ ▶ n. (pl. same) **1** a native or inhabitant of the Nicobar Islands. **2** a language spoken in the Nicobar Islands, distantly related to the Mon-Khmer and Munda families. It now has fewer than 20,000 speakers. ▶ adj. of or relating to the Nicobar Islands, their inhabitants, or their language.

Nic·o·bar Is·lands /'nikə,bär/ see **Andaman and Nicobar Islands**.

Ni·çois /nē'swä/ ▶ n. (fem. **Ni·çoise** /nē'swäz/) a native or inhabitant of the city of Nice, France. ▶ adj. of, relating to, or characteristic of Nice or its inhabitants. ■ [postpositive] denoting food that is characteristic of Nice or the surrounding region, typically garnished with tomatoes, capers, and anchovies: *salade Niçoise.*

Nic·ol prism /'nikəl/ ▶ n. a device for producing plane-polarized light, consisting of two pieces of optically clear calcite cemented together in the shape of a prism. [19th C.: William *Nicol* (died 1851), Scottish physicist.]

Nic·o·sia /,nikə'sēə/ the capital of Cyprus; pop. 186,000.

ni·co·ti·a·na /ni,kōsнē'änə; -'anə/ ▶ n. an ornamental plant (genus *Nicotiana*) of the nightshade family, related to tobacco, with tubular flowers that are particularly fragrant at night. [from mod. L. *nicotiana (herba)* 'tobacco (plant),' after Jean *Nicot*, 16th-C. French diplomat who introduced tobacco to France in 1560.]

nic·o·tin·a·mide /,nikə'tinə,mīd; -'tēn-/ ▶ n. Biochem. a compound, $(C_5H_4N)CONH_2$, that is the form in which nicotinic acid often occurs in nature.

nic·o·tin·a·mide ad·e·nine di·nu·cle·o·tide /'adn-in dī'n(y)ōōklēə,tīd/ ▶ n. see **NAD**.

nic·o·tine /'nikə,tēn/ ▶ n. a toxic colorless or yellowish oily liquid, $C_{10}H_{14}N_2$, that is the chief active constituent of tobacco. It acts as a stimulant in small doses, but in larger amounts blocks the action of autonomic nerve and skeletal muscle cells. [19th C.: from Fr., from **nicotiana** + **-ine**[4].]

nic·o·tine patch ▶n. a patch impregnated with nicotine and worn on the skin by a person trying to give up smoking. Nicotine is gradually absorbed into the bloodstream, helping reduce the craving for cigarettes.

nic·o·tin·ic ac·id /ˌnikəˈtinik; -ˈtēnik/ ▶n. Biochem. a vitamin of the B complex, $(C_5H_4N)COOH$, that is widely distributed in foods such as milk, wheat germ, and meat, and can be synthesized in the body from tryptophan. Its deficiency causes pellagra. — **nic·o·tin·ate** /-ˈtēˌnāt/ n.

nic·tate /ˈnikˌtāt/ (also **nic·ti·tate** /ˈniktiˌtāt/) ▶v. [intrans.] tech. (esp. of the eyelid) blink. — **nic·ta·tion** /ˈniktiˌtāt/ n. [17th C.: from L. *nictat-* 'blinked,' from the v. *nictare.*]

nic·ti·tat·ing mem·brane /ˈniktiˌtātiNG/ ▶n. Zool. a whitish or translucent membrane that forms an inner eyelid in birds, reptiles, and some mammals. It can be drawn across the eye to protect it from dust and keep it moist. Also called **THIRD EYELID**.

ni·da·tion /nīˈdāSHən/ ▶n. another term for **IMPLANTATION**. [19th C.: from L. *nidus* 'nest' + **-ATION**.]

nide /nīd/ ▶n. archaic a brood or nest of pheasants. [17th C.: from Fr. *nid* or L. *nidus* 'nest.']

ni·dic·o·lous /nīˈdikələs/ ▶adj. another term for **ALTRICIAL**. [20th C.: from L. *nidus* 'nest' + *-colus* 'inhabiting.']

nid·i·fi·ca·tion /ˌnidəfiˈkāSHən/ ▶n. Zool. nest-building. [17th C.: from L. *nidificat-* 'made into a nest' (from the v. *nidificare*, from *nidus* 'nest') + **-ATION**.]

ni·dif·u·gous /nīˈdifyəgəs/ ▶adj. another term for **PRECOCIAL**. [20th C.: from L. *nidus* 'nest' + *fugere* 'flee' + **-OUS**.]

ni·dus /ˈnīdəs/ ▶n. (pl. **-di** /-ˌdī/ or **-dus·es**) a place in which something is formed or deposited; a site of origin. ■ Med. a place in which bacteria have multiplied or may multiply; a focus of infection. [18th C.: from L., lit. 'nest.']

Nie·buhr /ˈnēˌbo͝or/, Reinhold (1892–1971), US theologian. He wrote *Moral Man and Immoral Society* (1932) and *The Irony of American History* (1952).

niece /nēs/ ▶n. a daughter of one's brother or sister, or of one's brother-in-law or sister-in-law. [ME: from OFr., based on L. *neptis* 'granddaughter,' fem. of *nepos* 'nephew, grandson.']

Nie·der·sach·sen /ˈnēdərˌsäksən/ German name for **LOWER SAXONY**.

ni·el·lo /nēˈelō/ ▶n. a black compound of sulfur with silver, lead, or copper, used for filling in engraved designs in silver or other metals. ■ such ornamental work: *plated objects were often further decorated with niello and gilding.* ■ objects decorated with this. — **ni·el·loed** adj. [19th C.: from Ital., from L. *nigellus*, dimin. of *niger* 'black.']

niels·bohr·i·um /ˌnēlzˈbôrēəm/ ▶n. a name proposed by the American Chemical Society for the chemical element of atomic number 107, now called **bohrium**. [mod. L., after *Niels Bohr* (see **BOHR**).]

Niel·sen /ˈnēlsən/, Carl August (1865–1931), Danish composer, best known for his six symphonies (1890–1925).

Nie·mey·er /ˈnēˌmīər/, Oscar (1907–), Brazilian architect; full name *Oscar Niemeyer Soares Filho.* He designed the main public buildings of Brasilia, 1950–60.

ni·en·te /nēˈentā/ ▶adv. & adj. Music (esp. as a direction) with a soft sound or tone gradually fading to nothing. [Ital., lit. 'nothing.']

Nier·stein·er /ˈni(ə)rˌstīnər; -ˌSHtīn-/ ▶n. a white Rhine wine produced in the region around Nierstein, a town in Germany.

Nietz·sche /ˈnēCHə; -CHē/, Friedrich Wilhelm (1844–1900), German philosopher. He repudiated Christianity's compassion for the weak and exalted the "will to power," formulating the idea of the *Übermensch* (superman). Notable works: *The Birth of Tragedy* (1872) and *Beyond Good and Evil* (1886). — **Nie·tzsche·an** /ˈnēCHēən/ adj. & n. **Ni·etzsche·an·ism** /ˈnēCHēəˌnizəm/ n.

ni·fed·i·pine /nīˈfedəpēn/ ▶n. Med. a synthetic compound that acts as a calcium antagonist and is used as a coronary vasodilator in the treatment of cardiac and circulatory disorders. [1970s: from *ni(tro-)* + *fe* (alt. of **PHENYL**) + **DI-**[1] + *p(yrid)ine.*]

Ni·fl·heim /ˈnivəlˌhām/ Scand. Mythol. an underworld of eternal cold, darkness, and mist inhabited by those who died of old age or illness. [from ON *Niflheimr.*]

nif·ty /ˈniftē/ ▶adj. (**-ti·er**, **-ti·est**) informal particularly good, skillful, or effective: *nifty footwork* | *a nifty little gadget.* ■ fashionable; stylish: *a nifty black shirt.* — **nif·ti·ly** adv. **nif·ti·ness** n. [19th C.: of unknown origin.]

Ni·ger /ˈnījər/ **1** a river in northwestern Africa that rises in Sierra Leone and flows in a great arc for 2,550 miles (4,100 km) into the Gulf of Guinea. **2** a landlocked country in West Africa. *See box.*

Ni·ger–Con·go ▶adj. denoting or belonging to a phylum of African languages, named after the rivers Niger and Congo. It comprises most of the languages spoken by the indigenous peoples of Africa south of the Sahara and includes the Bantu, Mande, Gur, and Kwa families.

Ni·ge·ri·a /nīˈji(ə)rēə/ a country on the coast of West Africa. *See box.* — **Ni·ge·ri·an** adj. & n.

nig·gard /ˈnigərd/ ▶n. a stingy or ungenerous person. ▶adj. archaic term for **NIGGARDLY**. [ME: alt. of earlier *nigon.*]

nig·gard·ly /ˈnigərdlē/ ▶adj. not generous; stingy: *the company was particularly niggardly with salaries* | *serving out the rations with a niggardly hand.* ■ meager; scanty: *their share is a niggardly 2.7 percent.* ▶adv. archaic in a stingy or meager manner. — **nig·gard·li·ness** n.

nig·ger /ˈnigər/ ▶n. offens. a contemptuous term for a black or dark-skinned person. [17th C. (as an adj.): from earlier *neger*, from Fr. *nègre*, from Sp. *negro* 'black' (see **NEGRO**).]
– USAGE The word **nigger** was used as an adjective denoting a black person as early as the 17th century and has long had strong offensive connotations. Today it remains one of the most racially offensive words in the language. Also referred to as 'the n-word,' **nigger** is sometimes used by black people in reference to other black people in a jocular or disparaging manner, or some variant in between (in somewhat the same way that *queer* has been adopted by some gay and lesbian people as a term of self-reference, acceptable only when used by those within the community).

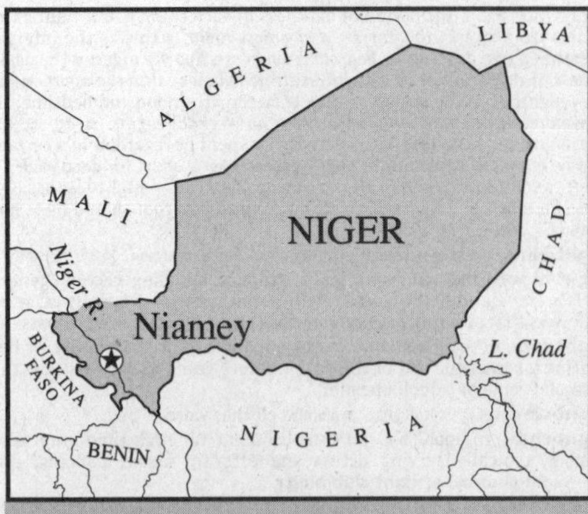

Niger

Official name: Republic of Niger
Location: West Africa, on the southern edge of the Sahara Desert
Area: 489,300 square miles (1,267,000 sq km)
Population: 11,360,000
Capital: Niamey
Languages: French (official), Hausa, other West African languages
Currency: CFA franc

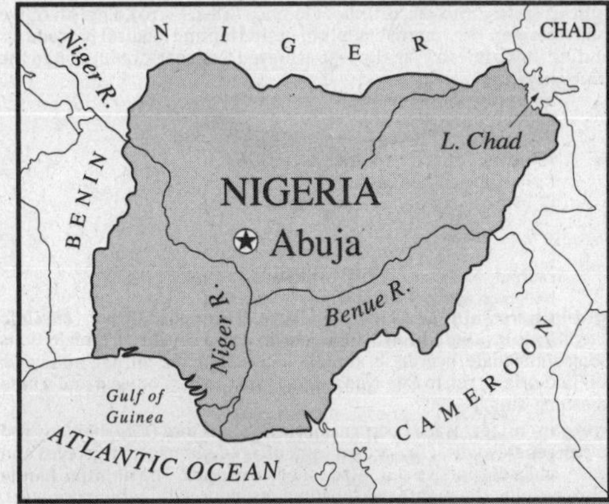

Nigeria

Official name: Federal Republic of Nigeria
Location: West Africa, bordered by Niger on the north and the Atlantic Ocean on the south
Area: 356,800 square miles (923,800 sq km)
Population: 137,253,000
Capital: Abuja
Languages: English (official), Hausa, Yoruba, Ibo, Fulani
Currency: naira

nig·gle /ˈnigəl/ ▶v. [intrans.] cause slight but persistent annoyance, discomfort, or anxiety: *a nasty leg wound which still **niggled at** him* | *a suspicion **niggled at** the back of her mind.* ■ [trans.] find fault with (someone) in a petty way: *he loved to niggle and criticize people.* ▶n. a trifling complaint, dispute, or criticism: *it is an excellent book except for my few niggles* | *I have a few niggles about design.* — **nig·gling·ly** adv. [17th C.: appar. of Scand. origin; cf. Norw. *nigla*.]

nigh /nī/ ▶adv., prep., & adj. **1** archaic or literary near: [as adj.] *departure time was nigh* | [as adv.] *they drew nigh unto the city.* **2** almost: [as adv.] *nigh on a thousand acres all told* | *a car weighing **nigh on** two tons* | *recovery will be **well nigh** impossible.* [OE *nēh, nēah*, of Gmc. origin; rel. to Du. *na*, Ger. *nah*.]

night /nīt/ ▶n. **1** the period of darkness in each twenty-four hours; the time from sunset to sunrise: *a moonless night.* ■ this as the interval between two days: *a two-bedroom cabin costs $90 per night.* ■ the darkness of night: *a line of watchfires stretched away into the night.* ■ literary nightfall. **2** the period of time between afternoon and bedtime; an evening: *he was not allowed to go out on weekday nights.* ■ [with adj.] an evening appointed for some activity, or spent or regarded in a certain way: *wasn't it a great **night out**?* ▶exclam. informal short for GOOD NIGHT.
– PHRASES **night and day** all the time; constantly. — **night·less** adj. [OE *neaht, niht*, rel. to Ger. *Nacht*, from an Indo-Eur. root shared by L. *nox* and Gk. *nux*.]

night blind·ness ▶n. less technical term for NYCTALOPIA.

night-bloom·ing ce·re·us ▶n. a tropical climbing cactus (genera *Hylocereus* and *Selenicereus*) with aerial roots and heavily scented flowers that open only at night and are typically pollinated by bats.

night·cap /ˈnītˌkap/ ▶n. **1** hist. a cap worn in bed. **2** an alcoholic or hot drink taken at the end of the day or before going to bed. **3** Baseball the second game of a doubleheader.

night·clothes /ˈnītˌklō(TH)z/ ▶plural n. clothes worn to bed.

night·club /ˈnītˌkləb/ ▶n. an establishment for nighttime entertainment, typically serving drinks and offering music, dancing, etc. — **night·club·ber** n. **night·club·bing** n.

night court ▶n. a criminal court that holds sessions at night for granting bail and quickly disposing of charges.

night crawl·er (also **night·crawl·er**) ▶n. an earthworm, in particular one that comes to the surface at night and is collected for use as fishing bait. ■ informal a person who is socially active at night.

night·dress /ˈnītˌdres/ ▶n. another term for NIGHTGOWN.

night·fall /ˈnītˌfôl/ ▶n. the onset of night; dusk.

night·gown /ˈnītˌgoun/ ▶n. **1** a light, loose garment worn by a woman or child in bed. **2** hist. a dressing gown.

night·hawk /ˈnītˌhôk/ ▶n. **1** an American nightjar with sharply pointed wings, in particular the **common nighthawk** (*Chordeiles minor*). **2** another term for NIGHT OWL.

night her·on ▶n. a small short-necked heron (genus *Nycticorax*) that is active mainly at night.

night·ie /ˈnītē/ ▶n. informal a nightgown.

Night·in·gale /ˈnītnˌgāl; ˈnītiNG-/, Florence (1820–1910), English nurse and reformer. Her improvements in sanitation and medical procedures during the Crimean War 1853–56 achieved a dramatic reduction in the mortality rate.

nightingale

night·in·gale /ˈnītnˌgāl; ˈnītiNG-/ ▶n. a small European thrush (*Luscinia megarhynchos*) with brownish plumage, noted for the rich melodious song of the male, heard esp. at night in breeding season. [OE *nihtegala*, of Gmc. origin; rel. to Ger. *Nachtigall*, from the base of NIGHT and a base meaning 'sing.']

night·jar /ˈnītˌjär/ ▶n. a nocturnal insectivorous bird (*Caprimulgus* and other genera) with gray-brown camouflaged plumage, large eyes and gape, and a distinctive call. Also called GOATSUCKER. The **nightjar family** also includes the nighthawks, pauraques, poor-wills, whip-poor-wills, and chuck-will's-widow.

night·life /ˈnītˌlīf/ ▶n. social activities or entertainment available at night in a town or city.

night·light /ˈnīt ˌlīt/ (also **night-light** or **night light**) ▶n. a small lamp, typically attached directly to an electrical outlet, providing a dim light during the night.

night·long /ˈnītˌlôNG/ ▶adj. lasting throughout the night: *a nightlong blizzard.*

night·ly /ˈnītlē/ ▶adj. **1** happening or done every night. **2** happening, done, or existing in the night. ▶adv. every night: *live music nightly.*

night·mare /ˈnītˌme(ə)r/ ▶n. a frightening or unpleasant dream. ■ a terrifying or very unpleasant experience or prospect. ■ a person, thing, or situation that is very difficult to deal with. — **night·mar·ish** adj. **night·mar·ish·ly** adv. [ME: from NIGHT + OE *mære* 'incubus.']

night owl ▶n. informal a person who is habitually active or wakeful at night.

night·rid·er /ˈnītˌrīdər/ ▶n. a member of a secret band of mounted men who committed nocturnal acts of violence and intimidation against blacks in the southern US during Reconstruction.

night·shade /ˈnītˌSHād/ ▶n. a plant (*Solanum* and other genera), typically having poisonous black or red berries. Its several species include the European **woody nightshade** (*S. dulcamara*), a climber with purple flowers and red berries.

night shift ▶n. the period of time scheduled for work at night, as in a factory or other institution. ■ the group of people working during this period.

night·shirt /ˈnītˌSHərt/ ▶n. a long, loose shirt worn to bed.

night·side /ˈnītˌsīd/ ▶n. **1** Astron. the side of a planet or moon that is facing away from the sun and is therefore in darkness. **2** the world at night; activities that take place during the night.

night soil ▶n. human excrement collected at night from buckets, and outhouses, sometimes used as manure.

night·spot /ˈnītˌspät/ ▶n. informal a nightclub.

night·stand /ˈnītˌstand/ (also **night table**) ▶n. a small low bedside table, typically having drawers.

night·stick /ˈnītˌstik/ ▶n. a police officer's club or billy.

night ter·rors ▶plural n. feelings of great fear experienced on suddenly waking in the night.

night·time /ˈnītˌtīm/ ▶n. the time between evening and morning; the time of darkness.

night vi·sion ▶n. the faculty of seeing in very low light, esp. after the eyes have become adapted. ▶adj. (**night-vi·sion**) denoting devices that enhance nighttime vision: *night-vision goggles.*

night watch·man ▶n. (pl. **-men**) a person whose job is to guard a building at night.

night·wear /ˈnītˌwe(ə)r/ ▶n. clothing suitable for wearing to bed.

ni·gres·cent /nīˈgresənt/ ▶adj. rare blackish. — **ni·gres·cence** n. [18th C.: from L. *nigrescent-* 'growing black,' from the v. *nigrescere*, from *niger, nigr-* 'black.']

nig·ri·tude /ˈnigriˌt(y)o͞od/ ▶n. rare blackness. [17th C.: from L. *nigritudo* 'blackness,' from *niger, nigr-* 'black.']

NIH ▶abbr. National Institutes of Health.

ni·hil·ism /ˈnīəˌlizəm; ˈnē-/ ▶n. the rejection of all religious and moral principles, often in the belief that life is meaningless. ■ Philos. extreme skepticism, according to which nothing in the world has a real existence. ■ hist. the doctrine of an extreme Russian revolutionary party *c.*1900, which found nothing to approve of in the established social order. — **ni·hil·ist** n. **ni·hil·is·tic** /ˌnīəˈlistik; ˌnēə-/ adj. [19th C.: from L. *nihil* 'nothing' + -ISM.]

ni·hil·i·ty /nīˈhilitē; ˈnē-/ ▶n. rare nonexistence; nothingness.

ni·hil ob·stat /ˈnīhil ˈäbstat/ ▶n. (in the Roman Catholic Church) a certification by an official censor that a book is not doctrinally or morally objectionable. [L., lit. 'nothing hinders.']

Ni·i·hau /ˈnē-ēˌhou/ an island in Hawaii.

Ni·jin·sky /nəˈZHinskē; -ˈjin-; nyi-/, Vaslav Fomich (1890–1950), Russian ballet dancer and choreographer.

-nik ▶suffix (forming nouns) denoting a person associated with a specified thing or quality: *beatnik.* [from Russ. (on the pattern of *(sput)nik*) and Yiddish.]

ni·kah /niˈkä/ ▶n. a Muslim marriage ceremony. [Urdu and Arab.]

Ni·ke /ˈnīkē/ Gk. Mythol. the goddess of victory.

Nik·kei in·dex /ˈnēkā/ a figure indicating the relative price of representative shares on the Tokyo Stock Exchange. Also called **Nikkei average**. [1970s: abbrev. of *Nihon Keizai Shimbun* 'Japanese Economic Journal.']

nil /nil/ ▶n. zero, esp. as a score in certain games. ▶adj. nonexistent: *his chances for survival were nil.* [19th C.: from L., contr. of *nihil* 'nothing.']

nil de·spe·ran·dum /ˈnil ˌdespəˈrändəm/ ▶exclam. do not despair; never despair. [from L. *nil desperandum Teucro duce* 'no need to despair with Teucer as your leader.']

Nile /nīl/ a river in eastern Africa, the longest river in the world, that rises near Lake Victoria and flows 4,160 miles (6,695 km) north to empty through a large delta into the Mediterranean Sea. See also BLUE NILE, ALBERT NILE, VICTORIA NILE, WHITE NILE.

Nile blue ▶n. a pale greenish blue.

Nile green ▶n. a pale bluish green.

nil·gai /ˈnilgī/ ▶n. a large Indian antelope (*Boselaphus tragocamelus*) the male of which has a blue-gray coat and short horns, and the female a tawny coat and no horns. [18th C.: from Hindi *nīlgāī*, from *nīl* 'blue' + *gāī* 'cow.']

Ni·lo-Sa·har·an /ˌnīlō səˈharən; -ˈhär-/ ▶adj. denoting or belonging to a phylum of languages that includes the Nilotic family together with certain other languages of northern and eastern Africa. ▶n. this phylum of languages.

Ni·lot·ic /nīˈlätik/ ▶adj. **1** of or relating to the Nile River or to the Nile region of Africa. **2** denoting or belonging to a subgroup of Nilo-Saharan languages spoken in Egypt, Sudan, Kenya, and Tanzania. [via L. from Gk. *Neilōtikos*, from *Neilos* 'Nile.']

nim /nim/ ▶n. a game in which two players alternately take one or more objects from one of a number of heaps, each trying to take, or to compel the other to take, the last remaining object. [20th C.: appar. from archaic *nim* 'to take' or from Ger. *nimm!* 'take!,' imper. of *nehmen*.]

nim·ble /ˈnimbəl/ ▶adj. (**-bler, -blest**) quick and light in movement or action; agile. ■ (of the mind) quick to comprehend. — **nim·ble·ness** n.

nim·bly adv. [OE *nǣmel* 'quick to seize or comprehend,' rel. to *niman* 'take,' of Gmc. origin.]

nim·bo·stra·tus /ˌnimbōˈstratəs; -ˈstrā-/ ▶n. a type of cloud forming a thick uniform gray layer at low altitude, from which rain or snow often falls. [19th C.: mod. L., from NIMBUS + STRATUS.]

nim·bus /ˈnimbəs/ ▶n. (pl. **-bi** /-ˌbī/ or **-bus·es**) **1** a luminous cloud or a halo surrounding a supernatural being or a saint. ■ a light, aura, color, etc., that surrounds someone or something. **2** a large gray rain cloud: [as adj.] *nimbus clouds.* [17th C.: from L., lit. 'cloud, aureole.']

NIMBY /ˈnimbē/ (also **Nimby**) ▶n. (pl. **NIMBYs**) acronym for *not in my backyard*, referring to those who object to the siting of something unpleasant or dangerous in their own neighborhood, such as a landfill. — **Nim·by·ism** n.

nim·i·ny-pim·i·ny /ˈniməne ˈpiməne/ ▶adj. affectedly prim or refined: *she had a niminy-piminy ladylike air.* [18th C.: fanciful coinage.]

Nimitz /ˈnimits/, Chester William (1885–1966), US admiral. He commanded the Pacific Fleet during World War II. A noted strategist, he introduced "island hopping."

nim·rod /ˈnimräd/ ▶n. esp. humorous a skillful hunter. [16th C.: from Heb. *Nimrōd*, great-grandson of Noah.]

Nim·rud /ˈnimˌro͞od/ modern name of an ancient Mesopotamian city on the east bank of the Tigris south of Nineveh, near the modern city of Mosul.

Nin /nin; nēn/, Anaïs (1903–77), US writer, noted for her diaries. Her novels include *House of Incest* (1936).

nin·com·poop /ˈninkəmˌpo͞op; ˈnING-/ ▶n. a foolish or stupid person. [17th C.: perh. from the given name *Nicholas*.]

nine /nīn/ ▶cardinal number equivalent to the product of three and three; one more than eight, or one less than ten; 9. (Roman numeral: **ix** or **IX**.) ■ a group or unit of nine individuals. ■ nine years old. ■ nine o'clock. ■ a size of garment or other merchandise denoted by nine. ■ a playing card with nine pips. ■ (**the Nine**) Gk. Mythol. the nine Muses.
– PHRASES **dressed to the nines** see DRESS. [OE *nigon*, rel. to Ger. *neun*, from an Indo-Eur. root shared by L. *novem* and Gk. *ennea*.]

9/11 /ˈnīn iˈlevən/ (also **September 11th**) ▶n. September 11, 2001. On this date, two hijacked commercial airliners were flown into the World Trade Center in lower Manhattan. A third hijacked airliner was crashed into the Pentagon, and a fourth went down in a field in Pennsylvania.

nine·fold /ˈnīnˌfōld/ ▶adj. nine times as great or as numerous. ■ having nine parts or elements. ▶adv. by nine times; to nine times the number or amount.

nine·pins /ˈnīnˌpinz/ ▶plural n. [usu. treated as sing.] a British game similar to bowling, using nine wooden pins and played in an alley. ■ [treated as pl.] the pins used in this game.

nine·teen /nīnˈtēn; ˈnīnˌtēn/ ▶cardinal number one more than eighteen; nine more than ten; 19. (Roman numeral: **xix** or **XIX**.) ■ nineteen years old. — **nine·teenth** /nīnˈtēnTH; ˈnīnˌtēnTH/ ordinal number. [OE *nigontȳne*.]

nine·teenth hole ▶n. informal the bar in a golf clubhouse, as reached after a standard round of eighteen holes.

nine-to-five ▶adj. used in reference to typical hours of work in an office, often to express an idea of routine or predictability: *a nine-to-five job.* ▶n. an occupation involving such hours. — **nine-to-fiv·er** n.

nine·ty /ˈnīntē/ ▶n. (pl. **-ties**) equivalent to the product of nine and ten; ten less than one hundred; 90. (Roman numeral: **xc** or **XC**.) ■ (**nineties**) the numbers from 90 to 99, esp. the years of a century or of a person's life. ■ ninety years old. ■ ninety miles an hour. — **nine·ti·eth** /-tēiTH/ ordinal number **nine·ty·fold** adj. & adv. [OE *nigontig*.]

Nin·e·veh /ˈninəvə/ an ancient city located on the eastern bank of the Tigris River, opposite the modern city of Mosul.

Ning·xia /ˈnINGˈSHä/ (also **Ning·sia**) an autonomous region of north central China; capital, Yinchuan.

nin·ja /ˈninjə/ ▶n. a person skilled in ninjutsu. [Japanese, lit. 'spy.']

nin·jut·su /ninˈjo͝otso͞o/ ▶n. the traditional Japanese technique of espionage, characterized by stealthy movement and camouflage. [Japanese, from *nin* 'stealth' + *jutsu* 'art, science.']

nin·ny /ˈninē/ ▶n. (pl. **-nies**) informal a foolish person. [16th C.: perh. from INNOCENT.]

ni·non /ˈnēnän/ ▶n. a lightweight sheer or silk fabric used for curtains and women's garments. [20th C.: from Fr.]

ninth /nīnTH/ ▶ordinal number constituting number nine in a sequence; 9th. ■ (**a ninth/one ninth**) each of nine equal parts into which something is or may be divided. ■ the ninth finisher or position in a race or competition. ■ the ninth and final inning of a regulation baseball game. ■ the ninth grade of a school. ■ Music an interval spanning nine consecutive notes in a diatonic scale. ■ Music the note that is higher by this interval than the tonic of a diatonic scale or root of a chord. ■ Music a chord in which the ninth note above the root forms an important component. — **ninth·ly** adv.

Ni·o·be /ˈnīəbē/ Gk. Mythol. the daughter of Tantalus. Apollo and Artemis, enraged because Niobe boasted herself superior to their mother Leto, slew her children and turned her to stone.

ni·o·bi·um /nīˈōbēəm/ ▶n. the chemical element of atomic number 41, a silver-gray metal of the transition series, used in superconducting alloys. (Symbol: **Nb**) [19th C.: mod. L., from NIOBE, by association with her father Tantalus (so named because the element was first found in TANTALITE).]

Nip /nip/ ▶n. offens. a Japanese person. [20th C.: abbrev. of the synonym *Nipponese*, from *Nippon*.]

nip[1] /nip/ ▶v. (**nipped, nip·ping**) [trans.] **1** pinch, squeeze, or bite sharply. ■ (of the cold or frost) cause sharp pain or harm to. ■ (**nip something off**) remove something by pinching or squeezing sharply. **2** informal defeat by a narrow margin. **3** informal steal or snatch (something). ▶n. a sharp pinch, squeeze, or bite. ■ a feeling of biting cold.
– PHRASES **nip something in the bud** suppress or destroy something, esp. at an early stage. [ME: prob. of Low Ger. or Du. origin.]

nip[2] ▶n. a small quantity or sip of liquor. ▶v. (**nipped, nip·ping**) [intrans.] take a sip or sips of liquor. [18th C.: prob. from *nipperkin* 'small measure'; cf. Du. *nippen* 'to sip.']

ni·pa /ˈnēpə/ (also **nipa palm**) ▶n. a palm tree (*Nypa fruticans*) with creeping roots, characteristic of mangrove swamps in India and the Pacific islands. [16th C.: via Sp. or Port. from Malay *nīpah*.]

nip and tuck ▶adv. & adj. neck and neck; closely contested. ▶n. informal a cosmetic surgical operation.

nip·per /ˈnipər/ ▶n. **1** informal a child, esp. a small boy. **2** (**nippers**) pliers, pincers, forceps, or a similar tool for gripping or cutting. **3** an insect or other creature that nips or bites. ■ (usu. **nippers**) the grasping claw of a crab or lobster.

nip·ple /ˈnipəl/ ▶n. **1** the small projection of a woman's or girl's breast in which the mammary ducts terminate and from which milk can be secreted. ■ the corresponding vestigial structure in a male. ■ the teat of a female animal. ■ the flexible tip of a baby's pacifier or bottle. **2** a small projection on a device or machine, esp. one from which oil, grease, or other fluid is dispensed in small amounts. ■ a short section of pipe with a screw thread at each end for coupling. [16th C.: perh. a dimin. of NEB.]

Nip·pon /niˈpän/ Japanese name for JAPAN. — **Nip·pon·ese** /ˌnipəˈnēz; -ˈnēs/ n. (dated or offens.) & adj.

nip·py /ˈnipē/ ▶adj. (**-pi·er, -pi·est**) informal **1** (of the weather) rather cold; chilly. **2** inclined to nip or bite. **3** esp. Brit. quick; nimble. — **nip·pi·ly** adv.

nir·va·na /nərˈvänə; nir-/ ▶n. Buddhism a transcendent state in which there is neither suffering, desire, nor sense of self, and the subject is released from the effects of karma and samsara. ■ Hinduism liberation of the soul from the effects of karma and from bodily existence. ■ a state of perfect happiness; an ideal or idyllic place. [from Sanskrit *nirvāṇa*, from *nirvā* 'be extinguished,' from *nis* 'out' + *vā-* 'to blow.']

Niš /nēSH/ (also **Nish**) a historically dominant industrial city in southeastern Serbia, on the Nišava River near its confluence with the Morava River; pop. 175,000.

Ni·san /ˈnisən; nēˈsän/ ▶n. (in the Jewish calendar) the seventh month of the civil and first of the religious year, usually coinciding with parts of March and April. [from Heb. *nīsān*.]

ni·sei /nēˈsā; ˈnēsā/ (also **Ni·sei**) ▶n. (pl. same or **-seis**) a person born in the US or Canada whose parents immigrated from Japan. Compare with ISSEI and SANSEI. [1940s: from Japanese, lit. 'second generation.']

ni·si /ˈnīsī/ ▶adj. [postpositive] Law (of a decree, order, or rule) taking effect or having validity only after certain specified conditions are met. [19th C.: from L., lit. 'unless.']

Nis·sen hut /ˈnisən/ ▶n. esp. Brit. a hut made of corrugated iron with a concrete floor, similar to a Quonset hut. [20th C.: Peter N. *Nissen* (1871–1930), British engineer.]

nit /nit/ ▶n. the egg or young form of a louse or other parasitic insect, esp. the egg of a head louse attached to a human hair.
– PHRASES **pick nits** look for and criticize small or insignificant faults or errors; nitpick. — **nit·ty** adj. [OE *hnitu*, of West Gmc. origin; rel. to Ger. *Nisse*.]

nite /nīt/ ▶n. informal simplified spelling of NIGHT.

ni·ter /ˈnītər/ (Brit. **ni·tre**) ▶n. another term for POTASSIUM NITRATE. [ME: from OFr., from L. *nitrum*, from Gk. *nitron*.]

Ni·te·rói /ˌnētəˈroi/ a city port on the coast of southeastern Brazil; pop. 455,000.

nit·er·y /ˈnītərē/ ▶n. informal (pl. **-er·ies**) a nightclub.

ni·ti·nol /ˈnitn-äl; -ôl/ ▶n. an alloy of nickel and titanium. [1960s: from NI and TI + *Naval Ordnance Laboratory*.]

nit·pick·ing /ˈnitˌpikING/ informal ▶adj. looking for small or unimportant errors or faults, esp. in order to criticize unnecessarily. ▶n. such fault-finding. — **nit·pick** v. **nit·pick·er** n.

ni·trate /ˈnītrāt/ ▶n. Chem. a salt or ester of nitric acid, containing the anion NO_3^- or the group $-NO_3$. ■ sodium nitrate, potassium nitrate, or ammonium nitrate, used as fertilizer. ▶v. [trans.] treat (a substance) with nitric acid to introduce nitro groups. — **ni·tra·tion** /nīˈtrāSHən/ n. [18th C.: from Fr. (see NITER, -ATE[1]).]

ni·tre ▶n. British spelling of NITER.

ni·tric /ˈnītrik/ ▶adj. Chem. of or containing nitrogen with a higher valence, often five. Compare with NITROUS. [18th C.: from Fr. *(acide) nitrique* (see NITER, -IC).]

ni·tric ac·id ▶n. Chem. a colorless or pale yellow liquid acid, HNO_3, that is corrosive and poisonous and has strong oxidizing properties, made in the laboratory by distilling nitrates with sulfuric acid.

ni·tric ox·ide ▶n. Chem. a colorless toxic gas, NO, formed in many reactions in which nitric acid is reduced, as in reaction with copper.

ni·tride /ˈnītrīd/ ▶n. Chem. a binary compound of nitrogen with a more electropositive element. ▶ **v.** [trans.] Metallurgy heat steel in the presence of ammonia to increase hardness and corrosion resistance.

ni·tri·fy /ˈnītrəˌfī/ ▶ **v.** **1** (**-fies, -fied**) [trans.] Chem. convert (ammonia or another nitrogen compound) into nitrites or nitrates. **2** impregnate with nitrogen or nitrogen compounds. — **ni·tri·fi·ca·tion** /ˌnītrəfiˈkāshən/ **n.**

ni·trile /ˈnītril; -trīl/ ▶ **n.** Chem. an organic compound containing a cyanide group –CN bound to an alkyl group.

ni·trite /ˈnītrīt/ ▶ **n.** Chem. a salt or ester of nitrous acid, containing the anion NO_2– or the group $-NO_2$.

ni·tro /ˈnītrō/ ▶ **n.** short for NITROGLYCERIN. ▶ **adj.** Chem. containing the NITRO GROUP.

nitro- ▶ **comb. form** of or containing nitric acid, nitrates, or nitrogen: *nitrogenous.* ■ Chem. containing a nitro group: *nitromethane.* [from NITER or NITROGEN.]

ni·tro·ben·zene /ˌnītrōˈbenzēn/ ▶ **n.** Chem. a yellow oily liquid, $C_6H_5NO_2$, made by nitrating benzene, used in chemical synthesis.

ni·tro·cel·lu·lose /ˌnītrōˈselyəˌlōs/ ▶ **n.** Chem. a highly flammable material made by treating cellulose with concentrated nitric acid, used to make explosives and celluloid. Also called CELLULOSE NITRATE.

ni·tro·fur·an·to·in /ˌnītrōˌfyo͝oˈrantōin/ ▶ **n.** Med. a synthetic compound, $C_8H_6N_4O_5$, with antibacterial properties, used to treat infections of the urinary tract.

ni·tro·gen /ˈnītrəjən/ ▶ **n.** the chemical element of atomic number 7, a colorless, odorless unreactive gas that forms about 78 percent of the earth's atmosphere. Liquid nitrogen (made by distilling liquid air) boils at 77.4 kelvins (–195.8°C) and is used as a coolant. (Symbol: **N**)

ni·tro·gen cy·cle ▶ **n.** Ecol. the series of processes by which nitrogen and its compounds are interconverted in the environment and in living organisms, including nitrogen fixation and decomposition.

ni·tro·gen di·ox·ide ▶ **n.** Chem. a reddish-brown poisonous gas, NO_2, used in the manufacture of nitric acid. It is also an air pollutant, a constituent of untreated automobile exhaust.

ni·tro·gen fix·a·tion ▶ **n.** Biol. the chemical processes by which atmospheric nitrogen is assimilated into organic compounds, esp. by certain microorganisms as part of the nitrogen cycle.

ni·tro·gen mon·ox·ide ▶ **n.** another term for NITRIC OXIDE.

ni·tro·gen mus·tard ▶ **n.** Chem. any of a group of organic compounds containing the group $-N(CH_2CH_2Cl)_2$. They are powerful cytotoxic alkylating agents, used in chemotherapy to treat cancer.

ni·tro·gen nar·co·sis ▶ **n.** Med. a drowsy state induced by breathing air under higher than atmospheric pressure, e.g., in deep-sea diving.

ni·trog·e·nous /nīˈträjənəs/ ▶ **adj.** containing nitrogen in chemical combination.

ni·tro·glyc·er·in /ˌnītrōˈglisərin/ (also **ni·tro·gly·ce·rine**) ▶ **n.** Chem. an explosive yellow liquid, $CH_2(NO_3)CH(NO_3)CH_2(NO_3)$, made by nitrating glycerol, used in explosives such as dynamite. It is also used in medicine as a vasodilator in the treatment of angina pectoris.

ni·tro group ▶ **n.** Chem. a group, $-NO_2$, attached to an organic group in a molecule.

ni·tro·meth·ane /ˌnītrōˈmeTHān/ ▶ **n.** Chem. an oily liquid, CH_3NO_2, used as a solvent and as a rocket fuel.

ni·tros·a·mine /nīˈtrōsəmēn/ ▶ **n.** Chem. a compound containing the group =NNO attached to two organic groups. Compounds of this kind are generally carcinogenic. [19th C.: from *nitroso-*.]

ni·trous /ˈnītrəs/ ▶ **adj.** **1** Chem. of or containing nitrogen with a lower valence, often three. Compare with NITRIC. **2** of nitrogen; nitrogenous.

ni·trous ac·id ▶ **n.** Chem. an unstable and weak acid, HNO_2, existing only in solution and in the gas phase, made by the action of acids on nitrites.

ni·trous ox·ide ▶ **n.** Chem. a colorless gas, N_2O, with a sweetish odor, prepared by heating ammonium nitrate. It produces exhilaration or anesthesia when inhaled and is used as an anesthetic and as an aerosol propellant. Also called LAUGHING GAS.

nit·ty-grit·ty /ˈnitēˈgritē/ ▶ **n.** (**the nitty-gritty**) informal the most important aspects or practical details of a subject or situation. [1960s: of unknown origin.]

nit·wit /ˈnitˌwit/ ▶ **n.** informal a silly or foolish person (often as a general term of abuse). — **nit·wit·ted adj. nit·wit·ted·ness n.** [20th C.: appar. from NIT + WIT[1].]

Ni·ue /nēˈo͞o/ an island territory in the South Pacific Ocean in free association with New Zealand; pop. 2,239; capital, Alofi.

NIV ▶ **abbr.** New International Version (of the Bible)

ni·val /ˈnīvəl/ ▶ **adj.** of, relating to, or characteristic of a region of perpetual snow. [17th C.: from L. *nivalis*, from *nix, niv-* 'snow.']

niv·e·ous /ˈnivēəs/ ▶ **adj.** literary snowy or resembling snow. [17th C.: from L. *niveus*.]

nix[1] /niks/ informal ▶ **n.** nothing. ▶ **v.** [trans.] put an end to; cancel: *he nixed the deal just before it was to be signed.* [18th C. (as a n.): from Ger., var. of *nichts* 'nothing.']

nix[2] ▶ **n.** (fem. **nix·ie** /ˈniksē/) (in Germanic mythology) a water sprite. [19th C.: from Ger.]

Nix·on /ˈniksən/, Richard Milhous (1913–94), 37th president of the US 1969–74. A Republican, he restored Sino-American diplomatic relations by his visit to China in 1972, and in 1973 he oversaw negotiations to end the Vietnam War. He was reelected in 1972 but was forced to resign after his involvement in the Watergate scandal was revealed.

Ni·zam /niˈzäm; -ˈzam/ ▶ **n.** hist. **1** the title of the hereditary ruler of Hyderabad. [abbrev. of Urdu *nizām-al-mulk* 'administrator of the realm.'] **2** (**the nizam**) the Turkish regular army. [abbrev. of Turk. *nizām askeri* 'regular soldier.']

Ni·za·ri /niˈzärē/ ▶ **n.** a member of a Muslim sect that split from the Ismaili branch in 1094 over disagreement about the succession to the caliphate.

Nizh·ni Nov·go·rod /ˈnizHnē ˈnôvgərəd/ a city in western Russia on the Volga River; pop. 1,443,000. Former name (1932–91): GORKY.

Nizh·ni Ta·gil /ˈnizHnē təˈgil/ a city in central Russia, in the Ural Mountains; pop. 440,000.

NJ ▶ **abbr.** New Jersey (in official postal use).

Nkru·mah /(ə)NGˈkro͞omə/, Kwame (1909–72), president of Ghana 1960–66.

NL ▶ **abbr.** Baseball National League.

NLF ▶ **abbr.** National Liberation Front.

NLP ▶ **abbr.** ■ natural language processing. ■ neurolinguistic programming.

NLRB ▶ **abbr.** National Labor Relations Board.

NM ▶ **abbr.** New Mexico (in official postal use).

nm ▶ **abbr.** ■ nanometer. ■ nautical mile.

n.m. ▶ **abbr.** nautical mile.

N.Mex. ▶ **abbr.** New Mexico.

NMI ▶ **abbr.** no middle initial.

NMR Physics ▶ **abbr.** nuclear magnetic resonance.

NNE ▶ **abbr.** north-north-east.

NNP ▶ **abbr.** net national product.

NNW ▶ **abbr.** north-northwest.

No[1] ▶ **symb.** the chemical element nobelium.

No[2] ▶ **n.** var. of NOH.

No. ▶ **abbr.** ■ North. ■ (also **no.**) number: *No. 27.*

no /nō/ ▶ **adj.** **1** not any: *there is no excuse.* **2** used to indicate that something is quite the opposite of what is being specified: *it was no easy task persuading her | Toby is no fool.* **3** hardly any: *you'll be back in no time.* **4** used in notices or slogans forbidding or rejecting something specified: *no nukes.* ▶ **exclam.** used to give a negative response: *"Is anything wrong?" "No."* ■ expressing disagreement or contradiction: *"This is boring." "No, it's not!"* ■ expressing agreement with or affirmation of a negative statement: *they would never cause a fuss, oh no.* ■ expressing shock or disappointment at something one has heard or discovered: ***oh no**, look at this!* ▶ **adv.** [with comparative] not at all; to no extent: *they were no more able to perform the task than I was.* ▶ **n.** (pl. **noes**) a negative answer or decision, as in voting.

– PHRASES **no can do** informal I am unable to do it. **the noes have it** the negative votes are in the majority. **no less** see LESS. **no longer** not now as formerly. **no more** see MORE. **no place** nowhere. **no sooner —— than** see SOON. **no way** informal under no circumstances; not at all: *You think she's alone? No way.* **or no** or not: *she'd have ridden there, winter or no.* **—— or no ——** regardless of the specified thing: *recession or no recession there is always going to be a shortage of good people.* [OE *nō, nā* (adv.), from *ne* 'not' + *ō, ā* 'ever.']

NOAA ▶ **abbr.** National Oceanic and Atmospheric Administration.

no-ac·count informal ▶ **adj.** of little or no importance, value, or use; worthless. ▶ **n.** such a person.

No·a·chi·an /nōˈākēən/ ▶ **adj.** **1** of or relating to the biblical patriarch Noah or his time. **2** Astron. of, relating to, or denoting an early geological period on the planet Mars.

No·ah /ˈnōə/ (in the Bible) a patriarch, who according to a story in Genesis, made the ark that saved his family and specimens of every animal from the Flood.

nob[1] /näb/ ▶ **n.** Brit., informal a person of wealth or high social position. — **nob·by adj.** [17th C.: of unknown origin.]

nob[2] ▶ **n.** informal a person's head. [17th C.: appar. a var. of KNOB.]

nob·ble /ˈnäbəl/ ▶ **v.** [trans.] Brit., informal **1** try to influence or thwart (someone or something) by underhanded or unfair methods: *an attempt to nobble the jury.* ■ accost (someone), esp. in order to persuade them to do something: *people always tried to nobble her at parties.* ■ tamper with (a racehorse or greyhound) to prevent it from winning a race, esp. by giving it a drug. **2** obtain dishonestly; steal. ■ seize. — **nob·bler n.** [19th C.: prob. a var. of dial. *knobble, knubble* 'knock.']

No·bel /nōˈbel/, Alfred Bernhard (1833–96), Swedish chemist, engineer, and philanthropist. He invented dynamite in 1866, making a large fortune that enabled him to endow the prizes that bear his name.

No·bel·ist /nōˈbelist/ ▶ **n.** a winner of a Nobel Prize.

no·bel·i·um /nōˈbelēəm/ ▶ **n.** the chemical element of atomic number 102, a radioactive metal of the actinide series. (Symbol: **No**) [1950s: mod. L., from the name NOBEL + -IUM.]

No·bel Prize /ˈnōbel/ ▶ **n.** any of six international prizes awarded annually for outstanding work in physics, chemistry, physiology or medicine, literature, economics (since 1969), and the promotion of peace. — **No·bel Prize win·ner n.**

Nob Hill /näb/ a commercial district of northern San Francisco in California, long noted for the homes of the wealthy ("nobs").

no·bil·i·ty /nōˈbilitē/ ▶ **n.** (pl. **-ties**) **1** the quality of being noble in character, mind, birth, or rank. **2** (usu. **the nobility**) the group of people belonging to the noble class in a country, esp. those with a hereditary or honorary title: *a member of the English nobility.* [ME: from OFr. *nobilite* or L. *nobilitas*, from *nobilis*.]

no·ble /'nōbəl/ ▶ **adj.** (**-bler, -blest**) **1** belonging to a hereditary class with high social or political status; aristocratic. **2** having or showing fine personal qualities or high moral principles and ideals. ■ of imposing or magnificent size or appearance. ■ of excellent or superior quality. ▶ **n. 1** (esp. in former times) a person of noble rank or birth. **2** hist. a former English gold coin. — **no·ble·ness n. no·bly adv.** [ME: from OFr., from L. *(g)nobilis* 'noted, highborn,' from an Indo-Eur. root shared by **KNOW**.]

no·ble gas ▶ **n.** Chem. any of the gaseous elements helium, neon, argon, krypton, xenon, and radon, occupying Group 0 (18) of the periodic table.

no·ble·man /'nōbəlmən/ ▶ **n.** (pl. **-men**) a man who belongs to the noble class.

no·ble met·al ▶ **n.** Chem. a metal (e.g., gold, silver, or platinum) that resists chemical action, does not corrode, and is not easily attacked by acids.

no·ble rot ▶ **n.** a gray mold (from the fungus *Botrytis cinerea*) that is deliberately cultivated on grapes to enhance the making of certain sweet wines.

no·ble sav·age ▶ **n.** (usu. **the noble savage**) a representative of primitive humankind as idealized in Romantic literature, symbolizing the innate goodness of humanity free from the corruption of civilization.

no·blesse /nō'bles/ ▶ **n.** the nobility.
– PHRASES **noblesse oblige** /nō'bles ō'blēzн/ the inferred responsibility of privileged people to act with generosity and nobility toward those less privileged. [Fr.]

no·ble·wom·an /'nōbəl,wo͝omən/ ▶ **n.** (pl. **-wom·en**) a woman who belongs to the noble class.

no·bod·y /'nō,bädē; -bədē/ ▶ **pron.** no person; no one: *nobody was at home.* ▶ **n.** (pl. **-bod·ies**) a person of no importance or authority: *they went from nobodies to superstars.*
– PHRASES **be nobody's fool** see **FOOL**. **like nobody's business** see **BUSINESS**. [ME: orig. as *no body*.]

no-brain·er ▶ **n.** informal something that requires or involves little or no mental effort.

no·ci·cep·tive /,nōsi'septiv/ ▶ **adj.** Physiol. of, relating to, or denoting pain arising from the stimulation of nerve cells. [20th C.: from L. *nocere* 'to harm' + **RECEPTIVE**.]

no·ci·cep·tor /,nōsi'septər/ ▶ **n.** Physiol. a sensory receptor for painful stimuli. [20th C.: from L. *nocere* 'to harm' + **RECEPTOR**.]

nock /näk/ ▶ **n.** Archery a notch at either end of a bow for holding the string. ■ a notch at the back end of an arrow into which the bowstring fits. ▶ **v.** [trans.] fit (an arrow) to the bowstring to ready it for shooting. [ME: perh. from MDu. *nocke* 'point, tip.']

no-'count (also **no-count**) ▶ **adj.** another term for **NO-ACCOUNT**.

noc·tam·bu·list /näk'tambyəlist/ ▶ **n.** rare a sleepwalker. — **noc·tam·bu·lism n.** [18th C.: from L. *nox, noct-* 'night' + *ambulare* 'walk' + **-IST**.]

noc·ti·lu·ca /,näktə'lo͞okə/ ▶ **n.** (pl. **-lu·cae** /-'lo͞o,sē/) a roughly spherical marine dinoflagellate (genus *Noctiluca*) that is strongly phosphorescent, esp. when disturbed. [mod. L., from L., lit. 'night light, lantern.']

noc·ti·lu·cent cloud /,näktə'lo͞osənt/ ▶ **n.** a high-altitude cloud that is luminous at night, esp. in summer in high latitudes. [19th C.: from L. *nox, noct-* 'night' + *lucere* 'to shine' + **-ENT**.]

noc·tu·id /'näkcнo͞owid/ ▶ **n.** Entomol. a moth of a large family (Noctuidae) whose members typically have dull forewings and pale or colorful hind wings. [19th C.: from mod. L. *Noctuidae* (pl.), based on L. *noctua* 'owl.']

noc·tule /'näkcнo͞ol/ ▶ **n.** a large golden-brown bat (*Nyctalus noctula*, family Vespertilionidae) native to Eurasia and North Africa with long slender wings, rounded ears, and a short muzzle. [18th C.: from Fr., from Ital. *nottola* 'bat,' lit. 'small night creature.']

noc·turn /'näktərn/ ▶ **n.** (in the Roman Catholic Church) a part of matins originally said at night. [ME: from OFr. *nocturne* or eccles. Latin *nocturnum*, neut. of L. *nocturnus* 'of the night.']

noc·tur·nal /näk'tərnl/ ▶ **adj.** done, occurring, or active at night: *most owls are nocturnal.* — **noc·tur·nal·ly adv.**

noc·tur·nal e·mis·sion ▶ **n.** an involuntary ejaculation of semen during sleep.

noc·turne /'näk,tərn/ ▶ **n. 1** Music a short composition of a romantic or dreamy character suggestive of night, typically for piano. **2** Art a picture of a night scene. [19th C.: Fr.]

noc·u·ous /'näkyo͞oəs/ ▶ **adj.** literary noxious, harmful, or poisonous. [17th C.: from L. *nocuus* (from *nocere* 'to hurt') + **-OUS**.]

nod /näd/ ▶ **v.** (**nod·ded, nod·ding**) **1** [intrans.] lower and raise one's head slightly and briefly, esp. in greeting, assent, or understanding, or to give someone a signal: *he nodded to Monica* | [trans.] *she nodded her head in agreement.* ■ [trans.] signify or express (greeting, assent, or understanding) in this way. ■ [intrans.] draw or direct attention to someone or something by moving one's head: *he nodded toward the corner of the room.* ■ [intrans.] move one's head up and down repeatedly: *he shut his eyes, nodding to the beat.* **2** [intrans.] have one's head fall forward when drowsy or asleep: *Anna nodded over her book.* ▶ **n.** an act of nodding the head. ■ fig. a gesture of acknowledgment or concession.
– PHRASES **a nodding acquaintance** a slight acquaintance with a person or cursory knowledge of a subject. **get the nod 1** be selected or approved. **2** receive a signal or information. **give someone/something the nod 1** select or approve someone or something. **2** give someone a signal.
– PHRASAL VERBS **nod off** informal fall asleep, esp. briefly or unintentionally. **nod out** informal fall asleep, esp. from the effects of a drug. [ME (as a v.): perh. of Low Ger. origin; cf. Mid. High Ger. *notten* 'move around, shake.']

nod·dle /'nädl/ ▶ **n.** informal, dated a person's head. [ME (denoting the back of the head): of unknown origin.]

nod·dy /'nädē/ ▶ **n.** (pl. **-ies**) **1** dated a silly or foolish person (esp. as a general term of abuse). **2** a tropical tern (genera *Anous* and *Procelsterna*) with mainly dark-colored plumage. [perh. from the v. **NOD** + **-Y**[1].]

node /nōd/ ▶ **n. 1** a point at which lines or pathways intersect or branch; a central or connecting point. ■ Comput. a piece of equipment, such as a PC or peripheral, attached to a network. ■ Math. a point at which a curve intersects itself. ■ Astron. either of the two points at which a planet's orbit intersects the plane of the ecliptic or the celestial equator. ■ (in generative grammar) a vertex or endpoint in a tree diagram. **2** Bot. the part of a plant stem from which one or more leaves emerge, often forming a slight swelling or knob. **3** Anat. a lymph node or other structure consisting of a small mass of differentiated tissue. **4** Physics & Math. a point at which the amplitude of vibration in a standing wave system is zero. ■ a point at which a harmonic function has the value zero, esp. a point of zero electron density in an orbital. ■ a point of zero current or voltage. — **nod·al** /'nōdl/ **adj.** [ME: from L. *nodus* 'knot.']

node of Ran·vier /'ränvyā/ (also **Ranvier's node**) ▶ **n.** Anat. a gap in the myelin sheath of a nerve, between adjacent Schwann cells. [19th C.: named after Louis Antoine *Ranvier* (1835–1922), Fr. histologist.]

nod·i·cal /'nōdikəl; 'nä-/ ▶ **adj.** Astron. of or relating to a node or the nodes of an orbit.

no·dose /'nōdōs/ ▶ **adj.** tech. having or characterized by hard or tight lumps; knotty. — **no·dos·i·ty** /nō'däsitē/ **n.** [18th C.: from L. *nodosus*, from *nodus* 'knot.']

nod·ule /'näjo͞ol/ ▶ **n. 1** a small swelling or aggregation of cells in the body, esp. an abnormal one. ■ (usu. **root nodule**) a swelling on a root of a leguminous plant, containing nitrogen-fixing bacteria. **2** a small rounded lump of matter distinct from its surroundings, e.g., of flint in chalk or carbon in cast iron. — **nod·u·lar** /'näjələr/ **adj. nod·u·lat·ed** /'näjə,lātid/ **adj. nod·u·la·tion** /,näjə'lāsнən/ **n. nod·u·lose** /'näjəlōs/ **adj. nod·u·lous** /'näjələs/ **adj.** [ME: from L. *nodulus*, dimin. of *nodus* 'knot.']

no·dus /'nōdəs/ ▶ **n.** (pl. **-di** /-dī/) rare a problem. [ME: from L., lit. 'knot.']

No·el /nō'el/ ▶ **n.** Christmas, esp. as a refrain in carols and on Christmas cards. [19th C.: from Fr. *noël*.]

no·et·ic /nō'etik/ ▶ **adj.** of or relating to mental activity or the intellect. [17th C.: from Gk. *noētikos*, from *noētos* 'intellectual,' from *noein* 'perceive.']

no-fault ▶ **adj.** [attrib.] not assigning fault or blame, in particular: ■ denoting an insurance policy that is valid regardless of whether the policyholder was at fault. ■ denoting an insurance or compensation plan whereby a complainant need not legally prove negligence against any party. ■ of or denoting a form of divorce granted without requiring one party to prove that the other is to blame for the breakdown of the marriage.

no-fly zone ▶ **n.** a designated area over which aircraft may not fly without risk of interception, esp. during a conflict.

no-frills ▶ **adj.** [attrib.] without unnecessary extras, esp. ones for decoration or additional comfort.

nog[1] /näg/ ▶ **n.** archaic a small block or peg of wood. [17th C.: of unknown origin.]

nog[2] ▶ **n.** short for **EGGNOG**. [17th C.: of unknown origin.]

No·gal·es /nō'galəs; -'gäles/ a city in northwestern Mexico, across from Nogales, Arizona; pop. 106,000.

nog·gin /'nägin/ ▶ **n.** informal **1** a person's head. **2** a small quantity of liquor, typically a quarter of a pint. [17th C.: of unknown origin.]

nog·ging /'nägiNG/ ▶ **n.** Building brickwork that fills the spaces between studs or framing members. [19th C.: from **NOG**[1] + **-ING**[1].]

no-go ▶ **adj.** informal not ready or not functioning properly. ■ impossible, hopeless, or forbidden: *no-go zones for cars.* ▶ **n.** a negative response; no.

no-go ar·e·a ▶ **n.** an area that is dangerous or impossible to enter or to which entry is restricted or forbidden.

no-good ▶ **adj.** [attrib.] informal (of a person) contemptible; worthless: *a no-good layabout.* ▶ **n.** a worthless or contemptible person.

No·gu·chi /nō'go͞ocнē/, Isamu (1904–88), US sculptor. His work includes a sculpture called "Red Cube" (1968) at the Marine Midland building in New York City.

Noh /nō/ (also **No** or **Nō**) ▶ **n.** traditional Japanese masked drama with dance and song, evolved from Shinto rites.

no-hit·ter ▶ **n.** Baseball a complete game in which a pitcher yields no hits to the opposing team.

no-hop·er ▶ **n.** informal a person who is not expected to be successful.

no·how /'nō,hou/ ▶ **adv.** used, esp. in jocular or dialectal speech, to emphasize a negative.

noil /noil/ ▶ **n.** (usu. **noils**) short strands and knots combed out of wool fiber before spinning. [17th C.: prob. from OFr. *noel*, from med. L. *nodellus*, dimin. of L. *nodus* 'knot.']

no-i·ron ▶ **adj.** (of clothes or fabric) wrinkle-resistant, and so not needing to be ironed after washing.

noise /noiz/ ▶ **n.** **1** a sound, esp. one that is loud or unpleasant or that causes disturbance: *making a noise like a pig in a trough* | *what's that rustling noise outside the door?* ■ a series or combination of loud, confused sounds, esp. when causing disturbance: *dazed with the heat and noise.* ■ (**noises**) conventional remarks or other sounds that suggest some emotion or quality: *Clarissa made encouraging noises.* **2** tech. irregular fluctuations that accompany a transmitted electrical signal but are not part of it and tend to obscure it. ■ random fluctuations that obscure or do not contain meaningful data or other information. ▶ **v.** [trans.] (usu. **be noised about**) dated talk about or make known publicly. ■ [intrans.] literary make much noise. [ME: from OFr., from L. *nausea* 'seasickness' (see NAUSEA).]

noise·less /'noizlis/ ▶ **adj.** silent; quiet. ■ tech. accompanied by or introducing no random fluctuations that would obscure the signal or data. — **noise·less·ly adv. noise·less·ness n.**

noise·mak·er /'noiz,mākər/ ▶ **n.** a device for making a loud noise, as at a party or sporting event.

noise pol·lu·tion ▶ **n.** harmful or annoying levels of noise, as from airplanes, industry, etc.

nois·es off ▶ **plural n.** sounds made offstage to be heard by the audience of a play. ■ distracting or intrusive background noise.

noi·sette /nwä'zet/ ▶ **n.** **1** a small round piece of lean meat, esp. lamb. **2** a chocolate made with hazelnuts. [Fr., dimin. of *noix* 'nut.']

noi·some /'noisəm/ ▶ **adj.** literary having an extremely offensive smell. ■ disagreeable; unpleasant. ■ harmful, noxious. — **noi·some·ness n.** [ME: from obs. *noy* (shortened form of ANNOY) + -SOME[1].]

nois·y /'noizē/ ▶ **adj.** (**nois·i·er, nois·i·est**) **1** making or given to making a lot of noise. ■ (of a person or group of people) stridently seeking to attract attention to their views. ■ (of a color or item of clothing) so gaudy as to attract attention. **2** full of or characterized by noise: *the bar was crowded and noisy.* ■ tech. accompanied by or introducing random fluctuations that obscure the real signal or data. — **nois·i·ly adv. nois·i·ness n.**

no-knock ▶ **adj.** denoting or relating to a search or raid by the police made without warning or identification: *during a no-knock raid.*

no·lens vo·lens /'nōlənz 'vōlənz/ ▶ **adv.** formal whether a person wants or likes something or not. [L., from *nolens* 'not willing' and *volens* 'willing.']

no·li me tan·ge·re /'nōlē ,mā 'täNGgə,rā/ ▶ **n.** a warning or prohibition against meddling or interference. [L., 'do not touch me.']

nol·le pros /,nôl 'präs/ (also **nol-pros**) (abbr.: **nol. pros.**) ▶ **v.** (**prossed, pros·sing**) [trans.] Law abandon or dismiss (a suit) by issuing a nolle prosequi.

nol·le pros·e·qui /,nälē 'präsi,kwē/ ▶ **n.** Law a formal notice of abandonment by a plaintiff or prosecutor of all or part of a suit or action. ■ the entry of this in a court record. [17th C.: L., 'be unwilling to pursue.']

no-load ▶ **adj.** (of shares in a mutual fund) sold without a commission being charged at the time of sale.

no·lo con·ten·de·re /,nōlō kən'tendərē/ ▶ **n.** (also **no·lo**) Law a plea by which a defendant in a criminal prosecution accepts conviction as though a guilty plea had been entered but does not admit guilt. [L., 'I do not wish to contend.']

nom. ▶ **abbr.** nominal.

no·mad /'nō,mad/ ▶ **n.** a member of a people who have no permanent abode and travel from place to place to find fresh pasture for their livestock. ■ a person who does not stay long in the same place; a wanderer. ▶ **adj.** relating to or characteristic of nomads. — **no·mad·ic** /nō'madik/ **adj. no·mad·i·cal·ly** /nō'madiklē/ **adv. no·mad·ism** /'nōma,dizəm/ **n.** [16th C.: from Fr. *nomade*, via L. from Gk. *nomas, nomad-* 'roaming in search of pasture,' from the base of *nemein* 'to pasture.']

no man's land ▶ **n.** land or area that is unowned, uninhabited, or undesirable.

nom·bril /'nämbrəl/ ▶ **n.** Heraldry the point halfway between fess point and the base of the shield. [16th C.: from Fr., lit. 'navel.']

nom de guerre /,näm də 'ger/ ▶ **n.** (pl. **noms de guerre** pronunc. same) an assumed name under which a person engages in combat or some other activity or enterprise. [Fr., lit. 'war name.']

nom de plume /,näm də 'plo͞om/ ▶ **n.** (pl. **noms de plume** pronunc. same) a pen name. [19th C.: formed in Engl. from Fr. words.]

Nome /nōm/ a city in western Alaska, on the southern coast of the Seward Peninsula; pop. 3,500.

nome /nōm/ ▶ **n.** one of the thirty-six territorial divisions of ancient Egypt. [18th C.: from Gk. *nomos* 'division,' from *nemein* 'to divide.']

no·men /'nōmen/ ▶ **n.** Roman History the second personal name of a citizen of ancient Rome, indicating the gens to which he belonged, e.g., Marcus *Tullius* Cicero. [L., 'name.']

no·men·cla·ture /'nōmən,klāCHər/ ▶ **n.** the devising or choosing of names for things, esp. in a science or other discipline. ■ the body or system of such names in a particular field: *the nomenclature of chemical compounds.* ■ formal the term or terms applied to someone or something: *"customers" was preferred to the original nomenclature "passengers."* — **no·men·cla·tur·al** /,nōmən'klāCHərəl/ **adj.** [17th C.: from Fr., from L. *nomenclatura*, from *nomen* 'name' + *clatura* 'calling, summoning' (from *calare* 'to call').]

no·men·kla·tu·ra /,nōmənklə't(y)o͝orə/ ▶ **n.** (in the former Soviet Union) a list of influential posts in government and industry to be filled by Communist Party appointees. ■ the holders of such posts collectively. [Russ., from L. *nomenclatura*.]

nom·i·nal /'näminl/ ▶ **adj.** **1** (of a role or status) existing in name only. ■ of, relating to, or consisting of names. ■ Gram. relating to, headed by, or having the function of a noun. **2** (of a price or amount of money) very small; far below the real value or cost. **3** (of a quantity or dimension, esp. of manufactured articles) stated or expressed but not necessarily corresponding exactly to the real value. ■ Econ. (of a rate or other figure) expressed in terms of a certain amount, without making allowance for changes in real value over time. **4** informal (chiefly in the context of space travel) functioning normally or acceptably. — **nom·i·nal·ly adv.** [15th C. (as a term in grammar): from L. *nominalis*, from *nomen, nomin-* 'name.']

nom·i·nal ac·count ▶ **n.** Finance an account recording the financial transactions of a business in a particular category, rather than with a person or other organization.

nom·i·nal·ism /'näminl,izəm/ ▶ **n.** Philos. the doctrine that general ideas are mere names without any corresponding reality and that only particular objects exist; properties, numbers, and sets are thought of as merely features of the way of considering the things that exist. Often contrasted with REALISM (sense 3). — **nom·i·nal·ist n. nom·i·nal·is·tic** /,nämənl,istik/ **adj.**

nom·i·nal·ize /'näminl,īz/ ▶ **v.** [trans.] Gram. convert (a word or phrase, as a verb or adjective) into a noun, e.g., *output* from *put out*; *the poor* from *poor*. — **nom·i·nal·i·za·tion** /,näminl-ə'zāSHən/ **n.**

nom·i·nal ledg·er ▶ **n.** Finance a ledger containing nominal accounts, or one containing both nominal and real accounts.

nom·i·nal val·ue ▶ **n.** Econ. the value that is stated on currency; face value. ■ the price of a share, bond, or security when it was issued, rather than its current market value.

nom·i·nate ▶ **v.** /'nämə,nāt/ [trans.] **1** propose or formally enter as a candidate for election or for an honor or award. ■ appoint to a job or position. **2** specify (something) formally, typically the date or place for an event: *a day was nominated for the exchange of contracts.* ▶ **adj.** /-nit/ Zool. Bot. denoting a race or subspecies that is given the same epithet as the species to which it belongs, e.g., *Homo sapiens sapiens.* — **nom·i·na·tor** /-,nātər/ **n.** [ME: from L. *nominat-* 'named,' from the v. *nominare*, from *nomen, nomin-* 'a name.']

nom·i·na·tion /,nämə'nāSHən/ ▶ **n.** the action of nominating or state of being nominated. ■ a person or thing nominated.

nom·i·na·tive /'nämənətiv/ ▶ **adj.** **1** Gram. relating to or denoting a case of nouns, pronouns, and adjectives (as in Latin) used for the subject of a verb. **2** /-,nātiv/ of or appointed by nomination as distinct from election. ▶ **n.** Gram. a word in the nominative case. ■ (**the nominative**) the nominative case.

nom·i·nee /,nämə'nē/ ▶ **n.** **1** a person who is proposed or formally entered as a candidate for an office or as the recipient of a grant or award. **2** a person or company whose name is given as having title to a stock, real estate, etc., but who is not the actual owner. [17th C.: from NOMINATE + -EE.]

nom·o·gram /'nämə,gram; 'nō-/ (also **nom·o·graph** /-,graf/) ▶ **n.** a diagram representing the relations between three or more variable quantities by means of a number of scales, so arranged that the value of one variable can be found by a simple geometric construction, e.g., by drawing a straight line intersecting the other scales at the appropriate values. — **nom·o·graph·ic** /,nämə'grafik; ,nō-/ **adj. nom·o·graph·i·cal·ly** /,nämə'grafik(ə)lē; ,nō-/ **adv. no·mog·ra·phy** /nə'mägrəfē/ **n.** [20th C.: from Gk. *nomos* 'law' + -GRAM[1].]

nom·o·log·i·cal /,nämə'läjikəl; ,nō-/ ▶ **adj.** relating to or denoting certain principles, such as laws of nature, that are neither logically necessary nor theoretically explicable, but are simply taken as true. ■ another term for NOMOTHETIC. — **nom·o·log·i·cal·ly adv.** [19th C.: from Gk. *nomos* 'law' + *-logical* (see -LOGY).]

nom·o·thet·ic /,nämə'THetik; ,nō-/ ▶ **adj.** of or relating to the study or discovery of general scientific laws. [17th C.: from obs. *nomothete* 'legislator' (from Gk. *nomothetēs*) + -IC.]

-nomy ▶ **comb. form** denoting a specified area of knowledge or the laws governing it: *astronomy* | *gastronomy.* [from Gk. *-nomia*; rel. to *nomos* 'law' and *nemein* 'distribute.']

non- ▶ **prefix** **1** not doing; not involved with: *nonaggression* | *nonrecognition.* **2** not of the kind or class described: *nonbeliever* | *nonconformist.* ■ also forming nouns used attributively (such as *nonunion* in *nonunion miners*). **3** not of the importance implied: *nonissue.* **4** a lack of: *nonsense.* **5** (**added to adverbs**) not in the way described: *nonuniformly.* **6** (added to verbs to form adjectives) not causing or requiring: *nonskid* | *noniron.* **7** expressing a neutral negative sense when a corresponding form beginning with *in-* or *un-* has a special connotation (such as *nonhuman* compared with *inhuman*). [from L. *non* 'not.']

nona- ▶ **comb. form** nine; having nine: *nonagon.* [from L. *nonus* 'ninth.']

non·age /'nänij; 'nō-/ ▶ **n.** [in sing.] formal the period of immaturity or youth. [ME: from OFr. *nonage*, from *non-* 'non-' + *age* 'age.']

non·a·ge·nar·i·an /,nänəjə'ne(ə)rēən; ,nōnə-/ ▶ **n.** a person who is from 90 to 99 years old. [19th C.: from L. *nonagenarius* (based on *nonaginta* 'ninety') + -AN.]

non·ag·gres·sion /,nänə'greSHən/ ▶ **n.** absence of the desire or intention to be aggressive, esp. on the part of nations or governments: [as adj.] *nonaggression pact.* — **non·ag·gres·sive adj.**

non·a·gon /'nänə,gän/ ▶ **n.** a plane figure with nine straight sides and nine angles. — **non·ag·o·nal** /nän'agənəl/ **adj.** [17th C.: from L. *nonus* 'ninth.']

non·al·co·hol·ic /,nän,alkə'hôlik; -'hälik/ ▶ **adj.** (of a drink) not containing alcohol.

non·a·ligned /ˌnänəˈlīnd/ ▶ **adj.** not aligned with something else. ■ (of countries) not aligned with a major power, esp. the former USSR or the US. — **non·a·lign·ment** /-ˈlīnmənt/ **n.**

no-name ▶ **adj.** (of a product) having no brand name. ■ (of a person) unknown, esp. in a particular profession. ▶ **n.** such a person.

no·nane /ˈnōnān/ ▶ **n.** Chem. a colorless liquid hydrocarbon, C_9H_{20}, of the alkane series.

non·ap·pear·ance /ˌnänəˈpi(ə)rəns/ ▶ **n.** failure to appear or be present, esp. at a gathering or engagement. ■ Law failure to appear or be present in a court of law, esp. as a witness, defendant, or plaintiff.

non·art /ˈnänˈärt/ ▶ **n.** something that is not art or that rejects the conventional forms or methods of art.

non·be·liev·er /ˌnänbəˈlēvər/ ▶ **n.** a person who does not believe in something, esp. in religion.

non·bi·o·log·i·cal /ˌnänbīəˈläjikəl/ ▶ **adj.** not involving or derived from biology or living organisms. ■ (of a detergent) not containing enzymes.

non·call·a·ble /nänˈkôləbəl/ ▶ **adj.** (of stocks and bonds) not subject to redemption before a certain date or until maturity.

non·cap·i·tal /nänˈkapitl/ ▶ **adj.** Law (of an offense) not punishable by death.

nonce /näns/ ▶ **adj.** (of a word or expression) coined for or used on one occasion: *a nonce usage.*
– PHRASES **for the nonce** for the present; temporarily. [ME: from *then anes* 'the one' (from *then*, form of THE + *ane* 'one' + -S[3]), alt. by misdivision.]

non·cha·lant /ˌnänshəˈlänt/ ▶ **adj.** (of a person or manner) feeling or appearing casually calm and relaxed. — **non·cha·lance n. non·cha·lant·ly adv.** [18th C.: from Fr., lit. 'not being concerned,' from the v. *nonchaloir*.]

non·clas·si·fied /nänˈklasəfīd/ ▶ **adj.** (of information or documents) not designated as officially secret; freely available (less forceful than **unclassified**).

non·cod·ing /nänˈkōdiNG/ ▶ **adj.** Biol. (of a section of a nucleic acid molecule) not directing the production of a peptide sequence.

non·com /ˈnänˌkäm/ ▶ **n.** Mil., informal a noncommissioned officer.

non·com·bat·ant /ˌnänkəmˈbatnt/ ▶ **n.** a person who is not engaged in fighting during a war, esp. a civilian, chaplain, or medical practitioner.

non·com·e·do·gen·ic /ˌnänˌkämədōˈjenik/ ▶ **adj.** denoting a skin-care product or cosmetic that is specially formulated so as not to cause blocked pores.

non·com·mis·sioned /ˌnankəˈmisHənd/ ▶ **adj.** Mil. (of an officer in the armed forces) ranking below warrant officer, as sergeant or petty officer.

non·com·mit·tal /ˌnänkəˈmitl/ ▶ **adj.** (of a person or a person's behavior) not expressing or revealing commitment to a definite opinion or course of action. — **non·com·mit·tal·ly adv.**

non·com·mu·ni·cant /ˌnänkəˈmyōōnikənt/ ▶ **n.** (in church use) a person who does not receive Holy Communion, esp. regularly or at a particular service.

non·com·pli·ance /ˌnänkəmˈplīəns/ ▶ **n.** failure to act in accordance with an agreement, law, contract, etc.

non com·pos men·tis /ˌnän ˈkämpəs ˈmentis/ (also **non com·pos**) ▶ **adj.** not sane or in one's right mind. [L., lit. 'not having control of one's mind.']

non·con·duc·tor /ˌnänkənˈdəktər/ ▶ **n.** a substance that does not conduct heat or electricity. — **non·con·duct·ing adj.**

non·con·form·ist /ˌnänkənˈfôrmist/ ▶ **n. 1** a person whose behavior or views do not conform to prevailing ideas or practices. **2** (**Nonconformist**) a member of a Protestant church in England that dissents from the established Anglican Church. ▶ **adj. 1** of or characterized by behavior or views that do not conform to prevailing ideas or practices. **2** (**Nonconformist**) of or relating to Nonconformists or their principles and practices. — **non·con·form·ism n.**

non·con·form·i·ty /ˌnänkənˈfôrmitē/ ▶ **n. 1** failure or refusal to conform to a prevailing rule or practice. ■ lack of similarity in form or type. **2** (**Nonconformity**) Nonconformists as a body, esp. Protestants in England dissenting from the Anglican Church. ■ the principles or practice of Nonconformists, esp. Protestant dissent.

non·con·tra·dic·tion /ˌnänkäntrəˈdiksHən/ ▶ **n.** a lack or absence of contradiction, esp. as a principle of logic that a proposition and its opposite cannot both be true. — **non·con·tra·dic·to·ry** /-ˈdiktərē/ **adj.**

non·con·trib·u·to·ry /ˌnänkənˈtribyəˌtôrē/ ▶ **adj. 1** not playing a part in bringing something about. **2** (of a pension or pension plan) funded by regular payments by the employer, not the employee.

non·co·op·er·a·tion /ˌnänkōˌäpəˈrāsHən/ ▶ **n.** failure or refusal to cooperate, esp. as a form of protest.

non·count /ˈnänˌkount/ ▶ **adj.** Gram. (of a noun) not countable.

non·cus·to·di·al /ˌnänˌkəˈstōdēəl/ ▶ **adj.** Law not having custody of one's children after a divorce.

non·dair·y /nänˈde(ə)rē/ ▶ **adj.** containing no milk or milk products: *a nondairy creamer.*

non·de·liv·er·y /ˌnändəˈlivərē/ ▶ **n.** esp. Law failure to provide or deliver goods.

non·de·nom·i·na·tion·al /ˌnändəˌnäməˈnāsHənəl/ ▶ **adj.** open or acceptable to people of any Christian denomination.

non·de·script /ˌnändəˈskript/ ▶ **adj.** lacking distinctive or interesting features or characteristics. ▶ **n.** a nondescript person or thing. — **non·de·script·ly adv. non·de·script·ness n.** [17th C.: from NON- + obs. *descript* 'described, engraved' (from L. *descriptus*).]

non·de·struc·tive /ˌnändəˈstrəktiv/ ▶ **adj.** tech. not involving damage or destruction, esp. of an object or material that is being tested.

non·di·rec·tion·al /ˌnändəˈreksHənəl/ ▶ **adj.** lacking directional properties. ■ (of sound, light, radio waves, etc.) equally sensitive, intense, etc., in every direction.

non·dis·junc·tion /ˌnändisˈjəNGksHən/ ▶ **n.** Genet. the failure of homologous chromosomes to separate normally during nuclear division.

non·drink·er /nänˈdriNGkər/ ▶ **n.** a person who does not drink alcohol.

none[1] /nən/ ▶ **pron.** not any: *none of you want to work.* ■ no person; no one: *none could match her looks.* ▶ **adv.** (**none the**) [with comparative] by no amount; not at all: *it is made none the easier by the differences in approach.*
– PHRASES **none the less** see NONETHELESS. **none other than** used to emphasize the surprising identity of a person or thing. **be none the wiser** see WISE[1]. **none the worse for** see WORSE. **none too** see TOO. [OE *nān*, from *ne* 'not' + *ān* 'one,' of Gmc. origin; cf. Ger. *nein* 'no!']

none[2] /nōn/ (also **nones**) ▶ **n.** a service forming part of the Divine Office of the Western Christian Church, traditionally said at the ninth hour of the day (3 p.m.). [19th C.: from Fr., from L. *nona*, fem. sing. of *nonus* 'ninth.']

non·en·ti·ty /nänˈentitē/ ▶ **n.** (pl. **-ties**) **1** an unimportant person or thing. **2** nonexistence.

nones /nōnz/ ▶ **plural n. 1** in the ancient Roman calendar, the ninth day before the ides by inclusive reckoning, i.e., the 7th day of March, May, July, and October, or the 5th of other months. **2** another term for NONE[2]. [via OFr. from L. *nonas*, fem. accusative pl. of *nonus* 'ninth.']

non·es·sen·tial /ˌnänəˈsencHəl/ ▶ **adj.** not absolutely necessary. ▶ **n.** (usu. **nonessentials**) a nonessential thing.

non est fac·tum /ˌnōn ˌest ˈfaktəm/ ▶ **n.** Law a plea that a written agreement is invalid because the defendant was mistaken about its character when signing it. [L., lit. 'it was not done.']

none·such /ˈnənˌsəcH/ (also **non·such**) ▶ **n. 1** a person or thing that is regarded as perfect or excellent. **2** another term for BLACK MEDICK (see MEDICK).

no·net /nōˈnet/ ▶ **n.** a group of nine people or things, esp. musicians. ■ a musical composition for nine voices or instruments. [19th C.: from Ital. *nonetto*, from *nono* 'ninth,' from L. *nonus*.]

none·the·less /ˌnənT͟Həˈles/ (also **none the less**) ▶ **adv.** in spite of that; nevertheless.

non-Eu·clid·e·an /ˌnän yōōˈklidēən/ ▶ **adj.** Geom. denying or going beyond Euclidean geometry, esp. in contravening the postulate that only one line through a given point can be parallel to a given line.

non·e·vent /ˌnäniˈvent/ ▶ **n.** a disappointing or insignificant event or occasion, esp. one that was expected or intended to be exciting or interesting. ■ a scheduled event that did not happen.

non·ex·ist·ent /ˌnänigˈzistənt/ ▶ **adj.** not existing, or not real or present. — **non·ex·ist·ence n.**

non·fat /ˈnänˈfat/ ▶ **adj.** (of a food) containing no fat; with all fat solids removed: *nonfat buttermilk.*

non·fea·sance /nänˈfēzəns/ ▶ **n.** Law failure to perform an act that is required by law.

non·fer·rous /nänˈferəs/ ▶ **adj.** relating to or denoting a metal other than iron or steel.

non·fic·tion /nänˈfiksHən/ ▶ **n.** prose writing based on facts, such as biography or history. — **non·fic·tion·al adj.**

non·fig·ur·a·tive ▶ **adj.** not figurative. ■ (of an artist or work of art) abstract.

non·fi·nite /nänˈfīnīt/ ▶ **adj.** not finite. ■ Gram. (of a verb form) not limited by tense, person, or number. Contrasted with FINITE.

non·flam·ma·ble /nänˈflaməbəl/ ▶ **adj.** not catching fire easily; not flammable.

non·ful·fill·ment /ˌnänfōōlˈfilmənt/ ▶ **n.** failure to fulfill something desired, planned, or promised.

non-Hodg·kin's lym·pho·ma ▶ **n.** Med. a form of malignant lymphoma distinguished from Hodgkin's disease only by the absence of binucleate giant cells.

non·hu·man /nänˈ(h)yōōmən/ ▶ **adj.** of, relating to, or characteristic of a creature that is not a human being. ▶ **n.** a creature that is not a human being.

non·in·flam·ma·ble /ˌnäninˈflaməbəl/ ▶ **adj.** not catching fire easily; not flammable.

non·in·su·lin-de·pend·ent /ˈnänˈinsəlin/ ▶ **adj.** Med. relating to or denoting a type of diabetes in which there is some insulin secretion. Such diabetes typically develops in adulthood and can frequently be managed by diet and hypoglycemic agents.

non·in·ter·ven·tion /ˌnänintərˈvensHən/ ▶ **n.** the principle or practice of not becoming involved in the affairs of others. ■ such a policy adopted by a country in its international relations. — **non·in·ter·ven·tion·ism n. non·in·ter·ven·tion·ist adj. & n.**

PRONUNCIATION KEY ə *ago, up*; ər *over, fur*; a *hat*; ā *ate*; ä *car*; e *let*; ē *see*; i *fit*; ī *by*; NG *sing*; ō *go*; ô *law, for*; oi *toy*; ōō *good*; ōō *goo*; ou *out*; TH *thin*; T͟H *then*; ZH *vision*

non·in·va·sive /ˌnänin'vāsiv/ ▶ **adj.** **1** (of medical procedures) not requiring the introduction of instruments into the body. **2** (of a cancerous disease) not tending to spread. ■ (of plants) not tending to spread undesirably.

non·i·on·ic /ˌnänī'änik/ ▶ **adj.** Chem. not ionic. ■ (of a detergent) not dissociating into ions in aqueous solution.

non·is·sue /'nän'isHōō/ ▶ **n.** a topic of little or no importance.

non·judg·men·tal /ˌnänjəj'mentl/ (also **non·judge·men·tal**) ▶ **adj.** avoiding moral judgments.

non·ju·ry /nän'jŏŏrē/ ▶ **adj.** Law denoting a trial or legal action not having or requiring a jury.

non li·cet /'nän 'līsit/ ▶ **adj.** not allowed; unlawful. [L.]

non·lin·e·ar /nän'linēər/ ▶ **adj.** **1** not denoting, involving, or arranged in a straight line. ■ Math. designating or involving an equation whose terms are not of the first degree. ■ Physics involving a lack of linearity between two related qualities such as input and output. ■ Math. involving measurement in more than one dimension. ■ not linear, sequential, or straightforward; random. **2** of or denoting digital editing whereby a sequence of edits is stored on computer as opposed to videotape, thus facilitating further editing.

non·log·i·cal /nän'läjikəl/ ▶ **adj.** not derived from or according to the rules of logic or formal argument (less forceful in meaning than **illogical**). — **non·log·i·cal·ly** **adv.**

non·mor·al /nän'môrəl; -'mär-/ ▶ **adj.** not holding or manifesting moral principles: *nonmoral value judgments.*

non·nat·u·ral /nän'nacHərəl/ ▶ **adj.** not involving or manifesting natural means or processes.

non·ne·go·ti·a·ble /ˌnän-nə'gōsHəbəl/ ▶ **adj.** not open to discussion or modification. ■ (of a document) not able to be transferred or assigned to the legal ownership of another person.

non·nu·cle·ar /nän'n(y)ōōklēər/ ▶ **adj.** **1** not involving or relating to nuclear energy or nuclear weapons. ■ (of a country) not possessing nuclear weapons. **2** Physics not involving, relating to, or forming part of a nucleus or nuclei.

no-no ▶ **n.** (pl. **-nos**) informal a thing that is not possible or acceptable.

non·ob·jec·tive /ˌnänəb'jektiv/ ▶ **adj.** **1** (of a person or their judgment) influenced by personal feeling or opinions in considering and representing facts. **2** of or relating to abstract art.

no-non·sense ▶ **adj.** simple and straightforward; sensible.

non·or·gan·ic /ˌnänôr'ganik/ ▶ **adj.** not organic, in particular: ■ not relating to or derived from living matter. ■ (esp. of food or farming methods) not involving or relating to production by organic methods.

non·pa·reil /ˌnänpə'rel/ ▶ **adj.** having no match or equal; unrivaled. ▶ **n.** **1** an unrivaled or matchless person or thing. **2** a flat round candy made of chocolate covered with white sugar sprinkles. **3** Print. an old type size equal to six points. [ME: from Fr., from *non-* 'not' + *pareil* 'equal' (from popular Latin *pariculus*, dimin. of L. *par* 'equal').]

non·par·tic·i·pat·ing /ˌnänpər'tisəˌpātiNG/ ▶ **adj.** **1** not involved or taking part in an activity. **2** (of an insurance policy) not allowing the holder a share of the profits made by the company.

non·par·ti·san /nän'pärtizən/ ▶ **adj.** not biased or partisan, esp. toward any particular political group.

non·par·ty ▶ **adj.** independent of any political party.

non·past /'nänˌpast/ ▶ **n.** Gram. a tense not expressing a past action or state.

non·pay·ment ▶ **n.** failure to pay an amount of money: *homes repossessed for nonpayment of mortgages.*

non·per·for·mance /ˌnänpər'fôrməns/ ▶ **n.** failure or refusal to perform or fulfill a condition, promise, etc. ■ the state of not being performed.

non·per·son /ˌnän'pərsən/ ▶ **n.** a person regarded as nonexistent or unimportant, or as having no rights; an ignored or forgotten person. Compare with **UNPERSON**.

non pla·cet /ˌnän 'plāsit/ ▶ **n.** a negative vote in a church or college assembly. [L., lit. 'it does not please.']

non·plus /nän'pləs/ ▶ **v.** (**-plussed, -plus·sing**) [trans.] (usu. **be nonplussed**) surprise and confuse (someone) so much that they are unsure how to react. ▶ **n.** a state of being surprised and confused in this way. [16th C.: from L. *non plus* 'not more.']

non·plussed /nän'pləst/ (also **non·plused**) ▶ **adj.** **1** (of a person) surprised and confused so much that they are unsure how to react. **2** informal (of a person) unperturbed.

non·pre·scrip·tion /ˌnänprə'skripsHən/ ▶ **adj.** (of a medicine) available for sale without a prescription. ■ denoting such sale or purchase.

non·pro·duc·tive /ˌnänprə'dəktiv/ ▶ **adj.** not producing goods, crops, or economic benefit (less forceful in meaning than **unproductive**). ■ achieving little. — **non·pro·duc·tive·ly** **adv.**

non·prof·it /'nän'präfit/ ▶ **adj.** [attrib.] not making or conducted primarily to make a profit.

non·pro·lif·er·a·tion /ˌnänprəˌlifə'rāsHən/ ▶ **n.** the prevention of an increase or spread of something, esp. the number of countries possessing nuclear weapons.

non·pro·pri·e·tar·y /ˌnänprə'prīəˌterē/ ▶ **adj.** (esp. of computer hardware or software) conforming to standards in the public domain or widely licensed. ■ not registered or protected as a trademark; generic.

non·pros (abbr.: **non pros.**) ▶ **v.** [trans.] Law adjudge (a plaintiff) in default.

non·res·i·dent /nän'rezidənt/ ▶ **adj.** not living in a particular place, esp. a country or a place of work. ■ (of a job or program of study) not requiring the holder or participant to reside at the place of work or instruction. ▶ **n.** a person not living in a particular place. — **non·res·i·dence** **n.**

non·res·i·den·tial /ˌnänrezə'dencHəl/ ▶ **adj.** not requiring or providing facilities for people to live on the premises. ■ (of land) containing or suitable for commercial premises rather than private houses.

non·re·sis·tance /ˌnänri'zistəns/ ▶ **n.** the practice or principle of not resisting authority, even when it is unjustly exercised.

non·re·stric·tive /ˌnänri'striktiv/ ▶ **adj.** **1** not involving restrictions or limitations. **2** Gram. (of a relative clause or descriptive phrase) giving additional information about a noun phrase whose particular reference has already been specified.

non·re·turn·a·ble /ˌnänri'tərnəbəl/ ▶ **adj.** (esp. of a deposit paid) not repayable in any circumstances. ■ (of bottles or other containers) not intended to be returned empty to the suppliers.

non·rig·id /nän'rijid/ ▶ **adj.** (esp. of materials) not rigid. ■ denoting an airship whose shape is maintained solely by the pressure of the gas inside.

non·sched·uled /'nän'skejəld; -jōōld/ ▶ **adj.** denoting or relating to an airline that operates without fixed or published flying schedules.

non·sec·tar·i·an /ˌnänsek'te(ə)rēən/ ▶ **adj.** not involving or relating to a specific religious sect or political group.

non·sense /'nänˌsens/ ▶ **n.** **1** spoken or written words that have no meaning or make no sense. ■ [as exclam.] used to show strong disagreement: *"Nonsense! No one can do that."* ■ [as adj.] denoting verse or other writing intended to be amusing by virtue of its absurd or whimsical language: *nonsense poetry.* **2** foolish or unacceptable behavior. ■ something that one disagrees with or disapproves of. — **non·sen·si·cal** /nän'sensikəl/ **adj.** **non·sen·si·cal·i·ty** /ˌnänsensə'kalitē/ **n.** **non·sen·si·cal·ly** /nän'sensik(ə)lē/ **adv.**

non·sense syl·la·ble ▶ **n.** an arbitrarily formed syllable with no meaning, esp. in songs or as used in memory experiments and tests.

non·sense word ▶ **n.** a word having no meaning.

non se·qui·tur /ˌnän 'sekwitər/ ▶ **n.** a conclusion or statement that does not logically follow from the previous argument or statement. [L., lit. 'it does not follow.']

non·skid /ˌnän'skid/ ▶ **adj.** designed to prevent sliding or skidding: *nonskid tires.*

non·smok·ing /nän'smōkiNG/ ▶ **adj.** denoting a place where smoking tobacco is forbidden. ■ denoting a person who does not smoke. ▶ **n.** the practice or habit of not smoking.

non·spe·cif·ic /ˌnänspə'sifik/ ▶ **adj.** not detailed or exact; general. ■ Med. not assignable to a particular cause, condition, or category.

non·spe·cif·ic u·re·thri·tis /ˌyōōrə'THrītis/ (abbr.: **NSU**) ▶ **n.** Med. inflammation of the urethra due to infection by organisms other than gonococci.

non·stand·ard /'nän'standərd/ ▶ **adj.** not average, normal, or usual. ■ (of language) not of the accepted standard.

non·start·er /'nän'stärtər/ ▶ **n.** a person or animal that fails to take part in a race. ■ informal a person, plan, or idea that has no chance of succeeding or being effective.

non·stick /'nän'stik/ ▶ **adj.** (of a pan or surface) covered with a substance that prevents food from sticking to it during cooking: *a nonstick frying pan.*

non·stop /'nän'stäp/ ▶ **adj.** continuing without stopping or pausing. ■ (of a passenger vehicle or journey) not having or making stops at intermediate places on the way to its destination. ■ oppressively constant; relentless. ▶ **adv.** without stopping or pausing: *working nonstop.* ▶ **n.** a nonstop flight or train.

non·such ▶ **n.** var. of **NONESUCH**.

non·suit /nän'sōōt/ Law ▶ **v.** [trans.] (of a judge or court) subject (a plaintiff) to the stoppage of their suit on the grounds of failure to make a legal case. ▶ **n.** the stoppage of a suit on such grounds. [ME (as a n.): from Anglo-Norman Fr., lit. 'not pursuing' (see **NON-**, **SUIT**).]

non·sup·port /ˌnänsə'pôrt/ ▶ **n.** Law failure to provide for the maintenance of a child, spouse, or other dependent as required by law.

non·trop·i·cal sprue /nän'träpikəl 'sprōō/ ▶ **n.** see **SPRUE**[2].

non-U /nän 'yōō/ ▶ **adj.** informal, esp. Brit. (of language or social behavior) not characteristic of the upper social classes. [1950s: from **NON-** + **U**[3].]

non·un·ion /nän'yōōnyən/ ▶ **adj.** not belonging or relating to a labor union. ■ (of a company) not having labor union members. ■ not done or produced by members of a labor union.

non·ver·bal /nän'vərbəl/ ▶ **adj.** not involving or using words or speech: *forms of nonverbal communication.* — **non·ver·bal·ly** **adv.**

non·vin·tage /nän'vintij/ ▶ **adj.** denoting a wine that is not made from the crop of a single identified district in a good year.

non·vi·o·lence /nän'vīələns/ ▶ **n.** the use of peaceful means, not force, to bring about political or social change. — **nonviolent** /ˌnän'vīələnt/ **adj.**

non·vol·a·tile /nän'välətl/ ▶ **adj.** not volatile. ■ Comput. (of a computer's memory) retaining data even if there is a break in the power supply.

non·white /ˌnän'(h)wīt/ ▶ **adj.** denoting or relating to a person whose origin is not predominantly European. ▶ **n.** a person whose origin is not predominantly European.

non·word /'nän'wərd/ ▶ **n.** a group of letters or speech sounds that looks or sounds like a word but is not accepted as such by native speakers.

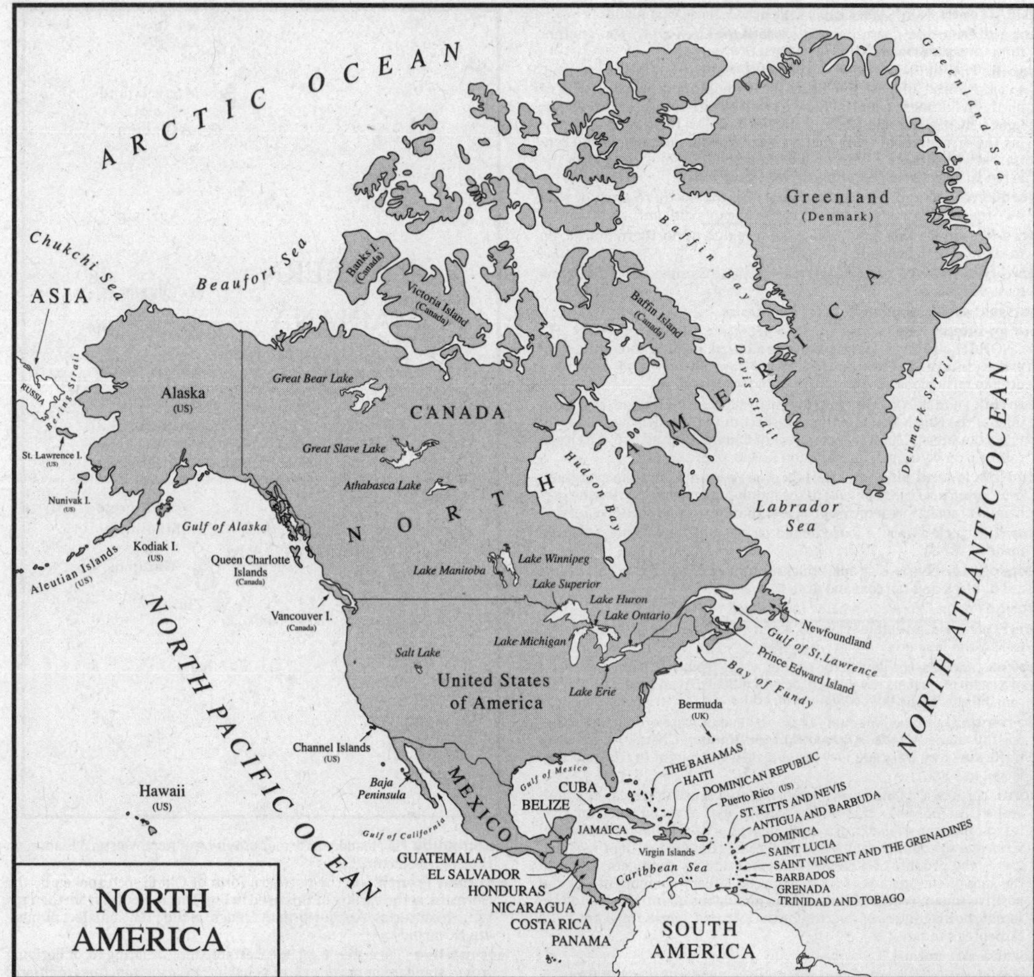

non·yl /'nänil; 'nō-/ ▶ n. [as adj.] Chem. of or denoting an alkyl radical $-C_9H_{19}$, derived from nonane.

non·ze·ro /nän'zērō/ ▶ adj. having a positive or negative value; not equal to zero.

noo·dle¹ /'no͞odl/ ▶ n. (usu. **noodles**) a strip, ring, or tube of pasta or a similar dough. [18th C.: from Ger. *Nudel*.]

noo·dle² ▶ n. informal a stupid or silly person. ■ a person's head. [18th C.: of unknown origin.]

noog·ie /'no͝ogē/ ▶ n. informal a hard poke or grind with the knuckles, esp. on a person's head. [1970s: origin unknown.]

nook /no͝ok/ ▶ n. a corner or recess, esp. one offering seclusion or security: *the nook beside the fire.* [ME: of unknown origin.]

nook·y /'no͝okē/ (also **nook·ie**) ▶ n. vulgar slang sexual activity or intercourse. [20th C.: perh. from NOOK.]

noon /no͞on/ ▶ n. twelve o'clock in the day; midday. [OE *nōn* 'the ninth hour from sunrise,' from L. *nona (hora)* 'ninth hour.']

noon·day /'no͞on,dā/ ▶ n. the middle of the day.

no one ▶ pron. no person; not a single person.

noon·er /'no͞onər/ ▶ n. informal an event that occurs in the middle of the day, esp. an act of sexual intercourse.

noon·ing /'no͞oniNG/ ▶ n. dialect a rest or meal at midday.

noon·tide /'no͞on,tīd/ (also **noon·time**/'no͞on,tīm/) ▶ n. literary noon.

noose /no͞os/ ▶ n. a loop with a running knot, tightening as the rope or wire is pulled and typically used to hang people or trap animals. ■ (**the noose**) death by hanging. ■ (**the noose**) fig. a difficult situation regarded as a restraint or bond. ▶ v. [trans.] put a noose on (someone). ■ catch (an animal) with a noose. ■ form (a rope) into a noose. [ME: prob. via OFr. *no(u)s* from L. *nodus* 'knot.']

no·o·sphere /'nōə,sfi(ə)r/ ▶ n. a postulated sphere or stage of evolutionary development dominated by consciousness, the mind, and interpersonal relationships (freq. with ref. to the writings of Teilhard de Chardin). [1940s: from Fr. *noösphere*, based on Gk. *noos* 'mind.']

Noot·ka /'no͞otkə; 'no͝ot-/ ▶ n. (pl. same or **-kas**) **1** a member of an American Indian people of Vancouver Island, Canada. **2** the Wakashan language of this people. ▶ adj. of or relating to this people or their language. [named after *Nootka* Sound, an inlet on the coast of Vancouver Island.]

n.o.p. (also **NOP**) ▶ abbr. not our publication.

no·pal /'nōpəl; nō'päl/ ▶ n. (pl. **-pa·les** /-'päles/) a cactus (genus *Nopalea*) that is a major food plant of the insects from which cochineal is obtained. ■ (**nopales**) the edible fleshy pads of this cactus, used as a staple in Mexican cuisine. [18th C.: via Fr. and Sp. from Nahuatl *nopalli* 'cactus.']

nope /nōp/ ▶ exclam. informal variant of NO.

nor /nôr/ ▶ conj. & adv. **1** used before the second or further of two or more alternatives (the first being introduced by a negative such as "neither" or "not") to indicate that they are each untrue or each do not happen: *they were neither cheap nor convenient.* ■ [as adv.] poetic/literary term for NEITHER: *nor God nor demon can undo the done.* **2** used to introduce a further negative statement: *the struggle did not end, nor was it diminished.* **3** [conj. or prep.] archaic dialect than: *she thinks she knows better nor me.* ▶ n. (usu. **NOR**) Electron. a Boolean operator that gives the value one if and only if all operands have a value of zero and otherwise has a value of zero. [ME: contr. of OE *nother* 'neither.']

nor' /nôr/ ▶ abbr. (esp. in compounds) north: *seek shelter from a raging nor'easter.*

nor- ▶ prefix Chem. denoting an organic compound derived from another, in particular by the shortening of a chain or ring by the removal of one methylene group or by the replacement of one or more methyl side chains by hydrogen atoms: *norepinephrine.* [from *nor(mal)*.]

NORAD ▶ abbr. North American Aerospace Defense Command.

nor·a·dren·a·line /ˌnôrəˈdrenəlin/ (also **nor·a·dren·a·lin**) ▶ n. another term for NOREPINEPHRINE.

Nor·dic /ˈnôrdik/ ▶ adj. of or relating to Scandinavia, Finland, Iceland, and the Faroe Islands. ■ relating to or denoting a physical type of northern European peoples characterized by tall stature, a bony frame, light coloring, and a dolichocephalic head. ■ Skiing relating to or denoting the disciplines of cross-country skiing or ski jumping. Often contrasted with ALPINE. ▶ n. a native of Scandinavia, Finland, Iceland, or the Faroe Islands. [from Fr. *nordique*, from *nord* 'north.']

Nord·kyn /ˈnŏŏrkin; -ˌkyn/ a promontory on the northern coast of Norway, the northernmost point on the European mainland.

Nord-Pas-de-Ca·lais /nôr ˌpä də käˈlā/ a region of northern France, on the border with Belgium.

Nord·rhein-West·fa·len /ˈnôrtˌrīn vestˈfälən/ German name for NORTH RHINE-WESTPHALIA.

nor'east·er ▶ n. another term for NORTHEASTER.

nor·ep·i·neph·rine /ˌnôrepəˈnefrin/ ▶ n. Biochem. a hormone, $(HO)_2C_6H_3$-$CHOHCH_2NH_2$, that is released by the adrenal medulla and by the sympathetic nerves and functions as a neurotransmitter. It is also used as a drug to raise blood pressure. Also called NORADRENALINE.

Nor·folk /ˈnôrfək/ **1** a county on the eastern coast of England, east of an inlet of the North Sea called the Wash; county town, Norwich. **2** a city in northeastern Nebraska, northwest of Omaha; pop. 23,516. **3** a city in southeastern Virginia, on Hampton Roads; pop. 234,403.

Nor·folk Is·land pine (also **Norfolk pine**) ▶ n. an Australian evergreen tree (*Araucaria heterophylla*) of the monkey puzzle family, having horizontal branches with upswept shoots that bear small scalelike leaves.

Nor·folk jack·et ▶ n. a loose belted jacket with box pleats, typically made of tweed.

Nor·folk ter·ri·er ▶ n. a small thickset terrier of a breed with a rough red or black-and-tan coat and drop ears.

Nor·ge /ˈnôrgə/ Norwegian name for NORWAY.

no·ri /ˈnôrē/ ▶ n. an edible seaweed, eaten either fresh or dried in sheets, esp. by the Japanese.

no·ri·a /ˈnôrēə/ ▶ n. a device for raising water from a stream, consisting of a chain of buckets revolving around a wheel driven by the water current. [via Sp. from Arab. *nāʿūra*.]

No·ri·e·ga /ˌnôrēˈāgə/, Manuel (1938–), head of state of Panama 1983–89; full name *Manuel Antonio Noriega Moreno*. Charged with drug trafficking by a US grand jury in 1988, he was brought to trial and convicted in 1992.

norm /nôrm/ ▶ n. **1** (**the norm**) something that is usual, typical, or standard. ■ (usu. **norms**) a standard or pattern, esp. of social behavior, that is typical or expected of a group: *the norms of good behavior in the civil service.* ■ a required standard; a level to be complied with or reached. **2** Math. the product of a complex number and its conjugate, equal to the sum of the squares of its real and imaginary components, or the positive square root of this sum. ■ an analogous quantity used to represent the magnitude of a vector. [19th C.: from L. *norma* 'precept, rule, carpenter's square.']

norm. ▶ abbr. normal.

nor·mal /ˈnôrməl/ ▶ adj. **1** conforming to a standard; usual, typical, or expected. ■ (of a person) free from physical or mental disorders. **2** tech. (of a line, ray, or other linear feature) intersecting a given line or surface at right angles. **3** Med. (of a salt solution) containing the same salt concentration as the blood. ■ Chem., dated (of a solution) containing one gram-equivalent of solute per liter. ▶ n. **1** the usual, average, or typical state or condition. ■ a person who is physically or mentally healthy. **2** tech. a line at right angles to a given line or surface. — **nor·mal·cy** /-məlsē/ n. **nor·mal·i·ty** /nôrˈmalitē/ n. [17th C.: from L. *normalis*, from *norma*.]

nor·mal dis·tri·bu·tion ▶ n. Stat. a function that represents the distribution of many random variables as a symmetrical bell-shaped graph.

nor·mal·ize /ˈnôrməˌlīz/ ▶ v. [trans.] bring or return to a normal condition or state: *Vietnam and China agreed to normalize diplomatic relations in 1991* | [intrans.] *the situation had normalized.* — **nor·mal·i·za·tion** /ˌnôrmələˈzāsнən/ n. **nor·mal·iz·er** n.

nor·mal·ly /ˈnôrməlē/ ▶ adv. **1** under normal or usual conditions; as a rule. **2** in a normal manner; in the usual way.

nor·mal school ▶ n. formerly, a school or college for the training of teachers.

Nor·man[1] /ˈnôrmən/ a city in central Oklahoma, south of Oklahoma City; pop. 95,694.

Nor·man[2] ▶ n. **1** a member of a people of mixed Frankish and Scandinavian origin who settled in Normandy from about AD 912. ■ in particular, any of the Normans who conquered England in 1066 or their descendants. ■ a native or inhabitant of modern Normandy. **2** the form of French spoken by the Normans. ▶ adj. of, relating to, or denoting the Normans. ■ denoting, relating to, or built in the style of Romanesque architecture used in Britain under the Normans. ■ of or relating to modern Normandy. — **Nor·man·esque** /ˌnôrməˈnesk/ adj. **Nor·man·ism** n. **Nor·man·ize** v. [ME: from OFr. *Normans*, pl. of *Normant*, from ON *Northmathr* 'Northman.']

Nor·man Con·quest the conquest of England by William of Normandy (William the Conqueror) after the Battle of Hastings in 1066.

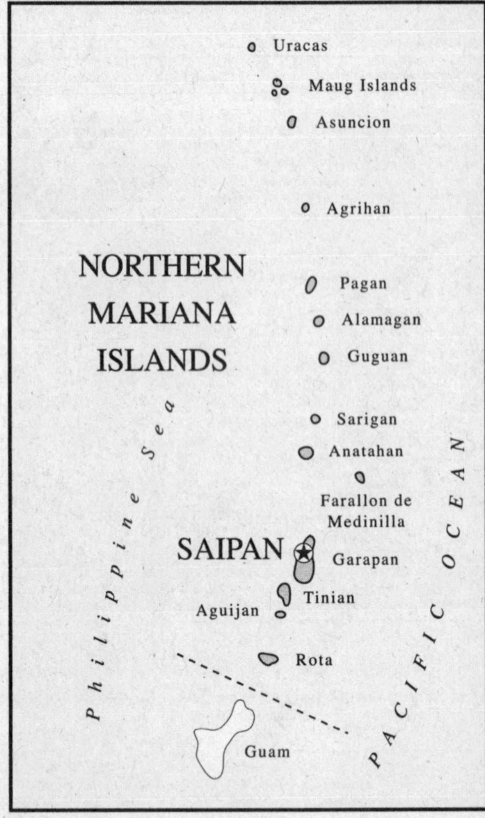

Nor·man·dy /ˈnôrməndē/ a former province of northwestern France, on the English Channel.

Nor·man French ▶ n. the northern form of Old French spoken by the Normans. ■ the variety of this used in English law courts from the 11th to 13th centuries; Anglo-Norman French. ■ the French dialect of modern Normandy.

nor·ma·tive /ˈnôrmətiv/ ▶ adj. formal establishing, relating to, or deriving from a standard or norm, esp. of behavior: *negative sanctions to enforce normative behavior.* — **nor·ma·tive·ly** adv. **nor·ma·tive·ness** n. [19th C.: from Fr. *normatif, -ive*, from L. *norma*.]

nor·mo·ten·sive /ˌnôrmōˈtensiv/ ▶ adj. Med. having or denoting a normal blood pressure.

Norn /nôrn/ ▶ n. a form of Norse formerly spoken in the Orkney and Shetland Islands. ▶ adj. of or relating to this language. [from ON *norrœnn* 'Norn, northern,' from *northr* 'north.']

Norns /nôrnz/ Scand. Mythol. the three virgin goddesses of destiny, who spin the web of fate. [from ON.]

Nor·plant /ˈnôrˌplant/ ▶ n. trademark a contraceptive for women consisting of small rods implanted under the skin that gradually release the hormone levonorgestrel over a number of years.

Nor·ris /ˈnôris/, Frank (1870–1902), US writer; full name *Benjamin Franklin Norris, Jr.* His fiction includes *The Octopus* (1901).

Norr·kö·ping /ˈnôrˌsнœpiɴg; -ˌsнœ-/ a city in southeastern Sweden; pop. 121,000.

Norse /nôrs/ ▶ n. **1** the Norwegian language, esp. in its medieval form. ■ the Scandinavian language group. **2** [treated as pl.] Norwegians or Scandinavians, esp. in medieval times. ▶ adj. of or relating to medieval Norway or Scandinavia, or their inhabitants or language. — **Norse·man** /ˈnôrsmən/ n. (pl. **-men**). [from Du. *noor(d)sch*, from *noord* 'north.']

nor·te·ño /nôrˈtānyō/ ▶ n. **1** (pl. **-ños**) an inhabitant or native of northern Mexico. **2** (also **nor·te·ña** /nôrˈtānyə/) a style of folk music of northern Mexico and Texas, typically featuring an accordion and using polkas of central European immigrants. [Sp., lit. 'northerner.']

North /nôrтн/, Frederick, Lord (1732–92), prime minister of Britain 1770–82. He was held responsible for the loss of the American colonies.

north /nôrтн/ ▶ n. (usu. **the north**) **1** the direction in which a compass needle normally points, toward the horizon on the left side of a person facing east, or the part of the horizon lying in this direction. ■ the compass point corresponding to this. ■ a direction in space parallel to the earth's axis of rotation and toward the point on the celestial sphere around which the stars appear to turn counterclockwise. **2** the north-

ern part of the world or of a specified country, region, or town: *cuisine from the north of Spain.* ■ (usu. **the North**) the northern part of the United States, esp. the northeastern states that fought to preserve the Union during the Civil War. **3** (**North**) [as name] Bridge the player occupying a designated position at the table, sitting opposite and partnering South. ▶ **adj.** [attrib.] **1** lying toward, near, or facing the north: *the north bank of the river | the north door.* ■ (of a wind) blowing from the north. **2** of or denoting the northern part of a specified area, city, or country or its inhabitants: *North African.* ▶ **adv.** to or toward the north: *the landscape became more dramatic as we drove north.*
– PHRASES **north by east** (or **west**) between north and north-northeast (or north-northwest). **up north** informal to or in the north of a country. [OE, of Gmc. origin; rel. to Ger. *nord.*]

North Af·ri·ca the northern part of the African continent, esp. the Mediterranean and Red Sea countries.

North A·mer·i·ca a continent comprising the northern half of the American landmass, connected to South America by the Isthmus of Panama. It contains Canada, the United States, Mexico, the countries of Central America, and usually Greenland. *See map on page 933.*

North A·mer·i·can ▶ **adj.** of or relating to North America. ▶ **n.** a native or inhabitant of North America, esp. a citizen of the US or Canada.

North A·mer·i·can Free Trade A·gree·ment (abbr.: **NAFTA**) an agreement that came into effect in January 1994 between the US, Canada, and Mexico to remove barriers to trade between the three countries over a ten-year period.

North·amp·ton /nôr'THamptən/ a town in southeast central England; pop. 178,000.

North At·lan·tic Drift a continuation of the Gulf Stream across the Atlantic Ocean and along the coast of northwestern Europe.

North At·lan·tic O·cean see ATLANTIC OCEAN.

North At·lan·tic Trea·ty Or·gan·i·za·tion (abbr.: **NATO**) an association of European and North American countries, formed in 1949 for the defense of Europe and the North Atlantic against the perceived threat of Soviet aggression. It includes most major Western powers although France withdrew from the military side of the alliance in 1966.

north·bound /'nôrTH,bound/ ▶ **adj.** traveling or leading toward the north: *northbound traffic.*

North Ca·na·di·an Riv·er (also **Beaver River**) a river that flows from northeastern New Mexico, through Texas and Oklahoma, to the Canadian River.

North Car·o·li·na a state in the east central US, on the Atlantic coast; pop. 8,049,313; capital, Raleigh; statehood, Nov. 21, 1789 (12). First settled by the English in the late 1600s, it was one of the original thirteen states. — **North Car·o·lin·i·an n. & adj.**

North Chan·nel the stretch of sea that separates southwestern Scotland from Northern Ireland.

North Da·ko·ta an agricultural state in the north central US, on the border with Canada; pop. 642,200; capital, Bismarck; statehood, Nov. 2, 1889 (39). Acquired partly by the Louisiana Purchase in 1803 and partly from Britain in 1818, it contains within its boundaries the geographical center of North America. — **North Da·ko·tan n. & adj.**

North·east /,nôrTH'ēst/ a region of the US including the six New England states, New Jersey, and the eastern portions of New York state and Pennsylvania.

north·east /,nôrTH'ēst/ ▶ **n. 1** (usu. **the northeast**) the point of the horizon midway between north and east. ■ the compass point corresponding to this. ■ the direction in which this lies: *the entrance was through a small door to the northeast.* **2** the northeastern part of a country, region, or town. ▶ **adj. 1** lying toward, near, or facing the northeast. ■ (of a wind) coming from the northeast: *there was a strong northeast wind.* **2** of or denoting the northeastern part of a specified country, region, or town, or its inhabitants: *northeast Baltimore.* ▶ **adv.** to or toward the northeast. — **north·east·ern** /-'ēstərn/ **adj.**

north·east·er /,nôrTH'ēstər/ (also **nor'east·er** /,nôr'ēstər/) ▶ **n.** a wind or storm blowing from the northeast.

north·east·er·ly /,nôrTH'ēstərlē/ ▶ **adj. & adv.** another term for NORTHEAST. ▶ **n.** another term for NORTHEASTER.

North-East Pas·sage a passage for ships along the northern coast of Europe and Asia, from the Atlantic Ocean to the Pacific Ocean via the Arctic Ocean.

north·east·ward /,nôrTH'ēstwərd/ ▶ **adv.** toward the northeast; in a northeast direction. ▶ **adj.** situated in, directed toward, or facing the northeast.

North E·qua·to·ri·al Cur·rent an ocean current that flows west across the North Atlantic Ocean just north of the equator.

north·er /'nôr<u>TH</u>ər/ ▶ **n.** a strong cold north wind blowing in autumn and winter over Texas, Florida, and the Gulf of Mexico.

north·er·ly /'nôr<u>TH</u>ərlē/ ▶ **adj. & adv.** in a northward position or direction. ■ (of wind) blowing from the north. ▶ **n.** (often **northerlies**) a wind blowing from the north.

north·ern /'nôr<u>TH</u>ərn/ ▶ **adj. 1** [attrib.] situated in the north, or directed toward or facing the north. ■ (of a wind) blowing from the north. **2** living in or originating from the north. ■ of, relating to, or characteristic of the north or its inhabitants. — **north·ern·most adj.**

North·ern blot ▶ **n.** Biol. an adaptation of the Southern blot procedure used to detect specific sequences of RNA by hybridization with complementary DNA.

North·ern·er /'nôr<u>TH</u>ərnər/ (also **north·ern·er**) ▶ **n.** a native or inhabitant of the north, esp. of the northern US.

north·ern har·ri·er ▶ **n.** a widespread harrier (*Circus cyaneus*) of open country, the male of which is mainly pale gray and the female brown. Also called MARSH HAWK.

north·ern hem·i·sphere the half of the earth that is north of the equator.

North·ern Ire·land a province of the United Kingdom in the northeastern part of Ireland; pop. 1,570,000; capital, Belfast.

north·ern lights another name for the aurora borealis. See AURORA.

North·ern Mar·i·an·a Is·lands /,merē'änə/ a self-governing commonwealth in union with the US, in the western Pacific, comprising the Mariana Islands with the exception of Guam; pop. 78,200; capital, Saipan. *See map on page 934.*

North·ern Rho·de·sia /rō'dēZHə/ former name (until 1964) of ZAMBIA.

North·ern States the states in the north of the US.

North·ern Ter·ri·to·ry a state in north central Australia; pop. 158,000; capital, Darwin.

North Fri·sian Is·lands see FRISIAN ISLANDS.

North Ger·man·ic ▶ **n.** the northern branch of the Germanic languages, descended from Old Norse and comprising Danish, Norwegian, Swedish, Icelandic, and Faeroese. ▶ **adj.** of or relating to North Germanic.

north·ing /'nôrTHiNG; -<u>TH</u>iNG/ ▶ **n.** distance traveled or measured northward, esp. at sea. ■ a figure or line representing northward distance on a map.

North Is·land the more northern of the two main islands of New Zealand.

North Ko·re·a a country in eastern Asia that occupies the northern part of the peninsula of Korea. *See box.* — **North Ko·re·an adj. & n.**

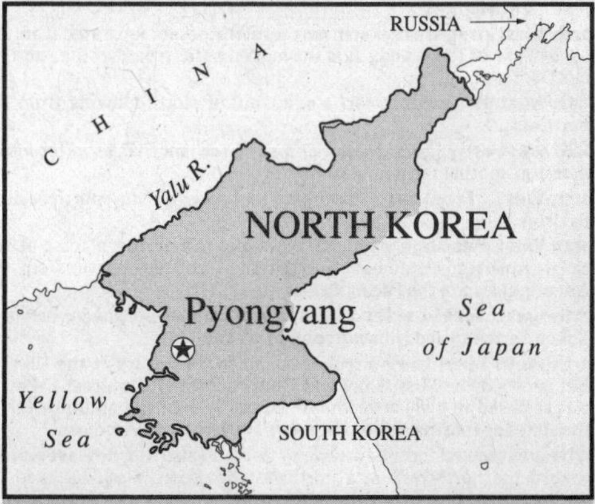

North Korea

Official name: Democratic People's Republic of Korea
Location: eastern Asia, in the northern part of the Korean peninsula
Area: 46,600 square miles (120,500 sq km)
Population: 22,227,000
Capital: Pyongyang
Language: Korean
Currency: North Korean won

north·land /'nôrTHlənd; -,land/ ▶ **n.** (also **northlands**) literary the northern part of a country or region.

North Las Ve·gas a city in southeastern Nevada, a northeastern suburb of Las Vegas; pop. 115,488.

north light ▶ **n.** good natural light without direct sun, esp. as desired by artists.

North·man /'nôrTHmən/ ▶ **n.** (pl. **-men**) archaic a native or inhabitant of Scandinavia, esp. of Norway.

north-north·east ▶ **n.** the compass point or direction midway between north and northeast.

north-north·west ▶ **n.** the compass point or direction midway between north and northwest.

North Os·se·tia an autonomous republic in European Russia; pop. 638,000; capital, Vladikavkaz. Since 1994 it has been called Alania. See also OSSETIA.

North Platte Riv·er a river that flows from northern Colorado to the Platte River in Nebraska.

North Pole ▶ n. see POLE[2].

North Rhine-West·pha·lia a state in west-central Germany; capital, Düsseldorf. German name **NORDRHEIN-WESTFALEN**.

North Sea an arm of the Atlantic Ocean that lies between the mainland of Europe and the coast of Britain.

North Slope a name for regions of Alaska that lie north of the Brooks Range and extend to the Arctic Ocean.

North Star Astron. another term for **POLARIS**.

Northumb. ▶ abbr. Northumberland.

North·um·ber·land /nôr'THəmbərlənd/ a county in northeastern England, on the Scottish border.

North·um·ber·land Strait an ocean passage in the Gulf of St. Lawrence.

North·um·bri·a /nôr'THəmbrēə/ an area of northeastern England. ■ an ancient Anglo-Saxon kingdom in northeastern England. — **North·um·bri·an** adj. & n.

North Vi·et·nam a former communist republic in Southeast Asia, in the northern part of Vietnam, created in 1954 when Vietnam was partitioned. After defeating noncommunist South Vietnam, it declared a reunited, socialist republic (1976).

north·ward /'nôrTHwərd/ ▶ adj. in a northerly direction. ▶ adv. (also **northwards**) toward the north. ▶ n. (**the northward**) the direction or region to the north. — **north·ward·ly** adj. & adv.

north·west /,nôrTH'west/ ▶ n. (usu. **the northwest**) **1** the point of the horizon midway between north and west. ■ the compass point corresponding to this. ■ the direction in which this lies. **2** the northwestern part of a country, region, or town. ▶ adj. **1** lying toward, near, or facing the northwest. ■ (of a wind) blowing from the northwest. **2** of or denoting the northwestern part of a country, region, or town, or its inhabitants. ▶ adv. to or toward the northwest. — **north·west·ern** /-'westərn/ adj.

North·west An·gle a region in northern Minnesota separated from the US by Lake of the Woods. It is the most northern part of the contiguous US.

north·west·er /,nôrTH'westər/ ▶ n. a wind or storm blowing from the northwest.

north·west·er·ly /,nôrTH'westərlē/ ▶ adj. & adv. another term for **NORTHWEST**. ▶ n. another term for **NORTHWESTER**.

North-West Fron·tier Prov·ince a province in northwestern Pakistan.

North-West Pas·sage a sea passage along the northern coast of the North American continent, through the Canadian Arctic from the Atlantic Ocean to the Pacific Ocean.

North·west Ter·ri·to·ries a territory of northern Canada, between Yukon Territory and Nunavut; capital, Yellowknife.

North·west Ter·ri·to·ry a region and former territory of the US that lies between the Mississippi and Ohio rivers and the Great Lakes. It was acquired in 1783 after the American Revolution and now forms the states of Indiana, Ohio, Michigan, Illinois, and Wisconsin.

north·west·ward /,nôrTH'westwərd/ ▶ adv. (also **north·west·wards**) toward the northwest; in a northwest direction. ▶ adj. situated in, directed toward, or facing the northwest.

Nor·walk /'nôr,wôk/ **1** a city in southwestern California, southeast of Los Angeles; pop. 94,279. **2** a city in southwestern Connecticut; pop. 82,951.

Nor·way /'nôr,wā/ a country in northwestern Europe. *See box.*

Nor·way lob·ster ▶ n. another term for **LANGOUSTINE**.

Nor·way ma·ple ▶ n. a large Eurasian maple, *Acer platanoides*, with yellow flowers that appear before the lobed leaves, widely planted as an ornamental shade tree.

Nor·way rat ▶ n. another term for **BROWN RAT**.

Nor·way spruce ▶ n. a long-coned European spruce (*Picea abies*) that is widely grown as an ornamental and for timber and pulp.

Nor·we·gian /nôr'wējən/ ▶ adj. of or relating to Norway or its people or language. ▶ n. **1** a native or national of Norway, or a person of Norwegian descent. **2** the North Germanic language of Norway. [from med. L. *Norvegia* 'Norway.']

Nor·we·gian Sea a sea between Iceland and Norway.

Nor·wich ter·ri·er ▶ n. a small thickset terrier of a breed with a rough coat and pricked ears.

n.o.s. ▶ abbr. not otherwise specified.

nos. ▶ abbr. numbers. [pl. of **No.**]

nose /nōz/ ▶ n. **1** the part projecting above the mouth on the face of a person or animal, containing the nostrils and used for breathing and smelling. ■ [in sing.] the sense of smell, esp. a dog's ability to track something by its scent. ■ [in sing.] fig. an instinctive talent for detecting something. ■ the aroma of a particular substance, esp. wine. **2** the front end of an aircraft, car, or other vehicle. ■ a projecting part of something: *the nose of the saddle.* **3** [in sing.] a look, esp. out of curiosity: *she wanted a good nose around the house.* ■ informal a police informer. ▶ v. **1** [no obj., with adverbial of place] (of an animal) thrust its nose against or into something, esp. in order to smell it: *the pony nosed at the straw.* ■ [trans.] smell or sniff (something). **2** [intrans.] investigate or pry into something: *she's always nosing into my business.* ■ [trans.] detect in such a way. **3** [no obj., with adverbial of direction] (of a vehicle or its driver) move cautiously forward: *he nosed into an empty parking space.* ■ (of a competitor) manage to achieve a winning or leading position, esp. by a small margin.
– PHRASES **by a nose** (of a victory) by a very narrow margin. **count noses** count people, typically in order to determine the numbers in a vote. **keep one's nose clean** informal stay out of trouble. **keep one's nose out of** refrain from interfering in (someone else's affairs). **keep one's nose to the grindstone** see **GRINDSTONE**. **nose to tail** (of vehicles) moving or standing close behind one another, esp. in heavy traffic. **not see further than one's** (or **the end of one's**) **nose** be unwilling or fail to consider different possibilities or to foresee the consequences of one's actions. **on the nose 1** to a person's sense of smell. **2** informal precisely. **3** informal (of betting) on a horse to win (as opposed to being placed). **put someone's nose out of joint** informal upset or annoy someone. **turn one's nose up at something** informal show distaste or contempt for something. **under someone's nose** informal directly in front of someone. ■ (of an action) committed openly and boldly, but without someone noticing or noticing in time to prevent it. **with one's nose in the air** haughtily. — **nosed** adj. [in comb.] *snub-nosed.* **nose·less** adj. [OE *nosu*, of West Gmc. origin; rel. Ger. *Nase*, L. *nasus*, and **NESS**.]

Norway

Official name: Kingdom of Norway
Location: northwestern Europe, on the northern and western coastline of Scandinavia, on the Norwegian Sea and the Arctic Ocean
Area: 125,200 square miles (324,200 sq km)
Population: 4,574,000
Capital: Oslo
Languages: Norwegian (official), small Sami- and Finnish-speaking minorities
Currency: Norwegian krone

nose·bag /'nōz,bag/ ▶ n. a strong canvas or leather bag containing grain, fastened over a horse's muzzle for feeding.

nose·band /'nōz,band/ ▶ n. the strap of a bridle or halter that passes over a horse's nose and under its chin.

nose·bleed /'nōz,blēd/ ▶ n. an instance of bleeding from the nose. ■ [as adj.] informal denoting cheap seating in an extremely high position in a sports stadium or concert hall.

nose can·dy ▶ n. informal an illegal drug that is inhaled, esp. cocaine.

nose cone ▶ n. the cone-shaped nose of a rocket or aircraft.

nose·dive /'nōz,dīv/ ▶ n. a steep downward plunge by an aircraft. ■ fig. a sudden dramatic deterioration. ▶ v. [intrans.] (of an aircraft) make a nosedive. ■ fig. deteriorate suddenly and dramatically. *massive strikes caused the economy to nosedive.*

no-see-um /nō 'sē əm/ ▶ n. a minute bloodsucking insect, esp. a biting midge.

nose·gay /'nōz,gā/ ▶ n. a small bunch of flowers, typically one that is sweet-scented.

nose guard ▶ n. another term for **NOSE TACKLE**.

nose job ▶ n. informal an operation involving rhinoplasty or cosmetic surgery on a person's nose.

nose leaf ▶ n. a fleshy leaf-shaped structure on the nose of many bats, used for echolocation.

nose·piece /ˈnōz,pēs/ ▶ **n.** **1** the part of a helmet or headdress that protects a person's nose. ■ another term for NOSEBAND. ■ the central part of a pair of glasses that fits over the bridge of the nose. **2** the part of a microscope to which the objective lenses are attached.

nose ring ▶ **n.** a ring fixed in the nose of an animal, typically a bull, for leading it. ■ a ring worn in a person's nose as a piece of jewelry.

nose tack·le ▶ **n.** Football a defensive lineman positioned opposite the center.

nose wheel ▶ **n.** a landing wheel under the nose of an aircraft.

nos·ey /ˈnōzē/ ▶ **adj. & v.** var. of NOSY.

nos·ey Par·ker ▶ **n.** var. of NOSY PARKER.

nosh /näsʜ/ informal ▶ **n.** food. ■ a small item of food. ■ a light meal; a snack. ▶ **v.** [intrans.] eat food enthusiastically or greedily: *you can nosh to your heart's content* | [trans.] *noshing my favorite food.* ■ eat between meals. [20th C.: Yiddish.]

no-show ▶ **n.** a person who has made a reservation or appointment but neither keeps nor cancels it.

nos·ing /ˈnōziNG/ ▶ **n.** a rounded edge of a step or molding. ■ a metal shield for such an edge.

nos·o·co·mi·al /,näsəˈkōmēəl/ ▶ **adj.** Med. (of a disease) originating in a hospital. [19th C.: from Gk. *nosokomos* 'person who tends the sick' + -IAL.]

no·sog·ra·phy /nōˈsägrəfē/ ▶ **n.** the systematic description of diseases. — **no·so·graph·ic** /,nōsəˈgrafik; ,nä-/ **adj.** [17th C.: from Gk. *nosos* 'disease' + -GRAPHY.]

no·sol·o·gy /nōˈsäləjē/ ▶ **n.** the branch of medical science dealing with the classification of diseases. — **nos·o·log·i·cal** /,näsəˈläjikəl/ **adj.** **no·sol·o·gist n.** [18th C.: from Gk. *nosos* 'disease' + -LOGY.]

nos·tal·gia /näˈstaljə; nə-/ ▶ **n.** a sentimental longing for the past, typically for a period or place with happy personal associations. ■ the evocation of these feelings or tendencies, esp. in commercialized form. — **nos·tal·gic** /-jik/ **adj.** **nos·tal·gi·cal·ly** /-jik(ə)lē/ **adv.** **nos·tal·gist** /-jist/ **n.** [18th C.: mod. L., from Gk. *nostos* 'return home' + *algos* 'pain.']

nos·tal·gie de la boue /,nôstälˈzʜēd lä ˈbo͞o/ ▶ **n.** a desire for degradation and depravity. [Fr., lit. 'nostalgia for mud.']

nos·toc /ˈnästäk/ ▶ **n.** Biol. a microorganism (genus *Nostoc*, division Cyanobacteria) composed of beaded filaments that aggregate to form a gelatinous mass, growing in water and damp places and able to fix nitrogen from the atmosphere. [name invented by Paracelsus.]

Nos·tra·da·mus /,nôstrəˈdäməs; ,nästrəˈdāməs/ (1503–66), French astrologer; Latinized name of *Michel de Nostredame*. His cryptic and apocalyptic predictions in rhyming quatrains appeared in two collections (1555, 1558).

Nos·trat·ic /näˈstratik/ ▶ **n.** a hypothetical phylum of languages comprising the Indo-European, Semitic, Altaic, and Dravidian families. ▶ **adj.** of or relating to this language phylum. [1960s: from Ger. *nostratisch*, based on L. *nostras, nostrat-* 'of our country.']

nos·tril /ˈnästrəl/ ▶ **n.** either of two external openings of the nasal cavity in vertebrates that admit air to the lungs and smells to the olfactory nerves. [OE *nosterl, nosthyrl*, from *nosu* 'nose' + *thȳr(e)l* 'hole.']

nos·trum /ˈnästrəm/ ▶ **n.** a medicine, esp. an ineffective one, prepared by an unqualified person. ■ a pet scheme, esp. one for bringing about some social or political reform or improvement. [17th C.: L., neut. of *noster* 'our.']

nos·y /ˈnōzē/ (also **nos·ey**) informal ▶ **adj.** (**nos·i·er, nos·i·est**) (of a person or their behavior) showing too much curiosity about other people's affairs. ▶ **v.** [no obj., with adverbial] pry into something: *they don't nosy into your business like some people.* — **nos·i·ly adv.** **nos·i·ness n.**

Nos·y Par·ker (also **nos·y Park·er**) ▶ **n.** informal an overly inquisitive person.

not /nät/ ▶ **adv.** **1** (also **n't** joined to a preceding verb) used with an auxiliary verb or "be" to form the negative: *he would not say.* ■ used in some constructions with other verbs: [with infin.] *he has been warned not to touch* | *the pain of not knowing.* **2** used as a short substitute for a negative clause: *maybe I'll regret it, but I hope not* | *"Don't you keep in touch?" "I'm afraid not."* **3** used to express the negative of other words: *not a single attempt was made* | *"How was it?" "Not so bad."* ■ used with a quantifier to exclude a person or part of a group: *not all the poems are serious.* ■ less than (used to indicate a surprisingly small quantity): *the brakes went on not ten feet from him.* **4** used in understatements to suggest that the opposite of a following word or phrase is true: *the not too distant future.* ■ informal, humorous following and emphatically negating a statement: *that sounds like quality entertainment—not.* ▶ **n.** (often **NOT**) Electron. a Boolean operator with only one variable that has the value one when the variable is zero and vice versa.

– PHRASES **not at all 1** used as a polite response to thanks. **2** definitely not. **not but what** archaic nevertheless: *not but what the picture has its darker side.* **not half** see HALF. **not least** see LEAST. **not quite** see QUITE. **not that** it is not to be inferred that: *I'll never be allowed back—not that I'd want to go back.* **not very** see VERY. [ME: contr. of the adv. NOUGHT.]

no·ta be·ne /ˈnōtə ˈbenē/ (abbr.: **n.b.** or **N.B.**) ▶ **v.** [in imper.] formal observe carefully or take special notice. [L., lit. 'note well!']

no·ta·bil·i·ty /,nōtəˈbilitē/ ▶ **n.** (pl. **-ties**) a famous or important person.

no·ta·ble /ˈnōtəbəl/ ▶ **adj.** worthy of attention or notice; remarkable. ▶ **n.** (usu. **notables**) a famous or important person. [ME: from OFr., from L. *notabilis* 'worthy of note,' from the v. *notare* 'to note, mark.']

no·ta·bly /ˈnōtəblē/ ▶ **adv.** especially; in particular. ■ in a way that is striking or remarkable.

no·ta·rize /ˈnōtə,rīz/ ▶ **v.** [trans.] have (a document) legalized by a notary.

no·ta·ry /ˈnōtərē/ (in full **notary public**) ▶ **n.** (pl. **-ries**) a person authorized to perform certain legal formalities, esp. to draw up or certify documents. — **no·tar·i·al** /nōˈterēəl/ **adj.** [ME: from L. *notarius* 'secretary,' from *nota* 'mark.']

no·tate /ˈnō,tāt/ ▶ **v.** [trans.] write (something, typically music) in notation. — **no·ta·tor** /-,tātər/ **n.** [20th C.: back-form. from NOTATION.]

no·ta·tion /nōˈtāsʜən/ ▶ **n.** **1** a series or system of written symbols used to represent numbers, amounts, or elements in something such as music or mathematics. **2** a note or annotation. **3** short for *SCALE OF NOTATION* (see SCALE[3] sense 2). — **no·ta·tion·al adj.** [16th C.: from L. *notatio(n-)*, from the v. *notare*, from *nota* 'mark.']

not·be·ing ▶ **n.** nonexistence.

notch /näcʜ/ ▶ **n.** **1** an indentation or incision on an edge or surface. ■ each of a series of holes for the tongue of a buckle. ■ a nick made on something in order to keep a score or record: *he had a six-gun with four notches in it for guys he had killed.* ■ a point or degree in a scale. **2** a deep, narrow mountain pass. ▶ **v.** [trans.] **1** make notches in. ■ secure or insert by means of notches: *she notched her belt tighter.* **2** score or achieve (something). — **notch·er n.** [16th C.: prob. from Anglo-Norman Fr. *noche*, var. of OFr. *osche*.]

notch·back /ˈnäcʜ,bak/ ▶ **n.** a car with a back that extends approximately horizontally from the bottom of the rear window so as to make a distinct angle with it.

note /nōt/ ▶ **n.** **1** a brief record of facts, topics, or thoughts, written down as an aid to memory. ■ a short comment on or explanation of a word or passage in a book or article; an annotation. **2** a short informal letter or written message. ■ an official letter sent from the representative of one government to another. ■ [usu. with adj.] a short official document that certifies a particular thing. **3** Brit. a banknote: *a ten-pound note.* **4** a single tone of definite pitch made by a musical instrument or the human voice. ■ a written sign representing the pitch and duration of such a sound. ■ a key of a piano or similar instrument: *black notes* | *white notes.* ■ a bird's song or call, or a single tone in this. **5** [in sing.] a particular quality or tone that reflects or expresses a mood or attitude: *there was a note of scorn in her voice.* ■ any of the basic components of fragrance or flavor: *the fresh note of bergamot.* ▶ **v.** [trans.] **1** notice or pay particular attention to (something): *noting his mother's unusual gaiety.* ■ remark upon (something), typically in order to draw someone's attention to it: *we noted the difficulties in this strategy.* **2** record (something) in writing: *he **noted down** her address on a piece of paper.*

– PHRASES **hit** (or **strike**) **the right** (or **wrong**) **note** say or do something in exactly the right (or wrong) way. **of note 1** worth paying attention to. **2** important; distinguished. **strike** (or **sound**) **a note of** express (a particular feeling or view) about something: *he sounded a note of caution.* **take note** pay attention. [ME: from OFr. *note* (n.), *noter* (v.), from L. *nota* 'a mark,' *notare* 'to mark.']

note·book /ˈnōt,bo͝ok/ ▶ **n.** a small book with blank or ruled pages for writing notes in. ■ a portable computer that is smaller than a laptop.

note·card /ˈnōt,kärd/ (also **note card**) ▶ **n.** a decorative card with a blank space for a short message.

note·case /ˈnōt,kās/ ▶ **n.** Brit., dated a small billfold or wallet.

note clus·ter ▶ **n.** Music a chord containing a number of closely adjacent notes. Also called TONE CLUSTER.

not·ed /ˈnōtid/ ▶ **adj.** well known; famous.

note·pad /ˈnōt,pad/ ▶ **n.** a pad of blank or ruled pages for writing notes on. ■ (also **notepad computer**) a pocket-sized personal computer that has a stylus with which the user writes on the screen to input text.

note·pa·per /ˈnōt,pāpər/ ▶ **n.** paper for writing letters on.

note·wor·thy /ˈnōt,wərt͟hē/ ▶ **adj.** interesting, significant, or unusual. — **note·wor·thi·ness n.**

not-for-prof·it ▶ **adj.** another term for NONPROFIT.

'noth·er /ˈnət͟hər/ ▶ **adj. & pron.** informal nonstandard spelling of ANOTHER, used to represent informal speech: *'nother thing just occurred to me.*

noth·ing /ˈnətʜiNG/ ▶ **pron.** not anything; no single thing: *I said nothing.* ■ something of no importance or concern: *they are nothing to him* | [as n.] *no longer could we be treated as nothings.* ■ (in calculations) no amount; zero. ▶ **adj.** [attrib.] informal having no prospect of progress; of no value: *he had a series of nothing jobs.* ▶ **adv.** not at all: *she cares nothing for others.* ■ [postpositive] informal used to contradict something emphatically: *"This is a surprise." "Surprise nothing."*

– PHRASES **be nothing to do with** see DO[1]. **for nothing 1** at no cost; without payment. **2** to no purpose. **have nothing on someone** see HAVE. **have nothing to do with** see DO[1]. **no nothing** informal (concluding a list of negatives) nothing at all: *how could you solve it with no clues, no witnesses, no nothing?* **not for nothing** for a very good reason. **nothing but** only: *nothing but the best will do.* **nothing daunted** see DAUNT. **nothing doing** informal **1** there is no prospect of success or agreement. **2** nothing is happening. **nothing** (or **nothing else**) **for it** Brit. no alternative. **nothing less than** used to emphasize how extreme something is: *it was nothing less than sexual harassment.* **nothing loath** quite willing. **there is nothing to it** there is no difficulty involved. **stop at nothing** see STOP. **sweet nothings** words of affection exchanged by lovers. **think nothing of it** do not apologize or feel bound to show gratitude (used as a polite response). **you ain't seen nothing yet** informal used to indicate that although something may be considered extreme or impressive, there is something even more extreme or impressive in store. [OE *nān thing* (see NO, THING).]

noth·ing·ness /'nəTHiNGnis/ ▶ **n.** the absence or cessation of life or existence. ■ worthlessness; unimportance.

no·tice /'nōtis/ ▶ **n.** **1** attention; observation: *their silence did not escape my notice.* **2** notification or warning of something, esp. to allow preparations to be made: *interest rates are subject to fluctuation without notice.* ■ a formal declaration of one's intention to end an agreement, typically one concerning employment or tenancy, at a specified time. **3** a displayed sheet or placard giving news or information. ■ a small advertisement or announcement in a newspaper or magazine. ■ (usu. **notices**) a short published review or comment about a new film, play, or book: *she had good notices in her first film.* ▶ **v.** [trans.] become aware of: *he noticed the youths behaving suspiciously* | [intrans.] *they were too drunk to notice.* ■ (usu. **be noticed**) treat (someone) with attention or recognition: *it was only last year that he began to be noticed.* ■ archaic remark upon: *she looked so much better that Sir Charles noticed it to Lady Harriet.*

– PHRASES **at short** (or **a moment's**) **notice** with little warning or time for preparation. **put someone on notice** (or **serve notice**) warn someone of something about or likely to occur, esp. in a formal or threatening manner. **take no notice** pay no attention to someone or something. **take notice** pay attention; show signs of interest. [ME (sense 2): from OFr., from L. *notitia* 'being known,' from *notus* 'known' (see NOTION).]

no·tice·a·ble /'nōtisəbəl/ ▶ **adj.** easily seen or noticed; clear or apparent. ■ noteworthy. — **no·tice·a·bly adv.**

no·ti·fi·a·ble /,nōtə'fīəbəl/ ▶ **adj.** denoting something, typically a serious infectious disease, that must be reported to the appropriate authorities.

no·ti·fy /'nōtə,fī/ ▶ **v.** (**-fies, -fied**) [trans.] inform (someone) of something, typically in a formal or official manner: *you will be **notified of** our decision as soon as possible.* ■ esp. Brit. give notice of or report (something) formally or officially. — **no·ti·fi·ca·tion** /,nōtəfi'kāSHən/ **n.** [ME: from OFr. *notifier*, from L. *notificare* 'make known,' from *notus* 'known' (see NOTION) + *facere* 'make.']

no·tion /'nōSHən/ ▶ **n.** **1** a conception of or belief about something. ■ a vague awareness or understanding of the nature of something. **2** an impulse or desire, esp. one of a whimsical kind. **3** (**notions**) items used in sewing, such as buttons, pins, and hooks. [ME: from L. *notio(n-)* 'idea,' from *notus* 'known,' past part. of *noscere*.]

no·tion·al /'nōSHənəl/ ▶ **adj.** **1** existing only in theory or as a suggestion or idea. ■ existing only in the imagination. **2** Ling. denoting or relating to an approach to grammar that is dependent on the definition of terminology (e.g., "a verb is an action word") as opposed to identification of structures and processes. — **no·tion·al·ly adv.**

no·to·chord /'nōtə,kôrd/ ▶ **n.** Zool. a cartilaginous skeletal rod supporting the body in all embryonic and some adult chordate animals. [19th C.: from Gk. *nōton* 'back' + CHORD[2].]

No·to·gae·a /,nōtə'jēə/ (also **No·to·ge·a**) Zool. a zoogeographical area comprising the Australian region. — **No·to·gae·an adj.** [19th C.: mod. L., from Gk. *notos* 'south wind' + *gaia* 'earth.']

no·to·ri·ous /nə'tôrēəs; nō-/ ▶ **adj.** famous or well known, typically for some bad quality or deed. — **no·to·ri·e·ty** /,nōtə'rīətē/ **n.** **no·to·ri·ous·ly adv.** [15th C.: from med. L. *notorius* (from L. *notus* 'known') + -OUS.]

no·to·un·gu·late /,nōtō'əNGgyəlit/ ▶ **n.** an extinct hoofed mammal (order Notoungulata) of a large and varied group that lived in South America throughout the Tertiary period, finally dying out in the Pleistocene. [20th C.: from mod. L. *Notoungulata*, from Gk. *notos* 'south' + L. *ungula* 'nail.']

No·tre Dame /,nōtrə 'däm; ,nōtər 'dām/ a Gothic cathedral in Paris, dedicated to the Virgin Mary, built between 1163 and 1250.

no-trump ▶ **n.** Bridge a situation in which no suit is designated as trump.

Not·ting·ham /'nätiNGəm/ a city in east central England; pop. 261,000.

Not·ting·ham·shire /'nätiNGəmSHər; -,SHi(ə)r/ a county in central England; county town, Nottingham.

Notts. ▶ **abbr.** Nottinghamshire.

no·tum /'nōtəm/ ▶ **n.** (pl. **-ta** /-tə/) Entomol. the dorsal exoskeleton of the thorax of an insect. — **no·tal** /'nōtl/ **adj.** [19th C.: from Gk. *nōton* 'back.']

not·with·stand·ing /,nätwiTH'standiNG; -wiTH-/ ▶ **prep.** in spite of. ▶ **adv.** nevertheless; in spite of this. ▶ **conj.** although; in spite of the fact that. [ME: from NOT + *withstanding*, pres. part. of WITHSTAND.]

Nouak·chott /nə'wäk,SHät/ the capital of Mauritania, on the Atlantic coast; pop. 850,000.

nou·gat /'no͞ogit/ ▶ **n.** a candy made from sugar or honey, nuts, and egg white. [19th C.: from Fr., from Provençal *nogat*, from *noga* 'nut.']

nought ▶ **n. & pron.** var. of NAUGHT.

Nou·mé·a /no͞o'mā ə/ the capital of New Caledonia; pop. 65,000. Former name PORT DE FRANCE.

nou·me·non /'no͞omə,nän/ ▶ **n.** (pl. **-na** /-nə/) (in Kantian philosophy) a thing as it is in itself, as distinct from a thing as it is knowable by the senses through phenomenal attributes. — **nou·me·nal** /-nəl/ **adj.** [18th C.: via Ger. from Gk., lit. '(something) conceived,' from *noien* 'conceive, apprehend.']

noun /noun/ ▶ **n.** Gram. a word (other than a pronoun) used to identify any of a class of people, places, or things (**common noun**), or to name a particular one of these (**proper noun**). — **noun·al** /'nounl/ **adj.** [ME: from Anglo-Norman Fr., from L. *nomen* 'name.']

noun phrase ▶ **n.** Gram. a word or group of words that functions in a sentence as subject, object, or prepositional object.

nour·ish /'nəriSH; 'nə-riSH/ ▶ **v.** [trans.] **1** provide with substances necessary for growth, health, and good condition. ■ enhance the fertility of (soil). **2** keep (a feeling or belief) in one's mind, typically for a long time. — **nour·ish·er n.** [ME: from OFr. *noriss-*, lengthened stem of *norir*, from L. *nutrire* 'feed, cherish.']

nour·ish·ing /'nəriSHiNG; 'nə-ri-/ ▶ **adj.** (of food) containing substances necessary for growth, health, and good condition: *a simple but nourishing meal.* — **nour·ish·ing·ly adv.**

nour·ish·ment /'nəriSHmənt; 'nə-riSH-/ ▶ **n.** the substances necessary for growth, health, and good condition. ■ food. ■ the action of nourishing someone or something.

nous /no͞os; nous/ ▶ **n.** **1** Philos. the mind or intellect. **2** informal, esp. Brit. common sense; practical intelligence: *if he had any nous at all, he'd sell the movie rights.* [17th C.: from Gk., 'mind.']

nou·veau /'no͞ovō; no͞o'vō/ ▶ **adj.** informal **1** short for NOUVEAU RICHE. **2** modern; up to date.

nou·veau riche /'no͞ovō 'rēSH/ ▶ **n.** [treated as pl.] (usu. **the nouveau riche**) people who have recently acquired wealth, typically those perceived as ostentatious or lacking in good taste. ▶ **adj.** of, relating to, or characteristic of such people. [Fr., lit. 'new rich.']

nou·velle /no͞o'vel/ ▶ **adj.** of, relating to, or specializing in nouvelle cuisine: *nouvelle bistros.*

Nou·velle-Ca·lé·do·nie /no͞o'vel ,kälədô'nē/ French name for NEW CALEDONIA.

nou·velle cui·sine /no͞o'vel kwi'zēn/ ▶ **n.** a modern style of cooking that avoids rich, heavy foods and emphasizes the freshness of the ingredients and the presentation of the dishes. [Fr., lit. 'new cooking.']

nou·velle vague /no͞o'vel 'väg/ ▶ **n.** a grouping of French movie directors in the late 1950s and 1960s who reacted against established French cinema and sought to make more innovative films. [Fr., lit. 'new wave.']

Nov. ▶ **abbr.** November.

no·va /'nōvə/ ▶ **n.** (pl. **-vae** /-vē; -,vī/ or **-vas**) Astron. a star showing a sudden large increase in brightness and then slowly returning to its original state over a few months. See also SUPERNOVA. [19th C.: from L., fem. of *novus* 'new.']

no·vac·u·lite /nō'vakyə,līt/ ▶ **n.** Geol. a hard, dense, fine-grained siliceous rock resembling chert, with a high content of microcrystalline quartz. [18th C.: from L. *novacula* 'razor' + -ITE[1].]

No·va Lis·bo·a /'nōvə lēzH'bōə; ,nôvə lēzH'vōə/ former name (until 1978) for HUAMBO.

No·va Sco·tia /'nōvə 'skōSHə/ **1** a peninsula on the southeastern coast of Canada that projects into the Atlantic Ocean. **2** a province in eastern Canada that consists of the Nova Scotia peninsula and adjoining Cape Breton Island; pop. 899,942; capital, Halifax. Settled as Acadia by the French in the early 18th century, it changed hands several times before being awarded to Britain in 1713. It became one of the original four provinces in the Dominion of Canada in 1867. — **No·va Sco·tian adj. & n.**

no·va·tion /nō'vāSHən/ ▶ **n.** Law the substitution of a new contract in place of an old one. — **no·vate** /'nōvāt; nō'vāt/ **v.** [16th C.: from late L. *novatio(n-)*, from the v. *novare* 'make new.']

No·va·ya Zem·lya /'nōvəyə ,zemlē'ä/ two large uninhabited islands in the Arctic Ocean off the northern coast of Siberian Russia.

nov·el[1] /'nävəl/ ▶ **n.** a fictitious prose narrative of book length, typically representing character and action with some degree of realism. ■ a book containing such a narrative. ■ (**the novel**) the literary genre represented or exemplified by such works. — **nov·el·is·tic** /,nävə'listik/ **adj.** [16th C.: from Ital. *novella (storia)* 'new (story).']

nov·el[2] ▶ **adj.** new or unusual in an interesting way: *a novel idea to make some money.* — **nov·el·ly adv.** [ME: from OFr., from L. *novellus*, from *novus* 'new.']

nov·el·ette /,nävə'let/ ▶ **n.** esp. derog. a short novel, typically one that is light and romantic or sentimental. — **nov·el·et·tish adj.**

nov·el·ist /'nävəlist/ ▶ **n.** a writer of novels.

nov·el·ize /'nävə,līz/ ▶ **v.** [trans.] [usu. as adj.] (**novelized**) convert (a story, movie, or screenplay) into a novel. — **nov·el·i·za·tion** /,nävəli'zāSHən/ **n.**

no·vel·la /nō'velə/ ▶ **n.** a short novel or long short story. [20th C.: from Ital., 'novel.']

nov·el·ty /'nävəltē/ ▶ **n.** (pl. **-ties**) **1** the quality of being new, original, or unusual. ■ a new or unfamiliar thing or experience. ■ [as adj.] denoting something intended to be amusing as a result of its new or unusual quality: *a novelty teapot.* **2** a small and inexpensive toy or ornament. [ME: from OFr. *novelte*, from *novel* 'new, fresh' (see NOVEL[2]).]

No·vem·ber /nō'vembər; nə-/ ▶ **n.** **1** the eleventh month of the year, in the northern hemisphere usually considered the last month of autumn. **2** a code word representing the letter N, used in radio communication. [OE, from L., from *novem* 'nine.']

no·ve·na /nō'vēnə/ ▶ **n.** (in the Roman Catholic Church) a form of devotion consisting of special prayers or services on nine successive days. [19th C.: from med. L., from L. *novem* 'nine.']

Nov·go·rod /'nôvgərət; 'nävgə,räd/ a city in northwestern Russia; pop. 232,000. It is Russia's oldest city.

nov·ice /ˈnävəs/ ▶ **n.** a person new to or inexperienced in a field or situation: *he was a complete novice in foreign affairs.* ■ a person who has entered a religious order and is under probation, before taking vows. ■ an animal, esp. a racehorse, that has not yet won a major prize or reached a level of performance to qualify for important events. [ME: from OFr., from late L. *novicius*, from *novus* 'new.']

No·vi Sad /ˌnōvē ˈsäd/ a city in Serbia, capital of of Vojvodina province; pop. 179,000.

no·vi·ti·ate /nōˈvisʜ(ē)ət; nə-/ (also **no·vi·ci·ate**) ▶ **n.** the period or state of being a novice, esp. in a religious order. ■ a place housing religious novices. ■ a novice, esp. in a religious order. [17th C.: from eccles. Latin *noviciatus*, from L. *novicius*.]

no·vo·caine /ˈnōvəˌkān/ (also trademark **No·vo·cain**) ▶ **n.** another term for PROCAINE. [20th C.: from L. *novus* 'new' + *-caine* (from COCAINE).]

No·vo·kuz·netsk /ˌnōvəko͝ozˈn(y)etsk/ a city in Russia, in central Siberia; pop. 601,000.

No·vo·si·birsk /ˌnōvəsiˈbirsk/ a city in Russia, in central Siberia, on the Ob River; pop. 1,443,000.

No·vot·ný /ˈnôvôtˌnē/, Antonín (1904–75), president of Czechoslovakia 1957–68. He was a founding member of the Czechoslovak Communist Party in 1921.

NOW ▶ **abbr.** National Organization for Women.

now /nou/ ▶ **adv.** **1** at the present time or moment: *where are you living now?* ■ at the time directly following the present moment; immediately: *if we leave now, we can be home by ten.* ■ under the present circumstances; as a result of something that has recently happened. *I didn't receive the letter, but it hardly matters now.* ■ on this further occasion, typically as the latest in a series of annoying situations or events: *what do you want now?* ■ used to emphasize a particular length of time: *they've been married four years now.* ■ (in a narrative or account of past events) at the time spoken of or referred to: *it had happened three times now.* **2** used, esp. in conversation, to draw attention to a particular statement or point in a narrative: *now, my first impulse was to run away.* ■ used when turning to a different subject or activity: *and **now for** something completely different* **3** used in or as a request, instruction, or question, typically to give a slight emphasis to one's words: *now, if you'll excuse me?* ■ used when pausing or considering one's next words: *let me see now; oh yes, I remember.* **4** used at the end of an ironic question echoing a previous statement: *"Mom says for you to give me some of your stamps." "Does she now?"* ▶ **conj.** as a consequence of the fact: *they spent a lot of time together **now that** he had retired.* ▶ **adj.** informal fashionable; up to date: *seventies disco dancing—very now.*

– PHRASES **for now** until a later time: *that's all the news for now.* **now now** used as an expression of mild remonstrance: *now now, that's not the way to behave.* **now then 1** used to get someone's attention or to invite a response: *now then, who's for a coffee?* **2** used as an expression of mild remonstrance or warning: *now then, Emily, I think Sarah has suffered enough.* **now you're talking** used to express one's enthusiastic approval of a statement or suggestion. — **now·ness n.** [OE. *nū*, rel. to Ger. *nun*, from an Indo-Eur. root shared by L. *nunc* and Gk. *nun*.]

now·a·days /ˈnouəˌdāz/ ▶ **adv.** at the present time, in contrast with the past.

no·way /ˈnōˌwā/ (also **noways**) ▶ **adv.** another term for NOWISE. See also *NO WAY* at NO.

no·where /ˈnōˌ(h)we(ə)r/ ▶ **adv.** not in or to any place; not anywhere: *Andrea is nowhere to be found.* ▶ **pron.** **1** no place: *there was nowhere for her to sit.* **2** a place that is remote, uninteresting, or nondescript: *a stretch of road between nowhere and nowhere* | [as n.] *the town is a particularly American nowhere.* ▶ **adj.** [attrib.] informal having no prospect of progress or success: *she's having a nowhere affair with a married man.*

– PHRASES **from** (or **out of**) **nowhere** appearing or happening suddenly and unexpectedly. **get** (or **go**) **nowhere** make no progress. **get someone nowhere** be of no use or benefit to someone: *being angry would get her nowhere.* **nowhere near** not nearly. **a road to nowhere** a situation or course of action offering no prospects of progress or advancement.

no·wheres /ˈnōˌ(h)w(ə)rz/ informal ▶ **adv.** nowhere.

no·wheres·ville /ˈnō(h)w(ə)rzˌvil/ (also **No·wheres·ville**) ▶ **n.** informal **1** a remote town or village. **2** a job or position that lacks prestige, recognition, or the opportunity for advancement. **3** anything that is impractical, unrealistic, or fruitless.

no-win ▶ **adj.** of or denoting a situation in which success or a favorable outcome is impossible.

no·wise /ˈnōˌwīz/ ▶ **adv.** archaic in no way or manner; not at all: *I can nowise accept the accusation.*

nowt /nout/ ▶ **pron. & adv.** N. English nothing.

NOx ▶ **n.** oxides of nitrogen, esp. as atmospheric pollutants.

nox·ious /ˈnäksʜəs/ ▶ **adj.** harmful, poisonous, or very unpleasant: *they were overcome by the noxious fumes.* — **nox·ious·ly adv. nox·ious·ness n.** [15th C.: from L. *noxius* (from *noxa* 'harm') + -OUS.]

no·yade /nwäˈyäd/ ▶ **n.** hist. an execution carried out by drowning. [19th C.: from Fr., lit. 'drowning,' from the v. *noyer*, from L. *necare* 'kill.']

no·yau /nwäˈyō; ˈnwäˌyō/ ▶ **n.** (pl. **-yaux** /-ˈyō(z); -ˌyō(z)/) a liqueur made of brandy flavored with fruit kernels. [Fr., lit. 'kernel,' based on L. *nux*, *nuc-* 'nut.']

noz·zle /ˈnäzəl/ ▶ **n.** a spout at the end of a pipe, hose, or tube, used to control a jet of gas or liquid. [17th C.: from NOSE + -LE[2].]

NP ▶ **abbr.** notary public.

Np ▶ **symb.** the chemical element neptunium.

n.p. ▶ **abbr.** ■ new paragraph. ■ no place of publication (used esp. in book classification).

NPR ▶ **abbr.** National Public Radio.

NRA ▶ **abbr.** ■ National Rifle Association.

NRC ▶ **abbr.** ■ National Research Council. ■ National Response Center. ■ Nuclear Regulatory Commission.

NRSV ▶ **abbr.** New Revised Standard Version (of the Bible).

NS ▶ **abbr.** ■ New Style. ■ Nova Scotia (in official postal use).

ns ▶ **abbr.** nanosecond.

n/s ▶ **abbr.** nonsmoker; nonsmoking (used in personal advertisements).

NSA ▶ **abbr.** National Security Agency.

NSC ▶ **abbr.** National Security Council.

nsec ▶ **abbr.** nanosecond.

NSF ▶ **abbr.** National Science Foundation.

n.s.f. ▶ **abbr.** not sufficient funds.

NSPCA ▶ **abbr.** National Society for the Prevention of Cruelty to Animals.

NSU Med. ▶ **abbr.** nonspecific urethritis.

NSW ▶ **abbr.** New South Wales.

NT ▶ **abbr.** ■ New Testament. ■ Northern Territory. ■ Northwest Territories (in official postal use).

n't ▶ **contr.** not, used with auxiliary verbs (e.g., *can't, won't, didn't*, and *isn't*).

nth /enᴛʜ/ ▶ **adj.** Math. denoting an unspecified member of a series of numbers or enumerated items: *systematic sampling by taking every nth name from the list.* ■ (in general use) denoting an unspecified item or instance in a series, typically the last or latest in a long series.

– PHRASES **to the nth degree** to the utmost: *the gullibility of the electorate was tested to the nth degree by such promises.*

NTP Chem. ▶ **abbr.** normal temperature and pressure.

NTSB ▶ **abbr.** National Transportation Safety Board.

nt. wt. ▶ **abbr.** net weight.

n-type ▶ **adj.** Electron. denoting a region in a semiconductor in which electrical conduction is due to the movement of electrons. Often contrasted with P-TYPE.

nu /n(y)o͞o/ ▶ **n.** the thirteenth letter of the Greek alphabet (Ν, ν), transliterated as 'n.' ▶ **symb.** (ν) frequency.

nu·ance /ˈn(y)o͞oˌäns/ ▶ **n.** a subtle difference in or shade of meaning, expression, or sound. ▶ **v.** [trans.] (usu. **be nuanced**) give nuances to. [18th C.: from Fr., 'shade, subtlety,' from *nuer* 'to shade,' based on L. *nubes* 'cloud.']

nub /nəb/ ▶ **n.** **1** (**the nub**) the crux or central point of a matter. **2** a small lump or protuberance. ■ a small chunk or nugget of metal or rock. [17th C.: appar. a var. of dial. *knub* 'protuberance,' from Mid. Low Ger. *knubbe, knobbe* 'knob.']

nub·bin /ˈnəbən/ ▶ **n.** a small lump or residual part. [17th C.: dimin. of NUB.]

nub·by /ˈnəbē/ (also **nub·bly** /ˈnəblē/) ▶ **adj.** (of fabric) coarse or knobbly in texture. ■ stubby; lumpy: *the nubby points of the new leaves.* [19th C.: deriv. of *nubble* 'small lump.']

Nu·bi·a /ˈn(y)o͞obēə/ an ancient region of southern Egypt and northern Sudan.

Nu·bi·an /ˈn(y)o͞obēən/ ▶ **adj.** of or relating to Nubia, its people, or their language. ▶ **n.** **1** a native or inhabitant of Nubia. **2** the Nilo-Saharan language of the Nubians. **3** a goat of a short-haired breed with long pendant ears and long legs, originally from Africa. [from med. L. *Nubianus*, from *Nubia* 'Nubia,' from L. *Nubae* 'Nubians.']

nu·bile /ˈn(y)o͞oˌbīl; -bəl/ ▶ **adj.** (of a girl or young woman) sexually mature; suitable for marriage. ■ (of a girl or young woman) sexually attractive. — **nu·bil·i·ty** /n(y)o͞oˈbilitē/ **n.** [17th C.: from L. *nubilis* 'marriageable,' from *nubere* 'cover or veil oneself for a bridegroom' (from *nubes* 'cloud').]

Nu·buck /ˈn(y)o͞oˌbək/ ▶ **n.** trademark cowhide leather that has been rubbed on the flesh side to give it a feel like that of suede.

nu·cel·lus /n(y)o͞oˈseləs/ ▶ **n.** (pl. **-cel·li** /-ˈselˌī; -ˈselē/) Bot. the central part of an ovule, containing the embryo sac. — **nu·cel·lar** /-ˈselər/ **adj.** [19th C.: mod. L., appar. dimin. of NUCLEUS.]

nu·chal /ˈn(y)o͞okəl/ ▶ **adj.** Anat. of or relating to the nape of the neck. [19th C.: from obs. *nucha* 'nape' (from med. L. *nucha* 'medulla oblongata,' from Arab. *nuḵāʿ* 'spinal marrow') + -AL.]

nuci- ▶ **comb. form** of a nut or nuts. [from L. *nux*, *nuc-* 'nut.']

nu·cle·ar /ˈn(y)o͞oklēər; -kli(ə)r/ ▶ **adj.** **1** of or relating to the nucleus of an atom. ■ denoting, relating to, or powered by the energy released in nuclear fission or fusion. ■ denoting, possessing, or involving weapons using this energy. **2** Biol. of or relating to the nucleus of a cell: *nuclear DNA.*

nu·cle·ar age ▶ **n.** the period in history usu. considered to have begun with the first use of the atomic bomb (1945). Also called ATOMIC AGE.

nu·cle·ar club ▶ **n.** the nations possessing nuclear weapons.

nu·cle·ar fam·i·ly ▶ n. a couple and their dependent children, regarded as a basic social unit.

nu·cle·ar fis·sion ▶ n. a nuclear reaction in which a heavy nucleus splits spontaneously or on impact with another particle, with the release of energy.

nu·cle·ar force ▶ n. Physics a strong attractive force between nucleons in the atomic nucleus that holds the nucleus together.

nu·cle·ar-free ▶ adj. (of a country or region) not having or allowing any nuclear weapons, materials, or power.

nu·cle·ar fuel ▶ n. a substance that will sustain a fission chain reaction so that it can be used as a source of nuclear energy.

nu·cle·ar fu·sion ▶ n. a nuclear reaction in which atomic nuclei of low atomic number fuse to form a heavier nucleus with the release of energy.

nu·cle·ar mag·net·ic res·o·nance (abbr.: **NMR**) ▶ n. the absorption of electromagnetic radiation by a nucleus having a magnetic moment when in an external magnetic field, used mainly as an analytical technique and in diagnostic body imaging.

nu·cle·ar med·i·cine ▶ n. the branch of medicine that deals with the use of radioactive substances in research, diagnosis, and treatment.

nu·cle·ar op·tion ▶ n. the most drastic or extreme response possible to a particular situation.

nu·cle·ar phys·ics ▶ plural n. [treated as sing.] the physics of atomic nuclei and their interactions, esp. in the generation of nuclear energy.

nu·cle·ar pow·er ▶ n. **1** electric or motive power generated by a nuclear reactor. **2** a country that has nuclear weapons. — **nu·cle·ar-pow·ered** adj.

nu·cle·ar reaction ▶ n. Physics a change in the identity or characteristics of an atomic nucleus that results when it is bombarded with an energetic particle, as in fission, fusion, or radioactive decay.

nu·cle·ar re·ac·tor ▶ n. see REACTOR.

nu·cle·ar thresh·old ▶ n. a point in a conflict at which nuclear weapons are or would be brought into use.

nu·cle·ar um·brel·la ▶ n. the supposed protection gained from an alliance with a country possessing nuclear weapons.

nu·cle·ar waste ▶ n. radioactive waste material, for example from the use or reprocessing of nuclear fuel.

nu·cle·ar win·ter ▶ n. a period of abnormal cold and darkness following a nuclear war, caused by smoke and dust in the atmosphere blocking the sun's rays.

nu·cle·ase /ˈn(y)o͞oklēˌās; -ˌāz/ ▶ n. Biochem. an enzyme that cleaves the chains of nucleotides in nucleic acids into smaller units.

nu·cle·ate ▶ adj. /ˈn(y)o͞oklēət; -ˌāt/ esp. Biol. having a nucleus. ▶ v. /ˈn(y)o͞okle ˌāt/ [intrans.] [usu. as adj.] (**nucleated**) form a nucleus. ■ form around a central area. — **nu·cle·a·tion** /ˌn(y)o͞oklēˈāshən/ n.

nu·cle·i /ˈn(y)o͞oklēˌī/ plural form of NUCLEUS.

nu·cle·ic ac·id /n(y)o͞oˈklē-ik/ ▶ n. Biochem. a complex organic substance present in living cells, esp. DNA or RNA, whose molecules consist of many nucleotides linked in a long chain.

nucleo- ▶ comb. form representing NUCLEUS, NUCLEAR, or NUCLEIC ACID.

nu·cle·o·cap·sid /ˌn(y)o͞oklē-ōˈkapsid/ ▶ n. Biol. the capsid of a virus with the enclosed nucleic acid.

nu·cle·o·lus /n(y)o͞oˈklēələs/ ▶ n. (pl. **-li** /-ˌlī; -ˌlē/) Biol. a small dense spherical structure in the nucleus of a cell during interphase. — **nu·cle·o·lar** /-lər/ adj. [19th C.: from late L., dimin. of L. *nucleus* 'inner part, kernel' (see NUCLEUS).]

nu·cle·on /ˈn(y)o͞oklēˌän/ ▶ n. Physics a proton or neutron.

nu·cle·on·ics /ˌn(y)o͞oklēˈäniks/ ▶ plural n. [treated as sing.] the branch of science and technology concerned with atomic nuclei and nucleons, esp. the exploitation of nuclear power. — **nu·cle·on·ic** adj. [1940s: from NUCLEAR.]

nu·cle·o·phil·ic /ˌn(y)o͞oklē-ōˈfilik/ ▶ adj. Chem. (of a molecule or group) having a tendency to donate electrons or react at electron-poor sites such as protons. Often contrasted with ELECTROPHILIC. — **nu·cle·o·phile** /ˈn(y)o͞oklēəˌfīl/ n.

nu·cle·o·plasm /ˈn(y)o͞oklēəˌplazəm/ ▶ n. Biol. the substance of a cell nucleus, esp. that not forming part of a nucleolus.

nu·cle·o·pro·tein /ˌn(y)o͞oklē-ōˈprōˌtēn/ ▶ n. Biochem. a complex consisting of a nucleic acid bonded to a protein.

nu·cle·o·side /ˈn(y)o͞oklēəˌsīd/ ▶ n. Biochem. a compound (e.g., adenosine or cytidine) commonly found in DNA or RNA, consisting of a purine or pyrimidine base linked to a sugar.

nu·cle·o·some /ˈn(y)o͞oklēəˌsōm/ ▶ n. Biol. a structural unit of a eukaryotic chromosome, consisting of a length of DNA coiled around a core of histones. — **nu·cle·o·so·mal** /ˌn(y)o͞oklēəˈsōməl/ adj.

nu·cle·o·syn·the·sis /ˌn(y)o͞oklē-ōˈsinTHəsis/ ▶ n. Astron. the cosmic formation of atoms more complex than the hydrogen atom. — **nu·cle·o·syn·thet·ic** /-sinˈTHetik/ adj.

nu·cle·o·tide /ˈn(y)o͞oklēəˌtīd/ ▶ n. Biochem. a compound consisting of a nucleoside linked to a phosphate group. Nucleotides form the basic structural unit of nucleic acids such as DNA.

nu·cle·us /ˈn(y)o͞oklēəs/ ▶ n. (pl. **-cle·i** /-klēˌī/) the central and most important part of an object, movement, or group, forming the basis for its activity and growth. ■ Physics the positively charged central core of an atom, containing most of its mass. ■ Biol. a dense organelle present in most eukaryotic cells, typically a single rounded structure bounded by a double membrane, containing the genetic material. ■ Astron. the solid part of the head of a comet. ■ Anat. a discrete mass of gray matter in the central nervous system. [18th C.: from L., lit. 'kernel, inner part,' dimin. of *nux, nuc-* 'nut.']

nu·clide /ˈn(y)o͞oˌklīd/ ▶ n. Physics a distinct kind of atom or nucleus characterized by a specific number of protons and neutrons. — **nu·clid·ic** /n(y)o͞oˈklidik/ adj. [1940s: from NUCLEUS + *-ide* (from Gk. *eidos* 'form').]

nude /n(y)o͞od/ ▶ adj. wearing no clothes; naked. ■ [attrib.] depicting or performed by naked people: *he acted in a frank nude scene.* ■ (esp. of hosiery) flesh-colored. ▶ n. a naked human figure, typically as the subject of a painting, sculpture, or photograph. ■ (**the nude**) the representation of the naked human figure as a genre in art. ■ flesh color.
– PHRASES **in the nude** in an unclothed state. [ME: from L. *nudus*.]

nudge /nəj/ ▶ v. [trans.] prod (someone) gently, typically with one's elbow, in order to draw their attention to something. ■ touch or push (something) gently or gradually. ■ fig. coax (someone) to do something. ■ approach (an age, figure, or level) very closely: *both men were nudging fifty.* ▶ n. a light touch or push. — **nudg·er** n. [17th C.: compare Norw. dial. *nugga, nyggja* 'to push.']

Nu·di·bran·chi·a /ˌn(y)o͞odəˈbrangkēə/ Zool. an order of shell-less marine mollusks (order Nudibranchia, class Gastropoda) that comprises the sea slugs. — **nu·di·branch** /ˈn(y)o͞odəˌbrangk/ n. [mod. L. (pl.), from L. *nudus* 'nude.']

nud·ie /ˈn(y)o͞odē/ ▶ n. (pl. **-ies**) informal a publication, entertainment, or venue featuring nude performers or models. ▶ adj. portraying, featuring, or including people in the nude.

nud·ist /ˈn(y)o͞odist/ ▶ n. a person who engages in the practice of going naked wherever possible. — **nud·ism** n.

nu·di·ty /ˈn(y)o͞odətē/ ▶ n. the state or fact of being naked: *scenes of full-frontal nudity.*

nud·nik /ˈno͝odˌnik/ (also **nud·nick**) ▶ n. informal a pestering, nagging, or irritating person; a bore. [20th C.: Yiddish, from Russ. *nudnyĭ* 'tedious.']

Nu·e·ces Riv·er /n(y)o͞oˈāsəs/ a river that flows from central Texas to the Gulf of Mexico.

nu·ée ar·dente /n(y)o͞oˈā ärˈdänt/ ▶ n. Geol. an incandescent cloud of gas, ash, and lava fragments ejected from a volcano, typically as part of a pyroclastic flow. [Fr., lit. 'burning cloud.']

Nu·er /ˈno͞oər/ ▶ n. (pl. same or **Nu·ers**) **1** a member of an African people of southeastern Sudan and Ethiopia. **2** the Nilotic language of this people. ▶ adj. of or relating to this people or their language. [the name in Dinka.]

Nue·vo La·re·do /ˈnwāvō ləˈrādō/ a city in eastern Mexico across from Laredo, Texas; pop. 218,000.

Nue·vo Le·ón /ˌnwāvō lāˈōn; lēˈōn/ a state in northeastern Mexico, on the US border; capital, Monterrey.

nue·vo sol /ˌnwāvō ˈsōl/ ▶ n. another term for SOL[3]. [Sp., 'new sol.']

nuff /nəf/ (also **'nuff**) ▶ adj., pron., & adv. nonstandard spelling of ENOUGH, representing informal speech.

nu·ga·to·ry /ˈn(y)o͞ogəˌtôrē/ ▶ adj. of no value or importance. ■ useless; futile. [17th C.: from L. *nugatorius*, from *nugari* 'to trifle,' from *nugae* 'jests.']

nug·get /ˈnəgət/ ▶ n. a small lump of gold or other precious metal found in the earth. ■ a small lump of another substance: *tiny nuggets of shrimp.* ■ a valuable idea or fact: *nuggets of information.* — **nug·get·y** adj. [19th C.: appar. from dial. *nug* 'lump.']

nui·sance /ˈn(y)o͞osəns/ ▶ n. a person, thing, or circumstance causing inconvenience or annoyance. ■ (also **private nuisance**) Law an unlawful interference with the use and enjoyment of a person's land. ■ Law see PUBLIC NUISANCE. [ME: from OFr., 'hurt,' from the v. *nuire*, from L. *nocere* 'to harm.']

nui·sance val·ue ▶ n. the significance of a person or thing arising from their capacity to cause inconvenience or annoyance.

nuke /n(y)o͞ok/ informal ▶ n. a nuclear weapon. ■ a nuclear power station. ■ a nuclear-powered vessel. ▶ v. [trans.] attack or destroy with nuclear weapons. ■ destroy; get rid of: *I fertilized the lawn and nuked the weeds.* ■ cook or heat (food) in a microwave oven: *I nuked a quick burger.* [1950s: abbrev. of NUCLEAR.]

Nu·ku·'a·lo·fa /ˌno͞oko͞oəˈlōfə/ the capital of Tonga, on the island of Tongatapu; pop. 30,000.

null /nəl/ ▶ adj. **1** [predic.] having no legal or binding force; invalid: *the interim government was declared null and void.* **2** having or associated with the value zero. ■ Math. (of a set or matrix) having no elements, or only zeros as elements. ■ lacking distinctive qualities; having no positive substance or content: *his null life.* ▶ n. literary a zero. ■ a dummy letter in a cipher. ■ Electron. a condition of no signal. ▶ v. [trans.] Electron. combine (a signal) with another in order to create a null; cancel out. [ME: from Fr. *nul, nulle*, from L. *nullus* 'none,' from *ne* 'not' + *ullus* 'any.']

nul·lah /ˈnələ/ ▶ n. Indian a dry riverbed or ravine. [18th C.: from Hindi *nālā*.]

null hy·poth·e·sis ▶ n. (in a statistical test) the hypothesis that there is no significant difference between specified populations, any observed difference being due to sampling or experimental error.

nul·li·fid·i·an /ˌnələˈfidēən/ rare ▶ n. a person having no faith or religious belief. ▶ adj. having no faith or religious belief. [16th C.: from med. L. *nullifidius* (from *nullus* 'no, none' + *fides* 'faith') + -AN.]

nul·li·fy /ˈnələˌfī/ ▶ v. (**-fies, -fied**) [trans.] make legally null and void; invalidate. ■ make of no use or value; cancel out. — **nul·li·fi·ca·tion** /ˌnələfəˈkāshən/ n. **nul·li·fi·er** n.

nul·lip·a·ra /,nəˈlipərə/ ▶ **n.** (pl. **-rae** /-,rē/) Med. Zool. a woman or female animal that has never given birth. Compare with PRIMIPARA. — **nul·lip·a·rous** /-ˈlip(ə)rəs/ **adj.** [19th C.: mod. L., from L. *nullus* 'none' + *-para* (fem. of *-parus*), from *parere* 'bear children.']

nul·li·ty /ˈnəlitē/ ▶ **n.** (pl. **-ties**) **1** Law an act or thing that is legally void. ■ the state of being legally void; invalidity, esp. of a marriage. **2** a thing of no importance or worth. ■ nothingness.

Num. ▶ **abbr.** Bible Numbers.

numb /nəm/ ▶ **adj.** deprived of the power of sensation. ▶ **v.** [trans.] deprive of feeling or responsiveness. ■ cause (a sensation) to be felt less intensely; deaden: *vodka might numb the pain in my hand.* — **numb·ly adv. numb·ness n.** [ME *nome(n)*, past part. of obs. *nim* 'take.']

num·bat /ˈnəm,bat/ ▶ **n.** a small termite-eating Australian marsupial (*Myrmecobius fasciatus*, family Myrmecobiidae) with a black-and-white striped back and a bushy tail. [20th C.: from Nyungar.]

num·ber /ˈnəmbər/ ▶ **n. 1** an arithmetical value, expressed by a word or symbol, representing a particular quantity and used in counting, calculating, and for showing order in a series or for identification. ■ (**numbers**) dated arithmetic: *the boy was adept at numbers.* **2** a quantity or amount: *the company increased the number of women on its staff.* ■ (**a number of**) several: *we discussed the matter on a number of occasions.* ■ a group or company of people: *there were distinguished names among our number.* ■ (**numbers**) a large quantity or amount, often in contrast to a smaller one; numerical preponderance: *the weight of numbers turned the battle against them.* **3** a single issue of a magazine. ■ a song, dance, piece of music, etc., esp. one of several in a performance. ■ [usu. with adj.] informal a thing, typically an item of clothing, regarded with approval or admiration: *Yvonne was wearing a little black number.* **4** Gram. a distinction of word form denoting reference to one person or thing or to more than one. See also SINGULAR (sense 2), PLURAL, COUNT NOUN, and MASS NOUN. ■ a particular form so classified. ▶ **v.** [trans.] **1** amount to (a specified figure or quantity); comprise: *the demonstrators numbered more than 5,000.* ■ include or classify as a member of a group: *the orchestra* **numbers** *Brahms* **among** *its past conductors.* **2** (often **be numbered**) mark with a number or assign a number to, typically to indicate position in a series: *each document was numbered consecutively.* ■ count: *strategies like ours can be numbered on the fingers of one hand.* ■ assess or estimate the size or quantity of (something) to be a specified figure: *he numbers the fleet at a thousand.*

– PHRASES **any number of** any particular whole quantity of: *the game can involve any number of players.* ■ a large and unlimited quantity or amount of: *the results can be read any number of ways.* **by numbers** following simple instructions identified by numbers or as if so identified: *paint by numbers.* **by the numbers** following standard operating procedure. ■ all together with a shouted-out count. **someone's/something's days are numbered** someone or something will not survive or remain in a position of power or advantage for much longer. **do a number on** informal treat someone badly, typically by deceiving, humiliating, or criticizing them in a calculated and thorough way. **have someone's number** informal understand a person's real motives or character and thereby gain some advantage. **have someone's number on it** informal (of a bomb, bullet, or other missile) be destined to find a specified person as its target. **someone's number is up** informal the time has come when someone is doomed to die or suffer some other disaster or setback. **without number** too many to count. [ME: from OFr. *nombre* (n.), *nombrer* (v.), from L. *numerus.*]

num·ber crunch·er (also **num·ber-crunch·er**) ▶ **n.** informal **1** a computer or software capable of performing rapid calculations with large amounts of data. **2** often derog. a statistician, accountant, or other person who deals with large amounts of numerical data. — **num·ber crunch·ing n.**

num·bered ac·count ▶ **n.** a bank account, esp. in a Swiss bank, identified only by a number and not bearing the owner's name.

num·ber·less /ˈnəmbərləs/ ▶ **adj.** too many to be counted; innumerable.

num·ber line ▶ **n.** Math. a line on which numbers are marked at intervals, used to illustrate simple numerical operations.

num·ber one informal ▶ **n. 1** oneself. **2** a person or thing that is the best or the most important in an activity or area. ■ a best-selling record or book. **3** used euphemistically to refer to urine, esp. in reference to children. ▶ **adj.** most important or prevalent: *number-one priority.* ■ best selling: *number-one album.*

Num·bers /ˈnəmbərz/ the fourth book of the Bible, relating the experiences of the Israelites in the wilderness after Moses led them out of Egypt.

num·bers game ▶ **n.** often derog. the use or manipulation of statistics or figures, esp. in support of an argument. ■ (also **the numbers** or **numbers racket**) an illegal lottery based on the occurrence of unpredictable numbers in the results of races, etc.

num·ber the·o·ry ▶ **n.** the branch of mathematics that deals with the properties and relationships of numbers, esp. the positive integers.

num·ber two ▶ **n.** informal **1** a second in command. ■ a person or thing ranked second in ability or size in an activity or area. **2** used euphemistically to refer to feces, esp. in reference to children.

numb·fish /ˈnəm,fisн/ ▶ **n.** (pl. same or **-fishes**) an electric ray, esp. a heavy-bodied Australian ray (*Hypnos monopterygium*) that lies partly buried in sand flats and estuaries and can give a severe electric shock.

num·bles /ˈnəmbəlz/ ▶ **plural n.** Brit., archaic the entrails of an animal, esp. a deer, used for food. [ME: from OFr., from L. *lumbulus*, dimin. of *lumbus* 'loin.']

numb·skull /ˈnəm,skəl/ (also **num·skull**) ▶ **n.** informal a stupid or foolish person.

nu·men /ˈn(y)o͞omən/ ▶ **n.** (pl. **-mi·na** /-mənə/) the spirit or divine power presiding over a thing or place. [17th C.: from L.]

nu·mer·a·ble /ˈn(y)o͞om(ə)rəbəl/ ▶ **adj.** able to be counted. [16th C.: from L. *numerabilis*, from *numerare* 'to number.']

nu·mer·a·cy /ˈn(y)o͞om(ə)rəsē/ ▶ **n.** the ability to understand and work with numbers.

nu·mer·al /ˈn(y)o͞om(ə)rəl/ ▶ **n.** a figure, symbol, or group of these denoting a number. ■ a word expressing a number. ▶ **adj.** of or denoting a number. [ME: from late L. *numeralis*, adj. from L. *numerus* (see NUMBER).]

nu·mer·ate /ˈn(y)o͞om(ə)rət/ ▶ **adj.** having a good basic knowledge of arithmetic.

nu·mer·a·tion /,n(y)o͞oməˈrāsнən/ ▶ **n.** the action or process of calculating or assigning a number to something. ■ a method or process of numbering, counting, or computing.

nu·mer·a·tor /ˈn(y)o͞omə,rātər/ ▶ **n.** the number above the line in a common fraction showing how many of the parts indicated by the denominator are taken, for example, 2 in $^2/_3$.

nu·mer·i·cal /n(y)o͞oˈmerikəl/ ▶ **adj.** of, relating to, or expressed as a number or numbers. — **nu·mer·i·cal·ly adv.**

nu·mer·i·cal a·nal·y·sis ▶ **n.** the branch of mathematics that deals with the development and use of numerical methods for solving problems.

nu·mer·i·cal con·trol ▶ **n.** Engin. computer control of machine tools, where operations are directed by numerical data.

nu·mer·ol·o·gy /,n(y)o͞oməˈräləjē/ ▶ **n.** the branch of knowledge that deals with the occult significance of numbers. — **nu·mer·o·log·i·cal** /-rəˈläjikəl/ **adj. nu·mer·ol·o·gist n.** [20th C.: from L. *numerus* 'a number' + -LOGY.]

nu·me·ro u·no /ˈn(y)o͞omərō ˈo͞onō/ ▶ **n.** (pl. **u·nos**) informal the best or most important person or thing. [Ital., lit. 'number one.']

nu·mer·ous /ˈn(y)o͞om(ə)rəs/ ▶ **adj.** great in number; many. ■ consisting of many members: *the orchestra and chorus were numerous.* — **nu·mer·ous·ly adv. nu·mer·ous·ness n.** [ME: from L. *numerosus*, from *numerus* 'a number.']

Nu·mid·i·a /n(y)o͞oˈmidēə/ an ancient kingdom, later a Roman province, located in North Africa, corresponding roughly to present-day Algeria. — **Nu·mid·i·an adj. & n.**

nu·mi·na /ˈn(y)o͞omənə/ plural form of NUMEN.

nu·mi·nous /ˈn(y)o͞omənəs/ ▶ **adj.** having a strong religious or spiritual quality; indicating or suggesting the presence of a divinity. [17th C.: from L. *numen, numin-* 'divine power' + -OUS.]

numis. ▶ **abbr.** numismatic; numismatics.

nu·mis·mat·ic /,n(y)o͞oməzˈmatik; -məs-/ ▶ **adj.** of, relating to, or consisting of coins, paper currency, and medals. — **nu·mis·mat·i·cal·ly adv.** [18th C.: from Fr. *numismatique*, via L. from Gk. *nomisma, nomismat-* 'current coin,' from *nomizein* 'use currently.']

nu·mis·mat·ics /,n(y)o͞oməzˈmatiks; -məs-/ ▶ **plural n.** [usu. treated as sing.] the study or collection of coins, paper currency, and medals. — **nu·mis·ma·tist** /n(y)o͞oˈmizmətist; -ˈmis-/ **n.**

num·mu·lar /ˈnəmyələr/ ▶ **adj.** resembling a coin or coins. [18th C.: from L. *nummulus* (dimin. of *nummus* 'coin') + -AR[1].]

num·mu·lite /ˈnəmyə,līt/ ▶ **n.** Paleontol. the flat disk-shaped calcareous shell of a foraminifer (*Nummulites* and other genera, family Nummulitidae), found commonly as a fossil up to 8 cm across in marine Tertiary deposits. [19th C.: from L. *nummulus* (dimin. of *nummus* 'coin') + -ITE[1].]

num·skull ▶ **n.** var. of NUMBSKULL.

nun /nən/ ▶ **n.** a member of a religious community of women, esp. a cloistered one, living under vows of poverty, chastity, and obedience. ■ a pigeon of a breed with a crest on its neck. — **nun·like adj. nun·nish adj.** [OE *nonne*, from eccles. L. *nonna*, fem. of *nonnus* 'monk.']

nun·a·tak /ˈnənə,tak/ ▶ **n.** an isolated peak of rock projecting above a surface of inland ice or snow. [19th C.: from Eskimo *nunataq.*]

Nu·na·vut /ˈno͝onə,vo͞ot/ a territory in northern Canada that includes the eastern part of the original Northwest Territories and most of the islands of the Arctic Archipelago; capital, Iqaluit.

nun bu·oy ▶ **n.** a buoy that is circular in the middle and tapering to each end. [18th C.: from obs. *nun* 'child's top.']

Nunc Di·mit·tis /ˈnəNGk dəˈmitis; ˈno͝oNGk/ ▶ **n.** the Song of Simeon (Luke 2:29–32) used as a canticle in Christian liturgy, esp. at compline and evensong. [L., '(Lord), now let (your servant) depart.']

nun·cha·ku /,nənˈcнäko͞o/ (also **nun·chuk** /ˈnən,cнək/) ▶ **n.** (pl. same or **-kus**) a Japanese martial arts weapon consisting of two hardwood sticks joined together by a chain, rope, or thong. [Japanese, from Okinawa dial.]

nun·ci·a·ture /ˈnənsēə,cнər; ˈno͞on-; -,cнo͝or/ ▶ **n.** the office of a nuncio in the Roman Catholic Church. [17th C.: from Ital. *nunziatura*, from *nunzio* (see NUNCIO).]

nun·ci·o /ˈnənsē,ō; ˈno͞on-/ ▶ **n.** (pl. **-os**) (in the Roman Catholic Church) a papal ambassador to a foreign court or government. [16th C.: from Ital., from L. *nuntius* 'messenger.']

nun·cle /'nəNGkəl/ ▶ **n.** archaic or dialect a person's uncle. [16th C.: by misdivision of *mine uncle*.]

nun·cu·pa·tive /'nəNGkyə,pātiv/ ▶ **adj.** Law (of a will or testament) declared orally as opposed to in writing. [16th C.: from late L. *nuncupativus*, from L. *nuncupat-* 'named, declared,' from the v. *nuncupare*.]

nun·ner·y /'nən(ə)rē/ ▶ **n.** (pl. **-ner·ies**) a building in which nuns live as a community; a convent.

nuoc mam /nə'wäk 'mäm/ ▶ **n.** a spicy Vietnamese fish sauce.

nup·tial /'nəpsHəl; -CHəl/ ▶ **adj.** of or relating to marriage or weddings. ■ Zool. denoting the characteristic breeding behavior, coloration, or structures of some animals. ▶ **n.** (usu. **nuptials**) a wedding. [15th C.: from OFr., or from L. *nuptialis*, from *nuptiae* 'wedding,' from *nubere* 'to wed.']

nup·tial mass ▶ **n.** (in the Roman Catholic Church) a mass celebrated as part of a wedding ceremony.

Nu·rem·berg /'n(y)o͝orəm,bərg/ a city in southern Germany, in Bavaria; pop. 497,000. In 1945–46 it was the site of the Nuremberg war trials. German name **NÜRNBERG**.

Nu·re·yev /no͝o'rāyef; -yev/, Rudolf (1939–93), Austrian ballet dancer and choreographer; born in Russia. He joined the Royal Ballet in London in 1961.

nurse /nərs/ ▶ **n.** a person trained to care for the sick or infirm, esp. in a hospital. ■ dated a person employed or trained to take charge of young children. ■ archaic a wet nurse. ■ [often as adj.] Forestry a tree or crop planted as a shelter to others. ■ Entomol. a worker bee, ant, or other social insect, caring for a young brood. ▶ **v.** [trans.] **1** give medical and other attention to (a sick person). ■ [intrans.] care for the sick and infirm, esp. as a profession: *she nursed at the hospital for 30 years.* ■ try to cure or alleviate (an injury or illness) by treating it carefully and protectively: *he has been nursing a cold* | fig. *he nursed his hurt pride.* ■ hold (a cup or glass) in one's hands, drinking from it occasionally: *nursing a brandy.* ■ harbor (a belief or feeling), esp. for a long time: *he still nurses resentment.* ■ take special care of, esp. to promote development or well-being: *our political unity needs to be protected and nursed.* ■ Billiards try to play strokes that keep (the balls) close together. **2** feed (a baby) at the breast. ■ [intrans.] be fed at the breast: *the baby snuffled as he nursed.* ■ (**be nursed in**) dated be brought up in (a specified condition). [ME: contr. of earlier *nourice*, from OFr., from late L. *nutricia*, fem. of L. *nutricius* '(person) that nourishes,' from *nutrix, nutric-* 'nurse,' from *nutrire* 'nourish.']

nurse·ling ▶ **n.** archaic spelling of **NURSLING**.

nurse·maid /'nərs,mād/ ▶ **n.** a woman or girl employed to look after a young child or children.

nurse prac·ti·tion·er (also **nurse-prac·ti·tion·er**) ▶ **n.** a registered nurse who has been specially trained to treat routine or minor ailments, and to perform many tasks ordinarily performed by a doctor.

nurs·er·y /'nərs(ə)rē/ ▶ **n.** (pl. **-er·ies**) a room in a house for the special use of young children. ■ a place where young children are cared for during the working day; a nursery school. ■ a place where young plants and trees are grown for sale or for planting elsewhere. ■ a place or natural habitat that breeds or supports animals. ■ an institution or environment in which certain types of people or qualities are fostered or bred.

nurs·er·y·man /'nərs(ə)rēmən/ ▶ **n.** (pl. **-men**) a worker in or owner of a plant or tree nursery.

nurs·er·y rhyme ▶ **n.** a simple traditional song or poem for children.

nurs·er·y school ▶ **n.** a school for young children, mainly between the ages of three and five.

nurse's aide ▶ **n.** (pl. **nurses' aides**) a person who assists professional nurses in a hospital or other medical facility by performing routine tasks, such a making beds and serving meals, that require little formal training.

nurse shark ▶ **n.** a shark (family Orectolobidae, or Ginglymostomatidae) with barbels on the snout. Its three species include *Ginglymostoma cirratum*, a slow-swimming brownish shark of warm Atlantic waters. [19th C.: *nurse* 'dogfish shark,' alt. of ME *nusse*.]

nurs·ing /'nərsiNG/ ▶ **n.** the profession or practice of providing care for the sick and infirm.

nurs·ing home ▶ **n.** a private institution providing residential accommodations with health care, esp. for the elderly.

nurs·ling /'nərsliNG/ ▶ **n.** a baby that is being breastfed. ■ any young animal or plant that is carefully tended.

nur·tur·ance /'nərCHərəns/ ▶ **n.** emotional and physical nourishment and care given to someone. ■ the ability to provide such care. — **nur·tur·ant adj.**

nur·ture /'nərCHər/ ▶ **v.** [trans.] care for and encourage the growth or development of. ■ cherish (a hope, belief, or ambition). ▶ **n.** the caring for and encouraging the growth of someone or something: *the nurture of ethics and integrity.* ■ upbringing, education, and environment, contrasted with inborn characteristics as an influence on or determinant of personality. Often contrasted with **NATURE**. — **nur·tur·er n.** [ME: from OFr. *noureture* 'nourishment,' based on L. *nutrire* 'feed, cherish.']

nut /nət/ ▶ **n.** **1** a fruit consisting of a hard or tough shell around an edible kernel. ■ the hard kernel of such a fruit. ■ informal a person's head. ■ (usu. **nuts**) vulgar slang testicles. **2** a small flat piece of metal or other material, typically square or hexagonal, with a threaded hole through it for screwing onto a bolt as a fastener. ■ Music the part at the lower end of the bow of a violin or similar instrument, with a screw for adjusting the tension of the hair. **3** informal a crazy or eccentric person. ■ [with adj.] a person who is excessively interested in or enthusiastic about a specified thing: *a football nut.* **4** the fixed ridge on the neck of a stringed instrument over which the strings pass. ▶ **v.** (**nut·ted, nut·ting**) [intrans.] [usu. as n.] (**nutting**) archaic gather nuts.
– PHRASES **nuts and bolts** informal the basic practical details. **off one's nut** informal out of one's mind; crazy. **a tough** (or **hard**) **nut** informal someone who is difficult to deal with. **a tough** (or **hard**) **nut to crack** informal a difficult problem or an opponent who is hard to beat. — **nut·like adj.** [OE *hnutu*, of Gmc. origin; rel. to Ger. *Nuss*.]

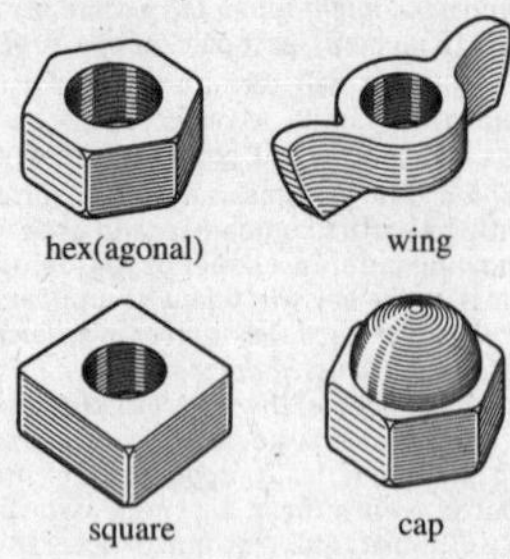

nuts

nu·ta·tion /n(y)o͞o'tāsHən/ ▶ **n.** a periodic variation in the inclination of the axis of a rotating object. ■ Astron. a periodic oscillation of the earth's axis that causes the precession of the poles to follow a wavy rather than a circular path. ■ Bot. the circular swaying movement of the tip of a growing shoot. [17th C.: from L. *nutatio(n-)*, from *nutare* 'to nod.']

nut-brown ▶ **adj.** of a rich dark brown color: *a nut-brown face.*

nut case (also **nut·case**) ▶ **n.** informal a crazy or foolish person.

nut·crack·er /'nət,krakər/ ▶ **n.** **1** a device for cracking nuts. **2** a crow (genus *Nucifraga*) that feeds on the seeds of conifers, found widely in Eurasia and in western North America.

nut·hatch /'nət,hacH/ ▶ **n.** a small songbird (genus *Sitta*, family Sittidae) with a long strong bill, a square-cut tail, and the habit of climbing down tree trunks head first.

white-breasted nuthatch

nuth·in /'nəTHin/ (also **nuth·in'**) ▶ **pron., adj., & adv.** informal nonstandard spelling of **NOTHING**, used to represent informal speech.

nut·house /'nət,hous/ ▶ **n.** informal, offens. a home or hospital for people with mental illnesses.

nut·let /'nətlət/ ▶ **n.** Bot. a small nut, esp. an achene.

nut loaf ▶ **n.** a baked vegetarian dish made from ground or chopped nuts, vegetables, and herbs.

nut meat (also **nut·meat**) ▶ **n.** the kernel of a nut, typically an edible one.

nut·meg /'nət,meg/ ▶ **n.** **1** the hard, aromatic, almost spherical seed of a tropical tree. ■ this seed grated and used as a spice. **2** the evergreen tree (*Myristica fragrans*, family Myristicaceae) that bears these seeds, native to the Moluccas. [ME *notemuge*, partial translation of OFr. *nois muguede*, based on L. *nux* 'nut' + late L. *muscus* 'musk.']

nut·pick /'nət,pik/ (also **nut pick**) ▶ **n.** a thin, sharp-pointed table implement used to dig out the edible meat from nuts.

nu·tra·ceu·ti·cal /,n(y)o͞otrə'so͞otikəl/ ▶ **n.** a food containing health-giving additives. [1990s: from L. *nutrire* 'nourish' + **PHARMACEUTICAL**.]

nu·tri·a /'n(y)o͞otrēə/ ▶ **n.** a large semiaquatic beaverlike rodent (*Myocastor coypus*, family Myocastoridae) native to South America. It is kept in captivity for its fur and has become naturalized in many other areas. ■ the pelt of this animal. [19th C.: from Sp., lit. 'otter.']

nu·tri·ent /'n(y)o͞otrēənt/ ▶ **n.** a substance that provides nourishment essential for growth and the maintenance of life. [17th C.: from L. *nutrient-* 'nourishing,' from the v. *nutrire*.]

nu·tri·ment /'n(y)o͞otrəmənt/ ▶ **n.** rare nourishment; sustenance. — **nu·tri·men·tal** /,n(y)o͞otrə'mentl/ **adj.** [ME: from L. *nutrimentum*, from *nutrire*.]

nu·tri·tion /n(y)o͞o'trisHən/ ▶ **n.** the process of providing or obtaining the food necessary for health and growth. ■ food; nourishment. ■ the branch of science that deals with nutrients and nutrition, particularly in humans. — **nu·tri·tion·al** /-sHənl/ **adj.** **nu·tri·tion·al·ly** /-sHənl-ē/ **adv.** [ME: from late L. *nutritio(n-)*, from *nutrire*.]

nu·tri·tion·ist /n(y)o͞o'trisH(ə)nist/ ▶ **n.** a person who studies or is an expert in nutrition.

nu·tri·tious /n(y)o͞o'trisHəs/ ▶ **adj.** nourishing; efficient as food. — **nu·tri·tious·ly adv. nu·tri·tious·ness n.** [17th C.: from L. *nutritius* 'that nourishes' (from *nutrex* 'a nurse') + **-OUS**.]

nu·tri·tive /'n(y)o͞otrətiv/ ▶ **adj.** of or relating to nutrition. ■ providing nourishment; nutritious.

nuts /nəts/ ▸ **adj.** [predic.] informal insane. ▸ **exclam.** informal an expression of contempt or derision.
– PHRASES **be nuts about** (or Brit. **on**) informal like very much: *I was nuts about him.*

nut·sedge /ˈnət,sej/ ▸ **n.** an invasive sedge (genus *Cyperus*) with small edible nutlike tubers.

nut·shell /ˈnət,sʜel/ ▸ **n.** the hard woody covering around the kernel of a nut.
– PHRASES **in a nutshell** in the fewest possible words.

nut·so /ˈnətsō/ informal ▸ **adj.** insane: *his nutso neighbors.* ▸ **n.** (pl. **-sos**) an insane or eccentric person.

nut·sy /ˈnətsē/ ▸ **adj.** (**-si·er, -si·est**) informal insane.

nut·ter /ˈnətər/ ▸ **n.** Brit., informal a crazy or eccentric person.

nut tree ▸ **n.** a tree that bears nuts, esp. the hazel.

nut·ty /ˈnətē/ ▸ **adj.** (**nut·ti·er, nut·ti·est**) **1** tasting like nuts. ▪ containing a lot of nuts. **2** informal peculiar; insane.
– PHRASES **be nutty about** informal like very much. (**as**) **nutty as a fruitcake** informal completely insane. — **nut·ti·ness n.**

Nuuk /no͝ok/ the capital of Greenland, on the Davis Strait; pop. 12,000. It was known as Godthåb until 1979.

nux vom·i·ca /ˈnəks ˈvämikə/ ▸ **n.** a spiny southern Asian tree (*Strychnos nux-vomica*, family Loganiaceae) with berrylike fruit and toxic seeds that are a commercial source of strychnine. ▪ a homeopathic preparation of this plant, used esp. for the treatment of symptoms of overeating and overdrinking. [ME: from med. L., from L. *nux* 'nut' + *vomica* 'causing vomiting.']

Nu·yor·i·can /n(y)o͞oˈyôrikən/ (also **New·yor·i·can**) ▸ **n.** a Puerto Rican living in the US, esp. in New York City.

nuz·zle /ˈnəzəl/ ▸ **v.** [trans.] rub or push against gently with the nose and mouth: *he nuzzled her hair* | [intrans.] *the foal nuzzled at its mother.* ▪ [intrans.] (**nuzzle up to/against**) lean or snuggle against. [ME: frequentative from NOSE.]

NV ▸ **abbr.** Nevada (in official postal use).

NW ▸ **abbr.** ▪ northwest. ▪ northwestern.

NWbN ▸ **abbr.** northwest by north.

NWbW ▸ **abbr.** northwest by west.

NWT ▸ **abbr.** Northwest Territories.

n.wt. ▸ **abbr.** net weight.

NY ▸ **abbr.** New York (in official postal use).

nya·la /ˈnyälə/ ▸ **n.** (pl. same) a southern African antelope (*Tragelaphus angasi*), with a conspicuous crest on the neck and back and lyre-shaped horns. [19th C.: from Zulu.]

Nyan·ja /ˈnyänjə; ˈnyan-/ ▸ **n.** (pl. same or **-jas**) **1** a member of a people of Malawi and eastern and central Zambia. **2** the Bantu language of this people. ▸ **adj.** of or relating to this people or their language. [a local name, lit. 'lake.']

Ny·as·a, Lake /ˈnyäsə; ˈnyasə/ a lake in east central Africa, about 350 miles (580 km) long. Also called MALAWI, LAKE.

Ny·as·a·land /ˈnyäsə,land; nīˈas-/ former name (until 1966) for MALAWI.

NYC ▸ **abbr.** New York City.

nyc·ta·lo·pi·a /,niktəˈlōpēə/ ▸ **n.** Med. the inability to see in dim light or at night. Also called NIGHT BLINDNESS. [17th C.: via late L. from Gk. *nuktalōps*, from *nux, nukt-* 'night' + *alaos* 'blind' + *ōps* 'eye.']

nyc·to·pho·bi·a /,niktəˈfōbēə/ ▸ **n.** extreme or irrational fear of the night or of darkness. [20th C.: from Gk. *nux, nukt-* 'night.']

Nye·re·re /nyəˈre(ə)rē; -ˈrerā/, Julius Kambarage (1922–99), president of Tanzania 1964–85.

ny·lon /ˈnī,län/ ▸ **n.** a tough, lightweight, elastic synthetic polymer with a proteinlike chemical structure, able to be produced as filaments, sheets, or molded objects. ▪ fabric or yarn made from nylon fibers. ▪ (**nylons**) stockings or hose made of nylon. [1930s: invented word.]

nymph /nimf/ ▸ **n.** **1** a mythological spirit of nature imagined as a beautiful maiden inhabiting rivers, woods, or other locations. ▪ esp. literary a beautiful young woman. **2** an immature form of an insect that does not change greatly as it grows, e.g., a dragonfly, mayfly, or locust. Compare with LARVA. ▪ an artificial fly made to resemble the aquatic nymph of an insect, used in fishing. **3** a mainly brown butterfly (subfamily Satyrinae, family Nymphalidae) that frequents woods and forest glades. — **nymph·al** /ˈnimfəl/ **adj.** **nym·phe·an** /ˈnimfēən/ **adj.** **nymph·like adj.** [ME: from OFr. *nimphe*, from L. *nympha*, from Gk. *numphē* 'nymph, bride.']

nym·pha·lid /nimˈfaləd; ˈnimfəlid/ ▸ **n.** Entomol. an insect of a large family (Nymphalidae) of strikingly marked butterflies that have small forelegs not used for walking, including many familiar butterflies of temperate regions, such as the monarch and viceroy. [19th C.: from mod. L. *Nymphalidae*, from L. *nympha* 'nymph.']

nymph·et /nimˈfet; ˈnimfit/ ▸ **n.** an attractive and sexually mature young girl. [1950s: from NYMPH + -ET[1].]

nym·pho /ˈnimˈfō/ ▸ **n.** informal a nymphomaniac.

nym·pho·lep·sy /ˈnimfə,lepsē/ ▸ **n.** literary passion aroused in men by beautiful young girls. ▪ frenzy caused by desire for an unattainable ideal. [18th C.: from NYMPHOLEPT.]

nym·pho·lept /ˈnimfə,lept/ ▸ **n.** a person affected by nympholepsy. — **nym·pho·lep·tic** /,nimfəˈleptik/ **adj.** [19th C.: from Gk. *numpholēptos* 'caught by nymphs,' from *numphē* 'nymph' + *lambanein* 'take.']

nym·pho·ma·ni·a /,nimfəˈmānēə/ ▸ **n.** uncontrollable or excessive sexual desire in a woman. — **nym·pho·ma·ni·ac** /-ˈmānē,ak/ **n. & adj.** **nym·pho·ma·ni·a·cal** /-məˈnīəkəl/ **adj.** [18th C.: mod. L., from L. *nympha* (see NYMPH).]

Ny·norsk /ˈno͞o,nôrsk; ,no͞oˈnôrsk/ ▸ **n.** a literary form of Norwegian, based on country dialects and constructed in the 19th century to serve as a national language more clearly distinct from Danish than Bokmål. [Norwegian, from *ny* 'new' + *Norsk* 'Norwegian.']

Nyo·man /ˈnyō,män/ Belorussian name for NEMAN.

NYP ▸ **abbr.** not yet published.

Ny·sa /ˈnisə/ Polish name for NEISSE.

NYSE ▸ **abbr.** New York Stock Exchange.

nys·tag·mus /nəˈstagməs/ ▸ **n.** rapid involuntary movements of the eyes. — **nys·tag·mic adj.** [19th C.: from Gk. *nustagmos* 'nodding, drowsiness,' from *nustazein* 'nod, be sleepy.']

nys·ta·tin /ˈnistətin; ˈnī-/ ▸ **n.** an antibiotic obtained from the bacterium *Streptomyces noursei*, used chiefly to treat fungal infections. [1950s: from *N(ew) Y(ork) Stat(e)*.]

Nyx /niks/ Gk. Mythol. the female personification of the night, daughter of Chaos.

NZ ▸ **abbr.** New Zealand.

Oo

O[1] /ō/ (also **o**) ▶ **n.** (pl. **Os** or **O's** /ōz/) **1** the fifteenth letter of the alphabet. ■ a human blood type (in the ABO system) lacking both the A and B antigens. In blood transfusion, a person with blood of this group is a potential universal donor. **2** (also **oh**) zero (in a sequence of numerals, esp. when spoken). **3** a shape like that of a capital O; a circle.

O[2] ▶ **abbr.** ■ Ocean. ■ (in prescriptions) a pint. ■ octavo. ■ October. ■ Ohio. ■ old. ■ Ontario. ■ Oregon. ▶ **symb.** the chemical element oxygen.

O[3] ▶ **exclam. 1** archaic spelling of OH[1]. **2** archaic used before a name in direct address, as in prayers and poetry: *give peace in our time, O Lord.* [natural exclamation: first recorded in ME.]

O' ▶ **prefix** in Irish patronymic names such as *O'Neill.* [18th C.: from Irish *ó, ua* 'descendant.']

o ▶ **abbr.** ■ pint. ■ octavo. ■ off. ■ old. ■ only. ■ order. ■ Baseball out; outs.

o' /ə; ō/ ▶ **prep.** short for OF, used to represent an informal pronunciation: *a cup o' coffee.*

o- ▶ **abbr.** [used in comb.] Chem. ortho-: o-*xylene.*

-o ▶ **suffix** forming chiefly informal or slang variants or derivatives such as *righto, wino.* [perh. from OH[1].]

-o- ▶ **suffix** used as the terminal vowel of combining forms: *chemico-* | *Gallo-.* [from Gk.]

o/a ▶ **abbr.** on or about.

oaf /ōf/ ▶ **n.** a stupid, uncultured, or clumsy person. — **oaf·ish adj. oaf·ish·ly adv. oaf·ish·ness n.** [17th C.: var. of obs. *auf,* from ON *álfr* 'elf.']

O·a·hu /ō'wähōō/ the third largest of the Hawaiian islands; pop. 838,500. Its principal town, Honolulu, is the capital of Hawaii, and it is the site of Pearl Harbor.

oak /ōk/ ▶ **n.** (also **oak tree**) a tree (genus *Quercus*) of the beech family that bears acorns and typically has lobed deciduous leaves and hard durable wood.

– PHRASES **mighty** (or **great**) **oaks from little acorns grow** proverb something of small or modest dimensions may grow into something very large or impressive. — **oak·en adj. oak·y adj.** [OE *āc,* of Gmc. origin; rel. to Du. *eik* and Ger. *Eiche.*]

oak ap·ple ▶ **n.** a spongy spherical gall that forms on oak trees in response to the developing larvae of a gall wasp, in particular the American *Amphibolips confluenta* and the European *Biorhiza pallida.*

oak ker·mes ▶ **n.** see KERMES (sense 2).

Oak·land /'ōklənd/ an industrial city in California; pop. 399,484.

oak leaf clus·ter ▶ **n.** an attachment to a military decoration depicting a twig with oak leaves and acorns, indicating distinguished action or a subsequent award of the same decoration.

Oak·ley /'ōklē/, Annie (1860–1926), US markswoman; full name *Phoebe Anne Oakley Mozee.* From 1885, she was the star of Buffalo Bill's Wild West Show.

Oak Ridge a city in eastern Tennessee, established in 1942 as part of US nuclear development; pop. 27,310.

oa·kum /'ōkəm/ ▶ **n.** esp. hist. loose fiber from untwisted rope, used esp. to caulk wooden ships. [OE *ācumbe,* lit. 'off-combings.']

oak wilt ▶ **n.** a disease of oaks and other trees that makes the foliage wilt and eventually kills the tree, cause by the fungus *Ceratocystis fagacearum.*

O. & M. ▶ **abbr.** ■ operations and maintenance. ■ organization and methods.

oar /ôr/ ▶ **n.** a pole with a flat blade, pivoting in an oarlock, used to row or steer a boat through the water. ■ a rower. ▶ **v.** [trans.] row; propel with or as with oars: *oaring the sea like madmen* | [intrans.] *oaring through the weeds.* ■ move (something, esp. the hands) like oars.

– PHRASES **put in one's oar** informal give an opinion without being asked. **rest on one's oars** relax one's efforts. — **oar·less adj.** [OE *ār,* of Gmc. origin; rel. to Dan. and Norw. *åre.*]

oar·fish /'ôr,fisH/ ▶ **n.** (pl. same or **-fish·es**) a very long, narrow, silvery marine fish (*Regalecus glesne,* family Regalecidae) of deep water, with a deep red dorsal fin running the length of the body. Also called RIBBONFISH.

oar·lock /'ôr,läk/ ▶ **n.** a fitting on the gunwale of a boat that serves as a fulcrum for an oar and keeps it in place.

oars·man /'ôrzmən/ ▶ **n.** (pl. **-men**) a rower, esp. as a member of a racing team. — **oars·man·ship n.**

oars·wom·an /'ôrz,wŏŏmən/ ▶ **n.** (pl. **-wom·en**) a female rower, esp. as a member of a racing team.

OAS ▶ **abbr.** ORGANIZATION OF AMERICAN STATES.

o·a·sis /ō'āsis/ ▶ **n.** (pl. **-ses** /-sēz/) a fertile spot in a desert where water is found. ■ fig. a pleasant or peaceful area or period in the midst of a difficult, troubled, or hectic place or situation. [17th C.: via late L. from Gk., appar. of Egyptian origin.]

oarlock

oast /ōst/ ▶ **n.** a kiln used for drying hops. [OE *āst* rel. to Du. *eest,* from an Indo-Eur. root meaning 'burn.']

oat /ōt/ ▶ **n.** a cereal plant (*Avena sativa*) cultivated chiefly in cool climates and widely used for animal feed as well as human consumption. ■ (**oats**) the grain yielded by this, used as food. ■ used in names of wild grasses related to the cultivated oat, e.g., **wild oat.**

– PHRASES **feel one's oats** informal feel lively and energetic. **sow one's wild oats** go through a period of wild or promiscuous behavior while young. — **oat·en adj.** (archaic) **oat·y adj.** [OE *āte,* pl. *ātan.*]

oat·cake /'ōt,kāk/ ▶ **n.** a thin, unleavened cake made of oatmeal.

oat·er /'ōtər/ ▶ **n.** informal a western movie or television show. [1950s: OAT.]

Oates[1] /ōts/, Joyce Carol (1938–) US writer. Her novels include *them* (1969) and *Black Girl/White Girl* (2006).

Oates[2], Titus (1649–1705), English clergyman. He fabricated the Popish Plot in 1678.

oat grass ▶ **n.** a wild grass (*Avenula* and other genera) that resembles the oat.

oath /ōTH/ ▶ **n.** (pl. **oaths** /ōTHs; ōTHz/) **1** a solemn promise, often invoking a divine witness, regarding one's future action or behavior. ■ a sworn declaration that one will tell the truth, esp. in a court of law. **2** a profane or offensive expression used to express anger or other strong emotions.

– PHRASES **under oath** having sworn to tell the truth, esp. in a court of law. [OE *āth,* of Gmc. origin; rel. to Du. *eed* and Ger. *Eid.*]

oat·meal /'ōt,mēl/ ▶ **n. 1** meal made from ground oats, used in breakfast cereals or other food. **2** a grayish-beige color flecked with brown.

OAU ▶ **abbr.** Organization of African Unity.

Oa·xa·ca /wä'häkə; -wə/ a state in southern Mexico. ■ its capital city; pop. 213,000. Full name OAXACA DE JUÁREZ.

OB ▶ **abbr.** ■ obstetrical. ■ obstetrician. ■ obstetrics.

Ob /äb; ôb/ a river in western Siberia in Russia. Rising in the Altai Mountains, it flows north and west for 3,481 miles (5,410 km) to the Kara Sea.

ob. ▶ **abbr.** he or she died: *ob. 1867.* [from L. *obiit.*]

ob- ▶ **prefix 1** denoting exposure or openness: *obverse.* ■ expressing meeting or facing: *observe.* **2** denoting opposition, hostility, or resistance: *obstacle.* ■ denoting hindrance, blocking, or concealment: *obliterate* | *obviate.* **3** denoting extensiveness, finality, or completeness: *obdurate* | *obsolete.* **4** (in modern technical words) inversely; in a direction or manner contrary to the usual: *obconical.* [from L. *ob* 'toward, against, in the way of.']

Obad. ▶ **abbr.** Bible Obadiah.

O·ba·di·ah /,ōbə'dīə/ (in the Bible) a Hebrew minor prophet. ■ the shortest book of the Bible, bearing his name.

ob·bli·ga·to /,äblə'gätō/ (also **ob·li·ga·to**) ▶ **n.** (pl. **-ga·tos** or **-ga·ti** /-'gätē/) [usu. with or as adj.] an instrumental part that is integral to a piece of music and should not be omitted in performance. [Ital., lit. 'obligatory,' from L. *obligatus,* past part. of *obligare* (see OBLIGE).]

ob·con·i·cal /äb'känikəl/ (also **ob·con·ic** /-'känik/) ▶ **adj.** Bot. in the form of an inverted cone.

ob·cor·date /äb'kôr,dāt/ ▶ **adj.** Bot. (of a leaf) in the shape of a heart with the pointed end at the base.

ob·du·rate /'äbd(y)ərit/ ▶ **adj.** stubbornly refusing to change one's opinion or course of action. — **ob·du·ra·cy** /-rəsē/ **n. ob·du·rate·ly adv. ob·du·rate·ness n.** [ME: from L. *obduratus,* past part. of *obdurare,* from *ob-* 'in opposition' + *durare* 'harden' (from *durus* 'hard').]

o·be·ah /'ōbēə/ (also **o·bi** /'ōbē/) ▶ **n.** a kind of sorcery practiced esp. in the Caribbean. [Twi, from *bayi* 'sorcery.']

o·be·di·ence /ō'bēdēəns/ ▶ **n.** compliance with someone's wishes or orders or acknowledgment of their authority. ■ submission to a law or rule. ■ observance of a monastic rule.

– PHRASES **in obedience to** in accordance with.

o·be·di·ent /ō'bēdēənt/ ▶ **adj.** complying with orders or requests; submissive to another's will. — **o·be·di·ent·ly adv.** [ME: via OFr. from L. *oboedient-* 'obeying,' from the v. *oboedire* (see OBEY).]

o·bei·sance /ō'bāsəns; ō'bē-/ ▶ **n.** deferential respect: *they paid obeisance to the prince.* ■ a gesture expressing deferential respect, such as a bow or curtsy. — **o·bei·sant** /ō'bāsənt/ **adj.** [ME: from OFr. *obeissance,* from *obeissant* 'obeying,' pres. part. of *obeir.*]

ob·e·li /'äbə,lī/ plural form of OBELUS.

ob·e·lisk /'äbə,lisk/ ▶ **n.** **1** a stone pillar, typically having a square or rectangular cross section and a pyramidal top, set up as a monument or landmark. **2** another term for OBELUS. [16th C.: via L. from Gk. *obeliskos,* dimin. of *obelos* 'pointed pillar.']

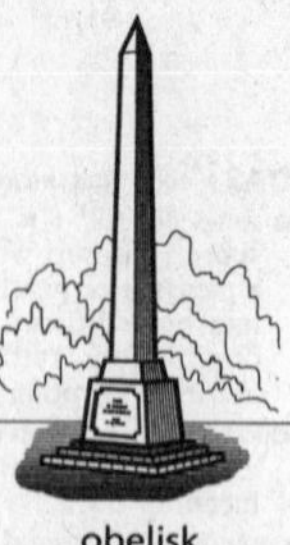

obelisk

ob·e·lize /'äbə,līz/ ▶ **v.** [trans.] mark (a word or passage) with an obelus to show that it is spurious, corrupt, or doubtful.

ob·e·lus /'äbələs/ ▶ **n.** (pl. **-li** /-,lī/) **1** a symbol (†) used as a reference mark in printed matter, or to indicate that a person is deceased. Also called DAGGER. **2** a mark (– or ÷) used in ancient texts to mark a word or passage as spurious, corrupt, or doubtful. [ME: via L. from Gk. *obelos* 'pointed pillar.']

O·ber·on /'ōbə,rän/ Astron. a satellite of Uranus, the furthest from the planet, discovered by W. Herschel in 1787.

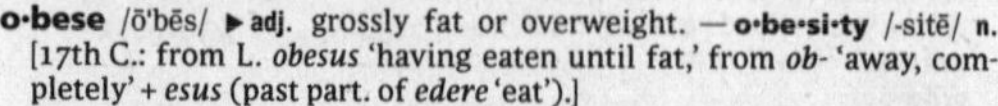

o·bese /ō'bēs/ ▶ **adj.** grossly fat or overweight. — **o·be·si·ty** /-sitē/ **n.** [17th C.: from L. *obesus* 'having eaten until fat,' from *ob-* 'away, completely' + *esus* (past part. of *edere* 'eat').]

o·bey /ō'bā/ ▶ **v.** [trans.] comply with the command, direction, or request of (a person or a law); submit to the authority of. ■ carry out (a command or instruction): *the officer was convicted for refusing to obey orders* | [intrans.] *when the order was repeated, he refused to obey.* ■ behave in accordance with (a general principle, natural law, etc.). — **o·bey·er n.** [ME: from OFr. *obeir,* from L. *oboedire,* from *ob-* 'in the direction of' + *audire* 'hear.']

ob·fus·cate /'äbfə,skāt/ ▶ **v.** [trans.] render obscure, unclear, or unintelligible. ■ bewilder (someone). — **ob·fus·ca·tion** /,äbfə'skāsʜən/ **n. ob·fus·ca·to·ry** /äb'fəskə,tôrē/ **adj.** [ME: from late L. *obfuscat-* 'darkened,' from the v. *obfuscare,* based on L. *fuscus* 'dark.']

ob-gyn /'ō'bē 'jē,wī'en/ ▶ **abbr.** obstetrics and gynecology.

o·bi[1] /'ōbē/ ▶ **n.** (pl. **o·bis**) a broad sash worn around the waist of a Japanese kimono. [Japanese, lit. 'belt.']

o·bi[2] ▶ **n.** var. of OBEAH.

o·bit /'ōbit; ō'bit/ ▶ **n.** informal an obituary. [ME: from L. *obitus* 'going down, death.']

ob·i·ter dic·tum /'ōbitər 'diktəm/ ▶ **n.** (pl. **dic·ta** /'diktə/) Law a judge's incidental expression of opinion, not essential to the decision and not establishing precedent. ■ an incidental remark. [L. *obiter* 'in passing' + *dictum* 'something that is said.']

o·bit·u·ar·y /ō'bicʜōō,erē/ ▶ **n.** (pl. **-ar·ies**) a notice of a death, esp. in a newspaper, typically including a brief biography of the deceased person. — **o·bit·u·ar·ist** /-ərist/ **n.** [18th C.: from med. L. *obituarius,* from L. *obitus* 'death,' from *obit-* 'perished,' from the v. *obire.*]

obj. ▶ **abbr.** ■ object. ■ objection. ■ objective.

ob·ject ▶ **n.** /'äbjəkt/ **1** a material thing that can be seen and touched. ■ Philos. a thing external to the thinking mind or subject. **2** a person or thing to which a specified action or feeling is directed. ■ a goal or purpose. ■ Gram. a noun or noun phrase governed by an active transitive verb or by a preposition. ■ Comput. a data construct that provides a description of something that may be used by a computer and defines its status, its method of operation, and how it interacts with other objects. ▶ **v.** /əb'jekt/ [reporting verb] say something to express one's disapproval of or disagreement with something: [intrans.] ***residents object to the volume of traffic.*** ■ [trans.] archaic adduce as a reason against something: *Bryant objects this very circumstance to the authenticity of the Iliad.* — **ob·ject·less** /'äbjəktləs/ **adj. ob·jec·tor** /əb'jektər/ **n.** [ME: from med. L. *objectum* 'thing presented to the mind,' neut. past part. (used as a n.) of L. *obicere,* from *ob-* 'in the way of' + *jacere* 'to throw'.]

ob·ject ball ▶ **n.** Billiards any ball other than the cue ball.

ob·ject code ▶ **n.** Comput. code produced by a compiler or assembler.

ob·ject glass (also **ob·ject-glass**) ▶ **n.** another term for OBJECTIVE (sense 3).

ob·jec·ti·fy /əb'jektə,fī/ ▶ **v.** (**-fies, -fied**) [trans.] express (something abstract) in a concrete form: *good poetry objectifies feeling.* ■ degrade to the status of a mere object. — **ob·jec·ti·fi·ca·tion** /əb,jektəfi'kāsʜən/ **n.**

ob·jec·tion /əb'beksʜən/ ▶ **n.** an expression or feeling of disapproval or opposition; a reason for disagreeing. ■ the action of challenging or disagreeing with something: *his view is open to objection.*

ob·jec·tion·a·ble /əb'jeksʜənəbəl/ ▶ **adj.** arousing distaste or opposition; unpleasant or offensive. — **ob·jec·tion·a·ble·ness n. ob·jec·tion·a·bly adv.**

ob·jec·tive /əb'jektiv/ ▶ **adj.** **1** (of a person or their judgment) not influenced by personal feelings or opinions in considering and representing facts. Contrasted with SUBJECTIVE. ■ not dependent on the mind for existence; actual: *objective fact.* **2** [attrib.] Gram. of, relating to, or denoting a case of nouns and pronouns used as the object of a transitive verb or a preposition. ▶ **n.** **1** a thing aimed at or sought; a goal. **2** (**the objective**) Gram. the objective case. **3** (also **objective lens**) the lens in a telescope or microscope nearest to the object observed. — **ob·jec·tive·ly adv. ob·jec·tive·ness n. ob·jec·tiv·i·ty** /,äbjek'tivitē/ **n. ob·jec·ti·vi·za·tion** /əb,jektəvi'zāsʜən/ **n. ob·jec·tiv·ize v.**

ob·jec·tive cor·rel·a·tive ▶ **n.** the artistic and literary technique of representing or evoking a particular emotion by means of symbols that objectify that emotion and are associated with it.

ob·jec·tiv·ism /əb'jektə,vizəm/ ▶ **n.** **1** the tendency to lay stress on what is external to or independent of the mind. **2** Philos. the belief that certain things, esp. moral truths, exist independently of human knowledge or perception of them. — **ob·jec·tiv·ist n. & adj. ob·jec·ti·vis·tic** /əb,jektə'vistik/ **adj.**

ob·ject lan·guage ▶ **n.** a language described by means of another language. Compare with METALANGUAGE, TARGET LANGUAGE.

ob·ject les·son ▶ **n.** a striking practical example of some principle or ideal.

ob·ject-o·ri·ent·ed ▶ **adj.** Comput. (of a programming language) using a methodology that enables a system to be modeled as a set of objects that can be controlled and manipulated in a modular manner. — **ob·ject o·ri·en·ta·tion n.**

ob·ject re·la·tions ▶ **n.** Psychoanal. a theory describing the relationship felt or the emotional energy directed by the self or ego toward a chosen object.

ob·jet d'art /,ôbzʜā'där/ ▶ **n.** (pl. **ob·jets d'art** pronunc. same) a small decorative or artistic object, typically when regarded as a collectible item. [Fr., lit. 'object of art.']

ob·jet trou·vé /ôb,zʜā trōō'vā/ ▶ **n.** (pl. **ob·jets trou·vés** pronunc. same) an object found or picked up at random and considered aesthetically pleasing. [Fr., lit. 'found object.']

ob·jur·gate /'äbjər,gāt/ ▶ **v.** [trans.] rebuke severely; scold. — **ob·jur·ga·tion** /,äbjər'gāsʜən/ **n. ob·jur·ga·tor n. ob·jur·ga·to·ry** /əb'jərgə,tôrē/ **adj.** [17th C.: from L. *objurgat-* 'chided, rebuked,' from the v. *objurgare,* based on *jurgium* 'strife.']

obl. ▶ **abbr.** ■ oblique. ■ oblong.

ob·lan·ce·o·late /äb'lansēə,lāt/ ▶ **adj.** tech. (esp. of leaves) lanceolate, with the more pointed end at the base.

o·blast /'ôbləst; 'äblast/ ▶ **n.** an administrative division or region in Russia and the former Soviet Union. [Russ.]

ob·late[1] /'äb,lāt; ō'blāt/ ▶ **adj.** Geom. (of a spheroid) flattened at the poles. Often contrasted with PROLATE. [18th C.: from mod. L. *oblatus* (from *ob-* 'inversely' + *-latus* 'carried').]

ob·late[2] ▶ **n.** a person dedicated to a religious life, but typically having not taken full monastic vows. [17th C.: from Fr., from L. *oblatus,* past part. of *offerre* 'to offer.']

ob·la·tion /ə'blāsʜən/ ▶ **n.** a thing presented or offered to God or a god. ■ Christian Church the presentation of bread and wine to God in the Eucharist. — **ob·la·tion·al** /-sʜənl; -sʜnəl/ **adj. ob·la·to·ry** /'äblə,tôrē/ **adj.**

ob·li·gate ▶ **v.** /'äbli,gāt/ **1** bind or compel (someone), esp. legally or morally. **2** [trans.] commit (assets) as security: *the money must be obligated within 30 days.* ▶ **adj.** [attrib.] Biol. restricted to a particular function or mode of life. Often contrasted with FACULTATIVE. — **ob·li·ga·tor n.** [ME: from L. *obligatus,* past part. of *obligare* (see OBLIGE).]

ob·li·ga·tion /,äbli'gāsʜən/ ▶ **n.** an act or course of action to which a person is morally or legally bound; a duty or commitment. ■ the condition of being morally or legally bound to do something. ■ a debt of gratitude for a service or favor. ■ Law a binding agreement committing a person to a payment or other action. ■ Law a document containing a binding agreement; a written contract or bond. — **ob·li·ga·tion·al** /-sʜənl; -sʜnəl/ **adj.**

ob·li·ga·to /,äbli'gätō/ ▶ **n.** var. of OBBLIGATO.

o·blig·a·to·ry /ə'bligə,tôrē/ ▶ **adj.** required by a legal, moral, or other rule; compulsory. ■ so customary or routine as to be expected of everyone or on every occasion: *after the obligatory preamble on the weather he got down to business.* ■ (of a ruling) having binding force. — **o·blig·a·to·ri·ly** /-,tôrəlē/ **adv.**

o·blige /ə'blīj/ ▶ **v.** [with obj. and infin.] make (someone) legally or morally bound to an action or course of action: *doctors are obliged by law to keep patients alive while there is a chance of recovery.* ■ [trans.] do as (someone) asks or desires in order to help or please them: ***oblige me by*** *not being sorry for yourself* | [intrans.] *tell me what you want to know and I'll see if I can oblige.* ■ (**be obliged**) be indebted or grateful. ■ [trans.] archaic bind (someone) by an oath, promise, or contract. — **o·blig·er n.** [ME: from OFr. *obliger,* from L. *obligare,* from *ob-* 'toward' + *ligare* 'to bind.']

ob·li·gee /,äbli'jē/ ▶ **n.** Law a person to whom another is bound by contract or another legal procedure. Compare with OBLIGOR.

o·blig·ing /ə'blījiɴɢ/ ▶ **adj.** willing to do a service or kindness; helpful. — **o·blig·ing·ly adv. o·blig·ing·ness n.**

ob·li·gor /,äbli'gôr/ ▶ **n.** Law a person who is bound to another by contract or another legal procedure. Compare with OBLIGEE.

o·blique /ə'blēk; ō'blēk/ ▶ **adj.** **1** neither parallel nor at a right angle to a specified or implied line; slanting. ■ not explicit or direct in addressing a point: *an oblique attack on the president.* ■ Geom. (of a line, plane figure, or surface) inclined at other than a right angle. ■ Geom. (of an angle) acute or obtuse. ■ Geom. (of a cone, cylinder, etc.) with an axis not perpendicular to the plane of its base. ■ Anat. (esp. of a muscle) neither parallel nor perpendicular to the long axis of a body or limb. **2** Gram. denoting any case other than the nominative or vocative. ▶ **n.** a muscle neither parallel nor perpendicular to the long axis of a body or limb. — **o•blique•ly** adv. **o•blique•ness** n. **o•bliq•ui•ty** /ə'blikwətē/ n. [ME: from L. *obliquus*.]

ob•lit•er•ate /ə'blitə,rāt/ ▶ **v.** [trans.] destroy utterly; wipe out. ■ cause to become invisible or indistinct; blot out. — **ob•lit•er•a•tion** /ə,blitə'rāsHən/ n. **ob•lit•er•a•tive** /-,rātiv/ adj. **o•blit•er•a•tor** n. [16th C.: from L. *obliterat-* 'struck out, erased,' from the v. *obliterare*, based on *littera* 'letter, something written.']

ob•liv•i•on /ə'blivēən/ ▶ **n. 1** the state of being unaware or unconscious of what is happening. ■ the state of being forgotten, esp. by the public. ■ fig. extinction. **2** Law, hist. amnesty or pardon. [ME: via OFr. from L. *oblivio(n-)*, from *oblivisci* 'forget.']

ob•liv•i•ous /ə'blivēəs/ ▶ **adj.** not aware of or not concerned about what is happening around one. — **ob•liv•i•ous•ly** adv. **ob•liv•i•ous•ness** n.

ob•long /'äb,lôNG; -,läNG/ ▶ **adj.** having an elongated shape, as a rectangle or an oval. ▶ **n.** an object or flat figure in this shape. [ME: from L. *oblongus* 'longish.']

ob•lo•quy /'äbləkwē/ ▶ **n.** strong public criticism or verbal abuse. ■ disgrace, esp. that brought about by public abuse. — **ob•lo•qui•al** /äb'lōkwēəl/ adj. **ob•lo•qui•ous** /äb'lōkwēəs/ adj. [ME: from late L. *obloquium* 'contradiction,' from L. *obloqui*, from *ob-* 'against' + *loqui* 'speak.']

ob•nox•ious /əb'näksHəs/ ▶ **adj.** extremely unpleasant. — **ob•nox•ious•ly** adv. **ob•nox•ious•ness** n. [16th C.: from L. *obnoxiosus*, from *obnoxius* 'exposed to harm,' from *ob-* 'toward' + *noxa* 'harm.']

ob•nu•bi•late /äb'n(y)o͞obə,lāt/ ▶ **v.** [trans.] literary darken or cover with or as if with a cloud; obscure. — **ob•nu•bi•la•tion** /äb,n(y)o͞obə'lāsHən/ n. [16th C.: from L. *obnubilat-* 'covered with clouds or fog,' from the v. *obnubilare*.]

obo (also **o.b.o.**) ▶ **abbr.** or best offer (used in advertisements): *$2,700 obo.*

oboe

o•boe /'ōbō/ ▶ **n.** a woodwind instrument with a slender, tubular body, played with a double-reed mouthpiece. ■ an organ stop resembling an oboe in tone. — **o•bo•ist** n. [18th C.: from Ital., or from Fr. *hautbois*, from *haut* 'high' + *bois* 'wood.']

ob•ol /'äbəl/ ▶ **n.** an ancient Greek coin worth one sixth of a drachma. [via L. from Gk. *obolos*, var. of *obelos* (see OBELUS).]

O•bo•te /ō'bōtā/, Milton (1924–2005), president of Uganda 1966–71, 1980–85; full name *Apollo Milton Opeto Obote.*

ob•o•vate /äb'ō,vāt/ ▶ **adj.** Bot. (of a leaf) ovate with the narrower end at the base.

obs. (also **Obs.**) ▶ **abbr.** ■ observation. ■ observatory. ■ obsolete.

ob•scene /əb'sēn/ ▶ **adj.** (of the portrayal or description of sexual matters) offensive or disgusting by accepted standards of morality and decency. ■ offensive to moral principles; repugnant. — **ob•scene•ly** adv. [16th C.: from Fr. *obscène* or L. *obscaenus* 'ill-omened or abominable.']

ob•scen•i•ty /əb'senitē/ ▶ **n.** (pl. **-ties**) the state or quality of being obscene; obscene behavior, language, or images. ■ an extremely offensive word or expression.

ob•scu•rant•ism /əb'skyo͝orən,tizəm; äb-/ ▶ **n.** the practice of deliberately preventing the facts or full details of something from becoming known. — **ob•scu•rant** /'äbskyərənt/ n. & adj. **ob•scu•rant•ist** n. & adj.

ob•scure /əb'skyo͝or/ ▶ **adj.** (**-scur•er**, **-scur•est**) not discovered or known about; uncertain. ■ not clearly expressed or easily understood. ■ not important or well known. ■ hard to make out or define; vague: fig. *I feel an obscure resentment.* ■ (of a color) not sharply defined; dim or dingy. ▶ **v.** [trans.] keep from being seen; conceal. ■ make unclear and difficult to understand. ■ overshadow: *none of this should obscure the perseverance of the workers.* — **ob•scu•ra•tion** /,äbskyə'rāsHən/ n. **ob•scure•ly** adv. [ME: from OFr. *obscur*, from L. *obscurus* 'dark,'.]

ob•scure vow•el ▶ **n.** another term for SCHWA.

ob•scu•ri•ty /əb'skyo͝oritē/ ▶ **n.** (pl. **-ties**) the state of being unknown, inconspicuous, or unimportant. ■ the quality of being difficult to understand. ■ a thing that is unclear or difficult to understand. [ME: from OFr. *obscurite*, from L. *obscuritas*, from *obscurus* 'dark.']

ob•se•cra•tion /,äbsə'krāsHən/ ▶ **n.** rare earnest pleading or supplication. [ME: from L. *obsecratio(n-)*, from *obsecrare* 'entreat,' based on *sacer, sacr-* 'sacred.']

ob•se•quies /'äbsəkwēz/ ▶ **plural n.** funeral rites. [ME: plural of obs. *obsequy*, from Anglo-Norman Fr. *obsequie*, from the med. L. pl. *obsequiae* (from L. *exsequiae* 'funeral rites,'.]

ob•se•qui•ous /əb'sēkwēəs/ ▶ **adj.** obedient or attentive to an excessive or servile degree. — **ob•se•qui•ous•ly** adv. **ob•se•qui•ous•ness** n. [15th C.: from L. *obsequiosus*, from *obsequium* 'compliance,' from *obsequi* 'comply with.']

ob•serv•ance /əb'zərvəns/ ▶ **n. 1** the action or practice of fulfilling or respecting the requirements of law, morality, or ritual. ■ (usu. **observances**) an act performed for religious or ceremonial reasons. ■ a rule to be followed by a religious order. ■ archaic respect; deference. **2** the action of watching or noticing something.

ob•serv•ant /əb'zərvənt/ ▶ **adj. 1** quick to notice things. **2** adhering strictly to the rules of a particular religion, esp. Judaism. ▶ **n.** (**Observant**) hist. a member of a branch of the Franciscan order that followed a strict rule. [ME (as a n.): from Fr., lit. 'watching,' pres. part. of *observer* (see OBSERVE).]

ob•ser•va•tion /,äbzər'vāsHən/ ▶ **n. 1** the action or process of observing something or someone carefully or in order to gain information. ■ the ability to notice things, esp. significant details. ■ the taking of the altitude of the sun or another celestial body for navigational purposes. **2** a remark, statement, or comment based on something one has seen, heard, or noticed. — **ob•ser•va•tion•al** /-sHənl/ adj. **ob•ser•va•tion•al•ly** /-sHənl-ē/ adv. [ME: from L. *observatio(n-)*, from *observare* (see OBSERVE).]

ob•ser•va•tion car ▶ **n.** a railroad car with large windows designed to provide a good view of passing scenery.

ob•ser•va•tion post ▶ **n.** Mil. a post for watching the movement of enemy forces or the effect of artillery fire.

ob•serv•a•to•ry /əb'zərvə,tôrē/ ▶ **n.** (pl. **-ries**) a room or building housing a telescope or other scientific equipment for the study of natural phenomena. ■ a position or building affording an extensive view. [17th C.; from mod. L. *observatorium*, from L. *observare* (see OBSERVE).]

ob•serve /əb'zərv/ ▶ **v.** [trans.] **1** notice or perceive (something) and register it as being significant. ■ watch (someone or something) carefully and attentively. ■ take note of or detect (something) in the course of a scientific study. ■ [reporting verb] make a remark or comment: [with direct speech] *"It's chilly," she observed* | [with clause] *a stockbroker once observed that dealers live and work in hell.* **2** fulfill or comply with (a social, legal, ethical, or religious obligation). ■ (usu. **be observed**) maintain (silence) in compliance with a rule or custom, or temporarily as a mark of respect. ■ perform or take part in (a ceremony). ■ celebrate or acknowledge (an anniversary). — **ob•serv•a•ble** adj. **ob•serv•a•bly** adv. [ME (sense 2): from OFr. *observer*, from L. *observare* 'to watch,' from *ob-* 'toward' + *servare* 'attend to, look at.']

ob•serv•er /əb'zərvər/ ▶ **n.** a person who watches or notices something. ■ a person who follows events, esp. political ones, closely and comments publicly on them. ■ a person posted to an area in an official capacity to monitor political or military events. ■ a person who attends a conference, inquiry, etc., to note the proceedings without participating in them. ■ (in science or art) a real or hypothetical person whose observation is regarded as having a particular viewpoint or effect.

ob•sess /əb'ses/ ▶ **v.** [trans.] (usu. **be obsessed**) preoccupy or fill the mind of (someone) continually, intrusively, and to a troubling extent: *he was obsessed with thoughts of suicide.* ■ [intrans.] (of a person) be preoccupied in this way: *her husband* ***obsessed about*** *the wrong she had done him.* — **ob•ses•sive** adj. & n. **ob•ses•sive•ly** adv. **ob•ses•sive•ness** n. [ME: from L. *obsess-* 'besieged,' from the v. *obsidere*, from *ob-* 'opposite' + *sedere* 'sit.']

ob•ses•sion /əb'sesHən/ ▶ **n.** the state of being obsessed with someone or something. ■ an idea or thought that continually preoccupies or intrudes on a person's mind. — **ob•ses•sion•al** /-sHənl/ adj. **ob•ses•sion•al•ly** /-sHənl-ē/ adv.

ob•ses•sive–com•pul•sive ▶ **adj.** Psychiatry denoting or relating to a disorder in which a person feels compelled to perform certain meaningless actions repeatedly in order to alleviate obsessive fears or intrusive thoughts, typically resulting in severe disruption of daily life. ▶ **n.** a person characterized by such obsessive behavior.

ob•sid•i•an /əb'sidēən; äb-/ ▶ **n.** a hard, dark, glasslike volcanic rock formed by the rapid solidification of lava without crystallization. [17th C.: from L. *obsidianus*, error for *obsianus*, from *Obsius*, discoverer of a similar stone.]

ob•so•les•cent /,äbsə'lesənt/ ▶ **adj.** becoming obsolete. — **ob•so•lesce** v. **ob•so•les•cence** n. [18th C.: from L. *obsolescent-* 'falling into disuse,' from the v. *obsolescere*.]

ob•so•lete /,äbsə'lēt/ ▶ **adj. 1** no longer produced or used; out of date. **2** Biol. (of a part or characteristic of an organism) less developed than formerly or in a related species; vestigial. ▶ **v.** [trans.] cause (a product or idea) to be or become obsolete by replacing it with something new: *we're obsoleting last year's designs.* — **ob•so•lete•ly** adv. **ob•so•lete•ness** n. **ob•so•let•ism** /-'lē,tizəm/ n. [16th C.: from L. *obsoletus* 'grown old, worn out,' past part. of *obsolescere* 'fall into disuse.']

ob•sta•cle /'äbstəkəl/ ▶ **n.** a thing that blocks one's way or prevents or hinders progress. [ME: via OFr. from L. *obstaculum*, from *obstare* 'impede,' from *ob-* 'against' + *stare* 'stand.']

ob•sta•cle course ▶ **n.** a course over which participants negotiate obstacles to be climbed, crawled under, crossed on suspended ropes, etc., as used for training soldiers. ■ fig. any situation that presents a series of challenges or obstacles.

ob•stet•ri•cal /əb'stetrikəl; äb-/ ▶ **adj.** of or relating to childbirth and the processes associated with it. — **ob•stet•ric** adj. **ob•stet•ri•cal•ly** adv. [18th C.: from mod. L. *obstetricus* for L. *obstetricius* (based on *obstetrix* 'midwife'), from *obstare* 'be present.']

ob•ste•tri•cian /,äbstə'trisHən/ ▶ **n.** a physician or surgeon qualified to practice in obstetrics.

ob•stet•rics /əb'stetriks; äb-/ ▶ **plural n.** [usu. treated as sing.] the branch of medicine and surgery concerned with childbirth and the care of women giving birth.

ob·sti·nate /'äbstənit/ ▶ **adj.** stubbornly refusing to change one's opinion or action, despite attempts to persuade one to do so. ■ (of an unwelcome phenomenon or situation) very difficult to change or overcome. — **ob·sti·na·cy** /-nəsē/ **n. ob·sti·nate·ly adv.** [ME: from L. *obstinatus*, past part. of *obstinare* 'persist.']

ob·sti·pa·tion /ˌäbstə'pāsHən/ ▶ **n.** Med. severe or complete constipation. [16th C.: alt. of CONSTIPATION.]

ob·strep·er·ous /əb'strepərəs; äb-/ ▶ **adj.** noisy and difficult to control: *the boy is cocky and obstreperous.* — **ob·strep·er·ous·ly adv. ob·strep·er·ous·ness n.** [16th C.: from L. *obstreperus* (from *obstrepere*, from *ob-* 'against' + *strepere* 'make a noise') + -OUS.]

ob·struct /əb'strəkt; äb-/ ▶ **v.** [trans.] block (an opening, path, road, etc.); be or get in the way of. ■ prevent or hinder (movement or someone or something in motion): *they had to obstruct the natural flow of the water.* ■ block (someone's view). ■ fig. put difficulties in the way of: *fears that the regime would obstruct the distribution of food.* ■ Law commit the offense of intentionally hindering (a legal process). ■ (in various sports) impede (a player on the opposing team) in a manner that constitutes an offense. — **ob·struc·tor n.** [16th C.: from L. *obstruct-* 'blocked up,' from the v. *obstruere*, from *ob-* 'against' + *struere* 'build, pile up.']

ob·struc·tion /əb'strəksHən; äb-/ ▶ **n.** the action of obstructing or the state of being obstructed. ■ a thing that impedes or prevents passage or progress; an obstacle or blockage: *the tractor hit an obstruction.* ■ (in various sports) the action of unlawfully obstructing a player on the opposing team. ■ Med. blockage of a bodily passageway, esp. the intestines. ■ Law deliberate hindrance of a legal process. [16th C.: from L. *obstructio(n-)*, from the v. *obstruere* (see OBSTRUCT).]

ob·struc·tion·ism /əb'strəksHəˌnizəm; äb-/ ▶ **n.** the practice of deliberately impeding or delaying the course of legal, legislative, or other procedures. — **ob·struc·tion·ist n. & adj.**

ob·struc·tive /əb'strəktiv; äb-/ ▶ **adj. 1** causing a blockage or obstruction. ■ of or relating to obstruction of a passage in the body, esp. the intestines or the bronchi. **2** causing or tending to cause deliberate difficulties and delays. — **ob·struc·tive·ly adv. ob·struc·tive·ness n.**

ob·stru·ent /'äbstrŏŏənt/ ▶ **n. 1** Phonet. a fricative or plosive speech sound. **2** Med. a medicine or substance that closes the natural passages or pores of the body. [17th C.: from L. *obstruent-* 'blocking up,' from the v. *obstruere*.]

ob·tain /əb'tān; äb-/ ▶ **v. 1** [trans.] get, acquire, or secure (something): *an opportunity to obtain advanced degrees.* **2** [intrans.] formal be prevalent, customary, or established: *the price of silver fell to that obtaining elsewhere.* — **ob·tain·a·bil·i·ty** /-nə'bilətē/ **n. ob·tain·a·ble adj. ob·tain·er n. ob·tain·ment n. ob·ten·tion** /-'tencHən/ **n.** [ME: from OFr. *obtenir*, from L. *obtinere* 'obtain, gain.']

ob·tect /əb'tekt/ (also **ob·tect·ed** /-'tektid/) ▶ **adj.** Entomol. (of an insect pupa or chrysalis) covered in a hard case with the legs and wings attached immovably against the body. [19th C.: from L. *obtectus*, past part. of *obtegere* 'cover over.']

ob·trude /əb'trŏŏd/ ▶ **v.** [intrans.] become noticeable in an unwelcome or intrusive way: *a sound from the hall obtruded into his thoughts.* ■ [trans.] impose or force (something) on someone in such a way: *I felt unable to obtrude my sorrow upon anyone.* — **ob·trud·er n. ob·tru·sion** /-'trŏŏzHən/ **n.** [16th C.: from L. *obtrudere*, from *ob-* 'toward' + *trudere* 'to push.']

ob·tru·sive /əb'trŏŏsiv; äb-/ ▶ **adj.** noticeable or prominent in an unwelcome or intrusive way. — **ob·tru·sive·ly adv. ob·tru·sive·ness n.** [17th C.: from L. *obtrus-* 'thrust forward,' from the v. *obtrudere* (see OBTRUDE).]

ob·tund /äb'tənd/ ▶ **v.** [trans.] dated, esp. Med. dull the sensitivity of; blunt; deaden. [ME: from L. *obtundere*, from *ob-* 'against' + *tundere* 'to beat.']

ob·tu·rate /'äbt(y)əˌrāt/ ▶ **v.** [trans.] formal or tech. block up; obstruct. — **ob·tu·ra·tion** /-'rāsHən/ **n.** [17th C.: from L. *obturat-* 'stopped up,' from the v. *obturare*.]

ob·tu·ra·tor /'äbt(y)əˌrātər/ ▶ **n.** Anat. either of two muscles covering the outer front part of the pelvis on each side and involved in movements of the thigh and hip. ■ [as adj.] relating to this muscle or to the obturator foramen.

ob·tu·ra·tor fo·ra·men ▶ **n.** Anat. a large opening in the hipbone between the pubis and the ischium.

ob·tuse /əb't(y)ŏŏs; äb-/ ▶ **adj. 1** annoyingly insensitive or slow to understand. ■ difficult to understand. **2** (of an angle) more than 90° and less than 180°. See illustration at ANGLE¹. ■ not sharp-pointed or sharp-edged; blunt. — **ob·tuse·ly adv. ob·tuse·ness n. ob·tu·si·ty** /-sitē/ **n.** [ME: from L. *obtusus*, past part. of *obtundere* (see OBTUND).]

Ob-U·gric /'äb '(y)ŏŏgrik; 'ōb/ (also **Ob-U·gri·an** /'(y)ŏŏgrēən/) ▶ **adj.** of or denoting a branch of the Finno-Ugric language family containing two languages of western Siberia related to Hungarian. ▶ **n.** this group of languages. [1930s: from *Ob*, a Siberian river.]

ob·verse ▶ **n.** /'äbˌvərs/ [usu. in sing.] **1** the side of a coin or medal bearing the head or principal design. ■ the design or inscription on this side. **2** the opposite or counterpart of a fact or truth: *true solitude is the obverse of true society.* ▶ **adj.** /əb'vərs; äb-/ [attrib.] **1** of or denoting the obverse of a coin or medal. **2** corresponding to something else as its opposite or counterpart. **3** Biol. narrower at the base or point of attachment than at the apex or top. — **ob·verse·ly** /əb'vərslē; äb-/ **adv.** [17th C.: from L. *obversus*, past part. of *obvertere*.]

ob·vert /əb'vərt; äb-/ ▶ **v.** [trans.] Logic alter (a proposition) so as to infer another proposition with a contradictory predicate, e.g., *"no men are immortal"* to *"all men are mortal."* — **ob·ver·sion** /əb'vərzHən; äb-/ **n.** [17th C.: from L. *obvertere*, from *ob-* 'toward' + *vertere* 'to turn.']

ob·vi·ate /'äbvēˌāt/ ▶ **v.** [trans.] remove (a need or difficulty): *the Venetian blinds obviated the need for curtains.* ■ avoid; prevent: *a parachute can obviate disaster.* — **ob·vi·a·tion** /äbvē'āsHən/ **n. ob·vi·a·tor n.** [16th C.: from late L. *obviat-* 'prevented,' from the v. *obviare*, based on L. *via* 'way.']

ob·vi·ous /'äbvēəs/ ▶ **adj.** easily perceived or understood; clear, self-evident, or apparent. ■ derog. predictable and lacking in subtlety. — **ob·vi·ous·ly adv. ob·vi·ous·ness n.** [16th C.: from L. *obvius* (from the phr. *ob viam* 'in the way') + -OUS.]

ob·vo·lute /'äbvəˌlŏŏt/ ▶ **adj.** Bot. (of a leaf) having a margin that alternately overlaps and is overlapped by that of an opposing leaf. — **ob·vo·lu·tion n.** /ˌäbvə'lŏŏsHən/ [18th C.: from L. *obvolutus*, past part. of *obvolvere* 'wrap around.']

oc. (also **Oc.**) ▶ **abbr.** ocean.

o.c. ▶ **abbr.** ■ Archit. on center. ■ in the work cited.

oc- ▶ **prefix** var. of OB- assimilated before *c* (as in *occasion, occlude*).

o/c ▶ **abbr.** overcharge.

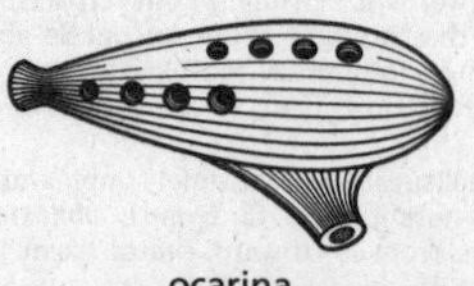

ocarina

oc·a·ri·na /ˌäkə'rēnə/ ▶ **n.** a small egg-shaped wind instrument with a mouthpiece and holes for the fingers. Also called SWEET POTATO. [19th C.: from Ital., from *oca* 'goose' (from its shape).]

O'Ca·sey /ō'kāsē/, Sean (1880–1964), Irish playwright. His plays include *The Shadow of a Gunman* (1923) and *Juno and the Paycock* (1924).

occ. ▶ **abbr.** ■ occasional; occasionally. ■ occident; occidental. ■ occupation.

Oc·cam, William of see WILLIAM OF OCCAM.

Oc·cam's ra·zor /'äkəmz/ (also **Ock·ham's ra·zor**) the principle (attributed to William of Occam) that in explaining a thing no more assumptions should be made than are necessary.

occas. ▶ **abbr.** ■ occasional; occasionally.

oc·ca·sion /ə'kāzHən/ ▶ **n. 1** a particular time or instance of an event. ■ a special or noteworthy event, ceremony, or celebration. ■ a suitable or opportune time for doing something. **2** formal reason; cause: [with infin.] *it's the first time that I've had occasion to complain.* ▶ **v.** [trans.] formal cause (something): *something vital must have occasioned this visit.*

– PHRASES **on occasion** (or esp. Brit. **occasions**) occasionally; from time to time. **rise to the occasion** perform very well in response to a special situation or event. **take occasion** archaic make use of an opportunity to do something. [ME: from L. *occasio(n-)* 'juncture, reason,' from *occidere* 'go down, set,' from *ob-* 'toward' + *cadere* 'to fall.']

oc·ca·sion·al /ə'kāzHənl/ ▶ **adj.** occurring, appearing, or done infrequently and irregularly. ■ (of furniture) made or adapted for use on a particular occasion or for irregular use. ■ (of a literary composition, speech, religious service, etc.) produced on or intended for a special occasion: *he wrote occasional verse for patrons.* ■ dated employed for a particular occasion or on an irregular basis: *occasional freelancer seeks full-time position.* — **oc·ca·sion·al·ly** /-zHənl-ē/ **adv.**

oc·ca·sion·al·ism /ə'kāzHənlˌizəm/ ▶ **n.** Philos. the doctrine ascribing the connection between mental and bodily events to the continuing intervention of God.

Oc·ci·dent /'äksidənt; -ˌdent/ ▶ **n.** (**the Occident**) formal literary the countries of the West, esp. Europe and the Americas (contrasted with ORIENT). [ME: via OFr. from L. *occident-* 'setting' (of the sun), from *occidere*.]

oc·ci·den·tal /ˌäksə'dentl/ ▶ **adj.** of or relating to the countries of the Occident. ▶ **n.** (**Occidental**) a native or inhabitant of the Occident. — **oc·ci·den·tal·ism n. oc·ci·den·tal·ize v.**

oc·cip·i·tal bone /äk'sipitl/ ▶ **n.** Anat. the bone that forms the back and base of the skull, and through which the spinal cord passes.

oc·cip·i·tal lobe ▶ **n.** Anat. the rearmost lobe in each cerebral hemisphere of the brain.

occipito- ▶ **comb. form** relating to the occipital lobe or the occipital bone: *occipitotemporal.* [from med. L. *occipitalis*, from L. *caput, capit-* 'head.']

oc·ci·put /'äksəpət/ ▶ **n.** (pl. **oc·ci·puts** or **oc·cip·i·ta** /äk'sipitə/) Anat. the back of the head or skull. — **oc·cip·i·tal** /äk'sipitl/ **adj.** [ME: from L. *occiput*, from *ob-* 'against' + *caput* 'head.']

Oc·ci·tan /'äksiˌtan/ ▶ **n.** the medieval or modern language of Languedoc, including literary Provençal of the 12th–14th centuries. ▶ **adj.** of or relating to this language. — **Oc·ci·ta·ni·an** /ˌäksə'tānēən/ **n. & adj.** [Fr. (see also LANGUE D'OC).]

oc·clude /ə'klŏŏd/ ▶ **v.** formal or tech. **1** [trans.] stop, close up, or obstruct (an opening, orifice, or passage). ■ shut (something) in: *they occluded the waterfront with buildings.* ■ cover (an eye) to prevent its use: *it is placed at eye level with one eye occluded.* ■ Chem. (of a solid) absorb and retain (a gas or impurity). **2** [intrans.] (of a tooth) close on or come into contact with another tooth in the opposite jaw. [16th C.: from L. *occludere* 'shut up.']

oc•clud•ed front ▶ n. Meteorol. a composite front produced by occlusion.

oc•clu•sal /ə'klo͞osəl/ ▶ adj. Dentistry of, relating to, or involved in the occlusion of teeth. ■ denoting a portion of a tooth that comes into contact with a tooth in the other jaw.

oc•clu•sion /ə'klo͞ozʜən/ ▶ n. 1 Med. the blockage or closing of a blood vessel or hollow organ. ■ Phonet. the momentary closure of the passage of breath during the articulation of a consonant. 2 Meteorol. a process in which the cold front of a rotating low pressure system overtakes the warm front, forcing the warm air upward above a wedge of cold air. ■ an occluded front. 3 Dentistry the position of the teeth when the jaws are closed. — **oc•clu•sive** adj.

oc•cult /ə'kəlt/ ▶ n. (**the occult**) supernatural, mystical, or magical beliefs, practices, or phenomena. ▶ adj. 1 of, involving, or relating to supernatural, mystical, or magical powers or phenomena. ■ beyond the range of ordinary knowledge or experience; mysterious. ■ communicated only to the initiated; esoteric. 2 Med. (of a disease or process) not accompanied by readily discernible signs or symptoms. ■ (of blood) abnormally present, e.g., in feces, but detectable only chemically or microscopically. ▶ v. [trans.] cut off from view by interposing something. ■ Astron. (of a celestial body) conceal (an apparently smaller body) from view by passing in front of it. — **oc•cul•ta•tion** /,äkəl'tāsʜən/ n. **oc•cult•ism** n. **oc•cult•ist** n. **oc•cult•ly** adv. **oc•cult•ness** n. [15th C. (v.): from L. *occultare* 'secrete,' frequentative of *occulere* 'conceal,' based on *celare* 'to hide'.]

oc•cult•ing light ▶ n. a light in a lighthouse or buoy that is cut off briefly at regular intervals.

oc•cu•pan•cy /'äkyəpənsē/ ▶ n. the action or fact of occupying a place. ■ the proportion of accommodations occupied or in use, typically in a hotel. ■ Law the action of taking possession of something having no owner, as constituting a title to it.

oc•cu•pant /'äkyəpənt/ ▶ n. a person who resides or is present in a house, vehicle, etc., at a given time. ■ the holder of a position or office: *the first occupant of the Oval Office.* ■ Law a person holding property, esp. land, in actual possession.

oc•cu•pa•tion /,äkyə'pāsʜən/ ▶ n. 1 a job or profession. ■ a way of spending time. 2 the action, state, or period of occupying or being occupied by military force. ■ the action of entering and taking control of a building: *the workers remained in occupation until October.* 3 the action or fact of living in or using a building or other place: *a property suitable for occupation by older people.* [ME: via OFr. from L. *occupatio(n-)*, from *occupare*.]

oc•cu•pa•tion•al /,äkyə'pāsʜənl/ ▶ adj. of or relating to a job or profession. — **oc•cu•pa•tion•al•ly** adv.

oc•cu•pa•tion•al haz•ard ▶ n. a risk accepted as a consequence of a particular occupation.

oc•cu•pa•tion•al ther•a•py ▶ n. therapy for those recuperating from illness that encourages rehabilitation by performing the activities of daily life. — **oc•cu•pa•tion•al ther•a•pist** n.

oc•cu•py /'äkyə,pī/ ▶ v. (**-pies, -pied**) [trans.] 1 reside or have one's place of business in (a building). ■ fill or take up (a space or time). ■ be situated in or at (a place or position in a system): *on the corporate ladder, they occupy the lowest rungs.* ■ hold (a position or job). 2 (often **be occupied with/in**) fill or preoccupy (the mind or thoughts). ■ keep (someone) busy and active. 3 take control of (a place, esp. a country) by military conquest or settlement. ■ enter, take control of, and stay in (a building) illegally and often forcibly, esp. as a form of protest. — **oc•cu•pi•er** /-,pīər/ n. [ME: from OFr. *occuper*, from L. *occupare* 'seize.']

oc•cur /ə'kər/ ▶ v. (**-curred, -cur•ring**) [no obj., with adverbial] happen; take place: *the accident occurred at about 3:30 p.m.* ■ exist in a place or under a particular set of conditions: *radon occurs in rocks such as granite.* ■ (**occur to**) (of a thought or idea) come into the mind of (someone): [with clause] *it occurred to him that he hadn't eaten.* [15th C.: from L. *occurrere* 'go to meet, present itself,' from *ob-* 'against' + *currere* 'to run.']

oc•cur•rence /ə'kərəns/ ▶ n. an incident or event. ■ the fact or frequency of something happening. ■ the fact of something existing or being found in a place or under a particular set of conditions.

oc•cur•rent /ə'kərənt/ ▶ adj. actually occurring or observable, not potential or hypothetical.

OCD ▶ abbr. obsessive-compulsive disorder.

o•cean /'ōsʜən/ ▶ n. a very large expanse of sea, in particular, each of the main areas into which the sea is divided geographically: *the Atlantic Ocean.* ■ (usu. **the ocean**) the sea: [as adj.] *the ocean floor.* ■ (**an ocean of/oceans of**) fig. a very large expanse or quantity. — **o•cean•ward** /-wərd/ (also **-wards**) adv. & adj. [ME: from OFr. *occean*, via L. from Gk. *ōkeanos* 'great stream encircling the earth's disk.']

o•cea•nar•i•um /,ōsʜə'ne(ə)rēəm/ ▶ n. (pl. **-nar•i•ums** or **-nar•i•a** /-'ne(ə)rēə/) a large seawater aquarium in which marine animals are kept.

o•cean bo•ni•to ▶ n. another term for SKIPJACK (sense 1).

o•cean•front /'ōsʜən,frənt/ ▶ n. the land that borders an ocean. — **o•cean•front** adj.

o•cean•go•ing /'ōsʜən,gō-iɴɢ/ (also **o•cean-go•ing**) ▶ adj. (of a ship) designed to cross oceans.

O•ce•an•i•a /,ōsʜē'anēə; -'änēə/ an area that encompasses the Pacific Ocean islands and adjacent seas. — **O•ce•an•i•an** adj. & n.

o•ce•an•ic /,ōsʜē'anik/ ▶ adj. 1 of or relating to the ocean. ■ of or inhabiting the part of the ocean beyond the edge of a continental shelf: *stocks of oceanic fish.* ■ (of a climate) governed by the proximity of the ocean. ■ fig. of enormous size or extent; huge; vast. 2 (**Oceanic**) of or relating to Oceania.

o•ce•an•ic crust ▶ n. Geol. the relatively thin part of the earth's crust that underlies the ocean basins.

O•ce•a•nid /ō'sēənid/ ▶ n. (pl. **O•ce•a•nids** or **O•ce•an•i•des** /,ōsē'anidēz/) Gk. Mythol. a sea nymph; one of the daughters of Oceanus.

O•cean Is•land another name for BANABA.

o•cean lin•er ▶ n. see LINER[1] (sense 1).

o•cea•nog•ra•phy /,ōsʜə'nägrəfē/ ▶ n. the branch of science that deals with the physical and biological properties and phenomena of the sea. — **o•cea•nog•ra•pher** n. **o•cea•no•graph•ic** /-nə'grafik/ adj. **o•cea•no•graph•i•cal** /-nə'grafəkəl/ adj.

o•cea•nol•o•gy /,ōsʜə'näləjē/ ▶ n. another term for OCEANOGRAPHY. ■ the branch of technology and economics dealing with human use of the sea. — **o•cea•no•log•i•cal** /-nə'läjikəl/ adj. **o•cea•nol•o•gist** n.

Ocean•side /'ōsʜən,sīd/ a city in southwestern California; pop. 128,398.

O•ce•a•nus /ō'sēənəs/ Gk. Mythol. the son of Uranus and Gaia, the personification of the great river believed to encircle the whole world.

oc•el•lat•ed /'äsə,lātid/ ▶ adj. (of an animal, or its plumage or body surface) having one or more ocelli, or eyelike markings.

o•cel•lus /ō'seləs/ ▶ n. (pl. **o•cel•li** /ō'selī; ō'selē/) Zool. 1 another term for SIMPLE EYE. 2 another term for EYESPOT (senses 1 and 2). — **o•cel•lar** /ō'selər/ adj. [19th C.: from L., dimin. of *oculus* 'eye.']

oc•e•lot /'äsə,lät; 'ōsə-/ ▶ n. a medium-sized wild cat (*Felis pardalis*, family Felidae) that has a tawny yellow coat marked with black blotches and spots. It ranges from southern Texas through South America. [18th C.: from Fr., from Nahuatl *tlatlocelotl*, lit. 'field tiger.']

o•cher /'ōkər/ (esp. Brit. also **o•chre**) ▶ n. an earthy pigment containing ferric oxide, typically with clay, varying from light yellow to brown or red. ■ a pale brownish yellow color. — **o•cher•ish** /'ōk(ə)risʜ/ adj. **o•cher•ous** /'ōk(ə)rəs/ adj. **o•cher•y** adj. **o•cher•oid** /'ōk(ə)roid/ adj. [ME: from OFr. *ocre*, via L. from Gk. *ōkhra* 'yellow ocher.']

och•loc•ra•cy /äk'läkrəsē/ ▶ n. government by a mob; mob rule. — **och•lo•crat** /'äklə,krat/ n. **och•lo•crat•ic** /,äklə'kratik/ adj. [16th C.: via Fr. from Gk. *okhlokratia*, from *okhlos* 'mob' + *-kratia* 'power.']

o•chone /ä'ᴋʜōn/ ▶ exclam. Irish & Scot., literary used to express regret or sorrow. [from Scot. Gael. *ochòin*, Irish *ochón*.]

o•chre ▶ n. esp. Brit. var. of OCHER.

Ochs /öks/, Adolph Simon (1858–1935), US publisher. He acquired *The New York Times* in 1896.

-ock ▶ suffix forming nouns originally with diminutive sense: *haddock* | *pollock.* ■ also occasionally forming words from other sources: *bannock* | *hassock.* [OE *-uc, -oc.*]

ock•er /'äkər/ informal ▶ n. Austral. a boorish or aggressive person, esp. an Australian man. [alt. of *Oscar*.]

Ock•ham's ra•zor ▶ n. var. of OCCAM'S RAZOR.

Ock•ham, William of see WILLIAM OF OCCAM.

o'clock /ə'kläk/ ▶ adv. used to specify the hour in telling time: *the gates will open at eight o'clock.* ■ used following a numeral to indicate direction or bearing with reference to an imaginary clock face, 12 o'clock being thought of as directly in front or overhead, or at the top of a circular target, etc.: *"I think we've got some action at 11 o'clock," he said, gesturing toward the eastern plains.*

O'Con•nell /ō'känl/, Daniel (1775–1847), Irish nationalist leader and social reformer; known as **the Liberator**. His election to Parliament in 1828 forced the British government to grant emancipation to Catholics in order to enable him to take his seat in the House of Commons.

O'Con•nor[1] /ō'känər/, Flannery (1925–64), US writer; full name *Mary Flannery O'Connor*. Noted for dark humor and grotesque characters, her short stories are in collections such as *A Good Man Is Hard to Find, and Other Stories* (1955). Her novels include *The Violent Bear It Away* (1960).

O'Connor[2], Sandra Day (1930–), US Supreme Court associate justice 1981–2006.

o•co•til•lo /,ōkə'tē(y)ō/ ▶ n. (pl. **-los**) a spiny, scarlet-flowered desert shrub (*Fouquieria splendens*, family Fouquieriaceae) of the southwestern US and Mexico, sometimes planted as a hedge. [19th C.: via Amer. Sp. (dimin. form) from Nahuatl *ocotl* 'torch.']

OCR ▶ abbr. ■ optical character reader. ■ optical character recognition.

Ocra•coke Is•land /'ōkrə,kōk/ a barrier island in eastern North Carolina, part of the Outer Banks.

oc•re•a /'äkrēə; 'ōkrēə/ (also **och•re•a**) ▶ n. (pl. **oc•re•ae** /'äkrē-ē; 'ōkrē-ē/ or **oc•re•as**) Bot. a sheath around a stem formed by the cohesion of two or more stipules, characteristic of the dock family. [19th C.: from L., lit. 'protective legging.']

OCS ▶ abbr. ■ Mil. officer candidate school. ■ Old Church Slavonic. ■ outer continental shelf.

Oct. ▶ abbr. October.

oct. ▶ abbr. octavo.

oct- ▶ comb. form var. of OCTA- and OCTO- assimilated before a vowel (as in *octennial*).

octa- (also **oct-** before a vowel) ▶ comb. form eight; having eight: *octahedron.* [from Gk. *oktō* 'eight.']

oc·tad /ˈäktad/ ▶ **n.** tech. a group or set of eight. [19th C.: via late L. from Gk. *oktas, oktad-*, from *oktō* 'eight.']

oc·ta·gon /ˈäktə,gän; -gən/ ▶ **n.** a plane figure with eight straight sides and eight angles. ■ an object or building with a plan or cross section of this shape. — **oc·tag·o·nal** /äkˈtagənl/ **adj.** **oc·tag·o·nal·ly** /äkˈtagən-lē/ **adv.** [16th C.: via L. from Gk. *octagōnos* 'eight-angled.']

oc·ta·he·drite /,äktəˈhēdrīt/ ▶ **n. 1** another term for ANATASE. **2** an iron meteorite containing plates of kamacite and taenite in an octahedral orientation. [19th C.: from OCTAHEDRON + -ITE[1].]

oc·ta·he·dron /,äktəˈhēdrən/ ▶ **n.** (pl. **-drons** or **-dra** /-drə/) a three-dimensional shape having eight plane faces, esp. a regular solid figure with eight equal triangular faces. ■ a body, esp. a crystal, in the form of a regular octahedron. — **oc·ta·he·dral** /-drəl/ **adj.** [16th C.: from Gk. *oktaedron*, neut. (used as a n.) of *oktaedros* 'eight-faced.']

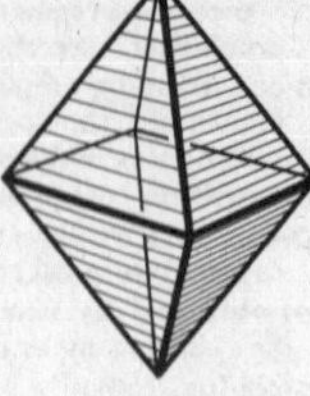
octahedron

oc·tal /ˈäktl/ ▶ **adj.** relating to or using a system of numerical notation that has 8 rather than 10 as a base. ▶ **n.** the octal system; octal notation.

oc·tam·er·ous /äkˈtamərəs/ ▶ **adj.** Bot. Zool. having parts arranged in groups of eight. ■ consisting of eight joints or parts.

oc·tam·e·ter /äkˈtamitər/ ▶ **n.** Pros. a line of verse consisting of eight metrical feet.

oc·tane /ˈäktān/ ▶ **n.** Chem. a colorless flammable hydrocarbon of the alkane series, C_8H_{18}, obtained in petroleum refining. [19th C.: from OCTO- 'eight' (denoting eight carbon atoms) + -ANE[2].]

oc·tane num·ber (also **octane rating**) ▶ **n.** a figure indicating the antiknock properties of a fuel, based on a comparison with a mixture of isooctane and heptane.

Oc·tans /ˈäktanz/ Astron. a faint southern constellation (the Octant), containing the south celestial pole. [L.]

oc·tant /ˈäktənt/ ▶ **n.** an arc of a circle equal to one eighth of its circumference, or the area enclosed by such an arc with two radii of the circle. ■ each of eight parts into which a space or solid body is divided by three planes that intersect (esp. at right angles) at a single point. ■ an obsolete instrument in the form of a graduated eighth of a circle, used in astronomy and navigation. [17th C.: from L. *octans, octant-* 'half-quadrant,' from *octo* 'eight.']

oc·tave /ˈäktəv; ˈäk,tāv/ ▶ **n. 1** Music a series of eight notes occupying the interval between two notes, one having twice or half the frequency of vibration of the other. ■ the interval between these two notes. ■ each of the two notes at the extremes of this interval. ■ these two notes sounding together. **2** a poem or stanza of eight lines; an octet. [ME: via OFr. from L. *octava dies* 'eighth day.']

Oc·ta·vi·an /äkˈtāvēən/ see AUGUSTUS.

oc·ta·vo /äkˈtävō/ (abbr.: **8vo**) ▶ **n.** (pl. **-vos**) a size of book page that results from the folding of each printed sheet into 8 leaves (16 pages). ■ a book of this size. [16th C.: from L. *in octavo* 'in an eighth,' from *octavus* 'eighth.']

oc·ten·ni·al /äkˈtenēəl/ ▶ **adj.** rare recurring every eight years. ■ lasting for or relating to a period of eight years. [17th C.: from late L. *octennium* 'period of eight years' + -AL.]

oc·tet /äkˈtet/ (also **oc·tette**) ▶ **n.** a group of eight people or things, in particular: ■ a group of eight musicians. ■ a musical composition for eight voices or instruments. ■ the first eight lines of a sonnet. [19th C.: from Ital. *ottetto* or Ger. *Oktett*.]

octo- (also **oct-** before a vowel) ▶ **comb. form** eight; having eight: *octosyllabic*. [from L. *octo* or Gk. *oktō* 'eight.']

Oc·to·ber /äkˈtōbər/ ▶ **n.** the tenth month of the year, in the northern hemisphere usually considered the second month of autumn. [OE, from L., from *octo* 'eight.']

Oc·to·ber Rev·o·lu·tion ▶ **n.** see RUSSIAN REVOLUTION.

Oc·to·ber War Arab name for YOM KIPPUR WAR.

oc·to·dec·i·mo /,äktōˈdesə,mō/ ▶ **n.** (pl. **-mos**) a size of book page that results from the folding of each printed sheet into 18 leaves (36 pages). ■ a book of this size. [19th C.: from L. *in octodecimo* 'in an eighteenth,' from *octodecimus* 'eighteenth.']

oc·to·ge·nar·i·an /,äktəjəˈne(ə)rēən/ ▶ **n.** a person who is from 80 to 89 years old. [19th C.: from L. *octogenarius* (based on *octoginta* 'eighty') + -AN.]

oc·to·nar·y /ˈäktə,nerē/ ▶ **adj.** rare relating to or based on the number eight.

Oc·top·o·da /äkˈtäpədə/ Zool. an order of cephalopods that comprises the octopuses. — **oc·to·pod** /ˈäktə,päd/ **n.** [mod. L. (pl.), from Gk. *oktōpous, oktōpod-*, from *oktō* 'eight' + *pous, pod-* 'foot.']

oc·to·pus /ˈäktəpəs/ ▶ **n.** (pl. **-pus·es**) **1** a cephalopod (*Octopus* and other genera, order Octopoda) with eight sucker-bearing arms, a soft saclike body, strong beaklike jaws, and no internal shell. **2** fig. an organization or system perceived to have far-reaching and typically harmful effects. — **oc·to·poid** **adj.** /-,poid/ [18th C.: from Gk. *oktōpous* (see also OCTOPODA).]

oc·to·roon /,äktəˈrōōn/ ▶ **n.** hist. a person whose parents are a quadroon and a white person and who is therefore one-eighth black by descent. [19th C.: from OCTO- on the pattern of *quadroon*.]

oc·to·syl·la·bic /,äktəsəˈlabik; ,äktō-/ ▶ **adj.** having or written in lines that have eight syllables. ▶ **n.** a line of verse that has eight syllables.

oc·to·syl·la·ble /ˈäktə,siləbəl/ ▶ **n.** a word or line of verse with eight syllables. ▶ **adj.** having eight syllables.

oc·to·thorp /ˈäktə,THôrp/ (also **oc·to·thorpe**) ▶ **n.** another term for the pound sign (#). [1970s: prob. from OCTO- + the surname *Thorpe*.]

oc·troi /ˈäktroi; äkˈtrwä/ ▶ **n.** a tax levied in some countries on various goods entering a town or city. [16th C.: from Fr. *octroyer* 'to grant,' based on med. L. *auctorizare* (see AUTHORIZE).]

oc·tu·ple /äkˈtəpəl; -ˈt(y)ōōpəl/ ▶ **adj.** [attrib.] consisting of eight parts or things. ■ eight times as many or as much. ▶ **v.** make or become eight times as numerous or as large. [17th C.: from Fr. *octuple* or L. *octuplus* (both adjectives), from *octo* 'eight' + *-plus* (as in *duplus* 'double').]

oc·tup·let /äkˈtəplit; -ˈt(y)ōō-/ ▶ **n.** (usu. in pl. **octuplets**) each of eight children born at one birth.

oc·tyl /ˈäktl/ ▶ **n.** [as adj.] Chem. of or denoting an alkyl radical $-C_8H_{17}$, derived from octane.

oc·u·lar /ˈäkyələr/ ▶ **adj.** [attrib.] Med. of or connected with the eyes or vision: *ocular trauma*. ▶ **n.** another term for EYEPIECE. — **oc·u·lar·ly** **adv.** [16th C.: from late L. *ocularis*, from L. *oculus* 'eye.']

oc·u·lar·ist /ˈäkyələrist/ ▶ **n.** a person who makes artificial eyes.

oc·u·list /ˈäkyəlist/ ▶ **n.** dated a person who specializes in the medical treatment of diseases or defects of the eye; an ophthalmologist. ■ an optometrist. [16th C.: from Fr. *oculiste*, from L. *oculus* 'eye.']

oculo- ▶ **comb. form** relating to the eye: *oculomotor*. [from L. *oculus* 'eye.']

oc·u·lo·mo·tor /,äkyəlōˈmōtər/ ▶ **adj.** of or relating to the motion of the eye.

oc·u·lo·mo·tor nerve ▶ **n.** Anat. each of the third pair of cranial nerves, supplying most of the muscles around and within the eyeballs.

oc·u·lus /ˈäkyələs/ ▶ **n.** (pl. **-li** /-,lī; -,lē/) Archit. a round or eyelike opening or design, in particular: ■ a circular window. ■ the central boss of a volute. ■ an opening at the apex of a dome. [19th C.: from L., lit. 'eye.']

OD informal ▶ **v.** (**OD's, OD'd, OD'ing**) [intrans.] take an overdose of a drug. ▶ **n.** an overdose of a narcotic drug.

Od /äd/ ▶ **n.** an archaic euphemism for God, used in exclamations: *Od damn it all!*

od /äd/ ▶ **n.** hist. a hypothetical power once thought to pervade nature and account for various phenomena, such as magnetism. [19th C.: arbitrary term coined in Ger.]

o.d. ▶ **abbr.** outer diameter.

o·da·lisque /ˈōdl,isk/ (also **o·da·lisk**) ▶ **n.** hist. a female slave or concubine in a harem. [17th C.: from Fr., from Turk. *odalık*, from *oda* 'chamber' + *lık* 'function.']

odd /äd/ ▶ **adj. 1** different from what is usual or expected; strange: *the neighbors thought him very odd*. **2** (of whole numbers such as 3 and 5) having one left over as a remainder when divided by two. ■ (of things numbered consecutively) represented or indicated by such a number. ■ [postpositive] [in comb.] in the region of or somewhat more than a particular number or quantity: *fifty-odd years*. **3** [attrib.] happening or occurring infrequently and irregularly; occasional. ■ spare; unoccupied. **4** separated from a usual pair or set and therefore out of place or mismatched. — **odd·ness** **n.** [ME (sense 2): from ON *odda-*, from *oddi* 'angle.']

odd·ball /ˈäd,bôl/ informal ▶ **n.** a strange person. ▶ **adj.** strange; bizarre: *oddball training methods*.

Odd Fel·low (also **Odd·fel·low**) ▶ **n.** a member of the Independent Order of Odd Fellows. — **Odd·fel·low·ship** **n.**

odd·i·ty /ˈäditē/ ▶ **n.** (pl. **-ties**) a strange or peculiar person, thing, or trait: *she was regarded as a bit of an oddity*. ■ the quality of being strange or peculiar.

odd job ▶ **n.** (usu. **odd jobs**) an isolated piece of work, esp. a routine or manual one. — **odd-job·ber** **n.** **odd-job·bing** **n.**

odd lot ▶ **n.** an incomplete set or random mixture of things. ■ Stock Ex. a transaction involving less than the usual round number of shares.

odd man out /ˈäd ,man ˈout/ ▶ **n.** a person differing from all other members of a group in some way.

odd·ment /ˈädmənt/ ▶ **n.** (usu. **oddments**) a remnant or part of something, typically left over from a larger piece or set: *a quilt made from oddments of silk*.

odd-pin·nate ▶ **adj.** Bot. (of a leaf) pinnate with an odd terminal leaflet.

odds /ädz/ ▶ **plural n.** the ratio between the amounts staked by the parties to a bet, based on the expected probability either way: *odds of 8-1*. ■ (usu. **the odds**) the chances or likelihood of something happening or being the case. ■ (usu. **the odds**) superiority in strength, power, or resources; advantage.

– PHRASES **at odds** in conflict or at variance. **by all odds** certainly; by far. **lay** (or **give**) **odds** offer a bet with odds favorable to the other bettor. ■ fig. be very sure about something. **take odds** offer a bet with odds unfavorable to the other bettor. [16th C.: appar. the pl. of the obs. n. *odd* 'odd number or odd person.']

odds and ends ▶ **plural n.** miscellaneous articles or remnants.

odds·mak·er /ˈädz,mākər/ ▶ **n.** a person who calculates or predicts the outcome of a contest, such as a horse race or an election, and sets betting odds.

odds-on ▶ **adj.** (esp. of a horse) rated as most likely to win: *the odds-on favorite*.

odd-toed un·gu·late ▶ **n.** a hoofed mammal of an order (Perissodactyla) that includes horses, rhinoceroses, and tapirs. Mammals of this group have either one or three toes on each foot. Compare with **EVEN-TOED UNGULATE.**

ode /ōd/ ▶ **n.** a lyric poem in the form of an address to a particular subject, often elevated in style or manner and written in varied or irregular meter. ■ hist. a poem meant to be sung. — **od·ic** /'ōdik/ **adj.** [16th C.: from Fr., from late L. *oda*, from Gk. *ōidē*, Attic form of *aoidē* 'song,' from *aeidein* 'sing.']

-ode[1] ▶ **comb. form** of the nature of a specified thing: *geode.* [from Gk. adjectival ending *-ōdēs*.]

-ode[2] ▶ **comb. form** in names of electrodes, or devices having them: *diode.* [from Gk. *hodos* 'way.']

O·der /'ōdər/ a river of central Europe that rises in the east of the Czech Republic and flows north to the Baltic Sea. Czech and Polish name **ODRA.**

O·des·sa /ō'desə/ a city in southern Ukraine; pop. 1,106,000. Ukrainian name **ODESA.**

O·dets /ō'dets/, Clifford (1906–63), US playwright. He wrote *Waiting for Lefty* (1935).

o·de·um /'ōdēəm/ ▶ **n.** (pl. **o·de·ums** or **o·de·a** /'ōdēə/) (esp. in ancient Greece or Rome) a building used for musical performances. [from Fr. *odéum* or L. *odeum*, from Gk. *ōideion* (see **ODE**).]

o·dif·er·ous /ō'difərəs/ ▶ **adj.** var. of **ODORIFEROUS.**

O·din /'ōdin/ (also **Wo·den** or **Wo·tan**) Scand. Mythol. the supreme god and creator, god of victory and the dead. Wednesday is named after him.

o·di·ous /'ōdēəs/ ▶ **adj.** extremely unpleasant; repulsive. — **o·di·ous·ly adv. o·di·ous·ness n.** [ME: from OFr. *odieus*, from L. *odiosus*, from *odium* 'hatred.']

o·di·um /'ōdēəm/ ▶ **n.** general or widespread hatred or disgust directed toward someone. ■ disgrace over something hated or shameful; opprobrium. [17th C.: from L., 'hatred.']

o·dom·e·ter /ō'dämitər/ ▶ **n.** an instrument for measuring the distance traveled by a vehicle. [18th C.: from Fr. *odomètre*, from Gk. *hodos* 'way' + **-METER.**]

O·do·na·ta /,ōdn'ätə; ō'dänə-/ Entomol. an order of predatory insects that comprises the dragonflies and damselflies. ■ [as pl. n.] (**odonata**) insects of this order; dragonflies and damselflies. — **o·do·nate** /'ōdn-it; -,āt/ **n. & adj.** [mod. L. (pl.), from Gk. *odōn* (var. of *odous*) 'tooth.']

odonto- ▶ **comb. form** relating to a tooth or teeth: *odontology.* [from Gk. *odous, odont-* 'tooth.']

o·don·to·blast /ō'däntə,blast/ ▶ **n.** Anat. a cell in the pulp of a tooth that produces dentin.

O·don·to·ce·ti /ō,däntə'sētē/ Zool. the taxonomic division (suborder Odontoceti, order Cetacea) that comprises the toothed whales. — **o·don·to·cete** /ō'dän(t)ə,sēt/ **n. & adj.** [mod. L. (pl.), from Gk. *odous, odont-* 'tooth' + *ceti* 'of a whale.']

o·don·toid /ō'däntoid/ (also **odontoid process**) ▶ **n.** Anat. a toothlike projection from the second cervical vertebra on which the first vertebra pivots. [19th C.: from Gk. *odontoeidēs*, from *odous, odont-* 'tooth' + *eidos* 'form.']

o·don·tol·o·gy /,ōdän'täləjē/ ▶ **n.** the scientific study of the structure and diseases of teeth. — **o·don·to·log·i·cal** /ō,däntl'äjəkəl/ **adj. o·don·tol·o·gist n.**

o·don·to·phore /ō'däntə,fôr/ ▶ **n.** Zool. a projection in the mouth of mollusks supporting the radula. — **o·don·toph·o·ral** /,ōdän'täfərəl/ **adj.**

o·dor /'ōdər/ (Brit. **o·dour**) ▶ **n.** a strong smell, esp. an unpleasant or distinctive one. ■ fig. a lingering quality, impression, or feeling attaching to something. ■ [with adj.] fig. the state of being held in a specified regard: *bad odor between Britain and France.*

– PHRASES **be in good** (or **bad**) **odor with someone** be in (or out of) favor with someone. — **o·dor·less adj.** [ME: from Anglo-Norman Fr., from L. *odor* 'smell, scent.']

o·dor·ant /'ōdərənt/ ▶ **n.** a substance giving off a smell, esp. one used to give a particular scent or odor to a product.

o·dor·if·er·ous /,ōdə'rifərəs/ ▶ **adj.** having or giving off a smell, esp. an unpleasant or distinctive one. — **o·dor·if·er·ous·ly adv.**

o·dor·ize /'ōdə,rīz/ ▶ **v.** [trans.] give an odor or scent to. — **o·dor·iz·er n.**

o·dor·ous /'ōdərəs/ ▶ **adj.** having or giving off a smell.

o·dour ▶ **n.** British spelling of **ODOR.**

O·dra /'ôdrə/ Polish name for **ODER.**

O·dys·se·us /ō'disēəs; ō'disyōōs/ Gk. Mythol. the king of Ithaca and central figure of the *Odyssey*. Roman name **ULYSSES.**

Od·ys·sey /'ädəsē/ a Greek epic poem traditionally ascribed to Homer, describing the travels of Odysseus. — **Od·ys·se·an** /ädə'sēən/ **adj.**

od·ys·sey /'ädəsē/ ▶ **n.** (pl. **-seys**) a long and eventful journey. — **od·ys·se·an adj.** [19th C.: via L. from Gk. *Odusseia* (see **ODYSSEY**).]

OE ▶ **abbr.** Old English.

Oe ▶ **abbr.** oersted(s).

Oe·a /'ēə/ ancient name for **TRIPOLI** (sense 1).

OECD ▶ **abbr.** Organization for Economic Cooperation and Development.

OED ▶ **abbr.** Oxford English Dictionary.

oe·de·ma ▶ **n.** variant British spelling of **EDEMA.**

Oed·i·pus /'edəpəs; 'ēdə-/ Gk. Mythol. the son of Jocasta and of Laius, king of Thebes. He unwittingly killed his father and married his mother.

Oed·i·pus com·plex ▶ **n.** Psychoanal. (in Freudian theory) the complex of emotions aroused in a young child by an unconscious sexual desire for the parent of the opposite sex and a wish to exclude the parent of the same sex. (The term was originally applied to boys, the equivalent in girls being the **Electra complex.**) — **Oed·i·pal** /-pəl/ **adj.** [20th C.: by association with **OEDIPUS.**]

oeil-de-boeuf /'oi də 'bœf/ ▶ **n.** (pl. **oeils-de-boeuf** pronunc. same) Archit. a small round window. [18th C.: Fr., lit. 'ox-eye.']

OEM ▶ **abbr.** original equipment manufacturer (an organization that makes devices from component parts bought from other organizations).

oe·nol·o·gy ▶ **n.** var. of **ENOLOGY.**

Oe·no·ne /ē'nōnē/ Gk. Mythol. a nymph of Mount Ida and lover of Paris, who deserted her for Helen.

oe·no·phile /'ēnə,fīl/ ▶ **n.** a connoisseur of wines. — **oe·noph·i·list** /ē'näfəlist/ **n.** [20th C.: from Gk. *oinos* 'wine' + **-PHILE.**]

OEO ▶ **abbr.** Office of Economic Opportunity.

o'er /ôr/ ▶ **adv. & prep.** archaic or poetic/literary contraction for **OVER.**

oer·sted /'ər,sted/ (abbr.: **Oe**) ▶ **n.** Physics a unit of magnetic field strength equivalent to 79.58 amperes per meter. [19th C.: named after H. C. *Oersted* (1777–1851).]

oe·soph·a·gus, etc. ▶ **n.** British spelling of **ESOPHAGUS,** etc.

oes·tra·di·ol ▶ **n.** British spelling of **ESTRADIOL.**

oes·tri·ol ▶ **n.** British spelling of **ESTRIOL.**

oes·tro·gen ▶ **n.** British spelling of **ESTROGEN.**

oes·trone ▶ **n.** British spelling of **ESTRONE.**

oes·trus ▶ **n.** esp. Brit. var. of **ESTRUS.**

oeu·vre /'œvrə/ ▶ **n.** the works of a painter, composer, or author regarded collectively: *the complete oeuvre of Mozart.* ■ a work of art, music, or literature. [19th C.: Fr., lit. 'work.']

OF ▶ **abbr.** Old French.

of /əv; äv/ ▶ **prep. 1** expressing the relationship between a part and a whole: *the sleeve of his coat.* **2** expressing the relationship between a scale or measure and a value: *an increase of 5 percent.* ■ expressing an age: *a boy of 15.* **3** indicating an association between two entities, typically one of belonging: *the son of a friend* | [with a possessive] *a former colleague of John's.* ■ expressing the relationship between an author, artist, or composer and their works collectively: *the plays of Shakespeare.* **4** expressing the relationship between a direction and a point of reference: *north of Chicago.* **5** expressing the relationship between a general category and the thing being specified which belongs to such a category: *the city of Prague* | *the idea of a just society.* ■ governed by a noun expressing the fact that a category is vague: *this type of book.* **6** indicating the relationship between a verb and an indirect object: ■ with a verb expressing a mental state: *they must be persuaded of the severity of the problem.* ■ expressing a cause: *he died of cancer.* **7** indicating the material or substance constituting something: *walls of stone.* **8** expressing time in relation to the following hour: *it was a quarter of three.*

– PHRASES **be of** possess intrinsically; give rise to: *this work is of great interest and value.* **of all** denoting the least likely or expected example: *Jordan, of all people, committed a flagrant foul.*

of- ▶ **prefix** var. of **OB-** assimilated before *f* (as in *offend*).

o·fay /'ō,fā/ ▶ **n.** derog. an offensive term for a white person, used by black people. [1920s: of unknown origin.]

Off. ▶ **abbr.** ■ Office. ■ Officer.

off /ôf; äf/ ▶ **adv. 1** away from the place in question; to or at a distance: *the man ran off.* ■ away from the main route: *turn off here.* **2** so as to be removed or separated: *he whipped off his coat.* ■ absent; away from work. **3** starting a journey or race; leaving: *he made off on foot.* **4** so as to bring to an end or be discontinued: *the party rounded off a successful year.* ■ canceled: *the wedding's off.* ■ Brit. informal (of a menu item) temporarily unavailable: *strawberries are off.* **5** (of an electrical appliance or power supply) not functioning or so as to cease to function. ▶ **prep. 1** moving away and often down from: *he rolled off the bed.* **2** situated or leading in a direction away from (a main route or intersection): *a back street off Olympic Boulevard.* ■ out at sea from (a place on the coast): *six miles off Dunkirk.* **3** so as to be removed or separated from: *knocking $20 off the price.* ■ absent from. ■ informal abstaining from. ▶ **adj. 1** [attrib.] characterized by someone performing or feeling worse than usual; unsatisfactory or inadequate: *having an off day.* **2** [predic.] (of food) no longer fresh: *the fish was a bit off.* **3** [attrib.] located on the side of a vehicle normally furthest from the curb; offside. Compare with **NEAR** (sense 4). ▶ **n.** (also **off side**) Cricket the half of the field toward which the batsman's feet are pointed when standing to receive the ball. The opposite of **LEG.** ▶ **v.** informal [trans.] kill; murder: *he was hired to off her stalker.*

– PHRASES **off and on** intermittently; now and then.

of·fa ▶ **prep.** informal off of; off from: *get offa your horse!*

off-air ▶ **adj. & adv. 1** not being broadcast. **2** of or relating to the reception of programs not broadcast by cable or satellite.

of·fal /'ôfəl; 'äfəl/ ▶ **n.** the entrails and internal organs of an animal used as food. ■ refuse or waste material. ■ decomposing animal flesh.

Of·fa·ly /'ôfəlē; 'äf-/ a county in the central part of the Republic of Ireland; county town, Tullamore.

off·beat ▶ **adj.** /'ôf,bēt; 'äf-/ **1** Music not coinciding with the beat. **2** informal

PRONUNCIATION KEY ə *ago, up*; ər *over, fur*; a *hat*; ā *ate*; ä *car*; e *let*; ē *see*; i *fit*; ī *by*; NG *sing*; ō *go*; ô *law, for*; oi *toy*; ŏŏ *good*; ōō *goo*; ou *out*; TH *thin*; TH *then*; ZH *vision*

unconventional; unusual. ▶ **n.** Music any of the normally unaccented beats in a bar.

off-brand ▶ **adj.** denoting or relating to an item of retail goods of an unknown, unpopular, or inferior brand. ▶ **n.** an unknown, unpopular, or inferior brand.

off-Broad·way (also **Off-Broad·way** or **off Broad·way** or **Off Broad·way**) ▶ **adj. & adv.** (of a theater, play, or performer) located in, appearing in, or associated with an area of New York City other than the Broadway theater district, typically with reference to experimental and less commercial productions. ▶ **n.** such theaters and productions collectively.

off-cam·pus ▶ **adj. & adv.** away from a university or college campus: *asked to live in an off-campus residence.*

off-cen·ter ▶ **adj. & adv.** not quite in the center of something. ■ [as adj.] strange or eccentric.

off-col·or (also **off col·or**) ▶ **adj. 1** somewhat indecent or in poor taste: *off-color jokes.* **2** of the wrong or an inferior color: *the new paint doesn't match: it's off-color.* ■ (of a diamond) neither white nor any definite color.

off-dry ▶ **adj.** (of wine) having a nearly dry flavor, with just a trace of sweetness.

Of·fen·bach /ˈôfən,bäk; ˈäf-/, Jacques (1819–80), German composer; born *Jacob Offenbach.* His operettas include *The Tales of Hoffmann* (1881).

of·fence ▶ **n.** British spelling of OFFENSE.

of·fend /əˈfend/ ▶ **v. 1** [trans.] (often **be offended**) cause to feel upset, annoyed, or resentful. ■ be displeasing to: *the smell of smoke offended him.* **2** [intrans.] commit an illegal act: *criminals who offend again and again.* ■ break a commonly accepted rule or principle: *those activities which **offend against** public order.* — **of·fend·ed·ly adv. of·fend·er n.** [ME: from OFr. *offendre*, from L. *offendere* 'strike against.']

of·fense /əˈfens/ (Brit. **of·fence**) ▶ **n. 1** a breach of a law or rule; an illegal act. ■ a thing that constitutes a violation of what is judged to be right or natural: *the outcome is an **offense to** justice.* **2** annoyance or resentment brought about by a perceived insult to or disregard for oneself or one's standards or principles: *I didn't intend to **give offense**.* **3** /ˈôfens; ˈäf-/ the action of attacking: [as adj.] *reductions in strategic offense arsenals.* ■ (in sports) the team or players who are attempting to score or advance the ball. ■ (in sports) the condition of possessing the ball or being on the team attempting to score.

– PHRASES **no offense** informal do not be offended. **take offense** be offended; feel resentment. [ME: from OFr. *offens* 'misdeed,' from Latin *offensus* 'annoyance,' reinforced by Fr. *offense*, from L. *offensa* 'a striking against, a hurt, or displeasure.']

of·fen·sive ▶ **adj. 1** /əˈfensiv/ causing someone to feel deeply hurt, upset, or angry: *offensive language.* ■ (of a sight or smell) disgusting; repulsive. **2** /ˈôfensiv; ˈäf-/ [attrib.] actively aggressive; attacking: *offensive operations against the insurgents.* ■ (of a weapon) meant for use in attack. ■ (in sports) of or relating to the team or player who is seeking to score. ▶ **n.** /əˈfensiv/ an attacking military campaign. ■ an organized and forceful campaign to achieve something, typically a political or social end.

– PHRASES **be on the offensive** act or be ready to act aggressively. **go on** (or **take**) **the offensive** take the initiative by beginning to attack or act aggressively. — **of·fen·sive·ly adv. of·fen·sive·ness n.**

of·fer /ˈôfər; ˈäfər/ ▶ **v.** [with two objs.] present or proffer (something) for (someone) to accept or reject as so desired: *may I offer you a drink?* ■ [reporting verb] express readiness or the intention to do something for or on behalf of someone: [with infin.] *he offered to fix the gate.* ■ [trans.] (usu. **be offered**) make available for sale: *the product is offered at a very competitive price.* ■ [trans.] provide (something): *the highway offers easy access to the public beaches.* ■ [trans.] present (something, esp. an opportunity) for consideration and possible exploitation: *a good understanding of what a particular career can offer.* ■ [trans.] present (a prayer or sacrifice) to a deity: *villagers have gone to offer prayers for the souls of the sailors.* ■ [trans.] make an attempt at or show one's readiness for (violence or resistance): *he had to offer some resistance to her tirade.* ■ [trans.] archaic give an opportunity for (battle) to an enemy: *Darius was about to meet him and to offer battle.* ▶ **n.** an expression of readiness to do or give something if desired. ■ an amount of money that someone is willing to pay for something: *the prospective purchaser who made the highest offer.* ■ a specially reduced price or terms for something on sale. ■ a proposal of marriage.

– PHRASES **have something to offer** have something available to be used or appreciated. **offer one's hand** extend one's hand to be shaken as a sign of friendship. **on offer** available. **open to offers** willing to sell something or do a job for a reasonable price. — **of·fer·er** (or **of·fer·or**) **n.** [OE *offrian* 'sacrifice (something) to a deity,' of Gmc. origin, from L. *offerre* 'bestow, present.']

of·fer·ing /ˈôf(ə)riNG; äf-/ ▶ **n.** a thing offered, esp. as a gift or contribution. ■ a thing produced or manufactured for entertainment or sale. ■ a contribution, esp. of money, to a church. ■ a thing offered as a religious sacrifice or token of devotion.

of·fer·to·ry /ˈôfər,tôrē; ˈäfər-/ ▶ **n.** (pl. **-ries**) Christian Church **1** the offering of the bread and wine at the Eucharist. ■ prayers or music accompanying this. **2** an offering or collection of money made at a religious service. ■ prayers or music accompanying this. [ME: from eccles. L. *offertorium* 'offering.']

off-glide ▶ **n.** Phonet. a glide produced just following the articulation of another speech sound. Compare with ON-GLIDE.

off·hand ▶ **adj.** /ˈôfˈhand; ˈäf-/ (also **off·hand·ed**) ungraciously or offensively nonchalant or cool in manner. ▶ **adv.** without previous thought or consideration. — **off·hand·ed·ly adv. off·hand·ed·ness n.**

off-hours ▶ **plural n.** the time when one is not at work; one's leisure time.

of·fice /ˈôfis; ˈäf-/ ▶ **n. 1** a room, set of rooms, or building used as a place for commercial, professional, or bureaucratic work. ■ the local center of a large business. ■ a room, department, or building used to provide a particular service. **2** a position of authority, trust, or service, typically one of a public nature: *the office of attorney general.* ■ tenure of an official position, esp. a government position. **3** (usu. **offices**) a service or kindness done for another person or group of people. ■ dated a duty attaching to one's position; a task or function: *the offices of a nurse.* **4** (**Office**) Christian Church the series of services of prayers and psalms said daily by Roman Catholic priests, members of religious orders, and other clergy. ■ one of these services: *the noon office.* [ME: via OFr. from L. *officium* 'performance of a task,' based on *opus* 'work' + *facere* 'do.']

of·fice boy (also **of·fice girl**) ▶ **n.** a young man (or woman) employed to do relatively unimportant jobs in a business office.

of·fice·hold·er /ˈôfis,hōldər/ ▶ **n.** a person who holds public office.

of·fice hours ▶ **plural n.** the hours during which business is normally conducted. ■ the hours set by a professional person for office consultation.

of·fice park ▶ **n.** an area where a number of office buildings are built together on landscaped grounds.

of·fi·cer /ˈôfisər; ˈäf-/ ▶ **n. 1** a person holding a position of command or authority in the armed services, in the merchant marine, or on a passenger ship. ■ a policeman or policewoman. ■ a bailiff. **2** a holder of a public, civil, or ecclesiastical office: *a probation officer.* ■ a holder of a post in a society, company, or other organization, esp. one who is involved at a senior level in its management. **3** a member of a certain grade in some honorary orders. ▶ **v.** [trans.] provide with military officers: *the aristocracy continued to officer the army.* ■ act as the commander of (a unit): *foreign mercenaries officered new regiments.*

of·fi·cial /əˈfisHəl/ ▶ **adj.** of or relating to an authority or public body and its duties, actions, and responsibilities. ■ having the approval or authorization of such a body: *French is the official language of Quebec.* ■ employed by such a body in a position of authority or trust. ■ emanating from or attributable to a person in office; properly authorized: *official statistics.* ■ often derog. perceived as characteristic of officials and bureaucracy; officious: *he sat up straight and became official.* ▶ **n.** a person holding public office or having official duties, esp. as a representative of an organization or government department: *a union official.* — **of·fi·cial·dom n. of·fi·cial·ism n. of·fi·cial·ize v.**

of·fi·cial·ese /ə,fisHəˈlēz/ ▶ **n.** derog. the formal and typically verbose style of writing considered characteristic of official documents, esp. when difficult to understand.

of·fi·cial·ly /əˈfisHəlē/ ▶ **adv.** in a formal and public way. ■ with the authority of the government or some other organization: *it was officially acknowledged that the economy was in recession.* ■ in public and for official purposes but not necessarily so in reality.

of·fi·ci·ant /əˈfisHēənt/ ▶ **n.** a person, typically a priest or minister, who performs a religious service.

of·fi·ci·ate /əˈfisHē,āt/ ▶ **v.** act as an official in charge of something, as a sporting event. ■ perform a religious service or ceremony. — **of·fi·ci·a·tion** /ə,fisHēˈāsHən/ **n. of·fi·ci·a·tor n.**

of·fic·i·nal /əˈfisənl/ ▶ **adj.** esp. hist. (of an herb or drug) standardly used in medicine. — **of·fic·i·nal·ly adv.** [17th C.: from med. L. *officinalis* 'storeroom for medicines,' from L. *officina* 'workshop.']

of·fi·cious /əˈfisHəs/ ▶ **adj.** assertive of authority in an annoyingly domineering way, esp. with regard to petty or trivial matters. ■ intrusively enthusiastic in offering help or advice; interfering. — **of·fi·cious·ly adv. of·fi·cious·ness n.** [15th C.: from L. *officiosus* 'obliging,' from *officium* (see OFFICE).]

off·ing /ˈôfiNG; ˈäf-/ ▶ **n.** the more distant part of the sea in view.

– PHRASES **in the offing** likely to happen or appear soon: *there are several initiatives in the offing.* [17th C.: perh. from OFF + -ING[1].]

off·ish /ˈôfisH; ˈäf-/ ▶ **adj.** informal aloof or distant in manner; not friendly: *he was being offish with her.* — **off·ish·ly adv. off·ish·ness n.**

off-is·land ▶ **adv.** away from an island. ▶ **n.** an island off the shore of a larger or central island. ▶ **adj.** located on or coming from such an island. — **off-is·land·er n.**

off-key ▶ **adj. & adv.** (of music or singing) not having the correct tone or pitch; out of tune. ■ not in accordance with what is appropriate or correct in the circumstances.

off-kil·ter ▶ **adj. & adv.** not aligned or balanced. ■ [as adj.] unconventional or eccentric: *an off-kilter comedy about living in mud.*

off-lim·its ▶ **adj.** not to be entered or used; out of bounds: *the place was off-limits to civilians.* ■ not to be mentioned or discussed.

off·line /ˈôfˈlīn; ˈäf-/ (also **off-line**) Comput. ▶ **adj.** not controlled by or directly connected to a computer or external network. ▶ **adv.** (also **off line**) while not directly controlled by or connected to a computer or external network.

off·load /ˈôf,lōd; ˈäf-/ (also **off-load**) ▶ **v.** [trans.] unload (a cargo). ■ rid oneself of (something) by selling or passing it on to someone else: *a dealer offloaded 5,000 of these shares on a client.* ■ relieve oneself of (a problem or worry) by talking to someone else. ■ Comput. move (data or a task) from one processor to another to free the first processor for other tasks.

off-off-Broad·way (also **off-off Broad·way** or **Off-Off-Broad·way** or **Off-Off Broad·way**) ▶ **adj. & adv.** denoting or relating to avant-garde, experimental theatrical productions in New York City taking place in small or informal venues. ▶ **n.** theatrical productions of this kind.

off-peak ▶ **adj. & adv.** at a time when demand is less.

off-price ▶ **n.** a method of retailing in which brand-name goods (esp. clothing) are sold below the usual retail price. ▶ **adv.** using this method: *selling goods off-price.*

off·print /'ôf,print; 'äf-/ ▶ **n.** a printed copy of an article that originally appeared as part of a larger publication.

off-put·ting ▶ **adj.** unpleasant, disconcerting, or repellent: *his scar is somewhat off-putting.* — **off-put·ting·ly adv.**

off-ramp ▶ **n.** a one-way road leading off a main highway.

off rhyme ▶ **n.** another term for NEAR RHYME.

off-road ▶ **adj.** away from a smooth road; on rough terrain. ■ (of a vehicle or bicycle) designed for use over rough terrain.

off-road·ing ▶ **n.** the activity or sport of driving a motor vehicle over rough terrain. — **off-road·er n.**

off·scour·ings /'ôf,skouriNGz; 'äf-/ (also **off-scour·ings**) ▶ **plural n.** refuse, rubbish, or dregs.

off-screen (also **off screen** or **off·screen**) ▶ **adj.** heard or implied, yet not appearing on a movie or television screen: *an off-screen narrator.* ■ [attrib.] happening in real life rather than fictionally on-screen: *off-screen lovers.* ▶ **adv.** outside what can be seen on a movie or television screen: *the girl is looking off-screen to the right.* ■ in real life rather than fictionally in a movie or on television.

off-sea·son (also **off·sea·son** or **off sea·son**) ▶ **n.** a time of year when a particular activity, typically a sport, is not engaged in. ■ a time of year when business in a particular sphere is slack. ▶ **adv.** in or during the off-season.

off·set ▶ **n.** /'ôf,set; 'äf-/ **1** a consideration or amount that diminishes or balances the effect of a contrary one. **2** the amount or distance by which something is out of line: *these wheels have an offset of four inches.* ■ Surveying a short distance measured perpendicularly from the main line of measurement. ■ Electron. a small deviation or bias in a voltage or current. **3** a side shoot from a plant serving for propagation. ■ a spur in a mountain range. **4** Archit. a sloping ledge in a wall or other feature where the thickness of the part above is diminished. **5** a bend in a pipe to carry it past an obstacle. **6** [often as adj.] a method of printing in which ink is transferred from a plate or stone to a uniform rubber surface and from that to the paper. ▶ **v.** /,ôf'set; ,äf-/ (**-set·ting**; past and past part. **-set**) **1** [trans.] (often **be offset**) counteract (something) by having an opposing force or effect: *the deficit was offset by capital inflows.* **2** [trans.] place out of line: *several places where the ridge was offset at right angles to its length.* **3** [intrans.] (of ink or a freshly printed page) transfer an impression to the next leaf or sheet.

off·shoot /'ôf,SHo͞ot; 'äf-/ ▶ **n.** a side shoot or branch on a plant. ■ a thing that originated or developed from something else.

off·shore /'ôf'SHôr; 'äf-/ ▶ **adj. & adv. 1** situated at sea some distance from the shore. ■ (of the wind) blowing toward the sea from the land. ■ of or relating to the business of extracting oil or gas from the seabed: *offshore drilling.* **2** made, situated, or conducting business abroad, esp. to take advantage of lower costs or less stringent regulation. ■ of, relating to, or derived from a foreign country: [as adj.] *offshore politics.* ▶ **v.** [trans.] [often as n.] (**offshoring**) move (some of a company's processes or services) overseas, esp. in order to take advantage of lower costs.

off·side /'ôf'sīd; 'äf-/ ▶ **adj. & adv.** (of a player in certain sports) occupying an illegal position on the field, in particular: ■ Ice Hockey moving into the attacking zone ahead of the puck. ■ (usu. **offsides**) Football over the scrimmage line or otherwise ahead of the ball before the play has begun. ■ Soccer in the attacking half ahead of the ball and having fewer than two defenders nearer the goal line at the moment the ball is played. ■ Field Hockey in the attacking half of the field when there are fewer than three defenders nearer the goal line at the moment the ball is played. ▶ **n.** the fact or an instance of being offside.

off-speed ▶ **adj.** slower than expected.

off·spring /'ôf,spriNG; 'äf-/ ▶ **n.** (pl. same) a person's child or children. ■ an animal's young. ■ fig. the product or result of something. [OE *ofspring* (see OFF, SPRING).]

off·stage /'ôf'stāj; 'äf-/ (also **off-stage**) ▶ **adj. & adv.** (in a theater) not on the stage and so not visible to the audience.

off-the-shoul·der ▶ **adj.** (esp. of a dress or blouse) not covering the shoulders.

off-track ▶ **adj.** (of betting on a race) situated or taking place away from a racetrack.

off-white ▶ **n.** a white color with a gray or yellowish tinge: [as adj.] *a frilly off-white blouse.*

off-world ▶ **n.** in science fiction, any place away from the earth, or from that world that is the location of a narrative or is regarded as the native world. ▶ **adj.** involving, located in, inhabiting, or coming from, a place outside the native world. ▶ **adv.** away from the native world. — **off-world·er n.**

off year ▶ **n. 1** a year in which there is no major election, esp. one in which there is a congressional election but no presidential election. **2** a year that is inferior or substandard compared to previous ones.

OFM ▶ **abbr.** Order of Friars Minor (Franciscans). [L. *Ordo Fratrum Minorum.*]

oft /ôft; äft/ ▶ **adv.** archaic, poetic/literary, or jocular form of OFTEN: in combination *an oft-quoted tenet.* [OE, of Gmc. origin; rel. to Ger. *oft.*]

of·ten /'ôf(t)ən; 'äf-/ ▶ **adv.** (**of·ten·er**, **of·ten·est**) frequently; many times: *how often do you have your hair cut?* ■ in many instances: *vocabulary often reflects social standing.*

– PHRASES **as often as not** quite frequently or commonly. **more often than not** usually. [ME: from OFT.]

of·ten·times /'ôf(t)ən,tīmz; 'äf-/ ▶ **adv.** often.

oft·times /'ôf(t),tīmz; 'äf(t)-/ ▶ **adv.** archaic or poetic/literary form of OFTEN.

OG ▶ **abbr.** officer of the guard.

O·ga·den /,ôgə'den; ,ägə-; ō'gäden/ (**the Ogaden**) a desert region in southeastern Ethiopia.

O·gal·la·la Aq·ui·fer /,ōgə'lälə/ a vast groundwater resource under eight US states, used esp. for crop irrigation, that stretches from South Dakota to Texas and New Mexico.

og·am /'ägəm/ ▶ **n.** var. of OGHAM.

Og·bo·mo·sho /,ägbə'mōSHō/ a city in southwestern Nigeria; pop. 661,000.

o·gee /'ōjē/ Archit. ▶ **adj.** having a double continuous S-shaped curve. ▶ **n.** an S-shaped line or molding. — **o·geed adj.** [ME: appar. from OGIVE.]

o·gee arch ▶ **n.** Archit. an arch with two ogee curves meeting at the apex.

og·ham /'ägəm/ (also **og·am**) ▶ **n.** an ancient Irish alphabet, consisting of twenty characters formed by parallel strokes on either side of or across a continuous line. ■ an inscription in this alphabet. ■ each of its characters. [18th C.: from Irish *ogam*, connected with *Ogma*, its mythical inventor.]

o·give /'ōjīv/ ▶ **n. 1** Archit. a pointed or Gothic arch. ■ one of the diagonal groins or ribs of a vault. ■ a thing having the profile of an ogive, esp. the head of a projectile or the nose cone of a rocket. **2** Stat. a cumulative frequency graph. — **o·gi·val** /ō'jīvəl/ **adj.** [ME: from Fr., of unknown origin.]

Og·la·la /äg'lälə/ (also **O·ga·la·la**) ▶ **n.** (pl. same or **-las** or **-las**) a member of the chief division of the Lakota people. ▶ **adj.** of or relating to this people. [the name in Lakota.]

o·gle /'ōgəl/ ▶ **v.** [trans.] stare at in a lecherous manner: *he was ogling her breasts* | [intrans.] *men who had turned up to ogle.* ▶ **n.** a lecherous look. — **o·gler** /'ōg(ə)lər/ **n.** [17th C.: prob. from Low German or Du.; cf. Low Ger. *oegeln*, frequentative of *oegen* 'look at.']

O·gle·thorpe /'ōgəl,THôrp/, James Edward (1696–1785), British politician. He founded the American colony of Georgia in 1732.

o·gre /'ōgər/ ▶ **n.** (in folklore) a man-eating giant. ■ a cruel or terrifying person. — **o·gre·ish** /'ōg(ə)risH/ (also **o·grish**) **adj.** [18th C.: from French, first used by the Fr. writer Perrault in 1697.]

o·gress /'ōgris/ ▶ **n.** a female ogre.

OH ▶ **abbr.** Ohio (in official postal use).

oh[1] /ō/ ▶ **exclam.** used to express a range of emotions including surprise, anger, disappointment, or joy, or when reacting to something that has just been said: *"Oh no," said Daisy, appalled.* [16th C.: var. of O[3].]

oh[2] ▶ **n.** var. of O[1] (sense 2).

O'Ha·ra[1] /ō'he(ə)rə; ō'harə/, Frank (1926–66), US poet; full name *Francis Russell O'Hara.* His poetry collections include *Lunch Poems* (1964).

O'Ha·ra[2], John Henry (1905–70), US writer. He wrote *BUtterfield 8* (1935) and *Pal Joey* (1940).

OHC ▶ **abbr.** overhead camshaft.

O'Hig·gins /ō'higinz; ô'ēgēns/, Bernardo (*c.*1778–1842), dictator of Chile 1817–23.

O·hi·o /ō'hī-ō/ a state in the northeastern US, bordering on Lake Erie; pop. 11,353,140; capital, Columbus; statehood, Mar. 1, 1803 (17). It was acquired by Britain from France in 1763 and by the US in 1783 after the American Revolution. — **O·hi·o·an adj. & n.**

O·hi·o Riv·er a river that flows for 980 miles (1,580 km) from Pennsylvania to the Mississippi River in Illinois.

ohm /ōm/ ▶ **n.** the SI unit of electrical resistance, expressing the resistance in a circuit transmitting a current of one ampere when subjected to a potential difference of one volt. (Symbol: Ω) — **ohm·ic** /'ōmik/ **adj. ohm·i·cal·ly** /'ōmik(ə)lē/ **adv.** [19th C.: named after G. S. *Ohm* (1789–1854).]

ohm·me·ter /'ō(m),mētər/ ▶ **n.** an instrument for measuring electrical resistance.

Ohm's law Physics a law stating that electric current is proportional to voltage and inversely proportional to resistance.

o·ho /ō'hō/ ▶ **exclam.** used to express pleased surprise or recognition. [ME: from O[3] + HO[2].]

oh-oh ▶ **exclam.** another spelling for UH-OH.

-oholic ▶ **suffix** var. of -AHOLIC.

oh-so ▶ **adv.** [as submodifier] informal extremely: *their oh-so-ordinary lives.*

-oid ▶ **suffix** forming adjectives and nouns: **1** Zool. denoting an animal belonging to a higher taxon with a name ending in *-oidea*: *hominoid* | *percoid.* **2** denoting form or resemblance: *asteroid* | *rhomboid.* — **-oidal suffix** forming corresponding adjectives **-oidally suffix** forming corresponding adverbs. [from mod. L. *-oides*, from Gk. *-oeidēs*; rel. to *eidos* 'form.']

oil /oil/ ▶ **n. 1** a viscous liquid derived from petroleum, esp. for use as a fuel or lubricant. ■ petroleum. ■ [with adj.] any of various thick, viscous, typically flammable liquids that are insoluble in water but soluble in organic solvents and are obtained from animals or plants. ■ a liquid preparation used on the hair or skin as a cosmetic. ■ Chem. any of a group of natural esters of glycerol and various fatty acids that are liquid at room temperature. Compare with FAT. **2** (often **oils**) oil paint. ▶ v. [trans.] lubricate or coat (something) with oil. ■ impregnate or treat (something) with oil. [ME: from Old North. Fr. *olie*, OFr. *oile*, from L. *oleum* '(olive) oil.']

oil bar·on ▶ n. derog. a magnate in the oil industry.

oil bee·tle ▶ n. a slow-moving flightless beetle (*Meloe* and other genera, family Meloidae) that releases a foul-smelling oily secretion when disturbed. The larvae develop as parasites in the nests of solitary bees.

oil·bird /'oil,bərd/ ▶ n. chiefly British term for GUACHARO.

oil cake ▶ n. a mass of compressed linseed or other plant material left after its oil has been extracted, used as fodder or fertilizer.

oil·can /'oil,kan/ ▶ n. a can containing lubricating oil, esp. one with a long nozzle.

oil·cloth /'oil,klôTH/ ▶ n. fabric treated on one side with oil to make it waterproof. ■ a canvas coated with linseed or other oil and used to cover a table or floor.

oil col·or ▶ n. another term for OIL PAINT.

oil·er /'oilər/ ▶ n. **1** a thing that holds or supplies oil, in particular: ■ an oil tanker. ■ an oilcan. ■ a person who oils machinery. ■ informal an oil well. **2** (**oilers**) informal oilskin garments.

oil field (also **oil·field**) ▶ n. an area of land or seabed underlain by strata yielding petroleum, esp. in amounts that justify commercial exploitation.

oil·man /'oil,man; -mən/ ▶ n. (pl. **-men**) a man who works in the oil industry, specifically: ■ one who owns or operates oil wells. ■ a high executive in an oil company. ■ one who sells or delivers fuel oil.

oil of cloves ▶ n. see CLOVE[1] (sense 1).

oil of tur·pen·tine ▶ n. see TURPENTINE (sense 1).

oil of vit·ri·ol ▶ n. archaic term for SULFURIC ACID.

oil paint ▶ n. a paste made with ground pigment and a drying oil such as linseed oil, used chiefly by artists.

oil paint·ing ▶ n. the art of painting with oil paints. ■ a picture painted with oil paints.

oil palm ▶ n. a widely cultivated tropical West African palm tree (*Elaeis guineensis*) that is the chief source of palm oil.

oil pan ▶ n. the bottom section of the crankcase of an internal combustion engine, serving as the reservoir for its lubricating oil.

oil·pa·per /'oil,pāpər/ (also **oil pa·per**) ▶ n. paper made transparent or waterproof by treatment with oil.

oil rig ▶ n. a structure with equipment for drilling and servicing an oil well.

oil·seed /'oil,sēd/ ▶ n. any of several seeds from cultivated crops yielding oil, e.g., rape, peanut, or soybean.

oil shale ▶ n. fine-grained sedimentary rock from which oil can be extracted.

oil·skin /'oil,skin/ ▶ n. heavy cotton cloth waterproofed with oil. ■ (also **oilskins**) a garment or set of garments made of such cloth.

oil slick ▶ n. a film or layer of oil floating on an expanse of water, esp. one that has leaked or been discharged from a ship.

oil·stone /'oil,stōn/ ▶ n. a fine-grained flat stone used with oil for sharpening cutting edges.

oil well ▶ n. a well or shaft drilled through rock, from which petroleum is drawn.

oil·y /'oilē/ ▶ adj. (**oil·i·er, oil·i·est**) **1** containing oil. ■ covered or soaked with oil: *an oily rag.* ■ resembling oil in appearance or behavior: *the oily swell of the river.* **2** fig. (of a person or their behavior) unpleasantly smooth and ingratiating: *his oily smile.* — **oil·i·ness** n.

oink /oiNGk/ ▶ n. the characteristic grunting sound of a pig. ▶ v. [intrans.] make such a sound. [1940s: imitative.]

oint·ment /'ointmənt/ ▶ n. a smooth oily preparation that is rubbed on the skin for medicinal purposes or as a cosmetic. [ME: alt. of OFr. *oignement*, from a pop. L. form of L. *unguentum* (see UNGUENT.)]

Oi·sin another name for OSSIAN.

OJ ▶ abbr. orange juice.

O·jib·wa /ō'jib,wā; -wə/ (also **O·jib·way** /-,wā/) ▶ n. (pl. same or **-was** or **-ways**) **1** a member of a North American Indian people native to the region around Lake Superior. Also called CHIPPEWA. **2** the Algonquian language of this people. ▶ adj. of or relating to this people or their language. [from Ojibwa *očipwē*, prob. 'puckered,' with ref. to their style of moccasins.]

OK[1] (also **o·kay** /'ō'kā/) informal ▶ exclam. used to express assent, agreement, or acceptance: *OK, I give in.* ■ used to introduce an utterance: *"OK, let's go."* ▶ adj. [predic.] satisfactory but not exceptionally or especially good: *the flight was OK.* ■ (of a person) in a satisfactory physical or mental state: *are you okay, Ben?* ■ permissible; allowable. ▶ adv. in a satisfactory manner or to a satisfactory extent. ▶ n. [in sing.] an authorization or approval: *when will she give us the OK?* ▶ v. (**OK's, OK'd, OK'ing**) [trans.] sanction or give approval to. [19th C.: prob. an abbrev. of *orl korrect*, humorous form of *all correct*, popularized as a slogan during President Van Buren's reelection campaign of 1840; his nickname *Old Kinderhook* provided the initials.]

OK[2] ▶ abbr. Oklahoma (in official postal use).

o·ka /'ōkə/ (also **oke**) ▶ n. **1** an Egyptian and former Turkish unit of weight, usually equal to approximately 2¾ pounds (1.3 kg). **2** an Egyptian and former Turkish unit of capacity equal to approximately ⅓ pint (0.2 l). [17th C.: via Ital. and Fr. *oque* from Turk. *okka*, from Arab. *ūkiya*, based on L. *uncia* 'ounce.']

o·ka·pi /ō'käpē/ ▶ n. (pl. same or **-pis**) a large browsing mammal (*Okapia johnstoni*) of the giraffe family that lives in the rain forests of the northern Democratic Republic of the Congo (formerly Zaire). It has a dark chestnut coat with stripes on the hindquarters and upper legs. [20th C.: a local word.]

O·ka·van·go /,ōkə'väNGgō/ a river in southwestern Africa that rises in Angola and flows 1,000 miles (1,600 km) south and then east to Namibia, where it turns east to the Okavango marshes. Also called CUBANGO.

o·kay /'ō'kā/ ▶ exclam., adj., adv., n., & v. var. of OK[1].

O.K. Cor·ral /'ō'kā kə'ral/ see TOMBSTONE, Arizona.

oke[1] ▶ n. var. of OKA.

oke[2] /ōk/ ▶ exclam., adj., adv., n., & v. another term for OKAY.

O·kee·cho·bee, Lake /,ōki'CHōbē/ a lake in southern Florida.

O'Keeffe /ō'kēf/, Georgia (1887–1986), US painter; wife of Alfred Stieglitz. Her best-known paintings depict enlarged studies, particularly of flowers.

O·ke·fe·no·kee Swamp /,ōkēfə'nōkē/ a swampland in southeastern Georgia and northeastern Florida.

o·key-doke /'ōkē 'dōk/ (also **o·key-do·key** /'dōkē/) ▶ exclam., adj., & adv. var. of OK[1].

O·khotsk, Sea of /ō'kätsk; ə'KHôtsk/ an inlet of the northern Pacific Ocean on the eastern coast of Russia.

O·kie /'ōkē/ ▶ n. (pl. **O·kies**) informal a native or inhabitant of Oklahoma. ■ hist., derog. a migrant agricultural worker from Oklahoma, who had been forced to leave during the Depression of the 1930s.

O·ki·na·wa /,ōkə'näwə/ an island in southern Japan, the largest of the Ryukyu Islands; chief town, Naha.

Okla. ▶ abbr. Oklahoma.

O·kla·ho·ma /,ōklə'hōmə/ a state in the southwestern central US, north of Texas; pop. 3,450,654; capital, Oklahoma City; statehood, Nov. 16, 1907 (46). In 1803, most of it was acquired from the French as part of the Louisiana Purchase. — **O·kla·ho·man** n. & adj.

O·kla·ho·ma Cit·y the capital of Oklahoma, in the central part of the state; pop. 444,719.

o·kra /'ōkrə/ ▶ n. a plant (*Abelmoschus esculentus*) of the mallow family with long ridged seedpods, native to the Old World tropics. ■ the immature seedpods of this plant eaten as a vegetable and also used to thicken soups and stews. Also called GUMBO. [18th C.: a West Afr. word, perh. from the root *nkru*; cf. *nkran*, the name of the town European-ized as *Accra*.]

Ok·to·ber·fest /äk'tōbər,fest/ ▶ n. a traditional autumn beer festival held in Munich, Germany every October. ■ any similar autumn festival.

-ol ▶ suffix Chem. **1** forming names of organic compounds: **2** denoting alcohols and phenols: *glycerol.* **3** denoting oils and oil-derived compounds: *benzol.* [sense 2 from *(alcoh)ol*; sense 3 from L. *oleum* 'oil.']

O·laf /'ōläf/ the name of five kings of Norway: ■ Olaf I Tryggvason (969–1000), reigned 995–1000. ■ Olaf II Haraldsson (*c.*995–1030), reigned 1016–30; canonized as **St. Olaf**, the patron saint of Norway. Feast day, July 29. ■ Olaf III Haraldsson (died 1093), reigned 1066–93. ■ Olaf IV Haakonson (1370–87), reigned 1380–87. ■ Olaf V (1903–91), reigned 1957–91; full name *Olaf Alexander Edmund Christian Frederik.*

Ö·land /'ə,länd; 'œ,länd/ a Swedish island in the Baltic Sea, off the southeastern coast.

old /ōld/ ▶ adj. (**old·er, old·est**) **1** having lived for a long time; no longer young. See also ELDER[1], ELDEST. ■ made or built long ago: *the old quarter of the town.* ■ possessed or used for a long time: *he gave his old clothes away.* ■ having the characteristics or showing the signs of age: *marble now so old that it has turned gray and chipped.* **2** [attrib.] belonging only or chiefly to the past; former or previous: *valuation under the old rating system was inexact.* ■ used to refer to the first of two or more similar things: *I was going to try to get my old job back.* ■ dating from far back; long-established or known: *old friends | the same old routine.* ■ (of a form of a language) as used in former or earliest times. **3** [in comb.] of a specified age: *he was 14 years old.* ■ [as n.] [in comb.] a person or animal of the age specified: *a nineteen-year-old.* **4** [attrib.] informal used to express affection, familiarity, or contempt: *it gets the old adrenaline going.*

– PHRASES **any old** any item of a specified type (used to show that no particular or special individual is in question): *any old room will do.* **any old way** in no particular order. **as old as the hills** of very long standing or very great age (often used in exaggerated statements): *that flannel shirt of yours is as old as the hills.* **for old times' sake** see SAKE[1]. **of old** **1** in or belonging to the past: *he was more reticent than of old.* **2** starting long ago; for a long time: *they knew him of old.* — **old·ish** adj. **old·ness** n. [OE *ald*, rel. to Ger. *alt*, L. *alere* 'nourish.']

Old Bai·ley the Central Criminal Court in London, England.

old bean ▶ n. see BEAN.

old boy ▶ n. Brit. a former male pupil of a school, college, or university. ■ a former male member of a sports team, company, or other organization.

old-boy net·work (also **old boy net·work**) ▶ n. an informal system of support and friendship through which men use their positions of influence to help others who went to the same school or college as they did or who share a similar social background.

Old Cath·o·lic ▶ n. a member of any of various religious groups that have separated from the Roman Catholic Church since the Reformation, esp. over the tenets of papal primacy and infallibility. ■ a member of an English family that has remained Roman Catholic since the Reformation.

Old Church Slav·ic (also **Old Church Sla·von·ic**) ▶ n. the oldest recorded Slavic language, surviving in texts from the 9th–12th centuries. It is related particularly to the South Slavic languages. See also CHURCH SLAVIC.

old coun·try ▶ n. (**the old country**) the native country of a person who has gone to live abroad.

Old Del·hi see DELHI.

olde ▶ adj. [attrib.] pseudoarchaic variant spelling of OLD, intended to be quaint: *Ye Olde Tea Shoppe.*

old·en /ˈōldən/ ▶ adj. [attrib.] archaic or jocular of or relating to former times: *the olden days.*

Ol·den·burg /ˈōldənˌbərg/, Claes Thure (1929–), US painter and sculptor; born in Sweden. During the 1960s he conducted "happenings," participational art events such as *Autobodys* (1964) in which he used actual cars and crowds of people.

Old Eng·lish ▶ n. the language of the Anglo-Saxons (up to about 1150), a highly inflected language with a largely Germanic vocabulary, very different from modern English. Also called ANGLO-SAXON.

Old English sheepdog

Old Eng·lish sheep·dog ▶ n. a large sheepdog of a breed with a shaggy blue-gray and white coat.

Old Faith·ful a geyser in Yellowstone National Park. Its eruptions, which rise to 175 feet (53.4 m), occur every 33 to 90 minutes.

old-fan·gled /ˈōldˈfaNGgəld/ ▶ adj. characterized by adherence to what is old; old-fashioned.

old-fash·ioned ▶ adj. in or according to styles or types no longer current or common; not modern. ■ (of a person or their views) favoring traditional and usually restrictive styles, ideas, or customs: *she's stuffy and old-fashioned.* ▶ n. a cocktail consisting chiefly of whiskey, bitters, water, and sugar. — **old-fash·ioned·ness** n.

Old French ▶ n. the French language up to *c.*1400.

Old Fri·sian ▶ n. the Frisian language up to *c.*1400, closely related to both Old English and Old Saxon.

old fus·tic ▶ n. see FUSTIC (sense 2).

Old Glo·ry an informal name for the US national flag.

old gold ▶ n. a dull brownish-gold color.

old guard (also **Old Guard**) ▶ n. (usu. **the old guard**) the original or long-standing members of a group or party, esp. ones who are unwilling to accept change or new ideas: *the aging right-wing old guard.* — **old guard·ism** n. **old guards·man** n. (pl. **-men**)

old hand ▶ n. a person with a lot of experience in something: *he was an old hand at red-tape cutting.*

old hat ▶ n. informal used to refer to something considered uninteresting, predictable, tritely familiar, or old-fashioned.

Old High Ger·man ▶ n. the language of southern Germany up to *c.*1200, from which modern standard German is derived. See GERMAN.

Old Ice·lan·dic ▶ n. the Icelandic language up to the 16th century, a form of Old Norse in which medieval sagas were composed.

old·ie /ˈōldē/ ▶ n. informal an old song, film, or television program that is still well known or popular.

Old I·rish ▶ n. the Irish Gaelic language up to *c.*1000, from which modern Irish and Scottish Gaelic are derived.

Old I·ron·sides nickname for the frigate Constitution, the oldest commissioned vessel in the US Navy. Launched in 1797, it defeated four British frigates in the War of 1812 and is permanently berthed at the Boston Navy Yard.

old la·dy ▶ n. informal, often derog. one's mother, wife, or girlfriend.

Old Lat·in ▶ n. Latin before about 100 BC.

old-line ▶ adj. **1** holding conservative views. **2** well established. — **old-lin·er** n.

Old Low Ger·man ▶ n. the language of northern Germany and the Netherlands up to *c.*1200, from which modern Dutch and modern Low German are derived.

old maid ▶ n. **1** derog. a single woman regarded as too old for marriage. ■ a prim and fussy person. **2** a card game in which players collect pairs and try not to be left with an odd penalty card, typically a black queen. — **old-maid·ish** adj.

old man ▶ n. informal, often derog. one's father, husband, or boyfriend. ■ (**the old man**) a man in authority over others, esp. an employer or commanding officer.

old mas·ter ▶ n. a great artist of former times, esp. of the 13th–17th century in Europe. ■ a painting by such an artist.

old mon·ey ▶ n. established, inherited wealth. ■ those whose families have been wealthy for many generations: *the list of Canada's wealthiest people, once dominated by old money, is no longer so exclusive.*

old moon ▶ n. the moon in its last quarter, before the new moon.

Old Nick /nik/ an informal name for the Devil. [17th C.: prob. from the name *Nicholas.*]

Old Norse ▶ n. the North Germanic (Scandinavian) language of medieval Norway, Iceland, Denmark, and Sweden up to the 14th century, from which the modern Scandinavian languages are derived. See also OLD ICELANDIC.

Old North Church an Episcopal church built in 1723 in Boston's North End. On April 18, 1775, two lanterns hung from the steeple meant that the British were moving up the Charles River, signaling Paul Revere to make his famous ride to Lexington.

Ol·do·wan /ˈōldəwən; ˈôl-/ ▶ adj. Archaeol. of, relating to, or denoting an early Lower Paleolithic culture of Africa, dated to about 2.0–1.5 million years ago. It is characterized by primitive stone tools that are associated chiefly with *Homo habilis.* ■ [as n.] (**the Oldowan**) the Oldowan culture or period. [1930s: from *Oldoway,* alt. of OLDUVAI GORGE, Tanzania, + -AN.]

Old Per·sian ▶ n. the Persian language up to the 3rd century BC, used in the ancient Persian empire and written in cuneiform.

Old Pre·tend·er see STUART[2].

Old Prus·sian ▶ n. a Baltic language, related to Lithuanian, spoken in Prussia until the 17th century.

old rose ▶ n. **1** a double-flowered rose of a variety or hybrid evolved before the development of the hybrid tea rose. **2** a shade of grayish or purplish pink. ▶ adj. (usu. **old-rose**) of this shade of pink.

Old Sax·on ▶ n. **1** a member of the Saxon peoples who remained in Germany, as opposed to an Anglo-Saxon. **2** the dialect of Old Low German spoken in Saxony up to *c.*1200. ▶ adj. of or relating to the Old Saxons or their language.

old school ▶ n. (often **of/from the old school**) used, usually approvingly, to refer to someone or something that is old-fashioned or traditional.

old school tie ▶ n. esp. Brit. a necktie with a characteristic pattern worn by the former students of an exclusive English public school. ■ used to refer to the group loyalty, mutual assistance, social class, and traditional attitudes associated with people who attended such schools.

Old Slav·ic (also **Old Sla·von·ic**) ▶ n. another name for CHURCH SLAVIC.

Old South ▶ n. (**the Old South**) the southern states of the US before the Civil War.

old·squaw /ˈōldˌskwô/ (also **old squaw** or **old squaw duck**) ▶ n. a marine diving duck (*Clangula hyemalis*) that breeds in Arctic Eurasia and North America, the male having very long tail feathers and mainly white plumage in winter.

old·ster /ˈōldstər/ ▶ n. informal an older person. [19th C.: from OLD, on the pattern of *youngster.*]

Old Stone Age the Paleolithic period.

Old Style (abbr.: **OS**) ▶ n. [often as adj.] the method of calculating dates using the Julian calendar.

old style ▶ n. a style that is no longer current, common, or fashionable. ■ Print. an early style of type characterized by strokes of relatively equal thickness and the use of serifs, often slanted. ▶ adj. [attrib.] denoting or according to such a style.

Old Tes·ta·ment ▶ n. the first part of the Christian Bible, comprising thirty-nine books and corresponding approximately to the Hebrew Bible.

old-time ▶ adj. [attrib.] used to refer to something old-fashioned in an approving or nostalgic way. ■ denoting traditional or folk styles of American popular music, such as gospel or bluegrass.

– PHRASES **for old times' sake** see SAKE[1].

old-tim·er ▶ n. informal a person who has had the same job, membership, or residence, etc., for a long time. ■ derog. an old person.

Ol·du·vai Gorge /ˈôldəˌvī; -ˌwā; -ˌvā/ a gorge in northern Tanzania, 30 miles (48 km) long and up to 300 feet (90 m) deep.

Old Vic /ˈvik/ the popular name of the Royal Victoria Theatre in London.

Old Welsh ▶ n. the Welsh language up to *c.*1150.

old·wife /ˈōldˌwīf/ ▶ n. **1** any of a number of deep-bodied edible marine fishes, including a brightly patterned tropical Atlantic triggerfish (*Balistes vetula*) and the black sea bream of European Atlantic waters (*Spondyliosoma cantharus*). **2** another term for OLDSQUAW.

old wives' tale ▶ n. a superstition or traditional belief that is regarded as unscientific or incorrect.

old wom·an ▶ n. **1** informal, often derog. one's mother, wife, or girlfriend. **2** derog. a fussy or timid person, esp. a man. — **old-wom·an·ish** adj. (in sense 2).

Old World Europe, Asia, and Africa, regarded collectively as the part of the world known before the discovery of the Americas. Compare with **New World**.

old-world (also **old world; Old World**) ▶ **adj.** belonging to or associated with former times, esp. when considered quaint and attractive. ■ characteristic of the Old World.

ole /ōl/ ▶ **adj.** informal or humorous old.

-ole ▶ **comb. form** in names of organic compounds, esp. heterocyclic compounds: *thiazole.* [from L. *oleum* 'oil.']

o·lé /ō'lā/ ▶ **exclam.** a cry of approval, joy, etc. [Sp., a cry used at bullfights.]

o·le·ag·i·nous /,ōlē'ajənəs/ ▶ **adj.** rich in, covered with, or producing oil; oily or greasy. ■ fig. exaggeratedly and distastefully complimentary; obsequious. [ME: from Fr. *oléagineux*, from L. *oleaginus* 'of the olive tree,' from *oleum* 'oil.']

o·le·an·der /'ōlē,andər/ ▶ **n.** a poisonous evergreen Old World shrub (*Nerium oleander*) of the dogbane family that is widely grown in warm countries for its clusters of white, pink, or red flowers. [16th C.: from med. L.]

o·le·as·ter /,ōlē'astər/ ▶ **n.** a Eurasian shrub or small tree (genus *Elaeagnus*, family Elaeagnaceae) often cultivated as an ornamental, in particular *E. angustifolia*, commonly called **Russian olive**, which bears edible yellow olive-shaped fruit. [ME: from L., from *olea* 'olive tree.']

o·lec·ra·non /ō'lekrə,nän; ,ōlə'krā-/ ▶ **n.** Anat. the bony prominence of the elbow, on the upper end of the ulna. [18th C.: from Gk. *ōle(no)kranon*, from *ōlenē* 'elbow' + *kranion* 'head.']

o·le·fin /'ōləfin/ (also **o·le·fine**) ▶ **n.** Chem. another term for **alkene**. — **o·le·fin·ic** /,ōlə'finik/ **adj.** [19th C.: from Fr. *oléfiant* 'oil-forming.']

o·le·ic ac·id /ō'lē-ik/ ▶ **n.** Chem. an unsaturated fatty acid, $CH_3(CH_2)_7CH=CH(CH_2)_7COOH$, present in many fats and soaps. [19th C.: *oleic* from L. *oleum* 'oil.']

o·le·if·er·ous /,ōlē'ifərəs/ ▶ **adj.** Bot. (of seeds, glands, etc.) producing oil. [19th C.: from L. *oleum* 'oil' + **-ferous**.]

o·le·o /'ōlēō/ ▶ **n.** another term for **margarine**.

oleo- ▶ **comb. form** relating to or containing oil: *oleoresin.* [from L. *oleum* 'oil.']

o·le·o·graph /'ōlēə,graf/ ▶ **n.** a lithographic print textured to resemble an oil painting. — **o·le·o·graph·ic** /,ōlēə'grafik/ **adj.** **o·le·og·ra·phy** /,ōlē'ägrəfē/ **n.**

o·le·o·mar·ga·rine /,ōlēō'märj(ə)rən/ ▶ **n.** another term for **margarine**.

o·le·o·res·in /,ōlēō'rezən/ ▶ **n.** a natural or artificial mixture of essential oils and a resin, e.g., balsam. — **o·le·o·res·in·ous** /-nəs/ **adj.**

O·les·tra /ō'lestrə/ (also **o·les·tra**) ▶ **n.** trademark a synthetic cooking oil used as a calorie-free fat substitute in various foods.

o·le·um /'ōlēəm/ ▶ **n.** a dense, corrosive liquid consisting of concentrated sulfuric acid containing excess sulfur trioxide in solution. [20th C.: from L., lit. 'oil.']

ol·fac·tion /äl'fakshən; ōl-/ ▶ **n.** tech. the action or capacity of smelling; the sense of smell. — **ol·fac·tive** **adj.**

ol·fac·tom·e·ter /,älfak'tämitər; ,ōl-/ ▶ **n.** an instrument for measuring the intensity of an odor or sensitivity to odor. — **ol·fac·tom·e·try** /-'tämitrē/ **n.**

ol·fac·to·ry /äl'fakt(ə)rē; ōl-/ ▶ **adj.** of or relating to the sense of smell: *the olfactory organs.* [17th C.: from L. *olfactare* (frequentative of *olfacere* 'to smell') + **-ory**[2].]

ol·fac·to·ry nerve ▶ **n.** Anat. each of the first pair of cranial nerves, transmitting impulses to the brain from the smell receptors in the mucous membrane of the nose.

o·lib·a·num /ō'libənəm/ ▶ **n.** another term for **frankincense**. [ME: from med. L., from late L. *libanus*, from Gk. *libanos* 'frankincense.']

ol·i·garch /'äli,gärk; 'ōli-/ ▶ **n.** a ruler in an oligarchy. [19th C.: from Gk. *oligarkhēs*, from *oligoi* 'few' + *arkhein* 'to rule.']

ol·i·gar·chy /'äli,gärkē; 'ōli-/ ▶ **n.** (pl. **-chies**) a small group of people having control of a country, organization, or institution. ■ a state governed by such a group. ■ government by such a group. — **ol·i·gar·chic** /,äli'gärkik; ,ōli-/ **adj.** **ol·i·gar·chi·cal** /,äli'gärkikəl; ,ōli-/ **adj.** **ol·i·gar·chi·cal·ly** /,äli'gärkik(ə)lē; ,ōli-/ **adv.**

oligo- ▶ **comb. form** having few; containing a relatively small number of units: *oligopoly | oligosaccharide.* [from Gk. *oligos* 'small,' *oligoi* 'few.']

Ol·i·go·cene /'äligō,sēn/ ▶ **adj.** Geol. of, relating to, or denoting the third epoch of the Tertiary period, between the Eocene and Miocene epochs. The Oligocene epoch lasted from 35.4 million to 23.3 million years ago. It was a time of falling temperatures, with evidence of the first primates. ■ [as n.] (**the Oligocene**) the Oligocene epoch or the system of rocks deposited during it. [19th C.: from **oligo-** 'few' + Gk. *kainos* 'new.']

Ol·i·go·chae·ta /,äligō'kētə/ Zool. a class of annelids that includes the earthworms. They have simple setae projecting from each segment and a small head lacking sensory appendages. — **ol·i·go·chaete** /'äligō,kēt/ **n.** [mod. L. (pl.), from **oligo-** 'few' + Gk. *khaitē* 'long hair.']

ol·i·go·clase /'äligō,klās/ ▶ **n.** a feldspar mineral common in siliceous igneous rocks, consisting of a sodium-rich plagioclase (with more calcium than albite). [19th C.: from **oligo-** + Gk. *klasis* 'breaking.']

ol·i·go·nu·cle·o·tide /,äligō'n(y)ōōklēə,tīd/ ▶ **n.** Biochem. a polynucleotide whose molecules contain a relatively small number of nucleotides.

ol·i·go·pep·tide /,äligō'pep,tīd/ ▶ **n.** Biochem. a peptide whose molecules contain a relatively small number of amino-acid residues.

ol·i·gop·o·ly /,äli'gäpəlē/ ▶ **n.** (pl. **-lies**) a state of limited competition, in which a market is shared by a small number of producers or sellers. — **ol·i·gop·o·list** **n.** **ol·i·gop·o·lis·tic** /,äli,gäpə'listik/ **adj.** [19th C.: from **oligo-**, on the pattern of *monopoly*.]

ol·i·gop·so·ny /,äli'gäpsənē/ ▶ **n.** (pl. **-nies**) a state of the market in which only a small number of buyers exists for a product. — **ol·i·gop·so·nis·tic** /,äli,gäpsə'nistik/ **adj.** [1940s: from **oligo-** + Gk. *opsōnein* 'buy provisions,' on the pattern of *monopsony*.]

ol·i·go·sac·cha·ride /,äligō'sakə,rīd/ ▶ **n.** Biochem. a carbohydrate whose molecules are composed of a relatively small number of monosaccharide units.

ol·i·go·troph·ic /,äligō'trōfik; -'träfik/ ▶ **adj.** Ecol. (esp. of a lake) relatively low in plant nutrients and containing abundant oxygen in the deeper parts. Compare with **dystrophic, eutrophic**. — **ol·i·got·ro·phy** /,äli'gätrəfē/ **n.**

ol·i·gu·ri·a /,äli'gyŏŏrēə/ ▶ **n.** Med. the production of abnormally small amounts of urine. — **ol·igu·ric** **adj.**

o·li·o /'ōlēō/ ▶ **n.** (pl. **-os**) another term for **olla podrida**. ■ a miscellaneous collection of things. ■ a variety act or show. [17th C.: from Sp. *olla* 'stew,' from L. *olla* 'cooking pot.']

ol·i·va·ceous /,älə'vāshəs/ ▶ **adj.** tech. of a dusky yellowish green color; olive green.

ol·i·va·ry /'älə,verē/ ▶ **adj.** Anat. relating to or denoting each of the pair of oval bodies of nerve tissue on the medulla oblongata of the brain. [ME: from L. *olivarius* 'relating to olives.']

ol·ive /'äliv/ ▶ **n.** **1** a small oval fruit with a hard pit and bitter flesh, green when unripe and brownish black when ripe, used as food and as a source of oil. **2** (also **olive tree**) the widely cultivated evergreen tree (*Olea europaea*) that yields this fruit, native to warm regions of the Old World. The **olive family** (Oleaceae) also includes the ash, lilac, jasmine, and privet. ■ used in names of other trees that are related to the olive, resemble it, or bear similar fruit, e.g., **Russian olive**. **3** (also **olive green**) a grayish-green color like that of an unripe olive. ▶ **adj.** grayish-green, like an unripe olive. ■ (of the complexion) yellowish brown; sallow. [ME: via OFr. from L. *oliva*, from Gk. *elaia*, from *elaion* 'oil.']

ol·ive branch ▶ **n.** the branch of an olive tree, traditionally regarded as a symbol of peace (in allusion to the story of Noah in Gen. 8:1, in which a dove returns with an olive branch after the Flood). ■ an offer of reconciliation.

ol·ive drab ▶ **n.** a dull olive-green color, used in some military uniforms.

ol·ive oil ▶ **n.** an oil pressed from ripe olives, used in cooking, medicines, soap, etc.

Ol·i·ver /'älәvər/ the companion of Roland in the *Chanson de Roland* (see **Roland**).

O·liv·i·er /ə'livēā; ō'livi-/, Laurence Kerr, Baron Olivier of Brighton (1907–89), English actor and director. He performed all the major Shakespearean roles and was director of the National Theatre (1963–73).

ol·i·vine /'älə,vēn/ ▶ **n.** an olive-green or brown mineral occurring in basalt, peridotite, and other basic igneous rocks. It is a silicate containing varying proportions of magnesium, iron, and other elements. [18th C.: from L. *oliva* (see **olive**) + **-ine**[1].]

ol·la po·dri·da /,älə pə'drēdə; ,ô(l)yə/ ▶ **n.** a highly spiced Spanish-style stew containing a mixture of meat and vegetables. ■ any miscellaneous assortment or collection. [Sp., lit. 'rotten pot,' from L. *olla* 'jar' + *putridus* 'rotten.']

Ol·mec /'äl,mek; 'ōl-/ ▶ **n.** (pl. same or **-mecs**) **1** a member of a prehistoric people inhabiting the coast of Veracruz and western Tabasco on the Gulf of Mexico (*c.*1200–400 BC), who established what was probably the first Meso-American civilization. **2** a native people living in the same general area during the 15th and 16th centuries. [from Nahuatl *Olmecatl*, (pl.) *Olmeca*, lit. 'inhabitants of the rubber country.']

Olm·sted /'ōm,sted/, Frederick Law (1822–1903) US landscape architect. He designed Central Park in New York City, and the Capitol grounds in Washington, DC.

ol·o·gy /'äləjē/ ▶ **n.** (pl. **-gies**) informal, humorous a subject of study; a branch of knowledge. — **ol·o·gist** /-jist/ **n.**

-ology ▶ **comb. form** common form of **-logy**.

o·lo·ro·so /,ōlə'rōsō/ ▶ **n.** a dry or medium-dry Spanish sherry. [Sp., lit. 'fragrant.']

O·lym·pi·a /ə'limpēə; ō'lim-/ **1** a plain in Greece, in the western Peloponnese, site of the sanctuary of Zeus, where the original Olympic Games were held. **2** the capital of Washington, a port on Puget Sound; pop. 33,840.

O·lym·pi·ad /ō'limpē,ad; ə'lim-/ ▶ **n.** a celebration of the ancient or modern Olympic Games. ■ a period of four years between Olympic Games, used by the ancient Greeks in dating events. [via Fr. or L. from Gk. *Olumpias, Olumpiad-*, from *Olumpios*.]

O·lym·pi·an /ə'limpēən; ō'lim-/ ▶ **adj.** **1** associated with Mount Olympus in northeastern Greece, or with the Greek gods whose home was there. ■ resembling or appropriate to a god, esp. in superiority and aloofness. **2** [attrib.] relating to the ancient or modern Olympic Games. ▶ **n.** **1** any of the twelve Greek gods regarded as living on Olympus. ■ a person of great attainments or exalted position. **2** a competitor in the Olympic Games.

O·lym·pic /ə'limpik; ō'lim-/ ▶ **adj.** [attrib.] of or relating to the ancient city of Olympia or the Olympic Games: *an Olympic champion.* ▶ **n.** (**the Olympics**) the Olympic Games.

O·lym·pic Games (also **the O·lym·pics**) a modern sports festival held every four years in different venues, instigated by the Frenchman Baron de Coubertin (1863–1937) in 1896. The Winter Olympics and Summer Olympics are now held two years apart. ■ an ancient Greek festival with athletic, literary, and musical competitions, held at Olympia every four years traditionally from 776 BC until abolished by the Roman emperor Theodosius I in AD 393.

Olym·pic Peninsula a region in northwestern Washington, on the Pacific Ocean and Juan de Fuca Strait.

O·lym·pic-sized (also **O·lym·pic-size**) ▶ **adj.** (of a swimming pool or other sports venue) of the dimensions prescribed for modern Olympic competitions.

O·lym·pus /ə'limpəs; ō'lim-/ Gk. Mythol. the home of the twelve principal gods, identified in later antiquity with Mount Olympus in northern Greece.

O·lym·pus, Mount **1** a mountain in northern Greece, rising to 9,570 feet (2,917 m). **2** the highest mountain in Cyprus, rising to 6,400 feet (1,951 m).

OM ▶ **abbr.** (in the UK) Order of Merit.

Om /ōm/ ▶ **n.** Hinduism & Tibetan Buddhism a mystic syllable, considered the most sacred mantra.

-oma ▶ **suffix** (forming nouns) denoting tumors and other abnormal growths: *carcinoma.* [mod. L., from a Gk. suffix denoting the result of verbal action.]

O·ma·ha[1] /'ōmə,hô; -,hä/ a city in eastern Nebraska; pop. 390,007.

O·ma·ha[2] ▶ **n.** (pl. same or **-has**) **1** a member of an American Indian people of northeastern Nebraska. **2** the Siouan language of this people. ▶ **adj.** of or relating to this people or their language. [from Omaha *uma-ha-* 'upstream.']

Oma·ha Beach the name used during the D-Day landing in June 1944 for one part of the Normandy coast where US troops landed.

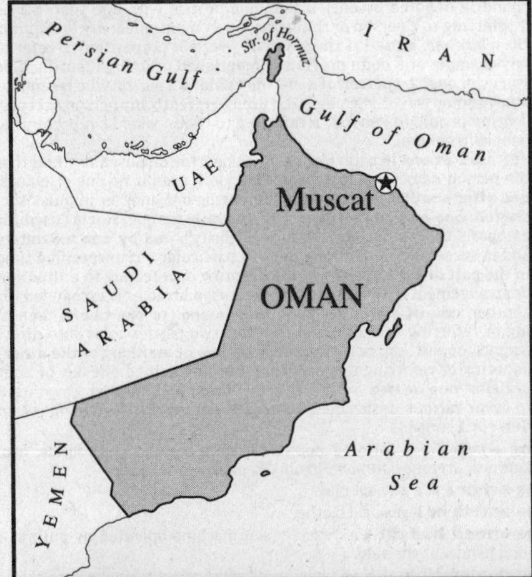

Oman

Official name: Sultanate of Oman
Location: Middle East, at the eastern corner of the Arabian peninsula
Area: 82,100 square miles (212,500 sq km)
Population: 2,903,000
Capital: Muscat
Languages: Arabic (official), English, Baluchi, Urdu, Indian dialects
Currency: Omani rial

O·man /ō'män/ a country at the eastern corner of the Arabian peninsula. *See box.* — **O·ma·ni** /ō'mänē/ **adj. & n.**

O·man, Gulf of an inlet of the Arabian Sea.

O·mar /'ō,mär/, Mullah Mohammad (1962–) head of the former Taliban government in Afghanistan. In 1996, Muslim clergymen named him the new Amirul Mumineen ("Supreme Leader of the Muslims"), and he established the Taliban regime with its headquarters at Kandahar.

O·mar Khay·yám /kī'äm; -'am/ (died 1123), Persian poet, mathematician, and astronomer. *The Rubáiyát of Omar Khayyám* was translated into English in 1859.

o·ma·sum /ō'māsəm/ ▶ **n.** (pl. **-sa** /-sə/) Zool. the muscular third stomach of a ruminant, between the reticulum and the abomasum. [18th C.: from L., lit. 'bullock's tripe.']

O·may·yad /ō'mī(y)ad/ var. of UMAYYAD.

OMB ▶ **abbr.** (in the federal government) Office of Management and Budget.

om·bre /'ämbər/ ▶ **n.** a trick-taking card game for three people using a pack of forty cards, popular in Europe in the 17th–18th centuries. [from Sp. *hombre* 'man.']

om·bré /'äm,brā/ ▶ **adj.** (of a fabric) having a dyed, printed, or woven design in which the color is graduated from light to dark. [Fr., past part. of *ombrer* 'to shade.']

om·buds·man /'ämbədzmən; -,bŏŏdz-/ ▶ **n.** (pl. **-men**) an official appointed to investigate individuals' complaints against maladministration, esp. that of public authorities. [1950s: from Swed., 'legal representative.']

om·buds·per·son /'ämbədz,pərsən; -bŏŏdz-/ ▶ **n.** a person acting as an ombudsman.

Om·dur·man /,ämdər'män/ a city in central Sudan; pop. 229,000.

-ome ▶ **suffix** esp. Biol. forming nouns denoting objects or parts having a specified nature: *rhizome.* [var. form of **-OMA**.]

o·me·ga /ō'māgə; ō'mē-; ō'megə/ ▶ **n.** the twenty-fourth, and last, letter of the Greek alphabet (Ω, ω), transliterated as 'o' or 'ō.' ■ the last of a series; the final development. ▶ **symb.** ■ (Ω) ohm(s): *a 100Ω resistor.* [from Gk. *ō mega* 'big O.']

o·me·ga-3 fat·ty ac·id ▶ **n.** an unsaturated fatty acid of a kind occurring chiefly in fish oils, with three double bonds at particular positions in the hydrocarbon chain.

om·e·let /'äm(ə)lit/ (also **om·e·lette**) ▶ **n.** a dish of beaten eggs cooked in a frying pan until firm, often with a filling added while cooking, and usually served folded over. [Fr. *omelette*, earlier *amelette*, alt. of *alumette*, var. of *alumelle*, from *lemele* 'knife blade,' from L. *lamella*.]

o·men /'ōmən/ ▶ **n.** an event regarded as a portent of good or evil. ■ prophetic significance: *a bird of evil omen.* [16th C.: from L.]

o·men·tum /ō'mentəm/ ▶ **n.** (pl. **-ta** /-tə/) Anat. a fold of peritoneum connecting the stomach with other abdominal organs. — **o·men·tal** /ō'mentl/ **adj.** [ME: from L.]

o·mer /'ōmər; 'ōmer/ ▶ **n.** **1** an ancient Hebrew dry measure, the tenth part of an ephah. **2** (**Omer**) Judaism a sheaf of corn or omer of grain presented as an offering on the second day of Passover. ■ the period of 49 days between this day and Shavuoth (Pentecost). [from Heb. *ōmer*.]

o·mer·tà /ō'me(ə)rtə; ,ōmer'tä/ ▶ **n.** (as practiced by the Mafia) a code of silence about criminal activity and a refusal to give evidence to authorities.

om·i·cron /'ämi,krän; 'ōmi-/ ▶ **n.** the fifteenth letter of the Greek alphabet (Ο, ο), transliterated as 'o.' [from Gk. *o mikron* 'little O.']

om·i·nous /'ämənəs/ ▶ **adj.** giving the impression that something bad or unpleasant is going to happen. — **om·i·nous·ly adv. om·i·nous·ness n.** [16th C.: from L. *ominosus*, from *omen, omin-* 'omen.']

o·mis·sion /ō'misʜən/ ▶ **n.** someone or something that has been left out or excluded. ■ the action of excluding or leaving out someone or something. ■ a failure to do something, esp. something that one has a moral or legal obligation to do. — **o·mis·sive** /ō'misiv/ **adj.** [ME: from late L. *omissio(n-)*, from the v. *omittere* (see **OMIT**).]

o·mit /ō'mit/ ▶ **v.** (**o·mit·ted, o·mit·ting**) [trans.] (often **be omitted**) leave out or exclude (someone or something), either intentionally or forgetfully. ■ fail or neglect to do (something); leave undone: *the final rinse is omitted.* — **o·mis·si·ble** /ō'misəbəl/ **adj.** [ME: from L. *omittere*, from *ob-* 'down' + *mittere* 'let go.']

om·ma·tid·i·um /,ämə'tideəm/ ▶ **n.** (pl. **-tid·i·a** /-'tideə/) Entomol. each of the optical units that make up a compound eye of an insect. — **om·ma·tid·i·al** /-'tideəl/ **adj.** [19th C.: mod. L., from Gk. *ommatidion*, dimin. of *omma, ommat-* 'eye.']

om·mat·o·phore /ə'matə,fôr/ ▶ **n.** Zool. a part of an invertebrate animal, esp. a stalk or tentacle, that bears an eye. [19th C.: from Gk. *omma, ommat-* 'eye' + **-PHORE**.]

omni- ▶ **comb. form** all; of all things: *omniscient.* ■ in all ways or places: *omnicompetent | omnipresent.* [from L. *omnis* 'all.']

om·ni·bus /'ämnə,bəs/ ▶ **n.** **1** a volume containing several novels or other items previously published separately. **2** dated a bus. ▶ **adj.** comprising several items. [19th C.: via Fr. from L., lit. 'for all,' dative pl. of *omnis*.]

om·ni·di·rec·tion·al /,ämni,di'reksʜənl/ ▶ **adj.** Telecom. receiving signals from or transmitting in all directions.

om·ni·far·i·ous /,ämnə'fe(ə)rēəs/ ▶ **adj.** formal comprising or relating to all sorts or varieties. — **om·ni·far·i·ous·ly adv. om·ni·far·i·ous·ness n.**

om·nip·o·tent /äm'nipətənt/ ▶ **adj.** (of a deity) having unlimited power; able to do anything. ■ having ultimate power and influence. ▶ **n.** (**the Omnipotent**) God. — **om·nip·o·tence n. om·nip·o·tent·ly adv.** [ME: via OFr. from L. *omnipotent-* 'all-powerful.']

om·ni·pres·ent /,ämnə'preznt/ ▶ **adj.** (of God) present everywhere at the same time. ■ widely or constantly encountered; common or widespread: *the omnipresent threat of natural disasters.* — **om·ni·pres·ence n.**

om·ni·range /'ämni,rānj/ ▶ **n.** a navigation system in which short-range omnidirectional VHF transmitters serve as radio beacons.

om·nis·cient /äm'nisʜənt/ ▶ **adj.** knowing everything. — **om·nis·cience**

n. **om·nis·cient·ly** adv. [17th C.: from med. L. *omniscient-* 'all-knowing,' based on *scire* 'to know.']

om·ni·sex·u·al /ˌämniˈsekSHo͞oəl/ ▶ adj. involving or characterized by a diverse sexual propensity. — **om·ni·sex·u·al·i·ty** /-ˌsekSHo͞oˈalitē/ n.

om·ni·um-gath·er·um /ˌämnēəm ˈgaTHərəm/ ▶ n. a collection of miscellaneous people or things. [16th C.: mock Latin, from Latin *omnium* 'of all' and GATHER + the L. suffix *-um*.]

om·ni·vore /ˈämnəˌvôr/ ▶ n. an animal or person that eats food of both plant and animal origin. [19th C.: from Fr., from L. *omnivorus* 'omnivorous.']

om·niv·o·rous /ämˈniv(ə)rəs/ ▶ adj. (of an animal or person) feeding on food of both plant and animal origin. ■ taking in or using whatever is available: *an omnivorous reader.* — **om·niv·o·rous·ly** adv. **om·niv·o·rous·ness** n. [17th C.: from L. *omnivorus* + -OUS.]

o·moph·a·gy /ōˈmäfəjē/ (also **o·mo·pha·gia** /ˌōməˈfāj(ē)ə/) ▶ n. the eating of raw food, esp. raw meat. — **o·mo·phag·ic** /ˌōməˈfajik/ adj. **o·moph·a·gist** n. **o·moph·a·gous** /-gəs/ adj. [18th C.: from Gk. *ōmophagia*, from *ōmos* 'raw' + *-phagia* (from *phagein* 'eat').]

O·mot·ic /ōˈmätik/ ▶ n. a subfamily of Afro-Asiatic languages spoken in Ethiopia, with over thirty members. ▶ adj. denoting or belonging to this subfamily. [1970s: from *Omo*, river in Ethiopia.]

omphalo- ▶ comb. form relating to the navel. [from Gk. *omphalos* 'navel.']

om·pha·los /ˈämfələs/ ▶ n. (pl. **-loi** /-ˌloi/) literary the center or hub of something. ■ a rounded stone (esp. that at Delphi) representing the navel of the earth in ancient Greek mythology. [Gk., lit. 'navel.']

Omsk /ômsk/ a city in south central Russia; pop. 1,159,000.

ON[1] ▶ abbr. Ontario (in official postal use).

ON[2] ▶ abbr. Old Norse.

on /än; ôn/ ▶ prep. **1** physically in contact with and supported by (a surface): *on the table was a water jug.* ■ located somewhere in the general surface area of (a place): *the house on the corner.* ■ as a result of accidental physical contact with. ■ supported by (a part of the body). ■ so as to be supported or held by. ■ in the possession of (the person referred to). **2** forming a distinctive or marked part of (the surface of something): *a smile on her face.* **3** having (the thing mentioned) as a topic. ■ having (the thing mentioned) as a basis. **4** as a member of (a committee, jury, or other body). **5** having (the place or thing mentioned) as a target. ■ having (the thing mentioned) as a target for visual focus: *her eyes were fixed on his dark profile.* **6** having (the thing mentioned) as a medium for transmitting or storing information. ■ being broadcast by (a radio or television channel). **7** in the course of (a journey). ■ while traveling in (a public conveyance): *John got some sleep on the plane.* ■ on to (a public conveyance) with the intention of traveling in it: *we got on the train.* **8** indicating the day or part of a day during which an event takes place: *reported on September 26.* ■ at the time of: *she was booed on arriving home.* **9** engaged in: *his attendant was out on errands.* **10** regularly taking (a drug or medicine): *on morphine.* **11** paid for by: *the drinks are on me.* **12** added to: *a few cents on the electric bill.* ▶ adv. **1** in contact with and supported by a surface. ■ (of clothing) being worn by a person: *she had her coat on.* **2** indicating continuation of a movement or action. ■ further forward; in an advanced state: *later on.* **3** (of an event) taking place or being presented. ■ due to take place as planned. **4** (of a power supply) functioning.

– PHRASES **on and off** intermittently. **on and on** continually; at tedious length. **what are you on?** informal said to express incredulity at someone's behavior, with the implication that they must be under the influence of drugs. **you're on** informal said by way of accepting a challenge or bet. [OE *on, an*; rel. to Ger. *an*, Gk. *ana*.]

-on ▶ suffix Physics, Biochem., & Chem. forming nouns: **1** denoting subatomic particles or quanta: *neutron.* **2** denoting molecular units: *codon.* **3** denoting substances: *interferon.* [sense 1 from ION; sense 3 is on the pattern of words such as *cotton* or from Ger. *-on*.]

on·a·ger /ˈänəjər/ ▶ n. an animal of a race of the Asian wild ass (*Equus hemionus onager*) native to northern Iran. [ME: via L. from Gk. *onagros*, from *onos* 'ass' + *agrios* 'wild.']

on-air ▶ adj. broadcasting: *his on-air antics.*

o·nan·ism /ˈōnəˌnizəm/ ▶ n. formal **1** masturbation. **2** coitus interruptus. — **o·nan·ist** n. **o·nan·is·tic** /ˌōnəˈnistik/ adj. [18th C.: from Fr. *onanisme* or mod. L. *onanismus*, from the biblical story of Onan (Gen. 38:8).]

O·nas·sis[1] /ōˈnasis/, Aristotle Socrates (1906–75), Greek businessman. He owned a shipping empire and founded Olympic Airways in 1957.

O·nas·sis[2], Jacqueline Lee Bouvier Kennedy (1929–94), US first lady 1961–63; wife of President Kennedy 1953–63 and of Aristotle Onassis 1968–75; known as **Jackie O.**

on-board ▶ adj. [attrib.] **1** available or situated on a ship, aircraft, or other vehicle. **2** Comput. denoting or controlled from a facility or feature incorporated into the main circuit board of a computer or computerized device.

once /wəns/ ▶ adv. **1** on one occasion or for one time. ■ [usu. with negative or **if**] at all; on even one occasion (used for emphasis): *he never once complained.* **2** at some time in the past; formerly. ▶ conj. as soon as; when.

– PHRASES **all at once 1** without warning; suddenly. **2** all at the same time. **at once 1** immediately. **2** simultaneously. **for once** (or **this once**) on this occasion only, as an exception. **once again** (or **more**) one more time. **once and for all** (or **once for all**) now and for the last time; finally. **once bitten, twice shy** see BITE. **once** (or **every once**) **in a while** from time to time; occasionally. **once or twice** a few times. **once upon a time** at some time in the past (used as a conventional opening of a story). ■ formerly. [ME *ones*, genitive of ONE.]

once-o·ver ▶ n. informal a rapid inspection or search. ■ a piece of work that is done quickly.

on·cho·cer·ci·a·sis /ˌäNGkōsərˈkīəsis/ ▶ n. technical term for RIVER BLINDNESS. [20th C.: from mod. L. *Onchocerca* (from Gk. *onkos* 'barb' + *kerkos* 'tail') + -IASIS.]

onco- ▶ comb. form of or relating to tumors: *oncology.* [from Gk. *onkos* 'mass.']

on·co·gene /ˈäNGkəˌjēn/ ▶ n. Med. a gene that in certain circumstances transforms a cell into a tumor cell.

on·co·gen·ic /ˌäNGkəˈjenik/ ▶ adj. Med. causing development of a tumor or tumors. — **on·co·gen·e·sis** /-ˈjenisis/ n. **on·co·ge·nic·i·ty** /-jəˈnisitē/ n.

on·col·o·gy /änˈkäləjē; äNG-/ ▶ n. Med. the study and treatment of tumors. — **on·co·log·ic** adj. **on·co·log·i·cal** /-kəˈläjikəl/ adj. **on·col·o·gist** /-ˈkäləjist/ n.

on·com·ing /ˈänˌkəmiNG; ˈôn-/ ▶ adj. [attrib.] approaching; moving toward. ■ fig. due to happen or occur in the near future. ▶ n. the fact of being about to happen in the near future.

one /wən/ ▶ cardinal number the lowest cardinal number; half of two; 1: *there's only room for one person.* (Roman numeral: **i**, **I**) ■ a single person or thing, viewed as taking the place of a group. ■ single; just one as opposed to any more or to none at all (used for emphasis). ■ denoting a particular item of a pair or number of items. ■ denoting a particular but unspecified occasion or period. ■ used before a name to denote a person who is not familiar or has not been previously mentioned; a certain: *he worked for one Mr. Ming.* ■ informal a noteworthy example of (used for emphasis). ■ identical; the same: *one common standard.* ■ identical and united; forming a unity: *the two things are one and the same.* ■ one year old. ■ one o'clock. ■ informal a one-dollar bill. ■ informal an alcoholic drink: *a cool one after a hot day.* ■ informal a joke or story: *the one about the chicken farmer.* ■ a size of garment or other merchandise denoted by one. ■ a domino or dice with one spot. ▶ pron. **1** referring to a person or thing previously mentioned: *her best apron, the white one.* ■ used as the object of a verb or preposition to refer to any example of a noun previously mentioned or easily identified: *do you want one?* **2** a person of a specified kind. ■ a person who is remarkable in some way. **3** [third person sing.] used to refer to any person as representing people in general. ■ referring to the speaker as representing people in general.

– PHRASES **at one** in agreement or harmony. **for one** used to stress that the person named holds the specified view, even if no one else does. **one after another** (or **the other**) following one another in quick succession. **one and all** everyone. **one and only** unique; single (used for emphasis or as a designation of a celebrity). **one by one** separately and in succession; singly. **one day** at a particular but unspecified time in the past or future. **one-for-one** denoting or referring to a situation or arrangement in which one thing corresponds to or is exchanged for another. **one of a kind** see KIND[1]. **one-on-one** (or **one-to-one**) denoting or referring to a situation in which two parties come into direct contact, opposition, or correspondence. **one or another** (or **the other**) denoting or referring to a particular but unspecified one out of a set of items. **one or two** informal a few. **one thing and another** informal used to cover various unspecified matters, events, or tasks. [OE *ān*, rel. to Ger. *ein*, L. *unus*.]

-one ▶ suffix Chem. forming nouns denoting various compounds, esp. ketones: *acetone* | *quinone.* [from Gk. patronymic *-ōnē*.]

one-act·er ▶ n. a one-act play.

one an·oth·er ▶ pron. each other.

one-armed ban·dit ▶ n. informal a slot machine operated by pulling a long handle at the side.

one-di·men·sion·al ▶ adj. having or relating to a single dimension: *one-dimensional curves.* ■ lacking depth; superficial. — **one-di·men·sion·al·i·ty** n.

one-down ▶ adj. informal at a psychological disadvantage in a game or a competitive situation.

O·ne·ga, Lake /ōˈnegə; əˈnyegə/ a lake in northwestern Russia, the second largest in Europe.

one-horse ▶ adj. drawn by or using a single horse. ■ informal small and insignificant: *a one-horse town.*

– PHRASES **one-horse race** a contest in which one candidate or competitor is clearly superior to all the others and seems certain to win.

O·nei·da /ōˈnīdə/ ▶ n. (pl. same or **-das**) **1** a member of an American Indian people formerly inhabiting upper New York state, one of the Five Nations. **2** the Iroquoian language of this people. ▶ adj. of or relating to this people or their language. [from Oneida *oneyóte'* 'erected stone.']

O'Neill /ōˈnēl/, Eugene Gladstone (1888–1953), US playwright. His plays include *Desire under the Elms* (1924) and *The Iceman Cometh* (1946). Nobel Prize for Literature (1936).

o·nei·ric /ōˈnīrik/ ▶ adj. formal of or relating to dreams or dreaming. [19th C.: from Gk. *oneiros* 'dream' + -IC.]

oneiro- ▶ comb. form relating to dreams or dreaming: *oneiromancy.* [from Gk. *oneiros* 'dream.']

o·nei·ro·man·cy /ōˈnīrəˌmansē/ ▶ n. the interpretation of dreams in order to foretell the future.

one-lin·er ▶ n. informal a short joke or witty remark.

one-lung·er /ˈləNGər/ ▶ n. informal a single-cylinder engine. ■ a vehicle or boat driven by such an engine.

one-man ▶ **adj.** [attrib.] involving, done, or operated by only one person: *a one-man show.*

one-man band ▶ **n.** a street entertainer who plays several instruments at the same time. ■ a person who runs a business alone.

one·ness /ˈwən-nis/ ▶ **n.** **1** the fact or state of being unified or whole, though composed of two or more parts. ■ identity or harmony with someone or something. **2** the fact or state of being one in number: *belief in the oneness of God.*

one-night stand ▶ **n. 1** informal (also **one-night·er**) a sexual relationship lasting only one night. ■ a person with whom one has such a relationship. **2** a single performance of a play or show in a particular place.

one-off informal, esp. Brit. ▶ **adj.** done, made, or happening only once and not repeated. ▶ **n.** something done, made, or happening only once, not as part of a regular sequence. ■ a person who is unusual or unique, esp. in an admirable way.

one-piece ▶ **adj.** [attrib.] (esp. of an article of clothing) made or consisting of a single piece. ▶ **n.** an article of clothing made or consisting of a single piece.

on·er·ous /ˈōnərəs; ˈänərəs/ ▶ **adj.** (of a task, duty, or responsibility) involving a burdensome amount of effort and difficulty. ■ Law involving heavy obligations. — **on·er·ous·ly adv. on·er·ous·ness n.** [ME: from OFr. *onereus*, from L. *onerosus*, from *onus, oner-* 'burden.']

one·self /wənˈself/ (also **one's self**) ▶ **pron.** [third person sing.] **1** [reflexive] a person's own self: *it is difficult to wrest oneself away.* **2** [emphatic] used to emphasize that one does something individually or unaided: *the idea of publishing a book oneself.* **3** in one's normal and individual state of body or mind; not influenced by others: *freedom to be oneself.*
– PHRASES **by oneself** see **BY.**

one-sid·ed ▶ **adj.** unfairly giving or dealing with only one side of a contentious issue or question; biased or partial. ■ (of a contest or conflict) having a gross inequality of strength or ability between the opponents. ■ (of a relationship or conversation) having all the effort or activity coming from one participant. ■ having or occurring on one side of something only. — **one-sid·ed·ly adv. one-sid·ed·ness n.**

one-star ▶ **adj.** (esp. of a hotel or restaurant) given one star in a grading system in which this denotes the lowest class or quality. ■ (in the US armed forces) having or denoting the rank of brigadier general, distinguished by one star on the uniform.

one-step ▶ **n.** a vigorous kind of ballroom dance in duple time.

one-stop ▶ **adj.** (of a store or other business) capable of supplying all a customer's needs within a particular range of goods or services: *one-stop shopping.*

one-time (also **one·time**) ▶ **adj. 1** former. **2** of or relating to a single occasion: *a one-time charge.*

one-track mind ▶ **n.** used in reference to a person whose thoughts are preoccupied with one subject or interest.

one-two ▶ **n.** a pair of punches in quick succession, esp. with alternate hands: [as adj.] *a one-two punch.*

one up informal ▶ **adj.** having a psychological advantage over someone. ▶ **v.** [trans.] **(one-up)** do better than (someone): *he one-upped the interrogator.*

one-up·man·ship /ˈwən ˈəpmən,SHip/ ▶ **n.** informal the technique or practice of gaining a feeling of superiority over another person.

one-way ▶ **adj.** moving or allowing movement in one direction only. ■ (of a road or system of roads) along which traffic may pass in one direction only. ■ (of a ticket) allowing a person to travel to a place but not back again. ■ (of glass or a mirror) seen as a mirror from one side but transparent from the other. ■ denoting a relationship in which all the action or contribution of a particular kind comes from only one member.

one-wom·an ▶ **adj.** involving, done, or operated by only one woman.

one-world ▶ **adj.** of, relating to, or holding the view that the world's inhabitants are interdependent and should behave accordingly. — **one-world·er n. one-world·ism n.**

on-glide ▶ **n.** Phonet. a glide produced just before the articulation of another speech sound. Compare with **OFF-GLIDE.**

on·go·ing /ˈän,gōiNG; ˈôn-/ ▶ **adj.** continuing; still in progress. — **on·go·ing·ness n.**

ONI ▶ **abbr.** Office of Naval Intelligence.

on·ion /ˈənyən/ ▶ **n. 1** an edible bulb with a pungent taste and smell, composed of several concentric layers, used in cooking. **2** the plant (*Allium cepa*) of the lily family that produces this bulb, with long rolled or straplike leaves and spherical heads of greenish-white flowers.
– PHRASES **know one's onions** informal be very knowledgeable about something. — **on·ion·y adj.** [ME: from OFr. *oignon*, based on L. *unio(n-)*, denoting a kind of onion.]

on·ion dome ▶ **n.** a dome that bulges in the middle and rises to a point, used esp. in Russian church architecture. — **on·ion-domed adj.**

on·ion·skin /ˈənyən,skin/ (also **onionskin paper**) ▶ **n.** very fine smooth translucent paper.

on·li·est /ˈōnlē-ist/ ▶ **adj.** dialectal or humorous emphatic form of **ONLY.**

on·line /ˈänlīn; ˈôn-/ (also **on-line**) Comput. ▶ **adj.** controlled by or connected to another computer or to a network. ■ connected to the Internet or World Wide Web. ▶ **adv.** (also **on line**) **1** while so connected or under computer control. ■ with processing of data carried out simultaneously with its production. **2** in or into operation or existence.

on·look·er /ˈän,lo͝okər; ˈôn-/ ▶ **n.** a nonparticipating observer; a spectator. — **on·look·ing adj.**

on·ly /ˈōnlē/ ▶ **adv. 1** and no one or nothing more besides; solely or exclusively: *there are only a limited number of tickets available.* ■ no more than (implying that more was hoped for or expected); merely: *she was still only in her mid-thirties.* ■ no longer ago than: *discovered only last year.* ■ not until: *a final report reached him only on May 15.* **2** [with infin.] with the negative or unfortunate result that: *she turned into the parking lot, only to find it full.* ■ [with modal] inevitably, although unfortunate or undesirable: *rebellion will only bring unhappiness.* ▶ **adj.** [attrib.] alone of its or their kind; single or solitary: *he was an only child.* ■ alone deserving consideration: *it's the only place to be seen these days.* ▶ **conj.** informal except that; but for the fact that: *he is still a young man, only he seems older.*
– PHRASES **only just** by a very small margin; almost not: *it survived the earthquake, but only just.* ■ very recently. **only too ——** used to emphasize that something is the case to an extreme or regrettable extent: *you should be only too glad to be rid of him.* [OE *ānlic* (adj.) (see **ONE, -LY**[1]).]

on-off ▶ **adj. 1** (of a switch) having two positions, "on" and "off." **2** (of a relationship) not continuous or steady.

on·o·ma·si·ol·o·gy /,änə,māsēˈäləjē; -,māzē-/ ▶ **n.** the branch of knowledge that deals with terminology, in particular contrasting terms for similar concepts. Compare with **SEMASIOLOGY.** — **on·o·ma·si·o·log·i·cal** /-əˈläjikəl/ **adj.** [20th C.: from Gk. *onomasia* 'term' + **-LOGY.**]

on·o·mast /ˈänə,mast/ ▶ **n.** a person who studies proper names, esp. personal names. [1980s: back-form. from **ONOMASTIC.**]

on·o·mas·tic /,änəˈmastik/ ▶ **adj.** of or relating to the study of the history and origin of proper names. [16th C.: from Gk. *onomastikos*, from *onoma* 'name.']

on·o·mas·tics /,änəˈmastiks/ ▶ **plural n.** [usu. treated as sing.] the study of the history and origin of proper names, esp. personal names.

on·o·mat·o·poe·ia /,änə,matəˈpēə; -,mätə-/ ▶ **n.** the formation of a word from a sound associated with what is named (e.g., *cuckoo, sizzle*). ■ the use of such words for rhetorical effect. — **on·o·mat·o·poe·ic** /-ˈpē-ik/ or **on·o·mat·o·po·et·ic** /-pōˈetik/ **adj. on·o·mat·o·poe·i·cal·ly** /-ˈpē-ik(ə)lē/ or **on·o·mat·o·po·et·i·cal·ly** /-pōˈetik(ə)lē/ **adv.** [16th C.: via late L. from Gk. *onomatopoiia* 'word-making,' from *onoma, onomat-* 'name' + *-poios* 'making' (from *poiein* 'to make').]

On·on·da·ga /,änənˈdôgə; ,ōnən-; -ˈdägə/ ▶ **n.** (pl. same or **-gas**) **1** a member of an Iroquois people, one of the Five Nations, formerly inhabiting an area near Syracuse, New York. **2** the Iroquoian language of this people. ▶ **adj.** of or relating to this people or their language. [from the Onondaga name of their main settlement, lit. 'on the hill.']

on-ramp ▶ **n.** a lane for traffic entering a turnpike or freeway.

on-road ▶ **adj.** denoting or relating to events or conditions on a road, esp. a vehicle's performance.

on·rush /ˈän,rəSH; ˈôn-/ ▶ **n.** a surging rush forward: *the onrush of the sea.* ▶ **v.** [intrans.] [usu. as adj.] **(onrushing)** move forward in a surging rush: *the onrushing white water.*

on-screen (also **on screen** or **on·screen**) ▶ **adj. & adv.** shown or appearing in a movie or television program. ■ making use of or performed with the aid of a video screen.

on·set /ˈän,set; ˈôn-/ ▶ **n.** the beginning of something, esp. something unpleasant. ■ archaic a military attack.

on·shore /ˈänˈSHôr; ˈôn-/ ▶ **adj. & adv.** situated or occurring on land: [as adj.] *an onshore oil field.* ■ (esp. of the direction of the wind) from the sea toward the land.

on·side /ˈänˈsīd; ˈôn-/ ▶ **adj. & adv.** (of a player, esp. in soccer or hockey) occupying a position on the field where playing the ball or puck is allowed; not offside.

on·side kick (also **on·sides kick**) ▶ **n.** Football an intentionally short kickoff that travels forward the required distance of 10 yards, which the kicking team can attempt to recover.

on-site ▶ **adj. & adv.** taking place or available on a particular site or premises.

on·slaught /ˈän,slôt; ˈôn-/ ▶ **n.** a fierce or destructive attack. ■ a large quantity of people or things that is difficult to cope with. [17th C. (also in the form *anslaight*): from MDu. *aenslag*, from *aen* 'on' + *slag* 'blow.']

on·stage /ˈänˈstāj; ˈôn-/ (also **on-stage**) ▶ **adj. & adv.** (in a theater) on the stage and so visible to the audience.

on-stream ▶ **adv.** in or into industrial production or useful operation. ▶ **adj.** of or relating to normal industrial production.

Ont. ▶ **abbr.** Ontario.

-ont ▶ **comb. form** Biol. denoting an individual or cell of a specified type: *schizont.* [from Gk. *ont-* 'being,' pres. part. of *einai* 'be.']

on tar·get ▶ **adj. & adv.** accurate; hitting a target or achieving an aim: *Saturday's forecast was on target.*

On·tar·i·o[1] /änˈte(ə)rē,ō/ a province in eastern Canada, between Hudson Bay and the Great Lakes; pop. 9,914,200; capital, Toronto. — **On·tar·i·an** /-ēən/ **adj. & n.**

On·tar·io[2] a city in southwestern California; pop. 133,179.

On·tar·i·o, Lake the smallest of the Great Lakes.

on·tic /ˈäntik/ ▶ **adj.** Philos. of or relating to entities and the facts about them; relating to real as opposed to phenomenal existence. [1940s: from Gk. *ōn, ont-* 'being' + **-IC.**]

on·to /ˈän,to͞o; ˈôn-/ ▶ **prep. 1** moving to a location on (the surface of something): *they went up onto the ridge.* **2** moving aboard (a public conveyance) with the intention of traveling in it: *we got onto the train.*
– PHRASES **be onto someone** informal be close to discovering the truth about an illegal or undesirable activity that someone is engaging in. **be onto something** informal have an idea or information that is likely to lead to an important discovery.

on·to·gen·e·sis /,äntəˈjenəsis/ ▶ **n.** Biol. the development of an individual organism or anatomical or behavioral feature from the earliest stage to maturity. Compare with PHYLOGENESIS. — **on·to·ge·net·ic** /-jəˈnetik/ **adj.** **on·to·ge·net·i·cal·ly** /-jəˈnetik(ə)lē/ **adv.** [19th C.: from Gk. *ōn, ont-* 'being' + *genesis* 'birth.']

on·tog·e·ny /änˈtäjənē/ ▶ **n.** the branch of biology that deals with ontogenesis. Compare with PHYLOGENY. ■ another term for ONTOGENESIS. — **on·to·gen·ic** /,äntəˈjenik/ **adj.** **on·to·gen·i·cal·ly** /,äntəˈjenik(ə)lē/ **adv.** [19th C.: from Gk. *ōn, ont-* 'being' + -GENY.]

on·to·log·i·cal ar·gu·ment /,äntəˈläjikəl/ ▶ **n.** Philos. the argument that God, being defined as most great or perfect, must exist, since a God who exists is greater than a God who does not. Compare with COSMOLOGICAL ARGUMENT and TELEOLOGICAL ARGUMENT.

on·tol·o·gy /änˈtäləjē/ ▶ **n.** the branch of metaphysics dealing with the nature of being. — **on·to·log·i·cal** /,äntəˈläjikəl/ **adj.** **on·to·log·i·cal·ly** /,äntəˈläjik(ə)lē/ **adv.** **on·tol·o·gist n.** [18th C.: from mod. L. *ontologia*, from Gk. *ōn, ont-* 'being' + -LOGY.]

o·nus /ˈōnəs/ ▶ **n.** (usu. as **the onus**) used to refer to something that is one's duty or responsibility: ***the onus is on you to show that you have suffered.*** [17th C.: from L., lit. 'load or burden.']

on·ward /ˈänwərd; ˈôn-/ ▶ **adv.** (also **on·wards**) in a continuing forward direction; ahead. ■ forward in time. ■ fig. so as to make progress or become more successful. ▶ **adj.** going further rather than coming to an end or halt; moving forward.

on·yx /ˈäniks/ ▶ **n.** a semiprecious variety of agate with different colors in layers. [ME: from OFr. *oniche, onix*, via L. from Gk. *onux* 'fingernail or onyx.']

oo- ▶ **comb. form** Biol. relating to or denoting an egg or ovum. [from Gk. *ōion* 'egg.']

o·o·cyst /ˈōə,sist/ ▶ **n.** Zool. a cyst containing a zygote formed by a parasitic protozoan such as the malaria parasite.

o·o·cyte /ˈōə,sīt/ ▶ **n.** Biol. a cell in an ovary that may undergo meiotic division to form an ovum.

OOD ▶ **abbr.** ■ officer of the day. ■ officer of the deck.

oo·dles /ˈo͞odlz/ ▶ **plural n.** informal a very great number or amount of something.

oof /o͞of/ ▶ **exclam.** expressing discomfort, as from sudden exertion or a blow to one's body. [natural exclamation: 19th C.]

o·og·a·mous /ōˈägəməs/ ▶ **adj.** Biol. relating to or denoting reproduction by the union of mobile male and immobile female gametes. — **o·og·a·mous·ly adv.** **o·og·a·my** /-gəmē/ **n.**

o·o·gen·e·sis /,ōəˈjenəsis/ ▶ **n.** Biol. the production or development of an ovum.

o·o·go·ni·um /,ōəˈgōnēəm/ ▶ **n.** (pl. **-ni·a** /-nēə/) **1** Bot. the female sex organ of certain algae and fungi, typically a rounded cell or sac containing one or more oospheres. **2** Biol. an immature female reproductive cell that gives rise to primary oocytes by mitosis. — **o·o·go·ni·al** /-nēəl/ **adj.** [19th C.: from **oo-** 'of an egg' + Gk. *gonos* 'generation' + -IUM.]

ooh /o͞o/ ▶ **exclam.** used to express a range of emotions including surprise, delight, or pain. ▶ **n.** an utterance of such an exclamation. ▶ **v.** (**oohed, ooh·ing**) [intrans.] utter such an exclamation. [natural exclamation: 20th C.]

o·o·lite /ˈōə,līt/ ▶ **n.** Geol. limestone consisting of a mass of rounded grains (ooliths) made up of concentric layers. — **o·o·lit·ic** /,ōəˈlitik/ **adj.**

o·o·lith /ˈōə,liTH/ ▶ **n.** Geol. any of the rounded grains making up oolite.

o·ol·o·gy /ōˈäləjē/ ▶ **n.** the study or collecting of birds' eggs. — **o·o·log·i·cal** /,ōəˈläjikəl/ **adj.** **o·ol·o·gist n.**

oo·long /ˈo͞o,lôNG; -,läNG/ ▶ **n.** a dark-colored China tea made by fermenting the withered leaves to about half the degree usual for black teas. [19th C.: from Chin. *wūlóng*, lit. 'black dragon.']

oom·pah /ˈo͞om,pä; ˈo͝om-/ (also **oom·pah-pah**) informal ▶ **n.** used to refer to the rhythmical sound of deep-toned brass instruments in a band. ▶ **v.** (**-pahed, -pah·ing**) [intrans.] make such a sound. [19th C.: imitative.]

oomph /o͝omf; o͞omf/ (also **umph**) ▶ **n.** informal the quality of being exciting, energetic, or sexually attractive. [1930s: perh. imitative.]

-oon ▶ **suffix** forming nouns, originally from French words having the final stressed syllable *-on*: *buffoon.* [from L. *-onis*, sometimes via Ital. *-one.*]

o·o·pho·rec·to·my /,ōəfəˈrektəmē/ ▶ **n.** (pl. **-mies**) surgical removal of one or both ovaries; ovariectomy. [19th C.: from mod. L. *oophoron* 'ovary' (from Gk. *ōophoros* 'egg-bearing') + -ECTOMY.]

o·o·pho·ri·tis /,ōəfəˈrītis/ ▶ **n.** Med. inflammation of an ovary; ovaritis.

oops /o͝ops; o͞ops/ ▶ **exclam.** informal used to show recognition of a mistake or minor accident, often as part of an apology. [natural exclamation: 1930s.]

oop·sy-dai·sy ▶ **exclam.** var. of UPSY-DAISY.

Oort cloud /ôrt/ Astron. a spherical cloud of small rocky and icy bodies postulated to orbit the sun beyond the orbit of Pluto and up to 1.5 light years from the sun, and to be the source of comets. Its existence was proposed by J. H. Oort (1900–92).

o·o·sphere /ˈōə,sfi(ə)r/ ▶ **n.** Bot. the female reproductive cell of certain algae or fungi, which is formed in the oogonium and when fertilized becomes the oospore.

o·o·spore /ˈōə,spôr/ ▶ **n.** Bot. the thick-walled zygote of certain algae and fungi, formed by fertilization of an oosphere. Compare with ZYGOSPORE.

o·o·the·ca /,ōəˈTHēkə/ ▶ **n.** (pl. **-cae** /-,sē; -,kē/) Entomol. the egg case of cockroaches, mantises, and related insects. [19th C.: from **oo-** 'of an egg' + Gk. *thēkē* 'receptacle.']

o·o·tid /ˈōə,tid/ ▶ **n.** Biol. a haploid cell formed by the meiotic division of a secondary oocyte, esp. the ovum, as distinct from the polar bodies. [20th C.: from **oo-** 'egg.']

ooze[1] /o͞oz/ ▶ **v.** [intrans.] (of a fluid) slowly trickle or seep out of something; flow in a very gradual way: ***honey oozed out of the comb.*** ■ [intrans.] slowly exude or discharge a viscous fluid. ■ [trans.] fig. give a powerful impression of (a quality): ***he oozed charm and poise.*** ▶ **n. 1** the sluggish flow of a fluid. **2** an infusion of oak bark or other vegetable matter, used in tanning. — **ooz·y** /ˈo͞ozē/ **adj.** [OE *wōs* 'juice or sap.']

ooze[2] ▶ **n.** wet mud or slime, esp. that found at the bottom of a river, lake, or sea. ■ Geol. a deposit of white or gray calcareous matter largely composed of foraminiferan remains, covering extensive areas of the ocean floor. — **ooz·y adj.** [OE *wāse*; rel. to ON *veisa* 'stagnant pool.']

OP ▶ **abbr.** ■ observation post. ■ organophosphate(s). ■ (in the Roman Catholic Church) *Ordo Praedicatorum* Order of Preachers (Dominican).

op. (also **op.**) ▶ **abbr.** Music opus.

op /äp/ ▶ **n.** informal a surgical or other operation.

op- ▶ **suffix** var. of OB- assimilated before *p* (as in *oppress, oppugn*).

o.p. ▶ **abbr.** ■ (of a book) out of print.

o·pac·i·ty /ōˈpasitē/ ▶ **n.** the condition of lacking transparency or translucence; opaqueness. ■ fig. obscurity of meaning. [16th C.: from Fr. *opacité*, from L. *opacitas*, from *opacus* 'darkened.']

o·pah /ˈōpə/ ▶ **n.** a large deep-bodied fish (*Lampris guttatus*, family Lampridae) with a deep blue back, silvery belly, and crimson fins, living in deep oceanic waters. Also called MOONFISH. [18th C.: from a West Afr. word.]

o·pal /ˈōpəl/ ▶ **n.** a gemstone consisting of hydrated silica, typically semitransparent and showing varying colors against a pale or dark ground. [16th C.: from Fr. *opale* or L. *opalus*, prob. based on Sanskrit *upala* 'precious stone.']

o·pal·es·cent /,ōpəˈlesənt/ ▶ **adj.** showing varying colors as an opal does. — **o·pal·es·cence n.**

o·pal·ine /ˈōpə,lēn; -,līn/ ▶ **adj.** another term for OPALESCENT. ▶ **n.** another term for MILK GLASS. ■ translucent glass of a color other than white.

o·paque /ōˈpāk/ ▶ **adj.** (**o·paqu·er, o·paqu·est**) not able to be seen through; not transparent. ■ fig. (esp. of language) hard or impossible to understand; unfathomable. ▶ **n.** an opaque thing or substance. ■ Photog. a substance for producing opaque areas on negatives. — **o·paque·ly adv.** **o·paque·ness n.** [ME *opake*, from L. *opacus* 'darkened.']

op art (also **op·ti·cal art**) ▶ **n.** a form of abstract art that gives the illusion of movement by the precise use of pattern and color, or in which conflicting patterns emerge and overlap.

op. cit. /ˈäp ,sit/ ▶ **adv.** in the work already cited. [from L. *opere citato.*]

ope /ōp/ ▶ **adj.** & **v.** poetic/literary or archaic form of OPEN.

OPEC /ˈōpek/ ▶ **abbr.** Organization of the Petroleum Exporting Countries.

op-ed /ˈäp ,ed/ (also **Op-Ed**) ▶ **adj.** denoting or printed on the page opposite the editorial page in a newspaper, devoted to commentary, feature articles, etc.

o·pen /ˈōpən/ ▶ **adj. 1** allowing access, passage, or a view through an empty space; not closed or blocked up: ***the door was wide open.*** ■ (of a container) not fastened or sealed. ■ (of a garment or its fasteners) not buttoned or fastened. ■ (of the mouth or eyes) with lips or lids parted. ■ free from obstructions: ***the pass is kept open all year by snowplows.*** ■ informal (of a car or house) unlocked. ■ Phonet. (of a vowel) produced with a relatively wide opening of the mouth and the tongue kept low. ■ Phonet. (of a syllable) ending in a vowel. ■ (of the bowels) not constipated. ■ (of a game or style of play) characterized by action that is spread out over the field. **2** [attrib.] exposed to the air or to view; not covered. ■ (of an area of land) not covered with buildings or trees. ■ having spaces or gaps between elements: ***air circulates more readily through an open tree.*** ■ (of a fabric) loosely knitted or woven. ■ (of a team member in a game) unguarded and therefore able to receive a pass. ■ (of a goalmouth or other object of attack in a game) unprotected; vulnerable. ■ (of a boat) without a deck. ■ [predic.] (**open to**) likely to suffer from or be affected by; vulnerable or subject to: ***the system is open to abuse.*** ■ (of a town or city) officially declared to be undefended, and so immune under international law from bombardment. ■ with the outer edges or sides drawn away from each other; unfolded: ***open flowers.*** ■ (of a book or file) with the covers parted or the contents in view, allowing it to be read. ■ (of a hand) not clenched into a fist. ■ [as complement] damaged or injured by a deep cut in the surface: ***he had his arm slashed open.*** **3** [predic.] (of a store, place of entertainment, etc.) available for business. ■ (of a bank account) available for transactions. ■ (of a telephone line) ready to take calls. ■ (of a choice, offer, or opportunity) still available; such that people can take advantage of it. **4** (of a person) frank and communicative; not given to deception or concealment. ■ not concealed; manifest: ***open admiration.*** ■ [attrib.] (of conflict) fully developed and unconcealed: ***open war.***

■ involving no concealment, restraint, or deception: *open discussion.* **5** (of a question, case, or decision) not finally settled. ■ (of the mind) accessible to new ideas; unprejudiced. ■ [predic.] (**open to**) receptive to: *open to suggestions.* ■ [predic.] (**open to**) admitting of; making possible: *the message is open to interpretation.* ■ freely available or accessible; offered without restriction. ■ with no restrictions on those allowed to attend or participate: *an open audition.* ■ (also **Open**) (of an award or the competition for it) unrestricted as to who may qualify to compete. ■ (of a ticket) not restricted as to day of travel. **6** Music (of a string) allowed to vibrate along its whole length. ■ (of a pipe) unstopped at each end. ■ (of a note) sounded from an open string or pipe. **7** (of an electrical circuit) having a break in the conducting path. **8** Math. (of a set) not containing any of its limit points. ▶**v.** [trans.] **1** move or adjust (a door or window) so as to leave a space allowing access and view. ■ [intrans.] (of a door or window) be moved or adjusted to leave a space allowing access and view: *the door opened.* ■ undo or remove the lid, cover, or fastener of (a container) to get access to the contents: *he opened a bottle.* ■ remove the covers or wrapping from: *can we open the presents?* ■ part the lips or lids of (a mouth or eye). ■ [intrans.] (of the mouth or eyes) have the lips or lids parted in this way: *her eyes slowly opened.* ■ [intrans.] (of a wound) lose or lack its protective covering. ■ improve or make possible access to or passage through: *his government would open the border.* ■ cause evacuation of (the bowels). ■ [intrans.] (**open onto/into**) (of a room, door, or window) give access to: *French doors opened onto a balcony.* ■ [intrans.] (of a panorama) come into view; spread out before someone: *the views that open out below.* ■ Naut. achieve a clear view of (a place) by sailing past a headland or other obstruction. **2** spread out; unfold. ■ [intrans.] be unfolded; spread out to the full extent: *the flowers never opened.* ■ part the covers or display the contents of (a book or file) to read it. ■ [intrans.] (**open out**) become wider or more spacious: *the path opened out into a glade.* **3** allow public access to: *she raised $731 by opening her home and selling tea.* ■ make available: *the plan proposed to **open up** opportunities to immigrants.* ■ make more widely known; reveal. ■ [intrans.] (**open up**) become more communicative or confiding. ■ make (one's mind or heart) more receptive or sympathetic. **4** establish (a new business, movement, etc.). ■ [intrans.] (of an enterprise) be established or become ready for business. ■ [intrans.] (of a meeting etc.) formally begin. ■ officially declare (a building, road, etc.) to be complete and ready for use. ▶**n.** (**Open**) a championship or competition with no restrictions on who may qualify to compete. [OE, of Gmc. origin.]

o·pen air ▶**n.** a free or unenclosed space outdoors. ▶**adj.** positioned or taking place out of doors.

o·pen bar ▶**n.** a bar at a special function at which the drinks have been paid for by the host or are prepaid through an admission fee.

o·pen book ▶**n.** a person or thing that is easily understood or interpreted: *my life's an open book.*

o·pen chain ▶**n.** Chem. a molecular structure consisting of a chain of atoms with no closed rings.

o·pen cir·cuit ▶**n.** an electrical circuit that is not complete. — **o·pen-cir·cuit·ed** **adj.**

o·pen classroom ▶**n.** an approach to elementary education that emphasizes spacious classrooms where learning is informal, flexible, and individualized. ■ a spacious instructional area shared by several groups of elementary students that facilitates such an approach.

o·pen clus·ter ▶**n.** Astron. a relatively loose grouping of stars.

o·pen com·mun·ion ▶**n.** Christian Church communion made available to any Christian believer.

o·pen date ▶**n.** a future date for which no event has yet been arranged.

o·pen door ▶**n.** [in sing.] a free or unrestricted means of admission or access. ■ the policy or practice by which a country does not restrict the admission of immigrants or foreign imports.

o·pen-end·ed (also **o·pen-end**) ▶**adj.** having no determined limit or boundary. ■ (of a question or set of questions) allowing the formulation of any answer, rather than a selection from a set of possible answers. — **o·pen-end·ed·ness n.**

o·pen en·roll·ment ▶**n.** the unrestricted enrollment of students at schools, colleges, or universities.

o·pen·er /ˈōp(ə)nər/ ▶**n.** **1** [usu. with adj.] a device for opening something, esp. a container. **2** the first of a series of games, cultural events, etc. ■ the first point or points scored in a sports event. ■ a remark used as an excuse to initiate a conversation. ■ Poker (**openers**) a hand of sufficient value to allow the opening of betting.

– PHRASES **for openers** informal to start with; first of all: *for openers, the car is roomier.*

o·pen-eyed ▶**adj.** with the eyes open or wide open. ■ fig. clear-sighted; perceptive; fully aware. ■ with a sense of wonder, awe, etc.

o·pen-faced ▶**adj.** **1** having a frank or ingenuous expression. **2** (of a watch) having no cover other than the glass. ■ (also **o·pen-face**) (of a sandwich or pie) without an upper layer of bread or pastry.

o·pen·hand·ed /ˈōpənˈhandid/ ▶**adj.** **1** (of a blow) delivered with the palm of the hand. **2** giving freely; generous. — **o·pen·hand·ed·ly adv.** **o·pen·hand·ed·ness n.**

o·pen-heart·ed (also **o·pen·heart·ed**) ▶**adj.** expressing or displaying one's warm and kindly feelings without concealment. — **o·pen-heart·ed·ness n.**

o·pen-hearth ▶**adj.** denoting a steelmaking process in which the charge is laid on a hearth in a shallow furnace and heated by burning gas.

o·pen-heart sur·ger·y ▶**n.** surgery in which the heart is exposed and the blood made to bypass it.

o·pen house ▶**n.** a place or situation in which all visitors are welcome. ■ a day when members of the public are invited to visit a place or institution, esp. one to which they do not normally have access. ■ an informal reception or party during which one's home is open to visitors. ■ a time when real estate offered for sale is open to prospective buyers.

o·pen·ing /ˈōp(ə)niNG/ ▶**n.** **1** an aperture or gap, esp. one allowing access. ■ fig. an opportunity to achieve something. ■ an available job or position. **2** a beginning; an initial part. ■ a formal or official beginning. ■ the occasion of the first performance of a play, movie, etc., or the start of an exhibition, marked by a celebratory gathering. ■ the occasion of a public building being officially ready for use, marked by a ceremony. ■ Chess a recognized sequence of moves at the beginning of a game. ■ an attorney's preliminary statement of a case in a court of law. ■ an open piece of ground in a wooded area; a clearing. ▶**adj.** [attrib.] coming at the beginning of something; initial.

o·pen·ing night ▶**n.** the first night of a theatrical play or other entertainment.

o·pen in·ter·est ▶**n.** Finance the number of contracts or commitments outstanding in futures and options that are trading on an official exchange at any one time.

o·pen let·ter ▶**n.** a letter addressed to a particular person or group but intended for publication.

o·pen line ▶**n.** a means of easy access or communication. ▶**adj.** denoting a radio or television program in which the public can participate by telephone.

o·pen·ly /ˈōpənlē/ ▶**adv.** without concealment, deception, or prevarication, esp. where these might be expected; frankly or honestly.

o·pen mar·ket ▶**n.** (often **the open market**) an unrestricted market with free access by and competition of buyers and sellers.

o·pen mike ▶**n.** a microphone that is in use. ■ [often as adj.] a session in a club during which anyone is welcome to sing or perform stand-up comedy.

o·pen-mind·ed ▶**adj.** willing to consider new ideas; unprejudiced. — **o·pen-mind·ed·ly adv.** **o·pen-mind·ed·ness n.**

o·pen-mouthed ▶**adj.** with the mouth open, as in surprise or excitement: *open-mouthed astonishment.*

o·pen-necked ▶**adj.** (of a dress shirt) worn with the collar unbuttoned and without a tie.

o·pen out·cry ▶**n.** a system of financial trading in which dealers shout their bids and contracts aloud.

o·pen-pit ▶**adj.** denoting a method of mining in which coal or ore is extracted at or from a level near the earth's surface, rather than from shafts.

o·pen-plan ▶**adj.** (of a building or floor plan) having large open areas with few or no internal dividing walls.

o·pen pri·ma·ry ▶**n.** a primary election in which voters are not required to declare party affiliation.

o·pen ques·tion ▶**n.** a matter on which differences of opinion are possible; a matter not yet decided.

o·pen range ▶**n.** a large area of grazing land without fences or other barriers.

o·pen-reel ▶**adj.** (of an audiotape recorder) having reels of tape requiring individual threading, as distinct from a cassette.

o·pen road ▶**n.** a road or highway allowing easy travel, esp. one outside an urban area. ■ a path or course of action without care or hindrance.

o·pen sea ▶**n.** (usu. **the open sea**) an expanse of sea away from land.

o·pen sea·son ▶**n.** [in sing.] a period when restrictions on the hunting of certain types of wildlife are lifted. ■ a period when all restrictions on a particular activity or product are abandoned or ignored.

o·pen se·cret ▶**n.** a supposed secret that is in fact known to many people.

o·pen ses·a·me ▶**n.** a free or unrestricted means of admission or access. [from the magic formula in the tale of Ali Baba and the Forty Thieves (see **Ali Baba**).]

o·pen shop ▶**n.** a system whereby employees in a place of work are not required to join a labor union. ■ a place of work following such a system.

o·pen so·ci·e·ty ▶**n.** a society characterized by freedom of belief and wide dissemination of information.

o·pen-source ▶**adj.** Computing denoting software for which the original source code is made freely available and may be redistributed with or without modification.

o·pen stock ▶**n.** merchandise, esp. china, silverware, and glassware, sold in sets and kept in stock so that customers can purchase or replace individual pieces.

o·pen sys·tem ▶**n.** **1** Comput. a system in which the components and protocols conform to standards independent of a particular supplier. **2** Physics a material system in which mass or energy can be lost to or gained from the environment.

o·pen ver·dict ▶**n.** Law a verdict of a coroner's jury affirming the occurrence of a suspicious death but not specifying the cause.

o·pen·work /'ōpən,wərk/ ▶ **n.** [usu. as adj.] ornamental work in cloth, metal, leather, or other material with regular patterns of openings and holes.

o·pe·ra[1] /'äp(ə)rə/ ▶ **n.** a dramatic work in one or more acts, set to music for singers and instrumentalists. ■ such works as a genre of classical music. ■ a building for the performance of opera. [17th C.: from Ital., from L., lit. 'labor, work.']

o·pe·ra[2] /'ōpərə; 'op-/ plural form of OPUS.

op·er·a·ble /'äp(ə)rəbəl/ ▶ **adj.** 1 able to be used. 2 able to be treated by means of a surgical operation. — **op·er·a·bil·i·ty** /,äp(ə)rə'bilitē/ **n.**

op·er·a glass·es (or **op·er·a glass**) ▶ **plural n.** small binoculars for use at the opera or theater.

op·er·a·go·er /'äp(ə)rə,gōər/ ▶ **n.** a person who attends opera performances.

op·er·a hat ▶ **n.** a collapsible top hat.

op·er·a house ▶ **n.** a theater designed for the performance of opera.

op·er·and /'äpə,rand/ ▶ **n.** Math. the quantity on which an operation is to be done. [19th C.: from L. *operandum*, neut. gerundive of *operari*.]

op·er·ant /'äpərənt/ Psychol. ▶ **adj.** involving the modification of behavior by the reinforcing or inhibiting effect of its own consequences (instrumental conditioning). ▶ **n.** an item of behavior that is initially spontaneous, rather than a response to a prior stimulus, but whose consequences may reinforce or inhibit recurrence of that behavior.

op·er·a queen ▶ **n.** informal a male homosexual who is fanatical about opera, esp. one characterized as being affectedly haughty and overrefined.

o·pe·ra se·ri·a /'äp(ə)rə 'si(ə)rēə; 'ōpe,rä 'serē,ä/ ▶ **n.** an opera, typically one of the 18th century in Italian, on a serious, usually classical or mythological theme. ■ such works as a genre. [Ital., lit. 'serious opera.']

op·er·ate /'äpə,rāt/ ▶ **v.** 1 [trans.] (of a person) control the functioning of (a machine, process, or system): *a shortage of workers to operate new machines.* ■ [intrans.] (of a machine, process, or system) function in a specified manner: *market forces operate freely.* ■ [intrans.] be in effect: *a law that operates in politics.* ■ (of a person or organization) manage and run (a business). ■ [intrans.] (of an organization) be managed and run in a specified way: *the company operated within the terms of its charter.* ■ [intrans.] (of an armed force) conduct military activities in a specified area or from a specified base. 2 [intrans.] perform a surgical operation: *the surgeon refused to operate.* 3 [intrans.] function; work. [17th C.: from L. *operat-* 'done by labor,' from the v. *operari*, from *opus, oper-* 'work.']

op·er·at·ic /,äpə'ratik/ ▶ **adj.** of, relating to, or characteristic of opera. ■ extravagantly theatrical; overly dramatic. — **op·er·at·i·cal·ly adv.**

op·er·at·ics /,äpə'ratiks/ ▶ **plural n.** [often treated as sing.] the production or performance of operas. ■ theatrically exaggerated or overemotional behavior.

op·er·at·ing room (abbr.: **OR**) (Brit.**operating theatre**) ▶ **n.** a room in a hospital specially equipped for surgical operations.

op·er·at·ing sys·tem ▶ **n.** the software that supports a computer's basic functions, such as scheduling tasks, executing applications, and controlling peripherals.

op·er·a·tion /,äpə'rāsнən/ ▶ **n.** 1 the fact or condition of functioning or being active. ■ an active process; a discharge of a function. ■ a business organization; a company. ■ an activity in which such an organization is involved. 2 an act of surgery performed on a patient. 3 [often with adj.] a piece of organized and concerted activity involving a number of people, esp. members of the armed forces or the police. ■ (**Operation**) preceding a code name for such an activity: *Operation Desert Storm.* 4 Math. a process in which a number, quantity, expression, etc., is altered or manipulated according to formal rules, such as those of addition, multiplication, and differentiation.

op·er·a·tion·al /,äpə'rāsнənl/ ▶ **adj.** in or ready for use. ■ of or relating to the routine functioning and activities of a business or organization. ■ engaged in or relating to active operations of the armed forces, police, or emergency services. — **op·er·a·tion·al·ly adv.**

op·er·a·tion·al·ism /äpə'rāsнənl,izəm/ ▶ **n.** (also **op·er·a·tion·ism**) Philos. a form of positivism that defines scientific concepts in terms of the operations used to determine or prove them. — **op·er·a·tion·al·ist n. & adj.**

op·er·a·tion·al·ize /,äpə'rāsнənl,īz/ ▶ **v.** [trans.] 1 put into operation or use. 2 Philos. express or define (something) in terms of the operations used to determine or prove it.

op·er·a·tions re·search ▶ **n.** the application of scientific principles to business management, providing a quantitative basis for complex decisions.

op·er·a·tive /'äp(ə)rətiv; 'äpə,rātiv/ ▶ **adj.** 1 functioning; having effect. ■ [attrib.] (of a word) having the most relevance or significance in a phrase or sentence: *a young man, and the operative word is young, should go into the armed services.* 2 [attrib.] of or relating to surgery. ▶ **n.** a worker, esp. a skilled one in a manufacturing industry. ■ a private detective or secret agent. — **op·er·a·tive·ly adv. op·er·a·tive·ness n.**

op·er·a·tor /'äpə,rātər/ ▶ **n.** 1 [often with adj.] a person who operates equipment or a machine. ■ (usu. **the operator**) a person who works for a telephone company assisting users, or who works at a telephone switchboard. 2 [usu. with adj.] a person or company that engages in or runs a business or enterprise. 3 [with adj.] informal a person who acts in a specified, esp. a manipulative, way: *a cool, clever operator.* 4 Math. a symbol or function denoting an operation (e.g., ×, +).

op·er·a win·dow ▶ **n.** a small fixed window usually behind the rear side window of an automobile.

o·per·cu·lum /ō'pərkyələm/ ▶ **n.** (pl. **-la** /-lə/) Zool. Bot. a structure that closes or covers an aperture, in particular: ■ technical term for GILL COVER. ■ a secreted plate that serves to close the aperture of a gastropod mollusk's shell when the animal is retracted. ■ a lidlike structure of the spore-containing capsule of a moss. — **o·per·cu·lar** /-lər/ **adj. o·per·cu·late** /-,lāt/ **adj. o·per·cu·li- comb. form.** [18th C.: from L., lit. 'lid, covering,' from *operire* 'to cover.']

op·er·et·ta /,äpə'retə/ ▶ **n.** a short opera, usually on a light or humorous theme and typically having spoken dialogue. [18th C.: from Ital., dimin. of *opera* (see OPERA[1]).]

op·er·on /'äpə,rän/ ▶ **n.** Biol. a unit made up of linked genes that is thought to regulate other genes responsible for protein synthesis. [1960s: from Fr. *opérer* 'to effect, work' + **-ON.**]

op·er·ose /'äpə,rōs/ ▶ **adj.** rare involving or displaying much industry or effort. [17th C.: from L. *operosus*, from *opus* 'work.']

oph·i·cleide /'äfi,klīd/ ▶ **n.** an obsolete bass brass instrument with keys, used in bands in the 19th century but superseded by the tuba. [19th C.: from Fr. *ophicléide*, from Gk. *ophis* 'serpent' + *kleis, kleid-* 'key.']

O·phid·i·a /ō'fidēə/ Zool. a group of reptiles (suborder Ophidia, order Squamata) that comprises the snakes. — **o·phid·i·an n. & adj.** [mod. L. (pl.), from Gk. *ophis, ophid-* 'snake.']

oph·i·o·lite /'äfēə,līt; 'ōfē-/ ▶ **n.** Geol. an igneous rock consisting largely of serpentine, believed to have been formed from the submarine eruption of oceanic crustal and upper mantle material. — **oph·i·o·lit·ic** /,äfēə'litik; ,ōfē-/ **adj.** [19th C.: from Gk. *ophis* 'snake' + -LITE.]

oph·i·ol·o·gy /,äfē'äləjē; ,ōfē-/ ▶ **n.** the branch of zoology that deals with snakes. — **oph·i·ol·o·gist n.** [19th C.: from Gk. *ophis* 'snake' + -LOGY.]

O·phir /'ōfər/ (in the Bible) an unidentified region, perhaps in southeastern Arabia, famous for its fine gold and precious stones.

oph·ite /'äfīt; 'ōfīt/ ▶ **n.** Geol. a green rock with spots or markings like a snake that can be either eruptive or metamorphic; serpentine. [17th C.: via L. from Gk. *ophitēs* 'serpentine stone,' from *ophis* 'snake,' + -ITE[1].]

o·phit·ic /ō'fitik/ ▶ **adj.** Geol. relating to or denoting a poikilitic rock texture in which crystals of feldspar are interposed between plates of augite.

Oph·i·u·chus /,äf(ē)'yōōkəs; ,ōf(ē)-/ Astron. a large constellation (the Serpent Bearer or Holder), said to represent a man in the coils of a snake. Both the celestial equator and the ecliptic pass through it.

Oph·i·u·roi·de·a /,äfēyōō'roidēə; ,ōfē-/ Zool. a class of echinoderms that comprises the brittle stars. — **oph·i·ur·oid** /-'yōōroid/ **n. & adj.** [mod. L. (pl.), based on Gk. *ophis* 'snake' + *oura* 'tail.']

oph·thal·mi·a /äf'тнalmēə; äp-/ ▶ **n.** Med. inflammation of the eye, esp. conjunctivitis. [ME: via late L. from Gk., from *ophthalmos* 'eye.']

oph·thal·mic /äf'тнalmik; äp-/ ▶ **adj.** [attrib.] of or relating to the eye and its diseases.

oph·thal·mi·tis /,äfтнəl'mītis; ,äp-/ ▶ **n.** Med. inflammation of the eye.

ophthalmo- ▶ **comb. form** Med. relating to the eyes. [from Gk. *ophthalmos* 'eye.']

oph·thal·mol·o·gy /,äfтнə(l)'mäləjē; ,äp-/ ▶ **n.** the branch of medicine concerned with the study and treatment of disorders and diseases of the eye. — **oph·thal·mo·log·i·cal** /-mə'läjikəl/ **adj. oph·thal·mol·o·gist n.**

oph·thal·mo·ple·gia /äf,тнalmə'plēj(ē)ə; äp-/ ▶ **n.** Med. paralysis of the muscles within or surrounding the eye. — **oph·thal·mo·ple·gic** /-'plējik/ **adj.**

oph·thal·mo·scope /äf'тнalmə,skōp; äp-/ ▶ **n.** an instrument for inspecting the retina and other parts of the eye. — **oph·thal·mo·scop·ic** /,äfтнəlmə'skäpik; ,äp-/ **adj. oph·thal·mos·co·py** /,äfтнəl'mäskəpē; ,äp-/ **n.**

-opia ▶ **comb. form** denoting a visual disorder: *myopia.* [from Gk. *ōps, ōp-* 'eye, face.']

o·pi·ate ▶ **adj.** /'ōpē-it; -,āt/ relating to, resembling, or containing opium. ■ fig., dated causing drowsiness or a dulling of the senses. ▶ **n.** /'ōpē-it; -,āt/ a drug with morphinelike effects, derived from opium. ■ fig. a thing that soothes or stupefies. ▶ **v.** /-,āt/ [trans.] [often as adj.] (**opiated**) impregnate with opium. [ME (as a noun): from med. L. *opiatus* (adj.), *opiatus* (n.), based on L. *opium* (see OPIUM).]

o·pine /ō'pīn/ ▶ **v.** [reporting verb] formal hold and state as one's opinion: [with direct speech] *"The man is a genius," he opined.* [ME: from L. *opinari* 'think, believe.']

o·pin·ion /ə'pinyən/ ▶ **n.** a view or judgment formed about something, not necessarily based on fact or knowledge. ■ the beliefs or views of a large number or majority of people about a particular thing. ■ (**opinion of**) an estimation of the quality or worth of someone or something. ■ a formal statement of advice by an expert on a professional matter. ■ Law a formal statement of reasons for a judgment given. ■ Law a lawyer's advice on the merits of a case.
– PHRASES **be of the opinion that** believe or maintain that. **a matter of opinion** something not capable of being proven either way. [ME: via OFr. from L. *opinio(n-)*, from the stem of *opinari* 'think, believe.']

o·pin·ion·at·ed /ə'pinyə,nātid/ ▶ **adj.** conceitedly assertive and dogmatic in one's opinions.

o·pin·ion poll ▶ **n.** an assessment of public opinion obtained by questioning a representative sample.

o·pi·oid /'ōpē,oid/ Biochem. ▶ **n.** an opiumlike compound that binds to one or more of the three opioid receptors of the body. ▶ **adj.** relating to or denoting such compounds. [1950s: from OPIUM + -OID.]

opistho- ▶ prefix behind; to the rear: *opisthosoma.* [from Gk. *opisthen* 'behind.']

op·is·thog·na·thous /ˈäpisˈTHägnəTHəs/ ▶ adj. Zool. (of an animal) having retreating jaws or teeth.

op·is·thot·o·nos /ˌäpisˈTHätnəs/ (also **op·is·thot·o·nus**) ▶ n. Med. spasm of the muscles causing backward arching of the head, neck, and spine, as in severe tetanus and some kinds of meningitis. [17th C.: via late L. from Gk. *opisthotonos* 'drawn backward.']

o·pi·um /ˈōpēəm/ ▶ n. a reddish-brown heavy-scented addictive drug prepared from the opium poppy, used as a narcotic and in medicine as an analgesic. [ME: via L. from Gk. *opion* 'poppy juice,' from *opos* 'juice,' from an Indo-Eur. root meaning 'water.']

o·pi·um den ▶ n. a place where opium is sold and smoked.

o·pi·um pop·py ▶ n. a Eurasian poppy (*Papaver somniferum*) with ornamental white, red, pink, or purple flowers. Its immature capsules yield a latex from which opium is obtained.

O·pi·um Wars two wars involving Britain and China regarding the question of trading rights.

O·por·to /ōˈpôrtō/ a city in northern Portugal, known for port wine; pop. 311,000. Portuguese name PORTO.

opossum

o·pos·sum /(ə)ˈpäsəm/ ▶ n. an American marsupial (family Didelphidae) that has a ratlike prehensile tail and hind feet with opposable thumbs. [17th C.: from Virginia Algonquian *opassom,* from *op* 'white' + *assom* 'dog.']

o·pos·sum shrimp ▶ n. a small, typically transparent, shrimplike crustacean (*Praunus* and other genera, order Mysidacea) that has a long abdomen and conspicuous eyes.

opp. ▶ abbr. opposite.

Op·pen·heim·er /ˈäpənˌhīmər/, Julius Robert (1904–67), US physicist. He was director of the laboratory at Los Alamos, New Mexico, during the development of the first atom bomb.

op·po·nens /əˈpōnənz/ ▶ n. Anat. another term for OPPONENT MUSCLE. [18th C.: from L., lit. 'setting against.']

op·po·nent /əˈpōnənt/ ▶ n. someone who competes against or fights another in a contest, game, or argument. ■ a person who disagrees with or resists a proposal or practice. [16th C.: from L. *opponent-* 'setting against,' from the v. *opponere,* from *ob-* 'against' + *ponere* 'place.']

op·po·nent mus·cle ▶ n. Anat. any of several muscles enabling the thumb to be moved toward a finger of the same hand.

op·por·tune /ˌäpərˈt(y)o͞on/ ▶ adj. (of a time) well-chosen or particularly favorable or appropriate. ■ done or occurring at a favorable or useful time; well-timed. — **op·por·tune·ly** adv. **op·por·tune·ness** n. [ME: from OFr. *opportun(e),* from L. *opportunus,* from *ob-* 'in the direction of' + *portus* 'harbor.']

op·por·tun·ist /ˌäpərˈt(y)o͞onist/ ▶ n. a person who exploits circumstances to gain immediate advantage rather than being guided by principles or plans. ▶ adj. opportunistic. — **op·por·tun·ism** n.

op·por·tun·is·tic /ˌäpərt(y)o͞oˈnistik/ ▶ adj. exploiting chances offered by immediate circumstances without reference to moral principle. ■ Ecol. (of a plant or animal) able to spread quickly in a previously unexploited habitat. ■ Med. (of a microorganism or an infection caused by it) rarely affecting patients except in unusual circumstances, typically when the immune system is depressed. — **op·por·tun·is·ti·cal·ly** adv.

op·por·tu·ni·ty /ˌäpərˈt(y)o͞onitē/ ▶ n. (pl. **-ties**) a set of circumstances that makes it possible to do something. ■ a chance for employment or promotion.

op·por·tu·ni·ty cost ▶ n. Econ. the loss of potential gain from other alternatives when one alternative is chosen.

op·pos·a·ble /əˈpōzəbəl/ ▶ adj. Zool. (of the thumb of a primate) capable of moving toward and touching the other digits on the same hand.

op·pose /əˈpōz/ ▶ v. [trans.] disapprove of and attempt to prevent, esp. by argument: *those who oppose capital punishment.* ■ actively resist or refuse to comply with (a person or a system). ■ compete against (someone) in a contest. — **op·pos·er** n. [ME: from OFr. *opposer,* from Latin *opponere* (see OPPONENT), but influenced by L. *oppositus* 'set against.']

op·posed /əˈpōzd/ ▶ adj. 1 [predic.] (**opposed to**) eager to prevent or put an end to; disagreeing with. ■ in conflict or disagreement with; hostile to: *groups opposed to communism.* 2 (of two or more things) contrasting or conflicting with each other: *doing two **diametrically opposed** things.*
– PHRASES **as opposed to** distinguished from or in contrast with.

op·pos·ing /əˈpōziNG/ ▶ adj. [attrib.] in conflict or competition with another. ■ (of two or more subjects) differing from or in conflict with each other: *fought on opposing sides in the war.* ■ facing; opposite.

op·po·site /ˈäpəzit; -sit/ ▶ adj. 1 [attrib.] having a position on the other or further side of something. ■ [postpositive] facing the speaker or a specified person or thing: *he went into the store opposite.* ■ Bot. (of leaves or shoots) arising in opposed pairs, one on each side of the stem. 2 diametrically different; of a contrary kind: *currents flowing in **opposite directions.*** ■ [attrib.] being the other of a contrasted pair: *the opposite ends of the price range.* ▶ n. a person or thing that is totally different from or the reverse of someone or something else. ▶ adv. in a position facing a specified or implied subject: *she was sitting opposite.* ▶ prep. in a position on the other side of a specific area from; facing: *they sat opposite one another.* ■ fig. (of someone taking a leading part in a play or movie) in a complementary role to (another performer). — **op·po·site·ly** adv. **op·po·site·ness** n. [ME: via OFr. from L. *oppositus,* past part. of *opponere* 'set against.']

op·po·site num·ber ▶ n. (**someone's opposite number**) a person whose position or rank in another group, organization, or country is equivalent to that held by someone already mentioned.

op·po·site sex ▶ n. women in relation to men or vice versa.

op·po·si·tion /ˌäpəˈzisHən/ ▶ n. resistance or dissent, expressed in action or argument. ■ (often **the opposition**) a group of adversaries or competitors, esp. a rival political party or athletic team. ■ (**the opposition**) the principal political party opposed to the one in office. ■ a contrast or antithesis. ■ Logic (of two propositions) the relation of having the same subject and predicate, but differing in quantity, quality, or both. ■ Astron. Astrol. the apparent position of two celestial objects that are directly opposite each other in the sky, esp. when a superior planet is opposite the sun.
– PHRASES **in opposition** in contrast or conflict: *they found themselves in opposition to federal policy.* — **op·po·si·tion·al** /-SHənl/ adj.

op·press /əˈpres/ ▶ v. [trans.] (often **be oppressed**) keep (someone) in subservience and hardship, esp. by the unjust exercise of authority. ■ cause (someone) to feel distressed, anxious, or uncomfortable: *he was oppressed by worry.* — **op·pres·sor** /əˈpresər/ n. [ME: from OFr. *oppresser,* from med. L. *oppressare,* from L. *oppress-* 'pressed against,' from the v. *opprimere.*]

op·pres·sion /əˈpresHən/ ▶ n. prolonged cruel or unjust treatment or control. ■ the state of being subject to such treatment or control. ■ mental pressure or distress.

op·pres·sive /əˈpresiv/ ▶ adj. unjustly inflicting hardship and constraint, esp. on a minority or other subordinate group. ■ weighing heavily on the mind or spirits; causing depression or discomfort. ■ (of weather) excessively hot and humid. — **op·pres·sive·ly** adv. **op·pres·sive·ness** n.

op·pro·bri·ous /əˈprōbrēəs/ ▶ adj. (of language) expressing opprobrium. ■ disgraceful; shameful. — **op·pro·bri·ous·ly** adv.

op·pro·bri·um /əˈprōbrēəm/ ▶ n. harsh criticism or censure. ■ the public disgrace arising from someone's shameful conduct. ■ archaic an occasion or cause of reproach or disgrace. [17th C.: from L., lit. 'infamy,' from *opprobrum,* from *ob-* 'against' + *probrum* 'disgraceful act.']

op·pugn /əˈpyo͞on/ ▶ v. [trans.] rare call into question the truth or validity of. — **op·pugn·er** n. [ME: from L. *oppugnare* 'attack, besiege,' from *ob-* 'against' + *pugnare* 'to fight.']

op·pug·nant /əˈpəgnənt/ ▶ adj. rare opposing; antagonistic. — **op·pug·nan·cy** /-nənsē/ n.

op·sin /ˈäpsin/ ▶ n. Biochem. a protein that forms part of the visual pigment rhodopsin and is released by the action of light. [1950s: shortening of RHODOPSIN.]

op·so·nin /ˈäpsənin/ ▶ n. Biochem. a substance that binds to foreign microorganisms or cells, making them more susceptible to phagocytosis. — **op·son·ic** /äpˈsänik/ adj. [20th C.: from L. *opsonare* 'buy provisions' (from Gk. *opsōnein*) + -IN[1].]

op·so·nize /ˈäpsəˌnīz/ ▶ v. [trans.] Med. make (a foreign cell) more susceptible to phagocytosis. — **op·so·ni·za·tion** /ˌäpsəˌniˈzāsHən/ n.

opt /äpt/ ▶ v. [intrans.] make a choice from a range of possibilities: *consumers will opt for low-priced goods.*
– PHRASAL VERBS **opt out** choose not to participate in or carry on with something. [19th C.: from Fr. *opter,* from L. *optare* 'choose, wish.']

opt. ▶ abbr. ■ optative. ■ optical. ■ optician. ■ optics. ■ optional.

op·ta·tive /ˈäptətiv/ Gram. ▶ adj. relating to or denoting a mood of verbs in Greek and other languages, expressing a wish, equivalent to English expressions *if only.* ▶ n. a verb in the optative mood. ■ (**the optative**) the optative mood. — **op·ta·tive·ly** adv.

op·tic /ˈäptik/ ▶ adj. of or relating to the eye or vision. ▶ n. 1 a lens or other optical component in an optical instrument. 2 archaic or humorous the eye. [ME: from Fr. *optique* or med. L. *opticus,* from Gk. *optikos,* from *optos* 'seen.']

op·ti·cal /ˈäptikəl/ ▶ adj. 1 of or relating to sight, esp. in relation to the physical action of light. ■ constructed to assist sight. ■ devised on the principles of optics. 2 Physics operating in or employing the visible part of the electromagnetic spectrum. ■ Electron. (of a device) requiring electromagnetic radiation for its operation. — **op·ti·cal·ly** adv.

op·ti·cal ac·tiv·i·ty ▶ n. Chem. the property of rotating the plane of polarization of plane-polarized light.

op·ti·cal art ▶ n. another term for OP ART.

op·ti·cal bench ▶ n. a straight rigid bar, typically marked with a scale, to which lenses, light sources, and other optical components can be attached.

op·ti·cal char·ac·ter rec·og·ni·tion (abbr.: **OCR**) ▶ n. the identification of printed characters using photoelectric devices and computer software.

op·ti·cal den·si·ty ▶ n. Physics the degree to which a refractive medium retards transmitted rays of light.

op·ti·cal disk ▶ n. see DISK (sense 1).

op·ti·cal dou·ble ▶ n. Astron. two stars that are in the same line of sight as seen from the earth, but that may be at far different distances. See also DOUBLE STAR.

op·ti·cal fi·ber ▶ n. a thin glass fiber through which light can be transmitted.

op·ti·cal glass ▶ n. a very pure kind of glass used for lenses.

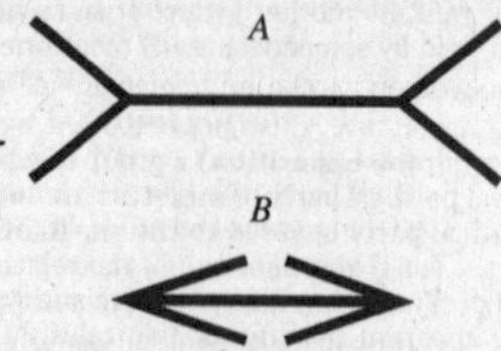

(horizontal line A appears to be longer than horizontal line B, but in fact, they are of equal length)

optical illusion

op·ti·cal il·lu·sion ▶ n. an experience of seeming to see something that does not exist or that is other than it appears. ■ something that deceives one's eyes and causes such an experience.

op·ti·cal i·so·mer ▶ n. Chem. each of two or more forms of a compound that have the same structure but are mirror images of each other and typically differ in optical activity. — **op·ti·cal i·som·er·ism** n.

op·ti·cal mi·cro·scope ▶ n. a microscope using visible light, typically viewed directly by the eye.

op·ti·cal ro·ta·tion ▶ n. Chem. the rotation of the plane of polarization of plane-polarized light by an optically active substance.

op·ti·cal scan·ner ▶ n. Electron. a device that performs optical character recognition and produces coded signals corresponding to the characters identified.

op·tic chi·as·ma ▶ n. (also **op·tic chi·asm**) Anat. the X-shaped structure formed at the point below the brain where the two optic nerves cross over each other.

op·tic cup ▶ n. Anat. a cuplike outgrowth of the brain of an embryo that develops into the retina.

op·tic disk ▶ n. (also **op·tic disc**) Anat. the raised disk on the retina at the point of entry of the optic nerve, lacking visual receptors and so creating a blind spot.

op·ti·cian /äp'tisHən/ ▶ n. a person qualified to make and supply eyeglasses and contact lenses for correction of vision. ■ rare a person who makes or sells optical instruments. [17th C.: from Fr. *opticien*, from med. L. *optica* 'optics.']

op·tic nerve ▶ n. Anat. each of the second pair of cranial nerves, transmitting impulses to the brain from the retina at the back of the eye.

op·tics /'äptiks/ ▶ plural n. [usu. treated as sing.] the scientific study of sight and the behavior of light, or the properties of transmission and deflection of other forms of radiation.

op·ti·ma /'äptəmə/ plural form of OPTIMUM.

op·ti·mal /'äptəməl/ ▶ adj. best or most favorable; optimum. — **op·ti·mal·i·ty** /,äptə'malitē/ n. **op·ti·mal·ly** adv.

op·ti·mism /'äptə,mizəm/ ▶ n. **1** hopefulness and confidence about the future or the successful outcome of something. **2** Philos. the doctrine, esp. as set forth by Leibniz, that this world is the best of all possible worlds. ■ the belief that good must ultimately prevail over evil in the universe. — **op·ti·mist** n. [18th C.: from Fr. *optimisme*, from L. *optimum* 'best thing' (see OPTIMUM).]

op·ti·mis·tic /,äptə'mistik/ ▶ adj. hopeful and confident about the future. ■ involving an overestimate: *previous estimates may be wildly optimistic.* — **op·ti·mis·ti·cal·ly** adv.

op·ti·mize /'äptə,mīz/ ▶ v. [trans.] make the best or most effective use of (a situation, opportunity, or resource). ■ Comput. rearrange or rewrite (data) to improve efficiency of retrieval or processing. — **op·ti·mi·za·tion** /,äptə,mī'zāsHən/ n. **op·ti·miz·er** n.

op·ti·mum /'äptəməm/ ▶ adj. most conducive to a favorable outcome; best. ▶ n. (pl. **-ma** /-mə/ or **-mums**) the most favorable conditions or level for growth, reproduction, or success. [19th C.: from L., neut. of *optimus* 'best.']

op·tion /'äpsHən/ ▶ n. **1** a thing that is or may be chosen. ■ [in sing.] the freedom, power, or right to choose something. ■ a right to buy or sell a particular thing at a specified price within a set time: *Columbia Pictures has an option on the script.* **2** Football an offensive play in which the ball carrier has the option to run, pass, hand off, or lateral. ▶ v. [trans.] buy or sell an option on (something): *his second script will have been optioned by the time you read this.* ■ Sports transfer a player (to a minor league team) with an option to recall him. [16th C.: from Fr., or from L. *optio(n-)*, from the stem of *optare* 'choose.']

op·tion·al /'äpsHənl/ ▶ adj. available to be chosen but not obligatory. — **op·tion·al·i·ty** /,äpsHə'nalitē/ n. **op·tion·al·ly** adv.

op·to·e·lec·tron·ics /'äptōəlek'träniks; -ē,lek-/ ▶ plural n. [treated as sing.] the branch of technology concerned with the combined use of electronics and light. ■ [treated as pl.] circuitry constructed using this technology. — **op·to·e·lec·tron·ic** adj.

op·tom·e·ter /äp'tämitər/ ▶ n. an instrument for testing the refractive power of the eye. [18th C.: from Gk. *optos* 'seen' + -METER.]

op·tom·e·trist /äp'tämitrist/ ▶ n. a person who practices optometry.

op·tom·e·try /äp'tämitrē/ ▶ n. the practice or profession of examining the eyes for visual defects and prescribing corrective lenses. — **op·to·met·ric** /,äptə'metrik/ adj.

opt-out ▶ n. an instance of choosing not to participate in something: *opt-outs from key parts of the treaty.*

op·tron·ics /äp'träniks/ ▶ plural n. [treated as sing.] short for OPTOELECTRONICS. — **op·tron·ic** adj.

op·u·lent /'äpyələnt/ ▶ adj. ostentatiously rich and luxurious or lavish. ■ wealthy. — **op·u·lence** n. **op·u·lent·ly** adv. [16th C.: from L. *opulent-* 'wealthy, splendid,' from *opes* 'wealth.']

o·pun·tia /ō'pənsH(ē)ə/ ▶ n. a cactus of a genus (genus *Opuntia*) that comprises the prickly pears. See illustration at PRICKLY PEAR. [17th C.: from L., a plant growing around *Opus* (stem *Opunt-*), a city in ancient Greece.]

o·pus /'ōpəs/ ▶ n. (pl. **o·pus·es** or **o·pe·ra** /'äp(ə)rə/) **1** Music a separate composition or set of compositions by a particular composer, usually ordered by date of publication. **2** any artistic work, esp. one on a large scale. [18th C.: from L., lit. 'work.']

o·pus·cule /ō'pəskyo͞ol/ (also **o·pus·cu·lum** /ō'pəskyələm/) ▶ n. (pl. **-cules** or **-cu·la** /-kyələ/) rare a small or minor literary or musical work. [17th C.: from Fr., from L. *opusculum*, dimin. of *opus* 'work.']

OR ▶ abbr. ■ operational research. ■ Oregon (in official postal use).

or[1] /ôr/ ▶ conj. **1** used to link alternatives: *a cup of tea or coffee | are you coming or not?* **2** introducing a synonym or explanation of a preceding word or phrase: *the espionage novel, or, as it is also known, the thriller.* **3** otherwise (used to introduce the consequences of something not being done or not being the case): *hurry up, or you'll miss it all.* **4** introducing an afterthought, usually in the form of a question: *John's indifference—or was it?—left her unsettled.* **5** literary either: *to love is the one way to know or God or man.* ▶ n. (often **OR**) Electron. a Boolean operator that gives the value one if at least one operand (or input) has a value of one, and otherwise has a value of zero.
– PHRASES **or else** see ELSE. **or so** (after a quantity) approximately: *a dozen or so people.* [ME: obs. conjunction *other*, prob. from OE *oththe.*]

or[2] ▶ n. gold or yellow, as a heraldic tincture: [postpositive] *a bend or.* [16th C.: from Fr., from L. *aurum* 'gold.']

-or[1] ▶ suffix (forming nouns) denoting a person or thing performing the action of a verb, or denoting another agent: *escalator | governor | resistor.* [from L., sometimes via Anglo-Norman Fr. *-eour* or OFr. *-eor.*]

-or[2] ▶ suffix forming nouns denoting a state or condition: *error | pallor | terror.* [from L., sometimes via OFr. *-or, -ur.*]

-or[3] ▶ suffix forming adjectives expressing a comparative sense: *minor | major.* [via Anglo-Norman Fr. from L.]

o·ra /'ôrə/ plural form of OS[2].

or·ache /'ôrəcH; 'är-/ (also **or·ach**) ▶ n. a plant (genus *Atriplex*) of the goosefoot family, with leaves that are sometimes covered in a white mealy substance. Several edible kinds are used as a substitute for spinach or sorrel. [ME *orage*, from Anglo-Norman Fr. *arasche*, from L. *atriplex*, from Gk. *atraphaxus.*]

or·a·cle /'ôrəkəl; 'är-/ ▶ n. **1** a priest or priestess acting as a medium through whom advice or prophecy was sought from the gods in classical antiquity. ■ a place at which such advice or prophecy was sought. ■ a person or thing regarded as an infallible authority or guide on something. **2** a response or message given by an oracle, typically one that is ambiguous or obscure. [ME: via OFr. from L. *oraculum*, from *orare* 'speak.']

o·rac·u·lar /ô'rakyələr/ ▶ adj. of or relating to an oracle. ■ (of an utterance, advice, etc.) hard to interpret; enigmatic. ■ holding or claiming the authority of an oracle. — **o·rac·u·lar·i·ty** /ô,rakyə'laritē/ n. **o·rac·u·lar·ly** adv. [17th C.: from L. *oraculum* (see ORACLE) + -AR[1].]

o·ra·cy /'ôrəsē/ ▶ n. the ability to express oneself fluently and grammatically in speech. [1960s: from L. *os, or-* 'mouth,' on the pattern of *literacy.*]

o·ral /'ôrəl/ ▶ adj. **1** by word of mouth; spoken rather than written. ■ relating to the transmission of information or literature by word of mouth rather than in writing: *oral literature.* ■ (of a society) not having reached the stage of literacy. **2** of or relating to the mouth: *oral hygiene.* ■ done or taken by the mouth. ■ Phonet. pronounced by the voice resonating in the mouth, as the vowels in English. Compare with NASAL (sense 2). ■ Psychoanal. (in Freudian theory) relating to or denoting a stage of infantile psychosexual development in which the mouth is the main source of pleasure and the center of experience. ▶ n. (often **orals**) a spoken examination or test. — **o·ral·ly** adv. [17th C.: from late L. *oralis*, from L. *os, or-* 'mouth.']

o·ral his·to·ry ▶ n. the collection and study of historical information using sound recordings of interviews with people having personal knowledge of past events. ▪ a record of this kind: *their own oral histories.*

o·ral·ism /ˈôrəˌlizəm/ ▶ **n.** the system of teaching the deaf to communicate by the use of speech and lip-reading rather than sign language.

o·ral·ist /ˈôrəlist/ ▶ **adj.** relating to or advocating oralism. ▶ **n.** a deaf person who uses speech and lip-reading to communicate, rather than sign language.

o·ral·i·ty /ôˈralitē/ ▶ **n. 1** the quality of being spoken or verbally communicated. ▪ preference for or tendency to use spoken forms of language. **2** Psychoanal. the focusing of sexual energy and feeling on the mouth.

o·ral sex ▶ **n.** sexual activity in which the genitals of one partner are stimulated by the mouth of the other; fellatio or cunnilingus.

O·ran /ōˈrän/ a city in northern Algeria; pop. 664,000.

o·rang /ôˈraNG/ ▶ **n.** short for ORANGUTAN.

Or·ange /ˈôrənj; ˈär-/ a city in southwestern California; pop. 110,658.

or·ange /ˈôrənj; ˈär-/ ▶ **n. 1** a round juicy citrus fruit with a tough bright reddish-yellow rind. **2** (also **orange tree**) the leathery-leaved evergreen tree (genus *Citrus*) of the rue family that bears this fruit, in particular the **sweet orange** (*C. sinensis*). Native to warm regions of south and Southeast Asia, oranges are a major commercial crop in many warm regions of the world. ▪ used in names of other plants with similar fruit or flowers, e.g., **mock orange**. **3** a bright reddish-yellow color like that of the skin of a ripe orange. ▶ **adj. 1** reddish yellow. **2** made from or flavored with oranges, or having an orangelike flavoring. — **or·ang·ey** (also **or·ang·y**) **adj. or·ang·ish** (also **or·ange·ish**) **adj.** [ME: from OFr. *orenge*, based on Arab. *nāranj*, from Pers. *nārang*.]

or·ange·ade /ˌôrənjˈād; ˌär-/ ▶ **n.** a drink made with orange juice, sweetener, and water.

or·ange blos·som ▶ **n. 1** flowers from an orange tree, traditionally worn by the bride at a wedding. **2** a cocktail made of gin, sugar, and orange juice.

or·ange flow·er wa·ter ▶ **n.** a solution of neroli in water, used in perfumery and as a food flavoring.

Or·ange Free State an area and former province in central South Africa. It became FREE STATE in 1995.

Or·ange, House of the Dutch royal house, originally a princely dynasty of the principality centered on the town of Orange in southern France in the 16th century.

Or·ange·man /ˈôrənjmən; ˈär-/ ▶ **n.** (pl. **-men**) a member of the Orange Order, a Protestant political society in Northern Ireland.

or·ange pe·koe ▶ **n.** a type of black tea made from young leaves.

Or·ange Riv·er a river that rises in northeastern Lesotho and flows west for 1,155 miles (1,859 km) across South Africa to the Atlantic Ocean.

or·ange·ry /ˈôrənjrē; ˈär-/ ▶ **n.** (pl. **-ries**) a greenhouse where orange trees are grown.

or·ange stick ▶ **n.** a thin stick, pointed at one end and typically made of orange wood, used for manicuring the fingernails.

Or·ange, William of William III of Great Britain and Ireland (see WILLIAM).

o·rang·u·tan /əˈraNG(g)əˌtan/ (also **o·rang·u·tang, o·rang-ou·tang** /ōˈraNG(g)əˌtaNG/, **o·rang-u·tan**) ▶ **n.** a large mainly solitary arboreal ape (*Pongo pygmaeus*, family Pongidae) with long reddish hair, long arms, and hooked hands and feet, native to Borneo and Sumatra. The mature male develops fleshy cheek pads and a throat pouch. [17th C.: from Malay *orang huan* 'forest person.']

orangutan

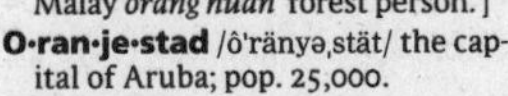

O·ran·je·stad /ôˈränyəˌstät/ the capital of Aruba; pop. 25,000.

o·rate /ôˈrāt; ˈôrˌāt/ ▶ **v.** [intrans.] make a speech, esp. pompously or at length. [17th C.: back-form. from ORATION.]

o·ra·tion /ôˈrāSHən/ ▶ **n.** a formal speech, esp. one given on a ceremonial occasion. ▪ the style or manner in which such a speech is given. [ME: from L. *oratio(n-)* 'discourse, prayer,' from *orare* 'speak, pray.']

or·a·tor /ˈôrətər; ˈär-/ ▶ **n.** a public speaker, esp. one who is eloquent or skilled. — **or·a·to·ri·al** /ˌôrəˈtôrēəl/ **adj.**

or·a·to·ri·o /ˌôrəˈtôrēˌō; ˌär-/ ▶ **n.** (pl. **-os**) a large-scale musical work for orchestra and voices, typically a narrative on a religious theme, performed without the use of costumes, scenery, or action. [Ital., from eccles. L. *oratorium* 'oratory,' from the musical services held in the Church of the Oratory of St. Philip Neri in Rome.]

or·a·to·ry[1] /ˈôrəˌtôrē; ˈär-/ ▶ **n.** (pl. **-ries**) **1** a small chapel, esp. for private worship. **2** (**Oratory**) (in the Roman Catholic Church) a religious society of secular priests founded in Rome in 1564 to provide plain preaching and popular services and established in various countries. — **Or·a·to·ri·an** /ˌôəˈtôrēən; ˈär-/ **n. & adj.** (sense 2).

or·a·to·ry[2] ▶ **n.** the art or practice of formal speaking in public. ▪ exaggerated, eloquent, or highly colored language. — **or·a·tor·i·cal** /ˌôrəˈtôrikəl; ˌär-/ **adj.** [16th C.: from L. *oratoria*, from *oratorius* 'relating to an orator.']

orb /ôrb/ ▶ **n.** a spherical body; a globe. ▪ a golden globe surmounted by a cross, forming part of the regalia of a monarch. ▪ literary a celestial body. ▪ (usu. **orbs**) literary an eyeball; an eye. ▪ Astrol. a circle of up to 10° radius around the position of a celestial object: *within an orb of 1° of Mars.* ▶ **v.** [trans.] literary encircle; enclose. ▪ form (something) into an orb; make circular or globular. [ME (denoting a circle): from L. *orbis* 'ring.']

or·bic·u·lar /ôrˈbikyələr/ ▶ **adj.** tech. **1** having the shape of a flat ring or disk. **2** having a rounded convex or globular shape. — **or·bic·u·lar·i·ty** /ôrˌbikyəˈlaritē/ **n. or·bic·u·lar·ly adv.** [ME: from late L. *orbicularis*, from L. *orbiculus*, dimin. of *orbis* 'ring.']

or·bit /ˈôrbit/ ▶ **n. 1** the curved path of a celestial object or spacecraft around a star, planet, or moon, esp. a periodic elliptical revolution. ▪ one complete circuit around an orbited body. ▪ the state of being on or moving in such a course: *the earth is in orbit around the sun.* ▪ the path of an electron around an atomic nucleus. **2** a sphere of activity, interest, or application. **3** Anat. the cavity in the skull of a vertebrate that contains the eye; the eye socket. ▪ the area around the eye of a bird or other animal. ▶ **v.** (**-bit·ed, -bit·ing**) [trans.] (of a celestial object or spacecraft) move in orbit around (a star, planet, or moon): *Mercury orbits the Sun.* ▪ [intrans.] fly or move around in a circle: *the mobile's disks spun and orbited slowly.* ▪ put (a satellite) into orbit. [16th C. (sense 3): from L. *orbita* 'course, track,' from *orbis* 'ring.']

or·bit·al /ˈôrbitl/ ▶ **adj.** of or relating to an orbit or orbits. ▶ **n.** Physics each of the actual or potential patterns of electron density that may be formed in an atom or molecule by one or more electrons, and that can be represented as a wave function.

or·bit·er /ˈôrbitər/ ▶ **n.** a spacecraft designed to go into orbit, esp. one not intended to land. Compare with LANDER.

orb web ▶ **n.** a generally circular, upright spider's web formed of threads radiating from a central point, crossed by radial links that spiral in from the edge.

orc /ôrk/ ▶ **n.** (in fantasy literature and games) a member of an imaginary race of humanlike creatures, characterized as ugly, warlike, and malevolent. [16th C.: perh. from L. *orcus* 'hell' or Ital. *orco* 'demon, monster.']

or·ca /ˈôrkə/ ▶ **n.** a large toothed whale (*Orcinus orca*, family Delphinidae) with distinctive black-and-white markings and a prominent dorsal fin. It lives in groups that cooperatively hunt fish, seals, and penguins. Also called KILLER WHALE. [19th C.: from Fr. *orque* or L. *orca*, a kind of whale.]

or·ce·in /ˈôrsēin/ ▶ **n.** Chem. a red dye obtained from orchil, used as a stain in microscopic study. [19th C.: alt. of *orcin*, another name for ORCINOL.]

orch. ▶ **abbr.** ▪ orchestra. ▪ orchestrated by.

or·chard /ˈôrCHərd/ ▶ **n.** a piece of land planted with fruit trees. — **or·char·dist n.** [OE *ortgeard*.]

or·ches·tra /ˈôrkistrə; -ˌkestrə/ ▶ **n. 1** a group of instrumentalists, esp. one combining string, woodwind, brass, and percussion sections and playing classical music. **2** (also **orchestra pit**) the part of a theater where the orchestra plays, typically in front of the stage and on a lower level than the audience. ▪ the seats on the ground floor in a theater. **3** the semicircular space in front of an ancient Greek theater stage where the chorus danced and sang. [17th C.: via L. from Gk. *orkhēstra*, from *orkheisthai* 'to dance.']

or·ches·tral /ôrˈkestrəl/ ▶ **adj.** written for an orchestra to play. ▪ of or relating to an orchestra. — **or·ches·tral·ly adv.**

or·ches·trate /ˈôrkiˌstrāt/ ▶ **v.** [trans.] **1** arrange or score (music) for orchestral performance. **2** arrange or direct the elements of (a situation) to produce a desired effect, esp. surreptitiously. — **or·ches·tra·tion** /ˌôrkəˈstrāSHən/ **n. or·ches·tra·tor n.**

or·ches·tri·on /ôrˈkestrēən/ (also **or·ches·tri·na** /ˌôrkiˈstrēnə/) ▶ **n.** a large mechanical musical instrument designed to imitate the sound of an orchestra. [19th C.: from ORCHESTRA.]

or·chid /ˈôrkid/ ▶ **n.** a plant (family Orchidaceae) with complex flowers that are typically showy or bizarrely shaped, having a large specialized lip (labellum) and frequently a spur. Orchids occur worldwide, esp. as epiphytes in tropical forests, and are valuable hothouse plants. — **or·chid·ist n.** [19th C.: from mod. L. *Orchid(ac)eae*, from L. *orchis*.]

or·chi·da·ceous /ˌôrkiˈdāSHəs/ ▶ **adj.** Bot. of, relating to, or denoting plants of the orchid family (Orchidaceae).

or·chi·ec·to·my /ˌôrkēˈektəmē/ (also **or·chi·dec·to·my** /ˌôrkiˈdektəmē/) ▶ **n.** surgical removal of one or both testicles. [19th C.: from Gk. *orkhis* 'testicle') + -ECTOMY.]

or·chil /ˈôrkəl; -CHil/ ▶ **n. 1** a red or violet dye obtained from certain lichens, used as a source of litmus, orcinol, and other pigments. **2** a lichen (*Roccella* and other genera) with flattened fronds from which such a dye can be obtained. [15th C.: from OFr. *orcheil*, rel. to Sp. *urchilla*; of uncert. origin.]

or·chis /ˈôrkis/ ▶ **n.** an orchid of (or formerly of) a genus (*Orchis* or *Dactylorhiza*) native to north temperate regions, characterized by a tuberous root and an erect fleshy stem bearing a spike of typically purple or pinkish flowers. [mod. L., based on Gk. *orkhis*, lit. 'testicle' (with ref. to the shape of its tuber).]

or·chi·tis /ôrˈkītis/ ▶ **n.** Med. inflammation of one or both of the testicles. [18th C.: mod. L., from Gk. *orkhis* 'testicle' + -ITIS.]

or·ci·nol /ˈôrsəˌnôl; -ˌnäl/ ▶ **n.** Chem. a crystalline compound, $C_7H_8O_2$, extracted from certain lichens and used to make dyes. [19th C.: from mod. L. *orcina*, from Ital. *orcello* 'orchil.']

ord. ▶ **abbr.** ▪ order. ▪ ordinary.

or·dain /ôr'dān/ ▶ **v.** [trans.] **1** make (someone) a priest or minister; confer holy orders on. **2** order or decree (something) officially: *equal punishment was ordained for the two crimes.* ■ (esp. of God or fate) prescribe; determine (something): *the path ordained by God.* — **or·dain·er** n. **or·dain·ment** n. [ME: from Anglo-Norman Fr. *ordeiner*, from L. *ordinare*, from *ordo, ordin-* (see ORDER).]

or·deal /ôr'dēl/ ▶ **n. 1** a painful or horrific experience, esp. a protracted one. **2** hist. an ancient test of guilt or innocence by subjection of the accused to severe pain, survival of which was taken as divine proof of innocence. [OE *ordāl, ordēl*, of Gmc. origin; rel. to Ger. *urteilen* 'give judgment,' from a base meaning 'share out.']

or·der /'ôrdər/ ▶ **n. 1** the arrangement or disposition of people or things in relation to each other according to a particular sequence, pattern, or method. ■ a state in which everything is in its correct or appropriate place. ■ a state in which the laws and rules regulating the public behavior of members of a community are observed and authority is obeyed: *the army was deployed to keep order.* ■ [with adj.] the overall state or condition of something: *the house was in good order.* ■ a particular social, political, or economic system: *the social order of Britain.* ■ the prescribed or established procedure followed by a meeting, legislative assembly, debate, or court of law. ■ a stated form of liturgical service, or of administration of a rite or ceremony, prescribed by ecclesiastical authority. **2** an authoritative command, direction, or instruction. ■ an oral or written request for something to be made, supplied, or served. ■ a thing made, supplied, or served as a result of such a request: *orders will be delivered the next business day.* ■ a written direction of a court or judge. ■ a written direction to pay money or deliver property. **3** (often **orders**) a social class: *the upper social orders.* ■ Biol. a principal taxonomic category that ranks below class and above family. ■ a grade or rank in the Christian ministry, esp. that of bishop, priest, or deacon. ■ (**orders**) the rank or position of a member of the clergy or an ordained minister of a church: *he took priest's orders.* See also HOLY ORDERS. ■ Theol. any of the nine grades of angelic beings in the celestial hierarchy. **4** (also **Order**) a society of monks, priests, nuns, etc., living according to religious and social regulations and discipline and at least some of whose members take solemn vows. ■ hist. a society of knights bound by a common rule of life and having a combined military and monastic character. ■ an institution founded by a monarch for the purpose of conferring an honor or honors for merit on those appointed to it. ■ the insignia worn by members of such an institution. ■ a Masonic or similar fraternal organization. **5** [in sing.] used to describe the quality, nature, or importance of something: *musical talent of a rare order.* **6** any of the five classical styles of architecture based on the proportions of columns, amount of decoration, etc. **7** [with adj.] Mil. equipment or uniform for a specified purpose or of a specified type: *drill order.* ■ (**the order**) the position in which a rifle is held after ordering arms. See *ORDER ARMS* below. **8** Math. the degree of complexity of an equation, expression, etc., as denoted by an ordinal number. ■ the number of differentiations required to reach the highest derivative in a differential equation. ■ the number of elements in a finite group. ■ the number of rows or columns in a square matrix. ▶ **v. 1** [trans.] give an authoritative direction or instruction to do something: *her father ordered her back home | the judge ordered a retrial.* ■ (**order someone around/about**) continually tell someone in an overbearing way what to do. ■ command (something) to be done or (someone) to be treated in a particular way: *he ordered the anchor dropped.* **2** [trans.] request (something) to be made, supplied, or served: *my friend ordered the tickets last week* | [intrans.] *Are you ready to order, sir?* **3** [trans.] arrange (something) in a methodical or appropriate way.
– PHRASES **by order of** according to directions given by the proper authority. **in order 1** according to a particular sequence. **2** in the correct condition for operation or use. **3** in accordance with the rules of procedure at a meeting, legislative assembly, etc. ■ appropriate in the circumstances: *a little bit of flattery was now in order.* **in order for** so that. **in order that** with the intention; so that. **in order to** as a means to. **of the order of 1** approximately: *sales increases are of the order of 20%.* **2** Math. having the order of magnitude specified by. **on order** (of goods) requested but not yet received from the supplier or manufacturer. **on the order of 1** another term for *OF THE ORDER OF* (sense 1) above. **2** along the lines of; similar to: *singers on the order of Janis Joplin.* **Order!** a call for silence or the observance of prescribed procedures by someone in charge of a trial, legislative assembly, etc. **order arms** Mil. hold a rifle with its butt on the ground close to one's right side. **order of battle** the units, formations, and equipment of a military force. **out of order 1** (of an electrical or mechanical device) not working properly or at all. **2** not in the correct sequence. **3** not according to the rules of a meeting etc. **to order** according to a customer's specific requirements. [ME: from OFr. *ordre*, from L. *ordo, ordin-* 'row, series, rank.']

or·dered pair ▶ **n.** Math. a pair of elements *a, b* having the property that $(a, b) = (u, v)$ if and only if $a = u, b = v$.

or·der·ly /'ôrdərlē/ ▶ **adj.** neatly and methodically arranged. ■ (of a person or group) well behaved; disciplined. ▶ **n.** (pl. **-lies**) **1** an attendant in a hospital responsible for the nonmedical care of patients and the maintenance of order and cleanliness. **2** a soldier who carries out orders or performs minor tasks for an officer. — **or·der·li·ness** n.

or·der·ly room ▶ **n.** Mil. the room used for regimental or company business.

or·der of busi·ness (pl. **or·ders of busi·ness**) ▶ **n.** a task assigned or a matter to be addressed.

or·der of mag·ni·tude ▶ **n.** a class in a system of classification determined by size, each class being a number of times (usually ten) greater or smaller than the one before. ■ relative size, quantity, quality, etc. ■ the arrangement of a number of items determined by their relative size.

or·der of the day ▶ **n.** (**the order of the day**) **1** the prevailing state of things. **2** something required or recommended. **3** a program or agenda.

Or·der of the Gar·ter the highest order of English knighthood, founded by Edward III *c.*1344.

or·di·nal /'ôrdn-əl/ ▶ **n. 1** short for ORDINAL NUMBER. **2** Christian Church, esp. hist. a service book, esp. one with the forms of service used at ordinations. ▶ **adj.** of or relating to a thing's position in a series: *ordinal position of birth.* ■ of or relating to an ordinal number. ■ Biol. of or relating to a taxonomic order. [ME: from late L. *ordinalis* 'relating to order in a series,' from L. *ordo, ordin-* (see ORDER).]

or·di·nal num·ber ▶ **n.** a number defining a thing's position in a series, such as "first," "second," or "third." Ordinal numbers are used as adjectives, nouns, and pronouns. Compare with CARDINAL NUMBER.

or·di·nance /'ôrdn-əns/ ▶ **n. 1** a piece of legislation enacted by a municipal authority. **2** an authoritative order; a decree. **3** a prescribed religious rite: *Talmudic ordinances.* [ME: from OFr. *ordenance*, from med. L. *ordinantia*, from L. *ordinare* 'put in order' (see ORDAIN).]

or·di·nand /'ôrdn,and/ ▶ **n.** a candidate for ordination. [19th C.: from L. *ordinandus*, gerundive of *ordinare* 'put in order' (see ORDAIN).]

or·di·nar·i·ly /,ôrdn'e(ə)rəlē/ ▶ **adv. 1** usually. **2** in a normal way.

or·di·nar·y /'ôrdn,erē/ ▶ **adj. 1** with no special or distinctive features; normal. ■ uninteresting; commonplace. **2** (esp. of a judge or bishop) exercising authority by virtue of office and not by delegation. ▶ **n.** (pl. **-nar·ies**) **1** [in sing.] what is commonplace or standard. **2** Law, Brit. a person, esp. a judge, exercising authority by virtue of office and not by delegation. ■ in some US states, a judge of probate. **3** (usu. **Ordinary**) those parts of a Roman Catholic service, esp. the Mass, that do not vary from day to day. ■ a rule or book giving the order for saying the Mass. **4** Heraldry any of the simplest principal charges used in coats of arms. **5** Brit., archaic a meal provided at a fixed time and price at an inn. ■ an inn providing this. **6** hist. an early type of bicycle with one large and one very small wheel; a penny-farthing.
– PHRASES **out of the ordinary** unusual. — **or·di·nar·i·ness** n. [ME: from L. *ordinarius* 'orderly,' from *ordo, ordin-* 'order.']

or·di·nar·y sea·man ▶ **n.** the lowest rank of merchant seaman, below able-bodied seaman.

or·di·nate /'ôrdn-it; -,āt/ ▶ **n.** Math. (in a system of coordinates) the *y*-coordinate, representing the distance from a point to the horizontal or *x*-axis measured parallel to the vertical or *y*-axis. See illustration at ABSCISSA. [17th C.: from L. *linea ordinata applicata* 'line applied parallel.']

or·di·na·tion /,ôrdn'āsʜən/ ▶ **n.** the action of ordaining or conferring holy orders on someone. ■ a ceremony in which someone is ordained.

ordn. ▶ **abbr.** ordnance.

ord·nance /'ôrdnəns/ ▶ **n. 1** mounted guns; artillery. ■ military weapons, ammunition, and equipment used with them. **2** a branch of the armed forces dealing with the supply and storage of weapons, ammunition, and related equipment. [ME: var. of ORDINANCE.]

or·don·nance /'ôrdn-əns; ,ôdô'näɴs/ ▶ **n.** the systematic or orderly arrangement of parts, esp. in art and architecture. [17th C.: from Fr., alt. of OFr. *ordenance* (see ORDINANCE).]

Or·do·vi·cian /,ôrdə'visʜən/ ▶ **adj.** Geol. of, relating to, or denoting the second period of the Paleozoic era, between the Cambrian and Silurian periods. ■ [as n.] (**the Ordovician**) the Ordovician period or the system of rocks deposited during it. [19th C.: from *Ordovices*, the L. name of an ancient British tribe in North Wales, + -IAN.]

or·dure /'ôrjər/ ▶ **n.** excrement; dung. ■ something regarded as vile or abhorrent. [ME: from OFr., from *ord* 'foul,' from L. *horridus* (see HORRID).]

Or·dzho·ni·kid·ze /,ôrjäni'kidzə; ərjənyi'kyēdzyə/ former name (1931–44, 1954–93) for VLADIKAVKAZ.

Ore. ▶ **abbr.** Oregon.

ore /ôr/ ▶ **n.** a naturally occurring solid material from which a metal or valuable mineral can be profitably extracted. [OE. *ōra* 'unwrought metal;' influenced by OE *ār* 'bronze' (rel. to L. *aes* 'crude metal, bronze').]

ø·re /'ərə; 'ɶrə/ ▶ **n.** (pl. same) a monetary unit of Denmark and Norway, equal to one hundredth of a krone.

ö·re /'ərə; 'ɶrə/ ▶ **n.** (pl. same) a monetary unit of Sweden, equal to one hundredth of a krona.

o·re·ad /'ôrē,ad/ ▶ **n.** Gk. & Rom. Mythol. a nymph believed to inhabit mountains. [from L. *Oreas, Oread-*, from Gk. *Oreias*, from *oros* 'mountain.']

ore·bod·y /'ôr,bädē/ ▶ **n.** a connected mass of ore in a mine or suitable for mining.

o·rec·chi·et·te /,ôri'kyetē/ ▶ **n.** a small ear-shaped pasta. [Ital., lit. 'little ears.']

o·rec·tic /ô'rektik/ ▶ **adj.** tech., rare of or concerning desire or appetite. [17th C.: from Gk. *orektikos*, from *oregein* 'stretch out, reach for.']

Oreg. ▶ **abbr.** Oregon.

o·reg·a·no /ə'regə,nō/ ▶ **n.** an aromatic plant (*Origanum vulgare*) of the mint family, related to marjoram, with leaves that are used fresh or dried as a culinary herb.

Or·e·gon /'ôrigən; 'är-; -,gän/ a state in the northwestern US, on the Pacific coast; pop. 3,421,399; capital, Salem; statehood, Feb. 14, 1859 (33). Many Americans arrived via the Oregon Trail during the early

1840s; by 1846, Britain formally ceded the territory to the US. — **Or·e·go·ni·an** /ˌôriˈgōnēən/ **adj. & n.**

Or·e·gon fir ▶ **n.** (also **Oregon pine**) another term for DOUGLAS FIR.

Or·e·gon grape (also **Oregon grape holly**) ▶ **n.** an evergreen shrub (*Mahonia aquifolium*) of the barberry family, bearing yellow flowers and edible blue berries, found on the western coast of the US.

Or·e·gon Trail a route across the central and western US used esp. 1840–60 by settlers moving west.

Ore Moun·tains another name for the ERZGEBIRGE.

O·ren·burg /ˈôrənbərg; əryinˈbo͝ork/ a city in southern Russia; pop. 552,000. Called CHKALOV 1938–57.

O·re·o /ˈôrēˌō/ ▶ **n.** (pl. **-os**) trademark a brand of chocolate sandwich cookie with a creamy white filling. ■ derog. an African-American who is seen, esp. by other blacks, as wishing to be part of the white establishment.

O·res·tes /ôˈrestēz/ Gk. Mythol. the son of Agamemnon and Clytemnestra. He killed his mother and her lover Aegisthus to avenge the murder of Agamemnon.

Ø·re·sund /ˈôrəˌso͞ond; ˈœrə-/ a narrow channel between Sweden and the Danish island of Zealand. Also called THE SOUND.

org /ôrg/ (usu **.org**) ▶ **abbr.** organization (in Internet addresses).

org. ▶ **abbr.** ■ organic. ■ organization. ■ organized.

or·gan /ˈôrgən/ ▶ **n.** **1** (also **pipe organ**) a large musical instrument having rows of tuned pipes sounded by compressed air, and played using one or more keyboards to produce a wide range of musical effects. ■ a smaller instrument without pipes, producing similar sounds electronically. See also REED ORGAN. **2** Biol. a part of an organism that is typically self-contained and has a specific vital function, such as the heart or liver in humans. ■ a department or organization that performs a specified function. ■ a medium of communication, esp. a newspaper or periodical that serves a particular organization, political party, etc.: *the People's Daily, the official organ of the Chinese Communist Party.* ■ (used euphemistically) the penis. ■ archaic a region of the brain formerly held to be the seat of a particular faculty. [OE, via L. from Gk. *organon* 'tool, instrument, sense organ.']

or·gan·dy /ˈôrgəndē/ (also **or·gan·die**) ▶ **n.** (pl. **-dies**) a fine translucent cotton or silk fabric that is usually stiffened and is used for women's clothing. [19th C.: from Fr. *organdi.*]

or·gan·elle /ˌôrgəˈnel/ ▶ **n.** Biol. any of a number of organized or specialized structures within a living cell. [20th C.: from mod. L. *organella*, dimin. of *organum* 'instrument, tool' (see ORGAN).]

or·gan grind·er ▶ **n.** a street musician who plays a barrel organ.

or·gan·ic /ôrˈganik/ ▶ **adj.** **1** of, relating to, or derived from living matter: *organic soils.* ■ Chem. of, relating to, or denoting compounds containing carbon (other than simple binary compounds and salts) and chiefly or ultimately of biological origin. Compare with INORGANIC. ■ (of food or farming methods) produced without chemical fertilizers, pesticides, or other artificial agents. **2** Physiol. of or relating to a bodily organ or organs. ■ Med. (of a disease) affecting the structure of an organ. **3** denoting a relation between elements of something such that they fit together as parts of a whole. ■ characterized by continuous or natural development. — **or·gan·i·cal·ly** **adv.**

or·gan·ic chem·is·try ▶ **n.** the chemistry of carbon compounds (other than simple salts such as carbonates, oxides, and carbides).

or·gan·i·cism /ôrˈganiˌsizəm/ ▶ **n.** **1** the doctrine that everything in nature has an organic basis or is part of an organic whole. **2** the use or advocacy of literary or artistic forms in which the parts are coordinated in the whole. — **or·gan·i·cist** **adj. & n.** **or·gan·i·cis·tic** /ôrˌganiˈsistik/ **adj.** [19th C.: from Fr. *organicisme.*]

or·gan·ism /ˈôrgəˌnizəm/ ▶ **n.** an individual animal, plant, or single-celled life form. ■ the material structure of such an individual. ■ a whole with interdependent parts, likened to a living being: *the upper strata of the American social organism.* — **or·gan·is·mal** /ˌôrgəˈnizməl/ **adj.** **or·gan·is·mic** /ˌôrgəˈnizmik/ **adj.**

or·gan·ist /ˈôrgənist/ ▶ **n.** a person who plays the organ.

or·gan·i·za·tion /ˌôrgəniˈzāsʜən/ ▶ **n.** **1** the action of organizing something. ■ the structure or arrangement of related or connected items. ■ an efficient and orderly approach to tasks. **2** an organized body of people with a particular purpose, esp. a business, society, association, etc. — **or·gan·i·za·tion·al** **adj.** **or·gan·i·za·tion·al·ly** /-sʜənl-ē/ **adv.**

or·gan·i·za·tion man ▶ **n.** derog. a man who lets his individuality and personal life be dominated by the organization he works for.

Or·gan·i·za·tion of Af·ri·can U·ni·ty (abbr.: **OAU**) an association of African states founded in 1963 for mutual cooperation and the elimination of colonialism in Africa. It is based in Addis Ababa, Ethiopia.

Or·gan·i·za·tion of A·mer·i·can States (abbr.: **OAS**) an association including most of the countries of North and South America, chartered in 1948 by members of the former Pan American Union. Its headquarters are in Washington, DC.

Or·gan·i·za·tion of the Pe·tro·le·um Ex·port·ing Coun·tries (abbr.: **OPEC**) an association of twelve major oil-producing countries, founded in 1960 to coordinate policies and prices, with headquarters in Vienna. Members are Algeria, Angola, Indonesia, Iran, Iraq, Kuwait, Libya, Nigeria, Qatar, Saudi Arabia, the United Arab Emirates, and Venezuela.

or·gan·ize /ˈôrgəˌnīz/ ▶ **v.** [trans.] **1** arrange into a structured whole; order: *organize lessons in a planned way.* ■ coordinate the activities of (a person or group) efficiently. ■ form (a number of people) into a labor union, political group, etc.: *an attempt to organize unskilled workers.* | [intrans.] *campaigns brought women together to organize.* ■ form (a labor union, political group, etc.). ■ archaic arrange or form into a living being or tissue. **2** make arrangements or preparations for (an event or activity); coordinate: *the union organized a 24-hour general strike.* ■ take responsibility for providing or arranging: *he is sometimes asked to organize transportation.* — **or·gan·iz·a·ble** **adj.**

or·gan·ized /ˈôrgəˌnīzd/ ▶ **adj.** arranged in a systematic way, esp. on a large scale. ■ having one's affairs in order so as to deal with them efficiently. ■ having formed a labor union, political group, etc.

or·gan·iz·er /ˈôrgəˌnīzər/ ▶ **n.** **1** a person who organizes. **2** a thing used for organizing. See also ELECTRONIC ORGANIZER, PERSONAL ORGANIZER.

or·gan loft ▶ **n.** a balcony in a church or concert hall for an organ.

organo- ▶ **comb. form** **1** esp. Biol. relating to bodily organs: *organogenesis.* **2** Chem. (forming names of classes of organic compounds containing a particular element or group) organic: *organochlorine* | *organophosphate.* [from Gk. *organon* 'organ'; sense 2 from ORGANIC.]

or·ga·no·chlo·rine /ˌôrgənōˈklôrēn/ ▶ **n.** [often as adj.] any of a large group of pesticides and other synthetic organic compounds with chlorinated aromatic molecules.

or·gan of Cor·ti /ˈkôrtē/ ▶ **n.** Anat. a structure in the cochlea of the inner ear that produces nerve impulses in response to sound vibrations. [19th C.: named after Alfonso *Corti* (1822–76), Ital. anatomist.]

or·ga·no·gen·e·sis /ˌôrgənōˈjenisis/ ▶ **n.** (also **or·ga·nog·e·ny** /ˌôrgəˈnäjənē/) Biol. the production and development of the organs of an animal or plant.

or·ga·no·lep·tic /ˌôrgənōˈleptik/ ▶ **adj.** acting on or involving the use of the sense organs. [19th C.: from Fr. *organoleptique*, from ORGANO- + *lēptikos* 'disposed to take.']

or·ga·no·me·tal·lic /ˌôrgənōməˈtalik/ ▶ **adj.** Chem. (of a compound) containing a metal atom bonded to an organic group or groups.

or·ga·non /ˈôrgəˌnän/ ▶ **n.** an instrument of thought, esp. a means of reasoning or a system of logic. [16th C.: from Gk., lit. 'instrument, organ.']

or·ga·no·phos·pho·rus /ˌôrgənəˈfäsf(ə)rəs; ôrˌganō'-/ ▶ **adj.** [attrib.] denoting synthetic organic compounds containing phosphorus, esp. pesticides and nerve gases of this kind. — **or·ga·no·phos·phate** /-ˈfäsˌfāt/ **n.**

or·ga·no·ther·a·py /ˌôrgənōˈᴛʜerəpē; ôrˌganō-/ ▶ **n.** the treatment of disease with extracts from animal organs, esp. glands. — **or·ga·no·ther·a·peu·tic** /-ˌᴛʜerəˈpyo͞otik/ **adj.**

or·gan stop ▶ **n.** a set of pipes of a similar tone in an organ. ■ the handle of the mechanism that brings such a set into action.

or·ga·num /ˈôrgənəm/ ▶ **n.** (pl. **-na** /-nə/) (in medieval music) a form of early polyphony based on an existing plainsong. [L., from Gk. *organon*, lit. 'instrument, organ.']

or·gan·za /ôrˈganzə/ ▶ **n.** a thin, stiff, transparent fabric made of silk or a synthetic yarn. [19th C.: prob. from *Lorganza*, a US trademark.]

or·gan·zine /ˈôrgənˌzēn/ ▶ **n.** a silk thread made of strands twisted together in the contrary direction to that of each individual strand. [17th C.: from Fr. *organsin*, from Ital. *organzino*, of unknown ultimate origin.]

or·gasm /ˈôrˌgazəm/ ▶ **n.** a climax of sexual excitement, characterized by pleasure centered in the genitals and (in men) accompanied by ejaculation. ▶ **v.** [intrans.] experience an orgasm. [17th C.: from Gk. *orgasmos*, from *organ* 'swell or be excited.']

or·gas·mic /ôrˈgazmik/ ▶ **adj.** of or relating to orgasm. ■ (of a person) able to achieve orgasm. ■ informal, fig. very enjoyable or exciting. — **or·gas·mi·cal·ly** **adv.** **or·gas·tic** /-ˈgastik/ **adj.** **or·gas·ti·cal·ly** /-ˈgastik(ə)lē/ **adv.**

or·geat /ˈôrˌzʜät; -ˌzʜä/ ▶ **n.** a cooling drink made from orange flower water and either barley or almonds. [Fr., from Provençal *orjat*, from *ordi* 'barley,' from L. *hordeum* 'barley.']

or·gi·as·tic /ˌôrjēˈastik/ ▶ **adj.** of or resembling an orgy. — **or·gi·as·ti·cal·ly** **adv.** [17th C.: from Gk. *orgiastikos*, from *orgiazein* 'hold an orgy.']

or·gone /ˈôrgōn/ ▶ **n.** (in the theory of Wilhelm Reich (1897–1957)) a supposed sexual energy or life force distributed throughout the universe that can be collected and stored (in an orgone box) for therapeutic use. [1940s: invented word.]

or·gu·lous /ˈôrg(y)ələs/ ▶ **adj.** literary haughty. [ME: from OFr. *orguillus*, from *orguill* 'pride.']

or·gy /ˈôrjē/ ▶ **n.** (pl. **-gies**) a wild party, esp. one involving excessive drinking and unrestrained sexual activity. ■ excessive indulgence in a specified activity: *an orgy of buying.* ■ (usu. **orgies**) hist. secret rites used in the worship of Bacchus, Dionysus, and other Greek and Roman deities, celebrated with dancing, drunkenness, and singing. [16th C.: from Fr. *orgies*, via L. from Gk. *orgia* 'secret rites or revels.']

or·i·bi /ˈôrəbē; ˈär-/ ▶ **n.** (pl. same or **-bis**) a small antelope (*Ourebia ourebi*) of the African savanna, having a reddish-beige back, white underparts, and short vertical horns. [18th C.: from Afrik., from Khoikhoi.]

or·i·chal·cum /ˌôriˈkalkəm/ (also **or·i·chalc** /ˈôriˌkalk/) ▶ **n.** a yellow metal prized in ancient times, probably a form of brass or a similar alloy. [ME: via L. from Gk. *oreikhalkon*, lit. 'mountain copper.']

o·ri·el /ˈôrēəl/ ▶ **n.** a projection from the wall of a building, typically supported from the ground or

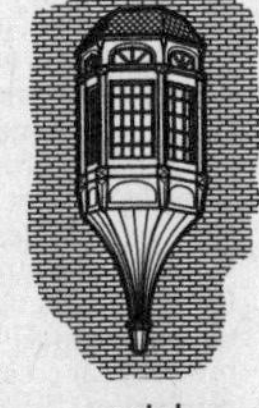
oriel

by corbels. ■ (also **oriel window**) a window in such a structure. ■ a projecting window, often on an upper story; a bay window. [ME: from OFr. *oriol* 'gallery,' of unknown origin.]

o·ri·ent ▶ **n.** /'ôrēˌənt/ **1** (**the Orient**) literary the countries of Asia, esp. eastern Asia. **2** the special luster of a pearl of the finest quality. ■ a pearl with such a luster. ▶ **adj.** literary situated in or belonging to the east; oriental. ■ (of the sun, daylight, etc.) rising. ■ (esp. of precious stones) lustrous (with reference to fine pearls from the East). ▶ **v.** /'ôrēˌent/ **1** [trans.] (often **be oriented**) align or position (something) relative to the points of a compass or other specified positions. ■ adjust or tailor (something) to specified circumstances or needs: *magazines oriented to the business community* | [as adj., in comb.] (**-oriented**) *market-oriented reforms.* ■ guide (someone) physically in a specified direction. **2** (**orient oneself**) find one's position in relation to new and strange surroundings. [ME: via OFr. from L. *orient-* 'rising or east,' from *oriri* 'to rise.']

o·ri·en·tal /ˌôrē'entl/ (also **O·ri·en·tal**) ▶ **adj.** **1** of, from, or characteristic of the Far East: *oriental countries.* ■ dated of, from, or characteristic of the countries of Asia. ■ (**Oriental**) Zool. of, relating to, or denoting a zoogeographical region comprising Asia south of the Himalayas and Indonesia west of Wallace's line. **2** (of a pearl or other jewel) orient. ▶ **n.** (**Oriental**) often offens. a person of Far Eastern descent. — **o·ri·en·tal·ize** **v.** **o·ri·en·tal·ly** **adv.**

– USAGE The term **Oriental**, which has many associations with European imperialism in Asia, is regarded as offensive by many Asians, esp. Asian Americans. **Asian** or, if appropriate, **East Asian** is preferred.

O·ri·en·ta·li·a /ˌôrē-en'tālēə/ ▶ **plural n.** books and other items relating to or characteristic of the Orient.

O·ri·en·tal·ism /ˌôrē'entlˌizəm/ ▶ **n.** something considered characteristic of the peoples and cultures of western, eastern, or central Asia. ■ the knowledge and study of these languages and cultures. — **O·ri·en·tal·ist** **n.**

o·ri·en·tal pop·py ▶ **n.** a southwestern Asian poppy (*Papaver orientale*) with coarse, deeply cut, hairy leaves and large scarlet flowers with a black mark at the base of each petal.

o·ri·en·tate /'ôrēənˌtāt/ ▶ **v.** another term for **ORIENT**. [19th C.: prob. a back-form. from **ORIENTATION**.]

o·ri·en·ta·tion /ˌôrēən'tāsʜən/ ▶ **n.** the determination of the relative position of something or someone (esp. oneself). ■ the relative physical position or direction of something. ■ Zool. an animal's change of position in response to an external stimulus, esp. with respect to compass directions. ■ familiarization with something. ■ a program of introduction for students new to a school or college. ■ the direction of someone's interest or attitude, esp. political or sexual. — **o·ri·en·ta·tion·al** **adj.** [19th C.: appar. from **ORIENT**.]

o·ri·en·teer /ˌôrēən'ti(ə)r/ ▶ **n.** a person who takes part in orienteering. ▶ **v.** [intrans.] take part in orienteering.

o·ri·en·teer·ing /ˌôriən'ti(ə)riɴɢ/ ▶ **n.** a competitive sport in which participants find their way to various checkpoints across rough country with the aid of a map and compass. [1940s: from Swed. *orientering*.]

or·i·fice /'ôrəfis/ ▶ **n.** an opening, as of a pipe or tube, or one in the body, such as a nostril or the anus. [ME: from Fr., from late L. *orificium*, from *os, or-* 'mouth' + *facere* 'make.']

or·i·flamme /'ôrəˌflam; 'är-/ ▶ **n.** literary (in historical use) a scarlet banner or knight's standard. ■ a principle or ideal that serves as a rallying point in a struggle. [ME: from OFr., from L. *aurum* 'gold' + *flamma* 'flame.']

orig. ▶ **abbr.** ■ origin. ■ original; originally.

o·ri·ga·mi /ˌôrə'gämē/ ▶ **n.** the Japanese art of folding paper into decorative shapes and figures. [Japanese, from *oru, -ori* 'fold' + *kami* 'paper.']

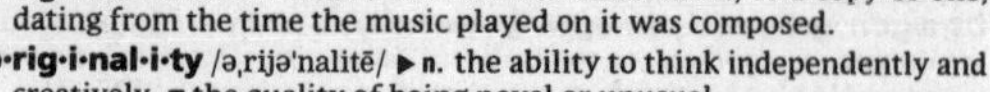

origami

Or·i·gen /'ôriˌjen; 'är-/ (*c.*185–*c.*254), Christian scholar and theologian, probably born in Alexandria, Egypt.

or·i·gin /'ôrəjən/ ▶ **n.** **1** the beginning of something's existence. ■ a person's social background or ancestry. ■ the place or situation from which something comes. **2** Anat. the place or point where a muscle, nerve, or other body part arises, in particular: ■ the more fixed end or attachment of a muscle. ■ a place where a nerve or blood vessel begins or branches from a main nerve or blood vessel. **3** Math. a fixed point from which coordinates are measured, as where axes intersect. [16th C.: from Fr. *origine*, from L. *origo, origin-*, from *oriri* 'to rise.']

o·rig·i·nal /ə'rijənl/ ▶ **adj.** **1** used or produced at the creation or earliest stage of something. ■ [attrib.] present or existing at the beginning of a series or process; first: *the original owner of the house.* **2** created directly and personally by a particular artist; not a copy or imitation: *original Rembrandts.* **3** not dependent on other people's ideas; inventive and unusual. ▶ **n.** **1** something serving as a model or basis for imitations or copies: *the portrait may be a copy of the original.* ■ (**the original**) the form or language in which something was first produced or created: *the study of Russian texts in the original.* ■ (**the original of**) a person or place on which a character or location in a literary work is based: *the paper where the original of the play's Walter Burns worked.* ■ a song, picture, etc., produced by a performer or artist personally. ■ a book or recording that has not been previously made available in a different form: *paperback originals.* ■ a garment made to order from a design specially prepared for a fashion collection. **2** an eccentric or unusual person: *he was one of the true originals.*

o·rig·i·nal in·stru·ment ▶ **n.** a musical instrument, or a copy of one, dating from the time the music played on it was composed.

o·rig·i·nal·i·ty /əˌrijə'nalitē/ ▶ **n.** the ability to think independently and creatively. ■ the quality of being novel or unusual.

o·rig·i·nal·ly /ə'rijənl-ē/ ▶ **adv.** **1** from or in the beginning; at first. **2** in a novel and inventive way.

o·rig·i·nal sin ▶ **n.** Christian Theol. the tendency to sin innate in all human beings, held to be inherited from Adam in consequence of the Fall.

o·rig·i·nate /ə'rijəˌnāt/ ▶ **v.** [intrans.] have a specified beginning: *the word originated as a marketing term.* ■ [trans.] create or initiate (something): *he originated this particular cliché.* — **o·rig·i·na·tion** /əˌrijə'nāsʜən/ **n.** **o·rig·i·na·tive** /-ˌnātiv/ **adj.** **o·rig·i·na·tor** /-ˌnātər/ **n.**

o·rig·i·na·tion fee /əˌrijə'nāsʜən/ ▶ **n.** Finance a fee charged by a lender on entering into a loan agreement to cover the cost of processing the loan.

Or·i·mul·sion /äri'məlsʜən/ ▶ **n.** trademark, a fuel consisting of an emulsion of bitumen in water.

O-ring ▶ **n.** a gasket in the form of a ring with a circular cross section, typically made of pliable material, used to seal connections in pipes, tubes, etc.

Or·i·no·co /ˌôrə'nōkō/ a river in northern South America that rises in Venezuela and flows 1,280 miles (2,060 km) to the Atlantic Ocean.

o·ri·ole /'ôrēˌōl/ ▶ **n.** **1** an Old World bird (genus *Oriolus*, family Oriolidae) related to the starlings that feeds on fruit and insects, the male typically having bright yellow and black plumage. **2** a New World bird (genus *Icterus*) of the American blackbird family, with black and orange or yellow plumage, including the **Baltimore oriole** (*I. galbula*). [18th C.: from med. L. *oriolus*, from L. *aureus* 'golden,' from *aurum* 'gold.']

O·ri·on /ə'rīən/ **1** Gk. Mythol. a giant and hunter who was changed into a constellation at his death. **2** Astron. a conspicuous constellation (the Hunter), said to represent a hunter holding a club and shield. It lies on the celestial equator and contains many bright stars, including Rigel, Betelgeuse, and a line of three that form **Orion's belt**.

or·i·son /'ôrisən; -zən; 'är-/ ▶ **n.** archaic a prayer. [ME: from OFr. *oreison*, from L. *oratio(n-)* 'speech' (see **ORATION**).]

O·ris·sa /ô'risə/ a state in eastern India, on the Bay of Bengal; capital, Bhubaneswar.

-orium ▶ **suffix** forming nouns denoting a place for a particular function: *auditorium* | *sanatorium.* [from L.; cf. **-ORY**[1].]

O·ri·ya /ô'rēə/ ▶ **n.** (pl. same or **-yas**) **1** a native or inhabitant of Orissa. **2** the Indic language of this people, closely related to Bengali. [from Hindi *Uriyā*.]

Ork·ney Is·lands /'ôrknē/ (also **Ork·ney** or **the Ork·neys**) a group of more than 70 islands off the northeastern tip of Scotland, an administrative region of Scotland; pop. 19,000; chief town, Kirkwall.

Or·lan·do /ôr'landō/ a city in central Florida; pop. 185,951.

orle /ôrl/ ▶ **n.** Heraldry a narrow border inset from the edge of a shield. [16th C.: from Fr. *ourle*, from *ourler* 'to hem,' based on L. *ora* 'edge.']

Or·le·an·ist /'ôrlēənist/ ▶ **n.** hist. a person supporting the claim to the French throne of the descendants of the Duke of Orleans (1640–1701), younger brother of Louis XIV.

Or·le·ans /ôr'lē(ə)nz; ôrlā'äɴ/ a city in central France; pop. 108,000. French name **Orléans**.

Or·lon /'ôrˌlän/ ▶ **n.** trademark a synthetic acrylic fiber used for textiles and knitwear, or a fabric made from it. [1950s: invented word.]

or·lop /'ôrˌläp/ (also **orlop deck**) ▶ **n.** the lowest deck of a wooden sailing ship with three or more decks. [ME: from Du. *overloop* 'covering,' from *overlopen* 'run over.']

Or·man·dy /'ôrməndē/, Eugene (1899–1985), US conductor; born in Hungary; born *Jeno Blau.* He conducted the Philadelphia Orchestra 1938–80.

Or·mazd /'ôrməzd/ (also **Or·muzd**) another name for **Ahura Mazda**.

or·mo·lu /'ôrməˌlo͞o/ ▶ **n.** a gold-colored alloy of copper, zinc, and sometimes tin, cast into desired shapes and often gilded, used esp. in the 18th century for decorating furniture and making ornaments. [18th C.: from Fr. *or moulu* 'powdered gold' (used in gilding).]

or·na·ment ▶ **n.** /'ôrnəmənt/ a thing used to adorn something but usually having no practical purpose, esp. a small object such as a figurine. ■ a quality or person adding grace, beauty, or honor to something. ■ decoration added to embellish something, esp. a building. ■ (**ornaments**) Music embellishments and decorations, such as trills or grace notes, added to a melody. ■ (usu. **ornaments**) Christian Church the accessories of worship, such as the altar, chalice, and sacred vessels. ▶ **v.** /'ôrnəˌment/ [trans.] adorn; beautify. [ME: from OFr. *ournement*, from L. *ornamentum* 'ornament,' from *ornare* 'adorn.']

or·na·men·tal /ˌôrnə'mentl/ ▶ **adj.** serving or intended as an ornament; decorative: *an ornamental fountain.* ▶ **n.** a plant or tree grown for its attractive appearance. — **or·na·men·tal·ism** **n.** **or·na·men·tal·ist** **n.** **or·na·men·tal·ly** **adv.**

or·na·men·ta·tion /ˌôrnəmən'tāsʜən/ ▶ **n.** things added to something to provide decoration. ■ the action of decorating something or making it more elaborate.

or·nate /ôr'nāt/ ▶ **adj.** made in an intricate shape or decorated with complex patterns. ■ (of literary style) using unusual words and complex constructions. ■ (of musical composition or performance) using many ornaments such as grace notes and trills. — **or·nate·ly** adv. **or·nate·ness** n. [ME: from L. *ornatus* 'adorned,' past part. of *ornare*.]

or·ner·y /'ôrn(ə)rē/ ▶ adj. informal bad-tempered and combative. ■ stubborn. — **or·ner·i·ness** n. [19th C.: dial. var. of ORDINARY.]

ornith. ▶ abbr. ■ ornithological. ■ ornithology.

or·ni·thine /'ôrnə,THēn/ ▶ n. Biochem. an amino acid, $NH_2(CH_2)_3CH(NH_2)$-COOH, produced by the body that is important in protein metabolism. [19th C.: from ORNITHO- (with ref. to a constituent found in bird excrement) + -INE[4].]

or·nith·is·chi·an /,ôrnə'THiskēən/ Paleontol. ▶ adj. of, relating to, or denoting herbivorous dinosaurs of an order (Ornithischia) distinguished by having a pelvic structure resembling that of birds. Compare with SAURISCHIAN. ▶ n. an ornithischian dinosaur. [20th C.: from mod. L. *Ornithischia*, from ORNITHO- + Gk.*iskhion* 'hip joint.']

ornitho- ▶ comb. form relating to or resembling a bird or birds: *ornithology* | *ornithopod*. [from Gk. *ornis, ornith-* 'bird.']

or·ni·thol·o·gy /,ôrnə'THäləjē/ ▶ n. the scientific study of birds. — **or·ni·tho·log·i·cal** /,ôrniTHə'läjikəl/ adj. **or·ni·tho·log·i·cal·ly** /,ôrniTHə'läjik(ə)lē/ adv. **or·ni·thol·o·gist** n.

or·ni·tho·pod /'ôrnəTHə,päd/ ▶ n. a mainly bipedal herbivorous dinosaur (infraorder Ornithopoda, order Ornithischia). [19th C.: from mod. L. *Ornithopoda*, from ORNITHO- + Gk. *pous, pod-* 'foot.']

or·ni·thop·ter /,ôrnə'THäptər/ ▶ n. esp. hist. a machine designed to achieve flight by means of flapping wings. [20th C.: coined in Fr. as *ornithoptère*.]

or·ni·tho·rhyn·chus /,ôrnəTHə'riNGkəs/ ▶ n. another term for PLATYPUS. [19th C.: mod. L., from ORNITHO- + Gk. *rhunkhos* 'bill.']

or·ni·tho·sis /,ôrnə'THōsis/ ▶ n. another term for PSITTACOSIS.

oro- ▶ comb. form of or relating to mountains: *orogeny*. [from Gk. *oros* 'mountain.']

or·o·gen /'ôrəjen; -jən/ ▶ n. Geol. a belt of the earth's crust involved in the formation of mountains.

o·rog·e·ny /ô'räjənē/ ▶ n. Geol. a process in which a section of the earth's crust is folded and deformed by lateral compression to form a mountain range. — **or·o·gen·e·sis** /,ôrō'jenəsis/ n. **or·o·gen·ic** /,ôrō'jenik/ adj.

or·o·graph·ic /,ôrə'grafik/ ▶ adj. of or relating to mountains, esp. with regard to their position and form. ■ (of clouds or rainfall) resulting from the effects of mountains in forcing moist air to rise. — **or·o·graph·i·cal** adj.

o·rog·ra·phy /ô'rägrəfē/ ▶ n. the branch of physical geography dealing with mountains.

O·ro·mo /ô'rōmō/ ▶ n. (pl. same or **-mos**) **1** a member of the largest ethnic group in Ethiopia. **2** the Cushitic language of this people. ▶ adj. of or relating to this people or their language. [the name in Oromo.]

O·ron·tes /ô'räntēz/ a river in southwestern Asia that rises in northern Lebanon and flows to the Mediterranean Sea.

o·ro·phar·ynx /,ôrō'fariNGks/ ▶ n. (pl. **-pha·ryn·ges** /-fə'rinjēz/ or **-phar·ynx·es**) Anat. the part of the pharynx that lies between the soft palate and the hyoid bone. — **o·ro·pha·ryn·ge·al** /-fə'rinj(ē)əl; -,farən'jēəl/ adj. [19th C.: from L. *os, -or* 'mouth' + PHARYNX.]

o·ro·tund /'ôrə,tənd/ ▶ adj. (of the voice or phrasing) full, round, and imposing. ■ (of writing, style, or expression) pompous; pretentious. — **o·ro·tun·di·ty** /,ôrə'təndité/ n. [18th C.: from L. *ore rotundo* 'with rounded mouth.']

or·phan /'ôrfən/ ▶ n. **1** a child whose parents are dead. ■ a person or thing bereft of protection, position, etc. **2** Print. the first line of a paragraph set as the last line of a page or column, considered undesirable. ▶ v. [trans.] (usu. **be orphaned**) make (a person or animal) an orphan: *John was orphaned at 12.* ▶ adj. denoting, of, or for an orphan or orphans. ■ bereft of protection, position, etc. — **or·phan·hood** n. [ME: via late L. from Gk. *orphanos* 'bereaved.']

or·phan·age /'ôrfənij/ ▶ n. a residential institution for the care and education of orphans. ■ archaic the state or condition of being an orphan.

or·phan drug ▶ n. a pharmaceutical that remains commercially undeveloped owing to limited potential for profitability.

Or·phe·us /'ôrfēəs/ Gk. Mythol. a poet and lyre player who went to the underworld after the death of his wife Eurydice and secured her release from the dead, but lost her because he disobeyed the condition that he not look back at her until they had reached the world of the living. — **Or·phe·an** /-fēən/ adj.

Or·phic /'ôrfik/ ▶ adj. of or concerning Orpheus or Orphism.

Or·phism /'ôr,fizəm/ ▶ n. **1** a mystic religion of ancient Greece, based on poems attributed to Orpheus, emphasizing the necessity for individuals to rid themselves of the evil part of their nature by ritual and moral purification throughout a series of reincarnations. **2** a short-lived art movement (*c.*1912) within cubism, pioneered by a group of French painters and emphasizing the lyrical use of color rather than the austere intellectual cubism of Picasso.

or·phrey /'ôrfrē/ ▶ n. (pl. **-phreys**) an ornamental stripe or border, esp. one on an ecclesiastical vestment such as a chasuble. [ME: from OFr. *orfreis*, from a med. L. alt. of *auriphrygium*, from L. *aurum* 'gold' + *Phrygius* 'Phrygian.']

or·pi·ment /'ôrpəmənt/ ▶ n. a bright yellow mineral consisting of arsenic trisulfide, formerly used as a dye and artist's pigment. [ME: via OFr. from L. *auripigmentum*, from *aurum* 'gold' + *pigmentum* 'pigment.']

or·pine /'ôrpən/ (also **or·pin**) ▶ n. a purple-flowered Eurasian plant (*Sedum telephium*) of the stonecrop family, a naturalized weed of North America. [ME: from OFr. *orpine*, prob. an alt. of ORPIMENT.]

Or·ping·ton /'ôrpiNGtən/ ▶ n. **1** a full-bodied breed of chicken of buff, white, or black color. **2** a duck of a buff or white breed, kept for its meat. [19th C.: from *Orpington*, England.]

Orr /ôr/, Bobby (1948–), Canadian hockey player; full name *Robert Gordon Orr*. He played for the Boston Bruins 1966–76.

or·rer·y /'ôrərē/ ▶ n. (pl. **-rer·ies**) a mechanical model of the solar system, or of just the sun, earth, and moon, used to represent their relative positions and motions. [18th C.: named after the fourth Earl of *Orrery*.]

or·ris /'ôris/ (also **or·ris·root**) ▶ n. a preparation of the fragrant rootstock of an iris (usu. *Iris* × *germanica* var. 'Florentina'), used in perfumery and formerly in medicine. [16th C.: appar. alt. of IRIS.]

ort /ôrt/ (usu. **orts**) ▶ n. archaic dialect a scrap or remainder of food from a meal. [ME: from Mid. Low Ger. *orte* 'food remains,' second element rel. to EAT.]

Or·te·ga /ôr'tāgə/, Daniel (1945–), president of Nicaragua 1985–90, 2007– ; full name *José Daniel Ortega Saavedra*.

orth. ▶ abbr. ■ orthopedic; orthopedics.

ortho- ▶ comb. form **1** straight; rectangular; upright: *orthodontics*. ■ right; correct: *orthoepy*. **2** Chem. denoting substitution at two adjacent carbon atoms in a benzene ring, e.g., in 1, 2 positions: *orthodichlorobenzene*. Compare with META- and PARA-[1]. **3** Chem. denoting a compound from which a *meta*-compound is formed by dehydration: *orthophosphoric acid*. [from Gk. *orthos* 'straight, right.']

or·tho·ce·phal·ic /,ôrTHōsə'falik/ ▶ adj. having a head with a medium ratio of breadth to height.

or·tho·chro·mat·ic /,ôrTHōkrə'matik/ ▶ adj. (of black-and-white photographic film) sensitive to all visible light except red. Often contrasted with PANCHROMATIC.

or·tho·clase /'ôrTHə,klās; -,klāz/ ▶ n. a common rock-forming mineral occurring typically as white or pink crystals. It is a potassium-rich alkali feldspar and is used in ceramics and glassmaking. [19th C.: from ORTHO- 'straight' + Gk. *klasis* 'breaking.']

or·tho·don·tics /,ôrTHə'däntiks/ (also **or·tho·don·tia** /-'dänsH(ē)ə/) ▶ plural n. [treated as sing.] the treatment of irregularities in the teeth (esp. of alignment and occlusion) and jaws, including the use of braces. — **or·tho·don·tic** adj. **or·tho·don·ti·cal·ly** adv. **or·tho·don·tist** n. [20th C.: from ORTHO- 'straight' + Gk. *odous, odont-* 'tooth.']

or·tho·dox /'ôrTHə,däks/ ▶ adj. **1** (of a person or their views, esp. religious or political ones) conforming to what is accepted as right or true: *orthodox Hindus.* ■ (of a person) not independent-minded; unoriginal: *a relatively orthodox artist.* **2** (of a thing) of the ordinary or usual type; normal: *they avoided orthodox jazz venues.* **3** (usu. **Orthodox**) (of the Jews or Judaism) strictly keeping to traditional doctrine and ritual. **4** (usu. **Orthodox**) of or relating to the Orthodox Church. — **or·tho·dox·ly** adv. [ME: from Gk. *orthodoxos*, from *orthos* 'straight or right' + *doxa* 'opinion.']

Or·tho·dox Church a Christian church or federation of churches originating in the Greek-speaking church of the Byzantine Empire, not accepting the authority of the pope.

Or·tho·dox Ju·da·ism a major branch within Judaism that teaches strict adherence to rabbinical interpretation of Jewish law and its traditional observances.

or·tho·dox·y /'ôrTHə,däksē/ ▶ n. (pl. **-dox·ies**) **1** authorized or generally accepted theory, doctrine, or practice. ■ the quality of conforming to such theories, doctrines, or practices. **2** the whole community of Orthodox Jews or Orthodox Christians.

or·tho·drom·ic /,ôrTHə'drämik/ ▶ adj. Physiol. (of an impulse) traveling in the normal direction in a nerve fiber. The opposite of ANTIDROMIC. [1940s: from ORTHO- 'right, correct' + Gk. *dromos* 'running' + -IC.]

or·tho·e·py /ôr'THōəpē/ ▶ n. the correct or accepted pronunciation of words. ■ the study of correct or accepted pronunciation. — **or·tho·ep·ic** /,ôrTHō'epik/ adj. **or·tho·e·pist** n. [17th C.: from Gk. *orthoepeia* 'correct speech,' from *orthos* 'right or straight' + *epos, epe-* 'word.']

or·tho·gen·e·sis /,ôrTHō'jenəsis/ ▶ n. Biol., esp. hist. a theory that variations in evolution follow a particular direction and are not merely sporadic. — **or·tho·gen·e·sist** n. **or·tho·ge·net·ic** /-jə'netik/ adj. **or·tho·ge·net·i·cal·ly** /-jə'netik(ə)lē/ adv.

or·thog·na·thous /ôr'THägnəTHəs/ ▶ adj. Anat. (esp. of a person) having a jaw that does not project or recede, so that the facial profile is nearly vertical. [19th C.: from ORTHO- 'straight' + Gk. *gnathos* 'jaw' + -OUS.]

or·thog·o·nal /ôr'THägənl/ ▶ adj. **1** of or involving right angles; at right angles. **2** Stat. (of variates) statistically independent. ■ (of an experiment) having variates that can be treated as statistically independent. — **or·thog·o·nal·i·ty** /ôr,THägə'nalitē/ n. **or·thog·o·nal·ly** adv. [16th C.: from Fr., based on Gk. *orthogōnios* 'right-angled.']

or·thog·o·nal pro·jec·tion ▶ n. Engin. a system of making engineering drawings showing two or more views of an object at right angles to each other on a single drawing. ■ a drawing made using this method.

or·tho·graph·ic pro·jec·tion /,ôrTHə'grafik/ ▶ n. a method of projection in which an object is depicted or a surface mapped using parallel lines to project its shape onto a plane. ■ a drawing or map made using this method.

or·thog·ra·phy /ôrˈTHägrəfē/ ▶ **n.** (pl. **-phies**) **1** the conventional spelling system of a language. ▪ the study of spelling and how letters combine to represent sounds and form words. **2** another term for ORTHOGRAPHIC PROJECTION. — **or·thog·ra·pher** n. (in sense 1). **or·tho·graph·ic** /ˌôrTHəˈgrafik/ adj. **or·tho·graph·i·cal** /ˌôrTHəˈgrafikəl/ adj. **or·tho·graph·i·cal·ly** /ˌôrTHəˈgrafik(ə)lē/ adv.

or·tho·pe·dics /ˌôrTHəˈpēdiks/ (Brit. **or·tho·pae·dics**) ▶ **plural n.** [treated as sing.] the branch of medicine dealing with the correction of deformities of bones or muscles. — **or·tho·pe·dic** adj. **or·tho·pe·di·cal·ly** adv. **or·tho·pe·dist** /-dist/ n. [19th C.: from Fr. *orthopédie*, from Gk. *orthos* 'right or straight' + *paideia* 'rearing of children.']

or·tho·psy·chi·a·try /ˌôrTHōˌsīˈkīətrē/ ▶ **n.** the branch of psychiatry concerned with the study and prevention of mental or behavioral disorders, with emphasis on child development and family life. — **or·tho·psy·chi·at·ric** /-ˌsīkēˈatrik/ adj. **or·tho·psy·chi·a·trist** n.

or·thop·ter /ôrˈTHäptər/ ▶ **n.** another term for ORNITHOPTER.

Or·thop·ter·a /ôrˈTHäptərə/ Entomol. an order of insects that comprises the grasshoppers, crickets, katydids, etc. They have a saddle-shaped thorax and hind legs that are typically long and modified for jumping. ▪ [as pl. n.] (**orthoptera**) insects of this order. — **or·thop·ter·an** n. & adj. **or·thop·ter·ous** /-tərəs/ adj. [mod. L. (pl.), from ORTHO- 'straight' + Gk. *pteros* 'wing.']

or·thop·ter·oid /ôrˈTHäptəˌroid/ ▶ **adj.** Entomol. of or relating to a group of insect orders related to the grasshoppers, including the stoneflies, stick insects, earwigs, cockroaches, mantises, and termites.

or·thop·tics /ôrˈTHäptiks/ ▶ **plural n.** [treated as sing.] the study or treatment of disorders of vision, esp. of eye movements or eye alignment. — **or·thop·tic** adj. **or·thop·tist** n. [19th C.: from ORTHO- 'correct' + Gk. *optikos* (see OPTIC).]

or·tho·py·rox·ene /ˌôrTHōpīˈräksēn/ ▶ **n.** a mineral of the pyroxene group crystallizing in the orthorhombic system.

or·tho·rhom·bic /ˌôrTHəˈrämbik/ ▶ **adj.** of or denoting a crystal system or three-dimensional geometric arrangement having three unequal axes at right angles.

or·tho·sis /ôrˈTHōsis/ ▶ **n.** (pl. **-ses** /-ˌsēz/) Med. the correction of disorders of the limbs or spine by use of braces and other devices to correct alignment or provide support. ▪ a brace or other such device; orthotic. [1950s: from Gk. *orthōsis* 'making straight,' from *orthoun* 'set straight.']

or·tho·stat·ic /ˌôrTHəˈstatik/ ▶ **adj.** Med. relating to or caused by an upright posture.

or·thot·ic /ôrˈTHätik/ ▶ **adj.** relating to orthotics. ▶ **n.** an artificial support or brace for the limbs or spine. [20th C.: from ORTHOSIS.]

or·thot·ics /ôrˈTHätiks/ ▶ **plural n.** [treated as sing.] the branch of medicine that deals with the provision and use of devices such as braces. ▪ a treatment prescribing such a device, esp. for the foot. — **or·thot·ist** n.

or·tho·trop·ic /ˌôrTHəˈtrōpik; -ˈträp-/ ▶ **adj.** **1** Bot. (of a shoot, stem, or axis) growing vertically. **2** Engin. (of a material) having elastic properties in two or three planes perpendicular to each other.

or·thot·ro·pous /ôrˈTHätrəpəs/ ▶ **adj.** Bot. (of a plant ovule) having the nucleus straight, i.e., not inverted, so that the micropyle is at the end opposite the base.

or·to·lan /ˈôrtl-ən/ (also **ortolan bunting**) ▶ **n.** a small Eurasian songbird (*Emberiza hortulana*) of the bunting family that was formerly eaten as a delicacy, the male having an olive-green head and yellow throat. [16th C.: from Fr., from Provençal, lit. 'gardener,' based on a dimin. of L. *hortus* 'garden.']

ORV ▶ **abbr.** off-road vehicle.

Or·vie·to /ôrˈvyetō/ ▶ **n.** a white wine made near Orvieto, Italy.

Or·well /ˈôrwel/, George (1903–50), British writer; born in India; pen name of *Eric Arthur Blair*. He wrote *Animal Farm* (1945) and *Nineteen Eighty-Four* (1949). — **Or·well·i·an** /ôrˈwelēən/ adj.

-ory[1] ▶ **suffix** (forming nouns) denoting a place for a particular function: *dormitory* | *repository*. — **-orial** suffix forming corresponding adjectives. [from L. *-oria*, *-orium*, sometimes via Anglo-Norman Fr. *-orie*, OFr. *-oire*.]

-ory[2] ▶ **suffix** forming adjectives (and occasionally nouns) relating to or involving a verbal action: *compulsory* | *directory* | *mandatory*. [from L. *-orius*, sometimes via Anglo-Norman Fr. *-ori(e)*.]

o·ryx /ˈôriks/ ▶ **n.** any of several species of antelope (genus *Oryx*) native to arid regions of Africa and Asia, having dark markings on the face and long, pointed horns. [ME: via L. from Gk. *orux* 'stonemason's pickax.']

or·zo /ˈôrzō/ ▶ **n.** a variety of pasta shaped like grains of barley or rice. [Ital., lit. 'barley.']

OS ▶ **abbr.** ▪ (in calculating dates) Old Style. ▪ Comput. operating system. ▪ Ordinary Seaman. ▪ out of stock.

Os ▶ **symb.** the chemical element osmium.

os[1] /äs/ ▶ **n.** (pl. **os·sa** /ˈäsə/) Anat. a bone (used chiefly in Latin names of bones, e.g., *os trapezium*). [L.]

os[2] ▶ **n.** (pl. **o·ra** /ˈôrə/) Anat. an opening or entrance to a passage, esp. one at either end of the cervix of the uterus. [18th C.: from L. *os* 'mouth.']

o.s. ▶ **abbr.** ▪ (in prescriptions) the left eye. [L., *oculus sinister*.]

OSA ▶ **abbr.** Order of St. Augustine (Augustinians).

O·sage /ˈōˌsāj/ ▶ **n.** (pl. same or **O·sages**) **1** a member of an American Indian people formerly inhabiting the Osage River valley in Missouri. **2** the Siouan language of this people. ▶ **adj.** of or relating to this people or their language. [via Fr., from Osage *Wazhazhe*.]

O·sage or·ange ▶ **n.** a small spiny North American deciduous tree (*Maclura pomifera*) of the mulberry family that bears inedible green orangelike fruit. Its durable yellowish-orange wood was formerly used by American Indians for bows and other weapons. Also called BOWWOOD.

O·sage Riv·er a river that flows for 360 miles (580 km) through Missouri to the Missouri River.

O·sa·ka /ōˈsäkə/ a city in central Japan; pop. 2,642,000.

OSB ▶ **abbr.** Order of St. Benedict (Benedictines).

Os·borne /ˈäzˌbôrn; -bərn/, John James (1929–94), English playwright. He wrote *Look Back in Anger* (1956).

Os·can /ˈäskən/ ▶ **n.** an extinct Italic language of southern Italy, related to Umbrian and surviving in inscriptions mainly of the 4th to 1st centuries BC. ▶ **adj.** of or relating to this language. [16th C.: from L. *Oscus* 'Oscan' + -AN.]

Os·car[1] /ˈäskər/ ▶ **n.** trademark the nickname for one of the golden statuettes given as an Academy Award. [one of the several speculative stories of its origin claims that the statuette reminded Margaret Herrick, an executive director of the Academy of Motion Picture Arts and Sciences, of her uncle Oscar.] ▪ (**the Oscars**) the annual presentation of the Academy Awards.

Os·car[2] ▶ **n.** a code word representing the letter O, used in radio communication.

os·car /ˈäskər/ (also **oscar cichlid**) ▶ **n.** a South American cichlid (*Astronotus ocellatus*) with velvety brown young and multicolored adults, popular in aquariums.

Os·ce·o·la /ˌäsēˈōlə; ˌōsē-/ (c.1804–38), Seminole Indian chief. He led his people in the Seminole Wars 1835–42.

os·cil·late /ˈäsəˌlāt/ ▶ **v.** [intrans.] **1** move or swing back and forth at a regular speed: *a pendulum oscillates about its lowest point*. ▪ [with adverbial] fig. waver between extremes of opinion, action, or quality: *he was oscillating between fear and bravery*. **2** Physics vary in magnitude or position in a regular manner around a central point. ▪ (of a circuit or device) cause the electric current or voltage running through it to behave in this way. — **os·cil·la·tion** /ˌäsəˈlāSHən/ n. **os·cil·la·to·ry** /əˈsiləˌtôrē/ adj. [18th C.: from L. *oscillat-* 'swung,' from the v. *oscillare*.]

os·cil·la·tor /ˈäsəˌlātər/ ▶ **n.** a device for generating oscillating electric currents or voltages by nonmechanical means.

oscillo- ▶ **comb. form** relating to oscillation, esp. of electric current: *oscilloscope*.

os·cil·lo·gram /əˈsiləˌgram/ ▶ **n.** a record produced by an oscillograph.

os·cil·lo·graph /əˈsiləˌgraf/ ▶ **n.** a device for recording oscillations, esp. those of an electric current. — **os·cil·lo·graph·ic** /əˌsiləˈgrafik/ adj. **os·cil·log·ra·phy** /ˌäsəˈlägrəfē/ n.

os·cil·lo·scope /əˈsiləˌskōp/ ▶ **n.** a device for viewing oscillations, as of electrical voltage or current, by a display on the screen of a cathode-ray tube. — **os·cil·lo·scop·ic** /əˌsiləˈskäpik/ adj.

os·cine /ˈäsin; ˈäˌsīn/ Ornithol. ▶ **adj.** of, relating to, or denoting passerine birds of a large division (suborder Oscines) that includes the songbirds. ▶ **n.** a bird of this division. [19th C.: from L. *oscen*, *oscin-* 'songbird' + -INE[1].]

Os·co-Um·bri·an /ˈäskō ˈəmbrēən/ ▶ **n.** **1** a group of ancient Italic languages including Oscan and Umbrian, spoken in Italy in the 1st millennium BC. **2** a member of any of the peoples who spoke a language of this group. ▶ **adj.** of or relating to these peoples or their languages.

os·cu·la /ˈäskyələ/ plural form of OSCULUM.

os·cu·lar /ˈäskyələr/ ▶ **adj.** **1** humorous of or relating to kissing. **2** Zool. of or relating to an osculum. [19th C.: from L. *osculum* 'mouth, kiss' (dimin. of *os* 'mouth') + -AR[1].]

os·cu·late /ˈäskyəˌlāt/ ▶ **v.** [trans.] **1** Math. (of a curve or surface) touch (another curve or surface) so as to have a common tangent at the point of contact. **2** formal humorous kiss. — **os·cu·lant** /-lənt/ adj. **os·cu·la·tion** /ˌäskyəˈlāSHən/ n. **os·cu·la·to·ry** /-ləˌtôrē/ adj. [17th C.: from L. *osculat-* 'kissed,' from the v. *osculari*, from *osculum*.]

os·cu·lum /ˈäskyələm/ ▶ **n.** (pl. **-la** /-lə/) Zool. a large aperture in a sponge through which water is expelled. [17th C.: from L., 'little mouth.']

-ose[1] ▶ **suffix** (forming adjectives) having a specified quality: *bellicose* | *comatose* | *verbose*. — **-osely** suffix forming corresponding adverbs **-oseness** suffix forming corresponding nouns. Compare with -OSITY. [from L. *-osus*.]

-ose[2] ▶ **suffix** Chem. forming names of sugars and other carbohydrates: *cellulose* | *glucose*. [on the pattern of *(gluc)ose*.]

OSF ▶ **abbr.** Order of St. Francis (Franciscans).

OSHA /ˈōSHə/ ▶ **abbr.** (in the US) Occupational Safety and Health Administration.

o·sier /ˈōZHər/ ▶ **n.** **1** a small Eurasian willow (*Salix viminalis*) that grows mostly in wet habitats and is a major source of the long flexible shoots (withies) used in basketwork. ▪ a shoot of a willow. ▪ dated any willow tree. **2** n. any of several North American dogwoods. [ME: from OFr.]

O·si·ris /ōˈsīris/ Egyptian Mythol. a god, husband of Isis and father of Horus, known chiefly through his death at the hands of his brother Seth and his restoration to a new life as ruler of the afterlife. — **O·si·ri·an** /-rēən/ adj.

-osis ▶ **suffix** (pl. **-oses**) denoting a process or condition: *metamorphosis*. ▪ denoting a pathological state: *neurosis* | *thrombosis*. [via L. from Gk. *-ōsis*, verbal n. ending.]

-osity ▶ **suffix** forming nouns from adjectives ending in *-ose* (such as *ver-*

bosity from *verbose*) and from adjectives ending in *-ous* (such as *pomposity* from *pompous*). [from Fr. *-osité* or L. *-ositas*.]

Os·lo /'äz,lō; 'äs-/ the capital of Norway, on the southern coast at the head of Oslofjord; pop. 450,000.

Os·man I /'äzmən; 'äs-; äs'män/ (also **Oth·man** /'äTH-/) (1259–1326), Turkish conqueror. He founded the Ottoman (Osmanli) dynasty and empire.

Os·man·li /äz'mänlē; äs-/ ▶ **adj.** & **n.** (pl. same or **-lis**) old-fashioned term for **OTTOMAN**. [Turk., from *Osman*, from Arab. *uṯmān* (see **OTTOMAN**).]

os·mic /'äzmik/ ▶ **adj.** relating to odors or the sense of smell. — **os·mi·cal·ly adv.** [20th C.: from Gk. *osmē* 'smell, odor' + **-IC**.]

os·mi·um /'äzmēəm/ ▶ **n.** the chemical element of atomic number 76, a hard, dense, silvery-white metal of the transition series. (Symbol: **Os**) [19th C.: mod. L., from Gk. *osmē* 'smell.']

osmo- ▶ **comb. form** representing **OSMOSIS**.

os·mom·e·ter /äz'mämitər/ ▶ **n.** an instrument for demonstrating or measuring osmotic pressure. — **os·mo·met·ric** /-mə'metrik/ **adj.** **os·mom·e·try n.**

os·mo·reg·u·la·tion /,äzmō,regyə'lāSHən/ ▶ **n.** Biol. the maintenance of constant osmotic pressure in the fluids of an organism by the control of water and salt concentrations. — **os·mo·reg·u·la·to·ry** /-'regyələ,tôrē/ **adj.**

os·mose /'äzmōs; 'äs-/ ▶ **v.** [intrans.] rare pass by or as if by osmosis. [19th C.: see **OSMOSIS**.]

os·mo·sis /äz'mōsis; äs-/ ▶ **n.** Biol. Chem. the tendency of molecules of a solvent to pass through a semipermeable membrane from a less concentrated solution into a more concentrated one, equalizing the concentrations on each side of the membrane. ■ fig. the process of gradual or unconscious assimilation of ideas, knowledge, etc. — **os·mot·ic** /-mätik/ **adj.** **os·mot·i·cal·ly** /-'mädik(ə)lē/ **adv.** [19th C.: Latinized form of *osmose*, from Gk. *ōsmos* 'a push.']

os·mot·ic pres·sure /äz'mätik/ ▶ **n.** Chem. the pressure to be applied to a pure solvent to prevent it from passing into a given solution by osmosis, often used to express the concentration of the solution.

os·mun·da /äz'məndə/ ▶ **n.** a fern of the genus *Osmunda* (family Osmundaceae), which includes the royal and cinnamon ferns. [Anglo-L., from Anglo-Norman Fr. *osmunde*, of unknown origin.]

os·na·burg /'äznə,bərg/ ▶ **n.** a kind of coarse, heavy linen or cotton used for such items as furnishings and sacks. [ME: alt. of *Osnabrück*, the German city where the cloth was made.]

os·prey /'äsprē; -prā/ ▶ **n.** (pl. **-preys**) a large fish-eating bird of prey (*Pandion haliaetus*, family Pandionidae) with long narrow wings and a white underside and crown, found throughout the world. Also called **FISH HAWK**. [ME: from OFr. *ospres*, appar. based on L. *ossifraga* (the lammergeier), from *os* 'bone' + *frangere* 'to break.']

OSS ▶ **abbr.** Office of Strategic Services, a US intelligence organization during World War II.

os·sa /'äsə/ plural form of **OS**[1].

Os·sa, Mount /'äsə/ a mountain in Thessaly, in northeastern Greece, south of Mount Olympus, that rises to a height of 6,489 feet (1,978 m).

os·se·in /'äsē-in/ ▶ **n.** Biochem. the collagen of bones, used for glues and gelatin, derived by dissolving the mineral content in an acid solution. [19th C.: from L. *osseus* 'bony' + **-IN**.]

os·se·ous /'äsēəs/ ▶ **adj.** esp. Zool. Med. consisting of or turned into bone; ossified. [ME: from L. *osseus* 'bony' + **-OUS**.]

Os·sete /'äsēt/ ▶ **n.** (also **Os·set**) **1** a native or inhabitant of Ossetia. **2** another term for **OSSETIAN** (the language). ▶ **adj.** of or relating to Ossetia or the Ossetes.

Os·se·tia /ô'sēSHə; ə'syetēə/ a region of the central Caucasus, divided into North Ossetia and South Ossetia.

Os·se·tian /ä'sēSHən/ ▶ **n.** **1** the Iranian language of the Ossetes. **2** a native or inhabitant of Ossetia. ▶ **adj.** of or relating to the Ossetes or their language. — **Os·set·ic** /ä'setik/ **adj.** & **n.**

Os·sian /'äsēən/ a legendary Irish warrior and bard, whose name became well known in 1760–63 when the Scottish poet James Macpherson (1736–96) published his own verse as an alleged translation of 3rd-century Gaelic tales. Irish name **OISIN**. — **Os·si·an·ic adj.**

os·si·cle /'äsikəl/ ▶ **n.** Anat. Zool. a very small bone, esp. one of those in the middle ear. ■ Zool. a small piece of calcified material forming part of the skeleton of an invertebrate animal such as an echinoderm. [16th C.: from L. *ossiculum*, dimin. of *os* 'bone.']

os·sif·er·ous /ä'sifərəs/ ▶ **adj.** Geol. (of a cave or stratum) containing or yielding deposits of bone, esp. fossil bone.

os·si·fy /'äsə,fī/ ▶ **v.** (**-fies, -fied**) [intrans.] turn into bone or bony tissue. ■ [often as adj.] (**ossified**) fig. cease developing; be stagnant or rigid. — **os·si·fi·ca·tion** /,äsəfi'kāSHən/ **n.**

os·so buc·co /'äsō 'bo͝okō; 'ōsō/ ▶ **n.** (also **os·so bu·co, os·so·bu·co**) an Italian dish made with veal shank stewed in wine with vegetables. [Ital., lit. 'marrowbone.']

os·su·ar·y /'äsHo͞o,erē; 'äs(y)o͞o-/ ▶ **n.** (pl. **-ar·ies**) a container or room into which the bones of dead people are placed. [17th C.: from late L. *ossuarium*, formed irregularly from L. *os, oss-* 'bone.']

Os·te·ich·thy·es /,ästē'ikTHē-ēz/ Zool. a class of fishes that includes those with a bony skeleton. Compare with **CHONDRICHTHYES**. [mod. L. (pl.), from Gk. *osteon* 'bone' + *ikhthus* 'fish.']

os·te·i·tis /,ästē'ītis/ ▶ **n.** Med. inflammation of the substance of a bone. [19th C.: from Gk. *osteon* 'bone' + **-ITIS**.]

os·ten·si·ble /ä'stensəbəl; ə'sten-/ ▶ **adj.** [attrib.] stated or appearing to be true, but not necessarily so. — **os·ten·si·bil·i·ty** /-,stensə'bilitē/ **n.** [18th C.: from Fr., from med. L. *ostensibilis* from L. *ostens-* 'stretched out to view,' from the v. *ostendere*, from *ob-* 'in view of' + *tendere* 'to stretch.']

os·ten·si·bly /ä'stensiblē; ə'sten-/ ▶ **adv.** [sentence adverb] apparently or purportedly, but perhaps not actually: *portrayed as a blue-collar type, ostensibly a carpenter.*

os·ten·sive /ä'stensiv; ə'sten-/ ▶ **adj.** directly or clearly demonstrative. ■ ostensible. ■ Ling. denoting a way of defining by direct demonstration, e.g., by pointing. — **os·ten·sive·ly adv.** **os·ten·sive·ness n.**

os·ten·ta·tion /,ästən'tāSHən/ ▶ **n.** vulgar display, esp. of wealth, to impress. [ME: via OFr. from L. *ostentatio(n-)*, from the v. *ostentare*, frequentative of *ostendere* 'stretch out to view.']

os·ten·ta·tious /,ästən'tāSHəs/ ▶ **adj.** characterized by vulgar or pretentious display. — **os·ten·ta·tious·ly adv.** **os·ten·ta·tious·ness n.**

osteo- ▶ **comb. form** of or relating to the bones: *osteoporosis*. [from Gk. *osteon* 'bone.']

os·te·o·ar·thri·tis /,ästēōär'THrītis/ ▶ **n.** Med. degeneration of joint cartilage and the underlying bone, most common from middle age onward. Compare with **RHEUMATOID ARTHRITIS**. — **os·te·o·ar·thrit·ic** /-'THritik/ **adj.**

os·te·o·blast /'ästēə,blast/ ▶ **n.** Physiol. a cell that secretes the matrix for bone formation. — **os·te·o·blas·tic** /,ästēə'blastik/ **adj.**

os·te·o·clast /'ästēə,klast/ ▶ **n.** Physiol. a large multinucleate bone cell that absorbs bone tissue during growth and healing. — **os·te·o·clas·tic** /,ästēə'klastik/ **adj.** [19th C.: from **OSTEO-** 'bone' + Gk. *klastēs* 'breaker.']

os·te·o·cyte /'ästēə,sīt/ ▶ **n.** Physiol. a bone cell, formed when an osteoblast becomes embedded in the matrix it has secreted. — **os·te·o·cyt·ic** /,ästēə'sitik/ **adj.**

os·te·o·gen·e·sis /,ästēō'jenəsis/ ▶ **n.** the formation of bone. — **os·te·o·ge·net·ic** /-jə'netik/ **adj.** **os·te·o·gen·ic** /'jenik/ **adj.**

os·te·o·gen·e·sis im·per·fec·ta /,impər'fektə/ ▶ **n.** Med. an inherited disorder characterized by extreme fragility of the bones. [L. *imperfecta* 'imperfect.']

os·te·oid /'ästē,oid/ Physiol. Med. ▶ **adj.** resembling bone in appearance or structure. ▶ **n.** the unmineralized organic component of bone.

os·te·ol·o·gy /,ästē'äləjē/ ▶ **n.** the study of the structure and function of the skeleton and bony structures. — **os·te·o·log·i·cal** /,ästēə'läjikəl/ **adj.** **os·te·o·log·i·cal·ly** /,ästēə'läjik(ə)lē/ **adv.** **os·te·ol·o·gist n.**

os·te·o·ma·la·cia /,ästēōmə'lāSH(ē)ə/ ▶ **n.** softening of the bones, typically through a deficiency of vitamin D or calcium. — **os·te·o·ma·lac·ic** /-'lasik/ **adj.** [19th C.: mod. L., from **OSTEO-** 'bone' + Gk. *malakos* 'soft.']

os·te·o·my·e·li·tis /,ästēō,mīə'lītis/ ▶ **n.** Med. inflammation of bone or bone marrow, usually due to infection.

os·te·op·a·thy /,ästē'äpəTHē/ ▶ **n.** a branch of medical practice that emphasizes the treatment of medical disorders through the manipulation and massage of the bones, joints, and muscles. — **os·te·o·path** /'ästēə,paTH/ **n.** **os·te·o·path·ic** /,ästēə'paTHik/ **adj.** **os·te·o·path·i·cal·ly** /,ästēə'paTHik(ə)lē/ **adv.**

os·te·o·phyte /'ästēə,fīt/ ▶ **n.** Med. a bony outgrowth associated with the degeneration of cartilage at joints. — **os·te·o·phyt·ic** /,ästēə'fitik/ **adj.**

os·te·o·po·ro·sis /,ästēōpə'rōsis/ ▶ **n.** a medical condition in which the bones become brittle and fragile from loss of tissue, typically as a result of hormonal changes, or deficiency of calcium or vitamin D. — **os·te·o·po·rot·ic** /-'rätik/ **adj.** [19th C.: from **OSTEO-** 'bone' + Gk. *poros* 'passage, pore' + **-OSIS**.]

os·te·o·sar·co·ma /,ästēōsär'kōmə/ ▶ **n.** (pl. **-mas** or **-ma·ta** /-mətə/) Med. a malignant tumor of bone in which there is a proliferation of osteoblasts.

os·te·o·tome /'ästēə,tōm/ ▶ **n.** a surgical instrument for cutting bone, typically resembling a chisel.

os·te·ot·o·my /,ästē'ätəmē/ ▶ **n.** (pl. **-mies**) the surgical cutting of a bone or removal of a piece of bone.

Os·tia /'ästēə/ an ancient Roman city situated on the western coast of Italy at the mouth of the Tiber River.

os·ti·na·to /,ästi'nätō/ ▶ **n.** (pl. **-tos** or **-ti** /-tē/) a continually repeated musical phrase or rhythm. [Ital., lit. 'obstinate.']

os·ti·ole /'ästē,ōl/ ▶ **n.** Bot. (in some small algae and fungi) a small pore through which spores are discharged. — **os·ti·o·lar** /-ələr/ **adj.** [19th C.: from L. *ostiolum*, dimin. of *ostium* 'opening.']

os·ti·um /'ästēəm/ ▶ **n.** (pl. **-ti·a** /-tēə/) Anat. Zool. an opening into a vessel or cavity of the body. [17th C.: from L., 'door, opening.']

ost·ler /'äslər/ ▶ **n.** var. of **HOSTLER**.

Ost·mark /'äst,märk/ ▶ **n.** hist. the basic monetary unit of the former German Democratic Republic, equal to 100 pfennigs. [Ger., lit. 'east mark' (see **MARK**[2]).]

os·tra·cize /'ästrə,sīz/ ▶ **v.** [trans.] exclude (someone) from a society or group. ■ (in ancient Athens) banish (an unpopular or too powerful citizen) from a city for five or ten years by popular vote. — **os·tra·cism n.** [17th C.: from Gk. *ostrakizein*, from *ostrakon* 'shell or potsherd' (on which names were written, in voting to banish unpopular citizens).]

Os·tra·co·da /,ästrə'kōdə/ Zool. a class of minute aquatic crustaceans that have a hinged shell from which the antennae protrude, and a reduced number of appendages. — **os·tra·cod** /ˈästrəˌkäd/ **n.** [mod. L. (pl.), from Gk. *ostrakōdēs* 'testaceous,' from *ostrakon* 'shell.']

os·tra·con /ˈästrəˌkän/ (also **os·tra·kon**) ▶ **n.** (pl. **-ca** /-kə/ or **-ka**) a potsherd used as a writing surface. [Gk., 'hard shell or potsherd.']

Os·tra·va /ˈästrəvə; ˈôsträvä/ an industrial city in the northeast of the Czech Republic, in the Moravian lowlands; pop. 328,000. It is located in the coal-mining region of Silesia.

os·trich /ˈästricH/ ▶ **n. 1** a flightless swift-running African bird (*Struthio camelus*, family Struthionidae) with a long neck, long legs, and two toes on each foot. It is the largest living bird, with males reaching an average height of 8 feet (2.5 m). **2** a person who refuses to face reality or accept facts. [ME: from OFr. *ostriche*, from L. *avis* 'bird' + late L. *struthio* (from Gk. *strouthiōn* 'ostrich,' from *strouthos* 'sparrow or ostrich').]

Os·tro·goth /ˈästrəˌgäTH/ ▶ **n.** a member of the eastern branch of the Goths, who conquered Italy in the 5th–6th centuries AD. — **Os·tro·goth·ic** /ˌästrəˈgäTHik/ **adj.** [from late L. *Ostrogothi* (pl.), from the Gmc. base of **EAST** + late L. *Gothi* 'Goths.']

OSU ▶ **abbr.** Order of St. Ursula (Ursulines).

Os·wald /ˈäzˌwôld/, Lee Harvey (1939–63), US alleged assassin of President John F. Kennedy. He was murdered by Jack Ruby, a Dallas nightclub owner, before he could be brought to trial.

Os·we·go tea /äsˈwēgō/ ▶ **n.** see **BERGAMOT** (sense 3). [18th C.: named after a river and town in New York.]

OT ▶ **abbr.** ■ occupational therapist. ■ occupational therapy. ■ Old Testament. ■ overnight telegram. ■ overtime.

-ot¹ ▶ **suffix** forming nouns that were originally diminutives: *ballot* | *parrot.* [from Fr.]

-ot² ▶ **suffix** (forming nouns) denoting a person of a particular type: *harlot* | *idiot.* ■ denoting a native of a place: *Cypriot.* [via Fr. and L. from Gk. *-ōtēs.*]

o·ta·ku /ōˈtäkōō/ ▶ **plural n.** (in Japan) young people who are highly skilled in or obsessed with computer technology to the detriment of their social skills. [Japanese, literally 'your house,' alluding to the reluctance of such young people to leave the house.]

o·tal·gi·a /ōˈtalj(ē)ə/ ▶ **n.** Med. earache. [17th C.: from Gk. *ōtalgia*, from *ous, ōt-* 'ear' + *algos* 'pain.']

OTB ▶ **abbr.** off-track betting.

OTC ▶ **abbr.** ■ over the counter.

oth·er /ˈəTHər/ ▶ **adj. & pron. 1** used to refer to a person or thing that is different or distinct from one already mentioned or known about: *other people found her difficult* | [as pron.] *a language unrelated to any other.* ■ the alternative of two: [as adj.] *the other side of the page* | [as pron.] *flinging up first one arm and then the other.* ■ those remaining in a group; those not already mentioned: [as adj.] *they took the other three away in an ambulance* | [as pron.] *Fred set off and the others followed.* **2** further; additional: [as adj.] *one other word of advice* | [as pron.] *reporting three stories and rewriting three others.* **3** (**the Other**) [pron.] Philos. Sociol. that which is distinct from, different from, or opposite to something or oneself.

– PHRASES **other than** [with negative or in questions] apart from; except. ■ differently or different from; otherwise than. **on the other hand** see **HAND. the other day** (or **night**, **week**, etc.) a few days (or nights, weeks, etc.) ago. **someone** (or **something** or **somehow**, etc.) **or other** some unspecified or unknown person, thing, manner, etc. (used to express vagueness or uncertainty). [OE *ōther*, of Gmc. origin; rel. to Du. and Ger. *ander*, from an Indo-Eur. root meaning 'different.']

oth·er-di·rect·ed ▶ **adj.** Psychol. (of a person or their behavior) governed by external circumstances.

oth·er half ▶ **n.** (**one's other half**) informal a person's wife, husband, or partner.

oth·er·ness /ˈəTHərnis/ ▶ **n.** the quality or fact of being different.

oth·er·where /ˈəTHərˌ(h)we(ə)r/ ▶ **adv. & pron.** archaic or literary elsewhere.

oth·er·wise /ˈəTHərˌwīz/ ▶ **adv. 1** in circumstances different from those present or considered: *the collection brings visitors who might not come to the college otherwise.* ■ [as conjunctive adv.] or else: *I'm not motivated by money, otherwise I would have quit.* **2** in other respects; apart from that: *an otherwise totally black cat with a single white whisker.* **3** in a different way: *pretending that they are* **otherwise engaged.** ■ as an alternative: *the mathematician Leonardo Pisano,* **otherwise known as** *Fibonacci.* ▶ **adj.** [predic.] in a different state or situation: *if it were otherwise, we would be unable to acquire knowledge.* [OE *on ōthre wisan* (see **OTHER, WISE²**).]

oth·er wom·an ▶ **n.** (**the other woman**) the lover of a married or similarly attached man.

oth·er world ▶ **n.** (**the other world**) the spiritual world or afterlife.

oth·er·world·ly /ˌəTHərˈwərldlē/ ▶ **adj.** of or relating to an imaginary or spiritual world. ■ unworldly. — **oth·er·world·li·ness n.**

Oth·man /ˈäTHmən; äTHˈmän/ var. of **OSMAN I.**

o·tic /ˈōtik; ˈätik/ ▶ **adj.** Anat. of or relating to the ear. [17th C.: from Gk. *ōtikos*, from *ous, ōt-* 'ear.']

-otic ▶ **suffix** forming adjectives and nouns corresponding to nouns ending in *-osis* (such as *neurotic* corresponding to *neurosis*). — **-otically suffix** forming corresponding adverbs. [from Fr. *-otique*, via L. from the Gk. adjectival ending *-ōtikos.*]

o·ti·ose /ˈōSHēˌōs; ˈōtēˌōs/ ▶ **adj.** serving no practical purpose or result. ■ archaic indolent; idle. — **o·ti·ose·ly adv.** [18th C.: from L. *otiosus*, from *otium* 'leisure.']

O·tis¹ /ˈōtis/, Elisha Graves (1811–61), US inventor. In 1852, he produced the first efficient elevator with a safety device.

O·tis², James (1725–83), American patriot. He opposed various revenue acts imposed by the British.

o·ti·tis /ōˈtītis/ ▶ **n.** Med. inflammation of the ear, esp. **otitis media** (of the middle ear). [18th C.: mod. L., from Gk. *ous, ōt-* 'ear' + **-ITIS.**]

oto- ▶ **comb. form** (used chiefly in medical terms) of or relating to the ears: *otoscope.* [from Gk. *ous, ōt-* 'ear.']

o·to·cyst /ˈōtəˌsist/ ▶ **n.** another term for **STATOCYST.**

o·to·lar·yn·gol·o·gy /ˌōtōˌlarəNGˈgäləjē/ ▶ **n.** the study of diseases of the ear and throat. — **o·to·la·ryn·go·log·i·cal** /-əNGgəˈläjikəl/ **adj. o·to·lar·yn·gol·o·gist n.**

o·to·lith /ˈōtlˌiTH/ ▶ **n.** Zool. each of three small oval calcareous bodies in the inner ear of vertebrates, involved in sensing gravity and movement. — **o·to·lith·ic** /ˌōtlˈiTHik/ **adj.**

o·tol·o·gy /ōˈtäləjē/ ▶ **n.** the study of the anatomy and diseases of the ear. — **o·to·log·i·cal** /ˌōtəˈläjəkəl/ **adj. o·tol·o·gist n.**

O·to·man·gue·an /ˌōtōˈmäNGgēən; -ˈmaNG-/ ▶ **adj.** of, relating to, or denoting a family of American Indian languages of central and southern Mexico, including Mixtec and Zapotec. [1940s: from **OTOMI** + *Mangue* (an extinct language of Costa Rica) + **-AN.**]

O·to·mi /ˌōtəˈmē/ ▶ **n.** (pl. same) **1** a member of an American Indian people inhabiting parts of central Mexico. **2** the Otomanguean language of this people. ▶ **adj.** of or relating to this people or their language. [via Amer. Sp. from Nahuatl *otomih*, lit. 'unknown.']

o·to·plas·ty /ˈōtəˌplastē/ ▶ **n.** (pl. **-ties**) a surgical operation to restore or enhance the appearance of an ear or the ears.

o·to·rhi·no·lar·yn·gol·o·gy /ˌōtōˌrīnōˌlarəNGˈgäləjē/ ▶ **n.** the study of diseases of the ear, nose, and throat. — **o·to·rhi·no·lar·yn·gol·o·gist n.**

o·to·scle·ro·sis /ˌōtōskləˈrōsis/ ▶ **n.** Med. a hereditary disorder causing progressive deafness due to overgrowth of bone in the inner ear. — **o·to·scle·rot·ic** /-ˈrätik/ **adj.**

o·to·scope /ˈōtəˌskōp/ ▶ **n.** an instrument designed for visual examination of the eardrum and the passage of the outer ear, typically having a light and a set of lenses. — **o·to·scop·ic** /ˌōtəˈskäpik/ **adj. o·to·scop·i·cal·ly** /ˌōtəˈskäpik(ə)lē/ **adv.**

o·to·tox·ic /ˌōtəˈtäksik/ ▶ **adj.** Med. having a toxic effect on the ear or its nerve supply. — **o·to·tox·ic·i·ty** /-täkˈsisitē/ **n.**

OTS (also **O.T.S.**) ▶ **abbr.** Officers' Training School.

ot·ta·va ri·ma /ōˈtävə ˈrēmə/ ▶ **n.** a form of poetry consisting of stanzas of eight lines of ten or eleven syllables, rhyming *abababcc.* [18th C.: from Ital., lit. 'eighth rhyme.']

Ot·ta·wa /ˈätəwə/ the federal capital of Canada, in southeastern Ontario; pop. 313,987.

ot·ter /ˈätər/ ▶ **n.** a fish-eating mammal (*Lutra* and other genera) of the weasel family, typically semiaquatic, with an elongated body, dense fur, and webbed feet. Its several species include the **river otter** (*L. canadensis*). See also **SEA OTTER.** [OE *otr, ot(t)or*, of Gmc. origin; rel. to Gk. *hudros* 'water snake.']

river otter

ot·ter·hound /ˈätərˌhound/ ▶ **n.** a large dog of a breed with a long rough coat, used in otter hunting.

ot·to /ˈätō/ ▶ **n.** another term for **ATTAR.**

ot·to·cen·to /ˌôtōˈCHentō/ ▶ **adj.** of or relating to the 19th century in Italy. [Ital., lit. '800' (shortened from *milottocento* '1800').]

Ot·to I /ˈätō/ (912–73), king of the Germans 936–973 and Holy Roman Emperor 962–973; known as **Otto the Great.**

Ot·to·man /ˈätəmən/ ▶ **adj.** hist. **1** of or relating to the Turkish dynasty of Osman I (Othman I). ■ of or relating to the branch of the Turks to which he belonged. ■ of or relating to the Ottoman Empire ruled by his successors. **2** Turkish. ▶ **n.** (pl. **-mans**) a Turk, esp. of the period of the Ottoman Empire. [based on Arab. *uṯmānī* (adj.), from *Uṯmān* 'Othman.']

ot·to·man /ˈätəmən/ ▶ **n.** (pl. **-mans**) **1** a low upholstered seat or footstool without a back or arms that typically serves also as a box, with the seat hinged to form a lid. **2** a heavy ribbed fabric made from silk and either cotton or wool, typically used for coats. [19th C.: from Fr. *ottomane*, fem. of *ottoman* 'Ottoman.']

Ot·to·man Em·pire the Turkish empire established by Osman I at the end of the 13th century and expanded by his successors to include Asia Minor and much of southeastern Europe. The Ottomans captured Constantinople in 1453, and the empire reached its zenith under Suleiman in the mid 16th century. It had declined by the 19th century and collapsed after World War I.

oua·bain /wäˈbī-in; -ˈbā-/ ▶ **n.** Chem. a toxic compound obtained from certain trees, used as a very rapid cardiac stimulant. It is a polycyclic glycoside. [19th C.: via Fr. from Somali *wabayo*, a tree.]

Ouach·i·ta Riv·er /ˈwäSHiˌtô/ a river that flows south from western Arkansas to the Red River.

Oua·ga·dou·gou /ˌwägəˈdōōgōō/ the capital of Burkina Faso; in the central part of the country; pop. 634,000.

oua·na·niche /ˌwänäˈnēSH/ ▶ **n.** (pl. same) Canadian a salmon of landlocked populations living in lakes in Labrador and Newfoundland. [19th C.: via Canad. Fr. from Algonquian.]

ou·bli·ette /ˌo͞oblēˈet/ ▶ **n.** a secret dungeon with access only through a trapdoor in its ceiling. [18th C.: from Fr., from *oublier* 'forget.']

ouch /oucH/ ▶ **exclam.** used to express pain. [natural exclamation: 17th C.]

oud /o͞od/ ▶ **n.** a form of lute or mandolin played principally in Arab countries. [18th C.: from Arab. *al-'ūd*.]

Oudh /oud/ (also **Audh** or **Awadh**) a former region in northern India, now in Uttar Pradesh.

ought[1] /ôt/ ▶ **modal verb** (3rd sing. pres. and past **ought**) [with infin.] **1** used to indicate duty or correctness, typically when criticizing someone's actions: *they ought to respect the law.* ■ used to indicate a desirable or expected state: *he ought to be able to take the initiative.* ■ used to give or ask advice: *you ought to go.* **2** used to indicate something that is probable: *five minutes ought to be enough time.* [OE *āhte*, past tense of *āgan* 'owe' (see OWE).]

ought[2] ▶ **n.** archaic term for AUGHT[2]. [19th C.: perh. from *an ought*, by wrong division of *a nought*.]

ought[3] ▶ **pron.** var. of AUGHT[1].

ought·n't /ˈôtnt/ ▶ **contr.** ought not.

ou·gui·ya /o͞oˈgēə/ (also **ou·gi·ya**) ▶ **n.** the basic monetary unit of Mauritania, equal to five khoums. [via Fr. from Mauritanian Arab., from Arab. *'ūkiyya*, from Gk. *ounkia*, from L. *uncia* 'ounce.']

Oui·ja board /ˈwējə; -jē/ ▶ **n.** trademark a board printed with letters, numbers, and other signs, to which a planchette points, in answer to questions from people at a seance.

ounce[1] /ouns/ ▶ **n.** **1** (abbr.: **oz**) a unit of weight of one sixteenth of a pound avoirdupois (approximately 28 grams). ■ a unit of one twelfth of a pound troy or apothecaries' measure, equal to 480 grains (approximately 31 grams). **2** a very small amount of something. **3** short for FLUID OUNCE. [ME: from OFr. *unce*, from L. *uncia* 'twelfth part.']

ounce[2] ▶ **n.** another term for SNOW LEOPARD. [ME: from OFr. *once*, earlier *lonce*, based on L. *lynx, lync-*.]

our /ou(ə)r; är/ ▶ **possessive adj.** **1** belonging to or associated with the speaker and one or more other people previously mentioned or easily identified: *Jo and I had our hair cut.* ■ belonging to or associated with people in general: *when we hear a sound, our brains identify the source quickly.* **2** used by a writer, editor, or monarch to refer to something belonging to or associated with himself or herself: *we want to know what you, our readers, think.* [OE *ūre*, of Gmc. origin; rel. to US and Ger. *unser*.]

-our[1] ▶ **suffix** esp. Brit. var. of -OR[1] (as in *saviour*).

-our[2] ▶ **suffix** esp. Brit. var. of -OR[2] surviving in some nouns such as *ardour, colour*.

Our La·dy Christian Church used as a title for the Virgin Mary.

ou·ro·bo·ros ▶ **n.** var. of UROBOROS.

ours /ˈou(ə)rz; ärz/ ▶ **possessive pron.** used to refer to a thing or things belonging to or associated with the speaker and one or more other people previously mentioned or easily identified: *ours was the ugliest house on the block | this chat of ours is strictly between us.*

our·self /ou(ə)rˈself; är-/ ▶ **pron.** [first person pl.] **1** used instead of "ourselves," typically when "we" refers to people in general rather than a definite group of people: [reflexive] *we must choose which aspects of ourself to express to the world* | [emphatic] *this is our affair—we deal with it ourself.* **2** archaic used instead of "myself" by a sovereign or other person in authority.

our·selves /ou(ə)rˈselvz; är-/ ▶ **pron.** [first person pl.] **1** [reflexive] used as the object of a verb or preposition when this is the same as the subject of the clause and the subject is the speaker and one or more other people considered together: *for this we can only blame ourselves.* **2** [emphatic] we or us personally (used to emphasize the speaker and one or more other people considered together): *we invented it ourselves.*

– PHRASES **(not) be ourselves** see *BE ONESELF, NOT BE ONESELF* at BE. **by ourselves** see *BY ONESELF* at BY.

-ous ▶ **suffix** forming adjectives: **1** characterized by; of the nature of: *dangerous | mountainous.* **2** Chem. denoting an element in a lower valence: *ferrous | sulfurous.* Compare with -IC. — **-ously suffix** forming corresponding adverbs **-ousness suffix** forming corresponding nouns. [from Anglo-Norman Fr., or OFr. *-eus*, from L. *-osus*.]

Ouse /o͞oz/ **1** (also **Great Ouse**) a river in eastern England that flows east and then north to the Wash near King's Lynn. **2** a river in northeastern England that flows southeast to the Humber estuary. **3** a river in southeastern England that flows southeast to the English Channel.

ou·sel /ˈo͞ozəl/ ▶ **n.** var. of OUZEL.

oust /oust/ ▶ **v.** [trans.] drive out or expel (someone) from a position or place. ■ Law deprive (someone) of or exclude (someone) from possession of something. [ME (as a legal term): from Anglo-Norman Fr. *ouster* 'take away,' from L. *obstare* 'oppose, hinder.']

oust·er /ˈoustər/ ▶ **n.** **1** dismissal or expulsion from a position. **2** Law ejection from a freehold or other possession; deprivation of an inheritance.

out /out/ ▶ **adv.** **1** moving or appearing to move away from a particular place, esp. one that is enclosed or hidden: *watch the stars come out.* ■ situated or operating in the open air, not in buildings: *they've been out looking for you.* ■ no longer detained in custody or in jail: *out on bail.* **2** away from one's usual base or residence: *the team put on a display out in Georgia.* ■ in a public place for purposes of pleasure or entertainment: *an evening out at a restaurant.* **3** to sea, away from the land: *the fleet put out from Cyprus.* ■ (of the tide) falling or at its lowest level: *the tide was going out.* **4** indicating a specified distance away from the goal line or finishing line: *he scored from 70 meters out.* **5** so as to be revealed or known: *find out what you can.* ■ aloud; so as to be heard: *Miss Beard cried out in horror.* **6** at or to an end: *the romance fizzled out.* ■ so as to be finished or complete: *I typed out the poem.* ■ (in various other completive uses): *the crowd had thinned out | he crossed out a word.* **7** (of a light or fire) so as to be extinguished or no longer burning: *the lights went out.* ■ (of a stain or mark) no longer visible; removed: *try to get the stain out.* **8** (of a party, politician, etc.) not in office. **9** (of a jury) considering its verdict in secrecy. ▶ **prep.** through to the outside: *he ran out the door.* ▶ **adj.** [predic.] **1** not at home or at one's place of work: *if he called, she'd pretend to be out.* **2** revealed or made public: *the secret was soon out.* ■ (of a flower) in bloom; open. ■ published: *the book should be out before the end of the month.* ■ informal in existence or in use: *it works as well as any system that's out.* ■ not concealing one's homosexuality: *I had been out since I was 17.* **3** no longer alight; extinguished: *the fire was out.* **4** at an end: *school was out for the summer.* ■ informal no longer in fashion: *life in the fast lane is out.* **5** not possible or worth considering: *a trip to the seaside is out.* **6** in a state of unconsciousness. ■ Boxing unable to rise before the count of ten. **7** mistaken; in error: *he was slightly out in his calculations.* **8** (of the ball in tennis and similar games) outside the designated playing area. **9** Baseball & Cricket no longer batting or on base, having had one's turn ended by the team in the field: *the Yankees are out in the ninth.* ▶ **n.** **1** informal a way of escaping from a problem or dilemma: *he was desperately looking for an out.* **2** Baseball an act of putting a player out. ■ (of a batter or base runner) a play ending in being put out. **3** (**the outs**) the political party or politicians not in office. ▶ **v.** **1** [intrans.] come or go out; emerge: *the truth will out.* **2** [trans.] informal reveal the homosexuality of (a prominent person).

– PHRASES **on the outs** in disagreement or dispute. **out and about** (of a person, esp. after inactivity) engaging in normal activity. **out for** intent on having: *he was out for a good time.* **out of** **1** moving or situated away from (a place, typically one that is enclosed or hidden). ■ situated a specified distance from (a place): *eight miles out of town.* ■ taken or appearing to be taken from (a particular type of writing, genre, or artistic performance): *a romance straight out of a fairy tale.* ■ eliminated from (a competition): *knocked out of the tournament.* **2** spoken by: *still not a word out of Pearsall.* **3** using (a particular thing) as raw material: *a bench fashioned out of a fallen tree trunk.* ■ using (a particular thing) as a source of some benefit: *you don't expect much out of life.* ■ having (the thing mentioned) as a motivation: *she did it out of spite.* ■ indicating the dam of a pedigree animal, esp. a horse. **4** from among (a number): *nine times out of ten.* **5** not having (a particular thing): *out of cash.* **out of it** informal **1** not included; rejected: *I hate feeling out of it.* **2** unaware of what is happening as a result of being uninformed. ■ unable to think or react properly as a result of being drowsy. **out to** keenly striving to: *they were out to impress.* **out with** an exhortation to expel or dismiss (an unwanted person or thing). **out with it** [as imper.] say what you are thinking. [OE *ūt* (adv.), *ūtian* (v.), of Gmc. origin; rel. to Du. *uit* and Ger. *aus*.]

out- ▶ **prefix** **1** to the point of surpassing or exceeding: *outfight | outperform.* **2** external; separate; from outside: *outbuildings | outpatient.* **3** away from; outward: *outbound | outpost.*

ou·ta /ˈoutə/ ▶ **prep.** var. of OUTTA.

out·age /ˈoutij/ ▶ **n.** a period when a power supply or other service is not available or when equipment is closed down.

out-and-out ▶ **adj.** [attrib.] in every respect; absolute; without question: *an out-and-out crook.*

out-and-out·er ▶ **n.** archaic, informal a person or thing that possesses a particular quality to an extreme degree.

out·a·sight /ˈoutəˈsīt/ ▶ **exclam.** informal var. of *OUT OF SIGHT* (see SIGHT).

out·back /ˈoutˌbak/ ▶ **n.** (**the outback**) the remote and usually uninhabited inland regions of Australia. ■ any remote or sparsely populated region. — **out·back·er n.**

out·bal·ance /ˌoutˈbaləns/ ▶ **v.** [trans.] be more valuable, important, or influential than; make up for.

out·bas·ket ▶ **n.** an out-box.

out·board /ˈoutˌbô(ə)rd/ ▶ **adj. & adv.** on, toward, or near the outside, esp. of a ship or other vehicle. ■ [as adj.] (of a motor) portable and usually mounted on the outside of the stern of a boat. ▶ **n.** an outboard motor. ■ a boat with such a motor.

out·bound /ˈoutˈbound/ ▶ **adj. & adv.** traveling away from a particular place, esp. on the first leg of a round trip: [as adj.] *an outbound flight* | [as adv.] *flying outbound.*

out·box ▶ **n.** a box or tray on someone's desk for outgoing memos, documents, etc., that have been dealt with.

out·brave /ˌoutˈbrāv/ ▶ **v.** [trans.] ■ face (something) with a show of brave defiance. ■ archaic outdo in bravery.

out·break /ˈoutˌbrāk/ ▶ **n.** the sudden or violent start of something unwelcome, such as war, disease, etc.

out·breed /ˌoutˈbrēd/ ▶ **v.** (past and past part. **-bred**) [trans.] [usu. as n.] (**outbreeding**) breed from parents not closely related: *many specific genetic factors regulate the degree of outbreeding.*

out·build·ing /ˈoutˌbildiNG/ ▶ **n.** a building, such as a shed, barn, or garage, on the same property but separate from a more important one, such as a house.

out·burst /ˈout,bərst/ ▶n. a sudden release of strong emotion. ■ a sudden outbreak of a particular activity: *a wild outburst of applause.* ■ a volcanic eruption. ■ Physics a sudden emission of energy or particles.

out·call /ˈout,kôl/ ▶n. a visit by an escort, prostitute, etc., to the address of the caller.

out·cast /ˈout,kast/ ▶n. a person who has been rejected by society or a social group. ▶adj. rejected or cast out: *made to feel outcast.*

out·caste /ˈout,kast/ ▶n. (in Hindu society) a person who has no caste or has been expelled from a caste.

out·class /,outˈklas/ ▶v. [trans.] be far superior to: *they totally outclassed us in the first half.*

out·come /ˈout,kəm/ ▶n. the way a thing turns out; a consequence: *it is the outcome of the vote that counts.*

out·crop /ˈout,kräp/ ▶n. a rock formation that is visible on the surface: *limestone outcrops.* ■ fig. a noticeable manifestation or occurrence. ▶v. (**-cropped, -crop·ping**) [intrans.] [often as n.] (**outcropping**) appear as an outcrop: *outcroppings of bedrock.*

out·cross ▶v. /,outˈkrôs; -ˈkräs/ [trans.] breed (an animal or plant) with one not closely related. ▶n. /ˈout,krôs; -ˈkräs/ an animal or plant produced as the result of such crossbreeding.

out·cry /ˈout,krī/ ▶n. (pl. **-cries**) an exclamation or shout. ■ a strong expression of public disapproval or anger.

out·dat·ed /,outˈdātid/ ▶adj. out of date; obsolete. — **out·dat·ed·ness** n.

out·dis·tance /,outˈdistəns/ ▶v. [trans.] leave (a competitor or pursuer) far behind: *she could maintain a fast enough pace to outdistance any pursuers.*

out·do /,outˈdo͞o/ ▶v. (**-does, -doing**; past **-did**; past part. **-done**) [trans.] be more successful than.

out·door /ˈoutˈdôr/ ▶adj. [attrib.] done, situated, or used out of doors: *a huge outdoor concert.* ■ (of a person) fond of the open air or open-air activities: *a rugged, outdoor type.*

out·doors /,outˈdôrz/ ▶adv. in or into the open air; outside a building or shelter. ▶n. (usu. **the outdoors**) any area outside buildings or shelter, typically far away from human habitation.

out·doors·man /,outˈdôrzmən/ ▶n. (pl. **-men**; fem. **out·doors·wom·an** /-,wo͝omən/ pl. **-wom·en**) a person who spends a lot of time outdoors or doing outdoor activities.

out·doors·y /,outˈdôrzē/ ▶adj. informal of, associated with, or fond of the outdoors.

out·drive /,outˈdrīv/ ▶v. (past **-drove**; past part. **-driven**) [trans.] **1** drive a golf ball farther than (another player). **2** drive a vehicle better or faster than (someone else). ▶n. /ˈout,drīv/ the portion of an inboard-outboard engine that is outside the hull, providing steering and propulsion.

out·er /ˈoutər/ ▶adj. [attrib.] outside; external. ■ further from the center or inside: *the outer hall at the main entrance.* ■ (esp. in place names) more remote: Outer Mongolia. ■ objective or physical; not subjective. [ME: from OUT + -ER².]

Out·er Banks a chain of barrier islands extending southward along the coast of North Carolina.

out·er·course /ˈoutər,kôrs/ ▶n. sexual stimulation that excludes penile penetration. [1980s: blend of OUTER and INTERCOURSE.]

Out·er Mon·go·li·a see MONGOLIA.

out·er·most /ˈoutər,mōst/ ▶adj. [attrib.] farthest from the center: *the outermost layer of the earth.* ▶pron. the one farthest from the center: *the orbit of the outermost of these eight planets.*

out·er plan·et ▶n. a planet whose orbit lies outside the asteroid belt, i.e., Jupiter, Saturn, Uranus, Neptune, or Pluto.

out·er space ▶n. the physical universe beyond the earth's atmosphere.

out·er·wear /ˈoutər,we(ə)r/ ▶n. clothing worn over other clothes, esp. for the outdoors.

out·face /,outˈfās/ ▶v. [trans.] disconcert or defeat (an opponent) by bold confrontation.

out·fall /ˈout,fôl/ ▶n. the place where a river, drain, or sewer empties into the sea, a river, or a lake.

out·field /ˈout,fēld/ ▶n. **1** the outer part of the field of play in various sports, in particular: ■ Baseball the grassy area beyond the infield. ■ Cricket the part of the field furthest from the wicket. ■ [treated as sing. or pl.] the players stationed in the outfield, collectively. **2** the outlying land of a farm. — **out·field·er** n.

out·fit /ˈout,fit/ ▶n. a set of clothes worn together, typically for a particular occasion or purpose. ■ [usu. with adj.] informal a group of people undertaking a particular activity together, such as a group of musicians, a military unit, or a business concern: *Tom was the brains of the outfit.* ■ [with adj.] a complete set of equipment or articles needed for a particular purpose: *a repair outfit.* ▶v. (**-fit·ted, -fit·ting**) [trans.] (usu. **be outfitted**) provide (someone) with a set of clothes. ■ provide with equipment.

out·fit·ter /ˈout,fitər/ (also **out·fit·ters**) ▶n. an establishment that sells clothing, equipment, and services, esp. for outdoor activities. ■ Brit., dated an establishment that sells men's clothing.

out·flank /,outˈflaNGk/ ▶v. [trans.] move around the side of (an enemy) so as to outmaneuver them. ■ fig. outwit: *an attempt to outflank the opposition.*

out·flow /ˈout,flō/ ▶n. a large amount of money, liquid, or people that moves or is transferred out of a place. ■ the flowing out of a liquid from a container or cavity.

out·fox /,outˈfäks/ ▶v. [trans.] informal defeat or deceive (someone) by being more clever; outwit.

out·gas /,outˈgas/ ▶v. (**-gas·es, -gas·sing, -gassed**) [trans.] release or give off (a substance) as a gas or vapor: *glue may outgas smelly volatile organic compounds* | [intrans.] *samples are heated and begin to outgas.*

out·gen·er·al /,outˈjen(ə)rəl/ ▶v. (**-gen·er·aled, -gen·er·al·ing**; Brit. **-gen·er·alled, -gen·er·al·ling**) [trans.] get the better of by superior strategy or tactics.

out·go ▶n. /ˈout,gō/ the outlay of money. ▶v. /,outˈgō/ (**-goes**; past **-went**; past part. **-gone**) [trans.] archaic go faster than: *he on horseback outgoes him on foot.*

out·go·ing /ˈout,gōiNG/ ▶adj. **1** friendly and socially confident. **2** [attrib.] leaving an office or position, esp. after an election defeat or completed term of office. ■ going out or away from a particular place: *incoming and outgoing calls.* ▶n. Brit. (**outgoings**) a person's regular expenditure.

out·gross /ˈoutˈgrōs/ ▶v. [trans.] surpass in gross income or profit: *the film has outgrossed all other movie comedies.*

out-group ▶n. Sociol. those people who do not belong to a specific in-group.

out·grow /,outˈgrō/ ▶v. (past **-grew**; past part. **-grown**) [trans.] grow too big for (something). ■ leave behind as one matures: *is it a permanent injury, or will the colt outgrow it?* ■ grow faster or taller than.

out·growth /ˈout,grōTH/ ▶n. something that grows out of something else. ■ a natural development or result of something. ■ the process of growing out: *with further outgrowth the radius and ulna develop.*

out·guess /,outˈges/ ▶v. [trans.] outwit (someone) by guessing correctly what they intend to do.

out·gun /,outˈgən/ ▶v. (**-gunned, -gun·ning**) [trans.] [often as adj.] (**outgunned**) have better or more weaponry than.

out·haul /ˈout,hôl/ ▶n. Sailing a rope used to haul out the clew of a boom sail or the tack of a jib.

out·house /ˈout,hous/ ▶n. an outbuilding containing a toilet, typically with no plumbing. ■ any outbuilding.

out·ing /ˈoutiNG/ ▶n. **1** a trip taken for pleasure, esp. one lasting a day or less. ■ a brief journey from home: *her daily outing to the stores.* ■ informal an appearance in something, such as an athletic event or show: *her first screen outing in three years.* **2** the act or practice of revealing the homosexuality of a person.

out·ing flan·nel ▶n. a type of flannelette with a short nap on both sides, used in infant clothing.

out·land /ˈout,land/ ▶n. (often **out·lands**) remote or distant territory. ▶adj. remote; distant. ■ foreign.

out·land·er /ˈout,landər/ ▶n. a foreigner; a stranger.

out·land·ish /outˈlandisH/ ▶adj. **1** looking or sounding bizarre or unfamiliar. **2** archaic foreign; alien. — **out·land·ish·ly** adv. **out·land·ish·ness** n. [OE *ūtlendisc* 'not native,' from *ūtland* 'foreign country.']

out·last /,outˈlast/ ▶v. [trans.] outlive; last longer than. ■ endure longer so as to overcome (an opponent or challenge).

out·law /ˈout,lô/ ▶n. a person who has broken the law, esp. one who remains at large or is a fugitive. ■ an intractable horse or other animal. ■ hist. a person deprived of the benefit and protection of the law. ▶v. [trans.] ban; make illegal. ■ hist. deprive (someone) of the benefit and protection of the law. — **out·law·ry** /-,lôrē/ n. [OE *ūtlaga*, from ON *útlagi*, from *útlagr* 'outlawed or banished.']

out·lay /ˈout,lā/ ▶n. an amount of money spent on something.

out·let /ˈout,let/ ▶n. a means by which something escapes, passes, or is released, in particular: ■ a pipe or hole through which water or gas may escape. ■ the mouth of a river. ■ a point in an electrical circuit from which current may be drawn. ■ a place from which goods are sold or distributed: *a fast-food outlet.* ■ a retail store that sells the goods of a specific manufacturer or brand: [as adj.] *an outlet store.* ■ a retail store offering discounted merchandise, esp. overstocked or irregular items. ■ a market for goods: *the indoor markets in Moscow were an outlet for surplus collective-farm produce.* ■ fig. a means of expressing one's talents, energy, or emotions: *writing became the main outlet for his energies.* [ME: from OUT- + the v. LET¹.]

out·let pass ▶n. Basketball a quick pass from a player who has just taken a rebound to a teammate who can initiate a fast break.

out·li·er /ˈout,līər/ ▶n. a person or thing situated away or detached from the main body or system. ■ a person or thing excluded from a group; an outsider. ■ Geol. a younger rock formation isolated among older rocks.

out·line /ˈout,līn/ ▶n. **1** a line or set of lines enclosing or indicating the shape of an object in a sketch or diagram. ■ a line or set of lines of this type, perceived as defining the contours or bounds of an object. **2** a general plan giving the essential features but not the detail. ■ a draft of a diagram, plan, proposal, etc., summarizing the main points. ■ the main features or general principles of something: *the main outlines of Elizabeth's career.* ▶v. [trans.] **1** draw, trace, or define the outer edge or shape of (something). **2** give a summary of (something).

out·live /,outˈliv/ ▶v. [trans.] (of a person) live longer than (another person). ■ survive or last beyond (a specified period or expected lifespan): *the organization had outlived its usefulness.* ■ archaic live through (an experience).

out·look /ˈout,lo͝ok/ ▶n. a person's point of view or general attitude to life. ■ a view. ■ a place from which a view is possible: *emerging onto a* *cliffy outlook over a river.* ■ the prospect for the future. ■ the weather as forecast for the near future.

out·ly·ing /ˈoutˌlī-iNG/ ▸ **adj.** [attrib.] situated far from a center; remote: *an outlying village.*

out·man /ˌoutˈman/ ▸ **v.** (**-manned, -man·ning**) [trans.] [usu. as adj.] (**out·manned**) outnumber. ■ overpower with skill or physical strength.

out·match /ˌoutˈmaCH/ ▸ **v.** [trans.] be superior to (an opponent or rival).

out·mi·grant /ˈoutˌmīgrənt/ ▸ **n.** a person who has migrated from one place to another, esp. within a country. — **out·mi·gra·tion** /-mīˌgrāSHən/ **n.**

out·mod·ed /ˌoutˈmōdid/ ▸ **adj.** old-fashioned. — **out·mod·ed·ness n.**

out·most /ˈoutˌmōst/ ▸ **adj.** farthest away. [ME: var. of *utmost* 'utmost.']

out·num·ber /ˌoutˈnəmbər/ ▸ **v.** [trans.] be more numerous than: *women outnumbered men by three to one.*

out-of-bod·y ex·pe·ri·ence ▸ **n.** a sensation of being outside one's own body, typically of floating and being able to observe oneself from a distance.

out-of-court ▸ **adj.** [attrib.] (of a settlement) made or done without a court decision.

out of date ▸ **adj.** old-fashioned. ■ no longer valid or relevant: *your passport is out of date.*

out of pock·et ▸ **adj.** (also **out-of-pock·et**) of, pertaining to, or requiring a cash expenditure: *out of pocket expenses.* ■ suffering from a financial loss: *even after our payment, he is still out of pocket.*

out-of-the-way ▸ **adj.** (also **out of the way**) (of a place) remote; secluded. ■ dealt with or finished: *economic recovery will begin once the election is out of the way.* ■ (of a person) no longer an obstacle or hindrance to someone's plans. ■ unusual, exceptional, or remarkable: *something very out of the way had happened.*

out-of-town ▸ **adj.** situated, originating from, or taking place outside a given or implied city or town. — **out-of-town·er n.**

out·pace /ˌoutˈpās/ ▸ **v.** [trans.] go faster than. ■ be more than; surpass.

out·pa·tient /ˈoutˌpāSHənt/ ▸ **n.** a patient who receives medical treatment without being admitted to a hospital: *attending a clinic as an outpatient.*

out·place·ment /ˈoutˌplāsmənt/ ▸ **n.** the provision of assistance to laid-off employees in finding new employment, either as a benefit provided by the employer directly, or through a specialist service.

out·point /ˌoutˈpoint/ ▸ **v.** [trans.] **1** defeat (an opponent) on points. **2** Naut. sail closer to the wind than (another ship).

out·port /ˈoutˌpôrt/ ▸ **n.** a subsidiary port built near an existing one.

out·post /ˈoutˌpōst/ ▸ **n.** a small military camp or position at some distance from the main force, used esp. as a guard against surprise attack. ■ a remote part of a country or empire. ■ fig. something regarded as an isolated or remote branch of something.

out·pour·ing /ˈoutˌpôriNG/ ▸ **n.** something that streams out rapidly. ■ (often **outpourings**) an outburst of strong emotion.

out·psych /ˌoutˈsīk/ (also **out·psyche**) ▸ **v.** [trans.] informal defeat by psychological influence or intimidation.

out·put /ˈoutˌpo͝ot/ ▸ **n. 1** the amount of something produced by a person, machine, or industry. ■ the action or process of producing something. ■ the power, energy, or other results supplied by a device or system. **2** Electron. a place where power or information leaves a system. ▸ **v.** (**-put·ting**; past and past part. **-put** or **-put·ted**) [trans.] produce, deliver, or supply (data) using a computer or other device.

out·race /ˌoutˈrās/ ▸ **v.** [trans.] exceed in speed, amount, or extent: *demand for clergy is outracing the supply.*

out·rage /ˈoutˌrāj/ ▸ **n.** an extremely strong reaction of anger, shock, or indignation. ■ an action or event causing such a reaction. ▸ **v.** [trans.] (usu. **be outraged**) arouse fierce anger, shock, or indignation in (someone): *he was outraged at this attempt to take his victory away from him.* ■ violate or infringe flagrantly (a principle, law, etc.). [ME: from OFr. *ou(l)trage,* based on L. *ultra* 'beyond.']

out·ra·geous /outˈrājəs/ ▸ **adj. 1** shockingly bad or excessive. ■ wildly exaggerated or improbable. **2** very bold, unusual, and startling: *her outrageous leotards.* — **out·ra·geous·ly adv. out·ra·geous·ness n.**

out·ran /ˌoutˈran/ past of OUTRUN.

out·range /ˌoutˈrānj/ ▸ **v.** (of a gun or its user) have a longer range than.

out·rank /ˌoutˈraNGk/ ▸ **v.** [trans.] have a higher rank than (someone else). ■ be better, more important, or more significant than.

ou·tré /o͞oˈtrā/ ▸ **adj.** unusual and startling. [Fr., lit. 'exceeded,' past part. of *outrer* (see OUTRAGE).]

out·reach ▸ **n.** /ˈoutˌrēCH/ the extent or length of reaching out. ■ an organization's involvement with or activity in the community, esp. in the context of social welfare: *her goal is to increase educational outreach.* ▸ **v.** /ˌoutˈrēCH/ [trans.] reach further than. ■ [intrans.] literary stretch out one's arms.

Ou·tre·mer /ˌo͞otrāˈmā/ a name applied to the medieval French crusader states, including Armenia, Antioch, Tripoli, and Jerusalem.

out·rid·er /ˈoutˌrīdər/ ▸ **n.** a person in a motor vehicle or on horseback who goes in front of or beside a vehicle as an escort or guard. ■ a person or thing that accompanies or precedes another, esp. as a precursor: *gray-white cumulus clouds—outriders of the storm.* ■ a mounted official who escorts racehorses to the starting post. ■ a cowhand who prevents cattle from straying beyond a certain limit. — **out·rid·ing** /ˌoutˈrīdiNG/ **n.**

out·rig·ger /ˈoutˌrigər/ ▸ **n.** a beam, spar, or framework projecting from or over the side of a ship or boat. ■ a float or secondary hull fixed parallel to a canoe or other boat to stabilize it. ■ a boat fitted with such a structure. ■ a similar projecting support in another structure or vehicle. — **out·rigged adj.** [18th C.: perh. influenced by the obs. nautical term *outligger,* in the same sense.]

outrigger

out·right ▸ **adv.** /ˈoutˌrīt/ **1** altogether; completely: *logging has been banned outright.* ■ without reservation; openly: *she couldn't ask him outright.* **2** immediately: *the impact killed four horses outright.* ■ not by degrees or installments: *they decided to buy the company outright.* ▸ **adj.** [attrib.] open and direct; not concealed: *an outright refusal.* ■ total; complete. ■ undisputed; clear: *an outright victory.*

out·run /ˌoutˈrən/ ▸ **v.** (**-run·ning**; past **-ran**; past part. **-run**) [trans.] run or travel faster or farther than. ■ escape from: *it's hard to outrun destiny.* ■ go beyond; exceed: *his courage outran his prudence.*

out·rush /ˈoutˌrəSH/ ▸ **n.** a rushing out of something; a sudden outpouring. — **out·rush·ing adj.**

out·sell /ˌoutˈsel/ ▸ **v.** (past and past part. **-sold**) [trans.] be sold in greater quantities than. ■ (of a person) sell more of something than (someone else): *Garth Brooks is outselling Michael Jackson.*

out·set /ˈoutˌset/ ▸ **n.** [in sing.] the start or beginning of something.

out·shine /ˌoutˈSHīn/ ▸ **v.** (past and past part. **-shone**) [trans.] shine more brightly than. ■ be much better than (someone) in a particular area.

out·shoot /ˌoutˈSHo͞ot/ ▸ **v.** (past and past part. **-shot**) [trans.] shoot better than (someone else). ■ Sports make or take more shots than (another player or team).

out·side ▸ **n.** /ˈoutˈsīd; -ˌsīd/ the external side or surface of something. ■ the side of a bend or curve where the edge or surface is longer in extent. ■ the side of a racetrack further from the center, where the lanes are longer. ■ the external appearance of someone or something. ■ (in basketball) the area beyond the perimeter of the defense: *he often set up the Lakers' plays from the outside.* ▸ **adj.** /ˌoutˈsīd/ [attrib.] **1** situated on or near the exterior or external surface of something: *put the outside lights on.* ■ Baseball (of a pitch) passing home plate on the side of the plate away from the batter, not in the strike zone. ■ (in soccer and other sports) denoting positions nearer to the sides of the field. ■ (in basketball) taking place beyond the perimeter of the defense. **2** not belonging to or coming from within a particular group: *outside help.* ■ beyond one's own immediate personal concerns: *I was able to face the outside world again.* **3** (of an estimate) the greatest or highest possible: *new monthly charges that, according to outside estimates, may total $8 per line.* ▸ **prep. & adv.** /ˌoutˈsīd/ **1** situated or moving beyond the boundaries of (a room, building, or other enclosed space): [as prep.] *a boy outside the door* | [as adv.] *the dog was still barking outside.* ■ situated beyond the boundaries of (a particular location): [as prep.] *just outside Paris* | [as adv.] *those in the territories and those outside.* ■ not being a member of (a particular group): [as prep.] *those outside the university.* ■ (in football, soccer, and other sports) closer to the side of the field than (another player): [as prep.] *Swift appeared outside him with Andrews on his left.* **2** [prep.] beyond the limits or scope of: *the cost of shipping put it outside their price range.*

– PHRASES **at the outside** (of an estimate) at the most. **on the outside** away from or not belonging to a particular circle or institution: *when you're on the outside, then you have a much better view of what they're doing.* **an outside chance** a remote possibility. **outside of** informal beyond the boundaries of: *a village 20 miles outside of New York.* ■ apart from: *outside of his family, nobody cares about him.*

out·side in·ter·est ▸ **n.** an interest or hobby not connected with one's work or studies. ■ curiosity about a place, situation, or thing on the part of people unconnected with it.

out·side line ▸ **n.** a telephone connection to an external dial tone, for outgoing calls.

out·side mon·ey ▸ **n.** Econ. money held in a form such as gold that is an asset for the holder and does not represent a corresponding liability for someone else. ■ money or investment from an independent source.

out·sid·er /ˌoutˈsīdər/ ▸ **n. 1** a person who does not belong to a particular group. ■ a person not accepted by or isolated from society. **2** a competitor, applicant, etc., thought to have little chance of success.

out·sid·er art ▸ **n.** art produced by self-taught artists who are not part of the artistic establishment. — **out·sid·er art·ist n.**

out·size /ˈoutˌsīz/ ▸ **adj.** (also **out·sized**) exceptionally large. ▸ **n.** an exceptionally large person or thing, esp. a garment made to measurements larger than the standard.

out·skirts /ˈoutˌskərts/ ▸ **plural n.** the outer parts of a town or city. ■ the fringes of something: *he likes to be on the outskirts of a discussion.*

out·smart /ˌoutˈsmärt/ ▸ **v.** [trans.] informal defeat or get the better of (someone) by being clever or cunning.

out·sold /ˌoutˈsōld/ past and past participle of OUTSELL.

out·sole /ˈoutˌsōl/ ▸ **n.** the outermost layer of the sole of a boot or shoe, esp. an athletic shoe.

out·source /ˈout,sôrs/ ▶v. [trans.] obtain (goods or a service) from an outside supplier, esp. in place of an internal source. ■ contract (work) out.

out·spo·ken /,outˈspōkən/ ▶adj. frank in stating one's opinions, esp. if they are critical or controversial. —**out·spok·en·ly** adv. **out·spok·en·ness** n.

out·spread /,outˈspred/ ▶adj. fully extended or expanded: *outspread arms.* ▶v. (past and past part. **-spread**) [trans.] literary spread out: *that eagle outspreading his wings for flight.*

out·stand·ing /,outˈstandiNG; ˈout-/ ▶adj. **1** exceptionally good. ■ clearly noticeable: *works of outstanding banality.* **2** remaining to be done or dealt with. ■ (of a debt) remaining to be paid or dealt with.

out·stand·ing·ly /,outˈstandiNGlē/ ▶adv. [usu. as submodifier] exceptionally: *outstandingly beautiful gardens.*

out·stare /,outˈste(ə)r/ ▶v. [trans.] stare at (someone) for longer than they can stare back, typically in order to intimidate or disconcert them.

out·sta·tion /ˈout,stāSHən/ ▶n. a branch of an organization situated at some distance from its headquarters.

out·stay /,outˈstā/ ▶v. [trans.] stay beyond the limit of (one's expected or permitted time).

out·step /,outˈstep/ ▶v. (**-stepped, -step·ping**) [trans.] rare exceed.

out·stretch /,outˈstreCH/ ▶v. [trans.] [usu. as adj.] (**outstretched**) extend or stretch out (something, esp. a hand or arm). ■ go beyond the limit of: *their good intentions outstretched their capacity to help.*

out·strip /,outˈstrip/ ▶v. (**-stripped, -strip·ping**) [trans.] move faster than and overtake (someone else). ■ exceed: *supply far outstripped demand.*

out·ta /ˈoutə/ (also **out·a**) ▶prep. an informal contraction of "out of," used in representing colloquial speech: *we'd better get outta here.*

out·take /ˈout,tāk/ ▶n. a scene or sequence filmed or recorded for a movie or program but not included in the final version.

out·talk ▶v. (also **out·talk**) [trans.] outdo or overcome in talking or argumentation.

out·turn /ˈout,tərn/ ▶n. the amount of something produced, esp. money; output: *the financial outturn.*

out·ward /ˈoutwərd/ ▶adj. [attrib.] **1** of, on, or from the outside: *the vehicle's outward appearance.* ■ relating to the external appearance of something rather than its true nature or substance: *an outward display of friendliness.* ■ archaic outer: *the outward physical body.* **2** going out or away from a place: *the outward voyage.* ▶adv. away from the center or a particular point; toward the outside: *a window that opens outward.* —**out·ward·ness** n.

out·ward-bound ▶adj. (of a ship or passenger) going away from home or point of origin.

out·ward·ly /ˈoutwərdlē/ ▶adv. [often as submodifier] on the surface: *an outwardly normal life.* ■ on or from the outside: *outwardly featureless modern offices.*

out·wards /ˈoutwərdz/ ▶adv.-esp. Brit. variant of **OUTWARD**.

out·wash /ˈout,wôSH; -,wäSH/ ▶n. material carried away from a glacier by meltwater and deposited beyond the moraine.

out·wear /,outˈwe(ə)r/ ▶v. (past **-wore**; past part. **-worn**) [trans.] last longer than. ■ exhaust; wear out; wear away.

out·weigh /,outˈwā/ ▶v. [trans.] be heavier than. ■ be greater or more significant than: *the advantages outweigh the disadvantages.*

out·went /,outˈwent/ past of **OUTGO**.

out·wit /,outˈwit/ ▶v. (**-wit·ted, -wit·ting**) [trans.] deceive or defeat by greater ingenuity.

out·work ▶n. /ˈout,wərk/ a section of a fortification or system of defense that is in front of the main part. ▶v. /,outˈwərk/ [trans.] work harder, faster, or longer than.

out·worn /,outˈwôrn/ past participle of **OUTWEAR**. ▶adj. out of date: *outworn prejudices.* ■ no longer usable or serviceable.

ou·zel /ˈo͞ozəl/ (also **ou·sel**) ▶n. a bird that resembles the blackbird, esp. the ring ouzel. See also **WATER OUZEL**. [OE *ōsle* 'blackbird,' of Gmc. origin; rel. to Ger. *Amsel* 'blackbird.']

ou·zo /ˈo͞ozō/ ▶n. a Greek anise-flavored liqueur. [mod. Gk.]

o·va /ˈōvə/ plural form of **OVUM**.

o·val /ˈōvəl/ ▶adj. having a rounded and slightly elongated outline or shape, like that of an egg. ▶n. a body, object, or design with such a shape or outline. ■ an oval playing field or racing track. —**o·val·i·ty** /ōˈvalitē/ n. **o·val·ness** n. [16th C.: from Fr., or mod. L. *ovalis,* from L. *ovum* 'egg.']

ov·al·bu·min /,ävəlˈbyo͞omən; ,ōvəl-/ ▶n. Biochem. albumin derived from the white of eggs. [19th C.: from L. *ovi albumen* 'albumen of egg,' alt. on the pattern of *albumin.*]

O·val Of·fice the office of the president of the US, in the White House. ■ fig. this office regarded as representing the power of the executive branch of the US government.

o·val win·dow ▶n. informal term for ***FENESTRA OVALIS*** (see **FENESTRA**).

Ov·am·bo /ōˈvambō/ ▶n. (pl. same or **-bos**) **1** a member of a people of northern Namibia. **2** the Bantu language of this people. ▶adj. of or relating to the Ovambo or their language. [a local name, from *ova-* (prefix denoting a pl.) + *ambo* 'man of leisure.']

Ov·am·bo·land /ōˈvämbō,land/ a semiarid region of northern Namibia, home to the Ovambo people.

o·var·i·an /ōˈve(ə)rēən/ ▶adj. of or relating to an ovary or the ovaries: *an ovarian cyst.*

o·var·i·an fol·li·cle ▶n. another term for **GRAAFIAN FOLLICLE**.

o·var·i·ec·to·my /ō,ve(ə)rēˈektəmē/ ▶n. (pl. **-mies**) surgical removal of one or both ovaries; oophorectomy.

o·var·i·ot·o·my /ō,ve(ə)rēˈätəmē/ ▶n. **1** surgical incision into an ovary. **2** another term for **OVARIECTOMY**.

o·va·ri·tis /,ōvəˈrītis/ ▶n. another term for **OOPHORITIS**.

o·va·ry /ˈōv(ə)rē/ ▶n. (pl. **-ries**) a female reproductive organ in which ova or eggs are produced, present in humans and other vertebrates as a pair. ■ Bot. the hollow base of the carpel of a flower, containing one or more ovules. [17th C.: from mod. L. *ovarium,* from L. *ovum* 'egg.']

o·vate /ˈō,vāt/ ▶adj. esp. Biol. having an oval outline or ovoid shape, like an egg.

o·va·tion /ōˈvāSHən/ ▶n. **1** a sustained show of appreciation from an audience, esp. by applause. **2** Roman History a processional entrance into Rome by a victorious commander, of lesser honor than a triumph. [16th C. (sense 2): from L. *ovatio(n-),* from *ovare* 'exult.']

ov·en /ˈəvən/ ▶n. an enclosed compartment, as in a kitchen range, for cooking and heating food. ■ a small furnace or kiln. ■ a cremation chamber in a Nazi concentration camp. [OE *ofen*; rel. to Ger. *Ofen,* Gk. *ipnos.*]

ov·en·bird /ˈəvən,bərd/ ▶n. **1** a small tropical American bird belonging to a diverse family (Furnariidae), many members of which make domed, ovenlike nests of mud. **2** a migratory brown North American warbler (*Seiurus aurocapillus*) that builds a domed, ovenlike nest on the ground.

ov·en·proof /ˈəvən,pro͞of/ ▶adj. (of cookware) suitable for use in an oven; heat-resistant.

ov·en-read·y ▶adj. (of food) prepared before sale so as to be ready for cooking in an oven.

ov·en·ware /ˈəvən,we(ə)r/ ▶n. dishes that can be used for cooking food in an oven.

o·ver /ˈōvər/ ▶prep. **1** extending directly upward from: *I saw flames over Berlin.* ■ above so as to cover or protect: *ladle this sauce over fresh pasta.* ■ extending above (a general area) from a vantage point: *views over Fairmount Park.* ■ at the other side of; beyond: *over the hill is a small village.* **2** expressing passage or trajectory across: *she trudged over the lawn.* ■ beyond and falling or hanging from: *it toppled over the cliff.* ■ expressing duration: *she told me over coffee.* ■ by means of; by the medium of: *over the loudspeaker.* **3** at a higher level or layer than: *a television over the bar.* ■ higher in grade or rank than. ■ expressing authority or control: *editorial control over what is included.* ■ expressing preference: *I'd choose this brand over that one.* ■ expressing greater number: *the predominance of Asian over African managers in the sample.* ■ higher in volume or pitch than: *he shouted over the noise of the taxis.* **4** higher than or more than (a specified number or quantity): *over 40 degrees C.* **5** on the subject of: *a debate over unemployment.* ▶adv. **1** expressing passage or trajectory across an area: *he leaned over and tapped me on the hand.* ■ beyond and falling or hanging from a point: *listing over at an acute angle.* **2** in or to the place mentioned or indicated: *over here.* **3** used to express action and result: *hand the money over.* ■ finished: *the game is over.* **4** used to express repetition of a process: *twice over.*

– PHRASES **be over** no longer be affected by: *we were over the worst.* **get something over with** do or undergo something unpleasant or difficult, so as to be rid of it. **over against** adjacent to: *over against the wall.* ■ in contrast with: *over against heaven is hell.* **over and above** in addition to. **over and done with** completely finished. **over and over** again and again. [OE *ofer,* of Gmc. origin.]

over- ▶prefix **1** excessively; to an unwanted degree: *overambitious* | *overcareful.* ■ completely; utterly: *overawe* | *overjoyed.* **2** upper; outer; extra: *overcoat* | *overtime.* ■ overhead; above: *overcast* | *overhang.*

o·ver·a·chieve /,ōvərəˈCHēv/ ▶v. [intrans.] do better than is expected, esp. in academic work. ■ be excessively dedicated to success in one's work. —**o·ver·a·chieve·ment** n. **o·ver·a·chiev·er** n.

o·ver·act /,ōvərˈakt/ ▶v. [intrans.] (of an actor) act a role in an exaggerated manner.

o·ver·age[1] /ˈōv(ə)rij/ ▶n. an excess or surplus, esp. the amount by which a sum of money is greater than a previous estimate.

o·ver·age[2] /,ōvərˈāj/ ▶adj. over a certain age limit.

o·ver·all ▶adj. /ˈōvər,ôl/ total. ■ taking everything into account: *the overall effect is impressive.* ▶adv. /ˈōvərˈôl/ [sentence adverb] in all parts; taken as a whole: *overall, 10,000 jobs will go.* ▶n. /ˈōvər,ôl/ (**overalls**) a garment consisting of trousers with a front flap over the chest held up by straps over the shoulders. Also called **bib overalls**. ■ Brit. a loose-fitting garment such as a smock worn typically over ordinary clothes for protection against dirt or heavy wear. —**o·ver·alled** /ˈōvər,ôld/ adj.

o·ver·arch /,ōvərˈärCH/ ▶v. [trans.] form an arch over.

o·ver·arch·ing /,ōvərˈärCHiNG/ ▶adj. [attrib.] forming an arch over something. ■ comprehensive; all-embracing: *a single overarching principle.*

o·ver·arm /ˈōvər,ärm/ ▶adj. & adv. done with the arm moving above the level of the shoulder.

o·ver·awe /,ōvərˈô/ ▶v. [trans.] (usu. **be overawed**) impress (someone) so much that they become silent or inhibited: *he used firepower to overawe the hostile tribes.*

o·ver·bal·ance /,ōvərˈbaləns/ ▶v. [trans.] outweigh. ■ fall or cause to fall over from loss of balance: [intrans.] *the ladder overbalanced on top of her.* ▶n. archaic excess of weight, value, or amount.

o•ver•bear /ˌōvərˈber/ ▶ v. (past **-bore**; past part. **-borne**) [trans.] overcome by emotional pressure or physical force.

o•ver•bear•ing /ˌōvərˈbe(ə)riNG/ ▶ adj. unpleasantly or arrogantly domineering. — **o•ver•bear•ing•ly** adv. **o•ver•bear•ing•ness** n.

o•ver•bid ▶ v. /ˌōvərˈbid/ (**-bid•ding**; past and past part. **-bid**) [intrans.] **1** (in an auction) make a higher bid than a previous bid. **2** (in competitive bidding, the auction in bridge, etc.) bid more than is warranted or manageable. ▶ n. /ˈōvərˌbid/ a bid that is higher than is justified. — **o•ver•bid•der** n.

o•ver•bite /ˈōvərˌbīt/ ▶ n. Dentistry the overlapping of the lower teeth by the upper.

o•ver•blouse /ˈōvərˌblous; -blouz/ ▶ n. a blouse to be worn without being tucked in at the waist.

o•ver•blow•ing /ˌōvərˈblōiNG/ ▶ n. a technique for playing a wind instrument so as to produce overtones.

o•ver•blown /ˌōvərˈblōn/ ▶ adj. **1** excessively inflated or pretentious. **2** (of a flower) past its prime.

o•ver•board /ˈōvərˌbôrd/ ▶ adv. from a ship into the water.

– PHRASES **go overboard 1** be very enthusiastic: *Gary went overboard for you.* **2** react in an immoderate way: *Chris can sometimes go overboard.* **throw something overboard** abandon or discard something.

o•ver•book /ˌōvərˈbo͝ok/ ▶ v. [trans.] accept more reservations for (a flight, hotel, etc.) than there is room for.

o•ver•boot /ˈōvərˌbo͞ot/ ▶ n. a boot worn over another boot or shoe to protect it or to provide extra warmth.

o•ver•bore /ˌovərˈbôr/ past of OVERBEAR.

o•ver•borne /ˌōvərˈbôrn/ past participle of OVERBEAR.

o•ver•bought /ˌōvərˈbôt/ ▶ v. past and past participle of OVERBUY. ▶ adj. Stock Market overvalued owing to excessive buying at unjustifiably high prices.

o•ver•brim•ming /ˌōvərˈbrimiNG/ ▶ adj. abundant, esp. excessively so: *overbrimming confidence.*

o•ver•build /ˌōvərˈbild/ ▶ v. (past and past part. **-built**) [trans.] **1** put up too many buildings in (an area). ■ build too many: *to overbuild hotels would destroy the setting.* ■ build (something) elaborately or to a very high standard, esp. unnecessarily. **2** [often as n.] (**overbuilding**) build on top of: *the preservation of the medieval field pattern by direct overbuilding.*

o•ver•bur•den ▶ v. /ˌōvərˈbərdn/ [trans.] (often **be overburdened**) load (someone) with too many things to carry. ■ give (someone) more work or pressure than they can deal with. ▶ n. /ˈōvərˌbərdn/ rock or soil overlying a mineral deposit, archaeological site, or other underground feature. ■ an excessive burden: *an overburden of costs.* — **o•ver•bur•den•some** adj.

o•ver•buy /ˌōvərˈbī/ ▶ v. (past and past part. **-bought**) [trans.] buy more of (something) than one needs.

o•ver•call Bridge ▶ v. /ˌōvərˈkôl/ [intrans.] make a higher bid than an opponent's bid. ▶ n. /ˈōvərˌkôl/ an act or instance of making such a bid.

o•ver•came /ˌōvərˈkām/ past of OVERCOME.

o•ver•ca•pac•i•ty /ˌōvərkəˈpasitē/ ▶ n. the situation in which an industry cannot sell as much as it can produce.

o•ver•cap•i•tal•ize /ˌōvərˈkapitlˌīz/ ▶ v. [trans.] [usu. as adj.] (**overcapitalized**) provide (a company) with more capital than is advisable or necessary. ■ estimate or set the capital value of (a company) at too high an amount. — **o•ver•cap•i•tal•i•za•tion** /ˈōvərˌkapitl-iˈzāsHən/ n.

o•ver•cast ▶ adj. /ˈōvərˌkast; ˌōvərˈkast/ **1** (of the sky or weather) marked by a covering of gray clouds; dull. **2** (in sewing) edged with stitching to prevent fraying. ▶ n. /ˈōvərˌkast/ clouds covering a large part of the sky: *the sky was leaden with overcast.* ▶ v. /ˌōvərˈkast/ (past and past part. **-cast**) [trans.] **1** cover with clouds or shade. **2** stitch over (an unfinished edge) to prevent fraying.

o•ver•charge ▶ v. /ˌōvərˈCHärj/ [trans.] **1** charge (someone) too high a price for goods or a service. ■ charge someone (a sum) beyond the correct amount: *the company overcharged the government $3 million.* **2** put too much electric charge into (a battery). ■ put exaggerated or excessive detail into (a text or work of art). ▶ n. /ˈōvərˌCHärj/ an excessive charge for goods or a service.

o•ver•class /ˈōvərˌklas/ ▶ n. a privileged, wealthy, or powerful subgroup in society.

o•ver•cloud /ˌōvərˈkloud/ ▶ v. [trans.] mar, dim, or obscure.

o•ver•coat /ˈōvərˌkōt/ ▶ n. **1** a long warm coat worn over other clothing. **2** a top, final layer of paint or a similar covering.

o•ver•come /ˌōvərˈkəm/ ▶ v. (past **-came**; past part. **-come**) [trans.] succeed in dealing with (a problem or difficulty). ■ defeat (an opponent); prevail: *they overcame the guards* | [intrans.] *we shall overcome.* ■ (usu. **be overcome**) (of an emotion) overpower or overwhelm: ***overcome** with excitement.*

o•ver•com•mit /ˌōvərkəˈmit/ ▶ v. (**-mit•ted, -mit•ting**) [trans.] oblige (oneself or others) to do more than one is capable of, esp. to repay a loan one cannot afford. ■ allocate more (resources) to a purpose than can be provided. — **o•ver•com•mit•ment** n.

o•ver•com•pen•sate /ˌōvərˈkämpənˌsāt/ ▶ v. [intrans.] take excessive measures in attempting to correct or make amends for an error, weakness, or problem. — **o•ver•com•pen•sat•ing•ly** /ˈōvərˌkämpənˈsātiNGlē/ adv. **o•ver•com•pen•sa•tion** /ˈōvərˌkämpənˈsāsHən/ n. **o•ver•com•pen•sa•to•ry** /ˈōvərkəmˈpensəˌtôrē/ adj.

o•ver•crop /ˌōvərˈkräp/ ▶ v. (**-cropped, -crop•ping**) [trans.] [usu. as n.] (**overcropping**) deplete (soil) by growing crops continuously on it.

o•ver•crowd /ˌōvərˈkroud/ ▶ v. [trans.] fill (accommodations or a space) beyond what is usual or comfortable: [as adj.] (**overcrowded**) *overcrowded dormitories.* ■ house (people or animals) in accommodations that are too confined.

o•ver•de•ter•mine /ˌōvərdiˈtərmən/ ▶ v. [trans.] tech. determine, account for, or cause (something) in more than one way or with more conditions than necessary. — **o•ver•de•ter•mi•na•tion** /ˈˌōvərdiˌtərməˈnāsHən/ n.

o•ver•de•vel•op /ˌōvərdəˈveləp/ ▶ v. (**-vel•oped, -vel•op•ing**) [trans.] develop too much or to excess. ■ Photog. treat with developer for too long. — **o•ver•de•vel•op•ment** n.

o•ver•do /ˌōvərˈdo͞o/ ▶ v. (**-does**; past **-did**; past part. **-done**) [trans.] carry to excess; exaggerate. ■ use too much of (something). ■ (**overdo it/things**) exhaust oneself by overwork or overexertion. ■ [often as adj.] (**overdone**) overcook (food).

o•ver•dose ▶ n. /ˈōvərˌdōs/ an excessive and dangerous dose of a drug. ▶ v. /ˈōvərˌdōs; ˌōvərˈdōs/ [intrans.] take an overdose of a drug. ■ [trans.] give an overdose to. — **o•ver•dos•age** /-ˈdōsij/ n.

o•ver•draft /ˈōvərˌdraft/ ▶ n. a deficit in a bank account caused by drawing more money than the account holds.

o•ver•draw /ˌōvərˈdrô/ ▶ v. (past **-drew**; past part. **-drawn**) [trans.] **1** (usu. **be overdrawn**) draw money from (one's bank account) in excess of what the account holds. ■ (**be overdrawn**) (of a person) have taken money out of an account in excess of what it holds. **2** exaggerate in describing or depicting (someone or something). **3** draw (a bow) too far.

o•ver•dress /ˌōvərˈdres/ ▶ v. [intrans.] (also **be overdressed**) dress with too much display or formality.

o•ver•drive ▶ n. /ˈōvərˌdrīv/ a gear in a motor vehicle providing a gear ratio higher than that of the drive gear or top gear, so that engine speed and fuel consumption are reduced in highway travel. ■ a state of high or excessive activity. ■ a mechanism that permits a higher than normal operating level in a piece of equipment, such as the amplifier of an electric guitar. ▶ v. /ˌōvərˈdrīv/ [trans.] [usu. as adj.] (**overdriven**) drive or work to exhaustion.

o•ver•dub ▶ v. /ˌōvərˈdəb/ (**-dubbed, -dubbing**) record (additional sounds) on an existing recording: [trans.] *she'd overdub her parts for a whole album in a single session.* | [intrans.] *a live tape that I overdubbed on.* ▶ n. /ˈōvərˌdəb/ an instance of overdubbing.

o•ver•due /ˌōvərˈd(y)o͞o/ ▶ adj. not yet having arrived, happened, or been done, though after the expected time: ***reform is now overdue.*** ■ (of a payment) not having been made, though required: ***the rent was overdue.*** ■ (of a woman) having gone beyond the expected time for a menstrual period. ■ (of a baby) not having been born, though beyond full gestation: *our daughter was six days overdue.* ■ having deserved or needed something for some time: *she was **overdue for** some leave.* ■ (of a library book) retained longer than the period allowed.

o•ver eas•y ▶ adj. (of a fried egg) turned over when the white is nearly done and fried lightly on the other side, so that the yolk remains slightly liquid.

o•ver•es•ti•mate ▶ v. /ˌōvərˈestəˌmāt/ [trans.] estimate (something) to be better, larger, or more important than it really is. ▶ n. /-mit/ an excessively high estimate. — **o•ver•es•ti•ma•tion** /ˈōvərˌestəˈmāsHən/ n.

o•ver•ex•pose /ˌōvərikˈspōz/ ▶ v. [trans.] expose too much, esp. to the public eye or to risk. ■ Photog. expose (film or a part of an image) for too long a time or for extra time. — **o•ver•ex•po•sure** /-ikˈspōzHər/ n.

o•ver•ex•tend /ˌōvərikˈstend/ ▶ v. [trans.] (usu. **be overextended**) **1** make too long. **2** impose on (someone) an excessive burden of work or commitments. — **o•ver•ex•ten•sion** /-ˈstensHən/ n.

o•ver•fa•mil•iar /ˌōvərfəˈmilyər/ ▶ adj. too well known. ■ [predic.] (**overfamiliar with**) too well acquainted with. ■ behaving or speaking in an inappropriately informal way. — **o•ver•fa•mil•i•ar•i•ty** /-fəˌmilēˈaritē/ n.

o•ver•fill /ˌōvərˈfil/ ▶ v. [trans.] put more into (a container) than it either should or can contain.

o•ver•fine /ˌōvərˈfīn/ ▶ adj. excessively or extremely fine or particular.

o•ver•fish /ˌōvərˈfisH/ ▶ v. [trans.] deplete the stock of fish in (a body of water) by too much fishing. ■ deplete the stock of (a fish): *tuna have been overfished.*

o•ver•flow ▶ v. /ˌōvərˈflō/ [intrans.] (esp. of a liquid) flow over the brim of a receptacle: *chemicals overflowed from a storage tank* | [trans.] *the river overflowed its banks.* ■ (of a container) be so full that the contents go over or extend above the sides. ■ (of a space) be so crowded that people cannot fit inside. ■ [trans.] flood or flow over (a surface or area): *her hair overflowed her shoulders.* ■ (**overflow with**) fig. be very full of (an emotion or quality): *her heart overflowed with joy.* ▶ n. /ˈōvərˌflō/ **1** [in sing.] the excess or surplus not able to be accommodated by an available space. ■ the flowing over of a liquid. **2** (also **overflow pipe**) (in a bathtub or sink) an outlet for excess water. **3** Comput. the generation of a number or some other data item that is too large for an assigned location or memory space.

– PHRASES **full to overflowing** completely full.

o•ver•fly /ˌōvərˈflī/ ▶ v. (**-flies**; past **-flew**; past part. **-flown**) [trans.] fly over (a place or territory). ■ fly beyond (a place or thing). — **o•ver•flight** /ˈōvərˌflīt/ n.

o•ver•gar•ment /ˈōvərˌgärmənt/ ▶ n. a garment that is worn over others.

o•ver•glaze /ˌōvərˈglāz/ ▶ n. decoration or a second glaze applied to glazed ceramic ware. ▶ adj. (of painting, printing, or other decoration) done on a glazed surface: *overglaze enamel.*

o·ver·graze /ˌōvərˈgrāz/ ▶ **v.** [trans.] graze (grassland) so heavily that the vegetation is damaged and the ground becomes liable to erosion.

o·ver·ground /ˈōvərˌground/ ▶ **adv. & adj.** on or above the ground.

o·ver·grow /ˌōvərˈgrō/ ▶ **v.** (past **-grew**; past part. **-grown**) [trans.] grow or spread over (something), esp. so as to choke or stifle it.

o·ver·grown /ˌōvərˈgrōn/ ▶ **adj. 1** covered with plants that have been allowed to grow wild. **2** grown too large or beyond its normal size. ■ esp. derog. used to describe an adult behaving in a childish manner.

o·ver·growth /ˈōvərˌgrōTH/ ▶ **n.** excessive growth.

o·ver·hand /ˈōvərˌhand/ ▶ **adj. & adv.** (chiefly of a throw or a stroke with a racket) made with the hand or arm passing above the level of the shoulder. ■ with the palm of the hand over what it grasps: [as adj.] *an overhand grip.* ■ Boxing (of a punch) passing over the other hand.

o·ver·hand knot ▶ **n.** a simple knot made by forming a loop and passing a free end around the standing part and through the loop. See illustration at KNOT[1].

o·ver·hang ▶ **v.** /ˌōvərˈhaNG/ (past and past part. **-hung**) [trans.] hang or extend outward over. ■ fig. loom over. ▶ **n.** /ˈōvərˌhaNG/ a part of something that sticks out or hangs over another thing.

o·ver·haul ▶ **v.** /ˌōvərˈhôl/ [trans.] **1** take apart (a piece of machinery or equipment) in order to examine it and repair it if necessary. **2** Brit. overtake (someone), esp. in a sporting event. ▶ **n.** /ˈōvərˌhôl/ a thorough examination of machinery or a system, with repairs or changes made if necessary.

o·ver·head ▶ **adv.** /ˈōvərˈhed/ above the level of the head; in the sky: *a helicopter overhead.* ▶ **adj.** /ˈōvərˌhed/ **1** situated above the level of the head: *overhead power cables.* **2** (of a driving mechanism) above the object driven: *an overhead cam four-cylinder engine.* **3** [attrib.] (of a cost or expense) incurred in the general upkeep or running of a plant, premises, or business, and not attributable to specific products or items. ▶ **n.** /ˈōvərˌhed/ **1** overhead cost or expense. **2** a transparency designed for use with an overhead projector. **3** short for OVERHEAD PROJECTOR. **4** an overhead compartment: *fits in most airline overheads.* **5** Tennis a shot directed sharply downward, hit while the ball is over the head; a smash.

o·ver·head pro·jec·tor ▶ **n.** a device that projects an enlarged image of a transparency placed on it onto a wall or screen by means of an overhead mirror.

o·ver·hear /ˌōvərˈhi(ə)r/ ▶ **v.** (past and past part. **-heard**) [trans.] hear (someone or something) without meaning to or without the knowledge of the speaker.

o·ver·heat /ˌōvərˈhēt/ ▶ **v.** make or become too hot. ■ make too excited: [as adj.] (**overheated**) *his overheated imagination.* ■ Econ. (of a country's economy) show marked inflation when increased demand results in rising prices rather than increased output: [intrans.] *lending rates could soar as the economy overheats* | [trans.] *credit expansion helped overheat the economy.*

O·ver·ijs·sel /ˌōvərˈīsəl/ a province in east central Netherlands; capital, Zwolle.

o·ver·is·sue /ˌōvərˈisHo͞o/ ▶ **v.** (**-is·sues, -is·sued, -is·suing**) [trans.] issue (bonds, shares of stock, etc.) beyond the authorized amount or the issuer's ability to pay them on demand. ▶ **n.** the action of overissuing bonds, shares of stock, etc.

o·ver·joyed /ˌōvərˈjoid/ ▶ **adj.** extremely happy.

o·ver·kill /ˈōvərˌkil/ ▶ **n.** the amount by which destruction or the capacity for destruction exceeds what is necessary. ■ excessive use, treatment, or action; too much of something: *animators now face technology overkill.*

o·ver·laid /ˌōvərˈlād/ past and past participle of OVERLAY[1].

o·ver·lain /ˌōvərˈlān/ past participle of OVERLIE.

o·ver·land /ˈōvərˌland/ ▶ **adj. & adv.** by land.

O·ver·land Park /ˈōvərlənd/ a city in northeastern Kansas; pop. 149,080.

o·ver·lap ▶ **v.** /ˌōvərˈlap/ (**-lapped, -lap·ping**) [trans.] extend over so as to cover partly: *the canopy overlaps the house roof* | [intrans.] *the curtains overlap at the center when closed.* ■ [intrans.] cover part of the same area of interest, responsibility, etc.: *their duties sometimes overlapped.* ■ [intrans.] partly coincide in time: *two new series overlapped.* ▶ **n.** /ˈōvərˌlap/ a part or amount that overlaps. ■ a common area of interest, responsibility, etc. ■ a period of time in which two events or activities happen together.

o·ver·lay[1] ▶ **v.** /ˌōvərˈlā/ (past and past part. **-laid**) [trans.] (often **be overlaid with**) cover the surface of (a thing) with a coating: *their fingernails were overlaid with gold.* ■ lie on top of: *a third screen which will overlay the others.* ■ fig. (of a quality or feeling) become more prominent than (a previous quality or feeling): *his openness had been overlaid by his self-confidence.* ▶ **n.** /ˈōvərˌlā/ something laid as a covering over something else: *a durable floor overlay.* ■ a transparency placed over artwork or something such as a map, marked with additional information or detail. ■ a graphical computer display that can be superimposed on another.

o·ver·lay[2] /ˌōvərˈlā/ past of OVERLIE.

o·ver·leaf /ˈōvərˌlēf/ ▶ **adv.** on the other side of the page: *an information sheet is printed overleaf.*

o·ver·leap /ˌōvərˈlēp/ ▶ **v.** (past and past part. **-leaped** or **-leapt**) [trans.] archaic jump over or across. ■ omit; ignore.

o·ver·lie /ˌōvərˈlī/ ▶ **v.** (**-ly·ing**; past **-lay**; past part. **-lain**) [trans.] lie on top of: *soft clays overlie the basalt.*

o·ver·look ▶ **v.** /ˌōvərˈlo͝ok/ [trans.] **1** fail to notice (something). ■ ignore or disregard (something, esp. a fault or offense): *she overlooks his faults.* ■ pass over (someone) in favor of another: *he was overlooked by the Nobel committee.* **2** have a view of from above: *the chateau overlooks fields.* **3** archaic supervise; oversee. **4** archaic bewitch with the evil eye: *they told them they were overlooked by some unlucky person.* ▶ **n.** /ˈōvərˌlo͝ok/ a commanding position or view.

o·ver·lord /ˈōvərˌlôrd/ ▶ **n.** a ruler, esp. a feudal lord. ■ a person of great power or authority. — **o·ver·lord·ship n.**

o·ver·ly /ˈōvərlē/ ▶ **adv.** excessively.

o·ver·ly·ing /ˈōvərˈlī-iNG/ present participle of OVERLIE.

o·ver·man ▶ **v.** /ˌōvərˈman/ (**-manned, -man·ning**) [trans.] provide with more people than necessary. ▶ **n.** /ˈōvərmən; -ˌman/ (pl. **-men**) **1** an overseer. **2** Philos. another term for SUPERMAN.

o·ver·man·tel /ˈōvərˌmantl/ ▶ **n.** an ornamental structure over a mantelpiece, typically of plaster or carved wood and sometimes including a mirror.

o·ver·mas·ter /ˌōvərˈmastər/ ▶ **v.** literary [trans.] overcome; conquer: *he was overmastered by events.*

o·ver·match /ˌōvərˈmacH/ ▶ **v.** [trans.] [usu. as adj.] (**overmatched**) be stronger, better armed, or more skillful than: *Bosnia's overmatched forces.*

o·ver·much /ˈōvərˈməcH/ ▶ **adv., adj., & pron.** too much.

o·ver·night ▶ **adv.** /ˈōvərˈnīt/ for the duration of a night. ■ during the course of a night: *you can recharge the battery overnight.* ■ very quickly; suddenly. ▶ **adj.** /ˈōvərˌnīt/ [attrib.] for use overnight: *an overnight bag.* ■ done or happening overnight: *an overnight stay.* ■ sudden, rapid, or instant. ▶ **v.** /ˌōvərˈnīt/ [intrans.] stay for the night in a particular place. ■ [trans.] ship for delivery the next day: *Forster overnighted the sample to headquarters by courier.* ▶ **n.** /ˈōvərˌnīt/ a stop or stay lasting one night.

o·ver·night·er /ˌōvərˈnītər/ ▶ **n.** a person who stops at a place overnight. ■ an overnight bag. ■ an overnight trip or stay.

o·ver·pass ▶ **n.** /ˈōvərˌpas/ a bridge by which a road or railroad passes over another. ▶ **v.** /ˌōvərˈpas/ [trans.] pass over; traverse. ■ surpass. ■ archaic come to the end of (something).

o·ver·play /ˌōvərˈplā/ ▶ **v.** [trans.] give undue importance to; overemphasize. ■ exaggerate the performance of (a dramatic role): *the uncontrollable urge of ham actors to overplay their parts.* ■ Sports play very aggressively.

– PHRASES **overplay one's hand 1** (in a card game) play or bet on one's hand with a mistaken optimism. **2** spoil one's chance of success through excessive confidence in one's position.

o·ver·plus /ˈōvərˌpləs/ ▶ **n.** dated a surplus or excess. [ME: partial translation of Fr. *surplus* or med. L. *superplus.*]

o·ver·pop·u·late /ˌōvərˈpäpyəˌlāt/ ▶ **v.** [trans.] populate (an area) in too large numbers: *the country was overpopulated.* ■ [intrans.] (of an animal) breed too rapidly: *without predators, deer would overpopulate.* — **o·ver·pop·u·la·tion** /ˈōvərˌpäpyəˈlāsHən/ **n.**

o·ver·pow·er /ˌōvərˈpouər/ ▶ **v.** [trans.] defeat or overcome with superior strength. ■ be too intense for; overwhelm. — **o·ver·pow·er·ing·ly adv.**

o·ver·price /ˌōvərˈprīs/ ▶ **v.** [trans.] [often as adj.] (**overpriced**) charge too high a price for: *overpriced hotels.*

o·ver·print ▶ **v.** /ˌōvərˈprint/ [trans.] **1** print additional matter on (a stamp or other surface already bearing print): *menus will be overprinted with company logos.* ■ print (additional matter) on something already printed. **2** print too many copies or too much of. ▶ **n.** /ˈōvərˌprint/ words or other matter printed onto something already bearing print. ■ an overprinted postage stamp.

o·ver·proof /ˈōvərˈpro͞of/ ▶ **adj.** containing more alcohol than proof spirit does: *overproof rum.*

o·ver·qual·i·fied /ˌōvərˈkwôləˌfīd/ ▶ **adj.** having qualifications that exceed the requirements of a particular job.

o·ver·ran /ˌōvərˈran/ past of OVERRUN.

o·ver·reach ▶ **v.** /ˌōvərˈrēcH/ **1** [intrans.] reach too far: *never overreach from a ladder.* ■ (**overreach oneself**) defeat one's own purpose by trying to do more than is possible. ■ (of a quadruped) bring the hind feet so far forward that they fall alongside or strike the forefeet: *the horse overreached jumping the first hurdle.* **2** [trans.] get the better of (someone) by cunning: *Faustus's lunacy in thinking he can overreach the devil.* ▶ **n.** /ˈovərˌrēcH/ an injury to a forefoot of a horse resulting from its having overreached.

o·ver·reach·er /ˌōvərˈrēcHər/ ▶ **n.** an excessively ambitious or haughty person.

o·ver·rep·re·sent /ˈovərˌreprəˈzent/ ▶ **v.** [trans.] include a disproportionately large number of (a particular category or type of person), as in a statistical study. ■ (**be overrepresented**) form a disproportionately large percentage. — **o·ver·rep·re·sen·ta·tion** /-zənˈtāsHən/ **n.**

o·ver·ride ▶ **v.** /ˌōvərˈrīd/ (past **-rode**; past part. **-rid·den**) [trans.] **1** use one's authority to reject or cancel (a decision, view, etc.). ■ interrupt the action of (an automatic device), typically in order to take manual control. ■ be more important than: *this commitment overrides all other considerations.* **2** tech. extend over; overlap. **3** travel or move over (a place or thing): *the deposit was overridden and covered by ice.* ▶ **n.** /ˈōvərˌrīd/ **1** a device for suspending an automatic function on a machine. ■ the action or process of suspending an automatic function. **2** an excess or increase on a budget, salary, or cost. ■ a commission paid to a manager on sales made by a subordinate or representative. **3** a cancellation of a decision by exertion of authority or winning of votes: *the House vote* *in favor of the bill was 10 votes short of the requisite majority for an override.*

o•ver•rid•ing /ˌōvərˈrīdiNG/ ▶ **adj.** **1** more important than any other considerations. **2** tech. extending or moving over something, esp. while remaining in close contact.

o•ver•ripe /ˈōvərˈrīp/ ▶ **adj.** too ripe; past its best. ■ fig. decadent.

o•ver•rule /ˌōvərˈro͞ol/ ▶ **v.** [trans.] reject or disallow by exercising one's superior authority. ■ reject the decision or argument of (someone).

o•ver•run ▶ **v.** /ˌōvərˈrən/ (**-run•ning**; past **-ran**; past part. **-run**) [trans.] **1** spread over or occupy (a place) in large numbers. ■ conquer or occupy (territory) by force. ■ move or extend over or beyond: *let the text overrun the right-hand margin.* ■ run over or beyond (a thing or place): *she overran third base.* ■ rotate faster than (another part of a machine). **2** continue beyond or above (an expected or allowed time or cost). ▶ **n.** /ˈōvərˌrən/ **1** an instance of something exceeding an expected or allowed time or cost. ■ the amount by which this happens. ■ a surplus in manufacturing. **2** the movement or extension of something beyond an allotted or particular position or space. ■ a clear area beyond the end of an airport runway. **3** the movement of a vehicle at a speed greater than is imparted by the engine.

o•ver•seas /ˈōvərˈsēz/ (Brit. also **o•ver•sea**) ▶ **adv.** in or to a foreign country, esp. one across the sea. ▶ **adj.** [attrib.] from, to, or relating to a foreign country, esp. one across the sea: *overseas trips.*

o•ver•see /ˌōvərˈsē/ ▶ **v.** (**-sees**; past **-saw**; past part. **-seen**) [trans.] supervise (a person or work), esp. in an official capacity.

o•ver•se•er /ˈōvərˌsi(ə)r; -ˌsēər/ ▶ **n.** a person who supervises others, esp. workers.

o•ver•sell /ˌōvərˈsel/ ▶ **v.** (past and past part. **-sold**) [trans.] sell more of (something) than exists or can be delivered. ■ exaggerate the merits of.

o•ver•set /ˌōvərˈset/ ▶ **v.** (**-set•ting**; past and past part. **-set**) [trans.] **1** upset emotionally. **2** esp. Brit. overturn: *he jumped up and overset the canoe.* **3** Print. set up (type) in excess of the available space.

o•ver•sew /ˌōvərˈsō/ ▶ **v.** (past part. **-sewn** or **-sewed**) [trans.] sew (the edges of two pieces of fabric) with every stitch passing over the join. ■ join the sections of (a book) in such a way.

o•ver•sexed /ˌōvərˈsekst/ ▶ **adj.** having unusually strong sexual desires.

o•ver•shad•ow /ˌōvərˈSHadō/ ▶ **v.** [trans.] tower above and cast a shadow over. ■ fig. cast a gloom over: *tragedy overshadows his story.* ■ appear much more prominent or important than: *his competitive nature often overshadows the other qualities.* ■ (often **be overshadowed**) be more impressive or successful than (another person).

o•ver•shoe /ˈōvərˌSHo͞o/ ▶ **n.** a shoe worn over a normal shoe, typically either of waterproof material to protect the normal shoe in wet weather or of fabric to protect a floor surface.

o•ver•shoot /ˌōvərˈSHo͞ot/ ▶ **v.** (past and past part. **-shot**) [trans.] go past (a point) unintentionally, esp. through traveling too fast or being unable to stop: *they overshot their destination* | [intrans.] *he had overshot by fifty yards.* ■ (of an aircraft) fly beyond or taxi too far along (the runway) when landing or taking off. ■ exceed (a target or limit). ▶ **n.** /ˈōvərˌSHo͞ot/ an act of going past or beyond a point, target, or limit. ■ an amount or distance by which a target is passed.

o•ver•shot /ˈōvərˌSHät/ past and past participle of OVERSHOOT. ▶ **adj.** **1** (of a waterwheel) turned by water falling onto it from an overhead channel. **2** denoting an upper jaw that projects beyond the lower jaw.

o•ver•sight /ˈōvərˌsīt/ ▶ **n.** **1** an unintentional failure to notice or do something. **2** the action of overseeing something.

o•ver•sim•pli•fy /ˌōvərˈsimpləˌfī/ ▶ **v.** (**-fies**, **-fied**) [trans.] [often as adj.] (**oversimplified**) simplify (something) so much that a distorted impression of it is given. — **o•ver•sim•pli•fi•ca•tion** /ˈōvərˌsimpləfiˈkāSHən/ **n.**

o•ver•sized /ˈōvərˈsīzd/ (also **o•ver•size**) ▶ **adj.** bigger than the usual size: *an oversized T-shirt.*

o•ver•skirt /ˈōvərˌskərt/ ▶ **n.** an outer skirt worn over the skirt of a dress.

o•ver•slaugh /ˌōvərˈslô/ ▶ **v.** [trans.] dated pass over (someone) in favor of another. [18th C.: from Du. *overslag* (n.), from *overslaan* 'pass over.']

o•ver•sleep /ˌōvərˈslēp/ ▶ **v.** (past and past part. **-slept**) [intrans.] sleep longer or later than one intended.

o•ver•sold /ˌōvərˈsōld/ past and past participle of OVERSELL. ▶ **adj.** Stock Market sold to a price below its true value: *technology stocks remain oversold and are ripe for buying.*

o•ver•soul /ˈōvərˌsōl/ ▶ **n.** [in sing.] a divine spirit pervading the universe and encompassing all human souls. The term is associated esp. with Transcendentalism.

o•ver•spend /ˌōvərˈspend/ ▶ **v.** (past and past part. **-spent**) [intrans.] spend too much: *she overspent on her husband's funeral.* ■ [trans.] spend more than (a specified amount): *the department overspent its budget.*

o•ver•spill /ˈōvərˌspil/ ▶ **n.** people or things that spill over or are in excess.

o•ver•spread /ˌōvərˈspred/ ▶ **v.** (past and past part. **-spread**) [trans.] cover the surface of; spread over.

o•ver•state /ˌōvərˈstāt/ ▶ **v.** [trans.] express or state too strongly; exaggerate. — **o•ver•state•ment** **n.**

o•ver•stay /ˌōvərˈstā/ ▶ **v.** [trans.] stay longer than the time, limits, or duration of.

o•ver•steer ▶ **v.** /ˌōvərˈsti(ə)r/ [intrans.] (of a motor vehicle) have a tendency to turn more sharply than was intended. ▶ **n.** /ˈōvərˌsti(ə)r/ the tendency of a vehicle to turn in such a way.

o•ver•step /ˌōvərˈstep/ ▶ **v.** (**-stepped**, **-step•ping**) pass beyond (a limit). ■ violate (a rule or standard of behavior).

o•ver•stock ▶ **v.** /ˌōvərˈstäk/ [trans.] supply with more of something than is necessary or required. ▶ **n.** /ˈōvərˌstäk/ (esp. in a manufacturing or retailing context) a supply or quantity in excess of demand or requirements.

o•ver•strung /ˈōvərˈstrəNG/ ▶ **adj.** dated (of a person) extremely nervous or tense.

o•ver•stuff /ˌōvərˈstəf/ ▶ **v.** [trans.] [usu. as adj.] (**overstuffed**) **1** force too much into (a container). **2** cover (furniture) completely with padded upholstery: *an overstuffed armchair.*

o•ver•sub•scribed /ˌōvərsəbˈskrībd/ ▶ **adj.** applied for in greater quantities than are available or expected. ■ (of a course, etc.) having more applications than available places.

o•vert /ōˈvərt; ˈōvərt/ ▶ **adj.** done or shown openly; plainly or readily apparent, not secret or hidden. — **o•vert•ly** **adv.** **o•vert•ness** **n.** [ME: from OFr., past part. of *ovrir* 'to open,' from L. *aperire*.]

o•ver•take /ˌōvərˈtāk/ ▶ **v.** (past **-took**; past part. **-tak•en**) [trans.] **1** catch up with and pass while traveling in the same direction. ■ become greater or more successful than: *Germany overtook Britain in industrial output.* **2** (esp. of misfortune) come suddenly or unexpectedly upon. ■ (of a feeling) affect (someone) suddenly and powerfully: *weariness overtook him.*

o•ver•task /ˌōvərˈtask/ ▶ **v.** [trans.] impose too much work on.

o•ver•throw ▶ **v.** /ˌōvərˈTHrō/ (past **-threw**; past part. **-thrown**) [trans.] **1** remove forcibly from power. ■ put an end to (something), typically by the use of force or violence. ■ archaic knock or throw to the ground. **2** throw (a ball) further or harder than intended. ■ throw a ball beyond (a receiving player). ▶ **n.** /ˈōvərˌTHrō/ **1** [in sing.] a removal from power; a defeat or downfall: *plotting the overthrow of the government.* **2** (in baseball and other games) a throw that sends a ball past its intended recipient or target.

o•ver•thrust /ˈōvərˌTHrəst/ Geol. ▶ **n.** the thrust of one series of rock strata over another, esp. along a fault line at a shallow angle to the horizontal.

o•ver•time /ˈōvərˌtīm/ ▶ **n.** time in addition to what is normal, esp. time worked beyond one's scheduled working hours. ■ payment for such extra work. ■ extra time played at the end of a game that is tied at the end of the regulation time: *they lost in overtime.* ▶ **adv.** in addition to normal working hours: *working overtime.*

o•ver•tone /ˈōvərˌtōn/ ▶ **n.** **1** a musical tone that is a part of the harmonic series above a fundamental note and may be heard with it. ■ Physics a component of any oscillation whose frequency is an integral multiple of the fundamental frequency. **2** (often **overtones**) a subtle or subsidiary quality, implication, or connotation.

o•ver•top /ˌōvərˈtäp/ ▶ **v.** (**-top•ped**, **-top•ping**) [trans.] exceed in height. ■ (esp. of water) rise over the top of (a barrier constructed to hold it back). ■ be superior to: *none can overtop him in goodness.*

o•ver•trade /ˌōvərˈtrād/ ▶ **v.** [intrans.] engage in more business than can be supported by the market or by the funds or resources available.

o•ver•trick /ˈōvərˌtrik/ ▶ **n.** Bridge a trick taken by the declarer in excess of the contract.

o•ver•trump /ˌōvərˈtrəmp/ ▶ **v.** [intrans.] (in bridge and similar card games) play a trump that is higher than one already played in the same trick.

o•ver•ture /ˈōvərCHər; -ˌCHo͝or/ ▶ **n.** **1** an introduction to something more substantial. ■ (usu. **overtures**) an approach or proposal made to someone with the aim of opening negotiations or establishing a relationship. **2** Music an orchestral piece at the beginning of an opera, suite, play, oratorio, or other extended composition. ■ an independent orchestral composition in one movement. [ME: from OFr., from L. *apertura* 'aperture.']

o•ver•turn ▶ **v.** /ˌōvərˈtərn/ [trans.] **1** tip (something) over so that it is on its side or upside down: *the crowd overturned cars.* ■ [intrans.] turn over and come to rest upside down, typically as the result of an accident. **2** abolish, invalidate, or turn around (an established fact, system, etc.). ■ reverse (a legal decision). ▶ **n.** /ˈōvərˌtərn/ rare an act of turning over or upsetting something. ■ Ecol. the occasional (typically twice yearly) mixing of the water of a thermally stratified lake.

o•ver•val•ue /ˌōvərˈvalyo͞o/ ▶ **v.** (**-val•ues**, **-val•ued**, **-val•uing**) [trans.] overestimate the importance of. ■ fix the value of (something, esp. a currency) at too high a level. — **o•ver•val•u•a•tion** /ˈōvərˌvalyo͞oˈāSHən/ **n.**

o•ver•view /ˈōvərˌvyo͞o/ ▶ **n.** a general review or summary of a subject.

o•ver•ween•ing /ˈōvərˈwēniNG/ ▶ **adj.** showing excessive confidence or pride: *overweening ambition.* — **o•ver•ween•ing•ly** **adv.**

o•ver•weight ▶ **adj.** /ˈōvərˈwāt/ above a weight considered normal or desirable. ■ above legal weight: *an overweight truck.* ▶ **n.** /ˈōvərˌwāt/ excessive or extra weight. ▶ **v.** /ˌōvərˈwāt/ [trans.] [usu. as adj.] (**overweighted**) put too much weight on; overload. ■ Finance invest in (a market sector, industry, etc.) to a greater than normal degree: *we have overweighted the banking sector.*

o•ver•whelm /ˌōvərˈ(h)welm/ ▶ **v.** [trans.] bury or drown beneath a huge mass. ■ defeat completely. ■ (often **be overwhelmed**) give too much of a thing to (someone); inundate: *they were overwhelmed by farewell messages.* ■ (usu. **be overwhelmed**) have a strong emotional effect on: *overwhelmed with guilt.* ■ be too strong for; overpower: *the wine doesn't overwhelm the flavor of the trout.*

o·ver·whelm·ing /,ōvər'(h)welmiNG/ ▶ **adj.** very great in amount: *elected by an overwhelming majority.* ■ (esp. of an emotion) very strong: *overwhelming gratitude.* — **o·ver·whelm·ing·ly adv. o·ver·whelm·ing·ness n.**

o·ver·win·ter /'ōvər'win(t)ər/ ▶ **v.** [intrans.] **1** [with adverbial of place] spend the winter: *many birds overwinter in equatorial regions.* **2** (of an insect, plant, etc.) live through the winter.

o·ver·work /'ōvər'wərk/ ▶ **v.** [trans.] exhaust with too much work: *executives who are overworked.* ■ [intrans.] (of a person) work too hard: *the doctor advised a complete rest because he had been overworking.* ■ [usu. as adj.] (**overworked**) make excessive use of: *the city's overworked sewer system.* ■ [usu. as adj.] (**overworked**) use (a word or idea) too much and so make it weaker in meaning or effect. ▶ **n.** excessive work.

o·ver·write /,ōvər'rīt/ ▶ **v.** (past **-wrote**; past part. **-writ·ten**) [trans.] **1** write on top of (other writing). ■ Comput. destroy (data) or the data in (a file) by entering new data in its place. **2** write too elaborately or ornately.

o·ver·wrought /'ōvə'rôt/ ▶ **adj.** **1** in a state of nervous excitement or anxiety. **2** (of a piece of writing or a work of art) too elaborate or complicated in design or construction. [ME: archaic past part. of OVERWORK.]

ovi- ▶ **comb. form** esp. Zool. of or relating to eggs or ova: *oviparous.* [from L. *ovum* 'egg.']

Ov·id /'ävid/ (43 BC–c.AD 17), Roman poet; full name *Publius Ovidius Naso.* He is known for his elegiac love poems and for the epic *Metamorphoses.*

o·vi·duct /'ōvi,dəkt/ ▶ **n.** Anat. Zool. the tube through which an ovum or egg passes from an ovary. — **o·vi·du·cal** /,ōvə'dōōkəl/ **adj.** **o·vi·duc·tal** /,ōvə'dəktəl/ **adj.**

O·vie·do /ō'vyedō/ a city in northwestern Spain, capital of the Asturias region; pop. 203,000.

o·vi·form /'ōvə,fôrm/ ▶ **adj.** egg-shaped.

O·vim·bun·du /,ōvim'bōōndōō/ see MBUNDU.

o·vine /'ō,vīn/ ▶ **adj.** of, relating to, or resembling sheep. [19th C.: from late L. *ovinus,* from L. *ovis* 'sheep.']

o·vip·a·rous /ō'vipərəs/ ▶ **adj.** Zool. (of a bird, etc.) producing young by means of eggs that are hatched after they have been laid by the parent. Compare with VIVIPAROUS and OVOVIVIPAROUS. — **o·vi·par·i·ty** /-'paritē/ **n.**

o·vi·pos·it /,ōvə'päzit/ ▶ **v.** (**-pos·it·ed, -pos·it·ing**) [intrans.] Zool. (esp. of an insect) lay an egg or eggs. — **o·vi·po·si·tion** /-pə'zisHən/ **n.** [19th C.: from OVI- 'egg' + L. *posit-* 'placed' (from the v. *ponere*).]

o·vi·pos·i·tor /,ōvə'päzitər/ ▶ **n.** Zool. a tubular organ through which a female insect or fish deposits eggs.

o·void /'ō,void/ ▶ **adj.** (of a solid or a three-dimensional surface) egg-shaped. ■ (of a plane figure) oval, esp. with one end more pointed than the other. ▶ **n.** an ovoid body or surface. [19th C.: from Fr. *ovoïde,* from mod. L. *ovoides,* from L. *ovum* 'egg.']

o·vo·lo /'ōvəlō/ ▶ **n.** (pl. **-li** /-,lī/) Archit. a rounded convex molding, in cross-section a quarter of a circle or ellipse. [17th C.: from Ital., dimin. of *ovo* 'egg,' from L. *ovum.*]

o·vo·tes·tis /,ōvō'testis/ ▶ **n.** (pl. **-tes·tes** /-'testēz/) Zool. an organ producing both ova and spermatozoa, as in some gastropod mollusks. [19th C.: from OVUM + TESTIS.]

o·vo·vi·vip·a·rous /,ōvōvī'vip(ə)rəs; -və'vip-/ ▶ **adj.** Zool. (of an animal) producing young by means of eggs that are hatched within the body of the parent, as in some snakes. Compare with OVIPAROUS and VIVIPAROUS. — **o·vo·vi·vi·par·i·ty** /-,vīvə'paritē/ **n.**

ov·u·late /'ōvyə,lāt; 'äv-/ ▶ **v.** [intrans.] discharge ova or ovules from the ovary. — **ov·u·la·tion** /,ōvyə'lāsHən; ,äv-/ **n.** **ov·u·la·to·ry** /-lə,tôrē/ **adj.**

ov·ule /'ōvyōōl; 'äv-/ ▶ **n.** a small or immature ovum. ■ Bot. the part of the ovary of seed plants that contains the female germ cell and after fertilization becomes the seed. — **ov·u·lar** /-lər/ **adj.** [19th C.: from Fr., from med. L. *ovulum,* dimin. of OVUM.]

o·vum /'ōvəm/ ▶ **n.** (pl. **o·va** /'ōvə/) Biol. a mature female reproductive cell, esp. of a human or other animal, that can divide to give rise to an embryo usually only after fertilization by a male cell. [18th C.: from L., lit. 'egg.']

ow /ou/ ▶ **exclam.** used to express sudden pain: *Ow! You're hurting me!*

owe /ō/ ▶ **v.** [trans.] have an obligation to pay or repay (something, esp. money) for something received. ■ owe something, esp. money, to (someone): *I owe you for the taxi.* ■ be under a moral obligation to give someone (gratitude, respect, etc.): [with two objs.] *I owe you an apology.* ■ (**owe something to**) have something because of (someone or something): *he owed his success to insight.* ■ be indebted to someone or something for (something): *I owe my life to you.*

– PHRASES **owe it to oneself** need to do something to protect one's own interests. **owe someone one** informal feel indebted to someone for a favor done: *thanks, I owe you one.* [OE *āgan* from an Indo-Eur. root shared by Sanskrit *īś* 'possess, own.']

Ow·ens /'ō(w)ənz/, Jesse (1913–80), US track and field athlete; born *James Cleveland Owens.* He won four gold medals at the 1936 Olympic Games in Berlin. The success of Owens, as a black man, outraged Hitler.

ow·ing /'ō-iNG/ ▶ **adj.** [predic.] (of money) yet to be paid.

– PHRASES **owing to** because of or on account of.

owl /oul/ ▶ **n.** a nocturnal bird of prey (order Strigiformes) with large forward-facing eyes surrounded by facial disks, a hooked beak, and typically a loud call. Two families: Strigidae (**typical owls**, such as saw-whet owls and the snowy owl) and Tytonidae (**barn owls** and their relatives). [OE *ūle,* of Gmc. origin; rel. to Du. *uil* and Ger. *Eule,* from a base imitative of the bird's call.]

owl·et /'oulit/ ▶ **n.** a small owl (genera *Glaucidium* and *Athene,* family Strigidae) found chiefly in Asia and Africa. ■ a young owl of any kind.

owl·ish /'oulisH/ ▶ **adj.** like an owl, esp. in acting or appearing wise or solemn. ■ (of eyeglasses) resembling the large round eyes of an owl. — **owl·ish·ly adv. owl·ish·ness n.**

owl par·rot ▶ **n.** another term for KAKAPO.

own /ōn/ ▶ **adj. & pron.** used with a possessive to emphasize that someone or something belongs or relates to the person mentioned: [as adj.] *they can't handle their own children* | [as pron.] *the Church would look after its own.* ■ done or produced by and for the person specified: [as adj.] *I design all my own clothes* | [as pron.] *they claimed the work as their own.* ■ particular to the person or thing mentioned; individual: [as adj.] *the style had its own charm* | [as pron.] *the film had a quality all its own.* ▶ **v.** **1** [trans.] have (something) as one's own; possess: *his father owns a restaurant.* **2** [intrans.] formal admit or acknowledge that something is the case or that one feels a certain way: *she owned to a feeling of jealousy.* ■ [trans.] archaic acknowledge paternity, authorship, or possession of: *he has published little, trivial things which he will not own.*

– PHRASES **be one's own man** (or **woman**) act independently and with confidence. ■ archaic be in full possession of one's faculties. **come into its** (or **one's**) **own** become fully effective, used, or recognized. **get one's own back** informal take action in retaliation for a wrongdoing or insult. **hold one's own** retain a position of strength in a challenging situation. **of one's own** belonging to oneself alone. **on one's own** unaccompanied by others; alone or unaided.

– PHRASAL VERBS **own up** admit or confess to having done something wrong or embarrassing: *he owns up to few mistakes.* [OE *āgen* (adj. and pronoun) 'owned, possessed,' past part. of *āgan* 'owe.']

own·er /'ōnər/ ▶ **n.** a person who owns something. — **own·er·less adj.** **own·er·ship n.**

own·er-oc·cu·pied ▶ **adj.** (of a house or apartment) used as a dwelling by the owner.

own goal ▶ **n.** (in soccer) a goal scored inadvertently when the ball is struck into the goal by a player on the defensive team.

ox /äks/ ▶ **n.** (pl. **ox·en** /'äksən/) a domesticated bovine animal kept for milk or meat; a cow or bull. See CATTLE (sense 1). ■ a castrated bull, formerly much used as a draft animal: [as adj.] *an ox cart.* ■ an animal of a group related to the domestic ox. See CATTLE (sense 2). [OE *oxa;* rel. to Ger. *Ochse,* Sanskrit *ukṣán* 'bull.']

ox- ▶ **comb. form** var. of OXY-², reduced before a vowel.

ox·a·cil·lin /,äksə'silin/ ▶ **n.** Med. an antibiotic drug made by chemical modification of penicillin and used to treat bacterial infections.

ox·al·ic ac·id /äk'salik/ ▶ **n.** Chem. a poisonous crystalline acid, $(COOH)_2$, with a sour taste, present in rhubarb leaves, wood sorrel, and other plants. Its uses include bleaching and cleansing. — **ox·a·late** /'äksə,lāt/ **n.** [18th C.: *oxalic* from Fr. *oxalique,* via L. from Gk. *oxalis* 'wood sorrel.']

ox·a·lis /'äksəlis; äk'salis/ ▶ **n.** a plant of the genus *Oxalis* (family Oxalidaceae), including the wood sorrel, and typically having three-lobed leaves and white, yellow, or pink flowers. [17th C.: via L. from Gk., from *oxus* 'sour' (because of its sharp-tasting leaves).]

ox·a·zole /'äksə,zōl/ ▶ **n.** Chem. a volatile liquid, C_3H_3NO, with weakly basic properties, whose molecule contains a five-membered ring that serves as the basis of a number of medicinal drugs.

ox·bow /'äks,bō/ ▶ **n.** **1** a U-shaped bend in the course of a river. ■ short for OXBOW LAKE. **2** a U-shaped collar of an ox-yoke.

ox·bow lake ▶ **n.** a curved lake formed at a former oxbow where the main stream of the river has cut across the narrow end and no longer flows around the loop of the bend.

Ox·bridge /'äks,brij/ ▶ **n.** Oxford and Cambridge universities regarded together: [as adj.] *Oxbridge colleges.* [19th C.]

ox·en /'äksən/ plural form of OX.

ox·eye /'äks,ī/ ▶ **n.** a yellow-flowered North American plant (*Heliopsis helianthoides*) of the daisy family.

ox·eye dai·sy ▶ **n.** an often-cultivated Eurasian daisy (*Leucanthemum vulgare*) that has large white flowers with yellow centers. Also called MARGUERITE.

Oxf. ▶ **abbr.** Oxford.

Ox·ford /'äksfərd/ a city in central England, on the Thames River; pop. 109,000.

ox·ford /'äksfərd/ ▶ **n.** **1** (also **oxford shoe**) a type of lace-up shoe with a low heel. **2** (also **oxford cloth**) a heavy cotton cloth chiefly used to make shirts.

Ox·ford Move·ment a Christian movement started in Oxford, England, in 1833, seeking to restore traditional Catholic teachings and ceremony within the Church of England. Also called TRACTARIANISM.

ox·herd /'äks,hərd/ ▶ **n.** archaic a cowherd. [OE, from OX + obs. *herd* 'herdsman.']

ox·hide /'äks,hīd/ ▶ **n.** leather made from the hide of an ox.

ox·ic /'äksik/ ▶ **adj.** designating a process or environment in which oxygen is involved or present. [1960s: from *ox(ide)* or *ox(ygen)* + -IC.]

ox·i·dant /'äksidənt/ ▶ **n.** an oxidizing agent.

ox·i·dase /'äksi,dās; -,dāz/ ▶ **n.** Biochem. an enzyme that promotes the transfer of a hydrogen atom from a particular substrate to an oxygen molecule, forming water or hydrogen peroxide.

ox·i·da·tion /,äksi'dāsHən/ ▶ **n.** Chem. the process or result of oxidizing or being oxidized. — **ox•i•da•tion•al** adj. **ox•i•da•tive** /'äksi,dātiv/ adj.

ox•i•da•tion num•ber (also **oxidation state**) ▶n. Chem. a number assigned to an element in chemical combination that represents the number of electrons lost (or gained, if the number is negative) by an atom of that element in the compound.

ox•ide /'äk,sīd/ ▶n. Chem. a binary compound of oxygen with another element or group.

ox•i•dize /'äksi,dīz/ ▶v. combine or become combined chemically with oxygen. ■ Chem. undergo or cause to undergo a reaction in which electrons are lost to another species. The opposite of REDUCE. — **ox•i•diz•a•ble** adj. **ox•i•di•za•tion** /,äksidi'zāsHən/ n. **ox•i•diz•er** n.

ox•i•diz•ing a•gent /'äksi,dīziNG/ ▶n. Chem. a substance that tends to bring about oxidation by being reduced and gaining electrons.

ox•lip /'äks,lip/ ▶n. a woodland Eurasian primula (*Primula elatior*) with yellow flowers that hang down one side of the stem. ■ (also **false oxlip**) a natural hybrid between a primrose and a cowslip. [OE *oxanslyppe*, from *oxa* 'ox' + *slyppe* 'slime.']

Ox•nard /'äks,närd/ a city in southwestern California; pop. 142,216.

Ox•on /'äksän/ ▶abbr. (esp. in degree titles) of Oxford University: *BA, Oxon.* [from med. L. *Oxoniensis*, from *Oxonia* (see OXONIAN).]

Ox•o•ni•an /äk'sōnēən; -'sōnyən/ ▶adj. of or relating to Oxford, England, or Oxford University. ▶n. a native or inhabitant of Oxford, England. ■ someone who attends or has a degree from Oxford University. [16th C.: from L. *Oxonia*.]

ox•peck•er /'äks,pekər/ ▶n. a brown African bird (genus *Buphagus*, family Sturnidae or Buphagidae) related to the starlings, feeding on parasites that infest the skins of large grazing mammals.

ox•tail /'äks,tāl/ ▶n. the tail of a cow. ■ meat from this, used esp. for making soup.

ox•ter /'äkstər/ ▶n. Scot. & N. English a person's armpit. [OE *ōhsta, ōxta*.]

ox-tongue ▶n. an Old World plant (genus *Picris*) of the daisy family with yellow dandelionlike flowers and prickly hairs on the stem and leaves.

Ox•us /'äksəs/ ancient name for AMU DARYA.

oxy-[1] ▶comb. form denoting sharpness: *oxytone*. [from Gk. *oxus* 'sharp.']

oxy-[2] (also **ox-**) ▶comb. form Chem. representing OXYGEN.

ox•y•a•cet•y•lene /,äksēə'setl-in; -,ēn/ ▶adj. [attrib.] of or denoting welding or cutting techniques using a very hot flame produced by mixing acetylene and oxygen.

ox•y•ac•id /,äksē'asid/ ▶n. Chem. an inorganic acid whose molecules contain oxygen, such as sulfuric or nitric acid.

ox•y•gen /'äksəjən/ ▶n. a colorless, odorless reactive gas, the chemical element of atomic number 8 and the life-supporting component of the air. Oxygen forms about 20 percent of the earth's atmosphere, and is the most abundant element in the earth's crust, mainly in the form of oxides, silicates, and carbonates. (Symbol: **O**) — **ox•yg•e•nous** /äk'sijənəs/ adj. [18th C.: from Fr. *(principe) oxygène* 'acidifying constituent.']

ox•y•gen•ate /'äksəjə,nāt/ ▶v. [trans.] supply, treat, charge, or enrich with oxygen. — **ox•y•gen•a•tion** /,äksəjə'nāsHən/ n.

ox•y•gen•a•tor /'äksəjə,nātər/ ▶n. Med. an apparatus for oxygenating the blood. ■ an aquatic plant that enriches the surrounding water with oxygen, esp. in a pond or aquarium.

ox•y•gen•ize /'äksəjə,nīz/ ▶v. alternate term for OXYGENATE.

ox•y•gen mask ▶n. a mask placed over the nose and mouth and connected to a supply of oxygen, used when the body is not able to gain enough oxygen by breathing air, for example at high altitudes or because of a medical condition.

oxygen mask

ox•y•gen tent ▶n. a tentlike enclosure within which the air supply can be enriched with oxygen to aid a patient's breathing.

ox•y•he•mo•glo•bin /,äksē'hēmə,glōbən/ ▶n. Biochem. a bright red substance formed by the combination of hemoglobin with oxygen, present in oxygenated blood.

ox•y•mo•ron /,äksə'môr,än/ ▶n. a figure of speech in which apparently contradictory terms appear in conjunction (e.g., *faith unfaithful kept him falsely true*). — **ox•y•mo•ron•ic** /-mə'ränik/ adj. [17th C.: from Gk. *oxumōron* 'pointedly foolish,' from OXY- + *mōros* 'foolish.']

ox•y•te•tra•cy•cline /,äksə,tetrə'sīklēn/ ▶n. Med. an antibiotic related to tetracycline, used to treat a variety of bacterial infections.

ox•y•to•cin /,äksə'tōsən/ ▶n. Biochem. a hormone released by the pituitary gland that causes increased contraction of the uterus during labor and stimulates the ejection of milk into the ducts of the breasts. [1920s: from Gk. *oxutokia* 'sudden delivery' (from OXY- + *tokos* 'childbirth') + -IN[1].]

ox•y•tone /'äksə,tōn/ ▶adj. (esp. in ancient Greek) having an acute accent on the last syllable. ▶n. a word of this kind. [18th C.: from Gk. *oxutonos*, from OXY- + *tonos* 'tone.']

oy /oi/ ▶exclam. see OY VEY.

o•yer and ter•mi•ner /'oi-ər and 'tərmənər/ ▶n. hist. a court authorized to hear certain criminal cases. [ME: from Anglo-Norman Fr. *oyer et terminer* 'hear and determine.']

o•yez /'ō'yā; 'ō'yez/ (also **o•yes**) ▶exclam. a call given by a court officer, or formerly by public criers, to command attention, typically before court is in session. [ME: from OFr. *oiez!, oyez!* 'hear!,' imper. pl. of *oir*, from L. *audire* 'hear.']

oys•ter /'oistər/ ▶n. **1** any of a number of bivalve mollusks with rough irregular shells. Several kinds are eaten (esp. raw) as a delicacy and may be farmed for food or pearls, in particular: ■ a true oyster (family Ostreidae), including the edible **American oyster** (*Crassostrea virginica*). ■ a similar bivalve of another family, esp. the **thorny oysters** (Spondylidae), **wing oysters** (Pteriidae), and **saddle oysters** (Anomiidae). **2** an oyster-shaped morsel of meat on each side of the backbone in poultry. **3** (also **oyster white**) a shade of grayish white. ▶v. [intrans.] raise, dredge, or gather oysters. ▶adj. [attrib.] of the color oyster white.

– PHRASES **the world is your oyster** you are in a position to take the opportunities that life has to offer. [ME: from OFr. *oistre*, via L. from Gk. *ostreon*; rel. to *osteon* 'bone' and *ostrakon* 'shell or tile.']

oys•ter bar ▶n. **1** a hotel bar, small restaurant, or other place where oysters are served. **2** (esp. in the southeastern US) an oyster bed.

oys•ter bed ▶n. a part of the sea bottom where oysters breed or are bred.

oys•ter•catch•er /'oistər,kacHər/ ▶n. a coastal wading bird (genus *Haematopus*, family Haematopodidae) with black-and-white or all-black plumage and a strong orange-red bill, feeding chiefly on shellfish.

oys•ter crab ▶n. a minute, soft-bodied crab (*Pinnotheres* and other genera, family Pinnotheridae) that lives inside the shell of a bivalve mollusk, where it filters food particles from the water drawn into the shell by its host.

oys•ter cracker ▶n. a small, round soda cracker served with soup, oysters, etc.

oys•ter farm ▶n. an area of the seabed used for breeding oysters.

oys•ter•man /'oistərmən/ ▶n. (pl. **-men**) a person who gathers, cultivates, or sells oysters. ■ a boat equipped for harvesting oysters.

oys•ter mush•room ▶n. a widely distributed edible fungus (*Pleurotus ostreatus*, family Pleurotaceae) that has a grayish-brown, oyster-shaped cap and a very short or absent stem, growing on the wood of broad-leaved trees and causing rot.

oys•ter plant ▶n. another term for SALSIFY.

oys•ter sauce ▶n. a sauce made with oysters and soy sauce, used esp. in oriental cooking.

oys•ters Rock•e•fel•ler ▶plural n. oysters covered with a mixture of spinach, butter, seasonings, and bread crumbs and cooked on the half shell.

oy vey /'oi 'vā/ (also **oy**) ▶exclam. indicating dismay or grief. [19th C.: Yiddish, lit. 'oh woe.']

Oz /äz/ Austral. informal ▶adj. Australian. ▶n. Australia. ■ a person from Australia. [1940s: representing a pronunc. of an abbrev. of AUSTRALIA.]

oz ▶abbr. ounce(s). [from Ital. *onza* 'ounce.']

Oz•a•lid /'äzə,lid/ ▶n. trademark a photocopy made by a process in which a diazonium salt and coupler are present in the paper coating, so that the image develops in the presence of ammonia.

oz ap ▶abbr. apothecaries' ounce.

O•zark Moun•tains /'ō,zärk/ (also **the O•zarks**) a highland plateau dissected by rivers, valleys, and streams, lying between the Missouri and Arkansas rivers in Missouri, Arkansas, Oklahoma, Kansas, and Illinois.

oz av ▶abbr. avoirdupois ounce.

O•za•wa /ō'zäwə/, Seiji (1935–), Japanese conductor, noted as the music director of the Boston Symphony Orchestra (1973–2002) and the Vienna State Opera (2002–).

o•zo•ce•rite /ō'zōkə,rīt; -sə,rīt; ,ōzō'si(ə)rīt/ (also **o•zo•ke•rite**) ▶n. a brown or black paraffin wax occurring naturally in some shales and sandstones and formerly used in candles, polishes, and electrical insulation. [19th C.: from Ger. *Ozokerit*, from Gk. *ozein* 'to smell' + *kēros* 'wax.']

o•zone /'ō,zōn/ ▶n. a colorless unstable toxic gas with a pungent odor and powerful oxidizing properties, formed from oxygen by electrical discharges or ultraviolet light. It differs from normal oxygen (O_2) in having three atoms in its molecule (O_3). ■ short for OZONE LAYER. ■ informal fresh invigorating air, esp. that blowing onto the shore from the sea. — **o•zon•ic** /ō'zänik/ adj. [19th C.: from Ger. *Ozon*, from Gk. *ozein* 'to smell.']

o•zone-friend•ly ▶adj. (of manufactured products) not containing chemicals that are destructive to the ozone layer.

o•zone hole ▶n. a region of marked thinning of the ozone layer in high latitudes, attributed to the chemical action of chlorofluorocarbons. The resulting increase in ultraviolet light at ground level gives rise to an increased risk of skin cancer.

o•zone lay•er ▶n. a layer in the earth's stratosphere at an altitude of about 10 km (6.2 miles) containing a high concentration of ozone, which absorbs most of the ultraviolet radiation from the sun.

o•zo•nide /'ōzə,nīd/ ▶n. Chem. any of a class of unstable cyclic compounds formed by the addition of ozone to a carbon–carbon double bond. ■ a salt of the anion O_3^-, derived from ozone.

o•zon•ize /'ōzə,nīz/ ▶v. [trans.] [often as adj.] (**ozonized**) convert (oxygen) into ozone. ■ enrich or treat with ozone: *ozonized air*. — **o•zon•i•za•tion** /,ōzəni'zāsHən/ n. **o•zon•iz•er** n.

o•zo•no•sphere /ō'zōnə,sfi(ə)r/ ▶n. technical term for OZONE LAYER.

oz t ▶abbr. troy ounce.

PRONUNCIATION KEY ə *ago, up*; ər *over, fur*; a *hat*; ā *ate*; ä *car*; e *let*; ē *see*; i *fit*; ī *by*; NG *sing*; ō *go*; ô *law, for*; oi *toy*; o͝o *good*; o͞o *goo*; ou *out*; TH *thin*; T̲H̲ *then*; ZH *vision*

Pp

P¹ /pē/ (also **p**) ▶ **n.** (pl. **Ps** or **P's** /pēz/) the sixteenth letter of the alphabet. ■ denoting the next after O (or N if O is omitted) in a set of items, categories, etc.
– PHRASES **mind one's Ps and Qs** see MIND.

P² ▶ **abbr.** ■ pastor. ■ father. [L. *pater*.] ■ (in tables of sports results) games played. ■ (on an automatic gearshift) park. ■ (on road signs and street plans) parking. ■ peseta. ■ peso. ■ [in comb.] (in units of measurement) peta- (1015): *27 PBq of radioactive material.* ■ Physics poise (unit of viscosity). ■ post. ■ president. ■ pressure. ■ priest. ■ prince. ■ proprietary. ■ progressive. ▶ **symb.** ■ the chemical element phosphorus.

p ▶ **abbr.** ■ page. ■ (*p-*) [in comb.] Chem. para-: *p-xylene.* ■ Brit. penny or pence. ■ Music piano (softly). ■ [in comb.] (in units of measurement) pico- (10–12): *a 220 pf capacitor.* ■ Chem. denoting electrons and orbitals possessing one unit of angular momentum. [from ***principal***, orig. applied to lines in atomic spectra.] ▶ **symb.** ■ Physics pressure. ■ Stat. probability.

PA ▶ **abbr.** ■ Pennsylvania (in official postal use). ■ Press Association. ■ public address.

Pa ▶ **abbr.** ■ pascal; pascals. ■ Pennsylvania. ▶ **symb.** the chemical element protactinium.

pa /pä/ ▶ **n.** informal father. [19th C.: abbrev. of PAPA.]

p.a. ▶ **abbr.** per annum.

pa'an·ga /'päNGgə; pä'äNGgə/ ▶ **n.** (pl. same) the basic monetary unit of Tonga, equal to 100 seniti. [Tongan.]

PABA ▶ **abbr.** para-aminobenzoic acid.

pab·lum /'pabləm/ ▶ **n.** (also **pab·u·lum** /'pabyələm/) bland or insipid intellectual fare, entertainment, etc.; pap. ■ (**Pablum**) trademark a soft breakfast cereal for infants. [17th C.: from L., from the stem of *pascere* 'to feed.']

PAC /pak/ ▶ **abbr.** ■ political action committee.

paca

pa·ca /'päkə; 'pakə/ ▶ **n.** a nocturnal South American rodent (genus *Agouti* or *Cuniculus*, family Dasyproctidae) that has a reddish-brown coat patterned with rows of white spots. It is hunted for its edible flesh. Also called SPOTTED CAVY. [17th C.: via Sp., Port. from Tupi.]

pace¹ /pās/ ▶ **n.** **1** a single step taken when walking or running. ■ a unit of length representing the distance between two successive steps in walking. ■ a gait of a horse or other animal. ■ literary a person's manner of walking or running. **2** consistent and continuous speed in walking, running, or moving. ■ the speed or rate at which something happens. ■ (in sports) the speed or force of a hit or pitched ball. ▶ **v.** [intrans.] walk at a steady and consistent speed, esp. back and forth and as an expression of one's anxiety or annoyance. ■ [trans.] measure (a distance) by walking it and counting the number of steps taken: *I **paced out** the dimensions of my new home.* ■ [trans.] lead (another runner in a race) in order to establish a competitive speed: *he paced us for four miles.* ■ (**pace oneself**) do something at a slow and steady rate in order to avoid overexerting oneself. ■ [trans.] move or develop (something) at a particular rate: *the action is paced to the beat of a march* | [as adj., in comb.] (**-paced**) *our fast-paced lives.* ■ [intrans.] (of a horse) move in a distinctive lateral gait in which both legs on the same side are lifted together.
– PHRASES **change of pace** a change from what one is used to. **keep pace with** move, develop, or progress at the same speed as. **off the pace** behind the leader or leading group in a race or contest. **put someone** (or **something**) **through their** (or **its**) **paces** make someone (or something) demonstrate their (or its) qualities or abilities. **set the pace** be the fastest runner in the early part of a race. ■ lead the way in doing or achieving something. [ME: from OFr. *pas*, from L. *passus* 'stretch,' from *pandere* 'to stretch.']

pace² /'pä,sē; 'pä,CHä/ ▶ **prep.** with due respect to (someone or their opinion), used to express polite disagreement or contradiction: *narrative history, pace some theorists, is by no means dead.* [L., lit. 'in peace,' ablative of *pax*.]

pace car ▶ **n.** Auto Racing a car that sets the pace and positions racers for a rolling start in a warm-up lap before a race.

pace·mak·er /'pās,mākər/ ▶ **n.** **1** an artificial device for stimulating the heart muscle and regulating its contractions. ■ the part of the heart muscle (the sinoatrial node) that normally performs this role. ■ the part of an organ or of the body that controls any other rhythmic physiological activity. **2** another term for PACESETTER. — **pace·mak·ing** **adj. & n.**

pac·er /'pāsər/ ▶ **n.** **1** a pacesetter. **2** a horse bred or trained to have a distinctive lateral gait in which both legs on the same side are lifted together.

pace·set·ter /'pās,setər/ ▶ **n.** a runner or competitor who sets the pace at the beginning of a race or competition, sometimes in order to help another runner break a record. ■ a person or organization viewed as taking the lead or setting standards of achievement for others. — **pace·set·ting** **adj. & n.**

pa·cha ▶ **n.** var. of PASHA.

pa·chin·ko /pə'CHiNGkō/ ▶ **n.** a Japanese form of pinball.

pa·chi·si /pə'CHēzē/ ▶ **n.** a four-person Indian board game in which cowrie shells are thrown to determine the movements of pieces around the board. ■ (also trademark **Par·chee·si** /pär'CHēzē/) a modern version of this game, using four marbles per player and dice. [from Hindi *paccīsī*, lit. '(throw) of 25.']

Pa·chu·ca de So·to /pä'CHōōkə de 'sōtō/ (also **Pa·chu·ca**) a city in central Mexico; pop. 179,000.

pach·y·derm /'pakə,dərm/ ▶ **n.** a very large mammal with thick skin, esp. an elephant, rhinoceros, or hippopotamus. — **pach·y·der·mal** /,pakə'dərməl/ **adj.** **pach·y·der·ma·tous** /,pakə'dərmətəs/ **adj.** **pach·y·der·mic** /,pakə'dərmik/ **adj.** [19th C.: ult. from Gk. ***pakhudermos***, from ***pakhus*** 'thick' + ***derma*** 'skin.']

pach·y·san·dra /,paki'sandrə/ ▶ **n.** an evergreen creeping shrubby plant (genus *Pachysandra*) of the box family. [from Gk. ***pakhus*** 'thick' + ***anēr***, ***andr-*** 'male.']

pach·y·tene /'pakə,tēn/ ▶ **n.** Biol. the third stage of the prophase of meiosis, following zygotene, during which the paired chromosomes shorten and thicken, the two chromatids of each separate, and exchange of segments between chromatids may occur. [20th C.: from Gk. ***pakhus*** 'thick' + ***tainia*** 'band.']

pa·cif·ic /pə'sifik/ ▶ **adj.** **1** peaceful in character or intent: *a pacific gesture.* **2** (**Pacific**) of or relating to the Pacific Ocean: *the Pacific War.* ▶ **n.** (**Pacific**) short for PACIFIC OCEAN. — **pa·cif·i·cal·ly** **adv.** [16th C.: ult. from L. *pacificus* 'peacemaking,' from *pax*, *pac-* 'peace.']

Pa·cif·ic Is·lands, Trust Ter·ri·to·ry of the a UN trusteeship under US administration 1947–94. It included the Caroline, Marshall, and Mariana islands.

Pa·cif·ic O·cean /pə'sifik/ the largest of the world's oceans. It lies between America on the east and Asia and Australasia on the west.

Pa·cif·ic Rim the countries and regions bordering the Pacific Ocean, esp. the small nations of eastern Asia.

Pa·cif·ic time the standard time in a zone including the Pacific coastal region of the US and Canada, specifically: ■ (**Pacific Standard Time**, abbrev.: **PST**) standard time based on the mean solar time at longitude 120° W, eight hours behind GMT. ■ (**Pacific Daylight Time**, abbrev.: **PDT**) Pacific time during daylight saving time, nine hours behind GMT.

pac·i·fi·er /'pasə,fīər/ ▶ **n.** a person or thing that pacifies. ■ a rubber or plastic nipple for a baby to suck on.

pac·i·fism /'pasə,fizəm/ ▶ **n.** the belief that war and violence are unjustifiable under any circumstances, and that all disputes should be settled by peaceful means. ■ the refusal to participate in war or military service because of such a belief. — **pac·i·fist** **n. & adj.** **pac·i·fis·tic** /,pasə'fistik/ **adj.** [20th C.: from Fr. *pacifisme*, from *pacifier* 'pacify.']

pac·i·fy /'pasə,fī/ ▶ **v.** (**-fies, -fied**) [trans.] quell the anger, agitation, or excitement of: ■ bring peace to (a country or warring factions), esp. by the use or threatened use of military force. — **pa·cif·i·ca·tion** /,pasifi'kāSHən/ **n.** **pa·cif·i·ca·to·ry** /pə'sifikə,tôrē/ **adj.** [15th C.: from OFr. *pacefier*, from L. *pacificare*, based on *pax*, *pac-* 'peace.']

pack¹ /pak/ ▶ **n.** **1** a small cardboard or paper container and the items contained within it: ***a pack of cigarettes.*** ■ a set of playing cards. ■ a knapsack or backpack. ■ a collection of related documents, esp. one kept in a folder. ■ (often **the pack**) a quantity of food packed or canned in a particular season or year. **2** a group of wild animals, esp. wolves. ■ a group of hounds used for hunting, esp. fox hunting. ■ an organized group of Cub Scouts. ■ (**the pack**) the main body of competitors following the leader in a race or competition: fig. ***innovations needed to keep ahead of the pack.*** ■ esp. derog. a group or set of similar things or people: ***the reports were a pack of lies.*** ■ short for PACK ICE. **3** a hot or cold pad of absorbent material, esp. as used for treating an injury. ■ **a cosmetic mask.** ▶ **v.** [trans.] fill (a suitcase or bag), esp. with clothes and other items needed when away from home: *I packed a bag with my favorite clothes* | [intrans.] *she had packed and checked out of the hotel.* ■ place (something) in a container, esp. for transportation or storage: *I packed up my stuff.* ■ [intrans.] be capable of being folded up for transportation or storage: *these blankets pack into a small area.* ■ (**pack something in**) store something perishable in (a specified substance) in order to preserve it: *the organs were packed in ice.* ■ informal carry (a gun): *pack a gun.* ■ (often **be packed**) cram a large number of things into (a container or space): *a large room, packed with beds.* ■ [often as adj.] (**packed**) (of a large number of people) crowd into and fill (a room, building, or place): *the room was packed.* ■ cover, surround, or fill (something): *he packed the wounds.*

– PHRASES **pack heat** informal carry a gun. **pack it in** informal stop what one is doing. **pack a punch** be capable of hitting with skill or force. ■ have a powerful effect: *wine packed quite a punch.* **send someone packing** informal make someone leave in an abrupt way.

– PHRASAL VERBS **pack something in** informal give up an activity or job. **pack someone off** informal send someone somewhere without much warning or notice. — **pack·a·ble** adj. [ME: from MDu., Mid. Low Ger. *pak* (n.), *pakken* (v.).]

pack² ▶ **v.** [trans.] fill (a jury, committee, etc.) with people likely to support a particular verdict or decision. [16th C.: prob. from obs. *pact* 'enter into an agreement with.']

pack·age /'pakij/ ▶ **n.** an object or group of objects wrapped in paper or plastic, or packed in a box. ■ the box or bag in which things are packed. ■ a packet. ■ (also **package deal**) a set of proposals or terms offered or agreed to as a whole. ■ informal a package tour. ■ Comput. a collection of programs or subroutines with related functionality. ▶ **v.** [trans.] (usu. **be packaged**) put into a box or wrapping, esp. for sale. ■ present (someone or something) in a particular way, esp. to make them more attractive: [as adj., with submodifier] (**packaged**) *a packaged photo opportunity.* ■ combine (various products) for sale as one unit. ■ commission and produce (a book, typically a highly illustrated one) to sell as a complete product to publishers. — **pack·ag·er** n. [16th C.: from v. PACK¹.]

pack·age store ▶ **n.** a liquor store.

pack·ag·ing /'pakijiNG/ ▶ **n.** materials used to wrap or protect goods. ■ the business or process of packing goods. ■ the presentation of a person, product, or action in a particular way: *diplomatic packaging of the key provisions.*

pack an·i·mal ▶ **n.** **1** an animal used to carry heavy loads. **2** an animal that lives and hunts in a pack.

pack·er /'pakər/ ▶ **n.** a person or machine that packs something, esp. someone who prepares and packs food for transportation and sale.

pack·et /'pakit/ ▶ **n.** **1** a paper or cardboard container, typically one in which goods are packed to be sold. ■ the contents of such a container. ■ a block of data transmitted across a network. **2** (also **packet boat**) dated a ship traveling at regular intervals between two ports, originally for the conveyance of mail. ▶ **v.** (**-et·ed, -et·ing**) [trans.] make up into or wrap up in a packet: *packet a basket of takeout.* [16th C.: dimin. of PACK¹, perh. from Anglo-Norman Fr.]

pack·et ra·di·o ▶ **n.** a method of broadcasting that makes use of radio signals carrying packets of data.

pack·et switch·ing ▶ **n.** Comput. Telecom. a mode of data transmission in which a message is broken into a number of parts that are sent independently, over whatever route is optimum for each packet, and reassembled at the destination.

pack·horse /'pak,hôrs/ ▶ **n.** a horse used to carry loads.

pack ice ▶ **n.** an expanse of large pieces of floating ice driven together into a nearly continuous mass, as occurs in polar seas.

pack·ing /'pakiNG/ ▶ **n.** the action or process of packing something. ■ material used to protect fragile goods, esp. in transit. ■ material used to seal a joint or assist in lubricating an axle.

pack·ing case (also **packing box** or **packing crate**) ▶ **n.** a large strong box, typically a wooden one, in which goods are packed for transportation or storage.

pack rat ▶ **n.** a ratlike rodent (*Neotoma* and other genera, family Muridae) that accumulates a mound of sticks and debris in the nest hole, native to North and Central America. ■ a person who saves unnecessary objects or hoards things.

pack·sack /'pak,sak/ ▶ **n.** a knapsack or backpack.

pack·sad·dle /'pak,sadl/ ▶ **n.** a horse's saddle adapted for supporting packs.

pack·thread /'pak,THred/ ▶ **n.** thick thread for sewing or tying up packages.

pact /pakt/ ▶ **n.** a formal agreement between individuals or parties. [ME: from OFr., from L. *pactum*, neut. past part. of *paciscere* 'agree.']

pad¹ /pad/ ▶ **n.** **1** a thick piece of soft material used to reduce friction or jarring, enlarge or change the shape of something, or hold or absorb liquid. ■ the fleshy underpart of an animal's foot or of a human finger. ■ a guard worn by a sports player for protection from blows. **2** a number of sheets of blank paper fastened together at one edge, used for writing or drawing on. **3** a flat-topped structure or area used for helicopter takeoff and landing or for rocket launching. ■ Electron. a flat area on a track of a printed circuit or on the edge of an integrated circuit to which wires or component leads can be attached to make an electrical connection. **4** informal a person's home. **5** short for LILY PAD. ▶ **v.** (**pad·ded, pad·ding**) [trans.] [often as adj.] (**padded**) fill or cover (something) with a soft material in order to give it a particular shape, protect it or its contents, or make it more comfortable: *a padded envelope.* ■ add false items to (an expense report or bill) in order to receive unjustified payment: *faked repairs and padded expenses.* [16th C. 'underpart' perh. rel. to Low Ger. *pad* 'sole of the foot.']

pad² ▶ **v.** (**pad·ded, pad·ding**) [intrans.] walk with steady steps making a soft dull sound. ■ [trans.] travel along (a road or route) on foot. ▶ **n.** [in sing.] the soft dull sound of steady steps. [16th C.: from Low Ger. *padden* 'to tread.']

Pa·dang /pä'däNG; 'pädäNG/ a city in Indonesia, on the west coast of Sumatra; pop. 481,000.

pa·dauk /pə'douk/ (also **pa·douk**) ▶ **n.** **1** timber from a tropical tree of the pea family, resembling rosewood. **2** the large hardwood tree (genus *Pterocarpus*) of the Old World tropics that is widely grown for this timber. Some kinds yield a red dye that is used for religious and ritual purposes. [19th C.: from Burmese.]

pad·ded cell ▶ **n.** a room in a psychiatric hospital with padding on the walls to prevent violent patients from injuring themselves.

pad·ding /'padiNG/ ▶ **n.** soft material such as foam or cloth used to pad or stuff something. ■ superfluous material in a book, speech, etc., introduced in order to make it reach a desired length.

pad·dle¹ /'padl/ ▶ **n.** a short pole with a broad blade at one or both ends, used without an oarlock to move a small boat or canoe through the water. ■ an act of using a paddle in a boat. ■ a short-handled bat used in various ball games, esp. table tennis. ■ a paddle-shaped instrument used for mixing food or for stirring or mixing in industrial processes. ■ another term for PEEL². ■ informal a paddle-shaped instrument used for administering corporal punishment. ■ each of the boards fitted around the circumference of a paddle wheel or mill wheel. ■ a flat array of solar cells projecting from a spacecraft. ■ the fin or flipper of an aquatic mammal or bird. ■ Med. a plastic-covered electrode used in cardiac stimulation. ■ short for BIDDING PADDLE. ▶ **v.** **1** [intrans.] move through the water in a boat using a paddle or paddles: *he paddled along the coast.* ■ [trans.] propel (a small boat or canoe) with a paddle or paddles. ■ [trans.] travel along (a stretch of water) using such a method. ■ (of a bird or other animal) swim with short fast strokes. **2** [trans.] informal beat (someone) with a paddle as a punishment.

– PHRASES **paddle one's own canoe** informal be independent and self-sufficient. — **pad·dler** n. [ME: of unknown origin.]

pad·dle² ▶ **v.** [intrans.] walk with bare feet in shallow water. ■ dabble the feet or hands in water. ▶ **n.** [in sing.] an act of walking barefoot in shallow water. — **pad·dler** n. [16th C.: cf. Low Ger. *paddeln* 'tramp around.']

pad·dle·ball /'padl,bôl/ ▶ **n.** a game played with a light ball and wooden bat in a four-walled handball court.

pad·dle·boat /'padl,bōt/ ▶ **n.** a small pleasure boat driven by pedals that in turn drive a paddle wheel.

pad·dle·fish /'padl,fiSH/ ▶ **n.** (pl. same or **-fish·es**) a large, mainly freshwater fish (family Polyodontidae) related to the sturgeon, with an elongated snout. Two species: the plankton-feeding *Polyodon spathula* of the Mississippi basin, and the fish-eating *Psephurus gladius* of the Yangtze River.

pad·dle steam·er ▶ **n.** a boat powered by steam and propelled by paddle wheels.

pad·dle ten·nis ▶ **n.** a type of tennis played in a small court with a rubber ball and a paddle.

paddle wheel

pad·dle wheel ▶ **n.** a steam-driven wheel with boards around its circumference, situated at the stern or side of a ship so as to propel the ship by its rotation.

pad·dock /'padək/ ▶ **n.** a small field or enclosure where horses are kept or exercised. ■ an enclosure adjoining a racetrack where horses are gathered and displayed before a race. ▶ **v.** [trans.] (usu. **be paddocked**) keep or enclose (a horse) in a paddock. [17th C.: appar. a var. of dial. *parrock*, of unknown ultimate origin.]

Pad·dy /'padē/ ▶ **n.** (pl. **-dies**) informal, often offens. an Irishman (often as a form of address). [18th C.: nickname for the Irish given name *Padraig.*]

pad·dy /'padē/ ▶ **n.** (pl. **-dies**) (also **rice paddy**) a field where rice is grown. ■ rice before threshing or in the husk. [17th C.: from Malay *pādī*.]

pad·dy wag·on ▶ **n.** informal a police van. [1930s: from PADDY.]

Pa·de·rew·ski /,padə'refskē; ,päd-/, Ignacy Jan (1860–1941), Polish pianist and composer. He was prime minister of Poland 1919.

pad·lock /'pad,läk/ ▶ **n.** a detachable lock hanging by a pivoted hook on the object fastened. ▶ **v.** [trans.] [usu. as adj.] (**padlocked**) secure with such a lock. [15th C.: from *pad-* (of unknown origin) + the n. LOCK¹.]

Pad·ma /ˈpadmə/ a river in southern Bangladesh.

pa·douk ▶ **n.** var. of PADAUK.

pa·dre /ˈpädrā/ ▶ **n.** father; the title of a priest or chaplain in some regions. ■ informal a chaplain (typically a Roman Catholic chaplain) in any of the armed services. [16th C.: from Ital., Sp., and Port., lit. 'father,' from L. *pater, patr-*.]

Pad·re Is·land /ˈpädrā/ a barrier island in southern Texas, on the Gulf of Mexico.

pa·dro·na /pəˈdrōnə/ ▶ **n.** (pl. **-nas**) a female boss or proprietress. [Ital.]

pa·dro·ne /pəˈdrōnā; pəˈdrōnē/ ▶ **n.** (pl. **-dro·nes** /-ˈdrōnāz; -ˈdrōnz/) a patron or master, in particular: ■ a Mafia boss. ■ informal an employer, esp. one who exploits immigrant workers. ■ (in Italy) the proprietor of a hotel. [Ital.]

pad thai /ˌpäd ˈtī/ ▶ **n.** a Thai dish based on rice noodles.

Pad·ua /ˈpajo͞oə/ a city in northeastern Italy; pop. 218,000. — **Pad·u·an adj.**

pad·u·a·soy /ˈpäjo͞oəˌsoi/ ▶ **n.** a heavy, rich corded or embossed silk fabric, popular in the 18th century. [16th C.: from Fr. *pou-de-soie*; influenced by *Padua say*, a cloth.]

pae·an /ˈpēən/ ▶ **n.** a song of praise or triumph. ■ a thing that expresses enthusiastic praise. [16th C.: via L. from Gk. *paian* 'hymn of thanksgiving to Apollo' (invoked by the name *Paian*).]

pae·di·at·rics ▶ **plural n.** British spelling of PEDIATRICS.

paedo- ▶ **comb. form** British spelling of PEDO-[1].

pa·el·la /päˈäyä; pīˈelə/ ▶ **n.** a Spanish dish of rice, saffron, chicken, seafood, etc. [Catalan, from OFr. *paele*, from L. *patella* 'pan.']

pae·on /ˈpēən/ ▶ **n.** Pros. a metrical foot of one long syllable and three short syllables in any order. — **pae·on·ic** /pēˈänik/ **adj.** [17th C.: via L. from Gk. *paiōn*, Attic form of *paian* (see PAEAN).]

Pa·gan /pəˈgän/ ruins in Myanmar (Burma), located on the Irrawaddy River southeast of Mandalay.

pa·gan /ˈpāgən/ ▶ **n.** a person holding religious beliefs other than those of the main world religions. ■ dated, derog. a non-Christian. ■ an adherent of neopaganism. ▶ **adj.** of or relating to such people or beliefs: *a pagan god.* — **pa·gan·ish adj. pa·gan·ism n. pa·gan·ize v.** [ME: from L. *paganus* 'villager,' from *pagus* 'country district.']

Pa·ga·ni·ni /ˌpagəˈnēnē; ˌpä-/, Niccolò (1782–1840), Italian violinist and composer. He was a major figure of the romantic movement.

page[1] /pāj/ ▶ **n.** one side of a sheet of paper as in a book, magazine, or newspaper. ■ the material written or printed on such a sheet of paper. ■ a sheet of paper of such a kind considered as a whole, comprising both sides. ■ [with adj.] a page of a newspaper or magazine set aside for a particular topic: *the editorial page.* ■ Print. the type set for the printing of a page. ■ Comput. a section of stored data, esp. that which can be displayed on a screen at one time. ■ a significant episode or period considered as a part of a longer history: *this transaction has no parallel on any page of our history.* ▶ **v.** [intrans.] (**page through**) leaf through (a book, magazine, or newspaper). ■ Comput. move through and display (text) one page at a time. ■ [usu. as n.] (**paging**) Comput. divide (a piece of software or data) into sections, keeping the most frequently accessed in main memory and storing the rest in virtual memory. ■ [trans.] assign numbers to the pages in (a book or periodical); paginate. ■ [as adj., in comb.] (**-paged**) having pages of a particular kind or number: *a many-paged volume.*
– PHRASES **on the same page** (of two or more people) in agreement. [16th C.: from Fr., from L. *pagina*, from *pangere* 'fasten.']

page[2] ▶ **n.** a young person, usually in uniform, employed to run errands, open doors, etc., as in a hotel. ■ hist. a boy in training for knighthood, ranking next below a squire in the personal service of a knight. ■ hist. a man or boy employed as the personal attendant of a person of rank. ▶ **v.** [trans.] summon (an individual) by name, typically over a public address system: *page the concierge.* ■ [often as n.] (**paging**) contact (someone) by means of a pager: *many systems have paging as a feature.* [ME: from OFr., perh. from Ital. *paggio*, from Gk. *paidion*, dimin. of *pais, paid-* 'boy.']

pag·eant /ˈpajənt/ ▶ **n.** a public entertainment consisting of a procession of people in costumes, or an outdoor performance of a historical scene. ■ (also **beauty pageant**) a beauty contest. ■ a thing that looks impressive, but is actually shallow and empty. ■ hist. a scene erected on a fixed stage or moving vehicle as a public show. [ME *pagyn*.]

pag·eant·ry /ˈpajəntrē/ ▶ **n.** elaborate display or ceremony.

page·boy /ˈpājˌboi/ ▶ **n.** a woman's hairstyle consisting of a shoulder-length bob with the ends rolled under.

page proof ▶ **n.** a printer's proof of a page to be published.

pag·er /ˈpājər/ ▶ **n.** an electronic device that receives messages and signals the user by beeping or vibrating.

Pag·et's dis·ease /ˈpajits/ ▶ **n.** **1** a chronic disease of the elderly characterized by alteration of bone tissue, esp. in the spine, skull, or pelvis, sometimes causing severe pain. Also called **osteitis deformans**. **2** an inflammation of the nipple associated with breast cancer. [19th C.: named after Sir James *Paget* (1814–99), Engl. surgeon.]

page-turn·er ▶ **n.** informal an exciting book.

pag·i·nal /ˈpajənəl/ ▶ **adj.** of or relating to the pages of a book or periodical. [17th C.: from late L. *paginalis*, from *pagina*.]

pag·i·na·tion /ˌpajəˈnāsʜən/ ▶ **n.** the sequence of numbers assigned to pages in a book or periodical. — **pag·i·nate** /ˈpajəˌnāt/ **v.**

pa·go·da /pəˈgōdə/ ▶ **n.** a Hindu or Buddhist temple or sacred building, typically a many-tiered tower, in India and the Far East. ■ an ornamental imitation of this. [16th C.: from Port. *pagode*, perh. based on Pers. *butkada* 'temple of idols.']

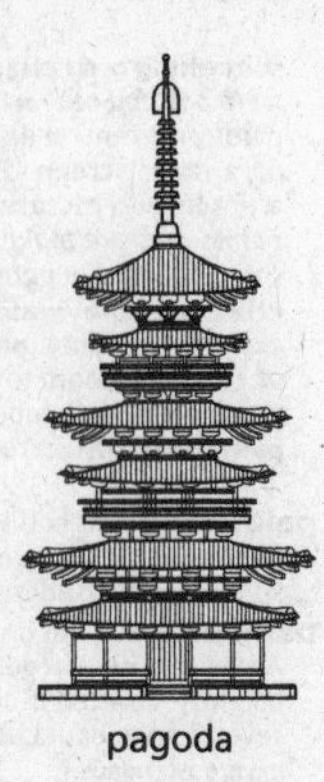
pagoda

Pa·go Pa·go /ˈpäɴɢ(g)ōˈpäɴɢ(g)ō; ˈpägōˈpägō/ the capital of American Samoa, on Tutuila Island; pop. 4,000.

pah /pä/ ▶ **exclam.** used to express disgust or contempt. [natural utterance: first recorded in Engl. in the 16th C.]

Pah·la·vi[1] /ˈpäləˌvē/ the name of two shahs of Iran: ■ Reza (1878–1944), ruled 1925–41; born *Reza Khan.* ■ Muhammad Reza (1919–80), ruled 1941–79; son of Reza Pahlavi; also known as **Reza Shah**. Opposition to his regime culminated in the Islamic revolution of 1979 under Ayatollah Khomeini.

Pah·la·vi[2] (also **Peh·le·vi**) ▶ **n.** an Aramaic-based writing system used in Persia from the 2nd century BC to the advent of Islam in the 7th century AD. ■ the form of the Middle Persian language written in this script. [from Pers. *pahlawī*, from *pahlav*, from *parthava* 'Parthia.']

pa·ho·e·ho·e /pəˈhōēˌhōē/ ▶ **n.** Geol. basaltic lava forming smooth undulating or ropy masses. Often contrasted with AA. [19th C.: from Hawaiian.]

paid /pād/ past and past participle of PAY[1]. ▶ **adj.** (of work or leave) for or during which one receives pay: *a one-month paid vacation.* ■ [attrib.] (of a person in a specified occupation) in receipt of pay: *a paid, anonymous informer.*

paid-up ▶ **adj.** [attrib.] (of a member of an organization, esp. a labor union) having paid all the necessary dues in full. ■ denoting the part of the subscribed capital of an undertaking that has actually been paid: *paid-up capital.* ■ denoting an endowment policy in which the policyholder has stopped paying premiums, resulting in the surrender value being used to purchase single-premium whole life insurance.

Paige /pāj/, Satchel (1906–82), US baseball player; born *Leroy Robert Paige.* A pitcher for the Negro leagues 1924–47 and the major leagues 1948–65, he threw 55 career no-hitters.

pail /pāl/ ▶ **n.** a bucket. — **pail·ful n.** (pl. **-fuls**) [ME: compare OE *pægel* 'small measure.']

pail·lette /pīˈyet; pā-; pəˈlet/ ▶ **n.** a piece of glittering material used to ornament clothing; a spangle. ■ a piece of bright metal used in enamel painting. [19th C.: ult. from L. *palea* 'straw.']

pain /pān/ ▶ **n.** **1** physical suffering or discomfort caused by illness or injury. ■ a feeling of marked discomfort in a particular part of the body. ■ mental suffering or distress: *the pain of loss.* ■ (also **pain in the neck** or vulgar slang **pain in the ass**) [in sing.] informal an annoying or tedious person or thing. **2** (**pains**) careful effort; great care or trouble: *she took pains to see that everyone ate well.* ▶ **v.** [trans.] cause mental or physical pain to: *it pains me to say this.* ■ [intrans.] (of a part of the body) hurt.
– PHRASES **for one's pains** informal as an unfairly bad return for efforts or trouble: *he was sued for his pains.* **no pain, no gain** suffering is necessary in order to achieve something. **on** (or **under**) **pain of** the penalty for disobedience or shortcoming being: *keep silent on pain of imprisonment.* [ME: from OFr. *peine*, from L. *poena* 'penalty.']

Paine /pān/, Thomas (1737–1809), English political writer. His pamphlet *Common Sense* (1776) called for American independence, and *The Rights of Man* (1791) defended the French Revolution.

pained /pānd/ ▶ **adj.** affected with pain, esp. mental pain; hurt or troubled: *a pained expression.*

pain·ful /ˈpānfəl/ ▶ **adj.** (of part of the body) affected with pain. ■ causing physical pain. ■ causing distress or trouble. — **pain·ful·ness n.**

pain·ful·ly /ˈpānfəlē/ ▶ **adv.** in a painful manner or to a painful degree: *she coughed painfully.* ■ [as submodifier] (with reference to something bad) exceedingly; acutely: *it was painfully obvious that she had no remorse.*

pain·kil·ler /ˈpānˌkilər/ ▶ **n.** a drug or medicine for relieving pain. — **pain·kill·ing adj.**

pain·less /ˈpānləs/ ▶ **adj.** not causing or suffering physical pain: *a painless death.* ■ involving little effort or stress: *a painless way to travel.* — **pain·less·ly adv. pain·less·ness n.**

pain·stak·ing /ˈpānzˌtākiɴɢ; ˈpānˌstākiɴɢ/ ▶ **adj.** done with or employing great care and thoroughness: *painstaking attention to detail.* — **pain·stak·ing·ly adv. pain·stak·ing·ness n.**

paint /pānt/ ▶ **n.** **1** a colored substance that is spread over a surface and dries to leave a thin decorative or protective coating. ■ an act of covering something with paint. ■ informal cosmetic makeup. ■ Basketball the rectangular area marked near the basket at each end of the court; the foul lane: *the two players jostled in the paint.* ■ Comput. the function or capability of producing graphics, esp. those that mimic the effect of real paint: [as adj.] *a paint program.* **2** a piebald horse: [as adj.] *a paint mare.* ▶ **v.** [trans.] **1** (often **be painted**) cover the surface of (something) with paint, as decoration or protection. ■ apply cosmetics to (the face or skin). ■ apply (a liquid) to a surface with a brush. ■ (**paint**

something out) efface something with paint: *the markings on the plane were painted out.* ■ Comput. create (a graphic or screen display) using a paint program. ■ display a mark representing (an aircraft or vehicle) on a radar screen. **2** depict (an object, person, or scene) with paint. ■ produce (a picture) in such a way: *Marr paints portraits* | [intrans.] *she paints and she makes sculptures.* ■ give a description of (someone or something): *I'm painted as a nut case.*
– PHRASES **like watching paint dry** (of an activity or experience) extremely boring. **paint oneself into a corner** leave oneself no means of escape or room to maneuver. **paint the town (red)** informal go out and enjoy oneself flamboyantly. — **paint·a·ble** adj. **paint·y** adj. (**paint·i·er, paint·i·est**). [ME: from *peint*, past part. of OFr. *peindre*, from L. *pingere* 'paint.']

paint·ball /ˈpānt,bôl/ ▶ n. a game in which participants simulate military combat using air guns to shoot capsules of paint at each other. ■ a capsule of paint used in this game. — **paint·ball·er** n.

paint·brush /ˈpānt,brəsʜ/ ▶ n. **1** a brush for applying paint. **2** a North American plant (genus *Castilleja*) of the figwort family that bears brightly colored flowering spikes with a brushlike appearance. Its several species include the **Indian paintbrush** (*C. coccinea*). See also DEVIL'S PAINTBRUSH.

paint-by-num·ber ▶ adj. denoting a child's picture marked out in advance into sections that are numbered according to the color to be used. ■ fig. denoting something mechanical or formulaic rather than imaginative, original, or natural.

paint chip ▶ n. a card showing a color or a range of related colors available in a type of paint.

paint·ed bunt·ing ▶ n. a bunting (*Passerina ciris*) with a violet head, red body, and green back, the only such multicolored songbird in North America.

Paint·ed Des·ert a region in northeastern Arizona that is noted for its colorful eroded landscapes.

painted lady

paint·ed la·dy ▶ n. **1** a migratory butterfly (genus *Cynthia*, family Nymphalidae) with predominantly orange-brown wings and darker markings. Species include the widely distributed *C. cardui*, with black and white markings, and the **American painted lady** (*C. virginiensis*), with eyemarks on the undersides of the wings. **2** (also **Painted Lady**) a Victorian house, the exterior of which is painted in three or more colors, effectively highlighting the architecture.

painted turtle

paint·ed tur·tle ▶ n. a small American freshwater turtle (*Chrysemys picta*, family Emydidae) with a smooth shell and colorful patterns of red, yellow, and black that appear along the border of the carapace and (in certain subspecies) on the plastron.

paint·er[1] /ˈpāntər/ ▶ n. **1** an artist who paints pictures. **2** a person who paints houses, esp. as a job.

paint·er[2] ▶ n. a rope attached to the bow of a boat for making it fast. [ME: compare OFr. *pentoir* 'something from which to hang things.']

paint·er·ly /ˈpāntərlē/ ▶ adj. of or appropriate to a painter; artistic: *she has a painterly eye.* ■ (of a painting or its style) characterized by qualities of color, stroke, and texture rather than of line. — **paint·er·li·ness** n.

pain thresh·old ▶ n. the point beyond which a stimulus causes pain. ■ the upper limit of tolerance to pain.

paint·ing /ˈpāntiɴɢ/ ▶ n. the process or art of using paint, either in a picture or as decoration. ■ a painted picture: *an oil painting.*

pair /pe(ə)r/ ▶ n. a set of two things used together or regarded as a unit. ■ an article or object consisting of two joined or corresponding parts not used separately: *a pair of jeans.* ■ two playing cards of the same denomination. ■ two people related in some way or considered together. ■ the second member of a pair in relation to the first: *each course member tries to persuade his pair of the merits of his model.* ■ a mated couple of animals. ■ two horses harnessed side by side. ■ either or both of two members of a legislative assembly on opposite sides who absent themselves from voting by mutual arrangement, leaving the relative position of the parties unaffected. ▶ v. [trans.] (often **be paired**) join or connect to form a pair: *a cardigan **paired with** a matching skirt.* ■ [intrans.] (of animals) mate. ■ [intrans.] (**pair off/up**) form a couple: *Rachel has **paired up with** Tommy.* ■ give (a member of a legislative assembly) another member as a pair, to allow both to absent themselves from a vote without affecting the result: *an absent member on one side is to be **paired with** an absentee on the other.*
– PHRASES **pair of hands** a person seen in terms of their participation in a task. — **pair·wise** adj. & adv. [ME: from OFr. *paire*, from L. *paria* neut. pl. of *par* 'equal.']

paired /pe(ə)rd/ ▶ adj. occurring in pairs or as a pair.

pair·ing /ˈpe(ə)riɴɢ/ ▶ n. an arrangement or match resulting from organizing or forming people or things into pairs. ■ the action of pairing things or people.

pair pro·duc·tion ▶ n. Physics the conversion of a radiation quantum into an electron and a positron.

pai·sa /ˈpīsä/ ▶ n. (pl. **-se** /-sā/) a monetary unit of Bangladesh, India, Pakistan, and Nepal, equal to one hundredth of a rupee. [from Hindi *paisā*.]

pai·san /pīˈzän/ ▶ n. informal (among people of Italian or Spanish descent) a fellow countryman or friend (often as a term of address). [from Ital. *paisano* 'peasant, rustic.']

pai·sa·no /pīˈzänō/ ▶ n. (pl. **-nos**) a peasant of Spanish or Italian ethnic origin. [Sp.]

pais·ley /ˈpāzlē/ ▶ n. [usu. as adj.] a distinctive intricate pattern of curved, feather-shaped figures based on a pine-cone design from India: *a paisley silk tie.* [19th C.: *Paisley*, Scotland.]

paisley

Pai·ute /ˈpī(y)o͞ot; pīˈ(y)o͞ot/ ▶ n. (pl. same or **-utes**) **1** a member of either of two culturally similar but geographically separate and linguistically distinct American Indian peoples, the **Southern Paiute** of the southwestern US and the **Northern Paiute** of Oregon and Nevada. **2** either of the Uto-Aztecan languages of these peoples. ▶ adj. of or relating to the Paiute or their languages. [from Sp. *Payuchi, Payuta*.]

pa·ja·mas /pəˈjäməz; -ˈjaməz/ (Brit. **py·ja·mas**) ▶ plural n. a suit of loose pants and shirt for sleeping in. ■ [in sing.] (**pajama**) a pair of loose pants tied by a drawstring around the waist, worn by both sexes in some Asian countries. [19th C.: from Urdu, Pers., from *pāy* 'leg' + *jāma* 'clothing.']

pak choi /,bäk ˈcʜoi/ ▶ n. another term for BOK CHOY.

Pak·i·stan /ˈpaki,stan; ,päkiˈstän/ a country in southern Asia. *See box.* — **Pak·i·sta·ni** /,pakəˈstanē; ,päkiˈstänē/ adj. & n.

Pa·ki·stan Peo·ple's Par·ty (abbr.: **PPP**) one of the main political parties in Pakistan. It was founded in 1967 by Zulfikar Ali Bhutto, and has been led since 1984 by his daughter Benazir Bhutto.

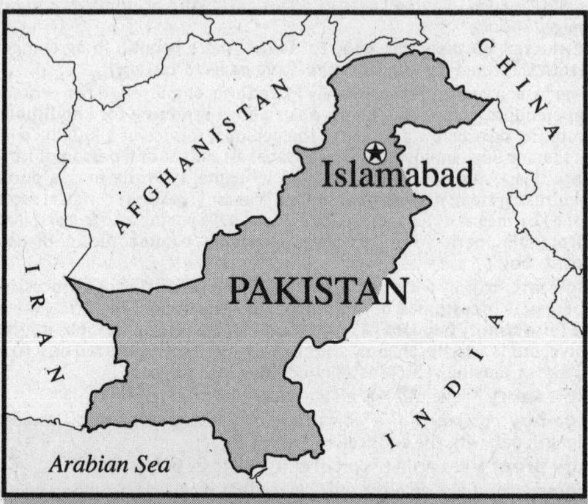

Pakistan

Official name: Islamic Republic of Pakistan
Location: southern Asia, bordered on south by Arabian Sea
Area: 310,500 square miles (803,900 sq km)
Population: 159,196,000
Capital: Islamabad
Languages: Urdu, English (both official), Punjabi, Sindhi, Pashto, and others
Currency: Pakistani rupee

pal /pal/ informal ▶ **n.** a friend. ■ used as a form of address, esp. to indicate anger or aggression: *back off, pal.* ▶ **v.** (**palled, pal·ling**) [intrans.] (**pal around**) spend time with a friend: *we never really palled around.* [17th C.: from Romany, 'brother, mate,' based on Sanskrit *bhrātr* 'brother.']

pal·ace /'palis/ ▶ **n.** the official residence of a sovereign, archbishop, bishop, or other exalted person. ■ informal a large, splendid house. [ME: from OFr. *paleis*, from L. *Palatium*, the Palatine hill in Rome, where the house of the emperor was situated.]

pal·ace coup (also **palace revolution**) ▶ **n.** the nonviolent overthrow of a sovereign or government by senior officials within the ruling group.

pal·a·din /'palədin/ ▶ **n.** hist. any of the twelve peers of Charlemagne's court, of whom the count palatine was the chief. ■ a knight renowned for heroism and chivalry. [16th C.: from Fr. *paladin*, ult. from L. *palatinus* (see PALATINE[1]).]

Pa·lae·arc·tic ▶ **adj.** British spelling of PALEARCTIC.

palaeo- ▶ **comb. form** British spelling of PALEO-.

pal·an·quin /,palən'kēn/ (also **pal·an·keen**) ▶ **n.** (in India and the East) a covered litter for one passenger, consisting of a large box carried on two horizontal poles by four or six bearers. [16th C.: from Port. *palanquim*, from Oriya *pālañki*, based on Sanskrit *palyanka* 'bed, couch.']

pal·at·a·ble /'palətəbəl/ ▶ **adj.** (of food or drink) pleasant to taste. ■ (of an action or proposal) acceptable or satisfactory. — **pal·at·a·bil·i·ty** /,palətə'bilətē/ **n.** **pal·at·a·bly adv.**

pal·a·tal /'palətl/ ▶ **adj.** tech. of or relating to the palate: *a palatal lesion.* ■ Phonet. (of a speech sound) made by placing the blade of the tongue against or near the hard palate (e.g., *y* in *yes*). ▶ **n.** Phonet. a palatal sound. — **pal·a·tal·ly adv.**

pal·a·tal·ize /'palətl,īz/ ▶ **v.** [trans.] Phonet. make (a speech sound) palatal, esp. by changing a velar to a palatal by moving the point of contact between tongue and palate further forward in the mouth. ■ [intrans.] (of a speech sound) become palatal. — **pal·a·tal·i·za·tion** /,palətl-i'zāsʜən/ **n.**

pal·ate /'palit/ ▶ **n.** **1** the roof of the mouth, separating the cavities of the nose and the mouth in vertebrates. **2** a person's appreciation of taste and flavor. ■ a person's taste or liking. ■ taste or flavor of wine or beer. [ME: from L. *palatum*.]

pa·la·tial /pə'lāsʜəl/ ▶ **adj.** resembling a palace in being spacious and splendid. — **pa·la·tial·ly adv.** [18th C.: from L. *palatium*.]

pa·lat·i·nate /pə'latn,āt; -,it/ ▶ **n.** hist. a territory under the jurisdiction of a count palatine. ■ (**the Palatinate**) the territory of the German Empire ruled by the count palatine of the Rhine.

pal·a·tine[1] /'palə,tīn/ ▶ **adj.** [usu. postpositive] esp. hist. (of an official or feudal lord) having local authority that elsewhere belongs only to a sovereign. ■ (of a territory) subject to this authority. [ME: from Fr. *palatin(e)*, from L. *palatinus* 'of the palace.']

pal·a·tine[2] esp. Anat. ▶ **adj.** of or relating to the palate or esp. the palatine bone. ▶ **n.** (also **palatine bone**) each of two bones within the skull forming parts of the eye socket, the nasal cavity, and the hard palate. [17th C.: from Fr. *palatin(e)*, from L. *palatum* 'palate.']

Pa·lau /pə'lou/ (also **Be·lau** /bə'lou/) a republic in the western Pacific Ocean. *See box.*

pa·lav·er /pə'lavər; -'läv-/ ▶ **n.** prolonged and idle discussion. ■ dated a parley or improvised conference between two sides. ▶ **v.** [intrans.] talk unnecessarily at length. [18th C.: from Port. *palavra* 'word,' from L. *parabola* 'comparison' (see PARABLE).]

Pa·la·wan /pə'läwən; pä-/ an island in the western Philippines.

pa·laz·zo /pə'lätsō/ ▶ **n.** (pl. **-laz·zos** or **-laz·zi** /-'lätsē/) a palatial building, esp. in Italy. [Ital., 'palace.']

pa·laz·zo pants ▶ **plural n.** a woman's loose, wide-legged pants.

pale[1] /pāl/ ▶ **adj.** light in color or having little color. ■ (of a person's face or complexion) having less color than usual, typically as a result of shock, fear, or ill health: *with pale skin and light eyes.* ■ [attrib.] (of a color or light) not strong or bright: *pale blue eyes* | *a pale dawn.* ■ fig. feeble and unimpressive: *a pale imitation of Bruce Springsteen.* ▶ **v.** [intrans.] **1** become pale in one's face from shock or fear: *I paled at the thought.* **2** seem less impressive or important. — **pale·ly adv.** **pale·ness n.** **pal·ish adj.** [ME: from OFr. *pale*, from L. *pallidus*.]

pale[2] ▶ **n.** **1** a wooden stake or post used as an upright along with others to form a fence. ■ fig. a boundary: *bring these things back within the pale of decency.* ■ archaic hist. an area within determined bounds, or subject to a particular jurisdiction. **2** Heraldry a broad vertical stripe down the middle of a shield.

– PHRASES **beyond the pale** outside the bounds of acceptable behavior: *the language my father used was beyond the pale.* **in pale** Heraldry arranged vertically. **per pale** Heraldry divided by a vertical line. [ME: from OFr. *pal*, from L. *palus* 'stake.']

pa·le·a /'pālēə/ ▶ **n.** (pl. **-le·ae** /-lē,ē; -lē,ī/) Bot. the upper bract of the floret of a grass. Compare with LEMMA[2]. [18th C.: from L., lit. 'chaff.']

Pa·le·arc·tic /,pālē'är(k)tik/ (Brit. **Pa·lae·arc·tic**) ▶ **adj.** Zool. of, relating to, or denoting a zoogeographical region comprising Eurasia north of the Himalayas, together with North Africa and the temperate part of the Arabian peninsula. Compare with HOLARCTIC. ■ [as n.] (**the Palearctic**) the Palearctic region.

pale·face /'pāl,fās/ ▶ **n.** a name supposedly used by North American Indians for a white person.

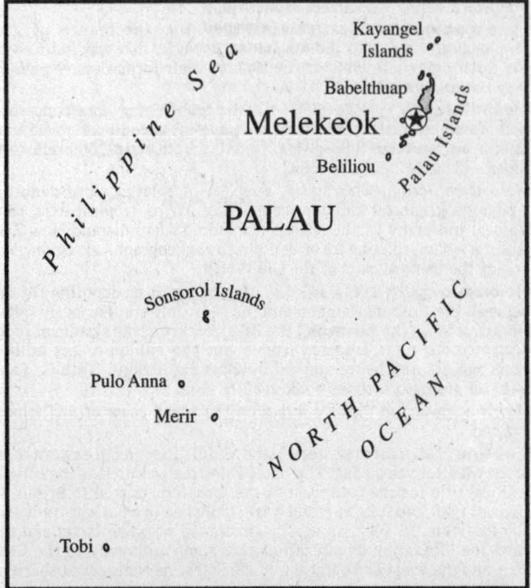

Palau

Official name: Republic of Palau
Location: western Pacific Ocean, a group of about 100 of the Caroline Islands
Area: 170 square miles (460 sq km)
Population: 20,000
Capital: Melekeok
Languages: English (official in all states), Palauan, Sonsorolese, Tobi, Angaur, Japanese
Currency: US dollar

Pa·lem·bang /pä'lem,bäɴɢ/ a city in Indonesia, in the southeastern part of Sumatra; pop. 1,141,000.

paleo- (Brit. **palaeo-**) ▶ **comb. form** older or ancient, esp. relating to the geological past: *Paleolithic.* [from Gk. *palaios* 'ancient.']

pa·le·o·an·thro·pol·o·gy /,pālēō,anᴛʜrə'päləjē/ ▶ **n.** the branch of anthropology concerned with fossil hominids. — **pa·le·o·an·thro·po·log·i·cal** /-pə'läjikəl/ **adj.** **pa·le·o·an·thro·pol·o·gist** /-jist/ **n.**

Pa·le·o·cene /'pālēə,sēn/ ▶ **adj.** Geol. of, relating to, or denoting the earliest epoch of the Tertiary period, between the Cretaceous period and the Eocene epoch. ■ [as n.] (**the Paleocene**) the Paleocene epoch or the system of rocks deposited during it, which lasted from 65 million to 56.5 million years ago. [19th C.: from PALEO- (relating to prehistoric times) + Gk. *kainos* 'new.']

pa·le·o·con /'pālēō,kän/ ▶ **n.** informal short for PALEOCONSERVATIVE.

pa·le·o·con·serv·a·tive /,pālēōkən'sərvətiv/ ▶ **n.** a person who advocates old or traditional forms of conservatism; an extremely right-wing conservative.

Pa·le·o·gene /'pālēəjēn/ ▶ **adj.** Geol. of, relating to, or denoting the earlier division of the Tertiary period, comprising the Paleocene, Eocene, and Oligocene epochs. Compare with NEOGENE. ■ [as n.] (**the Paleogene**) the Paleogene subperiod or the system of rocks deposited during it. It lasted from about 65 million to 23 million years ago. [19th C.: from PALEO- (relating to prehistoric times) + Gk. *genēs* 'of a specified kind' (see -GEN).]

pa·le·og·ra·phy /,pālē'ägrəfē/ (Brit. **pa·lae·og·ra·phy**) ▶ **n.** the study of ancient writing systems and the deciphering and dating of historical manuscripts. — **pa·le·og·ra·pher n.** **pa·le·o·graph·ic** /,pālēə'grafik/ **adj.** **pa·le·o·graph·i·cal** /,pālēə'grafikəl/ **adj.** **pa·le·o·graph·i·cal·ly** /,pālēə'grafik(ə)lē/ **adv.**

Pa·le·o-In·di·an ▶ **adj.** of, relating to, or denoting the earliest human inhabitants of the Americas, from as early as 40,000 years ago to *c.*5000 BC. ▶ **n.** **1** (**the Paleo-Indian**) the Paleo-Indian culture or period. **2** a member of the Paleo-Indian peoples.

pa·le·o·lat·i·tude /,pālēō'lati,t(y)o͞od/ ▶ **n.** the latitude of a place at some time in the past, measured relative to the earth's magnetic poles in the same period.

Pa·le·o·lith·ic /,pālēə'liᴛʜik/ ▶ **adj.** Archaeol. of, relating to, or denoting the early phase of the Stone Age, lasting about 2.5 million years, when primitive stone implements were used. ■ [as n.] (**the Paleolithic**) the Paleolithic period. Also called OLD STONE AGE. [19th C.: from PALEO- 'of

PRONUNCIATION KEY ə *ago, up*; ər *over, fur*; a *hat*; ā *ate*; ä *car*; e *let*; ē *see*; i *fit*; ī *by*; ɴɢ *sing*; ō *go*; ô *law, for*; oi *toy*; o͝o *good*; o͞o *goo*; ou *out*; ᴛʜ *thin*; T͟H *then*; ᴢʜ *vision*

prehistoric times' + Gk. *lithos* 'stone' + -IC.]

pa·le·o·mag·net·ism /ˌpālēōˈmagnəˌtizəm/ ▶ n. the branch of geophysics concerned with the magnetism in rocks that was induced by the earth's magnetic field at the time of their formation. — **pa·le·o·mag·net·ic** /-magˈnetik/ adj.

pa·le·on·tol·o·gy /ˌpālēənˈtäləjē/ ▶ n. the branch of science concerned with fossil animals and plants. — **pa·le·on·to·log·i·cal** /ˌpālēˌäntəˈläjikəl/ adj. **pa·le·on·tol·o·gist** n. [19th C.: from PALEO- 'of prehistoric times' + Gk. *onta* 'beings' + -LOGY.]

Pa·le·o·trop·i·cal /ˌpālēəˈträpikəl/ ▶ adj. Bot. of, relating to, or denoting a phytogeographical kingdom comprising Africa, tropical Asia, New Guinea, and many Pacific islands (excluding Australia and New Zealand). ■ Zool. of, relating to, or denoting a zoogeographical region comprising the tropical parts of the Old World.

Pa·le·o·zo·ic /ˌpālēəˈzōik/ ▶ adj. Geol. of, relating to, or denoting the era between the Precambrian eon and the Mesozoic era. Formerly called PRIMARY. ■ [as n.] **(the Paleozoic)** the Paleozoic era or the system of rocks deposited during it. It lasted from about 570 million to 245 million years ago, its end being marked by mass extinctions. [19th C.: from PALEO- 'of prehistoric times' + Gk. *zōē* 'life' + -IC.]

Pa·ler·mo /pəˈlərˌmō; -ˈle(ə)r-/ a city on the north coast of Sicily; pop. 734,000.

Pal·es·tine /ˈpaliˌstīn/ a territory in the Middle East on the eastern coast of the Mediterranean Sea. The name Palestine was used as the official political title for the land west of the Jordan mandated to Britain in 1920; in 1948, the state of Israel was established in what was traditionally Palestine. In 1993, an agreement signed between Israel and the Palestine Liberation Organization gave some autonomy to the Gaza Strip and the West Bank and set up the Palestine National Authority.

Pal·es·tine Lib·er·a·tion Or·gan·i·za·tion (abbr.: **PLO**) a political and military organization formed in 1964 to unite various Palestinian Arab groups and bring about an independent state of Palestine. It was led by Yasser Arafat from 1968 until 2004.

Pal·es·tin·i·an /ˌpaləˈstinēən/ ▶ adj. of or relating to Palestine or its peoples. ▶ n. a member of the native Arab population of the region of Palestine (including the modern state of Israel).

Pa·les·tri·na /ˌpaləˈstrēnə; ˌpäle-/, Giovanni Pierluigi da (*c.*1525–94), Italian composer. He is noted for his sacred music.

pal·ette /ˈpalit/ ▶ n. a thin board or slab on which an artist lays and mixes colors. ■ the range of colors used by a particular artist or in a particular picture. ■ fig. the range or variety of tonal or instrumental color in a musical piece. ■ (in computer graphics) the range of colors or shapes available to the user. [18th C.: from Fr., dimin. of *pale* 'shovel,' from L. *pala* 'spade.']

pal·ette knife ▶ n. a thin steel blade with a handle for mixing colors or applying or removing paint.

Pa·li /ˈpälē/ ▶ n. an Indic language, closely related to Sanskrit, in which the sacred texts of Theravada Buddhism are written. Pali developed in northern India in the 5th–2nd centuries BC. ▶ adj. of or relating to this language. [from Pali *pāli(-bhāsā)* 'canonical texts.']

pa·li /ˈpälē/ ▶ n. (pl. same or **pa·lis**) (in Hawaii) a cliff. [Hawaiian.]

pal·i·mo·ny /ˈpaləˌmōnē/ ▶ n. informal compensation made by one member of an unmarried couple to the other after separation. [1970s: from PAL + a shortened form of ALIMONY.]

pal·imp·sest /ˈpalimpˌsest/ ▶ n. a manuscript or piece of writing material on which the original writing has been effaced to make room for later writing. ■ fig. something reused or altered but still bearing visible traces of its earlier form. — **pal·imp·ses·tic** /ˌpalimpˈsestik/ adj. [17th C.: via L. from Gk. *palimpsēstos*, from *palin* 'again' + *psēstos* 'rubbed smooth.']

pal·in·drome /ˈpalinˌdrōm/ ▶ n. a word, phrase, or sequence that reads the same backward as forward, e.g., *madam* or *nurses run*. — **pal·in·drom·ic** /ˌpalinˈdrämik/ adj. **pa·lin·dro·mist** /pəˈlindrəmist/ n. [17th C.: from Gk. *palindromos* 'running back again,' from *palin* 'again' + *drom-* (from *dramein* 'to run').]

pal·ing /ˈpāliNG/ ▶ n. a fence made from pointed wooden or metal stakes. ■ a stake used in such a fence.

pal·in·gen·e·sis /ˌpalinˈjenəsis/ ▶ n. **1** Biol. the exact reproduction of ancestral characteristics in ontogenesis. **2** rebirth or regeneration. — **pal·in·ge·net·ic** /ˌpalinjəˈnetik/ adj. [19th C.: from Gk. *palin* 'again' + *genesis* 'birth.']

pal·i·node /ˈpaləˌnōd/ ▶ n. a poem in which a sentiment expressed in a former poem is retracted. [16th C.: via L. from Gk. *palinōidia*, from *palin* 'again' + *ōidē* 'song.']

pal·i·sade /ˌpaləˈsād/ ▶ n. a fence of wooden stakes or iron railings fixed in the ground, forming an enclosure or defense. ■ hist. a pointed wooden stake fixed deeply in the ground with others in a close row, used as a defense. ■ **(palisades)** a line of high cliffs. ▶ v. [trans.] [usu. as adj.] **(palisaded)** enclose or provide (a building or place) with a palisade. [17th C.: from Fr. *palissade*, based on L. *palus* 'stake.']

pal·i·sade lay·er ▶ n. Bot. a layer of parallel elongated cells below the epidermis of a leaf.

Pal·i·sades, the /ˌpaliˈsādz/ (also **Palisades of the Hudson**) a ridge of high basalt cliffs on the west bank of the Hudson River, in northeastern New Jersey.

Palk Strait /pôk; pôlk/ an inlet of the Bay of Bengal that separates northern Sri Lanka from the coast of Tamil Nadu in India.

pall[1] /pôl/ ▶ n. **1** a cloth spread over a coffin, hearse, or tomb. ■ fig. a dark cloud or covering of smoke, dust, or similar matter. ■ fig. something regarded as enveloping a situation with an air of gloom, heaviness, or fear. **2** an ecclesiastical pallium. ■ Heraldry a Y-shaped charge representing the front of an ecclesiastical pallium. [OE *pæll* 'rich cloth,' from L. *pallium* 'cloak.']

pall[2] ▶ v. [intrans.] become less appealing or interesting through familiarity: *the quiet life palled.* [ME: shortening of APPALL.]

Pal·la·di·an /pəˈlādēən/ ▶ adj. Archit. of, relating to, or denoting the neoclassical style of Andrea Palladio from *c.*1715. — **Pal·la·di·an·ism** n.

Pal·la·di·an win·dow ▶ n. a large window consisting of a central arched section flanked by two narrow rectangular sections.

pal·la·di·um /pəˈlādēəm/ ▶ n. the chemical element of atomic number 46, a rare silvery-white metal resembling platinum. (Symbol: **Pd**) [19th C.: mod. L., from *Pallas*, an asteroid.]

Pal·las /ˈpaləs/ **1** Gk. Mythol. (also **Pallas Athene**) one of the names (of unknown meaning) of ATHENA. **2** Astron. asteroid 2, discovered in 1802. It is the second largest (diameter 523 km).

pall·bear·er /ˈpôlˌbe(ə)rər/ ▶ n. a person helping to carry or officially escorting a coffin at a funeral.

pal·let[1] /ˈpalit/ ▶ n. a straw mattress. ■ a crude or makeshift bed. [ME: ult. from L. *palea*.]

pal·let[2] ▶ n. **1** a portable platform on which goods can be moved, stacked, and stored, esp. with the aid of a forklift. **2** a flat wooden blade with a handle, used to shape clay or plaster. **3** an artist's palette. **4** a projection on a machine part, serving to change the mode of motion of a wheel. ■ (in a clock or watch) a projection transmitting motion from an escapement to a pendulum or balance wheel. [ME: from Fr. *palette* 'little blade,' from L. *pala* 'spade.']

pal·let[3] ▶ n. Heraldry the diminutive of the pale, a narrow vertical strip, usually borne in groups of two or three. [15th C.: dimin. of n. PALE[2].]

pal·li·a /ˈpalēə/ plural form of PALLIUM.

pal·li·ate /ˈpalēˌāt/ ▶ v. [trans.] make (a disease or its symptoms) less severe or unpleasant without removing the cause. ■ allay or moderate (fears or suspicions). ■ disguise the seriousness or gravity of (an offense). — **pal·li·a·tion** /ˌpalēˈāSHən/ n. **pal·li·a·tor** /-ˌātər/ n. [ME: from late L. *palliat-* 'cloaked,' from the v. *palliare*, from *pallium* 'cloak.']

pal·li·a·tive /ˈpalēˌātiv; ˈpalēətiv/ ▶ adj. (of a treatment or medicine) relieving pain or alleviating a problem without dealing with the underlying cause. ▶ n. a remedy, medicine, etc., of such a kind. — **pal·li·a·tive·ly** adv.

pal·lid /ˈpalid/ ▶ adj. (of a person's face) pale, typically because of poor health. ■ derog. feeble or insipid. — **pal·lid·ly** adv. **pal·lid·ness** n. [16th C.: from L. *pallidus* 'pale.']

pal·li·um /ˈpalēəm/ ▶ n. (pl. **pal·li·a** /ˈpalēə/ or **pal·li·ums**) **1** a woolen vestment conferred by the pope on an archbishop, consisting of a narrow, circular band placed around the shoulders with a short lappet hanging from front and back. **2** hist. a man's large rectangular cloak, esp. as worn by Greek philosophical and religious teachers. **3** Zool. the mantle of a mollusk or brachiopod. **4** Anat. the outer wall of the mammalian cerebrum, corresponding to the cerebral cortex. — **pal·li·al** /ˈpalēəl/ adj. (in senses 3 and 4). [ME: from L., lit. 'covering.']

pal·lor /ˈpalər/ ▶ n. [in sing.] an unhealthy pale appearance. [ME: from L., from *pallere* 'be pale.']

pal·ly /ˈpalē/ ▶ adj. **(pal·li·er, pal·li·est)** [predic.] informal having a close, friendly relationship.

palm[1] /pä(l)m/ ▶ n. (also **palm tree**) an unbranched evergreen tree (family Palmae or Arecaceae) with a crown of long feathered or fan-shaped leaves, growing in tropical and warm regions. ■ a leaf of such a tree awarded as a prize or viewed as a symbol of victory or triumph. [OE *palm(a)*, of Gmc. origin; rel. to Du. *palm* and Ger. *Palme*, from L. *palma* 'palm (of a hand),' its leaf being likened to a spread hand.]

palm[2] ▶ n. the inner surface of the hand between the wrist and fingers. ■ a part of a glove that covers this part of the hand. ■ a hard shield worn on the hand by sailmakers to protect the palm in sewing. ■ the palmate part of an antler. ▶ v. **1** [trans.] conceal (a card or other small object) in the hand, esp. as part of a trick or theft. **2** [trans.] hit (something) with the palm of the hand. ■ Basketball illegally grip (the ball) with the hand while dribbling.

– PHRASES **have** (or **hold**) **someone in the palm of one's hand** have someone under one's influence. **read someone's palm** tell someone's fortune by looking at the lines on their palm.

– PHRASAL VERBS **palm someone off** informal persuade someone to accept something by deception. **palm something off** sell or dispose of something by misrepresentation or fraud. — **pal·mar** /ˈpalmər; ˈpä(l)mər/ adj. **palmed** adj. [in comb.] *sweaty-palmed.* **palm·ful** n. [ME: from OFr. *paume*, from L. *palma*.]

Pal·ma /ˈpälmə/ a city on the island of Majorca; pop. 309,000. Full name PALMA DE MALLORCA.

pal·mate /ˈpalˌmāt; ˈpä(l)-/ ▶ adj. **1** Bot. (of a leaf) having several lobes (typically 5–7) whose midribs all radiate from one point. See illustration at LEAF. **2** Zool. (of an antler) in which the angles between the tines are partly filled in to form a broad flat surface, as in fallow deer and moose. ■ web-footed. — **pal·mat·ed** adj. [18th C.: from L. *palmatus*, from *palma* 'palm.']

palm ball (also **palm·ball**) ▶ n. Baseball an off-speed pitch in which the ball is released from the palm and thumb rather than the fingers.

Palm Beach a town in southeastern Florida, noted as a resort; pop. 9,814.

palm·cord·er /'pä(l)m,kôrdər/ ▶ **n.** a small, hand-held camcorder. [1980s: blend of PALM² and RECORDER.]

Pal·me /'pälmə/, Olof (1927–86), prime minister of Sweden 1969–76, 1982–86. The leader of Sweden's Social Democratic Party, he was assassinated by an unknown assailant.

Pal·mer /'pä(l)mər/, Arnold Daniel (1929–), US golfer. During 1958–64, he won seven major championships.

Pal·mer·ston /'pä(l)mərstən/, Henry John Temple, 3rd Viscount (1784–1865), prime minister of Britain 1855–58, 1859–65.

pal·mette /pal'met/ ▶ **n.** Archaeol. an ornament of radiating petals that resemble the leaflets of a palm.

pal·met·to /pä(l)'metō; pal-/ ▶ **n.** (pl. **-tos**) a fan palm (*Sabal* and other genera), esp. one of a number occurring from the southern US to northern South America. Its several species include the **cabbage palmetto** (*S. palmetto*), which is the state tree of Florida (where it is better known as the **sabal palm**) and South Carolina. [16th C.: from Sp. *palmito*, lit. 'small palm,' dimin. of *palma*, assimilated to Ital. words ending in *-etto*.]

cabbage palmetto

palm·i·er /'pä(l)mēā/ ▶ **n.** (pl. pronunc. same) a sweet, crisp pastry shaped like a palm leaf. [Fr., lit. 'palm tree.']

palm·is·try /'pä(l)məstrē/ ▶ **n.** the art or practice of supposedly interpreting a person's character or predicting their future by examining the lines and other features of the hand, esp. the palm and fingers. — **palm·ist n.** [ME: from PALM² + *-estry* (of unknown origin).]

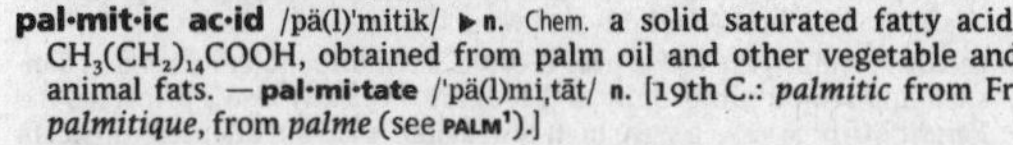

pal·mit·ic ac·id /pä(l)'mitik/ ▶ **n.** Chem. a solid saturated fatty acid, $CH_3(CH_2)_{14}COOH$, obtained from palm oil and other vegetable and animal fats. — **pal·mi·tate** /'pä(l)mi,tāt/ **n.** [19th C.: *palmitic* from Fr. *palmitique*, from *palme* (see PALM¹).]

palm oil ▶ **n.** oil from the fruit of certain palms, esp. the West African oil palm.

Palm Springs a city in the desert area of southern California, noted for its hot springs; pop. 40,181.

Palm Sun·day ▶ **n.** the Sunday before Easter, when the triumphal entry of Jesus into Jerusalem is celebrated in many Christian churches by processions in which palm fronds are carried.

palm·top /'pä(l)m,täp/ ▶ **n.** a computer small and lightweight enough to be held in one hand.

palm·y /'pä(l)mē/ ▶ **adj.** (**palm·i·er, palm·i·est**) **1** (esp. of a previous period of time) flourishing or successful. **2** covered with palms.

Pal·my·ra /pal'mīrə/ an ancient city in Syria, an oasis in the Syrian desert on the site of present-day Tadmur.

pal·my·ra /pal'mīrə/ ▶ **n.** an Asian fan palm (*Borassus flabellifer*) that yields a wide range of useful products, including timber, fiber, and fruit. [17th C.: from Port. *palmeira* 'palm tree.']

Pal·o Al·to /'palō 'altō/ a city in western California, south of San Francisco; pop. 55,900.

Pal·o·mar, Mount /'palə,mär/ a mountain in southern California, the site of an astronomical observatory.

pal·o·mi·no /,palə'mēnō/ ▶ **n.** **1** (pl. **-nos**) a pale golden or tan-colored horse with a white mane and tail, originally bred in the southwestern US. **2** a variety of white grape, used esp. to make sherry and fortified wines. [20th C.: from Latin Amer. Sp., from Sp. *palomino* 'young pigeon,' from L. *palumbinus* 'resembling a dove.']

pa·loo·ka /pə'lōōkə/ ▶ **n.** informal, dated an inferior or average prizefighter. ■ a stupid, uncouth person; a lout. [1920s: of unknown origin.]

pal·o·ver·de /,palō'vərd(ē)/ ▶ **n.** a thorny, yellow-flowered tree or shrub (genus *Cercidium*) of the pea family that grows along watercourses in the warm desert areas of America. [19th C.: from L. Amer. Sp., lit. 'green tree.']

palp /palp/ ▶ **n.** another term for PALPUS. [19th C.: from L. *palpus*, lit. 'feeler.']

pal·pa·ble /'palpəbəl/ ▶ **adj.** able to be touched or felt. ■ (esp. of a feeling or atmosphere) so intense as to be almost touched or felt. ■ clear to the mind or plain to see. — **pal·pa·bil·i·ty** /,palpə'bilitē/ **n.** **pal·pa·bly adv.** [ME: from late L. *palpabilis*, from L. *palpare* 'feel, touch gently.']

pal·pate /'pal,pāt/ ▶ **v.** [trans.] examine (a part of the body) by touch, esp. for medical purposes. — **pal·pa·tion** /pal'pāshən/ **n.** [19th C.: from L. *palpat-* 'touched gently,' from the v. *palpare*.]

pal·pe·bral /'palpəbrəl; pal'pē-/ ▶ **adj.** [attrib.] Anat. of or relating to the eyelids. [19th C.: from late L. *palpebralis*, from L. *palpebra* 'eyelid.']

pal·pi·tate /'palpi,tāt/ ▶ **v.** [intrans.] [often as adj.] (**palpitating**) (of the heart) beat rapidly, strongly, or irregularly. ■ shake; tremble. [17th C.: from L. *palpitat-* 'patted,' from the v. *palpitare*, frequentative of *palpare* 'touch gently.']

pal·pi·ta·tion /,palpi'tāshən/ ▶ **n.** (usu. **palpitations**) a noticeably rapid, strong, or irregular heartbeat due to agitation, exertion, or illness.

pal·pus /'palpəs/ (also **palp**) ▶ **n.** (pl. **pal·pi** /'palpī/ or **palps**) Zool. each of a pair of elongated segmented appendages near the mouth of an arthropod, usually concerned with the senses of touch and taste. — **pal·pal** /-pəl/ **adj.** [19th C.: L., from *palpare* 'to feel.']

pals·grave /'pôlz,grāv; 'palz-/ ▶ **n.** hist. a count palatine. [16th C.: from early mod. Du. *paltsgrave*, from *palts* 'palatinate' + *grave* 'count.']

pal·sy /'pôlzē/ ▶ **n.** (pl. **-sies**) dated paralysis, esp. that which is accompanied by involuntary tremors. ▶ **v.** (**-sies, -sied**) [trans.] (often **be palsied**) affect with paralysis and involuntary tremors. [ME: from OFr. *paralisie*, from an alt. of L. *paralysis*.]

pal·sy-wal·sy /'palzē 'walzē/ ▶ **adj.** informal very friendly or intimate. [1930s: from the n. PAL + -SY, by reduplication.]

pal·try /'pôltrē/ ▶ **adj.** (**pal·tri·er, pal·tri·est**) (of an amount) small or meager. ■ petty; trivial. — **pal·tri·ness n.** [16th C.: appar. based on dial. *pelt* 'trash, esp. rags'; cf. Low Ger. *paltrig* 'ragged.']

pa·lu·dal /pə'lōōdl; 'palyədl/ ▶ **adj.** Ecol. (of a plant, animal, or soil) living or occurring in a marshy habitat. [19th C.: from L. *palus, palud-* 'marsh' + -AL.]

pal·y /'pālē/ ▶ **adj.** Heraldry divided into equal vertical stripes: *paly of six, argent and gules*. [ME: from OFr. *pale* 'divided by stakes,' from *pal* 'pale, stake.']

pal·y·nol·o·gy /,palə'näləjē/ ▶ **n.** the study of pollen grains and other spores, esp. as found in archaeological or geological deposits. — **pal·y·no·log·i·cal** /-nə'läjikəl/ **adj.** **pal·y·nol·o·gist n.** [1940s: from Gk. *palunein* 'sprinkle.']

pam. ▶ **abbr.** pamphlet.

Pa·mir Moun·tains /pə'mi(ə)r/ (also **the Pa·mirs**) a mountain system of central Asia. The highest mountain is Communism Peak in Tajikistan.

Pam·li·co Sound /'pamli,kō/ an inlet of the Atlantic Ocean in eastern North Carolina.

pam·pas /'pampəz; -pəs/ ▶ **n.** [treated as sing. or pl.] large, treeless plains in South America. [18th C.: via Sp. from Quechua *pampa* 'plain.']

pam·pas grass /'pampəs/ ▶ **n.** a tall South American grass (*Cortaderia selloana*) with silky flowering plumes, widely cultivated as an ornamental plant.

pam·per /'pampər/ ▶ **v.** [trans.] indulge with every attention, comfort, and kindness; spoil. [ME: prob. of Low German or Du. origin; compare Ger. dial. *pampfen* 'cram.']

pam·pe·ro /päm'perō/ ▶ **n.** (pl. **-ros**) a strong, cold southwesterly wind in South America, blowing from the Andes across the pampas toward the Atlantic. [18th C.: from Sp. *pampas* 'plain.']

pam·phlet /'pamflit/ ▶ **n.** a small booklet or leaflet containing information about a single subject. ▶ **v.** (**-phlet·ed, -phlet·ing**) [trans.] distribute pamphlets to. [ME: from *Pamphilet*, a name of 12th-cent. L. poem *Pamphilus, seu de Amore*.]

pam·phlet·eer /,pamfli'ti(ə)r/ ▶ **n.** a writer of pamphlets, esp. ones of a political and controversial nature. ▶ **v.** [intrans.] [usu. as n.] (**pamphleteering**) write and issue such pamphlets.

Pam·phyl·i·a /pam'filēə/ an ancient coastal region of southern Asia Minor. — **Pam·phyl·i·an** /pam'filēən/ **adj. & n.**

Pam·plo·na /pam'plōnə; päm-/ a city in northern Spain; pop. 191,000. It is noted for annual running of bulls.

Pan /pan/ Gk. Mythol. a god of flocks and herds, typically represented with the horns, ears, and legs of a goat on a man's body. [prob. 'the feeder.']

pan¹ /pan/ ▶ **n.** **1** a container made of metal and used for cooking food in. ■ an amount of something contained in such a container. ■ a large container used in a technical or manufacturing process for subjecting a material to heat or a mechanical or chemical process. ■ a bowl fitted at either end of a balance, in which items to be weighed are set. ■ another term for STEEL DRUM. ■ a shallow bowl in which gold is separated from gravel and mud by agitation and washing. ■ a hollow in the ground in which water may collect or in which a deposit of salt remains after water has evaporated. ■ a small ice floe. ■ a part of the lock that held the priming in old types of guns. **2** informal a face. **3** a hard stratum of compacted soil. ▶ **v.** (**panned, pan·ning**) [trans.] **1** (often **be panned**) informal criticize (someone or something) severely. **2** wash gravel in a pan to separate out (gold).

– PHRASAL VERBS **pan out** (of gravel) yield gold. ■ turn out well. ■ end up; conclude. — **pan·ful n.** (pl. **-fuls**). [OE *panne*, of West Gmc. origin; or perh. based on L. *patina* 'dish.']

pan² ▶ **v.** (**panned, pan·ning**) [trans.] swing (a video or movie camera) in a horizontal or vertical plane, typically to give a panoramic effect or follow a subject. ■ [intrans.] (of a camera) be swung in such a way. ▶ **n.** a panning movement. [20th C.: abbrev. of PANORAMA.]

pan- ▶ **comb. form** all-inclusive, esp. in relation to the whole of a continent, racial group, religion, etc. [from Gk. *pan*, neut. of *pas* 'all.']

pan·a·ce·a /,panə'sēə/ ▶ **n.** a solution or remedy for all difficulties or diseases. — **pan·a·ce·an** /-'sēən/ **adj.** [16th C.: via L. from Gk. *panakeia*, from *panakēs* 'all-healing,' from *pan* 'all' + *akos* 'remedy.']

pa·nache /pə'nash; -'näsh/ ▶ **n.** **1** flamboyant confidence of style or manner. **2** hist. a tuft or plume of feathers, esp. as a headdress or on a helmet. [16th C.: from Fr., from Ital. *pennacchio*, from late L. *pinnaculum*, dimin. of *pinna* 'feather.']

pa·na·da /pə'nädə; -'nādə/ ▶ **n.** a simple dish consisting of bread boiled to a pulp and flavored. [16th C.: from Sp. and Port., based on L. *panis* 'bread.']

Pan·a·ma /'panə,mä; -,mô/ a country in Central America. *See box on next page.* — **Pan·a·ma·ni·an** /,panə'mānēən/ **adj. & n.**

pan·a·ma /'panə,mä/ (also **panama hat**) ▶ **n.** a wide-brimmed hat of strawlike material, originally made from the leaves of a particular tropical palm tree, worn chiefly by men. [19th C.: named after the country of PANAMA.]

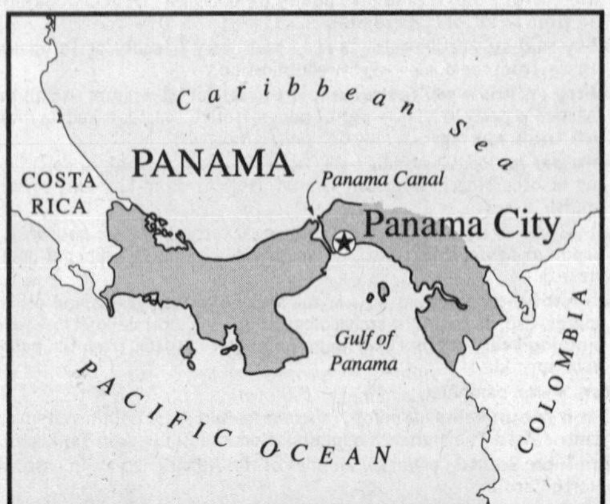

Panama

Official name: Republic of Panama
Location: southeasternmost Central America
Area: 30,200 square miles (78,200 sq km)
Population: 3,000,000
Capital: Panama City
Languages: Spanish (official), English
Currency: balboa, US dollar

Pan·a·ma Ca·nal a canal about 50 miles (80 km) long, across the Isthmus of Panama, that connects the Atlantic and Pacific oceans.

Pan·a·ma Cit·y the capital of Panama, on the Pacific coast close to the Panama Canal; pop. 585,000.

Pan·a·ma, Isth·mus of (formerly the **Isthmus of Darien**) in the narrowest sense, the site of the Panama Canal. More broadly, all of Panama, or the entire region that connects North and South America.

pan-A·mer·i·can /ˌpan əˈmerikən/ ▶ **adj.** of, relating to, or involving all the countries of North and South America.

Pan-American Highway a road system initiated in the 1920s to link nations of the western hemisphere from Alaska to Chile. Gaps remain in Panama and Colombia.

pan-A·mer·i·can·ism ▶ **n.** the principle or advocacy of political or commercial and cultural cooperation among all the countries of North and South America.

Pan·a·mint Range /ˈpanəmint/ a mountain range in east central California, west of Death Valley.

pan-Ar·ab·ism ▶ **n.** the principle or advocacy of political alliance or union of all the Arab states. — **pan-Ar·ab adj.**

pan·a·tel·a /ˌpanəˈtelə/ ▶ **n.** a long thin cigar. [19th C.: from Ital. *panatello* 'small loaf,' dimin. of *panata*.]

Pa·nay /pəˈnī/ an island in the central Philippines.

pan·cake /ˈpanˌkāk/ ▶ **n.** a thin, flat cake of batter, usually fried and turned in a pan. ■ (also **pancake makeup**) makeup consisting of a flat solid layer of compressed powder. ▶ **v. 1** [intrans.] (of an aircraft) make a pancake landing. ■ [trans.] (of a pilot) cause (an aircraft) to make such a landing. **2** informal flatten or become flattened.
– PHRASES **(as) flat as a pancake** completely flat. [ME: from PAN[1] + CAKE.]

pan·cake land·ing ▶ **n.** an emergency landing in which an aircraft levels out close to the ground and drops vertically with its undercarriage still retracted.

pan·cet·ta /panˈCHetə/ ▶ **n.** Italian cured belly of pork. [Ital., dimin. of *pancio* 'belly.']

Pan·chiao /ˈpanˈCHyou/ (also **Pan-ch'iao**; formerly **Pankiao**) a city in northern Taiwan; pop. 544,000.

pan·chro·mat·ic /ˌpankrōˈmatik/ ▶ **adj.** Photog. (of photographic film) sensitive to all visible colors of the spectrum. Often contrasted with ORTHOCHROMATIC.

pan·cre·as /ˈpaNGkrēəs; ˈpankrēəs/ ▶ **n.** (pl. **-cre·as·es**) a large gland behind the stomach that secretes digestive enzymes into the duodenum. Embedded in the pancreas are the islets of Langerhans, which secrete into the blood the hormones insulin and glucagon. — **pan·cre·at·ic** /-krēˈatik/ **adj.** [16th C.: mod. L., from Gk. *pankreas*, from *pan* 'all' + *kreas* 'flesh.']

pan·cre·a·tec·to·my /ˌpaNGkrēəˈtektəmē; ˌpan-/ ▶ **n.** (pl. **-mies**) surgical removal of the pancreas.

pan·cre·at·ic juice /ˌpaNGkrēˈatik; ˌpan-/ ▶ **n.** the clear alkaline digestive fluid secreted by the pancreas.

pan·cre·a·tin /ˈpaNGkrēətn; ˈpan-; ˌpanˈkrēətn/ ▶ **n.** a mixture of enzymes obtained from animal pancreases, given as a medicine to aid digestion.

pan·cre·a·ti·tis /ˌpaNGkrēəˈtītis; ˌpan-/ ▶ **n.** Med. inflammation of the pancreas.

pan·da /ˈpandə/ (also **giant panda**) ▶ **n.** a large bearlike black-and-white mammal (*Ailuropoda melanoleuca*) native to bamboo forests in China. See also RED PANDA. [19th C.: from Nepali.]

pan·da·nus /panˈdānəs; -ˈdanəs/ (also **pan·dan** /ˈpandən/) ▶ **n.** a tropical tree or shrub (genus *Pandanus*, family Pandanaceae) that has a twisted and branched stem, stilt roots, spiral tufts of long, narrow, typically spiny leaves, and fibrous edible fruit. Also called SCREW PINE. ■ fiber from the leaves of this plant, or material woven from this fiber. [mod. L., from Malay *pandan*.]

Pan·da·rus /ˈpandərəs/ Gk. Mythol. a Lycian fighting on the side of the Trojans.

pan·dect /ˈpanˌdekt/ ▶ **n.** esp. hist. a complete body of the laws of a country. ■ (usu. **the Pandects**) a compendium in 50 books of the Roman civil law made by order of Justinian in the 6th century. — **pan·dect·ist** /panˈdektist/ **n.** [16th C.: from Fr. *pandecte*, from L. *pandecta*, from Gk. *pandektēs* 'all-receiver,' from *pan* 'all' + *dektēs* (from *dekhesthai* 'receive').]

pan·dem·ic /panˈdemik/ ▶ **adj.** (of a disease) prevalent over a whole country or the world. ▶ **n.** an outbreak of such a disease. [17th C.: from Gk. *pandēmos* (from *pan* 'all' + *dēmos* 'people') + -IC.]

pan·de·mo·ni·um /ˌpandəˈmōnēəm/ ▶ **n.** wild and noisy disorder or confusion; uproar. [17th C.: mod. L., from PAN- + Gk. *daimōn* 'demon.']

pan·der /ˈpandər/ ▶ **v.** [intrans.] **(pander to)** gratify or indulge (an immoral or distasteful desire, need, or habit or a person with such a desire, etc.). ▶ **n.** dated a pimp. [ME: from *Pandare*, character in Chaucer's *Troilus and Criseyde* (see PANDARUS).]

Pan·dit /ˈpəndit; ˈpan-/, Vijaya Lakshmi (1900–90), Indian politician; sister of Jawaharlal Nehru. She was the first woman to serve as president of the UN General Assembly 1953–54.

pan·dit /ˈpəndit; ˈpan-/ (also **pun·dit**) ▶ **n.** a Hindu scholar learned in Sanskrit and Hindu philosophy and religion, typically also a priest: [as title] *Pandit Misir*. ■ Indian a wise man or teacher. ■ Indian a talented musician (used as a respectful title or form of address).

P & L ▶ **abbr.** profit and loss account.

Pan·do·ra /panˈdôrə/ Gk. Mythol. the first mortal woman. In one story she was created by Zeus and sent to earth with box of evils in revenge for Prometheus' having brought the gift of fire back to the world. Pandora let out the evils from the box to infect the earth; hope alone remained to assuage the lot of humankind. [from the Gk. name *Pandōra* 'all-gifted' (from *pan* 'all' + *dōron* 'gift').]

Pan·do·ra's box ▶ **n.** a process that generates many complicated problems as the result of unwise interference in something.

pan·dow·dy /panˈdoudē/ ▶ **n.** (pl. **-dies**) a kind of spiced apple pie baked in a deep dish. [of unknown origin.]

pane /pān/ ▶ **n.** a single sheet of glass in a window or door. ■ Comput. a separate defined area within a window for the display of, or interaction with, a part of that window's application or output. ■ a sheet or page of postage stamps. [ME: from OFr. *pan*, from L. *pannus* 'piece of cloth.']

pan·e·gyr·ic /ˌpanəˈjirik/ ▶ **n.** a public speech or published text in praise of someone or something. — **pan·e·gyr·i·cal** /-ˈjirikəl/ **adj.** **pan·e·gyr·i·cal·ly** /-ˈjirik(ə)lē/ **adv.** [17th C.: from Fr. *panégyrique*, via L. from Gk. *panēgurikos* 'of public assembly,' from *pan* 'all' + *aguris* 'agora, assembly.']

pan·el /ˈpanl/ ▶ **n. 1** a thin, typically rectangular piece of wood or glass forming or set into the surface of a door, wall, or ceiling. ■ a thin piece of metal forming part of the outer shell of a vehicle. ■ a flat board on which instruments or controls are fixed. ■ a decorated area within a larger design containing a separate subject. ■ one of several drawings making up a comic strip. ■ a piece of material forming part of a garment. **2** a small group of people brought together to discuss, investigate, or decide on a particular matter, esp. in the context of business or government. ■ a list of available jurors or a jury. **3** the soft underside of a saddle, typically of foam or wool. ▶ **v.** (**-eled**, **-el·ing**; Brit. **-elled**, **-el·ling**) [trans.] [usu. as adj.] **(paneled)** cover (a wall or other surface) with panels. [ME: from OFr., lit. 'piece of cloth,' based on L. *pannus* '(piece of) cloth.']

pan·el·ing /ˈpanl-iNG/ (Brit. **pan·el·ling**) ▶ **n.** panels collectively, when used to decorate a wall.

pan·el·ist /ˈpanl-ist/ (Brit. **pan·el·list**) ▶ **n.** a member of a panel, esp. in a formal public discussion.

pan·el stud·y ▶ **n.** an investigation of attitude changes using a constant set of people and comparing each individual's opinions at different times.

pan·el truck ▶ **n.** a small enclosed delivery truck.

pan·en·the·ism /paˈnenTHēˌizəm/ ▶ **n.** the belief or doctrine that God is greater than the universe and includes and interpenetrates it. — **pan·en·the·is·tic** /ˌpanenTHēˈistik/ **adj.**

pan·et·to·ne /ˌpanəˈtōnē/ ▶ **n.** (pl. **-ni** pronunc. same) a rich Italian bread made with eggs, fruit, and butter and typically eaten at Christmas. [Ital., from *panetto* 'cake,' dimin. of *pane* 'bread' (from L. *panis* 'bread').]

pan·fish /ˈpanˌfiSH/ ▶ **n.** (pl. same or **-fish·es**) a fish suitable for frying whole in a pan, esp. one caught by an angler rather than bought. ▶ **v.** [intrans.] [often as n.] **(panfishing)** catch, or try to catch, such fish.

pan-fry ▶ **v.** [trans.] [often as adj.] **(pan-fried)** fry in a pan in a small amount of fat.

pang /paNG/ ▶ **n.** a sudden sharp pain or painful emotion. [15th C.: perh. alt. of PRONG.]

pan·ga /ˈpänGgə/ ▸ **n.** a bladed African tool like a machete. [Kiswahili.]

Pan·gae·a /panˈjēə/ (also **Pan·ge·a**) a vast continental area or supercontinent comprising all the continental crust of the earth, postulated to have existed in late Paleozoic and Mesozoic times before breaking up into Gondwana and Laurasia. [20th C.: from **PAN-** + Gk. *gaia* 'earth.']

Pan·gloss /ˈpanglôs; -gläs/ ▸ **n.** a person who is optimistic regardless of the circumstances. — **Pan·gloss·i·an** /panˈglôsēən; -ˈgläs-/ **adj.** [19th C.: after the name of the tutor and philosopher in Voltaire's *Candide* (1759).]

pan·go·lin /ˈpanGgəlin; paNGˈgōlin/ ▸ **n.** a mammal (family Manidae) of Asia (genus *Manis*) and Africa (genus *Phataginus*) that has a body covered with horny overlapping scales, a small head with elongated snout, a long sticky tongue for catching ants and termites, and a thick, tapering tail. Also called **SCALY ANTEATER.** [18th C.: from Malay *peng-guling*, lit. 'roller' (from its habit of rolling into a ball).]

pan·han·dle /ˈpan,handl/ ▸ **n.** [often in place names] a narrow strip of territory projecting from the main territory of one state into another state: *the Oklahoma Panhandle.* ▸ **v.** [intrans.] informal beg in the street: *she went back to the streets to panhandle for money.* — **pan·han·dler n.**

pan·ic[1] /ˈpanik/ ▸ **n.** sudden uncontrollable fear or anxiety, often causing wildly unthinking behavior. ■ widespread financial or commercial apprehension provoking hasty action. ■ informal a frenzied hurry to do something. ▸ **v.** (**-icked, -ick·ing**) [intrans.] be affected by panic. ■ [trans.] cause to feel panic. — **pan·ick·y adj.** [17th C.: ult. from Gk. *panikos*, after **PAN**, noted for causing terror.]

pan·ic[2] (also **panic grass**) ▸ **n.** any of a number of cereal and fodder grasses (*Panicum* and related genera) related to millet. [ME: from L. *panicum*, from *panus* 'ear of millet,' based on Gk. *pēnos* 'web,' *pēnion* 'bobbin.']

pan·ic at·tack ▸ **n.** a sudden feeling of acute and disabling anxiety.

pan·ic but·ton ▸ **n.** a button for summoning help in an emergency.
– PHRASES **press** (or **push** or **hit**) **the panic button** informal respond to a situation by panicking or taking emergency measures.

pan·ic dis·or·der ▸ **n.** a psychiatric disorder in which debilitating anxiety and fear arise frequently and without reasonable cause.

pan·i·cle /ˈpanikəl/ ▸ **n.** Bot. a loose, branching cluster of flowers, as in oats. — **pan·i·cled adj.** [16th C.: from L. *panicula*, dimin. of *panus* (see **PANIC**[2]).]

pan·ic-strick·en (also **pan·ic-struck**) ▸ **adj.** affected with panic; very frightened.

pa·ni·no /pəˈnēnō/ ▸ **n.** (pl. **-ni** /-nē/) a sandwich, usu. toasted, made with a baguette or with Italian bread. [1950s: from Italian, literally 'bread roll.']

Pan·ja·bi /pənˈjäbē/ ▸ **n.** (pl. **-bis**) **& adj.** var. of **PUNJABI.**

pan·jan·drum /panˈjandrəm/ ▸ **n.** a person who has or claims to have a great deal of authority or influence. [19th C.: from *Grand Panjandrum*, an invented phr. in a nonsense verse (1755) by S. Foote.]

Pank·hurst /ˈpaNGk,hərst/ a family of English social activists. Emmeline (1858–1928) and her daughters Christabel (1880–1958) and Sylvia (1882–1960) founded the Women's Social and Political Union in 1903.

pan·mix·i·a /panˈmiksēə/ ▸ **n.** Zool. random mating within a breeding population. — **pan·mic·tic** /-ˈmiktik/ **adj.** [19th C.: mod. L., from Ger. *Panmixie*, from Gk. *pan* 'all' + *mixis* 'mixing.']

Pan·mun·jom /ˈpanˈmo͝onˈjôm/ a village in the demilitarized zone between North and South Korea.

panne /pan/ (also **panne velvet**) ▸ **n.** a lustrous fabric resembling velvet, made of silk or rayon and having a flattened pile. [18th C.: from Fr.]

pan·nier /ˈpanyər; ˈpanēər/ ▸ **n.** **1** a basket, esp. one of a pair carried by a beast of burden. ■ each of a pair of bags or boxes fitted on either side of the rear wheel of a bicycle or motorcycle. **2** hist. part of a skirt looped up around the hips. ■ a frame supporting this. [ME: from OFr. *panier*, from L. *panarium* 'breadbasket,' from *panis* 'bread.']

pan·nist /ˈpanist/ ▸ **n.** W. Indian a person who plays a pan in a steel band. See **PAN**[1] (sense 1).

Pan·no·ni·a /pəˈnōnēə/ an ancient country of southern Europe, south and west of the Danube River.

pan·o·ply /ˈpanəplē/ ▸ **n.** a complete or impressive collection of things: *their concerns range over the entire panoply of disciplinary functions.* ■ a splendid display. ■ hist. literary a complete set of arms or suit of armor. — **pan·o·plied** /-plēd/ **adj.** [16th C.]

pan·op·tic /paˈnäptik/ ▸ **adj.** showing or seeing the whole at one view. [19th C.: from Gk. *panoptos* 'seen by all,' from *panoptēs* 'all-seeing' + **-IC.**]

pan·op·ti·con /paˈnäpti,kän/ ▸ **n.** hist. a circular prison with cells arranged around a central well, from which prisoners could at all times be observed. [18th C.: from **PAN-** 'all' + Gk. *optikon*, neut. of *optikos* 'optic.']

pan·o·ram·a /,panəˈramə; -ˈrämə/ ▸ **n.** an unbroken view of the whole region surrounding an observer. ■ a picture or photograph containing a wide view. ■ a complete survey or presentation of a subject or sequence of events. — **pan·o·ram·ic** /-ˈramik/ **adj.** **pan·o·ram·i·cal·ly** /-ˈramik(ə)lē/ **adv.** [18th C.: from **PAN-** 'all' + Gk. *horama* 'view' (from *horan* 'see').]

pan-pan /ˈpan ,pan/ ▸ **n.** an international radio distress signal, of less urgency than a Mayday signal. [1920s: *pan* from Fr. *panne* 'breakdown.']

pan·pipes /ˈpan,pīps/ ▸ **plural n.** a musical instrument made from a row of short pipes of varying length fixed together and played by blowing across the top. [**PAN.**]

panpipes

pan·sex·u·al /panˈsekSHo͞oəl/ ▸ **adj.** not limited or inhibited in sexual choice with regard to gender or activity. ▸ **n.** a person who is sexually inclusive in this way. — **pan·sex·u·al·i·ty** /-,sekSHo͞oˈalitē/ **n.**

pan·sper·mi·a /panˈspərmēə/ ▸ **n.** the theory that life on the earth originated from microorganisms or chemical precursors of life present in outer space and able to initiate life on reaching a suitable environment. [19th C.: from Gk., from *panspermos* 'containing all kinds of seed.']

pan·sy /ˈpanzē/ ▸ **n.** **1** a popular cultivated viola with flowers in rich colors, esp. the familiar *Viola cornuta.* **2** informal, offens. an effeminate or homosexual man. [ME: from Fr. *pensée* 'thought, pansy,' from *penser* 'think,' from L. *pensare*, frequentative of *pendere* 'weigh, consider.']

pansy

pant /pant/ ▸ **v.** [intrans.] breathe with short, quick breaths, typically from exertion or excitement. ■ [with adverbial of direction] run or go in a specified direction while panting: *they panted up the stairs.* ■ [with direct speech] say something breathlessly: *"We'll never have time," she panted.* ■ long for, or long to do, something: *it makes you pant for more.* ■ literary (of the heart or chest) throb violently from strong emotions. ▸ **n.** a short, quick breath. ■ literary a throb or heave of a person's heart or chest. — **pant·ing·ly adv.** [ME: rel. to OFr. *pantaisier* 'be agitated, gasp,' based on Gk. *phantasioun* 'cause to imagine,' from *phantasia* (see **FANTASY**).]

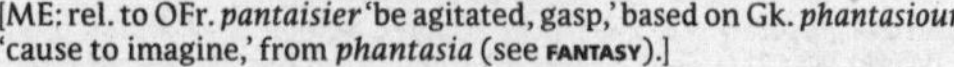

pan·ta·lets /,pantlˈets/ (also **pan·ta·lettes**) ▸ **plural n.** long underpants with a frill at the bottom of each leg, worn by women and girls in the 19th century.

pan·ta·loon /,pantlˈo͞on/ ▸ **n.** **1** (**pantaloons**) women's baggy trousers gathered at the ankles. ■ hist. men's close-fitting breeches fastened below the calf or at the foot. ■ informal pants. **2** (**Pantaloon**) a Venetian character in Italian commedia dell'arte represented as a foolish old man wearing pantaloons. [16th C. (sense 2): from Fr. *pantalon*, from Ital. *Pantalone* (see sense 2).]

pan·the·ism /ˈpanTHē,izəm/ ▸ **n.** a doctrine that identifies God with the universe, or regards the universe as a manifestation of God. — **pan·the·ist n.** **pan·the·is·tic** /,panTHēˈistik/ **adj.** **pan·the·is·ti·cal** /,panTHēˈistikəl/ **adj.** **pan·the·is·ti·cal·ly** /,panTHēˈistik(ə)lē/ **adv.** [18th C.: from **PAN-** + Gk. *theos* 'god.']

pan·the·on /ˈpanTHē,än; -THēən/ ▸ **n.** all the gods of a people or religion collectively. ■ (also **Pantheon**) (esp. in ancient Greece and Rome) a temple dedicated to all the gods. ■ a building in which the illustrious dead of a nation are buried or honored. ■ a group of particularly respected, famous, or important people. [ME: via L. from Gk. *pantheion*, from *pan* 'all' + *theion* 'holy' (from *theos* 'god').]

pan·ther /ˈpanTHər/ ▸ **n.** a leopard, esp. a black one. ■ a cougar. [ME: from OFr. *pantere*, from L. *panthera*, from Gk. *panthēr*.]

pant·ies /ˈpantēz/ ▸ **plural n.** informal legless underpants worn by women and girls.

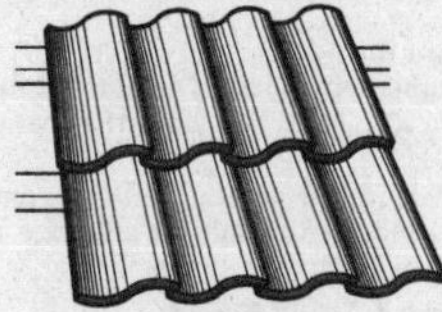

pantile

pan·tile /ˈpan,tīl/ ▸ **n.** a roof tile curved to form an S-shaped section, fitted to overlap its neighbor. — **pan·tiled adj.** [17th C.: from **PAN**[1] + **TILE.**]

panto- ▸ **comb. form** all; universal: *pantograph* | *pantomime.* [from Gk. *pas*, *pant-* 'all.']

pan·to·graph /ˈpantə,graf/ ▸ **n.** **1** an instrument for copying a drawing or plan on a different scale by a system of hinged and jointed rods. **2** a jointed framework conveying a current to a train, streetcar, or other electric vehicle from overhead wires. — **pan·to·graph·ic** /,pantəˈgrafik/ **adj.** [18th C.: from **PANTO-** + Gk. *-graphos* 'writing.']

pan·to·mime /ˈpantə,mīm/ ▸ **n.** a dramatic entertainment, originating in Roman mime, in which performers express meaning through gestures accompanied by music. ■ an absurdly exaggerated piece of behavior. ▪ informal a ridiculous or confused situation or event. ▶ **v.** [trans.] express or represent (something) by extravagant and exaggerated mime. — **pan·to·mim·ic** /ˌpantəˈmimik/ **adj.** **pan·to·mim·ist** **n.** [16th C.: from Gk. *pantomimos* 'imitator of all' (see PANTO-, MIME).]

Pan·tone /ˈpanˌtōn/ ▶ **n.** [usu. as adj.] trademark a system for matching colors, used in specifying printing inks.

pan·to·then·ic ac·id /ˌpantəˈTHenik/ ▶ **n.** Biochem. a vitamin of the B complex, found in rice, bran, and many other foods, and essential for the oxidation of fats and carbohydrates. — **pan·to·then·ate** /panˈtäTHənāt/ **n.** [1930s: from Gk. *pantothen* 'from every side.']

pan·try /ˈpantrē/ ▶ **n.** (pl. **-tries**) a small room or closet in which food, dishes, and utensils are kept. [ME: from Anglo-Norman Fr. *panterie*, from *paneter* 'baker,' based on late L. *panarius* 'bread seller,' from L. *panis* 'bread.']

pan·try·man /ˈpantrēmən/ ▶ **n.** (pl. **-men**) a butler or a butler's assistant.

pants /pants/ ▶ **plural n.** trousers.
– PHRASES **catch someone with their pants down** informal catch someone in an embarrassingly unprepared state. **fly** (or **drive**) **by the seat of one's pants** informal rely on instinct rather than logic or knowledge. **scare** (or **bore**, etc.) **the pants off someone** informal make someone extremely scared, bored, etc. **wear the pants** informal be the dominant partner in a relationship. [19th C.: abbrev. of *pantaloons* (see PANTALOON).]

pant·suit /ˈpantˌsōōt/ (also **pants suit**) ▶ **n.** a pair of pants and a matching jacket worn by women.

pant·y gir·dle ▶ **n.** a woman's elasticized undergarment combining girdle and panties.

pant·y·hose /ˈpantēˌhōz/ ▶ **plural n.** women's thin nylon tights.

pant·y raid ▶ **n.** dated a visit by a group of male students to a women's dormitory with the object of seizing panties.

pant·y·waist /ˈpantēˌwāst/ informal ▶ **n.** a feeble or effeminate person. ▶ **adj.** [attrib.] effeminate or feeble.

pan·za·nel·la /ˌpanzəˈnelə; ˌpansə-/ ▶ **n.** a type of Tuscan salad made with anchovies, chopped salad vegetables, and bread soaked in dressing. [Ital., from *pane* 'bread' + *zanella* 'small basket.']

pan·zer /ˈpanzər/ ▶ **n.** a German armored vehicle, esp. a tank used in World War II: [as adj.] *panzer divisions.* [from Ger. *Panzer*, lit. 'coat of mail.']

pap /pap/ ▶ **n.** often derog. bland soft or semiliquid food such as that suitable for babies or invalids. ▪ derog. reading matter or entertainment that is worthless or lacking in substance. [ME: probably from Mid. Low Ger., MDu. *pappe*, prob. based on L. *pappare* 'eat.']

pa·pa /ˈpäpə/ ▶ **n.** **1** one's father. **2** a code word representing the letter P, used in radio communication. [17th C.: from Fr., via late L. from Gk. *papas.*]

pa·pa·cy /ˈpāpəsē/ ▶ **n.** (pl. **-cies**) (usu. **the papacy**) the office or authority of the pope. ▪ the tenure of office of a pope. [ME: from med. L. *papatia*, from *papa* 'pope.']

Pap·a·go /ˈpapəˌgō; ˈpä-/ ▶ **n.** (pl. same or **-gos**) **1** a member of an American Indian people of southern Arizona and northern Sonora. **2** a dialect of the Uto-Aztecan Pima-Papago language. ▶ **adj.** of or relating to this people or their language. [via Sp. from an abbrev. of the Papago self-designation *bábawĭ'-o'odham.*]

pa·pa·in /pəˈpā-in; -ˈpī-/ ▶ **n.** a protein-digesting enzyme obtained from unripe papaya fruit, used to tenderize meat and as a food supplement to aid digestion. [19th C.: from PAPAYA + -IN[1].]

pa·pal /ˈpāpəl/ ▶ **adj.** of or relating to a pope or to the papacy. — **pa·pal·ist** /-ist/ **n. & adj.** **pa·pal·ly** **adv.** [ME: from OFr., from med. L. *papalis*, from eccles. L. *papa* 'bishop (of Rome).']

pa·pal in·fal·li·bil·i·ty ▶ **n.** see INFALLIBILITY.

Pa·pal States hist. the temporal dominions belonging to the pope, esp. in central Italy.

pa·pa·raz·zo /ˌpäpəˈrätsō/ ▶ **n.** (pl. **-raz·zi** /-ˈrätsē/) (usu. **paparazzi**) a freelance photographer who pursues celebrities to get photographs of them. [20th C.: from Ital., from the name of a character in Fellini's film *La Dolce Vita* (1960).]

pa·pav·er·ine /pəˈpavəˌrēn; -rin/ ▶ **n.** Chem. a compound, $C_{20}H_{21}NO_4$, present in opium used medicinally to alleviate muscle spasms and asthma. [19th C.: from L. *papaver* 'poppy.']

pa·paw /pəˈpô; ˈpôˌpô/ ▶ **n.** var. of PAWPAW.

pa·pa·ya /pəˈpīə/ ▶ **n.** **1** a tropical fruit shaped like an elongated melon, with edible orange flesh and small black seeds. Also called PAPAW or PAWPAW. **2** (also **papaya tree**) the fast-growing tree (*Carica papaya*, family Caricaceae) that bears this fruit, native to warm regions of America. [16th C.: from Sp. and Port. (see PAWPAW).]

Pa·pe·e·te /pəˈpētē; ˌpäpēˈātā/ the capital of French Polynesia, northwestern Tahiti; pop. 24,000.

pa·per /ˈpāpər/ ▶ **n.** **1** material manufactured in thin sheets from the pulp of wood or other fibrous substances, used for writing, drawing, or printing on, or as wrapping material. ▪ a newspaper. ▪ wallpaper. ▪ (usu. **papers**) a piece or sheet of paper with something written or drawn on it. ▪ (**papers**) significant or important documents belonging to a person. ▪ [as adj.] denoting something that is officially documented but has no real existence or little merit or use: *a paper profit.* ▪ a government report or policy document. ▪ (**papers**) documents attesting identity; credentials. ▪ a piece of paper used for wrapping or enclosing something or made into a packet. ▪ short for COMMERCIAL PAPER. **2** an essay or thesis, esp. one read at an academic lecture or seminar or published in an academic journal. **3** informal free passes of admission to a theater or other entertainment. ▶ **v.** [trans.] **1** (often **be papered**) apply wallpaper to (a wall or room). ▪ [intrans.] (**paper over**) cover (a hole or blemish) with wallpaper. ▪ (**paper over**) disguise (an awkward problem) instead of resolving it. **2** informal fill (a theater) by giving out free tickets.
– PHRASES **be not worth the paper it is written on** be of no value or validity whatsoever despite having been written down. **make the papers** be written about in newspapers and thus become famous or notorious. **on paper** in writing. ▪ in theory rather than in reality. — **pa·per·er** **n.** [ME: from Anglo-Norman Fr. *papir*, from L. *papyrus* 'paper reed' (see PAPYRUS).]

pa·per·back /ˈpāpərˌbak/ ▶ **adj.** (of a book) bound in stiff paper or flexible cardboard. ▶ **n.** a book bound in stiff paper or flexible cardboard.
– PHRASES **in paperback** in an edition bound in stiff paper or flexible cardboard.

pa·per birch (also **pa·per·bark birch**) ▶ **n.** a North American birch (*Betula papyrifera*) with large leaves and peeling white bark.

pa·per·board /ˈpāpərˌbôrd/ ▶ **n.** cardboard or pasteboard.

pa·per·boy /ˈpāpərˌboi/ ▶ **n.** a boy who delivers newspapers to people's homes.

pa·per chase ▶ **n.** **1** informal the action of processing forms and other paperwork, esp. when considered excessive. **2** informal the attempt to gain academic qualifications, esp. a law degree.

pa·per clip ▶ **n.** a piece of bent wire or plastic used for holding several sheets of paper together.

pa·per feed ▶ **n.** a device for inserting sheets of paper into a printer, typewriter, or similar machine.

pa·per·girl /ˈpāpərˌgərl/ ▶ **n.** a girl who delivers newspapers to people's homes.

pa·per·hang·er /ˈpāpərˌhaNGər/ ▶ **n.** a person who decorates with wallpaper, esp. professionally.

pa·per knife ▶ **n.** (pl. **pa·per knives**) a blunt knife used for cutting paper, such as when opening envelopes or slitting the uncut pages of books.

pa·per mon·ey ▶ **n.** money in the form of banknotes.

pa·per mul·ber·ry ▶ **n.** a small tree (*Broussonetia papyrifera*) of the mulberry family, the inner bark of which is used for making paper and tapa cloth, occurring from eastern Asia to Polynesia.

pa·per nau·ti·lus ▶ **n.** another term for ARGONAUT.

pa·per·push·er ▶ **n.** informal a bureaucrat or menial clerical worker. — **pa·per·push·ing** **n. & adj.**

pa·per route (Brit. **paper round**) ▶ **n.** a job of regularly delivering newspapers. ▪ a route taken doing this.

pa·per tape ▶ **n.** paper in the form of a long narrow strip. ▪ such tape having holes punched in it, used in older computer systems for conveying data or instructions.

pa·per ti·ger ▶ **n.** a person or thing that appears threatening but is ineffectual.

pa·per trail ▶ **n.** the total amount of written evidence of someone's activities.

pa·per-train ▶ **v.** [trans.] train a dog to defecate and urinate on paper placed on the floor.

paper wasp

pa·per wasp ▶ **n.** a social wasp (genus *Polistes*) that forms a small, umbrella-shaped nest made from wood pulp.

pa·per·weight /ˈpāpərˌwāt/ ▶ **n.** a small, heavy object for keeping loose papers in place.

pa·per·work /ˈpāpərˌwərk/ ▶ **n.** routine work involving written documents such as forms, records, or letters. ▪ such written documents.

pa·per·y /ˈpāpərē/ ▶ **adj.** thin and dry like paper: *wrapped in layers of papery pastry.*

Pa·pia·men·tu /ˌpäpyəˈmentōō/ (also **Pa·pia·men·to** /-tō/) ▶ **n.** a Spanish Creole language with admixtures of Portuguese and Dutch, spoken on the Caribbean islands of Aruba, Bonaire, and Curaçao. [from Sp. *Papiamento.*]

pa·pier col·lé /päpˈyā kōˈlā/ ▶ **n.** (pl. **pa·piers col·lés** pronunc. same) the technique of using paper for collage. ▪ a collage made from paper. [Fr., lit. 'glued paper.']

pa·pier mâ·ché /ˌpāpər məˈSHā; päˈp(y)ā/ ▶ **n.** a malleable mixture of paper and glue, or paper, flour, and water, that becomes hard when dry. [Fr., lit. 'chewed paper.']

pa·pil·i·o·na·ceous /pəˌpilēəˈnāSHəs/ ▶ **adj.** Bot. of, relating to, or denoting leguminous plants of a group (subfamily Papilionoideae or family Papilionaceae) with flowers that resemble a butterfly. [17th C.: from mod. L. *Papilionaceae* (pl.), based on L. *papilio* 'butterfly.']

pa·pil·la /pə'pilə/ ▸ **n.** (pl. **-pil·lae** /-'pil,ē; -'pil,ī/) a small rounded protuberance on a part of the body. ■ a small fleshy projection on a plant. — **pap·il·lar·y** /'papə,lerē/ **adj.** **pap·il·late** /'papə,lāt; pə'pilit/ **adj.** **pap·il·lose** /'päpə,lōs; -,lōz/ **adj.** [17th C.: from L., lit. 'nipple,' dimin. of *papula* 'small protuberance.']

pap·il·lo·ma /,papə'lōmə/ ▸ **n.** (pl. **-mas** or **-ma·ta** /-mətə/) Med. a wartlike growth on the skin or on a mucous membrane, derived from the epidermis and usually benign. [19th C.: from PAPILLA + -OMA.]

pap·il·lon /,päpē'yôn/ ▸ **n.** a dog of a toy breed with ears suggesting the form of a butterfly. [20th C.: from Fr., lit. 'butterfly,' from L. *papilio(n-)*.]

pa·pist /'pāpist/ esp. derog. ▸ **n.** a Roman Catholic. ▸ **adj.** of, relating to, or associated with the Roman Catholic Church. — **pa·pism** /-,pizəm/ **n.** **pa·pist·ry** **n.** [16th C.: from Fr. *papiste* or mod. L. *papista*, from eccles. L. *papa* 'bishop (of Rome).']

pa·poose /pa'pōōs; pə-/ ▸ **n.** **1** dated, offens. a young North American Indian child. **2** a type of bag used to carry a child on one's back. [17th C.: from Narragansett *papoos*.]

Papp /pap/, Joseph (1921–91), US producer and director; born *Joseph Papirofsky*. In 1954, he founded the Shakespearean Theatre Workshop, which became the New York Shakespeare Festival in 1960.

pap·par·del·le /,papär'delā/ ▸ **n.** pasta in the form of broad flat ribbons, usually served with a meat sauce. [Ital., from *pappare* 'eat hungrily.']

pap·pus /'papəs/ ▸ **n.** (pl. **pap·pi** /'pa,pī; -,pē/) Bot. the tuft of hairs on each seed of thistles, dandelions, and similar plants that assists dispersal by the wind. — **pap·pose** /'pa,pōs; 'pa,pōz/ **adj.** [18th C.: via L. from Gk. *pappos*.]

pap·py¹ /'papē/ ▸ **n.** (pl. **-pies**) [usu. as name] a child's word for father. [18th C.: from PAPA + -Y².]

pap·py² ▸ **adj.** of the nature of pap; soft and bland.

pap·ri·ka /pə'prēkə; pa-/ ▸ **n.** a powdered spice with a deep orange-red color and a mildly pungent flavor, made from the dried and ground fruits of certain varieties of sweet pepper. ■ a deep orange-red color like that of paprika. [19th C.: from Hungarian.]

Pap test /pap/ ▸ **n.** a test to detect cancer of the cervix or uterus, using a specimen of cellular material from the neck of the uterus spread on a microscope slide (**Pap smear**). [1960s: named after George N. *Papanicolaou* (1883–1962), Gk.-born Amer. scientist.]

Pap·u·a /'päpōōə; 'papyōōə/ **1** the southeastern part of New Guinea, now part of Papua New Guinea. **2** a province in eastern Indonesia on the western half of New Guinea and adjacent small islands; capital, Jayapura. Former name (1973-2002) IRIAN JAYA.

Pap·u·an /'päpōōən; 'papyōōən/ ▸ **n.** **1** a native or inhabitant of Papua, or of Papua New Guinea. **2** a heterogeneous group of around 750 languages spoken in Papua New Guinea and neighboring islands. ▸ **adj.** of or relating to Papua, its people, or languages.

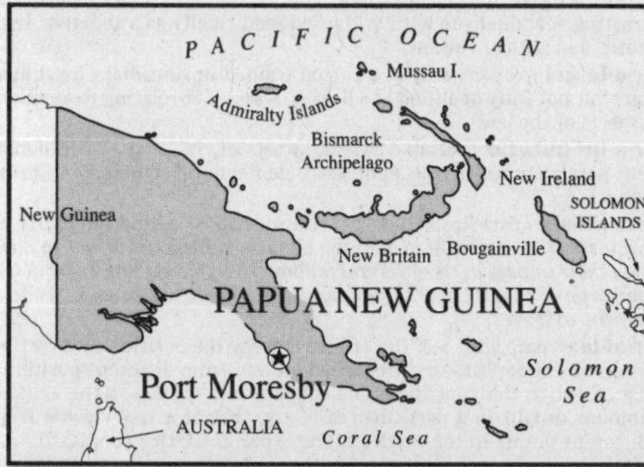

Papua New Guinea

Official name: Independent State of Papua New Guinea
Location: western Pacific Ocean, including the eastern half of the island of New Guinea as well as some neighboring islands
Area: 178,700 square miles (462,800 sq km)
Population: 5,420,000
Capital: Port Moresby
Languages: English (official), Tok Pisin, several hundred native Austronesian and Papuan languages
Currency: kina

Pap·u·a New Guin·ea a country in the western Pacific Ocean. *See box.* — **Pap·u·a New Guin·e·an** **adj.** & **n.**

pap·ule /'pap,yōōl/ (also **pap·u·la** /-yələ/) ▸ **n.** (pl. **-ules** or **-u·lae** /-yə,lē/) Med. a small, raised, solid pimple or swelling, often forming part of a rash on the skin and typically inflamed. — **pap·u·lar** /-yələr/ **adj.** **pap·u·lose** /-yəlōs; -lōz/ **adj.** **pap·u·lous** /-yələs/ **adj.** [18th C.: from L. *papula*.]

pap·y·rol·o·gy /,papə'räləjē/ ▸ **n.** the branch of study that deals with ancient papyri. — **pa·py·ro·log·i·cal** /pə,pīrə'läjikəl; -pi(ə)rə-/ **adj.** **pap·y·rol·o·gist** /,papə'räləjəst/ **n.**

pa·py·rus /pə'pīrəs/ ▸ **n.** (pl. **-py·ri** /-'pīrī/ or **-py·rus·es**) **1** a material prepared in ancient Egypt from the pithy stem of a water plant, used in sheets throughout the ancient Mediterranean world for writing or painting on and also for making rope, sandals, and boats. ■ a document written on papyrus. **2** the tall aquatic sedge (*Cyperus papyrus*) from which this material is obtained, native to central Africa and the Nile valley. [ME (sense 2): via L. from Gk. *papuros*.]

par¹ /pär/ ▸ **n.** **1** Golf the number of strokes a first-class player should normally require for a particular hole or course. ■ a score of this number of strokes at a hole. **2** Stock Market the face value of a stock or other security, as distinct from its market value. ■ (also **par of exchange**) the recognized value of one country's currency in terms of another's. ▸ **v.** (**parred**, **par·ring**) [trans.] Golf play (a hole) in par.
– PHRASES **above** (or **below** or **under**) **par** better (or worse) than is usual or expected. **on a par with** equal in importance or quality to; on an equal level with. **par for the course** what is normal or expected in any given circumstances. **up to par** at an expected or usual level or quality. [16th C.: from L., 'equal,' 'equality.']

par² /par/ ▸ **n.** informal a paragraph.

par. (also **para.**) ▸ **abbr.** paragraph.

par- ▸ **comb. form** var. of PARA-¹ shortened before a vowel or *h* (as in *paraldehyde, parody, parhelion*).

par·a¹ /'parə/ informal ▸ **n.** **1** a paratrooper. **2** a paragraph.

par·a² /'pärə/ ▸ **n.** (pl. same or **par·as**) a monetary unit of Bosnia–Herzegovina, Montenegro, and Serbia, equal to one hundredth of a dinar. [Turk., from Pers. *pāra* 'piece, portion.']

para-¹ (also **par-**) ▸ **prefix** **1** beside; adjacent to: *parameter* | *parataxis*. ■ Med. denoting a disordered function or faculty: *paresthesia*. ■ distinct from, but analogous to: *paramilitary*. ■ beyond: *paradox* | *paranormal*. ■ subsidiary; assisting: *paramedic*. **2** Chem. denoting substitution at diametrically opposite carbon atoms in a benzene ring, e.g., in 1, 4 positions: *paradichlorobenzene*. Compare with META- and ORTHO-. [from Gk. *para* 'beside.']

para-² ▸ **comb. form** denoting something that protects or wards off: *parachute* | *parasol*. [from Fr., from the Ital. imper. sing. of *parare* 'defend']

par·a·a·mi·no·ben·zo·ic ac·id /'parə ə,mēnōben'zōik/ (abbr.: **PABA**) ▸ **n.** Biochem. a crystalline acid, $NH_2C_6H_4COOH$, that is widely distributed in plant and animal tissue. It has been used to treat rickettsial infections and is used in sunscreens to absorb ultraviolet light.

par·a·bi·o·sis /,parəbī'ōsis/ ▸ **n.** Biol. the anatomical joining of two individuals, esp. artificially in physiological research. — **par·a·bi·ot·ic** /-'ätik/ **adj.** [20th C.: mod. L., from PARA-¹ 'beside, ' + Gk. *biōsis* 'mode of life' (from *bios* 'life').]

par·a·ble /'parəbəl/ ▸ **n.** a simple story used to illustrate a moral or spiritual lesson, as told by Jesus in the Gospels. [ME: from OFr. *parabole*, from L. *parabola* 'comparison,' from Gk. *parabolē* (see PARABOLA).]

pa·rab·o·la /pə'rabələ/ ▸ **n.** (pl. **-las** or **-lae** /-lē/) a symmetrical open plane curve formed by the intersection of a cone with a plane parallel to its side. The path of a projectile under the influence of gravity follows a curve of this shape. [16th C.: mod. L., from Gk. *parabolē* 'placing side by side,' from *para-* + *bolē* 'a throw'.]

par·a·bol·ic /,parə'bälik/ ▸ **adj.** **1** of or like a parabola or part of one. **2** of or expressed in parables. — **par·a·bol·i·cal** **adj.** **par·a·bol·i·cal·ly** **adv.**

pa·rab·o·loid /pə'rabə,loid/ ▸ **n.** **1** (also **paraboloid of revolution**) a solid generated by the rotation of a parabola around its axis of symmetry. **2** a solid having two or more nonparallel parabolic cross sections. — **pa·rab·o·loi·dal** /pə,rabə'loidl/ **adj.**

Pa·ra·cel Is·lands /,parə'sel/ (also **the Pa·ra·cels**) a group of about 130 small, barren coral islands and reefs in the South China Sea.

Par·a·cel·sus /,parə'selsəs/ (*c.*1493–1541), Swiss physician: born *Theophrastus Phillipus Aureolus Bombastus von Hohenheim*. His approach to medicine and philosophy was based on observation and experience.

par·a·cen·te·sis /,parəsen'tēsis/ ▸ **n.** (pl. **-ses** /-,sēz/) Med. the perforation of a cavity of the body or of a cyst or similar outgrowth, esp. with a hollow needle to remove fluid or gas. [16th C.: via L. from Gk. *parakentēsis*, from *parakentein* 'pierce at the side.']

par·a·chute /'parə,shōōt/ ▸ **n.** a cloth canopy that fills with air and allows a person or heavy object attached to it to descend slowly when dropped from an aircraft, or that is released from the rear of an aircraft on landing to act as a brake. ▸ **v.** drop or cause to drop from an aircraft by parachute. — **par·a·chut·ist** /-ist/ **n.** [18th C.: from Fr. *para-* 'protection against' + *chute* 'fall.']

parachute

Par·a·clete /'parə,klēt/ ▸ **n.** (in Christian theology) the Holy Spirit as advocate or counselor (John 14:16, 26). [via late L. from Gk. *paraklētos* 'called in aid,' from *para-* + *klētos* (from *kalein* 'to call').]

pa·rade /pə'rād/ ▸ **n.** **1** a public procession, esp.

one celebrating a special day or event and including marching bands and floats. ■ a formal march or gathering of troops for inspection or display. ■ a series of people or things appearing or being displayed one after the other. ■ a distasteful manifestation of a particular quality or kind of behavior. **2** a place where troops gather for parade; a parade ground. ▶ **v.** [intrans.] walk or march in public in a formal procession or in an ostentatious or attention-seeking way. ■ [trans.] walk or march in such a way along (the streets of a town): *men were parading the streets.* ■ [trans.] display (someone or something) while marching or moving around a place: *guards paraded him through the streets.* ■ [trans.] display (something) publicly in order to impress or attract attention: *he paraded his knowledge.* ■ (**parade as**) appear falsely as; masquerade as: *these untruths parading as history.* ■ (of troops) assemble for a formal inspection or ceremonial occasion: *recruits were due to parade that day.*
– PHRASES **on parade** taking part in a parade. ■ on public display. — **pa·rad·er n.** [17th C.: from Fr., lit. 'a showing,' based on L. *parare* 'prepare, furnish.']

par·a·did·dle /'parə,didl/ ▶ **n.** Music one of the basic patterns (rudiments) of drumming, consisting of four even strokes played in the order left-right-left-left or right-left-right-right. [1920s: imitative.]

par·a·digm /'parə,dīm/ ▶ **n. 1** tech. a typical example or pattern of something; a model. ■ a worldview underlying the theories and methodology of a particular scientific subject. **2** a set of linguistic items that form mutually exclusive choices in particular syntactic roles: *English determiners form a paradigm: we can say "a book" or "his book" but not "a his book."* ■ (in the traditional grammar of Latin, Greek, and other inflected languages) a table of all the inflected forms of a particular verb, noun, or adjective, serving as a model for other words of the same conjugation or declension. — **par·a·dig·mat·ic** /,parədig'matik/ **adj.** **par·a·dig·mat·i·cal·ly** /-(ə)lē/ **adv.** [15th C.: via late L. from Gk. *paradeigma*, from *paradeiknunai* 'show side by side,' from *para-* 'beside' + *deiknunai* 'to show.']

Par·a·dise /'parə,dīs/ a community in southeastern Nevada; pop. 124,682.

par·a·dise /'parə,dīs/ ▶ **n.** (in some religions) heaven as the ultimate abode of the just. ■ (**Paradise**) the abode of Adam and Eve before the Fall in the biblical account of the Creation; the Garden of Eden. ■ an ideal or idyllic place or state. — **par·a·dis·al** /,parə'dīsəl/ **adj.** **par·a·di·si·a·cal** /,parədi'sīəkəl/ (also **par·a·di·sa·i·cal** /,parədi'sā-ikəl/ or **par·a·di·si·cal** /,parə'dīsikəl/) **adj.** [ME: from OFr. *paradis*, ult. from Gk. *paradeisos* 'royal park,' from Avestan *pairidaēza* 'enclosure, park.']

pa·ra·dor /'parə,dôr/ ▶ **n.** (pl. **pa·ra·dors** or **pa·ra·do·res** /,parə'dôres/) a hotel in Spain owned and administered by the Spanish government.

par·a·dos /'parə,däs/ ▶ **n.** an elevation of earth behind a fortified place as a protection against attack from the rear, esp. a mound along the back of a trench. [19th C.: from Fr., from *para-* 'protection against' + *dos* 'back' (from L. *dorsum*).]

par·a·dox /'parə,däks/ ▶ **n.** a statement or proposition that, despite sound (or apparently sound) reasoning from acceptable premises, leads to a conclusion that seems senseless, logically unacceptable, or self-contradictory. ■ a seemingly absurd or self-contradictory statement or proposition that when investigated or explained may prove to be well founded or true. ■ a situation, person, or thing that combines contradictory features or qualities. [16th C.: via late L. from Gk. *paradoxon* 'contrary (opinion),' neut. adj., from *para-* 'distinct from' + *doxa* 'opinion.']

par·a·dox·i·cal /,parə'däksikəl/ ▶ **adj.** seemingly absurd or self-contradictory. — **par·a·dox·i·cal·ly adv.** [sentence adverb] *paradoxically, the more fuel a star starts off with, the sooner it runs out.*

par·a·drop /'parə,dräp/ ▶ **n.** a descent or delivery by parachute. ▶ **v.** (**-dropped, -drop·ping**) [trans.] drop (someone or something) by parachute. — **par·a·drop·per n.**

par·aes·the·sia ▶ **n.** British spelling of PARESTHESIA.

par·af·fin /'parəfin/ ▶ **n.** (also **paraffin wax**) a flammable, whitish, translucent, waxy solid consisting of a mixture of saturated hydrocarbons, obtained by distillation from petroleum or shale and used in candles, cosmetics, polishes, and sealing and waterproofing compounds. [19th C.: from Ger., from L. *parum* 'little' + *affinis* 'rel.' (from its low reactivity).]

par·a·gen·e·sis /,parə'jenəsis/ ▶ **n.** (pl. **-ses**) /-,sēz/ Geol. a set of minerals that were formed together, esp. in a rock, or with a specified mineral. — **par·a·ge·net·ic** /-jə'netik/ **adj.**

par·a·glid·ing /'parə,glīdiNG/ ▶ **n.** a sport in which a wide canopy resembling a parachute is attached to a person's body by a harness in order to allow them to glide through the air after jumping from or being lifted to a height. — **par·a·glide** /-,glīd/ **v.** **par·a·glid·er n.**

par·a·gon /'parə,gän; -gən/ ▶ **n.** a person or thing regarded as a perfect example of a particular quality. ■ a person or thing viewed as a model of excellence. ■ a perfect diamond of 100 carats or more. [16th C.: from obs. Fr., from Ital. *paragone* 'touchstone,' from med. Gk. *parakonē* 'whetstone.']

par·a·graph /'parə,graf/ ▶ **n.** a distinct section of a piece of writing, usually dealing with a single theme and indicated by a new line, indentation, or numbering. ▶ **v.** [trans.] arrange (a piece of writing) in paragraphs. — **par·a·graph·ic** /,parə'grafik/ **adj.** [15th C.: ult. from Gk. *paragraphos* 'short stroke,' from *para-* 'beside' + *graphein* 'write.']

par·a·graph mark (also **paragraph symbol**) ▶ **n.** a symbol (usually ¶) used in printed text to mark a new paragraph or as a reference mark.

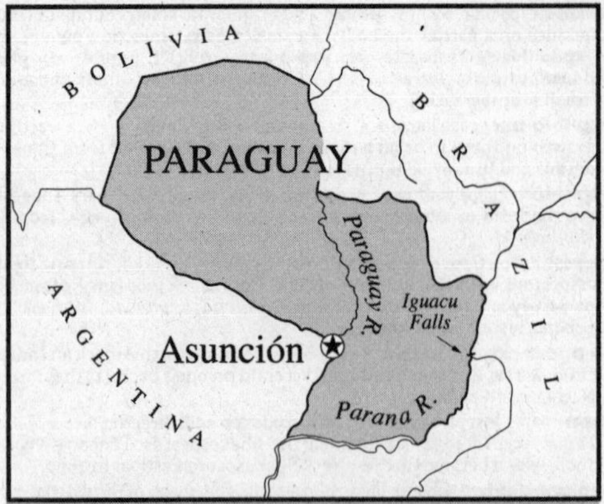

Paraguay

Official name: Republic of Paraguay
Location: central South America
Area: 157,100 square miles (406,800 sq km)
Population: 6,191,000
Capital: Asunción
Languages: Spanish, Guarani (both official)
Currency: guarani

Par·a·guay /'parə,gwī; -,gwā/ a landlocked country in central South America. *See box.* — **Par·a·guay·an** /,parə'gwīən; -'gwā-/ **adj. & n.**

Par·a·guay Riv·er a river that flows from western Brazil to the Paraná River in Paraguay.

par·a·in·flu·en·za /,parə,inflōō'enzə/ ▶ **n.** Med. a disease caused by any of a group of viruses that resemble the influenza viruses.

par·a·keet /'parə,kēt/ ▶ **n.** a small parrot (*Psittacula, Cyanoramphus*, and other genera) with predominantly green plumage and a long tail. [16th C.: from OFr. *paroquet*, Ital. *parrocchetto*, Sp. *periquito*; perh. based on a dimin., 'little wig.']

par·a·lan·guage /'parə,laNGgwij/ ▶ **n.** the nonlexical component of communication by speech, for example intonation, pitch and speed of speaking, hesitation noises, gesture, and facial expression.

par·al·de·hyde /pə'raldə,hīd/ ▶ **n.** Chem. a liquid, CH_3CHO, made by treating acetaldehyde with acid, used medicinally as a sedative, hypnotic, and anticonvulsant.

par·a·le·gal /,parə'lēgəl/ ▶ **n.** a person trained in subsidiary legal matters but not fully qualified as a lawyer. ▶ **adj.** of or relating to auxiliary aspects of the law.

par·a·lin·guis·tic /,paraliNG'gwistik/ ▶ **adj.** of, relating to, or denoting paralanguage or the nonlexical elements of communication by speech.

par·a·lip·sis /,parə'lipsis/ ▶ **n.** Rhet. the device of giving emphasis by professing to say little or nothing about a subject, as in *not to mention their unpaid debts of several million.* [16th C.: via late L. from Gk. *paraleipsis* 'passing over,' from *paraleipein* 'omit,' from *para-* 'aside' + *leipein* 'to leave.']

par·al·lax /'parə,laks/ ▶ **n.** the effect whereby the position or direction of an object appears to differ when viewed from different positions, e.g., through the viewfinder and the lens of a camera. ■ the angular amount of this in a particular case, esp. that of a star viewed from different points in the earth's orbit. — **par·al·lac·tic** /,parə'laktik/ **adj.** [16th C.: ult. from Gk. *parallaxis* 'a change,' from *parallassein* 'to alternate,' based on *allassein* 'to exchange' (from *allos* 'other').]

par·al·lel /'parə,lel; -ləl/ ▶ **adj.** (of lines, planes, surfaces, or objects) side by side and having the same distance continuously between them. ■ occurring or existing at the same time or in a similar way; corresponding. ■ Comput. involving the simultaneous performance of operations. ■ of or denoting electrical components or circuits connected to common points at each end, rather than one to another in sequence. The opposite of SERIES. ■ Music containing or denoting successive intervals of the same size in otherwise independent voices: *an answering phrase in parallel thirds.* ■ Gram. characterized by parallelism: *a parallel structure of transitive clauses.* ▶ **n. 1** a person or thing that is similar or analogous to another. ■ a similarity. ■ a comparison. **2** (also **parallel of latitude**) each of the imaginary parallel circles of constant latitude on the earth's surface. ■ a corresponding line on a map. **3** Print. two parallel lines (‖) as a reference mark. ▶ **v.** (**-leled, -lel·ing**) [trans.] (of something extending in a line) be side by side with (something extending in a line), always keeping the same distance: *a gutter that paralleled the road.* ■ be similar or corresponding to (something): *US naval and air superiority was paralleled by Soviet superiority in land-based missile systems.*
– PHRASES **in parallel** occurring at the same time and having some con-

nection. ■ (of electrical components or circuits) connected to common points at each end; not in series. [16th C.: ult. from Gk. *parallēlos*, from *para-* 'alongside' + *allēlos* 'one another.']

par·al·lel bars ▶ plural n. a pair of parallel rails mounted on posts, used in gymnastics.

par·al·lel cous·in ▶ n. the offspring of a parent's sibling; a first cousin.

par·al·lel·e·pi·ped /ˌparəˌleləˈpīpid; -ˈpipid/ ▶ n. Geom. a solid body of which each face is a parallelogram. [16th C.: from Gk. *parallēlepipedon*, from *parallēlos* 'beside another' + *epipedon* 'plane surface.']

par·al·lel·ism /ˈparəlelˌizəm/ ▶ n. the state of being parallel or of corresponding in some way. ■ the use of successive verbal constructions in poetry or prose that correspond in grammatical structure, sound, meter, meaning, etc. ■ the use of parallel processing in computer systems. — **par·al·lel·is·tic** /ˌparəlelˈistik/ adj.

par·al·lel·ize /ˈparələlˌīz; -lelˌīz/ ▶ v. [trans.] Comput. adapt (a program) to be suitable for running on a parallel processing system. — **par·al·lel·i·za·tion** /ˌparəˌleləˈzāsʜən/ n.

parallelograms

par·al·lel·o·gram /ˌparəˈleləˌgram/ ▶ n. a four-sided plane rectilinear figure with opposite sides parallel. [16th C.: ult. from Gk. *parallēlogrammon*, from *parallēlos* 'alongside another' + *grammē* 'line.']

par·al·lel park·ing ▶ n. the parking of a vehicle or vehicles parallel to the roadside. — **par·al·lel park** v.

par·al·lel port ▶ n. Comput. a connector for a device that sends or receives several bits of data simultaneously by using more than one wire.

par·al·lel pro·cess·ing ▶ n. a mode of computer operation in which a process is split into parts that execute simultaneously on different processors attached to the same computer.

pa·ral·o·gism /pəˈraləˌjizəm/ ▶ n. Logic a piece of illogical or fallacious reasoning, esp. one that appears superficially logical or that the reasoner believes to be logical. — **pa·ral·o·gist** n. [16th C.: ult. from Gk. *paralogismos*, from *paralogizesthai* 'reason falsely.']

Par·a·lym·pics /ˌparəˈlimpiks/ ▶ plural n. an international athletic competition for disabled athletes. — **Par·a·lym·pic** adj. [1950s: blend of *paraplegic* and *Olympics*.]

pa·ral·y·sis /pəˈraləsis/ ▶ n. (pl. **-ses** /-ˌsēz/) the loss of the ability to move (and sometimes to feel anything) in part or most of the body, typically as a result of illness, poison, or injury. ■ inability to act or function in a person, organization, or place. [OE, via L. from Gk. *paralusis*, from *paraluesthai* 'be disabled at the side,' from *para* 'beside' + *luein* 'loosen.']

pa·ral·y·sis ag·i·tans /ˈajəˌtanz/ ▶ n. less common term for PARKINSON'S DISEASE. [L., lit. 'shaking paralysis.']

par·a·lyt·ic /ˌparəˈlitik/ ▶ adj. of or relating to paralysis. ▶ n. a person affected by paralysis. — **par·a·lyt·i·cal·ly** adv. [ME: from Gk. *paralutikos*.]

par·a·lyze /ˈparəˌlīz/ (Brit. **par·a·lyse**) ▶ v. [trans.] (often **be paralyzed**) cause (a person or part of the body) to become partly or wholly incapable of movement. ■ render (someone) unable to think or act normally, esp. through panic or fear. ■ bring (a system, place, or organization) to a standstill by causing disruption or chaos. — **par·a·lyz·ing·ly** /-ˌlīzinglē/ adv. [19th C.: from Fr. *paralyser*, from *paralysie* 'paralysis.']

par·a·mag·net·ic /ˌparəmagˈnetik/ ▶ adj. (of a substance or body) very weakly attracted by the poles of a magnet, but not retaining any permanent magnetism. — **par·a·mag·net·ism** /-ˈmagnəˌtizəm/ n.

Par·a·mar·i·bo /ˌparəˈmarəˌbō/ the capital of Suriname, on the Atlantic coast; pop. 201,000.

par·a·me·ci·um /ˌparəˈmēsʜ(ē)əm; -sēəm/ ▶ n. Zool. a single-celled freshwater animal (genus *Paramecium*, phylum Ciliophora) that has a characteristic slipperlike shape and is covered with cilia. [18th C.: mod. L., from Gk. *paramēkēs* 'oval,' from *para-* 'against' + *mēkos* 'length.']

par·a·med·ic /ˌparəˈmedik/ ▶ n. a person who is trained to do medical work, esp. emergency first aid, but is not a fully qualified doctor.

par·a·med·i·cal /ˌparəˈmedikəl/ ▶ adj. of or relating to services and professions that supplement and support medical work but do not require a fully qualified doctor (such as nursing, radiography, etc.).

pa·ram·e·ter /pəˈramitər/ ▶ n. tech. a numerical or other measurable factor forming one of a set that defines a system or sets the conditions of its operation. ■ Math. a quantity whose value is selected for the particular circumstances and in relation to which other variable quantities may be expressed. ■ Stat. a numerical characteristic of a population, as distinct from a statistic of a sample. ■ (in general use) a limit or boundary that defines the scope of a particular process or activity. — **pa·ram·e·ter·i·za·tion** /pəˌramitəriˈzāsʜən/ n. **pa·ram·e·ter·ize** n. /pəˈramitəˌrīz/ v. [17th C.: mod. L., from Gk. *para-* 'beside' + *metron* 'measure.']

par·a·met·ric /ˌparəˈmetrik/ ▶ adj. of, relating to, or expressed in terms of a parameter or parameters. ■ Stat. assuming the value of a parameter for the purpose of analysis. ■ Electron. relating to or denoting a process in which amplification or frequency conversion is obtained using a device modulated by a pumping frequency, which enables power to be transferred from the pumping frequency to the signal.

par·a·mil·i·tar·y /ˌparəˈmiliˌterē/ ▶ adj. (of an unofficial force) organized similarly to a military force. ▶ n. (pl. **-tar·ies**) a member of an unofficial paramilitary organization.

par·am·ne·sia /ˌparamˈnēzʜə/ ▶ n. Psychiatry a condition or phenomenon involving distorted memory or confusions of fact and fantasy, such as déjà vu.

Par·a·mount a movie production and distribution company established in 1914.

par·a·mount /ˈparəˌmount/ ▶ adj. more important than anything else; supreme. ■ [attrib.] having supreme power. — **par·a·mount·cy** /-sē/ n. **par·a·mount·ly** adv. [16th C.: from Anglo-Norman Fr. *paramont*, from OFr. *par* 'by' + *amont* 'above.']

par·a·mour /ˈparəˌmo͝or/ ▶ n. archaic derog. a lover, esp. the illicit partner of a married person. [ME: from OFr. *par amour* 'by love.']

par·a·myx·o·vi·rus /ˌparəˈmiksəˌvīrəs/ ▶ n. Med. any of a group of RNA viruses similar to the myxoviruses but larger and hemolytic, including those causing mumps, measles, distemper, rinderpest, etc.

Pa·ra·ná /ˌpärəˈnä/ **1** a river in South America that rises in southeastern Brazil and flows to the Plate River estuary in Argentina. **2** a city in eastern Argentina; pop. 276,000.

pa·rang /ˈpäräng/ ▶ n. a Malayan machete. [Malay.]

par·a·noi·a /ˌparəˈnoiə/ ▶ n. a mental condition characterized by delusions of persecution, unwarranted jealousy, or exaggerated self-importance, typically worked into an organized system. ■ suspicion and mistrust of people or their actions without evidence or justification. — **par·a·noi·ac** /-ˈnoi-ak; -ˈnoi-ik/ adj. & n. **par·a·noi·a·cal·ly** /-ˈnoi-ik(ə)lē/ adv. **par·a·no·ic** /-ˈnoi-ik/ adj. **par·a·no·i·cal·ly** /-ˈnoi-ik(ə)lē/ adv. [19th C.: mod. L., from Gk., from *paranoos* 'distracted,' from *para* 'irregular' + *noos* 'mind.']

par·a·noid /ˈparəˌnoid/ ▶ adj. of, characterized by, or suffering from the mental condition of paranoia. ■ unreasonably or obsessively anxious, suspicious, or mistrustful. ▶ n. a person who is paranoid.

par·a·nor·mal /ˌparəˈnôrməl/ ▶ adj. denoting events or phenomena such as telekinesis or clairvoyance that are beyond the scope of normal scientific understanding. — **par·a·nor·mal·ly** adv.

par·a·pa·re·sis /ˌparəpəˈrēsis/ ▶ n. partial paralysis of the lower limbs. — **paraparetic** /-ˈretik/ adj.

par·a·pente /ˈparəˌpänt/ ▶ n. the activity of gliding by means of an airfoil parachute launched from high ground. ■ the parachute used for this purpose. ▶ v. [intrans.] glide using an airfoil parachute. — **par·a·pent·er** n. [1980s: from Fr., from *para(chute)* + *pente* 'slope.']

par·a·pet /ˈparəpit/ ▶ n. a low, protective wall along the edge of a roof, bridge, or balcony. ■ a protective wall or earth defense along the top of a trench or other place of concealment for troops. — **par·a·pet·ed** adj. [16th C.: from Fr., or from Ital. *parapetto* 'breast-high wall,' from *para-* 'protecting' + *petto* 'breast' (from L. *pectus*).]

par·aph /ˈparəf; pəˈraf/ ▶ n. a flourish after a signature, originally as a precaution against forgery. [ME: from Fr. *paraphe*, from med. L. *paraphus* (contr. of *paragraphus* 'stroke').]

par·a·pher·na·lia /ˌparəfə(r)ˈnālyə/ ▶ n. [treated as sing. or pl.] miscellaneous articles, esp. the equipment needed for a particular activity. ■ trappings associated with a particular institution or activity that are regarded as superfluous. [17th C.: from med. L., based on Gk. *parapherna* 'property apart from a dowry,' from *para* 'distinct from' + *pherna* (from *phernē* 'dowry').]

par·a·phil·i·a /ˌparəˈfilēə/ ▶ n. Psychiatry a condition characterized by abnormal sexual desires, typically involving extreme or dangerous activities. — **par·a·phil·i·ac** /-ˈfilēˌak/ adj. & n.

par·a·phrase /ˈparəˌfrāz/ ▶ v. [trans.] express the meaning of (the writer or speaker or something written or spoken) using different words, esp. to achieve greater clarity. ▶ n. a rewording of something written or spoken by someone else. — **par·a·phras·a·ble** adj. **par·a·phras·tic** /ˌparəˈfrastik/ adj. [16th C.: via L. from Gk. *paraphrasis*, from *paraphrazein*, from *para-* + *phrazein* 'tell.']

pa·raph·y·sis /pəˈrafəsəs/ ▶ n. (pl. **-ses** /-ˌsēz/) Bot. a sterile hairlike filament present among the reproductive organs in many lower plants, esp. bryophytes, algae, and fungi. [19th C.: mod. L., from Gk. *para-* 'beside' + *phusis* 'growth.']

Par·a·Plane /ˈparəˌplān/ (also **Par·a·plane**) ▶ n. trademark a motor-driven flying machine consisting of a parachute and a pair of fabric wings attached to a rigid framework.

par·a·ple·gi·a /ˌparəˈplēj(ē)ə/ ▶ n. paralysis of the legs and lower body. — **par·a·ple·gic** /-jik/ adj. & n. [17th C.: mod. L., from Gk. *paraplēgia*, from *paraplēssein* 'strike at the side,' from *para* 'beside' + *plēssein* 'to strike.']

par·a·pro·fes·sion·al /ˌparəprəˈfesʜənl/ ▶ n. a person to whom a particular aspect of a professional task is delegated but who is not licensed to practice as a fully qualified professional. ▶ adj. of, relating to, or denoting such a person.

par·a·psych·ic /ˌparəˈsīkik/ ▶ adj. of, relating to, or denoting mental phenomena for which no adequate scientific explanation exists.

par·a·psy·chol·o·gy /ˌparəsīˈkäləjē/ ▶ n. the study of mental phenomena that are excluded from or inexplicable by orthodox scientific psychology (such as hypnosis, telepathy, etc.). —**par·a·psy·cho·log·i·cal** /-ˌsīkəˈläjikəl/ **adj.** **par·a·psy·chol·o·gist** **n.**

par·a·quat /ˈparəˌkwät/ ▶**n.** a toxic, fast-acting herbicide that becomes deactivated in the soil. [1960s: from PARA-¹ + QUATERNARY.]

par·a·rhyme /ˈparəˌrīm/ ▶**n.** partial rhyme between words with the same pattern of consonants but different vowels, such as *light* and *late*. See also IMPERFECT RHYME.

par·a·sag·it·tal /ˌparəˈsajitl/ ▶**adj.** Anat. relating to or situated in a plane adjacent or parallel to the plane that divides the body into right and left halves. —**par·a·sag·it·tal·ly** **adv.**

par·a·sail /ˈparəˌsāl/ ▶**v.** [intrans.] [often as n.] (**parasailing**) glide through the air wearing an open parachute while being towed by a motorboat. ▶**n.** a parachute designed for parasailing.

par·a·se·le·ne /ˌparəsəˈlēnē/ ▶**n.** (pl. **-le·nae** pronunc. same) a bright spot in the sky similar to a parhelion but formed by moonlight. Also called MOCK MOON, MOON DOG. Compare with PARHELION. [17th C.: mod. L., from Gk. *para-* 'beside' + *selēnē* 'moon.']

par·a·site /ˈparəˌsīt/ ▶**n.** an organism that lives in or on another organism (its host) and benefits by deriving nutrients at the host's expense. ■ derog. a person who habitually relies on or exploits others and gives nothing in return. [16th C.: via L. from Gk. *parasitos* '(person) eating at another's table,' from *para-* 'alongside' + *sitos* 'food.']

par·a·sit·e·mi·a /ˌparəsīˈtēmēə/ (Brit. **par·a·sit·ae·mi·a**) ▶**n.** Med. the demonstrable presence of parasites in the blood.

par·a·sit·ic /ˌparəˈsitik/ ▶**adj.** (of an organism) living as a parasite. ■ resulting from infestation by a parasite. ■ derog. habitually relying on or exploiting others. ■ Phonet. (of a speech sound) inserted without etymological justification (e.g., the *b* in *thimble*); epenthetic. —**par·a·sit·i·cal** **adj.** **par·a·sit·i·cal·ly** **adv.** **par·a·sit·ism** /ˈparəsiˌtizəm; -ˌsī-/ **n.**

par·a·sit·i·cide /ˌparəˈsitəˌsīd/ ▶**n.** a substance used in medicine and veterinary medicine to kill parasites (esp. those other than bacteria or fungi).

par·a·si·tize /ˈparəsiˌtīz; -sī-/ ▶**v.** [trans.] infest or exploit (an organism or part) as a parasite. —**par·a·sit·i·za·tion** /ˌparəsiˌtīˈzāsʜən; -sī-/ **n.**

par·a·sit·oid /ˈparəsiˌtoid; -ˌsī-/ Entomol. ▶**n.** an insect (e.g., the ichneumon wasp) whose larvae live as parasites that eventually kill their hosts (typically other insects). ▶**adj.** of, relating to, or denoting such an insect.

par·a·si·tol·o·gy /ˌparəsiˈtäləjē; -sī-/ ▶**n.** the branch of biology or medicine concerned with the study of parasitic organisms. —**par·a·si·to·log·i·cal** /ˌparəˌsītlˈäjikəl; -ˌsitl-/ **adj.** **par·a·si·tol·o·gist** **n.**

par·a·ski /ˈparəˌskē/ ▶**v.** [intrans.] jump from an aircraft by parachute and ski from the landing place, as a sport or race. —**par·a·ski·ing** **n.**

par·a·sol /ˈparəˌsôl; -ˌsäl/ ▶**n.** a light umbrella used to give shade from the sun. [17th C.: from Fr., from Ital. *parasole*, from *para-* 'protecting against' + *sole* 'sun' (from L. *sol*).]

par·a·state /ˈparəˌstāt/ ▶**n.** a region that seeks or claims but does not have the status of a recognized independent state.

par·a·sym·pa·thet·ic /ˌparəˌsimpəˈᴛʜetik/ ▶**adj.** Physiol. of or relating to the part of the automatic nervous system that balances the action of the sympathetic nerves. It consists of nerves arising from the brain and the lower end of the spinal cord and supplying the internal organs, blood vessels, and glands.

par·a·tax·is /ˌparəˈtaksis/ ▶**n.** Gram. the placing of clauses or phrases one after another, without words to indicate coordination or subordination, as in *Tell me, how are you?* Contrasted with HYPOTAXIS. —**par·a·tac·tic** /-ˈtaktik/ **adj.** **par·a·tac·ti·cal·ly** /-ˈtaktik(ə)lē/ **adv.** [19th C.: from Gk. *parataxis*, from *para-* 'beside' + *taxis* 'arrangement' (from *tassein* 'arrange').]

par·a·thi·on /ˌparəˈᴛʜīˌän/ ▶**n.** a highly toxic synthetic compound containing phosphorus and sulfur, used as an agricultural insecticide. [1940s: from PARA-¹ + THIO-.]

par·a·thor·mone /ˌparəˈᴛʜôrˌmōn/ ▶**n.** Physiol. parathyroid hormone.

par·a·thy·roid /ˌparəˈᴛʜīˌroid/ ▶**n.** Anat. a gland next to the thyroid that secretes a hormone (**parathyroid hormone**) that regulates calcium levels in the body.

par·a·troop·er /ˈparəˌtro͞opər/ ▶**n.** a member of a paratroop regiment or airborne unit.

par·a·troops /ˈparəˌtro͞ops/ ▶**plural n.** troops equipped to be dropped by parachute from aircraft. [1940s: from an abbrev. of PARACHUTE + *troops*.]

par·a·ty·phoid /ˌparəˈtīˌfoid/ ▶**n.** a fever resembling typhoid but caused by different (though related) bacteria, specifically of the genus *Salmonella*. ▶**adj.** [attrib.] of or relating to such a fever or the bacteria causing it.

par·a·vane /ˈparəˌvān/ ▶**n.** a device towed behind a boat at a depth regulated by its vanes or planes, so that the cable to which it is attached can cut the moorings of submerged mines. [20th C.: from PARA-² + VANE.]

par a·vion /ˌpär äˈvyōn/ ▶**adv.** by airmail (written on a letter or parcel to indicate how it is to reach its destination). [Fr., lit. 'by airplane.']

par·a·wing /ˈparəˌwiɴɢ/ ▶**n.** a type of parachute or kite having a flattened shape like a wing, to give greater maneuverability.

par·boil /ˈpärˌboil/ ▶**v.** [trans.] partly cook (food) by boiling. [ME: from OFr. *parbouillir*, from late L. *perbullire* 'boil thoroughly,' from L. *per-* + *bullire* 'to boil.']

par·buck·le /ˈpärˌbəkəl/ ▶**n.** a loop of rope arranged like a sling, used for raising or lowering casks and other cylindrical objects along an inclined plane. ▶**v.** [trans.] raise or lower with such a device. [17th C.: from *parbunkle*.]

Par·cae /ˈpärsē/ Rom. Mythol. Roman name for *THE FATES* (see FATE).

par·cel /ˈpärsəl/ ▶**n.** **1** a thing or collection of things wrapped in paper in order to be carried or sent by mail. **2** a quantity or amount of something, in particular: ■ a piece of land, esp. one considered as part of an estate. ■ a quantity dealt with in one commercial transaction. ■ tech. a portion of a larger body of air or other fluid considered as a discrete element. ▶**v.** (**-celed, -cel·ing** ; Brit. **-celled, -cel·ling**) [trans.] make (something) into a parcel by wrapping it. ■ (**parcel something out**) divide into portions and then distribute. ■ Naut. wrap (rope) with strips of tarred canvas before binding it with yarn as part of a traditional technique to reduce chafing.

– PHRASES **be part and parcel of** see PART. [ME: from OFr. *parcelle*, from L. *particula* 'small part.']

par·cel post ▶**n.** mail consisting of parcels.

parch /pärcʜ/ ▶**v.** make or become dry through intense heat: [trans.] *grassland parched by the sun* | [intrans.] *his crops parched last summer.* ■ [trans.] roast (corn, peas, etc.) lightly. [ME: of unknown origin.]

parched /pärcʜt/ ▶**adj.** dried out with heat. ■ [predic.] informal extremely thirsty. ■ lightly roasted.

par·chee·si /pärˈcʜēzē/ ▶**n.** var. of PACHISI.

parch·ment /ˈpärcʜmənt/ ▶**n.** a stiff, flat, thin material made from the prepared skin of an animal and used as a durable writing surface in ancient and medieval times. ■ a manuscript written on this material. ■ (also **parchment paper**) a type of stiff translucent paper treated to resemble parchment and used for lampshades, as a writing surface, and in baking. ■ informal a diploma or other formal document. [ME: from OFr. *parchemin*, from a blend of late L. *pergamina* 'writing material from Pergamum' and *Parthica pellis* 'Parthian skin' (a kind of scarlet leather).]

pard·ner /ˈpärdnər/ ▶**n.** dated humorous var. of PARTNER, used to represent dialect speech.

par·don /ˈpärdn/ ▶**n.** the action of forgiving or being forgiven for an error or offense. ■ a remission of the legal consequences of an offense or conviction. ■ Christian Church, hist. an indulgence, as widely sold in medieval Europe. ▶**v.** [trans.] forgive or excuse (a person, error, or offense). ■ release (an offender) from the legal consequences of an offense or conviction, and often implicitly from blame. ■ (usu. **be pardoned**) used to indicate that the actions or thoughts of someone are justified or understandable given the circumstances. ▶**exclam.** a request to a speaker to repeat something because one did not hear or understand it.

– PHRASES **beg someone's pardon** express polite apology: *I beg your pardon for intruding.* **pardon me** (or **I beg your pardon**) used to indicate that one has not heard or understood something. ■ used to express one's anger or indignation at what someone has just said. —**par·don·a·ble** **adj.** **par·don·a·bly** /-əblē/ **adv.** [ME: from OFr. *pardun* (n.), *pardoner* (v.), from med. L. *perdonare* 'concede, remit,' from *per-* 'completely' + *donare* 'give.']

par·don·er /ˈpärdn-ər/ ▶**n.** hist. a person licensed to sell papal pardons or indulgences.

pare /pe(ə)r/ ▶**v.** [trans.] trim (something) by cutting away its outer edges. ■ cut off the outer skin of (something). ■ reduce (something) in size, extent, quantity, or number, usually in a number of small successive stages. —**par·er** **n.** [ME: from OFr. *parer* from L. *parare* 'prepare.']

par·e·gor·ic /ˌparəˈgôrik/ ▶**n.** a medicine consisting of opium flavored with camphor, aniseed, and benzoic acid, formerly used to treat diarrhea and coughing in children. [17th C.: via late L. from Gk. *parēgorikos* 'soothing,' from the v. *parēgorein*, lit. 'speak in the assembly,' hence 'soothe, console.']

pa·ren /pəˈren/ ▶**n.** (usu. **parens**) Print. a parenthesis.

paren. ▶**abbr.** parenthesis.

pa·ren·chy·ma /pəˈreɴɢkəmə/ ▶**n.** Anat. the functional tissue of an organ as distinguished from the connective and supporting tissue. ■ Bot. the cellular tissue, typically soft and succulent, found chiefly in the softer parts of leaves, pulp of fruits, bark and pith of stems, etc. ■ Zool. cellular tissue lying between the body wall and the organs of invertebrate animals lacking a coelom, such as flatworms. —**pa·ren·chy·mal** /-məl/ **adj.** (esp. Anat.). **pa·ren·chym·a·tous** /ˌperəɴɢˈkimətəs/ **adj.** (esp. Bot.). [17th C.: from Gk. *parenkhuma* 'something poured in beside,' from *para-* 'beside' + *enkhuma* 'infusion.']

par·ent /ˈpe(ə)rənt; ˈpar-/ ▶**n.** a father or mother. ■ archaic a forefather or ancestor. ■ an animal or plant from which younger ones are derived. ■ a source or origin of a smaller or less important part. ■ [often as adj.] an organization or company that owns or controls a number of subsidiary organizations or companies. ▶**v.** [trans.] [often as n.] (**parenting**) be or act as a mother or father to (someone). —**pa·ren·tal** /pəˈrentl/ **adj.** **pa·ren·tal·ly** /pəˈrentl-ē/ **adv.** **par·ent·hood** **n.** [ME (n.): from OFr., from L. *parent-* 'bringing forth,' from v. *parere*.]

par·ent·age /ˈpe(ə)rəntij; ˈpar-/ ▶**n.** the identity and origins of one's parents. ■ fig. the origin of something.

par·en·ter·al /pəˈrentərəl/ ▶**adj.** Med. administered or occurring elsewhere in the body than the mouth and alimentary canal: Often contrasted with ENTERAL. —**par·en·ter·al·ly** **adv.** [20th C.: from PARA-¹ 'beside' + Gk. *enteron* 'intestine' + -AL.]

pa·ren·the·sis /pəˈrenᴛʜəsis/ ▶**n.** (pl. **-ses** /-ˌsēz/) a word, clause, or sentence inserted as an explanation or afterthought into a passage that is grammatically complete without it, in writing usually marked off by curved brackets, dashes, or commas. ■ (usu. **parentheses**) one or both of a pair of marks ( ) used to include such a word, clause, or sentence. ■ an interlude or interval.

– PHRASES **in parenthesis** as a digression or afterthought. [16th C.: via late L. from Gk., from *parentithenai* 'put in beside.']

pa·ren·the·size /pəˈrenTHəˌsīz/ ▶ v. [trans.] [usu. as adj.] (**parenthesized**) put (a word, phrase, etc.) into parentheses. ■ express in parenthesis.

par·en·thet·i·cal /ˌparənˈTHetikəl/ ▶ adj. of, relating to, or inserted as a parenthesis. — **par·en·thet·ic** /-ˈTHetik/ adj. **par·en·thet·i·cal·ly** adv. [18th C.: from PARENTHESIS.]

Par·ent-Teach·er As·so·ci·a·tion (abbr.: **PTA**) ▶ n. a national organization devoted to furthering the safety and interests of children. ■ a local organization of parents and teachers for promoting closer relations and improving educational facilities at a school.

par·er·gon /pəˈrərˌgän/ ▶ n. (pl. **-ga** /-gə/) a piece of work that is supplementary to or a byproduct of a larger work. [17th C.: via L. from Gk. *parergon*, from *para-* 'beside' + *ergon* 'work.']

pa·re·sis /pəˈrēsis/ ▶ n. (pl. **-ses** /-sēz/) Med. a condition of muscular weakness caused by nerve damage or disease; partial paralysis. ■ (also **general paresis**) inflammation of the brain in the later stages of syphilis, causing progressive dementia and paralysis. — **pa·ret·ic** /-ˈretik/ adj. [17th C.: mod. L., from Gk. *parienai* 'let go,' from *para-* 'alongside' + *hienai* 'let go.']

par·es·the·sia /ˌparəsˈTHēZH(ē)ə/ (Brit. **par·aes·the·si·a**) ▶ n. (pl. **-si·ae** /-ZHē-ē/ or **-si·as**) Med. an abnormal sensation, typically tingling or pricking ("pins and needles"), caused chiefly by pressure on or damage to peripheral nerves. [19th C.: from PARA-[1] 'alongside, irregular' + Gk. *aisthēsis* 'sensation' + -IA[1].]

Pa·re·to /pəˈretō/ ▶ adj. [attrib.] denoting the theories and methods of Italian economist and sociologist Vilfredo Pareto (1848–1923), esp. a formula used to express the income distribution of a society.

pa·re·u /ˈpäräˌo͞o/ ▶ n. a kind of sarong made of a single straight piece of printed cotton cloth, worn by Polynesians. [Tahitian.]

pa·re·ve /ˈpär(ə)və/ (also **par·ve**) ▶ adj. Judaism prepared without meat, milk, or their derivatives and therefore permissible to be eaten with both meat and dairy dishes according to dietary laws.

par ex·cel·lence /ˌpär ˌeksəˈläns/ ▶ adj. [postpositive] better or more than all others of the same kind. [Fr., lit. 'by excellence.']

par·fait /pärˈfā/ ▶ n. **1** a dessert consisting of layers of ice cream, fruit, etc., served in a tall glass. **2** a rich cold dessert made with whipped cream, eggs, and often fruit. [from Fr. *parfait*, lit. 'perfect.']

par·fleche /ˈpärfleSH; pärˈfleSH/ ▶ n. (in American Indian culture) a hide, esp. a buffalo's hide, dried by being stretched on a frame after the hair has been removed. ■ an article, esp. a bag, made from this. [from Canad. Fr. *parflèche*, from Fr. *parer* 'ward off' + *flèche* 'arrow.']

par·fum·er·ie /pärˈfyo͞omərē/ ▶ n. (pl. **-er·ies**) a place where perfume is sold or made. [Fr.]

par·get /ˈpärjit/ (also **parge** /pärj/) ▶ v. (**-get·ed, -get·ing**) [trans.] cover (a part of a building, esp. a flue or an external brick wall) with plaster or mortar that typically bears an ornamental pattern. ▶ n. another term for PARGETING. [ME: from OFr. *parjeter*, from *par-* 'all over' + *jeter* 'to throw.']

par·get·ing /ˈpärjitiNG/ (also **parg·ing** /ˈpärjiNG/) ▶ n. plaster or mortar applied in a layer over a part of a building, esp. ornamental plasterwork.

par·he·li·on /pärˈhēlēən; -ˈhēlyən/ ▶ n. (pl. **-he·li·a** /-ˈhēlēə/) a bright spot in the sky appearing on either side of the sun, formed by refraction of sunlight through ice crystals high in the earth's atmosphere. Also called SUN DOG. [17th C.: from L. *parelion*, from Gk. *para-* 'beside' + *hēlios* 'sun.']

pa·ri·ah /pəˈrīə/ ▶ n. **1** an outcast. **2** hist. a member of an indigenous people of southern India originally functioning as ceremonial drummers but later having a low caste or no caste. [17th C.: from Tamil *paṟaiyar*, pl. of *paṟaiyan* '(hereditary) drummer,' from *paṟai* 'a drum.']

pa·ri·ah dog ▶ n. another term for PYE-DOG.

Par·i·an /ˈpe(ə)rēən; ˈpar-/ ▶ adj. of or relating to Paros or the fine white marble for which it is renowned. ■ denoting a form of fine white unglazed hard-paste porcelain likened to Parian marble. ▶ n. **1** a native or inhabitant of Paros. **2** Parian ware (porcelain).

pa·ri·e·tal /pəˈrīətəl/ ▶ adj. **1** Anat. Biol. of, relating to, attached to, or denoting the wall of the body or of a body cavity or hollow structure. ■ of the parietal lobe. **2** relating to residence in a college or university dormitory and esp. to visits from members of the opposite sex. **3** Archaeol. denoting prehistoric art found on rock walls. ▶ n. **1** Anat. Zool. a parietal structure. ■ short for PARIETAL BONE. **2** (**parietals**) informal dormitory rules governing visits from members of the opposite sex. [ME: from late L. *parietalis*, from L. *paries*, *pariet-* 'wall.']

pa·ri·e·tal bone ▶ n. a bone forming the central side and upper back part of each side of the skull.

pa·ri·e·tal cell ▶ n. an acid-secreting cell of the stomach wall.

pa·ri·e·tal lobe ▶ n. either of the paired lobes of the brain at the top of the head, including areas concerned with the reception and correlation of sensory information.

par·i·mu·tu·el /ˌparəˈmyo͞oCHo͞oəl/ (also **par·i·mu·tu·el**) ▶ n. [often as adj.] a form of betting in which those backing the first three places divide the losers' stakes (less the operator's commission). ■ a booth for placing bets under such a system. [Fr., lit. 'mutual stake.']

par·ing knife ▶ n. a small knife used mainly for peeling fruits and vegetables.

par·ings /ˈpe(ə)riNGz/ ▶ plural n. thin strips that have been pared off from something.

pa·ri pas·su /ˌpärē ˈpäˌso͞o/ ▶ adv. side by side; at the same rate or on an equal footing. [L., lit. 'with equal step.']

Par·is[1] /ˈparis/ the capital of France, on the Seine River; pop. 2,175,000.

Par·is[2] Gk. Mythol. a Trojan prince, the son of Priam and Hecuba.

Par·is[3], Matthew, see MATTHEW PARIS.

Par·is green ▶ n. a vivid green toxic crystalline salt of copper and arsenic, used as a preservative, pigment, and insecticide.

par·ish /ˈpariSH/ ▶ n. (in the Christian Church) a small administrative district typically having its own church and a priest or pastor. ■ (in Louisiana) a territorial division corresponding to a county in other states. [ME: from Anglo-Norman Fr., OFr. *paroche*, from Gk. *paroikia* 'sojourning,' + *oikos* 'dwelling.']

par·ish·ion·er /pəˈriSHənər/ ▶ n. an inhabitant of a parish, esp. one who belongs to or attends a particular church.

Pa·ri·sian /pəˈriZHən; -ˈrē-; -ˈrizē-/ ▶ adj. of or relating to Paris. ▶ n. a native or inhabitant of Paris.

Pa·ri·si·enne /pəˌrēzēˈen/ ▶ n. a Parisian girl or woman. ▶ adj. (esp. of a girl or woman) Parisian. [17th C.: Fr.]

Par·is, Trea·ty of the name of three peace treaties concluded in Paris, France: ■ signed in 1763 by Great Britain, France, and Spain, terminating the Seven Years' War in Europe (1756–63) and the French and Indian War (1754–60) in North America. ■ signed in 1783 by the US and Great Britain, terminating the American Revolution. ■ signed in 1898 by the US and Spain, terminating the Spanish-American War.

par·i·ty[1] /ˈparitē/ ▶ n. **1** the state or condition of being equal, esp. regarding status or pay. ■ the value of one currency in terms of another at an established exchange rate. ■ a system of providing farmers with consistent purchasing power by regulating prices of farm products, usually with government price supports. **2** Math. (of a number) the fact of being even or odd. ■ Physics the property of a spatial wave equation that either remains the same (**even parity**) or changes sign (**odd parity**) under a given transformation. ■ Physics the value of a quantum number corresponding to this property. ■ Comput. a function whose being even (or odd) provides a check on a set of binary values. [16th C.: from late L. *paritas*, from *par* 'equal.']

par·i·ty[2] ▶ n. Med. the fact or condition of having borne children. ■ the number of children previously borne. [19th C.: from -PAROUS.]

par·i·ty bit ▶ n. Comput. a bit that acts as a check on a set of binary values, calculated in such a way that the number of 1s in the set plus the parity bit should always be even (or occasionally, should always be odd).

Park /pärk/, Mungo (1771–1806), Scottish explorer. He explored in western Africa 1795–97, including the navigation of the Niger River.

park /pärk/ ▶ n. **1** a large public green area in a town, used for recreation. ■ a large area of land kept in its natural state for public recreational use. ■ (also **wildlife park**) a large enclosed area of land used to accommodate wild animals in captivity. ■ a stadium or enclosed area used for sports. ■ a large enclosed piece of ground, typically with woodland and pasture, attached to a large country house. ■ (in the western US) a broad flat area in a mountainous region. **2** [with adj.] an area devoted to a specified purpose: *an industrial park*. **3** (in a car with automatic transmission) the position of the gear selector in which the gears are locked, preventing the vehicle's movement. ▶ v. [trans.] bring (a vehicle that one is driving) to a halt and leave it temporarily, typically in a parking lot or by the side of the road. ■ [trans.] informal deposit and leave in a convenient place until required: *park your bag by the door*. ■ (**park oneself in/on**) informal sit down on or in: *we parked ourselves on the couch*. [ME: from OFr. *parc*, from med. L. *parricus*, of Gmc. origin; rel. to Ger. *Pferch* 'pen, fold,' also to PADDOCK.]

par·ka /ˈpärkə/ ▶ n. a large windproof jacket with a hood, designed to be worn in cold weather. ■ a hooded jacket made of animal skin, worn by Eskimos. [18th C.: via Aleut from Russ.]

park-and-ride ▶ n. [often as adj.] a system for reducing urban traffic congestion, in which drivers leave their cars in parking lots on the outskirts of a city and travel to the city center on public transportation.

Park Avenue a street in Manhattan in New York City, regarded as emblematic of worldly success.

Park Chung Hee /ˈCHəNG ˈhē/ (1917–79), president of South Korea 1963–79. Under his presidency, South Korea emerged as an industrial nation.

Par·ker[1] /ˈpärkər/, Bonnie Elizabeth (1910–34), US robber and murderer. She and her partner, Clyde Barrow, went on a criminal spree in which they shot and killed at least 13 people.

Par·ker[2], Charlie (1920–55), US saxophonist; full name *Charles Christopher Parker*; known as **Bird** or **Yardbird**. He was one of the key figures of the bebop movement.

Par·ker[3], Dorothy Rothschild (1893–1967), US writer, known for her scathing wit. From 1927, she wrote book reviews and short stories for the *New Yorker* magazine.

park·ing lot ▶ n. an area where cars or other vehicles may be left temporarily.

park·ing me·ter ▶ n. a machine next to a parking space in a street, into which the driver puts money so as to be authorized to park the vehicle for a particular length of time.

park·ing tick·et ▶ n. a notice telling a driver of a fine imposed for parking illegally, typically attached to a car windshield.

Par·kin·son·ism /'pärkinsən,izəm/ ▶ n. another term for PARKINSON'S DISEASE.

Par·kin·son's dis·ease /'pärkinsənz/ ▶ n. a progressive disease of the nervous system marked by tremor, muscular rigidity, and slow, imprecise movement, chiefly affecting middle-aged and elderly people. [19th C.: named after James *Parkinson* (1755–1824), Engl. surgeon.]

Par·kin·son's law the notion that work expands to fill the time available for its completion. [1950s: named after Cyril Northcote *Parkinson* (1909–93), Engl. writer.]

park·land /'pärk,land/ ▶ n. (also **parklands**) open land consisting of fields and scattered groups of trees. ■ land reserved for a public park.

Park·man /'pärkmən/, Francis (1823–93), US historian. He wrote an account of his journey along the Oregon Trail 1846 in *The California and Oregon Trail* (1849).

Park Range a range of the Rocky Mountains in southern Wyoming and northern Colorado.

Parks[1] /pärks/, Gordon Roger Alexander Buchanan (1912–2006), US photographer, writer, and director, noted for his photojournalism in *Life* magazine 1949–70, which chronicled the civil rights movement, and his direction of the movie *Shaft* (1971).

Parks[2], Rosa Louise McCauley (1913–2005), US civil rights activist. On December 1, 1955, her refusal to give up her bus seat to a white man in Montgomery, Alabama, inspired the civil rights movement.

park·way /'pärk,wā/ ▶ n. an open landscaped highway.

Parl. Brit. ▶ abbr. ■ Parliament. ■ Parliamentary.

par·lance /'pärləns/ ▶ n. a particular way of speaking or using words, esp. a way common to those with a particular job or interest. [16th C.: from OFr., from *parler* 'speak,' from L. *parabola* 'comparison.']

par·lan·do /pär'ländō/ Music ▶ adv. & adj. (with reference to singing) expressive or declamatory in the manner of speech. ▶ n. composition or performance in this manner. [Ital., lit. 'speaking.']

par·lay /'pär,lā; -lē/ ▶ v. [trans.] (**parlay something into**) turn an initial stake or winnings from a previous bet into (a greater amount) by gambling. ■ informal transform into (something greater or more valuable). ▶ n. a cumulative series of bets in which winnings accruing from each transaction are used as a stake for a further bet. [19th C.: from Fr. *paroli*, from Ital., from *paro* 'like,' from L. *par* 'equal.']

par·ley /'pärlē/ ▶ n. (pl. **-leys**) a conference between opposing sides in a dispute, esp. a discussion of terms for an armistice. ▶ v. (**-leys, -leyed**) [intrans.] hold a conference with the opposing side to discuss terms. [ME: (perh. from OFr. *parlee* 'spoken,' fem. past part. of v. *parler*.]

par·lia·ment /'pärləmənt/ ▶ n. (**Parliament**) (in the UK) the highest legislature, consisting of the sovereign, the House of Lords, and the House of Commons. ■ the members of this legislature for a particular period, esp. between one dissolution and the next. ■ a similar legislature in other nations and states. [ME: from OFr. *parlement* 'speaking,' from the v. *parler*.]

par·lia·men·tar·i·an /,pärləmen'te(ə)rēən/ ▶ n. 1 a member of a parliament, esp. one well versed in parliamentary procedure and experienced in debate. 2 hist. a supporter of Parliament in the English Civil War; a Roundhead. ▶ adj. 1 of or relating to Parliament or its members. 2 hist. of or relating to the Roundheads. — **par·lia·men·tar·i·an·ism** /-,nizəm/ n.

par·lia·men·ta·ry /,pärlə'mentərē/ ▶ adj. relating to, enacted by, or suitable for a parliament.

par·lia·men·ta·ry law ▶ n. the rules that govern the conduct of legislatures and other deliberative bodies.

par·lia·men·ta·ry pro·ce·dure ▶ n. 1 a rule that defines how a particular situation is to be handled, or a particular outcome achieved, in a legislature or deliberative body. 2 parliamentary law.

par·lor /'pärlər/ (Brit. **par·lour**) ▶ n. 1 dated a sitting room in a private house. ■ a room in a public building for receiving guests. ■ a room in a monastery or convent that is set aside for conversation. 2 [usu. with adj.] a shop or business providing specified goods or services. ▶ adj. [attrib.] dated, derog. denoting a person who professes but does not actively give support to a specified (esp. radical) political view. [ME: from Anglo-Norman Fr. *parlur* 'place for speaking,' from med. L. *parlare* 'speak.']

par·lor car ▶ n. a luxuriously fitted railroad car, typically with individually reserved seats.

par·lor game ▶ n. an indoor game, esp. a word game.

par·lor·maid /'pärlər,mād/ ▶ n. hist. a maid employed to serve at table.

par·lous /'pärləs/ ▶ adj. archaic humorous full of danger or uncertainty; precarious: *the parlous state of the economy.* ▶ adv. archaic greatly or excessively: *she is parlous handsome.* — **par·lous·ly** adv. **par·lous·ness** n. [ME: contr. of PERILOUS.]

Par·ma /'pärmə/ a city in northern Italy, southeast of Milan; pop. 194,000.

Par·ma vi·o·let ▶ n. a sweet violet of a variety with a heavy scent and lavender-colored flowers that are often crystallized and used for food decoration.

Par·men·i·des /pär'meni,dēz/ (*fl.* 5th century BC), Greek philosopher. He founded the Eleatic school of philosophers.

Par·men·tier /,pärmen'tyā/ ▶ adj. [postpositive] cooked or served with potatoes. [Antoine A. *Parmentier* (1737–1813), Fr. agriculturalist.]

Par·me·san /'pärmə,zän/ ▶ n. a hard, dry cheese used in grated form, esp. on Italian dishes. [16th C.: from Fr., from Ital. *parmigiano* 'of *Parma*.']

par·mi·gia·na /,pärmə'zHänə/ ▶ adj. [postpositive] cooked or served with Parmesan cheese. ▶ n. a dish cooked in this way. [Ital., fem. of *Parmigiano* 'of Parma.']

Par·nas·si·an /pär'nasēən/ ▶ adj. 1 relating to poetry; poetic. 2 of or relating to a group of French poets of the late 19th century who emphasized strictness of form, named from the anthology *Le Parnasse contemporain* (1866). ▶ n. a member of this group of French poets.

Par·nas·sus, Mount /pär'nasəs/ a mountain in central Greece, just north of Delphi. It was held to be sacred by the ancient Greeks. Greek name PARNASSÓS.

Par·nell /pär'nel; 'pärnl/, Charles Stewart (1846–91), Irish nationalist. He raised the profile of Irish affairs through obstructive parliamentary tactics. — **Par·nell·ite** /-'nelīt/ adj. & n.

pa·ro·chi·al /pə'rōkēəl/ ▶ adj. of or relating to a church parish. ■ having a limited or narrow outlook or scope. — **pa·ro·chi·al·ism** n. **pa·ro·chi·al·i·ty** /-,rōkē'alitē/ n. **pa·ro·chi·al·ly** adv. [ME: ult. from eccles. L. *parochialis*, from *parochia* (see PARISH).]

pa·ro·chi·al school ▶ n. a private school supported by a particular church or parish.

par·o·dy /'parədē/ ▶ n. (pl. **-dies**) an imitation of the style of a particular writer, artist, or genre with deliberate exaggeration for comic effect. ■ an imitation or a version of something that falls far short of the real thing; a travesty. ▶ v. (**-dies, -died**) [trans.] produce a humorously exaggerated imitation of (a writer, artist, or genre). ■ mimic humorously. — **pa·rod·ic** /pə'rädik/ adj. **par·o·dist** n. [16th C.: via late L. from Gk. *parōidia* 'burlesque poem,' from *para-* 'beside' (expressing alt.) + *ōidē* 'ode.']

par of ex·change ▶ n. see PAR[1] (sense 2).

pa·rol /pə'rōl; 'parəl/ ▶ adj. Law given or expressed orally. ■ (of a document) agreed orally, or in writing but not under seal.

– PHRASES **by parol** by oral declaration. [15th C.: from OFr. *parole*.]

pa·role /pə'rōl/ ▶ n. 1 the release of a prisoner temporarily (for a special purpose) or permanently before the completion of a sentence, on the promise of good behavior. ■ hist. a promise or undertaking given by a prisoner of war not to escape or, if released, to return to custody under stated conditions. 2 Ling. the actual linguistic behavior or performance of individuals, in contrast to the linguistic system of a community. Contrasted with LANGUE. ▶ v. [trans.] (usu. **be paroled**) release (a prisoner) on parole. — **pa·rol·ee** /-,rō'lē/ n. [15th C.: from OFr., lit. 'word,' from eccles. L. *parabola* 'speech.']

par·o·no·ma·sia /,parənō'māzH(ē)ə/ ▶ n. a play on words; a pun. [16th C.: via L. from Gk. *paronomasia*, from *para-* 'beside' + *onomasia* 'naming' (from *onomazein* 'to name,' from *onoma* 'a name').]

par·o·nym /'parənim/ ▶ n. Ling. a word that is a derivative of another and has a related meaning: *"wisdom" is a paronym of "wise."* ■ a word formed by adaptation of a foreign word: *"preface" is a paronym of Latin "prefatio."* Contrasted with HETERONYM. — **par·o·nym·ic** /,parə'nimik/ adj. **pa·ron·y·mous** /pə'ränəməs/ adj. **pa·ron·y·my** /pə'ränəmē/ n. [19th C.: from Gk. *parōnumon*, neut. (used as a n.) of *parōnumos* 'naming by modification,' from *para-* 'beside' + *onuma* 'a name.']

Pa·ros /'paräs; 'pärôs/ a Greek island in the southern Aegean Sea. Parian marble is quarried here.

pa·rot·id /pə'rätid/ Anat. ▶ adj. relating to, situated near, or affecting a parotid gland. ▶ n. short for PAROTID GLAND. [17th C.: via L. from Gk. *parōtis, parōtid-*, from *para-* 'beside' + *ous, ōt-* 'ear.']

pa·rot·id gland ▶ n. Anat. either of a pair of large salivary glands situated just in front of each ear.

par·o·ti·tis /,parə'tītis/ ▶ n. Med. inflammation of a parotid gland, esp. (**infectious parotitis**) mumps.

-parous ▶ comb. form Biol. bearing offspring of a specified number or reproducing in a specified manner. [from L. *-parus* '-bearing' (from *parere* 'bring forth, produce') + -OUS.]

Par·ou·si·a /pə'rōōzēə; ,pärōō'sēə/ ▶ n. Christian Theol. another term for SECOND COMING. [Gk., lit. 'being present.']

par·ox·ysm /'parək,sizəm/ ▶ n. a sudden attack or violent expression of a particular emotion or activity. ■ Med. a sudden recurrence or attack of a disease; a sudden worsening of symptoms. — **par·ox·ys·mal** /,parək'sizməl/ adj. [ME: ult. from Gk. *paroxusmos*, from *paroxunein* 'exasperate,' from *para-* 'beyond' + *oxunein* 'sharpen' (from *oxus* 'sharp').]

par·ox·y·tone /pə'räksi,tōn/ ▶ adj. (esp. in ancient Greek) having an acute accent on the penultimate syllable. ▶ n. a word with such an accent. [18th C.: from mod. L. *paroxytonus*, from Gk. *paroxutonos*, from *para-* 'alongside' + *oxutonos* 'sharp pitch.']

par·quet /pär'kā/ ▶ n. 1 (also **parquet flooring**) flooring composed of wooden blocks arranged in a geometric pattern. 2 the ground floor of a theater or auditorium. [17th C.: from Fr., lit. 'small park.']

par·quet·ry /'pärkitrē/ ▶ n. inlaid work of blocks of various woods arranged in a geometric pattern, esp. for flooring or furniture.

Parr /pär/, Katherine (1512–48), queen of England; sixth and last wife of Henry VIII.

parr /pär/ ▶ n. (pl. same) a young salmon (or trout) between the stages of fry and smolt, distinguished by dark rounded patches evenly spaced along its sides. [18th C.: of unknown origin.]

par·ra·keet ▶ n. var. of PARAKEET.

par·ri·cide /'parə,sīd/ ▶ n. the killing of a parent or other near relative. ■ a person who commits parricide. — **par·ri·cid·al** /ˌparəˈsīdl/ **adj.** [16th C.: from Fr., from L. *parricidium* 'murder of a parent'(first element of unknown origin).]

par·rot /ˈparət/ ▶ **n.** a mainly tropical bird (family Psittacidae), often vividly colored, with a short down-curved hooked bill and a raucous voice, some kinds of which are able to mimic the human voice. ▶ **v.** (**-rot·ed, -rot·ing**) [trans.] repeat mechanically: *parroting back information.* [16th C.: prob. from dial. Fr. *perrot*, dimin. of male name *Pierre* 'Peter.']

par·rot fe·ver ▶ **n.** less formal term for PSITTACOSIS.

par·rot·fish /ˈparətˌfisн/ ▶ **n.** (pl. same or **-fish·es**) **1** any of a number of brightly colored marine fish with a parrotlike beak, which they use to scrape food from coral and other hard surfaces, in particular: ■ a widespread fish (*Scarus* and other genera, family Scaridae) of warm seas that may secrete a mucous cocoon to deter predators. ■ an edible fish of the southern Indian Ocean (*Oplegnathus conwayi*, family Oplegnathidae). **2** Austral. a brightly colored marine fish, esp. one of the wrasse family.

par·ry /ˈparē/ ▶ **v.** (**-ies, -ied**) [trans.] ward off (a weapon or attack), esp. with a countermove. ■ answer (a question or accusation) evasively. ▶ **n.** (pl. **-ies**) an act of warding off a blow. ■ Fencing block or turn aside (an opponent's blade). ■ an evasive reply. [17th C.: prob. representing Fr. *parez!* 'ward off!,' imper. of *parer*, from Ital. *parare* 'ward off.']

parse /pärs/ ▶ **v.** [trans.] analyze (a sentence) into its component parts and describe their syntactic roles. ■ Comput. analyze (a string or text) into logical syntactic components, typically in order to test conformability to a logical grammar. ■ examine or analyze minutely. ▶ **n.** Comput. an act of or the result obtained by parsing a string or a text. [16th C.: perh. from ME *pars* 'parts of speech,' from OFr. 'parts.']

par·sec /ˈpärˌsek/ ▶ **n.** a unit of distance used in astronomy, equal to about 3.25 light years (3.08 × 1016 meters). [20th C.: blend of PARALLAX and SECOND[2].]

Par·see /pärˈsē; ˈpärsē/ (also **Par·si**) ▶ **n.** an adherent of Zoroastrianism, esp. a descendant of those Zoroastrians who fled to India from Muslim persecution in Persia during the 7th–8th centuries. [from Persian *pārsī* 'Pers.,' from *pārs* 'Persia.']

pars·er /ˈpärsər/ ▶ **n.** Comput. a program for parsing.

Par·si·fal /ˈpärsəfəl; -ˌfäl/ another name for PERCEVAL.

par·si·mo·ni·ous /ˌpärsəˈmōnēəs/ ▶ **adj.** unwilling to spend money or use resources; stingy or frugal. — **par·si·mo·ni·ous·ly adv. par·si·mo·ni·ous·ness n.**

par·si·mo·ny /ˈpärsəˌmōnē/ ▶ **n.** extreme unwillingness to spend money or use resources. [ME: from L. *parsimonia, parcimonia*, from *parcere* 'be sparing.']

pars·ley /ˈpärslē/ ▶ **n.** a biennial plant (*Petroselinum crispum*) with white flowers and aromatic leaves that are either crinkly or flat and used as a culinary herb and for garnishing food. [OE *petersilie*, via late L. based on Gk. *petroselinon*, from *petra* 'rock' + *selinon* 'parsley,' influenced in ME by OFr. *peresil*, of the same origin.]

pars·nip /ˈpärsnip/ ▶ **n.** **1** a long tapering cream-colored root with a sweet flavor. **2** the widely cultivated Eurasian plant (*Pastinaca sativa*) of the parsley family that yields this root. [ME: from OFr. *pasnaie*, from L. *pastinaca* (rel. to *pastinare* 'dig').]

par·son /ˈpärsən/ ▶ **n.** a beneficed member of the clergy; a rector or a vicar. ■ informal any member of the clergy, esp. a Protestant one. — **par·son·ic** /pärˈsänik/ **adj. par·son·i·cal** /pärˈsänikəl/ **adj.** [ME: from OFr. *persone*, from L. *persona* 'person.']

par·son·age /ˈpärsənij/ ▶ **n.** a church house provided for a member of the clergy.

part /pärt/ ▶ **n.** **1** a piece or segment of something such as an object, activity, or period of time, which combined with other pieces makes up the whole. ■ an element or constituent that belongs to something and is essential to its nature. ■ a component of a machine. ■ a measure allowing comparison between the amounts of different ingredients used in a mixture. ■ a specified fraction of a whole. ■ a division of a book treated as a unit in which a particular topic is discussed. ■ the amount of a serial that is published or broadcast at one time. ■ (**parts**) informal short for PRIVATE PARTS. **2** some but not all of something. ■ a point on or area of something. ■ (**parts**) informal a region, esp. one not clearly specified or delimited. **3** a character as represented in a play or movie; a role played by an actor or actress. ■ the words and directions to be learned and performed by an actor in such a role. ■ Music a melody or other constituent of harmony assigned to a particular voice or instrument in a musical work. ■ the contribution made by someone or something to an action or situation. ■ the behavior appropriate to or expected of a person in a particular role or situation; a person's duty. ■ the chance to be involved in something. **4** a line of scalp revealed in a person's hair by combing the hair away in opposite directions on either side. ▶ **v.** [intrans.] (of two things) move away from each other: *his lips parted in a smile.* ■ divide to leave a central space. ■ [trans.] cause to divide or move apart, leaving a central space. ■ leave someone's company. ■ (**be parted**) leave the company of someone. ■ (**part with**) give up possession of; hand over. ■ [trans.] separate (the hair of the head on either side of the part) with a comb. ▶ **adv.** to some extent; partly (often used to contrast different parts of something).
– PHRASES **be part and parcel of** be an essential feature or element of. **for my** (or **his, her**, etc.) **part** used to focus attention on one person or group and distinguish them from others involved in a situation. **in part** to some extent though not entirely. **look the part** have an appearance or style of dress appropriate to a particular role or situation. **a man of (many) parts** a man showing great ability in many different areas. **on the part of** (or **on my, their**, etc., **part**) used to ascribe responsibility for something to someone: *there was a series of errors on my part.* **part company** (of two or more people) cease to be together; go in different directions. ■ (of two or more parties) cease to associate with each other, esp. as the result of a disagreement. **take part** join in an activity; be involved. **take the part of** give support and encouragement to (someone) in a dispute. [OE ('part of speech'), from L. *pars, part-*.]

par·take /pärˈtāk/ ▶ **v.** (past **-took** /-ˈtŏŏk/; past part. **-tak·en** /-ˈtākən/) [intrans.] (**partake in**) formal join in (an activity). ■ (**partake of**) be characterized by (a quality). ■ (**partake of**) eat or drink (something). — **par·tak·er n.** [16th C.: back-form. from earlier *partaker* 'person who takes a part.']

part·er /ˈpärtər/ ▶ **n.** [in comb.] a broadcast or published work with a specified number of parts: *the first in a six-parter.*

par·terre /pärˈte(ə)r/ ▶ **n.** **1** a level space in a yard occupied by an ornamental arrangement of flower beds. **2** the part of the ground floor of an auditorium in the rear and on the sides, esp. the part beneath the balcony. [17th C.: from Fr., from *par terre* 'on the ground.']

par·the·no·car·py /ˈpärтнənōˌkärpē/ ▶ **n.** Bot. the development of a fruit without prior fertilization. — **par·the·no·car·pic** /ˌpärтнənōˈkärpik/ **adj.** [20th C.: from Ger. *Parthenocarpie*, from Gk. *parthenos* 'virgin' + *karpos* 'fruit.']

par·the·no·gen·e·sis /ˌpärтнənōˈjenəsis/ ▶ **n.** Biol. reproduction from an ovum without fertilization, esp. in some invertebrates and lower plants. — **par·the·no·ge·net·ic** /-jəˈnetik/ **adj. par·the·no·ge·net·i·cal·ly** /-jəˈnetik(ə)lē/ **adv.** [19th C.: mod. L., from Gk. *parthenos* 'virgin' + *genesis* 'creation.']

Par·the·non /ˈpärтнəˌnän/ the temple of Athena Parthenos, built on the Acropolis in 447–432 BC by Pericles to honor Athens' patron goddess and to commemorate the recent Greek victory over the Persians. [from Gk. *parthenos* 'virgin.']

Par·thi·a /ˈpärтнēə/ an ancient kingdom that lay southeast of the Caspian Sea in present-day Iran. — **Par·thi·an** /-тнēən/ **n. & adj.**

Par·thi·an shot ▶ **n.** another term for PARTING SHOT.

par·tial /ˈpärsнəl/ ▶ **adj.** **1** existing only in part; incomplete. **2** favoring one side in a dispute above the other; biased. ■ [predic.] (**partial to**) having a liking for. ▶ **n.** Music a component of a musical sound; an overtone or harmonic. — **par·tial·ly adv.** [as submodifier] *a partially open door.* **par·tial·ness n.** [ME ult. from late L. *partialis*, from *pars, part-* 'part.']

par·tial-birth a·bor·tion ▶ **n.** a late-term abortion of a fetus that has already died, or is killed before being completely removed from the mother.

par·tial de·riv·a·tive ▶ **n.** Math. a derivative of a function of two or more variables with respect to one variable, the other(s) being treated as constant.

par·tial dif·fer·en·tial e·qua·tion ▶ **n.** Math. an equation containing one or more partial derivatives.

par·tial frac·tion ▶ **n.** Math. each of two or more fractions into which a more complex fraction can be decomposed as a sum.

par·ti·al·i·ty /ˌpärsнēˈalitē/ ▶ **n.** unfair bias in favor of one thing or person compared with another; favoritism. ■ a particular liking or fondness for something.

par·tial pres·sure ▶ **n.** Chem. the pressure that would be exerted by one of the gases in a mixture if it occupied the same volume on its own.

par·tial prod·uct ▶ **n.** Math. the product of one term of a multiplicand and one term of its multiplier. ■ the product of the first *n* terms of a large or infinite series, where *n* is a finite integer (including 1).

par·ti·ble /ˈpärtəbəl/ ▶ **adj.** involving or denoting a system of inheritance in which a deceased person's estate is divided equally among the heirs. — **par·ti·bil·i·ty** /ˌpärtəˈbilətē/ **n.**

par·tic·i·pant /pärˈtisəpənt/ ▶ **n.** a person who takes part in something.

par·tic·i·pate /pärˈtisəˌpāt/ ▶ **v.** [intrans.] take part. — **par·tic·i·pa·tion** /pärˌtisəˈpāsнən/ **n. par·tic·i·pa·tive** /-ˌpātiv; -pətiv/ **adj. par·tic·i·pa·tor** /-ˌpātər/ **n. par·tic·i·pa·to·ry** /-pəˌtôrē/ **adj.** [16th C.: from L. *participat-* 'shared in,' from the v. *participare*, based on *pars, part-* 'part' + *capere* 'take.']

par·ti·cip·i·al ad·jec·tive /ˌpärtəˈsipēəl/ ▶ **n.** Gram. an adjective that is a participle in origin and form, such as *burned, cutting, engaged.*

par·ti·ci·ple /ˈpärtəˌsipəl/ ▶ **n.** Gram. a word formed from a verb (e.g., *going, gone, being, been*) and used as an adjective (e.g., *working woman, burned toast*) or a noun (e.g., *good breeding*). In English participles are also used to make compound verb forms (e.g., *is going, has been*). Compare with GERUND. — **par·ti·cip·i·al** /ˌpärtəˈsipēəl/ **adj. par·ti·cip·i·al·ly** /ˌpärtəˈsipēəlē/ **adv.** [ME: from OFr., ult. from L. *participium* from *participare* 'share in.']

par·ti·cle /ˈpärtikəl/ ▶ **n.** **1** a minute portion of matter. ■ (also **subatomic** or **elementary particle**) Physics any of numerous subatomic constituents of the physical world that interact with each other, including electrons, neutrinos, photons, and alpha particles. ■ [with negative] the least possible amount. ■ Math. a hypothetical object having mass but no physical size. **2** Gram. a minor function word that has comparatively little meaning and does not inflect, in particular: ■ (in English) any of the class of words such as *in, up, off, over*, used with verbs to make phrasal verbs. [ME: from L. *particula* 'little part,' dimin. of *pars, part-*.]

par·ti·cle ac·cel·er·a·tor ▶ n. an apparatus for accelerating subatomic particles to high velocities by means of electric or electromagnetic fields. The accelerated particles are generally made to collide with other particles, either as a research technique or for the generation of high-energy X-rays and gamma rays.

par·ti·cle beam ▶ n. **1** a concentrated stream of subatomic particles, generated with a view to causing collisions between particles that will shed new light on their nature and structure. **2** such a stream used in an antimissile defense weapon.

par·ti·cle·board /ˈpärtikəl,bôrd/ ▶ n. material made in rigid sheets or panels from compressed wood chips and resin, often coated or veneered, and used in furniture, buildings, etc.

par·ti·cle phys·ics ▶ plural n. [treated as sing.] the branch of physics that deals with the properties, relationships, and interactions of subatomic particles.

par·ti-col·ored /ˈpärtē,kələrd/ (also **par·ti·col·ored**) ▶ adj. having or consisting of two or more different colors. [16th C.: from the adj. PARTY[2].]

par·tic·u·lar /pə(r)ˈtikyələr/ ▶ adj. **1** [attrib.] used to single out an individual member of a specified group or class. ■ Logic denoting a proposition in which something is asserted of some but not all of a class. Contrasted with UNIVERSAL. **2** [attrib.] esp. great or intense. **3** insisting that something should be correct or suitable in every detail; fastidious. ▶ n. **1** Philos. an individual item, as contrasted with a universal quality. **2** a detail. ■ **(particulars)** detailed information about someone or something.

– PHRASES **in particular** especially (used to show that a statement applies to one person or thing more than any other). [ME: ult. from L. *particularis*.]

par·tic·u·lar in·te·gral ▶ n. Math. another term for PARTICULAR SOLUTION.

par·tic·u·lar·ism /pə(r)ˈtikyələ,rizəm/ ▶ n. exclusive attachment to one's own group, party, or nation. ■ the principle of leaving each state in an empire or federation free to govern itself and promote its own interests, without reference to those of the whole. ■ Theol. the doctrine that some but not all people are elected and redeemed. — **par·tic·u·lar·ist** n. & adj. **par·tic·u·lar·is·tic** /-,tikyələˈristik/ adj.

par·tic·u·lar·i·ty /pə(r),tikyəˈlaritē/ ▶ n. (pl. **-ties**) the quality of being individual. ■ fullness or minuteness of detail in the treatment of something. ■ **(particularities)** small details. ■ Christian Theol. God's incarnation as Jesus as a particular person at a particular time and place.

par·tic·u·lar·ize /pə(r)ˈtikyələ,rīz/ ▶ v. [trans.] formal mention or describe particularly; treat individually or in detail. — **par·tic·u·lar·i·za·tion** /-,tikyələriˈzāshən; -lə,rīˈzāshən/ n.

par·tic·u·lar·ly /pə(r)ˈtikyələrlē/ ▶ adv. **1** to a higher degree than is usual or average: *I don't particularly want to be reminded of that time.* ■ used to single out a subject to which a statement is especially applicable: *the team's defense is excellent, particularly their infield.* **2** so as to give special emphasis to a point; specifically.

par·tic·u·lar so·lu·tion ▶ n. Math. the most general form of the solution of a differential equation, containing arbitrary constants.

par·tic·u·late /pärˈtikyəlit; -,lāt/ ▶ adj. of, relating to, or in the form of minute separate particles. ▶ n. **(particulates)** matter in such a form.

part·ing /ˈpärting/ ▶ n. **1** the action of leaving or being separated from someone. ■ a leave-taking or departure. **2** the action of dividing something into parts.

– PHRASES **a** (or **the**) **parting of the ways** a point at which two people must separate or at which a decision must be taken.

part·ing shot ▶ n. a final remark, typically a cutting one, made by someone at the moment of departure.

par·ti pris /,pärtē ˈprē/ ▶ n. (pl. **par·tis pris** pronunc. same) a preconceived view; a bias. ▶ adj. prejudiced; biased. [Fr., lit. 'side taken.']

par·ti·san /ˈpärtəzən/ ▶ n. **1** a strong supporter of a party, cause, or person. **2** a member of an armed group formed to fight secretly against an occupying force, in particular one operating in enemy-occupied Yugoslavia, Italy, and parts of eastern Europe in World War II. ▶ adj. prejudiced in favor of a particular cause. — **par·ti·san·ship** n. [16th C.: from Fr., via Italian dial. from Ital. *partigiano*, from *parte* 'part' (from L. *pars, part-*).]

par·ti·ta /pärˈtētə/ ▶ n. (pl. **-ti·tas** or **-ti·te** /-ˈtētā/) Music a suite, typically for a solo instrument or chamber ensemble. [19th C.: from Ital., lit. 'divided off,' fem. past part. of *partire*.]

par·tite /ˈpär,tīt/ ▶ adj. [usu. in comb.] divided into parts. ■ Bot. Zool. (esp. of a leaf or an insect's wing) divided to or nearly to the base. [16th C.: from L. *partitus* 'divided up,' past part. of *partiri*.]

par·ti·tion /pärˈtishən; pər-/ ▶ n. (esp. with reference to a country with separate areas of government) the action or state of dividing or being divided into parts. ■ a structure dividing a space into two parts, esp. a light interior wall. ■ Comput. each of a number of portions into which some operating systems divide memory or storage. ▶ v. [trans.] divide into parts. ■ divide (a room) into smaller rooms or areas by erecting partitions. ■ **(partition something off)** separate a part of a room from the rest by erecting a partition. — **par·ti·tion·er** n. **par·ti·tion·ist** n.

par·ti·tion·er /pärˈtishənər/ ▶ n. Comput. a piece of software for apportioning space on a hard disk. A **hard partitioner** does this prior to formatting (i.e., permanently), while a **soft partitioner** does it after formatting.

par·ti·tive /ˈpärtitiv/ Gram. ▶ adj. (of a grammatical construction) referring to only a part of a whole, for example *a slice of bacon, a series of accidents, some of the children*. ▶ n. such a construction. ■ a noun or pronoun used as the first term in such a construction. — **par·ti·tive·ly** adv.

par·ti·tive gen·i·tive ▶ n. Gram. a genitive used to indicate a whole divided into or regarded in parts, expressed in English by *of* as in *most of us*.

par·ti·zan /ˈpärtəzən/ ▶ n. & adj. old-fashioned spelling of PARTISAN.

part·ly /ˈpärtlē/ ▶ adv. to some extent; not completely.

part·ner /ˈpärtnər/ ▶ n. **1** a person who takes part in an undertaking with another or others, esp. in a business or company with shared risks and profits: *a partner in a prosperous legal practice | a junior partner.* ■ a country or organization that has an agreement with another or others: *Britain has exasperated its European partners again | partners in the ruling coalition.* ■ either of two people dancing together or playing a game or sport on the same side: *arrange the children in pairs so that each person has a partner.* ■ either member of a married couple or of an established unmarried couple. ■ a person with whom one has sex; a lover: *make sure that you or your partner are using an effective method of contraception.* ■ dated dialect a friendly form of address by one man to another. **2** **(partners)** Naut. a timber framework secured to and strengthening the deck of a wooden ship around the holes for the mast. ▶ v. [trans.] be the partner of. *he partnered her for the waltz and the tango.* ■ [intrans.] associate as partners. [ME: alt. of *parcener* 'partner,' based on L. *partitio(n-)* 'partition.']

part·ner·ship /ˈpärtnər,ship/ ▶ n. the state of being a partner or partners. ■ an association of two or more people as partners. ■ a business or firm owned and run by two or more partners. ■ a position as one of the partners in a business or firm.

part of speech ▶ n. a category to which a word is assigned in accordance with its syntactic functions. In English the main parts of speech are noun, pronoun, adjective, determiner, verb, adverb, preposition, conjunction, and interjection.

par·took /pärˈto͝ok/ past of PARTAKE.

red-legged partridge

par·tridge /ˈpärtrij/ ▶ n. (pl. same or **-tridg·es**) a short-tailed Eurasian game bird (family Phasianidae) with mainly brown plumage. Its many species include the **gray partridge** (*Perdix perdix*), introduced into the northern US, and the **red-legged partridge** (*Alectoris rufa*), introduced into Colorado. ■ informal any of a number of birds, such as the bobwhite or ruffed grouse, that resemble the partridge. [ME *partrich*, from OFr. *pertriz, perdriz*, from L. *perdix*.]

par·tridge·ber·ry /ˈpärtrij,berē/ ▶ n. (pl. **-ries**) a creeping North American plant (*Mitchella repens*) of the bedstraw family, with red berries that are eaten chiefly by game birds. ■ the fruit of this plant.

par·tridge pea ▶ n. a yellow-flowered leguminous plant (*Cassia fasciculata*) with sensitive leaves.

part song ▶ n. an unaccompanied secular song with three or more voice parts, typically homophonic rather than contrapuntal in style.

part-time ▶ adj. & adv. for only part of the usual working day or week. — **part-tim·er** n.

par·tu·ri·ent /pärˈt(y)o͝orēənt/ ▶ adj. tech. (of a woman or female mammal) about to give birth; in labor. ▶ n. a parturient woman. [16th C.: from L. *parturient-* 'being in labor,' from the v. *parturire*, inceptive of *parere* 'bring forth.']

par·tu·ri·tion /,pärcho͝oˈrishən/ ▶ n. formal tech. the action of giving birth to young; childbirth. [17th C.: from late L. *parturitio(n-)*, from *parturire* 'be in labor' (see PARTURIENT).]

part·way /ˈpärt,wā; ˈpärtˈwā/ ▶ adv. part of the way.

par·ty[1] /ˈpärtē/ ▶ n. (pl. **-ties**) **1** a social gathering of invited guests, typically involving eating, drinking, and entertainment. **2** a formally constituted political group, typically operating on a national basis, that contests elections and attempts to form or take part in a government. ■ a group of people taking part in a particular activity or trip, esp. one for which they have been chosen. **3** a person or people forming one side in an agreement or dispute. ■ informal a person, esp. one with specified characteristics: *will you help the party on line 2?* ▶ v. **(-ties, -tied)** [intrans.] informal enjoy oneself at a party or other lively gathering, typically with drinking and music.

– PHRASES **be (a) party to** be involved in. [ME (denoting a body of people united in opposition to others, also in sense 2): from OFr. *partie*, based on L. *partiri* 'divide into parts.']

par·ty[2] ▶ adj. Heraldry divided into parts of different tinctures. [ME: from OFr. *parti* 'parted,' based on L. *partitus* 'divided into parts'.]

par·ty·go·er /ˈpärtē,gōər/ ▶ n. a person attending a party.

par·ty line ▶ n. **1** a policy, or the policies collectively, officially adopted by a political party. **2** a telephone line or circuit shared by two or more subscribers.

par·ty pol·i·tics ▶ plural n. [also treated as sing.] politics that relate to political parties rather than to the good of the general public.

par·ty poop·er ▶ n. informal a person who throws gloom over social enjoyment. — **par·ty-poop·ing** n.

par·ty wall ▶ n. a wall common to two adjoining buildings or rooms.

pa·rure /pəˈro͝or/ ▶ n. a set of jewels intended to be worn together. [19th C.: from Fr., from *parer* 'adorn.']

par val•ue ▶ **n.** the nominal value of a bond, share of stock, or a coupon as indicated in writing on the document or specified by charter.

Par•va•ti /ˈpärvətē/ Hinduism a benevolent goddess, wife of Shiva, mother of Ganesh and Skanda, often identified in her malevolent aspect with Durga and Kali. [from Sanskrit *Pārvatī*, lit. 'daughter of the mountain.']

par•ve /ˈpärvə/ ▶ **n.** var. of **PAREVE**.

par•ve•nu /ˈpärvəˌn(y)o͞o/ often derog. ▶ **n.** a person of obscure origin who has gained wealth, influence, or celebrity. ▶ **adj.** having recently achieved, or associated with someone who has recently achieved wealth, influence, or celebrity despite obscure origins. [19th C.: from Fr., lit. 'arrived,' past part. of *parvenir*, from L. *pervenire* 'come to, reach.']

par•vis /ˈpärvis/ ▶ **n.** an enclosed area in front of a cathedral or church, typically one that is surrounded with colonnades or porticoes. [ME: from OFr., based on late L. *paradisus* lit. 'paradise.']

par•vo•vi•rus /ˈpärvōˌvīrəs/ ▶ **n.** Med. any of a class of very small viruses chiefly affecting animals, esp. one (**canine parvovirus**) that causes contagious disease in dogs. [1960s: from L. *parvus* 'small' + **VIRUS**.]

pas /pä/ ▶ **n.** (pl. same) a step in dancing, esp. in classical ballet. [Fr.]

Pas•a•de•na /ˌpasəˈdēnə/ **1** a city in California, in the San Gabriel Mountains; pop. 131,591. **2** a city in southeastern Texas; pop. 141,674.

Pas•cal[1] /paˈskal/, Blaise (1623–62), French mathematician, physicist, and philosopher. He derived the principle that the pressure of a fluid at rest is transmitted equally in all directions.

Pas•cal[2] (also **PASCAL**) ▶ **n.** a high-level structured computer programming language used for teaching and general programming.

pas•cal /paˈskal; päˈskäl/ ▶ **n.** the SI unit of pressure, equal to one newton per square meter (approximately 0.000145 pounds per square inch, or 9.9×10^{-6} atmospheres). [1950s: named after B. *Pascal* (see **PASCAL[1]**).]

pas•chal /ˈpaskəl/ ▶ **adj.** formal **1** of or relating to Easter. **2** of or relating to the Jewish Passover. [ME: ult. from eccles. L. *paschalis*, from *pascha* 'feast of Passover,' Heb. *Pesah* 'Passover.']

pas•chal lamb ▶ **n.** **1** a lamb sacrificed at Passover. **2** Christ.

pas de chat /ˌpä də ˈshä/ ▶ **n.** (pl. same) Ballet a jump in which each foot in turn is raised to the opposite knee. [Fr., lit. 'step of a cat.']

pas de deux /ˌpä də ˈdo͞o/ ▶ **n.** (pl. same) a dance for two people, typically a man and a woman. [Fr., lit. 'step of two.']

pas de qua•tre /ˌpä də ˈkatrə/ ▶ **n.** (pl. same) a dance for four people. [Fr., lit. 'step of four.']

pas de trois /ˌpä də ˈt(r)wä/ ▶ **n.** (pl. same) a dance for three people. [Fr., lit. 'step of three.']

pa•se /päˈsā/ ▶ **n.** a maneuver with the cape in bullfighting, the purpose of which is to get the bull's attention.

pa•se•o /pəˈsāō/ ▶ **n.** (pl. **-os**) a leisurely walk or stroll, esp. one taken in the evening; a promenade (used with reference to the tradition of taking such a walk in Spain or Spanish-speaking communities). ■ (also **pa•se•o de cua•drill•as** /däkwäˈdrēlyäs; -ˈdrēäs/) a parade of bullfighters into the arena at the beginning of a bullfight. ■ a plaza or walkway for strolling. [Sp., lit. 'step.']

pash /pash/ ▶ **n.** informal, dated a brief infatuation: *Kath's got **a pash on him**.* [20th C.: abbrev. of **PASSION**.]

pa•sha /ˈpäshə; ˈpashə; pəˈshä/ ▶ **n.** (also **pa•cha**) hist. the title of a Turkish officer of high rank.

pash•ka /ˈpäshkə/ ▶ **n.** var. of **PASKHA**.

Pash•to /ˈpəshtō/ ▶ **n.** the Iranian language of the Pathans, also spoken in northern areas of Pakistan, that is an official language of Afghanistan. ▶ **adj.** of or relating to this language. [the name in Pashto.]

Pash•tun /pəshˈto͞on/ ▶ **n.** var. of **PATHAN**.

Pa•siph•a•ë /pəˈsifəˌē/ Gk. Mythol. the wife of Minos and mother of the Minotaur.

pas•kha /ˈpäskə/ (also **pash•ka** /ˈpäshkə/) ▶ **n.** a rich Russian dessert made with soft cheese, dried fruit, nuts, and spices, and traditionally eaten at Easter. [Russ., lit. 'Easter.']

pa•so do•ble /ˌpäsō ˈdōblā/ ▶ **n.** (pl. **pa•so do•bles**) a fast-paced ballroom dance based on a Latin American style of marching. ■ a piece of music for this dance, typically in duple time. ■ a quick, light march played at bullfights. [1920s: from Sp., lit. 'double step.']

pasque•flow•er /ˈpaskˌflouər/ ▶ **n.** a spring-flowering plant (genera *Anemone* and *Pulsatilla*) of the buttercup family, with purple or white flowers. Its several species include the North American *A. patens* and the Eurasian *P. vulgaris*. [16th C. (as *passeflower*): from Fr. *passe-fleur*, influenced by *pasque* 'Easter'.]

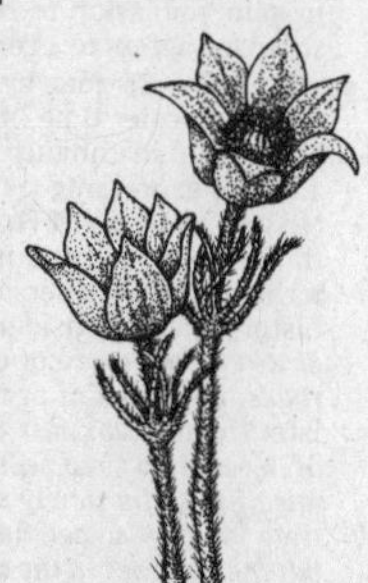
North American pasqueflower

pas•quin•ade /ˌpaskwəˈnād/ ▶ **n.** a satire or lampoon, originally one displayed or delivered publicly in a public place. [16th C.: from Ital. *pasquinata*, from *Pasquino*, a statue in Rome.]

pass[1] /pas/ ▶ **v.** **1** [intrans.] move in a specified direction: *he passed through towns.* ■ [trans.] cause (something) to move or lie in a specified direction or position: *he passed a hand across his forehead.* ■ change from one state or condition to another. ■ [intrans.] die (used euphemistically). **2** [trans.] go past or across; leave behind or on one side in proceeding. ■ go beyond the limits of; surpass; exceed. ■ Tennis hit a winning shot past (an opponent). **3** [intrans.] (of time or a point in time) elapse; go by. ■ happen; be done or said. ■ [trans.] spend or use up (a period of time): *this was how they **passed the time**.* ■ come to an end. **4** [trans.] transfer (something) to someone, esp. by handing or bequeathing it to the next person in a series: *please pass the fish.* ■ [intrans.] be transferred from one person or place to another, esp. by inheritance. ■ (in football, soccer, hockey, and other games) throw, kick, or hit (the ball or puck) to another player on one's own team. ■ put (something, esp. money) into circulation. ■ [intrans.] (esp. of money) circulate; be current. **5** [trans.] (of a candidate) be successful in (an examination, test, or course). ■ judge the performance or standard of (someone or something) to be satisfactory. ■ [intrans.] be accepted as adequate; go uncensured. ■ [intrans.] (**pass as/for**) be accepted as or taken for. **6** [trans.] (of a legislative or other official body) approve or put into effect (a proposal or law) by voting on it. ■ (of a proposal or law) be examined and approved by (a legislative body or process). ■ [intrans.] (of a proposal) be approved. **7** [trans.] pronounce (a judgment or judicial sentence). ■ utter (something, esp. criticism). **8** [trans.] discharge (something, esp. urine or feces) from the body. **9** [intrans.] forgo one's turn in a game or an offered opportunity. ■ [as exclam.] said when one does not know the answer to a question, for example in a quizzing game. ■ [trans.] (of a company) not declare or pay (a dividend). ■ Bridge make no bid when it is one's turn during an auction. ■ [trans.] Bridge make no bid in response to (one's partner's bid). ▶ **n.** **1** an act or instance of moving past or through something. ■ informal an amorous or sexual advance made to someone. ■ an act of passing the hands over anything, as in conjuring or hypnotism. ■ a thrust in fencing. ■ a juggling trick. ■ Bridge an act of refraining from bidding during the auction. ■ Comput. a single scan through a set of data or a program. **2** a successful completion of an examination or course, usually without honors. ■ the grade indicating this. **3** a card, ticket, or permit giving authorization for the holder to enter or have access to a place, form of transportation, or event. **4** (in football, soccer, hockey, and other games) an act of throwing, kicking, or hitting the ball or puck to another player on the same team. **5** a state or situation of a specified, usually bad or difficult, nature.

– PHRASES **pass the baton** see **BATON**. **pass the buck** see **BUCK[3]**. **pass one's eye over** read (a document) cursorily. **pass the hat** see **HAT**. **pass one's lips** see **LIP**. **pass muster** see **MUSTER**. **pass the time of day** see **TIME**. **pass water** urinate.

– PHRASAL VERBS **pass someone by** happen without being noticed or fully experienced by someone. **pass off** (of proceedings) happen or be carried through in a specified, usually satisfactory, way. **pass something off 1** evade or lightly dismiss an awkward remark. **2** Basketball throw the ball to a teammate who is unguarded. **pass someone/something off as** falsely represent a person or thing as (something else). **pass out** become unconscious. **pass someone over** ignore the claims of someone to promotion or advancement. **pass something over** avoid mentioning or considering something. **pass something up** refrain from taking up an opportunity. — **pass•er** **n.** *he's a good passer of the ball.* [ME: from OFr. *passer*, based on L. *passus* 'pace.']

pass[2] ▶ **n.** a route over or through mountains. ■ a passage for fish over or past a weir or dam. ■ a navigable channel, esp. at the mouth of a river.

– PHRASES **head** (or **cut**) **someone/something off at the pass** forestall someone or something. [ME: var. of **PACE[1]**.]

pass. ▶ **abbr.** ■ passenger. ■ passim. ■ passive.

pass•a•ble /ˈpasəbəl/ ▶ **adj.** **1** just good enough to be acceptable; satisfactory. **2** (of a route or road) clear of obstacles and able to be traveled along or on. — **pass•a•bly** **adv.**

pas•sa•ca•glia /ˌpäsəˈkälyə/ ▶ **n.** Music a composition similar to a chaconne, typically in slow triple time with variations over a ground bass. [Ital., from Sp. *pasacalle*, from *pasar* 'to pass' + *calle* 'street.']

pas•sade /pəˈsād/ ▶ **n.** a movement performed in advanced dressage and classical riding, in which the horse performs a 180° turn, with its forelegs describing a large circle and its hind legs a smaller one. [17th C.: Fr., based on med. L. *passare* 'to pass.']

pas•sage[1] /ˈpasij/ ▶ **n.** **1** the act or process of moving through, under, over, or past something on the way from one place to another. ■ the act or process of moving forward. ■ the right to pass through somewhere: *we obtained a permit for safe passage from the embassy.* ■ a journey or ticket for a journey by sea or air. ■ Ornithol. (of a migrating bird) the action of passing through a place en route to its final destination: [as adj.] *a passage migrant.* ■ Med. Biol. the process of propagating microorganisms or cells in a series of host organisms or culture media, so as to maintain them or modify their virulence. **2** a narrow way, typically having walls on either side, allowing access between buildings or to different rooms within a building; a passageway. ■ a duct, vessel, or other channel in the body. **3** the process of transition from one state to another. ■ the passing of a bill into law. **4** a short extract from a book or other printed material. ■ a section of a piece of music. ■ an episode in a longer activity such as a sporting event. ▶ **v.** [trans.] Med. Biol. subject (a strain of microorganisms or cells) to a passage: *each recombinant virus was passaged nine times successively.* [ME: from OFr., based on L. *passus* 'pace.']

pas•sage[2] ▶ **n.** a movement performed in advanced dressage and classical riding, in which the horse executes a slow elevated trot, giving the impression of dancing. [18th C.: from Fr. *passage*, from an alt. of Ital. *passeggiare* 'to walk, pace,' based on L. *passus* 'pace.']

pas·sage hawk ▶ n. a hawk caught for training while on migration, esp. as an immature bird of less than twelve months. Compare with HAGGARD.

pas·sage·way /'pasij,wā/ ▶ n. a long, narrow way, typically having walls on either side, that allows access between buildings or to different rooms within a building.

pas·sage·work /'pasij,wərk/ ▶ n. music notable chiefly for the scope it affords for virtuoso playing.

Pas·sa·ma·quod·dy /,pasəmə'kwädē/ ▶ n. (pl. same or **-dies**) **1** a member of a North American Indian people inhabiting parts of southeastern Maine and, formerly, southwestern New Brunswick. **2** the Algonquian language of this people. ▶ adj. of or relating to this people or their language. [from Passamaquoddy *pestəmokhatíyək*, 'place where pollack are plentiful.']

Pas·sa·ma·quod·dy Bay (also **Quod·dy Bay**) an inlet of the Bay of Fundy, noted for its powerful tides.

pas·sant /'pasənt/ ▶ adj. [usu. postpositive] Heraldry (of an animal) represented as walking, with the right front foot raised. The animal is depicted in profile facing the dexter (left) side with the tail raised, unless otherwise specified (e.g., as "passant guardant"). [ME: from OFr., lit. 'proceeding,' pres. part. of *passer*.]

pass·band /'pas,band/ ▶ n. a frequency band within which signals are transmitted by a filter without attenuation.

pass·book /'pas,bo͝ok/ ▶ n. a booklet issued by a bank to an account holder for recording sums deposited and withdrawn.

Pass·chen·dae·le, Battle of /'pasʜən,dāl/ (also **Passendale**) a prolonged episode of trench warfare involving appalling loss of life during World War I in 1917, near the village of Passchendaele in western Belgium. It is also known as the third Battle of Ypres.

pas·sé /pa'sā/ ▶ adj. [predic.] no longer fashionable; out of date. [Fr., lit. 'gone by,' past part. of *passer*.]

passed ball ▶ n. Baseball a pitch that the catcher fails to stop or control, enabling a base runner to advance.

pas·sel /'pasəl/ ▶ n. informal a large group of people or things of indeterminate number; a pack. [19th C.: from PARCEL.]

passe·men·terie /pas'mentrē/ ▶ n. decorative textile trimming consisting of gold or silver lace, gimp, or braid. [17th C.: from Fr., from *passement* 'gold lace.']

Pas·sen·dale, Battle of /'pasən,dāl/ var. of PASSCHENDAELE, BATTLE OF.

pas·sen·ger /'pasinjər/ ▶ n. a traveler on a public or private conveyance other than the driver, pilot, or crew. [ME: from the OFr. *passager* 'transitory,' from *passage* (see PASSAGE[1]).]

pas·sen·ger pi·geon ▶ n. an extinct long-tailed North American pigeon (*Ectopistes migratorius*), noted for its long migrations in huge flocks.

passe-par·tout /,pas pär'to͞o/ ▶ n. **1** a picture or photograph simply mounted between a piece of glass and a sheet of cardboard (or two pieces of glass) stuck together at the edges with adhesive tape. ■ adhesive tape or paper used in making such a frame. **2** archaic a master key. [17th C.: from Fr., lit. 'passes everywhere.']

passe·pied /päs'pyā/ ▶ n. a dance like a quick minuet, popular in the 17th and 18th centuries. [Fr., from *passer* 'to pass' + *pied* 'foot.']

pass·er·by /'pasər,bī/ (also **pass·er-by**) ▶ n. (pl. **pas·sers·by**) a person who happens to be going past something, esp. on foot.

pas·ser·ine /'pasərin; -,rīn/ Ornithol. ▶ adj. of, relating to, or denoting birds of a large order (Passeriformes) distinguished by feet that are adapted for perching, including all songbirds. ▶ n. a passerine bird; a perching bird. [18th C.: from L. *passer* 'sparrow.']

pas seul /,pä 'sœl/ ▶ n. a dance for one person. [Fr., lit. 'single step.']

pass-fail ▶ adj. denoting a class, course, or system of grading in which the only two grades given are "pass" and "fail."

pas·si·ble /'pasəbəl/ ▶ adj. Christian Theol. capable of feeling or suffering; susceptible to sensation or emotion. —**pas·si·bil·i·ty** /,pasə'bilitē/ n. [ME: from OFr., from late L. *passibilis*, from L. *pass-* 'suffered,' from v. *pati*.]

pas·sim /'pasim/ ▶ adv. (of allusions or references in a published work) to be found at various places throughout the text. [L., from *passus* 'scattered,' from v. *pandere*.]

pass·ing /'pasiɴɢ/ ▶ adj. [attrib.] **1** going past. **2** (of a period of time) going by. ■ carried out quickly and lightly. **3** meeting or surpassing the requirements of a course or examination. ▶ n. [in sing.] **1** the passage of something, esp. time. ■ the action of throwing, kicking, or hitting a ball or puck to another team member during a sports match. **2** used euphemistically to refer to a person's death. ■ the end of something.
– PHRASES **in passing** briefly and casually. —**pass·ing·ly** adv.

pass·ing note (also **passing tone**) ▶ n. Music a note not belonging to the harmony but interposed to secure a smooth transition from one chord to another.

pass·ing shot ▶ n. Tennis a winning shot beyond and out of reach of one's opponent.

pas·sion /'pasʜən/ ▶ n. **1** strong and barely controllable emotion. ■ a state or outburst of such emotion. ■ intense sexual love. ■ an intense desire or enthusiasm for something. ■ a thing arousing enthusiasm. **2** (**the Passion**) the suffering and death of Jesus. ■ a narrative of this from any of the Gospels. ■ a musical setting of any of these narratives. [ME: from OFr., from late L. *passio(n-)*, from L. *pati* 'suffer.']

pas·sion·al /'pasʜənl/ ▶ adj. rare of, relating to, or marked by passion. ▶ n. Christian Church a book about the sufferings of saints and martyrs, for reading on their feast days.

pas·sion·ate /'pasʜənit/ ▶ adj. showing or caused by strong feelings or a strong belief. ■ showing or caused by intense feelings of sexual love. ■ dominated by or easily affected by intense emotion. —**pas·sion·ate·ly** adv. **pas·sion·ate·ness** n.

pas·sion·flow·er /'pasʜən,flouər/ (also **pas·sion flow·er**) ▶ n. an evergreen climbing plant (genus *Passiflora*, family Passifloraceae) of warm regions that bears distinctive flowers with parts that supposedly resemble instruments of the Crucifixion.

pas·sion fruit (also **pas·sion·fruit**) ▶ n. the edible purple fruit of a kind of passionflower (*Passiflora edulis*) that is grown commercially, esp. in tropical America.

pas·sion play ▶ n. a dramatic performance representing Christ's Passion from the Last Supper to the Crucifixion.

Pas·sion Sun·day ▶ n. the fifth Sunday in Lent.

Pas·sion·tide /'pasʜən,tīd/ ▶ n. the last two weeks of Lent.

Pas·sion Week ▶ n. **1** the week between Passion Sunday and Palm Sunday. **2** older name for HOLY WEEK.

pas·si·vate /'pasə,vāt/ ▶ v. [trans.] [usu. as adj.] (**passivated**) make (a metal or other substance) unreactive by altering the surface layer or coating the surface with a thin inert layer. ■ Electron. coat (a semiconductor) with inert material to protect it from contamination. —**pas·si·va·tion** /,pasə'vāsʜən/ n.

pas·sive /'pasiv/ ▶ adj. **1** accepting or allowing what happens or what others do, without active response or resistance. ■ Chem. (of a metal) made unreactive by a thin inert surface layer of oxide. ■ (of a circuit or device) containing no source of electromotive force. ■ (of radar or a satellite) receiving or reflecting radiation from a transmitter or target rather than generating its own signal. ■ relating to or denoting heating systems that make use of incident sunlight as an energy source. **2** Gram. denoting or relating to a voice of verbs in which the subject undergoes the action of the verb (e.g., *they were killed* as opposed to *he killed them*). The opposite of ACTIVE. ▶ n. Gram. a passive form of a verb. ■ (**the passive**) the passive voice. —**pas·sive·ly** adv. **pas·sive·ness** n. **pas·siv·i·ty** /pa'sivitē/ n. [ME: from L. *passivus*, from *pass-* 'suffered,' from v. *pati*.]

pas·sive-ag·gres·sive ▶ adj. of or denoting a type of behavior or personality characterized by indirect resistance to the demands of others and an avoidance of direct confrontation, as in procrastinating, pouting, or misplacing important materials.

pas·sive im·mu·ni·ty ▶ n. Physiol. the short-term immunity that results from the introduction of antibodies from another person or animal. Compare with ACTIVE IMMUNITY.

pas·sive ma·trix ▶ n. Electron. a display system in which individual pixels are selected using two control voltages for the row and column.

pas·sive re·sist·ance ▶ n. nonviolent opposition to authority, esp. a refusal to cooperate with legal requirements.

pas·sive res·traint ▶ n. a car safety device that is activated by the force of a collision or other sudden stop and that aims to prevent injury to a passenger.

pas·sive smok·ing ▶ n. the involuntary inhaling of smoke from other people's cigarettes, cigars, or pipes.

pass·key /'pas,kē/ ▶ n. **1** a key to the door of a restricted area, given only to those who are officially allowed access. **2** a master key.

Pas·sos, John Dos, see DOS PASSOS.

Pass·o·ver /'pas,ōvər/ ▶ n. the major Jewish spring festival that commemorates the liberation of the Israelites from Egyptian bondage, lasting seven or eight days from the 15th day of Nisan. ■ another term for PASCHAL LAMB. [from the exemption of the Israelites from the death of their first born (Exod. 12).]

pass·port /'pas,pôrt/ ▶ n. an official document issued by a government, certifying the holder's identity and citizenship and entitling them to travel under its protection to and from foreign countries. ■ [in sing.] a thing that ensures admission to or the achievement of something. [15th C.: from Fr. *passeport*, from *passer* 'to pass' + *port* 'seaport.']

pass·word /'pas,wərd/ ▶ n. a secret word or phrase that must be used to gain admission to something. ■ a string of characters that allows someone access to a computer system.

past /past/ ▶ adj. gone by in time and no longer existing. ■ [attrib.] belonging to a former time. ■ [attrib.] (of a specified period of time) occurring before and leading up to the time of speaking or writing. ■ Gram. (of a tense) expressing an action that has happened or a state that previously existed. ▶ n. **1** (usu. **the past**) the time or a period of time before the moment of speaking or writing. ■ the events of an earlier time. ■ the history of a person, country, or institution. ■ a part of a person's history that is considered to be shameful. **2** Gram. a past tense or form of a verb. ▶ prep. to or on the further side of: *he rode on past the crossroads.* ■ in front of or from one side to the other of. ■ beyond in time; later than: *it was past 3:30.* ■ no longer capable of. ■ beyond the scope of. ▶ adv. **1** so as to pass from one side of something to the other: *large angelfish swim slowly past.* ■ used to indicate the lapse of time. **2** at a time later by a specified amount than a particular known hour: *we're having speeches in the dining room at half past.*
– PHRASES **not put it past someone** believe someone to be capable of doing something wrong or rash. —**past·ness** n. [ME: var. of *passed*, past part. of PASS[1].]

pas·ta /ˈpästə/ ▶ **n.** a dish originally from Italy consisting of dough made from durum wheat and water, extruded or stamped into various shapes and typically cooked in boiling water. [19th C.: from Ital., lit. 'paste.']

paste /pāst/ ▶ **n.** a thick, soft, moist substance, usually produced by mixing dry ingredients with a liquid. ■ a substance such as this that is used as an adhesive, esp. for sticking paper and other light materials. ■ a mixture consisting mainly of clay and water that is used in making ceramic ware, esp. a mixture of low plasticity based on kaolin for making porcelain. ■ a hard vitreous composition used in making imitation gems. ▶ **v.** [trans.] **1** coat with paste. ■ [trans.] fasten or stick (something) onto something with paste. ■ Comput. insert (text) into a document. **2** informal beat or defeat severely. [ME: from OFr., from late L. *pasta* 'medicinal preparation' prob. from Gk. *pastē*, *pasta* 'porridge.']

paste·board /ˈpās(t),bôrd/ ▶ **n.** a type of thin board made by pasting together sheets of paper.

pas·tel /paˈstel/ ▶ **n.** **1** a crayon made of powdered pigments bound with gum or resin. ■ a work of art created using such crayons. **2** a soft and delicate shade of a color. ▶ **adj.** of a soft and delicate shade or color. —**pas·tel·ist** (also **pas·tel·list**) **n.** [17th C.: via Fr. from Ital. *pastello*, dimin. of *pasta* 'paste.']

pas·tern /ˈpastərn/ ▶ **n.** the sloping part of a horse's foot between the fetlock and the hoof. ■ a corresponding part in some other domestic animals. [ME: from OFr. *pasturon*, from *pasture* 'strap for hobbling a horse.']

Pas·ter·nak /ˈpastər,nak/, Boris Leonidovich (1890–1960), Russian writer. His novel *Doctor Zhivago* (1957) describes the experience of the Russian intelligentsia during the Russian Revolution.

paste-up ▶ **n.** a document prepared for copying or printing by combining and pasting various sections on a backing.

Pas·teur /pasˈtər; päˈstœr/, Louis (1822–95), French chemist and bacteriologist. He introduced pasteurization and pioneered vaccination techniques.

pas·teur·ize /ˈpascHə,rīz/ ▶ **v.** [trans.] [often as adj.] (**pasteurized**) subject (milk, wine, or other products) to a process of partial sterilization, esp. one involving heat treatment or irradiation, thus making the product safe for consumption and improving its keeping quality: *pasteurized milk.* —**pas·teur·i·za·tion** /,pascHəriˈzāsHən/ **n.** **pas·teur·iz·er** **n.** [19th C.: from the name of L. PASTEUR.]

pas·tic·cio /päˈstēcHō/ ▶ **n.** (pl. **-cios**) another term for PASTICHE. [Ital.]

pas·tiche /paˈstēsH; pä-/ ▶ **n.** an artistic work in a style that imitates that of another work, artist, or period. ■ an artistic work consisting of a medley of pieces taken from various sources. ■ a confused mixture or jumble. ▶ **v.** [trans.] imitate the style of (an artist or work). [19th C.: from Fr., from Ital. *pasticcio*, based on late L. *pasta* 'paste.']

pas·ti·cheur /pasˈtēsHər/ ▶ **n.** an artist who creates a pastiche.

past·ie ▶ **n.** (pl. **-ies**) **1** /ˈpāstē/ (usu. **pasties**) informal a decorative covering for the nipple worn by a stripper. **2** /ˈpastē/ var. of PASTY[1].

pas·tille /paˈstēl/ ▶ **n.** a small candy or lozenge. ■ a small pellet of aromatic paste burned as a perfume or deodorizer. [17th C.: from Fr., from L. *pastillus* 'little loaf, lozenge,' from *panis* 'loaf.']

pas·time /ˈpas,tīm/ ▶ **n.** an activity that someone does regularly for enjoyment rather than work; a hobby. [15th C.: from the v. PASS[1] + TIME.]

past·ing /ˈpāstiNG/ ▶ **n.** informal a severe beating or defeat.

pas·tis /päˈstēs/ ▶ **n.** (pl. same) an aniseed-flavored aperitif. [Fr.]

past mas·ter ▶ **n.** **1** a person who is particularly skilled at a specified activity or art. **2** a person who has held the position of master in an organization.

pas·tor /ˈpastər/ ▶ **n.** a minister in charge of a Christian church or congregation. ▶ **v.** [trans.] be pastor of (a church or a congregation). —**pas·tor·ship** **n.** [ME: ult. from L. *pastor* 'shepherd,' from *past-* 'fed,' from v. *pascere*.]

pas·to·ral /ˈpastərəl; pasˈtôrəl/ ▶ **adj.** **1** (esp. of land or a farm) used for or related to the keeping or grazing of sheep or cattle. ■ associated with country life. ■ (of a work of art) portraying or evoking country life, typically in a romanticized or idealized form. **2** (in the Christian Church) concerning or appropriate to the giving of spiritual guidance. ▶ **n.** a work of literature portraying an idealized version of country life. —**pas·to·ral·ism** /ˈpastərə,lizəm/ **n.** **pas·to·ral·ly** **adv.**

pas·to·rale /,pastəˈräl; -ˈral/ ▶ **n.** (pl. **-rales** or **-ra·li** /-ˈrälē/) **1** a slow instrumental composition in compound time, usually with drone notes in the bass. **2** a simple musical play with a rural subject. [18th C.: from Ital., lit. 'pastoral.']

pas·to·ral·ist /ˈpastərəlist/ ▶ **n.** **1** a sheep or cattle farmer. **2** archaic a writer of pastorals.

pas·tor·ate /ˈpastərit/ ▶ **n.** the office or period of office of a pastor. ■ pastors collectively.

past par·ti·ci·ple ▶ **n.** Gram. the form of a verb, typically ending in *-ed* in English, that is used in forming perfect and passive tenses and sometimes as an adjective, e.g., *looked* in *have you looked?* and *lost* in *lost property*.

past per·fect ▶ **adj.** Gram. (of a tense) denoting an action completed prior to some past point of time specified or implied, formed in English by *had* and the past participle, as in *he had gone by then.* ▶ **n.** the past perfect tense.

pas·tra·mi /pəˈsträmē/ ▶ **n.** highly seasoned smoked beef, typically served in thin slices. [Yiddish.]

pas·try /ˈpāstrē/ ▶ **n.** (pl. **-tries**) a dough of flour, shortening, and water, used as a base and covering in baked dishes such as pies. ■ an item of food consisting of sweet pastry with a cream, jam, or fruit filling. [ME (as a collective term): from PASTE.]

pas·tur·age /ˈpascHərij/ ▶ **n.** land used for pasture. ■ the occupation or process of pasturing cattle, sheep, or other grazing animals.

pas·ture /ˈpascHər/ ▶ **n.** land covered with grass and other low plants suitable for grazing animals, esp. cattle or sheep. ■ the grass and herbage growing on such land. ■ fig. a place or activity regarded as offering new opportunities. ▶ **v.** [trans.] put (animals) in a pasture to graze. ■ [intrans.] (of animals) graze: *the livestock pastured and the crops grew.*
– PHRASES **put someone out to pasture** force someone to retire. [ME: from OFr., from late L. *pastura* 'grazing,' from *past-* 'grazed,' from v. *pascere*.]

pas·ture·land /ˈpascHər,land/ ▶ **n.** land used as pasture.

pas·ture rose ▶ **n.** a wild rose (*Rosa carolina*) of the eastern US with deep pink flowers and straight, thin thorns. Also called CAROLINA ROSE.

pasture rose

past·y[1] /ˈpastē/ (also **past·ie**) ▶ **n.** (pl. **past·ies**) esp. Brit. a folded pastry case filled with seasoned meat and vegetables. [ME: from OFr. *paste(e)*, based on late L. *pasta* 'paste.']

past·y[2] /ˈpāstē/ ▶ **adj.** (**past·i·er**, **past·i·est**) **1** (of a person's face) unhealthily pale. **2** of or like paste. —**past·i·ness** /-stēnis/ **n.**

Pat. ▶ **abbr.** Patent.

pat[1] /pat/ ▶ **v.** (**pat·ted**, **pat·ting**) [trans.] touch quickly and gently with the flat of the hand. ■ draw attention to (something) by tapping it gently. ■ [trans.] mold into shape or put in position with gentle taps. ▶ **n.** **1** a light stroke with the hand. **2** a compact mass of soft material: *a pat of butter*.
– PHRASES **a pat on the back** an expression of approval or congratulation. **pat someone on the back** express approval of or admiration for someone. [ME: prob. imitative.]

pat[2] ▶ **adj.** simple and somewhat glib or unconvincing. ▶ **adv.** at exactly the right moment or in the right way; conveniently or opportunely.
– PHRASES **down pat** see DOWN[1]. **stand pat** stick stubbornly to one's opinion or decision. ■ (in poker and blackjack) retain one's hand as dealt, without drawing other cards. —**pat·ly** **adv.** **pat·ness** **n.** [16th C.: rel. to PAT[1].]

pa·ta·gi·um /pəˈtājēəm/ ▶ **n.** (pl. **-gi·a** /-jēə/) Zool. a membrane or fold of skin between the forelimbs and hind limbs on each side of a bat or gliding mammal. ■ Entomol. a lobe that covers the wing joint in many moths. [19th C.: from L., 'gold edging', from Gk. *patageion*.]

Pat·a·go·ni·a /,patəˈgōnēə/ a region in South America, in southern Argentina and Chile. —**Pat·a·go·ni·an** **adj.** & **n.**

Pa·ta·li·pu·tra /,pätäləˈpo͞otrə/ ancient name for PATNA.

pa·ta·phys·ics /,pätəˈfiziks/ ▶ **plural n.** [usu. treated as sing.] the branch of philosophy that deals with an imaginary realm additional to metaphysics. [1940s: from Gk. *ta epi ta metaphusika*, lit. 'the (works) imposed on the Metaphysics.']

patch /pacH/ ▶ **n.** **1** a piece of cloth or other material used to mend or strengthen a torn or weak point. ■ a pad or shield worn over a sightless or injured eye or an eye socket. ■ a piece of cloth sewn onto clothing as a badge or distinguishing mark. ■ Comput. a small piece of code inserted into a program to improve its functioning or to correct a fault. ■ an adhesive piece of drug-impregnated material worn on the skin so that the drug can be absorbed gradually over a period of time. ■ (on an animal or bird) an area of hair or plumage different in color from that on most of the rest of the body. ■ a part of something marked out from the rest by a particular characteristic. ■ a small area or amount of something. ■ hist. a small disk of black silk attached to the face, esp. as worn by women in the 17th and 18th centuries for adornment. **2** a small piece of ground, esp. one used for gardening. **3** a temporary electrical or telephone connection. ■ a preset configuration or sound data file in an electronic musical instrument, esp. a synthesizer. ▶ **v.** [trans.] **1** mend or strengthen (fabric or an item of clothing) by putting a piece of material over a hole or weak point in it. ■ Med. place a patch over (a good eye) in order to encourage a lazy eye to work. ■ Comput. correct, enhance, or modify (a routine or program) by inserting a patch. ■ (usu. **be patched**) cover small areas of (a surface) with something different, causing it to appear variegated. ■ (**patch someone/something up**) informal treat someone's injuries or repair the damage to something, esp. hastily. ■ (**patch something together**) construct something hastily from unsuitable components. ■ (**patch something up**) informal restore peaceful or friendly relations after a quarrel or dispute. **2** [trans.] connect by a temporary electrical, radio, or telephonic connection. ■ [intrans.] become connected in this way. —**patch·er** **n.** [ME: perh. based on OFr. *piece* 'piece.']

patch·board /ˈpacH,bôrd/ ▶ **n.** another term for PATCH PANEL.

patch cord ▶ **n.** an insulated cord with a plug at each end, for use with a patch panel.

patch·ou·li /pəˈcHo͞olē/ ▶ **n.** **1** an aromatic oil obtained from a Southeast Asian shrub and used in perfumery, insecticides, and medicine. **2** the strongly scented shrub (*Pogostemon cablin*) of the mint family from which this oil is obtained. [19th C.: from Tamil.]

patch pan·el (also **patch·board**) ▶ **n.** a board in a switchboard, computer, or other device with a number of electric sockets that can be connected in various combinations.

patch pock·et ▶ **n.** a pocket made of a separate piece of cloth sewn on to the outside of a garment.

patch reef ▶ **n.** a small, isolated platform of coral.

patch test ▶ **n.** a test to discover whether a person is allergic to any of a range of substances that are applied to the skin in light scratches or under a patch.

patch·work /ˈpaCH,wərk/ ▶ **n.** needlework in which small pieces of cloth in different designs, colors, or textures are sewn together. ■ the craft of sewing in this way. ■ a thing composed of many different elements so as to appear variegated.

patch·y /ˈpaCHē/ ▶ **adj.** (**patch·i·er, patch·i·est**) existing or happening in small, isolated areas. ■ not of the same quality throughout; inconsistent. ■ incomplete. — **patch·i·ly adv. patch·i·ness n.**

patd. ▶ **abbr.** patented.

pate /pāt/ ▶ **n.** archaic humorous a person's head. [ME: of unknown origin.]

pâte /pät/ ▶ **n.** the paste of which porcelain is made. [19th C.: Fr., lit. 'paste.']

pâ·té /päˈtā/ ▶ **n.** a rich, savory paste made from finely minced or mashed ingredients, typically seasoned meat or fish. [Fr., from OFr. *paste* 'pie of seasoned meat.']

pâ·té de foie gras /päˈtā də ,fwä ˈgrä/ ▶ **n.** a smooth rich paste made from fattened goose liver. [Fr.]

pa·tel·la /pəˈtelə/ ▶ **n.** (pl. **-lae** /-lē/) Anat. the kneecap. — **pa·tel·lar** /-ˈtelər/ **adj. pa·tel·late** /-ˈtelit; -,lāt/ **adj.** [16th C.: from L., dimin. of *patina* 'shallow dish.']

pat·en /ˈpatn/ ▶ **n.** a plate, typically made of gold or silver, used for holding the bread during the Eucharist and sometimes as a cover for the chalice. ■ a shallow metal plate or dish. [ME: from OFr. *patene*, from L. *patina* 'shallow dish,' from Gk. *patanē* 'a plate.']

pa·ten·cy /ˈpatn-sē; ˈpātn-/ ▶ **n.** Med. the condition of being open, expanded, or unobstructed. ■ the condition of showing detectable parasite infection.

pat·ent ▶ **n.** /ˈpatnt/ **1** a government authority to an individual or organization conferring a right or title, esp. the sole right to make, use, or sell some invention. [Cf. LETTERS PATENT.] **2** short for PATENT LEATHER. ▶ **adj. 1** /ˈpātnt; ˈpat-/ easily recognizable; obvious. **2** Med. /ˈpātnt; ˈpat/ (of a vessel, duct, or aperture) open and unobstructed; failing to close. ■ (of a parasitic infection) showing detectable parasites in the tissues or feces. **3** /ˈpatnt/ [attrib.] made and marketed under a patent; proprietary. ▶ **v.** /ˈpatnt/ [trans.] obtain a patent for (an invention). — **pat·ent·a·ble adj. pat·ent·ly** /ˈpatntlē; ˈpā-/ **adv.** (in sense 1 of the **adjective**). [ME: from OFr., from L. *patent-* 'lying open,' from v. *patere*.]

pat·ent·ee /,patnˈtē/ ▶ **n.** a person or organization that obtains or holds a patent for something.

pat·ent leath·er ▶ **n.** leather with a glossy varnished surface, used chiefly for shoes, belts, and purses.

pat·ent med·i·cine ▶ **n.** a proprietary medicine made and marketed under a patent and available without prescription.

pat·ent of·fice ▶ **n.** an office from which patents are issued.

pat·ent right ▶ **n.** the exclusive right conferred by a patent: *one of the collaborators has agreed to waive its patent rights to the cowpea gene.*

pa·ter /ˈpātər; ˈpä-/ ▶ **n.** Anthropol. a person's legal father. Often contrasted with GENITOR. [L.]

pa·ter·fa·mil·i·as /,pātərfəˈmilēəs; ,pä-/ ▶ **n.** (pl. **pa·tres·fa·mil·i·as** /,pātrēzfə-; ,pä-/) the male head of a family or household. Compare with MATERFAMILIAS. [L., lit. 'father of the family.']

pa·ter·nal /pəˈtərnl/ ▶ **adj.** of or appropriate to a father. ■ showing a kindness and care associated with a father; fatherly. ■ [attrib.] related through the father. — **pa·ter·nal·ly adv.** [ME: from late L. *paternalis*, from L. *paternus* 'fatherly,' from *pater* 'father.']

pa·ter·nal·ism /pəˈtərnl,izəm/ ▶ **n.** the policy or practice on the part of people in positions of authority of restricting the freedom and responsibilities of those subordinate to them in the subordinates' supposed best interest. — **pa·ter·nal·ist n. & adj. pa·ter·nal·is·tic** /-,tərnlˈistik/ **adj. pa·ter·nal·is·ti·cal·ly** /-,tərnlˈistik(ə)lē/ **adv.**

pa·ter·ni·ty /pəˈternitē/ ▶ **n. 1** (esp. in legal contexts) the state of being someone's father. **2** paternal origin.

pa·ter·ni·ty suit ▶ **n.** a court case held to establish formally the identity of a child's father, typically in order to require the man to support the child financially.

pa·ter·ni·ty test ▶ **n.** a medical test, typically a blood test, to determine whether a man may be the father of a particular child.

pa·ter·nos·ter /ˈpätər,nästər; ˈpatər-/ ▶ **n. 1** (in the Roman Catholic Church) the Lord's Prayer, esp. in Latin. ■ any of a number of special beads occurring at regular intervals in a rosary, indicating that the Lord's Prayer is to be recited. **2** (also **paternoster lift**) an elevator consisting of a series of linked doorless compartments moving continuously on an endless belt. [OE, from L. *pater noster* 'our father.']

Pat·er·son[1] /ˈpatərsən/ a city in northeastern New Jersey; pop. 149,222.

Pat·er·son[2], William (1745–1806), US Supreme Court associate justice 1793–1806.

path /paTH/ ▶ **n.** (pl. **paths** /paT͟HZ; paTHS/) a way or track laid down for walking or made by continual treading. ■ [with adj.] such a way or track designed for a particular purpose: *a nature path.* ■ the course or direction in which a person or thing is moving. ■ a course of action or conduct. ■ Comput. a definition of the order in which an operating system or program searches for a file or executable program. ■ a schedule available for allocation to an individual railroad train over a given route. [OE *pæth*, of West Gmc. origin; rel. to Ger. *Pfad*.]

path. ▶ **abbr.** ■ pathological. ■ pathology.

-path ▶ **comb. form 1** denoting a practitioner of curative treatment: *homeopath.* **2** denoting a person who suffers from a disease: *psychopath.* [back-form. from -PATHY, or from Gk. *-pathēs* '-sufferer.']

Pa·than /pəˈtän/ (also **Pash·tun** /pəshˈto͞on/) ▶ **n.** a member of a Pashto-speaking people inhabiting northwestern Pakistan and southeastern Afghanistan. [from Hindi *Paṭhān*.]

path·break·ing /ˈpaTH,brākiNG/ (also **path-break·ing**) ▶ **adj.** pioneering; innovative. — **path·break·er n.**

pa·thet·ic /pəˈTHetik/ ▶ **adj.** arousing pity, esp. through vulnerability or sadness. ■ informal miserably inadequate. — **pa·thet·i·cal·ly adv.** [16th C.: via late L. from Gk. *pathētikos* 'sensitive,' based on *pathos* 'suffering.']

pa·thet·ic fal·la·cy ▶ **n.** the attribution of human feelings and responses to inanimate things or animals, esp. in art and literature.

Path·find·er /ˈpaTH,fīndər/ (in full **Mars Pathfinder**) an unmanned American spacecraft that landed on Mars in 1997, deploying a small robotic rover (*Sojourner*) to explore the surface and examine the rocks.

path·find·er /ˈpaTH,fīndər/ ▶ **n.** a person who goes ahead and discovers or shows others a path or way. ■ an aircraft or its pilot sent ahead to locate and mark the target area for bombing. ■ [usu. as adj.] an experimental plan or forecast.

path length ▶ **n.** Physics the overall length of the path followed by a light ray or sound wave.

path·name /ˈpaTH,nām/ (also **path name**) ▶ **n.** Comput. a description of where a file or other item is to be found in a hierarchy of directories.

patho- ▶ **comb. form** relating to disease: *pathogenesis.* [from Gk. *pathos* 'suffering.']

path·o·gen /ˈpaTHəjən; -,jen/ ▶ **n.** Med. a bacterium, virus, or other microorganism that can cause disease. — **path·o·gen·ic** /,paTHəˈjenik/ **adj. path·o·ge·nic·i·ty** /,paTHəjə,nisitē/ **n. pa·thog·e·nous** /pəˈTHäjənəs/ **adj.**

path·o·gen·e·sis /,paTHəˈjenəsis/ ▶ **n.** Med. the manner of development of a disease. — **path·o·ge·net·ic** /-jəˈnetik/ **adj.**

pa·thog·no·mon·ic /pə,THägnəˈmänik; ,paTHəgnə-/ ▶ **adj.** Med. (of a sign or symptom) specifically characteristic or indicative of a particular disease or condition. [17th C.: from Gk. *pathognōmonikos* 'skilled in diagnosis,' from *pathos* 'suffering' + *gnōmōn* 'judge.']

pa·thog·ra·phy /pəˈTHägrəfē/ ▶ **n.** (pl. **-phies**) a study of the life of an individual or the history of a community with regard to the influence of a particular disease or psychological disorder. ■ writing of such a type as a branch of literature.

path·o·log·i·cal /,paTHəˈläjikəl/ (also **path·o·log·ic**) ▶ **adj.** of or relating to pathology. ■ involving, caused by, or of the nature of a physical or mental disease. ■ informal compulsive; obsessive. — **path·o·log·i·cal·ly adv.**

pa·thol·o·gize /pəˈTHälə,jīz/ ▶ **v.** [trans.] regard or treat (someone or something) as psychologically abnormal or unhealthy. — **pa·thol·o·gi·za·tion** /pə,THäləjəˈzāSHən/ **n.**

pa·thol·o·gy /pəˈTHäləjē/ ▶ **n.** the science of the causes and effects of diseases, esp. the branch of medicine that deals with the laboratory examination of samples of body tissue for diagnostic or forensic purposes. ■ Med. pathological features considered collectively; the typical behavior of a disease. ■ Med. a pathological condition. ■ mental, social, or linguistic abnormality or malfunction. — **pa·thol·o·gist n.**

path·o·phys·i·ol·o·gy /,paTHə,fizēˈäləjē/ ▶ **n.** Med. the disordered physiological processes associated with disease or injury. — **path·o·phys·i·o·log·ic** /-,fizēəˈläjik/ **adj. path·o·phys·i·o·log·i·cal** /-,fizēəˈläjikəl/ **adj. path·o·phys·i·o·log·i·cal·ly** /,fizēəˈläjik(ə)lē/ **adv. path·o·phys·i·ol·o·gist n.**

pa·thos /ˈpā,THäs; -,THôs/ ▶ **n.** a quality that evokes pity or sadness. [17th C.: from Gk. 'suffering.']

path·way /ˈpaTH,wā/ ▶ **n.** a way that constitutes or serves as a path. ■ Physiol. a route, formed by a chain of nerve cells, along which impulses of a particular kind usually travel. ■ (also **metabolic pathway**) Biochem. a sequence of chemical reactions undergone by a compound or class of compounds in a living organism.

-pathy ▶ **comb. form 1** denoting feelings: *telepathy.* **2** denoting disorder in a particular part of the body: *neuropathy.* **3** relating to curative treatment of a specified kind: *hydropathy.* [from Gk. *patheia* 'suffering.']

pa·tience /ˈpāSHəns/ ▶ **n.** the capacity to accept or tolerate delay, trouble, or suffering without getting angry or upset.
– PHRASES **lose patience** (or **lose one's patience**) become unable to keep one's temper.

pa·tient /ˈpāSHənt/ ▶ **adj.** able to wait without becoming annoyed or anxious. ■ slow to lose one's temper with irritating people or situations. ▶ **n. 1** a person receiving or registered to receive medical treatment. **2** Ling. the semantic role of a noun phrase denoting something that is affected or acted upon by the action of a verb. — **pa·tient·ly adv.** [ME: from OFr., from L. *patient-* 'suffering,' from v. *pati*.]

pat·i·na /pəˈtēnə/ ▶ **n.** a green or brown film on the surface of bronze or similar metals, produced by oxidation over a long period. ■ a gloss or sheen on wooden furniture produced by age and polishing. ■ an acquired change in the appearance of a surface. ■ fig. an impression or appearance of something. — **pat·i·nat·ed** /ˈpatnˌātid/ **adj.** **pat·i·na·tion** /ˌpatnˈāsʜən/ **n.** [18th C.: from Ital., from L. *patina* 'shallow dish.']

pat·i·o /ˈpatēˌō/ ▶ **n.** (pl. **-os**) a paved outdoor area adjoining a house. ■ a roofless inner courtyard in a Spanish or Spanish-American house. [19th C.: from Sp., 'inner courtyard.']

pat·i·o rose ▶ **n.** a miniature floribunda rose.

pa·tis·se·rie /pəˈtisərē/ ▶ **n.** a shop where French pastries and cakes are sold. ■ French pastries and cakes collectively. [16th C.: from Fr. *pâtisserie*, from med. L. *pasticium* 'pastry,' from *pasta* 'paste.']

Pat·mos /ˈpatmäs; -məs; ˈpatmôs/ a Greek island in the Aegean Sea, one of the Dodecanese group.

Pat·na /ˈpatnə; ˈpət-/ a city in northeastern India, on the Ganges River; pop. 917,000. Former name **Pataliputra**.

pat·ois /ˈpaˌtwä; ˈpä-/ ▶ **n.** (pl. same) the dialect of the common people of a region, differing in various respects from the standard language of the rest of the country. ■ the jargon or informal speech used by a particular social group. [17th C.: Fr., lit. 'rough speech.']

Pa·ton /ˈpātn/, Alan Stewart (1903–88), South African writer. His novels include *Cry, the Beloved Country* (1948), an indictment of the apartheid system.

pa·tonce /pəˈtäns/ ▶ **adj.** [postpositive] Heraldry (of a cross) with limbs that broaden from the center and end in three pointed lobes: *a cross patonce*. [16th C.: prob. based on med. L. *potentia* 'crutch.']

pa·too·tie /pəˈto͞otē/ ▶ **n.** (pl. **-ties**) informal **1** dated a girlfriend or a pretty girl. **2** derog. a person's or animal's buttocks. [1920s: perh. an alt. of **potato**.]

Pa·tras /pəˈtras; ˈpatrəs/ a port in the northwestern Peloponnese, on the Gulf of Patras; pop. 155,000. Greek name **Pátrai**.

pa·tres·fa·mil·i·as /ˌpatrēzfəˈmilēəs; ˌpä-/ plural form of **paterfamilias**.

pa·tri·arch /ˈpātrēˌärk/ ▶ **n.** **1** the male head of a family or tribe. ■ a man who is the oldest or most venerable of a group. ■ a man who behaves in a commanding manner. ■ a person or thing that is regarded as the founder of something. **2** any of those biblical figures regarded as fathers of the human race, esp. Abraham, Isaac, and Jacob, their forefathers, or the sons of Jacob. **3** the title of a most senior Orthodox or Catholic bishop, in particular: ■ a bishop of one of the most ancient Christian sees (Alexandria, Antioch, Constantinople, Jerusalem, and formerly Rome). ■ the head of an autocephalous or independent Orthodox church. ■ a Roman Catholic bishop ranking above primates and metropolitans and immediately below the pope, often the head of a Uniate community. [ME: ult. from Gk. *patriarkhēs*, from *patria* 'family' + *arkhēs* 'ruling.']

pa·tri·ar·chal /ˌpātrēˈärkəl/ ▶ **adj.** **1** of, relating to, or characteristic of a patriarch. **2** of, relating to, or characteristic of a system of society or government controlled by men: *patriarchal values*. — **pa·tri·ar·chal·ly** **adv.**

pa·tri·arch·ate /ˈpātrēˌärkit; -ärˌkāt/ ▶ **n.** the office, see, or residence of an ecclesiastical patriarch.

pa·tri·arch·y /ˈpātrēˌärkē/ ▶ **n.** (pl. **-arch·ies**) a system of society or government in which the father or eldest male is head of the family and descent is traced through the male line. ■ a system of society or government in which men hold the power and women are largely excluded from it. ■ a society or community organized in this way.

pa·tri·ate /ˈpātrēˌāt/ ▶ **v.** [trans.] transfer control over (a constitution) from a mother country to its former dependency.

pa·tri·cian /pəˈtrisʜən/ ▶ **n.** an aristocrat or nobleman. ■ a member of a long-established wealthy family. ■ a member of a noble family or class in ancient Rome. ▶ **adj.** belonging to or characteristic of the aristocracy. ■ belonging to or characteristic of a long-established and wealthy family. ■ belonging to the nobility of ancient Rome. [ME: from OFr. *patricien*, from L. *patricius* 'having a noble father,' from *pater, patr-* 'father.']

pa·tri·ci·ate /pəˈtrisʜē-it; -ˌāt/ ▶ **n.** a noble order or class. ■ the position or rank of patrician in ancient Rome.

pat·ri·cide /ˈpatrəˌsīd/ ▶ **n.** the killing of one's father. ■ a person who kills their father. — **pat·ri·cid·al** /ˌpatrəˈsīdl/ **adj.** [17th C.: from late L. *patricidium*, alt. of L. *parricidium* (see **parricide**).]

Pat·rick, St. /ˈpatrik/ (5th century), patron saint of Ireland.

pat·ri·lin·e·al /ˌpatrəˈlinēəl/ ▶ **adj.** of, relating to, or based on relationship to the father or descent through the male line. [20th C.: from L. *pater, patr-* 'father.']

pat·ri·lo·cal /ˌpatrəˈlōkəl/ ▶ **adj.** of or relating to a pattern of marriage in which the couple settles in the husband's home or community. — **pat·ri·lo·cal·i·ty** /-lōˈkalətē/ **n.** [20th C.: from L. *pater, patr-* 'father.']

pat·ri·mo·ny /ˈpatrəˌmōnē/ ▶ **n.** (pl. **-nies**) property inherited from one's father or male ancestor. ■ heritage. ■ esp. hist. the estate or property belonging by ancient endowment or right to a church or other institution. — **pat·ri·mo·ni·al** /ˌpatrəˈmōnēəl/ **adj.** [ME: ult. from L. *patrimonium*, from *pater, patr-* 'father.']

pa·tri·ot /ˈpātrēət/ ▶ **n.** **1** a person who vigorously supports their country and is prepared to defend it against enemies or detractors. **2** (**Patriot**) trademark an automated surface-to-air missile system designed for early detection and interception of missiles or aircraft. ■ a missile deployed in this system. — **pa·tri·ot·ism** **n.** [16th C.: ult. from *patrios* 'of one's fathers,' from *patris* 'fatherland.']

pa·tri·ot·ic /ˌpātrēˈätik/ ▶ **adj.** having or expressing devotion to and vigorous support for one's country. — **pa·tri·ot·i·cal·ly** **adv.**

pa·tri·ot·ic front ▶ **n.** a militant nationalist political organization.

pa·tris·tic /pəˈtristik/ ▶ **adj.** of or relating to the early Christian theologians or to patristics. [19th C.: from Ger. *patristisch*, from L. *pater, patr-* 'father.']

pa·tris·tics /pəˈtristiks/ ▶ **plural n.** [treated as sing.] the branch of Christian theology that deals with the lives, writings, and doctrines of the early Christian theologians.

Pa·tro·clus /pəˈtrōkləs/ Gk. Mythol. a Greek hero of the Trojan War, the close friend of Achilles.

pa·trol /pəˈtrōl/ ▶ **n.** a person or group of people sent to keep watch over an area, esp. a detachment of guards or police. ■ the action of keeping watch over an area by walking or driving around it at regular intervals. ■ an expedition to carry out reconnaissance. ■ a detachment of troops sent out to reconnoiter. ■ a routine operational voyage of a ship or aircraft. ■ a unit of six to eight Girl Scouts or Boy Scouts forming part of a troop. ▶ **v.** (**-trolled**, **-trol·ling**) [trans.] keep watch over (an area) by regularly walking or traveling around or through it. — **pa·trol·ler** **n.** [17th C.: from Ger. *Patrolle*, from Fr. *patrouille*, from *patrouiller* 'paddle in mud,' from *patte* 'paw' + dial. *(gad)rouille* 'dirty water.']

pa·trol·man /pəˈtrōlmən/ ▶ **n.** (pl. **-men**) a patrolling police officer.

pa·trol·o·gy /pəˈträləjē/ ▶ **n.** another term for **patristics**. — **pa·trol·o·gist** **n.** [17th C.: from Gk. *patēr, patr-* 'father.']

pa·trol wag·on ▶ **n.** a police van for transporting prisoners.

pa·tron /ˈpātrən/ ▶ **n.** **1** a person who gives financial or other support to a person, organization, cause, or activity. **2** a customer, esp. a regular one, of a store, restaurant, or theater. **3** short for **patron saint**. **4** (in ancient Rome) a patrician in relation to a client. See also **client** (sense 3). ■ (in ancient Rome) the former owner and (frequently) protector of a freed slave. [ME: from OFr., from L. *patronus* 'defender,' from *pater, patr-* 'father.']

pa·tron·age /ˈpātrənij; ˈpat-/ ▶ **n.** **1** the support given by a patron. **2** the power to control appointments to office or the right to privileges. **3** a patronizing or condescending manner. **4** the regular business given to a store, restaurant, or public service by a person or group. **5** (in ancient Rome) the rights and duties or the position of a patron.

pa·tron·al /ˈpātrənl/ ▶ **adj.** of or relating to a patron saint.

pa·tron·ess /ˈpātrənis/ ▶ **n.** a female patron.

pa·tron·ize /ˈpātrəˌnīz; ˈpat-/ ▶ **v.** **1** [often as adj.] (**patronizing**) treat with an apparent kindness that betrays a feeling of superiority. **2** frequent (a store, theater, restaurant, or other establishment) as a customer. ■ give encouragement and financial support to (a person, esp. an artist, or a cause). — **pa·tron·i·za·tion** /ˌpātrəniˈzāsʜən; ˌpat-/ **n.** **pa·tron·iz·er** **n.** **pa·tron·iz·ing·ly** /-ˌnīzinɢlē/ **adv.**

pa·tron saint ▶ **n.** the protecting or guiding saint of a person or place.

Pa·trons of Hus·band·ry ▶ **n.** see **grange** (sense 2).

pat·ro·nym·ic /ˌpatrəˈnimik/ ▶ **n.** a name derived from the name of a father or ancestor, typically by the addition of a prefix or suffix, e.g., *Johnson, O'Brien, Ivanovich*. [17th C.: via late L. from Gk. *patrōnumikos*, from *patrōnumos*, from *patēr, patr-* 'father' + *onuma* 'name.']

pa·troon /pəˈtro͞on/ ▶ **n.** hist. a person given land and granted certain manorial privileges under the former Dutch governments of New York and New Jersey. [17th C.: from Du.]

pat·sy /ˈpatsē/ ▶ **n.** (pl. **-sies**) informal a person who is easily taken advantage of, esp. by being cheated or blamed for something. [20th C.: of unknown origin.]

pat·tée /pəˈtā/ ▶ **adj.** [postpositive] (of a cross) having almost triangular arms, narrow at the center and broadening to squared ends: *a cross pattée*. See illustration at **cross**. [15th C.: from Fr., from *patte* 'paw.']

pat·ten /ˈpatn/ ▶ **n.** hist. a shoe or clog with a raised sole or set on an iron ring, worn to raise one's feet above wet or muddy ground when walking outdoors. [ME: from OFr. *patin*, perh. from *patte* 'paw.']

pat·ter[1] /ˈpatər/ ▶ **v.** [intrans.] make a repeated light tapping sound. ■ run with quick light steps. ▶ **n.** [in sing.] a repeated light tapping. [17th C.: frequentative of **pat**[1].]

pat·ter[2] ▶ **n.** rapid or smooth-flowing continuous talk, such as that used by a comedian or salesman. ■ rapid speech included in a song, esp. for comic effect. ■ the special language or jargon of a profession or other group. ▶ **v.** [intrans.] talk at length without saying anything significant. [ME: from **paternoster**.]

pat·tern /ˈpatərn/ ▶ **n.** **1** a repeated decorative design. ■ an arrangement or sequence regularly found in comparable objects or events. ■ a regular and intelligible form or sequence discernible in certain actions or situations. **2** a model or design used as a guide in needlework and other crafts. ■ a set of instructions to be followed in making a sewn or knitted item. ■ a wooden or metal model from which a mold is made for a casting. ■ an example for others to follow. ■ a sample of cloth or wallpaper. ▶ **v.** [trans.] **1** [usu. as adj.] (**patterned**) decorate with a recurring design. **2** give a regular or intelligible form to. ■ (**pattern something on/after**) give something a form based on that of (something else). [ME *patron* 'something serving as a model,' from OFr. (see **patron**).]

Pat·ter·son /ˈpatərsən/, Floyd (1935–2006), US boxer. He was world heavyweight champion 1956–59, 1960–62.

Pat·ton /ˈpatn/, George Smith, Jr. (1885–1945), US general; known as **Old Blood and Guts**. During World War II, he commanded forces in the

PRONUNCIATION KEY ə *ago, up*; ər *over, fur*; a *hat*; ā *ate*; ä *car*; e *let*; ē *see*; i *fit*; ī *by*; ɴɢ *sing*; ō *go*; ô *law, for*; oi *toy*; o͝o *good*; o͞o *goo*; ou *out*; ᴛʜ *thin*; ᴛʜ *then*; ᴢʜ *vision* invasion of northwest Africa 1942–43, the invasion of Sicily 1943, and the drive through France 1944.

pat·ty /ˈpatē/ ▶ n. (pl. -ties) a small flat cake of minced or finely chopped food, esp. meat. ■ a small, round, flat chocolate-covered peppermint candy. ■ esp. Brit. a small pie or turnover. [17th C.: alt. of Fr. *pâté*, by association with PASTY[1].]

pat·ty-cake (also **pat-a-cake**) ▶ n. a children's game in which participants gently clap each other's hands and their own in time to the words of a rhyme.

pat·ty·pan /ˈpatē,pan/ (also **pattypan squash**) ▶ n. a squash of a saucer-shaped variety with a scalloped rim and creamy white flesh.

pat·ty shell ▶ n. a shell of puff pastry with a cooked meat or vegetable filling.

pat·u·lous /ˈpaCHələs/ ▶ adj. rare (esp. of the branches of a tree) spreading. [17th C.: from L. *patulus* (from *patere* 'be open.')]

pat·zer /ˈpätsər; ˈpat-/ ▶ n. a poor chess player. [1940s: perh. rel. to Ger. *patzen* 'to bungle.']

PAU ▶ abbr. Pan American Union.

pau·ci·ty /ˈpôsitē/ ▶ n. [in sing.] the presence of something only in small or insufficient quantities or amounts; scarcity. [ME: from OFr. *paucite* or L. *paucitas*, from *paucus* 'few.']

Paul /pôl/, Les (1915–), US guitarist; born *Lester Polfus*. His style of play influenced many jazz and rock guitarists.

Paul III (1468–1549), Italian pope 1534–49; born *Alessandro Farnese*. He excommunicated Henry VIII of England in 1538, instituted the order of the Jesuits in 1540, and initiated the Council of Trent in 1545.

Paul, St. (died *c.*64), one of the 12 Apostles; known as **Paul the Apostle**, **Saul of Tarsus**, or **the Apostle of the Gentiles**. His epistles form part of the New Testament.

Pau·li /ˈpôlē; ˈpou-/, Wolfgang (1900–58), US physicist; born in Austria. He made a major contribution to quantum theory. Nobel Prize for Physics (1945).

Pau·li ex·clu·sion prin·ci·ple (also **Pauli's exclusion principle**) Physics the assertion that no two fermions can have the same quantum number. [1920s: named after W. PAULI.]

Pau·line /ˈpô,līn; -,lēn/ ▶ adj. Christian Theol. of, relating to, or characteristic of St. Paul, his writings, or his doctrines. ■ (in the Roman Catholic Church) of or relating to Pope Paul VI, or the liturgical and doctrinal reforms pursued during his pontificate (1963–78) as a result of the Second Vatican Council.

Paul·ing /ˈpôliNG/, Linus Carl (1901–94), US chemist. His suggestion of a helical structure for proteins formed the foundation for the elucidation of the structure of DNA. Nobel Prize for Chemistry (1954).

pau·low·ni·a /pôˈlōnēə/ ▶ n. a small Southeast Asian tree (genus *Paulownia*) of the figwort family, with heart-shaped leaves and fragrant lilac flowers. [mod. L., named after Anna *Pavlovna* (1795–1865), a Russ. princess.]

paunch /pônCH; pänCH/ ▶ n. a large or protruding abdomen or stomach. — **paunch·i·ness** n. **paunch·y** adj. [ME: from Anglo-Norman Fr. *pa(u)nche*, based on L. *pantex*, *pantic-*, usually in the pl. in the sense 'intestines.']

pau·per /ˈpôpər/ ▶ n. a very poor person. ■ hist. a recipient of government relief or public charity. — **pau·per·dom** n. **pau·per·ism** n. **pau·per·i·za·tion** /,pôpəriˈzāSHən/ n. **pau·per·ize** /-,rīz/ v. [15th C.: from L., lit. 'poor.']

pau·piette /pōˈpyet/ ▶ n. a long, thin slice of fish or meat, rolled and stuffed with a filling. [Fr., prob. from Ital. *polpetta*, from L. *pulpa* 'pulp.']

pau·ra·que /pouˈräkā/ ▶ n. a long-tailed nightjar found in southern Texas, Mexico, and Central and South America, esp. the **common pauraque** (*Nyctidromus albicollis*. [prob. based on a local word.]

Pau·ro·po·da /,pôrəˈpādə/ Zool. a small class of myriapod invertebrates that resemble the centipedes. They are small, soft-bodied animals with one pair of legs per segment, living chiefly in forest litter. — **pau·ro·pod** /ˈpôrə,päd/ n. **pau·rop·o·dan** /pôˈräpədn/ n. & adj. [mod. L. (pl.), from Gk. *pauros* 'small' + *pous*, *pod-* 'foot.']

Pau·sa·ni·as /pôˈsānēəs/ (2nd century), Greek geographer and historian. His *Description of Greece* (also called the *Itinerary of Greece*) is a guide to the topography and remains of ancient Greece.

pause /pôz/ ▶ n. a temporary stop in action or speech. ■ Music a mark over a note or rest that is to be lengthened by an unspecified amount; fermata. ■ (also **pause button**) a control allowing the temporary interruption of an electronic (or mechanical) process, esp. video or audio recording or reproduction. ▶ v. [intrans.] interrupt action or speech briefly. ■ [trans.] temporarily interrupt the operation of (a videotape, audiotape, or computer program).

– PHRASES **give someone pause** cause someone to think carefully or hesitate before doing something. [ME: from OFr., from L. *pausa*, from Gk. *pausis*, from *pausein* 'to stop.']

pa·vane /pəˈvän/ (also **pa·van**) ▶ n. a stately dance in slow duple time, popular in the 16th and 17th centuries and performed in elaborate clothing. ■ a piece of music for this dance. [16th C.: from Fr. *pavane*, from Ital. *pavana*, fem. adj. from dial.*Pavo*, Padua.]

Pa·va·rot·ti /,pävəˈrätē; -väˈrôtē/, Luciano (1935–), Italian opera singer. A world-renowned tenor, he performed his last opera, Puccini's *Tosca*, in 2004.

pave /pāv/ ▶ v. [trans.] (often **be paved with**) cover (a piece of ground) with concrete, asphalt, stones, or bricks; lay paving over.

– PHRASES **pave the way for** create the circumstances to enable (something) to happen or be done. — **pav·er** n. [ME: from OFr. *paver* 'pave.']

pa·vé /pəˈvā; pa-/ ▶ n. a setting of precious stones placed so closely together that no metal shows. [Fr., lit. 'paved,' past part. of *paver*.]

pave·ment /ˈpāvmənt/ ▶ n. any paved area or surface. ■ the hard surface of a road or street. ■ Brit. a sidewalk. ■ Geol. a horizontal expanse of bare rock or cemented fragments.

– PHRASES **pound the pavement** see POUND[2]. [ME: from OFr., from L. *pavimentum* 'trodden-down floor,' from *pavire* 'tread down.']

pa·vil·ion /pəˈvilyən/ ▶ n. **1** a building or similar structure used for a specific purpose, in particular: ■ a summerhouse or other decorative building used as a shelter in a park or large garden. ■ in the names of buildings used for theatrical or other entertainments. ■ a detached or semidetached block at a hospital or other building complex. ■ a large tent with a peak and crenellated decorations, used esp. at a show or fair. ■ a temporary building, stand, or other structure in which items are displayed by a dealer or exhibitor at a trade exhibition. **2** a usually highly decorated projecting subdivision of a building. **3** the part of a cut gemstone below the girdle. [ME: from OFr. *pavillon*, from L. *papilio(n-)* 'butterfly or tent.']

pav·ing /ˈpāviNG/ ▶ n. pavement. ■ the materials used for a pavement.

pav·ior /ˈpāvyər/ (also Brit. **pav·iour**) ▶ n. a paving stone. ■ a person who lays paving stones. [ME: from OFr. *paveur*, from *paver* 'pave.']

Pa·vlov /ˈpav,läv; -lôf; -ləf/, Ivan Petrovich (1849–1936), Russian physiologist. He is known for his studies on the conditioned reflex. Nobel Prize for Physiology or Medicine (1904).

Pav·lo·va /pävˈlōvə; ˈpävləvə/ Anna Pavlovna (1881–1931), Russian ballet dancer. *The Dying Swan* was created for her by Michel Fokine in 1905.

pa·vlo·va /pävˈlōvə; ˈpavləvə/ ▶ n. a dessert consisting of a meringue base or shell filled with whipped cream and fruit. [A. PAVLOVA.]

Pav·lov·i·an /pavˈlōvēən; -ˈläv-/ ▶ adj. of or relating to classical conditioning as described by I. P. Pavlov.

Pa·vo /ˈpāvō/ Astron. a southern constellation (the Peacock), between Grus and Triangulum Australe. Its brightest star is itself sometimes called "the Peacock." [L.]

pav·o·nine /ˈpavə,nīn; -nin/ ▶ adj. literary, rare of or like a peacock. [17th C.: from L. *pavoninus*, from *pavo*, *pavon-* 'peacock.']

paw /pô/ ▶ n. an animal's foot having claws and pads. ■ esp. derog. a person's hand. ▶ v. [trans.] (of an animal) feel or scrape with a paw or hoof. ■ informal (of a person) touch or handle awkwardly or roughly. ■ (of a person) touch (someone) in a lascivious and offensive way. [ME: from OFr. *poue*, prob. of Gmc. origin and rel. to Du. *poot*.]

pawk·y /ˈpôkē/ ▶ adj. (**pawk·i·er**, **pawk·i·est**) esp. Brit. having or showing a sly sense of humor. ■ shrewd. — **pawk·i·ly** adv. **pawk·i·ness** n. [17th C.: from Scots, north. Engl. *pawk* 'trick.']

pawl /pôl/ ▶ n. a pivoted curved bar or lever whose free end engages with the teeth of a cogwheel or ratchet so that the wheel or ratchet can only turn or move one way. ■ each of a set of short stout bars that engage with the whelps and prevent a capstan, windlass, or winch from recoiling. [17th C.: perh. from Low Ger. Du. *pal* (rel. to *pal* 'fixed').]

pawn[1] /pôn/ ▶ n. a chess piece of the smallest size and value. ■ a person used by others for their own purposes. [ME: from Anglo-Norman Fr. *poun*, from med. L. *pedo*, *pedon-* 'foot soldier,' from L. *pes*, *ped-* 'foot.']

pawn[2] ▶ v. [trans.] deposit (an object) with a pawnbroker as security for money lent. ▶ n. archaic an object left as security for money lent.

– PHRASES **in pawn** (of an object) held as security by a pawnbroker.

– PHRASAL VERBS **pawn someone/something off** pass off someone or something unwanted. [15th C.: from OFr. *pan* 'pledge, security,' of West Gmc. origin; rel. to Ger. *Pfand*.]

pawn·brok·er /ˈpôn,brōkər/ ▶ n. a person who lends money at interest on the security of an article pawned. — **pawn·brok·ing** n.

Paw·nee /pôˈnē/ ▶ n. (pl. same or -nees) **1** a member of an American Indian confederacy formerly living in Nebraska, and now mainly in Oklahoma. **2** the Caddoan language of these peoples. ▶ adj. of or relating to these people or their language. [from Canad. Fr. *Pani*, from a Siouan name.]

pawn·shop /ˈpôn,SHäp/ ▶ n. a pawnbroker's shop, esp. one where unredeemed items are sold to the public.

pawn tick·et ▶ n. a ticket issued by a pawnbroker in exchange for an article pawned, bearing particulars of the loan.

paw·paw /ˈpôpô/ (also **pa·paw** /pəˈpô; ˈpôpô/) ▶ n. **1** another term for PAPAYA. **2** (also **pawpaw tree**) a North American tree (*Asimina triloba*) of the custard apple family, with purple flowers and edible oblong yellow fruit with sweet pulp. ■ the fruit of this tree. [17th C.: from Sp. and Port. *papaya*, of Carib origin. The change in spelling is unexplained.]

Pax /paks; päks/ Rom. Mythol. the goddess of peace. Greek equivalent EIRENE.

pax /paks; päks/ ▶ n. esp. hist. (in the Christian Church) the kissing by all the participants at a mass of a tablet depicting the Crucifixion or other sacred object; the kiss of peace. [L., lit. 'peace.']

Pax Ro·ma·na /ˈpäks rōˈmänə/ ▶ n. hist. the peace that existed between nationalities within the Roman Empire. [L., lit. 'Roman peace.']

pay[1] /pā/ ▶ v. (past **paid**) **1** [trans.] give (someone) money that is due for work done, goods received, or a debt incurred. ■ give (a sum of money) in exchange for goods or work done or in discharge of a debt. ■ hand over or transfer the amount due of (a debt, wages, etc.) to someone. ■ (of work, an investment, etc.) yield or provide someone with (a specified sum of money). ■ [intrans.] (of a business or undertaking, or an attitude) be profitable or advantageous to someone. **2** [intrans.] suffer a loss or other misfortune as a consequence of an action. ■ [trans.] give what is due or deserved to (someone); reward or punish. **3** [with two objs.] give or bestow (attention, respect, or a compliment) on (someone). ■ make (a visit or a call) to (someone). ▶ **n.** the money paid to someone for regular work.

– PHRASES **in the pay of** employed by. **pay one's compliments** see COMPLIMENT. **pay court to** see COURT. **pay dearly** obtain something at a high cost or great effort. ■ suffer for an error or failure. **pay one's dues** see DUE. **pay for itself** (of an object or system) earn or save enough money to cover the cost of its purchase. **pay its** (or **one's**) **way** (of an enterprise or person) earn enough to cover its (or one's) costs. **pay one's last respects** show respect toward a dead person by attending their funeral. **pay one's respects** make a polite visit to someone. **pay through the nose** informal pay much more than a fair price.

– PHRASAL VERBS **pay someone back** repay a loan to someone. ■ fig. take revenge on someone. ■ reward someone for something done earlier. **pay something back** repay a loan to someone. **pay something in** pay money into a bank account. **pay off** informal (of a course of action) yield good results; succeed. **pay someone off** dismiss someone with a final payment. **pay something off** pay a debt in full. **pay something out** (or **pay out**) **1** pay a large sum of money from funds under one's control. **2** let out (a rope) by slackening it. **pay up** (or **pay something up**) pay a debt in full. — **pay·er n.** [ME: from OFr. *paie* (n.), *payer* (v.), from L. *pacare* 'appease,' from *pax*, *pac-* 'peace.']

pay² ▶ **v.** (past and past part. **payed**) [trans.] Naut. seal (the deck or hull seams of a wooden ship) with pitch or tar to prevent leakage. [17th C.: from Old North. Fr. *peier*, from L. *picare*, from *pix*, *pic-* 'pitch.']

pay·a·ble /'pāəbəl/ ▶ **adj.** [predic.] **1** (of money) required to be paid; due. **2** able to be paid. ▶ **n.** (**payables**) debts owed by a business; liabilities.

pay-as-you-go ▶ **adj.** relating to a system of paying debts or meeting costs as they arise.

pay·back /'pā,bak/ ▶ **n.** **1** financial return or reward, esp. profit equal to the initial outlay of an investment. **2** an act of revenge or retaliation.

pay ca·ble ▶ **n.** a cable television service available on a subscription basis.

pay·check /'pā,CHek/ ▶ **n.** a check for salary or wages made out to an employee. ■ fig. a salary or income.

pay·day /'pā,dā/ ▶ **n.** a day on which someone is paid or expects to be paid their wages. ■ informal money or success won or earned.

pay dirt ▶ **n.** Mining ground containing ore in sufficient quantity to be profitably extracted. ■ profit; reward.

pay·ee /,pā'ē/ ▶ **n.** a person to whom money is paid or is to be paid, esp. the person to whom a check is made payable.

pay en·ve·lope ▶ **n.** an envelope containing an employee's wages. ■ fig. a salary or income.

pay·ess /'pā-is/ ▶ **plural n.** uncut sideburns worn by male Orthodox Jews. [20th C.: Yiddish, from Heb. *pē'ōt* 'corners' (see Lev. 19:27).]

pay·load /'pā,lōd/ ▶ **n.** the part of a vehicle's load, esp. an aircraft's, from which revenue is derived; passengers and cargo. ■ the total amount of bombs carried by a bomber. ■ an explosive warhead carried by a missile. ■ equipment, personnel, or satellites carried by a spacecraft.

pay·mas·ter /'pā,mastər/ ▶ **n.** an official who pays troops or workers.

pay·ment /'pāmənt/ ▶ **n.** **1** the action or process of paying someone or something, or of being paid. **2** an amount paid or payable. ■ fig. something given as a reward or in recompense for something done. [ME: from OFr. *paiement*, from *payer* 'to pay.']

pay·nim /'pānim/ ▶ **n.** archaic a pagan. ■ a non-Christian, esp. a Muslim. [ME: from OFr. *paienime*, from eccles. L. *paganismus* 'heathenism.']

pay·off /'pā,ôf; -,äf/ ▶ **n.** informal a payment made to someone, esp. as a bribe or reward, or on leaving a job. ■ the return on an investment or a bet. ■ a final outcome; a conclusion.

pay·o·la /pā'ōlə/ ▶ **n.** the practice of bribing someone to use their influence or position to promote a particular product or interest. [1930s: from PAY¹ + *-ola* as in *Victrola*, the name of a line of phonographs.]

pay·out /'pā,out/ ▶ **n.** a large payment of money, esp. as compensation or a dividend.

pay phone ▶ **n.** a public telephone that is operated by coins or by a credit or prepaid card.

pay·roll /'pā,rōl/ ▶ **n.** a list of a company's employees and the amount of money they are to be paid. ■ the total amount of wages and salaries paid by a company to its employees.

Pays Basque /'pā'bäsk/ French name for BASQUE COUNTRY.

pay·slip /'pā,slip/ ▶ **n.** a note given to an employee when they have been paid, detailing the amount of pay given and the tax and insurance deducted.

payt. ▶ **abbr.** payment.

Pay·ton /'pātn/, Walter (1954–99), US football player. A running back, he played for the Chicago Bears 1975–87.

pay TV (also **pay television**) ▶ **n.** television broadcasting in which viewers pay by subscription to watch a particular channel.

Paz /päz; päs/, Octavio (1914–98), Mexican poet. His poetry reflects a preoccupation with Aztec mythology. Nobel Prize for Literature (1990).

Pb ▶ **symb.** the chemical element lead. [from L. *plumbum*.]

pb ▶ **abbr.** paperback.

PBS ▶ **abbr.** Public Broadcasting Service.

PBX ▶ **abbr.** private branch exchange, a private telephone switchboard.

PC ▶ **abbr.** ■ Past Commander. ■ personal computer. ■ (also **pc**) politically correct; political correctness. ■ Post Commander. ■ professional corporation.

p.c. ▶ **abbr.** ■ percent. ■ postcard.

p/c (also **P/C**) ▶ **abbr.** ■ petty cash. ■ price current.

PCB ▶ **abbr.** ■ Electron. printed circuit board. ■ Chem. polychlorinated biphenyl.

PC card ▶ **n.** Comput. a printed circuit board for a personal computer, esp. one built to the PCMCIA standard.

P-Celt·ic /'keltik/ ▶ **n. & adj.** another term for BRYTHONIC. [*P*, from the development of the Indo-Eur. *kw* sound into *p* in this group of languages.]

PCI ▶ **n.** Comput. a standard for connecting computers and their peripherals. [20th C.: abbrev. of *peripheral component interconnect*.]

PCMCIA ▶ **abbr.** Comput. Personal Computer Memory Card International Association, denoting a standard specification for memory cards and interfaces in personal computers.

PCN ▶ **abbr.** personal communications network, a digital mobile telephone system.

PCP ▶ **abbr.** ■ pentachlorophenol. ■ phencyclidine. ■ pneumocystis carinii pneumonia. ■ primary care physician. ■ (in Canada) Progressive-Conservative Party.

PCS ▶ **abbr.** personal communications services, a digital mobile telephone system.

pct. ▶ **abbr.** percent.

PD ▶ **abbr.** ■ Police Department. ■ public domain.

Pd ▶ **symb.** the chemical element palladium.

p.d. ▶ **abbr.** ■ per diem. ■ potential difference.

pd ▶ **abbr.** paid.

PDA ▶ **n.** a palmtop computer used to store information such as addresses and telephone numbers, and for simple word processing and spreadsheeting. [20th C.: abbrev. of *personal digital assistant*.]

Pd.B. ▶ **abbr.** Bachelor of Pedagogy.

PDC ▶ **abbr.** program delivery control, a system for broadcasting a coded signal at the beginning and end of a television program which can be recognized by a video recorder and used to begin and end recording.

Pd.D. ▶ **abbr.** Doctor of Pedagogy.

PDF ▶ **n.** Comput. a file format that provides an electronic image of text or text and graphics that looks like a printed document and can be viewed, printed, and electronically tramsmitted. [abbr. of *portable document format*.]

Pd.M. ▶ **abbr.** Master of Pedagogy.

p.d.q. informal ▶ **abbr.** pretty damn quick.

PDT ▶ **abbr.** Pacific Daylight Time (see PACIFIC TIME).

PE ▶ **abbr.** ■ physical education. ■ Prince Edward Island (in official postal use).

pea /pē/ ▶ **n.** **1** a spherical green seed that is eaten as a vegetable. ■ [with adj.] any of a number of edible spherical seeds of the pea family, e.g., **chickpea** and **black-eyed pea**. **2** the Eurasian climbing leguminous plant (*Pisum sativum*) that yields pods containing peas. ■ used in names of similar or related plants or seeds, e.g. **sweet pea**.

– PHRASES **like peas** (or **two peas**) **in a pod** so similar as to be indistinguishable or nearly so. [17th C.: back-form. from *pease* (pl.), from OE *pise* 'pea.']

pea bean ▶ **n.** a variety of kidney bean with small rounded seeds.

pea·ber·ry /'pē,berē/ ▶ **n.** (pl. **-ries**) a coffee berry containing one rounded seed instead of the usual two, through nonfertilization of one ovule or subsequent abortion. Such beans are esteemed for their fine, strong flavor.

pea·brain /'pē,brān/ ▶ **n.** informal a stupid person.

pea-brained ▶ **adj.** informal stupid; foolish.

peace /pēs/ ▶ **n.** **1** freedom from disturbance; quiet and tranquility. ■ mental calm; serenity: *the peace of mind this insurance gives you.* **2** freedom from or the cessation of war or violence. ■ [in sing.] a period of this. ■ [in sing.] a treaty agreeing to the cessation of war between warring states. ■ freedom from civil disorder. ■ freedom from dispute or dissension between individuals or groups. **3** (**the peace**) a ceremonial handshake or kiss exchanged during a service in some churches (now usually only in the Eucharist), symbolizing Christian love and unity. ▶ **exclam.** **1** used as a greeting. **2** used as an order to remain silent.

– PHRASES **at peace 1** free from anxiety or distress. ■ dead (used to suggest that someone has escaped from the difficulties of life). **2** in a state of friendliness. **hold one's peace** remain silent about something. **keep the peace** refrain or prevent others from disturbing civil order. **make peace** (or **one's peace**) reestablish friendly relations; become reconciled. **no peace for the weary** see *NO REST FOR THE WEARY* at WEARY. [ME: from OFr. *pais*, from L. *pax*, *pac-* 'peace.']

peace·a·ble /'pēsəbəl/ ▶ **adj.** inclined to avoid argument or violent conflict. ■ free from argument or conflict; peaceful. — **peace·a·ble·ness n.** **peace·a·bly adv.**

Peace Corps /'pēs ,kôr/ an organization sponsored by the US government

PRONUNCIATION KEY ə *ago, up*; ər *over, fur*; a *hat*; ā *ate*; ä *car*; e *let*; ē *see*; i *fit*; ī *by*; NG *sing*; ō *go*; ô *law, for*; oi *toy*; o͝o *good*; o͞o *goo*; ou *out*; TH *thin*; T̲H̲ *then*; ZH *vision*

that sends young people to work as volunteers in developing countries.

peace div·i·dend ▶ n. a sum of public money that becomes available for other purposes when spending on defense is reduced.

peace·ful /'pēsfəl/ ▶ adj. **1** free from disturbance; tranquil. **2** not involving war or violence. ■ (of a person) inclined to avoid conflict; not aggressive. — **peace·ful·ness** n.

peace·ful·ly /'pēsfəlē/ ▶ adv. **1** without disturbance; tranquilly. ■ (of death) without pain. **2** without war or violence.

peace·keep·ing /'pēs,kēpiNG/ ▶ n. [usu. as adj.] the active maintenance of a truce between nations or communities, esp. by an international military force. — **peace·keep·er** n.

peace·mak·er /'pēs,mākər/ ▶ n. a person who brings about peace, esp. by reconciling adversaries. — **peace·mak·ing** n. & adj.

peace·nik /'pēs,nik/ ▶ n. informal, often derog. a member of a pacifist movement.

peace of·fer·ing ▶ n. **1** a propitiatory or conciliatory gift. **2** (in biblical use) an offering presented as a thanksgiving to God.

peace of·fi·cer ▶ n. a civil officer appointed to preserve law and order, such as a sheriff or police officer.

peace pipe ▶ n. a tobacco pipe offered and smoked as a token of peace among North American Indians.

Peace Riv·er a river in Canada that flows from northern British Columbia to the Slave River in Alberta.

peace sign ▶ n. **1** a sign of peace made by holding up the hand with palm turned outward and the first two fingers extended in a V-shape. **2** a figure representing peace, in the form of a circle with one line bisecting it from top to bottom and two shorter lines radiating downward on either side.

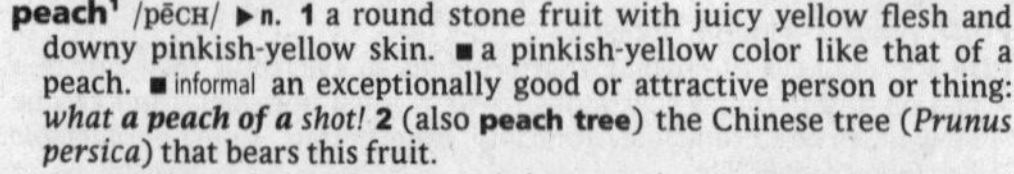

peace sign 2

peace talk ▶ n. (usu. **peace talks**) a discussion about peace or the ending of hostilities, esp. a conference or series of discussions aimed at achieving peace.

peace·time /'pēs,tīm/ ▶ n. a period when a country is not at war.

peach[1] /pēCH/ ▶ n. **1** a round stone fruit with juicy yellow flesh and downy pinkish-yellow skin. ■ a pinkish-yellow color like that of a peach. ■ informal an exceptionally good or attractive person or thing: *what a peach of a shot!* **2** (also **peach tree**) the Chinese tree (*Prunus persica*) that bears this fruit.
– PHRASES **peaches and cream 1** (of a person's complexion) of a cream color with downy pink cheeks. **2** fine; satisfactory: *it's not all peaches and cream.* [ME: from OFr. *pesche*, from med. L. *persica*, from L. *persicum (malum)*, lit. 'Persian apple.']

peach[2] ▶ v. [intrans.] (**peach on**) informal inform on. [ME: based on OFr. *empechier* 'impede' (see IMPEACH).]

peach-bloom ▶ n. a matte glaze of reddish pink, mottled with green and brown, used on fine Chinese porcelain since around 1700. ■ a delicate purplish-pink color.

peach-blow ▶ n. another term for PEACH-BLOOM. ■ a type of late 19th-century American colored glass.

peach fuzz ▶ n. informal the down on the chin of an adolescent boy whose beard has not yet developed.

pea·chick /'pē,CHik/ ▶ n. a young peafowl.

peach Mel·ba ▶ n. a dish of ice cream and peaches with liqueur or sauce. [named after Dame Nellie *Melba* (see MELBA).]

peach·y /'pēCHē/ ▶ adj. (**peach·i·er, peach·i·est**) informal of the nature or appearance of a peach. ■ fine; excellent. — **peach·i·ness** n.

peach·y-keen ▶ adj. informal attractive; outstanding.

pea·coat /'pē,kōt/ (also **pea coat**) ▶ n. another term for PEA JACKET.

pea·cock /'pē,käk/ ▶ n. a male peafowl, which has very long tail feathers that have eyelike markings and that can be erected and expanded in display like a fan. ■ an ostentatious strutting person. ▶ v. [intrans.] display oneself ostentatiously; strut like a peacock. [ME: from OE *pēa* (from L. *pavo*) 'peacock' + COCK[1].]

pea·cock blue ▶ n. a greenish-blue color like that of a peacock's neck.

pea·cock ore ▶ n. another term for BORNITE.

pea flour ▶ n. flour made from dried split peas.

pea·fowl /'pē,foul/ ▶ n. a large crested pheasant native to Asia, esp. the widely introduced **common peafowl** (*Pavo cristatus*).

pea green ▶ n. a yellowish green color like that of pea soup.

pea·hen /'pē,hen/ ▶ n. a female peafowl, having drabber colors and a shorter tail than the male.

pea jack·et (also **pea·coat**) ▶ n. a short, double-breasted overcoat of coarse woolen cloth, formerly worn by sailors. [18th C.: prob. from Du. *pijjakker*, from *pij* 'coat of coarse cloth' + *jekker* 'jacket.']

pea jacket

peak[1] /pēk/ ▶ n. the pointed top of a mountain. ■ a mountain, esp. one with a pointed top. ■ a projecting pointed part or shape. ■ a point in a curve or on a graph, or a value of a physical quantity, higher than those around it. ■ the point of highest activity, quality, or achievement. ■ esp. Brit. a stiff brim at the front of a cap. ■ the narrow part of a ship's hold at the bow or stern. ■ the upper, outer corner of a sail extended by a gaff. ▶ v. [intrans.] reach a highest point, either of a specified value or at a specified time. ▶ adj. [attrib.] greatest; maximum. ■ characterized by maximum activity or demand. — **peak·y** adj. **peak·i·ness** n. [16th C.: prob. back-form. from *peaked*, var. of dial. *picked* 'pointed.']

peak[2] ▶ v. [intrans.] archaic decline in health and spirits; waste away. [17th C.: of unknown origin.]

peaked[1] /pēkt/ ▶ adj. having a peak.

peak·ed[2] /'pē,kid/ ▶ adj. [predic.] (of a person) gaunt and pale from illness or fatigue.

peak load ▶ n. the maximum of electrical power demand.

peal /pēl/ ▶ n. **1** a loud ringing of a bell or bells. ■ Bell-ringing a series of unique changes (strictly, at least five thousand) rung on a set of bells. ■ a set of bells. **2** a loud repeated or reverberating sound of thunder or laughter. ▶ v. [intrans.] (of a bell or bells) ring loudly or in a peal. ■ (of laughter or thunder) sound in a peal. ■ [trans.] convey or give out by the ringing of bells. [ME: shortening of APPEAL.]

Peale[1] /pēl/ a family of US painters. Charles Willson (1741–1827) was known for his portraits of well-known Americans. His son Rembrandt (1778–1860) also painted portraits of well-known people, as well as historical scenes. Another son, Raphaelle (1774–1825), favored silhouettes and still-life paintings.

Peale[2], Norman Vincent (1898–1993), US clergyman. He encouraged people to think positively in *The Power of Positive Thinking* (1952).

pe·an /'pēən/ ▶ n. Heraldry fur resembling ermine but with gold spots on a black ground. [16th C.: of unknown origin.]

pea·nut /'pēnət/ ▶ n. **1** the oval seed of a South American plant, widely roasted and salted and eaten as a snack. ■ (**peanuts**) informal a paltry thing or amount, esp. a very small amount of money. ■ a small person (often used as a term of endearment). ■ (**peanuts**) small pieces of Styrofoam used for packing material. **2** the plant (*Arachis hypogaea*) of the pea family that bears these seeds, which develop in pods that ripen underground. It is widely cultivated, esp. in the southern US, and large quantities are used to make oil or animal feed.

pea·nut but·ter ▶ n. a paste of ground roasted peanuts, usually eaten spread on bread.

pea·nut gal·ler·y ▶ n. informal the top gallery in a theater where the cheaper seats are located. ■ a group of people who criticize someone, often by focusing on insignificant details.

pea·nut oil ▶ n. oil produced from peanuts and used mainly for culinary purposes, but also in some soaps and pharmaceuticals.

pear /pe(ə)r/ ▶ n. **1** a yellowish- or brownish-green edible fruit that is typically narrow at the stalk and wider toward the tip, with sweet, slightly gritty flesh. **2** (also **pear tree**) the Eurasian tree (genus *Pyrus*) of the rose family that bears this fruit. [OE *pere, peru*, of West Gmc. origin; from L. *pirum*.]

pearl /pərl/ ▶ n. a hard, lustrous spherical mass, typically white or bluish-gray, formed within the shell of a pearl oyster or other bivalve mollusk and highly prized as a gem. ■ an artificial imitation of this. ■ (**pearls**) a necklace of pearls. ■ something resembling a pearl in appearance. ■ short for MOTHER-OF-PEARL. ■ fig. a precious thing; the finest example of something. ■ a very pale bluish gray or white like the color of a pearl. ▶ v. [intrans.] **1** literary form pearllike drops. ■ [trans.] make bluish-gray like a pearl. **2** [usu. as n.] (**pearling**) dive or fish for pearl oysters.
– PHRASES **pearls before swine** valuable things offered or given to people who do not appreciate them. [with biblical allusion to Matt. 7:6.] — **pearl·er** n. [ME: from OFr. *perle*, perh. based on L. *perna* 'leg.']

pearl ash ▶ n. archaic commercial potassium carbonate.

pearl bar·ley ▶ n. barley reduced to small round grains by grinding.

pearl div·er ▶ n. a person who dives for pearl oysters.

pearled /pərld/ ▶ adj. **1** adorned with pearls. **2** literary bluish-gray, like a pearl. **3** formed into pearllike drops or grains.

pearl·es·cent /pər'lesənt/ ▶ adj. having a luster resembling that of mother-of-pearl.

Pearl Har·bor a harbor in Hawaii, on the island of Oahu, the site of a major US naval base, where a surprise attack on December 7, 1941, by Japanese aircraft brought the US into World War II.

pearl·ite /'pər,līt/ ▶ n. Metallurgy a finely laminated mixture of ferrite and cementite present in cast iron and steel, formed by the cooling of austenite.

pearl·ized /'pərlīzd/ ▶ adj. made to have or give a luster like that of mother-of-pearl.

pearl mil·let ▶ n. a tall tropical grain (*Pennisetum glaucum*) with long cylindrical ears, comprising an important food crop in the driest areas of Africa and the Indian subcontinent.

pearl on·ion ▶ n. a very small onion used esp. for pickling.

pearl oys·ter ▶ n. a tropical marine bivalve mollusk (genus *Pinctada*, family Pteriidae) that has a ridged scaly shell and produces pearls.

Pearl Riv·er 1 a river in southern China that flows south to the South China Sea. **2** a river that flows for 485 miles (780 km) across central Mississippi into the Gulf of Mexico.

pearl tea ▶ n. another term for BUBBLE TEA.

pearl·ware /'pərl,we(ə)r/ ▶ n. fine glazed earthenware pottery, typically white, of a type introduced by Josiah Wedgwood in 1779.

pearl·y /'pərlē/ ▶ adj. (**pearl·i·er, pearl·i·est**) resembling a pearl in luster or color. ■ containing or adorned with pearls or mother-of-pearl. – PHRASES **pearly whites** informal a person's teeth. — **pearl·i·ness** n.

pearl·y ev·er·last·ing ▶ n. an ornamental North American plant (*Anaphalis margaritacea*) of the daisy family, with gray-green foliage and pearly white flowerheads, used in dry flower arrangements.

Pearl·y Gates ▶ plural n. informal the gates of heaven.

pearl·y nau·ti·lus ▶ n. another term for CHAMBERED NAUTILUS (see NAUTILUS).

pear-shaped ▶ adj. shaped like a pear; tapering toward the top. ■ (of a person) having hips that are disproportionately wide in relation to the upper part of the body.

Pear·son[1] /'pi(ə)rsən/, Karl (1857–1936), English mathematician. He was the principal founder of 20th-century statistics.

Pear·son[2], Lester Bowles (1897–1972), prime minister of Canada 1963–68. He mediated the resolution of the Suez crisis in 1956. Nobel Peace Prize (1957).

peart /pərt/ ▶ adj. dialect lively; cheerful. [15th C.: var. of PERT.]

Pea·ry /'pi(ə)rē/, Robert Edwin (1856–1920), US explorer. On April 6, 1909, he became the first person to reach the North Pole.

Pea·ry Land a mountainous region on the Arctic coast of northern Greenland, named after Robert Peary.

peas·ant /'pezənt/ ▶ n. a poor farmer of low social status who owns or rents a small piece of land for cultivation (chiefly in historical use or with reference to subsistence farming in poorer countries). ■ informal an ignorant, rude, or unsophisticated person; a person of low social status. — **peas·ant·ry** n. **peas·ant·y** adj. [ME: from OFr. *paisent* 'country dweller,' from *pais* 'country,' based on L. *pagus* 'country district.']

peas·ant e·con·o·my ▶ n. an agricultural economy in which the family is the basic unit of production.

Peas·ants' Re·volt an uprising in 1381 among the peasant and artisan classes in England.

pea·shoot·er /'pē,SHōōtər/ ▶ n. a toy weapon consisting of a small tube that is blown through in order to shoot out dried peas.

pea soup ▶ n. **1** soup made from peas, esp. a thick, yellowish-green soup made from dried split peas. **2** a thick, yellowish fog.

peat /pēt/ ▶ n. a brown, soil-like material characteristic of boggy, acid ground, consisting of partly decomposed vegetable matter. It is widely cut and dried for use in gardening and as fuel. — **peat·y** adj. [ME: from Anglo-L. *peta*, perh. of Celtic origin.]

peat·land /'pēt,land/ ▶ n. (also **peatlands**) land consisting largely of peat or peat bogs.

peat moss ▶ n. **1** a large absorbent moss (genus *Sphagnum*, family Sphagnaceae) that grows in dense masses on boggy ground, where the lower parts decay slowly to form peat deposits. Peat moss is widely used in horticulture, esp. for packing plants and for compost. **2** a lowland peat bog.

peau de soie /'pōdə 'swä/ ▶ n. a smooth, finely ribbed satin fabric of silk or rayon. [19th C.: Fr., lit. 'skin of silk.']

peau d'or·ange /'pō dô'ränZH/ ▶ n. a pitted or dimpled appearance of the skin, esp. as characteristic of some cases of breast cancer or due to cellulite. [Fr., lit. 'orange skin.']

pea·vey /'pēvē/ (also **pea·vy**) ▶ n. (pl. **-veys** or **-vies**) a lumberjack's cant hook with a spike at the end. [19th C.: after the inventor.]

peb·ble /'pebəl/ ▶ n. a small stone made smooth and round by the action of water or sand. ▶ adj. [attrib.] informal (of an eyeglass lens) very thick and convex. — **peb·bled** adj. **peb·bly** adj. [OE: in*papel-stān* 'pebble-stone,' *pyppelrīpig* 'pebble-stream.']

peb·ble-dash ▶ n. esp. Brit. mortar with pebbles in it, used as a coating for external walls. — **peb·ble-dashed** adj.

pec /pek/ ▶ n. (usu. **pecs**) informal a pectoral muscle (esp. with reference to the development of these muscles in bodybuilding).

pe·can /pə'kän; -'kan; 'pē,kan/ ▶ n. a smooth brown nut with an edible kernel similar to a walnut, obtained from the hickory tree *Carya illinoensis*, native to the southern US. [18th C.: from Fr. *pacane*, from Illinois (an Amer. Ind. language).]

pec·ca·dil·lo /,pekə'dilō/ ▶ n. (pl. **-loes** or **-los**) a small, relatively unimportant offense or sin. [16th C.: from Sp. *pecadillo*, dimin. of *pecado* 'sin,' from L. *peccare* 'to sin.']

pec·cant /'pekənt/ ▶ adj. archaic **1** having committed a fault or sin; offending. **2** diseased or causing disease. — **pec·can·cy** /'pekənsē/ n. [16th C. (sense 2): from L. *peccant-* 'sinning,' from *peccare*.]

collared peccary

pec·ca·ry /'pekərē/ ▶ n. (pl. **-ries**) a gregarious piglike mammal (family Tayassuidae) that is found from the southwestern US to Paraguay. Its three species include the **collared peccary** (*Tayassu tajacu*). [17th C.: from Carib *pakira*.]

Pe·chen·ga /pə'CHENGgə; pyi'CHyengə/ a region of northwestern Russia that lies west of Murmansk on the border with Finland.

Pe·cho·ra /pə'CHôrə; pyi'CHyôrə/ a river in northern Russia that rises in the Ural Mountains and flows to the Barents Sea.

peck[1] /pek/ ▶ v. [intrans.] (of a bird) strike or bite something with its beak. ■ [trans.] make (a hole) by striking with the beak. ■ [trans.] remove or pluck out by biting with the beak. ■ [trans.] kiss (someone) lightly or perfunctorily. ■ (**peck at**) informal (of a person) eat (food) listlessly or daintily. ■ (**peck at**) criticize or nag. ■ [trans.] type (something) slowly and laboriously. ■ informal (of a horse) pitch forward or stumble as a result of striking the ground with the front rather than the flat of the hoof. ▶ n. a stroke or bite by a bird with its beak. ■ a light or perfunctory kiss. [ME: cf. Mid. Low Ger. *pekken* 'to peck.']

peck[2] ▶ n. a measure of capacity for dry goods, equal to a quarter of a bushel (8 US quarts = 8.81 liters). ■ archaic a large number or amount of something. [ME: from Anglo-Norman Fr. *pek*.]

peck·er /'pekər/ ▶ n. vulgar slang a penis.

peck·er·head /'pekər,hed/ ▶ n. vulgar slang an aggressive, objectionable person.

peck·er·wood /'pekər,wōōd/ ▶ n. informal, often derog. a white person, esp. a poor one. [1920s: alt. of *woodpecker*.]

Peck·ham /'pekəm/, Rufus Wheeler, Jr. (1838–1909), US Supreme Court associate justice 1895–1909.

peck·ing or·der (also **peck or·der**) ▶ n. a hierarchy of status seen among members of a group of people or animals, originally as observed among hens.

peck·ish /'pekiSH/ ▶ adj. informal, esp. Brit. hungry: *we were both feeling a bit peckish and there was nothing to eat.*

Peck·sniff·i·an /pek'snifēən/ ▶ adj. affecting benevolence or high moral principles. [19th C.: from *Pecksniff*, the name of a character in Dickens's *Martin Chuzzlewit*, + -IAN.]

Pe·con·ic Bay /pi'känik/ an inlet of the Atlantic Ocean at the eastern end of Long Island in New York.

pec·o·ri·no /pekə'rēnō/ ▶ n. (pl. **-nos**) an Italian cheese made from ewes' milk. [Ital., from *pecorino* 'of ewes,' from *pecora* 'sheep.']

Pe·cos Riv·er /'pā,kōs/ a river that flows from northern New Mexico to the Rio Grande.

pec·ten /'pektən/ ▶ n. (pl. **pec·tens** /'pektnz/ or **pec·ti·nes** /'pektnēz/) Zool. **1** any of a number of comblike structures occurring in animal bodies, in particular: ■ a pigmented vascular projection from the choroid in the eye of a bird. ■ an appendage of an insect consisting of or bearing a row of bristles or chitinous teeth. ■ a sensory appendage on the underside of a scorpion. **2** a scallop of the genus *Pecten*. — **pec·ti·nate** /'pektənit; -,nāt/ adj. **pec·ti·nat·ed** /-,nātid/ adj. **pec·ti·na·tion** /,pektə'nāSHən/ n. (all in sense 1). [ME: from L. *pecten, pectin-* 'a comb.']

pec·tin /'pektin/ ▶ n. a soluble gelatinous polysaccharide that is present in ripe fruits and is extracted for use as a setting agent in jams and jellies. — **pec·tic** /'pektik/ adj. [19th C.: from Gk. *pektos* 'congealed' (from *pēgnuein* 'make solid') + -IN[1].]

pec·to·ral /'pektərəl/ ▶ adj. of or relating to the breast or chest. ■ worn on the chest. ▶ n. (usu. **pectorals**) a pectoral muscle. ■ a pectoral fin. ■ an ornamental breastplate, esp. one worn by a Jewish high priest. [ME: from L. *pectorale* 'breastplate,' *pectoralis* 'of the breast,' from *pectus, pector-* 'breast.']

pec·to·ral fin ▶ n. Zool. each of a pair of fins situated on either side just behind a fish's head, helping to control the direction of movement during locomotion. They correspond to the forelimbs of other vertebrates.

pec·to·ral gir·dle ▶ n. (in vertebrates) the skeletal framework that provides attachment for the forelimbs or pectoral fins, usually consisting of the scapulas and clavicles.

pec·to·ral mus·cle ▶ n. (usu. **pectoral muscles**) each of the four large paired muscles that cover the front of the rib cage and serve to draw the forelimbs toward the chest.

pec·to·ral sand·pip·er ▶ n. a migratory sandpiper (*Calidris melanotos*) with dark streaks on the breast and a white belly, breeding chiefly in Arctic Canada.

pec·u·late /'pekyə,lāt/ ▶ v. [trans.] formal embezzle or steal (money, esp. public funds). — **pec·u·la·tion** /,pekyə'lāSHən/ n. **pec·u·la·tor** /-,lātər/ n. [18th C.: from L. *peculat-* 'embezzled,' from v. *peculari* (rel. to *peculium* 'property').]

pe·cu·liar /pə'kyōōlyər/ ▶ adj. **1** strange or odd; unusual. ■ [predic.] informal slightly and indefinably unwell; faint or dizzy. **2** [predic.] (**peculiar to**) belonging exclusively to. ■ formal particular; special. ▶ n. esp. Brit. a parish or church exempt from the jurisdiction of the diocese in which it lies, through being subject to the jurisdiction of the monarch or an archbishop. [ME (in the sense 'particular, special'): from L. *peculiaris* 'of private property,' from *peculium* 'property,' from *pecu* 'cattle.']

pe·cu·liar in·sti·tu·tion ▶ n. hist. the system of black slavery in the southern states of the US.

pe·cu·li·ar·i·ty /pə,kyōōlē'aritē/ ▶ n. (pl. **-ties**) an odd or unusual feature or habit. ■ a characteristic or quality that is distinctive of a particular person or place. ■ the quality or state of being peculiar.

pe·cu·liar·ly /pə'kyōōlyərlē/ ▶ adv. **1** [as submodifier] more than usually;

especially. **2** oddly: *the town is peculiarly built.* **3** used to emphasize restriction to an individual or group.

pe·cu·ni·ar·y /pi'kyōōnē,erē/ ▶ **adj.** formal of, relating to, or consisting of money. — **pe·cu·ni·ar·i·ly** /pə,kyōōnē'e(ə)rəlē/ **adv.** [16th C.: from L. *pecuniarius*, from *pecunia* 'money,' from *pecu* 'cattle, money.']

ped·a·gog·ic /,pedə'gäjik/ ▶ **adj.** of or relating to teaching. ■ rare of or characteristic of a pedagogue. — **ped·a·gog·i·cal adj. ped·a·gog·i·cal·ly adv.**

ped·a·gogue /'pedə,gäg/ ▶ **n.** archaic humorous a teacher, esp. a strict or pedantic one. [ME: via L. from Gk. *paidagōgos*, denoting a slave who accompanied a child to school (from *pais, paid-* 'boy' + *agōgos* 'guide').]

ped·a·go·gy /'pedə,gäjē; -,gōjē/ ▶ **n.** (pl. **-gies**) the method and practice of teaching, esp. as an academic subject or theoretical concept. — **ped·a·gog·ics** /,pedə'gäjiks/ **n.**

ped·al[1] /'pedl/ ▶ **n.** a foot-operated lever or control for a vehicle, musical instrument, or other mechanism, in particular: ■ each of a pair of cranks used for powering a bicycle or other vehicle propelled by leg power. ■ a foot-operated throttle, brake, or clutch control in a motor vehicle. ■ each of a set of two or three foot-operated levers on a piano, for sustaining or softening the tone. ■ Music (**ped·aled, ped·al·ing**; Brit. **ped·alled, ped·al·ling**) each key of an organ keyboard that is played with the feet. ■ Music short for PEDAL NOTE (sense 2). ▶ **v.** (**pedaled, pedaling**; Brit. **pedalled, pedalling**) [intrans.] move by working the pedals of a bicycle. ■ [trans.] move (a bicycle) by working its pedals. ■ [intrans.] work the pedals of a bicycle. ■ [intrans.] use the pedals of a piano, esp. in a particular style.
– PHRASES **with the pedal to the metal** informal with the accelerator of a car pressed to the floor. — **ped·al·er** (Brit. **ped·al·ler**) **n.** [17th C.: ult. from L. *pedalis* 'a foot in length,' from *pes, ped-* 'foot.']

ped·al[2] /'pēdl/ ▶ **adj.** esp. Med. Zool. of or relating to the foot or feet. [17th C.: from L. *pedalis*, from *pes, ped-* 'foot.']

ped·al·board /'pedl,bôrd/ ▶ **n.** the keyboard of pedals on an organ.

ped·al boat /'pedl/ ▶ **n.** another term for PADDLEBOAT.

ped·al note /'pedl/ ▶ **n.** (also **pedal tone**) Music **1** the lowest or fundamental note of a harmonic series in some brass and wind instruments. **2** (also **pedal point**) a note sustained in one part (usually the bass) through successive harmonies, some of which are independent of it.

ped·al push·er /'pedl/ ▶ **n.** **1** (**pedal pushers**) women's calf-length pants. **2** informal a cyclist.

ped·al steel gui·tar /'pedl/ (also **pedal steel**) ▶ **n.** a musical instrument played like the Hawaiian guitar, but set on a stand with pedals to adjust the tension of the strings.

ped·ant /'pednt/ ▶ **n.** a person who is excessively concerned with minor details and rules or with displaying academic learning. — **ped·ant·ry n.**

pe·dan·tic /pə'dantik/ ▶ **adj.** derog. of or like a pedant. — **pe·dan·ti·cal·ly adv.**

ped·dle /'pedl/ ▶ **v.** [trans.] try to sell (something, esp. small goods) by going from house to house or place to place. ■ sell (an illegal drug or stolen item). ■ derog. promote (an idea or view) persistently or widely. [16th C.: back-form. from PEDDLER.]

ped·dler /'pedlər; 'pedl-ər/ (also **ped·lar**) ▶ **n.** a person who goes from place to place selling small goods. ■ a person who sells illegal drugs or stolen goods. ■ a person who promotes an idea or view persistently or widely. [ME: perh. an alt. of dialect *pedder*, appar. from dial. *ped* 'basket.']

ped·er·ast /'pedə,rast/ ▶ **n.** a man who indulges in pederasty. [17th C.: from Gk. *paiderastēs*.]

ped·er·as·ty /'pedə,rastē/ ▶ **n.** sexual activity involving a man and a boy. — **ped·er·as·tic** /,pedə'rastik/ **adj.** [17th C.: from mod. L. *paederastia*, from Gk. *paiderastia*, from *pais, paid-* 'boy' + *erastēs* 'lover.']

pe·des /'pēdēz; 'pedēz/ plural form of PES.

ped·es·tal /'pedəstl/ ▶ **n.** the base or support on which a statue, obelisk, or column is mounted. ■ fig. a position in which one is greatly or uncritically admired: *the heroes they have* ***placed on pedestals.*** ■ each of the two supports of a kneehole desk or table, typically containing drawers. ■ the supporting column or base of a washbasin or toilet bowl. [16th C.: from Fr. *piédestal*, from Ital. *piedestallo*, from *piè* 'foot' (from L. *pes, ped-*) + *di* 'of' + *stallo* 'stall.']

pe·des·tri·an /pə'destrēən/ ▶ **n.** a person walking along a road or in a developed area. ▶ **adj.** lacking inspiration or excitement; dull. — **pe·des·tri·an·ly adv.** [18th C.: from Fr. *pédestre* or L. *pedester* 'going on foot,' also 'written in prose' + -IAN.]

pe·des·tri·an·ize /pə'destrēə,nīz/ ▶ **v.** [trans.] close (a street or area) to traffic, making it accessible only to pedestrians. — **pe·des·tri·an·i·za·tion** /pə,destrēəni'zāsʜən/ **n.**

pe·di·at·rics /,pēdē'atriks/ (Brit. **pae·di·at·rics**) ▶ **plural n.** [treated as sing.] the branch of medicine dealing with children and their diseases. — **pe·di·at·ric adj. pe·di·a·tri·cian** /,pēdēə'trisʜən/ **n.** [19th C.: from PEDO-[1] + Gk. *iatros* 'physician'.]

ped·i·cab /'pedikab/ ▶ **n.** a small pedal-operated vehicle, serving as a taxi in some countries.

ped·i·cel /'pedi,sel/ ▶ **n.** Bot. a small stalk bearing an individual flower in an inflorescence. Compare with PEDUNCLE. ■ Anat. Zool. another term for PEDICLE. — **ped·i·cel·late** /,pedi'selit; -'se,lāt/ **adj.** [17th C.: from mod. L. *pedicellus* 'small foot,' dimin. of *pes, ped-* 'foot.']

ped·i·cel·lar·i·a /,pedisə'le(ə)rēə/ ▶ **n.** (pl. **-lar·i·ae** /-'le(ə)rē,ē/) Zool. a defensive organ like a minute pincer present in large numbers on an echinoderm. [19th C.: mod. L., from L. *pediculus* 'small foot'.]

ped·i·cle /'pedikəl/ ▶ **n.** Anat. Zool. a small stalklike structure connecting an organ or other part to the human or animal body. Compare with PEDICEL. ■ Med. part of a graft, esp. a skin graft, left temporarily attached to its original site. [17th C.: from L. *pediculus* 'small foot,' dimin. of *pes, ped-*.]

pe·dic·u·li·cide /,pedi'kyōōlə,sīd/ ▶ **n.** a chemical used to kill lice. [20th C.: from L. *pediculus* 'louse' + -CIDE.]

pe·dic·u·lo·sis /pə,dikyə'lōsis/ ▶ **n.** Med. infestation with lice.

ped·i·cure /'pedi,kyŏŏr/ ▶ **n.** a cosmetic treatment of the feet and toenails. ▶ **v.** [trans.] give such a cosmetic treatment to (the feet). [19th C.: from Fr. *pédicure*, from L. *pes, ped-* 'foot' + *curare* 'attend to.']

ped·i·gree /'pedə,grē/ ▶ **n.** **1** the record of descent of an animal, showing it to be purebred. ■ informal a purebred animal. **2** the recorded ancestry, esp. upper-class ancestry, of a person or family. ■ the background or history of a person or thing, esp. as conferring distinction or quality. ■ a genealogical table. — **ped·i·greed adj.** [ME: from Anglo-Norman Fr. *pé de grue* 'crane's foot,' a mark used to denote succession in pedigrees.]

pediment

ped·i·ment /'pedəmənt/ ▶ **n.** the triangular upper part of the front of a building in classical style, typically surmounting a portico of columns. ■ a similar feature surmounting a door, window, front, or other part of a building in another style. ■ Geol. a broad, gently sloping expanse of rock debris extending outward from the foot of a mountain slope, esp. in a desert. — **ped·i·men·tal** /,pedə'mentl/ **adj. ped·i·ment·ed adj.** [16th C.: perh. an alt. of PYRAMID.]

ped·i·palp /'pedə,palp/ ▶ **n.** Zool. each of the second pair of appendages attached to the cephalothorax of most arachnids. They are variously specialized as pincers in scorpions, sensory organs in spiders, and locomotory organs in horseshoe crabs. [19th C.: from mod. L. *pedipalpi* (pl.), from L. *pes, ped-* 'foot' + *palpus* 'palp.']

ped·i·plain /'pedi,plān/ ▶ **n.** Geol. an extensive plain formed in a desert by the coalescence of neighboring pediments. — **ped·i·pla·na·tion** /,pediplə'nāsʜən/ **n.** [1930s: from PEDIMENT + PLAIN[1].]

ped·lar ▶ **n.** var. of PEDDLER.

pedo-[1] /'pēdō/ (Brit.**paedo-**) ▶ **comb. form** of a child; relating to children: *pedophile.* [from Gk. *pais, paid-* 'child, boy.']

pedo-[2] ▶ **comb. form** relating to soil or soil types: *pedogenic.* [from Gk. *pedon* 'ground.']

pe·do·don·tics /,pēdə'däntiks/ (Brit.**pae·do·don·tics**) ▶ **plural n.** [treated as sing.] the branch of dentistry that deals with children's teeth. — **pe·do·don·tic adj. pe·do·don·tist n.** [from PEDO-[1] + Gk. *odous, odont-* 'tooth.']

ped·o·gen·e·sis /,pēdō'jenəsəs/ ▶ **n.** Zool. see NEOTENY. — **ped·o·ge·net·ic adj.**

pe·do·gen·ic /,pedə'jenik/ ▶ **adj.** relating to or denoting processes occurring in soil or leading to the formation of soil.

pe·dol·o·gy /pə'däləjē/ ▶ **n.** another term for SOIL SCIENCE. — **ped·o·log·i·cal** /,pedə'läjikəl/ **adj. pe·dol·o·gist n.**

pe·dom·e·ter /pə'dämitər/ ▶ **n.** an instrument for estimating the distance traveled on foot by recording the number of steps taken. [18th C.: from Fr. *pédomètre*, from L. *pes, ped-* 'foot.']

ped·o·mor·pho·sis /,pēdə'môrfəsəs/ ▶ **n.** Zool. see NEOTENY. — **pe·do·mor·phic adj.**

pe·do·phile /'pedə,fīl/ (Brit.**pae·do·phile**) ▶ **n.** a person who is sexually attracted to children.

pe·do·phil·i·a /,pedə'filēə; ,pēdə-/ (Brit.**pae·do·phil·i·a**) ▶ **n.** sexual feelings directed toward children. — **pe·do·phil·i·ac** /-'filē,ak/ **n. & adj.**

Pe·dro Xi·me·nez /,pādrō hi'māniz/ (abbr.: **PX** or **px**) ▶ **n.** a variety of sweet white Spanish grape used in making sherry and sweet wine. ■ a sweet white wine made from this grape. [after the person who introduced the grape.]

pe·dun·cle /'pē,dəɴɢkəl; pə'dəɴɢkəl/ ▶ **n.** Bot. the stalk bearing a flower or fruit, or the main stalk of an inflorescence. Compare with PEDICEL. ■ Zool. a stalklike part by which an organ is attached to an animal's body, or by which a barnacle or other sedentary animal is attached to a substrate. ■ Anat. any of several bundles of nerve fibers connecting two parts of the brain. — **pe·dun·cu·lar** /pə'dəɴɢkyələr/ **adj. pe·dun·cu·late** /pə'dəɴɢkyə,lāt; -lit/ **adj.** [18th C.: from mod. L. *pedunculus*, from L. *pes, ped-* 'foot.']

pe·dun·cu·late oak ▶ **n.** the common or English oak.

pee /pē/ informal ▶ **v.** (**pees, peed, pee·ing**) [intrans.] urinate. ▶ **n.** [in sing.] an act of urinating: *I need to take a pee.* ■ urine. [18th C.: euphemistic use of the initial letter of PISS.]

Pee Dee Riv·er /'pē,dē/ a river that flows for 230 miles (370 km) through North Carolina and South Carolina to an inlet of the Atlantic Ocean.

peek /pēk/ ▶v. [intrans.] look quickly, typically in a furtive manner. ■ fig. protrude slightly so as to be just visible. ▶n. **1** a quick and typically furtive look. **2** (usu. **PEEK**) Comput. a statement or function in BASIC for reading the contents of a specified memory location. Compare with POKE[1] (sense 3).

peek·a·boo /'pēkə,bo͞o/ (also **peek-a-boo**) ▶n. a game played with a young child, which involves hiding behind something and suddenly reappearing, saying "peekaboo." ▶adj. [attrib.] (of a garment) revealing glimpses of the skin or body. ■ (of a hairstyle) concealing one eye with a fringe or wave of hair.

Peel /pēl/, Sir Robert (1788–1850), prime minister of Britain 1834–35, 1841–46.

peel[1] /pēl/ ▶v. **1** [trans.] remove the outer covering or skin from (a fruit, vegetable, or shrimp). ■ remove (the outer covering or skin) from a fruit or vegetable. ■ [intrans.] (of a fruit or vegetable) have a skin that can be removed. ■ (**peel something away/off**) remove or separate a thin covering or part from the outside or surface of something. ■ remove (an article of clothing). **2** [intrans.] (of a surface or object) lose parts of its outer layer or covering in small strips or pieces. ■ [with adverbial] (of an outer layer or covering) come off, esp. in strips or small pieces. ▶n. the outer covering or rind of a fruit or vegetable.
– PHRASAL VERBS **peel off** (of a member of a formation, esp. a flying formation) leave the formation by veering away to one side. **peel out** informal leave quickly, esp. in a motor vehicle. [ME: var. of dial. *pill*, from L. *pilare* 'to strip hair from,' from *pilus* 'hair.']

peel[2] ▶n. a flat, shovellike implement, esp. one used by baker for carrying loaves, pies, etc., into or out of an oven. [ME: from OFr. *pele*, from L. *pala*, from the base of *pangere* 'to fix, plant.']

peel[3] (also **pele** or **peel tower**) ▶n. a small square defensive tower of a kind built in the 16th century in the border counties of England and Scotland. [based on Anglo-Norman Fr. *pel* 'stake, palisade,' from L. *palus* 'stake.']

peel[4] ▶v. [trans.] Croquet send (another player's ball) through a wicket. [19th C.: from the name of Walter H. *Peel*, founder of the All England Croquet Association.]

peel·er /'pēlər/ ▶n. [usu. with adj.] a device for removing the skin from fruit and vegetables.

peel·ings /'pēliNGz/ ▶plural n. [usu. with adj.] strips of the outer skin of a vegetable or fruit.

peen /pēn/ ▶n. the end of a hammer head opposite the face, typically wedge-shaped, curved, or spherical. ▶v. [trans.] strike with a hammer or the peen of a hammer. [16th C.: prob. of Scand. origin; cf. Swed. dialect *pena (ut)*, Dan. dial. *pene (ud)* 'beat (out).']

peep[1] /pēp/ ▶v. [intrans.] look quickly and furtively at something, esp. through a narrow opening. ■ (**peep out**) be just visible; appear slowly or partly or through a small opening. ▶n. [usu. in sing.] a quick or furtive look. ■ a momentary or partial view of something. [15th C.: symbolic.]

peep[2] ▶n. a high-pitched feeble sound made by a young bird or mammal. ■ [with negative] a slight sound, utterance, or complaint: *not a peep out of them.* ■ (usu. **peeps**) informal a small sandpiper or similar wading bird. ▶v. [intrans.] make a cheeping or beeping sound. [ME: imitative.]

pee-pee ▶n. informal a child's word for an act of urinating. ■ urine. ■ a penis.

peep·er[1] /'pēpər/ ▶n. a person who peeps at someone or something, esp. in a voyeuristic way. ■ (**peepers**) informal a person's eyes.

peep·er[2] (also **spring peeper**) ▶n. a small North American tree frog (*Hyla crucifer*) that has brownish-gray skin with a dark cross on the back, the males of which sing in early spring.

peep·hole /'pēp,hōl/ ▶n. a small hole that may be looked through, esp. one in a door through which visitors may be identified before the door is opened.

peep·ing Tom ▶n. a person who gets sexual pleasure from secretly watching people undressing or engaging in sexual activity. [after the person said to have watched Lady GODIVA ride naked through Coventry.]

peep show ▶n. a sequence of pictures viewed through a lens or hole set into a box, traditionally offered as a public entertainment. ■ an erotic or pornographic film or show viewed from a coin-operated booth.

peep sight ▶n. a rear sight for rifles with a circular hole through which the front sight is brought into line with the object aimed at.

pee·pul /'pēpəl/ (also **pi·pal**) ▶n. another term for BO TREE. [18th C.: via Hindi from Sanskrit *pippala*.]

peer[1] /pi(ə)r/ ▶v. [intrans.] look keenly or with difficulty at someone or something. ■ be just visible: *the two towers peer over the roofs.* ■ archaic come into view; appear. [16th C.: perhaps a var. of dial. *pire*; perh. partly from a shortening of APPEAR.]

peer[2] ▶n. **1** a person of the same age, status, or ability as another specified person. **2** a member of the nobility in Britain or Ireland, comprising the ranks of duke, marquess, earl, viscount, and baron.
– PHRASES **without peer** unequaled; unrivaled. — **peer·less** adj. (in sense 1). [ME: from OFr. *peer*, from L. *par* 'equal.']

peer·age /'pi(ə)rij/ ▶n. the title and rank of peer or peeress. ■ (**the peerage**) those holding a hereditary or honorary title. ■ a book containing a list of peers and peeresses, with their genealogy and history.

peer·ess /'pi(ə)ris/ ▶n. a woman holding the rank of a peer in her own right. ■ the wife or widow of a peer.

peer group ▶n. a group of people of approximately the same age, status, and interests.

peer pres·sure ▶n. influence from members of one's peer group.

peer-to-peer ▶adj. [attrib.] denoting computer networks in which each computer can act as a server for the others, allowing shared access to files and peripherals without the need for a central server.

peeve /pēv/ informal ▶v. [trans.] (usu. **be peeved**) annoy; irritate. ▶n. a cause of annoyance: *his pet peeve is a noisy neighbor.* [20th C.: back-form. from PEEVISH.]

peev·ish /'pēviSH/ ▶adj. easily irritated, esp. by unimportant things. ■ querulous: *a peevish voice.* — **peev·ish·ly** adv. **peev·ish·ness** n.

pee·wee /'pē,wē/ ▶n. **1** [usu. as adj.] a level of amateur sports, involving children aged eight or nine. ■ a player at such a level of amateur sport. **2** var. of PEWEE. **3** a small marble.

pee·wit /'pē,wit/ ▶n. var. of PEWIT.

PEG ▶abbr. polyethylene glycol.

peg /peg/ ▶n. **1** a short cylindrical piece of wood, metal, or plastic, typically tapered at one end, that is used for holding things together, hanging things on, or marking a position. ■ such an object attached to a wall on which to hang garments. ■ (also **tent peg**) such an object driven into the ground to hold one of the ropes or corners of a tent in position. ■ such an object in the neck of a stringed musical instrument around which the strings are wound, and which are turned to adjust their tension and so tune the instrument. ■ a bung for stoppering a cask. ■ informal a person's leg. ■ a point or limit on a scale, esp. of exchange rates. **2** esp. Indian a measure of liquor: *have a peg of whiskey.* **3** informal a strong throw, esp. in baseball. ▶v. (**pegged, peg·ging**) [trans.] **1** fix or make fast with a peg or pegs. ■ mark (the score) with pegs on a cribbage board. **2** fix (a price, rate, or amount) at a particular level. ■ informal form a fixed opinion of; categorize: *she has us pegged as anarchists.* **3** informal throw (a ball) hard and low, esp. in baseball.
– PHRASES **a square peg in a round hole** a person in a situation unsuited to their abilities or character. **take someone down a peg or two** make someone realize that they are less talented or important than they think are.
– PHRASAL VERBS **peg away** informal continue working hard at or trying to achieve something, esp. over a long period. **peg out 1** informal, esp. Brit. die. **2** score the winning point at cribbage. **3** Croquet hit the peg with the ball as the final stroke in a game. **peg something out** mark the boundaries of an area of land: *I went out to peg out our assembly area.* [ME: prob. of Low Ger. origin; cf. Du. dial. *peg* 'plug, peg.']

Peg·a·sus /'pegəsəs/ **1** Gk. Mythol. a winged horse that sprang from the blood of Medusa when Perseus cut off her head. **2** Astron. a large northern constellation, said to represent a winged horse. The three brightest stars, together with one star of Andromeda, form the prominent **Square of Pegasus**. [via L. from Gk.]

peg·board /'peg,bôrd/ ▶n. a board having a regular pattern of small holes for pegs, used chiefly for games or the display of information.

peg·box /'peg,bäks/ ▶n. a structure at the head of a stringed instrument where the strings are attached to the tuning pegs.

pegged /pegd/ ▶adj. another term for PEGTOP.

peg leg ▶n. informal an artificial leg, esp. a wooden one. ■ a person with such an artificial leg.

peg·ma·tite /'pegmə,tīt/ ▶n. Geol. a coarsely crystalline granite or other igneous rock with crystals several centimeters in length. [19th C.: from Gk. *pēgma, pēgmat-* 'thing joined together' + -ITE[1].]

peg·top /'peg,täp/ ▶n. a pear-shaped spinning top with a metal pin or peg forming the point, spun by the rapid uncoiling of a string wound around it. ▶adj. dated (of a garment) wide at the top and narrow at the bottom.

Pe·gu /pe'go͞o/ a city in southern Myanmar (Burma), on the Pegu River; pop. 150,000.

Peh·le·vi /'pālə,vē/ ▶n. var. of PAHLAVI[2].

PEI ▶abbr. Prince Edward Island.

Pei /pā/, I. M. (1917–), US architect; born in China; full name *Ieoh Ming Pei.* He designed the John F. Kennedy Library 1979 in Boston and the pyramid entrance to the Louvre 1983–89 in Paris.

Pei·gan /'pēgən/ ▶n. (pl. same or **-gans**) & adj. var. of PIEGAN.

peign·oir /,pān'wär/ ▶n. a woman's light dressing gown or negligee. [Fr., from *peigner* 'to comb' (because the garment was orig. worn while combing the hair).]

Peirce /pi(ə)rs/, Charles Sanders (1839–1914), US philosopher. He was a founder of pragmatism.

Pei·sis·tra·tus var. of PISISTRATUS.

pe·jo·ra·tive /pə'jôrətiv; 'pejə,rātiv/ ▶adj. expressing contempt or disapproval. ▶n. a word expressing contempt or disapproval. — **pe·jo·ra·tive·ly** adv. [19th C.: from Fr. *péjoratif, -ive*, from late L. *pejorare* 'make worse,' from L. *pejor* 'worse.']

pek·an /'pekən/ ▶n. another term for FISHER (sense 2). [18th C.: from Canad. Fr., from Algonquian.]

peke /pēk/ ▶n. informal a Pekingese dog.

Pe·king duck /ˌpēˈkiNG; ˌpā-/ ▶ **n.** a Chinese dish consisting of strips of roast duck served with shredded vegetables and a sweet sauce.

Pekingese

Pe·king·ese /ˈpēkəˌnēz; -ˌnēs/ (also **Pe·kin·ese**) ▶ **n.** /ˈpēkəˌnēz/ (pl. same) a lapdog of a short-legged breed with long hair and a snub nose, originally brought to Europe from the Summer Palace at Beijing (Peking) in 1860. ▶ **adj.** /ˌpēkiNGˈēz; -ˈēs/ of or relating to Beijing, its citizens, or their culture or cuisine.

Pe·king man ▶ **n.** a fossil hominid of the middle Pleistocene period, identified from remains found near Beijing in 1926. It is a late form of *Homo erectus* (formerly *Sinanthropus pekinensis*).

pe·koe /ˈpēˌkō/ ▶ **n.** a high-quality black tea made from young leaves. [18th C.: from Chin. dial. *pekho*, from *pek* 'white' + *ho* 'down' (the leaves being picked young when covered with down).]

pel·age /ˈpelij/ ▶ **n.** Zool. the fur, hair, or wool of a mammal. [19th C.: from Fr., from OFr. *pel* 'hair.']

pe·lag·ic /pəˈlajik/ ▶ **adj.** tech. of or relating to the open sea. ■ (chiefly of fish) inhabiting the upper layers of the open sea. Often contrasted with DEMERSAL. [17th C.: via L. from Gk. *pelagikos*, from *pelagios* 'of the sea.']

Pe·la·gi·us /pəˈlāj(ē)əs/ (*c.*360–*c.*420), British or Irish monk. He denied the doctrines of original sin and predestination, defending innate goodness and free will. — **Pe·la·gi·an** /-jēən/ **adj.** & **n.** **Pe·la·gi·an·ism n.**

pel·ar·go·ni·um /ˌpelärˈgōnēəm/ ▶ **n.** a tender shrubby plant (genus *Pelargonium*, family Geraniaceae) that is widely cultivated for its red, pink, or white flowers. Some kinds have fragrant leaves that yield an essential oil. See also GERANIUM. [mod. L., from Gk. *pelargos* 'stork,' appar. on the pattern of *geranium* (based on Gk. *geranos* 'crane').]

Pe·las·gi·an /pəˈlazjēən/ ▶ **adj.** relating to or denoting an ancient people inhabiting the coasts and islands of the Aegean Sea and eastern Mediterranean before the arrival of Greek-speaking peoples in the Bronze Age. ▶ **n.** a member of this people. [15th C.: via L. from Gk. *Pelasgos* + -IAN.]

pe·lau /pəˈlou/ ▶ **n.** a spicy dish consisting of meat (typically chicken), rice, and pigeon peas. [from Fr. Creole *pêlao*.]

Pe·lé /ˈpāˌlā/ (1940–), Brazilian soccer player; born *Edson Arantes do Nascimento*. He is regarded as one of the greatest goal-scorers of all time.

pele ▶ **n.** var. of PEEL³.

pe·lec·y·pod /pəˈlesəˌpäd/ ▶ **n.** another term for BIVALVE. [19th C.: from mod. L. *Pelecypoda* (alternative class name), from Gk. *pelekus* 'hatchet' + *-podos* 'footed.']

Pe·lée, Mount /pəˈlā/ a volcano on the island of Martinique. Its 1902 eruption killed about 30,000 people.

pel·er·ine /ˌpeləˈrēn; ˈpelərin/ ▶ **n.** hist. a woman's cape of lace or silk with pointed ends at the center front, popular in the 19th century. [18th C.: from Fr. *pèlerine*, fem. of *pèlerin* 'pilgrim.']

Pe·le's hair /ˈpelāz/ ▶ **n.** fine threads of volcanic glass, formed when a spray of lava droplets cools rapidly in the air. [19th C.: after Pele, Hawaiian goddess of volcanoes.]

Pe·le·us /ˈpēlēəs/ Gk. Mythol. a king of Phthia in Thessaly, who was given as his wife the sea nymph Thetis; their child was Achilles.

pelf /pelf/ ▶ **n.** money, esp. when gained in a dishonest or dishonorable way. [ME: from a var. of OFr. *pelfre* 'spoils.']

pel·ham /ˈpeləm/ ▶ **n.** a horse's bit that combines the action of a curb bit and a snaffle. [19th C.: from the surname *Pelham*.]

pel·i·can /ˈpelikən/ ▶ **n.** a large gregarious waterbird (genus *Pelecanus*, family Pelecanidae) with a long bill, an extensible throat pouch for scooping up fish, and mainly white or gray plumage. ■ a heraldic or artistic representation of a pelican, typically depicted pecking its own breast as a symbol of Christ. [from an ancient legend that the pelican fed its young on its own blood.] [OE *pellicane*, via late L. from Gk. *pelekan*, prob. based on *pelekus* 'ax' (with ref. to its bill).]

Pe·li·on /ˈpēlēən/ a wooded mountain in Greece, near the coast of southeastern Thessaly, that rises to 5,079 feet (1,548 m).

pe·lisse /pəˈlēs/ ▶ **n.** hist. a woman's cloak with armholes or sleeves, reaching to the ankles. ■ a fur-lined cloak, esp. as part of a hussar's uniform. [18th C.: from Fr., from med. L. *pellicia (vestis)* '(garment) of fur,' from *pellis* 'skin.']

pe·lite /ˈpēˌlīt/ ▶ **n.** Geol. a sediment or sedimentary rock composed of very fine clay or mud particles. [19th C.: from Gk. *pēlos* 'clay, mud' + -ITE¹.]

pel·la·gra /pəˈlagrə; -ˈlāgrə; -ˈlägrə/ ▶ **n.** a deficiency disease caused by a lack of nicotinic acid or its precursor tryptophan in the diet. It is characterized by dermatitis, diarrhea, and mental disturbance, and is often linked to overdependence on corn as a staple food. — **pel·la·grous** /-grəs/ **adj.** [19th C.: from Ital., from *pelle* 'skin.']

pel·let /ˈpelit/ ▶ **n.** a small, rounded, compressed mass of a substance. ■ a piece of small shot or other lightweight bullet. ■ Ornithol. a small mass of bones and feathers regurgitated by a bird of prey or other bird. ■ a small round piece of animal feces, esp. from a rabbit or rodent. ▶ **v.** (**-let·ed**, **-let·ing**) [trans.] **1** form or shape (a substance, esp. animal food) into pellets. **2** hit with or as though with pellets: *drops of rain pelleting the windshield.* [ME: from OFr. *pelote* 'metal ball,' from a dimin. of L. *pila* 'ball.']

pel·let·ize /ˈpeliˌtīz/ ▶ **v.** [trans.] form or shape (a substance) into pellets.

Pel·li /ˈpelē/, César (1926–), US architect; born in Argentina. His designs include the World Financial Center 1981–87 (the buildings that surrounded the destroyed World Trade Center) in New York City and the Petronas Towers (1998) in Kuala Lumpur, Malaysia.

pel·li·cle /ˈpelikəl/ ▶ **n.** tech. a thin skin, cuticle, membrane, or film. — **pel·lic·u·lar** /pəˈlikyələr/ **adj.** [ME: ult. from L. *pellicula* 'small piece of skin,' dimin. of *pellis*.]

pel·li·to·ry /ˈpeliˌtôrē/ ▶ **n.** **1** (in full **pellitory of Spain**) a plant (*Anacyclus pyrethrum*) of the daisy family, with a pungent-flavored root, used as a local irritant, etc. **2** (also **pellitory of the wall**) a European plant (*Parietaria judaica*) of the nettle family with greenish flowers that grows on or at the foot of walls or in stony places. [ME: alt. of obs. *parietary*, from OFr. *paritaire*, based on L. *paries*, *pariet-* 'wall.']

pell-mell /ˈpel ˈmel/ ▶ **adv.** in a confused, rushed, or disorderly manner. ▶ **adj.** recklessly hasty or disorganized; headlong. ▶ **n.** [in sing.] a state of affairs or collection of things characterized by haste or confusion. [16th C.: from Fr. *pêle-mêle*, from earlier *pesle mesle*, *mesle pesle*, reduplication from *mesler* 'to mix.']

pel·lu·cid /pəˈlo͞osid/ ▶ **adj.** translucently clear. ■ lucid in style or meaning; easily understood. ■ (of music or other sound) clear and pure in tone. — **pel·lu·cid·ly adv.** [17th C.: from L. *pellucidus*, from *perlucere* 'shine through.']

pel·met /ˈpelmit/ ▶ **n.** a narrow border of cloth or wood, fitted across the top of a door or window to conceal the curtain fittings. [20th C.: prob. an alt. of Fr. *palmette*, lit. 'small palm.']

Pel·o·pon·ne·sian War /ˌpeləpəˈnēZHən/ the war of 431–404 BC fought between Athens and Sparta with their respective allies, occasioned largely by Spartan opposition to the Delian League. It ended in the total defeat of Athens and the transfer, for a brief period, of the leadership of Greece to Sparta.

Pel·o·pon·ne·sus /ˌpeləpəˈnēsəs/ (also **the Pel·o·pon·nese** /ˌpeləpəˈnēz; -ˈnēs/) the mountainous southern peninsula of Greece. Greek name PELOPÓNNISOS, also called PELOPONNESE.

Pel·ops /ˈpēˌläps/ Gk. Mythol. son of Tantalus, brother of Niobe, and father of Atreus. He was killed by his father and served up as food to the gods, but only one shoulder was eaten, and he was restored to life with an ivory shoulder replacing the one that was missing.

pe·lo·rus /pəˈlôrəs/ ▶ **n.** a sighting device on a ship for taking the relative bearings of a distant object. [19th C.: perh. from *Pelorus*, said to be the name of Hannibal's pilot.]

pe·lo·ta /pəˈlōtə/ ▶ **n.** a Basque or Spanish game played in a walled court with a ball and basketlike rackets attached to the hand. ■ the ball used in such a game. [Sp., lit. 'ball,' augmentative of *pella*, from L. *pila* 'ball.']

pel·o·ton /ˈpeləˌtän/ ▶ **n.** the main field or group of cyclists in a race. [1950s: from Fr., lit. 'small ball' (because of the concentrated grouping of the pack).]

pelt¹ /pelt/ ▶ **v.** [trans.] attack (someone) by repeatedly hurling things at them: *two boys pelted him with apples.* ■ hurl (something) at someone or something in this way. ■ [intrans.] (**pelt down**) (of rain, hail, or snow) fall quickly and very heavily. ■ [intrans.] informal run somewhere very quickly: *I pelted across the road.*

pelt² ▶ **n.** the skin of an animal with the fur, wool, or hair still on it. ■ an animal's coat of fur or hair. ■ the raw skin of a sheep or goat, stripped and ready for tanning. ■ informal a person's hair. [ME: either from obs. *pellet* 'skin,' based on L. *pellis* 'skin,' or a back-form. from PELTRY.]

pel·tate /ˈpelˌtāt/ ▶ **adj.** esp. Bot. shield-shaped. ■ (of a leaf) more or less circular, with the stalk attached at a point on the underside.

Pel·tier ef·fect /ˈpeltēā/ ▶ **n.** Physics an effect whereby heat is given out or absorbed when an electric current passes across a junction between two materials. [19th C.: named after Jean C. A. *Peltier* (1785–1845), Fr. scientist.]

pelt·ry /ˈpeltrē/ ▶ **n.** (also **peltries**) animal pelts collectively. [ME: from Anglo-Norman Fr. *pelterie*, based on OFr. *pel* 'skin,' from L. *pellis*.]

pel·vic /ˈpelvik/ ▶ **adj.** of, relating to, or situated within the bony pelvis. ■ of or relating to the renal pelvis.

pel·vic fin ▶ **n.** Zool. each of a pair of fins on the underside of a fish's body, attached to the pelvic girdle and helping to control direction. Also called VENTRAL FIN.

pel·vic floor ▶ **n.** the muscular base of the abdomen, attached to the pelvis.

pel·vic gir·dle ▶ **n.** (in vertebrates) the enclosing structure formed by the pelvis, providing attachment for the hind limbs or pelvic fins.

pel·vic in·flam·ma·to·ry dis·ease (abbr.: **PID**) ▶ **n.** inflammation of the female genital tract, accompanied by fever and lower abdominal pain.

pel·vis /ˈpelvis/ ▶ **n.** (pl. **-vis·es** or **-ves** /-vēz/) (also **renal pelvis**) the broadened top part of the ureter into which the kidney tubules drain. [17th C.: from L., lit. 'basin.']

Pem·ba /ˈpembə/ an island off the coast of Tanzania, in the western Indian Ocean, north of Zanzibar.

pem·mi·can /ˈpemikən/ ▶ **n.** a paste of dried and pounded meat mixed with melted fat and other ingredients, originally made by North American Indians and later adapted by Arctic explorers. [from Cree *pimikan*, from *pime* 'fat.']

pem·phi·gus /ˈpemfigəs; pemˈfīgəs/ ▶ **n.** Med. a skin disease in which watery blisters form on the skin. [18th C.: mod. L., from Gk. *pemphix, pemphig-* 'bubble.']

PEN ▶ **abbr.** International Association of Poets, Playwrights, Editors, Essayists, and Novelists.

Pen. ▶ **abbr.** Peninsula.

pen[1] /pen/ ▶ **n.** **1** an instrument for writing or drawing with ink, typically consisting of a metal nib or ball, or a nylon tip, fitted into a metal or plastic holder. ■ **(the pen)** the occupation or practice of writing. ■ an electronic penlike device used in conjunction with a writing surface to enter commands or data into a computer. **2** Zool. the tapering cartilaginous internal shell of a squid. ▶ **v.** **(penned, pen·ning)** [trans.] write or compose.

– PHRASES **the pen is mightier than the sword** proverb writing is more effective than military power or violence. **put** (or **set**) **pen to paper** write or begin to write something. [ME: from OFr. *penne*, from L. *penna* 'feather.']

pen[2] ▶ **n.** a small enclosure in which sheep, pigs, cattle, or other domestic animals are kept. ■ a number of animals in or sufficient to fill such an enclosure. ■ any small enclosure in which someone or something can be confined. ■ a covered dock for a submarine or other warship. ▶ **v.** **(penned, pen·ning)** [trans.] put or keep (an animal) in a pen. ■ **(pen someone up/in)** confine someone in a restricted space. [OE *penn*, of unknown origin.]

pen[3] ▶ **n.** a female swan. [16th C.: of unknown origin.]

pen[4] ▶ **n.** informal short for PENITENTIARY (sense 1).

pe·nal /ˈpēnl/ ▶ **adj.** of, relating to, or prescribing the punishment of offenders under the legal system. ■ used or designated as a place of punishment. ■ (of an act or offense) punishable by law. — **pe·nal·ly** **adv.** [ME: from OFr. *penal*, from L. *poenalis*, from *poena* 'penalty.']

pe·nal·ize /ˈpenl͵īz; ˈpē-/ ▶ **v.** [trans.] (often **be penalized**) subject to some form of punishment. ■ (in various sports) punish (a player or team) for a breach of the rules by awarding an advantage to the opposition. ■ put in an unfavorable position or at an unfair disadvantage. ■ Law make or declare (an act or offense) legally punishable. — **pe·nal·i·za·tion** /͵penl-iˈzāsʜən; ͵pē-/ **n.**

pe·nal ser·vi·tude ▶ **n.** imprisonment with hard labor.

pen·al·ty /ˈpenltē/ ▶ **n.** (pl. **-ties**) **1** a punishment imposed for breaking a law, rule, or contract. ■ a disadvantage or unpleasant experience suffered as the result of an action or circumstance. **2** (in sports and games) a disadvantage or handicap imposed on a player or team, typically for infringement of rules. ■ a kick or shot awarded to a team because of a serious infringement of the rules by an opponent. ■ Bridge points won by the defenders when a declarer fails to make the contract.

– PHRASES **under** (or **on**) **penalty of** under the threat of. [16th C.: based on med. L. *poenalitas* 'pain.']

pen·al·ty ar·e·a ▶ **n.** Soccer the rectangular area marked out in front of each goal, within which a foul by a defender involves the award of a penalty kick and outside which the goalkeeper is not allowed to handle the ball.

pen·al·ty box ▶ **n.** Ice Hockey an enclosure alongside the rink where players who have been assessed penalties must remain temporarily.

pen·al·ty kick ▶ **n.** **1** Soccer a free kick at the goal from the penalty spot (which only the goalkeeper is allowed to defend), awarded to the attacking team after a foul within the penalty area by an opponent. **2** Rugby a placekick awarded to a team after an offense by an opponent.

pen·al·ty kill·er ▶ **n.** Hockey a player specializing in preventing the opposing side from scoring while their own team's strength is reduced through penalties. — **pen·al·ty kill·ing** **n.**

pen·al·ty shoot-out ▶ **n.** see SHOOT-OUT.

pen·al·ty spot ▶ **n.** Soccer the point within the penalty area from which penalty kicks are taken.

pen·ance /ˈpenəns/ ▶ **n.** **1** voluntary self-punishment inflicted as an outward expression of repentance for having done wrong. **2** a Christian sacrament in which a member of the Church confesses sins to a priest and is given absolution. ■ a religious observance or other duty required of a person by a priest as part of this sacrament to indicate repentance. [ME: from OFr., from L. *paenitentia* 'repentance,' from *paenitere* 'be sorry.']

Pe·nang /pəˈnaɴɢ/ (also **Pi·nang**) an island in Malaysia, located off the western coast of the Malay Peninsula. ■ a state of Malaysia, consisting of this island and a coastal strip on the mainland; capital, George Town. ■ another name for GEORGE TOWN (sense 2).

pe·na·tes /pəˈnātēz; -ˈnä-/ ▶ **plural n.** Roman History household gods worshiped in conjunction with Vesta and the lares by the ancient Romans. [L., from *penus* 'provision of food.']

pence /pens/ plural form of PENNY.

pen·chant /ˈpencʜənt/ ▶ **n.** [usu. in sing.] a strong or habitual liking for something or tendency to do something. [17th C.: from Fr., 'leaning,' pres. part. of *pencher*.]

pen·cil /ˈpensəl/ ▶ **n.** an instrument for writing or drawing, consisting of a thin stick of graphite or a similar substance enclosed in a long thin piece of wood or fixed in a metal or plastic case. ■ used to refer to the composition, skill, or style of a drawing. ■ graphite or a similar substance used in such a way as a medium for writing or drawing. ■ a cosmetic in a long thin stick, designed to be applied to a particular part of the face. ■ something with the shape of a pencil: *a pencil of light.* ■ Physics Geom. a set of light rays, lines, etc., converging to or diverging narrowly from a single point. ▶ **v.** **(-ciled, -cil·ing;** Brit. **-cilled, -cil·ling)** [trans.] write, draw, or color (something) with a pencil.

– PHRASAL VERBS **pencil something in 1** fill in an area or shape with pencil strokes. **2** arrange, forecast, or note down something provisionally or tentatively. ■ **(pencil someone in)** make a provisional or tentative arrangement with or for someone: *I've penciled you in for next Tuesday.* — **pen·cil·er** **n.** [ME: from OFr. *pincel*, from diminutive of L. *peniculus* 'brush,' dimin. of *penis* 'tail.']

pen·cil push·er ▶ **n.** informal a person with a clerical job involving a lot of tedious and repetitive paperwork.

pend·ant /ˈpendənt/ ▶ **n.** **1** a piece of jewelry that hangs from a chain worn around the neck. ■ a necklace with such a piece of jewelry. ■ a light designed to hang from the ceiling. ■ the part of a pocket watch by which it is suspended. ■ Naut. a short rope hanging from the head of a ship's mast, yardarm, or clew of a sail, used for attaching tackles. **2** an artistic, literary, or musical composition intended to match or complement another. ▶ **adj.** hanging downward; pendent. [ME: from OFr., lit. 'hanging,' pres. part. of *pendre*, from L. *pendere*.]

pend·ent /ˈpendənt/ ▶ **adj.** **1** hanging down or overhanging. **2** undecided; pending. **3** Gram. (esp. of a sentence) incomplete; not having a finite verb. — **pen·den·cy** **n.**

pen·den·tive /penˈdentiv/ ▶ **n.** Archit. a curved triangle of vaulting formed by the intersection of a dome with its supporting arches. [18th C.: from Fr. *pendentif, -ive*, from L. *pendent-* 'hanging down,' from the v. *pendere*.]

Pen·de·rec·ki /͵pendəˈretskē/, Krzysztof (1933–), Polish composer. His music frequently features sounds drawn from extramusical sources and note clusters.

pend·ing /ˈpendiɴɢ/ ▶ **adj.** awaiting decision or settlement. ■ about to happen; imminent. ▶ **prep.** until (something) happens or takes place: *they were released on bail pending an appeal.* [17th C.: Anglicized spelling of Fr. *pendant* 'hanging.']

pen·drag·on /penˈdragən/ ▶ **n.** a title given to an ancient British or Welsh prince holding or claiming supreme power. [Welsh, lit. 'chief war-leader,' from *pen* 'head' + *dragon* 'standard.']

pen·du·lous /ˈpenjələs; ˈpendyə-/ ▶ **adj.** hanging down loosely. — **pen·du·lous·ly** **adv.** [17th C.: from L. *pendulus* 'hanging down' (from *pendere* 'hang') + **-ous**.]

pen·du·lum /ˈpenjələm; ˈpendyə-/ ▶ **n.** a weight hung from a fixed point so that it can swing freely backward and forward, esp. a rod with a weight at the end that regulates the mechanism of a clock. ■ fig. used to refer to the tendency of a situation or state of affairs to oscillate regularly etween one extreme and another. — **pen·du·lar** /-lər/ **adj.** [17th C.: from L., neut. of *pendulus* 'hanging down.']

pendulum

Pe·nel·o·pe /pəˈneləpē/ Gk. Mythol. the wife of Odysseus, who was beset by suitors when her husband did not return after the fall of Troy. See also ODYSSEY.

pe·ne·plain /ˈpēnə͵plān/ (also **pe·ne·plane**) ▶ **n.** Geol. a more or less level land surface produced by erosion over a long period, undisturbed by crustal movement. [19th C.: from L. *paene* 'almost' + PLAIN[1].]

pen·e·tra·li·a /͵peniˈtrālēə/ ▶ **plural n.** the innermost parts of a building; a secret or hidden place. [17th C.: from L., lit. 'innermost things,' neut. pl. of *penetralis* 'interior.']

pen·e·trance /ˈpenətrəns/ ▶ **n.** Genet. the extent to which a particular gene or set of genes is expressed in the phenotypes of individuals carrying it, measured by the proportion of carriers showing the characteristic phenotype. [1930s: from Ger. *Penetranz*.]

pen·e·trant /ˈpenətrənt/ ▶ **adj.** Genet. (of a gene or group of genes) producing characteristic effects in the phenotypes of individuals possessing it. ▶ **n.** a substance that can penetrate cracks, pores, and other surface defects.

pen·e·trate /ˈpeni͵trāt/ ▶ **v.** [trans.] succeed in forcing a way into or through (a thing). ■ (of a man) insert the penis into the vagina or anus of (a sexual partner). ■ infiltrate (an enemy group or rival organization) in order to spy on it. ■ (of a company) begin to sell its products in (a particular market or area). ■ succeed in understanding or gaining insight into (something complex or mysterious). ■ [intrans.] be fully understood or realized by someone. — **pen·e·tra·bil·i·ty** /ˌpenitrəˈbilitē/ **n. pen·e·tra·ble** /-trəbəl/ **adj.** [16th C.: from L. *penetrat-* 'placed into,' from the v. *penetrare*; rel. to *penitus* 'inner.']

pen·e·trat·ing /ˈpeniˌtrātiNG/ ▶ **adj.** able to make a way through or into something. ■ (of a voice or sound) clearly heard through or above other sounds. ■ (of a smell) strong; pungent. ■ (of a person's eyes or expression) reflecting an apparent ability to see into the mind of the person being looked at; piercingly intense. ■ having or showing clear insight. — **pen·e·trat·ing·ly adv.**

pen·e·tra·tion /ˌpeniˈtrāSHən/ ▶ **n. 1** the action or process of making a way through or into something. ■ the ability to do this: *the power and penetration of radiation.* ■ the insertion by a man of his penis into the vagina or anus of a sexual partner. ■ the infiltration of an enemy group or rival organization in order to spy on it. ■ the successful selling of a company's or country's products in a particular market or area. ■ the extent to which a product is recognized and bought by customers in a particular market: *a high degree of market penetration.* **2** the perceptive understanding of complex matters: *the survey shows subtlety and penetration.*

pen·e·tra·tive /ˈpeniˌtrātiv/ ▶ **adj. 1** able to make a way into or through something. ■ (in various sports) able to break through an opponent's defense. ■ (of sexual activity) in which a man inserts his penis into the vagina or anus of a sexual partner. **2** having or showing deep understanding and insight: *a thorough and penetrative survey.*

pen·e·tra·tor /ˈpeniˌtrātər/ ▶ **n.** a person or thing that penetrates something. ■ a missile containing a hard alloy rod, designed to penetrate the armor of tanks or fortifications.

pen·e·trom·e·ter /ˌpenəˈträmitər/ ▶ **n.** an instrument for determining the consistency or hardness of a substance by measuring the depth or rate of penetration of a rod or needle driven into it by a known force.

pen·gö /ˈpen-gō/ ▶ **n.** (pl. same or **-gös**) the basic monetary unit of Hungary from 1927 until 1946, when it was replaced by the forint. [Hungarian, lit. 'ringing.']

pen·guin /ˈpeNGgwin; ˈpengwin/ ▶ **n.** a large flightless seabird (family Spheniscidae) of the southern hemisphere, with black upper parts and white underparts and wings developed into flippers for swimming under water. See illustration at **Adélie penguin.** [16th C. (orig. denoting the great auk): of unknown origin.]

pen·i·cil·late /ˌpenəˈsilit; -ˈsilāt/ ▶ **adj.** Biol. having, forming, or resembling a small tuft or tufts of hair. [19th C.: from L. *penicillus* 'paintbrush' + **-ate**[2].]

pen·i·cil·lin /ˌpenəˈsilən/ ▶ **n. 1** an antibiotic or group of antibiotics produced naturally by certain blue molds, now usually prepared synthetically. **2** a blue mold (genus *Penicillium*, subdivision Deuteromycotina) of a type that produces these antibiotics.

pen·i·cil·lin·ase /ˌpenəˈsilənās/ ▶ **n.** Biochem. an enzyme that can inactivate penicillin, produced by certain bacteria.

pen·i·cil·li·um /ˌpenəˈsilēəm/ ▶ **n.** (pl. **-cil·li·a** /-ˈsilēə/) a blue mold that is common on food, being added to some cheeses and used sometimes to produce penicillin. [19th C.: mod. L., from L. *penicillus* 'paintbrush' (because of the brushlike fruiting bodies).]

pe·nile /ˈpēnəl; -nīl/ ▶ **adj.** [attrib.] esp. tech. of, relating to, or affecting the penis.

pen·in·su·la /pəˈninsələ/ ▶ **n.** a piece of land almost surrounded by water or projecting out into a body of water. — **pen·in·su·lar** /-lər/ **adj.** [16th C.: from L. *paeninsula*, from *paene* 'almost' + *insula* 'island.']

pe·nis /ˈpēnis/ ▶ **n.** (pl. **-nis·es** or **-nes** /-nēz/) the male genital organ of higher vertebrates, carrying the duct for the transfer of sperm during copulation. In humans and most other mammals, it consists largely of erectile tissue and serves also for the elimination of urine. ■ Zool. a type of male copulatory organ present in some invertebrates, such as gastropod mollusks. [17th C.: from L., 'tail, penis.']

pe·nis en·vy ▶ **n.** Psychoanal. supposed envy of the male's possession of a penis, postulated by Freud to account for some aspects of female behavior but controversial among modern theorists.

pen·i·tent /ˈpenitnt/ ▶ **adj.** feeling or showing sorrow and regret for having done wrong; repentant. ▶ **n.** a person who repents their sins or wrongdoings and (in the Christian Church) seeks forgiveness from God. ■ (in the Roman Catholic Church) a person who confesses their sins to a priest and submits to the penance that he imposes. — **pen·i·tence n. pen·i·tent·ly adv.** [ME: from OFr., from L. *paenitent-* 'repenting,' from the v. *paenitere*.]

pen·i·ten·tial /ˌpenəˈtenSHəl/ ▶ **adj.** relating to or expressing penitence or penance.

pen·i·ten·tia·ry /ˌpenəˈtenSHərē/ ▶ **n.** (pl. **-ries**) **1** a prison for people convicted of serious crimes. **2** (in the Roman Catholic Church) a priest charged with certain aspects of the administration of the sacrament of penance. ■ an office in the papal court forming a tribunal for deciding on questions relating to penance, dispensations, and absolution. [ME: from med. L. *paenitentiarius*, from L. *paenitentia* 'repentance.']

pen·knife /ˈpenˌnīf/ ▶ **n.** (pl. **-knives** /-ˌnīvz/) a small pocketknife with a blade that folds into the handle. [so named because orig. used for making and mending quill pens.]

pen·light /ˈpenˌlīt/ ▶ **n.** a small flashlight shaped like a fountain pen.

pen·man /ˈpenˌmən/ ▶ **n.** (pl. **-men**) esp. hist. a person who was skilled or professionally engaged in writing by hand, typically, as a clerk, on behalf of others. ■ an author.

pen·man·ship /ˈpenmənˌSHip/ ▶ **n.** the art or skill of writing by hand. ■ a person's handwriting.

Penn /pen/, William (1644–1718), English colonial administrator. He founded the colony of Pennsylvania as a sanctuary for Quakers and other nonconformists in 1682.

Penn. (also **Penna.**) ▶ **abbr.** Pennsylvania.

pen name ▶ **n.** an assumed name used by a writer instead of their real name.

pen·nant /ˈpenənt/ ▶ **n. 1** a flag denoting a sports championship or other achievement. **2** a tapering flag on a ship, esp. one flown at the masthead of a vessel in commission. Also called **pennon. 3** Naut. another term for **pendant. 4** Mil. another term for **pennon** (sense 1). [17th C.: blend of **pendant** and **pennon.**]

pen·nate /ˈpenāt/ ▶ **adj.** Bot. (of a diatom) bilaterally symmetrical. Compare with **centric.** [19th C.: from L. *pennatus* 'feathered, winged,' from *penna* 'feather.']

pen·ne /ˈpenā/ ▶ **n.** pasta in the form of short wide tubes. [Ital., pl. of *penna* 'quill.']

pen·ni /ˈpenē/ ▶ **n.** (pl. **pen·ni·ä** /ˈpenēə/) a monetary unit of Finland (until the introduction of the euro), equal to one hundredth of a markka.

pen·ni·less /ˈpenēlis/ ▶ **adj.** (of a person) having no money; very poor. — **pen·ni·less·ness n.**

Pen·nine Hills /ˈpenīn/ (also **Pen·nine Chain** or **the Pen·nines**) a range of hills in northern England.

pen·non /ˈpenən/ ▶ **n. 1** a long triangular or swallow-tailed flag, esp. as the military ensign of lancer regiments. Also called **pennant. 2** another term for **pennant** (sense 2). — **pen·noned adj.** [ME: from OFr., based on L. *penna* 'feather.']

Penn·syl·va·nia /ˌpensəlˈvānyə/ a state in the northeastern US, with a short coastline along Lake Erie in the far northwest; pop. 12,281,054; capital, Harrisburg; statehood, Dec. 12, 1787 (2). Founded 1682 by William Penn, it was one of the original thirteen states.

Penn·syl·vania Avenue a street in Washington, DC, along which the White House is situated.

Penn·syl·va·nia Dutch (also **Pennsylvania German**) ▶ **n. 1** a dialect of High German spoken in parts of Pennsylvania. **2** [as pl. n.] (**the Pennsylvania Dutch** or **Germans**) the German-speaking inhabitants of Pennsylvania, descendants of 17th- and 18th-century Protestant immigrants from the Rhineland. [*Dutch* from Ger. *Deutsch* 'German.']

Penn·syl·va·nian /ˌpensəlˈvānyən; -ˈvānēən/ ▶ **adj. 1** of or relating to the state of Pennsylvania. **2** Geol. of, relating to, or denoting the later part of the Carboniferous period in North America, following the Mississippian and preceding the Permian, and corresponding to the Upper Carboniferous of Europe. This period lasted from about 323 to 290 million years ago. ▶ **n. 1** a native or inhabitant of Pennsylvania. **2** (**the Pennsylvanian**) Geol. the Pennsylvanian period or the system of rocks deposited during it.

pen·ny /ˈpenē/ ▶ **n. 1** a one-cent coin equal to one hundredth of a dollar. ■ (pl. for separate coins **pen·nies**, for a sum of money **pence** /pens/) (abbr.: **p.**) a British bronze coin and monetary unit equal to one hundredth of a pound. ■ (abbr.: **d.**) a former British coin and monetary unit equal to one twelfth of a shilling and one 240th of a pound. ■ (**pennies**) a small sum of money: *a chance to save a few pennies.* ■ (in biblical use) a denarius. **2** [with negative] (**a penny**) used for emphasis to denote no money at all: *we didn't get paid a penny.*

– PHRASES **pinch** (or **count** or **watch**) (**one's**) **pennies** be careful about how much one spends. **pennies from heaven** unexpected benefits, esp. financial ones. **a penny for your thoughts** used in speech to ask someone what they are thinking about. [OE *penig, penning*, of Gmc. origin; rel. to Du. *penning*, Ger. *Pfennig*, perh. also to **pawn**[2].]

pen·ny an·te ▶ **n.** poker played for very small stakes. ■ [as adj.] informal petty; contemptible.

pen·ny ar·cade ▶ **n.** hist. an indoor area with coin-operated mechanical games, photography booths, picture shows, and other amusements.

pen·ny dread·ful ▶ **n.** a cheap, sensational comic or storybook.

pen·ny-far·thing ▶ **n.** hist. an early type of bicycle with a very large front wheel and a small rear wheel. Also called **ordinary.**

pen·ny loaf·er ▶ **n.** a casual leather shoe with a decorative slotted leather strip over the upper, in which a coin may be placed.

pen·ny-pinch·ing ▶ **adj.** unwilling to spend or share money; miserly; mean. ▶ **n.** unwillingness to spend or share money. — **pen·ny-pinch·er n.**

pen·ny·roy·al /ˈpenēˌroiəl/ ▶ **n.** either of two small-leaved plants of the mint family, used in herbal medicine: a creeping Eurasian plant (*Mentha pulegium*), and **American pennyroyal** (*Hedeoma pulegioides*). [16th C.: from Anglo-Norman Fr. *puliol* (based on L. *pulegium* 'thyme') + *real* 'royal.']

pen·ny stock ▶ **n.** a common stock valued at less than one dollar, and therefore highly speculative.

pen·ny·weight /ˈpenēˌwāt/ ▶ **n.** a unit of weight, 24 grains or one twentieth of an ounce troy.

pen·ny whis·tle ▶ **n.** another term for **tin whistle.**

pen·ny wise ▶ **adj.** extremely careful about the way one spends even small amounts of money.

– PHRASES **penny wise and pound foolish** careful and economical in small matters while being wasteful or extravagant in large ones.

pen·ny·wort /ˈpenēwərt; -ˌwôrt/ ▶ **n.** any of a number of plants with rounded leaves, in particular a creeping perennial of the parsley family belonging to the genus *Hydrocotyle*.

pen·ny·worth /'penē,wərTH/ ▶ **n.** esp. Brit. an amount of something that may be bought for a penny: *a pennyworth of chips.* ■ (**one's pennyworth**) a person's contribution to a discussion, esp. one that is unwelcome. ■ archaic value for one's money; a good bargain.

Pe·nob·scot /pə'näbskət; -,skät/ ▶ **n.** (pl. same) **1** a member of an American Indian people of the Penobscot River valley in Maine. **2** the Algonquian language of this people, a dialect of Eastern Abnaki. ▶ **adj.** of or relating to this people or their language. [from an Abnaki place name *panáwahpskek* 'where the rocks open out.']

Pe·nob·scot Riv·er a river that flows for 350 miles (560 km) through central Maine into Penobscot Bay.

pe·nol·o·gy /pē'näləjē/ ▶ **n.** the study of the punishment of crime and of prison management. — **pe·no·log·i·cal** /,pēnə'läjikəl/ **adj.** **pe·nol·o·gist n.** [19th C.: from L. *poena* 'penalty' + **-LOGY**.]

pen pal ▶ **n.** a person with whom one becomes friendly by exchanging letters, esp. someone in a foreign country whom one has never met.

pen-push·er ▶ **n.** another term for **PENCIL PUSHER**.

pen·sée /,pän'sā/ ▶ **n.** a thought or reflection put into literary form; an aphorism. [Fr.]

pen·sile /'pen,sīl; -sil/ ▶ **adj.** hanging down; pendulous. [17th C.: from L. *pensilis*, from the v. *pendere* 'hang.']

pen·sion[1] /'pensHən/ ▶ **n.** a regular payment made during a person's retirement from an investment fund to which that person or their employer has contributed during their working life. ■ a regular payment made by the government to people of or above the official retirement age and to some widows and disabled people. ■ esp. hist. a regular payment made to a royal favorite or to an artist or scholar to enable them to carry on work that is of public interest or value. ▶ **v.** [trans.] (**pension someone off**) dismiss someone from employment, typically because of age or ill health, and pay them a pension. [ME: from OFr., from L. *pensio(n-)* 'payment,' from *pendere* 'to pay.']

pen·sion[2] /pänsē'ōn/ ▶ **n.** a boardinghouse in France and other European countries, providing full or partial board at a fixed rate. [Fr.]

pen·sion·a·ble /'pensHənəbəl/ ▶ **adj.** entitling to or qualifying for a pension. — **pen·sion·a·bil·i·ty** /,pensHənə'bilitē/ **n.**

pen·sion·ar·y /'pensHə,nerē/ ▶ **adj.** of or concerning a pension. ▶ **n.** (pl. **-ar·ies**) **1** a pensioner. **2** a creature; a hireling.

pen·si·o·ne /pänsē'ōnā/ ▶ **n.** (pl. **-o·ni** /-'ōnē/) a small hotel or boardinghouse in Italy.

pen·sion·er /'pensHənər/ ▶ **n.** a person who receives a pension.

pen·sion fund ▶ **n.** a fund from which pensions are paid, accumulated from contributions from employers, employees, or both.

pen·sive /'pensiv/ ▶ **adj.** engaged in, involving, or reflecting deep or serious thought. — **pen·sive·ly adv.** **pen·sive·ness n.** [ME: from OFr. *pensif, -ive*, from *penser* 'think,' from L. *pensare* 'ponder,' frequentative of *pendere* 'weigh.']

pen·ste·mon /pen'stēmən; 'penstəmən/ (also **pent·ste·mon**) ▶ **n.** another term for **BEARDTONGUE**. [mod. L., from **PENTA-** 'five' + Gk. *stēmōn* 'warp,' used to mean 'stamen.']

pen·stock /'pen,stäk/ ▶ **n.** a sluice or floodgate for regulating the flow of a body of water. ■ a channel for conveying water to a waterwheel or turbine. [17th C.: from **PEN**[2] (in the sense 'milldam') + **STOCK**.]

pent /pent/ ▶ **adj.** esp. literary another term for **PENT-UP**: *with pent breath she waited out the meeting.*

penta- ▶ **comb. form** five; having five: *pentagram.* [from Gk. *pente* 'five.']

pen·ta·chlo·ro·phe·nol /,pentə,klôrə'fēnäl/ ▶ **n.** Chem. a colorless, crystalline, synthetic compound, C_6Cl_5OH, used in insecticides, fungicides, weed killers, and wood preservatives.

pen·ta·chord /'pentə,kôrd/ ▶ **n.** a musical instrument with five strings. ■ a series of five musical notes.

pen·ta·cle /'pentəkəl/ ▶ **n.** a talisman or magical object, typically disk-shaped and inscribed with a pentagram or other figure, and used as a symbol of the element of earth. ■ another term for **PENTAGRAM**. ■ (**pentacles**) one of the suits in some tarot packs, corresponding to coins in others. [16th C.: from med. L. *pentaculum*, appar. based on Gk. *penta-* 'five.']

pen·tad /'pen,tad/ ▶ **n.** tech. a group or set of five. [17th C.: from Gk. *pentas, pentad-*, from *pente* 'five.']

pen·ta·dac·tyl /,pentə'daktl/ ▶ **adj.** Zool. (of a vertebrate limb) having five toes or fingers, or derived from such a form, as characteristic of all tetrapods. — **pen·ta·dac·tyl·y n.** [19th C.: from **PENTA-** + Gk. *daktulos* 'finger.']

pen·ta·gon /'pentə,gän/ ▶ **n.** **1** a plane figure with five straight sides and five angles. **2** (**the Pentagon**) the pentagonal building serving as the headquarters of the US Department of Defense, near Washington, DC. ■ the US Department of Defense. — **pen·tag·o·nal** /pen'tagənəl/ **adj.** [16th C.: via L. from Gk. *pentagōnon*, neut. of *pentagōnos* 'five-angled.']

pen·ta·gram /'pentə,gram/ ▶ **n.** a five-pointed star that is formed by drawing a continuous line in five straight segments, often used as a mystic and magical symbol. Compare with **PENTACLE**. [19th C.: from Gk. *pentagrammon* (see **PENTA-**, **-GRAM**[1]).]

pentagram

pen·ta·he·dron /,pentə'hēdrən/ ▶ **n.** (pl. **-drons** or **-dra** /-drə/) a solid figure with five plane faces. — **pen·ta·he·dral** /-drəl/ **adj.**

pen·tam·er·al /pen'tamərəl/ ▶ **adj.** Zool. (of symmetry) fivefold, as typical of many echinoderms. Compare with **PENTAMEROUS**. — **pen·tam·er·al·ly adv.** **pen·tam·er·y** /-'tamərē/ **n.**

pen·tam·er·ous /pen'tamərəs/ ▶ **adj.** Bot. Zool. having parts arranged in groups of five. ■ consisting of five joints or parts. Compare with **PENTAMERAL**.

pen·tam·e·ter /pen'tamitər/ ▶ **n.** Pros. a line of verse consisting of five metrical feet, or (in Greek and Latin verse) of two halves each of two feet and a long syllable. [16th C.: via L. from Gk. *pentametros* (see **PENTA-**, **-METER**).]

pen·tam·i·dine /pen'tami,dēn/ ▶ **n.** Med. a synthetic antibiotic drug used chiefly in the treatment of pneumocystis carinii pneumonia (PCP) infection. [1940s: from **PENTANE** + **AMIDE** + **-INE**[4].]

pen·tane /'pen,tān/ ▶ **n.** Chem. a volatile liquid hydrocarbon, C_5H_{12}, of the alkane series, present in petroleum spirit. [19th C.: from Gk. *pente* 'five' + a shortened form of **ALKANE**.]

pen·tan·gle /'pen,taNGgəl/ ▶ **n.** another term for **PENTAGRAM**. [ME: perh. from med. L. *pentaculum* 'pentacle.']

pen·ta·no·ic ac·id /,pentə'nō-ik/ ▶ **n.** Chem. a colorless liquid fatty acid, $CH_3(CH_2)_3COOH$, present in various plant oils, used in making perfumes. Also called **VALERIC ACID**. [1920s: *pentanoic* from **PENTANE**.]

pen·ta·ploid /'pentə,ploid/ Genet. ▶ **adj.** (of a cell or nucleus) containing five homologous sets of chromosomes. ■ (of an organism or species) composed of pentaploid cells. ▶ **n.** a pentaploid organism, variety, or species.

Pen·ta·teuch /'pentə,t(y)o͞ok/ the first five books of the Hebrew Bible (Genesis, Exodus, Leviticus, Numbers, and Deuteronomy). Jewish name **TORAH**. — **Pen·ta·teuch·al** /-,t(y)o͞okəl/ **adj.** [ult. from eccles. Gk. *pentateukhos*, from *penta-* 'five' + *teukhos* 'implement, book.']

pen·tath·lon /pen'taTH(ə),län/ ▶ **n.** an athletic event comprising five different events for each competitor, in particular (also **modern pentathlon**) a men's event involving fencing, shooting, swimming, riding, and cross-country running. — **pen·tath·lete** /-'taTHlēt/ **n.** [17th C.: from Gk., from *pente* 'five' + *athlon* 'contest.']

pen·ta·thol ▶ **n.** var. of **PENTOTHAL**, regarded as a misspelling in technical use.

pen·ta·ton·ic /,pentə'tänik/ ▶ **adj.** Music relating to, based on, or denoting a scale of five notes, esp. one without semitones equivalent to an ordinary major scale with the fourth and seventh omitted. — **pen·ta·ton·i·cism** /-'tänəsizəm/ **n.**

pen·ta·va·lent /,pentə'vālənt/ ▶ **adj.** Chem. having a valence of five.

pen·taz·o·cine /pen'tazə,sēn/ ▶ **n.** Med. a synthetic compound, $C_{19}H_{27}NO$, that is a potent, nonaddictive analgesic, often given during childbirth. [1960s: from **PENTANE** + **AZO-** + **OCTA-** + **-INE**[4].]

Pen·te·cost /'pentə,kôst; -,käst/ **n.** **1** the Christian festival celebrating the descent of the Holy Spirit on the disciples of Jesus after his Ascension, held on the seventh Sunday after Easter. ■ the day on which this festival is held. Also called **WHITSUNDAY**. **2** the Jewish festival of Shavuoth. [OE *pentecosten*, ult. from Gk. *pentēkostē (hēmera)* 'fiftieth (day)' (because the Jewish festival is held on the fiftieth day after the second day of Passover).]

Pen·te·cos·tal /,pentə'kôstl; -'kästl/ ▶ **adj.** **1** of or relating to Pentecost. **2** of, relating to, or denoting any of a number of Christian sects and individuals emphasizing baptism in the Holy Spirit, evidenced by speaking in tongues, prophecy, healing, and exorcism. [with ref. to the baptism in the Holy Spirit at the first Pentecost (Acts 2: 9-11).] ▶ **n.** a member of a Pentecostal sect. — **Pen·te·cos·tal·ism n.** **Pen·te·cos·tal·ist adj. & n.**

pent·house /'pent,hous/ ▶ **n.** **1** an apartment on the top floor of a tall building, typically luxuriously fitted and offering fine views. ■ a structure on the roof of a building housing machinery or equipment. **2** archaic an outhouse or shelter built onto the side of a building, having a sloping roof.

pen·ti·men·to /,pentə'mentō/ ▶ **n.** (pl. **-men·ti** /-'mentē/) a visible trace of earlier painting beneath a layer or layers of paint on a canvas. [20th C.: from Ital., lit. 'repentance.']

Pent·land Firth /'pentlənd/ a channel that separates the Orkney Islands from the northern tip of mainland Scotland.

pent·land·ite /'pentlən,dīt/ ▶ **n.** a bronze-yellow mineral that consists of a sulfide of iron and nickel and is the principal ore of nickel. [19th C.: from the name of Joseph B. *Pentland* (1797–1873), Irish traveler.]

pen·to·bar·bi·tal /,pentə'bärbi,täl; -,tôl/ ▶ **n.** Med. a narcotic and sedative barbiturate drug formerly used to relieve insomnia. [1930s: from **PENTANE** + **BARBITAL**.]

pen·tode /'pentōd/ ▶ **n.** Electron. a thermionic tube having five electrodes. [20th C.: from Gk. *pente* 'five' + *hodos* 'way.']

pen·tose /'pentōs/ ▶ **n.** Chem. any of the class of simple sugars whose molecules contain five carbon atoms, such as ribose and xylose. They generally have the chemical formula $C_5H_{10}O_5$. [19th C.: from **PENTA-** + **-OSE**[2].]

Pen·to·thal /'pentə,THôl; -,THäl/ ▶ **n.** trademark for **THIOPENTAL**.

pent·ox·ide /pent'äksīd/ ▶ **n.** Chem. an oxide containing five atoms of oxygen in its molecule or empirical formula.

pent·ste·mon /pent'stēmən; 'pentstəmən/ ▶ **n.** var. of **PENSTEMON**.

pent-up ▶ **adj.** closely confined or held back: *pent-up frustrations.*

PRONUNCIATION KEY ə *ago, up*; ər *over, fur*; a *hat*; ā *ate*; ä *car*; e *let*; ē *see*; i *fit*; ī *by*; NG *sing*; ō *go*; ô *law, for*; oi *toy*; o͝o *good*; o͞o *goo*; ou *out*; TH *thin*; T͟H *then*; ZH *vision*

pen·tyl /'pentl/ ▶ **n.** [as adj.] Chem. of or denoting an alkyl radical $-C_5H_{11}$, derived from pentane. Compare with AMYL.

pe·nult /'pē,nəlt; pe'nəlt/ ▶ **n.** Ling. the penultimate syllable of a word. ▶ **adj.** archaic term for PENULTIMATE.

pe·nul·ti·mate /pe'nəltəmit/ ▶ **adj.** [attrib.] last but one in a series of things; second last: *the penultimate chapter of the book.* [17th C.: from L. *paenultimus*, from *paene* 'almost' + *ultimus* 'last.']

pe·num·bra /pe'nəmbrə/ ▶ **n.** (pl. **-brae** /-brē; -brī/ or **-bras**) the partially shaded outer region of the shadow cast by an opaque object. ■ Astron. the shadow cast by the earth or moon over an area experiencing a partial eclipse. ■ Astron. the less dark outer part of a sunspot, surrounding the dark core. ■ any area of partial shade. — **pe·num·bral** /-brəl/ **adj.** [17th C.: mod. L., from L. *paene* 'almost' + *umbra* 'shadow.']

pe·nu·ri·ous /pə'n(y)o͝orēəs/ ▶ **adj.** formal **1** extremely poor; poverty-stricken. ■ characterized by poverty or need. **2** parsimonious; mean. — **pe·nu·ri·ous·ly adv. pe·nu·ri·ous·ness n.**

pen·u·ry /'penyərē/ ▶ **n.** extreme poverty; destitution. [ME: from L. *penuria* 'need, scarcity.']

Pe·nu·ti·an /pə'no͞osʜən; -'no͞otēən/ ▶ **n.** a proposed phylum of American Indian languages including Chinook, Klamath, and Nez Percé, most of which are now extinct or nearly so. Some scholars include certain living languages of Central and South America, principally Mayan and Mapuche, in this group. ▶ **adj.** of, relating to, or denoting these languages or any of the peoples speaking them. [from *pen* and *uti*, words for 'two' in two groups of Penutian languages + -AN.]

pe·on /'pē,än; 'pēən/ ▶ **n. 1** a Spanish-American day laborer or unskilled farm worker. ■ hist. a debtor held in servitude by a creditor, esp. in the southern US and Mexico. ■ informal a person who does menial work; a drudge. **2** (in the Indian subcontinent and Southeast Asia) someone of low rank. ■ a foot soldier. ■ an attendant or messenger. ■ a person who does minor jobs in an office. — **pe·on·age** /'pēənij/ **n.** [from Port. *pea-o* and Sp. *peón*, from med. L. *pedo, pedon-* 'walker, foot soldier,' from L. *pes, ped-* 'foot.']

pe·o·ny /'pēənē/ ▶ **n.** a herbaceous or shrubby plant (genus *Paeonia*, family Paeoniaceae) of north temperate regions, which has long been cultivated for its showy flowers. [OE *peonie*, via L. from Gk. *paiōnia*, from *Paiōn*, physician of the gods.]

peo·ple /'pēpəl/ ▶ **plural n. 1** human beings in general or considered collectively. ■ (**the people**) the citizens of a country, esp. when considered in relation to those who govern them. ■ (**the people**) those without special rank or position in society; the populace. ■ (**one's people**) a person's parents or relatives. ■ (**one's people**) the supporters or employees of a person in a position of power or authority. ■ (**the People**) the state prosecution in a trial. **2** (pl. **peo·ples**) [treated as sing. or pl.] the men, women, and children of a particular nation, community, or ethnic group: *the native peoples of Canada.* ▶ **v.** [trans.] (usu. **be peopled**) (of a particular group of people) inhabit (an area or place). ■ fill or be present in (a place, environment, or domain): *the street is peopled with protestors.* ■ fill (an area or place) with a particular group of inhabitants. — **peo·ple·hood n.** (sense 2 of the **noun**). [ME: from Anglo-Norman Fr. *poeple*, from L. *populus* 'populace.']

peo·ple mov·er ▶ **n.** informal a means of transportation, in particular any of a number of automated systems for carrying large numbers of people over short distances.

peo·ple per·son ▶ **n.** informal a person who enjoys or is particularly good at interacting with others.

peo·ple's court ▶ **n.** informal a small-claims court.

Peo·ple's Lib·er·a·tion Ar·my (abbr.: **PLA**) the armed forces of the People's Republic of China, including all its land, sea, and air forces. The PLA traces its origins to an unsuccessful uprising by communist-led troops against pro-Nationalist forces in Jiangxi (Kiangsi) province on August 1, 1927, a date celebrated annually as its anniversary.

Peo·ple's par·ty ▶ **n.** another name for the Populist Party.

Peo·ple's Re·pub·lic ▶ **n.** used in the official title of several present or former communist or left-wing states. ■ (**the People's Republic**) short for PEOPLE'S REPUBLIC OF CHINA.

Peo·ple's Re·pub·lic of Chi·na official name (since 1949) of CHINA.

Pe·or·i·a /pē'ôrēə/ **1** a city in central Illinois, on the Illinois River; pop. 112,936. **2** a city in southwest central Arizona; pop. 108,364.

pep /pep/ informal ▶ **n.** energy and high spirits; liveliness: *he was an enthusiastic player, full of pep and fight.* ▶ **v.** (**pepped, pep·ping**) [trans.] (**pep someone/something up**) add liveliness or vigor to someone or something: *measures to pep up the economy.* [20th C.: abbrev. of PEPPER.]

pep·er·o·mi·a /,pepə'rōmēə/ ▶ **n.** a small, fleshy-leaved, tropical plant (genus *Peperomia*) of the pepper family. Many are grown as houseplants, chiefly for their decorative foliage. [mod. L., from Gk. *peperi*.]

pep·er·o·ni ▶ **n.** var. of PEPPERONI.

Pe·pin III /'pepin/ (c. 714–768) king of the Franks 751–768; called *Pepin the Short*; father of Charlemagne.

pe·pi·no /pe'pēnō/ ▶ **n.** (pl. **-nos**) a spiny plant (*Solanum muricatum*) of the nightshade family, with edible, purple-streaked yellow fruit, native to the Andes. [19th C.: from Sp., lit. 'cucumber.']

pep·los /'pepləs; 'pep,läs/ (also **pep·lus**) ▶ **n.** a loose outer robe or shawl worn by women in ancient Greece.

pep·lum /'pepləm/ ▶ **n.** a short flared, gathered, or pleated strip of fabric attached at the waist of a woman's jacket, dress, or blouse. ■ (in ancient Greece) a woman's loose outer tunic or shawl. [via L. from Gk. *peplos*.]

pe·po /'pēpō/ ▶ **n.** (pl. **-pos**) any fleshy, watery fruit of the melon or cucumber type, with numerous seeds and a firm rind. [19th C.: from L., lit. 'pumpkin,' from Gk. *pepōn* (from *pepōn sikuos* 'ripe gourd').]

pep·per /'pepər/ ▶ **n. 1** a pungent, hot-tasting powder prepared from dried and ground peppercorns, commonly used as a spice or condiment to flavor food. ■ a reddish and typically hot-tasting spice prepared from various forms of capsicum. See also CAYENNE. ■ a capsicum, esp. a sweet pepper. **2** a climbing vine (*Piper nigrum*, family Piperaceae) with berries that are dried as black or white peppercorns. ■ used in names of other plants that are related to this, have hot-tasting leaves, or have fruits used as a pungent spice. **3** Baseball a practice game in which fielders throw at close range to a batter who hits back to the fielders. ▶ **v.** [trans.] sprinkle or season (food) with pepper. ■ (usu. **be peppered with**) cover or fill with a liberal amount of scattered items. ■ hit repeatedly with small missiles or gunshot. [OE *piper, pipor*, of West Gmc. origin, via L. from Gk. *peperi*, from Sanskrit *pippalī* 'berry, peppercorn.']

pep·per-and-salt ▶ **adj.** another way of saying SALT-AND-PEPPER.

pep·per·box /'pepər,bäks/ ▶ **n. 1** a gun or piece of artillery with a revolving set of barrels. **2** archaic a pepper shaker.

pep·per·corn /'pepər,kôrn/ ▶ **n.** the dried berry of a climbing vine, used whole as a spice or crushed or ground to make pepper. See PEPPER (sense 2).

pep·per·grass /'pepər,gras/ ▶ **n.** a wild cress (genus *Lepidium*), particularly one with pungent leaves.

pep·per·idge /'pepərij/ ▶ **n.** another term for SOURGUM. [17th C.: alt. of dial. *pipperidge*, denoting the barberry and its fruit.]

pep·per mill ▶ **n.** a device for grinding peppercorns by hand to make pepper.

pep·per·mint /'pepər,mint/ ▶ **n. 1** the aromatic leaves of a plant of the mint family, or an essential oil obtained from them, used as a flavoring in food. ■ a candy flavored with such oil. **2** the cultivated Old World plant (*Mentha* × *piperita*) that yields these leaves or oil. — **pep·per·mint·y adj.**

pep·per·o·ni /,pepə'rōnē/ (also **pep·er·o·ni**) ▶ **n.** beef and pork sausage seasoned with pepper. [from Ital. *peperone* 'cayenne pepper plant.']

pep·per pot ▶ **n.** a West Indian dish consisting of stewed meat or fish with vegetables.

pep·per shak·er ▶ **n.** a container with a perforated top for sprinkling pepper.

pep·per spray ▶ **n.** an aerosol spray containing oils derived from cayenne pepper, irritating to the eyes and respiratory passages and used as a disabling weapon.

pep·per tree ▶ **n.** any of a number of shrubs or trees that have aromatic leaves or fruit with a pepperlike smell, in particular an evergreen Peruvian tree (*Schinus molle*) of the cashew family, widely grown as a shade tree in hot countries.

pep·per·wort /'pepər,wərt; -,wôrt/ ▶ **n.** another term for PEPPERGRASS.

pep·per·y /'pepərē/ ▶ **adj.** strongly flavored with pepper or other hot spices. ■ having a flavor or scent like that of pepper. ■ (of a person) irritable and sharp-tongued. — **pep·per·i·ness n.**

pep pill ▶ **n.** informal a pill containing a stimulant drug.

pep·py /'pepē/ ▶ **adj.** (**pep·pi·er, pep·pi·est**) informal lively and high-spirited. — **pep·pi·ly adv. pep·pi·ness n.**

pep ral·ly ▶ **n.** informal a meeting aimed at inspiring enthusiasm, esp. one held before a sporting event.

pep·sin /'pepsin/ ▶ **n.** Biochem. the chief digestive enzyme in the stomach, which breaks down proteins into polypeptides. [19th C.: from Gk. *pepsis* 'digestion.']

pep·sin·o·gen /pep'sinəjen/ ▶ **n.** Biochem. a substance that is secreted by the stomach wall and converted into the enzyme pepsin by gastric acid.

pep talk ▶ **n.** informal a talk intended to make someone feel more courageous or enthusiastic.

pep·tic /'peptik/ ▶ **adj.** of or relating to digestion, esp. that in which pepsin is concerned. [17th C.: from Gk. *peptikos* 'able to digest.']

pep·tic ul·cer ▶ **n.** a lesion in the lining (mucosa) of the digestive tract, typically in the stomach or duodenum, caused by the digestive action of pepsin and stomach acid.

pep·ti·dase /'pepti,dās/ ▶ **n.** Biochem. an enzyme that breaks down peptides into amino acids.

pep·tide /'peptīd/ ▶ **n.** Biochem. a compound consisting of two or more amino acids linked in a chain, the carboxyl group of each acid being joined to the amino group of the next by a bond of the type $-OC-NH-$. [20th C.: from Ger. *Peptid*, back-form. from *Polypeptid* 'polypeptide.']

pep·tone /'peptōn/ ▶ **n.** Biochem. a soluble protein formed in the early stage of protein breakdown during digestion. ■ (also **peptone water**) a solution of this in saline, used as a liquid medium for growing bacteria. [19th C.: from Ger. *Pepton*, from Gk. *pepton*, neut. of *peptos* 'cooked, digested.']

Pepys /pēps/, Samuel (1633–1703), English writer. He is noted for his *Diary* (1660–69), which describes events of his time.

Pé·quiste /,pā'kēst/ ▶ **n.** Canadian a member or supporter of the Parti Québecois, a political party originally advocating independent rule for Quebec. [from Fr. *PQ* + n. suffix *-iste*.]

Pe·quot /'pē,kwät/ ▶ **n.** (pl. same or **-quots**) **1** a member of an American

Indian people of southern New England. **2** the Algonquian language of this people, closely related to Mohegan. ▶ **adj.** of or relating to this people or their language. [from Narragansett *pequttôog*, perh. 'people of the shoals.']

per /pər/ ▶ **prep. 1** for each (used with units to express a rate). **2** archaic by means of: *send it per express.* **3** (**as per**) in accordance with. **4** Heraldry divided by a line in the direction of.
– PHRASES **as per usual** as usual. [L., 'through, by means of.']

per. ▶ **abbr.** ■ percentile. ■ period. ■ person.

per- ▶ **prefix 1** through; all over: *percuss* | *perforation* | *pervade.* ■ completely; very: *perfect* | *perturb.* ■ to destruction; to ill effect: *perdition* | *pervert.* **2** Chem. having the maximum proportion of some element in combination: *peroxide.* [from L. (see PER).]

per·ad·ven·ture /ˌpərəd'vencHər; ˌper-/ archaic or humorous ▶ **adv.** perhaps. ▶ **n.** uncertainty or doubt as to whether something is the case. [ME: from OFr. *per* (or *par*) *auenture* 'by chance.']

per·am·bu·late /pə'rambyəˌlāt/ ▶ **v.** [trans.] formal walk or travel through or around (a place or area), esp. for pleasure and in a leisurely way. ■ [intrans.] walk from place to place; walk about. — **per·am·bu·la·tion** /pəˌrambyə'lāsHən/ **n. per·am·bu·la·to·ry** /-ləˌtôrē/ **adj.** [ME: from L. *perambulat-* 'walked around,' from the verb *perambulare*, from *per-* + *ambulare* 'to walk.']

per·am·bu·la·tor /pə'rambyəˌlātər/ ▶ **n. 1** a person who perambulates; a pedestrian. **2** a machine, similar to an odometer, for measuring distances by means of a large wheel pushed along the ground by a long handle, with a mechanism for recording the revolutions. **3** Brit. a baby carriage.

per an·num /pər 'anəm/ ▶ **adv.** for each year (used in financial contexts). [17th C.: L.]

p/e ra·tio ▶ **abbr.** price–earnings ratio.

per·bo·rate /pər'bôrˌāt/ ▶ **n.** Chem. a salt that is an oxidized borate containing a peroxide linkage, esp. a sodium salt of this kind used as a bleach.

per·cale /pər'kāl; -'kal/ ▶ **n.** a closely woven fine cotton or polyester fabric used esp. for sheets. [17th C.: from Fr.]

per cap·i·ta /pər 'kapitə/ ▶ **adv. & adj.** for each person; in relation to people taken individually. [17th C.: L., lit. 'by heads.']

per·ceive /pər'sēv/ ▶ **v.** [trans.] **1** become aware or conscious of (something); come to realize or understand. ■ become aware of (something) by the use of one of the senses, esp. that of sight. **2** interpret or look on (someone or something) in a particular way; regard as. — **per·ceiv·a·ble adj. per·ceiv·er n.** [ME: from a var. of OFr. *perçoivre*, from L. *percipere* 'seize, understand,' from *per-* 'entirely' + *capere* 'take.']

per·cent /pər'sent/ (also esp. Brit. **per cent**) ▶ **adv.** by a specified amount in or for every hundred. ▶ **n.** one part in every hundred. ■ the rate, number, or amount in each hundred; percentage. [16th C.: from PER + CENT.]

per·cent·age /pər'sentij/ ▶ **n.** a rate, number, or amount in each hundred. ■ an amount, such as an allowance or commission, that is a proportion of a larger sum of money. ■ any proportion or share in relation to a whole. ■ [in sing.] informal personal benefit or advantage.
– PHRASES **play the percentages** (or **the percentage game**) informal choose a safe and methodical course of action when calculating the odds in favor of success.

-percenter ▶ **comb. form 1** denoting a member of a group forming a specified and usually small percentage of the population. **2** denoting a person who takes commission at a specified rate: *ten-percenters.*

per·cen·tile /pər'senˌtīl/ ▶ **n.** Stat. each of the 100 equal groups into which a population can be divided according to the distribution of values of a particular variable. ■ each of the 99 intermediate values of a random variable that divide a frequency distribution into 100 such groups.

per·cept /'pərsept/ ▶ **n.** Philos. an object of perception; something that is perceived. ■ a mental concept that is developed as a consequence of the process of perception. [19th C.: from L. *perceptum*, neut. past part. of *percipere*.]

per·cep·ti·ble /pər'septəbəl/ ▶ **adj.** (esp. of a slight movement or change of state) able to be seen or noticed. — **per·cep·ti·bil·i·ty** /pərˌseptə'bilitē/ **n. per·cep·ti·bly adv.**

per·cep·tion /pər'sepsHən/ ▶ **n.** the ability to see, hear, or become aware of something through the senses. ■ the state of being or process of becoming aware of something in such a way. ■ a way of regarding, understanding, or interpreting something; a mental impression. ■ intuitive understanding and insight. ■ Psychol. & Zool. the neurophysiological processes, including memory, by which an organism becomes aware of and interprets external stimuli. — **per·cep·tion·al** /-sHənl; -sHnəl/ **adj.** [ME: from L. *perceptio(n-)*, from *percipere* (see PERCEIVE).]

per·cep·tive /pər'septiv/ ▶ **adj.** having or showing sensitive insight. — **per·cep·tive·ly adv. per·cep·tive·ness n. per·cep·tiv·i·ty** /ˌpərsep'tivitē/ **n.**

per·cep·tron /pər'septrän/ ▶ **n.** a computer model or computerized machine devised to represent or simulate the ability of the brain to recognize and discriminate.

per·cep·tu·al /pər'sepcHo͞oəl/ ▶ **adj.** of or relating to the ability to interpret or become aware of something through the senses. — **per·cep·tu·al·ly adv.**

Per·ce·val /'pərsəvəl/ a legendary figure dating back to ancient times, found in French, German, and English poetry from the late 12th century onward. He is the father of Lohengrin and the hero of a number of legends, some of which are associated with the Holy Grail. Also called PARSIFAL.

perch[1] /pərcH/ ▶ **n.** a thing on which a bird alights or roosts, typically a branch or a horizontal rod or bar in a birdcage. ■ a place where someone or something rests or sits, esp. a place that is high or precarious. ▶ **v.** [intrans.] (of a bird) alight or rest on something. ■ (of a person) sit somewhere, esp. on something high or narrow. ■ (**be perched**) (of a building) be situated above or on the edge of something. ■ [trans.] (**perch someone/something on**) set or balance someone or something on (something). [ME: n. from PERCH[3]; v. from OFr. *percher*.]

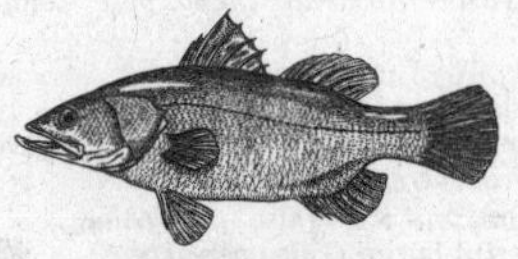

yellow perch

perch[2] ▶ **n.** (pl. same or **perch·es**) an edible freshwater fish (genus *Perca*) with a high spiny dorsal fin, dark vertical bars on the body, and orange lower fins. Its three species include the **yellow perch** (*P. flavescens*) of North America. The **perch family** also includes the pikeperches, ruffe, and darters. ■ used in names of other freshwater and marine fishes resembling or related to this, e.g., **climbing perch**. [ME: from OFr. *perche*, via L. from Gk. *perkē*.]

perch[3] ▶ **n.** hist., esp. Brit. a linear or square rod. [ME: from OFr. *perche*, from L. *pertica* 'pole.']

per·chance /pər'cHans/ ▶ **adv.** archaic literary by some chance; perhaps. [ME: from OFr. *par cheance* 'by chance.']

Per·che·ron /'pərsHəˌrän; 'pərcHə-/ ▶ **n.** a powerful draft horse of a gray or black breed, originally from France. [19th C.: from Fr., from le *Perche*, district in France.]

per·chlo·ric ac·id /pər'klôrik/ ▶ **n.** Chem. a fuming toxic liquid, $HClO_4$, with powerful oxidizing properties. — **per·chlo·rate** /-ˌrāt/ **n.**

per·cid /'pərsid/ ▶ **n.** Zool. a fish of the perch family (Percidae). [19th C.: from mod. L. *Percidae* (pl.), from L. *perca* 'perch.']

per·cip·i·ent /pər'sipēənt/ ▶ **adj.** (of a person) having a good understanding of things; perceptive. ▶ **n.** (esp. in philosophy or with reference to psychic phenomena) a person who is able to perceive things. — **per·cip·i·ence n. per·cip·i·ent·ly adv.** [17th C.: from L. *percipient-* 'seizing,' from *percipere*.]

per·coid /'pərkoid/ Zool. ▶ **n.** a fish of a large group (superfamily Percoidea) that includes the perches, basses, jacks, snappers, grunts, sea breams, and drums. ▶ **adj.** of or relating to fish of this group. [19th C.: from mod. L. *Percoïdes* (pl.), from L. *perca* 'perch.']

per·co·late /'pərkəˌlāt/ ▶ **v. 1** [intrans.] (of a liquid or gas) filter gradually through a porous surface or substance. ■ fig. (of information or an idea or feeling) spread gradually through an area or group of people. **2** [intrans.] (of coffee) be prepared in a percolator. ■ [trans.] prepare (coffee) in a percolator. ■ fig. be or become full of lively activity or excitement. — **per·co·la·tion** /ˌpərkə'lāsHən/ **n.** [17th C.: from L. *percolat-* 'strained through,' from v. *percolare*, from *per-* + *colare* 'to strain' (from *colum* 'strainer').]

per·co·la·tor /'pərkəˌlātər/ ▶ **n.** a machine for making coffee, consisting of a pot in which boiling water is circulated through a small chamber that holds the ground beans.

per con·tra /pər 'käntrə/ ▶ **adv.** formal on the other hand; on the contrary. ▶ **n.** the opposite side of an account or an assessment. [16th C.: from Ital.]

per cu·ri·am /pər 'kyo͝orēəm/ Law ▶ **adv.** by decision of a judge, or of a court in unanimous agreement. ▶ **n.** such a decision. [L., lit. 'by a court.']

per·cuss /pər'kəs/ ▶ **v.** [trans.] Med. gently tap (a part of the body) with a finger or an instrument as part of a diagnosis. [16th C.: from L. *percuss-* 'struck forcibly,' from the v. *percutere*, from *per-* + *quatere* 'to shake.']

per·cus·sion /pər'kəsHən/ ▶ **n. 1** musical instruments played by striking with the hand or with a hand-held or pedal-operated stick or beater, or by shaking, including drums, cymbals, xylophones, gongs, bells, and rattles. **2** the striking of one solid object with or against another with some degree of force. ■ Med. the action of tapping a part of the body as part of a diagnosis. — **per·cus·sion·ist n.** (in sense 1) **per·cus·sive** /-'kəsiv/ **adj. per·cus·sive·ly** /-'kəsivlē/ **adv. per·cus·sive·ness** /-'kəsivnis/ **n.**

per·cus·sion cap ▶ **n.** a small amount of explosive powder contained in metal or paper and exploded by striking. Percussion caps are used chiefly in toy guns and formerly in some firearms.

per·cu·ta·ne·ous /ˌpərkyo͞o'tānēəs/ ▶ **adj.** Med. made, done, or effected through the skin. — **per·cu·ta·ne·ous·ly adv.** [19th C.: from L. *per cutem* 'through the skin.']

per di·em /pər 'dēəm/ ▶ **adv. & adj.** for each day (used in financial contexts). ▶ **n.** an allowance or payment made for each day. [16th C.: L.]

per·di·tion /pər'disHən/ ▶n. (in Christian theology) a state of eternal punishment and damnation into which a sinful and unpenitent person passes after death. [ME: ult. from eccles. Latin *perditio(n-)*, from L. *perdere* 'destroy,' from *per-* 'completely' + base of *dare* 'put.']

per·dur·a·ble /pər'd(y)o͝orəbəl/ ▶adj. formal enduring continuously; imperishable. —**per·dur·a·bil·i·ty** /-,d(y)o͝orə'bilitē/ n. **per·dur·a·bly** adv.

per·dure /pər'd(y)o͝or/ ▶v. [intrans.] formal remain in existence throughout a substantial period of time; endure. —**per·dur·ance** /-'d(y)o͝orəns/ n. [15th C.: from OFr. *perdurer*, ult. 'endure,' from *per-* 'through' + *durare* 'to last.']

père /pe(ə)r/ ▶n. used after a surname to distinguish a father from a son of the same name: *Alexandre Dumas père.* Compare with FILS[2]. [Fr., lit. 'father.']

per·e·gri·nate /'perigrə,nāt/ ▶v. [intrans.] archaic humorous travel or wander around from place to place. —**per·e·gri·na·tion** /,perigrə'nāsHən/ n. **per·e·gri·na·tor** n. [16th C.: from L. *peregrinat-* 'traveled abroad,' from v. *peregrinari*, from *peregrinus* 'foreign.']

per·e·grine /'perəgrin/ ▶n. (also **peregrine falcon**) a powerful falcon (*Falco peregrinus*) found on most continents, breeding chiefly on mountains and coastal cliffs and much used for falconry. ▶adj. archaic coming from another country; foreign or outlandish: *peregrine species of grass.* [ME: from L. *peregrinus* 'foreign,' from *peregre* 'abroad,' from *per-* 'through' + *ager* 'field.']

peregrine

Perel·man /'pərlmən; 'perəl-/, S. J. (1904–79), US humorist and writer; full name *Sidney Joseph Perelman.* From 1934, his name was linked with the *New Yorker* magazine, for which he wrote most of his short stories and sketches.

per·emp·to·ry /pə'remptərē/ ▶adj. (esp. of a person's manner or actions) insisting on immediate attention or obedience, esp. in a brusquely imperious way: *"Just do it!" came the peremptory reply.* ■ Law not open to appeal or challenge; final. —**per·emp·to·ri·ly** /-tərəlē/ adv. **per·emp·to·ri·ness** n. [ME: ult. from L. *peremptorius* 'deadly,' from *perempt-* 'destroyed,' from v. *perimere*, from *per-* 'completely' + *emere* 'take.']

per·emp·to·ry chal·lenge ▶n. Law a defendant's or lawyer's objection to a proposed juror, made without needing to give a reason.

per·en·nate /'perə,nāt; pə'renāt/ ▶v. [intrans.] [usu. as adj.] (**perennating**) Bot. (of a plant or part of a plant) live through a number of years, usually with an annual quiescent period. —**per·en·na·tion** /,perə'nāsHən/ n. [17th C.: from L. *perennat-* 'continued for many years' (from v. *perennare*).]

per·en·ni·al /pə'renēəl/ ▶adj. lasting or existing for a long or apparently infinite time; enduring. ■ (of a plant) living for several years. Compare with ANNUAL, BIENNIAL. ■ (esp. of a problem or difficult situation) continually occurring. ■ [attrib.] (of a person) apparently permanently engaged in a specified role or way of life. ■ (of a stream or spring) flowing throughout the year. ▶n. a perennial plant. —**per·en·ni·al·ly** adv. [17th C.: from L. *perennis* 'lasting the year through.']

Pe·res /'perez/, Shimon (1923–), prime minister of Israel 1984–86, 1995–96; born in Poland; Polish name *Szymon Perski.* He played a major role in negotiating the PLO–Israeli peace accord of 1993. Nobel Peace Prize (1994, shared with Yitzhak Rabin and Yasser Arafat).

pe·re·stroi·ka /,perə'stroikə/ ▶n. (in the former Soviet Union) the policy of restructuring or reforming the economic and political system, practiced in the 1980s under Mikhail Gorbachev. See also GLASNOST. [Russ., lit. 'restructuring.']

Pé·rez de Cué·llar /'pārās də 'kwāyär/, Javier (1920–), Peruvian diplomat. He was secretary-general of the UN 1982–91.

per·fect ▶adj. /'pərfikt/ **1** having all the required or desirable elements, qualities, or characteristics; as good as it is possible to be. ■ free from any flaw or defect in condition or quality; faultless. ■ precisely accurate; exact. ■ highly suitable for someone or something; exactly right. ■ Print. denoting a way of binding books in which pages are glued to the spine rather than sewn together. ■ dated thoroughly trained in or conversant with. **2** [attrib.] absolute; complete (used for emphasis): *a perfect stranger.* **3** Math. (of a number) equal to the sum of its positive divisors, e.g., the number 6, whose divisors (1, 2, 3) also add up to 6. **4** Gram. (of a tense) denoting a completed action or a state or habitual action that began in the past, formed in English with *have* or *has* and the past participle, as in *they have eaten.* **5** Bot. (of a flower) having both stamens and carpels present and functional. ■ Bot. denoting the stage or state of a fungus in which the sexually produced spores are formed. ■ Entomol. (of an insect) fully adult and (typically) winged. ▶v. /pər'fekt/ [trans.] make (something) completely free from faults or defects, or as close to such a condition as possible: *he's perfecting his bowling technique.* ■ complete (a printed sheet of paper) by printing the second side. ■ Law satisfy the necessary conditions or requirements for the transfer of (a gift, title, etc.). ▶n. /'pərfikt/ (**the perfect**) Gram. the perfect tense. —**per·fect·er** /pər'fektər/ n. **per·fect·i·bil·i·ty** /pər,fektə'bilitē/ n. **per·fect·i·ble** /pər'fektəbəl/ adj. **per·fect·ness** /'pərfək(t)nəs/ n. [ME: from OFr. *perfet*, from L. *perfectus* 'completed,' from the v. *perficere*, from *per-* 'through' + *facere* 'do.']

per·fec·ta /pər'fektə/ ▶n. another term for EXACTA. [1970s: from L. Amer. Sp. *quiniela perfecta* 'perfect quinella.']

per·fect ca·dence ▶n. Music a cadence in which the chord of the dominant immediately precedes that of the tonic.

per·fect fifth ▶n. Music see FIFTH.

per·fect fourth ▶n. Music see FOURTH.

per·fect game ▶n. **1** Bowling a game in which a player bowls twelve consecutive strikes, earning the maximum score of 300. **2** Baseball a game in which all the batters from one team are retired in order, with no one reaching base.

per·fect gas ▶n. another term for IDEAL GAS.

per·fec·tion /pər'feksHən/ ▶n. the condition, state, or quality of being free or as free as possible from all flaws or defects. ■ a person or thing perceived as the embodiment of such a condition, state, or quality. ■ the action or process of improving something until it is faultless or as faultless as possible.
– PHRASES **to perfection** in a manner or way that could not be better; perfectly. [ME: via OFr. from L. *perfectio(n-)*, from *perficere* (see PERFECT).]

per·fec·tion·ism /pər'feksHə,nizəm/ ▶n. refusal to accept any standard short of perfection. ■ Philos. a doctrine holding that religious, moral, social, or political perfection is attainable, esp. the theory that human moral or spiritual perfection should be or has been attained. —**per·fec·tion·ist** n. & adj. **per·fec·tion·is·tic** /-,feksHən'istik/ adj.

per·fec·tive /pər'fektiv/ Gram. ▶adj. denoting or relating to an aspect of verbs, esp. in Slavic languages that expresses completed action. The opposite of IMPERFECTIVE. ▶n. a perfective form of a verb. ■ (**the perfective**) the perfective aspect.

per·fect·ly /'pərfik(t)lē/ ▶adv. in a manner or way that could not be better. ■ [as submodifier] used for emphasis, esp. in order to assert something that has been challenged or doubted: *you know perfectly well I can't stay.*

per·fec·to /pər'fektō/ ▶n. (pl. **-tos**) a type of cigar that is thick in the center and tapered at each end. [19th C.: from Sp., lit. 'perfect.']

per·fect pitch ▶n. the ability to recognize the pitch of a note or to produce any given note; a sense of absolute pitch.

per·fect rhyme ▶n. **1** the rhyme exemplified by homonyms, such as *bear/bare* or *wear/where.* **2** rhyme in which different consonants are followed by identical vowel and consonant sounds, such as in *moon* and *June.*

per·fect square ▶n. the product of a rational number multiplied by itself. ■ the product of a polynomial multiplied by itself.

per·fect storm ▶n. a particularly violent storm arising from a rare combination of adverse meteorological factors. ■ a particularly bad or critical state of affairs, arising from a number of negative and unpredictable factors: *the past two years have been a perfect storm for the travel industry.*

per·fer·vid /pər'fərvid/ ▶adj. literary intense and impassioned. —**per·fer·vid·ly** adv. [19th C.: from mod. L. *perfervidus*, from L. *per-* 'utterly' + *fervidus* 'fiery.']

per·fid·i·ous /pər'fidēəs/ ▶adj. literary deceitful and untrustworthy. —**per·fid·i·ous·ly** adv.

per·fi·dy /'pərfidē/ ▶n. literary deceitfulness; untrustworthiness. [16th C.: via Fr. from L. *perfidia*, from *perfidus* 'treacherous,' based on *per-* 'to ill effect' + *fides* 'faith.']

per·fo·li·ate /pər'fōlē,āt; -it/ ▶adj. Bot. (of a stalkless leaf or bract) extended at the base to encircle the node, so that the stem apparently passes through it. ■ (of a plant) having such leaves. [17th C.: from mod. L. *perfoliatus*, from L. *per-* 'through' + *foliatus* 'leaved.']

per·fo·rate ▶v. /'pərfə,rāt/ [trans.] pierce and make a hole or holes in. ■ make a row of small holes in (paper) so that a part may be torn off easily. ▶adj. /'pərfərit; -,rāt/ Biol. Med. perforated. —**per·fo·ra·tor** /-,rātər/ n. [ME: from L. *perforat-* 'pierced through,' from v. *perforare*, from *per-* + *forare* 'pierce.']

per·fo·ra·tion /,pərfə'rāsHən/ ▶n. a hole made by boring or piercing; an aperture passing through or into something. ■ a small hole or row of small holes punched in a sheet of paper, e.g., of postage stamps, so that a part can be torn off easily. ■ the action or state of perforating or being perforated.

per·force /pər'fôrs/ ▶adv. formal used to express necessity or inevitability: *amateurs, perforce, have to settle for less expensive solutions.* [ME: from OFr. *par force* 'by force.']

per·form /pər'fôrm/ ▶v. [trans.] **1** carry out, accomplish, or fulfill (an action, task, or function). ■ [intrans.] work, function, or do something to a specified standard. ■ [intrans.] (of an investment) yield a profitable return. ■ [intrans.] informal have successful or satisfactory sexual intercourse with someone. **2** present (a form of entertainment) to an audience. ■ [intrans.] entertain an audience, typically by acting, singing, or dancing on stage. —**per·form·a·bil·i·ty** /-,fôrmə'bilitē/ n. **per·form·a·ble** adj. **per·form·er** n. [ME: based on OFr. *parfournir*, from *par* 'through' + *fournir* 'provide.']

per·for·mance /pər'fôrməns/ ▶n. **1** an act of staging or presenting a play, concert, or other form of entertainment. ■ a person's rendering of a dramatic role, song, or piece of music. ■ [in sing.] informal a display of exaggerated behavior or a process involving a great deal of unnecessary time and effort; a fuss. **2** the action or process of carrying out or accomplishing an action, task, or function. ■ an action, task, or operation, seen in terms of how successfully it was performed. ■ the capabilities of a machine or product, esp. when observed under particular conditions. ■ a vehicle's capacity to gain speed rapidly and move efficiently and safely at high speed. ■ the extent to which an investment is profitable, esp. in relation to other investments. ■ (also **linguistic performance**) Ling. an individual's use of a language, i.e., what a speaker actually says, including hesitations, false starts, and errors. Often contrasted with COMPETENCE.

per·for·mance art ▶ n. an art form that combines visual art with dramatic performance. — **per·for·mance art·ist** n.

per·for·ma·tive /pər'fôrmətiv/ Ling. Philos. ▶ adj. relating to or denoting an utterance by means of which the speaker performs a particular act (e.g., *I bet, I apologize, I promise*). Often contrasted with CONSTATIVE. ▶ n. a performative verb, sentence, or utterance.

per·form·ing arts ▶ plural n. forms of creative activity that are performed in front of an audience, such as drama, music, and dance.

per·fume /'pər,fyo͞om; ,pər'fyo͞om/ ▶ n. a fragrant liquid typically made from essential oils extracted from flowers and spices, used to impart a pleasant smell to one's body or clothes. ■ a pleasant smell. ▶ v. [trans.] impart a pleasant smell to. ■ (usu. **be perfumed**) impregnate (something) with perfume or a sweet-smelling ingredient. ■ apply perfume to (someone or something). — **per·fum·y** /-mē/ adj. [16th C.: from Fr. *parfum* (n.), *parfumer* (v.), from obs. Ital. *parfumare*, lit. 'to smoke through.']

per·fumed /,pər'fyo͞omd/ ▶ adj. naturally having or producing a sweet, pleasant smell. ■ impregnated with a sweet-smelling substance. ■ denoting something to which perfume has been applied.

per·fum·er /pər'fyo͞omər/ ▶ n. a producer or seller of perfumes.

per·fum·er·y /pər'fyo͞omərē/ ▶ n. (pl. **-er·ies**) the action or business of producing or selling perfumes. ■ a store or store department that sells perfumes.

per·func·to·ry /pər'fəNGktərē/ ▶ adj. (of an action or gesture) carried out with a minimum of effort or reflection. — **per·func·to·ri·ly** /-'fəNGktərəlē/ adv. **per·func·to·ri·ness** n. [16th C.: from late L. *perfunctorius* 'careless,' from L. *perfunct-* 'done with,' from v. *perfungi*.]

per·fuse /pər'fyo͞oz/ ▶ v. [trans.] permeate or suffuse (something) with a liquid, color, quality, etc. ■ Med. supply (an organ, tissue, or body) with a fluid, typically treated blood or a blood substitute, by circulating it through blood vessels or other natural channels. — **per·fu·sion** /-ZHən/ n. **per·fu·sion·ist** /-ZHənist/ n. [ME: from L. *perfus-* 'poured through,' from the v. *perfundere*, from *per-* + *fundere* 'pour.']

Per·ga·mum /'pərgəməm/ a city in ancient Mysia, in western Asia Minor, north of Izmir, famed for its library and other cultural institutions. The city later became a province of Rome. — **Per·ga·mene** /-,mēn/ adj. & n.

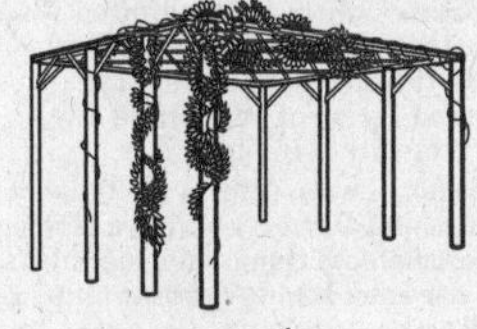
pergola

per·go·la /'pərgələ/ ▶ n. an archway in a garden or park consisting of a framework covered with trained climbing or trailing plants. [17th C.: from Ital., from L. *pergula* 'projecting roof,' from *pergere* 'come forward.']

per·haps /pər'(h)aps/ ▶ adv. used to express uncertainty or possibility: *perhaps I should have been frank with him*. ■ used when one does not wish to be too definite or assertive in the expression of an opinion. ■ used when making a polite request, offer, or suggestion. ■ used to express reluctant or qualified agreement or acceptance: *"She understood him better than his wife ever did." "Perhaps so, but ..."* [15th C.: from PER + HAP.]

pe·ri /'pi(ə)rē/ ▶ n. (pl. **pe·ris**) (in Persian mythology) a mythical superhuman being, originally represented as evil but subsequently as a good or graceful genie or fairy. [from Pers. *perī*.]

peri- ▶ prefix **1** around; about: *pericardium* | *perimeter*. **2** Astron. denoting the point nearest to a specified celestial body: *perihelion* | *perilune*. Compare with APO-. [from Gk. *peri* 'about, around.']

per·i·anth /'perē,anTH/ ▶ n. Bot. the outer part of a flower, consisting of the calyx (sepals) and corolla (petals). [18th C.: ult. from mod. L. *perianthium*, from Gk. *peri* 'around' + *anthos* 'flower.']

per·i·ap·sis /,perē'apsis/ ▶ n. (pl. **-ses** /-,sēz/) Astron. the point in the path of an orbiting body at which it is nearest to the body that it orbits.

per·i·as·tron /,perē'astrən/ ▶ n. Astron. the point nearest to a star in the path of a body orbiting that star. [19th C.: from PERI- + Gk. *astron* 'star.']

per·i·car·di·tis /,perikär'dītis/ ▶ n. Med. inflammation of the pericardium.

per·i·car·di·um /,peri'kärdēəm/ ▶ n. (pl. **-car·di·a** /-'kärdēə/) Anat. the membrane enclosing the heart, consisting of an outer fibrous layer and an inner double layer of serous membrane. — **per·i·car·di·al** /-'kärdēəl/ adj. [ME: mod. L., from Gk. *perikardion*, from *peri* 'around' + *kardia* 'heart.']

per·i·carp /'peri,kärp/ ▶ n. Bot. the part of a fruit formed from the wall of the ripened ovary. [17th C.: from Gk. *perikarpion* 'shell,' from *peri-* 'around' + *karpos* 'fruit.']

per·i·chon·dri·um /,peri'kändrēəm/ ▶ n. Anat. the connective tissue that envelops cartilage where it is not at a joint. [18th C.: mod. L., from PERI- + Gk. *khondros* 'cartilage.']

Per·i·cles /'peri,klēz/ (*c*.495–429 BC), Athenian statesman and general. He masterminded Athenian strategy in the Peloponnesian War.

per·i·cli·nal /,peri'klīnl/ ▶ adj. Bot. (of a cell wall) parallel to the surface of the meristem. ■ (of cell division) taking place by the formation of periclinal walls. — **per·i·cli·nal·ly** adv. [19th C.: from Gk. *periklinēs* 'sloping on all sides,' from *peri-* + *klinēs* 'sloping' (from v. *klinein*).]

pe·ric·o·pe /pə'rikəpē/ ▶ n. an extract from a text, esp. a passage from the Bible. [17th C.: via late L. from Gk. *perikopē* 'section,' from *peri-* 'around' + *kopē* 'cutting' (from *koptein* 'to cut').]

per·i·cra·ni·um /,peri'krānēəm/ ▶ n. Anat. the periosteum enveloping the skull. [ME: mod. L., from Gk. *peri-* 'around' + *kranion* 'skull.']

per·i·cy·cle /'peri,sīkəl/ ▶ n. Bot. a thin layer of plant tissue between the endodermis and the phloem. [19th C.: from Gk. *perikuklos* 'spherical,' from *perikukloun* 'encircle.']

per·i·derm /'peri,dərm/ ▶ n. Bot. the corky outer layer of a plant stem formed in secondary thickening or as a response to injury or infection. — **per·i·der·mal** /,peri'dərməl/ adj. [19th C.: from PERI- + Gk. *derma* 'skin.']

pe·rid·i·um /pə'ridēəm/ ▶ n. (pl. **-rid·i·a** /-'ridēə/) Bot. the outer skin of a sporangium or other fruiting body of a fungus. [19th C.: from Gk. *pēridion*, lit. 'small wallet,' dimin. of *pēra*.]

per·i·dot /'peri,dät/ ▶ n. a green semiprecious variety of olivine. [18th C.: from Fr., from OFr. *peritot*.]

per·i·do·tite /'peridə,tīt; pə'ridə,tīt/ ▶ n. Geol. a dense, coarse-grained plutonic rock containing a large amount of olivine, believed to be the main constituent of the earth's mantle. — **per·i·do·tit·ic** /,peridə'titik; pə,ridə-/ adj.

per·i·gee /'perə,jē/ ▶ n. Astron. the point in the orbit of the moon or a satellite at which it is nearest to the earth. The opposite of APOGEE. [16th C.: ult. from Gk. *perigeion* 'close around the earth,' from *peri-* 'around' + *gē* 'earth.']

per·i·gla·cial /,perə'glāSHəl/ ▶ adj. Geol. relating to or denoting an area adjacent to a glacier or ice sheet or otherwise subject to repeated freezing and thawing.

pe·rig·y·nous /pə'rijənəs/ ▶ adj. Bot. (of a plant or flower) having the stamens and other floral parts at the same level as the carpels. Compare with EPIGYNOUS, HYPOGYNOUS. — **pe·rig·y·ny** /-'rijənē/ n. [19th C.: from mod. L. *perigynus* (from Gk. *peri-* 'around' + *gunē* 'woman').]

per·i·he·li·on /,perə'hēlyən; -'hēlēən/ ▶ n. (pl. **-he·li·a** /-'hēlyə; -'hēlēə/ or **-he·li·ons**) Astron. the point in the orbit of a planet, asteroid, or comet at which it is closest to the sun. The opposite of APHELION. [17th C.: alt. of mod. L. *perihelium*, from Gk. *peri-* 'around' + *hēlios* 'sun.']

per·il (**per·iled, per·il·ing**; Brit. **per·illed, per·il·ling**) 'perəl ▶ n. serious and immediate danger. ■ (**perils**) the dangers or difficulties that arise from a particular situation or activity.

– PHRASES **at one's peril** at one's own risk (used esp. in warnings). **in** (or **at**) **peril of** very likely to incur or to suffer from. ■ at risk of losing or injuring. [ME: from OFr., from L. *peric(u)lum* 'danger,' from base of *experiri* 'to try.']

per·il·ous /'perələs/ ▶ adj. full of danger or risk. ■ exposed to imminent risk of disaster or ruin. — **per·il·ous·ly** adv. **per·il·ous·ness** n.

per·i·lune /'peri,lo͞on/ ▶ n. the point at which a spacecraft in lunar orbit is closest to the moon. The opposite of APOLUNE. [1960s: from PERI- + L. *luna* 'moon.']

per·i·lymph /'peri,limf/ ▶ n. Anat. the fluid between the membranous labyrinth of the ear and the bone that encloses it. — **per·i·lym·phat·ic** /,perilim'fatik/ adj.

pe·rim·e·ter /pə'rimitər/ ▶ n. **1** the continuous line forming the boundary of a closed geometric figure. ■ the length of such a line. ■ the outermost parts or boundary of an area or object. ■ a defended boundary of a military position or base. ■ Basketball an area away from the basket, beyond the reach of the defensive team. **2** an instrument for measuring the extent and characteristics of a person's field of vision. — **per·i·met·ric** /,perə'metrik/ adj. [ME: via L. from Gk. *perimetros*, based on *peri-* 'around' + *metron* 'measure.']

pe·rim·e·try /pə'rimətrē/ ▶ n. measurement of a person's field of vision.

per·i·my·si·um /,perə'mizēəm; -'mizH-/ ▶ n. Anat. the sheath of connective tissue surrounding a bundle of muscle fibers. — **per·i·my·si·al** /-'mizēəl; -'mizH-/ adj. [19th C.: mod. L., from Gk. *peri-* 'around' + *mus* 'muscle.']

per·i·na·tal /,perə'nātl/ ▶ adj. Med. of or relating to the time, usually a number of weeks, immediately before and after birth. — **per·i·na·tal·ly** adv.

per·i·na·tol·o·gy /,perinā'täləjē/ ▶ n. Med. the branch of obstetrics dealing with the period of time around childbirth. — **per·i·na·tol·o·gist** n.

per·i·ne·um /,perə'nēəm/ ▶ n. Anat. the area between the anus and the scrotum or vulva. — **per·i·ne·al** /-'nēəl/ adj. [ME: ult. from Gk. *perinaion*.]

per·i·neu·ri·um /,perə'n(y)o͝orēəm/ ▶ n. Anat. the sheath of connective tissue surrounding a bundle (fascicle) of nerve fibers within a nerve. — **per·i·neu·ri·al** /-ˈn(y)o͝orēəl/ **adj.** [19th C.: mod. L., from Gk. *peri-* 'around' + *neuron* 'sinew.']

pe·ri·od /ˈpi(ə)rēəd/ ▶**n.** **1** a length or portion of time. ■ a portion of time in the life of a person, nation, or civilization characterized by the same prevalent features or conditions: *the medieval period.* ■ one of the set divisions of the day in a school allocated to a lesson or other activity. ■ [with adj.] a set period of time during which a particular activity takes place: *the training period.* ■ each of the intervals into which the playing time of a sporting event is divided. ■ a major division of geological time that is a subdivision of an era and is itself subdivided into epochs, corresponding to a system in chronostratigraphy. **2** a punctuation mark (.) used at the end of a sentence or an abbreviation. ■ informal added to the end of a statement to indicate that no further discussion is possible or desirable: *he is the sole owner of the trademark, period.* **3** Physics the interval of time between successive occurrences of the same state in an oscillatory or cyclic phenomenon, such as a mechanical vibration, an alternating current, a variable star, or an electromagnetic wave. ■ Astron. the time taken by a celestial object to rotate around its axis, or to make one circuit of its orbit. ■ Math. the interval between successive equal values of a periodic function. **4** (also **menstrual period**) a flow of blood and other material from the lining of the uterus, lasting for several days and occurring in sexually mature women (who are not pregnant) at intervals of about one lunar month until the onset of menopause. **5** Chem. a set of elements occupying a horizontal row in the periodic table. **6** Rhet. a complex sentence, esp. one consisting of several clauses, constructed as part of a formal speech or oration. ■ Music a complete idea, typically consisting of two or four phrases. ▶**adj.** [attrib.] belonging to, or characteristic of, a past historical time, esp. in style or design: *period furniture.* [ME: from OFr. *periode*, via L. from Gk. *periodos* 'orbit,' from *peri-* 'around' + *hodos* 'course.']

pe·ri·od·ic /ˌpi(ə)rēˈädik/ ▶**adj.** **1** appearing or occurring at intervals. **2** Chem. relating to the periodic table of the elements or the pattern of chemical properties that underlies it. **3** of or relating to a rhetorical period. See PERIOD (sense 6).

pe·ri·od·ic ac·id /ˌpərīˈädik/ ▶**n.** Chem. a hygroscopic solid acid, H_5IO_6, with strong oxidizing properties. — **per·i·o·date** /pəˈrīəˌdāt/ **n.** [19th C.: from PER- + IODIC ACID.]

pe·ri·od·i·cal /ˌpi(ə)rēˈädikəl/ ▶**n.** a magazine or newspaper published at regular intervals. ▶**adj.** [attrib.] occurring or appearing at intervals; occasional. ■ (of a magazine or newspaper) published at regular intervals. — **pe·ri·od·i·cal·ly adv.**

pe·ri·od·i·cal ci·ca·da ▶**n.** an American cicada (genus *Magicicada*) whose nymphs emerge from the soil in large numbers periodically. The nymphs of the northern species (**seventeen-year locust**) emerge every seventeen years; those of the southern species emerge every thirteen years.

pe·ri·od·ic func·tion /ˌpi(ə)rēˈädik/ ▶**n.** Math. a function returning to the same value at regular intervals.

pe·ri·o·dic·i·ty /ˌpi(ə)rēəˈdisitē/ ▶**n.** esp. tech. the quality or character of being periodic; the tendency to recur at intervals: *the periodicity of the sunspot cycle.*

pe·ri·od·ic ta·ble /ˌpi(ə)rēˈädik/ ▶**n.** Chem. a table of the chemical elements arranged in order of atomic number, usually in rows, so that elements with similar atomic structure (and hence similar chemical properties) appear in vertical columns.

pe·ri·od·ize /ˈpi(ə)rēəˌdīz/ ▶**v.** [trans.] formal divide (a portion of time) into periods. — **pe·ri·od·i·za·tion** /ˌpi(ə)rēədəˈzāshən/ **n.**

per·i·o·don·tics /ˌperēəˈdäntiks/ (also **per·i·o·don·tia** /ˈdänshə/) ▶**plural n.** [treated as sing.] the branch of dentistry concerned with the structures surrounding and supporting the teeth. — **per·i·o·don·tal** /-ˈdäntl/ **adj.** **per·i·o·don·tist** /-ˈdäntist/ **n.** [1940s: from PERI- + Gk. *odous, odont-* 'tooth.']

per·i·o·don·ti·tis /ˌperēədänˈtītis/ ▶**n.** Med. inflammation of the tissue around the teeth, often causing shrinkage of the gums and loosening of the teeth.

per·i·o·don·tol·o·gy /ˌperēədänˈtäləjē/ ▶**n.** another term for PERIODONTICS.

pe·ri·od piece ▶**n.** an object or work that is set in or strongly reminiscent of an earlier historical period.

per·i·os·te·um /ˌperēˈästēəm/ ▶**n.** (pl. **-os·te·a** /-ˈästēə/) Anat. a dense layer of vascular connective tissue enveloping the bones except at the surfaces of the joints. — **per·i·os·te·al** /-ˈästēəl/ **adj.** [16th C.: mod. L., from Gk. *periosteon*, from *peri-* 'around' + *osteon* 'bone.']

per·i·os·ti·tis /ˌpereäˈstītis/ ▶**n.** Med. inflammation of the membrane enveloping a bone.

per·i·pa·tet·ic /ˌperipəˈtetik/ ▶**adj.** **1** traveling from place to place, esp. working or based in various places for relatively short periods. **2** (**Peripatetic**) Aristotelian. ▶**n.** **1** a person who travels from place to place. **2** (**Peripatetic**) an Aristotelian philosopher. — **per·i·pa·tet·i·cal·ly adv.** **per·i·pa·tet·i·cism** /-ˈtetəˌsizəm/ **n.** [ME: ult. from Gk. *peripatētikos* 'walking up and down,' from v. *peripatein*.]

per·i·pe·tei·a /ˌperipəˈtēə; -ˈtīə/ ▶**n.** formal a sudden reversal of fortune or change in circumstances, esp. in reference to fictional narrative. [16th C.: from Gk., from *peri-* 'around' + stem of *piptein* 'to fall.']

pe·riph·er·al /pəˈrifərəl/ ▶**adj.** of, relating to, or situated on the edge or periphery of something. ■ of secondary or minor importance; marginal. ■ [attrib.] (of a device) able to be attached to and used with a computer, although not an integral part of it. ■ Anat. near the surface of the body, with special reference to the circulation and nervous system. ▶**n.** Comput. a peripheral device. — **pe·riph·er·al·i·za·tion** /pəˌrifərəliˈzāshən/ **n.** **pe·riph·er·al·ize v.** **pe·riph·er·al·ly adv.**

pe·riph·er·al nerv·ous sys·tem ▶**n.** Anat. the nervous system outside the brain and spinal cord.

pe·riph·er·al vi·sion ▶**n.** side vision; what is seen on the side by the eye when looking straight ahead.

pe·riph·er·y /pəˈrifərē/ ▶**n.** (pl. **-er·ies**) the outer limits or edge of an area or object. ■ a marginal or secondary position in, or part or aspect of, a group, subject, or sphere of activity. [16th C.: via late L. from Gk. *periphereia* 'circumference,' from *peripherēs* 'revolving around,' from *peri-* + *pherein* 'to bear.']

pe·riph·ra·sis /pəˈrifrəsis/ ▶**n.** (pl. **-ses** /-ˌsēz/) the use of indirect and circumlocutory speech or writing. ■ an indirect and circumlocutory phrase. ■ Gram. the use of separate words to express a grammatical relationship that is otherwise expressed by inflection, e.g., *did go* as opposed to *went* and *more intelligent* as opposed to *smarter.* [16th C.: via L. from Gk., from *periphrazein*, from *peri-* 'around' + *phrazein* 'declare.']

per·i·phras·tic /ˌperəˈfrastik/ ▶**adj.** (of speech or writing) indirect and circumlocutory. ■ Gram. (of a case or tense) formed by a combination of words rather than by inflection (such as *did go* and *of the people* rather than *went* and *the people's*). — **per·i·phras·ti·cal·ly adv.**

pe·riph·y·ton /pəˈrifiˌtän/ ▶**n.** Ecol. freshwater organisms attached to or clinging to plants and other objects projecting above the bottom sediments. — **per·i·phyt·ic** /ˌperəˈfitik/ **adj.** [1960s: from Gk. *peri-* 'around' + *phuton* 'plant.']

pe·rique /pəˈrēk/ ▶**n.** a strong dark tobacco from Louisiana. [19th C.: Louisiana Fr., appar. from the nickname of Pierre Chenet.]

per·i·scope /ˈperəˌskōp/ ▶**n.** an apparatus consisting of a tube attached to a set of mirrors or prisms, by which an observer (typically in a submerged submarine or behind a high obstacle) can see things that are otherwise out of sight.

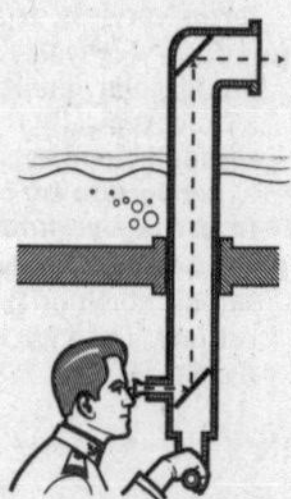
periscope

per·i·scop·ic /ˌperəˈskäpik/ ▶**adj.** of or relating to a periscope. ■ (of a lens or an optical instrument) giving a wide field of view. — **per·i·scop·i·cal·ly adv.**

per·ish /ˈperish/ ▶**v.** [intrans.] suffer death, typically in a violent, sudden, or untimely way. ■ suffer complete ruin or destruction. ■ (of rubber, a foodstuff, or other organic substance) lose its normal qualities; rot or decay.
– PHRASES **perish the thought** informal used, often ironically, to show that one finds a suggestion or idea completely ridiculous or unwelcome. [ME: from OFr. *periss-*, stem of *perir*, from L. *perire* 'pass away,' from *per-* + *ire* 'go.']

per·ish·a·ble /ˈperishəbəl/ ▶**adj.** (esp. of food) likely to decay or go bad quickly. ■ (of something abstract) having a brief life or significance; transitory. ▶**n.** (**perishables**) things, esp. foodstuffs, likely to decay or go bad quickly. — **per·ish·a·bil·i·ty** /ˌperishəˈbilitē/ **n.**

Pe·ris·so·dac·ty·la /pəˌrisəˈdaktələ/ Zool. an order of mammals that comprises the odd-toed ungulates. Compare with ARTIODACTYLA. — **pe·ris·so·dac·tyl n. & adj.** [mod. L. (pl.), from Gk. *perissos* 'uneven' + *daktulos* 'finger, toe.']

per·i·stal·sis /ˌperəˈstôlsis; -ˈstal-/ ▶**n.** Physiol. the involuntary constriction and relaxation of the muscles of the intestine or another canal, creating wavelike movements that push the contents of the canal forward. — **per·i·stal·tic** /-ˈstôltik/ **adj.** **per·i·stal·ti·cal·ly** /-ˈstôltik(ə)lē/ **adv.** [19th C.: mod. L., from Gk. *peristallein* 'wrap around,' from *peri-* + *stallein* 'to place.']

per·i·stome /ˈperəˌstōm/ ▶**n.** Zool. the parts surrounding the mouth of various invertebrates. ■ Bot. a fringe of small projections around the mouth of a capsule in mosses and certain fungi. [18th C.: from mod. L. *peristoma*, from Gk. *peri-* 'around' + *stoma* 'mouth.']

per·i·style /ˈperəˌstīl/ ▶**n.** Archit. a row of columns surrounding a space within a building such as a court or internal garden or edging a veranda or porch. ■ an architectural space such as a court or porch that is surrounded or edged by such columns. [17th C.: ult. from Gk. *peristulon*, from *peri-* 'around' + *stulos* 'pillar.']

per·i·the·ci·um /ˌperəˈthēsh(ē)əm; -sēəm/ ▶**n.** (pl. **-the·ci·a** /-ˈthēsh(ē)ə; -sēə/) Bot. (in some fungi) a round or flask-shaped fruiting body with a pore through which the spores are discharged. [19th C.: mod. L., from PERI- + Gk. *thēkē* 'case.']

per·i·to·ne·um /ˌperitnˈēəm/ ▶**n.** (pl. **-ne·ums** or **-ne·a** /-ˈnēə/) Anat. the serous membrane lining the cavity of the abdomen and covering the abdominal organs. — **per·i·to·ne·al** /-ˈēəl/ **adj.** [ME: via late L. from Gk. *peritonaion*, from *peritonos* 'stretched around,' from *peri-* + *-tonos* 'stretched.']

per·i·to·ni·tis /ˌperitnˈītis/ ▶**n.** Med. inflammation of the peritoneum, typically caused by bacterial infection either via the blood or after rupture of an abdominal organ.

pe·ri·tus /pəˈrētōos/ ▶**n.** (pl. **-ti** /-tē/) a theological adviser or consultant to a council of the Roman Catholic Church. [1960s: from L.]

periwig

per·i·wig /ˈperiˌwig/ ▶**n.** a highly styled wig worn

formerly as a fashionable headdress by both women and men. ■ archaic term for WIG[1]. — **per·i·wigged** adj. [16th C.: alt. of PERUKE.]

per·i·win·kle[1] /ˈperi,wiNGkəl/ ▶ n. a plant (genera *Vinca* and *Catharanthus*) of the dogbane family with flat, five-petaled flowers and glossy leaves. Some kinds are grown as ornamentals, and some contain alkaloids used in medicine. [OE *peruince*, from late L. *pervinca*.]

per·i·win·kle[2] ▶ n. another term for WINKLE. [16th C.: of unknown origin.]

per·jure /ˈpərjər/ ▶ v. (**perjure oneself**) Law willfully tell an untruth when giving evidence to a court; commit perjury. — **per·jur·er** n. [from OFr. *parjurer*, from L. *perjurare* 'swear falsely,' from *per-* + *jurare* 'swear.']

per·jured /ˈpərjərd/ ▶ adj. Law (of evidence) involving willfully told untruths. ■ (of a person) guilty of perjury.

per·ju·ry /ˈpərjərē/ ▶ n. (pl. **-ries**) Law the offense of willfully telling an untruth in a court after having taken an oath or affirmation. — **per·ju·ri·ous** /pərˈjo͝orēəs/ adj.

perk[1] /pərk/ ▶ v. [intrans.] (**perk up**) become more cheerful, lively, or interesting. ■ [trans.] (**perk someone/something up**) make someone or something more cheerful, lively, or interesting. ▶ adj. dialect perky; pert. [ME: perh. from OFr. dial. var. of *percher* 'to perch.']

perk[2] ▶ n. (usu. **perks**) informal money, goods, or other benefit to which one is entitled as an employee or as a shareholder of a company. [19th C.: abbrev. of PERQUISITE.] ■ an advantage or benefit following from a job or situation.

perk[3] informal ▶ v. [intrans.] (of coffee) percolate. ■ [trans.] percolate (coffee).

Per·kins /ˈpərkənz/, Frances (1882–1965), US secretary of labor 1933–45; born *Fannie Coralie Perkins*. She was the first woman to hold a federal cabinet post.

perk·y /ˈpərkē/ ▶ adj. (**perk·i·er, perk·i·est**) cheerful and lively. — **perk·i·ly** adv. **perk·i·ness** n.

per·lite /ˈpərlīt/ ▶ n. a form of obsidian consisting of glassy globules, used as insulation or in plant growth media. [19th C.: from Fr., from *perle* 'pearl.']

Perl·man /ˈpərlmən/, Itzhak (1945–), Israeli violinist and teacher. He has appeared with most of the world's major orchestras.

per·lo·cu·tion /,pərləˈkyo͞osHən/ ▶ n. Philos. Ling. an act of speaking or writing that has an action as its aim but that in itself does not effect or constitute the action, for example persuading or convincing. Compare with ILLOCUTION. — **per·lo·cu·tion·ar·y** /-,nerē/ adj. [1950s: from mod. L. *perlocutio(n-)*, from *per-* 'throughout' + *locutio(n-)* 'speaking.']

Perm /pərm; pyerm/ an industrial city in Russia, in the western foothills of the Ural Mountains; pop. 1,094,000. Former name (1940–57) MOLOTOV[1]

perm /pərm/ ▶ n. (also **permanent wave**) a method of setting the hair in waves or curls and then treating it with chemicals so that the style lasts for several months. ▶ v. [trans.] (often **be permed**) treat (the hair) in such a way. [1920s: abbrev. of PERMANENT.]

perm. ▶ abbr. permanent.

per·ma·cul·ture /ˈpərmə,kəlcHər/ ▶ n. the development of agricultural ecosystems intended to be sustainable and self-sufficient. [1970s: blend of PERMANENT and AGRICULTURE.]

per·ma·frost /ˈpərmə,frôst; -,fräst/ ▶ n. a thick subsurface layer of soil that remains frozen throughout the year, occurring chiefly in polar regions. [1940s: from PERMANENT.]

perm·al·loy /ˈpərmə,loi; ,pərmˈaloi/ ▶ n. an alloy of nickel and iron that is easily magnetized and demagnetized, used in electrical equipment. [1920s: from PERMEABLE.]

per·ma·nence /ˈpərmənəns/ ▶ n. the state or quality of lasting or remaining unchanged indefinitely. — **per·ma·nen·cy** /-sē/ n.

per·ma·nent /ˈpərmənənt/ ▶ adj. lasting or intended to last or remain unchanged indefinitely. ■ lasting or continuing without interruption. ▶ n. a perm for the hair. — **per·ma·nent·ly** adv. [ME: from L. *permanent-* 'remaining to the end,' from *per-* + *manere* 'remain.']

per·ma·nent mag·net ▶ n. a magnet that retains its magnetic properties in the absence of an inducing field or current.

per·ma·nent rev·o·lu·tion ▶ n. the state or condition, envisaged by Leon Trotsky, of a country's continuing revolutionary progress being dependent on a continuing process of revolution in other countries.

per·ma·nent tooth ▶ n. a tooth in a mammal that replaces a temporary milk tooth and lasts for most of the mammal's life.

per·ma·nent wave ▶ n. see PERM.

per·man·ga·nate /pərˈmaNGgə,nāt/ ▶ n. Chem. a salt containing the anion MnO_4^-, typically deep purplish-red and with strong oxidizing properties.

per·me·a·bil·i·ty /,pərmēəˈbilitē/ ▶ n. **1** the state or quality of a material or membrane that causes it to allow liquids or gases to pass through it. **2** Physics a quantity measuring the influence of a substance on the magnetic flux in the region it occupies.

per·me·a·ble /ˈpərmēəbəl/ ▶ adj. (of a material or membrane) allowing liquids or gases to pass through it.

per·me·ance /ˈpərmēəns/ ▶ n. Physics the property of allowing the passage of lines of magnetic flux.

per·me·ate /ˈpərmē,āt/ ▶ v. [trans.] spread throughout (something); pervade. — **per·me·a·tion** /,pərmēˈāsHən/ n. [17th C.: from L. *permeat-* 'passed through,' from v. *permeare*, from *per-* + *meare* 'go.']

per·meth·rin /pərˈmēTHrin/ ▶ n. a synthetic insecticide of the pyrethroid class, used chiefly against disease-carrying insects. [1970s: from PER- + *(res)methrin*.]

Per·mi·an /ˈpərmēən/ ▶ adj. Geol. of, relating to, or denoting the last period of the Paleozoic era, between the Carboniferous and Triassic periods. See also PERMO–TRIASSIC. ■ [as n.] (**the Permian**) the Permian period or the system of rocks deposited during it. [16th C.: PERM.]

Per·mi·an Basin /ˈpərmēən/ a region in western Texas and the geologic structure underlying it, a major oil and gas reservoir.

per mill (also **per mil**) ▶ n. one part in every thousand. [17th C.: L.]

per·mis·si·ble /pərˈmisəbəl/ ▶ adj. permitted; allowed. — **per·mis·si·bil·i·ty** /-,misəˈbilitē/ n. **per·mis·si·bly** adv. [ME: from med. L. *permissibilis*, from *permittere*.]

per·mis·sion /pərˈmisHən/ ▶ n. consent; authorization. ■ an official document giving authorization. [ME: from L. *permissio(n-)*, from *permittere* (see PERMIT[1]).]

per·mis·sive /pərˈmisiv/ ▶ adj. **1** allowing or characterized by great or excessive freedom of behavior. **2** Law allowed but not obligatory; optional. **3** Biol. allowing a biological or biochemical process to occur. ■ allowing the infection and replication of viruses. — **per·mis·sive·ly** adv. **per·mis·sive·ness** n.

per·mit[1] ▶ v. /pərˈmit/ (**-mit·ted, -mit·ting**) [trans.] give authorization or consent to (someone) to do something. ■ [trans.] authorize or give permission for (something). ■ [trans.] (of a thing, circumstance, or condition) provide an opportunity or scope for (something) to take place; make possible. ▶ n. /ˈpərmit/ [often with adj.] an official document giving someone authorization to do something. ■ official or formal permission to do something.

– PHRASES **permit me** dated used for politeness before making a suggestion or expressing an intention. —— **permitting** if the specified thing does not prevent one from doing something: *weather permitting, guests can dine outside*. — **per·mit·tee** /,pərmiˈtē/ n. **per·mit·ter** /pərˈmitər/ n. [ME: from L. *permittere*, from *per-* 'through' + *mittere* 'send.']

per·mit[2] /ˈpərmit/ ▶ n. a deep-bodied fish (*Trachinotus falcatus*) of the jack family, found in warm waters of the western Atlantic and Caribbean and caught for food and sport. [alt. of Sp. *palometa* 'little dove.']

per·mit·tiv·i·ty /,pərmiˈtivitē/ ▶ n. Physics the ability of a substance to store electrical energy in an electric field.

Per·mo–Car·bon·if·er·ous /,pərmō ,kärbəˈnifərəs/ ▶ adj. Geol. of, relating to, or linking the Permian and Carboniferous periods or rock systems together.

Per·mo–Tri·as·sic /,pərmō ,trīˈasik/ ▶ adj. Geol. of, relating to, or occurring at the boundary of the Permian and Triassic periods, about 245 million years ago. Mass extinctions occurred at this time, marking the end of the era. ■ of or relating to the Permian and Triassic periods or rock systems considered as a unit. ■ [as n.] (**the Permo–Triassic** or **Permo–Trias**) the Permian and Triassic periods together or the system of rocks deposited during them.

per·mu·tate /ˈpərmyo͝o,tāt/ ▶ v. [trans.] change the order or arrangement of. [19th C.: prob. back-form. from PERMUTATION.]

per·mu·ta·tion /,pərmyo͝oˈtāsHən/ ▶ n. a way, esp. one of several possible variations, in which a set or number of things can be ordered or arranged. ■ Math. the action of changing the arrangement, esp. the linear order, of a set of items. — **per·mu·ta·tion·al** /-ˈtāsHənəl/ adj. [ME: via OFr. from L. *permutatio(n-)*, from *permutare*.]

per·mute /pərˈmyo͞ot/ ▶ v. [trans.] tech. submit to a process of alteration, rearrangement, or permutation. [ME: from L. *permutare* 'change completely,' from *per-* + *mutare* 'to change.']

Per·nam·bu·co /,pərnəmˈb(y)o͞okō; ,pernämˈ-/ a state of eastern Brazil, on the Atlantic coast; capital, Recife. ■ former name for RECIFE.

per·ni·cious /pərˈnisHəs/ ▶ adj. having a harmful effect, esp. in a gradual or subtle way. — **per·ni·cious·ly** adv. **per·ni·cious·ness** n. [ME: from L. *perniciosus* 'destructive,' from *pernicies* 'ruin,' based on *nex, nec-* 'death.']

per·ni·cious a·ne·mi·a ▶ n. a deficiency in the production of red blood cells through a lack of vitamin B_{12}.

Per·nod /perˈnō/ ▶ n. trademark an anise-flavored liqueur. [named after the manufacturing firm *Pernod* Fils.]

pe·ro·gi ▶ n. var. of PIROGI.

Pe·rón /peˈrōn/ an Argentine political family. Juan Domingo (1895–1974) was president of Argentina 1946–55, 1973–74. The faltering economy and conflict with the Roman Catholic Church led to his removal and his exile until 1973. His second wife, Eva (1919–52), full name *María Eva Duarte de Perón*, was popularly known as **Evita**. An outspoken first lady 1946–52 with political aspirations, she wielded extraordinary power and influence. Juan's third wife, Isabel Martínez de (1931–), full name *María Estela Martínez de Perón*, became first lady in 1961 and was vice president 1973–74. She succeeded to the presidency in 1974 and was deposed in 1976. — **Pe·ro·nism** /-,nizəm/ n. **Pe·ro·nist** /-nist/ adj. & n.

per·o·ne·al /,perəˈnēəl/ ▶ adj. Anat. relating to or situated in the outer side of the calf of the leg. [19th C.: from mod. L. *peronaeus* 'peroneal muscle' (based on Gk. *peronē*).]

per·o·rate /ˈperə,rāt/ ▶v. [intrans.] formal speak at length. ■ archaic sum up and conclude a speech: *the following innocent conclusion with which she perorates.* [17th C.: from L. *perorat-* 'spoken at length,' from v. *perorare*, from *per-* + *orare* 'speak.']

per·o·ra·tion /,perəˈrāsʜən/ ▶n. the concluding part of a speech, typically intended to inspire enthusiasm in the audience.

per·ox·i·dase /pəˈräksə,dās/ ▶n. Biochem. an enzyme that catalyzes the oxidation of a particular substrate by hydrogen peroxide.

per·ox·ide /pəˈräksīd/ ▶n. Chem. a compound containing two oxygen atoms bonded together in its molecule or as the anion $O_2 2-$. ■ hydrogen peroxide, esp. as used as a bleach for the hair. ▶v. [trans.] bleach (hair) with peroxide.

per·ox·i·some /pəˈräksi,sōm/ ▶n. Biol. a small organelle that is present in the cytoplasm of many cells and that contains the reducing enzyme catalase and usually some oxidases. — **per·ox·i·so·mal** /-,räksiˈsōməl/ **adj.** [1960s: from PEROXIDE.]

perp /pərp/ ▶n. informal the perpetrator of a crime. [1980s: abbrev.]

perp. ▶abbr. perpendicular.

per·pend /pərˈpend/ ▶n. a vertical layer of mortar between two bricks.

per·pen·dic·u·lar /,pərpənˈdikyələr/ ▶adj. **1** at an angle of 90° to a given line, plane, or surface. ■ at an angle of 90° to the ground; vertical. ■ (of something with a slope) so steep as to be almost vertical. **2** (**Perpendicular**) denoting the latest stage of English Gothic church architecture, prevalent from the late 14th to mid 16th centuries and characterized by broad arches, elaborate fan vaulting, and large windows with vertical tracery: *the handsome Perpendicular church of St. Andrew.* ▶n. a straight line at an angle of 90° to a given line, plane, or surface. ■ (usu. **the perpendicular**) perpendicular position or direction. ■ an instrument for indicating the vertical line from any point, as a spirit level or plumb line. — **per·pen·dic·u·lar·i·ty** /-,dikyəˈlaritē/ **n.** **per·pen·dic·u·lar·ly** **adv.** [ME: via OFr. from L. *perpendicularis*, from *perpendiculum* 'plumb line,' from *per-* 'through' + *pendere* 'to hang.']

per·pe·trate /ˈpərpə,trāt/ ▶v. [trans.] carry out or commit (a harmful, illegal, or immoral action). — **per·pe·tra·tion** /,pərpəˈtrāsʜən/ **n.** **per·pe·tra·tor** /-,trātər/ **n.** [16th C.: from L. *perpetrat-* 'performed,' from v. *perpetrare*, from *per-* 'to completion' + *patrare* 'bring about.']

per·pet·u·al /pərˈpecʜo͞oəl/ ▶adj. **1** never ending or changing. ■ [attrib.] denoting a position, job, or trophy held for life rather than a limited period, or the person holding it. ■ (of an investment) having no fixed maturity date; irredeemable. **2** occurring repeatedly; so frequent as to seem endless and uninterrupted. ■ (of a plant) blooming or fruiting several times in one season. ▶n. a perpetual plant, esp. a hybrid rose. — **per·pet·u·al·ly** **adv.** [ME: ult. from L. *perpetualis*, from *perpetuus* 'continuing throughout,' from *perpes, perpet-* 'continuous.']

per·pet·u·al cal·en·dar ▶n. a calendar that can be adjusted to show any combination of day, month, and year, and is therefore usable year after year. ■ a set of tables from which the day of the week can be reckoned for any date.

per·pet·u·al check ▶n. Chess the situation of play when a draw is obtained by repeated checking of the king.

per·pet·u·al mo·tion ▶n. a state in which movement or action is or appears to be continuous and unceasing. ■ the motion of a hypothetical machine that, once activated, would run forever unless subject to an external force or to wear.

per·pet·u·ate /pərˈpecʜo͞o,āt/ ▶v. [trans.] make (something, typically an undesirable situation or an unfounded belief) continue indefinitely. ■ preserve (something valued) from oblivion or extinction. — **per·pet·u·ance** /-o͞oəns/ **n.** **per·pet·u·a·tion** /pər,pecʜo͞oˈāsʜən/ **n.** **per·pet·u·a·tor** /-,ātər/ **n.** [16th C.: from L. *perpetuat-* 'made permanent,' from the v. *perpetuare*, from *perpetuus.*]

per·pe·tu·i·ty /,pərpiˈt(y)o͞oitē/ ▶n. (pl. **-ties**) **1** a thing that lasts forever or for an indefinite period, in particular: ■ a bond or other security with no fixed maturity date. ■ Law a restriction making an estate inalienable perpetually or for a period beyond certain limits fixed by law. ■ Law an estate so restricted. **2** the state or quality of lasting forever.
– PHRASES **in** (or **for**) **perpetuity** forever. [ME: ult. from L. *perpetuitas*, from *perpetuus.*]

Per·pi·gnan /,perpēˈnyäɴ/ a city in southern France, in the northeastern foothills of the Pyrenees, close to the border with Spain; pop. 108,000.

per·plex /pərˈpleks/ ▶v. [trans.] (often **be perplexed**) (of something complicated or unaccountable) cause (someone) to feel completely baffled. ■ dated complicate or confuse (a matter). — **per·plex·ed·ly** /-ˈpleksidlē/ **adv.** **per·plex·ing·ly** **adv.** [15th C.: ult. from L. *perplexus* 'entangled,' based on *plexus* 'interwoven,' from v. *plectere.*]

per·plex·i·ty /pərˈpleksitē/ ▶n. (pl. **-ties**) inability to deal with or understand something complicated or unaccountable. ■ (usu. **perplexities**) a complicated or baffling situation or thing.

per pro. /pər ˈprō/ ▶abbr. per procurationem (used when signing a letter on behalf of someone else; now usually abbreviated to **pp**). See usage at PP. [L.]

per·qui·site /ˈpərkwəzit/ ▶n. formal another term for PERK². ■ a thing regarded as a special right or privilege enjoyed as a result of one's position. ■ hist. a thing that has served its primary use and is then given to a subordinate or employee as a customary right. [ME: from med. L. *perquisitum* 'acquisition,' from L. *perquirere* 'search diligently for,' from *per-* + *quaerere* 'seek.']

Per·rault /pəˈrō/, Charles (1628–1703), French writer, noted for creating the best known version of *Cinderella* (1697). His *Tales of Mother Goose* (1697) helped introduce the literary genre of fairy tales.

Per·ri·er /ˈperē,yā/ (also **Perrier water**) ▶n. trademark an effervescent natural mineral water sold as a drink. [after a spring at Vergèze, France.]

Per·rin /ˈperən; peˈraɴ/, Jean Baptiste (1870–1942), French chemist. He proved the existence of atoms. Nobel Prize for Physics (1926).

per·ron /ˈperən; pəˈrōn/ ▶n. Archit. an exterior set of steps and a platform at the main entrance to a large building such as a church or mansion. [ME: from OFr., lit. 'large stone,' from L. *petra* 'stone.']

Per·ry /ˈperē/ a family of US naval officers. Oliver Hazard (1785–1819) led US forces in a decisive victory at the Battle of Lake Erie during the War of 1812. His brother, Matthew Calbraith (1794–1858), was Commodore of the US Navy when he opened Japan to Western relations in 1854.

per·ry /ˈperē/ ▶n. (pl. **-ries**) an alcoholic drink made from the fermented juice of pears. [ME: from OFr. *pere*, based on L. *pirum* 'pear.']

per se /pər ˈsā/ ▶adv. by or in itself or themselves; intrinsically: *it is not these facts per se that are important.* [L.]

per·se·cute /ˈpərsə,kyo͞ot/ ▶v. [trans.] (often **be persecuted**) subject (someone) to hostility and ill-treatment, esp. because of their race or political or religious beliefs. ■ harass or annoy (someone) persistently. — **per·se·cu·tion** /,pərsəˈkyo͞osʜən/ **n.** **per·se·cu·tor** /-,kyo͞otər/ **n.** **per·se·cu·to·ry** /-kyo͞o,tôrē/ **adj.** [ME: from OFr. *persecuter*, from L. *persecut-* 'followed with hostility,' from v. *persequi*, from *per-* 'utterly' + *sequi* 'follow.']

per·se·cu·tion com·plex ▶n. an irrational and obsessive feeling or fear that one is the object of collective hostility or ill-treatment on the part of others.

Per·se·ids /ˈpərsēidz/ Astron. an annual meteor shower radiating from a point in the constellation Perseus, reaching a peak about August 12.

Per·seph·o·ne /pərˈsefənē/ Gk. Mythol. a goddess, the daughter of Zeus and Demeter. Roman name PROSERPINA.

Per·sep·o·lis /pərˈsepəlis/ a city in ancient Persia, northeast of Shiraz. It was founded in the late 6th century BC by Darius I.

Per·se·us /ˈpərsēəs; -syo͞os/ **1** Gk. Mythol. the son of Zeus and Danae. He cut off the head of the Gorgon Medusa and gave it to Athena; he also rescued and married Andromeda, and became king of Tiryns in Greece. **2** Astron. a large northern constellation that includes a dense part of the Milky Way. It contains several star clusters and the variable star Algol.

per·se·ver·ance /,pərsəˈvi(ə)rəns/ ▶n. **1** steadfastness in doing something despite difficulty or delay in achieving success. **2** Theol. continuance in a state of grace leading finally to a state of glory.

per·sev·er·ate /pərˈsevə,rāt/ ▶v. [intrans.] Psychol. repeat or prolong an action, thought, or utterance after the stimulus that prompted it has ceased. — **per·sev·er·a·tion** /pər,sevəˈrāsʜən/ **n.** [20th C.: from L. *perseverat-* 'strictly abided by,' from *perseverare.*]

per·se·vere /,pərsəˈvi(ə)r/ ▶v. [intrans.] continue in a course of action even in the face of difficulty or with little or no indication of success. — **per·se·ver·ance** /-ˈvi(ə)rəns/ **n.** **per·se·ver·ing·ly** **adv.** [ME: ult. from L. *perseverare* 'abide by strictly,' from *perseverus* 'very strict,' from *per-* + *severus* 'severe.']

Per·shing¹ /ˈpərsʜiɴg; -zʜiɴg/, John Joseph (1860–1948), US general; known as **Black Jack**. He commanded the American Expeditionary Force 1917–19 in World War I and served as US Army chief of staff 1921–24.

Per·shing² (also **Pershing missile**) ▶n. a US short-range surface-to-surface ballistic missile, capable of carrying a nuclear or conventional warhead. [1950s: John J. *Pershing* (1860–1948), Amer. general.]

Per·sia /ˈpərzʜə/ a former country in southwestern Asia, called Iran since 1935. It became the center of a powerful empire under the Achaemenid dynasty in the 6th century BC, but this was overthrown by Alexander the Great in 330 BC.

Per·sian /ˈpərzʜən/ ▶n. **1** a native or national of ancient or modern Persia (or Iran), or a person of Persian descent. ■ (also **Per·sian cat**) a long-haired domestic cat of a breed originating in Persia, having a broad round head, stocky body, and short thick legs. **2** the Iranian language of modern Iran, written in Arabic script. Also called FARSI. ■ an earlier form of this language spoken in ancient or medieval Persia. ▶adj. of or relating to ancient Persia or modern Iran or its people or language. [ME: from OFr. *persien*, based on Old Pers. *pārsa* 'Persia.']

Per·sian car·pet (also **Persian rug**) ▶n. a carpet or rug woven in Iran in a traditional design using stylized symbolic imagery, or made elsewhere in such a style.

Per·sian Gulf an arm of the Arabian Sea, to which it is connected by the Strait of Hormuz and the Gulf of Oman. Also called ARABIAN GULF; informally *THE GULF* (see GULF).

Per·sian Gulf War ▶n. another name for GULF WAR

Per·sian lamb ▶n. a silky, tightly curled fur made from or resembling the fleece of a young karakul, used to make clothing.

Per·sian Wars the wars fought between Greece and Persia in the 5th century BC, in which the Persians sought to extend their territory over the Greek world.

per·si·flage /ˈpərsə,fläzʜ/ ▶n. formal light and slightly contemptuous mockery or banter. [18th C.: from Fr. *persifler* 'to banter,' based on *siffler* 'to whistle.']

per·sim·mon /pərˈsimən/ ▶n. **1** an edible fruit that resembles a large tomato and has very sweet flesh. **2** the tree (genus *Diospyros*, family

Ebenaceae) that yields this fruit, related to ebony. Its several species include the North American *D. virginiana*, an evergreen with dark red fruit, and the **Japanese persimmon** (*D. kaki*), cultivated for its orange fruit. [17th C.: alt. of Virginia Algonquian *pessemmins*.]

per·sist /pər'sist/ ▶ **v.** [intrans.] continue firmly or obstinately in an opinion or a course of action in spite of difficulty, opposition, or failure. ■ continue to exist; be prolonged. [16th C.: from L. *persistere*, from *per-* 'through' + *sistere* 'to stand.']

per·sist·ence /pər'sistəns/ ▶ **n.** firm or obstinate continuance in a course of action in spite of difficulty or opposition. ■ the continued or prolonged existence of something. — **per·sist·en·cy n.**

per·sist·ent /pər'sistənt/ ▶ **adj. 1** continuing firmly or obstinately in a course of action in spite of difficulty or opposition. ■ [attrib.] characterized by a specified habitual behavior pattern, esp. a dishonest or undesirable one. **2** continuing to exist or endure over a prolonged period. ■ occurring repeatedly over a prolonged period. ■ (of a chemical or radioactivity) remaining within the environment for a long time after its introduction. **3** Bot. Zool. (of a part of an animal or plant, such as a horn, leaf, etc.) remaining attached instead of falling off in the normal manner. — **per·sist·ent·ly adv.**

per·snick·et·y /pər'snikətē/ ▶ **adj.** informal placing too much emphasis on trivial or minor details; fussy. ■ requiring a particularly precise or careful approach. [19th C.: of unknown origin.]

per·son /'pərsən/ ▶ **n.** (pl. **peo·ple** /'pēpəl/ or **per·sons**) **1** a human being regarded as an individual. ■ used in legal or formal contexts to refer to an unspecified individual. ■ [in sing.] [with adj.] an individual characterized by a preference or liking for a specified thing. ■ an individual's body. ■ a character in a play or story. **2** Gram. a category used in the classification of pronouns, possessive determiners, and verb forms, according to whether they indicate the speaker (**first person**), the addressee (**second person**), or a third party (**third person**). **3** Christian Theol. each of the three modes of being of God, namely the Father, the Son, or the Holy Spirit, who together constitute the Trinity.
– PHRASES **be one's own person** do or be what one wishes or in accordance with one's own character rather than as influenced by others. **in person** with the personal presence or action of the individual specified. **in the person of** in the physical form of. [ME: from OFr. *persone*, from L. *persona* 'actor's mask, character in a play.']

-person ▶ **comb. form** used as a neutral alternative to *-man* in nouns denoting professional status, a position of authority, etc.: *chairperson* | *salesperson.*

per·so·na /pər'sōnə/ ▶ **n.** (pl. **-so·nas** or **-so·nae** /-'sōnē/) the aspect of someone's character that is presented to or perceived by others. In psychology, often contrasted with **ANIMA**. ■ a role or character adopted by an author or an actor. [20th C.: L. (see **PERSON**).]

per·son·a·ble /'pərsənəbəl/ ▶ **adj.** (of a person) having a pleasant appearance and manner. — **per·son·a·ble·ness n. per·son·a·bly adv.**

per·son·age /'pərsənij/ ▶ **n.** a person (often used to express their significance, importance, or elevated status). ■ a character in a play or other work.

per·so·na gra·ta /pər'sōnə 'grätə/ ▶ **n.** (pl. **per·so·nae gra·tae** /pər'sōnē 'grätē/) a person, esp. a diplomat, acceptable to certain others. [L., from *persona* (see **PERSON**) + *grata*, fem. of *gratus* 'pleasing.']

per·son·al /'pərsənl/ ▶ **adj. 1** [attrib.] of, affecting, or belonging to a particular person rather than to anyone else. ■ done or made by a particular person; involving the actual presence or action of a particular individual. ■ done, intended, or made for a particular person. **2** of or concerning one's private life, relationships, and emotions rather than matters connected with one's public or professional career. ■ referring to an individual's character, appearance, or private life, esp. in a hostile or critical way. **3** [attrib.] of or relating to a person's body. **4** [attrib.] Gram. of or denoting one of the three persons. See **PERSON** (sense 2). **5** existing as a self-aware entity, not as an abstraction or an impersonal force. ▶ **n.** an advertisement or message in the personal column of a newspaper; personal ad. ■ (**personals**) another term for **PERSONAL COLUMN**. [ME: from OFr., from L. *personalis*, from *persona* (see **PERSON**).]

per·son·al ad ▶ **n.** informal a private advertisement or message placed in a newspaper, esp. by someone searching for a romantic partner.

per·son·al as·sis·tant ▶ **n.** a secretary or administrative assistant working exclusively for one person.

per·son·al col·umn ▶ **n.** (usu. **personal columns**) a section of a newspaper devoted to personal ads.

per·son·al com·pu·ter ▶ **n.** a microcomputer designed for use by one person at a time.

per·son·al es·tate ▶ **n.** Law another term for **PERSONAL PROPERTY**.

per·son·al foul ▶ **n.** Sports a rule violation involving illegal contact, as (in basketball) touching a player who is in the act of shooting.

per·son·al i·den·ti·fi·ca·tion num·ber (abbr.: **PIN**) ▶ **n.** a number allocated to an individual and used to validate electronic transactions.

per·son·al·ism /'pərsənl,izəm/ ▶ **n.** the quality of being personal, esp. a theory or system based on subjective ideas or applications. — **per·son·al·ist n. per·son·al·is·tic** /,pərsənl'istik/ **adj.**

per·son·al·i·ty /,pərsə'nalitē/ ▶ **n.** (pl. **-ties**) **1** the combination of characteristics or qualities that form an individual's distinctive character. ■ qualities that make someone interesting or popular. **2** a famous person, esp. in entertainment or sports. **3** (**personalities**) archaic disparaging remarks about an individual.

per·son·al·i·ty dis·or·der ▶ **n.** Psychiatry a deeply ingrained and maladaptive pattern of behavior of a specified kind, typically manifest by adolescence and causing long-term difficulties.

per·son·al·i·ty in·ven·to·ry ▶ **n.** a type of questionnaire designed to reveal the respondent's personality traits.

per·son·al·i·ty type ▶ **n.** Psychol. a collection of personality traits that are thought to occur together consistently.

per·son·al·ize /'pərsənl,īz/ ▶ **v.** [trans.] **1** (usu. **be personalized**) design or produce (something) to meet someone's individual requirements. ■ make (something) identifiable as belonging to a particular person, esp. by marking it with their name or initials. **2** cause (something, esp. an issue, argument, or debate) to become concerned with personalities or feelings rather than with general or abstract matters. **3** (often **be personalized**) personify (something, esp. a deity or spirit). — **per·son·al·i·za·tion** /,pərsənəli'zāsHən/ **n.**

per·son·al·ly /'pərsənəlē/ ▶ **adv. 1** with the personal presence or action of the individual specified; in person. ■ used to indicate that a specified person and no other is involved in something. ■ used to indicate that one knows or has contact with someone in person rather than indirectly through their work, reputation, or a third party. **2** from someone's personal standpoint or according to their particular nature; in a subjective rather than an objective way. ■ [sentence adverb] used to emphasize that one is expressing one's personal opinion: *personally, I think he made a sensible move.* ■ with regard to one's personal and private rather than public or professional capacity.
– PHRASES **take something personally** interpret a remark or action as directed against oneself and be upset or offended by it, even if that was not the speaker's intention: *I took it personally when he yelled at the class.*

per·son·al or·gan·iz·er ▶ **n.** a loose-leaf notebook that includes a calendar and pages for recording addresses and telephone numbers. ■ a hand-held microcomputer for the same purpose.

per·son·al pro·noun ▶ **n.** each of the pronouns in English (*I, you, he, she, it, we, they, me, him, her, us,* and *them*) comprising a set that shows contrasts of person, gender, number, and case.

per·son·al pro·per·ty ▶ **n.** Law all of someone's property except land and those interests in land that pass to their heirs. Compare with **REAL PROPERTY**.

per·son·al space ▶ **n.** the physical space immediately surrounding someone, into which any encroachment feels threatening to or uncomfortable for them. ■ space designated for the use of an individual within a larger communal area such as an office. ■ time in which someone is undisturbed and free to concentrate on their own thoughts and needs.

per·son·al ster·e·o ▶ **n.** a small portable electronic device for playing music, used with lightweight headphones.

per·son·al touch ▶ **n.** an element or feature contributed by someone to make something less impersonal.

per·son·al·ty /'pərsənltē/ ▶ **n.** Law a person's personal, movable property. The opposite of **REALTY**. [16th C.: from Anglo-Norman Fr. *personaltie*, from med. L. *personalitas*, based on L. **PERSONA**.]

per·son·al wa·ter·craft ▶ **n.** (abbr.: **PW** or **PWC**) a small, jet-powered craft, resembling a snowmobile in appearance and ridden like a motorcycle or astraddle, for individual use on water.

per·so·na non gra·ta /pər'sōnə nän 'grätə/ ▶ **n.** (pl. **per·so·nae non gra·tae** /pər'sōnē nän 'grätē/) an unacceptable or unwelcome person. [L., from *persona* (see **PERSON**) + *non* 'not' + *grata*, fem. of *gratus* 'pleasing.']

per·son·ate /'pərsə,nāt/ ▶ **v.** [trans.] formal play the part of (a character in a drama). ■ pretend to be (someone else), esp. for fraudulent purposes, such as casting a vote in another person's name. — **per·son·a·tion** /,pərsə'nāsHən/ **n. per·son·a·tor** /-,nātər/ **n.**

per·son·hood /'pərsən,ho͝od/ ▶ **n.** the quality or condition of being an individual person.

per·son·i·fi·ca·tion /pər,sänəfi'kāsHən/ ▶ **n.** the attribution of a personal nature or human characteristics to something nonhuman, or the representation of an abstract quality in human form. ■ a figure intended to represent an abstract quality. ■ [in sing.] a person, animal, or object regarded as representing or embodying a quality, concept, or thing.

per·son·i·fy /pər'sänə,fī/ ▶ **v.** (**-fies, -fied**) [trans.] represent (a quality or concept) by a figure in human form. ■ (usu. **be personified**) attribute a personal nature or human characteristics to (something nonhuman). ■ represent or embody (a quality, concept, or thing) in a physical form. — **per·son·i·fi·er** /-,fī(ə)r/ **n.**

per·son·nel /,pərsə'nel/ ▶ **plural n.** people employed in an organization or engaged in an organized undertaking such as military service. ■ short for **PERSONNEL DEPARTMENT**. [19th C.: from Fr. (adj.).]

per·son·nel car·ri·er ▶ **n.** an armored vehicle for transporting troops.

per·son·nel de·part·ment ▶ **n.** the part of an organization concerned with the appointment, training, and welfare of employees.

per·son of col·or ▶ **n.** a person who is not white or of European parentage.
– USAGE The term **person of color** is first recorded at the end of the 18th century. It has been revived in the 1990s as the recommended

term to use in some official contexts, esp. in US English, to refer to a person who is not white. The term is not common in general use, however, where terms such as **nonwhite** are still used. See also usage at BLACK and COLORED.

per·son-to-per·son ▶ adj. & adv. taking place directly between individuals. ■ denoting a phone call made through the operator to a specified person and paid for from the time that person answers the phone.

per·spec·tive /pərˈspektiv/ ▶ n. **1** the art of drawing solid objects on a two-dimensional surface so as to give the right impression of their height, width, depth, and position in relation to each other when viewed from a particular point. See also LINEAR PERSPECTIVE. ■ a picture drawn in such a way, esp. one appearing to enlarge or extend the actual space, or to give the effect of distance. ■ a view or prospect. ■ Geom. the relation of two figures in the same plane, such that pairs of corresponding points lie on concurrent lines, and corresponding lines meet in collinear points. **2** a particular attitude toward or way of regarding something; a point of view. ■ true understanding of the relative importance of things; a sense of proportion. **3** an apparent spatial distribution in perceived sound.
– PHRASES **in** (or **out of**) **perspective** showing the right (or wrong) relationship between visible objects. ■ correctly (or incorrectly) regarded in terms of relative importance. — **per·spec·ti·val** adj. [ME: from med. L. *perspectiva (ars)* 'science of optics,' from *perspect-* 'looked at closely,' from v. *perspicere*, from *per-* + *specere* 'to look.']

per·spec·tiv·ism /pərˈspekti,vizəm/ ▶ n. **1** Philos. the theory that knowledge of a subject is inevitably partial and limited by the individual perspective from which it is viewed. See also RELATIVISM. **2** the practice of regarding and analyzing a situation or work of art from different points of view. — **per·spec·tiv·ist** n.

Per·spex /ˈpərspeks/ ▶ n. trademark (often **per·spex**) solid transparent plastic made of polymethyl methacrylate (the same material as plexiglas or lucite). [1930s: from L. *perspicere* 'look through,' from *per-* + *specere* 'to look.']

per·spi·ca·cious /,pərspiˈkāsнəs/ ▶ adj. having a ready insight into and understanding of things. — **per·spi·ca·cious·ly** adv. **per·spi·cac·i·ty** /-ˈkasitē/ n. [17th C.: from L. *perspicax, perspicac-* 'seeing clearly.']

per·spic·u·ous /pərˈspikyo͞oəs/ ▶ adj. formal (of an account or representation) clearly expressed and easily understood; lucid. ■ (of a person) able to give an account or express an idea clearly. — **per·spi·cu·i·ty** /,pərspiˈkyo͞oitē/ n. **per·spic·u·ous·ly** adv. [15th C.: from L. *perspicuus* 'clear' (from *perspicere* 'look at closely').]

per·spi·ra·tion /,pərspəˈrāsнən/ ▶ n. the process of sweating. ■ sweat. — **per·spir·a·to·ry** /pərˈspīrə,tôrē/ adj.

per·spire /pərˈspī(ə)r/ ▶ v. [intrans.] give out sweat through the pores of the skin as the result of heat, physical exertion, or stress. [17th C.: ult. from L. *perspirare*, from *per-* 'through' + *spirare* 'breathe.']

per·suade /pərˈswād/ ▶ v. [trans.] cause (someone) to do something through reasoning or argument. ■ [trans.] cause (someone) to believe something, esp. after a sustained effort; convince. ■ (of a situation or event) provide a sound reason for (someone) to do something. — **per·suad·a·bil·i·ty** /-,swādəˈbilitē/ n. **per·suad·a·ble** /-əbəl/ adj. **per·sua·si·ble** adj. [15th C.: from L. *persuadere*, from *per-* 'through' + *suadere* 'advise.']

per·suad·er /pərˈswādər/ ▶ n. a person who persuades someone to do something. ■ informal a thing used to compel submission or obedience, typically a gun or other weapon.

per·sua·sion /pərˈswāzнən/ ▶ n. **1** the action or fact of persuading someone or of being persuaded to do or believe something. ■ a means of persuading someone to do or believe something; an argument or inducement. **2** a belief or set of beliefs, esp. religious or political ones. ■ a group or sect holding a particular religious belief. ■ humorous any group or type of person or thing linked by a specified characteristic, quality, or attribute. [ME: from L. *persuasio(n-)*, from *persuadere*.]

per·sua·sive /pərˈswāsiv; -ziv/ ▶ adj. good at persuading someone to do or believe something through reasoning or the use of temptation. — **per·sua·sive·ly** adv. **per·sua·sive·ness** n.

pert /pərt/ ▶ adj. (of a girl or young woman) sexually attractive because lively or saucy. ■ (of a bodily feature or garment) attractive because neat and jaunty. ■ (of a young person or their speech or behavior) impudent. ■ another term for PEART. — **pert·ly** adv. **pert·ness** n. [ME: from OFr. *apert*, from L. *apertus* 'opened,' past part. of *aperire*.]

per·tain /pərˈtān/ ▶ v. [intrans.] be appropriate, related, or applicable. ■ esp. Law belong to something as a part, appendage, or accessory. ■ [with adverbial] be in effect or existence in a specified place or at a specified time. [ME: from OFr. *partenir*, from L. *pertinere* 'extend to,' from *per-* 'through' + *tenere* 'to hold.']

Perth /pərтн/ the capital of the state of Western Australia, in western Australia, on the Indian Ocean; pop. 1,019,000 (including the port of Fremantle).

per·ti·na·cious /,pərtnˈāsнəs/ ▶ adj. formal holding firmly to an opinion or a course of action. — **per·ti·na·cious·ly** adv. **per·ti·na·cious·ness** n. **per·ti·nac·i·ty** /-ˈasitē/ n. [17th C.: from L. *pertinax, pertinac-* 'holding fast.']

per·ti·nent /ˈpərtn-ənt/ ▶ adj. relevant or applicable to a particular matter; apposite. — **per·ti·nence** n. **per·ti·nen·cy** n. **per·ti·nent·ly** adv. [ME: ult. from L. *pertinent-*, from *pertinere* (see PERTAIN).]

per·turb /pərˈtərb/ ▶ v. [trans.] **1** (often **be perturbed**) make (someone) anxious or unsettled. **2** subject (a system, moving object, or process) to an influence tending to alter its normal or regular state or path. — **per·turb·a·ble** adj. **per·tur·ba·tive** /ˈpərtər,bātiv; pərˈtərbətiv/ adj. (sense 2) **per·turb·ing·ly** adv. [ME: ult. from L. *perturbare*, from *per-* 'completely' + *turbare* 'disturb.']

per·tur·ba·tion /,pərtərˈbāsнən/ ▶ n. **1** anxiety; mental uneasiness. ■ a cause of such anxiety or uneasiness. **2** a deviation of a system, moving object, or process from its regular or normal state of path, caused by an outside influence. ■ Physics a slight alteration of a physical system, for example of the electrons in an atom, caused by a secondary influence. ■ Astron. a minor deviation in the course of a celestial body, caused by the attraction of a neighboring body.

per·tus·sis /pərˈtəsis/ ▶ n. medical term for WHOOPING COUGH. [18th C.: mod. L., from PER- + L. *tussis* 'a cough.']

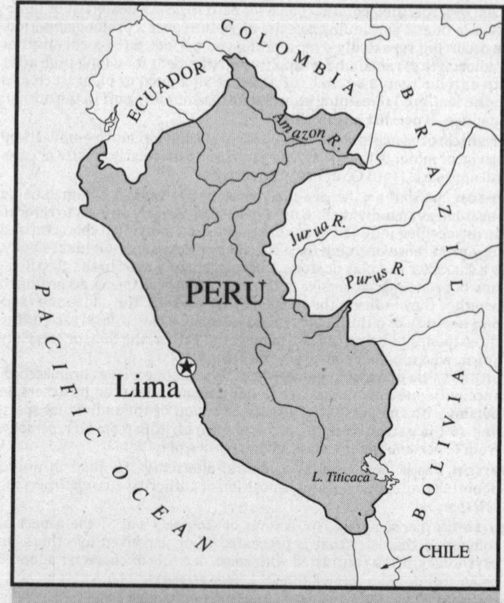

Peru

Official name: Republic of Peru
Location: South America, on the Pacific coast, crossed throughout its length by the Andes
Area: 496,400 square miles (1,285,200 sq km)
Population: 27,544,000
Capital: Lima
Languages: Spanish, Quechua (both official), Aymara
Currency: sol

Pe·ru /pəˈro͞o/ a country in South America on the Pacific coast. *See box.* — **Pe·ru·vi·an** /-vēən/ adj. & n.

Pe·ru·gia /pəˈro͞oj(ē)ə/ a city in central Italy, the capital of Umbria; pop. 151,000.

pe·ruke /pəˈro͞ok/ ▶ n. archaic term for PERIWIG. ■ archaic term for WIG[1]. [16th C.: from Fr. *perruque*, from Ital. *perrucca*.]

pe·rus·al /pəˈro͞ozəl/ ▶ n. formal the action of reading or examining something.

pe·ruse /pəˈro͞oz/ ▶ v. [trans.] formal read thoroughly or carefully. ■ examine carefully or at length. — **pe·rus·er** n. [15th C.: perh. from PER- + USE.]

Pe·ru·vi·an bark /pəˈro͞ovēən/ ▶ n. cinchona bark.

perv /pərv/ informal ▶ n. (also **perv·o** /ˈpər,vō/) a sexual pervert.

per·vade /pərˈvād/ ▶ v. [trans.] (esp. of a smell) spread through and be perceived in every part of. ■ (of an influence, feeling, or quality) be present and apparent throughout. — **per·va·sion** /pərˈvāzнən/ n. [17th C.: from L. *pervadere*, from *per-* 'throughout' + *vadere* 'go.']

per·va·sive /pərˈvāsiv/ ▶ adj. (esp. of an unwelcome influence or physical effect) spreading widely throughout an area or a group of people. — **per·va·sive·ly** adv. **per·va·sive·ness** n. [18th C.: from L. *pervas-* 'passed through' (from *pervadere*).]

per·verse /pərˈvərs/ ▶ adj. (of a person or their actions) showing a deliberate and obstinate desire to behave in a way that is unreasonable or unacceptable, often in spite of the consequences. ■ contrary to the accepted or expected standard or practice. ■ Law (of a verdict) against the weight of evidence or the direction of the judge on a point of law. ■ sexually perverted. — **per·verse·ly** adv. **per·verse·ness** n. **per·ver·si·ty** /-ˈvərsitē/ n. (pl. **-ties**). [ME: from OFr. *pervers(e)*, from L. *perversus* 'turned around,' from *pervertere*.]

per·ver·sion /pərˈvərzнən/ ▶ n. the alteration of something from its original course, meaning, or state to a distortion or corruption of what was first intended. ■ sexual behavior or desire that is considered abnormal or unacceptable.

per·vert ▶ v. /pər'vərt/ [trans.] alter (something) from its original course, meaning, or state to a distortion or corruption of what was first intended. ■ lead (someone) away from what is considered right, natural, or acceptable. ▶ n. /'pərvərt/ a person whose sexual behavior is regarded as abnormal and unacceptable. — **per·vert·er** n. [ME: from OFr. *pervertir*, from L. *pervertere*, from *per-* 'thoroughly' + *vertere* 'to turn.']

per·vert·ed /pər'vərtid/ ▶ adj. (of a person or their actions) characterized by sexually abnormal and unacceptable practices or tendencies. ■ (of a thing) having been corrupted or distorted from its original course, meaning, or state. — **per·vert·ed·ly** adv.

per·vi·ous /'pərvēəs/ ▶ adj. (of a substance) allowing water to pass through; permeable. — **per·vi·ous·ness** n. [17th C.: from L. *pervius* 'having a passage through' (based on *via* 'way').]

per·vo /'pər,vō/ ▶ n. (pl. **-vos**) variant of PERV.

pes /pēs; pās/ ▶ n. (pl. **pe·des** /'pēdēz; 'pedēz/) tech. the human foot, or the corresponding terminal segment of the hind limb of a vertebrate animal. [19th C.: from L., 'foot.']

Pe·sach /'pā,säk/ ▶ n. Jewish term for the Passover festival. [from Heb. *Pesah*]

pe·se·ta /pə'sātə/ ▶ n. the basic monetary unit of Spain (until the introduction of the euro), equal to 100 centimos. ■ hist. a silver coin. [Sp., dimin. of *pesa* 'weight.']

pe·se·wa /pā'sāwä/ ▶ n. a monetary unit of Ghana, equal to one hundredth of a cedi. [Akan, lit. 'penny.']

Pe·sha·war /pə'sʜäwər/ a city in northwestern Pakistan, near the Khyber Pass; pop. 555,000.

pes·ky /'peskē/ ▶ adj. (**-ki·er**, **-ki·est**) informal causing trouble; annoying. — **pesk·i·ly** adv. **pesk·i·ness** n. [18th C.: perh. rel. to PEST.]

pe·so /'pāsō/ ▶ n. (pl. **-sos**) the basic monetary unit of Mexico, several other Latin American countries, and the Philippines, equal to 100 centésimos in Uruguay and 100 centavos elsewhere. [Sp., lit. 'weight', from L. *pensum* 'something weighed.']

pes·sa·ry /'pesərē/ ▶ n. (pl. **-ries**) a small soluble block that is inserted into the vagina to treat infection or as a contraceptive. ■ an elastic or rigid device that is inserted into the vagina to support the uterus. [ME: from late L. *pessarium*, based on Gk. *pessos* 'oval stone.']

pes·si·mism /'pesə,mizəm/ ▶ n. a tendency to see the worst aspect of things or believe that the worst will happen; a lack of hope or confidence in the future. ■ Philos. a belief that this world is as bad as it could be or that evil will ultimately prevail over good. — **pes·si·mist** n. [18th C.: from L. *pessimus* 'worst.']

pest /pest/ ▶ n. a destructive insect or other animal that attacks crops, food, livestock, etc. ■ informal an annoying person or thing; a nuisance. ■ (**the pest**) archaic bubonic plague. [15th C.: from Fr. *peste* or L. *pestis* 'plague.']

pes·ter /'pestər/ ▶ v. [trans.] trouble or annoy (someone) with frequent or persistent requests or interruptions: *she constantly pestered him with telephone calls.* — **pes·ter·er** n. [16th C.: from Fr. *empestrer* 'encumber.']

pest·house /'pest,hous/ ▶ n. hist. a hospital for people suffering from infectious diseases, esp. the plague.

pes·ti·cide /'pestə,sīd/ ▶ n. a substance used for destroying insects or other organisms harmful to cultivated plants or to animals. — **pes·ti·cid·al** /,pestə'sīdl/ adj.

pes·tif·er·ous /pe'stifərəs/ ▶ adj. literary harboring infection and disease. ■ humorous constituting a pest or nuisance; annoying. [ME: from L. *pestifer* 'bringing pestilence.']

pes·ti·lence /'pestləns/ ▶ n. archaic a fatal epidemic disease, esp. bubonic plague.

pes·ti·lent /'pestlənt/ ▶ adj. destructive to life; deadly. ■ informal, dated causing annoyance; troublesome. — **pes·ti·lent·ly** adv. [ME: from L. *pestilens*, *pestilent-* 'unhealthy,' from *pestis* 'plague.']

pes·ti·len·tial /,pestl'ensʜəl/ ▶ adj. harmful or destructive to crops or livestock. ■ dated of, relating to, or tending to cause infectious diseases. ■ informal annoying. — **pes·ti·len·tial·ly** adv.

pes·tle /'pestl; 'pesəl/ ▶ n. a heavy tool with a rounded end, used for crushing and grinding substances such as spices or drugs, usually in a mortar. ■ a mechanical device for grinding, pounding, or stamping something. [ME: from OFr. *pestel*, from L. *pistillum*, from *pist-* 'pounded,' from the v. *pinsere*.]

pes·to /'pestō/ ▶ n. a sauce of crushed basil leaves, pine nuts, garlic, Parmesan cheese, and olive oil, typically served with pasta. [Ital., from *pestare* 'pound, crush.']

PET /pet/ ▶ abbr. ■ polyethylene terephthalate. ■ positron emission tomography, a form of tomography used esp. for brain scans.

Pet. ▶ abbr. Bible Peter.

pet[1] /pet/ ▶ n. a domestic or tamed animal or bird kept for companionship or pleasure and treated with care and affection. ■ a person treated with special favor, esp. in a way that others regard as unfair. ■ used as an affectionate form of address. ▶ adj. [attrib.] (of an animal or bird) kept as a pet: *a pet cat.* ■ of or relating to pet animals. ■ denoting a thing that one devotes special attention to or feels particularly strongly about. ■ denoting a person or establishment that one regards with particular favor or affection. ▶ v. (**pet·ted**, **pet·ting**) [trans.] stroke or pat (an animal) affectionately. ■ treat (someone) with affection or favoritism; pamper. ■ [intrans.] engage in sexually stimulating caressing and touching. — **pet·ter** n. [16th C.: of unknown origin.]

pet[2] ▶ n. [in sing.] a fit of sulking or ill humor: *Mother's **in a pet**.* [16th C.: of unknown origin.]

PETA /pētə/ ▶ abbr. People for the Ethical Treatment of Animals.

peta- ▶ comb. form (used in units of measurement) denoting a factor of 10^{15}: *petabytes.* [from *pe(n)ta-* (see PENTA-).]

Pé·tain /pe'ten; pā'tan/, Henri Philippe Omer (1856–1951), French general; head of state 1940–42. In 1940, he established the French government at Vichy (effectively a puppet regime for the Third Reich) until the German occupation in 1942.

pet·al /'petl/ ▶ n. each of the segments of the corolla of a flower, which are modified leaves and are typically colored. — **pet·al·ine** /'petl,īn; -in/ adj. **pet·aled** adj. [in comb.] *pink-petaled.* **pet·al·oid** /-,oid/ adj. [18th C.: from mod. L. *petalum*, from Gk. *petalon* 'leaf,' neut. of *petalos* 'outspread.']

pe·tard /pi'tärd/ ▶ n. hist. a small bomb made of a metal or wooden box filled with powder, used to blast down a door or to make a hole in a wall. ■ a kind of firework that explodes with a sharp report.

– PHRASES **hoist with** (or **by**) **one's own petard** have one's plans to cause trouble for others backfire on one. [16th C.: from Fr. *pétard*, from *péter* 'break wind.']

pet·a·sus /'petəsəs/ (also **pet·a·sos**) ▶ n. a hat with a low crown and broad brim, worn in ancient Greece. ■ Gk. Mythol. a winged hat of such a type worn by the god Hermes. [via L. from Gk. *petasos*.]

pet·cock /'pet,käk/ ▶ n. a small valve, esp. in the pipe of a steam boiler or cylinder of a steam engine for drainage or testing.

pe·te·chi·a /pə'tēkēə/ ▶ n. (pl. **-chi·ae** /-kē,ē/) Med. a small red or purple spot caused by bleeding into the skin. — **pe·te·chi·al** /-kēəl/ adj. [18th C.: mod. L., from Ital. *petecchia*, 'freckle', from L. *petigo* 'scab.']

Pe·ter /'pētər/ ▶ n. either of two books of the New Testament, epistles ascribed to St. Peter.

pe·ter[1] /'pētər/ ▶ v. [intrans.] decrease or fade gradually before coming to an end: *the storm had **petered out**.* [19th C.: of unknown origin.]

pe·ter[2] ▶ n. informal a man's penis. [ME: from the given name *Peter*.]

Pe·ter I (1672–1725), czar of Russia 1682–1725; known as **Peter the Great**. He modernized the armed forces and expanded Russia's territory.

Pe·ter, St. one of the 12 apostles; born *Simon*. He is regarded by Roman Catholics as the first bishop of the Church at Rome.

Pe·ter Pan /,pētər 'pan/ the hero of J. M. Barrie's play of the same name (1904), a boy with magical powers who never grew up. ■ [as n.] (**a Peter Pan**) a person, esp. a male who retains youthful features, or who is immature.

Pe·ter Pan col·lar ▶ n. a flat collar with rounded ends that meet at the front.

Pe·ter Prin·ci·ple the principle that members of a hierarchy are promoted until they reach the level at which they are no longer competent. [1960s: Laurence J. *Peter* (1919–90), Amer. educationalist.]

Pe·ters·burg /'pētərz,bərg/ a city in southeastern Virginia, scene of heavy fighting during the Civil War; pop. 38,386.

pe·ter·sham /'pētər,sʜam; -sʜəm/ ▶ n. **1** hist. a kind of heavy overcoat with a short shoulder cape. ■ the thick woolen fabric used to make such coats. **2** a corded tape used for stiffening, esp. in the making of belts and hatbands. [19th C.: Lord *Petersham* (1790–1851), Engl. army officer.]

Pe·ter·son, Roger Tory (1908–96), US ornithologist and artist. The format of his field guides for the identification of birds has become standard in field guides.

Pe·ter's pence ▶ plural n. **1** hist. an annual tax of one penny from every English householder having land of a certain value, paid to the papal see at Rome from Anglo-Saxon times until discontinued in 1534 after Henry VIII's break with Rome. **2** a voluntary payment by Roman Catholics to the papal treasury, made since 1860. [St. *Peter*, (see PETER, ST.)]

Pe·ters pro·jec·tion a world map projection in which areas are shown in correct proportion at the expense of distorted shape, using a rectangular decimal grid to replace latitude and longitude. [named after Arno *Peters* (born 1916), Ger. historian.]

Pe·ter the Her·mit (*c.*1050–1115), French monk. His preaching on the First Crusade rallied thousands of Europe's peasants throughout Europe to journey to the Holy Land.

pé·til·lant /,pāti'yän/ ▶ adj. (of wine) slightly sparkling. [Fr.]

pet·i·ole /'petē,ōl/ ▶ n. Bot. the stalk that joins a leaf to a stem; leafstalk. ■ Zool. a slender stalk between two structures, esp. that between the abdomen and thorax of a wasp or ant. — **pet·i·o·lar** /,petē'ōlər/ adj. **pet·i·o·late** /'petēə,lāt/ adj. [18th C.: from Fr. *pétiole*, from L. *petiolus* 'little foot, stalk.']

pet·it /'petē/ ▶ adj. Law (of a crime) petty: *petit larceny.* [ME: from OFr., 'small.']

pet·it batte·ment /pə'tē ,batmä/ ▶ n. Ballet a movement in which one leg is extended and lightly moved forward and backward from the ankle of the supporting leg.

pet·it bour·geois /'petē bo͝or'zʜwä; pə'tē/ ▶ adj. of or characteristic of the lower middle class, esp. with reference to a perceived conventionalism and conservatism. ▶n. (pl. **pet·its bour·geois** pronunc. same) a member of the lower middle class, esp. when perceived as conventional and conservative. [Fr., lit. 'little citizen.']

pe·tite /pəˈtēt/ ▶adj. (of a woman) having a small and attractively dainty build. ■ (of a size of women's clothing) smaller than standard. [18th C.: Fr., fem. of *petit* 'small.']

pe·tite bour·geoi·sie /pəˈtēt ˌbo͝orzʜwäˈzē/ (also **petit bourgeoisie**) ▶n. (**the petite bourgeoisie**) [treated as sing. or pl.] the lower middle class. [Fr., lit. 'little townsfolk.']

pe·tit four /ˈpetē ˈfôr/ ▶n. (pl. **pe·tits fours** /ˈpetē ˈfôrz/ or **pe·tit fours** /ˈpetē ˈfôrz/) a very small fancy cake, cookie, or confection, typically made with marzipan. [Fr., lit. 'little oven.']

pe·ti·tion /pəˈtisʜən/ ▶n. a formal written request, typically one signed by many people, appealing to authority with respect to a particular cause. ■ an appeal or request, esp. a solemn or humble one to a deity or a superior. ■ Law an application to a court for a writ, judicial action in a suit, etc. ▶v. [trans.] make or present a formal request to (an authority) with respect to a particular cause. ■ make a solemn or humble appeal to (a figure of authority). ■ Law make a formal application to (a court) for a writ, judicial action in a suit, etc. — **pe·ti·tion·ar·y** /-ˌnerē/ adj. **pe·ti·tion·er** n. [ME: from L. *petitio(n-)*, from *petit-* 'sought,' from the verb *petere*.]

pe·ti·ti·o prin·ci·pi·i /pəˈtisʜēˌō prinˈsipēˌī/ ▶n. Logic a fallacy in which a conclusion is taken for granted in the premises; begging the question. [L., lit. 'laying claim to a principle.']

pe·tit je·té /pəˈtē zʜəˈtā/ ▶n. Ballet a jump in which a dancer brushes one leg out to the side in the air then brings it back in again and lands on it with the other leg lifted and bent behind the body.

pe·tit mal /ˈpetē ˈmäl/ ▶n. a mild form of epilepsy characterized by brief spells of unconsciousness without loss of posture. Compare with GRAND MAL. ■ an epileptic fit of this kind. [19th C.: from Fr., lit. 'little sickness.']

pe·tit point /ˈpetē ˌpoint/ ▶n. a type of embroidery on canvas, consisting of small, diagonal, adjacent stitches. [19th C.: from Fr., lit. 'little stitch.']

pe·tits pois /pəˈtē ˈpwä; pəˈtē ˈpwä/ ▶plural n. young peas that are picked before they are grown to full size. [Fr., lit. 'small peas.']

pet name ▶n. a name that is used instead of someone's usual first name to express fondness or familiarity.

Pe·tra /ˈpetrə; ˈpē-/ an ancient city in southwestern Asia, in present-day Jordan. Its extensive ruins are accessible only through narrow gorges.

Pe·trarch /ˈpēträrk; ˈpet-/ (1304–74), Italian poet; Italian name *Francesco Petrarca*. His reputation is chiefly based on the *Canzoniere* (*c.*1351–53), a sonnet sequence in praise of a woman he calls Laura.

Pe·trar·chan /pəˈträrkən/ ▶adj. denoting a sonnet of the kind used by the Italian poet Petrarch, with an octave rhyming *abbaabba*, and a sestet typically rhyming *cdcdcd* or *cdecde*.

pet·rel /ˈpetrəl/ ▶n. a seabird (order Procellariiformes, esp. families Procellariidae and Hydrobatidae) related to the shearwaters, typically flying far from land. [17th C.: assoc with St Peter, from the bird's habit of flying low with legs dangling, and so appearing to walk on the water (Matt. 14:30).]

pe·tri dish /ˈpētrē/ ▶n. a shallow, circular, transparent dish with a flat lid, used for the culture of microorganisms. [19th C.: named after Julius R. *Petri* (1852–1922), Ger. bacteriologist.]

Pe·trie /ˈpetrē; ˈpētrē/, Sir William Matthew Flinders (1853–1942), English archaeologist. He began excavating the Great Pyramid in Egypt in 1880 and established the system of sequence dating.

pet·ri·fac·tion /ˌpetrəˈfaksʜən/ ▶n. another term for PETRIFICATION.

pet·ri·fi·ca·tion /ˌpetrəfiˈkāsʜən/ ▶n. the process by which organic matter exposed to minerals over a long period is turned into a stony substance. ■ a state of extreme fear, making someone unable to move. ■ an organic object that has been been turned to stone.

Pet·ri·fied Forest a highland area in east central Arizona, noted for its agates and plant fossils, now a national park.

pet·ri·fy /ˈpetrəˌfī/ ▶v. (**-fies, -fied**) [trans.] **1** make (someone) so frightened that they are unable to move or think. **2** change (organic matter) into a stony concretion by encrusting or replacing its original substance with a calcareous, siliceous, or other mineral deposit. ■ [intrans.] (of organic matter) become converted into stone or a stony substance in such a way. ■ fig. deprive or become deprived of vitality or the capacity for change. [ME: from Fr. *pétrifier*, from med. L. *petrificare*, from L. *petra* 'rock,' from Gk.]

Pe·trine /ˈpēˌtrīn/ ▶adj. **1** Christian Theol. of or relating to St. Peter or his writings or teachings. ■ of or relating to the authority of the pope over the Church, in his role as the successor of St. Peter. **2** of or relating to Peter I of Russia.

petro- ▶comb. form **1** of rock; relating to rocks: *petrography*. **2** relating to petroleum: *petrodollar*. [sense 1 from Gk. *petros* 'stone,' *petra* 'rock'; sense 2 from PETROLEUM.]

pet·ro·chem·i·cal /ˌpetrōˈkemikəl/ ▶adj. relating to or denoting substances obtained by the refining and processing of petroleum or natural gas. ■ of or relating to petrochemistry. ▶n. (usu. **petrochemicals**) a chemical obtained from petroleum and natural gas.

pet·ro·chem·is·try /ˌpetrōˈkeməstrē/ ▶n. **1** the branch of chemistry concerned with the composition and formation of rocks (as distinct from minerals and ore deposits). **2** the branch of chemistry concerned with petroleum and natural gas, and with their refining and processing.

pet·ro·dol·lar /ˈpetrōˌdälər/ ▶n. a notional unit of currency earned by a country from the export of petroleum: *petrodollars were pouring into the kingdom*.

pet·ro·glyph /ˈpetrəˌglif/ ▶n. a rock carving, esp. a prehistoric one. [19th C.: from PETRO- + Gk. *gluphē* 'carving.']

Pet·ro·grad /ˈpetrəˌgrad; pyitrəˈgrät/ former name (1914–24) for ST. PETERSBURG.

pe·trog·ra·phy /pəˈträgrəfē/ ▶n. the branch of science concerned with the composition and properties of rocks. — **pe·trog·ra·pher** n. **pet·ro·graph·ic** /ˌpetrəˈgrafik/ adj. **pet·ro·graph·i·cal** /ˌpetrəˈgrafikəl/ adj.

pet·rol /ˈpetrəl/ ▶n. British term for GASOLINE. [19th C.: from Fr. *pétrole*, from med. L. *petroleum*.]

pet·ro·la·tum /ˌpetrəˈlātəm/ ▶n. another term for PETROLEUM JELLY. [19th C.: mod. L., from PETROL + L. suffix *-atum*.]

pe·tro·le·um /pəˈtrōlēəm/ ▶n. a liquid mixture of hydrocarbons that is present in suitable rock strata and can be extracted and refined to produce fuels including gasoline, kerosene, and diesel oil; oil. [ME: from med. L., from Latin *petra* 'rock' (from Gk.) + L. *oleum* 'oil.']

pe·tro·le·um jel·ly ▶n. a translucent jelly consisting of a mixture of hydrocarbons, used as a lubricant or ointment.

pet·ro·lif·er·ous /ˌpetrəˈlifərəs/ ▶adj. (of rock) yielding or containing petroleum.

pe·trol·o·gy /pəˈträləjē/ ▶n. the branch of science concerned with the origin, structure, and composition of rocks. Compare with LITHOLOGY. — **pet·ro·log·ic** /ˌpetrəˈläjik/ adj. **pet·ro·log·i·cal** /ˌpetrəˈläjikəl/ adj. **pe·trol·o·gist** n.

Pet·ro·nas Towers /peˈtrōnəs/ twin commercial towers in Kuala Lumpur, Malaysia, completed in 1998, when they were the tallest buildings in the world. The towers are 1,482 feet (452 m) above street level, contain 88 stories topped by steel spires 155 feet (47.2 m) high, and are connected by a double-decked skywalk at the forty-first and forty-second levels.

Pe·tro·ni·us /piˈtrōnēəs/, Gaius (died AD 66), Roman writer; known as **Petronius Arbiter**. He wrote *Satyricon*, a work that satirizes the excesses of Roman society.

Pet·ro·pav·lovsk /ˌpetrəˈpavlôfsk; pyitrəˈpävləfsk/ **1** (also **Petropavlovsk-Kamchatsky**) a city in eastern Siberia in Russia; pop. 245,000. **2** (also **Pet·ro·pavl** /ˌpetrəˈpävəl/) a city in northern Kazakhstan; pop. 248,000.

pet·ro·phys·ics /ˌpetrōˈfiziks/ ▶plural n. [treated as sing.] the branch of geology concerned with the physical properties and behavior of rocks. — **pet·ro·phys·i·cal** /-ˈfizikəl/ adj. **pet·ro·phys·i·cist** /-ˈfizəsist/ n.

pe·tro·sal /pəˈtrōsəl/ Anat. ▶n. the dense part of the temporal bone at the base of the skull, surrounding the inner ear. ▶adj. relating to or denoting this part of the temporal bone, or the nerves that pass through it. [18th C.: from L. *petrosus* 'stony, rocky' (from *petra* 'rock').]

pet·rous /ˈpetrəs/ ▶adj. Anat. another term for PETROSAL. [ME: from L. *petrosus* 'stony,' from *petra* 'rock,' from Gk.]

Pet·sa·mo /ˈpetsəˌmō/ former name (1920–44) for PECHENGA.

pet·ti·coat /ˈpetēˌkōt/ ▶n. a woman's light, loose undergarment hanging from the shoulders or the waist, worn under a skirt or dress. ■ [as adj.] informal, often derog. used to denote female control of something regarded as more commonly dominated by men. — **pet·ti·coat·ed** adj. [ME: from *petty coat*, lit. 'small coat.']

pet·ti·fog /ˈpetēˌfôg; ˈpetēˌfäg/ ▶v. (**-fogged, -fog·ging**) [intrans.] rare quibble about petty points. ■ archaic practice legal deception or trickery. — **pet·ti·fog·ger·y** /ˌpetēˈfôgərē; -ˈfäg-/ n. [17th C.: back-form. from PETTIFOGGER.]

pet·ti·fog·ger /ˈpetēˌfôgər; -ˌfäg-/ ▶n. archaic an inferior legal practitioner, esp. one who deals with petty cases or employs dubious practices. [16th C.: from PETTY + obs. *fogger* 'underhanded dealer,' prob. from *Fugger*, family of merchants in Germany in the 15th and 16th cents.]

pet·ti·fog·ging /ˈpetēˌfôgiɴɢ; -ˌfäg-/ ▶adj. petty; trivial. ■ (of a person) placing undue emphasis on petty details.

pet·tish /ˈpetisʜ/ ▶adj. (of a person or their behavior) childishly bad-tempered and petulant. — **pet·tish·ly** adv. **pet·tish·ness** n.

Pet·ty /ˈpetē/, Richard Lee (1937–), US race car driver, noted for winning a record 200 races during his career 1960–92, including seven NASCAR Championships.

pet·ty /ˈpetē/ ▶adj. (**pet·ti·er, pet·ti·est**) **1** of little importance; trivial. ■ (of behavior) characterized by an undue concern for trivial matters, esp. in a small-minded or spiteful way. **2** [attrib.] of secondary or lesser importance, rank, or scale; minor. ■ Law (of a crime) of lesser importance. Compare with GRAND. — **pet·ti·ly** /ˈpetl-ē/ adv. **pet·ti·ness** n. [ME: from Fr. *petit* 'small.']

pet·ty bour·geois ▶n. another term for PETIT BOURGEOIS.

pet·ty bour·geoi·sie ▶n. another term for PETITE BOURGEOISIE.

pet·ty cash ▶n. an accessible store of money kept by an organization for expenditure on small items.

pet·ty lar·ce·ny ▶n. Law theft of personal property having a value less than a legally specified amount.

pet·ty of·fi·cer ▶n. a noncommissioned officer in a navy, in particular an NCO in the US Navy or Coast Guard ranking above seaman and below chief petty officer.

pet·ty trea·son ▶n. see TREASON.

pet·u·lant /ˈpecHələnt/ ▸ **adj.** (of a person or their manner) childishly sulky or bad-tempered. — **pet·u·lance** n. **pet·u·lant·ly** adv. [16th C.: ult. from L. *petulant-* 'impudent' (rel. to *petere* 'seek').]

pe·tu·nia /pəˈt(y)o͞onyə/ ▸ **n.** a plant (*Petunia* × *hybrida*) of the nightshade family with brightly colored funnel-shaped flowers. Native to tropical America, it has been widely developed as an ornamental hybrid, with numerous varieties. [mod. L., from Fr. *petun*, from Guarani *petyn* 'tobacco.']

pew /pyo͞o/ ▸ **n.** a long bench with a back, placed in rows in the main part of some churches to seat the congregation. ■ an enclosure or compartment containing a number of seats, used in some churches to seat a particular worshiper or group of worshipers. ■ **(the pews)** the congregation of a church. [ME: from OFr. *puye* 'balcony,' from L. *podia*, pl. of *podium* 'elevated place.']

pe·wee /ˈpēˌwē/ (also **pee·wee**) ▸ **n.** a North American tyrant flycatcher (genus *Contopus*) with dark olive-gray plumage and a call that sounds like "pee-a-wee." [18th C.: imitative.]

pe·wit /ˈpēwit; ˈpyo͞oit/ (also **pee·wit**) ▸ **n.** the northern lapwing. [16th C.: imitative.]

pew·ter /ˈpyo͞otər/ ▸ **n.** a gray alloy of tin with copper and antimony (formerly, tin and lead). ■ utensils made of this. ■ a shade of bluish or silver gray. — **pew·ter·er** n. [ME: from OFr. *peutre*.]

pe·yo·te /pāˈyōtē/ ▸ **n.** a small, soft, blue-green, spineless cactus (*Lophophora williamsii*), native to Mexico and the southern US. Also called MESCAL. ■ a hallucinogenic drug prepared from this cactus, containing mescaline. [19th C.: from L. Amer. Sp., from Nahuatl *peyotl*.]

pe·yo·te but·tons ▸ **plural n.** the disk-shaped dried tops of the peyote cactus, eaten or chewed for their hallucinogenic effects. Also called MESCAL BUTTONS.

Pf. ▸ **abbr.** pfennig.

pf ▸ **abbr.** ■ perfect. ■ pfennig. ■ pianoforte; piano. ■ preferred (stock). ■ proof.

PFC (also **Pfc.**) ▸ **abbr.** Private First Class.

PFD ▸ **abbr.** personal flotation device, a life jacket or similar buoyancy aid.

pfd. ▸ **abbr.** preferred (stock).

pfen·nig /ˈfenig/ ▸ **n.** a monetary unit of Germany (until the introduction of the euro), equal to one hundredth of a mark. [from Ger. *Pfennig*; rel. to PENNY.]

pfft /ft/ ▸ **exclam.** used to represent a dull abrupt sound as of a slight impact or explosion.

pfg. ▸ **abbr.** pfennig.

pfu·i /ˈfo͞oē/ ▸ **exclam.** var. of PHOOEY. [19th C.: from Ger.]

PG ▸ **abbr.** ■ parental guidance suggested, a rating in the Voluntary Movie Rating System that some material may not be suitable for children. ■ paying guest.

pg. ▸ **abbr.** page.

PG-13 ▸ **symb.** parents strongly cautioned, a rating in the Voluntary Movie Rating System that some material may be inappropriate for children under 13.

PGA ▸ **abbr.** Professional Golfers' Association (of America).

PH (also **P.H.**) ▸ **abbr.** ■ Public Health. ■ Purple Heart.

pH ▸ **n.** Chem. a figure expressing the acidity or alkalinity of a solution on a logarithmic scale on which 7 is neutral, lower values are more acid, and higher values more alkaline. [20th C.: *p* from Ger. *Potenz* 'power' + H^+, hydrogen.]

ph. ▸ **abbr.** ■ phase. ■ phone.

PHA ▸ **abbr.** Public Housing Administration.

Phae·a·cian /fēˈāsHən/ ▸ **n.** (in the *Odyssey*) an inhabitant of Scheria (Corfu), whose people were noted for their hedonism. [from L. *Phaeacia*, Gk. *Phaiakia*, Scheria.]

Phae·dra /ˈfēdrə; ˈfedrə/ Gk. Mythol. the wife of Theseus. She fell in love with her stepson Hippolytus, who rejected her, whereupon she hanged herself, leaving behind a letter that accused him of raping her. Theseus would not believe his son's protestations of innocence and banished him.

Pha·e·thon /ˈfāəTHən; -ˌTHän/ Gk. Mythol. the son of Helios the sun god. He asked to drive his father's solar chariot for a day, but could not control the immortal horses and the chariot plunged too near to the earth until Zeus killed Phaethon with a thunderbolt in order to save the earth from destruction.

phaeton

pha·e·ton /ˈfā-itn/ ▸ **n.** hist. a light, open, four-wheeled horse-drawn carriage. ■ a vintage touring car. [18th C.: ult. from Gk. *Phaethōn* (see PHAETHON).]

phage /fāj/ ▸ **n.** short for BACTERIOPHAGE.

phag·o·cyte /ˈfagəˌsīt/ ▸ **n.** Physiol. a type of cell within the body capable of engulfing and absorbing bacteria and other small cells and particles. — **phag·o·cyt·ic** /ˌfagəˈsitik/ **adj.** [19th C.: from Gk. *phago-* 'eating' (from v. *phagein*).]

phag·o·cy·to·sis /ˌfagəsīˈtōsis/ ▸ **n.** Biol. the ingestion of bacteria or other material by phagocytes and ameboid protozoans. — **phag·o·cyt·ize** /ˈfagəsiˌtīz/ **v.** **phag·o·cy·tose** /ˈfagəˌsītōs; ˈfagəˌsītōz/ **v.**

phag·o·some /ˈfagəˌsōm/ ▸ **n.** Biol. a vacuole in the cytoplasm of a cell, containing a phagocytosed particle enclosed within a part of the cell membrane. — **phag·o·so·mal** /ˌfagəˈsōməl/ **adj.**

-phagous ▸ **comb. form** feeding or subsisting on a specified food: *coprophagous*. [from L. *-phagus*, Gk. *-phagos* (from *phagein* 'eat') + **-ous**.]

-phagy ▸ **comb. form** denoting the practice of eating a specified food: *anthropophagy*. [from Gk. *-phagia*, from *phagein* 'eat.']

phal·ange /fəˈlanj; ˈfāˌlanj/ ▸ **n.** **1** Anat. another term for PHALANX (sense 2). [19th C.: back-form. from *phalanges*, pl. of PHALANX.] **2** **(Phalange)** a right-wing Maronite party in Lebanon founded in 1936 by Pierre Gemayel (1905–84). [20th C.: shortened from Fr. *Phalanges Libanaises* 'Lebanese phalanxes.'] — **Phalangiste** /ˌfālanˈzHēst; fəˈlanjist/ **n. & adj.** (in sense 2).

pha·lan·ge·al /fəˈlanjēəl/ ▸ **adj.** Anat. of or relating to a phalanx or the phalanges.

pha·lan·ger /fəˈlanjər/ ▸ **n.** a lemurlike tree-dwelling marsupial (*Phalanger*, *Spilocuscus*, and other genera) native to Australia and New Guinea. The **phalanger family** (Phalangeridae) includes the cuscuses. [18th C.: from Fr., from Gk. *phalangion* 'spider's web.']

pha·lan·ges /fəˈlanjēz/ plural form of PHALANX (sense 2).

phal·an·ster·y /ˈfalənˌsterē/ ▸ **n.** (pl. **-ster·ies**) a group of people living together in community, free of external regulation and holding property in common. [19th C.: from Fr. *phalanstère*, blend of L. *phalanx* 'band' and Fr. *monastère* 'monastery.']

pha·lanx /ˈfālaNGks; ˈfal-/ ▸ **n.** **1** (pl. **pha·lanx·es**) a group of people or things of a similar type forming a compact body or brought together for a common purpose. ■ a body of troops or police officers, standing or moving in close formation. ■ (in ancient Greece) a body of Macedonian infantry drawn up in close order with shields touching and long spears overlapping. **2** (pl. **pha·lan·ges** /fəˈlanjēz; fāˈlanjēz/) Anat. a bone of the finger or toe. [16th C.: via L. from Gk.]

phal·a·rope /ˈfaləˌrōp/ ▸ **n.** a small wading or swimming bird of the sandpiper family, with a straight bill and lobed feet, unusual in that the female is more brightly colored than the male. [18th C.: ult. from mod. L. *Phalaropus*, from Gk. *phalaris* 'coot' + *pous*, *pod-* 'foot.']

phal·li /ˈfalī/ plural form of PHALLUS.

phal·lic /ˈfalik/ ▸ **adj.** of, relating to, or resembling a phallus or erect penis. ■ Psychoanal. of or denoting the genital phase of psychosexual development, esp. in males. — **phal·li·cal·ly** adv.

phal·lo·cen·tric /ˌfalōˈsentrik/ ▸ **adj.** focused on or concerned with the phallus or penis as a symbol of male dominance. — **phal·lo·cen·tric·i·ty** /-senˈtrisitē/ **n.** **phal·lo·cen·trism** /-ˈsentrizəm/ **n.**

phal·lo·plas·ty /ˈfaləˌplastē/ ▸ **n.** plastic surgery performed to construct, repair, or enlarge the penis. [19th C.: from Gk. *phallos* 'phallus.']

phal·lus /ˈfaləs/ ▸ **n.** (pl. **phal·li** /ˈfalī/ or **phal·lus·es**) a penis, esp. when erect (typically used with reference to male potency or dominance). ■ an image or representation of an erect penis, typically symbolizing fertility or potency. — **phal·li·cism** **n.** **phal·lism** **n.** [17th C.: via late L. from Gk. *phallos*.]

phan·er·o·gam /ˈfanərəˌgam/ ▸ **n.** Bot. old-fashioned term for SPERMATOPHYTE. — **phan·er·o·gam·ic** /ˌfanərəˈgamik/ **adj.** **phan·er·og·a·mous** /ˌfanəˈrägəməs/ **adj.** [19th C.: from Fr. *phanérogame*, from Gk. *phaneros* 'visible' + *gamos* 'marriage.']

Phan·er·o·zo·ic /ˌfanərəˈzōik/ ▸ **adj.** Geol. of, relating to, or denoting the eon covering the whole of time since the beginning of the Cambrian period, and comprising the Paleozoic, Mesozoic, and Cenozoic eras. Compare with CRYPTOZOIC. ■ [as n.] **(the Phanerozoic)** the Phanerozoic eon or the system of rocks deposited during it. [19th C.: from Gk. *phaneros* 'visible,' + *zōion* 'animal' + -IC.]

phan·ta·size ▸ **v.** var. of FANTASIZE (restricted to archaic uses or, in modern use, to the fields of psychology and psychiatry).

phan·tasm /ˈfantazəm/ ▸ **n.** literary a figment of the imagination; an illusion or apparition. ■ archaic an illusory likeness of something. — **phan·tas·mal** /fanˈtazməl/ **adj.** **phan·tas·mic** /fanˈtazmik/ **adj.** [ME: from OFr. *fantasme*, via L. from Gk. *phantasma*, from *phantazein* 'make visible,' from *phainein* 'to show.']

phan·tas·ma·go·ri·a /fanˌtazməˈgôrēə/ ▸ **n.** a sequence of real or imaginary images like that seen in a dream. — **phan·tas·ma·gor·ic** /-ˈgôrik/ **adj.** **phan·tas·ma·gor·i·cal** /-ˈgôrikəl/ **adj.** [19th C.: prob. from Fr. *fantasmagorie*, from *fantasme* 'phantasm' + fanciful suffix.]

phan·tast ▸ **n.** var. of FANTAST.

phan·ta·sy ▸ **n.** var. of FANTASY (restricted to archaic uses or, in modern use, to the fields of psychology and psychiatry).

phan·tom /ˈfantəm/ ▸ **n.** a ghost. ■ a figment of the imagination. ■ [as adj.] denoting a financial arrangement or transaction that has been invented for fraudulent purposes but that does not really exist. ■ [as adj.] denoting something, esp. something illegal, that is done by an unknown person. [ME: from OFr. *fantosme*, based on Gk. *phantasma* (see PHANTASM).]

phar. (also **Phar.**) ▶ abbr. ■ pharmaceutical. ■ pharmacology. ■ pharmacopoeia. ■ pharmacy.

Phar·aoh /'fe(ə)r,ō; 'far,ō; 'fā,rō/ (also **phar·aoh**) ▶ n. a ruler in ancient Egypt. — **phar·a·on·ic** /,fe(ə)rā'änik; ,far-/ adj. [ME: via eccles. L. from Gk. *Pharaō*, from Heb. *par ōh*, from Egyptian *pr-o* 'great house.']

phar·aoh ant (also **pharaoh's ant**) ▶ n. a small red or yellowish African ant (*Monomorium pharaonis*), established worldwide and living as a pest in heated buildings.

Phar·aoh hound ▶ n. a hunting dog of a short-coated tan-colored breed with large, pointed ears.

Phar.B. ▶ abbr. Bachelor of Pharmacy.

Phar.D. ▶ abbr. Doctor of Pharmacy.

Phar·i·see /'farəsē/ ▶ n. a member of an ancient Jewish sect, distinguished by strict observance of the traditional and written law, and commonly held to have pretensions to superior sanctity. ■ a self-righteous person; a hypocrite. — **Phar·i·sa·ic** /,farə'sāik/ adj. **Phar·i·sa·i·cal** /,farə'sāikəl/ adj. **Phar·i·sa·ism** /-sā,izəm/ n. [ult. from Gk. *Pharisaios*, from Aramaic *prīš ayyā* 'separated ones.']

Phar.M. ▶ abbr. Master of Pharmacy.

phar·ma·ceu·ti·cal /,färmə'sōōtikəl/ ▶ adj. of or relating to medicinal drugs. ▶ n. (usu. **pharmaceuticals**) a compound manufactured for use as a medicinal drug. ■ (**pharmaceuticals**) companies manufacturing medicinal drugs. — **phar·ma·ceu·ti·cal·ly** adv. **phar·ma·ceu·tics** /-sōōtiks/ n. [17th C.: via late L. from Gk. *pharmakeutikos* (from *pharmakeutēs* 'druggist,' from *pharmakon* 'drug').]

phar·ma·cist /'färməsist/ ▶ n. a person who is professionally qualified to prepare and dispense medicinal drugs.

pharmaco- ▶ comb. form relating to drugs. [from Gk. *pharmakon* 'drug, medicine.']

phar·ma·co·dy·nam·ics /,färməkōdī'namiks/ ▶ plural n. [treated as sing.] the branch of pharmacology concerned with the effects of drugs and the mechanism of their action. — **phar·ma·co·dy·nam·ic** /-mik/ adj.

phar·ma·co·ge·net·ics /,färməkōjə'netiks/ ▶ plural n. [treated as sing.] the branch of pharmacology concerned with the effect of genetic factors on reactions to drugs.

phar·ma·cog·no·sy /,färmə'kägnəsē/ ▶ n. the branch of knowledge concerned with medicinal drugs obtained from plants or other natural sources. — **phar·ma·cog·no·sist** n. [19th C.: from PHARMACO- + *gnōsis* 'knowledge.']

phar·ma·co·ki·net·ics /,färməkōki'netiks/ ▶ plural n. [treated as sing.] the branch of pharmacology concerned with the movement of drugs within the body. — **phar·ma·co·ki·net·ic** adj.

phar·ma·col·o·gy /,färmə'käləjē/ ▶ n. the branch of medicine concerned with the uses, effects, and modes of action of drugs. — **phar·ma·co·log·ic** /,färməkə'läjik/ adj. **phar·ma·co·log·i·cal** /-'läjikəl/ adj. **phar·ma·co·log·i·cal·ly** /,färməkə'läjik(ə)lē/ adv. **phar·ma·col·o·gist** /-'käləjist/ n. [18th C.: from mod. L. *pharmacologia*, from Gk. *pharmakon* 'drug.']

phar·ma·co·poe·ia /,färməkə'pēə/ (also **pharmacopeia**) ▶ n. a book, esp. an official publication, containing a list of medicinal drugs with their effects and directions for their use. ■ a stock of medicinal drugs. [17th C.: mod. L., from Gk. *pharmakopoiia* 'art of preparing drugs,' based on *pharmakon* 'drug' + *-poios* 'making.']

phar·ma·co·ther·a·py /,färməkō'THerəpē/ ▶ n. medical treatment by means of drugs.

phar·ma·cy /'färməsē/ ▶ n. (pl. **-cies**) a store where medicinal drugs are dispensed and sold. ■ the science or practice of the preparation and dispensing of medicinal drugs. [ME: ult. from Gk. *pharmakeia* 'practice of the druggist,' based on *pharmakon* 'drug.']

Pha·ros /'fe(ə)rōs/ a lighthouse, often considered one of the Seven Wonders of the World, erected by Ptolemy II (308–246 BC) in *c.*280 BC on the island of Pharos, off the coast of Alexandria. ■ [as n.] (**pharos**) a lighthouse or a beacon to guide sailors.

pha·ryn·ge·al /fə'rinj(ē)əl; ,farin'jēəl/ ▶ adj. of or relating to the pharynx. ■ Phonet. (of a speech sound) produced by articulating the root of the tongue with the pharynx, a feature of certain consonants in Arabic, for example. ▶ n. Phonet. a pharyngeal consonant. [19th C.: from mod. L. *pharyngeus* (from Gk. *pharunx, pharung-* 'throat').]

phar·yn·gi·tis /,farin'jītis/ ▶ n. Med. inflammation of the pharynx, causing a sore throat.

pharyngo- ▶ comb. form of or relating to the pharynx. [from mod. L. *pharynx, pharyng-*.]

phar·ynx /'fariNGks/ ▶ n. (pl. **pha·ryn·ges** /fə'rinjēz/ or **phar·ynx·es**) Anat. Zool. the membrane-lined cavity behind the nose and mouth, connecting them to the esophagus. ■ Zool. the part of the alimentary canal immediately behind the mouth in invertebrates. [17th C.: mod. L., from Gk. *pharunx, pharung-*.]

phase /fāz/ ▶ n. **1** a distinct period or stage in a process of change or forming part of something's development. ■ a stage in a person's psychological development, esp. a period of temporary unhappiness or difficulty during adolescence or a particular stage during childhood. ■ each of the aspects of the moon or a planet, according to the amount of its illumination, esp. the new moon, the first quarter, the full moon, and the last quarter. **2** Zool. a genetic or seasonal variety of an animal's coloration. ■ a stage in the life cycle or annual cycle of an animal. **3** Chem. a distinct and homogeneous form of matter (i.e., a particular solid, liquid, or gas) separated by its surface from other forms. **4** Physics the relationship in time between the successive states or cycles of an oscillating or repeating system (such as an alternating electric current or a light or sound wave) and either a fixed reference point or the states or cycles of another system with which it may or may not be in synchrony. ▶ v. [trans.] (usu. **be phased**) **1** carry out (something) in gradual stages. ■ (**phase something in/out**) introduce into (or withdraw from) use in gradual stages. **2** Physics adjust the phase of (something), esp. so as to synchronize it with something else.
– PHRASES **in** (or **out of**) **phase** being or happening in (or out of) synchrony or harmony: *the cabling work should be carried out in phase with the building work.* [19th C.: from Fr., based on Gk. *phasis* 'appearance,' from base of *phainein* 'to show.']

phase con·trast ▶ n. the technique in microscopy of introducing a phase difference between parts of the light supplied by the condenser so as to enhance the outlines of the sample, or the boundaries between parts differing in optical density.

phase di·a·gram ▶ n. Chem. a diagram representing the limits of stability of the various phases in a chemical system at equilibrium, with respect to variables such as composition and temperature.

phase-lock ▶ v. [trans.] Electron. fix the frequency of (an oscillator or a laser) relative to a stable oscillator of lower frequency by a method that utilizes a correction signal derived from the phase difference generated by any shift in the frequency.

phase mod·u·la·tion /,mäjə'lāSHən/ ▶ n. Electron. variation of the phase of a radio or other wave as a means of carrying information such as an audio signal.

phase·out /'fā,zout/ ▶ n. an act of discontinuing a process, project, or service in phases.

phas·er /'fāzər/ ▶ n. **1** an instrument that alters a sound signal by phasing it. **2** (in science fiction) a weapon that delivers a beam that can stun or annihilate.

phase rule ▶ n. Chem. a rule relating the possible numbers of phases, constituents, and degrees of freedom in a chemical system.

phase shift ▶ n. Physics a change in the phase of a waveform.

phase space ▶ n. Physics a multidimensional space in which each axis corresponds to one of the coordinates required to specify the state of a physical system, all the coordinates being thus represented so that a point in the space corresponds to a state of the system.

pha·sic /'fāzik/ ▶ adj. of or relating to a phase or phases. ■ esp. Physiol. characterized by occurrence in phases rather than continuously.

phas·ing /'fāziNG/ ▶ n. the relationship between the timing of two or more events, or the adjustment of this relationship. ■ the modification of the sound signal from an electric guitar or other electronic instrument by introducing a phase shift into either of two copies of it and then recombining them. ■ the action of dividing a large task or process into several stages.

Phas·mi·da /'fazmidə/ **1** Entomol. an order of insects that comprises the stick insects and leaf insects. They have very long bodies that resemble twigs or leaves. **2** Zool. a class of nematodes that includes the parasitic hookworms and roundworms. — **phas·mid** n. & adj. [mod. L. (pl.), from L. *phasma* 'apparition,' from Gk.]

phat /fat/ ▶ adj. black slang excellent. [1970s: of uncert. origin.]

phat·ic /'fatik/ ▶ adj. denoting or relating to language used for general purposes of social interaction, rather than to convey information or ask questions. Utterances such as *hello, how are you?* are phatic. [1920s: from Gk. *phatos* 'spoken' or *phatikos* 'affirming.']

Ph.B ▶ abbr. Bachelor of Philosophy. [L. *Philosophiae Baccalaureus*.]

Ph.C. ▶ abbr. Pharmaceutical Chemist.

PhD ▶ abbr. Doctor of Philosophy. [from L. *philosophiae doctor*.]

ring-necked pheasant

pheas·ant /'fezənt/ ▶ n. a large long-tailed game bird (family Phasianidae) native to Asia, the male of which typically has very showy plumage. Its several species include the widely introduced **ring-necked pheasant** (*Phasianus colchicus*). [ME: from OFr. *fesan*, via L. from Gk. *phasianos* '(bird) of *Phasis*,' river in the Caucasus.]

phen- ▶ comb. form var. of PHENO- shortened before a vowel (as in *phenacetin*).

phe·nac·e·tin /fə'nasitən/ ▶ n. Med. a synthetic compound used as a painkilling and antipyretic drug. [19th C.: from PHENO- + *acet(yl)*.]

phe·nan·threne /fə'nanTHrēn/ ▶ n. Chem. a crystalline hydrocarbon, $C_{14}H_{10}$, present in coal tar, used esp. in making dyes and synthetic drugs.

phen·cy·cli·dine /fen'sīkli,dēn; -'sik-/ (abbr.: **PCP**) ▶ n. a synthetic compound derived from piperidine, used as a veterinary anesthetic and in hallucinogenic drugs such as angel dust. [1950s: from PHENO- + CYCLO- + shortened form of PIPERIDINE.]

pheno- (also **phen-** before a vowel) ▶**comb. form** **1** Chem. derived from benzene: *phenobarbital.* **2** showing: *phenotype.* [ult. from Gk. *phainein* 'to show.']

phe·no·bar·bi·tal /ˌfēnōˈbärbiˌtôl/ ▶**n.** Med. a narcotic and sedative barbiturate drug used chiefly to treat epilepsy.

phe·no·cop·y /ˈfēnəˌkäpē/ ▶**n.** (pl. **-cop·ies**) Genet. an individual showing features characteristic of a genotype other than its own, but produced environmentally rather than genetically.

phe·no·cryst /ˈfēnəˌkrist/ ▶**n.** Geol. a large or conspicuous crystal in a porphyritic rock, distinct from the groundmass. [19th C.: from Fr. *phénocryste*, from Gk. *phainein* 'to show' + *krustallos* 'crystal.']

phe·nol /ˈfēˌnôl; -ˌnäl/ ▶**n.** Chem. a mildly acidic toxic white crystalline solid, C_6H_5OH, obtained from coal tar and used in chemical manufacture, and in dilute form (under the name **carbolic**) as a disinfectant. ■ any compound with a hydroxyl group linked directly to a benzene ring. — **phe·no·lic** /fiˈnälik/ **adj.** [19th C.: from Fr. *phénole.*]

phe·nol·o·gy /fiˈnäləjē/ ▶**n.** the study of cyclic and seasonal natural phenomena, esp. in relation to climate and plant and animal life. — **phe·no·log·i·cal** /ˌfēnəˈläjikəl/ **adj.** [19th C.: from PHENOMENON.]

phe·nol·phthal·ein /ˌfēnəlˈTHălē(i)n/ ▶**n.** Chem. a colorless crystalline solid, $C_{20}H_{14}O_4$, (pink in alkaline solution) used as an acid–base indicator and medicinally as a laxative. [19th C.: from PHENOL + *-phthal-* (from NAPHTHALENE) + -IN[1].]

phe·nom /ˈfēˌnäm; fiˈnäm/ ▶**n.** informal a person who is outstandingly talented or admired; a star. [19th C.: abbrev. of PHENOMENON.]

phe·nom·e·na /fəˈnämənə/ plural form of PHENOMENON.

phe·nom·e·nal /fəˈnämənəl/ ▶**adj.** **1** very remarkable; extraordinary. **2** perceptible by the senses or through immediate experience. — **phe·nom·e·nal·ize** **v.** (in sense 2). **phe·nom·e·nal·ly** **adv.**

phe·nom·e·nal·ism /fəˈnämənəlˌizəm/ ▶**n.** Philos. the doctrine that human knowledge is confined to or founded on the realities or appearances presented to the senses. — **phe·nom·e·nal·ist** **n. & adj.** **phe·nom·e·nal·is·tic** /-ˌnämənəlˈistik/ **adj.**

phe·nom·e·nol·o·gy /fiˌnäməˈnäləjē/ ▶**n.** Philos. the science of phenomena as distinct from that of the nature of being. ■ an approach that concentrates on the study of consciousness and the objects of direct experience. — **phe·nom·e·no·log·i·cal** /-ˌnämənəˈläjikəl/ **adj.** **phe·nom·e·no·log·i·cal·ly** /-ˌnämənəˈläjik(ə)lē/ **adv.** **phe·nom·e·nol·o·gist** /-ˈnäləjist/ **n.**

phe·nom·e·non /fəˈnäməˌnän; -nən/ ▶**n.** (pl. **-na** /-nə/) **1** a fact or situation that is observed to exist or happen, esp. one whose cause or explanation is in question. ■ a remarkable person, thing, or event. **2** Philos. the object of a person's perception; what the senses or the mind notice. [16th C.: via late L. from Gk. *phainomenon* 'thing appearing to view,' based on *phainein* 'to show.']

phe·no·thi·a·zine /ˌfēnəˈTHīəˌzēn/ ▶**n.** Chem. a synthetic compound, $C_{12}H_9NS$, that is used in veterinary medicine to treat parasitic infestations of animals. ■ Psychiatry any of a group of derivatives of this compound with tranquilizing properties, used in the treatment of mental illness.

phe·no·type /ˈfēnəˌtīp/ ▶**n.** Biol. the set of observable characteristics of an individual resulting from the interaction of its genotype with the environment. — **phe·no·typ·ic** /ˌfēnəˈtipik/ **adj.** **phe·no·typ·i·cal** /ˌfēnəˈtipikəl/ **adj.** **phe·no·typ·i·cal·ly** /ˌfēnəˈtipik(ə)lē/ **adv.**

phen·tol·a·mine /fenˈtäləˌmēn/ ▶**n.** Med. a synthetic compound, $C_{17}H_{19}N_3O$, used as a vasodilator, esp. in certain cases of hypertension. [1950s: from PHEN- + *tol(yl).*]

phen·yl /ˈfenl; ˈfē-/ ▶**n.** [as adj.] Chem. of or denoting the radical $-C_6H_5$, derived from benzene by removal of a hydrogen atom. [19th C.: from Fr. *phényle*, from Gk. *phaino-* 'shining'.]

phen·yl·al·a·nine /ˌfenlˈaləˌnēn; ˌfēnl-/ ▶**n.** Biochem. an amino acid, $C_6H_5CH_2CH(NH_2)COOH$, widely distributed in plant proteins. It is an essential nutrient in the diet of vertebrates.

phen·yl·bu·ta·zone /ˌfenəlˈbyo͞otəˌzōn; ˌfēnəl-/ ▶**n.** a synthetic compound used as an analgesic drug, esp. in the treatment of horses. [1950s: from PHENYL + *but(yl)* + AZO-.]

phen·yl·eph·rine /ˌfēnlˈefrin; ˌfenl-/ ▶**n.** Med. a synthetic compound related to epinephrine, used as a vasoconstrictor and nasal decongestant. [1940s: from PHENYL + contr. of EPINEPHRINE.]

phen·yl·ke·to·nu·ri·a /ˌfenlˌkētōˈn(y)o͝orēə; ˌfēnl-/ (abbr.: **PKU**) ▶**n.** Med. an inherited inability to metabolize phenylalanine that causes brain and nerve damage if untreated.

phen·y·to·in /ˌfeniˈtō-in; fəˈnitō-in/ ▶**n.** Med. a synthetic compound, $C_{15}H_{12}N_2O_2$, used as an anticonvulsant in the treatment of epilepsy.

pher·o·mone /ˈferəˌmōn/ ▶**n.** Zool. a chemical substance produced and released into the environment by an animal, esp. a mammal or an insect, affecting the behavior or physiology of others of its species. — **pher·o·mo·nal** /ferəˈmōnl/ **adj.** [1950s: from Gk. *pherein* 'convey' + HORMONE.]

phew /fyo͞o/ ▶**exclam.** informal expressing a strong reaction of relief. [17th C.: imitative.]

phi /fī/ ▶**n.** the twenty-first letter of the Greek alphabet (Φ, φ), transliterated as 'ph.' ▶**symb.** ■ (φ) a plane angle. ■ (φ) a polar coordinate.

phi·al /ˈfīəl/ ▶**n.** another term for VIAL. [ME: ult. from Gk. *phialē*, 'container.']

Phi Be·ta Kap·pa /ˈfī ˈbātə ˈkapə/ ▶**n.** an honorary society of college and university undergraduates and some graduates to which members are elected on the basis of high academic achievement. ■ a member of this society. [from Gk. *philosophia biou kubernētēs* 'philosophy is the guide to life.']

Phid·i·as /ˈfidēəs/ (5th century BC), Athenian sculptor. He is noted for the Elgin Marbles and his statue of Zeus at Olympia (*c.*430), one of the Seven Wonders of the World.

Phil. ▶**abbr.** ■ Bible Philippians. ■ Bible Philemon. ■ Philadelphia. ■ Philharmonic. ■ Philippine.

phil- ▶**comb. form** var. of PHILO- shortened before a vowel or *h* (as in *philharmonic*).

-phil ▶**comb. form** having a chemical affinity for a substance: *acidophil* | *neutrophil.* [see -PHILE.]

Phil·a·del·phi·a /ˌfiləˈdelfēə/ a city in southeastern Pennsylvania, on the Delaware River; pop. 1,517,550. — **Phil·a·del·phi·an** **n. & adj.**

Phil·a·del·phi·a law·yer ▶**n.** a very shrewd lawyer who is expert in the exploitation of legal technicalities.

phil·a·del·phus /ˌfiləˈdelfəs/ ▶**n.** a mock orange. [18th C.: mod. L., from Gk. *philadelphos* 'loving one's brother.']

phi·lan·der /fəˈlandər/ ▶**v.** [intrans.] (of a man) readily or frequently enter into casual sexual relationships with women. — **phi·lan·der·er** **n.** [18th C.: from *philander* 'man,' from Gk. *philandros* 'fond of men,' from *philein* 'to love' + *anēr* 'man.']

phil·an·throp·ic /ˌfilənˈTHräpik/ ▶**adj.** (of a person or organization) seeking to promote the welfare of others, esp. by donating money to good causes; generous and benevolent. — **phil·an·throp·i·cal·ly** **adv.**

phi·lan·thro·pist /fəˈlanTHrəpist/ ▶**n.** a person who seeks to promote the welfare of others, esp. by the generous donation of money to good causes.

phi·lan·thro·py /fəˈlanTHrəpē/ ▶**n.** the desire to promote the welfare of others, expressed esp. by the generous donation of money to good causes. ■ a philanthropic institution; a charity. — **phi·lan·thro·pism** **n.** **phi·lan·thro·pize** **v.**

phi·lat·e·ly /fəˈlatl-ē/ ▶**n.** the collection and study of postage stamps. — **phil·a·tel·ic** /ˌfiləˈtelik/ **adj.** **phil·a·tel·i·cal·ly** /ˌfiləˈtelik(ə)lē/ **adv.** **phi·lat·e·list** **n.** [19th C.: from Fr. *philatélie*, from *philo-* 'loving' + Gk. *ateleia* 'exemption from payment' (from *a-* 'not' + *telos* 'toll, tax').]

-phile ▶**comb. form** denoting fondness for a specified thing: *bibliophile.* [from Gk. *philos* 'loving.']

Philem. ▶**abbr.** Bible Philemon.

Phi·le·mon[1] /fəˈlēmən; fī-/ Gk. Mythol. a good old countryman living with his wife Baucis in Phrygia who offered hospitality to Zeus and Hermes when the two gods came to earth, without revealing their identities, to test people's piety. Philemon and Baucis were subsequently saved from a flood that covered the district.

Phi·le·mon[2] a book of the New Testament, an epistle of St. Paul to a well-to-do Christian living probably at Colossae in Phrygia.

phil·har·mon·ic /ˌfilərˈmänik; ˌfilhär-/ ▶**adj.** devoted to music (chiefly used in the names of orchestras). ▶**n.** a philharmonic orchestra or the society that sponsors it (chiefly used in names). [18th C.: from Fr. *philharmonique*, from Ital. *filarmonico* 'loving harmony.']

phil·hel·lene /filˈhelēn/ ▶**n.** a lover of Greece and Greek culture: *a romantic philhellene.* ■ hist. a supporter of Greek independence. — **phil·hel·len·ic** /ˌfilheˈlenik/ **adj.** **phil·hel·len·ism** /filˈheləˌnizəm/ **n.** [19th C.: from Gk. *philellēn* 'loving the Greeks.']

-philia ▶**comb. form** denoting fondness, esp. an abnormal love for a specified thing: *pedophilia.* ■ denoting undue inclination: *spasmophilia.* — **-philiac** **comb. form** in corresponding nouns and adjectives **-philic** **comb. form** in corresponding adjectives **-philous** **comb. form** in corresponding adjectives. [from Gk. *philia* 'fondness.']

Phil·ip[1] /ˈfilip/ the name of five kings of ancient Macedonia, notably: ■ Philip II (382–336 BC), reigned 359–336 BC; known as **Philip II of Macedon**; father of Alexander the Great. ■ Philip V (238–179 BC), reigned 221–179 BC.

Phil·ip[2] the name of six kings of France: ■ Philip I (1052–1108), reigned 1059–1108. ■ Philip II (1165–1223), reigned 1180–1223; known as **Philip Augustus**; son of Louis VII. ■ Philip III (1245–1285), reigned 1270–85; known as **Philip the Bold.** ■ Philip IV (1268–1314), reigned 1285–1314; known as **Philip the Fair**; son of Philip III. ■ Philip V (1293–1322), reigned 1316–1322; known as **Philip the Tall.** ■ Philip VI (1293–1350), reigned 1328–50; known as **Philip of Valois.** His claim to the throne was challenged by Edward III of England, and the dispute developed into the Hundred Years War.

Phil·ip[3] the name of five kings of Spain: ■ Philip I (1478–1506), reigned 1504–06; known as **Philip the Handsome.** ■ Philip II (1527–98), reigned 1556–98. His armada against England 1588 ended in defeat. ■ Philip III (1578–1621), reigned 1598–1621. ■ Philip IV (1605–1665), reigned 1621–65. ■ Philip V (1683–1746), reigned 1700–46; grandson of Louis XIV.

Phil·ip[4], King (c.1639–1676) Wampanoag Indian chief; Indian name Metacomet; son of Massasoit. He waged King Philip's War 1675–76 on the New England colonists.

Phil·ip, Prince, Duke of Edinburgh (1921–); husband of Elizabeth II of the United Kingdom.

Phil·ip, St.[1], one of the 12 apostles.

Phil·ip, St.[2], leader of the early Christian Church; known as **St. Philip the Evangelist**.

Phil·ip II of Mac·e·don, Philip II of Macedonia (see PHILIP[1]).

Phil·ip Au·gus·tus, Philip II of France (see PHILIP[2]).

Phil·ip of Va·lois, Philip VI of France (see PHILIP[2]).

Phi·lip·pi /fəˈlipī; ˈfiləˌpī/ a city in ancient Macedonia, in northeastern Greece, near the port of Kaválla (ancient Neapolis). Greek name FILIPPOI.

Phi·lip·pi·ans /fəˈlipēənz/ a book of the New Testament, an epistle of St. Paul to the Church at Philippi in Macedonia.

phi·lip·pic /fəˈlipik/ ▶n. literary a bitter attack or denunciation, esp. a verbal one. [16th C.: via L. from Gk. *philippikos*, name given to Demosthenes' speeches against Philip II of Macedon, also to those of Cicero against Mark Antony.]

Phil·ip·pine /ˈfiləˌpēn/ ▶adj. of or relating to the Philippines. See also FILIPINO.

Phil·ip·pine ma·hog·a·ny ▶n. **1** reddish-brown timber from a tropical tree, used for paneling, cabinetry, and furniture. It resembles mahogany, but is softer and less expensive. **2** the tree (genus *Shorea*, family Dipterocarpaceae) that produces this timber, harvested chiefly in Indonesia and the Philippines. Also called LAUAN.

Philippines

Official name: Republic of the Philippines

Location: Southeast Asia, an archipelago of over 7,000 islands, including Luzon, Mindanao, Mindoro, Leyte, Samar, Negros, and Panay, separated from the Asian mainland by the South China Sea

Area: 115,900 square miles (300,000 sq km)

Population: 86,241,000

Capital: Manila

Languages: Filipino, English (both official)

Currency: Philippine peso

Phil·ip·pines /ˈfiləˌpēnz/ a country in Southeast Asia that consists of an archipelago of over 7,000 islands. *See box.*

Phil·ip·pine Sea a section of the western Pacific on the east side of the Philippine Islands that extends north to Japan. During World War II, several major battles, including that at LEYTE GULF, were fought here.

Phil·ip·pop·o·lis /ˌfiləˈpäpəlis/ ancient Greek name for PLOVDIV.

Phil·ip the Bold, Philip III of France (see PHILIP[2]).

Phil·ip the Fair, Philip IV of France (see PHILIP[2]).

Phil·ip the Hand·some, Philip I of Spain (see PHILIP[3]).

Phil·ip the Tall, Philip V of France (see PHILIP[2]).

Phil·is·tine /ˈfiləˌstēn; -ˌstīn/ ▶n. **1** a member of a non-Semitic (perhaps originally Anatolian) people of southern Palestine in ancient times, who came into conflict with the Israelites during the 12th and 11th centuries BC. **2** (usu. **philistine**) a person who is hostile or indifferent to culture and the arts, or who has no understanding of them. —**phil·is·tin·ism** /ˈfiləstēˌnizəm; fəˈlistə-/ n. [ult. from Gk. *Philistinos*, from Heb. *pĕlištī*.]

Phil·lips /ˈfiləps/ ▶adj. trademark denoting a screw with a cross-shaped slot for turning, the head of such a screw, or a corresponding screwdriver. [1930s: Henry F. *Phillips* (died 1958).]

phil·lu·men·ist /fəˈlo͞omənist/ ▶n. a collector of matchboxes or matchbooks. —**phil·lu·men·y** /-mənē/ n. [1940s: from PHIL- + L. *lumen* 'light.']

Phil·ly /ˈfilē/ ▶n. informal Philadelphia.

Phil·ly cheese·steak ▶n. see CHEESESTEAK.

philo- (also **phil-** before a vowel or *h*) ▶comb. form denoting a liking for a specified thing: *philogynist.* [from Gk. *philein* 'to love' or *philos* 'loving.']

phil·o·den·dron /ˌfiləˈdendrən/ ▶n. (pl. **-drons** or **-dra** /-drə/) a tropical American climbing plant (genus *Philodendron*) of the arum family that is widely grown as a greenhouse or indoor plant. [19th C.: from PHILO- + Gk. *dendron* 'tree.']

phi·log·y·nist /fəˈläjənist/ ▶n. formal a person who likes or admires women. —**phi·log·y·ny** /-ˈläjənē/ n. [19th C.: from PHILO- + Gk. *gunē* 'woman.']

phi·lol·o·gy /fəˈläləjē/ ▶n. the branch of knowledge that deals with the structure, historical development, and relationships of a language or languages. ■ literary or classical scholarship. —**phil·o·lo·gi·an** /ˌfiləˈlōjēən/ n. **phil·o·log·i·cal** /ˌfiləˈläjikəl/ adj. **phil·o·log·i·cal·ly** /ˌfiləˈläjik(ə)lē/ adv. **phi·lol·o·gist** n. [ME: current usage (late 17th C.) ult. from Gk. *philologia* 'love of learning.']

Phil·o·me·la /ˌfiləˈmēlə/ (also **Phil·o·mel** /ˈfiləˌmel/) Gk. Mythol. the daughter of Pandion, king of Athens. She was turned into a swallow and her sister Procne into a nightingale (or, in Latin versions, into a nightingale with Procne the swallow) when they were being pursued by the cruel Tereus, who had married Procne and raped Philomela.

phil·o·pat·ric /ˌfiləˈpatrik/ ▶adj. Zool. (of an animal or species) tending to return to or remain near a particular site or area. —**phil·op·a·try** /fəˈläpətrē/ n. [1940s: from PHILO- + Gk. *patra* 'fatherland.']

phil·o·pro·gen·i·tive /ˌfilōprōˈjenitiv/ ▶adj. formal having many offspring. ■ showing love toward one's offspring. —**phil·o·pro·gen·i·tive·ness** n.

phi·los·o·pher /fəˈläsəfər/ ▶n. a person engaged or learned in philosophy, esp. as an academic discipline. [ME: ult. from Gk. *philosophos*, from *philein* 'to love' + *sophos* 'wise.']

phi·los·o·pher's stone ▶n. (**the philosopher's stone**) a mythical substance supposed to change any metal into gold or silver and, according to some, to cure all diseases and prolong life indefinitely. Its discovery was the supreme object of alchemy.

phil·o·soph·i·cal /ˌfiləˈsäfikəl/ ▶adj. **1** of or relating to the study of the fundamental nature of knowledge, reality, and existence. ■ devoted to the study of such issues. **2** having or showing a calm attitude toward disappointments or difficulties. —**phil·o·soph·ic** /-ˈsäfik/ adj. **phil·o·soph·i·cal·ly** adv.

phi·los·o·phize /fəˈläsəˌfīz/ ▶v. [intrans.] speculate or theorize about fundamental or serious issues, esp. in a tedious or pompous way. ■ [trans.] explain or argue (a point or idea) in terms of one's philosophical theories. —**phi·los·o·phiz·er** n.

phi·los·o·phy /fəˈläsəfē/ ▶n. (pl. **-phies**) the study of the fundamental nature of knowledge, reality, and existence, esp. when considered as an academic discipline. See also NATURAL PHILOSOPHY. ■ a set of views and theories of a particular philosopher concerning such study or an aspect of it. ■ the study of the theoretical basis of a particular branch of knowledge or experience. ■ a theory or attitude held by a person or organization that acts as a guiding principle for behavior. [ME: from OFr. *philosophie*, via L. from Gk. *philosophia* 'love of wisdom.']

phil·ter /ˈfiltər/ (Brit. **phil·tre**) ▶n. a drink supposed to excite sexual love in the drinker. [16th C.: from Fr. *philtre*, via L. from Gk. *philtron*, from *philein* 'to love.']

-phily ▶comb. form equivalent to -PHILIA.

phi·mo·sis /fīˈmōsis/ ▶n. Med. a congenital narrowing of the opening of the foreskin so that it cannot be retracted. —**phi·mot·ic** /fīˈmätik/ adj. [17th C.: mod. L., from Gk., lit. 'muzzling.']

phish·ing /ˈfisHiNG/ ▶n. the fraudulent practice of sending e-mails purporting to be from legitimate companies in order to induce individuals to reveal personal information, such as credit-card numbers, online. —**phish** v. [1990s: respelling of FISHING, on the pattern of PHREAKING.]

phle·bi·tis /fləˈbītis/ ▶n. Med. inflammation of the walls of a vein. —**phle·bit·ic** /-ˈbitik/ adj. [19th C.: mod. L., from Gk., from *phleps*, *phleb-* 'vein.']

phle·bot·o·my /fləˈbätəmē/ ▶n. (pl. **-mies**) the surgical opening or puncture of a vein in order to withdraw blood or introduce a fluid, or (historically) as part of the procedure of letting blood. —**phle·bot·o·mist** n. **phle·bot·o·mize** /-ˈbätəˌmīz/ v. (archaic). [ME: via OFr. from late L. *phlebotomia*, from Gk., from *phleps*, *phleb-* 'vein' + *-tomia* 'cutting.']

phlegm /flem/ ▶n. the thick viscous substance secreted by the mucous membranes of the respiratory passages, esp. when produced in excessive or abnormal quantities, e.g., when someone is suffering from a cold. ■ (in medieval science and medicine) one of the four bodily humors, believed to be associated with a calm, stolid, or apathetic temperament. ■ calmness of temperament. —**phlegm·y** adj. [ME *fleem*, *fleume*, based on Gk. *phlegma* 'inflammation,' from *phlegein* 'to burn.']

phleg·mat·ic /fleg'matik/ ▶ **adj.** (of a person) having an unemotional and stolidly calm disposition. — **phleg·mat·i·cal·ly adv.**

phlo·em /'flō,em/ ▶ **n.** Bot. the vascular tissue in plants that conducts sugars and other metabolic products downward from the leaves. [19th C.: from Gk. *phloos* 'bark' + passive suffix *-ēma.*]

phlo·gis·ton /flō'jistän; -tən/ ▶ **n.** a substance supposed by 18th-century chemists to exist in all combustible bodies, and to be released in combustion. [18th C.: mod. L., from Gk. *phlogizein* 'set on fire,' from *phlox, phlog-* 'flame,' from base of *phlegein* 'to burn.']

phlog·o·pite /'flägə,pīt/ ▶ **n.** a brown micaceous mineral that occurs chiefly in metamorphosed limestone and magnesium-rich igneous rocks. [19th C.: from Gk. *phlogōpos* 'fiery' (from base of *phlegein* 'to burn') + *ōps, ōp-* 'face.']

phlox /fläks/ ▶ **n.** a North American plant (genus *Phlox*, family Polemoniaceae) that typically has dense clusters of colorful scented flowers, widely grown as a rock-garden or border plant. [mod. L., from L., a flower, from Gk., lit. 'flame.']

Ph.M. ▶ **abbr.** Master of Philosophy.

Phnom Penh /(pə),näm 'pen/ the capital of Cambodia, a port at the junction of the Mekong and Tonlé Sap rivers; pop. 920,000.

-phobe ▶ **comb. form** denoting a person having a fear or dislike of what is specified: *homophobe.* [from Fr., via L. *-phobus* from Gk. *-phobos* 'fearing,' from *phobos* 'fear.']

pho·bi·a /'fōbēə/ ▶ **n.** an extreme or irrational fear of or aversion to something: *he had a* ***phobia about*** *being under water* | *a* ***phobia of*** *germs* | *a snake phobia.* — **pho·bic** /'fōbik/ **adj. & n.** [18th C.: independent usage of **-PHOBIA.**]

-phobia ▶ **comb. form** extreme or irrational fear or dislike of a specified thing or group: *arachnophobia.* — **-phobic comb. form** in corresponding adjectives. [via L. from Gk.]

Pho·bos /'fōbəs; 'fōbäs/ Astron. the inner, and larger, of the two satellites of Mars, discovered in 1877. Heavily cratered, it has a diameter of 13 miles (21 km). Compare with **DEIMOS.** [after son of war god **ARES.**]

pho·cine /'fōsīn; 'fōsin/ ▶ **adj.** Zool. of, relating to, or affecting the true (earless) seals. [19th C.: from mod. L. *Phocinae*, from Gk. *phōkē* 'seal.']

pho·co·me·li·a /,fōkō'mēlyə; -'mēlēə/ ▶ **n.** Med. a rare congenital deformity in which the hands or feet are attached close to the trunk, the limbs being grossly underdeveloped or absent. This condition was a side effect of the drug thalidomide taken during early pregnancy. [19th C.: mod. L., from Gk. *phōkē* 'seal' + *melos* 'limb.']

Phoe·be /'fēbē/ **1** Gk. Mythol. a Titaness, daughter of Uranus (Heaven) and Gaia (Earth). She became the mother of Leto and thus the grandmother of Apollo and Artemis. In the later Greek writers, her name was often used for Selene (Moon). **2** Astron. a satellite of Saturn, the furthest from the planet and with an eccentric retrograde orbit, discovered in 1898. [from Gk. *Phoibē*, lit. 'bright one.']

phoe·be /'fēbē/ ▶ **n.** an American tyrant flycatcher (genus *Sayornis*) with mainly gray-brown or blackish plumage. [18th C.: imitative.]

Phoe·bus /'fēbəs/ Gk. Mythol. an epithet of Apollo, used in contexts where the god was identified with the sun. [from Gk. *Phoibos*, lit. 'bright one.']

Phoe·ni·cia /fə'nisнə; -'nēsнə/ an ancient country on the shores of the eastern Mediterranean Sea, corresponding to modern Lebanon and part of Syria.

Phoe·ni·cian /fə'nēsнən/ ▶ **n.** **1** a member of a Semitic people inhabiting ancient Phoenicia and its colonies. The Phoenicians prospered from trade and manufacturing until the capital, Tyre, was sacked by Alexander the Great in 332 BC. **2** the Semitic language of this people, written in an alphabet that was the ancestor of the Greek and Roman alphabets. ▶ **adj.** of or relating to Phoenicia or its colonies, or its people, language, or alphabet.

Phoe·nix[1] /'fēniks/ Astron. a southern constellation (the Phoenix), west of Grus. [L.]

Phoe·nix[2] the capital of Arizona, in the central part of the state; pop. 1,321,045.

phoe·nix /'fēniks/ ▶ **n.** (in classical mythology) a unique bird that lived for five or six centuries in the Arabian desert, after this time burning itself on a funeral pyre and rising from the ashes with renewed youth to live through another cycle. ■ a person or thing regarded as uniquely remarkable in some respect. [from OFr. *fenix*, via L. from Gk. *phoinix* 'Phoenician, reddish purple, or phoenix.']

Phoe·nix Is·lands a group of eight islands that form a part of Kiribati.

Phol·i·do·ta /,fäli'dätə/ Zool. a small order of mammals that comprises the pangolins. [mod. L. (pl.), from Gk. *pholidōtos* 'scaly,' from *pholis, pholid-* 'scale.']

phon /fän/ ▶ **n.** a unit of the perceived loudness of sounds. [1930s: from Gk. *phōnē* 'sound.']

pho·na·tion /fō'nāsнən/ ▶ **n.** Phonet. the production or utterance of speech sounds. — **pho·nate** /'fō,nāt/ **v.** **pho·na·to·ry** /'fōnə,tôrē/ **adj.** [19th C.: from Gk. *phōnē* 'sound.']

phone[1] /fōn/ ▶ **n.** short for **TELEPHONE.** ■ **(phones)** informal headphones or earphones. ▶ **v.** short for **TELEPHONE.**

phone[2] ▶ **n.** Phonet. a speech sound; the smallest discrete segment of sound in a stream of speech. [19th C.: from Gk. *phōnē* 'sound, voice.']

-phone ▶ **comb. form** **1** denoting an instrument using or connected with sound: *megaphone.* **2** denoting a person who uses a specified language: *francophone.* [from Gk. *phōnē* 'sound, voice.']

phone bank ▶ **n.** a battery of telephones.

phone book ▶ **n.** a telephone directory.

phone card ▶ **n.** another term for **CALLING CARD** (sense 2).

phone-in ▶ **n. & adj.** another term for **CALL-IN.**

pho·neme /'fōnēm/ ▶ **n.** Phonet. any of the perceptually distinct units of sound in a specified language that distinguish one word from another, for example *p, b, d,* and *t* in the English words *pad, pat, bad,* and *bat.* Compare with **ALLOPHONE.** — **pho·ne·mic** /fə'nēmik; fō-/ **adj.** **pho·ne·mics** /fə'nēmiks; fō-/ **n.** [19th C.: from Fr. *phonème*, from Gk. *phōnēma* 'sound, speech,' from *phōnein* 'speak.']

pho·net·ic /fə'netik/ ▶ **adj.** Phonet. of or relating to speech sounds. ■ (of a system of writing) having a direct correspondence between symbols and sounds. ■ of or relating to phonetics. — **pho·net·i·cal·ly adv.** **pho·net·i·cism** /-'neti,sizəm/ **n.** **pho·net·i·cist** /-'netisist/ **n.** [19th C.: from mod. L. *phoneticus*, from Gk. *phōnētikos*, from *phōnein* 'speak.']

pho·net·ics /fə'netiks/ ▶ **plural n.** [treated as sing.] the study and classification of speech sounds. — **pho·ne·ti·cian** /,fōnə'tisнən/ **n.**

pho·ney ▶ **adj. & n.** var. of **PHONY.**

phon·ic /'fänik/ ▶ **adj.** of or relating to speech sounds. ■ of or relating to phonics. — **phon·i·cal·ly adv.** [19th C.: from Gk. *phōnē* 'voice' + **-IC.**]

phon·ics /'fäniks/ ▶ **plural n.** [treated as sing.] a method of teaching people to read by correlating sounds with letters or groups of letters in an alphabetic writing system.

pho·no /'fōnō/ ▶ **n.** short for **PHONOGRAPH.** ▶ **adj.** [attrib.] denoting a type of plug, and the corresponding socket, used with audio and video equipment, in which one conductor is cylindrical and the other is a central prong that extends beyond it. [1940s: abbrev. of **PHONOGRAPH.**]

phono- ▶ **comb. form** relating to sound: *phonograph.* [from Gk. *phōnē* 'sound, voice.']

pho·no·gram /'fōnə,gram/ ▶ **n.** Phonet. a symbol representing a vocal sound.

pho·no·graph /'fōnə,graf/ ▶ **n.** a record player. ■ esp. hist. an early sound-reproducing machine that used cylinders to record as well as reproduce sound. — **pho·no·graph·ic** /,fōnə'grafik/ **adj.**

pho·no·graph rec·ord ▶ **n.** fuller form of **RECORD** (sense 4).

pho·no·lite /'fōnə,līt/ ▶ **n.** Geol. a fine-grained volcanic igneous rock composed of alkali feldspars and nepheline.

pho·nol·o·gy /fə'näləjē; fō-/ ▶ **n.** the branch of linguistics that deals with systems of sounds (including or excluding phonetics), esp. in a particular language. ■ the system of relationships among the speech sounds that constitute the fundamental components of a language. — **pho·no·log·i·cal** /,fōnə'läjikəl/ **adj.** **pho·no·log·i·cal·ly** /,fōnə'läjik(ə)lē/ **adv.** **pho·nol·o·gist n.**

pho·non /'fōnän/ ▶ **n.** Physics a quantum of energy or a quasiparticle associated with a compressional wave such as sound or a vibration of a crystal lattice. [1930s: from Gk. *phōnē* 'sound.']

pho·no·tac·tics /,fōnō'taktiks/ ▶ **plural n.** [treated as sing.] the study of the rules governing the possible phoneme sequences in a language. — **pho·no·tac·tic adj.**

pho·ny /'fōnē/ (also **pho·ney**) informal ▶ **adj.** (**-ni·er, -ni·est**) not genuine; fraudulent. ▶ **n.** (pl. **-nies**) a fraudulent person or thing. — **pho·ni·ly adv.** **pho·ni·ness n.** [19th C.: of unknown origin.]

pho·ny war the period of comparative inaction at the beginning of World War II between the German invasion of Poland (September 1939) and that of Norway (April 1940).

phoo·ey /'fōōē/ informal ▶ **exclam.** (also **pfu·i**) used to express disdain or disbelief. ▶ **n.** nonsense. [1920s: imitative.]

-phore ▶ **comb. form** denoting an agent or bearer of a specified thing: *ionophore.* — **-phorous comb. form** in corresponding adjectives. [from mod. L. *-phorus*, from Gk. *-phoros, -phoron* 'bearing, bearer,' from *pherein* 'to bear.']

Pho·ron·i·da /fə'ränədə/ Zool. a small phylum of wormlike marine invertebrates. — **pho·ro·nid** /fə'rōnid/ **n.** [mod. L. (pl.), from L. *Phoronis, Phoronid-*, the name of a character in Gk. mythology.]

phos·gene /'fäsjēn/ ▶ **n.** Chem. a colorless poisonous gas, $COCl_2$, made by the reaction of chlorine and carbon monoxide. It was used as a poison gas, notably in World War I. [19th C.: from Gk. *phōs* 'light' + **-GEN,** with ref. to its original production by the action of sunlight on chlorine and carbon monoxide.]

phos·pha·tase /'fäsfə,tās/ ▶ **n.** Biochem. an enzyme that catalyzes the hydrolysis of organic phosphates in a specified (acid or alkaline) environment.

phos·phate /'fäsfāt/ ▶ **n.** **1** Chem. a salt or ester of phosphoric acid, containing PO_43- or a related anion or a group such as $-OPO(OH)_2$. **2** an effervescent soft drink containing phosphoric acid, soda water, and flavoring. [18th C.: from Fr., from *phosphore* 'phosphorus.']

phos·phat·ic /fäs'fatik/ ▶ **adj.** (chiefly of rocks and fertilizer) containing or consisting of phosphates.

phos·pha·tide /'fäsfə,tīd/ ▶ **n.** Biochem. any of a class of compounds that are fatty acid esters of glycerol phosphate with a nitrogen base linked to the phosphate group.

phos·pha·ti·dyl·cho·line /,fäsfə,tīdl'kōlēn; fäs,fatədl-/ ▶ **n.** Biochem. another term for **LECITHIN.**

phos·phene /ˈfäsfēn/ ▶ **n.** a ring or spot of light produced by pressure on the eyeball or direct stimulation of the visual system other than by light. [19th C.: formed irregularly from Gk. *phōs* 'light' + *phainein* 'to show.']

phos·phide /ˈfäsfīd/ ▶ **n.** Chem. a binary compound of phosphorus with another element or group.

phos·phine /ˈfäsfēn/ ▶ **n.** Chem. a colorless foul-smelling gaseous compound, PH_3, of phosphorus and hydrogen, analogous to ammonia. [19th C.: from PHOSPHO- 'relating to phosphorus' + -INE[4], on the pattern of *amine*.]

phos·phite /ˈfäsfīt/ ▶ **n.** Chem. old-fashioned term for *PHOSPHONATE* (see PHOSPHONIC ACID).

phospho- ▶ **comb. form** representing PHOSPHORUS.

phos·pho·cre·a·tine /ˌfäsfōˈkrēətin/ ▶ **n.** Biochem. a phosphate ester of creatine found in vertebrate muscle, where it serves to store phosphates to provide energy for muscular contraction.

phos·pho·li·pase /ˌfäsfōˈlīpās/ ▶ **n.** Biochem. an enzyme that hydrolyzes lecithin or a similar phospholipid.

phos·pho·lip·id /ˌfäsfōˈlipid/ ▶ **n.** Biochem. a lipid containing a phosphate group in its molecule, e.g., lecithin.

phos·phon·ic ac·id /fäsˈfänik/ ▶ **n.** Chem. a crystalline acid, $HPO(OH)_2$, obtained by the reaction of phosphorus trioxide with water. — **phos·pho·nate** /ˈfäsfəˌnāt/ **n.** [19th C.: *phosphonic* from PHOSPHO- 'relating to phosphorus,' on the pattern of *sulfonic*.]

phos·pho·ni·um /fäsˈfōnēəm/ ▶ **n.** see PHOSPHINE. [19th C.: blend of PHOSPHORUS and AMMONIUM.]

phos·pho·pro·tein /ˌfäsfōˈprōtēn/ ▶ **n.** Biochem. a protein that contains phosphorus (other than in a nucleic acid or a phospholipid).

phos·phor /ˈfäsfər/ ▶ **n.** a synthetic fluorescent or phosphorescent substance, esp. any of those used to coat the screens of cathode-ray tubes. ■ old-fashioned term for PHOSPHORUS. [17th C.: from L. *phosphorus*.]

phos·pho·rat·ed /ˈfäsfəˌrātid/ ▶ **adj.** combined or impregnated with phosphorus.

phos·pho·resce /ˌfäsfəˈres/ ▶ **v.** [intrans.] emit light or radiation by phosphorescence.

phos·pho·res·cence /ˌfäsfəˈresəns/ ▶ **n.** light emitted by a substance without combustion or perceptible heat. ■ Physics the emission of radiation in a similar manner to fluorescence but on a longer timescale, so that emission continues after excitation ceases. — **phos·pho·res·cent** **adj.**

phos·phor·ic /fäsˈfôrik/ ▶ **adj.** relating to or containing phosphorus. ■ Chem. of phosphorus with a valence of five. Compare with PHOSPHOROUS.

phos·phor·ic ac·id ▶ **n.** Chem. a crystalline acid, H_3PO_4, obtained, e.g., by treating phosphates with sulfuric acid, and used in fertilizer and soap manufacture and in food processing.

phos·pho·rite /ˈfäsfəˌrīt/ ▶ **n.** a sedimentary rock containing a high proportion of calcium phosphate.

phos·pho·rous /ˈfäsfərəs; fäsˈfôrəs/ ▶ **adj.** relating to or containing phosphorus. Compare with PHOSPHORIC. ■ Chem. of phosphorus with a valence of three. ■ phosphorescent.

phos·pho·rous ac·id ▶ **n.** another term for PHOSPHONIC ACID.

phos·pho·rus /ˈfäsfərəs/ ▶ **n.** the chemical element of atomic number 15, a poisonous, combustible nonmetal that exists in two common allotropic forms, **white phosphorus**, a yellowish waxy solid that ignites spontaneously in air and glows in the dark, and **red phosphorus**, a less reactive form used in making matches. (Symbol: **P**) [17th C.: from L., from Gk. *phōsphoros*, from *phōs* 'light' + *-phoros* '-bringing.']

phos·pho·ryl·ase /ˈfäsfərəˌlās; fäsˈfôrəˌlās/ ▶ **n.** Biochem. an enzyme that introduces a phosphate group into an organic molecule, notably glucose.

phos·pho·ryl·ate /ˈfäsfərəˌlāt; fäsˈfôrə-/ ▶ **v.** [trans.] (often **be phosphorylated**) esp. Biochem. introduce a phosphate group into (a molecule or compound). — **phos·pho·ryl·a·tion** /ˈfäsfərəˈlāshən/ **n.**

phot /fōt/ ▶ **n.** a unit of illumination equal to one lumen per square centimeter. [20th C.: from Gk. *phōs, phōt-* 'light.']

pho·tic /ˈfōtik/ ▶ **adj.** tech. of or relating to light, esp. as an agent of chemical change or physiological response. ■ Ecol. denoting the layers of the ocean reached by sufficient sunlight to allow plant growth.

pho·ti·no /fōˈtēnō/ ▶ **n.** (pl. **-nos**) Physics the hypothetical supersymmetric counterpart of the photon, with spin −12. [1970s: from PHOTON + *-ino* from NEUTRINO.]

pho·to /ˈfōtō/ ▶ **n.** (pl. **-tos**) a photograph. ■ informal a photo finish.

photo- ▶ **comb. form** **1** relating to light. **2** relating to photography. [sense 1 from Gk. *phōs, phōt-* 'light'; sense 2, abbrev. of PHOTOGRAPHY.]

pho·to·ac·tive /ˌfōtōˈaktiv/ ▶ **adj.** (of a substance) capable of a chemical or physical change in response to illumination.

pho·to·bi·ol·o·gy /ˌfōtōbīˈäləjē/ ▶ **n.** the study of the effects of light on living organisms.

pho·to·cath·ode /ˌfōtōˈkathōd/ ▶ **n.** a cathode that emits electrons when illuminated, causing an electric current.

pho·to CD ▶ **n.** a compact disc from which still photographs can be displayed on a television screen or computer monitor. ■ the storing and reproducing of photographs in this way.

pho·to·cell /ˈfōtōˌsel/ ▶ **n.** short for PHOTOELECTRIC CELL.

pho·to·chem·i·cal /ˌfōtōˈkemikəl/ ▶ **adj.** of, relating to, or caused by the chemical action of light. ■ of or relating to photochemistry. — **pho·to·chem·i·cal·ly** **adv.**

pho·to·chem·is·try /ˌfōtōˈkeməstrē/ ▶ **n.** the branch of chemistry concerned with the chemical effects of light.

pho·to·chro·mic /ˌfōtəˈkrōmik/ ▶ **adj.** (of a substance) undergoing a reversible change in color or shade when exposed to light of a particular frequency or intensity. — **pho·to·chro·mism** **n.** [1950s: from PHOTO- + Gk. *khrōma* 'color.']

pho·to·co·ag·u·la·tion /ˌfōtōkōˌagyəˈlāshən/ ▶ **n.** Med. the use of a laser beam or other intense light source to coagulate and destroy or fuse small areas of tissue, esp. in the retina.

pho·to·com·po·si·tion /ˌfōtōˌkämpəˈzishən/ ▶ **n.** Print. the setting of material to be printed by projecting it onto photographic film from which the printing surface is prepared.

pho·to·con·duc·tiv·i·ty /ˌfōtōˌkändəkˈtivitē/ ▶ **n.** increased electrical conductivity caused by the presence of light. — **pho·to·con·duc·tive** /-kənˈdəktiv/ **adj.** **pho·to·con·duc·tor** /-kənˈdəktər/ **n.**

pho·to·cop·i·er /ˈfōtəˌkäpēər/ ▶ **n.** a machine for making photocopies.

pho·to·cop·y /ˈfōtəˌkäpē/ ▶ **n.** (pl. **-cop·ies**) a photographic copy of printed or written material produced by a process involving the action of light on a specially prepared surface. ▶ **v.** (**-cop·ies**, **-cop·ied**) [trans.] make a photocopy of. — **pho·to·cop·i·a·ble** /-ˌkäpēəbəl/ **adj.**

pho·to·cur·rent /ˌfōtōˈkərənt/ ▶ **n.** an electric current induced by the action of light.

pho·to·de·grad·a·ble /ˌfōtōdəˈgrādəbəl/ ▶ **adj.** capable of being decomposed by the action of light, esp. sunlight.

pho·to·de·tec·tor /ˌfōtōdəˈtektər/ ▶ **n.** a device that detects or responds to incident light by using the electrical effect of individual photons.

pho·to·di·ode /ˈfōtōˌdīōd/ ▶ **n.** a semiconductor diode that, when exposed to light, generates a potential difference or changes its electrical resistance.

pho·to·dis·so·ci·a·tion /ˌfōtōdiˌsōsēˈāshən/ ▶ **n.** Chem. dissociation of a chemical compound by the action of light.

pho·to·dy·nam·ic /ˌfōtōdīˈnamik/ ▶ **adj.** Med. denoting treatment for cancer involving the injection of a cytotoxic compound that is relatively inactive until activated by a laser beam after collecting in the tumor.

pho·to·e·lec·tric /ˌfōtō-iˈlektrik/ ▶ **adj.** characterized by or involving the emission of electrons from a surface by the action of light. — **pho·to·e·lec·tric·i·ty** /ˌfōtō-ilekˈtrisitē/ **n.**

pho·to·e·lec·tric cell ▶ **n.** a device that generates an electric current or voltage dependent on the degree of illumination.

pho·to·e·lec·tron /ˌfōtō-iˈlekˌträn/ ▶ **n.** an electron emitted from an atom by interaction with a photon, esp. an electron emitted from a solid surface by the action of light. — **pho·to·e·lec·tron·ic** /-ilekˈtränik/ **adj.**

pho·to·e·mis·sion /ˌfōtō-iˈmishən/ ▶ **n.** the emission of electrons from a surface caused by the action of light striking it. — **pho·to·e·mit·ter** /-iˈmitər/ **n.**

pho·to fin·ish ▶ **n.** a close finish of a race in which the winner is identifiable only from a photograph taken as the competitors cross the finish line.

pho·tog /fəˈtäg/ ▶ **n.** informal a photographer.

pho·to·gen·ic /ˌfōtəˈjenik/ ▶ **adj.** **1** (esp. of a person) looking attractive in photographs or on film. **2** Biol. (of an organism or tissue) producing or emitting light. — **pho·to·gen·i·cal·ly** **adv.**

pho·to·ge·ol·o·gy /ˌfōtōjēˈäləjē/ ▶ **n.** the field of study concerned with the geological interpretation of aerial photographs. — **pho·to·ge·o·log·i·cal** /-ˌjēəˈläjikəl/ **adj.** **pho·to·ge·ol·o·gist** **n.**

pho·to·gram /ˈfōtəˌgram/ ▶ **n.** a picture produced with photographic materials, such as light-sensitive paper, but without a camera.

pho·to·gram·me·try /ˌfōtəˈgramitrē/ ▶ **n.** the use of photography in surveying and mapping to ascertain measurements between objects. — **pho·to·gram·met·ric** /-grəˈmetrik/ **adj.** **pho·to·gram·me·trist** **n.**

pho·to·graph /ˈfōtəˌgraf/ ▶ **n.** a picture made using a camera, in which an image is focused onto film or other light-sensitive material and then made visible and permanent by chemical treatment. ▶ **v.** [trans.] take a photograph of. ■ [intrans.] appear in a particular way when in a photograph. — **pho·to·graph·a·ble** **adj.** **pho·tog·ra·pher** /fəˈtägrəfər/ **n.** **pho·to·graph·ic** /ˌfōtəˈgrafik/ **adj.** **pho·to·graph·i·cal·ly** /ˌfōtəˈgrafik(ə)lē/ **adv.**

pho·to·graph·ic mem·o·ry /ˌfōtəˈgrafik/ ▶ **n.** the ability to remember information or visual images in great detail.

pho·tog·ra·phy /fəˈtägrəfē/ ▶ **n.** the art or practice of taking and processing photographs.

pho·to·gra·vure /ˌfōtəgrəˈvyo͝or/ ▶ **n.** an image produced from a photographic negative transferred to a metal plate and etched in. ■ the production of images in this way. [19th C.: from Fr., from *photo-* + *gravure* 'engraving.']

pho·to·i·o·ni·za·tion /ˌfōtōˌīəniˈzāshən/ ▶ **n.** Physics ionization produced in a medium by the action of electromagnetic radiation.

pho·to·jour·nal·ism /ˌfōtōˈjərnəˌlizəm/ ▶ **n.** the art or practice of communicating news by photographs, esp. in magazines. — **pho·to·jour·nal·ist** **n.**

pho·to·li·thog·ra·phy /ˌfōtōliˈthägrəfē/ ▶ **n.** lithography using plates made photographically. — **pho·to·lith·o·graph·ic** /-ˌlithəˈgrafik/ **adj.** **pho·to·lith·o·graph·i·cal·ly** /-ˌlithəˈgrafik(ə)lē/ **adv.**

pho·tol·y·sis /fōˈtäləsis/ ▶ **n.** Chem. the decomposition or separation of molecules by the action of light. — **pho·to·lyze** /ˈfōtl,īz/ **v.** **pho·to·lyt·ic** /,fōtlˈitik/ **adj.**

pho·to·map /ˈfōtō,map/ ▶ **n.** a map made from or drawn on photographs of the area concerned.

pho·to·mask /ˈfōtō,mask/ ▶ **n.** Electron. a photographic pattern used in making microcircuits, ultraviolet light being shone through the mask onto a photoresist in order to transfer the pattern.

pho·to·me·chan·i·cal /,fōtōməˈkanikəl/ ▶ **adj.** relating to or denoting processes in which photography is involved in the making of a printing plate. — **pho·to·me·chan·i·cal·ly** **adv.**

pho·tom·e·ter /fōˈtämitər/ ▶ **n.** an instrument for measuring the intensity of light. — **pho·to·met·ric** /,fōtəˈmetrik/ **adj.** **pho·to·met·ri·cal·ly** /,fōtōˈmetrik(ə)lē/ **adv.** **pho·tom·e·try** /-ˈtämətrē/ **n.**

pho·to·mi·cro·graph /,fōtōˈmīkrō,graf/ ▶ **n.** a photograph of a microscopic object, taken with the aid of a microscope. — **pho·to·mi·crog·ra·pher** /-mīˈkrägrəfər/ **n.** **pho·to·mi·crog·ra·phy** /,fōtō,mīˈkrägrəfē/ **n.**

pho·to·mon·tage /,fōtōmänˈtäZH/ ▶ **n.** a montage constructed from photographic images. ■ the technique of constructing such a montage.

pho·to·mul·ti·pli·er /,fōtōˈməltəplīər/ ▶ **n.** an instrument containing a photoelectric cell and a series of electrodes, used to detect and amplify the light from very faint sources.

pho·to·mur·al /,fōtōˈmyo͝orəl/ ▶ **n.** a mural consisting of a single enlarged photograph or a collection of photographs covering a wall.

pho·ton /ˈfōtän/ ▶ **n.** Physics a particle representing a quantum of light or other electromagnetic radiation. A photon carries energy proportional to the radiation frequency but has zero rest mass. [20th C.: from Gk. *phōs, phōt-* 'light.']

pho·to·neg·a·tive /,fōtōˈnegətiv/ ▶ **adj.** **1** Biol. (of an organism) tending to move away from light. **2** Physics (of a substance) exhibiting a decrease in electrical conductivity under illumination.

pho·ton·ics /fōˈtäniks/ ▶ **plural n.** [treated as sing.] the branch of technology concerned with the properties and transmission of photons, for example in fiber optics.

pho·to-off·set ▶ **n.** offset printing using plates made photographically.

pho·to op /ˈfōtō äp/ ▶ **n.** informal term for PHOTO OPPORTUNITY.

pho·to op·por·tu·ni·ty ▶ **n.** an occasion on which famous people pose for photographers by arrangement.

pho·to·pe·ri·od /ˈfōtō,pi(ə)rēəd/ ▶ **n.** Bot. Zool. the period of time each day during which an organism receives illumination; day length. — **pho·to·pe·ri·od·ic** /,fōtō,pi(ə)rēˈädik/ **adj.**

pho·to·pe·ri·od·ism /,fōtōˈpi(ə)rēə,dizəm/ (also **pho·to·pe·ri·o·dic·i·ty** /-,pi(ə)rēəˈdisitē/) ▶ **n.** Bot. Zool. the response of an organism to seasonal changes in day length.

pho·to·pho·bi·a /,fōtəˈfōbēə/ ▶ **n.** extreme sensitivity to light. — **pho·to·pho·bic** /,fōtəˈfōbik/ **adj.**

pho·to·phore /ˈfōtə,fôr/ ▶ **n.** Zool. a light-producing organ in certain fishes and other animals. [19th C.: from Gk. *phōtophoros* 'light-bearing.']

pho·top·ic /fōˈtäpik/ ▶ **adj.** Physiol. relating to or denoting vision in daylight or other bright light, believed to involve chiefly the cones of the retina. Often contrasted with SCOTOPIC. [20th C.: from PHOTO- + -OPIA.]

pho·to·pig·ment /,fōtōˈpigmənt/ ▶ **n.** a pigment whose chemical state depends on its degree of illumination, such as those in the retina of the eye.

pho·to·po·lar·im·e·ter /,fōtə,pōləˈrimitər/ ▶ **n.** a telescopic apparatus for photographing stars, galaxies, etc., and measuring the polarization of light from them.

pho·to·pol·y·mer /,fōtōˈpäləmər/ ▶ **n.** a light-sensitive polymeric material, esp. one used in printing plates or microfilms.

pho·to·pos·i·tive /,fōtōˈpäzitiv/ ▶ **adj.** **1** Biol. (of an organism) tending to move toward light. **2** Physics (of a substance) exhibiting an increase in electrical conductivity under illumination.

pho·to·re·cep·tor /,fōtōriˈseptər/ ▶ **n.** a structure in a living organism, esp. a sensory cell or sense organ, that responds to light falling on it. — **pho·to·re·cep·tive** /ˈseptiv/ **adj.**

pho·to·re·con·nais·sance /,fōtōriˈkänəsəns/ ▶ **n.** military reconnaissance carried out by means of aerial photography.

pho·to·re·sist /,fōtōriˈzist/ ▶ **n.** a photosensitive resist that, when exposed to light, loses its resistance or its susceptibility to attack by an etchant or solvent. Such materials are used in making microcircuits.

pho·to·res·pi·ra·tion /,fōtō,respəˈrāSHən/ ▶ **n.** Bot. a respiratory process in many higher plants by which they take up oxygen in the light and give out some carbon dioxide, contrary to the general pattern of photosynthesis.

pho·to·sen·si·tive /,fōtəˈsensitiv/ ▶ **adj.** having a chemical, electrical, or other response to light. — **pho·to·sen·si·tiv·i·ty** /-,sensəˈtivitē/ **n.**

pho·to·shop /ˈfōtō,SHäp/ (also **Pho·to·shop**) ▶ **v.** (**-shopped, -shop·ping**) [trans.] alter (a photographic image) digitally using computer software: [as adj.] (**photoshopped**) *goofy photoshopped pictures of politicians.* [1990s: from *Adobe Photoshop*, the proprietary name for a software package for the digital editing of photographic images.]

pho·to·sphere /ˈfōtə,sfi(ə)r/ ▶ **n.** Astron. the luminous envelope of a star from which its light and heat radiate. — **pho·to·spher·ic** /,fōtəˈsfi(ə)rik; ˈsferik/ **adj.**

pho·to·stat /ˈfōtō,stat/ (also **Pho·to·stat**) ▶ **n.** trademark a type of machine for making photocopies on special paper. ■ a copy made by this means. ▶ **v.** (**-stat·ed, -stat·ing**) [trans.] make a copy of (a document) using a photostat machine. — **pho·to·stat·ic** /,fōtōˈstatik/ **adj.**

pho·to·syn·the·sis /,fōtōˈsinTHəsis/ ▶ **n.** the process by which green plants and some other organisms use sunlight to synthesize foods from carbon dioxide and water. It generally involves the green pigment chlorophyll and generates oxygen as a byproduct. — **pho·to·syn·thet·ic** /-,sinˈTHetik/ **adj.** **pho·to·syn·thet·i·cal·ly** /-,sinˈTHetik(ə)lē/ **adv.**

pho·to·syn·the·size /,fōtōˈsinTHə,sīz/ ▶ **v.** [intrans.] (of a plant) synthesize sugars or other substances by means of photosynthesis.

pho·to·sys·tem /ˈfōtō,sistəm/ ▶ **n.** a biochemical mechanism in plants by which chlorophyll absorbs light energy for photosynthesis. There are two such mechanisms (**photosystems I** and **II**) involving different chlorophyll–protein complexes.

pho·to·tax·is /,fōtōˈtaksis/ ▶ **n.** (pl. **-tax·es** /-ˈtaksēz/) Biol. the bodily movement of a motile organism in response to light, either toward the source of light (**positive phototaxis**) or away from it (**negative phototaxis**). Compare with PHOTOTROPISM. ■ a movement of this kind. — **pho·to·tac·tic** /-ˈtaktik/ **adj.**

pho·to·ther·a·py /,fōtōˈTHerəpē/ ▶ **n.** the use of light in the treatment of physical or mental illness.

pho·to·tran·sis·tor /,fōtō,tranˈzistər/ ▶ **n.** a transistor that responds to light striking it by generating and amplifying an electric current.

pho·to·troph /ˈfōtə,träf/ ▶ **n.** Biol. a phototrophic organism.

pho·to·troph·ic /,fōtəˈträfik/ ▶ **adj.** Biol. (of an organism) obtaining energy from sunlight to synthesize organic compounds for nutrition.

pho·tot·ro·pism /,fōtəˈtrōpizəm; fōˈtätrə,pizəm/ ▶ **n.** Biol. the orientation of a plant or other organism in response to light, either toward the source of light (**positive phototropism**) or away from it (**negative phototropism**). Compare with HELIOTROPISM, PHOTOTAXIS. — **pho·to·trop·ic** /,fōtəˈtrōpik; -ˈträpik/ **adj.**

pho·to·tube /ˈfōtō,t(y)o͞ob/ ▶ **n.** Electron. a photocell in the form of an electron tube with a photoemissive cathode.

pho·to·type·set·ter /,fōtōˈtīp,setər/ ▶ **n.** a machine for photocomposition. — **pho·to·type·set** **adj.** **pho·to·type·set·ting** **n.**

pho·to·vol·ta·ic /,fōtəvōlˈtāik; ,fōtōväl-/ ▶ **adj.** relating to the production of electric current at the junction of two substances exposed to light.

pho·to·vol·ta·ics /,fōtəvōlˈtāiks; ,fōtōväl-/ ▶ **plural n.** [treated as sing.] the branch of technology concerned with the production of electric current at the junction of two substances. ■ [treated as pl.] devices having such a junction.

phr. ▶ **abbr.** phrase.

phrag·mi·tes /fragˈmītēz/ ▶ **n.** a common and invasive tall reed (genus *Phragmites*), esp. the **common reed** (*P. communis*). [mod. L., from Gk. *phragmitēs* 'growing in hedges,' from *phragma* 'hedge.']

phras·al /ˈfrāzəl/ ▶ **adj.** [attrib.] Gram. consisting of a phrase or phrases. — **phras·al·ly** **adv.**

phras·al verb ▶ **n.** Gram. an idiomatic phrase consisting of a verb and another element, typically either an adverb, as in *break down*, or a preposition, for example *see to*, or a combination of both, such as *look down on*.

phrase /frāz/ ▶ **n.** a small group of words standing together as a conceptual unit, typically forming a component of a clause. ■ an idiomatic or short pithy expression. ■ Music a group of notes forming a distinct unit within a longer passage. ■ Ballet a group of steps within a longer sequence or dance. ▶ **v.** [trans.] put into a particular form of words. ■ divide (music) into phrases in a particular way, esp. in performance.
– PHRASES **turn of phrase** a manner of expression: ***an awkward turn of phrase.*** [16th C.: via late L. from Gk. *phrasis*, from *phrazein* 'declare, tell.']

phra·se·ol·o·gy /,frāzēˈäləjē/ ▶ **n.** (pl. **-gies**) a mode of expression, esp. one characteristic of a particular speaker or writer. — **phra·se·o·log·i·cal** /-zēəˈläjikəl/ **adj.** [17th C.: from mod. L. *phraseologia*, from Gk. *phraseōn*, genitive pl. of *phrasis* 'a phrase' + *-logia* (see -LOGY).]

phra·try /ˈfrātrē/ ▶ **n.** (pl. **-tries**) Anthropol. a descent group or kinship group in some tribal societies. [19th C.: from Gk. *phratria*, from *phratēr* 'clansman.']

phreak·ing /ˈfrēkiNG/ ▶ **n.** informal the action of hacking into telecommunications systems, esp. to obtain free calls. — **phreak** **n.** **phreak·er** /ˈfrēkər/ **n.** [1970s: alt. of *freaking*.]

phre·at·ic /frēˈatik/ ▶ **adj.** Geol. relating to or denoting underground water in the zone of saturation (beneath the water table). Compare with VADOSE. ■ (of a volcanic eruption) caused by the heating and expansion of groundwater. [19th C.: from Gk. *phrear, phreat-* 'a well.']

phre·at·o·phyte /frēˈatə,fīt/ ▶ **n.** Bot. a plant with a deep root system that draws its water supply from near the water table. — **phre·at·o·phyt·ic** /-,atəˈfitik/ **adj.** [1920s: from Gk. *phrear, phreat-* 'a well.']

phren·ic /ˈfrenik/ ▶ **adj.** [attrib.] **1** Anat. of or relating to the diaphragm. **2** of or relating to the mind or mental activity. [18th C.: from Fr. *phrénique*, from Gk. *phrēn, phren-* 'diaphragm, mind.']

phre·nol·o·gy /freˈnäləjē/ ▶ **n.** esp. hist. the detailed study of the shape and size of the cranium as a supposed indication of character and mental abilities. — **phre·no·log·i·cal** /,frenlˈäjikəl/ **adj.** **phre·nol·o·gist** **n.** [19th C.: from Gk. *phrēn, phren-* 'mind.']

Phryg·i·a /ˈfrijēə/ an ancient region in west central Asia Minor, to the south of Bithynia.

Phryg·i·an /ˈfrijēən/ ▶ **adj.** of or relating to Phrygia, its people, or their language. ▶ **n. 1** a native or inhabitant of ancient Phrygia. **2** the extinct Indo-European language of the ancient Phrygians, related to Greek and Armenian, of which only a few inscriptions survive.

Phryg·i·an cap ▶ **n.** a soft conical cap with the top bent forward, worn in ancient times and now identified with the liberty cap.

PHS ▶ **abbr.** Public Health Service.

phthal·ic ac·id /ˈTHalik/ ▶ **n.** Chem. a crystalline acid, $C_6H_4(COOH)_2$, derived from benzene, with two carboxylic acid groups attached to the benzene ring. — **phthal·ate** /ˈTHalˌāt/ **n.** [19th C.: shortening of *naphthalic.*]

phthal·ic an·hy·dride ▶ **n.** Chem. a crystalline compound, $C_6H_4(CO)_2O$, made by oxidizing naphthalene, used as an intermediate in the manufacture of plastics, resins, and dyes.

phthal·o·cy·a·nine /ˌTHaləˈsīəˌnēn/ ▶ **n.** Chem. a greenish-blue crystalline dye, $C_{32}H_{18}N_8$, of the porphyrin group. ■ any of a large class of green or blue pigments and dyes that are chelate complexes of this compound or one of its derivatives with a metal (in particular, copper). [1930s: from *phthalic* (see PHTHALIC ACID) + Gk. *kuan(e)os* 'dark blue.']

Phthi·rap·ter·a /THīˈraptərə/ Entomol. an order of insects comprising the sucking lice and the biting lice. [mod. L. (pl.), from Gk. *phtheir* 'louse' + *pteron* 'wing.']

phthi·sis /ˈTHīsis; ˈtī-/ ▶ **n.** Med., archaic pulmonary tuberculosis or a similar progressive systemic disease. — **phthis·ic** /ˈtizik; ˈTHizik/ **adj.** **phthis·i·cal** /ˈtizikəl; ˈTHiz-/ **adj.** [16th C.: via L. from Gk., from *phthinein* 'to decay.']

phyco- ▶ **comb. form** relating to seaweed: *phycology.* [from Gk. *phukos* 'seaweed.']

phy·col·o·gy /fīˈkäləjē/ ▶ **n.** the branch of botany concerned with seaweeds and other algae. — **phy·co·log·i·cal** /ˌfīkəˈläjikəl/ **adj.** **phy·col·o·gist n.**

Phyfe /fīf/, Duncan (1768–1854) US cabinetmaker; born in Scotland. His furniture is noted for its graceful proportions and precisely carved simple ornaments.

phy·la /ˈfīlə/ plural form of PHYLUM.

phy·lac·ter·y /fīˈlaktərē/ ▶ **n.** (pl. **-ter·ies**) a small leather box containing Hebrew texts on vellum, worn by Jewish men at morning prayer as a reminder to keep the law. [ME: via late L. from Gk. *phulaktērion* 'amulet,' from *phulassein* 'to guard.']

phylactery

phy·let·ic /fīˈletik/ ▶ **adj.** Biol. relating to or denoting the evolutionary development of a species or other group. — **phy·let·i·cal·ly adv.** [19th C.: from Gk. *phuletikos*, from *phuletēs* 'tribesman,' from *phulē* 'tribe.']

phyl·lite /ˈfilīt/ ▶ **n.** Geol. a fine-grained metamorphic rock with a well-developed laminar structure, intermediate between slate and schist. [19th C.: from Gk. *phullon* 'leaf.']

phyl·lo /ˈfēlō/ (also **fi·lo**) ▶ **n.** a kind of dough that can be stretched into thin sheets, used in layers to make pastries, esp. in eastern Mediterranean cooking. [1950s: from mod. Gk. *phullo* 'leaf.']

phyllo- ▶ **comb. form** of a leaf; relating to leaves. [from Gk. *phullon* 'leaf.']

phyl·lo·pod /ˈfiləˌpäd/ ▶ **n.** Zool. a branchiopod crustacean. [from mod. L. *Phyllopoda*, from Gk. *phullon* 'leaf' + *pous, pod-* 'foot.']

phyl·lo·qui·none /ˌfilōˈkwinōn; -kwiˈnōn/ ▶ **n.** Biochem. one of the K vitamins, found in cabbage, spinach, and other leafy green vegetables, and essential for the blood-clotting process. Also called VITAMIN K_1.

phyl·lo·tax·is /ˌfiləˈtaksis/ (also **phyl·lo·tax·y** /ˈfiləˌtaksē/) ▶ **n.** Bot. the arrangement of leaves on an axis or stem. — **phyl·lo·tac·tic** /-ˈtaktik/ **adj.**

phyl·lox·e·ra /fiˈläksərə; ˌfiləkˈsi(ə)rə/ ▶ **n.** a plant louse (*Phylloxera vitifoliae*, family Phylloxeridae) that is a pest of vines. [19th C.: mod. L., from Gk. *phullon* 'leaf' + *xēros* 'dry.']

phy·lo·gen·e·sis /ˌfīləˈjenəsis/ ▶ **n.** Biol. the evolutionary development and diversification of a species or group of organisms, or of a particular feature of an organism. Compare with ONTOGENESIS. — **phy·lo·ge·net·ic** /-jəˈnetik/ **adj.** **phy·lo·ge·net·i·cal·ly** /-jəˈnetik(ə)lē/ **adv.** [19th C.: from Gk. *phulon, phulē* 'race, tribe.']

phy·log·e·ny /fīˈläjənē/ ▶ **n.** the branch of biology that deals with phylogenesis. Compare with ONTOGENY. ■ another term for PHYLOGENESIS. — **phy·lo·gen·ic** /ˌfīləˈjenik/ **adj.** **phy·lo·gen·i·cal·ly** /ˌfīləˈjenik(ə)lē/ **adv.** [19th C.: from Gk. *phulon, phulē* 'race, tribe.']

phy·lum /ˈfīləm/ ▶ **n.** (pl. **-la** /-lə/) Zool. a principal taxonomic category that ranks above class and below kingdom. ■ Ling. a group of languages related to each other less closely than those forming a family, esp. one in which the relationships are disputed or unclear. [19th C.: mod. L., from Gk. *phulon* 'race.']

phys. ▶ **abbr.** ■ physical. ■ physician. ■ physics. ■ physiological. ■ physiology.

phy·sa·lis /ˈfīsəlis; ˈfis-/ ▶ **n.** a nightshade-family plant of a genus (*Physalis*) that includes the cape gooseberry and Chinese lantern, which have an inflated, lanternlike calyx. [mod. L., from Gk. *phusallis* 'bladder.']

phys ed /ˈfiz ˈed/ ▶ **n.** informal short for PHYSICAL EDUCATION.

phys·i·at·rics /ˌfizēˈatriks/ ▶ **plural n.** [treated as sing.] another term for PHYSICAL THERAPY. — **phys·i·at·rist** /ˌfizēˈatrist; fiˈzīəˌtrist/ **n.**

phys·ic /ˈfizik/ archaic ▶ **n.** medicine, esp. a cathartic. ■ the art of healing. ▶ **v.** (**phys·icked** /ˈfizikt/, **phys·ick·ing** /ˈfizikiNG/) [trans.] treat with a medicine. [ME: from OFr. *fisique* 'medicine,' from L. *physica*, from Gk. *phusikē (epistēmē)* '(knowledge) of nature.']

phys·i·cal /ˈfizikəl/ ▶ **adj. 1** of or relating to the body as opposed to the mind. ■ involving bodily contact or activity. ■ sexual. **2** of or relating to things perceived through the senses as opposed to the mind; tangible or concrete. ■ of or relating to physics or the operation of natural forces generally. ▶ **n.** (also **physical examination**) a medical examination to determine a person's bodily fitness.

– PHRASES **get physical** informal become aggressive or violent. ■ become sexually intimate with someone. — **phys·i·cal·i·ty** /ˌfiziˈkalitē/ **n.** **phys·i·cal·ly adv.** **phys·i·cal·ness n.** [ME: from med. L. *physicalis*, from L. *physica.*]

phys·i·cal an·thro·pol·o·gy ▶ **n.** see ANTHROPOLOGY.

phys·i·cal chem·is·try ▶ **n.** the branch of chemistry concerned with the application of the techniques and theories of physics to the study of chemical systems.

phys·i·cal ed·u·ca·tion ▶ **n.** instruction in physical exercise and games, esp. in schools.

phys·i·cal ge·og·ra·phy ▶ **n.** the branch of geography dealing with natural features.

phys·i·cal·ism /ˈfizikəˌlizəm/ ▶ **n.** Philos. the doctrine that the real world consists simply of the physical world. — **phys·i·cal·ist n. & adj.** **phys·i·cal·is·tic** /ˌfizikəˈlistik/ **adj.**

phys·i·cal·ize /ˈfizikəˌlīz/ ▶ **v.** [trans.] express or represent by physical means or in physical terms. — **phys·i·cal·i·za·tion** /ˌfizikəliˈzāsHən/ **n.**

phys·i·cal med·i·cine ▶ **n. 1** the branch of medicine concerned with the treatment of disease by physical means such as manipulation, heat, electricity, or radiation, rather than by medication or surgery. **2** the branch of medicine that treats biomechanical disorders and injuries.

phys·i·cal sci·ences ▶ **plural n.** the sciences concerned with the study of inanimate natural objects, including physics, chemistry, astronomy, and related subjects. Often contrasted with LIFE SCIENCES.

phys·i·cal the·a·ter ▶ **n.** a form of theater that emphasizes the use of physical movement, as in dance and mime, for expression.

phys·i·cal ther·a·py ▶ **n.** the treatment of disease, injury, or deformity by physical methods such as massage, heat treatment, and exercise rather than by drugs or surgery. — **phys·i·cal ther·a·pist n.**

phys·i·cal train·ing ▶ **n.** the systematic use of exercises to promote bodily fitness and strength.

phy·si·cian /fiˈzisHən/ ▶ **n.** a person qualified to practice medicine. ■ a healer. [ME: from OFr. *fisicien*, based on L. *physica* (see PHYSIC).]

phys·i·cian's as·sis·tant ▶ **n.** someone qualified to assist a physician and carry out routine clinical procedures under the supervision of a physician.

phys·i·cist /ˈfizəsist/ ▶ **n.** an expert in or student of physics.

physico- ▶ **comb. form** physical; physical and ...: *physico-mental.* [from PHYSICS.]

phys·i·co·chem·i·cal /ˌfizikōˈkemikəl/ ▶ **adj.** of or relating to physics and chemistry or to physical chemistry.

phys·ics /ˈfiziks/ ▶ **plural n.** [treated as sing.] the branch of science concerned with the nature and properties of matter and energy. The subject matter of physics, distinguished from that of chemistry and biology, includes mechanics, heat, light and other radiation, sound, electricity, magnetism, and the structure of atoms. ■ the physical properties and phenomena of something: *the physics of plasmas.* [15th C. (denoting natural science in general, esp. the Aristotelian system): pl. of obs. *physic* 'physical (thing).']

physio- ▶ **comb. form 1** relating to nature and natural phenomena: *physiography.* **2** representing PHYSIOLOGY. [from Gk. *phusis* 'nature.']

phys·i·o·chem·i·cal /ˌfizēōˈkemikəl/ ▶ **adj.** of or relating to physiological chemistry.

phys·i·o·crat /ˈfizēəˌkrat/ ▶ **n.** a member of an 18th-century group of French economists who believed that agriculture was the source of all wealth and that agricultural products should be highly priced. Advocating adherence to a supposed natural order of social institutions, they also stressed the necessity of free trade. — **phys·i·oc·ra·cy** /ˌfizēˈäkrəsē/ **n.** **phys·i·o·crat·ic** /ˌfizēəˈkratik/ **adj.** [18th C.: from Fr. *physiocrate*, from *physiocratie* 'physiocracy.']

phys·i·og·no·mist /ˌfizēˈä(g)nəmist/ ▶ **n.** a person supposedly able to judge character (or, formerly, to predict the future) from facial characteristics. [16th C.: from OFr. *physionomiste.*]

phys·i·og·no·my /ˌfizēˈä(g)nəmē/ ▶ **n.** (pl. **-mies**) a person's facial features or expression, esp. when regarded as indicative of character or ethnic origin. ■ the supposed art of judging character from facial characteristics. ■ the general form or appearance of something. — **phys·i·og·nom·ic** /ˌfizēəˈnämik/ **adj.** **phys·i·og·nom·i·cal** /ˌfizēəˈnämikəl/ **adj.** **phys·i·og·nom·i·cal·ly** /ˌfizēəˈnämik(ə)lē/ **adv.** [ME: ult. from Gk. *phusiognōmonia* 'judging of a man's nature,' based on *gnōmōn* 'a judge.']

phys·i·og·ra·phy /ˌfizēˈägrəfē/ ▶ **n.** another term for PHYSICAL GEOGRAPHY. — **phys·i·og·ra·pher** /-fər/ **n.** **phys·i·o·graph·ic** /ˌfizēəˈgrafik/ **adj.** **phys·i·o·graph·i·cal** /ˌfizēəˈgrafikəl/ **adj.** **phys·i·o·graph·i·cal·ly** /ˌfizēəˈgrafik(ə)lē/ **adv.** [19th C.: from Fr. *physiographie* (see PHYSIO-, -GRAPHY).]

phys·i·o·log·i·cal sa·line /ˌfizēəˈläjikəl/ ▶ **n.** a solution of salts that is isotonic with the body fluids.

phys·i·ol·o·gy /ˌfizēˈäləjē/ ▶ **n.** the branch of biology that deals with the normal functions of living organisms and their parts. ■ the way in which a living organism or bodily part functions. — **phys·i·o·log·ic** /ˌfizēəˈläjik/ **adj.** **phys·i·o·log·i·cal** /ˌfizēəˈläjikəl/ **adj.** **phys·i·o·log·i·cal·ly** /ˌfizēəˈläjik(ə)lē/ **adv.** **phys·i·ol·o·gist** **n.** [17th C.: ult. from Gk. *phusiologia* (see PHYSIO-, -LOGY).]

phys·i·o·ther·a·py /ˌfizēōˈTHerəpē/ ▶ **n.** British term for PHYSICAL THERAPY. — **phys·i·o·ther·a·pist** /-pist/ **n.**

phy·sique /fiˈzēk/ ▶ **n.** the form, size, and development of a person's body. [19th C.: from Fr., lit. 'physical.']

phy·so·stig·mine /ˌfīsōˈstigˌmēn/ ▶ **n.** Chem. a compound, $C_{15}H_{21}N_3O_2$, that is the active ingredient of the Calabar bean and is used medicinally in eye drops because of its anticholinergic activity. [19th C.: from mod. L. *Physostigma*, a genus.]

-phyte ▶ **comb. form** denoting a plant or plantlike organism: *epiphyte*. — **-phytic** **comb. form** in corresponding adjectives. [from Gk. *phuton* 'a plant,' from *phuein* 'come into being.']

phyto- ▶ **comb. form** of a plant; relating to plants: *phytogeography*. [from Gk. *phuton* (see -PHYTE).]

phy·to·a·lex·in /ˌfītōəˈleksin/ ▶ **n.** Bot. a substance that is produced by plant tissues in response to contact with a parasite and that specifically inhibits the growth of that parasite. [1940s: from PHYTO- + *alexin*.]

phy·to·chem·is·try /ˌfītōˈkeməstrē/ ▶ **n.** the branch of chemistry concerned with plants and plant products. — **phy·to·chem·i·cal** /-ˈkemikəl/ **adj.** **phy·to·chem·ist** **n.**

phy·to·chrome /ˈfītəˌkrōm/ ▶ **n.** Biochem. a blue-green pigment found in many plants, in which it regulates various developmental processes. [19th C.: from PHYTO- + Gk. *khrōma* 'color.']

phy·to·ge·o·graph·i·cal king·dom /ˌfītōjēəˈgrafikəl/ ▶ **n.** Bot. each of a number of major areas of the earth distinguished on the basis of the characteristic plants present. They usually include the Boreal, Paleotropical, Neotropical, Australian, and Antarctic kingdoms.

phy·to·ge·og·ra·phy /ˌfītōjēˈägrəfē/ ▶ **n.** the branch of botany that deals with the geographical distribution of plants. Also called **geobotany**. — **phy·to·ge·og·ra·pher** **n.** **phy·to·ge·o·graph·ic** /ˌfītōˌjēəˈgrafik/ **adj.** **phy·to·ge·o·graph·i·cal** /ˈfītōˌjēəˈgrafikəl/ **adj.** **phy·to·ge·o·graph·i·cal·ly** /ˌfītōˌjēəˈgrafik(ə)lē/ **adv.**

phy·to·he·mag·glu·ti·nin /ˌfītōˌhēməˈglo͞otn-in/ (Brit. **phy·to·hae·mag·glu·ti·nin**) ▶ **n.** Biochem. a toxic plant protein, esp. that extracted from the red kidney bean. It has important medical applications, esp. in immunology, because it can induce mitosis and also causes red blood cells to clump together.

phy·to·lith /ˈfītəlith/ ▶ **n.** Bot. a minute mineral particle formed inside a plant. ■ Paleontol. a fossilized particle of plant tissue.

phy·to·pa·thol·o·gy /ˌfītōpəˈTHäləjē/ ▶ **n.** the study of plant diseases. — **phy·to·path·o·log·i·cal** /-ˌpaTHəˈläjikəl/ **adj.** **phy·to·path·ol·o·gist** /-jist/ **n.**

phy·toph·a·gous /fīˈtäfəgəs/ ▶ **adj.** Zool. (esp. of an insect or other invertebrate) feeding on plants. — **phy·toph·a·gy** **n.**

phy·to·plank·ton /ˌfītōˈplaNGktən/ ▶ **n.** Biol. plankton consisting of microscopic plants.

phy·to·tox·ic /ˌfītəˈtäksik/ ▶ **adj.** Bot. poisonous to plants. ■ of or relating to a poisonous substance derived from a plant. — **phy·to·tox·ic·i·ty** /-ˌtäkˈsisitē/ **n.**

phy·to·tox·in /ˌfītəˈtäksin/ ▶ **n.** Bot. a poisonous substance derived from a plant. ■ a substance that is phytotoxic, esp. one produced by a parasite.

PI ▶ **abbr.** private investigator

pi /pī/ ▶ **n.** the sixteenth letter of the Greek alphabet (Π, π), transliterated as 'p.' ■ the numerical value of the ratio of the circumference of a circle to its diameter (approximately 3.14159). ■ Chem. Physics relating to or denoting an electron or orbital with one unit of angular momentum about an internuclear axis. ▶ **symb.** ■ (π) the numerical value of pi. ■ (Π) osmotic pressure. ■ (Π) mathematical product. [Gk.]

pi·a /ˈpīə; ˈpēə/ ▶ **n.** short for PIA MATER. — **pi·al** /ˈpīəl; ˈpēəl/ **adj.**

Piaf /ˈpēäf; pyäf/, Edith (1915–63), French singer; born *Edith Giovanna Gassion*. She became known as a cabaret and music-hall singer in the late 1930s.

piaffe /pyaf/ ▶ **n.** a movement performed in advanced dressage and classical riding, in which the horse executes a slow, elevated trot without moving forward. ▶ **v.** [intrans.] (of a horse) perform such a movement. [18th C.: from Fr. *piaffer* 'to strut.']

Pia·get /ˌpēəˈZHā; pyä-/, Jean (1896–1980), Swiss psychologist. He studied human thought processes.

pi·a ma·ter /ˈpīə ˈmātər; ˈpēə ˈmätər/ ▶ **n.** Anat. the delicate innermost membrane enveloping the brain and spinal cord. See also MENINGES. [19th C.: from med. L., lit. 'tender mother.']

pia·ni /pēˈänē/ plural form of PIANO².

pi·a·nism /ˈpēəˌnizəm/ ▶ **n.** technical skill or artistry in playing the piano, or in composing piano music. — **pi·a·nis·tic** /ˌpēəˈnistik/ **adj.** **pi·a·nis·ti·cal·ly** /ˌpēəˈnistik(ə)lē/ **adv.**

pi·a·nis·si·mo /ˌpēəˈnisiˌmō/ Music ▶ **adv. & adj.** (esp. as a direction) very soft or softly. ▶ **n.** (pl. **-mos** or **-mi** /-ˌmī/) a passage marked to be performed very softly. [Ital., superlative of *piano* 'soft.']

pi·an·ist /ˈpēənist; pēˈanist/ ▶ **n.** a person who plays the piano, esp. professionally.

pi·an·o¹ /pēˈanō/ ▶ **n.** (pl. **-os**) a large keyboard musical instrument with a wooden case enclosing a soundboard and metal strings, which are struck by hammers when the keys are depressed. The strings' vibration is stopped by dampers when the keys are released, and it can be regulated for length and volume by two or three pedals. [19th C.: from Ital., abbrev. of PIANOFORTE.]

grand piano

pi·an·o² /pēˈänō; pēˈanō/ Music ▶ **adv. & adj.** (esp. as a direction) soft or softly. ▶ **n.** (pl. **-nos** or **-ni** /-nē/) a passage marked to be performed softly. [Ital., lit. 'soft.']

pi·a·no bar ▶ **n.** a bar that features live piano music.

pi·an·o·forte /pēˌanōˈfôrtā; pēˈanōˌfôrt/ ▶ **n.** formal term for PIANO¹. [18th C.: from Ital., earlier *piano e forte* 'soft and loud.']

pi·a·no·la /ˌpēəˈnōlə/ ▶ **n.** trademark a piano equipped to be played automatically using a piano roll. [19th C.: appar. dimin. of PIANO¹.]

pi·an·o roll /pēˈänō/ ▶ **n.** a roll of perforated paper that controls the movement of the keys in a player piano or similar instrument, so producing a particular melody.

pi·as·ter /pēˈastər/ (also **pi·as·tre**) ▶ **n.** a monetary unit of several Middle Eastern countries, equal to one hundredth of a pound. [from Fr., from Ital. *piastra (d'argento)* 'plate (of silver).']

pi·az·za /pēˈätsə; pēˈazə/ ▶ **n.** **1** /pēˈätsə/ a public square or marketplace, esp. in an Italian town. **2** /pēˈazə/ the veranda of a house.

pi·broch /ˈpēbräk/ ▶ **n.** a form of music for the Scottish bagpipes involving elaborate variations on a theme, typically of a martial or funerary character. ■ a piece of such music. [18th C.: from Scot. Gael. *piobaireachd* 'art of piping,' from *piobair* 'piper,' from *piob*, from Engl. PIPE.]

pic /pik/ ▶ **n.** (pl. **pics** or **pix** /piks/) informal a photograph or movie; a picture. [19th C.: abbrev.]

pi·ca¹ /ˈpīkə/ ▶ **n.** Print. a unit of type size and line length equal to 12 points (about 16 inch or 4.2 mm). ■ a size of letter in typewriting, with 10 characters to the inch (about 3.9 to the centimeter). [16th C.: from Anglo-L. *pica* (lit. 'magpie').]

pi·ca² ▶ **n.** Med. a tendency or craving to eat substances other than normal food (such as clay, plaster, or ashes), occurring during childhood or pregnancy, or as a symptom of disease. [16th C.: mod. L., from L., lit. 'magpie,' prob. translating Gk. *kissa* 'magpie.']

pi·ca·dor /ˈpikəˌdôr/ ▶ **n.** a bullfighter on horseback who pricks the bull with a lance to weaken it and goad it. [Sp., from *picar* 'to prick.']

pi·can·te /piˈkantā/ ▶ **adj.** (of food) spicy. [Sp., lit. 'pricking.']

Pic·ar·dy /ˈpikərdē/ a region and former province of northern France. French name PICARDIE.

pic·a·resque /ˌpikəˈresk/ ▶ **adj.** of or relating to an episodic style of fiction dealing with the adventures of a rough and dishonest but appeal-ing hero. [19th C.: from Fr., from Sp. *picaresco*, from *pícaro* 'rogue.']

pic·a·ro /ˈpēkəˌrō/ ▶ **n.** (pl. **-ros**) a rogue. [17th C.: from Sp.]

Pi·cas·so /piˈkäsō; -ˈkasō/, Pablo (1881–1973), Spanish painter. He was the dominant figure in avant-garde art in the first half of the 20th century. — **Pi·cas·so·esque** /-ˌkäsōˈesk; -ˌkasō-/ **adj.**

pic·a·yune /ˌpikiˈyo͞on/ ▶ **adj.** informal petty; worthless. ▶ **n.** a small coin of little value, esp. a 5-cent piece. ■ informal an insignificant person or thing. [19th C.: from Fr. *picaillon*, a coin, from Provençal *picaioun*.]

Pic·ca·dil·ly /ˌpikəˈdilē; ˈpikəˌdilē/ a street in central London, from Hyde Park to Piccadilly Circus.

pic·ca·lil·li /ˈpikəˌlilē/ ▶ **n.** (pl. **-lies** or **-lis**) a relish of chopped vegetables, mustard, and hot spices. [18th C.: prob. from blend of PICKLE and CHILI.]

pic·ca·nin·ny ▶ **n.** chiefly British spelling of PICKANINNY.

pic·ca·ta /piˈkätə/ ▶ **adj.** cooked in a sauce of lemon, parsley and butter.

pic·co·lo /ˈpikəˌlō/ ▶ **n.** (pl. **-los**) a small flute sounding an octave higher than the ordinary one. ■ a player of this instrument in an orchestra. [19th C.: from Ital., 'small (flute).']

pice /pīs/ ▶ **n.** (pl. same) a former monetary unit in the Indian subcontinent, equal to one quarter of an anna. [from Hindi *paisā*.]

pich·i·ci·a·go /ˌpiCHəsēˈāgō/ (also **pich·i·ci·e·go**) ▶ **n.** (pl. **-gos**) another term for FAIRY ARMADILLO. [19th C.: from Spanish, perh. from Guarani *pichey* 'armadillo' + Sp. *ciego* 'blind.']

pick¹ /pik/ ▶ **v.** **1** [trans.] take hold of and remove (a flower, fruit, or vegetable) from where it is growing. ■ [trans.] take hold of and lift or move. ■ [intrans.] (**pick up**) Golf take hold of and lift up one's ball, esp. when conceding a hole. **2** [trans.] choose (someone or something) from a number of alternatives, typically after careful thought. ■ (**pick one's way**) [with adverbial of direction] walk slowly and carefully, selecting the best or safest places to put one's feet. **3** [intrans.] repeatedly pull at something with one's fingers. ■ [trans.] make (a hole) in fabric by doing this. ■ eat food or a meal in small amounts or without much appetite. ■ criticize someone in a niggling way. ■ [trans.] remove unwanted matter from (one's nose or teeth) by using one's finger or a pointed instrument. ■ [trans.] pluck the strings of (a guitar or banjo). ■ [trans.] (**pick something out**) play a tune on such an instrument slowly or with difficulty. ▶ **n.** **1** [in sing.] an act or the right of selecting something from among a group of alternatives. ■ (**the pick of**) informal the person or thing perceived as the best in a particular group. ■ someone or something that has been selected. **2** Basketball an act of blocking

or screening a defensive player from the ball handler, allowing an open shot.
– PHRASES **pick and choose** select only the best or most desirable from among a number of alternatives. **pick someone's brains** (or **brain**) informal obtain information by questioning someone who is better informed about a subject than oneself. **pick something clean** completely remove the flesh from a bone or carcass. **pick a fight** (or **quarrel**) talk or behave in such a way as to provoke an argument or fight. **pick holes in** find fault with. **pick a lock** open a lock with an instrument other than the proper key. **pick someone's pockets** steal something surreptitiously from another person's pocket. **pick someone/something to pieces** (or **apart**) criticize someone or something severely and in detail. **pick up the pieces** restore one's life or a situation to a more normal state, typically after a shock or disaster. **pick up speed** (or **steam**) (of a vehicle) go faster; accelerate.
– PHRASAL VERBS **pick someone/something off** shoot a member of a group of people or things, aiming carefully from a distance. ■ Baseball put out a runner by a pickoff. **pick on** repeatedly single (someone) out for blame, criticism, or unkind treatment in a way perceived to be unfair. **pick someone/something out** distinguish someone or something among a group of people or things. ■ (of a light) illuminate an object by shining directly on it. ■ (usu. **be picked out**) distinguish shapes or letters from their surroundings by painting or fashioning them in a contrasting color or medium. **pick something over** (or **pick through**) examine or sort through a number of items carefully. **pick up** become better; improve. ■ become stronger; increase. **pick oneself up** stand up again after a fall. **pick someone up** go somewhere to collect someone, typically in one's car and according to a prior arrangement. ■ stop for someone and take them into one's vehicle or vessel. ■ informal arrest someone. ■ informal casually strike up a relationship with someone one has never met before, as a sexual overture. **pick something up 1** collect something that has been left elsewhere. ■ informal pay the bill for something, esp. when others have contributed to the expense. ■ tidy a room or building. **2** obtain, acquire, or learn something, esp. without formal arrangements or instruction. ■ catch an illness or infection. **3** detect or receive a signal or sound, esp. by means of electronic apparatus. ■ (also **pick up on**) become aware of or sensitive to something. ■ find and take a particular road or route. **4** (also **pick up**) resume something. ■ (also **pick up on**) refer to or develop a point or topic mentioned earlier. ■ (of an object or color) attractively accentuate the color of something else by being of a similar shade. **pick up after** tidy up things left strewn around by (someone). — **pick·a·ble** adj. [ME: of unknown origin.]

pick[2] ▶n. **1** a tool consisting of a long handle set at right angles in the middle of a curved iron or steel bar with a point at one end and a chisel edge or point at the other, used for breaking up hard ground or rock. ■ short for ICE PICK. **2** an instrument for picking. ■ informal a plectrum. ■ short for TOOTHPICK. [ME: var. of PIKE[2].]

pick·a·back /'pikə,bak/ ▶n., adv., adj., & v. old-fashioned term for PIGGYBACK.

pick·a·nin·ny /'pikə,ninē/ (also **pic·a·nin·ny** or esp. Brit. **pic·ca·nin·ny**) ▶n. (pl. **-nies**) offens. a small black child. [17th C.: from W. Ind. Creole, from Sp. *pequeño* or Port. *pequeno* 'little,' *pequenino* 'tiny.']

pick·ax /'pik,aks/ (also **pick·axe**) ▶n. another term for PICK[2] (sense 1). ▶v. [trans.] break or strike with a pickax. [ME *pikoys*, from OFr. *picois*; rel. to PIKE[2].]

pick·er /'pikər/ ▶n. [usu. with adj.] a person or machine that gathers or collects something. ■ a person who plays a plucked instrument, esp. a guitar, banjo, or mandolin.

pick·er·el /'pik(ə)rəl/ ▶n. (pl. same or **-els**) a small North American pike. Its several species include the **grass** (or **redfin**) **pickerel** (*Esox americanus*). ■ a young pike. [ME: dimin. of PIKE[1].]

pick·er·el·weed /'pik(ə)rəl,wēd/ ▶n. a freshwater plant (*Pontederia cordata*, family Pontederiaceae) with broad arrow-shaped leaves and spikes of blue flowers that was formerly believed to give rise to, or provide food for, young pike.

Pick·er·ing /'pik(ə)riNG/, John (1777–1846), US lexicographer; son of Timothy Pickering. He wrote the first dictionary of Americanisms 1816.

pick·et /'pikit/ ▶n. **1** a person or group of people standing outside a place of work or other venue, protesting about something or trying to persuade others not to enter during a strike. ■ a blockade of a workplace or other venue staged by such a person or group. **2** esp. hist. a small body of troops or a single soldier sent out to watch for the enemy. ■ a soldier or party of soldiers performing a particular duty. **3** [usu. as adj.] a pointed wooden stake driven into the ground, typically to form a fence or palisade or to tether a horse. See also PICKET FENCE. ▶v. (**-et·ed**, **-et·ing**) [trans.] **1** act as a picket outside (a place of work or other venue). **2** tether (an animal). — **pick·et·er** n. [17th C.: from Fr. *piquet* 'pointed stake,' from *piquer* 'to prick,' from *pic* 'pike.']

pick·et fence ▶n. a wooden fence made of spaced uprights connected by two or more horizontal rails.

pick·et line ▶n. a boundary established by workers on strike, esp. at the entrance to the place of work, that others are asked not to cross.

Pick·ett /'pikit/, George Edward (1825–75), Confederate general in the American Civil War. In 1863, at Gettysburg, he led a disastrously miscalculated infantry assault that became known as "Pickett's Charge."

Pick·ford /'pikfərd/, Mary (1893–1979), US actress; born in Canada; born *Gladys Mary Smith*; known as **America's Sweetheart**. A star of silent movies, she usually played the innocent young heroine, as in *Rebecca of Sunnybrook Farm* (1917). She and future husband Douglas Fairbanks were cofounders of United Artists in 1919.

pick·ings /'pikiNGz/ ▶plural n. **1** profits or gains that are made effortlessly or dishonestly, as by picking. **2** remaining scraps or leftovers.

pick·le /'pikəl/ ▶n. **1** a small cucumber preserved in vinegar, brine, or a similar solution. ■ any food preserved in this way and used as a relish. ■ the liquid used to preserve food or other perishable items. ■ an acid solution for cleaning metal objects. **2** [in sing.] informal a difficult or messy situation. ▶v. [trans.] preserve (food or other perishable items) in vinegar, brine, or a similar solution. ■ immerse (a metal object) in an acid or other chemical solution for cleaning. [ME: from MDu., Mid. Low Ger. *pekel*.]

pick·led /'pikəld/ ▶adj. (of food) preserved in vinegar or brine. ■ [predic.] informal drunk.

pick·ler /'pik(ə)lər/ ▶n. a vegetable or fruit suitable for pickling.

pick·ling /'pik(ə)liNG/ ▶adj. [attrib.] (of food) suitable for being pickled or used in making pickles.

pick·lock /'pik,läk/ ▶n. a person who picks locks. ■ an instrument for picking locks.

pick-me-up ▶n. informal a thing that makes one feel more energetic or cheerful. ■ an alcoholic drink.

pick·ney /'piknē/ ▶n. black English a child: *me and the pickney have to survive some way.* Compare with PICKANINNY. [contr. of PICKANINNY.]

pick·off /'pik,ôf; 'pik,äf/ ▶n. Baseball the putout of a runner leading off base, involving an unexpected throw to a base by the pitcher or the catcher while the batter is still at bat.

pick·pock·et /'pik,päkət/ ▶n. a person who steals from other people's pockets. ▶v. [trans.] steal from the pockets of (someone). ■ [intrans.] steal from other people's pockets.

Pick's dis·ease /piks/ ▶n. a rare form of progressive dementia, typically occurring in late middle age and often familial, involving localized atrophy of the brain. [20th C.: named after Arnold *Pick* (1851–1924), Bohemian neurologist.]

pick·up /'pik,əp/ ▶n. **1** (also **pickup truck**) a small truck with an enclosed cab and open back. **2** an act of collecting a person or goods, esp. in a vehicle. **3** the reception of signals, esp. interference or noise, by electrical apparatus. **4** informal a casual encounter with someone, with a view to having a sexual relationship. ■ a person met in such an encounter. **5** an improvement in an economic indicator. **6** a device that produces an electrical signal in response to some other kind of signal or change, in particular: ■ the cartridge of a record player, carrying the stylus. ■ a device on a musical instrument, particularly an electric guitar, that converts sound vibrations into electrical signals for amplification. **7** Music a series of introductory notes leading into the opening part of a tune. **8** Fishing a semicircular loop of metal for guiding the line back onto the spool as it is reeled in. ▶adj. informal and spontaneous.

Pick·wick·i·an /pik'wikēən/ ▶adj. of or like Mr. Pickwick in Dickens's *Pickwick Papers*, esp. in being jovial, plump, or generous. ■ (of words or their senses) misunderstood or misused; not literally meant, esp. to avoid offense.

pick·y /'pikē/ ▶adj. (**pick·i·er**, **pick·i·est**) informal fastidious, esp. excessively so. — **pick·i·ness** n.

pic·nic /'pik,nik/ ▶n. an outing or occasion that involves taking a packed meal to be eaten outdoors. ■ a meal eaten outdoors on such an occasion. ▶v. (**-nicked**, **-nick·ing**) [intrans.] have or take part in a picnic.
– PHRASES **no picnic** informal used of something difficult or unpleasant. — **pic·nick·er** n. [18th C.: from Fr. *pique-nique*.]

pico- ▶comb. form (used in units of measurement) denoting a factor of 10–12: *picosecond*. [from Sp. *pico*, lit. 'beak, peak, little bit.']

Pi·co de O·ri·za·ba /'pēkō de ,ôrē'säbä/ Spanish name for CITLALTÉPETL.

pi·cor·na·vi·rus /pi'kôrnə,vīrəs/ ▶n. any of a group of very small RNA viruses that includes enteroviruses, rhinoviruses, and the virus of foot-and-mouth disease. [1960s: from PICO- + **RNA** + VIRUS.]

pi·cot /'pēkō/ ▶n. [often as adj.] a small loop or series of small loops of twisted thread in lace or embroidery, typically decorating the border of a fabric. [17th C.: from Fr., lit. 'small peak or point,' dimin. of *pic*.]

pic·o·tee /,pikə'tē/ ▶n. a type of carnation whose light-colored flowers have dark-edged petals. [18th C.: from Fr. *picoté(e)*, past part. of *picoter* 'to prick.']

pic·quet /pi'kāt; -'ket/ ▶n. var. of PIQUET.

pic·ric ac·id /'pikrik/ ▶n. Chem. a bitter yellow compound, $C_6H_2(NO_2)_3OH$, obtained by nitrating phenol, used as a dye and in the manufacture of explosives. — **pic·rate** /'pikrāt/ n. [19th C.: from Gk. *pikros* 'bitter.']

pic·rite /'pik,rīt/ ▶n. Geol. a dark basaltic igneous rock rich in olivine. — **pic·rit·ic** /pik'ritik/ adj. [19th C.: from Gk. *pikros* 'bitter.']

pic·ro·tox·in /,pikrə'täksin/ ▶n. Med. a bitter compound obtained from the seeds of the shrub *Anamirta cocculus* (family Menispermaceae), used to stimulate the respiratory and nervous systems, esp. in treating barbiturate poisoning. [19th C.: from Gk. *pikros* 'bitter.']

Pict /pikt/ ▶n. a member of an ancient people inhabiting northern Scotland in Roman times. — **Pict·ish** adj. & n. [from late L. *Picti*, perh. from *pict-* 'painted' (from *pingere* 'to paint').]

pic·to·graph /'piktə,graf/ (also **pic·to·gram** /-,gram/) ▶n. a pictorial symbol for a word or phrase. Pictographs were used as the earliest known form of writing, examples having been discovered in Egypt and Mesopotamia from before 3000 BC. ■ a pictorial representation of statistics on a chart, graph, or computer screen. — **pic·to·graph·ic**

/ˌpiktəˈgrafik/ **adj.** **pic·tog·ra·phy** /pikˈtägrəfē/ **n.** [19th C.: from L. *pict-* 'painted' (from the v. *pingere*).]

Pic·tor /ˈpiktər/ Astron. an inconspicuous southern constellation (the Easel or Painter), close to the star Canopus in Puppis. [L.]

pic·to·ri·al /pikˈtôrēəl/ ▶ **adj.** of or expressed in pictures; illustrated. ■ suggestive of pictures. ▶ **n.** a newspaper or periodical with pictures as a main feature. — **pic·to·ri·al·ly** **adv.** [17th C.: from late L. *pictorius* (from L. *pictor* 'painter,' from *pingere* 'to paint').]

pic·ture /ˈpikCHər/ ▶ **n.** a painting or drawing. ■ a photograph. ■ a portrait. ■ archaic a person or thing resembling another closely. ■ fig. an impression of something formed from an account or description. ■ an image on a television screen. ■ a movie. ■ (**the pictures**) the movies. ▶ **v.** [trans.] (often **be pictured**) represent (someone or something) in a photograph or picture. ■ describe (someone or something) in a certain way. ■ form a mental image of.
– PHRASES **be in pictures** act in movies or work for the motion-picture industry. **get the picture** informal understand a situation. **in the picture** fully informed about something. **out of the picture** no longer involved; irrelevant. **the picture of ——** the embodiment of a specified state or emotion. [ME: from L. *pictura*, from *pict-* 'painted' (from the verb *pingere*).]

pic·ture book ▶ **n.** a book containing many illustrations, esp. one for children.

pic·ture card ▶ **n.** an illustrated card, used esp. in games. ■ another term for FACE CARD.

pic·ture el·e·ment ▶ **n.** see PIXEL.

pic·ture hat ▶ **n.** a woman's highly decorated hat with a wide brim, as shown in pictures by 18th-century English painters such as Reynolds and Gainsborough.

pic·ture plane ▶ **n.** in perspective, the imaginary plane corresponding to the surface of a picture, perpendicular to the viewer's line of sight.

pic·tur·esque /ˌpikCHəˈresk/ ▶ **adj.** visually attractive, esp. in a quaint or pretty style. ■ (of language) unusual and vivid. — **pic·tur·esque·ly** **adv.** **pic·tur·esque·ness** **n.** [18th C.: from Fr. *pittoresque*, from Ital. *pittoresco*, from *pittore* 'painter' (from L. *pictor*).]

pic·ture tube ▶ **n.** Electron. the cathode-ray tube of a television set designed for the reproduction of television pictures.

pic·ture win·dow ▶ **n.** a large window consisting of one pane of glass, typically in a living room.

pic·ture writ·ing ▶ **n.** a mode of recording events by pictorial symbols; pictography.

PID ▶ **abbr.** pelvic inflammatory disease.

pid·dle /ˈpidl/ informal ▶ **v.** [intrans.] urinate. ▶ **n.** [in sing.] an act of urinating. ■ urine.
– PHRASAL VERBS **piddle around** (or **about**) spend time in trifling activities. [16th C.: cf. synonym *peddle*.] — **pid·dler** **n.** [18th C.: prob. from a blend of PISS and PUDDLE.]

pid·dling /ˈpidliNG/ ▶ **adj.** informal pathetically trivial; trifling: *piddling little questions.*

pid·dock /ˈpidək/ ▶ **n.** a bivalve mollusk (*Pholas* and other genera, family Pholadidae) that bores into soft rock or other firm surfaces. The valves of the shell have a conspicuous gap between them and rough frontal ridges to aid in boring. [19th C.: of unknown origin.]

pidg·in /ˈpijən/ ▶ **n.** [often as adj.] a grammatically simplified form of a language with elements taken from local languages, used for communication between people not sharing a common language. ■ (**Pidgin**) another term for TOK PISIN. [19th C.: Chin. alt. of Engl. *business*.]

pie[1] /pī/ ▶ **n.** a baked dish of fruit, or meat and vegetables, typically with a top and base of pastry. ■ a pizza.
– PHRASES **(as) easy as pie** informal very easy. **(as) nice** (or **sweet**) **as pie** extremely pleasant or polite. **a piece** (or **slice**) **of the pie** a share of an amount of money or business available to be claimed or distributed. **pie in the sky** informal used to describe or refer to something that is pleasant to contemplate but is very unlikely to be realized. [ME: prob. the same word as PIE[2].]

pie[2] ▶ **n.** short for MAGPIE. [ME: from OFr., from L. *pica*.]

pie[3] ▶ **n.** a former monetary unit in the Indian subcontinent, equal to one twelfth of an anna. [from Hindi *pā'ī*.]

pie·bald /ˈpīˌbôld/ ▶ **adj.** (of a horse) having irregular patches of two colors, typically black and white. ▶ **n.** a piebald horse or other animal.

piece /pēs/ ▶ **n.** a portion of an object or of material, produced by cutting, tearing, or breaking the whole. ■ one of the items that were put together to make something and into which it naturally divides. ■ an item of a particular type, esp. one forming one of a set. ■ an instance or example. ■ a financial share. ■ a written, musical, or artistic creation or composition. ■ [with adj.] a coin of specified value. ■ a figure or token used to make moves in a board game. ■ Chess a king, queen, bishop, knight, or rook, as opposed to a pawn. ■ informal a firearm. ■ informal, offens. a woman. ▶ **v.** [trans.] (**piece something together**) assemble something from individual parts. ■ slowly make sense of something from separate facts and pieces of evidence.
– PHRASES **a piece of ass** (or **tail**) vulgar slang a person, usually a woman, regarded as a sexual partner. **a piece of cake** see CAKE. **a piece of the action** informal a share in the excitement of something. ■ a share in the profits accruing from something. **go to pieces** become so nervous or upset that one is unable to behave or perform normally. **in one piece** unharmed or undamaged, esp. after a dangerous experience. **(all) of a piece (with something)** (entirely) consistent (with something). **piece by piece** in slow and small stages. **say one's piece** give one's opinion or make a prepared statement. **tear** (or **rip**) **someone/something to pieces** criticize someone or something harshly. [ME: from OFr.]

pièce de ré·sis·tance /pēˈes də ˌrəziˈstäns; -räziˈstäNs/ ▶ **n.** [in sing.] (esp. with reference to creative work or a meal) the most important or remarkable feature. [Fr., lit. 'piece of resistance.']

piece goods ▶ **plural n.** fabrics woven in standard lengths for sale.

piece·meal /ˈpēsˌmēl/ ▶ **adj. & adv.** characterized by unsystematic partial measures taken over a period of time. [ME: from the n. PIECE + *-meal* from OE *mǣlum*, 'measure.']

piece of eight ▶ **n.** hist. a Spanish dollar, equivalent to 8 reals.

piece rate ▶ **n.** a rate of payment for piecework.

piece·work /ˈpēsˌwərk/ ▶ **n.** work paid for according to the amount produced. — **piece·work·er** **n.**

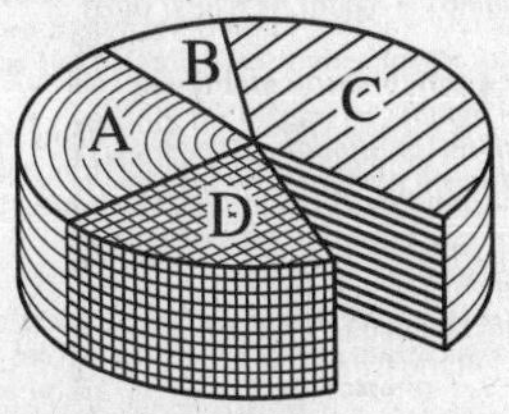

pie chart

pie chart ▶ **n.** a type of graph in which a circle is divided into sectors that each represent a proportion of the whole.

pie crust (also **pie·crust**) ▶ **n.** the baked pastry crust of a pie. ■ the dough used to make pie crusts.

pied /pīd/ ▶ **adj.** having two or more different colors: *pied dogs from the Pyrenees.* [ME: from PIE[2].]

pied-à-terre /ˈpyād ə ˈter/ ▶ **n.** (pl. **pieds-à-terre** pronunc. same) a small apartment, house, or room kept for occasional use. [19th C.: Fr., lit. 'foot to earth.']

Pied·mont /ˈpēdˌmänt/ **1** a region in northwestern Italy; capital, Turin. Italian name PIEMONTE. **2** a hilly highland region in the US, between the Appalachian Mountains and the Atlantic coast. — **Pied·mon·tese** /ˌpēdmänˈtēz; -ˈtēs/ **n. & adj.**

pied·mont /ˈpēdmänt/ ▶ **n.** a gentle slope leading from the base of mountains to a region of flat land. ■ (**the Piedmont**) a hilly region of the eastern US, between the Appalachians and the coastal plain. [19th C.: from Ital. *piemonte* 'mountain foot.']

Pied Pip·er /ˈpīd ˈpīpər/ the hero of *The Pied Piper of Hamelin*, a poem by Robert Browning (1842), based on an old German legend. The piper rid the town of Hamelin of rats by enticing them away with his music, and when refused the promised payment, he lured away the town's children. ■ [as n.] (**a Pied Piper**) a person who entices people to follow them, esp. to their doom.

pie-eyed ▶ **adj.** informal very drunk.

pie-faced ▶ **adj.** informal having a roundish face and typically a blank or stupid expression.

Pie·gan /pēˈgan/ (also **Pei·gan**) ▶ **n.** (pl. same or **-gans**) a member of a North American Indian people of the Blackfoot confederacy. ▶ **adj.** of or relating to this people. [via Cree, from Blackfoot *piikáni* 'Piegan band.']

Pie·mon·te /pyeˈmônte/ Italian name for PIEDMONT.

pier /pi(ə)r/ ▶ **n.** **1** a structure leading out from the shore into a body of water, in particular: ■ a platform supported on pillars or girders, used as a landing stage for boats. ■ a similar structure leading out to sea and used as an entertainment area, typically incorporating arcades and places to eat. ■ a breakwater or mole. **2** a solid support designed to sustain vertical pressure, in particular: ■ a pillar supporting an arch or a bridge. ■ a wall between windows or other adjacent openings. [ME: from med. L. *pera*.]

Pierce /pi(ə)rs/, Franklin (1804–69), 14th president of the US 1853–57. A New Hampshire Democrat, he served as US congressman 1833–37 and US senator 1837–42. His presidency saw the rise of divisions within the country over slavery and the encouragement of settlement in the northwest.

pierce /pi(ə)rs/ ▶ **v.** [trans.] (of a sharp pointed object) go into or through (something). ■ prick (something) with a sharp instrument. ■ make (a hole) with a sharp instrument. ■ make a hole in (the ears, nose, or other part of the body) so as to wear jewelry in them. ■ (usu. **be pierced**) bore a hole or tunnel through. ■ force or cut a way through. — **pierc·er** **n.** [ME: from OFr. *percer*, based on L. *pertus-* 'bored through,' from the v. *pertundere*, from *per* + *tundere* 'thrust.']

pierc·ing /ˈpi(ə)rsiNG/ ▶ **adj.** (of eyes or a look) appearing to see through someone; searching. ■ (of a voice or sound) extremely high, loud, or shrill. ■ (of wind or extreme temperature) seeming to cut through one. ■ (of a feeling) affecting one keenly or deeply. ■ (of mental attributes) sharp; profound. — **pierc·ing·ly** **adv.**

PRONUNCIATION KEY ə *ago, up*; ər *over, fur*; a *hat*; ā *ate*; ä *car*; e *let*; ē *see*; i *fit*; ī *by*; NG *sing*; ō *go*; ô *law, for*; oi *toy*; o͝o *good*; o͞o *goo*; ou *out*; TH *thin*; T̲H̲ *then*; ZH *vision*

pier glass ▶ n. a large mirror, used originally to fill wall space between windows.

pie·ro·gi ▶ n. var. of PIROGI.

Pierre /'pi(ə)r; pē'e(ə)r/ the capital of South Dakota, in the central part of the state; pop. 13,876.

Pi·er·rot /,pēə'rō/ ▶ n. a stock male character in French pantomime, with a sad white-painted face, a loose white costume, and a pointed hat. [Fr., dimin. *Pierre* 'Peter.']

pie·tà /,pēā'tä/ (often **Pie·tà**) ▶ n. a picture or sculpture of the Virgin Mary holding the dead body of Christ on her lap or in her arms. [Ital., from L. *pietas* 'dutifulness.']

Pie·ter·mar·itz·burg /,pētər'marits,bərg/ a city in eastern South Africa; pop. 229,000.

pi·e·tism /'pī-i,tizəm/ ▶ n. pious sentiment, esp. of an exaggerated or affected nature. ■ (usu. **Pietism**) a 17th-century movement for the revival of piety in the Lutheran Church. — **pi·e·tist** n. **pi·e·tis·tic** /,pī-i'tistik/ adj. **pi·e·tis·ti·cal** /,pīə'tistikəl/ adj. **pi·e·tis·ti·cal·ly** /,pīə'tistik(ə)lē/ adv.

pi·e·ty /'pī-itē/ ▶ n. (pl. **-ties**) the quality of being religious or reverent. ■ the quality of being dutiful. ■ a belief or point of view that is accepted with unthinking conventional reverence. [16th C.: ult. from L. *pietas* 'dutifulness,' from *pius* (see PIOUS).]

pi·e·zo /pī'ēzō; pē'āzō/ ▶ adj. piezoelectric.

pi·e·zo·e·lec·tric·i·ty /pē,āzō,ilek'trisitē; pī,ēz-/ ▶ n. electric polarization in a substance (esp. certain crystals) resulting from the application of mechanical stress. — **pi·e·zo·e·lec·tric** /-trik/ adj. **pi·e·zo·e·lec·tri·cal·ly** /-trik(ə)lē/ adv. [19th C.: from Gk. *piezein* 'press, squeeze.']

pi·e·zom·e·ter /,pēə'zämitər; ,pīə'zämitər/ ▶ n. an instrument for measuring the pressure of a liquid or gas, or something related to pressure (such as the compressibility of liquid). Piezometers are often placed in boreholes to monitor the pressure or depth of groundwater. [19th C.: from Gk. *piezein* 'press, squeeze.']

pif·fle /'pifəl/ ▶ n. & exclam. informal nonsense. [19th C.: dimin. of imitative *piff*-.]

pif·fling /'pifliNG/ ▶ adj. informal trivial; unimportant.

Chester white pig

pig /pig/ ▶ n. **1** an omnivorous domesticated hoofed mammal (numerous varieties of *Sus domesticus*) with sparse bristly hair and a flat snout for rooting in the soil, kept for its meat. The **pig family** (Suidae) also includes the warthog and babirusa. ■ a wild animal of this family. ■ a young pig; a piglet. ■ the flesh of a pig, esp. a young one, as food. ■ informal derog. a greedy, dirty, or unpleasant person. ■ informal derog. a police officer. **2** an oblong mass of iron or lead from a smelting furnace. See also PIG IRON. ■ a device that fits snugly inside an oil or gas pipeline and is sent through it to clean or test the inside, or to act as a barrier. ▶ v. (**pigged, pig·ging**) [intrans.] **1** informal gorge oneself with food: *don't pig out on chips.* **2** informal crowd together with other people in disorderly or dirty conditions. **3** (of a sow) give birth to piglets; farrow. **4** operate a pig within an oil or gas pipeline.
– PHRASES **bleed like a pig** bleed copiously. **in a pig's eye** informal expressing scornful disbelief at a statement. **a pig in a poke** something that is bought or accepted without knowing its value or seeing it first. [ME: prob. from the first element of OE *picbrēd* 'acorn,' lit. 'pig bread.']

pi·geon[1] /'pijən/ ▶ n. **1** a stout seed- or fruit-eating bird (family Columbidae) with a small head, short legs, and a cooing voice, typically having gray and white plumage. ■ (also **domestic** or **feral pigeon**) a pigeon descended from the wild rock dove, kept for racing, showing, and carrying messages, and common as a feral bird in towns. **2** informal a gullible person, esp. someone swindled in gambling or the victim of a confidence game. **3** military slang an aircraft from one's own side. [ME: from OFr. *pijon* 'young bird,' based on late L. *pipio(n-)*.]

pi·geon[2] ▶ n. archaic spelling of PIDGIN.

pi·geon breast (also **pigeon chest**) ▶ n. a deformed human chest with a projecting breastbone. — **pi·geon-breast·ed** (also **pi·geon-chest·ed**) adj.

pi·geon hawk ▶ n. another term for MERLIN.

pi·geon-heart·ed ▶ adj. timid; cowardly.

pi·geon·hole /'pijən,hōl/ ▶ n. a small recess for a domestic pigeon to nest in. ■ a small compartment, open at the front and forming part of a set, where letters or messages may be left for someone. ■ a similar compartment built into a desk for keeping documents in. ■ fig. a category to which someone or something is assigned. ▶ v. [trans.] deposit (a document) into a pigeonhole. ■ assign to a particular category or class, esp. in a manner that is too rigid or exclusive. ■ put aside for future consideration.

pi·geon pea ▶ n. **1** a dark red tropical pealike seed. **2** the woody Old World plant (*Cajanus cajan*) of the pea family that yields these seeds, with pods and foliage that are used as fodder.

pi·geon-toed ▶ adj. having the toes or feet turned inward.

pig·fish /'pig,fisH/ ▶ n. (pl. same or **-fish·es**) **1** a deep-bodied scaleless fish (family Congiopodidae) with a protuberant snout, living in the cooler seas of the southern hemisphere. **2** [usu. with adj.] any of a number of other marine fishes, esp. one that grunts.

pig·ger·y /'pigərē/ ▶ n. (pl. **-er·ies**) **1** a farm where pigs are bred or kept. ■ a pigpen. **2** behavior regarded as characteristic of pigs in greed or unpleasantness.

pig·gish /'pigisH/ ▶ adj. resembling a pig, esp. in being greedy or unpleasant. — **pig·gish·ness** n.

pig·gy /'pigē/ ▶ n. (pl. **-gies**) (used by or when talking to children) a pig or piglet. ▶ adj. resembling a pig, esp. in features or appetite.

pig·gy·back /'pigē,bak/ ▶ n. a ride on someone's back and shoulders. ▶ adv. on the back and shoulders of another person. ■ on top of something else. ▶ v. [trans.] carry by or as if by piggyback. ■ mount on or attach to (an existing object or system). ■ [intrans.] use existing work or an existing product as a basis or support. ▶ adj. on the back and shoulders of another person. ■ attached to or riding on a larger object. [16th C.: origin unknown.]

pig·gy bank ▶ n. a container for saving money in, esp. one shaped like a pig, with a slit in the top through which coins are dropped. ■ fig. savings.

pig·head·ed /'pig,hedid/ ▶ adj. stupidly obstinate. — **pig·head·ed·ly** adv. **pig·head·ed·ness** n.

pig i·ron ▶ n. crude iron as first obtained from a smelting furnace, in the form of oblong blocks.

pig Lat·in ▶ n. a version of language formed from English by transferring the initial consonant or consonant cluster of each word to the end of the word and adding a vocalic syllable (usually /ā/): so *chicken soup* would be translated to *ickenchay oupsay*.

pig·let /'piglit/ ▶ n. a young pig.

pig·ment /'pigmənt/ ▶ n. the natural coloring matter of animal or plant tissue. ■ a substance used for coloring or painting, esp. a dry powder that, when mixed with oil, water, or another medium, constitutes a paint or ink. ▶ v. [trans.] [usu. as adj.] (**pigmented**) color (something) with or as if with pigment. — **pig·men·tar·y** /-mən,terē/ adj. [ME, from L. *pigmentum*, from *pingere* 'to paint.']

pig·men·ta·tion /,pigmən'tāsHən/ ▶ n. the natural coloring of animal or plant tissue. ■ the coloring of a person's skin, esp. when abnormal or distinctive.

pig·my ▶ n. var. of PYGMY.

pig·nut /'pig,nət/ ▶ n. **1** a hickory tree that bears nuts with thin husks. Its four North American species include the **pignut hickory** (*C. glabra*). **2** another term for EARTHNUT (sense 1).

pig-out ▶ n. informal a bout of eating a large amount of food.

pig·pen /'pig,pen/ ▶ n. a pen or enclosure for a pig or pigs. ■ a very dirty or untidy house or room.

Pigs, Bay of a bay on the southwestern coast of Cuba, scene of an unsuccessful invasion in 1961 by US-backed Cuban exiles to overthrow Fidel Castro.

pig·skin /'pig,skin/ ▶ n. **1** the hide of a domestic pig. ■ leather made from this. **2** informal a football.

pig·stick·er /'pig,stikər/ ▶ n. informal a long sharp knife or weapon.

pig·stick·ing /'pig,stikiNG/ ▶ n. the sport of hunting wild boar with a spear, typically on horseback.

pig·sty /'pig,stī/ ▶ n. (pl. **-sties**) a pigpen.

pig·tail /'pig,tāl/ ▶ n. **1** a braid or gathered hank of hair hanging from the back of the head, or either of a pair at the sides. **2** a short length of flexible braided wire connecting a stationary part to a moving part in an electrical device. **3** a thin twist of tobacco. — **pig·tailed** adj.

pig·weed /'pig,wēd/ ▶ n. **1** an amaranth (esp. *Amaranthus retroflexus* and *A. albus*) that grows as a weed or is used for fodder. **2** another term for LAMB'S-QUARTERS.

pi·ka /'pīkə; 'pē-/ ▶ n. a small mammal (genus *Ochotona*, family Ochotonidae) related to the rabbits, having rounded ears, short limbs, and a very small tail. [19th C.: from Tungus *piika*.]

Pike /pīk/, Zebulon Montgomery (1779–1813), US soldier and explorer. He led several expeditions into the Louisiana Purchase region, where he came upon (but never climbed) Pike's Peak in Colorado.

northern pike

pike[1] /pīk/ ▶ n. (pl. same) a long-bodied predatory freshwater fish (genus *Esox*, family Esocidae) with a pointed snout and large teeth, of North America and Eurasia. Its five species include the widespread **northern pike** (*E. lucius*). ■ any fish with similar characteristics, such as the walleye. [ME: from PIKE[2].]

pike[2] ▶ n. hist. an infantry weapon with a pointed steel or iron head on a long wooden shaft. ■ esp. Brit. (in names) a hill with a peaked top: *Scafell Pike.* [appar. of Scand. origin; compare Norw. dial. *pīk*.] ▶ v. [trans.] hist. kill or thrust (someone) through with a pike. [16th C.: from Fr. *pique*, based on *pic* 'pick, pike.']

pike[3] ▶ n. short for TURNPIKE.

– PHRASES **come down the pike** appear on the scene; come to notice.

pike[4] (also **pike position**) ▶ n. [often as adj.] a position in diving or gymnastics in which the body is bent at the waist but the legs remain straight. [1920s: of unknown origin.]

pike·man /'pīkmən/ ▶ n. (pl. **-men**) hist. a soldier armed with a pike.

pike·perch /'pīk,pərCH/ ▶ n. (pl. same) a predatory pikelike freshwater fish (genus *Stizostedion*) of the perch family, esp. the walleye.

pik·er /'pīkər/ ▶ n. informal a gambler who makes only small bets. ■ a stingy or cautious person. [19th C.: from *pike* 'withdraw from an agreement.']

Pikes Peak /'pīks/ a mountain in Colorado, in the Front Range of the southern Rocky Mountains.

pike·staff /'pīk,staf/ ▶ n. hist. the wooden shaft of a pike. [16th C.: from PIKE[2] + STAFF[1].]

Pik Po·be·dy /'pēk päb'yedē/ a mountain in eastern Kyrgyzstan, situated close to the border with China. Rising to a height of 24,406 feet (7,439 m), it is the highest peak in the Tien Shan range.

pi·laf /pə'läf; 'pēläf/ (also **pi·laff** or **pi·lau** /-'lô; -'lou; -lô; -lou/ or **pu·lao**) ▶ n. a Middle Eastern or Indian dish of rice or wheat, with vegetables and spices, typically having added meat or fish. [from Turk. *pilâv*.]

pi·las·ter /pə'lastər/ ▶ n. a rectangular column, esp. one projecting from a wall. — **pi·las·tered** adj. [16th C.: from Fr. *pilastre*, based on L. *pila* 'pillar.']

Pi·late /'pīlət/, Pontius (died c.AD 36), Roman procurator of Judaea *c.*26–*c.*36. He presided at the trial of Jesus Christ and authorized his crucifixion.

Pi·la·tes /pi'lätēz/ ▶ n. a system of exercises using special apparatus, designed to improve physical strength, flexibility, and posture, and enhance mental awareness. [1960s: named after German physical fitness specialist Joseph *Pilates* (1880–1967), who devised the system.]

pil·chard /'pilCHərd/ ▶ n. a small, edible, commercially valuable marine fish (*Sardinops* and other genera) of the herring family. [16th C.: of unknown origin.]

Pil·co·ma·yo Riv·er /,pilkə'māyō/ a river that flows from western Bolivia to the Paraguay River.

pile[1] /pīl/ ▶ n. a heap of things laid or lying one on top of another. ■ informal a large amount of something. ■ informal a lot of money. ■ a large imposing building or group of buildings. ■ a series of plates of dissimilar metals laid one on another alternately to produce an electric current. ■ dated term for NUCLEAR REACTOR. ■ archaic a funeral pyre. ▶ v. 1 [trans.] place (things) one on top of another. ■ (**be piled with**) be stacked or loaded with. ■ (**pile up**) [intrans.] increase in quantity: *the work has piled up.* ■ (**pile something up**) cause to increase in quantity. ■ (**pile something on**) informal intensify or exaggerate something for effect. 2 [intrans.] (**pile in/out**) (of a group of people) get into or out of a vehicle in a disorganized manner. ■ (**pile into**) (of a vehicle) crash into.

– PHRASES **pile it on** informal exaggerate the seriousness of a situation or of someone's behavior to increase guilt or distress. [ME: from OFr., from L. *pila* 'pillar, pier.']

pile[2] ▶ n. 1 a heavy beam or post driven vertically into the bed of a river, soft ground, etc., to support the foundations of a superstructure. 2 Heraldry a triangular charge or ordinary formed by two lines meeting at an acute angle, usually pointing down from the top of the shield. ▶ v. [trans.] strengthen or support (a structure) with piles. [OE *pīl* 'dart, arrow,' of Gmc. origin.]

pile[3] ▶ n. the soft projecting surface of a carpet or a fabric such as velvet or flannel, consisting of many small threads. ▶ v. [trans.] [usu. in comb.] (**-piled**) furnish with a pile. [ME: from L. *pilus* 'hair.']

pi·le·at·ed wood·peck·er /'pīlē,ātid; 'pil-/ ▶ n. a large North American woodpecker (*Dryocopus pileatus*) with mainly black plumage and a red cap and crest. [18th C.: from L. *pileatus* 'capped,' from *pileus* 'felt cap.']

pile driv·er (also **pile-driv·er**) ▶ n. a machine for driving piles into the ground. — **pile-driv·ing** n. & adj.

piles /pīlz/ ▶ plural n. hemorrhoids. [ME: prob. from L. *pila* 'ball.']

pile·up /'pīl,əp/ (also **pile-up**) ▶ n. informal 1 a crash involving several vehicles. ■ a confused mass of people fallen on top of one another, esp. in a team game. 2 an accumulation of a specified thing.

pi·le·us /'pīlēəs; 'pil/ ▶ n. (pl. **-le·i** /-lē,ī/) Bot. the cap of a mushroom or toadstool. [18th C.: from L., lit. 'felt cap.']

pile·wort /'pīl,wərt; -,wôrt/ ▶ n. 1 a plant (*Erechtites hieracifolia*) of the daisy family with clusters of rayless, brush-shaped white flowers and strong-smelling stems. Also called FIREWEED. 2 another term for *LESSER CELANDINE* (see CELANDINE). [ME: from PILES.]

pil·fer /'pilfər/ ▶ v. [trans.] steal (typically things of relatively little value). — **pil·fer·age** n. **pil·fer·er** n. [ME: from OFr. *pelfrer* 'to pillage.']

pil·grim (**-grimed, -grim·ing**)'pilgrəm ▶ n. a person who journeys to a sacred place for religious reasons. ■ (usu. **Pilgrim**) a member of a group of English Puritans fleeing religious persecution who sailed in the *Mayflower* and founded the colony of Plymouth, Massachusetts, in 1620. ■ a person who travels on long journeys. ■ esp. literary a person whose life is compared to a journey. — **pil·grim·ize** v. (archaic). [ME: from Provençal *pelegrin*, from L. *peregrinus* 'foreign' (see PEREGRINE).]

pil·grim·age /'pilgrəmij/ ▶ n. a pilgrim's journey. ■ a journey to a place associated with someone or something well known or respected. ■ life viewed as a journey: *life's pilgrimage.* ▶ v. [intrans.] go on a pilgrimage.

Pil·i·pi·no /,pilə'pēnō/ ▶ n. & adj. variant of FILIPINO.

pill[1] /pil/ ▶ n. a small round mass of solid medicine to be swallowed whole. ■ (**the pill** or **the Pill**) a contraceptive pill. ■ informal a tedious or unpleasant person. ■ informal (in some sports) a humorous term for a ball.

– PHRASES **a bitter pill (to swallow)** an unpleasant or painful necessity (to accept). — **pil·u·lar** /'pilyələr/ adj. [ME: ult. from L. *pilula* 'little ball,' dimin. of *pila*.]

pill[2] ▶ v. [intrans.] (of knitted fabric) form small balls of fluff on its surface. [1960s: from L. *pilare* 'make bald' and 'pillage.']

pil·lage /'pilij/ ▶ v. [trans.] rob (a place) using violence, esp. in wartime. ■ steal (something) using violence, esp. in wartime. ▶ n. the action of pillaging a place or property, esp. in wartime. — **pil·lag·er** n. [ME: from OFr., from *piller* 'to plunder.']

pil·lar /'pilər/ ▶ n. a tall vertical structure of stone, wood, or metal, used as a support for a building, or as an ornament or monument. ■ something shaped like such a structure. ■ a person or thing regarded as reliably providing essential support for something.

– PHRASES **from pillar to post** from one place to another in an unceremonious or fruitless manner. — **pil·lared** adj. [ME: from Anglo-Norman Fr. *piler*, based on L. *pila* 'pillar.']

Pil·lars of Her·cu·les an ancient name for two promontories on either side of the Strait of Gibraltar (the Rock of Gibraltar and Mount Acho in Ceuta), held to have been parted by the arm of Hercules.

pill·box /'pil,bäks/ ▶ n. a small shallow cylindrical box for holding pills. ■ (usu. **pillbox hat**) a hat of a similar shape. ■ a small, enclosed, partly underground concrete fort used as an outpost.

pill·bug /'pil,bəg/ (also **pill bug**) ▶ n. a wood louse (genus *Armadillidium*) that has a thick cuticle and is able to roll up into a ball when threatened.

pil·lion /'pilyən/ ▶ n. a seat for a passenger behind a motorcyclist. ■ hist. a woman's light saddle. ■ hist. a cushion attached to the back of a saddle for an additional passenger. [15th C.: from Scot. Gael. *pillean*, Irish *pillín* 'small cushion,' based on L. *pellis* 'skin.']

pil·lock /'pilək/ ▶ n. Brit., informal a stupid person. [16th C.: var. of archaic *pillicock* 'penis,' the early sense of *pillock* in north. Engl.]

pillory

pil·lo·ry /'pilərē/ hist. ▶ n. (pl. **-ries**) a wooden framework with holes for the head and hands, in which an offender was imprisoned and exposed to public abuse. ▶ v. (**-ries, -ried**) [trans.] put (someone) in the pillory. ■ fig. attack or ridicule publicly. [ME: from OFr. *pilori*, prob. from Provençal *espilori*.]

pil·low /'pilō/ ▶ n. a rectangular cloth bag stuffed with feathers, foam rubber, or other soft materials, used to support the head when lying down or sleeping. ■ a piece of wood or metal used as a support; a block or bearing. ▶ v. [trans.] rest (one's head) as if on a pillow. ■ literary serve as a pillow for. — **pil·low·y** adj. [OE *pyle, pylu*, of West Gmc. origin, based on L. *pulvinus* 'cushion.']

pil·low·case /'pilō,kās/ ▶ n. a removable cloth cover for a pillow.

pil·low lace ▶ n. lace made by hand using a lace pillow.

pil·low la·va ▶ n. lava that has solidified as rounded masses, characteristic of eruption under water.

pil·low sham ▶ n. a decorative pillowcase for covering a pillow when it is not in use.

pil·low·slip /'pilō,slip/ ▶ n. a pillowcase.

pil·low talk ▶ n. intimate conversation in bed.

pill pop·per ▶ n. informal a person who regularly takes large amounts of pills, esp. barbiturates or amphetamines. — **pill-pop·ping** n. & adj.

pill push·er ▶ n. informal a person, specifically a doctor, who resorts too readily to advocating the use of medication to cure illness rather than considering other treatments. — **pill-push·ing** n. & adj.

pi·lo·car·pine /,pīlə'kär,pēn/ ▶ n. Chem. a volatile alkaloid obtained from jaborandi leaves, used to contract the pupils and to relieve pressure in the eye in glaucoma patients. [19th C.: from mod. L. *Pilocarpus*, a genus.]

pi·lose /'pīlōs/ (also **pi·lous**) ▶ adj. Bot. Zool. covered with long soft hairs. — **pi·los·i·ty** /pī'läsitē/ n. [18th C.: from L. *pilosus*, from *pilus* 'hair.']

pi·lot /'pīlət/ ▶ n. 1 a person who operates the flying controls of an aircraft. ■ a person with expert local knowledge qualified to take charge of a ship entering or leaving confined waters; a helmsman. ■ [often as adj.] Telecom. an unmodulated reference signal transmitted with another signal for the purposes of control or synchronization. 2 a television program made to test audience reaction with a view to the production of a series. 3 another term for COWCATCHER. 4 short for PILOT LIGHT (sense

1). ▶ **adj.** [attrib.] **1** done as an experiment or test before introducing something more widely. **2** leading or guiding: *a pilot boat.* ▶ **v.** (**-lot·ed, -lot·ing**) [trans.] **1** act as a pilot of (an aircraft or ship). ■ [trans.] guide; steer. **2** test (a plan, project, etc.) before introducing it more widely. — **pi·lot·age** /ˈpīlətij/ **n.** [16th C.: from Fr. *pilote*, from med. L. *pilotus*, alt. of *pedota*, based on Gk. *pēdon* 'oar,' (pl.) 'rudder.']

pi·lot bal·loon ▶ **n.** a small meteorological balloon used to track air currents.

pi·lot bis·cuit ▶ **n.** another term for HARDTACK.

pi·lot·fish /ˈpīlət,fisH/ ▶ **n.** (pl. same or **-fish·es**) a fish (*Naucrates ductor*) of the jack family, often seen swimming close to large fish and said to lead sharks to prey. ■ fig. someone who guides someone else.

pi·lot·house /ˈpīlət,hous/ ▶ **n.** another term for WHEELHOUSE.

pi·lot jack·et ▶ **n.** another term for PEA JACKET.

pi·lot light ▶ **n.** **1** a small gas burner kept continuously burning to light a larger burner when needed, esp. on a gas stove or water heater. **2** an electric indicator light or control light.

pi·lot whale ▶ **n.** a toothed whale (genus *Globicephala*, family Delphinidae) that has black skin with a gray anchor-shaped marking on the chin, a low dorsal fin, and a square bulbous head. Also called BLACKFISH.

pi·lous /ˈpīləs/ ▶ **adj.** another term for PILOSE.

Pils /pilz/ (also **pils**) ▶ **n.** short for PILSNER.

Pil·sen /ˈpilzən/ a city in western Czech Republic; pop. 173,000. Czech name PLZEŇ.

Pil·sner /ˈpilznər/ (also **pil·sner, Pil·sen·er,** or **pil·sen·er**) ▶ **n.** a lager beer with a strong hop flavor, originally brewed at Pilsen (Plzeň) in the Czech Republic.

Pilt·down man /ˈpilt,doun/ ▶ **n.** a fraudulent fossil composed of a human cranium and an ape jaw, allegedly discovered in England and presented in 1912 as a genuine hominid of the early Pleistocene, but shown to be a hoax in 1953. [*Piltdown*, village in England.]

Pi·ma /ˈpēmə/ ▶ **n.** (pl. same or **Pi·mas**) **1** a member of either of two American Indian peoples, the **(Upper) Pima** living chiefly along the Gila and Salt rivers of southern Arizona, and the **Lower Pima** of central Sonora. **2** the Uto-Aztecan languages of these peoples. See PAPAGO. ▶ **adj.** of or relating to this people or their language. [Sp., shortening of *Pima Ayto*, from Pima *pimaha'icu* 'nothing.']

pi·men·to /pəˈmentō/ ▶ **n.** (pl. **-tos**) **1** var. of PIMIENTO. **2** esp. W. Indian another term for ALLSPICE (sense 2). [17th C.: from Sp. *pimiento*.]

pi me·son /ˈpī ˈmāsän; -,zän/ ▶ **n.** another term for PION.

pi·mien·to /pəˈm(y)entō/ (also **pi·men·to**) ▶ **n.** (pl. **-tos**) a red sweet pepper. ■ a piece of pimiento used as a garnish, esp. stuffed inside a pitted green olive. [17th C.: from Sp., from med. L. *pigmentum* 'spice,' from L., 'pigment.']

pimp /pimp/ ▶ **n.** a man who controls prostitutes and arranges clients for them, taking a percentage of their earnings in return. ▶ **v.** [intrans.] [often as n.] **(pimping)** act as a pimp. ■ [trans.] provide (someone) as a prostitute. [16th C.: of unknown origin.]

pim·per·nel /ˈpimpər,nel; -pərnl/ ▶ **n.** a small plant (genera *Anagallis* and *Lysimachia*) of the primrose family, with creeping stems and flat five-petaled flowers. [ME: from OFr. *pimpernelle*, based on L. *piper* 'pepper.']

pim·ple /ˈpimpəl/ ▶ **n.** a small hard inflamed spot on the skin. — **pim·pled adj. pim·ply adj.** [ME: rel. to OE *piplian* 'break out in pustules.']

PIN /pin/ (also **PIN number**) ▶ **abbr.** personal identification number.

pin /pin/ ▶ **n.** **1** a small piece of metal or wood for fastening or attaching things, in particular: ■ a thin piece of metal with a sharp point at one end and a round head at the other, used esp. for fastening pieces of cloth. ■ a small brooch or badge. ■ Med. a steel rod used to join the ends of fractured bones while they heal. ■ a metal peg that holds down the activating lever of a hand grenade, preventing its explosion. ■ short for HAIRPIN. ■ Music a peg around which one string of a musical instrument is fastened. **2** a short piece of wood or metal for various purposes, in particular: ■ (in bowling) one of a set of bottle-shaped wooden pieces that are arranged in an upright position at the end of a lane in order to be toppled by a rolling ball. ■ a metal projection from a plug or an integrated circuit that makes an electrical connection with a socket or another part of a circuit. ■ Golf a stick with a flag placed in a hole to mark the hole's position. **3 (pins)** informal legs. **4** Chess an attack on a piece or pawn, which is thereby pinned. ▶ **v.** (**pinned, pin·ning**) [trans.] attach with a pin or pins. ■ fasten (something) with a pin or pins in a specified position. ■ **(pin something on)** fix blame or responsibility for something on (someone). ■ hold someone firmly in a specified position so they are unable to move. ■ [trans.] transfix (something) with a pin or other pointed instrument. ■ [trans.] Chess hinder or prevent (a piece or pawn) from moving because of the danger to a more valuable piece standing behind it along the line of an attack.
– PHRASES **on pins and needles** in an agitated state of suspense. **pin one's ears back** listen carefully. **pin one's hopes (as) on** rely heavily on.
– PHRASAL VERBS **pin someone down** restrict the actions or movement of an enemy by firing at them. ■ force someone to be specific and make their intentions clear. **pin something down** define something precisely. [OE *pinn*, of West Gmc. origin, from L. *pinna* 'point, edge.']

pi·ña /ˈpēnyə/ ▶ **n.** a sheer fabric made from the fibers of pineapple leaves.

pi·ña co·la·da /ˈpēnyə kəˈlädə/ ▶ **n.** a cocktail made with rum, pineapple juice, and coconut. [Sp., lit. 'strained pineapple.']

pin·a·fore /ˈpinə,fôr/ ▶ **n.** a sleeveless apronlike garment worn over a child's dress. ■ a collarless sleeveless dress, tied or buttoned in the back and typically worn as a jumper, over a blouse or sweater. [18th C.: from PIN + AFORE.]

child's pinafore

Pi·nang var. of PENANG.

pi·ña·ta /pēnˈyätə/ ▶ **n.** (esp. in Spanish-speaking communities) a brightly decorated figure of an animal, usually made of papier mâché, containing toys and candy, and hung in the air so that blindfolded children, taking turns swinging sticks and bats, can smash the figure and share the scattered contents as part of a celebration.

Pin·a·tu·bo, Mount /,pinəˈtoobō/ a volcano on the island of Luzon, in the Philippines. It erupted in 1991, killing more than 300 people.

pin·ball /ˈpin,bôl/ ▶ **n.** a game in which small metal balls are shot across a sloping board and score points by striking various targets.

pince-nez /ˈpans,nā; ˈpins/ ▶ **n.** [treated as sing. or pl.] a pair of eyeglasses with a nose clip instead of earpieces. [19th C.: from Fr., lit. '(that) pinches (the) nose.']

pince-nez

pin·cer /ˈpinsər/ ▶ **n.** (usu. **pincers**) (also **a pair of pincers**) a tool made of two pieces of metal bearing blunt concave jaws that are arranged like the blades of scissors, used for gripping and pulling things. ■ a front claw of a lobster, crab, or similar crustacean. [ME: from Anglo-Norman Fr., from OFr. *pincier* 'to pinch.']

pin·cer move·ment ▶ **n.** a movement by two separate bodies of troops converging on the enemy.

pinch /pincH/ ▶ **v.** [trans.] **1** grip (the skin of someone's body) tightly and sharply between finger and thumb. ■ grip the skin of a part of the body of (someone) in such a way. ■ (of a shoe) hurt (a foot) by being too tight. ■ compress (the lips), esp. with worry or tension. ■ remove (a bud, leaves, etc.) to encourage bushy growth. **2** [intrans.] live in a frugal way. **3** informal arrest (someone). ■ informal steal. **4** Sailing sail (a boat) so close to the wind that the sails begin to lose power. ▶ **n.** **1** an act of gripping the skin of someone's body between finger and thumb. ■ an amount of an ingredient that can be held between fingers and thumb. **2** informal an arrest. ■ an act of theft or plagiarism.
– PHRASES **in a pinch** in a critical situation; if absolutely necessary. **feel the pinch** experience hardship, esp. financial. **pinch (one's) pennies** see PENNY. — **pinch·er n.** [ME: based on OFr. *pincier* 'to pinch.']

pinch·beck /ˈpincH,bek/ ▶ **n.** an alloy of copper and zinc resembling gold, used in watchmaking and costume jewelry. ▶ **adj.** appearing valuable, but actually cheap or tawdry. [18th C.: Christopher *Pinchbeck* (died 1732), Engl. watchmaker.]

pinched /pincHt/ ▶ **adj.** **1** (of a person or their face) tense and pale from cold, worry, or hunger. **2** hurt by financial hardship.

pinch ef·fect ▶ **n.** Physics the constriction of a plasma through which a large electric current is flowing, caused by the attractive force of the current's own magnetic field.

pin cher·ry ▶ **n.** see BIRD CHERRY.

pinch-hit ▶ **v.** [intrans.] Baseball bat in place of another player, typically at a critical point in the game. ■ (of a team manager or coach) delegate a player to pinch-hit in place of another. ■ informal act as a substitute for someone, esp. in an emergency. — **pinch hit·ter n.**

Pin·chot /ˈpinsHō/, Gifford (1865–1946), US forester. The first professional US forester, he was a leader in the land conservation movement.

pinch·pen·ny /ˈpincH,penē/ ▶ **n.** (pl. **-nies**) [usu. as adj.] a miserly person.

pinch-run ▶ **v.** [intrans.] Baseball substitute for another as a base runner, typically at a critical point in the game. — **pinch run·ner n.**

Pinck·ney /ˈpiNGknē/, Charles Cotesworth (1746–1825), US diplomat and politician. As minister to France in 1797, he was one of the proposed recipients of the bribery attempts made by the French to US officials in what became known as the XYZ Affair.

pin curl ▶ **n.** a curl that is held by a hairpin while setting.

pin·cush·ion /ˈpin,koosHən/ ▶ **n.** a small cushion into which pins are stuck for convenient storage. ■ (also **pincushion distortion**) a form of optical distortion in which straight lines along the edge of a screen or a lens bulge toward the center.

Pin·dar /ˈpindər; -,där/ (*c.*518–*c.*438 BC), Greek poet. His odes (the *Epinikia*) celebrate victories in athletic contests at Olympia. — **Pin·dar·ic** /pinˈdarik/ **adj.**

Pin·dus Moun·tains /ˈpindəs/ a mountain range in west central Greece. Greek name PÍNDHOS.

pine[1] /pīn/ ▶ **n.** **1** (also **pine tree**) an evergreen coniferous tree (genus *Pinus*, family Pinaceae) that has clusters of long needle-shaped leaves, grown for its soft timber or for tar and turpentine. See illustration at

RED PINE. ■ used in names of coniferous trees of other families, e.g., **Norfolk Island pine.** ■ used in names of unrelated plants that resemble the pines in some way, e.g., **ground pine.** ■ [as adj.] having the scent of pine needles. **2** informal a pineapple. [OE, from L. *pinus*.]

pine² ▶v. [intrans.] suffer a mental and physical decline, esp. because of a broken heart. ■ (**pine for**) miss and long for the return of. [OE *pīnian* '(cause to) suffer,' of Gmc. origin, based on L. *poena* 'punishment.']

pin·e·al /ˈpinēəl; ˈpī-/ (also **pineal gland, pineal body**) ▶n. a pea-sized conical mass of tissue behind the third ventricle of the brain, secreting a hormonelike substance in some mammals. ▶adj. of, denoting, or relating to the pineal. [17th C.: from Fr. *pinéal*, from L. *pinea* 'pine cone.']

pin·e·al eye ▶n. Zool. (in some reptiles and lower vertebrates) an eyelike structure on the top of the head, covered by almost transparent skin and derived from or linked to the pineal body.

pine·ap·ple /ˈpīnˌapəl/ ▶n. **1** a large juicy tropical fruit consisting of aromatic edible yellow flesh surrounded by a tough segmented skin and topped with a tuft of stiff leaves. **2** the widely cultivated tropical American plant (*Ananas comosus*, family Bromeliaceae) that bears this fruit. It is low-growing, with a spiral of spiny sword-shaped leaves on a thick stem. **3** informal a hand grenade.

pineapple

pine cone ▶n. the conical or rounded woody fruit of a pine tree, with scales that open to release the seeds.

pine mar·ten ▶n. a marten with a dark brown coat, a yellowish throat, and a bushy tail. Two species: *Martes martes* of northern Eurasia, and *M. americana* of North America, esp. Canada and Alaska.

pi·nene /ˈpīˌnēn/ ▶n. Chem. a colorless flammable liquid, $C_{10}H_{16}$, present in turpentine, juniper oil, and other natural extracts. [19th C.: from L. *pinus* 'pine.']

pine nut ▶n. the edible seed of various pine trees.

Pine Ridge a village in southwestern South Dakota, headquarters of the Pine Ridge Indian Reservation.

pine·sap /ˈpīnˌsap/ ▶n. a woodland plant of the wintergreen family, lacking chlorophyll and bearing one or more waxy bell-shaped flowers. Two species: the yellow or reddish *Monotropa hypopithys* (also called **false beechdrops**), and the pinkish or purplish violet-scented *Monotropsis odorata* (also called **sweet pinesap**).

pine snake ▶n. a large harmless North American snake (*Pituophis melanoleucus*, family Colubridae) with dark markings. When disturbed it hisses loudly and vibrates its tail.

pine tar ▶n. a thick, sticky liquid obtained from the destructive distillation of pinewood, used in soap, roofing, and medicinally for skin infections.

pi·ne·tum /pīˈnētəm/ ▶n. (pl. **-ta** /-tə/) an arboretum of pine trees or other conifers for scientific or ornamental purposes. [19th C.: from L., from *pinus* 'pine.']

pine·wood /ˈpīnˌwo͝od/ ▶n. **1** [usu. as adj.] the timber of the pine. **2** (usu. **pinewoods**) a forest of pines.

pine·y /ˈpīnē/ (also **pin·y**) ▶adj. of, like, or full of pines.

pin·feath·er /ˈpinˌfeT͟Hər/ ▶n. Ornithol. an immature feather, before the veins have expanded and while the shaft is full of fluid.

pin·fold /ˈpinˌfōld/ hist. ▶n. a pound for stray animals. ▶v. [trans.] confine (a stray animal) in such a pound. [OE *pundfald*, from a base shared by **POND + FOLD²**.]

ping /piNG/ ▶n. a short high-pitched ringing sound, as of a tap on a crystal glass. ■ a percussive knocking sound, esp. in an internal combustion engine. ▶v. **1** [intrans.] make such a sound. ■ [trans.] cause (something) to make a such a sound. **2** [trans.] query (another computer) on a network to determine whether there is a connection to it. ■ send a brief electronic message to (someone). [19th C.: imitative.]

ping·er /ˈpiNGər/ ▶n. a device that transmits short high-pitched signals at brief intervals for purposes of detection, measurement, or identification.

pin·go /ˈpiNGgō/ ▶n. (pl. **-gos**) Geol. a dome-shaped mound consisting of a layer of soil over a large core of ice, occurring in permafrost areas. [1920s: from Inuit *pinguq* 'nunatak.']

Ping-Pong /ˈpiNG ˌpôNG; -ˌpäNG/ ▶n. trademark another term for **TABLE TENNIS.** [20th C.: imitative.]

pin·guid /ˈpiNGgwid/ ▶adj. formal of the nature of or resembling fat; oily or greasy. —**pin·guid·i·ty** /piNGˈgwiditē/ n. [17th C.: from L. *pinguis* 'fat.']

pin·head /ˈpinˌhed/ ▶n. **1** the flattened head of a pin. ■ [often as adj.] a very small rounded object. **2** informal a stupid or foolish person.

pin·head·ed /ˈpinˌhedəd/ ▶adj. informal stupid; foolish. —**pin·head·ed·ness** n.

pin·hole /ˈpinˌhōl/ ▶n. a very small hole.

pin·ion¹ /ˈpinyən/ ▶n. the outer part of a bird's wing including the flight feathers. ■ literary a bird's wing as used in flight. ▶v. [trans.] **1** tie or hold the arms or legs of (someone). ■ bind (the arms or legs) of someone. **2** cut off the pinion of (a wing or bird) to prevent flight. [ME: from OFr. *pignon*, based on L. *pinna*, *penna* 'feather.']

pin·ion² ▶n. a small gear or spindle engaging with a large gear. [17th C.: from Fr. *pignon*, based on L. *pinea* 'pine cone,' from *pinus* 'pine.']

pink¹ /piNGk/ ▶adj. **1** of a color intermediate between red and white, as of coral or salmon. ■ (of wine) rosé. **2** informal, often derog. having or showing left-wing tendencies. **3** of or associated with homosexuals. ▶n. **1** pink color or pigment. ■ pink clothes or material. ■ (also **hunting pink**) the red clothing or material worn by fox hunters. **2** a pink thing, such as a rosé wine. **3** the best condition or degree. **4** informal, often derog. a person with left-wing tendencies. See also **PINKO.**
– PHRASES **in the pink** informal in extremely good health and spirits. **turn** (or **go**) **pink** blush. —**pink·ish** adj. **pink·ly** adv. **pink·ness** n. **pink·y** adj. [17th C.: from **PINK²**.]

pink² ▶n. a herbaceous Eurasian plant (genus *Dianthus*) with sweet-smelling pink or white flowers and slender, typically gray-green leaves. The **pink family** (Caryophyllaceae) includes the campions, chickweeds, stitchworts, and the cultivated carnations. [16th C.: perh. short for *pink eye*, lit. 'small eye.']

pink³ ▶v. [trans.] cut a scalloped or zigzag edge on. ■ pierce or nick (someone) slightly with a weapon or missile. [16th C.: cf. Low Ger. *pinken* 'strike, peck.']

pink⁴ ▶n. hist. a small square-rigged sailing ship, typically with a narrow, overhanging stern. [15th C.: from MDu. *pin(c)ke*.]

pink-col·lar ▶adj. of or relating to work traditionally associated with women.

Pin·ker·ton /ˈpiNGkərtən/, Allan (1819–84), US detective; born in Scotland. In 1850, he established the first US private detective agency.

pink·eye /ˈpiNGkˌī/ ▶n. **1** conjunctivitis in humans and some livestock. **2** a disease of horses, symptoms of which include fever, spontaneous abortion, and redness of the eyes, caused by a virus (genus *Arterivirus*).

pink·ie /ˈpiNGkē/ (also **pink·y**) ▶n. informal the little finger. [19th C.: partly from Du. *pink* 'the little finger,' reinforced by **PINK¹**.]

pink·ing shears ▶plural n. shears with a serrated blade, used to cut a zigzag edge in fabric to prevent it from fraying.

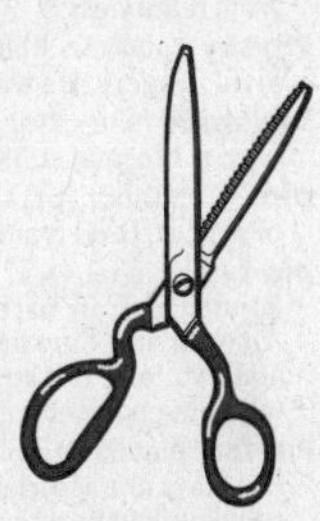

pinking shears

pink noise ▶n. Physics random noise having equal energy per octave, and so having more low-frequency components than white noise.

pink·o /ˈpiNGkō/ ▶n. (pl. **-os** or **-oes**) informal, derog. a person with left-wing or liberal views.

pink salm·on ▶n. a small salmon (*Oncorhynchus gorbuscha*) with dark spots on the back, native to the North Pacific and introduced into the northwestern Atlantic. ■ its pale pink flesh used as food.

pink slip informal ▶n. a notice of dismissal from employment. ▶v. (**pink-slip**) [trans.] dismiss (someone) from employment.

Pink·ster /ˈpiNGkstər/ ▶n. dialect Whitsuntide. [18th C.: from Du., 'Pentecost.']

pin mon·ey ▶n. a small sum of money for spending on inessentials. ■ hist. an allowance to a woman from her husband for clothing and other personal expenses.

pin·na /ˈpinə/ ▶n. (pl. **pin·nae** /ˈpinē/) **1** Anat. Zool. the external part of the ear in humans and other mammals; the auricle. **2** Bot. a primary division of a pinnate leaf, esp. of a fern. **3** Zool. any of a number of animal structures resembling fins or wings. [18th C.: mod. L., from var. of L. *penna* 'feather.']

pin·nace /ˈpinis/ ▶n. esp. hist. a small boat, typically with sails and/or oars, forming part of the equipment of a warship or other large vessel. [16th C.: from Fr. *pinace*, prob. based on L. *pinus* 'pine.']

pin·na·cle /ˈpinəkəl/ ▶n. a high pointed piece of rock. ■ a small pointed turret built as an ornament on a roof. ■ the most successful point; the culmination. ▶v. [trans.] literary set on or as if on a pinnacle. ■ form the culminating point or example of. —**pin·na·cled** adj. [ME: from OFr., from late L. *pinnaculum*, dimin. of *pinna* 'point.']

pin·nae /ˈpinē/ plural form of **PINNA.**

pin·nate /ˈpināt; -it/ ▶adj. Bot. (of a compound leaf) having leaflets arranged on either side of the stem, typically in pairs opposite each other. See illustration at **LEAF.** ■ Zool. (esp. of an invertebrate animal) having branches, tentacles, etc., on each side of an axis, like the vanes of a feather. —**pin·nat·ed** adj. **pin·nate·ly** adv. **pin·na·tion** /piˈnāSHən/ n. [18th C.: from L. *pinnatus* 'feathered,' from *pinna*, *penna* (see **PINNA**).]

pinni- ▶comb. form relating to wings or fins: *pinniped*. [from L. *pinna*, *penna* 'wing, fin.']

Pin·ni·pe·di·a /ˌpinəˈpēdēə/ Zool. an order (Pinnipedia) of carnivorous aquatic mammals that comprises the seals, sea lions, and walrus. They are distinguished by their flipperlike limbs. —**pin·ni·ped** /ˈpinəˌped/ n. & adj. [mod. L. (pl.), from L. *pinna* 'wing, fin' + *pes*, *ped-* 'foot.']

pin·nule /ˈpinˌyo͞ol/ ▶n. Bot. a secondary division of a pinnate leaf, esp. of a fern. ■ Zool. a part or organ like a small wing or fin, esp. a side branch on the arm of a crinoid. [16th C.: from L. *pinnula* 'small wing,' dimin. of *pinna*.]

PIN num·ber ▶n. see **PIN.**

pin oak ▶n. a North American oak (*Quercus palustris*) with deeply lobed, toothed leaves. Its dead branches remain in position and resemble pegs fixed in the trunk.

Pi·no·chet /'pēnə,SHā; ,pēnō'CHet/, Augusto (1915–2006), president of Chile 1974–90; full name *Augusto Pinochet Ugarte*.

pi·noch·le /'pē,nəkəl; -,nakəl/ ▶ **n.** a card game for two or more players using a 48-card deck consisting of two of each card from nine to ace, the object being to score points for various combinations and to win tricks. ■ the combination of queen of spades and jack of diamonds in this game. [19th C.: of unknown origin.]

pin·o·cy·to·sis /,pinəsī'tōsis; pīnə-/ ▶ **n.** Biol. the ingestion of liquid into a cell by the budding of small vesicles from the cell membrane. — **pin·o·cy·tot·ic** /-tätik/ **adj.** [19th C.: from Gk. *pino* 'drink' + *-cytosis*.]

pi·no·le /pi'nōlē/ ▶ **n.** a sweetened flour made from ground dried corn mixed with flour made of mesquite beans, sugar, and spices. [19th C.: from L. Amer. Sp., from Nahuatl *pinolli*.]

pi·ñon /'pinyən; ,pin'yōn/ (also **pi·nyon** or **pi·ñon pine**) ▶ **n.** a small pine tree (*Pinus cemebroides*) with edible seeds, native to Mexico and the southwestern US. ■ (also **piñon nut**) a pine nut obtained from this tree. [19th C.: from Sp., from L. *pinea* 'pine cone.']

Pi·not /'pēnō; pē'nō/ ▶ **n.** any of several varieties of wine grape, esp. the chief varieties **Pinot Noir**, a black grape, and **Pinot Blanc**, a white grape. ■ a wine made from these grapes. [var. of *Pineau*, dimin. of *pin* 'pine.']

pi·no·tage /'pēnō,täZH/ ▶ **n.** a variety of red wine grape grown in South Africa, produced by crossing Pinot Noir and other varieties. ■ red wine made from this grape. [blend of *Pinot (Noir)* and *Hermitage*, types of grape.]

pin·point /'pin,point/ ▶ **n.** a tiny dot or point. ▶ **adj.** [attrib.] absolutely precise; to the finest degree. ■ tiny. ▶ **v.** [trans.] find or locate exactly.

pin·prick /'pin,prik/ ▶ **n.** a prick caused by a pin. ■ a cause of minor irritation.

pins and nee·dles ▶ **plural n.** a tingling sensation in a limb recovering from numbness.

Pin·sky /'pinskē/, Robert (1940–), US poet and writer, noted for his vivid imagery. He was US poet laureate 1997–2000.

pin·stripe /'pin,strīp/ ▶ **n.** a very narrow stripe in cloth, esp. of the type used for formal suits. ■ a pinstripe suit. — **pin·striped adj.**

pint /pīnt/ (abbr.: **pt**) ▶ **n.** a unit of liquid or dry capacity equal to one half of a quart. [ME: from OFr. *pinte*.]

pin·tail /'pin,tāl/ ▶ **n.** a mainly migratory duck (genus *Anas*) with a pointed tail, in particular the **common pintail** (*A. acuta*) of North America and Eurasia, the male of which has boldly marked plumage and two long tail streamers. ■ informal any of a number of other birds with long pointed tails, esp. a grouse.

Pin·ter /'pintər/, Harold (1930–), English playwright and screenwriter. His plays are associated with the Theater of the Absurd and are typically marked by a sense of menace. Nobel Prize for Literature (2005).

pin·tle /'pintl/ ▶ **n.** one of the pins (on the forward edge of a rudder) that fit into the gudgeons and so suspend the rudder. [OE *pintel* 'penis,' perh. dimin.; compare Ger. *Pint* 'penis.']

pin·to /'pintō/ ▶ **adj.** piebald. ▶ **n.** (pl. **-tos**) a piebald horse. [19th C.: from Sp., lit. 'mottled,' based on L. *pictus*, past part. of *pingere* 'to paint.']

pin·to bean ▶ **n.** a medium-sized speckled variety of kidney bean. [20th C.: from PINTO.]

pint-sized (also **pint-size**) ▶ **adj.** informal very small.

pin tuck ▶ **n.** (in sewing) a very narrow ornamental tuck.

pin·up /'pin,əp/ ▶ **n.** a poster showing a famous person or sex symbol, designed to be displayed on a wall. ■ a person shown in such a poster.

pin·wheel /'pin,(h)wēl/ ▶ **n.** a child's toy consisting of a stick with colored vanes that twirl in the wind. ■ a fireworks device that whirls and emits colored fire. ■ something shaped or rotating like a pinwheel. ▶ **v.** [intrans.] spin or rotate like a pinwheel.

pin·worm /'pin,wərm/ ▶ **n.** a small nematode (family Oxyuridae, class Phasmida) that is an internal parasite of vertebrates.

pin·y /'pīnē/ ▶ **adj.** var. of PINEY.

Pin·yin /'pin'yin/ (also **pin·yin**) ▶ **n.** the standard system of romanized spelling for transliterating Chinese. [1960s: from Chin. *pīn-yīn*, lit. 'spell-sound.']

pin·yon ▶ **n.** var. of PIÑON.

pi·on /'pī,än/ ▶ **n.** Physics a meson having a mass approximately 270 times that of an electron. Also called PI MESON. — **pi·on·ic** /pī'änik/ **adj.** [1950s: from PI.]

Pi·o·neer /,pīə'ni(ə)r/ a series of American space probes launched between 1958 and 1973, two of which provided the first clear pictures of Jupiter and Saturn (1973–79).

pi·o·neer /,pīə'ni(ə)r/ ▶ **n.** a person who is among the first to explore or settle a new country or area. ■ a person who is among the first to research and develop a new area of knowledge or activity. ■ a member of an infantry group preparing roads or terrain for the main body of troops. ■ (also **pioneer species**) a plant or animal that establishes itself in an unoccupied area. ▶ **v.** [trans.] develop or be the first to use or apply (a new method, area of knowledge, or activity). ■ open up (a road or terrain) as a pioneer. [16th C.: from Fr. *pionnier* 'foot soldier, pioneer,' OFr. *paonier*, from *paon*, from L. *pedo*, *pedon-* (see PAWN[1]).]

pi·o·neer·ing /,pīə'ni(ə)riNG/ ▶ **adj.** involving new ideas or methods.

pi·ous /'pīəs/ ▶ **adj.** devoutly religious. ■ making a hypocritical display of virtue. ■ [attrib.] (of a hope) sincere but unlikely to be fulfilled. ■ (of a deception) with good or religious intentions, whether professed or real. — **pi·ous·ly adv. pi·ous·ness n.** [ME: from L. *pius* 'dutiful, pious.']

pip[1] /pip/ ▶ **n.** a small hard seed in a fruit. — **pip·less adj.** [18th C.: abbrev. of PIPPIN.]

pip[2] ▶ **n.** a small shape or symbol, in particular: ■ any of the spots on playing cards, dice, or dominoes. ■ a single blossom of a clustered head of flowers. ■ a diamond-shaped segment of the surface of a pineapple. ■ an image of an object on a radar screen; blip. [16th C.: of unknown origin.]

pip[3] ▶ **n.** a disease of poultry or other birds causing thick mucus in the throat and white scale on the tongue. [ME: from MDu. *pippe*, based on L. *pituita* 'slime.']

pip[4] ▶ **v.** (**pipped, pip·ping**) [trans.] (of a young bird) crack (the shell of the egg) when hatching. [19th C.: perh. imitative.]

pi·pa /'pē,pä/ ▶ **n.** a shallow-bodied, four-stringed Chinese lute. [Chin.]

pi·pal /'pēpəl/ ▶ **n.** var. of PEEPUL.

pipe /pīp/ ▶ **n. 1** a tube of metal, plastic, or other material used to convey water, gas, oil, or other fluid substances. ■ a cylindrical vein of ore or rock, esp. one in which diamonds are found. ■ a cavity in cast metal. ■ informal a duct, vessel, or tubular structure in the body, or in an animal or plant. **2** a narrow tube made from wood, clay, etc., with a bowl at one end for containing burning tobacco, the smoke from which is drawn into the mouth. ■ a quantity of tobacco held by this. **3** a wind instrument consisting of a single tube with holes along its length that are covered by the fingers to produce different notes. ■ (usu. **pipes**) bagpipes. ■ (**pipes**) a set of pipes joined together, as in panpipes. ■ a tube by which sound is produced in an organ. ■ [in sing.] a high-pitched cry or song, esp. of a bird. ■ a boatswain's whistle. **4** a cask for wine, esp. as a measure equal to two hogsheads, usually equivalent to 105 gallons (about 477 liters). ▶ **v. 1** [trans.] convey (water, gas, oil, or other fluid substances) through a pipe or pipes. ■ transmit (music, a radio or television program, signals, etc.) by wire or cable. **2** [trans.] play (a tune) on a pipe or pipes. ■ [intrans.] (of a bird) sing in a high or shrill voice. ■ [with direct speech] say something in a high, shrill voice. ■ [trans.] use a boatswain's whistle to summon (the crew) to work or a meal. **3** [trans.] decorate (clothing or soft furnishings) with a thin cord covered in fabric. ■ put (a decorative line or pattern) on a cake or similar dish using icing, whipped cream, etc.

– PHRASES **put that in one's pipe and smoke it** informal used to indicate that someone should accept what one has said, even if it is unwelcome.

– PHRASAL VERBS **pipe down** [often in imper.] informal stop talking; be less noisy. **pipe up** say something suddenly. — **pipe·ful n.** (pl. **-fuls**) [OE *pīpe* 'musical tube,' *pīpian* 'play a pipe,' of Gmc. origin, based on L. *pipare* 'to chirp.']

pipe bomb ▶ **n.** a homemade bomb, the components of which are contained in a pipe.

pipe-clay (also **pipe·clay** or **pipe clay**) ▶ **n.** a fine white clay, used esp. for making tobacco pipes or for whitening leather. ▶ **v.** (**pipe-clay** or **pipe·clay**) [trans.] whiten (leather) with such clay.

pipe clean·er ▶ **n.** a piece of wire covered with tufted fiber, used to clean a tobacco pipe and for a variety of handicrafts.

pipe dream ▶ **n.** an unattainable or fanciful hope or scheme.

pipe·fish /'pīp,fiSH/ ▶ **n.** (pl. same or **-fish·es**) a narrow, elongated, chiefly marine fish (*Syngnathus* and other genera, family Syngnathidae) with segmented bony armor beneath the skin and a long tubular snout.

pipe·line /'pīp,līn/ ▶ **n.** a long pipe, typically underground, for conveying oil, gas, etc., over long distances. ■ fig. a channel supplying goods or information. ■ (in surfing) the hollow formed by the breaking of a large wave. ■ Comput. a linear sequence of specialized modules used for pipelining. ▶ **v.** [trans.] convey (a substance) by a pipeline. ■ [trans.] [often as adj.] (**pipelined**) Comput. design or execute (a computer or instruction) using the technique of pipelining.

– PHRASES **in the pipeline** awaiting completion or processing; being developed.

pipe·lin·ing /'pīp,līniNG/ ▶ **n. 1** the laying of pipelines. ■ transportation by means of pipelines. **2** Comput. a form of computer organization in which successive steps of an instruction sequence are executed in turn by a sequence of modules able to operate concurrently, so that another instruction can be begun before the previous one is finished.

pipe or·gan ▶ **n.** Music see ORGAN (sense 1).

pip·er /'pīpər/ ▶ **n. 1** a bagpipe player. **2** a person who plays a pipe, esp. an itinerant musician.

– PHRASES **pay the piper** bear the consequences of an action or activity that one has enjoyed.

pi·per·a·zine /pi'perə,zēn; pī-; 'pipərə-/ ▶ **n.** Chem. a synthetic crystalline compound, $C_4H_{10}N_2$, with basic properties, sometimes used as an anthelmintic and insecticide. [19th C.: from PIPERIDINE.]

pi·per·i·dine /pi'peri,dēn; pī-; 'pipərə-/ ▶ **n.** Chem. a peppery-smelling liquid, $C_5H_{11}N$, formed by the reduction of pyridine. [19th C.: from L. *piper* 'pepper' + -IDE.]

pipe stem (also **pipe·stem**) ▶ **n.** the shaft of a tobacco pipe. ■ [as adj.] used to describe anything resembling this, such as a very narrow pants leg.

pipe·stone /'pīp,stōn/ ▶ **n.** hard red clay (catlinite) used by North American Indians for tobacco pipes.

pi·pette /pī'pet/ (also **pi·pet**) ▶ **n.** a slender tube attached to or incorporating a bulb, for transferring or measuring out small quantities of liquid, esp. in a laboratory. ▶ **v.** [trans.] pour, convey, or draw off using a pipette. [19th C.: from Fr., lit. 'little pipe,' dimin. of *pipe*.]

pip·ing /ˈpīpiNG/ ▶ **n.** **1** lengths of pipe, or a network of pipes, made of metal, plastic, or other materials. **2** ornamentation on food consisting of lines of icing, whipped cream, etc. ■ thin cord covered in fabric, used to decorate clothing or soft furnishings and reinforce seams. **3** the action or art of playing a pipe or pipes. ▶ **adj.** [attrib.] **1** (of a voice or sound) high-pitched. **2** (of a time) peaceful; characterized by the playing of pipes.
– PHRASES **piping hot** (of food or water) very hot.

pip·i·strelle /ˌpipəˈstrel; ˈpipəˌstrel/ (also **pip·i·strel**) ▶ **n.** a small insectivorous Old World bat (genus *Pipistrellus*, family Vespertilionidae) with jerky, erratic flight. [18th C.: from Fr., from Ital. *pipistrello*, from L. *vespertilio(n-)* 'bat,' from *vesper* 'evening.']

pip·it /ˈpipit/ ▶ **n.** a mainly ground-dwelling songbird (*Anthus* and other genera, family Motacillidae) of open country, typically having brown streaky plumage. [18th C.: prob. imitative.]

pip·pin /ˈpipin/ ▶ **n.** a red and yellow dessert apple. ■ an apple grown from seed. ■ informal an excellent person or thing. [ME: from OFr. *pepin*.]

pip·sis·se·wa /pipˈsisəˌwô; -wə/ ▶ **n.** a North American plant (*Chimaphila umbellata*) of the wintergreen family, with whorled evergreen leaves that yield a diuretic and tonic. [18th C.: from Abnaki, lit. 'flower of the woods.']

pip·squeak /ˈpipˌskwēk/ ▶ **n.** informal a person considered to be insignificant, esp. because they are small or young. [20th C.: symbolic and imitative.]

pi·quant /ˈpēkənt; -känt/ ▶ **adj.** having a pleasantly sharp taste or appetizing flavor. ■ pleasantly stimulating or exciting to the mind. — **pi·quan·cy** /-kənsē/ **n.** **pi·quant·ly** **adv.** [16th C.: from Fr., lit. 'stinging,' pres. part. of *piquer*.]

pique /pēk/ ▶ **n.** a feeling of irritation or resentment resulting from a slight, esp. to one's pride. ▶ **v.** (**piques** /pēks/, **piqued** /pēkt/, **piqu·ing** /ˈpēkiNG/) **1** [trans.] stimulate (interest or curiosity). **2** (**be piqued**) feel irritated or resentful. [16th C.: from Fr. *piquer* 'prick, irritate.']

pi·qué /pēˈkā; pi-/ ▶ **n.** stiff fabric, typically cotton, woven in a strongly ribbed or raised pattern. [19th C.: from Fr., lit. 'backstitched,' past part. of *piquer*.]

pi·quet /piˈkā; ˈket/ (also **pic·quet**) ▶ **n.** a trick-taking card game for two players, using a 32-card deck consisting of cards from the seven to the ace. [17th C.: from Fr.]

pi·ra·cy /ˈpīrəsē/ ▶ **n.** the practice of attacking and robbing ships at sea. ■ a similar practice in other contexts, esp. hijacking. ■ the unauthorized use or reproduction of another's work. [16th C.: via med. L. from Gk. *pirateia*, from *peiratēs* (see PIRATE).]

Pi·rae·us /pəˈrāəs; pīˈrēəs/ a city in southeastern Greece on the Saronic Gulf; pop. 183,000. Greek name PIRAIÉVS or PIRAIÉUS.

Pi·ran·del·lo /ˌpirənˈdelō/, Luigi (1867–1936), Italian playwright and writer. His plays challenged the conventions of naturalism. Nobel Prize for Literature (1934).

red piranha

pi·ra·nha /pəˈränə/ ▶ **n.** (pl. same or **-nhas**) a deep-bodied South American freshwater fish (*Serrasalmus* and other genera, family Characidae) having very sharp teeth that it uses to tear flesh from prey. [18th C.: via Port. from Tupi *pirá* 'fish' + *sainha* 'tooth.']

pi·rate /ˈpīrət/ ▶ **n.** a person who attacks and robs ships at sea. ■ a person who appropriates or reproduces the work of another for profit without permission, usually in contravention of patent or copyright. ■ a person or organization that broadcasts radio or television programs without official authorization. ▶ **v.** [trans.] **1** dated rob or plunder (a ship). **2** [often as adj.] (**pirated**) use or reproduce (another's work) for profit without permission, usually in contravention of patent or copyright. — **pi·rat·ic** /pīˈratik; pi-/ **adj.** **pi·rat·i·cal** /pīˈratikəl; pi-/ **adj.** **pi·rat·i·cal·ly** /pīˈratiklē; pi-/ **adv.** [ME: from L. *pirata*, from Gk. *peiratēs*, from *peirein* 'to attack' (from *peira* 'an attempt').]

pir·i·form ▶ **adj.** var. of PYRIFORM.

pi·ro·gi /piˈrōgē/ (also **pe·ro·gi**) ▶ **n.** (pl. same or **-gies**) a dough dumpling stuffed with a filling such as potato or cheese. [from Pol. *pieróg* or Ukrainian *pyrih*.]

pi·rogue /piˈrōg/ ▶ **n.** a long narrow canoe made from a single tree trunk, esp. in Central America and the Caribbean. [17th C.: from Fr., prob. from Galibi.]

pir·o·plas·mo·sis /ˌpi(ə)rəplazˈmōsis/ ▶ **n.** another term for BABESIOSIS.

pi·rosh·ki /piˈrôshkē; -ˈräsh-/ (also **pi·rozh·ki**) ▶ **plural n.** small Russian pastries or patties, filled with meat or fish and rice. [from Russ. *pirozhki*, pl. of *pirozhok*.]

pir·ou·ette /ˌpirōōˈet/ ▶ **n.** esp. Ballet an act of spinning on one foot, typically with the raised foot touching the knee of the supporting leg. ■ a movement performed in advanced dressage and classical riding, in which the horse makes a circle by pivoting on a hind leg while cantering. ▶ **v.** [intrans.] perform a pirouette. [17th C.: from Fr., lit. 'spinning top.']

Pi·sa /ˈpēzə/ a city in west central Italy, in Tuscany; pop. 101,000. It is noted for the **Leaning Tower of Pisa**.

pis al·ler /ˌpēz äˈlā/ ▶ **n.** a course of action followed as a last resort. [Fr., from *pis* 'worse' + *aller* 'go.']

Pi·sa·no /pəˈzänō/ Nicola (*c.*1220–*c.*1278), Italian sculptor.

pis·ca·ry /ˈpiskərē/ ▶ **n.** (in phrase **common of piscary**) esp. hist. the right of fishing in another's water. [15th C.: from med. L. *piscaria*, neut. pl. of L. *piscarius* 'relating to fishing,' from *piscis* 'fish.']

pis·ca·to·ri·al /ˌpiskəˈtôrēəl/ ▶ **adj.** formal of or concerning fishermen or fishing. [19th C.: from L. *piscatorius* (from *piscator* 'fisherman,' from *piscis* 'fish').]

pis·ca·to·ry /ˈpiskəˌtôrē/ ▶ **adj.** another term for PISCATORIAL.

Pis·ces /ˈpīsēz; ˈpisēz/ **1** Astron. a large constellation (the Fish or Fishes), said to represent a pair of fish tied together by their tails. **2** Astrol. the twelfth sign of the zodiac, which the sun enters about February 20. ■ (**a Pisces**) (pl. same) a person born when the sun is in this sign. — **Pis·ce·an** /-sēən/ **n. & adj.** (in sense 2). [L., pl. of *piscis* 'fish.']

pis·ci·cul·ture /ˈpisiˌkəlCHər/ ▶ **n.** the controlled breeding and rearing of fish. — **pis·ci·cul·tur·al** /ˌpisiˈkəlCHərəl/ **adj.** **pis·ci·cul·tur·ist** /ˌpisiˈkəlCHərist/ **n.** [19th C.: from L. *piscis* 'fish.']

pis·ci·na /piˈsēnə; -ˈsīnə/ ▶ **n.** (pl. **-nas** or **-nae** /-nē/) **1** a stone basin near the altar in Catholic and pre-Reformation churches for draining water used in the Mass. **2** (in ancient Roman architecture) a pool or pond for bathing or swimming. [16th C.: from L., 'fishpond,' from *piscis* 'fish.']

pis·cine /ˈpīsēn; ˈpisīn/ ▶ **adj.** of or concerning fish. [18th C.: from L. *piscis* 'fish.']

Pis·cis Aus·tri·nus /ˈpīsis ôˈstrīnəs/ (also **Pis·cis Aus·tra·lis** /ôˈstrālis/) Astron. a southern constellation (the Southern Fish), south of Aquarius and Capricornus. [L.]

pis·civ·o·rous /piˈsivərəs/ ▶ **adj.** Zool. (of an animal) feeding on fish. — **piscivore** /ˈpisiˌvôr/ **n.** [17th C.: from L. *piscis* 'fish.']

pis·co /ˈpēskō; ˈpiskō/ ▶ **n.** a white brandy made in Peru from muscat grapes. [after a port in Peru.]

pish /pish/ ▶ **exclam.** dated used to express annoyance, impatience, or disgust. [natural utterance: first recorded in Engl. in the 16th C.]

pish·er /ˈpishər/ ▶ **n.** informal an insignificant or contemptible person. [1940s: Yiddish, lit. 'pisser,' from the v. *pissen*.]

Pish·pek /pishˈpek; pishˈpyek/ former name (until 1926) of BISHKEK.

Pi·sid·i·a /pəˈsidēə; pī-/ an ancient region in Asia Minor, between Pamphylia and Phrygia. — **Pi·sid·i·an** **adj. & n.**

pi·si·form /ˈpīsəˌfôrm/ (also **pisiform bone**) ▶ **n.** a small rounded carpal bone situated where the palm of the hand meets the outer edge of the wrist. [18th C.: from mod. L. *pisiformis* 'pea-shaped,' from *pisum* 'pea' + *forma* 'shape.']

Pi·sis·tra·tus /piˈsistrətəs/ (also **Pei·sis·tra·tus**) (*c.*600–*c.*527 BC), tyrant of Athens.

piss /pis/ vulgar slang ▶ **v.** [intrans.] urinate. ■ [trans.] wet with urine. ■ [trans.] discharge (something, esp. blood) when urinating. ▶ **n.** urine. ■ [in sing.] an act of urinating.
– PHRASES **not have a pot to piss in** be very poor. **piss in the wind** do something that is ineffective or a waste of time. **take a piss** urinate.
– PHRASAL VERBS **piss something away** waste something, esp. money or time. **piss off** [usu. in imper.] go away (usually used to angrily dismiss someone). **piss someone off** annoy someone. **piss on** show complete contempt for. [ME: from OFr. *pisser*, prob. imitative.]

piss and vin·e·gar ▶ **n.** vulgar slang aggressive energy.

piss·ant /ˈpisˌant/ vulgar slang ▶ **n.** an insignificant or contemptible person or thing. ▶ **adj.** worthless; contemptible. [17th C.: from n. PISS.]

Pis·sar·ro /piˈsärō; pēsäˈrō/, Camille (1830–1903), French painter. He was a leading figure of the Impressionist movement.

pissed /pist/ vulgar slang ▶ **adj.** (also **pissed off**) very annoyed; angry.

piss·er /ˈpisər/ ▶ **n.** vulgar slang **1** [in sing.] an annoying or disappointing event or circumstance. **2** an unpleasant person; a person who causes difficulties.

pis·soir /pēˈswär/ ▶ **n.** a public urinal. [Fr.]

piss-poor ▶ **adj.** vulgar slang of a very low standard.

piss·y /ˈpisē/ ▶ **adj.** (**piss·i·er**, **piss·i·est**) vulgar slang **1** of, relating to, or suggestive of urine. ■ inferior; contemptible. **2** arrogantly argumentative.

pis·tach·i·o /pəˈstashēˌō/ ▶ **n.** (pl. **-os**) **1** (also **pistachio nut**) the edible pale green seed of an Asian tree. ■ (also **pistachio green**) a pale green color. **2** the evergreen tree (*Pistacia vera*) of the cashew family that produces this nut, with small brownish-green flowers and reddish wrinkled fruit borne in heavy clusters. [ME *pistace*, based on Gk. *pistakion*, from Old Pers.]

piste /pēst/ ▶ **n.** **1** a ski run of compacted snow. **2** the specially marked-out rectangular playing area in fencing. [Fr., lit. 'racetrack.']

pis·til /ˈpistl/ ▶ **n.** Bot. the female organs of a flower, comprising the stigma, style, and ovary. [18th C.: from Fr. *pistile* or L. *pistillum* 'pestle.']

pis·til·late /ˈpistəlit; -ˌlāt/ ▶ **adj.** Bot. (of a plant or flower) having pistils but no stamens. Compare with STAMINATE.

pis·tol (**-toled, -tol·ing**; Brit. **-tolled, -tol·ling**)ˈpistl ▶ **n.** a small firearm designed to be held in one hand. [16th C.: from obs. Fr. *pistole*, from Ger. *Pistole*, from Czech *píšťala* orig. 'whistle.']

pis·tole /piˈstōl/ ▶ **n.** any of various gold coins used in Europe in the 17th and 18th centuries. [16th C.: from Fr., abbrev. of *pistolet*.]

pis·to·le·ro /pistəˈle(ə)rō/ ▶ **n.** (pl. **-ros**) (in Spanish-speaking regions) a gunman or gangster.

pis·tol-whip ▶ **v.** [trans.] hit or beat (someone) with a pistol.

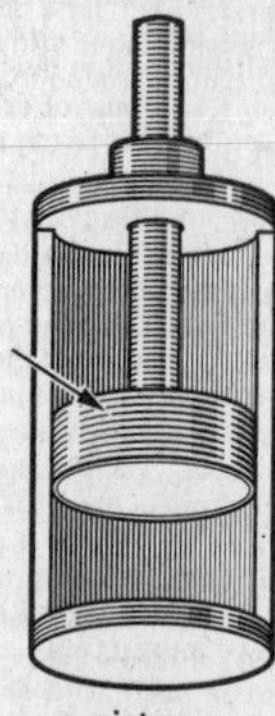

piston

pis·ton /ˈpistn/ ▶ **n.** a disk or short cylinder fitting closely within a tube in which it moves up and down against a liquid or gas, used in an internal combustion engine to derive motion, or in a pump to impart motion. ■ a valve in a brass musical instrument in the form of a piston, depressed to alter the pitch of a note. [18th C.: from Fr., from Ital. *pistone*, var. of *pestone*, augmentative of *pestello* 'pestle.']

pis·ton en·gine ▶ **n.** an engine in which power is derived from cylinders and pistons. — **pis·ton-en·gined** /ˈpistn ˌenjənd/ **adj.**

pis·ton ring ▶ **n.** a ring on a piston sealing the gap between the piston and the cylinder wall.

pis·ton rod ▶ **n.** a rod or crankshaft attached to a piston to drive a wheel or to impart motion.

pit¹ /pit/ ▶ **n. 1** a large hole in the ground. ■ a large deep hole from which stones or minerals are dug. ■ a coal mine. ■ a sunken enclosure in which certain animals are kept in captivity. ■ short for ***ORCHESTRA PIT*** (see **ORCHESTRA**). ■ a sunken area in a workshop floor allowing access to a car's underside. ■ fig. a low or wretched psychological state. ■ (**the pit**) literary hell. **2** an area reserved or enclosed for a specific activity, in particular: ■ (usu. **pits**) an area at the side of a track where race cars are serviced and refueled. ■ a part of the floor of an exchange in which a particular stock or commodity is traded, typically by open outcry. ■ esp. hist. an enclosure in which animals are made to fight. **3** a hollow or indentation in a surface. ■ a small indentation left on the skin after smallpox, acne, or other diseases; a pockmark. ▶ **v.** (**pit·ted, pit·ting**) [trans.] **1** (**pit someone/something against**) set someone or something in conflict or competition with. ■ hist. set an animal to fight against (another animal) for sport. **2** make a hollow or indentation in the surface of. ■ [intrans.] sink in or contract so as to form a pit or hollow. **3** [intrans.] drive a race car into the pits for fuel or maintenance.
– PHRASES **be the pits** informal be extremely bad or the worst of its kind. **the pit of one's** (or **the**) **stomach** an ill-defined region of the lower abdomen regarded as the seat of strong feelings, esp. anxiety. [OE *pytt*, of West Gmc. origin, based on L. *puteus* 'well, shaft.']

pit² ▶ **n.** the stone of a fruit. ▶ **v.** (**pit·ted, pit·ting**) [trans.] remove the pit from (fruit). [19th C.: appar. from Du.; rel. to **PITH**.]

pi·ta /ˈpētə/ (also **pita bread**) ▶ **n.** flat hollow unleavened bread that can be split open to hold a filling. [mod. Gk., lit. 'cake or pie.']

pit·a·ha·ya /ˌpitəˈhīə/ ▶ **n.** any tall cactus of Mexico and the southwestern US, in particular the saguaro. ■ the edible fruit of such cacti. [18th C.: from Sp., from Haitian Creole.]

pit-a-pat /ˈpit ə ˌpat/ (also **pit·a·pat**) ▶ **adv.** with a sound like quick light steps or taps. ▶ **n.** [in sing.] a sound of this kind. [16th C.: imitative.]

pit bull (in full **pit bull terrier**) ▶ **n.** the American Staffordshire terrier, popularly associated with ferocity and often provoked because of this belief.

Pit·cairn Is·lands /ˈpitˌke(ə)rn/ a British dependency that consists of a group of volcanic islands in the South Pacific Ocean, east of French Polynesia. The islands were settled in 1790 by mutineers from HMS *Bounty*.

pitch¹ /picH/ ▶ **n. 1** the quality of a sound governed by the rate of vibrations producing it; the degree of highness or lowness of a tone. ■ a standard degree of highness or lowness used in performance. See also **CONCERT PITCH**. **2** the steepness of a slope, esp. of a roof. ■ Climbing a section of a climb, esp. a steep one. ■ the height to which a hawk soars before swooping on its prey. **3** [in sing.] the level of intensity of something. ■ (**a pitch of**) a very high degree of. **4** Baseball a legal delivery of the ball by the pitcher. ■ (also **pitch shot**) Golf a high approach shot onto the green. ■ Football short for **PITCHOUT** sense 2. ■ Cricket the strip of ground between the two sets of stumps. **5** a form of words used when trying to persuade someone to buy or accept something. **6** a swaying or oscillation of a ship, aircraft, or vehicle around a horizontal axis perpendicular to the direction of motion. ■ the degree of slope or angle, as of a roof. **7** tech. the distance between successive corresponding points or lines, e.g., between the teeth of a cogwheel. ■ a measure of the angle of the blades off a screw propeller, equal to the distance forward a blade would move in one revolution if it exerted no thrust on the medium. ■ the density of typed or printed characters on a line, typically expressed as numbers of characters per inch. ▶ **v. 1** [trans.] Baseball throw (the ball) for the batter to try to hit. ■ Baseball assign (a player) to pitch. ■ [intrans.] be a pitcher. ■ Golf hit (the ball) onto the green with a pitch shot. ■ [intrans.] Golf (of the ball) strike the ground in a particular spot. **2** [trans.] throw or fling roughly or casually. ■ [intrans.] fall heavily, esp. headlong. **3** [trans.] set (one's voice or a piece of music) at a particular pitch. ■ express at a particular level of difficulty. ■ aim (a product) at a particular section of the market. **4** [intrans.] make a bid to obtain a contract or other business. **5** [trans.] set up and fix in a definite position. **6** [intrans.] (of a moving ship, aircraft, or vehicle) rock or oscillate around a lateral axis, so that the front and back move up and down. ■ (of a vehicle) move with a vigorous jogging motion. **7** [trans.] cause (a roof) to slope downward from the ridge. ■ [intrans.] slope downward.
– PHRASES **make a pitch** make a bid to obtain a contract or other business.
– PHRASAL VERBS **pitch in** informal vigorously join in to help with a task or activity. ■ join in a fight or dispute. **pitch into** informal vigorously tackle or begin to deal with. ■ forcefully assault. **pitch out** throw a pitchout. [ME: perh. rel. to OE *picung* 'stigmata.']

pitch² ▶ **n.** a sticky resinous black or dark brown substance that is semiliquid when hot, hard when cold. It is obtained by distilling tar or turpentine and is used for waterproofing. ■ any of various similar substances, such as asphalt or bitumen. ▶ **v.** [trans.] cover, coat, or smear with pitch. — **pitch·y adj.** [OE *pic* (n.), *pician* (v.), of Gmc. origin, based on L. *pix, pic-*.]

pitch-black (also **pitch-dark**) ▶ **adj.** completely dark; as black as pitch. — **pitch-black·ness n.**

pitch·blende /ˈpicHˌblend/ ▶ **n.** a form of the mineral uraninite occurring in brown or black pitchlike masses. [18th C.: from Ger. *Pechblende*, from *Pech* 'pitch' + *Blende* (see **BLENDE**).]

pitch cir·cle ▶ **n.** Mech. an imaginary circle concentric to a toothed wheel, along which the pitch of the teeth is measured.

pitch con·trol ▶ **n. 1** control of the pitch of a helicopter's rotors or an aircraft's propellers. **2** control of the pitching motion of an aircraft.

pitched bat·tle /ˈpicHt ˈbatl/ ▶ **n.** a planned military encounter on a prearranged battleground. ■ a violent or vigorous confrontation involving large numbers of people.

pitch·er¹ /ˈpicHər/ ▶ **n.** a large container, typically earthenware, glass, or plastic, with a handle and a lip, used for holding and pouring liquids. ■ the contents of such a container. ■ the modified leaf of a pitcher plant. — **pitch·er·ful n.** (pl. **-fuls**). [ME: from OFr. *pichier* 'pot,' based on late L. *picarium*.]

pitch·er² ▶ **n.** Baseball the player who delivers the ball to the batter.

pitch·er plant ▶ **n.** a plant (families Nepenthaceae, Sarraceniaceae, and Droseraceae) with a pitcher-shaped pouch that contains fluid into which insects are attracted and trapped.

pitch·fork /ˈpicHˌfôrk/ ▶ **n.** a farm tool with a long handle and sharp metal prongs, used esp. for lifting hay. ▶ **v.** [trans.] lift with a pitchfork. ■ fig. thrust (someone) suddenly into an unexpected and difficult situation.

pitch·man /ˈpicHmən/ ▶ **n.** (pl. **-men**) informal a person delivering a sales pitch.

pitch·out /ˈpicHˌout/ ▶ **n. 1** Baseball a pitch thrown intentionally away from the reach of the batter to allow the catcher a clear throw to put out a base runner who is stealing or leading off too far. **2** (also **pitch**) Football a lateral, esp. from the quarterback to a running back.

pitch pine ▶ **n.** a pine tree that is a source of pitch or turpentine, and typically yielding hard, heavy, resinous timber that is used in building, esp. the longleaf *Pinus rigida* of the Appalachians and northeastern US.

California pitcher plant

pitch pipe ▶ **n.** Music a small reed pipe or set of pipes blown to set the pitch for singing or tuning an instrument.

pitch·pole /ˈpicHˌpōl/ ▶ **v.** [intrans.] dialect somersault. ■ Naut. (of a boat) be overturned so that its stern pitches forward over its bow. [17th C.: from the verb **PITCH¹** + **POLL**.]

pitch·stone /ˈpicHˌstōn/ ▶ **n.** Geol. a dull vitreous rock resembling hardened pitch, formed by weathering of obsidian.

pitch·y /ˈpicHē/ ▶ **adj.** (**pitch·i·er, pitch·i·est**) of, like, or as dark as pitch.

pit·e·ous /ˈpitēəs/ ▶ **adj.** deserving or arousing pity. — **pit·e·ous·ly adv. pit·e·ous·ness n.** [ME: from OFr. *piteus*, from L. *pietas* 'piety, pity' (see **PIETY**).]

pit·fall /ˈpitˌfôl/ ▶ **n.** a hidden or unsuspected danger or difficulty. ■ a covered pit used as a trap.

pith /piTH/ ▶ **n.** **1** soft or spongy tissue in plants or animals, in particular: ■ spongy white tissue lining the rind of an orange, lemon, and other citrus fruits. ■ Bot. the spongy cellular tissue in the stems and branches of many higher plants. **2** fig. the essence of something. **3** fig. forceful and concise expression. ▶ **v.** [trans.] **1** dated, esp. fig. remove the pith from. **2** rare pierce or sever the spinal cord of (an animal) so as to kill or immobilize it. [OE *pitha*, of West Gmc. origin.]

Pith·e·can·thro·pus /ˌpiTHəˈkanTHrəpəs/ ▶ **n.** a former genus name applied to some fossilized hominids found in Java in 1891. See JAVA MAN. [19th C.: mod. L., from Gk. *pithēkos* 'ape' + *anthrōpos* 'man.']

pith·y /ˈpiTHē/ ▶ **adj.** (**pith·i·er, pith·i·est**) **1** (of language or style) concise and forcefully expressive. **2** (of a fruit or plant) containing much pith. — **pith·i·ly** /ˈpiTHəlē/ **adv.** **pith·i·ness n.**

pit·i·a·ble /ˈpitēəbəl/ ▶ **adj.** deserving or arousing pity. ■ contemptibly poor or small. — **pit·i·a·ble·ness n.** **pit·i·a·bly adv.**

pit·i·ful /ˈpitifəl/ ▶ **adj.** deserving or arousing pity. ■ very small or poor; inadequate. — **pit·i·ful·ly adv.** **pit·i·ful·ness n.**

pit·i·less /ˈpitēlis/ ▶ **adj.** showing no pity; cruel. — **pit·i·less·ly adv.** **pit·i·less·ness n.**

pit·man /ˈpitmən/ ▶ **n.** **1** (pl. **-men**) a coal miner. **2** (pl. **-mans**) a connecting rod in machinery.

Pit·ney /ˈpitnē/, Mahlon (1858–1924), US Supreme Court associate justice 1912–22.

pi·ton /ˈpētän/ ▶ **n.** a peg or spike driven into a rock or crack to support a climber or a rope. [19th C.: from Fr., lit. 'eye bolt.']

piton

pi·tot tube /ˈpētō; pēˈtō/ (also **pi·tot**) ▶ **n.** an open-ended right-angled tube pointing in opposition to the flow of a fluid and used to measure pressure. ■ (also **pitot-static tube, pitot head**) a device consisting of a pitot tube inside or adjacent to a parallel tube closed at the end but with holes along its length, the pressure difference between them being a measure of the relative velocity of the fluid or the airspeed of an aircraft. [19th C.: named after Henri *Pitot* (1695–1771), Fr. physicist.]

pit saw (also **pit·saw**) ▶ **n.** hist. a large saw with handles at each end, used in a vertical position by two persons, one standing above the timber to be cut, the other in a pit below it.

pit stop ▶ **n.** Auto Racing a stop in the pits for servicing and refueling, esp. during a race. ■ a brief rest, esp. during a journey. ■ informal a place where one takes such a rest.

Pitt /pit/ a family of British leaders. William, 1st Earl of Chatham (1708–78), known as **Pitt the Elder**, headed coalition governments 1756–61, 1766–68. His son, William (1759–1806), known as **Pitt the Younger**, served as prime minister in 1783 and 1801–04.

pit·tance /ˈpitns/ ▶ **n.** [usu. in sing.] a very small or inadequate amount of money paid to someone as an allowance or wage. [ME: from OFr. *pitance*, from med. L. *pitantia*, from L. *pietas* 'pity.']

pit·ted /ˈpitid/ ▶ **adj.** **1** having a hollow or indentation on the surface. **2** (of a fruit) having had the stone removed.

pit·ter-pat·ter /ˈpitər ˈpatər/ ▶ **n.** a sound as of quick light steps or taps. ▶ **adv.** with this sound. [ME: reduplication of the v. PATTER[1].]

Pitt Is·land see CHATHAM ISLANDS.

pit·tos·po·rum /pəˈtäspərəm; ˌpitəˈspôrəm/ ▶ **n.** an evergreen shrub or small tree (genus *Pittosporum*, family Pittosporaceae) that typically has small fragrant flowers and is native chiefly to Australasia.

Pitts·burgh /ˈpitsˌbərg/ a city in southwestern Pennsylvania; pop. 334,563.

pi·tu·i·tar·y /pəˈt(y)ōōəˌterē/ ▶ **n.** (pl. **-tar·ies**) (in full **pituitary gland** or **pituitary body**) the major endocrine gland. A pea-sized body attached to the base of the brain, the pituitary is important in controlling growth and development and the functioning of the other endocrine glands. Also called HYPOPHYSIS. ▶ **adj.** of or relating to this gland. [17th C.: from L. *pituitarius* 'secreting phlegm,' from *pituita* 'phlegm.']

pit vi·per ▶ **n.** a viper of a group (subfamily Crotalinae) distinguished by visible sensory pits on the head that can detect prey by heat.

pit·y /ˈpitē/ ▶ **n.** (pl. **pit·ies**) **1** the feeling of sorrow and compassion caused by the suffering and misfortunes of others. **2** [in sing.] a cause for regret or disappointment. ▶ **v.** (**pit·ies, pit·ied**) [trans.] feel sorrow for the misfortunes of.
– PHRASES **for pity's sake** informal used to express impatience or make an urgent appeal. **more's the pity** informal used to express regret about a fact that has just been stated. **take** (or **have**) **pity** show compassion. — **pit·y·ing·ly adv.** [ME: from OFr. *pite* 'compassion,' from L. *pietas* 'piety.']

pit·y·ri·a·sis /ˌpitəˈrīəsis/ ▶ **n.** [with adj.] Med. a skin disease characterized by the shedding of fine flaky scales. [17th C.: mod. L., from Gk. *pituriasis* 'scurf,' from *pituron* 'bran.']

piu /pyōō/ ▶ **adj.** Music (esp. as a direction) more.

più mos·so /ˈpyōō ˈmōsō/ ▶ **adv. & adj.** Music (esp. as a direction) more quickly. [Ital.]

Pi·us XII /ˈpīəs/ (1876–1958), pope 1939–58; born *Eugenio Pacelli*. He upheld the neutrality of the Roman Catholic Church during World War II.

piv·ot /ˈpivət/ ▶ **n.** the central point, pin, or shaft on which a mechanism turns or oscillates. ■ [usu. in sing.] a person or thing that plays a central part in an activity or organization. ■ the person or people about whom a body of troops wheels. ■ (also **pivotman**) a player in a central position in a team sport. ■ Basketball a movement in which the player holding the ball may move in any direction with one foot, while keeping the other (the **pivot foot**) in contact with the floor. ▶ **v.** (**piv·ot·ed, piv·ot·ing**) [intrans.] turn on or as if on a pivot. ■ (**pivot on**) fig. depend on. ■ [trans.] provide (a mechanism) with a pivot; fix (a mechanism) on a pivot. — **piv·ot·a·bil·i·ty** /ˌpivətəˈbilitē/ **n.** **piv·ot·a·ble adj.** [ME: from Fr., prob. from the root of dial. *pue* 'tooth of a comb.']

piv·ot·al /ˈpivətl/ ▶ **adj.** of crucial importance in relation to the development or success of something else. ■ fixed on or as if on a pivot.

pix[1] /piks/ ▶ **plural n.** informal pictures, esp. photographs. [1930s: pluralized abbrev.]

pix[2] ▶ **n.** var. of PYX.

pix·el /ˈpiksəl/ ▶ **n.** Electron. a minute area of illumination on a display screen, one of many from which an image is composed. [1960s: acronym from *picture element*.]

pixe·late /ˈpiksəlāt/ (also **pix·el·late** or **pix·il·ate**) ▶ **v.** [trans.] divide (an image) into pixels, typically for display or storage in a digital format. ■ display an image of (someone or something) on television as a small number of large pixels, typically in order to disguise someone's identity. — **pix·e·la·tion** /ˌpiksəˈlāSHən/ **n.**

pix·ie /ˈpiksē/ (also **pix·y**) ▶ **n.** (pl. **pix·ies**) a supernatural being in folklore and children's stories, typically portrayed as small and humanlike in form, with pointed ears and a pointed hat, and mischievous in character. — **pix·ie·ish adj.** [17th C.: of unknown origin.]

pix·i·late /ˈpiksəˌlāt/ ▶ **v.** var. of PIXELATE.

pix·i·lat·ed /ˈpiksəˌlātid/ (Brit. also **pix·il·lat·ed**) ▶ **adj.** crazy; confused. [19th C.: var. of *pixie-led*, lit. 'led astray by pixies,' or from PIXIE.]

pix·i·la·tion /ˌpiksəˈlāSHən/ (Brit. also **pix·il·la·tion**) ▶ **n.** **1** a technique used in film whereby the movements of real people are made to appear like artificial animations. **2** the state of being crazy or confused. **3** var. of *PIXELATION* (see PIXELATE).

Pi·zar·ro /piˈzärō; pēˈsä-; -ˈTHä-/, Francisco (*c.*1478–1541), Spanish conquistador. He defeated the Inca empire.

pizz. ▶ **abbr.** Music pizzicato.

piz·za /ˈpētsə/ ▶ **n.** a dish of Italian origin consisting of a flat base of dough baked with a topping of tomato sauce and cheese, typically with added meat or vegetables. [Ital., lit. 'pie.']

piz·za box ▶ **n.** a computer casing that is not very tall and has a square cross section.

piz·zazz /pəˈzaz/ (also **pi·zazz**) ▶ **n.** informal an attractive combination of vitality and glamour. [unknown.]

piz·ze·ri·a /ˌpētsəˈrēə/ ▶ **n.** a place where pizzas are made or sold; a pizza restaurant. [Ital.]

piz·zi·ca·to /ˌpitsiˈkätō/ Music ▶ **adv.** (often as a direction) plucking the strings of a violin or other stringed instrument with one's finger. ▶ **adj.** performed in this way. ▶ **n.** (pl. **-tos** or **-ti** /-tē/) this technique of playing. ■ a note or passage played in this way. [Ital., lit. 'pinched,' past part. of *pizzicare*, based on *pizza* 'point.']

piz·zle /ˈpizəl/ ▶ **n.** the penis of an animal, esp. a bull. [15th C.: from Low Ger. *pēsel* or Flemish *pezel* (diminutives).]

PJs ▶ **plural n.** informal pajamas.

PK ▶ **abbr.** ■ psychokinesis.

pK ▶ **n.** Chem. a figure expressing the acidity or alkalinity of a solution of a weak electrolyte in a similar way to pH, equal to $-\log_{10} K$ where K is the dissociation (or ionization) constant of the electrolyte. [from *p* as in *pH* and *K* 'constant.']

pk ▶ **abbr.** ■ (also **Pk**) park. ■ peak. ■ peck(s).

pkg. ▶ **abbr.** (pl. **pkgs.**) package.

pkt. ▶ **abbr.** ■ packet. ■ pocket.

PKU ▶ **abbr.** phenylketonuria.

pkwy ▶ **abbr.** (also **pky**) parkway.

PL ▶ **abbr.** ■ Comput. programming language.

pl. ▶ **abbr.** ■ (also **Pl.**) place. ■ plate (referring to illustrations in a book). ■ esp. Mil. platoon. ■ Gram. plural.

PL/1 ▶ **n.** Comput. a high-level programming language used in science, engineering, business, and data processing. [from P(rogramming) L(anguage)/1.]

PLA ▶ **abbr.** People's Liberation Army.

plac·a·ble /ˈplakəbəl/ ▶ **adj.** archaic easily calmed; gentle and forgiving. — **plac·a·bil·i·ty** /ˌplakəˈbilitē/ **n.** **plac·a·bly adv.** [ME: ult. from L. *placabilis*, from *placare* 'appease.']

plac·ard /ˈplakärd; -ərd/ ▶ **n.** a poster or sign for public display, either fixed to a wall or carried during a demonstration. ▶ **v.** [trans.] cover with placards. [15th C.: from OFr. *placquart*, from *plaquier* 'to plaster,' from MDu. *placken*.]

pla·cate /ˈplākāt/ ▶ **v.** [trans.] make (someone) less angry or hostile. — **pla·cat·er n.** **pla·cat·ing·ly** /pləˈkātiNG-lē/ **adv.** **pla·ca·tion** /plāˈkāSHən/ **n.** **pla·ca·to·ry** /-kəˌtôrē; ˈplakə-/ **adj.** [17th C.: from L. *placat-* 'appeased,' from the v. *placare*.]

place /plās/ ▶ **n.** **1** a particular position or point in space. ■ used to refer to an area already identified (giving an impression of informality). ▪ a particular point on a larger surface or in a larger object or area. ▪ a building or area used for a specified purpose or activity. ▪ informal a person's home. ▪ a point in a book or other text reached by a reader at a particular time. **2** a portion of space occupied by someone. ▪ a portion of space available or designated for someone. ▪ a vacancy or available position. ▪ the regular or proper position of something. ▪ [often with negative] somewhere where it is appropriate or prudent for someone to be or for something to occur. ▪ a chance to be accepted or to be of use. ▪ a person's rank or status. ▪ [usu. with negative] a right or privilege resulting from someone's role or position. ▪ the role played by or importance attached to someone or something in a particular context. **3** a position in a sequence, in particular: ▪ a position in a contest. ▪ the second position, esp. in a horse race. ▪ the degree of priority given to something. ▪ the position of a figure in a series indicated in decimal or similar notation, esp. one after the decimal point. **4** [in place names] a square or a short street. ▪ a country house with its grounds. ▶ v. [trans.] **1** [trans.] put in a particular position. ▪ cause to be in a particular situation. ▪ used to express the attitude someone has toward someone or something. ▪ (**be placed**) used to indicate the degree of advantage or convenience enjoyed by someone or something as a result of their position or circumstances. **2** [trans.] find a home or employment for. ▪ dispose of (something, esp. shares) by selling to a customer. ▪ arrange for the recognition and implementation of (an order, bet, etc.). ▪ order or obtain a connection for (a telephone call) through an operator. **3** [trans.] identify or classify as being of a specified type or as holding a specified position in a sequence or hierarchy. ▪ [trans.] [usu. with negative] remember where one has seen or how one comes to recognize (someone or something). ▪ [intrans.] be among the first three in a race.

– PHRASES **give place to** be succeeded or replaced by. **go places** informal visit places; travel. ▪ be increasingly successful. **in place 1** working or ready to work; established. **2** not traveling any distance. **in place of** instead of. **keep someone in his** (or **her**) **place** keep someone from becoming presumptuous. **out of place** not in the proper position; disarranged. ▪ in a setting where one is or feels inappropriate or incongruous. **place in the sun** a position of favor or advantage. **put someone in his** (or **her**) **place** deflate or humiliate someone regarded as being presumptuous. **take place** occur. **take one's place** take up the physical position or status in society that is correct or due for one. **take the place of** replace. [ME: from OFr., from an alt. of L. *platea* 'open space,' from Gk. *plateia (hodos)* 'broad (way).']

pla·ce·bo /plə'sēbō/ ▶ n. (pl. **-bos**) a harmless pill, medicine, or procedure prescribed more for the psychological benefit to the patient than for any physiological effect. ▪ a substance that has no therapeutic effect, used as a control in testing new drugs. ▪ fig. a measure designed merely to calm or please someone. [18th C.: from L., lit. 'I shall please,' from *placere* 'to please.']

place card ▶ n. a card bearing a person's name and used to mark their place at a dining or meeting table.

place·hold·er /'plās,hōldər/ ▶ n. **1** Math. a significant zero in the decimal representation of a number. ▪ a symbol or piece of text used in a mathematical expression or in an instruction in a computer program to denote a missing quantity or operator. **2** Ling. an element of a sentence that is required by syntactic constraints but carries little or no semantic information, for example the word *it* as a subject in *it is a pity that she left*, where the true subject is *that she left*.

place·kick /'plās,kik/ Football ▶ n. a kick made with the ball held on the ground or on a tee. ▶ v. [intrans.] [often as n.] (**placekicking**) take such a kick. — **place·kick·er** n.

place mat (also **place·mat**) ▶ n. a small mat underneath a person's place setting at a dining table.

place·ment /'plāsmənt/ ▶ n. the action of putting someone or something in a particular place or the fact of being placed. ▪ the action of finding a home, job, or school for someone. ▪ Football another term for PLACEKICK. ▪ Football the act of holding the ball for a placekick.

pla·cen·ta /plə'sentə/ ▶ n. (pl. **-tae** /-tē/ or **-tas**) **1** a flattened circular organ in the uterus of pregnant eutherian mammals, nourishing and maintaining the fetus through the umbilical cord. **2** Bot. (in flowers) part of the ovary wall to which the ovules are attached. [17th C.: from L., from Gk. *plakous, plakount-* 'flat cake,' based on *plax, plak-* 'flat plate.']

pla·cen·tal /plə'sentl/ ▶ adj. of or relating to a placenta. ▪ Zool. relating to or denoting mammals that possess a placenta; eutherian. ▶ n. Zool. a placental mammal. See EUTHERIA.

plac·en·ta·tion /,plasən'tāsʜən/ ▶ n. Anat. Zool. the formation or arrangement of a placenta or placentae in a woman's or female animal's uterus. ▪ Bot. the arrangement of the placenta or placentae in the ovary of a flower.

plac·er[1] /'plāsər/ ▶ n. [often as adj.] a deposit of sand or gravel in the bed of a river or lake, containing particles of valuable minerals. [19th C.: from L. Amer. Sp., lit. 'deposit'; rel. to *placel* 'sandbank,' from *plaza* 'a place.']

plac·er[2] ▶ n. **1** [with adj.] a person or animal gaining a specified position in a competition or race. **2** a person who positions, sets, or arranges something.

place set·ting ▶ n. a complete set of dishes and cutlery provided for one person at a meal.

pla·cet /'plāsit/ ▶ n. an affirmative vote, indicated by an utterance of 'placet.' [L., lit. 'it pleases.']

place val·ue ▶ n. the numerical value that a digit has by virtue of its position in a number.

plac·id /'plasid/ ▶ adj. (of a person or animal) not easily upset or excited. ▪ (esp. of a place or stretch of water) calm and peaceful, with little movement or activity. — **pla·cid·i·ty** /plə'siditē/ n. **plac·id·ly** adv. [17th C.: from Fr. *placide*, from L. *placidus*, from *placere* 'to please.']

plack·et /'plakit/ ▶ n. an opening or slit in a garment, covering fastenings or giving access to a pocket, or the flap of fabric under such an opening. [17th C.: var. of PLACARD.]

plac·oid /'plakoid/ ▶ adj. Zool. (of fish scales) toothlike, being made of dentin with a pointed backward projection of enamel, as in sharks and rays. Compare with CTENOID and GANOID. [19th C.: from Gk. *plax, plak-* 'flat plate.']

Plac·o·zo·a /,plakə'zōə/ Zool. a minor phylum that contains a single minute marine invertebrate (*Trichoplax adhaerens*), which has a flattened body with two cell layers and is the simplest known metazoan. [mod. L. (pl.), from Gk. *plakos* 'flat' + *zōia* 'animals.']

pla·fond /plə'fänd/ ▶ n. an ornately decorated ceiling. ▪ a painting or decoration on a ceiling. [Fr., from *plat* 'flat' + *fond* 'bottom.']

pla·gal /'plāgəl/ ▶ adj. Music (of a church mode) containing notes between the dominant and the note an octave higher, having the final in the middle. Compare with AUTHENTIC. [16th C.: from med. L. *plagalis*, based on med. Greek *plagios (hēkhos)* 'plagal (mode),' from Gk. *plagos* 'side.']

plage /pläzʜ/ ▶ n. **1** dated a beach by the sea, esp. at a fashionable resort. **2** Astron. an unusually bright region on the sun. [19th C.: from Fr.]

pla·gia·rism /'plājə,rizəm/ ▶ n. the practice of taking someone else's work or ideas and passing them off as one's own. — **pla·gia·rist** n. **pla·gia·ris·tic** /,plājə'ristik/ adj. [17th C.: from L. *plagiarius* 'kidnapper' (from *plagium* 'a kidnapping,' from Gk. *plagion*).]

pla·gia·rize /'plājə,rīz/ ▶ v. [trans.] take (the work or an idea of someone else) and pass it off as one's own. ▪ copy from (someone) in such a way. — **pla·gia·riz·er** n.

plagio- ▶ comb. form oblique. [from Gk. *plagios* 'slanting,' from *plagos* 'side.']

pla·gi·o·clase /'plājēə,klās/ (also **plagioclase feldspar**) ▶ n. a form of feldspar consisting of aluminosilicates of sodium and/or calcium, common in igneous rocks and typically white. [19th C.: from PLAGIO- + Gk. *klasis* 'cleavage.']

plague /plāg/ ▶ n. a contagious bacterial disease characterized by fever and delirium, typically with the formation of buboes (see BUBONIC PLAGUE) and sometimes infection of the lungs (**pneumonic plague**). ▪ a contagious disease that spreads rapidly and kills many people. ▪ an unusually large number of insects or animals infesting a place and causing damage. ▪ [in sing.] a thing causing trouble or irritation. ▪ a widespread affliction regarded as divine punishment. ▪ [in sing.] archaic used as a curse or an expression of despair or disgust. ▶ v. (**plagues, plagued, pla·guing**) [trans.] cause continual trouble or distress to. ▪ pester or harass (someone) continually. [ME: from L. *plaga* 'stroke, wound,' prob. from Gk. *plēgē, plaga*, from base meaning 'strike.']

pla·guy /'plāgē/ (also **pla·guey**) ▶ adj. [attrib.] informal troublesome; annoying.

plaice /plās/ ▶ n. (pl. same) a North Atlantic flatfish (family Pleuronectidae) that is a commercially important food fish. [ME: from OFr. *plaiz*, from late L. *platessa*, from Gk. *platus* 'broad.']

plaid /plad/ ▶ n. checkered or tartan twilled cloth, typically made of wool. ▪ any cloth with a tartan pattern. ▪ a long piece of plaid worn over the shoulder as part of Scottish Highland dress. — **plaid·ed** adj. [16th C.: from Scot. Gael. *plaide* 'blanket.']

plain[1] /plān/ ▶ adj. **1** not decorated or elaborate; simple or ordinary in character. ▪ without a pattern; in only one color. ▪ bearing no indication as to contents or affiliation. ▪ (of a person) having no pretensions; not remarkable or special. ▪ [attrib.] (of a person) without a special title or status. **2** easy to perceive or understand; clear. ▪ [attrib.] (of written or spoken usage) clearly expressed, without the use of technical or abstruse terms. ▪ not using concealment or deception; frank. **3** (of a person) not beautiful or attractive. **4** [attrib.] sheer; simple (used for emphasis). **5** (of a knitting stitch) made using a knit rather than a purl stitch. ▶ adv. [as submodifier] informal clearly; unequivocally (used for emphasis). ▶ n. a large area of flat land with few trees. ▪ (**the Plains**) another term for GREAT PLAINS.

– PHRASES **as plain as the nose on one's face** informal very obvious. **plain and simple** informal used to emphasize the statement preceding or following. **plain as day** informal very clearly. — **plain·ness** n. [ME: from OFr. *plain*, from L. *planus*, from a base meaning 'flat.']

plain[2] ▶ v. [intrans.] archaic mourn; lament. ▪ complain. ▪ emit a mournful or plaintive sound. [ME: from OFr. *plaindre*, from L. *plangere* 'to lament.']

plain·chant /'plān,cʜant/ ▶ n. another term for PLAINSONG.

plain clothes ▶ plural n. ordinary clothes rather than uniform, esp. when worn as a disguise by police officers. ▶ adj. [attrib.] (**plainclothes**) (esp. of a police officer) wearing such clothes.

plain-laid ▶ adj. denoting a rope consisting of three strands twisted to the right.

plain·ly /'plānlē/ ▶ adv. **1** [as submodifier] able to be perceived easily. ▪ [sentence adverb] used to state one's belief that something is obviously or undeniably true. ▪ in a frank and direct way; unequivocally. **2** in a style that is simple and without decoration.

Plain Peo·ple ▶ plural n. the Amish, the Mennonites, and the Dunkers, three strict Christian sects emphasizing a simple way of life.

plain sail·ing ▶ n. used to describe a process or activity that goes well and is easy and uncomplicated.

plain-saw ▶ v. (past part. **-sawed** /-sôd/ or **-sawn** /-sôn/) [trans.] saw (timber) tangential to the growth rings, so that the rings make angles of less than 45° with the faces of the boards produced. — **plain saw·ing** n.

Plains In·di·an ▶ n. a member of any of various North American Indian peoples who formerly inhabited the Great Plains.

plains·man /ˈplānzmən/ ▶ n. (pl. **-men**) a person who lives on a plain, esp. a frontiersman who lived on the Great Plains of North America.

Plains of A·bra·ham a plateau beside the city of Quebec, overlooking the St. Lawrence River. In 1759 it was the scene of a British victory over the French.

plain·song /ˈplānˌsôNG; -säNG/ ▶ n. unaccompanied church music sung in unison in medieval modes and in free rhythm corresponding to the accentuation of the words, which are taken from the liturgy. Compare with GREGORIAN CHANT.

plain-spo·ken (also **plain·spo·ken**) ▶ adj. outspoken; blunt. — **plain-spok·en·ness** n.

Plains States the US states dominated by the Great Plains, generally including North and South Dakota, Nebraska, Kansas, and sometimes Iowa and Missouri.

plaint /plānt/ ▶ n. esp. literary a complaint; a lamentation. [ME: from Old Fr. *plainte*, fem. past part. of *plaindre* 'complain,' or from OFr. *plaint*, from L. *planctus* 'beating of the breast.']

plain·text /ˈplānˌtekst/ ▶ n. Comput. an original readable text, as opposed to a coded version.

plain·tiff /ˈplāntif/ ▶ n. Law a person who brings a case against another in a court of law. Compare with DEFENDANT. [ME: from OFr. *plaintif* 'plaintive.']

plain·tive /ˈplāntiv/ ▶ adj. sounding sad and mournful. — **plain·tive·ly** adv. **plain·tive·ness** n. [ME: from OFr. *plaintif, -ive*, from *plainte* (see PLAINT).]

plain weave ▶ n. a common and basic style of weave in which the weft alternates over and under the warp.

plait /plāt; plat/ ▶ n. a single length of hair or other flexible material made up of three or more interlaced strands; a braid. ■ archaic term for PLEAT. ▶ v. [trans.] form (hair or other material) into a plait or plaits. ■ make (something) by forming material into a plait or plaits. [ME: from OFr. *pleit* 'a fold,' based on L. *plicare* 'to fold.']

plan /plan/ ▶ n. **1** a detailed proposal for doing or achieving something. ■ [with adj.] a scheme for the regular payment of contributions toward a pension, savings account, or insurance policy. **2** (usu. **plans**) an intention or decision about what one is going to do. **3** a detailed diagram, drawing, or program, in particular: ■ a fairly large-scale map of a town or district. ■ a drawing or diagram made by projection on a horizontal plane, esp. one showing the layout of a building or one floor of a building. Compare with ELEVATION (sense 3). ■ a diagram showing how something will be arranged. ▶ v. (**planned, pla·nning**) [trans.] **1** decide on and arrange in advance. ■ [intrans.] make preparations for an anticipated event or time. **2** design or make a plan of (something to be made or built). [17th C.: from Fr., from earlier *plant* 'ground plan.']

pla·nar /ˈplānər/ ▶ adj. Math. of, relating to, or in the form of a plane: *planar surfaces.*

pla·nar·i·an /pləˈne(ə)rēən/ ▶ n. a free-living flatworm (order Tricladida, class Turbellaria) that has a three-branched intestine and a tubular pharynx, typically located halfway down the body. [19th C.: from mod. L. *Planaria* (fem. of L. *planarius* 'lying flat').]

pla·na·tion /plāˈnāSHən/ ▶ n. the leveling of a landscape by erosion. [19th C.: from PLANE[1].]

planch·et /ˈplanCHit/ ▶ n. a plain metal disk from which a coin is made. [17th C.: dimin. of *planch* 'slab of metal,' from OFr. *planche* 'plank.']

plan·chette /planˈSHet/ ▶ n. a small board supported on casters, typically heart-shaped and fitted with a vertical pencil, used for automatic writing and in seances. [19th C.: from Fr., lit. 'small plank,' dimin. of *planche*.]

Planck /plaNGk; läNGk/, Max Karl Ernst Ludwig (1858–1947), German physicist. He was the founder of the quantum theory. Nobel Prize for Physics (1918).

Planck's con·stant (also **Planck constant**) Physics a fundamental constant, equal to the energy of a quantum of electromagnetic radiation divided by its frequency, with a value of $6.626 \times 10{-}34$ joules.

plane[1] /plān/ ▶ n. **1** a flat surface on which a straight line joining any two points on it would wholly lie. ■ an imaginary flat surface through or joining material objects. ■ a flat or level surface of a material object. ■ a flat surface producing lift by the action of air or water over and under it. **2** a level of existence, thought, or development. ▶ adj. [attrib.] completely level or flat. ■ of or relating to only two-dimensional surfaces or magnitudes. ▶ v. [intrans.] (of a bird or an airborne object) soar without moving the wings; glide. ■ [intrans.] (of a boat, surfboard, etc.) skim over the surface of water as a result of lift produced hydrodynamically. [17th C.: from L. *planum* 'flat surface,' neut. of adj. *planus* 'plain.']

plane[2] ▶ n. an airplane. [20th C.: shortened form.]

plane[3] ▶ n. a tool consisting of a block with a projecting steel blade, used to smooth a wooden or other surface by paring shavings from it. ▶ v. [trans.] smooth (wood or other material) with a plane. ■ [trans.] reduce or remove (redundant material) with a plane: ***high areas can be planed down.*** [ME: from var. of obs. Fr. *plaine* 'planing instrument,' based on L. *planare* 'make level,' from *planus* 'level.']

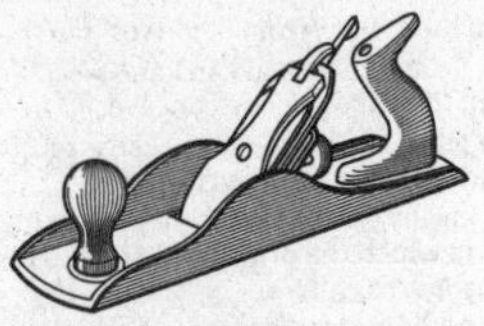
plane[3]

plane[4] (also **plane tree**) ▶ n. a tall spreading tree (genus *Platanus*, family Platanaceae) of the northern hemisphere, with maplelike leaves and bark that peels in uneven patches. See also SYCAMORE. [ME: from OFr., from L. *platanus*, from Gk. *platanos*, from *platus* 'broad.']

plane po·lar·i·za·tion /ˌpōlərəˈzāSHən/ ▶ n. a process restricting the vibrations of electromagnetic radiation, esp. light, to one direction. — **plane-po·lar·ized** adj.

plan·er /ˈplānər/ ▶ n. another term for PLANE[3].

plan·et /ˈplanit/ ▶ n. a celestial body moving in an elliptical orbit around a star. ■ (**the planet**) the earth. ■ esp. Astrol., hist. a celestial body distinguished from the fixed stars by having an apparent motion of its own (including the moon and sun), esp. with reference to its supposed influence on people and events. — **plan·e·tol·o·gy** /ˌplaniˈtäləjē/ n. [ME: ult. from Gk. *planētēs* 'wanderer, planet,' from *planan* 'wander.']

plan·e·tar·i·um /ˌplaniˈte(ə)rēəm/ ▶ n. (pl. **-tar·i·ums** or **-tar·i·a** /-ˈte(ə)rēə/) **1** a domed building in which images of stars, planets, and constellations are projected for public entertainment or education. ■ a device used to project such images. **2** another term for ORRERY. [18th C.: mod. L., from L. *planetarius* 'relating to the planets.']

plan·e·tar·y /ˈplaniˌterē/ ▶ adj. of, relating to, or belonging to a planet or planets. ■ of or relating to the earth as a planet.

plan·e·tar·y neb·u·la ▶ n. Astron. a ring-shaped nebula formed by an expanding shell of gas around an aging star.

plan·e·tes·i·mal /ˌplaniˈtesəməl/ Astron. ▶ n. a minute planet; a body that could come together with many others under gravitation to form a planet. ▶ adj. [attrib.] denoting or relating to such bodies. [20th C.: from PLANET.]

plan·et·oid /ˈplaniˌtoid/ ▶ n. another term for ASTEROID.

plan·form /ˈplanˌfôrm/ ▶ n. the shape or outline of an aircraft wing as projected onto a horizontal plane.

plan·gent /ˈplanjənt/ ▶ adj. esp. literary (of a sound) loud, reverberating, and often melancholy. — **plan·gen·cy** n. **plan·gent·ly** adv. [19th C.: from L. *plangent-* 'lamenting,' from the v. *plangere*.]

pla·nim·e·ter /pləˈnimitər/ ▶ n. an instrument for mechanically measuring the area of a plane figure. — **plan·i·met·ric** /ˌplānəˈmetrik/ adj. **plan·i·met·ri·cal·ly** /-ˈmetrik(ə)lē/ adv. **pla·nim·e·try** /-ˈnimətrē/ n. [19th C.: from Fr. *planimètre*, from L. *planus* 'level' + *-mètre* 'measuring.']

plan·ish /ˈplanisH/ ▶ v. [trans.] flatten (sheet metal) with a smooth-faced hammer or between rollers. — **plan·ish·er** n. [ME: from obs. Fr. *planiss-*, stem of *planir* 'to smooth,' from *plain* 'smooth.']

plan·i·sphere /ˈplanəˌsfi(ə)r/ ▶ n. a map formed by the projection of a sphere or part of a sphere on a plane, esp. an adjustable circular star map that shows the appearance of the heavens at a specific time and place. — **plan·i·spher·ic** /ˌplanəˈsfi(ə)rik; -ˈsfer-/ adj. [ME *planisperie*, based on L. *planus* 'level' + *sphaera* 'sphere.']

plank /plaNGk/ ▶ n. **1** a long, thin, flat piece of timber, used esp. in building and flooring. **2** a fundamental point of a political or other program. ▶ v. [trans.] **1** make, provide, or cover with planks. **2** informal another term for PLUNK (sense 3). **3** cook and serve (meat or fish) on a plank.
– PHRASES **walk the plank** (formerly) be forced by pirates to walk blindfold along a plank over the side of a ship to one's death in the sea. ■ informal lose one's job or position. [ME: from Old North. Fr. *planke*, from late L. *planca* 'board,' fem. of *plancus* 'flatfooted.']

plank·ing /ˈplaNGkiNG/ ▶ n. planks collectively, esp. when used for flooring or as part of a boat. ■ the act or process of laying planks.

plank·ton /ˈplaNGktən/ ▶ n. the small and microscopic organisms drifting or floating in the sea or fresh water, consisting chiefly of diatoms, protozoans, small crustaceans, and the eggs and larval stages of larger animals. Compare with NEKTON. — **plank·tic** /-tik/ adj. **plank·ton·ic** /-ˈtänik/ adj. [19th C.: from Ger., from Gk. *planktos* 'wandering,' from the base of *plazein* 'wander.']

planned e·con·o·my ▶ n. another term for COMMAND ECONOMY.

Planned Par·ent·hood trademark a nonprofit organization that does research into and gives advice on contraception, family planning, and reproductive problems.

plan·ner /ˈplanər/ ▶ n. **1** a person who makes plans. ■ a person who controls or plans urban development. **2** [usu. with adj.] a list or chart with information that is an aid to planning.

plan·ning /ˈplaniNG/ ▶ n. the process of making plans for something. ■ [often as adj.] the control of urban development by a local government authority, from which a license must be obtained to build a new property or change an existing one.

Pla·no /ˈplānō/ a city in northeastern Texas, northeast of Dallas; pop. 222,030.

plano- ▶ comb. form level; flat. [from L. *planus* 'flat.']

pla·no-con·cave /ˌplānōˌkän'kāv; -'känˌkāv/ ▶ adj. (of a lens) with one surface plane and the opposite one concave.

pla·no-con·vex /ˌplānōˌkän'veks; -'känˌveks/ ▶ adj. (of a lens) with one surface plane and the opposite one convex.

pla·no·graph·ic /ˌplānə'grafik/ ▶ adj. Print. relating to or denoting a printing process in which the printing surface is flat, as in lithography. — **pla·nog·ra·phy** /plə'nägrəfē/ n.

plant /plant/ ▶ n. **1** a living organism of the kind exemplified by trees, shrubs, herbs, grasses, ferns, and mosses, typically growing in a permanent site, absorbing water and inorganic substances through its roots, and synthesizing nutrients in its leaves by photosynthesis using the green pigment chlorophyll. ■ a small organism of this kind, as distinct from a shrub or tree: *garden plants.* **2** a place where an industrial or manufacturing process takes place. ■ machinery used in an industrial or manufacturing process. ■ any system that is analyzed and controlled, e.g., the dynamic equations of an aircraft or the equations governing chemical processes. **3** a person placed in a group as a spy or informer. ■ a thing put among someone's belongings to incriminate or compromise them. ▶ v. [trans.] **1** place (a seed, bulb, or plant) in the ground so that it can grow. ■ place a seed, bulb, or plant in (a place) to grow. ■ informal bury (someone). **2** [trans.] place or fix in a specified position. ■ (**plant oneself**) position oneself. ■ establish (an idea) in someone's mind. ■ secretly place (a bomb that is set to go off at a later time). ■ put or hide (something) among someone's belongings to compromise or incriminate the owner. ■ send (someone) to join a group or organization to act as a spy or informer. ■ found or establish (a colony, city, or community). ■ deposit (young fish, spawn, oysters, etc.) in a river or lake. — **plant·a·ble** adj. **plant·let** /-lit/ n. [OE *plante* 'seedling,' *plantian* (v.), from L. *planta* 'sprout,' *plantare* 'plant, fix.']

Plan·tag·e·net /plan'tajənit/ ▶ adj. of or relating to the English royal dynasty that held the throne from the accession of Henry II in 1154 until the death of Richard III in 1485. ▶ n. a member of this dynasty. [from L. *planta genista* 'sprig of broom.']

plan·tain[1] /'plantən/ ▶ n. a low-growing plant (genus *Plantago*, family Plantaginaceae) that typically has a rosette of leaves and a slender green flower spike, widely growing as a weed of lawns. [ME: from OFr., from L. *plantago, plantagin-*, from *planta* 'sole of the foot.']

plan·tain[2] ▶ n. **1** a banana (*Musa × paradisiaca*) containing high levels of starch and little sugar, harvested green and widely used as a cooked vegetable in the tropics. **2** the plant that bears this fruit. [16th C.: from Sp. *plá(n)tano.*]

plan·tain lil·y ▶ n. another term for HOSTA.

plan·tar /'plantər/ ▶ adj. Anat. of or relating to the sole of the foot. [18th C.: from L. *plantaris*, from *planta* 'sole.']

plan·ta·tion /plan'tāsHən/ ▶ n. [often with adj.] an estate on which crops such as coffee, sugar, and tobacco are cultivated by resident labor. ■ an area in which trees have been planted, esp. for commercial purposes. ■ hist. a colony.

plant·er /'plantər/ ▶ n. **1** [often with adj.] a manager or owner of a plantation: *sugar planters.* **2** a decorative container in which plants are grown. **3** a machine or person that plants seeds, bulbs, etc.

plan·ti·grade /'plantiˌgrād/ ▶ adj. (of a mammal) walking on the soles of the feet, like a human or a bear. Compare with DIGITIGRADE. [19th C.: from Fr., based on L. *planta* 'sole' + *-gradus* '-walking.']

plant louse ▶ n. a small bug that infests plants and feeds on the sap or tender shoots, esp. an aphid.

plan·u·la /'planyələ/ ▶ n. (pl. **-lae** /-ˌlē/) Zool. a free-swimming coelenterate larva with a flattened, ciliated, solid body. [19th C.: mod. L., dimin. of L. *planus* 'plane, flat.']

plaque /plak/ ▶ n. **1** an ornamental tablet, typically of metal, porcelain, or wood, that is fixed to a wall or other surface in commemoration of a person or event. **2** a sticky deposit on teeth in which bacteria proliferate. **3** Med. a small, distinct, typically raised patch or region resulting from local damage or deposition of material, such as a fatty deposit on an artery wall in atherosclerosis or a site of localized damage of brain tissue in Alzheimer's disease. ■ Microbiol. a clear area in a cell culture caused by the inhibition of growth or destruction of cells by an agent such as a virus. [19th C.: from Fr., from Du. *plak* 'tablet,' from *plakken* 'to stick.']

plash /plasH/ literary ▶ n. [in sing.] a sound produced by liquid striking something or being struck. ■ a pool or puddle. ▶ v. [intrans.] splash: *gray curtains of rain plashed down.* ■ [trans.] strike the surface of (water) with a splashing sound. — **plash·y** adj. [16th C.: prob. imitative.]

plas·ma /'plazmə/ (also **plasm** /'plazəm/) ▶ n. **1** the colorless fluid part of blood, lymph, or milk, in which corpuscles or fat globules are suspended. ■ this substance taken from donors or donated blood for administering in transfusions. **2** an ionized gas consisting of positive ions and free electrons in proportions resulting in more or less no overall electric charge, typically at low pressures (as in the upper atmosphere and in fluorescent lamps) or at very high temperatures (as in stars and nuclear fusion reactors). ■ an analogous substance consisting of mobile charged particles (such as a molten salt or the electrons within a metal). **3** a dark green, translucent variety of quartz used in mosaic and for other decorative purposes. **4** another term for CYTOPLASM or PROTOPLASM. — **plas·mat·ic** /plaz'matik/ adj. **plas·mic** /-mik/ adj. [18th C.: from late L., lit. 'mold,' from Gk., from *plassein* 'to shape.']

plas·ma cell ▶ n. Physiol. a fully differentiated B cell that produces a single type of antibody.

plas·ma mem·brane ▶ n. Biol. a microscopic membrane of lipids and proteins that forms the external boundary of the cytoplasm of a cell or encloses a vacuole, and that regulates the passage of molecules in and out of the cytoplasm.

plas·ma·pher·e·sis /ˌplazməfə'rēsis/ ▶ n. Med. a method of removing blood plasma from the body by withdrawing blood, separating it into plasma and cells, and transfusing the cells back into the bloodstream. It is performed esp. to remove antibodies in treating autoimmune conditions. [1920s: from PLASMA + Gk. *aphairesis* 'taking away' (from *apo-* 'from' + *hairein* 'take').]

plas·ma screen ▶ n. a flat display screen using an array of cells containing a gas plasma to produce different colors in each cell.

plas·mid /'plazmid/ ▶ n. Biol. a genetic structure in a cell that can replicate independently of the chromosomes, typically a small circular DNA strand in the cytoplasm of a bacterium or protozoan. Plasmids are much used in the laboratory manipulation of genes. Compare with EPISOME. [1950s: from PLASMA.]

plas·min /'plazmin/ ▶ n. Biochem. an enzyme, formed in the blood in some circumstances, that destroys blood clots by attacking fibrin. [19th C.: from Fr. *plasmine*, from late L. *plasma* 'mold.']

plas·min·o·gen /plaz'minəjen/ ▶ n. Biochem. the inactive precursor of the enzyme plasmin, present in blood.

plas·mo·des·ma /ˌplazmə'desmə/ ▶ n. (pl. **-des·ma·ta** /-'desmətə/) Bot. a narrow thread of cytoplasm that passes through the cell walls of adjacent plant cells and allows communication between them. [20th C.: from Ger. *Plasmodesma*, from late L. *plasma* 'mold' + Gk. *desma* 'bond.']

plas·mo·di·um /plaz'mōdēəm/ ▶ n. (pl. **-di·a** /-dēə/) **1** a parasitic protozoan of a genus (*Plasmodium*) that includes those causing malaria. **2** Biol. a form within the life cycle of some simple organisms such as slime molds, typically consisting of a mass of naked protoplasm containing many nuclei. — **plas·mo·di·al** /-mōdēəl/ adj. [19th C.: mod. L., based on late L. *plasma* 'mold.']

plas·mol·y·sis /plaz'mäləsis/ ▶ n. Bot. contraction of the protoplast of a plant cell as a result of loss of water from the cell. [19th C.: mod. L., based on late L. *plasma* 'mold' + Gk. *lusis* 'loosening.']

plas·mo·lyze /'plazməˌlīz/ (Brit. **plas·mo·lyse**) ▶ v. [trans.] Bot. subject to plasmolysis.

plas·ter /'plastər/ ▶ n. **1** a soft mixture of lime with sand or cement and water for spreading on walls, ceilings, or other structures to form a smooth hard surface when dried. ■ (also **plaster of Paris**) a hard white substance made by the addition of water to powdered and partly dehydrated gypsum, used for holding broken bones in place and making sculptures and casts. [so called because prepared from the gypsum of Paris, France.] ■ the powder from which such a substance is made. **2** dated a bandage on which a poultice or liniment is spread for application. See MUSTARD PLASTER. ▶ v. [trans.] cover (a wall, ceiling, or other structure) with plaster. ■ (**plaster something with/in**) coat or cover something with (a substance), esp. to an extent considered excessive. ■ [trans.] make (hair) lie flat by applying a liquid to it. ■ apply a plaster cast or medical plaster to (a part of the body). ■ (**plaster something with**) cover a surface with (large numbers of pictures or posters). ■ (**plaster something over**) present a story or picture conspicuously and sensationally in (a newspaper or magazine). ■ informal, dated bomb or shell (a target) heavily. — **plas·ter·er** n. **plas·ter·y** adj. [OE, 'a bandage,' from med. L. *plastrum* (shortening of L. *emplastrum*, from Gk. *emplastron* 'daub, salve').]

plas·ter·board /'plastərˌbôrd/ ▶ n. a type of drywall made of plaster set between two sheets of paper.

plas·ter cast ▶ n. see CAST[1] (sense 1).

plas·tered /'plastərd/ ▶ adj. **1** informal very drunk. **2** covered with or made of plaster.

plas·ter saint ▶ n. a person who makes a show of being without moral faults or human weakness, esp. in a hypocritical way.

plas·ter·work /'plastərˌwərk/ ▶ n. plaster as part of the interior of a building, esp. covering the surface of a wall or formed into decorative shapes and patterns.

plas·tic /'plastik/ ▶ n. a synthetic material made from a wide range of organic polymers such as polyethylene, PVC, nylon, etc., that can be molded into shape while soft and then set into a rigid or slightly elastic form. ■ informal credit cards or other types of plastic card that can be used as money. ▶ adj. **1** made of plastic. ■ looking or tasting artificial. **2** (of substances or materials) easily shaped or molded. ■ (in art) of or relating to molding or modeling in three dimensions, or producing three-dimensional effects. ■ (in science and technology) of or relating to the permanent deformation of a solid without fracture by the temporary application of force. ■ offering scope for creativity. ■ Biol. exhibiting adaptability to change or variety in the environment. — **plas·ti·cal·ly** adv. [17th C.: ult. from Gk. *plastikos*, from *plassein* 'to mold.']

plas·tic arts ▶ plural n. art forms that involve modeling or molding, such as sculpture and ceramics, or art involving the representation of solid objects with three-dimensional effects.

plas·tic ex·plo·sive ▶ n. a puttylike explosive capable of being molded by hand.

plas·ti·cine /'plastəˌsēn/ (also **Plas·ti·cine**) ▶ n. trademark a soft modeling material, used esp. by children.

plas·tic·i·ty /pla'stisitē/ ▶ n. the quality of being easily shaped or molded. ■ Biol. the adaptability of an organism to changes in its environment or differences between its various habitats.

plas·ti·cize /ˈplastəˌsīz/ ▶**v.** [trans.] [often as adj.] (**plasticized**) make plastic or moldable, esp. by the addition of a plasticizer. ■ treat or make with plastic: *plasticized cotton.* — **plas·ti·ci·za·tion** /ˌplastəsiˈzāshən/ **n.**

plas·ti·ciz·er /ˈplastəˌsīzər/ ▶**n.** a substance (typically a solvent) added to a synthetic resin to produce or promote plasticity and flexibility and to reduce brittleness.

plas·tick·y /ˈplastikē/ ▶**adj.** resembling plastic. ■ seeming artificial or of inferior quality.

plas·tic sur·ger·y ▶**n.** the process of reconstructing or repairing parts of the body, esp. by the transfer of tissue, either in the treatment of injury or for cosmetic reasons. — **plas·tic sur·geon n.**

plas·tic wrap ▶**n.** a thin, transparent plastic film that adheres to surfaces and to itself, used chiefly as a wrapping or covering for food.

plas·tid /ˈplastid/ ▶**n.** Bot. any of a class of small organelles in the cytoplasm of plant cells, containing pigment or food. [19th C.: from Ger., based on Gk. *plastos* 'shaped.']

plas·tique /plaˈstēk/ ▶**n. 1** plastic explosive. **2** statuesque poses or slow graceful movements in dancing. ■ the art or technique of performing such movements. [20th C.: Fr., lit. 'plastic.']

plas·ti·sol /ˈplastəˌsôl; -ˌsäl/ ▶**n.** a liquid substance that can be converted into a solid plastic simply by heating, consisting of particles of synthetic resin dispersed in a nonvolatile liquid. [1940s: from the n. PLASTIC.]

plas·tron /ˈplastrən/ ▶**n. 1** a large pad worn by a fencer to protect the chest. ■ hist. a lancer's breast covering. **2** an ornamental front of a women's bodice or shirt consisting of colorful material with lace or embroidery, fashionable in the late 19th century. ■ a man's starched shirtfront without pleats. **3** Zool. the part of a tortoise's or turtle's shell forming the underside. ■ a similar ventral plate in some invertebrate animals. — **plas·tral** /ˈplastrəl/ **adj.** [16th C.: from Fr., from Ital. *piastrone*, augmentative of *piastra* 'breastplate,' from L. *emplastrum* (see PLASTER).]

-plasty ▶**comb. form** molding, grafting, or formation of a specified part, esp. a part of the body: *rhinoplasty.* [based on Gk. *plastos* 'formed.']

plat[1] /plat/ ▶**n.** a plot of land. ■ a map or plan of an area of land showing actual or proposed features. ▶**v.** [trans.] plan out or make a map of (an area of land, esp. a proposed site for construction). [ME: var. of the n. PLOT.]

plat[2] ▶**n. & v.** var. of PLAIT.

Pla·tae·a, Battle of /pləˈtēə/ a battle in 479 BC, during the Persian Wars, in which the Persian forces were defeated by the Greeks near the city of Plataea in Boeotia.

plat du jour /ˌplä də ˈzhŏŏr/ ▶**n.** (pl. **plats du jour** pronunc. same) a dish specially prepared by a restaurant on a particular day, in addition to the usual menu. [Fr., lit. 'dish of the day.']

plate /plāt/ ▶**n. 1** a flat dish, typically circular and made of china, from which food is eaten or served. ■ an amount of food on such a dish. ■ a similar dish, typically made of metal or wood, passed around a church congregation in order to collect donations of money. ■ a course of a meal, served on one plate. ■ an individual meal, with reference to its cost. ■ Biol. a shallow glass dish on which a culture of cells or microorganisms may be grown. ■ dishes, bowls, cups, and other utensils made of gold, silver, or other metal. ■ a silver or gold dish or trophy awarded as a prize in a race or competition. **2** a thin, flat sheet or strip of metal or other material, typically one used to join or strengthen things or forming part of a machine. ■ a small, flat piece of metal or other material bearing a name or inscription and attached to a door or other object. ■ (usu. **plates**) short for LICENSE PLATE. ■ Bot. Zool. a thin, flat organic structure or formation. ■ Geol. each of the several rigid pieces of the earth's lithosphere that together make up the earth's surface. (See also PLATE TECTONICS.) ■ Baseball short for HOME PLATE. ■ a horizontal timber laid along the top of a wall to support the ends of joists or rafters. **3** a sheet of metal, plastic, or some other material bearing an image of type or illustrations from which multiple copies are printed. ■ a printed photograph, picture, or illustration, esp. one on superior-quality paper in a book. ■ a thin sheet of metal, glass, or other substance coated with a light-sensitive film on which an image is formed, used in larger or older types of cameras. **4** a thin piece of plastic molded to the shape of a person's mouth and gums, to which artificial teeth or another orthodontic appliance are attached. ■ informal a complete denture or orthodontic appliance. **5** a thin piece of metal that acts as an electrode in a capacitor, battery, or cell. ■ the anode of a thermionic tube. ▶**v.** [trans.] **1** cover (a metal object) with a thin coating or film of a different metal. ■ cover (an object) with plates of metal for decoration, protection, or strength. **2** serve or arrange (food) on a plate or plates before a meal. **3** Baseball score (a run or runs); cause (someone) to score. **4** Biol. inoculate (cells or infective material) onto a culture plate, esp. with the object of isolating a particular strain of microorganisms or estimating viable cell numbers.
– PHRASES **on one's plate** occupying one's time or energy: *you've got a lot on your plate at the moment.* — **plate·ful n.** (pl. **-fuls**) [from OFr., from med. L. *plata* 'plate armor,' based on Gk. *platus* 'flat.']

plate ap·pear·ance ▶**n.** Baseball a player's turn at the plate, the total of which for any player includes all official at bats plus appearances that resulted in a walk, sacrifice, etc. Compare with AT BAT.

plate ar·mor ▶**n.** protective armor of metal plates, esp. as worn in medieval times by mounted knights.

pla·teau /plaˈtō/ ▶**n.** (pl. **-teaus** or **-teaux** /-ˈtōz/) an area of fairly level high ground. ■ fig. a state of little or no change following a period of activity or progress. ■ [as adj.] denoting a group of American Indian peoples of the high plains of western Canada and the US, including the Nez Percé. ▶**v.** (**-teaus, -teaued, -teau·ing**) [intrans.] reach a state of little or no change after a time of activity or progress. [18th C.: from Fr., from OFr. *platel*, dimin. of *plat* 'level.']

plate glass ▶**n.** [often as adj.] (**plate-glass**) thick fine-quality glass, typically used for doors and store windows and originally cast in plates.

plate·let /ˈplāt-lit/ ▶**n.** Physiol. a small colorless disk-shaped cell fragment without a nucleus, found in large numbers in blood and involved in clotting. Also called THROMBOCYTE.

plat·en /ˈplatn/ ▶**n. 1** the plate in a small letterpress printing press that presses the paper against the type. **2** the cylindrical roller in a typewriter against which the paper is held. [16th C.: from Fr. *platine* 'flat piece,' from *plat* 'flat.']

Plate Riv·er /plāt/ a wide estuary on the Atlantic coast of South America between Argentina and Uruguay that is formed by the confluence of the Paraná and Uruguay rivers. Spanish name RÍO DE LA PLATA.

plate tec·ton·ics ▶**plural n.** [treated as sing.] a theory explaining the structure of the earth's crust and many associated phenomena as resulting from the interaction of rigid lithospheric plates that move slowly over the underlying mantle. — **plate-tec·ton·ic adj.**

plat·form /ˈplatfôrm/ ▶**n. 1** a raised level surface on which people or things can stand. ■ a raised floor or stage used by public speakers or performers so that they can be seen by their audience. ■ a raised structure along the side of a railroad track where passengers get on and off trains at a station. ■ a raised structure standing in the sea from which oil or gas wells can be drilled or regulated. ■ [usu. with adj.] a raised structure or orbiting satellite from which rockets or missiles may be launched. ■ Comput. a standard for the hardware of a computer system, determining what kinds of software it can run. **2** [usu. in sing.] the declared policy of a political party or group. ■ an opportunity to voice one's views or initiate action. **3** (**platforms**) shoes with very thick soles. [16th C.: from Fr. *plateforme* 'ground plan,' lit. 'flat shape.']

plat·form bed ▶**n.** a bed consisting of a mattress supported by a platform, which sometimes contains drawers for storage.

Plath /plath/, Sylvia (1932–63), US poet; wife of Ted Hughes. Her work, notable for its treatment of extreme and painful states of mind, includes *The Bell Jar* (1963).

plat·ing /ˈplāting/ ▶**n. 1** a thin coating of gold, silver, or other metal. ■ the process of applying such a layer. **2** an outer covering of broad, flattish sections, typically of metal. **3** the process of knitting two yarns together so that each yarn appears mainly on one side of the finished piece.

plat·i·nize /ˈplatnˌīz/ ▶**v.** [trans.] [usu. as adj.] (**platinized**) coat (something) with platinum. — **plat·i·ni·za·tion** /ˌplatn-iˈzāshən/ **n.**

plat·i·noid /ˈplatnˌoid/ ▶**n.** an alloy of copper with zinc, nickel, and sometimes tungsten, used for its high electrical resistance.

plat·i·num /ˈplatn-əm/ ▶**n.** a precious silvery-white metal, the chemical element of atomic number 78. It is used in jewelry, electrical contacts, laboratory equipment, and industrial catalysts. (Symbol: **Pt**) ■ the grayish-white or silvery color of platinum. ▶**adj. 1** of a platinum color. **2** (of a recording) having sold enough copies to merit a platinum disk.
– PHRASES **go platinum** (of a recording) achieve sales meriting a platinum disk. [19th C.: alt. of *platina*, from Sp., dimin. of *plata* 'silver.']

plat·i·num black ▶**n.** platinum in the form of a finely divided black powder, used as a catalyst and absorbent for gases.

plat·i·num blonde ▶**n.** a woman with silvery-blond hair. ▶**adj.** (of a woman's hair) silvery blond.

plat·i·num disk ▶**n.** a framed disk of platinum awarded to a recording artist or group for sales of a recording exceeding one million copies (for albums) or two million copies (for singles).

plat·i·num met·als ▶**plural n.** Chem. the six metals platinum, palladium, ruthenium, osmium, rhodium, and iridium, which have similar properties and tend to occur together in nature.

plat·i·tude /ˈplatiˌt(y)ōōd/ ▶**n.** a remark or statement, esp. one with a moral content, that has been used too often to be interesting or thoughtful. ■ the quality of being dull, ordinary, or trite. — **plat·i·tu·di·nize** /ˌplatiˈt(y)ōōdnˌīz/ **v. plat·i·tu·di·nous** /ˌplatiˈt(y)ōōdn-əs/ **adj.** [19th C.: from Fr., from *plat* 'flat.']

Pla·to /ˈplātō/ (*c.*429–*c.*347 BC), Greek philosopher. A disciple of Socrates and the teacher of Aristotle, he founded the Academy in Athens. His philosophical writings are presented in the form of dialogues, and his political theories appear in the *Republic*.

Pla·ton·ic /pləˈtänik/ ▶**adj.** of or associated with the Greek philosopher Plato or his ideas. ■ (**platonic**) (of love or friendship) intimate and affectionate but not sexual. ■ (**platonic**) confined to words, theories, or ideals, and not leading to practical action. — **pla·ton·i·cal·ly adv.** [16th C.: via L. from Gk. *Platōnikos*, from *Platōn* 'Plato.']

Pla·ton·ic sol·id ▶**n.** one of five regular solids (a tetrahedron, cube, octahedron, dodecahedron, or icosahedron).

Pla·to·nism /ˈplātnˌizəm/ ▶**n.** the philosophy of Plato or his followers. See PLATO. ■ any of various revivals of Platonic doctrines or related ideas, esp. Neoplatonism and Cambridge Platonism (a 17th-century attempt to reconcile Christianity with humanism and science). ■ the theory that numbers or other abstract objects are objective, timeless entities, independent of the physical world and of the symbols used to represent them. — **Pla·to·nist** n.

pla·toon /plə'to͞on/ ▶ n. a subdivision of a company of soldiers, usually forming a tactical unit that is commanded by a lieutenant and divided into several sections. ■ a group of people acting together. ■ (in baseball and other sports) a pairing of two or more teammates who play the same position at different times. ▶ v. [trans.] (in baseball and other sports) have (an athlete) play in rotation with one or more teammates at the same position. ■ [intrans.] play a sport in this way. [17th C.: from Fr. *peloton* 'platoon,' lit. 'small ball,' dimin. of *pelote*.]

pla·toon ser·geant ▶ n. a noncommissioned officer in the US Army intermediate in rank between a staff sergeant and a first sergeant.

Platt·deutsch /'plät,doicн/ ▶ n. & adj. another term for **Low German**. [German, from Du. *Platduits*, from *plat* 'flat, low' + *Duits* 'Ger.']

plat·ter /'platər/ ▶ n. **1** a large flat dish or plate, typically oval or circular in shape, used for serving food. ■ a quantity of food served on such a dish. ■ a meal or selection of food placed on a platter, esp. one served in a restaurant. **2** something shaped like such a dish or plate, esp. of a circular shape, in particular: ■ informal, dated a phonograph record. ■ the rotating metal disk forming the turntable of a record player. ■ Comput. a rigid rotating disk on which data is stored in a disk drive; a hard disk (considered as a physical object).

– PHRASES **on a (silver) platter** informal used to indicate that someone receives or achieves something with little or no effort. [ME: from Anglo-Norman Fr. *plater*, from *plat* 'large dish' (see **plate**).]

Platte Riv·er /'plat/ a river in southwestern Nebraska that joins the Missouri River near Omaha.

platy- ▶ comb. form broad; flat: *platypus*. [from Gk. *platus*.]

Plat·y·hel·min·thes /,platēhel'minтнēz/ Zool. a phylum of invertebrates that comprises the flatworms. — **plat·y·hel·minth** /-'helminтн/ n. [mod. L. (pl.), from **platy-** 'flat' + Gk. *helminth* 'worm.']

plat·y·kur·tic /,plati'kərtik/ ▶ n. Stat. (of a frequency distribution or its graphical representation) having less kurtosis than the normal distribution. Compare with **leptokurtic**, **mesokurtic** — **plat·y·kur·to·sis** /-ikər'tōsis/ n. [20th C.: from **platy-** + Gk. *kurtos* 'bulging.']

plat·y·pus /'platəpəs; -,po͝os/ ▶ n. (pl. **-pus·es**) a semiaquatic egg-laying mammal (*Ornithorhynchus anatinus*, family Ornithorhynchidae) that frequents lakes and streams in eastern Australia. It has a sensitive pliable bill shaped like that of a duck, webbed feet with venomous spurs, and dense fur. [18th C.: mod. L., from Gk. *platupous* 'flatfooted,' from *platus* 'flat' + *pous* 'foot.']

plat·yr·rhine /'platə,rīn; -rin/ Zool. ▶ adj. of or relating to primates of a group (families Cebidae and Callitrichidae, infraorder Platyrrhini) that comprises the New World monkeys, marmosets, and tamarins. They are distinguished by having nostrils that are far apart and directed forward or sideways, and typically have a prehensile tail. Compare with **catarrhine**. ▶ n. a platyrrhine primate. [19th C.: from **platy-** + Gk. *rhis, rhin-* 'nose.']

plau·dits /'plôdits/ ▶ plural n. praise. ■ the applause of an audience. [17th C.: *plaudit* shortened from L. *plaudite* 'applaud!', imper. pl. of *plaudere*.]

plau·si·ble /'plôzəbəl/ ▶ adj. (of an argument or statement) seeming reasonable or probable. ■ (of a person) skilled at producing persuasive arguments, esp. ones intended to deceive. — **plau·si·bil·i·ty** /,plôzə'bilitē/ n. **plau·si·bly** adv. [16th C.: from L. *plausibilis*, from *plaus-* 'applauded,' from v. *plaudere*.]

Plau·tus /'plôtəs/, Titus Maccius (*c*.250–184 BC), Roman playwright. Fantasy and imagination are more important than realism in his plots.

play /plā/ ▶ v. **1** [intrans.] engage in activity for enjoyment and recreation rather than a serious or practical purpose. ■ [trans.] engage in (a game or activity) for enjoyment. ■ amuse oneself by engaging in imaginative pretense. ■ **(play at)** engage in without proper seriousness or understanding. ■ **(play with)** treat inconsiderately for one's own amusement. ■ **(play with)** handle without skill so as to damage or prevent from working. **2** [trans.] take part in (a sport) on a regular basis. ■ participate in (an athletic match or contest). ■ compete against (another player or team) in an athletic match or contest. ■ [intrans.] [usu. with negative] fig. be cooperative. ■ [intrans.] be part of a team, esp. in a specified position, in a game. ■ strike (a ball) or execute (a stroke) in a game. ■ assign to take part in an athletic contest, esp. in a specified position. ■ move (a piece) or display (a playing card) in one's turn in a game. ■ bet or gamble at or on. **3** [trans.] represent (a character) in a theatrical performance or on film. ■ [intrans.] perform in a theatrical production or on film. ■ put on or take part in (a theatrical performance or concert). ■ give a dramatic performance at (a particular theater or place). ■ behave as though one were (a specified type of person). ■ **(play someone for)** treat someone as being of (a specified type). ■ **(play a trick/joke on)** behave in a deceptive or teasing way toward. **4** [trans.] perform on (a musical instrument). ■ possess the skill of performing upon (a musical instrument). ■ produce (notes) from a musical instrument; perform (a piece of music): *they played a violin sonata*. ■ make (an audiotape, CD, radio, etc.) produce sounds. ■ [intrans.] (of a musical instrument, audiotape, CD, radio, etc.) produce sounds. ■ [trans.] accompany (someone) with music as they are moving in a specified direction. **5** [intrans.] move lightly and quickly, so as to appear and disappear; flicker. ■ (of a fountain or similar source of water) emit a stream of gently moving water. **6** [trans.] allow (a fish) to exhaust itself pulling against a line before reeling it in. ▶ n. **1** activity engaged in for enjoyment and recreation, esp. by children. ■ behavior or speech that is not intended seriously. ■ [as adj.] designed to be used in games of pretense; not real. **2** the conducting of an athletic match or contest. ■ the action or manner of engaging in a sport or game. ■ the status of the ball in a game as being available to be played according to the rules. ■ fig. the state of being active, operative, or effective. ■ a move or maneuver in a sport or game. **3** a dramatic work for the stage or to be broadcast. **4** the space in or through which a mechanism can or does move. ■ fig. scope or freedom to act or operate. ■ light and constantly changing movement.

– PHRASES **make a play for** informal attempt to attract or attain. **make (great) play of** (or **with**) draw attention to in an ostentatious manner, typically to gain prestige or advantage. **not playing with a full deck** see **deck**. **play ball** see **ball**[1]. **play both ends against the middle** keep one's options open by supporting or favoring opposing sides. **play something by ear** perform music without having to read from a score. ■ **(play it by ear)** informal proceed instinctively according to results and circumstances rather than according to rules or a plan. **play by the rules** follow what is generally held to be the correct line of behavior. **play one's cards close to one's chest** see **chest**. **play one's cards right** (or **well**) see **card**[1]. **play fair** observe principles of justice; avoid cheating. **play someone false** prove treacherous or deceitful toward someone. **play fast and loose** behave irresponsibly or immorally. **play favorites** show favoritism toward someone or something. **play the field** see **field**. **play for time** use specious excuses or unnecessary maneuvers to gain time. **play the game** see **game**[1]. **play God** see **God**. **play havoc with** see **havoc**. **play hookey** see **hookey**. **play a** (or **one's**) **hunch** make an instinctive choice. **play into someone's hands** act in such a way as unintentionally to give someone an advantage. **play it cool** informal make an effort to be or appear to be calm and unemotional. **play the market** speculate in stocks. **a play on words** a pun. **play** (or **play it**) **safe** take precautions; avoid risks. **play to the gallery** see **gallery**. **play truant** see **truant**. **play with oneself** informal masturbate. **play with fire** take foolish risks.

– PHRASAL VERBS **play around** (or **about**) behave in a casual, foolish, or irresponsible way. ■ informal (of a married person) have a love affair. **play along** pretend to cooperate. **play someone along** informal deceive or mislead someone over a period of time. **play something back** play sounds that one has recently recorded, esp. to monitor recording quality. **play something down** represent something as being less important than it in fact is. **play someone off** bring people into conflict or competition for one's own advantage: *China can no longer play one superpower off against the other*. **play off** (of two teams or competitors) play an extra game or match to decide a draw or tie. **play on** exploit (a weak or vulnerable point in someone). **play someone out** (usu. **be played out**) drain someone of strength or life. **play something out** act the whole of a drama; enact a scene or role. **play something up** emphasize the extent or importance of something. **play up to** humor or flatter, esp. to win favor. — **play·a·bil·i·ty** /,plāə'bilitē/ n. **play·a·ble** adj. [OE *pleg(i)an* 'to exercise,' *plega* 'brisk movement,' rel. to MDu. *pleien* 'leap for joy.']

pla·ya /'plīə/ ▶ n. an area of flat, dried-up land, esp. a desert basin from which water evaporates quickly. [19th C.: Sp., 'beach,' from late L. *plagia*.]

play·act /'plā,akt/ ▶ v. [intrans.] act in a play. ■ [trans.] act (a scene, role, etc.). ■ [usu. as n.] **(playacting)** engage in histrionic pretense. — **play·ac·tor** n.

play·back /'plā,bak/ ▶ n. the reproduction of previously recorded sounds or moving images.

play·bill /'plā,bil/ ▶ n. a poster announcing a theatrical performance. ■ a theater program.

play·boy /'plā,boi/ ▶ n. a wealthy man who spends his time enjoying himself, esp. one who behaves irresponsibly or is sexually promiscuous.

play-by-play ▶ n. a detailed running commentary on an athletic contest.

play date ▶ n. a date and time set by parents for children to play together.

Play·er /'plāər/, Gary (1936–), South African golfer. He won numerous championships between 1961 and 1978.

play·er /'plāər/ ▶ n. **1** a person taking part in a sport or game. ■ a person or body that is involved and influential in an area or activity. **2** a person who plays a musical instrument. ■ a device for playing compact discs, audiocassettes, etc. **3** an actor.

play·er pi·an·o ▶ n. a piano fitted with an apparatus enabling it to be played automatically.

play·fel·low /'plā,felō/ ▶ n. a playmate.

play·ful /'plāfəl/ ▶ adj. fond of games and amusement; lighthearted. ■ intended for one's own or others' amusement rather than seriously. ■ giving or expressing pleasure and amusement. — **play·ful·ly** adv. **play·ful·ness** n.

play·go·er /'plā,gōər/ ▶ n. a person who goes to the theater, esp. regularly.

play·ground /'plā,ground/ ▶ n. an outdoor area provided for children to play on, esp. at a school or public park. ■ a place where a particular group of people choose to enjoy themselves.

play·house /'plā,hous/ ▶ n. **1** a theater. **2** a toy house for children to play in.

play·ing card ▶ n. each of a set of rectangular pieces of cardboard or other material with an identical pattern on one side and different numbers and symbols on the other, used to play various games, some involving gambling. A standard deck contains 52 cards divided into four suits.

play·let /'plālit/ ▶ n. a short play or dramatic piece.

play·list /'plā,list/ ▶ n. a list of recorded songs or pieces of music chosen to be broadcast on a radio show or by a particular radio station.

play·mak·er /ˈplā,mākər/ ▶ **n.** a player in a team game who leads attacks or brings other players on the same side into a position from which they could score. — **play·mak·ing** /-mākiNG/ **n.**

play·mate /ˈplā,māt/ ▶ **n.** **1** a friend with whom a child plays. **2** used euphemistically to refer to a person's lover.

play·off /ˈplā,ôf; -,äf/ ▶ **n.** an additional game or period of play that decides the outcome of a tied contest. ■ **(playoffs)** a series of contests played to determine the winner of a championship, as between the leading teams in different divisions or leagues.

play·pen /ˈplā,pen/ ▶ **n.** a small portable enclosure in which a baby or small child can play safely.

play·room /ˈplā,ro͞om; -,ro͝om/ ▶ **n.** a room in a house that is set aside for children to play in.

play·scape /ˈplā,skāp/ ▶ **n.** a designed and integrated set of playground equipment, often made of wood.

play ther·a·py ▶ **n.** therapy in which emotionally disturbed children are encouraged to act out their fantasies and express their feelings through play, aided by a therapist's interpretations. — **play ther·a·pist n.**

play·thing /ˈplā,THiNG/ ▶ **n.** a toy. ■ fig. a person treated as amusing but unimportant by someone else.

play·time /ˈplā,tīm/ ▶ **n.** time for play or recreation.

play·wright /ˈplā,rīt/ ▶ **n.** a person who writes plays.

play·writ·ing /ˈplā,rītiNG/ ▶ **n.** the activity or process of writing plays.

pla·za /ˈplazə; ˈpläzə/ ▶ **n.** **1** a public square, marketplace, or similar open space in a built-up area. **2** a shopping center. ■ a service area on a highway, typically with a gas station and restaurants. [17th C.: from Sp., lit. 'place.']

plea /plē/ ▶ **n.** **1** a request made in an urgent manner. ■ a claim that one should not be blamed for or should not be forced to do something. **2** Law a formal statement by or on behalf of a defendant or prisoner, stating guilt or innocence. [ME: from OFr. *plait, plaid* 'agreement,' from L. *placitum* 'a decree,' neut. past part. of *placere* 'to please.']

plea bar·gain·ing ▶ **n.** Law an arrangement between a prosecutor and a defendant whereby the defendant pleads guilty to a lesser charge in the hopes of leniency. — **plea-bar·gain v. plea bar·gain n.**

plead /plēd/ ▶ **v.** (past **plead·ed** or **pled** /pled/) **1** [reporting verb] make an emotional appeal. **2** [trans.] present and argue for (a position), esp. in court or in another public context. ■ [intrans.] Law address a court as an advocate on behalf of a party. ■ [intrans.] Law state formally in court whether one is guilty or not guilty of the offense with which one is charged. ■ Law invoke (a reason or a point of law) as an accusation or defense. ■ offer or present as an excuse for doing or not doing something. — **plead·er n. plead·a·ble adj. plead·ing·ly adv.** [ME: from OFr. *plaidier* 'resort to legal action,' from *plaid* (see PLEA).]

plead·ing /ˈplēdiNG/ ▶ **n.** **1** the action of making an emotional or earnest appeal to someone. **2** (usu. **pleadings**) Law a formal statement of the cause of an action or defense.

pleas·ance /ˈplezəns/ ▶ **n.** a secluded enclosure or part of a garden, esp. one attached to a large house.

pleas·ant /ˈplezənt/ ▶ **adj.** (**pleas·ant·er, pleas·ant·est**) giving a sense of happy satisfaction or enjoyment. ■ (of a person or their manner) friendly and considerate; likable. — **pleas·ant·ly adv. pleas·ant·ness n.** [ME: from OFr. *plaisant* 'pleasing,' from the v. *plaisir* (see PLEASE).]

pleas·ant·ry /ˈplezəntrē/ ▶ **n.** (pl. **-ries**) (usu. **pleasantries**) a remark made in polite conversation. ■ a mild joke.

please /plēz/ ▶ **v.** [trans.] **1** cause to feel happy and satisfied: *he arranged a fishing trip to please his son.* ■ [intrans.] give satisfaction. ■ satisfy aesthetically. **2** (**please oneself**) take only one's own wishes into consideration in deciding how to act or proceed. ■ [intrans.] wish or desire to do something: *as you please.* ■ (**it pleases, pleased,** etc., **someone to do something**) dated it is someone's choice to do something. ▶ **adv.** used in polite requests or questions. ■ used to add urgency and emotion to a request. ■ used to agree politely to a request. ■ used in polite or emphatic acceptance of an offer. ■ used to ask someone to stop doing something of which the speaker disapproves.

– PHRASES **as —— as you please** informal used to emphasize the manner in which someone does something, esp. when this is seen as surprising. **if you please 1** used in polite requests. **2** used to express indignation at something perceived as unreasonable. — **pleas·er n. pleas·ing·ly** /ˈplēziNGlē/ **adv.** [ME: from OFr. *plaisir* 'to please,' from L. *placere.*]

pleased /plēzd/ ▶ **adj.** feeling or showing pleasure and satisfaction, esp. at an event or a situation. ■ [trans.] willing or glad to do something. ■ (**pleased with oneself**) proud of one's achievements, esp. excessively so; self-satisfied.

– PHRASES (**as**) **pleased as Punch** see PUNCH[4]. **pleased to meet you** said on being introduced to someone.

pleas·ur·a·ble /ˈplezHərəbəl/ ▶ **adj.** pleasing. — **pleas·ur·a·ble·ness n. pleas·ur·a·bly** /-blē/ **adv.** [16th C.: from PLEASURE, on the pattern of *comfortable.*]

pleas·ure /ˈplezHər/ ▶ **n.** a feeling of happy satisfaction and enjoyment: *she smiled with pleasure at being praised.* ■ enjoyment and entertainment, contrasted with things done out of necessity. ■ an event or activity from which one derives enjoyment. ■ sensual gratification. ▶ **adj.** [attrib.] used or intended for entertainment. ▶ **v.** [trans.] give sexual enjoyment or satisfaction to. ■ [intrans.] (**pleasure in**) derive enjoyment from.

– PHRASES **at someone's pleasure** as and when someone wishes. **have the pleasure of something** used in formal requests and descriptions: *the pleasure of taking her to lunch.* **my pleasure** used as a polite reply to thanks. **take pleasure in** derive happiness or enjoyment from. **what's your pleasure?** what would you like? **with pleasure** gladly (used to express polite agreement or acceptance). [ME: from OFr. *plaisir* 'to please.']

pleas·ure prin·ci·ple ▶ **n.** Psychoanal. the instinctive drive to seek pleasure and avoid pain.

pleat /plēt/ ▶ **n.** a double or multiple fold in a garment. ▶ **v.** [trans.] fold into pleats: [as adj.] (**pleated**) *a short pleated skirt.* — **pleat·er n.** [ME: var. of PLAIT.]

plebe /plēb/ ▶ **n.** informal a newly entered cadet or freshman, esp. at a military academy. [17th C.: perh. abbrev. of PLEBEIAN.]

ple·be·ian /pliˈbēən/ ▶ **n.** (in ancient Rome) a commoner. ■ a member of the lower social classes. ▶ **adj.** of or belonging to the commoners of ancient Rome. ■ of or belonging to the lower social classes. ■ lacking in refinement: *he is a man of plebeian tastes.* [16th C.: from L. *plebeius* (from *plebs, pleb-* 'the common people').]

pleb·i·scite /ˈplebə,sīt/ ▶ **n.** the direct vote of all the members of an electorate. — **ple·bis·ci·tar·y** /pləˈbisi,terē/ **adj.** [16th C. (referring to Roman history): from Fr. *plébiscite,* from L. *plebiscitum,* from *plebs, pleb-* 'the common people' + *scitum* 'decree.']

Ple·cop·ter·a /pləˈkäptərə/ Entomol. an order of insects that comprises the stoneflies. ■ [as pl. n.] (**plecoptera**) insects of this order; stoneflies. — **ple·cop·ter·an** /-tərən/ **n. & adj.** [mod. L. (pl.), from Gk. *plekos* 'wickerwork' (from *plekein* 'to plait') + *pteron* 'wing.']

plec·trum /ˈplektrəm/ ▶ **n.** (pl. **-trums** or **-tra** /-trə/) a thin flat piece of plastic or other slightly flexible material held by or worn on the fingers and used to pluck the strings of a musical instrument. ■ the corresponding mechanical part that plucks the strings of an instrument such as a harpsichord. [ME: via L. from Gk. *plēktron,* from *plēssein* 'to strike.']

pled /pled/ past and past participle of PLEAD.

pledge /plej/ ▶ **n.** **1** a solemn promise or undertaking. ■ a promise of a donation to charity. ■ (**the pledge**) a solemn undertaking to abstain from alcohol. **2** Law a thing that is given as security for the fulfillment of a contract or the payment of a debt. ■ a thing given as a token of love, favor, or loyalty. **3** one who promises to join a fraternity or sorority. ▶ **v.** **1** [trans.] commit (a person or organization) by a solemn promise. ■ [with clause] formally declare or promise that something is or will be the case. ■ [intrans.] solemnly undertake to do something: *they pledged to continue the campaign.* ■ [trans.] undertake formally to give. **2** [trans.] Law give as security on a loan. **3** [trans.] promise to join (a fraternity or sorority).

– PHRASES **pledge one's troth** see TROTH. — **pledg·er n. pledg·or** /ˈplejər/ **n.** (Law). [ME: from OFr. *plege,* from med. L. *plebium,* perh. akin to Gmc. base of PLIGHT[1].]

pledg·ee /pleˈjē/ ▶ **n.** a person to whom a pledge is given.

Pledge of Al·le·giance an oath of loyalty to the US.

pledg·et /ˈplejit/ ▶ **n.** a small wad of soft material used to stop up a wound or an opening in the body. [16th C.: of unknown origin.]

Ple·ia·des /ˈplēədēz/ **1** Gk. Mythol. the seven daughters of the Titan Atlas and the Oceanid Pleione. **2** Astron. an open cluster of stars in the constellation Taurus. [via L. from Gk.]

plein-air /ˈplān ˈe(ə)r/ ▶ **adj.** [attrib.] denoting or in the manner of a 19th-century style of painting outdoors that was a central feature of French Impressionism. [from Fr. *en plein air* 'in the open air.']

plei·ot·ro·py /plīˈätrəpē/ ▶ **n.** Genet. the production by a single gene of two or more unrelated effects. — **plei·o·trop·ic** /,plīəˈtrōpik; -ˈträpik/ **adj. plei·ot·ro·pism** /,plīˈätrə,pizəm/ **n.** [1930s: from Gk. *pleiōn* 'more' + *tropē* 'turning.']

Pleis·to·cene /ˈplīstə,sēn/ ▶ **adj.** Geol. of, relating to, or denoting the first epoch of the Quaternary period. ■ [as n.] (**the Pleistocene**) the Pleistocene epoch or the system of deposits laid down during it. [19th C.: from Gk. *pleistos* 'most' + *kainos* 'new.']

ple·na·ry /ˈplenərē/ ▶ **adj.** **1** unqualified; absolute. **2** (of a meeting) to be attended by all participants at an assembly, who otherwise meet in smaller groups. ▶ **n.** a meeting or session of this type. [ME: from late L. *plenarius* 'complete,' from *plenus* 'full.']

plen·i·po·ten·ti·ar·y /,plenəpəˈtensHē,erē; -ˈtensHərē/ ▶ **n.** (pl. **-ar·ies**) one with the full power of independent action on behalf of one's government. ▶ **adj.** having full power to take independent action. ■ (of power) absolute. [17th C.: from med. L. *plenipotentiarius,* from *plenus* 'full' + *potentia* 'power.']

plen·i·tude /ˈpleni,t(y)o͞od/ ▶ **n.** an abundance. ■ the condition of being full or complete. [ME: from OFr., from late L. *plenitudo,* from *plenus* 'full.']

plen·te·ous /ˈplentēəs/ ▶ **adj.** literary plentiful. — **plen·te·ous·ly adv. plen·te·ous·ness n.** [ME: from OFr. *plentivous,* from *plentif, -ive,* from *plente* 'plenty.' Cf. BOUNTEOUS.]

plen·ti·ful /ˈplentəfəl/ ▶ **adj.** existing in or yielding great quantities; abundant: *the wine is plentiful.* — **plen·ti·ful·ly adv. plen·ti·ful·ness n.**

plen·ty /ˈplentē/ ▶ **pron.** a large or sufficient amount or quantity; more than enough. ▶ n. a situation in which food and other necessities are available in sufficiently large quantities. ▶ adv. [usu. as submodifier] informal used to emphasize the degree of something: *she has **plenty more** ideas.* [ME: from OFr. *plente,* from L. *plenitas,* from *plenus* 'full.']

ple·num /ˈplenəm; ˈplēnəm/ ▶ n. 1 an assembly of all the members of a group or committee. 2 Physics a space completely filled with matter. [17th C.: from L., lit. 'full space,' neut. of *plenus* 'full.']

pleo- ▶ comb. form having more than the usual or expected number: *pleomorphism.* [from Gk. *pleōn* 'more.']

ple·o·chro·ic /ˌplēəˈkrōik/ ▶ adj. (of a crystal) absorbing different wavelengths of light differently depending on the direction of incidence of the rays or their plane of polarization. — **ple·och·ro·ism** /-ˈkrōˌizəm/ n. [19th C.: from PLEO- + *khrōs* 'color.']

ple·o·mor·phism /ˌplēəˈmôrˌfizəm/ ▶ n. the occurrence of more than one form of a natural object. — **ple·o·mor·phic** /-fik/ adj. [19th C.: from Gk. *pleiōn* 'more' + *morphē* 'form.']

ple·o·nasm /ˈplēəˌnazəm/ ▶ n. the use of more words than are necessary to convey meaning (e.g., *see with one's eyes*), either as a fault of style or for emphasis. — **ple·o·nas·tic** /ˌplēəˈnastik/ adj. **ple·o·nas·ti·cal·ly** /ˌplēəˈnastik(ə)lē/ adv. [16th C.: via late L. from Gk. *pleonasmos,* from *pleonazein* 'be superfluous.']

ple·o·pod /ˈplēəˌpäd/ ▶ n. Zool. a forked swimming limb of a crustacean, five pairs of which are typically attached to the abdomen. Also called SWIMMERET. [19th C.: from Gk. *plein* 'swim, sail' + *pous, pod-* 'foot.']

ple·ro·ma /pləˈrōmə/ ▶ n. [in sing.] 1 (in Gnosticism) the spiritual universe as the abode of God and of the totality of the divine powers and emanations. 2 (in Christian theology) the totality or fullness of the Godhead that dwells in Christ. — **ple·ro·mat·ic** /ˌplerəˈmatik/ adj. [18th C.: from Gk. *plērōma* 'that which fills,' from *plēroun* 'make full,' from *plērēs* 'full.']

ple·si·o·saur /ˈplēsēəˌsôr/ ▶ n. a large extinct marine reptile (Plesiosauridae and other families, infraorder Plesiosauria, superorder Sauropterygia) of the Mesozoic era, with a broad flat body, large paddlelike limbs, and typically a long flexible neck and small head. [19th C.: from mod. L. *Plesiosaurus,* from Gk. *plēsios* 'near' + *sauros* 'lizard.']

ples·sor /ˈplesər/ ▶ n. var. of PLEXOR.

pleth·o·ra /ˈpleTHərə/ ▶ n. (**a plethora of**) an excess of. ■ Med. an excess of a bodily fluid, particularly blood. — **ple·thor·ic** /ˈpleTHərik; pləˈTHôrik/ adj. (archaic or Med.). [16th C.: via late L. from Gk. *plēthōrē,* from *plēthein* 'be full.']

ple·thys·mo·graph /pləˈTHizməˌgraf/ ▶ n. Med. an instrument for recording and measuring variation in the volume of a part of the body. — **ple·thys·mo·graph·ic** /pləˌTHizməˈgrafik/ adj. **pleth·ys·mog·ra·phy** /ˌpleTHizˈmägrəfē/ n. [19th C.: from Gk. *plēthusmos* 'enlargement' (based on *plēthus* 'fullness').]

pleu·ra /ˈplo͝orə/ ▶ n. (pl. **pleu·rae** /ˈplo͝orē/) 1 each of a pair of serous membranes lining the thorax and enveloping the lungs in humans and other mammals. 2 Zool. a lateral part in an animal body or structure. Compare with PLEURON. — **pleu·ral** adj. [ME: via med. L. from Gk., lit. 'side of the body.']

pleu·ri·sy /ˈplo͝orəsē/ ▶ n. Med. inflammation of the pleurae, which causes pain when breathing. — **pleu·rit·ic** /plo͝oˈritik/ adj. [ME: from OFr. *pleurisie,* from late L. *pleurisis,* based on Gk. *pleura* 'side of the body.']

pleuro- ▶ comb. form of or relating to the pleura or pleurae: *pleuropneumonia.* [from Gk. *pleura* 'side,' *pleuron* 'rib.']

pleu·ron /ˈplo͝oˌrän/ ▶ n. (pl. **pleu·ra** /ˈplo͝orə/) Zool. the sidewall of each segment of the body of an arthropod. [18th C.: from Gk., lit. 'side of the body.']

pleu·ro·pneu·mo·nia /ˌplo͝orəˌn(y)o͞oˈmōnyə/ ▶ n. pneumonia complicated with pleurisy.

Ple·ven /ˈplevən/ a city northern Bulgaria; pop. 168,000.

plew /plo͞o/ ▶ n. hist. a beaver skin, used as a standard unit of value in the fur trade. [19th C.: from Canad. Fr. *pélu* 'hairy,' from Fr. *poil* 'hair, bristle.']

Plex·i·glas /ˈpleksiˌglas/ (also **plex·i·glas** or **plex·i·glass**) ▶ n. trademark a solid transparent plastic made of polymethyl methacrylate. [1930s: from Gk. *plēxis* 'percussion' + GLASS.]

plex·or /ˈpleksər/ (also **ples·sor**) ▶ n. Med. a small hammer with a rubber head used to test reflexes. [19th C.: formed irregularly from Gk. *plēxis* 'percussion' (from *plēssein* 'to strike').]

plex·us /ˈpleksəs/ ▶ n. (pl. same or **plex·us·es**) Anat. a network of nerves or vessels in the body. ■ an intricate network or weblike formation. — **plex·i·form** /ˈpleksəˌfôrm/ adj. [17th C.: from L., lit. 'plaited formation,' past part. of *plectere* 'to plait.']

pli·a·ble /ˈplīəbəl/ ▶ adj. easily bent; flexible. ■ fig. easily influenced: *pliable teenage minds.* — **pli·a·bil·i·ty** /ˌplīəˈbilitē/ n. **pli·a·bly** /-əblē/ adv. [ME: from Fr., from *plier* 'to bend' (see PLY¹).]

pli·ant /ˈplīənt/ ▶ adj. pliable: *pliant willow stems.* — **pli·an·cy** /ˈplīənsē/ n. **pli·ant·ly** adv. [ME: from OFr., lit. 'bending,' pres. part. of *plier.*]

pli·ca /ˈplīkə/ ▶ n. 1 (pl. **-cae** /-kē; -sē/ or **-cas**) Anat. a fold or ridge of tissue. ■ Bot. a small lobe between the petals of a flower. 2 Med. a densely matted condition of the hair. [17th C.: mod. L., from med. L., 'fold,' from *plicare* 'to fold.']

pli·cate /ˈplīkāt; -kit/ ▶ adj. Biol. Geol. folded, crumpled, or corrugated. — **pli·cat·ed** adj. [18th C.: from L. *plicatus* 'folded,' past part. of *plicare.*]

pli·ca·tion /plīˈkāSHən/ ▶ n. a fold or corrugation. ■ the manner of folding or condition of being folded. [ME: via OFr. from med. L. *plicatio(n-),* from L. *plicare* 'to fold.']

pli·é /plēˈā/ Ballet ▶ n. a movement in which a dancer bends the knees and straightens them again. ▶ v. [intrans.] perform a plié. [Fr., lit. 'bent,' past part. of *plier* (see also PLY¹).]

pli·ers /ˈplīərz/ (also **a pair of pliers**) ▶ plural n. pincers with parallel, flat, and typically serrated surfaces, used for gripping small objects or bending wire. [16th C.: from dial. *ply* 'bend,' from Fr. *plier* 'to bend,' from L. *plicare* 'to fold.']

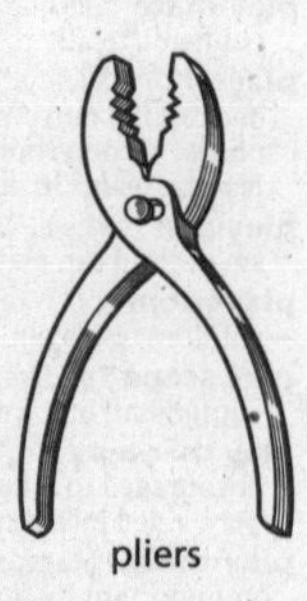
pliers

plight¹ /plīt/ ▶ n. a dangerous, difficult, or otherwise unfortunate situation: *the plight of poor children.* [ME: from Anglo-Norman Fr. *plit* 'fold.']

plight² ▶ v. [trans.] archaic pledge or promise solemnly. ■ (**be plighted to**) be engaged to be married to.

— PHRASES **plight one's troth** see TROTH. [OE *plihtan* 'endanger,' of Gmc. origin; rel. to Ger. *Pflicht* 'duty.']

Plim·soll line /ˈplimsəl; -sōl/ (also **Plimsoll mark**) ▶ n. a marking on a ship's side showing the limit of submersion legal under various conditions. [Samuel *Plimsoll* (1824–98), the Engl. politician.]

plink /pliNGk/ ▶ v. [intrans.] emit a short, sharp, metallic or ringing sound. ■ play a musical instrument in such a way as to produce such sounds. ■ [trans.] shoot at (a target) casually. ▶ n. a short, sharp, metallic or ringing sound. — **plink·y** adj. [1940s: imitative.]

plinth /plinTH/ ▶ n. a base supporting a statue or vase. ■ Archit. the lower slab at the base of a column. [16th C.: from L. *plinthus,* from Gk. *plinthos* 'tile.']

Plin·y¹ /ˈplinē; ˈplīnē/ (23–79), Roman statesman and scholar; Latin name *Gaius Plinius Secundus*; known as **Pliny the Elder**. His *Natural History* (77) is a vast encyclopedia of the natural and human worlds.

Plin·y² (*c.*61–*c.*112), Roman senator and writer; Latin name *Gaius Plinius Caecilius Secundus*; known as **Pliny the Younger**; nephew of Pliny the Elder. He is noted for his books of letters.

Pli·o·cene /ˈplīəˌsēn/ ▶ adj. Geol. of, relating to, or denoting the last epoch of the Tertiary period. ■ [as n.] (**the Pliocene**) the Pliocene epoch or the system of rocks deposited during it. [19th C.: from Gk. *pleiōn* 'more' + *kainos* 'new.']

plis·sé /plēˈsā; pli-/ ▶ adj. (of fabric) treated to give a permanent puckered or crinkled effect. ▶ n. material treated in this way. [19th C.: Fr., lit. 'pleated,' past part. of *plisser.*]

PLO ▶ abbr. Palestine Liberation Organization.

plod /pläd/ ▶ v. (**plod·ded, plod·ding**) [no obj., with adverbial of direction] walk slowly with heavy steps. ■ work slowly and perseveringly at a dull task. ▶ n. a slow, heavy walk: *he settled down to a steady plod.* ■ the sound of a heavy, dull tread; a thud. — **plod·der** n. [16th C.: prob. symbolic.]

plod·ding /ˈplädiNG/ ▶ adj. slow and unexciting. ■ (of a person) thorough and hardworking but lacking in imagination or intelligence. — **plod·ding·ly** adv.

-ploid ▶ comb. form Biol. denoting the number of sets of chromosomes in a cell: *triploid.* [based on *(ha)ploid* and *(di)ploid.*]

ploi·dy /ˈploidē/ ▶ n. Genet. the number of sets of chromosomes in a cell, or in the cells of an organism. [1940s: from *(di)ploidy, (poly)ploidy,* etc.]

Plo·ieș·ti /plôˈyesHt(ē)/ a city in central Romania, north of Bucharest; pop. 254,000.

plonk¹ /pläNGk/ informal ▶ v. 1 [with obj. and adverbial of place] set down heavily or carelessly. ■ (**plonk oneself**) sit down heavily, without ceremony. 2 [intrans.] play on a musical instrument laboriously or unskillfully. ▶ n. a sound as of something being set down heavily. [19th C.: imitative.]

plonk² ▶ n. informal cheap wine of inferior quality. [1930s: prob. alt. of Fr. *vin blanc* 'white wine.']

plop /pläp/ ▶ n. a short sound as of a small, solid object dropping into water without a splash. ▶ v. (**plopped, plop·ping**) fall or cause to fall with such a sound: *she plopped into the pond.* ■ (**plop oneself down**) sit or lie down clumsily. [19th C.: imitative.]

plo·sion /ˈplōZHən/ ▶ n. Phonet. the sudden release of air in the pronunciation of a plosive consonant. [20th C.: shortening of EXPLOSION.]

plo·sive /ˈplōsiv/ Phonet. ▶ adj. denoting a consonant that is produced by stopping the airflow using the lips, teeth, or palate, followed by a sudden release of air. ▶ n. a plosive speech sound. The basic plosives in English are *t, k,* and *p* (voiceless) and *d, g,* and *b* (voiced). [19th C.: shortening of EXPLOSIVE.]

plot /plät/ ▶ n. 1 a plan made in secret by a group of people to do something illegal or harmful. 2 the main events of a play, novel, movie, or similar work, presented as an interrelated sequence. 3 a small piece of ground marked out for a purpose: *a vegetable plot.* 4 a graph showing the relation between two variables. ■ a diagram, chart, or map. ▶ v. (**plot·ted, plot·ting**) [trans.] 1 secretly make plans to carry out (an illegal or harmful action). 2 devise the sequence of events in (a play, novel, etc.). 3 mark (a route or position) on a chart. ■ mark out or allocate (points) on a graph. ■ make (a curve) by marking out a number of such points. ■ illustrate by use of a graph.

— PHRASES **the plot thickens** see THICKEN. — **plot·less** adj. **plot·ter** /ˈplätər/ n. [OE: of unknown origin.]

Plo·ti·nus /plō'tīnəs/ (c.205–270), Roman philosopher; born in Egypt. He founded Neoplatonism.

plot line ▶ n. the course or main features of a narrative.

plotz /pläts/ ▶ v. [intrans.] informal collapse or be beside oneself with frustration or other strong emotion. [1960s: from Yiddish *platsen*, lit. 'to burst,' from Mid. High Ger. *platzen*.]

plough·man's lunch /'ploumənz/ ▶ n. Brit. a meal of bread and cheese, typically with pickled vegetables and salad.

Plov·div /'plôv,dif/ a city in southern Bulgaria; pop. 379,000. It was known to the ancient Greeks as Philippopolis and to the Romans as Trimontium.

plov·er /'pləvər; 'plō-/ ▶ n. a short-billed gregarious wading bird, typically found by water but sometimes frequenting grassland, tundra, and mountains. The **plover family** (Charadriidae) includes several genera, esp. *Charadrius* (ringed plovers), *Pluvialis* (golden plovers), and *Vanellus* (lapwings). [ME: from Anglo-Norman Fr., based on L. *pluvia* 'rain.']

plow /plou/ (Brit. **plough**) ▶ n. a large farming implement with one or more blades fixed in a frame, drawn by a tractor or by animals and used for cutting furrows in the soil and turning it over. ■ a snowplow. ▶ v. [trans.] **1** turn up earth with a plow. ■ cut (a furrow or line) with or as if with a plow. ■ (of a ship or boat) travel through (an area of water). **2** [intrans.] (esp. of a vehicle) move in a fast and uncontrolled manner. ■ advance or progress laboriously or forcibly. ■ (**plow on**) continue steadily despite difficulties or warnings to stop. **3** clear snow from (a road) using a snowplow.
– PHRASES **plow a lonely** (or **one's own**) **furrow** follow a course of action in which one is isolated or can act independently. **put** (or **set**) **one's hand to the plow** embark on a task.
– PHRASAL VERBS **plow something in/back** plow grass or other material into the soil to enrich it. ■ invest money in a business or reinvest profits in the enterprise producing them. **plow under** bury in the soil by plowing. **plow up** till (soil) completely or thoroughly. ■ uncover by plowing. — **plow·a·ble** adj. **plow·er** n. [OE *plōh*, of Gmc. origin; rel. to Ger. *Pflug*.]

plow·man /'ploumən/ (Brit. **plough·man**) ▶ n. (pl. **-men**) a person who uses a plow.

plow·share /'plou,sнe(ə)r/ (Brit. **plough·share**) ▶ n. the main cutting blade of a plow, behind the coulter. [ME: from *plowgh*, an earlier spelling of PLOW + OE *scær*, *scear* 'plowshare' (rel. to SHEAR).]

ploy /ploi/ ▶ n. a cunning plan or action designed to turn a situation to one's own advantage. [17th C.: of unknown origin.]

plu. ▶ abbr. plural.

pluck /plək/ ▶ v. [trans.] take hold of (something) and quickly remove it from its place; pick. ■ catch hold of and pull quickly. ■ quickly or suddenly remove someone from a dangerous or unpleasant situation. ■ pull the feathers from (a bird's carcass) to prepare it for cooking. ■ pull some of the hairs from (one's eyebrows) to make them look neater. ■ sound (a musical instrument or its strings) with one's finger or a plectrum. ▶ n. **1** spirited and determined courage: *it took a lot of pluck to face him.* **2** the heart, liver, and lungs of an animal as food.
– PHRASAL VERBS **pluck up courage** see COURAGE. — **pluck·er** n. [usu. in comb.] *a goose-plucker.* [OE *ploccian*, *pluccian*, of Gmc. origin, prob. from the base of OFr. *(es)peluchier* 'to pluck.']

pluck·y /'pləkē/ ▶ adj. (**pluck·i·er**, **pluck·i·est**) having or showing determined courage in the face of difficulties. — **pluck·i·ly** /'pləkəlē/ adv. **pluck·i·ness** n.

plug /pləg/ ▶ n. **1** a piece of solid material fitting tightly into a hole and blocking it up. ■ a circular piece of metal, rubber, or plastic used to stop the drain of a bathtub or basin. ■ informal a baby's pacifier. ■ a mass of solidified lava filling the neck of a volcano. ■ (in gardening) a young plant with a small mass of soil protecting its roots. **2** a device for making an electrical connection, consisting of an insulated casing with metal pins that fit into holes in a outlet. ■ short for SPARK PLUG. **3** informal a piece of publicity promoting something. **4** a piece of tobacco. ■ (also **plug tobacco**) tobacco in large cakes designed to be cut for chewing. **5** Fishing a lure with one or more hooks attached. **6** short for FIREPLUG. **7** informal a tired or old horse. ▶ v. (**plugged**, **plug·ging**) [trans.] **1** block or fill in (a hole or cavity). ■ insert (something) into an opening so as to fill it. **2** informal mention (a product, event, or establishment) publicly in order to promote it: *plug a new record.* **3** informal shoot or hit (someone or something). **4** [no obj., with adverbial] informal proceed steadily and laboriously with a journey or task.
– PHRASES **pull the plug** see PULL.
– PHRASAL VERBS **plug something in** connect an electrical appliance to a power supply by inserting a plug into a outlet. **plug into** (of an electrical appliance) be connected to another appliance by a plug inserted in a outlet. ■ gain or have access to a system of computerized information. ■ fig. become knowledgeable about and involved with. — **plug·ger** n. [17th C.: from MDu., Mid. Low Ger. *plugge*.]

Plug and Play (also **plug and play**) ▶ n. a standard for the connection of peripherals to personal computers, whereby a device only needs to be connected to a computer in order to be configured to work perfectly.

plug·board /'pləg,bôrd/ ▶ n. a board containing several sockets into which plugs can be inserted.

plug-com·pat·i·ble ▶ adj. relating to or denoting computing equipment that is compatible with devices or systems produced by different manufacturers. ▶ n. computing equipment designed in this way.

plug fuse ▶ n. a fuse designed to be pushed into a socket in a panel or board.

plugged-in informal ▶ adj. aware of what is going on or what is up to date; alert: *plugged-in politicians.*

plug-in ▶ adj. able to be connected by means of a plug. ■ Comput. (of a module or software) able to be added to a system to give extra features or functions. ▶ n. **1** Comput. a module or software of this kind. **2** Canadian an electric socket in a garage for plugging in the block heater of a vehicle to prevent from freezing.

plug-ug·ly informal ▶ n. (pl. **-lies**) a thug or villain. ▶ adj. very ugly: *that was one plug-ugly dress.* [from PLUG.]

plum /pləm/ ▶ n. **1** an oval fleshy fruit that is purple, reddish, or yellow when ripe and contains a flattish pointed pit. **2** (also **plum tree**) the deciduous tree (genus *Prunus*) of the rose family that bears this fruit. **3** a reddish-purple color: [as adj.] *a plum blazer.* **4** [usu. as adj.] informal a thing, typically a job, considered to be highly desirable: *he landed a plum assignment.* ▶ adv. var. of PLUMB[1]. [OE *plūme*, from med. L. *pruna*, from L. *prunum* (see PRUNE[1]).]

plum·age /'ploomij/ ▶ n. a bird's feathers collectively. — **plum·aged** adj. [ME: from OFr., from *plume* 'feather.']

plumb[1] /pləm/ ▶ v. [trans.] **1** measure (the depth of a body of water). ■ [intrans.] (of water) be of a specified depth. ■ explore or experience fully or to extremes: *plumb the depths of depravity.* **2** test (an upright surface) to determine the vertical. ▶ n. a plumb bob. ▶ adv. informal exactly: *plumb in the middle.* ■ [as submodifier] to a very high degree; extremely. ■ [as submodifier] completely: *plumb worn out.* ▶ adj. vertical.
– PHRASES **out of plumb** not exactly vertical. [ME: via OFr. from L. *plumbum* 'lead.']

plumb[2] ▶ v. [trans.] install and connect water and drainage pipes in (a building or room). [19th C.: back-form. from PLUMBER.]

plum·ba·go /pləm'bāgō/ ▶ n. (pl. **-gos**) **1** old-fashioned term for GRAPHITE. [17th C.: from L. *plumbum* 'lead.' The sense 'graphite' arose through its use for pencil leads.] **2** an evergreen flowering shrub or climber (*Plumbago*, family Plumbaginaceae) widely distributed in warm regions and grown elsewhere as an indoor plant. Also called LEADWORT.

plumb bob ▶ n. a bob of lead or other heavy material forming the weight of a plumb line.

plum·be·ous /'pləmbēəs/ ▶ adj. esp. Ornithol. of the dull gray color of lead. [16th C.: from L. *plumbeus* 'leaden' (from *plumbum* 'lead').]

plumb·er /'pləmər/ ▶ n. a person who fits and repairs the pipes, fittings, and other apparatus of water supply, sanitation, or heating systems. [ME: from OFr. *plommier*, from L. *plumbarius*, from *plumbum* 'lead.']

plumb·er's help·er ▶ n. informal a plunger.

plumb·er's snake ▶ n. see SNAKE.

plum·bic /'pləmbik/ ▶ adj. Chem. of lead with a valence of four; of lead (IV). Compare with PLUMBOUS. ■ Med. caused by the presence of lead. [18th C.: from L. *plumbum* 'lead.']

plumb·ing /'pləmiNG/ ▶ n. the system of pipes, tanks, fittings, and other apparatus required for the water supply, heating, and sanitation in a building. ■ the work of installing and maintaining such a system. ■ informal used as a humorous euphemism for the excretory tracts and urinary system.

plum·bism /'pləm,bizəm/ ▶ n. technical term for LEAD POISONING.

plumb line ▶ n. a line with a plumb attached to it, used for finding the depth of water or determining the vertical of an upright surface.

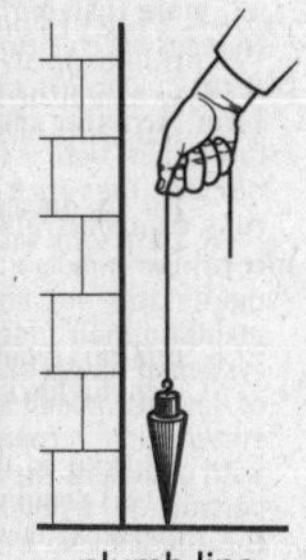

plumb line

plum·bous /'pləmbəs/ ▶ adj. Chem. of lead with a valence of two; of lead (II). Compare with PLUMBIC. [17th C.: from L. *plumbosus* 'full of lead.']

plumb rule ▶ n. a plumb line attached to a board.

plume /ploom/ ▶ n. a long, soft feather or arrangement of feathers on a bird or worn for ornament. ■ Zool. a part of an animal's body that resembles a feather. ■ a long cloud of smoke or vapor resembling a feather. ■ (also **mantle plume**) Geol. a localized column of hot magma rising by convection in the mantle. ▶ v. [intrans.] spread out in a shape resembling a feather: *smoke plumed from the chimneys.* ■ [trans.] decorate with or as if with feathers: [as adj.] (**plumed**) *a plumed cap.* — **plume·less** adj. **plume·like** /-,līk/ adj. **plum·er·y** /-mərē/ n. [ME: from OFr., from L. *pluma* 'down.']

Plumed Ser·pent ▶ n. a mythical creature depicted as part bird, part snake, in particular Quetzalcóatl, a god of the Toltec and Aztec civilizations having this form.

plu·me·ri·a /ploo'mi(ə)rēə/ ▶ n. a fragrant flowering tropical tree of the dogbane family, of a genus (*Plumeria*) that includes frangipani. [mod. L., named after Charles *Plumier* (1646–1704), Fr. botanist.]

plum·met /'pləmit/ ▶ v. (**-met·ed**, **-met·ing**) [intrans.] fall or drop straight down at high speed. ■ decrease rapidly in value or amount. ▶ n. **1** a steep and rapid fall or drop. **2** a plumb or plumb line. [ME: from OFr. *plommet* 'small sounding lead,' dimin. of *plomb* 'lead.']

plu·mose /'ploo,mōs/ ▶ adj. esp. Biol. having many fine filaments or branches that give a feathery appearance. [18th C.: from L. *plumosus* 'full of down,' from *pluma* 'down.']

plump[1] /pləmp/ ▶ **adj.** having a full rounded shape. ■ slightly fat. ▶ **v.** [trans.] shake or pat (a cushion or pillow) to adjust its stuffing and make it rounded and soft. ■ [intrans.] (**plump up**) become rounder and fatter. — **plump·ish adj. plump·ly adv. plump·ness n. plump·y adj.** [15th C.: rel. to MDu. *plomp*, 'blunt.']

plump[2] ▶ **v.** [trans.] set down heavily or unceremoniously. ■ (**plump oneself**) sit down in this way. ▶ **n.** archaic an abrupt plunge; a heavy fall. ▶ **adv.** informal **1** with a sudden or heavy fall. **2** dated directly and bluntly: *tell her plump and plain.* [ME: rel. to Mid. Low Ger. *plumpen* 'fall into water,' prob. of imitative origin.]

plum pud·ding ▶ **n.** a rich boiled or steamed pudding containing raisins, currants, and spices.

plum to·ma·to ▶ **n.** a tomato of an Italian variety that is shaped like a plum.

plu·mule /'plo͞omyo͞ol/ ▶ **n. 1** Bot. the rudimentary shoot or stem of an embryo plant. **2** Ornithol. a bird's down feather. [18th C.: ult. from L. *plumula* 'small feather,' dimin. of *pluma* 'down.']

plum·y /'plo͞omē/ ▶ **adj.** (**plum·i·er, plum·i·est**) resembling or decorated with feathers.

plun·der /'pləndər/ ▶ **v.** [trans.] steal goods from, (typically using force and in a time of war or civil disorder. ■ steal (goods) in such a way. ■ take material from (artistic or academic work) for one's own purposes. ▶ **n.** the violent and dishonest acquisition of property. ■ property acquired illegally and violently. — **plun·der·er n.** [17th C.: from Ger. *plündern*, lit. 'rob of household goods,' from Mid. High Ger. *plunder* 'household effects.']

plunge /plənj/ ▶ **v. 1** [no obj., with adverbial] jump or dive quickly and energetically. ■ fall suddenly and uncontrollably. ■ embark impetuously on a speech or course of action. ■ suffer a rapid decrease in value: *plunged 25%.* ■ (of a ship) pitch. **2** [trans.] push or thrust quickly. ■ put (something) in liquid so as to immerse it completely. ■ (often **be plunged into**) suddenly bring into a specified condition or state: *for a moment the scene was plunged back into darkness.* ▶ **n.** an act of jumping or diving into water. ■ a swift and drastic fall in value or amount.
– PHRASES **take the plunge** informal commit oneself to a course of action about which one is nervous. [ME: from OFr. *plungier* 'thrust down,' based on L. *plumbum* 'lead.']

plunge pool ▶ **n. 1** a deep basin excavated at the foot of a waterfall by the action of the falling water. **2** esp. Brit. a small, deep swimming pool.

plung·er /'plənjər/ ▶ **n. 1** a rubber cup on a long handle, used to suction out blocked pipes. ■ a part of a device or mechanism that works with a plunging or thrusting movement. **2** informal a person who spends money recklessly.

plunk /pləngk/ informal ▶ **v. 1** [intrans.] play a keyboard or plucked stringed instrument. **2** [trans.] hit (someone) abruptly. **3** (also **plank**) [trans.] put or set (something) down heavily or abruptly. ■ pay (money) on the spot or abruptly. ■ (**plunk oneself down**) sit down in an undignified way. ▶ **n. 1** the sound made by abruptly plucking a string of a stringed instrument. **2** a heavy blow. **3** an act of setting something down heavily. — **plunk·er n.** [19th C.: prob. imitative.]

plu·per·fect /,plo͞o'pərfikt/ ▶ **adj. & n.** another term for PAST PERFECT. ■ [as adj.] more than perfect. [15th C.: from mod. L. *plusperfectum*, from L. *(tempus praeteritum) plus quam perfectum* 'more than perfect.']

plu·ral /'plo͝orəl/ ▶ **adj.** more than one in number. ■ Gram. (of a word or form) denoting more than one, or (in languages with dual number) more than two. ▶ **n.** Gram. a plural word or form. ■ [in sing.] the plural number: *the verb is in the plural.* — **plu·ral·ly adv.** [ME: ult. from L. *pluralis*, from *plus, plur-* 'more.']

plu·ral·ism /'plo͝orə,lizəm/ ▶ **n. 1** a condition or system in which two or more states, etc., coexist. ■ a form of society in which minority groups maintain their independent cultural traditions. ■ a political theory or system of power-sharing among political parties. ■ a theory or system of devolution and autonomy for individual bodies. ■ Philos. a theory or system that recognizes more than one ultimate principle. Compare with MONISM. **2** the practice of holding more than one office or church benefice at a time. — **plu·ral·ist n. & adj. plu·ral·is·tic adj. plu·ral·is·ti·cal·ly adv.**

plu·ral·i·ty /plo͞o'ralitē/ ▶ **n.** (pl. **-ties**) **1** the fact or state of being plural. ■ [in sing.] a large number of people or things. **2** the number of votes cast for a candidate who receives more than any other but not an absolute majority. ■ the number by which this exceeds the number of votes cast for the candidate who placed second. **3** esp. hist. another term for PLURALISM (sense 2).

plu·ral·ize /'plo͝orə,līz/ ▶ **v.** [trans.] **1** cause to become more numerous. ■ cause to be made up of several different elements. **2** give a plural form to (a word). — **plu·ral·i·za·tion** /,plo͝orəli'zāsнən/ **n.**

pluri- ▶ **comb. form** several: *pluripotent.* [from L. *plus, plur-* 'more,' *plures* 'several.']

plu·ri·po·tent /,plo͝ori'pōtnt/ ▶ **adj.** Biol. (of an immature or stem cell) capable of giving rise to several different cell types. [1940s: from PLURI- 'several' + L. *potent-* 'being able' (see POTENT).]

plus /pləs/ ▶ **prep.** with the addition of. ■ informal together with. ▶ **adj. 1** [postpositive] (after a number or amount) at least. ■ (after a grade) better than: *B plus.* **2** (before a number) above zero; positive: *plus 60 degrees.* **3** having a positive electric charge. ▶ **n. 1** short for PLUS SIGN. ■ a mathematical operation of addition. **2** an advantage: *knowing the language is a plus* | [as adj.] *on the plus side, the employees are enthusiastic.* ▶ **conj.** informal furthermore; also.
– PHRASES **plus or minus** used to define the margin of error of an estimate or calculation. [16th C.: from L., lit. 'more.']

plus fours /'pləs 'fôrz/ ▶ **plural n.** dated baggy knickers reaching below the knee, worn esp. for playing golf.

plush /pləsн/ ▶ **n.** a rich fabric with a long, soft nap. ▶ **adj.** informal richly luxurious and expensive. — **plush·ly adv. plush·ness n. plush·y (plush·i·er, plush·i·est) adj.** [16th C.: from obs. Fr. *pluche*, ult. fromOFr. *peluchier* 'to pluck,' based on L. *pilus* 'hair.']

plus sign ▶ **n.** the symbol +, indicating addition or a positive value.

plus-size ▶ **adj.** (of clothing or people) of a size larger than the normal range.

Plu·tarch /'plo͞o,tärk/ (*c.*46–*c.*120), Greek writer and philosopher; Latin name *Lucius Mestrius Plutarchus.* He wrote *Parallel Lives.*

plu·te·us /'plo͞otēəs/ ▶ **n.** (pl. **-te·i** /-tē,ī/) Zool. the planktonic larva of some echinoderms, being somewhat triangular with lateral projections. [19th C.: from L., lit. 'barrier.']

Plu·to /'plo͞otō/ **1** Gk. Mythol. the god of the underworld. Also called HADES. **2** Astron. a dwarf planet, formerly considered the ninth planet in order from the sun. [via L. from Gk. *Ploutōn.*]

plu·toc·ra·cy /plo͞o'täkrəsē/ ▶ **n.** (pl. **-cies**) government by the wealthy. ■ a country or society governed in this way. ■ an elite class of people whose power derives from wealth. — **plu·to·crat·ic** /,plo͞otə'kratik/ **adj. plu·to·crat·i·cal·ly** /,plo͞otə'kratiklē/ **adv.** [17th C.: from Gk. *ploutokratia*, from *ploutos* 'wealth' + *kratos* 'strength.']

plu·to·crat /'plo͞otə,krat/ ▶ **n.** a person whose power derives from their wealth.

plu·ton /'plo͞o,tän/ ▶ **n.** Geol. a body of intrusive igneous rock. [1930s: back-form. from PLUTONIC.]

Plu·to·ni·an /plo͞o'tōnēən/ ▶ **adj. 1** of or associated with the underworld. **2** of or relating to the planet Pluto.

plu·ton·ic /plo͞o'tänik/ ▶ **adj. 1** Geol. relating to or denoting igneous rock formed by solidification at considerable depth beneath the earth's surface. **2** (**Plutonic**) relating to the underworld or the god Pluto.

plu·to·nism /'plo͞otn,izəm/ ▶ **n.** Geol. the formation of intrusive igneous rock by solidification of magma beneath the earth's surface. ■ (**Plutonism**) hist. the theory (now accepted) that rocks such as granite were formed by solidification from the molten state.

plu·to·ni·um /plo͞o'tōnēəm/ ▶ **n.** the chemical element of atomic number 94, a dense silvery radioactive metal of the actinide series, used in nuclear reactors and nuclear fission weapons. (Symbol: **Pu**) [18th C.: from Gk. *Ploutōn* 'Pluto.']

plu·vi·al /'plo͞ovēəl/ esp. Geol. ▶ **adj.** relating to or characterized by rainfall. ▶ **n.** a period marked by increased rainfall. [17th C.: from L. *pluvialis*, from *pluvia* 'rain.']

ply[1] /plī/ ▶ **n.** (pl. **plies**) **1** a thickness or layer of a folded or laminated material. ■ [usu. in comb.] a strand of yarn or rope. ■ the number of multiple layers or strands of which something is made. ■ [usu. in comb.] a reinforcing layer of fabric in a tire. **2** short for PLYWOOD. **3** (in game theory) the number of levels at which branching occurs in a tree of possible outcomes. ■ a half-move (one player's move) in computer chess. [ME: from Fr. *pli* 'fold,' from the v. *plier*, from L. *plicare.*]

ply[2] ▶ **v.** (**plies, plied**) [trans.] **1** work with (a tool, esp. one requiring steady, rhythmic movements). ■ work steadily at (one's business or trade); conduct: *he plied a profitable export trade.* **2** [intrans.] (of a vessel or vehicle) travel regularly over a route. ■ [trans.] travel over (a route) in this way. **3** (**ply someone with**) provide someone with (food or drink) in a continuous or insistent way. ■ direct (numerous questions) at someone. [ME: shortening of APPLY.]

Ply·mouth /'pliməтн/ **1** a city in southwestern England; pop. 239,000. **2** a town in southeastern Massachusetts; pop. 45,608. It was the earliest permanent European settlement in New England. **3** the capital of Montserrat; pop. 3,500.

Plym·outh Breth·ren a strict Calvinistic religious body formed at Plymouth in England *c.*1830, having no formal creed and no official order of ministers.

Ply·mouth Rock[1] a granite boulder at Plymouth, Massachusetts, on to which the Pilgrim Fathers are said to have first stepped in the New World.

Plym·outh Rock[2] ▶ **n.** a chicken of a large domestic breed of American origin.

ply·wood /'plī,wo͝od/ ▶ **n.** a type of strong thin wooden board consisting of two or more layers glued and pressed together with the direction of the grain alternating.

Pl·zeň /'pəl,zenyə/ Czech name for PILSEN.

PM ▶ **abbr.** ■ Past Master. ■ Paymaster. ■ Postmaster. ■ post-mortem. ■ Prime Minister. ■ Provost Marshal.

Pm ▶ **symb.** the chemical element promethium.

p.m. ▶ **abbr.** after noon, used after times of day between noon and midnight: *at 3:30 p.m.* [from L. *post meridiem.*]

PMG ▶ **abbr.** ■ paymaster general. ■ postmaster general.

PMS ▶ **abbr.** premenstrual syndrome.

pmt. ▶ **abbr.** payment.

p.n. ▶ **abbr.** promissory note.

PNdB ▶ **abbr.** perceived noise decibel(s).

pneum. ▶ **abbr.** ■ pneumatic. ■ pneumatics.

pneu·ma /'n(y)o͞omə/ ▶ **n.** Philos. (in Stoic thought) the vital spirit, soul, or creative force of a person. [Gk., lit. 'that which is breathed.']

pneu·mat·ic /n(y)o͝o'matik/ ▶ **adj. 1** containing or operated by air or gas under pressure. ■ Zool. (chiefly of cavities in the bones of birds) containing air. **2** of or relating to the spirit. ▶ **n.** (usu. **pneumatics**) an item of pneumatic equipment. — **pneu·mat·i·cal·ly** /n(y)o͝o'matik(ə)lē/ **adv.** **pneu·ma·tic·i·ty** /ˌn(y)o͞omə'tisətē/ **n.** [17th C.: ult. from Gk. *pneumatikos*, from *pneuma* 'wind,' from *pnein* 'breathe.']

pneu·mat·ic drill ▶ **n.** a large, heavy mechanical drill driven by compressed air.

pneu·mat·ics /n(y)o͝o'matiks/ ▶ **plural n.** [treated as sing.] the branch of physics or technology concerned with the mechanical properties of gases.

pneumato- ▶ **comb. form 1** of or containing air: *pneumatophore.* **2** relating to the spirit: *pneumatology.* [from Gk. *pneuma, pneumat-* 'wind, breath.']

pneu·ma·tol·o·gy /ˌn(y)o͞omə'täləjē/ ▶ **n.** the branch of Christian theology concerned with the Holy Spirit. — **pneu·ma·to·log·i·cal** /ˌn(y)o͞omədə'läjəkəl/ **adj.**

pneu·ma·tol·y·sis /ˌn(y)o͞omə'täləsis/ ▶ **n.** Geol. the chemical alteration of rocks and the formation of minerals by the action of hot magmatic gases and vapors. — **pneu·mat·o·lyt·ic adj.**

pneu·mat·o·phore /ˌn(y)o͝o'matəˌfô(ə)r/ ▶ **n. 1** Zool. the gas-filled float of some colonial coelenterates. **2** Bot. (in mangroves and other swamp plants) an aerial root specialized for gaseous exchange.

pneumo- /'n(y)o͞omō/ ▶ **comb. form 1** of or relating to the lungs: *pneumogastric.* **2** of or relating to the presence of air or gas: *pneumothorax.* [sense 1 from Gk. *pneumōn* 'lung'; sense 2 from Gk. *pneuma* 'air.']

pneu·mo·coc·cus /ˌn(y)o͞omō'käkəs/ ▶ **n.** (pl. **-coc·ci** /-'käksī; -'käksē/) a bacterium (*Streptococcus pneumoniae*) associated with pneumonia and some forms of meningitis. — **pneu·mo·coc·cal adj.**

pneu·mo·co·ni·o·sis /ˌn(y)o͞omōˌkōnē'ōsəs/ ▶ **n.** Med. a disease of the lungs due to inhalation of dust. [19th C.: from PNEUMO- + Gk. *konis* 'dust'.]

pneu·mo·cys·tis /'n(y)o͞omōˌsistis/ ▶ **n.** Med. a parasitic protozoan (*Pneumocystis carinii*) that can cause fatal pneumonia in people affected with immunodeficiency disease.

pneu·mo·en·ceph·a·log·ra·phy /ˌn(y)o͞omōenˌsefə'lägrəfē/ ▶ **n.** Med. a radiographic technique (now largely superseded) for examining the brain. It involved displacing the cerebrospinal fluid in the ventricles of the brain. — **pneu·mo·en·ceph·a·lo·gram n.** **pneu·mo·en·ceph·a·lo·graph·ic adj.**

pneu·mo·gas·tric /ˌn(y)o͞omō'gastrik/ ▶ **adj.** of or relating to the lungs and stomach.

pneu·mo·nec·to·my /ˌn(y)o͞omō'nektəmē/ ▶ **n.** (pl. **-mies**) surgical removal of a lung or part of a lung.

pneu·mo·nia /n(y)o͝o'mōnēə; -'mōnyə/ ▶ **n.** lung inflammation caused by bacterial or viral infection. — **pneu·mon·ic** /n(y)o͝o'mänik/ **adj.** [17th C.: via L. from Gk., from *pneumōn* 'lung.']

pneu·mo·ni·tis /ˌn(y)o͞omə'nītis/ ▶ **n.** Med. inflammation of the walls of the alveoli in the lungs.

pneu·mo·tho·rax /ˌn(y)o͞omō'THôrˌaks/ ▶ **n.** Med. the presence of air or gas in the cavity between the lungs and the chest wall, causing collapse of the lung.

PNG ▶ **abbr.** Papua New Guinea.

p-n junc·tion ▶ **n.** Electron. a boundary between p-type and n-type material in a semiconductor device, functioning as a rectifier.

PNP ▶ **adj.** Electron. denoting a semiconductor device in which an n-type region is between two p-type regions. ▶ **abbr.** (in computing) Plug and Play.

PO ▶ **abbr.** ■ Petty Officer. ■ postal order. ■ Post Office. ■ purchase order.

Po[1] /pō/ a river in northern Italy that rises in the Alps and flows 405 miles (652 km) to the Adriatic Sea.

Po[2] ▶ **symb.** the chemical element polonium.

po' /pō; po͞oə; pô/ ▶ **adj.** short for POOR, used to represent dialectal speech.

poach[1] /pōCH/ ▶ **v.** [trans.] cook (an egg), without its shell, in or over boiling water. ■ cook by simmering in a small amount of liquid. [ME: from OFr. *pochier*, earlier 'enclose in a bag,' from *poche* 'bag.']

poach[2] ▶ **v.** [trans.] **1** illegally hunt or catch (game or fish) on land that is not one's own or is under official protection. ■ take or acquire in an unfair or clandestine way. ■ [intrans.] (in ball games) take a shot that a partner or teammate would have expected to take. **2** (of an animal) trample or cut up (turf) with its hoofs. ■ [intrans.] (of land) become sodden by being trampled.

– PHRASES **poach on someone's territory** encroach on someone else's rights. [16th C.: appar. rel. to POKE[1].]

poach·er[1] /'pōCHər/ ▶ **n.** [usu. with adj.] a pan for cooking eggs or other food by poaching: *an egg poacher.*

poach·er[2] ▶ **n.** a person who hunts game illegally.

POB ▶ **abbr.** post office box.

po·bla·no /pō'blänō/ ▶ **n.** a dark green chili pepper. [Sp.]

Po·ca·hon·tas /ˌpōkə'häntəs/ (*c.*1595–1617), American Indian; daughter of Powhatan. She rescued John Smith from death at the hands of her father and later married colonist John Rolfe.

po·chard /'pōCHərd/ ▶ **n.** (pl. same or **-chards**) a diving duck (genera *Aythya* and *Netta*), the male of which typically has a reddish-brown head and a black breast. [16th C.: of unknown origin.]

pock /päk/ ▶ **n.** a pockmark. — **pocked adj. pock·y adj.** (archaic). [OE *poc* 'pustule,' of Gmc. origin; rel. to Du. *pok* and Ger. *Pocke.*]

pock·et /'päkət/ ▶ **n. 1** a small bag sewn into or on clothing, used for carrying small articles. ■ a pouchlike compartment providing separate storage space. ■ informal (often **pockets**) a person or organization's financial resources. ■ Baseball the hollow in the center of a baseball glove or mitt. ■ an opening on the corner or side of a billiard table into which balls are struck. **2** a small patch of something: *pockets of dirty snow.* ■ a small, isolated group or area. ■ Football the protected area behind the offensive line from which the quarterback throws passes. ■ (in bowling) the space between the head pin and the pin immediately behind it on the left or right. ■ a cavity in a rock or stratum filled with ore or other distinctive component. ■ Aeron. an air pocket. ▶ **adj.** [attrib.] of a suitable size for carrying in a pocket: *pocket dictionary.* ▶ **v.** (**pock·et·ed, pock·et·ing**) [trans.] put into one's pocket. ■ take or receive (money or other valuables) for oneself, esp. dishonestly. ■ Billiards drive (a ball) into a pocket. ■ enclose as though in a pocket: *the fillings can be pocketed in a pita bread.* ■ suppress (one's feelings) and proceed despite them. ■ block passage of (a bill) by a pocket veto.

– PHRASES **in pocket** having enough money or money to spare. ■ (of money) gained by someone from a transaction. **in someone's pocket 1** dependent on someone financially and therefore under their influence. **2** very close to and closely involved with someone. **line one's pockets** see LINE[2]. **out of pocket** having lost money in a transaction. ■ (**out-of-pocket**) [as adj.] [attrib.] (of an expense or cost) paid for directly rather than being put on account. **put one's hand in one's pocket** spend or provide one's own money. — **pock·et·a·ble adj. pock·et·ful** /-ˌfo͝ol/ (pl. **-fuls**) **n. pock·et·less adj.** [ME: from Anglo-Norman Fr. *poket(e)*, dimin. of *poke* 'pouch.']

pock·et bat·tle·ship ▶ **n.** any of a class of cruisers with large-caliber guns, operated by the German navy in World War II.

pock·et bil·liards ▶ **plural n.** a form of billiards played on a table with six pockets. Also called POOL.

pock·et·book /'päkətˌbo͝ok/ ▶ **n. 1** a handbag. ■ one's financial resources. **2** (**pocket book**) a paperback edition of a book.

pock·et·book plant ▶ **n.** another term for CALCEOLARIA.

pock·et go·pher ▶ **n.** see GOPHER (sense 1).

pock·et·knife /'päkətˌnīf/ ▶ **n.** (pl. **pocketknives**) a knife with folding blades, suitable for a pocket.

pock·et mon·ey ▶ **n.** a small amount of money suitable for minor expenses. ■ Brit. a child's allowance.

pock·et mouse ▶ **n.** a small nocturnal rodent (genus *Perognathus*, family Heteromyidae) with large cheek pouches for carrying food, native to the deserts of North and Central America.

pock·et ve·to ▶ **n.** an indirect veto of a legislative bill by the president or a governor by retaining the bill unsigned until after the legislative session is over.

pock·et watch ▶ **n.** a watch on a chain, intended to be carried in the pocket of a jacket or vest.

pock·mark /'päkˌmärk/ ▶ **n.** a pitted scar or mark on the skin left by a pustule or pimple. ■ a scar, mark, or pitted area disfiguring a surface. ▶ **v.** [trans.] (usu. **be pockmarked**) cover or disfigure with such marks: *the area is pockmarked by gravel pits.*

po·co /'pōkō; 'pô-/ ▶ **adv.** Music (in directions) a little. [Ital.]

po·co a po·co /'pōkō ä 'pōkō/ ▶ **adv.** Music (esp. as a direction) little by little; gradually.

Po·co·ma·ni·a /ˌpōkə'mānēə/ ▶ **n.** a Jamaican folk religion combining revivalism with ancestor worship and spirit possession. [1930s: prob. based on a local word.]

Po·co·no Moun·tains /'pōkəˌnō/ a mountain range in northeastern Pennsylvania, noted for its resorts.

pod[1] /päd/ ▶ **n. 1** an elongated seed vessel of a leguminous plant, splitting open on both sides when ripe. ■ the egg case of a locust. ■ Geol. a body of rock or sediment whose length greatly exceeds its other dimensions. ■ a purse seine for catching eels. **2** [often with adj.] a detachable or self-contained unit on an aircraft, spacecraft, vehicle, or vessel. ▶ **v.** (**pod·ded, pod·ding**) **1** [intrans.] (of a plant) bear or form pods: *the peas have failed to pod.* **2** [trans.] remove (peas or beans) from their pods. [17th C.: back-form. from dial. *podware, podder* 'field crops.']

pod[2] /päd/ ▶ **n.** a small herd or school of marine animals, esp. whales. [19th C.: of unknown origin.]

po·dag·ra /pə'dagrə/ ▶ **n.** Med. gout of the foot, esp. the big toe. — **po·dag·ral** /-rəl/ **adj. po·dag·ric** /-rik/ **adj. po·dag·rous** /-rəs/ **adj.** [ME: from L., from Gk. *pous, pod-* 'foot' + *agra* 'seizure.']

pod·cast /'pädˌkast/ ▶ **n.** a multimedia digital file made available on the Internet for downloading to a portable media player, personal computer, etc. — **pod·cast·ing n.** [21st C.: from *iPod*, a proprietary name for a personal audio player.]

Pod·go·ri·ca /'pôdgôˌrētsə/ the capital of Montenegro. It was named Titograd 1946–93.

po·di·a·try /pə'dīətrē/ ▶ **n.** the treatment of the feet. — **po·di·a·trist** /-trəst/ **n.** [20th C.: from Gk. *pous, pod-* 'foot' + *iatros* 'physician.']

po·di·um /'pōdēəm/ ▶ **n.** (pl. **-di·ums** or **-di·a** /-dēə/) a small platform on which a person may stand, as when making a speech or conducting an orchestra. ■ a lectern. ■ a continuous projecting base or pedestal under a building. [18th C.: via L. from Gk. *podion*, dimin. of *pous*, *pod-* 'foot.']

pod·o·carp /'pädə,kärp/ ▶ **n.** a coniferous tree or shrub (genus *Podocarpus*, family Podocarpaceae) that is chiefly native to the southern hemisphere, widely grown as an ornamental or timber tree. [19th C.: from mod. L. *Podocarpus*, from Gk. *pous*, *pod-* 'foot' + *karpos* 'fruit.']

Po·dunk /'pō,dəNGk/ ▶ **n.** [usu. as adj.] informal a hypothetical small town regarded as dull or insignificant. [19th C.: place name of New England, of Algonquian origin.]

pod·zol /'päd,zôl; -,zäl/ (also **pod·sol**) ▶ **n.** Soil Science an infertile acidic soil having an ashlike subsurface layer and a lower dark stratum. — **pod·zol·ic** /-'zôlik; -'zälik/ **adj.** **pod·zol·i·za·tion** /,pädzələ'zāSHən/ **n.** **pod·zol·ize** /'pädzə,līz/ **v.** [20th C.: from Russ., from *pod* 'under' + *zola* 'ashes.']

Poe /pō/, Edgar Allan (1809–49), US writer, poet, and critic. His poetry includes "The Raven" (1845).

po·em /'pōəm/ ▶ **n.** a piece of writing that partakes of the nature of both speech and song, and that is usually rhythmical and metaphorical. [15th C.: ult. from Gk. *poēma*, var. of *poiēma* 'fiction,' from *poiein* 'create.']

po·e·sy /'pōəsē; -zē/ ▶ **n.** archaic literary poetry: *they were enamored of poesy and the fine arts.* ■ the art or composition of poetry. [ME: ult. from Gk. *poēsis*, var. of *poiēsis* 'poetry,' from *poiein*.]

po·et /'pōət/ ▶ **n.** a person who writes poems. [ME: from OFr. *poete*, via L. from Gk. *poētēs*, var. of *poiētēs*, from *poiein* 'create.']

poet. ▶ **abbr.** ■ poetic; poetical. ■ poetry.

po·et·as·ter /'pōət,astər/ ▶ **n.** a person who writes inferior poetry. [16th C.: mod. L., from L. *poeta* 'poet.']

po·et·ess /'pōətəs/ ▶ **n.** dated a female poet.

po·et·ic /pō'etik/ ▶ **adj.** of, relating to, or used in poetry. ■ written in verse rather than prose: *a poetic drama.* ■ having an imaginative or sensitively emotional style of expression. — **po·et·i·cal** /pō'etikəl/ **adj.** **po·et·i·cal·ly** /-ik(ə)lē/ **adv.**

po·et·i·cize /pō'etə,sīz/ ▶ **v.** [trans.] make poetic in character. ■ [intrans.] write or speak poetically. — **po·et·i·cism** /-,sizəm/ **n.**

po·et·ic jus·tice ▶ **n.** the fact of experiencing a fitting or deserved retribution for one's actions.

po·et·ic li·cense ▶ **n.** the freedom to depart from the facts or conventional rules of language when speaking or writing in order to create an effect.

po·et·ics /pō'etiks/ ▶ **plural n.** [treated as sing.] the art of writing poetry. ■ writing that deals with the art of poetry or presents a theory of poetry or literary discourse.

po·et·ize /'pōə,tīz/ ▶ **v.** [intrans.] dated write or speak in verse or in a poetic style. ■ [trans.] represent in poetic form.

po·et lau·re·ate /'lôrēət/ ▶ **n.** (pl. **po·ets lau·re·ate**) a poet appointed to, or regarded unofficially as holding, an honorary representative position in a particular country, region, or group.

po·et·ry /'pōətrē/ ▶ **n.** literary work in which special intensity is given to the expression of feelings and ideas by the use of distinctive style and rhythm; poems collectively or as a genre of literature. ■ a quality of beauty and intensity of emotion regarded as characteristic of poems: *poetry and fire are nicely balanced in the music.* ■ something regarded as comparable to poetry in its beauty. [ME: from med. L. *poetria*, from L. *poeta* 'poet.']

Pog /päg; pôg/ ▶ **n.** (usu. **Pogs**) trademark a cardboard or plastic disk printed with a design or picture, used in a children's game. ■ (**Pogs**) a game played with these disks. [1990s: from *passion fruit, orange, guava*.]

po·go /'pōgō/ ▶ **n.** (also **po·go stick**) (pl. **-gos**) a toy for jumping around on, consisting of a long, spring-loaded pole with a handle and rests for a person's feet. ▶ **v.** (**-goes, -goed**) [intrans.] informal jump up and down as if on such a toy. [1920s: of unknown origin.]

Po·go·noph·o·ra /,pōgə'näfərə/ Zool. a small phylum of long deep-sea worms that live in upright tubes of protein and chitin. — **po·go·noph·o·ran** /-rən/ **n. & adj.** [mod. L. (pl.), from Gk. *pōgōn* 'beard' + *pherein* 'to bear.']

po·grom /'pōgrəm; pə'gräm/ ▶ **n.** an organized massacre of a particular ethnic group. [20th C.: from Russ., lit. 'devastation,' from *gromit'* 'destroy.']

Po Hai /'bō'hī/ variant of **Bo Hai**.

poi /poi/ ▶ **n.** a Hawaiian dish made from the fermented root of the taro, baked and pounded to a paste. [of Polynesian origin.]

poign·ant /'poinyənt/ ▶ **adj.** evoking a keen sense of sadness or regret: *a poignant reminder.* ■ keenly felt: *the sensation was most poignant in winter.* ■ archaic sharp or pungent in taste or smell. — **poign·ance** **n.** **poign·an·cy** /-yənsē/ **n.** **poign·ant·ly** /-yəntlē/ **adv.** [ME: from OFr., lit. 'pricking,' pres. part. of *poindre*, from L. *pungere* 'to prick.']

poi·ki·lit·ic /,poikə'litik/ ▶ **adj.** Geol. relating to the texture of an igneous rock in which small crystals of one mineral occur within crystals of another. [19th C.: from Gk. *poikilos* 'variegated' + **-ITE**[1].]

poikilo- ▶ **comb. form** variegated: *poikiloblastic.* ■ variable: *poikilotherm.* [from Gk. *poikilos* 'variegated, varied.']

poi·ki·lo·therm /poi'kēlə,THərm; -kil-/ ▶ **n.** Zool. an organism that cannot regulate its body temperature except by behavioral means. Often contrasted with **HOMEOTHERM**; compare with **COLD-BLOODED**. — **poi·ki·lo·ther·mal** /,poi,kēlə'THərməl; -,kil-/ **adj.** **poi·ki·lo·ther·mic** /,poi,kēlə'THərmik; -,kilə-/ **adj.** **poi·ki·lo·ther·my** **n.**

poi·lu /pwäl'(y)o͞o/ ▶ **n.** hist., informal an infantry soldier in the French army, esp. one in World War I. [Fr., lit. 'hairy.']

poin·ci·an·a /,poinsē'anə/ ▶ **n.** a tropical tree (genera *Caesalpinia* and *Delonix*) of the pea family, with showy red or red and yellow flowers. [18th C.: mod. L., M. de *Poinci*, 17th-cent. governor of the Antilles.]

poin·set·ti·a /poin'set(ē)ə/ ▶ **n.** a small Mexican shrub (*Euphorbia pulcherrima*, formerly *Poinsettia pulcherrima*) of the spurge family, with large showy scarlet bracts surrounding the small yellow flowers, popular as a Christmas houseplant. [19th C.: mod. L., Joel R. *Poinsett* (1779–1851), Amer. diplomat.]

point /point/ ▶ **n.** **1** the tapered, sharp end of a tool, weapon, or other object: *the point of his dagger.* ■ Archaeol. a pointed flake or blade, esp. one that has been worked. ■ see **GLAZIER'S POINT**. ■ Ballet another term for **POINTE**. ■ the prong of a deer's antler. **2** a dot or other punctuation mark, esp. a period. ■ a decimal point: *fifty-five point nine.* ■ a dot or small stroke used in the alphabets of Semitic languages to indicate vowels or distinguish particular consonants. ■ a very small dot or mark on a surface. **3** a particular spot, place, or position in an area or on a map, object, or surface. ■ a particular moment in time or stage in a process. ■ (usu. **the point**) the critical or decisive moment. ■ (**the point of**) the verge or brink of (doing or being something): *she was on the point of leaving.* ■ [usu. with adj.] a stage or level at which a change of state occurs: *it is packed to the bursting point.* ■ any of the twenty-four triangles on a backgammon board. ■ (in geometry) something having position but not spatial extent, magnitude, dimension, or direction, for example the intersection of two lines. **4** a single item or detail in a discussion, list, or text. ■ an argument or idea put forward by a person in discussion. ■ an interesting or convincing idea. ■ (usu. **the point**) the significant or essential element of what is intended or being discussed. ■ [in sing.] [usu. with negative or in questions] advantage or purpose that can be gained from doing something. ■ relevance or effectiveness. ■ a distinctive feature or characteristic, typically a good one, of a person or thing. **5** (in sports and games) a mark or unit of scoring. ■ (in craps) the combination total of the two thrown dice (4, 5, 6, 8, 9, or 10) that permits a shooter to keep throwing until the shooter throws the same number again and wins. ■ a unit used in measuring value, achievement, or extent. ■ an advantage or success in an argument or discussion. ■ a unit of credit toward an award or benefit. ■ a percentage of the profits from a movie or recording offered to certain people involved in its production. ■ a punishment awarded by the courts for a driving offense and recorded cumulatively on a person's driver's license. ■ a unit of weight (one hundredth of a carat, or 2 mg) for diamonds. ■ a unit of varying value, used in quoting the price of stocks, bonds, or futures. ■ Bridge a value assigned to certain cards (4 points for an ace, 3 for a king, 2 for a queen, and 1 for a jack, sometimes with extra points for long or short suits) by a player in assessing the strength of a hand. ■ (**point of**) (in piquet) the longest suit in a player's hand, containing a specified number of up to eight cards. **6** each of thirty-two directions marked at equal distances around a compass. ■ the corresponding direction toward the horizon. ■ the angular interval between two successive points of a compass, i.e., one eighth of a right angle (11° 15'). ■ (**points ——**) unspecified places considered in terms of their direction from a specified place. **7** a piece of land jutting out into a body of water. **8** (usu. **points**) Brit. another term for **SWITCH** (sense 4). **9** Print. a unit of measurement for type sizes and spacing, which in the US and UK is one twelfth of a pica, or 0.013835 inch (0.351 mm), and in Europe is 0.015 inch (0.376 mm). **10** Basketball a frontcourt position. ■ Ice Hockey either of two areas in each attacking zone, just inside the blue line where it meets the boards. **11** (usu. **points**) each of a set of electrical contacts in the distributor of a motor vehicle. **12** a small leading party of an advanced guard of troops. ■ the position at the head of a column or wedge of troops. ■ short for **POINT MAN**. **13** (usu. **points**) the extremities of an animal, typically a horse or cat. **14** (usu. **points**) hist. a tagged piece of ribbon or cord used for lacing a garment. **15** a short piece of cord for tying up a reef in a sail. **16** the action or position of a dog in pointing. **17** Music an important phrase or subject, esp. in a contrapuntal composition. ▶ **v.** **1** [intrans.] direct attention to the position or direction of something, typically by extending one's finger. ■ [with adverbial of direction] indicate a particular time, direction, or reading. ■ [trans.] direct or aim (something) at someone or something. ■ [with adverbial of direction] face or be turned in a particular direction. ■ [with adverbial] cite or put forward a fact or situation as evidence of something. ■ (**point to**) (of a situation) be evidence or an indication that (something) is likely to happen or be the case. ■ [trans.] (of a dog) indicate the presence of (game) by acting as pointer. ■ [trans.] esp. Ballet extend (the toes or feet) by tensing the foot and ankle so as to form a point. **2** [trans.] give force or emphasis to (words or actions). **3** [trans.] fill in or repair the joints of (brickwork, a brick structure, or tiling) with smoothly finished mortar or cement. **4** [trans.] give a sharp, tapered point to: *he twisted and pointed his mustache.* **5** [trans.] insert points in (written Hebrew). ■ mark (Psalms) with signs for chanting. **6** [intrans.] Naut. (of a sailing vessel) sail close to the wind.

– PHRASES **beside the point** irrelevant. **case in point** an instance or example that illustrates what is being discussed. **in point of fact** see **FACT**. **make one's point** put across a proposition clearly and convincingly. **make a point of** make a special and noticeable effort to do (a specified thing). **off the point** irrelevant. **point the finger** openly accuse someone or apportion blame. **the point of no return** the point in a journey or enterprise at which it becomes essential or more practical to continue to the end instead of returning to the point of departure. **point of sailing** a sailboat's heading in relation to the wind. **score points** deliberately make oneself appear superior to someone else by making clever remarks. **take someone's point** esp. Brit. accept the validity of someone's idea or argument. **to the point** relevant. **up to a point** to some extent but not completely. **win on points** Boxing win by scoring more points than one's opponent (as awarded by the judges and/or the referee) rather than by a knockout.

– PHRASAL VERBS **point something out** direct someone's gaze or attention toward something, esp. by extending one's finger. ■ [reporting verb] say something to make someone aware of a fact or circumstance. [ME: the n. partly from OFr. *point*, from L. *punctum* 'something that is pricked'; partly from OFr. *pointe*, from L. *puncta* 'pricking'; the v. is from OFr. *pointer*.]

point af·ter touch·down ▶ n. another term for EXTRA POINT.

point-blank ▶ adj. & adv. (of a shot, bullet, or other missile) fired from very close to its target. ■ [as adj.] (of the range of a shot, bullet, or other missile) so close as to allow no possibility of missing. ■ (of a statement or question) blunt and direct; without explanation or qualification. [16th C.: prob. from POINT + BLANK.]

point d'ap·pui /ˌpwaN däˈpwē/ ▶ n. (pl. **points d'ap·pui** pronunc. same) a support or prop; a strategic point. [Fr., lit. 'point of support.']

pointe /point; pwaNt/ ▶ n. (pl. pronunc. same) Ballet the tips of the toes. ■ (also **pointe work**) dance performed on the tips of the toes.

– PHRASES **on** (or **en**) **pointe** /äN; än; ôn/ on the tips of the toes. [Fr., lit. 'tip.']

point·ed /ˈpointid/ ▶ adj. **1** having a sharpened or tapered tip or end: *his face tapers to a pointed chin.* **2** (of a remark or look) expressing criticism in a direct and unambiguous way: *pointed comments.* — **point·ed·ly** adv. (in sense2). **point·ed·ness** n.

point·ed arch ▶ n. an arch with a pointed crown.

poin·telle /poinˈtel/ (also trademark **Poin·telle**) ▶ n. a type of knitwear or woolen fabric with small eyelet holes that create a lacy effect. [1950s: prob. from *point* 'lace' + the Fr. *-elle*.]

Pointe-Noire /pwaNt ˈnwär/ a city in the Republic of Congo; pop. 576,000.

English pointer

point·er /ˈpointər/ ▶ n. **1** a long thin piece of metal on a scale or dial that moves to indicate a figure or position. ■ a rod used for pointing to features on a map or chart. ■ a hint as to what might happen in the future: *the figures were a* **pointer** *to gradual economic recovery.* ■ a small piece of advice; a tip: *here are some* **pointers on** *how to go about the task.* ■ Comput. another term for CURSOR. ■ Comput. a variable whose value is the address of another variable; a link. **2** a dog of a breed that on scenting game stands rigid looking toward it.

Point·ers /ˈpointərz/ (**the Pointers**) Astron. (in the northern hemisphere) two stars of the Big Dipper in Ursa Major, through which a line points nearly to Polaris. ■ (in the southern hemisphere) two stars in the Southern Cross, through which a line points nearly to the south celestial pole.

point guard ▶ n. Basketball the backcourt player who directs the team's offense.

poin·til·lism /ˈpwaNtēˌyizəm; ˈpointlˌizəm/ ▶ n. a technique of neo-Impressionist painting using tiny dots, which become blended in the viewer's eye. — **poin·til·list** /ˌpwaNtēˈyēst; ˈpointl-ist/ n. & adj. **poin·til·list·ic** /ˌpwaNtēˈyistik; ˌpointlˈistik/ adj. [20th C.: from Fr. *pointillisme*, from *pointiller* 'mark with dots.']

point·ing /ˈpointiNG/ ▶ n. cement or mortar used to fill the joints of brickwork, esp. when added externally to a wall to improve its appearance and weatherproofing. ■ the process of adding such cement or mortar.

point lace ▶ n. lace made with a needle on a parchment pattern.

point·less /ˈpointlis/ ▶ adj. **1** having little or no sense, use, or purpose. **2** (of a contest or competitor) without a point scored. — **point·less·ly** adv. **point·less·ness** n.

point man ▶ n. the soldier at the head of a patrol. ■ (esp. in a political context) a person at the forefront of an activity or endeavor.

point mu·ta·tion ▶ n. Genet. a mutation affecting only one or very few nucleotides in a gene sequence.

point of de·par·ture ▶ n. the starting point of a line of thought or course of action; an initial assumption.

point of hon·or ▶ n. an action or circumstance that affects one's reputation or conscience.

point of or·der ▶ n. a query in a formal debate or meeting as to whether correct procedure is being followed.

point of sale (abbr.: **POS**) ▶ n. the place at which goods are retailed: *refunds will be provided at the point of sale.*

point of view ▶ n. a particular attitude or way of considering a matter: *change his point of view.* ■ (in fictional writing) the narrator's position in relation to the story being told. ■ the position from which something or someone is observed.

point source ▶ n. Physics a source of energy, such as light or sound, that can be regarded as having negligible dimensions.

point spread ▶ n. **1** a forecast of the number of points by which a stronger team is expected to defeat a weaker one, used for betting purposes. **2** Physics Physiol. the spread of energy from a point source, esp. with respect to light coming into an optical instrument or eye.

point sys·tem ▶ n. a system for distributing or allocating resources or for ranking or evaluating candidates or claimants on the basis of points.

point-to-point ▶ n. (pl. **point-to-points**) an amateur steeplechase for horses used in hunting. ▶ adj. (of a route or journey) from one place to the next without stopping or changing; direct. ■ (of a telecommunications or computer link) directly from the sender to the receiver. — **point-to-point·er** n. **point-to-point·ing** n.

point·y /ˈpointē/ ▶ adj. (**point·i·er, point·i·est**) informal having a pointed tip or end: *a pointy goatee.*

point·y-head·ed ▶ adj. informal, esp. derog. intellectual; expert: *some pointy-headed college professor.*

poise[1] /poiz/ ▶ n. **1** graceful and elegant bearing in a person. ■ composure and dignity of manner. **2** archaic balance; equilibrium. ▶ v. be or cause to be balanced or suspended. ■ (**be poised**) (of a person or organization) be ready to do something: [with infin.] *poised to resume.* [ME (in the sense 'weight'): from OFr. *pois, peis* (n.), *peser* (verb), from an alt. of L. *pensum* 'weight,' from the v. *pendere* 'weigh.']

poise[2] ▶ n. Physics a unit of dynamic viscosity, such that a tangential force of one dyne per second per square centimeter causes a velocity change one centimeter per second between two parallel planes separated by one centimeter in a liquid. [20th C.: from the name of Jean L. M. *Poiseuille* (1799–1869), Fr. physician.]

poised /poizd/ ▶ adj. having a self-assured manner. ■ having a graceful and elegant bearing.

poi·sha /ˈpoiSHə/ ▶ n. (pl. same) a monetary unit of Bangladesh, equal to one hundredth of a taka. [Bengali.]

poi·son /ˈpoizən/ ▶ n. a substance that, when introduced into or absorbed by a living organism, causes death or injury, esp. one that kills by rapid action. ■ Chem. a substance that reduces the activity of a catalyst. ■ Physics an additive or impurity in a nuclear reactor that slows a reaction by absorbing neutrons. ■ a person, idea, action, or situation that is considered to have a destructive or corrupting effect or influence. ▶ v. [trans.] administer poison to (a person or animal), either deliberately or accidentally. ■ adulterate or contaminate (food or drink) with poison. ■ [usu. as adj.] (**poisoned**) treat (a weapon or missile) with poison in order to augment its lethal effect. ■ (of a dangerous substance) kill or cause to become very ill. ■ contaminate or pollute (an area, the air, or water). ■ fig. prove harmful or destructive to. ■ Chem. (of a substance) reduce the activity of (a catalyst).

– PHRASES **what's your poison?** informal used to ask someone what they would like to drink. — **poi·son·er** /ˈpoizənər/ n. [ME: from OFr. *poison* 'magic potion,' from L. *potio(n-)* 'potion,' rel. to *potare* 'to drink.']

poi·son gas ▶ n. poisonous gas or vapor, used esp. to disable an enemy in warfare.

poison ivy

poi·son i·vy ▶ n. a North American climbing plant (*Rhus radicans*) of the cashew family that secretes an irritant oil from its leaves, which can cause dermatitis.

poi·son oak ▶ n. a North American climbing shrub (*Rhus toxicodendron*) of the cashew family, closely related to poison ivy and having similar properties.

poi·son·ous /ˈpoiz(ə)nəs/ ▶ adj. (of an animal or insect) producing poison to attack enemies or prey. ■ (of a plant or substance) causing or capable of causing death or illness if taken into the body. ■ fig. extremely unpleasant or malicious. — **poi·son·ous·ly** adv.

poi·son-pen let·ter ▶ n. a letter, typically anonymous, that is libelous, abusive, or malicious.

poi·son pill ▶ n. Finance a tactic used to make a company unattractive to an unwelcome takeover bidder.

poi·son su·mac ▶ n. see SUMAC.

Pois·son dis·tri·bu·tion /pwä'sôN/ ▶ n. Stat. a discrete frequency distribution that gives the probability of a number of independent events occurring in a fixed time.

Pois·son's ra·tio /pwä'sôNz/ ▶ n. Physics the ratio of the proportional decrease in a lateral measurement to the proportional increase in length in a sample of material that is elastically stretched.

Poi·tou /pwä'to͞o/ a former province in west central France, now part of Poitou-Charentes.

poke[1] /pōk/ ▶ v. **1** [trans.] jab or prod (someone or something), esp. with one's finger. ■ [trans.] jab (one's finger) at someone or into something. ■ prod and stir (a fire) with a poker to make it burn more fiercely. ■ make (a hole) in something by prodding or jabbing at it. ■ [trans.] thrust (something, such as one's head) in a particular direction. ■ [intrans.] protrude and be or become visible. ■ vulgar slang (of a man) have sexual intercourse with (another person). **2** [intrans.] move slowly; dawdle: *I was poking along.* ▶ n. **1** an act of poking someone or something. ■ (**a poke around**) informal a look or search around a place. **2** (also **poke bonnet**) a woman's bonnet with a projecting brim, popular esp. in the early 19th century. **3** (usu. **POKE**) Comput. a statement or function in BASIC for altering the contents of a specified memory location. Compare with PEEK (sense 2).
– PHRASES **poke fun at** tease or make fun of. **poke one's nose into** informal take an intrusive interest in. **take a poke at someone** informal hit or punch someone. ■ criticize someone.
– PHRASAL VERBS **poke around/about** look around a place, typically in search of something. [ME: cf. MDu.*poken*.]

poke[2] ▶ n. dialect a bag or small sack. ■ informal a purse or wallet.
– PHRASES **a pig in a poke** see PIG. [ME: ult. from OFr. *poche* 'pocket.']

poke[3] ▶ n. **1** another term for POKEWEED. **2** (**Indian poke**) another term for FALSE HELLEBORE. [18th C.: from Algonquian *poughkone* (see PUCCOON).]

pok·er[1] /'pōkər/ ▶ n. a metal rod with a handle, used for prodding and stirring an open fire.

pok·er[2] ▶ n. a card game played by two or more people who bet on the value of the hands dealt to them. [19th C.: perh. rel. to Ger. *pochen* 'to brag.']

pok·er face ▶ n. an impassive expression that hides one's true feelings. ■ a person with such an expression. — **pok·er-faced** adj.

pok·er·work /'pōkər,wərk/ ▶ n. British term for PYROGRAPHY.

poke·weed /'pōk,wēd/ ▶ n. a North American plant (*Phytolacca americana*, family Phytolaccaceae) with red stems, spikes of cream flowers, and purple berries. [18th C.: *poke* from Algonquian *poughkone*.]

pok·ey /'pōkē/ ▶ n. (usu. **the pokey**) informal prison. [20th C.: of unknown origin.]

pok·y /'pōkē/ (also **pok·ey**) ▶ adj. (**pok·i·er, pok·i·est**) **1** annoyingly slow or dull: *his poky old horse.* **2** (of a room or building) small and cramped. — **pok·i·ly** /-kəlē/ adv. **pok·i·ness** n. [19th C.: from POKE[1].]

pol /päl/ ▶ n. informal a politician.

pol. ▶ abbr. ■ political. ■ politics.

Po·lack /'pō,läk; -,lak/ (also **po·lack**) derog. ▶ n. a person from Poland or of Polish descent. ▶ adj. of Polish origin or descent. [16th C.: from Pol. *Polak*.]

Po·land /'pōlənd/ a country in central Europe. *See box.*

Po·land Chi·na ▶ n. a US breed of hog that is black with white markings.

Po·lan·ski /pə'lanskē/, Roman Raymond (1933–), French movie director. His movies include *Rosemary's Baby* (1968) and *Chinatown* (1974).

po·lar /'pōlər/ ▶ adj. **1** of or relating to the North or South Pole: *the polar regions.* ■ (of an animal or plant) living in the north or south polar region. ■ Astron. of or relating to the poles of a celestial body. ■ Astron. of or relating to a celestial pole. ■ Geom. of or relating to the poles of a sphere. See POLE[2]. ■ Biol. of or relating to the poles of a cell, organ, or part. **2** Physics Chem. having electrical or magnetic polarity. ■ (of a liquid, esp. a solvent) consisting of molecules with a dipole moment. ■ (of a solid) ionic. **3** directly opposite in character or tendency. ▶ n. **1** Geom. the straight line joining the two points at which tangents from a fixed point touch a conic section. **2** Astron. a variable binary star that emits strongly polarized light, one component being a strongly magnetic white dwarf.

po·lar ax·is ▶ n. Astron. the axis of an equatorially mounted telescope that is at right angles to the declination axis and parallel to the earth's axis of rotation.

po·lar bear ▶ n. a large white arctic bear (*Thalarctos maritimus*) that lives mainly on the pack ice. It is a powerful swimmer and feeds chiefly on seals.

po·lar bod·y ▶ n. Biol. each of the small cells that bud off from an oocyte at the two meiotic divisions and do not develop into ova.

po·lar cap ▶ n. Astron. a region of ice or other frozen matter surrounding a pole of a planet.

po·lar co·or·di·nates ▶ plural n. Geom. a pair of coordinates locating the position of a point in a plane, the first being the length of the straight line (r) connecting the point to the origin, and the second the angle (θ) made by this line with a fixed line. ■ the coordinates in a three-dimensional extension of this system.

Poland

Official name: Republic of Poland
Location: central Europe, with a coastline on the Baltic Sea
Area: 120,800 square miles (312,700 sq km)
Population: 38,183,000
Capital: Warsaw
Language: Polish
Currency: zloty

polar bear

po·lar dis·tance ▶ n. Geom. the angular distance of a point on a sphere from the nearest pole.

po·lar·im·e·ter /,pōlə'rimitər/ ▶ n. an instrument for measuring the polarization of light, and esp. (in chemical analysis) for determining the effect of a substance in rotating the plane of polarization of light. — **po·lar·i·met·ric** /pō,larə'metrik/ adj. **po·lar·im·e·try** /-trē/ n. [19th C.: from med. L. *polaris* 'polar.']

Po·lar·is /pə'larəs/ **1** Astron. a fairly bright star located within one degree of the north celestial pole, in the constellation Ursa Minor. Also called NORTH STAR, POLESTAR. **2** a type of submarine-launched ballistic missile.

po·lar·i·scope /pə'larə,skōp/ ▶ n. another term for POLARIMETER. — **po·lar·i·scop·ic** /pə,larə'skäpik/ adj.

po·lar·i·ty /pō'laritē; pə-/ ▶ n. (pl. **-ties**) the property of having poles or being polar. ■ the relative orientation of poles; the direction of a magnetic or electric field. ■ the state of having two opposite or contradictory tendencies, opinions, or aspects: *the polarity between male and female.* ■ Biol. the tendency of living organisms or parts to develop with distinct anterior and posterior (or uppermost and lowermost) ends.

po·lar·i·ty ther·a·py ▶ n. a system of treatment used in alternative medicine, intended to restore a balanced distribution of the body's energy, and incorporating manipulation, exercise, and dietary restrictions.

po·lar·ize /'pōlə,rīz/ ▶ v. **1** [trans.] Physics restrict the vibrations of (a transverse wave, esp. light) wholly or partially to one direction. **2** [trans.] Physics cause (something) to acquire polarity. **3** divide or cause to divide into two sharply contrasting groups or sets of opinions or beliefs. — **po·lar·iz·a·bil·i·ty** /,pōlə,rīzə'bilətē/ n. **po·lar·iz·a·ble** adj. **po·lar·i·za·tion** /,pōlərə'zāsHən/ n. **po·lar·iz·er** n.

po·lar·og·ra·phy /,pōlə'rägrəfē/ ▶ n. Chem. a method of analysis in which a sample is subjected to electrolysis using a special electrode and a range of applied voltages, a plot of current against voltage showing steps corresponding to particular chemical species and proportional to their concentration. — **po·lar·o·graph·ic** /pō,larə'grafik; pə-/ adj. [1930s: from *polarization*.]

Po·lar·oid /'pōlə,roid/ ▶ n. trademark **1** material in thin plastic sheets that produces a high degree of plane polarization in light passing through it. ■ (**Polaroids**) sunglass lenses of this material. **2** a photograph taken with a Polaroid camera. ▶ adj. Photog. denoting a type of camera with internal processing that produces a finished print rapidly after each exposure. ■ denoting a photograph taken with such a camera.

pol·der /'pōldər/ ▶ n. a piece of low-lying land reclaimed from a sea or river, protected by dikes. [17th C.: from Du., from MDu. *polre*.]

Pole /pōl/ ▶ n. a native or national of Poland, or a person of Polish descent. [via Ger. from Pol. *Polanie*, lit. 'field-dwellers,' from *pole* 'field.']

pole[1] /pōl/ ▶ **n.** a long, slender, rounded piece of wood or metal, typically used with one end placed in the ground as a support for something: *a tent pole.* ■ Track & Field a long, slender, flexible rod of wood or fiberglass used in pole-vaulting. ■ short for SKI POLE. ■ a wooden shaft fitted to the front of a cart or carriage drawn by animals and attached to their yokes or collars. ■ a simple fishing rod. ▶ **v.** [trans.] propel (a boat) by pushing a pole against the bottom of a river, canal, or lake.
– PHRASES **under bare poles** Sailing with no sail set. [OE *pāl*, of Gmc. origin; based on L. *palus* 'stake.']

pole[2] ▶ **n.** either of the two locations (**North Pole** or **South Pole**) on the surface of the earth (or of a celestial object) that are the northern and southern ends of the axis of rotation. See also CELESTIAL POLE, MAGNETIC POLE. ■ Geom. either of the two points at which the axis of a sphere intersects its surface. ■ Geom. a fixed point to which other points or lines are referred. ■ Biol. an extremity of the main axis of a cell, organ, or part. ■ each of the two opposite points on the surface of a magnet at which magnetic forces are strongest. ■ each of two terminals (positive and negative) of an electric cell, battery, or machine. ■ fig. one of two opposed or contradictory principles or ideas.
– PHRASES **be poles apart** have nothing in common. — **pole·ward** /-wərd/ **adj.** **pole·wards** /-wərdz/ **adj. & adv.** [ME: from L. *polus* 'end of an axis,' from Gk. *polos* 'pivot, axis, sky.']

pole·ax /'pō,laks/ (also **pole·axe**) ▶ **n.** another term for BATTLE-AX (sense 1). ■ a short-handled ax with a spike at the back. ■ a butcher's ax with a hammerhead at the back, used to slaughter animals. ▶ **v.** [trans.] hit, kill, or knock down with or as if with a poleax. [ME: rel. to MDu. *pol(l)aex* (see POLL, AX).]

pole bean ▶ **n.** a variety of bean plant that climbs up a wall, tree, or trellis. Compare with BUSH BEAN. ■ the edible bean from such a plant.

pole·cat /'pōl,kat/ ▶ **n.** a Eurasian mammal (genus *Mustela*) of the weasel family, with mainly dark brown fur and a darker mask across the eyes, noted for ejecting a fetid-smelling fluid when threatened. ■ another term for SKUNK. [ME: perh. from OFr. *pole* 'chicken.']

po·lem·ic /pə'lemik/ ▶ **n.** a strong verbal or written attack on someone or something. ■ (usu. **polemics**) the art or practice of engaging in controversial debate or dispute. — **po·lem·i·cist** /pə'leməsist/ **n.** **po·lem·i·cize** /pə'lemə,sīz/ **v.** **po·lem·i·cal adj.** [17th C.: via med. L. from Gk. *polemikos*, from *polemos* 'war.']

po·len·ta /pō'lentə/ ▶ **n.** cornmeal as used in Italian cooking. ■ a paste or dough made from cornmeal. [16th C.: Ital., from L., 'pearl barley.']

pole·star /'pōl,stär/ ▶ **n.** Astron. (also **Pole Star**) another term for POLARIS. ■ fig. a thing or principle that guides or attracts.

pole vault ▶ **n.** (**the pole vault**) an athletic event in which competitors attempt to vault over a high bar with the end of an extremely long flexible pole held in the hands. ■ a vault performed in this way. ▶ **v.** (**pole-vault**) [intrans.] perform a pole vault. — **pole-vault·er n.** **pole-vault·ing n.**

po·lice /pə'lēs/ ▶ **n.** [treated as pl.] (usu. **the police**) the civil force of a federal or local government, responsible for the prevention and detection of crime and the maintenance of public order. ■ members of a police force. ■ [with adj.] an organization engaged in the enforcement of official regulations in a specified domain: *transit police.* ■ a group of people who aim or are seen as aiming at monitoring the actions or beliefs of others: *morality police | thought police.* ▶ **v.** [trans.] [often as n.] (**policing**) (of a police force) have the duty of maintaining law and order. ■ enforce regulations or an agreement in (a particular area or domain). ■ enforce the provisions of (a law, agreement, or treaty). [15th C.: from Fr., from med. L. *politia* 'citizenship, government' (see POLICY[1]).]

po·lice dog ▶ **n.** a dog, esp. a German shepherd, trained for use in police work. ■ informal a German shepherd.

po·lice force ▶ **n.** an organized body of police officers.

po·lice·man /pə'lēsmən/ ▶ **n.** (pl. **-men**) a member of a police force.

po·lice of·fi·cer ▶ **n.** a policeman or policewoman.

po·lice pro·ce·dur·al ▶ **n.** a crime novel in which the emphasis is on the procedures used by the police in solving the crime.

po·lice state ▶ **n.** a totalitarian state controlled by a political secret police force.

po·lice sta·tion ▶ **n.** the headquarters of a police force.

po·lice·wom·an /pə'lēs,wo͝omən/ ▶ **n.** (pl. **-wom·en**) a female member of a police force.

po·li·cier /pō,lēs'yā/ ▶ **n.** a movie based on portraying crime and its detection by police. [Fr., from *roman policier* 'detective novel.']

pol·i·cy[1] /'päləsē/ ▶ **n.** (pl. **-cies**) a proposed or adopted course or principle of action. ■ archaic prudent or expedient conduct or action. [ME: from OFr. *policie* 'civil administration,' via L. from Gk. *politeia* 'citizenship,' from *politēs* 'citizen,' from *polis* 'city.']

pol·i·cy[2] ▶ **n.** (pl. **-cies**) **1** a contract of insurance. **2** an illegal lottery or numbers game. [16th C.: from Fr. *police* 'bill of lading,' prob. based on Gk. *apodeixis* 'evidence, proof,' from *apodeiknunai* 'demonstrate, show.']

pol·i·cy·hold·er /'päləsē,hōldər/ ▶ **n.** a person or group in whose name an insurance policy is held.

po·li·o /'pōlē,ō/ ▶ **n.** short for POLIOMYELITIS.

po·li·o·my·e·li·tis /,pōlēō,mīə'lītis/ ▶ **n.** Med. an infectious viral disease that affects the central nervous system and can cause paralysis. [19th C.: mod. L., from Gk. *polios* 'gray' + *muelos* 'marrow.']

po·li·o·vi·rus /'pōlēō,vīrəs/ ▶ **n.** Med. any of a group of enteroviruses, including poliomyelitis.

po·lis /'pōləs; 'pä-/ ▶ **n.** (pl. **po·leis** /'päl,ās/) a city-state in ancient Greece. [Gk.]

Po·li·sa·ri·o /,pōlə'särē,ō/ (also **Polisario Front**) ▶ **n.** an independence movement in Western (formerly Spanish) Sahara, formed in 1973. [Sp. acronym, from *Frente Popular para la Liberación de Sagnia el-Hamra y Río de Oro* 'Popular Front for the Liberation of Sagnia el-Hamra and Rio de Oro.']

Po·lish /'pōlisн/ ▶ **adj.** of or relating to Poland, its inhabitants, or their language. ▶ **n.** the West Slavic language of Poland.

pol·ish /'pälisн/ ▶ **v.** [trans.] make the surface of (something) smooth and shiny by rubbing it. ■ improve, refine, or add the finishing touches to. ▶ **n.** a substance used to give something a smooth and shiny surface when rubbed in: *furniture polish.* ■ [in sing.] an act of rubbing something to give it a shiny surface. ■ smoothness or glossiness produced by rubbing or friction. ■ refinement or elegance in a person or thing.
– PHRASAL VERBS **polish something off** finish or consume something quickly: *they polished off most of the sausages.* — **pol·ish·a·ble adj.** **pol·ish·er n.** [ME: from OFr. *poliss-*, lengthened stem of *polir* 'to polish,' from L. *polire.*]

Po·lish Cor·ri·dor a former region of Poland that extended north to the Baltic coast and separated East Prussia from the rest of German.

pol·ished /'pälisнt/ ▶ **adj.** shiny due to being rubbed. ■ accomplished and skillful. ■ refined, sophisticated, or elegant. ■ (of rice) having had the outer husk removed during milling.

Po·lish no·ta·tion ▶ **n.** Logic Comput. a system of formula notation without brackets or special punctuation, frequently used to represent the order in which arithmetical operations are performed in many computers and calculators. In the usual form (**reverse Polish notation**), operators follow rather than precede their operands.

polit. ▶ **abbr.** ■ political. ■ politics.

po·lit·bu·ro /'pälət,byo͝orō; 'pō-/ ▶ **n.** (pl. **-ros**) the principal policymaking committee of a Communist Party. ■ (**Politburo**) this committee in the former Soviet Union. Also called (1952–66) the PRESIDIUM. [from Russ. *politbyuro*, from *polit(icheskoe) byuro* 'political bureau.']

po·lite /pə'līt/ ▶ **adj.** (**-lit·er, -lit·est**) having or showing respectful and considerate behavior. ■ [attrib.] of or relating to people who regard themselves as more refined than others: *polite society.* — **po·lite·ly adv.** **po·lite·ness n.** [ME: from L. *politus* 'polished, made smooth,' past part. of *polire.*]

pol·i·tesse /,pälə'tes/ ▶ **n.** formal politeness or etiquette. [18th C.: Fr., from Ital. *politezza, pulitezza*, from *pulito* 'polite.']

pol·i·tic /'pälə,tik/ ▶ **adj.** (of an action) seeming sensible and judicious under the circumstances. ■ (also **pol·i·tick**) archaic (of a person) prudent and sagacious. ▶ **v.** (**-ticked, -ticking**) [intrans.] [often as n.] (**politicking**) often derog. engage in political activity. — **pol·i·tic·ly adv.** (rare). [ME: from OFr. *politique* 'political,' via L. from Gk. *politikos*, from *politēs* 'citizen,' from *polis* 'city.']

po·lit·i·cal /pə'litikəl/ ▶ **adj.** of or relating to the government or the public affairs of a country. ■ of or relating to the ideas or strategies of a particular party or group in politics. ■ interested in or active in politics. ■ motivated or caused by a person's beliefs or actions concerning politics. ■ esp. derog. relating to, affecting, or acting according to the interests of status or authority within an organization rather than matters of principle. — **po·lit·i·cal·ly** /-ik(ə)lē/ **adv.**

po·lit·i·cal ac·tion com·mit·tee (abbr.: **PAC**) ▶ **n.** an organization that raises money privately and employs lobbyists to influence legislation.

po·lit·i·cal a·sy·lum ▶ **n.** see ASYLUM.

po·lit·i·cal cor·rect·ness (also **po·lit·i·cal cor·rec·ti·tude**) ▶ **n.** the avoidance of forms of expression or action that are perceived to exclude, marginalize, or insult certain groups of people.

po·lit·i·cal·ly cor·rect /pə'litik(ə)lē/ (or **in·correct**) ▶ **adj.** exhibiting (or not exhibiting) political correctness.

po·lit·i·cal pris·on·er ▶ **n.** a person imprisoned for their political beliefs or actions.

po·lit·i·cal ref·u·gee ▶ **n.** a refugee from an oppressive government.

po·lit·i·cal sci·ence ▶ **n.** the branch of knowledge that deals with systems of government. — **po·lit·i·cal sci·en·tist n.**

pol·i·ti·cian /,pälə'tisнən/ ▶ **n.** a person who is professionally involved in politics. ■ a person who acts in a manipulative and devious way, typically to gain advancement.

po·lit·i·cize /pə'litə,sīz/ ▶ **v.** [trans.] [often as adj.] (**politicized**) cause (an activity or event) to become political in character: *art was becoming politicized.* ■ make (someone) politically aware. — **po·lit·i·ci·za·tion** /pə,litəsi'zāsнən/ **n.**

po·lit·i·co /pə'liti,kō/ ▶ **n.** (pl. **-cos**) informal term for POLITICIAN. [Sp. and Ital., 'politic' or 'political person.']

politico- ▶ **comb. form** politically: *politico-ethical.* ■ political and ...: *politico-economic.* [from Gk. *politikos* 'civic, political.']

pol·i·tics /'pälə,tiks/ ▶ **plural n.** [usu. treated as sing.] the activities associated with the governance of a country or area. ■ the activities of governments concerning the political relations between countries. ■ the academic study of government and the state. ■ activities within an organization that are aimed at improving someone's status or position and are typically considered to be devious or divisive. ■ a particular set of

political beliefs or principles. ■ (often **the politics of**) the assumptions or principles relating to or inherent in a sphere, theory, or thing, esp. when concerned with power and status in a society.
– PHRASES **play politics** act for political or personal gain rather than from principle.

pol·i·ty /'pälətē/ ▶ n. (pl. **-ties**) a form or process of civil government or constitution. ■ an organized society; a state as a political entity. [16th C.: from obs. Fr. *politie*, via L. from Gk. *politeia* 'citizenship, government,' from *politēs* 'citizen,' from *polis* 'city.']

Polk /pōk/, James Knox (1795–1849), 11th president of the US 1845–49. A Democrat, his administration oversaw major territorial additions to the US when Texas was admitted to the Union in 1845, and California and other parts of the Southwest were annexed two years later.

pol·ka /'pō(l)kə/ ▶ n. a lively dance of Bohemian origin. ■ a piece of music for this dance or in its rhythm. ▶ v. (**pol·kas, pol·kaed** or **pol·ka'd, pol·ka·ing**) [intrans.] dance the polka. [19th C.: via Fr. and Ger. from Czech *půlka* 'half step,' from *půl* 'half.']

pol·ka dot ▶ n. one of a number of large round dots repeated to form a regular pattern on fabric. — **pol·ka-dot·ted** adj.

poll /pōl/ ▶ n. **1** (often **the polls**) the process of voting in an election: *the country went to the polls on March 10.* ■ a record of the number of votes cast in an election. ■ (**the polls**) the places where election votes are cast. **2** dialect a person's head. ■ the part of the head on which hair grows; the scalp. ▶ v. [trans.] **1** (often **be polled**) record an opinion or vote. ■ [intrans.] (of a candidate in an election) receive a specified number of votes. ■ Telecom. Comput. check the status of (a measuring device, part of a computer, or a node in a network). **2** cut the horns off (an animal, esp. a young cow). — **poll·ee** /pō'lē/ n. (sense 1 of the verb). [ME (in the sense 'head'): perh. of Low Ger. origin]

Pol·lack /'päläk/, Sidney (1934–), US director. His movies include *The Way We Were* (1973) and *Out of Africa* (1985).

pol·lack /'päläk/ (also **pol·lock**) ▶ n. (pl. same or **-lacks**) an edible greenish-brown fish (*Pollachius pollachius*) of the cod family, with a protruding lower jaw. Found in the northeastern Atlantic, it is popular with anglers. [ME: perh. of Celtic origin.]

pol·lard /'pälərd/ ▶ v. [trans.] [often as adj.] (**pollarded**) cut off the top and branches of (a tree) to encourage new growth at the top. ▶ n. **1** a tree whose top and branches have been cut off for this reason. **2** archaic an animal, e.g., a sheep or deer, that has lost its horns or cast its antlers. [17th C.: from the v. POLL + -ARD.]

polled /pōld/ ▶ adj. (of cattle, sheep, or goats) lacking horns, either naturally or because of removal.

pol·len /'pälən/ ▶ n. a fine powdery substance, typically yellow, of microscopic grains discharged from the male part of a flower or from a male cone transported to the female ovule by the wind, insects, or other animals. [18th C.: from L., lit. 'fine powder.']

pol·len count ▶ n. an index of the amount of pollen in the air, published for those allergic to it.

pol·len grain ▶ n. each of the microscopic particles, typically single cells, of which pollen is composed.

pol·len tube ▶ n. Bot. a hollow tube that develops from a pollen grain when deposited on the stigma of a flower.

pol·lex /'päl,eks/ ▶ n. (pl. **pol·li·ces** /'pälə,sēz/) Anat. Zool. the innermost digit of a forelimb. [19th C.: from L., lit. 'thumb or big toe.']

pol·li·nate /'pälə,nāt/ ▶ v. [trans.] deposit pollen on (a stigma, ovule, flower, or plant) and so allow fertilization. — **pol·li·na·tion** /,pälə'nāSHən/ n. **pol·li·na·tor** /-,nātər/ n.

poll·ing place (also **polling station**) ▶ n. a building where voting takes place during an election.

pol·lin·i·um /pə'linēəm/ ▶ n. (pl. **pol·lin·ia** /pə'linēə/) Bot. a coherent mass of pollen grains that is the product of each anther lobe of some flowers, esp. orchids. [19th C.: mod. L., from L. *pollen, pollin-* 'pollen.']

pol·li·wog /'pälē,wäg; -,wôg/ (also **pol·ly·wog**) ▶ n. a tadpole. [ME (earlier as *pollywiggle*): from POLL in the sense 'head' + the v. WIGGLE.]

Pol·lock /'päläk/, Jackson (1912–56), US painter; full name *Paul Jackson Pollock.* A leading figure in the abstract expressionist movement, he became the chief exponent of the style known as action painting from 1947.

pol·lock /'päläk/ ▶ n. **1** a commercially valuable food fish (*Pollachius virens*) of the cod family, occurring in the North Atlantic. **2** var. of POLLACK.

poll·ster /'pōlstər/ ▶ n. a person who conducts or analyzes opinion polls.

poll tax ▶ n. a tax levied on every adult, without reference to their income or resources.

pol·lute /pə'lo͞ot/ ▶ v. [trans.] contaminate (water, air, or a place) with harmful or poisonous substances. ■ fig. defile; corrupt: *a society polluted by racism.* — **pol·lu·tant** /-'lo͞otnt/ adj. & n. **pol·lut·er** n. [ME: from L. *pollut-* 'soiled, defiled,' from the v. *polluere*, based on the root of *lutum* 'mud.']

pol·lu·tion /pə'lo͞oSHən/ ▶ n. the presence in or introduction into the environment of a substance or thing that has harmful or poisonous effects.

Pol·lux /'päləks/ **1** Gk. Mythol. the twin brother of Castor. Also called POLYDEUCES. See DIOSCURI. **2** Astron. the brightest star in the constellation Gemini, close to Castor.

Pol·ly·an·na /,pälē'anə/ ▶ n. an excessively cheerful or optimistic person. — **Pol·ly·an·na·ish** /-iSH/ adj. **Pol·ly·an·na·ism** /-,izəm/ n. [20th C.: after the heroine created by Eleanor Hodgman Porter (1868–1920), US author.]

pol·ly·wog ▶ n. var. of POLLIWOG.

Po·lo, Marco, see MARCO POLO.

po·lo /'pōlō/ ▶ n. a game resembling field hockey, played on horseback with a long-handled mallet. [19th C.: from Balti, 'ball.']

pol·o·naise /,pälə'nāz; ,pō-/ ▶ n. **1** a slow dance of Polish origin in triple time. ■ a piece of music for this dance or in its rhythm. **2** hist. a woman's dress with a tight bodice and a skirt open from the waist downward, looped up to show a decorative underskirt. ▶ adj. (of a dish, esp. vegetable) garnished with chopped hard-boiled egg yolk, breadcrumbs, and parsley. [18th C.: from Fr., fem. of *polonais* 'Pol.,' from med. L. *Polonia* 'Poland.']

po·lo·ni·um /pə'lōnēəm/ ▶ n. the chemical element of atomic number 84, a radioactive metal occurring in nature only as a product of radioactive decay of uranium. (Symbol: **Po**) [19th C.: mod. L., from med. L. *Polonia* 'Poland.']

po·lo shirt ▶ n. a casual cotton shirt with a collar and several buttons at the neck.

Pol Pot /päl 'pät; pôl/ (*c.*1925–98), Cambodian communist leader of the Khmer Rouge; prime minister 1976–79; born *Saloth Sar.* Overthrown in 1979, he led the Khmer Rouge in a guerrilla war.

Pols·ka /'pôlskä/ Polish name for POLAND.

Pol·ta·va /pəl'tävə/ a city in east central Ukraine; pop. 317,000.

pol·ter·geist /'pōltər,gīst/ ▶ n. a ghost or other supernatural being supposedly responsible for physical disturbances such as throwing objects around. [19th C.: from Ger. *Poltergeist*, from *poltern* 'create a disturbance' + *Geist* 'ghost.']

Pol·to·ratsk /pəltə'rätsk/ former name (1919–27) of ASHGABAT.

pol·troon /päl'tro͞on/ ▶ n. archaic literary a coward. — **pol·troon·er·y** /-'tro͞onərē/ n. [16th C.: from Fr. *poltron*, from Ital. *poltrone*, perh. from *poltro* 'sluggard.']

pol·y /'pälē/ ▶ n. (pl. **pol·ys**) informal short for: ■ polyester. ■ polytechnic. ■ polyethylene.

poly- ▶ comb. form many; much: *polyandry* | *polychrome.* ■ Chem. denoting the presence of many atoms or groups of a particular kind in a molecule: *polycarbonate.* [from Gk. *polus* 'much,' *polloi* 'many.']

pol·y·ad·ic /,pälē'adik/ ▶ adj. involving three or more quantities, elements, or individuals. [20th C.: from POLY- 'many.']

pol·y·am·ide /,pälē'amīd/ ▶ n. a synthetic polymer of a type made by the linkage of an amino group of one molecule and a carboxylic acid group of another.

pol·y·an·dry /'pälē,andrē/ ▶ n. polygamy in which a woman has more than one husband. Compare with POLYGYNY. ■ Zool. a pattern of mating in which a female animal has more than one male mate. — **pol·y·an·drous** /,pälē'andrəs/ adj. [17th C.: from POLY- 'many' + Gk. *anēr, andr-* 'male.']

pol·y·an·thus /,pälē'anTHəs/ ▶ n. (pl. same) a herbaceous flowering plant (*Primula* × *polyantha*) that is a complex hybrid between the wild primrose and primulas. [18th C.: mod. L., from POLY- 'many' + Gk. *anthos* 'flower.']

pol·y·car·bon·ate /,päli'kärbə,nāt; -nət/ ▶ n. a synthetic resin in which the polymer units are linked through carbonate groups.

Pol·y·carp, St. /'pälē,kärp/ (*c.*69–*c.*155), Greek bishop of Smyrna and martyr.

Pol·y·chae·ta /,päli'kētə/ Zool. a class of marine annelids that comprises the bristle worms. — **pol·y·chaete** /'pälē,kēt/ n. & adj. [mod. L. (pl.), from Gk. *polu-* 'many' + *khaitē* 'mane' (taken to mean 'bristle').]

pol·y·chlo·rin·at·ed bi·phen·yl /,pälē'klôrə,nātid bī'fenəl/ (abbr.: **PCB**) ▶ n. Chem. any of a class of toxic aromatic compounds whose molecules contain two benzene rings in which hydrogen atoms have been replaced by chlorine atoms.

pol·y·chro·mat·ic /,pälikrō'matik/ ▶ adj. of two or more colors; multicolored. — **pol·y·chro·ma·tism** /-'krōmə,tizəm/ n.

pol·y·chrome /'päli,krōm/ ▶ adj. painted, printed, or decorated in several colors. ▶ n. varied coloring. ■ a work of art in several colors, esp. a statue. ▶ v. [trans.] [usu. as adj.] (**polychromed**) execute or decorate (a work of art) in several colors. [19th C.: from Fr., from Gk. *polukhrōmos*, from *polu-* 'many' + *khrōma* 'color.']

pol·y·chro·my /'päli,krōmē/ ▶ n. the art of painting in several colors.

pol·y·cy·clic /,päli'siklik; -'sīklik/ ▶ adj. of, relating to, or resulting from many cycles. ■ Chem. (of an organic compound) having several rings of atoms in the molecule. ■ Geol. (of a landform or deposit) having undergone two or more cycles of erosion and deposition.

pol·y·cy·the·mi·a /,päli,sī'THēmēə/ (Brit. **pol·y·cy·thae·mi·a**) ▶ n. Med. an abnormally increased concentration of hemoglobin in the blood. [19th C.: from mod. L. *polycythaemia*, from POLY- 'many' + -CYTE 'cell' + Gk. *haima* 'blood' + -IA[1].]

pol·y·dac·ty·ly /,päli'daktəlē/ ▶ n. a condition in which there are more than five fingers or toes on a hand or foot. — **pol·y·dac·tyl** adj. & n. [19th C.: from Gk. *poludaktulos* (from *polu-* 'many' + *daktulos* 'finger') + -Y[3].]

Pol·y·deu·ces /,päli'd(y)o͞o,sēz/ another name for POLLUX (sense 1).

pol·y·e·lec·tro·lyte /,pälēə'lektrə,līt/ ▶ n. Chem. a polymer that has several ionizable groups along the molecule.

pol·y·em·bry·o·ny /,pālē'embrēənē; -em'brīənē/ ▶ n. Biol. the formation of more than one embryo from a single fertilized ovum or in a single seed. — **pol·y·em·bry·on·ic** /-,embrē'änik/ adj.

pol·y·ene /ˈpälēˌēn/ ▶ **n.** Chem. a hydrocarbon with several carbon–carbon double bonds.

pol·y·es·ter /ˈpälēˌestər/ ▶ **n.** a synthetic resin in which the polymer units are linked by ester groups. ■ a fabric made from polyester fiber.

pol·y·eth·yl·ene /ˌpälēˈeᴛʜəˌlēn/ ▶ **n.** a tough, light, flexible synthetic resin made by polymerizing ethylene.

pol·y·eth·yl·ene gly·col ▶ **n.** a synthetic resin made by polymerizing ethylene glycol, including polymers used chiefly as solvents or waxes.

pol·y·eth·yl·ene ter·eph·thal·ate /ˌterə(f)ˈᴛʜalˌāt/ (abbr.: **PET**) ▶ **n.** a synthetic resin made by copolymerizing ethylene glycol and terephthalic acid, widely used to make polyester fibers.

po·lyg·a·my /pəˈligəmē/ ▶ **n.** the practice or custom of having more than one wife or husband at the same time. ■ Zool. a pattern of mating in which an animal has more than one mate of the opposite sex. — **po·lyg·a·mist** /-mist/ **n.** **po·lyg·a·mous** **adj.** [16th C.: from Fr. *polygamie*, via late L. from Gk. *polugamia*, from *polugamos* 'often marrying.']

pol·y·gene /ˈpäliˌjēn/ ▶ **n.** Genet. a gene whose individual effect on a phenotype is too small to be observed. [1940s: back-form. from POLYGENIC.]

pol·y·gen·e·sis /ˌpäliˈjenəsəs/ ▶ **n.** origination from several independent sources, in particular: ■ Biol. the hypothetical origination of a race or species from a number of independent stocks. ■ the hypothetical origination of language or of a surname from a number of independent sources in different places at different times.

pol·y·gen·ic /ˌpäliˈjenik/ ▶ **adj.** Genet. of, relating to, or determined by polygenes. — **pol·y·gen·i·cal·ly** /-ik(ə)lē/ **adv.** [1940s: from Gk. *polugenēs* 'of many kinds' + -IC.]

po·lyg·e·nism /pəˈlijəˌnizəm/ ▶ **n.** the doctrine of polygeny. — **po·lyg·e·nist** /ˌpəˈlijənist/ **n. & adj.**

pol·y·glot /ˈpäliˌglät/ ▶ **adj.** knowing or using several languages. ▶ **n.** a person who knows several languages. — **pol·y·glot·ism** /-ˌglätˌizəm/ **n.** [17th C.: from Fr. *polyglotte*, from Gk. *poluglōttos*, from *polu-* 'many' + *glōtta* 'tongue.']

pol·y·gon /ˈpäliˌgän/ ▶ **n.** Geom. a plane figure with at least three straight sides and angles, and typically five or more. — **po·lyg·o·nal** /pəˈligənl/ **adj.** [16th C.: via late L. from Gk. *polugōnon*, neut. (used as a n.) of *polugōnos* 'many-angled.']

po·lyg·o·num /pəˈligənəm/ ▶ **n.** a plant of a genus (*Polygonum*) that includes knotgrass and knotweed. Some are weeds and some are ornamentals. [mod. L., from Gk. *polu-* 'many' + *gonu* 'knee, joint' (because of the swollen joints sheathed by stipules).]

pol·y·graph /ˈpäliˌgraf/ ▶ **n.** a machine designed to detect and record changes in physiological characteristics, used esp. as a lie detector. ■ a lie-detector test using a machine of this type. — **pol·y·graph·ic** /ˌpäliˈgrafik/ **adj.**

pol·y·gyne /ˈpäliˌjīn/ ▶ **adj.** Entomol. (of a social insect) having more than one egg-laying queen in each colony.

po·lyg·y·ny /pəˈlijənē/ ▶ **n.** polygamy in which a man has more than one wife. Compare with POLYANDRY. — **po·lyg·y·nous** /pəˈlijənəs/ **adj.** [18th C.: from POLY- 'many' + Gk. *gunē* 'woman.']

pol·y·he·dron /ˌpäliˈhēdrən/ ▶ **n.** (pl. **-he·drons** or **-he·dra** /-ˈhēdrə/) Geom. a solid figure with many plane faces, typically more than six. — **pol·y·he·dral** /-ˈhēdrəl/ **adj.** **pol·y·he·dric** /-ˈhēdrik/ **adj.** [16th C.: from Gk. *poluedron*, neut. (used as a n.) of *poluedros* 'many-sided.']

pol·y·his·tor /ˌpäliˈhistər/ ▶ **n.** another term for POLYMATH. [16th C.: from Gk. *poluistōr* 'very learned,' from *polu-* 'much, very' + *histōr* 'wise man.']

Pol·y·hym·ni·a /ˌpäliˈhimnēə/ Greek Rom. Mythol. the Muse of the art of mime.

pol·y·math /ˈpäliˌmaᴛʜ/ ▶ **n.** a person of wide-ranging knowledge or learning. — **pol·y·math·ic** /ˌpäliˈmaᴛʜik/ **adj.** **po·lym·a·thy** /pəˈliməᴛʜē; ˈpäliˌmaᴛʜē/ **n.** [17th C.: from Gk. *polumathēs* 'having learned much,' from *polu-* 'much' + the stem of *manthanein* 'learn.']

pol·y·mer /ˈpäləmər/ ▶ **n.** Chem. a substance that has a molecular structure built up chiefly or completely from a large number of similar units bonded together. — **pol·y·mer·ic** /ˌpäləˈmerik/ **adj.** [19th C.: from Ger., from Gk. *polumeros* 'having many parts,' from *polu-* 'many' + *meros* 'a share.']

pol·y·mer·ase /pəˈliməˌrās; -ˌrāz/ ▶ **n.** Biochem. an enzyme that brings about the formation of a particular polymer. See also TRANSCRIPTASE.

po·lym·er·ize /pəˈliməˌrīz; ˈpäləməˌrīz/ ▶ **v.** Chem. combine or cause to combine to form a polymer. — **po·lym·er·iz·a·ble** /pəˌliməˈrīzəbəl; päləmə-/ **adj.** **po·lym·er·i·za·tion** /pəˌlimərəˈzāsʜən; ˌpäləmərə-/ **n.**

po·lym·er·ous /pəˈlimərəs/ ▶ **adj.** Biol. having or consisting of many parts.

pol·y·meth·yl meth·ac·ry·late /ˈpäliˌmeᴛʜəl meᴛʜˈakrəˌlāt/ ▶ **n.** a glassy synthetic resin obtained by polymerizing methyl methacrylate, used to make perspex, plexiglas, and lucite.

pol·y·morph /ˈpäliˌmôrf/ ▶ **n.** an organism or inorganic object or material that takes various forms. ■ Physiol. a polymorphonuclear leukocyte. [19th C.: from Gk. *polumorphos*, from *polu-* 'many' + *morphē* 'form.']

pol·y·mor·phism /ˌpäliˈmôrˌfizəm/ ▶ **n.** the occurrence of something in different forms, in particular: ■ Biol. the occurrence of different forms among the members of a population or colony. ■ Biochem. the occurrence of a number of alternative forms within a section of a nucleic acid or protein molecule. — **pol·y·mor·phic** /-ˈmôrfik/ **adj.** **pol·y·mor·phous** /-ˈmôrfəs/ **adj.**

pol·y·mor·pho·nu·cle·ar /ˌpäliˌmôrfōˈn(y)o͞oklēər/ ▶ **adj.** Physiol. (of a leukocyte) having a nucleus with several lobes and a cytoplasm that contains granules, as in an eosinophil or basophil.

pol·y·myx·in /ˌpäliˈmiksən/ ▶ **n.** Med. any of a group of polypeptide antibiotics that are active chiefly against Gram-negative bacteria. Polymyxins are obtained from soil bacteria of the genus *Bacillus*, in particular *B. polymyxa*. [1940s: from mod. L. *polymyxa*, from Gk. *polu-* 'much' + *muxa* 'slime' + -IN[1].]

Pol·y·ne·sia /ˌpäləˈnēzʜə/ a region of the central Pacific Ocean that lies east of Micronesia and Melanesia.

Pol·y·ne·sian /ˌpäləˈnēzʜən/ ▶ **adj.** of or relating to Polynesia, its people, or their languages. ▶ **n.** **1** a native or inhabitant of Polynesia, or a person of Polynesian descent. **2** a group of Austronesian languages spoken in Polynesia, including Maori, Hawaiian, and Samoan.

pol·y·neu·ri·tis /ˌpälin(y)o͝oˈrītis/ ▶ **n.** Med. any disorder that affects the peripheral nerves collectively. — **pol·y·neu·rit·ic** /-n(y)o͝oˈritik/ **adj.**

pol·y·no·mi·al /ˌpäləˈnōmēəl/ ▶ **adj.** consisting of several terms. ▶ **n.** Math. an expression of more than two algebraic terms. ■ Biol. a Latin name with more than two parts. [17th C.: from POLY- 'many,' on the pattern of *multinomial*.]

pol·y·nu·cle·ar /ˌpäliˈn(y)o͞oklēər/ ▶ **adj.** Chem. (of a complex) containing more than one metal atom. ■ (of a compound) polycyclic.

pol·y·nu·cle·o·tide /ˌpäliˈn(y)o͞oklēəˌtīd/ ▶ **n.** Biochem. a linear polymer whose molecule is composed of many nucleotide units, constituting a section of a nucleic acid molecule.

po·lyn·ya /ˌpälənˈyä/ ▶ **n.** a stretch of open water surrounded by ice, esp. in Arctic seas. [19th C.: from Russ., from the base of *pole* 'field.']

pol·y·o·ma vi·rus /ˌpälēˈōmə/ ▶ **n.** Med. any of a group of DNA that are usually endemic in their host species without causing disease but that can cause tumors when injected into other species.

pol·yp /ˈpäləp/ ▶ **n.** **1** Zool. a solitary or colonial sedentary form of a coelenterate, typically having a columnar body with the mouth uppermost surrounded by a ring of tentacles. Compare with MEDUSA. **2** Med. a small growth, typically benign and with a stalk, protruding from a mucous membrane. — **pol·yp·ous** /ˈpäləpəs/ **adj.** (in sense 2). [ME (sense 2): from OFr. *polipe*, from L. *polypus* (see POLYPUS).]

pol·y·par·y /ˈpäləˌperē/ ▶ **n.** (pl. **-par·ies**) Zool. the common stem of a polyp colony, to which zooids are attached. [18th C.: from mod. L. *polyparium*, from L. *polypus* (see POLYPUS).]

pol·y·pep·tide /ˌpäliˈpepˌtīd/ ▶ **n.** Biochem. a linear organic polymer consisting of a large number of amino-acid residues bonded together in a chain, forming part of (or the whole of) a protein molecule. [20th C.: from POLY- 'many' + PEPTONE + -IDE.]

pol·y·phase /ˈpäliˌfāz/ ▶ **adj.** consisting of or occurring in a number of separate stages. — **pol·y·pha·sic** /ˌpäliˈfāzik/ **adj.**

Pol·y·phe·mus /ˌpäləˈfēməs/ Gk. Mythol. a Cyclops.

pol·y·phe·nol /ˌpäliˈfēˌnôl; -ˌnōl/ ▶ **n.** Chem. a compound containing more than one phenolic hydroxyl group.

pol·y·phon·ic /ˌpäliˈfänik/ ▶ **adj.** producing many sounds simultaneously; many-voiced. ■ Music (esp. of vocal music) in two or more parts, each having a melody of its own; contrapuntal. Compare with HOMOPHONIC. ■ Music (of an instrument) capable of producing more than one note at a time. — **pol·y·phon·i·cal·ly** /-ik(ə)lē/ **adv.** [18th C.: from Gk. *poluphōnos* (from *polu-* 'many' + *phōnē* 'voice, sound') + -IC.]

po·lyph·o·ny /pəˈlifənē/ ▶ **n.** (pl. **-nies**) Music the style of simultaneously combining a number of individual parts that harmonize with each other. ■ a composition written, played, or sung in this style. — **pol·y·pho·nist** /-fənist/ **n.** **pol·y·pho·nous** /-fənəs/ **adj.**

pol·y·phy·let·ic /ˌpälifīˈletik/ ▶ **adj.** Biol. (of a group of organisms) derived from more than one common evolutionary ancestor or ancestral group.

pol·y·pi /ˈpäləˌpī; -pē/ plural form of POLYPUS.

pol·y·ploid /ˈpäliˌploid/ Biol. ▶ **adj.** (of a cell or nucleus) containing more than two homologous sets of chromosomes. ▶ **n.** a polyploid organism, variety, or species. — **pol·y·ploi·dy** **n.**

pol·y·pod /ˈpäləˌpäd/ ▶ **adj.** Zool. having many feet or footlike appendages. [18th C. (as a n. denoting an animal having many feet): from Fr. *polypode* 'many-footed,' from Gk. *polupous*, *polupod-*, from *polu-* 'many' + *pous*, *pod-* 'foot.']

pol·y·po·dy /ˈpäləˌpōdē/ ▶ **n.** (pl. **-dies**) a widely distributed fern (genus *Polypodium*, family Polypodiaceae) that has stout scaly creeping rhizomes and remains green during the winter, growing on trees, walls, and stones, esp. in limestone areas.

pol·yp·oid /ˈpäliˌpoid/ ▶ **adj.** **1** Zool. of, relating to, or resembling a polyp or hydra. ■ of, relating to, or denoting the polyp stage in the life cycle of a coelenterate. Also called HYDROID. Compare with MEDUSOID. **2** Med. (of a growth) resembling or in the form of a polyp.

pol·yp·o·sis /ˌpäliˈpōsəs/ ▶ **n.** Med. a condition characterized by the presence of numerous internal polyps, esp. a hereditary disease (**familial adenomatous polyposis**) that affects the colon and in which the polyps may become malignant.

pol·y·pro·pyl·ene /ˌpäliˈprōpəˌlēn/ ▶ **n.** a synthetic resin that is a polymer of propylene.

pol·yp·tych /ˈpälipˌtik/ ▶ **n.** a painting consisting of more than three leaves or joined panels. [19th C.: from late L. *polyptycha* (neut. pl.)

'registers,' from Gk. *poluptukhos* 'having many folds,' from *polu-* 'many' + *ptukhē* 'fold.']

pol·y·pus /'päləpəs/ ▶ **n.** (pl. **-pi** /-,pī; -,pē/) archaic or technical term for **POLYP.** [ME: via L. from a var. of Gk. *polupous* 'cuttlefish, polyp,' from *polu-* 'many' + *pous, pod-* 'foot.']

pol·y·rhythm /'päli,riT͟Həm/ ▶ **n.** Music a rhythm that makes use of two or more different rhythms at once. — **pol·y·rhyth·mic** /,päli'riT͟Hmik/ **adj.**

pol·y·ri·bo·some /,päli'rībə,sōm/ ▶ **n.** another term for **POLYSOME.**

pol·y·sac·cha·ride /,päli'sakə,rīd/ ▶ **n.** Biochem. a carbohydrate whose molecules consist of a number of sugar molecules bonded together.

po·ly·se·my /'päli,semē/ ▶ **n.** Ling. the coexistence of many possible meanings for a word or phrase. — **po·ly·se·mic** /,päli'sēmik/ **adj.** **po·ly·se·mous** /,päli'sēməs/ **adj.** [20th C.: from **POLY-** 'many' + Gk. *sēma* 'sign.']

pol·y·some /'päli,sōm/ ▶ **n.** Biol. a cluster of ribosomes held together by a strand of messenger RNA.

pol·y·sty·rene /,päli'stīrēn/ ▶ **n.** a synthetic resin that is a polymer of styrene.

pol·y·sul·fide /,päli'səl,fīd/ ▶ **n.** Chem. a compound containing two or more sulfur atoms bonded together as an anion or group. ■ a synthetic rubber or other polymer in which the units are linked through such groups.

pol·y·syl·lab·ic /,pälisə'labik/ ▶ **adj.** (of a word) having more than one syllable. ■ using or characterized by words of many syllables. — **pol·y·syl·lab·i·cal·ly** /-sə'labək(ə)lē/ **adv.**

pol·y·syl·la·ble /'päli,siləbəl; ,päli'siləbəl/ ▶ **n.** a polysyllabic word.

pol·y·symp·to·mat·ic /,päli,simptə'matik/ ▶ **adj.** (of a disease) involving or exhibiting many symptoms.

pol·y·syn·thet·ic /,pälisin'THetik/ ▶ **adj.** denoting or relating to a language characterized by complex words consisting of several morphemes, in which a single word may function as a whole sentence.

pol·y·tech·nic /,päli'teknik/ ▶ **n.** an institution of higher education offering courses in vocational or technical subjects. ▶ **adj.** dealing with or devoted to these subjects. [19th C.: from Fr. *polytechnique*, from Gk. *polutekhnos*, from *polu-* 'many' + *tekhnē* 'art.']

pol·y·tet·ra·fluor·o·eth·y·lene /,päli,tetrə,flo͝orō'eTHə,lēn/ ▶ **n.** a tough translucent synthetic resin made by polymerizing tetrafluoroethylene, chiefly used to make seals and bearings and to coat nonstick cooking utensils.

pol·y·the·ism /'päliTHē,izəm/ ▶ **n.** the belief in or worship of more than one god. — **pol·y·the·ist** /-,THēist/ **n.** **pol·y·the·is·tic** /,päliTHē'istik/ **adj.**

pol·y·thene /'päləTHēn/ ▶ **n.** esp. Brit. another term for **POLYETHYLENE.** [1930s: contr. of **POLYETHYLENE.**]

pol·y·to·nal·i·ty /,päli,tō'nalətē/ ▶ **n.** the simultaneous use of two or more keys in a musical composition. — **pol·y·ton·al** /,päli'tōnl/ **adj.**

pol·y·type /'päli,tīp/ ▶ **n.** Crystallog. any of a number of forms of a crystalline substance that differ in only one of the dimensions of the unit cell. — **pol·y·typ·ic** /,päli'tipik/ **adj.** **pol·y·typ·ism** /,päli'tī,pizəm/ **n.**

pol·y·un·sat·u·rat·ed /,pälēən'saCHə,rātid/ ▶ **adj.** Chem. (of an organic compound, esp. a fat or oil molecule) containing several double or triple bonds between carbon atoms.

pol·y·un·sat·u·rates /,pälēən'saCHərits/ ▶ **plural n.** polyunsaturated fats or fatty acids.

pol·y·u·re·thane /,päli'yo͝orə,THān/ ▶ **n.** a synthetic resin in which the polymer units are linked by urethane groups, used chiefly in paints and varnishes. ▶ **v.** [trans.] [usu. as adj.] (**polyurethaned**) coat or protect with paint or varnish of this kind.

pol·y·u·ri·a /,päli'yo͝orēə/ ▶ **n.** Med. production of too much dilute urine. Compare with **DIURESIS.** — **pol·y·u·ric** /-'yo͝orik/ **adj.**

pol·y·va·lent /,päli'vālənt/ ▶ **adj.** Chem. having a valence of three or more. ■ Med. having the property of counteracting several related poisons or affording immunity against different strains of a microorganism. ■ Med. another term for **MULTIVALENT.** ■ fig. having many different functions, forms, or facets. — **pol·y·va·lence n.**

pol·y·vi·nyl /,päli'vīnl/ ▶ **adj.** [attrib.] denoting materials or objects made from polymers of vinyl compounds.

pol·y·vi·nyl ac·e·tate (abbr.: **PVA**) ▶ **n.** a synthetic resin made by polymerizing vinyl acetate.

pol·y·vi·nyl chlo·ride (abbr.: **PVC**) ▶ **n.** a tough, chemically resistant synthetic resin made by polymerizing vinyl chloride.

pol·y·vi·nyl·pyr·rol·i·done /,päli,vīnl-pi'rälə,dōn/ ▶ **n.** Chem. a water-soluble polymer of vinyl pyrrolidone, used as a synthetic blood plasma substitute and in the cosmetic, drug, and food-processing industries.

Pol·y·zo·a /,päli'zōə/ Zool. British term for **BRYOZOA.** — **pol·y·zo·an n. & adj.** [mod. L. (pl.), from **POLY-** 'many' + *zōion* 'animal.']

Pom /päm/ ▶ **n.** **1** short for **POMERANIAN.** **2** short for **POMMY.**

pom·ace /'pəməs; 'päm-/ ▶ **n.** (esp. in cider making) the pulpy residue remaining after fruit has been crushed in order to extract its juice. ■ the pulpy matter remaining after some other substance has been pressed or crushed. [16th C.: appar. from med. L. *pomacium* 'cider,' from L. *pomum* 'apple.']

po·made /pä'mād; -'mäd; pō-/ dated ▶ **n.** a scented ointment applied to the hair or scalp. ▶ **v.** [trans.] [often as adj.] (**pomaded**) apply pomade to. [16th C.: from Fr. *pommade*, based on L. *pomum* 'apple' (from which it was orig. made).]

po·man·der /'pō'mandər; 'pō,mandər/ ▶ **n.** a ball or perforated container of sweet-smelling substances used to perfume the air or (formerly) carried as a supposed protection against infection. ■ a piece of fruit, typically an orange or apple, studded with cloves and hung in a closet by a ribbon for a similar purpose. [15th C.: from OFr. *pome d'embre*, from med. L. *pomum de ambra* 'apple of ambergris.']

pom·be /'päm,bā/ ▶ **n.** (in central and eastern Africa) a fermented drink made from various kinds of grain and fruit. [Kiswahili.]

pome /pōm/ ▶ **n.** Bot. a fruit such as an apple or pear, with a central core containing the seeds. [ME: from OFr., based on L. *poma*, pl. of *pomum* 'apple.']

pome·gran·ate /'päm(ə),granit; 'pəm-/ ▶ **n.** **1** an orange-sized fruit with a tough reddish outer skin and sweet red gelatinous flesh containing many seeds. **2** the widely cultivated tree (*Punica granatum*, family Punicaceae) that bears this fruit, which is native to North Africa and western Asia. [ME: from OFr. *pome grenate*, from *pome* 'apple' + *grenate* 'pomegranate.']

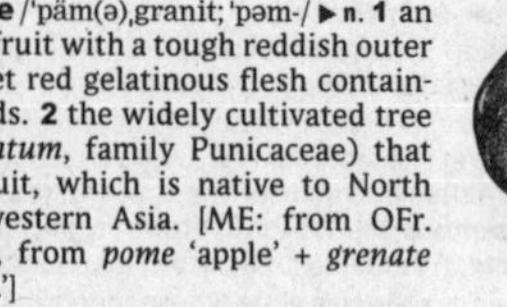

pomegranate 1

pom·e·lo /'pämə,lō; 'pəm-/ (also **pum·me·lo**) ▶ **n.** (pl. **-los**) **1** the largest of the citrus fruits, with a thick yellow skin and bitter pulp that resembles grapefruit in flavor. **2** the tree (*Citrus maxima*) that bears this fruit.

Pom·er·a·ni·a /,pämə'rānēə/ a region of north central Europe that extends along the southern shore of the Baltic Sea in northeastern Germany and Poland.

Pomeranian

Pom·er·a·ni·an /,pämə'rānēən/ ▶ **n.** a small dog of a breed with long silky hair, a pointed muzzle, and pricked ears.

Pom·e·rol /'pämə,rôl; -,rōl/ ▶ **n.** a red Bordeaux wine produced in Pomerol, a region in the Gironde, France.

pom·fret /'pämfrət; 'pəm-/ ▶ **n.** a deep-bodied fish (family Bramidae) of open seas that typically has scales on the dorsal and anal fins. [18th C.: appar. from Port. *pampo.*]

pom·mel /'pəməl; 'päməl/ ▶ **n.** **1** a rounded knob on the end of a sword, dagger, or gun handle. **2** the upward curving or projecting part of a saddle in front of the rider. ▶ **v.** /'pəməl; 'päməl/ (**-meled, -mel·ing**; Brit. **-melled, -mel·ling**) another term for **PUMMEL.** [ME: from OFr. *pomel*, from a dimin. of L. *pomum* 'fruit, apple.']

pom·mel horse ▶ **n.** a vaulting horse fitted with a pair of curved handgrips, used for a gymnastic exercise. ■ [in sing.] exercises performed on this.

pommes frites /,pəm 'frēt/ ▶ **plural n.** (esp. in recipes or on menus) French fries. [Fr., from *pommes de terre frites*, lit. 'fried potatoes.']

Pom·my /'pämē/ (also **Pom·mie**) ▶ **n.** (pl. **-mies**) Austral./NZ, informal derog. a British person. [20th C.: of unknown origin.]

Po·mo /'pōmō/ ▶ **n.** (pl. same or **-mos**) **1** a member of an American Indian people of northern California. **2** any of the languages of this people. ▶ **adj.** of or relating to this people or their languages. [from Pomo *phōmō phó'ma'* 'dweller at the red earth hole.']

po-mo informal ▶ **abbr.** postmodern.

po·mol·o·gy /pō'mäləjē/ ▶ **n.** the science of growing fruit. — **po·mo·log·i·cal** /,pōmə'läjikəl/ **adj.** **po·mol·o·gist** /-jist/ **n.** [19th C.: from L. *pomum* 'fruit' + **-LOGY.**]

Po·mo·na /pə'mōnə/ a city in southwestern California; pop. 131,723.

pomp /pämp/ ▶ **n.** ceremony and splendid display. [ME: from OFr. *pompe*, via L. from Gk. *pompē* 'procession, pomp,' from *pempein* 'send.']

Pom·pa·dour /'pämpə,dôr; -,do͝or; pôNpä'do͝or/, Jeanne Antoinette Poisson, Marquise de (1721–64), French noblewoman; known as **Madame de Pompadour.** In 1744, she became the mistress of Louis XV.

pom·pa·dour /'pämpə,dôr/ ▶ **n.** a man's hairstyle in which the hair is combed up from the forehead. ■ a woman's hairstyle in which the hair is turned back off the forehead in a roll. ▶ **v.** [trans.] [usu. as adj.] (**pompadoured**) arrange (hair) in a pompadour. [19th C.: named after Madame de **POMPADOUR.**]

pom·pa·no /'pämpə,nō/ ▶ **n.** (pl. **-nos**) an edible butterfish (*Peprillus simillimus*) that lives in shoals along the east coast of North America.

Pom·pe·ii /päm'pā(ē)/ an ancient city in western Italy, southeast of Naples. It was buried by an eruption of Mount Vesuvius in AD 79.

Pom·pey /'pämpē/ (106–48 BC), Roman general; Latin name *Gnaeus Pompeius Magnus*; known as **Pompey the Great.** He founded the First Triumvirate.

Pom·pi·dou /'pämpi,do͞o; pôNpē'do͞o/, Georges Jean Raymond (1911–74), president of France 1969–74.

pom-pom[1] /'päm ,päm/ (also **pom·pom** or **pom·pon**) ▶ **n.** a small woolen ball attached to a garment as a decoration. ■ a cluster of brightly colored strands of yarn or plastic, waved in pairs by cheerleaders. ■ a dahlia, chrysanthemum, or aster with tightly clustered petals. [18th C.: Fr. *pompon*.]

pom·pom[2] (also **pom·pom**) ▶ n. an automatic quick-firing two-pounder cannon. [19th C.: imitative.]

pomp·ous /ˈpämpəs/ ▶ adj. affectedly and irritatingly grand, solemn, or self-important: *a pompous ass.* ■ archaic characterized by pomp or splendor: *there were many processions and other pompous shows.* — **pom·pos·i·ty** /pämˈpäsətē/ n. **pomp·ous·ly** adv. **pomp·ous·ness** n. [ME: from OFr. *pompeux* 'full of grandeur,' from late L. *pomposus*, from *pompa* 'pomp.']

Pon·ca /ˈpäNGkə; ˈpôNGkə/ ▶ n. (pl. same or **-cas**) **1** a member of a Siouan people. **2** the Siouan language of this people. ▶ adj. of or relating to this people or their language. [via Fr., from the Ponca name *pa-ka*.]

Pon·ce /ˈpônsā/ a city in southern Puerto Rico; pop. 159,151.

Ponce de Le·ón /ˈpäns də ˈlēän; ˌpônsā de lāˈôn/, Juan (*c.*1460–1521), Spanish explorer. He a landed on the coast of Florida near what became St. Augustine in 1513, claiming the area for Spain.

pon·cho /ˈpäncHō/ ▶ n. (pl. **-chos**) a garment of a type originally worn in South America, made of a thick piece of woolen cloth with a slit in the middle for the head. ■ a garment in this style, esp. a waterproof one worn as a raincoat. [18th C.: from South Amer. Sp., from Araucanian.]

pond /pänd/ ▶ n. a fairly small body of still water. ■ (**the pond**) informal the Atlantic Ocean. ▶ v. [trans.] hold back or dam up (flowing water or another liquid) to form a small lake. ■ [intrans.] (of flowing liquids) form such a lake. [ME: alt. of **POUND**[3].]

pon·der /ˈpändər/ ▶ v. [trans.] think about (something) carefully, esp. before deciding or concluding. — **pon·der·a·tion** /ˌpändəˈrāsHən/ n. (rare). [ME: from OFr. *ponderer* 'consider,' from L. *ponderare* 'weigh, reflect on,' from *pondus, ponder-* 'weight.']

pon·der·a·ble /ˈpändərəbəl/ ▶ adj. literary having appreciable weight or significance. — **pon·der·a·bil·i·ty** /ˌpändərəˈbilətē/ n.

pon·der·o·sa /ˌpändəˈrōsə/ (also **ponderosa pine**) ▶ n. a tall slender pine tree (*Pinus ponderosa*), the most widespread conifer of western North America. [19th C.: fem. of L. *ponderosus* 'massive, ponderous.']

pon·der·ous /ˈpändərəs/ ▶ adj. slow and clumsy because of great weight: *her footsteps were ponderous.* ■ dull, laborious, or excessively solemn. — **pon·der·os·i·ty** /ˌpändəˈräsətē/ n. **pon·der·ous·ly** adv. **pon·der·ous·ness** n.

Pon·di·cher·ry /ˌpändiˈcHerē; -ˈsHerē/ a Union Territory of southeastern India, on the Coromandel Coast. ■ its capital city; pop. 203,000.

pond·weed /ˈpändˌwēd/ ▶ n. a submerged aquatic plant (genus *Potamogeton*, family Potamogetonaceae) that grows in still or running water and sometimes has floating leaves.

pone /pōn/ ▶ n. (also **corn pone** or **pone bread**) unleavened cornbread in the form of flat oval cakes. [Algonquian, 'bread.']

pon·gee /pänˈjē; ˈpänjē/ ▶ n. a soft and typically unbleached type of Chinese plain-woven fabric, originally made from raw silk. [18th C.: from Chin. (Mandarin dial.) *běnjī*, literally 'own loom' or *běnzhì*, lit. 'home-woven.']

pon·gid /ˈpänjəd; -gəd/ ▶ n. Zool. a primate of a family (Pongidae) that comprises the great apes. See also **HOMINID**. [1950s: from mod. L. *Pongidae* (pl.), from *Pongo*, from Congolese *mpongo*.]

pon·iard /ˈpänyərd/ ▶ n. hist. a small, slim dagger. [16th C.: from Fr. *poignard*, based on L. *pugnus* 'fist.']

Pons /pänz/, Lily (1904–76), US opera singer; born in France; born *Alice-Josephine Pons*. A coloratura soprano, she made her debut at the Metropolitan Opera in 1931.

pons /pänz/ (in full **pons Va·ro·li·i** /vəˈrōlēˌī/) ▶ n. (pl. **pon·tes** /ˈpänˌtēz/) Anat. the part of the brainstem that links the medulla oblongata and the thalamus. [17th C.: from L., lit. 'bridge,' (in full) 'bridge of Varolius,' named after C. Varoli (1543–75), Ital. anatomist.]

Pont·char·train, Lake /ˈpäncHərˌtrān/ a shallow lake in southeastern Louisiana.

pon·tes /ˈpänˌtēz/ plural form of **PONS**.

Pon·ti·ac /ˈpäntēˌak/ (c.1720–69), Ottawa Indian chief. He led a yearlong siege of Fort Detroit 1763–64.

Pon·ti·a·nak /ˌpäntēˈänək/ a city in Indonesia, on the western coast of Borneo; pop. 305,000.

Pon·tic /ˈpäntik/ ▶ adj. of or relating to ancient Pontus.

pon·ti·fex /ˈpäntəˌfeks/ ▶ n. (pl. **pon·tif·i·ces** /pänˈtifəˌsēz/) (in ancient Rome) a member of the principal college of priests. [L., from *pons, pont-* 'bridge' + *-fex* from *facere* 'make.']

Pon·ti·fex Max·i·mus /ˈmaksəməs/ ▶ n. (in ancient Rome) the head of the principal college of priests. ■ (in the Roman Catholic Church) a title of the pope. [*Maximus*, superlative of L. *magnus* 'great.']

pon·tiff /ˈpäntəf/ (also **sovereign** or **supreme pontiff**) ▶ n. the pope. [17th C.: from Fr. *pontife*, from L. *pontifex* (see **PONTIFEX**).]

pon·tif·i·cal /pänˈtifikəl/ ▶ adj. **1** (in the Roman Catholic Church) of or relating to the pope. **2** characterized by a superior air of infallibility. ▶ n. rare (in the Roman Catholic Church) an office book of the Western Church containing rites to be performed by the pope or bishops. ■ (**pontificals**) the vestments and insignia of a bishop, cardinal, or abbot: *a bishop in full pontificals.* — **pon·tif·i·cal·ly** /-ik(ə)lē/ adv. [ME: from L. *pontificalis*, from *pontifex*.]

pon·tif·i·cate ▶ v. /pänˈtifiˌkāt/ [intrans.] **1** (in the Roman Catholic Church) officiate as bishop, esp. at Mass. **2** express one's opinions in a way considered annoyingly pompous and dogmatic. ▶ n. /-kət/ (also **Pontificate**) (in the Roman Catholic Church) the office of pope or bishop. ■ the period of such an office. — **pon·tif·i·ca·tor** /-ˌkātər/ n.

pon·tif·i·ces /pänˈtifəˌsēz/ plural form of **PONTIFEX**.

pon·til /ˈpäntl/ ▶ n. another term for **PUNTY**. [19th C.: from Fr., appar. from Ital. *pontello* 'small point,' dimin. of *punto*.]

Pon·tine Marsh·es /ˈpänˌtēn; -ˌtīn/ an area of marshland in western Italy, south of Rome. Italian name **AGRO PONTINO**.

pontoon[1]

pon·toon /ˌpänˈtōōn/ ▶ n. a flat-bottomed boat or hollow metal cylinder used with others to support a temporary bridge or floating landing stage. ■ a bridge or landing stage supported by pontoons. ■ a large flat-bottomed barge or lighter equipped with cranes. ■ either of two floats fitted to an aircraft to enable it to land on water. [17th C.: from Fr. *ponton*, from L. *ponto, ponton-*, from *pons, pont-* 'bridge.']

Pon·tus /ˈpäntəs/ an ancient region in northern Asia Minor, on the Black Sea coast north of Cappadocia.

po·ny /ˈpōnē/ ▶ n. (pl. **-nies**) **1** a horse of a small breed. ■ (**the ponies**) informal racehorses: ***playing the ponies.*** **2** informal a small drinking glass or the drink in it. **3** a literal translation of a foreign-language text, used illicitly by students; a trot. **4** Brit., informal twenty-five pounds sterling. ▶ v. (**-nies, -nied**) [intrans.] (**pony up**) informal pay (money). [17th C.: prob. from Fr. *poulenet* 'small foal,' dimin. of *poulain*, from late L. *pullanus*, from L. *pullus* 'young animal.']

Po·ny Ex·press a system of mail delivery operating from 1860–61 between St. Joseph, Missouri, and Sacramento, California, using horse riders.

po·ny·tail /ˈpōnēˌtāl/ ▶ n. a hairstyle in which the hair is drawn back and tied at the back of the head. — **po·ny·tailed** adj.

poo ▶ exclam., n., & v. var. of **POOH**.

pooch[1] /pōōcH/ ▶ n. informal a dog. [1920s: of unknown origin.]

pooch[2] ▶ v. informal protrude or cause to protrude. [17th C.: from the n. **POUCH**.]

poo·dle /ˈpōōdl/ ▶ n. a dog of a breed with a curly coat that is usually clipped. The numerous varieties of poodle include standard, miniature, and toy. [19th C.: from Ger. *Pudel(hund)*, from Low Ger. *pud(d)eln* 'splash in water.']

poo·dle skirt ▶ n. a long full skirt in a solid color with a chenille poodle on it, popular in the 1950s.

poof[1] /pōōf; po͝of/ (also **pouf**) ▶ exclam. used to convey the suddenness with which someone or something disappears. [19th C.: symbolic.]

poof[2] (also **pouf** or **poove**) ▶ n. Brit., informal derog. an effeminate or homosexual man. — **poof·y** adj. [19th C.: perh. an alt. of the archaic n. *puff* in the sense 'braggart.']

pooh /pōō; po͝o/ (also **poo**) informal ▶ exclam. used to express disgust at an unpleasant smell. ■ used to express impatience or contempt. ▶ n. excrement. ■ [in sing.] an act of defecating. ▶ v. [intrans.] defecate. [natural exclamation: first recorded in Engl. in the late 16th C.]

pooh-bah /ˈpōō ˌbä/ (also **Pooh-Bah**) ▶ n. a person having much influence or holding many offices at the same time. [after a character in W. S. Gilbert's *The Mikado* (1885).]

pooh-pooh /ˈpōō ˌpōō; ˌpōō ˈpōō/ ▶ v. [trans.] informal dismiss (an idea or suggestion) as being foolish. [18th C.: reduplication of **POOH**.]

poo·ka /ˈpōōkə/ ▶ n. (in Irish mythology) a hobgoblin. [from Irish *púca*.]

pool[1] /pōōl/ ▶ n. a small area of still water. ■ a small, shallow patch of liquid lying on a surface. ■ a swimming pool. ■ a deep place in a river. ▶ v. [intrans.] (of water or another liquid) form a pool on the ground or another surface: *the oil pooled.* ■ (of blood) accumulate in parts of the venous system. [OE *pōl*, of West Gmc. origin; rel. to Ger. *Pfuhl*.]

pool[2] ▶ n. **1** a supply of vehicles or goods available for use when needed: *the oldest vehicle in the motor pool.* ■ a group of people available for work when required. ■ a group of people considered as a resource. ■ an arrangement, illegal in many countries, between competing parties to fix prices or rates and share business in order to eliminate competition. ■ a common fund into which all contributors pay and from which financial backing is provided. ■ a source of common funding for speculative operations on financial markets. ■ the collective amount of players' stakes in gambling or sweepstakes; a kitty. **2** Billiards a game played on a table using fifteen colored and numbered balls and a white cue ball. ■ another term for **POCKET BILLIARDS**. ■ short for **STRAIGHT POOL**. ▶ v. [trans.] (of two or more people or organizations) put (money or other assets) into a common fund. ■ share (things) for the benefit of all those involved: [as n.] (**pooling**) *a pooling of ideas.* — **pool·er** n. [17th C.: from Fr. *poule* in the sense 'stake, kitty,' associated with POOL[1].]

Poole[1] /pōōl/ a city on the southern coast of England; pop. 131,000.

Poole[2], Elijah, see MUHAMMAD[2].

pool·room /'pōōl,rōōm; -,rŏŏm/ ▶ n. (also **pool hall**) a commercial establishment where pool is played.

pool·side /'pōōl,sīd/ ▶ n. the area adjoining a swimming pool: [as adj.] *the poolside bar.* ▶ adv. toward or beside a swimming pool.

poon /pōōn/ ▶ n. **1** any large Indo-Malayan evergreen tree of the genus *Calophyllum.* **2** short for POONTANG.

Poo·na /'pōōnə/ (also **Pu·ne**) a city in western India, southeast of Bombay; pop. 1,560,000

poon·tang /'pōōn,taNG/ (also **poon**) ▶ n. vulgar slang sexual activity. ■ a woman or women regarded solely in terms of potential sexual gratification. [1920s: perh. from Limba (a West Afr. language of Sierra Leone) *puntu* 'vagina.']

poop[1] /pōōp/ ▶ n. (also **poop deck**) the aftermost and highest deck of a ship. ▶ v. [trans.] (usu. **be pooped**) (of a wave) break over the stern of (a ship), sometimes causing it to capsize. [ME: from OFr. *pupe*, from a var. of L. *puppis* 'stern.']

poop[2] ▶ v. [trans.] (usu. **be pooped**) informal exhaust.
– PHRASAL VERBS **poop out** stop functioning. [1930s: of unknown origin.]

poop[3] informal ▶ n. excrement. ▶ v. [intrans.] defecate. [18th C.: imitative.]

poop[4] ▶ n. informal up-to-date or inside information. [1940s: of unknown origin.]

poop[5] ▶ n. informal a stupid or ineffectual person. — **poop·y** adj. [20th C.: perh. a shortening of NINCOMPOOP.]

poop·er-scoop·er /'pōōpər ,skōōpər/ (also **poop·er scoop·er**) ▶ n. a tool for picking up dog excrement.

poor /pŏŏr; pôr/ ▶ adj. **1** lacking enough money to live comfortably in a society. ■ (of a place) inhabited by people without sufficient money: *a poor area.* **2** worse than is usual, expected, or desirable; of a low or inferior standard or quality: *her work was poor.* ■ [predic.] (**poor in**) deficient or lacking in. **3** [attrib.] (of a person) considered to be deserving of pity or sympathy: *they inquired after poor Dorothy.*
– PHRASES **(as) poor as a church mouse** (or **as church mice**) extremely poor. **the poor man's ——** an inferior or cheaper substitute for the thing specified. **poor relation** a person or thing that is considered inferior or subordinate to others of the same type or group. **take a poor view of** regard with disfavor or disapproval. [ME: from OFr. *poure*, from L. *pauper.*]

poor box ▶ n. hist. a collection box, esp. one in a church, for gifts to relieve the poor.

poor boy (also **poor-boy**) ▶ n. another term for SUBMARINE SANDWICH.

poor·house /'pŏŏr,hous; 'pôr-/ ▶ n. hist. an institution where paupers were supported.

Poor Law ▶ n. Brit., hist. a law relating to the support of the poor.

poor·ly /'pŏŏrlē; 'pôr-/ ▶ adv. in a way or at a level that is considered inadequate: *schools were performing poorly.* ■ with insufficient money or resources. ▶ adj. unwell: *she looked poorly.*

poor-mouth ▶ v. informal **1** [trans.] talk disparagingly about. **2** [intrans.] claim to be poor.

poor-spir·it·ed ▶ adj. archaic timid; cowardly.

poor white ▶ n. derog. a member of a group of white people regarded as socially inferior.

poor-will /'pŏŏr,wil/ (also **poor·will**) ▶ n. a small nightjar, found mainly in central and western North America, esp. the **common poor-will** (*Phalaenoptilus nuttallii*), which hibernates in cold weather. [19th C.: imitative of its call.]

poove /pōōv; pŏŏv/ ▶ n. var. of POOF[2].

pop[1] /päp/ ▶ v. (**popped, pop·ping**) **1** [intrans.] make a sudden, sharp, explosive sound. ■ [trans.] cause (something) to burst, making such a sound: *they were popping balloons with darts.* ■ (of a person's ears) make a small popping sound within the head as pressure is equalized, typically because of a change of altitude. ■ [trans.] heat (popcorn or another foodstuff) until it bursts open. ■ [intrans.] (of popcorn or another foodstuff) burst open in such a way. ■ (of a person's eyes) bulge or appear to bulge when opened wide. ■ [trans.] shoot (a gun). ■ [trans.] shoot (something) with a gun. **2** [intrans.] go somewhere, typically for a short time and often without notice. ■ [trans.] put or move (something) somewhere quickly. **3** [intrans.] Baseball (of a batter) hit a pop fly. ■ [trans.] (of a pitcher) cause (a batter) to pop up. **4** [trans.] informal take or inject (a drug). ▶ n. **1** a sudden sharp explosive sound. **2** informal short for SODA POP. **3** (also **pop fly** or **pop-up**) Baseball a ball hit high in the air but not deep, providing an easy catch. **4** an attempt: *he grabs about two hundred berries at a pop.* ▶ adv. with a sudden explosive sound. ▶ adj. sudden or unexpected: *a pop quiz.*
– PHRASES **—— a pop** informal costing a specified amount per item: *$50 a pop.* **have** (or **take**) **a pop at** informal esp. Brit. attack physically or verbally. **make someone's eyes pop (out)** informal cause great astonishment to someone. **pop for something** pay for something, esp. a treat for someone else. **pop the question** informal propose marriage.
– PHRASAL VERBS **pop off** informal **1** die. **2** speak spontaneously and at length, typically angrily. **pop out** make an out in a baseball game by hitting a pop fly that is caught. **pop up 1** appear or occur suddenly and unexpectedly. **2** hit a baseball high into the air but not deep, providing an easy catch. [ME: imitative.]

pop[2] ▶ adj. [attrib.] **1** of or relating to commercial popular music: *a pop star* | *a pop group.* ■ of, denoting, or relating to pop art. **2** often derog. made accessible to the general public; popularized: *pop psychology.* ▶ n. (also **pop music**) commercial popular music. ■ dated a pop record or song. [19th C.: abbrev. of POPULAR.]

pop[3] (also **pops**) ▶ n. informal term for FATHER. [19th C.: abbrev. of *poppa*, from PAPA.]

pop. ▶ abbr. population.

pop art ▶ n. art based on modern popular culture and the mass media.

pop·corn /'päp,kôrn/ ▶ n. corn of a variety with hard kernels that swell up and burst open when heated. ■ these kernels when popped.

pop cul·ture ▶ n. commercial culture based on popular taste.

Pope[1] /pōp/, Alexander (1688–1744), English poet. His verse includes *The Rape of the Lock* (1712).

Pope[2], John Russell (1874–1937), US architect. He designed the Jefferson Memorial 1937–43 in Washington, DC.

pope /pōp/ ▶ n. (usu. **the pope** or **the Pope**) the head of the Roman Catholic Church. ■ the head of the Coptic Church, the bishop or patriarch of Alexandria. — **pope·dom** /-dəm/ n. [OE, via ecclesiastical L. from eccles. Greek *papas* 'bishop, patriarch,' var. of Gk. *pappas* 'father.']

pope·mo·bile /'pōpmə,bēl; -mō,bēl/ ▶ n. informal a bulletproof vehicle, used by the pope on official visits.

pop·er·y /'pōpərē/ ▶ n. derog., esp. archaic the doctrines, practices, and ceremonies of Roman Catholicism.

pop-eyed ▶ adj. informal (of a person) having bulging eyes.

pop fly ▶ n. Baseball see POP[1] (sense 3).

pop·gun /'päp,gən/ ▶ n. a child's toy gun that shoots a pellet or cork. ■ a small, inefficient, or antiquated gun.

pop·in·jay /'päpən,jā/ ▶ n. **1** dated a vain or conceited person, esp. one who dresses or behaves extravagantly. **2** archaic a parrot. [ME: from OFr. *papingay*, via Sp. from Arab. *babbaġā.*]

pop·ish /'pōpisH/ ▶ adj. derog. Roman Catholic. — **pop·ish·ly** adv.

Pop·ish Plot a fictitious Jesuit plot concocted by Titus Oates in 1678, to put the Catholic Duke of York on the English throne.

pop·lar /'päplər/ ▶ n. **1** a tall, fast-growing tree (genus *Populus*) of the willow family, widely grown in shelter belts and for timber and pulp. **2** (**yellow poplar**) another term for TULIP TREE. [ME: from OFr. *poplier*, from L. *populus* 'poplar.']

pop·lin /'päplən/ ▶ n. a plain-woven fabric, typically a lightweight cotton, with a corded surface. [18th C.: from obs. Fr. *papeline*, perh. from Ital. *papalina* (fem.) 'papal.']

pop·lit·e·al /päp'litēəl; ,päplə'tēəl/ ▶ adj. Anat. relating to or situated in the hollow at the back of the knee. [18th C.: from mod. L. *popliteus* (from L. *poples, poplit-* 'hollow of the knee') + -AL.]

pop mu·sic ▶ n. fuller form of POP[2].

Po·po·ca·té·petl /,pōpə'katə,petl; pō,pōkä'tā,petl/ an active volcano in southeastern Mexico.

pop-out ▶ n. Baseball an act of being put out by a caught fly ball. ▶ adj. denoting something designed or made so that it is easily removable for use: *a pop-out panel.*

pop·o·ver /'päp,ōvər/ ▶ n. a light muffin, which rises to form a hollow shell when baked.

Pop·per /'päpər/, Sir Karl Raimund (1902–94), British philosopher; born in Austria. He wrote *The Logic of Scientific Discovery* (1934).

pop·per /'päpər/ ▶ n. a thing that makes a popping sound, in particular: ■ a utensil for popping corn. ■ informal a small vial of amyl nitrite used for inhalation that makes a popping sound when opened.

pop·pet /'päpət/ ▶ n. **1** (also **poppet valve**) Engin. a mushroom-shaped valve with a flat end piece that is lifted in and out of an opening by an axial rod. **2** esp. hist. a small figure of a human being used in sorcery and witchcraft. **3** Brit., informal an endearingly sweet or pretty child or young girl. [ME: based on L. *pup(p)a* 'girl, doll.']

pop·ple /'päpəl/ archaic ▶ v. [intrans.] (of water) flow in a tumbling or rippling way. ▶ n. [in sing.] a rolling or rippling of water. — **pop·ply** /'päplē/ adj. [ME: prob. from MDu. *popelen* 'to murmur,' of imitative origin.]

pop·py /'päpē/ ▶ n. a herbaceous plant (*Papaver, Eschscholzia*, and other genera) with showy flowers, milky sap, and rounded seed capsules. Many poppies contain alkaloids and are a source of drugs such as morphine and codeine. The **poppy family** (Papaveraceae) also includes the corydalis, greater celandine, and bloodroot. [OE *popig, papæg*, from a med. L. alt. of L. *papaver.*]

pop·py·cock /'päpē,käk/ ▶ n. informal nonsense. [19th C.: from Du. dial. *pappekak*, from *pap* 'soft' + *kak* 'dung.']

pop·py·head /'päpē,hed/ ▶ n. an ornamental top on the end of a church pew.

pop quiz ▶ n. a short test given to students without prior warning. ■ any unexpected question or set of questions.

Pop·si·cle /'päp,sikəl/ ▶ n. trademark a piece of flavored ice or ice cream on a stick. [1920s: fanciful formation.]

pop-top ▶ adj. (of a can) having a ring or tab that is pulled to open its seal: *a pop-top beer can.* ▶ n. **1** the ring or tab from a pop-top can. ■ a pop-top can. **2** the top of something that pops up or open.

pop·u·lace /'päpyələs/ ▶ n. [treated as sing. or pl.] the people living in a particular country or area. [16th C.: from Fr., from Ital. *popolaccio* 'common people.']

pop·u·lar /'päpyələr/ ▶ adj. **1** liked, admired, or enjoyed by many people or by a particular person or group. **2** [attrib.] (of cultural activities or products) intended for or suited to the taste, understanding, or means of the general public rather than specialists or intellectuals. ■ (of a belief or attitude) held by the majority of the general public. 3 [attrib.] (of political activity) of or carried on by the people as a whole rather than restricted to politicians or political parties. — **pop·u·lar·ism** /-ˌrizəm/ n. [ME: from L. *popularis*, from *populus* 'people.']

pop·u·lar et·y·mol·o·gy ▶ n. another term for FOLK ETYMOLOGY.

pop·u·lar front ▶ n. a party or coalition representing left-wing elements such as in France and Spain in the 1930s.

pop·u·lar·i·ty /ˌpäpyəˈlaritē/ ▶ n. the state or condition of being liked, admired, or supported by many people.

pop·u·lar·ize /ˈpäpyələˌrīz/ ▶ v. [trans.] cause (something) to become generally liked. ■ make (something technical, scientific, or academic) accessible or interesting to the general public by presenting it in a readily understandable form. — **pop·u·lar·i·za·tion** /ˌpäpyələrəˈzāsHən/ n. **pop·u·lar·iz·er** n.

pop·u·lar·ly /ˈpäpyələrlē/ ▶ adv. by many or most people; generally. ■ (of a term, name, or title) in informal, common, or nonspecialist use. ■ (of a politician or government) chosen by the majority of the voters; democratically: *a popularly elected governor.*

pop·u·lar mu·sic ▶ n. music appealing to the popular taste.

pop·u·late /ˈpäpyəˌlāt/ ▶ v. [trans.] (usu. **be populated**) form the population of (a town, area, or country). ■ fig. fill or be present in (a place, environment, or domain): *the characters who populate its pages.* ■ cause people to settle in (an area or place). [16th C.: from med. L. *populat-* 'supplied with people,' from the v. *populare*, from *populus* 'people.']

pop·u·la·tion /ˌpäpyəˈlāsHən/ ▶ n. all the inhabitants of a particular town, area, or country. ■ [with adj.] a particular section, group, or type of people or animals living in an area or country. ■ [with adj.] the specified extent or degree to which an area is or has been populated. ■ the action of populating an area. ■ Biol. a community of animals, plants, or humans among whose members interbreeding occurs. ■ Stat. a finite or infinite collection of items under consideration.

pop·u·la·tion ex·plo·sion ▶ n. a sudden large increase in the size of a population.

pop·u·la·tion in·ver·sion ▶ n. see INVERSION (sense 1).

pop·u·list /ˈpäpyələst/ ▶ n. a member or adherent of a political party that represents the interests of ordinary people. ■ a person who holds, or who is concerned with, the views of ordinary people. ■ (**Populist**) a member of the Populist Party, a formed in 1891. ▶ adj. of or relating to a populist or populists. — **pop·u·lism** /-ˌlizəm/ n. **pop·u·lis·tic** /ˌpäpyəˈlistik/ adj.

pop·u·lous /ˈpäpyələs/ ▶ adj. having a large population; densely populated. — **pop·u·lous·ly** adv. **pop·u·lous·ness** n.

pop-up ▶ adj. [attrib.] (of a book or greeting card) containing folded cutout pictures that rise up to form a three-dimensional scene or figure. ■ (of an electric toaster) operating so as to push up a piece of toast quickly when it is ready. ■ Computing (of a menu or other utility) able to be superimposed on the current window and suppressed rapidly. ▶ n. 1 a pop-up picture in a book. ■ a book containing such pictures. 2 Baseball see POP[1] (sense 3). 3 Computing a pop-up menu or other utility. ■ an unrequested browser window, esp. one generated for the purpose of advertising.

por·bea·gle /ˈpôrˌbēgəl/ ▶ n. a large active shark (*Lamna nasus*, family Lamnidae) that is found chiefly in the open seas of the North Atlantic and in the Mediterranean. [18th C.: from Cornish dial., perh. from Cornish *porth* 'harbor, cove' + *bugel* 'shepherd.']

por·ce·lain /ˈpôrs(ə)lən/ ▶ n. a white vitrified translucent ceramic; china. See also HARD-PASTE, SOFT-PASTE. ■ (usu. **porcelains**) articles made of this. ■ such articles collectively: *a collection of Chinese porcelain.* — **por·ce·la·ne·ous** /ˌpôrsəˈlānēəs/ adj. **por·cel·la·nous** /-əs/ adj. [16th C.: from Fr. *porcelaine*, from Ital. *porcellana* 'cowrie shell,' hence 'chinaware.']

por·ce·lain clay ▶ n. another term for KAOLIN.

porch /pôrcH/ ▶ n. a covered shelter projecting in front of the entrance of a building. ■ a veranda. — **porched** adj. **porch·less** adj. [ME: from OFr. *porche*, from L. *porticus* 'colonnade,' from *porta* 'passage.']

por·cine /ˈpôrˌsīn/ ▶ adj. of, affecting, or resembling a pig or pigs. [17th C.: from Fr. *porcin* or L. *porcinus*, from *porcus* 'pig.']

por·ci·ni /pôrˈcHēnē/ ▶ n. (pl. same) the cęp (a wild mushroom), esp. as an item on a menu. [Ital., lit. 'little pigs.']

por·cu·pine /ˈpôrkyəˌpīn/ ▶ n. a large rodent (Old World family Hystricidae and New World family Erethizontidae) with defensive spines or quills on the body and tail. The common North American species is *Erethizon dorsatum* [ME: from OFr. *porc espin*, from Provençal *porc espi(n)*, from L. *porcus* 'pig' + *spina* 'thorn.']

por·cu·pine fish ▶ n. a tropical marine fish (family Diodontidae) that has a parrotlike beak and is covered with sharp spines. It inflates itself like a balloon when threatened.

Por·cu·pine River /ˈpôrkyəˌpīn/ a river that flows from the Yukon Territory into northeastern Alaska to join the Yukon River.

pore[1] /pôr/ ▶ n. esp. Biol. a minute opening in a surface, esp. the skin, through which gases, liquids, or microscopic particles can pass. [ME: from OFr., via L. from Gk. *poros* 'passage, pore.']

pore[2] ▶ v. [intrans.] (**pore over/through**) be absorbed in the reading or study of: *hours poring over cookbooks.* [ME: perh. rel. to PEER[1].]

por·gy /ˈpôrgē/ ▶ n. (pl. same or **-gies**) a deep-bodied fish (*Calamus* and other genera) of the sea bream family, typically silvery but sometimes changing to a blotched pattern. [17th C.: alt. of Sp. and Port. *pargo*.]

Po·rif·er·a /pəˈrifərə/ Zool. n. a phylum of aquatic invertebrate animals that comprises the sponges. — **po·rif·er·an** adj. & n. [mod. L. (pl.), from L. *porus* 'pore' + *-fer* 'bearing.']

po·rin /ˈpôrən/ ▶ n. Biochem. any of a class of proteins whose molecules can form channels (for small ions and molecules) through cellular membranes. [1970s: from Gk. *poros* 'pore' + -IN[1].]

pork /pôrk/ ▶ n. 1 the flesh of a pig used as food. 2 short for PORK BARREL. [ME: from OFr. *porc*, from L. *porcus* 'pig.']

pork bar·rel ▶ n. informal the use of government funds for projects designed to win votes. — **pork-bar·rel·ing** n.

pork·er /ˈpôrkər/ ▶ n. a pig raised for food. ■ informal, derog. a fat person.

pork·pie hat /ˈpôrkˌpī/ ▶ n. a hat with a flat crown and a brim turned up all around.

pork·y[1] /ˈpôrkē/ ▶ adj. (**pork·i·er**, **pork·i·est**) 1 informal (of a person or part of their body) fleshy or fat. 2 of or resembling pork.

pork·y[2] ▶ n. (pl. **pork·ies**) informal a porcupine.

porn /pôrn/ (also **porn·o** /ˈpôrnō/) informal ▶ n. pornography. ▶ adj. pornographic.

por·nog·ra·phy /pôrˈnägrəfē/ ▶ n. printed or visual material containing the explicit description or display of sexual organs or activity. — **por·nog·ra·pher** /-fər/ n. **por·no·graph·ic** /ˌpôrnəˈgrafik/ adj. **por·no·graph·i·cal·ly** /ˌpôrnəˈgrafik(ə)lē/ adv. [19th C.: from Gk. *pornographos* 'writing about prostitutes,' from *pornē* 'prostitute' + -GRAPHY.]

po·rous /ˈpôrəs/ ▶ adj. (of a rock or other material) having minute holes through which liquid or air may pass. ■ fig. not retentive or secure: *he ran through a porous defense to score easily.* — **po·ros·i·ty** /pəˈräsətē; pôˈräs-/ n. **po·rous·ness** n. [ME: from OFr. *poreux*, based on L. *porus* 'pore.']

por·phyr·i·a /pôrˈfi(ə)rēə/ ▶ n. Med. a rare hereditary disease in which the blood pigment hemoglobin is abnormally metabolized. [1920s: mod. L., from PORPHYRIN.]

por·phy·rin /ˈpôrfərin/ ▶ n. Biochem. any of a class of pigments (including heme and chlorophyll) whose molecules contain four linked heterocyclic groups. [20th C.: from Gk. *porphura* 'purple' + -IN[1].]

por·phy·rit·ic /ˌpôrfəˈritik/ ▶ adj. Geol. relating to or denoting a rock texture containing distinct embedded crystals or crystalline particles.

por·phy·ro·blast /pôrˈfi(ə)rəˌblast; ˈpôrfərō-/ ▶ n. Geol. a larger recrystallized grain occurring in a finer groundmass in a metamorphic rock. — **por·phy·ro·blas·tic** /pôrˌfi(ə)rəˈblastik; ˌpôrfərō-/ adj.

por·phy·ry /ˈpôrfərē/ ▶ n. (pl. **-ries**) a hard igneous rock containing crystals, usually of feldspar, in a fine-grained, typically reddish groundmass. [ME: via med. L. from Gk. *porphuritēs*, from *porphura* 'purple.']

por·poise /ˈpôrpəs/ ▶ n. a small toothed whale with a low triangular dorsal fin and a blunt rounded snout. Its several species include the **common** (or **harbor**) **porpoise** (*Phocoena phocoena*) of the North Atlantic and North Pacific. ▶ v. [intrans.] move through the water like a porpoise, alternately rising above it and submerging. [ME: from OFr. *porpois*, based on L. *porcus* 'pig' + *piscis* 'fish.']

por·ridge /ˈpôrij; ˈpär-/ ▶ n. a dish consisting of oatmeal or another meal or cereal boiled in water or milk. — **por·ridg·y** adj. [16th C.: alt. of POTTAGE.]

por·rin·ger /ˈpôrənjər; ˈpär-/ ▶ n. hist. a small bowl, typically with a handle, used for soup or a similar dish. [ME: from OFr. *potager*, from *potage* 'contents of a pot.']

port[1] /pôrt/ ▶ n. a town or city with a harbor where ships load or unload. ■ a harbor. ■ (also **inland port**) an inland town or city whose connection to the coast by a river or other body of water enables it to act as a port.

– PHRASES **any port in a storm** proverb in adverse circumstances one welcomes any source of relief or escape. **port of entry** a harbor or airport by which people and goods may enter a country. [OE, from L. *portus* 'harbor.']

port[2] (also **port wine**) ▶ n. a strong, sweet, typically dark red fortified wine, originally from Portugal, typically drunk as a dessert wine. [shortened form of OPORTO, a major port from which the wine is shipped.]

port[3] ▶ n. the side of a ship or aircraft on the left when one is facing forward. The opposite of STARBOARD. ▶ v. [trans.] turn (a ship or its helm) to port. [16th C.: prob. from PORT[1].]

port[4] ▶ n. an aperture or opening, in particular: ■ a socket in a computer network into which a device can be plugged. ■ an opening for the passage of steam, liquid, or gas. ■ a gunport. ■ a porthole. ■ an opening in the side of a ship for boarding or loading. [OE: from L. *porta* 'gate.']

port[5] ▶ v. 1 [with obj. and adverbial of direction] Comput. transfer (software) from one system to another. 2 [trans.] [often in imper.] Mil. carry (a rifle or other weapon) diagonally across and close to the body with the barrel or blade near the left shoulder. ▶ n. 1 Mil. the position required by an order to port a rifle or other weapon: *Parker had his rifle at the port.* 2 literary a person's carriage or bearing. 3 Comput. a transfer of software from one system or machine to another. [ME: from OFr. *port* 'bearing, gait,' from the v. *porter*, from L. *portare* 'carry.']

port·a·ble /ˈpôrtəbəl/ ▶ adj. able to be easily carried or moved. ■ Comput. (of software) able to be transferred from one machine or system to another. ▶ n. a version of something that can be easily carried. ■ a small transportable building used as a classroom. — **port·a·bil·i·ty**

/ˌpôrtəˈbilətē/ **n.** **port•a•bly** /-blē/ **adv.** [ME: from OFr. *portable,* from late L. *portabilis,* from L. *portare* 'carry.']

por•tage /ˈpôrtij/ ▶**n.** the carrying of a boat or its cargo between two navigable waters. ■ a place at which this is necessary. ■ archaic the action of carrying or transporting something. ▶**v.** [trans.] carry (a boat) between navigable waters: *they are incapable of portaging a canoe* | [intrans.] *they would only run the rapid if they couldn't portage.* ■ [intrans.] (of a boat) be carried between navigable waters: *boats had to portage onto the Lualaba.* [ME: from Fr., from *porter* 'carry.']

por•tal¹ /ˈpôrtl/ ▶**n.** **1** a doorway, gate, or other entrance. **2** Computing an Internet site providing access or links to other sites. [ME: from OFr., from med. L. *portale,* neut. of *portalis* 'like a gate,' from L. *porta* 'door, gate.']

por•tal² ▶**adj.** [attrib.] Anat. of or relating to an opening in an organ through which major blood vessels pass. [19th C.: from mod. L. *portalis,* from L. *porta* 'gate.']

por•ta•men•to /ˌpôrtəˈmenˌtō/ ▶**n.** (pl. **-tos** or **-ti** /-tē/) Music a slide from one note to another, esp. in singing or playing a bowed string instrument. ■ this as a technique or style. [Ital., lit. 'carrying.']

Port Ar•thur former name (1898–1905) for **Lushun.**

por•ta•tive or•gan /ˈpôrtədiv/ ▶**n.** esp. hist. a small portable pipe organ. [16th C.: *portative* from OFr. *portatif, -ive,* based on L. *portare* 'carry.']

Port-au-Prince /ˌpôrt ōˈprins; ˈpraNs/ the capital of Haiti, on the western coast of Hispaniola; pop. 1,255,080.

Port Blair /ˈble(ə)r/ the capital of the Andaman and Nicobar Islands; pop. 75,000.

port•cul•lis /pôrtˈkələs/ ▶**n.** a strong, heavy grating sliding up and down in vertical grooves, lowered to block a gateway to a fortress or town. — **port•cul•lised** **adj.** [ME: from OFr. *porte coleice* 'sliding door,' from *porte* 'door' + *coleice* 'sliding.']

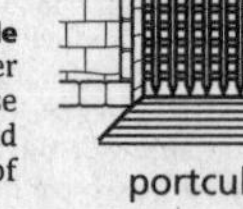
portcullis

port de bras /ˌpôr də ˈbrä/ ▶**n.** (pl. **ports de bras** pronunc. same) esp. Ballet an act or manner of moving and posing the arms. ■ an exercise designed to develop graceful movement and disposition of the arms. [Fr., lit. 'bearing of (the) arms.']

Port de France /ˌpôrt də ˈfrans/ former name for **Nouméa.**

Porte /pôrt/ (also **the Sublime Porte**) hist. the Ottoman court at Constantinople. [17th C.: from Fr. *la Sublime Porte* 'the exalted gate.']

porte co•chère /ˌpôrt kōˈsHe(ə)r/ ▶**n.** Archit. a covered entrance large enough for vehicles to pass through. ■ a porch where vehicles stop to discharge passengers. [17th C.: Fr., lit. 'coach gateway.']

Port E•liz•a•beth a city and port in southern South Africa; pop. 853,000.

por•tend /pôrˈtend/ ▶**v.** [trans.] be a sign or warning that (something, esp. something momentous or calamitous) is likely to happen. ■ be a signal of. [ME: from L. *portendere,* based on *pro-* 'forth' + *tendere* 'stretch.']

por•tent /ˈpôrˌtent/ ▶**n.** a sign or warning that something, esp. something momentous or calamitous, is likely to happen. ■ future significance: *an omen of grave portent for the tribe.* [16th C.: from L. *portentum* 'omen, token,' from the v. *portendere* (see **portend**).]

por•ten•tous /pôrˈtentəs/ ▶**adj.** of or like a portent. ■ done in a pompously or overly solemn manner. — **por•ten•tous•ly** **adv.** **por•ten•tous•ness** **n.**

Por•ter¹ /ˈpôrtər/, Cole (1892–1964), US songwriter. His songs include "Night and Day" (1932) and "Begin the Beguine" (1935).

Por•ter², Katherine Anne (1890–1980), US writer. Her novels include *Ship of Fools* (1962).

por•ter¹ /ˈpôrtər/ ▶**n.** **1** a person employed to carry luggage and other loads, esp. in an airport or a hotel. ■ a person employed to carry supplies on a mountaineering expedition. ■ an attendant in a railroad sleeping car or parlor car. **2** dark brown bitter beer brewed from malt partly charred or browned by drying at a high temperature. [ME: from OFr. *porteour,* from med. L. *portator,* from L. *portare* 'carry.']

por•ter² ▶**n.** an employee in charge of the entrance of a hotel, apartment complex, or other large building. [ME: from OFr. *portier,* from late L. *portarius,* from *porta* 'gate, door.']

por•ter•age /ˈpôrtərij/ ▶**n.** the work done by porters or laborers.

por•ter•house /ˈpôrtərˌhous/ ▶**n.** short for **porterhouse steak.** ■ hist. an establishment at which porter and sometimes steaks were served. [18th C.: from **porter¹**.]

por•ter•house steak ▶**n.** a choice steak.

port•fo•li•o /pôrtˈfōlēˌō/ ▶**n.** (pl. **-os**) **1** a large, thin, flat case for loose sheets of paper such as drawings or maps. ■ a set of pieces of creative work collected by someone to display their skills, esp. to a potential employer. ■ a varied set of photographs of a model or actor. **2** a range of investments held by someone. ■ a range of products or services offered by an organization, esp. when considered as a business asset. **3** the position and duties of a minister of state or a member of a cabinet: *the Foreign Affairs portfolio.* [18th C.: from Ital. *portafogli,* from *portare* 'carry' + *foglio* 'leaf' (from L. *folium*).]

Port Har•court /ˈhärˌkôrt; -kərt/ a city in southeastern Nigeria; pop. 371,000.

port•hole /ˈpôrtˌhōl/ ▶**n.** a small exterior window in a ship or aircraft. ■ hist. an opening for firing a cannon through.

portico

por•ti•co /ˈpôrtiˌkō/ ▶**n.** (pl. **-coes** or **-cos**) a structure consisting of a roof supported by columns at regular intervals, typically attached as a porch to a building. [17th C.: from Ital., from L. *porticus* 'porch.']

por•tière /ˌpôrtēˈer; -ˈtye(ə)r/ (also **por•tiere**) ▶**n.** a curtain hung over a door or doorway. [19th C.: Fr., from *porte* 'door.']

Por•ţi•le de Fier /pôrˌsēlə də ˈfyer/ Romanian name for **Iron Gate.**

por•tion /ˈpôrsHən/ ▶**n.** a part of a whole; an amount, section, or piece of something. ■ a part of something divided between two or more people; a share. ■ an amount of food suitable for or served to one person. ■ Law the part or share of an estate given or descending by law to an heir. ■ archaic a person's future as allotted by fate; one's destiny or lot. ■ (also **marriage portion**) archaic a dowry given to a bride at her marriage. ▶**v.** [trans.] (usu. **be portioned**) divide (something) into shares to be distributed among two or more people. ■ [usu. as adj., with submodifier] (**portioned**) serve (food) in an amount suitable for one person: *generously portioned lunches.* ■ archaic give a dowry to (a bride at her marriage). [ME: from OFr. *porcion,* from L. *portio(n-),* from *pro portione* 'in proportion.']

Port•land /ˈpôrtlənd/ **1** a city in southwestern Maine, on Casco Bay; pop. 64,249. **2** a city in northwestern Oregon; pop. 529,121.

Port•land ce•ment (also **port•land ce•ment**) ▶**n.** cement that is manufactured from limestone and clay and that hardens under water. [1810s: named after the Isle of *Portland* in Dorset, England.]

Port Lou•is /ˈlo͞o-is; ˈlo͞o-ē/ the capital of Mauritius, a port on the northwestern coast; pop. 144,000.

port•ly /ˈpôrtlē/ ▶**adj.** (**-li•er**, **-li•est**) (esp. of a man) having a stout body; somewhat fat. — **port•li•ness** **n.** [15th C.: from **port⁵**.]

port•man•teau /pôrtˈmantō; ˌpôrtmanˈtō/ ▶**n.** (pl. **-teaus** or **-teaux** /-tōz/) a large trunk or suitcase opening into two equal parts. [16th C.: from Fr. *portemanteau,* from *porter* 'carry' + *manteau* 'mantle.']

port•man•teau word ▶**n.** a word blending the sounds and combining the meanings of two others, for example *motel* (from 'motor' and hotel'). [*portmanteau* coined by Lewis Carroll in *Through the Looking Glass* (1871).]

Port Mores•by /ˈmôrzbē/ the capital of Papua New Guinea, on south New Guinea; pop. 193,000.

Port Na•tal former name (until 1835) for **Durban.**

Por•to /ˈpôrto͞o/ Portuguese name for **Oporto.**

Pôr•to A•le•gre /ˈpôrto͞o äˈlegrə/ a city in southeastern Brazil; pop. 1,263,000.

por•to•bel•lo /ˌpôrtəˈbelō/ (also **portobello mushroom**) ▶**n.** a large mature edible mushroom with an open flat cap.

port of call ▶**n.** a place where a ship stops on a voyage. ■ any of the places that a person visits in succession.

Port-of-Spain the capital of Trinidad and Tobago, on northwestern Trinidad; pop. 46,000.

Por•to No•vo /ˈpôrtō ˈnōvō/ the capital of Benin, on the Gulf of Guinea; pop. 179,000.

Port Or•ford ce•dar /ˈôrfərd/ ▶**n.** a slender cypress (*Chamaecyparis lawsoniana*) with dense foliage and lower branches arising at ground level. Native to a small area of northwestern California and southwestern Oregon, it is widely grown for timber and as an ornamental.

Pôr•to Vel•ho /ˈpôrto͞o ˈvelyo͞o/ a city in western Brazil; pop. 286,000.

Port Pe•trovsk /piˈtrôfsk/ former name (until 1922) for **Makhachkala.**

por•trait /ˈpôrtrət; -ˌtrāt/ ▶**n.** **1** a painting, drawing, photograph, or engraving of a person. ■ a representation or impression of someone or something in language or on film. **2** [as adj.] (of a page, book, or illustration, or the manner in which it is set or printed) higher than it is wide. Compare with **landscape** (sense 2). — **por•trait•ist** /ˈpôrtrətist; -ˌtrātist/ **n.** (in sense 1). [16th C.: from Fr., past part. of OFr. *portraire* 'portray.']

por•trai•ture /ˈpôrtricHər; -ˌcHo͝or/ ▶**n.** the art of creating portraits. ■ graphic and detailed description, esp. of a person. ■ formal a portrait.

por•tray /pôrˈtrā/ ▶**v.** [trans.] depict (someone or something) in a work of art or literature. ■ (of an actor) represent or play the part of (someone) on film or stage. ■ [trans.] describe (someone or something) in a particular way. — **por•tray•a•ble** **adj.** **por•tray•al** /-ˈtrā(ə)l/ **n.** **por•tray•er** **n.** [ME: from OFr. *portraire,* based on *traire* 'to draw,' from L. *trahere.*]

Port Sa•id /sīˈēd/ a city in Egypt, at the northern end of the Suez Canal; pop. 461,000.

Port Sa•lut /ˌpôr səˈl(y)o͞o/ ▶**n.** a pale, mild type of cheese. [named after the Trappist monastery in France, where it was first produced.]

Ports•mouth /ˈpôrtsməTH/ **1** a city on the southern coast of England; pop. 175,000. **2** a city in southeastern Virginia, on Hampton Roads; pop. 100,565.

Port Su•dan a city in northeastern Sudan; pop. 206,000.

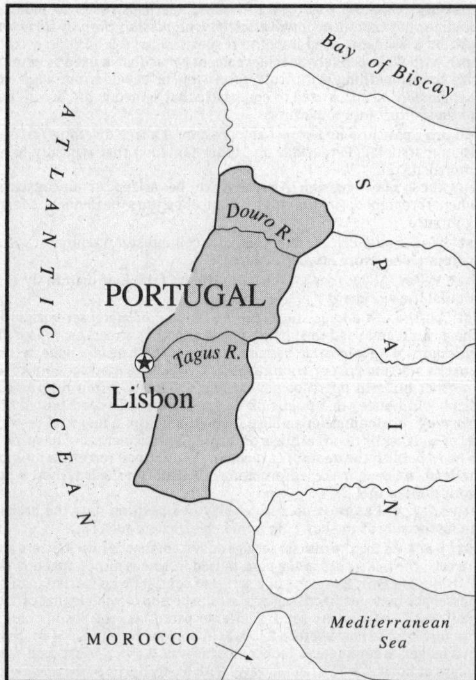

Portugal

Official name: Portuguese Republic
Location: southwestern Europe, in the western part of the Iberian peninsula
Area: 35,700 square miles (92,400 sq km)
Population: 10,393,000
Capital: Lisbon
Language: Portuguese
Currency: euro

port tack ▶ **n.** a sailboat's heading when the wind is coming from the left, or port, side.

Por·tu·gal /'pôrCHəgəl/ a country in southwestern Europe. *See box.*

Por·tu·guese /'pôrCHə,gēz; -,gēs/ ▶ **adj.** of or relating to Portugal or its people or language. ▶ **n.** (pl. same) **1** a native or national of Portugal, or a person of Portuguese descent. **2** the Romance language of Portugal and Brazil.

Por·tu·guese man-of-war ▶ **n.** a floating colonial coelenterate (*Physalia physalis*, order Siphonophora, class Hydrozoa) with a number of polyps and a conspicuous float. It bears long tentacles that are able to inflict painful stings.

Port Vi·la another name for **Vila**.

port watch ▶ **n.** see **watch** (sense 2).

port wine ▶ **n.** see **port²**.

port wine stain ▶ **n.** a deep red birthmark, a persistent hemangioma or nevus, typically on the face.

POS ▶ **abbr.** point of sale.

pos. ▶ **abbr.** ■ position. ■ positive. ■ possession. ■ possessive.

po·sa·da /pə'sädə/ ▶ **n.** (in Spanish-speaking regions) a hotel or inn. ■ (also **Las Posadas**) a ritual reenactment of Mary and Joseph's search for a lodging in Bethlehem. [Sp., from *posar* 'to lodge.']

pose¹ /pōz/ ▶ **v.** **1** [trans.] present or constitute (a problem, danger, or difficulty). ■ raise (a question or matter for consideration). **2** [intrans.] assume a particular attitude or position in order to be photographed, painted, or drawn. ■ [trans.] place (someone) in a particular attitude or position in order to be photographed, painted, or drawn: *he posed her on the sofa.* ■ (**pose as**) set oneself up as or pretend to be (someone or something). ■ behave affectedly in order to impress others. ▶ **n.** a particular way of standing or sitting, usually adopted for effect or in order to be photographed, painted, or drawn. ■ a particular way of behaving adopted in order to give others a false impression or to impress others. [ME: from OFr. *poser* (v.), from late L. *pausare* 'to pause.']

pose² ▶ **v.** [trans.] archaic puzzle or perplex (someone) with a question or problem: *we have thus posed the mathematician and the historian.* [16th C.: shortening of obs. *appose*, from OFr. *aposer*, var. of *oposer* 'oppose.']

Po·sei·don /pə'sīdn/ Gk. Mythol. the god of the sea, water, earthquakes, and horses, son of Cronus and Rhea and brother of Zeus. Roman equivalent **Neptune**.

Po·sen /'pōzən/ German name for **Poznań**.

pos·er¹ /'pōzər/ ▶ **n.** a person who acts in an affected manner in order to impress others.

pos·er² ▶ **n.** a difficult or perplexing question or problem.

po·seur /pō'zər/ ▶ **n.** another term for **poser¹**. [Fr., from *poser* 'to place.']

po·sey /'pōzē/ (also **po·sy**) ▶ **adj.** informal (of a person or their behavior) affected and attempting to impress others; pretentious.

posh /päsH/ informal ▶ **adj.** elegant or stylishly luxurious. ■ esp. Brit. typical of or belonging to upper-class society. ▶ **n.** Brit. the quality or state of being elegant, stylish, or upper class. — **posh·ly adv. posh·ness n.** [20th C.: perh. from slang *posh*, denoting a dandy. There is no evidence to support the folk etymology that *posh* is formed from the initials of *port out starboard home*.]

pos·it /'päzit/ ▶ **v.** (**pos·it·ed, pos·it·ing**) **1** [trans.] assume as a fact; put forward as a basis of argument. ■ (**posit something on**) base something on the truth of (a particular assumption): *posited on a false premise.* **2** [trans.] put in position; place. ▶ **n.** Philos. a statement made on the assumption that it will prove to be true. [17th C.: from L. *posit-* 'placed,' from the v. *ponere*.]

po·si·tion /pə'zisHən/ ▶ **n.** **1** a place where someone or something is located or has been put: *the ship's position.* ■ the location where someone or something should be; the correct place: *the lid was put into position.* ■ (often **positions**) a place where part of a military force is posted for strategic purposes. **2** a particular way in which someone or something is placed or arranged: *a reclining position.* ■ in a game of chess, the configuration of the pieces and pawns on the board at any point. ■ Music a particular location of the hand on the fingerboard of a stringed instrument: *the first six positions across the four strings.* ■ Music a particular location of the slide of a trombone. ■ Music the arrangement of the constituent notes of a chord. **3** a situation or set of circumstances, esp. one that affects one's power to act: *the company's financial position is grim.* ■ a job: *her position as marketing director.* ■ the state of being placed where one has an advantage over one's rivals in a competitive situation. ■ a person's place or rank in relation to others, esp. in a competitive situation: *in second position.* ■ high rank or social standing. ■ (in team games) a set of functions considered as the responsibility of a particular player based on the location in which they play. **4** a person's particular point of view or attitude toward something: *the official US position on Palestine.* **5** an investor's net holdings in one or more markets at a particular time; the status of an individual or institutional trader's open contracts: *traders were covering short positions.* **6** Logic a proposition laid down or asserted. ▶ **v.** [trans.] put or arrange (someone or something) in a particular place or way. ■ promote (a product, service, or business) within a particular sector of a market, or as the fulfillment of that sector's specific requirements. ■ fig. portray or regard (someone) as a particular type of person. [ME: from OFr., from L. *positio(n-)*, from *ponere* 'to place.']

po·si·tion·al /pə'zisHənl/ ▶ **adj.** of, relating to, or determined by position: *make several positional changes.* — **po·si·tion·al·ly adv.**

po·si·tion pa·per ▶ **n.** (in business and politics) a written report outlining someone's attitude or intentions regarding a particular matter.

pos·i·tive /'päzətiv; 'päztiv/ ▶ **adj.** **1** consisting in or characterized by the presence or possession of features or qualities rather than their absence. ■ (of a statement or decision) expressing or implying affirmation, agreement, or permission: *a positive response.* ■ (of the results of a test or experiment) indicating the presence of something: *tested positive for cocaine use.* ■ constructive in intention or attitude: *a positive approach.* ■ showing optimism and confidence: *feeling positive about our chances.* ■ showing pleasing progress, gain, or improvement: *rescuing that cat has had a positive effect on her.* **2** with no possibility of doubt; clear and definite: *a positive identification.* ■ convinced or confident in one's opinion; certain: *I'm positive it was the same man.* ■ [attrib.] informal downright; complete (used for emphasis): *the dog is a positive delight.* **3** of, containing, producing, or denoting an electric charge opposite to that carried by electrons. **4** (of a photographic image) showing lights and shades or colors true to the original. **5** Gram. (of an adjective or adverb) expressing a quality in its basic, primary degree. Contrasted with **comparative** and **superlative**. **6** esp. Philos. dealing only with matters of fact and experience; not speculative or theoretical. Compare with **positivism** (sense 1). **7** (of a quantity) greater than zero. **8** Astrol. of, relating to, or denoting any of the air or fire signs, considered active in nature. ▶ **n.** **1** a good, affirmative, or constructive quality or attribute: *translate your weakness into positives.* **2** a photographic image showing lights and shades or colors true to the original. **3** a result of a test or experiment indicating the presence of something: *the distribution of those positives.* **4** the part of an electric circuit that is at a higher electrical potential than another point designated as having zero electrical potential. **5** Gram. an adjective or adverb in the positive degree. **6** a number greater than zero. — **pos·i·tive·ness n. pos·i·tiv·i·ty** /,päzə'tivətē/ **n.** [ME: from OFr. *positif, -ive* or L. *positivus*, from *posit-* 'placed,' from the v. *ponere*.]

pos·i·tive feed·back ▶ **n.** esp. Biol. the enhancement or amplification of an effect by its own influence on the process that gives rise to it. ■ Electron. the return of part of an output signal to the input, which is in phase with it, so that the amplifier gain is increased and often the output is distorted.

pos·i·tive·ly /ˈpäzətivlē; ˈpäztivlē; ˌpäzəˈtivlē/ ▶ **adv.** in a positive way, in particular: ■ in a constructive or affirmative way. ■ with optimism or confidence: *it's time I got down to thinking positively.* ■ with certainty; so as to leave no room for doubt. ■ [as submodifier] used to emphasize that something is the case, even though it may seem surprising or unlikely. ■ [sentence adverb] used to emphasize that someone means what they are saying.

pos·i·tive pole ▶ **n.** Physics a north-seeking pole of a magnet. ■ an anode.

pos·i·tive sign ▶ **n.** Math. term for PLUS SIGN.

pos·i·tiv·ism /ˈpäzətivˌizəm; ˈpäztiv-/ ▶ **n.** Philos. **1** a philosophical system that holds that every rationally justifiable assertion can be scientifically verified or is capable of logical or mathematical proof. ■ a humanistic religious system founded on this. ■ another term for LOGICAL POSITIVISM. **2** the theory that laws are to be understood as social rules, valid because they are enacted by authority or derive logically from existing decisions, and that ideal or moral considerations (e.g., that a rule is unjust) should not limit the scope or operation of the law. **3** the state or quality of being positive. — **pos·i·tiv·ist n. & adj. pos·i·tiv·is·tic** /ˌpäzətəˈvistik/ **adj. pos·i·tiv·is·ti·cal·ly** /ˌpäzətəˈvistik(ə)lē/ **adv.**

pos·i·tron /ˈpäzəˌträn/ ▶ **n.** Physics a subatomic particle with the same mass as an electron and a numerically equal but positive charge. [1930s: from POSITIVE + -TRON.]

po·sol·o·gy /pəˈzäləjē/ ▶ **n.** rare the part of medicine concerned with dosage. — **pos·o·log·i·cal** /ˌpäzəˈläjikəl/ **adj.** [19th C.: from Fr. *posologie*, from Gk. *posos* 'how much' + *-logia* (see -LOGY).]

poss. ▶ **abbr.** ■ possession. ■ possessive. ■ possible; possibly.

pos·se /ˈpäsē/ ▶ **n.** hist. a body of men, typically armed, summoned by a sheriff to enforce the law. ■ (also **pos·se com·i·ta·tus** /ˌkämiˈtätəs; -ˈtātəs/) hist. the body of men in a county whom the sheriff could summon to enforce the law. ■ informal a group of people who have a common characteristic, occupation, or purpose. ■ informal a gang of youths involved in (usually drug-related) crime. ■ informal a group of people who socialize together, esp. to go to clubs or raves. [17th C.: from med. L., lit. 'power,' from L. *posse* 'be able.']

pos·sess /pəˈzes/ ▶ **v.** [trans.] **1** have as belonging to one; own: *I do not possess a television set.* ■ Law have possession of as distinct from ownership. ■ have as an ability, quality, or characteristic. **2** (usu. **be possessed**) (supposedly of a demon or spirit, esp. an evil one) have complete power over (someone) and be manifested through their speech or actions. ■ (of an emotion, idea, etc.) dominate the mind of; have an overpowering influence on.

– PHRASES **what possessed you?** used to express surprise at an action regarded as extremely unwise. [ME: from OFr. *possesser*, from L. *possess-* 'occupied, held,' from the v. *possidere*, from *potis* 'able, capable' + *sedere* 'sit.']

pos·ses·sion /pəˈzesʜən/ ▶ **n.** **1** the state of having, owning, or controlling something. ■ Law visible power or control over something, as distinct from lawful ownership; holding or occupancy. ■ informal the state of possessing an illegal drug: *charged with possession.* ■ (in football, basketball, and other ball games) temporary control of the ball by a particular player or team. **2** (usu. **possessions**) an item of property; something belonging to one: *I was alone with no possessions.* ■ a territory or country controlled or governed by another. **3** the state of being controlled by a demon or spirit. ■ the state of being completely under the influence of an idea or emotion: *fear took possession of my soul.* — **pos·ses·sion·less adj.**

pos·ses·sive /pəˈzesiv/ ▶ **adj.** **1** demanding someone's total attention and love. ■ showing a desire to own things and an unwillingness to share what one already owns. **2** Gram. relating to or denoting the case of nouns and pronouns expressing possession. ▶ **n.** Gram. a possessive word or form. ■ (**the possessive**) the possessive case. — **pos·ses·sive·ly adv. pos·ses·sive·ness n.**

pos·ses·sive pro·noun ▶ **n.** Gram. a pronoun indicating possession, for example *mine, yours, hers, theirs.*

pos·ses·sor /pəˈzesər/ ▶ **n.** a person who owns something or has a particular quality. ■ Law a person who takes, occupies, or holds something without necessarily having ownership, or as distinguished from the owner. — **pos·ses·so·ry adj.**

pos·set /ˈpäsət/ ▶ **n.** hist. a drink made of hot milk curdled with ale, wine, or other alcoholic liquor and typically flavored with spices. [ME: of unknown origin.]

pos·si·bil·i·ty /ˌpäsəˈbilətē/ ▶ **n.** (pl. **-ties**) a thing that may happen or be the case. ■ the state or fact of being likely or possible; likelihood. ■ a thing that may be chosen or done out of several possible alternatives. ■ (**possibilities**) unspecified qualities of a promising nature; potential.

pos·si·ble /ˈpäsəbəl/ ▶ **adj.** able to be done; within the power or capacity of someone or something. ■ able to happen although not certain to; denoting a fact, event, or situation that may or may not occur or be so: *it's possible we may not find her.* ■ [attrib.] able to be or become; potential: *a possible future customer.* ■ [with superlative] having as much or as little of a specified quality as can be achieved: *the shortest possible route.* ■ [attrib.] (of a number or score) as high as is achievable in a test, competition, or game: *scored 723 out of a possible 900.* ▶ **n.** a person or thing that has the potential to become or do something. [ME: from OFr., or from L. *possibilis*, from *posse* 'be able.']

pos·si·bly /ˈpäsəblē/ ▶ **adv.** **1** [sentence adverb] perhaps (used to indicate doubt or hesitancy): *he found himself alone, possibly the only surviving officer.* ■ [with modal] used in polite requests. **2** [usu. with modal] in accordance with what is likely or achievable, in particular: ■ used to emphasize that something is difficult, surprising, or bewildering: *what can you possibly mean?* ■ used to emphasize that someone has or will put all their effort into something.

pos·sum /ˈpäsəm/ ▶ **n.** **1** informal an opossum. **2** a tree-dwelling Australasian marsupial (Petauridae and other families) that typically has a prehensile tail.

– PHRASES **play possum** **1** pretend to be asleep or unconscious when threatened (in imitation of an opossum's behavior). **2** feign ignorance.

Post¹ /pōst/, Emily Price (1873–1960), US columnist. An arbiter of social manners, she wrote *Etiquette* (1922).

Post², Wiley (1899–1935), US aviator. He was the first man to fly solo around the world 1933.

post¹ /pōst/ ▶ **n.** **1** a long, sturdy piece of timber or metal set upright in the ground and used to support something or as a marker: *follow the blue posts.* ■ a goalpost: *Robertson, at the near post, headed wide.* ■ (**the post**) a starting post or winning post. **2** Computing a message sent to an Internet bulletin board or newsgroup. ▶ **v.** [trans.] (often **be posted**) display (a notice) in a public place: *the exam results were posted this morning.* ■ announce or publish (something, esp. a financial result). ■ (of a player or team) achieve or record (a particular score or result). ■ [trans.] publish the name of (a member of the armed forces) as missing or dead. ■ Comput. make (information) available on the Internet. ■ put notices on or in.

– PHRASAL VERBS **post up** Basketball play in a position near the basket, along the side of the key. [OE, from L. *postis* 'doorpost.']

post² ▶ **n.** **1** esp. Brit. the official service or system that delivers letters and parcels: *the tickets are in the post.* ■ used in names of newspapers: *the Washington Post.* **2** hist. one of a series of couriers who carried mail on horseback between fixed stages. ■ archaic a person or vehicle that carries mail. ▶ **v.** **1** [trans.] esp. Brit. send (a letter or parcel) via the postal system: *I've just been to post a letter.* **2** [trans.] (in bookkeeping) enter (an item) in a ledger. ■ complete (a ledger) in this way. **3** [intrans.] hist. travel with relays of horses. ■ [trans.] archaic travel with haste; hurry. ▶ **adv.** archaic with haste; hurry.

– PHRASES **keep someone posted** keep someone informed of the latest developments or news. [16th C.: from Fr. *poste*, from Ital. *posta*, from a contr. of L. *posita*, fem. past part. of *ponere* 'to place.']

post³ ▶ **n.** **1** a position of paid employment; a job. **2** a place where someone is on duty or where a particular activity is carried out: *a worker asleep at his post.* ■ a place where a soldier, guard, or police officer is stationed or which they patrol. ■ a force stationed at a permanent position or camp; a garrison. ■ a local group in an organization of military veterans. ▶ **v.** [with trans.] (usu. **be posted**) send (someone) to a particular place to take up an appointment. ■ station (someone, esp. a soldier, guard, or police officer) in a particular place: *a guard was posted.* [16th C.: from Fr. *poste*, from Ital. *posto*, from a contr. of pop. L. *positum*, neut. past part. of *ponere* 'to place.']

post- ▶ **prefix** after in time or order: *postdate.* [from L. *post* 'after, behind.']

post·age /ˈpōstij/ ▶ **n.** the sending or conveying of letters and parcels by mail: *the free postage.* ■ the amount required to send a letter or parcel by mail: *$15.95 including postage and handling.*

post·age due ▶ **n.** the balance of postage not prepaid.

post·age me·ter ▶ **n.** a machine that prints an official mark or signature on a letter or parcel to indicate that postage has been paid or does not need to be paid.

post·age stamp ▶ **n.** a small adhesive piece of paper of specified value issued by a postal authority to indicate the amount of postage paid.

post·al /ˈpōstl/ ▶ **adj.** [attrib.] of or relating to the post office or the mail: *increased postal rates | postal services.* ■ esp. Brit. done through the mail: *a postal ballot.* ▶ **n.** (in full **postal card**) another term for POSTCARD.

– PHRASES **go postal** become crazed and violent, esp. as the result of stress. — **post·al·ly adv.** [19th C.: from Fr., from *poste* 'postal service.']

post-and-beam ▶ **adj.** (of a building or a method of construction) having or using a framework of upright and horizontal beams.

post·bel·lum /pōstˈbeləm/ ▶ **adj.** occurring or existing after a war, in particular the American Civil War. [19th C.: from L. *post* 'after' + *bellum* 'war.']

post·box /ˈpōstˌbäks/ ▶ **n.** British term for MAILBOX.

post·card /ˈpōstˌkärd/ ▶ **n.** a card for sending a message by mail without an envelope.

post-chaise /ˈsʜāz/ ▶ **n.** (pl. **post-chaises** pronunc. same or /-ˌsʜāziz/) hist. a horse-drawn carriage used for transporting passengers or mail. [17th C.: from POST² + CHAISE.]

post·clas·si·cal /ˌpōstˈklasəkəl/ ▶ **adj.** of or relating to a time after the classical period.

post·date /pōstˈdāt/ ▶ **v.** [trans.] **1** [usu. as adj.] (**postdated**) affix or assign a date later than the actual one. **2** occur or come at a later date than.

post·doc /ˈpōstˌdäk/ ▶ **n.** informal a person engaged in postdoctoral research. ■ postdoctoral research. ■ a postdoctoral research fellowship.

post·doc·tor·al /pōstˈdäktərəl/ ▶ **adj.** of, relating to, or denoting research undertaken after the completion of doctoral research: *a postdoctoral fellowship.*

post·er /ˈpōstər/ ▶ **n.** a large printed picture used for decoration. ■ a large printed picture, notice, or advertisement displayed in a public place: [as adj.] *a poster campaign.*

post·er child (or **poster boy** or **poster girl**) ▶ **n.** a person or thing that epitomizes or represents a specified quality, cause, etc.: *the organization is the poster child for bad business deals.* [from the use of appealing children in charitable print advertisements.]

poste res·tante /ˌpōst ˌresˈtänt/ ▶ **n.** an indication that a letter should be kept at a specified post office until collected by the addressee. [18th C.: from Fr., lit. 'mail remaining.']

pos·te·ri·or /päˈsti(ə)rēər; pō-/ ▶ **adj. 1** esp. Anat., tech. further back in position; of or nearer the rear or hind end. The opposite of ANTERIOR. **2** formal coming after in time or order; later: *a date posterior to the first Reform Bill.* ▶ **n.** humorous a person's buttocks. — **pos·te·ri·or·i·ty** /päˌsti(ə)rēˈôritē; pō-/ **n. pos·te·ri·or·ly adv.** [16th C.: from L., compar. of *posterus* 'following,' from *post* 'after.']

pos·ter·i·ty /päˈsteritē/ ▶ **n.** all future generations.

pos·tern /ˈpōstərn; ˈpäs-/ ▶ **n.** a back or side entrance. [ME: from OFr. *posterne,* alt. of *posterle,* from late L. *posterula,* dimin. of *posterus* 'following.']

post ex·change (abbr.: **PX**) ▶ **n.** a store at a US military base selling food, clothing, and other items.

post·face /ˈpōstˌfās/ ▶ **n.** a brief explanatory comment or note at the end of a book or other piece of writing.

post·fem·i·nist /pōstˈfemənist/ ▶ **adj.** coming after the feminism of the 1960s and subsequent decades. — **post·fem·i·nism n.**

post·fix ▶ **v.** /pōstˈfiks/ **1** [trans.] (usu. **be postfixed**) Biol. treat (a biological substance or specimen) with a second fixative. **2** Ling., rare append as a suffix. ▶ **n.** a suffix.

post·fron·tal /ˌpōstˈfrəntl/ ▶ **n.** Zool. a bone behind the orbit of the eye in some vertebrates.

post·gla·cial /pōstˈglāsHəl/ ▶ **adj.** Geol. of or relating to the period since the last continental glaciation from the sudden rise in temperature about 10,000 years ago. Compare with LATE-GLACIAL. ■ [as n.] (**the postglacial**) the postglacial period.

post·grad /ˈpōstˈgrad/ ▶ **adj. & n.** informal short for POSTGRADUATE.

post·grad·u·ate /pōstˈgrajo͞oit/ ▶ **adj.** denoting study undertaken after completing a first degree. ▶ **n.** a student engaged in such a course of study.

post·haste /ˈpōstˈhāst/ ▶ **adv.** with great speed. [16th C.: from the direction "haste, post, haste."]

post hoc /ˈpōst ˈhäk/ ▶ **adj. & adv.** occurring or done after the event: *a post hoc justification for the changes.* [L., 'after this.']

post·hu·mous /ˈpäsCHəməs; -CHo͞o-/ ▶ **adj.** occurring or appearing after the death of the originator. ■ (of a child) born after the death of its father. — **post·hu·mous·ly adv.** [17th C.: from L. *postumus* 'last' (superlative from *post* 'after').]

post·hyp·not·ic /ˌpōst(h)ipˈnätik/ ▶ **adj.** relating to or denoting the giving of ideas or instructions to a subject under hypnosis that are intended to affect behavior after the hypnotic trance ends.

pos·til·ion /pəˈstilyən; pō-/ (also **pos·til·lion**) ▶ **n.** a person who rides the leading left-hand horse of a team or pair drawing a coach or carriage. [16th C.: from Fr. *postillon,* from Ital. *postiglione* 'post boy,' from *posta* (see POST²).]

post-Im·pres·sion·ism (also **Post-Im·pres·sion·ism**) ▶ **n.** the work or style of a varied group of late 19th-century and early 20th-century artists who reacted against the naturalism of the Impressionists. — **post-Im·pres·sion·ist n. & adj. post-Im·pres·sion·is·tic adj.**

post·ing /ˈpōstiNG/ ▶ **n.** esp. Brit. an appointment to a job, esp. one abroad or in the armed forces. ■ the location of such an appointment.

Post-it (also **Post-it note**) ▶ **n.** trademark a piece of paper with an adhesive strip on one side, designed to be stuck prominently to an object or surface and easily removed.

post·lude /ˈpōstˌlo͞od/ ▶ **n.** Music a concluding piece of music. ■ a written or spoken epilogue; an afterword. [19th C.: from POST- 'later, after,' on the pattern of *prelude.*]

post·man /ˈpōstmən/ ▶ **n.** (pl. **-men**) a mail carrier.

post·mark /ˈpōstˌmärk/ ▶ **n.** an official mark stamped on a letter or other postal package, giving the place, date, and time of posting, and canceling the stamp. ▶ **v.** [trans.] (usu. **be postmarked**) stamp (a letter or other postal package) officially with such a mark.

post·mas·ter /ˈpōstˌmastər/ ▶ **n.** a person in charge of a post office.

post·mas·ter gen·er·al ▶ **n.** (pl. **post·mas·ters gen·er·al**) the head of a country's postal service.

post·mil·len·ni·al /ˌpōstməˈlenēəl/ ▶ **adj.** (esp. in Christian doctrine) following the millennium.

post·mil·len·ni·al·ism /ˌpōstməˈlenēəˌlizəm/ ▶ **n.** (among some Christian Protestants) the doctrine that the Second Coming of Christ will be the culmination of the prophesied millennium of blessedness. Compare with PREMILLENNIALISM. — **post·mil·len·ni·al·ist** /-ist/ **n.**

post·mis·tress /ˈpōstˌmistris/ ▶ **n.** a woman in charge of a post office.

post·mod·ern·ism /pōstˈmädərˌnizəm/ ▶ **n.** a late 20th-century style in the arts, architecture, and criticism that represents a departure from modernism. — **post·mod·ern adj. post·mod·ern·ist n. & adj. post·mod·er·ni·ty** /ˌpōstməˈdərnətē/ **n.**

post·mor·tem /pōstˈmôrtəm/ ▶ **n.** (also **post-mor·tem**) an examination of a dead body to determine the cause of death. ■ an analysis or discussion of an event held soon after it has occurred: *an election postmortem.* ▶ **adj.** [attrib.] of or relating to a postmortem. ■ happening after death: *postmortem changes in his body.* [18th C.: from L., lit. 'after death.']

post·na·tal /pōstˈnātl/ ▶ **adj.** of, relating to, characteristic of, or denoting the period after childbirth. — **post·na·tal·ly adv.**

post·nup·tial /pōstˈnəpsHəl; -CHəl/ ▶ **adj.** occurring or relating to the period after marriage.

post-o·bit ▶ **adj.** archaic taking effect after death. [18th C.: from L. *post obitum,* from *post* 'after' + *obitus* 'decease' (from *obire* 'to die').]

post of·fice ▶ **n. 1** the public department or corporation responsible for postal services. ■ a building where postal business is carried on. **2** a game, played esp. by children, in which imaginary letters are delivered in exchange for kisses.

post of·fice box ▶ **n.** a numbered box in a post office assigned to a person or organization for mail.

post-op ▶ **abbr.** postoperative.

post·op·er·a·tive /pōstˈäp(ə)rətiv/ ▶ **adj.** during, relating to, or denoting the period following surgery.

post·or·bit·al /pōstˈôrbətl/ esp. Zool. ▶ **adj.** [attrib.] situated at the back of the orbit or eye socket. ▶ **n.** a postorbital bone.

post·paid /pōstˈpād/ ▶ **adj. & adv.** (with reference to a letter or parcel) on which postage has been paid.

post·par·tum /pōstˈpärtəm/ ▶ **adj.** Med. & Vet. following childbirth or the birth of young. [19th C.: from L. *post partum* 'after childbirth.']

post·par·tum de·pres·sion ▶ **n.** depression suffered by a mother following childbirth.

post·pone /pōstˈpōn/ ▶ **v.** [trans.] cause or arrange for (something) to take place at a time later than that first scheduled. — **post·pon·a·ble adj. post·pone·ment n. post·pon·er n.** [15th C.: from L. *postponere,* from *post* 'after' + *ponere* 'to place.']

post·po·si·tion /ˌpōstpəˈzisHən/ ▶ **n.** Gram. a word or morpheme placed after the word it governs, for example *-ward* in *homeward.* — **post·po·si·tion·al** /-sHənl/ **adj.** [19th C.: from PREP..]

post·pos·i·tive /ˌpōstˈpäzətiv/ ▶ **adj.** (of a word) placed after or as a suffix on the word that it relates to. ▶ **n.** a postpositive word. — **post·pos·i·tive·ly adv.**

post·pran·di·al /pōstˈprandēəl/ ▶ **adj.** formal humorous during or relating to the period after dinner or lunch. ■ Med. occurring after a meal. [19th C.: from POST- 'after' + L. *prandium* 'a meal' + -AL.]

post·pro·duc·tion /ˌpōstprəˈdəksHən/ ▶ **n.** [often as adj.] work done on a film or recording after filming or recording has taken place: *postproduction editing.*

post·script /ˈpōs(t)ˌskript/ ▶ **n.** an additional remark at the end of a letter. ■ an additional statement or action that provides further information on or a sequel to something. [16th C.: from L. *postscriptum,* neut. past part. of *postscribere* 'write under, add,' from *post* 'after, later' + *scribere* 'write.']

post time ▶ **n.** the time at which a race is scheduled to start and entrants must be at their starting positions.

post-trau·mat·ic stress dis·or·der ▶ **n.** Med. a condition of persistent mental and emotional stress occurring as a result of injury or severe psychological shock.

pos·tu·lant /ˈpäsCHələnt/ ▶ **n.** a candidate, esp. one seeking admission into a religious order.

pos·tu·late ▶ **v.** /ˈpäsCHəˌlāt/ [trans.] **1** suggest or assume the existence, fact, or truth of (something) as a basis for reasoning, discussion, or belief. **2** (in ecclesiastical law) nominate or elect (someone) to an ecclesiastical office subject to the sanction of a higher authority. ▶ **n.** /ˈpäsCHələt/ formal a thing suggested or assumed as true as the basis for reasoning, discussion, or belief. ■ Math. an assumption used as a basis for mathematical reasoning. — **pos·tu·la·tion** /ˌpäsCHəˈlāsHən/ **n.** [ME (sense 2): from L. *postulat-* 'asked,' from the v. *postulare.*]

pos·tu·la·tor /ˈpäsCHəˌlātər/ ▶ **n. 1** a person who postulates something. **2** a person who presents a case for canonization or beatification in the Roman Catholic Church.

pos·ture /ˈpäsCHər/ ▶ **n.** a position of a person's body when standing or sitting: *good posture will protect your spine.* ■ Zool. a particular pose adopted by a bird or other animal, interpreted as a signal of a specific pattern of behavior. ■ fig. a particular way of dealing with or considering something; an approach or attitude: *a defiant posture.* ■ fig. a particular way of behaving that is intended to convey a false impression; a pose. ▶ **v.** [intrans.] [often as n.] (**posturing**) behave in a way that is intended to impress or mislead others. ■ [trans.] adopt (an attitude) to impress or mislead. — **pos·tur·al** /-CHərəl/ **adj. pos·tur·er n.** [16th C.: from Fr., from Ital. *postura,* from L. *positura* 'position,' from *posit-* 'placed,' from the v. *ponere.*]

po·sy¹ /ˈpōzē/ ▶ **n.** (pl. **-sies**) **1** a small bunch of flowers. **2** archaic a short saying inscribed inside a ring. [ME (sense 2): contr. of POESY.]

po·sy² ▶ **adj.** var. of POSEY.

pot¹ /pät/ ▶ **n. 1** a container, typically rounded and of metal, used for storage or cooking. ■ short for TEAPOT, FLOWERPOT, LOBSTER POT, CHAMBER POT, etc. ■ (**the pot**) a toilet. ■ the contents of any of such containers: *a pot of coffee.* **2** (**the pot**) the total sum of the bets made on a round in poker and other card games: *Jim raked in the pot.* ■ all the money contributed by a group of people for a particular purpose. **3** informal a potbelly. ▶ **v.** (**pot·ted, pot·ting**) [trans.] plant in a flowerpot: *pot the individual cuttings.*

– PHRASES **for the pot** for food or cooking: *at the age of fifteen weeks, the snails are ready for the pot.* **go to pot** informal deteriorate through neglect. **the pot calling the kettle black** used to convey that the criticisms a person is aiming at someone else could equally well apply to themselves. — **pot·ful** /-ˌfo͝ol/ **n.** (pl. **-fuls**). [OE *pott*.]

pot[2] ▶ **n.** informal cannabis. [1930s: prob. from Mex. Sp. *potiguaya* 'cannabis leaves.']

po·ta·ble /ˈpōtəbəl/ ▶ **adj.** formal safe to drink; drinkable. — **po·ta·bil·i·ty** /ˌpōtəˈbilətē/ **n.** [ME: from Fr. *potable*, from late L. *potabilis*, from L. *potare* 'to drink.']

po·tage /pôˈtäzʜ/ ▶ **n.** thick soup. [16th C.: from Fr. Cf. POTTAGE.]

pot·ash /ˈpätˌasʜ/ ▶ **n.** an alkaline potassium compound, esp. potassium carbonate or hydroxide. [17th C.: from *pot-ashes*, from obs. Du. *potasschen*.]

po·tas·si·um /pəˈtasēəm/ ▶ **n.** the chemical element of atomic number 19, a soft, silvery-white reactive metal of the alkali metal group. (Symbol: **K**) — **po·tas·sic** /-ˈtasik/ **adj.** (Mineral.). [19th C.: Latinization of POTASH or *potass* (from Fr. *potasse*).]

po·tas·si·um–ar·gon dat·ing ▶ **n.** Geol. a method of dating rocks from the relative proportions of radioactive potassium-40 and its decay product, argon-40.

po·tas·si·um hy·drox·ide ▶ **n.** a strongly alkaline white deliquescent compound, KOH, used in many industrial processes, e.g., soap manufacture.

po·tas·si·um ni·trate ▶ **n.** a white crystalline salt, KNO_3, occurring naturally and produced synthetically, used in fertilizer, as a meat preservative, and as a constituent of gunpowder. Also called SALTPETER and NITER.

po·ta·tion /pōˈtāsʜən/ ▶ **n.** archaic humorous a drink. ■ the action of drinking something, esp. alcohol. ■ (often **potations**) a drinking bout. [ME: from OFr., from L. *potatio(n-)*, from *potare* 'to drink.']

po·ta·to /pəˈtātō/ ▶ **n.** (pl. **-toes**) **1** a starchy plant tuber that is one of the most important food crops, cooked and eaten as a vegetable. ■ see SWEET POTATO. **2** the plant (*Solanum tuberosum*) of the nightshade family that produces these tubers on underground runners. [16th C.: from Sp. *patata*, var. of Taino *batata* 'sweet potato.']

po·ta·to chip ▶ **n.** a wafer-thin slice of potato fried until crisp and eaten as a snack.

pot-au-feu /ˌpôt ō ˈfœ/ ▶ **n.** a French soup of meat, typically boiled beef, and vegetables cooked in a large pot. [Fr., lit. 'pot on the fire.']

Pot·a·wat·o·mi /ˌpätəˈwätəmē/ ▶ **n.** (pl. same or **-mis**) **1** a member of an American Indian people living originally around Lake Michigan. **2** the Algonquian language of this people. ▶ **adj.** of or relating to this people or their language. [Ojibwa.]

pot·bel·ly /ˈpätˌbelē/ (also **pot bel·ly**) ▶ **n.** a large, protruding, rotund stomach. — **pot·bel·lied adj.**

pot·bel·ly stove (also **pot·bel·lied stove**) ▶ **n.** a small, bulbous-sided wood-burning stove.

pot·boil·er ▶ **n.** informal a book, painting, or recording produced merely to make the writer or artist a living.

pot·bound /ˈpätˌbound/ ▶ **adj.** (of a plant) having roots that fill the flowerpot, leaving no room for expansion.

pot cheese ▶ **n.** a coarse type of cottage cheese.

po·teen /pəˈtēn; -ˈcʜēn; pō -/ (also **po·theen**) ▶ **n.** esp. Irish alcohol made illicitly, typically from potatoes. [19th C.: from Irish *(fuisce) poitín* 'little pot (of whiskey),' dimin. of *pota* 'pot.']

Po·tem·kin /pəˈtemkin/ ▶ **adj.** informal having a false or deceptive appearance, esp. one for the purpose of propaganda. [1930s: from Grigori Aleksandrovich *Potyomkin* (1739–91), a favorite of Empress Catherine II of Russia, said to have ordered sham villages to be built for the empress's tour of the Crimea.]

potbelly stove

po·ten·cy /ˈpōtnsē/ ▶ **n.** (pl. **-cies**) **1** power or influence. ■ the strength of an intoxicant, as measured by the amount needed to produce a certain response: *the unexpected potency of the rum punch.* ■ (in homeopathy) the number of times a remedy has been diluted and succussed, taken as a measure of the strength of the effect it will produce. ■ Genet. the extent of the contribution of an allele toward the production of a phenotypic characteristic. ■ Biol. a capacity in embryonic tissue for developing into a particular specialized tissue or organ. **2** a male's ability to achieve erection or reach orgasm.

po·tent /ˈpōtnt/ ▶ **adj. 1** having great power, influence, or effect. **2** (of a male) able to achieve erection or reach an orgasm. — **po·tence n. po·tent·ly adv.** [ME: from L. *potent-* 'being powerful, being able,' from the v. *posse*.]

po·ten·tate /ˈpōtnˌtāt/ ▶ **n.** a monarch or ruler.

po·ten·tial /pəˈtencʜəl/ ▶ **adj.** [attrib.] having or showing the capacity to develop into something in the future. ▶ **n. 1** latent qualities or abilities that may be developed and lead to future success or usefulness. ■ (often **potential for/to do something**) the possibility of something happening or of someone doing something in the future: *the potential for accidents.* **2** Physics the quantity determining the energy of mass in a gravitational field or of charge in an electric field. — **po·ten·ti·al·i·ty** /pəˌtencʜēˈalətē/ **n. po·ten·tial·ize** /-ˌlīz/ **v. po·ten·tial·ly adv.**

po·ten·tial bar·ri·er ▶ **n.** Physics a region within a force field in which the potential is significantly higher than at points either side of it, so that a particle requires energy to pass through it.

po·ten·tial dif·fer·ence ▶ **n.** Physics the difference of electrical potential between two points.

po·ten·tial di·vid·er ▶ **n.** another term for VOLTAGE DIVIDER.

po·ten·tial en·er·gy ▶ **n.** Physics the energy possessed by a body by virtue of its position relative to others, stresses within itself, electric charge, and other factors. Compare with KINETIC ENERGY.

po·ten·ti·ate /pəˈtencʜēˌāt/ ▶ **v.** [trans.] tech. increase the power, effect, or likelihood of (something).

po·ten·ti·a·tion /pəˌtencʜēˈāsʜən/ ▶ **n.** Physiol. the increase in strength of nerve impulses along pathways that have been used previously, either short-term or long-term.

po·ten·til·la /ˌpōtnˈtilə/ ▶ **n.** a plant of the rose family belonging to a genus (*Potentilla*) that includes the cinquefoils, esp. (in gardening) a small shrub with bright yellow, red, orange, or pink flowers. [mod. L., based on L. *potent-* 'being powerful' + the dimin. suffix *-illa*.]

po·ten·ti·om·e·ter /pəˌtencʜēˈämətər/ ▶ **n. 1** an instrument for measuring an electromotive force by balancing it against the potential difference produced by passing a known current through a known variable resistance. **2** a variable resistor with a third adjustable terminal.

pot·head /ˈpätˌhed/ ▶ **n.** informal a person who smokes marijuana, esp. habitually.

po·theen ▶ **n.** esp. Irish var. of POTEEN.

poth·er /ˈpät͟hər/ ▶ **n.** [in sing.] literary a commotion. [16th C.: of unknown origin.]

pot·herb /ˈpätˌ(h)ərb/ ▶ **n.** any herb grown for culinary use.

pot·hold·er /ˈpätˌhōldər/ ▶ **n.** a piece of quilted or thick fabric for handling hot dishes and pans.

pot·hole /ˈpätˌhōl/ ▶ **n.** a deep natural underground cavity formed by the erosion of rock. ■ a deep circular hole in a riverbed formed by the erosion of the rock by the rotation of stones in an eddy. ■ a depression or hollow in a road surface caused by wear or subsidence. — **pot·holed adj.** [19th C.: from ME *pot* 'pit' (perh. of Scand. origin) + HOLE.]

pot·hook /ˈpätˌho͝ok/ ▶ **n. 1** esp. hist. a hook used for hanging a pot over a hearth or for lifting a hot pot. **2** dated a curved stroke in handwriting.

pot·hunt·er /ˈpätˌhəntər/ ▶ **n. 1** esp. archaic a person who hunts solely to achieve a kill. ■ a contestant only interested in the prize. **2** an amateur archaeologist.

po·tion /ˈpōsʜən/ ▶ **n.** a liquid with healing, magical, or poisonous properties: *a love potion.* [ME: from OFr., from L. *potio(n-)* '(poisonous) drink,' rel. to *potare* 'to drink.']

pot·latch /ˈpätˌlacʜ/ ▶ **n.** (among North American Indian peoples of the northwest coast) an opulent ceremonial feast at which possessions are given away or destroyed to display wealth or enhance prestige. ▶ **v.** [intrans.] hold such a feast or ceremony. [Chinook Jargon *pálač*, *pátłačč*, prob. from Nootka.]

pot lik·ker ▶ **n.** informal nonstandard spelling of POT LIQUOR, used in the southern US.

pot liq·uor ▶ **n.** liquid in which meat, fish, or vegetables have been boiled; stock.

pot·luck /ˈpätˈlək/ ▶ **n.** used in reference to a situation in which one must take a chance that whatever is available will prove to be good or acceptable. ■ a meal to which each guest contributes food: *a potluck supper.*

Po·tok /ˈpōtäk/, Chaim (1929–2002), US writer and theologian. A rabbi, his novels include *The Chosen* (1967).

Po·to·mac /pəˈtōmək/ a river in the eastern US that rises in the Appalachian Mountains in West Virginia and flows into Chesapeake Bay.

Po·to·sí /ˌpôtôˈsē/ a city in southern Bolivia, at an altitude of about 13,758 feet (4,205 m); pop. 112,000.

pot pie ▶ **n. 1** a meat and vegetable pie baked in a deep dish, often with a top crust only. **2** a stew with dumplings.

pot·pour·ri /ˌpōpəˈrē; ˌpōpo͝oˈrē/ ▶ **n.** (pl. **-ris**) a mixture of dried petals and spices. ■ a mixture of things, esp. a musical medley. [17th C.: from Fr., lit. 'rotten pot.']

pot roast ▶ **n.** meat covered and cooked slowly. ▶ **v.** (**pot-roast**) [trans.] cook (covered meat) slowly.

Pots·dam /ˈpätsˌdam/ a city in eastern Germany, southwest of Berlin, on the Havel River; pop. 95,000.

pot·sherd /ˈpätˌsʜərd/ ▶ **n.** a broken piece of ceramic material, esp. one found on an archaeological site.

pot·shot /ˈpätˌsʜät/ ▶ **n.** a shot aimed unexpectedly or at random at someone or something. ■ fig. a criticism, esp. a random or unfounded one. ■ a shot at a game bird or other animal purely to kill it for food, without regard to the rules of the sport. [19th C.: orig. a *shot* at an animal intended for the *pot*.]

pot·stick·er /ˈpätˌstikər/ ▶ **n.** a filled Chinese dumpling, typically crescent-shaped, esp. one that is pan-fried until brown on one side, then turned and simmered in a small amount of broth.

pot·tage /ˈpätij/ ▶ **n.** archaic soup or stew. [ME (as *potage*): from OFr. *potage* 'that which is put into a pot.']

pot·ted /ˈpätid/ ▶ **adj.** **1** (of a plant) planted or grown in a flowerpot. **2** [predic.] informal intoxicated by drink or drugs.

Pot·ter /ˈpätər/, Beatrix (1866–1943), English writer and illustrator. Her stories for children include *The Tale of Peter Rabbit* (1902).

pot·ter ▶ **n.** a person who makes pottery.

pot·ter's field ▶ **n.** hist. a burial place for paupers and strangers. [with biblical allusion to Matt. 27:7.]

pot·ter's wheel ▶ **n.** a horizontal revolving disk on which wet clay is shaped into pots or other round ceramic objects.

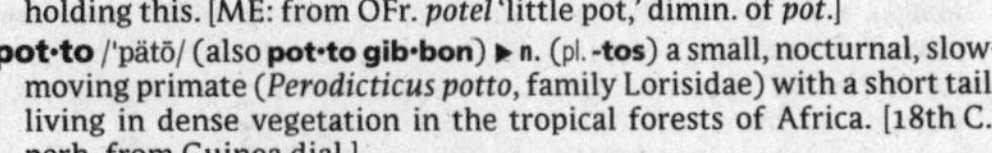

potter's wheel

pot·ter wasp ▶ **n.** a solitary wasp (genus *Eumenes*, family Eumenidae) that builds a flask-shaped nest of mud into which it seals an egg and a supply of food for the larva.

pot·ter·y /ˈpätərē/ ▶ **n.** (pl. **-er·ies**) pots, dishes, and other articles made of earthenware or baked clay. ■ the craft or profession of making such ware. ■ a factory or workshop where such ware is made.

pot·tle /ˈpätl/ ▶ **n.** archaic a measure for liquids equal to a half gallon. ■ a pot or container holding this. [ME: from OFr. *potel* 'little pot,' dimin. of *pot*.]

pot·to /ˈpätō/ (also **pot·to gib·bon**) ▶ **n.** (pl. **-tos**) a small, nocturnal, slow-moving primate (*Perodicticus potto*, family Lorisidae) with a short tail, living in dense vegetation in the tropical forests of Africa. [18th C.: perh. from Guinea dial.]

pot·ty[1] /ˈpätē/ ▶ **n.** (pl. **-ties**) informal a child's toilet. ■ informal a toilet.

pot·ty[2] ▶ **adj.** (**pot·ti·er**, **pot·ti·est**) informal, esp. Brit. **1** foolish; crazy: *he felt she really had gone potty.* ■ [predic.] extremely enthusiastic about or fond of. **2** [attrib.] insignificant or feeble: *that potty little mower.* — **pot·ti·ness n.** [19th C.: of unknown origin.]

pot·ty-mouthed ▶ **adj.** informal using or characterized by bad language: *a potty-mouthed rapper.* — **pot·ty mouth n.**

pot·ty-train ▶ **v.** [trans.] train (a child) to use a potty.

POTUS ▶ **abbr.** President of the United States.

pot-val·iant ▶ **adj.** archaic (of a person) courageous as a result of being drunk. — **pot-val·or n.**

pouch /pouch/ ▶ **n.** **1** a small bag, typically carried in a pocket or attached to a belt: *a tobacco pouch.* ■ a lockable bag for mail or dispatches. **2** a pocketlike abdominal receptacle in which marsupials carry their young during lactation. ■ any of a number of similar animal structures, such as those in the cheeks of rodents. ▶ **v.** [trans.] **1** put into a pouch. **2** make (part of a garment) hang like a pouch: *the muslin is lightly pouched over the belt.* — **pouched adj. pouch·y adj.** [ME (as a n.): from Old North. Fr. *pouche*, var. of OFr. *poche* 'bag.']

pouf[1] /po͝of/ ▶ **n.** var. of POOF[2]. ▶ **exclam.** var. of POOF[1].

pouf[2] ▶ **n.** a dress or part of a dress in which material has been gathered and stands away from the body. ■ a bouffant hairstyle. [19th C.: from Fr., of imitative origin.]

Pouil·ly-Fuis·sé /po͞o͞,yē fwēˈsā/ ▶ **n.** a dry white Chardonnay wine from Burgundy.

poult[1] /pōlt/ ▶ **n.** Farming a young domestic chicken, turkey, pheasant, or other fowl being raised for food. [ME: contr. of PULLET.]

poult[2] /po͞o(lt)/ (also **poult-de-soie** /də ˈswä/) ▶ **n.** a fine corded silk or taffeta, typically colored and used as a dress fabric. [1930s: from Fr. *poult-de-soie*, from *poult* (of unknown origin) + *de soie* 'of silk.']

poul·ter·er /ˈpōltərər/ ▶ **n.** a dealer in poultry and, typically, game. [16th C.: from archaic *poulter*, from OFr. *pouletier*.]

poul·tice /ˈpōltəs/ ▶ **n.** a soft, moist mass of material, typically of plant material or flour, applied to the body to relieve soreness and inflammation. ▶ **v.** [trans.] apply a poultice to: *he poulticed the wound.* [ME: from L. *pultes* (pl.), from *puls, pult-* 'porridge, pap.']

poul·try /ˈpōltrē/ ▶ **n.** domestic fowl, such as chickens. [ME: from OFr. *pouletrie*, from *poulet* 'pullet.']

pounce[1] /pouns/ ▶ **v.** [intrans.] (of an animal or bird of prey) spring or swoop suddenly so as to catch prey. ■ (of a person) spring forward suddenly so as to attack or seize someone or something. ■ fig. take sudden decisive action so as to grasp an opportunity. ■ fig. notice and take swift and eager advantage of a mistake, remark, or sign of weakness. ▶ **n.** a sudden swoop or spring. — **pounc·er n.** [ME: perh. from PUNCHEON[1].]

pounce[2] ▶ **n.** a fine resinous powder formerly used to prevent ink from spreading on unglazed paper or to prepare parchment to receive writing. ■ powdered charcoal or other fine powder dusted over a perforated pattern to transfer the design to the object beneath. ▶ **v.** [trans.] **1** smooth down by rubbing with pounce or pumice. **2** transfer (a design) by the use of pounce. — **pounc·er n.** [16th C. (as a v.): from Fr. *poncer*, based on L. *pumex* 'pumice.']

poun·cet box /ˈpounsət/ ▶ **n.** archaic a small box with a perforated lid used for holding perfume. [16th C.: perh. from *pounced box*.]

Pound /pound/, Ezra Weston Loomis (1885–1972), US poet. A modernist, his works include *Cantos* (series, 1917–70).

pound[1] /pound/ ▶ **n.** **1** (abbr.: **lb**) a unit of weight equal to 16 oz. avoirdupois (0.4536 kg), or 12 oz. troy (0.3732 kg). **2** (also **pound ster·ling**) (pl. **pounds ster·ling**)) the basic monetary unit of the UK, equal to 100 pence. ■ another term for PUNT[4]. ■ the basic monetary unit of several Middle Eastern countries, equal to 100 piastres. ■ the basic monetary unit of Cyprus, equal to 100 cents. ■ a monetary unit of the Sudan, equal to one tenth of a dinar.
– PHRASES **one's pound of flesh** something that one is strictly or legally entitled to, but that it is ruthless or inhuman to demand. [with allusion to Shakespeare's *Merchant of Venice*.] [OE *pund*, of Gmc. origin; from L. *(libra) pondo*, denoting a Roman 'pound weight' of 12 ounces.]

pound[2] ▶ **v.** [trans.] strike or hit heavily and repeatedly. ■ crush or grind (something) into a powder or paste. ■ [intrans.] beat, throb, or vibrate with a strong regular rhythm. ■ [intrans., with adverbial of direction] walk or run with heavy steps. ■ informal defeat (an opponent) in a resounding way.
– PHRASES **pound the beat** (of a police officer) patrol an allocated route or area. **pound the pavement** walk the streets in an effort to accomplish something. ■ search diligently for something, typically for a job.
– PHRASAL VERBS **pound something out** type something with heavy keystrokes: *she pounded out her poems.* ■ produce music by striking an instrument heavily and repeatedly. [OE *pūnian*; rel. to Du. *puin* 'rubble.']

pound[3] ▶ **n.** a building or other enclosure run by public officials where stray animals, esp. dogs, are held. ■ a place where illegally parked motor vehicles removed by the police are kept until their owners pay a fine in order to reclaim them. ▶ **v.** [trans.] archaic shut (an animal) in a pound. [ME: of uncert. origin.]

pound·age /ˈpoundij/ ▶ **n.** weight, esp. when regarded as excessive: *reduce excess poundage.*

pound·al /ˈpoundəl/ ▶ **n.** Physics a unit of force equal to that required to give a mass of one pound an acceleration of one foot per second per second. [19th C.: from POUND[1] + the suffix *-al*.]

pound cake ▶ **n.** a rich cake containing a pound, or equal weights, of each chief ingredient.

pound coin ▶ **n.** a coin worth one British pound sterling.

pound·er /ˈpoundər/ ▶ **n.** [usu. in comb.] **1** a person or thing weighing a specified number of pounds. ■ a gun designed to fire a shell weighing a specified number of pounds. **2** a person or thing that pounds something.

pound·ing /ˈpoundiNG/ ▶ **n.** repeated and heavy striking or hitting of someone or something: *the pounding of the surf* | fig. *technology stocks took a pounding.* ■ informal a resounding defeat: *a 100-86 pounding of the Rockets.*

pound note ▶ **n.** a banknote worth one British pound sterling, now replaced by the pound coin in England and Wales.

pound sign ▶ **n.** **1** the sign (#), representing a pound as a unit of weight or mass. ■ used to refer to this sign, esp. as represented on a telephone keypad or a computer keyboard. **2** the sign (£), representing a British pound sterling.

pound ster·ling ▶ **n.** see POUND[1] (sense 2).

pour /pôr/ ▶ **v.** [no obj., with adverbial of direction] (esp. of a liquid) flow rapidly in a steady stream. ■ [trans.] cause (a liquid) to flow from a container in a steady stream. ■ [trans.] serve (a drink) in this way. ■ [intrans.] (of rain) fall heavily. ■ (of people or things) come or go in a steady stream and in large numbers: *letters poured in.* ■ [trans.] (**pour something into**) donate something, esp. money, to (a particular enterprise or project) in large amounts. ■ [trans.] (**pour something out**) express one's feelings or thoughts in a full and unrestrained way. ■ (**pour oneself into**) humorous dress oneself in (a tight-fitting piece of clothing).
– PHRASES **when it rains it pours** proverb misfortunes or difficult situations tend to follow each other in rapid succession or to arrive all at the same time. **pour cold water on** see COLD. **pour it on** informal progress or work quickly or with all one's energy. **pour oil on troubled waters** try to settle a disagreement or dispute with words intended to placate or pacify those involved. **pour scorn on** see SCORN. — **pour·a·ble adj. pour·er n.** [ME: of unknown origin.]

pour·boire /po͝orˈbwär/ ▶ **n.** a gratuity; a tip. [Fr., from *pour boire*, lit. '(money) for drinking.']

pousse-ca·fé /ˌpo͞os kaˈfā/ ▶ **n.** (pl. pronunc. same) a glass of various liqueurs or cordials poured in successive layers, drunk immediately after coffee. [from Fr., lit. 'push coffee.']

Pous·sin /po͞oˈsan; -ˈsaN/, Nicolas (1594–1665), French painter. His work included biblical scenes, classical mythology, and historical landscapes.

pout[1] /pout/ ▶ **v.** [intrans.] push one's lips or one's bottom lip forward as an expression of petulant annoyance or in order to make oneself look attractive ■ (of a person's lips) be pushed forward in such a way. ▶ **n.** a pouting expression. — **pout·ing·ly adv. pout·y adj.** [ME (as a v.): perh. from the base of Swed. dial. *puta* 'be inflated.' Cf. POUT[2].]

pout[2] ▶ **n.** another term for EELPOUT. [OE *pūta* (only in *ǣlepūta* 'eelpout'); rel. to Du. *puit* 'frog, chub,' *puitaal* 'eelpout,' and perh. to POUT[1].]

pout·er /ˈpoutər/ ▶ **n.** a kind of pigeon able to inflate its crop considerably.

POV ▶ **abbr.** point of view.

pov·er·ty /ˈpävərtē/ ▶ **n.** the state of being extremely poor. ■ the state of being inferior in quality or insufficient in amount. ■ the renunciation of the right to individual ownership of property as part of a religious vow. [ME: from OFr. *poverte*, from L. *paupertas*, from *pauper* 'poor.']

pov·er·ty line ▶ **n.** the estimated minimum level of income needed to secure the necessities of life.

pov·er·ty-strick·en ▶ **adj.** extremely poor.

POW ▶ abbr. prisoner of war.

pow /pou/ ▶ exclam. expressing the sound of a blow or explosion: *Pow! Bombs went off on six beaches at once.* [19th C. (orig. US): imitative.]

pow·der /'poudər/ ▶ n. fine dry particles produced by the grinding, crushing, or disintegration of a substance. ■ (also **face powder**) a cosmetic in this form designed to be applied to a person's face. ■ dated a medicine or drug in this form, usually designed to be dissolved in a liquid. ■ (also **powder snow**) light, dry, newly fallen snow. ■ short for GUNPOWDER (sense 1). ▶ v. [trans.] **1** apply powder to (the face or body). ■ sprinkle or cover (a surface) with powder or a powdery substance: *broken glass powdered the floor.* **2** reduce (a substance) to a powder by drying or crushing it.
– PHRASES **take a powder** informal depart quickly. [ME: from OFr. *poudre*, from L. *pulvis, pulver-* 'dust.']

pow·der blue ▶ n. a soft, pale blue.

pow·der-coat ▶ v. [trans.] cover (an object) with a polyester or epoxy powder, which is then heated to fuse into a protective layer.

pow·dered sug·ar ▶ n. another term for CONFECTIONERS' SUGAR.

pow·der flask ▶ n. hist. a small container with a nozzle for carrying and dispensing gunpowder.

pow·der horn ▶ n. hist. the horn of an ox, cow, or similar animal used to hold gunpowder.

pow·der keg ▶ n. a barrel of gunpowder. ■ fig. a dangerous or volatile situation.

Pow·der·ly /'poudərlē/, Terence Vincent (1849–1924), US labor leader. Under his leadership 1879–93, the Knights of Labor was one of the first successful national labor unions in the US.

pow·der met·al·lur·gy ▶ n. the production and working of metals as fine powders.

pow·der mon·key ▶ n. hist. a boy employed on a sailing warship to carry powder to the guns. ■ informal a person who works with explosives.

pow·der puff (also **pow·der-puff**) ▶ n. a soft pad for applying powder to the skin, esp. the face. ▶ adj. [attrib.] **1** (of sports) played by women or girls only. **2** informal (of a person or thing) ineffectual.

Pow·der Riv·er a river that flows from northeastern Wyoming to join the Yellowstone River in Montana.

pow·der room ▶ n. used euphemistically to refer to a women's toilet in a public building.

pow·der·y /'poudərē/ ▶ adj. consisting of or resembling powder: *powdery snow.* ■ covered with powder: *her pale powdery cheeks.*

pow·der·y mil·dew ▶ n. mildew on a plant that is marked by a white floury covering consisting of conidia.

Pow·ell[1] /'pouəl/, Adam Clayton, Jr. (1908–72), US politician. A New York Democrat, he served in the US House of Representatives 1945–67, 1969–71.

Pow·ell[2], Anthony Dymoke (1905–2000), English writer. He wrote a sequence of 12 novels, *A Dance to the Music of Time* (1951–75).

Pow·ell[3], Colin Luther (1937–), US secretary of state 2001–05. The first black American to become chairman of the Joint Chiefs of Staff 1989–93, he commanded the 1990–91 US military operations (Desert Shield and Desert Storm) against Iraq.

Pow·ell[4], John Wesley (1834–1902), US geologist. He directed the US Geological Survey 1881–94.

Pow·ell[5], Lewis Franklin, Jr. (1907–98), US Supreme Court associate justice 1972–87.

pow·er /'pouər/ ▶ n. **1** the ability to do something or act in a particular way, esp. as a faculty or quality. **2** the capacity or ability to direct or influence the behavior of others or the course of events. ■ political or social authority or control, esp. that exercised by a government. ■ a right or authority that is given or delegated to a person or body: *emergency powers.* ■ the military strength of a state: *the sea power of Venice.* ■ a state or country, esp. one viewed in terms of its international influence and military strength: *a great colonial power.* ■ a person or organization that is strong or influential within a particular context. ■ a supernatural being, deity, or force. ■ [as adj.] informal denoting something associated with people who hold authority and influence, esp. in the context of business or politics: *a power suit.* ■ [with adj.] used in the names of movements aiming to enhance the status of a specified group: *gay power.* **3** physical strength and force exerted by something or someone: *the power of the storm.* ■ capacity or performance of an engine or other device. ■ the capacity of something to affect the emotions or intellect strongly: *the power of reason.* ■ [as adj.] denoting a sports player, team, or style of play that makes use of power rather than finesse: *a power pitcher.* ■ the magnifying capacity of a lens. **4** energy that is produced by mechanical, electrical, or other means and used to operate a device. ■ electrical energy supplied to an area, building, etc. ■ [as adj.] driven by such energy: *a power drill.* ■ [as adj.] power-assisted: *power brakes.* ■ Physics the time-rate of doing work, measured in watts or less frequently horsepower. **5** Math. the product obtained when a number is multiplied by itself a certain number of times: *2 to the power of 4 equals 16.* ▶ v. **1** [trans.] supply (a device) with mechanical or electrical energy. ■ (**power something up/down**) switch a device on or off: *the officer powered up the fighter's radar.* **2** [intrans., with adverbial of direction] move or travel with great speed or force: *they powered past the dock.* ■ [trans.] direct (something, esp. a ball) with great force: *he powered a header into the net.*
– PHRASES **power behind the throne** a person who exerts authority or influence without having formal status. **the powers that be** the authorities. [ME: from Anglo-Norman Fr. *poeir*, from an alt. of L. *posse* 'be able.']

pow·er base ▶ n. a source of authority, influence, or support, esp. in politics or negotiations.

pow·er·beads /'pouər,bēdz/ ▶ n. a bracelet or necklace of round beads that are purported to enhance the spiritual well-being of the wearer.

pow·er bloc (also **block**) ▶ n. an association of groups, esp. nations, acting as a single political force.

pow·er·boat /'pouər,bōt/ ▶ n. a motorboat designed for racing or recreation.

pow·er·bro·ker /'pouər,brōkər/ (also **pow·er brok·er**) ▶ n. a person who affects the distribution of political or economic power by exerting influence. — **pow·er·bro·ker·ing** (also **pow·er·brok·ing**) n. & adj.

pow·er dive ▶ n. a steep dive of an aircraft with the engines providing thrust. ▶ v. (**pow·er-dive**) [intrans.] perform a power dive.

pow·er for·ward ▶ n. Basketball a forward who plays in the low post and typically has good rebounding skills.

pow·er·ful /'pouərfəl/ ▶ adj. having great power or strength: *a fast, powerful car.* ■ (of a person, organization, or country) having control and influence over people and events. ■ having a strong effect on people's feelings or thoughts: *his photomontages are powerful antiwar images.* ▶ adv. [as submodifier] esp. dialect very. — **pow·er·ful·ly** /-f(ə)lē/ adv. **pow·er·ful·ness** n.

pow·er·house /'pouər,hous/ ▶ n. a person or thing of great energy, strength, or power. ■ another term for POWER PLANT.

pow·er·less /'pouərləs/ ▶ adj. [often with infin.] without ability, influence, or power. — **pow·er·less·ly** adv. **pow·er·less·ness** n.

pow·er·lift·ing /'pouər,lifting/ ▶ n. a form of competitive weightlifting. — **pow·er·lift·er** /-tər/ n.

pow·er line ▶ n. a cable carrying electrical power.

pow·er of at·tor·ney ▶ n. Law the authority to act for another person in legal or financial matters. ■ a legal document giving such authority to someone.

pow·er pack ▶ n. a self-contained and typically transportable unit that stores and supplies electrical power. ■ a transformer for converting an alternating current to a direct current at a different voltage.

pow·er plant ▶ n. an installation where electrical power is generated for distribution. ■ an engine or other apparatus that provides power.

pow·er play ▶ n. **1** tactics exhibiting or intended to increase a person's power or influence. ■ the use of physical strength to defeat one's opponent. **2** tactics in a team sport involving the concentration of players at a particular point. ■ Ice Hockey a situation in which a team has a numerical advantage over its opponents while one or more players is serving a penalty.

pow·er pol·i·tics ▶ plural n. [treated as sing. or pl.] political action by a person or group that makes use of or is intended to increase their power or influence.

pow·er se·ries ▶ n. Math. an infinite series of the form $\Sigma a_n x^n$ (where n is a positive integer). ■ a generalization of this for more than one variable.

pow·er-shar·ing ▶ n. a policy agreed between political parties or within a coalition to share responsibility for decision-making and political action.

pow·er sta·tion ▶ n. another term for POWER PLANT.

pow·er struc·ture ▶ n. **1** the hierarchy that encompasses the most powerful people in an organization. **2** the people in such a hierarchy.

pow·er take·off ▶ n. a device that transfers mechanical power from an engine to another piece of equipment.

pow·er train ▶ n. the mechanism that transmits the drive from the engine of a vehicle to its axle. ■ this mechanism, the engine, and the axle.

pow·er trip ▶ n. a self-aggrandizing quest for ever-increasing control over others.

pow·er us·er ▶ n. Comput. a user who needs products having the most features and the fastest performance.

pow·er walk·ing ▶ n. a form of cardiopulmonary exercise consisting of fast walking with rhythmic swinging of the arms.

Pow·ha·tan[1] /,pouə'tan; pou'hatn/ ▶ n. (pl. same or **-tans**) **1** a member of an American Indian people of eastern Virginia. **2** the Algonquian language of this people. ▶ adj. of or relating to this people or their language. [from the chief nicknamed *Powhatan*, from Virginia Algonquian *pawatan* 'river falls.']

Pow·ha·tan[2] (c. 1550–1618), Algonquian Indian chief; Indian name **Wahun-sen-a-cawh** or **Wahunsonacock**. He made peace with the colonists after his daughter Pocahontas married John Rolfe in 1614.

pow·wow /'pou,wou/ ▶ n. a North American Indian ceremony involving feasting, singing, and dancing. ■ a conference or meeting for discussion. ▶ v. [intrans.] informal hold a powwow; confer. [17th C.: from Narragansett *powáw* 'magician' (lit. 'he dreams').]

Pow·ys /'pōis/ a former Welsh kingdom.

pox /päks/ ▶ n. any of several viral diseases producing a rash of pimples that become pus-filled and leave pockmarks on healing. ■ (**the pox**) informal syphilis. ■ (**the pox**) hist. smallpox. ■ a plant disease that causes pocklike spots.
– PHRASES **a pox on** archaic used to express anger or intense irritation with someone or something. [ME: alt. of *pocks*, pl. of POCK.]

pox·vi·rus /'päks,vīrəs/ ▶ n. Med. any of a group of large DNA viruses that cause smallpox and similar infectious diseases in vertebrates.

Poz·nan' /'pōznan; 'pôz,nänyə/ a city in northwestern Poland; pop. 590,000. German name **Posen**.

Po·zsony /'pô,zhônyə/ Hungarian name for **Bratislava**.

poz·zo·la·na /,pätsə'länə/ ▶ **n.** a type of volcanic ash used for mortar or for cement that sets under water. [18th C.: from Ital., from *pozz(u)olana* '(earth) of *Pozzuoli*,' a town near Naples.]

pp ▶ **abbr.** ■ pages: *pp 71—73.* ■ parcel post. ■ past participle. ■ per person. ■ per procurationem (used when signing a letter on someone else's behalf). [L.] ■ Music pianissimo. ■ postpaid. ■ privately printed.

PPA ▶ **abbr.** phenylpropanolamine.

p.p.a. ▶ **abbr.** per power of attorney.

ppb (also **p.p.b.**) ▶ **abbr.** ■ (in publishing) paper, printing, and binding. ■ parts per billion.

ppd. ▶ **abbr.** ■ postpaid. ■ prepaid.

ppi Comput. ▶ **abbr.** pixels per inch, a measure of the resolution of display screens, scanners, and printers.

PPLO ▶ **abbr.** pleuropneumonia-like organism.

ppm ▶ **abbr.** ■ part(s) per million: *water containing 1 ppm fluoride.* ■ Comput. page(s) per minute.

PPO ▶ **abbr.** preferred-provider organization.

PPP ▶ **abbr.** ■ Pakistan People's Party. ■ (in computing) point to point protocol, which allows data conforming to the Internet protocol IP to be handled on a serial line. ■ purchasing power parity (a way of measuring what an amount of money will buy in different countries).

PPS ▶ **abbr.** ■ additional postscript.

PPV ▶ **abbr.** pay-per-view.

PR ▶ **abbr.** ■ parliamentary report. ■ press release. ■ prize ring. ■ proportional representation. ■ public relations. ■ Puerto Rico.

Pr. ▶ **abbr.** ■ preferred (stock). ■ Priest. ■ Prince. ■ Provençal. ▶ **symb.** the chemical element praseodymium.

pr ▶ **abbr.** ■ pair. ■ price.

prac·ti·ca·ble /'praktikəbəl/ ▶ **adj.** able to be done or put into practice successfully. ■ able to be used; useful. —**prac·ti·ca·bil·i·ty** /,praktikə'bilətē/ **n.** **prac·ti·ca·bly** /-blē/ **adv.**

prac·ti·cal /'praktikəl/ ▶ **adj.** **1** of or concerned with the actual doing or use of something. ■ (of an idea, plan, or method) likely to succeed or be effective in real circumstances; feasible. ■ suitable for a particular purpose: *a practical kitchen.* ■ (of a person) sensible and realistic in their approach to a situation or problem. **2** so nearly the case that it can be regarded as so; virtual: *a practical certainty.*

– PHRASES **for all practical purposes** virtually, or essentially. [16th C.: from archaic *practic* 'practical' (from OFr. *practique*, via late L. from Gk. *praktikos* 'concerned with action,' from *prattein* 'do, act') + **-al**.]

prac·ti·cal·i·ty /,prakti'kalətē/ ▶ **n.** (pl. **-ties**) **1** the quality or state of being practical. **2** (**practicalities**) the aspects of a situation that involve the actual doing or experience of something rather than theories or ideas: *the practicalities of living at sea.*

prac·ti·cal joke ▶ **n.** a trick played on someone in order to make them look foolish and to amuse others. —**prac·ti·cal jok·er n.**

prac·ti·cal·ly /'praktik(ə)lē/ ▶ **adv.** **1** virtually; almost. **2** in a practical manner.

prac·ti·cal nurse ▶ **n.** a nurse who has completed a training course of a lower standard than a registered nurse, esp. one who is licensed by the state.

prac·tice (Brit. **prac·tise**) /'praktəs/ ▶ **n.** **1** the actual application or use of an idea, belief, or method as opposed to theories about such application or use. ■ the customary, habitual, or expected procedure of something: *modern child-rearing practices.* ■ the carrying out or exercise of a profession, esp. that of a doctor or lawyer. ■ the business or premises of a doctor or lawyer: *Dr. Reamer has a practice in Pottsville.* ■ an established method of legal procedure. **2** repeated exercise in or performance of an activity or skill so as to acquire or maintain proficiency in it. ■ a period of time spent doing this: *daily choir practice.* ▶ **v.** [trans.] **1** perform (an activity) or exercise (a skill) repeatedly or regularly in order to improve or maintain one's proficiency. **2** carry out or perform (a particular activity, method, or custom) habitually or regularly. ■ actively pursue or be engaged in (a particular profession or occupation): *he began to practice law.* ■ observe the teaching and rules of (a particular religion): *you're free to practice your religion here.*

– PHRASES **in practice** in reality (used to refer to what actually happens as opposed to what is meant or believed to happen). **out of practice** not currently proficient in a particular activity or skill due to not having exercised or performed it for some time. **practice makes perfect** used to convey that regular exercise of an activity or skill is the way to become proficient in it. **practice what one preaches** do what one advises others to do. —**prac·tic·er n.** [ME: the v. from OFr. *practiser* or med. L. *practizare*, alt. of *practicare* 'perform, carry out,' from *practica* 'practice,' from Gk. *praktikē*, from *praktikos* (see **practical**).]

prac·ticed /'praktəst/ (Brit. **prac·tised**) ▶ **adj.** expert, typically as the result of much experience.

prac·ti·cum /'praktikəm/ ▶ **n.** (pl. **-cums**) a practical section of a course of study. [20th C.: from late L., neut. of *practicus* 'practical.']

prac·tise ▶ **v.** British spelling of **practice**.

prac·ti·tion·er /prak'tishənər/ ▶ **n.** a person actively engaged in a discipline, or profession, esp. medicine. [16th C.: extension of obs. *practitian*.]

prae- ▶ **prefix** (used esp. in words regarded as Latin or relating to Roman antiquity, e.g., *praenomen*) equivalent to **pre-**. [from L.]

prae·mu·ni·re /,prēmyōō'nīrē/ ▶ **n.** hist. the offense of maintaining papal jurisdiction in England. ■ a writ charging a sheriff to summon a person accused of this offense. [ME: from med. L., 'forewarn,' for L. *praemonere*, from *prae* 'beforehand' + *monere* 'warn.']

prae·no·men /prē'nōmən/ ▶ **n.** an ancient Roman's first or personal name. [L., from *prae* 'before' + *nomen* 'name.']

Prae·se·pe /prī'sēpē/ Astron. a large open cluster of stars in the constellation Cancer; the Beehive. [L., lit. 'manger, hive.']

prae·sid·i·um /pri'sidēəm; prī-/ ▶ **n.** Brit. var. of **presidium**.

prae·tor /'prētər/ (also **pre·tor**) ▶ **n.** Roman History each of two ancient Roman magistrates ranking below consul. —**prae·to·ri·al** /prē'tôrēəl/ **adj.** **prae·tor·ship** /'prētər,ship/ **n.** [from L. *praetor*, perh. from *prae* 'before' + *it-* 'gone' (from the v. *ire*).]

prae·to·ri·an /prē'tôrēən/ (also **pre·to·ri·an**) ▶ **adj.** Roman History of or having the powers of a praetor. ▶ **n.** a man of praetorian rank.

prae·to·ri·an guard ▶ **n.** Roman History the bodyguard of the Roman emperor.

prag·mat·ic /prag'matik/ ▶ **adj.** dealing with things sensibly and realistically in a way that is based on practical rather than theoretical considerations. ■ relating to philosophical or political pragmatism. ■ Ling. of or relating to pragmatics. —**prag·mat·i·cal·ly** /-ik(ə)lē/ **adv.** [16th C.: via L. from Gk. *pragmatikos* 'relating to fact,' from *pragma* 'deed' (from the stem of *prattein* 'do').]

prag·mat·ics /prag'matiks/ ▶ **plural n.** [usu. treated as sing.] the branch of linguistics dealing with language in use and the contexts in which it is used.

prag·mat·ic sanc·tion ▶ **n.** hist. an imperial or royal ordinance or decree that has the force of law.

prag·ma·tism /'pragmə,tizəm/ ▶ **n.** **1** a pragmatic attitude or policy: *ideology was tempered with pragmatism.* **2** Philos. an approach that assesses the truth of meaning of theories or beliefs in terms of the success of their practical application. —**prag·ma·tist n.** **prag·ma·tis·tic** /,pragmə'tistik/ **adj.**

Prague /präg/ the capital of the Czech Republic, in the northeastern part of the country, on the Vltava River; pop. 1,212,000. Czech name **Praha**.

pra·hu /'prou; 'prä,ōō/ ▶ **n.** var. of **proa**.

Prai·a /'prīə/ the capital of the Cape Verde Islands, on the island of São Tiago; pop. 62,000.

prai·rie /'pre(ə)rē/ ▶ **n.** a large open area of grassland, esp. in the Mississippi River valley. [18th C.: from Fr., from OFr. *praerie*, from L. *pratum* 'meadow.']

prai·rie chick·en (also **prairie hen**) ▶ **n.** a large North American grouse (genus *Tympanuchus*) found on the prairies, the male being noted for the display dance in which it inflates two orange neck pouches and makes a booming sound.

prai·rie dog ▶ **n.** a gregarious ground squirrel (genus *Cynomys*) that lives in interconnected burrows that may cover many acres. It is native to the grasslands of North America.

prai·rie oys·ter ▶ **n.** **1** a drink made with a raw egg and seasoning, drunk as a cure for a hangover. **2** (**prairie oysters**) the cooked testicles of a calf.

prai·rie schoon·er ▶ **n.** a covered wagon used by the 19th-century pioneers in crossing the North American prairies.

prai·rie wolf ▶ **n.** another term for **coyote**.

praise /prāz/ ▶ **v.** [trans.] express warm approval or admiration of: *we can't praise Christine enough.* ■ express one's respect and gratitude toward (a deity), esp. in song: *we praise God for past blessings.* ▶ **n.** the expression of approval or admiration for someone or something: *the audience was full of praise.* ■ the expression of respect and gratitude as an act of worship: *give praise to God.*

– PHRASES **praise be** archaic used as an expression of relief, joy, or gratitude. **sing the praises of** express enthusiastic approval or admiration of. —**praise·ful** /-fəl/ **adj.** [ME: from OFr. *preisier* 'to prize, praise,' from late L. *pretiare*, from L. *pretium* 'price.']

praise·wor·thy /'prāz,wər<u>th</u>ē/ ▶ **adj.** deserving approval and admiration. —**praise·wor·thi·ly** /-,wər<u>th</u>əlē/ **adv.** **praise·wor·thi·ness n.**

Pra·krit /'präk,rit/ ▶ **n.** any of the ancient or medieval vernacular dialects of northern and central India. [from Sanskrit *prākṛta* 'unrefined, natural.']

pra·line /'prä,lēn/ ▶ **n.** a smooth, sweet substance made by boiling nuts in sugar and grinding the mixture. ■ a crisp or semicrisp candy made by a similar process. [18th C.: from Fr., after Marshal de Plessis-*Praslin* (1598–1675), French soldier.]

prall·tril·ler /'präl,trilər/ ▶ **n.** a musical ornament consisting of one rapid alternation of the written note with the note immediately above it. [19th C.: from Ger., from *prallen* 'rebound' + *Triller* 'a trill.']

pram[1] /pram/ ▶ **n.** short for **perambulator** (sense 3). [19th C.]

pram[2] /präm; pram/ ▶ **n.** a flat-bottomed sailboat. ■ a small, flat-bottomed rowboat for fishing. [ME: from MDu. *prame*, Mid. Low Ger. *prâme*, perh. from Czech *prám* 'raft.']

PRONUNCIATION KEY ə *ago, up*; ər *over, fur*; a *hat*; ā *ate*; ä *car*; e *let*; ē *see*; i *fit*; ī *by*; NG *sing*; ō *go*; ô *law, for*; oi *toy*; ŏŏ *good*; ōō *goo*; ou *out*; TH *thin*; <u>TH</u> *then*; ZH *vision*

prance /prans/ ▶ v. [intrans.] (of a horse) move with high springy steps: *the pony was prancing.* ■ (of a person) walk or move around with ostentatious, exaggerated movements. ▶ n. an act or instance of prancing. — **pranc·er** n. [ME (as a v.): of unknown origin.]

pran·di·al /ˈprandēəl/ ▶ adj. [attrib.] formal, often humorous during or relating to dinner or lunch. ■ Med. during or relating to the eating of food. [19th C.: from L. *prandium* 'meal' + -AL.]

prank /praNGk/ ▶ n. a practical joke or mischievous act. — **prank·ish** adj. **prank·ish·ness** n. [16th C. (denoting a wicked deed): of unknown origin.]

prank·ster /ˈpraNGkstər/ ▶ n. a person fond of playing pranks.

prase /ˈprāz; prās/ ▶ n. a translucent, greenish variety of chalcedony. [18th C.: from Fr., via L. from Gk. *prasios* 'leek-green,' from *prason* 'leek.']

pra·se·o·dym·i·um /ˌprāzēōˈdimēəm/ ▶ n. the chemical element of atomic number 59, a soft silvery-white metal of the lanthanide series. (Symbol: **Pr**) [19th C.: mod. L., from Ger. *Praseodym*, from Gk. *prasios* 'leek-green' + Ger. *Didym* 'didymium.']

prat /prat/ ▶ n. informal a person's buttocks. [16th C.: of unknown origin.]

prate /prāt/ ▶ v. [intrans.] talk foolishly or at tedious length about something. — **prat·er** n. (rare). [ME: from MDu., Mid. Low Ger. *praten*, prob. of imitative origin.]

prat·fall /ˈpratˌfôl/ ▶ n. informal a fall on the buttocks. ■ a stupid and humiliating action.

prat·in·cole /ˈpratnˌkōl; ˈpratiNG-/ ▶ n. a long-winged, fork-tailed, insectivorous bird (genera *Glareola* and *Stiltia*, family Glareolidae) related to the plovers, resembling a swallow in flight and typically living near water. [18th C.: from mod. L. *pratincola*, from L. *pratum* 'meadow' + *incola* 'inhabitant.']

pra·tique /praˈtēk/ ▶ n. hist. permission granted to a ship to have dealings with a port. [17th C.: from Fr., lit. 'practice,' via Ital. from med. L. *practica*, fem. of *practicus* 'practical.']

Pra·to /ˈprätō/ a city in west central Italy; pop. 167,000.

prat·tle /ˈpratl/ ▶ v. [intrans.] talk at length foolishly. ▶ n. foolish or inconsequential talk: *this childish prattle.* — **prat·tler** /ˈpratlər; ˈpratl-ər/ n. [16th C.: from Mid. Low Ger. *pratelen*, from *praten* (see PRATE).]

prau /prou/ ▶ n. var. of PROA.

Prav·da /ˈprävdə/ a Russian daily newspaper 1912–91 of the Soviet Communist Party. [Russ., lit. 'truth.']

prawn /prôn/ ▶ n. a marine crustacean (*Leander* and other genera, class Malacostraca) that resembles a large shrimp. [ME: of unknown origin.]

prax·is /ˈpraksəs/ ▶ n. formal practice, as distinguished from theory: *praxis of Marxism.* ■ accepted practice or custom. [16th C.: via med. L. from Gk., lit. 'doing,' from *prattein* 'do.']

Prax·it·e·les /prakˈsitlˌēz/ (mid 4th century BC), Athenian sculptor. Only one of his works, *Hermes Carrying the Infant Dionysus*, survives.

pray /prā/ ▶ v. [intrans.] address a solemn request of thanks to a deity or other object of worship. ■ wish or hope strongly for a particular outcome. ▶ adv. formal archaic used as a preface to polite requests or instructions: *pray continue.* ■ used as a way of adding ironic or sarcastic emphasis to a question: *and what, pray, was the purpose of that?* [ME: from OFr. *preier*, from late L. *precare*, alt. of L. *precari* 'entreat.']

prayer /pre(ə)r/ ▶ n. a solemn request for help or expression of thanks addressed to God or an object of worship. ■ (**prayers**) a religious service, esp. a regular one, at which people gather in order to pray together. ■ an earnest hope or wish. [ME: from OFr. *preiere*, based on L. *precarius* 'obtained by entreaty,' from *prex, prec-* 'prayer.']

prayer beads ▶ n. a string of beads used in prayer, esp. a rosary.

prayer book ▶ n. a book containing the forms of prayer regularly used in Christian worship, esp. the Book of Common Prayer.

prayer·ful /ˈpre(ə)rfəl/ ▶ adj. (of an action or event) characterized by or expressive of prayer: *prayerful self-examination.* ■ (of a person) given to praying; devout. — **prayer·ful·ly** adv. **prayer·ful·ness** n.

prayer plant ▶ n. a Brazilian plant (*Maranta leuconeura*, family Marantaceae) with variegated leaves that are erect at night but lie flat during the day, grown as a houseplant.

prayer rug ▶ n. a small carpet used by Muslims for kneeling on when praying.

prayer shawl ▶ n. Judaism another term for TALLITH.

prayer wheel ▶ n. a revolving cylinder inscribed with or containing prayers, a revolution of which symbolizes the repetition of a prayer, used by Tibetan Buddhists.

pray·ing man·tis ▶ n. see MANTIS.

PRC ▶ abbr. People's Republic of China.

pre- ▶ prefix before (in time, place, order, degree, or importance): *preadolescent* | *precaution* | *precede.* [from L. *prae-*.]

preach /prēCH/ ▶ v. [intrans.] deliver a sermon or religious address to an assembled group of people, typically in church: *he preached to a large congregation* | [trans.] *our pastor will preach the sermon.* ■ [trans.] publicly proclaim or teach (a religious message or belief). ■ [trans.] earnestly advocate (a belief or course of action): *my parents have always preached toleration.* ■ give moral advice to someone in an annoying way: *viewers want to be entertained, not preached at.* [ME: from OFr. *prechier*, from L. *praedicare* 'proclaim,' in eccles. L. 'preach,' from *prae* 'before' + *dicare* 'declare.']

preach·er /ˈprēCHər/ ▶ n. a person who preaches, esp. a minister of religion.

preach·i·fy /ˈprēCHiˌfī/ ▶ v. (**-fies, -fied**) [intrans.] informal preach or moralize tediously.

preach·ment /ˈprēCHmənt/ ▶ n. dogmatic instruction and exhortation.

preach·y /ˈprēCHē/ ▶ adj. (**preach·i·er, preach·i·est**) informal having or revealing a tendency to give moral advice in a tedious or self-righteous way. — **preach·i·ness** n.

pre·a·dapt /ˌprēəˈdapt/ ▶ v. [trans.] Biol. adapt (an organism) for life in conditions it has yet to encounter. — **pre·ad·ap·ta·tion** /ˈprēˌadˌapˈtāSHən/ n.

pre·ad·o·les·cent /ˈprēˌadlˈesənt/ ▶ adj. (of a child) having nearly reached adolescence. ■ of, relating to, or occurring in the two or three years preceding adolescence. ▶ n. a preadolescent child. — **pre·ad·o·les·cence** n.

pre·ag·ri·cul·tur·al /ˈprēˌagriˈkəlCHərəl/ ▶ adj. denoting a people, tribe, or culture that has not developed agriculture as a means of subsistence.

pre-AIDS ▶ adj. following infection with HIV but before the full development of AIDS. ■ before the recognition of AIDS as a disease.

Preak·ness /ˈprēknis/ ▶ n. an annual horse race for three-year-olds at Pimlico racetrack in Baltimore, Maryland.

pre·am·ble /ˈprēˌambəl/ ▶ n. a preliminary or preparatory statement; an introduction. ■ Law the introductory part of a statute or deed, stating its purpose, aims, and justification. — **pre·am·bu·lar** /prēˈambyələr/ adj. (formal). [ME: from OFr. *preambule*, from med. L. *praeambulum*, from late L. *praeambulus* 'going before.']

pre·amp /ˈprēˌamp/ ▶ n. short for PREAMPLIFIER.

pre·am·pli·fi·er /prēˈampləˌfīər/ ▶ n. an electronic device that amplifies a very weak signal, for example from a microphone or pickup, and transmits it to a main amplifier.

preb·end /ˈprebənd/ ▶ n. hist. the portion of the revenues of a cathedral or collegiate church formerly granted to a canon or member of the chapter as his stipend. ■ the property from which such a stipend was derived. ■ the tenure of this as a benefice. ■ another term for PREBENDARY. [ME: from OFr. *prebende*, from late L. *praebenda*, neut. pl. gerundive of L. *praebere* 'to grant,' from *prae* 'before' + *habere* 'hold, have.']

pre·ben·dal /priˈbendəl; ˈprebəndəl/ ▶ adj. of or relating to a prebend or a prebendary: *the prebendal manor.*

preb·en·dar·y /ˈprebənˌderē/ ▶ n. (pl. **-dar·ies**) an honorary canon. ■ hist. a canon of a cathedral or collegiate church whose income originally came from a prebend. — **preb·en·dar·y·ship** /-ˌSHip/ n.

pre·bi·ot·ic /ˈprēˌbīˈätik/ ▶ adj. existing or occurring before the emergence of life.

Pre·bo·re·al /prēˈbôrēəl/ ▶ adj. Geol. of, relating to, or denoting the first climatic stage of the postglacial period in northern Europe, between the Younger Dryas and Boreal stages (about 10,000 to 9,000 years ago). ■ [as n.] (**the Preboreal**) the Preboreal climatic stage.

prec. ▶ abbr. ■ preceded. ■ preceding.

pre·cal·cu·lus /prēˈkalkyələs/ ▶ n. a course in mathematics that prepares a student for calculus.

Pre·cam·bri·an /prēˈkambrēən; -kām-/ ▶ adj. Geol. of, relating to, or denoting the earliest eon, preceding the Cambrian period and the Phanerozoic eon. Compare with CRYPTOZOIC. ■ [as n.] (**the Precambrian**) the Precambrian eon or the system of rocks deposited during it.

pre·can·cer·ous /prēˈkansərəs/ ▶ adj. Med. (of a cell or medical condition) likely to develop into cancer if untreated: *precancerous skin lesions.*

pre·car·i·ous /priˈke(ə)rēəs/ ▶ adj. **1** not securely held or in position; dangerously likely to fall or collapse. **2** dependent on chance; uncertain. — **pre·car·i·ous·ly** adv. **pre·car·i·ous·ness** n. [17th C.: from L. *precarius* 'obtained by entreaty' (from *prex, prec-* 'prayer') + -OUS.]

pre·cast /ˈprēˈkast/ ▶ v. (past and past part. **pre·cast**). [trans.] [usu. as adj.] (**precast**) cast (an object or material, typically concrete) in its final shape before positioning: *precast concrete beams.*

prec·a·to·ry /ˈprekəˌtôrē/ ▶ adj. formal of, relating to, or expressing a wish or request. ■ Law (in a will) expressing a wish or intention of the testator. [17th C.: from late L. *precatorius*, from *precat-* 'prayed,' from the v. *precari*.]

pre·cau·tion /priˈkôSHən/ ▶ n. a measure taken in advance to prevent something dangerous, unpleasant, or inconvenient from happening. — **pre·cau·tion·ar·y** /-ˌnerē/ adj. [16th C.: from Fr. *précaution*, from late L. *praecautio(n-)*, from L. *praecavere*, from *prae* 'before' + *cavere* 'take heed.']

pre·cede /priˈsēd/ ▶ v. [trans.] come before (something) in time. ■ come before in order or position: *read the chapters that precede the recipes.* ■ go in front or ahead of. ■ (**precede something with**) preface or introduce something with: *he preceded the book with a collection of poems.* [ME: from OFr. *preceder*, from L. *praecedere*, from *prae* 'before' + *cedere* 'go.']

prec·e·dence /ˈpresədəns; priˈsēdns/ ▶ n. the condition of being considered more important than someone or something else; priority in rank. ■ the order to be observed by people of different rank, according to an acknowledged or legally determined system.

prec·e·dent ▶ n. /ˈpresid(ə)nt/ an earlier event or action regarded as an example or guide to be considered in subsequent similar circumstances. ■ Law a previous case or legal decision that may be or (**binding precedent**) must be followed in subsequent similar cases. ▶ adj. /priˈsēd(ə)nt/ preceding in time, order, or importance: *a precedent case.*

pre·cen·tor /pri'sentər/ ▶ **n.** a person who leads a congregation in its singing or (in a synagogue) prayers. — **pre·cent v. pre·cen·tor·ship** /-,sHip/ **n.** [17th C.: from Fr. *précenteur* or L. *praecentor*, from *praecent-* 'sung before,' from the v. *praecinere*, from *prae* 'before' + *canere* 'sing.']

pre·cept /'prē,sept/ ▶ **n.** **1** a general rule intended to regulate behavior or thought. **2** a writ or warrant. — **pre·cep·tive** /pri'septiv/ **adj.** [ME: from L. *praeceptum*, neut. past part. of *praecipere* 'warn, instruct,' from *prae* 'before' + *capere* 'take.']

pre·cep·tor /'prē,septər; pri'septər/ ▶ **n.** a teacher or instructor. — **pre·cep·to·ri·al** /pri,sep'tôrēəl; 'prē-/ **adj. pre·cep·tor·ship** /-,sHip/ **n.**

pre·ces·sion /prə'sesHən/ ▶ **n.** Physics the slow movement of the axis of a spinning body around another axis due to a torque (such as gravitational influence) acting to change the direction of the first axis. It is seen in the circle slowly traced out by the pole of a spinning gyroscope. — **pre·cess** /prē'ses; 'prē,ses/ **v. pre·ces·sion·al** /pri'sesHənl/ **adj.** [16th C.: from late L. *praecessio(n-)*, from *praecedere* (see PRECEDE).]

pre·ces·sion of the e·qui·noxes ▶ **n.** Astron. the slow retrograde, or westward, motion of equinoctial points along the ecliptic. ■ the resulting earlier occurrence of equinoxes in each successive sidereal year.

pre-Chris·tian /prē'krisCHən/ ▶ **adj.** of or relating to a time before Christ or the advent of Christianity.

pre·cinct /'prē,siNGkt/ ▶ **n.** **1** a district of a city or town as defined for police purposes. ■ the police station situated in such a subdivision. ■ an electoral district of a city or town served by a single polling place. **2** (usu. **precincts**) the area within the walls or perceived boundaries of a particular building or place. ■ an enclosed or clearly defined area of ground around a cathedral, church, or college. [ME: from med. L. *praecinctum*, neut. past part. of *praecingere* 'encircle,' from *prae* 'before' + *cingere* 'gird.']

pre·ci·os·i·ty /,presHē'äsətē/ ▶ **n.** overrefinement in art, music, or language, esp. in the choice of words.

pre·cious /'presHəs/ ▶ **adj.** **1** (of an object, substance, or resource) of great value; not to be wasted or treated carelessly. ■ greatly loved or treasured by someone. ■ [attrib.] informal used to express the speaker's contempt for someone or something greatly valued by another person: *you and your precious schedule.* ■ [attrib.] informal used for emphasis, often in an ironic context: *a precious lot you know about dogs!* **2** derog. affectedly concerned with elegant or refined behavior, language, or manners. ▶ **n.** used as a term of address to a beloved person.
– PHRASES **precious little/few** extremely little or few (used for emphasis). — **pre·cious·ly adv. pre·cious·ness n.** [ME: from OFr. *precios*, from L. *pretiosus* 'of great value,' from *pretium* 'price.']

pre·cious cor·al ▶ **n.** another term for RED CORAL.

pre·cious met·als ▶ **plural n.** gold, silver, and platinum.

pre·cious stone ▶ **n.** a highly attractive and valuable piece of mineral or rock, used esp. in jewelry.

prec·i·pice /'presəpəs/ ▶ **n.** a very steep rock face or cliff, typically a tall one. [16th C.: from Fr. *précipice* or L. *praecipitium* 'abrupt descent,' from *praeceps, praecip(it)-* 'steep, headlong.']

pre·cip·i·tan·cy /pri'sipətənsē/ ▶ **n.** rashness or suddenness of action.

pre·cip·i·tant /pri'sipətənt/ ▶ **n.** a cause of a particular action or event. ■ esp. Psychol. a cause or stimulus that precipitates a particular condition. ■ Chem. a substance that causes the precipitation of a specified substance. — **pre·cip·i·tance n.**

pre·cip·i·tate ▶ **v.** /pri'sipə,tāt/ [trans.] **1** cause (an event or situation, typically a bad one) to happen suddenly, unexpectedly, or prematurely: *the incident precipitated a political crisis.* ■ cause to move suddenly and with force: *suddenly the ladder broke, precipitating them down into a heap.* ■ (**precipitate someone/something into**) send someone or something suddenly into a particular state or condition: *they were precipitated into a conflict.* **2** (usu. **be precipitated**) Chem. cause (a substance) to be deposited in solid form from a solution. ■ cause (drops of moisture or particles of dust) to be deposited from the atmosphere or from a vapor or suspension. ▶ **adj.** /pri'sipətit/ done, made, or acting suddenly or without careful consideration. ■ (of an event or situation) occurring suddenly or abruptly. ▶ **n.** /pri'sipətit; -ə,tāt/ Chem. a substance precipitated from a solution. — **pre·cip·i·ta·ble** /pri'sipətəbəl/ **adj. pre·cip·i·tate·ly** /pri'sipətətlē/ **adv. pre·cip·i·tate·ness** /pri'sipətətnəs/ **n.** [16th C.: from L. *praecipitat-* 'thrown headlong,' from the v. *praecipitare*, from *praeceps, praecip(it)-* 'headlong,' from *prae* 'before' + *caput* 'head.']

pre·cip·i·ta·tion /pri,sipə'tāsHən/ ▶ **n.** **1** Chem. the action or process of precipitating a substance from a solution. **2** rain, snow, sleet, or hail that falls to the ground. **3** archaic the fact or quality of acting suddenly and rashly.

pre·cip·i·ta·tor /pri'sipə,tātər/ ▶ **n.** an apparatus for causing precipitation, esp. a device for removing dust from a gas.

pre·cip·i·tin /pri'sipətin/ ▶ **n.** Biochem. an antibody that produces a visible precipitate when it reacts with its antigen. [20th C.: from the v. PRECIPITATE + -IN[1].]

pre·cip·i·tous /pri'sipətəs/ ▶ **adj.** **1** dangerously high or steep. ■ (of a change for the worse) sudden and dramatic. **2** (of an action) done suddenly and without careful consideration. — **pre·cip·i·tous·ly adv. pre·cip·i·tous·ness n.** [17th C.: from obs. Fr. *précipiteux*, from L. *praeceps, praecip(it)-* 'steep, headlong' (see PRECIPITATE).]

pré·cis /prā'sē; 'prāsē/ ▶ **n.** (pl. same) a summary or abstract of a text or speech. ▶ **v.** (**pré·cises** /prā'sēz; 'prāsēz/, **pré·cised, pré·cis·ing**) [trans.] make a précis of (a text or speech). [18th C.: from Fr. *précis*, lit. 'precise.']

pre·cise /pri'sīs/ ▶ **adj.** marked by exactness and accuracy of expression or detail. ■ (of a person) exact, accurate, and careful about details. ■ [attrib.] used to emphasize that one is referring to an exact and particular thing. — **pre·cise·ness n.** [ME: from OFr. *prescis*, from L. *praecis-* 'cut short,' from the v. *praecidere*, from *prae* 'in advance' + *caedere* 'to cut.']

pre·cise·ly /pri'sīslē/ ▶ **adv.** in exact terms; without vagueness. ■ exactly (used to emphasize the complete accuracy or truth of a statement). ■ used as a reply to assert emphatic agreement with or confirmation of a statement: *"You mean it was a conspiracy?" "Precisely."*

pre·ci·sion /pri'sizHən/ ▶ **n.** the quality, condition, or fact of being exact and accurate. ■ [as adj.] marked by or adapted for accuracy and exactness: *a precision instrument.* ■ tech. refinement in a measurement, calculation, or specification, esp. as represented by the number of digits given. Compare with ACCURACY.

pre·clas·si·cal /prē'klasəkəl/ ▶ **adj.** of or relating to a time before a period regarded as classical, esp. in music, literature, or history.

pre·clin·i·cal /prē'klinikəl/ ▶ **adj.** Med. relating to or denoting a stage preceding a clinical stage, in particular: ■ relating to or denoting the first, chiefly theoretical, stage of a medical education. ■ relating to or denoting the stage in a disease prior to the appearance of symptoms that make a diagnosis possible. ■ relating to or denoting the stage of drug testing that precedes the clinical stage.

pre·clude /pri'klo͞od/ ▶ **v.** [trans.] prevent from happening; make impossible. ■ (**preclude someone from**) (of a situation or condition) prevent someone from doing something. — **pre·clu·sion** /-'klo͞ozHən/ **n. pre·clu·sive** /-'klo͞osiv; -ziv/ **adj.** [15th C.: from L. *praecludere*, from *prae* 'before' + *claudere* 'to shut.']

pre·co·cial /pri'kōsHəl/ Zool. ▶ **adj.** (of a young bird or other animal) hatched or born in an advanced state and able to feed itself almost immediately. Also called NIDIFUGOUS. Often contrasted with ALTRICIAL. ■ (of a particular species) having such young. ▶ **n.** a precocial bird. [19th C.: from mod. L. *Praecoces* (pl. of L. *praecox* 'mature before its time') + -IAL.]

pre·co·cious /pri'kōsHəs/ ▶ **adj.** (of a child) having developed certain abilities or proclivities at an earlier age than usual. ■ (of behavior or ability) indicative of such development: *a precocious talent for computing.* ■ (of a plant) flowering or fruiting earlier than usual. — **pre·co·cious·ly adv. pre·co·cious·ness n. pre·coc·i·ty** /pri'käsətē/ **n.** [17th C.: from L. *praecox, praecoc-* (from *praecoquere* 'ripen fully,' from *prae* 'before' + *coquere* 'to cook') + -IOUS.]

pre·cog·ni·tion /,prēkäg'nisHən/ ▶ **n.** foreknowledge of an event, esp. foreknowledge of a paranormal kind. — **pre·cog·ni·tive** /prē'kägnətiv/ **adj.** [ME: from late L. *praecognitio(n-)*, based on L. *cognoscere* 'know.']

pre-Co·lum·bi·an /kə'ləmbēən/ ▶ **adj.** of or relating to the history and cultures of the Americas before the arrival of Columbus in 1492.

pre·con·ceived /,prēkən'sēvd/ ▶ **adj.** (of an idea or opinion) formed before having the evidence for its truth or usefulness.

pre·con·cep·tion /,prēkən'sepsHən/ ▶ **n.** a preconceived idea or prejudice.

pre·con·cert /,prēkən'sərt/ ▶ **v.** [trans.] archaic arrange or organize (something) in advance.

pre·con·di·tion /,prēkən'disHən/ ▶ **n.** a condition that must be fulfilled before other things can happen or be done. ▶ **v.** [trans.] **1** (usu. **be preconditioned**) condition (an action) to happen in a certain way: *inquiries are always preconditioned by cultural assumptions.* ■ condition or influence (a person or animal) by exposing them to stimuli or information prior to the relevant behavioral situation. **2** bring (something) into the desired state for use.

pre-Con·quest ▶ **adj.** occurring or existing before the Norman Conquest of England.

pre·con·scious /prē'känCHəs/ ▶ **adj.** Psychoanal. of or associated with a part of the mind below the level of immediate conscious awareness, from which unrepressed memories and emotions can be recalled. ▶ **n.** (**one's/the preconscious**) Psychol. the part of the mind in which preconscious thoughts or memories reside. — **pre·con·scious·ness n.**

pre·cor·di·um /prē'kôrdēəm/ ▶ **n.** Anat. the region or the thorax immediately in front of the heart. — **pre·cor·dial** /-'kôrdēəl/ **adj.** [19th C.: sing. of L. *praecordia* 'diaphragm, entrails.']

pre·cur·sor /'prē,kərsər; pri'kər-/ ▶ **n.** a person or thing that comes before another of the same kind; a forerunner. ■ Biochem. a substance from which another is formed, esp. by metabolic reaction. [ME: from L. *praecursor*, from *praecurs-* 'preceded,' from *praecurrere*, from *prae* 'beforehand' + *currere* 'to run.']

pre·cur·so·ry /pri'kərsərē/ ▶ **adj.** preceding something in time, development, or position; preliminary.

pred. ▶ **abbr.** predicate.

pre·da·cious /pri'dāsHəs/ (also **pre·da·ceous**) ▶ **adj.** (of an animal) predatory. — **pre·da·cious·ness n. pre·dac·i·ty** /pri'dasətē/ **n.** [18th C.: from L. *praeda* 'booty' + -ACIOUS.]

pre·date /prē'dāt/ ▶ **v.** [trans.] exist or occur at a date earlier than (something): *this letter predates her illness.*

pre·da·tion /pri'dāsHən/ ▶ **n.** Zool. the preying of one animal on others. [15th C.: from L. *praedatio(n-)* 'taking of booty,' from the v. *praedari* 'seize as plunder,' from *praeda* 'booty.']

pred·a·tor /'predətər/ ▶ **n.** an animal that naturally preys on others. ■ fig. a rapacious, exploitative person or group. ■ fig. a company that tries to take over another.

pred·a·to·ry /'predə,tôrē/ ▶ **adj.** relating to or denoting an animal or animals preying naturally on others. ■ fig. seeking to exploit or oppress others. — **pred·a·to·ri·ly** /,predə'tôrəlē/ **adv.** **pred·a·to·ri·ness n.**

pred·a·to·ry pric·ing ▶ **n.** the pricing of goods or services at such a low level that other suppliers cannot compete and are forced to leave the market.

pre·de·cease /,prēdi'sēs/ formal ▶ **v.** [trans.] die before (another person, typically someone related by blood or marriage): *his second wife predeceased him.*

pred·e·ces·sor /'predə,sesər; 'prē-/ ▶ **n.** a person who held a job or office before the current holder. ■ a thing followed or replaced by another. [ME: from late L. *praedecessor*, from L. *prae* 'beforehand' + *decessor* 'retiring officer' (from *decedere* 'depart').]

pre·des·ti·nar·i·an /prē,destə'ne(ə)rēən/ ▶ **n.** a person who believes in the doctrine of predestination. ▶ **adj.** upholding, affirming, or relating to the doctrine of predestination.

pre·des·ti·nate ▶ **v.** /prē'destə,nāt/ [trans.] predestine. ▶ **adj.** predestined.

pre·des·ti·na·tion /prē,destə'nāsʜən/ ▶ **n.** (as a doctrine in Christian theology) the divine foreordaining of all that will happen, esp. with regard to the salvation of some and not others. It has been particularly associated with St. Augustine of Hippo and Calvin.

pre·des·tine /prē'destin/ ▶ **v.** [trans.] (usu. **be predestined**) (of God) destine (someone) for a particular fate or purpose. ■ determine (an outcome or course of events) in advance by divine will or fate. [ME: from OFr. *predestiner* or eccles. L. *praedestinare* (see PREDESTINATE).]

pre·de·ter·mine /,prēdi'tərmən/ ▶ **v.** [trans.] establish or decide in advance. ■ (usu. **be predetermined**) predestine (an outcome or course of events). — **pre·de·ter·min·a·ble adj.** **pre·de·ter·mi·nate** /-'tərmənit/ **adj.** **pre·de·ter·mi·na·tion** /-,tərmə'nāsʜən/ **n.**

pre·de·ter·min·er /,prēdi'tərmənər/ ▶ **n.** Gram. a word or phrase that occurs before a determiner, quantifying the noun phrase, e.g. *both* or *a lot of*.

pre·di·al /'prēdēəl/ ▶ **adj.** archaic of, relating to, or consisting of land or farming. ■ hist. relating to or denoting a slave or tenant attached to farms or the land. ■ hist. (of a tithe) consisting of agricultural produce. ▶ **n.** hist. a predial slave. [ME: from med. L. *praedialis*, from L. *praedium* 'farm.']

predic. ▶ **abbr.** predicate.

pred·i·ca·ble /'predikəbəl/ ▶ **adj.** that may be predicated or affirmed. ▶ **n.** a thing that is predicable. ■ (usu. **predicables**) (in Aristotelian logic) each of the classes to which predicates belong, usually listed as: genus, species, difference, property, and accident. — **pred·i·ca·bil·i·ty** /,predikə'bilətē/ **n.** [16th C.: from med. L. *praedicabilis*, from L. *praedicare*.]

pre·dic·a·ment /pri'dikəmənt/ ▶ **n.** **1** a difficult, unpleasant, or embarrassing situation. **2** Philos., archaic (in Aristotelian logic) each of the ten "categories," often listed as: substance or being, quantity, quality, relation, place, time, posture, having or possession, action, and passion. [ME: from late L. *praedicamentum*, from L. *praedicare*.]

pred·i·cate ▶ **n.** /'predikət/ Gram. the part of a sentence or clause containing a verb and stating something about the subject (e.g., *went home* in *John went home*). ■ Logic something that is affirmed or denied concerning an argument of a proposition. ▶ **v.** /'predə,kāt/ [trans.] **1** Gram. Logic state, affirm, or assert (something) about the subject of a sentence or an argument of proposition: *aggression is predicated of those who act aggressively.* **2** (**predicate something on/upon**) found or base something on: *the theory of structure on which later chemistry was predicated.* — **pred·i·ca·tion** /,predə'kāsʜən/ **n.** [ME: from L. *praedicatum* 'something declared,' neut. of *praedicatus* 'declared,' past part. of the v. *praedicare*, from *prae* 'beforehand' + *dicare* 'make known.']

pred·i·cate cal·cu·lus /'predəkət/ ▶ **n.** the branch of symbolic logic that deals with propositions containing predicates, names, and quantifiers.

pred·i·cate nom·i·na·tive ▶ **n.** Gram. a word in the nominative case that completes a copulative verb, such as *son* in the sentence *Charlie is my son*.

pred·i·ca·tive /'predə,kātiv; -ikətiv/ ▶ **adj.** **1** Gram. (of an adjective or noun) forming or contained in the predicate, as *old* in *the dog is old* (but not in *the old dog*). Contrasted with ATTRIBUTIVE. ■ denoting a use of the verb *to be* to assert something about the subject. **2** Logic acting as a predicate. — **pred·i·ca·tive·ly adv.**

pred·i·ca·tor /'predə,kātər/ ▶ **n.** (in systemic grammar) a verb phrase considered as a constituent of clause structure, along with subject, object, and adjunct.

pre·dict /pri'dikt/ ▶ **v.** [trans.] say or estimate that (a specified thing) will happen in the future or will be a consequence of something. — **pre·dic·tor** /-tər/ **n.** [17th C.: from L. *praedict-* 'made known beforehand, declared,' from the v. *praedicere*, from *prae-* + *dicere* 'say.']

pre·dict·a·ble /pri'diktəbəl/ ▶ **adj.** able to be predicted. ■ esp. derog. behaving or occurring in a way that is expected. — **pre·dict·a·bil·i·ty** /-,diktə'bilətē/ **n.** **pre·dict·a·bly** /-blē/ **adv.**

pre·dic·tion /pri'diksʜən/ ▶ **n.** a thing predicted; a forecast. ■ the action of predicting something.

pre·dic·tive /pri'diktiv/ ▶ **adj.** relating to or having the effect of predicting an event or result: *rules are not predictive of behavior.* — **pre·dic·tive·ly adv.**

pre·di·gest /,prēdī'jest; ,prēdə-/ ▶ **v.** (of an animal) treat (food) by a process similar to digestion in order to make it more digestible when subsequently eaten. ■ fig. make (language, ideas, etc.) easier to understand or appreciate, typically by simplification. — **pre·di·ges·tion** /-'jescʜən/ **n.**

pre·di·lec·tion /,predl'eksʜən; ,prēdl-/ ▶ **n.** a preference or special liking for something; a bias in favor of something. [18th C.: from Fr. *prédilection*, from L. *praedilect-* 'preferred,' from the v. *praediligere*, from *prae* 'in advance' + *diligere* 'to select.']

pre·dis·pose /,prēdi'spōz/ ▶ **v.** [trans.] (**predispose someone to/to do something**) make someone liable or inclined to a specified attitude, action, or condition.

pre·dis·po·si·tion /,prē,dispə'zisʜən/ ▶ **n.** a liability or tendency to suffer from a particular condition, hold a particular attitude, or act in a particular way.

pred·ni·sone /'prednə,sōn; -,zōn/ ▶ **n.** Med. a synthetic drug similar to cortisone, used to relieve rheumatic and allergic conditions and to treat leukemia. [1950s: perh. from *pre(gnane)* + *d(ie)n(e)* + *(cort)isone*.]

pre·dom·i·nance /pri'dämənəns/ ▶ **n.** the state or condition of being greater in number or amount. ■ the possession or exertion of control or power.

pre·dom·i·nant /pri'dämənənt/ ▶ **adj.** present as the strongest or main element. ■ having or exerting control or power. [16th C.: from OFr., from med. L. *predominant-*, from *predominari*.]

pre·dom·i·nant·ly /pri'dämənəntlē/ ▶ **adv.** mainly; for the most part.

pre·dom·i·nate /pri'dämə,nāt/ ▶ **v.** [intrans.] be the strongest or main element; be greater in number or amount: *small-scale producers predominate in the south.* ■ have or exert control or power. [16th C.: from med. L. *predominat-* 'predominated,' from the v. *predominari* (see PRE-, DOMINATE).]

pre·dom·i·nate·ly /pri'dämənətlē/ ▶ **adv.** another term for PREDOMINANTLY.

pre·e·clamp·si·a /,prē-i'klampsēə/ ▶ **n.** a condition in pregnancy characterized by high blood pressure, sometimes with fluid retention and proteinuria. — **pre·e·clamp·tic** /-'klamptik/ **adj. & n.**

pre·em·bry·o /prē'embrē,ō/ ▶ **n.** tech. a human embryo or fertilized ovum in the first fourteen days after fertilization, before implantation in the uterus has occurred. — **pre·em·bry·on·ic adj.**

pree·mie /'prēmē/ ▶ **n.** (pl. **-mies**) informal a baby born prematurely. [1920s (as *premy*): from PREMATURE + -IE.]

pre·em·i·nent /prē'emənənt/ ▶ **adj.** surpassing all others; very distinguished in some way. — **pre·em·i·nence n.** [ME: from L. *praeeminent-* 'towering above, excelling,' from the v. *praeeminere*, from *prae* 'before' + *eminere* 'stand out.']

pre·em·i·nent·ly /prē'emənəntlē/ ▶ **adv.** [sentence adverb] above all; in particular.

pre·empt /prē'empt/ ▶ **v.** [trans.] **1** take action in order to prevent (an event) from happening; forestall. ■ act in advance of (someone) to prevent them from doing something. ■ (of a broadcast) interrupt or replace (a scheduled program). **2** acquire or appropriate (something) in advance. ■ take (something, esp. public land) for oneself so as to have the right of preemption. **3** [intrans.] Bridge make a preemptive bid. ▶ **n.** Bridge a preemptive bid. — **pre·emp·tor** /-tər/ **n.** [19th C.: back-form. from PREEMPTION.]

pre·emp·tion /prē'empsʜən/ ▶ **n.** **1** the purchase of goods or shares by one person or party before the opportunity is offered to others. ■ hist. the right to purchase public land in this way. **2** the action of preempting or forestalling, esp. of making a preemptive attack. ■ the interruption or replacement of a scheduled radio or television program. [17th C.: from med. L. *praeemptio(n-)*, from the v. *praeemere*, from *prae* 'in advance' + *emere* 'buy.']

pre·emp·tive /prē'emptiv/ ▶ **adj.** serving or intended to forestall something, esp. to prevent attack by disabling the enemy: *a preemptive strike.* ■ relating to the purchase of goods or shares by one person or party before the opportunity is offered to others: *preemptive rights.* ■ Bridge denoting a bid, typically an opening bid, intended to be so high that it prevents or interferes with effective bidding by the opponents.

preen /prēn/ ▶ **v.** [intrans.] (of a bird) straighten and clean its feathers with its beak: *robins preened at the pool's edge* | [trans.] *the pigeon preened her feathers.* ■ (of a person) devote effort to making oneself look attractive and then admire one's appearance. ■ (**preen oneself**) congratulate or pride oneself. — **preen·er n.** [ME: appar. a var. of obs. *prune* (based on L. *ungere* 'anoint').]

pre·ex·ist /,prē-ig'zist/ ▶ **v.** [intrans.] [usu. as adj.] (**preexisting**) exist at or from an earlier time. ■ [trans.] exist at or from an earlier time than (something). — **pre·ex·ist·ence** /-'zistəns/ **n.** **pre·ex·ist·ent** /-'zistənt/ **adj.**

pre·ex·ist·ing con·di·tion ▶ **n.** a medical condition existing at a time when new insurance is applied for, for which treatment is not covered by the insurance.

pre·ex·po·sure /,prē-ik'spōzʜər/ ▶ **n.** previous or premature exposure to something. ▶ **adj.** occurring or existing before exposure, esp. exposure to a disease or infection: *preexposure vaccination.*

pref. ▶ **abbr.** ■ preface. ■ preferred (with reference to a preferred stock).

pre·fab /prē'fab; 'prē,fab/ informal ▶ **n.** a prefabricated building. ▶ **adj.** prefabricated. [1930s: abbrev.]

pre·fab·ri·cate /prē'fabri,kāt/ ▶ **v.** [trans.] [usu. as adj.] (**prefabricated**) manufacture sections of (a building or piece of furniture) to enable quick or easy assembly on site: *prefabricated homes.* — **pre·fab·ri·ca·tion** /-ˌfabrəˈkāshən/ **n.**

pref·ace /ˈprefəs/ ▶**n.** an introduction to a book, typically stating its subject, scope, or aims. ■ the introduction or preliminary part of a speech or event. ■ Christian Church the introduction to the central part of the Eucharist, forming the first part of the canon or prayer of consecration. ▶**v.** [trans.] provide (a book) with a preface. ■ (**preface something with/by**) introduce or begin (a speech or event) with or by doing something. — **pref·a·to·ry** /ˈprefəˌtôrē/ **adj.** [ME: via OFr. from med. L. *praefatia*, alt. of L. *praefatio(n-)* 'words spoken beforehand,' from the v. *praefari*, from *prae* 'before' + *fari* 'speak.']

pre·fect /ˈprēˌfekt/ ▶**n.** **1** a chief officer, magistrate, or regional governor in certain countries. ■ a senior magistrate in the ancient Roman world. **2** esp. Brit. in some schools, a senior student authorized to enforce discipline. — **pre·fec·tor·al** /prēˈfektərəl/ **adj.** **pre·fec·to·ri·al** /ˌprēˌfekˈtôrēəl/ **adj.** [ME (sense 2): from OFr., from L. *praefectus*, past part. of *praeficere* 'set in authority over,' from *prae* 'before' + *facere* 'make.']

pre·fec·ture /ˈprēˌfekchər/ ▶**n.** a district under the government of a prefect. ■ a prefect's office or tenure. ■ the official residence or headquarters of a prefect. — **pre·fec·tur·al** /prēˈfekchərəl/ **adj.**

pre·fer /priˈfər/ ▶**v.** (**pre·ferred, pre·fer·ring**) [trans.] **1** like (one thing or person) better than another or others; tend to choose: *I prefer Venice to Rome.* **2** formal submit (a charge or a piece of information) for consideration: *the police will prefer charges.* **3** archaic promote (someone) to a prestigious position: *he was preferred to the post.* [ME: from OFr. *preferer*, from L. *praeferre*, from *prae* 'before' + *ferre* 'to bear, carry.']

pref·er·a·ble /ˈpref(ə)rəbəl/ ▶**adj.** more desirable or suitable. — **pref·er·a·bil·i·ty** /ˌpref(ə)rəˈbilətē/ **n.**

pref·er·a·bly /ˈpref(ə)rəblē/ ▶**adv.** [sentence adverb] ideally; if possible.

pref·er·ence /ˈpref(ə)rəns/ ▶**n.** **1** a greater liking for one alternative over another or others. ■ a thing preferred. ■ favor shown to one person or thing over another or others. **2** Law a prior right or precedence, esp. in connection with the payment of debts: *debts owed to the community should be accorded a preference.*

pre·fer·ment /priˈfərmənt/ ▶**n.** promotion or appointment to a position or office.

pre·ferred stock ▶**n.** stock that entitles the holder to a fixed dividend, whose payment takes priority over that of common-stock dividends.

pre·fig·ure /prēˈfigyər/ ▶**v.** [trans.] **1** be an early indication or version of (something). **2** archaic imagine beforehand. — **pre·fig·u·ra·tion** /prēˌfigyəˈrāshən/ **n.** **pre·fig·ur·a·tive** /prēˈfigyərətiv/ **adj.** **pre·fig·ure·ment n.** [ME: from eccles. L. *praefigurare* 'represent beforehand,' from *prae* 'before' + *figurare* 'to form, fashion.']

pre·fix /ˈprēˌfiks/ ▶**n.** a word, letter, or number placed before another. ■ an element placed at the beginning of a word to adjust or qualify its meaning, e.g., *ex-*, *non-*, *re-* or (in some languages) as an inflection. ■ a title placed before a name, e.g., *Mr.* ▶**v.** [trans.] add (something) at the beginning as a prefix or introduction. ■ add a prefix or introduction to (something). — **pre·fix·a·tion** /ˌprēfikˈsāshən/ **n.** [16th C. (as a v.): from OFr. *prefixer*, from L. *praefixus* 'fixed in front,' from the verb *praefigere*, from *prae* 'before' + *figere* 'to fix.']

pre·form /ˈprēˈfôrm/ ▶**v.** [trans.] [usu. as adj.] (**preformed**) form (something) beforehand: *a preformed pool.*

pre·for·ma·tion /ˌprēfôrˈmāshən/ ▶**n.** the action or process of preforming something. ■ Biol., hist. the theory, now discarded, that an embryo develops from a complete miniature version of the organism. Often contrasted with EPIGENESIS. — **pre·for·ma·tion·ist** /-ist/ **n. & adj.**

pre·fron·tal /prēˈfrəntl/ ▶**adj.** [attrib.] **1** Anat. in or relating to the foremost part of the frontal lobe of the brain. **2** Zool. relating to or denoting a bone in front of the eye socket in some lower vertebrates. ▶**n.** Zool. a prefrontal bone.

preg·gers /ˈpregərz/ ▶**adj.** [predic.] esp. Brit. informal pregnant.

preg·na·ble /ˈpregnəbəl/ ▶**adj.** vulnerable to attack; not impregnable: *the fort's pregnable approaches.* [ME: from OFr. *prenable*, lit. 'takable,' from L. *prehendere* 'seize.']

preg·nan·cy /ˈpregnənsē/ ▶**n.** (pl. **-cies**) the condition or period of being pregnant. ■ a case or situation of being pregnant.

preg·nant /ˈpregnənt/ ▶**adj.** **1** (of a woman or female animal) having a child or young developing in the uterus. ■ having been in such a condition for a specified time: *she was six months pregnant.* **2** full of meaning; significant or suggestive: *a pregnant pause.* — **preg·nant·ly adv.** [ME: from L. *praegnant-*, prob. from *prae* 'before' + the base of *gnasci* 'be born.']

pre·heat /prēˈhēt/ ▶**v.** [trans.] heat (something, esp. an oven or grill) beforehand: *preheat the oven to 350°.*

pre·hen·sile /prēˈhensəl; -ˌsīl/ ▶**adj.** (chiefly of an animal's limb or tail) capable of grasping. — **pre·hen·sil·i·ty** /prēˌhenˈsilətē/ **n.** [18th C.: from Fr. *préhensile*, from L. *prehens-* 'grasped,' from the v. *prehendere*, from *prae* 'before' + *hendere* 'to grasp.']

pre·hen·sion /prēˈhenchən/ ▶**n.** **1** Zool. Psychol. the action of grasping or seizing. **2** Philos. an interaction of a subject with an event or entity that involves perception but not necessarily cognition.

pre·his·tor·ic /ˌprē(h)iˈstôrik/ ▶**adj.** of, relating to, or denoting the period before written records. ■ informal very old, primitive, or out of date. — **pre·his·to·ri·an** /-ˈstôrēən/ **n.** **pre·his·tor·i·cal·ly** /-ik(ə)lē/ **adv.**

pre·his·to·ry /prēˈhist(ə)rē/ ▶**n.** the period of time before written records. ■ the events or conditions leading up to a particular occurrence or phenomenon: *the prehistory of capitalism.*

pre·ig·ni·tion /ˌprē-igˈnishən/ ▶**n.** the premature combustion of the fuel–air mixture in an internal combustion engine.

pre·im·plan·ta·tion /ˌprē-imˌplanˈtāshən/ (also **pre-im·plan·ta·tion**) ▶**adj.** Zool. Med. occurring or existing between the fertilization of an ovum and its implantation in the wall of the uterus.

pre·judge /prēˈjəj/ ▶**v.** [trans.] form a judgment on (an issue or person) prematurely and without adequate information. — **pre·judg·ment** (also **pre·judge·ment**) **n.**

prej·u·dice /ˈprejədəs/ ▶**n.** **1** preconceived opinion not based on reason or experience. ■ dislike, hostility, or unjust behavior formed on such a basis: *racial prejudice.* **2** esp. Law harm or injury that results or may result from some action or judgment. ▶**v.** [trans.] **1** give rise to prejudice in (someone); make biased: *the statement might prejudice the jury.* **2** esp. Law cause harm to (a state of affairs): *delay is likely to prejudice the child's welfare.* [ME (sense 2 of the **n.**): from OFr., from L. *praejudicium*, from *prae* 'in advance' + *judicium* 'judgment.']

prej·u·diced /ˈprejədəst/ ▶**adj.** having or showing a dislike or distrust that is derived from prejudice; bigoted.

prej·u·di·cial /ˌprejəˈdishəl/ ▶**adj.** harmful to someone or something; detrimental. — **prej·u·di·cial·ly adv.**

pre·kin·der·gar·ten /prēˈkindərˌgärtn; -ˌgärdn/ (abbr.: **pre-K.**) ▶**n.** day care with some educational content for children younger than five, provided by elementary schools or preschools.

prel·a·cy /ˈpreləsē/ ▶**n.** (pl. **-cies**) esp. archaic the government of the Christian Church by clerics of high social rank and power. ■ the office or rank of a prelate. ■ (**the prelacy**) prelates collectively. [ME: from Anglo-Norman Fr. *prelacie*, from med. L. *prelatia*, from *praelatus* (see PRELATE).]

pre·lap·sar·i·an /ˌprēlapˈse(ə)rēən/ ▶**adj.** Theol. or literary characteristic of the time before the Fall of Man; innocent and unspoiled. [19th C.: from PRE- 'before,' on the pattern of *sublapsarian*.]

prel·ate /ˈprelət/ ▶**n.** formal hist. a bishop or other high ecclesiastical dignitary. — **pre·lat·ic** /priˈlatik/ **adj.** **pre·lat·i·cal** /priˈlatikəl/ **adj.** [ME: from OFr. *prelat*, from med. L. *praelatus* 'civil dignitary,' past part. of L. *praeferre* 'carry before.']

prel·a·ture /ˈprelәchər; -ˌchŏŏr/ ▶**n.** the office, rank, or sphere of authority of a prelate. ■ (**the prelature**) prelates collectively.

pre·lim /ˈprēˌlim/ ▶**n.** informal **1** an event that precedes or prepares for another, in particular: ■ a preliminary examination, esp. at a university. ■ a preliminary round in an athletic competition. **2** (**prelims**) the pages preceding the main text of a book, including the title, contents, and preface.

pre·lim·i·nar·y /priˈliməˌnerē/ ▶**adj.** denoting an action or event preceding or done in preparation for something fuller or more important: *preliminary talks.* ▶**n.** (pl. **-nar·ies**) an action or event preceding or preparing for something fuller or more important. ■ (**preliminaries**) business or talk, esp. of a formulaic or polite nature, taking place before an action or event. ■ a preliminary round in a sporting competition. ■ (**preliminaries**) fuller form of PRELIMS (see PRELIM (sense 2)). — **pre·lim·i·nar·i·ly** /-ˌliməˈnerəlē/ **adv.** [17th C.: from mod. L. *praeliminaris* or Fr. *préliminaire*, from L. *prae* 'before' + *limen, limin-* 'threshold.']

pre·lin·guis·tic /ˌprēlingˈgwistik/ ▶**adj.** of or at a stage before the development of language (by the human species) or the acquisition of speech (by a child).

pre·lit·er·ate /prēˈlitərət/ ▶**adj.** of, relating to, or denoting a society or culture that has not developed the use of writing.

pre·load /prēˈlōd/ ▶**v.** [trans.] load beforehand. ■ give (a mechanical component) an internal load independent of any working load, to reduce distortion or noise in operation. ▶**n.** something loaded or applied as a load beforehand.

prel·ude /ˈprelˌ(y)o͞od; ˈprāˌl(y)o͞od/ ▶**n.** **1** an action or event serving as an introduction to something more important. **2** an introductory piece of music, most commonly an orchestral opening to an act of an opera, the first movement of a suite, or a piece preceding a fugue. ■ a short piece of music of a similar style, esp. for the piano. ■ the introductory part of a poem or other literary work. ▶**v.** [trans.] serve as a prelude or introduction to. — **pre·lu·di·al** /priˈlo͞odēəl; prā-/ **adj.** [16th C.: from Fr. *prélude*, from med. L. *praeludium*, from L. *praeludere* 'play beforehand,' from *prae* 'before' + *ludere* 'to play.']

prem. ▶**abbr.** premium.

pre·ma·lig·nant /ˌprēməˈlignənt/ ▶**adj.** another term for PRECANCEROUS.

pre·ma·ture /ˌprēməˈchŏŏr; -ˈt(y)ŏŏr/ ▶**adj.** occurring or done before the usual or proper time; too early. ■ (of a baby) born before the end of the full term of gestation, esp. three or more weeks before. — **pre·ma·ture·ly adv.** **pre·ma·tu·ri·ty** /-ˈchŏŏritē; -ˈt(y)ŏŏr-/ **n.** [ME: from L. *praematurus* 'very early,' from *prae* 'before' + *maturus* 'ripe.']

pre·max·il·lar·y /prēˈmaksəˌlerē/ ▶**adj.** Anat. situated in front of the maxilla.

pre·med /ˈprēˈmed/ ▶**n.** **1** a program of premedical studies. ■ a student in such a program. **2** short for PREMEDICATION. ▶**adj.** short for PREMEDICAL.

pre·med·i·cal /prēˈmedikəl/ ▶**adj.** of, relating to, or engaged in study in preparation for medical school.

pre·med·i·ca·tion /ˌprēˌmedəˈkāshən/ ▶**n.** medication that is given in preparation for an operation or other treatment.

PRONUNCIATION KEY ə *ago, up*; ər *over, fur*; a *hat*; ā *ate*; ä *car*; e *let*; ē *see*; i *fit*; ī *by*; NG *sing*; ō *go*; ô *law, for*; oi *toy*; o͝o *good*; o͞o *goo*; ou *out*; TH *thin*; T̲H̲ *then*; ZH *vision*

pre·med·i·tate /pri'medə,tāt; prē-/ ▶ **v.** [trans.] [usu. as adj.] (**premeditated**) think out or plan (an action, esp. a crime) beforehand: *premeditated murder.* — **pre·med·i·ta·tion** /-,medə'tāsʜən/ **n.** [16th C.: from L. *praemeditat-* 'thought out before,' from the v. *praemeditari,* from *prae* 'before' + *meditari* 'meditate.']

pre·men·stru·al syn·drome /prē'menstr(ōō)əl/ (abbr.: **PMS**) ▶ **n.** any of a complex of symptoms (including emotional tension and fluid retention) experienced by some women in the days immediately before menstruation.

pre·mier /prē'm(y)i(ə)r; 'prēmēər; 'prē,mi(ə)r/ ▶ **adj.** [attrib.] first in importance, order, or position; leading. ■ of earliest creation. ▶ **n.** a Prime Minister or other head of government. ■ (in Australia and Canada) the chief minister of a government of a state or province. [15th C.: from OFr., 'first,' from L. *primarius* 'principal.']

pre·mier cru /prə'myā 'kry; 'krē/ ▶ **n.** (pl. **pre·miers crus** /prə'myā 'kry; 'krē(z)/) (chiefly in French official classifications) a wine of a superior grade, or the vineyard that produces it. Compare with **GRAND CRU.** [Fr., lit. 'first growth.']

pre·miere /prē'myer; -'mi(ə)r/ ▶ **n.** the first performance of a musical or theatrical work or the first showing of a movie. ▶ **v.** [trans.] give the first performance of. ■ [intrans.] (of a musical or theatrical work or a film) have its first performance. [19th C.: Fr. *première,* fem. of *premier.*]

pre·mier·ship /prē'm(y)ir,sʜip; 'prēmēər-; 'prē,mi(ə)r-/ ▶ **n.** the office or position of a Prime Minister or other head of government.

pre·mil·len·ni·al /,prēmə'lenēəl/ ▶ **adj.** existing or occurring before a new millennium. ■ Christian Theol. relating to or believing in premillennialism.

pre·mil·len·ni·al·ism /,prēmə'lenēə,lizəm/ ▶ **n.** (among some Christian Protestants) the doctrine that the prophesied millennium of blessedness will begin with the imminent Second Coming of Christ. Compare with **POSTMILLENNIALISM.** — **pre·mil·len·ni·al·ist n.**

Prem·in·ger /'preminjər/, Otto Ludwig (1906–86), US director, born in Austria. His movies include *Exodus* (1960).

prem·ise ▶ **n.** /'premis/ Logic a previous statement or proposition from which another is inferred or follows as a conclusion. ■ an assertion or proposition that forms the basis for a work or theory. ▶ **v.** [trans.] (**premise something on/upon**) base an argument, theory, or undertaking on: *the reforms were premised on our findings.* ■ state or presuppose (something) as a premise: [with clause] *one thought premised that the cosmos is indestructible.* [ME: from OFr. *premisse,* from med. L. *praemissa (propositio)* '(proposition) set in front,' from L. *praemittere,* from *prae* 'before' + *mittere* 'send.']

prem·is·es /'preməsəz/ ▶ **plural n.** a house or building, together with its land and outbuildings, occupied by a business or considered in an official context.

pre·mi·um /'prēmēəm/ ▶ **n.** (pl. **-ums**) **1** an amount to be paid for an insurance policy. **2** a sum added to an ordinary price or charge. ■ a sum added to interest or wages; a bonus. ■ [as adj.] relating to or denoting a commodity or product of superior quality and therefore a higher price. ■ Stock Market the amount by which the price of a share or other security exceeds its issue price, its nominal value, or the value of the assets it represents: *the fund has traded at a premium of 12%.* **3** something given as a reward, prize, or incentive.
– PHRASES **at a premium 1** scarce and in demand. **2** above the usual or nominal price. **put** (or **place**) **a premium on** regard or treat as particularly valuable or important. [17th C.: from L. *praemium* 'booty, reward,' from *prae* 'before' + *emere* 'buy, take.']

pre·mix /'prē'miks/ ▶ **v.** [trans.] mix in advance. ▶ **n.** a mixture that is provided already mixed, in particular: ■ a ready-mixed feed for cattle or horses. ■ a preparation of the dry components of a building material such as concrete or plaster.

pre·mo·lar /prē'mōlər/ ▶ **n.** a tooth situated between the canine and the molar teeth. An adult human normally has eight.

pre·mo·ni·tion /,prēmə'nisʜən; ,prem-/ ▶ **n.** a strong feeling of something about to happen, esp. something unpleasant. — **pre·mon·i·to·ry** /prē'mänə,tôrē/ **adj.** [16th C.: from Fr. *prémonition,* from late L. *praemonitio(n-),* from L. *praemonere,* from *prae* 'before' + *monere* 'warn.']

pre·mor·bid /prē'môrbəd/ ▶ **adj.** Med. Psychiatry preceding the symptoms of disease or disorder.

pre·mo·tor /'prē'mōtər/ ▶ **adj.** [attrib.] Anat. relating to or denoting the anterior part of the motor cortex in the frontal lobe of the brain, which is concerned with coordinating voluntary movement.

pre·na·tal /prē'nātl/ ▶ **adj.** before birth; during or relating to pregnancy: *prenatal development.* — **pre·na·tal·ly** /-'nātl-ē/ **adv.**

pre-need ▶ **adj.** denoting a scheme in which one pays in advance for a service or facility: *pre-need funeral sales.*

pre·nup /prē'nəp/ ▶ **n.** informal a prenuptial agreement. [1990s: abbrev.]

pre·nup·tial /prē'nəpsʜəl; -cʜəl/ ▶ **adj.** existing or occurring before marriage: *prenuptial pregnancy.* ■ Zool. existing or occurring before mating.

pre·nup·tial a·gree·ment ▶ **n.** an agreement made by a couple before they marry concerning the ownership of their respective assets should the marriage fail.

pre·oc·cu·pa·tion /,prē,äkyə'pāsʜən/ ▶ **n.** the state or condition of being preoccupied or engrossed with something. ■ a subject or matter that engrosses someone.

pre·oc·cu·py /prē'äkyə,pī/ ▶ **v.** (**-pies, -pied**) [trans.] (of a matter or subject) dominate or engross the mind of (someone) to the exclusion of other thoughts: *she was **preoccupied with** paying the bills.* [16th C.: from **PRE-** + **OCCUPY.**]

pre-op /'prē,äp/ informal ▶ **adj.** short for **PREOPERATIVE.** ▶ **n.** a tranquilizing injection or other treatment administered in preparation for a surgical operation.

pre·op·er·a·tive /prē'äpərətiv/ ▶ **adj.** denoting, administered in, or occurring in the period before a surgical operation. — **pre·op·er·a·tive·ly adv.**

pre·or·bit·al /prē'ôrbətl/ ▶ **adj.** esp. Zool. situated in front of the orbit or eye socket.

pre·or·dain /,prēôr'dān/ ▶ **v.** [trans.] (usu. **be preordained**) decide or determine (an outcome or course of action) beforehand.

pre-owned /prē'ōnd/ ▶ **adj.** secondhand.

prep[1] /prep/ ▶ **n.** informal a student or graduate of a preparatory school.

prep[2] informal ▶ **v.** (**prepped, prep·ping**) [trans.] prepare (something); make ready. ■ [intrans.] prepare oneself for an event. ▶ **n.** preparation.

prep. ▶ **abbr.** preposition.

pre·pack·age /prē'pakij/ ▶ **v.** [trans.] [usu. as adj.] (**prepackaged**) pack or wrap (goods, esp. food) on the site of production or before sale: *prepackaged lasagnas.*

pre·paid /prē'pād/ past and past participle of **PREPAY.**

prep·a·ra·tion /,prepə'rāsʜən/ ▶ **n.** the action of making ready or being made ready for use. ■ (usu. **preparations**) something done to get ready for an event or undertaking. ■ a substance specially made up and usually sold, esp. a medicine or food. ■ a specimen prepared for scientific or medical examination: *a microscope preparation.* ■ Music (in conventional harmony) the sounding of the discordant note in a chord in the preceding chord where it is not discordant, lessening the effect of the discord.

pre·par·a·tive /prē'pe(ə)rətiv; -'par-/ ▶ **adj.** preparatory. ▶ **n.** a thing that acts as a preparation. — **pre·par·a·tive·ly adv.**

pre·par·a·to·ry /pri'pe(ə)rə,tôrē; -'parə-; 'prep(ə)rə-/ ▶ **adj.** serving as or carrying out preparation for a task or undertaking: *more preparatory work is needed.*

pre·par·a·to·ry school ▶ **n.** a private school that prepares students for college.

pre·pare /pri'pe(ə)r/ ▶ **v.** [trans.] **1** make (something) ready for use or consideration. ■ make (food or a meal) ready for cooking or eating. ■ make (someone) ready or able to do or deal with something: *schools should **prepare** children **for** life.* ■ [intrans.] make oneself ready to do or deal with something: *time off to **prepare for** her exams.* ■ (**be prepared to do something**) be willing to do something: *I wasn't prepared to go along with that.* ■ make (a chemical product) by a reaction or series of reactions. **2** Music (in conventional harmony) lead up to (a discord) by means of preparation. — **pre·par·er n.** [ME: from Fr. *préparer* or L. *praeparare,* from *prae* 'before' + *parare* 'make ready.']

pre·par·ed·ness /prə'pe(ə)r(ə)dnis/ ▶ **n.** a state of readiness, esp. for war.

pre·pay /prē'pā/ ▶ **v.** (past and past part. **pre·paid**) [trans.] [usu. as adj.] (**prepaid**) pay for in advance. — **pre·pay·a·ble adj. pre·pay·ment n.**

prepd. ▶ **abbr.** prepared.

pre·pense /pri'pens/ ▶ **adj.** [usu. postpositive] esp. Law, dated deliberate; intentional: *malice prepense.* — **pre·pense·ly adv.** [18th C.: alt. of *prepensed,* past part. of obs. *prepense,* from OFr. *purpenser,* from *por-* 'beforehand' + *penser* 'think.']

pre·pon·der·ant /pri'pändərənt/ ▶ **adj.** predominant in influence, number, or importance. — **pre·pon·der·ance n. pre·pon·der·ant·ly adv.** [ME: from L. *praeponderant-,* from *praeponderare.*]

pre·pon·der·ate /pri'pändə,rāt/ ▶ **v.** [intrans.] be greater in number, influence, or importance. [17th C.: from L. *praeponderat-* 'of greater weight,' from the v. *praeponderare,* from *prae* 'before' + *ponderare* 'weigh, consider.']

pre·pose /prē'pōz/ ▶ **v.** [trans.] Ling. place (an element or word) in front of another. [15th C.: from Fr. *préposer,* suggested by L. *praeponere* 'put before.']

prep·o·si·tion /,prepə'zisʜən/ ▶ **n.** Gram. a word governing, and usually preceding, a noun or pronoun and expressing a relation to another word or element in the clause, as in "the man *on* the platform." — **prep·o·si·tion·al** /-sʜənl/ **adj. prep·o·si·tion·al·ly** /-sʜənl-ē/ **adv.** [ME: from L. *praepositio(n-),* from the v. *praeponere,* from *prae* 'before' + *ponere* 'to place.']

prep·o·si·tion·al ob·ject /,prepə'zisʜənl 'äbjəkt; -jekt/ ▶ **n.** Gram. a noun phrase governed by a preposition.

prep·o·si·tion·al phrase ▶ **n.** a modifying phrase consisting of a preposition and its object.

pre·pos·i·tive /prē'päzətiv/ ▶ **adj.** Gram. (of a word, particle, etc.) placed in front of the word that it governs or modifies.

pre·pos·sess·ing /,prēpə'zesiɴɢ/ ▶ **adj.** [often with negative] attractive or appealing in appearance. — **pre·pos·ses·sion** /-'zesʜən/ **n.**

pre·pos·ter·ous /pri'päst(ə)rəs/ ▶ **adj.** contrary to reason or common sense; utterly absurd or ridiculous. — **pre·pos·ter·ous·ly adv. pre·pos·ter·ous·ness n.** [16th C.: from L. *praeposterus* 'reversed, absurd' (from *prae* 'before' + *posterus* 'coming after') + **-OUS.**]

pre·po·tent /prē'pōtnt/ ▶ **adj.** greater than others in power or influence. ■ (of a breeding animal) effective in transmitting hereditary characteristics to its offspring. — **pre·po·tence n. pre·po·ten·cy n.** [ME: from L. *praepotent-* 'having greater power,' from *prae* 'before, ahead' + *posse* 'be able.']

prep·py /'prepē/ (also **prep·pie**) informal ▶ **n.** (pl. **-pies**) a student or graduate of an expensive preparatory school or a person resembling such a student in dress or appearance. ▶ **adj.** (**-pi·er**, **-pi·est**) of or typical of such a person, esp. with reference to their dress. [20th C.: from PREP SCHOOL + -Y².]

pre·pran·di·al /prē'prandēəl/ ▶ **adj.** formal humorous done or taken before dinner. ■ Med. before a main meal. [19th C.: from PRE- 'before' + L. *prandium* 'a meal' + -AL.]

pre·preg /'prē'preg/ ▶ **n.** a fibrous material preimpregnated with a particular synthetic resin, used in making reinforced plastics. [1950s: from PRE- 'before' + *(im)preg(nated)*.]

pre·press /'prē'pres/ ▶ **adj.** of or relating to typesetting, page layout, and other work done on a publication before it is actually printed.

pre·print /prē'print/ ▶ **v.** [trans.] [usu. as adj.] (**preprinted**) print (something) in advance. ▶ **n.** /'prē,print/ something printed in advance, esp. a part of a work printed and issued before general publication of that work.

pre·proc·ess /prē'präs,es; prē'prōs,es; -əs/ ▶ **v.** [trans.] subject (data) to preliminary processing.

pre·proc·es·sor /prē'präs,esər; -'prōs,esər; -əsər/ ▶ **n.** a computer program that modifies data to conform with the input requirements of another program.

pre·pro·duc·tion /,prēprə'dəksHən/ ▶ **n.** work done on a product, esp. a film or broadcast program, before full-scale production begins.

pre·pro·gram /prē'prō,gram; -grəm/ ▶ **v.** [trans.] [usu. as adj.] (**preprogrammed**) program (a computer or other electronic device) in advance for ease of use. ■ program (something) into a computer or other electronic device before use.

prep school ▶ **n.** another term for PREPARATORY SCHOOL.

pre·pu·bes·cent /,prēpyo͞o'besənt/ ▶ **adj.** relating to or in the period preceding puberty. ▶ **n.** a prepubescent boy or girl. — **pre·pu·bes·cence** **n.**

pre·puce /'prē,pyo͞os/ ▶ **n.** Anat. **1** technical term for FORESKIN. **2** the fold of skin surrounding the clitoris. — **pre·pu·tial** /prē'pyo͞osHəl/ **adj.** [ME: from Fr. *prépuce*, from L. *praeputium*.]

pre·quel /'prēkwəl; -kwil/ ▶ **n.** a story or movie containing events that precede those of an existing work. [1970s: from PRE- 'before' + SEQUEL.]

Pre-Raph·a·el·ite /'rafēə,līt; -rāfē-; -'räfē-/ ▶ **n.** a member of a group of English 19th-century artists, including Holman Hunt, Millais, and D. G. Rossetti, who sought to emulate the simplicity and sincerity of the work of Italian artists from before Raphael. ▶ **adj.** of or relating to the Pre-Raphaelites. ■ of a style or appearance associated with the later Pre-Raphaelites or esp. with the women they frequently used as models, with long, thick, wavy auburn hair, pale skin, and a fey demeanor. — **Pre-Raph·a·el·it·ism** /-,līt,izəm/ **n.**

pre·re·cord /,prēri'kôrd/ ▶ **v.** [trans.] [often as adj.] (**prerecorded**) record (sound or film) in advance. ■ record sound on (a tape) beforehand.

pre·re·lease /,prērə'lēs; 'prērə,lēs/ ▶ **adj.** of, relating to, or denoting a record, movie, or other product that has not yet been generally released. ■ of or relating to the period before the release of a suspect or prisoner. ▶ **n.** a movie, record, or other product given restricted availability before being generally released.

pre·req·ui·site /prē'rekwəzət/ ▶ **n.** a thing required as a prior condition for something else to happen. ▶ **adj.** required as a prior condition.

pre·rog·a·tive /pri'rägətiv; pə'räg-/ ▶ **n.** a right or privilege exclusive to a particular individual or class. ■ a faculty or property distinguishing a person or class. ■ (also **royal prerogative**) the right of the sovereign, which in British law is theoretically subject to no restriction. [ME: via OFr. from L. *praerogativa*, fem. of *praerogativus* 'asked first,' from *prae* 'before' + *rogare* 'ask.']

Pres. ▶ **abbr.** President.

pres·age /'presij; pri'sāj/ ▶ **v.** [trans.] (of an event) be a sign or warning that (something, typically something bad) will happen: *the outcome of the game presaged the coming year.* ▶ **n.** a sign or warning that something, typically something bad, will happen; an omen or portent. [ME (as a n.): via Fr. from L. *praesagium*, from *praesagire* 'forebode,' from *prae* 'before' + *sagire* 'perceive keenly.']

Presb. (also **Presby.**) ▶ **abbr.** Presbyterian.

pres·by·o·pi·a /,prezbē'ōpēə; ,pres-/ ▶ **n.** farsightedness caused by loss of elasticity of the lens of the eye, occurring typically in middle and old age. — **pres·by·op·ic** /-'äpik/ **adj.** [18th C.: mod. L., from Gk. *presbus* 'old man' + *ōps*, *ōp-* 'eye.']

pres·by·ter /'prezbitər; 'pres-/ ▶ **n.** hist. an elder or minister of the Christian Church. ■ formal (in Presbyterian churches) an elder. ■ formal (in Episcopal churches) a minister of the second order, under the authority of a bishop; a priest. — **pres·byt·er·al** /prez'bitərəl; pres-/ **adj.** **pres·byt·er·ate** /prez'bitə,rāt; pres-/ **n.** **pres·by·te·ri·al** /,prezbi'ti(ə)rēəl; ,pres-/ **adj.** **pres·by·ter·ship** /-,SHip/ **n.** [16th C.: via eccles. L. from Gk. *presbuteros* 'elder', compar. of *presbus* 'old (man).']

Pres·by·te·ri·an /,prezbə'ti(ə)rēən; ,pres-/ ▶ **adj.** of, relating to, or denoting a Christian Church or denomination governed by elders according to Presbyterianism. ▶ **n.** a member of a Presbyterian Church. ■ an advocate of the Presbyterian system.

Pres·by·te·ri·an·ism /,prezbə'ti(ə)rēə,nizəm; ,pres-/ ▶ **n.** a form of Protestant Church government in which the Church is administered locally by the minister with a group of elected elders, and regionally and nationally by representative courts of ministers and elders.

pres·by·ter·y /'prezbə,terē; 'pres-; -bətrē/ ▶ **n.** (pl. **-ter·ies**) **1** [treated as sing. or pl.] a body of church elders and ministers, esp. (in Presbyterian churches) an administrative body representing the local congregations of a district. ■ a district represented by such a body of elders and ministers. **2** the house of a Roman Catholic parish priest. **3** esp. Archit. the eastern part of a church chancel beyond the choir; the sanctuary.

pre·school ▶ **adj.** /'prē'sko͞ol/ [attrib.] of or relating to the time before a child is old enough to go to school. ■ (of a child) under the age at which compulsory schooling begins. ▶ **n.** /'prē,sko͞ol/ a nursery school. — **pre·school·er** **n.**

pre·scient /'presH(ē)ənt; 'prē-/ ▶ **adj.** having or showing knowledge of events before they take place. — **pre·science** /-əns/ **n.** **pre·scient·ly** **adv.** [17th C.: from L. *praescient-* 'knowing beforehand,' from the v. *praescire*, from *prae* 'before' + *scire* 'know.']

pre·scind /pri'sind/ ▶ **v.** [intrans.] (**prescind from**) formal leave out of consideration: *we have prescinded from many vexing issues.* ■ [trans.] cut off or separate from something: *his is an idea entirely prescinded from all of the others.* [17th C.: from L. *praescindere*, from *prae* 'before' + *scindere* 'to cut.']

pre·scribe /pri'skrīb/ ▶ **v.** [trans.] (of a medical practitioner) advise and authorize the use of (a medicine or treatment) for someone, esp. in writing. ■ recommend (a substance or action) as something beneficial. ■ state authoritatively or as a rule that (an action or procedure) should be carried out. — **pre·scrib·er** **n.** [ME: from L. *praescribere* 'direct in writing,' from *prae* 'before' + *scribere* 'write.']

pre·script /'prē,skript; pri'skript/ ▶ **n.** formal dated an ordinance, law, or command. [16th C.: from L. *praescriptum*, neut. past part. of *praescribere*.]

pre·scrip·tion /pri'skripsHən/ ▶ **n.** **1** an instruction written by a medical practitioner that authorizes a patient to be issued with a medicine or treatment. ■ the action of prescribing a medicine or treatment. ■ a medicine or remedy that is prescribed. **2** a recommendation authoritatively put forward. ■ the authoritative recommendation of an action or procedure. **3** (also **positive prescription**) Law the establishment of a claim founded on a long or indefinite period of uninterrupted use or of long-standing custom. [ME: via OFr. from L. *praescriptio(n-)*, from *praescribere*.]

pre·scrip·tive /pri'skriptiv/ ▶ **adj.** **1** of or relating to the imposition or enforcement of a rule or method. ■ Ling. attempting to impose rules of correct usage on the users of a language. Often contrasted with DESCRIPTIVE. **2** (of a right, title, or institution) having become legally established or accepted by long usage: *a prescriptive right of way.* — **pre·scrip·tive·ly** **adv.** **pre·scrip·tive·ness** **n.** **pre·scrip·tiv·ism** /-'skriptə,vizəm/ **n.** **pre·scrip·tiv·ist** /-vist/ **n. & adj.**

pres·ence /'prezəns/ ▶ **n.** the state or fact of existing, occurring, or being present in a place or thing. ■ a person or thing that exists or is present in a place but is not seen: *the monks became aware of a strange presence.* ■ [in sing.] a group of people, esp. soldiers or police, stationed in a particular place. ■ the impressive manner or appearance of a person.

– PHRASES **presence of mind** the ability to remain calm and take quick, sensible action.

pres·ence cham·ber ▶ **n.** a room, esp. one in a palace, in which a monarch or other distinguished person receives visitors.

pre·se·nile /prē'sē,nīl; -'sen,īl/ ▶ **adj.** occurring in or characteristic of the period of life preceding old age.

pres·ent¹ /'prezənt/ ▶ **adj.** **1** [predic.] (of a person) in a particular place. ■ (often **present in**) (of a thing) existing or occurring in a place or thing: *organic molecules are present in comets.* **2** [attrib.] existing or occurring now. ■ now being considered or discussed: *the present article cannot answer every question.* ■ Gram. (of a tense or participle) expressing an action now going on or habitually performed or a condition now existing. ▶ **n.** [in sing.] (usu. **the present**) the period of time now occurring. ■ Gram. a present tense. See also HISTORIC PRESENT.

– PHRASES **at present** now. **for the present** for now; temporarily. **these presents** Law, formal this document. [ME: via OFr. from L. *praesent-* 'being at hand,' pres. part. of *praeesse*, from *prae* 'before' + *esse* 'be.']

pre·sent² /pri'zent/ ▶ **v.** [trans.] **1** (**present something to**) give something to (someone) formally or ceremonially. ■ (**present someone with**) give someone (something) in such a way. ■ show or offer (something) for others to scrutinize or consider: *he presented his passport.* ■ formally introduce (someone) to someone else. ■ proffer (compliments or good wishes) in a formal manner: *may I present the greetings of my master?* ■ formally deliver (a check or bill) for acceptance or payment. ■ Law bring (a complaint, petition, or evidence) formally to the notice of a court. ■ (of a company or producer) put (a show or exhibition) before the public. **2** bring about or be the cause of (a problem or difficulty): *this should not present much difficulty.* ■ exhibit (a particular state or appearance) to others: *the EC presented a united front over the crisis.* ■ represent (someone) to others in a particular way, typically false or exaggerated: *he presented himself as a hardworking man.* ■ (**present oneself**) come forward into the presence of another or others, esp. for a formal occasion; appear. ■ (**present itself**) (of an opportunity or idea) occur and be available for use or exploitation. ■ [intrans.] (**present with**) Med. (of a patient) come forward for initial medical examination for a condition or symptom: *the patient presented with mild clinical encephalopathy.* ■ [intrans.] Med. (of a part of a fetus) be directed toward the cervix during labor. ■ [intrans.] Med. (of an illness) manifest itself. **3** hold out or aim (a firearm) at something so as to be ready to fire.

– PHRASES **present arms** hold a rifle vertically in front of the body as a salute. — **pre·sent·er** n. [ME: from OFr. *presenter*, from L. *praesentare* 'place before' (in med. L. 'present as a gift'), from *praesent-* 'being at hand' (see PRESENT[1]).]

pres·ent[3] /'prezənt/ ▶ n. a thing given to someone as a gift: *a Christmas present.* [ME: from OFr.]

pre·sent·a·ble /pri'zentəbəl/ ▶ adj. clean, well-dressed, or decent enough to be seen in public. — **pre·sent·a·bil·i·ty** /-,zentə'bilətē/ n. **pre·sent·a·bly** /-blē/ adv.

pres·en·ta·tion /,prē,zen'tāsʜən; ,prezən-; ,prēzən-/ ▶ n. **1** the proffering or giving of something to someone, esp. as part of a formal ceremony. ■ the manner or style in which something is given, offered, or displayed. ■ a formal introduction of someone, esp. at court. ■ the official submission of something for consideration in a law court. ■ esp. hist. the action or right of formally proposing a candidate for a church benefice or other position. ■ a demonstration or display of a product or idea. ■ an exhibition or theatrical performance. **2** Med. the position of a fetus in relation to the cervix at the time of delivery. ■ the coming forward of a patient for initial examination and diagnosis. **3** (**Presentation of Christ**) another term for CANDLEMAS. — **pres·en·ta·tion·al** /-sʜənl/ adj. **pres·en·ta·tion·al·ly** /-sʜənl-ē/ adv.

pre·sen·ta·tive /pri'zentətiv/ ▶ adj. hist. (of a benefice) to which a patron has the right of presentation.

pres·ent-day ▶ adj. [attrib.] of or relating to the current period of time: *present-day developments.*

pres·en·tee /,prezən'tē; pri,zen'tē/ ▶ n. a person nominated or recommended for an office or position, esp. a church benefice.

pre·sen·tient /prē'sencʜənt/ ▶ adj. rare having a presentiment. [19th C.: from L. *praesentient-* 'perceiving beforehand,' from the v. *praesentire*, from *prae* 'before' + *sentire* 'to feel.']

pre·sen·ti·ment /pri'zentəmənt/ ▶ n. an intuitive feeling about the future, esp. one of foreboding. [18th C.: from obs. Fr. *présentiment*.]

pres·ent·ism /'prezen,tizəm/ ▶ n. uncritical adherence to present-day attitudes, esp. the tendency to interpret past events in terms of modern values and concepts. — **pres·en·tist** adj.

pres·ent·ly /'prezəntlē/ ▶ adv. **1** after a short time; soon. **2** at the present time; now.

pre·sent·ment /pri'zentmənt/ ▶ n. Law, esp. hist. a formal presentation of information to a court, esp. by a sworn jury regarding an offense or other matter.

pres·ent par·ti·ci·ple ▶ n. Gram. the form of a verb, ending in *-ing* in English, which is used in forming continuous tenses, e.g., in *I'm thinking*, alone in nonfinite clauses, e.g., in *sitting here, I haven't a care in the world*, as a noun, e.g., in *good thinking*, and as an adjective, e.g., in *running water*.

pres·ent val·ue (also **net present value**) ▶ n. Finance the value in the present of a sum of money, in contrast to some future value it will have when it has been invested at compound interest.

pres·er·va·tion /,prezər'vāsʜən/ ▶ n. the action of preserving something. ■ the state of being preserved, esp. to a specified degree.

pres·er·va·tion·ist /,prezər'vāsʜənəst/ ▶ n. a supporter or advocate of the preservation of something, esp. of historic buildings and artifacts.

pre·serv·a·tive /pri'zərvətiv/ ▶ n. a substance used to preserve foodstuffs, wood, or other materials against decay. ▶ adj. acting to preserve something.

pre·serve /pri'zərv/ ▶ v. [trans.] maintain (something) in its original or existing state. ■ retain (a condition or state of affairs). ■ maintain or keep alive (a memory or quality). ■ keep safe from harm or injury: *preserving endangered species.* ■ treat or refrigerate (food) to prevent its decomposition or fermentation. ■ prepare (fruit) for long-term storage by boiling it with sugar. ■ keep (game or an area where game is found) undisturbed to allow private hunting or shooting. ▶ n. **1** (usu. **preserves**) food made with fruit preserved in sugar, such as jam or marmalade. **2** a sphere of activity regarded as being reserved for a particular person or group. **3** a place where game is protected and kept for private hunting or shooting. — **pre·serv·a·ble** adj. **pre·serv·er** n. [ME: from OFr. *preserver*, from late L. *praeservare*, from *prae-* 'before, in advance' + *servare* 'to keep.']

pre·serv·ice /'prē'sərvəs/ ▶ adj. of or relating to the period before a person takes a job that requires training, esp. in teaching: *preservice training.*

pre·set /prē'set/ ▶ v. (**-set·ting** ; past and past part. **-set**) [trans.] [usu. as adj.] (**preset**) set (a value that controls a device) in advance of its use. ▶ n. a control on electronic equipment that is set or adjusted beforehand to facilitate use.

pre·shrunk /prē'sʜrəngk/ ▶ adj. (of a fabric or garment) having undergone a shrinking process during manufacture to prevent further shrinking in use. — **pre·shrink** /-'sʜringk/ v.

pre·side /pri'zīd/ ▶ v. [intrans.] **1** be in the position of authority in a meeting or gathering: *Bishop Herbener presided at the meeting.* ■ (**preside over**) be in charge of (a place or situation). **2** (**preside at**) play (a musical instrument, esp. a keyboard instrument) at a public gathering. [17th C.: from Fr. *présider*, from L. *praesidere*, from *prae* 'before' + *sedere* 'sit.']

pres·i·den·cy /'prez(ə)dənsē/ ▶ n. (pl. **-cies**) the office of president. ■ the period of this. ■ Christian Church the role of the priest or minister who conducts a Eucharist. ■ (also **First Presidency**) (in the Mormon church) a council of three officers forming the highest administrative body.

pres·i·dent /'prez(ə)dənt; 'prezə,dent/ ▶ n. **1** the elected head of a republican state. ■ the head of a society, council, or other organization. ■ the head of a college or university. ■ the head of a company. **2** Christian Church the celebrant at a Eucharist. — **pres·i·den·tial** /,prezə'dencʜəl/ adj. **pres·i·den·tial·ly** /,prezə'dencʜəlē/ adv. [ME: via OFr. from L. *praesident-* 'sitting before' (see PRESIDE).]

pres·i·dent-e·lect ▶ n. (pl. **pres·i·dents-e·lect**) a person elected president but not yet in office.

Pres·i·den·tial Med·al of Free·dom /,prezə'dencʜəl/ ▶ n. (in the US) a medal constituting the highest award given to a civilian in peacetime.

Pres·i·den·tial Range a mountain range in northern New Hampshire's White Mountains that includes Mount Washington, which rises 6,288 feet (1,918 m).

pres·i·dent pro tem·po·re /'prō 'tempə,rē/ (also **pres·i·dent pro tem** /'prō 'tem/) ▶ n. a high-ranking senator of the majority party who presides over the US Senate in the absence of the vice president.

pre·sid·i·o /pri'sidē,ō; -se'dē-/ ▶ n. (pl. **-os**) (in Spain and Spanish America) a fortified military settlement. [Sp., from L. *praesidium* 'garrison.']

pre·sid·i·um /pri'sidēəm; -'zid-/ (also **prae·sid·i·um**) ▶ n. a standing executive committee in a communist country. ■ (**Presidium**) the committee of this type in the former USSR, which functioned as the legislative authority when the Supreme Soviet was not sitting. [1920s: from Russ. *prezidium*, from L. *praesidium* 'protection, garrison' (see PRESIDE).]

Pres·ley /'prezlē; 'pres-/, Elvis Aron (1935–77), US singer and actor; known as the **King of Rock and Roll**. The dominant personality of his music genre, he also made numerous movies.

pre-So·crat·ic ▶ adj. of, relating to, or denoting the philosophers active in the ancient Greek world in the 6th and 5th centuries BC, who attempted to find rational explanations for natural phenomena. ▶ n. a pre-Socratic philosopher.

pre·sort /prē'sôrt/ ▶ v. [trans.] sort outgoing mail by zip code to take advantage of cheaper postage.

press[1] /pres/ ▶ v. **1** move or cause to move into a position of contact with something by exerting continuous physical force: [trans.] *he pressed his face to the glass* | [intrans.] *her body pressed against his.* ■ [trans.] exert continuous physical force on (something), to operate a device or machine: *he pressed a button and the doors opened.* ■ [trans.] squeeze (someone's arm or hand) as a sign of affection. ■ [intrans.] move in a specified direction by pushing: *the mob pressed forward.* ■ fig. (of an enemy or opponent) attack persistently and fiercely: [intrans.] *their enemies pressed in on all sides* | [trans.] *two assailants were pressing Agrippa.* ■ [intrans.] (**press on/ahead**) fig. continue in one's action: *he pressed on with his work.* ■ [trans.] Weightlifting raise (a specified weight) by first lifting it to shoulder height and then gradually pushing it upward above the head. **2** [trans.] apply pressure to (something) to flatten, shape, or smooth it, typically by ironing. ■ apply pressure to (a flower or leaf) between sheets of paper in order to dry and preserve it. ■ extract (juice or oil) by crushing or squeezing fruit, vegetables, etc. ■ squeeze or crush (fruit, vegetables, etc.) to extract the juice or oil. ■ manufacture (something, esp. a phonograph record) by molding under pressure. **3** [trans.] forcefully put forward (an opinion, claim, or course of action): *Rose did not press the point.* ■ make strong efforts to persuade or force (someone) to do or provide something: *I pressed him for precise figures* | [intrans.] *they pressed for changes in legislation.* ■ [intrans.] Golf try too hard to achieve distance with a shot, at the risk of inaccuracy. ■ (**press something on/upon**) insist that (someone) accept an offer or gift: *he pressed dinner invitations on her.* ■ [intrans.] (of something, esp. time) be in short supply and so demand immediate action. ■ (**be pressed**) have barely enough of something, esp. time: *I'm pressed for time.* ■ (**be pressed to do something**) have difficulty doing or achieving something. ▶ n. **1** a device for applying pressure to something in order to flatten or shape it or to extract juice or oil. ■ a machine that applies pressure to a workpiece by means of a tool, in order to punch shapes. **2** a printing press. ■ [often in names] a business that prints or publishes books. ■ the process of printing: *the book is ready to go to press.* **3** (**the press**) [treated as sing. or pl.] newspapers or journalists viewed collectively. ■ coverage in newspapers and magazines. **4** an act of pressing something. ■ [in sing.] a closely packed crowd or mass of people or things. ■ dated pressure of business. ■ Weightlifting an act of raising a weight up to shoulder height and then gradually pushing it upward above the head. ■ Basketball any of various forms of close guarding by the defending team.

– PHRASES **press charges** see CHARGE. **press something home** see HOME. **press (the) flesh** informal (of a celebrity or politician) greet people by shaking hands. [ME: from OFr. *presse* (n.), *presser* (v.), from L. *pressare* 'keep pressing,' frequentative of *premere*.]

press[2] ▶ v. [trans.] (**press someone/something into**) put (someone or something) to a specified use, esp. as a temporary or makeshift measure: *many of these stones have been pressed into service as gateposts.* ■ hist. force (a man) to enlist in the army or navy. ▶ n. hist. a forcible enlistment of men, esp. for the navy. [16th C.: alt. (by association with PRESS[1]) of obs. *prest* 'pay given on enlistment, enlistment by such payment,' from OFr. *prest* 'loan, advance pay,' based on L. *praestare* 'provide.']

press a·gent ▶ n. a person employed to organize advertising and publicity in the press on behalf of an organization or well-known person.

press·board /'pres,bôrd/ ▶ n. a hard, dense kind of board with a smooth finish, typically made from wood or textile pulp or laminated wastepaper, and used as an electrical insulator and for making light furniture.

press box ▶ n. an area reserved for journalists at a sports event.

Press·burg /'pres,bərg/ German name for BRATISLAVA.

press card ▶ n. an official authorization carried by a reporter, esp. one that gives admission to an event.

press clipping ▶ n. a paragraph or short article cut out of a newspaper or magazine.

press con·fer·ence ▶ n. an interview given to journalists by a prominent person in order to make an announcement or answer questions.

press gal·ler·y ▶ n. a place reserved for journalists observing the proceedings in a legislature or court of law.

press gang ▶ n. hist. a body of men employed to enlist men forcibly into service in the army or navy. ▶ v. [trans.] (**press-gang**) esp. hist. forcibly enlist (someone) into service in the army or navy. ■ (**press-gang someone into**) force someone to do something.

press·ing /'presiNG/ ▶ adj. (of a problem, need, or situation) requiring quick or immediate action or attention. ■ (of an engagement or activity) important and requiring one's attendance or presence. ■ (of an invitation) strongly expressed. ▶ n. a thing made by the application of force or weight, esp. a record. ■ a series of such things made at one time: *the first pressing of the live album.* ■ an act or instance of applying force or weight to something. — **press·ing·ly** adv.

press kit ▶ n. a package of promotional material provided to members of the press to brief them, esp. about a product, service, or candidate.

press·man /'pres,mən; ,man/ ▶ n. (pl. **-men**) **1** esp. Brit. a journalist. **2** a person who operates a printing press.

press·mark /'pres,märk/ ▶ n. esp. Brit. a call number.

pres·sor /'presər/ ▶ adj. [attrib.] Physiol. producing an increase in blood pressure by stimulating constriction of the blood vessels: *a pressor response.*

press re·lease ▶ n. an official statement issued to newspapers giving information on a particular matter.

press run ▶ n. the operation of a printing press for a single job (the number or entire set of items produced).

press time ▶ n. the moment when a magazine or other publication goes to press.

pres·sure /'presHər/ ▶ n. **1** the continuous physical force exerted on or against an object by something in contact with it. ■ the force exerted per unit area. **2** the use of persuasion, influence, or intimidation to make someone do something. ■ the influence or effect of someone or something. ■ the feeling of stressful urgency caused by the necessity of doing or achieving something, esp. with limited time. ▶ v. [trans.] attempt to persuade or coerce (someone) into doing something: *it might now be possible to* ***pressure*** *him* ***into*** *resigning.* [ME: from OFr., from L. *pressura*, from *press-* 'pressed,' from the v. *premere* (see PRESS[1]).]

pres·sure cook·er ▶ n. an airtight pot in which food can be cooked quickly under steam pressure. ■ fig. a highly stressful situation or assignment. — **pres·sure-cook** v.

pres·sure gauge ▶ n. an instrument indicating pressure: *an oil pressure gauge.*

pres·sure group ▶ n. a group that tries to influence public policy in the interest of a particular cause.

pres·sure point ▶ n. a point on the surface of the body sensitive to pressure. ■ a point where an artery can be pressed against a bone to inhibit bleeding. ■ a place in which trouble or difficulty is likely to be found.

pres·sure suit ▶ n. an inflatable suit that protects the wearer against low pressure, e.g., when flying at a high altitude.

pres·sur·ize /'presHə,rīz/ ▶ v. [trans.] **1** produce or maintain raised pressure artificially in (a gas or its container): *the mixture was pressurized to 1,900 atmospheres.* ■ maintain a tolerable atmospheric pressure in (an aircraft cabin) at a high altitude. **2** [trans.] attempt to persuade or coerce (someone) into doing something: *the protests were an attempt to* ***pressurize*** *the government* ***into*** *stopping the violence.* — **pres·sur·i·za·tion** /,presHərə'zāsHən/ n.

pres·sur·ized-wa·ter re·ac·tor (abbr.: **PWR**) ▶ n. a nuclear reactor in which the fuel is uranium oxide clad in zircaloy and the coolant and moderator is water maintained at high pressure so that it does not boil at the operating temperature of the reactor.

press·work /'pres,wərk/ ▶ n. **1** the process of using a printing press. ■ printed matter, esp. with regard to its quality. **2** the shaping of metal by pressing or drawing it into a shaped hollow die.

Pres·ter John /'prestər 'jän/ a legendary medieval Christian king of Asia.

pres·ti·dig·i·ta·tion /,prestə,dijə'tāsHən/ ▶ n. formal magic tricks performed as entertainment. — **pres·ti·dig·i·ta·tor** /-'dijə,tātər/ n. [19th C.: from Fr., from *preste* 'nimble' + L. *digitus* 'finger' + -ATION.]

pres·tige /pres'tēzH; -'tēj/ ▶ n. respect and admiration felt for someone or something on the basis of their achievements or quality. ■ [as adj.] denoting something that arouses such respect or admiration. [17th C. (in the sense 'illusion, conjuring trick'): from Fr., lit. 'illusion, glamour.']

pres·tig·ious /pre'stijəs; -'stē-/ ▶ adj. inspiring respect and admiration; having high status. — **pres·tig·i·ous·ly** adv. **pres·tig·i·ous·ness** n. [16th C.: from late L. *praestigiosus*, from *praestigiae* 'conjuring tricks.']

pres·tis·si·mo /pre'stisə,mō/ Music ▶ adv. & adj. (esp. as a direction) in a very quick tempo. ▶ n. (pl. **-mos**) a movement or passage marked to be performed in a very quick tempo. [Ital., superlative of *presto* 'quick, quickly' (see PRESTO).]

pres·to /'prestō/ ▶ adv. & adj. Music (esp. as a direction) in a quick tempo. ▶ n. (pl. **-tos**) Music a movement or passage marked to be performed in a quick tempo. ▶ exclam. a phrase announcing the successful completion of a trick, or suggesting that something has been done so easily that it seems to be magic. [Ital., 'quick, quickly,' from late L. *praestus* 'ready,' from L. *praesto* 'at hand.']

pre·stressed /prē'strest/ ▶ adj. strengthened by the application of stress during manufacture, esp. (of concrete) by means of rods or wires inserted under tension before the material is set. — **pre·stress·ing** /-'stresiNG/ n.

pre·sum·a·bly /pri'zōōməblē/ ▶ adv. [sentence adverb] used to convey that what is asserted is very likely though not known for certain.

pre·sume /pri'zōōm/ ▶ v. **1** [with clause] suppose that something is the case on the basis of probability: *I presumed that the man had been escorted from the building* | [trans.] *the two men were presumed dead.* ■ take for granted that something exists or is the case. **2** [intrans.] be audacious enough to do something: *don't presume to issue me orders in my own house.* ■ [intrans.] make unjustified demands; take liberties: *forgive me if I have presumed.* ■ [intrans.] (**presume on/upon**) unjustifiably regard (something) as entitling one to privileges: *she knew he regarded her as his protegée, but was determined not to presume on that.* — **pre·sum·a·ble** adj. [ME: from OFr. *presumer*, from L. *praesumere* 'anticipate' (in late L. 'take for granted'), from *prae* 'before' + *sumere* 'take.']

pre·sum·ing /pri'zōōmiNG/ ▶ adj. archaic presumptuous. — **pre·sum·ing·ly** adv.

pre·sump·tion /pri'zəmpsHən/ ▶ n. **1** an act or instance of taking something to be true or adopting a particular attitude toward something, esp. at the start of a chain of argument or action. ■ an idea that is taken to be true, and often used as the basis for other ideas, although it is not known for certain. ■ esp. Law an attitude adopted in law or as a matter of policy toward an action or proposal in the absence of acceptable reasons to the contrary: *the policy shows a* ***presumption in favor of*** *development.* **2** behavior perceived as arrogant, disrespectful, and transgressing the limits of what is permitted or appropriate. [ME: from OFr. *presumpcion*, from L. *praesumptio(n)*, from *praesumere* (see PRESUME).]

pre·sump·tive /pri'zəmptiv/ ▶ adj. of the nature of a presumption; presumed in the absence of further information. ■ Law giving grounds for the inference of a fact or of the appropriate interpretation of the law. ■ another term for PRESUMPTUOUS. — **pre·sump·tive·ly** adv.

pre·sump·tu·ous /pri'zəmpcH(ōō)əs/ ▶ adj. (of a person or their behavior) failing to observe the limits of what is permitted or appropriate. — **pre·sump·tu·ous·ly** adv. **pre·sump·tu·ous·ness** n. [ME: from OFr. *presumptueux*, from late L. *praesumptuosus*, from *praesumptio*.]

pre·sup·pose /,prēsə'pōz/ ▶ v. [trans.] (of an action, process, or argument) require as a precondition of possibility or coherence. ■ [with clause] tacitly assume at the beginning of a line of argument or course of action that something is the case: *your argument presupposes that it does not matter who is in power.* [ME: from OFr. *presupposer*, suggested by med. L. *praesupponere*, from *prae* 'before' + *supponere* 'place under' (see SUPPOSE).]

pre·sup·po·si·tion /,prē,səpə'zisHən/ ▶ n. a thing tacitly assumed beforehand at the beginning of a line of argument or course of action. ■ the action or state of presupposing or being presupposed.

pre·syn·ap·tic /,prēsə'naptik/ ▶ adj. Physiol. relating to or denoting a nerve cell that releases a transmitter substance into a synapse during transmission of an impulse. — **pre·syn·ap·ti·cal·ly** /-ik(ə)lē/ adv.

pret. ▶ abbr. preterite.

prêt-à-por·ter /,pret ä pôr'tā/ ▶ adj. (of designer clothes) sold ready-to-wear as opposed to made to measure. ▶ n. designer clothes sold ready-to-wear. [Fr., lit. 'ready to wear.']

pre·tax /'prē'taks/ ▶ adj. (of income or profits) considered or calculated before the deduction of taxes.

pre·teen /'prē'tēn/ ▶ adj. [attrib.] of or relating to a child just under the age of thirteen. ▶ n. a child of such an age.

pre·tence ▶ n. British spelling of PRETENSE.

pre·tend /pri'tend/ ▶ v. **1** [with clause or infin.] speak and act so as to make it appear that something is the case when in fact it is not: *I pretended I was asleep* | *she pretended to read.* ■ engage in a game or fantasy that involves supposing something that is not the case to be so: *children pretending to be grownups.* ■ [trans.] give the appearance of feeling or possessing (an emotion or quality); simulate: *she pretended a greater surprise than she felt.* **2** [intrans.] (**pretend to**) lay claim to (a quality or title): *he cannot pretend to sophistication.* ▶ adj. [attrib.] informal not really what it is represented as being; used in a game or deception: *the children are pouring pretend tea for the dolls.* [ME: from L. *praetendere* 'stretch forth, claim,' from *prae* 'before' + *tendere* 'stretch.']

pre·tend·er /pri'tendər/ ▶ n. a person who claims or aspires to a title or position.

pre·tense /'prē,tens; pri'tens/ (Brit. **pre·tence**) ▶ n. **1** an attempt to make something that is not the case appear true. ■ a false display of feelings, attitudes, or intentions. ■ the practice of inventing imaginary situations in play. ■ affected and ostentatious speech and behavior. **2** (**pretense to**) a claim, esp. a false or ambitious one. [ME: from Anglo-Norman Fr. *pretense*, based on med. L. *pretensus* 'pretended,' alt. of L.

praetentus, from the v. *praetendere* (see PRETEND).]

pre·ten·sion[1] /pri'tencHən/ ▸ **n.** **1** (**pretension to**) a claim or the assertion of a claim to something. ■ (often **pretensions**) an aspiration or claim to a certain status or quality. **2** the use of affectation to impress; ostentatiousness.

pre·ten·sion[2] /prē'tencHən/ ▸ **v.** [trans.] apply tension to (an object) before some other process or event. ■ strengthen (reinforced concrete) by applying tension to the reinforcing rods before the concrete has set.

pre·ten·tious /pri'tencHəs/ ▸ **adj.** attempting to impress by affecting greater importance, talent, culture, etc., than is actually possessed. — **pre·ten·tious·ly** adv. **pre·ten·tious·ness** n. [19th C.: from Fr. *prétentieux*, based on L. *praetendere*.]

preter- ▸ **comb. form** more than: *preternatural*. [from L. *praeter* 'past, beyond.']

pret·er·ite /'pretərit/ (also **pret·er·it**) Gram. ▸ **adj.** expressing a past action or state. ▸ **n.** a simple past tense or form. [ME (in the sense 'bygone, former'): from L. *praeteritus* 'gone by,' past part. of *praeterire*, from *praeter* 'past, beyond' + *ire* 'go.']

pret·er·i·tion /,pretə'risHən/ ▸ **n.** **1** the action of passing over or disregarding a matter, esp. the rhetorical technique of making summary mention of something by professing to omit it. **2** (in Calvinist theology) omission from God's elect; nonelection to salvation.

pre·term /prē'tərm/ Med. ▸ **adj.** born or occurring after a pregnancy significantly shorter than normal, esp. after no more than 37 weeks of pregnancy. ▸ **adv.** after a short pregnancy; prematurely.

pre·ter·nat·u·ral /,prētər'nacH(ə)rəl/ ▸ **adj.** beyond what is normal or natural. — **pre·ter·nat·u·ral·ism** /-'nacH(ə)rə,lizəm/ **n.** **pre·ter·nat·u·ral·ly** adv.

pre·text /'prē,tekst/ ▸ **n.** a reason given in justification of a course of action that is not the real reason. [16th C.: from L. *praetextus* 'outward display,' from the v. *praetexere* 'to disguise,' from *prae* 'before' + *texere* 'weave.']

pre·tor /'prētər/ ▸ **n.** var. of PRAETOR.

Pre·to·ri·a /prə'tôrēə/ the administrative capital of South Africa; pop. 1,080,000.

pre·to·ri·an /pri'tôrēən/ ▸ **adj. & n.** var. of PRAETORIAN.

pret·ti·fy /'pritə,fī/ ▸ **v.** (**-fies, -fied**) [trans.] make (someone or something) appear superficially attractive. — **pret·ti·fi·ca·tion** /,pritəfə'kāsHən/ **n.** **pret·ti·fi·er** n.

pret·ty /'pritē/ ▸ **adj.** (**-ti·er, -ti·est**) attractive in a delicate way without being beautiful. ■ [attrib.] informal used ironically in expressions of annoyance or disgust: *a pretty state of affairs!* ▸ **adv.** [as submodifier] informal to a moderately high degree; fairly: *he looked pretty fit for his age.* ▸ **n.** (pl. **-ties**) informal an attractive thing, typically a pleasing but unnecessary accessory: *he buys her lots of pretties—rings and things.* ■ used to refer in a condescending way to an attractive person, usually a girl or a woman. ▸ **v.** (**-ties, -tied**) [trans.] make pretty or attractive: *she'll be all prettied up in an hour.*
– PHRASES **pretty much** (or **nearly** or **well**) informal very nearly. **be sitting pretty** informal be in an advantageous position or situation. — **pret·ti·ly** /'pritl-ē/ adv. **pret·ti·ness** n. **pret·ty·ish** adj. [OE *prættig*; rel. to MDu. *pertich* 'brisk, clever,' obs. Du. *prettig* 'humorous, sporty,' from a West Gmc. base meaning 'trick.']

pret·zel /'pretsəl/ ▸ **n.** a crisp biscuit baked in the form of a knot or stick and flavored with salt. ▸ **v.** (**-zeled, -zel·ing**) [trans.] twist, bend, or contort. [19th C.: from Ger. *Pretzel*.]

prev. ▸ **abbr.** ■ previous; previously.

pre·vail /pri'vāl/ ▸ **v.** [intrans.] prove more powerful than opposing forces; be victorious: *it is hard for logic to prevail over emotion.* ■ be widespread in a particular area at a particular time; be current: *an atmosphere of crisis prevails.* ■ (**prevail on/upon**) persuade (someone) to do something: *she was prevailed upon to give an account of her work.* — **pre·vail·ing·ly** adv. [ME: from L. *praevalere* 'have greater power,' from *prae* 'before' + *valere* 'have power.']

pre·vail·ing wind ▸ **n.** a wind from the direction that is most usual at a particular place or season.

prev·a·lent /'prevələnt/ ▸ **adj.** widespread in a particular area at a particular time. ■ archaic predominant; powerful. — **prev·a·lence** n. **prev·a·lent·ly** adv. [16th C.: from L. *praevalent-* 'having greater power,' from *praevalere*.]

pre·var·i·cate /pri'vari,kāt/ ▸ **v.** [intrans.] speak or act in an evasive way: *he prevaricated when journalists asked questions.* — **pre·var·i·ca·tion** /pri,vari'kāsHən/ **n.** **pre·var·i·ca·tor** /-,kātər/ **n.** [16th C.: from L. *praevaricat-* 'walked crookedly, deviated,' from the v. *praevaricari*, from *prae* 'before' + *varicari* 'straddle' (from *varus* 'bent, knock-kneed').]

pre·ven·ient /pri'vēnēənt/ ▸ **adj.** formal preceding in time or order; antecedent. [17th C.: from L. *praevenient-* 'coming before,' from the v. *praevenire*, from *prae* 'before' + *venire* 'come.']

pre·vent /pri'vent/ ▸ **v.** [trans.] keep (something) from happening or arising: *action must be taken to prevent further accidents.* ■ make (someone or something) unable to do something: *window locks won't prevent a burglary.* — **pre·vent·a·bil·i·ty** /pri,ventə'bilətē/ **n.** **pre·vent·a·ble** (also **pre·vent·i·ble**) adj. **pre·vent·er** n. [ME: from L. *praevent-* 'preceded, hindered,' from the v. *praevenire*, from *prae* 'before' + *venire* 'come.']

pre·ven·ta·tive /prē'ventətiv/ ▸ **adj. & n.** another term for PREVENTIVE. — **pre·ven·ta·tive·ly** adv.

pre·ven·tion /pri'vencHən/ ▸ **n.** the action of stopping something from happening or arising.

pre·ven·tive /pri'ventiv/ ▸ **adj.** designed to keep something undesirable such as illness, harm, or accidents from occurring: *preventive medicine.* ▸ **n.** a medicine or other treatment designed to stop disease or ill health from occurring. — **pre·ven·tive·ly** adv.

pre·ver·bal /'prē'vərbəl/ ▸ **adj.** **1** existing or occurring before the development of speech. **2** Gram. occurring before a verb: *preverbal particles.*

pre·view /'prē,vyo͞o/ ▸ **n.** an inspection or viewing of something before it is bought or becomes generally known and available. ■ a showing of a movie, play, exhibition, etc., before its official opening. ■ a short extract shown in a movie theater as publicity for a forthcoming film. ■ a commentary on or appraisal of a forthcoming film, play, book, etc., based on an advance viewing. ■ Comput. a facility for inspecting the appearance of a document prepared in a word-processing program before it is printed. ▸ **v.** [trans.] display (a product, movie, play, etc.) before it officially goes on sale or opens to the public. ■ see or inspect (something) before it is used or becomes generally available. ■ comment on or appraise (a forthcoming event) in advance.

Prev·in /'prevən/, André George (1929–), US conductor and composer; born in Germany; born *Andreas Ludwig Priwin*. He conducted the London Symphony Orchestra 1968–79 and the Pittsburgh Symphony Orchestra 1976–86.

pre·vi·ous /'prēvēəs/ ▸ **adj.** **1** [attrib.] existing or occurring before in time or order. **2** informal overly hasty in acting or drawing a conclusion: *I admit I may have been a bit previous.*
– PHRASES **previous to** before. — **pre·vi·ous·ly** adv. [17th C.: from L. *praevius* 'going before' (from *prae* 'before' + *via* 'way') + **-ous**.]

pre·vise /pri'vīz/ ▸ **v.** [trans.] literary foresee or predict (an event). — **pre·vi·sion** /-'vizHən/ **n.** **pre·vi·sion·al** /-'vizHənl/ adj. [16th C.: from L. *praevis-* 'foreseen, anticipated,' from the v. *praevidere*, from *prae* 'before' + *videre* 'to see.']

pre·vo·cal·ic /,prēvō'kalik/ ▸ **adj.** occurring immediately before a vowel. — **pre·vo·cal·i·cal·ly** /-ik(ə)lē/ adv.

pre·vue /'prē,vyo͞o/ ▸ **n.** var. of PREVIEW.

prex·y /'preksē/ (also **prex**) ▸ **n.** (pl. **prex·ies**) informal a president, esp. the president of a college or society. [19th C. (as *prex*): college slang.]

prey /prā/ ▸ **n.** an animal hunted and killed by another for food. ■ a person or thing easily injured or taken advantage of. ■ a person vulnerable to distressing emotions or beliefs. ■ archaic plunder or (in biblical use) a prize. ▸ **v.** [intrans.] (**prey on/upon**) hunt and kill for food: *small birds that prey on insects.* ■ take advantage of; exploit or injure. ■ cause constant trouble and distress to. — **prey·er** n. [ME: n. from OFr. *preie*, from L. *praeda* 'booty.']

prez /prez/ ▸ **n.** informal term for PRESIDENT.

prf. ▸ **abbr.** proof.

Pri·am /'prīəm/ Gk. Mythol. the king of Troy at the time of its destruction by the Greeks under Agamemnon; the father of Paris and Hector.

pri·ap·ic /prī'apik; -'āpik/ ▸ **adj.** of, relating to, or resembling a phallus. ■ of or relating to male sexuality and sexual activity. ■ Med. (of a male) having a persistently erect penis.

pri·a·pism /'prīə,pizəm/ ▸ **n.** Med. persistent and painful erection of the penis. [ME: via late L. from Gk. *priapismos*, from *priapizein* 'be lewd,' from *Priapos* (see PRIAPUS).]

Pri·ap·u·li·da /,prīə'pyo͞olədə/ Zool. a small phylum of burrowing wormlike marine invertebrates. — **pri·ap·u·lid** /prī'apyələd/ **n. & adj.** [mod. L. (pl.), from *Priapulus* (genus name), dimin. of PRIAPUS.]

Pri·a·pus /prī'āpəs/ Gk. Mythol. a god of fertility, whose cult spread to Greece (and, later, Italy) from Turkey after Alexander's conquests.

Prib·i·lof Is·lands /'pribə,lôf/ a group of four islands in the Bering Sea, off the coast of southwestern Alaska.

Price /prīs/, Leontyne (1927–), US opera singer; full name *Mary Violet Leontyne Price*. A soprano acclaimed for her role as Aida, she sang with the Metropolitan Opera 1961–85.

price /prīs/ ▸ **n.** the amount of money expected, required, or given in payment for something. ■ fig. an unwelcome experience, event, or action involved as a condition of achieving a desired end: *the price of success.* ■ the odds in betting. ■ archaic value; worth: *a pearl of great price.* ▸ **v.** [trans.] (often **be priced**) decide the amount required as payment for (something offered for sale).
– PHRASES **at any price** no matter what expense, sacrifice, or difficulty is involved. **at a price** requiring great expense or involving unwelcome consequences. **a price on someone's head** a reward offered for someone's capture or death. **price oneself out of the market** become unable to compete commercially. **put a price on** determine the value of. [ME: the n. from OFr. *pris*, from L. *pretium* 'value, reward.']

price con·trol ▸ **n.** a government regulation establishing a maximum price to be charged for specified goods and services, esp. during periods of war or inflation.

price-earn·ings ra·tio (also **price-earnings multiple**) ▸ **n.** Finance the current market price of a company share divided by the earnings per share of the company.

price-fix·ing (also **price fix·ing**) ▸ **n.** the maintaining of prices at a certain level by agreement between competing sellers.

price·less /'prīsləs/ ▸ **adj.** so precious that its value cannot be determined. ■ informal used to express great and usually affectionate amusement. — **price·less·ly** adv. **price·less·ness** n.

price list ▸ **n.** a list of current prices of items on sale.

price point ▸ **n.** a point on a scale of possible prices at which something might be marketed.

price-sen·si·tive ▶ adj. denoting a product whose sales are greatly influenced by the price. ■ (of information) likely to affect share prices if it were made public.

price sup·port ▶ n. Econ. government assistance in maintaining the levels of market prices regardless of supply or demand.

price tag ▶ n. the label on an item for sale, showing its price. ■ fig. the cost of a company, enterprise, or undertaking.

price-tak·er ▶ n. Econ. a company that must accept the prevailing market prices of its products, its own transactions being unable to affect market price. — **price-tak·ing** n. & adj.

price war ▶ n. a fierce competition in which retailers cut prices to increase their share of the market.

pric·ey /ˈprīsē/ (also **pric·y**) ▶ adj. (**pric·i·er, pric·i·est**) informal expensive. — **pric·i·ness** n.

prick /prik/ ▶ v. [trans.] **1** make a small hole in (something) with a sharp point; pierce slightly. ■ [intrans.] feel a sensation as though a sharp point were sticking into one: *she felt her scalp prick.* ■ (of tears) cause the sensation of imminent weeping in (a person's eyes): *tears were pricking her eyelids.* ■ [intrans.] (of a person's eyes) experience such a sensation. ■ cause mental or emotional discomfort to: *her conscience pricked her as she told the lie.* ■ arouse or provoke to action: *the police were pricked into action.* **2** (usu. **be pricked**) (esp. of a horse or dog) make (the ears) stand erect when on the alert: *the dog's ears were pricked.* ▶ n. **1** an act of piercing something with a fine, sharp point. ■ a small hole or mark made by piercing something with a fine, sharp point. ■ a sharp pain caused by being pierced with a fine point. ■ a sudden feeling of distress, anxiety, or some other unpleasant emotion. **2** vulgar slang a penis. ■ a man regarded as stupid, unpleasant, or contemptible.
– PHRASES **prick up one's ears** (esp. of a horse or dog) make the ears stand erect when on the alert. ■ (of a person) become suddenly attentive.
– PHRASAL VERBS **prick something out** (or **off**) transplant seedlings to a container or bed that provides adequate room for growth. — **prick·er** n. **prick·ing** n. [OE *pricca* (n.), *prician* (v.), prob. of West Gmc. origin and rel. to Low Ger. and Du. *prik* (n.), *prikken* (v.).]

prick·et /ˈprikit/ ▶ n. **1** a male fallow deer in its second year, having straight, unbranched horns. **2** hist. a spike for holding a candle. [ME: from PRICK + -ET[1].]

prick·le /ˈprikəl/ ▶ n. a short, slender, sharp-pointed outgrowth on the bark or epidermis of a plant; a small thorn. ■ a small spine or pointed outgrowth on the skin of certain animals. ■ a tingling sensation on someone's skin, typically caused by strong emotion. ▶ v. [intrans.] (of a person's skin or a part of the body) experience a tingling sensation, esp. as a result of strong emotion: *the sound made her skin prickle.* ■ [trans.] cause a tingling or mildly painful sensation in: *the fibers prickle your skin.* ■ (of a person) react defensively or angrily to something: *she prickled at the implication that she had led a soft life.* [OE *pricel* 'instrument for pricking'; rel. to MDu. *prickel*, from the Gmc. base of PRICK.]

prick·ly /ˈprik(ə)lē/ ▶ adj. (**-li·er, -li·est**) **1** covered in prickles. ■ resembling or feeling like prickles. ■ having or causing a tingling or itching sensation. **2** (of a person) ready to take offense. ■ liable to cause someone to take offense. — **prick·li·ness** n.

prick·ly-ash ▶ n. a spiny North American shrub or tree (genus *Zanthoxylum*) of the rue family, with prickly branches and bark that can be used medicinally. Two species: the **northern prickly-ash** (*Z. americanum*) (also called TOOTHACHE TREE), and the **southern prickly-ash** (see HERCULES-CLUB). ■ a medicinal preparation of the bark of these trees.

prick·ly heat ▶ n. an itchy inflammation of the skin, typically with a rash of small vesicles, common in hot moist weather. Also called MILIARIA.

prick·ly pear ▶ n. a cactus (genus *Opuntia*) with jointed stems and oval flattened segments, having barbed bristles and large pear-shaped, prickly fruits. ■ the edible orange or red fruit of this plant.

prickly pear

prick·ly pop·py ▶ n. a Central American poppy (*Argemone mexicana*) with prickly leaves and large scented yellow flowers. It has become a weed in many tropical regions, but is cultivated in cooler regions as an ornamental.

pric·y /ˈprīsē/ ▶ adj. var. of PRICEY.

pride /prīd/ ▶ n. **1** a feeling of pleasure from one's own achievements, the achievements of those with whom one is associated, or from qualities or possessions that are widely admired. ■ the consciousness of one's own dignity: *he swallowed his pride and asked for help.* ■ the quality of having an excessively high opinion of oneself or one's importance. ■ a person or thing that is the object or source of a feeling of deep pleasure or satisfaction. ■ literary the best state or condition of something; the prime. **2** a group of lions forming a social unit. ▶ v. (**pride oneself on/upon**) be especially proud of a particular quality or skill.
– PHRASES **pride of place** the most prominent or important position among a group of things. — **pride·ful** /-fəl/ adj. **pride·ful·ly** /-fəlē/ adv. [OE *prȳde* 'excessive self-esteem,' var. of *prȳtu, prȳte*, from *prūd* (see PROUD).]

prie-dieu /prē ˈdyə(r); -ˈdyœ/ ▶ n. (pl. **prie-dieux** /ˈdyə(r)(z); -ˈdyœ(z)/) a piece of furniture for use during prayer, consisting of a kneeling surface and a narrow upright front with a rest for the elbows. [18th C.: Fr., lit. 'pray God.']

priest /prēst/ ▶ n. an ordained minister of the Catholic, Orthodox, or Anglican Church having the authority to perform rites and administer sacraments. ■ a person who performs religious ceremonies and duties in a non-Christian religion. ▶ v. [trans.] (usu. **be priested**) formal ordain to the priesthood. [OE *prēost*, of Gmc. origin; based on eccles. L. *presbyter* 'elder' (see PRESBYTER).]

priest·craft /ˈprēst,kraft/ ▶ n. often derog. the knowledge and work of a priest.

priest·ess /ˈprēstis/ ▶ n. a female priest of a non-Christian religion.

priest·hood /ˈprēst,(h)o͝od/ ▶ n. (often **the priesthood**) the office or position of a priest. ■ priests in general.

Priest·ley[1] /ˈprēstlē/, J. B. (1894–1984), English writer; full name *John Boynton Priestley*. His novels include *The Good Companions* (1929).

Priest·ley[2], Joseph (1733–1804), English scientist and theologian. He discovered oxygen and demonstrated its importance.

priest·ly /ˈprēstlē/ ▶ adj. of, relating to, or befitting a priest or priests. — **priest·li·ness** n. [OE *prēostlic* (see PRIEST, -LY[1]).]

prig /prig/ ▶ n. a self-righteously moralistic person who behaves as if superior to others. — **prig·ger·y** /ˈprigərē/ n. **prig·gish** adj. **prig·gish·ly** adv. **prig·gish·ness** n. [16th C.: of unknown origin.]

prill /pril/ ▶ n. a pellet or solid globule formed by the congealing of a liquid during an industrial process. — **prilled** adj. [18th C.: of unknown origin.]

prim /prim/ ▶ adj. (**prim·mer, prim·mest**) stiffly formal and respectable. ▶ v. (**primmed, prim·ming**) [trans.] purse (the mouth or lips) into a prim expression: *Larry primmed up his mouth.* — **prim·ly** adv. **prim·ness** n. [17th C. (as a v.): prob. ult. from OFr. *prin*, Provençal *prim* 'excellent, delicate,' from L. *primus* 'first.']

prim. ▶ abbr. ■ primary. ■ primitive.

pri·ma bal·le·ri·na /ˈprēmə/ ▶ n. the chief female dancer in a ballet or ballet company. [19th C.: Ital., lit. 'first ballerina.']

pri·ma·cy /ˈprīməsē/ ▶ n. **1** the fact of being primary, preeminent, or more important. **2** the office, period of office, or authority of a primate of the Church.

pri·ma don·na /,primə ˈdänə; ,prēmə/ ▶ n. the chief female singer in an opera or opera company. ■ a very temperamental person with an inflated view of their own talent or importance. — **pri·ma don·na·ish** adj. [18th C.: Ital., lit. 'first lady.']

pri·mae·val /prīˈmēvəl/ ▶ adj. Brit. var. of PRIMEVAL.

pri·ma fa·ci·e /,prīmə ˈfāshə; ˈfāshē; ˈfāshē,ē/ ▶ adj. & adv. Law based on the first impression; accepted as correct until proved otherwise. [L., from *primus* 'first' + *facies* 'face.']

pri·mal /ˈprīməl/ ▶ adj. essential; fundamental. ■ relating to an early stage in evolutionary development; primeval. ■ Psychol. of, relating to, or denoting the needs, fears, or behavior postulated to form the origins of emotional life. See also PRIMAL SCENE. — **pri·mal·ly** adv. [17th C.: from med. L. *primalis*, from L. *primus* 'first.']

pri·mal scene ▶ n. Psychol. (in Freudian theory) the occasion on which a child becomes aware of its parents' sexual intercourse.

pri·mal scream ▶ n. a release of intense basic frustration, anger, and aggression, esp. that rediscovered by means of primal therapy.

pri·mal ther·a·py ▶ n. a form of psychotherapy that focuses on a patient's earliest emotional experiences and encourages verbal expression of childhood suffering.

pri·ma·quine /ˈprīmə,kwēn; ˈprē-/ ▶ n. Med. a synthetic compound derived from quinoline and used in the treatment of malaria. [1940s: appar. from L. *prima* (fem. of *primus* 'first') + *quin(olin)e*.]

pri·ma·ri·ly /prīˈme(ə)rəlē/ ▶ adv. for the most part.

pri·ma·ry /ˈprī,merē; ˈprīm(ə)rē/ ▶ adj. **1** of chief importance; principal. **2** earliest in time or order of development. ■ not derived from, caused by, or based on anything else: *the research involved the use of primary source materials.* **3** [attrib.] of or relating to education for children between the ages of about five and ten: *a primary school.* **4** Biol. & Med. belonging to or directly derived from the first stage of development or growth: *a primary bone tumor.* **5** (**Primary**) Geol. former term for PALEOZOIC. **6** relating to or denoting the input side of a device using electromagnetic induction, esp. in a transformer. **7** Chem. (of an organic compound) having its functional group located on a carbon atom that is bonded to no more than one other carbon atom. ■ (chiefly of amines) derived from ammonia by replacement of one hydrogen atom by an organic group. ▶ n. (pl. **-ries**) **1** (also **primary election**) a preliminary election to appoint delegates to a party conference or to select the candidates for a principal, esp. presidential, election. **2** short for: ■ a primary color. ■ a primary coil or winding in an electrical transformer. **3** Astron. the body orbited by a smaller satellite or companion. **4** (**the Primary**) Geol., dated the Primary or Paleozoic era. [ME: from L. *primarius*, from *primus* 'first.']

pri·ma·ry ac·cent ▶ n. another term for PRIMARY STRESS.

pri·ma·ry care (also **primary health care**) ▶ n. health care at a basic level for people making an initial approach to a doctor or nurse for treatment.

pri·ma·ry cell ▶ n. an electric cell that produces current by an irreversible chemical reaction.

pri·ma·ry col·or ▶ n. any of a group of colors from which all other colors can be obtained by mixing.

pri·ma·ry plan·et ▶ n. a planet that directly orbits the sun.

pri·ma·ry proc·ess ▶ n. Psychoanal. an unconscious thought process that arises from the pleasure principle and is irrational and not subject to compulsion.

pri·ma·ry stress ▶ n. Phonet. the strongest accent in a word or breath group. Compare with SECONDARY STRESS.

pri·ma·ry struc·ture ▶ n. Biochem. the characteristic sequence of amino acids forming a protein or polypeptide chain, considered as the most basic element of its structure.

pri·mate[1] /ˈprīˌmāt; ˈprīmət/ ▶ n. Christian Church the chief bishop or archbishop of a province. — **pri·ma·tial** /prīˈmāSHəl/ adj. [ME: from OFr. *primat*, from L. *primas, primat-* 'of the first rank,' from *primus* 'first.']

pri·mate[2] /ˈprīˌmāt/ ▶ n. Zool. a mammal of an order (Primates) that includes the lemurs, bush babies, tarsiers, marmosets, monkeys, apes, and humans. They are distinguished by having hands, handlike feet, and forward-facing eyes, and, with the exception of humans, are typically agile tree-dwellers. [19th C.: (see PRIMATE[1]).]

pri·ma·tol·o·gy /ˌprīməˈtäləjē/ ▶ n. the branch of zoology that deals with primates. — **pri·ma·to·log·i·cal** /ˌprīmətəˈläjikəl/ adj. **pri·ma·tol·o·gist** /-jist/ n.

pri·ma·ve·ra /ˌprēməˈve(ə)rə/ ▶ adj. [postpositive] (of a pasta dish) made with lightly sautéed spring vegetables: *linguine primavera*. [19th C.: from Sp., denoting the season of spring, from L. *primus* 'first, earliest' + *ver* 'spring.']

prime[1] /prīm/ ▶ adj. **1** of first importance; main. ■ from which another thing may derive or proceed: *Diogenes' conclusion that air is the prime matter.* **2** [attrib.] of the best possible quality; excellent. ■ having all the expected or typical characteristics of something: *the novel is a prime example of the genre.* ■ most suitable or likely: *it's the prime contender for best comedy of the year.* **3** Math. (of a number) evenly divisible only by itself and one (e.g., 2, 3, 5, 7, 11). ■ [predic.] (of two or more numbers in relation to each other) having no common factor but one. ▶ n. **1** [in sing.] a state or time of greatest strength, vigor, or success in a person's life. **2** Christian Church a service forming part of the Divine Office, traditionally said (or chanted) at the first hour of the day (i.e., 6 a.m.), but now little used. ■ archaic this time of day. **3** a prime number. **4** Print. a symbol (′) written after a letter or symbol as a distinguishing mark or after a figure as a symbol for minutes or feet. **5** Fencing the first of eight standard parrying positions. **6** short for PRIME RATE. — **prime·ness** n. [OE *prīm*, from L. *prima (hora)* 'first (hour);' adj. via OFr. from L. *primus* 'first.']

prime[2] ▶ v. [trans.] **1** make (something) ready for use or action, in particular: ■ prepare (a firearm or explosive device) for firing or detonation. ■ cover (wood, canvas, or metal) with a preparatory coat of paint to prevent the absorption of subsequent layers of paint. ■ pour or spray liquid into (a pump) before starting, to seal the moving parts and facilitate its operation. ■ inject extra fuel into (the cylinder or carburetor of an internal combustion engine) to facilitate starting. ■ [intrans.] (of a steam engine or its boiler) mix water with the steam being passed into the cylinder. ■ Biochem. serve as a starting material for (a polymerization process). **2** prepare (someone) for a situation or task, typically by supplying them with relevant information: [with infin.] *the sentries were primed to admit him without challenge.*
– PHRASES **prime the pump** stimulate the growth or success of something by supplying it with money. [16th C.: prob. based on L. *primus* 'first.']

prime cost ▶ n. the direct cost of a commodity in terms of the materials and labor involved in its production, excluding fixed costs.

prime me·rid·i·an ▶ n. a planet's meridian adopted as the zero of longitude. ■ (usu. **the prime meridian**) the earth's zero of longitude, which by convention passes through Greenwich, England. See also GREENWICH MERIDIAN.

prime min·is·ter ▶ n. the head of an elected government; the principal minister of a sovereign or state. — **prime min·is·ter·ship** n.

prime mov·er ▶ n. a person or establishment that is chiefly responsible for the creation or execution of a plan or project. ■ an initial natural or mechanical source of motive power.

prim·er[1] /ˈprīmər/ ▶ n. a substance used as a preparatory coat on previously unpainted wood, metal, or canvas, esp. to prevent the absorption of subsequent layers of paint or the development of rust. ■ a cap or cylinder containing a compound that responds to friction or an electrical impulse and ignites the charge in a cartridge or explosive. ■ a small pump for pumping fuel to prime an internal combustion engine, esp. in an aircraft. ■ Biochem. a molecule that serves as a starting material for a polymerization process.

prim·er[2] /ˈprimər/ ▶ n. an elementary textbook that serves as an introduction to a subject of study or is used for teaching children to read. [ME: from med. L. *primarius, primarium* 'primary.']

prime rate ▶ n. the lowest rate of interest at which money may be borrowed commercially.

prime rib ▶ n. a roast or steak cut from the seven ribs immediately before the loin.

prime time ▶ n. the regularly occurring time at which a television or radio audience is expected to be greatest, generally regarded as between 8 and 11 p.m.

pri·me·val /prīˈmēvəl/ (Brit. also **pri·mae·val**) ▶ adj. of or resembling the earliest ages in the history of the world. ■ (of feelings or actions) based on primitive instinct; raw and elementary: *a primeval desire.* — **pri·me·val·ly** adv. [17th C.: from L. *primaevus* (from *primus* 'first' + *aevum* 'age') + -AL.]

prim·ing /ˈprīmiNG/ ▶ n. a substance that prepares something for use or action, in particular: ■ another term for PRIMER[1]. ■ gunpowder placed in the pan of a firearm to ignite a charge.

pri·mip·a·ra /prīˈmipərə/ ▶ n. (pl. **-ras** or **-rae** /-rē; -ˌrī/) Med. a woman who is giving birth for the first time. — **pri·mip·a·rous** /-rəs/ adj. [19th C.: mod. L. (fem.), from *primus* 'first' + *-parus* 'bringing forth' (from the verb *parere*).]

prim·i·tive /ˈprimətiv/ ▶ adj. **1** relating to, denoting, or preserving an early stage in the evolutionary or historical development of something. ■ relating to or denoting a preliterate, nonindustrial society characterized by simple social and economic organization. ■ having a quality or style that offers a basic level of comfort, convenience, or efficiency. ■ (of behavior, thought, or emotion) apparently originating in unconscious needs or desires and unaffected by reasoning. ■ of or denoting a simple, direct style of art that deliberately rejects sophisticated artistic techniques. **2** not developed or derived from anything else. ■ Ling. denoting a word, base, or root from which another is historically derived. ■ Ling. denoting an irreducible form. ■ Math. (of an algebraic or geometric expression) from which another is derived, or which is not itself derived from another. **3** Biol. (of a part or structure) in the first or early stage of formation or growth; rudimentary. See also PRIMITIVE STREAK. ▶ n. **1** a person belonging to a preliterate, nonindustrial society or culture. **2** a pre-Renaissance painter. ■ a modern painter who imitates the pre-Renaissance style. ■ an artist employing a simple, naive style that deliberately rejects conventional techniques. ■ a painting by a primitive artist, or an object in a primitive style. **3** Ling. a word, base, or root from which another is historically derived. ■ Ling. an irreducible form. ■ Math. an algebraic or geometric expression from which another is derived; a curve of which another is the polar or reciprocal. — **prim·i·tive·ly** adv. **prim·i·tive·ness** n. **prim·i·tiv·i·ty** /ˌpriməˈtivətē/ n. [ME: from OFr. *primitif, -ive*, from L. *primitivus* 'first of its kind,' from *primus* 'first.']

prim·i·tive streak ▶ n. Embryol. the faint streak that is the earliest trace of the embryo in the fertilized ovum of a higher vertebrate.

prim·i·tiv·ism /ˈprimətivˌizəm/ ▶ n. **1** a belief in the value of what is simple and unsophisticated, expressed as a philosophy of life or through art or literature. **2** unsophisticated behavior that is unaffected by objective reasoning. — **prim·i·tiv·ist** n. & adj.

pri·mo /ˈprēmō/ ▶ n. (pl. **-mos**) Music the leading or upper part in a duet. ▶ adj. informal of top quality or importance. [18th C.: Ital., lit. 'first.']

pri·mo·gen·i·tor /ˌprīmōˈjenətər/ ▶ n. an ancestor, esp. the earliest ancestor of a people; a progenitor. [17th C.: var. of PROGENITOR.]

pri·mo·gen·i·ture /ˌprīmōˈjeniˌCHər; -ˌCHo͝or/ ▶ n. the state of being the firstborn child. ■ (also **right of primogeniture**) the right of succession belonging to the firstborn child, esp. the feudal rule by which the whole real estate of an intestate passed to the eldest son. — **pri·mo·gen·i·tal** /-ˈjenitl/ adj. **pri·mo·gen·i·tar·y** /-ˈjeniˌterē/ adj. [17th C.: from med. L. *primogenitura*, from L. *primo* 'first' + *genitura* 'geniture.']

pri·mor·di·al /prīˈmôrdēəl/ ▶ adj. existing at or from the beginning of time; primeval. ■ (esp. of a state or quality) basic and fundamental. ■ Biol. (of a cell, part, or tissue) in the earliest stage of development. — **pri·mor·di·al·i·ty** /ˌprīˌmôrdēˈalətē/ n. **pri·mor·di·al·ly** adv. [ME: from late L. *primordialis* 'first of all,' from *primordius* 'original' (see PRIMORDIUM).]

pri·mor·di·al soup ▶ n. a solution rich in organic compounds in the primitive oceans of the earth, from which life is thought to have originated.

pri·mor·di·um /prīˈmôrdēəm/ ▶ n. (pl. **-di·a** /-dēə/) Biol. an organ, structure, or tissue in the earliest stage of development. [19th C.: from L.]

primp /primp/ ▶ v. [trans.] spend time making minor adjustments to (one's hair, makeup, or clothes). [16th C.: rel. to PRIM.]

prim·rose /ˈprimˌrōz/ ▶ n. a cultivated plant (*Primula vulgaris*) of European woodlands that produces pale yellow flowers in the early spring. The **primrose family** (Primulaceae) also includes the cowslips, pimpernels, and cyclamens. ■ (also **primrose yellow**) a pale yellow color.
– PHRASES **primrose path** the pursuit of pleasure, esp. when it is seen to bring disastrous consequences. [ME: compare OFr. *primerose*, lit. 'first rose.']

prim·u·la /ˈprimyələ/ ▶ n. a plant of a genus (*Primula*) that includes primroses, cowslips, and cyclamens. Many kinds are cultivated as ornamentals, bearing flowers in a wide variety of colors in the spring. [mod. L., from med. L., fem. of *primulus*, dimin. of *primus* 'first.']

prim·u·la·ceous /ˌprimyəˈlāSHəs/ ▶ adj. Bot. of, relating to, or denoting plants of the primrose family (Primulaceae).

pri·mum mo·bi·le /ˌprīməm ˈmōbəˌlē; ˌprē-/ ▶ n. **1** the central or most important source of motion or action. **2** (in the Ptolemaic system) an outer sphere supposed to move around the earth in 24 hours, carrying the inner spheres with it. [from med. L., lit. 'first moving thing.']

pri·mus in·ter pa·res /ˈprīməs ˌintər ˈparˌēz/ ▶ n. a first among equals. [L.]

prin. ▶ abbr. ■ principal. ■ principally. ■ principle.

prince /prins/ ▶ n. the son of a monarch. ■ a close male relative of a monarch, esp. a son's son. ■ a male royal ruler of a small state subject to a king or emperor. ■ (in France, Germany, and other European countries) a nobleman, usually ranking next below a duke. ■ **(prince of/among)** a man or thing outstanding in a particular sphere or group. — **prin·ce·dom** /-dəm/ **n.** [ME: via OFr. from L. *princeps, princip-* 'first, chief, sovereign,' from *primus* 'first' + *capere* 'take.']

Prince Charm·ing (also **prince charm·ing**) an ideal male lover who is both handsome and of admirable character.

prince con·sort ▶ **n.** (pl. **princ·es con·sort**) the husband of a reigning female sovereign who is himself a prince.

Prince Ed·ward Is·land an island in the Gulf of St. Lawrence, in eastern Canada, the country's smallest province; capital, Charlottetown.

prince·ling /'prinsliNG/ ▶ **n.** esp. derog. the ruler of a small principality or domain. ■ a young prince.

prince·ly /'prinslē/ ▶ **adj.** of or held by a prince. ■ sumptuous and splendid. ■ (of a sum of money) large or generous (often used ironically). — **prince·li·ness n.**

Prince of Dark·ness ▶ **n.** a name for the Devil.

Prince of Peace ▶ **n.** a title given to Jesus Christ (in allusion to Isa. 9:6).

Prince of the Church ▶ **n.** hist. a dignitary in the Church, esp. a wealthy or influential cardinal or bishop.

Prince of Wales ▶ **n.** a title granted to the heir apparent to the British throne (usually the eldest son of the sovereign).

Prince of Wales Is·land **1** an island in the Canadian Arctic, in the Northwest Territories. **2** former name for **PENANG**. **3** the largest island in the Alexander Archipelago, in southeastern Alaska, home to the Haida people.

prince roy·al ▶ **n.** the eldest son of a reigning monarch.

Prince Ru·pert's Land another name for **RUPERT'S LAND**.

prin·cess /'prinsəs; 'prin,ses; prin'ses/ ▶ **n.** the daughter of a monarch. ■ a close female relative of monarch, esp. a son's daughter. ■ the wife or widow of a prince. ■ the female ruler of a small state, or subject to a king or emperor. ■ informal a spoiled young woman.

prin·cess roy·al ▶ **n.** the eldest daughter of a reigning monarch (esp. as a title conferred by the British monarch).

Prince·ton U·ni·ver·si·ty /'prinstən/ an Ivy League university at Princeton, New Jersey, founded in 1746.

Prince Wil·liam Sound /'wilyəm/ an inlet of the Pacific Ocean in south central Alaska.

prin·ci·pal /'prinsəpəl/ ▶ **adj.** [attrib.] **1** first in order of importance; main. **2** (of money) denoting an original sum invested or lent. ▶ **n.** **1** the person with the highest authority or most important position in an organization. ■ the head of a school, college, or other educational institution. ■ the leading performer in a concert, play, ballet, or opera. ■ Music the leading player in each section of an orchestra. **2** a sum of money lent or invested on which interest is paid. **3** a person for whom another acts as an agent or representative. ■ Law the person directly responsible for a crime. ■ hist. each of the combatants in a duel. **4** a main rafter supporting purlins. **5** an organ stop sounding a main register of open flue pipes typically an octave above the diapason. — **prin·ci·pal·ship** /-,SHip/ **n.** [ME: via OFr. from L. *principalis* 'first, original,' from *princeps, princip-* 'first, chief.']

prin·ci·pal di·ag·o·nal ▶ **n.** Math. the set of elements of a matrix that lie on the line joining the top left corner to the bottom right corner.

prin·ci·pal·i·ty /,prinsə'palətē/ ▶ **n.** (pl. **-ties**) **1** a state ruled by a prince. ■ **(the Principality)** Brit. Wales. **2** **(principalities)** (in traditional Christian angelology) the fifth highest order of the ninefold celestial hierarchy.

prin·ci·pal·ly /'prinsəp(ə)lē/ ▶ **adv.** [sentence adverb] for the most part; chiefly.

prin·ci·pal parts ▶ **plural n.** Gram. the forms of a verb from which all other inflected forms can be deduced, for example, *swim, swam, swum*.

prin·ci·pate /'prinsə,pāt; -pət/ ▶ **n.** the rule of the early Roman emperors, during which some features of republican government were retained. ■ supreme office or authority.

prin·ci·ple /'prinsəpəl/ ▶ **n.** **1** a fundamental truth or proposition that serves as the foundation for a system of belief or behavior or for a chain of reasoning. ■ (usu. **principles**) a rule or belief governing one's personal behavior. ■ morally correct behavior and attitudes. ■ a general scientific theorem or law that has numerous special applications across a wide field. ■ a natural law forming the basis for the construction or working of a machine. **2** a fundamental source or basis of something: *the first principle of all things was water.* ■ a fundamental quality or attribute determining the nature of something; an essence: *the combination of male and female principles.* ■ [with adj.] Chem. an active or characteristic constituent of a substance, obtained by simple analysis or separation: *the active principle in the medulla is epinephrine.*

– PHRASES **in principle** as a general idea or plan, although the details are not yet established or clear. ■ used to indicate that although something is theoretically possible, it may not actually happen. **on principle** because of or in order to demonstrate one's adherence to a particular belief. [ME: from OFr., from L. *principium* 'source,' *principia* (pl.) 'foundations,' from *princeps, princip-* 'first, chief.']

prin·ci·pled /'prinsəpəld/ ▶ **adj.** **1** (of a person or their behavior) acting in accordance with morality and showing recognition of right and wrong. **2** (of a system or method) based on a given set of rules.

prink /priNGk/ ▶ **v.** **(prink oneself)** spend time making minor adjustments to one's appearance; primp. [16th C.: rel. to Mid. Low Ger. *prank* 'pomp.']

print /print/ ▶ **v.** [trans.] (often **be printed**) **1** produce (books, newspapers, etc.), esp. in large quantities, by a mechanical process involving the transfer of text or designs to paper. ■ produce (text or a picture) in such a way: *the words had been printed in blue type.* ■ (of a newspaper or magazine) publish (a piece of writing) within its pages: *the article was printed in the first edition.* ■ (of a publisher or printer) arrange for (a book, manuscript, etc.) to be reproduced in large quantities. ■ produce a paper copy of (information stored on a computer). ■ produce (a photographic print) from a negative. ■ write (text) clearly without joining the letters: *print your name and address* | [intrans.] *it will be easier to read if I print.* **2** mark (a surface, typically a textile or a garment) with a colored design or pattern: *a delicate fabric printed with roses.* ■ transfer (a colored design or pattern) to a surface. ■ make (a mark or indentation) on a surface or in a soft substance by pressing something onto it: *he printed a mark on her soft skin.* ■ mark or indent (the surface of a soft substance) in such a way: *we printed the butter with carved wooden butter molds.* ■ fig. fix (something) firmly or indelibly in someone's mind. ▶ **n.** **1** the text appearing in a book, newspaper, or other printed publication, esp. with reference to its size, form, or style. ■ the state of being available in published form: *the news will never get into print.* ■ a newspaper or magazine: [as adj.] *the print media.* ■ [as adj.] of or relating to the printing industry or the printed media. **2** an indentation or mark left on a surface or soft substance by pressure, esp. that of a foot or hand. ■ **(prints)** fingerprints. **3** a picture or design printed from a block or plate or copied from a painting by photography. ■ a photograph printed on paper from a negative or transparency. ■ a copy of a motion picture on film, esp. a particular version of it. **4** a piece of fabric or clothing with a decorative colored pattern or design printed on it. ■ such a pattern or design.

– PHRASES **appear in print** (of an author) have one's work published. **in print** **1** (of a book) available from the publisher. **2** in printed or published form. **out of print** (of a book) no longer available from the publisher: *the title I want is out of print.* **the printed word** language or ideas as expressed in books, newspapers, or other publications. [ME: from OFr. *preinte* 'pressed,' fem. past part. of *preindre*, from L. *premere* 'to press.']

print·a·bil·i·ty /,printə'bilətē/ ▶ **n.** the ability of paper to take print.

print·a·ble /'printəbəl/ ▶ **adj.** suitable or fit to be printed or published. ■ Comput. (of text) able to be printed.

print·ed cir·cuit ▶ **n.** an electronic circuit consisting of thin strips of a conducting material etched from a layer fixed to a flat insulating sheet called a **printed circuit board**, to which integrated circuits and other components are attached.

print·er /'printər/ ▶ **n.** a person whose job or business is commercial printing. ■ a machine for printing text or pictures onto paper, esp. one linked to a computer.

print·er's dev·il ▶ **n.** hist. a person, typically a young boy, serving at or below the level of apprentice in a printing establishment.

print·er's mark ▶ **n.** a logo serving as a printer's trademark.

print·er·y /'printərē/ ▶ **n.** (pl. **-ter·ies**) a print shop.

print·head /'print,hed/ (also **print head**) ▶ **n.** Comput. a component in a printer that assembles and holds the characters and from which the images of the characters are transferred to the printing medium.

print·ing /'printiNG/ ▶ **n.** the production of books, newspapers, or other printed material. ■ a single impression of a book. ■ handwriting in which the letters are written separately rather than being joined together.

print·ing press ▶ **n.** a machine for printing text or pictures from type or plates.

print·mak·er /'print,mākər/ ▶ **n.** a person who makes pictures or designs by printing them from specially prepared plates or blocks. — **print·mak·ing** /-,mākiNG/ **n.**

print·out /'print,out/ ▶ **n.** Comput. a page or set of pages of printed material produced by a computer's printer.

print queue ▶ **n.** Comput. a series of print jobs waiting to use a printer.

print run ▶ **n.** the number of copies of a book, magazine, etc., printed at one time.

print shop (also **print·shop**) ▶ **n.** an establishment where the printing of newspapers, books, and other materials takes place.

pri·on /'prē,än/ ▶ **n.** Microbiol. a protein particle that is believed to be the cause of brain diseases such as BSE, scrapie, and Creutzfeldt–Jakob disease. Prions contain no nucleic acid and are highly resistant to destruction. [1980s: from *pro(teinaceous) in(fectious particle)*.]

pri·or[1] /'prīər/ ▶ **adj.** [attrib.] existing or coming before in time, order, or importance. ▶ **n.** informal a previous criminal conviction: *he had no priors.*

– PHRASES **prior to** before a particular time or event. [18th C.: from L., lit. 'former, elder,' rel. to *prae* 'before.']

pri·or[2] ▶ **n.** a man who is head of a house or group of houses of certain religious orders, in particular: ■ the man next in rank below an abbot. ■ the head of a house of friars. — **pri·or·ate** /'prīərət/ **n.** **pri·or·ship** /-,SHip/ **n.** [OE, from L. *prior* 'elder, former' (see **PRIOR**[1]).]

pri·or·ess /'prīərəs/ ▶ **n.** a woman who is head of a house of certain orders of nuns. ■ the woman next in rank below an abbess.

pri·or·i·tize /prī'ôrə,tīz; -'är-/ ▶**v.** [trans.] designate or treat (something) as more important than other things: *prioritize your credit card debt.* ■ determine the order for dealing with (a series of items or tasks) according to their relative importance: *people prioritize their goals* | [intrans.] *are you able to prioritize?* — **pri·or·i·ti·za·tion** /,prī,ôrətə'zāsʜən/ **n.**

pri·or·i·ty /prī'ôrətē; -'är-/ ▶**n.** (pl. **-ties**) a thing that is regarded as more important than another. ■ the fact or condition of being regarded or treated as more important. ■ the right to take precedence or to proceed before others: *priority is given to those with press passes.*

pri·o·ry /'prīərē/ ▶**n.** (pl. **-ries**) a small monastery or nunnery that is governed by a prior or prioress. [ME: from Anglo-Norman Fr. *priorie*, med. L. *prioria*, from L. *prior* 'elder, superior' (see **PRIOR**[2]).]

Pri·pyat /'prēpyit/ (also **Pri·pet** /'pripit; -et/) a river in northwestern Ukraine and southern Belarus that flows through the Pripyat Marshes to join the Dnieper River.

Pri·scian /'prisʜ(ē)ən/ (6th century AD), Byzantine grammarian; full name *Priscianus Caesariensis.*

prise ▶**v.** var. of **PRIZE**[2].

prism /'prizəm/ ▶**n.** Geom. a solid geometric figure whose two end faces are similar, equal, and parallel rectilinear figures, and whose sides are parallelograms. ■ Optics a glass or other transparent object in this form, esp. one that is triangular with refracting surfaces at an acute angle with each other and that separates white light into a spectrum of colors. ■ used figuratively with reference to the clarification or distortion afforded by a particular viewpoint. [16th C.: via late L. from Gk. *prisma* 'thing sawn,' from *prizein* 'to saw.']

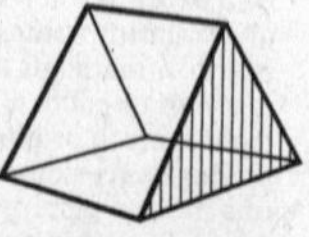
geometric prism

pris·mat·ic /priz'matik/ ▶**adj.** of, relating to, or having the form of a prism or prisms. ■ (of colors) formed, separated, or distributed by an optical prism or something acting as one. ■ (of colors) varied and brilliant. ■ (of an instrument) incorporating a prism or prisms. — **pris·mat·i·cal·ly** /-ik(ə)lē/ **adv.**

pris·moid /'priz,moid/ ▶**n.** Geom. a solid geometric figure like a prism, in which the end faces have the same number of sides but are not equal.

pris·on /'prizən/ ▶**n.** a building to which people are legally committed as a punishment for crimes they have committed or while awaiting trial. ■ confinement in such a building. ▶**v.** (**-oned, -on·ing**) [trans.] literary imprison. [OE, from OFr. *prisun*, from L. *prensio(n-)*, var. of *prehensio(n-)* 'laying hold of,' from the verb *prehendere.*]

pris·on camp ▶**n.** a camp where prisoners of war or political prisoners are kept under guard. ■ a minimum-security prison, typically where prisoners have outdoor work assignments.

pris·on·er /'priz(ə)nər/ ▶**n.** a person legally committed to prison as a punishment for crimes committed or while awaiting trial. ■ a person captured and kept confined by an enemy, opponent, or criminal. ■ fig. a person who is or perceives themselves to be confined or trapped by a situation or set of circumstances.
– PHRASES **take no prisoners** be ruthlessly aggressive or uncompromising in the pursuit of one's objectives.

pris·on·er of con·science ▶**n.** a person imprisoned for holding political or religious views not tolerated by the government of the state in which they live.

pris·on·er of war (abbr.: **POW**) ▶**n.** a person who has been captured and imprisoned by the enemy in war.

pris·on·er's base ▶**n.** a chasing game played by two groups of children each occupying a distinct base.

pris·on·er's di·lem·ma ▶**n.** (in game theory) a situation in which two players each have two options whose outcome depends on the simultaneous choice made by the other, often formulated in terms of two prisoners separately deciding whether to confess to a crime.

pris·sy /'prisē/ ▶**adj.** (**-si·er, -si·est**) (of a person or their manner) fussily and excessively respectable. ■ (of clothes) overadorned with details such as ruffles and bows. — **pris·si·ly** /'prisəlē/ **adv.** **pris·si·ness** **n.** [19th C.: perh. a blend of **PRIM** and **SISSY**.]

Priš·ti·na /'prisʜti,nä/ a city in southern Serbia, the capital of the autonomous province of Kosovo; pop. 108,000.

pris·tine /'pris,tēn; pri'stēn/ ▶**adj.** in its original condition; unspoiled. ■ clean and fresh as if new; spotless. — **pris·tine·ly** **adv.** [16th C.: from L. *pristinus* 'former.']

Pritch·ett /'pricʜət/, Sir V. S. (1900–97), English writer; full name *Victor Sawdon Pritchett.* His short-story collections include *The Spanish Virgin and Other Stories* (1930).

prith·ee /'priᴛʜē/ ▶**exclam.** archaic please (used to convey a polite request): *prithee, Jack, answer me honestly.* [16th C.: abbrev. of *I pray thee.*]

priv. ▶**abbr.** ■ private. ■ privative.

pri·va·cy /'prīvəsē/ ▶**n.** the state or condition of being free from being observed or disturbed by other people. ■ the state of being free from public attention.

pri·vate /'prīvit/ ▶**adj.** **1** belonging to or for the use of one particular person or group of people only. ■ (of a situation, activity, or gathering) affecting or involving only one person or group of people. ■ (of thoughts and feelings) not to be shared with or revealed to others. ■ (of a person) not choosing to share thoughts and feelings with others. ■ (of a meeting or discussion) involving only a small number of people and dealing with matters not to be disclosed to others. ■ (of a place) quiet and free from people who can interrupt. **2** (of a person) having no official or public role or position. ■ not connected with one's work or official position. **3** (of a service or industry) provided or owned by an individual or an independent, commercial company rather than by the government. ■ of or relating to a system of education or medical treatment conducted outside the government and charging fees to the individuals using it. ■ of, relating to, or denoting a transaction between individuals and not involving commercial organizations. ▶**n.** **1** an enlisted person in the armed forces of the lowest rank, in particular an enlisted person in the US Army or Marine Corps ranking below private first class. **2** (**privates**) informal short for **PRIVATE PARTS**.
– PHRASES **in private** with no one else present. [ME: from L. *privatus* 'withdrawn from public life,' a use of the past part. of *privare* 'bereave, deprive,' from *privus* 'single, individual.']

pri·vate de·tec·tive ▶**n.** another term for **PRIVATE INVESTIGATOR**.

pri·vate en·ter·prise ▶**n.** business or industry that is managed by independent companies or private individuals rather than by the state.

pri·va·teer /,prīvə'ti(ə)r/ ▶**n.** esp. hist. an armed ship owned and officered by private individuals holding a government commission and authorized for use in war, esp. in the capture of enemy merchant shipping. ■ (also **privateersman**) a commander or crew member of such a ship, often regarded as a pirate. ▶**v.** [intrans.] engage in the activities of a privateer. — **pri·va·teer·ing** **n.**

pri·vate eye ▶**n.** informal a private investigator.

pri·vate first class ▶**n.** an enlisted person in the armed forces, in particular (in the US Army) an enlisted person ranking above private and below corporal or (in the US Marine Corps) an enlisted person ranking above private and below lance corporal.

pri·vate in·ves·ti·ga·tor (also **private detective**) ▶**n.** a freelance detective who carries out covert investigations on behalf of private clients.

pri·vate key ▶**n.** see **PUBLIC KEY**.

pri·vate law ▶**n.** a branch of the law that deals with the relations between individuals or institutions, rather than relations between these and the government.

pri·vate·ly /'prīvitlē/ ▶**adv.** in a private way, manner, or capacity. ■ [often sentence adverb] used to refer to a situation in which someone's thoughts and feelings are not disclosed to others: *privately, Republicans worried about the polls.*

pri·vate nui·sance ▶**n.** Law see **NUISANCE**.

pri·vate parts ▶**plural n.** used euphemistically to refer to a person's genitals.

pri·vate prac·tice ▶**n.** the work of a professional, such as a doctor or lawyer, who is self-employed.

pri·vate school ▶**n.** **1** a school supported by a private organization or private individuals rather than by the government. **2** Brit. a school supported wholly by the payment of fees.

pri·vate sec·re·tar·y ▶**n.** a secretary who deals with the personal and confidential concerns of a business person or public figure.

pri·vate sec·tor ▶**n.** the part of the national economy that is not under direct government control.

pri·vate sol·dier ▶**n.** a soldier of the lowest rank.

pri·va·tion /prī'vāsʜən/ ▶**n.** a state in which things essential for human well-being such as food and warmth are scarce or lacking. ■ formal the loss or absence of a quality normally present. [ME: from L. *privatio(n-)*, from *privat-* 'deprived,' from the verb *privare* (see **PRIVATE**).]

pri·va·tism /'prīvə,tizəm/ ▶**n.** a tendency to be concerned with ideas or issues only insofar as they affect one as an individual. — **pri·va·tist** **adj.**

pri·va·tive /'privətiv/ ▶**adj.** (of an action or state) marked by the absence, removal, or loss of some quality normally present. ■ (of a statement or term) denoting the absence or loss of an attribute: *the wording of the privative clause.* ■ Gram. (of a particle or affix) expressing absence or negation, for example, the Greek *a-*, meaning "not," in *atypical.* ▶**n.** a privative attribute, quality, or proposition.

pri·va·tize /'prīvə,tīz/ ▶**v.** [trans.] transfer (a business, industry, or service) from public to private ownership and control: *a plan for privatizing education.* — **pri·va·ti·za·tion** /,prīvətə'zāsʜən/ **n.** **pri·va·tiz·er** **n.**

priv·et /'privit/ ▶**n.** a shrub (genus *Ligustrum*) of the olive family, with small white, heavily scented flowers and poisonous black berries. Its several species include the semievergreen **common privet** (*L. vulgare*), often grown as a hedge. [16th C.: of unknown origin.]

priv·i·lege /'priv(ə)lij/ ▶**n.** a special right, advantage, or immunity granted or available only to one person or group of people. ■ something regarded as a rare opportunity and bringing particular pleasure. ■ the right of a lawyer or official to refuse to divulge confidential information. ▶**v.** [trans.] formal grant a privilege or privileges to: *English inheritance law privileged the eldest son.* ■ (usu. **be privileged from**) exempt (someone) from a liability or obligation to which others are subject. [ME: via OFr. from L. *privilegium* 'bill or law affecting an individual,' from *privus* 'private' + *lex, leg-* 'law.']

priv·i·leged /'priv(ə)lijd/ ▶**adj.** having special rights, advantages, or immunities. ■ [with infin.] having the rare opportunity to do something that brings particular pleasure: *I felt privileged to compete in such a race.* ■ (of information) legally protected from being made public: *the reports are privileged.*

priv·i·ty /'privitē/ ▶**n.** (pl. **-ties**) Law a relation between two parties that is recognized by law, such as that of blood, lease, or service.

priv·y /ˈprivē/ ▶ **adj.** [predic.] (**privy to**) sharing in the knowledge of (something secret or private): *he was not privy to her thoughts.* ▶ **n.** (pl. **priv·ies**) **1** a toilet located in a small shed outside a house or other building; an outhouse. **2** Law a person having a part or interest in any action, matter, or thing. — **priv·i·ly** /ˈprivəlē/ **adv.** [ME: from OFr. *prive* 'private,' from L. *privatus* 'withdrawn from public life' (see PRIVATE).]

priv·y coun·cil ▶ **n.** a body of advisers or private counselors appointed by a sovereign or a governor general. — **priv·y coun·ci·lor n.**

prix fixe /prē ˈfēks; ˈfiks/ ▶ **n.** a meal consisting of several courses served at a total fixed price. [Fr., lit. 'fixed price.']

prize[1] /prīz/ ▶ **n.** a thing given as a reward to the winner of a competition or race or in recognition of another outstanding achievement. ▪ a thing, esp. money or a valuable object, that can be won in a lottery or other game of chance. ▪ something of great value that is worth struggling to achieve. ▪ esp. hist. an enemy ship captured during the course of naval warfare. ▶ **adj.** [attrib.] (esp. of something entered in a competition) having been or likely to be awarded a prize. ▪ denoting something for which a prize is awarded. ▪ excellent of its kind; outstanding. ▪ complete; utter: *I'm a prize idiot.* ▶ **v.** [trans.] (often **be prized**) value extremely highly: *the berries were prized for their healing properties.* [ME: the noun, a var. of PRICE; the verb from OFr. *pris-*, stem of *preisier* 'to praise, appraise' (see PRAISE).]

prize[2] (also **prise**) ▶ **v.** another term for PRY[2]. [17th C.: from dial. *prise* 'lever,' from OFr. *prise* 'grasp, taking hold.']

prize court ▶ **n.** a naval court that adjudicates on the distribution of ships and property captured in the course of naval warfare.

prize·fight /ˈprīzˌfīt/ (also **prize fight**) ▶ **n.** a boxing match fought for prize money. — **prize·fight·er n. prize·fight·ing n.**

prize ring ▶ **n.** a ring used for prizefighting. ▪ (**the prize ring**) the practice of prizefighting; boxing.

p.r.n. ▶ **abbr.** (in prescriptions) as the occasion arises; as needed. [L. *pro re nata.*]

PRO ▶ **abbr.** public relations officer.

pro[1] /prō/ ▶ **n.** (pl. **pros**) informal a professional, esp. in sports: *a tennis pro.* ▶ **adj.** (of a person or an event) professional. [19th C.: abbrev.]

pro[2] ▶ **n.** (pl. **pros**) (usu. **pros**) an advantage of something or an argument in favor of a course of action: *the pros and cons of joint ownership.* ▶ **prep. & adv.** in favor of. [ME (as a n.): from L., lit. 'for, on behalf of.']

pro-[1] ▶ **prefix 1** favoring; supporting: *pro-life.* **2** acting as a substitute or deputy for; on behalf of; for: *procure.* **3** denoting motion forward, out, or away: *propel.* [from L. *pro* 'in front of, on behalf of, instead of, on account of.']

pro-[2] ▶ **prefix** before in time, place, order, etc.: *prognosis.* [from Gk. *pro* 'before.']

pro·a /ˈprōə/ (also **pra·hu** /ˈpräˌo͞o/ or **prau** /prou/) ▶ **n.** a type of sailing boat originating in Malaysia and Indonesia that may be sailed with either end at the front, typically having a large triangular sail and an outrigger. [16th C.: from Malay *perahu.*]

pro·ac·tive /prōˈaktiv/ ▶ **adj.** (of a person, policy, or action) creating or controlling a situation by causing something to happen rather than responding to it after it has happened. — **pro·ac·tion** /prōˈakshən/ **n. pro·ac·tive·ly adv. pro·ac·tiv·i·ty** /ˌprōˌakˈtivətē/ **n.** [1930s: from PRO-[2].]

pro·ac·tive in·hi·bi·tion ▶ **n.** Psychol. the tendency of previously learned material to hinder subsequent learning.

pro-am /ˈprō ˈam/ ▶ **adj.** (of a sports event) involving both professionals and amateurs. ▶ **n.** an event of this type.

prob /präb/ ▶ **n.** informal problem: *there's no prob.*

prob. ▶ **abbr.** ▪ probable or probably. ▪ probate. ▪ problem.

prob·a·bi·lis·tic /ˌpräbəbəˈlistik/ ▶ **adj.** based on or adapted to a theory of probability. — **prob·a·bi·lism** /ˈpräbəbəˌlizəm/ **n.**

prob·a·bil·i·ty /ˌpräbəˈbilətē/ ▶ **n.** (pl. **-ties**) the extent to which something is probable. ▪ a probable event: *revolution was a strong probability.* ▪ the most probable thing. ▪ Math. the extent to which an event is likely to occur, measured by the ratio of the favorable cases to the whole number of cases possible.
– PHRASES **in all probability** used to convey that something is very likely.

prob·a·bil·i·ty den·si·ty func·tion ▶ **n.** Stat. a function of a continuous random variable, whose integral across an interval gives the probability that the value of the variable lies within the same interval.

prob·a·bil·i·ty dis·tri·bu·tion ▶ **n.** Stat. a function of a discrete variable whose integral over any interval is the probability that the random variable specified by it will lie within that interval.

prob·a·bil·i·ty the·o·ry ▶ **n.** the branch of mathematics that deals with quantities having random distributions.

prob·a·ble /ˈpräbəbəl/ ▶ **adj.** [often with clause] likely to be the case or to happen. [ME (in the sense 'worthy of belief'): via OFr. from L. *probabilis*, from *probare* 'to test, demonstrate.']

prob·a·ble cause ▶ **n.** Law reasonable grounds (for making a search, pressing a charge, etc.).

prob·a·bly /ˈpräbəblē/ ▶ **adv.** almost certainly; as far as one knows or can tell.

pro·band /ˈprōˌband; prōˈband/ ▶ **n.** a person serving as the starting point for the genetic study of a family (used esp. in medicine and psychiatry). [1920s: from L. *probandus* 'to be proved,' gerundive of *probare* 'to test.']

pro·bang /ˈprōˌbaNG/ ▶ **n.** Med. a strip of flexible material with a sponge or tuft at the end, used to remove an object from the throat or apply medication to it. [17th C.: origin unknown.]

pro·bate /ˈprōˌbāt/ ▶ **n.** the official proving of a will. ▪ a verified copy of a will with a certificate as handed to the executors. ▶ **v.** [trans.] establish the validity of (a will). [ME: from L. *probatum* 'something proved,' neut. past part. of *probare* 'to test, prove.']

pro·ba·tion /prōˈbāshən/ ▶ **n.** Law the release of an offender from detention, subject to a period of good behavior under supervision. ▪ the process or period of testing or observing the character or abilities of a person in a certain role, for example, a new employee. — **pro·ba·tion·ar·y** /-ˌnerē/ **adj.**

pro·ba·tion·er /prōˈbāshənər/ ▶ **n.** a person who is serving a probationary or trial period in a job or position to which they are newly appointed. ▪ an offender on probation.

pro·ba·tion of·fi·cer ▶ **n.** a person appointed to supervise offenders who are on probation.

pro·ba·tive /ˈprōbətiv/ ▶ **adj.** esp. Law having the quality or function of proving or demonstrating something.

probe /prōb/ ▶ **n.** a blunt-ended surgical instrument used for exploring a wound or part of the body. ▪ a small device, esp. an electrode, used for measuring, testing, or obtaining information. ▪ a projecting device for engaging in a drogue, either on an aircraft for use in in-flight refueling or on a spacecraft for use in docking with another craft. ▪ (also **space probe**) an unmanned exploratory spacecraft designed to transmit information about its environment. ▪ an investigation into a crime or other matter. ▶ **v.** [trans.] physically explore or examine (something) with the hands or an instrument. ▪ [intrans.] seek to uncover information about someone or something: *he began to probe into Donald's whereabouts* | [trans.] *police are probing another murder.* — **prob·er n. prob·ing·ly adv.** [ME (as a n.): from late L. *proba* 'proof,' from L. *probare* 'to test.']

pro·ben·e·cid /prōˈbenəsid/ ▶ **n.** Med. a synthetic sulfur-containing compound that promotes increased excretion of uric acid and is used to treat gout. [1950s: from *pro(pyl)* + *ben(zoic)* + *-e-* + *(a)cid.*]

pro·bi·ot·ic /ˌprōbīˈätik/ ▶ **adj.** denoting a substance that stimulates the growth of microorganisms, especially those with beneficial properties (such as those of the intestinal flora). ▶ **n.** a probiotic substance or preparation. ▪ a microorganism introduced into the body for its beneficial qualities.

pro·bi·ty /ˈprōbitē/ ▶ **n.** formal the quality of having strong moral principles; honesty and decency. [ME: from L. *probitas*, from *probus* 'good.']

prob·lem /ˈpräbləm/ ▶ **n. 1** a matter or situation regarded as unwelcome or harmful and needing to be dealt with and overcome. ▪ a thing difficult to achieve or accomplish. **2** Physics & Math. an inquiry starting from given conditions to investigate a fact, result, or law. ▪ Geom. a proposition in which something has to be constructed. Compare with THEOREM. ▪ (in various games, esp. chess) an arrangement of pieces in which the solver has to achieve a specified result.
– PHRASES **have a problem with** disagree with or have an objection to. **no problem** used to express one's agreement or acquiescence. [ME: from OFr. *probleme*, via L. from Gk. *problēma*, from *proballein* 'put forth,' from *pro* 'before' + *ballein* 'to throw.']

prob·lem·at·ic /ˌpräbləˈmatik/ ▶ **adj.** constituting or presenting a problem or difficulty. ▪ doubtful or questionable. ▪ Logic enunciating or supporting what is possible but not necessarily true. ▶ **n.** a thing that constitutes a problem or difficulty: *the problematics of artificial intelligence.* — **prob·lem·at·i·cal adj. prob·lem·at·i·cal·ly** /-ik(ə)lē/ **adv.**

prob·lem·a·tize /ˈpräbləməˌtīz/ ▶ **v.** [trans.] make into or regard as a problem requiring a solution. — **prob·lem·a·ti·za·tion** /ˌpräbləmətəˈzāshən; -ˌmatə-/ **n.**

pro bo·no pu·bli·co /ˌprō ˈbōnō ˈpo͞obliˌkō; ˈbōnō ˈpəbliˌkō/ ▶ **adv. & adj.** for the public good. ▪ (usu. **pro bono**) denoting work undertaken for the public good without charge, esp. legal work for a client with a low income. [L.]

Pro·bos·cid·e·a /ˌprōbəˈsidēə; prəˌbäˈsidēə/ Zool. an order of large mammals that comprises the elephants and their extinct relatives. — **pro·bos·cid·e·an** /ˌprōbəˈsidēən; prəˌbäsəˈdēən/ (also **pro·bos·cid·i·an**) **n. & adj.** [mod. L. (pl.), from PROBOSCIS.]

pro·bos·cis /prəˈbäsəs; -ˈbäskəs/ ▶ **n.** (pl. **-bos·cis·es, -bos·ci·des** /-ˈbäsəˌdēz/, or **-bos·ces** /-ˈbäsēz/) the nose of a mammal, esp. when it is long and mobile, such as the trunk of an elephant. ▪ Entomol. (in many insects) an elongated sucking mouthpart that is typically tubular and flexible. ▪ Zool. (in some worms) an extensible tubular sucking organ. [17th C.: via L. from Gk. *proboskis* 'means of obtaining food,' from *pro* 'before' + *boskein* '(cause to) feed.']

pro·bos·cis mon·key ▶ **n.** a leaf-eating monkey (*Nasalis larvatus*, family Cercopithecidae) native to the forests of Borneo, the male of which is twice the weight of the female and has a large pendulous nose.

proc. ▶ **abbr.** ▪ procedure. ▪ proceedings. ▪ process. ▪ proclamation. ▪ proctor.

pro·caine /ˈprōˌkān/ ▶ **n.** a synthetic compound derived from benzoic acid, used as a local anesthetic, esp. in dentistry. [20th C.: from PRO-[1] (denoting substitution) + *-caine* (from COCAINE).]

pro·caine pen·i·cil·lin ▶ **n.** Med. an antibiotic made from a salt of procaine and a form of penicillin.

pro·car·y·ote ▶ n. var. of PROKARYOTE.

pro·ce·dure /prəˈsējər/ ▶ n. an established or official way of doing something. ■ a series of actions conducted in a certain order or manner. ■ a surgical operation. ■ Comput. another term for SUBROUTINE. — **pro·ce·dur·al** /-jərəl/ adj. **pro·ce·dur·al·ly** /-jərəlē/ adv. [16th C.: from Fr. *procédure*, from *procéder* (see PROCEED).]

pro·ceed /prəˈsēd; prō-/ ▶ v. [intrans.] begin or continue a course of action: *proceed with the investigation.* ■ move forward, esp. after reaching a certain point: *the ship proceeded to Milwaukee.* ■ [with infin.] do something as a natural or seemingly inevitable next step: *opposite the front door was a staircase, which I proceeded to climb.* ■ Law start a lawsuit against someone: *he can **proceed against** the contractor under the common law negligence rules.* ■ (of an action) be started: *negotiations must proceed without delay.* ■ (of an action) be carried on or continued: *as the excavation proceeds, the visible layers can be recorded and studied.* ■ originate from: *his claim that all power **proceeded from** God.* [ME: from OFr. *proceder*, from L. *procedere*, from *pro-* 'forward' + *cedere* 'go.']

pro·ceed·ings /prəˈsēdiNGz; prō-/ ▶ plural n. an event or a series of activities involving a set procedure. ■ Law action taken in a court to settle a dispute: *criminal proceedings.* ■ a published report of a set of meetings or a conference.

pro·ceeds /ˈprōˌsēdz/ ▶ plural n. money obtained from an event or activity.

proc·ess[1] /ˈpräˌses; ˈpräsəs; ˈprō-/ ▶ n. **1** a series of actions or steps taken to achieve an end. ■ a natural or involuntary series of changes: *the aging process.* ■ a systematic series of operations performed to produce or manufacture something: *the printer needs to accommodate all the processes in one shop.* ■ [as adj.] Print. relating to or denoting printing using ink in three colors (cyan, magenta, and yellow) and black to produce a complete range of color: *process inks.* **2** Law a summons or writ requiring a person to appear in court. **3** Biol. & Anat. a natural appendage or outgrowth on or in an organism, such as a protuberance on a bone. ▶ v. [trans.] perform a series of mechanical or chemical operations on (something) in order to change or preserve it: *the stages in processing the wool.* ■ Comput. operate on (data) by means of a program. ■ deal with (someone) using an official and established procedure: *the immigration authorities who processed him.* ■ another term for CONK[3].
– PHRASES **in the process** as an unintended part of a course of action. **in process of time** as time goes on. — **proc·ess·a·ble** adj. [ME: from OFr. *proces*, from L. *processus*, from *procedere*.]

pro·cess[2] /prəˈses/ ▶ v. [intrans.] walk or march in procession: *they processed down the aisle.* [19th C.: back-form. from PROCESSION.]

pro·ces·sion /prəˈseSHən/ ▶ n. **1** a number of people or vehicles moving forward in an orderly fashion, esp. as part of a ceremony or festival. ■ the action of moving forward in such a way: *the dignitaries walk in procession.* ■ fig. a relentless succession of people or things: *his path was paved by **a procession of** industry executives.* **2** Theol. the emanation of the Holy Spirit.

pro·ces·sion·al /prəˈseSHənl/ ▶ adj. of, for, or used in a religious or ceremonial procession. ▶ n. a book containing litanies and hymns for use in religious processions. ■ a hymn or other musical composition sung or played during a procession.

proc·es·sor /ˈpräˌsesər; ˈpräsəsər; ˈprō-/ ▶ n. a machine that processes something. ■ Comput. another term for CENTRAL PROCESSING UNIT. ■ short for FOOD PROCESSOR.

proc·ess print·ing /ˈpräˌses; ˈpräsəs; ˈprō-/ ▶ n. a full-color printing method using four templates of magenta, cyan, yellow, and black.

proc·ess serv·er ▶ n. a person, esp. a sheriff or deputy, who serves writs, warrants, subpoenas, etc.

pro·cès-ver·bal /prōˌsā vərˈbäl/ ▶ n. (pl. **pro·cès-ver·baux** /vərˈbō/) a written report of proceedings. ■ a written statement of facts in support of a charge. [17th C.: Fr.]

pro-choice /prōˈCHois/ (also **pro·choice**) ▶ adj. advocating legalized abortion: *a pro-choice demonstration.* — **pro-choic·er** n.

pro·claim /prəˈklām; prō-/ ▶ v. [with clause] announce officially or publicly: *the manifesto proclaimed that imperialism would be the coalition's chief objective* | [trans.] *army commanders proclaimed a state of emergency.* ■ declare something one considers important with due emphasis. ■ [trans.] declare officially or publicly to be: *he proclaimed James III as King of England.* ■ [trans.] demonstrate or indicate clearly: *the decor proclaimed good taste.* — **pro·claim·er** n. **pro·clam·a·to·ry** /-ˈklaməˌtôrē/ adj. [ME *proclame*, from L. *proclamare* 'cry out,' from *pro-* 'forth' + *clamare* 'to shout.']

proc·la·ma·tion /ˌprākləˈmāSHən/ ▶ n. a public or official announcement, esp. one dealing with a matter of great importance. ■ the public or official announcement of such a matter. ■ a clear declaration of something. [ME: via OFr. from L. *proclamatio(n-)*, from *proclamare*.]

pro·clit·ic /prōˈklitik/ Ling. ▶ n. a word pronounced with so little emphasis that it is shortened and forms part of the following word, for example, *you* in *y'all.* Compare with ENCLITIC. ▶ adj. being or relating to such a word. — **pro·clit·i·cal·ly** /-ik(ə)lē/ adv. [19th C.: from mod. L. *procliticus* (from Gk. *proklinein* 'lean forward'), on the pattern of late L. *encliticus* (see ENCLITIC).]

pro·cliv·i·ty /prōˈklivətē; prə-/ ▶ n. (pl. **-ties**) a tendency to choose or do something regularly. [16th C.: from L. *proclivitas*, from *proclivis* 'inclined,' from *pro-* 'forward, down' + *clivus* 'slope.']

Proc·ne /ˈpräknē/ Gk. Mythol. the sister of Philomela.

pro·co·ag·u·lant /ˌprōkōˈagyələnt/ Biochem. ▶ adj. relating to or denoting substances that promote the conversion in the blood of the inactive protein prothrombin to the clotting enzyme thrombin. ▶ n. a substance of this kind.

Pro·con·sul /prōˈkänsəl/ ▶ n. a fossil hominoid primate (genus *Proconsul*, family Pongidae) found in Lower Miocene deposits in East Africa, one of the last common ancestors of both humans and the great apes.

pro·con·sul /prōˈkänsəl/ ▶ n. **1** a governor of a province in ancient Rome, having much of the authority of a consul. **2** a governor or deputy consul of a modern colony. — **pro·con·su·lar** /-ˈkäns(y)ələr/ adj. **pro·con·su·late** /-ˈkäns(y)ələt/ n. **pro·con·sul·ship** /-ˌSHip/ n. [from L. *pro consule* '(one acting) for the consul.']

pro·cras·ti·nate /prəˈkrastəˌnāt; prō-/ ▶ v. [intrans.] delay or postpone action; put off doing something. — **pro·cras·ti·na·tion** /prəˌkrastəˈnāSHən; prō-/ n. **pro·cras·ti·na·tor** /-ˌnātər/ n. **pro·cras·ti·na·to·ry** /-nəˌtôrē/ adj. [16th C.: from L. *procrastinat-* 'deferred till the morning,' from the verb *procrastinare*, from *pro-* 'forward' + *crastinus* 'belonging to tomorrow' (from *cras* 'tomorrow').]

pro·cre·ate /ˈprōkrēˌāt/ ▶ v. [intrans.] (of people or animals) produce young; reproduce. — **pro·cre·ant** /-krēənt/ adj. (archaic). **pro·cre·a·tion** /ˌprōkrēˈāSHən/ n. **pro·cre·a·tive** /-krēˌātiv/ adj. **pro·cre·a·tor** /-ˌātər/ n. [ME: from L. *procreat-* 'generated, brought forth,' from the verb *procreare*, from *pro-* 'forth' + *creare* 'create.']

Pro·crus·te·an /prōˈkrəstēən; prō-/ ▶ adj. (esp. of a framework or system) enforcing uniformity or conformity without regard to natural variation or individuality. [19th C.: from the name PROCRUSTES + -AN.]

Pro·crus·tes /prōˈkrəstēz; prō-/ Gk. Mythol. a robber who forced travelers to lie on a bed and made them fit it by stretching their limbs or cutting off the appropriate length of leg. Theseus killed him in like manner. [from Gk. *prokroustēs*, lit. 'stretcher,' from *prokrouein* 'beat out.']

proc·ti·tis /präkˈtītis/ ▶ n. Med. inflammation of the rectum and anus. [19th C.: from Gk. *prōktos* 'anus' + -ITIS.]

proc·tol·o·gy /präkˈtäləjē/ ▶ n. the branch of medicine concerned with the anus and rectum. — **proc·to·log·i·cal** /ˌpräktəˈläjikəl/ adj. **proc·tol·o·gist** /-jist/ n. [19th C.: from Gk. *prōktos* 'anus' + -LOGY.]

proc·tor /ˈpräktər/ ▶ n. **1** a person who monitors students during an examination. **2** Brit. an officer at certain universities, appointed annually and having mainly disciplinary functions. ▶ v. [trans.] monitor students during (an examination). — **proc·to·ri·al** /präkˈtôrēəl/ adj. **proc·tor·ship** /-ˌSHip/ n. [ME: contr. of PROCURATOR.]

proc·to·scope /ˈpräktəˌskōp/ ▶ n. a medical instrument with an integral lamp for examining the anus and lower part of the rectum or carrying out minor medical procedures. — **proc·to·scop·ic** /ˌpräktəˈskäpik/ adj. **proc·tos·co·py** /präkˈtäskəpē/ n. [19th C.: from Gk. *prōktos* 'anus' + -SCOPE.]

pro·cum·bent /prōˈkəmbənt/ ▶ adj. Bot. (of a plant or stem) growing along the ground without setting forth roots. [17th C.: from L. *procumbent-* 'falling forward,' from the verb *procumbere*, from *pro-* 'forward, down' + a verb rel. to *cubare* 'to lie.']

proc·u·ra·tion /ˌpräkyəˈrāSHən/ ▶ n. Law, dated the appointment, authority, or action of an attorney. ■ archaic the action of procuring or obtaining something.

proc·u·ra·tor /ˈpräkyəˌrātər/ ▶ n. Law an agent representing others in a court of law in countries retaining Roman civil law. ■ hist. a treasury officer in a province of the Roman Empire. — **proc·u·ra·to·ri·al** /ˌpräkyərəˈtôrēəl/ adj. **proc·u·ra·tor·ship** /-ˌSHip/ n.

pro·cure /prəˈkyo͝or; prō-/ ▶ v. [trans.] **1** obtain (something), esp. with care or effort: *food procured for the rebels.* ■ obtain (someone) as a prostitute for another person: *he was charged with procuring a minor.* **2** [trans.] Law persuade or cause (someone) to do something: *he procured his wife to sign the agreement.* — **pro·cur·a·ble** adj. **pro·cure·ment** n. [ME: from OFr. *procurer*, from L. *procurare* 'take care of, manage,' from *pro-* 'on behalf of' + *curare* 'see to.']

pro·cure·ment /prəˈkyo͝ormənt; prō-/ ▶ n. the action of obtaining or procuring something. ■ the action or occupation of acquiring military equipment and supplies.

pro·cur·er /prəˈkyo͝orər; prō-/ ▶ n. a person who obtains a woman as a prostitute for another person.

pro·cur·ess /prəˈkyo͝oris; prō-/ ▶ n. a female procurer.

Pro·cy·on /ˈprōsēˌän; -sēən/ Astron. the eighth brightest star in the sky, and the brightest in the constellation Canis Minor. [Gk., lit. 'before the dog' (because it rises before Sirius, the Dog Star).]

prod /präd/ ▶ v. (**prod·ded, prod·ding**) [trans.] poke (someone) with a finger, foot, or pointed object: *he prodded her in the ribs* | [intrans.] *he **prods at** a tiger with a stick.* ■ stimulate or persuade (someone who is reluctant or slow) to do something. ▶ n. **1** a poke with a finger, foot, or pointed object. ■ an act of stimulating or reminding someone to do something. **2** a pointed implement, typically one discharging an electric current and used as a goad. — **prod·der** n. [16th C. (as a v.): perh. symbolic.]

prod. ▶ abbr. ■ produce. ■ produced. ■ producer. ■ product. ■ production.

prod·i·gal /ˈprädigəl/ ▶ adj. **1** spending money or resources freely and recklessly; wastefully extravagant. **2** having or giving something on a lavish scale. ▶ n. a person who spends money in a recklessly extravagant way. ■ (also **prodigal son** or **daughter**) a person who leaves home and behaves in such a way, but later makes a repentant return. — **prod·i·gal·i·ty** /ˌprädəˈgalətē/ n. **prod·i·gal·ly** /-g(ə)lē/ adv. [ME: from late L. *prodigalis*, from L. *prodigus* 'lavish.']

pro·di·gious /prəˈdijəs/ ▶ **adj.** **1** remarkably or impressively great in extent, size, or degree. **2** archaic unnatural or abnormal. — **pro·di·gious·ly** **adv.** **pro·di·gious·ness** **n.**

prod·i·gy /ˈprädəjē/ ▶ **n.** (pl. **-gies**) [often with adj.] a person, esp. a young one, endowed with exceptional abilities. ■ an impressive or outstanding example of a particular quality. ■ an amazing or unusual thing, esp. one out of the ordinary course of nature. [15th C.: from L. *prodigium* 'portent.']

pro·drome /ˈprōˌdrōm/ ▶ **n.** Med. an early symptom indicating the onset of a disease or illness. — **prod·ro·mal** /prōˈdrōməl/ **adj.** **pro·drom·ic** /prōˈdrämik/ **adj.** [17th C.: from Fr., from mod. L. *prodromus*, from Gk. *prodromos* 'precursor,' from *pro* 'before' + *dromos* 'running.']

pro·drug /ˈprōˌdrəg/ ▶ **n.** a biologically inactive compound that can be metabolized in the body to produce a drug.

pro·duce ▶ **v.** /prəˈd(y)o͞os; prō-/ [trans.] **1** make or manufacture from components or raw materials. ■ (of a region, country, or process) yield, grow, or supply: *the California vineyards produce excellent wines.* ■ create or form (something) as part of a physical, biological, or chemical process: *the plant produces blue flowers in late autumn.* ■ make (something) using creative or mental skills. **2** cause (a particular result or situation) to happen or come into existence: *no conventional drugs had produced any significant change.* **3** show or provide (something) for consideration, inspection, or use: *he produced a sheet of paper from his pocket.* **4** administer the financial and managerial aspects of (a movie or broadcast) or the staging of (a play, opera, etc.). ■ supervise the making of a (musical recording), esp. by determining the overall sound. **5** Geom., dated extend or continue (a line): *one side of the triangle was produced.* ▶ **n.** /ˈpräd(y)o͞os; ˈprō-/ things that have been produced or grown, esp. by farming: *dairy produce.* — **pro·duc·i·bil·i·ty** /prəˌd(y)o͞osəˈbilətē; prō-/ **n.** **pro·duc·i·ble** **adj.** [ME: from L. *producere*, from *pro-* 'forward' + *ducere* 'to lead.']

pro·duc·er /prəˈd(y)o͞osər; prō-/ ▶ **n.** **1** a person, company, or country that makes, grows, or supplies goods or commodities for sale. ■ a person or thing that makes or causes something. **2** a person responsible for the financial and managerial aspects of making a movie or broadcast or for staging a play, opera, etc. ■ a person who supervises the making of a musical recording, esp. by determining the overall sound.

pro·duc·er gas ▶ **n.** a low-grade fuel gas consisting largely of nitrogen and carbon monoxide, formed by passing air, or air and steam, through red-hot carbon.

prod·uct /ˈprädəkt/ ▶ **n.** **1** an article or substance that is manufactured or refined for sale. ■ a substance produced during a natural, chemical, or manufacturing process: *waste products.* ■ a thing or person that is the result of an action or process: *his daughter, the product of his first marriage.* ■ a person whose character and identity have been formed by a particular period or situation. ■ commercially manufactured articles, esp. recordings, viewed collectively. **2** Math. a quantity obtained by multiplying quantities together, or from an analogous algebraic operation. [ME (as a mathematical term): from L. *productum*, neut. past part. of *producere*.]

pro·duc·tion /prəˈdəkSHən; prō-/ ▶ **n.** **1** the action of making or manufacturing from components or raw materials, or the process of being so manufactured. ■ the harvesting or refinement of something natural. ■ the total amount of something that is manufactured, harvested, or refined. ■ the creation or formation of something as part of a physical, biological, or chemical process: *excess production of collagen by the liver.* ■ [as adj.] denoting a car or other vehicle that has been manufactured in large numbers. **2** the process of or financial and administrative management involved in making a movie, play, or record: *the movie was still in production* | [as adj.] *a production company.* ■ a movie, play, or record, esp. when viewed in terms of its making or staging: *this production updates the play and sets it in the sixties.* ■ [in sing.] the overall sound of a musical recording; the way a record is produced.
– PHRASES **make a production of** do (something) in an unnecessarily elaborate or complicated way.

pro·duc·tion line ▶ **n.** an arrangement in a factory in which a thing being manufactured is passed through a set linear sequence of mechanical or manual operations. Compare with ASSEMBLY LINE.

pro·duc·tion num·ber ▶ **n.** a spectacular musical item, typically including song and dance and involving all or most of the cast, in a theatrical show or motion picture.

pro·duc·tion plat·form ▶ **n.** a platform housing equipment necessary to keep an oil or gas field in production, with facilities for temporarily storing the output of several wells.

pro·duc·tive /prəˈdəktiv; prō-/ ▶ **adj.** producing or able to produce large amounts of goods, crops, or other commodities. ■ relating to or engaged in the production of goods, crops, or other commodities. ■ achieving or producing a significant amount or result. ■ [predic.] (**productive of**) producing or giving rise to: *the unconscious is limitlessly productive of dreams, myths, stories.* ■ Ling. (of a morpheme or other linguistic unit) currently used in forming new words or expressions. ■ Med. (of a cough) that raises mucus from the respiratory tract. — **pro·duc·tive·ly** **adv.** **pro·duc·tive·ness** **n.** **pro·duc·tiv·i·ty** /ˌprōˌdəkˈtivətē; ˌprädək-; prəˌdək-/ **n.**

prod·uct li·a·bil·i·ty ▶ **n.** the legal liability a manufacturer or trader incurs for producing or selling a faulty product.

prod·uct place·ment ▶ **n.** a practice in which manufacturers of goods or providers of a service gain exposure for their products by paying for them to be featured in movies and television programs.

pro·em /ˈprōˌem; -əm/ ▶ **n.** formal a preface or preamble to a book or speech. — **pro·e·mi·al** /prōˈemēəl/ **adj.** [ME: from OFr. *proeme*, via L. from Gk. *prooimion* 'prelude,' from *pro* 'before' + *oimē* 'song.']

pro·en·zyme /prōˈenˌzīm/ ▶ **n.** Biochem. a biologically inactive substance that is metabolized into an enzyme.

pro-Eur·o·pe·an /ˌprōˌyərəˈpēən, -ˌyo͝orə-/ ▶ **adj.** (of a person, attitude, or policy) supporting closer links with the European Union. ▶ **n.** a person who favors or supports closer links with the European Union.

Prof. ▶ **abbr.** professor: [as title] *Prof. Smith.*

prof /präf/ ▶ **n.** informal a professor.

pro-fam·i·ly /prōˈfam(ə)lē/ ▶ **adj.** promoting family life and traditional moral values.

pro·fane /prəˈfān; prō-/ ▶ **adj.** **1** relating or devoted to that which is not sacred or biblical; secular. ■ (of a person) not initiated into religious rites or any esoteric knowledge. **2** (of a person or their behavior) not respectful of orthodox religious practice; irreverent. ■ (of language) blasphemous or obscene. ▶ **v.** [trans.] treat (something sacred) with irreverence or disrespect. — **prof·a·na·tion** /ˌpräfəˈnāSHən; ˌprō-/ **n.** **pro·fane·ly** **adv.** **pro·fane·ness** **n.** **pro·fan·er** **n.** [ME (in the sense 'heathen'): from OFr. *prophane*, from L. *profanus* 'outside the temple, not sacred,' from *pro-* (from *pro* 'before') + *fanum* 'temple.']

pro·fan·i·ty /prəˈfanətē; prō-/ ▶ **n.** (pl. **-ties**) blasphemous or obscene language. ■ a swear word; an oath. ■ irreligious or irreverent behavior.

pro·fess /prəˈfes; prō-/ ▶ **v.** [trans.] **1** claim openly but often falsely that one has (a quality or feeling): *he had professed his love for her* | [with complement] (**profess oneself**) *he professed himself amazed at the boy's ability.* **2** affirm one's faith in or allegiance to (a religion or set of beliefs). ■ (**be professed**) be received into a religious order under vows: *she was professed in 1943.* **3** dated or humorous teach (a subject) as a professor: *a professor—what does he profess?* **4** archaic have or claim knowledge or skill in (a subject or accomplishment). [ME: from L. *profess-* 'declared publicly,' from the verb *profiteri*, from *pro-* 'before' + *fateri* 'confess.']

pro·fessed /prəˈfest; prō-/ ▶ **adj.** **1** (of a quality, feeling, or belief) claimed or asserted openly but often falsely. **2** (of a person) self-acknowledged or openly declared to be. ■ (of a monk or nun) having taken the vows of a religious order. ■ archaic claiming to be qualified as a particular specialist; professional.

pro·fess·ed·ly /prəˈfesədlē; -ˈfestlē/ ▶ **adv.** ostensibly; apparently.

pro·fes·sion /prəˈfeSHən/ ▶ **n.** **1** a paid occupation, esp. one that involves prolonged training and a formal qualification. ■ [treated as sing. or pl.] a body of people engaged in a particular profession. **2** an open but often false declaration or claim. ■ a declaration of belief in a religion. ■ the declaration or vows made on entering a religious order. ■ the ceremony or fact of being professed in a religious order.
– PHRASES **the oldest profession** humorous the practice of working as a prostitute. [ME: via OFr. from L. *professio(n-)*, from *profiteri* 'declare publicly' (see PROFESS).]

pro·fes·sion·al /prəˈfeSHənl/ ▶ **adj.** **1** [attrib.] of, relating to, or connected with a profession. **2** (of a person) engaged in a specified activity as one's main paid occupation rather than as a pastime. ■ having or showing the skill appropriate to a professional person; competent or skillful. ■ worthy of or appropriate to a professional person. ■ informal, derog. denoting a person who persistently makes a feature of a particular activity or attribute: *a professional naysayer.* ▶ **n.** a person engaged or qualified in a profession. ■ a person engaged in a specified activity, esp. a sport or branch of the performing arts, as a main paid occupation rather than as a pastime. ■ a person competent or skilled in a particular activity. — **pro·fes·sion·al·ly** /-SHənl-ē/ **adv.**

pro·fes·sion·al·ism /prəˈfeSHənlˌizəm/ ▶ **n.** the competence or skill expected of a professional. ■ the practicing of an activity, esp. a sport, by professional rather than amateur players.

pro·fes·sion·al·ize /prəˈfeSHənlˌīz/ ▶ **v.** [trans.] give (an occupation, activity, or group) professional qualities, typically by increasing training or raising required qualifications. — **pro·fes·sion·al·i·za·tion** /prəˌfeSHənləˈzāSHən/ **n.**

pro·fes·sor /prəˈfesər/ ▶ **n.** **1** (also **full professor**) a teacher of the highest rank in a college or university. ■ an associate professor or an assistant professor. ■ informal any instructor, esp. in a specialized field. **2** a person who affirms a faith in or allegiance to something: *the professors of true religion.* — **pro·fes·sor·ate** /-rət/ **n.** **pro·fes·so·ri·al** /ˌpräfəˈsôrēəl/ **adj.** **pro·fes·so·ri·al·ly** /ˌpräfəˈsôrēəlē/ **adv.** **pro·fes·so·ri·ate** /ˌpräfəˈsôrēət/ **n.** **pro·fes·sor·ship** /-ˌSHip/ **n.**

prof·fer /ˈpräfər/ ▶ **v.** [trans.] hold out (something) to someone for acceptance; offer. ▶ **n.** literary an offer or proposal. [ME: from Anglo-Norman Fr. *proffrir*, from L. *pro-* 'before' + *offerre* 'to offer.']

pro·fi·cient /prəˈfiSHənt/ ▶ **adj.** competent or skilled in doing or using something. ▶ **n.** rare a person who is proficient. — **pro·fi·cien·cy** **n.** **pro·fi·cient·ly** **adv.** [16th C.: from L. *proficient-* 'advancing,' from the verb *proficere*, from *pro-* 'on behalf of' + *facere* 'do, make.']

pro·file /ˈprōˌfīl/ ▶ **n.** **1** an outline of something, esp. a person's face, as seen from one side: *the man turned and she caught his profile.* ■ a drawing or other representation of such an outline. ■ a vertical cross section of a structure: *skillfully made vessels with an S-shaped profile.* ■ Geog. an outline of part of the earth's surface, e.g., the course of a river, as seen in a vertical section. ■ Theater a flat piece of scenery or stage property that has been cut so as to form an outline or silhouette of an object. ■ a graphical or other representation of information relating to particular characteristics of something, recorded in quantified form: *the blood profiles of cancer patients.* ■ a short article giving a description of a person or organization, esp. a public figure. **2** [in sing.] the extent to which a person or organization attracts public notice or comment. ▶ **v.** [trans.] **1** describe (a person or organization, esp. a public figure) in a short article. **2** (usu. **be profiled**) represent in outline from one side. ■ (**be profiled**) have a specified shape or appearance in outline. ■ shape (something), esp. by means of a tool guided by a template. — **pro·fil·er** **n.** [17th C.: from obs. Ital. *profilo*, from the verb *profilare*, from *pro-* 'forth' + *filare* 'to spin,' formerly 'draw a line' (from L. *filare*, from *filum* 'thread').]

pro·fil·ing /ˈprōˌfīliNG/ ▶ **n.** the recording and analysis of a person's psychological and behavioral characteristics, so as to assess or predict their capabilities in a certain sphere or to assist in identifying a particular subgroup of people.

prof·it /ˈpräfit/ ▶ **n.** a financial gain, esp. the difference between the amount earned and the amount spent in buying, operating, or producing something. ■ advantage; benefit. ▶ **v.** (**-it·ed**, **-it·ing**) [intrans.] obtain a financial advantage or benefit, esp. from an investment: *the only people to profit from the entire episode were the lawyers.* ■ obtain an advantage or benefit: *not all children would profit from this kind of schooling.* ■ [trans.] be beneficial to: *it would profit us to change our plans.* [ME: from OFr., from L. *profectus* 'progress, profit,' from *proficere* 'to advance,' from *pro-* 'on behalf of' + *facere* 'do.']

prof·it·a·ble /ˈpräfitəbəl/ ▶ **adj.** **1** (of a business or activity) yielding profit or financial gain. **2** beneficial; useful. — **prof·it·a·bil·i·ty** /ˌpräfitəˈbilətē/ **n.** **prof·it·a·bly** /-blē/ **adv.**

prof·it·eer /ˌpräfəˈti(ə)r/ ▶ **v.** [intrans.] make or seek to make an excessive or unfair profit, esp. illegally or in a black market. ▶ **n.** a person who profiteers.

pro·fit·er·ole /prəˈfitəˌrōl/ ▶ **n.** a small cream puff. [Fr., dimin. of *profit* 'profit.']

prof·it mar·gin ▶ **n.** the amount by which revenue from sales exceeds costs in a business.

prof·it-shar·ing (also **prof·it shar·ing**) ▶ **n.** a system in which the people who work for a company receive a direct share of the profits.

prof·it-tak·ing (also **prof·it tak·ing**) ▶ **n.** Stock Market the sale of securities that have risen in price.

prof·li·gate /ˈpräfligət; -ləˌgāt/ ▶ **adj.** recklessly extravagant or wasteful in the use of resources. ■ licentious; dissolute. ▶ **n.** a licentious, dissolute person. — **prof·li·ga·cy** /ˈpräfligəsē/ **n.** **prof·li·gate·ly** **adv.** [16th C.: from L. *profligatus* 'dissolute,' past part. of *profligare* 'overthrow, ruin,' from *pro-* 'forward, down' + *fligere* 'strike down.']

pro-form /ˈprōˌfôrm/ ▶ **n.** Ling. a word or lexical unit dependent for its meaning on reference to some other part of the context in which it occurs, e.g., a pronoun replacing a noun or noun phrase, or a verb replacing a clause, such as *do* in *she likes chocolate and so do I.*

pro for·ma /prō ˈfôrmə/ ▶ **adv.** as a matter of form or politeness. ▶ **adj.** done or produced as a matter of form. ■ [attrib.] denoting a standard document or form, esp. an invoice sent in advance of or with goods supplied. ▶ **n.** a standard document or form of such a type. [16th C.: from L.]

pro·found /prəˈfound; prō-/ ▶ **adj.** (**-found·er**, **-found·est**) **1** (of a state, quality, or emotion) very great or intense. ■ (of a disease or disability) very severe; deep-seated. **2** (of a person or statement) having or showing great knowledge or insight. ■ (of a subject or thought) demanding deep study or thought. **3** archaic at, from, or extending to a great depth; very deep: *he opened the door with a profound bow.* ▶ **n.** (**the profound**) literary the vast depth of the ocean or of the mind. — **pro·found·ly** **adv.** **pro·found·ness** **n.** [ME: from OFr. *profund*, from L. *profundus* 'deep,' from *pro* 'before' + *fundus* 'bottom.']

pro·fun·di·ty /prəˈfəndətē/ ▶ **n.** (pl. **-ties**) deep insight; great depth of knowledge or thought. ■ great depth or intensity of a state, quality, or emotion. ■ a statement or idea that shows great knowledge or insight. [ME: ult. from late L. *profunditas*, from L. *profundus*.]

pro·fuse /prəˈfyo͞os; prō-/ ▶ **adj.** (esp. of something offered or discharged) exuberantly plentiful; abundant. ■ archaic (of a person) lavish; extravagant. — **pro·fuse·ly** **adv.** **pro·fuse·ness** **n.** [ME (in the sense 'extravagant'): from L. *profusus* 'lavish, spread out,' past part. of *profundere*, from *pro-* 'forth' + *fundere* 'pour.']

pro·fu·sion /prəˈfyo͞oZHən; prō-/ ▶ **n.** [in sing.] an abundance or large quantity of something.

prog /präg/ informal ▶ **adj.** [attrib.] (of rock music) progressive: *prog rock bands.*

pro·gen·i·tive /prəˈjenətiv; prō-/ ▶ **adj.** formal having reproductive power.

pro·gen·i·tor /prəˈjenətər; prō-/ ▶ **n.** a person or thing from which a person, animal, or plant is descended or originates; an ancestor or parent. ■ a person who originates an artistic, political, or intellectual movement. — **pro·gen·i·to·ri·al** /-ˌjenəˈtôrēəl/ **adj.** [ME: from OFr. *progeniteur*, from L. *progenitor*, from *progenit-* 'begotten,' from the verb *progignere*, from *pro-* 'forward' + *gignere* 'beget.']

prog·e·ny /ˈpräjənē/ ▶ **n.** [treated as sing. or pl.] a descendant or the descendants of a person, animal, or plant; offspring: *the progeny of mixed marriages.* [ME: from OFr. *progenie*, from L. *progenies*, from *progignere* 'beget' (see **PROGENITOR**).]

pro·ge·ri·a /prōˈji(ə)rēə; prə-/ ▶ **n.** Med. a rare syndrome in children characterized by physical signs and symptoms suggestive of premature old age. [20th C.: mod. L., from Gk. *progērōs* 'prematurely old.']

pro·ges·ter·one /prōˈjestəˌrōn; prə-/ ▶ **n.** Biochem. a steroid hormone released by the corpus luteum that stimulates the uterus to prepare for pregnancy. [1930s: blend of **PROGESTIN** and the Ger. synonym *Luteosteron* (from **CORPUS LUTEUM** + **STEROL**).]

pro·ges·tin /prōˈjestin/ ▶ **n.** Biochem. a natural or synthetic steroid hormone, such as progesterone, that maintains pregnancy and prevents further ovulation during pregnancy.

pro·ges·to·gen /prōˈjestəjən/ ▶ **n.** Biochem. another term for **PROGESTIN.** [1940s: from **PROGESTIN** + **-GEN.**]

pro·glot·tid /prōˈglätid/ (also **pro·glot·tis** /-ˈglätis/) ▶ **n.** Zool. each segment in the strobila of a tapeworm, containing a complete sexually mature reproductive system. [19th C.: from Gk. *proglōssis*, *proglōssid-* 'point of the tongue,' based on *glōssa*, *glōtta* 'tongue' (because of its shape).]

prog·na·thous /ˈprägnəTHəs; prägˈnā-/ ▶ **adj.** (esp. of a person) having a projecting lower jaw or chin. — **prog·nath·ic** /prägˈnaTHik/ **adj.** **prog·na·thism** /-ˌTHizəm/ **n.** [19th C.: from **PRO-**[2] 'before' + Gk. *gnathos* 'jaw' + **-OUS.**]

prog·no·sis /prägˈnōsəs/ ▶ **n.** (pl. **-ses** /-ˌsēz/) the likely course of a disease or ailment. ■ a forecast of the likely course of a disease or ailment. ■ a forecast of the likely outcome of a situation. [17th C.: via late L. from Gk. *prognōsis*, from *pro-* 'before' + *gignōskein* 'know.']

prog·nos·tic /prägˈnästik/ ▶ **adj.** predicting the likely outcome of a disease; of or relating to a prognosis. ▶ **n.** archaic an advance indication or portent of a future event. — **prog·nos·ti·cal·ly** /-ik(ə)lē/ **adv.** [ME: from L. *prognosticus*, from Gk. *prognōstikos*, from *prognōsis* (see **PROGNOSIS**).]

prog·nos·ti·cate /prägˈnästəˌkāt/ ▶ **v.** [trans.] foretell or prophesy (an event in the future). — **prog·nos·ti·ca·tor** /-ˌkātər/ **n.** **prog·nos·ti·ca·to·ry** /-kəˌtôrē/ **adj.**

prog·nos·ti·ca·tion /prägˌnästəˈkāSHən/ ▶ **n.** the action of foretelling or prophesying future events. ■ a prophecy.

pro·grade /ˈprōˈgrād/ ▶ **adj.** Astron. (of planetary motion) proceeding from west to east; direct. The opposite of **RETROGRADE.** — **pro·gra·da·tion** /ˌprōˌgrāˈdāSHən; ˌprōgrə-/ **n.** [20th C. (as a v.): from **PRO-**[1] 'forward' + **RETROGRADE.**]

pro·gram /ˈprōˌgram; -grəm/ (Brit. **pro·gramme**) ▶ **n.** **1** a planned series of future events, items, or performances. ■ a set of related measures, events, or activities with a particular long-term aim: *the nuclear power program.* **2** a sheet or booklet giving details of items or performers at an event or performance. **3** a presentation or item on radio or television, esp. one broadcast regularly between stated times. ■ dated a radio or television service or station providing a regular succession of programs on a particular frequency; a channel. **4** (**program**) a series of coded software instructions to control the operation of a computer or other machine. ▶ **v.** (**-grammed**, **-gram·ming**; or **-gramed**, **-gram·ing**) [trans.] **1** (**program**) provide (a computer or other machine) with coded instructions for the automatic performance of a particular task. ■ input (instructions for the automatic performance of a task) into a computer or other machine. ■ (often **be programmed**) fig. cause (a person or animal) to behave in a predetermined way. **2** arrange according to a plan or schedule. ■ schedule (an item) within a framework: *the next stage is programmed for 1996.* ■ broadcast (an item).
– PHRASES **get with the program** [often in imper.] informal do what is expected of one; adopt the prevailing viewpoint. — **pro·gram·ma·bil·i·ty** /-əˈbilətē/ **n.** **pro·gram·ma·ble** /ˈprōˌgraməbəl; prōˈgram-/ **adj.** [17th C. (in the sense 'written notice'): via late L. from Gk. *programma*, from *prographein* 'write publicly,' from *pro* 'before' + *graphein* 'write.']

pro·gram·mat·ic /ˌprōgrəˈmatik/ ▶ **adj.** of the nature of or according to a program, schedule, or method. ■ of the nature of program music. — **pro·gram·mat·i·cal·ly** /-ik(ə)lē/ **adv.**

pro·gram·mer /ˈprōˌgramər/ ▶ **n.** a person who writes computer programs. ■ a device that automatically controls the operation of something in accordance with a prescribed program.

pro·gram·ming /ˈprōˌgramiNG/ ▶ **n.** **1** the action or process of writing computer programs. ■ fig. predetermined behavior. **2** the action or process of scheduling something, esp. radio or television programs. ■ radio or television programs that are scheduled or broadcast.

pro·gram mu·sic ▶ **n.** music that is intended to evoke images or convey the impression of events. Compare with **ABSOLUTE MUSIC.**

pro·gram trad·ing ▶ **n.** the simultaneous purchase and sale of many different stocks, or of stocks and related futures contracts, with the use of a computer program to exploit price differences in different markets.

pro·gress ▶ **n.** /ˈprägrəs; ˈprägˌres; ˈprōˌgres/ forward or onward movement toward a destination. ■ advance or development toward a better, more complete, or more modern condition. ▶ **v.** /prəˈgres/ [intrans.] move forward or onward in space or time: *as the century progressed, the quality of telescopes improved.* ■ advance or develop toward a better, more complete, or more modern state.
– PHRASES **in progress** in the course of being done or carried out: *a meeting was in progress.* [ME (as a n.): from L. *progressus* 'an advance,' from the verb *progredi*, from *pro-* 'forward' + *gradi* 'to walk.']

pro·gres·sion /prəˈgreSHən/ ▶ **n.** a movement or development toward a destination or a more advanced state, esp. gradually or in stages. ■ a succession; a series. ■ Music a passage or movement from one note or chord to another: *a blues progression.* ■ Math. short for **ARITHMETIC PROGRESSION, GEOMETRIC PROGRESSION,** or **HARMONIC PROGRESSION.** — **pro·gres·sion·al** /-SHənl/ **adj.**

pro·gres·sive /prəˈgresiv/ ▶ **adj.** **1** happening or developing gradually or in stages; proceeding step by step. ■ (of a disease or ailment) increasing in severity or extent. ■ (of taxation or a tax) increasing as a proportion of the sum taxed as that sum increases. **2** (of a group, person, or idea) favoring or implementing social reform or new, liberal ideas. ■ favoring or promoting change or innovation: *a progressive art school.* ■ relating to or denoting a style of rock music popular esp. in the 1980s and characterized by classical influences. **3** Gram. denoting an aspect or tense of a verb that expresses an action in progress, e.g., *am writing, was writing.* Also called CONTINUOUS. ▶ **n. 1** a person advocating or implementing social reform or new, liberal ideas. **2** Gram. a progressive tense or aspect. **3** (also **progressive proof**) (usu. **progressives**) Print. each of a set of proofs of color work, showing all the colors separately and the cumulative effect of overprinting them. — **pro•gres•sive•ly** adv. **pro•gres•sive•ness** n. **pro•gres•siv•ism** /-ˈgresəˌvizəm/ n. **pro•gres•siv•ist** /-ˈgresəvist/ n. & adj.

Pro•gres•sive Con•ser•va•tive Par•ty a Canadian political party advocating free trade and holding moderate views on social policies.

Pro•gres•sive Par•ty ▶ n. any of three related political parties active in the first half of the twentieth century that favored social reform. The most prominent was that formed under Theodore Roosevelt in 1912.

pro•hib•it /prəˈhibit; prō-/ ▶ v. (**-hib•it•ed, -hib•it•ing**) [trans.] formally forbid (something) by law, rule, or other authority. ■ (**prohibit someone/something from doing something**) formally forbid a person or group from doing something. ■ (of a fact or situation) prevent (something); make impossible. — **pro•hib•it•er** n. **pro•hib•i•tor** /-itər/ n. **pro•hib•i•to•ry** /-ˌtôrē/ adj. [ME: from L. *prohibit-* 'kept in check,' from the verb *prohibere*, from *pro-* 'in front' + *habere* 'to hold.']

pro•hi•bi•tion /ˌprō(h)əˈbisHən/ ▶ n. **1** the action of forbidding something, esp. by law. ■ a law or regulation forbidding something. **2** (**Prohibition**) the prevention by law of the manufacture and sale of alcohol, esp. in the US between 1920 and 1933. — **pro•hi•bi•tion•ar•y** /-sHəˌnerē/ adj. **Pro•hi•bi•tion•ist** /-nist/ n.

pro•hib•i•tive /prəˈhibitiv; prō-/ ▶ adj. **1** (of a price or charge) excessively high; difficult or impossible to pay. **2** (esp. of a law or rule) forbidding or restricting something. ■ (of a condition or situation) preventing someone from doing something: *a wind over force 5 is prohibitive.* — **pro•hib•i•tive•ly** adv. **pro•hib•i•tive•ness** n.

pro•in•su•lin /prōˈinsələn/ ▶ n. Biochem. a substance produced by the pancreas that is converted to insulin.

pro•ject ▶ n. /ˈpräjˌekt; -ikt/ **1** an individual or collaborative enterprise planned and designed to achieve an aim. ■ a school assignment undertaken by a student or group of students, typically as a long-term task that requires independent research. ■ a proposed or planned undertaking. **2** (also **housing project**) a government-subsidized housing development with relatively low rents. ▶ v. /prəˈjekt; prōˈjekt/ [trans.] **1** (usu. **be projected**) estimate or forecast (something) on the basis of present trends: *spending was **projected** at $72 million.* ■ [often as adj.] (**projected**) plan (a scheme or undertaking): *a projected exhibition of contemporary art.* **2** [intrans.] extend outward beyond something else; protrude: *a slip of paper **projecting from** the book.* **3** throw or cause to move forward or outward: *seeds are projected from the tree.* ■ cause (light, shadow, or an image) to fall on a surface: *the one light projected shadows on the wall.* ■ cause (a sound, esp. the voice) to be heard at a distance: *being audible depends on your ability to project your voice.* ■ imagine (oneself, a situation, etc.) as having moved to a different place or time: *people **project** the present **into** the past.* **4** present or promote (a particular view or image): *he projects an image of youth.* ■ present (someone or something) in a way intended to create a favorable impression: *she projects herself more as a friend than a doctor.* ■ display (an emotion or quality) in one's behavior: *everyone would be amazed that a young girl could project such depths of emotion.* ■ (**project something onto**) transfer or attribute one's own emotion or desire to (another person), esp. unconsciously: *men may sometimes project their own fears onto women.* **5** Geom. draw straight lines from a center of or parallel lines through every point of (a given figure) to produce a corresponding figure on a surface or a line by intersecting the surface. ■ draw (such lines). ■ produce (such a corresponding figure). **6** make a projection of (the earth, sky, etc.) on a plane surface. — **pro•ject•a•ble** /prəˈjektəbəl/ adj. [ME (in the sense 'preliminary design, tabulated statement'): from L. *projectum* 'something prominent,' neut. past part. of *proicere* 'throw forth,' from *pro-* 'forth' + *jacere* 'to throw.']

pro•jec•tile /prəˈjektl; -ˌtīl/ ▶ n. a missile designed to be fired from a rocket or gun. ■ an object propelled through the air, esp. one thrown as a weapon. ▶ adj. [attrib.] of or relating to such a missile or object. ■ impelled with great force.

pro•jec•tion /prəˈjeksHən/ ▶ n. **1** an estimate or forecast of a future situation or trend based on a study of present ones. **2** the presentation of an image on a surface, esp. a movie screen. ■ an image projected in such a way. ■ the ability to make a sound, esp. the voice, heard at a distance. **3** the presentation or promotion of someone or something in a particular way. ■ a mental image viewed as reality. ■ the unconscious transfer of one's own desires or emotions to another person. **4** a thing that extends outward from something else. **5** Geom. the action of projecting a figure. **6** the representation on a plane surface of any part of the surface of the earth or a celestial sphere. ■ (also **map projection**) a method by which such representation may be done. — **pro•jec•tion•ist** /-sHəˌn/ n. (in sense 2).

pro•jec•tion tel•e•vi•sion (also **pro•jec•tion TV**) ▶ n. a large television receiver in which the image is projected optically onto a large viewing screen.

pro•jec•tive /prəˈjektiv/ ▶ adj. **1** Geom. relating to or derived by projection: *projective transformations.* ■ (of a property of a figure) unchanged by projection. **2** Psychol. relating to the unconscious transfer of one's own desires or emotions to another person. ■ relating to or exploiting the unconscious expression or introduction of one's impressions or feelings. — **pro•jec•tive•ly** adv. **pro•jec•tiv•i•ty** /ˌprōˌjekˈtivətē; ˌpräjˌek-/ n.

pro•jec•tive ge•om•e•try ▶ n. the study of the projective properties of geometric figures.

pro•jec•tive test ▶ n. a psychological test in which words, images, or situations are presented to a person and the responses analyzed for the unconscious expression of elements of personality that they reveal.

pro•jec•tor /prəˈjektər/ ▶ n. **1** an object used to project rays of light, esp. an apparatus with a system of lenses for projecting slides or film onto a screen. **2** archaic a person who plans and sets up an enterprise. ■ a promoter of a dubious or fraudulent enterprise.

pro•kar•y•ote /prōˈkarēˌōt/ (also **pro•car•y•ote**) ▶ n. Biol. a microscopic single-celled organism that has neither a distinct nucleus with a membrane nor other specialized organelles, including the bacteria and cyanobacteria. Compare with EUKARYOTE. — **pro•kar•y•ot•ic** /prōˌkarēˈätik/ adj. [1960s: from PRO-[2] 'before' + Gk. *karuon* 'nut, kernel' + *-ote* as in ZYGOTE.]

Pro•ko•fi•ev /prōˈkôfēˌef/, Sergei Sergeevich (1891–1953), Russian composer. He composed the music for *Romeo and Juliet* (1935–36) and *Peter and the Wolf* (1936).

pro•lac•tin /prōˈlaktən/ ▶ n. Biochem. a hormone released from the anterior pituitary gland that stimulates milk production after childbirth. [1930s: from PRO-[2] 'before' + LACTATION.]

pro•lapse ▶ n. /prōˈlaps; ˈprōˌlaps/ a slipping forward or down of one of the parts or organs of the body. ■ a prolapsed part or organ, esp. a uterus or rectum. ▶ v. /prōˈlaps/ [intrans.] [usu. as adj.] (**prolapsed**) (of a part or organ of the body) slip forward or down. [18th C.: from L. *prolaps-* 'slipped forward,' from the verb *prolabi*, from *pro-* 'forward, down' + *labi* 'to slip.']

pro•lap•sus /prōˈlapsəs/ ▶ n. technical term for PROLAPSE. [18th C.: mod. L.]

pro•late /ˈprōˌlāt/ ▶ adj. Geom. (of a spheroid) lengthened in the direction of a polar diameter. Often contrasted with OBLATE[1]. [17th C.: from L. *prolatus* 'carried forward,' past part. of *proferre* 'prolong,' from *pro-* 'forward' + *ferre* 'carry.']

prole /prōl/ informal, derog. ▶ n. a member of the working class; a worker. ▶ adj. working-class. [19th C.: abbrev. of PROLETARIAT.]

pro•leg /ˈprōˌleg/ ▶ n. Entomol. a fleshy abdominal limb of a caterpillar or similar insect larva.

pro•le•gom•e•non /ˌprōləˈgäməˌnän; -nən/ ▶ n. (pl. **-na** /-nə/) a critical or discursive introduction to a book. — **pro•le•gom•e•nous** /-nəs/ adj. [17th C.: via L. from Gk., passive pres. part. (neut.) of *prolegein* 'say beforehand,' from *pro* 'before' + *legein* 'say.']

pro•lep•sis /prōˈlepsəs/ ▶ n. (pl. **-ses** /-ˌsēz/) **1** Rhet. the anticipation and answering of possible objections in rhetorical speech. ■ literary anticipation. **2** the representation of a thing as existing before it actually does or did so, as in *he was a dead man when he entered.* — **pro•lep•tic** /-ˈleptik/ adj. **pro•lep•ti•cal•ly** /-ˈleptik(ə)lē/ adv. [ME (as a term in rhetoric): via late L. from Gk. *prolēpsis*, from *prolambanein* 'anticipate,' from *pro* 'before' + *lambanein* 'take.']

pro•le•tar•i•an /ˌprōliˈte(ə)rēən/ ▶ adj. of or relating to the proletariat: *a proletarian ideology.* ▶ n. a member of the proletariat. — **pro•le•tar•i•an•ism** /-əˌnizəm/ n. **pro•le•tar•i•an•i•za•tion** /-ˌte(ə)rēənəˈzāsHən/ n. **pro•le•tar•i•an•ize** /-əˌnīz/ v. [17th C.: from L. *proletarius* (from *proles* 'offspring').]

pro•le•tar•i•at /ˌprōliˈte(ə)rēət/ (also archaic **pro•le•tar•i•ate**) ▶ n. [treated as sing. or pl.] workers or working-class people, regarded collectively (often used with reference to Marxism). ■ the lowest class of citizens in ancient Rome. [19th C.: from Fr. *prolétariat*, from L. *proletarius* (see PROLETARIAN).]

pro-life /prōˈlīf/ ▶ adj. opposing abortion and euthanasia. — **pro-lif•er** n.

pro•lif•er•ate /prəˈlifəˌrāt/ ▶ v. [intrans.] increase rapidly in numbers; multiply: *magazines proliferated in the 1920s.* ■ (of a cell, structure, or organism) reproduce rapidly. ■ [trans.] cause (cells, tissue, structures, etc.) to reproduce rapidly: *electromagnetic radiation can only proliferate cancers already present.* ■ [trans.] produce (something) in large or increasing quantities. — **pro•lif•er•a•tive** /-ˌrātiv/ adj. **pro•lif•er•a•tor** /-ˌrātər/ n. [19th C.: back-form. from PROLIFERATION.]

pro•lif•er•a•tion /prəˌlifəˈrāsHən/ ▶ n. rapid increase in numbers. ■ rapid reproduction of a cell, part, or organism. ■ [in sing.] a large number of something. [19th C.: from Fr. *prolifération*, from *prolifère* 'proliferous.']

pro•lif•er•ous /prəˈlifərəs/ ▶ adj. Biol. (of a plant) producing buds or side shoots from a flower or other terminal part. ■ (of a plant or invertebrate) propagating or multiplying by means of buds or offsets.

pro•lif•ic /prəˈlifik/ ▶ adj. **1** (of a plant, animal, or person) producing much fruit or foliage or many offspring. ■ (of an artist, author, or composer) producing many works. ■ (of a sports player) high-scoring. **2** present in large numbers or quantities; plentiful. — **pro•lif•i•ca•cy** /-ikəsē/ n. **pro•lif•i•cal•ly** /-ik(ə)lē/ adv. **pro•lif•ic•ness** n. [17th C.: from med. L. *prolificus*, from L. *proles.*]

pro·line /'prō,lēn/ ▶ **n.** Biochem. an amino acid, $C_5H_9NO_2$, that is a constituent of most proteins, esp. collagen. [20th C.: contr. of *p(yr)rol(id)ine-*2-carboxylic acid.]

pro·lix /prō'liks/ ▶ **adj.** (of speech or writing) using or containing too many words; tediously lengthy. — **pro·lix·i·ty** /-'liksətē/ **n. pro·lix·ly adv.** [ME: from OFr. *prolixe* or L. *prolixus* 'poured forth, extended,' from *pro-* 'outward' + *liquere* 'be liquid.']

pro·loc·u·tor /prō'läkyətər/ ▶ **n. 1** a chairperson of the lower house of convocation in a province of the Church of England. **2** archaic or formal a spokesperson. [ME (sense 2): from L., from *prolocut-* 'spoken out,' from the verb *proloqui*, from *pro-* 'before' + *loqui* 'speak.']

pro·logue /'prō,lôg; -,läg/ ▶ **n.** a separate introductory section of a literary or musical work. ■ an event or action that leads to another event or situation. ■ the actor who delivers the prologue in a play. [ME: from OFr., via L. from Gk. *prologos*, from *pro-* 'before' + *logos* 'saying.']

pro·long /prə'lôNG; -'läNG/ (also **pro·lon·gate** /-'lôNGgāt; -'läNG-/) ▶ **v.** [trans.] extend the duration of: *an idea that prolonged the life of the engine by many years.* ■ (usu. **be prolonged**) rare extend in spatial length. — **pro·lon·ga·tion** /prō,lôNG'gāSHən; prə-/ **n. pro·long·er n.** [ME: from OFr. *prolonguer*, from late L. *prolongare*, from *pro-* 'forward, onward' + *longus* 'long.']

pro·longed /prə'lôNGd; -'läNGd/ ▶ **adj.** continuing for a long time or longer than usual; lengthy. — **pro·long·ed·ly** /-'lôNG(ə)dlē; -'läNG-/ **adv.**

pro·lu·sion /prō'lo͞oZHən/ ▶ **n.** archaic or formal a preliminary action or event; a prelude. ■ a preliminary essay or article. [17th C.: from L. *prolusio(n)*, from *prolus-* 'practiced beforehand,' from the verb *proludere*, from *pro* 'before' + *ludere* 'to play.']

PROM ▶ **n.** Comput. a memory chip that can be programmed only once by the manufacturer or user. [from *p(rogrammable) r(ead-)o(nly) m(emory).*]

prom /präm/ ▶ **n.** informal a formal dance, esp. one held by a class in high school or college at the end of a year.

prom. ▶ **abbr.** promontory.

prom·e·nade /,prämə'nād; -'näd/ ▶ **n.** a paved public walk, typically one along a waterfront at a resort. ■ a leisurely walk, typically taken in a public place so as to meet or be seen by others. ■ (in country dancing) a movement in which couples follow one another in a given direction, each couple having both hands joined. ▶ **v.** [intrans.] take a leisurely walk in public, esp. to meet or be seen by others. ■ [trans.] take such a walk through (a place): *people began to promenade the streets.* ■ [trans.] dated escort (someone) about a place, esp. so as to be seen by others: *the governor of Utah promenades the daughter of the Maryland governor.* — **prom·e·nad·er n.** [16th C.: from Fr., from *se promener* 'to walk,' reflexive of *promener* 'take for a walk.']

prom·e·nade deck ▶ **n.** an upper deck on a passenger ship for the use of passengers who wish to enjoy the open air.

Pro·me·the·us /prə'mēTHēəs; -,TH(y)o͞os/ Gk. Mythol. a Titan worshiped by craftsmen. When Zeus hid fire from man, Prometheus stole it by trickery and returned it to earth. As punishment, Zeus chained him to a rock where an eagle fed each day on his liver, which grew again each night. — **Pro·me·the·an** /-THēən/ **adj.**

pro·me·thi·um /prō'mēTHēəm/ ▶ **n.** the chemical element of atomic number 61, a radioactive metal of the lanthanide series. It was first produced artificially in a nuclear reactor and occurs in nature in traces as a product of uranium fission. (Symbol: **Pm**) [1940s: mod. L., after PROMETHEUS.]

prom·i·nence /'prämənəns/ ▶ **n. 1** the state of being important or famous. **2** the fact or condition of standing out from something by physically projecting or being particularly noticeable. ■ a thing that projects from something, esp. a projecting feature of the landscape or a protuberance on a part of the body. ■ Astron. a stream of incandescent gas projecting above the sun's chromosphere.

prom·i·nent /'prämənənt/ ▶ **adj. 1** important; famous. **2** projecting from something; protuberant. ■ situated so as to catch the attention; noticeable. — **prom·i·nen·cy n. prom·i·nent·ly adv.** [ME: from L. *prominent-* 'jutting out,' from the verb *prominere.*]

pro·mis·cu·ous /prə'miskyo͞oəs/ ▶ **adj. 1** derog. (of a person) having many sexual relationships, esp. transient ones. ■ (of sexual behavior or a society) characterized by such relationships. **2** demonstrating an undiscriminating approach; indiscriminate or casual: *the city fathers were promiscuous with their honors.* ■ consisting of a wide range of different things: *Americans are free to pick and choose from a promiscuous array of values and behavior.* — **prom·is·cu·i·ty** /,prämə'skyo͞oitē; prə,mis'kyo͞o-/ **n. prom·is·cu·ous·ly adv. prom·is·cu·ous·ness n.** [17th C.: from L. *promiscuus* 'indiscriminate' (based on *miscere* 'to mix') + -OUS.]

prom·ise /'präməs/ ▶ **n.** a declaration or assurance that one will do a particular thing or that guarantees that a particular thing will happen. ■ the quality of potential excellence: *he showed great promise as a junior officer.* ■ [in sing.] an indication that something specified is expected or likely to occur: *the promise of peace.* ▶ **v. 1** [reporting verb] assure someone that one will definitely do, give, or arrange something; undertake or declare that something will happen: [with infin.] *he promised to forward my mail* | [with two objs.] *he promised her the job.* ■ [trans.] (usu. **be promised**) archaic pledge (someone, esp. a woman) to marry someone else; betroth: *I've been promised to him for years.* **2** [trans.] give good grounds for expecting (a particular occurrence or situation): *forthcoming concerts promise a feast of music from around the world.* ■ (of a person, publication, institution, etc.) announce (something) as being expected to happen: *China yesterday promised a record grain harvest.* ■ (**promise oneself**) contemplate the pleasant expectation of. — **prom·is·er n.** [ME: from L. *promissum* 'something promised,' neut. past part. of *promittere* 'put forth, promise,' from *pro-* 'forward' + *mittere* 'send.']

Prom·ised Land ▶ **n.** (in the Bible) the land of Canaan, promised to Abraham and his descendants (Gen. 12:7). ■ (**promised land**) a place or situation in which someone expects to find great happiness.

prom·is·ee /,prämə'sē/ ▶ **n.** Law a person to whom a promise is made.

prom·is·ing /'präməsiNG/ ▶ **adj.** showing signs of future success: *a promising actor.* — **prom·is·ing·ly adv.**

prom·i·sor /'präməsər/ ▶ **n.** Law a person who makes a promise.

prom·is·so·ry /'prämə,sôrē/ ▶ **adj.** esp. Law conveying or implying a promise. ■ archaic indicative of something to come; full of promise: *the glow of evening is **promissory of** the splendid days to come.* [ME: from med. L. *promissorius*, from *promittere.*]

prom·is·so·ry note ▶ **n.** a signed document containing a written promise to pay a stated sum to a specified person or the bearer at a specified date or on demand.

pro·mo /'prōmō/ informal ▶ **n.** (pl. **-mos**) a piece of promotional publicity or advertising, esp. in the form of a short film or video: *taping a two-minute promo* | [as adj.] *a promo video.* [1960s: abbrev. of PROMOTION.]

prom·on·to·ry /'prämən,tôrē/ ▶ **n.** (pl. **-ries**) a point of high land that juts out into the sea or a large lake; a headland. ■ Anat. a prominence or protuberance on an organ or other structure in the body. [16th C.: from L. *promontorium*, var. of *promunturium.*]

Prom·on·to·ry Moun·tains a range that forms a peninsula in the northern Great Salt Lake, in northern Utah.

pro·mote /prə'mōt/ ▶ **v.** [trans.] **1** further the progress of (something, esp. a cause, venture, or aim); support or actively encourage. ■ give publicity to (a product, organization, or venture) so as to increase sales or public awareness: *they are using famous personalities to promote the library nationally.* ■ Chem. act as a promoter of (a catalyst). **2** (often **be promoted**) advance or raise (someone) to a higher position or rank. ■ transfer (a sports team) to a higher division of a league: *they were promoted from the Third Division last season.* ■ Chess exchange (a pawn) for a more powerful piece of the same color, typically a queen, as part of the move in which it reaches the opponent's end of the board. — **pro·mot·a·bil·i·ty** /prə,mōtə'bilətē/ **n. pro·mot·a·ble adj. pro·mo·tive** /-tiv/ **adj.** [ME: from L. *promot-* 'moved forward,' from the verb *promovere*, from *pro-* 'forward, onward' + *movere* 'to move.']

pro·mot·er /prə'mōtər/ ▶ **n.** a person or thing that promotes something, in particular: ■ a person or company that finances or organizes a sporting event or theatrical production. ■ a person involved in setting up and funding a new company. ■ a supporter of a cause or aim. ■ (also **pro·mo·tor**) Chem. an additive that increases the activity of a catalyst. ■ Biol. a region of a DNA molecule that forms the site at which transcription of a gene starts.

pro·mo·tion /prə'mōSHən/ ▶ **n. 1** activity that supports the furtherance of a cause, venture, or aim. ■ the publicization of a product, organization, or venture to increase sales or public awareness. ■ a publicity campaign for a particular product, organization, or venture. ■ [often as adj.] (**promotions**) the activity or business of organizing such publicity or campaigns: *she's the promotions manager for the museum.* ■ a sporting event, esp. a series of boxing matches, staged for profit. **2** the action of raising someone to a higher position or rank or the fact of being so raised. ■ the transfer of a sports team to a higher division of a league: *they won promotion last season.*

pro·mo·tion·al /prə'mōSHənl/ ▶ **adj.** of or relating to the publicizing of a product, organization, or venture so as to increase sales or public awareness: *she was on a promotional tour for her books.*

prompt /prämpt/ ▶ **v.** [trans.] **1** (of an event or fact) cause or bring about (an action or feeling): *his death prompted an investigation of safety violations.* ■ cause (someone) to take a course of action: *a demonstration prompted the government to step up security.* **2** assist or encourage (a hesitating speaker) to say something. ■ supply a forgotten word or line to (an actor) during the performance of a play. ■ Comput. (of a computer) request input from (a user). ▶ **n. 1** an act of assisting or encouraging a hesitating speaker. ■ the word or phrase spoken as a reminder to an actor of a forgotten word or line. ■ Comput. a word or symbol on a monitor to show that the system is waiting for input. ■ another term for PROMPTER. **2** the time limit for the payment of an account, as stated on a prompt note. ▶ **adj.** done without delay; immediate. ■ (of a person) acting without delay. ■ (of goods) for immediate delivery and payment. — **promp·ti·tude** /'prämptə,t(y)o͞od/ **n. prompt·ly adv. prompt·ness n.** [ME (as a v.): based on OFr. *prompt* or L. *promptus* 'brought to light,' also 'prepared, ready,' past part. of *promere* 'to produce,' from *pro-* 'out, forth' + *emere* 'take.']

prompt·book /'prämpt ,bo͝ok/ ▶ **n.** an annotated copy of a play for the use of a prompter during a performance.

prompt·er /'prämptər/ ▶ **n.** a person seated out of sight of the audience who supplies a forgotten word or line to an actor during the performance of a play.

prompt·ing /'prämptiNG/ ▶ **n.** the action of saying something to persuade, encourage, or remind someone to do or say something.

prom·ul·gate /'präməl,gāt; prō'məl-/ ▶ **v.** [trans.] promote or make widely known (an idea or cause). ■ put (a law or decree) into effect by official proclamation. — **prom·ul·ga·tion** /,präməl'gāSHən; ,prōməl-/ **n. prom·ul·ga·tor** /-,gātər/ **n.** [16th C.: from L. *promulgat-* 'exposed to public view,' from the verb *promulgare*, from *pro-* 'out, publicly' + *mulgere* 'cause to come forth' (lit. 'to milk').]

pro·mulge /prō'məlj/ ▶ **v.** archaic variant of PROMULGATE. [15th C.: from L. *promulgare*.]

pron. ▶ **abbr.** ■ pronominal. ■ pronoun. ■ pronounced. ■ pronunciation.

pro·nate /'prō,nāt/ ▶ **v.** [trans.] tech. put or hold (a hand, foot, or limb) with the palm or sole turned downward. Compare with SUPINATE. — **pro·na·tion** /prō'nāsHən/ **n.** [19th C.: back-form. from *pronation*, based on L. *pronus* 'leaning forward.']

pro·na·tor /'prō,nātər/ ▶ **n.** Anat. a muscle whose contraction produces or assists in the pronation of a limb or part of a limb. ■ any of several specific muscles in the forearm.

prone /prōn/ ▶ **adj. 1** [predic.] (**prone to/prone to do something**) likely to or liable to suffer from, do, or experience something, typically something regrettable or unwelcome: *he is prone to jump to conclusions.* **2** lying flat, esp. face downward or on the stomach. ■ tech. denoting the position of the forearm with the palm of the hand facing downward. **3** archaic with a downward slope or direction. — **prone·ness n.** [ME: from L. *pronus* 'leaning forward,' from *pro* 'forward.']

prong /prôNG; präNG/ ▶ **n.** each of two or more projecting pointed parts at the end of a fork. ■ a projecting part on various other devices. ■ fig. each of the separate parts of an attack or operation. ▶ **v.** [trans.] pierce or stab with a fork. — **pronged** /prôNGd; präNGd/ **adj.** [15th C.: perh. rel. to Mid. Low Ger. *prange* 'pinching instrument.']

prong·horn /'prôNG,hôrn; 'präNG-/ (also **pronghorn antelope**) ▶ **n.** a deerlike North American mammal (*Antilocapra americana*) with a stocky body, long slim legs, and black horns that are shed and regrown annually.

pro·nom·i·nal /prō'nämənl/ ▶ **adj.** of, relating to, or serving as a pronoun: *a pronominal form.* — **pro·nom·i·nal·i·za·tion** /,prō,nämənl-ə'zāsHən/ **n. pro·nom·i·nal·ize** /-,īz/ **v. pro·nom·i·nal·ly adv.** [17th C.: from late L. *pronominalis* 'belonging to a pronoun,' from L. *pronomen* (see PRONOUN).]

pro·noun /'prō,noun/ ▶ **n.** a word that can function as a noun phrase used by itself and that refers either to the participants in the discourse (e.g., *I, you*) or to someone or something mentioned elsewhere in the discourse (e.g., *she, it, this*). [ME: from PRO-[1] 'on behalf of' + NOUN.]

pro·nounce /prə'nouns/ ▶ **v.** [trans.] **1** make the sound of (a word or part of a word), typically in the correct or a particular way. **2** declare or announce, typically formally or solemnly: *allow history to pronounce the verdict* | [with clause] *the doctors pronounced that he would never improve.* ■ [intrans.] (**pronounce on**) pass judgment or make a decision on: *the secretary of state will shortly pronounce on alternative measures.* — **pro·nounce·a·bil·i·ty** /prə,nounsə'bilətē/ **n. pro·nounce·a·ble adj. pro·nounce·ment n. pro·nounc·er n.** [ME: from OFr. *pronuncier*, from L. *pronuntiare*, from *pro-* 'out, forth' + *nuntiare* 'announce' (from *nuntius* 'messenger').]

pro·nounced /prə'nounst/ ▶ **adj.** very noticeable or marked; conspicuous: *he had a pronounced squint.* — **pro·nounc·ed·ly** /-'nounsədlē; -'nounstlē/ **adv.**

pron·to /'präntō/ ▶ **adv.** informal promptly; quickly. [20th C.: from Sp., from L. *promptus* (see PROMPT).]

pro·nu·cle·us /prō'n(y)ōōklēəs/ ▶ **n.** (pl. **-cle·i** /-klē,ī/) Biol. either of a pair of gametic nuclei, in the stage following meiosis but before their fusion leads to the formation of the nucleus of the zygote. — **pro·nu·cle·ar** /-klēər/ **adj.**

pro·nun·ci·a·men·to /prō,nənsēə'mentō/ ▶ **n.** (pl. **-tos**) (esp. in Spain and Spanish-speaking countries) a political manifesto or proclamation. [Sp. *pronunciamiento*, from *pronunciar* 'pronounce.']

pro·nun·ci·a·tion /prə,nənsē'āsHən/ ▶ **n.** the way in which a word is pronounced. [ME: from L. *pronuntiatio(n-)*, from *pronuntiare*.]

proof /prōōf/ ▶ **n. 1** evidence or argument establishing or helping to establish a fact or the truth of a statement. ■ Law the spoken or written evidence in a trial. ■ the action or process of establishing the truth of a statement: *it shifts the onus of proof in convictions from the police to the public.* ■ archaic a test or trial. ■ a series of stages in the resolution of a mathematical or philosophical problem. **2** a trial print of something, in particular: ■ Print. a trial impression of a page, taken from type or film and used for making corrections before final printing. ■ a trial photographic print made for initial selection. ■ each of a number of impressions from an engraved plate, esp. (in commercial printing) of a limited number before the ordinary issue is printed and before an inscription or signature is added. ■ any of various preliminary impressions of coins struck as specimens. **3** the strength of distilled alcoholic liquor, relative to proof spirit taken as a standard of 100: [in comb.] *powerful 132-proof rum.* ▶ **adj. 1** able to withstand something damaging; resistant. **2** [attrib.] denoting a trial impression of a page or printed work: *a proof copy is sent up for checking.* ▶ **v.** [trans.] **1** make (fabric) waterproof: [as adj.] (**proofed**) *the tent is made from proofed nylon.* **2** make a proof of (a printed work, engraving, etc.): [as n.] (**proofing**) *proofing could be done on a low-cost printer.* ■ proofread (a text). **3** activate (yeast) by the addition of liquid. ■ knead (dough) until light and smooth. ■ [intrans.] (of dough) prove: *shape into a baguette and let proof for a few minutes.* [ME *preve*, from OFr. *proeve*, from late L. *proba*, from L. *probare* 'to test, prove.']

proof pos·i·tive ▶ **n.** evidence taken to be final or absolute proof of the existence of something.

proof·read /'prōōf,rēd/ (also **proof-read**) ▶ **v.** (past and past part. **-read** /-,red/) [trans.] read (printer's proofs or other written or printed material) and mark any errors. — **proof·read·er n.**

proof spir·it ▶ **n.** a mixture of alcohol and water containing 50 percent alcohol by volume, used as a standard of strength of distilled alcoholic liquor.

prop[1] /präp/ ▶ **n.** a pole or beam used as a support or to keep something in position, typically not an integral part of the thing supported. ■ fig. a person or thing that is a major source of support or assistance. ■ Gram. a word used to fill a syntactic role without any specific meaning of its own, for example *one* in *it's a nice one* and *it* in *it is raining.* ▶ **v.** (**propped, prop·ping**) [trans.] position something underneath (someone or something) for support: *she propped her chin in the palm of her right hand.* ■ position (something or someone) more or less upright by leaning it against something else. ■ use an object to keep (something) in position: *the door to the office was propped open.*

– PHRASAL VERBS **prop someone/something up** provide support or assistance for someone or something that would otherwise fail or decline: *foreign aid tends to prop up incompetent governments.* [ME: prob. from MDu. *proppe* 'support (for vines).']

prop[2] ▶ **n.** (usu. **props**) a portable object other than furniture or costumes used on the set of a play or movie. [19th C.: abbrev. of PROPERTY.]

prop[3] ▶ **n.** informal an aircraft propeller.

prop. ▶ **abbr.** ■ proposition. ■ proprietor.

pro·pae·deu·tic /,prōpi'd(y)ōōtik/ ▶ **adj.** formal (of an area of study) serving as a preliminary instruction or as an introduction to further study. — **pro·pae·deu·ti·cal adj.** [18th C.: from PRO-[2] 'before' + Gk. *paideutikos* 'of or for teaching.']

prop·a·gan·da /,präpə'gandə/ ▶ **n. 1** esp. derog. information, esp. of a biased or misleading nature, used to promote or publicize a particular political cause or point of view. ■ the dissemination of such information as a political strategy. **2** (**Propaganda**) a committee of cardinals of the Roman Catholic Church responsible for foreign missions, founded in 1622 by Pope Gregory XV. [Ital., from mod. L. *congregatio de propaganda fide* 'congregation for propagation of the faith'.]

prop·a·gan·dist /,präpə'gandist/ esp. derog. ▶ **n.** a person who promotes or publicizes a particular organization or cause. ▶ **adj.** consisting of or spreading propaganda. — **prop·a·gan·dism** /-,dizəm/ **n. prop·a·gan·dis·tic** /-,gan'distik/ **adj. prop·a·gan·dis·ti·cal·ly** /-,gan'distik(ə)lē/ **adv.**

prop·a·gan·dize /,präpə'gan,dīz/ ▶ **v.** [intrans.] esp. derog. promote or publicize a particular cause or view, esp. in a biased or misleading way. ■ [trans.] (often **be propagandized**) attempt to influence (someone) in such a way.

prop·a·gate /'präpə,gāt/ ▶ **v.** [trans.] **1** breed specimens of (a plant, animal, etc.) by natural processes from the parent stock. ■ [intrans.] (of a plant, animal, etc.) reproduce in such a way: *the plant propagates from stem cuttings.* ■ cause (something) to increase in number or amount: *operational error includes errors propagated during digitizing.* **2** spread and promote (an idea, theory, knowledge, etc.) widely. **3** transmit (motion, light, sound, etc.) in a particular direction or through a medium: *electromagnetic effects can be propagated at a finite velocity only through material substances.* ■ [intrans.] (of motion, light, sound, etc.) be transmitted or travel in such a way: *a hydraulic fracture generally propagates in a vertical plane.* — **prop·a·ga·tion** /,präpə'gāsHən/ **n. prop·a·ga·tive** /-,gātiv/ **adj. prop·a·ga·tor** /-,gātər/ **n.** [ME: from L. *propagat-* 'multiplied from layers or shoots,' from the verb *propagare*; rel. to *propago* 'young shoot' (from a base meaning 'fix').]

prop·a·gule /'präpə,gyōōl/ ▶ **n.** Bot. a vegetative structure that can become detached from a plant and give rise to a new plant, e.g., a bud, sucker, or spore. [19th C.: from mod. L. *propagulum* 'small shoot,' dimin. of *propago* 'shoot, runner.']

pro·pane /'prō,pān/ ▶ **n.** Chem. a flammable hydrocarbon gas, C_3H_8, of the alkane series, present in natural gas and used as bottled fuel. [19th C.: from PROPIONIC ACID + -ANE[2].]

pro·pa·nol /'prōpə,nôl; -,näl/ ▶ **n.** Chem. each of two isomeric liquid alcohols, $CH_3CH_2CH_2OH$ and $CH_3CH(OH)CH_3$, used as solvents; propyl alcohol.

pro·pel /prə'pel/ ▶ **v.** (**-pelled, -pel·ling**) [trans.] drive, push, or cause to move in a particular direction, typically forward: *the boat is propelled by paddle.* ■ [trans.] fig. spur or drive into a particular situation: *fear propelled her out of her stillness.* [ME): from L. *propellere*, from *pro-* 'forward' + *pellere* 'to drive.']

pro·pel·lant /prə'pelənt/ ▶ **n.** a thing or substance that causes something to move or be driven forward or outward, in particular: ■ an inert fluid, liquefied under pressure, in which the active contents of an aerosol are dispersed. ■ an explosive that fires bullets from a firearm. ■ a substance used as a reagent in a rocket engine to provide thrust. ▶ **adj.** another term for PROPELLENT. [17th C.: orig. from L. *propellent-* 'driving ahead (of oneself),' from the v. *propellere*, later from PROPEL.]

pro·pel·lent /prə'pelənt/ ▶ **adj.** capable of driving, pushing, or moving something in a particular direction.

pro·pel·ler /prə'pelər/ ▶ **n.** a mechanical device for propelling a boat or aircraft, consisting of a revolving shaft with two or more broad, angled blades attached to it. *See illustration on next page.*

pro·pel·ler-head (also **pro·pel·ler head** or **pro·pel·ler·head**) ▶ **n.** informal a person who has an obsessive interest in computers or technology.

pro·pene /'prō,pēn/ ▶ **n.** Chem. another term for PROPYLENE. [19th C.: blend of PROPANE and ALKENE.]

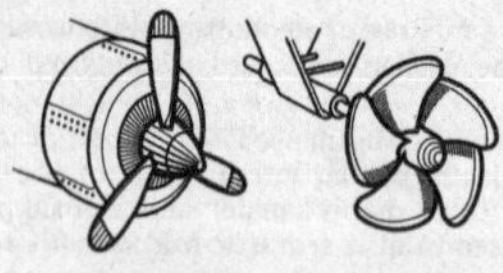

propellers

pro·pen·si·ty /prə'pensətē/ ▶n. (pl. **-ties**) an inclination or natural tendency to behave in a particular way. [16th C.: from archaic *propense* (from L. *propensus* 'inclined,' past part. of *propendere*, from *pro-* 'forward, down' + *pendere* 'hang') + **-ITY**.]

prop·er /'präpər/ ▶adj. **1** [attrib.] truly what something is said or regarded to be; genuine: *a proper meal.* ■ [postpositive] strictly so called; in its true form: *some of the dos and don'ts in espionage proper.* ■ informal, esp. Brit. used as an intensifier, often in derogatory contexts: *she looked like a proper harlot.* **2** [attrib.] of the required type; suitable or appropriate. ■ according to what is correct or prescribed for a particular situation or thing: *proper procedures.* ■ according to or respecting recognized social standards or conventions; respectable, esp. excessively so. **3** [predic.] (**proper to**) belonging or relating exclusively or distinctively to; particular to: *elephants proper to Africa.* ■ (of a psalm, lesson, prayer, etc.) appointed for a particular day, occasion, or season. ■ archaic belonging to oneself or itself; own: *to judge with my proper eyes.* **4** [usu. postpositive] Heraldry in the natural colors. **5** archaic (of a person) good-looking. **6** Math. denoting a subset or subgroup that does not constitute the entire set or group, esp. one that has more than one element. ▶adv. Brit., informal or dialect satisfactorily or correctly: *my eyes were all blurry and I couldn't see proper.* ■ thoroughly: *I had been fooled good and proper.* ▶n. the part of a church service that varies with the season or festival. — **prop·er·ly** /'präpərlē/ adv. **prop·er·ness** n. [ME: from OFr. *propre*, from L. *proprius* 'one's own, special.']

prop·er ad·jec·tive ▶n. an adjective, typically capitalized, derived from a proper noun.

prop·er·din /prō'pərdn/ ▶n. Biochem. a protein present in the blood, involved in the body's response to certain kinds of infection. [1950s: from **PRO-**[2] 'before' + L. *perdere* 'destroy' + **-IN**[1].]

prop·er frac·tion ▶n. a fraction that is less than one, with the numerator less than the denominator.

prop·er noun (also **proper name**) ▶n. a name used for an individual person, place, or organization, spelled with initial capital letters, e.g., *Larry* or *Mexico*. Often contrasted with **COMMON NOUN**.

prop·er·tied /'präpərtēd/ ▶adj. (of a person or group) owning property and land, esp. in large amounts.

Pro·per·tius /prō'pərsh(ē)əs/, Sextus (*c.*50–*c.*16 BC), Roman poet.

prop·er·ty /'präpərtē/ ▶n. (pl. **-ties**) **1** a thing or things belonging to someone; possessions collectively. ■ a building or buildings and the land belonging to it or them. ■ Law the right to the possession, use, or disposal of something; ownership. ■ old-fashioned term for **PROP**[2]. **2** an attribute, quality, or characteristic of something. [ME: from an Anglo-Norman Fr. var. of OFr. *propriete*, from L. *proprietas*, from *proprius* 'one's own, particular' (see **PROPER**).]

prop·er·ty man ▶n. dated a man in charge of theatrical props.

prop·er·ty mis·tress ▶n. dated a woman in charge of theatrical props.

pro·phage /'prō,fāj/ ▶n. Microbiol. the genetic material of a bacteriophage, incorporated into the genome of a bacterium and able to produce phages if specifically activated.

pro·phase /'prō,fāz/ ▶n. Biol. the first stage of cell division, before metaphase, during which the chromosomes become visible as paired chromatids and the nuclear envelope disappears. The first prophase of meiosis includes the reduction division.

proph·e·cy /'präfəsē/ ▶n. (pl. **-cies**) a prediction of what will happen in the future. ■ the faculty, function, or practice of prophesying. [ME: from OFr. *profecie*, via late L. from Gk. *prophēteia*, from *prophētēs* (see **PROPHET**).]

proph·e·sy /'präfə,sī/ ▶v. (**-sies, -sied**) [trans.] say that (a specified thing) will happen in the future: *Jacques was prophesying a bumper harvest.* ■ [intrans.] speak or write by divine inspiration; act as a prophet: *when a man prophesies, it is because the Spirit of the Lord comes upon him.* — **proph·e·si·er** /-,sīər/ n. [ME: from OFr. *profecier*, from *profecie* (see **PROPHECY**).]

proph·et /'präfit/ ▶n. **1** a person regarded as an inspired teacher or proclaimer of the will of God: *the Old Testament prophet Jeremiah.* ■ (**the Prophet**) (among Muslims) Muhammad. ■ (**the Prophet**) (among Mormons) Joseph Smith or one of his successors. ■ a person who advocates or speaks in a visionary way about a new belief, cause, or theory. ■ a person who predicts, or claims to be able to predict, what will happen in the future: *the anti-technology prophets of doom.* **2** (**the Prophets**) the prophetic writings of the Old Testament or Hebrew scriptures, in particular: ■ (in Christian use) the books of Isaiah, Jeremiah, Ezekiel, Daniel, and the twelve minor prophets. ■ (in Jewish use) one of the three canonical divisions of the Hebrew Bible, comprising the books of Joshua, Judges, Samuel, Kings, Jeremiah, Ezekiel, Isaiah, and the twelve minor prophets. — **proph·et·hood** /-,ho͝od/ n. [ME: from OFr. *prophete*, via L. from Gk. *prophētēs* 'spokesman,' from *pro* 'before' + *phētēs* 'speaker' (from *phēnai* 'speak').]

proph·et·ess /'präfətəs/ ▶n. a female prophet.

pro·phet·ic /prə'fetik/ ▶adj. **1** accurately describing or predicting what will happen in the future. **2** of, relating to, or characteristic of a prophet or prophecy. — **pro·phet·i·cal** adj. **pro·phet·i·cal·ly** /-ik(ə)lē/ adv.

pro·phy·lac·tic /,prōfə'laktik/ ▶adj. intended to prevent disease. ▶n. a medicine or course of action used to prevent disease. ■ a condom. — **pro·phy·lac·ti·cal·ly** /-ik(ə)lē/ adv. [16th C.: from Fr. *prophylactique*, from Gk. *prophulaktikos*, from *pro* 'before' + *phulassein* 'to guard.']

pro·phy·lax·is /,prōfə'laksəs/ ▶n. action taken to prevent disease, esp. by specified means or against a specified disease. [19th C.: mod. L., from **PRO-**[2] 'before' + Gk. *phulaxis* 'act of guarding.']

pro·pin·qui·ty /prə'piNGkwətē/ ▶n. **1** the state of being close to someone or something; proximity. **2** tech. close kinship. [ME: from OFr. *propinquité*, from L. *propinquitas*, from *propinquus* 'near,' from *prope* 'near to.']

pro·pi·on·i·bac·te·ri·um /,prōpē,änə,bak'ti(ə)rēəm/ ▶n. (pl. **-te·ri·a** /-'ti(ə)rēə/) a bacterium (genus *Propionibacterium*) that metabolizes carbohydrate, some kinds being involved in the fermentation of dairy products and the etiology of acne. [mod. L., from *propionic* (see **PROPIONIC ACID**).]

pro·pi·on·ic ac·id /,prōpē'änik/ ▶n. Chem. a colorless pungent liquid organic acid, C_2H_5COOH, produced in some forms of fermentation and used for inhibiting the growth of mold in bread. — **pro·pi·o·nate** /'prōpēə,nāt/ n. [19th C.: from Fr. *propionique*, from Gk. *pro* 'before' + *piōn* 'fat.']

pro·pi·ti·ate /prə'pishē,āt/ ▶v. [trans.] win or regain the favor of (a god, spirit, or person) by doing something that pleases them. — **pro·pi·ti·a·tor** /-,ātər/ n. **pro·pi·ti·a·to·ry** /-'pishēə,tôrē/ adj. [16th C.: from L. *propitiat-* 'made favorable,' from the verb *propitiare*, from *propitius* 'favorable, gracious' (see **PROPITIOUS**).]

pro·pi·ti·a·tion /prə,pishē'āshən/ ▶n. the action of propitiating or appeasing a god, spirit, or person. ■ atonement, esp. that of Christ.

pro·pi·tious /prə'pishəs/ ▶adj. giving or indicating a good chance of success; favorable. ■ archaic favorably disposed toward someone. — **pro·pi·tious·ly** adv. **pro·pi·tious·ness** n. [ME: from OFr. *propicieus* or L. *propitius* 'favorable, gracious.']

prop jet ▶n. a turboprop aircraft or engine.

prop·o·lis /'präpələs/ ▶n. a resinous substance collected by honeybees from tree buds, used to fill crevices and to seal and varnish honeycombs. [17th C.: via L. from Gk. *propolis* 'suburb,' also 'bee glue,' from *pro* 'before' + *polis* 'city.']

pro·po·nent /prə'pōnənt/ ▶n. a person who advocates a theory, proposal, or project. [16th C.: from L. *proponent-* 'putting forth,' from the verb *proponere* (see **PROPOUND**).]

Pro·pon·tis /prə'päntəs/ ancient name for the Sea of Marmara (see **MARMARA, SEA OF**).

pro·por·tion /prə'pôrshən/ ▶n. a part, share, or number considered in comparative relation to a whole. ■ the relationship of one thing to another in terms of quantity, size, or number; the ratio. ■ (**proportions**) the comparative measurements or size of different parts of a whole. ■ (**proportions**) dimensions; size. ■ the correct, attractive, or ideal relationship in size or shape between one thing and another or between the parts of a whole. ▶v. [trans.] formal adjust or regulate (something) so that it has a particular or suitable relationship to something else: *a life in which happiness was proportioned to virtue.*
– PHRASES **in proportion** according to a particular relationship in size, amount, or degree. ■ in comparison with; in relation to. ■ in the correct or appropriate relation to the size, shape, or position of other things. ■ correctly or realistically regarded in terms of relative importance or seriousness. **out of proportion** in the wrong relation to the size, shape, or position of other things. ■ greater or more serious than is necessary or appropriate. ■ wrongly or unrealistically regarded in terms of relative importance or seriousness. **sense of proportion** the ability to judge the relative importance or seriousness of things. [ME: from OFr., from L. *proportio(n-)*, from *pro portione* 'with respect to (its or a person's) share.']

pro·por·tion·a·ble /prə'pôrshənəbəl/ ▶adj. archaic term for **PROPORTIONAL**. — **pro·por·tion·a·bly** /-blē/ adv.

pro·por·tion·al /prə'pôrshənl/ ▶adj. corresponding in size or amount to something else. ■ Math. (of a variable quantity) having a constant ratio to another quantity. — **pro·por·tion·al·i·ty** /prə,pôrshə'nalətē; pər,pôrshə'nalədē/ n. **pro·por·tion·al·ly** /-shənl-ē/ adv.

pro·por·tion·al rep·re·sen·ta·tion (abbr.: **PR**) ▶n. an electoral system in which parties gain seats in proportion to the number of votes cast for them.

pro·por·tion·ate /prə'pôrshənət/ ▶adj. another term for **PROPORTIONAL**. — **pro·por·tion·ate·ly** adv.

pro·por·tioned /prə'pôrshənd/ ▶adj. [with submodifier] having dimensions or a comparative relationship of parts of a specified type.

pro·pos·al /prə'pōzəl/ ▶n. **1** a plan or suggestion put forward for consideration or discussion by others. ■ the action of putting forward such a plan or suggestion. **2** an offer of marriage.

pro·pose /prə'pōz/ ▶v. **1** [trans.] put forward (an idea or plan) for consideration or discussion by others: *he proposed a new peace plan.* ■ nominate (someone) for an elected office or as a member of a society. ■ put forward (a motion) to a legislature or committee: *the government proposed a vote of confidence.* **2** [intrans.] make an offer of marriage to someone. — **pro·pos·er** n. [ME: from OFr. *proposer*, from L. *proponere* (see **PROPONENT**), influenced by L. *propositus* 'put forth.']

prop·o·si·tion /ˌpräpəˈzisʜən/ ▶n. **1** a statement or assertion that expresses a judgment or opinion. ■ Logic a statement that expresses a concept that can be true or false. ■ Math. a formal statement of a theorem or problem, typically including the demonstration. **2** a suggested plan of action, esp. in a business context: *a detailed investment proposition.* ■ a constitutional proposal; a bill. ■ informal an offer of sexual intercourse made to a person with whom one is not sexually involved, esp. one that is made in an unsubtle or offensive way. **3** [with adj.] a project, task, or idea considered in terms of its likely success or difficulty, esp. in a commercial context. ■ a person considered in terms of the likely success or difficulty of one's dealings with them: *as a potential manager, Sandy is a better proposition than Dave.* ▶v. [trans.] informal make a suggestion of sexual intercourse to (someone with whom one is not sexually involved), esp. in an unsubtle or offensive way. ■ make an offer or suggestion to (someone). — **prop·o·si·tion·al** /-ʜənl/ **adj.** (esp. Logic).

pro·pound /prəˈpound/ ▶v. [trans.] put forward (an idea, theory, or point of view) for consideration. — **pro·pound·er** n. [16th C.: alt. of archaic *propone*, from L. *proponere* 'set forth,' from *pro-* 'forward' + *ponere* 'put.']

pro·pox·y·phene /prōˈpäksəˌfēn/ ▶n. Med. a synthetic compound chemically related to methadone, used as a mild narcotic analgesic. [1950s: from PROPYL + OXY-[2] + *-phene* (from PHENYL).]

propr. ▶abbr. proprietor.

pro·pran·o·lol /prōˈpranlˌôl; -ˌäl/ ▶n. Med. a synthetic compound, $C_{16}H_{21}NO_2$, that acts as a beta blocker and is used mainly in the treatment of cardiac arrhythmia. [1960s: from *pro(pyl)* + *pr(op)anol.*]

pro·pri·e·tar·y /prəˈprī-iˌterē/ ▶adj. of or relating to an owner or ownership. ■ (of a product) marketed under and protected by a registered trade name. ■ behaving as if one were the owner of someone or something. ▶n. an owner; proprietor. ■ hist. esp. in North America, a grantee or owner of a colony who has been granted, as an individual or as part of a group, the full rights of self-government. [ME: from late L. *proprietarius* 'proprietor,' from *proprietas* (see PROPERTY).]

pro·pri·e·tar·y name ▶n. a name of a product or service registered by its owner as a trademark and not usable by others without permission.

pro·pri·e·tor /prəˈprīətər/ ▶n. the owner of a business. ■ a holder of property. — **pro·pri·e·to·ri·al** /prəˌprīəˈtôrēəl/ **adj.** **pro·pri·e·to·ri·al·ly** /prəˌprīəˈtôrēəlē/ **adv.** **pro·pri·e·tor·ship** /-ˌsʜip/ n.

pro·pri·e·tress /prəˈprīətrəs/ ▶n. a female proprietor.

pro·pri·e·ty /prəˈprīətē/ ▶n. (pl. **-ties**) the state or quality of conforming to conventionally accepted standards of behavior or morals. ■ **(proprieties)** the details or rules of behavior considered correct: *she's a great one for the proprieties.* ■ the condition of being right, appropriate, or fitting. [ME: from OFr. *propriete*, from L. *proprietas* (see PROPERTY).]

pro·pri·o·cep·tive /ˌprōprēəˈseptiv/ ▶adj. Physiol. relating to stimuli that are produced and perceived within an organism, esp. those connected with the position and movement of the body. Compare with EXTEROCEPTIVE and INTEROCEPTIVE. — **pro·pri·o·cep·tion** /-ˈsepsʜən/ n. **pro·pri·o·cep·tive·ly** adv. [20th C.: from L. *proprius* 'own' + RECEPTIVE.]

pro·pri·o·cep·tor /ˌprōprēəˈseptər/ ▶n. Physiol. a sensory receptor that receives stimuli from within the body, esp. one that responds to position and movement. [20th C.: from L. *proprius* 'own' + RECEPTOR.]

prop·to·sis /präpˈtōsəs/ ▶n. Med. abnormal protrusion or displacement of an eye or other body part. [17th C.: via late L. from Gk. *proptōsis*, from *pro* 'before' + *piptein* 'to fall.']

pro·pul·sion /prəˈpəlsʜən/ ▶n. the action of driving or pushing forward. — **pro·pul·sive** /-siv/ **adj.** [17th C. (in the sense 'expulsion'): from med. L. *propulsio(n-)*, from L. *propellere* 'drive before (oneself).']

pro·pyl /ˈprōpəl/ ▶n. [as adj.] Chem. of or denoting the alkyl radical $-C_3H_7$, derived from propane. Compare with ISOPROPYL.

prop·y·lae·um /ˌpräpəˈlēəm; ˌprō-/ ▶n. (pl. **-lae·a** /-ˈlēə/) the structure forming the entrance to a temple. [via L. from Gk. *propulaion*, neut. (used as a n.) of *propulaios* 'before the gate,' from *pro* 'before' + *pulē* 'gate.']

pro·pyl·ene /ˈprōpəˌlēn/ ▶n. Chem. a gaseous hydrocarbon of the alkene series, C_3H_6, made by cracking alkanes.

pro·pyl·ene gly·col ▶n. Chem. a liquid alcohol, $C_3H_6(OH)_2$, that is used as a solvent, in antifreeze, and in the food, plastics, and perfume industries.

pro ra·ta /prō ˈrātə; ˈrätə; ˈratə/ ▶adj. proportional. ▶adv. proportionally. [16th C.: L., lit. 'according to the rate.']

pro·rate /prōˈrāt; ˈprōˌrāt/ ▶v. [trans.] (usu. **be prorated**) allocate, distribute, or assess pro rata. — **pro·ra·tion** /prōˈrāsʜən/ n.

pro·rogue /prəˈrōg/ ▶v. (**-rogues, -rogued, -rogu·ing**) [trans.] discontinue a session of (a legislative assembly) without dissolving it. ■ [intrans.] (of such an assembly) be discontinued in this way. — **pro·ro·ga·tion** /ˌprōrəˈgāsʜən/ n. [ME: from OFr. *proroger*, from L. *prorogare* 'prolong, extend,' from *pro-* 'in front of, publicly' + *rogare* 'ask.']

pros. ▶abbr. ■ proscenium. ■ prosody.

pro·sa·ic /prōˈzāik/ ▶adj. having the style or diction of prose; lacking poetic beauty. ■ commonplace; unromantic. — **pro·sa·i·cal·ly** /-ik(ə)lē/ **adv.** **pro·sa·ic·ness** n. [16th C.: from late L. *prosaicus*, from L. *prosa* 'straightforward (discourse)' (see PROSE).]

Pros. Atty. ▶abbr. prosecuting attorney.

pro·sau·ro·pod /prōˈsôrəˌpäd/ ▶n. an elongated, partly bipedal herbivorous dinosaur (infraorder Prosauropoda, order Saurischia) of the late Triassic and early Jurassic periods, related to the ancestors of sauropods.

pro·sce·ni·um /prəˈsēnēəm; prō-/ ▶n. (pl. **-ni·ums** or **-ni·a** /-nēə/) the part of a theater stage in front of the curtain. ■ short for PROSCENIUM ARCH. ■ the stage of an ancient theater. [17th C.: via L. from Gk. *proskēnion*, from *pro* 'before' + *skēnē* 'stage.']

pro·sce·ni·um arch ▶n. an arch framing the opening between the stage and the auditorium in some theaters.

pro·sciut·to /prəˈsʜōōtō/ ▶n. Italian ham cured by drying and typically served in very thin slices. [Ital.]

pro·scribe /prōˈskrīb/ ▶v. [trans.] forbid, esp. by law. ■ denounce or condemn. ■ hist. outlaw (someone). — **pro·scrip·tion** /-ˈskripsʜən/ n. **pro·scrip·tive** /-ˈskriptiv/ **adj.** [ME: from L. *proscribere*, from *pro-* 'in front of' + *scribere* 'write.']

prose /prōz/ ▶n. **1** written or spoken language in its ordinary form, without metrical structure. ■ fig. plain or dull writing, discourse, or expression: *medical and scientific prose.* **2** another term for SEQUENCE (sense 4). ▶v. **1** [intrans.] talk tediously: *prosing on about female beauty.* **2** [trans.] dated compose or convert into prose. — **pros·er** n. [ME: via OFr. from L. *prosa (oratio)* 'straightforward (discourse),' fem. of *prosus*, earlier *prorsus* 'direct.']

pro·sec·tor /prōˈsektər/ ▶n. a person who dissects dead bodies for anatomical demonstration. [19th C.: from late L., lit. 'anatomist,' based on L. *secare* 'to cut,' perh. via Fr. *prosecteur.*]

pros·e·cute /ˈpräsiˌkyōōt/ ▶v. [trans.] **1** institute legal proceedings against (a person or organization): *they were prosecuted for obstructing the highway.* ■ institute legal proceedings in respect of (a claim or offense): *the state's attorney's office decided this was a case worth prosecuting* | [intrans.] *the company didn't prosecute because of his age.* ■ [intrans.] (of a lawyer) conduct the case against the party being accused or sued in a lawsuit. **2** continue with (a course of action) with a view to its completion: *the government's ability to prosecute the war.* — **pros·e·cut·a·ble** adj. [ME (sense 2): from L. *prosecut-* 'pursued, accompanied,' from the verb *prosequi*, from *pro-* 'onward' + *sequi* 'follow.']

pros·e·cu·tion /ˌpräsiˈkyōōsʜən/ ▶n. **1** the institution and conducting of legal proceedings against someone in respect of a criminal charge. ■ **(the prosecution)** [treated as sing. or pl.] the party instituting or conducting legal proceedings against someone in a lawsuit. **2** the continuation of a course of action with a view to its completion.

pros·e·cu·tor /ˈpräsiˌkyōōtər/ ▶n. a person, esp. a public official, who institutes legal proceedings against someone. ■ a lawyer who conducts the case against a defendant in a criminal court. Also called **prosecuting attorney.** — **pros·e·cu·to·ri·al** /ˌpräsikyəˈtôrēəl/ **adj.**

pros·e·lyte /ˈpräsəˌlīt/ ▶n. a person who has converted from one opinion, religion, or party to another, esp. recently. ■ a Gentile convert to Judaism. ▶v. another term for PROSELYTIZE. — **pros·e·lyt·ism** /-lə,tizəm/ n. [ME: via late L. from Gk. *prosēluthos* 'stranger, convert,' from *prosēluth-*, past stem of *proserkhesthai* 'approach.']

pros·e·lyt·ize /ˈpräsələˌtīz/ ▶v. [trans.] convert or attempt to convert (someone) from one religion, belief, or opinion to another: *the program had a tremendous effect, proselytizing many* | [intrans.] *proselytizing for converts.* ■ advocate or promote (a belief or course of action): *Davis wanted to proselytize his ideas.* — **pros·e·lyt·iz·er** n.

pro·sem·i·nar /prōˈseməˌnär/ ▶n. a seminar that accepts graduate and advanced undergraduate students alike.

pros·en·ceph·a·lon /ˌpräsˌenˈsefəˌlän; -lən/ ▶n. another term for FOREBRAIN. [19th C.: from Gk. *prosō* 'forward' + *enkephalos* 'brain.']

pros·en·chy·ma /präsˈeɴɢkəmə/ ▶n. Biol. a plant tissue consisting of elongated cells with interpenetrating tapering ends, occurring esp. in vascular tissue. — **pros·en·chym·a·tous** /ˌpräsənˈkimətəs/ **adj.** [19th C.: from Gk. *pros* 'toward' + *enkhuma* 'infusion,' on the pattern of *parenchyma.*]

prose po·em ▶n. a piece of writing in prose whose poetic qualities, including intensity, compactness, prominent rhythms, and imagery, are self-evident. — **prose po·et·ry** n.

Pro·ser·pi·na /prōˈsərpənə/ (also **Pro·ser·pi·ne** /-pənē/) Rom. Mythol. Roman name for PERSEPHONE.

pro shop ▶n. a retail outlet at a golf club, typically run by the resident professional, where golfing equipment can be purchased or repaired.

pro·sim·i·an /prōˈsimēən/ Zool. ▶n. a primitive primate of a group (suborder Prosimii) that includes the lemurs, lorises, bush babies, and tarsiers. ▶adj. of or relating to the prosimians. Compare with SIMIAN.

pro·sit /ˈprōzət; -sət/ ▶exclam. an expression used as a toast when drinking to a person's health. [Ger., from L., lit. 'may it benefit.']

Pros·o·bran·chi·a /ˌpräsəˈbraɴɢkēə/ Zool. a group of mollusks (subclass Prosobranchia) that includes the limpets, abalones, and many terrestrial and aquatic snails. They all have a shell, and many have an operculum. — **pros·o·branch** /ˈpräsəˌbraɴɢk/ n. [mod. L. (pl.), from Gk. *prosō* 'forward' + *brankhia* 'gills.']

pros·o·dy /ˈpräsədē/ ▶n. the patterns of rhythm and sound used in poetry. ■ the theory or study of these patterns, or the rules governing them. ■ the patterns of stress and intonation in a language. — **pro·sod·ic** /prəˈsädik; -ˈzädik/ or **pro·sod·i·cal** /prəˈsädikəl; -ˈzäd-/ **adj.** **pros·o·dist** /ˈpräsədist; ˈpräz-/ n. [15th C.: from L. *prosodia* 'accent of a syllable,' from Gk. *prosōidia* 'song sung to music, tone of a syllable,' from *pros* 'toward' + *ōidē* 'song.']

pro·so·ma /prō'sōmə/ ▶ **n.** (pl. **-mas** or **-ma·ta** /-mətə/) another term for CEPHALOTHORAX. [19th C.: from PRO-² 'before' + Gk. *sōma* 'body.']

pros·o·pag·no·sia /,präsəpag'nōzн(ē)ə/ ▶ **n.** Psychiatry an inability to recognize the faces of familiar people, typically as a result of damage to the brain. — **pros·o·pag·nos·ic** /-'nōzik; -'nōsik/ **n.** [1950s: mod. L., from Gk. *prosōpon* 'face' + *agnōsia* 'ignorance.']

pros·o·pog·ra·phy /,präsə'pägrəfē/ ▶ **n.** (pl. **-phies**) a description of a person's social and family connections, career, etc., or a collection of such descriptions. — **pros·o·pog·ra·pher** /-fər/ **n.** **pros·o·po·graph·i·cal** /-pə'grafikəl/ **adj.** [1920s: from mod. L. *prosopographia*, from Gk. *prosōpon* 'face, person' + *-graphia* 'writing.']

pro·so·po·poe·ia /prə,sōpə'pēə; ,präsə-/ ▶ **n.** **1** a figure of speech in which an abstract thing is personified. **2** a figure of speech in which an imagined or absent person or thing is represented as speaking. [16th C.: via L. from Gk. *prosōpopoiia*, from *prosōpon* 'person' + *poiein* 'to make.']

pros·pect ▶ **n.** /'präs,pekt/ **1** the possibility or likelihood of some future event occurring. ■ [in sing.] a mental picture of a future or anticipated event. ■ (usu. **prospects**) chances or opportunities for success or wealth. **2** a person regarded as a potential customer or subscriber to something. ■ a person regarded as likely to succeed, esp. in a sporting event. ■ a place likely to yield mineral deposits. ■ a place being explored for mineral deposits. **3** an extensive view of landscape. ▶ **v.** [intrans.] search for mineral deposits in a place, esp. by means of experimental drilling and excavation: *the company is also* ***prospecting for*** *gold.* ■ (**prospect for**) fig. look out for; search for: *the responsibilities of salespeople to prospect for customers.* — **pros·pec·tor** /-tər/ **n.** [ME (as a noun denoting the action of looking toward a distant object): from L. *prospectus* 'view,' from *prospicere* 'look forward.']

pro·spec·tive /prə'spektiv/ ▶ **adj.** [attrib.] (of a person) expected or expecting to be something particular in the future. ■ likely to happen at a future date; concerned with or applying to the future. — **pro·spec·tive·ly** **adv.** **pro·spec·tive·ness** **n.**

pro·spec·tus /prə'spektəs/ ▶ **n.** (pl. **-tus·es**) a printed document that advertises or describes a school, commercial enterprise, forthcoming book, etc., in order to attract or inform clients, members, buyers, or investors. [18th C.: from L., lit. 'view, prospect.']

pros·per /'präspər/ ▶ **v.** [intrans.] succeed in material terms; be financially successful: *his business prospered.* ■ flourish physically; grow strong and healthy. ■ [trans.] archaic make successful. [ME: from OFr. *prosperer*, from L. *prosperare*, from *prosperus* 'doing well.']

pros·per·i·ty /prä'speritē/ ▶ **n.** the state of being prosperous.

pros·per·ous /'präspərəs/ ▶ **adj.** successful in material terms; flourishing financially. ■ bringing wealth and success. — **pros·per·ous·ly** **adv.** **pros·per·ous·ness** **n.**

pros·ta·cy·clin /,prästə'sīklin/ ▶ **n.** Biochem. a compound of the prostaglandin type that is produced in arterial walls and that functions as an anticoagulant and vasodilator. [1970s: from PROSTAGLANDIN + CYCLIC + -IN¹.]

pros·ta·glan·din /,prästə'glandin/ ▶ **n.** Biochem. any of a group of cyclic fatty acids with hormonelike effects, notably the promotion of uterine contractions. [1930s: from PROSTATE + GLAND¹ + -IN¹.]

pros·tate /'präs,tāt/ (also **prostate gland**) ▶ **n.** a gland surrounding the neck of the bladder in male mammals and releasing a fluid component of semen. — **pros·tat·ic** /prä'statik/ **adj.** [17th C.: via Fr. from mod. L. *prostata*, from Gk. *prostatēs* 'one that stands before,' from *pro* 'before' + *statos* 'standing.']

pros·ta·tec·to·my /,prästə'tektəmē/ ▶ **n.** (pl. **-mies**) surgery to remove all or part of the prostate gland.

pros·ta·ti·tis /,prästə'tītəs/ ▶ **n.** Med. inflammation of the prostate gland.

pros·the·sis /präs'тнēsis/ ▶ **n.** (pl. **-ses** /-sēz/) **1** an artificial body part, such as a leg, a heart, or a breast implant. **2** (also **prothesis**) the addition of a letter or syllable at the beginning of a word, as in Spanish *escribo* derived from Latin *scribo*. — **pros·thet·ic** /-'тнetik/ **adj.** **pros·thet·i·cal·ly** /-'тнetik(ə)lē/ **adv.** [16th C. (sense 2): via late L. from Gk., from *prostithenai*, from *pros* 'in addition' + *tithenai* 'to place.']

pros·thet·ic group ▶ **n.** Biochem. a nonprotein group forming part of or combined with a protein.

pros·thet·ics /präs'тнetiks/ ▶ **plural n.** artificial body parts; prostheses. ■ [treated as sing.] the making and fitting of artificial body parts.

pros·the·tist /'präsтнətist/ ▶ **n.** a specialist in prosthetics.

pros·tho·don·tics /,präsтнə'däntiks/ ▶ **plural n.** [treated as sing.] the branch of dentistry concerned with the design, manufacture, and fitting of artificial replacements for teeth and other parts of the mouth. — **pros·tho·don·tist** /-'däntist/ **n.** [1940s: from PROSTHESIS, on the pattern of *orthodontics*.]

pros·ti·tute /'prästə,t(y)o͞ot/ ▶ **n.** a person, typically a woman, who engages in sex for payment. ■ fig. a person who misuses their talents or sacrifices their self-respect for personal or financial gain. ▶ **v.** [trans.] offer (someone, typically a woman) for sex for payment: *she never prostituted herself.* ■ fig. put (oneself or one's talents) to a corrupt use for personal or financial gain. — **pros·ti·tu·tor** /-,t(y)o͞otər/ **n.** [16th C. (as a verb): from L. *prostitut-* 'exposed publicly, offered for sale,' from the verb *prostituere*, from *pro-* 'before' + *statuere* 'set up, place.']

pros·ti·tu·tion /,prästə't(y)o͞osнən/ ▶ **n.** the practice or occupation of engaging in sex with someone for payment. ■ fig. the corrupt use of one's talents for personal or financial gain.

pros·trate ▶ **adj.** /'präs,trāt/ lying stretched out on the ground with one's face downward. ■ [predic.] fig. completely overcome or helpless, esp. with distress or exhaustion. ■ Bot. growing along the ground. ▶ **v.** [trans.] (**prostrate oneself**) lay oneself flat on the ground face downward, esp. in reverence or submission. ■ (often **be prostrated**) (of distress, exhaustion, or illness) reduce (someone) to extreme physical weakness. — **pros·tra·tion** /prä'strāsнən/ **n.** [ME: from L. *prostratus* 'thrown down,' past part. of *prosternere*, from *pro-* 'before' + *sternere* 'lay flat.']

pro·style /'prō,stīl/ ▶ **n.** Archit. a portico with a maximum of four columns. [17th C.: from L. *prostylos* '(building) having pillars in front,' from Gk. *pro* 'before' + *stulos* 'column.']

pros·y /'prōzē/ ▶ **adj.** (**pros·i·er**, **pros·i·est**) (esp. of speech or writing) showing no imagination; dull. — **pros·i·ly** /-əlē/ **adv.** **pros·i·ness** **n.**

prot- ▶ **comb. form** var. of PROTO- before a vowel (as in *protamine*).

prot·ac·tin·i·um /,prō,tak'tinēəm/ ▶ **n.** the chemical element of atomic number 91, a radioactive metal of the actinide series, occurring in small amounts as a product of the natural decay of uranium. (Symbol: **Pa**)

pro·tag·o·nist /prō'tagənist; prō-/ ▶ **n.** the leading character or a major character in a drama, movie, novel, or other fictional text. ■ the main figure or one of the most prominent figures in a real situation. ■ an advocate or champion of a particular cause or idea. [17th C.: from Gk. *prōtagōnistēs*, from *prōtos* 'first in importance' + *agōnistēs* 'actor.']

prot·a·mine /'prōtə,mēn/ ▶ **n.** Biochem. any of a group of simple proteins found combined with nucleic acids, esp. in fish sperm.

pro·ta·nope /'prōtə,nōp/ ▶ **n.** a person suffering from protanopia.

pro·ta·no·pi·a /,prōtə'nōpēə/ ▶ **n.** color-blindness resulting from insensitivity to red light, causing confusion of greens, reds, and yellows. Also called DALTONISM. Compare with DEUTERANOPIA, TRITANOPIA.

prot·a·sis /'prätəsəs/ ▶ **n.** (pl. **-ses** /-,sēz/) Gram. the clause expressing the condition in a conditional sentence (e.g., *if you asked me* in *if you asked me I would agree*). Often contrasted with APODOSIS. [16th C.: via L. from Gk. *protasis* 'proposition,' from *pro* 'before' + *teinein* 'to stretch.']

pro·te·a /'prōtēə/ ▶ **n.** an evergreen shrub or small tree (genus *Protea*, family Proteaceae) with large nectar-rich conelike flowerheads surrounded by brightly colored bracts, chiefly native to South Africa. [mod. L., from PROTEUS.]

pro·te·an /'prōtēən; prō'tēən/ ▶ **adj.** tending or able to change frequently or easily. ■ able to do many different things; versatile. — **pro·te·an·ism** /-ə,nizəm/ **n.** [16th C.: from PROTEUS + -AN.]

pro·te·ase /'prōtē,āz; -,ās/ ▶ **n.** Biochem. an enzyme that breaks down proteins and peptides. [20th C.: from PROTEIN + -ASE.]

pro·te·ase in·hib·i·tor ▶ **n.** a substance that breaks down protease, thereby inhibiting the replication of certain cells and viruses, including HIV.

protec. ▶ **abbr.** protectorate.

pro·tect /prə'tekt/ ▶ **v.** [trans.] keep safe from harm or injury: ***he protected her from the attack*** | [intrans.] ***certain vitamins may protect against heart disease.*** ■ [often as adj.] (**protected**) aim to preserve (a threatened plant or animal species) by legislating against collecting or hunting. ■ [often as adj.] (**protected**) restrict by law access to or development of (land) so as to preserve its natural state. ■ Econ. shield (a domestic industry) from competition by imposing import duties on foreign goods. ■ Comput. restrict access to or use of (data or a memory location). ■ provide funds to meet (a bill of exchange or commercial draft). — **pro·tect·a·ble** **adj.** [ME: from L. *protect-* 'covered in front,' from the verb *protegere*, from *pro-* 'in front' + *tegere* 'to cover.']

pro·tect·ant /prə'tektənt/ ▶ **n.** a substance that provides protection, e.g., against disease.

pro·tec·tion /prə'teksнən/ ▶ **n.** the action of protecting someone or something, or the state of being protected. ■ a person or thing that prevents someone or something from suffering harm or injury. ■ the cover provided by an insurance policy. ■ (usu. **protections**) a legal or other formal measure intended to preserve civil liberties and rights. ■ a document guaranteeing immunity from harm to the person specified in it. ■ the practice of paying money to criminals so as to prevent them from attacking oneself or one's property. ■ (also **protection money**) the money so paid to criminals, esp. on a regular basis. ■ archaic used euphemistically to refer to the keeping of a mistress by her lover in a separate establishment.

pro·tec·tion·ism /prə'teksнə,nizəm/ ▶ **n.** Econ. the theory or practice of shielding a country's domestic industries from foreign competition by taxing imports. — **pro·tec·tion·ist** **n. & adj.**

pro·tec·tive /prə'tektiv/ ▶ **adj.** capable of or intended to protect someone or something. ■ having or showing a strong wish to keep someone or something safe from harm. ■ Econ. of or relating to the protection of domestic industries from foreign competition. — **pro·tec·tive·ly** **adv.** **pro·tec·tive·ness** **n.**

pro·tec·tive col·or·a·tion (also **pro·tec·tive col·or·ing**) ▶ **n.** coloring that disguises or camouflages a plant or animal.

pro·tec·tive cus·to·dy ▶ **n.** the detention of a person for their own protection.

pro·tec·tor /prə'tektər/ ▶ **n.** **1** a person who protects or defends someone or something. **2** [often with adj.] a thing that protects someone or something from injury. **3** (chiefly **Protector**) hist. a regent in charge of a kingdom during the minority, absence, or incapacity of the sovereign. ■ (also **Lord Protector**) the title of the head of state in England during the later period of the Commonwealth between 1653 and 1659, first

Oliver Cromwell (1653–58), then his son Richard (1658–59). — **pro·tec·tor·al** /-rəl/ **adj.** **pro·tec·tor·ship** /-,SHip/ **n.**

pro·tec·tor·ate /prə'tektərət/ ▶**n.** **1** a state controlled and protected by another. ■ the relationship between a state of this kind and the one that controls it. **2** (usu. **Protectorate**) hist. the position or period of office of a Protector, esp. that in England of Oliver and Richard Cromwell.

pro·tect·ress /'prōtektres/ ▶**n.** a female protector.

pro·té·gé /'prōtə,ZHā; ,prōtə'ZHā/ (also **pro·te·ge**) ▶**n.** a person who is guided and supported by an older and more experienced or influential person. [18th C.: Fr., lit. 'protected,' past part. of *protéger*, from L. *protegere* 'cover in front' (see **PROTECT**).]

pro·té·gée /'prōtə,ZHā; ,prōtə'ZHā/ (also **pro·te·gee**) ▶**n.** a female protégé.

pro·tein /'prō,tē(ə)n/ ▶**n.** any of a class of nitrogenous organic compounds that consist of large molecules composed of one or more long chains of amino acids and are an essential part of all living organisms, esp. as structural components of body tissues, and as enzymes and antibodies. ■ such substances collectively, esp. as a dietary component. — **pro·tein·a·ceous** /,prō,tē(ə)'nāSHəs; ,prōtn'ā-/ **adj.** [19th C.: from Fr. *protéine*, Ger. *Protein*, from Gk. *prōteios* 'primary,' from *prōtos* 'first.']

pro·tein·ase /'prōtn,ās; 'prō,tēn-; -,āz/ ▶**n.** another term for **ENDOPEPTIDASE**.

pro·tein·oid /'prōtn,oid; 'prō,tēn-/ ▶**n.** Biochem. a polypeptide or mixture of polypeptides obtained by heating a mixture of amino acids.

pro·tein·u·ri·a /,prōtn'(y)o͝orēə; ,prō,tēn-/ ▶**n.** Med. the presence of abnormal quantities of protein in the urine, which may indicate damage to the kidneys.

pro tem /prō 'tem/ ▶**adv. & adj.** for the time being. [abbrev. of L. *pro tempore*.]

pro·te·o·gly·can /,prōtēə'glī,kan/ ▶**n.** Biochem. a compound consisting of a protein bonded to glycosaminoglycan groups, present esp. in connective tissue.

pro·te·ol·y·sis /,prōtē'äləsəs/ ▶**n.** Biochem. the breakdown of proteins or peptides into amino acids by the action of enzymes. — **pro·te·o·lyt·ic** /-ə'litik/ **adj.** **pro·te·o·lyt·i·cal·ly** /-ə'litik(ə)lē/ **adv.** [19th C.: mod. L., from **PROTEIN** + **-LYSIS**.]

Prot·er·o·zo·ic /,prōtərə'zōik/ ▶**adj.** Geol. of, relating to, or denoting the eon that constitutes the later part of the Precambrian, between the Archean eon and the Cambrian period, in which the earliest forms of life evolved. ■ [as n.] (**the Proterozoic**) the Proterozoic eon or the system of rocks deposited during it. [20th C.: from Gk. *proteros* 'former' + *zōē* 'life,' *zōos* 'living' + **-IC**.]

pro·test ▶**n.** /'prō,test/ **1** a statement or action expressing disapproval of or objection to something. ■ an organized public demonstration expressing strong objection to a policy or course of action adopted by those in authority. **2** Law a written declaration, typically by a notary public, that a bill has been presented and payment or acceptance refused. ▶**v.** /prə'test; prō'test; 'prō,test/ **1** [intrans.] express an objection to what someone has said or done: *she paid, and he didn't protest.* ■ publicly demonstrate objection to a policy or course of action adopted by those in authority: *doctors **protested against** plans to cut services at the hospital.* ■ [trans.] publicly demonstrate such objection to (a policy or course of action): *the workers were protesting economic measures enacted.* **2** [reporting verb] declare (something) firmly and emphatically in the face of stated or implied doubt or in response to an accusation: [trans.] *she has always protested her innocence.* **3** [trans.] Law write or obtain a protest in regard to (a bill).

– PHRASES **under protest** after expressing one's objection or reluctance; unwillingly. — **pro·test·er n. pro·test·ing·ly adv. pro·tes·tor** /'prō,testər; prə'tes-/ **n.** [ME: from OFr. *protester*, from L. *protestari*, from *pro-* 'forth, publicly' + *testari* 'assert' (from *testis* 'witness').]

Prot·es·tant /'prätəstənt/ ▶**n.** a member or follower of any of the Western Christian churches that are separate from the Roman Catholic Church and follow the principles of the Reformation, including the Baptist, Presbyterian, and Lutheran churches. ▶**adj.** of, relating to, or belonging to any of the Protestant churches. — **Prot·es·tant·i·za·tion** /,prätəstəntə'zāSHən/ **n.** **Prot·es·tant·ize** /-īz/ **v.**

Prot·es·tant eth·ic (also **Protestant work ethic**) ▶**n.** the view that a person's duty is to achieve success through hard work and thrift, such success being a sign that one is saved.

Prot·es·tant·ism /'prätəstən,tizəm/ ▶**n.** the faith, practice, and church order of the Protestant churches. ■ adherence to the forms of Christian doctrine regarded as Protestant rather than Catholic or Eastern Orthodox.

prot·es·ta·tion /,prätə'stāSHən; ,prō,tes'tā-/ ▶**n.** an emphatic declaration that something is or is not the case. ■ an objection or protest.

Pro·te·us /'prōtēəs; 'prō,t(y)o͞os/ Gk. Mythol. a minor sea god who had the power of prophecy but who would assume different shapes to avoid answering questions.

pro·te·us /'prōtēəs/ ▶**n.** a bacterium (genus *Proteus*) found in the intestines of animals and in the soil. [19th C.: from **PROTEUS**.]

pro·tha·la·mi·on /,prōTHə'lāmēən/ (also **pro·tha·la·mi·um** /-mēəm/) ▶**n.** (pl. **-mi·a** /-mēə/) literary a song or poem celebrating an upcoming wedding. [16th C.: from *Prothalamion*, a poem by Spenser.]

pro·thal·lus /prō'THaləs/ ▶**n.** (pl. **-thal·li** /-'THalē; 'THal,ī/) Bot. the gametophyte of ferns and related plants. — **pro·thal·li·al** /-'THalēəl/ **adj.** [19th C.: mod. L., from **PRO-**[2] 'before, earlier' + Gk. *thallos* 'green shoot.']

proth·e·sis /'präTHəsəs/ ▶**n.** (pl. **-ses** /-,sēz/) **1** Christian Church (esp. in the Orthodox Church) the action of placing the Eucharistic elements on the credence table. ■ a credence table. ■ the part of a church where the credence table stands. **2** another term for **PROSTHESIS** (sense 2). — **pro·thet·ic** /prə'THetik/ **adj.** [16th C. (sense 2): from Gk., 'placing before or in public view,' from *pro* 'before' + *thesis* 'placing.']

pro·thon·o·tar·y /prō'THänə,terē; ,prōTHə'nōtərē/ ▶**n.** var. of **PROTONOTARY**.

pro·thon·o·tar·y war·bler ▶**n.** a North American warbler (*Protonotaria citrea*), the male of which has a golden-yellow head, breast, and underparts. [18th C.: from *prothonotary*, var. of **PROTONOTARY**.]

pro·tho·rax /prō'THôr,aks/ ▶**n.** (pl. **-tho·rax·es** or **-tho·ra·ces** /-'THôrə,sēz/) Entomol. the anterior segment of the thorax of an insect, not bearing any wings. — **pro·tho·rac·ic** /,prōTHə'rasik/ **adj.**

pro·throm·bin /prō'THrämbən/ ▶**n.** Biochem. a protein present in blood plasma that is converted into active thrombin during coagulation.

Pro·tis·ta /prō'tistə/ Biol. a kingdom or large grouping that comprises mostly single-celled organisms such as the protozoa, simple algae and fungi, slime molds, and (formerly) the bacteria. — **pro·tist** /'prōtəst; 'prō,tist/ **n.** **pro·tis·tan** /prō'tistən/ **adj. & n.** **pro·tis·tol·o·gy** /,prōtə'stäləjē; ,prō,tis'täl-/ **n.** [mod. L. (plural), from Gk. *prōtista*, neut. pl. of *prōtistos* 'very first,' superlative of *prōtos* 'first.']

pro·ti·um /'prōtēəm; 'prōSH(ē)əm/ ▶**n.** Chem. the common, stable isotope of hydrogen, as distinct from deuterium and tritium. [1930s: mod. L., from Gk. *prōtos* 'first.']

proto- (usu. **prot-** before a vowel) ▶**comb. form** original; primitive: *prototype.* ■ first; anterior; relating to a precursor: *protomartyr.* [from Gk. *prōtos* 'first.']

pro·to·cer·a·tops /,prōtə'serə,täps/ ▶**n.** a small quadrupedal dinosaur (genus *Protoceratops*, infraorder Ceratopsia, order Ornithischia) of the late Cretaceous period, having a bony frill above the neck and probably ancestral to triceratops. The remains of many individuals and their eggs have been found in Mongolia.

pro·to·col /'prōtə,kôl; -,käl/ ▶**n.** **1** the official procedure governing affairs of state or diplomatic occasions. ■ the established code of procedure or behavior in any group, organization, or situation. ■ Comput. a set of rules governing the exchange or transmission of data electronically between devices. **2** the original draft of a diplomatic document, esp. of the terms of a treaty agreed to in conference and signed by the parties. ■ an amendment or addition to a treaty or convention. **3** a formal or official record of scientific experimental observations. ■ a procedure for carrying out a scientific experiment or a course of medical treatment. [ME (denoting the original record of an agreement): from OFr. *prothocole*, via med. L. from Gk. *prōtokollon* 'first page, flyleaf.']

Pro·toc·tis·ta /,prōtäk'tistə/ Biol. a kingdom or large grouping that is either synonymous with the Protista or equivalent to the Protista together with their multicellular descendants. — **pro·toc·tist** /'prōtäk,tist/ **n.** [mod. L. (pl.), based on Gk. *prōtos* 'first.']

pro·to·hu·man /,prōtō'(h)yo͞omən/ Anthropol. ▶**n.** a hypothetical prehistoric primate, resembling humans and thought to be their ancestor. ▶**adj.** relating to or denoting such a primate.

Pro·to-In·do-Eu·ro·pe·an ▶**n.** the unrecorded language from which all Indo-European languages are hypothesized to derive. See **INDO-EUROPEAN**. ▶**adj.** of or relating to this language.

pro·to·lan·guage /'prōtō,laNG(g)wij/ ▶**n.** a hypothetical lost parent language from which actual languages are derived.

pro·to·mar·tyr /'prōtō,märtər/ ▶**n.** the first martyr for a cause, esp. the first Christian martyr, St. Stephen.

pro·ton /'prō,tän/ ▶**n.** Physics a stable subatomic particle occurring in all atomic nuclei, with a positive electric charge equal in magnitude to that of an electron. — **pro·ton·ic** /prō'tänik/ **adj.** [1920s: from Gk., neut. of *prōtos* 'first.']

pro·ton·ate /'prōtn,āt/ ▶**v.** [trans.] (often **be protonated**) Chem. transfer a proton to (a molecule, group, or atom), so that a coordinate bond to the proton is formed. — **pro·to·na·tion** /,prō¯tn'āSHən/ **n.**

pro·ton·o·tar·y /prō'tänə,terē; ,prōtə'nōtərē/ (also **pro·thon·o·tar·y**) ▶**n.** (pl. **-tar·ies**) esp. hist. a chief clerk in some courts of law, originally in the Byzantine court. [ME: via med. L. from late Gk. *prōtonotarios*, from *prōtos* 'first' + *notarios* 'notary.']

Pro·ton·o·tar·y Ap·os·tol·ic ▶**n.** (pl. **Pro·ton·o·tar·ies Ap·os·tol·ic**) a member of the Roman Catholic college of prelates who register papal acts.

pro·to·path·ic /,prōtə'paTHik/ ▶**adj.** Physiol. relating to or denoting those sensory nerve fibers of the skin that are capable of discriminating only between such relatively coarse stimuli as heat, cold, and pain. Often contrasted with **EPICRITIC**. [19th C.: from **PROTO-** 'primitive' + Gk. *pathos* 'suffering, feeling' + **-IC**.]

pro·to·plasm /'prōtə,plazəm/ ▶**n.** Biol. the colorless material comprising the living part of a cell, including the cytoplasm, nucleus, and other organelles. — **pro·to·plas·mic** /,prōtə'plazmik/ **adj.** [19th C.: from Gk. *prōtoplasma* (see **PROTO-**, **PLASMA**).]

pro·to·plast /'prōtə,plast/ ▶**n.** esp. Bot. the protoplasm of a living plant or bacterial cell whose cell wall has been removed. — **pro·to·plas·tic** /,prōtə'plastik/ **adj.** [19th C.: from Gk. *prōtoplastos* 'first formed,' from *prōtos* 'first' + *plassein* 'to mold.']

pro·to·star /ˈprōtəˌstär/ ▶n. Astron. a contracting mass of gas that represents an early stage in the formation of a star, before nucleosynthesis has begun.

pro·to·stome /ˈprōtəˌstōm/ ▶n. Zool. a multicellular organism whose mouth develops from a primary embryonic opening, such as an annelid or mollusk. [1950s: from PROTO- 'primitive' + Gk. *stoma* 'mouth.']

Pro·to·the·ri·a /ˌprōtəˈTHi(ə)rēə/ Zool. a group of mammals (subclass Prototheria) that comprises the monotremes and their extinct relatives. Compare with THERIA. — **pro·to·the·ri·an** n. & adj. [mod. L. (pl.), from PROTO- 'first, original' + Gk. *thēr* 'wild beast.']

pro·to·type /ˈprōtəˌtīp/ ▶n. a first or preliminary model of something, esp. a machine, from which other forms are developed or copied. ■ a typical example of something. ■ the archetypal example of a class of living organisms, astronomical objects, or other items. ■ a building, vehicle, or other object that acts as a pattern for a full-scale model. ▶v. [trans.] make a prototype of (a product). — **pro·to·typ·al** /ˌprōtəˈtīpəl/ adj. **pro·to·typ·ic** /ˌprōtəˈtipik/ adj. **pro·to·typ·i·cal** /ˌprōtəˈtipikəl/ adj. **pro·to·typ·i·cal·ly** /ˌprōtəˈtipik(ə)lē/ adv. [16th C.: via Fr. or late L. from Gk. *prōtotupos* (see PROTO-, TYPE).]

Pro·to·zo·a /ˌprōtəˈzōə/ Zool. a phylum or grouping of phyla that comprises the single-celled microscopic animals, which include amebas, flagellates, ciliates, and sporozoans. They are now usually treated as a number of phyla belonging to the kingdom Protista. ■ [as pl. n.] (**protozoa**) organisms of this group. — **pro·to·zo·al** adj. **pro·to·zo·an** n. & adj. **pro·to·zo·ic** /-ˈzōik/ adj. **pro·to·zo·on** /-ˈzōˌän/ n. [mod. L. (pl.), from PROTO- 'first' + Gk. *zōion* 'animal.']

pro·tract /prəˈtrakt; prō-/ ▶v. [trans.] **1** prolong. **2** extend a part of the body. **3** draw (a plan, etc.) to scale. — **pro·trac·tion** /-ˈtrakSHən/ n. [16th C.: from L. *protract-* 'prolonged,' from the verb *protrahere*, from *pro-* 'out' + *trahere* 'to draw.']

pro·tract·ed /prəˈtraktəd; prō-/ ▶adj. lasting for a long time or longer than expected or usual. — **pro·tract·ed·ly** adv. **pro·tract·ed·ness** n.

pro·trac·tile /prəˈtraktl; prō-; -ˈtrakˌtīl/ ▶adj. another term for PROTRUSIBLE.

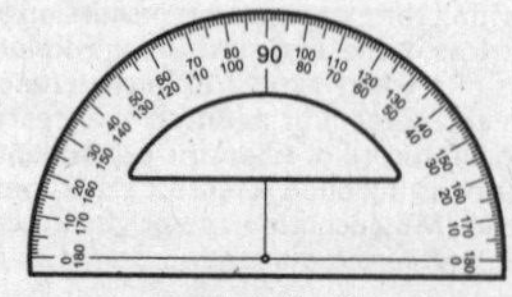

protractor 1

pro·trac·tor /ˈprōˌtraktər/ ▶n. **1** an instrument for measuring angles, typically in the form of a flat semicircle marked with degrees along the curved edge. **2** (also **protractor muscle**) esp. Zool. a muscle serving to extend a part of the body. Compare with RETRACTOR.

pro·trude /prəˈtro͞od; prō-/ ▶v. [intrans.] extend beyond or above a surface: *a fin protruded from the water.* ■ [trans.] (of an animal) cause (a body part) to do this. — **pro·tru·sion** /-ˈtro͞oZHən/ n. **pro·tru·sive** /-ˈtro͞osiv; -ziv/ adj. [17th C.: from L. *protrudere*, from *pro-* 'forward, out' + *trudere* 'to thrust.']

pro·tru·si·ble /prəˈtro͞osəbəl; prō-; -zəbəl/ ▶adj. Zool. (of a body part, such as the jaws of a fish) capable of being protruded or extended. [19th C.: from L. *protrus-* 'extended or thrust forward' (from the verb *protrudere*) + -IBLE.]

pro·tru·sile /prəˈtro͞osəl; prō-; -zəl/ ▶adj. (of a limb or other body part) able to be thrust forward.

pro·tu·ber·ance /prəˈt(y)o͞ob(ə)rəns; prō-/ ▶n. a thing that protrudes from something else. ■ the fact or state of protruding.

pro·tu·ber·ant /prəˈt(y)o͞ob(ə)rənt; prō-/ ▶adj. protruding; bulging: *his protuberant eyes fluttered open.* [17th C.: from late L. *protuberant-* 'swelling out,' from the verb *protuberare*, from *pro-* 'forward, out' + *tuber* 'bump.']

Pro·tu·ra /prəˈt(y)o͝orə/ Entomol. an order (Protura) of minute white wingless insects with slender bodies. They lack eyes and antennae, using the first pair of legs as sensory organs. — **pro·tu·ran** n. & adj. [mod. L. (pl.), from Gk. *prōtos* 'first, primitive.']

proud /proud/ ▶adj. **1** feeling or showing pride: *a proud grandma of three boys.* ■ (of an event, achievement, etc.) causing someone to feel this way: *a proud history of innovation.* ■ having or showing a consciousness of one's own dignity: *I was too proud to go home.* ■ having or showing an excessively high opinion of oneself or one's importance: *a proud, arrogant man.* ■ imposing; splendid. **2** [attrib.] (of flesh) overgrown around a healing wound.
– PHRASES **do someone proud** informal act in a way that gives someone cause to feel pride. ■ treat someone very well, typically by lavishly feeding or entertaining them. — **proud·ly** adv. **proud·ness** n. [OE *prūt*, *prūd* 'having a high opinion of one's own worth,' from OFr. *prud* 'valiant,' based on L. *prodesse* 'be of value.']

proud·heart·ed /ˈproudˈhärtəd/ ▶adj. arrogant.

Prou·dhon /pro͞oˈdôN/, Pierre Joseph (1809–65), French social philosopher and journalist. His pamphlet *What Is Property?* (1840) argues against private property.

Proust /pro͞ost/, Marcel (1871–1922), French writer. He devoted his life to writing his 16-volume novel *À la recherche du temps perdu* (1913–27), some of which was published after his death.

Prov. ▶abbr. ■ Bible Proverbs. ■ esp. Canadian Province or Provincial. ■ Provost.

prove /pro͞ov/ ▶v. (past part. **proved** or **prov·en** /ˈpro͞ovən/) **1** [trans.] demonstrate the truth or existence of (something) by evidence or argument: *the concept is difficult to prove.* ■ demonstrate by evidence or argument (someone or something) to be: *innocent until proven guilty.* ■ Law establish the genuineness and validity of (a will). ■ [intrans.] be seen or found to be: *the plan has proved a great success.* ■ (**prove oneself**) demonstrate one's abilities or courage: *a new lieutenant, desperate to prove himself.* ■ rare test the accuracy of (a mathematical calculation). ■ subject (a gun or other item) to a testing process. **2** [intrans.] (of bread dough) become aerated by the action of yeast; rise. — **prov·a·bil·i·ty** /ˌpro͞ovəˈbilətē/ n. **prov·a·ble** adj. **prov·a·bly** /-blē/ adv. **prov·er** n. [ME: from OFr. *prover*, from L. *probare* 'test, approve, demonstrate,' from *probus* 'good.']

prov·e·nance /ˈprävənəns/ ▶n. the place of origin or earliest known history of something: *a rug of Iranian provenance.* ■ the beginning of something's existence; something's origin. ■ a record of ownership of a work of art or an antique, used as a guide to authenticity or quality. [18th C.: from Fr., from the verb *provenir* 'come or stem from,' from L. *provenire*, from *pro-* 'forth' + *venire* 'come.']

Pro·ven·çal /ˌprävənˈsäl; ˌprōvən-; ˌprōväN-/ ▶adj. of, relating to, or denoting Provence or its people or language. ▶n. **1** a native or inhabitant of Provence. **2** the Romance language of Provence. [Fr., from L. *provincialis* 'provincial.']

pro·ven·çale /ˌprävənˈsäl; ˌprō-; ˌprōväN-/ ▶adj. [postpositive] denoting a dish cooked in a sauce made with tomatoes, garlic, and olive oil: *chicken provençale.* [from Fr. *à la provençale* 'in the Provençal style.']

Pro·vence /prōˈväns/ a former province of southeastern France, on the Mediterranean coast.

Pro·vence–Al·pes–Côte d'A·zur /prəˈväNs ˌälp ˌkōt däˈzHo͝or/ a mountainous region in southeastern France that includes the French Riviera.

prov·en·der /ˈprävəndər/ ▶n. often humorous food. ■ dated animal fodder. [ME: from OFr. *provendre*, based on an alt. of L. *praebenda* 'things to be supplied' (see PREBEND).]

pro·ve·ni·ence /prəˈvinyəns/ ▶n. another term for PROVENANCE.

pro·ven·tric·u·lus /ˌprōvenˈtrikyələs/ ▶n. (pl. **-li** /-ˌlī; -ˌlē/) Zool. the narrow glandular first region of a bird's stomach between the crop and the gizzard. ■ the thick-walled muscular expansion of the esophagus above the stomach of crustaceans and insects. [19th C.: from PRO-[2] 'before' + L. *ventriculus* 'small belly,' dimin. of *venter, ventr-* 'belly.']

pro·verb /ˈprävərb/ ▶n. a short pithy saying in general use, stating a general truth or piece of advice. [ME: from OFr. *proverbe*, from L. *proverbium*, from *pro-* '(put) forth' + *verbum* 'word.']

pro·ver·bi·al /prəˈvərbēəl/ ▶adj. (of a word or phrase) referred to in a proverb or idiom. ■ well known, esp. so as to be stereotypical. — **pro·ver·bi·al·i·ty** /-ˌvərbēˈalətē/ n. **pro·ver·bi·al·ly** adv.

Prov·erbs /ˈprävərbz/ (also **Book of Proverbs**) a book of the Bible containing maxims attributed mainly to Solomon.

pro·vide /prəˈvīd/ ▶v. **1** [trans.] make available for use; supply. ■ (**provide someone with**) equip or supply someone with (something useful or necessary): *we were provided with a map.* ■ present or yield (something useful). **2** [intrans.] (**provide for**) make adequate preparation for (a possible event): *we must provide for changes in technology.* ■ supply sufficient money to ensure the maintenance of (someone): *Emma was provided for in Frank's will.* ■ (of a law) enable or allow (something to be done). **3** [with clause] stipulate in a legal document: *the order provided that there would be no contact with the father.* [ME: from L. *providere* 'foresee, attend to,' from *pro-* 'before' + *videre* 'to see.']

pro·vid·ed /prəˈvīdid/ ▶conj. on the condition or understanding that.

Prov·i·dence /ˈprävəˌdens; -dəns/ the capital of Rhode Island, a port near the head of the Providence River, on the Atlantic coast; pop. 173,618.

prov·i·dence /ˈprävədəns; -ˌdens/ ▶n. the protective care of God or of nature as a spiritual power. ■ (**Providence**) God or nature as providing such care. ■ timely preparation for future eventualities.

Prov·i·dence Plan·ta·tions the mainland portion of the state of Rhode Island.

prov·i·dent /ˈprävədənt; -ˌdent/ ▶adj. making or indicative of timely preparation for the future. — **prov·i·dent·ly** adv. [ME: from L. *provident-*, from *providere*.]

prov·i·den·tial /ˌprävəˈdenCHəl/ ▶adj. **1** occurring at a favorable time; opportune. **2** involving divine foresight or intervention. — **prov·i·den·tial·ly** adv.

pro·vid·er /prəˈvīdər/ ▶n. a person or thing that provides something. ■ a breadwinner.

pro·vid·ing /prəˈvīdiNG/ ▶conj. on the condition or understanding that.

prov·ince /ˈprävins/ ▶n. **1** a principal administrative division of certain countries or empires. ■ (**the provinces**) the whole of a country outside the capital, esp. when regarded as lacking in sophistication or culture. ■ an area of the world with respect to its flora, fauna, or physical characteristics: *the inaccessibility of underwater igneous provinces.* ■ Christian Church a district under an archbishop or a metropolitan. ■ Roman History a territory outside Italy under a Roman governor. **2** (**one's province**) an area of special knowledge, interest, or responsibility. [ME: from OFr., from L. *provincia* 'charge, province.']

pro·vin·cial /prəˈvinSHəl/ ▶adj. **1** of or concerning a province of a country or empire. ■ of or pertaining to a style of architecture or furniture in fashion in the provinces of various European countries. 2 of or concerning the regions outside the capital city of a country. ■ unsophisticated or narrow-minded, esp. when considered as typical of such regions. ▶ n. 1 an inhabitant of a province of a country or empire. 2 an inhabitant of the regions outside the capital city of a country, esp. when regarded as unsophisticated or narrow-minded. 3 Christian Church the head or chief of a province or of a religious order in a province. — **pro·vin·ci·al·i·ty** /prə,vinsHē'alətē/ n. **pro·vin·cial·i·za·tion** /prə,vinsHələ'zāsHən/ n. **pro·vin·cial·ly** adv.

pro·vin·cial·ism /prə'vincHə,lizəm/ ▶ n. 1 the way of life or mode of thought characteristic of the regions outside the capital city of a country, esp. when regarded as unsophisticated or narrow-minded. ■ narrow-mindedness, insularity, or lack of sophistication. 2 concern for one's own area or region at the expense of national or supranational unity. 3 a word or phrase peculiar to a local area. — **pro·vin·cial·ist** n. & adj.

prov·ing ground ▶ n. an environment that serves to demonstrate whether something, such as a theory or product, really works.

pro·vi·rus /prō'vīrəs/ ▶ n. Microbiol. the genetic material of a virus as incorporated into, and able to replicate with, the genome of a host cell. — **pro·vi·ral** /-rəl/ adj.

pro·vi·sion /prə'vizHən/ ▶ n. 1 the action of providing or supplying something for use. ■ **(provision for/against)** financial or other arrangements for future eventualities or requirements. ■ an amount set aside out of profits in the accounts of an organization for a known liability, esp. a bad debt or the diminution in value of an asset. 2 an amount or thing supplied or provided. ■ **(provisions)** supplies of food, drink, or equipment, esp. for a journey. 3 a condition or requirement in a legal document. 4 Christian Church, hist. an appointment to a benefice, esp. directly by the pope. ▶ v. 1 [trans.] supply with food, drink, or equipment, esp. for a journey: *civilian contractors were responsible for provisioning these armies.* 2 [intrans.] set aside an amount in an organization's accounts for a known liability: *financial institutions have to provision against loan losses.* — **pro·vi·sion·er** n. [ME: via OFr. from L. *provisio(n-)*, from *providere* 'foresee, attend to' (see PROVIDE).]

pro·vi·sion·al /prə'vizHənl/ ▶ adj. 1 arranged or existing for the present, possibly to be changed later. ■ (of a postage stamp) put into circulation temporarily, usually owing to the unavailability of the definitive issue. 2 **(Provisional)** [attrib.] of or relating to the unofficial wings of the Irish Republican Army and Sinn Fein established in 1969 and advocating terrorism. ▶ n. 1 a provisional postage stamp. 2 **(Provisional)** a member of the Provisional wings of the Irish Republican Army or Sinn Fein. — **pro·vi·sion·al·i·ty** /prə,vizHə'nalətē/ n. **pro·vi·sion·al·ly** /-zHənl-ē/ adv.

pro·vi·so /prə'vīzō/ ▶ n. (pl. -sos) a condition attached to an agreement. [ME: from the med. L. phr. *proviso (quod)* 'it being provided (that),' from L. *providere* 'foresee, provide.']

pro·vi·so·ry /prə'vīzərē/ ▶ adj. 1 rare subject to a proviso; conditional. 2 another term for PROVISIONAL (sense 1).

pro·vi·ta·min /prō'vītəmən/ ▶ n. Biochem. a substance converted into a vitamin within an organism.

Pro·vo[1] /'prōvō/ a city in north central Utah; pop. 105,166.

Pro·vo[2] ▶ n. (pl. -vos) informal term for PROVISIONAL (sense 2).

prov·o·ca·tion /,prävə'kāsHən/ ▶ n. 1 action or speech that provokes someone, esp. deliberately. ■ Law action or speech held to be likely to prompt physical retaliation. 2 Med. testing to elicit a particular response or reflex. [ME: from OFr., from L. *provocatio(n-)*, from *provocare*.]

pro·voc·a·tive /prə'väkətiv/ ▶ adj. causing provocation, esp. deliberately: *a provocative article.* ■ arousing sexual desire or interest, esp. deliberately. — **pro·voc·a·tive·ly** adv. **pro·voc·a·tive·ness** n.

pro·voke /prə'vōk/ ▶ v. [trans.] stimulate or give rise to (a reaction or emotion, typically a strong or unwelcome one) in someone: *the decision provoked a storm of protest.* ■ stimulate or incite (someone) to do or feel something, esp. by arousing anger in them: *a teacher can provoke you into working harder.* ■ deliberately make (someone) annoyed or angry. — **pro·vok·a·ble** adj. **pro·vok·er** n. **pro·vok·ing·ly** adv. [ME: from OFr. *provoquer*, from L. *provocare* 'challenge,' from *pro-* 'forth' + *vocare* 'to call.']

pro·vo·lo·ne /,prōvə'lōnē/ ▶ n. an Italian soft smoked cheese made from cow's milk. [Ital., from *provola* 'buffalo-milk cheese.']

pro·vost /'prō,vōst/ ▶ n. 1 a senior administrative officer in certain colleges and universities. ■ Brit. the head of certain university colleges and public schools. 2 the head of a chapter in a cathedral. ■ the Protestant minister of the principal church of a town or district in Germany and certain other European countries. ■ hist. the head of a Christian community. 3 short for PROVOST MARSHAL. 4 Scottish term for MAYOR. — **pro·vost·ship** /-,sHip/ n. [OE *profost* 'head of a chapter, prior,' from med. L. *propositus*, synonym of L. *praepositus* 'head, chief'.]

pro·vost mar·shal ▶ n. the head of military police in camp or on active service.

prow /prou/ ▶ n. the portion of a ship's bow above water. ■ the projecting front part of something such as a car or building. [16th C.: from OFr. *proue*, from Provençal *proa*, prob. via L. from Gk. *prōira*, akin to L. *pro* 'in front.']

prow·ess /'prou-əs; 'prōəs/ ▶ n. 1 skill or expertise in an activity or field. 2 bravery in battle. [ME (sense 2): from OFr. *proesce*, from *prou* 'valiant.']

prowl /proul/ ▶ v. [trans.] (of a person or animal) move around (a place) in search of or as if in search of prey: *black bears prowl the canyons.* ■ [intrans.] (of a person or animal) move stealthily or restlessly as or like a hunter: *committee members prowling around the offices.* ▶ n. an act of prowling.
– PHRASES **on the prowl** (of a person or animal) moving around in search or as if in search of prey. [ME: of unknown origin.]

prowl car ▶ n. a police squad car.

prowl·er /'proulər/ ▶ n. a person who moves stealthily around a place with a view to committing a crime.

prox. ▶ abbr. proximo.

prox·e·mics /präk'sēmiks/ ▶ plural n. [treated as sing.] the branch of knowledge that deals with the amount of space that people feel it necessary to set between themselves and others. — **prox·e·mic** adj. [1960s: from PROXIMITY, on the pattern of words such as *phonemics*.]

Prox·i·ma Cen·tau·ri /'präksəmə ,sen'tôrē; -'tôr,ī/ Astron. a faint red dwarf star associated with the bright binary star Alpha Centauri. It is the closest known star to the solar system (distance 4.24 light years).

prox·i·mal /'präksəməl/ ▶ adj. Anat. situated nearer to the center of the body or the point of attachment. The opposite of DISTAL. — **prox·i·mal·ly** adv. [19th C.: from L. *proximus* 'nearest' + -AL.]

prox·i·mate /'präksəmit/ ▶ adj. 1 (esp. of a cause of something) closest in relationship; immediate. ■ closest in space or time. 2 nearly accurate; approximate: *he would try to change her speech into proximate ladylikeness.* — **prox·i·mate·ly** adv. **prox·i·ma·tion** /,präksə'māsHən/ n. [16th C.: from L. *proximatus* 'drawn near,' past part. of *proximare*, from *proximus* 'nearest.']

prox·im·i·ty /präk'simətē/ ▶ n. nearness in space, time, or relationship.

prox·im·i·ty fuse ▶ n. an electronic detonator that causes a projectile to explode when it comes within a preset distance of its target.

prox·i·mo /'präksə,mō/ ▶ adj. [postpositive] dated of next month: *he must be in San Francisco on 1st proximo.* [from L. *proximo mense* 'in the next month.']

prox·y /'präksē/ ▶ n. (pl. prox·ies) 1 the authority to represent someone else, esp. in voting. ■ a person authorized to act on behalf of another. ■ a document authorizing a person to vote on another's behalf. 2 a figure that can be used to represent the value of something in a calculation: *the use of a US wealth measure as a **proxy for** the true worldwide measure.* [ME: contr. of obs. *procuracy* 'letter of attorney.']

prox·y war ▶ n. a war instigated by a major power that does not itself become involved.

Pro·zac /'prō,zak/ ▶ n. trademark for FLUOXETINE. [1980s: an invented name.]

prude /prōōd/ ▶ n. a person who is or claims to be easily shocked by matters relating to sex or nudity. — **prud·er·y** /'prōōdərē/ n. **prud·ish** adj. **prud·ish·ly** adv. **prud·ish·ness** n. [18th C.: from Fr., back-form. from *prudefemme*, fem. of *prud'homme* 'good man and true,' from *prou* 'worthy.']

pru·dent /'prōōdnt/ ▶ adj. acting with or showing care and thought for the future. — **pru·dence** n. **pru·dent·ly** adv. [ME: from OFr., or from L. *prudent-*, contr. of *provident-* 'foreseeing, attending to' (see PROVIDENT).]

pru·den·tial /prōō'dencHəl/ ▶ adj. involving or showing care and forethought, typically in business. — **pru·den·tial·ly** adv.

Prud·hoe Bay /'prōōd(h)ō/ an inlet of the Arctic Ocean, on the northern coast of Alaska.

pru·i·nose /'prōōə,nōs/ ▶ adj. esp. Bot. (of a surface, such as that of a grape) covered with white powdery granules; frosted in appearance. [19th C.: from L. *pruinosus*, from *pruina* 'hoarfrost.']

prune[1] /prōōn/ ▶ n. a plum preserved by drying, having a black, wrinkled appearance. ■ informal an unpleasant or disagreeable person. [ME: from OFr., via L. from Gk. *prou(m)non* 'plum.']

prune[2] ▶ v. [trans.] trim (a tree, shrub, or bush) by cutting away dead or overgrown branches or stems, esp. to increase fruitfulness and growth. ■ cut away (a branch or stem) in this way. ■ reduce the extent of (something) by removing superfluous or unwanted parts. ■ remove (superfluous or unwanted parts) from something. — **prun·er** n. [15th C.: from OFr. *pro(o)ignier*, possibly based on L. *rotundus* 'round.']

pru·nel·la[1] /prōō'nelə/ ▶ n. a plant of the mint family belonging to a genus (*Prunella*) that includes self-heal. Several kinds are cultivated as ground cover and rock garden plants. [mod. L., lit. 'quinsy,' in med. L. *brunella*, dimin. of *brunus* 'brown.']

pru·nel·la[2] ▶ n. a strong silk or worsted twill fabric used formerly for legal robes and the uppers of women's shoes. [17th C.: perh. from Fr. *prunelle* 'sloe.']

prun·ing hook ▶ n. a cutting tool used for pruning, consisting of a hooked blade on a long handle.

prun·ing knife ▶ n. a knife designed for pruning, having a slightly curved blade and a hooked end.

pru·nus /'prōōnəs/ ▶ n. a tree or shrub of the rose family belonging to a large genus (*Prunus*) that includes many varieties grown for their spring blossom (cherry and almond) or for their fruit (plum, peach, and apricot). [mod. L., from L., 'plum tree.']

pru·ri·ent /'prōōrēənt/ ▶ adj. having or encouraging an excessive interest in sexual matters. — **pru·ri·ence** n. **pru·ri·en·cy** n. **pru·ri·ent·ly** adv.

[16th C.: from L. *prurient-* 'itching, longing' and 'being wanton,' from the verb *prurire*.]

pru·ri·go /pro͞oˈrīgō; -ˈrēgō/ ▶ **n.** Med. a chronic skin disease causing severe itching. — **pru·rig·i·nous** /pro͞orˈijənəs/ **adj.** [17th C.: from L., from *prurire* 'to itch.']

pru·ri·tus /pro͞oˈrītəs/ ▶ **n.** Med. severe itching of the skin, as a symptom of various ailments. — **pru·rit·ic** /-ˈritik/ **adj.** [17th C.: from L., 'itching' (see PRURIGO).]

Prus·sia /ˈprəsнə/ a former kingdom of Germany. Originally a small country on the southeastern shores of the Baltic Sea, it became a major European power, covering much of modern northeastern Germany and Poland, under Frederick the Great. After the Franco-Prussian War of 1870–71, it became the center of Bismarck's new German Empire. — **Prus·sian adj. & n.**

Prus·sian blue /ˈprəsнən/ ▶ **n.** a deep blue pigment used in painting and dyeing, made from or in imitation of ferric ferrocyanide. ■ the deep blue color of this pigment.

prus·sic ac·id /ˈprəsik/ ▶ **n.** old-fashioned term for HYDROCYANIC ACID. — **prus·si·ate** /ˈprəsēˌāt/ **n.** [18th C.: *prussic* from Fr. *prussique* 'relating to Prussian blue.']

Prut /pro͞ot/ (also **Pruth**) a river in southeastern Europe that rises in southern Ukraine and flows southeast to join the Danube River in Romania.

pry[1] /prī/ ▶ **v.** **(pries, pried)** [intrans.] inquire too inquisitively into a person's private affairs: *I'm sick of you prying into my personal life.* — **pry·ing·ly adv.** [ME: of unknown origin.]

pry[2] ▶ **v.** **(pries, pried)** [trans.] use force in order to move or open (something) or to separate (something) from something else: *he pried open the window.* ■ **(pry something out of/from)** obtain something from (someone) with effort or difficulty. [19th C.: from the verb PRIZE[2], interpreted as *pries*, third person sing. of the present tense.]

pry bar ▶ **n.** a small, flattish iron bar used in the same way as a crowbar.

Prze·wal·ski's horse /ˌpərzнəˈvälskēz/ ▶ **n.** a stocky wild Mongolian horse (*Equus ferus*) with a dun-colored coat and a dark brown erect mane, now extinct in the wild. It is the only true wild horse, and is the ancestor of the domestic horse. [19th C.: named after Nikolai M. *Przheval'sky* (1839–88), Russian explorer.]

PS ▶ **abbr.** ■ passenger steamer. ■ permanent secretary. ■ police sergeant. ■ postscript. ■ private secretary. ■ Public School.

Ps. (pl. **Pss.**) ▶ **abbr.** Bible Psalm or Psalms.

psalm /sä(l)m/ (also **Psalm**) ▶ **n.** a sacred song or hymn, in particular any of those contained in the biblical Book of Psalms and used in Christian and Jewish worship. ■ **(the Psalms** or **the Book of Psalms)** a book of the Bible comprising a collection of religious verses, sung or recited in both Jewish and Christian worship. — **psalm·ic** /ˈsä(l)mik/ **adj.** [OE *(p)sealm*, via eccles. L. from Gk. *psalmos* 'song sung to harp music,' from *psallein* 'to pluck.']

psalm·book /ˈsä(l)mˌbo͝ok/ ▶ **n.** a book containing psalms, esp. with metrical settings for worship.

psalm·ist /ˈsä(l)mist/ ▶ **n.** the author or composer of a psalm, esp. of any of the biblical Psalms.

psal·mo·dy /ˈsä(l)mədē/ ▶ **n.** the singing of psalms or similar sacred canticles, esp. in public worship. ■ psalms arranged for singing. — **psal·mod·ic** /säˈ(l)ˈmädik/ **adj.** **psal·mo·dist** /-dist/ **n.** [ME: via late L. from Gk. *psalmōidia* 'singing to a harp,' from *psalmos* (see PSALM) + *ōidē* 'song.']

psal·ter /ˈsôltər/ ▶ **n.** **(the psalter** or **the Psalter)** the Book of Psalms. ■ a copy of the biblical Psalms, esp. for liturgical use. [OE *(p)saltere*, via L. *psalterium* from Gk. *psaltērion* 'stringed instrument.']

psal·te·ri·um /ˌsôlˈti(ə)rēəm/ ▶ **n.** another term for OMASUM. [19th C.: from L., lit. 'psalter' (see PSALTER).]

psal·ter·y /ˈsôltərē/ ▶ **n.** (pl. **-ter·ies**) an ancient and medieval musical instrument like a dulcimer but played by plucking the strings with the fingers or a plectrum.

PSAT ▶ **abbr.** Preliminary Scholastic Aptitude Test.

psec. (also **ps**) ▶ **abbr.** picosecond; picoseconds.

pse·phol·o·gy /sēˈfäləjē/ ▶ **n.** the statistical study of elections and trends in voting. — **pse·pho·log·i·cal** /ˌsēfəˈläjikəl/ **adj.** **pse·pho·log·i·cal·ly** /-ik(ə)lē/ **adv.** **pse·phol·o·gist** /-jist/ **n.** [1950s: from Gk. *psēphos* 'pebble, vote' + -LOGY.]

pseud /so͞od/ informal ▶ **adj.** intellectually or socially pretentious. ▶ **n.** a pretentious person; a poseur. [1960s: abbrev. of PSEUDO.]

pseud. ▶ **abbr.** pseudonym.

pseud- ▶ **comb. form** var. of PSEUDO- reduced before a vowel (as in *pseudepigrapha*).

pseud·e·pig·ra·pha /ˌso͞odəˈpigrəfə/ ▶ **plural n.** spurious or pseudonymous writings, esp. Jewish writings ascribed to various patriarchs and prophets but composed within 200 years of the birth of Christ. — **pseud·e·pig·ra·phal adj.** **pseud·e·pi·graph·ic** /ˌso͞odˌepiˈgrafik/ **adj.** [17th C.: neut. pl. of Gk. *pseudepigraphos* 'with false title' (see PSEUDO-, EPIGRAPH).]

pseu·do /ˈso͞odō/ ▶ **adj.** not genuine; sham. [ME: independent use of PSEUDO-.]

pseudo- (also **pseud-** before a vowel) ▶ **comb. form** **1** supposed or purporting to be but not really so; false; not genuine: *pseudonym* | *pseudoscience.* **2** resembling or imitating: *pseudo-French.* [from Gk. *pseudēs* 'false,' *pseudos* 'falsehood.']

pseu·do·carp /ˈso͞odōˌkärp/ ▶ **n.** technical term for FALSE FRUIT. [19th C.: from PSEUDO- 'false' + Gk. *karpos* 'fruit.']

pseu·do·cho·lin·es·ter·ase /ˌso͞odōˌkōləˈnestəˌrās; -ˌrāz/ ▶ **n.** Biochem. an enzyme present in the blood and certain organs that hydrolyzes acetylcholine more slowly than acetylcholinesterase.

pseu·do·clas·si·cal /ˌso͞odōˈklasikəl/ ▶ **adj.** having a false or spurious classical style: *a pretentious pseudoclassical building.*

pseu·do·cy·e·sis /ˌso͞odōsīˈēsis/ ▶ **n.** technical term for FALSE PREGNANCY. [19th C.: from PSEUDO- 'false' + Gk. *kuēsis* 'conception.']

Pseu·do-Di·o·ny·si·us /ˈso͞odōˌdīəˈnisēəs/ (6th century AD), the unidentified author of theological works formerly attributed to Dionysius the Areopagite.

pseu·do·e·vent ▶ **n.** informal an event arranged or brought about merely for the sake of the publicity or entertainment value it generates.

pseu·do·gene /ˈso͞odōˌjēn/ ▶ **n.** Genet. a section of a chromosome that is an imperfect copy of a functional gene.

pseu·do·her·maph·ro·dit·ism /ˌso͞odō-hərˈmafrəˌdītˌizəm/ ▶ **n.** Med. the condition in which an individual of one sex has external genitalia superficially resembling those of the other sex. — **pseu·do·her·maph·ro·dite** /-ˈmafrəˌdīt/ **n.**

pseu·dom·o·nas /ˌso͞odōˈmōnəs/ ▶ **n.** Microbiol. a bacterium (genus *Pseudomonas*) of a genus that occurs in soil and detritus, including a number that are pathogens of plants or animals. — **pseu·dom·o·nad** /-ˈmōˌnad/ **n.** [mod. L., from PSEUDO- 'false' + *monas* 'monad.']

pseu·do·morph /ˈso͞odəˌmôrf/ Crystallog. ▶ **n.** a crystal consisting of one mineral but having the form of another. — **pseu·do·mor·phic** /ˌso͞odōˈmôrfik/ **adj.** **pseu·do·mor·phism** /ˌso͞odōˈmôrˌfizəm/ **n.** **pseu·do·mor·phous** /ˌso͞odōˈmôrfəs/ **adj.** [19th C.: from PSEUDO- 'false' + Gk. *morphē* 'form.']

pseu·do·nym /ˈso͞odn-im/ ▶ **n.** a fictitious name, esp. one used by an author. — **pseu·do·nym·i·ty** /ˌso͞odnˈimətē/ **n.** [19th C.: from Fr. *pseudonyme*, from Gk. *pseudōnymos*, from *pseudēs* 'false' + *onoma* 'name.']

pseu·don·y·mous /so͞oˈdänəməs/ ▶ **adj.** writing or written under a false name. — **pseu·don·y·mous·ly adv.**

pseu·do·pod /ˈso͞odəˌpäd/ ▶ **n.** another term for PSEUDOPODIUM.

pseu·do·po·di·um /ˌso͞odəˈpōdēəm/ ▶ **n.** (pl. **-po·di·a** /-ˈpōdēə/) Biol. a temporary protrusion of the surface of an ameboid cell for movement and feeding.

pseu·do·preg·nan·cy /ˌso͞odōˈpregnənsē/ ▶ **n.** (pl. **-cies**) another term for FALSE PREGNANCY. — **pseu·do·preg·nant** /-ˈpregnənt/ **adj.**

pseu·do·ran·dom /ˌso͞odōˈrandəm/ ▶ **adj.** (of a number, a sequence of numbers, or any digital data) satisfying one or more statistical tests for randomness but produced by a definite mathematical procedure. — **pseu·do·ran·dom·ly adv.**

pseu·do·sci·ence /ˌso͞odōˈsīəns/ ▶ **n.** a collection of beliefs or practices mistakenly regarded as being based on scientific method. — **pseu·do·sci·en·tif·ic** /-ˌsīənˈtifik/ **adj.** **pseu·do·sci·en·tist** /-ˈsīəntist/ **n.**

pseu·do·scor·pi·on /ˌso͞odōˈskôrpēən/ ▶ **n.** a minute arachnid (order Pseudoscorpiones) that has pincers but no long abdomen or sting, occurring abundantly in leaf litter.

pseu·do·u·ri·dine /ˌso͞odōˈyo͝orəˌdēn/ ▶ **n.** Biochem. a nucleoside present in transfer RNA and differing from uridine in having the sugar residue attached at a carbon atom instead of nitrogen.

pshaw /(p)sнô/ dated or humorous ▶ **exclam.** an expression of contempt or impatience. ▶ **v.** [intrans.] utter such an exclamation: *when I suggested that free trade might dilute Canadian culture, he pshawed.* [natural exclamation: first recorded in Engl. in the late 17th C.]

psi /(p)sī/ ▶ **n.** **1** the twenty-third letter of the Greek alphabet (Ψ, ψ), transliterated as 'ps.' **2** supposed parapsychological or psychic faculties or phenomena.

p.s.i. ▶ **abbr.** pounds per square inch.

psil·o·cy·bin /ˌsīləˈsībin/ ▶ **n.** Chem. a hallucinogenic alkaloid, found in some toadstools. [1950s: from mod. L. *Psilocybe* (genus name), from Gk. *psilos* 'bald' + *kubē* 'head.']

psi·on·ic /sīˈänik/ ▶ **adj.** relating to or denoting the practical use of psychic powers or paranormal phenomena: *psionic communication.* — **psi·on·i·cal·ly** /-ik(ə)lē/ **adv.** [1950s: from PSI, on the pattern of *electronic*.]

psit·ta·cine /ˈsitəˌsīn/ Ornithol. ▶ **adj.** of, relating to, or denoting birds of the parrot family. ▶ **n.** a bird of the parrot family. [19th C.: from L. *psittacinus* 'of a parrot,' from *psittacus*, from Gk. *psittakos* 'parrot.']

psit·ta·co·sau·rus /ˌsitəkōˈsôrəs/ ▶ **n.** a partly bipedal herbivorous dinosaur (genus *Psittacosaurus*, infraorder Ceratopsia, order Ornithischia) of the mid Cretaceous period, having a parrotlike beak and probably ancestral to other ceratopsians. [mod. L., from Gk. *psittakos* 'parrot' + *sauros* 'lizard.']

psit·ta·co·sis /ˌsitəˈkōsəs/ ▶ **n.** a disease of birds, caused by chlamydiae and transmissible (esp. from parrots) to human beings as a form of pneumonia.

pso·as /ˈsōəs/ (also **psoas major**) ▶ **n.** Anat. each of a pair of large muscles that run from the lumbar spine through the groin on either side and which assist in flexing the hip. [17th C.: from Gk., accusative pl. of *psoa*, interpreted as sing.]

pso·cid /ˈsōsəd/ ▶ **n.** Entomol. a small or minute insect of an order (Psocoptera) that includes the booklice. Many psocids are wingless and somewhat resemble lice or aphids, and most live on bark and among foliage. [19th C.: from mod. L. *Psocidae* (pl.), from *Psocus* (genus name), from Gk. *psōkhein* 'to grind.']

Pso·cop·ter·a /sōˈkäptərə/ Entomol. an order of insects that comprises the booklice and other psocids. — **pso·cop·ter·an** n. & adj. [mod. L. (pl.), from *Psocus* (genus name) + *pteron* 'wing.']

pso·ra·len /'sôrələn; -,len/ ▶ n. Chem. a compound, $C_{11}H_6O_3$, present in certain plants, that is used in perfumery and (in combination with ultraviolet light) to treat psoriasis and other skin disorders. [1930s: from mod. L. *Psorolea* (former genus name), from Gk. *psōraleos* 'itchy' (from *psōra* 'itch') + the suffix *-en* (cf. -ENE).]

pso·ri·a·sis /sə'rīəsəs/ ▶ n. Med. a skin disease marked by red, itchy, scaly patches. — **pso·ri·at·ic** /,sôrē'atik/ adj. [17th C.: mod. L., from Gk. *psōriasis*, from *psōrian* 'have an itch,' from *psōra* 'itch.']

psst /pst/ ▶ exclam. used to attract someone's attention surreptitiously. [1920s: imitative.]

PST ▶ abbr. Pacific Standard Time (see PACIFIC TIME).

psych /sīk/ (also **psyche**) ▶ v. [trans.] informal mentally prepare (someone) for a testing task or occasion. ▶ n. informal short for PSYCHIATRIST or PSYCHOLOGIST. ■ short for PSYCHIATRY or PSYCHOLOGY. ▶ adj. [attrib.] 1 informal short for PSYCHIATRIC. 2 short for PSYCHEDELIC.
– PHRASAL VERBS **psych someone out** informal intimidate an opponent or rival by appearing confident or aggressive. **psych something out** informal analyze something in psychological terms.

psych. ▶ abbr. ■ psychological. ■ psychologist. ■ psychology.

Psy·che /'sīkē/ Gk. Mythol. a Hellenistic personification of the soul as female, or sometimes as a butterfly. The allegory of Psyche's love for Cupid is told in *The Golden Ass* by Apuleius.

psy·che[1] /'sīkē/ ▶ n. the human soul, mind, or spirit. [17th C.: via L. from Gk. *psukhē* 'breath, life, soul.']

psy·che[2] /sīk/ ▶ v., n., & adj. var. of PSYCH.

psych·e·de·lia /,sīkə'dēlyə/ ▶ n. music, culture, or art based on the experiences produced by psychedelic drugs. [1960s: back-form. from PSYCHEDELIC.]

psy·che·del·ic /,sīkə'delik/ ▶ adj. relating to or denoting drugs (esp. LSD) that produce hallucinations and apparent expansion of consciousness. ■ relating to or denoting a style of rock music originating in the mid-1960s, characterized by musical experimentation and drug-related lyrics. ■ denoting or having an intense, vivid color or a swirling abstract pattern. ▶ n. a psychedelic drug. — **psy·che·del·i·cal·ly** /-ik(ə)lē/ adv. [1950s: formed irregularly from PSYCHE[1] + Gk. *dēlos* 'clear, manifest' + -IC.]

psy·chi·at·ric /,sīkē'atrik/ ▶ adj. of or relating to mental illness or its treatment. — **psy·chi·at·ri·cal·ly** /-rik(ə)lē/ adv.

psy·chi·a·trist /sə'kīətrist; sī-/ ▶ n. a medical practitioner specializing in the diagnosis and treatment of mental illness.

psy·chi·a·try /sə'kīətrē; sī-/ ▶ n. the study and treatment of mental illness, emotional disturbance, and abnormal behavior. [19th C.: from Gk. *psukhē* 'soul, mind' + *iatreia* 'healing' (from *iatros* 'healer').]

psy·chic /'sīkik/ ▶ adj. 1 relating to or denoting faculties or phenomena apparently inexplicable by natural laws, esp. involving telepathy or clairvoyance. ■ (of a person) appearing or considered to have powers of telepathy or clairvoyance. 2 of or relating to the soul or mind. ▶ n. a person considered or claiming to have psychic powers; a medium. ■ (**psychics**) [treated as sing. or pl.] the study of psychic phenomena. — **psy·chi·cal** adj. (usu. in sense 1). **psy·chi·cal·ly** /'sīkik(ə)lē/ adv. **psy·chism** /'sī,kizəm/ n. (in sense 1). [19th C.: from Gk. *psukhikos* (see PSYCHE[1]).]

psy·cho /'sīkō/ informal ▶ n. (pl. **-chos**) a psychopath. ▶ adj. psychopathic.

psycho- ▶ comb. form relating to the mind or psychology: *psychobabble*. [from Gk. *psukhē* 'breath, soul, mind.']

psy·cho·a·cous·tics /,sīkōə'kōōstiks/ ▶ plural n. [treated as sing.] the branch of psychology covering the perception of sound and its physiological effects. — **psy·cho·a·cous·tic** adj.

psy·cho·ac·tive /,sīkō'aktiv/ ▶ adj. (chiefly of a drug) affecting the mind.

psy·cho·a·nal·y·sis /,sīkōə'naləsəs/ ▶ n. a system of psychological theory and therapy that aims to treat mental disorders by investigating the interaction of conscious and unconscious elements in the mind and bringing repressed fears and conflicts into the conscious mind. — **psy·cho·an·a·lyze** /,sīkō'anl,īz/ v. **psy·cho·an·a·lyt·ic** /,sīkō,anl'itik/ adj. **psy·cho·an·a·lyt·i·cal** /,sīkō,anl'itikəl/ adj. **psy·cho·an·a·lyt·i·cal·ly** /,sīkō,anl'itik(ə)lē/ adv.

psy·cho·an·a·lyst /,sīkō'anl-əst/ ▶ n. a person who practices psychoanalysis.

psy·cho·bab·ble /'sīkō,babəl/ ▶ n. informal, derog. jargon used in popular psychology.

psy·cho·bi·ol·o·gy /,sīkō,bī'äləjē/ ▶ n. the branch of science that deals with the biological basis of behavior and mental phenomena. — **psy·cho·bi·o·log·i·cal** /-,bīə'läjəkəl/ adj. **psy·cho·bi·ol·o·gist** /-jist/ n.

psy·cho·dra·ma /,sī'kō'drämə; -'dramə/ ▶ n. a form of psychotherapy in which patients act out events from their past. — **psy·cho·dra·mat·ic** /-drə'matik/ adj.

psy·cho·dy·nam·ics /,sīkōdī'namiks/ ▶ plural n. [treated as sing.] the interrelation of the unconscious and conscious mental and emotional forces that determine personality and motivation. ■ the branch of psychology that deals with this. — **psy·cho·dy·nam·ic** adj. **psy·cho·dy·nam·i·cal·ly** /-ik(ə)lē/ adv.

psy·cho·gen·e·sis /,sīkō'jenəsis/ ▶ n. [in sing.] the psychological cause to which a mental disturbance may be attributed (as distinct from a physical cause).

psy·cho·gen·ic /,sīkō'jenik/ ▶ adj. having a psychological origin or cause rather than a physical one.

psy·cho·graph·ics /,sīkō'grafiks/ ▶ plural n. [treated as sing.] the study and classification of people according to their attitudes, aspirations, and other psychological criteria, esp. in market research. — **psy·cho·graph·ic** adj.

psy·cho·his·to·ry /'sīkō,hist(ə)rē/ ▶ n. (pl. **-ries**) the interpretation of historical events with the aid of psychological theory. ■ a work that interprets historical events in such a way. ■ a psychological history of an individual. — **psy·cho·his·to·ri·an** /,sīkō(h)i'stôrēən/ n. **psy·cho·his·to·ri·cal** /,sīkō(h)i'stôrikəl/ adj.

psy·cho·ki·ne·sis /,sīkōkə'nēsis/ ▶ n. the supposed ability to move objects by mental effort alone. — **psy·cho·ki·net·ic** /-'netik/ adj.

psychol. ▶ abbr. ■ psychological. ■ psychologist. ■ psychology.

psy·cho·lin·guis·tics /,sīkōliNG'gwistiks/ ▶ plural n. [treated as sing.] the study of the relationships between linguistic behavior and psychological processes, including the process of language acquisition. — **psy·cho·lin·guist** /-'liNGgwist/ n. **psy·cho·lin·guis·tic** adj.

psy·cho·log·i·cal /,sīkə'läjəkəl/ ▶ adj. of, affecting, or arising in the mind; related to the mental and emotional state of a person. ■ of or relating to psychology. ■ (of an ailment or problem) having a mental rather than a physical cause. — **psy·cho·log·i·cal·ly** /-ik(ə)lē/ adv.

psy·cho·log·i·cal mo·ment ▶ n. [in sing.] the moment at which something will or would have the greatest psychological effect.

psy·cho·log·i·cal war·fare ▶ n. actions intended to reduce an opponent's morale.

psy·chol·o·gism /sī'käləjizəm/ ▶ n. Philos. a tendency to interpret events or arguments in subjective terms, or to exaggerate the relevance of psychological factors.

psy·chol·o·gist /sī'käləjist/ ▶ n. an expert or specialist in psychology.

psy·chol·o·gize /sī'kälə,jīz/ ▶ v. [trans.] analyze or regard in psychological terms, esp. in an uninformed way. ■ [intrans.] theorize or speculate concerning the psychology of something or someone.

psy·chol·o·gy /sī'käləjē/ ▶ n. the scientific study of the human mind and its functions, esp. those affecting behavior in a given context. ■ [in sing.] the mental characteristics or attitude of a person or group. ■ [in sing.] the mental and emotional factors governing a situation or activity.

psy·cho·met·ric /,sīkə'metrik/ ▶ adj. of, relating to, or deriving from psychometry or psychometrics. — **psy·cho·met·ri·cal·ly** /-rik(ə)lē/ adv.

psy·cho·met·rics /,sīkə'metriks/ ▶ plural n. [treated as sing.] the science of measuring mental capacities and processes. — **psy·chom·e·tri·cian** /-mə'trisHən/ n.

psy·chom·e·try /sī'kämətrē/ ▶ n. 1 the supposed ability to discover facts about an event or person by touching inanimate objects associated with them. 2 another term for PSYCHOMETRICS. — **psy·chom·e·trist** /-trist/ n.

psy·cho·mo·tor /,sīkō'mōtər/ ▶ adj. [attrib.] of or relating to the origination of movement in conscious mental activity.

psy·cho·neu·ro·im·mu·nol·o·gy /,sīkō,n(y)ōōrō,imyə'näləjē/ ▶ n. Med. the study of the effect of the mind on health and resistance to disease.

psy·cho·neu·ro·sis /,sīkō-n(y)ōō'rōsəs/ ▶ n. (pl. **-ro·ses** /-'rō,sēz/) another term for NEUROSIS. — **psy·cho·neu·rot·ic** /-,n(y)ōō'rätik/ adj.

psy·cho·path /'sīkə,paTH/ ▶ n. a person suffering from chronic mental disorder with abnormal or violent social behavior. — **psy·cho·path·ic** /,sīkə'paTHik/ adj. **psy·cho·path·i·cal·ly** /,sīkə'paTHik(ə)lē/ adv.

psy·cho·pa·thol·o·gy /,sīkōpə'THäləjē; -paTH'äl-/ ▶ n. the scientific study of mental disorders. ■ features of people's mental health considered collectively. ■ mental or behavioral disorder. — **psy·cho·path·o·log·i·cal** /-paTHə'läjikəl/ adj. **psy·cho·pa·thol·o·gist** /-THäləjist/ n.

psy·chop·a·thy /sī'käpəTHē/ ▶ n. mental illness or disorder.

psy·cho·phar·ma·col·o·gy /,sīkō,färmə'käləjē/ ▶ n. the branch of psychology concerned with the effects of drugs on the mind and behavior. — **psy·cho·phar·ma·co·log·i·cal** /-,färməkə'läjikəl/ adj. **psy·cho·phar·ma·col·o·gist** /-jist/ n.

psy·cho·phys·ics /,sīkō'fiziks/ ▶ plural n. [treated as sing.] the branch of psychology that deals with the relationships between physical stimuli and mental phenomena. — **psy·cho·phys·i·cal** /-'fizikəl/ adj.

psy·cho·phys·i·ol·o·gy /,sīkō,fizē'äləjē/ ▶ n. Psychol. the study of the relationship between physiological and psychological phenomena. ■ the way in which the mind and body interact. — **psy·cho·phys·i·o·log·i·cal** /-,fizēə'läjikəl/ adj. **psy·cho·phys·i·ol·o·gist** /-jist/ n.

psy·cho·sex·u·al /,sīkō'seksHōōəl/ ▶ adj. of or involving the psychological aspects of the sexual impulse. — **psy·cho·sex·u·al·ly** adv.

psy·cho·sis /sī'kōsəs/ ▶ n. (pl. **-ses** /-,sēz/) a severe mental disorder in which thought and emotions are so impaired that contact is lost with external reality.

psy·cho·so·cial /,sīkō'sōsHəl/ ▶ adj. of or relating to the interrelation of social factors and individual thought and behavior. — **psy·cho·so·cial·ly** adv.

psy·cho·so·mat·ic /,sīkōsə'matik/ ▶ adj. (of a physical illness or other condition) caused or aggravated by a mental factor such as internal conflict or stress. ■ of or relating to the interaction of mind and body. — **psy·cho·so·mat·i·cal·ly** /-ik(ə)lē/ adv.

psy·cho·sur·ger·y /,sīkō'sərjərē/ ▶ n. brain surgery, such as lobotomy, used to treat mental disorder. — **psy·cho·sur·gi·cal** /-'sərjikəl/ adj.

psy·cho·syn·the·sis /ˌsīkōˈsinᴛʜəsəs/ ▶ **n.** Psychoanal. the integration of separated elements of the psyche or personality.

psy·cho·ther·a·py /ˌsīkōˈᴛʜerəpē/ ▶ **n.** the treatment of mental disorder by psychological rather than medical means. — **psy·cho·ther·a·peu·tic** /-ˌᴛʜerəˈpyo͞otik/ **adj.** **psy·cho·ther·a·pist** /-ˈᴛʜerəpist/ **n.**

psy·chot·ic /sīˈkätik/ ▶ **adj.** of, denoting, or suffering from a psychosis: *a psychotic disturbance.* ▶ **n.** a person suffering from a psychosis. — **psy·chot·i·cal·ly** /-ik(ə)lē/ **adv.**

psy·chot·o·mi·met·ic /ˌsīˌkätōməˈmetik/ ▶ **adj.** relating to or denoting drugs that are capable of producing an effect on the mind similar to a psychotic state. ▶ **n.** a drug of this kind.

psy·cho·tron·ic /ˌsīkəˈtränik/ ▶ **adj. 1** denoting or relating to a genre of movies, typically with a science fiction, horror, or fantasy theme, that were made on a low budget or poorly received by critics. **2** of or relating to psychotronics.

psy·cho·tro·pic /ˌsīkəˈtrōpik; -ˈträpik/ ▶ **adj.** relating to or denoting drugs that affect a person's mental state. ▶ **n.** a drug of this kind.

psy·chrom·e·ter /sīˈkrämətər/ ▶ **n.** a hygrometer consisting of a wet-bulb and a dry-bulb thermometer, the difference in the two thermometer readings being used to determine atmospheric humidity. [18th C.: from Gk. *psukhros* 'cold' + **-METER**.]

psyl·la /ˈsilə/ (also **psyl·lid** /ˈsilid/) ▶ **n.** Entomol. a minute insect of a family (Psyllidae) that comprises the jumping plant lice. [19th C.: from mod. L. *Psyllidae* (pl.), from Gk. *psulla* 'flea.']

psyl·li·um /ˈsilēəm/ ▶ **n.** a leafy-stemmed Eurasian plantain (*Plantago psafra*), the seeds of which are used as a laxative and as a bulking agent in the treatment of obesity. [16th C.: via L. from Gk. *psullion*, from *psulla* 'flea' (because the seeds resemble fleas).]

PT ▶ **abbr.** ■ Pacific Time. ■ physical therapy. ■ physical training. ■ postal telegraph. ■ pupil teacher.

Pt ▶ **symb.** the chemical element platinum.

pt. ▶ **abbr.** ■ part. ■ payment. ■ pint; pints. ■ point. ■ Print. point (as a unit of measurement). ■ (denoting a side of a ship or aircraft) port. ■ preterit.

p.t. ▶ **abbr.** ■ past tense. ■ post town. ■ pro tempore.

PTA ▶ **abbr.** ■ parent–teacher association.

pta. (also **Pta.**) ▶ **abbr.** (pl. **ptas.**) peseta.

Ptah /tä/ Egyptian Mythol. an ancient deity of Memphis, creator of the universe, god of artisans, and husband of Sekhmet.

ptar·mi·gan /tärməgən/ ▶ **n.** (pl. same or **-gans**) a northern grouse, esp. the **rock ptarmigan** (*Lagopus mutus*) of Eurasia and North America, with feathered legs and feet and plumage that typically changes to white in winter. [16th C.: from Scot. Gael. *tàrmachan*.]

PT boat ▶ **n.** a motorboat equipped with torpedoes and used by the military, esp. during World War II. [1940s: from *P(atrol) T(orpedo) boat*.]

PTC ▶ **abbr.** Biochem. phenylthiocarbamide.

pter·an·o·don /təˈranəˌdän; -dən/ ▶ **n.** a large tailless pterosaur (genus *Pteranodon*) of the Cretaceous period, with a long toothless beak, a long bony crest, and a wingspan of up to 23 feet (7 m). [mod. L., from Gk. *pteron* 'wing' + *an-* 'without' + *odous, odont-* 'tooth.']

pter·i·dol·o·gy /ˌterəˈdäləjē/ ▶ **n.** the study of ferns and related plants. — **pter·i·do·log·i·cal** /-dlˈäjikəl/ **adj.** **pter·i·dol·o·gist** /-jist/ **n.** [19th C.: from Gk. *pteris, pterid-* 'fern' + **-LOGY**.]

Pter·i·doph·y·ta /ˌterəˈdäfitə/ Bot. a division (Pteridophyta) of flowerless green plants that comprises the ferns and their relatives. Three classes: Filicopsida (ferns), Sphenopsida (horsetails), and Lycopsida (club mosses). — **pte·rid·o·phyte** /təˈridəˌfīt; ˈteridə-/ **n.** [mod. L. (pl.), from Gk. *pteris, pterid-* 'fern' + *phuton* 'plant.']

pte·rid·o·sperm /təˈridəˌspərm; ˈteridə-/ ▶ **n.** an extinct plant that is intermediate between the ferns and seed-bearing plants, dying out in the Triassic period. Formerly placed in their own taxon (class Pteridospermeae), pteridosperms are now included with the gymnosperms. [20th C.: from mod. L. *pteridospermeae*, from Gk. *pteris, pterid-* 'fern.']

ptero- ▶ **comb. form** relating to wings; having wings. [from Gk. *pteron* 'feather, wing.']

pter·o·dac·tyl /ˌterəˈdaktəl/ ▶ **n.** a pterosaur (*Pterodactylus* and other genera, family Pterodactylidae) of the late Jurassic period, with a long slender head and neck and a very short tail. See illustration at **DINOSAUR**. ■ (in general use) any pterosaur. [19th C.: from mod. L. *Pterodactylus* (genus name), from Gk. *pteron* 'wing' + *daktulos* 'finger.']

pter·o·pod /ˈterəˌpäd/ ▶ **n.** Zool. a small mollusk (class Gastropoda) with winglike extensions to its body that it uses for swimming. Two orders: Thecosomata (with shells) and Gymnosomata (lacking shells). [19th C.: from mod. L. *Pteropoda* (pl.), from Gk. *pteron* 'wing' + *pous, pod-* 'foot.']

pter·o·saur /ˈterəˌsôr/ ▶ **n.** an extinct warm-blooded flying reptile (order Pterosauria, subdivision Archosauria) of the Jurassic and Cretaceous periods, with membranous wings supported by a greatly lengthened fourth finger, and probably covered with fur. Its several families include the pterodactyls and pteranodons. [19th C.: from mod. L. *Pterosauria* (pl.), from Gk. *pteron* 'wing' + *sauros* 'lizard.']

pter·o·yl·glu·tam·ic ac·id /ˌterōilˌglo͞oˈtamik/ ▶ **n.** another term for **FOLIC ACID**. — **pter·o·yl·glu·ta·mate** /-ˈglo͞otəˌmāt/ **n.** [1940s: initial element from Gk. *pteron* 'wing.']

pter·y·goid proc·ess /ˈteriˌgoid ˈpräˌses; ˈpräsəs/ ▶ **n.** Anat. each of a pair of projections from the sphenoid bone in the skull. [18th C.: from mod. L. *pterygoides* (pl.), from Gk. *pterux, pterug-* 'wing.']

Pter·y·go·ta /ˌterəˈgōtə/ Entomol. a large group of insects (subclass Pterygota, class Insecta or Hexapoda) that comprises those that have wings or winged ancestors, including the majority of modern species. — **pter·y·gote** /ˈterəˌgōt/ **n.** [mod. L. (pl.), from Gk. *pterugōtos* 'winged,' from *pterux, pterug-* 'wing.']

ptg. ▶ **abbr.** printing.

PTH ▶ **abbr.** parathyroid hormone.

PTO ▶ **abbr.** ■ please turn over (written at the foot of a page to indicate that the text continues on the reverse). ■ (also **pto**) (in a tractor or other vehicle) power takeoff. ■ Parent-Teacher Organization.

Ptol·e·ma·ic /ˌtäləˈmā-ik/ ▶ **adj. 1** of or relating to the Greek astronomer Ptolemy or his theories. **2** of or relating to the Ptolemies of Egypt (see **PTOLEMY**[1].)

Ptol·e·ma·ic sys·tem (also **Ptolemaic theory**) ▶ **n.** Astron., hist. the theory that the earth is the stationary center of the universe, with the planets moving in epicyclic orbits within surrounding concentric spheres. Compare with **COPERNICAN SYSTEM**.

Ptol·e·my[1] /ˈtäləmē/ the name of all the Macedonian rulers of Egypt, a dynasty founded by Ptolemy, a close friend and general of Alexander the Great, who took charge of Egypt after the latter's death and declared himself king (Ptolemy I) in 304 BC. The dynasty ended with the death of Cleopatra in 30 BC.

Ptol·e·my[2] (2nd century) Greek astronomer and geographer. His teachings influenced medieval thought, the geocentric view of the cosmos being adopted as Christian doctrine until the late Renaissance.

pto·maine /ˈtōˌmān; tōˈmān/ ▶ **n.** Chem., dated any of a group of amine compounds of unpleasant taste and odor formed in putrefying animal and vegetable matter and formerly thought to cause food poisoning. [19th C.: from Fr. *ptomaïne*, from Ital. *ptomaina*, formed irregularly from Gk. *ptōma* 'corpse.']

P2P /ˈpētəˈpē/ ▶ **abbr.** Computing peer-to-peer; denoting a network or data communications in which no dedicated server is involved.

pto·sis /ˈtōsəs/ ▶ **n.** Med. drooping of the upper eyelid due to paralysis or disease, or as a congenital condition. — **pto·tic** /ˈtōˌtik; ˈtätik/ **adj.** [18th C.: from Gk. *ptōsis*, from *piptein* 'to fall.']

PTSD ▶ **abbr.** post-traumatic stress disorder.

pty. ▶ **abbr.** proprietary.

pty·a·lin /ˈtīələn/ ▶ **n.** Biochem. a form of amylase found in the saliva of humans and some other animals. [19th C.: from Gk. *ptualon* 'spittle' + **-IN**[1].]

p-type ▶ **adj.** Electron. denoting a region in a semiconductor in which electrical conduction is due chiefly to the movement of positive holes. Often contrasted with **N-TYPE**.

Pu ▶ **symb.** the chemical element plutonium.

pub /pəb/ Brit. ▶ **n.** a tavern or bar. [19th C.: abbrev. of **PUBLIC HOUSE**.]

pub. ▶ **abbr.** ■ publication(s). ■ published. ■ publisher.

pub crawl informal, esp. Brit. ▶ **n.** a tour taking in several pubs or bars, with one or more drinks at each. ▶ **v.** [intrans.] (**pub-crawl**) go on a pub crawl.

pu·ber·ty /ˈpyo͞obərtē/ ▶ **n.** the period during which adolescents reach sexual maturity and become capable of reproduction. — **pu·ber·tal** /-bərtl/ **adj.** [ME: from L. *pubertas*, from *puber* 'adult,' rel. to *pubes* (see **PUBES**).]

pu·bes /ˈpyo͞obēz; pyo͞obz/ ▶ **n. 1** (pl. same) the lower part of the abdomen at the front of the pelvis, covered with hair from puberty. **2** plural form of **PUBIS**. [16th C.: from L., 'pubic hair, groin, genitals.']

pu·bes·cence /pyo͞oˈbesəns/ ▶ **n. 1** the time when puberty begins. **2** Bot. & Zool. soft down or fine short hairs on the leaves and stems of plants or on various parts of animals, esp. insects.

pu·bes·cent /pyo͞oˈbesənt/ ▶ **adj. 1** relating to or denoting a person at or approaching the age of puberty. **2** Bot. & Zool. covered with short soft hair; downy. ▶ **n.** a person at or approaching the age of puberty. [17th C.: from Fr., or from L. *pubescent-* 'reaching puberty,' from the verb *pubescere*.]

pu·bic /ˈpyo͞obik/ ▶ **adj.** [attrib.] of or relating to the pubes or pubis: *pubic hair.*

pu·bic louse ▶ **n.** another term for **CRAB**[1] (sense 2).

pu·bis /ˈpyo͞obəs/ ▶ **n.** (pl. **-bes** /-bēz/) either of a pair of bones forming the two sides of the pelvis. [16th C.: from L. *os pubis* 'bone of the pubes.']

publ. ▶ **abbr.** ■ public. ■ publication. ■ publicity. ■ published. ■ publisher.

pub·lic /ˈpəblik/ ▶ **adj. 1** of or concerning the people as a whole. ■ open to or shared by all the people of an area or country. ■ of or provided by the government rather than an independent, commercial company. ■ of or involved in the affairs of the community, esp. in government: *his public career was destroyed by tenacious reporters.* ■ known to many people; famous. **2** done, perceived, or existing in open view. ▶ **n.** (**the public**) [treated as sing. or pl.] ordinary people in general; the community. ■ [with adj.] a section of the community having a particular interest or connection: *the reading public.* ■ (**one's public**) the people who watch or are interested in an artist, writer, or performer.

– PHRASES **go public 1** become a public company. **2** reveal details about a previously private concern. **in public** in view of other people; when others are present. **the public eye** the state of being known or of interest to people in general, esp. through the media. [ME: from OFr., from L. *publicus*, blend of *poplicus* 'of the people' (from *populus* 'people') and *pubes* 'adult.']

pub·lic act ▶ n. an act of legislation affecting the public as a whole.

pub·lic-ad·dress sys·tem ▶ n. a system of microphones, amplifiers, and loudspeakers used to amplify speech or music in a large building or at an outdoor gathering.

pub·li·can /'pəblikən/ ▶ n. **1** Brit. a person who owns or manages a pub. **2** (in ancient Roman and biblical times) a collector of taxes.

pub·lic as·sis·tance ▶ n. government benefits provided to the needy, usually in the form of cash or vouchers.

pub·li·ca·tion /,pəbli'kāsHən/ ▶ n. the preparation and issuing of a book, journal, piece of music, or other work for public sale. ■ a book, journal, etc. issued for public sale. ■ the action of making something generally known.

pub·lic com·pa·ny ▶ n. a company whose shares are traded freely on a stock exchange.

pub·lic de·fend·er ▶ n. Law a lawyer employed at public expense in a criminal trial to represent a defendant who is unable to afford legal assistance.

pub·lic do·main ▶ n. the state of belonging or being available to the public as a whole. ■ not subject to copyright. ■ public land.

pub·lic en·e·my ▶ n. a notorious wanted criminal. ■ fig. a person or thing regarded as the greatest threat to a group or community.

pub·lic good ▶ n. **1** Econ. a commodity or service provided without profit to all members of a society, either by the government or a private individual or organization. **2** the benefit or well-being of the public.

pub·lic house ▶ n. esp. Brit. a tavern.

pub·li·cist /'pəbləsist/ ▶ n. **1** a person responsible for publicizing a product, person, or company. **2** dated a journalist, esp. one concerned with current affairs. — **pub·li·cis·tic** /,pəblə'sistik/ adj.

pub·lic·i·ty /pə'blisətē/ ▶ n. the notice or attention given to someone or something by the media. ■ public exposure; notoriety. ■ the giving out of information about a product, person, or company for advertising or promotional purposes. ■ material or information used for such a purpose.

pub·lic·i·ty a·gent ▶ n. another term for PUBLICIST (sense 1).

pub·li·cize /'pəblə,sīz/ ▶ v. [trans.] make (something) widely known. ■ give out publicity about (a product, person, or company) for advertising or promotional purposes.

pub·lic key ▶ n. a cryptographic key that can be obtained and used by anyone to encrypt messages intended for a particular recipient, such that the encrypted messages can be deciphered only by using a second key that is known only to the recipient (the **private key**).

pub·lic law ▶ n. the law of relationships between individuals and the government.

pub·lic·ly /'pəbliklē/ ▶ adv. so as to be seen by other people; in public. ■ [often sentence adverb] used in reference to views expressed to others and not necessarily genuinely felt. ■ by a government or the public rather than an independent, commercial company.

pub·lic nui·sance ▶ n. an act, condition, or thing that is illegal because it interferes with the rights of the public generally. ■ informal an obnoxious or dangerous person or group of people.

pub·lic o·pin·ion ▶ n. views prevalent among the general public.

pub·lic pol·i·cy ▶ n. **1** the principles, often unwritten, on which social laws are based. **2** Law the principle that injury to the public good is a basis for denying the legality of a contract or other transaction.

pub·lic pros·e·cu·tor ▶ n. a law officer who conducts criminal proceedings on behalf of the government or in the public interest.

pub·lic purse ▶ n. the funds raised by a government by taxation or other means.

pub·lic re·la·tions ▶ plural n. [also treated as sing.] the professional maintenance of a favorable public image by an organization or a famous person. ■ the state of the relationship between the public and a company or other organization or a famous person.

pub·lic school ▶ n. (chiefly in North America) a school supported by public funds.

pub·lic sec·tor ▶ n. the part of an economy that is controlled by the government.

pub·lic serv·ant ▶ n. a government official.

pub·lic-serv·ice cor·po·ra·tion ▶ n. a public utility.

pub·lic spir·it ▶ n. willingness to do things that help the public. — **pub·lic-spir·it·ed** adj. **pub·lic-spir·it·ed·ly** adv. **pub·lic-spir·it·ed·ness** n.

pub·lic trans·por·ta·tion ▶ n. buses, trains, subways, and other forms of transportation that charge set fares, run on fixed routes, and are available to the public.

pub·lic u·til·i·ty ▶ n. an organization supplying a community with electricity, gas, water, or sewerage.

pub·lic works ▶ plural n. the work of building such things as roads, schools, and reservoirs, carried out by the government for the community.

pub·lish /'pəblisH/ ▶ v. [trans.] **1** (of an author or company) prepare and issue (a book, journal, piece of music, or other work) for public sale. ■ print (something) in a book or journal to make it generally known. ■ [usu. as adj.] (**published**) prepare and issue the works of (a particular writer). ■ formally announce (an edict or marriage banns). **2** Law communicate (a libel) to a third party. — **pub·lish·a·ble** adj. [ME: from the stem of OFr. *puplier*, from L. *publicare* 'make public,' from *publicus* (see PUBLIC).]

pub·lish·er /'pəblisHər/ ▶ n. (also **publishers**) a person or company that prepares and issues books, journals, music, or other works for sale.

pub·lish·ing /'pəblisHiNG/ ▶ n. the occupation or activity of preparing and issuing books, journals, and other material for sale.

Puc·ci·ni /pōō'CHēnē/, Giacomo (1858–1924), Italian composer. His operas include *La Bohème* (1896), *Tosca* (1900), and *Madama Butterfly* (1904).

puc·coon /pə'kōōn/ ▶ n. a North American plant (genus *Lithospermum*) of the borage family that yields a pigment from which dye or medicinal products are obtained, esp. formerly. ■ another term for BLOODROOT. [17th C.: from Algonquian *poughkone*.]

puce /pyōōs/ ▶ adj. of a dark red or purple-brown color. ▶ n. a dark red or purple-brown color. [18th C.: from Fr., lit. 'flea(-color),' from L. *pulex, pulic-*.]

puck[1] /pək/ ▶ n. a mischievous or evil sprite. [OE *pūca*; it is unclear whether the word is of Celtic or Gmc. origin.]

puck[2] ▶ n. **1** a black disk made of hard rubber, the focus of play in ice hockey. **2** Comput. an input device similar to a mouse that is dragged across a sensitive surface, which notes the puck's position to move the cursor on the screen. [19th C.: of unknown origin.]

puck·a ▶ adj. var. of PUKKA.

puck·er /'pəkər/ ▶ v. [intrans.] (esp. of a person's face or a facial feature) tightly gather or contract into wrinkles or small folds: *her brows puckered in a frown.* ■ [trans.] cause to do this: *the baby puckered its tiny face.* ▶ n. a tightly gathered wrinkle or small fold, esp. on a person's face.

– PHRASES **pucker up** contract one's lips as in preparation for a kiss. — **puck·er·y** /'pəkərē/ adj. [16th C. (as a v.): prob. frequentative, from the base of POKE[2].]

puck·ish /'pəkisH/ ▶ adj. playful, esp. in a mischievous way. — **puck·ish·ly** adv. **puck·ish·ness** n.

pud·ding /'pōōdiNG/ ▶ n. **1** a dessert with a creamy consistency. **2** a sweet or savory steamed dish made with flour: *Yorkshire pudding.* ■ the intestines of a pig or sheep stuffed with oatmeal, spices, and meat and boiled. See also BLACK PUDDING, BLOOD PUDDING. — **pud·ding·y** adj. [ME: appar. from OFr. *boudin* 'black pudding,' from L. *botellus* 'sausage, small intestine.']

pud·ding·stone /'pōōdiNG,stōn/ ▶ n. a conglomerate rock in which dark-colored rounded pebbles contrast with a paler fine-grained matrix.

pud·dle /'pədl/ ▶ n. **1** a small pool of liquid, esp. of rainwater on the ground. **2** clay and sand mixed with water and used as a watertight covering for embankments. ▶ v. [trans.] **1** wet or cover (a surface) with water, esp. rainwater. ■ [intrans.] (of liquid) form a small pool. **2** line (a hole) with puddle. ■ knead (clay and sand) into puddle. ■ work (mixed water and clay) to separate gold or opal. ■ [usu. as n.] (**puddling**) esp. hist. stir (molten iron) with iron oxide in a furnace, to produce wrought iron by oxidizing carbon. — **pud·dler** /'pədlər; 'pədl-ər/ n. **pud·dly** /'pədlē; 'pədl-ē/ adj. [ME: dimin. of OE *pudd* 'ditch, furrow'; cf. Ger. dial. *Pfudel* 'pool.']

pud·dle jump·er (also **pud·dle-jump·er**) ▶ n. informal a small light airplane that is fast and highly maneuverable and used for short trips.

pu·den·cy /'pyōōdn-sē/ ▶ n. literary modesty; shame. [17th C.: from late L. *pudentia*.]

pu·den·dum /pyōō'dendəm/ ▶ n. (pl. **-den·da** /-'dendə/) (often **pudenda**) a person's external genitals, esp. a woman's. — **pu·den·dal** /-'dendl/ adj. **pu·dic** /'pyōōdik/ adj. [17th C.: from L. *pudenda*, neut. pl. of the gerundive of *pudere* 'be ashamed.']

pu·deur /pyōō'dər/ ▶ n. a sense of shame or embarrassment, esp. with regard to matters of a sexual or personal nature. [20th C.: Fr., lit. 'modesty.']

pudg·y /'pəjē/ ▶ adj. (**pudg·i·er, pudg·i·est**) informal (of a person or part of their body) slightly fat: *his pudgy fingers.* — **pudg·i·ly** /'pəjəlē/ adv. **pudg·i·ness** n. [19th C. (denoting a fat person): of unknown origin.]

pu·du /'pōōdōō/ ▶ n. a very small and rare deer (genus *Pudu*) found in the lower Andes of South America. [19th C.: from Araucanian.]

Pue·bla /'pweblä/ a state in south central Mexico. ■ its capital city; pop. 1,055,000. Full name **Puebla de Zaragoza**.

Pueb·lo /'pweblō/ a city in south central Colorado; pop. 102,121.

pueb·lo /'pweblō/ ▶ n. (pl. **-los**) **1** an American Indian settlement of the southwestern US, esp. one consisting of multistoried adobe houses built by the Pueblo people. ■ (in Spanish-speaking regions) a town or village. **2** (**Pueblo**) (pl. same or **-los**) a member of any of various American Indian peoples, including the Hopi, occupying pueblo settlements chiefly in New Mexico and Arizona. ▶ adj. (**Pueblo**) of, relating to, or denoting the Pueblos or their culture. [Sp., lit. 'people,' from L. *populus*.]

pu·er·ile /'pyōōərəl; 'pyōōr,īl/ ▶ adj. childishly silly and trivial. — **pu·er·ile·ly** adv. **pu·er·il·i·ty** /pyōōə-; pyōō'rilətē/ n. (pl. **-ties**) [16th C. (in the sense 'like a boy'): from Fr. *puéril* or L. *puerilis*, from *puer* 'boy.']

pu·er·per·al fe·ver /pyōō'ərpərəl/ ▶ n. fever caused by uterine infection following childbirth.

pu·er·pe·ri·um /,pyōōər'pi(ə)rēəm/ ▶ n. Med. the period of about six weeks after childbirth during which the mother's reproductive organs return to their original nonpregnant condition. — **pu·er·per·al** /pyo͞o'ərpərəl/ **adj.** [17th C.: from L., from *puerperus* 'parturient' (from *puer* 'child' + *-parus* 'bearing').]

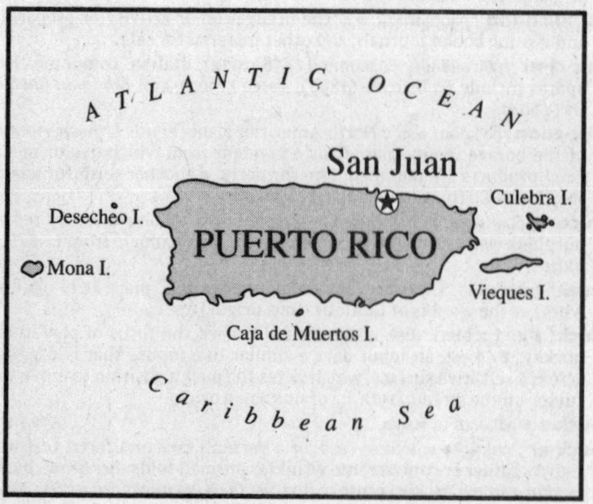

Puer·to Ri·co /'pôrtə 'rēkō; 'pwertō/ an island in the Greater Antilles in the Caribbean Sea; pop. 3,808,610; capital, San Juan. In 1952 it became a commonwealth in voluntary association with the US with full powers of local government. — **Puer·to Ri·can** /'rēkən/ **adj. & n.**

puff /pəf/ ▶**n. 1** a short, explosive burst of breath or wind. ■ the sound of air or vapor escaping suddenly. ■ a small quantity of vapor or smoke, emitted in one blast. ■ an act of drawing quickly on a pipe, cigarette, or cigar. **2** [usu. with adj. or in comb.] a light pastry case, typically one made of puff pastry, containing a sweet or savory filling. ■ a gathered mass of material in a dress or other garment. ■ a rolled protuberant mass of hair. ■ a powder puff. ■ a soft quilt. **3** informal a review of a work of art, book, or theatrical production, esp. an excessively complimentary one. ▶**v. 1** [intrans.] breathe in repeated short gasps. ■ [with adverbial] (of a person, engine, etc.) move with short, noisy breaths or bursts of air or steam: *the train came puffing in.* ■ smoke a pipe, cigarette, or cigar. ■ [trans.] blow (dust, smoke, or a light object) in a specified direction with a quick breath or blast of air. ■ move through the air in short bursts. **2** (**puff something out/up** or **puff out/up**) cause to swell or become swollen: [trans.] *he sucked his stomach in and puffed his chest out* | [intrans.] *his cheeks puffed up.* ■ [trans.] (usu. **be puffed up**) fig. cause to become conceited: *he was never puffed up about his writing.* **3** [trans.] advertise with exaggerated or false praise: *publishers have puffed the book.* [ME: imitative, perh. from OE *pyf* (n.), *pyffan* (v.).]

puff ad·der ▶**n.** a large, sluggish, mainly nocturnal African viper (*Bitis arietans*) that inflates the upper part of its body and hisses loudly in threat. ■ another term for HOGNOSE SNAKE.

puff·back /'pəf,bak/ (also **puff-back shrike**) ▶**n.** a small black-and-white African shrike (genus *Dryoscopus*), the male of which displays by puffing up the feathers of the lower back.

puff·ball /'pəf,bôl/ ▶**n. 1** a fungus (*Lycoperdon* and other genera, family Lycoperdaceae) that produces a spherical or pear-shaped fruiting body that ruptures when ripe to release a cloud of spores. **2** anything round and fluffy, such as a powder puff.

puff·bird /'pəf,bərd/ ▶**n.** a stocky large-headed bird (family Bucconidae) somewhat resembling a kingfisher, found in tropical American forests.

puffed /pəft/ ▶**adj.** (also **puffed up**) swollen. ■ (of a sleeve or other part of a garment) gathered so as to have a rounded shape.

puff·er /'pəfər/ ▶**n. 1** informal a person or thing that puffs, esp. a person who smokes. **2** short for PUFFERFISH.

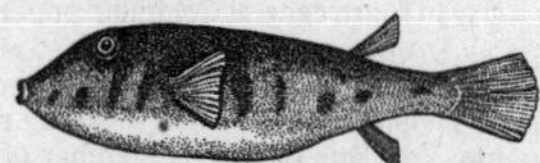

northern pufferfish

puff·er·fish /'pəfər,fisʜ/ (also **puff·er fish**) ▶**n.** (pl. same or **-fish·es**) a stout-bodied marine or freshwater fish (family Tetraodontidae) that typically has spiny skin and inflates itself like a balloon when threatened. It is sometimes used as food, but some parts are highly toxic.

puff·er·y /'pəfərē/ ▶**n.** exaggerated or false praise.

puf·fin /'pəfən/ ▶**n.** a hole-nesting auk (genera *Fratercula* and *Lunda*) of northern and Arctic waters, with a large head and a massive brightly colored triangular bill, in particular the **Atlantic puffin** (*F. arctica*). [ME: appar. from PUFF + -ING[3].]

puff pas·try ▶**n.** light flaky pastry, used for pie crusts, canapés, etc.

puff piece ▶**n.** informal a newspaper article or item on a television show using exaggerated praise to advertise or promote a celebrity, book, or event.

puff·y /'pəfē/ ▶**adj.** (**puff·i·er**, **puff·i·est**) **1** (esp. of part of the body) swollen and soft. ■ soft, rounded, and light: *small puffy clouds.* ■ (of a garment or part of a garment) padded or gathered to give a rounded shape. ■ fig. (of a piece of writing) overembellished and pompous. **2** (of wind or breath) coming in short bursts. — **puff·i·ly** /'pəfəlē/ **adv. puff·i·ness n.**

pug dog

pug[1] /pəg/ ▶**n.** (also **pug dog**) a dog of a dwarf breed like a bulldog with a broad flat nose and deeply wrinkled face. — **pug·gish adj. pug·gy** /'pəgē/ **adj.** [18th C.: perh. of Low Ger. origin.]

pug[2] ▶**n.** loam or clay mixed and worked into a soft, plastic condition without air pockets for making bricks or pottery. ▶**v.** (**pugged**, **pug·ging**) [trans.] **1** [usu. as adj.] (**pugged**) prepare (clay) in this way. **2** [usu. as n.] (**pugging**) pack (a space under a floor) with pug, sawdust, or other material in order to deaden sound. [19th C.: of unknown origin.]

pug[3] ▶**n.** informal a boxer. [19th C.: abbrev. of PUGILIST.]

pug[4] ▶**n.** the footprint of an animal. ▶**v.** (**pugged**, **pug·ging**) [trans.] track (an animal) by its footprints. [19th C.: from Hindi *pag* 'footprint.']

pug dog ▶**n.** another term for PUG[1].

Pu·get Sound /'pyo͞ojit/ an inlet of the Pacific Ocean on the coast of the state of Washington.

pug·ga·ree /'pəg(ə)rē/ ▶**n.** an Indian turban. ■ a thin muslin scarf tied around a sun helmet so as to hang down over the wearer's neck and shield it from the sun. [from Hindi *pagṛī* 'turban.']

pu·gi·list /'pyo͞ojəlist/ ▶**n.** dated or humorous a boxer, esp. a professional one. — **pu·gi·lism** /-,lizəm/ **n. pu·gi·lis·tic** /,pyo͞ojə'listik/ **adj.** [18th C.: from L. *pugil* 'boxer' + -IST.]

pug·na·cious /pəg'nāsнəs/ ▶**adj.** eager or quick to argue, quarrel, or fight. ■ having the appearance of a willing fighter. — **pug·na·cious·ly adv. pug·nac·i·ty** /,pəg'nasətē/ **n.** [17th C.: from L. *pugnax*, *pugnac-* (from *pugnare* 'to fight,' from *pugnus* 'fist') + -IOUS.]

pug nose ▶**n.** a short nose with an upturned tip. — **pug-nosed adj.**

puis·ne /'pyo͞onē/ ▶**adj.** [attrib.] Law (in the UK and some other countries) denoting a judge of a superior court inferior in rank to chief justices. [16th C.: from OFr., from *puis* (from L. *postea* 'afterwards') + *ne* 'born' (from L. *natus*).]

pu·is·sance /'pwisəns; 'pwē-; pyo͞o'isəns/ ▶**n.** archaic or literary great power, influence, or prowess.

pu·is·sant /'pwisənt; 'pwēsənt; 'pyo͞oəsənt/ ▶**adj.** archaic or literary having great power or influence. — **pu·is·sant·ly adv.** [ME: via OFr. from L. *posse* 'be able.']

puke /pyo͞ok/ informal ▶**v.** vomit: [intrans.] *I had eaten to the point of puking* | [trans.] *he puked up his pizza.* ▶**n.** vomit. — **puk·ey adj.** [16th C.: prob. imitative.]

puk·ka /'pəkə/ (also **puk·kah**) ▶**adj.** genuine. ■ of or appropriate to high or respectable society. ■ informal excellent. [17th C.: from Hindi *pakkā* 'cooked, ripe, substantial.']

pul /po͞ol/ ▶**n.** (pl. **puls** or **pu·li** /'po͞olē/) a monetary unit of Afghanistan, equal to one hundredth of an afghani. [Pashto, from Pers. *pūl* 'copper coin.']

pu·la /'p(y)o͞olə/ ▶**n.** (pl. same) the basic monetary unit of Botswana, equal to 100 thebe. [Setswana, lit. 'rain.']

pu·lao /pə'lou; pə'lō; 'pərlo͞o/ ▶**n.** var. of PILAF.

Pu·las·ki[1] /pə'laskē/, Casimir (*or* Kazimierz) (1747–79) Polish general who commanded American forces during the Revolutionary War. Invaluable in the defense of Charleston 1779, he was mortally wounded at the siege of Savannah.

Pu·las·ki[2] ▶**n.** (pl. **-kis**) an ax with a head that forms an ax blade on one side and an adze on the other. [1920s: named after Edward C. *Pulaski* (1866–1931), Amer. forest ranger.]

Pu·lau Se·ri·bu /,po͞olou 'seribo͞o/ Indonesian name for THOUSAND ISLANDS (sense 2).

pul·chri·tude /'pəlkrə,t(y)o͞od/ ▶**n.** literary beauty. — **pul·chri·tu·di·nous** /,pəlkrə't(y)o͞odn-əs/ **adj.** [ME: from L. *pulchritudo*, from *pulcher*, *pulchr-* 'beautiful.']

pule /pyo͞ol/ ▶**v.** [intrans.] [often as adj.] (**puling**) literary cry querulously or weakly: *she's no puling infant.* [ME: prob. imitative.]

pu·li /'po͞olē/ ▶**n.** (pl. **pu·lik** /'po͞olik/) a sheepdog of a black, gray, or white breed with a long thick coat. [20th C.: from Hungarian.]

Pul·it·zer /'po͞olitsər; 'pyo͞ol-/, Joseph (1847–1911), US publisher and philanthropist; born in Hungary. He owned several newspapers and made provisions in his will for the establishment of the annual Pulitzer Prizes.

Pu·litz·er Prize ▶ **n.** an award for an achievement in American journalism, literature, or music. There are thirteen awarded each year.

pull /po͝ol/ ▶ **v.** [trans.] **1** exert force on (someone or something), typically by taking hold of them, to move or try to move them toward oneself or the origin of the force: *he pulled the car door handle* | [intrans.] *the boy pulled at her skirt.* ■ (of an animal or vehicle) be attached to the front and be the source of forward movement of (a vehicle). ■ take hold of and exert force on (something) to move it from a specified position or in a specified direction: *I pulled up some onions.* ■ informal bring out (a weapon) to attack or threaten someone: *one man pulled a gun and demanded cash.* ■ [intrans.] **(pull at/on)** inhale deeply while smoking (a pipe or cigar). ■ damage (a muscle, ligament, etc.) by abnormal strain. ■ print (a proof). ■ Comput. retrieve (an item of data) from the top of a stack. **2** [intrans.] (of a vehicle or person) move steadily in a specified direction or to reach a specified point: *the bus was about to pull away.* ■ **(pull oneself)** move in a specified direction with effort, esp. by taking hold of something and exerting force: *he pulled himself into the saddle.* ■ [intrans.] move one's body in a specified direction, esp. against resistance: *she tried to pull away from him.* ■ [intrans.] (of an engine) exert propulsive force; deliver power: *the engine pulled well.* ■ [intrans.] work oars to cause a boat to move. **3** cause (someone) to patronize, buy, or show interest in something; attract: *attractions that pull in foreign visitors.* ■ influence in favor of a particular course of action: *they are pulled in incompatible directions by external factors.* ■ informal carry out or achieve (something requiring skill, luck, or planning): *the magazine pulled its trick of producing the right issue at the right time.* **4** informal cancel or withdraw (an entertainment or advertisement). ■ withdraw (a player) from a game: *four of the leading eight runners were pulled.* ■ check the speed of (a horse), esp. so as to make it lose a race. **5** esp. Baseball & Golf strike (a ball) in the direction of one's follow-through so that it travels to the left (or, with a left-handed player, to the right). **6** [intrans.] Football (of a lineman) withdraw from position and cross parallel to and behind the line of scrimmage to block opposing players for a runner. ▶ **n. 1** an act of taking hold of something and exerting force to draw it toward one. ■ a handle to hold while performing such an action. ■ a deep draft of a drink. ■ an act of sucking at a cigar or pipe. ■ an injury to a muscle or ligament caused by abnormal strain. ■ a printer's proof. **2** [in sing.] a force drawing someone or something in a particular direction. ■ a powerful influence or compulsion. ■ something exerting an influence or attraction. ■ the condition of being able to exercise influence.

– PHRASES **like pulling teeth** informal used to convey that something is extremely difficult to do. **pull a face** (or **faces**) see FACE. **pull a fast one** see FAST[1]. **pull someone's leg** deceive someone playfully; tease someone. **pull out all the stops** see STOP. **pull the plug 1** informal prevent something from happening or continuing. **2** informal remove (a patient) from life support. **pull (one's) punches** [usu. with negative] be less forceful, severe, or violent than one could be. **pull rank** see RANK[1]. **pull one's socks up** see SOCK. **pull strings** make use of one's influence and contacts to gain an advantage unofficially or unfairly. **pull the strings** be in control of events or of other people's actions. **pull together** cooperate in a task or undertaking. **pull oneself together** recover control of one's emotions. **pull one's weight** do one's fair share of work. **pull wires** another way of saying *PULL STRINGS* above. **pull the wool over someone's eyes** see WOOL.

– PHRASAL VERBS **pull back** (or **pull someone/something back**) retreat or cause troops to retreat from an area. ■ **(pull back)** withdraw from an undertaking. **pull something down 1** demolish a building. **2** informal earn a sum of money. **pull in 1** (of a vehicle or its driver) move to the side of or off the road. **2** (of a bus or train) arrive to take passengers. **pull someone/something in 1** succeed in securing or obtaining something. ■ informal earn a sum of money. **2** informal arrest someone. **3** use reins to check a horse. **pull something off** informal succeed in achieving or winning something difficult. **pull out 1** withdraw from an undertaking. ■ retreat or cause to retreat from an area. **2** (of a bus or train) leave with its passengers. **3** (of a vehicle or its driver) move out from the side of the road, or from its normal position in order to pass. **pull over** (of a vehicle or its driver) move to the side of or off the road. **pull someone over** cause a driver to move to the side of the road to be charged for a traffic offense. **pull through** (or **pull someone/something through**) get through or enable someone or something to get through an illness or other difficult situation. **pull up 1** (of a vehicle or its driver) come to a halt. **2** increase the altitude of an aircraft. **pull someone up** cause someone to stop or pause; check someone. ■ reprimand someone. — **pull·er n.** [OE *pullian* 'pluck, snatch.']

pull·back /ˈpo͝olˌbak/ ▶ **n. 1** an act of withdrawing troops. **2** a reduction in price or demand.

pull-down ▶ **adj.** [attrib.] designed to be worked or made operable by being pulled down. ■ Comput. (of a menu) appearing below a menu title only while selected. Compare with DROP-DOWN. ▶ **n.** Comput. a pull-down menu.

pul·let /ˈpo͝olət/ ▶ **n.** a young hen, esp. one less than one year old. [ME: from OFr. *poulet*, dimin. of *poule*, from the fem. of L. *pullus* 'chicken, young animal.']

pul·ley /ˈpo͝olē/ ▶ **n.** (pl. **-leys**) (also **pulley wheel**) a wheel with a grooved rim around which a cord passes. It acts to change the direction of a force applied to the cord and is chiefly used to raise heavy weights. ■ (on a bicycle) a wheel with a toothed rim around which the chain passes. ■ a wheel or drum fixed on a shaft and turned by a belt, used esp. to increase speed or power. ▶ **v.** (**-leys, -leyed**) [trans.] hoist with a pulley. [ME: from OFr. *polie*, prob. from a med. Gk. dimin. of *polos* 'pivot, axis.']

pulley

pul·ley block ▶ **n.** a block or casing in which one or more pulleys are mounted.

pull hit·ter ▶ **n.** Baseball a hitter who normally drives the ball in the direction of the follow-through of the bat.

Pull·man[1] /ˈpo͝olmən/, George Mortimer (1831–97), US industrialist. He founded his own company in 1867 for converting railroad coaches into sleeping cars and also designed the first railroad dining car.

Pull·man[2] ▶ **n.** (pl. **-mans**) [usu. as adj.] a railroad car affording special comfort, esp. one with sleeping berths. ■ a train consisting of such cars. ■ **(pullman)** a large suitcase designed to fit under the seat in a Pullman car. [19th C.: named after George M. *Pullman*.]

pull-off ▶ **n.** an area on the side of a road where a motorist may park, typically in a scenic area.

pull-on ▶ **adj.** [attrib.] (of a garment) designed to be put on without the need to undo any fastenings. ▶ **n.** a garment of this type.

pull·out /ˈpo͝olˌout/ (also **pull-out**) ▶ **n. 1** a section of a magazine or newspaper designed to be detached and kept for rereading. **2** a withdrawal, esp. from military involvement or participation in a commercial venture. ▶ **adj.** [attrib.] designed to be pulled out of the usual position: *pull-out wire baskets at the bottom of one cupboard.* ■ (of a section of a magazine, newspaper, or other publication) designed to be detached and kept.

pull·o·ver /ˈpo͝olˌōvər/ ▶ **n.** a garment, esp. a sweater or jacket, put on over the head and covering the top half of the body. ▶ **adj.** (of a sweater, jacket, or shirt) designed to be put on by pulling over the head.

pull-quote ▶ **n.** a brief, attention-catching quotation, typically in a distinctive typeface, taken from the main text of an article and used as a subheading.

pull tab ▶ **n. 1** a ring or tab that is pulled to open a can. **2** a gambling card with a tab that can be pulled back to reveal a row or rows of symbols, with prizes for matching symbols.

pul·lu·late /ˈpəlyəˌlāt/ ▶ **v.** [intrans.] [often as adj.] **(pullulating)** breed or spread so as to become extremely common. ■ be very crowded; be full of life and activity. — **pul·lu·la·tion** /ˌpəlyəˈlāsHən/ **n.** [17th C.: from L. *pullulat-* 'sprouted,' from the verb *pullulare*, from *pullulus*, dimin. of *pullus* 'young animal.']

pull-up ▶ **n. 1** an exercise involving raising oneself with one's arms by pulling up against a horizontal bar fixed above one's head. **2** an act of pulling up; a sudden stop.

pul·mo·nar·y /ˈpo͝olməˌnerē; ˈpəl-/ ▶ **adj.** [attrib.] of or relating to the lungs: *pulmonary blood flow.* [17th C.: from L. *pulmonarius*, from *pulmo*, *pulmon-* 'lung.']

pul·mo·nar·y ar·ter·y ▶ **n.** the artery carrying blood from the right ventricle of the heart to the lungs for oxygenation.

pul·mo·nar·y tu·ber·cu·lo·sis ▶ **n.** see TUBERCULOSIS.

pul·mo·nar·y vein ▶ **n.** a vein carrying oxygenated blood from the lungs to the left atrium of the heart.

Pul·mo·na·ta /ˌpo͝olməˈnätə; pəl-; -ˈnātə/ Zool. a group of mollusks (subclass Pulmonata) that includes the land snails and slugs and many freshwater snails. They have a modified mantle cavity that acts as a lung for breathing air. — **pul·mo·nate** /ˈpo͝olməˌnāt; ˈpəl-/ **n. & adj.** [mod. L. (pl.), from L. *pulmo, pulmon-* 'lung.']

pul·mon·ic /po͝olˈmänik; pəl-/ ▶ **adj.** another term for PULMONARY.

pulp /pəlp/ ▶ **n.** a soft, wet, shapeless mass of material. ■ the soft fleshy part of a fruit. ■ a soft wet mass of fibers derived from rags or wood, used in papermaking. ■ vascular tissue filling the interior cavity and root canals of a tooth. ■ Mining pulverized ore mixed with water. ■ [usu. as adj.] fig. popular or sensational writing that is generally regarded as being of poor quality: *the story is a mix of pulp fiction and Greek tragedy.* ▶ **v.** [trans.] crush into a soft, shapeless mass. ■ withdraw (a publication) from the market and recycle the paper. — **pulp·er n. pulp·i·ness n. pulp·y adj.** [ME: from L. *pulpa*.]

pulp cav·i·ty ▶ **n.** the space in the interior of a tooth that contains the pulp.

pul·pit /ˈpo͝olpit; ˈpəl-/ ▶ **n.** a raised platform or lectern in a church or chapel from which the preacher delivers a sermon. ■ **(the pulpit)** religious teaching as expressed in sermons; preachers collectively. ■ a raised platform in the bow of a fishing boat or whaler. ■ a guard rail enclosing a small area at the bow of a yacht. [ME: from L. *pulpitum* 'scaffold, platform,' in med. L. 'pulpit.']

pulp·wood /ˈpəlpˌwo͝od/ ▶ **n.** timber suitable for making into pulp.

pul·que /ˈpo͝olˌkā; -kē/ ▶ **n.** a Mexican alcoholic drink made by fermenting sap from the maguey. [via Amer. Sp. from Nahuatl *puliúhki* 'decomposed.']

pul·sar /ˈpəlˌsär/ ▶ **n.** Astron. a celestial object, thought to be a rapidly rotating neutron star, that emits regular pulses of radio waves at rates of up to one thousand pulses per second. [from *puls(ating st)ar*, on the pattern of *quasar*.]

PRONUNCIATION KEY ə *ago, up*; ər *over, fur*; a *hat*; ā *ate*; ä *car*; e *let*; ē *see*; i *fit*; ī *by*; NG *sing*; ō *go*; ô *law, for*; oi *toy*; o͝o *good*; o͞o *goo*; ou *out*; TH *thin*; T͟H *then*; ZH *vision*

pul·sate /ˈpəlˌsāt/ ▶ v. [intrans.] expand and contract with strong regular movements. ■ [often as adj.] (**pulsating**) produce a regular throbbing sensation or sound. ■ [usu. as adj.] (**pulsating**) be very exciting. — **pul·sa·tion** /ˌpəlˈsāsHən/ n. **pul·sa·tor** /-ˌsātər/ n. **pul·sa·to·ry** /-səˌtôrē/ adj. [18th C.: from L. *pulsat-* 'throbbed, pulsed,' from the verb *pulsare*, frequentative of *pellere* 'to drive, beat.']

pul·sa·tile /ˈpəlsətl; -səˌtīl/ ▶ adj. esp. Physiol. pulsating; relating to pulsation: *pulsatile tinnitus*.

pul·sa·til·la /ˌpəlsəˈtilə/ ▶ n. a plant of the buttercup family belonging to the genus *Pulsatilla*, which includes the pasqueflower. [mod. L., dimin. of *pulsatus* 'battered.']

pulse[1] /pəls/ ▶ n. a rhythmical throbbing of the arteries as blood is propelled through them. ■ the rate of this throbbing, used to ascertain the rate of someone's heartbeat and so their state of health or emotions. ■ (usu. **pulses**) each successive throb of the arteries or heart. ■ a single vibration or short burst of sound, electric current, light, or other wave: *radio pulses*. ■ a musical beat or other regular rhythm. ■ fig. the central point of energy and organization in an area or activity: *those close to the financial pulse maintain that there have been fundamental changes*. ■ Biochem. a measured amount of an isotopic label given to a culture of cells. ▶ v. [intrans.] throb rhythmically; pulsate. ■ [trans.] transmit in rhythmical beats: *the sun pulsed fire into her eyes*. ■ [trans.] modulate (a wave or beam) so that it becomes a series of pulses. ■ [trans.] apply a pulsed signal to (a device). — **puls·er** n. [ME: from L. *pulsus* 'beating,' from *pellere* 'to drive, beat.']

pulse[2] ▶ n. (usu. **pulses**) the edible seeds of various leguminous plants, for example chickpeas, lentils, and beans. ■ the plant or plants producing such seeds. [ME: from OFr. *pols*, from L. *puls* 'porridge of meal or pulse'; rel. to POLLEN.]

pulse di·al·ing ▶ n. a method of telephone dialing in which each digit is transmitted as a corresponding number of electronic pulses.

pulse jet ▶ n. a type of jet engine in which combustion is intermittent, with the ignition and expulsion of each charge of mixture causing the intake of a fresh charge.

pulse mod·u·la·tion ▶ n. Electron. a type of modulation in which pulses are varied in some respect, such as width or amplitude, to represent the amplitude of a signal.

pul·trude /po͝olˈtro͞od; pəl-/ ▶ v. [trans.] [usu. as adj.] (**pultruded**) make (a reinforced plastic article) by drawing resin-coated glass fibers through a heated die. — **pul·tru·sion** /-ˈtro͞ozHən/ n. [1960s: from *pul(ling)* + EXTRUDE.]

pul·ver·ize /ˈpəlvəˌrīz/ ▶ v. [trans.] reduce to fine particles. ■ informal defeat utterly. — **pul·ver·iz·a·ble** adj. **pul·ver·i·za·tion** /ˌpəlvərəˈzāsHən/ n. **pul·ver·iz·er** n. [ME: from late L. *pulverizare*, from *pulvis*, *pulver-* 'dust.']

pul·ver·u·lent /ˌpəlˈver(y)ələnt/ ▶ adj. archaic consisting of fine particles; powdery or crumbly. [17th C.: from L. *pulverulentus*, from *pulvis*, *pulver-* 'dust.']

pul·vi·nus /pəlˈvīnəs; -ˈvēnəs/ ▶ n. (pl. **-ni** /-ˌnī; -nē/) Bot. an enlarged section at the base of a leaf stalk in some plants that is subject to changes of turgor, leading to movements of the leaf or leaflet. [19th C.: from L., lit. 'cushion.']

pu·ma /ˈp(y)o͞omə/ ▶ n. another term for COUGAR. [18th C.: via Sp. from Quechua.]

pum·ice /ˈpəməs/ ▶ n. a very light and porous volcanic rock formed when a gas-rich froth of glassy lava solidifies rapidly. ■ (also **pumice stone**) a piece of such rock used as an abrasive, esp. for removing hard skin. ▶ v. [trans.] rub with pumice to smooth or clean. — **pu·mi·ceous** /pyo͞oˈmisHəs; ˌpəmˈisH-/ adj. [ME: from OFr. *pomis*, from a L. dial. var. of *pumex*, *pumic-*.]

pum·mel /ˈpəməl/ ▶ v. (**-meled**, **-mel·ing** ; Brit. **-melled**, **-mel·ling**) [trans.] strike repeatedly, typically with the fists. ■ informal criticize adversely. [16th C.: var. of POMMEL.]

pum·me·lo ▶ n. var. of POMELO.

pump[1] /pəmp/ ▶ n. a mechanical device using suction or pressure to raise or move liquids, compress gases, or force air into inflatable objects such as tires. ■ [in sing.] an instance of moving something or being moved by or as if by such a machine. ■ [with adj.] Physiol. an active transport mechanism in living cells by which specific ions are moved through the cell membrane against a concentration gradient. ■ a pump-action shotgun. ▶ v. **1** [trans.] force (liquid, gas, etc.) to move in a specified direction by or as if by means of a pump: *the blood is pumped around the body* | [intrans.] *if we pump long enough, we should bring the level up*. ■ [intrans.] move in spurts as though driven by a pump. ■ fill with something: *my veins had been pumped full of glucose*. ■ shoot (bullets) into a target. ■ (**pump something in/into**) informal invest a large amount of money in (something). ■ informal try to elicit information from (someone) by persistent questioning. **2** [trans.] move (something) vigorously up and down. ■ [intrans.] move vigorously up and down or back and forth: *that's superb running—look at his legs pumping*. ■ apply and release (a brake pedal or lever) several times in quick succession, typically to prevent skidding. ■ [intrans.] move one's arm as if throwing a ball held in the hand, but without releasing the ball.
– PHRASES **pump someone's hand** shake a person's hand vigorously. **pump iron** informal exercise with weights.
– PHRASAL VERBS **pump something up** inflate a tire, balloon, etc. ■ informal increase something. ■ give inappropriate support and encouragement to. [ME: rel. to Du. *pomp* 'ship's pump.']

pump[2] ▶ n. a light shoe, in particular: ■ a woman's plain, lightweight shoe that has a low-cut upper, no fastening, and typically a medium heel. ■ a man's slip-on patent leather shoe for formal wear. [16th C.: of unknown origin.]

pump-ac·tion ▶ adj. [attrib.] **1** denoting a repeating firearm, typically a shotgun, in which a new round is brought from the magazine into the breech by a slide action in line with the barrel. **2** denoting an unpressurized spray dispenser for a liquid such as deodorant or cooking oil that is worked by finger action rather than by internal pressure (as in an aerosol).

pumped /pəmpt/ (also **pumped up**) ▶ adj. informal (of a person) stimulated or filled with excitement.

pump·er /ˈpəmpər/ ▶ n. a fire engine that carries a hose and pumps water.

pum·per·nick·el /ˈpəmpərˌnikəl/ ▶ n. dark, dense German bread made from coarsely ground whole-grain rye. [18th C.: from Ger. *Pumpernickel* 'lout, bumpkin.']

pump gun ▶ n. a pump-action rifle with a tubular magazine.

pump jock·ey ▶ n. informal a service station attendant.

pump·kin /ˈpəm(p)kin; ˈpəNGkin/ ▶ n. **1** a large rounded orange-yellow fruit with a thick rind, edible flesh, and many seeds. ■ the flesh of this fruit, esp. used as food. ■ informal used as an affectionate term of address, esp. to a child. **2** the plant (genus *Cucurbita*) of the gourd family that produces this fruit, having tendrils and large lobed leaves and native to warm regions of America. ■ Brit. another term for SQUASH[2]. [17th C.: alt. of earlier *pumpion*, from obs. Fr. *pompon*, via L. from Gk. *pepōn* 'large melon' (see PEPO).]

pump·kin·seed /ˈpəm(p)kinˌsēd; ˈpəNGkin-/ ▶ n. (pl. same or **-seeds**) a small, edible, brightly colored fish (*Lepomis gibbosus*) of the freshwater sunfish family, native to North America and popular as an aquarium fish.

pump-prim·ing ▶ n. **1** the introduction of fluid into a pump to prepare it for working. **2** the stimulation of economic activity by investment. — **pump-prim·er** n.

pun /pən/ ▶ n. a joke exploiting the different possible meanings of a word or the fact that there are words that sound alike but have different meanings: *the pigs were a squeal (if you'll forgive the pun)*. ▶ v. (**punned**, **pun·ning**) [intrans.] make a joke exploiting the different possible meanings of a word. — **pun·ning·ly** adv. **pun·ster** /ˈpənstər/ n. [17th C.: perh. an abbrev. of obs. *pundigrion*, as a fanciful alt. of PUNCTILIO.]

pu·na /ˈpo͞onə/ ▶ n. **1** a high treeless plateau in the Peruvian Andes. **2** another term for ALTITUDE SICKNESS. [via Amer. Sp. from Quechua.]

punch[1] /pənCH/ ▶ v. [trans.] **1** strike with the fist. ■ drive with a blow from the fist: *he punched the ball into his own goal*. **2** press (a button or key on a machine). ■ (**punch something in/into**) enter information by this action. **3** drive (cattle) by prodding them with a stick. ▶ n. a blow with the fist. ■ informal the strength needed to deliver such a blow: *he has the punch to knock out anyone in his division*. ■ [in sing.] informal the power to impress or startle: *photos give their arguments an extra visual punch*.
– PHRASES **beat someone to the punch** informal anticipate or forestall someone's actions. **punch the (time) clock** (of an employee) punch in or out. ■ be employed in a conventional job with regular hours. **punch someone's lights out** beat someone up; knock someone unconscious. **punch something up 1** use a computer keyboard to call something to the screen. **2** informal enliven: *he needed to punch up his presentation*.
– PHRASAL VERBS **punch in** (or **out**) register one's arrival at (or departure from) work, esp. by means of a time clock. — **punch·er** n. [ME (as a v. in the sense 'puncture, prod'): var. of POUNCE[1].]

punch[2] ▶ n. **1** a device or machine for making holes in materials such as paper, leather, metal, and plaster. **2** a tool or machine for impressing a design or stamping a die on a material. ▶ v. [trans.] pierce a hole in (metal, paper, leather, etc.) with or as if with a punch. ■ pierce (a hole) with or as if with a punch. [16th C.: perh. an abbrev. of PUNCHEON[1], or from the verb PUNCH[1].]

punch[3] ▶ n. a drink made with fruit juices, soda, spices, and sometimes liquor, typically served in small cups from a large bowl. [17th C.: appar. from Sanskrit *pañca* 'five, five kinds of.']

punch[4] ▶ n. (**Punch**) a grotesque, hook-nosed, humpbacked buffoon, the chief male character of the Punch and Judy show. Also called PUNCHINELLO.
– PHRASES **pleased as Punch** feeling great delight or pride. [17th C.: abbrev. of PUNCHINELLO.]

Punch and Ju·dy /ˈpənCH and ˈjo͞odē/ a puppet show in which Punch nags, beats, and often kills a series of characters—baby, wife (Judy), priest, doctor, policeman, hangman.

punch·ball /ˈpənCHˌbôl/ ▶ n. a team ball game in which a rubber ball is punched or headed.

punch·board /ˈpənCHˌbôrd/ ▶ n. a board with holes containing slips of paper that are punched out as a form of gambling, with the object of locating a winning slip.

punch bowl ▶ n. a bowl used for mixing and serving punch.

punch-drunk ▶ adj. stupefied by or as if by a series of heavy blows.

punched card (also **punch card**) ▶ n. a card perforated according to a code, for controlling the operation of a machine, used in voting machines and formerly in programming computers.

punched tape ▶ n. a paper tape perforated according to a code, formerly used for conveying instructions or data to a data processor.

pun·cheon[1] /ˈpənCHən/ ▶ **n.** **1** a short post, esp. one used for supporting the roof in a coal mine. ■ a rough board or other length of wood, used for flooring or building. **2** another term for PUNCH[2]. [ME: from OFr. *poinchon*, prob. based on L. *punct-* 'punctured,' from the v. *pungere*.]

pun·cheon[2] ▶ **n.** hist. a large cask for liquids or other commodities holding from 72 to 120 gallons. [ME: from OFr. *poinchon*.]

Pun·chi·nel·lo /ˌpənCHəˈnelō/ ▶ **n.** (pl. **-los**) another name for PUNCH[4]. [17th C.: alt. of Neapolitan dial. *Polecenella*, perh. a dimin. of *pollecena* 'young turkey cock with a hooked beak,' from *pulcino* 'chicken,' from L. *pullus*.]

punch·ing bag ▶ **n.** a stuffed or inflated bag, typically cylindrical or pear-shaped, suspended so it can be punched for exercise or training, esp. by boxers. ■ a person on whom another person vents their anger.

punch line ▶ **n.** the final phrase or sentence of a joke, providing the humor or some other crucial element.

punch press ▶ **n.** a press that is designed to drive a punch for shaping metal.

punch·y /ˈpənCHē/ ▶ **adj.** (**punch·i·er**, **punch·i·est**) **1** having an immediate impact; forceful. **2** another term for PUNCH-DRUNK. — **punch·i·ly** /ˈpənCHəlē/ **adv.** **punch·i·ness** **n.**

punc·ta /ˈpəNGktə/ plural form of PUNCTUM.

punc·tate /ˈpəNGkˌtāt/ ▶ **adj.** Biol. studded with or denoting dots or tiny holes. — **punc·ta·tion** /ˌpəNGkˈtāSHən/ **n.** [18th C.: from L. *punctum* 'point' + -ATE[2].]

punc·til·i·o /ˌpəNGkˈtilēˌō/ ▶ **n.** (pl. **-os**) a fine or petty point of conduct or procedure. [16th C.: from Ital. *puntiglio(n-)* and Sp. *puntillo*, dimin. of *punto* 'a point.']

punc·til·i·ous /ˌpəNGkˈtilēəs/ ▶ **adj.** showing great attention to detail or correct behavior. — **punc·til·i·ous·ly** **adv.** **punc·til·i·ous·ness** **n.**

punc·tu·al /ˈpəNGkCHo͞oəl/ ▶ **adj.** happening or doing something at the agreed or proper time; on time. ■ Gram. denoting or relating to an action that takes place at a particular point in time. Contrasted with DURATIVE. — **punc·tu·al·i·ty** /ˌpəNGkCHo͞oˈalitē/ **n.** **punc·tu·al·ly** **adv.** [17th C.: from med. L. *punctualis*, from L. *punctum* 'a point.']

punc·tu·ate /ˈpəNGkCHo͞oˌāt/ ▶ **v.** [trans.] **1** (often **be punctuated**) occur at intervals throughout (a continuing event or a place): *the country's history has been punctuated by coups.* ■ (**punctuate something with**) interrupt or intersperse (an activity) with: *she punctuates her conversation with snatches of song.* **2** insert punctuation marks in (text). **3** accentuate; emphasize. [17th C. (in the sense 'point out'): from med. L. *punctuat-* 'brought to a point,' from the verb *punctuare*, from *punctum* 'a point.']

punc·tu·at·ed e·qui·lib·ri·um ▶ **n.** Biol. the hypothesis that evolutionary development is marked by isolated episodes of rapid speciation between long periods of little or no change.

punc·tu·a·tion /ˌpəNGkCHo͞oˈāSHən/ ▶ **n.** **1** the marks, such as period, comma, and parentheses, used in writing to separate sentences and their elements and to clarify meaning. **2** Biol. rapid or sudden speciation, as suggested by the theory of punctuated equilibrium. — **punc·tu·a·tion·al** /-SHənl/ **adj.**

punc·tu·a·tion·ist /ˌpəNGkCHo͞oˈāSHənist/ ▶ **n.** Biol. a person who believes in or advocates the hypothesis of punctuated equilibrium. — **punc·tu·a·tion·al·ism** /-ˈāSHənlˌizəm/ **n.** **punc·tu·a·tion·al·ist** /-ˈāSHənl-ist/ **adj.** **punc·tu·a·tion·ism** /-ˈāSHəˌnizəm/ **n.**

punc·tum /ˈpəNGktəm/ ▶ **n.** (pl. **-ta** /-tə/) tech. a small, distinct point. ■ Anat. the opening of a tear duct. [16th C.: from L., lit. 'a point.']

punc·ture /ˈpəNGkCHər/ ▶ **n.** a small hole in a tire resulting in an escape of air. ■ a small hole in something such as the skin, caused by a sharp object. ▶ **v.** [trans.] make such a hole in (something). ■ [intrans.] sustain such a small hole: *the tire had punctured.* ■ fig. bring about a dramatic reversal in (mood or behavior) resembling a sudden deflation or collapse: *the earlier mood of optimism was punctured.* [ME: from L. *punctura*, from *punct-* 'pricked,' from the verb *pungere*.]

pun·dit /ˈpəndit/ ▶ **n.** **1** an expert in a particular subject or field who is frequently called on to give opinions about it to the public: *a globe-trotting financial pundit.* **2** var. of PANDIT. — **pun·dit·ry** /-ditrē/ **n.** (in sense 1). [from Sanskrit *paṇḍita* 'learned.']

Pu·ne var. of POONA.

pun·gent /ˈpənjənt/ ▶ **adj.** having a sharply strong taste or smell. ■ (of comment, criticism, or humor) having a sharp and caustic quality. — **pun·gen·cy** /ˈpənjənsē/ **n.** **pun·gent·ly** **adv.** [16th C.: from L. *pungent-* 'pricking,' from the verb *pungere*.]

Pu·nic /ˈpyo͞onik/ ▶ **adj.** of or relating to Carthage. ▶ **n.** the language of ancient Carthage, related to Phoenician. [from L. *Punicus* (earlier *Poenicus*), from *Poenus*, from Gk. *Phoinix* 'Phoenician.']

Pu·nic Wars three wars between ancient Rome and Carthage that led to the unquestioned dominance of Rome in the western Mediterranean.

pun·ish /ˈpəniSH/ ▶ **v.** [trans.] inflict a penalty or sanction on (someone) as retribution for an offense, esp. a transgression of a legal or moral code. ■ inflict a penalty or sanction on someone for (such an offense): *fraud is punished by up to two years in prison.* ■ treat (someone) in an unfairly harsh way: *a rise in prescription charges would punish the poor.* ■ [usu. as adj.] (**punishing**) subject (someone or something) to severe and debilitating treatment. — **pun·ish·a·ble** **adj.** **pun·ish·er** **n.** **pun·ish·ing·ly** **adv.** [ME: from OFr. *puniss-*, lengthened stem of *punir* 'punish,' from L. *punire*, from *poena* 'penalty.']

pun·ish·ment /ˈpəniSHmənt/ ▶ **n.** the infliction or imposition of a penalty as retribution for an offense. ■ the penalty inflicted. ■ informal rough treatment or handling inflicted on or suffered by a person or thing.

pu·ni·tive /ˈpyo͞onətiv/ ▶ **adj.** inflicting or intended as punishment. ■ (of a tax or other charge) extremely high. — **pu·ni·tive·ly** **adv.** **pu·ni·tive·ness** **n.** [17th C.: from Fr. *punitif, -ive* or med. L. *punitivus*, from L. *punit-* 'punished,' from the verb *punire* (see PUNISH).]

pu·ni·tive damages ▶ **plural n.** Law damages exceeding simple compensation and awarded to punish the defendant.

Pun·jab /ˈpənˌjäb; pənˈjäb/ (also **the Punjab**) a region in northwestern India and Pakistan. ■ a province of Pakistan; capital, Lahore. ■ a state of India; capital, Chandigarh.

Pun·ja·bi /ˌpənˈjäbē; po͞on-/ (also **Pan·ja·bi** /ˌpən-/) ▶ **n.** (pl. **-bis**) **1** a native or inhabitant of Punjab. **2** the Indic language of Punjab. ▶ **adj.** of or relating to Punjab or its people or language. [from Hindi *pa-jābī*.]

pun·ji stick /ˈpənjē/ (also **punji stake**) ▶ **n.** a sharpened bamboo stake, typically one tipped with poison, set in a camouflaged hole in the ground as a means of defense, esp. in Southeast Asia. [19th C.: *punji* prob. of Tibeto-Burman origin.]

punk /pəNGk/ ▶ **n.** **1** informal a worthless person (often used as a general term of abuse). ■ a criminal or hoodlum. ■ derog. (in prison slang) a passive male homosexual. ■ an inexperienced young person; a novice. **2** (also **punk rock**) a loud, fast-moving, and aggressive form of rock music, popular in the late 1970s and early 1980s. ■ (also **punk rock·er**) an admirer or player of such music, typically characterized by colored spiked hair and clothing decorated with safety pins or zippers. **3** soft, crumbly wood that has been attacked by fungus, widely used as tinder. ▶ **adj.** **1** informal in poor or bad condition: *I felt too punk to eat.* **2** of or relating to punk rock and its associated subculture. — **punk·ish** **adj.** **punk·y** **adj.** [17th C. (sense 3): perh., in some senses, rel. to archaic *punk* 'prostitute,' also to SPUNK.]

pun·kah /ˈpəNGkə/ ▶ **n.** esp. hist. (in India) a large cloth fan on a frame suspended from the ceiling, moved backward and forward by pulling on a cord. [via Hindi from Sanskrit *pakṣaka*, from *pakṣa* 'wing.']

punk·er /ˈpəNGkər/ ▶ **n.** a punk rocker.

punk·ette /ˌpəNGˈket/ ▶ **n.** a female punk rocker.

punt[1] /pənt/ ▶ **n.** a long, narrow, flat-bottomed boat, square at both ends and propelled with a long pole, used on inland waters chiefly for recreation. ▶ **v.** [intrans.] travel in such a boat. ■ [trans.] convey in such a boat. [OE, from L. *ponto*, denoting a flat-bottomed ferryboat.]

punt[2] ▶ **v.** **1** [trans.] Football & Rugby kick (the ball) after it is dropped from the hands and before it reaches the ground. ■ [intrans.] (of an offensive team) turn possession over to the defensive team by punting the ball after failing to make a first down: *the Raiders had to punt.* ■ (of a player) act as the punter. **2** [intrans.] delay in answering or taking action; equivocate: *he would continue to punt on questions of Medicare.* ▶ **n.** a kick of this kind. [19th C.: prob. from dial. *punt* 'push forcibly.']

punt[3] ▶ **v.** [intrans.] (in some gambling card games) place a bet against the bank. [18th C.: from Fr. *ponte* 'player against the bank,' from Sp. *punto* 'a point.']

punt[4] ▶ **n.** the basic monetary unit of the Republic of Ireland (until replaced by the euro), equal to 100 Irish pence. [Irish, lit. 'pound.']

punt·er /ˈpəntər/ ▶ **n.** **1** Football & Rugby a player who punts. **2** a person who propels or travels in a punt.

pun·ty /ˈpəntē/ (also **pon·til** /ˈpäntil/) ▶ **n.** (pl. **-ties**) (in glassmaking) an iron rod used to hold or shape soft glass. [17th C.: from Fr. *pontil* (see PONTIL).]

pu·ny /ˈpyo͞onē/ ▶ **adj.** (**-ni·er**, **-ni·est**) small and weak. ■ poor in quality, amount, or size. — **pu·ni·ly** /ˈpyo͞onl-ē/ **adv.** **pu·ni·ness** **n.** [16th C.: phonetic spelling of PUISNE.]

pup /pəp/ ▶ **n.** a young dog. ■ a young wolf, seal, rat, or other mammal. ▶ **v.** (**pupped**, **pup·ping**) [intrans.] (of female dogs and certain other animals) give birth to young. [16th C.: back-form. from PUPPY, interpreted as a dimin.]

pu·pa /ˈpyo͞opə/ ▶ **n.** (pl. **-pae** /-ˌpē; -ˌpī/) an insect in its inactive immature form between larva and adult, e.g., a chrysalis. — **pu·pal** **adj.** [18th C.: mod. L., from L. *pupa* 'girl, doll.']

pu·pate /ˈpyo͞oˌpāt/ ▶ **v.** [intrans.] (of a larva) become a pupa. — **pu·pa·tion** /pyo͞oˈpāSHən/ **n.**

pup·fish /ˈpəpˌfiSH/ ▶ **n.** (pl. same or **-fish·es**) a small fish (genus *Cyprinodon*, family Cyprinodontidae) found in fresh or brackish water in the deserts of the southwestern US and northern Mexico.

pu·pil[1] /ˈpyo͞opəl/ ▶ **n.** a student in school. [ME (in the sense 'orphan, ward'): from OFr. *pupille*, from L. *pupillus* (diminutive of *pupus* 'boy') and *pupilla* (dimin. of *pupa* 'girl').]

pu·pil[2] ▶ **n.** the dark circular opening in the center of the iris of the eye, varying in size to regulate the amount of light reaching the retina. — **pu·pil·lar·y** /ˈpyo͞opəˌlerē/ (also **pu·pil·ar·y**) **adj.** [ME: from OFr. *pupille* or L. *pupilla*, dimin. of *pupa* 'doll.']

pu·pil·age /ˈpyo͞opəlij/ (also **pu·pil·lage**) ▶ **n.** the state of being a pupil or student.

pu·pip·a·rous /pyo͞oˈpipərəs/ ▶ **adj.** Entomol. (of certain flies, e.g., the tsetse) producing young that are already ready to pupate. [19th C.:

from mod. L. *pupipara* (neut. pl. of *pupiparus* 'bringing forth young') + -OUS.]

pup·pet /ˈpəpət/ ▶ **n.** a movable model of a person or animal used in entertainment and typically moved either by strings from above or by a hand inside it. ■ fig. a person, party, or state under the control of another person, group, or power. — **pup·pet·ry** /-trē/ **n.** [16th C. (denoting a doll): later form of POPPET.]

pup·pet·eer /ˌpəpəˈti(ə)r/ ▶ **n.** a person who works puppets. — **pup·pet·eer·ing n.**

Pup·pis /ˈpəpis/ Astron. a southern constellation (the Poop or Stern), lying partly in the Milky Way south of Canis Major and originally part of Argo. [L.]

pup·py /ˈpəpē/ ▶ **n.** (pl. **-pies**) a young dog. ■ informal, dated a conceited or arrogant young man. — **pup·py·hood** /-ˌho͝od/ **n. pup·py·ish adj.** [15th C.: perh. from OFr. *poupee* 'doll, plaything.']

pup·py dog ▶ **n.** a child's word for a puppy. ■ fig. a gentle or devotedly loyal person.

pup·py love ▶ **n.** an intense but relatively shallow romantic attachment, typically associated with adolescents.

pup tent ▶ **n.** a small triangular tent, esp. one with a pole at either end and room for one or two people.

pur- ▶ **prefix** equivalent to PRO-[1] (as in *purloin, pursue*). [from Anglo-Norman Fr., from L. *por-, pro-*.]

Pu·ra·na /po͝oˈränə/ ▶ **n.** (usu. **Puranas**) any of a class of Sanskrit sacred writings containing Hindu legends and folklore of varying date and origin, the most ancient of which dates from the 4th century AD. — **Pu·ra·nic** /-ˈränik/ **adj.** [from Sanskrit *purāṇ* 'ancient (legend),' from *purā* 'formerly.']

pur·blind /ˈpərˌblīnd/ ▶ **adj.** having impaired or defective vision. ■ fig. slow or unable to understand; dim-witted. — **pur·blind·ness n.** [ME: from the adv. PURE.]

pur·chase /ˈpərCHəs/ ▶ **v.** [trans.] **1** acquire (something) by paying for it; buy. ■ archaic obtain or achieve with effort or suffering: *the victory was purchased by the death of Rhiwallon.* **2** Naut. haul in (a rope or cable) or haul up (an anchor) by means of a pulley, lever, etc. ▶ **n. 1** the action of buying something. ■ a thing that has been bought. ■ Law the acquisition of property by means other than inheritance. **2** a hold or position on something for applying power advantageously, or the advantage gained by such application. ■ a block and tackle. — **pur·chas·a·ble adj. pur·chas·er n.** [ME: from OFr. *pourchacier* 'seek to obtain or bring about.']

pur·dah /ˈpərdə/ ▶ **n.** the practice among women in certain Muslim and Hindu societies of living in a separate room or behind a curtain, or of dressing in all-enveloping clothes, to stay out of the sight of men or strangers. ■ the state of living in such a place or dressing in this way. ■ fig. isolation or hiding. ■ a curtain used for screening off women in this way. [19th C.: from Urdu and Pers. *parda* 'veil, curtain.']

pure /pyo͝or/ ▶ **adj.** not mixed or adulterated with any other substance or material. ■ without any extraneous and unnecessary elements: *pure art devoid of social responsibility.* ■ free of any contamination: *the pure, clear waters of Montana.* ■ wholesome and untainted by immorality, esp. that of a sexual nature. ■ (of a sound) perfectly in tune and with a clear tone. ■ (of an animal or plant) of unmixed origin or descent. ■ (of a subject of study) dealing with abstract concepts and not practical application. Compare with APPLIED. ■ Phonet. (of a vowel) not joined with another to form a diphthong. ■ [attrib.] involving or containing nothing else but; sheer (used for emphasis): *a shout of pure anger.* — **pure·ness n.** [ME: from OFr. *pur* 'pure,' from L. *purus*.]

pure·bred /ˈpyo͝orˌbred/ ▶ **adj.** (of an animal) bred from parents of the same breed or variety. ▶ **n.** an animal of this kind.

pu·rée /pyo͝oˈrā; -ˈrē/ ▶ **n.** a smooth, creamy substance made of liquidized or crushed fruit or vegetables. ▶ **v.** (**pu·rées, pu·réed, pu·rée·ing**) [trans.] make a purée of (fruit or vegetables). [18th C.: Fr., lit. 'purified,' fem. past part. of *purer*.]

pure line ▶ **n.** Biol. an inbred line of genetic descent.

pure·ly /ˈpyo͝orlē/ ▶ **adv.** in a pure manner. ■ entirely; exclusively.

pure math·e·mat·ics plural n. see MATHEMATICS.

pure sci·ence ▶ **n.** a science depending on deductions from demonstrated truths, such as mathematics or logic, without regard to practical applications.

pur·fle /ˈpərfəl/ ▶ **n.** an ornamental border, typically one inlaid on the back or belly of a violin. ■ archaic an ornamental or embroidered edge of a garment. ▶ **v.** [trans.] [often as n.] (**purfling**) decorate (something) with an ornamental border. [ME (as a verb): from OFr. *porfil* (n.), *porfiler* (v.), based on L. *pro* 'forward' + *filum* 'thread.']

pur·ga·tion /ˌpərˈgāSHən/ ▶ **n.** the purification or cleansing of someone or something. ■ (in Roman Catholic doctrine) the spiritual cleansing of a soul in purgatory. ■ hist. the action of clearing oneself of accusation or suspicion by an oath or ordeal. ■ evacuation of the bowels brought about by laxatives. [ME: from OFr. *purgacion*, from L. *purgatio(n-)*, from *purgare* 'purify' (see PURGE).]

pur·ga·tive /ˈpərgətiv/ ▶ **adj.** strongly laxative in effect. ■ fig. having the effect of ridding someone of unwanted feelings or memories. ▶ **n.** a laxative. ■ fig. a thing that rids someone of unwanted feelings or memories.

pur·ga·to·ry /ˈpərgəˌtôrē/ ▶ **n.** (pl. **-ries**) (in Roman Catholic doctrine) a place or state of suffering inhabited by the souls of sinners who are expiating their sins before going to heaven. ■ mental anguish or suffering. ▶ **adj.** archaic having the quality of cleansing or purifying. — **pur·ga·to·ri·al** /ˌpərgəˈtôrēəl/ **adj.** [ME: from Anglo-Norman Fr. *purgatorie* or med. L. *purgatorium*, neut. (used as a n.) of late L. *purgatorius* 'purifying,' from the verb *purgare* (see PURGE).]

purge /pərj/ ▶ **v.** [trans.] rid (someone) of an unwanted feeling, memory, or condition, typically giving a sense of cathartic release. ■ remove (an unwanted feeling, memory, or condition) in such a way. ■ remove (a group of people considered undesirable) from an organization or place, typically in an abrupt or violent manner: *he purged all of the committee members.* ■ remove someone from (an organization or place) in such a way. ■ Law atone for or wipe out (contempt of court). ■ physically remove (something) completely. ■ [intrans.] [often as n.] (**purging**) evacuate one's bowels, esp. as a result of taking a laxative. ▶ **n.** an abrupt or violent removal of a group of people from an organization or place: *the Stalinist purges.* ■ dated a laxative. — **purg·er n.** [ME: from OFr. *purgier*, from L. *purgare* 'purify,' from *purus* 'pure.']

pu·ri /ˈpo͝orē/ (also **poo·ri**) ▶ **n.** (pl. **pu·ris**) (in Indian cooking) a small, round, flat piece of bread made of unleavened wheat flour, deep-fried and served with meat or vegetables. [via Hindi from Sanskrit *pūrikā*.]

pu·ri·fy /ˈpyo͝orəˌfī/ ▶ **v.** (**-fies, -fied**) [trans.] remove contaminants from. ■ make ceremonially clean: *a ritual bath to purify the soul.* ■ rid (something) of an unwanted element. ■ (**purify something from**) extract something from: *genomic DNA was purified from whole blood.* — **pu·ri·fi·ca·tion** /ˌpyo͝orəfiˈkāSHən/ **n. pu·rif·i·ca·to·ry** /pyo͝oˈrifikəˌtôrē/ **adj. pu·ri·fi·er n.** [ME: from OFr. *purifier*, from L. *purificare*, from *purus* 'pure.']

Pu·rim /ˈpo͝orim; po͝oˈrēm/ ▶ **n.** a lesser Jewish festival held in spring (on the 14th or 15th day of Adar) to commemorate the defeat of Haman's plot to massacre the Jews as recorded in the book of Esther. [Heb., pl. of *pūr*, explained in the book of Esther (3:7, 9:24) as meaning 'lot.']

pu·rine /ˈpyo͝orˌēn/ ▶ **n.** Chem. a colorless crystalline compound, $C_5H_4N_4$, with basic properties, forming uric acid on oxidation. ■ (also **purine base**) a substituted derivative of this, esp. the bases adenine and guanine present in DNA and RNA. [19th C.: from Ger. *Purin*, from L. *purus* 'pure' + *uricum* 'uric acid' + -INE[4].]

pur·ism /ˈpyo͝orˌizəm/ ▶ **n.** scrupulous or exaggerated observance of or insistence on traditional rules or structures, esp. in language or style. — **pur·ist n. pu·ris·tic** /pyo͝oˈristik/ **adj.**

Pu·ri·tan /ˈpyo͝oritn/ ▶ **n.** a member of a group of English Protestants of the late 16th and 17th centuries who regarded the Reformation of the Church of England under Elizabeth I as incomplete and sought to simplify and regulate forms of worship. ■ (**puritan**) a person with censorious moral beliefs, esp. about pleasure and sex. ▶ **adj.** of or relating to the Puritans. ■ (**puritan**) having or displaying censorious moral beliefs, esp. about pleasure and sex. — **Pu·ri·tan·ism** /-ˌizəm/ (also **pu·ri·tan·ism**) **n.** [16th C.: from late L. *puritas* 'purity' + -AN.]

pu·ri·tan·i·cal /ˌpyo͝oriˈtanikəl/ ▶ **adj.** often derog. practicing or affecting strict religious or moral behavior. — **pu·ri·tan·i·cal·ly** /-ik(ə)lē/ **adv.**

pu·ri·ty /ˈpyo͝oritē/ ▶ **n.** freedom from adulteration or contamination. ■ freedom from immorality, esp. of a sexual nature. [ME: from OFr. *purete*, later assimilated to late L. *puritas*, from L. *purus* 'pure.']

Pur·kin·je cell /pərˈkinjē/ ▶ **n.** Anat. a nerve cell of a large, branched type found in the cortex of the cerebellum. [19th C.: named after Jan E. *Purkinje* (1787–1869), Bohemian physiologist.]

purl[1] /pərl/ ▶ **adj.** [attrib.] denoting or relating to a knitting stitch made by putting the needle through the front of the stitch from right to left. Compare with KNIT. ▶ **n.** a purl stitch. ▶ **v.** [trans.] knit with a purl stitch: *knit one, purl one.* [17th C. (as a n.): of uncert. origin.]

purl[2] ▶ **v.** [intrans.] (of a stream or river) flow with a swirling motion and babbling sound. ▶ **n.** [in sing.] a motion or sound of this kind. [16th C.: prob. imitative.]

pur·lieu /ˈpərl(y)o͞o/ ▶ **n.** (pl. **-lieus** or **-lieux** /-l(y)o͞o(z)/) the area near or surrounding a place. ■ fig. a person's usual haunts. ■ Brit., hist. a tract on the border of a forest, esp. one earlier included in it and still partly subject to forest laws. [15th C.: prob. an alt. (suggested by Fr. *lieu* 'place') of Anglo-Norman Fr. *puralee* 'a going around to settle the boundaries.']

pur·lin /ˈpərlən/ ▶ **n.** a horizontal beam along the length of a roof, resting on a main rafter and supporting the common rafters or boards. [ME: perh. of Fr. origin.]

pur·loin /pərˈloin/ ▶ **v.** [trans.] steal (something). — **pur·loin·er n.** [ME: from Anglo-Norman Fr. *purloigner* 'put away,' from *pur-* 'forth' + *loign* 'far.']

pu·ro·my·cin /ˌpyo͝orəˈmīsin/ ▶ **n.** Med. an antibiotic produced by the bacterium *Streptomyces alboniger*, used to treat sleeping sickness and amebic dysentery. [1950s: from PURINE + -MYCIN.]

pur·ple /ˈpərpəl/ ▶ **n.** a color intermediate between red and blue. ■ purple clothing or material. ■ (also **Tyrian purple**) a crimson dye obtained from some mollusks, formerly used for fabric worn by an emperor or senior magistrate in ancient Rome or Byzantium. ■ (**the purple**) (in ancient Rome or Byzantium) clothing of this color. ■ (**the purple**) (in ancient Rome) a position of rank, authority, or privilege: *he was too young to assume the purple.* ■ (**the purple**) the scarlet official dress of a cardinal. ▶ **adj.** of a color intermediate between red and blue. ▶ **v.** become or make purple in color: [intrans.] *Ed's cheeks purpled* | [trans.] *the neon was purpling the horizon above the highway.*

– PHRASES **born in** (or **to**) **the purple** born into a reigning family or privileged class. — **pur·ple·ness n. pur·plish** /ˈpərp(ə)liSH/ **adj. pur·ply**

/ˈpərp(ə)lē/ **adj.** [OE, alt. of *purpre*, from L. *purpura* 'purple,' from Gk. *porphura*, denoting mollusks that yielded a crimson dye.]

pur·ple gal·li·nule ▶**n.** **1** another term for GALLINULE. **2** a marsh bird (*Porphyrio porphyrio*) of the rail family, with a purplish-blue head and breast and a large red bill, found throughout the Old World.

Pur·ple Heart ▶**n.** (in the US) a military decoration for those wounded or killed in action, established in 1782 and reestablished in 1932.

pur·ple mar·tin ▶**n.** a martin (*Progne subis*) with purplish-blue plumage. It is the largest North American swallow, and the male is the only swallow with uniform dark plumage on its belly.

pur·ple pas·sage ▶**n.** an elaborate or excessively ornate passage in a literary composition.

pur·ple prose ▶**n.** prose that is too elaborate or ornate.

pur·port ▶**v.** /pərˈpôrt/ [with infin.] appear or claim to be or do something, esp. falsely; profess. ▶**n.** /ˈpərˌpôrt/ the meaning or substance of something, typically a document or speech. ■ the purpose of a person or thing. —**pur·port·ed·ly** **adv.** [ME: from OFr. *purporter*, from med. L. *proportare*, from L. *pro-* 'forth' + *portare* 'carry, bear.']

pur·pose /ˈpərpəs/ ▶**n.** the reason for which something is done or created or for which something exists. ■ a person's sense of resolve or determination. ■ (usu. **purposes**) a particular requirement or consideration, typically one that is temporary or restricted in scope or extent: *pensions are considered as earned income for tax purposes.* ▶**v.** [trans.] formal have as one's intention or objective: *God has allowed suffering, even purposed it.*
– PHRASES **on purpose** intentionally. **to no purpose** with no result or effect; pointlessly. **to the purpose** relevant or useful. [ME: from OFr. *porpos*, from the verb *porposer*, var. of *proposer* (see PROPOSE).]

pur·pose·ful /ˈpərpəsfəl/ ▶**adj.** having or showing determination or resolve. ■ having a useful purpose. ■ intentional. —**pur·pose·ful·ly** **adv.** **pur·pose·ful·ness** **n.**

pur·pose·less /ˈpərpəslis/ ▶**adj.** done or made with no discernible point or purpose: *purposeless vandalism.* ■ having no aim or plan: *his purposeless life.* —**pur·pose·less·ly** **adv.** **pur·pose·less·ness** **n.**

pur·pose·ly /ˈpərpəslē/ ▶**adv.** on purpose; intentionally.

pur·pos·ive /ˈpərpəsiv; pərˈpō-/ ▶**adj.** having, serving, or done with a purpose. —**pur·pos·ive·ly** **adv.** **pur·pos·ive·ness** **n.**

pur·pu·ra /ˈpərp(y)ərə/ ▶**n.** Med. a rash of purple spots on the skin caused by internal bleeding from small blood vessels. ■ [with adj.] any of a number of diseases characterized by such a rash: *psychogenic purpura.* —**pur·pu·ric** /pərˈpyo͝orik/ **adj.** [18th C.: from L., from Gk. *porphura* 'purple.']

pur·pure /ˈpərpyər/ ▶**n.** purple, as a heraldic tincture. [OE, from L. *purpura* (see PURPURA).]

pur·pu·rin /ˈpərpyərin/ ▶**n.** Chem. a red dye originally extracted from madder and also prepared artificially by the oxidation of alizarin. [19th C.: from L. *purpura* 'purple' + -IN[1].]

purr /pər/ ▶**v.** [intrans.] (of a cat) make a low continuous vibratory sound usually expressing contentment. ■ (of a vehicle or machine) make such a sound when running smoothly at low speed. ■ (of a vehicle or engine) move smoothly while making such a sound. ■ speak in a low soft voice, esp. when expressing contentment or acting seductively: [with direct speech] *"Would you like coffee?" she purred* | [trans.] *she purred her lines seductively.* ▶**n.** a low continuous vibratory sound, typically that made by a cat or vehicle. [17th C.: imitative.]

purse /pərs/ ▶**n.** a small bag used esp. by a woman to carry everyday personal items. ■ a small pouch of leather or plastic used for carrying money, typically by a woman. ■ the money possessed or available to a person or country. ■ a sum of money given as a prize in a sporting contest, esp. a boxing match. ▶**v.** (with reference to the lips) pucker or contract, typically to express disapproval or irritation: [trans.] *Marianne pursed her lips disgustedly* | [intrans.] *under stress his lips would purse slightly.*
– PHRASES **hold the purse strings** have control of expenditure. **tighten** (or **loosen**) **the purse strings** restrict (or increase) the amount of money available to be spent. [OE, alt. of late L. *bursa* 'purse,' from Gk. *bursa* 'hide, leather.']

purs·er /ˈpərsər/ ▶**n.** an officer on a ship who keeps the accounts, esp. the head steward on a passenger vessel.

purse seine ▶**n.** [usu. as adj.] a fishing net or seine that can be drawn into the shape of a bag, used for catching shoal fish. —**purse sein·er** **n.**

purs·lane /ˈpərslən; -ˌslān/ ▶**n.** any of a number of small, typically fleshy-leaved plants (family Portulacaceae) that grow in damp habitats or waste places, in particular *Portulaca oleracea*, a prostrate North American plant with tiny yellow flowers. [ME: from OFr. *porcelaine*, prob. from L. *porcil(l)aca*, var. of *portulaca*.]

pur·su·ance /pərˈso͞oəns/ ▶**n.** formal the carrying out of a plan or action. ■ the action of trying to achieve something.

pur·su·ant /pərˈso͞oənt/ ▶**adv.** (**pursuant to**) formal in accordance with (a law or a legal document). ▶**adj.** archaic following; going in pursuit: *the pursuant lady.* —**pur·su·ant·ly** **adv.**

pur·sue /pərˈso͞o/ ▶**v.** (**-sues, -sued, -su·ing**) [trans.] **1** follow (someone or something) to catch or attack them. ■ seek to form a sexual relationship with (someone) in a persistent way. ■ seek to attain or accomplish (a goal), esp. over a long period. ■ archaic or literary (of something unpleasant) persistently afflict (someone): *mercy lasts as long as sin pursues man.* **2** (of a person or way) continue or proceed along (a path or route). ■ engage in (an activity or course of action). ■ continue to investigate, explore, or discuss (a topic, idea, or argument). —**pur·su·a·ble** **adj.** **pur·su·er** **n.** [ME: from Anglo-Norman Fr. *pursuer*, from an alt. of L. *prosequi* 'prosecute.']

pur·suit /pərˈso͞ot/ ▶**n.** **1** the action of following or pursuing someone or something. **2** [with adj.] (often **pursuits**) an activity of a specified kind, esp. a recreational or athletic one.
– PHRASES **give pursuit** (of a person, animal, or vehicle) start to chase another. [ME: from Anglo-Norman Fr. *purseute* 'following after,' from *pursuer* (see PURSUE).]

pur·sy /ˈpərsē/ ▶**adj.** archaic **1** (esp. of a horse) short of breath; asthmatic. **2** (of a person) fat. —**pur·si·ness** **n.** [ME: reduction of Anglo-Norman Fr. *porsif*, alt. of OFr. *polsif*, from *polser* 'breathe with difficulty,' from L. *pulsare* 'set in violent motion.']

pu·ru·lent /ˈpyo͝or(y)ələnt/ ▶**adj.** Med. consisting of, containing, or discharging pus. [ME: from L. *purulentus* 'festering,' from *pus, pur-* (see PUS).]

Pu·rus Riv·er /pəˈro͞os/ a river that flows from eastern Peru to join the Amazon River in northwestern Brazil.

pur·vey /pərˈvā/ ▶**v.** [trans.] provide or supply (food, drink, or other goods) as one's business. —**pur·vey·or** /-ˈvāər/ **n.** [ME: from Anglo-Norman Fr. *purveier*, from L. *providere* 'foresee, attend to' (see PROVIDE).]

pur·vey·ance /pərˈvāəns/ ▶**n.** the action of purveying something.

pur·view /ˈpərˌvyo͞o/ ▶**n.** [in sing.] the scope of the influence or concerns of something. ■ a range of experience or thought. [ME: from Anglo-Norman Fr. *purveu* 'foreseen,' past part. of *purveier* (see PURVEY).]

pus /pəs/ ▶**n.** a thick yellowish or greenish liquid produced in infected tissue, consisting of dead white blood cells and bacteria with tissue debris and serum. [ME: from L.]

Pu·san /ˈpo͞oˈsän/ a city on the southeastern coast of South Korea; pop. 3,798,000.

Pu·sey /ˈpyo͞ozē/, Edward Bouverie (1800–82), English theologian. In 1833, he founded the Oxford Movement.

push /po͝osн/ ▶**v.** **1** [trans.] exert force on (someone or something), typically with one's hand, in order to move them away from oneself or the origin of the force: *she pushed her glass toward him* | [intrans.] *he pushed at the skylight, but it wouldn't budge.* ■ hold and exert force on (something) so as to cause it to move in front of one: *pushing a stroller.* ■ move one's body or a part of it into a specified position, esp. forcefully or with effort: *she pushed her hands into her pockets.* ■ press (a part of a machine or other device): *he pushed the button for the tenth floor.* ■ fig. affect (something) so that it reaches a specified level or state: *the huge crop will push down prices.* **2** [intrans.] move forward by using force to pass people or cause them to move aside: *he pushed past an old woman in his haste.* ■ (of an army) advance over territory. ■ exert oneself to attain something or surpass others. ■ (**push for**) demand persistently. ■ [trans.] compel or urge (someone) to do something, esp. to work hard: *she believed he was pushing their daughter too hard.* ■ (**be pushed**) informal have very little of something, esp. time. ■ (**be pushing**) informal be nearly (a particular age): *she must be pushing forty.* **3** [trans.] informal promote the use, sale, or acceptance of. ■ put forward (an argument or demand) with undue force or in too extreme a form. ■ sell (a narcotic drug) illegally. **4** [trans.] Comput. prepare (a stack) to receive a piece of data on the top. ■ transfer (data) to the top of a stack. **5** [trans.] Photog. develop (film) so as to compensate for deliberate underexposure. ▶**n.** **1** an act of exerting force on someone or something to move them away from oneself. ■ an act of pressing a part of a machine or device. ■ fig. something that encourages or assists something else: *the fall in prices was given a push by official policy.* **2** a vigorous effort to do or obtain something: *a fund-raising push.* ■ a military attack in force: *a push against guerrilla strongholds.* ■ forcefulness and enterprise.
– PHRASES **get** (or **give someone**) **the push** (or **shove**) informal be dismissed (or dismiss someone) from a job. ■ be rejected in (or end) a relationship. **push the boat out** see BOAT. **push someone's buttons** see BUTTON. **pushing up daisies** see DAISY. **push one's luck** informal take a risk on the assumption that one will continue to be successful or in favor. **when push comes to shove** informal when one must commit oneself to an action or decision.
– PHRASAL VERBS **push ahead** proceed with a course of action or policy. **push someone around** informal treat someone roughly or inconsiderately. **push off** use an oar, boathook, etc., to exert pressure so as to move a boat out from a bank or away from another vessel. **push on** continue on a journey. **push something through** get a proposed measure completed or accepted quickly. [ME (as a v.): from OFr. *pousser*, from L. *pulsare* 'to push, beat, pulse' (see PULSE[1]).]

push·back /ˈpo͝osнˌbak/ ▶**n.** **1** a negative or unfavorable response: *there's been some strong pushback from Republicans on this.* **2** (at an airport) the action or an instance of moving an airplane from a passenger terminal to a runway or taxiway.

push broom ▶**n.** a broom with a handle attached at an angle to a wide brush worked by pushing.

push but·ton ▶**n.** a button that is pushed to operate an electrical device.

push·cart /ˈpo͝osнˌkärt/ ▶**n.** a small handcart or barrow.

push·er /ˈpo͝osнər/ ▶**n.** **1** informal a person who sells illegal drugs. **2** a person or thing that pushes something. ■ informal a forceful or pushy person.

push·ful /ˈpŏŏshfəl/ ▶ adj. arrogantly self-assertive; pushy. — **push·ful·ly** adv. **push·ful·ness** n.

Push·kin /ˈpŏŏshkin; -kyin/, Aleksandr Sergeevich (1799–1837), Russian poet, writer, and playwright. His works include *Boris Godunov* (1831).

push·o·ver /ˈpŏŏsh,ōvər/ ▶ n. informal a person who is easy to overcome or influence. ■ a thing easily done.

push·pin /ˈpŏŏsh,pin/ ▶ n. a thumbtack with a head of colored plastic, used to fasten papers to a bulletin board or to indicate positions on charts and maps.

push-pull ▶ adj. [attrib.] operated by pushing and pulling. ■ Electron. having or involving two matched tubes or transistors that operate 180 degrees out of phase, conducting alternately for increased output.

push·rod /ˈpŏŏsh,räd/ ▶ n. a rod operated by cams that opens and closes the valves in an internal combustion engine.

push-start ▶ v. [trans.] start (a motor vehicle) by pushing it in order to make the engine turn. ▶ n. an act of starting a motor vehicle in this way.

Push·tu /ˈpəshtōō/ ▶ n. variant of PASHTO.

push·up /ˈpŏŏsh,əp/ (also **push-up**) ▶ n. an exercise in which a person lies facing the floor and, keeping their back straight, raises their body by pressing down on their hands. ▶ adj. (**push-up**) denoting a padded or underwired bra or similar garment that gives uplift to the breasts.

push·y /ˈpŏŏshē/ ▶ adj. (**push·i·er, push·i·est**) excessively or unpleasantly self-assertive or ambitious. — **push·i·ly** /ˈpŏŏshəlē/ adv. **push·i·ness** n.

pu·sil·lan·i·mous /,pyōōsəˈlanəməs/ ▶ adj. showing a lack of courage or determination; timid. — **pu·sil·la·nim·i·ty** /-ləˈnimətē/ n. **pu·sil·lan·i·mous·ly** adv. [ME: from eccles. L. *pusillanimis*, from *pusillus* 'very small' + *animus* 'mind,' + -OUS.]

puss[1] /pŏŏs/ ▶ n. informal a cat (esp. as a form of address). ■ [usu. with adj.] a playful or coquettish girl or young woman. [16th C.: prob. from Mid. Low Ger. *pūs* (also *pūskatte*) or Du. *poes*, of unknown origin.]

puss[2] ▶ n. informal a person's face or mouth. [19th C.: from Irish *pus* 'lip, mouth.']

pus·sy /ˈpŏŏsē/ ▶ n. (pl. **-sies**) **1** (also **pus·sy·cat**) informal a cat. **2** vulgar slang a woman's genitals. ■ offens. women in general, considered sexually. ■ offens. sexual intercourse with a woman. ■ informal a weak, cowardly, or effeminate man.

pus·sy·foot /ˈpŏŏsē,fŏŏt/ ▶ v. [intrans.] act in a cautious or noncommittal way. ■ move stealthily or warily. — **pus·sy·foot·er** /-,fŏŏtər/ n.

pus·sy-whip ▶ v. [trans.] [usu. as adj.] (**pussy-whipped**) vulgar slang henpeck (a man).

pus·sy wil·low ▶ n. a willow with soft fluffy silvery or yellow catkins that appear before the leaves, esp. the North American *Salix discolor*. [19th C.: a child's word.]

pussy willow

pus·tu·late ▶ v. /ˈpəschə,lāt; ˈpəstyə-/ [intrans.] form into pustules. ▶ adj. esp. Biol. having or covered with pustules. — **pus·tu·la·tion** /,pəschəˈlāshən; ,pəstyə-/ n.

pus·tule /ˈpəschōōl; ˈpəst(y)ōōl/ ▶ n. Med. a small blister or pimple on the skin containing pus. ■ Biol. a small raised spot or rounded swelling, esp. one on a plant resulting from fungal infection. — **pus·tu·lar** /ˈpəschələr; ˈpəstyə-/ adj. [ME: from L. *pustula*.]

put /pŏŏt/ ▶ v. (**put·ting** ; past **put**) [trans.] **1** move to or place in a particular position: *Harry put down his cup.* ■ cause (someone or something) to go to a particular place and remain there for a time: *India has put three satellites into space.* ■ [intrans.] (of a ship or the people on it) proceed in a particular direction: *the boat put out to sea.* ■ write or print (something) in a particular place. ■ [intrans.] archaic (of a river) flow in a particular direction. **2** bring into a particular state or condition: *they put me at ease.* ■ (**put oneself in**) imagine oneself in (a particular situation): *put yourself in his place.* ■ express (a thought or comment) in a particular way, form, or language: *to put it bluntly, he was not divorced.* **3** (**put something on/on to**) cause (someone or something) to carry or be subject to something: *commentators put some of the blame on Congress.* ■ assign a particular value, figure, or limit to: *it is difficult to put a figure on the size of the budget.* ■ (**put something at**) estimate something to be (a particular amount). **4** throw (a shot or weight) as an athletic sport. ▶ n. **1** a throw of the shot or weight. **2** Stock Market short for PUT OPTION.

– PHRASES **put something behind one** get over a bad experience by distancing oneself from it. **put the clocks back** (or **forward**) adjust clocks or watches backward (or forward) to take account of official changes in time. **put someone's eyes out** blind someone, typically in a violent way. **put one's hands together** applaud; clap. **put one's hands up** raise one's hands in surrender. **put it there** [in imper.] informal used to indicate that the speaker wishes to shake hands with someone in agreement or congratulation. **put it to** [with clause] make a statement or allegation to (someone) and challenge them to deny it: *I put it to him that he was just a political groupie.* **put one over on** informal deceive (someone) into accepting something false. **put up or shut up** informal justify oneself or remain silent.

– PHRASAL VERBS **put about** Naut. (of a ship) turn on the opposite tack. **put something about** (often **be put about**) spread information or rumors. **put something across** (or **over**) communicate something effectively. **put something aside 1** save money for future use. **2** forget or disregard something, typically a feeling or a past difference. **put someone away** (often **be put away**) informal confine someone in a prison or psychiatric hospital. **put something away 1** save money for future use. **2** informal consume food or drink in large quantities. **3** another way of saying PUT SOMETHING DOWN (sense 3 below). **4** informal (in sports) dispatch or deal with a goal or shot. **put something back** reschedule a planned event to a later time or date. ■ delay something. **put something by** another way of saying PUT SOMETHING ASIDE (sense 1 above). **put someone down 1** informal lower someone's self-esteem by criticizing them in front of others. **2** lay a baby down to sleep. **put something down 1** record something in writing. **2** suppress a rebellion, riot, or other disturbance by force. **3** (usu. **be put down**) kill an animal because it is sick, injured, or old. **4** pay a specified sum as a deposit. **5** preserve or store food or wine for future use. **6** (also **put down**) land an aircraft. **put someone down as** consider or judge someone or something to be: *I'd have put you down as a Vivaldi man.* **put something down to** attribute something to: *if I forget anything, put it down to old age.* **put someone forward** recommend someone as a suitable candidate for a job or position. **put something forward** submit a plan, proposal, or theory for consideration. **put in** [with direct speech] interrupt a conversation or discussion: *"But you're a sybarite, Roger," put in Isobel.* **put in at/into** (of a ship) enter (a port or harbor). **put someone in** appoint someone to fulfill a particular role or job. ■ (in team sports) send a player out to participate in a game. **put something in/into 1** present or submit something formally: *put in a claim for damages.* ■ (**put in for**) apply formally for: *Adam put in for six months' leave.* **2** devote time or effort to something. **3** invest money or resources in. **put someone off 1** cancel or postpone an appointment with someone. **2** cause someone to lose interest or enthusiasm. ■ cause someone to feel dislike or distrust: *she had a coldness that just put me off.* **3** distract someone: *you're just trying to put me off my game.* **put something off** postpone something. **put someone on** informal deceive or hoax someone. **put something on 1** place a garment, glasses, or jewelry on part of one's body. ■ attach or apply something. **2** cause a device to operate. ■ start cooking something: *he hadn't put the dinner on.* ■ play recorded music or a video. **3** organize or present a play, exhibition, or event. ■ provide a public transportation service: *an extra flight had to be put on.* **4** add a specified amount to (the cost of something): *the news put 12 cents on the share price.* ■ increase in body weight; become heavier by a specified amount. **5** assume a particular expression, accent, etc.: *he put on a lugubrious look.* ■ behave deceptively: *she put on an act.* **6** bet a specified amount of money on: *he put $1,000 on the horse to win.* **put someone on to** draw someone's attention to (someone or something useful, notable, or interesting). **put out** vulgar slang be willing to have sexual intercourse. **put someone out 1** cause someone trouble or inconvenience: *would it put you out too much to let her visit you?* ■ (often **be put out**) upset or annoy someone: *he was not put out by the rebuff.* **2** (in sports) defeat a player or team and so cause them to be out of a competition. **3** make someone unconscious, typically by means of drugs or an anesthetic. **put something out 1** extinguish something that is burning. ■ turn off a light. **2** lay something out ready for use: *she put out glasses and napkins.* **3** issue or broadcast something. **4** dislocate a joint: *she put her shoulder out.* **5** (of a company) allocate work to a contractor or freelancer to be done off the premises. **6** (of an engine or motor) produce a particular amount of power: *the new motor puts out about 250 h.p.* **put something over 1** another way of saying PUT SOMETHING ACROSS above. **2** postpone something: *let's put the case over for a few weeks.* **put someone through 1** connect someone by telephone to another person or place. **2** subject someone to an unpleasant or demanding experience. **3** pay for someone to attend school or college. **put something through** initiate something and see it to a successful conclusion: *he put through a reform program.* **put someone to** cause inconvenience or difficulty to someone: *I don't want to put you to any trouble.* **put something to 1** submit something to (someone) for consideration or attention: *we are putting an offer to the shareholders.* **2** devote something to (a particular use or purpose). **put something together** make something by assembling different parts or people. ■ assemble things or people to make something. **put someone under** another way of saying PUT SOMEONE OUT (sense 3 above). **put up 1** offer or show (resistance, effort, or skill) in a fight or competitive situation: *he put up a brave fight.* **2** stay temporarily in lodgings other than one's own home. **put someone up 1** accommodate someone temporarily. **2** propose someone for election or adoption. **put something up 1** construct or erect something. **2** raise one's hand to signal that one wishes to answer or ask a question. **3** display a notice, sign, or poster. ■ present a proposal, theory, or argument for discussion or consideration. **4** provide money as backing for an enterprise. **5** (often **be put up for**) offer something for sale or auction. **put upon** [often as adj.] (**put-upon**) informal take advantage of (someone) by exploiting their good nature: *a put-upon drudge who slaved for her employer.* **put someone up to** informal encourage someone to do (something wrong or unwise): *Rose put him up to it.* **put up with** tolerate; endure. [OE, cf. dial. *pote* 'to push, thrust.']

pu·ta·men /pyōōˈtāmən/ ▶ n. (pl. **-tam·i·na** /-ˈtamənə/ or **-ta·mens**) Anat. the outer part of the lentiform nucleus of the brain. — **pu·tam·i·nal** /-ˈtamənl/ adj. [19th C.: from L., lit. 'shell remaining after pruning.']

pu·ta·tive /ˈpyōōtətiv/ ▶ adj. [attrib.] generally considered or reputed to be: *the putative father of a boy of two.* — **pu·ta·tive·ly** adv. [ME: from

OFr. *putatif, -ive* or late L. *putativus*, from L. *putat-* 'thought,' from the verb *putare*.]

put-down ▶ **n.** informal a remark intended to humiliate or criticize someone.

Pu·tin /ˈpo͞otn/, Vladimir (1952–); president of Russia 1999– .

put·log /ˈpo͝ot,lôg; -,läg/ (also **put·lock** /-,läk/) ▶ **n.** a short horizontal pole projecting from a wall, on which the floorboards of scaffolding rest. [17th C.: of unknown origin.]

put-off ▶ **n.** informal **1** an evasive reply. **2** an unpleasant or deterrent quality or feature.

put-on ▶ **n.** informal a deception; a hoax.

pu·tong·hua /ˈpo͞oˈto͝onGˈhwä/ ▶ **n.** the standard spoken form of modern Chinese, based on the dialect of Beijing. [Chin., lit. 'common spoken language.']

put op·tion ▶ **n.** Stock Market an option to sell assets at an agreed price on or before a particular date.

put·out /ˈpo͝ot,out/ ▶ **n.** Baseball an act of a fielder in retiring a batter or runner.

pu·tre·fac·tion /,pyo͞otrəˈfakSHən/ ▶ **n.** the process of decay or rotting in a body or other organic matter. [ME: from OFr., or from late L. *putrefactio(n-)*, from *putrefacere* 'make rotten' (see **PUTREFY**).]

pu·tre·fac·tive /,pyo͞otrəˈfaktiv/ ▶ **adj.** relating to or causing decay.

pu·tre·fy /ˈpyo͞otrə,fī/ ▶ **v.** (**-fies, -fied**) [intrans.] (of a body or other organic matter) decay or rot and produce a fetid smell. [ME: via Fr. from L. *putrefacere*, from *puter, putr-* 'rotten.']

pu·tres·cent /pyo͞oˈtresənt/ ▶ **adj.** undergoing the process of decay; rotting. — **pu·tres·cence n.** [18th C.: from L. *putrescent-* 'beginning to go rotten,' inceptive of *putrere* 'to rot' (see **PUTRID**).]

pu·tres·ci·ble /pyo͞oˈtresəbəl/ ▶ **adj.** liable to decay; subject to putrefaction. ▶ **n.** (usu. **putrescibles**) something liable to decay.

pu·trid /ˈpyo͞otrid/ ▶ **adj.** (of organic matter) decaying or rotting and emitting a fetid smell. ■ of or characteristic of rotting matter. ■ informal very unpleasant; repulsive. — **pu·trid·i·ty** /pyo͞oˈtridətē/ **n.** **pu·trid·ly adv.** **pu·trid·ness n.** [ME: from L. *putridus*, from *putrere* 'to rot,' from *puter, putr-* 'rotten.']

putsch /po͝oCH/ ▶ **n.** a violent attempt to overthrow a government. [1920s: from Swiss Ger., lit. 'thrust, blow.']

putt /pət/ ▶ **v.** (**put·ted, put·ting**) [intrans.] try to hit a golf ball into a hole by striking it gently so that it rolls across the green: *Nicklaus putted for eagle on 11 of the 16 par 5s* | [trans.] *putt the balls into the hole.* ▶ **n.** a stroke of this kind made to hole the ball. [17th C. (orig. Scots): differentiated from **PUT**.]

put·tee /,pəˈtē/ ▶ **n.** a long strip of cloth wound spirally around the leg from ankle to knee for protection and support. ■ a leather legging. [19th C.: from Hindi *paṭṭī* 'band, bandage.']

put·ter¹ /ˈpətər/ ▶ **n.** **1** a golf club designed for use in putting, typically with a flat-faced malletlike head. **2** [with adj.] a golfer considered in terms of putting ability: *you'll need to be a good putter to break par.*

put·ter² ▶ **n.** & **v.** another term for **PUTT-PUTT**. [1940s: imitative.]

put·ter³ ▶ **v.** [intrans.] occupy oneself in a desultory but pleasant manner, doing a number of small tasks. ■ move or go in a casual, unhurried way: *the duck putters on the surface of the pond.* — **put·ter·er n.** [19th C. (orig. US).]

put·ting green /ˈpətiNG/ ▶ **n.** a smooth area of short grass surrounding a hole, either as part of a golf course or as a separate area for putting.

put·to /ˈpo͞otō/ ▶ **n.** (pl. **put·ti** /ˈpo͞otē/) a representation of a naked child, esp. a cherub or a cupid in Renaissance art. [Ital., lit. 'boy,' from L. *putus*.]

putt-putt (also **put-put**) ▶ **n.** the rapid intermittent sound of a small gasoline engine. ▶ **v.** [intrans.] make such a sound. ■ move under the power of an engine that makes such a sound: *the car putt-putted down the hill.* [20th C.: imitative.]

put·ty /ˈpətē/ ▶ **n.** **1** a soft paste, made from whiting and raw linseed oil, used chiefly for sealing glass panes in window frames. ■ [usu. with adj.] any of a number of similar substances used inside and outside buildings, e.g., **plumber's putty**. **2** a polishing powder, usually made from tin oxide, used in jewelry work. ▶ **v.** (**-ties, -tied**) [trans.] seal or cover (something) with putty.

– PHRASES **be (like) putty in someone's hands** be easily manipulated or dominated by someone. [17th C.: from Fr. *potée*, lit. 'potful,' from *pot* 'pot.']

Put·u·ma·yo Riv·er /,po͞otəˈmī-ō/ a river that flows from southwestern Colombia to join the Amazon River in northwestern Brazil.

put-up ▶ **adj.** [attrib.] arranged beforehand in order to deceive someone: *the whole thing could be a put-up job.*

putz /ˈpəts; ˈpo͝ots/ informal ▶ **n.** **1** a stupid or worthless person. **2** vulgar slang a penis. ▶ **v.** [intrans.] engage in inconsequential or unproductive activity: *too much putzing around.* [1960s: Yiddish, lit. 'penis.']

Pu·zo /ˈpo͞ozō/, Mario (1920–99), US writer. He wrote the novel *The Godfather* (1969).

puz·zle /ˈpəzəl/ ▶ **v.** [trans.] cause (someone) to feel confused because they cannot understand or make sense of something: *one remark he made puzzled me.* ■ [intrans.] think hard about something difficult to understand or explain: *she puzzled over this problem.* ■ (**puzzle something out**) solve or understand something by thinking hard. ▶ **n.** a game, toy, or problem designed to test ingenuity or knowledge. ■ short for **JIGSAW PUZZLE** (see **JIGSAW**). ■ [usu. in sing.] a person or thing difficult to understand or explain; an enigma. — **puz·zle·ment n.** **puz·zling·ly** /ˈpəz(ə)liNGlē/ **adv.** [16th C. (as a v.): of unknown origin.]

puz·zler /ˈpəz(ə)lər/ ▶ **n.** a difficult question or problem. ■ a person who solves puzzles as a pastime. ■ informal a computer game in which the player must solve puzzles.

PV ▶ **abbr.** polyvinyl.

PVA ▶ **abbr.** polyvinyl acetate.

PVC ▶ **abbr.** polyvinyl chloride.

Pvt. (also **PVT**) ▶ **abbr.** ■ (in the US Army) private. ■ (in company names) private.

p.w. ▶ **abbr.** per week.

PWA ▶ **abbr.** person with AIDS.

PWC ▶ **abbr.** personal watercraft.

PWR ▶ **abbr.** pressurized-water reactor.

pwr. ▶ **abbr.** power.

PX ▶ **abbr.** ■ post exchange.

pya /pēˈä/ ▶ **n.** a monetary unit of Myanmar (Burma), equal to one hundredth of a kyat.

py·ae·mi·a ▶ **n.** British spelling of **PYEMIA**.

pyc·no·cline /ˈpiknə,klīn/ ▶ **n.** Geog. a layer in an ocean or other body of water in which water density increases rapidly with depth. [1950s: from Gk. *puknos* 'thick' + **CLINE**.]

pye-dog /ˈpī,dôg/ ▶ **n.** a stray mongrel, esp. in Asia. [19th C.: from Anglo-Ind. *pye*, Hindi *pāhī* 'outsider' + **DOG**.]

py·e·li·tis /,pīəˈlītis/ ▶ **n.** Med. inflammation of the renal pelvis. [19th C.: from Gk. *puelos* 'trough, basin' + **-ITIS**.]

py·e·log·ra·phy /,pīəˈlägrəfē/ ▶ **n.** Med. an X-ray technique for producing an image of the renal pelvis and urinary tract by the introduction of a radiopaque fluid. Also called **UROGRAPHY**. — **py·e·lo·gram** /ˈpīəlō,gram; pīˈelə-/ **n.**

py·e·lo·ne·phri·tis /,pīə,lōniˈfrītis/ ▶ **n.** Med. inflammation of the substance of the kidney as a result of bacterial infection. — **py·e·lo·ne·phrit·ic** /-ˈfritik/ **adj.**

py·e·mi·a /pīˈēmēə/ (Brit. **py·ae·mi·a**) ▶ **n.** blood poisoning caused by the spread in the bloodstream of pus-forming bacteria released from an abscess. — **py·e·mic** /pīˈēmik/ **adj.** [19th C.: mod. L., from Gk. *puon* 'pus' + *haima* 'blood.']

py·gid·i·um /pīˈjidēəm/ ▶ **n.** (pl. **-gid·i·a** /-ˈjidēə/) Zool. the terminal part or hind segment of the body in certain invertebrates. [19th C.: mod. L., from Gk. *pugē* 'rump.']

Pyg·ma·li·on /pigˈmālyən; -lēən/ Gk. Mythol. a king of Cyprus who fashioned an ivory statue of a beautiful woman and loved it so deeply that in answer to his prayer Aphrodite gave it life.

Pyg·my /ˈpigmē/ (also **Pig·my**) ▶ **n.** (pl. **-mies**) a member of certain peoples of very short stature in equatorial Africa and parts of Southeast Asia. ■ (**pygmy**) esp. derog. a very small person, animal, or thing. ■ (**pygmy**) [usu. with adj.] an insignificant person, esp. one deficient in one respect. ▶ **adj.** [attrib.] of, relating to, or denoting the Pygmies. ■ (**pygmy**) (of a person or thing) very small. ■ (**pygmy**) used in names of animals and plants that are much smaller than more typical kinds, e.g., **pygmy hippopotamus, pygmy water lily**. [ME: via L. from Gk. *pugmaios* 'dwarf,' from *pugmē* 'the length measured from elbow to knuckles.']

pyg·my chim·pan·zee ▶ **n.** another term for **BONOBO**.

pyg·my owl ▶ **n.** a very small owl (genus *Glaucidium*, family Strigidae) found in America and northern Eurasia.

pyg·my pos·sum ▶ **n.** a very small Australasian marsupial (family Burramyidae) that feeds on insects and nectar, with handlike feet and a prehensile tail.

pyg·my shrew ▶ **n.** a shrew (genus *Sorex*) that is one of the smallest known mammals.

py·jam·as /pəˈjäməz; -jaməz/ ▶ **plural n.** British spelling of **PAJAMAS**.

pyk·nic /ˈpiknik/ ▶ **adj.** Anthropol. of, relating to, or denoting a stocky physique with a rounded body and head, thickset trunk, and a tendency to be fat. [1920s: from Gk. *puknos* 'thick' + **-IC**.]

Pyle /pīl/, Ernie (1900–1945), US journalist; full name *Ernest Taylor Pyle*. A syndicated war correspondent, he was noted for his firsthand reports from the perspectives of World War II soldiers.

py·lon /ˈpī,län; -lən/ ▶ **n.** an upright structure that is used for support or navigation, in particular: ■ (also **electricity pylon**) a tall towerlike structure used for carrying power lines high above the ground. ■ a pillarlike structure on the wing of an aircraft used for carrying an engine, weapon, fuel tank, or other load. ■ a tower or post marking a path for light aircraft, cars, or other vehicles, esp. in racing. ■ a monumental gateway to an ancient Egyptian temple formed by two truncated pyramidal towers. [19th C.: from Gk. *pulōn*, from *pulē* 'gate.']

py·lo·rus /pīˈlôrəs; pə-/ ▶ **n.** (pl. **-lo·ri** /-ˈlôr,ī; -ˈlôrē/) Anat. the opening from the stomach into the duodenum (small intestine). — **py·lor·ic** /pīˈlôrik; pə-/ **adj.** [17th C.: via late L. from Gk. *pulouros* 'gatekeeper,' from *pulē* 'gate' + *ouros* 'warder.']

Pyn·chon /ˈpinCHən/, Thomas Ruggles (1937–), US writer. His novels include *Vineland* (1990) and *Against the Day* (2006).

py·o·der·ma /,pīəˈdərmə/ ▶ **n.** Med. a skin infection with formation of pus. [1930s: from Gk. *puo-* (from *puon* 'pus') + *derma* 'skin.']

py·o·gen·ic /,pīə'jenik/ ▶ **adj.** Med. involving or relating to the production of pus.

Pyong·yang /'pyäNG'yäNG; -'yaNG; 'pyäNG-/ the capital of North Korea, in the western part of the country; pop. 2,000,000.

py·or·rhe·a /,pīə'rēə/ (also **pyorrhea alveolaris**, Brit. **py·or·rhoe·a**) ▶ **n.** another term for PERIODONTITIS. [19th C.: from Gk. *puo-* (from *puon* 'pus') + *rhoia* 'flux' (from *rhein* 'to flow').]

py·ra·can·tha /,pīrə'kanTHə/ ▶ **n.** a thorny evergreen Eurasian shrub (genus *Pyracantha*) of the rose family, with white flowers and bright red or yellow berries that is a popular ornamental. [mod. L., via L. from Gk. *purakantha*, a plant, from *pur* 'fire' + *akantha* 'thorn.']

pyr·a·lid /'pīrə,lid/ ▶ **n.** Entomol. an insect of a family (Pyralidae) of small delicate moths with narrow forewings. [19th C.: from mod. L. *Pyralidae* (pl.), based on Gk. *puralis*, denoting a mythical fly said to live in fire.]

pyr·a·mid /'pirə,mid/ ▶ **n. 1** a monumental structure with a square or triangular base and sloping sides that meet in a point at the top, esp. one built of stone as a royal tomb in ancient Egypt. **2** a thing, shape, or graph with such a form. ■ Geom. a polyhedron of which one face is a polygon of any number of sides, and the other faces are triangles with a common vertex. ■ a pile of things with such a form. ■ Anat. a structure of more or less pyramidal form, esp. in the brain or the renal medulla. ■ an organization or system structured with fewer people or things at each level as one approaches the top. ■ a system of financial growth achieved by a small initial investment, with subsequent investments being funded by using unrealized profits as collateral. ▶ **v.** [trans.] heap or stack in the shape of a pyramid. ■ achieve a substantial return on (money or property) after making a small initial investment. — **py·ram·i·dal** /pi'ramidl/ **adj.** **py·ram·i·dal·ly** **adv.** **pyr·a·mid·i·cal** /,pirə'midikəl/ **adj.** **pyr·a·mid·i·cal·ly** /,pirə'midik(ə)lē/ **adv.** [ME: via L. from Gk. *puramis, puramid-*.]

pyr·a·mid scheme ▶ **n.** a system of selling goods in which agency rights are sold to an increasing number of distributors at successively lower levels.

Pyr·a·mus /'pirəməs/ Rom. Mythol. a Babylonian youth, lover of Thisbe.

py·rar·gy·rite /pī'rärjə,rīt/ ▶ **n.** a dark red mineral consisting of a sulfide of silver and antimony. [19th C.: from Gk. *puro-* (from *pur* 'fire') + *arguros* 'silver' + -ITE[1].]

pyre /pī(ə)r/ ▶ **n.** a heap of combustible material, esp. one for burning a corpse as part of a funeral ceremony. [17th C.: via L. from Gk. *pura*, from *pur* 'fire.']

py·rene /'pī,rēn/ ▶ **n.** Chem. a crystalline aromatic hydrocarbon, $C_{16}H_{10}$, present in coal tar. [19th C.: from Gk. *pur* 'fire' + -ENE.]

Pyr·e·nees /'pirə,nēz/ a mountain range between France and Spain. — **Pyr·e·ne·an** /,pirə'nēən/ **adj.**

py·re·thrin /pī'rēTHrən; -'reTHrən/ ▶ **n.** Chem. any of a group of insecticidal compounds present in pyrethrum flowers. [1920s: from PYRETHRUM + -IN[1].]

py·re·throid /pī'rēTH,roid; pī'reTH-/ ▶ **n.** Chem. a pyrethrin or related insecticidal compound.

py·re·thrum /pī'rēTHrəm; -'reTHrəm/ ▶ **n.** an aromatic plant (genus *Tanacetum*, formerly *Chrysanthemum* or *Pyrethrum*) of the daisy family, typically having feathery foliage and brightly colored flowers. ■ an insecticide made from the dried flowers of these plants. [ME: from L., from Gk. *purethron* 'feverfew.']

py·ret·ic /pī'retik/ ▶ **adj.** rare fevered, feverish, or inducing fever. [18th C.: from mod. L. *pyreticus*, from Gk. *puretos* 'fever.']

Py·rex /'pī,reks/ ▶ **n.** [usu. as adj.] trademark a hard heat-resistant type of glass, typically used for ovenware. [20th C.: an invented word.]

py·rex·i·a /pī'reksēə/ ▶ **n.** Med. raised body temperature; fever. — **py·rex·i·al** **adj.** **py·rex·ic** /-sik/ **adj.** [18th C.: mod. L., from Gk. *purexis*, from *puressein* 'be feverish,' from *pur* 'fire.']

pyr·i·dine /'pirə,dēn/ ▶ **n.** Chem. a colorless volatile liquid, C_5H_5N, with an unpleasant odor, present in coal tar and used chiefly as a solvent. [19th C.: from Gk. *pur* 'fire' + -IDE + -INE[4].]

pyr·i·dox·al /,piri'däksəl/ ▶ **n.** Biochem. an oxidized derivative of pyridoxine that acts as a coenzyme in transamination and other processes. [1940s: from PYRIDOXINE + -AL.]

pyr·i·dox·ine /,piri'däk,sēn/ ▶ **n.** Biochem. a colorless weakly basic solid, $C_8H_{11}NO_3$, present chiefly in cereals, liver oils, and yeast, and important in the metabolism of unsaturated fatty acids. Also called VITAMIN B_6. [1930s: from *pyrid(ine)* + **ox-** 'oxygen' + -INE[4].]

pyr·i·form /'pirə,fôrm/ ▶ **adj.** Anat. & Biol. pear-shaped: *the pyriform fossa*. [18th C.: from mod. L. *pyriformis*, from *pyrum* (misspelling of *pirum* 'pear') + -IFORM.]

py·ri·meth·a·mine /,pirə'meTHə,mēn/ ▶ **n.** Med. a synthetic compound derived from pyrimidine, used to treat malaria.

py·rim·i·dine /pə'rimə,dēn; pī-/ ▶ **n.** Chem. a colorless crystalline compound, $C_4H_4N_2$, with basic properties. ■ (also **pyrimidine base**) a substituted derivative of this, esp. the bases thymine and cytosine present in DNA. [19th C.: from Ger. *Pyrimidin*, from PYRIDINE, with the insertion of *-im-* from IMIDE.]

py·rite /'pī,rīt/ (also **py·ri·tes** /pə'rītēz; pī-/) ▶ **n.** a shiny yellow mineral consisting of iron disulfide and typically occurring as intersecting cubic crystals. — **py·rit·ic** /pī'ritik; pə-/ **adj.** **py·rit·i·za·tion** /pə,rītə'zāSHən; pī-/ **n.** **py·ri·tize** /'pīrīt,īz/ **v.** **py·ri·tous** /pə'rītəs; pī-/ **adj.** [ME (denoting a mineral used for kindling fire): via L. from Gk. *puritēs* 'of fire,' from *pur* 'fire.']

py·ro /'pīrō/ ▶ **n.** (pl. **-ros**) informal a pyromaniac.

pyro. ▶ **abbr.** pyrotechnics.

pyro- ▶ **comb. form 1** of or relating to fire: *pyromania*. **2** Chem. & Mineral. denoting a compound or mineral that is formed or affected by heat or has a fiery color: *pyrophosphate* | *pyrope*. [from Gk. *pur* 'fire.']

py·ro·clas·tic /,pīrō'klastik/ Geol. ▶ **adj.** relating to, consisting of, or denoting fragments of rock erupted by a volcano. — **py·ro·clast** /'pīrō,klast/ **n.**

py·ro·clas·tic flow ▶ **n.** Geol. a dense, destructive mass of very hot ash, lava fragments, and gases ejected explosively from a volcano and typically flowing at great speed.

py·ro·e·lec·tric /,pīrō-i'lektrik/ ▶ **adj.** having the property of becoming electrically charged when heated. ■ of, relating to, or utilizing this property. — **py·ro·e·lec·tric·i·ty** /-i,lek'trisitē/ **n.**

py·ro·gal·lol /,pīrō'gal,ôl; -,ōl/ ▶ **n.** Chem. a weakly acid crystalline compound, $C_6H_3(OH)_3$, chiefly used as a developer in photography.

py·ro·gen /'pīrəjən/ ▶ **n.** Med. a substance, typically produced by a bacterium, that produces fever when introduced or released into the blood.

py·ro·gen·ic /,pīrō'jenik/ ▶ **adj.** Med. inducing fever. ■ caused or produced by combustion or heat. — **py·ro·ge·nic·i·ty** /,pīrōjə'nisitē/ **n.**

py·rog·ra·phy /pī'rägrəfē/ ▶ **n.** the art or technique of decorating wood or leather by burning a design on the surface with a heated metallic point.

py·ro·lu·site /,pīrō'lōō,sīt/ ▶ **n.** a black or dark gray mineral with a metallic luster, consisting of manganese dioxide. [19th C.: from PYRO- 'fire, heat' + Gk. *lousis* 'washing.']

py·rol·y·sis /pī'räləsəs/ ▶ **n.** Chem. decomposition brought about by high temperatures. — **py·ro·lyt·ic** /,pīrə'litik/ **adj.**

py·ro·ma·ni·a /,pīrō'mānēə/ ▶ **n.** an obsessive desire to set fire to things. — **py·ro·ma·ni·ac** /-'mānē,ak/ **n.** **py·ro·ma·ni·a·cal** /-mə'nīəkəl/ **adj.** **py·ro·man·ic** /-'manik/ **adj.**

py·ro·met·al·lur·gy /,pīrō'metl,ərjē/ ▶ **n.** the branch of science and technology concerned with the use of high temperatures to extract and purify metals. — **py·ro·met·al·lur·gi·cal** /-,metl'ərjikəl/ **adj.**

py·rom·e·ter /pī'rämitər/ ▶ **n.** an instrument for measuring high temperatures, esp. in furnaces and kilns. — **py·ro·met·ric** /,pīrō'metrik/ **adj.** **py·ro·met·ri·cal·ly** /,pīrō'metrik(ə)lē/ **adv.** **py·rom·e·try** /-trē/ **n.**

py·ro·mor·phite /,pīrə'môr,fīt/ ▶ **n.** a mineral consisting of a chloride and phosphate of lead, typically occurring as green, yellow, or brown crystals in the oxidized zones of lead deposits. [19th C.: from PYRO- 'fire, heat' + Gk. *morphē* 'form' + -ITE[1].]

py·rope /'pī,rōp/ (also **pyrope garnet**) ▶ **n.** a deep red variety of garnet. [19th C.: from Ger. *Pyrop*, via L. from Gk. *purōpos* 'gold-bronze,' lit. 'fiery-eyed,' from *pur* 'fire' + *ōps* 'eye.']

py·ro·phor·ic /,pīrə'fôrik/ ▶ **adj.** liable to ignite spontaneously on exposure to air. ■ (of an alloy) emitting sparks when scratched or struck. [19th C.: from mod. L. *pyrophorus*, from Gk. *purophoros* 'fire-bearing,' from *pur* 'fire' + *pherein* 'to bear.']

py·ro·phos·phor·ic ac·id /,pīrō,fäs'fôrik; -'fäsfərik/ ▶ **n.** Chem. a glassy solid, $H_4P_2O_7$, obtained by heating phosphoric acid. — **py·ro·phos·phate** /-'fäs,fāt/ **n.**

py·ro·sis /pī'rōsəs/ ▶ **n.** another term for HEARTBURN. [18th C.: mod. L., from Gk. *purōsis*, from *puroun* 'set on fire,' from *pur* 'fire.']

py·ro·tech·nic /,pīrə'teknik/ ▶ **adj.** of or relating to fireworks. ■ brilliant or sensational. — **py·ro·tech·ni·cal** **adj.** **py·ro·tech·nist** /-nist/ **n.** [19th C.: from PYRO- 'fire' + Gk. *tekhnē* 'art' + -IC.]

py·ro·tech·nics /,pīrə'tekniks/ ▶ **plural n.** a fireworks display. ■ [usu. with adj.] a brilliant performance or display. ■ [treated as sing.] the art of making or displaying fireworks.

py·ro·tech·ny /'pīrə,teknē/ ▶ **n.** hist. the use of fire in alchemy. ■ another term for PYROTECHNICS. [16th C.: from Fr. *pyrotechnie* or mod. L. *pyrotechnia*.]

py·rox·ene /pī'räk,sēn; pə-/ ▶ **n.** any of a large class of rock-forming silicate minerals, generally containing calcium, magnesium, and iron and typically occurring as prismatic crystals. [19th C.: from PYRO- 'fire' + Gk. *xenos* 'stranger.']

py·rox·e·nite /pī'räksə,nīt; pə-/ ▶ **n.** Geol. a dark, greenish, granular intrusive igneous rock consisting chiefly of pyroxenes and olivine.

py·rox·y·lin /pī'räksələn; pə-/ ▶ **n.** Chem. a form of nitrocellulose that is less highly nitrated and is soluble in ether and alcohol. [19th C.: from Fr. *pyroxyline*, from Gk. *pur* 'fire' + *xulon* 'wood.']

Pyr·rha /'pirə/ Gk. Mythol. the wife of Deucalion.

Pyr·rhic /'pirik/ (also **pyr·rhic**) ▶ **adj.** [attrib.] (of a victory) won at too great a cost to have been worthwhile for the victor. [19th C.: from the name PYRRHUS + -IC.]

pyr·rhic /'pirik/ ▶ **n.** a metrical foot of two short or unaccented syllables. ▶ **adj.** written in or based on such a measure. [17th C.: via L. from Gk. *purrhikhios (pous)* 'pyrrhic (foot).']

Pyr·rho /'pirō/ (*c.*365–*c.*270 BC), Greek philosopher. He is regarded as the founder of skepticism. — **Pyr·rho·nism** /'pirə,nizəm/ **n.** **Pyr·rho·nist** /'pirə,nist/ **n. & adj.**

pyr·rho·tite /'pirə,tīt/ ▶ **n.** a reddish-bronze mineral consisting of iron sulfide, typically forming massive or granular deposits. [19th C.: from Gk. *purrhotēs* 'redness' + -ITE[1].]

Pyr·rhus /'pirəs/ (*c.*318–272 BC), king of Epirus *c.*307–272. He defeated the Romans at Asculum in 279.

pyr·role /'pir,ōl/ ▶ **n.** Chem. a weakly basic sweet-smelling liquid compound, C_4H_4NH, present in coal tar. [19th C.: from Gk. *purrhos* 'reddish' + L. *oleum* 'oil.']

pyr·rol·i·dine /pə'rōlə,dēn/ ▶ **n.** Chem. a pungent liquid, C_4H_8NH, made by reduction of pyrrole.

pyr·rol·i·done /pə'rōlə,dōn/ ▶ **n.** Chem. a colorless weakly basic solid, C_4H_7NO, that is a keto derivative of pyrrolidine.

py·ru·vic ac·id /pī'ro͞ovik/ ▶ **n.** Biochem. a yellowish organic acid, $CH_3COCOOH$, that occurs as an intermediate in many metabolic processes, esp. glycolysis. — **pyr·u·vate** /-,vāt/ **n.** [19th C.: from mod. L. *acidum pyruvicum*, from *acidum* 'acid' + *pyruvicum* based on **PYRO-** (denoting an acid) + L. *uva* 'grape.']

Py·thag·o·ras /pi'THagərəs/ *c.*580–500 BC, Greek philosopher; known as **Pythagoras of Samos**. Pythagoras sought to interpret the entire physical world in terms of numbers. He is best known for the theorem of the right-angled triangle. — **Py·thag·o·re·an** /pi,THagə'rēən; pī-/ **adj. & n.**

Py·thag·o·re·an the·o·rem /pə,THagə'rēən; pī-/ a theorem attributed to Pythagoras that the square of the hypotenuse of a right triangle is equal to the sum of the squares of the other two sides.

Pyth·i·a /'piTHēə/ the priestess of Apollo at Delphi in ancient Greece. See **DELPHI**. — **Pyth·i·an adj.**

Pyth·i·as /'piTHēəs/ see **DAMON**.

py·thon /'pī,THän; 'pīTHən/ ▶ **n.** a large heavy-bodied nonvenomous snake (genera *Python*, *Morelia*, and *Aspidites*, family Pythonidae) occurring throughout the Old World tropics, killing prey by constriction and asphyxiation. — **py·thon·ic** /pī'THänik/ **adj.** [16th C.: via L. from Gk. *Puthōn*, a serpent.]

Py·thon·esque /,pīTHə'nesk/ ▶ **adj.** after the style of or resembling the humor of *Monty Python's Flying Circus*, a British television comedy series (1969–74).

py·tho·ness /'pīTHənəs; 'piTH-/ ▶ **n.** archaic a female soothsayer or conjuror of spirits. [ME: from OFr. *phitonise*, from an alt. of late L. *pythonissa*, based on Gk. *puthōn* 'soothsaying demon.']

py·u·ri·a /pī'yo͝orēə/ ▶ **n.** Med. the presence of pus in the urine, typically from bacterial infection. [19th C.: from Gk. *puon* 'pus' + **-URIA**.]

pyx /piks/ ▶ **n.** **1** Christian Church the container in which the consecrated bread of the Eucharist is kept. **2** a box at a mint in which specimen gold and silver coins are deposited to be tested. [ME: from L. *pyxis*, from Gk. *puxis* 'box.']

pyx·id·i·um /pik'sidēəm/ ▶ **n.** (pl. **-i·a** /-ēə/) Bot. a seed capsule that splits open so that the top comes off like the lid of a box. [19th C.: mod. L., from Gk. *puxidion*, dimin. of *puxis* 'box.']

Pyx·is /'piksis/ Astron. a small and inconspicuous southern constellation (the Compass Box or Mariner's Compass), lying in the Milky Way between Vela and Puppis. [L.]

pzazz /pə'zaz/ ▶ **n.** var. of **PIZZAZZ**.

Qq

Q[1] /kyōō/ (also **q**) ▸ **n.** (pl. **Qs** or **Q's**) the seventeenth letter of the alphabet. ▪ denoting the next after P in a set of items, categories, etc.

Q[2] ▸ **abbr.** ▪ quarter (used to refer to a specified quarter of the fiscal year): *an exceptional Q4.* ▪ question.

q ▸ **symb.** Physics electric charge. [19th C.: from *quantity.*]

QA ▸ **abbr.** quality assurance.

Qab·a·lah /kə'bälə/ ▸ **n.** var. of KABBALAH.

Qae·da, al see AL QAEDA.

qa·nat /kə'nät/ ▸ **n.** (in the Middle East) a gently sloping underground channel or tunnel constructed to lead water from the interior of a hill to a village below. [Pers., from Arab. *ḳanāt* 'reed.']

q and a /kyōō' ən ā'/ ▸ **abbr.** informal a question and answer period or exchange.

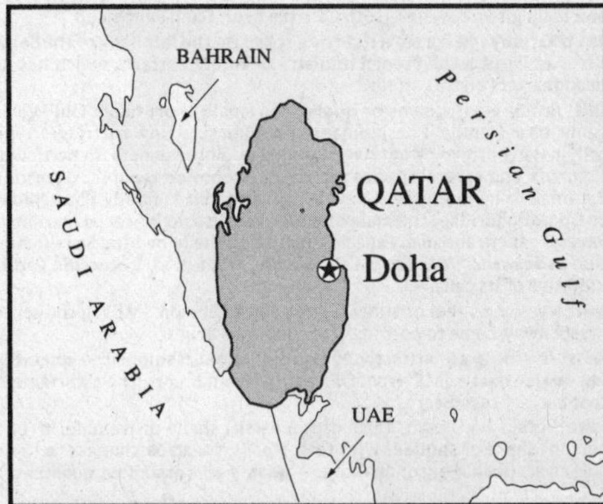

Qatar

Official name: State of Qatar
Location: Middle East, on a peninsula off Saudi Arabia, in the Persian Gulf
Area: 4,400 square miles (11,400 sq km)
Population: 840,000
Capital: Doha
Languages: Arabic (official), English
Currency: Qatari rial

Qa·tar /'kätär; kə'tär/ a sheikhdom on the western coast of the Persian Gulf. *See box.* — **Qa·tar·i** /'kätärē; kə'tärē/ **adj. & n.**

Qat·ta·ra De·pres·sion /kə'tärə/ an extensive, low-lying, and largely impassable area of desert in northeastern Africa, west of Cairo.

QB ▸ **abbr.** ▪ Football quarterback. ▪ Chess queen's bishop.

QC ▸ **abbr.** ▪ quality control. ▪ Quebec (in official postal use).

QCD ▸ **abbr.** quantum chromodynamics.

Q-Celtic /'keltik/ ▸ **n. & adj.** another term for GOIDELIC. [Q, from the retention of the Indo-Eur. *kw* sound as *q* or *c.*]

QED ▸ **abbr.** quantum electrodynamics.

Q fe·ver ▸ **n.** an infectious fever caused by rickettsiae and transmitted to humans from cattle, sheep, and goats by unpasteurized milk. [1930s: from *query.*]

qi /CHē/ (also **chi** or **ki**) ▸ **n.** the circulating life force whose existence and properties are the basis of much Chinese philosophy and medicine. [from Chin. (Mandarin) *qì*, lit. 'air, breath.']

qib·la /'kiblə/ (also **kib·lah**) ▸ **n.** [in sing.] the direction of the Kaaba (the sacred building at Mecca), to which Muslims turn at prayer. [17th C.: from Arab. *ḳibla* 'that which is opposite.']

q.i.d. ▸ **abbr.** (in prescriptions) four times a day. [L. *quater in die.*]

qi·gong /'CHē'gäNG; -'gôNG/ ▸ **n.** a Chinese system of physical exercises and breathing control related to tai chi.

Qin /CHin/ (also **Ch'in**) a dynasty that ruled China 221–206 BC and was the first to establish rule over a united China.

Qing /CHING/ (also **Ch'ing**) a dynasty established by the Manchus that ruled China 1644–1912 until overthrown by Sun Yat-sen and his supporters.

Qing·dao /'CHING'dou/ a city in eastern China, on the Yellow Sea coast; pop. 2,040,000.

Qing·hai /'CHING'hī/ (also **Tsing·hai**) a province in north central China; capital, Xining.

qin·tar /kin'tär/ ▸ **n.** (pl. same, **qin·tars**, or **qin·dar·ka** /kin'darkə/) a monetary unit of Albania, equal to one hundredth of a lek. [from Albanian *qindar*, from *qind* 'hundred.']

Qi·qi·har /'CHē'CHē'här/ a port city in Heilongjiang province, in northeastern China; pop. 1,370,000.

QM ▸ **abbr.** quartermaster.

QMC ▸ **abbr.** Quartermaster Corps.

QMG ▸ **abbr.** quartermaster general.

Qom /kōōm/ (also **Qum** or **Kum**) a city in central Iran; pop. 780,000.

q.p. ▸ **abbr.** (in prescriptions) as much as you please. [L. *quantum placet.*]

qq. ▸ **abbr.** questions.

qq.v. ▸ **abbr.** which (words, etc.) see. [L. *quae vide.*]

qr. ▸ **abbr.** quarter(s).

q.s. ▸ **abbr.** ▪ (in prescriptions) enough; as much as is sufficient. [L. *quantum sufficit.*] ▪ quarter section.

QSO ▸ **abbr.** quasi-stellar object, a quasar.

QT (also **q.t.**) ▸ **n.** (in phrase **on the QT**) informal secretly; stealthily: *she'd better get there on the QT.* [19th C.: abbrev. of QUIET.]

qt. ▸ **abbr.** quart(s).

qto. ▸ **abbr.** quarto.

qty. ▸ **abbr.** quantity.

qua /kwä/ ▸ **conj.** in the capacity of; as being: *his views on music qua music.* [L., ablative fem. sing. of *qui* 'who.']

quack[1] /kwak/ ▸ **n.** [in sing.] the characteristic harsh sound made by a duck. ▸ **v.** [intrans.] (of a duck) make this sound. ▪ informal talk loudly and foolishly. [16th C. (as a v.): imitative.]

quack[2] ▸ **n.** a person who dishonestly claims to have special knowledge in some field, typically in medicine. — **quack·er·y** /'kwakərē/ **n.** **quack·ish adj.** [17th C.: abbrev. of *quacksalver*, from Du., prob. from obs. *quacken* 'prattle' + *salf* 'salve.']

quack grass ▸ **n.** another term for COUCH GRASS. [19th C.: *quack*, var. of *quick*, north. Engl. form of QUITCH.]

quad /kwäd/ ▸ **n.** **1** informal short for: ▪ a quadrangle. ▪ QUADRUPLET (sense 1). ▪ a quadriceps. ▪ a quad bike. ▪ quadraphonic sound. ▪ a quadriplegic. **2** (in telephony) a group of four insulated conductors twisted together, usually forming two circuits. [abbrev. of *quadraplex.*] **3** a radio antenna in the form of a square or rectangle broken in the middle of one side. [abbrev. of QUADRILATERAL.] ▸ **adj.** [attrib.] informal short for: ▪ quadruple. ▪ quadraphonic.

quad. ▸ **abbr.** ▪ quadrangle. ▪ quadrant.

quad bike ▸ **n.** a motorcycle with four large tires, typically used for racing.

quad chair (also **quad chair·lift** or **quad**) ▸ **n.** a chairlift with seats for four people at a time.

quad·plex /'kwäd,pleks/ ▸ **n.** another term for QUADRAPLEX.

quad·ra·ge·nar·i·an /,kwädrəjə'ne(ə)rēən/ ▸ **n.** a person who is from 40 to 49 years old. [19th C.: from late L. *quadragenarius* (based on L. *quadraginta* 'forty') + -AN.]

Quad·ra·ges·i·ma /,kwädrə'jesəmə/ (also **Quadragesima Sunday**) **n.** the first Sunday in Lent. [from L. *quadragesimus* 'fortieth,' from *quadraginta* 'forty' (Lent lasting 40 days).]

quad·ra·min·i·um ▸ **n.** var. of QUADROMINIUM.

quad·ran·gle /'kwä,draNGgəl/ ▸ **n.** Geom. a four-sided plane figure, esp. a square or rectangle. ▪ a square or rectangular space or courtyard enclosed by buildings. ▪ the area shown on a standard topographic map sheet of the US Geological Survey. — **quad·ran·gu·lar** /kwä'draNGgyələr/ **adj.** [ME: ult. from late L. *quadrangulum* 'square,' neut. of *quadrangulus*, from L. 'four' + *angulus* 'angle.']

quad·rant /'kwädrənt/ ▸ **n.** tech. each of four quarters of a circle. See illustration at GEOMETRIC. ▪ each of four parts of a plane, sphere, space, or body divided by two lines or planes at right angles. ▪ hist.

an instrument used for taking angular measurements of altitude in astronomy and navigation, typically consisting of a graduated quarter circle and a sighting mechanism. ■ a frame fixed to the head of a ship's rudder, to which the steering mechanism is attached. — **quad·ran·tal** /kwä'drantl/ **adj.** [ME (denoting the astronomical instrument): from L. *quadrans, quadrant-* 'quarter,' from *quattuor* four.]

quad·ra·phon·ic /ˌkwädrə'fänik/ (also **quad·ro·phon·ic**) ▶ **adj.** (of sound reproduction) transmitted through four channels. — **quad·ra·phon·i·cal·ly** /-ik(ə)lē/ **adv.** **quad·ra·phon·ics plural n.** **qua·draph·o·ny** /kwä'dräfənē/ **n.** [1960s: from QUADRI- 'four' + a shortened form of STEREOPHONIC.]

quad·ra·plex /'kwädrəˌpleks/ (also **quadriplex**) ▶ **n.** a building divided into four self-contained residences. Also called QUADPLEX.

quad·rat /'kwädrət/ ▶ **n.** Ecol. each of a number of small areas of habitat, typically of one square meter, selected at random to act as samples for assessing the local distribution of plants or animals.

quad·rate ▶ **n.** /'kwäˌdrāt; -rət/ **1** (also **quadrate bone**) Zool. (in the skull of a bird or reptile) a squarish bone with which the jaw articulates. **2** Anat. another term for QUADRATUS. ▶ **adj.** roughly square or rectangular. [ME: from L. *quadrat-* 'made square,' from *quadrare*, from *quattuor* 'four.']

quad·rat·ic /kwä'dratik/ ▶ **adj.** Math. involving the second and no higher power of an unknown quantity or variable: *a quadratic equation.* ▶ **n.** a quadratic equation.

quad·ra·ture /'kwädrəˌcʜər; -ˌcʜo͝or/ ▶ **n.** **1** Math. the process of constructing a square with an area equal to that of a circle, or of another figure bounded by a curve. **2** Astron. the position of the moon or a planet when it is 90° from the sun as viewed from the earth. ■ the point in space or time when this occurs.

qua·dra·tus /kwä'drātəs/ ▶ **n.** (pl. **-dra·ti** /-'drāˌtī/) Anat. any of several roughly square or rectangular muscles, e.g., in the abdomen, thigh, and eye socket. [18th C.: from L., lit. 'made square.']

quad·ren·ni·al /kwä'drenēəl/ ▶ **adj.** recurring every four years. ■ lasting for or relating to a period of four years. — **quad·ren·ni·al·ly adv.**

quad·ren·ni·um /kwä'drenēəm/ ▶ **n.** (pl. **-dren·ni·a** /-'drenēə/ or **-dren·ni·ums**) a specified period of four years.

quadri- ▶ **comb. form** four; having four: *quadriplegia.* [from L. *quattuor* 'four.']

quad·ric /'kwädrik/ Geom. ▶ **adj.** (of a surface or curve) described by an equation of the second degree. ▶ **n.** a quadric surface or curve.

quad·ri·ceps /'kwädrəˌseps/ ▶ **n.** (pl. same) Anat. the large muscle at the front of the thigh, which is divided into four distinct portions and acts to extend the leg. [16th C.: from L., lit. 'four-headed.']

quad·ri·lat·er·al /ˌkwädrə'latərəl/ ▶ **n.** a four-sided figure. See illustration at GEOMETRIC. ▶ **adj.** having four straight sides.

quad·rille[1] /kwä'dril; k(w)ə-/ ▶ **n.** a square dance performed typically by four couples and containing five figures, each of which is a complete dance in itself. ■ a piece of music for this dance. [Fr., from Sp. *cuadrilla* or Ital. *quadriglia* 'troop, company.']

quad·rille[2] ▶ **n.** a card game for four players using a deck of forty cards, fashionable in the 18th century. [18th C.: from Fr., perh. from Sp. *cuartillo* (from *cuarto* 'fourth').]

quad·rille[3] ▶ **n.** a ruled grid of small squares, esp. on paper. [19th C.: from Fr. *quadrillé*, from *quadrille* 'small square,' from Sp. *cuadrillo* 'small block.']

quad·ril·lion /kwä'drilyən/ ▶ **cardinal number** (pl. **-lions** or (with numeral or quantifying word) same) a thousand raised to the power of five (10^{15}). — **quad·ril·lionth** /-'drilyənᴛʜ/ **ordinal number.**

quad·ri·par·tite /ˌkwädrə'pärtīt/ ▶ **adj.** consisting of four parts. ■ shared by or involving four parties. [ME: from L. *quadripartitus*, from *quadri-* 'four' + *partitus* 'divided.']

quad·ri·ple·gi·a /ˌkwädrə'plēj(ē)ə/ ▶ **n.** Med. paralysis of all four limbs; tetraplegia. — **quad·ri·ple·gic** /-'plējik/ **adj. & n.** [1920s: from QUADRI- 'four' + a shortened form of PARAPLEGIA.]

quad·ri·plex ▶ **n.** var. of QUADRAPLEX.

quad·ri·va·lent /ˌkwädrə'vālənt/ ▶ **adj.** Chem. another term for TETRAVALENT.

quad·riv·i·um /kwä'drivēəm/ ▶ **n.** hist. a medieval university curriculum involving the "mathematical arts" of arithmetic, geometry, astronomy, and music. Compare with TRIVIUM. [L., lit. 'the place where four roads meet' from *quadri-* 'four' + *via* 'road.']

quad·ro·min·i·um /ˌkwädrə'minēəm/ (also **quad·ra·min·i·um**) ▶ **n.** a condominium consisting of four apartments. [1970s: blend of QUADRI- 'four' and CONDOMINIUM.]

quad·roon /kwä'dro͞on/ ▶ **n.** a person whose parents are a mulatto and a white, and who is therefore one-quarter black. [18th C.: via Fr. *quarteron* from Sp. *cuarterón*, from *cuarto* 'quarter,' from L. *quartus*.]

quad·ro·phon·ic /ˌkwädrə'fänik/ ▶ **adj.** var. of QUADRAPHONIC.

quad·ru·ma·nous /kwä'dro͞omənəs/ ▶ **adj.** Zool., dated (of primates other than humans) having all four feet modified as hands, i.e., having opposable digits. [17th C.: from mod. L. *Quadrumana*, ult. from *quadru-* 'four' + L. *manus* 'hand.']

quad·ru·ped /'kwädrəˌped/ ▶ **n.** an animal that has four feet, esp. an ungulate mammal. — **quad·ru·pe·dal** /ˌkwädrə'pedl; kwä'dro͞opədl/ **adj.** [17th C.: ult. from L. *quadrupes, quadruped-*, from *quadru-* 'four' + *pes, ped-* 'foot.']

quad·ru·ple /kwä'dro͞opəl/ ▶ **adj.** [attrib.] consisting of four parts or elements: *a quadruple murder.* ■ consisting of four times as much or as many as usual. ■ (of time in music) having four beats in a bar. ▶ **v.** increase or be increased fourfold: [intrans.] *prices quadrupled.* ▶ **n.** a quadruple thing, number, or amount. — **quad·ru·ply** /-p(ə)lē/ **adv.**

quad·ru·plet /kwä'dro͞oplit/ ▶ **n.** **1** (usu. **quadruplets**) each of four children born at one birth. **2** Music a group of four notes to be performed in the time of three.

quad·ru·pli·cate ▶ **adj.** /kwä'dro͞opləkit/ consisting of four parts or elements. ■ of which four copies are made. ▶ **v.** /kwä'dro͞opləˌkāt/ [trans.] multiply (something) by four. ■ [usu. as adj.] (**quadruplicated**) make or provide in quadruplicate. — **quad·ru·pli·ca·tion** /kwäˌdro͞oplə'kāsʜən/ **n.**

quaes·tor /'kwestər/ ▶ **n.** (in ancient Rome) any of a number of officials who had charge of public revenue and expenditure. — **quaes·to·ri·al** /kwe'stôrēəl/ **adj.** **quaes·tor·ship** /-sʜip/ **n.** [L., from an old form of *quaesit-* 'sought,' from the v. *quaerere*.]

quaff /kwäf/ ▶ **v.** [trans.] drink (something, esp. an alcoholic drink) heartily. — **quaff·a·ble adj.** **quaff·er n.** [16th C.: prob. imitative.]

quag /kwag/ ▶ **n.** archaic a marshy or boggy place. — **quag·gy adj.** [16th C.: rel. to dialect *quag* 'shake.']

quag·ga /'kwagə/ ▶ **n.** an extinct South African zebra (*Equus quagga*) that had a yellowish-brown coat with darker stripes, exterminated in 1883. [South Afr. Du., prob. from Khoikhoi, imitative of its braying.]

quag·mire /'kwagˌmī(ə)r/ ▶ **n.** a soft boggy area of land that gives way underfoot. ■ an awkward, complex, or hazardous situation: *a legal quagmire.*

qua·hog /'kwôˌhôg; -ˌhäg; 'kwō-; 'kō-/ (also **qua·haug**) ▶ **n.** a large, rounded edible clam (*Venus mercenaria*, family Veneridae) of the Atlantic coast of North America. Also called HARD CLAM, HARD-SHELL CLAM. [18th C.: from Narragansett *poquaûhock*.]

quaich /kwāk/ ▶ **n.** Scot. a shallow drinking cup, typically made of wood and having two handles. [16th C.: from Scot. Gael. *cuach* 'cup.']

Quai d'Or·say /'kē dôr'sā/ a riverside street on the left bank of the Seine River in Paris. ■ the French ministry of foreign affairs, which has its headquarters on this street.

quail[1] /kwāl/ ▶ **n.** (pl. same or **quails**) **1** a small, short-tailed Old World game bird (family Phasianidae) resembling a tiny partridge, typically having brown camouflaged plumage. Three genera, in particular *Coturnix*, and several species include the **common quail** (*C. coturnix*). **2** a small or medium-sized New World game bird (family Phasianidae or Odontophoridae) the male of which has distinctive facial markings. Several genera and many species, including the bobwhite. See illustration at BOBWHITE. [ME: from OFr. *quaille*, from med. L. *coacula* (prob. imitative of its call).]

quail[2] ▶ **v.** [intrans.] feel or show fear or apprehension. [ME (in the sense 'waste away, come to nothing'): of unknown origin.]

quaint /kwānt/ ▶ **adj.** attractively unusual or old-fashioned. — **quaint·ly adv.** **quaint·ness n.** [ME: from OFr. *cointe*, from L. *cognitus* 'ascertained,' past part. of *cognoscere*.]

quake /kwāk/ ▶ **v.** [intrans.] (esp. of the earth) shake or tremble. ■ (of a person) shake or shudder with fear. ▶ **n.** informal an earthquake. ■ [usu. in sing.] an act of shaking or quaking. — **quak·y adj.** (**quak·i·er, quak·i·est**). [OE *cwacian*.]

Quak·er /'kwākər/ ▶ **n.** a member of the Religious Society of Friends, a Christian movement founded by George Fox *c.*1650 and devoted to peaceful principles. — **Quak·er·ish adj.** **Quak·er·ism** /-izəm/ **n.** [from QUAKE + -ER[1], perh. alluding to George Fox's direction to his followers to "tremble at the name of the Lord."]

quak·ing grass ▶ **n.** a slender-stalked grass (genus *Briza*, several species) with oval or heart-shaped flowerheads.

qua·le /'kwälē/ ▶ **n.** (pl. **qua·li·a** /'kwälēə/) (usu. **qualia**) Philos. a quality or property as perceived or experienced by a person. [17th C.: from L., neut. of *qualis* 'of what kind.']

qual·i·fi·ca·tion /ˌkwäləfə'kāsʜən/ ▶ **n.** **1** a quality or accomplishment that makes someone suitable for a particular job or activity. ■ the action or fact of becoming qualified as a practitioner of a particular profession or activity: *an opportunity to share experiences before qualification.* ■ a condition that must be fulfilled before a right can be acquired; an official requirement: *a residency qualification.* **2** the action or fact of qualifying or being eligible for something: *qualification for the World Cup finals.* **3** a statement or assertion that makes another less absolute: *they have renounced without qualification all terrorism.* ■ Gram. the attribution of a quality to a word, esp. a noun. — **qual·i·fi·ca·to·ry** /'kwäləfikəˌtôrē/ **adj.**

qual·i·fi·er /'kwäləˌfīər/ ▶ **n.** **1** a person or team that qualifies for a competition: *the youngest qualifier for a PGA Tour.* ■ a match or contest to decide which individuals or teams qualify for a competition or its final rounds. **2** Gram. a word or phrase, esp. an adjective, used to attribute a quality to another word, esp. a noun. ■ (in systemic grammar) a word or phrase added after a noun to qualify its meaning.

qual·i·fy /'kwäləˌfī/ ▶ **v.** (**-fies, -fied**) **1** [intrans.] be entitled to a particular benefit or privilege by fulfilling a necessary condition: *we qualify for compensation.* ■ become eligible for a competition or its final rounds, by reaching a certain standard or defeating a competitor. **2** [intrans.] become officially recognized as a practitioner of a particular profession or activity by satisfying the relevant requirements. ■ [trans.] officially recognize or establish (someone) as a practitioner of a particular profession or activity: [as adj.] (**qualified**) *qualified teachers.* ■ [trans.] make (someone) competent or knowledgeable enough to do something: *I'm not qualified to write on the subject.* **3** [trans.] make (a statement or assertion) less absolute; add reservations to: *the authors later qualified their findings.* ■ [trans.] Gram. (of a word or phrase) attribute a quality to (another word, esp. a preceding noun). — **qual·i·fi·a·ble** adj. [ME: from Fr. *qualifier*, from med. L. *qualificare*, from L. *qualis* 'of what kind.']

qual·i·ta·tive /'kwälə,tātiv/ ▶ adj. relating to, measuring, or measured by the quality of something rather than its quantity: *a qualitative change in the curriculum.* Often contrasted with QUANTITATIVE. ■ Gram. (of an adjective) describing the quality of something in size, appearance, value, etc. Such adjectives can be submodified by words such as *very* and have comparative and superlative forms. — **qual·i·ta·tive·ly** adv.

qual·i·ta·tive a·nal·y·sis ▶ n. Chem. identification of the constituents present in a substance.

qual·i·ty /'kwälətē/ ▶ n. (pl. **-ties**) **1** the standard of something as measured against other things of a similar kind; the degree of excellence of something: *quality of life.* ■ general excellence of standard or level: [as adj.] *quality beers.* **2** a distinctive attribute or characteristic possessed by someone or something: *leadership qualities.* ■ Phonet. the distinguishing characteristic or characteristics of a speech sound. ■ Music another term for TIMBRE. [ME: from OFr. *qualite*, from L. *qualitas* (translating Gk. *poiotēs*), from *qualis* 'of what kind.']

qual·i·ty as·sur·ance ▶ n. the maintenance of a desired level of quality in a service or product.

qual·i·ty con·trol ▶ n. a system of maintaining standards in manufactured products by testing samples. — **qual·i·ty con·trol·ler** n.

qual·i·ty time ▶ n. time spent in giving another person one's undivided attention to strengthen a relationship, esp. with reference to working parents.

qualm /kwä(l)m; kwô(l)m/ ▶ n. an uneasy feeling of doubt, worry, or fear; a misgiving. ■ a momentary faint or sick feeling. — **qualm·ish** adj. [16th C.: perh. rel. to OE *cw(e)alm* 'pain,' of Gmc. origin.]

quam·ash /'kwä,mash/ ▶ n. var. of CAMAS.

quan·da·ry /'kwänd(ə)rē/ ▶ n. (pl. **-ries**) perplexity or uncertainty over what to do in a difficult situation: *Jim is in a quandary.* ■ a difficult situation; a practical dilemma. [16th C.: perh. from L. *quando* 'when.']

quan·dong /'kwän,däng/ ▶ n. either of two Australian trees: a small tree (*Eucarya acuminata*) of the sandalwood family. ■ (also **blue quandong**) a large tree of the subtropical rain forest (*Elaeocarpus grandis*, family Elaeocarpaceae). [19th C.: from Wiradhuri.]

Quant /kwänt/, Mary (1934–), English fashion designer; a principal creator of the "1960s look."

quan·tal /'kwäntl/ ▶ adj. tech. composed of discrete units; varying in steps rather than continuously: *a quantal release of neurotransmitter.* ■ Physics of or relating to a quantum or quanta, or to quantum theory. ■ esp. Physiol. relating to or denoting an all-or-none response or state. — **quan·tal·ly** /'kwäntl-ē/ adv. [20th C.: from QUANTUM + -AL.]

quan·tic /'kwäntik/ ▶ n. Math. a homogeneous function of two or more variables having rational and irrational coefficients. [19th C.: from L. *quantus* 'how great, how much' + -IC.]

quan·ti·fi·er /'kwäntə,fīər/ ▶ n. Logic an expression (e.g., *all, some*) that indicates the scope of a term to which it is attached. ■ Gram. a determiner or pronoun indicative of quantity (e.g., *all, both*).

quan·ti·fy /'kwäntə,fī/ ▶ v. (**-fies, -fied**) [trans.] **1** express or measure the quantity of. **2** Logic define the application of (a term or proposition) by the use of *all, some,* etc., e.g., "for all *x* if *x* is A then *x* is B." — **quan·ti·fi·a·bil·i·ty** /,kwäntə,fīə'bilətē/ n. **quan·ti·fi·a·ble** /'kwäntə,fīəbəl/ adj. **quan·ti·fi·ca·tion** /,kwäntəfi'kāshən/ n. [16th C.: from med. L. *quantificare*, from L. *quantus* 'how much.']

quan·tile /'kwän,tīl/ ▶ n. Stat. each of any set of values of a variate that divide a frequency distribution into equal groups, each containing the same fraction of the total population. ■ any of the groups so produced, e.g., a quartile or percentile.

quan·ti·tate /'kwäntə,tāt/ ▶ v. [trans.] Med. Biol. determine the quantity or extent of something, esp. in numerical terms. — **quan·ti·ta·tion** /,kwäntə'tāshən/ n.

quan·ti·ta·tive /'kwäntə,tātiv/ ▶ adj. relating to, measuring, or measured by the quantity of something. Often contrasted with QUALITATIVE. ■ denoting or relating to verse whose meter is based on the length of syllables as opposed to the stress. — **quan·ti·ta·tive·ly** adv.

quan·ti·ta·tive a·nal·y·sis ▶ n. Chem. measurement of the quantities of particular constituents present in a substance.

quan·ti·ta·tive lin·guis·tics ▶ plural n. [treated as sing.] the comparative study of the frequency and distribution of words and syntactic structures in different texts.

quan·ti·ty /'kwäntətē/ ▶ n. (pl. **-ties**) **1** the amount or number of a material or immaterial thing not usually estimated by spatial measurement: *the quantity of the fruit can be controlled.* ■ Logic the property of a proposition of being universal or particular. ■ a certain amount or number of something: *a small quantity of food.* ■ (often **quantities**) a considerable number or amount of something: *Joe was able to drink quantities of beer.* **2** Phonet. the perceived length of a vowel sound or syllable. **3** Math. & Physics a value or component that may be expressed in numbers. [ME: from OFr. *quantite*, from L. *quantitas* (translating Gk. *posotēs*), from *quantus* 'how great.']

quan·tize /'kwän,tīz/ ▶ v. [trans.] Physics apply quantum theory to, in particular restrict the number of possible values of (a quantity) or states of (a system). — **quan·ti·za·tion** /,kwäntə'zāshən/ n.

quan·tum /'kwäntəm/ ▶ n. (pl. **-ta** /-tə/) **1** Physics a discrete quantity of energy proportional in magnitude to the frequency of the radiation it represents. ■ an analogous discrete amount of any other physical quantity, such as momentum or electric charge. **2** a required or allowed amount, esp. an amount of money legally payable in damages. ■ a share or portion. [16th C.: from L., neut. of *quantus* 'how great.']

quan·tum chro·mo·dy·nam·ics (abbr.: **QCD**) ▶ plural n. [treated as sing.] Physics a quantum theory of interaction of quarks mediated by gluons, both being assigned a quantum number called "color."

quan·tum e·lec·tro·dy·nam·ics (abbr.: **QED**) ▶ plural n. [treated as sing.] a quantum theory that deals with the electromagnetic field and its interaction with electrically charged particles.

quan·tum field the·o·ry ▶ n. Physics a field theory that incorporates quantum mechanics and the principles of the theory of relativity.

quan·tum grav·i·ty ▶ n. Physics a theory that attempts to explain gravitational physics in terms of quantum mechanics.

quan·tum jump ▶ n. Physics an abrupt transition of an electron, atom, or molecule from one quantum state to another, with absorption or emission of a quantum.

quan·tum me·chan·ics ▶ plural n. [treated as sing.] Physics the branch of mechanics that deals with the mathematical description of the motion and interaction of subatomic particles. — **quan·tum-me·chan·i·cal** adj.

quan·tum num·ber ▶ n. Physics a number that occurs in the theoretical expression for the value of some quantized property of a subatomic particle, atom, or molecule.

quan·tum state ▶ n. Physics a state of a quantized system that is described by a set of quantum numbers.

quan·tum the·o·ry ▶ n. Physics a theory of matter and energy based on the concept of quanta, esp. quantum mechanics.

Qua·paw /'kwô,pô/ ▶ n. (pl. same or **-paws**) **1** a member of an American Indian people of the Arkansas River region, now living mainly in northeastern Oklahoma. **2** the Siouan language of this people. ▶ adj. of or relating to this people or their language.

quar. ▶ abbr. ■ quarter. ■ quarterly.

quar·an·tine /'kwôrən,tēn; 'kwär-/ ▶ n. a state, period, or place of isolation in which people or animals that have been exposed to infectious or contagious disease are placed. ▶ v. [trans.] impose such isolation on; put in quarantine. [17th C.: from Ital. *quarantina* 'forty days,' from *quaranta* 'forty.']

quar·an·tine flag ▶ n. another term for YELLOW FLAG.

quark /kwôrk; kwärk/ ▶ n. Physics any of a number of subatomic particles carrying a fractional electric charge, postulated as building blocks of the hadrons. [1960s: invented by Murray GELL-MANN; from *quork*, changed by association with "Three quarks for Muster Mark" in Joyce's *Finnegans Wake* (1939).]

quar·rel[1] /'kwôrəl; 'kwär-/ ▶ n. an angry argument or disagreement, typically between people who are usually on good terms. ■ [usu. with negative] a reason for disagreement with a person, group, or principle: *we have no quarrel with you.* ▶ v. (**-reled, -rel·ing** ; Brit. **-relled, -rel·ling**) [intrans.] have an angry argument or disagreement. — **quar·rel·er** n. [ME: from OFr. *querele*, from L. *querel(l)a* 'complaint,' from *queri* 'complain.']

quar·rel[2] ▶ n. **1** hist. a short, heavy, square-headed arrow or bolt used in a crossbow or arbalest. **2** another term for QUARRY[3]. [ME: from OFr., based on late L. *quadrus* 'square.']

quar·rel·some /'kwôrəlsəm; 'kwär-/ ▶ adj. given to or characterized by quarreling. — **quar·rel·some·ly** adv. **quar·rel·some·ness** n.

quar·ry[1] /'kwôrē; 'kwär-/ ▶ n. (pl. **-ries**) a place, typically a large, deep pit, from which stone or other materials are or have been extracted. ▶ v. (**-ries, -ried**) [trans.] extract (stone or other materials) from a quarry. ■ cut into (rock or ground) to obtain stone or other materials. [ME: from OFr. *quarriere*, based on L. *quadrum* 'a square.']

quar·ry[2] ▶ n. (pl. **-ries**) an animal pursued by a hunter, hound, predatory mammal, or bird of prey. ■ a thing or person that is chased or sought. [ME: from OFr. *cuiree*, alt., influenced by *cuir* 'leather' and *curer* 'clean, disembowel,' of *couree*, based on L. *cor* 'heart.']

quar·ry[3] ▶ n. (pl. **-ries**) **1** (also **quar·rel**) a diamond-shaped pane of glass as used in lattice windows. **2** (also **quarry tile**) an unglazed floor tile.

quart /kwôrt/ ▶ n. **1** a unit of liquid capacity equal to a quarter of a gallon or two pints, equivalent in the US to approximately 0.94 liter and in Britain to approximately 1.13 liters. ■ a unit of dry capacity equivalent to approximately 1.10 liters. **2** (also **quarte**) Fencing the fourth of eight standard parrying positions. [ME: from OFr. *quarte*, from L. *quarta (pars)* 'fourth (part),' from *quartus* 'fourth,' from *quattuor* 'four.']

quar·tan /'kwôrtn/ ▶ adj. [attrib.] Med. denoting a mild form of malaria causing a fever that recurs every third day: *quartan fever.* [ME: from L. *(febris) quartana*, based on *quartus* 'fourth' (because, by inclusive reckoning, the fever recurs every fourth day).]

quar·ter /'kwôrtər/ ▶ n. **1** each of four equal or corresponding parts into which something is or can be divided: *she cut each apple into quarters.* ■ a period of three months regarded as one fourth of a year. ■ a period of fifteen minutes or a point of time marking the transition from one fifteen-minute period to the next: *a quarter past nine.* ■ a coin representing 25 cents, one fourth of a US or Canadian dollar. ■ each of the four parts into which an animal's or bird's carcass may be divided, each including a leg or wing. ■ (**quarters**) the haunches or hindquarters of a horse. ■ one fourth of a lunar month. ■ (in various sports) each of four equal periods into which a game is divided. ■ one of four terms into which a school or college year may be divided. **2** one fourth of a measure of weight. **3** [usu. with adj. or n.] a part of a town or city having a specific character or use: *the Italian quarter.* **4** the direction of one of the points of the compass, esp. as a direction from which the wind blows. ■ a particular but unspecified person, group of people, or area: *help from an unexpected quarter.* ■ either side of a ship aft of the beam: *the starboard quarter.* **5** (**quarters**) rooms or lodgings, esp. those allocated to servicemen or to staff in domestic service. **6** [usu. with neg.] pity or mercy shown toward an enemy or opponent: *the riot squad gave no quarter.* **7** Heraldry each of four or more roughly equal divisions of a shield separated by vertical and horizontal lines. ■ a square charge that covers the top left (dexter chief) quarter of the field. ▸**v.** [trans.] **1** divide into four equal or corresponding parts. ■ hist. cut (the body of an executed person) into four parts. **2** (**be quartered**) [with adverbial of place] be stationed or lodged in a specified place: *many were quartered in tents.* **3** range over or traverse (an area) in every direction. ■ [intrans.] move at an angle; go in a diagonal or zigzag direction: *the dog quartered back and forth.* **4** Heraldry display (different coats of arms) in quarters of a shield. ■ divide (a shield) into four or more parts. [ME: from OFr. *quartier*, from L. *quartarius* 'fourth part of a measure,' from *quartus* 'fourth,' from *quattuor* 'four.']

quar·ter·back /ˈkwôrtərˌbak/ ▸**n.** Football a player positioned behind the center who directs a team's offensive play. ■ fig. a person who directs or coordinates an operation or project. ▸**v.** [trans.] Football play as a quarterback for (a particular team). ■ fig. direct or coordinate (an operation or project).

quar·ter·deck /ˈkwôrtərˌdek/ ▸**n.** the part of a ship's upper deck near the stern, traditionally for officers. ■ the officers of a ship or the navy.

quar·ter·fi·nal /ˈkwôrtərˌfīnl/ ▸**n.** a match or round of a tournament that precedes the semifinal.

Quar·ter Horse (also **quar·ter horse**) ▸**n.** a horse of a small, stocky breed noted for agility and speed over short distances, esp. a quarter of a mile.

quar·ter-hour (also **quarter of an hour**) ▸**n.** a period of 15 minutes. ■ a point of time 15 minutes before or after any hour.

quar·ter·ing /ˈkwôrtəriNG/ ▸**n.** **1** (**quarterings**) Heraldry the coats of arms marshaled on a shield to denote the marriages into a family of the heiresses of others. **2** the provision of accommodations or lodgings, esp. for troops. **3** the action of dividing something into four parts.

quar·ter·ly /ˈkwôrtərlē/ ▸**adj.** [attrib.] done, produced, or occurring once every quarter of a year. ▸**adv.** once every quarter of a year: *paid quarterly.* ▸**n.** (pl. **-lies**) a magazine or journal that is published four times a year.

quar·ter·mas·ter /ˈkwôrtərˌmastər/ ▸**n.** **1** a military officer responsible for providing quarters, rations, clothing, and other supplies. **2** a naval petty officer with particular responsibility for steering and signals.

quar·ter·mas·ter gen·er·al ▸**n.** (pl. **quar·ter·mas·ters gen·er·al** or **quar·ter·mas·ter gen·er·als**) the head of the army department in charge of the quartering and equipment of troops.

quar·ter note ▸**n.** Music a musical note having the time value of a quarter of a whole note or half a half note.

quar·ter-pipe ▸**n.** a ramp with a slightly convex surface, used by skateboarders, rollerbladers, or snowboarders to perform jumps and other maneuvers.

quar·ter-saw ▸**v.** [trans.] [usu. as adj.] (**quarter-sawn**) saw (a log) radially into quarters and then into boards. ■ produce (a board) using this technique.

quar·ter sec·tion ▸**n.** a quarter of a square mile of land; 160 acres (approximately 64.7 hectares).

quar·ter·staff /ˈkwôrtərˌstaf/ ▸**n.** hist. a stout pole 6–8 feet (2–2.5 m) long, tipped with iron, used as a weapon.

quar·ter-tone ▸**n.** Music half a semitone.

quar·tet /kwôrˈtet/ ▸**n.** a group of four people playing music or singing together. ■ a composition for such a group. ■ a set of four people or things. [17th C.: from Fr. *quartette*, from Ital. *quartetto*, from *quarto* 'fourth,' from L. *quartus*.]

quar·tic /ˈkwôrtik/ Math. ▸**adj.** involving the fourth and no higher power of an unknown quantity or variable. ▸**n.** a quartic equation, function, curve, or surface.

quar·tile /ˈkwôrˌtīl; ˈkwôrtl/ ▸**n.** **1** Stat. each of four equal groups into which a population can be divided according to a particular variable. ■ each of the three values of the random variable that divide a population into four such groups. **2** the aspect between two planets that are 90 degrees apart in the sky.

quar·to /ˈkwôrtō/ (abbr.: **4to**) ▸**n.** (pl. **-tos**) Print. a size of book page resulting from folding each printed sheet into four leaves (eight pages). ■ a book of this size. ■ a size of writing paper, 10 in. × 8 in. (254 mm × 203 mm).

quartz /kwôrts/ ▸**n.** a hard white or colorless mineral consisting of silicon dioxide, found widely in igneous, metamorphic, and sedimentary rocks. It is often colored by impurities (as in amethyst, citrine, and cairngorm). [18th C.: from Ger. *Quarz*, from Polish dial. *kwardy*, corresponding to standard Pol. *twardy* 'hard.']

quartz-hal·o·gen ▸**adj.** (of a high-intensity electric lamp) using a quartz bulb containing the vapor of a halogen, usually iodine.

quartz·ite /ˈkwôrtˌsīt/ ▸**n.** Geol. an extremely compact, hard, granular rock consisting essentially of quartz. It often occurs as silicified sandstone, as in sarsen stones.

quartz lamp ▸**n.** an electric lamp in which the envelope is made of quartz, which allows ultraviolet light to pass through it. It may be a bulb containing a halogen or a tube containing mercury vapor.

qua·sar /ˈkwāˌzär/ ▸**n.** Astron. a massive and extremely remote celestial object, emitting exceptionally large amounts of energy, and typically having a starlike image in a telescope. It has been suggested that quasars contain massive black holes and may represent a stage in the evolution of some galaxies. [1960s: contr. of *quasi-stellar*.]

quash /kwôSH; kwäSH/ ▸**v.** [trans.] reject as invalid, esp. by legal procedure: *his conviction was quashed on appeal.* ■ put an end to; suppress: *a hospital executive quashed rumors that nursing staff will lose jobs.* [ME: from OFr. *quasser* 'annul,' from late L. *cassare* (med. L. also *quassare*), from *cassus* 'null, void.' Cf. SQUASH[1].]

quasi- ▸**comb. form** seemingly; apparently but not really: *quasi-American* | *quasi-scientific.* ■ being partly or almost: *quasicrystalline.* [from L. *quasi* 'as if, almost.']

qua·si con·tract /ˈkwāˌzī; ˈkwäzē/ ▸**n.** an obligation of one party to another imposed by law independently of an agreement between the parties. — **qua·si-con·trac·tu·al** **adj.**

qua·si·crys·tal /ˌkwāˌzīˈkristəl; ˌkwäzē-/ ▸**n.** Physics a locally regular aggregation of molecules resembling a crystal in certain properties (such as that of diffraction) but not having a consistent spatial periodicity. — **qua·si·crys·tal·line** /-ˈkristəlēn/ **adj.**

Qua·si·mo·do[1] /ˌkwäzēˈmōdō/ the name of the hunchback in Victor Hugo's novel *Notre-Dame de Paris* (1831).

Qua·si·mo·do[2], Salvatore (1901–68), Italian poet. His early work was influenced by French symbolism but his later work was more concerned with political and social issues. Notable works: *Water and Land* (1930) and *And It's Suddenly Evening* (1942). Nobel Prize for Literature (1959).

qua·si·par·ti·cle /ˌkwāzīˈpärtəkəl; ˌkwäzē-/ ▸**n.** Physics a quantum of energy in a crystal lattice or other system of bodies that has momentum and position and can in some respects be regarded as a particle.

quas·sia /ˈkwäSH(ē)ə/ ▸**n.** a South American shrub or small tree (genera *Quassia* and *Picrasma*, family Simaroubaceae) related to ailanthus. ■ the wood, bark, or root of this tree, yielding a bitter medicinal tonic, insecticide, and vermifuge. [named after Graman *Quassi*, an 18th-cent. Surinamese slave who discovered its medicinal properties in 1730.]

quat·er·cen·ten·ar·y /ˌkwätərsenˈtenərē; -ˈsentnˌerē/ ▸**n.** (pl. **-ar·ies**) the four-hundredth anniversary of a significant event. ▸**adj.** of or relating to such an anniversary. [19th C.: from L. *quater* 'four times' + CENTENARY.]

quat·er·nar·y /ˈkwätərˌnerē/ ▸**adj.** **1** fourth in order or rank; belonging to the fourth order. **2** (**Quaternary**) Geol. of, relating to, or denoting the most recent period in the Cenozoic era, following the Tertiary period and comprising the Pleistocene and Holocene epochs (and thus including the present). **3** Chem. denoting an ammonium compound containing a cation of the form NR_4^+, where R represents organic groups or atoms other than hydrogen. ■ (of a carbon atom) bonded to four other carbon atoms. ▸**n.** (**the Quaternary**) Geol. the Quaternary period or the system of deposits laid down during it. It began about 1,640,000 years ago. Humans and other mammals evolved into their present forms and were strongly affected by the ice ages of the Pleistocene. [ME (as a n. denoting a set of four): from L. *quaternarius*, from *quaterni* 'four at once,' from *quater* 'four times,' from *quattuor* 'four.']

qua·ter·ni·on /kwəˈtərnēən; kwä-/ ▸**n.** **1** Math. a complex number of the form $w + xi + yj + zk$, where w, x, y, z are real numbers and i, j, k are imaginary units that satisfy certain conditions. **2** rare a set of four people or things. [19th C.: from late L. *quaternio(n-)*, from L. *quarterni* (see QUATERNARY).]

qua·torze /kəˈtôrz/ ▸**n.** (in piquet) a set of four aces, kings, queens, jacks, or tens held in one hand. [18th C.: Fr., lit. 'fourteen,' from L. *quattuordecim*.]

quat·rain /ˈkwäˌtrān/ ▸**n.** a stanza of four lines, esp. one having alternate rhymes. [16th C.: from Fr., from *quatre* 'four.']

quat·re·foil /ˈkatərˌfoil; ˈkatrə-/ ▸**n.** an ornamental design of four lobes or leaves as used in architectural tracery, resembling a flower or four-leaf clover. [15th C.: from Anglo-Norman Fr., from OFr. *quatre* 'four' + *foil* 'leaf.']

quat·tro·cen·to /ˌkwätrōˈCHentō/ ▸**n.** (**the quattrocento**) the 15th century as a period of Italian art or architecture. [Ital., lit. '400' (shortened from *milquattrocento* '1400'), used with ref. to the years 1400–99.]

qua·ver /ˈkwāvər/ ▸**v.** [intrans.] (of a person's voice) shake or tremble in speaking, typically through nervousness or emotion. ▸**n.** **1** a shake or tremble in a person's voice. **2** Music, esp. Brit. another term for EIGHTH NOTE. — **qua·ver·ing·ly** **adv.** **qua·ver·y** **adj.** [ME (as a v. in the general sense 'tremble'): from dial. *quave* 'quake, tremble,' prob. from an OE word rel. to QUAKE. The n. is first recorded (16th C.) as a musical term.]

quay /kē; k(w)ā/ ▸**n.** a concrete, stone, or metal platform lying alongside or projecting into water for loading and unloading ships. — **quay·age** /ˈkēij; ˈk(w)āij/ **n.** [ME *key*, from OFr. *kay*, of Celtic origin. The change of spelling in the late 17th C. was influenced by the mod. Fr. spelling *quai*.]

quay·side /ˈkēˌsīd; ˈk(w)ā-/ ▸**n.** a quay and the area around it.

Que. ▸**abbr.** Quebec.

quean /kwēn/ ▸**n.** archaic an impudent or badly behaved girl or woman. ■ a prostitute. [OE *cwene* 'woman,' of Gmc. origin; rel. to Du. *kween* 'barren cow,' from an Indo-Eur. root shared by Gk. *gunē* 'woman.']

quea·sy /'kwēzē/ ▶ **adj.** (**queas·i·er, queas·i·est**) nauseated; feeling sick: *in the morning he was still pale and queasy.* ■ inducing a feeling of nausea: *the queasy swell of the boat.* ■ fig. slightly nervous or worried about something. — **quea·si·ly** /-zəlē/ **adv. quea·si·ness n.** [ME *queisy, coisy* 'causing nausea,' of uncert. origin; perh. rel. to OFr. *coisier* 'to hurt.']

Que·bec /k(w)ə'bek; kā-/ **1** a heavily forested province in eastern Canada; pop. 6,845,700. Settled by the French in 1608, it was ceded to the British in 1763 and became one of the original four provinces in the Dominion of Canada in 1867. The majority of its residents are French-speaking, and it is a focal point of the French-Canadian nationalist movement, which advocates independence for Quebec. French name **Québec.** ■ (also **Quebec City**) its capital city, a port on the St. Lawrence River; pop. 167,517. Founded in 1608, it is Canada's oldest city. It was captured from the French by the British in 1759 after the battle of the Plains of Abraham and became capital of Lower Canada (later Quebec) in 1791. **2** a code word representing the letter Q, used in radio communication. — **Que·beck·er** (also **Que·bec·er**) **n.**

que·bra·cho /kā'brä,chō; kə-/ ▶ **n.** (pl. **-chos**) a South American tree of the dogbane family (genus *Aspidosperma*) or of the cashew family (genus *Schinopsis*), whose timber and bark are a rich source of tannin. [19th C.: from Sp., from *quebrar* 'to break' + *hacha* 'ax.']

Quech·ua /'kechwə/ (also **Quech·a** /'kechə/, **Quich·ua**) ▶ **n.** (pl. same or **Quech·uas**) **1** a member of an American Indian people of Peru and parts of Bolivia, Chile, Colombia, and Ecuador. **2** the language or group of languages of this people. ▶ **adj.** of or relating to this people or their language. — **Quech·uan** /-wən/ (also **Quech·an** /'kechən/) **adj. & n.** [Sp., abbrev. of Quechua *qheswa simi* 'valley speech,' the designation of a Quechua dial.]

Queen /kwēn/, Ellery, writer and fictional detective of mystery novels; joint pseudonym of US cousins *Frederic Dannay* (1905–82), born *Daniel David Nathan*, and *Manfred Bennington Lee* (1905–71), born *Manford Emanuel Lepofsky*. The first of the numerous Ellery Queen mysteries was *The Roman Hat Mystery* (1929).

queen /kwēn/ ▶ **n. 1** the female ruler of an independent state, esp. one who inherits the position by right of birth. ■ (also **queen consort**) a king's wife. ■ a woman or thing regarded as excellent or outstanding of its kind: *the queen of romance novelists | Venice: Queen of the Adriatic.* ■ a woman or girl chosen to hold the most important position in a festival or event: *football stars and homecoming queens.* ■ (**the Queen**) dated (in the UK) the national anthem when there is a female sovereign. ■ informal a man's wife or girlfriend. **2** the most powerful chess piece that each player has, able to move any number of unobstructed squares in any direction along a rank, file, or diagonal on which it stands. **3** a playing card bearing a representation of a queen, normally ranking next below a king and above a jack. **4** Entomol. a reproductive female in a colony of social ants, bees, wasps, etc. **5** an adult female cat that has not been spayed. **6** informal a male homosexual, typically one regarded as ostentatiously effeminate. ■ [with modifier] used as part of a figurative compound for a person obsessed, typically sexually, with a specified appetite. A 'drag queen' is a professional female impersonator or a male homosexual transvestite; a 'leather queen' is a male homosexual leather fetishist. ▶ **v.** [trans.] **1** (**queen it over**) (of a woman) behave in an unpleasant and superior way toward. **2** Chess convert (a pawn) into a queen when it reaches the opponent's back rank on the board. — **queen·dom** /-dəm/ **n. queen·like** /-,līk/ **adj. queen·ship** /-,ship/ **n.** [OE *cwēn*, of Gmc. origin; rel. to **quean**.]

Queen Anne ▶ **adj.** denoting a style of English furniture or architecture characteristic of the early 18th century. The furniture is noted for its simple, proportioned style and for its cabriole legs and walnut veneer; the architecture is characterized by the use of red brick in simple, basically rectangular designs.

Queen Anne's lace ▶ **n.** the uncultivated form of the carrot (*Daucus carota*), with broad round heads of tiny white flowers that resemble lace. Also called **wild carrot.**

queen bee ▶ **n.** the single reproductive female in a hive or colony of honeybees. See illustration at **honeybee.** ■ informal a woman who has a dominant or controlling position in a particular group or sphere.

queen cake ▶ **n.** a small, soft, typically heart-shaped currant cake.

Queen Char·lotte Is·lands a group of more than 150 islands off the western coast of Canada, in British Columbia.

Queen Cit·y ▶ **n.** the preeminent city of a region.

queen con·sort /'kän,sôrt/ ▶ **n.** see **queen** (sense 1)

queen·ly /'kwēnlē/ ▶ **adj.** (**-li·er, -li·est**) fit for or appropriate to a queen. — **queen·li·ness** /-lēnis/ **n.**

Queen Maud Land /môd/ a part of Antarctica that borders the Atlantic Ocean, claimed since 1939 by Norway.

queen of pud·dings ▶ **n.** a pudding made with bread, jam, and meringue.

Queens /kwēnz/ a borough of New York City, at the western end of Long Island; pop. 1,951,598.

Queens·ber·ry rules /'kwēnz,berē; -bərē/ the standard rules of boxing, originally drawn up in 1867 to govern the sport in Britain. ■ standard rules of polite or acceptable behavior. [19th C.: named after John Sholto Douglas (1844–1900), 8th Marquess of *Queensberry*, who supervised the preparation of the rules.]

queen scal·lop ▶ **n.** a small, edible European scallop (*Chlamys opercularis*, family Pectinidae).

Queen's Eng·lish ▶ **n.** (**the Queen's English**) standard English language as written and spoken by educated people in Britain.

queen·side /'kwēn,sīd/ ▶ **n.** Chess the half of the board on which both queens stand at the start of a game (the left-hand side for White, right for Black).

Queens·land /'kwēnzlənd; -,land/ a state that comprises the northeastern part of Australia; pop. 2,922,000; capital, Brisbane. Originally established in 1824 as a penal colony, Queensland was constituted a separate colony in 1859, having previously formed part of New South Wales, and was federated with the other states of Australia in 1901. — **Queens·land·er n.**

Queens·land nut ▶ **n.** another term for **macadamia.**

queen's pawn ▶ **n.** Chess the pawn occupying the square immediately in front of each player's queen at the start of a game.

queens·ware /'kwēnz,we(ə)r/ ▶ **n.** a type of fine, cream-colored Wedgwood pottery. [18th C. (as *Queen's ware*): named in honor of Queen Charlotte (wife of George III), who had been presented with a set in 1765.]

queer /kwi(ə)r/ ▶ **adj. 1** strange; odd: *she had a queer feeling that they were being watched.* ■ [predic.] dated slightly ill. **2** informal usu. offens. (esp. of a man) homosexual. ▶ **n.** informal usu. offens. a homosexual man. ▶ **v.** [trans.] informal spoil or ruin (an agreement, event, or situation): *Reg didn't want someone meddling and queering the deal at the last minute.* — **queer·ish adj. queer·ly adv. queer·ness n.** [16th C.: considered to be from Ger. *quer* 'oblique, perverse,' but the origin is doubtful.]

– USAGE The word **queer** was first used to mean 'homosexual' in the early 20th century: it was originally, and often still is, a deliberately offensive and aggressive term when used by heterosexual people. In recent years, however, many gay people have taken the word **queer** and deliberately used it in place of **gay** or **homosexual**, in an attempt, by using the word positively, to deprive it of its negative power. This use of **queer** is now well established and widely used among gay people (esp. as an adjective or noun modifier, as in *queer rights; queer theory*) and at present exists alongside the other, deliberately offensive, use. (This use is similar to the way in which a racial epithet may be used *within* a racial group, but not by outsiders.) See also usage at **nigger.**

queer·core /'kwi(ə)r,kôr/ ▶ **n.** a cultural movement among young homosexuals that deliberately rebels against and dissociates itself from the established gay scene, having as its primary form of expression an aggressive type of punk-style music.

que·le·a /'kwēlēə/ ▶ **n.** a brownish weaverbird (genus *Quelea*) found in Africa, the male of which has either a black face or a red head. [mod. L., perh. from med. L. *qualea* 'quail.']

quell /kwel/ ▶ **v.** [trans.] put an end to (a rebellion or other disorder), typically by the use of force: *extra police were called to quell the disturbance.* ■ subdue or silence (someone): *Connor quelled him with a look.* ■ suppress (a feeling, esp. an unpleasant one): *he spoke up again to quell any panic among the assembled youngsters.* — **quell·er n.** [OE *cwellan* 'kill,' of Gmc. origin; rel. to Ger. *quälen* 'torture.']

quench /kwench/ ▶ **v.** [trans.] **1** satisfy (one's thirst) by drinking. ■ satisfy (a desire): *he only pursued her to quench an aching need.* **2** extinguish (a fire): *firemen hauled on hoses in a desperate bid to quench the flames.* ■ stifle or suppress (a feeling): *fury rose in him, but he quenched it.* ■ rapidly cool (red-hot metal or other material), esp. in cold water or oil. ■ Physics Electron. suppress or damp (an effect such as luminescence, or an oscillation or discharge). ▶ **n.** an act of quenching something very hot. — **quench·a·ble adj. quench·er n.** (esp. Physics & Metallurgy) **quench·less adj.** (literary). [OE *-cwencan* (in *acwencan* 'put out, extinguish'), of Gmc. origin.]

que·nelle /kə'nel/ ▶ **n.** (usu. **quenelles**) a small seasoned ball of pounded fish or meat. [Fr., prob. from Alsatian Ger. *knödel*.]

quer·ce·tin /'kwərsətin/ ▶ **n.** Chem. a yellow crystalline pigment, $C_{15}H_{10}O_7$, present in plants, used as a food supplement to reduce allergic responses or boost immunity. [19th C.: prob. from L. *quercetum* 'oak grove' (from *quercus* 'oak') + **-in**[1].]

Quer·cia, Jacopo della, see **della Quercia.**

Que·ré·ta·ro /ke'rātä,rō/ a state in central Mexico. ■ its capital city; pop. 454,000. In 1847, it was the scene of the signing of the treaty that ended the US–Mexican war.

que·rist /'kwi(ə)rist/ ▶ **n.** esp. archaic a person who asks questions; a questioner. [17th C.: from L. *quaerere* 'ask' + **-ist.**]

quern /kwərn/ ▶ **n.** a simple hand mill for grinding grain, typically consisting of two circular stones, the upper of which is rotated or rubbed to and fro on the lower one. [OE *cweorn(e)*, of Gmc. origin; rel. to ON *kvern* and Du. *kweern*.]

quer·u·lous /'kwer(y)ələs/ ▶ **adj.** complaining in a petulant or whining manner: *she became querulous and demanding.* — **quer·u·lous·ly adv. quer·u·lous·ness n.** [15th C.: from late L. *querulosus*, from L. *querulus*, from *queri* 'complain.']

que·ry /'kwi(ə)rē/ ▶ **n.** (pl. **-ries**) a question, esp. one addressed to an official or organization: *a spokeswoman said queries could not be answered until Monday.* ■ used in writing or speaking to question the accuracy of a following statement or to introduce a question. ■ esp. Print. a question mark. ▶ **v.** (**-ries, -ried**) [reporting verb] ask a question about something, esp. in order to express one's doubts about it or to check its validity or accuracy: [with clause] *many people queried whether any harm had been done* | [trans.] *he queried the medical database.* | [with direct speech] *"Why not?" he queried.* ■ [trans.] put a question or questions to (someone): *when these officers were queried, they felt unhappy.* [17th C.: Anglicized form of the L. imper. *quaere!*, used in the 16th C. in Engl. as a v. in the sense 'inquire' and as a n. meaning 'query,' from L. *quaerere* 'ask, seek.']

que·ry lan·guage ▶ **n.** Comput. a language for the specification of procedures for the retrieval (and sometimes also modification) of information from a database.

ques. ▶ **abbr.** question.

que·sa·dil·la /ˌkāsəˈdēyə/ ▶ **n.** a tortilla filled with cheese and heated. [Sp.]

quest /kwest/ ▶ **n.** a long or arduous search for something: *the quest for a reliable vaccine has intensified.* ■ (in medieval romance) an expedition made by a knight to accomplish a prescribed task. ▶ **v.** [intrans.] search for something: *he was a real scientist, questing after truth.* ■ [trans.] literary search for; seek out. — **quest·er** (also **ques·tor**) **n.** **quest·ing·ly adv.** [ME: from OFr. *queste* (n.), *quester* (v.), based on L. *quaerere* 'ask, seek.' See also INQUEST.]

ques·tion /ˈkweschən/ ▶ **n.** a sentence worded or expressed so as to elicit information: *we hope this leaflet has been helpful in answering your questions.* ■ a doubt about the truth or validity of something: *there is no question that America faces the threat of Balkanization.* ■ the raising of a doubt about or objection to something: *Edward was the only one she obeyed* **without question** | *her loyalty is really* **beyond question**. ■ a matter forming the basis of a problem requiring resolution: *we have kept an eye on the question of political authority.* ■ a matter or concern depending on or involving a specified condition or thing: *it was not simply* **a question of** *age and hierarchy.* ▶ **v.** [trans.] ask questions of (someone), esp. in an official context: *four men were being questioned about the killings* | [as n.] (**questioning**) *the young lieutenant escorted us to the barracks for questioning.* ■ feel or express doubt about; raise objections to: *members had questioned the cost of the scheme.*
– PHRASES **be (just** or **only) a question of time** be certain to happen sooner or later. **bring something into question** raise an issue for further consideration or discussion: *technology had brought into question the whole future of work.* **come into question** become an issue for further consideration or discussion: *our Sunday Trading laws have come into question.* **in question 1** being considered or discussed: *on the day in question, there were several serious emergencies.* **2** in doubt: *all of the old certainties are in question.* **no question of** no possibility of. **out of the question** too impracticable or unlikely to merit discussion. **question of fact** Law, an issue to be decided by a jury. **question of law** Law, an issue to be decided by a judge. **put the question** (in a formal debate or meeting) require supporters and opponents of a proposal to record their votes. — **ques·tion·er n.** **ques·tion·ing·ly adv.** [ME: from OFr. *question* (n.), *questionner* (v.), from L. *quaestio(n-)*, from *quaerere* 'ask, seek.']

ques·tion·a·ble /ˈkweschənəbəl/ ▶ **adj.** doubtful as regards truth or quality: [with clause] *it is questionable whether any of these exceptions is genuine.* ■ not clearly honest, honorable, or wise: *a few men of allegedly questionable character.* — **ques·tion·a·bil·i·ty** /ˌkweschənəˈbilətē/ **n.** **ques·tion·a·ble·ness n.** **ques·tion·a·bly** /-əblē/ **adv.**

ques·tion·ar·y /ˈkweschəˌnerē/ ▶ **n.** (pl. **-ar·ies**) a questionnaire. [19th C.: from Fr. *questionnaire* (see QUESTIONNAIRE).]

ques·tion mark ▶ **n.** a punctuation mark (?) indicating a question. ■ fig. used to express doubt or uncertainty about something: *there's a question mark over his future.*

ques·tion·naire /ˌkweschəˈne(ə)r/ ▶ **n.** a set of printed or written questions with a choice of answers, devised for the purposes of a survey or statistical study. [19th C.: from Fr., from *questionner* 'to question.']

Quet·ta /ˈkwetə/ a city in western Pakistan, the capital of Baluchistan province; pop. 350,000.

quet·zal /ketˈsäl/ ▶ **n. 1** a bird (genus *Pharomachrus*) of the trogon family, with iridescent green plumage and typically red underparts, found in the forests of tropical America. The male **resplendent quetzal** (*P. mocinno*) has very long tail coverts and was venerated by the Aztecs. **2** the basic monetary unit of Guatemala, equal to 100 centavos. [19th C. (sense 1): from Sp., from Aztec *quetzalli* 'brightly colored tail feather.']

Quet·zal·co·a·tl /ˌketsälkōˈätl/ the plumed serpent god of the Toltec and Aztec civilizations. Traditionally the god of the morning and evening star, he later became known as the patron of priests, inventor of books and of the calendar, and as the symbol of death and resurrection.

quet·zal·co·a·tlus /ˌketsəlkōˈätləs/ ▶ **n.** a giant pterosaur (genus *Quetzalcoatlus*, family Azhdarchidae) of the late Cretaceous period. It was the largest ever flying animal, with a wingspan of up to 50 feet (15 m). [mod. L., from the name of the Aztec god QUETZALCOATL.]

queue /kyo͞o/ ▶ **n. 1** esp. Brit. a line or sequence of people or vehicles awaiting their turn to be attended to or to proceed. **2** Comput. a list of data items, commands, etc., stored so as to be retrievable in a definite order, usually the order of insertion. **3** archaic a braid of hair worn at the back. ▶ **v.** (**queues, queued, queu·ing** or **queue·ing**) [intrans.] esp. Brit. **1** take one's place in a queue: *in the war they had queued for food* | [with infin.] fig. *companies are queuing up to move to the bay.* **2** [trans.] Comput. arrange in a queue. [16th C. (as a heraldic term denoting the tail of an animal): from Fr., based on L. *cauda* 'tail.' Cf. CUE². Sense 1 dates from the 19th C.]

Que·zon Cit·y /ˈkāzän; -sōn/ a city on the island of Luzon in the northern Philippines; pop. 1,667,000. Established in 1940, it was the capital of the Philippines 1948–76.

quib·ble /ˈkwibəl/ ▶ **n. 1** a slight objection or criticism: *the only quibble about this book is the price.* **2** archaic a play on words; a pun. ▶ **v.** [intrans.] argue or raise objections about a trivial matter: *they are always quibbling about the amount they are prepared to pay.* — **quib·bler n.** **quib·bling·ly adv.** [17th C.: dimin. of obs. *quib* 'a petty objection,' prob. from L. *quibus*, dative and ablative pl. of *qui, quae, quod* 'who, what, which,' frequently used in legal documents.]

Qui·ché /kēˈchä/ ▶ **n.** (pl. same or **-chés**) **1** a member of a people inhabiting the western highlands of Guatemala. **2** the Mayan language of this people. ▶ **adj.** of or relating to this people or their language. [the name in Quiché.]

quiche /kēsh/ ▶ **n.** a baked flan or tart with a savory filling thickened with eggs. [Fr., from Alsatian dial. *Küchen*; rel. to Ger. *Kuchen* 'cake.']

Quich·ua /ˈkichwə/ ▶ **n. & adj.** var. of QUECHUA.

quick /kwik/ ▶ **adj. 1** moving fast or doing something in a short time: *some children are particularly quick learners* | *I was much quicker than he was and held him at bay for several laps* | [with infin.] *he was always quick to point out her faults.* ■ lasting or taking a short time: *she took a quick look through the drawers* | *we went to the pub for a quick drink.* ■ happening with little or no delay; prompt: *children like to see quick results from their efforts.* **2** (of a person) prompt to understand, think, or learn; intelligent: *it was quick of him to spot the mistake.* ■ (of a person's eye or ear) keenly perceptive; alert. ■ (of a person's temper) easily roused. ▶ **adv.** informal at a fast rate; quickly: *he'll find some place where he can make money quicker* | [as exclam.] *Get out, quick!* ▶ **n. 1** (**the quick**) the soft, tender flesh below the growing part of a fingernail or toenail. ■ fig. the central or most sensitive part of someone or something. **2** [as pl. n.] (**the quick**) archaic those who are living: *the quick and the dead.*
– PHRASES **cut someone to the quick** cause someone deep distress by a hurtful remark or action. **(as) quick as a flash** see FLASH. **quick on the draw** see DRAW. **quick with child** archaic at a stage of pregnancy when movements of the fetus have been felt. — **quick·ly adv.** **quick·ness n.** [OE *cwic, cwicu* 'alive, animated, alert,' of Gmc. origin.]

quick-and-dirt·y ▶ **adj.** informal makeshift; done or produced hastily: *a quick-and-dirty synopsis of their work.*

quick·en /ˈkwikən/ ▶ **v. 1** make or become faster or quicker: [trans.] *she quickened her pace, desperate to escape* | [intrans.] *I felt my pulse quicken.* **2** [intrans.] spring to life; become animated: *her interest quickened* | [as adj.] (**quickening**) *he looked with quickening curiosity through the smoke.* ■ [trans.] stimulate: *the coroner's words suddenly quickened his own memories.* ■ [trans.] give or restore life to: *on the third day after his death the human body of Jesus was quickened by the Spirit.* ■ archaic (of a woman) reach a stage in pregnancy when movements of the fetus can be felt. ■ archaic (of a fetus) begin to show signs of life. ■ [trans.] archaic make (a fire) burn brighter.

quick-freeze ▶ **v.** [trans.] freeze (food) rapidly so as to preserve its nutritional value.

quick·ie /ˈkwikē/ informal ▶ **n.** a thing done or made quickly or hastily, in particular: ■ a rapidly consumed alcoholic drink. ■ a brief act of sexual intercourse. ▶ **adj.** done or made quickly: *his wife cooperated with a quickie divorce.*

quick·lime /ˈkwikˌlīm/ ▶ **n.** see LIME¹.

quick march ▶ **n.** a brisk military march. ▶ **exclam.** a command to begin marching quickly.

quick-re·lease ▶ **adj.** (of a device) designed for rapid release: *a quick-release button.*

quick·sand /ˈkwikˌsand/ ▶ **n.** (also **quicksands**) loose wet sand that yields easily to pressure and sucks in anything resting on or falling into it: fig. *John found himself sinking fast in financial quicksand.*

quick·sil·ver /ˈkwikˌsilvər/ ▶ **n.** the liquid metal mercury. ■ used in similes and metaphors to describe something that moves or changes very quickly, or that is difficult to hold or contain: *his mood changed like quicksilver.*

quick·step /ˈkwikˌstep/ ▶ **n.** a fast foxtrot in 4/4 time. ▶ **v.** (**-stepped, -step·ping**) [intrans.] dance the quickstep.

quick·thorn /ˈkwikˌthôrn/ ▶ **n.** another term for HAWTHORN.

quick time ▶ **n.** Mil. marching that is conducted at about 120 paces per minute.

quick trick ▶ **n.** (usu. **quick tricks**) Bridge a card such as an ace (or a king in a suit where the ace is also held) that can normally be relied on to win a trick.

quick-wit·ted ▶ **adj.** showing or characterized by an ability to think or respond quickly or effectively. — **quick-wit·ted·ness n.**

quid¹ /kwid/ ▶ **n.** (pl. same) Brit., informal one pound sterling: *we paid him four hundred quid.* [17th C.: of obscure origin.]

quid² ▶ **n.** a lump of tobacco for chewing. [18th C.: var. of CUD.]

quid·di·ty /ˈkwiditē/ ▶ **n.** (pl. **-ties**) esp. Philos. the inherent nature or essence of someone or something. ■ a distinctive feature; a peculiarity: *his quirks and quiddities.* [ME: from med. L. *quidditas*, from L. *quid* 'what.']

quid·nunc /ˈkwidˌnəngk/ ▶ **n.** archaic an inquisitive and gossipy person. [18th C.: from L. *quid nunc?* 'what now?']

quid pro quo /ˈkwid ˌprō ˈkwō/ ▶ **n.** (pl. **quos**) a favor or advantage granted in return for something: *the pardon was a quid pro quo for their help in releasing hostages.* [16th C. (denoting a medicine substituted for another): L., 'something for something.']

qui·es·cent /kwē'esnt; kwī-/ ▶ **adj.** in a state or period of inactivity or dormancy: *strikes were headed by groups of workers who had previously been quiescent | quiescent ulcerative colitis.* — **qui·es·cence n. qui·es·cent·ly adv.** [17th C.: from L. *quiescent-* 'being still,' from the v. *quiescere*, from *quies* 'quiet.']

qui·et /'kwīət/ ▶ **adj.** (**qui·et·er, qui·et·est**) **1** making little or no noise: *the car has a quiet, economical engine | I was as quiet as I could be, but he knew I was there.* ■ (of a place, period of time, or situation) without much activity, disturbance, or excitement: *the street below was quiet, little traffic braving the snow.* ■ without being disturbed or interrupted: *all he wanted was a quiet drink.* **2** carried out discreetly, secretly, or with moderation: *we wanted a quiet wedding | I'll have a quiet word with him.* ■ (of a person) tranquil and reserved by nature; not brash or forceful: *his quiet, middle-aged parents.* ■ [attrib.] expressed in a restrained or understated way: *Molly spoke with quiet confidence.* ■ (of a color or garment) unobtrusive; not bright or showy. ▶ **n.** absence of noise or bustle; silence; calm: *the ringing of the telephone shattered the early morning quiet.* ■ freedom from disturbance or interruption by others: *he understood her wish for* ***peace and quiet.*** ■ a peaceful or settled state of affairs in social or political life: *after several months of comparative quiet, the scandal reerupted in August.* ▶ **v.** make or become silent, calm, or still: [trans.] *there are ways of* ***quieting*** *kids* ***down*** | [intrans.] *the journalists* ***quieted down*** *as Judy stepped on to the dais.*

– PHRASES **do anything for a quiet life** see LIFE. **keep quiet** (or **keep someone quiet**) refrain or prevent someone from speaking or from disclosing something secret. **keep something quiet** (or **keep quiet about something**) refrain from disclosing information about something; keep something secret. **on the quiet** informal without anyone knowing or noticing; secretly or unobtrusively. **(as) quiet as the grave** see GRAVE[1]. **(as) quiet as a mouse** (of a person or animal) extremely quiet or docile. — **qui·et·ly adv. qui·et·ness n.** [ME (orig. as a n. denoting peace as opposed to war): via OFr., based on L. *quies, quiet-* 'repose, quiet.']

qui·et·en /'kwīətn/ ▶ **v.** esp. Brit. make or become quiet and calm: [trans.] *her mother was trying to quieten her* | [intrans.] *things seemed to have quietened down.*

qui·et·ism /'kwīə,tizəm/ ▶ **n.** (in the Christian faith) devotional contemplation and abandonment of the will as a form of religious mysticism. ■ calm acceptance of things as they are without attempts to resist or change them: *political quietism.* — **qui·et·ist n. & adj. qui·et·is·tic** /,kwīə'tistik/ **adj.** [17th C. (denoting the religious mysticism based on the teachings of the Sp. priest Miguel de Molinos (*c.*1640–97)): from Ital. *quietismo*, based on L. *quies, quiet-* 'quiet.']

qui·e·tude /'kwīə,t(y)o͞od/ ▶ **n.** a state of stillness, calmness, and quiet in a person or place. [16th C.: from Fr. *quiétude* or med. L. *quietudo*, from L. *quietus* 'quiet.']

qui·e·tus /'kwīətəs/ ▶ **n.** (pl. **qui·et·us·es**) death or something that causes death, regarded as a release from life. ■ archaic something that has a calming or soothing effect. [ME: abbrev. of med. L. *quietus est* 'he is quit', orig. used as a form of receipt or discharge on payment of a debt.]

quiff /kwif/ ▶ **n.** esp. Brit. a piece of hair, esp. on a man, brushed upward and backward from the forehead. [19th C. (orig. denoting a lock of hair plastered down on the forehead, esp. as worn by soldiers): of unknown origin.]

quill /kwil/ ▶ **n. 1** (also **quill feather**) any of the main wing or tail feathers of a bird. ■ the hollow shaft of a feather, esp. the lower part or calamus that lacks barbs. ■ (also **quill pen**) a pen made from a main wing or tail feather of a large bird. **2** an object in the form of a thin tube, in particular: ■ the hollow sharp spines of a porcupine, hedgehog, or other spiny mammal. ■ a weaver's spindle. ▶ **v.** [trans.] **1** form (fabric) into small cylindrical folds. **2** pierce or cover (fabric or bark) with quills. [ME (in the senses 'hollow stem' and 'shaft of a feather'): prob. from Mid. Low Ger. *quiele.*]

quill·ing /'kwiliNG/ ▶ **n.** a piece of quilled lace or other fabric used as a trim. ■ a type of ornamental handicraft involving the shaping of paper, fabric, or glass into delicate pleats or folds.

quill·work /'kwil,wərk/ ▶ **n.** a decoration for clothing and possessions characteristic of certain North American Indian peoples, using softened and dyed porcupine quills.

quill·wort /'kwil,wərt; -,wôrt/ ▶ **n.** a plant (genus *Isoetes*, family Isoetaceae) related to the club mosses, occurring typically as a submerged aquatic.

quilt /kwilt/ ▶ **n.** a warm bed covering made of padding enclosed between layers of fabric and kept in place by lines of stitching. ■ a knitted or fabric bedspread with decorative stitching. ■ a layer of padding used for insulation. ▶ **v.** [trans.] join together (layers of fabric or padding) with lines of stitching to form a bed covering. — **quilt·er n.** [ME: from OFr. *cuilte*, from L. *culcita* 'mattress, cushion.']

quilt·ed /'kwiltid/ ▶ **adj.** (of a garment, bed covering, or sleeping bag) made of two layers of cloth filled with padding held in place by lines of stitching.

quilt·ing /'kwiltiNG/ ▶ **n.** the making of quilts as an activity. ■ the work so produced; quilted material. ■ the pattern of stitching used for such work.

qui·nac·ri·done /kwə'nakrə,dōn/ ▶ **n.** Chem. any of a group of synthetic organic compounds whose molecules contain three benzene and two pyridine rings arranged alternately. [20th C.: from *quin(oline)* + *acrid(ine)* + -ONE.]

quin·a·crine /'kwinə,krin/ ▶ **n.** Med. a synthetic compound derived from acridine, used as an anthelmintic and antimalarial drug. ■ (in full **quinacrine mustard**) Biochem. a nitrogen mustard derived from this, used as a fluorescent stain for chromosomes. [1930s: blend of QUININE and ACRIDINE.]

qui·na·ry /'kwī,nerē/ ▶ **adj.** of or relating to the number five, in particular: ■ of the fifth order or rank. ■ Zool., hist. relating to or denoting a former system of classification in which the animal kingdom is divided into five subkingdoms, and each subkingdom into five classes. [17th C.: from L. *quinarius*, from *quini* 'set of five,' from *quinque* 'five.']

quince /kwins/ ▶ **n. 1** a hard, acid, pear-shaped fruit used in preserves or as flavoring. **2** the shrub or small tree (*Cydonia oblonga*) of the rose family that bears this fruit, native to western Asia. ■ (**Japanese quince**) another term for JAPONICA. [ME: from OFr. *cooin*, from L. *(malum) cotoneum*, var. of *(malum) cydonium* 'apple of *Cydonia* (= Canea, in Crete).']

quin·cen·ten·ni·al /,kwinsen'tenēəl/ ▶ **n.** the five-hundredth anniversary of a significant event. ▶ **adj.** of or relating to such an anniversary. [19th C.: from L. *quinque* 'five' + CENTENNIAL.]

Quin·cey, Thomas De, see **DE QUINCEY**.

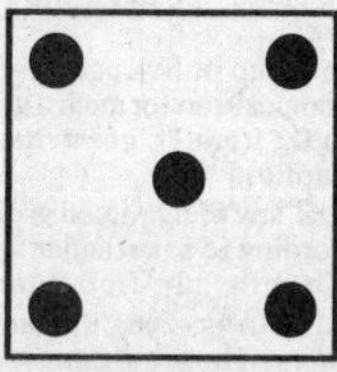

quincunx 1

quin·cunx /'kwin,kəNGks/ ▶ **n.** (pl. **quin·cunx·es**) an arrangement of five objects with four at the corners of a square or rectangle and the fifth at its center, used for the five on dice or playing cards, and in planting trees. — **quin·cun·cial** /,kwin'kənSHəl/ **adj. quin·cun·cial·ly** /,kwin'kənSHəlē/ **adv.** [17th C.: from L., lit. 'five twelfths,' from *quinque* 'five' + *uncia* 'twelfth.']

Quin·cy /'kwinzē/ a historic city in eastern Massachusetts, on Boston Harbor; pop. 88,025.

Quine /kwīn/, Willard Van Orman (1908–2000), US philosopher. He argued that even the principles of logic themselves can be questioned and replaced.

qui·nel·la /kwi'nelə/ (also **qui·niel·a** /kēn'yelə/) ▶ **n.** a bet in which the first two places in a race must be predicted, in any order. Compare with EXACTA. [1940s: from L. Amer. Sp. *quiniela.*]

quin·i·dine /'kwinə,dēn/ ▶ **n.** Med. a compound obtained from cinchona bark and used to treat irregularities of heart rhythm. It is an isomer of quinine.

qui·nine /'kwī,nīn/ ▶ **n.** a bitter crystalline compound, $C_{20}H_{24}N_2O_2$, present in cinchona bark, used as a tonic and formerly as an antimalarial drug. [19th C.: from Sp. *quina* 'cinchona bark' (from Quechua *kina* 'bark') + -INE[4].]

qui·noa /'kēnwä/ ▶ **n.** a goosefoot (*Chenopodium quinoa*) found in the Andes, where it was widely cultivated for its edible starchy seeds before the introduction of Old World grains. ■ the grainlike seeds of this plant, used as food and in the production of alcoholic drinks. [17th C.: Sp. spelling of Quechua *kinua, kinoa.*]

quin·o·line /'kwinəlin/ ▶ **n.** Chem. a pungent oily liquid, C_9H_7N, present in coal tar and bone oil.

qui·none /'kwinōn/ ▶ **n.** Chem. another term for 1,4-benzoquinone (see BENZOQUINONE). ■ any compound with the same ring structure as 1,4-benzoquinone.

Quin·qua·ges·i·ma /,kwiNGkwə'jesəmə/ (also **Quinquagesima Sunday**) **n.** the Sunday before the beginning of Lent. [ult. from L. *quinquagesimus* 'fiftieth,' (because it is ten days before the forty penitential days of Lent).]

quinque- ▶ **comb. form** five; having five: *quinquevalent.* [from L. *quinque* 'five.']

quin·quen·ni·al /kwin'kwenēəl/ ▶ **adj.** recurring every five years. ■ lasting for or relating to a period of five years. — **quin·quen·ni·al·ly adv.** [15th C.: from L. *quinquennis* (from *quinque* 'five' + *annus* 'year') + -AL.]

quin·quen·ni·um /kwin'kwenēəm/ ▶ **n.** (pl. **-quen·ni·a** /-'kwenēə/ or **-quen·ni·ums**) a specified period of five years.

quin·que·va·lent /,kwiNGkwə'vālənt/ ▶ **adj.** Chem. another term for PENTAVALENT.

quin·sy /'kwinzē/ ▶ **n.** inflammation of the throat, esp. an abscess in the region of the tonsils. [ME: from OFr. *quinencie*, from med. L. *quinancia*, from Gk. *kunankhē* 'canine quinsy,' from *kun-* 'dog' + *ankhein* 'throttle.']

quint /kwint/ ▶ **n.** short for QUINTUPLET.

quin·tain /ˈkwintn/ ▶ **n.** hist. a post set up as a mark in tilting with a lance, typically with a sandbag attached that swung around and struck an unsuccessful tilter. ■ (**the quintain**) the medieval military exercise of tilting at such a post.

quin·tal /ˈkwintl/ ▶ **n.** a unit of weight equal to a hundredweight (112 lb) or formerly, 100 lb. ■ a unit of weight equal to 100 kg. [ME: via OFr. from med. L. *quintale*, from Arab. *ḳinṭār*, based on L. *centenarius* 'containing a hundred.']

Quin·ta·na Roo /kēnˈtänä ˈrō͞o/ a state in southeastern Mexico, on the Yucatán Peninsula.

quinte /kant/ ▶ **n.** Fencing the fifth of eight standard parrying positions.

quin·tes·sence /kwinˈtesəns/ ▶ **n.** the most perfect or typical example of a quality or class: *the quintessence of professionalism.* ■ the aspect of something regarded as the intrinsic and central constituent of its character: *advertising is the quintessence of marketing.* ■ a refined essence or extract of a substance. ■ (in classical and medieval philosophy) a fifth substance in addition to the four elements, thought to compose the heavenly bodies and to be latent in all things. [ME (as a term in philosophy): via Fr. from med. L. *quinta essentia* 'fifth essence.']

quin·tes·sen·tial /ˌkwintəˈsenCHəl/ ▶ **adj.** representing the most perfect or typical example of a quality or class: *the quintessential tough guy.* — **quin·tes·sen·tial·ly** **adv.**

quin·tet /kwinˈtet/ ▶ **n.** a group of five people playing music or singing together. ■ a musical composition for such a group. ■ any group of five people or things. [18th C.: from Fr. *quintette* or Ital. *quintetto*, from *quinto* 'fifth,' from L. *quintus*.]

quin·tile /ˈkwinˌtīl/ ▶ **n.** Stat. any of five equal groups into which a population can be divided according to a particular variable. [17th C.: from L. *quintilis (mensis)* 'fifth month, July,' from *quintus* 'fifth.']

Quin·til·ian /kwinˈtilēən/ (C.AD 35–c.96), Roman rhetorician; Latin name *Marcus Fabius Quintilianus*. He wrote *Education of an Orator*.

quin·til·lion /kwinˈtilyən/ ▶ **cardinal number** (pl. **-lions** or (with numeral) same) a thousand raised to the power of six (10^{18}). — **quin·til·lionth** /-yənTH/ **ordinal number.** [17th C.: from Fr., from *million*, by substitution of the prefix *quinti-* 'five' (from L. *quintus* 'fifth') for the initial letters.]

quin·tu·ple /kwinˈt(y)o͞opəl; -ˈtəpəl/ ▶ **adj.** [attrib.] consisting of five parts or things. ■ five times as much or as many. ■ (of time in music) having five beats in a bar. ▶ **v.** increase or cause to increase fivefold. ▶ **n.** a fivefold number or amount; a set of five. — **quin·tu·ply** /-(ə)lē/ **adv.**

quin·tu·plet /kwinˈtəplət; -ˈt(y)o͞oplət/ ▶ **n.** (usu. **quintuplets**) each of five children born to the same mother at one birth.

quin·tu·pli·cate ▶ **adj.** /kwinˈt(y)o͞opləˌkit/ fivefold. ■ of which five copies are made. ▶ **v.** /kwinˈt(y)o͞opləˌkāt/ [trans.] multiply by five.
– PHRASES **in quintuplicate** in five identical copies. ■ in groups of five.

quip /kwip/ ▶ **n.** a witty remark. ▶ **v.** (**quipped, quip·ping**) [intrans.] make a witty remark. — **quip·ster** /-stər/ **n.** [16th C.: perh. from L. *quippe* 'indeed.']

qui·pu /ˈkēpo͞o; ˈkwipo͞o/ ▶ **n.** an ancient Inca device for recording information, consisting of variously colored threads knotted in different ways. [from Quechua *khipu* 'knot.']

quire /kwī(ə)r/ ▶ **n.** four sheets of paper or parchment folded to form eight leaves. ■ any collection of leaves one within another in a manuscript or book. ■ 25 (formerly 24) sheets of paper; one twentieth of a ream. [ME: from OFr. *quaier*, from L. *quaterni* 'set of four.']

quirk /kwərk/ ▶ **n.** 1 a peculiar behavioral habit: *his annoying quirks.* ■ a strange chance occurrence: *a strange quirk of fate.* 2 Archit. an acute hollow between convex or other moldings. — **quirk·ish** **adj.** [16th C. (as a v.): of unknown origin.]

quirk·y /ˈkwərkē/ ▶ **adj.** (**quirk·i·er, quirk·i·est**) characterized by peculiar or unexpected traits: *quirky charm.* — **quirk·i·ly** /-kəlē/ **adv.** **quirk·i·ness** /-kēnis/ **n.**

quirt /kwərt/ ▶ **n.** a short-handled riding whip with a braided leather lash. ▶ **v.** [trans.] hit with a whip of this kind. [19th C. (orig. US): from Sp. *cuerda* 'cord' (from L. *chorda* 'cord') or from Mex. Sp. *cuarta* 'whip.']

quis·ling /ˈkwizliNG/ ▶ **n.** a traitor who collaborates with an enemy force occupying their country. [World War II: after Major Vidkun *Quisling* (1887–1945), the Norwegian army officer who ruled Norway on behalf of the German occupying forces 1940–45.]

quit[1] /kwit/ ▶ **v.** (**quit·ting**; past and past part. **quit·ted** or **quit**) [trans.] leave (a place), usually permanently. ■ informal resign from (a job). ■ informal stop or discontinue (an action or activity): *quit moaning!* [ME: from OFr. *quiter* (v.), *quite* (adj.), from L. *quietus*, past part. of *quiescere* 'be still,' from *quies* 'quiet.']

quit[2] ▶ **n.** [in comb.] used in names of various small songbirds found in the Caribbean area, e.g., **bananaquit.** [19th C.: prob. imitative.]

quitch /kwiCH/ (also **quitch grass**) ▶ **n.** another term for COUCH GRASS.

quit·claim /ˈkwitˌklām/ ▶ **n.** Law a formal renunciation or relinquishing of a claim. ▶ **v.** [trans.] renounce or relinquish a claim.

quite /kwīt/ ▶ **adv.** [usu. as submodifier] 1 to the utmost or most absolute extent or degree; absolutely; completely: *it's quite out of the question.* ■ very; really (used as an intensifier): *I'm quite sorry.* 2 to a certain or fairly significant extent or degree; fairly: *it's quite warm outside.* ▶ **exclam.** (also **quite so**) Brit. expressing agreement with or understanding of a remark or statement.
– PHRASES **not quite** not completely or entirely. **quite a ——** (also often ironic **quite the ——**) used to indicate that the specified person or thing is perceived as particularly notable, remarkable, or impressive: *it's been quite a year.* **quite a few** see FEW. **quite a lot** (or **a bit**) a considerable number or amount of something: *quite a bit older.* **quite some** a considerable amount of: *hasn't been seen for quite some time.* **quite something** see SOMETHING. **quite the thing** dated socially acceptable: *she was quite the thing in heels.* [ME: from the obs. adj. *quite*, var. of QUIT[1].]

Qui·to /ˈkētō/ the capital of Ecuador; pop. 1,401,000. It is situated in the Andes at an altitude of 9,350 feet (2,850 m).

quit·rent ▶ **n.** hist. a rent paid by a freeholder or copyholder in lieu of services required of them.

quits /kwits/ ▶ **adj.** [predic.] (of two people) on even terms, esp. because a debt or score has been settled.
– PHRASES **call it quits** agree or acknowledge that terms are now equal, esp. on the settlement of a debt. ■ decide to abandon an activity or venture. [15th C.: perh. a colloq. abbrev. of med. L. *quittus*, from L. *quietus*.]

quit·tance /ˈkwitns/ ▶ **n.** archaic or literary a release or discharge from a debt or obligation. ■ a document certifying this; a receipt. [ME: from OFr. *quitance*, from *quiter* 'to release' (see QUIT[1]).]

quit·ter /ˈkwitər/ ▶ **n.** [usu. with negative] informal a person who gives up easily or does not finish a task.

quiv·er[1] /ˈkwivər/ ▶ **v.** [intrans.] tremble or shake with a slight rapid motion. ■ (of a person, a part of their body, or their voice) tremble with sudden strong emotion. ▶ **n.** a slight trembling movement or sound, esp. one caused by a sudden strong emotion: *a quiver of fear.* — **quiv·er·ing·ly** **adv.** **quiv·er·y** **adj.** [ME: from OE *cwifer* 'nimble, quick.']

archer's quiver

quiv·er[2] ▶ **n.** an archer's case for holding arrows. [ME: from Anglo-Norman Fr. *quiveir*, of West Gmc. origin; rel. to Du. *koker* and Ger. *Köcher*.]

qui vive /ˌkēˈvēv/ ▶ **n.** (in phrase **on the qui vive**) on the alert or lookout. [16th C.: from Fr., literally '(long) live who?,' i.e., 'on whose side are you?,' used as a sentry's challenge.]

Qui·xo·te /kēˈhōtē/ see DON QUIXOTE.

quix·ot·ic /kwikˈsätik/ ▶ **adj.** exceedingly idealistic; unrealistic and impractical: *a vast and quixotic project.* — **quix·ot·i·cal·ly** /-ik(ə)lē/ **adv.** **quix·o·tism** /ˈkwiksəˌtizəm/ **n.** **quix·o·try** /ˈkwiksətrē/ **n.** [18th C.: from DON QUIXOTE + -IC.]

quiz[1] /kwiz/ ▶ **n.** (pl. **quiz·zes**) a test of knowledge, esp. a brief, informal written or oral test given to students. ▶ **v.** (**quiz·zes, quizzed, quiz·zing**) [trans.] (often **be quizzed**) ask (someone) questions. ■ give (a student or class) an informal written test or examination. [19th C. (as a v.; orig. US): possibly from QUIZ[2], influenced by INQUISITIVE.]

quiz[2] archaic ▶ **v.** (**quiz·zes, quizzed, quiz·zing**) [trans.] 1 look curiously or intently at (someone) through or as if through an eyeglass. 2 make fun of. ▶ **n.** (pl. **quiz·zes**) 1 a practical joke or hoax; a piece of banter or ridicule. ■ a person who ridicules another; a hoaxer. 2 a person who is odd or eccentric. — **quiz·zer** **n.** [18th C.: origin unknown.]

quiz·mas·ter /ˈkwizˌmastər/ ▶ **n.** a person who asks the questions in a television or radio quiz program.

quiz show ▶ **n.** a television or radio program in which people compete in a quiz, typically for prizes.

quiz·zi·cal /ˈkwizəkəl/ ▶ **adj.** (of a person's expression or behavior) indicating mild or amused puzzlement: *a quizzical look.* — **quiz·zi·cal·i·ty** /ˌkwiziˈkalətē/ **n.** **quiz·zi·cal·ly** **adv.** **quiz·zi·cal·ness** **n.**

Qum /ko͝om/ var. of QOM.

Qum·ran /ko͝omˈrän/ a region on the western shore of the Dead Sea. The Dead Sea scrolls were found 1947–56 in caves at nearby Khirbet Qumran.

quod·li·bet /ˈkwädləˌbet/ ▶ **n.** 1 archaic a topic for or exercise in philosophical or theological discussion. 2 literary a medley of well-known tunes. — **quod·li·be·tar·i·an** /ˌkwädləbiˈte(ə)rēən/ **n.** [ME: from L., from *quod* 'what' + *libet* 'it pleases.']

quoin /k(w)oin/ ▶ **n.** 1 an external angle of a wall or building. ■ (also **quoin stone**) any of the stones or bricks forming such an angle; a cornerstone. 2 Print. a wedge or expanding mechanical device used for locking a letterpress form into a chase. ▶ **v.** [trans.] 1 provide (a wall) with quoins or corners. 2 Print. lock up (a form) with a quoin. [ME: var. of COIN, used earlier in the sense 'cornerstone' and 'wedge.']

quoin·ing /ˈk(w)oiniNG/ ▶ **n.** the stone or brick used to form a quoin of a wall or building.

quoit /k(w)oit/ ▶ **n.** 1 a ring of iron, rope, or rubber thrown in a game to encircle or land as near as possible to an upright peg. ■ (**quoits**) [treated as sing.] a game consisting of aiming and throwing such rings. 2 the flat covering stone of a dolmen. ■ [often in place names] the dolmen itself. [ME: prob. of Fr. origin.]

quok·ka /ˈkwäkə/ ▶ **n.** a small, short-tailed wallaby (*Setonix brachyurus*) native to Western Australia. [19th C.: from Nyungar *kwaka*.]

quoll /kwäl/ ▶ **n.** a catlike, carnivorous marsupial (genus *Dasyurus*, family Dasyuridae) with short legs and a white-spotted coat, native to the forests of Australia and New Guinea.

quon·dam /ˈkwändəm; -ˌdam/ ▶ **adj.** [attrib.] formal that once was; former: *its quondam popularity.* [16th C.: from L., 'formerly.']

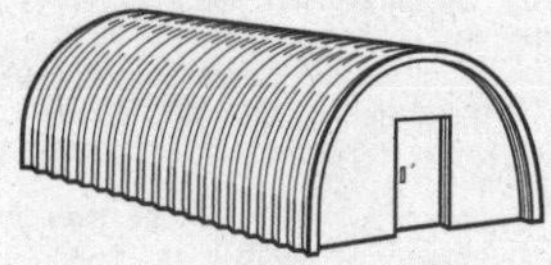

Quonset hut

Quon·set /ˈkwänsət/ (usu. **Quonset hut**) ▶ **n.** trademark a semicylindrical building made of corrugated metal. [World War II: after *Quonset* Point, Rhode Island, where such huts were first made.]

quo·rum /ˈkwôrəm/ ▶ **n.** (pl. **quo·rums**) the minimum number of members of an assembly that must be present to make a meeting valid. [ME (referring to justices of the peace): from L., 'of whom,' used in commissions for committee members.]

quot. ▶ **abbr.** quotation.

quo·ta /ˈkwōtə/ ▶ **n.** a limited or fixed number or amount of people or things, in particular: ■ a limited quantity of a particular product that under official controls can be produced, exported, or imported: *an import quota on oil.* ■ a fixed share of something that a person or group is entitled to receive from a total: *the island's salmon quota.* ■ a person's share of something that must be done: *the quota of arrests the police had to make.* ■ a fixed minimum or maximum number of a particular group of people allowed to do something, e.g., immigrants to enter a country, workers to undertake a job, or students to enroll for a course. ■ (in a system of proportional representation) the minimum number of votes required to elect a candidate. [17th C.: from med. L. *quota (pars)* 'how great (a part),' fem. of *quotus*, from *quot* 'how many.']

quot·a·ble /ˈkwōtəbəl/ ▶ **adj.** (of a person or remark) suitable for or worth quoting. — **quot·a·bil·i·ty** /ˌkwōtəˈbilətē/ **n.**

quo·ta·tion /ˌkwōˈtāsʜən/ ▶ **n.** **1** a group of words taken from a text or speech and repeated by someone other than the original author or speaker: *a quotation from Mark Twain.* ■ a short musical passage or visual image taken from one piece of music or work of art and used in another. ■ the action of quoting from a text, speech, piece of music, or work of art. **2** a formal statement setting out the estimated cost for a particular job or service: *a written quotation for the repairs.* ■ Stock Market a price offered by a broker for the sale or purchase of a stock or other security. ■ Stock Market a registration granted to a company enabling their shares to be officially listed and traded.

quo·ta·tion mark ▶ **n.** each of a set of punctuation marks, single (' ') or double (" "), used either to mark the beginning and end of a title or quoted passage or to indicate that a word or phrase is slang or is being discuss rather than used within the sentence.

quote /kwōt/ ▶ **v.** [trans.] **1** repeat or copy out (a group of words from a text or speech), typically with an indication that one is not the original author or speaker: *he **quoted** a passage **from** Shakespeare.* ■ repeat a passage from (a work or author) or statement by (someone): *he quoted Goethe and other poets.* **2** give someone (the estimated price of something). ■ (usu. **be quoted**) Stock Market give (a company) a quotation or listing on a stock exchange. ▶ **n.** **1** a quotation from a text or speech: *a quote from Darwin.* **2** a quotation giving the estimated cost for a particular job or service. ■ Stock Market a price offered by a broker for the sale or purchase of a stock or other security. ■ Stock Market a quotation or listing of a company on a stock exchange. **3** (**quotes**) quotation marks. [ME: from med. L. *quotare*, from *quot* 'how many,' or from med. L. *quota* (see QUOTA).]

quoth /kwōᴛʜ/ ▶ **v.** [with direct speech] archaic or humorous said (used only in first and third person singular before the subject): *"Well, the tide is going out" quoth the sailor.* [ME: past tense of obs. *quethe* 'say, declare,' of Gmc. origin.]

quo·tid·i·an /kwōˈtidēən/ ▶ **adj.** [attrib.] of or occurring every day; daily. ■ ordinary or everyday, esp. when mundane. ■ Med. denoting the malignant form of malaria. [ME: via OFr. from L. *quotidianus*, earlier *cotidianus*, from *cotidie* 'daily.']

quo·tient /ˈkwōsʜənt/ ▶ **n.** **1** Math. a result obtained by dividing one quantity by another. **2** [usu. with adj.] a degree or amount of a specified quality or characteristic: *an increase in our cynicism quotient.* [ME: from L. *quotiens* 'how many times' (from *quot* 'how many').]

quo war·ran·to /ˌkwō wəˈränˌtō; -ˈran-/ ▶ **n.** [usu. as adj.] Law a writ or legal action requiring a person to show by what warrant an office or franchise is held. [Law L., lit. 'by what warrant.']

Qu·r'an /kəˈrän; -ˈran/ (also **Qu·ran**) ▶ **n.** Arabic spelling of KORAN.

qursh /kərsʜ/ ▶ **n.** (pl. same) a monetary unit of Saudi Arabia, equal to one twentieth of a riyal. [from Arab. *ḳirsh*, from Slavic *grossus*.]

q.v. ▶ **abbr.** used to direct a reader to another part of a book or article for further information. [from L. *quod vide*, lit. 'which see.']

qwerty /ˈkwərtē/ ▶ **adj.** denoting the standard layout on English-language typewriters and keyboards, having *q, w, e, r, t,* and *y* as the first keys from the left on the top row of letters.

R[1] /är/ (also **r**) ▶ **n.** (pl. **Rs** or **R's**) the eighteenth letter of the alphabet.
– PHRASES **the three Rs** reading, writing, and arithmetic.

R[2] ▶ **abbr.** ■ rand. ■ Réaumur. ■ Regina or Rex: *Elizabeth R.* ■ (also ®) registered as a trademark. ■ Republican. ■ restricted, a movie rating that children under 17 require an accompanying parent or adult guardian for admission. ■ reverse. ■ river. ■ roentgen(s). ▶ **symb.** ■ Chem. an unspecified alkyl or other organic radical or group. [abbrev. of RADICAL.] ■ electrical resistance. ■ Chem. the gas constant.

r ▶ **abbr.** ■ recto. ■ right. ■ Law rule. ▶ **symb.** ■ radius: $2\pi r$. ■ Stat. correlation coefficient.

RA ▶ **abbr.** ■ regular army. ■ Astron. right ascension.

Ra[1] /rä/ (also **Re**) Egyptian Mythol. the sun god, worshiped as the creator of all life. From earliest times he was associated with the pharaoh.

Ra[2] ▶ **symb.** the chemical element radium.

Ra. ▶ **abbr.** range.

Ra·bat /rəˈbät/ the capital of Morocco, a port on the Atlantic coast; pop. 1,220,000.

Ra·baul /räˈboul/ a town in Papua New Guinea, on the island of New Britain; pop. 17,000.

rab·bet /ˈrabit/ ▶ **n.** a step-shaped recess cut along the edge or in the face of a piece of wood, typically forming a match to the edge or tongue of another piece: [as adj.] *a rabbet joint.* ▶ **v.** (**-bet·ed, -bet·ing**) [trans.] make a rabbet in (a piece of wood). ■ [with obj. and adverbial] join or fix (a piece of wood) to another with a rabbet. [ME: from OFr. *rabbat* 'abatement.']

rab·bet plane ▶ **n.** a plane for making a rabbet in a piece of wood.

rab·bi /ˈrab,ī/ ▶ **n.** (pl. **-bis**) a Jewish scholar or teacher, esp. one who studies or teaches Jewish law. ■ a person appointed as a Jewish religious leader. — **rab·bin·ate** /ˈrabənət; -,nāt/ **n.** [OE, via eccles. L. and Gk. from Heb. *rabbī* 'my master,' from *raḇ* 'master.']

rab·bin·i·cal /rəˈbinikəl; ra-/ ▶ **adj.** [attrib.] of or relating to rabbis or to Jewish law or teachings. — **rab·bin·ic** /-ik/ **adj. rab·bin·i·cal·ly** /-ik(ə)lē/ **adv.**

rab·bit /ˈrabit/ ▶ **n.** a burrowing, gregarious, plant-eating mammal (family Leporidae) with long ears, long hind legs, and a short tail. ■ the fur of the rabbit. ■ another term for HARE. ■ a runner who acts as pacesetter in the first laps of a race. ▶ **v.** (**-bit·ed, -bit·ing**) [intrans.] hunt rabbits.
– PHRASES **pull a rabbit out of the hat** used to describe an action that is fortuitous, and may involve sleight of hand or deception. — **rab·bit·y** **adj.** [ME: appar. from OFr. (compare Fr. dial. *rabotte* 'young rabbit'), perh. of Du. origin (compare Flemish *robbe*).]

rab·bit·brush /ˈrabit,brəsh/ (also **rab·bit·bush** /-,bo͝osh/) ▶ **n.** a North American shrub (*Chrysothamnus nauseosus*) of the daisy family, with clusters of pungent small yellow flowers, native esp. to the western US.

rab·bit fe·ver ▶ **n.** informal term for TULAREMIA.

rab·bit food ▶ **n.** informal salad.

rab·bit punch ▶ **n.** a sharp chop to the back of the neck.

rab·bit's foot ▶ **n.** the foot of a rabbit carried as a good luck charm.

rab·ble /ˈrabəl/ ▶ **n.** a disorderly crowd; a mob. ■ (**the rabble**) ordinary people; the masses. [ME ('string of meaningless words,' 'pack of animals'): perh. akin to dial. *rabble* 'to gabble.']

rab·ble-rous·er ▶ **n.** a person who speaks with the intention of inflaming the emotions of a crowd. — **rab·ble-rous·ing adj. & n.**

Rab·e·lais /ˈrabə,lā; ,rabəˈlā/, François (*c.*1494–1553), French writer. His works are noted for their earthy humor.

rab·id /ˈrabəd; ˈrā-/ ▶ **adj.** **1** having or proceeding from a fanatical belief in something: *a rabid feminist.* **2** (of an animal) affected with rabies. — **rab·id·i·ty** /rəˈbidətē; ra-; rā-/ **n. rab·id·ly adv. rab·id·ness n.** [17th C. ('furious'): from L. *rabidus*, from *rabere* 'to rave.']

ra·bies /ˈrābēz/ ▶ **n.** a contagious and fatal viral disease of dogs and other mammals, transmissible through the saliva to humans and causing madness and convulsions. Also called HYDROPHOBIA. [16th C.: from L., from *rabere* 'rave.']

Ra·bin /räˈbēn/, Yitzhak (1922–95), prime minister of Israel 1974–77, 1992–95. In 1993, he negotiated a PLO–Israeli peace accord with Yasser Arafat. Nobel Peace Prize (1994, shared with Arafat and Shimon Peres).

rac·coon /raˈko͞on; rə-/ (also **ra·coon**) ▶ **n.** a grayish-brown American mammal (esp. the **common raccoon**, *Procyon lotor*) that has a foxlike face with a black mask, a ringed tail, and the habit of washing its food in water. The **raccoon family** (Procyonidae) also includes the coati, kinkajou, and cacomistle. [17th C.: from Virginia Algonquian *aroughcun*.]

common raccoon

rac·coon dog ▶ **n.** a small wild dog (*Nyctereutes procyonoides*) of raccoonlike appearance, with a black facial mask and long brindled fur, native to the forests of south and eastern Asia.

race[1] /rās/ ▶ **n.** **1** a competition between runners, horses, vehicles, boats, etc., to see which is the fastest in covering a set course. ■ (**the races**) a series of such competitions for horses or dogs, held at a fixed time on a set course. ■ [in sing.] a situation in which individuals or groups compete to be first to achieve a particular objective: *the race for nuclear power.* **2** a strong or rapid current flowing through a narrow channel in the sea or a river. **3** a groove, channel, or passage, in particular: ■ a water channel, esp. one built to lead water to or from a point where its energy is utilized, as in a mill or mine. See also MILLRACE. ■ a smooth, ring-shaped groove or guide in which a ball bearing runs. ■ a fenced passageway in a stockyard through which animals pass singly for branding, loading, washing, etc. ■ (in weaving) the channel along which the shuttle moves. ▶ **v.** **1** [intrans.] compete with another or others to see who is fastest at covering a set course or achieving an objective. ■ compete regularly in races as a sport or leisure activity. ■ [trans.] prepare and enter (an animal or vehicle) in races as a sport or leisure activity. **2** move or progress swiftly or at full speed. ■ [intrans.] (of an engine or other machinery) operate at excessive speed. ■ [intrans.] (of a person's heart or pulse) beat faster than usual because of fear or excitement. ■ [intrans.] (of a person's mind) think very rapidly when faced with a demanding situation: *he tried to reassure her, but Carrie's mind was racing.* ■ [trans.] cause to move, progress, or operate swiftly or at excessive speed: *she'd driven like a madwoman, racing the engine.*
– PHRASES **a race against time** a situation in which something must be done before a particular point in time. [OE, from ON *rás* 'current.']

race[2] ▶ **n.** each of the major divisions of humankind, having distinct physical characteristics. ■ a group of people sharing the same culture, history, language, etc.; an ethnic group: *we Scots were a bloodthirsty race then.* ■ the fact or condition of belonging to such a division or group. ■ a group or set of people or things with a common feature or features: *the new race of photographers tried to seize the fleeting moment.* ■ Biol. a population within a species that is distinct in some way, esp. a subspecies. ■ (in nontechnical use) each of the major divisions of living creatures: *the human race.* ■ literary a group of people descended from a common ancestor: *a prince of the race of Solomon.* [16th C. ('a group with common features'): via Fr. from Ital. *razza.*]

race car ▶ **n.** an automobile built or modified for racing.

race·course /ˈrās,kôrs/ ▶ **n.** a racetrack.

race driv·er ▶ **n.** a person who drives race cars as a profession.

race·horse /ˈrās,hôrs/ ▶ **n.** a horse bred, trained, and kept for racing.

race·mate /ˈrās,māt/ ▶ **n.** Chem. a racemic mixture.

ra·ceme /rāˈsēm; rə-/ ▶ **n.** Bot. a flower cluster with the separate flowers attached by short equal stalks at equal distances along a central stem. Compare with CYME and SPIKE[2]. [18th C.: from L. *racemus* 'bunch of grapes.']

ra·ce·mic /rāˈsēmik; rə-/ ▶ **adj.** Chem. composed of dextrorotatory and levorotatory forms of a compound in equal proportion. — **rac·e·mize** /ˈrāsē,mīz; rəˈsē-; ˈrasə-/ **v.** [19th C. ('derived from grape juice'): from Fr. *racémique*.]

rac·e·mose /ˈrasə,mōs; ˈrasə,mōz/ ▶ **adj.** Bot. (of a flower cluster) taking the form of a raceme. ■ Anat. (esp. of compound glands) having the form of a cluster.

race mu·sic ▶ n. dated music popular among or played by black people, esp. jazz and blues.

rac·er /ˈrāsər/ ▶ n. **1** an animal or means of transportation bred or designed esp. for racing. ■ a person who competes in races. **2** a fast-moving, harmless, and typically slender-bodied snake (*Coluber* and other genera, family Colubridae).

rac·er·back /ˈrāsər,bak/ ▶ n. [as adj.] denoting an article of clothing with a T-shaped back to allow ease of movement in sporting activities.

race ri·ot ▶ n. a public outbreak of violence due to racial antagonism.

race·run·ner /ˈrās,rənər/ ▶ n. any of a number of fast-moving active lizards with longitudinal markings and a pointed snout, in particular an American lizard (genus *Cnemidophorus*, family Teiidae).

race·track /ˈrās,trak/ ▶ n. a ground or track for horse, dog, or auto racing.

race·way /ˈrās,wā/ ▶ n. **1** a track or channel along which something runs, in particular: ■ a water channel, esp. one in which fish are reared. ■ a groove in which bearings run. ■ a pipe enclosing electric wires. **2** a track for horse or auto racing.

ra·chis /ˈrākis; ˈrak-/ ▶ n. (pl. **rach·i·des** /ˈrakə,dēz; ˈrā-/) **1** Bot. a stem of a plant, esp. a grass, bearing flower stalks at short intervals. ■ the midrib of a compound leaf or frond. **2** Anat. the vertebral column or the cord from which it develops. **3** Ornithol. the shaft of a feather. [18th C.: ult. from Gk. *rhakhis* 'spine.']

ra·chi·tis /rəˈkītis/ ▶ n. old-fashioned medical term for RICKETS. — **ra·chit·ic** /rəˈkitik/ adj. [18th C.: mod. L., from Gk. *rhakhitis*, from *rhakhis* 'spine.']

Rach·ma·ni·nov /räkˈmänənôf; rəKHˈmänyinəf/, Sergei Vasilevich (1873–1943), Russian composer, noted for his piano compositions.

ra·cial /ˈrāSHəl/ ▶ adj. of or relating to race or difference in race. — **ra·cial·ly** adv.

ra·cial·ism /ˈrāSHə,lizəm/ ▶ n. another term for RACISM.

ra·cial pro·fil·ing ▶ n. the practice of substituting skin color for evidence as grounds for suspicion.

Ra·cine¹ /rəˈsēn; rā-/ a city in southeastern Wisconsin, on Lake Michigan; pop. 81,855.

Ra·cine² /rəˈsēn; rä-/, Jean (1639–99), French playwright. He wrote *Andromaque* (1667) and *Phèdre* (1677).

rac·ing /ˈrāsiNG/ ▶ n. short for HORSE RACING. ■ any sport that involves competing in races. ▶ adj. **1** moving swiftly: *his racing thoughts.* **2** (of a person) following horse racing.

rac·ism /ˈrā,sizəm/ ▶ n. the belief that all members of each race possess characteristics or abilities specific to that race, esp. so as to distinguish it as inferior or superior to another race or races. ■ prejudice or discrimination directed against someone of a different race based on such a belief. — **rac·ist** n. & adj.

rack¹ /rak/ ▶ n. **1** a framework, typically with rails, bars, hooks, or pegs, for holding or storing things. ■ an overhead shelf on a bus, train, or plane for stowing luggage. ■ a fixed or movable framework, usually consisting of a horizontal rail set at chest height on vertical supports, for transporting and displaying items of clothing for sale. ■ a vertically barred frame or wagon for holding animal fodder: *a hay rack.* ■ a lift used for elevating and repairing motor vehicles. ■ a set of antlers. ■ informal a bed. **2** a cogged or toothed bar or rail engaging with a wheel or pinion, or using pegs to adjust the position of something: *a steering rack.* **3** (**the rack**) hist. an instrument of torture consisting of a frame on which the victim was stretched by turning rollers to which the wrists and ankles were tied. ■ a triangular structure for positioning the balls in pool. ■ the triangular arrangement of balls set up for the beginning of a game of pool. **4** a digital effects unit for a guitar or other instrument, typically giving many different sounds. ▶ v. [trans.] **1** (also **wrack**) (often **be racked**) cause extreme physical or mental pain to; subject to extreme stress: *he was racked with guilt.* ■ hist. torture (someone) on the rack. **2** [trans.] place in or on a rack: *the shoes were racked neatly beneath the dresses.* ■ [trans.] put (pool balls) in a rack.
– PHRASES **go to rack** (or **wrack**) **and ruin** gradually deteriorate in condition because of neglect; fall into disrepair. **off the rack** (of clothes) ready-made rather than made to order. **rack** (or **wrack**) **one's brains** (or **brain**) make a great effort to think of or remember something.
– PHRASAL VERBS **rack something up** accumulate or achieve something, typically a score or amount. [ME: from MDu. *rec*, Mid. Low Ger. *rek* 'horizontal bar or shelf,' prob. from *recken* 'to stretch, reach.']

rack² ▶ n. a horse's gait in which both hoofs on either side in turn are lifted almost simultaneously, and all four hoofs are off the ground together at certain moments. ▶ v. [intrans.] (of a horse) move with such a gait. [16th C.: of unknown origin.]

rack³ ▶ n. a joint of meat that includes the front ribs. [16th C.: of unknown origin.]

rack⁴ ▶ v. [trans.] draw off (wine, beer, etc.) from the sediment in the barrel. [15th C.: from Provençal *arracar*, from *raca* 'stems and husks of grapes, dregs.']

rack⁵ (also **wrack**) ▶ n. a mass of high, thick, fast-moving clouds. [ME ('a rush'): prob. of Scand. origin.]

rack-and-pin·ion ▶ adj. [attrib.] denoting a mechanism using a fixed cogged or toothed bar or rail engaging with a smaller cog: *rack-and-pinion steering.*

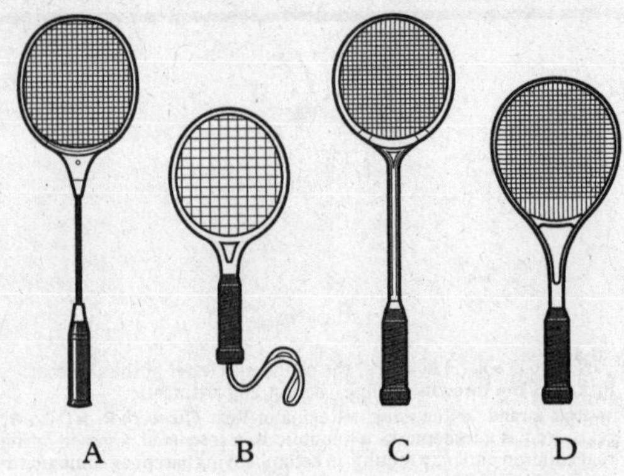

A. badminton racket
B. racquetball racket
C. squash racket
D. tennis racket

rackets

rack·et¹ /ˈrakit/ (also **rac·quet**) ▶ n. a type of bat with a round or oval frame strung with catgut, nylon, etc., used esp. in tennis, badminton, and squash. ■ a snowshoe resembling such a bat. [16th C.: from Fr. *raquette* (see RACKETS).]

rack·et² ▶ n. **1** [in sing.] a loud unpleasant noise; a din. **2** informal an illegal scheme for obtaining money. ■ a person's line of business or way of life. ▶ v. (**rack·et·ed, rack·et·ing**) [intrans.] make a loud unpleasant noise: *trains racketed by.* ■ (**racket around**) enjoy oneself socially; pursue pleasure. [16th C.: perh. imitative.]

rack·et·eer /,rakiˈti(ə)r/ ▶ n. a person who engages in dishonest and fraudulent business dealings. — **rack·et·eer·ing** n.

rack·ets /ˈrakits/ ▶ plural n. [treated as sing.] a ball game played with rackets in a plain, four-walled court. [ME (also *racket*): from Fr. *raquette*, via Ital. from Arab. *rāḥa, rāḥat-* 'palm of the hand.']

rack rail·way ▶ n. another term for COG RAILWAY.

rack rent ▶ n. an extortionate or very high rent, esp. an annual rent equivalent to the full value of the property.

ra·clette /raˈklet; rä-/ ▶ n. a Swiss dish of melted cheese, typically eaten with potatoes. [Fr., lit. 'small scraper,' because the cheese is scraped as it melts.]

ra·con /ˈrā,kän/ ▶ n. a radar beacon that can be identified by its response to a specific radar signal. [1940s: blend of RADAR and BEACON.]

rac·on·teur /,rak,änˈtər; -ən-/ ▶ n. a person who tells anecdotes in a skillful and amusing way. [19th C.: Fr., from *raconter* 'recount.']

ra·coon ▶ n. var. of RACCOON.

rac·quet /ˈrakit/ ▶ n. var. of RACKET¹.

rac·quet·ball /ˈrakit,bôl/ ▶ n. a game played with a small hard ball and a short-handled racket in a four-walled handball court.

rac·y /ˈrāsē/ ▶ adj. (**rac·i·er, rac·i·est**) lively, entertaining, and sexually titillating. ■ (of a wine, flavor, etc.) having a characteristic quality in a high degree. ■ (of a vehicle or animal) designed or bred to be suitable for racing. — **rac·i·ly** /-səlē/ adv. **rac·i·ness** n.

rad¹ ▶ abbr. radian(s).

rad² /rad/ ▶ n. informal a political radical.

rad³ ▶ n. Physics a unit of absorbed dose of ionizing radiation, corresponding to the absorption of 0.01 joule per kilogram of absorbing material. [20th C.: acronym from *radiation absorbed dose*.]

rad⁴ ▶ adj. informal excellent; impressive. [1980s: prob. an abbrev. of RADICAL.]

rad. ▶ abbr. Math. ■ radical. ■ radix.

ra·dar /ˈrādär/ ▶ n. a system for detecting the presence, direction, distance, and speed of aircraft, ships, and other objects, by sending out pulses of high-frequency electromagnetic waves that are reflected off the object back to the source. ■ used to indicate that someone or something has or has not come to the attention of a person or group: *he's off the radar in the US but in Europe he's a well-known figure.* [1940s: from *ra(dio) d(etection) a(nd) r(anging)*.]

Rad·cliffe /ˈrad,klif/, Mrs. Ann (1764–1823), English writer. Her Gothic novels include *The Mysteries of Udolpho* (1794).

rad·dled /ˈradld/ ▶ adj. (of a person or their face) showing signs of age or fatigue. [rel. to obs. *rud* 'red color.']

Ra·dha /ˈrädə/ Hinduism the favorite consort of the god Krishna, and an incarnation of Lakshmi. [from Sanskrit, lit. 'prosperity.']

Ra·dha·krish·nan /,rädəˈkrishnən/, Sir Sarvepalli (1888–1975), president of India 1962–67. He introduced classical Indian philosophy to the West.

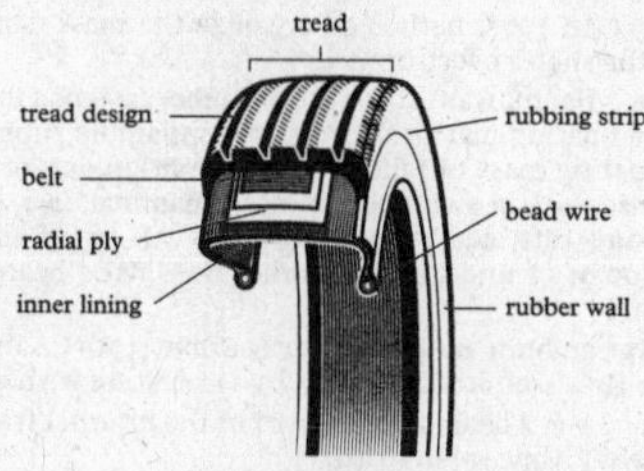

radial tire

ra·di·al /ˈrādēəl/ ▶ **adj.** **1** of or arranged like rays or the radii of a circle. ■ (of a road or route) running directly from a city center to an outlying district. ■ denoting a tire in which the layers of fabric have their cords running at right angles to the circumference of the tire. Compare with BIAS-PLY. ■ denoting an internal combustion engine with its cylinders fixed like spokes around a rotating crankshaft. **2** Anat. & Zool. of or relating to the radius. ▶ **n.** a radial tire. — **ra·di·al·ly adv.** [16th C.: from med. L. *radialis*, from L. *radius* 'ray.']

ra·di·al sym·me·try ▶ **n.** chiefly Biol. symmetry around a central axis, as in a starfish or a tulip flower.

ra·di·an /ˈrādēən/ ▶ **n.** Geom. a unit of angle, equal to an angle at the center of a circle whose arc is equal in length to the radius.

ra·di·ance /ˈrādēəns/ ▶ **n.** **1** light or heat as emitted or reflected by something: *the radiance of the sunset.* ■ great joy or love, apparent in someone's expression or bearing. ■ a glowing quality of the skin, esp. as indicative of good health or youth. **2** Physics the flux of radiation emitted per unit solid angle in a given direction by a unit area of a source.

ra·di·ant /ˈrādēənt/ ▶ **adj.** **1** sending out light; shining or glowing brightly. ■ (of a person or their expression) clearly emanating great joy, love, or health. ■ (of an emotion or quality) emanating powerfully from someone or something: *radiant self-confidence.* **2** [attrib.] (of electromagnetic energy, esp. heat) transmitted by radiation, rather than conduction or convection. ■ (of an appliance) designed to emit such energy, esp. for cooking or heating. ▶ **n.** a point or object from which light or heat radiates. — **ra·di·an·cy** /-ənsē/ **n.** **ra·di·ant·ly adv.** [ME: from L. *radiant-* 'emitting rays,' from *radiare* (see RADIATE).]

ra·di·ate ▶ **v.** /ˈrādēˌāt/ **1** [trans.] emit (energy, esp. light or heat) in the form of rays or waves. ■ [intrans.] (of light, heat, or other energy) be emitted in such a way. ■ (of a person) clearly emanate (a strong feeling or quality). ■ **(radiate from)** (of a feeling or quality) emanate clearly from: *confidence radiates from her.* **2** [intrans.] diverge from a central point. ■ Biol. (of an animal or plant group) evolve into a variety of forms adapted to new situations or ways of life. — **ra·di·a·tive** /-ˌātiv/ **adj.** (in sense 1). [17th C.: from L. *radiat-* 'emitted in rays,' from the v. *radiare*, from *radius* 'ray.']

ra·di·a·tion /ˌrādēˈāshən/ ▶ **n.** **1** Physics the emission of energy as electromagnetic waves or as moving subatomic particles. ■ the energy transmitted in this way. **2** chiefly Biol. evolution from an ancestral animal or plant group into a variety of new forms. — **ra·di·a·tion·al** /-ˈāshənl/ **adj.** [ME (denoting the action of sending out rays of light): from L. *radiatio(n-)*, from *radiare* 'emit rays' (see RADIATE).]

ra·di·a·tion sick·ness ▶ **n.** illness caused by exposure of the body to ionizing radiation, characterized by nausea, hair loss, diarrhea, bleeding, and damage to the bone marrow and central nervous system.

ra·di·a·tion ther·a·py (also **ra·di·a·tion treat·ment**) ▶ **n.** the treatment of disease, esp. cancer, using X-rays or similar forms of radiation.

ra·di·a·tor /ˈrādēˌātər/ ▶ **n.** **1** a thing that radiates or emits light, heat, or sound. ■ a device for heating a room consisting of a metal case connected by pipes through which hot water is pumped by a central heating system. **2** an engine-cooling device in a motor vehicle or aircraft consisting of a bank of thin tubes in which circulating water is cooled by the surrounding air.

rad·i·cal /ˈradikəl/ ▶ **adj.** **1** (esp. of change or action) relating to or affecting the fundamental nature of something; far-reaching or thorough. ■ forming an inherent or fundamental part of the nature of someone or something. ■ (of surgery or medical treatment) thorough and intended to be completely curative. ■ characterized by departure from tradition; innovative or progressive. **2** advocating thorough political or social reform. **3** of or relating to the root of something, in particular: ■ Math. of the root of a number or quantity. ■ Bot. of the root or stem base of a plant. **4** [usu. as exclam.] informal very good; excellent. ▶ **n.** **1** a person who advocates thorough or complete political or social reform. **2** Chem. a group of atoms behaving as a unit in a number of compounds. See also FREE RADICAL. **3** the root or base form of a word. ■ any of the basic set of 214 Chinese characters. **4** Math. a quantity forming or expressed as the root of another. ■ a radical sign. — **rad·i·cal·ism** /-ˌlizəm/ **n.** **rad·i·cal·ly** /-ik(ə)lē/ **adv.** **rad·i·cal·ness n.** [ME ('forming the root,' 'inherent'): from late L. *radicalis*, from L. *radix, radic-* 'root.']

rad·i·cal chic ▶ **n.** the fashionable affectation of radical left-wing views. ■ the dress, lifestyle, or people associated with this.

rad·i·cal·ize /ˈradikəˌlīz/ ▶ **v.** [trans.] cause (someone) to become an advocate of radical reform. — **rad·i·cal·i·za·tion** /ˌradikələˈzāshən/ **n.**

rad·i·cal sign ▶ **n.** Math. the sign $\sqrt{}$, indicating the square root of the number following (or a higher root indicated by a preceding superscript numeral).

ra·dic·chi·o /raˈdēkēˌō; rə-/ ▶ **n.** (pl. **-os**) chicory of a variety that has dark red leaves. [Ital.]

rad·i·ces /ˈradəˌsēz; ˈrā-/ plural form of RADIX.

rad·i·cle /ˈradikəl/ ▶ **n.** Bot. the part of a plant embryo that develops into the primary root. ■ Anat. a rootlike subdivision of a nerve or vein. [17th C.: from L. *radicula*, dimin. of *radix, radic-* 'root.']

ra·di·i /ˈrādēˌī/ plural form of RADIUS.

ra·di·o /ˈrādēˌō/ ▶ **n.** (pl. **-os**) the transmission and reception of electromagnetic waves of radio frequency, esp. those carrying sound messages. ■ the activity or industry of broadcasting sound programs to the public: [as adj.] *a radio station.* ■ radio programs. ■ an apparatus for receiving such programs. ■ an apparatus capable of both receiving and transmitting radio messages. ▶ **v.** **(-oes, -oed)** [intrans.] communicate by radio. ■ [trans.] communicate with (a person) by radio. [20th C.: abbrev. of *RADIOTELEPHONY* (see RADIOTELEPHONE).]

radio- ▶ **comb. form** **1** denoting radio waves. **2** Physics connected with rays or radioactivity. ■ denoting artificially prepared radioisotopes. [from RADIO or RADIUS.]

ra·di·o·ac·tive /ˌrādēōˈaktiv/ ▶ **adj.** emitting or relating to the emission of ionizing radiation or particles. — **ra·di·o·ac·tive·ly adv.** **ra·di·o·ac·tiv·i·ty** /ˌrādēōakˈtivətē/ **n.**

ra·di·o as·tron·o·my ▶ **n.** the branch of astronomy concerned with radio emissions from celestial objects.

ra·di·o·bi·ol·o·gy /ˌrādēˌōbīˈäləjē/ ▶ **n.** the branch of biology concerned with the effects of ionizing radiation on organisms and the application in biology of radiological techniques. — **ra·di·o·bi·o·log·i·cal** /-ˌbīəˈläjikəl/ **adj.** **ra·di·o·bi·ol·o·gist** /-jist/ **n.**

ra·di·o but·ton ▶ **n.** Comput. (in a graphical display) an icon representing one of a set of options, only one of which can be selected at any time.

ra·di·o·car·bon /ˌrādēōˈkärbən/ ▶ **n.** Chem. a radioactive isotope of carbon.

ra·di·o·car·bon dat·ing ▶ **n.** another term for CARBON DATING.

ra·di·o·chem·is·try /ˌrādēōˈkemistrē/ ▶ **n.** the branch of chemistry concerned with radioactive substances. — **ra·di·o·chem·i·cal** /-ˈkemi-kəl/ **adj.**

ra·di·o-con·trolled ▶ **adj.** controllable from a distance by radio.

ra·di·o·el·e·ment /ˌrādēōˈeləmənt/ ▶ **n.** a radioactive element or isotope.

ra·di·o fre·quen·cy ▶ **n.** a frequency or band of frequencies in the range 104 to 1011 or 1012 Hz, suitable for use in telecommunications.

ra·di·o gal·ax·y ▶ **n.** a galaxy emitting radiation in the radio-frequency range of the electromagnetic spectrum.

ra·di·o·gen·ic /ˌrādēōˈjenik/ ▶ **adj.** produced by radioactivity.

ra·di·o·gram /ˈrādēōˌgram/ ▶ **n.** **1** another term for RADIOGRAPH. **2** a message sent by radiotelegraphy.

ra·di·o·graph /ˈrādēōˌgraf/ ▶ **n.** an image produced on a sensitive film by X-rays, gamma rays, or similar radiation, and typically used in medical examination. ▶ **v.** [trans.] produce an image of (something) on a sensitive film by X-rays, gamma rays, or similar radiation. — **ra·di·og·ra·pher** /ˌrādēˈägrəfər/ **n.** **ra·di·o·graph·ic** /ˌrādēōˈgrafik/ **adj.** **ra·di·o·graph·i·cal·ly** /-ik(ə)lē/ **adv.** **ra·di·og·ra·phy** /ˌrādēˈägrəfē/ **n.**

ra·di·o·im·mu·no·as·say /ˌrādēōˌimyənōˈaˌsā/ ▶ **n.** Med. a technique for determining antibody levels by introducing an antigen labeled with a radioisotope and measuring the subsequent radioactivity of the antibody component.

ra·di·o·i·so·tope /ˌrādēōˈīsəˌtōp/ ▶ **n.** Chem. a radioactive isotope. — **ra·di·o·i·so·top·ic** /-ˌīsəˈtäpik/ **adj.**

ra·di·o·lar·i·an /ˌrādēəˈle(ə)rēən/ Zool. ▶ **n.** a single-celled aquatic animal (phylum Actinopoda) that has a spherical, amebalike body with a spiny skeleton of silica. Their skeletons can accumulate as a slimy deposit on the seabed. ▶ **adj.** of, relating to, or formed from radiolarians.

ra·di·ol·o·gy /ˌrādēˈäləjē/ ▶ **n.** the science of X-rays and other high-energy radiation, esp. the use of such radiation for the diagnosis and treatment of disease. — **ra·di·o·log·ic** /ˌrādēəˈläjik/ **adj.** **ra·di·o·log·i·cal** /ˌrādēəˈläjikəl/ **adj.** **ra·di·o·log·i·cal·ly** /ˌrādēəˈläjik(ə)lē/ **adv.** **ra·di·ol·o·gist** /-jist/ **n.**

ra·di·o·lu·cent /ˌrādēōˈlo͞osnt/ ▶ **adj.** transparent to X-rays. — **ra·di·o·lu·cen·cy n.**

ra·di·ol·y·sis /rādēˈäləsis/ ▶ **n.** (pl. **-ses** /-sēz/) Chem. the molecular decomposition of a substance by ionizing radiation.

ra·di·om·e·ter /ˌrādēˈämitər/ ▶ **n.** an instrument for detecting or measuring the intensity or force of radiation. — **ra·di·om·e·try** /-trē/ **n.**

radiometer

ra·di·o·met·ric /ˈˌrādēəˈmetrik/ ▶ **adj.** Physics of or relating to the measurement of radioactivity. — **ra·di·o·met·ri·cal·ly** /-ik(ə)lē/ **adv.**

ra·di·o·met·ric dat·ing ▶ **n.** a method of dating geological specimens by determining the proportions of particular radioactive isotopes present in a sample.

ra·di·o·nu·clide /ˌrādēōˈn(y)o͞oˌklīd/ ▶ **n.** a radioactive nuclide.

ra·di·o·paque /ˌrādēōˈpāk/ ▶ **adj.** (of a substance) opaque to X-rays or similar radiation. — **ra·di·o·pac·i·ty** /ˌrādēōˈpasətē/ **n.**

ra·di·o·phar·ma·ceu·ti·cal /ˌrādēōˌfärməˈsōōtikəl/ ▶ **n.** a radioactive compound used for diagnostic or therapeutic purposes.

ra·di·os·co·py /ˌrādēˈäskəpē/ ▶ **n.** Physics the examination by X-rays or similar radiation of objects opaque to light. — **ra·di·o·scop·ic** /ˈˌrādēəˈskäpik/ **adj.**

ra·di·o·sonde /ˈrādēōˌsänd/ ▶ **n.** dated an instrument carried by balloon or other means into the atmosphere and transmitting measurements by radio. [1930s: from RADIO- + Ger. *Sonde* 'probe.']

ra·di·o·te·leg·ra·phy /ˌrādēōtəˈlegrəfē/ ▶ **n.** telegraphy using radio transmission. — **ra·di·o·tel·e·graph** /-ˈteləˌgraf/ **n.**

ra·di·o·tel·e·phone /ˌrādēōˈteləˌfōn/ ▶ **n.** a telephone that uses radio transmission. — **ra·di·o·te·leph·o·ny** /-təˈlefənē/ **n.**

ra·di·o tel·e·scope ▶ **n.** Astron. an instrument used to detect radio emissions from the sky, whether from natural celestial objects or from artificial satellites.

ra·di·o·ther·a·py /ˌrādēōˈTHerəpē/ ▶ **n.** another term for RADIATION THERAPY.

ra·di·o wave ▶ **n.** an electromagnetic wave of a frequency between about 104 and 1011 or 1012 Hz, as used for long-distance communication.

rad·ish /ˈradisH/ ▶ **n.** **1** a pungent-tasting edible root, esp. a variety that is small, spherical, and red. **2** the plant (*Raphanus sativus*) of the cabbage family that yields this root. [OE *rædic*, from L. *radix*, *radic-* 'root.']

ra·di·um /ˈrādēəm/ ▶ **n.** the chemical element of atomic number 88, a rare radioactive metal of the alkaline earth series. (Symbol: **Ra**) [19th C.: from L. *radius* 'ray.']

ra·di·us /ˈrādēəs/ ▶ **n.** (pl. **ra·di·i** /ˈrādēˌī/ or **ra·di·us·es**) **1** a straight line from the center to the circumference of a circle or sphere. See also illustration at GEOMETRIC. ■ a radial line from the focus to any point of a curve. ■ the length of the radius of a circle or sphere. ■ a specified distance from a center in all directions: *a two-mile radius.* **2** Anat. the thicker and shorter of the two bones in the human forearm. Compare with ULNA. ■ Zool. the corresponding bone in a vertebrate's foreleg or a bird's wing. ■ Zool. (in an echinoderm or coelenterate) any of the primary axes of radial symmetry. ■ Entomol. any of the main veins in an insect's wing. [16th C. (sense 2): from L., lit. 'ray.']

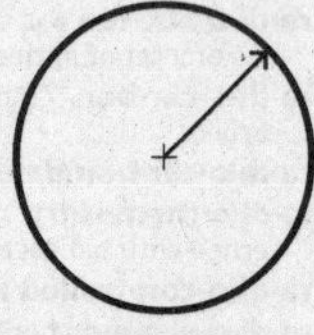

radius 1

ra·di·us vec·tor ▶ **n.** Math. a line of variable length drawn from a fixed origin to a curve. ■ Astron. such a line joining a satellite or other celestial object to its primary.

ra·dix /ˈrādiks; ˈrad-/ ▶ **n.** (pl. **ra·di·ces** /ˈradəˌsēz; ˈrā-/) Math. the base of a system of numeration. See also BASE[1] (sense 8). [18th C.: from L., lit. 'root.']

RADM (also **RAdm**) ▶ **abbr.** rear admiral.

Ra·dom /ˈräˌdôm/ a city in central Poland; pop. 228,000.

ra·dome /ˈrāˌdōm/ ▶ **n.** a dome protecting radar equipment and made from material transparent to radio waves, esp. one on the outer surface of an aircraft. [1940s: blend of RADAR and DOME.]

ra·don /ˈrāˌdän/ ▶ **n.** the chemical element of atomic number 86, a rare radioactive gas belonging to the noble gas series. (Symbol: **Rn**) [20th C.: from RADIUM.]

rad·u·la /ˈrajələ/ ▶ **n.** (pl. **-lae** /-lē; -ˌlī/) Zool. (in a mollusk) a rasplike structure of tiny teeth used for scraping food particles off a surface and drawing them into the mouth. — **rad·u·lar** /-lər/ **adj.** [19th C.: from L., lit. 'scraper,' from *radere* 'to scrape.']

RAF informal ▶ **abbr.** (in the UK) Royal Air Force.

raf·fi·a /ˈrafēə/ ▶ **n.** a palm tree (*Raphia ruffia*) native to tropical Africa and Madagascar, with a short trunk and leaves that may be up to 60 feet (18 m) long. ■ the fiber from these leaves, used for making items such as hats, baskets, and mats. [18th C.: from Malagasy.]

raf·fi·nose /ˈrafəˌnōs; -ˌnōz/ ▶ **n.** Chem. a sugar present in sugar beet, cotton seed, and many grains. It is a trisaccharide with glucose, galactose, and fructose units. [19th C.: from Fr. *raffiner* 'refine.']

raf·fish /ˈrafisH/ ▶ **adj.** unconventional and slightly disreputable, esp. in an attractive manner. — **raf·fish·ly** **adv.** **raf·fish·ness** **n.** [19th C.: from RIFFRAFF.]

raf·fle[1] /ˈrafəl/ ▶ **n.** a means of raising money by selling numbered tickets, one of which is subsequently drawn at random, the holder of such ticket winning a prize. ▶ **v.** [trans.] (usu. **be raffled**) offer (something) as a prize in such a lottery: *a work that will be **raffled off** for a fine arts scholarship.* [ME (denoting a kind of dice game): from OFr., of unknown origin. The current sense dates from the 18th C.]

raf·fle[2] ▶ **n.** rubbish; refuse: *the raffle of the yard below.* [ME ('rabble'): perh. from OFr. *ne rifle ne rafle* 'nothing at all.']

Raf·fles /ˈrafəlz/, Sir Thomas Stamford (1781–1826), British colonial administrator. He persuaded the East India Company to purchase Singapore in 1819.

raf·fle·sia /rəˈflēzHə; ra-/ ▶ **n.** a parasitic plant (genus *Rafflesia*, family Rafflesiaceae) that lacks chlorophyll and bears a single, very large flower that smells of carrion, native to Malaysia and Indonesia. [mod. L., after Sir T. Stamford RAFFLES.]

Raf·san·ja·ni /ˌräfsänˈjänē/, Ali Akbar Hashemi (1934–), president of Iran 1989–97. In 1978, he helped organize the mass demonstrations that led to the shah's overthrow.

raft[1] /raft/ ▶ **n.** a flat buoyant structure of timber fastened together, used as a boat or floating platform. ■ a small, inflatable rubber or plastic boat. ■ a floating mass of fallen trees, vegetation, ice, or other material. ■ a dense flock of swimming birds or mammals. ▶ **v.** [intrans.] travel on or as if on a raft. ■ [trans.] transport on a raft. ■ (of an ice floe) be driven on top of or underneath another floe. [ME ('beam'): from ON *raptr* 'rafter.']

raft[2] ▶ **n.** a large amount: ***a raft of investigations.*** [19th C.: alt. of dial. *raff* 'abundance' (perh. of Scand. origin), by association with RAFT[1].]

raft·er[1] /ˈraftər/ ▶ **n.** a beam forming part of the internal framework of a roof. [OE *ræfter*, Gmc.; akin to RAFT[1].]

raft·er[2] ▶ **n.** a person who travels on a raft.

raft·ing /ˈraftiNG/ ▶ **n.** the sport or pastime of traveling down a river on a raft.

rafts·man /ˈraftsmən/ ▶ **n.** (pl. **-men**) a man who works on a raft.

rag[1] /rag/ ▶ **n.** **1** a piece of old cloth, esp. one torn from a larger piece, used typically for cleaning things. ■ (**rags**) old or tattered clothes. **2** informal a newspaper, typically one regarded as being of low quality: *the local rag.*

– PHRASES **be on the rag** informal be menstruating. **in rags** (of clothes) tattered and torn. ■ (of a person) wearing such clothes. [ME: prob. back-form. from RAGGED.]

rag[2] ▶ **v.** (**ragged** /ragd/, **rag·ging**) [trans.] **1** make fun of (someone) in a loud, boisterous manner. **2** rebuke severely. [18th C.: origin unknown.]

rag[3] ▶ **n.** a large, coarse roofing slate. [ME ('a hard rock'): origin unknown.]

rag[4] ▶ **n.** a ragtime composition or tune. [19th C.: perh. from RAGGED.]

ra·ga /ˈrägə/ ▶ **n.** (in Indian music) a pattern of notes having characteristic intervals, rhythms, and embellishments, used as a basis for improvisation. ■ a piece using a particular raga. [18th C.: from Sanskrit, lit. 'color, tone.']

rag·a·muf·fin /ˈragəˌməfən/ ▶ **n.** a person, typically a child, in ragged, dirty clothes. [ME: prob. based on RAG[1].]

rag-and-bone man ▶ **adj.** an itinerant dealer in old clothes, furniture, and small, cheap secondhand items.

rag·bag /ˈragˌbag/ ▶ **n.** a bag in which scraps of fabric and old clothes are kept for use. ■ a miscellaneous collection of something.

rag doll ▶ **n.** a soft doll made from pieces of cloth.

rage /rāj/ ▶ **n.** violent, uncontrollable anger. ■ aggressive behavior or violent anger caused by a stressful situation: *office rage.* ■ fig. the violent action of a natural agency: *the rage of the sea.* ■ [in sing.] a vehement desire or passion. ■ (**the rage**) a widespread temporary enthusiasm or fashion. ▶ **v.** [intrans.] feel or express violent uncontrollable anger. ■ (of a natural agency or a conflict) continue violently or with great force: *the argument raged for days.* ■ (of an illness) spread very rapidly or uncontrollably. ■ (of an emotion) have or reach a high degree of intensity. [ME (also 'madness'): from OFr. *rage* (n.), *rager* (v.), from a var. of L. *rabies* (see RABIES).]

rag·ged /ˈragid/ ▶ **adj.** **1** (of cloth or clothes) old and torn. ■ (of a person) wearing such clothes: *a ragged child.* **2** having a rough, irregular, or uneven surface, edge, or outline: *a ragged coastline.* ■ lacking finish, smoothness, or uniformity: *the ragged discipline of the players.* ■ (of a sound) rough or uneven. ■ (of an animal) having a rough, shaggy coat. ■ Print. (esp. of a right margin) uneven because the lines are unjustified. **3** suffering from exhaustion or stress.

– PHRASES **run someone ragged** exhaust someone by making them undertake a lot of physical activity. [ME: of Scand. origin; compare ON *rǫgvathr* 'tufted.']

rag·ged·y /ˈragədē/ ▶ **adj.** informal scruffy; shabby.

rag·ged·y-ass (also **rag·ged·y-assed**) ▶ **adj.** [attrib.] informal shabby; miserably inadequate: *a raggedy-ass house.* ■ (of a person) new and inexperienced.

rag·gle-tag·gle /ˈragəl ˌtagəl/ ▶ **adj.** scruffy. [20th C.: appar. from RAGTAG.]

rag·head /ˈragˌhed/ ▶ **n.** informal, offens. a person who wears a kaffiyeh or turban.

rag·ing /ˈrājiNG/ ▶ **adj.** showing violent anger. ■ (of a natural agency) continuing with overpowering force: *a raging storm.* ■ (of a feeling, illness, process, or activity) so powerful as to seem out of control: *raging thirst.* ■ informal tremendous: *a raging success.*

rag·lan /ˈraglən/ ▶ **adj.** (of a sleeve) continuing in one piece up to the neck of a garment, without a shoulder seam. ■ (of a garment) having sleeves of this type. [19th C.: Lord *Raglan* (1788–1855), British commander in the Crimean War.]

raglan sleeves

rag·man /ˈragˌman/ ▶ **n.** (pl. **-men**) a person who collects or deals in rags, old clothes, and other items.

Rag·na·rök /ˈragnəˌräk; -rək/ Scand. Mythol. the final battle between the gods and the powers of evil. [from ON *ragnarǫkr* 'twilight of the gods.']

ra·gout /raˈgōō/ ▶ **n.** a highly seasoned dish of meat cut into small pieces and stewed with vegetables. [from Fr. *ragoût*, from *ragoûter* 'revive the taste of.']

rag pa·per ▶ **n.** paper made from cotton, originally from cotton rags, but now from cotton linters.

rag·pick·er /'rag,pikər/ ▶ **n.** hist. a person who collected and sold rags.

rag rug ▶ **n.** a rug made from strips of fabric hooked into or pushed through a base material such as burlap.

rag·tag /'rag,tag/ ▶ **adj.** [attrib.] untidy, disorganized, or incongruously varied in character: *a ragtag group.* [19th C.: superseding earlier *tag-rag.*]

rag·time /'rag,tīm/ ▶ **n.** music characterized by a syncopated melodic line and regularly accented accompaniment, evolved by black American musicians in the 1890s and played esp. on the piano. [prob. from RAG[4] (from the syncopation).]

rag·top /'rag,täp/ ▶ **n.** a car with a convertible roof.

rag trade ▶ **n.** informal the clothing or fashion industry.

Ra·gu·sa /rə'go͞ozə; rä'go͞ozä/ Italian name of DUBROVNIK.

rag·weed /'rag,wēd/ ▶ **n.** a North American plant (*Ambrosia artemisia*) of the daisy family. Its tiny green flowers produce copious amounts of pollen, making it a major causative agent of hay fever.

rag·wort /'rag,wərt; -,wôrt/ ▶ **n.** a yellow-flowered plant (genus *Senecio*) of the daisy family that is a common weed of grazing land. It is toxic to livestock, esp. when dried.

rah /rä/ ▶ **exclam.** informal a cheer of encouragement or approval. [19th C.: shortening of HURRAH.]

Rah·man see ABDUL RAHMAN, MUJIBUR RAHMAN.

rah-rah informal ▶ **adj.** marked by great or uncritical enthusiasm or excitement: *his rah-rah style.* [20th C.: reduplication of RAH.]

Rah·way /'rô,wā; 'rä-/ a city in northeastern New Jersey; pop. 25,325.

raid /rād/ ▶ **n.** a rapid surprise attack on an enemy by troops, aircraft, or other armed forces in warfare. ■ a rapid surprise attack to commit a crime, esp. to steal from business premises. ■ a surprise visit by police to arrest suspected people or seize illicit goods. ■ Stock Market a hostile attempt to buy a major or controlling interest in the shares of a company. ▶ **v.** [trans.] conduct a raid on: *officers raided thirty homes.* ■ quickly and illicitly take something from (a place). — **raid·er** n. [ME (n.): Scots var. of ROAD 'foray.']

rail[1] /rāl/ ▶ **n. 1** a bar or series of bars, typically fixed on upright supports, serving as part of a fence or barrier or used to hang things on. ■ (**the rails**) the inside boundary fence of a racecourse. ■ the edge of a surfboard or sailboard. ■ the rim of a billiard or pool table. **2** a steel bar or continuous line of bars laid on the ground as one of a pair forming a railroad track. ■ [often as adj.] railroads as a means of transportation. **3** a horizontal piece in the frame of a paneled door or sash window. Compare with STILE[2]. ▶ **v.** [trans.] provide or enclose (a space or place) with a rail or rails: *the altar is railed off from the nave.*
– PHRASES **go off the rails** informal begin behaving in a strange way. [ME: from OFr. *reille* 'iron rod,' from L. *regula* 'straight stick.']

rail[2] ▶ **v.** [intrans.] (**rail against/at/about**) complain or protest strongly and persistently about: *he railed at human fickleness.* [ME: from Fr. *railler*, from Provençal *ralhar* 'to jest,' based on an alt. of L. *rugire* 'to bellow.']

rail[3] ▶ **n.** a secretive bird (*Rallus* and other genera) with drab gray and brown plumage, typically having a long bill and found in dense waterside vegetation. The **rail family** (Rallidae) also includes the crakes, gallinules, moorhens, and coots. [ME: from Old North. Fr. *raille*, perh. imitative.]

rail·bird /'rāl,bərd/ ▶ **n.** a spectator at a horse race.

rail·head /'rāl,hed/ ▶ **n.** a point on a railroad from which roads and other transportation routes begin. ■ the furthest point reached in constructing a railroad.

rail·ing /'rāliNG/ ▶ **n.** (usu. **railings**) a fence or barrier made of rails.

rail·ler·y /'rālərē/ ▶ **n.** good-humored teasing. [17th C.: from Fr. *raillerie*, from *railler* (see RAIL[2]).]

rail·road /'rāl,rōd/ ▶ **n. 1** a track or set of tracks made of steel rails along which passenger and freight trains run. **2** a system of such tracks with the trains, organization, and personnel required for its working. ▶ **v. 1** [trans.] informal press (someone) into doing something by rushing or coercing them: *she hesitated, unwilling to be **railroaded into** a decision.* ■ cause (a measure) to be passed or approved quickly by applying pressure: *the Bill had been **railroaded through** the House.* ■ send (someone) to prison without a fair trial or by means of false evidence. **2** [intrans.] [usu. as n.] (**railroading**) travel or work on the railroads.

rail·way /'rāl,wā/ ▶ **n.** chiefly British term for RAILROAD.

rai·ment /'rāmənt/ ▶ **n.** archaic or literary clothing. [ME: shortening of obs. *arrayment* 'dress, outfit.']

rain /rān/ ▶ **n.** the condensed moisture of the atmosphere falling visibly in separate drops. ■ (**rains**) falls of rain. ■ [in sing.] a large or overwhelming quantity of things that fall or descend: *a **rain of** debris.* ▶ **v.** [intrans.] (**it rains, it is raining**, etc.) rain falls. ■ [with adverbial of direction] (of objects) fall in large or overwhelming quantities: *bombs rained down.* ■ [trans.] (**it rains ——, it is raining ——**, etc.) used to convey that a specified thing is falling in large or overwhelming quantities: *it was just raining glass.* ■ [with obj. and adverbial of direction] send down in large or overwhelming quantities: *she rained blows onto him.*
– PHRASES **be as right as rain** (of a person) be perfectly fit and well. **when it rains it pours** see POUR. **rain cats and dogs** rain very hard. [18th C.: earlier (17th C.) as *rain dogs and polecats.*]
– PHRASAL VERBS **rain something out** (usu. **be rained out**) cause an event to be terminated or canceled because of rain. — **rain·less** adj. [OE *regn* (n.), *regnian* (v.), from Gmc.; akin to Ger. *Regen.*]

rain·bow /'rān,bō/ ▶ **n.** an arch of colors formed in the sky in certain circumstances, caused by the refraction and dispersion of the sun's light by rain or other water droplets in the atmosphere. ■ any display of the colors of the spectrum produced by dispersion of light. ■ a wide range or variety of related and typically colorful things: ***a rainbow of** medals decorated his chest.* ■ short for RAINBOW TROUT. [OE *regnboga* (see RAIN, BOW[1]).]

Rain·bow Bridge a natural rock bridge in southern Utah. Its span is 278 feet (86 m).

rain·bow trout ▶ **n.** a large, partly migratory trout (*Salmo gairdneri*) native to the Pacific seaboard of North America. It has been widely introduced elsewhere, both as a farmed food fish and as a sporting fish.

rain check ▶ **n.** a ticket given for later use when an outdoor event is postponed by rain. ■ a coupon issued to a customer by a store, guaranteeing that a sale item that is out of stock may be purchased at a later date at the same reduced price.

rain·coat /'rān,kōt/ ▶ **n.** a long coat made from waterproofed or water-resistant fabric.

rain dance ▶ **n.** a ritual done to summon rain, as practiced by some Pueblo Indians and other peoples.

rain date ▶ **n.** an alternative date for an event in case of inclement weather.

rain·drop /'rān,dräp/ ▶ **n.** a single drop of rain.

rain·fall /'rān,fôl/ ▶ **n.** the fall of rain. ■ the quantity of rain falling within a given area in a given time.

rain for·est (also **rain·for·est**) ▶ **n.** a luxuriant, dense forest, found typically in tropical areas with consistently heavy rainfall.

rain gauge ▶ **n.** a device for collecting and measuring the amount of rain that falls.

Rai·nier, Mount /rə'ni(ə)r; rā-/ a volcanic peak in southwestern Washington state that rises to 14,410 feet (4,395 m).

rain·mak·er /'rān,mākər/ ▶ **n.** a person who attempts to cause rain to fall, either by rituals or by a scientific technique such as seeding clouds with crystals. ■ informal a person who is highly successful, esp. in business. — **rain·mak·ing** /-,mākiNG/ **n.**

rain·out /'rān,out/ ▶ **n.** a cancellation or premature ending of an event because of rain.

rain·proof /'rān,pro͞of/ ▶ **adj.** impervious to rain.

rain shad·ow ▶ **n.** a region having little rainfall because it is sheltered from prevailing rain-bearing winds by a range of hills.

rain stick ▶ **n.** a percussion instrument made from a dried cactus branch that is hollowed out, capped at both ends, and filled with small pebbles so that it makes the sound of falling rain when slightly tilted.

rain·storm /'rān,stôrm/ ▶ **n.** a storm with heavy rain.

rain·wa·ter /'rān,wôtər; -,wätər/ ▶ **n.** water that has fallen as or been obtained from rain.

rain·wear /'rān,we(ə)r/ ▶ **n.** waterproof or water-resistant clothes suitable for wearing in the rain.

rain·y /'rānē/ ▶ **adj.** (**rain·i·er, rain·i·est**) (of weather, a period of time, or an area) having a great deal of rainfall.
– PHRASES **a rainy day** used in reference to a possible time in the future when something, esp. money, will be needed: *invest and save for a rainy day.* — **rain·i·ness** n.

Rai·pur /'rīpo͝or/ a city in central India; pop. 438,000.

raise /rāz/ ▶ **v.** [trans.] **1** lift or move to a higher position or level: *she raised both arms above her head.* ■ lift or move to a vertical position; set upright: *Melody managed to raise him to his feet.* ■ construct or build (a structure): *a fence was being raised around the property.* ■ cause to rise or form: *the galloping horse raised a cloud of dust.* ■ bring to the surface (something that has sunk). ■ cause (bread) to rise, esp. by the action of yeast: [as adj.] (**raised**) *raised doughnuts.* ■ make a (nap) on cloth. **2** increase the amount, level, or strength of: *the bank raised interest rates | an effort to raise awareness.* ■ promote (someone) to a higher rank: *the king **raised** him **to** the title of Count Torre Bella.* ■ [usu. as n.] (**raising**) Ling. (in transformational grammar) move (an element) from a lower structure to a higher one. ■ (**raise something to**) Math. multiply a quantity to (a specified power): *3 raised to the 7th power is 2,187.* ■ [with two objs.] (in poker or brag) bet (a specified amount) more than (another player): *I'll raise you another hundred dollars.* ■ Bridge make a higher bid in the same suit as that bid by (one's partner). ■ increase (a bid) in this way. **3** cause to be heard, considered, or discussed: *the alarm was raised | doubts have been raised.* ■ cause to occur, appear, or be felt: *recent sightings have raised hopes that otters are making a return.* ■ generate (an invoice or other document). **4** collect, levy, or bring together (money or resources): *she was attempting to raise $20,000.* **5** bring up (a child). ■ breed or grow (animals or plants): *they raised pigs.* **6** bring (someone) back from death: *God **raised** Jesus **from the dead.*** **7** abandon or force an enemy to abandon (a siege, blockade, or embargo). **8** drive (an animal) from its lair. ■ cause (a ghost or spirit) to appear: fig. *the piece raises the ghosts of a number of twentieth-century art* *ideas.* ■ (of someone at sea) come in sight of (land or another ship). **9** Immunol. stimulate production of (an antiserum, antibody, or other biologically active substance) against the appropriate target cell or substance. ▶ **n. 1** an increase in salary. **2** (in poker or brag) an increase in a stake. ■ Bridge a higher bid in the suit that one's partner has bid. **3** [usu. with adj.] Weightlifting an act of lifting or raising a part of the body while holding a weight: *bent-over raises.* — **rais·a·ble adj. rais·er n.** [ME: from ON *reisa*; akin to REAR².]

rai·sin /'rāzən/ ▶ **n.** a partially dried grape. — **rai·sin·y adj.** [ME: from OFr., 'grape,' from an alt. of L. *racemus* 'grape bunch.']

rai·son d'é·tat /rā'zôN dā'tä/ ▶ **n.** (pl. **rai·sons d'é·tat** /rā'zôN(z)/) a purely political reason for action on the part of a ruler or government, esp. where a departure from openness, justice, or honesty is involved. [Fr., lit. 'reason of state.']

rai·son d'ê·tre /rā'zôN 'detr(ə)/ ▶ **n.** (pl. **rai·sons d'ê·tre** /rā'zôn(z)/) the most important reason or purpose for someone or something's existence. [Fr., lit. 'reason for being.']

rai·ta /'rītə/ ▶ **n.** an Indian side dish of yogurt containing chopped cucumber or other vegetables, and spices. [from Hindi *rāytā*.]

Raj /räj/ ▶ **n.** (**the Raj**) hist. British sovereignty in India: *the last days of the Raj.* [from Hindi *rāj* 'reign.']

ra·jah /'räjə; 'räzHə/ (also **ra·ja**) ▶ **n.** hist. an Indian king or prince. ■ a Malay or Javanese ruler or chief. [from Hindi *rājā*, Sanskrit *rājan* 'king.']

Ra·ja·sthan /'räjə,stän/ a state in western India, on the Pakistani border; capital, Jaipur. — **Ra·ja·stha·ni** /,räjə'stänē/ **n. & adj.**

Raj·kot /'räjkōt/ a city in western India; pop. 556,000.

Raj·put /'räj,po͝ot/ ▶ **n.** a member of a Hindu military caste claiming Kshatriya descent. [from Hindi *rājpūt*, from Sanskrit *rājan* 'king' + *putra* 'son.']

Raj·sha·hi /räj'sHä,hē/ a city in western Bangladesh; pop. 325,000.

rake¹ /rāk/ ▶ **n.** an implement consisting of a pole with a crossbar toothed like a comb at the end, or with several tines held together by a crosspiece, used esp. for drawing together cut grass or smoothing loose soil. ■ a similar implement used for other purposes, e.g., by a croupier drawing in money at a gaming table. ▶ **v.** [trans.] collect, gather, or move with a rake. ■ make (a stretch of ground) tidy or smooth with a rake. ■ scratch or scrape (something, esp. a person's flesh) with a long sweeping movement: *her fingers raked Bill's face.* ■ draw or drag (something) with a long sweeping movement: *she raked a comb through her hair.* ■ sweep (something) from end to end with gunfire, a look, or a beam of light: *his high beams raked the shrubbery.* ■ [intrans.] move across something with a long sweeping movement: *his icy gaze raked mercilessly over Lissa's slender figure.*

– PHRASES (**as**) **thin as a rake** (of a person) very thin.

– PHRASAL VERBS **rake in something** informal make a lot of money, typically very easily: *he was now raking in $250 million.* — **rak·er n.** [OE *raca*, from Gmc.; akin to Ger. *Rechen*, from a base meaning 'heap up'; v. partly from ON *raka* 'to scrape.']

rake² ▶ **n.** a fashionable or wealthy man of dissolute or promiscuous habits.

– PHRASES **a rake's progress** a progressive deterioration, esp. through self-indulgence. [a series of engravings (1735) by Hogarth.] [17th C.: abbrev. of archaic *rakehell*.]

rake³ ▶ **v.** [trans.] (often **be raked**) set (something, esp. a stage or the floor of an auditorium) at a sloping angle. ■ [intrans.] (of a ship's mast or funnel) incline from the perpendicular toward the stern. ■ [intrans.] (of a ship's bow or stern) project at its upper part beyond the keel. ▶ **n. 1** [in sing.] the angle at which a thing slopes. **2** the angle of the edge or face of a cutting tool. [17th C.: prob. akin to Ger. *ragen* 'to project.']

rake-off ▶ **n.** informal a commission or share of the profits from a deal, esp. one that is disreputable.

ra·ki /rä'kē; 'rakē; 'räkē/ ▶ **n.** a strong alcoholic spirit made in eastern Europe or the Middle East. [from Turk. *rakı*.]

rak·ish¹ /'rākisH/ ▶ **adj.** having or displaying a dashing, jaunty, or slightly disreputable quality or appearance. — **rak·ish·ly adv. rak·ish·ness n.**

rak·ish² ▶ **adj.** (esp. of a boat or car) trim and fast-looking, with streamlined angles and curves. [19th C.: from RAKE³ + (n.).]

Rá·ko·si /'räkôsHē/, Mátyás (1892–1971), prime minister of Hungary 1952–53, 1955–56.

ra·ku /'rä,ko͞o/ ▶ **n.** [usu. as adj.] a kind of lead-glazed Japanese earthenware, used esp. for the tea ceremony. [Japanese, lit. 'enjoyment.']

rale /räl; ral/ ▶ **n.** (usu. **rales**) Med. an abnormal rattling sound heard when examining unhealthy lungs. [19th C.: from Fr. *râle*, from *râler* 'to rattle.']

Ra·leigh¹ /'rôlē; 'rä-/ the capital of North Carolina, in the east central part of the state; pop. 276,093.

Ra·leigh² (also **Ra·legh**), Sir Walter (*c.*1552–1618), English explorer. A favorite of Elizabeth I, he organized several voyages to the Americas.

rall. Music ▶ **abbr.** rallentando.

ral·len·tan·do /,rälən'tändō; ,ralən'tandō/ Music ▶ **adv., adj., & n.** (pl. **-dos** or **-di** /-dē/) Music another term for RITARDANDO. [Ital., lit. 'slowing down,' from the v. *rallentare*.]

ral·ly /'ralē/ ▶ **v.** (**-lies, -lied**) [intrans.] **1** (of troops) come together again in order to continue fighting after a defeat or dispersion. ■ [trans.] bring together (forces) again in order to continue fighting. ■ assemble in a mass meeting. ■ come together in order to support a person or cause or for concerted action. ■ [trans.] bring together (forces or support) in such a way. ■ Sports come from behind in scoring. ■ (of a person) recover their health, spirits, or poise. ■ [trans.] revive (a person or their health or spirits). ■ (of share, currency, or commodity prices) increase after a fall. **2** drive in a rally. ■ (in tennis and other racket sports) engage in a rally. ▶ **n.** (pl. **-lies**) **1** a mass meeting of people making a political protest or showing support for a cause. ■ an open-air event for people who own a particular kind of vehicle: *a traction engine rally.* **2** (also **rallye**) a competition for motor vehicles in which they are driven a long distance over public roads or rough terrain, typically in stages. **3** a quick or marked recovery after a reverse or a period of weakness. ■ (in baseball and football) a renewed offensive, usually by the losing team, that ties or wins the game. **4** (in tennis and other racket sports) an extended exchange of strokes between players. [17th C. ('bring together again'): from Fr. *rallier*, from *re-* + *allier* 'to ally.']

ral·ly·ing /'ralēiNG/ ▶ **n.** **1** [often as adj.] the action or process of coming together to support a person or cause or take concerted action: *a rallying cry.* **2** the sport or action of participating in a motor rally.

RAM /ram/ ▶ **abbr.** Comput. random-access memory.

ram /ram/ ▶ **n.** **1** an uncastrated male sheep. See illustration at BIGHORN. ■ (**the Ram**) the zodiacal sign or constellation Aries. **2** short for BATTERING RAM. ■ the falling weight of a pile-driving machine. ■ hist. a beak or other projecting part of the bow of a warship, for piercing the hulls of other ships. **3** a hydraulic water-raising or lifting machine. ■ the piston of a hydraulic press. ■ the plunger of a force pump. ▶ **v.** (**rammed, ramming**) [trans.] roughly force (something) into place. ■ [trans.] (of a vehicle or vessel) be driven violently into (something, typically another vehicle or vessel) in an attempt to stop or damage it. ■ [intrans.] crash violently against something. ■ [trans.] [often as adj.] (**rammed**) beat (earth or the ground) with a heavy implement to make it hard and firm: *rammed earth.* ■ (**ram through**) [trans.] force (something) to be accepted. — **rammer n.** [OE *ram(m)*, from Gmc.; akin to Du. *ram*.]

Ra·ma /'rämə/ the hero of the Ramayana and the seventh incarnation of Vishnu.

ra·ma·da /rə'mädə; -'madə/ ▶ **n.** an arbor or porch. [19th C.: from Sp.]

Ram·a·dan /'rämə,dän; 'ramə,dan/ ▶ **n.** the ninth month of the Muslim year, during which strict fasting is observed from sunrise to sunset. [from Arab. *ramaḍān*, from *ramaḍa* 'be hot.' The lunar reckoning of the Muslim calendar brings the fast earlier each year; orig. Ramadan was supposed to be in one of the hot months.]

Ra·man /'rämən/, Sir Chandrasekhara Venkata (1888–1970), Indian physicist. Nobel Prize for Physics (1930).

Ra·ma·pith·e·cus /,ramə'piTHikəs; ,rä-/ ▶ **n.** an extinct anthropoid ape (genus *Ramapithecus*, family Pongidae) of the Miocene epoch. [mod. L., from RAMA + Gk. *pithēkos* 'ape.']

Ra·ma·ya·na /,rämə'yänə; rə'mäyənə/ one of the two great Sanskrit epics of the Hindus, composed 300 BC. [Sanskrit, lit. 'exploits of Rama.']

ram·ble /'rambəl/ ▶ **v.** [intrans.] **1** walk for pleasure in the countryside, typically without a definite route. ■ (of a plant) put out long shoots and grow over walls or other plants. **2** talk or write at length in a confused or inconsequential way: ***he rambled on about his acting career.*** ▶ **n.** a walk taken for pleasure in the countryside. [ME (sense 2): prob. akin to MDu. *rammelen* '(of animals) wander around in heat,' also to RAM (n.).]

ram·bler /'ramb(ə)lər/ ▶ **n.** **1** a person who walks in the countryside for pleasure. **2** a straggling or climbing rose. **3** another term for *RANCH HOUSE* (see RANCH).

ram·bling /'ramb(ə)liNG/ ▶ **adj.** **1** (of writing or speech) lengthy and confused or inconsequential. **2** (of a plant) putting out long shoots and growing over walls or other plants; climbing: *rambling roses.* ■ (of a building or path) spreading or winding irregularly in various directions: *a big old rambling house.* ■ (of a person) traveling from place to place; wandering. — **ram·bling·ly adv.**

Ram·bouil·let /,rambə'lā; -bo͞o'yā/ ▶ **n.** (pl. same) a sheep of a hardy breed developed from the Spanish merino.

ram·bunc·tious /ram'bəNGksHəs/ ▶ **adj.** informal uncontrollably exuberant; boisterous. — **ram·bunc·tious·ly adv. ram·bunc·tious·ness n.** [19th C.: origin unknown.]

ram·bu·tan /ram'bo͞otn/ ▶ **n.** **1** a red, plum-sized tropical fruit with soft spines and a slightly acidic taste. **2** the Malaysian tree (*Nephelium lappaceum*) of the soapberry family that bears this fruit. [18th C.: from Malay *rambūtan*, from *rambut* 'hair,' from the fruit's spines.]

ram·e·kin /'ramikən/ ▶ **n.** (also **ram·e·kin dish**) a small dish for baking and serving an individual portion of food. ■ a small quantity of cheese baked with breadcrumbs and eggs served in such a dish. [17th C.: from Fr. *ramequin*, of Low Ger. or Du. origin; compare obs. Flemish *rameken* 'toast.']

ra·men /'rämən/ ▶ **plural n.** (in oriental cuisine) quick-cooking noodles, typically served in a broth. [Japanese, from Chin. *lā* 'to pull' + *miàn* 'noodles.']

ram·ie /'ramē; 'rä-/ ▶ **n.** **1** a vegetable fiber noted for its length and toughness. **2** the plant (*Boehmeria nivea*) of the nettle family that yields this fiber, native to tropical Asia and cultivated elsewhere. [19th C.: from Malay *rami*.]

ram·i·fi·ca·tion /,raməfə'kāsHən/ ▶ **n.** (usu. **ramifications**) a consequence of an action or event, esp. when complex or unwelcome. ■ a subdivision of a complex structure or process. ■ formal or tech. the action or state of ramifying or being ramified. [17th C.: from Fr., from *ramifier* 'form branches' (see RAMIFY).]

ram·i·fy /'ramə,fī/ ▶v. (-fies, -fied) [intrans.] formal tech. form branches or offshoots; spread or branch out. ■ [trans.] [often as adj.] (**ramified**) cause to branch or spread out: *a ramified genealogical network.* [ME: from OFr. *ramifier*, from med. L. *ramificare*, from L. *ramus* 'branch.']

ram·jet /'ram,jet/ ▶n. a type of jet engine in which the air drawn in for combustion is compressed solely by the forward motion of the aircraft.

Ra·món y Ca·jal /rə'mōn ē kə'häl/, Santiago (1852–1934), Spanish physician. He was a founder of the science of neurology. Nobel Prize for Physiology or Medicine (1906, shared with Camillo Golgi).

ramp /ramp/ ▶n. **1** a slope or inclined plane for joining two different levels, as at the entrance or between floors of a building. ■ a movable set of steps for entering or leaving an aircraft. ■ an inclined road leading onto or off a main road or highway. **2** an upward bend in a stair rail. ▶v. **1** [trans.] provide or build (something) with a ramp. **2** [intrans.] archaic (of an animal) rear up on its hind legs in a threatening posture. ■ rush about violently or uncontrollably. ■ (of a plant) grow or climb luxuriantly.
– PHRASAL VERBS **ramp something up** (or **ramp up**) (esp. in reference to the production of goods) increase or cause to increase in amount: *they ramped up production.* [ME 'rear up': from OFr. *ramper* 'creep, crawl.']

ram·page /,ram'pāj/ ▶v. [no obj., with adverbial of direction] (esp. of a large group of people) rush around in a violent and uncontrollable manner. ▶n. a period of violent and uncontrollable behavior, typically involving a large group of people. [17th C.: perh. based on RAMP (v.) and RAGE (n.).]

ramp·ant /'rampənt/ ▶adj. **1** (esp. of something unpleasant) flourishing or spreading unchecked: *rampant inflation.* ■ (of a person or activity) violent or unrestrained in action or performance. ■ (of a plant) lush in growth. **2** [usu. postpositive] Heraldry (of an animal) represented standing on one hind foot with its forefeet in the air. **3** Archit. (of an arch) springing from a level of support at one height and resting on the other support at a higher level. [ME (as a heraldic term): from OFr., lit. 'crawling,' from the v. *ramper* 'crawl.']

ram·part /'ram,pärt/ ▶n. (usu. **ramparts**) a defensive wall of a castle or walled city, having a broad top with a walkway and typically a stone parapet. ■ a defensive or protective barrier. [16th C.: from Fr. *rempart*, from *remparer* 'fortify, take possession of again,' based on L. *ante* 'before' + *parare* 'prepare.']

ram·pi·on /'rampēən/ ▶n. a Eurasian plant of the bellflower family, some kinds of which have a root that can be eaten in salads, in particular the Mediterranean *Campanula rapunculus*, with a long narrow spike of bluish flowers and a thick taproot. [16th C.: from a var. of med. L. *rapuncium*; compare Ger. *Rapunzel* 'corn salad.']

ram·rod /'ram,räd/ ▶n. a rod for ramming down the charge of a muzzle-loading firearm. ■ used in similes and metaphors to describe someone's erect or rigid posture: *he held himself ramrod straight.* ■ a manager, esp. one who is a strict disciplinarian. ▶v. (**-rod·ded, -rod·ding**) [trans.] (**ramrod something through**) force a proposed measure to be accepted or completed quickly.

Ram·say /'ramzē/, Sir William (1852–1916), Scottish chemist. He discovered the noble gases. Nobel Prize for Chemistry (1904).

Ram·ses /'ramsēz/ (also **Ram·e·ses** /'ramə,sēz/) the name of 11 Egyptian pharaohs, notably: ■ Ramses II (died *c.*1225 BC), reigned *c.*1292–*c.*1225 BC; known as **Ramses the Great**. He built the two rock temples at Abu Simbel. ■ Ramses III (died *c.*1167 BC), reigned *c.*1198–*c.*1167 BC.

ram·shack·le /'ram,SHakəl/ ▶adj. (esp. of a house or vehicle) in a state of severe disrepair. [19th C. (dial., meaning 'irregular'): alt. of *ramshackled*, obs. *ransackled* 'ransacked.']

ra·mus /'rāməs/ ▶n. (pl. **-mi** /-,mī/) Anat. an arm or branch of a bone or nerve. [17th C.: from L., lit. 'branch.']

ran /ran/ past of RUN.

ranch /ranCH/ ▶n. a large farm, esp. in the western US and Canada, where cattle or other animals are bred. ■ (also **ranch house**) a single-story, sometimes split-level, house, typically with a low-pitched roof. ▶v. [intrans.] run a ranch. ■ [trans.] [often as adj.] (**ranched**) breed (animals) on a ranch. ■ [trans.] use (land) as a ranch. [19th C.: from Sp. *rancho* 'group of persons eating together.']

ranch dress·ing ▶n. a type of thick white salad dressing made with sour cream or buttermilk.

ranch·er /'ranCHər/ ▶n. a person who owns or runs a ranch.

ran·cher·a /ran'CHerə; rän-/ ▶n. a type of Mexican country music, often played with guitars and horns. [20th C.: from Sp. *cancion ranchera* 'farmers' songs.']

ran·che·ria /,ranCHə'rēə/ ▶n. (in Spanish America and the western US) a small Indian settlement. [Sp., from *rancho* (see RANCH).]

ran·che·ro /ran'CHerō/ ▶n. (pl. **-ros**) a person who farms or works on a ranch, esp. in the southwestern US and Mexico. [Sp., from *rancho* (see RANCH).]

ran·cid /'ransid/ ▶adj. (of foods containing fat or oil) smelling or tasting unpleasant as a result of being old and stale. — **ran·cid·i·ty** /ran'sidətē/ n. [17th C.: from L. *rancidus* 'stinking.']

ran·cor /'raNGkər/ (Brit. **ran·cour**) ▶n. bitterness or resentfulness, esp. when long-standing: *he spoke without rancor.* — **ran·cor·ous** /-rəs/ adj. **ran·cor·ous·ly** /-k(ə)rəslē/ adv. [ME: via OFr. from late L. *rancor* 'rankness,' akin to L. *rancidus* 'stinking.']

Rand[1] /rand/ (**the Rand**) another name for WITWATERSRAND.

Rand[2], Ayn (1905–82), US writer; born in Russia; born *Alissa Rozenbaum*. She wrote *The Fountainhead* (1943) and *Atlas Shrugged* (1957).

rand[1] /rand; ränd; ränt/ ▶n. the basic monetary unit of South Africa, equal to 100 cents. [from *the Rand*, the name of a goldfield district near Johannesburg.]

rand[2] /rand/ ▶n. a strip of leather placed under the back part of a shoe or boot to make it level before the lifts of the heel are attached. [OE ('border):' Gmc.; akin to Ger. *Rand* 'edge.']

R & B ▶abbr. rhythm and blues.

R & D ▶abbr. research and development.

Ran·dolph /'ran,dôlf; -,dälf/, A. Philip (1889–1979), US labor and civil rights leader; full name *Asa Philip Randolph*. He founded the Brotherhood of Sleeping Car Porters in 1925.

ran·dom /'randəm/ ▶adj. made, done, happening, or chosen without method or conscious decision: *a random sample of 100 households.* ■ Stat. governed by or involving equal chances for each item. ■ (of masonry) with stones of irregular size and shape. — **ran·dom·ly** adv. **ran·dom·ness** n. [ME ('headlong rush'): from OFr. *randon* 'great speed,' from *randir* 'gallop,' from Gmc.; akin to RAND[2].]

ran·dom ac·cess Comput. ▶n. the process of transferring information to or from memory in which every memory location can be accessed directly rather than being accessed in a fixed sequence.

ran·dom·ize /'randə,mīz/ ▶v. [trans.] tech. make unpredictable, unsystematic, or random in order or arrangement; employ random selection or sampling in (an experiment or procedure). — **ran·dom·i·za·tion** /,randəmi'zāSHən/ n.

ran·dom var·i·a·ble ▶n. Stat. a quantity having a numerical value for each member of a group, esp. one whose values occur according to a frequency distribution. Also called VARIATE.

ran·dom walk ▶n. Physics the movements of an object or changes in a variable that follow no discernible pattern or trend.

R & R ▶abbr. ■ informal rest and recreation. ■ Med. rescue and resuscitation.

rand·y /'randē/ ▶adj. (**rand·i·er, rand·i·est**) informal sexually aroused or excited. [17th C.: perh. from obsolete *rand* 'to rant' from obs. Du. *randen*.]

rang /raNG/ past of RING[2].

range /rānj/ ▶n. **1** the area of variation between upper and lower limits on a particular scale. ■ a set of different things of the same general type: *a wide range of activities.* ■ the scope of a person's knowledge or abilities. ■ the compass of a person's voice or of a musical instrument: *an incredible vocal range.* ■ the extent of time covered by something such as a forecast. See also LONG-RANGE, SHORT-RANGE. ■ the area or extent covered by or included in something: *the range of debate.* ■ Math. the set of values that a given function can take as its argument varies. **2** the distance within which a person can see or hear: *range of vision.* ■ the maximum distance at which a radio transmission can be effectively received: *planets within radio range.* ■ the distance that can be covered by a vehicle or aircraft without refueling. ■ the maximum distance to which a gun will shoot or over which a missile will travel: *a duck came within range.* ■ the distance between a gun, missile, shot, or blow and its objective. ■ the distance between a camera and the subject to be photographed. ■ Surveying the horizontal direction and length of a survey line determined by at least two fixed points. **3** a line or series of mountains or hills: *the coastal ranges.* ■ a series of townships extending north and south parallel to the principal meridian of a survey. ■ Naut. a line defined by landmarks or beacons, used to locate something offshore, esp. a navigable channel or a hazard. **4** a large area of open land for grazing or hunting. ■ an area of land or sea used as a testing ground for military equipment. ■ an open or enclosed area with targets for shooting practice. ■ the area over which a thing, esp. a plant or animal, is distributed. **5** an electric or gas stove with several burners and one or more ovens. **6** Building a course of masonry extending from end to end at one height. ■ a row of buildings. ▶v. **1** [no obj., with adverbial] vary or extend between specified limits: *patients whose ages ranged from 13 to 25.* **2** [with obj. and adverbial] (usu. **be ranged**) place or arrange in a row or rows or in a specified order or manner: *a table with half a dozen chairs ranged around it.* ■ [no obj., with adverbial of direction] run or extend in a line in a particular direction: *benches that ranged along the path.* **3** [no obj., with adverbial of direction] (of a person or animal) travel or wander over a wide area: *patrols ranged thousands of miles.* ■ (of a person's eyes) pass from one person or thing to another: *his eyes ranged over them.* ■ (of something written or spoken) cover or embrace a wide number of different topics: *tutorials ranged over a variety of subjects.* **4** [intrans.] obtain the range of a target by adjustment after firing past it or short of it, or by the use of radar or laser equipment: *radar-type transmissions which appeared to be ranging on our convoys.* ■ [with adverbial] (of a projectile) cover a specified distance. ■ [with adverbial] (of a gun) send a projectile over a specified distance. [ME ('line of people or animals'):

from OFr. *range* 'row,' from *rangier* 'put in order,' from *rang* 'rank.']

range·find·er /'rānj,fīndər/ ▶ n. an instrument for estimating the distance of an object, esp. for use with a camera or gun.

range·land /'rānj,land/ ▶ n. (also **rangelands**) open country used for grazing or hunting animals.

Rang·er /'rānjər/ a series of nine American moon probes launched between 1961 and 1965.

rang·er /'rānjər/ ▶ n. **1** a keeper of a park, forest, or area of countryside. **2** a member of a body of armed men, in particular: ■ a mounted soldier. ■ a commando or highly-trained infantryman. **3** a person or thing that wanders or ranges.

Ran·goon /raNG'goon; ran-/ the capital of Myanmar (Burma), a port in the Irrawaddy delta; pop. 2,495,000. For centuries it was a Buddhist religious center. Burmese name **Yangon**.

rang·y /'rānjē/ ▶ adj. (**rang·i·er, rang·i·est**) **1** (of a person or animal) tall and slim with long, slender limbs. **2** (of land) having a large, open range.

ra·ni /'rānē; rä'nē/ ▶ n. (pl. **ra·nis**) hist. a Hindu queen, either by marriage to a raja or in her own right. [from Hindi *rānī*, Sanskrit *rājñī*, fem. of *rājan* 'king.']

rank¹ /raNGk/ ▶ n. **1** a position in the hierarchy of the armed forces: *the rank of Captain.* ■ a position within the hierarchy of an organization or society: *ministerial rank.* ■ high social position: *persons of rank and breeding.* ■ Stat. a number specifying position in a numerically ordered series. **2** a single line of soldiers or police officers drawn up abreast. ■ (**the ranks**) common soldiers as opposed to officers. ■ (**ranks**) the people belonging to or constituting a group or class: *the ranks of the unemployed.* ■ a regular row or line of things or people: *trees growing in ranks.* ■ Chess each of the eight rows of eight squares running from side to side across a chessboard. Compare with **file²**. ▶ v. [with obj. and adverbial] **1** give (someone or something) a rank or place within a grading system: *rank them in order of preference.* ■ [no obj., with adverbial] have a specified rank or place within a grading system: *he ranks with Newman as one of the outstanding English theologians* ■ [trans.] take precedence over (someone) in respect to rank; outrank. **2** arrange in a rank or ranks.
– PHRASES **break rank** (of soldiers or police officers) fail to remain in line. ■ fig. fail to maintain solidarity. **close ranks** (of soldiers or police officers) come closer together in a line. ■ fig. unite in order to defend common interests. **pull rank** take unfair advantage of one's seniority or privileged position. [ME: from OFr. *ranc*, from Gmc.; akin to **ring¹**.]

rank² ▶ adj. **1** (of vegetation) growing too thickly and coarsely. **2** (esp. of air or water) having a foul or offensive smell. **3** [attrib.] (esp. of something bad or deficient) complete and utter (used for emphasis): *rank stupidity.* — **rank·ly** adv. **rank·ness** n. [OE *ranc* 'proud, sturdy,' 'fully grown,' from Gmc.]

rank and file ▶ n. [treated as pl.] the ordinary members of an organization as opposed to its leaders. [from the "ranks" and "files" into which privates and noncommissioned officers form on parade.]

rank·ing ▶ n. /'raNGkiNG/ a position in a scale of achievement or status; a classification. ■ the action or process of giving a specified rank or place within a grading system. ▶ adj. [in comb.] having a specified position in a scale of achievement or status: *high-ranking army officers.* ■ [attrib.] having a high position in such a scale: *two ranking PLO figures.*

ran·kle /'raNGkəl/ ▶ v. [intrans.] **1** archaic (of a wound or sore) continue to be painful; fester. **2** (of a comment, event, or fact) cause annoyance or resentment that persists. ■ [trans.] annoy or irritate (someone). [ME: from OFr. *rancler*, from *rancle*, *draoncle* 'festering sore,' ult. from med. L. *dracunculus*, dimin. of *draco* 'serpent.']

Rann of Kutch see **Kutch, Rann of.**

ran·sack /'ran,sak; ran'sak/ ▶ v. [trans.] go hurriedly through (a place) stealing things and causing damage. — **ran·sack·er** /'ran,sakər/ n. [ME: from ON *rannsaka*, from *rann* 'house' + element akin to *sœkja* 'seek.']

Ran·som /'ransəm/, John Crowe (1888–1974), US poet and critic. His essays are collected in *The New Criticism* (1941).

ran·som /'ransəm/ ▶ n. a sum of money or other payment demanded or paid for the release of a prisoner. ■ the holding or freeing of a prisoner in return for payment of such money: *the capture and ransom of the king.* ▶ v. [trans.] obtain the release of (a prisoner) by making a payment demanded: *the lord was captured in war and had to be ransomed.* ■ hold (a prisoner) and demand payment for their release: *mercenaries burned the village and ransomed the inhabitants.* ■ release (a prisoner) after receiving payment.
– PHRASES **hold someone/something at** (or **for**) **ransom** hold someone prisoner and demand payment for their release. ■ demand concessions from a person or organization by threatening damaging action. [ME: from OFr. *ransoun* (n.), *ransouner* (v.), from L. *redemptio(n-)* 'ransoming, releasing' (see **redemption**). Early use also occurred in theological contexts expressing 'deliverance' and 'atonement.']

rant /rant/ ▶ v. [intrans.] speak or shout at length in a wild, impassioned way. ▶ n. a spell of ranting; a tirade.
– PHRASES **rant and rave** shout and complain angrily and at length. — **rant·er** n. **rant·ing·ly** adv. [16th C. ('behave in a boisterous way'): from Du. *ranten* 'talk nonsense, rave.']

ra·nun·cu·lus /rə'nəNGkyələs/ ▶ n. (pl. **-lus·es** or **-li** /-,lē; -,lī/) a temperate plant (genus *Ranunculus*) of the buttercup family, typically having yellow or white bowl-shaped flowers and lobed or toothed leaves. [mod. L., from L., dimin. of *rana* 'frog.']

Ran·vier's node /rän'vyāz; 'ranvi(ə)rz/ ▶ n. see **node of Ranvier.**

Rao /rou/, P. V. Narasimha (1921–2004); prime minister of India 1991–96; full name *Pamulaparti Venkata Narasimha Rao.*

rap¹ /rap/ ▶ v. (**rapped, rap·ping**) **1** [trans.] strike (a hard surface) with a series of rapid audible blows, esp. in order to attract attention: *he stood up and rapped the table* | [intrans.] *she **rapped** angrily **on the** window.* ■ strike (something) against a hard surface in such a way. ■ strike (someone or something) sharply with a stick or similar implement. ■ informal rebuke or criticize sharply. ■ say sharply or suddenly: *the ambassador **rapped out** an order.* **2** [intrans.] informal talk or chat in an easy and familiar manner. **3** [intrans.] perform rap music. ▶ n. **1** a quick, sharp knock or blow. **2** a type of popular music of US black origin in which words are recited rapidly and rhythmically over a prerecorded, typically electronic instrumental backing. ■ a piece of music performed in this style, or the words themselves. **3** informal a talk or discussion, esp. a lengthy or impromptu one: *a rap over a beer.* **4** [usu. with adj.] informal a criminal charge, esp. of a specified kind: *a murder rap.* ■ a person or thing's reputation, typically a bad one: *there's no reason why drag queens should get a bad rap.*
– PHRASES **beat the rap** informal escape punishment for or be acquitted of a crime. **take the rap** informal be punished or blamed. [ME ('severe blow,' and 'deliver a blow'): prob. imitative and of Scand. origin; compare Swed. *rappa* 'beat.']

rap² ▶ n. [in sing., with negative] the smallest amount (used to add emphasis to a statement): *he doesn't care a rap.* [19th C.: from Irish *ropaire* 'robber'; in 18th-cent. Ireland a counterfeit coin.]

ra·pa·cious /rə'pāsHəs/ ▶ adj. aggressively greedy or grasping: *rapacious landlords.* — **ra·pa·cious·ly** adv. **ra·pa·cious·ness** n. **ra·pac·i·ty** /rə'pasətē/ n. [17th C.: from L. *rapax, rapac-*, from *rapere* 'to snatch.']

rape¹ /rāp/ ▶ n. the crime, committed by a man, of forcing another person to have sexual intercourse with him, esp. by the threat or use of violence. ■ fig. the wanton destruction or spoiling of a place or area: *the rape of the Russian countryside.* ▶ v. [trans.] (of a man) force (another person) to have sexual intercourse with him, esp. by the threat or use of violence against them. ■ fig. spoil or destroy (a place). — **rap·er** n. [ME ('seizure of property': ult. from L. *rapere* 'seize.']

rape² ▶ n. a plant (genus *Brassica*) of the cabbage family with bright yellow, heavily scented flowers, esp. a variety (**oilseed rape**) grown for its oil-rich seed and as stockfeed. Also called **cole, colza.** [ME ('turnip plant'): from L. *rapum, rapa* 'turnip.']

rape³ ▶ n. (often **rapes**) the stalks and skins of grapes left after winemaking, used in making vinegar. [17th C. (as *rape wine*): from Fr. *râpe*, med. L. *raspa* 'bunch of grapes.']

rape oil (also **rape·seed oil**) ▶ n. an oil obtained from rapeseed, used as a lubricant and in foodstuffs.

rape·seed /'rāp,sēd/ ▶ n. seeds of the rape plant, used chiefly for oil. See **rape²**.

Raph·a·el¹ /'rafēəl; 'rā-/ (in the Bible) one of the seven archangels in the apocryphal Book of Enoch.

Raph·a·el² /'rafēəl; 'rāfēəl; ,räfī'el/ (1483–1520), Italian painter; Italian name *Raffaello Sanzio.* He is particularly noted for his madonnas, including his altarpiece, the *Sistine Madonna* (c.1513).

ra·phe /'rāfē/ ▶ n. (pl. **ra·phae** pronunc. same) Anat. & Biol. a groove, ridge, or seam in an organ or tissue, typically marking the line where two halves fused in the embryo. [18th C.: mod. L., from Gk. *rhaphē* 'seam.']

rap·id /'rapid/ ▶ adj. happening in a short time or at a great rate: *rapid economic decline.* ■ (of movement or activity) characterized by great speed: *his breathing was rapid and jerky.* ▶ n. (usu. **rapids**) a fast-flowing and turbulent part of the course of a river. — **ra·pid·i·ty** /rə'pidətē/ n. **rap·id·ly** adv. [17th C.: from L. *rapidus*, from *rapere* 'take by force.']

Rap·id Cit·y a city in southwestern South Dakota; pop. 59,607.

rap·id eye move·ment ▶ n. a jerky motion of a person's eyes occurring in REM sleep.

rap·id-fire ▶ adj. [attrib.] (esp. of something said in dialogue or done in a sequence) unhesitating and rapid. ■ (of a gun) able to fire shots in rapid succession.

rap·id tran·sit ▶ n. [usu. as adj.] a form of high-speed urban passenger transportation such as an elevated railroad system.

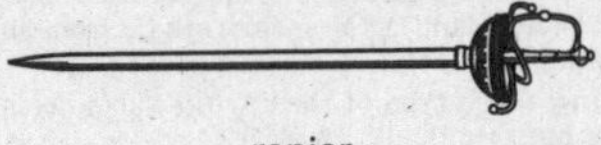

rapier

ra·pi·er /'rāpēər/ ▶ n. a thin, light, sharp-pointed sword used for thrusting. ■ [as adj.] (esp. of speech or intelligence) quick and incisive: *rapier wit.* [16th C.: from Fr. *rapière*, from *râpe* 'rasp, grater' (because the perforated hilt resembles a rasp or grater).]

rap·ine /'rapən; -īn/ ▶ n. literary the violent seizure of someone's property. [ME: ult. from L. *rapina*, from *rapere* 'seize.']

rap·ist /'rāpist/ ▶ n. a man who commits rape.

Rap·pa·han·nock Riv·er /,rapə'hanək/ a river that flows for 210 miles (340 km) across eastern Virginia.

rap·pel /rə'pel/ ▶ v. (**-pelled, -pel·ling**) [intrans.] descend a rock face by using a doubled rope coiled around the body and fixed at a higher point. ▶ n. a descent made by rappeling. [1930s: from Fr., lit. 'a recalling,' from *rappeler* 'to recall.']

rap·pen /'rapən/ ▶ **n.** (pl. same) a monetary unit in Switzerland, equal to one hundredth of the Swiss franc. [from Ger. *Rappe* 'raven,' with ref. to the depiction of the head of a raven, on a medieval coin.]

rap·per /'rapər/ ▶ **n.** a person who performs rap music.

rap·port /ra'pôr; rə-/ ▶ **n.** a close and harmonious relationship in which the people or groups concerned understand each other's feelings or ideas and communicate well: *a good rapport with children.* [17th C.: Fr., from *rapporter* 'bring back.']

rap·por·teur /,rapôr'tər/ ▶ **n.** a person appointed by an organization to report on its proceedings. [18th C.: Fr., from *rapporter* 'bring back.']

rap·proche·ment /,rap,rōsн'män; -,rôsн-/ ▶ **n.** (esp. in international relations) an establishment or resumption of harmonious relations: *a growing rapprochement between the two countries.* [Fr., from *rapprocher*, from *re-* (intensive) + *approcher* 'to approach.']

rap·scal·lion /rap'skalyən/ ▶ **n.** archaic or humorous a mischievous person: *they were the rapscallions behind this practical joke.* [17th C.: alt. of *rascallion*, perh. from RASCAL.]

rap sheet ▶ **n.** informal a criminal record.

rapt /rapt/ ▶ **adj. 1** completely fascinated by what one is seeing or hearing: *Andrew looked at her, rapt.* ■ indicating or characterized by such a state of fascination: *rapt attention.* ■ filled with an intense and pleasurable emotion; enraptured. **2** archaic or literary having been carried away bodily or transported to heaven: *he was rapt on high.* — **rapt·ly adv. rapt·ness n.** [ME ('transported by religious feeling'): from L. *raptus* 'seized,' past part. of *rapere.*]

rap·tor /'raptər/ ▶ **n.** a bird of prey, e.g., an eagle, hawk, falcon, or owl. [ME: from L., lit. 'plunderer,' from *rapt-* 'seized,' from the v. *rapere.*]

rap·ture /'rapcнər/ ▶ **n. 1** a feeling of intense pleasure. ■ **(raptures)** expressions of intense pleasure or enthusiasm about something. **2** (**the Rapture**) (according to some millenarian teaching) the transporting of believers to heaven at the Second Coming of Christ. ▶ **v.** [trans.] (usu. **be raptured**) (according to some millenarian teaching) transport (a believer) from earth to heaven at the Second Coming of Christ. [16th C. ('seizing and carrying off'): from obs. Fr., or from med. L. *raptura* 'seizing.']

rap·ture of the deep ▶ **n.** informal term for NITROGEN NARCOSIS.

rap·tur·ous /'rapcнərəs/ ▶ **adj.** characterized by, feeling, or expressing great pleasure or enthusiasm: *he was greeted with rapturous applause.* — **rap·tur·ous·ly adv. rap·tur·ous·ness n.**

ra·ra a·vis /,re(ə)rə 'āvis; ,rärə 'äwis/ ▶ **n.** (pl. **ra·rae a·ves** /,re(ə)rē 'āvēs; ,rärī 'äwes/) another term for RARE BIRD. [L.]

rare[1] /re(ə)r/ ▶ **adj.** (**rar·er, rar·est**) (of an event, situation, or condition) not occurring very often. ■ (of a thing) not found in large numbers and consequently of interest or value. ■ unusually good or remarkable: *he plays with rare strength and sensitivity.* — **rare·ness n.** [ME ('infrequent'): from L. *rarus.*]

rare[2] ▶ **adj.** (**rar·er, rar·est**) (of meat, esp. beef) lightly cooked, so that the inside is still red. [18th C.: var. of obs. *rear* '(of eggs) half-cooked.']

rare bird ▶ **n.** an exceptional person or thing; a rarity. [translating L. *rara avis* (Juvenal's *Satires*).]

rare·bit /'re(ə)rbit/ (also **Welsh rare·bit**) ▶ **n.** a dish of melted and seasoned cheese on toast. [18th C.: alt. of *rabbit* in *Welsh rabbit.*]

rare earth (also **rare earth el·e·ment** or **rare earth met·al**) ▶ **n.** Chem. any of a group of chemically similar metallic elements comprising the lanthanide series and (usually) scandium and yttrium. They are not esp. rare, but they tend to occur together in nature and are difficult to separate from one another.

rar·e·fied /'re(ə)rə,fīd/ (also **rar·i·fied**) ▶ **adj.** (of air, esp. that at high altitudes) containing less oxygen than usual. ■ fig. esoterically distant from the lives and concerns of ordinary people: *rarefied rituals.*

rare gas ▶ **n.** another term for NOBLE GAS.

rare·ly /'re(ə)rlē/ ▶ **adv.** not often; seldom: *I rarely drive above 60 mph.*

rar·ing /'re(ə)riNG/ ▶ **adj.** [with infin.] informal very enthusiastic and eager to do something: *she was raring to go.* [1920s: pres. part. of *rare*, dial. var. of ROAR or REAR[2].]

Rar·i·tan Riv·er /'raritn/ a river in central New Jersey that flows into Raritan Bay, which is an arm of New York Bay and the Atlantic Ocean.

rar·i·ty /'re(ə)ritē/ ▶ **n.** (pl. **-ties**) the state or quality of being rare: *the rarity of the condition.* ■ a thing that is rare, esp. one having particular value as a result of this: *to take the morning off was a rarity.*

Ra·ro·tong·a /,rarə'täNGgə/ a mountainous island in the South Pacific Ocean, the chief island of the Cook Islands. — **Ra·ro·tong·an n. & adj.**

Ras al Khai·mah /'räs al 'kīmə/ a member state of the United Arab Emirates; pop. 144,000. ■ its capital, a port on the Persian Gulf; pop. 42,000.

ras·cal /'raskəl/ ▶ **n.** a mischievous or cheeky person. — **ras·cal·i·ty** /ras'kalətē/ **n.** (pl. **-ties**) **ras·cal·ly adj.** [ME ('a mob,' 'member of the rabble'): from OFr. *rascaille* 'rabble.']

rash[1] /rasн/ ▶ **adj.** displaying or proceeding from a lack of careful consideration of the possible consequences of an action: *a rash decision.* — **rash·ly adv. rash·ness n.** [ME (also Scots, north. Engl. 'nimble'): Gmc.; akin to Ger. *rasch.*]

rash[2] ▶ **n.** an area of reddening of a person's skin, sometimes with raised spots, appearing esp. as a result of illness. ■ a series of things of the same type, esp. when unpleasant or undesirable, occurring or appearing within a short space of time: *a rash of auto accidents.* [18th C.: prob. akin to OFr. *rasche* 'eruptive sores'; compare Ital. *raschia* 'itch.']

rash·er /'rasнər/ ▶ **n.** a thin slice of bacon. ■ a serving of several such slices. [16th C.: origin unknown.]

rasp /rasp/ ▶ **n. 1** a coarse file or similar metal tool with a roughened surface for scraping, filing, or rubbing down objects of metal, wood, or other hard material. **2** [in sing.] a harsh, grating noise: *the rasp of the engine.* ▶ **v. 1** [trans.] scrape (something) with a rasp in order to make it smoother. ■ (of a rough surface or object) scrape (something, esp. someone's skin) in a painful or unpleasant way. **2** [intrans.] make a harsh, grating noise: *my breath rasped in my throat.* — **rasp·ing·ly adv. rasp·y adj.** [ME (v.): from OFr. *rasper*, perh. Gmc.]

rasp·ber·ry /'raz,berē; -b(ə)rē/ ▶ **n. 1** an edible soft fruit related to the blackberry, consisting of a cluster of reddish-pink drupelets. **2** the plant (*Rubus idaeus*) of the rose family that yields this fruit, forming tall, stiff, prickly stems (canes). **3** a deep reddish-pink color like that of a ripe raspberry. **4** informal a sound made with the tongue and lips in order to express derision or contempt. [from *raspberry tart*, rhyming slang for 'fart.'] [17th C.: from dial. *rasp*, abbrev. of obs. *raspis* 'raspberry' + BERRY.]

Ra·spu·tin /ras'pyōōtn/, Grigori Efimovich (1871–1916), Russian monk. He exerted great influence over Czar Nicholas II and his family during World War I.

Ras·ta·far·i /,rastə'fe(ə)rē; -'färē/ ▶ **n.** [usu. as adj.] the Rastafarian movement. [from *Ras Tafari*, the name by which Haile Selassie was known (1916–30).]

Ras·ta·far·i·an /,rastə'fe(ə)rēən; -'färēən/ ▶ **adj.** of or relating to a religious movement of Jamaican origin holding that blacks are the chosen people, that Emperor Haile Selassie of Ethiopia was the Messiah, and that black people will eventually return to their Africa. ▶ **n.** a member of the Rastafarian religious movement. — **Ras·ta·far·i·an·ism n.** [from *Ras Tafari*, the name by which Haile Selassie was known (1916–30).]

ras·ter /'rastər/ ▶ **n.** a rectangular pattern of parallel scanning lines followed by the electron beam on a television screen or computer monitor. [20th C.: from Ger. *Raster*, lit. 'screen,' from L. *rastrum* 'rake,' from *ras-* 'scraped,' from the v. *radere.*]

Rast·ya·pi·no /räst'yäpi,nō/ former name (1919–29) of DZERZHINSK.

rat /rat/ ▶ **n. 1** a rodent (*Rattus* and other genera, family Muridae) that resembles a large mouse, typically having a pointed snout and a long, sparsely haired tail. Some kinds have become cosmopolitan and are sometimes responsible for transmitting diseases. **2** informal a person regarded as despicable, esp. a man who has been deceitful or disloyal. ■ an informer. **3** [with adj.] a person who is associated with or frequents a specified place: *mall rats.* **4** a pad used to give shape or fullness to a woman's hair. ▶ **exclam.** (**rats**) informal used to express mild annoyance or irritation. ▶ **v.** (**rat·ted, rat·ting**) [intrans.] **1** [usu. as n.] (**ratting**) (of a person, dog, or cat) hunt or kill rats. **2** informal desert one's party, side, or cause. **3** give (hair) shape or fullness with a rat. [OE *ræt*, prob. of Romance origin.]

rat·a·ble /'rātəbəl/ ▶ **adj.** able to be rated or estimated. — **rat·a·bil·i·ty** /,rātə'bilətē/ **n.**

rat·a·ma·cue /'ratəmə,kyōō/ ▶ **n.** Music one of the basic patterns (rudiments) of drumming, consisting of a two-beat figure, the first beat of which is played as a triplet and preceded by two grace notes. [1940s: imitative.]

rat·a·plan /'rätə,plan/ ▶ **n.** [in sing.] a drumming or beating sound. [19th C.: from Fr., of imitative origin.]

rat-a-tat /'rat ə ,tat/ ▶ **n.** a rapping sound. [17th C.: imitative.]

ra·ta·touille /,ratə'tōō-ē; ,rä,tä-/ ▶ **n.** a vegetable dish consisting of onions, zucchini, tomatoes, eggplant, and peppers, fried and stewed in oil and sometimes served cold. [a Fr. dial. word.]

rat-bite fe·ver ▶ **n.** Med. a disease contracted from the bite of a rat that causes inflammation of the skin and fever or vomiting. It can be caused by either the bacterium *Spirillum minus* or the fungus *Streptobacillus moniliformis.*

ratch·et /'racнit/ ▶ **n.** a device consisting of a bar or wheel with a set of angled teeth in which a pawl, cog, or tooth engages, allowing motion in one direction only. ■ a bar or wheel that has such a set of teeth. ▶ **v.** (**ratch·et·ed, ratch·et·ing**) [trans.] operate by means of a ratchet. ■ (**ratchet something up/down**) fig. cause something to rise (or fall) as a step in what is perceived as a steady and irreversible process: *the Bank of Japan ratcheted up interest rates again.* [17th C.: from Fr. *rochet*, 'blunt lance head,' akin to Ital. *rocchetto* 'rocket' (see ROCKET).]

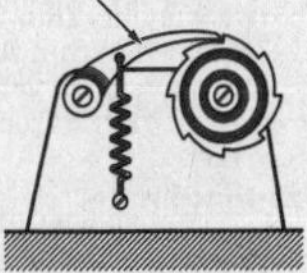

ratchet

rate[1] /rāt/ ▶ **n. 1** a measure, quantity, or frequency, typically one measured against some other quantity or measure: *the crime rate.* ■ the speed with which something moves, happens, or changes: *your heart rate.* **2** a fixed price paid or charged for something, esp. goods or services: *the basic rate of pay.* ■ the amount of a charge or payment expressed as a percentage of some other amount, or as a basis of calculation: *interest rates.* ■ (usu. **rates**) (in the UK) a tax on land and buildings paid to the local authority by a business, and formerly also by occupants of private property. ▶ **v. 1** [trans.] assign a standard or value to (something) according to a particular scale: *we rated the cameras.* ■ [with obj. and adverbial] assign a standard, optimal, or limiting rating to (a piece of equipment): *its fuel economy is* **rated** *at 25 miles a gallon.* **2** consider to be of a certain quality, standard, or rank: *he rates the stock a "buy."* ■ [no obj., with adverbial] be regarded in a specified way: *Jeff still rates as one of the nicest people I have ever met.* ■ [trans.] be worthy of; merit: *the ambassador rated a bulletproof car and a police escort.*

– PHRASES **at any rate** whatever happens or may have happened: *for the moment, at any rate, he was safe.* [ME ('estimated value'): from OFr., ult. from L. *(pro) rata (parte)* 'according to the proportional share,' from *ratus* 'reckoned.']

rate[2] ▶ **v.** [trans.] archaic scold (someone) angrily. [ME: origin unknown.]

ra·tel /'rätl; 'rātl/ ▶ **n.** a badgerlike mammal (*Mellivora capensis*) of the weasel family, with a white or gray back and black underparts, native to Africa and Asia. Also called **HONEY BADGER.** [18th C.: from Afrik.]

rate of ex·change ▶ **n.** another term for **EXCHANGE RATE.**

rate·pay·er /'rāt,pāər/ ▶ **n.** a customer of a public utility.

rat·fish /'rat,fisH/ ▶ **n.** (pl. same or **-fish·es**) a blunt-nosed chimaera (genera *Chimaera* and *Hydrolagus*, family Chimaeridae) with rodentlike front teeth and a long thin tail, found chiefly in cooler waters.

Rat·haus /'rät,hous/ ▶ **n.** (pl. **-häu·ser** /-,hoizər/) a town hall in a German-speaking country. [Ger., from *Rat* 'council' + *Haus* 'house.']

rathe /rāTH; raTH/ ▶ **adj.** archaic or literary (of a person or their actions) prompt and eager. ■ (of flowers or fruit) blooming or ripening early in the year. [OE *hræth, hræd*, from Gmc.; perh. akin to **RASH[1]**.]

rath·er /'raTHər; 'räTHər; 'rəTHər/ ▶ **adv. 1** (**would rather**) used to indicate one's preference in a particular matter: *would you like some wine, or would you rather stick to sherry?* | *she'd* **rather** *die* **than** *cause a scene* | [with clause] *I'd rather you not tell him.* **2** [as submodifier] to a certain or significant extent or degree: *she's been behaving rather strangely.* ■ used before verbs as a way of making the expression of a feeling or opinion less assertive: *I rather think he wants me to marry him* | *we were rather hoping you might do that for us.* **3** on the contrary (used to suggest that the opposite of what has just been implied or stated is the case): [sentence adverb] *There is no shortage of basic skills in the workplace. Rather, the problem is poor management.* ■ more precisely (used to modify or clarify something previously stated): *I walked,* **or rather** *limped, the two miles home.* ■ instead of; as opposed to: *she seemed indifferent* **rather than** *angry.* ▶ **exclam.** esp. Brit., dated used to express emphatic affirmation, agreement, or acceptance: *"You are glad to be home, aren't you?" "Rather!"*

– PHRASES **had rather** would rather: *I had rather not see him.* [OE *hrathor* 'earlier' compar. of *hræthe* 'without delay,' from *hræth* (see **RATHE**).]

rat·hole /'rat,hōl/ ▶ **n. 1** informal a cramped or squalid room or building. **2** informal used to refer to the waste of money or resources.

raths·kel·ler /'rät,skelər; 'rat-; 'raTH-/ ▶ **n.** a beer hall or restaurant in a basement. [20th C.: from obs. Ger., from *Rathaus* 'town hall' + *Keller* 'cellar,' denoting the place where beer and wine were sold.]

rat·i·fy /'ratə,fī/ ▶ **v.** (**-fies, -fied**) [trans.] sign or give formal consent to (a treaty, contract, or agreement), making it officially valid. — **rat·i·fi·a·ble** /'ratə,fīəbəl/ **adj. rat·i·fi·ca·tion** /,ratəfə'kāsHən/ **n. rat·i·fi·er n.** [ME: from OFr. *ratifier*, from med. L. *ratificare*, from L. *ratus* (see **RATE[1]**).]

rat·ing[1] /'rātiNG/ ▶ **n.** a classification or ranking of someone or something based on a comparative assessment of their quality, standard, or performance: *the hotel regained its five-star rating.* ■ (**ratings**) the estimated audience size of a particular television or radio program. ■ the value of a property or condition that is claimed to be standard, optimal, or limiting for a substance, material, or item of equipment: *fuel with a low octane rating.* ■ any of the classes into which racing yachts are assigned according to dimensions.

rat·ing[2] ▶ **n.** dated an angry reprimand.

ra·tio /'rāsHō; 'rāsHē,ō/ ▶ **n.** (pl. **-tios**) the quantitative relation between two amounts showing the number of times one value contains or is contained within the other: *the ratio of men's jobs to women's is 8 to 1.* ■ the relative value of silver and gold in a bimetallic system of currency. [17th C.: from L., lit. 'reckoning,' from *rat-* 'reckoned,' from the v. *reri*.]

ra·ti·oc·i·nate /,ratē'ōsə,nāt; ,rasHē-/ ▶ **v.** [intrans.] formal form judgments by a process of logic; reason. — **ra·ti·oc·i·na·tion** /-,ōsə'nāsHən/ **n. ra·ti·oc·i·na·tive** /-'ōsə,nātiv; 'äs-/ **adj. ra·ti·oc·i·na·tor** /-'ōsə,nātər; -'äs-/ **n.** [17th C.: from L. *ratiocinat-* 'calculated,' from the v. *ratiocinari*, from *ratio* (see **RATIO**).]

ra·tion /'rasHən; 'rā-/ ▶ **n.** a fixed amount of a commodity officially allowed to each person during a time of shortage, as in wartime: *the bread ration.* ■ (usu. **rations**) an amount of food supplied on a regular basis, esp. to members of the armed forces during a war. ■ (**rations**) food; provisions. ■ fig. a fixed amount of a particular thing: *their daily ration of fresh air.* ▶ **v.** [trans.] (usu. **be rationed**) allow each person to have only a fixed amount of (a particular commodity): *shoes were rationed from 1943.* ■ (**ration someone to**) allow someone to have only (a fixed amount of a certain commodity): *they rationed themselves to one glass of wine each.* [18th C.: from Fr., from L. *ratio(n-)* 'reckoning.']

ra·tion·al /'rasHənl; 'rasHnəl/ ▶ **adj. 1** based on or in accordance with reason or logic: *a rational explanation.* ■ (of a person) able to think clearly, sensibly, and logically. ■ endowed with the capacity to reason: *man is a rational being.* **2** Math. (of a number, quantity, or expression) expressible, or containing quantities that are expressible, as a ratio of whole numbers. When expressed as a decimal, a rational number has a finite or recurring expansion. ▶ **n.** Math. a rational number. — **ra·tion·al·i·ty** /,rasHə'nalətē/ **n. ra·tion·al·ly** /'rasHənl-ē; 'rasHnəlē/ **adv.** [ME ('able to reason'): from L. *rationalis*, from *ratio(n-)* (see **RATIO**).]

ra·tion·ale /,rasHə'nal/ ▶ **n.** a set of reasons or a logical basis for a course of action or a particular belief: *he explained the rationale behind the change.* [17th C.: mod. L., neut. of L. *rationalis* 'endowed with reason' (see **RATIONAL**).]

ra·tion·al·ism /'rasHənl,izəm; 'rasHnə,lizəm/ ▶ **n.** a belief or theory that opinions and actions should be based on reason and knowledge rather than on religious belief or emotional response. ■ Philos. the theory that reason rather than experience is the foundation of certainty in knowledge. — **ra·tion·al·ist n. ra·tion·al·is·tic** /,rasHənl'istik; ,rasHnə'listik/ **adj. ra·tion·al·is·ti·cal·ly** /,rasHənl'istik(ə)lē; ,rasHnə'listik(ə)lē/ **adv.**

ra·tion·al·ize /'rasHənl,īz; 'rasHnə,līz/ ▶ **v.** [trans.] **1** attempt to explain or justify (one's own or another's behavior or attitude) with logical, plausible reasons, even if these are not true or appropriate: *she couldn't rationalize her urge to return to the cottage.* **2** Brit. make (a company, process, or industry) more efficient by reorganizing it in such a way as to dispense with unnecessary personnel or equipment. **3** Math. convert (a function or expression) to a rational form. — **ra·tion·al·i·za·tion** /,rasHənl-ə'zāsHən; ,rasHnələ-/ **n. ra·tion·al·iz·er n.**

Rat Is·lands an island group in southwestern Alaska, part of the Aleutian Islands.

rat·ite /'ra,tīt/ Ornithol. ▶ **adj.** (of a bird) having a flat breastbone without a keel, and so unable to fly. Contrasted with **CARINATE.** ▶ **n.** any of the mostly large, flightless birds with such a breastbone, e.g., the ostrich, emu, cassowary, and kiwi. [19th C.: from L. *ratis* 'raft.']

rat kan·ga·roo ▶ **n.** a small ratlike Australian marsupial (family Potoroidae) with long hind limbs used for hopping.

rat·lines /'ratlənz/ ▶ **plural n.** a series of small ropes fastened across a sailing ship's shrouds like the rungs of a ladder, used for climbing the rigging. [ME: origin unknown.]

ratlines

ra·toon /rə'to͞on; ra-/ ▶ **n.** a new shoot or sprout springing from the base of a crop plant, esp. sugar cane, after cropping. ▶ **v.** [intrans.] (of sugar cane) produce ratoons. [17th C. (n.): from Sp. *retoño* 'a sprout.']

rat race ▶ **n.** informal a way of life in which people are caught up in a fiercely competitive struggle for wealth or power.

rats·bane /'rats,bān/ ▶ **n.** literary rat poison.

rat snake ▶ **n.** a harmless constricting snake (family Colubridae) that feeds on rats and other small mammals.

rat·tan /ra'tan; rə-/ ▶ **n. 1** the thin pliable stems of a palm, used to make furniture. ■ a length of such a stem used as a walking stick. **2** the tropical Old World climbing palm (genus *Calamus*) that yields this product, with long, spiny, jointed stems. [17th C.: from Malay *rotan*, prob. from *raut* 'pare, trim.']

rat·ter /'ratər/ ▶ **n.** a dog or other animal that is used for hunting rats.

rat·tle /'ratl/ ▶ **v. 1** [intrans.] make a rapid succession of short, sharp knocking sounds, typically as a result of being shaken and striking repeatedly against a hard surface or object: *a sound of bottles rattling.* ■ [trans.] cause (something) to make such sounds. ■ [with adverbial of direction] (of a vehicle or its driver or passengers) move or travel somewhere while making such sounds: *trains rattled past.* ■ (**rattle around in**) fig. be in or occupy (an unnecessarily or undesirably spacious room or building). **2** [trans.] (often **be rattled**) informal cause (someone) to feel nervous, worried, or irritated: *she turned quickly, rattled by his presence.* ▶ **n. 1** a rapid succession of short, sharp, hard sounds: *the rattle of teacups on the tray.* ■ a gurgling sound in the throat of a dying person. **2** a thing used to make a rapid succession of short, sharp sounds, in particular: ■ a baby's toy consisting of a container filled with small pellets that makes a noise when shaken. ■ the set of horny rings at the end of a rattlesnake's tail, shaken with a dry buzzing sound as a warning.

– PHRASAL VERBS **rattle something off** say, perform, or produce something quickly and effortlessly. [ME (v.): akin to MDu. and Low Ger. *ratelen*, of imitative origin.]

rat·tler /'ratl-ər; 'ratlər/ ▶ **n.** informal a rattlesnake.

rat·tle·snake /'ratl,snāk/ ▶ **n.** a heavy-bodied American pit viper (genera *Crotalus* and *Sistrurus*) with a series of horny rings on the tail that, when vibrated, produce a characteristic rattling sound as a warning.

rat·tle·trap /'ratl,trap/ ▶ **n.** informal an old or rickety vehicle.

rat·tling /'ratl-iNG; 'ratliNG/ ▶ **adj. 1** making a series of short, sharp knocking sounds: *a rattling old bus.* **2** informal, dated denoting something very good of its kind (used for emphasis): *a rattling good story.*

rat·trap /'rat,trap/ ▶ **n.** informal **1** a shabby, squalid, or ramshackle building or establishment. **2** an unpleasant situation with no hope for improvement.

rat·ty /'ratē/ ▶ **adj.** (**-ti·er, -ti·est**) resembling or characteristic of a rat: *his ratty eyes glittered.* ■ (of a place) infested with rats. ■ informal shabby, untidy or in bad condition: *a ratty old armchair.* — **rat·ti·ly** /'ratl-ē/ **adv.**

rat·ti·ness n.

rau·cous /ˈrôkəs/ ▶ **adj.** making or constituting a disturbingly harsh and loud noise: *raucous youths.* — **rau·cous·ly** adv. **rau·cous·ness** n. [18th C.: from L. *raucus* 'hoarse' + -OUS.]

raunch /rônCH; ränCH/ ▶ **n.** informal energetic earthiness; vulgarity: *the raunch of his first album.* [1960s: back-form. from RAUNCHY.]

raun·chy /ˈrônCHē; ˈrän-/ ▶ **adj.** (**-chi·er, -chi·est**) informal **1** energetically earthy and sexually explicit. **2** (esp. of a person or place) slovenly; grubby. — **raunch·i·ly** /-CHəlē/ **adv.** **raunch·i·ness** n. [1930s: origin unknown.]

Rau·schen·berg /ˈrousHən,bərg/, Robert (1925–), US painter. Some of his paintings incorporate three-dimensional objects.

rau·wol·fi·a /rouˈwŏŏlfēə; rôˈwŏŏl-/ (also **rau·vol·fi·a**) ▶ **n.** a tropical shrub or tree (genus *Rauwolfia*) of the dogbane family, some kinds of which are cultivated for their medicinal properties. Many species include the Indian snakeroot (*R. serpentina*), from which the drug reserpine is obtained. [mod. L., after Leonhard *Rauwolf* (died 1596), Ger. botanist.]

rav·age /ˈravij/ ▶ **v.** [trans.] cause severe and extensive damage to: *fears that a war could ravage their country.* ▶ **n.** (**ravages**) the severely damaging or destructive effects of something: *his face had withstood the ravages of time.* ■ acts of destruction: *the ravages committed by man.* — **rav·ag·er** n. [17th C.: from Fr. *ravager*, from *ravage* 'destruction', alt. of *ravine* 'rush of water.']

rave /rāv/ ▶ **v.** [intrans.] **1** talk wildly or incoherently, as if one were delirious or insane. ■ address someone in an angry, uncontrolled way: [with direct speech] *"Never mind!" Melissa raved.* **2** speak or write about someone or something with great enthusiasm or admiration. **3** informal attend or take part in a rave party. ▶ **n.** **1** informal an extremely enthusiastic recommendation or appraisal of someone or something. **2** informal a lively party or gathering involving dancing and drinking. ■ a party or event attended by large numbers of young people, involving drug use and dancing to fast, electronic music. ■ electronic dance music of the kind played at such events. [ME ('show signs of madness'): prob. from Old North. Fr. *raver*; akin to (Middle) Low Ger. *reven* 'be senseless.']

Rav·el /rəˈvel/, Maurice Joseph (1875–1937), French composer. His works include *Daphnis and Chloë* (1912) and *Boléro* (1928).

rav·el /ˈravəl/ ▶ **v.** (**rav·eled, rav·el·ing** ; Brit. **rav·el·led, rav·el·ling**) [trans.] **1** (**ravel something out**) untangle or unravel something: *he raveled out his herring net.* **2** confuse or complicate (a question or situation). ▶ **n.** rare a tangle, cluster, or knot. [ME ('entangle'): prob. from Du. *ravelen* 'fray out, tangle.']

rav·el·ing /ˈrav(ə)liNG/ ▶ **n.** a thread from a woven or knitted fabric that has frayed or started to unravel.

rav·en[1] /ˈrāvən/ ▶ **n.** a large heavily built crow, esp. the all-black **common raven** (*Corvus corax*), feeding chiefly on carrion. ▶ **adj.** (esp. of hair) of a glossy black color. [OE *hræfn*, from Gmc.; akin to Ger. *Rabe*.]

rav·en[2] /ˈravən/ ▶ **v.** [intrans.] archaic (of a ferocious wild animal) hunt for prey. ■ [trans.] devour voraciously. [15th C. ('take as spoil'): from OFr. *raviner* 'to ravage,' based on L. *rapina* 'pillage.']

rav·en·ing /ˈravəniNG/ ▶ **adj.** (of a ferocious wild animal) extremely hungry and hunting for prey.

Ra·ven·na /rəˈvenə/ a city in northeast central Italy; pop. 137,000.

rav·en·ous /ˈravənəs/ ▶ **adj.** extremely hungry. ■ (of hunger or need) very great; voracious. — **rav·en·ous·ly** adv. **rav·en·ous·ness** n. [ME: from OFr. *ravineus*, from *raviner* (see RAVEN[2]).]

rav·er /ˈrāvər/ ▶ **n.** **1** informal a person who goes to raves. **2** a person who talks wildly or incoherently.

rave-up ▶ **n.** informal a fast, loud, or danceable piece of pop music.

Ra·vi /ˈrävē/ a river in the northern Indian subcontinent, one of the headwaters of the Indus River.

rav·in /ˈravən/ ▶ **n.** archaic or literary violent seizure of prey or property; plunder. [ME: from OFr. *ravine*, from L. *rapina* 'pillage' (see RAPINE).]

ra·vine /rəˈvēn/ ▶ **n.** a deep, narrow gorge with steep sides. — **ra·vined** adj. [18th C.: from Fr., 'violent rush (of water),' ult. from L. *rapina* (see RAPINE).]

rav·ing /ˈrāviNG/ ▶ **n.** (usu. **ravings**) wild, irrational, or incoherent talk: *the ravings of a madwoman.* ▶ **adj.** informal used to emphasize the bad or extreme quality of someone or something: *a raving beauty.*

ra·vi·o·li /,ravēˈōlē/ ▶ **n.** small pasta envelopes containing ground meat, cheese, or vegetables. [Ital.]

rav·ish /ˈravisH/ ▶ **v.** [trans.] **1** archaic seize and carry off (someone) by force. ■ dated (of a man) force (a woman or girl) to have sexual intercourse against her will. **2** (often **be ravished**) literary fill (someone) with intense delight; enrapture. — **rav·ish·er** n. **rav·ish·ment** n. [ME: from OFr. *raviss-*, lengthened stem of *ravir*, from an alt. of L. *rapere* 'seize.']

rav·ish·ing /ˈravisHiNG/ ▶ **adj.** delightful; entrancing: *she looked ravishing.* — **rav·ish·ing·ly** adv.

raw /rô/ ▶ **adj.** (**raw·er, raw·est**) **1** (of food) uncooked: *raw eggs.* ■ (of a material or substance) in its natural state; not yet processed or purified: *raw silk | raw sewage.* ■ (of information) not analyzed, evaluated, or processed for use. ■ (of the edge of a piece of cloth) not having a hem or selvage. ■ (of a person) new to an activity or job and therefore lacking experience or skill. **2** (of a part of the body) red and painful, esp. as the result of skin abrasion. **3** (of the weather) bleak, cold, and damp: *a raw night.* **4** (of an emotion or quality) strong and undisguised: *he exuded an air of raw, vibrant masculinity.* ■ frank and realistic in the depiction of unpleasant facts or situations: *a raw, uncompromising portrait.* ■ informal (of language) coarse or crude, typically in relation to sexual matters.
– PHRASES **in the raw** **1** in its true state; not made to seem better or more palatable than it actually is: *nature in the raw.* **2** informal (of a person) naked. — **raw·ly** adv. **raw·ness** n. [OE *hrēaw*, 'raw,' from Indo-Eur.; akin to Ger. *roh*, Gk. *kreas* 'raw flesh.']

raw bar ▶ **n.** a bar or counter that sells raw oysters and other seafood.

raw·boned /ˈrôˈbōnd/ ▶ **adj.** having a bony or gaunt physique.

raw·hide /ˈrô,hīd/ ▶ **n.** stiff untanned leather. ■ a whip or rope made of such leather.

Rawl·ings /ˈrôliNGz/, Marjorie Kinnan (1896–53), US writer. She wrote *The Yearling* (1938) for young adults.

raw ma·te·ri·al ▶ **n.** the basic material from which a product is made.

Ray[1] /rā/, Man (1890–1976), US painter; born *Emmanuel Rudnitsky*. He was a leading figure in the New York and European Dada movements.

Ray[2] /rī; rā/, Satyajit (1921–92), Indian director. He brought Indian movies to Western audiences.

ray[1] /rā/ ▶ **n.** **1** each of the lines in which light (and heat) may seem to stream from the sun or any luminous body, or pass through a small opening: *a ray of sunlight.* ■ the straight line in which light or other electromagnetic radiation travels to a given point. ■ [with adj.] (**rays**) a specified form of nonluminous radiation. ■ Math. any of a set of straight lines passing through one point. ■ (**rays**) informal, sunlight considered in the context of sunbathing. ■ fig. an initial or slight indication of a positive or welcome quality in a time of difficulty or trouble. **2** a thing that is arranged radially, in particular: ■ Bot. (in a composite flowerhead of the daisy family) an array of ray florets arranged radially around the central disc, forming the white part of the flowerhead of a daisy. ■ (also **fin ray**) Zool. each of the long, slender bony protuberances supporting the fins of most bony fishes. ■ Zool. each radial arm of a starfish. ▶ **v.** [no obj., with adverbial of direction] spread from or as if from a central point: *delicate lines rayed out.* ■ [with obj. and adverbial of direction] literary radiate (light): *the sun rays forth its natural light.* — **ray·less** adj. (esp. Bot.). [ME: from OFr. *rai*, based on L. *radius* 'spoke, ray.']

ray[2] ▶ **n.** a broad, flat marine or freshwater fish (Rajidae and other families) with a cartilaginous skeleton, winglike pectoral fins, and a long slender tail. Many rays have venomous spines or electric organs. [ME: from OFr. *raie*, from L. *raia*.]

Ray·burn /ˈrā,bərn/, Samuel Taliaferro (1882–1961), US politician. A Democrat, he was Speaker of the House 1940–46, 1949–53, 1955–61.

rayed /rād/ ▶ **adj.** [in comb.] esp. Biol. having rays of a specified number or kind: *white-rayed daisies.*

ray-finned fish ▶ **n.** a fish of a large group (subclass Actinopterygii) having thin fins strengthened by slender rays, including all bony fishes apart from the coelacanth and lungfishes. Compare with LOBE-FINNED FISH, TELEOST.

ray flo·ret ▶ **n.** Bot. (in a composite flowerhead of the daisy family) any of a number of strap-shaped and typically sterile florets that form the ray. In plants such as dandelions, the flowerhead is composed entirely of ray florets. Compare with DISK FLORET.

ray gun ▶ **n.** (in science fiction) a gun causing injury or damage by the emission of rays.

Ray·leigh /ˈrālē/, John William Strutt, 3rd Baron (1842–1919), English physicist. Nobel Prize for Physics (1904).

Ray·leigh scat·ter·ing ▶ **n.** Physics the scattering of light by particles in a medium, without change in wavelength. It accounts, for example, for the blue color of the sky, since blue light is scattered slightly more efficiently than red.

Ray·leigh wave ▶ **n.** Physics an undulating wave that travels over the surface of a solid, esp. of the ground in an earthquake, with a speed independent of wavelength, the motion of the particles being in ellipses.

Ray·naud's dis·ease /rāˈnōz/ ▶ **n.** a disease characterized by spasm of the arteries in the extremities, esp. the fingers (**Raynaud's phenomenon**). It is typically brought on by constant cold or vibration, and leads to pallor, pain, numbness, and in severe cases, gangrene. [19th C.: Maurice *Raynaud* (1834–81), French physician.]

ray·on /ˈrā,än/ ▶ **n.** a textile fiber made from regenerated cellulose (viscose). ■ fabric or cloth made from this fiber. [1920s: arbitrary formation.]

raze /rāz/ ▶ **v.** [trans.] (usu. **be razed**) completely destroy (a building, town, or other site): *villages were razed to the ground.* [ME ('incise'): from OFr. *raser* 'shave closely,' from L. *ras-* 'scraped,' from the v. *radere*.]

ra·zor /ˈrāzər/ ▶ **n.** an instrument with a sharp blade or combination of blades, used to remove unwanted hair from the face or body. ▶ **v.** [trans.] cut with a razor. [ME: from OFr. *rasor*, from *raser* (see RAZE).]

ra·zor·back /ˈrāzər,bak/ ▶ **n.** **1** (also **ra·zor·back hog**) a pig of a half-wild breed common in the southern US, with the back formed into a high, narrow ridge. **2** (also **ra·zor·back ridge**) a steep-sided, narrow ridge of land.

ra·zor·bill /ˈrāzər,bil/ ▶ **n.** a black-and-white auk (*Alca torda*) with a deep bill that is said to resemble a straight razor, found in the North Atlantic and Baltic Sea.

ra·zor clam ▶ **n.** a burrowing bivalve mollusk (*Ensis* and other genera, family Solenidae) with a long, slender shell that resembles the handle of a straight razor.

razz /raz/ informal ▶ **v.** [trans.] tease (someone) playfully. ▶ **n.** another term for RASPBERRY (sense 4). [20th C.: from *razzberry*, alt. of RASPBERRY.]

raz·zi·a /ˈrazēə/ ▶ **n.** hist. a hostile raid for purposes of conquest, plunder, and capture of slaves, esp. one carried out by Moors in North Africa. [19th C.: via Fr. from Algerian Arab. *ġāziya* 'raid.']

raz·zle-daz·zle /ˌrazəl ˈdazəl/ ▶ **n.** informal noisy, showy, and exciting activity and display designed to attract and impress. ■ Football unusual and showy offensive maneuvers. [19th C.: reduplication of DAZZLE.]

razz·ma·tazz /ˈrazməˌtaz/ ▶ **n.** another term for RAZZLE-DAZZLE. [19th C.: prob. alt. of RAZZLE-DAZZLE.]

RBC ▶ **abbr.** red blood cell.

RBI Baseball ▶ **abbr.** run batted in (a run credited to the batter's hitting statistics for enabling a runner to score during his at bat).

RC ▶ **abbr.** ■ Electron. radio-controlled. ■ Red Cross. ■ Electron. resistance/capacitance (or resistor/capacitor). ■ Roman Catholic.

RCAF ▶ **abbr.** Royal Canadian Air Force.

RCCh ▶ **abbr.** Roman Catholic Church.

RCMP ▶ **abbr.** Royal Canadian Mounted Police.

rcpt. ▶ **abbr.** receipt.

rct. (also **Rct.**) ▶ **abbr.** ■ receipt. ■ recruit.

Rd ▶ **abbr.** Road (used in street names).

rd. ▶ **abbr.** rod; rods.

RDA ▶ **abbr.** recommended daily (or dietary) allowance, the quantity of a particular nutrient which should be consumed daily in order to maintain good health.

RDBMS Comput. ▶ **abbr.** relational database management system.

Re[1] /rā/ var. of RA[1].

Re[2] ▶ **symb.** the chemical element rhenium.

Re. (also **re.**) ▶ **abbr.** rupee.

re[1] /rē; rā/ ▶ **prep.** in the matter of (used typically as the first word in the heading of an official document or to introduce a reference in an official letter): *re: invoice 87.* ■ about; concerning: *I saw the deputy re the incident.* [L., ablative of *res* 'thing.']

re[2] /rā/ ▶ **n.** Music (in solmization) the second note of a major scale. ■ the note D in the fixed-do system. [ME *re*, from first syllable of *resonare*, taken from a L. hymn.]

re- ▶ **prefix 1** once more; afresh; anew: *reaccustom* | *reactivate.* ■ with return to a previous state: *restore* | *revert.* **2** (also **red-**) in return; mutually: *react* | *resemble.* ■ in opposition: *repel* | *resistance.* **3** behind or after: *relic* | *remain.* ■ in a withdrawn state: *recluse* | *reticent.* ■ back and away; down: *recede* | *relegation.* **4** with frequentative or intensive force: *redouble* | *resound.* **5** with negative force: *rebuff* | *recant.* [from L. *re-*, *red-* 'again, back.']

're informal ▶ **abbr.** are (usually after the pronouns you, we, and they): *we're a bit worried.*

reach /rēCH/ ▶ **v. 1** [no obj., with adverbial of direction] stretch out an arm in a specified direction in order to touch or grasp something: *he reached over and turned off his bedside light.* ■ (**reach for**) make a movement with one's hand or arm in an attempt to touch or grasp (something): *Carl reached for the phone.* ■ [trans.] (**reach something out**) stretch out one's hand or arm: *he reached out a hand.* ■ [with two objs.] hand (something) to (someone): *reach me those glasses.* ■ [intrans.] be able to touch something with an outstretched arm or leg: *I had to stand on tiptoe and even then I could hardly reach.* ■ (**reach out**) extend help, understanding, or influence: *he felt such an urge to reach out to his fellow sufferer.* **2** [trans.] arrive at; get as far as: *they reached the door.* ■ attain or extend to (a specified point, level, or condition): *unemployment reached a peak* | [intrans.] *it will* **reach to** *about 6 m in height.* ■ succeed in achieving: *they reached agreement.* ■ make contact or communicate with (someone) by telephone or other means. ■ (of a broadcast or other communication) be received by. **3** [intrans.] Sailing sail with the wind blowing from the side, or from slightly behind the side, of the ship. ▶ **n. 1** an act of reaching out with one's arm: *she made a reach for him.* ■ [in sing.] the distance to which someone can stretch out their hand (used esp. of a boxer). ■ the extent or range of application, effect, or influence: *the diameter and the reach of the spark plug.* **2** (often **reaches**) a continuous extent of land or water, esp. a stretch of river between two bends, or the part of a canal between locks. **3** Sailing a distance traversed in reaching. — **reach·a·ble adj.** [OE *rǣcan*, from West Gmc.; akin to Ger. *reichen*.]

reach-me-down Brit., informal, dated ▶ **adj.** [attrib.] (of a garment) ready-made or secondhand. ▶ **n.** a secondhand or ready-made garment. ■ (**reach-me-downs**) trousers.

re·act /rēˈakt/ ▶ **v.** [intrans.] respond or behave in a particular way in response to something: *Iraq* **reacted** *angrily* **to** *Jordan's shift in policy* | *the market reacted by falling a further 3.1%.* ■ (**react against**) respond with hostility, opposition, or a contrary course of action to: *they reacted against the elite art music of their time.* ■ (of a person) suffer from adverse physiological effects after ingesting, breathing, or touching a substance: *many babies react to soy-based formulas.* ■ Chem. Physics interact and undergo a chemical or physical change: *the sulfur in the coal* **reacts with** *the limestone during combustion.* ■ [trans.] Chem. cause (a substance) to undergo such a change by interacting with another substance. ■ Stock Market (of stock prices) fall after rising. [17th C.: from RE- + ACT, suggested by med. L. *react-* 'done again,' from the v. *reagere*.]

re·ac·tance /rēˈaktəns/ ▶ **n.** Physics the nonresistive component of impedance in an AC circuit, arising from the effect of inductance or capacitance or both and causing the current to be out of phase with the electromotive force causing it.

re·ac·tant /rēˈaktənt/ ▶ **n.** Chem. a substance that takes part in and undergoes change during a reaction.

re·ac·tion /rēˈakSHən/ ▶ **n.** an action performed or a feeling experienced in response to a situation or event: *Carrie's immediate reaction was one of relief.* ■ (**reactions**) a person's ability to respond physically and mentally to external stimuli. ■ an adverse physiological response to a substance that has been breathed in, ingested, or touched: *allergic reactions.* ■ a chemical process in which two or more substances act mutually on each other and are changed into different substances, or one substance changes into two or more other substances. ■ Physics an analogous transformation of atomic nuclei or other particles. ■ a mode of thinking or behaving that is deliberately different from previous modes of thought and behavior: *the work of these painters was a* **reaction against** *fauvism.* ■ opposition to political or social progress or reform. ■ Physics repulsion or resistance exerted in opposition to the impact or pressure of another body; a force equal and opposite to the force giving rise to it. — **re·ac·tion·ist** /-nist/ **n. & adj.**

re·ac·tion·ar·y /rēˈakSHəˌnerē/ ▶ **adj.** (of a person or a set of views) opposing political or social liberalization or reform. ▶ **n.** (pl. **-ar·ies**) a person who holds such views.

re·ac·tion for·ma·tion ▶ **n.** Psychoanal. the tendency of a repressed wish or feeling to be expressed at a conscious level in a contrasting form.

re·ac·tive /rēˈaktiv/ ▶ **adj.** showing a response to a stimulus: *pupils are reactive to light.* ■ acting in response to a situation rather than creating or controlling it: *a proactive rather than a reactive approach.* ■ having a tendency to react chemically: *nitrogen dioxide is a highly reactive gas.* ■ Physiol. showing an immune response to a specific antigen. ■ (of a disease or illness) caused by a reaction to something: *reactive arthritis* | *reactive depression.* ■ Physics of or relating to reactance: *a reactive load.* — **re·ac·tiv·i·ty** /ˌrēˌakˈtivətē/ **n.**

re·ac·tor /rēˈaktər/ ▶ **n. 1** (also **nu·cle·ar re·ac·tor**) an apparatus or structure in which fissile material can be made to undergo a controlled, self-sustaining nuclear reaction with the consequent release of energy. ■ a container or apparatus in which substances are made to react chemically, esp. one in an industrial plant. **2** Med. a person who shows an immune response to a specific antigen or an adverse reaction to a drug or other substance. **3** Physics a coil or other component that provides reactance in a circuit.

read /rēd/ ▶ **v.** (past **read** /red/) [trans.] **1** look at and comprehend the meaning of (written or printed matter) by mentally interpreting the characters or symbols of which it is composed. ■ speak (the written or printed matter that one is reading) aloud, typically to another person. ■ [intrans.] have the ability to look at and comprehend the meaning of written or printed matter: *only three of the girls could read.* ■ habitually read (a particular newspaper or journal). ■ discover (information) by reading it in a written or printed source: *he was arrested yesterday—I read it in the paper* | [intrans.] *I read about the course in a magazine.* ■ [as adj., with submodifier] (**read**) (of a person) knowledgeable and informed as a result of extensive reading: *Ada was* **well read** *in French literature.* ■ discern (a fact, emotion, or quality) in someone's eyes or expression: *he read fear on her face.* ■ understand or interpret the nature or significance of: *he didn't dare look away, in case this was read as a sign of weakness.* ■ [no obj., with adverbial] (of a piece of writing) convey a specified impression to the reader: *the brief note read like a cry for help.* ■ [no obj., with complement] (of a passage, text, or sign) contain or consist of specified words; have a certain wording: *the placard read "We want justice."* ■ used to indicate that a particular word in a text or passage is incorrect and that another should be substituted for it: *for madam read madman.* ■ proofread (written or typeset material). ■ [intrans.] (**read for**) (of an actor) audition for (a part in a play or film). ■ (of a device) obtain data from (light or other input). **2** inspect and record the figure indicated on (a measuring instrument): *I've come to read the gas meter.* ■ [no obj., with complement] (of such an instrument) indicate a specified measurement or figure: *the thermometer read 0° C.* **3** esp. Brit. study (an academic subject) at a university: *I'm reading English at Cambridge.* **4** (of a computer) copy or transfer (data). ■ [with obj. and adverbial] enter or extract (data) in an electronic storage device: *the commonest way of reading a file into the system.* **5** hear and understand the words of (someone speaking on a radio transmitter): *"Do you read me? Over."* ■ interpret the words formed by (a speaking person's lips) by watching rather than listening. ▶ **n.** [usu. in sing.] a person's interpretation of something: *their read on the national situation may be correct.* ■ [with adj.] informal a book considered in terms of its readability: *the book is a thoroughly entertaining read.*

— PHRASES **read between the lines** look for or discover a meaning that is hidden or implied rather than explicitly stated. **read my lips** informal listen carefully (used to emphasize the importance of the speaker's words or the earnestness of their intent).

— PHRASAL VERBS **read something into** attribute a meaning or significance to (something) that it may not in fact possess: *was I reading too much into his behavior?* **read someone out of** formally expel someone from (an organization or body). [from the reading of the formal sentence of expulsion.] **read up on something** acquire information about a particular subject by studying it intensively or systematically: *she spent the time reading up on antenatal care.* [OE *rǣdan* from Gmc.; akin to Ger. *raten* 'advise, guess.']

read·a·ble /'rēdəbəl/ ▶ **adj.** (of a text, script, or code) able to be read or deciphered; legible. ■ easy or enjoyable to read: *a marvelously readable book.* — **read·a·bil·i·ty** /,rēdə'bilətē/ **n.** **read·a·bly** /-blē/ **adv.**

re·ad·dress /,rēə'dres/ ▶ **v.** [trans.] **1** change the address written or printed on (a letter or parcel). **2** look at or attend to (an issue or problem) once again.

read·er /'rēdər/ ▶ **n.** **1** a person who reads or who is fond of reading. ■ a person who reads a particular newspaper, magazine, or text: *Times readers.* ■ short for LAY READER. ■ a person entitled to use a particular library. ■ a person who reads and reports to a publisher or producer on the merits of manuscripts submitted for publication or production, or who provides critical comments on the text prior to publication. ■ a person who reads and grades examinations and papers for a professor. ■ short for *PROOFREADER* (see PROOFREAD). ■ a person who interprets the significance of tarot cards, horoscopes, lines in the palm of a hand, etc., so as to predict the future: *a tarot reader.* **2** a person who inspects and records the figure indicated on a measuring instrument: *a meter reader.* **3** a book containing extracts of a particular author's work or passages of text designed to give learners of a language practice in reading. **4** (usu. **Reader**) Brit. a university lecturer of the highest grade below professor. **5** a machine for producing on a screen a magnified, readable image of any desired part of a microfiche or microfilm. ■ Comput. a device or piece of software used for reading or obtaining data stored on tape, cards, or other media.

read·er·ly /'rēdərlē/ ▶ **adj.** of or relating to a reader: *he tries one's readerly patience to breaking point.*

read·er·ship /'rēdər,sHip/ ▶ **n.** **1** [treated as sing. or pl.] the readers of a newspaper, magazine, or book regarded collectively: *it has a readership of 100 million.* **2** (usu. **Readership**) Brit. the position of Reader at a university.

read·i·ly /'redl-ē/ ▶ **adv.** without hesitation or reluctance; willingly: *he readily admits his guilt.* ■ without delay or difficulty; easily: [as submodifier] *illegal fireworks are readily available.*

read-in /'rēd,in/ ▶ **n.** Comput. the input or entry of data to a computer or storage device.

read·i·ness /'redēnis/ ▶ **n.** **1** [in sing.] [with infin.] willingness to do something: *a readiness to accept his terms.* **2** the state of being fully prepared for something. **3** immediacy, quickness, or promptness: *readiness of speech.*

Read·ing /'rediNG/ **1** a town in southern England, on the Kennet River; pop. 123,000. **2** a city in southeastern Pennsylvania; pop. 81,207.

read·ing /'rēdiNG/ ▶ **n.** **1** the action or skill of reading written or printed matter silently or aloud: *suggestions for further reading* | [as adj.] *reading skills.* ■ written or printed matter that can be read: *his main reading was detective stories.* ■ [with adj.] used to convey the specified quality of such written or printed matter: *his file certainly makes interesting reading.* ■ [usu. with adj.] knowledge of literature: *a man of wide reading.* ■ the formal reading aloud of a legal document to an audience. ■ an occasion at which poetry or other pieces of literature are read aloud to an audience. ■ a piece of literature or passage of scripture read aloud to a group of people. **2** an interpretation: *feminist readings of Goethe.* ■ a form in which a given passage appears in a particular edition of a text. **3** a figure or amount shown by a meter or other measuring instrument: *radiation readings.* **4** a stage of debate in a parliament through which a bill must pass before it can become law.

re·ad·just /,rēə'jəst/ ▶ **v.** [trans.] set or adjust (something) again: *I readjusted the rear-view mirror.* ■ [intrans.] adjust or adapt to a changed environment or situation: [as adj.] (**readjusted**) *she wondered if she could ever become readjusted to this sort of life.* — **re·ad·just·ment** **n.**

read-on·ly mem·o·ry /rēd/ (abbr.: **ROM**) ▶ **n.** Comput. memory read at high speed but not capable of being changed by program instructions.

read·out /'rēd,out/ ▶ **n.** a visual record or display of the output from a computer or scientific instrument. ■ the process of transferring or displaying such data.

read-write /'rēd 'rīt/ ▶ **adj.** Comput. capable of reading existing data and accepting alterations or further input.

read·y /'redē/ ▶ **adj.** (**read·i·er, read·i·est**) **1** [predic.] in a suitable state for an activity, action, or situation; fully prepared: *are you ready, Carrie?* ■ (of a thing) made suitable and available for immediate use: *dinner's ready!* ■ (**ready with**) keen or quick to give: *ready with a wisecrack.* ■ (**ready for**) in need of or having a desire for: *ready for a drink.* ■ [with infin.] eager, inclined, or willing to do something: *she is ready to die.* ■ [with infin.] in such a condition as to be likely to do something: *he was ready to drop.* **2** easily available or obtained; within reach: *there was a ready supply of drink.* ■ [attrib.] immediate, quick, or prompt: *a ready smile.* ▶ **v.** (**read·ies, read·ied**) [trans.] prepare (someone or something) for an activity or purpose: *the spare transformer was readied for shipment* | [with obj. and infin.] *she had readied herself to speak first.* [ME: from OE *rǣde* (from Gmc. 'arrange, prepare'; akin to Du. *gereed*) + -Y[1].]

read·y-made ▶ **adj.** (esp. of products such as clothes and curtains) made to a standard size or specification rather than to order. ■ available straight away; not needing to be specially created or devised: *we have no ready-made answers.* ■ (of food) ready to be served without further preparation: *a ready-made Christmas cake.* ▶ **n.** (usu. **ready-mades**) a ready-made article. ■ a mass-produced article selected by an artist and displayed as a work of art.

read·y-mix ▶ **n.** ready-mixed concrete.

read·y mon·ey (also **read·y cash**) ▶ **n.** money in the form of cash that is immediately available.

read·y-to-wear ▶ **adj.** (of clothes) made for the general market and sold through stores rather than made to order for an individual customer.

re·af·firm /,rēə'fərm/ ▶ **v.** [reporting verb] state again as a fact; assert again strongly: *the prime minister reaffirmed his commitment.* ■ [trans.] confirm the validity or correctness of (something previously established): *the election reaffirmed his position as leader.* — **re·af·fir·ma·tion** /,rē,afər'māsHən/ **n.**

Rea·gan /'rāgən/, Ronald Wilson (1911–2004), 40th president of the US 1981–89. He was a movie actor before serving as governor of California 1967–74. A conservative Republican president, he signed an intermediate nuclear forces nonproliferation treaty in 1987. — **Rea·gan·ism** /-,nizəm/ **n.**

re·a·gent /rē'ājənt/ ▶ **n.** a substance or mixture for use in chemical analysis or other reactions.

re·a·gin /rē'ājən; -gən/ ▶ **n.** Immunol. the antibody that is involved in allergic reactions, causing the release of histamine when it combines with antigen in tissue. — **re·a·gin·ic** /,rēə'jinik; -'ginik/ **adj.** [20th C.: coined in Ger. from *reagieren* 'react.']

re·al[1] /'rē(ə)l/ ▶ **adj.** **1** actually existing as a thing or occurring in fact; not imagined or supposed: *Julius Caesar was a real person.* ■ used to emphasize the significance or seriousness of a situation or circumstance: *a real danger of civil war.* ■ Philos. relating to something as it is, not merely as it may be described or distinguished. **2** (of a substance or thing) not imitation or artificial; genuine: *real gold.* ■ true or actual: *his real name is James.* ■ [attrib.] (of a person or thing) rightly so called; proper: *a real man.* **3** [attrib.] informal complete; utter (used for emphasis): *the tour turned out to be a real disaster.* **4** [attrib.] adjusted for changes in the value of money; assessed by purchasing power: *real incomes had fallen.* **5** Math. (of a number or quantity) having no imaginary part. See IMAGINARY. **6** Optics (of an image) of a kind in which the light that forms it actually passes through it; not virtual. ▶ **adv.** [as submodifier] informal really; very: *my head hurts real bad.* — **real·ness** **n.** [ME ('relating to things (in law)'): from Anglo-Norman Fr., from late L. *realis*, from L. *res* 'thing.']

real[2] /rā'äl/ ▶ **n.** (pl. **re·als** or **reis** /rāsH; rās/) the basic monetary unit of Brazil since 1994, equal to 100 centavos. ■ (pl. **re·a·les** /rā'äles/ or **re·als**) a former coin and monetary unit of various Spanish-speaking countries. [Port. and Sp., lit. 'royal.']

real es·tate ▶ **n.** another term for REAL PROPERTY.

re·al·gar /rē'algər; -,gär/ ▶ **n.** a soft, reddish mineral consisting of arsenic sulfide, formerly used as a pigment and in fireworks. [ME: via med. L. from Arab. *rahj al-ġār* 'arsenic,' lit. 'dust of the cave.']

re·a·li·a /rē'ālēə; -'älēə/ ▶ **n.** objects and material from everyday life, esp. when used as teaching aids. [1950s: from late L., neut. pl. of *realis* (see REAL[1]).]

re·a·lign /,rēə'līn/ ▶ **v.** [trans.] change or restore to a different or former position or state. ■ (**realign oneself with**) change one's position or attitude with regard to (a person, organization, or cause): *he wished to realign himself with Bagehot's more pessimistic position.* — **re·a·lign·ment** **n.**

re·al·ism /'rēə,lizəm/ ▶ **n.** **1** the attitude or practice of accepting a situation as it is and being prepared to deal with it accordingly: *a new mood of realism.* ■ the view that the subject matter of politics is political power, not matters of principle. **2** the quality or fact of representing a person, thing, or situation accurately or in a way that is true to life. ■ (in art and literature) the movement or style of representing familiar things as they actually are. Often contrasted with IDEALISM (sense 1). **3** Philos. the doctrine that universals or abstract concepts have an objective or absolute existence. Often contrasted with NOMINALISM. ■ the doctrine that matter as the object of perception has real existence and is neither reducible to universal mind or spirit nor dependent on a perceiving agent. Often contrasted with IDEALISM (sense 2). — **re·al·ist** /'rēəlist/ **n.**

re·al·is·tic /,rēə'listik/ ▶ **adj.** **1** having or showing a sensible and practical idea of what can be achieved or expected: *jobs are scarce, so you've got to be realistic.* **2** representing familiar things in a way that is accurate or true to life: *a realistic human drama.* — **re·al·is·ti·cal·ly** /-ik(ə)lē/ **adv.** [sentence adverb] *realistically, you can't expect to win.*

re·al·i·ty /rē'alətē/ ▶ **n.** (pl. **-ties**) **1** the world or the state of things as they actually exist, as opposed to an idealistic or notional idea of them: *he refuses to face reality.* ■ a thing that is actually experienced or seen, esp. when this is grim or problematic: *the harsh realities of life.* ■ a thing that exists in fact, having previously only existed in one's mind: *the paperless office may yet become a reality.* ■ the quality of being lifelike or resembling an original: *the reality of Marryat's detail.* **2** the state or quality of having existence or substance: *youth, when death has no reality.* ■ Philos. existence that is absolute, self-sufficient, or objective, and not subject to human decisions or conventions.

re·al·i·ty check ▶ **n.** [usu. in sing.] informal an occasion on which one is reminded of the state of things in the real world.

QR

re·al·i·ty prin·ci·ple ▶ **n.** Psychoanal. the ego's control of the pleasure-seeking activity of the id in order to meet the demands of the external world.

re·al·i·za·ble /ˌrēəˈlīzəbəl/ ▶ **adj.** **1** able to be achieved or made to happen: *a realizable dream.* **2** in or able to be converted into cash: *realizable assets.* — **re·al·iz·a·bil·i·ty** /ˌrēəlīzəˈbilətē/ **n.**

re·al·i·za·tion /ˌrē(ə)ləˈzāshən/ ▶ **n.** **1** [in sing.] an act of becoming fully aware of something as a fact. **2** the fulfillment or achievement of something desired or anticipated: *the realization of his dream.* ■ an actual, complete, or dramatic form given to a concept or work: *a perfect realization of Bartók's music.* **3** the action of converting an asset into cash. ■ a sale of goods: *auction realizations.*

re·al·ize /ˈrē(ə)ˌlīz/ ▶ **v.** [trans.] **1** become fully aware of (something) as a fact; understand clearly: *he realized his mistake at once.* **2** cause (something desired or anticipated) to happen: *his worst fears have been realized.* ■ fulfill: *she is beginning to realize her potential.* **3** (usu. **be realized**) give actual or physical form to: *the stage designs have been beautifully realized.* ■ use (a linguistic feature) in a particular spoken or written form. ■ Music add to or complete (a piece of music left sparsely notated by the composer). **4** make (money or a profit) from a transaction: *she realized a profit of $100,000.* ■ (of goods) be sold for (a specified price); fetch: *the drawings are expected to realize $500,000.* ■ convert (an asset) into cash: *he realized all the assets in her trust fund.* [17th C.: from REAL[1], on the pattern of Fr. *réaliser.*]

re·al·lo·cate /rēˈaləˌkāt/ ▶ **v.** [trans.] allocate in a different way: *they reallocated their resources overseas.* — **re·al·lo·ca·tion** /ˌrēˌaləˈkāshən/ **n.**

re·al·ly /ˈrē(ə)lē/ ▶ **adv.** **1** in actual fact, as opposed to what is said or imagined to be true or possible: *what really happened?* | [sentence adverb] *really, there are only three options.* ■ used to add strength, sincerity, or seriousness to a statement or opinion: *I really want to go.* ■ seriously (used in questions and exclamations with an implied negative answer): *do you really expect me to believe that?* **2** [as submodifier] very; thoroughly: *a really cold day.* ▶ **exclam.** used to express interest, surprise, or doubt. ■ used to express mild protest. ■ used to express agreement.

realm /relm/ ▶ **n.** archaic, literary, or Law a kingdom: *the peers of the realm.* ■ a field or domain of activity or interest: *the realm of applied chemistry* | *it is beyond the realms of possibility.* ■ Zool. a primary biogeographical division of the earth's surface. [ME *rewme*, from Old Fr. *reaume*, from L. *regimen* 'government' (see REGIMEN); spelling influenced by OFr. *reiel* 'royal.']

re·al·po·li·tik /rāˈälˌpōliˌtēk/ ▶ **n.** a system of politics or principles based on practical rather than moral or ideological considerations. [20th C.: from Ger. *Realpolitik* 'practical politics.']

real pres·ence ▶ **n.** Christian Theol. the actual presence of Christ's body and blood in the Eucharistic elements.

real prop·er·ty ▶ **n.** Law property consisting of land or buildings. Compare with PERSONAL PROPERTY.

real time ▶ **n.** the actual time during which a process or event occurs: *information updated in real time.* ■ [as adj.] Comput. of or relating to a system in which input data is processed within milliseconds so that it is available virtually immediately as feedback, e.g., in a missile guidance or airline booking system. ■ informal a two-way conversation, as opposed to the delay of written correspondence.

re·al·tor /ˈrē(ə)ltər; -ˌtôr/ ▶ **n.** a person who acts as an agent for the sale and purchase of buildings and land; a real estate agent. [20th C.: from REALTY.]

re·al·ty /ˈrē(ə)ltē/ ▶ **n.** Law a person's real property. The opposite of PERSONALTY.

ream[1] /rēm/ ▶ **n.** 500 (formerly 480) sheets of paper. ■ a large quantity of something, typically paper or writing on paper. [ME: from OFr. *raime*, based on Arab. *rizma* 'bundle.']

ream[2] ▶ **v.** [trans.] widen (a bore or hole) with a special tool. ■ widen a bore or hole in (a gun or other metal object) in such a way. ■ clear out or remove (material) from something. ■ informal rebuke someone fiercely. [19th C.: origin unknown.]

ream·er /ˈrēmər/ ▶ **n.** a tool for widening or finishing drilled holes. ■ an instrument for scraping the burrs off the inside of water pipes. ■ a blade for scraping the carbon layer from the inside of the bowl of a smoking pipe. ■ another term for JUICER (sense 1).

re·an·i·mate /rēˈanəˌmāt/ ▶ **v.** [trans.] restore to life or consciousness; revive. ■ give fresh vigor or impetus to: *his dislike was reanimated.* — **re·an·i·ma·tion** /ˌrēˌanəˈmāshən/ **n.**

reap /rēp/ ▶ **v.** [trans.] cut or gather (a crop or harvest). ■ harvest the crop from (a piece of land). ■ fig. receive (a reward or benefit) as a consequence of one's own or other people's actions.

– PHRASES **you reap what you sow** proverb you eventually have to face up to the consequences of your actions. [OE *ripan.*]

reap·er /ˈrēpər/ ▶ **n.** a person or machine that harvests a crop. ■ (**the Reaper**) short for GRIM REAPER.

re·ap·por·tion /ˌrēəˈpôrshən/ ▶ **v.** [trans.] assign or distribute (something) again or in a different way. — **re·ap·por·tion·ment n.**

re·ap·praise /ˌrēəˈprāz/ ▶ **v.** [trans.] appraise or assess (something) again or in a different way. — **re·ap·prais·al** /-ˈprāzəl/ **n.**

rear[1] /ri(ə)r/ ▶ **n.** [in sing.] the back part of something, esp. a building or vehicle. ■ the space or position at the back of something or someone: *the field at the rear of the church.* ■ the hindmost part of an army, fleet, or line of people. ■ (also **rear end**) informal a person's buttocks. ▶ **adj.** [attrib.] at the back: *the car's rear window.* [ME (first used as a military term): from OFr. *rere*, based on L. *retro* 'back.']

rear[2] ▶ **v.** **1** [trans.] (usu. **be reared**) bring up and care for (a child) until they are fully grown, esp. in a particular manner or place: *he was reared in New York City.* ■ (of an animal) care for (its young) until they are fully grown. ■ breed and raise (animals): *the calves are reared for beef.* ■ grow or cultivate (plants): [as adj., in comb.] (**-reared**) *laboratory-reared plantlets.* **2** [intrans.] (of a horse or other animal) raise itself upright on its hind legs. ■ [with adverbial of place] (of a building, mountain, etc.) extend or appear to extend to a great height: *houses reared up on either side.* ■ [trans.] archaic set (something) upright. [OE *rǣran* 'set upright, construct,' from Gmc. akin to RAISE and RISE.]

rear ad·mir·al ▶ **n.** an officer in the US Navy or Coast Guard ranking above commodore and below vice admiral.

rear·guard /ˈri(ə)rˌgärd/ ▶ **n.** the soldiers positioned at the rear of a body of troops, esp. those protecting an army when it is in retreat. ■ a defensive or conservative element in an organization or community. [ME ('rear part of an army'): from OFr. *rereguarde.*]

rear·guard ac·tion ▶ **n.** a defensive action carried out by a retreating army.

re·arm /rēˈärm/ ▶ **v.** [trans.] provide with a new supply of weapons: *his plan to rearm Germany.* ■ [intrans.] acquire or build up a new supply of weapons. — **re·ar·ma·ment** /rēˈärməmənt/ **n.**

rear·most /ˈri(ə)rˌmōst/ ▶ **adj.** furthest back: *the rearmost door.*

re·ar·range /ˌrēəˈrānj/ ▶ **v.** [trans.] move (something) into a more acceptable position or state: *she rearranged her skirt.* ■ change (the position, time, or order of something): *he had rearranged his schedule.* — **re·ar·range·ment n.**

rear·view mir·ror /ˈri(ə)rˌvyo͞o/ ▶ **n.** a small angled mirror fixed inside the windshield of a motor vehicle, enabling the driver to see the vehicle or road behind.

rear·ward /ˈri(ə)rwərd/ ▶ **adj.** directed toward the back: *a slight rearward movement.* [17th C.: from REAR[1] + -WARD.] ▶ **adv.** (also esp. Brit. **rear·wards**) toward the back: *the engine nozzles point rearward.*

rear-wheel drive ▶ **n.** a transmission system that provides power to the rear wheels of a motor vehicle: [as adj.] *a rear-wheel drive coupé.*

rea·son /ˈrēzən/ ▶ **n.** **1** a cause, explanation, or justification for an action or event. ■ good or obvious cause to do something: *we have reason to celebrate.* ■ Logic a premise of an argument in support of a belief, esp. a minor premise when given after the conclusion. **2** the power of the mind to think, understand, and form judgments by a process of logic. ■ what is right, practical, or possible; common sense: *people are willing, **within reason**, to pay for schooling.* ■ (**one's reason**) one's sanity. ▶ **v.** [intrans.] think, understand, and form judgments by a process of logic: *humans do not reason entirely from facts* | [as n.] (**reasoning**) *the reasoning behind the review.* ■ [trans.] (**reason something out**) find an answer to a problem by considering various possible solutions. ■ (**reason with**) persuade (someone) with rational argument: *I tried to reason with her.*

– PHRASES **beyond (all) reason** to a foolishly excessive degree. **by reason of** formal because of: *persons who, by reason of age, are in need of care.* **(it) stands to reason** it is obvious or logical. — **rea·son·er** /ˈrēz(ə)nər/ **n.** **rea·son·less adj.** (archaic). [ME: from OFr. *reisun* (n.), *raisoner* (verb), from a var. of L. *ratio(n-)*, from the v. *reri* 'consider.']

rea·son·a·ble /ˈrēz(ə)nəbəl/ ▶ **adj.** **1** (of a person) having sound judgment; fair and sensible. ■ based on good sense: *a reasonable request.* ■ archaic (of a person or animal) able to think, understand, or form judgments by a logical process: *man is by nature reasonable.* **2** as much as is appropriate or fair; moderate: *a police officer may use reasonable force.* ■ fairly good; average: *the carpet is in reasonable condition.* ■ (of a price or product) not too expensive. — **rea·son·a·ble·ness n.**

rea·son·a·bly /ˈrēz(ə)nəblē/ ▶ **adv.** **1** in a fair and sensible way. ■ by fair or sensible standards of judgment; rightly or justifiably. **2** to a moderate or acceptable degree: fairly; quite: [as submodifier] *she played the piano reasonably well.* ■ inexpensively.

rea·soned /ˈrēzənd/ ▶ **adj.** underpinned by logic or good sense: *a reasoned judgment.*

re·as·sess /ˌrēəˈses/ ▶ **v.** [trans.] consider or assess again, esp. while paying attention to new or different factors: *we have decided to reassess our timetable.* — **re·as·sess·ment n.**

re·as·sign /ˌrēəˈsīn/ ▶ **v.** [trans.] appoint (someone) to a different job or task. ■ allocate or distribute (work or resources) differently. — **re·as·sign·ment n.**

re·as·sume /ˌrēəˈs(y)o͞om/ ▶ **v.** [trans.] take on or gain (something) again: *he reassumed the title of Governor.* — **re·as·sump·tion** /ˌrēəˈsəmpshən/ **n.**

re·as·sur·ance /ˌrēəˈsho͝orəns/ ▶ **n.** the action of removing someone's doubts or fears: *children need reassurance and praise.* ■ a statement or comment that removes someone's doubts or fears.

re·as·sure /ˌrēəˈsho͝or/ ▶ **v.** [trans.] say or do something to remove the doubts and fears of someone. — **re·as·sur·ing·ly adv.**

Ré·au·mur scale /ˌrāōˈmyo͝or; rāˈōˌmyo͝or/ ▶ **n.** an obsolete scale of temperature at which water freezes at 0° and boils at 80° under standard conditions. [18th C.: René A. F. de *Réaumur* (1683–1757), Fr. naturalist.]

reave /rēv/ ▶ **v.** (past and past part. **reft** /reft/) [intrans.] archaic carry out raids in order to plunder. ■ [trans.] rob (a person or place) of something by force. ■ [trans.] steal (something). — **reav·er n.** [OE *rēafian*, Gmc.; akin to Ger. *rauben* and ROB.]

re·a·wak·en /ˌrēəˈwākən/ ▶ **v.** [trans.] restore (a feeling or state): *his departure reawakened deep divisions.* ■ [intrans.] (of a feeling or state) emerge again; return.

Reb[1] /reb/ ▶ n. a traditional Jewish title or form of address, corresponding to Sir, for a man who is not a rabbi (used preceding the forename or surname). [Yiddish.]

Reb[2] (also **John·ny Reb**) ▶ n. informal a Confederate soldier in the American Civil War. [abbrev. of REBEL.]

re·bar /'rē,bär/ ▶ n. a steel reinforcing rod in concrete.

re·bar·ba·tive /rə'bärbətiv/ ▶ adj. formal unattractive and objectionable: *rebarbative modern buildings.* [19th C.: from Fr. *rébarbatif, -ive*, from OFr. *se rebarber* 'face each other "beard to beard" aggressively,' from *barbe* 'beard.']

re·base /rē'bās/ ▶ v. [trans.] establish a new base level for (a tax level, price index, etc.).

re·bate[1] ▶ n. /'rē,bāt/ a partial refund to someone who has paid too much money for tax, rent, or a utility. ■ a deduction or discount on a sum of money due. ▶ v. /'rē,bāt; ri'bāt/ [trans.] pay back (such a sum of money). — **re·bat·a·ble** /'rē,bātəbəl; ri'bā-/ adj. [ME ('diminish (a sum)'): from Anglo-Norman Fr. *rebatre* 'beat back.']

re·bate[2] /'rabit; 'rē,bāt/ ▶ n. & v. another term for RABBET. [17th C.: alt.]

reb·be /'rebə; -bē/ ▶ n. Judaism a rabbi, esp. a religious leader of the Hasidic sect. [Yiddish, from Heb. *rabbī* 'rabbi.']

reb·betz·in /'rebətsin; 'rebət-/ (also **reb·bitz·in**) ▶ n. Judaism the wife of a rabbi. ■ a female religious teacher. [Yiddish, fem. of *rebbe* (see REBBE).]

re·bec /'rē,bek; 'reb,ek/ (also **re·beck**) ▶ n. a medieval stringed instrument played with a bow, typically having three strings. [ME: from Fr., based on Arab. *rabāb*.]

reb·el ▶ n. /'rebəl/ a person who rises in armed resistance against an established government or ruler. ■ a person who resists authority, control, or convention. ▶ v. /ri'bel/ (**re·bel·led, re·bel·ling**) [intrans.] rise in opposition or armed resistance to an established government or ruler. *the Earl of Pembroke subsequently rebelled against Henry III.* ■ (of a person) resist authority, control, or convention. ■ show or feel repugnance for or resistance to something: *my legs rebelled—I could walk no further.* [ME: ult. from L. *rebellis* 'rebellious,' based on *bellum* 'war.']

re·bel·lion /ri'belyən/ ▶ n. an act of violent or open resistance to an established government or ruler. ■ the action or process of resisting authority, control, or convention: *an act of teenage rebellion.*

re·bel·lious /ri'belyəs/ ▶ adj. showing a desire to resist authority, control, or convention. ■ (of a person, city, or state) engaged in opposition or armed resistance to an established government or ruler. ■ (of a thing) not easily handled or kept in place: *a rebellious lock of hair.* — **re·bel·lious·ly** adv. **re·bel·lious·ness** n.

re·bind /rē'bīnd/ ▶ v. (past and past part. **-bound**) [trans.] give a new binding to (a book).

re·birth /rē'bərTH; 'rē,bərTH/ ▶ n. the process of being reincarnated or born again. ■ the action of reappearing or starting to flourish or increase after a decline; revival.

re·blo·chon /rə,blô'SHōN/ ▶ n. a kind of soft French cheese, made originally and chiefly in Savoy.

re·bore ▶ v. /rē'bôr/ [trans.] make a new boring in (the cylinders of an internal combustion engine), typically in order to widen them. ▶ n. an act of reboring an engine's cylinders. ■ an engine with rebored cylinders.

re·born /rē'bôrn/ ▶ adj. brought back to life or activity. ■ having experienced a complete spiritual change.

re·bound[1] ▶ v. /ri'bound; 'rē,bound/ [intrans.] bounce back through the air after hitting a hard surface or object. ■ [intrans.] recover in value, amount, or strength after a previous decrease or decline. ■ [intrans.] (**rebound on/upon**) (of an event or situation) have an unexpected adverse consequence for (someone, esp. the person responsible for it). ■ [intrans.] Basketball gain possession of a missed shot after it bounces off the backboard or basket rim. ▶ n. /'rē,bound/ (in sporting contexts) a ball or shot that bounces back after striking a hard surface. ■ Basketball a recovery of possession of a missed shot. ■ an instance of increasing in value, amount, or strength after a previous decline: *a big rebound in profits.* ■ [usu. as adj.] the recurrence of a medical condition, esp. after withdrawal of medication: *rebound hypertension.*
– PHRASES **on the rebound** in the process of bouncing back after striking a hard surface. ■ still affected by the emotional distress caused by the ending of a romantic or sexual relationship. [ME: from OFr. *rebondir*, from *re-* 'back' + *bondir* 'bounce up.']

re·bound[2] /rē'bound/ past and past participle of REBIND.

re·bound·er /'rē,boundər; ri'boun-/ ▶ n. Basketball a player who rebounds the ball or is especially proficient at doing so.

re·bo·zo /ri'bōzō; -sō/ ▶ n. (pl. **-zos**) a long scarf covering the head and shoulders, traditionally worn by Spanish-American women. [Sp.]

re·brand /rē'brand/ ▶ v. [trans.] [usu. as n.] (**rebranding**) change the corporate image of (a company or organization).

re·broad·cast /rē'brôd,kast/ ▶ v. (past **-cast** or **-cast·ed**; past part. **-cast**) [trans.] broadcast or relay (a program or signal) again. ▶ n. a repeated or relayed broadcast. — **re·broad·cast·er** n.

re·buff /ri'bəf/ ▶ v. [trans.] reject (someone or something) in an abrupt or ungracious manner. ▶ n. an abrupt or ungracious refusal or rejection of an offer, request, or friendly gesture. [16th C.: from obs. Fr. *rebuffer* (v.), *rebuffe* (n.), from Ital. *ri-* ('back') + *buffo* 'a gust' of imitative origin.]

re·build ▶ v. /rē'bild/ (past and past part. **-built** /-'bilt/) [trans.] build (something) again after it has been damaged or destroyed. ▶ n. /'rē,bild/ an instance or rebuilding something, esp. a vehicle or other machine. ■ a thing that has been rebuilt, esp. a part of a motor vehicle, e.g., a motor or an alternator. — **re·build·a·ble** adj. **re·build·er** n.

re·buke /ri'byo͞ok/ ▶ v. [trans.] express sharp disapproval or criticism of (someone) because of their behavior or actions. ▶ n. an expression of sharp disapproval or criticism. — **re·buk·er** n. **re·buk·ing·ly** adv. [ME ('force back'): from Anglo-Norman Fr. and Old North. Fr. *rebuker*, from *re-* 'back' + *bukier* 'to beat' (orig. 'cut down wood,' from OFr. *busche* 'log').]

re·bus /'rēbəs/ ▶ n. (pl. **-bus·es**) a puzzle in which words are represented by combinations of pictures and individual letters; for instance, *apex* might be represented by a picture of an ape followed by a letter *X*. ■ hist. an ornamental device associated with a person to whose name it punningly alludes. [17th C.: from Fr. *rébus*, from L. *rebus*, ablative pl. of *res* 'thing.']

"To be or not to be"
rebus

re·but /ri'bət/ ▶ v. (**-but·ted, -but·ting**) [trans.] **1** claim or prove that (evidence or an accusation) is false. **2** archaic drive back or repel (a person or attack). — **re·but·ta·ble** adj. [ME ('rebuke'): from Anglo-Norman Fr. *rebuter*, from OFr. *re-* 'back' + *boter* 'to butt.']

re·but·tal /ri'bətl/ ▶ n. a refutation or contradiction. ■ another term for REBUTTER.

re·but·ter /ri'bətər/ ▶ n. Law, archaic a defendant's reply to the plaintiff's surrejoinder.

rec /rek/ ▶ n. informal recreation: [as adj.] *the rec center.* [1920s: abbrev.]

rec. ▶ abbr. ■ receipt. ■ (in prescriptions) fresh. [from L. *recens*.] ■ recipe. ■ record. ■ recorder. ■ recording.

re·cal·ci·trant /ri'kalsətrənt/ ▶ adj. having an obstinately uncooperative attitude toward authority. ▶ n. a person with such an attitude. — **re·cal·ci·trance** n. **re·cal·ci·trant·ly** adv. [19th C.: from L. *recalcitrant-* 'kicking out with the heels,' from the v. *recalcitrare*, based on *calx, calc-* 'heel.']

re·cal·cu·late /rē'kalkyə,lāt/ ▶ v. [trans.] calculate again, typically using different data. — **re·cal·cu·la·tion** /,rē,kalkyə'lāSHən/ n.

re·call ▶ v. /ri'kôl/ [trans.] **1** bring (a fact, event, or situation) back into one's mind, esp. so as to recount it to others; remember. ■ cause one to remember or think of. ■ (**recall someone/something to**) bring the memory or thought of someone or something to (a person or their mind). ■ call up (stored computer data) for processing or display. **2** officially order (someone) to return to a place. ■ select (a sports player) as a member of a team from which they have previously been dropped. ■ (of a manufacturer) request all the purchasers of (a certain product) to return it, as the result of the discovery of a fault. ■ bring (someone) out of a state of inattention or reverie: *she recalled him to the present.* ■ archaic revoke or annul (an action or decision). ▶ n. /'rē,kôl; ri'kôl; rē'kôl/ **1** an act or instance of officially recalling someone or something: *a recall of Parliament.* ■ a request for the return of a faulty product, issued by a manufacturer to all those who have purchased it. ■ the removal of an elected government official from office by a petition followed by voting. **2** the action or faculty of remembering something learned or experienced. ■ the proportion of the number of relevant documents retrieved from a database in response to an inquiry. — **re·call·a·ble** adj. [16th C. (v.): from RE- + CALL.]

re·cant /ri'kant/ ▶ v. [intrans.] say that one no longer holds an opinion or belief, esp. one considered heretical: *heretics were burned if they would not recant* | [trans.] *Galileo was forced to recant his assertion.* — **re·can·ta·tion** /,rē,kan'tāSHən/ n. **re·cant·er** n. [16th C.: from L. *recantare* 'revoke,' from *re-* 'back' + *cantare* 'sing.']

re·cap informal ▶ v. /'rē'kap/ (**-capped, -cap·ping**) state again as a summary; recapitulate. ▶ n. /'rē,kap/ a summary of what has been said; a recapitulation. [1950s: abbrev.]

re·cap·i·tal·ize /rē'kapətl,īz/ ▶ v. [trans.] provide (a business) with more capital, esp. by replacing debt with stock. — **re·cap·i·tal·i·za·tion** /rē,kapətl-ə'zāSHən/ n.

re·ca·pit·u·late /,rēkə'picHə,lāt/ ▶ v. [trans.] summarize and state again the main points of: *he began to recapitulate his argument with care.* ■ Biol. repeat (an evolutionary or other process) during development and growth. — **re·ca·pit·u·la·to·ry** /-lə,tôrē/ adj. [16th C.: from late L. *recapitulat-* 'gone through heading by heading,' from *re-* 'again' + *capitulum* 'chapter' (dimin. of *caput* 'head').]

re·ca·pit·u·la·tion /,rēkə,picHə'lāSHən/ ▶ n. an act or instance of summarizing the main points of something. ■ Biol. the repetition of an evolutionary or other process during development or growth. ■ Music a part of a movement (esp. one in sonata form) in which themes from the exposition are restated.

re·cap·ture /rē'kapCHər/ ▶**v.** [trans.] capture (a person or animal that has escaped). ■ recover (something previously captured by an enemy): *Edward I recaptured the castle.* ■ regain (something that has been lost): *Democrats might recapture both the House and the Senate.* ■ recreate or experience again (a past time, event, or feeling): *they want to recapture their own childhoods.* ▶**n.** [in sing.] an act of recapturing.

re·cast /rē'kast/ ▶**v.** (past and past part. **-cast**) [trans.] **1** give (a metal object) a different form by melting it down and reshaping it. ■ present or organize in a different form or style: *his doctoral thesis has been recast for the general reader.* **2** allocate the parts in (a play or film) to different actors: *there were moves to recast the play.*

recd ▶**abbr.** received.

re·cede /ri'sēd/ ▶**v.** [intrans.] go or move back or further away from a previous position: *the flood waters receded.* ■ (of a quality, feeling, or possibility) gradually diminish: *the prospects of an early end to the war receded.* ■ (of a man's hair) cease to grow at the temples and above the forehead. ■ (of a man) begin to go bald in such a way. ■ [usu. as adj.] (**receding**) (of a facial feature) slope backward: *a slightly receding chin.* ■ (**recede from**) archaic withdraw from (an undertaking, promise, or agreement). [15th C. ('depart from'): from L. *recedere*, from *re-* 'back' + *cedere* 'go.']

re·ceipt /ri'sēt/ ▶**n.** **1** the action of receiving something or the fact of its being received: *receipt of this letter.* ■ a written or printed statement acknowledging that something has been paid for or that goods have been received. ■ (**receipts**) an amount of money received during a particular period by an organization or business: *box-office receipts.* **2** archaic a recipe. ▶**v.** [trans.] [usu. as adj.] (**receipted**) mark (a bill) as paid: *the receipted hotel bill.* ■ write a receipt for (goods or money): *all fish shall be receipted at time of purchase.* [ME: from Anglo-Norman Fr. *receite*, from med. L. *recepta* 'received,' fem. past part. of L. *recipere*.]

re·ceiv·a·ble /ri'sēvəbəl/ ▶**adj.** able to be received. ▶**plural n.** (**receivables**) amounts owed to a business, regarded as assets.

re·ceive /ri'sēv/ ▶**v.** [trans.] **1** be given, presented with, or paid (something): *most businesses will receive a tax cut.* ■ take delivery of (something sent or communicated): *he received fifty inquiries.* ■ buy or accept goods in the knowledge that they have been stolen. ■ detect or pick up (broadcast signals). ■ form (an idea or impression) as a result of perception or experience: *the impression she received was one of unhurried leisure.* ■ (in tennis and similar games) be the player to whom the server serves (the ball). ■ (in Christian services) eat or drink (the Eucharistic bread or wine). ■ consent to formally hear (an oath or confession). ■ serve as a receptacle for. **2** suffer, experience, or be subject to (specified treatment): *the event received wide press coverage | he received an eight-year prison sentence | she received only cuts and bruises.* ■ [with obj. and adverbial] (usu. **be received**) respond to (something) in a specified way: *her first poem was not well received.* ■ meet with (a specified response or reaction): *the rulings have received widespread acceptance.* ■ [as adj.] (**received**) widely accepted as authoritative or true: *received wisdom.* ■ meet and have to withstand: *the slopes receive the full force of the wind.* **3** greet or welcome (a visitor) formally. ■ be visited by: *she received visitors.* ■ admit as a member: *hundreds of converts were received into the Church.* ■ provide space or accommodations for.

– PHRASES **be at** (or **on**) **the receiving end** be the person to whom a telephone call is made. ■ informal be subjected to something unpleasant. [ME: from Anglo-Norman Fr. *receivre*, based on L. *recipere*, from *re-* 'back' + *capere* 'take.']

re·ceived pro·nun·ci·a·tion (also **re·ceived stand·ard**) ▶**n.** the standard form of British English pronunciation, based on educated speech in southern England, widely accepted as a standard elsewhere.

re·ceiv·er /ri'sēvər/ ▶**n.** **1** the part of a telephone apparatus contained in the earpiece, in which electrical signals are converted into sounds. ■ a complete telephone handset. ■ a piece of radio or television apparatus that detects broadcast signals and converts them into visible or audible form. **2** a person who gets or accepts something that has been sent or given to them. ■ (in tennis and similar games) the player to whom the ball is served to begin play. ■ Football a player who is eligible to catch a pass. ■ a person who buys or accepts stolen goods in the knowledge that they have been stolen. **3** a person or company appointed by a court to manage the financial affairs of a business or person that has gone bankrupt. **4** Chem. a container for collecting the products of distillation, chromatography, or other process. **5** the part of a firearm that houses the action and to which the barrel and other parts are attached.

re·ceiv·er·ship /ri'sēvər,SHip/ ▶**n.** the state of being dealt with by an official receiver: *the company went into receivership last week.*

re·ceiv·ing line ▶**n.** a collection of people who gather in a row to greet guests as they arrive at a formal social event.

re·cen·sion /ri'senCHən/ ▶**n.** a revised edition of a text; an act of making a revised edition of a text. [17th C. ('survey'): from L. *recensio(n-)*, from *recensere* 'revise,' from *re-* 'again' + *censere* 'to review.']

re·cent /'rēsənt/ ▶**adj.** **1** having happened, begun, or been done not long ago or not long before; belonging to a past period of time comparatively close to the present: *his recent visit to Britain.* **2** (**Recent**) Geol. another term for HOLOCENE. ▶**n.** (**the Recent**) Geol. the Holocene epoch. — **re·cen·cy n. re·cent·ly adv. re·cent·ness n.** [ME (in the sense 'fresh'): from L. *recens, recent-* or Fr. *récent*.]

re·cep·ta·cle /ri'septikəl/ ▶**n.** **1** an object or space used to contain something: *trash receptacles.* ■ esp. Zool. an organ or structure that receives a secretion, eggs, sperm, etc. ■ an electrical outlet into which the plug of an electrical device may be inserted. **2** Bot. an enlarged area at the apex of a stem that bears the organs of a flower or the florets of a flowerhead. ■ a structure supporting the sexual organs in some algae, mosses, and liverworts. [ME: from L. *receptaculum*, from *receptare* 'receive back,' frequentative of *recipere* (see RECEIVE).]

re·cep·tion /ri'sepSHən/ ▶**n.** **1** the action or process of receiving something sent, given, or inflicted: *the reception of the sacrament.* ■ the way in which a person or group of people reacts to someone or something: *a lukewarm reception.* ■ the receiving of broadcast signals. ■ the quality of this: *poor radio reception.* ■ the action of admitting someone to a place, group, or institution or the process of being admitted. ■ the formal or ceremonious welcoming of a guest. ■ Football an act of catching a pass. **2** a formal social occasion held to welcome someone or to celebrate a particular event: *a wedding reception.* **3** the area in a hotel, office, or other establishment where guests and visitors are greeted and dealt with: [as adj.] *the reception desk.* [ME: ult. from L. *receptio(n-)*, from the v. *recipere* (see RECEIVE).]

re·cep·tion·ist /ri'sepSHənist/ ▶**n.** a person employed in an office or other establishment to greet and deal with clients and visitors.

re·cep·tion room ▶**n.** a room in a hotel or other building used for functions such as parties and meetings.

re·cep·tive /ri'septiv/ ▶**adj.** able or willing to receive something, esp. signals or stimuli. ■ willing to consider or accept new suggestions and ideas. ■ (of a female animal) ready to mate. — **re·cep·tive·ly adv. re·cep·tive·ness n. re·cep·tiv·i·ty** /,rē,sep'tivətē/ **n.**

re·cep·tor /ri'septər/ ▶**n.** Physiol. an organ or cell able to respond to light, heat, or other external stimulus and transmit a signal to a sensory nerve. ■ a region of tissue, or a molecule in a cell membrane, that responds specifically to a particular neurotransmitter, hormone, antigen, or other substance.

re·cess /'rē,ses; ri'ses/ ▶**n.** **1** a small space created by building part of a wall further back from the rest: *a table set into a recess.* ■ a hollow space inside something: *the concrete block has a recess in its base.* ■ (usu. **recesses**) a remote, secluded, or secret place. **2** a period of time when the proceedings of a parliament, committee, court of law, or other official body are temporarily suspended. ■ a break between school classes. ▶**v.** **1** [trans.] [often as adj.] (**recessed**) attach (a piece of equipment or furniture) by setting it back into the wall or surface to which it is fixed: *recessed ceiling lights.* **2** [intrans.] (of formal proceedings) be temporarily suspended: *the talks recessed at 2:15.* ■ [trans.] suspend (such proceedings) temporarily. ■ (of an official body) suspend its proceedings for a period of time. [16th C. ('withdrawal'): from L. *recessus*, from *recedere* (see RECEDE).]

re·ces·sion /ri'seSHən/ ▶**n.** **1** a period of temporary economic decline during which trade and industrial activity are reduced, generally identified by a fall in GDP in two successive quarters. **2** esp. Astron. the action of receding; motion away from an observer. — **re·ces·sion·ar·y** /-,nerē/ **adj.**

re·ces·sion·al /ri'seSHənl; ri'seSHnəl/ ▶**adj.** of or relating to an economic recession: *recessional times.* ■ esp. Astron. relating to or denoting motion away from the observer. ■ Geol. (of a moraine or other deposit) left during a pause in the retreat of a glacier or ice sheet. ▶**n.** a hymn sung while the clergy and choir process out of church at the end of a service.

re·ces·sive /ri'sesiv/ ▶**adj.** **1** Genet. relating to or denoting heritable characteristics controlled by genes that are expressed in offspring only when inherited from both parents, i.e., when not masked by a dominant characteristic inherited from one parent. Often contrasted with DOMINANT. **2** undergoing an economic recession. **3** Phonet. (of the stress on a word or phrase) tending to fall on the first syllable. ▶**n.** Genet. a recessive trait or gene. — **re·ces·sive·ly adv. re·ces·sive·ness n. re·ces·siv·i·ty** /,rē,se'sivətē/ **n.**

re·charge ▶**v.** /rē'CHärj/ [trans.] restore an electric charge to (a battery or a battery-operated device) by connecting it to a device that draws power from another source of electricity. ■ [intrans.] (of a battery or battery-operated device) be refilled with electrical power in such a way. ■ refill (a container, lake, or aquifer) with water. ■ [intrans.] be refilled: *the aquifer recharges naturally.* ■ [intrans.] fig. (of a person) return to a normal state of mind or strength after a period of physical or mental exertion: *she needs time to recharge.* ▶**n.** the replenishment of an aquifer by the absorption of water. — **re·charge·a·ble adj. re·charg·er n.**

re·cher·ché /rə,SHer'SHā; rə'SHer,SHā/ ▶**adj.** rare, exotic, or obscure. [Fr., lit. 'carefully sought out,' past part. of *rechercher*.]

re·chris·ten /rē'krisən/ ▶**v.** [with obj. and complement] give a new name to: *he rechristened Zaire the Democratic Republic of the Congo.*

re·cid·i·vist /ri'sidəvist/ ▶**n.** a convicted criminal who reoffends, esp. repeatedly. ▶**adj.** denoting such a person: *recidivist male prisoners | women are rarely recidivist.* — **re·cid·i·vism** /-,vizəm/ **n. re·cid·i·vis·tic** /ri,sidə'vistik/ **adj.** [19th C.: from Fr. *récidiviste*, from *récidiver* 'fall back,' based on L. *recidivus* 'falling back,' from the v. *recidere*, from *re-* + *cadere* 'to fall.']

Re·ci·fe /re'sēfā/ a city in northeastern Brazil; pop. 1,298,000. Former name PERNAMBUCO.

recip. ▶**abbr.** ■ reciprocal. ■ reciprocity.

rec·i·pe /'resə,pē/ ▶**n.** a set of instructions for preparing a particular dish, including a list of the ingredients required. ■ fig. something which is likely to lead to a particular outcome: *sky-high interest rates are a recipe for disaster.* ■ archaic a medical prescription. [ME: from L., lit.

'receive!' (instruction in medical prescriptions), imper. of *recipere*.]

re·cip·i·ent /ri'sipēənt/ ▸ **n.** a person or thing that receives or is awarded something. ▸ **adj.** [attrib.] receiving or capable or receiving something: *a recipient country.* [16th C.: from L. *recipient-* 'receiving,' from the v. *recipere*.]

re·cip·ro·cal /ri'siprəkəl/ ▸ **adj. 1** given, felt, or done in return: *a reciprocal comment or gesture.* **2** (of an agreement or obligation) bearing on or binding each of two parties equally. ■ Gram. (of a pronoun or verb) expressing mutual action or relationship. **3** (of a course or bearing) differing from a given course or bearing by 180 degrees. **4** Math. (of a quantity or function) related to another so that their product is one. ▸ **n. 1** tech. a mathematical expression or function so related to another that their product is one; the quantity obtained by dividing the number one by a given quantity. **2** Gram. a pronoun or verb expressing mutual action or relationship, e.g., *each other, fight.* — **re·cip·ro·cal·i·ty** /ri,siprə'kalətē/ **n.** **re·cip·ro·cal·ly** /-ək(ə)lē/ **adv.** [16th C.: from L. *reciprocus* (based on *re-* 'back' + *pro-* 'forward.']

re·cip·ro·cate /ri'siprə,kāt/ ▸ **v. 1** [trans.] respond to (a gesture or action) by making a corresponding one: *the favor was reciprocated* | [intrans.] *I reciprocated with a remark of my own.* ■ experience the same (love, liking, or affection) for someone as that person does for oneself: *her passion for him was not reciprocated.* **2** [intrans.] [usu. as adj.] (**reciprocating**) (of a part of a machine) move backward and forward in a straight line: *a reciprocating blade.* — **re·cip·ro·ca·tion** /ri,siprə'kāsHən/ **n.** **re·cip·ro·ca·tor** /-,kātər/ **n.**

re·cip·ro·cat·ing en·gine ▸ **n.** an engine in which one or more pistons move up and down in cylinders; a piston engine.

rec·i·proc·i·ty /,resə'präsətē/ ▸ **n.** the practice of exchanging things with others for mutual benefit, esp. privileges granted by one country or organization to another.

re·cit·al /ri'sītl/ ▸ **n. 1** the performance of a program of music by a solo instrumentalist or singer or by a small group: *a piano recital.* **2** an enumeration or listing of connected names, facts, or elements; *a recital of their misfortunes.* **3** (usu. **recitals**) Law the part of a legal document that explains the purpose of the deed and gives factual information. — **re·cit·al·ist** /-ist/ **n.**

rec·i·ta·tive /,res(ə)tə'tēv/ ▸ **n.** musical declamation of the kind usual in the narrative and dialogue parts of opera and oratorio, sung in the rhythm of ordinary speech with many words on the same note. [17th C.: from Ital. *recitativo*, from L. *recitare* (see **RECITE**).]

rec·i·ta·ti·vo /,resətə'tēvō/ ▸ **n.** (pl. **-vos**) another term for **RECITATIVE**. [Ital.]

re·cite /ri'sīt/ ▸ **v.** [trans.] repeat aloud or declaim (a poem or passage) from memory before an audience. ■ state (names, facts, etc.) in order. — **rec·i·ta·tion** /,resi'tāsHən/ **n.** **re·cit·er** **n.** [ME ('(in law) state in a document'): ult. from L. *recitare* 'read out,' from *re-* (intensive) + *citare* 'cite.']

reck /rek/ ▸ **v.** [intrans.] archaic pay heed to something. ■ (**it recks**) it is of importance: *what recks it?* [OE, from Gmc., 'care'; akin to **RECKLESS**.]

reck·less /'rekləs/ ▸ **adj.** (of a person or their actions) without thinking or caring about the consequences of an action: *reckless driving.* — **reck·less·ly** **adv.** **reck·less·ness** **n.** [OE *recceléas*, from the Gmc. base ('care') of **RECK**.]

reck·on /'rekən/ ▸ **v. 1** [trans.] establish by counting or calculation; calculate. ■ (**reckon someone/something among**) include in (a class or group): *he was reckoned among the brainiest.* **2** [with clause] informal conclude after calculation; be of the opinion: *I reckon I can manage that.* ■ [with obj. and complement] (often **be reckoned**) consider or regard in a specified way: *it was generally reckoned a failure.* **3** [intrans.] (**reckon on**) rely on or be sure of doing, having, or dealing with: *they had reckoned on privacy.* ■ [with infin.] informal expect to do a particular thing: *I reckon to get away by two-thirty.*

– PHRASES **a —— to be reckoned with** (or **to reckon with**) a thing or person of considerable importance or ability that is not to be ignored or underestimated: *the trade unions were a political force to be reckoned with.*

– PHRASAL VERBS **reckon with** (or **without**) **1** take (or fail to take) into account: *it must reckon with two great challenges.* **2** (**reckon with**) archaic settle accounts with. [OE *(ge)recenian* 'recount, relate'; rel. to Du. *rekenen* and Ger. *rechnen* 'to count (up).']

reck·on·ing /'rekəniNG/ ▸ **n.** the action or process of calculating or estimating something: *last year was not, by any reckoning, a good one.* ■ a person's view, opinion, or judgment. ■ archaic a bill or account, or its settlement. ■ the avenging or punishing of past mistakes or misdeeds: *a terrible reckoning.*

re·claim /rē'klām/ ▸ **v.** [trans.] **1** retrieve or recover (something previously lost, given, or paid); obtain the return of: *I reclaimed my room.* ■ redeem (someone) from a state of vice; reform. ■ archaic tame or civilize (an animal or person). **2** bring (waste land or land formerly under water) under cultivation. ■ recover (material) for reuse; recycle. ▸ **n.** the action or process of reclaiming or being reclaimed: *beyond reclaim.* — **re·claim·a·ble** **adj.** **re·claim·er** **n.** **rec·la·ma·tion** /,reklə'māsHən/ **n.** [ME '(in falconry) recall': from OFr. *reclamer*, from L. *reclamare* 'cry out against,' from *re-* + *clamare* 'to shout.']

ré·clame /rā'klām/ ▸ **n.** public acclaim; notoriety. ■ a hunger for publicity or flair for getting attention. [19th C.: Fr., from *réclamer* 'to claim,' from OFr. *reclamer* (see **RECLAIM**).]

re·clas·si·fy /rē'klasə,fī/ ▸ **v.** (**-fies, -fied**) [trans.] (often **be reclassified**) assign to a different class or category. — **re·clas·si·fi·ca·tion** /rē,klasəfə'kāsHən/ **n.**

re·cline /ri'klīn/ ▸ **v.** [intrans.] lean or lie back in a relaxed position with the back supported. ■ (of a seat) be able to have the back moved into a sloping position. ■ [trans.] move the back of (a seat) into a sloping position. — **re·clin·a·ble** **adj.** [ME ('cause to lean back'): from OFr. L. *reclinare* 'bend back,' from *re-* + *clinare* 'to bend.']

re·clin·er /ri'klīnər/ ▸ **n. 1** a person who reclines. **2** an upholstered armchair that can be tilted backward, esp. one with a footrest that simultaneously extends from the front.

re·clothe /rē'klōTH/ ▸ **v.** [trans.] dress again, esp. in different clothes.

rec·luse /'rek,lo͞os; ri'klo͞os; 'rek,lo͞oz/ ▸ **n.** a person who lives a solitary life and tends to avoid other people. — **re·clu·sion** /ri'klo͞ozHən/ **n.** [ME: from OFr. *reclus*, past part. of *reclure*, from L. *recludere* 'enclose,' from *re-* 'again' + *claudere* 'to shut.']

re·clu·sive /ri'klo͞osiv; -ziv/ ▸ **adj.** avoiding the company of other people; solitary: *a reclusive life in rural Ireland.* — **re·clu·sive·ness** **n.**

re·code /rē'kōd/ ▸ **v.** [trans.] put (something, esp. a computer program) into a different code. ■ assign a different code to.

rec·og·ni·tion /,rekig'nisHən/ ▸ **n.** the action or process of recognizing or being recognized, in particular: ■ identification of a thing or person from previous encounters or knowledge: *she saw him pass by without a sign of recognition.* ■ acknowledgment of something's existence, validity, or legality. ■ appreciation or acclaim for an achievement, service, or ability. ■ (also **dip·lo·mat·ic rec·og·ni·tion**) formal acknowledgment by a country that another political entity fulfills the conditions of statehood and is eligible to be dealt with as a member of the international community. — **re·cog·ni·to·ry** /ri'kägnə,tôrē/ **adj.** (rare). [15th C. ('acknowledgment'): from L. *recognitio(n-)*, from *recognoscere* (see **RECOGNIZE**).]

rec·og·niz·a·ble /,rekig'nīzəbəl/ ▸ **adj.** able to be recognized or identified from previous encounters or knowledge. — **rec·og·niz·a·bil·i·ty** /-,nīzə'bilətē/ **n.** **rec·og·niz·a·bly** /-blē/ **adv.**

re·cog·ni·zance /ri'kägnəzəns; -'känəzəns/ ▸ **n.** Law a bond by which a person undertakes before a court or magistrate to observe some condition, esp. to appear when summoned: *he was released on his own recognizance.* [ME: from OFr. *reconnissance*, from *reconnaistre* 'recognize.']

rec·og·nize /'rekig,nīz; 'rekə(g),nīz/ ▸ **v.** [trans.] **1** identify (someone or something) from having encountered them before; know again: *I recognized her when her wig fell off* | *Julia hardly recognized Jill when they met.* ■ identify from knowledge of appearance or character: *Pat is good at recognizing wildflowers.* ■ (of a computer or other machine) automatically identify and respond correctly to (a sound, printed character, etc.). **2** acknowledge the existence, validity, or legality of: *he was recognized as an international authority.* ■ officially regard (a qualification) as valid or proper. ■ grant diplomatic recognition to (a country or government). ■ show official appreciation of; reward formally. ■ (of a person presiding at a meeting or debate) call on (someone) to speak. — **rec·og·niz·er** **n.** [ME (Scots law term): from OFr. *reconniss-*, stem of *reconnaistre*, from L. *recognoscere* 'know again,' from *re-* + *cognoscere* 'learn.']

re·coil ▸ **v.** /ri'koil/ [intrans.] suddenly spring or flinch back in fear, horror, or disgust: *he recoiled in horror.* ■ feel fear, horror, or disgust at the thought or prospect of something; shrink mentally. ■ (of a gun) move abruptly backward as a reaction on firing a bullet, shell, or other missile. ■ rebound or spring back through force of impact or elasticity: *the muscle has the ability to recoil.* ■ (**recoil on/upon**) (of an action) have an adverse reactive effect on (the originator). ▸ **n.** /'rē,koil; ri'koil/ the action of recoiling. [ME ('act of retreating'): from OFr. *reculer* 'move back,' based on L. *culus* 'buttocks.']

rec·ol·lect /,rekə'lekt/ ▸ **v.** [trans.] remember (something); call to mind: *he could not recollect the reason.* [16th C. ('gather'): from L. *recollect-* 'gathered back,' from the v. *recolligere*, from *re-* + *colligere* 'collect.']

re·col·lect /,rēkə'lekt/ ▸ **v.** [trans.] collect or gather together again.

rec·ol·lec·tion /,rekə'leksHən/ ▸ **n.** the action or faculty of remembering something: *to the best of my recollection no one ever had a bad word to say about him.* ■ a thing recollected; a memory. — **rec·ol·lec·tive** /-tiv/ **adj.**

re·col·o·nize /rē'kälə,nīz/ ▸ **v.** [trans.] (chiefly of a plant or animal species) colonize (a region or habitat) again. — **re·col·o·ni·za·tion** /,rē,kälənə'zāsHən/ **n.**

re·com·bi·nant /rē'kämbənənt; ri-/ Genet. ▸ **adj.** [attrib.] of, relating to, or denoting an organism, cell, or genetic material formed by recombination. ▸ **n.** a recombinant organism, cell, or piece of genetic material.

re·com·bi·nant DNA ▸ **n.** DNA that has been formed artificially by combining constituents from different organisms.

re·com·bi·na·tion /rē,kəmbə'nāsHən/ ▸ **n.** the process of recombining things. ■ Genet. the rearrangement of genetic material, esp. by crossing over in chromosomes or by the artificial joining of segments of DNA from different organisms.

rec·om·mend /,rekə'mend/ ▸ **v.** [trans.] put forward (someone or something) with approval as being suitable for a particular purpose or role: *George had recommended some local architects.* ■ advise or suggest (something) as a course of action. ■ [with obj. and infin.] advise (someone) to do something: *you are strongly recommended to seek professional advice.* ■ make (someone or something) appealing or desirable: *the house had much to recommend it.* — **rec·om·mend·a·ble** adj. **rec·om·men·da·tion** /ˌrekəmənˈdāsHən; -ˌmen-/ n. **rec·om·mend·a·to·ry** /-ˈmendəˌtôrē/ adj. **rec·om·mend·er** n. [ME (sense 2): from med. L. *recommendare*, from L. *re-* (intensive) + *commendare* 'commit to the care of.']

re·com·mit /ˌrēkəˈmit/ ▶v. (**-mit·ted, -mit·ting**) [trans.] commit again. ■ return (a motion, proposal, or legislative bill) to a committee for further consideration. — **re·com·mit·ment** n. **re·com·mit·tal** /-ˈmitl/ n.

rec·om·pense /ˈrekəmˌpens/ ▶v. [trans.] make amends to (someone) for loss or harm suffered; compensate. ■ pay or reward (someone) for effort or work: *he was handsomely recompensed.* ■ make amends to or reward someone for (loss, harm, or effort): *he thought his loyalty had been inadequately recompensed.* ▶n. compensation or reward given for loss or harm suffered or effort made: *substantial damages were paid in recompense.* ■ archaic restitution made or punishment inflicted for a wrong or injury. [ME: from OFr., from *recompenser* 'do a favor to requite a loss,' from L. *re-* 'again' + *compensare* 'weigh one thing against another.']

re·com·pose /ˌrēkəmˈpōz/ ▶v. [trans.] compose again or differently: *a marble panel recomposed from fragments.* — **re·com·po·si·tion** /ˌrēˌkämpəˈzisHən/ n.

re·con /ˈrēˌkän; riˈkän/ ▶n. informal short for RECONNAISSANCE.

rec·on·cile /ˈrekənˌsīl/ ▶v. [trans.] (often **be reconciled**) restore friendly relations between: *she wanted to be reconciled with her father.* ■ cause to coexist in harmony; make or show to be compatible. ■ make (one account) consistent with another, esp. by allowing for transactions begun but not yet completed. ■ settle (a disagreement). ■ (**reconcile someone to**) make someone accept (a disagreeable or unwelcome thing): *he was reconciled to leaving.* — **rec·on·cil·a·bil·i·ty** /ˌrekənˌsīləˈbilətē/ n. **rec·on·cil·a·ble** /ˌrekənˈsīləbəl/ adj. **rec·on·cile·ment** n. **rec·on·cil·er** n. **rec·on·cil·i·a·tion** /ˌrekənˌsilēˈāsHən/ n. **rec·on·cil·i·a·to·ry** /ˌrekənˈsilēəˌtôrē/ adj. [ME: ult. from L. *reconciliare*, from *re-* 'back' + *conciliare* 'bring together.']

rec·on·dite /ˈrekənˌdīt; riˈkän-/ ▶adj. (of a subject or knowledge) little known; abstruse: *recondite information.* [17th C.: from L. *reconditus* 'hidden,' past part. of *recondere*, from *re-* 'back' + *condere* 'put together.']

re·con·di·tion /ˌrēkənˈdisHən/ ▶v. [trans.] condition again. ■ overhaul or renovate (a vehicle engine or piece of equipment).

re·con·nais·sance /riˈkänəzəns; -səns/ ▶n. military observation of a region to locate an enemy or ascertain strategic features: *low-level reconnaissance.* ■ preliminary surveying or research. [19th C.: from Fr., from *reconnaître* (see RECONNOITER).]

re·con·nect /ˌrēkəˈnekt/ ▶v. [trans.] connect back together: *surgeons reconnected tendons, nerves, and veins.* ■ [intrans.] reestablish a bond of communication or emotion. — **re·con·nec·tion** /ˌrēkəˈneksHən/ n.

re·con·noi·ter /ˌrēkəˈnoitər; ˌrek-/ (Brit. **re·con·noi·tre**) ▶v. [trans.] make a military observation of (a region): *they reconnoitered the beach before the landing* | [intrans.] *the raiders were reconnoitering for further attacks.* ▶n. informal an act of reconnoitering. [18th C.: from obs. Fr. *reconnoître*, from L. *recognoscere* (see RECOGNIZE).]

re·con·sid·er /ˌrēkənˈsidər/ ▶v. [trans.] consider (something) again, esp. for a possible change of decision regarding it: *they called on the government to reconsider its policy* | [intrans.] *I beg you to reconsider.* — **re·con·sid·er·a·tion** /ˌrēkənˌsidəˈrāsHən/ n.

re·con·sti·tute /rēˈkänstəˌt(y)o͞ot/ ▶v. [trans.] build up again from parts; reconstruct. ■ change the form and organization of (an institution). ■ restore (something dried, esp. food) to its original state by adding water to it. — **re·con·sti·tu·tion** /ˌrēˌkänstəˈt(y)o͞osHən/ n.

re·con·struct /ˌrēkənˈstrəkt/ ▶v. [trans.] build or form (something) again after it has been damaged or destroyed. ■ reorganize (something). ■ form an impression, model, or reenactment of (a past event or thing) from the available evidence: *it is possible to reconstruct the sequence of events.* ■ reenact (a crime or other incident) with the aim of discovering the culprit or cause. — **re·con·struct·a·ble** (also **re·con·struct·i·ble**) adj. **re·con·struc·tive** /-tiv/ adj. **re·con·struc·tor** /-tər/ n.

re·con·struc·tion /ˌrēkənˈstrəksHən/ ▶n. the action or process of reconstructing or being reconstructed: *the economic reconstruction of Russia.* ■ a thing that has been rebuilt after being damaged or destroyed: *comparison between the original and the reconstruction.* ■ an impression, model, or reenactment of a past event formed from the available evidence: *a reconstruction of the accident.* ■ (**Reconstruction**) the period 1865–77 following the Civil War, during which the states of the Confederacy were controlled by federal government and the granting of new rights to freed slaves was introduced.

re·con·vene /ˌrēkənˈvēn/ ▶v. convene or cause to convene again, esp. after a pause in proceedings: [intrans.] *the Senate reconvenes next month* | [trans.] *it was agreed to reconvene the permanent commission.*

re·con·vert /ˌrēkənˈvərt/ ▶v. [trans.] convert back to a former state: *she reconverted the basement back into an apartment.* — **re·con·ver·sion** /-ˈvərZHən/ n.

rec·ord ▶n. /ˈrekərd/ **1** a thing constituting a piece of evidence about the past, esp. an account of an act or occurrence kept in writing or some other permanent form: *dental records.* ■ (also **court rec·ord**) Law an official report of the proceedings and judgment in a court. ■ Comput. a number of related items of information that are handled as a unit. **2** the sum of the past achievements or actions of a person or organization; a person or thing's previous conduct or performance: *the safety record.* ■ short for CRIMINAL RECORD. **3** (esp. in sports) the best performance or most remarkable event of its kind that has been officially measured and noted. **4** a thin plastic disk carrying recorded sound, esp. music, in grooves on each surface, for reproduction by a record player. ■ a piece or collection of music reproduced on such a disk or on another medium, such as compact disc. ▶v. /riˈkôrd/ [trans.] **1** set down in writing or some other permanent form for later reference, esp. officially. ■ state or express publicly or officially; make an official record of: *he recorded a verdict of accidental death.* ■ (of an instrument or observer) show or register (a measurement or result): *the temperature was the lowest recorded since 1926.* ■ achieve (a certain score or result): *they recorded their first win of the season.* **2** convert (sound or a broadcast) into permanent form for later reproduction: *they recorded a guitar recital.* ■ produce (a piece or collection of music or a program) by such means.

– PHRASES **for the record** so that the true facts are recorded or known: *for the record, I have never been to the apartment.* **a matter of record** a thing that is established as a fact through being officially recorded. **off the record** not made as an official or attributable statement. **on the record** used in reference to the making of an official or public statement: *he seems shadowy because he rarely speaks on the record.* — **re·cord·a·ble** /rəˈkôrdəbəl; rē-/ adj. [ME: from OFr. *record* 'remembrance,' from *recorder* 'bring to remembrance,' from L. *recordari* 'remember,' based on *cor, cord-* 'heart.']

recorder 3

re·cord·er /riˈkôrdər/ ▶n. **1** an apparatus for recording sound, pictures, or data, esp. a tape recorder. **2** a person who keeps records: *a poet and recorder of rural and industrial life.* **3** a simple woodwind instrument with finger holes and no keys, held vertically and played by blowing air through a shaped mouthpiece against a sharp edge. **4** (**Recorder**) (in England and Wales) a barrister appointed to serve as a part-time judge. ■ Brit., hist. a judge in certain courts. — **re·cord·er·ship** /-ˌsHip/ n. (in sense 4).

re·cord·ing /riˈkôrdiNG/ ▶n. a recorded sound or picture. ■ a tape or disc on which sounds or visual images have been recorded.

re·cord·ist /riˈkôrdist/ ▶n. a person who makes recordings, esp. of sound.

rec·ord play·er ▶n. an apparatus for reproducing sound from phonograph records, comprising a turntable that spins the record at a constant speed and a stylus that slides along in the groove and picks up the sound, together with an amplifier and a loudspeaker.

re·count[1] /riˈkount/ ▶v. [reporting verb] tell someone about something; give an account of an event or experience. [ME: from Old North. Fr. *reconter* 'tell again,' based on OFr. *counter* (see COUNT[1]).]

re·count[2] ▶v. /rēˈkount; ˈrē-/ [trans.] count again. ▶n. /ˈrēˌkount/ an act of counting something again, esp. votes in an election.

re·coup /riˈko͞op/ ▶v. [trans.] regain (something lost): *rains have helped recoup water levels.* ■ regain (money spent or lost), esp. through subsequent profits. ■ reimburse or compensate (someone) for money spent or lost. ■ Law deduct or keep back (part of a sum due). ■ regain (lost physical or mental resources): *sleep was what she needed to recoup her strength* | [intrans.] *he's recouping from the trial.* — **re·coup·a·ble** adj. **re·coup·ment** n. [17th C. (legal term): from Fr. *recouper* 'retrench, cut back,' from *re-* + *couper* 'to cut.']

re·course /ˈrēˌkôrs; riˈkôrs/ ▶n. [in sing.] a source of help in a difficult situation: *surgery may be the only recourse.* ■ (**recourse to**) the use of someone or something as a source of help in a difficult situation: *all three countries **had recourse to** the loans.* ■ the legal right to demand compensation or payment.

– PHRASES **without recourse** Finance a formula used to disclaim responsibility for future nonpayment, esp. of a negotiable financial instrument. [ME ('running or flowing back'): from OFr. *recours*, from L. *recursus*, from *re-* 'back' + *cursus* 'course, running.']

re·cov·er /riˈkəvər/ ▶v. **1** [intrans.] return to a normal state of health, mind, or strength: *Neil is still **recovering from** shock* | *the economy has begun to recover.* ■ (**be recovered**) (of a person) be well again. **2** [trans.] find or regain possession of (something stolen or lost). ■ regain control of (oneself or of a physical or mental state): *I regained consciousness.* ■ regain or secure (compensation) by means of a legal process or subsequent profits: *many companies recovered their costs within six months.* ■ make up for (a loss in position or time): *the French recovered the lead.* ■ remove or extract (an energy source or industrial chemical) for use, reuse, or waste treatment. ▶n. (**the recover**) a defined position of a firearm forming part of a military drill. — **re·cov·er·er** n. [ME: from Anglo-Norman Fr. *recoverer*, from L. *recuperare* 'get again.']

re-cov·er /rē ˈkəvər; ˈrē-/ ▶v. [trans.] put a new cover or covering on: *the cost of re-covering the armchair.*

re·cov·er·a·ble /riˈkəvərəbəl/ ▶adj. **1** (of something lost) able to be regained or retrieved. ■ (of compensation or money spent or lost) able to be regained or secured by means of a legal process or subsequent profits. **2** (of an energy source or a supply of it) able to be economically extracted from the ground or sea. — **re·cov·er·a·bil·i·ty** /-ˌkəvərəˈbilətē/ n.

re·cov·er·y /riˈkəvərē/ ▶n. (pl. **-er·ies**) **1** a return to a normal state of health, mind, or strength: *signs of recovery in the housing market.* **2** the action or process of regaining possession or control of something stolen or lost: *the recovery of his sight.* ■ the action of regaining or securing compensation or money lost or spent by means of a legal process or subsequent profits: *debt recovery.* ■ an object or amount of money recovered: *the recoveries included gold jewelry.* ■ the process of removing or extracting an energy source or industrial chemical for use, reuse, or waste treatment. ■ (also **re·cov·er·y shot**) Golf a stroke bringing the ball from the rough or from a hazard back on to the fairway or the green. ■ Football an act of taking possession of a fumbled ball. ■ (in rowing, cycling, or swimming) the action of returning the paddle, leg, or arm to its initial position ready to make a new stroke.

rec·re·ant /ˈrekrēənt/ archaic ▶ **adj.** **1** cowardly. **2** unfaithful to a belief; apostate. ▶ **n.** **1** a coward. **2** a person who is unfaithful to a belief; an apostate. — **rec·re·an·cy** /-ənsē/ **n.** **rec·re·ant·ly adv.** [ME: from OFr., lit. 'surrendering,' pres. part. of *recroire*, from med. L. *(se) recredere* 'surrender (oneself),' from *re-* 'back' + *credere* 'entrust.']

re·cre·ate /ˌrēkrēˈāt/ (also **re-cre·ate**) ▶ **v.** [trans.] create again: *a single German state was recreated.* ■ reproduce; reenact: *he recreated Mallory's 1942 climb.*

rec·re·a·tion[1] /ˌrekrēˈāsʜən/ ▶ **n.** activity done for enjoyment when one is not working. [ME (also 'consolation'): ult. from L. *recreatio(n-)*, from *recreare* 'create again.']

rec·re·a·tion[2] /ˈˌrēkrēˈāsʜən/ (also **re-cre·a·tion**) ▶ **n.** the action or process of creating something again: *the periodic destruction and recreation of the universe.* ■ a reenactment or simulation of something. [16th C.: from **RE-** + **CREATION**.]

rec·re·a·tion·al /ˌrekrēˈāsʜənl/ ▶ **adj.** relating to or denoting activity done for enjoyment when one is not working: *recreational facilities | recreational cycling in the countryside.* ■ relating to or denoting drugs taken on an occasional basis for enjoyment, esp. when socializing: *recreational drug use.* — **rec·re·a·tion·al·ly adv.**

rec·re·a·tion room /ˌrekrēˈāsʜən/ ▶ **n.** a room in an institution or place of work in which people can relax and play games. ■ another term for **REC ROOM**.

rec·re·a·tive /ˈrekrēˌātiv/ ▶ **adj.** another term for **RECREATIONAL**.

re·crim·i·nate /riˈkriməˌnāt/ ▶ **v.** [intrans.] archaic make counteraccusations: *his party would never recriminate, never return evil for evil.* [17th C.: from med. L. *recriminat-* 'accused in return,' from the v. *recriminari*, from *re-* + *criminare* 'accuse' (from *crimen* 'crime').]

re·crim·i·na·tion /riˌkriməˈnāsʜən/ ▶ **n.** (usu. **recriminations**) an accusation in response to one from someone else.

re·crim·i·na·tive /riˈkriməˌnātiv/ ▶ **adj.** archaic term for **RECRIMINATORY**.

re·crim·i·na·to·ry /riˈkrimənəˌtôrē/ ▶ **adj.** involving or of the nature of mutual accusations or counteraccusations.

rec room (also chiefly dated **rec·re·a·tion room**) ▶ **n.** a room in a private house, esp. in the basement, used for recreation and entertainment.

re·cru·desce /ˌrēkro͞oˈdes/ ▶ **v.** [intrans.] formal break out again; recur. — **re·cru·des·cence** /-ˈdesns/ **n.** **re·cru·des·cent** /-ˈdesənt/ **adj.** [19th C.: back-form. from *recrudescence* 'recurrence,' from L. *recrudescere* 'become raw again,' from *re-* + *crudus* 'raw.']

re·cruit /riˈkro͞ot/ ▶ **v.** [trans.] enlist (someone) in the armed forces. ■ form (an army or other force) by enlisting new people: *recruiting an army.* ■ enroll (someone) as a member or worker in an organization or as a supporter of a cause. ■ informal persuade (someone) to do or assist in doing something: *she recruited her children to help run the racket.* ▶ **n.** a person newly enlisted in the armed forces and not yet fully trained: *army recruits.* ■ a new member of an organization or a new supporter of a cause. — **re·cruit·a·ble adj.** **re·cruit·er n.** [17th C. ('fresh body of troops' and 'to supplement'): from obs. Fr. dial. *recrute*, based on L. *recrescere* 'grow again,' from *re-* + *crescere* 'grow.']

rect. ▶ **abbr.** ■ receipt. ■ rectangle. ■ rectangular. ■ (in prescriptions) rectified. [from L. *rectificatus*.] ■ rector. ■ rectory.

rec·ta /ˈrektə/ plural form of **RECTUM**.

rec·tal /ˈrektəl/ ▶ **adj.** [attrib.] of, relating to, or affecting the rectum: *rectal cancer.* — **rec·tal·ly adv.**

rec·tan·gle /ˈrekˌtaɴggəl/ ▶ **n.** a plane figure with four straight sides and four right angles, esp. one with unequal adjacent sides, in contrast to a square. [16th C.: from med. L. *rectangulum*, ult. from L. *rectus* 'straight' + *angulus* 'angle.']

rec·tan·gu·lar /rekˈtaɴggyələr/ ▶ **adj.** **1** denoting or shaped like a rectangle: *a neat rectangular area.* ■ (of a solid) having a base, section, or side shaped like a rectangle: *a rectangular prism.* **2** placed or having parts placed at right angles. — **rec·tan·gu·lar·i·ty** /rekˌtaɴggyəˈlaritē/ **n.** **rec·tan·gu·lar·ly adv.**

rec·tan·gu·lar hy·per·bo·la ▶ **n.** a hyperbola with rectangular asymptotes.

rec·ti /ˈrekˌtī; -ˌtē/ plural form of **RECTUS**.

rec·ti·fi·er /ˈrektəˌfīər/ ▶ **n.** an electrical device that converts an alternating current into a direct one by allowing a current to flow through it in one direction only.

rec·ti·fy /ˈrektəˌfī/ ▶ **v.** (**-fies**, **-fied**) [trans.] **1** put (something) right; correct: *mistakes made now cannot be rectified later.* ■ [usu. as adj.] (**rectified**) purify or refine (a substance), esp. by repeated distillation: *rectified alcohol.* **2** convert (alternating current) to direct current: [as adj.] (**rectified**) *rectified AC power systems.* **3** find a straight line equal in length to (a curve). — **rec·ti·fi·a·ble adj.** **rec·ti·fi·ca·tion** /ˌrektəfiˈkāsʜən/ **n.** [ME: from OFr. *rectifier*, from med. L. *rectificare*, from L. *rectus* 'right.']

rec·ti·lin·e·ar /ˌrektəˈlinēər/ (also **rec·ti·lin·e·al** /-ēəl/) ▶ **adj.** contained by, consisting of, or moving in a straight line or lines: *a rectilinear waveform.* ■ Photog. of or relating to a straight line or lines: *rectilinear distortion.* ■ Photog. (of a wide-angle lens) corrected as much as possible, so that straight lines in the subject appear straight in the image. — **rec·ti·lin·e·ar·i·ty** /-ˌlinēˈaritē/ **n.** **rec·ti·lin·e·ar·ly adv.** [17th C.: from late L. *rectilineus*, from L. *rectus* 'straight' + *linea* 'line.']

rec·ti·tude /ˈrektəˌt(y)o͞od/ ▶ **n.** formal morally correct behavior or thinking; righteousness. [ME ('straightness'): ult. from late L. *rectitudo*, from L. *rectus* 'right, straight.']

rec·to /ˈrektō/ ▶ **n.** (pl. **-tos**) a right-hand page of an open book, or the front of a loose document. Contrasted with **VERSO**. [19th C.: from L. *recto (folio)* 'on the right (leaf).']

rec·to·cele /ˈrektəˌsēl/ ▶ **n.** Med. a prolapse of the wall between the rectum and the vagina. [19th C.: from **RECTUM**.]

rec·tor /ˈrektər/ ▶ **n.** **1** (in the Episcopal Church) a member of the clergy who has charge of a parish. ■ (in the Roman Catholic Church) a priest in charge of a church or of a religious institution. ■ (in the Church of England) the incumbent of a parish where all tithes formerly passed to the incumbent. Compare with **VICAR**. **2** the head of certain universities, colleges, and schools. — **rec·tor·ate** /-rət/ **n.** **rec·to·ri·al** /rekˈtôrēəl/ **adj.** **rec·tor·ship** /-ˌsʜip/ **n.** [ME: from L. *rector* 'ruler,' from *rect-* 'ruled,' from the v. *regere*.]

rec·to·ry /ˈrektərē/ ▶ **n.** (pl. **-ries**) a rector's house. ■ a Church of England benefice held by a rector.

rec·trix /ˈrekˌtriks/ ▶ **n.** (pl. **-tri·ces** /-ˌtrəsēz/) Ornithol. any of the larger feathers in a bird's tail, used for steering in flight. Compare with **REMEX**. [18th C.: from L., fem. of *rector* (see **RECTOR**).]

rec·tum /ˈrektəm/ ▶ **n.** (pl. **-tums** or **-ta** /-tə/) the final section of the large intestine, terminating at the anus. [16th C.: from L. *rectum (intestinum)* 'straight (intestine).']

rec·tus /ˈrektəs/ ▶ **n.** (pl. **-ti** /-tī/) Anat. any of several straight muscular structures, in particular, those in the abdomen and the eye. [18th C.: from L., lit. 'straight.']

re·cum·bent /riˈkəmbənt/ ▶ **adj.** (esp. of a person or human figure) lying down: *recumbent statues.* ■ denoting a bicycle designed to be ridden lying almost flat on one's back or sitting up with the legs stretched out in front. ■ (of a plant) growing close to the ground. ▶ **n.** a recumbent bicycle. — **re·cum·ben·cy n.** **re·cum·bent·ly adv.** [17th C.: from L. *recumbent-* 'reclining,' from the verb *recumbere*, from *re-* 'back' + v. akin to *cubare* 'to lie.']

re·cu·per·ate /riˈko͞opəˌrāt/ ▶ **v.** **1** [intrans.] recover from illness or exertion. **2** [trans.] recover or regain (something lost or taken): *they will recuperate the returns that go with investment.* — **re·cu·per·a·ble** /-pərəbəl/ **adj.** **re·cu·per·a·tion n.** **re·cu·per·a·tive adj.** [16th C.: from L. *recuperat-* 'regained,' from the v. *recuperare*, from *re-* 'back' + *capere* 'take.']

re·cu·per·a·tor /riˈko͞opəˌrātər/ ▶ **n.** a form of heat exchanger in which hot waste gases from a furnace are conducted continuously along a system of flues where they impart heat to incoming air or gaseous fuel.

re·cur /riˈkər/ ▶ **v.** (**-curred**, **-cur·ring**) [intrans.] occur again, periodically, or repeatedly: *the symptoms recurred.* ■ (of a thought, image, or memory) come back to one's mind. ■ (**recur to**) go back to (something) in thought or speech. — **re·cur·rence** /riˈkərəns; -ˈkə-rəns/ **n.** [ME (in the sense 'return to'): from L. *recurrere*, from *re-* 'back' + *currere* 'run.']

– USAGE **Recur** and **recurrence** are generally regarded as better style than *reoccur* and *reoccurrence*.

re·cur·rent /riˈkərənt; -ˈkə-rənt/ ▶ **adj.** **1** occurring often or repeatedly, esp. (of a disease or symptom) recurring after apparent cure or remission: *a recurrent dream about falling | recurrent fever.* **2** Anat. (of a nerve or blood vessel) turning back so as to reverse direction. — **re·cur·rent·ly adv.** [16th C. (sense 2): from L. *recurrent-* 'running back,' from the v. *recurrere* (see **RECUR**).]

re·cur·ring dec·i·mal ▶ **n.** a repeating decimal.

re·cur·sion /riˈkərzʜən/ ▶ **n.** Math. Ling. the repeated application of a recursive procedure or definition. ■ a recursive definition. [1930s: from late L. *recursio(n-)*, from *recurrere* (see **RECUR**).]

re·cur·sion for·mu·la ▶ **n.** Math. an equation relating the value of a function for a given value of its argument (or arguments) to its values for other values of the argument(s).

re·cur·sive /riˈkərsiv/ ▶ **adj.** characterized by recurrence or repetition, in particular: ■ Math. Ling. relating to or involving the repeated application of a rule, definition, or procedure to successive results. ■ Comput. relating to or involving a program or routine of which a part requires the application of the whole, so that its explicit interpretation requires in general many successive executions. — **re·cur·sive·ly adv.**

re·curve /rēˈkərv/ ▶ **v.** [intrans.] esp. Biol. bend backward: [as adj.] (**recurved**) *large recurved tusks.* ▶ **n.** Archery a bow that curves forward at the ends, which straighten out under tension when the bow is drawn. — **re·cur·va·ture** /-vəcʜər/ **n.** [16th C.: from L. *recurvare* 'bend (something) back,' from *re-* + *curvare* 'to bend.']

rec·u·sant /ˈrekyəzənt; riˈkyo͞ozənt/ ▶ **n.** a person who refuses to submit to an authority or to comply with a regulation. ■ esp. hist. a Roman

Catholic in England who refused to attend services of the Church of England. ▶ adj. of or denoting a recusant. — **rec·u·sance** n. **rec·u·san·cy** /-zənsē/ n. [16th C.: from L. *recusant-* 'refusing,' from the v. *recusare* (see RECUSE).]

re·cuse /ri'kyo͞oz/ ▶ v. [trans.] challenge (a judge, prosecutor, or juror) as unqualified to perform legal duties because of a possible conflict of interest or lack of impartiality: *a motion to recuse the prosecutor.* ■ **(recuse oneself)** (of a judge) excuse oneself from a case because of a possible conflict of interest or lack of impartiality. — **re·cus·al** /-zəl/ n. [ME ('reject'): from L. *recusare* 'to refuse,' from *re-* + *causa* 'a cause.']

re·cy·cle /rē'sīkəl/ ▶ v. [trans.] convert (waste) into reusable material. ■ return (material) to a previous stage in a cyclic process. ■ use again: *he recycled his own text.* — **re·cy·cla·bil·i·ty** /-,sīk(ə)lə'bilətē/ n. **re·cy·cla·ble** /rē'sīk(ə)ləbəl/ adj. & n. **re·cy·cler** /-k(ə)lər/ n.

red /red/ ▶ adj. **(red·der, red·dest) 1** of a color at the end of the spectrum next to orange and opposite violet, as of blood, fire, or rubies: *her red lips.* ■ (of a person or their face or complexion) flushed or rosy, esp. with embarrassment, anger, or a healthy glow. ■ (of a person's eyes) bloodshot or having pink rims, esp. with tiredness or crying. ■ (of hair or fur) of a reddish-brown color. ■ dated, offens. (of a people) having or regarded as having reddish skin. ■ of or denoting the suits hearts and diamonds in a deck of cards. ■ (of wine) made from dark grapes and colored by their skins. ■ denoting a red light or flag used as a signal to stop. ■ used to denote something forbidden, dangerous, or urgent: *the force went on red alert.* ■ (of a ski run) of the second highest level of difficulty, as indicated by colored markers. ■ Physics denoting one of three colors of quark. **2 (Red)** informal, esp. derog. communist or socialist (used esp. during the Cold War with reference to the Soviet Union). Contrasted with WHITE (sense 3). **3** stained or covered with blood. ■ archaic or literary involving bloodshed or violence: *red battle stamps his foot and nations feel the shock.* ▶ n. **1** red color or pigment: *the reds and browns of wood.* ■ red clothes or material: *she could not wear red.* **2** a red thing or person, in particular: ■ a red wine. ■ a red ball in billiards. ■ a red light. **3** (also **Red**) informal, esp. derog. a communist or socialist. **4 (the red)** the situation of owing money or showing a debit: *the company was $4,000,000 in the red.* [from the use of *red* to indicate debt items.]

– PHRASES **the red planet** a name for Mars. **see red** informal become very angry suddenly: *the mere thought of Peter with Nicole made her see red.* — **red·dish** adj. **red·dy** adj. **red·ly** adv. **red·ness** n. [OE *rēad*, of Gmc. origin.]

red. ▶ abbr. reduction.

red- ▶ prefix var. of RE- before a vowel (as in *redeem, redolent*).

re·dact /ri'dakt/ ▶ v. [trans.] rare edit (text) for publication. — **re·dac·tor** /-tər/ n. [19th C.: back-form. from REDACTION.]

re·dac·tion /ri'dakSHən/ ▶ n. the process of editing text for publication. ■ a version of a text, such as a new edition or an abridged version. — **re·dac·tion·al** /-SHənl/ adj. [18th C.: ult. from late L. *redactio(n-)*, from *redigere* 'bring back.']

red admiral

red ad·mi·ral ▶ n. a migratory butterfly (genus *Vanessa*, subfamily Nymphalinae, family Nymphalidae) that has dark wings marked with red-orange bands and white spots.

red al·gae ▶ n. a large group of algae (division Rhodophyta) that includes many seaweeds that are mainly red in color. Some kinds yield useful products (agar, alginates) or are used as food (laver, dulse, carrageen).

red-bait ▶ v. [trans.] [often as n.] **(red-baiting)** informal harass or persecute (someone) on account of known or suspected communist sympathies. — **red-bait·er** n.

red blood cell ▶ n. less technical term for ERYTHROCYTE.

red-blood·ed ▶ adj. (of a man) vigorous or virile, esp. in having strong heterosexual appetites: *a red-blooded male.* — **red-blood·ed·ness** n.

red·bone /'red,bōn/ ▶ n. a dog with a red or red and tan coat of an American breed formerly used to hunt raccoons.

red·breast /'red,brest/ ▶ n. informal a robin.

red·bud /'red,bəd/ ▶ n. a North American tree (genus *Cercis*) of the pea family, with pink flowers that grow from the trunk, branches, and twigs.

red·cap /'red,kap/ ▶ n. **1** a railroad porter. [19th C.: from the cap with a red strip worn by John Williams, New York City porter.] **2** Brit., informal a member of the military police.

red car·pet ▶ n. a long, narrow red carpet laid on the ground for a distinguished visitor to walk on when arriving. ■ **(the red carpet)** privileged treatment of a distinguished visitor.

red ce·dar ▶ n. a North American tree of the cypress family with red-dish-brown bark. Two species: the **western red cedar** (*Thuja plicata*), which yields strong, lightweight timber, and the **eastern red cedar** (*Juniperus virginiana*), found chiefly in the eastern US.

red cell ▶ n. less technical term for ERYTHROCYTE.

red cent ▶ n. a one-cent coin; a penny. ■ [usu. with negative] the smallest amount of money: *some of the people don't deserve a single red cent.* [19th C.: because it was made of copper.]

Red Cloud (1822–1909), Oglala Sioux Indian chief; Indian name *Mahpiua Luta* or *Makhpiya-luta.* He opposed, in what is known as Red Cloud's War 1865–68, government attempts to build forts along the Bozeman Trail in Wyoming and Montana.

red·coat /'red,kōt/ ▶ n. hist. a British soldier. [16th C.: from the color of the uniform.]

red cor·al ▶ n. a branching pinkish-red horny coral (genus *Corallium*, order Gorgonacea) that is used in jewelry.

Red Cres·cent a national branch in Muslim countries of the International Movement of the Red Cross and the Red Crescent.

Red Cross the International Movement of the Red Cross and the Red Crescent, a humanitarian organization that brings relief to victims of war or natural disaster.

red cur·rant (Brit. also **red·cur·rant**) ▶ n. **1** a small, sweet, edible red berry. **2** the shrub (genus *Ribes*) of the gooseberry family that produces this fruit.

redd[1] /red/ ▶ v. (past and past part. **redd**) [trans.] **(redd something up)** dialect put something in order; tidy: *you take this baby while I redd the room up.* [ME ('clear (space)'): perh. akin to RID.]

redd[2] ▶ n. a hollow in a riverbed made by a trout or salmon to spawn in. [17th C. (Scots, north. Engl. 'spawn'): origin unknown.]

red deer ▶ n. a deer (*Cervus elaphus*) with a rich red-brown summer coat that turns dull brownish-gray in winter, the male having large branched antlers. It is native to North America, Eurasia, and North Africa.

Red De·li·cious ▶ n. a widely grown dessert apple of a soft-fleshed red-skinned variety.

red·den /'redn/ ▶ v. make or become red: [trans.] *bare arms reddened by sun* | [intrans.] *the sky is reddening.* ■ [intrans.] (of a person) blush: *Lynn reddened at the description of herself.* ■ [intrans.] (of the eyes) become pink at the rims as a result of crying.

Red·ding /'rediNG/ a city in northern California; pop. 66,462.

red dwarf ▶ n. Astron. a small, old, relatively cool star.

rede /rēd/ archaic ▶ n. advice or counsel given by one person to another. ▶ v. [trans.] **1** advise (someone). **2** interpret (a riddle or dream). [OE *rǣd*, from Gmc.; akin to Ger. *Rat*; v., var. of READ.]

re·dec·o·rate /rē'dekə,rāt/ ▶ v. [trans.] decorate (a room or building) again, typically differently. — **re·dec·o·ra·tion** /,rē,dekə'rāSHən/ n.

re·deem /ri'dēm/ ▶ v. [trans.] **1** compensate for the faults or bad aspects of (something): *a disappointing debate redeemed by an outstanding speech.* ■ **(redeem oneself)** do something that compensates for poor past performance or behavior. ■ (of a person) atone or make amends for (error or evil): *the thief who redeemed a life of evil.* ■ save (someone) from sin, error, or evil: *he was a sinner, redeemed by the grace of God.* **2** gain or regain possession of (something) in exchange for payment: *his best suit had been redeemed from the pawnbrokers.* ■ Finance repay (a stock, bond, or other instrument) at the maturity date. ■ exchange (a coupon, voucher, or trading stamp) for merchandise, a discount, or money. ■ pay the necessary money to clear (a debt). ■ exchange (paper money) for gold or silver. ■ fulfill or carry out (a pledge or promise). ■ archaic buy the freedom of. — **re·deem·a·ble** adj. [ME ('buy back'): ult. from L. *redimere*, from *re(d)-* 'back' + *emere* 'buy.']

re·deem·er /ri'dēmər/ ▶ n. a person who redeems someone or something. ■ (often **the Redeemer**) Christ.

re·demp·tion /ri'dempSHən/ ▶ n. **1** the action of saving or being saved from sin, error, or evil: *God's plans for the redemption of his world.* ■ [in sing.] fig. a thing that saves someone from error or evil: *his marginalization from the Hollywood jungle proved to be his redemption.* **2** the action of regaining or gaining possession of something in exchange for payment, or clearing a debt. ■ archaic the action of buying one's freedom. [ME: from OFr., from L. *redemptio(n-)*, from *redimere* (see REDEEM).]

re·demp·tion yield ▶ n. Finance the yield of a stock calculated as a percentage of the redemption price with an adjustment made for any capital gain or loss the price represents relative to the current price.

re·demp·tive /ri'demptiv/ ▶ adj. acting to save someone from error or evil: *redemptive love.*

red en·sign ▶ n. a red flag with the Union Jack in the top corner next to the flagstaff, flown by British-registered ships.

re·de·ploy /,rēdə'ploi/ ▶ v. [trans.] assign (troops, employees, or resources) to a new place or task. — **re·de·ploy·ment** n.

re·de·vel·op /,rēdi'veləp/ ▶ v. [trans.] develop (something) again or differently. ■ erect new buildings in (an urban area), typically after demolishing the existing buildings. — **re·de·vel·op·er** n. **re·de·vel·op·ment** n.

red-eye ▶ n. **1** the undesirable effect in flash photography of people appearing to have red eyes, caused by a reflection from the retina when the flashgun is too near the camera lens. **2** (also **red-eye flight**) [in sing.] informal an overnight or late-night flight on a commercial airline. **3** a freshwater fish with red eyes, in particular a rock bass. See illustration at ROCK BASS. **4** informal cheap whiskey.

red-eye gra·vy ▶ n. gravy made by adding liquid to the fat from cooked ham.

red-faced ▶ adj. (of a person) having a red face, esp. as a result of exertion, embarrassment, or shame.

red·fish /'red,fisн/ ▶ n. (pl. same or **-fish·es**) a bright red edible marine fish, in particular: ■ a North Atlantic rockfish (genus *Sebastes*), in particular the commercially important *S. marinus*). ■ the red drum (*Sciaenops ocellatus*) of the western Atlantic, popular as a game fish.

red flag ▶ n. a red flag as a warning of danger or a problem: fig. *red flags that should have alerted them to the disastrous investment.* ■ a red flag as the symbol of socialist revolution.

red flan·nel hash ▶ n. a type of hash made with beets.

red fox ▶ n. a common fox (*Vulpes vulpes*) with a reddish coat, native to both Eurasia and North America and living from the Arctic tundra to the southern temperate regions.

red fox

red gi·ant ▶ n. Astron. a very large star of high luminosity and low surface temperature.

red gold ▶ n. an alloy of gold and copper.

red grouse ▶ n. a bird of a race of the willow ptarmigan (*Lagopus lagopus scoticus*), having entirely reddish-brown plumage, native to the British Isles.

Red Guard ▶ n. a militant youth movement in China (1966–76) that carried out attacks as part of Mao Zedong's Cultural Revolution.

red gum ▶ n. an Australian gum tree (genera *Eucalyptus* and *Angophora*) with smooth bark and hard dark red timber. ■ astringent reddish kino obtained from some of these trees, used for medicinal purposes and for tanning.

red-hand·ed ▶ adj. used to indicate that a person has been discovered in or just after the act of doing something wrong or illegal: *I caught him red-handed.*

red hat ▶ n. a cardinal's hat, esp. as the symbol of a cardinal's office.

red·head /'red,hed/ ▶ n. **1** a person with reddish hair. **2** a North American diving duck (*Aythya americana*) with a reddish-brown head, related to and resembling the pochard.

red-head·ed ▶ adj. [attrib.] (of a person) having reddish-brown hair: *a redheaded man.* ■ used in names of birds, insects, and other animals with red heads, e.g., **red-headed woodpecker**.

red heat ▶ n. the temperature or state of something so hot that it emits red light.

red her·ring ▶ n. **1** a dried smoked herring, which is turned red by the smoke. **2** something, esp. a clue, that is or is intended to be misleading or distracting: *the book is fast-paced and full of red herrings.* [because the scent of red herring is used in training hounds.]

red-hot ▶ adj. **1** (of a substance) so hot as to glow red. ■ very hot, esp. too hot to touch. **2** extremely exciting or popular: *red-hot jazz.* ■ very passionate: *a red-hot lover.*

red-hot pok·er ▶ n. a South African plant (*Kniphofia uvaria*) of the lily family, with tall erect spikes of tubular flowers, the upper ones of which are typically red and the lower ones yellow.

re·di·al ▶ v. /rē'dīl/ (**-di·aled, -di·al·ing**; Brit. **-di·alled, -di·al·ling**) [trans.] dial (a telephone number) again. ▶ n. /-'rē,dīl/ the facility on a telephone by which the number just dialed may be automatically redialed by pressing a single button.

Red In·di·an ▶ n. offens., esp. Brit. old-fashioned term for AMERICAN INDIAN.
– USAGE See usage at REDSKIN.

red·in·gote /'rediNG,gōt/ ▶ n. a woman's long coat with a cutaway or contrasting front. ■ a man's double-breasted topcoat with a full skirt. [18th C.: Fr., from Engl. *riding coat*.]

red·in·te·grate /ri'dintə,grāt/ ▶ v. [trans.] archaic restore (something) to a state of wholeness, or perfection. — **red·in·te·gra·tion** /ri,dintə'grāsHən/ n. **red·in·te·gra·tive** /-,grātiv/ adj. [ME: from L. *redintegrat-* 'made whole,' from the v. *redintegrare*, from *re(d)-* 'again' + *integrare* 'restore.']

re·di·rect /,rēdə'rekt; -,dī-/ ▶ v. [trans.] direct (something) to a new or different place or purpose: *get the post office to redirect your mail.* — **re·di·rec·tion** /-'reksHən/ n.

re·dis·count Finance /rē'dis,kount/ ▶ v. [trans.] (of a central bank) discount (a bill of exchange or similar instrument) that has already been discounted by a commercial bank. ▶ n. the action of rediscounting something.

re·dis·cov·er /,rēdis'kəvər/ ▶ v. [trans.] discover (something forgotten or ignored) again: *he was trying to rediscover his Gaelic roots.* — **re·dis·cov·er·y** /-'kəv(ə)rē/ n. (pl. **-er·ies**).

re·dis·tri·bute /,rēdə'strib,yōōt/ ▶ v. [trans.] distribute (something) differently or again, typically to achieve greater social equality: *redistribute income from rich to poor.* — **re·dis·tri·bu·tion** /,rē,distrə'byōōsHən/ n. **re·dis·trib·u·tive** /-'stribyətiv/ adj.

red·i·vi·vus /,redə'vīvəs; -'vēvəs/ ▶ adj. [postpositive] literary come back to life; reborn. [16th C.: from L., from *re(d)-* 'again' + *vivus* 'living.']

Red Jack·et (*c.*1758–1830), Seneca Indian chief; Indian name *Sagoyewatha*. He was noted as an orator and for fighting for the rights of his people.

Red·lands /'redləndz/ a city in southern California, near the San Bernardino Mountains; pop. 60,394.

red lead ▶ n. a red form of lead oxide used as a pigment.

red-let·ter day ▶ n. a day that is pleasantly noteworthy or memorable. [18th C.: from the practice of highlighting a festival in red on a calendar.]

red light ▶ n. a red traffic light or similar signal that instructs moving vehicles to stop. ■ fig. a refusal, or an order to stop an action. ■ a red light used as a signal of warning, danger, or, on a machine, operation.

red-light dis·trict ▶ n. an area of a town or city containing many brothels, strip clubs, and other sex businesses. [from the use of a red light as the sign of a brothel.]

red·line /'red,līn/ informal ▶ v. [trans.] **1** drive with (a car engine) at or above its rated maximum rpm: *both his engines were redlined now.* **2** refuse (a loan or insurance) to someone because they live in an area deemed to be a poor financial risk. ■ cancel (a project). ▶ n. the maximum number of revolutions per minute for a car engine. [from the use of *red* as a limit marker.]

red man ▶ n. dated, offens. American Indian.
– USAGE See usage at REDSKIN.

red meat ▶ n. meat that is red when raw, for example beef or lamb. Often contrasted with WHITE MEAT.

red·neck /'red,nek/ ▶ n. informal, offens. a working-class white person, esp. a politically reactionary one from a rural area: [as adj.] *a place of redneck biases.* — **red·necked** adj. [from the back of the neck being sunburned from outdoor work.]

red o·cher ▶ n. a variety of ocher, esp. used for coloring or dyeing.

red·o·lent /'redl-ənt/ ▶ adj. **1** [predic.] (**redolent of/with**) strongly reminiscent or suggestive of (something): *names redolent of history and tradition.* ■ literary strongly smelling of something: *the church was old, dark, and redolent of incense.* **2** archaic or literary fragrant or sweet-smelling: *a rich, inky, redolent wine.* — **red·o·lence** n. **red·o·lent·ly** adv. [ME ('fragrant'): ult. from L. *redolent-* 'giving out a strong smell,' from *re(d)-* 'back' + *olere* 'to smell.']

Re·don /rə'dôN/, Odilon (1840–1916), French painter. He was a leading exponent of symbolism.

re·dou·ble /rē'dəbəl/ ▶ v. [trans.] make much greater, more intense, or more numerous: *we will redouble our efforts.* ■ [intrans.] become greater or more intense or numerous: *pressure to solve the problem has redoubled.* ■ [intrans.] Bridge double a bid already doubled by an opponent. ▶ n. Bridge a call that doubles a bid already doubled by an opponent.

re·doubt /ri'dout/ ▶ n. Mil. a temporary or supplementary fortification, typically square or polygonal and without flanking defenses. ■ an entrenched stronghold or refuge. [17th C.: from Fr. *redoute*, ult. from med. L. *reductus* 'refuge,' from L. *reducere* 'withdraw.']

re·doubt·a·ble /ri'doutəbəl/ ▶ adj. often humorous (of a person) formidable, esp. as an opponent: *a redoubtable debater.* — **re·doubt·a·bly** /-blē/ adv. [ME: from OFr. *redoutable*, from *redouter* 'to fear,' from *re-* (intensive) + *douter* 'to doubt.']

re·dound /ri'dound/ ▶ v. [intrans.] **1** (**redound to**) formal contribute greatly to (a person's credit or honor): *his latest diplomatic effort will redound to his credit.* **2** (**redound upon**) archaic come back upon; rebound on: *may his sin redound upon his head!* [ME ('surge up'): from OFr. *redonder*, from L. *redundare* 'to surge,' from *re(d)-* 'again' + *unda* 'wave.']

red·out /'red,out/ ▶ n. a reddening of the vision resulting from congestion of blood in the eyes when the body is accelerated downward, sometimes followed by loss of consciousness.

re·dox /'rē,däks/ ▶ n. [usu. as adj.] Chem. a process in which one substance or molecule is reduced and another oxidized; oxidation and reduction considered together as complimentary processes. [1920s: blend.]

red pan·da ▶ n. a raccoonlike mammal (*Ailurus fulgens*) with thick reddish-brown fur and a bushy tail, native to high bamboo forests from the Himalayas to southern China. It is variously placed with the raccoon family, the bear family, or its own family (Ailurudae).

red pep·per ▶ n. the ripe red fruit of a sweet pepper. ■ another term for CAYENNE.

red phos·pho·rus ▶ n. see PHOSPHORUS.

red pine ▶ n. any of a number of coniferous trees that yield reddish timber, in particular *Pinus resinosa*, a North American pine.

red·poll /'red,pōl/ ▶ **n.** **1** a mainly brown finch (*Acanthis flammea*) with a red forehead, related to the linnet and widespread in Eurasia and North America. **2** (**Red Poll**) an animal of a breed of red-haired polled cattle.

re·draft ▶ **v.** /rē'draft/ [trans.] draft (a document, text, or map) again in a different way. ▶ **n.** /'rē,draft/ a document, text, or map that has been redrafted.

re·dress /ri'dres; 'rē,dres/ ▶ **v.** [trans.] remedy or set right (an undesirable or unfair situation): *the power to redress the grievances of our citizens.* ■ archaic set upright again: *redress a leaning wall.* ▶ **n.** remedy or compensation for a wrong or grievance.

– PHRASES **redress the balance** take action to restore equality in a situation. — **re·dress·a·ble** **adj.** **re·dress·al** /-əl/ **n.** **re·dress·er** **n.** [ME: v., from OFr. *redresser*; n., via Anglo-Norman Fr. *redresse*.]

re-dress /rē'dres; 'rē-/ ▶ **v.** [trans.] dress (someone or something) again: *he re-dressed the wound.*

Red Riv·er **1** a river in Southeast Asia that flows 730 miles (1,175 km) to the Gulf of Tonkin. Chinese name **Yuan Jiang**; Vietnamese name **Song Hong**. **2** a river in the southern US that rises in northern Texas and flows 1,222 miles (1,966 km) southeast to enter the Mississippi River in Louisiana. Also called **Red River of the South**. **3** a river in the northern US and Canada that rises in North Dakota and flows 545 miles (877 km) north to Canada's Lake Winnipeg. Also called **Red River of the North**.

Red Riv·er cart ▶ **n.** hist. a strong two-wheeled cart formerly used on the Canadian prairies.

red roan ▶ **adj.** denoting an animal's coat consisting of bay or chestnut mixed with white or gray. ▶ **n.** a red roan animal.

red salm·on ▶ **n.** another term for **sockeye**. ■ the reddish-pink flesh of the sockeye salmon used as food.

Red Sea a long, narrow, landlocked sea that separates Africa from the Arabian peninsula.

red set·ter ▶ **n.** less formal term for **Irish setter**.

red·shank /'red,shaNGk/ ▶ **n.** a large Eurasian sandpiper (esp. *Tringa totanus*) with long red legs and brown, gray, or blackish plumage.

red·shift /'red'shift/ ▶ **n.** Astron. the displacement of spectral lines toward longer wavelengths (the red end of the spectrum) in radiation from distant galaxies and celestial objects. This is interpreted as a Doppler shift that is proportional to the velocity of recession and thus to distance. Compare with **blueshift**. — **red·shift·ed** **adj.**

red·shirt /'red,shərt/ ▶ **n.** informal a college athlete who is withdrawn from college sporting events during one year in order to develop skills and extend the period of playing eligibility by a further year. ▶ **v.** [trans.] (usu. **be redshirted**) keep (an athlete) out of college competition for a year. [from the red shirts worn by such athletes.]

red-shoul·dered hawk ▶ **n.** a common North American hawk (*Buteo lineatus*) having reddish-brown shoulders and dark wings with white spots.

red·skin /'red,skin/ ▶ **n.** dated, offens. an American Indian.

– USAGE **Redskin** is first recorded in the late 17th century and was applied to the Algonquian peoples generally, but specifically to the Delaware (who lived in what is now southern New York State and New York City, New Jersey, and eastern Pennsylvania). **Redskin** referred not to the natural skin color of the Delaware, but to their use of vermilion face paint and body paint. In time, however, through a process that in linguistics is called *pejoration*, by which a neutral term acquires an unfavorable connotation or denotation, **redskin** lost its neutral, accurate descriptive sense and became a term of disparagement. **Red man** is first recorded in the early 17th century and was originally neutral in tone. **Red Indian** is first recorded in the early 19th century and was used by the British, far more than by Americans, to distinguish the Indians of the subcontinent from the Indians of the Americas. All three terms are dated or offensive or derogatory. **American Indian** and **Native American** are now the standard umbrella terms. Of course, if it is possible or appropriate, one can also use specific names (**Cheyenne**, **Nez Percé**, etc.).

red snap·per ▶ **n.** a reddish marine fish that is of commercial value as a food fish, in particular: ■ a tropical fish (genus *Lutjanus*) of the snapper family. ■ a North Pacific rockfish (*Sebastes ruberrimus*).

red spi·der (also **red spi·der mite**) ▶ **n.** see **spider mite**.

Red Square a large square in Moscow next to the Kremlin.

red squir·rel ▶ **n.** a small tree squirrel with a reddish coat, in particular the North American *Tamiasciurus hudsonicus*, which has a pale belly and a black line along the sides during the summer.

red·start /'red,stärt/ ▶ **n.** **1** an American warbler (genera *Setophaga* and *Myioborus*), the male of which is black with either a red belly or orange markings. **2** a Eurasian and North African songbird (*Phoenicurus* and other genera, family Muscicapidae) related to the chats, having a reddish tail and underparts.

red state ▶ **n.** a US state that predominantly votes for or supports the Republican Party. Compare with **blue state**. [from the typical color used to represent the Republican Party on maps during elections.]

red-tailed hawk ▶ **n.** the most common and most widespread hawk (*Buteo jamaicensis*) of North and Central America, with a reddish tail.

red tape ▶ **n.** excessive bureaucracy or adherence to rules and formalities, esp. in public business: *this law will just create more red tape.* [18th C.: from the red or pink tape used to bind official documents.]

red tide ▶ **n.** a discoloration of seawater caused by a bloom of toxic red dinoflagellates.

re·duce /ri'd(y)o͞os/ ▶ **v.** [trans.] **1** make smaller or less in amount, degree, or size: *the need to reduce costs* | [as adj.] (**reduced**) *a reduced risk of coronary disease.* ■ [intrans.] become smaller or less in size, amount, or degree. ■ boil (a sauce or other liquid) in cooking so that it becomes thicker and more concentrated. ■ [intrans.] (of a person) lose weight, typically by dieting: *by May she had reduced to 125 pounds.* ■ archaic conquer (a place), in particular besiege and capture (a town or fortress). ■ Photog. make (a negative or print) less dense. ■ Phonet. articulate (a speech sound) in a way requiring less muscular effort. In vowels, this gives rise to a more central articulatory position. **2** (**reduce someone/something to**) bring someone or something to (a lower or weaker state, condition, or role): *the church was reduced to rubble.* ■ (**be reduced to doing something**) (of a person) be forced by difficult circumstances into doing something desperate: *ordinary soldiers are reduced to begging.* ■ make someone helpless with (an expression of emotion, esp. with hurt, shock, or amusement): *Olga was reduced to stunned silence.* ■ force into (obedience or submission). **3** (**reduce something to**) change a substance to (a different or more basic form): *lava was reduced to dust.* ■ present a problem or subject in (a simplified form): *he reduces unimaginable statistics to manageable proportions.* ■ convert a fraction to (the form with the lowest terms). **4** Chem. cause to combine chemically with hydrogen. ■ undergo or cause to undergo a reaction in which electrons are gained from another substance or molecule. The opposite of **oxidize**. **5** restore (a dislocated part) to its proper position by manipulation or surgery. ■ remedy (a dislocation) in such a way.

– PHRASES **reduced circumstances** used euphemistically to refer to the state of being poor after being relatively wealthy: *a divorcée living in reduced circumstances.* **reduce someone to the ranks** demote a noncommissioned officer to an ordinary soldier. — **re·duc·er** **n.** [ME: from L. *reducere*, from *re-* 'back, again' + *ducere* 'bring, lead.']

re·duc·i·ble /ri'd(y)o͞osəbəl/ ▶ **adj.** **1** [predic.] (of a subject or problem) capable of being simplified in presentation or analysis: *Shakespeare's major soliloquies are not reducible to categories.* **2** Math. (of a polynomial) able to be factorized into two or more polynomials of lower degree. ■ (of a group) expressible as the direct product of two of its subgroups. — **re·duc·i·bil·i·ty** /ri,d(y)o͞osə'bilətē/ **n.**

re·duc·ing a·gent ▶ **n.** Chem. a substance that tends to bring about reduction by being oxidized and losing electrons.

re·duc·tant /ri'dəktənt/ ▶ **n.** Chem. a reducing agent.

re·duc·tase /ri'dək,tās; -,tāz/ ▶ **n.** [usu. with adj.] Biochem. an enzyme that promotes the chemical reduction of a specified substance.

re·duc·ti·o ad ab·sur·dum /rə'dəktē,ō,ad əb'sərdəm; -'dəkshē,ō/ ▶ **n.** Philos. a method of proving the falsity of a premise by showing that its logical consequence is absurd or contradictory. [L., lit. 'reduction to the absurd.']

re·duc·tion /ri'dəkshən/ ▶ **n.** **1** the action or fact of making a specified thing smaller or less in amount, degree, or size: ***a reduction in the number of casualties.*** ■ the amount by which something is made smaller, less, or lower in price: *special reductions on knitwear.* ■ the simplification of a subject or problem to a particular form in presentation or analysis: *the reduction of classical genetics to molecular biology.* ■ Math. the process of converting an amount from one denomination to a smaller one, or of bringing down a fraction to its lowest terms. ■ Biol. the halving of the number of chromosomes per cell that occurs at one of the two anaphases of meiosis. **2** a thing that is made smaller or less in size or amount, in particular: ■ an arrangement of an orchestral score for piano or for a smaller group of performers. ■ a thick and concentrated liquid or sauce made by boiling. ■ a copy of a picture or photograph made on a smaller scale than the original. **3** the action of remedying a dislocation or fracture by returning the affected part of the body to its normal position. **4** Chem. the process or result of reducing or being reduced. **5** Phonet. substitution of a sound that requires less muscular effort to articulate. [ME ('action of bringing back'): ult. from L. *reductio(n-)*, from *reducere* (see **reduce**).]

re·duc·tion gear ▶ **n.** a system of gearwheels in which the driven shaft rotates more slowly than the driving shaft.

re·duc·tion·ism /ri'dəkshə,nizəm/ ▶ **n.** often derog. the practice of analyzing and describing a complex phenomenon, esp. a mental, social, or biological phenomenon, in terms of phenomena that are held to represent a simpler or more fundamental level, esp. when this is said to provide a sufficient explanation. — **re·duc·tion·ist** **n. & adj.** **re·duc·tion·is·tic** /ri,dəkshə'nistik/ **adj.**

re·duc·tive /ri'dəktiv/ ▶ **adj.** **1** tending to present a subject or problem in a simplified form, esp. one viewed as crude. ■ (with reference to art) minimal: *reductive abstract shapes.* **2** of or relating to chemical reduction. — **re·duc·tive·ly** **adv.** **re·duc·tive·ness** **n.**

re·duc·tiv·ism /ri'dəktə,vizəm/ ▶ **n.** **1** another term for **minimalism**. **2** another term for **reductionism**.

re·dun·dan·cy /ri'dəndənsē/ ▶ **n.** (pl. **-cies**) the state of being no longer needed or useful: *the redundancy of 19th-century heavy plant machinery.* ■ the use of words or data that could be omitted without loss of meaning or function; repetition or superfluity of information. ■ Engin. the inclusion of extra components that are not strictly necessary to functioning, in case of failure in other components. ■ esp. Brit. the state of being no longer in employment because there is no more work available.

re·dun·dant /ri'dəndənt/ ▶ **adj.** no longer needed or useful; superfluous. ■ (of words or data) able to be omitted without loss of meaning or function. ■ Engin. (of a component) not strictly necessary to functioning but included in case of failure in another component. ■ esp. Brit. (of a person) no longer in employment because there is no more work available. — **re·dun·dant·ly** adv. [16th C. ('abundant'): from L. *redundant-* 'surging up,' from *redundare* (see REDOUND).]

re·du·pli·cate /ri'd(y)o͞opli,kāt; 'rē-/ ▶ **v.** [trans.] repeat or copy so as to form another of the same kind: *the upper parts may be reduplicated at the octave above.* ■ repeat (a syllable or other linguistic element) exactly or with a slight change, e.g., *hurly-burly, see-saw.* — **re·du·pli·ca·tion** /ri,d(y)o͞opli'kāsHən; ,rē-/ **n. re·du·pli·ca·tive** /-,kātiv/ **adj.**

re·dux /rē'dəks; 'rē'dəks/ ▶ **adj.** [postpositive] brought back; revived: *the 1980s were more than the 50s redux.* [19th C.: from L., from *reducere* 'bring back.']

red va·le·ri·an ▶ **n.** see VALERIAN.

red wig·gler ▶ **n.** another term for RED WORM (sense 1).

red·wing /'red,wiNG/ ▶ **n.** **1** a small migratory thrush (*Turdus iliacus*) that breeds mainly in northern Europe, with red underwings showing in flight. **2** any of a number of other red-winged birds, esp. the American red-winged blackbird.

red wolf ▶ **n.** a fairly small wolf (*Canis rufus*) with a cinnamon or tawny-colored coat, native to the southeastern US but possibly extinct in the wild.

red·wood /'red,wo͝od/ ▶ **n.** a giant conifer (family Taxodiaceae) with thick fibrous bark, native to California and Oregon. Two species: the **California** (or **coast**) **redwood** (*Sequoia sempervirens*) and the **giant redwood** (*Sequoiadendron giganteum*). Growing to heights of 325 feet (110 m), they are the world's tallest trees. ■ used in names of other, chiefly tropical, trees with reddish timber.

red worm ▶ **n.** **1** a red earthworm (*Lumbricus rubellus*) used in composting and as fishing bait. Also called RED WIGGLER. **2** a parasitic strongyle (genus *Strongylus*) occurring in the intestines of horses.

ree·bok ▶ **n.** var. of RHEBOK.

Reed /rēd/, Stanley Forman (1884–1980), US Supreme Court associate justice 1938–57.

reed /rēd/ ▶ **n.** **1** a tall, slender-leaved plant (genera *Phragmites* and *Arundo*) of the grass family that grows in water or on marshy ground. ■ used in names of similar plants growing in wet habitats, e.g., **bur reed.** ■ a tall, thin, straight stalk of such a plant, used esp. as material for thatching. ■ [often as adj.] such plants growing in a mass or used as material, esp. for making thatch or household items. ■ literary a rustic musical pipe made from such plants or from straw. **2** a thing or person resembling or likened to such plants, in particular: ■ a weak or impressionable person. ■ literary an arrow. ■ a weaver's comblike implement for separating the threads of the warp and correctly positioning the weft. ■ (**reeds**) a set of semicylindrical adjacent moldings like reeds laid together. **3** a piece of thin cane or metal, sometimes doubled, that vibrates in a current of air to produce the sound of various musical instruments. ■ a wind instrument played with a reed. ■ an organ stop with reed pipes. **4** an electrical contact used in a magnetically operated switch or relay. [OE *hrēod*, from West Gmc.; akin to Ger. *Ried*.]

reed·buck /'rēd,bək/ ▶ **n.** an African antelope (genus *Redunca*) with a distinctive whistling call and high bouncing jumps.

reed·ed /'rēdid/ ▶ **adj.** **1** shaped into or decorated with semicylindrical adjacent moldings. **2** (of a wind instrument) having a reed or reeds.

reed·ing /'rēdiNG/ ▶ **n.** a small semicylindrical molding or ornamentation. ■ the making of such moldings.

reed mace ▶ **n.** another term for CATTAIL.

reed or·gan ▶ **n.** a keyboard instrument similar to a harmonium, in which air is drawn upward past metal reeds.

reed pipe ▶ **n.** a simple wind instrument made from a reed or with the sound produced by a reed. ■ an organ pipe with a reed.

reed stop ▶ **n.** an organ stop controlling reed pipes.

re·ed·u·cate /rē'ejə,kāt/ ▶ **v.** [trans.] educate or train (someone) in order to change their beliefs or behavior. — **re·ed·u·ca·tion** /,rē,ejə'kāsHən/ **n.**

reed·y /'rēdē/ ▶ **adj.** (**reed·i·er, reed·i·est**) **1** (of a voice, sound, or instrument) high and thin in tone. **2** (of water or land) full of or edged with reeds. **3** (of a person) tall and thin. — **reed·i·ness n.**

reef[1] /rēf/ ▶ **n.** a ridge of jagged rock, coral, or sand just above or below the surface of the sea. ■ a vein of ore in the earth, esp. one containing gold. [16th C. (as *riff*): from Mid. Low Ger. and MDu. *rif*, from ON *rif*, lit. 'rib'; cf. REEF[2].]

reef[2] Sailing ▶ **n.** each of the several strips across a sail that can be taken in or rolled up to reduce the area exposed to the wind. ▶ **v.** [trans.] take in one or more reefs of (a sail). [ME: from MDu. *reef, rif*, from ON *rif*, lit. 'rib'; cf. REEF[1].]

reef·er[1] /'rēfər/ ▶ **n.** informal a marijuana cigarette. ■ marijuana. [1930s: perh. rel. to Mex. Sp. *grifo* '(smoker of) cannabis.']

reef·er[2] ▶ **n.** short for REEFER JACKET.

reef·er[3] ▶ **n.** informal a refrigerated truck, railroad car, or ship. [20th C.: abbrev.]

reef·er jack·et ▶ **n.** a thick, close-fitting, double-breasted jacket.

reef knot ▶ **n.** a square knot, originally used for reefing sails.

reek /rēk/ ▶ **v.** [intrans.] smell strongly and unpleasantly; stink. ■ fig. be suggestive of something unpleasant or disapproved of. ▶ **n.** **1** [in sing.] a foul smell. **2** esp. Scot. smoke. — **reek·y adj.** [OE *rēocan* 'give out smoke or vapor,' *rēc* (n.) 'smoke,' from Gmc.; akin to Ger. *riechen* 'to smell,' *Rauch* 'smoke.']

reel /rēl/ ▶ **n.** **1** a cylinder on which film, wire, thread, or other flexible materials can be wound. ■ a length of something wound on to such a device. ■ a part of a movie. ■ a device for winding and unwinding a line as required, in particular a fishing reel. **2** a lively Scottish or Irish folk dance. ■ a piece of music for such a dance, typically in simple or duple time. ■ short for VIRGINIA REEL. ▶ **v.** **1** [trans.] (**reel something in**) wind a line on to a reel by turning the reel. ■ bring something attached to a line, esp. a fish, toward one by turning a reel and winding in the line. **2** [intrans.] lose one's balance and stagger or lurch violently. ■ feel very giddy, disoriented, or bewildered, typically as a result of an unexpected setback. ■ [with adverbial of direction] walk in a staggering or lurching manner, esp. while drunk. **3** [intrans.] dance a reel.

– PHRASAL VERBS **reel (something) off** say or recite something rapidly and without apparent effort. — **reel·er n.** [OE *hrēol*.]

re·e·lect /,rēə'lekt/ ▶ **v.** [trans.] (usu. **be reelected**) elect (someone) to a further term of office. — **re·e·lec·tion** /-'leksHən/ **n.**

reel-to-reel ▶ **adj.** denoting a tape recorder in which the tape passes between two reels mounted separately rather than within a cassette.

re·e·merge /,rēə'mərj/ ▶ **v.** [intrans.] emerge again; come into sight or prominence once more. — **re·e·mer·gence** /-jəns/ **n. re·e·mer·gent** /-jənt/ **adj.**

re·en·act /,rēə'nakt/ ▶ **v.** [trans.] **1** act out (a past event). **2** bring (a law) into effect again when the original statute has been repealed. — **re·en·act·ment n.**

re·en·gi·neer /,rē,enjə'ni(ə)r/ ▶ **v.** [trans.] redesign (a device or machine). ■ [often as n.] (**reengineering**) restructure (a company or part of its operations), esp. by exploiting information technology.

re·en·trant /rē'entrənt/ ▶ **adj.** (of an angle) pointing inward. The opposite of SALIENT. ■ having an inward-pointing angle or angles. ▶ **n.** **1** a reentrant angle. ■ an indentation or depression in terrain. **2** a person who has reentered something, esp. the labor force.

re·en·try /rē 'entrē/ ▶ **n.** (pl. **-tries**) **1** the action or process of entering something again. ■ the return of a spacecraft or missile into the earth's atmosphere. **2** Law the action of retaking or repossession. **3** a visible duplication of part of the design for a postage stamp due to an inaccurate first impression. ■ a stamp displaying such a duplication.

reeve[1] /rēv/ ▶ **n.** Canadian the president of a village or town council. ■ esp. hist. a local official, in particular the chief magistrate of a town or district in Anglo-Saxon England. [OE *rēfa*.]

reeve[2] ▶ **v.** (past and past part. **rove** /rōv/ or **reeved**) [trans.] Naut. thread (a rope or rod) through a ring or other aperture, esp. in a block. ■ fasten (a rope or block) in this way. [17th C.: prob. from Du. *reven* 'reef (a sail).']

reeve[3] ▶ **n.** a female ruff. See RUFF[1] (sense 3). [17th C.: var. of dial. *ree*.]

ref /ref/ ▶ **n.** informal (in sports) a referee.

ref. ▶ **abbr.** ■ reference. ■ refer to.

re·face /rē'fās/ ▶ **v.** [trans.] put a new facing on (a building).

re·fec·tion /ri'feksHən/ ▶ **n.** literary refreshment by food or drink. ■ a meal, esp. a light one. ■ Zool. the eating of partly digested fecal pellets, as practiced by rabbits. [ME: ult. from L. *refectio(n-)*, from *reficere* (see REFECTORY).]

re·fec·to·ry /ri'fekt(ə)rē/ ▶ **n.** (pl. **-ries**) a room used for communal meals, esp. in an educational or religious institution. [ME: from late L. *refectorium*, from L. *reficere* 'refresh,' from *re-* 'back' + *facere* 'make.']

re·fec·to·ry ta·ble ▶ **n.** a long, narrow table.

re·fer /ri'fər/ ▶ **v.** (**-ferred, -fer·ring**) **1** [intrans.] (**refer to**) mention or allude to. ■ [trans.] (**refer someone to**) direct the attention of someone to. ■ (**refer to**) (of a word or phrase) describe or denote; have as a referent. **2** [trans.] (**refer something to**) pass a matter to (another body, typically one with more authority or expertise) for a decision. ■ send or direct (someone) to a medical specialist. ■ [intrans.] (**refer to**) read or otherwise use (a source of information) in order to ascertain something; consult. **3** [trans.] (**refer something to**) archaic trace or attribute something to (someone or something) as a cause or source. ■ regard something as belonging to (a certain period, place, or class). — **ref·er·a·ble** /'ref(ə)rəbəl; ri'fər-/ **adj. re·fer·rer n.** [ME: ult. from L. *referre* 'carry back,' from *re-* + *ferre* 'bring.']

ref·er·ee /,refə'rē/ ▶ **n.** **1** an official who watches a game or match closely to ensure that the rules are adhered to and (in some sports) to arbitrate on matters arising from the play. **2** a person whose opinion or judgment is sought in some connection, or who is referred to for a decision in a dispute. ■ a person willing to testify in writing about the character or ability of someone, esp. an applicant for a job. ■ a person appointed to examine and assess for publication a scientific or other academic work. ▶ **v.** (**-er·ees, -er·eed, -er·ee·ing**) **1** [trans.] officiate as referee at (a game or match). **2** act as referee.

ref·er·ence /'ref(ə)rəns/ ▶ **n.** **1** the action of mentioning or alluding to something. ■ a mention or citation of a source of information in a book or article. ■ a book or passage cited in such a way. **2** use of a source of information in order to ascertain something. ■ the sending of a matter for decision or consideration to some authority. **3** a letter from a previous employer testifying to someone's ability or reliability, used when applying for a new job. ■ a person giving this. ▶ **v.** [trans.] provide (a book or article) with citations of authorities. ▶ **adj.** of, denoting, or pertaining to a reference library.

– PHRASES **with** (or **in**) **reference to** in relation to; as regards: *war can only be explained with reference to complex social factors.*

ref·er·ence book ▶ **n.** a book intended to be consulted for information on specific matters rather than read from beginning to end.

ref·er·ence frame ▶ **n.** see FRAME OF REFERENCE.

ref·er·ence li·brar·y ▶ **n.** a library, typically one holding many reference books, in which the books are not for loan but may be read on site.

ref·er·ence point ▶ **n.** a basis or standard for evaluation, assessment, or comparison; a criterion.

ref·er·en·dum /ˌrefəˈrendəm/ ▶ **n.** (pl. **-dums** or **-da** /-də/) a general vote by the electorate on a single political question that has been referred to them for a direct decision. ■ the process of referring a political question to the electorate for this purpose. [19th C.: from L., gerund or neut. gerundive of *referre* (see REFER).]

ref·er·ent /ˈref(ə)rənt/ ▶ **n.** Ling. the thing that a word or phrase denotes or stands for. [19th C.: from L. *referent-* 'bringing back,' from *referre* (see REFER).]

ref·er·en·tial /ˌrefəˈrenCHəl/ ▶ **adj.** **1** containing or of the nature of references or allusions. **2** Ling. of or relating to a referent, in particular having the external world rather than a text or language as a referent. — **ref·er·en·ti·al·i·ty** /ˌrefəˌrenCHēˈalətē/ **n.** **ref·er·en·tial·ly** **adv.**

re·fer·ral /riˈfərəl/ ▶ **n.** an act of referring someone or something for consultation, review, or further action. ■ the directing of a patient to a medical specialist by a primary care physician. ■ a person whose case has been referred to a specialist doctor or a professional body.

re·ferred pain ▶ **n.** Med. pain felt in a part of the body other than its actual source.

re·fill ▶ **v.** /rēˈfil/ [trans.] fill (a container) again. ■ replenish the supply of (medicine called for in a prescription). ■ [intrans.] (of a container) become full again. ▶ **n.** /ˈrēˌfil/ an act of filling a container again. ■ a container, esp. a glass, that is so filled. ■ a replenished supply of medicine called for in a prescription. — **re·fill·a·ble** **adj.**

re·fi·nance /ˌrēfəˈnans; rēˈfīˌnans/ ▶ **v.** [trans.] finance (something) again, typically with a new loan at a lower rate of interest.

re·fine /riˈfīn/ ▶ **v.** [trans.] remove impurities or unwanted elements from (a substance), typically as part of an industrial process. ■ improve (something) by making small changes, in particular make (an idea, theory, or method) more subtle and accurate. — **re·fin·er** **n.** [16th C.: from RE- + FINE[1] (v.).]

re·fined /riˈfīnd/ ▶ **adj.** with impurities or unwanted elements having been removed by processing. ■ elegant and cultured in appearance, manner, or taste. ■ precise; subtle.

re·fine·ment /riˈfīnmənt/ ▶ **n.** the process of removing impurities or unwanted elements from a substance. ■ the improvement or clarification of something by the making of small changes. ■ cultured elegance in behavior or manner. ■ sophisticated and superior good taste.

re·fin·er·y /riˈfīnərē/ ▶ **n.** (pl. **-er·ies**) an industrial installation where a substance is refined.

re·fin·ish /rēˈfiniSH/ ▶ **v.** [trans.] apply a new finish to (a surface or object). ▶ **n.** an act of refinishing a surface or object.

re·fit ▶ **v.** /rēˈfit/ (**-fit·ted**, **-fit·ting**) [trans.] replace or repair machinery, equipment, and fittings in (a ship, building, etc.). ▶ **n.** /ˈrēˌfit; rēˈfit/ a restoration or repair of machinery, equipment, or fittings.

re·flag /rēˈflag/ ▶ **v.** (**-flagged**, **-flag·ging**) [trans.] change the national registry of (a ship).

re·flate /riˈflāt/ ▶ **v.** [trans.] expand the level of output of (an economy) by government stimulus, using either fiscal or monetary policy. — **re·fla·tion** /riˈflāSHən/ **n.** **re·fla·tion·ar·y** /riˈflāSHəˌnerē/ **n.** [1930s: from RE- + *-flate*, as in *inflate*.]

re·flect /riˈflekt/ ▶ **v.** **1** [trans.] (of a surface or body) throw back (heat, light, or sound) without absorbing it. ■ (of a mirror or shiny surface) show an image of. ■ embody or represent (something) in a faithful or appropriate way. ■ (of an action or situation) bring (credit or discredit) to the relevant parties. ■ [intrans.] (**reflect well/badly on**) bring about a good or bad impression of. **2** [intrans.] (**reflect on/upon**) think deeply or carefully about. [ME: ult. from L. *reflectere*, from *re-* 'back' + *flectere* 'to bend.']

re·flect·ance /riˈflektəns/ ▶ **n.** Physics the measure of the proportion of light or other radiation striking a surface that is reflected off it.

re·flect·ing tel·e·scope ▶ **n.** a telescope in which a mirror is used to collect and focus light.

re·flec·tion /riˈflekSHən/ ▶ **n.** **1** the throwing back by a body or surface of light, heat, or sound without absorbing it. ■ an amount of light, heat, or sound that is thrown back in such a way. ■ an image seen in a mirror or shiny surface. ■ a thing that is a consequence of or arises from something else. ■ [in sing.] a thing bringing discredit to someone or something. ■ Math. the conceptual operation of inverting a system or event with respect to a plane, each element being transferred perpendicularly through the plane to a point the same distance the other side of it. **2** serious thought or consideration. ■ an idea about something, esp. one that is written down or expressed. [ME: ult. from late L. *reflexio (n-)*, from L. *reflex-* 'bent back,' from the v. *reflectere*.]

re·flec·tion co·ef·fi·cient ▶ **n.** another term for REFLECTANCE.

re·flec·tive /riˈflektiv/ ▶ **adj.** **1** providing a reflection; capable of reflecting light or other radiation. ■ produced by reflection. **2** relating to or characterized by deep thought; thoughtful. — **re·flec·tive·ly** **adv.** **re·flec·tive·ness** **n.**

re·flec·tiv·i·ty /riˌflekˈtivətē; ˌrēˌflek-/ ▶ **n.** Physics the property of reflecting light or radiation, esp. reflectance as measured independently of the thickness of a material.

re·flec·tor /riˈflektər/ ▶ **n.** a piece of glass, metal, or other material for reflecting light in a required direction, e.g., a red one on the back of a motor vehicle or bicycle. ■ an object or device that reflects radio waves, seismic vibrations, sound, or other waves. ■ a reflecting telescope.

re·flex /ˈrēˌfleks/ ▶ **n.** **1** an action that is performed without conscious thought as a response to a stimulus. ■ (**reflexes**) a person's ability to perform such actions, esp. quickly. ■ (in reflexology) a response in a part of the body to stimulation of a corresponding point on the feet, hands, or head. **2** a thing that is determined by and reproduces the essential features or qualities of something else. ■ a word formed by development from an earlier stage of a language. ▶ **adj.** **1** (of an action) performed without conscious thought as an automatic response to a stimulus. **2** (of an angle) exceeding 180°. ■ (also **re·flexed**) (esp. of flower petals) bent or turned backward. — **re·flex·ly** /ˈrēˌfleksle̅; riˈflekslē/ **adv.** [16th C. ('reflection'): from L. *reflexus* 'a bending back,' from *reflectere* (see REFLECT).]

re·flex arc ▶ **n.** Physiol. the nerve pathway involved in a reflex action.

re·flex cam·er·a ▶ **n.** a camera with a ground glass focusing screen on which the image is formed by a combination of lens and mirror, enabling the scene to be correctly composed and focused.

re·flex·i·ble /riˈfleksəbəl/ ▶ **adj.** esp. tech. capable of being reflected. — **re·flex·i·bil·i·ty** /riˌfleksəˈbilətē/ **n.**

re·flex·ive /riˈfleksiv/ ▶ **adj.** **1** Gram. denoting a pronoun that refers back to the subject of the clause in which it is used, e.g., *myself*, *themselves*. ■ (of a verb or clause) having a reflexive pronoun as its object, e.g., *wash oneself*. **2** (of an action) performed as a reflex, without conscious thought. **3** Logic (of a relation) always holding between a term and itself. ▶ **n.** a reflexive word or form, esp. a pronoun. — **re·flex·ive·ly** **adv.** **re·flex·ive·ness** **n.** **re·flex·iv·i·ty** /riˌflekˈsivətē; ˌrēˌflek/ **n.**

re·flex·ol·o·gy /ˌrēˌflekˈsäləjē/ ▶ **n.** **1** a system of massage used to relieve tension and treat illness, based on the theory that there are reflex points on the feet, hands, and head linked to every part of the body. **2** Psychol. the scientific study of reflex action as it affects behavior. — **re·flex·ol·o·gist** /-jist/ **n.** (usu. in sense 1).

re·flow ▶ **n.** /ˈrēˌflō/ (in word processing) the action of rearranging text on a page having varied such features as type size, line length, and spacing. ▶ **v.** /ˈrēˌflō; rēˈflō/ [trans.] (in word processing) rearrange (text) on a page having varied such features as type size, line length, and spacing.

ref·lu·ent /ˈrefˌlo͞oənt; refˈlo͞o-/ ▶ **adj.** literary flowing back; ebbing. — **re·flu·ence** **n.** [ME: from L. *refluent-* 'flowing back,' from the v. *refluere*, from *re-* + *fluere* 'to flow.']

re·flux /ˈrēˌfləks/ ▶ **n.** tech. the flowing back of a liquid, esp. that of a fluid in the body. ▶ **v.** [intrans.] tech. (of a liquid, esp. a bodily fluid) flow back.

re·fo·cus /rēˈfōkəs/ ▶ **v.** (**-fo·cused**, **-fo·cus·ing** or **-fo·cussed**, **-fo·cus·sing**) [trans.] adjust the focus of (a lens or one's eyes). ■ focus (attention or resources) on something new or different.

re·for·est /rēˈfôrəst; -ˈfärəst/ ▶ **v.** [trans.] replant with trees; cover again with forest. — **re·for·est·a·tion** /rēˌfôrəˈstāSHən; -ˈfärə-/ **n.**

re·form /riˈfôrm/ ▶ **v.** [trans.] **1** make changes in (something, typically a social, political, or economic institution or practice) in order to improve it. ■ bring about a change in (someone) so that they no longer behave in an immoral, criminal, or self-destructive manner. ■ [intrans.] (of a person) change oneself in such a way: *I've totally reformed—no more smoking, drinking, or drugging.* **2** Chem. subject (hydrocarbons) to a catalytic process in which straight-chain molecules are converted to branched forms for use as gasoline. ▶ **n.** the action or process of reforming an institution or practice. ▶ **adj.** (**Reform**) of, denoting, or pertaining to Reform Judaism. — **re·form·a·ble** **adj.** **re·form·a·tive** /-mətiv/ **adj.** **re·form·er** **n.** [ME ('restore'): ult. from L. *reformare*, from *re-* 'back' + *formare* 'to form.']

re-form /ˈrēˈfôrm/ ▶ **v.** form or cause to form again. — **re-for·ma·tion** /ˌrēˌfôrˈmāSHən/ **n.**

ref·or·ma·tion /ˌrefərˈmāSHən/ ▶ **n.** **1** the action or process of reforming an institution or practice. **2** (**the Reformation**) a 16th-century movement for the reform of abuses in the Roman Catholic Church ending in the establishment of the Reformed and Protestant Churches. — **ref·or·ma·tion·al** /-SHənl/ **adj.** [ME: from L. *reformatio(n-)*, from *reformare* 'shape again' (see REFORM).]

re·form·a·to·ry /riˈfôrməˌtôrē/ ▶ **n.** (pl. **-ries**) an institution to which youthful offenders are sent as an alternative to prison; a reform school. ▶ **adj.** tending or intended to produce reform.

Re·formed Church ▶ **n.** a church that has accepted the principles of the Reformation, esp. a Calvinist church (as distinct from Lutheran).

re·form·ist /riˈfôrmist/ ▶ **adj.** supporting or advancing gradual reform rather than abolition or revolution. ▶ **n.** a person who advocates gradual reform rather than abolition or revolution. — **re·form·ism** /-ˌmizəm/ **n.**

Re·form Ju·da·ism ▶ n. a form of Judaism, initiated in Germany by the philosopher Moses Mendelssohn (1729–86), that has reformed or abandoned aspects of Orthodox Jewish worship and ritual in an attempt to adapt to modern life. — **Re·form Jew** n.

re·form school ▶ n. an institution to which youthful offenders are sent as an alternative to prison.

re·fract /ri'frakt/ ▶ v. [trans.] (usu. **be refracted**) (of water, air, or glass) make (a ray of light) change direction when it enters at an angle. ■ measure the focusing characteristics of (an eye) or of the eyes of (someone). [17th C.: from L. *refract-* 'broken up,' from the v. *refringere*, from *re-* 'back' + *frangere* 'to break.']

re·fract·ing tel·e·scope ▶ n. a telescope that uses a converging lens to collect light.

re·frac·tion /ri'fraksʜən/ ▶ n. Physics the fact or phenomenon of light, radio waves, etc., being deflected in passing obliquely through the interface between one medium and another or through a medium of varying density. ■ change in direction of propagation of any wave as a result of its traveling at different speeds at different points along the wave front. ■ measurement of the focusing characteristics of an eye or eyes. — **re·frac·tive** /-tiv/ adj. **re·frac·tive·ly** /-tivlē/ adv.

re·frac·tive in·dex ▶ n. the ratio of the velocity of light in a vacuum to its velocity in a specified medium.

re·frac·tor /ri'fraktər/ ▶ n. a lens or other object that causes refraction. ■ a refracting telescope.

re·frac·to·ry /ri'fraktərē/ ▶ adj. formal **1** stubborn or unmanageable. **2** resistant to a process or stimulus. ■ Med. (of a person, illness, or diseased tissue) not yielding to treatment. ■ tech. (of a substance) resistant to heat; hard to melt or fuse. ▶ n. (pl. **-ries**) tech. a substance that is resistant to heat. — **re·frac·to·ri·ness** n. [17th C.: alt. of obs. *refractary*, from L. *refractarius* 'stubborn' (see also REFRACT).]

re·frain¹ /ri'frān/ ▶ v. [intrans.] stop oneself from doing something. [ME ('restrain (a thought)'): ult. from L. *refrenare*, from *re-* (intensive force) + *frenum* 'bridle.']

re·frain² ▶ n. a repeated line or number of lines in a poem or song, typically at the end of each verse. ■ the musical accompaniment for such a line or number of lines. ■ a comment or complaint that is often repeated. [ME: from OFr., from *refraindre* 'break,' based on L. *refringere* 'break up' (because the refrain "broke" the sequence).]

re·fran·gi·ble /ri'franjəbəl/ ▶ adj. able to be refracted. — **re·fran·gi·bil·i·ty** /ri,franjə'bilətē/ n. [17th C.: from mod. L. *refrangibilis*, from *refrangere* (see REFRACT).]

re·fresh /ri'fresʜ/ ▶ v. [trans.] give new strength or energy to; reinvigorate. ■ stimulate or jog (someone's memory) by checking or going over previous information. ■ revise or update (skills or knowledge). ■ Comput. update the display on (a screen). ■ pour more (drink) for someone or refill (a container) with drink. ■ place or keep (food) in cold water so as to cool it or maintain its freshness. ▶ n. Comput. an act or function of updating the display on a screen. [ME: from OFr. *refreschier*, from *re-* 'back' + *fres(che)* 'fresh.']

re·fresh·er /ri'fresʜər/ ▶ n. a thing that refreshes, in particular: ■ [usu. as adj.] an activity that revises or updates one's skills or knowledge. ■ dated a drink.

re·fresh·er course ▶ n. a short course reviewing or updating previous studies or training.

re·fresh·ing /ri'fresʜiɴɢ/ ▶ adj. serving to refresh or reinvigorate someone. ■ welcome or stimulating because new or different. — **re·fresh·ing·ly** adv.

re·fresh·ment /ri'fresʜmənt/ ▶ n. **1** (usu. **refreshments**) a light snack or drink, esp. one provided in a public place or at a public event. **2** the giving of fresh mental or physical strength or energy.

re·fried beans /'rē,frīd/ ▶ plural n. pinto beans boiled and fried in advance and reheated when required, used esp. in Mexican cooking.

re·frig·er·ant /ri'frijərənt/ ▶ n. a substance used for refrigeration. ▶ adj. causing cooling or refrigeration.

re·frig·er·ate /ri'frijə,rāt/ ▶ v. [trans.] subject (food or drink) to cold in order to chill or preserve it, typically by placing it in a refrigerator. — **re·frig·er·a·tion** /ri,frijə'rāsʜən/ n. **re·frig·er·a·to·ry** /ri'frijərə,tôrē/ adj. [ME: from L. *refrigerat-* 'made cool,' from the v. *refrigerare*, from *re-* 'back' + *frigus, frigor-* 'cold.']

re·frig·er·at·ed /ri'frijə,rātid/ ▶ adj. (of food or drink) chilled, esp. in a refrigerator. ■ (of a vehicle or container) used to keep or transport food or drink in a chilled condition.

re·frig·er·a·tor /ri'frijə,rātər/ ▶ n. an appliance or compartment that is artificially kept cool and used to store food and drink.

re·frin·gent /ri'frinjənt/ ▶ adj. Physics refractive. — **re·frin·gence** n. [18th C.: from L. *refringent-*, lit. 'breaking again,' from the v. *refringere*.]

reft /reft/ past and past participle of REAVE.

re·fuel /rē'fyōō(ə)l/ ▶ v. (**-fu·eled**, **-fu·el·ing** ; Brit. **-fu·elled**, **-fu·el·ling**) [trans.] supply (a vehicle) with more fuel. ■ [intrans.] (of a vehicle) be supplied with more fuel.

ref·uge /'ref,yōōj; -,yōōzʜ/ ▶ n. a condition of being safe or sheltered from pursuit, danger, or trouble. ■ something providing such shelter. ■ an institution providing safe accommodations for women who have suffered violence from a husband or partner. [ME: from OFr., from L. *refugium*, from *re-* 'back' + *fugere* 'flee.']

ref·u·gee /,refyŏŏ'jē; 'refyŏŏ,jē/ ▶ n. a person who has been forced to leave their country in order to escape war, persecution, or natural disaster. [17th C.: from Fr. *réfugié* 'gone in search of refuge,' past part. of *(se) réfugier*, from *refuge* (see REFUGE).]

re·fu·gi·um /ri'fyōōjēəm/ ▶ n. (pl. **-gi·a** /-jēə/) Biol. an area in which organisms can survive through a period of unfavorable conditions, esp. glaciation. [1950s: from L., lit. 'place of refuge.']

re·ful·gent /ri'fŏŏljənt; -'fəl-/ ▶ adj. literary shining brightly. — **re·ful·gence** n. **re·ful·gent·ly** adv. [15th C.: from L. *refulgent-* 'shining out,' from the v. *refulgere*, from *re-* (intensive force) + *fulgere* 'to shine.']

re·fund¹ ▶ v. /ri'fənd; 'rē,fənd/ [trans.] pay back (money), typically to a customer who is not satisfied with goods or services bought. ■ pay back money to (someone). ▶ n. /'rē,fənd/ a repayment of a sum of money, typically to a dissatisfied customer. — **re·fund·a·ble** adj. [ME ('pour back,' 'restore'): ult. from L. *refundere*, from *re-* + *fundere* 'pour.']

re·fund² /rē'fənd; 'rē-/ ▶ v. fund (a debt, etc.) again.

re·fur·bish /ri'fərbisʜ/ ▶ v. [trans.] (usu. **be refurbished**) renovate and redecorate (something, esp. a building). — **re·fur·bish·ment** n.

re·fus·al /ri'fyōōzəl/ ▶ n. [usu. with infin.] an act or an instance of refusing; the state of being refused. ■ see FIRST REFUSAL.

ref·use¹ /ri'fyōōz/ ▶ v. [intrans.] indicate or show that one is not willing to do something. ■ [trans.] indicate that one is not willing to accept or grant (something offered or requested). ■ informal (of a thing) fail to perform a required action. ■ [trans.] dated decline to accept an offer of marriage from (someone). ■ [trans.] (of a horse) stop short or run alongside (a fence or other obstacle) instead of jumping it. — **re·fus·er** n. [ME: from OFr. *refuser*, prob. an alt. of L. *recusare* 'to refuse,' influenced by *refutare* 'refute.']

ref·use² /'ref,yōōs; -,yōōz/ ▶ n. matter thrown away or rejected as worthless; trash. [ME: perh. from OFr. *refusé* 'refused,' past part. of *refuser* (see REFUSE¹).]

re·fuse·nik /ri'fyōōznik/ ▶ n. **1** a person in the former Soviet Union who was refused permission to emigrate, in particular, a Jew forbidden to emigrate to Israel. **2** a person who refuses to follow orders or obey the law. [1970s: from REFUSE¹.]

re·fute /ri'fyōōt/ ▶ v. [trans.] prove (a statement or theory) to be wrong or false; disprove. ■ prove that (someone) is wrong. ■ deny or contradict (a statement or accusation). — **re·fut·a·ble** adj. **re·fut·al** /-'fyōōtl/ n. (rare) **ref·u·ta·tion** /,refyŏŏ'tāsʜən/ n. **re·fut·er** n. [16th C.: from L. *refutare* 'repel, rebut.']

re·gain /ri'gān/ ▶ v. [trans.] obtain possession or use of (something, typically something abstract) again after losing it. ■ reach (a place, position, or thing) again; get back to. [16th C.: from Fr. *regagner* (see RE-, GAIN).]

re·gal /'rēgəl/ ▶ adj. of, resembling, or fit for a monarch, esp. in being magnificent or dignified. — **re·gal·ly** adv. [ME: ult. from L. *regalis*, from *rex, reg-* 'king.']

re·gale /ri'gāl/ ▶ v. [trans.] entertain or amuse (someone) with talk. ■ lavishly supply (someone) with food or drink. [17th C.: from Fr. *régaler*, from *re-* (intensive force) + OFr. *gale* 'pleasure.']

re·ga·li·a /ri'gālyə/ ▶ plural n. [treated as sing. or pl.] the emblems or insignia of royalty, esp. the crown, scepter, and other ornaments used at a coronation. ■ the distinctive clothing worn and ornaments carried at formal occasions as an indication of status. ■ distinctive, elaborate clothing. [16th C. ('royal powers'): from med. L., lit. 'royal privileges,' from L., neut. pl. of *regalis* 'regal.']

re·gal·i·ty /ri'galətē/ ▶ n. (pl. **-ties**) the state of being a king or queen. ■ the demeanor or dignity appropriate to a king or queen.

re·gard /ri'gärd/ ▶ v. [trans.] consider or think of (someone or something) in a specified way. ■ gaze at steadily in a specified fashion. ■ [trans.] (of a thing) have relation to or connection with; concern. ▶ n. **1** attention to or concern for something. ■ high opinion; liking and respect; esteem. ■ [in sing.] a gaze; a steady or significant look. **2** (**regards**) best wishes (used to express friendliness in greetings, esp. at the end of letters). [ME: from OFr. *regarder* 'to watch,' from *re-* 'back' + *garder* 'to guard.']

re·gard·ant /ri'gärdnt/ ▶ adj. [usu. postpositive] Heraldry looking backward. [ME: from Anglo-Norman Fr. and OFr., pres. part. of *regarder* 'look (again).']

re·gard·ful /ri'gärdfəl/ ▶ adj. [predic.] (**regardful of**) formal paying attention to; mindful of. — **re·gard·ful·ly** adv.

re·gard·ing /ri'gärdiɴɢ/ ▶ prep. with respect to; concerning.

re·gard·less /ri'gärdləs/ ▶ adv. without paying attention to the present situation; despite the prevailing circumstances. — **re·gard·less·ly** adv.

re·gat·ta /ri'gätə; ri'gatə/ ▶ n. a sporting event consisting of a series of boat or yacht races. [17th C.: from Ital. (Venetian dial.), lit. 'a fight, contest.']

re·gen·cy /'rējənsē/ ▶ n. (pl. **-cies**) the office or period of government by a regent. ■ a commission acting as regent. ■ (**the Regency**) the particular period of a regency, esp. (in Britain) from 1811 to 1820 and (in France) from 1715 to 1723. ▶ adj. (**Regency**) relating to or denoting British architecture, clothing, and furniture of the Regency or, more widely, of the late 18th and early 19th centuries. [ME: from med. L. *regentia*, from L. *regent-* 'ruling' (see REGENT).]

re·gen·er·ate ▶ v. /riˈjenəˌrāt/ [trans.] (of a living organism) regrow (new tissue) to replace lost or injured tissue. ■ [intrans.] (of an organ or tissue) regrow. ■ bring into renewed existence; generate again. ■ bring new and more vigorous life to (an area or institution), esp. in economic terms; revive. ■ (esp. in Christian use) give a new and higher spiritual nature to. ■ [usu. as adj.] (**regenerated**) Chem. precipitate (a natural polymer such as cellulose) in a different form following chemical processing, esp. in the form of fibers. ▶ adj. /riˈjenərət/ reformed or reborn, esp. in a spiritual or moral sense. — **re·gen·er·a·tor** /-ˌrātər/ n. [ME (adj.): from L. *regeneratus* 'created again,' past part. of *regenerare*, from *re-* + *generare* 'create.']

re·gen·er·a·tion /riˌjenəˈrāsʜən; ˌrē-/ ▶ n. the action or process of regenerating or being regenerated, in particular the formation of new animal or plant tissue. ■ Electron. positive feedback. ■ Chem. the action or process of regenerating polymer fibers.

re·gen·er·a·tive /riˈjenərətiv; -ˌrātiv/ ▶ adj. tending to or characterized by regeneration. ■ denoting a method of braking in which energy is extracted from the parts braked, to be stored and reused. — **re·gen·er·a·tive·ly** adv.

re·gent /ˈrējənt/ ▶ n. **1** a person appointed to administer a country because the monarch is a minor or is absent or incapacitated. **2** a member of the governing body of a university or other academic institution. ▶ adj. [postpositive] acting as regent for a monarch. [ME: ult. from L. *regent-* 'ruling,' from the v. *regere*.]

reg·gae /ˈregā; ˈrāgā/ ▶ n. a style of popular music with a strongly accented subsidiary beat, originating in Jamaica. It evolved in the late 1960s from ska and other local variations on calypso and rhythm and blues. [perh. akin to Jamaican Engl. *rege-rege* 'quarrel.']

reg·gae·ton /ˈregāˌtōn/ ▶ n. a form of dance music of Puerto Rican origin, characterized by a fusion of Latin rhythms, dancehall, and hip-hop or rap. [21st C.: from REGGAE and Sp. *-ton*, on the pattern of *marathon*.]

Reg·gio di Ca·la·bri·a /ˈrej(ē)ōdē käˈlābrēä/ a port at the southern tip of Italy, on the Strait of Messina; pop. 183,000.

reg·i·cide /ˈrejəˌsīd/ ▶ n. the action of killing a king. ■ a person who kills or takes part in killing a king. — **reg·i·cid·al** /ˌrejəˈsīdl/ adj. [16th C.: from L. *rex, reg-* 'king.']

re·gift /rēˈgift/ ▶ v. [trans.] give (a gift one has received) to someone else. ▶ n. an item that has been regifted. — **re·gift·er** n.

re·gime /riˈzʜēm; rā-/ (also **ré·gime**) ▶ n. **1** a government, esp. an authoritarian one. **2** a system or planned way of doing things, esp. one imposed from above. ■ a coordinated program for the promotion or restoration of health; a regimen. ■ the conditions under which a scientific or industrial process occurs. [15th C. ('regimen'): Fr. *régime*, from L. *regimen* 'rule' (see REGIMEN).]

reg·i·men /ˈrejəmən; ˈrezʜ-/ ▶ n. a prescribed course of medical treatment, way of life, or diet for the promotion or restoration of health. [ME ('action of governing'): from L., from *regere* 'to rule.']

reg·i·ment ▶ n. /ˈrejəmənt/ a permanent unit of an army typically commanded by a colonel and divided into several companies, squadrons, or batteries and often into two battalions. ■ an operational unit of artillery. ■ a large array or number of people or things. ▶ v. /ˈrejəˌment/ [trans.] (usu. **be regimented**) **1** organize according to a strict, sometimes oppressive system or pattern. **2** rare form (troops) into a regiment or regiments. — **reg·i·men·tal** /ˌrejəˈmentl/ adj. **reg·i·men·tal·ly** /ˌrejəˈmentl-ē/ adv. **reg·i·men·ta·tion** /ˌrejəmənˈtāsʜən; -ˌmen-/ n. [ME ('rule or government'): via OFr. from late L. *regimentum* 'rule,' from *regere* 'to rule.']

Re·gi·na[1] /rəˈjīnə/ the capital of Saskatchewan, in south central Canada; pop. 179,178.

Re·gi·na[2] /rəˈjēnə/ ▶ n. (in the UK) the reigning queen (used following a name or in the titles of lawsuits, e.g., *Regina v. Jones*, the Crown versus Jones). [L., lit. 'queen.']

Re·gi·o·mon·ta·nus /ˌrāgē-ōˌmônˈtānəs; ˌrējē-ōˌmänˈtānəs/, Johannes (1436–76), German astronomer and mathematician; born *Johannes Müller*. He translated Ptolemy's *Mathematical Syntaxis* and wrote four monumental works on mathematics and astronomy.

re·gion /ˈrējən/ ▶ n. an area or division, esp. part of a country or the world having definable characteristics but not always fixed boundaries. ■ an administrative district of a city or country. ■ a part of the body, esp. around or near an organ. ■ fig. the sphere or realm of something.
– PHRASES **in the region of** approximately. [ME: ult. from L. *regio(n-)* 'direction, district,' from *regere* 'to rule.']

re·gion·al /ˈrējənl; ˈrējnəl/ ▶ adj. of, relating to, or characteristic of a region. ▶ n. (**regionals**) an athletic contest involving competitors from a particular region. — **re·gion·al·ly** adv.

re·gion·al·ism /ˈrējənlˌizəm; ˈrējnə-/ ▶ n. **1** the theory or practice of regional rather than central systems of administration or economic, cultural, or political affiliation. **2** a linguistic feature peculiar to a particular region and not part of the standard language of a country. — **re·gion·al·ist** n. & adj.

re·gion·al·ize /ˈrējənlˌīz; ˈrējnəˌlīz/ ▶ v. [trans.] [usu. as adj.] (**regionalized**) organize (a country, area, or enterprise) on a regional basis. — **re·gion·al·i·za·tion** /ˌrējənl-əˈzāsʜən; ˌrējnələ-/ n.

re·gis·seur /ˌrāzʜēˈsər/ ▶ n. a person who stages a theatrical production, esp. a ballet. [from Fr. *régisseur*.]

reg·is·ter /ˈrejəstər/ ▶ n. **1** an official list or record, for example of births, marriages, and deaths, of shipping, or of historic places. ■ a book or record of attendance, for example of students in a class or school or guests in a hotel. **2** a particular part of the range of a voice or instrument. ■ a sliding device controlling a set of organ pipes that share a tonal quality. ■ a set of organ pipes so controlled. **3** Ling. a variety of a language or a level of usage, as determined by degree of formality and choice of vocabulary, pronunciation, and syntax, according to the communicative purpose, social context, and social status of the user. **4** Print. & Photog. the exact correspondence of the position of color components in a printed positive. ■ Print. the exact correspondence of the position of printed matter on the two sides of a page. **5** (in electronic devices) a location in a store of data, used for a specific purpose and with quick access time. **6** an adjustable plate for widening or narrowing an opening and regulating a draft, esp. in a fire grate. **7** short for CASH REGISTER. **8** Art one of a number of bands or sections into which a design is divided. ▶ v. [trans.] **1** enter or record in an official list as being in a particular category, having a particular eligibility or entitlement, or in keeping with a requirement. ■ [intrans.] put one's name on an official list under such terms. ■ [intrans.] put one's name in a register as a guest in a hotel. ■ [intrans.] (of a couple to be married) have a list of wedding gifts compiled and kept at a store for consultation by gift buyers. ■ entrust (a letter or parcel) to a post office for transmission by registered mail. ■ express (an opinion or emotion). **2** (of an instrument) detect and show (a reading) automatically. ■ [intrans.] (of an event) give rise to a specified reading on an instrument. ■ [usu. with negative] properly notice or become aware of (something). ■ [intrans.] [usu. with negative] make an impression on a person's mind. ■ [intrans.] (of an emotion) show in a person's face or gestures. ■ indicate or convey (a feeling or emotion) by facial expression or gestures. **3** Print. & Photog. correspond or cause to correspond exactly in position. — **reg·is·tra·ble** /-st(ə)rəbəl/ adj. [ME: from OFr. *regestre* or med. L. *registrum*, alt. of *regestum*, sing. of late L. *regesta* 'things recorded,' from *regerere* 'enter, record.']

reg·is·tered mail ▶ n. prepaid first class mail that is recorded by the post office at each point along its route to safeguard against loss or damage.

reg·is·tered nurse (abbr.: **RN**) ▶ n. a fully trained nurse with an official certificate of competence.

reg·is·ter ton ▶ n. see TON[1] (sense 1).

reg·is·trant /ˈrejəstrənt/ ▶ n. a person who registers.

reg·is·trar /ˈrejəˌsträr/ ▶ n. an official responsible for keeping a register or official records. ■ an official in a college or university who is responsible for keeping student records. — **reg·is·trar·ship** /-ˌsʜip/ n. [17th C.: from med. L. *registrarius*, from *registrum* (see REGISTER).]

reg·is·tra·tion /ˌrejəˈstrāsʜən/ ▶ n. the action or process of registering or of being registered. ■ a certificate that attests to the registering of (a person, automobile, etc.). ■ Music a combination of stops used when playing the organ.

reg·is·try /ˈrejəstrē/ ▶ n. (pl. **-tries**) **1** a place or office where registers or records are kept. **2** an official list or register. **3** registration. **4** the nationality of a merchant ship.

reg·let /ˈreglit/ ▶ n. **1** Print. a thin strip of wood or metal used to separate type. **2** Archit. a narrow strip used to separate moldings or panels from one another. [17th C.: from Fr. *réglet*, dimin. of *règle* 'rule.']

reg·nant /ˈregnənt/ ▶ adj. **1** [often postpositive] reigning; ruling. **2** currently having the greatest influence; dominant. [17th C.: from L. *regnant-* 'reigning,' from the v. *regnare*.]

reg·o·lith /ˈregəˌlitʜ/ ▶ n. Geol. the layer of unconsolidated solid material covering the bedrock of a planet. [19th C.: from Gk. *rhēgos* 'rug, blanket' + -LITH.]

re·gorge /rēˈgôrj/ ▶ v. [intrans.] gush or flow back again. [17th C.: from Fr. *regorger*, or from RE- 'again' + the v. GORGE.]

re·gress ▶ v. /riˈgres/ **1** [intrans.] return to a former or less developed state. ■ return mentally to a former stage of life or a supposed previous life, esp. through hypnosis or mental illness. **2** [trans.] Stat. calculate the coefficient or coefficients of regression of (a variable) against or on another variable. **3** [intrans.] Astron. move in a retrograde direction. ▶ n. /ˈrēˌgres/ **1** the action of returning to a former or less developed state. **2** Philos. a series of statements in which a logical procedure is continually reapplied to its own result without approaching a useful conclusion (e.g., defining something in terms of itself). [ME (n.): from L. *regressus*, from *regredi* 'go back,' from *re-* + *gradi* 'walk.']

re·gres·sion /riˈgresʜən/ ▶ n. **1** a return to a former or less developed state. ■ a return to an earlier stage of life or a supposed previous life, esp. through hypnosis or mental illness, or as a means of escaping present anxieties. ■ a lessening of the severity of a disease or its symptoms. **2** Stat. a measure of the relation between the mean value of one variable (e.g., output) and corresponding values of other variables (e.g., time and cost).

re·gres·sive /riˈgresiv/ ▶ adj. **1** becoming less advanced; returning to a former or less developed state. ■ of, relating to, or marked by psychological regression. **2** (of a tax) taking a proportionally greater amount from those on lower incomes. **3** Philos. proceeding from effect to cause or from particular to universal. — **re·gres·sive·ly** adv. **re·gres·sive·ness** n.

re·gret /riˈgret/ ▶ v. (**-gret·ted, -gret·ting**) [trans.] feel sad, repentant, or disappointed over (something that has happened or been done, esp. a loss or missed opportunity). ■ used in polite formulas to express apology for or sadness over something unfortunate or unpleasant. ▶ n. a feeling of sadness, repentance, or disappointment over something that has happened or been done. ■ (often **regrets**) an instance or cause of such a feeling. ■ (often **one's regrets**) used in polite formulas to express apology for or sadness at an occurrence or an inability to accept an invitation. [ME: from OFr. *regreter* 'bewail (the dead),' perh. from the Gmc. base of GREET.]

re·gret·ful /ri'gretfəl/ ▶ **adj.** feeling or showing regret. — **re·gret·ful·ness** n.

re·gret·ful·ly /ri'gretfəlē/ ▶ **adv.** in a regretful manner. ■ [sentence adverb] regrettably.

re·gret·ta·ble /ri'gretəbəl/ ▶ **adj.** (of conduct or an event) giving rise to regret; undesirable; unwelcome.

re·gret·ta·bly /ri'gretəblē/ ▶ **adv.** [sentence adverb] unfortunately (used to express apology for or sadness at something).

re·group /rē'groop/ ▶ **v.** [intrans.] (of troops) reassemble into organized groups, typically after being attacked or defeated. ■ [trans.] cause to reassemble in this way. ■ [trans.] rearrange (something) into a new group or groups. — **re·group·ment** n.

regs /regz/ informal ▶ **abbr.** regulations.

Regt ▶ **abbr.** ■ Regent. ■ Regiment.

reg·u·la·ble /'regyələbəl/ ▶ **adj.** able to be regulated.

reg·u·lar /'regyələr/ ▶ **adj.** **1** arranged in or constituting a constant or definite pattern, esp. with the same space between individual instances. ■ happening in such a pattern with the same time between individual instances; recurring at short uniform intervals. ■ (of a person) doing the same thing or going to the same place with the same time between individual instances. ■ (of a structure or arrangement) arranged in or constituting a symmetrical or harmonious pattern. ■ (of a person) defecating or menstruating at predictable times. **2** done or happening frequently. ■ (of a person) doing the same thing or going to the same place frequently. **3** conforming to or governed by an accepted standard of procedure or convention. ■ [attrib.] of or belonging to the permanent professional armed forces of a country. ■ (of a person) properly trained or qualified and pursuing a full-time occupation. ■ Christian Church subject to or bound by religious rule; belonging to a religious or monastic order. Contrasted with SECULAR (sense 2). ■ informal rightly so called; complete; absolute (used for emphasis). **4** used, done, or happening on a habitual basis; usual; customary. ■ of a normal or ordinary kind; not special. ■ (chiefly in commercial use) denoting merchandise, esp. food or clothing, of average, medium, or standard size. ■ (of a person) not pretentious or arrogant; ordinary and friendly. ■ (of coffee) of a specified type, such as caffeinated, or prepared in a specified way, such as black or with cream. ■ (in surfing and other board sports) with the left leg in front of the right on the board. **5** Gram. (of a word) following the normal pattern of inflection. **6** Geom. (of a figure) having all sides and all angles equal. ■ (of a solid) bounded by a number of equal figures. **7** Bot. (of a flower) having radial symmetry. ▶ **n.** a regular customer or member, for example of a bar, store, or team. ■ a regular member of the armed forces. ■ a member of a political party who is faithful to that party. ■ Christian Church one of the regular clergy. — **reg·u·lar·ly** adv. [ME: from OFr. *reguler*, from L. *regularis*, from *regula* 'rule.']

reg·u·lar·i·ty /,regyə'laritē/ ▶ **n.** (pl. **-ties**) the state or quality of being regular.

reg·u·lar·ize /'regyələ,rīz/ ▶ **v.** [trans.] make (something) regular. ■ establish (a hitherto temporary or provisional arrangement) on an official or correct basis. — **reg·u·lar·i·za·tion** /,regyələrə'zāsнən/ n.

reg·u·late /'regyə,lāt/ ▶ **v.** [trans.] control or maintain the rate or speed of (a machine or process) so that it operates properly. ■ control or supervise (something, esp. a company or business activity) by means of rules and regulations. ■ set (a clock or other apparatus) according to an external standard. — **reg·u·la·tive** /-,lātiv/ adj. [ME ('control by rules'): from late L. *regulat-* 'directed,' from the v. *regulare*, from L. *regula* 'rule.']

reg·u·la·tion /,regyə'lāsнən/ ▶ **n.** **1** a rule or directive made and maintained by an authority. ■ [as adj.] in accordance with regulations; of the correct type. ■ [as adj.] informal of a familiar or predictable type; formulaic; standardized. **2** the action or process of regulating or being regulated.

reg·u·la·tor /'regyə,lātər/ ▶ **n.** a person or thing that regulates something, in particular: ■ a person or body that supervises a particular industry or business activity. ■ a device for controlling the rate of working of machinery or for controlling fluid flow, in particular a handle controlling the supply of steam to the cylinders of a steam engine. ■ a device for adjusting the balance of a clock or watch in order to regulate its speed.

reg·u·la·to·ry /'regyələ,tôrē/ ▶ **adj.** serving or intended to regulate something.

Reg·u·lus /'regyələs/ Astron. the brightest star in the constellation Leo. It is a triple system of which the primary is a hot dwarf star. [L., lit. 'little king.']

re·gur·gi·tate /ri'gərjə,tāt/ ▶ **v.** [trans.] bring (swallowed food) up again to the mouth. ■ fig. repeat (information) without analyzing or comprehending it. — **re·gur·gi·ta·tion** /ri,gərjə'tāsнən/ n. [16th C.: from med. L. *regurgitat-*, from the v. *regurgitare*, from L. *re-* 'again, back' + *gurges, gurgit-* 'whirlpool.']

re·hab /'rē,hab/ informal ▶ **n.** rehabilitation. ■ a thing, esp. a building, that has been rehabilitated or restored. ▶ **v.** (**-habbed, -hab·bing**) [trans.] rehabilitate or restore. — **re·hab·ber** n.

re·ha·bil·i·tate /,rē(h)ə'bilə,tāt/ ▶ **v.** [trans.] restore (someone) to health or normal life by training and therapy after imprisonment, addiction, or illness. ■ restore (someone) to former privileges or reputation after a period of critical or official disfavor. ■ return (something, esp. an environmental feature) to its former condition. — **re·ha·bil·i·ta·tion** /-,bilə'tāsнən/ n. **re·ha·bil·i·ta·tive** /-,tātiv/ adj. [16th C. ('restore to former privileges'): from med. L. *rehabilitat-*, from the v. *rehabilitare* (see RE-, HABILITATE).]

re·hang ▶ **v.** /rē'haNG/ (past and past part. **-hung** /-'həNG/) [trans.] hang (something) again or differently. ▶ **n.** /'rē,haNG/ an act of rehanging works of art in a gallery.

re·hash ▶ **v.** /rē'hasн/ [trans.] put (old ideas or material) into a new form without significant change or improvement. ■ consider or discuss (something) at length after it has happened. ▶ **n.** /'rē,hasн/ a reuse of old ideas or material without significant change or improvement.

re·hear /rē'hi(ə)r/ ▶ **v.** (past and past part. **-heard** /-'hərd/) hear or listen to again. ■ Law hear (a case or plaintiff) in a court again.

re·hears·al /ri'hərsəl/ ▶ **n.** a practice or trial performance of a play or other work for later public performance. ■ the action or process of rehearsing.

re·hearse /ri'hərs/ ▶ **v.** [trans.] practice (a play, piece of music, or other work) for later public performance. ■ supervise (a performer or group) that is practicing in this way. ■ mentally prepare or recite (words one intends to say). ■ state (a list of points, esp. those that have been made many times before); enumerate. — **re·hears·er** n. [ME ('repeat aloud'): from OFr. *rehercier* (see HEARSE).]

re·heat ▶ **v.** /rē'hēt/ [trans.] heat (something, esp. cooked food) again. ▶ **n.** the process of using the hot exhaust to burn extra fuel in a jet engine and produce extra power. ■ an afterburner. — **re·heat·er** n.

re·heel /rē'hēl/ ▶ **v.** [trans.] fit (a shoe) with a new heel.

Rehn·quist /'ren,kwist/, William Hubbs (1924–2005), Chief Justice of the US 1986–2005. He was appointed by President Nixon as an associate justice to the US Supreme Court in 1972.

re·ho·bo·am /,rē(h)ə'bōəm/ ▶ **n.** a wine bottle of about six times the standard size. [19th C.: from *Rehoboam*, king of Israel *c.*915 BC.]

re·house /rē'houz/ ▶ **v.** [trans.] (usu. **be rehoused**) provide (someone) with new housing.

re·hung /rē'həNG/ past and past participle of REHANG.

re·hy·drate /rē'hī,drāt/ ▶ **v.** absorb or cause to absorb moisture after dehydration. — **re·hy·drat·a·ble** adj. **re·hy·dra·tion** /,rēhī'drāsнən/ n.

Reich /rīk; rīкн/ the former German state, most often used to refer to the Third Reich, the Nazi regime from 1933 to 1945. The **First Reich** was the Holy Roman Empire, 962–1806, and the **Second Reich** the German Empire, 1871–1918, but neither of these terms is part of normal historical terminology. [Ger., lit. 'empire.']

Reichs·mark /'rīks,märk; 'rīкнs-/ ▶ **n.** the basic monetary unit of the Third Reich, replaced in 1948 by the Deutschmark. [Ger.]

Reichs·tag /'rīks,täg; 'rīкнs-/ the main legislature of the German state under the Second and Third Reichs. ■ the building in which this met. [Ger., from *Reichs* 'of the empire' + *Tag* 'diet' (see DIET[2]).]

Reid /rēd/, Whitelaw (1837–1912), US journalist. He was the owner and editor-in-chief of the *New York Tribune* 1872–1905.

re·i·fy /'rēə,fī/ ▶ **v.** (**-fies, -fied**) [trans.] formal make (something abstract) more concrete or real. — **re·i·fi·ca·tion** /,rēəfə'kāsнən/ n. **re·if·i·ca·to·ry** /rē'ifəkə,tôrē/ adj. [19th C.: from L. *res, re-* 'thing.']

reign /rān/ ▶ **v.** [intrans.] hold royal office; rule as king or queen. ■ [usu. as adj.] (**reigning**) (of an athlete or team) currently hold a particular title. ■ (of a quality or condition) prevail; predominate. ▶ **n.** the period during which a sovereign rules. ■ the period of prevalence or domination of a specified thing. ■ the period during which an athlete or team holds a specified title. [ME: from OFr. *reignier* 'to reign,' *reigne* 'kingdom,' from L. *regnum*, rel. to *rex, reg-* 'king.']

reign of ter·ror ▶ **n.** a period of remorseless repression or bloodshed, in particular (**Reign of Terror**), the period of the Terror during the French Revolution.

re·im·burse /,rē-im'bərs/ ▶ **v.** [trans.] (often **be reimbursed**) repay (a person who has spent or lost money). ■ repay (a sum of money that has been spent or lost). — **re·im·burs·a·ble** adj. **re·im·burse·ment** n. [17th C.: from RE- 'back, again' + obs. *imburse* 'put in a purse,' from med. L. *imbursare*, from *in-* 'into' + late L. *bursa* 'purse.']

re·im·port ▶ **v.** /,rē-im'pôrt/ [trans.] import (goods processed or made from exported materials). ▶ **n.** /,rē-impôrt/ the action of reimporting something. ■ a reimported item. — **re·im·por·ta·tion** /,rē,impôr'tāsнən/ n.

re·im·pose /,rē-im'pōz/ ▶ **v.** [trans.] impose (something, esp. a law or regulation) again after a lapse. — **re·im·po·si·tion** /,rēimpə'zisнən/ n.

Reims /rēmz; rans/ (also **Rheims**) a city in northern France; pop. 185,000. It was the traditional coronation place for most French kings.

rein /rān/ ▶ **n.** (usu. **reins**) a long, narrow strap attached at one end to a horse's bit, typically used in pairs to control a horse in riding or driving. ■ fig. the power to direct and control. ▶ **v.** [trans.] cause (a horse) to stop or slow down by pulling on its reins. ■ cause (a horse) to change direction by pulling on its reins. ■ keep under control; restrain.

– PHRASES **draw rein** stop one's horse. **(a) free rein** freedom of action or expression: *he was given free rein to work out his designs.* **keep a tight rein on** exercise strict control over; allow little freedom to. [ME: from OFr. *rene*, based on L. *retinere* 'retain.']

re·in·car·nate ▶ v. /ˌrē-inˈkärˌnāt/ [trans.] (often **be reincarnated**) cause (someone) to undergo rebirth in another body. ■ [intrans.] (of a person) be reborn in this way. ▶ adj. /-nət/ [usu. postpositive] reborn in another body.

re·in·car·na·tion /ˌrē-inkärˈnāsHən/ ▶ n. the rebirth of a soul in a new body. ■ a person or animal in whom a particular soul is believed to have been reborn. ■ fig. the newest version or closest match of something from the past.

rein·deer /ˈrānˌdi(ə)r/ ▶ n. (pl. same or **-deers**) a deer (genus *Rangifer*) of the tundra and subarctic regions of Eurasia and North America, both sexes of which have large branching antlers. Most Eurasian reindeer are domesticated and used for drawing sleds and as a source of milk, flesh, and hide. [ME: from ON *hreindýri*, from *hreinn* 'reindeer' + *dýr* 'deer.']

rein·deer moss ▶ n. a large branching bluish-gray lichen (*Cladonia rangiferina*, order Cladoniales) that grows in arctic and subarctic regions, sometimes providing the chief winter food of reindeer.

re·in·force /ˌrē-inˈfôrs/ ▶ v. [trans.] strengthen or support, esp. with additional personnel or material. ■ strengthen (an existing feeling, idea, or habit). — **re·in·forc·er** n. [ME: from Fr. *renforcer*, influenced by *inforce*, obs. spelling of ENFORCE.]

re·in·forced con·crete ▶ n. concrete in which wire or metal bars are embedded to increase its tensile strength.

re·in·force·ment /ˌrē-inˈfôrsmənt/ ▶ n. the action or process of reinforcing or strengthening. ■ the process of encouraging or establishing a belief or pattern of behavior, esp. by encouragement or reward. ■ (**reinforcements**) extra personnel sent to increase the strength of an army or similar force. ■ the strengthening structure or material employed in reinforced concrete or plastic.

re·in·state /ˌrē-inˈstāt/ ▶ v. [trans.] (often **be reinstated**) restore (someone or something) to their former position or condition. — **re·in·state·ment** n.

re·in·sure /ˌrē-inˈsHŏŏr/ ▶ v. [trans.] (of an insurer) transfer (all or part of a risk) to another insurer to provide protection against the risk of the first insurance. — **re·in·sur·ance** /-ˈsHŏŏrəns/ n. **re·in·sur·er** n.

re·in·te·grate /rēˈintəˌgrāt/ ▶ v. [trans.] restore (elements regarded as disparate) to unity. ■ restore to a position as a part fitting easily into a larger whole. — **re·in·te·gra·tion** /ˌrēintəˈgrāsHən/ n.

re·in·tro·duce /ˌrē-intrəˈd(y)o͞os/ ▶ v. [trans.] bring (something, esp. a law or system) into existence or effect again. ■ put (a species of animal or plant) back into a region where it formerly lived. — **re·in·tro·duc·tion** /-ˈdəksHən/ n.

re·in·vent /ˌrē-inˈvent/ ▶ v. [trans.] change (something) so much that it appears to be entirely new. ■ (**reinvent oneself**) take up a radically new job or way of life.
– PHRASES **reinvent the wheel** waste a great deal of time or effort in creating something that already exists. — **re·in·ven·tion** /-ˈvencHən/ n.

re·in·vest /ˌrē-inˈvest/ ▶ v. [trans.] put (the profit on a previous investment) back into the same place. — **re·in·vest·ment** /-ˈvestmənt/ n.

re·is·sue /rēˈisHo͞o/ ▶ v. (**-is·sues**, **-is·sued**, **-is·su·ing**) [trans.] make a new supply or different form of (a product, esp. a book or record) available for sale. ▶ n. a new issue of such a product.

REIT ▶ abbr. real-estate investment trust.

re·it·er·ate /rēˈitəˌrāt/ ▶ v. [reporting verb] say something again or a number or times, typically for emphasis or clarity. — **re·it·er·a·tion** /rēˌitəˈrāsHən/ n. **re·it·er·a·tive** /-ˌrātiv; -rətiv/ adj. [ME ('do repeatedly'): from L. *reiterat-* 'gone over again,' from the v. *reiterare*, from *re-* + *iterare* 'do a second time.']

reive /rēv/ ▶ v. [intrans.] [usu. as n.] (**reiving**) esp. Scot. another term for REAVE. — **reiv·er** n. [ME: var.]

re·ject ▶ v. /riˈjekt/ [trans.] dismiss as inadequate, inappropriate, or not to one's taste. ■ refuse to agree to (a request). ■ fail to show due affection or concern for (someone); rebuff. ■ Med. show an immune response to (a transplanted organ or tissue) so that it fails to survive. ▶ n. /ˈrēˌjekt/ a person or thing dismissed as failing to meet standards or satisfy tastes. — **re·ject·ee** /riˌjekˈtē; ˌrē-/ n. **re·jec·tion** /riˈjeksHən/ n. **re·jec·tor** /-tər/ n. [ME: from L. *reject-* 'thrown back,' from the v. *reicere*, from *re-* 'back' + *jacere* 'to throw.']

re·jec·tion·ist /riˈjeksHənist/ ▶ n. [often as adj.] a person who rejects a proposed policy, esp. an Arab who refuses to accept a negotiated peace with Israel.

re·jec·tion slip ▶ n. a formal notice sent by an editor or publisher to an author with a rejected manuscript or typescript.

re·jig·ger /rēˈjigər/ (Brit. **re·jig**) ▶ v. [trans.] organize (something) differently; rearrange.

re·joice /riˈjois/ ▶ v. [intrans.] feel or show great joy or delight. — **re·joic·er** n. **re·joic·ing·ly** adv. [ME ('cause joy to'): from OFr. *rejoiss-*, lengthened stem of *rejoir*, from *re-* (intensive force) + *joir* 'experience joy.']

re·join[1] /rēˈjoin; ˈrē-/ ▶ v. [trans.] join together again; reunite. ■ return to (a companion, organization, or route that one has left).

re·join[2] /riˈjoin/ ▶ v. [reporting verb] say something in answer to a remark, typically rudely or in a discouraging manner. [ME (in the sense '(in law) reply to a charge'): from OFr. *rejoindre*, from *re-* 'again' + *joindre* 'to join.']

re·join·der /riˈjoindər/ ▶ n. a reply, esp. a sharp or witty one. ■ Law, dated a defendant's answer to the plaintiff's reply or replication. [ME: from Anglo-Norman Fr. *rejoindre* (infinitive) (see REJOIN[2]).]

re·ju·ve·nate /riˈjo͞ovəˌnāt/ ▶ v. [trans.] make (someone or something) look or feel younger, fresher, or more lively. ■ [often as adj.] (**rejuvenated**) restore (a river or stream) to a condition characteristic of a younger landscape. — **re·ju·ve·na·tion** /riˌjo͞ovəˈnāsHən/ n. **re·ju·ve·na·tor** /-ˌnātər/ n. [19th C.: from RE- + L. *juvenis* 'young.']

re·ju·ve·nes·cence /riˌjo͞ovəˈnesəns/ ▶ n. the renewal of youth or vitality. ■ Biol. the reactivation of vegetative cells, resulting in regrowth from old or injured parts. — **re·ju·ve·nes·cent** /-ˈnesənt/ adj. [17th C.: from late L. *rejuvenescere*, from L. *re-* 'again' + *juvenis* 'young.']

rel. ▶ abbr. ■ relating. ■ relative. ■ relatively. ■ released. ■ religion. ■ religious.

-rel ▶ suffix forming nouns with diminutive or derogatory force such as *cockerel*, *pickerel*, *scoundrel*. [from OFr. *-erel(le)*.]

re·laid /rēˈlād; ˈrē-/ past and past participle of RELAY[2].

re·lapse /riˈlaps; ˈrēˌlaps/ ▶ v. [intrans.] (of someone suffering from a disease) suffer deterioration after a period of improvement. ■ (**relapse into**) return to (a less active or a worse state). ▶ n. /ˈrēˌlaps/ a deterioration in someone's state of health after a temporary improvement. — **re·laps·er** n. [ME: from L. *relaps-* 'slipped back,' from the v. *relabi*, from *re-* 'back' + *labi* 'to slip.' Early senses referred to a return to heresy or wrongdoing.]

re·laps·ing fe·ver ▶ n. an infectious bacterial disease marked by recurrent fever, caused by spirochetes of the genus *Borrelia*.

re·late /riˈlāt/ ▶ v. [trans.] **1** give an account of (a sequence of events); narrate. **2** (**be related**) be connected by blood or marriage. ■ be causally connected. ■ (**relate something to**) discuss something in such a way as to indicate its connections with (something else). ■ [intrans.] (**relate to**) have reference to; concern. ■ [intrans.] (**relate to**) feel sympathy with; identify with. — **re·lat·a·ble** adj. [16th C.: from L. *relat-* 'brought back,' from the v. *referre* (see REFER).]

re·lat·ed /riˈlātid/ ▶ adj. belonging to the same family, group, or type; connected. ■ [in comb.] associated with the specified item or process, esp. causally: *income-related benefits*. — **re·lat·ed·ness** n.

re·la·tion /riˈlāsHən/ ▶ n. **1** the way in which two or more concepts, objects, or people are connected; a thing's effect on or relevance to another. ■ (**relations**) the way in which two or more people, countries, or organizations feel about and behave toward each other. ■ (**relations**) esp. formal sexual intercourse. **2** a person who is connected by blood or marriage; a kinsman or kinswoman. **3** the action of telling a story.
– PHRASES **in relation to** in the context of; in connection with. [ME: ult. from L. *relatio(n-)*, from *referre* 'bring back' (see RELATE).]

re·la·tion·al /riˈlāsHənl/ ▶ adj. concerning the way in which two or more people or things are connected. — **re·la·tion·al·ly** adv.

rela·tion·al da·ta·base ▶ n. Comput. a database structured to recognize relations between stored items of information.

re·la·tion·ship /riˈlāsHənˌsHip/ ▶ n. the way in which two or more concepts, objects, or people are connected, or the state of being connected. ■ the state of being connected by blood or marriage. ■ the way in which two or more people or organizations regard and behave toward each other. ■ an emotional and sexual association between two people.

rel·a·tive /ˈrelətiv/ ▶ adj. **1** considered in relation or in proportion to something else: *the relative effectiveness of the mechanism is not known*. ■ existing or possessing a specified characteristic only in comparison to something else; not absolute. **2** Gram. denoting a pronoun, determiner, or adverb that refers to an expressed or implied antecedent and attaches a subordinate clause to it, e.g., *which, who*. ■ (of a clause) attached to an antecedent by a relative word. **3** Music (of major and minor keys) having the same key signature. **4** (of a service rank) corresponding in grade to another in a different service. ▶ n. **1** a person connected by blood or marriage. ■ a species related to another by common origin. **2** Gram. a relative pronoun, determiner, or adverb. **3** Philos. a term, thing, or concept that is dependent on something else.
– PHRASES **relative to 1** in comparison with. ■ in terms of a connection to. **2** in connection with; concerning. — **rel·a·tiv·al** /ˌreləˈtīvəl/ adj. (in sense 2 of the noun).

rel·a·tive hu·mid·i·ty ▶ n. the amount of water vapor present in air expressed as a percentage of the amount needed for saturation at the same temperature.

rel·a·tive·ly /ˈrelətivlē/ ▶ adv. [sentence adverb] in relation, comparison, or proportion to something else. ■ [as submodifier] viewed in comparison with something else rather than absolutely: *relatively affluent people*.

rel·a·tiv·ism /ˈrelətəˌvizəm/ ▶ n. the doctrine that knowledge, truth, and morality exist in relation to culture, society, or historical context, and are not absolute. — **rel·a·tiv·ist** n.

rel·a·tiv·is·tic /ˌrelətəˈvistik/ ▶ adj. **1** Physics accurately described only by the theory of relativity. **2** of or relating to the doctrine of relativism. — **rel·a·tiv·is·ti·cal·ly** /-ik(ə)lē/ adv.

rel·a·tiv·i·ty /ˌreləˈtivətē/ ▶ n. **1** the absence of standards of absolute and universal application. **2** Physics the dependence of various physical phenomena on relative motion of the observer and the observed objects, esp. regarding the nature and behavior of light, space, time, and gravity.

rel·a·tiv·ize /ˈrelətəˌvīz/ ▶ v. [trans.] esp. Ling. & Philos. make or treat as relative to or dependent on something else. ■ Gram. & Ling. make into a relative clause. ■ Physics treat (a phenomenon or concept) according to the principles of the theory of relativity. — **rel·a·tiv·i·za·tion** /ˌrelətəvəˈzāsHən/ n.

re·la·tor /riˈlātər/ ▶ n. Law a person who brings a public lawsuit, typically in the name of the attorney general, regarding the abuse of an office or franchise.

re•launch ▶ **v.** /rēˈlôncH; -ˈläncH/ [trans.] cause to start again with renewed vigor after a period of inactivity. ■ reintroduce (a product). ▶ **n.** an instance of reintroducing or restarting something, esp. a product.

re•lax /riˈlaks/ ▶ **v.** make or become less tense or anxious. ■ [intrans.] rest or engage in an enjoyable activity so as to become less tired or anxious. ■ [trans.] cause (a limb or muscle) to become less rigid. ■ make (something) less firm or tight. ■ [trans.] make (a rule or restriction) less strict while not abolishing it. — **re•lax•er n.** [ME: from L. *relaxare*, from *re-* (intensive force) + *laxus* 'loose.']

re•lax•ant /rəˈlaksənt/ ▶ **n.** a drug used to promote relaxation or reduce tension. ■ a thing having a relaxing effect. ▶ **adj.** causing relaxation.

re•lax•a•tion /ˌrilakˈsāsHən; rē-/ ▶ **n. 1** the state of being free from tension and anxiety. ■ recreation or rest, esp. after a period of work. ■ the loss of tension in a part of the body, esp. in a muscle when it ceases to contract. ■ the action of making a rule or restriction less strict. **2** Physics the restoration of equilibrium following disturbance.

re•laxed /riˈlakst/ ▶ **adj.** free from tension and anxiety. ■ (of a muscle or other body part) not tense. — **re•lax•ed•ly** /riˈlaksədlē/ **adv.** **re•lax•ed•ness** /riˈlaksədnəs/ **n.**

re•lax•in /rəˈlaksin/ ▶ **n.** Biochem. a hormone secreted by the placenta that causes the cervix to dilate and prepares the uterus for the contractions during labor.

re•lay[1] ▶ **n.** /ˈrēˌlā/ **1** a group of people or animals engaged in a task or activity for a fixed period of time and then replaced by a similar group. ■ [usu. as adj.] a race between teams usually of sprinters or swimmers, each team member in turn covering part of the total distance. **2** an electrical device, typically incorporating an electromagnet, that is activated by a current or signal in one circuit to open or close another circuit. **3** a device to receive, reinforce, and retransmit a broadcast or program. ■ a message or program transmitted by such a device. ▶ **v.** /riˈlā; ˈrēˌlā/ [trans.] receive and pass on (information or a message). ■ broadcast (something) by passing signals received from elsewhere through a transmitting station. [ME ('(in hunting) fresh hounds'): from OFr. *relai* (n.), *relayer* (v.), based on L. *laxare* 'slacken.']

re•lay[2] /rēˈlā/ ▶ **v.** (past and past part. **-laid**) [trans.] lay again or differently.

re•lease /riˈlēs/ ▶ **v.** [trans.] **1** allow or enable to escape from confinement; set free. ■ remove restrictions or obligations from (someone or something) so that they become available for other activity. ■ allow (information) to be generally available. ■ make (a movie or recording) available for general viewing or purchase. ■ allow (something concentrated in a small area) to spread and work freely. ■ remove (part of a machine or appliance) from a fixed position, allowing something else to move or function. ■ allow (something) to return to its resting position by ceasing to put pressure on it. **2** Law remit or discharge (a debt). ■ surrender (a right). ■ make over (property or money) to another. ▶ **n. 1** the action or process of releasing or being released. ■ the action of making a movie, recording, or other product available for general viewing or purchase. ■ a movie or other product issued for viewing or purchase. ■ a press release. ■ a handle or catch that releases part of a mechanism. **2** Law the action of releasing property, money, or a right to another. ■ a document effecting this. — **re•leas•a•ble adj. re•leas•ee** /riˌlēˈsē/ **n.** (Law). **re•leas•er n. re•leas•or** /riˈlēsər/ **n.** (Law). [ME: from OFr. *reles* (n.), *relesser* (v.), from L. *relaxare* 'stretch out again, slacken' (see RELAX).]

rel•e•gate /ˈreləˌgāt/ ▶ **v.** [trans.] consign or dismiss to an inferior rank or position. — **rel•e•ga•tion** /ˌreləˈgāsHən/ **n.** [ME ('send into exile'): from L. *relegat-* 'sent away,' from the v. *relegare*, from *re-* 'again' + *legare* 'send.']

re•lent /riˈlent/ ▶ **v.** [intrans.] abandon or mitigate a harsh intention or cruel treatment. ■ (esp. of bad weather) become less severe or intense. [ME ('dissolve, melt'): based on L. *re-* 'back' + *lentare* 'to bend' (from *lentus* 'flexible').]

re•lent•less /riˈlentləs/ ▶ **adj.** oppressively constant; incessant. ■ harsh or inflexible. — **re•lent•less•ly adv. re•lent•less•ness n.**

rel•e•vant /ˈreləvənt/ ▶ **adj.** closely connected or appropriate to the matter at hand. — **rel•e•vance n. rel•e•van•cy** /-vənsē/ **n. rel•e•vant•ly adv.** [16th C. ('(Scots law) legally pertinent'): from med. L. *relevant-* 'raising up,' from L. *relevare*.]

re•le•vé /ˌreləˈvā/ ▶ **n. 1** Ballet a movement in which the dancer rises on the tips of the toes. **2** Ecol. each of a number of small plots of vegetation, analyzed as a sample of a wider area. [Fr., lit. 'raised up.']

re•li•a•ble /riˈlīəbəl/ ▶ **adj.** consistently good in quality or performance; able to be trusted. ▶ **n.** a person or thing with such trustworthy qualities. — **re•li•a•bil•i•ty** /riˌlīəˈbilətē/ **n. re•li•a•ble•ness n. re•li•a•bly** /-blē/ **adv.**

re•li•ance /riˈlīəns/ ▶ **n.** dependence on or trust in someone or something. — **re•li•ant** /-ənt/ **adj.**

rel•ic /ˈrelik/ ▶ **n.** an object surviving from an earlier time, esp. one of historical or sentimental interest. ■ a part of a deceased holy person's body or belongings kept as an object of reverence. ■ an object, custom, or belief that has survived from an earlier time but is now outmoded. ■ (**relics**) all that is left of something. [ME: from OFr. *relique*, from L. *reliquiae* (see RELIQUIAE).]

rel•ict /ˈrelikt/ ▶ **n. 1** a thing that has survived from an earlier period or in a primitive form. ■ an animal or plant that has survived while others of its group have become extinct, e.g., the coelacanth. ■ a species or community that formerly had a wider distribution but now survives in only a few localities such as refugia. [20th C.: from L. *relictus* 'left behind,' from v. *relinquere*.] **2** archaic a widow. [ME: from OFr. *relicte* '(woman) left behind,' from late L. *relicta*, from *relinquere*.]

re•lief /riˈlēf/ ▶ **n. 1** a feeling of reassurance and relaxation following release from anxiety or distress. ■ a cause of or occasion for such a feeling. ■ the alleviation of pain, discomfort, or distress. ■ a temporary break in a generally tense or tedious situation. **2** assistance, esp. in the form of food, clothing, or money, given to those in special need or difficulty. ■ a remission of tax normally due. ■ esp. Law the redress of a hardship or grievance. ■ the action of raising the siege of a besieged town. **3** a person or group of people replacing others who have been on duty. ■ Baseball the role of a relief pitcher. **4** the state of being clearly visible or obvious due to being accentuated in some way. ■ a method of molding, carving, or stamping in which the design stands out from the surface, to a greater (**high relief**) or lesser (**bas-relief**) extent. ■ a piece of sculpture in relief. ■ a representation of relief given by an arrangement of line or color or shading. ■ Geog. difference in height from the surrounding terrain. [via Fr. from Ital. *rilievo*, from *rilevare* 'raise,' from L. *relevare*.]

– PHRASES **in relief 1** Art carved, molded, or stamped so as to stand out from the surface. **2** Baseball acting as a replacement pitcher. **on relief** receiving government assistance because of need. [ME: from OFr., from *relever* 'raise up,' from L. *relevare* 'raise again.']

re•lief map ▶ **n.** a map indicating hills and valleys by shading rather than by contour lines alone. ■ a map model with elevations and depressions representing hills and valleys, typically on an exaggerated relative scale.

re•lief pitch•er ▶ **n.** Baseball a pitcher who enters the game in place of the previous pitcher.

re•lief print•ing ▶ **n.** printing from raised images, as in letterpress and flexography.

re•lieve /riˈlēv/ ▶ **v.** [trans.] **1** cause (pain, distress, or difficulty) to become less severe or serious. ■ (usu. **be relieved**) cause (someone) to stop feeling distressed or anxious about something. ■ make less tedious or monotonous by the introduction of variety or of something striking or pleasing. **2** release (someone) from duty by taking their place. ■ bring military support for (a besieged place). ■ Baseball (of a relief pitcher) take the place of (another pitcher) during a game. **3** (**relieve someone of**) take (a burden) from someone. ■ free someone from (a tiresome responsibility). ■ used euphemistically to indicate that someone has been deprived of something. **4** (**relieve oneself**) urinate or defecate (used euphemistically). — **re•liev•a•ble adj. re•liev•ed•ly** /riˈlēvədlē/ **adv. re•liev•er n.** [ME: from OFr. *relever*, from L. *relevare*, from *re-* (intensive force) + *levare* 'raise' (from *levis* 'light').]

re•lie•vo /riˈlēvō; rēlˈyāvō/ (also **ri•lie•vo**) ▶ **n.** (pl. **-vos**) esp. Art another term for RELIEF (sense 4). [Ital. *rilievo*.]

religio- ▶ **comb. form** religious and ...: *religio-political*. [from RELIGION or RELIGIOUS.]

re•li•gion /riˈlijən/ ▶ **n.** the belief in and worship of a superhuman controlling power, esp. a personal God or gods. ■ details of belief as taught or discussed. ■ a particular system of faith and worship. ■ a pursuit or interest to which someone ascribes supreme importance. [ME ('life under monastic vows'): ult. from L. *religio(n-)* 'scruple, reverence,' perh. from *religare* 'to bind.']

re•li•gion•ism /riˈlijəˌnizəm/ ▶ **n.** excessive religious zeal. — **re•li•gion•ist n.**

re•li•gi•ose /riˈlijēˌōs/ ▶ **adj.** excessively religious. — **re•li•gi•os•i•ty** /riˌlijēˈäsətē/ **n.** [19th C.: from L. *religiosus*, from *religio* 'reverence.']

re•li•gious /riˈlijəs/ ▶ **adj.** believing in and worshiping a superhuman controlling power or powers, esp. a personal God or gods. ■ (of a belief or practice) forming part of someone's thought about or worship of a divine being. ■ of or relating to the worship of or a doctrine concerning a divine being or beings. ■ belonging or relating to a monastic order or other group of people who are united by their practice of religion. ■ treated or regarded with a devotion and scrupulousness appropriate to worship. ▶ **n.** (pl. same) a person bound by monastic vows. — **re•li•gious•ly adv. re•li•gious•ness n.** [ME: ult. from L. *religiosus*, from *religio* (see RELIGION).]

Re•li•gious So•ci•e•ty of Friends official name for the Quakers (see QUAKER).

re•line /rēˈlīn; ˈrē-/ ▶ **v.** [trans.] replace the lining of. ■ attach a new backing canvas to (a painting).

re•lin•quish /riˈliNGkwisH/ ▶ **v.** [trans.] voluntarily cease to keep or claim; give up. — **re•lin•quish•ment n.** [ME: from OFr. *relinquiss-*, lengthened stem of *relinquir*, from L. *relinquere*, from *re-* (intensive force) + *linquere* 'to leave.']

rel•i•quar•y /ˈreləˌkwerē/ ▶ **n.** (pl. **-quar•ies**) a container for holy relics. [16th C.: from Fr. *reliquaire*, from OFr. *relique* (see RELIC).]

re•liq•ui•ae /rəˈlikwēˌī; -wēˌē/ ▶ **plural n.** remains. ■ Geol. fossil remains of animals or plants. [17th C.: L., fem. pl. of *reliquus* 'remaining,' based on *linquere* 'to leave.']

rel•ish /ˈrelisH/ ▶ **n. 1** great enjoyment. ■ liking for or pleasurable anticipation of something. **2** a condiment eaten with plain food to add flavor. ■ chopped sweet pickles used as such a condiment. ▶ **v.** [trans.] enjoy greatly. ■ be pleased by or about. — **re·lish·a·ble** adj. [ME: alt. of obs. *reles*, from OFr., 'remainder,' from *relaisser* 'to release.']

re·live /rē'liv; 'rē-/ ▶ v. [trans.] live through (an experience or feeling, esp. an unpleasant one) again in one's imagination or memory.

rel·le·no /rə(l)'yānō/ ▶ n. (pl. **-nos**) short for CHILE RELLENO.

re·lo·cate /rē'lō,kāt; ,rēlō'kāt/ ▶ v. [intrans.] move to a new place and establish one's home or business there. — **re·lo·ca·tion** /,rēlō'kāsHən/ n.

re·luc·tance /ri'ləktəns/ ▶ n. unwillingness or disinclination to do something. ■ Physics the property of a magnetic circuit of opposing the passage of magnetic flux lines, equal to the ratio of the magnetomotive force to the magnetic flux.

re·luc·tant /ri'ləktənt/ ▶ adj. unwilling and hesitant; disinclined. — **re·luc·tant·ly** adv. [17th C. ('struggling'): from L. *reluctant-* 'struggling against,' from the v. *reluctari*, from *re-* + *luctari* 'to struggle.']

re·ly /ri'lī/ ▶ v. (**-lies, -lied**) [intrans.] (**rely on/upon**) depend on with full trust or confidence. ■ be dependent on. [ME ('gather together'): from OFr. *relier* 'bind together,' from L. *religare*, from *re-* (intensive force) + *ligare* 'bind.']

REM ▶ abbr. rapid eye movement.

rem /rem/ ▶ n. (pl. same) a unit of effective absorbed dose of ionizing radiation in human tissue, equivalent to one roentgen of X-rays. [1940s: acronym from *roentgen equivalent man*.]

re·made /rē'mād; 'rē-/ past and past participle of REMAKE.

re·main /ri'mān/ ▶ v. [intrans.] continue to exist, esp. after other similar or related people or things have ceased to exist. ■ stay in the place that one has been occupying. ■ [with complement] continue to possess a particular quality or fulfill a particular role. ■ be left over after others or other parts have been completed, used, or dealt with.
– PHRASES **remain to be seen** used to express the notion that something is not yet known or certain. [ME: from OFr. *remain-*, stressed stem of *remanoir*, from L. *remanere*, from *re-* (intensive force) + *manere* 'to stay.']

re·main·der /ri'māndər/ ▶ n. **1** a part, number, or quantity that is left over. ■ a part that is still to come. ■ the number that is left over in a division in which one quantity does not exactly divide another. ■ a copy of a book left unsold when demand has fallen. **2** Law an interest in an estate that becomes effective in possession only when a prior interest (devised at the same time) ends. ▶ v. [trans.] (often **be remaindered**) dispose of (a book left unsold) at a reduced price. [ME (sense 2): from Anglo-Norman Fr., from L. *remanere* (see REMAIN).]

re·mains /ri'mānz/ ▶ plural n. the parts left over after other parts have been removed, used, or destroyed. ■ historical or archaeological relics. ■ a person's body after death. [ME: from OFr. *remain*, from *remaindre* 'to remain,' ult. from L. *remanere* (see REMAIN).]

re·make ▶ v. /rē'māk; 'rē-/ (past and past part. **-made**) [trans.] make (something) again or differently. ▶ n. /'rē,māk/ a movie or piece of music that has been filmed or recorded again and rereleased.

re·man /rē'man; 'rē-/ ▶ v. (**-manned, -man·ning**) [trans.] **1** equip with new personnel. **2** literary make (someone) manly or courageous again.

re·mand /ri'mand/ Law ▶ v. [trans.] place (a defendant) on bail or in custody, esp. when a trial is adjourned. ■ return (a case) to a lower court for reconsideration. ▶ n. a committal to custody. [ME ('send back again'): from late L. *remandare*, from *re-* + *mandare* 'commit.']

rem·a·nent /'remənənt/ ▶ adj. tech. remaining; residual. ■ (of magnetism) remaining after the magnetizing field has been removed. — **rem·a·nence** n. [ME: from L. *remanent-* 'remaining,' from the v. *remanere*.]

re·map /rē'map; 'rē-/ ▶ v. (**-mapped, -map·ping**) [trans.] Comput. assign (a function) to a different key.

re·mark /ri'märk/ ▶ v. **1** [reporting verb] say something as a comment; mention. **2** [trans.] regard with attention; notice. ▶ n. a written or spoken comment. ■ notice or comment. [16th C. (sense 2): from Fr. *remarquer* 'note again,' from *re-* + *marquer* 'to mark.']

re-mark /rē 'märk; 'rē/ ▶ v. [trans.] mark (an examination paper or piece of academic work) again. ▶ n. [in sing.] an act of marking an examination or piece of academic work again.

re·mark·a·ble /ri'märkəbəl/ ▶ adj. worthy of attention; striking. — **re·mark·a·ble·ness** n. **re·mark·a·bly** /-blē/ adv.

Re·marque /rə'märk/, Erich Maria (1898–1970), US writer; born in Germany. His first novel, *All Quiet on the Western Front* (1929), was made into a movie in 1930.

re·mas·ter /rē'mastər/ ▶ v. [trans.] make a new master of (a recording), typically in order to improve the sound quality.

re·match /'rē,macH/ ▶ n. a second match or game between two teams or players.

Rem·brandt /'rem,brant/ (1606–69), Dutch painter; full name *Rembrandt Harmensz van Rijn*. He established his reputation as a portrait painter with the *Anatomy Lesson of Dr. Tulp* (1632).

re·me·di·al /ri'mēdēəl/ ▶ adj. giving or intended as a remedy or cure. ■ provided or intended for students who are experiencing learning difficulties. — **re·me·di·al·ly** adv. [17th C.: from late L. *remedialis*, from L. *remedium* (see REMEDY).]

re·me·di·a·tion /ri,mēdē'āsHən/ ▶ n. the action of remedying something, in particular of reversing or stopping environmental damage. ■ the giving of remedial teaching or therapy. — **re·me·di·ate** /ri'mēdē,āt/ v.

rem·e·dy /'remədē/ ▶ n. (pl. **-dies**) **1** a medicine or treatment for a disease or injury. ■ a means of counteracting or eliminating something undesirable. ■ a means of legal reparation. **2** the margin within which coins as minted may differ from the standard fineness and weight. ▶ v. (**-dies, -died**) [trans.] set right (an undesirable situation). — **re·me·di·a·ble** /ri'mēdēəbəl/ adj. [ME: from Anglo-Norman Fr. *remedie*, from L. *remedium*, from *re-* 'back' + *mederi* 'heal.']

re·mem·ber /ri'membər/ ▶ v. [trans.] have in or be able to bring to one's mind an awareness of (someone or something that one has seen, known, or experienced in the past). ■ [with infin.] do something that one has undertaken to do or that is necessary or advisable. ■ [with clause] used to emphasize the importance of what is asserted. ■ bear (someone) in mind by making them a gift or making provision for them. ■ (**remember someone to**) convey greetings from one person to (another). ■ pray for the success or well-being of. ■ (**remember oneself**) recover one's manners after a lapse. — **re·mem·ber·er** n. [ME: from OFr. *remembrer*, from late L. *rememorari* 'call to mind,' from *re-* (intensive force) + L. *memor* 'mindful.']

re·mem·brance /ri'membrəns/ ▶ n. the action of remembering something. ■ the action of remembering the dead, esp. in a ceremony. ■ a memory or recollection. ■ a thing kept or given as a reminder or in commemoration of someone.

re·mem·branc·er /ri'membrənsər/ ▶ n. a person with the job or responsibility of reminding others of something; a chronicler.

re·mex /'rē,meks/ ▶ n. (pl. **remiges** /'rēmi,jēz/) Ornithol. a flight feather. Compare with RECTRIX. [18th C.: from L., lit. 'rower,' based on *remus* 'oar.']

re·mind /ri'mīnd/ ▶ v. [trans.] cause (someone) to remember someone or something. ■ (**remind someone of**) cause someone to think of (something) because of a resemblance or likeness. ■ bring something, esp. a commitment or necessary course of action, to the attention of (someone). [17th C.: from RE- + MIND (v.).]

re·mind·er /ri'mīndər/ ▶ n. a thing that causes someone to remember something. ■ a message or communication designed to ensure that someone remembers something. ■ a letter sent to remind someone of an obligation, esp. to pay a bill.

re·mind·ful /ri'mīndfəl/ ▶ adj. acting as a reminder.

re·min·er·al·ize /rē'minərə,līz/ ▶ v. [trans.] restore the depleted mineral content of (a part of the body, esp. the bones or teeth). — **re·min·er·al·i·za·tion** /-,minərələ'zāsHən/ n.

Rem·ing·ton[1] /'remingtən/, Frederic (1861–1909), US painter and sculptor. He painted scenes of the American West. His bronze sculptures include "Bronco Buster" (1895).

Rem·ing·ton[2] ▶ n. trademark **1** a make of firearm. **2** a typewriter, esp. a large manual one formerly used in offices. [19th C.: named after Eliphalet *Remington* (1793–1861) and his son Philo (1816–89), gunsmiths of Ilion, New York.]

rem·i·nisce /,remə'nis/ ▶ v. [intrans.] indulge in enjoyable recollection of past events. — **rem·i·nis·cer** n. [19th C.: back-form. from REMINISCENCE.]

rem·i·nis·cence /,remə'nisəns/ ▶ n. a story told about a past event remembered by the narrator. ■ the enjoyable recollection of past events. ■ (**reminiscences**) a collection in literary form of incidents and experiences that someone remembers. ■ a characteristic of one thing reminding or suggestive of another.

rem·i·nis·cent /,remə'nisənt/ ▶ adj. tending to remind one of something. ■ suggesting something by resemblance. ■ (of a person or their manner) absorbed in or suggesting absorption in memories. — **rem·i·nis·cent·ly** adv. [18th C.: from L. *reminiscent-* 'remembering,' from the v. *reminisci*.]

re·miss /ri'mis/ ▶ adj. [predic.] lacking care or attention to duty; negligent. — **re·miss·ly** adv. **re·miss·ness** n. [ME ('dilute'): from L. *remissus* 'slackened,' past part. of *remittere*.]

re·mis·si·ble /ri'misəbəl/ ▶ adj. (esp. of sins) able to be pardoned.

re·mis·sion /ri'misHən/ ▶ n. the cancellation of a debt, charge, or penalty. ■ a diminution of the seriousness or intensity of disease or pain; a temporary recovery. ■ formal forgiveness of sins. [ME: ult. from L. *remissio(n-)*, from *remittere* (see REMIT).]

re·mit ▶ v. /ri'mit/ (**-mit·ted, -mit·ting**) [trans.] **1** cancel or refrain from exacting or inflicting (a debt or punishment). ■ Theol. pardon (a sin). **2** send (money) in payment or as a gift. **3** refer (a matter for decision) to some authority. ■ Law send back (a case) to a lower court. ■ Law send (someone) from one tribunal to another for a trial or hearing. ▶ n. /ri'mit; 'rē,mit/ **1** the task or area of activity officially assigned to an individual or organization. **2** an item referred to someone for consideration. — **re·mit·ta·ble** adj. **re·mit·tal** /-'mitl/ n. **re·mit·ter** n. [ME: from L. *remittere* 'send back,' from *re-* + *mittere* 'send.']

re·mit·tance /ri'mitns/ ▶ n. a sum of money sent, esp. by mail, in payment for goods or services or as a gift. ■ the action of sending money in such a way.

re·mit·tent /ri'mitnt/ ▶ adj. (of a fever) characterized by fluctuating body temperatures. [17th C.: from L. *remittent-* 'sending back,' from *remittere* (see REMIT).]

re·mix ▶ v. /rē'miks; 'rē-/ [trans.] mix (something) again. ■ produce a different version of (a musical recording) by altering the balance of the separate tracks. ▶ n. /'rē,miks/ a different version of a musical recording produced in such a way. — **re·mix·er** n.

rem·nant /'remnənt/ ▶ n. a small remaining quantity of something. ■ a piece of cloth or carpeting left when the greater part has been used or sold. ■ a surviving trace. ■ Christian Theol. a small minority of people who will remain faithful to God and so be saved (in allusion to biblical prophecies concerning Israel). ▶ adj. [attrib.] remaining. [ME: contr. of obs. *remenant*, from OFr., from *remenoir*, *remanoir* 'remain.']

re·mod·el /rē'mädl/ ▶ v. (**-mod·eled**, **-mod·el·ing**; Brit. **-mod·elled**, **-mod·el·ling**) [trans.] change the structure or form of (something, esp. a building, policy, or procedure). ■ fashion or shape (a figure or object) again or differently.

re·mod·el·er /rē'mädl-ər/ ▶ n. a person who carries out structural alterations to an existing building, such as adding a new room.

re·mold /rē'mōld/ (Brit. **re·mould**) ▶ v. [trans.] change or refashion the appearance, structure, or character of.

re·mon·strance /ri'mänstrəns/ ▶ n. a forcefully reproachful protest.

re·mon·strate /ri'män,strāt; 'remən-/ ▶ v. [intrans.] make a forcefully reproachful protest. — **re·mon·stra·tion** /ri,män'strāsʜən; ,remən-/ n. **re·mon·stra·tive** /-strətiv/ adj. **re·mon·stra·tor** /-,strātər/ n. [16th C. ('make plain'): from med. L. *remonstrat-* 'demonstrated,' from the v. *remonstrare*, from *re-* (intensive force) + *monstrare* 'to show.']

rem·o·ra /'remərə; ri'môrə/ ▶ n. a slender marine fish (family Echeneidae) that attaches itself to large fish by means of a sucker on top of its head. It generally feeds on the host's external parasites. Also called SHARKSUCKER, SUCKERFISH. See illustration at SHARKSUCKER. [16th C.: from L., lit. 'hindrance,' from *re-* 'back' + *mora* 'delay' (from the belief that the fish slowed down ships).]

re·morse /ri'môrs/ ▶ n. deep regret or guilt for a wrong committed. — **re·morse·ful** /-fəl/ adj. **re·morse·ful·ly** /-fəlē/ adv. [ME: from OFr. *remors*, from med. L. *remorsus*, from L. *remordere* 'vex,' from *re-* (intensive force) + *mordere* 'to bite.']

re·morse·less /ri'môrsləs/ ▶ adj. without regret or guilt. ■ (of something unpleasant) never ending or improving; relentless. — **re·morse·less·ly** adv. **re·morse·less·ness** n.

re·mort·gage /rē'môrgij/ ▶ v. [trans.] take out another or a different kind of mortgage on (a property). ▶ n. a different or additional mortgage.

re·mote /ri'mōt/ ▶ adj. (**-mot·er**, **-mot·est**) **1** (of a place) far away; distant. ■ (of a place) situated far from the main centers of population in a country. ■ (of an electronic device) operating or operated by means of radio or infrared signals. ■ distant in time. ■ distantly related. ■ having very little connection with or relationship to. ■ (of a person) aloof and unfriendly in manner. ■ Comput. denoting a device that can only be accessed by means of a network. Compare with LOCAL. **2** (of a chance or possibility) unlikely to occur. ▶ n. a remote control device. — **re·mote·ness** n. [ME ('far apart'): from L. *remotus* 'removed,' past part. of *removere* (see REMOVE).]

re·mote con·trol ▶ n. control of a machine or apparatus from a distance by means of signals transmitted from a radio or electronic device. ■ (also **re·mote con·trol·ler**) a device that controls an apparatus, esp. a television or VCR, in such a way. — **re·mote-con·trolled** adj.

re·mote·ly /ri'mōtlē/ ▶ adv. **1** from a distance; without physical contact. **2** [as submodifier] [usu. with negative] in the slightest degree: *he had never been remotely jealous.*

ré·mou·lade /,rāmə'läd/ (also **re·mou·lade**) ▶ n. salad or seafood dressing made with hard-boiled egg yolks, oil, and vinegar, and flavored with mustard, capers, and herbs. [Fr., from Ital. *remolata*.]

re·mould /rē'mōld/ ▶ v. British spelling of REMOLD.

re·mount ▶ v. /rē'mount; 'rē-/ [trans.] mount (something) again, in particular: ■ get on (something) in order to ride it again. ■ attach to a new frame or setting. ■ produce (a play or exhibition) again. ■ organize and embark on (a significant course of action) again. ▶ n. /'rē,mount/ a fresh horse for a rider. ■ hist. a supply of fresh horses for a regiment.

re·mov·al /ri'mōōvəl/ ▶ n. the action of removing someone or something, in particular: ■ the taking away of something unwanted. ■ the abolition of something. ■ the dismissal of someone from a job or office.

re·move /ri'mōōv/ ▶ v. [trans.] take away (something unwanted or unnecessary) from the position it occupies. ■ take (something) from a place in order to take it to another location. ■ eliminate or get rid of (someone or something). ■ take off (clothing). ■ abolish. ■ dismiss from a job or office. ■ [intrans.] (**remove to**) dated change one's home or place of residence by moving to (another place or area). ■ (**be removed**) be very different from. ■ [as adj.] (**removed**) separated by a particular number of steps of descent: *his second cousin once removed.* ▶ n. a degree of remoteness or separation: *at this remove, the incident seems insane.* — **re·mov·a·bil·i·ty** /ri,mōōvə'bilətē/ n. **re·mov·a·ble** adj. **re·mov·er** n. [ME (v.): from OFr. *remov-*, from L. *removere*, from *re-* 'back' + *movere* 'to move.']

REM sleep /rem/ ▶ n. a kind of sleep that occurs at intervals during the night and is characterized by rapid eye movements, more dreaming and bodily movement, and faster pulse and breathing.

re·mu·da /ri'm(y)ōōdə/ ▶ n. a herd of horses that have been saddle-broken, from which ranch hands choose their mounts for the day. [19th C.: via Amer. Sp. from Sp., lit. 'exchange.']

re·mu·ner·ate /ri'myōōnə,rāt/ ▶ v. [trans.] pay (someone) for services rendered or work done. — **re·mu·ner·a·tive** /-rətiv; -,rātiv/ adj. [16th C.: from L. *remunerat-* 'rewarded,' from v. *remunerari*, from *re-* (intensive force) + *munus, muner-* 'gift.']

re·mu·ner·a·tion /ri,myōōnə'rāsʜən/ ▶ n. money paid for work or a service.

Re·mus /'rēməs/ Rom. Mythol. the twin brother of Romulus.

Ren·ais·sance /'renə,säns; -,zäns/ the revival of art and literature under the influence of classical models in the 14th–16th centuries. ■ the culture and style of art and architecture developed during this era. ■ [as n.] (**a renaissance**) a revival of or renewed interest in something. [from Fr. *renaissance*, from *re-* 'again' + *naissance* 'birth' (from L. *nascentia*, from *nasci* 'be born').]

Ren·ais·sance man (or **wom·an**) ▶ n. a person with many talents or interests, esp. in the humanities.

re·nal /'rēnl/ ▶ adj. tech. of or relating to the kidneys. [17th C.: from Fr. *rénal*, from late L. *renalis*, from L. *renes* 'kidneys.']

re·nal pel·vis ▶ n. see PELVIS (sense 2).

re·nas·cence /ri'nasəns; -'nāsəns/ ▶ n. formal the revival of something that has been dormant. ■ (**Renascence**) another term for RENAISSANCE.

re·nas·cent /ri'nasənt; -'nāsənt/ ▶ adj. becoming active or popular again. [18th C.: from L. *renascent-* 'being born again,' from the v. *renasci*, from *re-* + *nasci* 'be born.']

rend /rend/ ▶ v. (past **rent** /rent/) [trans.] tear (something) into two or more pieces. ■ literary cause great emotional pain to (a person or their heart). [OE *rendan*; akin to Mid. Low Ger. *rende*.]

rend·er /'rendər/ ▶ v. [trans.] **1** provide (a service). ■ give (help). ■ submit or present for inspection or consideration. ■ literary hand over. ■ deliver (a verdict or judgment). **2** [trans.] cause to be or become; make. **3** represent or depict artistically. ■ translate. ■ Music perform (a piece). ■ Comput. process (an outline image) using color and shading in order to make it appear solid and three-dimensional. **4** melt down (fat), typically in order to clarify it. ■ process (the carcass of an animal) in order to extract proteins, fats, and other usable parts. **5** cover (stone or brick) with a coat of plaster. ▶ n. a first coat of plaster applied to a brick or stone surface. — **ren·der·er** n. [ME ('recite,' 'translate'): from OFr. *rendre*, from an alt. of L. *reddere* 'give back,' from *re-* + *dare* 'give.']

rend·er·ing /'rendəriɴɢ/ ▶ n. **1** a performance of a piece of music or drama. ■ a translation. ■ a work of visual art, esp. a detailed architectural drawing. ■ Comput. the processing of an outline image using color and shading to make it appear solid and three-dimensional. **2** the action of applying plaster to a wall. ■ the coating applied in such a way. **3** formal the action of giving, yielding, or surrendering something.

ren·dez·vous /'rändi,vōō; -dā-/ ▶ n. (pl. same) a meeting at an agreed time and place, typically between two people. ■ a place used for such a meeting. ■ a place, typically a bar or restaurant, that is used as a popular meeting place. ■ a meeting up of troops, ships, or aircraft at an agreed time and place. ■ a prearranged meeting between spacecraft in space. ▶ v. (**-vouses** /-,vōōz/, **-voused** /-,vōōd/, **-vous·ing** /-,vōōiɴɢ/) [intrans.] meet at an agreed time and place. [16th C.: from Fr. *rendez-vous!* 'present yourselves!,' imper. of *se rendre*.]

ren·di·tion /ren'disʜən/ ▶ n. **1** a performance or interpretation, esp. of a dramatic role or piece of music. ■ a visual representation or reproduction. ■ a translation or transliteration. **2** (also **extraordinary rendition**) the practice of sending a foreign criminal or terrorist suspect covertly to be interrogated in a country with less rigorous regulations for the humane treatment of prisoners. [17th C.: from obs. Fr., from *rendre* 'give back, render.']

Ren·do·va /ren'dōvə/ an island in the west central Solomon Islands, the scene of fighting between US and Japanese forces in 1943.

ren·e·gade /'reni,gād/ ▶ n. a person who deserts and betrays an organization, country, or set of principles. ■ a person who behaves in a rebelliously unconventional manner. ▶ adj. having treacherously changed allegiance. [15th C.: from Sp. *renegado*, from med. L. *renegatus* 'renounced,' past part. of *renegare*, from *re-* (intensive force) + L. *negare* 'deny.']

re·nege /ri'neg; -'nig/ (also **re·negue**) ▶ v. [intrans.] go back on a promise, undertaking, or contract. ■ another term for REVOKE (sense 2). — **re·neg·er** n. [16th C. ('desert'): from med. L. *renegare*, from L. *re-* (intensive force) + *negare* 'deny.']

re·ne·go·ti·ate /,rēnə'gōsʜē,āt/ ▶ v. [trans.] negotiate (something) again in order to change the original agreed terms. — **re·ne·go·ti·a·ble** /-'gōsʜ(ē)əbəl/ adj. **re·ne·go·ti·a·tion** /-,gōsʜē'āsʜən; -,gōsē-/ n.

re·new /ri'n(y)ōō/ ▶ v. [trans.] resume (an activity) after an interruption. ■ reestablish (a relationship). ■ repeat (an action or statement). ■ give fresh life or strength to. ■ extend for a further period the validity of (a license, subscription, or contract). ■ replace (something that is broken or worn out). — **re·new·er** n.

re·new·a·ble /ri'n(y)ōōəbəl/ ▶ adj. capable of being renewed. ■ (of energy or its source) not depleted when used. ▶ n. (usu. **renewables**) a source of energy that is not depleted by use, such as water, wind, or solar power. — **re·new·a·bil·i·ty** /ri,n(y)ōōə'bilətē/ n.

re·new·al /ri'n(y)ōōəl/ ▶ n. the action of extending the period of validity of a license, subscription, or contract. ■ an instance of resuming an activity or state after an interruption. ■ the replacing or repair of something that is worn out, run-down, or broken. ■ (among charismatic Christians) the state or process of being made spiritually new in the Holy Spirit.

ren·i·form /'rēnə,fôrm; 'ren-/ ▶ adj. esp. Mineral. Bot. kidney-shaped. [18th C.: from L. *ren* 'kidney.']

re·nin /'rēnin; 'ren-/ ▶ n. Biochem. an enzyme secreted by and stored in the kidneys that promotes the production of the protein angiotensin. [19th C.: from L. *ren* 'kidney.']

ren·min·bi /'ren'min'bē/ ▶ **n.** (pl. same) the name of the national currency of the People's Republic of China, introduced in 1948. ■ the yuan. [from Chin. *rénmínbì*, from *rénmín* 'people' + *bì* 'currency.']

Rennes /ren(s)/ a city in northwestern France; pop. 204,000.

ren·net /'renit/ ▶ **n.** curdled milk from the stomach of an unweaned calf, containing rennin and used in curdling milk for cheese. ■ any preparation containing rennin. [15th C.: prob. akin to RUN.]

ren·nin /'renin/ ▶ **n.** an enzyme secreted into the stomach of unweaned mammals causing the curdling of milk. [19th C.: from RENNET.]

Re·no[1] /'rēnō/ a city in western Nevada; pop. 180,480. It is noted as a gambling resort and for its liberal laws for divorces.

Re·no[2], Janet (1938–), US attorney general 1993–2001, the first woman to hold that office.

Re·noir[1] /'ren,wär; rən'wär/, Auguste (1841–1919), French painter; full name *Pierre Auguste Renoir*. His works include *Le Moulin de la galette* (1876) and *The Judgment of Paris* (*c.*1914).

Re·noir[2], Jean (1894–1979), French director; son of Auguste Renoir. His movies include *La Grande Illusion* (1937).

re·nounce /ri'nouns/ ▶ **v.** [trans.] formally declare one's abandonment of (a claim, right, or possession). ■ refuse to recognize or abide by any longer. ■ declare that one will no longer engage in or support. ■ reject and stop using or consuming. ■ [intrans.] Law refuse or resign a right or position, esp. one as an heir or trustee. — **re·nounce·a·ble** **adj.** **re·nounce·ment** **n.** **re·nounc·er** **n.** [ME: from OFr. *renoncer*, from L. *renuntiare* 'protest against,' from *re-* + *nuntiare* 'announce.']

ren·o·vate /'renə,vāt/ ▶ **v.** [trans.] restore (something old, esp. a building) to a good state of repair. — **ren·o·va·tion** /,renə'vāshən/ **n.** **ren·o·va·tor** /-,vātər/ **n.** [16th C.: from L. *renovat-* 'made new again,' from the v. *renovare*, from *re-* + *novus* 'new.']

re·nown /ri'noun/ ▶ **n.** the condition of being known or talked about by many people; fame. [ME: from Anglo-Norman Fr. *renoun*, from OFr. *renomer* 'make famous,' from *re-* (intensive force) + *nomer* 'to name,' from L. *nominare*.]

re·nowned /ri'nound/ ▶ **adj.** known or talked about by many people; famous.

rent[1] /rent/ ▶ **n.** a tenant's regular payment to a landlord for the use of property or land. ■ a sum paid for the hire of equipment. ▶ **v.** [trans.] pay someone for the use of (something, typically property, land, or a car). ■ (of an owner) let someone use (something) in return for payment. ■ [intrans.] be let or hired out at a specified rate. — **rent·a·bil·i·ty** /,rentə'bilətē/ **n.** **rent·a·ble** **adj.** [ME: from OFr. *rente*, akin to RENDER.]

rent[2] ▶ **n.** a large tear in a piece of fabric. ■ an opening or gap resembling such a tear. [16th C.: from obs. *rent* 'to tear,' var. of REND.]

rent[3] past and past participle of REND.

ren·tal /'rentl/ ▶ **n.** an amount paid or received as rent. ■ the action of renting something. ■ a rented house or car. ▶ **adj.** of, relating to, or available for rent.

rent·er /'rentər/ ▶ **n.** **1** a person who rents an apartment, a car, or other object. **2** a rented car or videocassette.

rent-free ▶ **adj.** & **adv.** with exemption from rent.

ren·tier /rän'tyā/ ▶ **n.** a person living on income from property or investments. [Fr., from *rente* 'dividend.']

re·nun·ci·a·tion /ri,nənsē'āshən/ ▶ **n.** the formal rejection of something, typically a belief, claim, or course of action. ■ Law a document expressing renunciation. — **re·nun·ci·ant** /ri'nənsēənt/ **n.** & **adj.** [ME: from late L. *renuntiatio(n-)*, from L. *renuntiare* (see RENOUNCE).]

re·or·der /rē'ôrdər/ ▶ **v.** [trans.] **1** request (something) to be made, supplied, or served again. **2** arrange (something) again. ▶ **n.** a renewed or repeated order for goods.

re·org /'rē,ôrg; rē'ôrg/ informal ▶ **n.** a reorganization. ▶ **v.** reorganize.

re·or·gan·ize /rē'ôrgə,nīz/ ▶ **v.** [trans.] change the way in which (something) is organized. — **re·or·gan·i·za·tion** /,rē,ôrgənə'zāshən/ **n.** **re·or·gan·iz·er** **n.**

re·o·ri·ent /rē'ôrē,ent/ ▶ **v.** [trans.] change the focus or direction of. ■ (**reorient oneself**) find one's position again in relation to one's surroundings. — **re·o·ri·en·tate** /-ēən,tāt/ **v.** **re·o·ri·en·ta·tion** /,rē,ôrēən'tāshən/ **n.**

re·o·vi·rus /'rēō,vīrəs/ ▶ **n.** any of a group of RNA viruses that are sometimes associated with respiratory and enteric infection. [20th C.: from *respiratory*, *enteric*, *orphan* (not identified with a disease) + VIRUS.]

Rep. ▶ **abbr.** ■ (in the US Congress) Representative. ■ Republic. ■ a Republican.

rep[1] /rep/ informal ▶ **n.** a representative. ■ a sales representative. ▶ **v.** (**repped, rep·ping**) [intrans.] act as a sales representative for a company or product.

rep[2] ▶ **n.** informal repertory. ■ a repertory theater or company.

rep[3] (also **repp**) ▶ **n.** a fabric with a ribbed surface, used in curtains and upholstery. [19th C.: from Fr. *reps*.]

rep[4] ▶ **n.** informal short for REPUTATION.

rep[5] ▶ **n.** (in bodybuilding) a repetition of a set of exercises. ▶ **v.** [trans.] (in knitting patterns) repeat (stitches or part of a design).

re·pack·age /rē'pakij/ ▶ **v.** [trans.] package again or differently. ■ present in a new way.

re·paid /rē'pād/ past and past participle of REPAY.

re·pair[1] /ri'pe(ə)r/ ▶ **v.** [trans.] fix or mend (a thing suffering from damage or a fault). ■ make good (such damage) by fixing or repairing it. ■ put right (a damaged relationship or unwelcome situation). ▶ **n.** the action of fixing or mending something. ■ a result of such fixing or mending. ■ the relative physical condition of an object: *in a bad state of repair*. — **re·pair·a·ble** **adj.** **re·pair·er** **n.** [ME: from OFr. *reparer*, from L. *reparare*, from *re-* 'back' + *parare* 'make ready.']

re·pair[2] ▶ **v.** [intrans.] (**repair to**) formal humorous go to (a place), esp. in company. ▶ **n.** archaic frequent or habitual visiting of a place: *she exhorted repair to the church*. ■ a place that is frequently visited or occupied: *the repairs of wild beasts*. [ME: from OFr. *repairer*, from late L. *repatriare* (see REPATRIATE).]

re·pair·man /ri'pe(ə)r,man; -mən/ ▶ **n.** (pl. **-men**) a person who repairs vehicles, machinery, or appliances.

re·pap·er /rē'pāpər/ ▶ **v.** [trans.] apply new wallpaper to (a wall or room).

rep·a·ra·ble /'rep(ə)rəbəl/ ▶ **adj.** (esp. of an injury or loss) possible to rectify or repair.

rep·a·ra·tion /,repə'rāshən/ ▶ **n.** **1** the making of amends for a wrong one has done, by paying money to or otherwise helping those who have been wronged. ■ (**reparations**) the compensation for war damage paid by a defeated state. **2** archaic the action of repairing something. — **re·par·a·tive** /ri'parətiv/ **adj.** [ME: ult. from late L. *reparatio(n-)*, from *reparare* (see REPAIR[1]).]

rep·ar·tee /,repər'tē; ,repär'tē; -'tā/ ▶ **n.** conversation or speech characterized by quick, witty comments. [17th C.: from Fr. *repartie* 'replied promptly,' fem. past part. of *repartir*, from *re-* 'again' + *partir* 'divide, depart.']

re·par·ti·tion /,rē,pär'tishən/ ▶ **v.** [trans.] divide (something) up, or partition or divide (something) again.

re·past /ri'past; 'rē,past/ ▶ **n.** formal a meal. [ME: from OFr., based on late L. *repascere*, from *re-* (intensive force) + *pascere* 'to feed.']

re·pa·tri·ate /rē'pātrē,āt; rē'pat-/ ▶ **v.** [trans.] send (someone) back to their own country. ■ send or bring (money) back to one's own country. ▶ **n.** a person who has been repatriated. — **re·pa·tri·a·tion** /,rē,pātrē'āshən; ,rē,pa-/ **n.** [17th C.: from late L. *repatriat-* 'returned to one's country,' from the v. *repatriare*, from *re-* 'back' + L. *patria* 'native land.']

re·pay /rē'pā/ ▶ **v.** (past and past part. **-paid** /rē'pād/) [trans.] pay back (a loan, debt, or sum of money). ■ pay back money borrowed from (someone). ■ do or give something as recompense for (a favor or kindness received). — **re·pay·a·ble** **adj.** **re·pay·ment** **n.**

re·peal /ri'pēl/ ▶ **v.** [trans.] revoke or annul (a law or congressional act). ▶ **n.** the action of revoking or annulling a law or congressional act. — **re·peal·a·ble** **adj.** [ME: from Anglo-Norman Fr. *repeler*, from OFr. *re-* 'back' + *apeler* 'to call, appeal.']

re·peat /ri'pēt/ ▶ **v.** **1** [reporting verb] say again something one has already said. ■ say again (something said or written by someone else). ■ (**repeat oneself**) say or do the same thing again. ■ used for emphasis: *force was not—repeat, not—to be used*. **2** [trans.] do (something) again, either once or a number of times. ■ broadcast (a television or radio program) again. ■ undertake (a course or period of instruction) again. ■ (**repeat itself**) occur again in the same way or form. ■ [intrans.] illegally vote more than once in an election. ■ [intrans.] attain a particular success or achievement again, esp. by winning a championship for the second consecutive time. ■ [trans.] (of a watch or clock) strike (the last hour or quarter) over again when required. **3** [intrans.] (of food) be tasted intermittently for some time after being swallowed as a result of belching or indigestion. ▶ **n.** an action, event, or other thing that occurs or is done again. ■ a repeated broadcast of a television or radio program. ■ [as adj.] occurring, done, or used more than once. ■ a consignment of goods similar to one already received. ■ a decorative pattern that is repeated uniformly over a surface. ■ Music a passage intended to be repeated. ■ a mark indicating this. — **re·peat·a·bil·i·ty** /ri,pētə'bilətē/ **n.** **re·peat·a·ble** **adj.** **re·peat·ed·ly** **adv.** [ME: ult. from L. *repetere*, from *re-* 'back' + *petere* 'seek.']

re·peat·er /ri'pētər/ ▶ **n.** a person or thing that repeats something, in particular: ■ a firearm that fires several shots without reloading. ■ a watch or clock that repeats its last strike when required. ■ a device for the automatic retransmission or amplification of an electrically transmitted message.

re·peat·ing /ri'pēting/ ▶ **adj.** **1** (of a firearm) capable of firing several shots in succession without reloading. **2** (of a pattern) recurring uniformly over a surface.

re·peat·ing dec·i·mal ▶ **n.** a decimal fraction in which a figure or group of figures is repeated indefinitely, as in *0.666 ...* or as in *1.851851851 ...*.

re·pel /ri'pel/ ▶ **v.** (**-pelled, -pel·ling**) [trans.] **1** drive or force (an attack or attacker) back or away. ■ [trans.] (of a magnetic pole or electric field) force (something similarly magnetized or charged) away from itself. ■ (of a substance) resist mixing with or be impervious to (another substance). **2** be repulsive or distasteful to. **3** formal refuse to accept (something, esp. an argument or theory). — **re·pel·ler** **n.** [ME: from L. *repellere*, from *re-* 'back' + *pellere* 'to drive.']

re·pel·lent /ri'pelənt/ (also **re·pel·lant**) ▶ **adj.** **1** [often in comb.] able to repel a particular thing; impervious to a particular substance. **2** causing disgust or distaste. ▶ **n.** **1** a substance that dissuades particular insects or other pests from approaching or settling. **2** a substance used to treat something, esp. fabric or stone, so as to make it impervious to water.

—**re·pel·lence** n. **re·pel·len·cy** n. **re·pel·lent·ly** adv. [17th C.: from L. *repellent-* 'driving back,' from *repellere* (see REPEL).]

re·pent /ri'pent/ ▶v. [intrans.] feel or express sincere regret or remorse about one's wrongdoing or sin. ■ [trans.] view or think of (an action or omission) with deep regret or remorse. —**re·pent·ance** /ri'pentns/ n. **re·pent·ant** /ri'pentnt/ adj. **re·pent·er** n. [ME: from OFr. *repentir*, from *re-* (intensive force) + *pentir*, from L. *paenitere* 'cause to repent.']

re·per·cus·sion /ˌrēpər'kəsHən; ˌrep-/ ▶n. **1** (usu. **repercussions**) an unintended consequence occurring some time after an event or action, esp. an unwelcome one. **2** archaic the recoil of something after impact. **3** archaic an echo or reverberation. —**re·per·cus·sive** /-'kəsiv/ adj. [ME ('repressing of infection'): ult. from L. *repercussio(n-)*, from *repercutere* 'push back,' from *re-* + *percutere* 'to strike.']

rep·er·toire /'repə(r),twär/ ▶n. a stock of plays, dances, or pieces that a company or a performer knows or is prepared to perform. ■ the whole body of items that are regularly performed. ■ a stock of skills or types of behavior that a person habitually uses. [19th C.: from Fr. *répertoire*, from late L. *repertorium* (see REPERTORY).]

rep·er·to·ry /'repə(r),tôrē/ ▶n. (pl. **-ries**) **1** the performance of various plays, operas, or ballets by a company at regular short intervals. ■ repertory theaters regarded collectively. ■ a repertory company. **2** another term for REPERTOIRE. ■ a repository or collection, esp. of information or retrievable examples. —**rep·er·to·ri·al** /ˌrepə(r)'tôrēəl/ adj. [16th C. ('index'): from late L. *repertorium*, from L. *repert-* 'discovered,' from the v. *reperire*.]

rep·er·to·ry com·pa·ny ▶n. a theatrical company that performs works from its repertoire for regular, short periods of time, moving on from one work to another.

ré·pé·ti·teur /ˌrāpāti'tər/ ▶n. a tutor or coach of ballet dancers or musicians, esp. opera singers. [Fr.]

rep·e·ti·tion /ˌrepə'tisHən/ ▶n. the action of repeating something that has already been said or written. ■ [often with negative] the recurrence of an action or event. ■ a thing repeated. ■ a training exercise that is repeated, esp. a series of repeated raisings and lowerings of the weight in weight training. ■ Music the repeating of a passage or note. —**rep·e·ti·tion·al** /-sHənl/ adj. [ME: ult. from L. *repetitio(n-)*, from *repetere* (see REPEAT).]

rep·e·ti·tious /ˌrepə'tisHəs/ ▶adj. another term for REPETITIVE. —**rep·e·ti·tious·ly** adv. **rep·e·ti·tious·ness** n.

re·pet·i·tive /ri'petətiv/ ▶adj. containing or characterized by repetition, esp. when unnecessary or tiresome. —**re·pet·i·tive·ly** adv. **re·pet·i·tive·ness** n.

re·pet·i·tive-mo·tion dis·or·der ▶n. work-related physical symptoms caused by excessive and repeated use of the upper extremities, esp. when typing on a computer keyboard. Also called **repetitive injury**.

re·pet·i·tive strain in·ju·ry (abbr.: **RSI**) ▶n. a condition in which the prolonged performance of repetitive actions, typically with the hands, causes pain or impairment of function in those tendons and muscles.

re·phrase /rē'frāz/ ▶v. [trans.] express (an idea or question) in an alternative way, esp. with the purpose of changing the detail or perspective of the original idea or question.

re·pine /ri'pīn/ ▶v. [intrans.] literary feel or express discontent; fret. [16th C.: from RE- + PINE[2].]

re·place /ri'plās/ ▶v. [trans.] **1** take the place of. ■ provide or find a substitute for (something that is broken, old, or inoperative). ■ fill the role of (someone or something) with a substitute. **2** put (something) back in a previous place or position. —**re·plac·er** n.

re·place·a·ble /ri'plāsəbəl/ ▶adj. able to be replaced. ■ Chem. denoting those hydrogen atoms in an acid that can be displaced by metal atoms when forming salts. —**re·place·a·bil·i·ty** /-ˌplāsə'bilətē/ n.

re·place·ment /ri'plāsmənt/ ▶n. the action or process of replacing someone or something. ■ a person or thing that takes the place of another.

re·plant /rē'plant; 'rē-/ ▶v. [trans.] plant (a tree or plant that has been dug up) again, esp. when transferring it to a larger pot or new site. ■ provide (an area) with new plants or trees. ■ surgically reattach to the body a part that has been removed or severed.

re·plan·ta·tion /ˌrē,plan'tāsHən/ ▶n. permanent reattachment to the body of a part that has been removed or severed.

re·play ▶v. /rē'plā; 'rē-/ [trans.] **1** play back (a recording on tape, video, or film). ■ fig. repeat (something, esp. an event or sequence of events). **2** play (a game or contest) again to decide a winner after the original encounter ended in a draw or contentious result. ▶n. /'rē,plā/ **1** the playing again of a section of a recording, esp. so as to be able to watch an incident more closely. ■ fig. an occurrence that closely follows the pattern of a previous event. **2** a replayed game or contest.

re·plen·ish /ri'plenisH/ ▶v. [trans.] fill (something) up again. ■ restore (a stock or supply of something) to the former level or condition. —**re·plen·ish·er** n. **re·plen·ish·ment** n. [ME ('supply abundantly'): from OFr. *repleniss-*, lengthened stem of *replenir*, from *re-* 'again' + *plenir* 'fill' (from L. *plenus* 'full').]

re·plete /ri'plēt/ ▶adj. [predic.] filled or well-supplied with something. ■ very full of or sated by food. —**re·ple·tion** /ri'plēsHən/ n. [ME: ult. from L. *repletus* 'filled up,' past part. of *replere*, from *re-* 'again' + *plere* 'fill.']

rep·li·ca /'replikə/ ▶n. an exact copy or model of something, esp. one on a smaller scale. ■ a duplicate of an original artistic work. [18th C. ('(in music) a repeat'): from Ital., from *replicare* 'to reply.']

rep·li·cant /'replikənt/ ▶n. **1** (in science fiction) a genetically engineered or artificial being created as an exact replica of a particular human being. **2** a disparaging term for something that imitates or resembles another. [from *replica* + *-ant*: first used in the movie *Blade Runner* (1982).]

rep·li·cate ▶v. /'repli,kāt/ [trans.] make an exact copy of; reproduce. ■ (**replicate itself**) (of genetic material or a living organism) reproduce or give rise to a copy of itself. ■ repeat (a scientific experiment or trial) to obtain a consistent result. ▶adj. /-kit/ [attrib.] of the nature of a copy. ■ of the nature of a repetition of a scientific experiment or trial. ▶n. /-kit/ **1** a close or exact copy; a replica. ■ a repetition of an experimental test or procedure. **2** Music a tone one or more octaves above or below the given tone. —**rep·li·ca·bil·i·ty** /ˌreplikə'bilətē/ n. **rep·li·ca·ble** /'replikəbəl/ adj. [ME ('repeat'): from L. *replicat-*, from the v. *replicare*, from *re-* 'again' + *plicare* 'to fold.']

rep·li·ca·tion /ˌrepli'kāsHən/ ▶n. **1** the action of copying or reproducing something. ■ a copy. ■ the repetition of a scientific experiment or trial to obtain a consistent result. ■ the process by which genetic material or a living organism gives rise to a copy of itself. **2** Law, dated a plaintiff's reply to the defendant's plea.

rep·li·ca·tive /'repli,kātiv/ ▶adj. Biol. relating to or involving the replication of genetic material or living organisms.

rep·li·ca·tor /'repli,kātər/ ▶n. a thing that replicates or copies something. ■ Biol. a structural gene at which replication of a specific replicon is believed to be initiated.

rep·li·con /'repli,kän/ ▶n. Biol. a nucleic acid molecule, or part of one, that replicates as a unit, beginning at a specific site within it. [1960s: from REPLICATION + -ON.]

re·ply /ri'plī/ ▶v. (**-plies, -plied**) [reporting verb] say something in response to something someone has said. ■ [intrans.] write back to someone one has received a letter from. ■ [intrans.] respond by a similar action or gesture. ▶n. (pl. **-plies**) a verbal or written answer. ■ the action of answering someone or something. ■ a response in the form of a gesture, action, or expression. ■ Law a plaintiff's response to the defendant's plea. —**re·pli·er** n. [ME (v.): from OFr. *replier*, from L. *replicare* (see REPLICATE).]

re·po /'rē,pō/ informal ▶n. (pl. **-pos**) **1** another term for REPURCHASE AGREEMENT. [1960s: abbrev.] **2** a car or other item that has been repossessed. ▶v. (**-po's, -po'd**) [trans.] repossess (a car or other item) when a buyer defaults on payments.

re·point /rē'point/ ▶v. [trans.] fill in or repair the joints of (brickwork) again.

re·po man ▶n. informal a repossessor.

re·port /ri'pôrt/ ▶v. **1** [reporting verb] give a spoken or written account of something that one has observed, heard, done, or investigated. ■ [intrans.] cover an event or subject as a journalist or a reporter. ■ (**be reported**) used to indicate that something has been stated, although one cannot confirm its accuracy. ■ [trans.] make a formal statement or complaint about (someone or something) to the necessary authority. ■ [trans.] (of a legislative committee) formally announce that the committee has dealt with (a bill). See also REPORT A BILL OUT below. **2** [intrans.] present oneself formally as having arrived at a particular place or as ready to do something. **3** [intrans.] (**report to**) be responsible to (a superior or supervisor). ▶n. **1** an account given of a particular matter, esp. in the form of an official document, after thorough investigation or consideration by an appointed person or body. ■ a spoken or written description of an event or situation, esp. one intended for publication or broadcast in the media. ■ a teacher's written assessment of a student's work, progress, and conduct, issued at the end of a term or academic year. ■ Law a detailed formal account of a case heard in a court, giving the main points in the judgment, esp. as prepared for publication. ■ a piece of information that is unsupported by firm evidence and that the speaker feels may or may not be true. ■ dated rumor. **2** a sudden loud noise of or like an explosion or gunfire.
– PHRASES **on report** (esp. of a prisoner or member of the armed forces) on a disciplinary charge.
– PHRASAL VERBS **report back** (or **report something back**) **1** deliver a spoken or written account of something one has been asked to do or investigate. **2** return to work or duty after a period of absence. **report a bill out** (of a committee of Congress) return a bill to the legislative body for action. —**re·port·a·ble** adj. [ME: from OFr. *reporter* (v.), *report* (n.), from L. *reportare* 'bring back,' from *re-* 'back' + *portare* 'carry.']

re·port·age /rə'pôrtij; ˌrepôr'täzH/ ▶n. the reporting of news, for the press and the broadcast media. ■ factual presentation in a book or other text, esp. when this adopts a journalistic style. [17th C.: Fr., from OFr. *reporter* (see REPORT).]

re·port card ▶n. a teacher's written assessment of a student's work, progress, and conduct, sent home to a parent or guardian. ■ an evaluation of performance.

re·port·ed·ly /ri'pôrtədlē/ ▶adv. [sentence adverb] according to what some say (used to express the speaker's belief that the information given is not necessarily true).

re·port·ed speech ▶n. a speaker's words reported in subordinate clauses governed by a reporting verb, with the required changes of person and tense (e.g., *he said that he would go*, based on *I will go*). Also called **INDIRECT SPEECH**. Contrasted with **DIRECT SPEECH**.

re·port·er /ri'pôrtər/ ▶ n. a person who reports, esp. one employed to report news or conduct interviews for newspapers or broadcasts.

re·port·ing verb ▶ n. a verb belonging to a class of verbs conveying the action of speaking and used with both direct and reported speech. Reporting verbs may also be used with a direct object and with an infinitive construction.

rep·or·to·ri·al /ˌrepər'tôrēəl; ˌrē-/ ▶ adj. of or characteristic of newspaper reporters. — **rep·or·to·ri·al·ly** adv. [19th C.: from **REPORTER**.]

re·pose[1] /ri'pōz/ ▶ n. temporary rest from activity, excitement, or exertion, esp. sleep or the rest given by sleep. ■ a state of peace. ■ composure. ■ Art harmonious arrangement of colors and forms, providing a restful visual effect. ▶ v. [intrans.] be lying, situated, or kept in a particular place. ■ lie down in rest. ■ [trans.] (**repose something on/in**) literary lay something to rest in or on (something). — **re·pose·ful** /-fəl/ adj. **re·pose·ful·ly** /-fəlē/ adv. [ME: from OFr. *repos* (n.), *reposer* (v.), from late L. *repausare*, from *re-* (intensive force) + *pausare* 'to pause.']

re·pose[2] ▶ v. [trans.] (**repose something in**) place something, esp. one's confidence or trust, in. [ME ('put back'): from **RE-** + **POSE**[1] (v.), suggested by L. *reponere* 'replace,' from *re-* (intensive force) + *ponere* 'to place.']

re·po·si·tion /ˌrēpə'zisʜən/ ▶ v. [trans.] place in a different position; adjust or alter the position of. ■ change the image of (a company, product, etc.) to target a new or wider market.

re·pos·i·to·ry /ri'päzəˌtôrē/ ▶ n. (pl. **-ries**) a place, building, or receptacle where things are or may be stored. ■ a place in which something, esp. a natural resource, has accumulated or where it is found in significant quantities. ■ a person or thing regarded as a store of information or in which something abstract is held to exist or be found. [15th C.: ult. from L. *repositorium*, from *reposit-* 'placed back,' from *reponere* (see **REPOSE**[2]).]

re·pos·sess /ˌrēpə'zes/ ▶ v. [trans.] retake possession of (something) when a buyer defaults on payments. — **re·pos·ses·sion** /-'zesʜən/ n.

re·pos·ses·sor /ˌrēpə'zesər/ ▶ n. a person hired by a credit company to repossess an item when the buyer defaults on payments.

re·pous·sé /rəˌpoo͞'sā/ ▶ adj. (of metalwork) hammered into relief from the reverse side. ▶ n. ornamental metalwork fashioned in this way. [19th C.: Fr., lit. 'pushed back,' past part. of *repousser*, from *re-* + *pousser* 'to push.']

repp /rep/ ▶ n. var. of **REP**[3].

repr. ▶ abbr. reprint or reprinted.

rep·re·hend /ˌrepri'hend/ ▶ v. [trans.] reprimand. — **rep·re·hen·sion** /-'hencʜən/ n. [ME: from L. *reprehendere* from *re-* (intensive force) + *prehendere* 'seize.']

rep·re·hen·si·ble /ˌrepri'hensəbəl/ ▶ adj. deserving censure or condemnation. — **rep·re·hen·si·bil·i·ty** /-ˌhensə'bilətē/ n. **rep·re·hen·si·bly** /-blē/ adv. [ME: from late L. *reprehensibilis*, from *reprehens-* 'rebuked,' from *reprehendere* (see **REPREHEND**).]

rep·re·sent /ˌrepri'zent/ ▶ v. [trans.] **1** be entitled or appointed to act or speak for (someone), esp. in an official capacity. ■ (of a competitor) participate in a sports event or other competition on behalf of (one's club, town, region, or country). ■ be an elected member of a legislature for (a particular constituency, party, or group). ■ (usu. **be represented**) act as a substitute for (someone), esp. on an official or ceremonial occasion. **2** constitute; amount to. ■ be a specimen or example of; typify. ■ (**be represented**) (of a group or type of person or thing) be present or found in something, esp. to a particular degree. **3** depict (a particular subject) in a picture or other work of art. ■ [trans.] describe or depict (someone or something) as being of a certain nature; portray in a particular way. ■ (of a sign or symbol) have a particular signification; stand for. ■ be a symbol or embodiment of (a particular quality or thing). ■ play the part of (someone) in a theatrical production. **4** formal state or point out (something) clearly. ■ [with clause] allege; claim. — **rep·re·sent·a·bil·i·ty** /ˌrepriˌzentə'bilətē/ n. **rep·re·sent·a·ble** adj. [ME: ult. from L. *repraesentare*, from *re-* (intensive force) + *praesentare* 'to present.']

re-pre·sent /ˌrēpri'zent/ ▶ v. [trans.] present (something) again, esp. for further consideration or in an altered form. ■ present (a check or bill) again for payment. — **re-pres·en·ta·tion** /ˌrēˌprezən'tāsʜən; -ˌprēˌzen-/ n.

rep·re·sen·ta·tion /ˌrepriˌzen'tāsʜən; -zən-/ ▶ n. **1** the action of speaking or acting on behalf of someone or the state of being so represented. **2** the description or portrayal of someone or something in a particular way or as being of a certain nature. ■ the depiction of someone or something in a picture or other work of art. ■ a thing, esp. a picture or model, that depicts a likeness or reproduction of someone or something. ■ (in some theories of perception) a mental state or concept regarded as corresponding to a thing perceived. **3** (**representations**) formal statements made to a higher authority, esp. so as to communicate an opinion or register a protest. ■ a statement or allegation.

rep·re·sen·ta·tion·al /ˌrepriˌzen'tāsʜənl/ ▶ adj. of, relating to, or characterized by representation. ■ relating to or denoting art that aims to depict the physical appearance of things. Contrasted with **ABSTRACT**.

rep·re·sen·ta·tion·al·ism /ˌrepriˌzen'tāsʜənlˌizəm/ ▶ n. **1** the practice or advocacy of representational art. **2** Philos. another term for **REPRESENTATIONISM**. — **rep·re·sen·ta·tion·al·ist** adj. & n.

rep·re·sen·ta·tion·ism /ˌrepriˌzen'tāsʜəˌnizəm; -zən-/ ▶ n. Philos. the doctrine that thought is the manipulation of mental representations that (somehow) correspond to external states or objects. — **rep·re·sen·ta·tion·ist** n.

rep·re·sen·ta·tive /ˌrepri'zentətiv/ ▶ adj. **1** typical of a class, group, or body of opinion. ■ containing typical examples of many or all types. **2** (of a legislative or deliberative assembly) consisting of people chosen to act and speak on behalf of a wider group. ■ (of a government or political system) based on representation of the people by such deputies. **3** serving as a portrayal or symbol of something. ■ (of art) representational. **4** Philos. of or relating to mental representation. ▶ n. **1** a person chosen or appointed to act or speak for another or others, in particular: ■ an agent of a firm who travels to potential clients to sell its products. ■ an employee of a travel company who looks after the needs of its vacationing clients. ■ a person chosen or elected to speak and act on behalf of others in a legislative assembly or deliberative body. ■ a delegate who attends a conference, negotiations, legal hearing, etc., so as to represent the interests of another person or group. ■ a person who takes the place of another on a ceremonial or official occasion. **2** an example of a class or group. — **rep·re·sent·a·tive·ly** adv. **rep·re·sent·a·tive·ness** n.

re·press /ri'pres/ ▶ v. [trans.] subdue (someone or something) by force. ■ restrain or prevent (the expression of a feeling). ■ suppress (a thought, feeling, or desire) in oneself so that it becomes or remains unconscious. ■ inhibit the natural development or self-expression of (someone or something). ■ Biol. prevent the transcription of (a gene). — **re·press·er** n. **re·press·i·ble** adj. **re·pres·sion** /ri'presʜən/ n. [ME ('keep back'): from L. *repress-* 'pressed back,' from the v. *reprimere*, from *re-* + *premere* 'to press.']

re·pressed /ri'prest/ ▶ adj. restrained, inhibited, or oppressed. ■ (of a thought, feeling, or desire) kept suppressed and unconscious in one's mind. ■ having or characterized by a large number of thoughts, feelings, or desires, esp. sexual ones, that are suppressed in this way.

re·pres·sive /ri'presiv/ ▶ adj. (esp. of a social or political system) inhibiting or restraining the freedom of a person or group of people. ■ inhibiting or preventing the awareness of certain thoughts or feelings. — **re·pres·sive·ly** adv. **re·pres·sive·ness** n.

re·pres·sor /ri'presər/ ▶ n. Biochem. a substance that acts on an operon to inhibit messenger RNA synthesis.

re·prieve /ri'prēv/ ▶ v. [trans.] cancel or postpone the punishment of (someone, esp. someone condemned to death). ■ abandon or postpone plans to close or put an end to (something). ▶ n. a cancellation or postponement of a punishment. ■ a temporary escape from an undesirable fate or unpleasant situation. [15th C. (as the past participle *repryed*): from Anglo-Norman Fr. *repris*, past part. of *reprendre*, from L. *re-* 'back' + *prehendere* 'seize.']

rep·ri·mand /'reprəˌmand/ ▶ n. a rebuke, esp. an official one. ▶ v. [trans.] rebuke (someone), esp. officially. [17th C.: from Fr. *réprimande*, via Sp. from L. *reprimenda*, neut. pl. gerundive of *reprimere* (see **REPRESS**).]

re·print ▶ v. /rē'print; 'rē-/ [trans.] print again or in a different form. ▶ n. /'rēˌprint/ an act of printing more copies of a work. ■ a copy of a book or other material that has been reprinted. ■ an offprint. — **re·print·er** n.

re·pris·al /ri'prīzəl/ ▶ n. an act of retaliation. ■ hist. the forcible seizure of a foreign subject or their goods as an act of retaliation. [ME: from Anglo-Norman Fr. *reprisaille*, from med. L. *reprisalia* (neut. pl.), based on L. *repraehens-* 'seized,' from *repraehendere* (see **REPREHEND**).]

re·prise /ri'prēz/ ▶ n. a repeated passage in music. ■ a repetition or further performance of something. ▶ v. [trans.] repeat (a piece of music or a performance). [18th C.: Fr., lit. 'taken up again,' fem. past part. of *reprendre* (see **REPRIEVE**).]

re·pro /'rēˌprō/ ▶ n. (pl. **-pros**) [usu. as adj.] informal **1** a reproduction or copy, particularly of a piece of furniture. **2** the action or process of copying a document or image. [1940s: abbrev.]

re·proach /ri'prōcʜ/ ▶ v. [trans.] address (someone) in such a way as to express disapproval or disappointment. ■ (**reproach someone with**) accuse someone of. ▶ n. the expression of disapproval or disappointment. ■ (**a reproach to**) a thing that makes the failings of someone or something else more apparent. ■ (**Reproaches**) (in the Roman Catholic Church) a set of antiphons and responses for Good Friday representing the reproaches of Christ to his people.

– PHRASES **above** (or **beyond**) **reproach** such that no criticism can be made; perfect. — **re·proach·a·ble** adj. **re·proach·er** n. **re·proach·ing·ly** adv. [ME: from OFr. *reprochier* (v.), from a base meaning 'bring back close,' based on L. *prope* 'near.']

re·proach·ful /ri'prōcʜfəl/ ▶ adj. expressing disapproval or disappointment. — **re·proach·ful·ly** adv. **re·proach·ful·ness** n.

rep·ro·bate /'reprəˌbāt/ ▶ n. an unprincipled person (often used humorously or affectionately). ▶ adj. unprincipled (often used as a humorous or affectionate reproach). — **rep·ro·ba·tion** /ˌreprə'bāsʜən/ n. [ME (verb): from L. *reprobat-* 'disapproved,' from the v. *reprobare*, from *re-* + *probare* 'approve.']

re·proc·ess /rē'präsˌes; -'präsəs; -'prō-/ ▶ v. [trans.] process (something, esp. spent nuclear fuel) again or differently, typically in order to reuse it.

re·pro·duce /ˌrēprə'd(y)oo͞s/ ▶ v. [trans.] produce again. ■ produce a copy or representation of. ■ create something very similar to (something else), esp. in a different medium or context. ■ (of an organism) produce offspring by a sexual or asexual process. ■ [intrans.] be copied with a specified degree of success. — **re·pro·duc·er** n. **re·pro·duc·i·bil·i·ty** /-ˌd(y)oo͞sə'bilətē/ n. **re·pro·duc·i·ble** adj. **re·pro·duc·i·bly** /-əblē/ adv.

re·pro·duc·tion /ˌrēprəˈdəkSHən/ ▶ **n.** the action or process of making a copy of something. ■ the production of offspring by a sexual or asexual process. ■ a copy of a work of art, esp. a print or photograph of a painting. ■ [as adj.] made to imitate the style of an earlier period or of a particular artist or craftsman. ■ the quality of reproduced sound. — **re·pro·duc·tive** /-ˈdəktiv/ **adj. re·pro·duc·tive·ly** /-ˈdəktivlē/ **adv. re·pro·duc·tive·ness** /-ˈdəktivnis/ **n.**

re·pro·graph·ics /ˌreprəˈgrafiks; ˈrē-/ ▶ **plural n.** [treated as sing.] reprography.

re·prog·ra·phy /riˈprägrəfē/ ▶ **n.** the science and practice of copying and reproducing documents and graphic material. — **re·prog·ra·pher** /-fər/ **n. re·pro·graph·ic** /ˌreprəˈgrafik; ˌrē-/ **adj.** [1960s: from REPRODUCE + -GRAPHY.]

re·prove /riˈpro͞ov/ ▶ **v.** [trans.] reprimand or censure someone. — **re·prov·a·ble adj. re·prov·er n. re·prov·ing·ly adv.** [ME: from OFr. *reprover*, from late L. *reprobare* 'disapprove' (see REPROBATE).]

rep·tile /ˈreptəl; ˈrepˌtīl/ ▶ **n. 1** a cold-blooded vertebrate animal of a class (Reptilia) that includes snakes, lizards, crocodiles, turtles, and tortoises. They are distinguished by having a dry scaly skin and typically laying soft-shelled eggs on land. **2** informal a person regarded with loathing and contempt. ▶ **adj.** [attrib.] belonging to a reptile or to the class of reptiles. — **rep·til·i·an** /repˈtilēən; -ˈtilyən/ **adj. & n.** [ME: from late L., neut. of *reptilis*, from L. *rept-* 'crawled,' from the v. *repere*.]

re·pub·lic /riˈpəblik/ ▶ **n.** a state in which supreme power is held by the people and their elected representatives, and which has an elected or nominated president rather than a monarch. [16th C.: from Fr. *république*, from L. *respublica*, from *res* 'concern' + *publicus* 'of the people.']

re·pub·li·can /riˈpəblikən/ ▶ **adj.** (of a form of government, constitution, etc.) belonging to or characteristic of a republic. ■ advocating or supporting republican government. ▶ **n. 1** a person advocating or supporting republican government. **2** (**Republican**) a member or supporter of the Republican Party. — **re·pub·li·can·ism** /-ˌnizəm/ **n.**

Re·pub·li·can Par·ty one of the two main US political parties (the other being the Democratic Party), favoring a conservative stance, limited central government, and a strong national defense.

Re·pub·li·can Riv·er a river that flows for 445 miles (715 km) from northeastern Colorado to join the Smoky Hill River and form the Kansas River.

Re·pub·lic of Kal·myk·i·a-Khalmg Tangch official name for KALMYKIA.

re·pub·lish /rēˈpəblisH; ˈrē-/ ▶ **v.** [trans.] (often **be republished**) publish (a text) again, esp. in a new edition. — **re·pub·li·ca·tion** /ˌrēˌpəbləˈkāsHən/ **n.**

re·pu·di·ate /riˈpyo͞odēˌāt/ ▶ **v.** [trans.] refuse to accept or be associated with. ■ deny the truth or validity of. ■ esp. Law refuse to fulfill or discharge (an agreement, obligation, or debt). ■ (esp. in the past or in non-Christian religions) divorce (one's wife). — **re·pu·di·a·tion** /riˌpyo͞odēˈāsHən/ **n. re·pu·di·a·tor** /-ˌātər/ **n.** [ME (adj., 'divorced'): from L. *repudiatus* from *repudium* 'divorce.']

re·pug·nance /riˈpəgnəns/ ▶ **n. 1** intense disgust. **2** (also **repugnancy**) inconsistency or incompatibility of ideas or statements.

re·pug·nant /riˈpəgnənt/ ▶ **adj. 1** extremely distasteful; unacceptable. **2** [predic.] (**repugnant to**) in conflict with; incompatible with. — **re·pug·nant·ly adv.** [ME ('opposing resistance'): ult. from L. *repugnant-* 'oppose,' from *re-* 'back' + *pugnare* 'to fight.']

re·pulse /riˈpəls/ ▶ **v.** [trans.] **1** drive back (an attack or attacking enemy) by force. ■ fail to welcome (friendly advances or the person making them); rebuff. ■ refuse to accept (an offer). **2** (usu. **be repulsed**) cause (someone) to feel intense distaste and aversion. ▶ **n.** the action of driving back an attacking force or of being driven back. ■ a discouraging response to friendly advances. [ME: from L. *repuls-* 'driven back,' from *repellere* (see REPEL).]

re·pul·sion /riˈpəlsHən/ ▶ **n. 1** a feeling of intense distaste or disgust. **2** Physics a force under the influence of which objects tend to move away from each other, e.g., through having the same magnetic polarity or electric charge.

re·pul·sive /riˈpəlsiv/ ▶ **adj. 1** arousing intense distaste or disgust. **2** of or relating to repulsion between physical objects. — **re·pul·sive·ly adv. re·pul·sive·ness n.**

re·pur·chase /rēˈpərCHəs/ ▶ **v.** [trans.] buy (something) back. ▶ **n.** the action of buying something back. — **re·pur·chas·er n.**

re·pur·chase a·gree·ment ▶ **n.** Finance a contract in which the vendor of a security agrees to repurchase it from the buyer at an agreed price.

re·pur·pose /rēˈpərpəs/ ▶ **v.** [trans.] adapt for use in a different purpose.

rep·u·ta·ble /ˈrepyətəbəl/ ▶ **adj.** having a good reputation. — **rep·u·ta·bly** /-blē/ **adv.**

rep·u·ta·tion /ˌrepyəˈtāsHən/ ▶ **n.** the beliefs or opinions that are generally held about someone or something. ■ a widespread belief that someone or something has a particular habit or characteristic. [ME: from L. *reputatio(n-)*, from *reputare* (see REPUTE).]

re·pute /riˈpyo͞ot/ ▶ **n.** the opinion generally held of someone or something; the state of being generally regarded in a particular way. ■ the state of being highly thought of; fame. ▶ **v.** (**be reputed**) be generally said or believed to do something or to have particular characteristics. ■ [usu. as adj.] (**reputed**) be generally said or believed to exist or be of a particular type, despite not being so. ■ [usu. as adj.] (**reputed**) be widely known and well thought of. — **re·put·ed·ly adv.** [ME: ult. from L. *reputare* 'think over,' from *re-* (intensive force) + *putare* 'think.']

req. ▶ **abbr.** ■ require. ■ required. ■ requisition.

reqd. ▶ **abbr.** required.

re·quest /riˈkwest/ ▶ **n.** an act of asking politely or formally for something. ■ a thing that is asked for. ■ an instruction to a computer to provide information or perform another function. ■ a tune or song played on a radio program in response to a letter or call asking for it. ▶ **v.** [trans.] politely or formally ask for. ■ [with infin.] politely ask (someone) to do something.
– PHRASES **by** (or **on**) **request** in response to an expressed wish.
— **re·quest·er n.** [ME: from OFr. *requeste* (n.), based on L. *requirere* (see REQUIRE).]

req·ui·em /ˈrekwēəm; ˈrā-/ ▶ **n.** (also **req·ui·em Mass**) (esp. in the Roman Catholic Church) a Mass for the repose of the souls of the dead. ■ a musical composition setting parts of such a Mass, or of a similar character. ■ an act or token of remembrance. [ME: from L. (first word of the mass), accusative of *requies* 'rest.']

req·ui·em shark ▶ **n.** a migratory, livebearing shark (family Carcharhinidae) of warm seas, sometimes also found in brackish or fresh water. [17th C.: from obs. Fr. *requiem*, var. of *requin* 'shark,' influenced by REQUIEM.]

re·qui·es·cat /ˌrekwēˈesˌkät; ˌrā-/ ▶ **n.** a wish or prayer for the repose of a dead person. [L., from *requiescat in pace* (see RIP).]

re·quin·to /rāˈkēntō/ ▶ **n.** (pl. **-tos**) (in Spanish-speaking regions) a small guitar, typically tuned a fifth higher than a standard guitar. [Sp., lit. 'second fifth subtracted from a quantity.']

re·quire /riˈkwī(ə)r/ ▶ **v.** [trans.] need for a particular purpose; depend on for success or survival. ■ cause to be necessary. ■ specify as compulsory. ■ [trans.] (of someone in authority) instruct or expect (someone) to do something. ■ (**require something of**) regard an action, ability, or quality as due from (someone) by virtue of their position. ■ wish to have. — **re·quire·ment n. re·quir·er n.** [ME: from OFr. *requere*, from L. *requirere*, from *re-* (intensive force) + *quaerere* 'seek.']

req·ui·site /ˈrekwəzət/ ▶ **adj.** made necessary by particular circumstances or regulations. ▶ **n.** a thing that is necessary for the achievement of a specified end. — **req·ui·site·ly adv.** [ME: from L. *requisitus* 'searched for,' past part. of *requirere* (see REQUIRE).]

req·ui·si·tion /ˌrekwəˈzisHən/ ▶ **n.** an official order laying claim to the use of property or materials. ■ a formal written demand that some duty should be performed or something be put into operation. ■ the appropriation of goods, esp. for military or public use. ▶ **v.** [trans.] demand the use or supply of, esp. by official order and for military or public use. ■ demand the performance or occurrence of. — **req·ui·si·tion·er n.** [ME (n., 'demand'): ult. from L. *requisitio(n-)*, from *requirere* (see REQUIRE).]

re·quite /riˈkwīt/ ▶ **v.** [trans.] formal make appropriate return for (a favor or service); reward. ■ avenge or retaliate for (an injury or wrong). ■ return a favor to (someone). ■ respond to (love or affection); return. — **re·quit·al** /-ˈkwītl/ **n.** [16th C.: from RE- 'back' + obs. *quite*, var. of the v. QUIT[1].]

re·ran /rēˈran/ past of RERUN.

re·re·cord /ˌrē riˈkôrd/ ▶ **v.** [trans.] record (sound, esp. music) again.

rere·dos /ˈrerəˌdäs; ˈri(ə)rə-/ ▶ **n.** (pl. same) Christian Church an ornamental screen covering the wall at the back of an altar. [ME: from Anglo-Norman Fr., from OFr. *areredos*, from *arere* 'behind' + *dos* 'back.']

re·re·lease /ˌrē-riˈlēs/ (also **re-re·lease**) ▶ **v.** [trans.] release (a recording or movie) again. ▶ **n.** the action of releasing a recording or movie again. ■ a recording or movie that is released for a second or subsequent time.

re·run ▶ **v.** /rēˈrən/ (**-run·ning**; past **-ran**; past part. **-run**) [trans.] show or perform (something, esp. a television program) again. ▶ **n.** /ˈrēˌrən/ a program, event, or competition that occurs or is run again.

RES ▶ **abbr.** reticuloendothelial system.

res. ▶ **abbr.** ■ research. ■ reserve. ■ residence or resident(s). ■ resigned. ■ resolution.

re·sale /ˈrēˌsāl/ ▶ **n.** the sale of a thing previously bought. — **re·sal·a·ble** /rēˈsāləbəl/ (also **re·sale·a·ble**) **adj.**

re·sched·ule /rēˈskejo͞o(ə)l/ ▶ **v.** [trans.] change the time of (a planned event). ■ arrange a new scheme of repayments of (a debt).

re·scind /riˈsind/ ▶ **v.** [trans.] revoke, cancel, or repeal (a law, order, or agreement). — **re·scind·a·ble adj.** [16th C.: from L. *rescindere*, from *re-* (intensive force) + *scindere* 'to divide.']

re·scis·sion /riˈsizHən/ ▶ **n.** formal the revocation, cancellation, or repeal of a law, order, or agreement. [17th C.: from late L. *rescissio(n-)*, from *resciss-* 'split again,' from *rescindere* (see RESCIND).]

re·script /ˈrēˌskript/ ▶ **n.** an official edict or announcement. ■ hist. a Roman emperor's written reply to an appeal for guidance, esp. on a legal point. ■ the pope's decision on a question of Roman Catholic doctrine or papal law. [ME ('papal decision'): from L. *rescriptum*, neut. past part. of *rescribere* 'write back,' from *re-* + *scribere* 'write.']

res·cue /ˈreskyo͞o/ ▶ **v.** (**-cues, -cued, -cu·ing**) [trans.] save (someone) from a dangerous or distressing situation. ■ informal keep from being lost or abandoned; retrieve. ▶ **n.** an act of saving or being saved from danger or distress. ■ [as adj.] denoting the emergency excavation of archaeological sites threatened by imminent building or road development. — **res·cu·a·ble** adj. **res·cu·er** n. [ME: from OFr. *rescoure*, from L. *re-* (intensive force) + *excutere* 'shake out.']

re·search /ˈrēˌsərCH; riˈsərCH/ ▶n. the systematic investigation into and study of materials and sources in order to establish facts and reach new conclusions. ■ (**researches**) acts or periods of such investigation. ■ [as adj.] engaged in or intended for use in such investigation and discovery. ▶v. [trans.] investigate systematically. ■ discover facts by investigation for use in (a book, program, etc.). — **re·search·a·ble** adj. **re·search·er** n. [16th C.: from obs. Fr. *recerche* (n.), *recercher* (v.), from OFr. *re-* (intensive force) + *cerchier* 'to search.']

re·search and de·vel·op·ment ▶n. (in industry) work directed toward the innovation, introduction, and improvement of products and processes.

re·seat /rēˈsēt/ ▶v. [trans.] **1** cause (someone) to sit down again after they have risen. ■ cause to sit in a new position. ■ realign or repair (a tap, valve, or other object) in order to fit it into its correct position. **2** equip with new seats.

ré·seau /rāˈzō; ri-/ ▶n. (pl. **-seaux** /-ˈzōz/) a network or grid. ■ a plain net ground used in lacemaking. ■ a reference marking pattern on a photograph, used in astronomy and surveying. [16th C. (as a term in lacemaking): Fr., lit. 'net, web.']

re·sect /riˈsekt/ ▶v. [trans.] [often as adj.] (**resected**) Surg. cut out (tissue or part of an organ). — **re·sect·a·ble** adj. **re·sec·tion** /riˈsekSHən/ n. **re·sec·tion·al** /-SHənl/ adj. **re·sec·tion·ist** /-SHənist/ n. [17th C. ('remove'): from L. *resect-* 'cut off,' from the v. *resecare*, from *re-* 'back' + *secare* 'to cut.']

re·se·da /rəˈsēdə; ˈrāzəˌdä/ ▶n. **1** a plant of the genus *Reseda* (family Resedaceae), esp. (in gardening) a mignonette. **2** the pale green color of mignonette flowers. ▶adj. pale green. [18th C.: from L., interpreted as 'assuage!,' imper. of *resedare*, from its supposed curative powers.]

re·sem·blance /riˈzembləns/ ▶n. the state of resembling or being alike. ■ a way in which two or more things are alike.

re·sem·ble /riˈzembəl/ ▶v. [trans.] have qualities or features, esp. those of appearance, in common with (someone or something); look or seem like. — **re·sem·bler** /-blər/ n. (rare). [ME: from OFr. *resembler*, based on L. *similare* (from *similis* 'like').]

re·sent /riˈzent/ ▶v. [trans.] feel bitterness or indignation at (a circumstance, action, or person). [16th C. ('to experience'): from obs. Fr. *resentir*, from *re-* (intensive force) + *sentir* 'feel' (from L. *sentire*).]

re·sent·ful /riˈzentfəl/ ▶adj. feeling or expressing bitterness or indignation at having been treated unfairly. — **re·sent·ful·ly** adv. **re·sent·ful·ness** n.

re·sent·ment /riˈzentmənt/ ▶n. bitter indignation at having been treated unfairly.

res·er·pine /riˈsərˌpēn; -pən/ ▶n. Med. a compound of the alkaloid class obtained from Indian snakeroot and other plants and used in the treatment of hypertension. [1950s: from mod. L. *R(auwolfia) serp(entina)*, named after Leonhard *Rauwolf* (see RAUWOLFIA).]

res·er·va·tion /ˌrezərˈvāSHən/ ▶n. **1** the action of reserving something. ■ an arrangement whereby something, esp. a seat or room, is booked or reserved for a particular person. ■ an area of land set aside for occupation by North American Indians or Australian Aboriginals. ■ Law a right or interest retained in an estate being conveyed. ■ (in the Roman Catholic Church) the practice of retaining a portion of the consecrated elements after mass for communion of the sick or as a focus for devotion. **2** a qualification to an expression of agreement or approval; a doubt. **3** (in the Roman Catholic Church) the action of a superior of reserving to himself the power of absolution. ■ a right reserved to the pope of nomination to a vacant benefice.

re·serve /riˈzərv/ ▶v. [trans.] refrain from using or disposing of (something); retain for future use. ■ arrange for (a room, seat, ticket, etc.) to be kept for the use of a particular person and not given to anyone else. ■ retain or hold (an entitlement to something), esp. by formal or legal stipulation. ■ refrain from delivering (a judgment or decision) immediately or without due consideration or evidence. ■ (**reserve something for**) use or engage in something only in or at (a particular circumstance or time). ■ (in church use) retain (a portion of the consecrated elements) after mass for communion of the sick or as a focus for devotion. ▶n. **1** (often **reserves**) a supply of a commodity not needed for immediate use but available if required. ■ a force or body of troops kept back from action to reinforce or protect others, or additional to the regular forces and available in an emergency. ■ a member of the military reserve. ■ an extra player who is a possible substitute in a team. ■ (**the reserves**) the second-choice team. ■ funds kept available by a bank, company, or government. ■ a part of a company's profits added to capital rather than paid as a dividend. **2** a place set aside for special use, in particular: ■ an area designated as a habitat for a native people. ■ a protected area for wildlife. **3** a lack of warmth or openness in manner or expression. ■ qualification or doubt attached to some statement or claim. **4** short for RESERVE PRICE. **5** (in the decoration of ceramics or textiles) an area that still has the original color of the material or the color of the background.
– PHRASES **in reserve** unused and available if required. — **re·serv·a·ble** adj. **re·serv·er** n. [ME: from OFr. *reserver*, from L. *reservare* 'keep back,' from *re-* + *servare* 'to keep.']

re-serve /rēˈsərv; ˈrē-/ ▶v. [intrans.] (in various sports) serve again.

re·serve bank ▶n. a regional bank operating under and implementing the policies of the US Federal Reserve.

re·served /riˈzərvd/ ▶adj. **1** slow to reveal emotion or opinions. **2** kept specially for a particular purpose or person. — **re·serv·ed·ly** /riˈzərvədlē/ adv. **re·serv·ed·ness** /riˈzərvədnəs/ n.

re·served word ▶n. Comput. a word in a programming language that has a fixed meaning and cannot be redefined by the programmer.

re·serve price ▶n. the price stipulated as the lowest acceptable by the seller for an item sold at auction.

re·serv·ist /riˈzərvist/ ▶n. a member of the military reserve forces.

res·er·voir /ˈrezə(r)ˌvwär; -ˌv(w)ôr/ ▶n. a large natural or artificial lake used as a source of water supply. ■ a supply or source of something. ■ [usu. with adj.] a place where fluid collects, esp. in rock strata or in the body. ■ a receptacle or part of a machine designed to hold fluid. ■ Med. a population, tissue, etc., that is chronically infested with the causative agent of a disease and can act as a source of further infection. [17th C.: from Fr. *réservoir*, from *réserver* 'to reserve.']

re·set /rēˈset/ ▶v. (**-set·ting**; past and past part. **-set**) [trans.] set again or differently. ■ Electron. cause (a binary device) to enter the state representing the numeral 0. — **re·set·ta·bil·i·ty** /ˌrēˌsetəˈbilətē/ n. **re·set·ta·ble** adj.

re·set·tle /rēˈsetl/ ▶v. settle or cause to settle in a different place. — **re·set·tle·ment** n.

res ges·tae /ˈrās ˈgesˌtī; ˈrēz ˈjestē/ ▶plural n. Law the events, circumstances, remarks, etc., that relate to a particular case, esp. as constituting admissible evidence in a court of law. [L., lit. 'things done.']

re·shuf·fle /rēˈSHəfəl/ ▶v. [trans.] interchange the positions of (government appointees, members of a team, etc.). ■ put in a new order; rearrange. ▶n. an act of reorganizing or rearranging something.

re·side /riˈzīd/ ▶v. [intrans.] have one's permanent home in a particular place. ■ be situated. ■ (of power or a right) belong by right to a person or body. ■ (of a quality) be present or inherent in something. [ME ('be in residence as an official'): prob. a back-form. from RESIDENT.]

res·i·dence /ˈrez(ə)dəns; ˈrezəˌdens/ ▶n. a person's house, esp. a large and impressive one. ■ the official house of a government minister or other public and official figure. ■ the fact of living in a particular place.

res·i·dence time ▶n. tech. the average length of time during which a substance, a portion of material, or an object is in a given location or condition, such as adsorption or suspension.

res·i·den·cy /ˈrez(ə)dənsē; ˈrezəˌdensē/ ▶n. (pl. **-cies**) **1** the fact of living in a place. ■ a residential post held by a writer, musician, or artist, typically for teaching purposes. **2** hist. the official residence of the British governor general's representative or other government agent, esp. at the court of an Indian state. ■ a group or organization of intelligence agents in a foreign country. **3** a period of specialized medical training in a hospital; the position of a resident: *Cora is in residency.*

res·i·dent /ˈrez(ə)dənt; ˈrezəˌdent/ ▶n. **1** a person who lives somewhere permanently or on a long-term basis. ■ a bird, butterfly, or other animal of a species that does not migrate. ■ a person who boards at a boarding school. **2** a medical graduate engaged in specialized practice under supervision in a hospital. ▶adj. living somewhere on a long-term basis. ■ having quarters on the premises of one's work. ■ attached to and working regularly for a particular institution. ■ (of a bird, butterfly, or other animal) nonmigratory; remaining in an area throughout the year. ■ (of a computer program, file, etc.) immediately available in computer memory, rather than having to be loaded from elsewhere. — **res·i·dent·ship** /-ˌSHip/ n. (hist.). [ME: from L. *resident-* 'remaining,' from the v. *residere*, from *re-* 'back' + *sedere* 'sit.']

res·i·dent com·mis·sion·er ▶n. a delegate elected to represent a dependency, such as Puerto Rico, in the US House of Representatives. They may speak in the House and serve on committees, but may not vote.

res·i·den·tial /ˌrezəˈdenCHəl/ ▶adj. designed for people to live in. ■ providing accommodations in addition to other services. ■ occupied by private houses. ■ concerning or relating to residence. — **res·i·den·tial·ly** adv.

res·i·den·ti·ar·y /ˌrezəˈdenCHēˌerē; -ˈdenCHərē/ ▶adj. required to live officially in a cathedral or collegiate church. ■ relating to or involving residence in an establishment or place. ▶n. (pl. **-ar·ies**) a residentiary canon. [16th C. (n.): from med. L. *residentiarius*, from L. *resident-* (see RESIDENT).]

re·sid·u·a /riˈzijo͞oə/ plural form of RESIDUUM.

re·sid·u·al /riˈzijo͞oəl/ ▶adj. remaining after the greater part or quantity has gone. ■ (of a quantity) left after other things have been subtracted. ■ (of a physical state or property) remaining after the removal of or present in the absence of a causative agent. ■ (of an experimental or arithmetical error) not accounted for or eliminated. ■ (of a soil or other deposit) formed in situ by weathering. ▶n. a quantity remaining after other things have been subtracted or allowed for. ■ a difference between a value measured in a scientific experiment and the theoretical or true value. ■ a royalty paid to a performer, writer, etc., for a repeat of a play, television show, etc. ■ Geol. a portion of rocky or high ground remaining after erosion. ■ the resale value of a new car or other item at a specified time after purchase, expressed as a percentage of its purchase price. — **re·sid·u·al·ly** /-o͞oəlē/ adv.

re·sid·u·ar·y /riˈzijo͞oˌerē/ ▶adj. tech. residual. ■ Law of or relating to the residue of an estate.

res·i·due /ˈrezəˌd(y)o͞o/ ▶n. a small amount of something that remains after the main part has gone or been taken or used. ■ Law the part of an estate that is left after the payment of charges, debts, and bequests. ■ a substance that remains after a process such as combustion or evaporation. [ME: from OFr. *residu*, from L. *residuum* (see RESIDUUM).]

re·sid·u·um /riˈzijo͞oəm/ ▶**n.** (pl. **-sid·u·a** /-ˈzijo͞oə/) tech. a substance or thing that remains or is left behind, in particular, a chemical residue. [17th C.: from L., neut. of *residuus* 'remaining,' from the v. *residere*.]

re·sign /riˈzīn/ ▶**v. 1** [intrans.] voluntarily leave a job or other position. ■ [trans.] give up (an office, power, privilege, etc.). ■ [intrans.] Chess end a game by conceding defeat without being checkmated. **2** (**be resigned**) accept that something undesirable cannot be avoided. —**re·sign·ed·ly** /riˈzīnədlē/ **adv. re·sign·ed·ness** /riˈzīnədnəs/ **n. re·sign·er n.** [ME: from OFr. *resigner*, from L. *resignare* 'unseal,' from *re-* 'back' + *signare* 'sign, seal.']

re-sign /rēˈsīn/ ▶**v.** [trans.] sign (a document) again. ■ engage (a sports player) to play for a team for a further period. ■ [intrans.] (of a sports player) commit oneself to play for a team for a further period.

res·ig·na·tion /ˌrezigˈnāsʜən/ ▶**n. 1** an act of retiring or giving up a position. ■ a document conveying someone's intention of retiring. ■ Chess an act of ending a game by conceding defeat without being checkmated. **2** the acceptance of something undesirable but inevitable.

re·sile /riˈzīl/ ▶**v.** [intrans.] formal abandon a position or a course of action. [16th C.: ult. from L. *resilire* 'to recoil,' from *re-* 'back' + *salire* 'to jump.']

re·sil·ient /riˈzilyənt/ ▶**adj.** (of a substance or object) able to recoil or spring back into shape after bending, stretching, or being compressed. ■ (of a person or animal) able to withstand or recover quickly from difficult conditions. —**re·sil·ience n. re·sil·ien·cy n. re·sil·ient·ly adv.** [17th C.: from L. *resilient-* 'leaping back,' from *resilire* (see **RESILE**).]

res·i·lin /ˈrezələn/ ▶**n.** Biochem. an elastic material formed of cross-linked protein chains, found in insect cuticles, esp. in the hinges and ligaments of wings. [1960s: from L. *resilire* 'leap back.']

res·in /ˈrezən/ ▶**n.** a sticky flammable organic substance, insoluble in water, exuded by some trees and other plants (notably fir and pine). Compare with **GUM**[1] (sense 1). ■ (also **syn·the·tic res·in**) a solid or liquid synthetic organic polymer used as the basis of plastics, adhesives, varnishes, or other products. ▶**v.** (**res·ined, res·in·ing**) [trans.] [usu. as adj.] (**resined**) rub or treat with resin. —**res·in·ous** /ˈrezənəs/ **adj.** [ME: from L. *resina*; akin to Gk. *rhētinē* 'pine resin.']

res·in·ate ▶**v.** /ˈrezəˌnāt/ [trans.] impregnate or flavor with resin. ▶**n.** Chem. a salt of an acid derived from resin.

res ip·sa lo·qui·tur /ˌrēz ˌipsə ˈläkwitər; ˌrās; ˈlōkwəˌto͝or/ ▶**n.** Law the principle that the occurrence of an accident implies negligence. [L., lit. 'the matter speaks for itself.']

re·sist /riˈzist/ ▶**v.** [trans.] withstand the action or effect of. ■ try to prevent by action or argument. ■ succeed in ignoring the attraction of (something wrong or unwise). ■ [intrans.] struggle against someone or something. ▶**n.** a resistant substance applied as a coating to protect a surface during some process, for example to prevent dye or glaze adhering. —**re·sist·er n. re·sist·i·ble adj. re·sist·i·bil·i·ty** /riˌzistəˈbilətē/ **n.** [ME: from OFr. *resister* or L. *resistere*, from *re-* 'back' + *sistere* 'stop' (reduplication of *stare* 'to stand').]

re·sist·ance /riˈzistəns/ ▶**n. 1** the refusal to accept or comply with something; the attempt to prevent something by action or argument. ■ armed or violent opposition. ■ (also **re·sist·ance move·ment**) [in sing.] a secret organization resisting authority, esp. in an occupied country. ■ (**the Resistance**) the underground movement formed in France during World War II to fight the German occupying forces and the Vichy government. Also called **MAQUIS**. ■ the impeding, slowing, or stopping effect exerted by one material thing on another. **2** the ability not to be affected by something, esp. adversely. ■ Med. Biol. lack of sensitivity to a drug, insecticide, etc., esp. as a result of continued exposure or genetic change. **3** the degree to which a substance or device opposes the passage of an electric current, causing energy dissipation. Ohm's law resistance (measured in ohms) is equal to the voltage divided by the current. ■ a resistor or other circuit component that opposes the passage of an electric current.

re·sist·ant /riˈzistənt/ ▶**adj.** offering resistance to something or someone.

re·sis·tive /riˈzistiv/ ▶**adj.** tech. able to withstand the action or effect of something. ■ Physics of or concerning electrical resistance.

re·sis·tiv·i·ty /riˌzisˈtivətē/ ▶**n.** Physics a measure of the resisting power of a specified material to the flow of an electric current.

re·sis·tor /riˈzistər/ ▶**n.** Physics a device having resistance to the passage of an electric current.

re·size /rēˈsīz/ ▶**v.** [trans.] alter the size of (something, esp. a computer window or image).

res ju·di·ca·ta /ˌrēz jo͞odiˈkätə; ˌrās/ ▶**n.** (pl. **res ju·de·ca·tae** /ˌjo͞odiˈkätē; -tī/) Law a matter that has been adjudicated by a competent court and may not be pursued further by the same parties. [L., lit. 'judged matter.']

re·skin /rēˈskin/ ▶**v.** (**-skinned, -skin·ning**) [trans.] replace or repair the skin of (an aircraft or motor vehicle).

Res·nais /rəˈnā; rəˈne/, Alain (1922–), French director. He directed the movie *Hiroshima mon amour* (1959).

res·o·lute /ˈrezəˌlo͞ot; -lət/ ▶**adj.** admirably purposeful, determined, and unwavering. —**res·o·lute·ly adv. res·o·lute·ness n.** [ME ('(of a rent) paid'): from L. *resolutus* 'loosened,' past part. of *resolvere* (see **RESOLVE**).]

res·o·lu·tion /ˌrezəˈlo͞osʜən/ ▶**n. 1** a firm decision to do or not to do something. ■ a formal expression of opinion or intention agreed on by a legislative body, committee, or other formal meeting, typically after taking a vote. ■ the quality of being determined or resolute. **2** the action of solving a problem, dispute, or contentious matter. ■ Music the passing of a discord into a concord during the course of changing harmony. ■ Med. the disappearance of inflammation, or of any symptom or condition. **3** esp. Chem. the process of reducing or separating something into constituent parts or components. ■ Physics the replacing of a single force or other vector quantity by two or more jointly equivalent to it. ■ the conversion of something abstract into another form. ■ Pros. the substitution of two short syllables for one long one. **4** the smallest interval measurable by a scientific (esp. optical) instrument; the resolving power. ■ the degree of detail visible in a photographic or television image. [ME: from L. *resolutio(n-)*, from *resolvere* 'loosen' (see **RESOLVE**).]

re·solve /riˈzälv; -ˈzôlv/ ▶**v. 1** [trans.] settle or find a solution to (a problem, dispute, or contentious matter). ■ [trans.] Med. cause (a symptom or condition) to disperse, subside, or heal. ■ [intrans.] (of a symptom or condition) disperse, subside, or heal. ■ [intrans.] Music (of a discord) lead into a concord during the course of harmonic change. ■ [trans.] Music cause (a discord) to pass into a concord. **2** [intrans.] decide firmly on a course of action. ■ [with clause] (of a legislative body, committee, or other formal meeting) make a decision by a formal vote. **3** esp. Chem. separate or cause to be separated into constituent parts or components. ■ [trans.] (**resolve something into**) reduce a subject, statement, etc., by mental analysis into (separate elements or a more elementary form). ■ [intrans.] (of something seen at a distance) turn into a different form when seen more clearly. ■ [trans.] (of optical or photographic equipment) separate or distinguish between (closely adjacent objects). ■ [trans.] separately distinguish (peaks in a graph or spectrum). ■ [trans.] Physics analyze (a force or velocity) into components acting in particular directions. ▶**n.** firm determination to do something. ■ a formal resolution by a legislative body or public meeting. —**re·solv·a·bil·i·ty** /riˌzälvəˈbilətē; -ˈzôlvə-/ **n. re·solv·a·ble adj. re·solv·er n.** [ME ('dissolve,' 'solve'): from L. *resolvere*, from *re-* (intensive force) + *solvere* 'loosen.']

re·solved /riˈzälvd; -ˈzôlvd/ ▶**adj.** [predic., with infin.] firmly determined to do something. —**re·solv·ed·ly** /riˈzälvədlē; -ˈzôlvədlē/ **adv.**

re·sol·vent /riˈzälvənt; -ˈzôl-/ Math. ▶**adj.** denoting an equation, function, or expression that is introduced in order to reach or complete a solution. ▶**n.** an equation, function, or expression of this type.

res·o·nance /ˈrezənəns/ ▶**n.** the quality in a sound of being deep, full, and reverberating. ■ fig. the ability to evoke or suggest images, memories, and emotions. ■ Physics the reinforcement or prolongation of sound by reflection from a surface or by the synchronous vibration of a neighboring object. ■ Mech. the condition in which an object or system is subjected to an oscillating force having a frequency close to its own natural frequency. ■ the condition in which an electric circuit or device produces the largest possible response to an applied oscillating signal, esp. when its inductive and its capacitative reactances are balanced. ■ Physics a short-lived subatomic particle that is an excited state of a more stable particle. ■ Astron. the occurrence of a simple ratio between the periods of revolution of two bodies about a single primary. ■ Chem. the state attributed to certain molecules of having a structure that cannot adequately be represented by a single structural formula but is a composite of two or more structures of higher energy.

res·o·nant /ˈrezənənt/ ▶**adj.** (of sound) deep, clear, and continuing to sound or ring. ■ tech. of, relating to, or bringing about resonance in a circuit, atom, or other object. ■ (of a room, a musical instrument, or a hollow body) tending to reinforce or prolong sounds, esp. by synchronous vibration. ■ (of a color) enhancing or enriching another color or colors by contrast. ■ [predic.] (**resonant with**) (of a place) filled or resounding with (the sound of something). ■ fig. having the ability to evoke or suggest enduring images, memories, or emotions. —**res·o·nant·ly adv.**

res·o·nate /ˈrezəˌnāt/ ▶**v.** [intrans.] produce or be filled with a deep, full, reverberating sound. ■ fig. evoke or suggest images, memories, and emotions. ■ (of an idea or action) meet with someone's agreement. ■ tech. produce electrical or mechanical resonance. [19th C.: from L. *resonat-* 'resounded,' from *resonare* (see **RESOUND**).]

res·o·na·tor /ˈrezənˌātər/ ▶**n.** an apparatus that increases the resonance of a sound, esp. a hollow part of a musical instrument. ■ a musical or scientific instrument responding to a single sound or note, used for detecting it when it occurs in combination with other sounds. ■ Physics a device that displays electrical resonance, esp. one used for the detection of radio waves. ■ Physics a hollow enclosure with conducting walls capable of containing electromagnetic fields having particular frequencies of oscillation and exchanging electrical energy with them, used to detect or amplify microwaves.

re·sorb /rēˈsôrb; -ˈzôrb/ ▶**v.** [trans.] tech. absorb (something) again. ■ Physiol. remove (cells, or a tissue or structure) by gradual breakdown into its component materials and dispersal in the circulation. [17th C.: from L. *resorbere*, from *re-* (intensive force) + *sorbere* 'absorb.']

res·or·cin·ol /rəˈzôrsəˌnôl; -ˌnōl/ ▶**n.** Chem. a crystalline compound, $C_6H_4(OH)_2$, originally obtained from galbanum resin, used in the production of dyes, resins, and cosmetics. [19th C.: from *resorcin*.]

re·sorp·tion /rēˈsôrpsʜən; -ˈzôrp-/ ▶**n.** the process or action by which something is reabsorbed. ■ Physiol. the absorption into the circulation of cells or tissue. — **re·sorp·tive** /-tiv/ **adj.** [19th C.: from **RESORB**, on the pattern of the pair *absorb, absorption*.]

re·sort /ri'zôrt/ ▶ **n.** **1** a place that is a popular destination for vacations or recreation, or which is frequented for a particular purpose. **2** the action of turning to and adopting a strategy or course of action, esp. a disagreeable or undesirable one, so as to resolve a difficult situation. ■ [in sing.] a strategy or course of action that may be adopted in a difficult situation. ▶ **v.** [intrans.] (**resort to**) turn to and adopt (a strategy or course of action, esp. a disagreeable or undesirable one) so as to resolve a difficult situation.
– PHRASES **as a first** (or **last** or **final**) **resort** before anything else is attempted (or when all else has failed). — **re·sort·er n.** [ME ('something one can turn to for assistance'): from OFr. *resortir*, from *re-* 'again' + *sortir* 'go out.']

re-sort /rē 'sôrt/ ▶ **v.** [trans.] sort (something) again or differently.

re·sound /ri'zound/ ▶ **v.** [intrans.] (of a sound, voice, etc.) fill a place with sound; be loud enough to echo. ■ (of a place) be filled or echo with a particular sound or sounds. ■ fig. (of fame, a person's reputation, etc.) be much talked of. ■ [trans.] literary sing (the praises) of. ■ [trans.] literary (of a place) reecho (a sound). [ME: from **RE-** 'again' + the v. **SOUND**[1], suggested by OFr. *resoner* or L. *resonare* 'sound again.']

re·sound·ing /ri'zoundiNG/ ▶ **adj.** **1** (of a sound) loud enough to reverberate. **2** [attrib.] unmistakable; emphatic. — **re·sound·ing·ly adv.**

re·source /'rē,sôrs; 'rē'zôrs; ri'sôrs; ri'zôrs/ ▶ **n.** **1** (usu. **resources**) a stock or supply of money, materials, staff, and other assets that can be drawn on by a person or organization in order to function effectively. ■ (**resources**) a country's collective means of supporting itself or becoming wealthier, as represented by its reserves of minerals, land, and other assets. ■ (**resources**) available assets. **2** an action or strategy that may be adopted in adverse circumstances. ■ (**resources**) one's personal attributes and capabilities regarded as able to help or sustain one in adverse circumstances. ■ the ability to find quick and clever ways to overcome difficulties. ■ a teaching aid. ▶ **v.** [trans.] provide (a person or organization) with materials, money, staff, and other assets necessary for effective operation. [17th C.: from obs. Fr. *ressourse*, fem. past part. of OFr. dial. *resourdre* 'rise again' (based on L. *surgere* 'to rise').]

re·source·ful /ri'sôrsfəl; -'zôrs-/ ▶ **adj.** having the ability to find clever ways to overcome difficulties. — **re·source·ful·ly adv. re·source·ful·ness n.**

resp. ▶ **abbr.** ■ respective. ■ respectively. ■ respelled; respelling. ■ respondent.

re·spect /ri'spekt/ ▶ **n.** **1** a feeling of deep admiration for someone or something elicited by their abilities, qualities, or achievements. ■ the state of being admired in such a way. ■ due regard for the feelings, wishes, rights, or traditions of others. ■ (**respects**) a person's polite greetings. **2** a particular aspect, point, or detail. ▶ **v.** [trans.] admire (someone or something) deeply, as a result of their abilities, qualities, or achievements. ■ have due regard for the feelings, wishes, rights, or traditions of. ■ avoid harming or interfering with. ■ agree to recognize and abide by (a legal requirement).
– PHRASES **with respect to** as regards; with reference to. **pay one's respects, pay one's last respects** see **PAY**[1]. **with** (or **with all due**) **respect** used as a polite formula preceding, and intended to mitigate the effect of, an expression of disagreement or criticism: *with all due respect, Father, I think you've got to be more broad-minded.* [ME: from L. *respectus*, from *respicere* 'look back at,' from *re-* + *specere* 'look at.']

re·spect·a·bil·i·ty /ri,spektə'bilətē/ ▶ **n.** the state or quality of being proper, correct, and socially acceptable. ■ the state or quality of being accepted as valid or important within a particular field.

re·spect·a·ble /ri'spektəbəl/ ▶ **adj.** **1** regarded by society to be good, proper, or correct. ■ (of a person's appearance, clothes, or behavior) decent or presentable. **2** of some merit or importance. ■ adequate or acceptable in number, size, or amount. — **re·spect·a·bly** /-blē/ **adv.**

re·spect·er /ri'spektər/ ▶ **n.** [usu. with negative] a person who has a high regard for someone or something.

re·spect·ful /ri'spektfəl/ ▶ **adj.** feeling or showing deference and respect. — **re·spect·ful·ly adv. re·spect·ful·ness n.**

re·spect·ing /ri'spektiNG/ ▶ **prep.** dated formal with reference or regard to.

re·spec·tive /ri'spektiv/ ▶ **adj.** [attrib.] belonging or relating separately to each of two or more people or things.

re·spec·tive·ly /ri'spektivlē/ ▶ **adv.** separately or individually and in the order already mentioned (used when enumerating two or more items or facts that refer back to a previous statement): *they received sentences of one year and eight months, respectively.*

re·spell /rē'spel/ ▶ **v.** (past and past part. **-spelled** or esp. Brit. **-spelt**) [trans.] spell (a word) again or differently, esp. phonetically in order to indicate its pronunciation.

res·pi·ra·ble /'respərəbəl; ri'spīrəbəl/ ▶ **adj.** (of the air or a gas) able or fit to be breathed. ■ (of particles in the air) able to be breathed in.

res·pi·rate /'respə,rāt/ ▶ **v.** [trans.] Med. Biol. assist (a person or animal) to breathe by means of artificial respiration. [17th C.: back-form. from **RESPIRATION**.]

res·pi·ra·tion /,respə'rāSHən/ ▶ **n.** the action of breathing. ■ esp. Med. a single breath. ■ Biol. a process in living organisms involving the production of energy, typically with the intake of oxygen and the release of carbon dioxide from the oxidation of complex organic substances. [ME: from L. *respiratio(n-)*, from *respirare* (see **RESPIRE**).]

res·pi·ra·tor /'respə,rātər/ ▶ **n.** an apparatus worn over the mouth and nose or the entire face to prevent the inhalation of dust, smoke, or other noxious substances. ■ an apparatus used to induce artificial respiration.

res·pi·ra·to·ry /'respərə,tôrē; ri'spīrə-/ ▶ **adj.** of, relating to, or affecting respiration or the organs of respiration.

res·pi·ra·to·ry dis·tress syn·drome ▶ **n.** another term for **HYALINE MEMBRANE DISEASE**.

res·pi·ra·to·ry pig·ment ▶ **n.** Biochem. a substance (such as hemoglobin or hemocyanin) with a molecule consisting of protein with a pigmented prosthetic group, involved in the physiological transport of oxygen or electrons.

res·pi·ra·to·ry quo·tient ▶ **n.** Physiol. the ratio of the volume of carbon dioxide evolved to that of oxygen consumed by an organism, tissue, or cell in a given time.

res·pi·ra·to·ry tract ▶ **n.** the passage formed by the mouth, nose, throat, and lungs, through which air passes during breathing.

re·spire /ri'spī(ə)r/ ▶ **v.** [intrans.] breathe. ■ (of a plant) carry out respiration, esp. at night when photosynthesis has ceased. ■ literary recover hope, courage, or strength after a time of difficulty. [ME: ult. from L. *respirare* 'breathe out,' from *re-* 'again' + *spirare* 'breathe.']

res·pi·rom·e·ter /,respə'rämətər/ ▶ **n.** Biol. a device that measures the rate of consumption of oxygen by a living organism or organic system. ■ Med. an instrument for measuring the air capacity of the lungs.

res·pite /'respət; ri'spīt/ ▶ **n.** a short period of rest or relief from something difficult or unpleasant. ■ a short delay permitted before an unpleasant obligation is met or a punishment is carried out. [ME: from OFr. *respit*, from L. *respectus* 'refuge, consideration.']

res·pite care ▶ **n.** temporary institutional care of a dependent elderly, ill, or handicapped person, providing relief for their usual caregivers.

re·splend·ent /ri'splendənt/ ▶ **adj.** attractive and impressive through being richly colorful or sumptuous. — **re·splend·ence n. re·splend·en·cy n. re·splend·ent·ly adv.** [ME: from L. *resplendent-* 'shining out,' from the v. *resplendere*, from *re-* (intensive force) + *splendere* 'to glitter.']

re·spond /ri'spänd/ ▶ **v.** [reporting verb] say something in reply. ■ (of a congregation) say or sing the response in reply to a priest. ■ [intrans.] (of a person) act or behave in reaction to someone or something. ■ react quickly or positively to a stimulus or treatment. ■ [trans.] Bridge make (a bid) in answer to one's partner's preceding bid. ▶ **n.** **1** Archit. a half-pillar or half-pier attached to a wall to support an arch, esp. at the end of an arcade. **2** (in church use) a responsory; a response to a versicle. — **re·spond·er n.** [ME ('responsory'): from OFr., from *respondre* 'to answer,' from L. *respondere*, from *re-* 'again' + *spondere* 'to pledge.']

re·spond·ent /ri'spändənt/ ▶ **n.** **1** a defendant in a lawsuit, esp. one in an appeals or divorce case. **2** a person who replies to something, esp. one supplying information for a survey or questionnaire or responding to an advertisement. ▶ **adj.** [attrib.] **1** in the position of defendant in a lawsuit. **2** replying to something, esp. a survey or questionnaire. **3** Psychol. involving or denoting a response, esp. a conditioned reflex, to a specific stimulus.

re·sponse /ri'späns/ ▶ **n.** a verbal or written answer. ■ a written or verbal answer to a question in a test, questionnaire, survey, etc. ■ a reaction to something. ■ Psychol. Physiol. an excitation of a nerve impulse caused by a change or event; a physical reaction to a specific stimulus or situation. ■ the way in which a mechanical or electrical device responds to a stimulus or range of stimuli. ■ (usu. **responses**) a part of a religious liturgy said or sung by a congregation in answer to a minister or cantor. ■ Bridge a bid made in answer to one's partner's preceding bid. [ME: ult. from L. *responsum*, neut. past part. of *respondere* (see **RESPOND**).]

re·sponse time ▶ **n.** the length of time it takes to react to a given stimulus or event.

re·spon·si·bil·i·ty /ri,spänsə'bilətē/ ▶ **n.** (pl. **-ties**) the state or fact of having a duty to deal with something. ■ the state or fact of being accountable or to blame for something. ■ the opportunity or ability to act independently and make decisions without authorization. ■ (often **responsibilities**) a thing that one is required to do as part of a job, role, or legal obligation. ■ [in sing.] (**responsibility to/toward**) a moral obligation to behave correctly toward or in respect of.

re·spon·si·ble /ri'spänsəbəl/ ▶ **adj.** [predic.] having an obligation to do something as part of a job or role. ■ being the primary cause of something and so able to be blamed or credited for it. ■ [attrib.] (of a job or position) involving important duties, independent decision-making, or control over others. ■ [predic.] (**responsible to**) having to report to (a superior or someone in authority) and be answerable to them. ■ capable of being trusted. ■ morally accountable for one's behavior. — **re·spon·si·ble·ness n. re·spon·si·bly** /-blē/ **adv.**

re·spon·sive /ri'spänsiv/ ▶ **adj.** **1** reacting quickly and positively. ■ responding readily and with interest or enthusiasm. **2** answering. ■ (of a section of liturgy) using responses. — **re·spon·sive·ly adv. re·spon·sive·ness n.**

re·spon·so·ri·al /ri,spän'sôrēəl/ ▶ **adj.** (of a psalm or liturgical chant) recited in parts with a congregational response between each part.

re·spon·so·ry /ri'spänsərē/ ▶ **n.** (pl. **-ries**) (in the Christian Church) an anthem said or sung after a lesson. [ME: from late L. *responsorium*, from L. *respons-* 'answered,' from *respondere* (see **RESPOND**).]

res pu·bli·ca /rās 'po͞obli,kä; 'pəblikə/ ▶ **n.** the state, republic, or commonwealth. [L., lit. 'public matter.']

res·sen·ti·ment /rə,säNtē'mäN/ ▶ **n.** a psychological state arising from suppressed feelings of envy and hatred that cannot be acted upon. [via Ger. from Fr. *ressentiment* 'feeling.']

rest[1] /rest/ ▶**v.** [intrans.] **1** cease work or movement in order to relax, refresh oneself, or recover strength. ■ [trans.] allow to be inactive in order to regain strength, health, or energy. ■ (of a dead person or body) lie buried. ■ (of a problem or subject) be left without further investigation, discussion, or treatment: *allow the matter to rest.* ■ [trans.] allow (land) to lie fallow. ■ conclude the case for the prosecution or the defense in a law case. See also REST ONE'S CASE below. **2** [intrans.] be placed or supported so as to stay in a specified position: *resting on the sofa.* ■ [trans.] place (something) so that it is supported in a specified position. ■ **(rest on/upon)** (of a look) alight or be steadily directed on. ■ **(rest on/upon)** be based on or grounded in; depend on. ■ [trans.] **(rest something in/on)** place hope, trust, or confidence in or on: *she rested her hopes in her attorney.* ■ belong or be located at a specified place or with a specified person: *ultimate control rested with the founders.* ▶**n. 1** an instance or period of relaxing or ceasing to engage in strenuous or stressful activity. ■ refreshment through sleep. ■ a motionless state. ■ Music an interval of silence of a specified duration. ■ Music the sign denoting such an interval. ■ a pause in elocution. ■ a caesura in verse. ■ [in place names] a place where people can stay. **2** [in comb.] an object that supports something: *a chin-rest.*

– PHRASES **at rest** not moving or exerting oneself. ■ not agitated or troubled; tranquil. ■ dead and buried. **come to rest** stop moving; settle. **give it a rest** informal used to ask someone to stop doing something or talking about something that the speaker finds irritating or tedious. **no rest for the weary** see WEARY. **put** (or **set**) **someone's mind** (or **doubts** or **fears**) **at rest** relieve someone of anxiety or uncertainty; reassure someone. **rest one's case** conclude one's presentation of evidence and arguments in a lawsuit. ■ humorous said to show that one believes one has presented sufficient evidence for one's views. **rest on one's laurels** see LAUREL. **rest** (or **God rest**) **his** (or **her**) **soul** used to express a wish that God should grant someone's soul peace. **rest on one's oars** see OAR. [OE *rest* (n.), *restan* (v.), from Gmc., orig. 'league' or 'mile' (a distance after which one rests).]

rest[2] ▶**n.** [in sing.] the remaining part of something. ■ [treated as pl.] the remaining people or things; the others: *the rest of us were experienced skiers.* ▶**v.** [intrans.] remain or be left in a specified condition: *rest assured.*

– PHRASES **the rest is history** see HISTORY. [ME: from OFr. *reste* (n.), *rester* (v.), from L. *restare* 'remain,' from *re-* 'back' + *stare* 'to stand.']

re·state /rē'stāt/ ▶**v.** [trans.] state (something) again or differently, esp. more clearly or convincingly. — **re·state·ment n.**

res·tau·rant /'rest(ə)rənt; 'restə,ränt; 'res,tränt/ ▶**n.** a place where people pay to eat meals. [19th C.: from Fr., from *restaurer* 'provide food for' (lit. 'restore').]

res·tau·ra·teur /,restərə'tər/ ▶**n.** a person who owns and manages a restaurant. [18th C.: Fr., from the v. *restaurer* (see RESTAURANT).]

rest cure ▶**n.** a period spent in inactivity with the intention of improving one's physical or mental health.

re·ste·no·sis /,rēstə'nōsəs/ ▶**n.** Med. the recurrence of abnormal narrowing of an artery or valve after corrective surgery. [1950s: from RE- 'again' + STENOSIS.]

rest·ful /'restfəl/ ▶**adj.** having a soothing quality. — **rest·ful·ly adv. rest·ful·ness n.**

rest home ▶**n.** a residential institution where old or frail people are cared for.

rest·ing po·ten·tial ▶**n.** Physiol. the electrical potential of a neuron or other excitable cell relative to its surroundings when at rest.

res·ti·tu·tion /,restə't(y)o͞oSHən/ ▶**n. 1** the restoration of something lost or stolen to its proper owner. **2** recompense for injury or loss. **3** the restoration of something to its original state. ■ Physics the resumption of an object's original shape or position through elastic recoil. — **res·ti·tu·tive** /'restə,t(y)o͞otiv/ **adj.** [ME: ult. from L. *restitutio(n-)*, from *restituere* 'restore,' from *re-* 'again' + *statuere* 'establish.']

res·tive /'restiv/ ▶**adj.** (of a person) unable to keep still or silent and becoming increasingly difficult to control. ■ (of a horse) refusing to advance, stubbornly standing still, or moving backward or sideways. — **res·tive·ly adv. res·tive·ness n.** [16th C. ('inactive'): from OFr. *restif, -ive*, from L. *restare* 'remain.']

rest·less /'restləs/ ▶**adj.** (of a person or animal) unable to rest or relax as a result of anxiety or boredom. ■ offering no physical or emotional rest; involving constant activity or motion: *a restless night.* — **rest·less·ly adv. rest·less·ness n.**

rest mass ▶**n.** Physics the mass of a body when at rest.

re·stock /rē'stäk/ ▶**v.** [trans.] replenish (a store) with fresh stock or supplies: *restock the fishery.*

res·to·ra·tion /,restə'rāSHən/ ▶**n. 1** the return of something to a former owner, place, or condition. ■ the process of repairing or renovating a building, work of art, etc., so as to restore it to its original condition. ■ the reinstatement of a previous practice, right, custom, or situation. ■ Dentistry a structure provided to replace or repair dental tissue so as to restore its form and function. ■ a model or drawing representing the supposed original form of an extinct animal, ruined building, etc. **2** the return of a hereditary monarch to a throne, a head of state to government, or a regime to power. ■ **(the Restoration)** the reestablishment of Charles II as King of England in 1660. ■ **(Restoration)** [usu. as adj.] the period following this.

Res·to·ra·tion com·e·dy ▶**n.** a style of drama that flourished in London after the Restoration in 1660.

re·stor·a·tive /ri'stôrətiv/ ▶**adj.** having the ability to restore health, strength, or a feeling of well-being. ■ Surg. Dentistry relating to or concerned with the restoration of form or function to a damaged tooth or other part of the body. ▶**n.** something, esp. a medicine or drink, that restores health, strength, or well-being. — **re·stor·a·tive·ly adv.**

re·store /ri'stôr/ ▶**v.** [trans.] bring back; reinstate. ■ return (someone or something) to a former condition, place, or position. ■ repair or renovate (a building, work of art, vehicle, etc.) so as to return it to its original condition. ■ give (something previously stolen, taken away, or lost) back to the original owner or recipient. — **re·stor·a·ble adj. re·stor·er n.** [ME: from OFr. *restorer*, from L. *restaurare* 'rebuild, restore.']

re·strain /ri'strān/ ▶**v.** [trans.] prevent (someone or something) from doing something; keep under control. ■ prevent oneself from displaying or giving way to (a strong urge or emotion. ■ deprive (someone) of freedom of movement or personal liberty. ■ (of a seat belt) hold (a person or part of their body) down and back while in a vehicle seat. — **re·strain·a·ble adj. re·strain·er n.** [ME: from OFr. *restreign-*, stem of *restreindre*, from L. *restringere*, from *re-* 'back' + *stringere* 'to tie, pull tight.']

re·strained /ri'strānd/ ▶**adj.** characterized by reserve or moderation; unemotional or dispassionate. ■ (of color, clothes, decoration, etc.) understated and subtle; not excessively showy or ornate. ■ kept under control; prevented from freedom of movement or action. ■ (of a person) held down and back in a vehicle seat by a seat belt. — **re·strain·ed·ly** /ri'strānidlē/ **adv.**

re·straint /ri'strānt/ ▶**n. 1** (often **restraints**) a measure or condition that keeps someone or something under control or within limits: *financial restraints.* ■ the action of keeping someone or something under control. ■ deprivation or restriction of personal liberty or freedom of movement. ■ a device that limits or prevents freedom of movement: *car safety restraints.* **2** unemotional or moderate behavior; self-control. ■ understatement, esp. of artistic expression. [ME: from OFr. *restreinte*, fem. past part. of *restreindre* (see RESTRAIN).]

re·straint of trade ▶**n.** Law action that interferes with free competition in a market.

re·strict /ri'strikt/ ▶**v.** [trans.] put a limit on; control. ■ deprive (someone or something) of freedom of movement or action. ■ **(restrict someone to)** limit someone to only doing or having (a particular thing) or staying in (a particular place). ■ **(restrict something to)** limit something, esp. an activity, to (a particular place, time, or category of people). ■ withhold (information) from general circulation or disclosure: *restrict news.* [16th C.: from L. *restrict-* 'confined,' from *restringere* (see RESTRAIN).]

re·strict·ed /ri'striktid/ ▶**adj.** [attrib.] limited in extent, number, scope, or action: *restricted access to the site.* ■ (of a document or information) for limited circulation and not to be revealed to the public for reasons of national security. — **re·strict·ed·ly adv. re·strict·ed·ness n.**

re·stric·tion /ri'strikSHən/ ▶**n.** (often **restrictions**) a limiting condition or measure, esp. a legal one. ■ the limitation or control of someone or something, or the state of being limited or restricted. — **re·stric·tion·ism** /-,nizəm/ **n. re·stric·tion·ist** /-nist/ **adj. & n.**

re·stric·tion en·zyme (also **re·stri·ction en·do·nu·cle·ase**) ▶**n.** Biochem. an enzyme produced chiefly by certain bacteria, having the property of cleaving DNA molecules at or near a specific sequence of bases.

re·stric·tion frag·ment ▶**n.** Biochem. a fragment of a DNA molecule cleaved by a restriction enzyme.

re·stric·tive /ri'striktiv/ ▶**adj. 1** imposing restrictions or limitations on someone's activities or freedom. **2** Gram. (of a relative clause or descriptive phrase) serving to specify the particular instance or instances being mentioned. — **re·stric·tive·ly adv. re·stric·tive·ness n.**

re·stric·tive cov·e·nant ▶**n.** Law a covenant imposing a restriction on the use of land so that the value and enjoyment of adjoining land will be preserved.

re·string /rē'striNG; 'rē-/ ▶**v.** (past and past part. **-strung**) [trans.] **1** fit new or different strings to (a musical instrument or sports racket). **2** thread (objects such as beads) on a new string.

rest·room /'rest,ro͞om; -,ro͝om/ (also **rest room**) ▶**n.** a bathroom in a public building.

re·struc·ture /rē'strəkCHər/ ▶**v.** [trans.] organize differently: *restructure the department.* ■ Finance convert (the debt of a business in difficulty) into another kind of debt.

re·style ▶**v.** /rē'stīl/ [trans.] **1** rearrange or remake in a new shape or layout: *Nick restyled her hair.* **2** give a new designation to. ▶**n.** an instance of reshaping or rearranging something. ■ a new shape or arrangement.

re·sult /ri'zəlt/ ▶**n.** a consequence, effect, or outcome of something. ■ an item of information obtained by experiment or some other scientific method; a quantity or formula obtained by calculation. ■ (often **results**) a final score, mark, or placing in a sporting event or examination. ■ (often **results**) a satisfactory or favorable outcome of an undertaking or contest. ■ (usu. **results**) the outcome of a business's trading over a given period, expressed as a statement of profit or loss.

▶v. [intrans.] occur or follow as a consequence. ■ (**result in**) have (a specified end or outcome).
– PHRASES **without result** in vain. [ME (v.): from L. *resultare* 'spring back,' from *re-* + *saltare* (frequentative of *salire* 'to jump').]

re·sult·ant /ri'zəltnt/ ▶adj. [attrib.] occurring or produced as a result or consequence of something. ▶n. tech. a force, velocity, or other vector quantity that is equivalent to the combined effect of two or more component vectors acting at the same point.

re·sult·a·tive /ri'zəltətiv/ Gram. ▶adj. expressing, indicating, or relating to the outcome of an action. ▶n. a resultative verb, conjunction, or clause.

re·sume /ri'zo͞om/ ▶v. [trans.] begin to do or pursue (something) again after a pause or interruption. ■ [intrans.] begin to be done, pursued, or used again. ■ [intrans.] begin speaking again after a pause or interruption. ■ take, pick up, or put on again; return to the use of. ▶n. var. of RÉSUMÉ. — **re·sum·a·ble** adj. **re·sump·tion** /ri'zəmpsHən/ n. [ME: ult. from L. *resumere*, from *re-* 'back' + *sumere* 'take.']

ré·su·mé /'rezə,mā ,rezə'mā/ (also **re·su·mé** or **re·su·me**) ▶n. **1** a curriculum vitae. **2** a summary. [19th C.: Fr., lit. 'resumed,' past part. of *résumer*.]

re·su·pi·nate /ri'so͞opə,nāt/ ▶adj. Bot. (of a leaf, flower, fruiting body, etc.) upside down. — **re·su·pi·na·tion** /ri,so͞opə'nāsHən/ n. [18th C.: from L. *resupinatus* 'bent back,' past part. of *resupinare*, based on *supinus* 'lying on the back.']

re·sur·face /rē'sərfəs/ ▶v. **1** [trans.] put a new coating on or reform (a surface such as a road, a floor, or ice). **2** [intrans.] come back up to the surface. ■ arise or become evident again. ■ (of a person) come out of hiding or obscurity.

re·sur·gent /ri'sərjənt/ ▶adj. increasing or reviving after a period of little activity, popularity, or occurrence. — **re·sur·gence** n. [19th C. (as n.): from L. *resurgent-* 'rising again,' from the v. *resurgere*, from *re-* + *surgere* 'to rise.']

res·ur·rect /,rezə'rekt/ ▶v. [trans.] restore (a dead person) to life. ■ revive the practice, use, or memory of (something); bring new vigor to. [18th C.: back-form. from RESURRECTION.]

res·ur·rec·tion /,rezə'reksHən/ ▶n. the action or fact of resurrecting or being resurrected. ■ (**the Resurrection**) (in Christian belief) Christ's rising from the dead. ■ (**the Resurrection**) (in Christian belief) the rising of the dead at the Last Judgment. ■ the revitalization or revival of something: *resurrections of scandals.* [ME: ult. from OFr., from late L. *resurrectio(n-)*, from *resurgere* (see RESURGENT).]

res·ur·rec·tion plant ▶n. any of a number of plants that are able to survive drought, typically folding up when dry and unfolding when moistened, in particular: ■ a fern (*Polypodium polypodioides*, family Polypodiaceae) of tropical and warm-temperate America. ■ a California club moss (*Selaginella lepidophylla*, family Selaginellaceae). ■ the rose of Jericho.

re·sus·ci·tate /ri'səsə,tāt/ ▶v. [trans.] revive (someone) from unconsciousness or apparent death. ■ fig. make (something such as an idea or enterprise) active or vigorous again. — **re·sus·ci·ta·tion** /ri,səsə'tāsHən/ n. **re·sus·ci·ta·tive** /-,tātiv/ adj. **re·sus·ci·ta·tor** /-,tātər/ n. [16th C.: from L. *resuscitat-* 'raised again,' from the v. *resuscitare*, from *re-* + *suscitare* 'raise.']

ret /ret/ ▶v. (**ret·ted, ret·ting**) [trans.] soak (flax or hemp) in water to soften it and separate the fibers. [ME: rel. to Du. *reten*, also to ROT.]

ret. ▶abbr. retired.

re·ta·ble /'rē,tābəl; 'retəbəl/ (also **re·ta·blo** /ri'täblō/) ▶n. (pl. **-ta·bles** or **-ta·blos**) a frame or shelf enclosing decorated panels or revered objects above and behind an altar. ■ a painting or other image in such a position. [19th C.: from Fr. *rétable*, from Sp. *retablo*, from med. L. *retrotabulum* 'rear table,' from L. *retro* 'backward' + *tabula* 'table.']

re·tail /'rē,tāl/ ▶n. the sale of goods to the public for use or consumption rather than for resale. ▶adv. being sold in such a way: *it is not available retail.* ▶v. [trans.] sell (goods) to the public in such a way: *the difficulties in retailing new products.* ■ [intrans.] (**retail at/for**) (of goods) be sold in this way for (a specified price): *the product retails for $20.* — **re·tail·er** n. [ME: ult. from OFr. *retaille* 'a piece cut off,' from *retaillier*, from *re-* (intensive force) + *tailler* 'to cut.']

re·tain /ri'tān/ ▶v. continue to have (something); keep possession of: *the house retains many original features.* ■ not abolish, discard, or alter. ■ keep in one's memory. ■ absorb and continue to hold (a substance). ■ [often as adj.] (**retaining**) keep (something) in place; hold fixed. ■ keep (someone) engaged in one's service. ■ secure the services of (a person, esp. an attorney) with a preliminary payment. — **re·tain·a·bil·i·ty** /ri,tānə'bilətē/ n. **re·tain·a·ble** adj. **re·tain·ment** n. [ME: ult. from OFr. *retenir*, from L. *retinere*, from *re-* 'back' + *tenere* 'hold.']

re·tain·er /ri'tānər/ ▶n. **1** a thing that holds something in place: *a guitar string retainer.* ■ an appliance for keeping a loose tooth or orthodontic prosthesis in place. **2** a fee paid in advance to someone, esp. an attorney, in order to secure or keep their services when required. **3** a servant or follower of a noble or wealthy person.

re·tain·ing wall ▶n. a wall that holds back earth or water on one side of it.

re·take ▶v. /rē'tāk; 'rē-/ (past **-took**; past part. **-taken**) [trans.] take again, in particular: ■ take (a test or examination) again. ■ recapture. ■ regain possession of (something left or lost). ▶n. /'rē,tāk/ a thing that is retaken. ■ an instance of filming a scene or recording a piece of music again.

re·tal·i·ate /ri'talē,āt/ ▶v. [intrans.] make an attack or assault in return for a similar attack. ■ [trans.] archaic repay (an injury or insult) in kind. — **re·tal·i·a·tion** /ri,talē'āsHən/ n. **re·tal·i·a·tive** /ri'talē,ātiv; -ētiv/ adj. **re·tal·i·a·tor** /-,ātər/ n. **re·tal·i·a·to·ry** /ri'talēə,tôrē/ adj. [17th C.: from L. *retaliat-* 'returned in kind,' from the v. *retaliare*, from *re-* 'back' + *talis* 'such.']

re·tard ▶v. /ri'tärd/ [trans.] delay or hold back in terms of progress, development, or accomplishment. ▶n. /'rē,tärd/ offens. a mentally handicapped person (often used as a general term of abuse). — **re·tar·da·tion** /,rē,tär'dāsHən; ri-/ n. **re·tard·er** n. [15th C.: ult. from L. *retardare*, from *re-* 'back' + *tardus* 'slow.']

re·tar·dant /ri'tärdnt/ ▶adj. [in comb.] (chiefly of a synthetic or treated fabric or substance) not readily susceptible to fire. ▶n. a fabric or substance that prevents or inhibits something, esp. the outbreak of fire. — **re·tard·an·cy** /-'tärdnsē/ n.

re·tar·da·taire /ri,tärdə'ter/ ▶adj. (of a work of art or architecture) executed in an earlier or outdated style. [Fr.]

re·tar·date /ri'tär,dāt/ ▶n. dated offens. a mentally handicapped person.

re·tard·ed /ri'tärdid/ ▶adj. less advanced, esp. mentally, than is usual for one's age.

retch /recH/ ▶v. [intrans.] make the sound and movement of vomiting. ■ vomit. ▶n. a movement or sound of vomiting. [19th C.: var. of dial. *reach*, from Gmc., 'spittle.']

retd (also **ret.**) ▶abbr. retired.

re·te /'rētē; 'rātē/ ▶n. (pl. **-ti·a** /-tēə/) Anat. an elaborate network of blood vessels or nerve cells. [16th C.: from L., 'net.']

re·ten·tion /ri'tencHən/ ▶n. the continued possession, use, or control of something. ■ the fact of keeping something in one's memory. ■ the action of absorbing and continuing to hold a substance. ■ failure to eliminate a substance from the body. [ME ('power to retain something'): ult. from L. *retentio(n-)*, from *retinere* (see RETAIN).]

re·ten·tive /ri'tentiv/ ▶adj. **1** (of a person's memory) able to remember facts and impressions easily. **2** (of a substance) able to absorb and hold moisture. ■ esp. Med. serving to keep something in place. — **re·ten·tive·ly** adv. **re·ten·tive·ness** n. [ME: ult. from med. L. *retentivus*, from *retent-* 'held back,' from *retinere* (see RETAIN).]

re·ten·tiv·i·ty /,rē,ten'tivətē; ri-/ ▶n. (pl. **-ties**) Physics the ability of a substance to retain or resist magnetization, frequently measured as the strength of the magnetic field that remains after removal of an inducing field.

re·think ▶v. /rē'THiNGk/ (past and past part. **-thought**) [trans.] think again about, esp. in order to make changes to it. ▶n. /'rē,THiNGk/ [in sing.] a reassessment of something.

re·tia /'rētēə; 'rā-/ plural form of RETE.

re·ti·ar·i·us /,rēsHē'e(ə)rēəs/ ▶n. (pl. **-ar·i·i** /-'e(ə)rē,ē; -ē,ī/) an ancient Roman gladiator who used a net to trap his opponent. [L., from *rete* 'net.']

ret·i·cent /'retəsənt/ ▶adj. not revealing one's thoughts or feelings readily. — **ret·i·cence** n. **ret·i·cent·ly** adv. [19th C.: from L. *reticent-* 'remaining silent,' from the v. *reticere*, from *re-* (intensive force) + *tacere* 'be silent.']

ret·i·cle /'retikəl/ ▶n. a series of fine lines or fibers in the eyepiece of an optical device. [18th C.: from L. *reticulum* 'net.']

re·tic·u·la /ri'tikyələ/ plural form of RETICULUM.

re·tic·u·late ▶v. /ri'tikyə,lāt/ [trans.] rare divide or mark (something) to resemble a net or network. ▶adj. /-lət; -,lāt/ esp. Bot. Zool. reticulated. [17th C.: from L. *reticulatus* 'reticulated,' from *reticulum* (see RETICULUM).]

re·tic·u·lat·ed /ri'tikyə,lātid/ ▶adj. [attrib.] constructed, arranged, or marked like a net or network. ■ (of porcelain) having a pattern of interlacing lines, esp. of pierced work, forming a net or web. ■ Archit. relating to or denoting a style of decorated tracery in a netlike framework. ■ divided into small squares or sections.

re·tic·u·la·tion /ri,tikyə'lāsHən/ ▶n. a pattern or arrangement of interlacing lines resembling a net. ■ Photog. the formation of a network of wrinkles or cracks in a photographic emulsion.

ret·i·cule /'reti,kyo͞ol/ ▶n. **1** esp. hist. a woman's small handbag, typically having a drawstring. **2** var. of RETICLE. [18th C.: from Fr. *réticule*, from L. *reticulum* (see RETICULUM).]

re·tic·u·lo·cyte /ri'tikyələ,sīt/ ▶n. Physiol. an immature red blood cell without a nucleus. [1920s: from RETICULATED + -CYTE.]

re·tic·u·lo·en·do·the·li·al /ri,tikyə,lō,endō'THēlēəl/ ▶adj. [attrib.] Physiol. relating to or denoting a diverse system of fixed and circulating phagocytic cells (macrophages and monocytes) involved in the immune response. Also called LYMPHORETICULAR. [1920s: from RETICULUM + *endothelial* (see ENDOTHELIUM).]

Re·tic·u·lum /ri'tikyələm/ Astron. a small southern constellation (the Net). [L., dimin. of *rete* 'net.']

re·tic·u·lum /ri'tikyələm/ ▶n. (pl. **-la** /-lə/) **1** a fine network or netlike structure. See also ENDOPLASMIC RETICULUM. **2** Zool. the second stomach of a ruminant, having a honeycomblike structure. — **re·tic·u·lar** /-lər/ adj. [17th C.: from L., dimin. of *rete* 'net.']

re·ti·form /'retə,fôrm/ ▶adj. rare netlike. [17th C.: from L. *rete* 'net.']

Ret·in-A /'retn 'ā/ ▶n. Trademark a brand of tretinoin, used to treat acne and to reduce wrinkles.

ret·i·na /'retn-ə/ ▶n. (pl. **ret·i·nas** or **ret·i·nae** /'retn,ē; 'retn,ī/) a layer at the back of the eyeball containing cells that are sensitive to light and that trigger nerve impulses that pass via the optic nerve to the brain. — **ret·i·nal** /ˈretn-əl/ **adj.** [ME: from med. L., from L. *rete* 'net.']

ret·i·ni·tis /ˌretnˈītis/ ▶ **n.** Med. retinal inflammation.

ret·i·ni·tis pig·men·to·sa /ˌpigmənˈtōsə; -zə/ ▶ **n.** Med. a chronic hereditary eye disease characterized by gradual degeneration of the retina. [19th C.: fem. of L. *pigmentosus*, from *pigmentum* 'pigment.']

ret·ino·blas·to·ma /ˌretnˌō-blaˈstōmə/ ▶ **n.** Med. a rare malignant retinal tumor, affecting children.

ret·i·noid /ˈretnˌoid/ ▶ **n.** Biochem. any of a group of compounds having effects like those of vitamin A.

ret·i·nol /ˈretnôl; -ˌōl/ ▶ **n.** Biochem. a yellow compound, $C_{20}H_{29}OH$, found in green and yellow vegetables, egg yolk, and fish-liver oil. It is essential for growth and vision in dim light. Also called **VITAMIN A.** [1960s: from **RETINA** + **-OL.**]

ret·i·nop·a·thy /ˌretnˈäpəᴛʜē/ ▶ **n.** Med. disease of the retina that results in impairment or loss of vision.

ret·i·nue /ˈretnˌ(y)o͞o/ ▶ **n.** a group of advisers, assistants, or others accompanying an important person. [ME: from OFr. *retenue*, fem. past part. of *retenir* 'keep back, retain.']

re·tire /riˈtī(ə)r/ ▶ **v. 1** [intrans.] leave one's job and cease to work, typically upon reaching a certain age. ■ [trans.] compel (an employee) to leave their job, esp. before they have reached such an age. ■ (of an athlete) cease to play competitively. ■ (of an athlete) withdraw from a race or match, typically as a result of accident or injury. ■ [trans.] Baseball put out (a batter); cause (a side) to end a turn at bat. ■ [trans.] Econ. withdraw (a bill or note) from circulation or currency. ■ Finance pay off or cancel (a debt). **2** withdraw to or from a particular place. ■ (of a military force) retreat from an enemy or an attacking position. ■ [trans.] order (a military force) to retreat. ■ (of a jury) leave the courtroom to decide the verdict of a trial. ■ go to bed. — **re·tir·er n.** [16th C. ('withdraw'): from Fr. *retirer*, from *re-* 'back' + *tirer* 'draw.']

re·tired /riˈtī(ə)rd/ ▶ **adj. 1** [attrib.] having left one's job and ceased to work. **2** archaic (of a place) quiet and secluded; not seen or frequented by many people. ■ (of a person's way of life) quiet and involving little contact with other people. ■ (of a person) reserved; uncommunicative.

re·tir·ee /riˌtīˈrē/ ▶ **n.** a person who has retired from full-time work.

re·tire·ment /riˈtī(ə)rmənt/ ▶ **n. 1** the action or fact of leaving one's job and ceasing to work. ■ the period of one's life after leaving one's job and ceasing to work. ■ the action or fact of ceasing to play a sport competitively. **2** the withdrawal of a jury from the courtroom to decide their verdict. ■ the time during which a jury decides their verdict. **3** seclusion: *he lived in retirement in Miami.* ■ archaic a secluded or private place.

re·tire·ment home ▶ **n.** a house or apartment in which a person lives in old age. ■ an institution for elderly people needing care.

re·tir·ing /riˈtī(ə)riɴɢ/ ▶ **adj.** shy and reclusive. — **re·tir·ing·ly adv.**

re·took /rēˈto͝ok/ past of **RETAKE.**

re·tool /rēˈto͞ol/ ▶ **v.** [trans.] equip (a factory) with tools. ■ adapt or alter (someone or something) to make them more useful or suitable. ■ [intrans.] adapt or prepare oneself for something.

re·tort[1] /riˈtôrt/ ▶ **v. 1** [reporting verb] say something in answer to a remark or accusation, typically in a sharp, angry, or wittily incisive manner. **2** [trans.] archaic repay (an insult or injury). ■ turn (an insult or accusation) back on the person who has issued it. ■ use (an opponent's argument) against them: *the answer may very easily be retorted.* ▶ **n.** a sharp, angry, or wittily incisive reply to a remark. [15th C.: from L. *retort-* 'twisted back, cast back,' from the v. *retorquere*, from *re-* 'in return' + *torquere* 'to twist.']

re·tort[2] ▶ **n. 1** a container or furnace for carrying out a chemical process on a large or industrial scale. **2** hist. a glass container with a long neck. ▶ **v.** [trans.] heat in a retort in order to separate or purify. [17th C. (sense 2): ult. from med. L. *retorta*, fem. past part. of *retorquere* 'twist back' (recurved neck).]

retort[2] 2

re·touch /rēˈtəcʜ/ ▶ **v.** [trans.] improve or repair by making slight additions or alterations. — **re·touch·er n.** [17th C.: prob. from Fr. *retoucher*.]

re·tract /riˈtrakt/ ▶ **v.** [trans.] draw or pull (something) back or back in: *she retracted her hand.* ■ withdraw (a statement or accusation) as untrue or unjustified. ■ withdraw or go back on (an undertaking or promise). ■ (of an animal) draw (a part of itself) back into its body. ■ draw (the undercarriage or the wheels) up into the body of an aircraft. ■ [intrans.] be drawn back into something. — **re·tract·a·ble adj. re·trac·tion** /riˈtraksʜən/ **n. re·trac·tive** /-tiv/ **adj.** [ME: from L. *retract-* 'drawn back,' from the v. *retrahere* (from *re-* + *trahere* 'drag'); 'withdraw (a statement),' 'go back on' via OFr. from *retractare* 'reconsider' (based on *trahere* 'drag').]

re·trac·tile /riˈtraktəl; -ˌtīl/ ▶ **adj.** Zool. capable of being retracted: *a long retractile proboscis.* — **re·trac·til·i·ty** /ˌrēˌtrakˈtilətē/ **n.**

re·trac·tor /riˈtraktər/ ▶ **n.** a device for retracting something. ■ (also **re·trac·tor mus·cle**) esp. Zool. a muscle serving to retract a part of the body. Compare with **PROTRACTOR.**

re·train /rēˈtrān/ ▶ **v.** [trans.] teach (someone) new skills. ■ [intrans.] learn new skills, esp. for a different job.

re·trans·late /ˌrētransˈlāt; -tranz-/ ▶ **v.** [trans.] translate (a translation) back into its original language. — **re·trans·la·tion** /-ˈlāsʜən/ **n.**

re·tread ▶ **v.** /rēˈtred/ **1** (past **-trod**; past part. **-trod·den**) [trans.] go back over (a path or one's steps): *they never retread the same ground.* **2** (past and past part. **-tread·ed**) [trans.] put a new tread on (a worn tire). ▶ **n.** /ˈrēˌtred/ a tire that has been given a new tread. ■ informal a person retrained or recalled for service. ■ informal a superficially altered version of an original.

re·treat /riˈtrēt/ ▶ **v.** [intrans.] (of an army) withdraw from enemy forces as a result of their superior power or after a defeat. ■ move back or withdraw, esp. so as to remove oneself from a difficult or uncomfortable situation. ■ withdraw to a quiet or secluded place. ■ (of an expanse of ice or water) become smaller in size or extent. ■ change one's decisions, plans, or attitude, as a result of criticism from others. ■ (of shares of stock) decline in value: [with complement] *shares retreated 32 points.* ■ [trans.] Chess move (a piece) back from a forward position on the board. ▶ **n. 1** an act of moving back or withdrawing. ■ an act of changing one's decisions, plans, or attitude, esp. as a result of criticism from others. ■ a decline in the value of shares of stock. **2** a signal for a military force to withdraw: *the bugle sounded a retreat.* ■ a military musical ceremony carried out at sunset to tell soldiers to return to camp for the night. **3** a quiet or secluded place in which one can relax. ■ a period of seclusion for the purposes of prayer and meditation.
– PHRASES **beat a retreat** see **BEAT.** [ME: from OFr. *retret* (n.), *retraiter* (v.), from L. *retrahere* (see **RETRACT**).]

re·trench /riˈtrencʜ/ ▶ **v.** [intrans.] (of a company, government, or individual) reduce costs or spending in response to economic difficulty. ■ [trans.] formal reduce or diminish (something). — **re·trench·ment n.** [16th C. ('diminish'): from obs. Fr. *retrencher*, from *re-* + *trancher* 'to cut.']

re·tri·al /rēˈtrīəl; ˈrēˌtrīəl/ ▶ **n.** Law a second or further trial.

ret·ri·bu·tion /ˌretrəˈbyo͞osʜən/ ▶ **n.** punishment that is considered to be morally right and fully deserved. — **re·trib·u·tive** /riˈtribyətiv/ **adj. re·trib·u·to·ry** /riˈtribyəˌtôrē/ **adj.** [ME (also 'recompense'): from late L. *retributio(n-)*, from *retribut-* 'assigned again,' from the v. *retribuere*, from *re-* + *tribuere* 'assign.']

re·triev·al /riˈtrēvəl/ ▶ **n.** the process of getting something back from somewhere. ■ the obtaining or consulting of material stored in a computer system.

re·trieve /riˈtrēv/ ▶ **v.** [trans.] get (something) back; regain possession of. ■ pick (something) up. ■ (of a dog) find and bring back (game that has been shot). ■ bring (something) back into one's mind: *retrieve forgotten memories.* ■ find or extract (information stored in a computer). ■ put right or improve (an unwelcome situation). ■ [intrans.] reel or bring in a fishing line. ▶ **n. 1** an act of retrieving something, esp. game that has been shot. ■ an act of reeling or drawing in a fishing line. **2** archaic the possibility of recovery: ***beyond retrieve.*** — **re·triev·a·bil·i·ty** /riˌtrēvəˈbilətē/ **n. re·triev·a·ble adj.** [ME: from OFr. *retroeve-*, stressed stem of *retrover* 'find again.']

re·triev·er /riˈtrēvər/ ▶ **n. 1** a dog of a breed used for retrieving game. **2** a person or thing that retrieves something.

ret·ro /ˈretrō/ ▶ **adj.** imitative of a style, fashion, or design from the recent past: *retro 60s fashions.* ▶ **n.** clothes or music whose style or design is imitative of those of the recent past. [1960s: from Fr. *rétro*, abbrev. of *rétrograde* 'retrograde.']

retro- ▶ **comb. form 1** denoting action that is directed backward or is reciprocal: *retrocede* | *retroject.* **2** denoting location behind: *retrochoir.* [from L. *retro* 'backward.']

ret·ro·ac·tive /ˌretrōˈaktiv/ ▶ **adj.** (esp. of legislation) taking effect from a date in the past. — **ret·ro·ac·tion** /-ˈaksʜən/ **n. ret·ro·ac·tive·ly adv. ret·ro·ac·tiv·i·ty** /-ˌakˈtivətē/ **n.**

ret·ro·bul·bar /ˌretrōˈbəlbər; -ˌbär/ ▶ **adj.** [attrib.] Anat. & Med. situated or occurring behind the eyeball.

ret·ro·cede /ˌretrəˈsēd/ ▶ **v.** [trans.] rare cede (territory) back again: *Hong Kong, retroceded to China.* — **ret·ro·ces·sion** /-ˈsesʜən/ **n.** [19th C.: from Fr. *rétrocéder*.]

ret·ro·choir /ˈretrōˌkwī(ə)r/ ▶ **n.** the interior of a cathedral or large church behind the high altar. [19th C.: from med. L. *retrochorus* (see **RETRO-, CHOIR**).]

re·trod /rēˈträd/ past of **RETREAD** (sense 1).

re·trod·den /rēˈträdn/ past participle of **RETREAD** (sense 1).

ret·ro·fit /ˌretrōˈfit/ ▶ **v.** (**-fit·ted, -fit·ting**) [trans.] add (a component or accessory) to something that did not have it when manufactured. ■ provide (something) with a component or accessory not fitted to it during manufacture. ▶ **n.** an act of adding a component or accessory to something that did not have it when manufactured. ■ a component or accessory added after manufacture. [1950s: blend of **RETROACTIVE** and **REFIT.**]

ret·ro·flex /ˈretrəˌfleks/ (also **ret·ro·flexed**) ▶ **adj.** Anat. Med. turned backward. ■ Phonet. pronounced with the tip of the tongue curled up toward the hard palate: *the retroflex /r/.* — **ret·ro·flex·ion** /ˌretrəˈfleksʜən/ **n.** [18th C.: from L. *retroflex-* 'bent backward,' from the v. *retroflectere*, from *retro* + *flectere* 'to bend.']

ret·ro·gra·da·tion /ˌretrōgrāˈdāsʜən/ ▶ **n.** Astron. Astrol. the apparent temporary reverse motion of a planet (from east to west). ■ the orbiting or rotation of a planet or planetary satellite in a reverse direction.

ret·ro·grade /'retrə,grād/ ▶ **adj.** directed or moving backward: *a retrograde flow.* ■ reverting to an earlier and inferior condition. ■ (of the order of something) reversed; inverse. ■ (of amnesia) involving the period immediately preceding the causal event. ■ Geol. (of a metamorphic change) resulting from a decrease in temperature or pressure. ■ Astron. Astrol. (of the apparent motion of a planet) in a reverse direction from normal (from east to west), resulting from the relative orbital progress of the earth and the planet. The opposite of **PROGRADE**. ■ Astron. (of the orbit or rotation of a planet or planetary satellite) in a reverse direction from that normal in the solar system. ▶ **n.** rare a degenerate person. ▶ **v.** [intrans.] **1** archaic go back in position or time. ■ revert to an earlier and usually inferior condition. **2** Astron. show retrogradation. [ME (astronomical term): from L. *retrogradus*, from *retro* 'backward' + *gradus* 'step' (from *gradi* 'to walk').]

ret·ro·gress /,retrə'gres/ ▶ **v.** [intrans.] go back to an earlier state, typically a worse one. [19th C.: from **RETRO-** + *-gress*, from *progress*.]

ret·ro·gres·sion /,retrə'greshən/ ▶ **n. 1** the process of returning to an earlier state, typically a worse one. **2** Astron. another term for **RETROGRADATION**. — **ret·ro·gres·sive** /-'gresiv/ **adj.**

ret·ro·ject /'retrə,jekt/ ▶ **v.** [trans.] rare project backward. [19th C.: from **RETRO-** + *-ject*, from *project*.]

ret·ro·re·flec·tor /,retrōri'flektər/ ▶ **n.** a device that reflects light back along the incident path. — **ret·ro·re·flec·tive** /-'flektiv/ **adj.**

ret·ro·rock·et /'retrō,räkit/ ▶ **n.** a small auxiliary rocket on a spacecraft or missile, fired in the direction of travel to slow the craft down.

re·trorse /'rē,trôrs/ ▶ **adj.** Biol. turned or pointing backward: *retrorse spines.* [19th C.: from L. *retrorsus*, contr. of *retroversus*, from *retro* 'backward' + *versus* 'turned' (past part. of *vertere*).]

ret·ro·spect /'retrə,spekt/ ▶ **n.** a survey or review of a past course of events or period of time.

– PHRASES **in retrospect** when looking back on a past event or situation; with hindsight. [17th C.: from **RETRO-** + *-spect*, from *prospect*.]

ret·ro·spec·tion /,retrə'spekshən/ ▶ **n.** the action of looking back on or reviewing past events or situations. [17th C.: prob. from **RETROSPECT** (as v.).]

ret·ro·spec·tive /,retrə'spektiv/ ▶ **adj.** looking back on or dealing with past events or situations. ■ (of an exhibition or compilation) showing the development of an artist's work over time. ■ (of a statute or legal decision) taking effect from a past date. ▶ **n.** an exhibition or compilation showing the development of the work of a particular artist over time. — **ret·ro·spec·tive·ly adv.**

ret·ro·ster·nal /,retrō'stərnl/ ▶ **adj.** Anat. Med. behind the breastbone.

ret·rous·sé /rə,troo'sā ,retroo-/ ▶ **adj.** (of a person's nose) turned up at the tip, esp. in an attractive way. [19th C.: Fr., lit. 'tucked up,' past part. of *retrousser*.]

ret·ro·vert·ed /,retrə'vərtəd/ ▶ **adj.** Anat. (of the uterus) tilted abnormally backward. — **ret·ro·ver·sion** /-'vərzhən/ **n.** [18th C.: from L. *retrovertere* 'turn backward' + **-ED**[2].]

Ret·ro·vir /'retrō,vi(ə)r/ ▶ **n.** trademark for **ZIDOVUDINE**. [1980s: abbrev. of **RETROVIRUS**.]

ret·ro·vi·rus /,retrō'vīrəs; 'retrō,vīrəs/ ▶ **n.** Biol. any RNA virus that inserts a DNA copy of its genome into the host cell in order to replicate, e.g., HIV. [1970s: mod. L., from the initial letters of *reverse transcriptase* + **VIRUS**.]

re·try /rē'trī/ ▶ **v.** (**-tries, -tried**) **1** [trans.] Law try (a defendant or case) again. **2** [intrans.] Comput. reenter a command. ■ (of a system) transmit data again. ▶ **n.** an instance of reentering a command or retransmitting data.

ret·si·na /ret'sēnə/ ▶ **n.** a Greek white or rosé wine flavored with resin.

re·turn /ri'tərn/ ▶ **v. 1** [intrans.] come or go back to. ■ (**return to**) go back to (a particular state or activity). ■ (**return to**) divert one's attention back to (something). ■ (esp. of a feeling) come back or recur. **2** [trans.] give or send back to a place or person. ■ feel, say, or do (the same feeling, action, etc.) in response. ■ (in tennis and other sports) hit or send (the ball) back to an opponent. ■ Football run upfield with the ball after fielding (a kick), intercepting (a pass), or recovering (a fumble). ■ (of a judge or jury) state or present (a verdict) in response to a formal request. ■ Bridge lead (a card of a suit led earlier by one's partner). ■ Archit. continue (a wall) in a changed direction, esp. at right angles. **3** [trans.] yield or make (a profit). **4** [trans.] (of an electorate) reelect to office. ▶ **n. 1** an act of coming or going back to something. ■ [in sing.] an act of going back to an earlier state or condition. ■ the action of giving, sending, or putting something back. ■ Football a play in which the ball is caught after a kick or pass interception and is advanced by running; an advance of this kind. ■ (in tennis and other sports) a stroke played in response to a serve or other stroke by one's opponent. ■ (also **re·turn tick·et**) esp. Brit. a ticket that allows someone to travel to a place and back again; a round trip ticket. ■ an electrical conductor bringing a current back to its source. ■ (also **re·turn game**) a second contest between the same opponents. **2** (often **returns**) a profit from an investment. ■ a good rate of return. **3** an official report or statement submitted in response to a formal demand: *census returns.* ■ Law an endorsement or report by a court officer or sheriff on a writ. **4** election to office: *we campaigned for his return.* ■ an official report of the results of an election. **5** (also **car·riage re·turn**) a key pressed to move the carriage of an electric typewriter back to a fixed position. ■ (also **re·turn key**) a key pressed on a computer keyboard to end a command or data string. **6** Archit. a part receding from the line of the front.

– PHRASES **in return** as a response, exchange, or reward for something. **many happy returns (of the day)** used as a greeting to someone on their birthday. — **re·turn·a·ble adj. re·turn·er n.** [ME: v., from OFr. *returner*, from L. *re-* 'back' + *tornare* 'to turn'; n., via Anglo-Norman Fr.]

re·turn·ee /ri,tər'nē/ ▶ **n.** a person who returns, esp. after a prolonged absence.

Reu·ben /'roobən/ (in the Bible) a Hebrew patriarch, eldest son of Jacob and Leah. ■ the tribe of Israel traditionally descended from him.

re·u·ni·fy /rē'yoonə,fī/ ▶ **v.** (**-fies, -fied**) [trans.] restore political unity to (a divided place or group). — **re·u·ni·fi·ca·tion** /,rē,yoonəfi'kāshən/ **n.**

Ré·union /rē'yoonyən; rā-Y'nyôN/ an island in the Indian Ocean, east of Madagascar, one of the Mascarene Islands; pop. 597,000; capital, Saint-Denis. It became an administrative region of France in 1974.

re·un·ion /rē'yoonyən/ ▶ **n.** an instance of two or more people coming together again after separation. ■ a social gathering attended by members of a certain group of people who have not seen each other for some time: *a school reunion.* ■ the act or process of being brought together again as a unified whole. [17th C.: from Fr. *réunion* or Anglo-Latin *reunio(n-)*, from L. *reunire* 'unite.']

re·u·nite /,rēyoo'nīt/ ▶ **v.** come together or cause to come together again after separation or disunity.

re·up·hol·ster /,rēəp'hōlstər; ,rēə'pōl-/ ▶ **v.** [trans.] upholster with new materials. — **re·up·hol·ster·y** /-stərē/ **n.**

re·use ▶ **v.** /rē'yooz/ [trans.] use more than once. ▶ **n.** /re'yoos/ the action of using something again. — **re·us·a·ble** /rē'yoozəbəl/ **adj.**

Reu·ters /'roitərz/ an international news agency founded in London in 1851 by Paul Julius Reuter (1816–99). The agency pioneered the use of telegraphy.

Reu·ther /'roothər/, Walter Philip (1907–70), US labor leader. He was president of the United Automobile Workers 1946–70 and of the Congress of Industrial Organizations 1952–55.

Rev. ▶ **abbr.** ■ Bible the book of Revelation. ■ (as the title of a priest) Reverend.

rev /rev/ informal ▶ **n.** (usu. **revs**) a revolution of an engine per minute. ■ an act of increasing the speed of revolution of a vehicle's engine by pressing the accelerator, esp. while the clutch is disengaged. ▶ **v.** (**revved, rev·ving**) [trans.] increase the running speed of (an engine) or the engine speed of (a vehicle) by pressing the accelerator, esp. while the clutch is disengaged. ■ [intrans.] (of an engine or vehicle) operate with increasing speed when the accelerator is pressed, esp. while the clutch is disengaged. [20th C.: abbrev. of **REVOLUTION**.]

re·val·ue /rē'valyoo/ ▶ **v.** (**-val·ues, -val·ued, -val·u·ing**) [trans.] assess the value of (something) again. ■ Econ. adjust the value of (a currency) in relation to other currencies. — **re·val·u·a·tion** /rē,valyoo'āshən/ **n.**

re·vamp /rē'vamp/ ▶ **v.** [trans.] give new and improved form, structure, or appearance to: *revamp her image.* ▶ **n.** [usu. in sing.] an act of improving the form, structure, or appearance of something. ■ a new and improved version.

re·vanch·ism /rə'väN,shizəm/ ▶ **n.** a policy of seeking to retaliate, esp. to recover lost territory. — **re·vanch·ist adj. & n.** [1950s: from Fr. *revanche*, lit. 'revenge.']

Revd ▶ **abbr.** (as the title of a priest) Reverend.

re·veal[1] /ri'vēl/ ▶ **v.** [trans.] make (previously unknown or secret information) known to others. ■ cause or allow (something) to be seen. ■ make known to humans by divine or supernatural means. — **re·veal·a·ble adj. re·veal·er n.** [ME: ult. from L. *revelare*, from *re-* 'back' + *velum* 'veil.']

re·veal[2] ▶ **n.** either side surface of an aperture in a wall for a door or window. [17th C.: from obs. *revale* 'to lower,' from OFr. *revaler*, from *re-* 'back' + *avaler* 'go down.']

re·vealed re·li·gion ▶ **n.** religion based on divine revelation rather than reason.

re·veal·ing /ri'vēliNG/ ▶ **adj.** making interesting or significant information known. ■ (of an item of clothing) allowing more of the wearer's body to be seen than is usual. — **re·veal·ing·ly adv.**

re·veg·e·tate /rē'vejə,tāt/ ▶ **v.** [trans.] produce a new growth of vegetation on (disturbed or barren ground). — **re·veg·e·ta·tion** /rē,vejə'tāshən/ **n.**

rev·eil·le /'revəlē/ ▶ **n.** [in sing.] a signal sounded esp. on a bugle or drum to wake personnel in the armed forces. [17th C.: from Fr. *réveillez!* 'wake up!,' imper. pl. of *réveiller*, based on L. *vigilare* 'keep watch.']

rev·el /'revəl/ ▶ **v.** (**rev·eled, rev·el·ing**; esp. Brit. **rev·elled, rev·el·ling**) [intrans.] engage in lively and noisy festivities, esp. those that involve drinking and dancing. ■ (**revel in**) get great pleasure from. ▶ **n.** (**revels**) lively and noisy festivities, esp. those that involve drinking and dancing. — **rev·el·er** or **rev·el·ler n.** [ME: from OFr. *reveler* 'rise up in rebellion,' from L. *rebellare* 'to rebel.']

rev·e·la·tion /,revə'lāshən/ ▶ **n. 1** a surprising and previously unknown fact, esp. one made in a dramatic way. ■ the making known of a secret or the unknown. ■ used to emphasize the surprising or remarkable quality of someone or something. **2** the divine or supernatural disclosure to humans of something relating to human existence or the world. ■ (**Revelation** or informal **Revelations**) (in full **the Revelation of St. John the Divine**) the last book of the New Testament. — **rev·e·la·tion·al** /-shənl/ **adj.** [ME (theological term): ult. from late L. *revelatio(n-)*, from *revelare* (see REVEAL[1]).]

rev·e·la·tion·ist /ˌrevəˈlāSHənist/ ▶ **n.** a believer in divine revelation.

re·vel·a·to·ry /ˈrevələˌtôrē; riˈvel-/ ▶ **adj.** revealing something hitherto unknown.

rev·el·ry /ˈrevəlrē/ ▶ **n.** (pl. **-ries**) (also **revelries**) lively and noisy festivities, esp. when these involve drinking a large amount of alcohol.

rev·e·nant /ˈrevəˌnäN; -nənt/ ▶ **n.** a person who has returned, esp. supposedly from the dead. [19th C.: Fr., lit. 'coming back,' pres. part. of *revenir*.]

re·venge /riˈvenj/ ▶ **n.** the action of inflicting hurt or harm on someone for a wrong suffered at their hands. ■ the desire to inflict such retribution. ■ (in sports) the defeat of a person or team by whom one was beaten in a previous encounter. ▶ **v.** (**revenge oneself** or **be revenged**) chiefly archaic literary inflict hurt or harm on someone for an injury or wrong done to oneself. ■ [trans.] inflict such retribution on behalf of (someone else). ■ inflict retribution for (a wrong or injury done to oneself or another): *she revenged his death.* — **re·veng·er n.** (literary). [ME: from OFr. *revencher*, from late L. *revindicare*, from *re-* (intensive force) + *vindicare* 'claim, avenge.']

re·venge·ful /riˈvenjfəl/ ▶ **adj.** eager for revenge. — **re·venge·ful·ly adv. re·venge·ful·ness n.**

rev·e·nue /ˈrevəˌn(y)o͞o/ ▶ **n.** income, esp. when of a company or organization and of a substantial nature. ■ a state's annual income. ■ (**revenues**) items or amounts constituting such income. ■ the government department collecting such income. [ME: from OFr. *revenu(e)* 'returned,' past part. of *revenir*, from L. *revenire*, from *re-* 'back' + *venire* 'come.']

rev·e·nue shar·ing ▶ **n.** the distribution of a portion of federal tax revenues to state and local governments.

rev·e·nue stamp ▶ **n.** a stamp showing that a government tax has been paid.

rev·e·nue tar·iff ▶ **n.** a tariff imposed principally to raise government revenue.

re·verb /ˈrēˌvərb; riˈvərb/ ▶ **n.** an effect whereby the sound produced by an amplifier or an amplified musical instrument is made to reverberate slightly. ■ a device for producing such an effect. [1960s: abbrev.]

re·ver·ber·ate /riˈvərbəˌrāt/ ▶ **v.** [intrans.] (of a loud noise) be repeated several times as an echo. ■ (of a place) appear to vibrate or be disturbed because of a loud noise. ■ [trans.] archaic return or reecho (a sound). ■ have continuing and serious effects. — **re·ver·ber·ant** /-rənt/ **adj. re·ver·ber·ant·ly** /-rəntlē/ **adv. re·ver·ber·a·tion** /riˌvərbəˈrāSHən/ **n. re·ver·ber·a·tive** /-rətiv/ **adj. re·ver·ber·a·tor** /-ˌrātər/ **n. re·ver·ber·a·to·ry** /-rəˌtôrē/ **adj.** [15th C. ('drive back'): from L. *reverberat-* 'struck again,' from the v. *reverberare*, from *re-* + *verberare* 'to lash' (from *verbera* (pl.) 'scourge').]

Re·vere, Paul (1735–1818), American patriot and silversmith. In 1775 he rode from Boston to Lexington to warn of the approach of British troops.

re·vere /riˈvi(ə)r/ ▶ **v.** [trans.] (often **be revered**) feel deep respect or admiration for (something). [17th C.: ult. from L. *revereri*, from *re-* (intensive force) + *vereri* 'to fear.']

rev·er·ence /ˈrev(ə)rəns/ ▶ **n.** deep respect for. ■ (**His/Your Reverence**) a title given to a member of the clergy, or used in addressing them. ▶ **v.** [trans.] regard or treat with deep respect.

rev·er·end /ˈrev(ə)rənd/ ▶ **adj.** (usu. **Reverend**) used as a title or form of address to members of the clergy. ■ dated (of a person) deserving respect or reverence. ▶ **n.** informal a clergyman. [ME: ult. from L. *reverendus*, gerundive of *revereri* (see REVERE).]

rev·er·ent /ˈrev(ə)rənt/ ▶ **adj.** feeling or showing deep and solemn respect: *a reverent silence.* — **rev·er·ent·ly adv.** [ME: from L. *reverent-* 'revering,' from *revereri* (see REVERE).]

rev·er·en·tial /ˌrevəˈrenCHəl/ ▶ **adj.** of the nature of, due to, or characterized by reverence. — **rev·er·en·tial·ly adv.**

rev·er·ie /ˈrevərē/ ▶ **n.** a state of being pleasantly lost in one's thoughts; a daydream: *I slipped into reverie.* ■ Music an instrumental piece suggesting a dreamy or musing state. ■ archaic a fanciful or impractical idea. [17th C.: from obs. Fr. *resverie*, from OFr. *reverie* 'revelry,' from *rever* 'be delirious.']

re·vers /riˈvi(ə)r; -ˈve(ə)r/ ▶ **n.** (pl. same) the turned-back edge of a garment revealing the undersurface. [19th C.: from Fr., lit. 'reverse.']

re·ver·sal /riˈvərsəl/ ▶ **n.** a change to an opposite direction, position, or course of action. ■ Law an annulment of a judgment, sentence, or decree made by a lower court or authority. ■ an adverse change of fortune. ■ Photog. direct production of a positive image from an exposed film or plate; direct reproduction of a positive or negative image.

re·verse /riˈvərs/ ▶ **v.** [intrans.] move backward. ■ [trans.] cause (a vehicle) to move backward. ■ [trans.] turn (something) the other way around or up or inside out. ■ [trans.] make (something) the opposite of what it was. ■ [trans.] exchange (the position or function) of two people or things: *reversed roles.* ■ [trans.] Law revoke or annul (a judgment, sentence, or decree made by a lower court or authority). ■ (of an engine) work in a contrary direction. ■ [trans.] Print. make (type or a design) print as white in a block of solid color or a halftone. ▶ **adj.** [attrib.] going in or turned toward the direction opposite to that previously stated. ■ operating, behaving, or ordered in a way contrary or opposite to that which is usual or expected. ■ Electron. (of a voltage applied to a semiconductor junction) in the direction that does not allow significant current to flow. ■ Geol. denoting a fault or faulting in which a relative downward movement occurred in the strata situated on the underside of the fault plane. ▶ **n. 1** a complete change of direction or action. ■ reverse gear on a motor vehicle; the position of a gear lever or selector corresponding to this. See also *IN REVERSE* below. ■ (**the reverse**) the opposite or contrary to that previously stated. ■ an adverse change of fortune; a setback or defeat. ■ Football a play in which the ballcarrier reverses the direction of attack by lateraling or handling the ball to a teammate moving in the opposite direction. **2** the opposite side or face to the observer. ■ a left-hand page of an open book, or the back of a loose document. ■ the side of a coin or medal bearing the value or secondary design. ■ the design or inscription on this side. See also OBVERSE (sense 1).

– PHRASES **in** (or **into**) **reverse** (of a motor vehicle) in reverse gear so as to travel backward. ■ in the opposite direction or manner from usual: *do the route in reverse.* **reverse the charges** make the recipient of a telephone call responsible for payment. — **re·verse·ly adv. re·vers·er n.** [ME: ult. from L. *reversus* 'turned back,' past part. of *revertere*, from *re-* + *vertere* 'to turn.']

re·verse dis·crim·i·na·tion ▶ **n.** (in the context of the allocation of resources or employment) the practice or policy of favoring individuals belonging to groups known to have been discriminated against previously.

re·verse en·gi·neer·ing ▶ **n.** the reproduction of another manufacturer's product following detailed examination of its construction or composition.

re·verse gear ▶ **n.** a gear used to make a vehicle or piece of machinery move or work backward.

re·verse os·mo·sis ▶ **n.** Chem. a process by which a solvent passes through a porous membrane in the direction opposite to that for natural osmosis.

re·verse tran·scrip·tase ▶ **n.** an enzyme that catalyzes the formation of DNA from an RNA template in reverse transcription. See also TRANSCRIPTASE.

re·vers·i·ble /riˈvərsəbəl/ ▶ **adj.** able to be reversed, in particular: ■ (of a garment, fabric, or bedclothes) faced on both sides so as to be worn or used with either outside. ■ able to be turned the other way around. ■ (of the effects of a process or condition) capable of being reversed so that the previous state or situation is restored. ■ Chem. (of a reaction) occurring together with its converse, and so yielding an equilibrium mixture of reactants and products. ■ Physics (of a change or process) capable of complete and detailed reversal, esp. denoting or undergoing an ideal change in which a system is in thermodynamic equilibrium at all times. ■ Chem. (of a colloid) capable of being changed from a gel into a sol by a reversal of the treatment that turns the sol into a gel. — **re·vers·i·bil·i·ty** /riˌvərsəˈbilətē/ **n. re·vers·i·bly** /-blē/ **adv.**

re·ver·sion /riˈvərZHən/ ▶ **n. 1** a return to a previous state, practice, or belief. ■ Biol. the action of reverting to a former type. **2** Law the right, esp. of the original owner or their heirs, to possess or succeed to property on the death of the present possessor or at the end of a lease. ■ a property to which someone has such a right. ■ the right of succession to an office or post after the death or retirement of the holder. — **re·ver·sion·ar·y** /-ˌnerē/ **adj.** (in sense 2). [ME ('action of returning'): ult. from L. *reversio(n-)*, from *revertere* (see REVERSE).]

re·ver·sion·er /riˈvərZHənər/ ▶ **n.** Law a person who possesses the reversion to a property or privilege.

re·vert /riˈvərt/ ▶ **v.** [intrans.] (**revert to**) return to (a previous state, condition, practice, etc.). ■ return to (a previous topic). ■ Biol. return to (a former or ancestral type). ■ Law (of property) return or pass to (the original owner) by reversion. ■ [trans.] archaic turn (one's eyes or steps) back. — **re·vert·er n.** (Law). [ME: from OFr. *revertir* or L. *revertere* 'turn back.']

re·ver·tant /riˈvərtnt/ Biol. ▶ **adj.** (of a cell, organism, or strain) having reverted to normal from abnormal. ▶ **n.** a cell, organism, or strain of this type.

re·vet /riˈvet/ ▶ **v.** (**-vet·ted, -vet·ting**) [trans.] [usu. as adj.] (**revetted**) face (a rampart, wall, etc.) with masonry, esp. in fortification. [19th C.: from Fr. *revêtir*, from late L. *revestire*, from *re-* 'again' + *vestire* 'clothe' (from *vestis* 'clothing').]

re·vet·ment /riˈvetmənt/ ▶ **n.** (esp. in fortification) a retaining wall or facing of masonry or other material. ■ a barricade of earth or sandbags set up to provide protection from blast or to prevent planes from overrunning when landing.

re·view /riˈvyo͞o/ ▶ **n. 1** a formal assessment or examination of something. ■ a critical appraisal of a book, play, movie, exhibition, etc., published in a newspaper or magazine. ■ [often in names] a periodical publication with critical articles on current events, the arts, etc. ■ Law a reconsideration of a judgment, sentence, etc., by a higher court or authority. Compare with JUDICIAL REVIEW. ■ a retrospective survey or report on past events. ■ a survey or evaluation of a particular subject. **2** a ceremonial display and formal inspection of military or naval forces. ▶ **v.** [trans.] **1** examine or assess (something) with the possibility or intention of instituting change if necessary. ■ write a critical appraisal of (a book, play, movie, etc.) for publication in a newspaper or magazine. ■ Law submit (a sentence, case, etc.) for reconsideration by a higher court or authority. ▪ make a retrospective assessment or survey of (past events). ▪ survey or evaluate (a particular subject). **2** (of a sovereign, commander in chief, or high-ranking visitor) make a ceremonial and formal inspection of (military or naval forces). **3** view or inspect visually for a second time or again. — **re·view·a·ble** adj. **re·view·al** /-ˈvyo͞oəl/ n. [ME ('inspection of forces'): from obs. Fr. *reveue*, from *revoir* 'see again.']

re·view·er /riˈvyo͞oər/ ▸ n. a person who writes critical appraisals of books, plays, movies, etc., for publication. ▪ a person who formally assesses or examines something with a view to changing it if necessary.

re·vile /riˈvīl/ ▸ v. [trans.] (usu. **be reviled**) criticize in an abusive or angrily insulting manner. — **re·vile·ment** n. **re·vil·er** n. [ME: from OFr. *reviler*, based on *vil* 'vile.']

re·vise /riˈvīz/ ▸ v. [trans.] reconsider and alter (something) in the light of further evidence. ▪ reexamine and make alterations to (written or printed matter). ▪ alter so as to make more efficient or realistic. ▸ n. Print. a proof including corrections made in an earlier proof. — **re·vis·a·ble** adj. **re·vis·al** /-ˈvīzəl/ n. **re·vis·er** n. **re·vi·so·ry** /-ˈvīzərē/ adj. [16th C. ('look again'): ult. from L. *revisere* 'look at again,' from *re-* + *visere* (intensive form of *videre* 'to see').]

Re·vised Stand·ard Ver·sion (abbr.: **RSV**) ▸ n. a modern English translation of the Bible, published 1946–57.

Re·vised Ver·sion (abbr.: **RV**) ▸ n. an English translation of the Bible, published 1881–95.

re·vi·sion /riˈvizʜən/ ▸ n. the action of revising. ▪ a revised edition or form of something. — **re·vi·sion·ar·y** /-ˌnerē/ adj.

re·vi·sion·ism /riˈvizʜəˌnizəm/ ▸ n. often derog. a policy of revision or modification, esp. of Marxism on evolutionary socialist (rather than revolutionary) or pluralist principles. ▪ the theory or practice of revising one's attitude to a previously accepted situation or point of view. — **re·vi·sion·ist** n. & adj.

re·vis·it /rēˈvizit/ ▸ v. (**-vis·it·ed, -vis·it·ing**) [trans.] come back to or visit again.

re·vi·tal·ize /rēˈvītlˌīz/ ▸ v. [trans.] imbue (something) with new life and vitality: *revitalize the economy.* — **re·vi·tal·i·za·tion** /rēˌvītl-əˈzāsʜən/ n.

re·viv·al /riˈvīvəl/ ▸ n. an improvement in the condition or strength of something: *an economic revival.* ▪ an instance of something becoming popular, active, or important again. ▪ a new production of an old play or similar work. ▪ a reawakening of religious fervor, esp. by means of a series of evangelistic meetings. ▪ such a meeting or series of meetings. ▪ a restoration to bodily or mental vigor, to life or consciousness, or to sporting success.

re·viv·al·ism /riˈvīvəˌlizəm/ ▸ n. belief in or the promotion of a revival of religious fervor. ▪ a tendency or desire to revive a former practice. — **re·viv·al·ist** n. & adj. **re·viv·al·is·tic** /-ˌvīvəˈlistik/ adj.

re·vive /riˈvīv/ ▸ v. [trans.] restore to life or consciousness: *both men collapsed, but were revived.* ▪ [intrans.] regain life, consciousness, or strength. ▪ give new strength or energy to. ▪ restore interest in or the popularity of. ▪ improve the position or condition of. — **re·viv·a·ble** adj. **re·viv·er** n. [ME: ult. from late L. *revivere*, from L. *re-* 'back' + *vivere* 'live.']

re·viv·i·fy /rēˈvivəˌfī/ ▸ v. (**-fies, -fied**) [trans.] give new life or vigor to: *they revivified a wine industry.* — **re·viv·i·fi·ca·tion** /ˌrēˌvivəfəˈkāsʜən/ n. [17th C.: ult. from late L. *revivificare* (see **RE-**, **VIVIFY**).]

rev·o·ca·ble /ˈrevəkəbəl; riˈvōkəbəl/ ▸ adj. capable of being revoked or canceled. — **rev·o·ca·bil·i·ty** /ˌrevəkəˈbilətē; riˌvōkə-/ n.

re·voke /riˈvōk/ ▸ v. **1** [trans.] put an end to the validity or operation of (a decree, decision, or promise). **2** [intrans.] (in bridge, whist, and other card games) fail to follow suit despite being able to do so. — **rev·o·ca·tion** /ˌrevəˈkāsʜən; riˌvō-/ n. **rev·o·ca·to·ry** /ˈrevəkəˌtôrē; riˈvōkə-/ adj. **re·vok·er** n. [ME: ult. from L. *revocare*, from *re-* 'back' + *vocare* 'to call.']

re·volt /riˈvōlt/ ▸ v. **1** [intrans.] rise in rebellion. **2** [trans.] (often **be revolted**) cause to feel disgust. ▸ n. an attempt to put an end to the authority of a person or body by rebelling: *the peasants rose in revolt.* ▪ a refusal to continue to obey or conform. — **re·volt·ing·ly** adv. [16th C.: ult. from Ital. *rivoltare*, based on L. *revolvere* (see **REVOLVE**).]

rev·o·lute /ˈrevəˌlo͞ot/ ▸ adj. Bot. (esp. of the edge of a leaf) curved or curled back. [18th C.: from L. *revolutus*, past part. of *revolvere* (see **REVOLVE**).]

rev·o·lu·tion /ˌrevəˈlo͞osʜən/ ▸ n. **1** a forcible overthrow of a government or social order for a new system. ▪ (**the Revolution**) (in Marxism) the class struggle that is expected to lead to political change and the triumph of communism. ▪ a dramatic and wide-reaching change in the way something works or is organized or in people's ideas about it. **2** an instance of revolving: *one revolution a second.* ▪ motion in orbit or a circular course or around an axis or center. ▪ the single completion of an orbit or rotation. — **rev·o·lu·tion·ism** /-ˌnizəm/ n. **rev·o·lu·tion·ist** /-nist/ n. [ME: ult. from late L. *revolutio(n-)*, from *revolvere* (see **REVOLVE**).]

rev·o·lu·tion·ar·y /ˌrevəˈlo͞osʜəˌnerē/ ▸ adj. engaged in or promoting political revolution. ▪ (**Revolutionary**) of or relating to the American Revolution. ▪ involving a complete or dramatic change. ▸ n. (pl. **-ar·ies**) a person engaged in political revolution.

rev·o·lu·tion·ize /ˌrevəˈlo͞osʜəˌnīz/ ▸ v. [trans.] change (something) radically or fundamentally.

re·volve /riˈvälv; riˈvôlv/ ▸ v. [intrans.] move in a circle on a central axis: *the fan revolved slowly.* ▪ (**revolve around/about**) move in a circular orbit around. ▪ (**revolve around**) treat as the most important point or element. [ME ('turn (the eyes) back'): from L. *revolvere*, from *re-* + *volvere* 'roll.']

revolver

re·volv·er /riˈvälvər; -ˈvôl-/ ▸ n. a pistol with revolving chambers enabling several shots to be fired without reloading.

re·volv·ing cred·it ▸ n. credit that is automatically renewed as debts are paid off.

re·volv·ing door ▸ n. an entrance to a large building in which four partitions turn about a central axis. ▪ used to refer to a situation in which the same events or problems recur in a continuous cycle. ▪ [usu. as adj.] a place or organization that people tend to enter and leave very quickly. ▪ used to refer to a situation in which someone moves from an influential government position to a position in a private company, or vice versa.

re·volv·ing fund ▸ n. a fund that is continually replenished as withdrawals are made.

re·vue /riˈvyo͞o/ ▸ n. a light theatrical entertainment consisting of short sketches, songs, and dances. [Fr., lit. 'review.']

re·vul·sion /riˈvəlsʜən/ ▸ n. a sense of disgust. [16th C.: ult. from L. *revulsio(n-)*, from *revuls-* 'torn out,' from the v. *revellere* (from *re-* 'back' + *vellere* 'pull').]

Rev. Ver. ▸ abbr. Revised Version (of the Bible).

re·ward /riˈwôrd/ ▸ n. a thing given in recognition of service, effort, or achievement. ▪ a fair return for good or bad behavior. ▪ a sum offered for the detection of a criminal, the restoration of lost property, or the giving of information. ▸ v. [trans.] make a gift of something to (someone) in recognition of their services, efforts, or achievements. ▪ show one's appreciation of (an action or quality) by making a gift. ▪ (**be rewarded**) receive what one deserves.
– PHRASES **go to one's (final) reward** used euphemistically to indicate that someone has died. — **re·ward·less** adj. [ME (also 'regard, heed'): from Anglo-Norman Fr., var. of OFr. *reguard* 'regard.']

re·ward·ing /riˈwôrdiɴɢ/ ▸ adj. providing satisfaction; gratifying. — **re·ward·ing·ly** adv.

re·wind ▸ v. /rēˈwīnd/ (past and past part. **-wound** /-ˈwound/) [trans.] wind (a tape or film) back to the beginning. ▸ n. /ˈrēˌwīnd/ a mechanism for rewinding a tape or film. — **re·wind·er** /rēˈwīndər/ n.

re·word /rēˈwərd/ ▸ v. put (something) into different words.

re·work /rēˈwərk/ ▸ v. [trans.] (often **be reworked**) make changes to something, esp. in order to make it more up to date: *he reworked the orchestral score.*

re·wound /rēˈwound/ past and past participle of **REWIND**.

re·writ·a·ble /rēˈrītəbəl/ ▸ adj. Comput. (of a storage device) supporting overwriting of previously recorded data.

re·write ▸ v. /rēˈrīt/ (past **-wrote**; past part. **-writ·ten**) [trans.] write (something) again so as to alter or improve it. ▸ n. /ˈrēˌrīt/ an instance of writing something again so as to alter or improve it. ▪ a piece of text that has been altered or improved in such a way.
– PHRASES **rewrite history** select or interpret events from the past in a way that suits one's own particular purposes. **rewrite the record books** (of an athlete) break a record or several records.

Rex[1] /reks/ ▸ n. the reigning king (used following a name or in the titles of lawsuits, e.g., *Rex v. Jones*). [L., lit. 'king.']

Rex[2] ▸ n. a cat with curly fur that lacks guard hairs. [1960s: from L., lit. 'king.']

Reye's syn·drome /rīz; rāz/ ▸ n. a life-threatening metabolic disorder in young children, of uncertain cause but sometimes precipitated by aspirin. [1960s: named after Ralph D. K. *Reye* (1912–78), Australian pediatrician.]

Rey·kja·vik /ˈrākyəˌvik; -vēk/ the capital of Iceland, a port on the western coast; pop. 98,000.

Reyn·ard /ˈrāˌnärd; ˈrānərd; ˈrenərd/ ▸ n. literary a name for a fox. [from OFr. *renart*; influenced by MDu. *Reynaerd*.]

Reyn·olds /ˈrenəldz/, Sir Joshua (1723–92), English painter. He was a noted portrait painter.

Re·za Shah /riˈzä ˈsʜä/ see **PAHLAVI**[1].

Rf ▸ symb. the chemical element rutherfordium.

r.f. ▸ abbr. radio frequency.

rf. ▸ abbr. Baseball right fielder.

RFC ▸ abbr. ▪ (in computing) request for comment.

RFD (also **R.F.D.**) ▸ abbr. rural free delivery.

RFP ▸ abbr. request for proposal.

Rg ▸ symb. the chemical element roentgenium.

Rh ▸ abbr. Rhesus (factor). ▸ symb. the chemical element rhodium.

r.h. ▸ abbr. right hand.

rhab·dom /ˈrabˌdäm; -dəm/ (also **rhab·dome** /-ˌdōm/) ▸ n. Zool. a translucent cylinder forming part of the light-sensitive receptor in an arthropod's eye. [19th C.: from late Gk. *rhabdōma*, from *rhabdos* 'rod.']

rhab·do·man·cy /ˈrabdəˌmansē/ ▶ **n.** formal dowsing with a rod or stick. — **rhab·do·man·cer** /-sər/ **n.** [17th C.: from Gk. *rhabdomanteia*, from *rhabdos* 'rod.']

rhab·do·my·o·sar·co·ma /ˌrabdōˌmīōˌsärˈkōmə/ ▶ **n.** (pl. **-co·mas** or **-co·ma·ta** /-ˈkōmətə/) Med. a rare malignant tumor involving striated muscle tissue. [19th C.: from Gk. *rhabdos* 'rod' + MYO- + SARCOMA.]

Rhad·a·man·thine /ˌradəˈmanTHən; -ˌTHīn/ ▶ **adj.** literary showing stern and inflexible judgment. [17th C.: from RHADAMANTHUS.]

Rhad·a·man·thus /ˌradəˈmanTHəs/ Gk. Mythol. a ruler and judge in the underworld, known for his justice.

Rhae·to-Ro·man·ic /ˌrētōˌrōˈmanik/ (also **Rhae·to-Ro·mance**) ▶ **adj.** of, relating to, or denoting the Romance dialects spoken in parts of southeastern Switzerland, northeastern Italy, and Tyrol. ▶ **n.** any of these dialects. [from L. *Rhaetus* 'of *Rhaetia*' (a Roman province in the Alps) + ROMANIC.]

rham·nose /ˈramˌnōs; -ˌnōz/ ▶ **n.** Chem. a sugar of the hexose class that occurs widely in plants. [19th C.: from mod. L. *rhamnus*.]

rhap·sode /ˈrapˌsōd/ ▶ **n.** a person who recites epic poems, esp. one of a group in ancient Greece. [from Gk. *rhapsōidos*, from *rhapsōidia* (see RHAPSODY).]

rhap·so·dist /ˈrapsədist/ ▶ **n.** **1** one who rhapsodizes. **2** another term for RHAPSODE.

rhap·so·dize /ˈrapsəˌdīz/ ▶ **v.** [intrans.] speak or write about someone or something with great enthusiasm.

rhap·so·dy /ˈrapsədē/ ▶ **n.** (pl. **-dies**) **1** an effusively enthusiastic or ecstatic expression of feeling. ▪ Music a free instrumental composition in one extended movement. **2** (in ancient Greece) an epic poem, or part of it, of a suitable length for recitation at one time. — **rhap·sod·ic** /rapˈsädik/ **adj.** [16th C. (sense 2): via L. from Gk. *rhapsōidia*, from *rhaptein* 'to stitch' + *ōidē* 'song, ode.']

rhat·a·ny /ˈratn-ē/ ▶ **n.** **1** an astringent extract of the root of a South American shrub, used in medicine. **2** the partially parasitic South American shrub (genus *Krameria*, family Krameriaceae) that yields this root, which is also used as a source of dye. [19th C.: from mod. L. *rhatania*, via Port. and Sp. from Quechua *ratánya*.]

Rhe·a /ˈrēə/ **1** Gk. Mythol. one of the Titans, wife of Cronus and mother of Zeus, Demeter, Poseidon, Hera, and Hades. **2** Astron. a satellite of Saturn, the fourteenth closest to the planet, discovered by Cassini in 1672.

rhe·a /ˈrēə/ ▶ **n.** a large flightless bird (family Rheidae) of South American grasslands, resembling a small ostrich, with grayish-brown plumage. Two species: *Rhea americana* and *Pterocnemia pennata*. [19th C.: mod. L., after RHEA.]

rhe·bok /ˈrēˌbäk/ ▶ **n.** a small South African antelope (*Pelea capreolus*) with a woolly brownish-gray coat, a long slender neck, and short straight horns. [18th C.: from Du. *reebok* 'roebuck.']

Rhee /rē/, Syngman (1875–1975), president of South Korea 1948–60. Amid social and political unrest, he resigned one month into his fourth term.

Rhein /rīn/ German name for RHINE.

Rhein·land /ˈrīnˌlänt/ German name for RHINELAND.

Rhein·land-Pfalz /(p)fälts/ German name for RHINELAND-PALATINATE.

Rhen·ish /ˈrenisH; ˈrē-/ ▶ **adj.** of the Rhine and the regions adjoining it. ▶ **n.** wine from this area. [ME: from Anglo-Norman Fr. *reneis*, ult. from L. *Rhenanus*, from *Rhenus* 'Rhine.']

rhe·ni·um /ˈrēnēəm/ ▶ **n.** the chemical element of atomic number 75, a rare silvery-white metal that occurs in trace amounts in ores of molybdenum and other metals. (Symbol: **Re**) [1920s: mod. L., from L. *Rhenus* 'Rhine.']

rhe·ol·o·gy /rēˈäləjē/ ▶ **n.** the branch of physics that deals with the deformation and flow of matter. — **rhe·o·log·i·cal** /ˌrēəˈläjikəl/ **adj.** **rhe·ol·o·gist** /-jist/ **n.** [1920s: from Gk. *rheos* 'stream.']

rhe·o·stat /ˈrēəˌstat/ ▶ **n.** an electrical instrument used to control a current by varying the resistance. — **rhe·o·stat·ic** /ˌrēəˈstatik/ **adj.** [19th C.: from Gk. *rheos* 'stream.']

Rhe·sus fac·tor /ˈrēsəs/ (abbr.: **Rh fac·tor**) ▶ **n.** [in sing.] an antigen occurring on the red blood cells of many humans and some other primates. [1940s: from RHESUS MONKEY, in which it was first observed.]

rhe·sus mon·key (also **rhe·sus ma·caque**) ▶ **n.** a small brown macaque (*Macaca mulatta*) with red skin on the face and rump, native to southern Asia. It is often kept in captivity and is widely used in medical research. [19th C.: mod. L. *rhesus*, from L. *Rhesus*, mythical king of Thrace, from Gk. *Rhēsos*.]

Rhe·sus neg·a·tive (abbr.: **Rh neg·a·tive**) ▶ **adj.** lacking the Rhesus factor.

Rhe·sus pos·i·tive (abbr.: **Rh pos·i·tive**) ▶ **adj.** having the Rhesus factor.

rhet. ▶ **abbr.** ▪ rhetoric. ▪ rhetorical.

rhe·tor /ˈretər/ ▶ **n.** (in ancient Greece and Rome) a teacher of rhetoric. ▪ an orator. [via L. from Gk. *rhētōr*.]

rhet·o·ric /ˈretərik/ ▶ **n.** the art of effective or persuasive speaking or writing. ▪ language designed to have a persuasive or impressive effect on its audience, but often regarded as lacking in sincerity or meaningful content. [ME: from OFr. *rethorique*, via L. from Gk. *rhētorikē (tekhnē)* '(art) of rhetoric,' from *rhētōr* 'rhetor.']

rhe·tor·i·cal /rəˈtôrikəl/ ▶ **adj.** of, relating to, or concerned with the art of rhetoric. ▪ expressed in terms intended to persuade or impress. ▪ (of a question) asked to produce an effect or to make a statement rather than to elicit information. — **rhe·tor·i·cal·ly** /-ik(ə)lē/ **adv.**

rhet·o·ri·cian /ˌretəˈrisHən/ ▶ **n.** an expert in formal rhetoric. ▪ a speaker whose words are primarily intended to impress or persuade.

rheum /ro͞om/ ▶ **n.** esp. literary a watery fluid that collects in or drips from the nose or eyes. [ME: from OFr. *reume*, via L. from Gk. *rheuma* 'stream' (from *rhein* 'to flow').]

rheu·mat·ic /ro͝oˈmatik/ ▶ **adj.** of, relating to, or caused by rheumatism: *rheumatic pains*. ▪ (of a person or part of the body) suffering from or affected by rheumatism. ▶ **n.** a person suffering from rheumatism. — **rheu·mat·i·cal·ly** /-ik(ə)lē/ **adv.** **rheu·ma·tick·y** /ro͝oˈmatikē; ˈro͞oməˌtikē/ **adj.** (informal). [ME ('characterized by rheum'): ult. from Gk. *rheumatikos*, from *rheuma* (see RHEUM).]

rheu·mat·ic fe·ver ▶ **n.** a noncontagious acute fever marked by inflammation and pain in the joints.

rheu·ma·tism /ˈro͞oməˌtizəm/ ▶ **n.** any disease marked by inflammation and pain in the joints, muscles, or fibrous tissue, esp. rheumatoid arthritis. [17th C.: ult. from Gk. *rheumatismos*, from *rheumatizein* 'to snuffle,' from *rheuma* 'stream.']

rheu·ma·toid /ˈro͞oməˌtoid/ ▶ **adj.** Med. relating to, affected by, or resembling rheumatism.

rheu·ma·toid ar·thri·tis ▶ **n.** a chronic progressive disease causing inflammation in the joints. Compare with OSTEOARTHRITIS.

rheu·ma·tol·o·gy /ˌro͞oməˈtäləjē/ ▶ **n.** Med. the study of rheumatism, arthritis, and other such disorders. — **rheu·ma·to·log·i·cal** /ˌro͞omətl'äjikəl/ **adj.** **rheu·ma·tol·o·gist** /-jist/ **n.**

rheum·y /ˈro͞omē/ ▶ **adj.** (esp. of the eyes) full of rheum; watery.

rhi·nal /ˈrīnl/ ▶ **adj.** Anat. of or relating to the nose or the olfactory part of the brain. [19th C.: from Gk. *rhis, rhin-* 'nose.']

Rhine /rīn/ a river in western Europe that rises in the Swiss Alps and flows for 820 miles (1,320 km) to the North Sea. German name RHEIN; French name RHIN.

Rhine·land /ˈrīnˌland/ the region of western Germany through which the Rhine River flows. German name RHEINLAND.

Rhine·land-Pa·lat·i·nate a state in western Germany; capital, Mainz. German name RHEINLAND-PFALZ.

rhine·stone /ˈrīnˌstōn/ ▶ **n.** an imitation diamond. [19th C.: translating Fr. *caillou du Rhin*, lit. 'pebble of the Rhine.']

rhi·ni·tis /rīˈnītis/ ▶ **n.** Med. inflammation of the mucous membrane of the nose.

rhi·no /ˈrīnō/ ▶ **n.** (pl. same or **-nos**) informal a rhinoceros.

rhino- ▶ **comb. form** of or relating to the nose: *rhinoplasty*. [from Gk. *rhis, rhin-* 'nose.']

rhi·noc·er·os /rīˈnäs(ə)rəs/ ▶ **n.** (pl. same or **-os·es**) a large, heavily built plant-eating endangered mammal (family Rhinocerotidae) with one or two horns on the nose and thick folded skin, native to Africa and South Asia. All kinds have become endangered through hunting. [ME: via L. from Gk. *rhinokerōs*, from *rhis, rhin-* 'nose' + *keras* 'horn.']

rhi·noc·er·os bee·tle ▶ **n.** a very large mainly tropical beetle (family Scarabaeidae), the male of which has a curved horn extending from the head and typically another from the thorax. In some parts of Asia, males are put to fight as a spectator sport.

rhi·noc·er·os bird ▶ **n.** another term for OXPECKER.

rhi·noc·er·os horn ▶ **n.** a mass of keratinized fibers that comprises the horn of a rhinoceros.

rhi·no·plas·ty /ˈrīnōˌplastē/ ▶ **n.** (pl. **-ties**) plastic surgery performed on the nose. — **rhi·no·plas·tic** /ˌrīnōˈplastik/ **adj.**

rhi·no·vi·rus /ˌrīnōˈvīrəs; ˈrīnōˌvī-/ ▶ **n.** Med. any of a group of picornaviruses.

rhizo- ▶ **comb. form** Bot. relating to a root or roots. [from Gk. *rhiza* 'root.']

rhi·zo·bi·um /rīˈzōbēəm/ ▶ **n.** a nitrogen-fixing bacterium (genus *Rhizobium*) that is common in the soil, esp. in the root nodules of leguminous plants. [1920s: mod. L., from RHIZO- 'root' + Gk. *bios* 'life.']

rhi·zoc·to·ni·a /ˌrīˌzäkˈtōnēə/ ▶ **n.** a common soil fungus (genus *Rhizoctonia*) that sometimes causes plant diseases such as damping off and foot rot. [19th C.: mod. L., from Gk. *rhiza* 'root' + *ktonos* 'murder.']

rhi·zoid /ˈrīˌzoid/ ▶ **n.** Bot. a filamentous outgrowth or root hair on the underside of the thallus in some lower plants, esp. mosses and liverworts. — **rhi·zoi·dal** /rīˈzoidl/ **adj.**

rhi·zome /ˈrīˌzōm/ ▶ **n.** Bot. a continuously growing horizontal underground stem that puts out lateral shoots and adventitious roots at intervals. Compare with BULB (sense 1), CORM. [19th C.: from Gk. *rhizōma*, from *rhizousthai* 'take root,' based on *rhiza* 'root.']

rhi·zo·morph /ˈrīzəˌmôrf/ ▶ **n.** Bot. a rootlike aggregation of hyphae in certain fungi.

Rhi·zop·o·da /rīˈzäpədə/ Zool. a phylum of single-celled animals that have extensible pseudopodia. — **rhi·zo·pod** /ˈrīzəˌpäd/ **n.** [mod. L. (pl.), from RHIZO- + Gk. *pous, pod-* 'foot.']

rhi·zo·sphere /ˈrīzəˌsfi(ə)r/ ▶ **n.** Ecol. the region of soil in the vicinity of plant roots.

rho /rō/ ▶ **n.** the seventeenth letter of the Greek alphabet (Ρ, ρ), transliterated as 'r.'

rho·da·mine /ˈrōdəˌmēn/ ▶ **n.** Chem. any of a number of synthetic dyes derived from xanthene. [19th C.: from RHODO- + AMINE.]

Rhode Is·land /rōd/ a state in the northeastern US, on the coast of the Atlantic Ocean, one of the six New England states; pop. 1,048,319; capital, Providence; statehood, May 29, 1790 (13). It is the smallest and most densely populated US state. — **Rhode Is·land·er n.**

Rhode Is·land Red ▶ **n.** a bird of an American breed of reddish-black domestic chicken.

Rhodes[1] /rōdz/ a Greek island in the southeastern Aegean Sea, off the Turkish coast; pop. 98,000. Greek name **Ródhos.** ■ its capital, a port on the northern tip; pop. 42,000.

Rhodes[2], Cecil John (1853–1902), prime minister of Cape Colony in South Africa 1890–96; born in Britain. By 1890, he had acquired 90 percent of the world's production of diamonds.

Rho·de·sia /rōˈdēzhə/ the former name of a large territory in central and southern Africa that is now Zambia and Zimbabwe. — **Rho·de·sian adj. & n.**

Rho·de·sian ridge·back /rōˈdēzhən/ ▶ **n.** a dog with a short light brown coat and a ridge of hair growing in the opposite direction along the back.

Rhodes Schol·ar·ship ▶ **n.** any of several scholarships awarded annually for study at Oxford University. — **Rhodes schol·ar n.** [named after Cecil *Rhodes* (see RHODES[2]).]

rho·di·um /ˈrōdēəm/ ▶ **n.** the chemical element of atomic number 45, a hard silvery-white metal of the transition series. (Symbol: **Rh**) [17th C.: mod. L., from Gk. *rhodon* 'rose' (from the color of the solution of its salts).]

rhodo- ▶ **comb. form** esp. Mineral. Chem. rose-colored: *rhodochrosite.* [from Gk. *rhodon* 'rose.']

rho·do·chro·site /ˌrōdəˈkrōˌsīt; rəˈdäkrə-/ ▶ **n.** a mineral consisting of manganese carbonate. [19th C.: from Gk. *rhodokhrōs* 'rose-colored' + -ITE[1].]

rho·do·den·dron /ˌrōdəˈdendrən/ ▶ **n.** a shrub or small tree (genus *Rhododendron*) of the heath family, with large clusters of bell-shaped flowers and typically with large evergreen leaves, widely grown as an ornamental. [via L. from Gk., from *rhodon* 'rose' + *dendron* 'tree.']

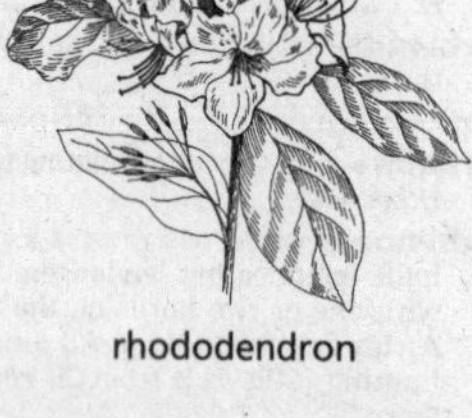

rhododendron

rho·do·lite /ˈrōdlˌīt/ ▶ **n.** a pale violet or red variety of garnet, used as a gemstone.

rho·do·nite /ˈrōdnˌīt/ ▶ **n.** a brownish or rose-pink mineral containing a silicate of manganese. [19th C.: from Gk. *rhodon* 'rose.']

Rhod·o·pe Moun·tains /ˈrädəpē/ a mountain system in the Balkans, in southeastern Europe.

Rho·doph·y·ta /rōˈdäfətə/ Bot. a division of lower plants that comprises the red algae. — **rho·do·phyte** /ˈrōdəˌfīt/ **n.** [mod. L. (pl.), from RHODO- + Gk. *phuta* 'plants.']

rho·dop·sin /rōˈdäpsən/ ▶ **n.** a purplish-red light-sensitive pigment present in the retinas. [19th C.: from Gk. *rhodon* 'rose' + *opsis* 'sight' + -IN[1].]

rho·do·ra /rəˈdôrə/ ▶ **n.** a pink-flowered North American shrub (*Rhododendron canadense*) of the heath family. [18th C.: mod. L., based on Gk. *rhodon* 'rose.']

rhomb /räm(b)/ ▶ **n.** a rhombohedral crystal. ■ a rhombus. — **rhom·bic** /ˈrämbik/ **adj.** [19th C.: from L. *rhombus* (see RHOMBUS).]

rhomb. ▶ **abbr.** rhombic.

rhom·ben·ceph·a·lon /ˌrämˌbenˈsefəˌlän; -lən/ ▶ **n.** Anat. another term for HINDBRAIN. [19th C.: from RHOMB + ENCEPHALON.]

rhom·bi /ˈrämˌbī; -ˌbē/ plural form of RHOMBUS.

rhom·bo·he·dral /ˌrämbōˈhēdrəl/ ▶ **adj.** (chiefly of a crystal) shaped like a rhombohedron.

rhom·bo·he·dron /ˌrämbōˈhēdrən/ ▶ **n.** (pl. **-drons** or **-dra** /-drə/) a solid figure whose faces are six equal rhombuses. ■ a crystal or other solid object of this form. [19th C.: from RHOMBUS.]

rhom·boid /ˈrämˌboid/ ▶ **adj.** having or resembling the shape of a rhombus. ▶ **n. 1** a quadrilateral of which only the opposite sides and angles are equal. **2** (also **rhom·boid mus·cle**) another term for RHOMBOIDEUS. — **rhom·boi·dal** /rämˈboidl/ **adj.** [16th C. (n.): ult. from Gk. *rhomboeidēs*, from *rhombos* 'rhombus.']

rhomboid 1

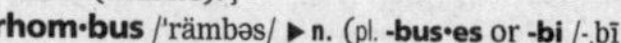

rhom·boi·de·us /rämˈboidēəs/ ▶ **n.** (pl. **-de·i** /-dēˌī/) Anat. a muscle connecting the shoulder blade to the vertebrae. [19th C.: mod. L., from *rhomboideus (musculus)*, lit. 'rhomboid (muscle).']

rhombus

rhom·bus /ˈrämbəs/ ▶ **n.** (pl. **-bus·es** or **-bi** /-ˌbī; -ˌbē/) a parallelogram with opposite equal acute and obtuse angles and four equal sides. ■ any parallelogram with equal sides. [16th C.: via L. from Gk. *rhombos.*]

Rhône /rōn/ a river in southwestern Europe that rises in the Swiss Alps and flows 505 miles (812 km) to the Mediterranean Sea.

rho·ta·ci·za·tion /ˌrōtəsəˈzāshən/ ▶ **n.** Ling. change of an original *s* or *z* to *r*, as in *was* and *were.* ■ Phonet. pronunciation of a vowel to reflect a following *r* in the orthography, e.g., in *farm, bird.* — **rho·ta·cized** /ˈrōtəˌsīzd/ **adj.** [1970s: from *rhotacize*, from Gk. *rhōtakizein.*]

rho·tic /ˈrōtik/ ▶ **adj.** Phonet. of, relating to, or denoting a dialect or variety of English in which *r* is pronounced before a consonant (as in 'farm') and at the end of a word (as in 'favor'). — **rho·tic·i·ty** /rōˈtisətē/ **n.** [1960s: from Gk. *rhot-*, stem of *rho* (see RHO) + -IC.]

rhu·barb /ˈro͞oˌbärb/ ▶ **n. 1** the thick leaf stalks of a cultivated plant of the dock family, which are reddish or green and eaten as a fruit after cooking. **2** the large-leaved Eurasian plant (*Rheum rhaponticum*) that produces these stems. **3** esp. Brit. informal the noise made by a group of actors to give the impression of indistinct background conversation or to represent the noise of a crowd, esp. by the random repetition of the word "rhubarb" with different intonations. ■ nonsense. ■ a heated dispute. [ME: from OFr. *reubarbe*, from a shortening of med. L. *rheubarbarum*, alt. (by association with *rheum* 'rhubarb') of *rhabarbarum* 'foreign rhubarb,' from Gk. *rha* (also meaning 'rhubarb') + *barbaros* 'foreign.']

rhumb /rəm(b)/ ▶ **n.** Naut. **1** (also **rhumb line**) an imaginary line on the earth's surface cutting all meridians at the same angle. **2** any of the 32 points of the compass. [16th C.: from Fr. *rumb*, prob. from Du. *ruim* 'space, room.']

rhum·ba ▶ **n.** var. of RUMBA.

rhyme /rīm/ ▶ **n.** correspondence of sound between words or the endings of words, esp. when these are used at the ends of lines of poetry. ■ a short poem in which the sound of the word or syllable at the end of each line corresponds with that at the end of another. ■ poetry or verse marked by such correspondence of sound. ■ a word that has the same sound as another. ▶ **v.** [intrans.] (of a word, syllable, or line) have or end with a sound that corresponds to another. ■ (of a poem or song) be composed of lines that end in words or syllables with sounds that correspond with those at the ends of other lines. ■ [trans.] (**rhyme something with**) put a word together with (another having a corresponding sound), as when writing poetry. ■ literary compose poetry.
– PHRASES **rhyme or reason** [with negative] logical explanation or reason: *without rhyme or reason his mood changed.* — **rhym·er n.** [ME *rime*, ult. from med. L. *rithmus*, via L. from Gk. *rhuthmos* (see RHYTHM).]

rhyme scheme ▶ **n.** the ordered pattern of rhymes.

rhym·ing slang ▶ **n.** a type of slang, typically in Cockney, that replaces words with rhyming words or phrases, typically with the rhyming element omitted.

rhy·o·lite /ˈrīəˌlīt/ ▶ **n.** Geol. a pale fine-grained volcanic rock of granitic composition. — **rhy·o·lit·ic** /ˌrīəˈlitik/ **adj.** [19th C.: from Ger. *Rhyolit*, from Gk. *rhuax* 'lava stream' + *lithos* 'stone.']

Rhys /rēs/, Jean (1890–1979), British writer, born in Dominica; pen name of *Ella Gwendolen Rees Williams*. Her novels include *Wide Sargasso Sea* (1966).

rhythm /ˈri<u>th</u>əm/ ▶ **n.** a strong, regular, repeated pattern of movement or sound. ■ the systematic arrangement of musical sounds, principally according to duration and periodic stress. ■ a particular type of pattern formed by such arrangement. ■ a person's natural feeling for such arrangement. ■ the measured flow of words and phrases in verse or prose as determined by the relation of long and short or stressed and unstressed syllables. ■ a regularly recurring sequence of events, actions, or processes. ■ Art a harmonious sequence or correlation of colors or elements. [16th C. (also orig. in the sense 'rhyme'): from Fr. *rhythme*, or via L. from Gk. *rhuthmos* (rel. to *rhein* 'to flow').]

rhythm and blues (abbr.: **R & B**) ▶ **n.** a form of popular music of African-American origin that arose during the 1940s from blues and jazz.

rhyth·mic /ˈri<u>th</u>mik/ ▶ **adj.** having or relating to rhythm. ■ occurring regularly: *rhythmic changes in our bodies.* — **rhyth·mi·cal adj. rhyth·mi·cal·ly** /-ik(ə)lē/ **adv.**

rhyth·mic gym·nas·tics ▶ **plural n.** [usu. treated as sing.] a form of gymnastics emphasizing dancelike rhythmic routines, typically accentuated by the use of ribbons or hoops. — **rhyth·mic gym·nast n.**

rhyth·mic·i·ty /ˌri<u>th</u>ˈmisətē/ ▶ **n.** rhythmical quality or character.

rhythm meth·od ▶ **n.** a method of avoiding conception by which sexual intercourse is restricted to the times when ovulation is least likely to occur.

rhythm sec·tion ▶ **n.** the part of a pop or jazz group supplying the rhythm.

rhy·ton /ˈrīˌtän/ ▶ **n.** (pl. **rhy·tons** or **rhy·ta** /ˈrītə/) a type of drinking vessel used in ancient Greece. [from Gk. *rhuton*, neut. of *rhutos* 'flowing'; rel. to *rhein* 'to flow.']

RI ▶ **abbr.** ■ Rex et Imperator (King and Emperor) or Regina et Imperatrix (Queen and Empress). [L.] ■ Rhode Island (in official postal use).

RIA ▶ **abbr.** ■ radioimmunoassay.

ri·a /ˈrēə/ ▶ **n.** Geog. a long narrow river inlet. [19th C.: from Sp. *ría* 'estuary.']

ri·al /rē'ôl; rē'äl/ ▶ **n.** **1** (also **ri·yal**) the basic monetary unit of Iran and Oman, equal to 100 dinars in Iran and 1000 baiza in Oman. **2** var. of RIYAL. [via Pers. from Arab. *riyāl* (see RIYAL).]

rib /rib/ ▶ **n.** **1** each of a series of slender curved bones articulated in pairs to the spine, protecting the thoracic cavity. ■ a rib of an animal with meat adhering to it used as food. **2** a long raised piece of stronger or thicker material across a surface or through a structure, in particular: ■ Archit. a curved member supporting a vault or defining its form. ■ any of the curved transverse pieces of metal or timber in a ship, forming part of the framework of the hull. ■ each of the curved pieces of wood forming the body of a lute or the sides of a violin. ■ each of the hinged rods supporting the fabric of an umbrella. ■ Aeron. a structural member in an airfoil, serving to define its contour. ■ a vein of a leaf or an insect's wing. ■ a ridge of rock or land. ■ Knitting a combination of alternate knit (plain) and purl stitches, used esp. for the cuffs and bottom edges of sweaters. ▶ **v.** (**ribbed, rib·bing**) [trans.] **1** (usu. **be ribbed**) mark with or form into raised bands or ridges. **2** informal tease good-naturedly. [OE *rib, ribb* (n.), of Gmc. origin.]

rib·ald /'ribəld; 'rib,ôld; 'rī,bôld/ ▶ **adj.** referring to sexual matters in an amusingly rude or irreverent way. [ME (n., 'lowly retainer'): from OFr. *ribauld*, from *riber* 'pursue licentious pleasures,' from Gmc., 'prostitute.']

rib·ald·ry /'ribəldrē; 'rī-/ ▶ **n.** ribald talk or behavior.

rib·and /'ribənd/ ▶ **n.** archaic a ribbon. [ME: from OFr. *riban*, prob. from Gmc. compound of (n.) BAND[1].]

ribbed /ribd/ ▶ **adj.** (esp. of a fabric or garment) having a pattern of raised bands. ■ Archit. (of a vault or other structure) strengthened with ribs.

rib·bie /'ribē/ ▶ **n.** (pl. **-bies**) Baseball, informal a run batted in. See **RBI**. [20th C.: elaboration of **RBI**.]

rib·bing /'ribiNG/ ▶ **n.** **1** a riblike structure or pattern. **2** informal good-natured teasing.

rib·bon /'ribən/ ▶ **n.** a long, narrow strip of fabric, used esp. for tying something or for decoration. ■ a strip of fabric of a special color or design awarded as a prize or worn to indicate the holding of an honor. ■ a long, narrow strip of something. ■ a narrow band of inked material forming the inking agent in some typewriters and computer printers. ▶ **v.** [intrans.] extend or move in a long narrow strip like a ribbon.
– PHRASES **cut a** (or **the**) **ribbon** perform an opening ceremony, typically by formally cutting a ribbon across the entrance to somewhere. **cut** (or **tear**) **something to ribbons** cut (or tear) something so badly that only ragged strips remain. ■ fig. damage something severely. — **rib·boned adj.** [16th C.: var. of RIBAND.]

rib·bon·fish /'ribən,fisH/ ▶ **n.** (pl. same or **-fish·es**) any of a number of long slender fishes that typically have a dorsal fin running the length of the body, in particular a dealfish, cutlassfish, or oarfish.

rib·bon grass ▶ **n.** another term for TAPE GRASS.

rib·bon worm ▶ **n.** a chiefly aquatic worm (phylum Nemertea) with an elongated, unsegmented, flattened body that is typically brightly colored and tangled in knots, and a long proboscis for catching food.

rib·by /'ribē/ ▶ **adj.** having prominent ribs.

rib cage ▶ **n.** the bony frame formed by the ribs around the chest.

rib eye (also **rib·eye** or **rib-eye steak**) ▶ **n.** a cut of beef from the outer side of the ribs.

ri·bo·fla·vin /,rībə'flāvin; 'rībə,flā-/ ▶ **n.** Biochem. a yellow vitamin of the B complex that is essential for metabolic energy production. Also called VITAMIN B_2. [1930s: from RIBOSE + L. *flavus* 'yellow.']

ri·bo·nu·cle·ase /,rībō'n(y)o͞oklē,ās; -,āz/ ▶ **n.** another term for **RNase**.

ri·bo·nu·cle·ic ac·id /,rībōn(y)o͞o'klē-ik; -'klā-ik/ ▶ **n.** see **RNA**. [1930s: from RIBOSE + NUCLEIC ACID.]

ri·bose /'rī,bōs; -,bōz/ ▶ **n.** Chem. a sugar of the pentose class that occurs widely in nature as a constituent of nucleosides and several vitamins and enzymes. [19th C.: alt. of ARABINOSE.]

ri·bo·some /'rībə,sōm/ ▶ **n.** Biochem. a minute particle consisting of RNA and associated proteins, found in large numbers in the cytoplasm of living cells. — **ri·bo·so·mal** /,rībə'sōməl/ **adj.** [1950s: from RIBONUCLEIC ACID.]

ri·bo·zyme /'rībə,zīm/ ▶ **n.** Biochem. an RNA molecule capable of acting as an enzyme. [1980s: blend of *ribonucleic* and ENZYME.]

rib-tick·ler ▶ **n.** informal an amusing joke or story. — **rib-tick·ling adj. rib-tick·ling·ly adv.**

ri·bu·lose /'rībyə,lōs; -,lōz/ ▶ **n.** Chem. a sugar of the pentose class that is an important intermediate in carbohydrate metabolism and photosynthesis. [1930s: from RIBOSE + *-ulose*.]

rib·wort /'rib,wərt; -,wôrt/ (also **rib·wort plan·tain**) ▶ **n.** a plantain (*Plantago lanceolata*) with erect ribbed leaves and a rounded flower spike.

Ri·car·di·an /ri'kärdēən/ ▶ **adj.** relating to or denoting the doctrines of the political economist David Ricardo (1772–1823).

RICE ▶ **abbr.** rest, ice, compression, and elevation (treatment method for bruises, strains, and sprains).

Rice[1] /rīs/, Anne (1941–), US writer; born *Howard Allen O'Brien*. Known for her fictional series *The Vampire Chronicles* (1976–2003), she later renounced its dark themes and began writing Christ-centered fiction.

Rice[2], Condoleezza (1954–), US secretary of state 2005–. She was President George W. Bush's chief security advisor 2001–05.

Rice[3], Sir Tim (1944–), English lyricist and entertainer; full name *Timothy Miles Bindon Rice*. With Andrew Lloyd Webber, he cowrote musicals, including *Jesus Christ Superstar* (1971).

rice /rīs/ ▶ **n.** a swamp grass (*Oryza sativa*) that is widely cultivated as a source of food, esp. in Asia. ■ the grains of this cereal used as food. ▶ **v.** [trans.] force (cooked potatoes or other vegetables) through a sieve or ricer. [ME: from OFr. *ris*, from Ital. *riso*, from Gk. *oruza*.]

rice bowl ▶ **n.** a dish from which rice is eaten. ■ fig. one's livelihood. ■ an area in which large quantities of rice are grown (used esp. to refer to Asia).

rice burn·er ▶ **n.** derog. a Japanese motorcycle.

rice pa·per ▶ **n.** thin translucent edible paper made from the flattened and dried pith of a shrub, used in painting (esp. oriental) and in baking biscuits and cakes.

ric·er /'rīsər/ ▶ **n.** a utensil with small holes through which boiled potatoes or other soft food can be pushed to form particles of a similar size to grains of rice.

ri·cer·car /,rēCHər'kär/ (also **ri·cer·ca·re** /-'kärā/) ▶ **n.** (pl. **-cars** or **-ca·ri** /-'kärē/) Music an elaborate instrumental composition in fugal or canonic style, typically of the 16th to 18th centuries. [from Ital. *ricercare* 'search out.']

rich /riCH/ ▶ **adj.** **1** having a great deal of money or assets; wealthy. ■ (of a country or region) having valuable natural resources or a successful economy. ■ of expensive materials or workmanship; demonstrating wealth. ■ generating wealth; valuable. **2** plentiful; abundant. ■ having (a particular thing) in large amounts. ■ (of food) containing a large amount of fat, spices, sugar, etc. ■ (of drink) full-bodied. ■ (of the mixture in an internal combustion engine) containing a high proportion of fuel. ■ (of a color or sound) pleasantly deep and strong. ■ (of a smell or taste) pleasantly smooth and mellow. ■ fig. interesting because full of diversity or complexity. **3** producing a large quantity of something. ■ (of soil or a piece of land) having the properties necessary to produce fertile growth. ■ (of a mine or mineral deposit) yielding a large quantity or proportion of precious metal. **4** informal (of a remark) causing ironic amusement or indignation: *these comments are a bit rich.* — **rich·ness n.** [OE *rice* 'powerful, wealthy,' from Gmc., akin to Ger. *reich*; ult. from Celtic.]

-rich ▶ **comb. form** containing a large amount of something specified: *protein-rich.*

Rich·ard /'riCHərd/ the name of three kings of England: ■ Richard I (1157–99), reigned 1189–99; son of Henry II; known as **Richard Coeur de Lion** or **Richard the Lionheart**. He led the Third Crusade. ■ Richard II (1367–1400), reigned 1377–99; son of the Black Prince. ■ Richard III (1452–85), reigned 1483–85; brother of Edward IV.

Rich·ards /'riCHərdz/, I. A. (1893–1979), English critic; full name *Ivor Armstrong Richards*.

Rich·ard·son /'riCHərdsən/, Samuel (1689–1761), English novelist, author of *Pamela* (1740–41), written in the form of letters and journals.

Rich·ard the Li·on·heart /'līən,härt/, Richard I of England (see RICHARD).

Rich·e·lieu /'rēsHə,lo͞o; rēsH'lœ/, Armand Jean du Plessis, duc de (1585–1642), French cardinal. He was chief minister to Louis XIII 1624–42.

rich·en /'riCHən/ ▶ **v.** [trans.] make richer.

rich·es /'riCHiz/ ▶ **plural n.** material wealth. ■ valuable natural resources: *the riches of the world.* [ME: var. (later interpreted as a pl. form) of archaic *richesse*, from OFr. *richeise* (from *riche* 'rich').]

Ri·chler /'riCHlər/, Mordecai (1931–2001), Canadian writer. His novels include *The Apprenticeship of Duddy Kravitz* (1959).

rich·ly /'riCHlē/ ▶ **adv.** in an elaborate, generous, or plentiful way: *she was richly dressed.* ■ [as submodifier] fully (used esp. to indicate that someone or something merits a particular thing): *a richly deserved vacation.*

Rich·mond /'riCHmənd/ the capital of Virginia, a port on the James River; pop. 197,790.

Rich·ter scale /'riktər/ ▶ **n.** Geol. a numerical scale for expressing the magnitude of an earthquake on the basis of seismograph oscillations. [1930s: named after Charles F. *Richter* (1900–85), American geologist.]

Richt·ho·fen /'riKHt,hōfən; 'rik,tōvən/, Manfred Albrecht Freiherr von (1892–1918), German aviator; known as **the Red Baron**. Flying a bright red aircraft, he shot down 80 enemy planes.

ri·cin /'rīsən; 'ris-/ ▶ **n.** Chem. a highly toxic protein obtained from the pressed seeds of the castor-oil plant. [19th C.: from mod. L. *Ricinus communis* ('castor-oil plant').]

rick[1] /rik/ ▶ **n.** a stack of hay, corn, straw, or similar material, esp. one shaped and thatched. ■ a pile of firewood somewhat smaller than a cord. ■ a set of shelving for storing barrels. ▶ **v.** [trans.] form into rick or ricks; stack. [OE *hrēac*, of Gmc. origin; rel. to Du. *rook*.]

rick[2] ▶ **n.** a slight sprain or strain, esp. in a person's neck or back. ▶ **v.** [trans.] strain (one's neck or back) slightly. [18th C. (v.): of dial. origin.]

rick·ets /'rikits/ ▶ **n.** [treated as sing. or pl.] Med. a disease of children caused by vitamin D deficiency. [17th C.: perh. an alt. of Gk. *rhakhitis* (see RACHITIS).]

rick·ett·si·a /ri'ketsēə/ ▶ **n.** (pl. **-si·ae** /-sē,ē; -sē,ī/ or **-si·as**) any of a group of very small bacteria (genus *Rickettsia*, order Rickettsiales) that includes the causative agents of typhus and various other febrile diseases in humans. Like viruses, many of them can only grow inside living cells, and they are frequently transmitted by mites, ticks, or lice. — **rick·ett·si·al** adj. [mod. L., named after Howard Taylor *Ricketts* (1871–1910), US pathologist.]

rick·et·y /ˈrikitē/ ▶adj. **1** (of a structure or piece of equipment) poorly made and likely to collapse. **2** (of a person) suffering from rickets. — **rick·et·i·ness** n. [17th C.: from RICKETS + -Y[1].]

rick·ey /ˈrikē/ ▶n. (pl. **-eys**) a drink made of liquor, typically gin, lime or lemon juice, carbonated water, and ice. [19th C.: prob. from the surname *Rickey*.]

Rick·ov·er /ˈrik,ōvər/, Hyman George (1900–1986), US admiral; born in Russia (now part of Poland). He was most responsible for creating the US nuclear-powered navy.

rick·rack /ˈrik,rak/ ▶n. braided trimming in a zigzag pattern.

rick·sha /ˈrik,SHô/ (also **rick·shaw**) ▶n. a light two-wheeled hooded vehicle drawn by one or more people. ■ a similar vehicle like a three-wheeled bicycle, having a seat for passengers behind the driver. [19th C.: abbrev. of JINRIKISHA.]

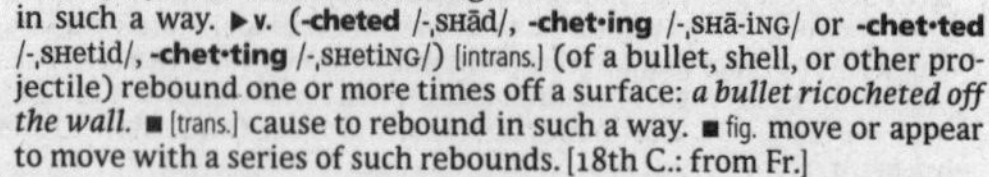

ricksha

RICO /ˈrēkō/ ▶abbr. (in the US) Racketeer Influenced and Corrupt Organizations Act.

ric·o·chet /ˈrikə,SHā; -,SHet/ ▶n. a shot or hit that rebounds one or more times off a surface. ■ the action or movement of a bullet, shell, or other projectile when rebounding in such a way. ▶v. (**-cheted** /-,SHād/, **-chet·ing** /-,SHā-iNG/ or **-chet·ted** /-,SHetid/, **-chet·ting** /-,SHetiNG/) [intrans.] (of a bullet, shell, or other projectile) rebound one or more times off a surface: *a bullet ricocheted off the wall.* ■ [trans.] cause to rebound in such a way. ■ fig. move or appear to move with a series of such rebounds. [18th C.: from Fr.]

ri·cot·ta /riˈkätə/ ▶n. a soft white Italian cheese. [Ital., lit. 'recooked.']

ric·tus /ˈriktəs/ ▶n. a fixed grimace or grin. — **ric·tal** /ˈriktəl/ adj. [19th C.: from L., lit. 'open mouth,' from *rict-* 'gaped,' from the v. *ringi*.]

rid /rid/ ▶v. (**rid·ding**; past and past part. **rid** or archaic **rid·ded**) [trans.] (**rid someone/something of**) make someone or something free of (a troublesome or unwanted person or thing): *rid the world of nuclear weapons.* ■ (**be rid of**) be freed or relieved from.
– PHRASES **be well rid of** be in a better state for having removed or disposed of (something troublesome). **get rid of** take action to be free of (something troublesome). [ME ('to clear (a path)'): from ON *rythja*.]

rid·dance /ˈridns/ ▶n. the action of getting rid of something troublesome.
– PHRASES **good riddance** said to express relief at being free of something troublesome.

rid·den /ˈridn/ past participle of RIDE.

rid·dle[1] /ˈridl/ ▶n. a question intentionally phrased to require ingenuity in ascertaining its answer. ■ a person, event, or fact that is difficult to understand.
– PHRASES **talk** (or **speak**) **in riddles** express oneself in an ambiguous or puzzling manner. — **rid·dler** /ˈridlər; ˈridl-ər/ n. [OE *rǣdelse* 'riddle, opinion'; akin to Ger. *Rätsel* and READ.]

rid·dle[2] ▶v. [trans.] **1** (usu. **be riddled**) make many holes in (someone or something), esp. with gunshot. ■ fill or permeate (someone or something), esp. with something unpleasant or undesirable. **2** pass (a substance) through a large coarse sieve. ■ remove ashes or other unwanted material from (something, esp. a fire or stove) in such a way. ▶n. a large coarse sieve, esp. one used for separating ashes from cinders or sand from gravel. [OE *hriddel*, from Indo-Eur.; akin to L. *cribrum* 'sieve,' *cernere* 'separate,' Gk. *krinein* 'decide.']

Ride /rīd/, Sally Kristen (1951–), US astronaut and physicist. She was the first US woman to travel in space 1983.

ride /rīd/ ▶v. (past **rode** /rōd/; past part. **rid·den** /ˈridn/) [trans.] **1** sit on and control the movement of (an animal, esp. a horse). ■ [intrans.] travel on a horse or other animal. ■ sit on and control (a bicycle or motorcycle). ■ [intrans.] (**ride in/on**) travel in or on (a vehicle) as a passenger. ■ travel in (a vehicle) or on (a public transport system) as a passenger. ■ go through or over (an area) on horseback, a bicycle, etc. ■ compete in (a race) on horseback or on a bicycle or motorcycle. ■ travel up or down in (an elevator). ■ [intrans.] (of a vehicle, animal, racetrack, etc.) be of a particular character for riding on or in: *the van rode well.* **2** be carried or supported by (something with a great deal of momentum): *ride the waves.* ■ [intrans.] project or overlap: *when two lithospheric plates collide, one tends to ride over the other.* ■ [intrans.] (of a vessel) sail or float: *ride at anchor.* ■ [intrans.] float or seem to float: *the moon was riding high in the sky.* ■ vulgar slang have sexual intercourse with. ■ (of a supernatural being) take spiritual possession of (someone). ■ annoy, pester, or tease. **3** (**be ridden**) be full of or dominated by. ▶n. **1** a journey made on horseback, on a bicycle or motorcycle, or in a vehicle. ■ a person giving someone a lift in their vehicle. ■ informal a motor vehicle: *that's my ride.* ■ the quality of comfort or smoothness offered by a vehicle while it is being driven, as perceived by the driver or passenger. ■ a path, typically one through woods, for riding horses. **2** a roller coaster, merry-go-round, or other amusement ridden at a fair or amusement park. **3** vulgar slang an act of sexual intercourse. **4** (also **ride cym·bal**) a cymbal used for keeping up a continuous rhythm.
– PHRASES **be riding for a fall** informal be acting in a reckless or arrogant way that invites defeat or failure. **for the ride** for pleasure or interest, rather than any serious purpose. **let something ride** take no immediate action over something. **ride herd on** keep watch over. **ride high** be successful. **ride the pine** (or **bench**) informal (of an athlete) sit on the sidelines. **ride the rods** esp. Canadian, informal ride on a freight train surreptitiously without paying. **ride roughshod over** carry out one's own plans or wishes with arrogant disregard for (others or their wishes). —— **rides again** used to indicate that someone or something has reappeared unexpectedly and with new vigor. **ride shotgun** travel as a guard in the seat next to the driver of a vehicle. ■ ride in the passenger seat of a vehicle. ■ fig. act as a protector. **ride to hounds** esp. Brit. go hunting (esp. fox hunting) on horseback with a pack of dogs. **a rough** (or **easy**) **ride** a difficult (or easy) time doing something. **take someone for a ride 1** informal deceive or cheat someone. **2** informal drive someone out somewhere in a car and then kill them.
– PHRASAL VERBS **ride someone down** trample or overtake someone while on horseback. **ride on** depend on: *there is money riding on the results of these studies.* **ride something out** come safely through something. **ride up** (of a garment) gradually work or move upward out of its proper position. — **ride·a·ble** (also **rid·a·ble**) adj. [OE *ridan*, of Gmc. origin; rel. to Du. *rijden* and Ger. *reiten*.]

Ri·deau Ca·nal /riˈdō/ a waterway in eastern Ontario in Canada, created in the 1820s.

ride-off ▶n. (in a riding competition) a round held to resolve a tie or determine qualifiers.

rid·er /ˈrīdər/ ▶n. **1** a person who is riding or who can ride something, esp. a horse or bicycle. **2** a condition or proviso added to something already said or decreed: *one rider to the deal.* ■ an addition or amendment to a document. **3** a small weight positioned on the beam of a balance for fine adjustment. — **rid·er·less** adj.

rid·er·ship /ˈrīdər,SHip/ ▶n. the number of passengers using a particular form of public transportation.

Ridge, Thomas Joseph (1945–), the first US secretary of homeland security 2003–05. A Republican, he was governor of Pennsylvania 1995–2001 and assistant to the president for homeland security 2001–03.

ridge /rij/ ▶n. a long narrow hilltop, mountain range, or watershed. ■ the line or edge formed where the two sloping sides of a roof meet at the top. ■ Meteorol. an elongated region of high atmospheric pressure. ■ a narrow raised band running along or across a surface. ■ a raised strip of arable land. ▶v. [trans.] [often as adj.] (**ridged**) mark with or form into narrow raised bands: *the ridged sand of the beach.* ■ [intrans.] (of a surface) form into or rise up as a narrow raised band. ■ form (arable land) into raised strips separated by furrows. — **ridg·y** adj. [OE *hrycg* 'spine, crest,' from Gmc.; akin to Ger. *Rücken* 'back.']

ridge·back /ˈrij,bak/ ▶n. short for RHODESIAN RIDGEBACK.

ridge·piece /ˈrij,pēs/ ▶n. another term for RIDGEPOLE.

ridge·pole /ˈrij,pōl/ ▶n. **1** a horizontal beam along the ridge of a roof, into which the rafters are fastened. **2** the horizontal pole of a long tent.

ridge run·ner ▶n. informal a mountain farmer of the Southern states.

ridge tile ▶n. a semicircular or curved tile used in making a roof ridge.

ridge·way /ˈrij,wā/ ▶n. a road or track along a ridge.

rid·i·cule /ˈridi,kyo͞ol/ ▶n. the subjection of someone or something to mockery and derision. ▶v. [trans.] subject to mockery and derision. [17th C.: ult. from L. *ridiculum*, neut. of *ridiculus* 'laughable,' from *ridere* 'to laugh.']

ri·dic·u·lous /riˈdikyələs/ ▶adj. deserving or inviting derision or mockery; absurd. — **ri·dic·u·lous·ly** adv. **ri·dic·u·lous·ness** n. [16th C.: from L. *ridiculosus*, from *ridiculus* 'laughable' (see RIDICULE).]

ri·ding /ˈrīdiNG/ ▶n. the activity of riding horses. ▶adj. **1** associated with the sport of riding. **2** (of a machine or device) designed to be operated while riding on it: *a riding mower.*

rid·ing crop ▶n. a short flexible whip with a loop for the hand, used in riding horses.

rid·ing hab·it ▶n. a woman's riding dress.

rid·ing light ▶n. a light shown by a ship at anchor.

Rid·ley /ˈridlē/, Nicholas (c.1500–55), English bishop and martyr. A Protestant, he opposed the Catholic policies of Mary I.

rid·ley /ˈridlē/ (also **rid·ley tur·tle**) ▶n. (pl. **-leys**) a small turtle (genus *Lepidochelys*, family Cheloniidae) of tropical seas.

rie·beck·ite /ˈrē,bek,īt/ ▶n. a dark blue or black mineral of the amphibole group. [19th C.: from the name of Emil *Riebeck* (died 1885), German explorer.]

Ri·el /rēˈel/, Louis (1844–85), Canadian political leader. He led the rebellion of the Metis in 1869, later negotiating terms for the union of Manitoba with Canada.

ri·el /rēˈel/ ▶n. the basic monetary unit of Cambodia, equal to 100 sen. [Khmer.]

Rie·mann·i·an ge·om·e·try /rēˈmänēən; -ˈman-/ ▶n. a form of differential non-Euclidean geometry developed by Bernard Riemann (1826–66), used to describe curved space.

Ries·ling /ˈrēzliNG; ˈrēs-/ ▶n. a variety of wine grape grown in Germany, Austria, and elsewhere. ■ a dry white wine made from this grape.

ri·fam·pin /riˈfampin/ (also **ri·fam·pi·cin** /riˈfampəsin/) ▶n. Med. a reddish-brown antibiotic (obtained from the bacterium *Nocardia mediterranei*) used chiefly to treat tuberculosis and leprosy. [1960s: from *rifam(yci)n* (an antibiotic first isolated from the bacterium *Streptomyces mediterranei*) + *pi-* from PIPERAZINE.]

rife /rīf/ ▶ **adj.** [predic.] (esp. of something undesirable or harmful) of common occurrence; widespread. ■ (**rife with**) full of: *the streets were rife with rumor.* ▶ **adv.** in an unchecked or widespread manner. [OE *rȳfe*, prob. from ON *rīfr* 'acceptable.']

riff /rif/ ▶ **n.** (in popular music and jazz) a short repeated phrase, frequently played over changing chords or used as a background to a solo improvisation. ▶ **v.** [intrans.] play such phrases. [1930s: abbrev. of the n. RIFFLE.]

rif·fle /'rifəl/ ▶ **v.** turn over something, esp. the pages of a book, quickly and casually. ■ (**riffle through**) search quickly through (something), esp. so as to cause disorder. ■ [trans.] disturb the surface of; ruffle. ■ [trans.] shuffle (playing cards) by flicking up and releasing the corners or sides of two piles of cards so that they intermingle. ▶ **n.** **1** [usu. in sing.] a quick or casual leaf or search through something. ■ the rustle of paper being leafed through in such a way. ■ a shuffle performed by riffling playing cards. **2** a rocky or shallow part of a stream or river where the water flows brokenly. ■ a patch of waves or ripples. [18th C.: perh. from a var. of the v. RUFFLE, influenced by RIPPLE.]

rif·fler /'riflər/ ▶ **n.** a narrow elongated tool used to file concave surfaces. [18th C.: from Fr. *rifloir*, from OFr. *rifler* 'to scrape.']

riff·raff /'rif,raf/ ▶ **n.** disreputable or undesirable people: *I don't think they talk to riffraff off the street.* [15th C. (as *riff and raff*): from OFr. *rif et raf* 'one and all,' of Gmc. origin.]

rifle[1]

ri·fle[1] /'rīfəl/ ▶ **n.** a gun, esp. one fired from shoulder level, having a long spirally grooved barrel intended to make a bullet spin and thereby have greater accuracy over a long distance. ■ (**rifles**) troops armed with rifles. ▶ **v.** **1** [trans.] [usu. as adj.] (**rifled**) make spiral grooves in (a gun or its barrel or bore) to make a bullet spin and thereby have greater accuracy over a long distance. **2** [trans.] hit, throw, or kick (a ball or puck) hard and straight. [17th C.: from Fr. *rifler* 'graze, scratch,' of Gmc. origin.]

ri·fle[2] ▶ **v.** [intrans.] search through something in a hurried way in order to find or steal something. [ME: from OFr. *rifler* 'graze, plunder,' of Gmc. origin.]

ri·fle bird ▶ **n.** a bird of paradise (genus *Ptiloris*), the male of which has mainly velvety-black plumage and a display call that sounds like a whistling bullet.

ri·fle·man /'rīfəlmən/ ▶ **n.** (pl. **-men**) **1** a soldier armed with a rifle, esp. a private in a rifle regiment. ■ a person skilled at using a rifle. **2** a very small, short-tailed, greenish-yellow songbird (*Acanthisitta chloris*) that feeds on insects on tree bark, native to New Zealand. [perh. from a comparison between its plumage and a military uniform.]

ri·fle range ▶ **n.** a place for practicing shooting with rifles. ■ an attraction at a fairground in which people fire rifles at targets in order to win prizes.

ri·fling /'rīf(ə)liNG/ ▶ **n.** the arrangement of spiral grooves on the inside of a rifle barrel.

Rif Moun·tains /rif/ (also **Er Rif** /er 'rif/) a mountain range in northern Morocco that runs parallel to the Mediterranean Sea.

rift /rift/ ▶ **n.** a crack, split, or break in something. ■ Geol. a major fault separating blocks of the earth's surface; a rift valley. ■ fig. a serious break in friendly relations: ***a rift between the town and gown.*** ▶ **v.** [intrans.] esp. Geol. form fissures, cracks, or breaks, esp. through large-scale faulting; move apart. ■ [trans.] [usu. as adj.] (**rifted**) tear or force (something) apart: *the nascent rifted margins of the Red Sea.* [ME: of Scand. origin.]

rift val·ley ▶ **n.** a large elongated depression with steep walls formed by the downward displacement of a block of the earth's surface between nearly parallel faults or fault systems.

rig[1] /rig/ ▶ **v.** (**rigged, rig·ging**) [trans.] make (a sailing ship or boat) ready for sailing by providing it with sails and rigging. ■ assemble and adjust (the equipment of a sailboat, aircraft, etc.) to make it ready for operation. ■ set up (equipment or a device or structure), typically hastily or in makeshift fashion. ■ provide (someone) with clothes of a particular style or type. ▶ **n.** **1** the particular way in which a sailboat's masts, sails, and rigging are arranged. ■ the sail, mast, and boom of a sailboard. **2** an apparatus, device, or piece of equipment designed for a particular purpose: *a lighting rig.* ■ an oil rig or drilling rig. ■ (in CB and shortwave radio) a transmitter and receiver. ■ a particular type of construction for fishing tackle that bears the bait and hook. **3** a person's costume, outfit, or style of dress. **4** a tractor-trailer. ■ another type of vehicle, such as a horse-drawn carriage.

– PHRASES (**in**) **full rig** informal (wearing) fancy or ceremonial clothes. [15th C. (in nautical use): perh. of Scand. origin.]

rig[2] ▶ **v.** (**rigged, rig·ging**) manage or conduct (something) fraudulently so as to produce an advantageous result. ■ cause an artificial rise or fall in prices in (a market, esp. the stock market) with a view to personal profit. [18th C.: of unknown origin.]

Ri·ga /'rēgə/ a city on the Baltic Sea, the capital of Latvia; pop. 915,000.

rig·a·to·ni /,rigə'tōnē/ ▶ **n.** pasta in the form of short hollow fluted tubes. [Ital.]

Ri·gel /'rījəl; -gəl/ Astron. the seventh brightest star in the sky, and the brightest in the constellation Orion. [from Arab. *rijl* 'foot (of Orion).']

rig·ger[1] /'rigər/ ▶ **n.** a person who rigs or attends to the rigging of a sailing ship, aircraft, or parachute. ■ a person who erects and maintains scaffolding, lifting tackle, cranes, etc. ■ a person who works on or helps construct an oil rig.

rig·ger[2] ▶ **n.** a person who manipulates something so as to produce a result or situation to their advantage.

rig·ging /'rigiNG/ ▶ **n.** **1** the system of ropes, cables, or chains employed to support a ship's masts (**standing rigging**) and to control or set the yards and sails (**running rigging**). ■ the action of providing a sailing ship with sails, stays, and braces. **2** the ropes and wires supporting the structure of an airship, biplane, hang glider, or parachute. ■ the system of cables and fittings controlling the flight surfaces and engines of an aircraft. ■ the action of assembling and adjusting such rigging.

right /rīt/ ▶ **adj.** **1** morally good, justified, or acceptable. **2** true or correct as a fact. ■ [predic.] correct in one's opinion or judgment. ■ used as an interrogative at the end of a statement as a way of inviting agreement, approval, or confirmation: *you went to see Angie on Monday, right?* ■ according to what is correct for a particular situation or thing. ■ the best or most suitable of a number of possible choices. ■ socially fashionable or important: *he was seen at all the right places.* ■ [predic.] in a satisfactory, sound, or normal state or condition: *that sausage doesn't smell right.* **3** denoting or worn on the side of a person's body which is toward the east when they are facing north. ■ denoting the corresponding side of any other object. ■ on this side from the point of view of a spectator. **4** of or relating to a person or political party or grouping favoring conservative views. ▶ **adv.** **1** [with prep. phr.] to the furthest or most complete extent or degree: *the car spun right off the track.* ■ exactly; directly (used to emphasize the precise location or time of something): *Harriet was standing right behind her.* ■ informal immediately; without delay. **2** correctly: *he had guessed right.* ■ in the required or necessary way; properly; satisfactorily: *nothing's going right for me this season.* **3** on or to the right side: *turn right at Main Street.* ▶ **n.** **1** that which is morally correct, just, or honorable: *the difference between right and wrong.* **2** a moral or legal entitlement to have or obtain something or to act in a certain way: [with infin.] *she had every right to be angry.* ■ (**rights**) the authority to perform, publish, film, or televise a particular work, event, etc. **3** (**the right**) the right-hand part, side, or direction: *take the first turning on the right.* ■ (in football or a similar sport) the right-hand half of the field when facing the opponent's goal. ■ (**right**) Baseball short for RIGHT FIELD. ■ the right wing of an army. ■ a right turn. ■ a road or entrance on the right. ■ (esp. in the context of boxing) a person's right fist. ■ a blow given with this. **4** (often **the Right**) [treated as sing. or pl.] a grouping or political party favoring conservative views and supporting capitalist economic principles. ■ the section of a group or political party adhering particularly strongly to such views. [see RIGHT WING.] ▶ **v.** [trans.] restore to a normal or upright position. ■ restore to a normal or correct condition or situation: *righting the economy demanded major spending cuts.* ■ redress or rectify (a wrong or mistaken action). ▶ **exclam.** informal used to indicate one's agreement with a suggestion or to acknowledge a statement or order. ■ used as a filler in speech or as a way of confirming that someone is listening to or understanding what one is saying. ■ used to introduce an utterance, exhortation, or suggestion: *right, let's have a drink.*

– PHRASES **be in the right** be morally or legally justified in one's views, actions, or decisions. **by rights** if things had happened or been done fairly or correctly. **do right by** treat (someone) fairly. **in one's own right** as a result of one's own claims, qualifications, or efforts, rather than an association with someone else. (**not**) **in one's right mind** (not) sane. **not right in the head** informal (of a person) not completely sane. **put** (or **set**) **someone right 1** restore someone to health. **2** make someone understand the true facts of a situation. **put** (or **set**) **something to rights** restore something to its correct or normal state or condition. (**as**) **right as rain** informal (of a person) feeling completely well or healthy, typically after an illness or minor accident. **right** (or **straight**) **away** (or informal **off**) immediately. **right on** informal used as an expression of strong support, approval, or encouragement. See also RIGHT-ON. — **right·a·ble** **adj.** **right·ness** **n.** [OE *riht* (adj. and n.), *rihtan* (v.), *rihte* (adv.), of Gmc. origin; rel. to L. *rectus* 'ruled,' from an Indo-Eur. root denoting movement in a straight line.]

right-a·bout (also **right-a·bout face**) ▶ **n.** Mil. a right turn continued through 180° so as to face in the opposite direction.

right an·gle ▶ **n.** an angle of 90°, as in a corner of a square. See illustration at ANGLE[1].

– PHRASES **at right angles** (or **a right angle**) **to** forming an angle of 90° with (something).

right-an·gled ▶ **adj.** containing or being a right angle.

right arm ▶ **n.** dated one's most reliable helper.

right as·cen·sion (abbr.: **RA**) ▶ **n.** Astron. the distance of a point east of the First Point of Aries, measured along the celestial equator and expressed in hours, minutes, and seconds. Compare with DECLINATION and CELESTIAL LONGITUDE.

Right Bank a district in the city of Paris, on the right bank of the Seine River.

right brain ▶ n. the right-hand side of the human brain, believed to be associated with creativity and emotion. — **right-brain** adj. **right-brained** adj.

right·eous /ˈrīCHəs/ ▶ adj. **1** (of a person or conduct) morally right or justifiable; virtuous. **2** informal perfectly wonderful; fine and genuine. — **right·eous·ly** adv. **right·eous·ness** n. [OE *rihtwīs*, from *riht* 'right' + *wīs* 'manner, state,' associated with words such as *bounteous*.]

right field (also **right**) ▶ n. Baseball the part of the outfield to the right of center field from the perspective of home plate: *a ball hit to right field.* ■ the position of the defensive player stationed there. — **right field·er** n.

right-foot·ed ▶ adj. (of a person) using the right foot more naturally than the left. ■ (of a kick) done with the right foot.

right·ful /ˈrītfəl/ ▶ adj. [attrib.] having a legitimate right to property, position, or status. ■ legitimately claimed; fitting. — **right·ful·ly** adv. **right·ful·ness** n.

right hand ▶ n. the hand of a person's right side. ■ the region or direction on the right side of a person or thing. ■ the most important position next to someone. ■ an efficient or indispensable assistant. ▶ adj. [attrib.] on or toward the right side of a person or thing: *the top right-hand corner.* ■ done with or using the right hand.

right-hand·ed ▶ adj. **1** (of a person) using the right hand more naturally than the left. ■ (of a tool or item of equipment) made to be used with the right hand or by right-handed people. ■ made or done with the right hand, or in a manner natural to right-handed people. **2** going toward or turning to the right, in particular: ■ (of a screw) advanced by turning clockwise. ■ Biol. (of a spiral shell or helix) dextral. ■ (of a racecourse) turning clockwise. ▶ adv. with the right hand, or in a manner natural to right-handed people: *Jackson bats right-handed.* — **right-hand·ed·ly** adv.

right-hand·er /ˈhandər/ ▶ n. a right-handed person, esp. a right-handed baseball pitcher. ■ a blow struck with the right hand.

right·ist /ˈrītist/ ▶ n. a person who supports the political views or policies of the right. ▶ adj. supportive of the political views or policies of the right: *rightist doctrine.* — **right·ism** /-ˌizəm/ n.

right·ly /ˈrītlē/ ▶ adv. correctly. ■ with good reason. ■ in accordance with justice or what is morally right.

right-mind·ed ▶ adj. having sound views and principles.

right·most /ˈrītˌmōst/ ▶ adj. [attrib.] situated furthest to the right.

right of way (also **right-of-way**) ▶ n. **1** the legal right, established by usage or grant, to pass along a specific route through property belonging to another. ■ a path or thoroughfare subject to such a right. **2** the legal right of a pedestrian, rider, or driver to proceed before other road users at a particular point. ■ the right of a ship, boat, or aircraft to proceed with precedence over others in a particular situation. **3** the right to build and operate a railroad line, road, or utility on land belonging to another. ■ the land on which a railroad line, road, or utility is built.

right-on ▶ adj. often derog. in keeping with fashionable liberal or left-wing opinions and values.

right side ▶ n. the side of something, esp. a garment or fabric, intended to be uppermost or foremost.
– PHRASES **on the right side of** on the safe, appropriate, or desirable side of. ■ in a position to be viewed with favor by. ■ somewhat less than (a specified age). **right side out** with the side intended to be seen or used uppermost: *turn the skirt right side out.*

right·size /ˈrītˌsīz/ ▶ v. [trans.] convert (something) to an appropriate or optimum size. ■ reduce the size of (a company or organization).

rights of man ▶ plural n. rights held to be justifiably belonging to any person; human rights.

right-think·ing ▶ adj. right-minded.

right-to-die ▶ adj. pertaining to, expressing, or advocating the right to refuse extraordinary measures intended to prolong someone's life when they are terminally ill or comatose.

right-to-know ▶ adj. of or pertaining to laws or policies that make certain government or company records available to any individual who can demonstrate a right or need to know their contents.

right-to-life ▶ adj. another term for PRO-LIFE. — **right-to-lif·er** /ˈlīfər/ n.

right tri·an·gle ▶ n. a triangle with a right angle.

right turn ▶ n. a turn that brings a person's front to face the way their right side did before.

right·ward /ˈrītwərd/ ▶ adv. (also **right·wards** /-wərdz/) toward the right: *the party began to shift rightward.* ▶ adj. going toward or situated on the right.

right whale ▶ n. a baleen whale (family Balaenidae) with a large head and a deeply curved jaw, of Arctic and temperate waters.

right wing ▶ n. (**the right wing**) **1** the conservative or reactionary section of a political party or system. [with ref. to the National Assembly in France (1789–91), where the nobles sat to the president's right and the commons to the left.] **2** the right side of a team on the field in soccer, rugby, and field hockey. ■ the right side of an army. ▶ adj. conservative or reactionary: *a right-wing Republican.* — **right-wing·er** n.

right·y /ˈrītē/ ▶ n. (pl. **right·ies**) informal a right-handed person. ▶ adv. with the right hand or as customary for a right-handed person: *he bats righty.*

rig·id /ˈrijid/ ▶ adj. unable to bend or be forced out of shape; not flexible: *a seat of rigid orange plastic.* ■ (of a person or part of the body) stiff and unmoving, esp. as a result of shock or fear. ■ fig. not able to be changed or adapted. ■ fig. (of a person or their behavior) not adaptable in outlook, belief, or response. — **ri·gid·i·fy** /rəˈjidəˌfī/ v. **ri·gid·i·ty** /rəˈjidətē/ n. **rig·id·ly** adv. **rig·id·ness** n. [ME: from L. *rigidus*, from *rigere* 'be stiff.']

rig·ma·role /ˈrig(ə)məˌrōl/ ▶ n. [usu. in sing.] a lengthy and complicated procedure. ■ a long, rambling story or statement. [18th C.: appar. alt. of *ragman roll*, orig. denoting a legal document recording a list of offenses.]

rig·or /ˈrigər/ ▶ n. **1** the quality of being extremely thorough, exhaustive, or accurate. ■ severity or strictness: *the full rigor of the law.* ■ (**rigors**) demanding, difficult, or extreme conditions. **2** Med. shivering accompanied by a rise in temperature, often with copious sweating, esp. at the onset or height of a fever. ■ short for RIGOR MORTIS. [ME: from L., lit. 'stiffness,' from *rigere* 'be stiff.']

rig·or·ism /ˈrigəˌrizəm/ ▶ n. extreme strictness in interpreting or enforcing a law, precept, or principle. — **rig·or·ist** n. & adj.

rig·or mor·tis /ˌrigər ˈmôrtəs/ ▶ n. Med. stiffening of the joints and muscles of a body after death. [19th C.: from L., lit. 'stiffness of death.']

rig·or·ous /ˈrigərəs/ ▶ adj. extremely thorough, exhaustive, or accurate: *the rigorous testing of consumer products.* ■ (of a rule, system, etc.) strictly applied or adhered to. ■ (of a person) adhering strictly or inflexibly to a belief, opinion, or way of doing something: *a rigorous teetotaler.* ■ (of an activity) physically demanding. ■ (of the weather or climate) harsh. — **rig·or·ous·ly** adv. **rig·or·ous·ness** n.

Rig Ve·da /rig ˈvādə; ˈvēdə/ Hinduism the oldest and principal of the Vedas. See VEDA. [from Sanskrit *ṛgveda*, from *ṛc* '(sacred) stanza' + *veda* '(sacred) knowledge.']

Riis /rēs/, Jacob August (1849–1914), US journalist and social activist; born in Denmark. His photojournalism exposed the worst conditions of New York City slums.

Ri·je·ka /riˈyekə/ a city on the Adriatic coast of Croatia; pop. 168,000. Italian name FIUME.

rijst·ta·fel /ˈrīˌstäfəl/ ▶ n. a meal of Southeast Asian food consisting of a selection of spiced rice dishes. [Du., from *rijst* 'rice' + *tafel* 'table.']

rik·i·shi /ˈrikəˌSHē/ ▶ n. (pl. same) a sumo wrestler.

Riks·mål /ˈrikˌsmôl; ˈrēk-/ ▶ n. another term for BOKMÅL. [Norw., from *rike* 'state' + *mål* 'language.']

rile /rīl/ ▶ v. [trans.] informal make (someone) annoyed or irritated: *he's getting you all riled up.* [19th C.: var. of ROIL.]

Ri·ley[1] /ˈrīlē/, Bridget Louise (1931–), English painter. She was a leading exponent of op art.

Ri·ley[2], James Whitcomb (1849–1916), US poet; known as **the Hoosier poet**; pen name **Benj. F. Johnson of Boone**. Noted for his popular sentimental verse, he wrote "Little Orphant Annie" (1885).

ri·lie·vo ▶ n. var. of RELIEVO.

Ril·ke /ˈrilkə/, Rainer Maria (1875–1926), Austrian poet; born in Bohemia; born *René Karl Wilhelm Josef Maria Rilke*. He wrote *Duino Elegies* and *Sonnets to Orpheus* (both 1923).

rill /ril/ ▶ n. a small stream. ■ a shallow channel cut in the surface of soil or rocks by running water. ■ var. of RILLE. ▶ v. [intrans.] (of water) flow in or as in a rill. ■ [as adj.] (**rilled**) indented with small grooves. [16th C.: prob. of Low Ger. origin.]

rille /ˈrilə/ (also **rill**) ▶ n. Astron. a fissure or narrow channel on the moon's surface. [19th C.: from Ger. (see RILL).]

ril·lettes /rēˈyet/ ▶ plural n. pâté made of minced pork or other light meat, seasoned and combined with fat. [Fr., dimin. (pl.) of OFr. *rille* 'strip of pork.']

rim[1] /rim/ ▶ n. the upper or outer edge of an object, typically something circular: *an egg cup with a gold rim.* ■ (also **wheel rim**) the outer edge of a wheel, on which the tire is fitted. ■ the metal hoop from which a basketball net is suspended. ■ (often **rims**) the part of a glasses frame surrounding the lenses. ■ an encircling stain or deposit: *a thick rim of suds.* ▶ v. (**rimmed, rim·ming**) [trans.] form or act as an outer edge or rim for: *a huge lake rimmed by glaciers.* ■ (usu. **be rimmed**) mark with an encircling stain or deposit: *his collar was rimmed with dirt.* [OE *rima* 'a border, coast'; akin to ON *rimi* 'ridge, strip of land.']

rim[2] ▶ v. (**rimmed, rim·ming**) [trans.] vulgar slang lick or suck the anus of (someone) as a means of sexual stimulation.

Rim·baud /ramˈbō; raNˈbō/, Arthur (1854–91), French poet; full name *John Nicholas Arthur Rimbaud*. He was known for his symbolist prose poems.

rime[1] /rīm/ ▶ n. (also **rime ice**) frost formed on cold objects by the rapid freezing of water vapor. ▶ v. [trans.] literary cover (an object) with hoarfrost: *he does not brush away the frost that rimes his beard.* [OE *hrīm*, of Gmc. origin; rel. to Du. *rijm*.]

rime[2] ▶ n. & v. archaic spelling of RHYME.

rim·fire /ˈrimˌfī(ə)r/ ▶ adj. [attrib.] (of a cartridge) having the primer around the edge of the base.

Rim·i·ni /ˈrimənē/ a city on the Adriatic coast of northeastern Italy; pop. 131,000.

Rim·mon /ˈrimən/ (in the Bible) a deity worshiped in ancient Damascus (2 Kings 5:18).

rim·rock /ˈrimˌräk/ ▶ n. an outcrop of resistant rock forming a margin to a gravel deposit.

rim shot ▶**n.** a drum stroke in which the stick strikes the rim and the head of the drum simultaneously.

Rim·sky-Kor·sa·kov /'rimskē 'kôrsə,kôf/, Nikolai Andreevich (1844–1908), Russian composer. He wrote the orchestral suite *Scheherazade* (1888).

rind /rīnd/ ▶**n.** the tough outer layer of something, in particular: ■ the tough outer skin of certain fruit, esp. citrus fruit. ■ the hard outer edge of cheese or bacon, usually removed before eating. ■ the bark of a tree or plant. ▶**v.** [trans.] strip the bark from (a tree). [OE *rind(e)* 'bark of a tree'; rel. to Ger. *Rinde*.]

rin·der·pest /'rindər,pest/ ▶**n.** Vet. Med. an infectious disease of ruminants, esp. cattle. [19th C.: from Ger., from *Rinder* 'cattle' + *Pest* 'plague.']

ring[1] /riNG/ ▶**n.** **1** a small circular band, typically of precious metal and often set with one or more gemstones, worn on a finger as an ornament or token. ■ a circular band of any material: *fried onion rings.* ■ Astron. a thin band or disk of rock and ice particles around a planet. ■ a circular marking or pattern. **2** an enclosed space, in which a sport, performance, or show takes place: *a circus ring.* ■ a roped enclosure for boxing or wrestling. **3** a group of people or things arranged in a circle. ■ (**in a ring**) arranged or grouped in a circle: *everyone sat in a ring, holding hands.* ■ [usu. with adj.] a group of people drawn together due to a shared interest or goal, esp. one involving unscrupulous activity. ■ Chem. another term for **CLOSED CHAIN**. **4** a circular or spiral course: *they were dancing energetically in a ring.* **5** Math. a set of elements with two binary operations, addition and multiplication, the second being distributive over the first and associative. ▶**v.** [trans.] **1** (often **be ringed**) surround (someone or something), esp. for protection or containment. ■ form a line around the edge of (something circular): *dark shadows ringed his eyes.* ■ draw a circle around (something), esp. to focus attention on it: *an area of Tribeca had been ringed in red.* **2** put a circular band through the nose of (a bull, pig, or other farm animal) to lead or otherwise control it.
– PHRASES **run rings around someone** informal outclass or outwit someone very easily. — **ringed** adj. [in comb.] *the five-ringed Olympic emblem.* **ring·less** adj. [OE *hring*, of Gmc. origin; rel. to Du. *ring*, Ger. *Ring* and **RANK**[1].]

ring[2] ▶**v.** (past **rang** /raNG/; past part. **rung** /rəNG/) **1** [intrans.] make a clear resonant or vibrating sound: *a shot rang out* | [as n.] (**ringing**) *the ringing of fire alarms.* ■ [trans.] cause (a bell or alarm) to make such a sound. ■ (of a telephone) produce a series of resonant or vibrating sounds to signal an incoming call. ■ call for service or attention by sounding a bell. ■ (of a person's ears) be filled with a continuous buzzing or humming sound. ■ (**ring with/to**) (of a place) resound or reverberate with (a sound or sounds): *the room rang with laughter.* ■ [intrans.] convey a specified impression or quality: *the author's honesty rings true.* ■ [trans.] sound (the hour, a peal, etc.) on a bell or bells: *a bell ringing the hour.* **2** esp. Brit. call by telephone: *I rang her this morning.* ▶**n.** an act of causing a bell to sound, or the resonant sound caused by this: *there was a ring at the door.* ■ each of a series of resonant or vibrating sounds signaling an incoming telephone call. ■ [in sing.] a loud clear sound or tone: *the ring of sledgehammers on metal.* ■ [in sing.] a particular quality conveyed by something heard or expressed: *the song had a curious ring of nostalgia to it.*
– PHRASES **ring a bell** see **BELL**[1]. **ring down** (or **up**) **the curtain** cause a theater curtain to be lowered (or raised). ■ fig. mark the end (or the beginning) of an enterprise or event. **ring in one's ears** (or **head**) linger in the memory. **ring in** (or **out**) **the new** (or **old**) **year** commemorate the new year (or the end of the previous year) with boisterous celebration. **ring off the hook** (of a telephone) be constantly ringing.
– PHRASAL VERBS **ring someone/something in** (or **out**) usher someone or something in (or out) by or as if by ringing a bell. **ring something up** record an amount on a cash register. ■ fig. make, spend, or announce a particular amount in sales, profits, or losses. [OE *hringan*, of Gmc. origin, perh. imitative.]

ring-a·round-a·ro·sy ▶**n.** a singing game played by children, in which the players hold hands and dance in a circle, falling down at the end of the song. [said to refer to the inflamed ("rose-colored") ring of buboes, symptomatic of the plague; the final part of the game is symbolic of death.]

ring bear·er ▶**n.** the person, typically a young boy, who ceremoniously bears the rings at a wedding.

ring bind·er ▶**n.** a loose-leaf binder with ring-shaped clasps.

ring·bolt /'riNG,bōlt/ ▶**n.** a bolt with a ring attached for passing a rope through.

ring·bone /'riNG,bōn/ ▶**n.** osteoarthritis of the pastern joint of a horse, causing swelling and lameness.

ring cir·cuit ▶**n.** an electric circuit serving a number of outlets, with one fuse in the supply to the circuit.

ring·dove /'riNG,dəv/ ▶**n.** a dove or pigeon with a ringlike mark on the neck, in particular: ■ a captive or feral African collared dove (*Streptopelia roseogrisea*). ■ Brit. the wood pigeon.

ringed plov·er ▶**n.** a small plover (genus *Charadrius*) found chiefly in Eurasia, with white underparts and a black collar, breeding on sand or shingle beaches.

ring·er /'riNGər/ ▶**n.** **1** informal an athlete or horse fraudulently substituted for another in a competition. ■ a person's or thing's double, esp. an impostor: *he's a ringer for the French actor Fernandel.* ■ a person who is highly proficient at a particular skill or sport and is brought in to supplement a team or group of people. **2** a person who rings something, esp. a bell-ringer. ■ a device for ringing a bell, esp. on a telephone.

Ring·er's so·lu·tion /'riNGərz/ ▶**n.** Biol. a physiological saline solution that typically contains, in addition to sodium chloride, salts of potassium and calcium. [19th C.: Sydney *Ringer* (1834–1910), English physician.]

ring fin·ger ▶**n.** the finger next to the little finger, esp. of the left hand, on which the wedding band is worn.

ring flash ▶**n.** Photog. a circular electronic flash tube that fits around a camera lens to give shadowless lighting of a subject near the lens.

ring·git /'riNGgit/ ▶**n.** (pl. same or **-gits**) the basic monetary unit of Malaysia, equivalent to 100 sen. [Malay.]

ring·hals /'riNG,hals/ (also **rink·hals** /'riNG,kals/) ▶**n.** a large nocturnal spitting cobra (*Hemachatus haemachatus*) of southern Africa, with one or two white rings across the throat. [18th C.: from Afrik. *rinkhals*, from *ring* 'ring' + *hals* 'neck.']

ring·ing /'riNGiNG/ ▶**adj.** [attrib.] having or emitting a clear resonant sound: *a ringing voice.* ■ fig. (of a statement) forceful and unequivocal. — **ring·ing·ly** adv.

ring·lead·er /'riNG,lēdər/ ▶**n.** a person who initiates or leads an illicit or illegal activity.

ring·let /'riNGlit/ ▶**n.** **1** a lock of hair hanging in a corkscrew-shaped curl. **2** a brown butterfly (*Aphantopus*, *Erebia*, and other genera, family Nymphalidae) that has wings bearing eyespots that are typically highlighted by a paler color. — **ring·let·ed** adj. **ring·let·y** adj.

ring·mas·ter /'riNG,mastər/ ▶**n.** the person directing a circus performance.

ring mod·u·la·tor ▶**n.** an electronic circuit, esp. in a musical instrument, that incorporates a closed loop of four diodes and can be used for the balanced mixing and modulation of signals.

ring-neck (also **ring·neck**) ▶**n.** any of a number of ring-necked birds, in particular a ring-necked pheasant (see **PHEASANT**) and a ring-necked duck (*Aythya collaris*).

ring-necked ▶**adj.** used in names of birds and reptiles with a band or bands of color around the neck.

Ring of Fire the zone of volcanic activity surrounding the Pacific Ocean.

ring ou·zel (also **ring ou·sel**) ▶**n.** a European thrush (*Turdus torquatus*) that resembles a blackbird with a white crescent across the breast, inhabiting upland moors and mountainous country.

ring pull ▶**n.** a ring-shaped pull tab on a can.

ring road ▶**n.** a bypass encircling a town.

ring·side /'riNG,sīd/ ▶**n.** [often as adj.] the area immediately beside a boxing ring or circus ring. ■ fig. an advantageous position from which to observe or monitor something: *a ringside seat.* — **ring·sid·er** n.

ring·ster /'riNGstər/ ▶**n.** archaic **1** a member of a political or price-fixing ring. **2** a boxer.

ring·tail /'riNG,tāl/ ▶**n.** **1** any of a number of mammals or birds having a tail marked with a ring or rings, in particular: ■ a ring-tailed cat or lemur. ■ a female hen harrier or related harrier. ■ a golden eagle up to its third year. **2** (also **ring·tail** or **ring-tailed pos·sum**) a nocturnal tree-dwelling Australian possum (*Pseudocheirus* and other genera, family Petauridae) that habitually curls its prehensile tail into a ring or spiral. Its several species include the **common ringtail** (*P. peregrinus*) of southern Australia and Tasmania.

ring-tailed ▶**adj.** used in names of mammals and birds that have the tail banded in contrasting colors.

ring-tailed cat ▶**n.** a North American cacomistle (*Bassariscus astutus*), with a dark-ringed tail.

ring-tailed le·mur ▶**n.** a gregarious lemur (*Lemur catta*) with a gray coat, black rings around the eyes, and distinctive black-and-white banding on the tail.

ring-tailed lemur

ring·tone /'riNG,tōn/ ▶**n.** a sound made by a mobile phone when an incoming call is received.

ring·toss /'riNG,tôs; -,täs/ ▶**n.** a game in which rings are tossed at an upright peg.

ring·work /'riNG,wərk/ ▶**n.** Archaeol. the circular entrenchment of a minor medieval castle.

ring·worm /'riNG,wərm/ ▶**n.** a contagious itching skin disease occurring in small circular patches, caused by any of a number of fungi and affecting chiefly the scalp or the feet. Also called **TINEA**.

rink /riNGk/ ▶**n.** (also **ice rink** or **hock·ey rink**) an enclosed area of ice for skating, ice hockey, or curling. ■ (also **rol·ler rink**) a smooth enclosed floor for roller skating. ■ a building containing either of these. ■ (also **bowl·ing rink**) the strip of a bowling green used for playing a match. [ME (orig. Scots, 'jousting ground'): perh. from OFr. *renc* 'rank.']

rink·hals /'riNG,kals/ ▶**n.** var. of **RINGHALS**.

rink rat ▶ n. informal a young person who spends time around an ice-hockey rink in the hope of meeting players, watching practice, and spending time on the ice.

rink·y-dink /ˈriNGkē ˌdiNGk/ ▶ adj. informal old-fashioned, amateurish, or shoddy. [19th C.: origin unknown.]

rinse /rins/ ▶ v. wash (something) with clean water to remove soap, detergent, dirt, or impurities. ■ wash (something) quickly, esp. without soap. ■ clean (one's mouth) by swilling around and then spitting out a mouthful of water or mouthwash. ▶ n. **1** an act of rinsing something. **2** an antiseptic solution for cleansing the mouth. **3** a preparation for conditioning or temporarily tinting the hair. [ME (v.): from OFr. *rincer*.]

Ri·o Bran·co /ˈrē-ō ˈbräNGkō; ˈrē-o͝o ˈbräNGko͝o/ a city in western Brazil; pop. 197,000.

Ri·o de Ja·nei·ro /ˈrē-ō ˌdā zHəˈne(ə)rō; -jə-; ˌdē/ a state in eastern Brazil, on the Atlantic coast. ■ (also **Rio**) its capital; pop. 5,481,000. The chief port of Brazil, it was the country's capital from 1763 until 1960, when it was replaced by Brasília.

Rí·o de la Pla·ta /ˈrē-ō dā lä ˈplätä/ Spanish name for **Plate River**.

Rí·o de O·ro /ˈrē-ō dē ˈôrō/ an arid region of northwestern Africa that forms the southern part of Western Sahara. It was united with Saguia el Hamra in 1958 to form the province of Spanish Sahara (now Western Sahara).

Ri·o Grande /ˌrē-ō ˈgrand(ē)/ a river in North America that rises in the Rocky Mountains of southwestern Colorado and flows 1,880 miles (3,030 km) southeast to the Gulf of Mexico.

Ri·o Mu·ni /ˈrē-ō ˈmo͞onē/ the part of Equatorial Guinea that lies on the mainland of West Africa.

Ri·o Ne·gro /ˈrē-ō ˈnāgrō/ a river in South America that rises as the Guainia in eastern Colombia and flows for about 1,400 miles (2,255 km) to join the Amazon River near Manaus.

Rio Ran·cho /ˈrē-ō ˈrancHō/ a city in north central New Mexico; pop. 51,765.

ri·ot /ˈrīət/ ▶ n. **1** a violent disturbance of the peace by a crowd: *riots broke out in the capital.* ■ [as adj.] concerned with or used in the suppression of such disturbances: *riot police.* ■ fig. an uproar: *the film's sex scenes caused a riot.* ■ fig. an outburst of uncontrolled feelings: *a riot of emotions.* ■ archaic uncontrolled revelry; rowdy behavior. **2** [in sing.] an impressively large or varied display of something: *the garden was a riot of color.* **3** [in sing.] informal a highly amusing or entertaining person or thing: *everyone thought she was a riot.* ▶ v. [intrans.] take part in a violent public disturbance: *students rioted in Paris* | [as n.] (**rioting**) *a night of rioting.* ■ fig. behave in an unrestrained way: *another set of emotions rioted through him.*
– PHRASES **run riot** behave in a violent and unrestrained way. ■ (of a mental faculty or emotion) function or be expressed without restraint: *her imagination ran riot.* ■ proliferate or spread uncontrollably: *traditional prejudices were allowed to run riot.* — **ri·ot·er** n. [ME ('dissolute living'): from OFr. *riote* 'debate,' from *rioter* 'to quarrel.']

Ri·ot Act a law passed by the British government in 1715 and repealed in 1967, designed to prevent civil disorder.
– PHRASES **read the Riot Act** (or **riot act**) give someone a warning that they must improve their behavior.

ri·ot gear ▶ n. protective clothing and equipment worn by police or prison officers in violent crowds.

ri·ot girl (also **riot grrrl**) ▶ n. a member of a movement of young feminists expressing their resistance to the sexual harassment and exploitation of women.

ri·ot·ous /ˈrīətəs/ ▶ adj. marked by or involving public disorder: *a riotous crowd.* ■ characterized by wild and uncontrolled behavior: *a riotous party.* ■ having a vivid, varied appearance: *a riotous display of vegetables.* ■ hilariously funny. — **ri·ot·ous·ly** adv. **ri·ot·ous·ness** n.

RIP ▶ abbr. rest in peace (used on grave markers). [from L. *requiescat* (or pl. *requiescant*) *in pace*.]

rip[1] /rip/ ▶ v. (**ripped, rip·ping**) **1** [trans.] tear or pull (something) quickly or forcibly away from something or someone. ■ [trans.] make a long tear or cut in: *you've ripped my jacket* | [as adj.] (**ripped**) *ripped jeans.* ■ make (a hole) by force. ■ [intrans.] come violently apart; tear. ■ cut (wood) in the direction of the grain. **2** [no obj., with adverbial of direction] move forcefully and rapidly: *fire ripped through her bungalow.* **3** [trans.] use a program to copy (a sound sequence on a compact disc) on to a computer's hard drive. ▶ n. **1** a long tear or cut. ■ [in sing.] an act of tearing something forcibly. **2** a fraud or swindle; a rip-off.
– PHRASES **let rip** informal do something or proceed vigorously or without restraint. ■ express oneself vehemently or angrily. **let something rip** informal allow something, esp. a vehicle, to go at full speed. ■ allow something to happen forcefully or without interference. ■ utter or express something forcefully and noisily.
– PHRASAL VERBS **rip into** informal make a vehement verbal attack on. **rip someone off** informal cheat someone, esp. financially. **rip something off** informal steal. ■ copy; plagiarize. **rip something up** tear something violently into small pieces so as to destroy it. [ME (v.): origin unknown.]

rip[2] ▶ n. a stretch of fast-flowing and rough water. ■ short for **rip current**. [18th C.: perh. akin to **rip**[1].]

ri·par·i·an /riˈpe(ə)rēən; rī-/ ▶ adj. esp. Law of, relating to, or situated on the banks of a river. ■ Ecol. of or relating to wetlands adjacent to rivers and streams. [19th C.: from L. *riparius*, from *ripa* 'bank.']

rip·cord /ˈripˌkôrd/ ▶ n. a cord that is pulled to open a parachute.

rip cur·rent ▶ n. an intermittent strong surface current.

ripe /rīp/ ▶ adj. (of fruit or grain) developed to the point of readiness for harvesting and eating. ■ (of a cheese or wine) fully matured: *a ripe Brie.* ■ (of a smell or flavor) rich, intense, or pungent: *rich, ripe flavors.* ■ (of a female fish or insect) ready to lay eggs or spawn. ■ [predic.] (**ripe for**) arrived at the fitting stage or time for (a particular action or purpose): *land ripe for development.* ■ [predic.] (**ripe with**) full of: *a population ripe with discontent.* ■ [attrib.] (of a person's age) advanced: *she lived to a ripe old age.* ■ informal (of a person's language) coarse.
– PHRASES **the time is ripe** a suitable time has arrived: *the time was ripe to talk about peace.* — **ripe·ly** adv. **ripe·ness** n. [OE *rīpe*, from West Gmc., akin to Ger. *reif*.]

rip·en /ˈrīpən/ ▶ v. become or make ripe.

Rip·ken /ˈripkin/, Cal, Jr. (1960–), US baseball player; full name *Calvin Edwin Ripken, Jr.* An infielder for the Baltimore Orioles 1981–2001, he holds the record for most consecutive games played (2,632).

rip-off ▶ n. informal a fraud or swindle, esp. something that is grossly overpriced. ■ an inferior imitation of something.

ri·poste /riˈpōst/ ▶ n. **1** a quick clever reply to an insult or criticism. **2** Fencing a quick return thrust following a parry. ▶ v. **1** [with direct speech] make a quick clever reply to an insult or criticism: *"You've got a strange sense of humor," Grant riposted.* **2** [intrans.] make a quick return thrust in fencing. [18th C.: from Fr. *risposte* (n.), *risposter* (v.), from Ital. *risposta* 'response.']

rip·per /ˈripər/ ▶ n. **1** a tool that is used to tear or break something. ■ a murderer who mutilates victims' bodies. **2** informal a thing that is particularly admirable.

rip·ple /ˈripəl/ ▶ n. **1** a small wave or series of waves on the surface of water. ■ a thing resembling such a wave or series of waves in appearance or movement: *the sand undulated and was ridged with ripples.* ■ a gentle rising and falling sound, esp. of laughter or conversation, that spreads through a group of people: *a ripple of laughter ran around the room.* ■ a particular feeling or effect that spreads through or to someone or something: *his words set off a ripple of excitement within her.* ■ Physics a wave on a fluid surface, the restoring force for which is provided by surface tension rather than gravity, and that consequently has a wavelength shorter than that corresponding to the minimum speed of propagation. ■ small periodic, usually undesirable, variations in electrical voltage superposed on a direct voltage or on an alternating voltage of lower frequency. **2** a type of ice cream with wavy lines of colored flavored syrup running through it: *raspberry ripple.* ▶ v. [intrans.] (of water) form or flow with small waves on the surface: *the Mediterranean rippled and sparkled.* ■ [trans.] cause (the surface of water) to form small waves: *a cool wind rippled the surface of the estuary.* ■ move or cause to move in a way resembling such waves. ■ [intrans.] (of a sound or feeling) spread through a person, group, or place. ■ [as adj.] (**rippled**) having the appearance of small waves. — **rip·ply** /ˈrip(ə)lē/ adj. [17th C. (v.): origin unknown.]

rip·ple ef·fect ▶ n. the continuing and spreading results of an event or action.

rip·rap /ˈripˌrap/ ▶ n. loose stone used to form a foundation for a breakwater or other structure. ▶ v. (**-rapped, -rap·ping**) [trans.] strengthen with such a structure. [19th C.: reduplication of **rap**[1].]

rip-roar·ing ▶ adj. [attrib.] full of energy and vigor. — **rip-roar·ing·ly** adv.

rip·saw /ˈripˌsô/ ▶ n. a coarse saw for cutting wood along the grain.

rip·snort·ing /ˈripˈsnôrtiNG/ ▶ adj. [attrib.] informal showing great vigor or intensity: *a ripsnorting editorial.* — **rip·snort·er** /-ˈsnôrtər/ n. **rip·snort·ing·ly** adv.

rip·stop /ˈripˌstäp/ ▶ n. nylon fabric that is woven so that a tear will not spread.

rip·tide /ˈripˌtīd/ ▶ n. another term for **rip current**.

Rip Van Win·kle /ˌrip ˌvan ˈwiNGkəl/ the hero of a story in Washington Irving's *Sketch Book* (1819–20), who fell asleep in the Catskill Mountains and awoke twenty years later.

RISC /risk/ ▶ n. [usu. as adj.] Comput. a computer based on a processor or processors designed to perform a limited set of operations extremely quickly. ■ computing using this kind of computer. [1980s: from *reduced instruction set computer* (or *computing*).]

rise /rīz/ ▶ v. (past **rose** /rōz/; past part. **ris·en** /ˈrizən/) [intrans.] **1** move from a lower position to a higher one. ■ (of the sun, moon, or another celestial body) appear above the horizon: *the sun had just risen.* ■ (of a fish) come to the surface of water. ■ (of a voice) become higher in pitch. ■ reach a higher position in society or one's profession: *the officer had risen from the ranks.* ■ (**rise above**) succeed in not being limited or constrained by (a restrictive environment or situation): *he struggled to rise above his humble background.* ■ (**rise above**) be superior to: *I try to rise above pettiness.* **2** get up from lying, sitting, or kneeling. ■ get out of bed, esp. in the morning. ■ be restored to life: *your sister has risen from the dead.* ■ (of a wind) start to blow or to blow more strongly. ■ (of a river) have its source: *the Euphrates rises in Turkey.* ■ cease to be submissive, obedient, or peaceful. ■ (**rise to**) (of a person) react with annoyance or argument to (provocation): *he didn't rise to my teasing.* ■ (**rise to**) find the strength or ability to respond adequately to. **3** (of land or a feature following the contours of the land) incline upward; become higher. ■ (of a building, mountain, or other high object or structure) be much taller than the surrounding landscape: *the cliff rose more than a hundred feet above us.* ■ (of someone's hair) stand on end. ■ (of a building) undergo construction from the foundations. ■ (of dough) swell by the action of yeast: *leave the dough in a warm place to rise.* ■ (of a bump, blister, or weal) appear as a swelling on the skin: *blisters rose on his burned hand.* ■ (of a person's stomach) become nauseated. **4** increase in number, size, amount, or quality: *land prices had risen.* ■ (of the sea, a river, or other body of water) increase in height, typically through tidal action or flooding. ■ (of an emotion) develop and become more intense. ■ (of a sound) become louder; be audible above other sounds: *her voice rose above the clamor.* ■ (of a person's mood) become more cheerful. ■ (of the color in a person's face) become deeper. ■ (of a barometer or other instrument) give a higher reading. ▶ **n. 1** an upward movement; an instance of becoming higher: *the bird has a display flight of steep flapping rises.* ■ an act of a fish moving to the surface to take a fly or bait. ■ an increase in sound or pitch: *the rise and fall of his voice.* ■ an instance of social, commercial, or political advancement. ■ an upward slope or hill. ■ the vertical height of a step, arch, or incline. **2** an increase in amount, extent, size, or number. ■ Brit. an increase in salary or wages. **3** [in sing.] a source; an origin: *it was here that the brook had its rise.*

– PHRASES **get** (or **take**) **a rise out of** informal provoke an angry or irritated response from (someone), esp. by teasing. **on the rise** becoming greater or more numerous; increasing. ■ becoming more successful. **rise and shine** [usu. in imper.] informal get out of bed smartly; wake up. **rise to the bait** see BAIT. **rise with the sun** (or **lark**) get up early in the morning. [OE *risan* 'make an attack,' 'wake, get out of bed,' of Gmc. origin; rel. to Du. *rijzen* and Ger. *reisen*.]

ris·er /'rīzər/ ▶ **n. 1** [with adj.] a person who habitually gets out of bed at a particular time of the morning. **2** a vertical section between the treads of a staircase. See illustration at STAIR. **3** a vertical pipe for the upward flow of liquid or gas. **4** a low platform on a stage or in an auditorium.

ris·i·ble /'rizəbəl/ ▶ **adj.** such as to provoke laughter: *a risible scene of lovemaking in a tent.* — **ris·i·bil·i·ty** /ˌrizə'bilətē/ **n. ris·i·bly** /-blē/ **adv.** [16th C. ('inclined to laughter'): from late L. *risibilis*, from L. *ris-* 'laughed,' from the v. *ridere*.]

ris·ing /'rīziNG/ ▶ **adj. 1** going up; getting higher. ■ increasing: *rising costs.* ■ advancing to maturity or high standing: *the rising generation of American writers.* ■ approaching a higher level, grade, age, etc.: *a rising senior at North Carolina State.* ■ (of ground) sloping upward. ■ Astrol. (of a sign) ascendant. **2** [postpositive] Heraldry (of a bird) depicted with the wings open but not fully displayed, as if preparing for flight. ▶ **n.** an armed protest against authority; a revolt.

risk /risk/ ▶ **n.** a situation involving exposure to danger: *flouting the law was too much of a risk.* ■ [in sing.] the possibility that something unpleasant or unwelcome will happen: ***reduce the risk of heart disease*** | [as adj.] *a high consumption of caffeine was suggested as a* ***risk factor*** *for loss of bone mass.* ■ [usu. in sing.] [with adj.] a person or thing regarded as likely to turn out well or badly, as specified, in a particular context or respect: *Western banks regarded Romania as a good risk.* ■ [with adj.] a person or thing regarded as a threat to something in need of protection. ■ [with adj.] a thing regarded as likely to result in a specified danger: *gloss paint can burn strongly and pose a fire risk.* ■ (usu. **risks**) a possibility of harm or damage against which something is insured. ■ the possibility of financial loss. ▶ **v.** [trans.] expose (someone or something valued) to danger, harm, or loss: *he risked his life to save his dog.* ■ act or fail to act in such a way as to bring about the possibility of. ■ incur the chance of unfortunate consequences by engaging in (an action).

– PHRASES **at risk** exposed to harm or danger. **at one's (own) risk** used to indicate that if harm befalls a person or their possessions, it is their own responsibility: *they undertook the adventure at their own risk.* **at the risk of doing something** although there is the possibility of something unpleasant resulting. **risk one's neck** put one's life in danger. **run the risk** (or **run risks**) expose oneself to the possibility of something unpleasant occurring. **take a risk** (or **take risks**) proceed in the knowledge that there is a chance of something unpleasant occurring. [17th C.: from Fr. *risque* (n.), *risquer* (v.); from Ital. *risco* 'danger.']

risk·y /'riskē/ ▶ **adj.** (**risk·i·er**, **risk·i·est**) full of the possibility of danger, failure, or loss.

Ri·sor·gi·men·to /rēˌzôrjə'menˌtō; -ˌsôr-/ a movement for the unification and independence of Italy, which was achieved in 1870. [Ital., lit. 'resurrection.']

ri·sot·to /ri'zôtō; -'sôtō/ ▶ **n.** (pl. **-tos**) an Italian dish of rice cooked in stock with other ingredients. [Ital., from *riso* 'rice.']

ris·qué /ri'skā/ ▶ **adj.** slightly indecent or liable to shock, esp. by being sexually suggestive. [19th C.: Fr., past part. of *risquer* 'to risk.']

ris·sole /ri'sōl; 'risˌōl/ ▶ **n.** a compressed mixture of meat and spices, coated in breadcrumbs and fried. [18th C.: from Fr., from OFr. dial. *ruissole*, from a fem. form of late L. *russeolus* 'reddish,' from L. *russus* 'red.']

Ris·so's dol·phin /'risōz/ ▶ **n.** a gray dolphin (*Grampus griseus*) that has long black flippers and a rounded snout with no beak, living mainly in temperate seas. Also called GRAMPUS. [19th C.: Giovanni A. *Risso* (1777–1845), Italian naturalist.]

rit. Music ▶ **abbr.** ritardando.

Rit·a·lin /'ritl-in/ ▶ **n.** trademark for METHYLPHENIDATE.

ri·tar·dan·do /ˌrētär'dändō/ (also **ri·tard** /ri'tärd/) ▶ **adv. & adj.** (esp. as a direction) with a gradual decrease of tempo. ▶ **n.** (pl. **-dan·dos** or **-dan·di** /-'dändē/) a gradual decrease in tempo. [Ital.]

rite /rīt/ ▶ **n.** a religious or other solemn ceremony or act: *the rite of communion* | *fertility rites.* ■ a body of customary observances characteristic of a church or a part of it. ■ a social custom, practice, or conventional act: *the family Christmas rite.*

– PHRASES **rite of passage** a ceremony or event marking an important stage in someone's life. [ME: from L. *ritus* '(religious) usage.']

ri·tor·nel·lo /ˌritər'nelō/ ▶ **n.** (pl. **-nel·los** or **-nel·li** /-'nelē/) Music a short instrumental refrain or interlude in a vocal work. ■ a recurring tutti section in a concerto. [Ital., dimin. of *ritorno* 'return.']

rit·u·al /'riCHōōəl/ ▶ **n.** a religious or solemn ceremony consisting of a series of actions performed according to a prescribed order: *the ancient rituals of Christian worship.* ■ a prescribed order of performing such a ceremony, esp. one characteristic of a particular religion or church. ■ a series of actions or type of behavior regularly and invariably followed by someone. ▶ **adj.** [attrib.] of, relating to, or done as a religious or solemn rite: *ritual burial.* ■ (of an action) arising from convention or habit: *the players gathered for the ritual pregame huddle.* — **rit·u·al·ly** **adv.** [16th C. (adj.): from L. *ritualis*, from *ritus* (see RITE).]

rit·u·al·ism /'riCHōōəˌlizəm/ ▶ **n.** the regular observance or practice of ritual, esp. when excessive or without regard to its function. — **rit·u·al·ist** **n. rit·u·al·is·tic** /ˌriCHōōə'listik/ **adj. rit·u·al·is·ti·cal·ly** /ˌriCHōōə'listik(ə)lē/ **adv.**

rit·u·al·i·za·tion /ˌriCHōōələ'zāSHən/ ▶ **n.** the action or process of ritualizing something, in particular: ■ the formalization of certain actions expressing a particular emotion or state of mind, whether abnormally or as part of the symbolism of religion or culture. ■ Zool. the evolutionary process by which an action or behavior pattern in an animal loses its original function but is retained for its role in display or other social interaction.

rit·u·al·ize /'riCHōōəˌlīz/ ▶ **v.** [trans.] [usu. as adj.] (**ritualized**) make (something) into a ritual by following a pattern of actions or behavior. ■ Zool. cause (an action or behavior pattern) to undergo ritualization.

ritz /rits/ ▶ **n.** informal ostentatious luxury and glamour: *removed from all the ritz and glitz.*

– PHRASES **put on the ritz** make a show of luxury or extravagance. [20th C.: from *Ritz*, associated with luxury hotels, after César *Ritz* (1850–1918), Swiss hotel owner.]

ritz·y /'ritsē/ ▶ **adj.** (**ritz·i·er**, **ritz·i·est**) informal expensively stylish: *the ritzy Plaza Hotel.*

ri·val /'rīvəl/ ▶ **n.** a person or thing competing with another for the same objective or for superiority in the same field of activity. ■ [with negative] a person or thing that equals another in quality: *she has no rivals as a female rock singer.* ▶ **v.** (**-valed**, **-val·ing**; Brit. **-valled**, **-val·ling**) [trans.] compete for superiority with; be or seem to be equal or comparable to. [16th C.: from L. *rivalis*, lit. 'person using the same stream,' from *rivus* 'stream.']

ri·val·rous /'rīvəlrəs/ ▶ **adj.** prone to or subject to rivalry: *rivalrous presidential aspirants.*

ri·val·ry /'rīvəlrē/ ▶ **n.** (pl. **-ries**) competition for the same objective or for superiority in the same field.

rive /rīv/ ▶ **v.** (past **rived** /rīvd/; past part. **riv·en** /'rivən/) (usu. **be riven**) split or tear apart violently: *the party was riven by disagreements over Europe.* [ME: from ON *rífa*.]

riv·er /'rivər/ ▶ **n.** a large natural stream of water flowing in a channel to the sea, a lake, or another stream. ■ a large quantity of a flowing substance: *great rivers of molten lava* | fig. *the trickle of disclosures has grown into a river of revelations.*

– PHRASES **sell someone down the river** informal betray someone, esp. so as to benefit oneself. **up the river** informal to or in prison. [ME: from Anglo-Norman Fr., based on L. *riparius*, from *ripa* 'bank of a river.']

Ri·ve·ra /ri'vе(ə)rə/, Diego (1886–1957), Mexican painter and muralist; husband of Frida Kahlo. He inspired a revival of fresco painting in Latin America and the US.

riv·er birch ▶ **n.** a North American birch (*Betula nigra*) with shaggy reddish-brown or orange bark.

riv·er blind·ness ▶ **n.** a tropical skin disease caused by a parasitic filarial worm (*Onchocerca volvulus*), transmitted by the bite of blackflies (*Simulium damnosum*) that breed in fast-flowing rivers. The larvae of the parasite can migrate into the eye and cause blindness.

riv·er·boat /'rivərˌbōt/ ▶ **n.** a boat with a shallow draft, designed for use on rivers.

riv·er dol·phin ▶ **n.** a solitary dolphin (family Platanistidae) with a long slender beak, a small dorsal fin, and very poor eyesight. It lives in rivers and coastal waters of South America, India, and China, using echolocation to find its prey.

riv·er·front /'rivərˌfrənt/ ▶ **n.** the land or property along a river: *a distinctive feature of Quebec's riverfront.* ▶ **adj.** located along a river: *a lovely riverfront park.*

riv·er·ine /'rivəˌrīn; -ˌrēn/ ▶ **adj.** tech. literary of, relating to, or situated on a river or riverbank.

riv·er·scape /'rivərˌskāp/ ▶ **n.** a picturesque view or prospect of a river.

Riv·er·side /'rivərˌsīd/ a city in southern California, east of Los Angeles; pop. 255,166.

riv·er·side /'rivərˌsīd/ ▶ **n.** [often as adj.] the ground along a riverbank: *in one of the better riverside hotels.*

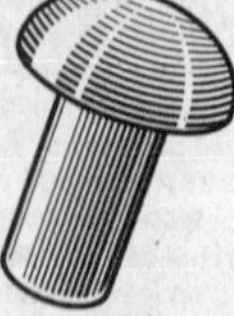
rivet

riv·et /'rivit/ ▶ **n.** a short metal pin or bolt for holding together two plates of metal, its headless end being beaten out or pressed down when in place. ■ a similar device for holding seams together. ▶ **v.** (**riv·et·ed, riv·et·ing**) [trans.] join or fasten (plates of metal or other material) with a rivet or rivets. ■ hold (someone or something) fast so as to make them incapable of movement. ■ attract and completely engross (someone): *he was riveted by the reports shown on television* | [as adj.] (**riveting**) *a riveting story.* — **riv·et·er n. riv·et·ing·ly adv.** [ME: from OFr., from *river* 'fix, clinch.']

riv·i·er·a /,rivē'e(ə)rə; ri'vye(ə)rə/ ▶ **n.** a coastal region with a subtropical climate and vegetation, esp.: ■ (**the Riviera**) a Mediterranean coastal region from Marseilles in France to La Spezia in Italy, site of many resorts. See also **Côte d'Azur.** [18th C.: from Ital., lit. 'seashore.']

Ri·vi·era Beach /ri'vi(ə)rə/ a city in southeastern Florida; pop. 27,639.

Riv·ne /'rivnə/ a city in western Ukraine northeast of Lviv; pop. 233,000. Russian name **Rovno.**

riv·u·let /'riv(y)ələt/ ▶ **n.** a very small stream: *sweat ran in rivulets down his back.* [16th C.: alt. of obs. *riveret* (from Fr., lit. 'small river'), perh. suggested by Ital. *rivoletto,* ult. from L. *rivus* 'stream.']

riv·u·lus /'rivyələs/ ▶ **n.** a small tropical American fish (genus *Rivulus,* family Rivulidae) of shallow fresh and brackish water. Often mistaken for a killifish or topminnow, the rivulus is distinguished by its tubular nostrils. [mod. L., from L., lit. 'small stream.']

Ri·yadh /rē'yäd/ the capital of Saudi Arabia; pop. 2,000,000. It is located in the center of the country.

ri·yal /rē'(y)ôl; rē'(y)äl/ ▶ **n.** (also **ri·al**) the basic monetary unit of Saudi Arabia, Qatar, and Yemen. [via Pers. from Arab. *riyāl,* from Sp. *real* 'royal.']

RKO a movie production and distribution company 1928–53, which produced classic movies such as *King Kong* (1933) and *Citizen Kane* (1941). [abbrev. of *Radio-Keith-Orpheum.*]

rm. ▶ **abbr.** room.

RMA ▶ **abbr.** Royal Military Academy.

RMP ▶ **abbr.** Royal Military Police.

r.m.s. Math. ▶ **abbr.** root mean square.

RN ▶ **abbr.** ■ (chiefly in North America) Registered Nurse. ■ (in the UK) **Royal Navy.**

Rn ▶ **symb.** the chemical element radon.

RNA ▶ **n.** Biochem. ribonucleic acid, a nucleic acid present in all living cells. Its principal role is to act as a messenger carrying instructions from DNA for controlling the synthesis of proteins.

RNase /'är'en,ās; -,āz/ ▶ **n.** Biochem. an enzyme that promotes the breakdown of RNA into oligonucleotides and smaller molecules. [1950s: from **RNA.**]

RNA vi·rus ▶ **n.** a virus in which the genetic information is stored in the form of RNA (as opposed to DNA).

RNP ▶ **abbr.** Biochem. ribonucleoprotein.

ro. ▶ **abbr.** ■ recto. ■ roan. ■ rood.

roach[1] /rōch/ ▶ **n.** informal **1** a cockroach. [19th C.: shortened form.] **2** the butt of a marijuana cigarette. [1930s: of unknown origin.]

roach[2] ▶ **n.** (pl. same) an edible Eurasian freshwater fish (*Rutilus rutilus*) of the minnow family, popular with anglers. It can hybridize with related fishes, notably rudd and bream. [ME: from OFr. *roche.*]

roach[3] ▶ **n.** Sailing a curve, in or out, in the edge off a sail. [18th C.: of unknown origin.]

roach clip ▶ **n.** informal a clip for holding the butt of a marijuana cigarette.

roached /rōcht/ ▶ **adj. 1** (esp. of an animal's back) having an upward curve. **2** (of a person's hair) brushed upward or forward into a roll. ■ (of a horse's mane) clipped or trimmed short so that the hair stands on end.

road /rōd/ ▶ **n. 1** a wide way leading from one place to another, esp. one that vehicles can use. ■ the part of such a way intended for vehicles, esp. in contrast to a shoulder or sidewalk. ■ [with adj.] hist. a regular trade route for a particular commodity: *the Silk Road across Asia to the West.* ■ Mining an underground passage or gallery in a mine. ■ a railroad. **2** fig. a series of events or course of action that will lead to a particular outcome: ***on the road to recovery.*** ■ a particular course or direction taken or followed. **3** [often in place names] (usu. **roads**) another term for **roadstead:** *Boston Roads.*
– PHRASES **by road** in or on a road vehicle. **down the road** informal in the future. **the end of the road** see **end. hit the road** see **hit. in** (or **out of**) **the** (or **one's**) **road** [often in imper.] informal in (or out of) someone's way. **one for the road** informal a final drink, esp. an alcoholic one, before leaving for home. **on the road 1** on a long journey or series of journeys. ■ (of a person) without a permanent home and moving from place to place. **2** (of a car) in use; able to be driven. **a road to nowhere** see **nowhere.** [OE *rād* 'journey on horseback,' 'foray'; of Gmc. origin; rel. to the v. **ride.**]

road a·gent ▶ **n.** hist. a highwayman or bandit, esp. along stagecoach routes in the western US.

road·bed /'rōd,bed/ ▶ **n.** the material laid down to form a road. ■ the part of a road on which vehicles travel. ■ the foundation on which railroad tracks are laid.

road bike ▶ **n. 1** a motorcycle that meets the legal requirements for use on ordinary roads. **2** a bicycle that is suitable for use on ordinary roads.

road·block /'rōd,bläk/ ▶ **n.** a barrier or barricade on a road, esp. one set up by the authorities. ■ fig. any hindrance: *the tax has become a roadblock.*

road hog ▶ **n.** informal a motorist who drives recklessly or inconsiderately, making it difficult for others to pass.

road·house /'rōd,hous/ ▶ **n.** a tavern, inn, or club on a country road.

road·ie /'rōdē/ informal ▶ **n.** a person employed by a touring band of musicians to set up and maintain equipment.

road kill ▶ **n.** a killing of an animal on the road by a vehicle. ■ animals killed in such a way.

road map ▶ **n.** a map, esp. one designed for motorists, showing the roads of a country or area. ■ a document or plan setting out the procedure for achieving a goal: *a road map for peace.*

road met·al ▶ **n.** see **metal** (sense 2).

road mov·ie ▶ **n.** a movie of a genre in which the main character travels and has adventures along the way.

road noise ▶ **n.** noise resulting from the movement of a vehicle's tires over the road surface.

road rage ▶ **n.** violent anger caused by the stress and frustration involved in driving a motor vehicle.

road·run·ner /'rōd,rənər/ ▶ **n.** a slender fast-running bird (genus *Geococcyx*) of the cuckoo family, found chiefly in arid country from the southern US to Central America, esp. the **greater roadrunner** (*G. californianus*). [prob. a calque from Sp. *correcamino.*]

road show (also **road·show**) ▶ **n.** a touring show of performers, esp. pop musicians. ■ a touring political or promotional campaign. ■ a radio or television program broadcast on location.

road·side /'rōd,sīd/ ▶ **n.** [often as adj.] the strip of land beside a road: *roadside cafes.*

road sign ▶ **n.** a sign giving information or instructions to road users.

road·stead /'rōd,sted/ ▶ **n.** a partly sheltered stretch of water near the shore in which ships can ride at anchor. [16th C.: from **road** + obs. *stead* 'a place.']

road·ster /'rōdstər/ ▶ **n.** an open-top automobile with two seats.

road test ▶ **n.** a test of the performance of a vehicle or engine on the road. ■ fig. a test of equipment carried out in working conditions. ■ a test of a person's competence in driving a motor vehicle. ▶ **v.** (**road-test**) [trans.] test (a vehicle, etc.) on the road. ■ fig. try out (something) in working conditions for review or prior to purchase or release.

Road Town the capital of the British Virgin Islands, on the island of Tortola; pop. 6,000.

road·way /'rōd,wā/ ▶ **n.** a road. ■ the part of a road intended for vehicles, in contrast to the sidewalk or median. ■ the part of a bridge or railroad used by traffic.

road·work /'rōd,wərk/ ▶ **n. 1** work done in building or repairing roads. **2** running on roads for athletic exercise or training. ■ time spent traveling while working or on tour.

road·wor·thy /'rōd,wər<u>th</u>ē/ ▶ **adj.** (of a motor vehicle or bicycle) fit to be used on the road.

roam /rōm/ ▶ **v.** [intrans.] move about or travel aimlessly or unsystematically, esp. over a wide area: *tigers once **roamed over** most of Asia.* ■ [trans.] travel unsystematically over, through, or around (a place): *gangs of youths roamed the streets unopposed.* ■ (of a person's eyes or hands) pass lightly over something without stopping: *her eyes roamed over the chattering women.* ■ [intrans.] (of a person's mind or thoughts) drift along without dwelling on anything in particular: *he let his mind roam.* ■ [trans.] move from site to site on (the Internet); browse. ▶ **n.** [in sing.] an aimless walk. — **roam·er n.** [ME: of unknown origin.]

roam·ing /'rōming/ ▶ **n.** [usually as modifier] the use of a cellular phone outside of its local area: *the roaming charges were too high.*

roan[1] /rōn/ ▶ **adj.** denoting an animal, esp. a horse or cow, having a coat of a main color thickly interspersed with hairs of another color, typically white. ▶ **n.** an animal with such a coat: *the roan is a stallion.* [16th C.: from OFr.]

roan[2] ▶ **n.** soft flexible leather made from sheepskin, used in bookbinding as a substitute for morocco. [19th C.: perh. from *Roan,* the old name of Rouen, a city in northwestern France.]

Ro·a·noke /'rōə,nōk/ a city in west central Virginia; pop. 94,911.

Ro·a·noke Is·land an island in eastern North Carolina, inside the Outer Banks, site of the first English settlement in America that was established in 1585 and had mysteriously disappeared by 1591.

Ro·a·noke Riv·er a river that flows for 410 miles (660 km) from southwestern Virginia to Albemarle Sound.

roar /rôr/ ▶ **n.** a full, deep, prolonged cry uttered by a lion or other large wild animal. ■ a loud, deep sound uttered by a person or crowd, generally to express pain, anger, or approval. ■ a loud, prolonged sound made by something inanimate, such as an engine or traffic: *the roar of the sea.* ▶ **v. 1** [intrans.] (of a lion or other large wild animal) utter a full, deep, prolonged cry. ■ (of something inanimate) make a loud, deep, prolonged sound. ■ (of a person or crowd) utter a loud, deep, prolonged sound, typically because of anger, pain, or excitement. ■ [trans.] utter or express in a loud tone: *the crowd roared its approval.* ■ (of a horse) make a loud breathing noise as a symptom of disease of the larynx. **2** [intrans.] (esp. of a vehicle) move at high speed making a loud prolonged sound. ■ proceed, act, or happen fast and decisively or conspicuously: *the Clippers came roaring back.* [OE *rārian* (v.), imitative of a deep prolonged cry, of West Gmc. origin; rel. to Ger. *röhren*. The n. dates from ME.]

roar·ing /ˈrôriNG/ ▶ **adj.** [attrib.] **1** (of a person, crowd, or animal) making a loud and deep sound, esp. as an expression of pain, anger, or approval. ■ (of something inanimate, esp. a natural phenomenon) making a loud, deep, or harsh prolonged sound: *a roaring river.* ■ (of a fire) burning fiercely and noisily. ■ (of a period of time) characterized by optimism, buoyancy, or excitement: *the roaring twenties.* ■ (of business) lively; brisk. **2** informal obviously or unequivocally the thing mentioned (used for emphasis): *a roaring success.* — **roar·ing·ly adv.**

roast /rōst/ ▶ **v.** [trans.] **1** cook (food, esp. meat) by prolonged exposure to heat in an oven or over a fire. ■ [intrans.] (of food) be cooked in such a way: *meat roasting in the oven.* ■ process (a foodstuff, metal ore, etc.) by subjecting it to intense heat. ■ make (someone or something) very warm, esp. by exposure to the heat of the sun or a fire. ■ [intrans.] become very hot: *Jessica could feel her face begin to roast.* **2** criticize or reprimand severely. ■ offer a mocking tribute to (someone) at a roast. ▶ **adj.** [attrib.] (of food) having been cooked in an oven or over an open fire: *a plate of cold roast beef.* ▶ **n. 1** a cut of meat that has been roasted or that is intended for roasting: *carving the Sunday roast.* ■ a dish or meal of roasted food. ■ the process or result of roasting something. ■ [with adj.] a particular type of roasted coffee: *continental roasts.* ■ an outdoor party at which meat is roasted. **2** a banquet to honor a person at which the honoree is subjected to good-natured ridicule. [ME: from OFr. *rostir*, of West Gmc. origin.]

roast·er /ˈrōstər/ ▶ **n.** a container, oven, furnace, or apparatus for roasting something. ■ a foodstuff that is particularly suitable for roasting. ■ a person or company that processes coffee beans.

roast·ing /ˈrōstiNG/ ▶ **adj.** [attrib.] (of a container) used for roasting food: *a roasting pan.* ■ (of a foodstuff) particularly suitable for roasting. ■ (of food) undergoing roasting: *the aroma of a roasting pig.* ■ informal very hot and dry: *a roasting day.* ▶ **n.** the action of cooking something in an oven or over an open fire. ■ [in sing.] informal a severe criticism or reprimand.

rob /räb/ ▶ **v.** (**robbed, rob·bing**) [trans.] take property unlawfully from (a person or place) by force or threat of force. ■ (usu. **be robbed**) informal overcharge (someone) for something. ■ deprive (someone or something) of something needed, deserved, or significant: *poor health has robbed her of a normal social life.*

– PHRASES **rob Peter to pay Paul** take something away from one person to pay another; discharge one debt only to incur another. [prob. with ref. to the saints and apostles *Peter* and *Paul*; the allusion is uncert., the phr. often showing variations such as 'unclothe Peter and clothe Paul,' 'borrow from Peter ...,' etc.] **rob someone blind** see BLIND. [ME: from OFr. *rober*, of Gmc. origin; rel. to the V. REAVE.]

Robbe-Gril·let /ˌrôb grēˈyā/, Alain (1922–), French writer and filmmaker. His novel *The Erasers* (1953) was an early example of the *nouveau roman.* His movies include *C'est Gradiva qui vous appelle* (2006).

rob·ber crab ▶ **n.** another term for COCONUT CRAB.

rob·ber fly ▶ **n.** a large, powerful, predatory fly (family Asilidae) that darts out and grabs insect prey on the wing.

rob·ber·y /ˈräb(ə)rē/ ▶ **n.** (pl. **-ber·ies**) the action of robbing a person or place. ■ Law the felonious taking of personal property from someone using force or the threat of force.

Rob·bia /ˈrōbēə; ˈräb-/ see DELLA ROBBIA.

Rob·bins[1] /ˈräbənz/, Harold (1916–97), US writer. His novels include *The Carpetbaggers* (1961).

Rob·bins[2], Jerome (1918–98), US choreographer for stage musicals such as *The King and I* (1951) and *West Side Story* (1957).

robe /rōb/ ▶ **n.** a long, loose outer garment. ■ (often **robes**) such a garment worn, esp. on ceremonial occasions, to indicate the wearer's rank, office, or profession. ■ a dressing gown or bathrobe. ▶ **v.** [trans.] [usu. as adj.] (**robed**) clothe in a long, loose outer garment: *a circle of robed figures.* ■ [intrans.] put on robes, esp. for a formal or ceremonial occasion: *I went into the vestry and robed for the Mass.* [ME: from OFr., from the Gmc. base (sense 'booty') of ROB.]

Rob·ert /ˈräbərt/ the name of three kings of Scotland: ■ Robert I (1274–1329), reigned 1306–29; known as **Robert the Bruce**. He reestablished Scotland as a separate kingdom. ■ Robert II (1316–90), reigned 1371–90; grandson of Robert the Bruce. He was the first of the Stuarts. ■ Robert III (c.1337–1406) reigned 1390–1406; son of Robert II; born *John.*

Ro·berts[1] /ˈräbərts/, John Glover, Jr. (1955–), Chief Justice of the US 2005– .

Ro·berts[2], Julia (1967–), US actress. Her movies include *Pretty Woman* (1990) and *Erin Brockovich* (2000).

Ro·berts[3], Owen Josephus (1875–1955), US Supreme Court associate justice 1930–45.

Rob·ert·son /ˈräbərtsən/, Oscar (1938–), US basketball player, considered one of the most versatile players ever. He played professionally 1960–74.

Robe·son /ˈrōb(ə)sən/, Paul Bustill (1898–1976), US singer and actor, noted for his onstage portrayal of Othello. His black activism and communist sympathies led to ostracism in the 1950s.

Robes·pierre /ˈrōbzˌpi(ə)r; -ˌpye(ə)r/, Maximilien François Marie Isidore de (1758–94), French revolutionary. He led the radical Jacobins in the National Assembly and initiated the Terror. When he fell from favor, he was guillotined.

robins

rob·in /ˈräbən/ ▶ **n. 1** (also **American robin**) a large New World thrush (genus *Turdus*) that typically has a reddish breast. **2** a bird that resembles the American robin, in particular a small Old World thrush (*Erithacus* and other genera), typically having a brown back with red on the breast or other colorful markings. [16th C.: from OFr., nickname for the given name *Robert*.]

Rob·in Hood /ˈräbən ˌho͝od/ a semilegendary English medieval outlaw, reputed to have robbed the rich and helped the poor. ■ [as n.] (**a Robin Hood**) a person considered to be taking from the wealthy and giving to the poor.

rob·in red·breast ▶ **n.** informal a robin.

ro·bin's-egg (also **rob·in's-egg blue** or **rob·in-egg**) ▶ **n.** a greenish-blue color.

Rob·in·son[1] /ˈräbinsən/, Edward Arlington (1869–1935), US poet. His verse includes "Miniver Cheevy" (1910) and "Tristram" (1927).

Rob·in·son[2], Jackie (1919–72), US baseball player; full name *Jack Roosevelt Robinson.* Joining the Brooklyn Dodgers in 1947, he became the first black player in the major leagues.

Rob·in·son[3], Mary Terese Winifred (1944–), president of Ireland 1990–1997, the first woman to hold that office.

Rob·in·son[4], Sugar Ray (1920–89), US boxer; born *Walker Smith, Jr.* He was world welterweight champion 1946–51 and seven times the middleweight champion between 1951 and 1960.

Rob·in·son Cru·soe /ˈkro͞osō/ the title hero of Daniel Defoe's 1719 novel. He survives a shipwreck and lives on a desert island.

ro·bot /ˈrōˌbät; ˈrōbət/ ▶ **n.** a machine capable of carrying out a complex series of actions automatically. ■ (esp. in science fiction) a machine resembling a human being and able to replicate certain human movements and functions. ■ used to refer to a person who behaves in a mechanical or unemotional manner. [from Czech, from *robota* 'forced labor.']

ro·bot·ic /rōˈbätik/ ▶ **adj.** of or relating to robots. ■ (of a person) mechanical, stiff, or unemotional. — **ro·bot·i·cal·ly** /-ik(ə)lē/ **adv.**

ro·bot·ics /rōˈbätiks/ ▶ **plural n.** [treated as sing.] the branch of technology that deals with the design, construction, operation, and application of robots. — **ro·bot·i·cist** /-ˈbätəsist/ **n.**

ro·bot·ize /ˈrōbəˌtīz/ ▶ **v.** [trans.] convert (a production system, factory, etc.) to operation by robots. — **ro·bot·i·za·tion** /ˌrōbətəˈzāSHən; ˌrō ˌbätə-/ **n.**

Rob Roy[1] /ˈräb ˈroi/ (1671–1734), Scottish outlaw; born *Robert Macgregor.*

Rob Roy[2] ▶ **n.** a cocktail made of Scotch whisky and vermouth.

ro·bust (**-bust·er, -bust·est**) /rōˈbəst; ˈrōˌbəst/ ▶ **adj.** (of a person, animal, or plant) strong and healthy; vigorous. ■ (of an object) sturdy in construction. ■ (of a process or system, esp. an economic one) able to withstand or overcome adverse conditions: *California's robust property market.* ■ (of an intellectual approach or the person taking or expressing it) not perturbed by or attending to subtleties or difficulties; uncompromising and forceful. ■ (of action) involving physical force or energy: *a robust game of football.* ■ (of wine or food) strong and rich in flavor or smell. — **ro·bust·ly adv. ro·bust·ness n.** [16th C.: from L. *robustus* 'hard,' from *robus*, earlier form of *robur* 'oak, strength.']

roc /räk/ ▶ **n.** a gigantic mythological bird described in the Arabian Nights. [16th C.: ult. from Pers. *ruḳ*.]

ro·caille /rōˈkī; rä-/ ▶ **n. 1** an 18th-century artistic or architectural style of decoration characterized by elaborate ornamentation with pebbles and shells. **2** (**rocailles**) tiny beads. [Fr., from *roc* 'rock.']

roc·am·bole /ˈräkəmˌbōl/ ▶ **n.** a Eurasian plant (*Allium scorodoprasum*) of the lily family, closely related to garlic and sometimes used as a flavoring. [17th C.: from Fr., from Ger. *Rockenbolle*.]

Roche lim·it /rōSH; rôSH/ (also **Roch·e's lim·it**) ▶ **n.** Astron. the closest distance from the center of a planet that a satellite can approach without being pulled apart by the planet's gravitational field. [19th C.: Edouard Albert *Roche* (1820–83), French mathematician.]

roche mou·ton·née /ˈrôSH ˌmo͞otnˈā; rôSH/ ▶ **n.** (pl. **roches mou·ton·nées** pronunc. same or /ˌmo͞otnˈāz/) Geol. a small bare outcrop of rock shaped by glacial erosion, with one side smooth and gently sloping and the other steep, rough, and irregular. [19th C.: Fr., lit. 'fleecy rock.']

Roch·es·ter /ˈräCHəstər; ˈräˌCHes-/ **1** a city in southeastern Minnesota, home to the Mayo Clinic; pop. 85,806. **2** a city in northwestern New York; pop. 219,773.

Roch·es·ter Hills /ˈräˌCHestər/ a city in southeastern Michigan; pop. 61,766.

roch·et /ˈräCHit/ ▶ **n.** Christian Church a vestment resembling a surplice, used chiefly by bishops and abbots. [ME: from OFr., a dimin. from a Gmc. base shared by Ger. *Rock* 'coat.']

rock[1] /räk/ ▶ **n. 1** the solid mineral material forming part of the surface of the earth and other planets. ■ a mass of such material projecting above the earth's surface or out of the sea. ■ Geol. any natural material, hard or soft (e.g., clay), having a distinctive mineral composition. ■ (**the Rock**) Gibraltar. **2** a large piece of such material that has become detached from a cliff or mountain; a boulder. ■ a stone of any size, esp. one small enough to be picked up and used as a projectile. ■ informal a precious stone, esp. a diamond. ■ informal a small piece of crack cocaine. **3** used in similes and metaphors to refer to someone or something that is extremely strong, reliable, or hard. ■ (usu. **rocks**) (esp. with allusion to shipwrecks) a source of danger or destruction: *the new system is heading for the rocks.*
– PHRASES **between a rock and a hard place** informal in a situation where one is faced with two equally difficult alternatives. **get one's rocks off** vulgar slang have an orgasm. ■ obtain pleasure or satisfaction. **on the rocks** informal **1** (of a relationship or enterprise) experiencing difficulties and likely to fail. **2** (of a drink) served undiluted and with ice cubes. — **rock·less adj. rock·like** /-ˌlīk/ **adj.** [ME: from OFr. *rocque*, from med. L. *rocca*.]

rock[2] ▶ **v. 1** [trans.] cause (someone or something) to move gently to and fro or from side to side. ■ [intrans.] move in such a way: *the vase rocked back and forth on its base.* ■ (with reference to a building or region) shake or cause to shake or vibrate, esp. because of an impact, earthquake, or explosion. ■ cause great shock or distress to (someone or something), esp. so as to weaken or destabilize them or it: *diplomatic upheavals that rocked the British Empire.* **2** [intrans.] informal dance to or play rock music. ■ fig. (of a place) have an atmosphere of excitement or much social activity: *the new club really rocks.* ▶ **n. 1** rock music: [as adj.] *a rock star.* ■ rock and roll. **2** [in sing.] a gentle movement to and fro or from side to side: *she gave the cradle a rock.*
– PHRASAL VERBS **rock out** informal perform rock music loudly and vigorously. ■ enjoy oneself in an enthusiastic and uninhibited way, esp. by dancing to rock music. [OE *roccian*, prob. from a Gmc. base meaning 'remove, move'; rel. to Du. *rukken* 'jerk, tug' and Ger. *rücken* 'move.' The n. dates from the early 19th C.]

rock·a·bil·ly /ˈräkəˌbilē/ ▶ **n.** a type of popular music, originating in the southeastern US in the 1950s, combining elements of rock and roll and country music. [1950s: blend of ROCK AND ROLL and HILLBILLY.]

rock and roll (also **rock 'n' roll**) ▶ **n.** a type of popular dance music originating in the 1950s, characterized by a heavy beat and simple melodies. — **rock and roll·er n.**

rock bass

rock bass /bas/ ▶ **n.** a red-eyed North American fish (*Ambloplites rupestris*) of the freshwater sunfish family, found chiefly in rocky streams. Also called RED-EYE.

rock-bot·tom ▶ **adj.** at the lowest possible level. ■ fundamental: *a pure, rock-bottom kind of realism.* ▶ **n.** (**rock bot·tom**) the lowest possible level.

rock-bound ▶ **adj.** (of a coast or shore) rocky and inaccessible.

rock can·dy ▶ **n.** sugar crystallized in large masses onto a string or stick, eaten as candy.

rock climb·ing ▶ **n.** the sport or pastime of climbing rock faces.

rock cod ▶ **n.** any of a number of marine fishes that frequent rocky habitats, chiefly in the scorpionfish and sea bass families.

rock crys·tal ▶ **n.** transparent quartz, typically in the form of colorless hexagonal crystals.

rock cy·cle ▶ **n.** Geol. an idealized cycle of processes undergone by rocks in the earth's crust.

rock dove ▶ **n.** a mainly gray Old World pigeon (*Columba livia*) that frequents coastal and inland cliffs. It is the ancestor of domestic and feral pigeons.

Rock·e·fel·ler /ˈräkəˌfelər/, John Davison (1839–1937), US industrialist and philanthropist. He founded the Standard Oil Company in 1870.

Rock·e·fel·ler Center a business building complex in midtown Manhattan in New York City.

rock·er /ˈräkər/ ▶ **n. 1** a person who performs, dances to, or enjoys rock music, esp. of a particular type: *a punk rocker.* ■ a rock song. **2** a thing that rocks, in particular: ■ a rocking chair. ■ a rocking device forming part of a mechanism, esp. one for controlling the positions of brushes in a generator. **3** a curved bar or similar support on which something such as a chair or cradle can rock. **4** the amount of curvature in the longitudinal contour of a boat or surfboard.
– PHRASES **off one's rocker** informal insane.

rock·er arm ▶ **n.** a rocking lever in an engine, esp. one in an internal combustion engine that serves to work a valve and is operated by a pushrod from the camshaft.

rock·er pan·el ▶ **n.** (in a motor vehicle) a panel forming part of the bodywork below the level of the passenger door.

rock·et[1] /ˈräkit/ ▶ **n.** a cylindrical projectile that can be propelled to a great height or distance by the combustion of its contents. ■ (also **rock·et en·gine** or **rock·et mo·tor**) an engine operating on the same principle, providing thrust as in a jet engine but without depending on the intake of air for combustion. ■ an elongated rocket-propelled missile or spacecraft. ■ used, esp. in similes and comparisons, to refer to a person or thing that moves very fast or to an action that is done with great force. ▶ **v.** (**rock·et·ed, rock·et·ing**) **1** [intrans.] (of an amount, price, etc.) increase very rapidly and suddenly. ■ move or progress very rapidly: *he rocketed to national stardom.* ■ [trans.] cause to move or progress very rapidly. **2** [trans.] attack with rocket-propelled missiles. [17th C.: from Fr. *roquette*, from Ital. *rocchetto*, dimin. of *rocca* 'distaff (for spinning),' from its cylindrical shape.]

rock·et[2] ▶ **n.** (also **gar·den rock·et** or **sal·ad rock·et**) an edible Mediterranean plant (*Eruca vesicaria* subsp. *sativa*) of the cabbage family, sometimes eaten in salads. ■ used in names of other fast-growing plants of this family, e.g., **dame's rocket**. [15th C.: from Fr. *roquette*, from Ital. *ruchetta*, dimin. of *ruca*, from L. *eruca* 'downy-stemmed plant.']

rock·e·teer /ˌräkiˈti(ə)r/ ▶ **n.** a person who works with space rockets; a rocket enthusiast.

rock·et·ry /ˈräkətrē/ ▶ **n.** the branch of science that deals with rockets and rocket propulsion. ■ the use of rockets.

rock·et sci·en·tist ▶ **n.** a specialist in rocketry. ■ [usu. with negative] informal an extremely intelligent person: *he's not a rocket scientist, but he should come out okay.*

rock face ▶ **n.** a bare vertical surface of natural rock.

rock·fall /ˈräkˌfôl/ (also **rock fall**) ▶ **n.** a descent of loose rocks. ■ a mass of fallen rock.

rock·fish /ˈräkˌfiSH/ ▶ **n.** (pl. same or **-fish·es**) a marine fish (genus *Sebastes*) of the scorpionfish family with a laterally compressed body. It is generally a bottom-dweller in rocky areas and is frequently of sporting or commercial value.

Rock·ford /ˈräkfərd/ a city in north central Illinois; pop. 150,115.

Rock Hill a city in northern South Carolina; pop. 49,765.

rock·hop·per /ˈräkˌhäpər/ (also **rock·hop·per pen·guin**) ▶ **n.** a small penguin (*Eudyptes chrysocome*) with a yellowish crest, breeding on subantarctic coastal cliffs that it ascends by hopping from rock to rock.

rock·hound /ˈräkˌhound/ ▶ **n.** informal a geologist or amateur collector of mineral specimens. — **rock·hound·ing n.**

rock hy·rax ▶ **n.** an African hyrax (genus *Procavia*) that lives on rocky outcrops and cliffs and feeds mainly on grass. Also called DASSIE.

Rock·ies another name for the ROCKY MOUNTAINS.

rock·ing chair ▶ **n.** a chair mounted on rockers or springs, so as to rock back and forth.

rocking horse

rock·ing horse ▶ **n.** a model of a horse mounted on rockers or springs for a child to sit on and rock back and forth.

Rock Is·land a city in northwestern Illinois, on the Mississippi River; pop. 40,552.

rock jock ▶ **n.** informal a mountaineer.

rock liz·ard ▶ **n.** a small climbing lizard living in mountains and arid rocky habitats, in particular: ■ (also **banded rock lizard**) a North American lizard (*Streptosaurus mearnsi*, family Iguanidae). ■ a European and African lizard (genus *Lacerta*, family Lacertidae).

rock lob·ster ▶ **n.** another term for SPINY LOBSTER.

rock ma·ple ▶ **n.** another term for SUGAR MAPLE.

rock mu·sic ▶ **n.** a form of popular music that evolved from rock and roll and pop music during the mid- and late 1960s. It was initially characterized by experimentation and drug-related or anti-Establishment lyrics. ■ another term for ROCK AND ROLL.

Rock·ne /ˈräknē/, Knute Kenneth (1888–1931), US football coach; born in Norway. He coached at the University of Notre Dame in Indiana 1918–31.

rock 'n' roll ▶ **n.** var. of ROCK AND ROLL.

Rock of Gi·bral·tar see GIBRALTAR.

rock pi·geon ▶ **n.** another term for ROCK DOVE.

rock plant ▶ **n.** a plant that grows on or among rocks.

rock py·thon ▶ **n.** a large dark-skinned constricting snake (genera

Python and *Morelia*) with paler markings and a distinctive pale mark on the crown.

rock rab·bit ▶ n. **1** another term for HYRAX. **2** another term for PIKA.

rock-ribbed ▶ adj. having ribs or elevations of rock. ■ resolute or uncompromising, esp. with respect to political allegiance: *rock-ribbed communists.*

rock·rose /ˈräkˌrōz/ ▶ n. **1** a herbaceous or shrubby plant (genera *Cistus* and *Helianthemum*, family Cistaceae) with saucer-shaped, roselike flowers, native to temperate and warm regions. See also LABDANUM. **2** another term for BITTERROOT.

rock salt ▶ n. common salt occurring naturally as a mineral; halite.

rock·slide /ˈräkˌslīd/ ▶ n. an avalanche of rock or other stony material. ■ a mass of stony material deposited by such an avalanche.

rock snake ▶ n. the Asian rock python.

rock sol·id ▶ adj. unlikely to change, fail, or collapse: *her love was rock solid.*

rock stead·y (also **rock·stead·y** /ˈräkˈstedē/) ▶ n. an early form of reggae music originating in Jamaica in the 1960s, characterized by a slow tempo.

rock·u·men·ta·ry /ˌräkyəˈment(ə)rē/ ▶ n. informal a documentary about rock music and musicians. [1970s: from ROCK² + DOCUMENTARY.]

Rock·ville /ˈräkˌvil/ a city in central Maryland, NW of Washington, DC; pop. 47,381.

rock wal·la·by ▶ n. an agile Australian wallaby (genus *Petrogale*) that lives among cliffs and rocks, having feet with thick pads and a long cylindrical tail.

Rock·well /ˈräkˌwel; -wəl/, Norman Percevel (1894–1978), US illustrator. He was known for his sentimental portraits of small-town life in the US.

rock wool ▶ n. inorganic material made into matted fiber used esp. for insulation or soundproofing.

rock·y¹ /ˈräkē/ ▶ adj. (**rock·i·er, rock·i·est**) consisting or formed of rock, esp. when exposed to view: *a rocky crag.* ■ full of rocks. ■ fig. difficult; full of obstacles.

rock·y² ▶ adj. (**rock·i·er, rock·i·est**) tending to rock or shake; unsteady. ■ fig. not stable or firm; full of problems. — **rock·i·ly** /ˈräkəlē/ adv.

Rocky Mount /ˈräkē/ a city in east central North Carolina; pop. 55,893.

Rock·y Moun·tain goat ▶ n. see MOUNTAIN GOAT (sense 1).

Rock·y Moun·tains (also **the Rockies**) the chief mountain system in North America. It extends from the US–Mexico border to the Yukon Territory of northern Canada. It separates the Great Plains from the Pacific coast and forms the Continental Divide.

Rock·y Moun·tain spot·ted fe·ver ▶ n. a rickettsial disease transmitted by ticks.

ro·co·co /rəˈkōkō; ˌrōkəˈkō/ ▶ adj. (of furniture or architecture) of or characterized by an elaborately ornamental late baroque style of decoration prevalent in 18th-century Continental Europe. ■ extravagantly or excessively ornate. ▶ n. the rococo style of art, decoration, or architecture. [19th C.: from Fr., alt. of ROCAILLE.]

rod /räd/ ▶ n. **1** a thin straight bar, esp. of wood or metal. ■ a wand or staff as a symbol of office, authority, or power. ■ a slender straight stick or shoot growing on or cut from a tree or bush. ■ a stick used for caning or flogging. ■ (**the rod**) the use of such a stick as punishment. ■ vulgar slang a penis. **2** a fishing rod. **3** hist. a linear measure, esp. for land, equal to 5½ yards (approximately 5.029 m). ■ (also **square rod**) a square measure, esp. for land, equal to 160th of an acre or 30¼ square yards (approximately 25.29 sq m). **4** informal a pistol or revolver. **5** Anat. a light-sensitive cell of one of the two types present in large numbers in the retina of the eye. Compare with CONE (sense 3).
– PHRASES **spare the rod and spoil the child** proverb if children are not physically punished when they do wrong their personal development will suffer. [OE *rodd* 'shoot,' 'stick for flogging'; prob. akin to ON *rudda* 'club.']

rode¹ /rōd/ past of RIDE.

rode² ▶ n. Naut. a rope, esp. one securing an anchor or trawl. [17th C.: of unknown origin.]

ro·dent /ˈrōdnt/ ▶ n. a gnawing mammal of an order (Rodentia) that includes rats, mice, squirrels, hamsters, porcupines, and their relatives, distinguished by strong constantly growing incisors and no canine teeth. They constitute the largest order of mammals. ▶ adj. of or relating to mammals of this order. [19th C.: from L. *rodent-* 'gnawing,' from the v. *rodere.*]

ro·den·ti·cide /rōˈdentəˌsīd/ ▶ n. a poison used to kill rodents.

ro·de·o /ˈrōdēˌō; rəˈdāō/ ▶ n. (pl. **-de·os**) **1** an exhibition or contest in which cowboys show their skill at riding broncos, roping calves, wrestling steers, etc. **2** a roundup of cattle on a ranch for branding, counting, etc. ▶ v. (**-de·oed, -de·o·ing**) [intrans.] compete in a rodeo. [19th C.: from Sp., from *rodear* 'go around,' based on L. *rotare* 'rotate.']

Rodg·ers /ˈräjərz/, Richard Charles (1902–79), US composer. He worked with librettist Lorenz Hart (1895–1942) before collaborating with Oscar Hammerstein II on a succession of popular musicals that included *Oklahoma!* (1943) and *South Pacific* (1949).

rodg·er·si·a /räˈjərzēə/ ▶ n. an Asian plant (genus *Rodgersia*, family Saxifragaceae) that is sometimes cultivated for its attractive foliage. [mod. L., named after John Rodgers (1812–82), American admiral.]

Ró·dhos /ˈrôT͟Hôs/ Greek name for RHODES¹.

Ro·din /rōˈdaN/, Auguste (1840–1917), French sculptor. Chiefly concerned with the human form, his works include *The Thinker* (1880).

rod·o·mon·tade /ˌrädəmənˈtād; ˌrōd-; -ˈtäd/ ▶ n. boastful or inflated talk or behavior. [17th C.: from Fr., from obs. Italian *rodomontada*, from Ital. *rodomonte*, after a character in the med. *Orlando* epics.]

roe¹ /rō/ ▶ n. (also **hard roe**) the mass of eggs contained in the ovaries of a female fish or shellfish, typically including the ovaries themselves, esp. when ripe and used as food. ■ (**soft roe**) the ripe testes of a male fish, esp. when used as food. [ME: rel. to Mid. Low Ger., MDu. *roge.*]

roe² (also **roe deer**) ▶ n. (pl. same or **roes**) a small Eurasian deer (genus *Capreolus*) that lacks a visible tail and has a reddish summer coat that turns grayish in winter. [OE *rā(ha)*, from Gmc.; akin to Ger. *Reh.*]

roe·buck /ˈrōˌbək/ ▶ n. a male roe deer.

roent·gen /ˈrentgən; ˈrənt-; -jən/ (abbr.: **R**) ▶ n. a unit of ionizing radiation, the amount producing one electrostatic unit of positive or negative ionic charge in one cubic centimeter of air under standard conditions. [1920s: Wilhelm Conrad *Röntgen* (1845–1923), German physicist, discoverer of X-rays.]

roent·gen·i·um /rentˈgenēəm; rənt-/ ▶ n. the chemical element of atomic number 111, a radioactive element produced artificially. (Symbol: **Rg**) [21st C.: named after Wilhelm Conrad *Röntgen* (see ROENTGEN).]

roent·gen·o·gram /ˈrentgənəˌgram; ˈrənt-; -jə- ;/ ▶ n. esp. Med. an X-ray photograph.

roent·gen·og·ra·phy /ˌrentgəˈnägrəfē; ˌrənt-; -jə-/ ▶ n. esp. Med. X-ray photography. — **roent·gen·o·graph·ic** /-gənəˈgrafik/ adj. **roent·gen·o·graph·i·cal·ly** /-gənəˈgrafik(ə)lē/ adv.

roent·gen·ol·o·gy /ˌrentgəˈnäləjē; ˌrənt-; -jə-/ ▶ n. esp. Med. another term for RADIOLOGY. — **roent·gen·o·log·ic** /-gənəˈläjik/ adj.

ro·ga·tion /rōˈgāSHən/ ▶ n. [usu. as adj.] (in the Christian Church) a solemn supplication consisting of the litany of the saints chanted on the three days before Ascension Day. [ME: from L. *rogatio(n-)*, from *rogare* 'ask.']

Ro·ga·tion Days (in the Western Christian Church) the three days before Ascension Day, traditionally marked by fasting and prayer, particularly for the blessing of the harvest (after the pattern of pre-Christian rituals).

Ro·ga·tion Sun·day ▶ n. the Sunday preceding the Rogation Days.

rog·er /ˈräjər/ ▶ exclam. your message has been received and understood (used in radio communication). ■ informal used to express assent or understanding: *"Go light the stove." "Roger, Mister Bossman," Frank replied.* [16th C.: from the name *Roger.*]

Rog·ers¹ /ˈräjərz/ a resort city in northwestern Arkansas, north of Fayetteville; pop. 38,829.

Rog·ers², Fred (1928–2003), US educator and television host; full name *Frederick McFeely Rogers.* He created and starred in the children's program "Mister Rogers' Neighborhood" 1968–2001.

Rog·ers³, Roy (1912–98), US actor and singer; born *Leonard Franklin Slye.* He starred in many singing cowboy movies, with his horse Trigger and, from 1944, Dale Evans (1912–2001), whom he married in 1947.

Rog·ers⁴, Will (1879–1935), US humorist; full name *William Penn Adair Rogers.* He was a vaudeville headliner with his rope twirling and homespun humor. He died in a plane crash with aviator Wiley Post in Alaska.

Ro·get /rōˈZHā; ˈrōˌZHā/, Peter Mark (1779–1869), English scholar. He compiled *Roget's Thesaurus of English Words and Phrases* (1852).

rogue /rōg/ ▶ n. **1** a dishonest or unprincipled man. ■ a person whose behavior one disapproves of but who is nonetheless likable or attractive. **2** [usu. as adj.] an elephant or other large wild animal driven away or living apart from the herd and having savage or destructive tendencies: *a rogue elephant.* ■ a person or thing that behaves in an aberrant, faulty, or unpredictable way. ■ an inferior or defective specimen among many satisfactory ones. ▶ v. [trans.] remove inferior or defective plants or seedlings from (a crop). [16th C. ('vagrant'): prob. from L. *rogare* 'beg, ask,' and akin to obs. *roger* 'beggar.']

Rogue Riv·er /rōg/ a river that flows west for 200 miles (320 km) across southern Oregon to the Pacific Ocean.

ro·guer·y /ˈrōgərē/ ▶ n. (pl. **-guer·ies**) conduct characteristic of a rogue, esp. acts of dishonesty or playful mischief.

rogues' gal·ler·y ▶ n. informal a collection of photographs of known criminals. ■ a collection of people or creatures notable for a certain shared quality or characteristic, typically a disreputable one.

ro·guish /ˈrōgiSH/ ▶ adj. characteristic of a dishonest or unprincipled person: *he led a roguish existence.* ■ playfully mischievous, esp. in a way that is sexually attractive: *he gave her a roguish smile.* — **ro·guish·ly** adv. **ro·guish·ness** n.

Roh Moo-hyun /ˈrō ˈmo͞o ˈhyən/ (1946–), president of South Korea 2003– .

Rohn·ert Park /ˈrōnərt/ a city in northwestern California; pop. 36,326.

ROI Finance ▶ abbr. return on investment.

roil /roil/ ▶ v. **1** [trans.] make (a liquid) turbid or muddy by disturbing the sediment: *winds roil these waters.* ■ [intrans.] (of a liquid) move in a turbulent, swirling manner: *the sea roiled below her.* **2** another term for

RILE (sense 1). [16th C.: perh. from OFr. *ruiler* 'mix mortar,' from late L. *regulare* 'regulate.']

roil·y /'roilē/ ▸ **adj.** (chiefly of water) muddy; turbulent.

roist·er /'roistər/ ▸ **v.** [intrans.] enjoy oneself or celebrate in a noisy or boisterous way. — **roist·er·er n. roist·er·ous** /'roist(ə)rəs/ **adj.** [16th C.: from obs. *roister* 'roisterer,' from Fr. *rustre* 'ruffian,' ult. from L. *rusticus* 'rustic.']

Ro·land /'rōlənd/ the most famous of Charlemagne's paladins, hero of the *Chanson de Roland* (12th cent.).

role /rōl/ ▸ **n.** an actor's part in a play, movie, etc. ■ the function assumed or part played by a person or thing in a particular situation. [17th C.: from obs. Fr. *roule* 'roll,' from the paper roll on which an actor's part was written.]

role mod·el ▸ **n.** a person looked to by others as an example to be imitated.

role-play·ing (also **role-play**) ▸ **n. 1** esp. Psychol. the acting out of a particular role, either consciously or unconsciously, in accordance with the perceived expectations of society with regard to a person's behavior in a particular context. **2** participation in a role-playing game. — **role-play v. role-play·er n.**

role-play·ing game ▸ **n.** a game in which players take on the roles of imaginary characters who engage in adventures, typically in a computerized setting.

role re·ver·sal ▸ **n.** a situation in which someone adopts a role the reverse of that which they normally assume in relation to someone else, who typically assumes their role in exchange.

Rolfe /rälf/, John (1585–1622), English colonizer. In Virginia, he perfected the process of curing tobacco. In 1614, he married Pocahontas.

Rolf·ing /'rôlfiNG; 'räl-/ ▸ **n.** trademark a massage technique aimed at the vertical realignment of the body, deep enough to release muscular tension at skeletal level. — **Rolf** /rôlf; rälf/ **v.** [1970s: Ida P. *Rolf* (1897–1979), American physiotherapist.]

roll /rōl/ ▸ **v. 1** move or cause to move in a particular direction by turning over and over on an axis. ■ turn or cause to turn over to face a different direction. ■ [trans.] turn (one's eyes) upward, typically to show surprise or disapproval. ■ [trans.] make (something cylindrical) revolve between two surfaces. ■ [intrans.] (of a person or animal) lie down and turn over and over while remaining in the same place. ■ [intrans.] (of a moving ship, aircraft, or vehicle) rock or oscillate around an axis parallel to the direction of motion: *the ship pitched and rolled.* ■ [intrans.] move along or from side to side unsteadily or uncontrollably: *they were rolling about with laughter.* ■ [trans.] informal overturn (a vehicle): *he rolled his Mercedes in a 100 mph crash.* ■ [trans.] throw (a die or dice). ■ [trans.] obtain (a particular score) by doing this. **2** [intrans.] (of a vehicle) move or run on wheels: *the van was rolling along the highway.* ■ [trans.] move or push (a wheeled object): *Pat rolled the cart back and forth.* ■ (**roll something up/down**) make a car window or a window blind move up or down. ■ (of time) elapse steadily: *the years rolled by.* ■ (of a drop of liquid) flow. ■ (**roll off**) (of a product) issue from (an assembly line or machine). ■ (of waves, smoke, cloud, or fog) move or flow forward with an undulating motion. ■ [intrans.] [usu. as adj.] (**rolling**) (of land) extend in gentle undulations: *the rolling countryside.* ■ [intrans.] (of credits for a movie or television program) be displayed as if moving on a roller up the screen. ■ [intrans.] (of a machine, esp. a camera) operate or begin operating. ■ [trans.] cause (a machine, esp. a camera) to begin operating. **3** [trans.] turn (something flexible) over and over on itself to form a cylinder, tube, or ball. ■ [trans.] make by forming material into a cylinder or ball. ■ [intrans.] (of a person or animal) curl up tightly: *the shock made the armadillo roll into a ball.* **4** [trans.] flatten (something) by passing a roller over it or by passing it between rollers: *roll out the dough.* **5** [intrans.] (of a loud, deep sound such as that of thunder or drums) reverberate. ■ [trans.] pronounce (a consonant, typically an *r*) with a trill: *when he wanted to emphasize a point he rolled his rrrs.* ■ [trans.] utter (a word or words) with a reverberating or vibratory effect: *he rolled the word around his mouth.* ■ (of words) flow effortlessly or mellifluously: *the names of his colleagues rolled off his lips.* **6** informal rob (someone, typically when they are intoxicated or asleep). ▸ **n. 1** a cylinder formed by winding flexible material around a tube or by turning it over and over on itself. ■ a cylindrical mass of something or a number of items arranged in a cylindrical shape: *a roll of mints.* ■ [with adj.] an item of food that is made by wrapping a flat sheet of pastry, cake, meat, or fish around a sweet or savory filling: *salmon and rice rolls.* ■ money, typically a quantity of banknotes rolled together. **2** a movement in which someone or something turns or is turned over on itself: *a roll of the dice.* ■ a gymnastic exercise in which the body is rolled into a tucked position and turned in a forward or backward circle. ■ a swaying or oscillation of a ship, aircraft, or vehicle around an axis parallel to the direction of motion: *the car corners capably with a minimum of roll.* **3** a prolonged, deep, reverberating sound: *thunder exploded, roll after roll.* ■ Music one of the basic patterns (rudiments) of drumming, consisting of a sustained, rapid alternation of single or double strokes of each stick. **4** a very small loaf of bread, typically eaten with butter or a filling: *a sausage roll.* **5** an official list or register of names. ■ the total numbers on such a list. ■ a document, typically an official record, in scroll form.
– PHRASES **a roll in the hay** (or **the sack**) informal an act of sexual intercourse. **be rolling** (**in money**) informal be very rich. **on a roll** informal experiencing a prolonged spell of success or good luck. **rolled into one** (of characteristics drawn from different people or things) combined in one person or thing. **rolling in the aisles** informal (of an audience) laughing uncontrollably. **roll of the dice** see DICE. **roll one's own** informal make one's own cigarettes from loose tobacco. **roll up one's sleeves** prepare to fight or work. **roll with the punches** (of a boxer) move one's body away from an opponent's blows so as to lessen the impact. ■ fig. adapt oneself to adverse circumstances.
– PHRASAL VERBS **roll something back** reverse the progress or reduce the power or importance of something. **roll in** informal be received in large amounts: *the money was rolling in.* ■ arrive at a place in a casual way, typically in spite of being late: *Steve rolled in about lunchtime.* **roll something on** apply something with a roller. **roll something out** officially launch or unveil a new product or service: *the firm rolled out its new computer.* **roll up** informal arrive: *we rolled up at the same time.* — **roll·a·ble adj.** [ME: from OFr. *rolle* (n.), *roller* (v.), from L. *rotulus* 'a roll,' var. of *rotula*, dimin. of *rota* 'wheel.']

Rol·land /rô'läN/, Romain (1866–1944), French writer. He wrote *Jean-Christophe* (1904–12), a cycle of 10 novels about a German composer. Nobel Prize for Literature (1915).

roll·a·way /'rōlə,wā/ ▸ **n.** a bed fitted with wheels or casters, allowing it to be moved easily: [as adj.] *a rollaway bed.*

roll·back /'rōl,bak/ ▸ **n. 1** a reduction or decrease. ■ a reversion to a previous state or situation. **2** Comput. the process of restoring a database or program to a previously defined state. ▸ **v.** [trans.] Comput. restore (a database) to a previously defined state.

roll bar

roll bar ▸ **n.** a metal bar running up the sides and across the top of a vehicle, strengthening its frame and protecting the occupants should the vehicle overturn.

roll cage ▸ **n.** a framework of reinforcements protecting a car's passenger cabin.

roll call ▸ **n.** the process of calling out a list of names to establish who is present. ■ fig. a list or group of people or things that are notable in some specified way.

rolled oats ▸ **plural n.** oats that have been husked and crushed.

roll·er /'rōlər/ ▸ **n. 1** a cylinder that rotates around a central axis and is used in various machines and devices to move, flatten, or spread something. ■ an absorbent revolving cylinder attached to a handle, used to apply paint. ■ a small cylinder on which hair is rolled in order to produce curls. ■ a long swelling wave that appears to roll steadily toward the shore. ■ [as adj.] of, relating to, or involving roller skates. **2** a brightly colored crow-sized bird (genera *Coracias* and *Eurystomus*, family Coraciidae) with predominantly blue plumage, having a characteristic tumbling display flight. **3** a bird of a breed of canary with a trilling song.

roll·er·ball /'rōlər,bôl/ ▸ **n. 1** a ballpoint pen using thinner ink than other ballpoints. **2** Comput. an input device containing a ball that is moved with the fingers to control the cursor.

roll·er bear·ing ▸ **n.** a bearing similar to a ball bearing but using small cylindrical rollers instead of balls. ■ a roller used in such a bearing.

roller bearing

Roll·er·blade /'rōlər,blād/ ▸ **n.** trademark an in-line skate. ▸ **v.** [intrans.] skate using Rollerblades. — **roll·er·blad·er n. roll·er·blad·ing n.**

roll·er coast·er ▸ **n.** an amusement park attraction that consists of a light railroad track with many tight turns and steep slopes, on which people ride in open cars. ■ fig. a thing that contains or goes through wild and unpredictable changes: *a terrific roller coaster of a book.* ▸ **v.** (**roll·er-coast·er**) (also **roll·er-coast**) [intrans.] move, change, or occur in the dramatically changeable manner of a roller coaster.

Roll·er Der·by (also **roll·er der·by**) ▸ **n.** trademark a team roller skating competition, held on a banked oval track.

roll·er rink ▸ **n.** see RINK.

roll·er skate ▸ **n.** each of a pair of boots, or metal frames attached to shoes, with four or more small wheels. ▸ **v.** [intrans.] (**roller-skate**) glide across a hard surface wearing roller skates. — **roll·er skat·er n. roll·er-skat·ing** (also **roll·er skat·ing**) **n.**

roll film ▸ **n.** photographic film with protective lightproof backing paper wound onto a spool.

rol·lick /'rälik/ ▸ **v.** [intrans.] rare act or behave in a jovial and exuberant fashion. [19th C.: prob. dial., perh. a blend of ROMP and FROLIC.]

rol·lick·ing /'räliking/ ▸ **adj.** [attrib.] exuberantly lively and amusing: *good rollicking fun.*

roll·ing hitch ▸ **n.** a kind of hitch used to attach a rope to a spar or larger rope. See illustration at KNOT[1].

roll·ing mill ▸ **n.** a factory or machine for rolling steel or other metal into sheets.

roll·ing pin ▸ n. a cylinder rolled over pastry or dough to flatten or shape it.

roll·ing stock ▸ n. locomotives, carriages, wagons, or other vehicles used on a railroad. ■ the road vehicles of a trucking company.

roll·ing stone ▸ n. a person who is unwilling to settle for long in one place.
– PHRASES **a rolling stone gathers no moss** proverb a person who does not settle in one place will not accumulate wealth, status, responsibilities, or commitments.

roll-in roll-out ▸ n. Comput. a method or the process of switching data or code between main and auxiliary memories in order to process several tasks at once.

roll·mop /ˈrōl,mäp/ ▸ n. a rolled uncooked pickled herring fillet. [20th C.: from Ger. *Rollmops.*]

roll-on ▸ adj. [attrib.] (of deodorant or cosmetic) applied by means of a rotating ball in the neck of the container. ▸ n. a roll-on deodorant or cosmetic.

roll-on roll-off ▸ adj. [attrib.] denoting a passenger ferry or other method of transportation in which vehicles are driven directly on at the start and off at the end.

roll·out /ˈrōl,out/ (also **roll-out**) ▸ n. **1** the unveiling of a new aircraft or spacecraft. ■ the official launch of a new product or service. **2** Aeron. the stage of an aircraft's landing during which it travels along the runway while losing speed. **3** Football a play in which the quarterback runs toward the sideline before attempting to pass or advance.

roll·o·ver /ˈrōl,ōvər/ ▸ n. **1** Finance the extension or transfer of a debt or other financial arrangement. ■ (in a lottery) the accumulative carryover of prize money to the following drawing. **2** informal the overturning of a vehicle.

roll·top desk /ˈrōl,täp/ ▸ n. a writing desk with a flexible cover sliding in curved grooves.

roll-up ▸ n. an article of food rolled up and sometimes stuffed with a filling: *ham roll-ups.* ▸ adj. [attrib.] denoting something that can be rolled up. ■ Comput. denoting a menu that will display only its title to save screen space.

Ro·lo·dex /ˈrōlə,deks/ ▸ n. trademark a desktop card index used to record names, addresses, and telephone numbers.

ro·ly-po·ly /ˈrōlēˈpōlē/ ▸ adj. (of a person) having a round, plump appearance: *a roly-poly young boy.* [17th C.: from ROLL.]

ROM /räm/ ▸ abbr. Comput. read-only memory.

Rom /rōm/ ▸ n. (pl. **Ro·ma** /ˈrōmə/) a gypsy, esp. a man. [19th C.: abbrev. of ROMANY.]

Rom. ▸ abbr. Bible Romans.

rom. ▸ abbr. roman (type).

Ro·ma /ˈrōmə/ Italian name for ROME.

Ro·ma·ic /rōˈmāik/ dated ▸ adj. of or relating to the vernacular language of modern Greece. ▸ n. this language. [from mod. Gk. *romaiikos* 'Roman,' referring to the Eastern Roman Empire.]

ro·maine /rōˈmān/ ▸ n. a lettuce of a variety with crisp narrow leaves that form a tall head. [20th C.: from Fr., fem. of *romain* 'Roman.']

Ro·man /ˈrōmən/ ▸ adj. **1** of or relating to ancient Rome or its empire or people: *an old Roman road.* ■ of or relating to medieval or modern Rome. **2** denoting the alphabet (or any of the letters in it) used for writing Latin, English, and most European languages, developed in ancient Rome. ■ **(roman)** (of type) of a plain upright style; not italic. See illustration at TYPE. ▸ n. **1** a citizen or soldier of the ancient Roman Republic or modern Rome. **2 (roman)** roman type. [ME: ult. from L. *Romanus*, from *Roma* 'Rome.']

ro·man à clef /rō,män ä ˈklā/ (also **ro·man-à-clef**) ▸ n. (pl. **ro·mans à clef** pronunc. same) a novel in which real people or events appear with invented names. [Fr., lit. 'novel with a key.']

Ro·man can·dle ▸ n. a firework giving off a series of flaming colored balls and sparks.

Ro·man Cath·o·lic ▸ adj. of or relating to the Roman Catholic Church: *a Roman Catholic bishop.* ▸ n. a member of this church. — **Ro·man Ca·thol·i·cism** n.

Ro·man Cath·o·lic Church the part of the Christian Church that acknowledges the pope as its head, esp. as it has developed since the Reformation.

Ro·mance /rōˈmans; ˈrō,mans/ ▸ n. the group of Indo-European languages descended from Latin, including French, Spanish, Portuguese, and Italian. ▸ adj. of, relating to, or denoting this group of languages. [ME ('French' language): from OFr. *romanz*, based on L. *Romanicus* 'Roman.']

ro·mance /rōˈmans; ˈrō,mans/ ▸ n. **1** a feeling of excitement and mystery associated with love. ■ love, esp. when sentimental or idealized. ■ an exciting, enjoyable love affair, esp. one that is not serious or long-lasting. ■ a book or movie dealing with love in a sentimental or idealized way. ■ a genre of fiction dealing with love in such a way. **2** a quality or feeling of mystery, excitement, and remoteness from everyday life: *the romance of the night.* ■ wild exaggeration; picturesque falsehood: *she slammed the claims as "pure romance, complete fiction."* ■ a work of fiction dealing with events remote from real life. **3** a medieval tale dealing with a hero of chivalry, of the kind common in the Romance languages. ■ the literary genre of such works. **4** Music a short informal piece. ▸ v. [trans.] **1** court; woo: *the wealthy owner romanced her.* ■ informal seek the attention or patronage of (someone), esp. by use of flattery: *he is being romanced by the big boys in New York.* ■ [intrans.] engage in a love affair. **2** another term for ROMANTICIZE: *to a certain degree I am romancing the past.* [ME: from ROMANCE.]

ro·manc·er /rōˈmansər; ˈrō,mansər/ ▸ n. **1** a person prone to wild exaggeration or falsehood. **2** a writer of medieval romances.

Ro·man Em·pire the empire established by Augustus in 27 BC and divided by Theodosius in AD 395 into the Western or Latin and Eastern or Greek Empires.

Ro·man·esque /,rōməˈnesk/ ▸ adj. of or relating to a style of architecture that prevailed in Europe c.900–1200. ▸ n. Romanesque architecture, characterized by round arches and massive vaulting, and heavy piers, columns, and walls with small windows.

ro·man-fleuve /rō,mäɴ ˈflœv/ ▸ n. (pl. **ro·mans-fleuves** pronunc. same) a novel featuring the leisurely description of the lives of closely related people. ■ a sequence of related, self-contained novels. [Fr., lit. 'river novel.']

Ro·man hol·i·day ▸ n. literary an occasion on which enjoyment or profit is derived from others' suffering. [19th C.: from Byron's *Childe Harold.*]

Romania

Location: southeastern Europe, on the Black Sea
Area: 91,700 square miles (237,500 sq km)
Population: 22,355,000
Capital: Bucharest
Languages: Romanian (official), Hungarian, German
Currency: leu

Ro·ma·ni·a /rōˈmānēə/ (also **Ru·ma·ni·a** /ro͝o-/) a country in southeastern Europe. *See box.*

Ro·ma·ni·an /rōˈmānēən/ (also **Ru·ma·ni·an** /ro͝o-/) ▸ adj. of or relating to Romania or its people or language. ▸ n. **1** a native or national of Romania, or a person of Romanian descent. **2** the language of Romania.

Ro·man·ic /rōˈmanik/ ▸ n. & adj. less common term for ROMANCE. [18th C.: from L. *Romanicus*, from *Romanus* 'Roman.']

Ro·man·ism /ˈrōmə,nizəm/ ▸ n. dated Roman Catholicism.

Ro·man·ist /ˈrōmənist/ ▸ n. **1** an expert in or student of Roman antiquities or law, or of the Romance languages. **2** usu. derog. a member or supporter of the Roman Catholic Church. ▸ adj. usu. derog. belonging or adhering to the Roman Catholic Church.

ro·man·ize /ˈrōmə,nīz/ (also **Ro·man·ize**) ▸ v. [trans.] **1** hist. bring (something, esp. a region or people) under Roman influence or authority. **2** make Roman Catholic in character. **3** put (text) into the Roman alphabet or roman type. — **ro·man·i·za·tion** /,rōmənəˈzāsʜən/ n.

Ro·man law ▸ n. the law code of the ancient Romans, which forms the basis of modern civil law.

Ro·man nose ▸ n. a nose with a high bridge.

Ro·man num·er·al ▸ n. any of the letters representing numbers in the Roman numerical system: I = 1, V = 5, X = 10, L = 50, C = 100, D = 500, M = 1,000.

Ro·ma·no /rəˈmänō/ ▸ n. a strong-tasting hard cheese, originally made in Italy. [Ital., lit. 'Roman.']

Romano- ▸ comb. form Roman; Roman and ...: *Romano-Celtic.*

Ro·ma·nov /rōˈmänəf; ˈrōmə,nôf; -,näf/ a dynasty that ruled in Russia from the accession of Michael Romanov (1596–1645) in 1613 until the overthrow of the last czar, Nicholas II, in 1917.

Ro·man Re·pub·lic the ancient Roman state 509–27 BC.

Ro·mans /ˈrōmənz/ a book of the New Testament, an epistle of St. Paul to the Christian Church at Rome.

Ro·mansh /rōˈmänsH; -ˈmansH/ ▶ **n.** the Rhaeto-Romanic language that is spoken in the Swiss canton of Grisons and is an official language of Switzerland. ▶ **adj.** of or relating to this language. [from Romansh *Roman(t)sch*, from med. L. *romanice* 'in the Romanic manner.']

ro·man·tic /rōˈmantik; rə-/ ▶ **adj. 1** inclined toward or suggestive of the feeling of excitement and mystery associated with love. ■ relating to love, esp. in a sentimental or idealized way. **2** of, characterized by, or suggestive of an idealized view of reality: *a romantic view of history.* **3** (usu. **Romantic**) of, relating to, or denoting the artistic and literary movement of Romanticism. ▶ **n.** a person with romantic beliefs or attitudes. ■ (usu. **Romantic**) a writer or artist of the Romantic movement. — **ro·man·ti·cal·ly** /-ik(ə)lē/ **adv.** [17th C. (of a narrative 'like a romance'): from archaic *romaunt* 'tale of chivalry,' from an OFr. var. of *romanz* (see ROMANCE).]

ro·man·ti·cism /rōˈmantəˌsizəm; rə-/ ▶ **n. 1** (often **Romanticism**) a movement in the arts and literature that originated in the late 18th century, emphasizing inspiration, subjectivity, and the primacy of the individual. **2** the state or quality of being romantic.

ro·man·ti·cist /rōˈmantəsist; rə-/ ▶ **n.** a writer, artist, or musician of the Romantic movement. ■ a person who subscribes to the ideas of Romanticism.

ro·man·ti·cize /rōˈmantəˌsīz; rə-/ ▶ **v.** [trans.] deal with or describe in an idealized or unrealistic fashion: *the tendency to romanticize nonindustrial societies.* — **ro·man·ti·ci·za·tion** /rōˌmantəsəˈzāsHən; rə-/ **n.**

Rom·a·ny /ˈrämənē; ˈrō-/ (also **Rom·a·ni**) ▶ **n.** (pl. **-nies**) **1** the Indic language of the gypsies. **2** a gypsy. ▶ **adj.** of or relating to gypsies or their language. [19th C.: from Romany *Romani*, fem. and pl. of the adj. *Romano*, from *Rom* 'man.']

Rom·berg /ˈrämˌbərg/, Sigmund (1887–1951), US composer; born in Hungary. He wrote a succession of operettas, including *The Student Prince* (1924) and *The Desert Song* (1926).

Rome /rōm/ **1** the capital of Italy, in the west central part of the country, on the Tiber River; pop. 2,791,000. According to tradition, the ancient city was founded by Romulus in 753 BC on the Palatine Hill; as it grew it spread to the other six hills of Rome. Italian name ROMA. ■ used allusively to refer to the Roman Catholic Church. **2** a city in central New York; pop. 44,350.
– PHRASES **all roads lead to Rome** proverb there are many different ways of reaching the same goal or conclusion. **Rome was not built in a day** proverb a complex task should not be rushed. **when in Rome (do as the Romans do)** proverb when in an unfamiliar environment, you should adopt the customs or behavior of those around you.

Ro·me·o /ˈrōmēˌō/ ▶ **n. 1** (pl. **-os**) an attractive, passionate male seducer or lover. **2** a code word representing the letter R, used in radio communication. [the hero of Shakespeare's romantic tragedy *Romeo and Juliet*.]

Rom·ish /ˈrōmisH/ ▶ **adj.** esp. derog. Roman Catholic: *Romish ideas.*

Rom·mel /ˈräməl/, Erwin (1891–1944), German field marshal; known as **the Desert Fox**. As commander of the Afrika Korps, he captured Tobruk in 1942, but was defeated at El Alamein later that year.

Rom·ney /ˈrämnē/, George (1734–1802), English painter. From the early 1780s, he produced more than 50 portraits of Lady Hamilton.

romp /rämp; rômp/ ▶ **v.** [intrans.] (esp. of a child or animal) play roughly and energetically. ■ [with adverbial] informal proceed without effort to achieve something: *the Vikings romped to victory.* ■ informal engage in sexual activity, esp. illicitly. ▶ **n.** a spell of rough, energetic play: *a romp in the snow.* ■ a lighthearted movie or other work: *an enjoyably gross sci-fi romp.* ■ informal an easy victory. ■ informal a spell of sexual activity, esp. an illicit one: *three-in-a-bed sex romps.* [18th C.: perh. alt. of RAMP.]

romp·er /ˈrämpər; ˈrôm-/ ▶ **n. 1** (also **romp·er suit** or **romp·ers**) a young child's one-piece outer garment. ■ a similar item of clothing for adults, typically worn as overalls or as sports clothing. **2** a person who romps.

Rom·u·lus /ˈrämyələs/ Rom. Mythol. the traditional founder of Rome, one of the twin sons of Mars by the Vestal Virgin Rhea Silvia. See also REMUS.

ronde /ränd/ ▶ **n.** a dance in which the dancers move in a circle. [1930s: Fr., fem. of *rond* 'round.']

ron·deau /ˈrändō; ränˈdō/ ▶ **n.** (pl. **-deaux** /-dōz; ˈdōz/) a thirteen-line poem, divided into three stanzas of 5, 3, and 5 lines, with only two rhymes throughout and with the opening words of the first line used as a refrain at the end of the second and third stanzas. [16th C.: Fr., later form of *rondel* (see RONDEL).]

ron·del /ˈrändəl; ränˈdel/ ▶ **n. 1** a rondeau, esp. one of three stanzas of thirteen or fourteen lines, with the first two lines of the opening quatrain recurring at the end of the second quatrain and the concluding sestet. **2** a circular object. [ME: from OFr., from *rond* 'round.']

ron·do /ˈrändō; ränˈdō/ ▶ **n.** (pl. **-dos**) a musical form with a recurring leading theme, often found in the final movement of a sonata or concerto. [18th C.: Ital., from Fr. *rondeau* (see RONDEAU).]

Rong·e·lap /ˈränGəˌlap/ an atoll in the western Pacific, in the northern Marshall Islands.

Rönt·gen /ˈrentgən; -jən; ˈrənt-/, Wilhelm Conrad (1845–1923), German physicist. He discovered X-rays. Nobel Prize for Physics (1901).

rönt·gen, etc. ▶ **n.** var. of ROENTGEN, etc.

rood /ro͞od/ ▶ **n. 1** a crucifix, esp. one positioned above the rood screen of a church or on a beam over the entrance to the chancel. **2** hist., esp. Brit. a measure of land area equal to a quarter of an acre. [OE *rōd*; akin to Ger. *Rute* 'rod.']

rood screen ▶ **n.** a screen, typically of richly carved wood or stone, separating the nave from the chancel of a church.

roof /ro͞of; ro͝of/ ▶ **n.** (pl. **roofs**) the structure forming the upper covering of a building or vehicle. ■ the top inner surface of a covered area or space; the ceiling. ■ used to signify a house or other building, esp. in the context of hospitality or shelter: *helping those without a roof over their heads.* ■ (**roof of the mouth**) the palate. ▶ **v.** [trans.] (usu. **be roofed**) cover with a roof: *the yard had been roughly roofed over with corrugated iron.* ■ function as the roof of: *fan vaults roof these magnificent buildings.*
– PHRASES **go through the roof** informal **1** (of prices or figures) reach extreme or unexpected heights. **2** another way of saying HIT THE ROOF. **hit the roof** informal suddenly become very angry. — **roof·less adj.** [OE *hrōf*, from Gmc.; akin to ON *hróf* 'boat shed.']

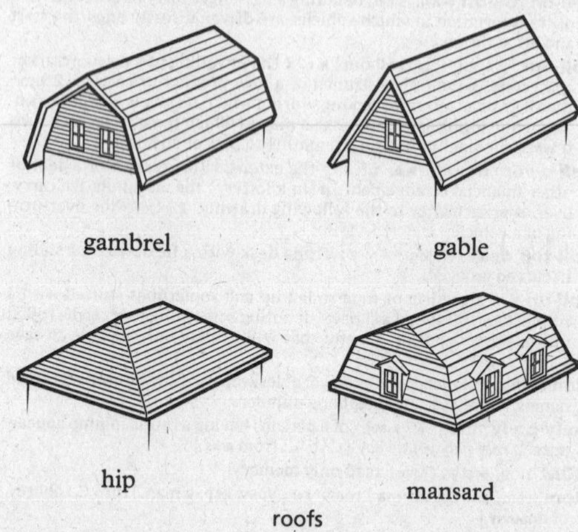

roofs

roof·er /ˈro͞ofər; ˈro͝of-/ ▶ **n.** a person who constructs or repairs roofs.

roof·ing /ˈro͞ofiNG; ˈro͝of-/ ▶ **n.** material for constructing a building's roof: *a house with corrugated tin roofing.* ■ the process of constructing a roof or roofs.

roof·line /ˈro͞ofˌlīn; ˈro͝of-/ ▶ **n.** the design or proportions of the roof of a building or vehicle.

roof prism ▶ **n.** a reflecting prism in which the reflecting surface is in two parts that are angled like the two sides of a pitched roof.

roof rack ▶ **n.** a framework for carrying luggage or equipment on the roof of a vehicle.

roof rat ▶ **n.** another term for BLACK RAT.

roof·top /ˈro͞ofˌtäp; ˈro͝of-/ ▶ **n.** the outer surface of a building's roof.

roof·tree /ˈro͞ofˌtrē; ˈro͝of-/ ▶ **n.** the ridgepole of a roof.

rook[1] /ro͝ok/ ▶ **n.** a gregarious Eurasian crow (*Corvus frugilegus*) with black plumage and a bare face, nesting in colonies in treetops. ▶ **v.** [trans.] informal take money from (someone) by cheating, defrauding, or overcharging them. [OE *hrōc*, from Gmc., prob. imitative; akin to Du. *roek*.]

rook[2] ▶ **n.** a chess piece with its top in the shape of a battlement that can move in any direction along a rank or file on which it stands. See also CASTLE. [ME: from OFr. *rock*, based on Arab. *rukk*.]

rook·er·y /ˈro͝okərē/ ▶ **n.** (pl. **-er·ies**) a breeding colony of rooks, typically seen as a collection of nests. ■ a breeding colony of seabirds, seals, or turtles. ■ fig. a dense collection of housing, esp. in a slum.

rook·ie /ˈro͝okē/ ▶ **n.** informal a new recruit. ■ a member of an athletic team in his or her first full season in that sport. [19th C.: perh. an alt. of RECRUIT.]

room /ro͞om; ro͝om/ ▶ **n. 1** space that can be occupied or where something can be done, esp. viewed in terms of whether there is enough: *there's only room for a single bed in there* | [with infin.] *she was trapped without room to move.* ■ fig. opportunity or scope for something to happen or be done, esp. without causing trouble or damage: *there is plenty of room.* **2** a part or division of a building enclosed by walls, floor, and ceiling: *he wandered from room to room.* ■ (**rooms**) a set of rooms, typically rented, in which a person, couple, or family live. ■ [in sing.] the people present in a room: *the whole room burst into an uproar of approval.* ▶ **v.** [intrans.] share a room or house or flat, esp. a rented one. ■ [trans.] provide with a shared room or lodging: *they roomed us together.*
– PHRASES **make room** move aside or move something aside to allow someone to enter or pass or to clear space for something. **smoke-filled**

room used to refer to political bargaining or decision-making that is conducted privately by a small group of influential people. — **roomed** adj. [in comb.] *a four-roomed house.* **room•ful** /-ˌfo͝ol/ n. (pl. **-fuls**). [OE *rūm*, of Gmc. origin; rel. to Du. *ruim*, Ger. *Raum*.]

room and board ▶n. lodging and food.

room•er /ˈro͞omər; ˈro͝om-/ ▶n. a renter of a room in another person's house.

room•ie /ˈro͞omē; ˈro͝omē/ ▶n. informal a roommate.

room•ing house ▶n. a private house in which rooms are rented for living or staying temporarily.

room•mate /ˈro͞om,māt; ˈro͝om-/ ▶n. a person occupying the same room, apartment, or house as another.

room serv•ice ▶n. hotel service allowing guests to order food and drink in their rooms.

room tem•per•a•ture ▶n. a comfortable ambient temperature, generally taken as about 70°F.

room•y /ˈro͞omē; ˈro͝omē/ ▶adj. (**room•i•er, room•i•est**) (esp. of accommodations) having plenty of room. — **room•i•ly** /-məlē/ adv.

Roo•se•velt[1] /ˈrōzə,velt; -vəlt/, Eleanor (1884–1962), US first lady, humanitarian, and diplomat; full name *Anna Eleanor Roosevelt*; wife of Franklin D. Roosevelt and niece of Theodore Roosevelt. She served as the first chairman of the UN Commission on Human Rights.

Roo•se•velt[2], Franklin Delano (1882–1945), 32nd president of the US 1933–45; known as **FDR**. His New Deal programs of the 1930s helped to lift the US out of the Great Depression, and he played an important part in Allied policy during World War II. A New York Democrat, he was the only president to be elected to a third, and then a fourth, term in office.

Roo•se•velt[3], Theodore (1858–1919), 26th president of the US 1901–09; nicknamed **Teddy**. He initiated many antitrust laws, and he successfully engineered the US bid to build the Panama Canal (1904–14). He also negotiated the end of the Russo-Japanese War in 1905. Nobel Peace Prize (1906).

Roo•se•velt Is•land /ˈrōzə,velt/ an island in the East River in New York City.

roost /ro͞ost/ ▶n. a place where birds regularly settle or congregate to rest. ▶v. [intrans.] (of a bird or bat) settle or congregate for rest or sleep: *migrating martins were settling to roost.*

– PHRASES **come home to roost** (of a scheme, etc.) recoil unfavorably upon the originator. **rule the roost** see **RULE**. [OE *hrōst*, akin to Du. *roest*.]

roost•er /ˈro͞ostər/ ▶n. a male domestic fowl; a cock.

rooster

roost•er tail ▶n. informal the spray of water thrown up behind a speedboat or surfboard.

root[1] /ro͞ot; ro͝ot/ ▶n. **1** the part of a plant that attaches it to the ground or to a support, conveying water and nourishment to the rest of the plant: *cacti have deep and spreading roots.* ■ the persistent underground part of a plant, esp. when fleshy and enlarged and used as a vegetable. ■ any plant grown for such a root. ■ the embedded part of a bodily organ or structure such as a hair, tooth, or nail. ■ the part of a thing attaching it to a greater or more fundamental whole; the end or base. **2** the basic cause, source, or origin of something: *jealousy was at the root of it* | [as adj.] *the root cause.* ■ the essential substance or nature of something. ■ (**roots**) family, ethnic, or cultural origins, esp. as the reasons for one's long-standing emotional attachment to a place or community: *it's always nice to return to my roots.* ■ [as adj.] (**roots**) denoting or relating to something, esp. music, from a particular ethnic or cultural origin, esp. a non-Western one. ■ (in biblical use) a scion; a descendant: *the root of David.* ■ Ling. a morpheme, not necessarily surviving as a word in itself, from which words have been made by the addition of prefixes or suffixes or by other modification. ■ Music the fundamental note of a chord. **3** Math. a number or quantity that when multiplied by itself, typically a specified number of times, gives a specified number or quantity: *find the cube root.* ■ short for **SQUARE ROOT**. ■ a value of an unknown quantity satisfying a given equation. ▶v. [trans.] **1** cause (a plant or cutting) to grow roots. ■ [intrans.] (of a plant or cutting) establish roots. **2** (usu. **be rooted**) establish deeply and firmly: *vegetarianism is rooted in Indian culture.* ■ (**be rooted in**) have as an origin or cause. ■ [with obj. and adverbial] [often as adj.] (**rooted**) cause (someone) to stand immobile through fear or amazement: *she found herself rooted to the spot in disbelief.*

– PHRASES **at root** basically; fundamentally: *it is a moral question at root.* **put down roots** (of a plant) begin to draw nourishment from the soil through its roots. ■ (of a person) begin to have a settled life in a particular place. **strike at the root** (or **roots**) **of** affect in a vital area with potentially destructive results: *the proposals struck at the roots of community life.* **take root** (of a plant) begin to grow and draw nourishment from the soil. ■ become fixed or established. — **root•ed•ness** n. **root•let** /-lət/ n. **root•like** /-ˌlīk/ adj. **root•y** adj. [OE *rōt*, from ON *rót*; akin to L. *radix* and **WORT**.]

root[2] ▶v. [intran.] (of an animal) turn up the ground with its snout in search of food. ■ search unsystematically through an untidy mass or area; rummage: *she was rooting through a pile of papers.* ■ [trans.] (**root something out**) find or extract something by rummaging: *he managed to root out the cleaning kit.*

– PHRASAL VERBS **root for** informal support or hope for the success of (a person or group): *the whole club is rooting for him.* **root someone on** informal cheer or spur someone on. [OE *wrōtan*, of Gmc. origin; rel. to OE *wrōt* 'snout,' Ger. *Rüssel* 'snout.']

root•ball /ˈro͞ot,bôl; ˈro͝ot-/ (also **root ball**) ▶n. the mass formed by a plant's roots and the surrounding soil.

root beer ▶n. an effervescent drink made from an extract of the roots and bark of certain plants.

root ca•nal ▶n. the pulp-filled cavity in a tooth root. ■ a procedure to replace infected pulp in a root canal.

root cel•lar ▶n. a domestic cellar used for storing root vegetables.

root crop ▶n. a crop that is a root vegetable or other root, e.g., sugar beet.

root di•rec•to•ry ▶n. Comput. the directory at the highest level of a hierarchy.

root•er /ˈro͞otər/ ▶n. informal a supporter or fan.

root fly ▶n. a dark slender fly (family Anthomyiidae) whose larvae may cause serious damage to the roots of crops.

root hair ▶n. Bot. each of a large number of microscopic outgrowths from the outer layer of cells in a root.

root-knot ▶n. a disease of cultivated flowers and vegetables caused by eelworm infestation, resulting in galls on the roots. The eelworms belong to the genus *Meloidogyne*, class Nematoda.

root•less /ˈro͞otlis; ˈro͝ot-/ ▶adj. **1** having no settled home or social or family ties: *a rootless nomad.* **2** (of a plant) not having roots: *a rootless flowering plant.*

root mean square ▶n. Math. the square root of the arithmetic mean of the squares of a set of values.

root sign ▶n. Math. another term for **RADICAL SIGN**.

roots mu•sic ▶n. music springing from and identified with a particular culture, esp. the West Indies.

root•stock /ˈro͞ot,stäk; ˈro͝ot-/ ▶n. a rhizome. ■ a plant onto which another variety is grafted. ■ a primary form or source from which offshoots have arisen: *the rootstock of all post-Triassic ammonites.*

root veg•e•ta•ble ▶n. the fleshy enlarged root of a plant used as a vegetable, e.g., a carrot, rutabaga, or beet.

rope /rōp/ ▶n. **1** a length of strong cord made by twisting together strands of natural fibers such as hemp or artificial fibers such as polypropylene. ■ a lasso. ■ (**the ropes**) the ropes enclosing a boxing or wrestling ring. **2** a quantity of roughly spherical objects such as onions or pearls strung together: *a rope of pearls.* **3** (**the ropes**) informal the established procedures: *I want you to show her the ropes.* ▶v. [trans.] catch, fasten, or secure with rope: *the calves must be roped and led out of the stockade.* ■ (**rope someone in/into**) persuade someone to take part in (an activity). ■ (**rope something off**) enclose or separate an area with a rope or tape: *police roped off the area.*

– PHRASES **the end of one's rope** see **END**. **give a man enough rope and he will hang himself** proverb given enough freedom of action a person will bring about their own downfall. **on the ropes** Boxing forced against the ropes by the opponent's attack. ■ in state of near collapse or defeat: *the company was on the ropes.* — **rop•er** n. [OE *rāp*, of Gmc. origin; akin to Ger. *Reif*.]

rope-a-dope /ˈrōp ə ˌdōp/ ▶n. informal a boxing tactic of pretending to be trapped against the ropes, goading an opponent to throw tiring ineffective punches. [1970s: coined by Muhammad Ali.]

rope lad•der ▶n. two long ropes connected by short crosspieces, typically made of wood or metal, used as a ladder.

rope•walk•er /ˈrōp,wôkər/ ▶n. dated a performer on a tightrope. — **rope•walk•ing** /-kiNG/ n.

rope•y ▶adj. var. of **ROPY**.

rope yarn ▶n. loosely twisted fibers used for making the strands of rope.

rop•ing /ˈrōpiNG/ ▶n. **1** the action of catching or securing something with ropes: *calf roping.* **2** ropes collectively.

rop•y /ˈrōpē/ (also **rop•ey**) ▶adj. (**rop•i•er, rop•i•est**) resembling a rope in being long, strong, and fibrous. ■ (of a liquid) resembling a rope in forming viscous or gelatinous threads. — **rop•i•ly** /ˈrōpəlē/ adv. **rop•i•ness** n.

roque /rōk/ ▶n. a form of croquet played on a hard court surrounded by a bank. [19th C.: alt. of **ROQUET**.]

Roque•fort /ˈrōkfərt/ ▶n. trademark a soft blue cheese made from ewes' milk. It is ripened in limestone caves and has a strong flavor. [after a village in southern France.]

Roq•ue•laure /rōkəˈlôr/, A. N., see **RICE**[1].

ro•quet /rōˈkā/ Croquet ▶v. (**-queted** /-ˈkād/, **-quet•ing** /-ˈkāiNG/) [trans.] strike (another ball) with one's own. ▶n. an act of roqueting. [19th C.: appar. alt. of **CROQUET**.]

ror•qual /ˈrôrkwəl; -ˌkwôl/ ▶n. a baleen whale (family Balaenopteridae) of streamlined appearance with pleated skin on the underside. Its six species include the **FINBACK**. [19th C.: via Fr. from Norw. *røyrkval*, from ON *reythr* 'rorqual' + *hvalr* 'whale.']

Ror·schach test /'rôr,shäk/ ▶ n. Psychol. a type of test in which a standard set of symmetrical ink blots is presented one by one to the subject, who is asked to describe what they resemble. [1920s: Hermann *Rorschach* (1884–1922), Swiss psychiatrist.]

ro·sace /rō'zās; rō'zäs/ ▶ n. an ornamentation resembling a rose, in particular a rose window. [19th C.: from Fr., from L. *rosaceus* 'roselike' (see ROSACEOUS).]

ro·sa·ce·a /rō'zāsh(ə)ə/ (also **ac·ne ro·sa·ce·a**) ▶ n. Med. a condition in which facial blood vessels enlarge. [19th C.: from L., fem. of *rosaceus* in the sense 'rose-colored.']

ro·sa·ceous /rō'zāshəs/ ▶ adj. Bot. of, relating to, or denoting plants of the rose family (Rosaceae). [18th C.: from mod. L. *Rosaceae* (based on L. *rosa* 'rose').]

ros·an·i·line /rō'zanl-in/ ▶ n. Chem. a reddish-brown synthetic compound, $C_{20}H_{19}N_3$, that is a base used in making a number of red dyes, notably fuchsin. [19th C.: from ROSE[1] + ANILINE.]

ro·sar·i·an /rō'ze(ə)rēən/ ▶ n. one who cultivates roses. [19th C.: from L. *rosarium* 'rose garden.']

Ro·sa·ri·o /rō'särē,ō; -,zär-/ a city in east central Argentina; pop. 1,096,000.

ro·sar·i·um /rō'ze(ə)rēəm/ ▶ n. (pl. **-sar·i·ums** or **-sar·i·a** /-'ze(ə)rēə/) formal a rose garden. [19th C.: from L. (see ROSARY).]

ro·sa·ry /'rōzərē/ ▶ n. (pl. **-ries**) (in the Roman Catholic Church) a form of devotion in which five (or fifteen) decades of Hail Marys are repeated, each decade preceded by an Our Father and followed by a Glory Be. ■ a string of beads for keeping count in such a devotion or in the devotions of some other religions. ■ a book containing such a devotion. [ME ('rose garden'): from L. *rosarium*, based on *rosa* 'rose.']

rose[1] /rōz/ ▶ n. **1** a prickly bush or shrub (genus *Rosa*) that typically bears red, pink, yellow, or white fragrant flowers, native to north temperate regions and widely grown as an ornamental. ■ the flower of such a plant: [as adj.] *a rose garden.* ■ used in names of other plants whose flowers resemble roses, e.g., **rose of Sharon**. ■ used in similes and comparisons in reference to the rose flower's beauty or its typical rich red color. **2** a thing representing or resembling the flower, in particular: ■ a stylized representation of the flower in heraldry or decoration, typically with five petals (esp. as a national emblem of England): *the Tudor rose.* ■ short for COMPASS ROSE. ■ short for ROSE WINDOW. **3** a perforated cap attached to a shower, the spout of a watering can, or the end of a hose to produce a spray. **4** a warm pink or light crimson color. ■ (usu. **roses**) used in reference to a rosy complexion: *the fresh air will soon put the roses back in her cheeks.* ▶ v. [trans.] literary make rosy.
– PHRASES **a bed of roses** see BED. **come up roses** (of a situation) develop in a very favorable way. [OE *rōse*, from Gmc., from L. *rosa*.]

rose[2] past of RISE.

ro·sé /rō'zā/ ▶ n. any light pink wine, colored by only brief contact with red grape skins. [Fr., lit. 'pink.']

ro·se·ate /'rōzēət; -,āt/ ▶ adj. **1** rose-colored. ■ used in names of birds with partly pink plumage, e.g., **roseate tern, roseate spoonbill**. **2** optimistic; promising good fortune: *his letters home give a somewhat roseate idea of how he lived.* [ME: from L. *roseus* 'rosy,' from *rosa* 'rose.']

Ro·seau /rō'zō/ the capital of Dominica in the Caribbean; pop. 16,000.

rose·bay /'rōz,bā/ ▶ n. **1** a rhododendron, esp. the **great rhododendron** (*R. maximum*) of eastern North America. **2** (also **rose·bay wil·low herb**) esp. Brit. the pink-flowered willow herb *Epilobium angustifolium*, a common fireweed.

rose-breast·ed gros·beak ▶ n. a North American grosbeak (*Pheucticus ludovicianus*) of the bunting family, the male of which is black and white with a pinkish-red breast patch.

rose·bud /'rōz,bəd/ ▶ n. an unopened flower of a rose.

rose chaf·er ▶ n. a brilliant green or copper-colored day-flying chafer (beetle) (genus *Marodactylus*, family Scarabaeidae) that feeds on roses and other flowers.

rose-col·ored ▶ adj. of a warm pink color. ■ used in reference to a naively optimistic or unfoundedly favorable viewpoint: *you are still seeing the profession through rose-colored glasses.*

rose·fish /'rōz,fish/ ▶ n. (pl. same or **-fish·es**) the redfish of the North Atlantic (*Sebastes marinus*).

rose ge·ra·ni·um ▶ n. a pink-flowered pelargonium (*Pelargonium graveolens*) with fragrant leaves.

rose hip ▶ n. see HIP[2].

ro·sel·la /rō'zelə/ ▶ n. an Australian parakeet (genus *Platycercus*) with vivid green, red, yellow, or blue plumage. [19th C.: alt. of *Rosehill*, New South Wales.]

rose mad·der ▶ n. a pale shade of pink.

rose mal·low ▶ n. a plant (genus *Hibiscus*) of the mallow family, often cultivated for its large pink or white flowers. Wild species include the showy pink-flowered **swamp rose mallow** (*H. palustris*), found esp. in coastal marshes of the eastern US.

swamp rose mallow

rose·mar·y /'rōz,me(ə)rē/ ▶ n. an evergreen aromatic shrub (*Rosmarinus officinalis*) of the mint family, native to southern Europe. The narrow leaves are used as a culinary herb, in perfumery, and as an emblem of remembrance. [ME *rosmarine*, based on L. *ros marinus*, from *ros* 'dew' + *marinus* 'of the sea'; influenced by ROSE[1] and MARY.]

Rose·mead /'rōz,mēd/ a city in southwestern California, east of Los Angeles; pop. 51,638.

Ros·en·berg /'rōzən,bərg/ US spies. Julius (1918–53) and his wife Ethel Greenglass (1915–53) were Communist Party members who were tried and convicted of espionage in 1951. They were executed in 1953.

rose of Jer·i·cho ▶ n. an annual desert plant (*Anastatica hierochuntica*) of the cabbage family whose dead branches fold inward around the mature seeds forming a ball that is blown about, native to North Africa and the Middle East.

rose of Shar·on ▶ n. **1** a shrub (*Hibiscus syriacus*) of the mallow family, with rose, lavender, or white flowers. **2** a St. John's wort (*Hypericum calycinum*) with dense foliage and large golden-yellow flowers, native to southeastern Europe and Asia Minor and widely cultivated for ground cover. **3** (in biblical use) a flowering plant of unknown identity.

ro·se·o·la /,rōzē'ōlə; rō'zēələ/ ▶ n. Med. a rose-colored rash. ■ (in full **roseola infantum** /in'fantəm/) a disease of young children in which a fever is followed by a rash. [19th C.: mod. var. of RUBEOLA, from L. *roseus* 'rose-colored.']

rose quartz ▶ n. a translucent pink variety of quartz.

Ro·set·ta Stone /rō'zetə/ an inscribed stone found near Rosetta on the western mouth of the Nile in 1799. Its deciphering led to the interpretation of many other early records of Egyptian civilization. ■ [as n.] (**a Rosetta stone**) a key to some previously undecipherable mystery.

ro·sette /rō'zet/ ▶ n. **1** a rose-shaped decoration. **2** a design, arrangement, or growth resembling a rose, in particular: ■ Archit. a carved or molded ornament resembling a rose. ■ Biol. markings resembling a rose. ■ a roselike cluster of parts, esp. a radiating arrangement of horizontally spreading leaves at the base of a low-growing plant. — **ro·set·ted** /rō'zetəd/ adj. [18th C.: from Fr., dimin. of *rose* (see ROSE[1]).]

Rose·ville /'rōz,vil/ **1** a city in northeastern California; pop. 44,685. **2** a city in southeastern Michigan; pop. 51,412.

rose wa·ter ▶ n. scented water made with rose petals.

rose win·dow ▶ n. a circular window with mullions or tracery radiating in a form suggestive of a rose.

rose·wood /'rōz,wŏŏd/ ▶ n. **1** fragrant close-grained tropical timber with a distinctive fragrance, used particularly for making furniture and musical instruments. **2** the tree (genus *Dalbergia*) of the pea family that produces this timber.

Rosh Ha·sha·nah /,rōsh (h)ə'shōnə; ,räsh; -'shänə/ (also **Rosh Ha·sha·na**) ▶ n. the Jewish New Year festival, held on the first (also sometimes the second) day of Tishri (in September). [Heb., lit. 'head (i.e., beginning) of the year.']

Ro·si·cru·cian /,rōzə'krōōshən; -,räzə-/ ▶ n. a member of a secretive 17th- and 18th-century society devoted to the study of metaphysical, mystical, and alchemical lore. ■ a member of any of a number of later organizations deriving from this. ▶ adj. of or relating to the Rosicrucians. — **Ro·si·cru·cian·ism** /-,nizəm/ n. [from mod. L. *rosa crucis* (or *crux*), Latinization of Ger. *Rosenkreuz*.]

ros·in /'räzən/ ▶ n. resin, esp. the solid amber residue obtained after the distillation of crude turpentine oleoresin, or of naphtha extract from pine stumps. ▶ v. (**ros·ined, ros·in·ing**) [trans.] rub (something, esp. the bow of a stringed instrument) with rosin. — **ros·in·y** adj. [ME: from med. L. *rosina*, from L. *resina* (see RESIN).]

Ross[1] /rôs; räs/, Betsy (1752–1836), US patriot and upholsterer; full name *Elizabeth Griscom Ross*. Although the legend is disputed, she is credited with having made the first flag of the US in June 1776.

Ross[2], Sir James Clark (1800–62), British explorer. He discovered the north magnetic pole 1831 and Ross Island, Ross Dependency, and the Ross Sea 1839–43.

Ross[3], Sir John (1777–1856), British explorer. He searched for the Northwest Passage 1829–33.

Ross[4], Sir Ronald (1857–1932), British physician. He confirmed that the *Anopheles* mosquito transmits the malarial parasite. Nobel Prize for Physiology or Medicine (1902).

Ross De·pend·en·cy part of Antarctica administered by New Zealand, consisting of everything lying south of latitude 60° south between longitudes 160° east and 150° west.

Ros·set·ti /rə'zetē/ a family of English poets. Dante Gabriel (1828–82), born *Gabriel Charles Dante Rossetti*, was also a painter. His poem *The Blessed Damozel* (1846) became the subject of his same-titled painting 1875–78. His sister Christina Georgina (1830–94) wrote religious and love poetry and children's verse.

Ros·si·ni /rə'sēnē/, Gioacchino Antonio (1792–1868), Italian composer. He wrote the operas *The Barber of Seville* (1816) and *William Tell* (1829).

Ross Sea a large arm of the Pacific Ocean that forms a deep indentation in the coast of Antarctica.

Ross's goose ▶ n. a small Arctic goose (*Anser rossi*) that breeds in northern Canada.

Ross's gull ▶ n. a pinkish-white Arctic gull (*Rhodostethia rosea*).

Ros·tand /'räs,tand; rô'stäN/, Edmond (1868–1918), French playwright and poet. He wrote *Cyrano de Bergerac* (1897).

ros·ter /ˈrästər; ˈrôs-/ ▶ **n.** a list or plan showing turns of duty or leave for individuals or groups in an organization: *next week's duty roster.* ■ a list of members of a team or organization, in particular of athletes available for team selection. [18th C.: from Du. *rooster* 'list,' earlier 'gridiron,' from *roosten* 'to roast,' from its parallel lines.]

Ros·tock /ˈrästäk; ˈrôstôk/ a city on the Baltic coast of Germany; pop. 244,000.

Ro·stov /rəˈstôf; -ˈstäf/ a city in southwestern Russia, on the Don River; pop. 1,025,000. Full name **Rostov-on-Don**.

ros·tral /ˈrästrəl; ˈrô-/ ▶ **adj.** **1** Anat. situated or occurring near the front end of the body, esp. in the region of the nose and mouth or (in an embryo) near the hypophyseal region: *the rostral portion of the brain.* **2** Zool. of or on the rostrum. **3** (of a column, etc.) adorned with the rams of ancient warships or with representations of these. — **ros·tral·ly** **adv.** [19th C.: from **rostrum**.]

Ros·tro·po·vich /ˌrästrəˈpōvich/, Mstislav Leopoldovich (1927–2007), Russian-American cellist and conductor. He was conductor of the National Symphony Orchestra 1977–94.

ros·trum /ˈrästrəm; ˈrôs-/ ▶ **n.** (pl. **ros·tra** /ˈrästrə; ˈrô-/ or **ros·trums**) **1** a raised platform on which a person stands to make a public speech, receive an award or medal, play music, or conduct an orchestra. ■ a similar platform for supporting a movie or television camera. **2** esp. Zool. a beaklike projection. — **ros·trate** /ˈräs,trāt; ˈrô,strāt/ **adj.** (in sense 2). [16th C.: from L., lit. 'beak' (from *rodere* 'gnaw'); orig. used to denote an orator's platform in the Forum in Rome, which was decorated with the beaks of captured galleys.]

Ros·well /ˈräzwel; -wəl/ **1** a city in northwestern Georgia; pop. 79,334. **2** a town in southeastern New Mexico, the scene of a mysterious crash in July 1947, thought by some to have been a UFO; pop. 45,293.

ros·y /ˈrōzē/ ▶ **adj.** (**ros·i·er, ros·i·est**) **1** (esp. of a person's skin) colored like a pink or red rose. **2** promising or suggesting good fortune or happiness. ■ easy and pleasant: *life could never be rosy for them.* — **ros·i·ly** /ˈrōzəlē/ **adv.** **ros·i·ness** **n.**

ros·y finch ▶ **n.** a finch (genus *Leucosticte*) found in Asia and western North America, the male of which has pinkish underparts and rump.

rot /rät/ ▶ **v.** (**rot·ted, rot·ting**) [intrans.] decompose by the action of bacteria and fungi; decay. ■ [trans.] cause to decay. ■ fig. gradually deteriorate through lack of attention or opportunity. ▶ **n.** **1** the process of decaying. ■ rotten or decayed matter. ■ (**the rot**) a process of deterioration; a decline in standards: *it was when they moved back home that the rot set in.* ■ [usu. with adj.] any of a number of fungal or bacterial diseases that cause tissue deterioration, esp. in plants. **2** informal nonsense; rubbish: *don't talk rot.* [OE *rotian* (v.), from Gmc.; akin to Du. *rotten*.]

Ro·ta·ry /ˈrōtərē/ (in full **Ro·ta·ry In·ter·na·tion·al**) a worldwide charitable society of businessmen, businesswomen, and professional people, formed in 1905. — **Ro·tar·i·an** /rōˈte(ə)rēən/ **n. & adj.** [because members hosted events in rotation.]

ro·ta·ry /ˈrōtərē/ ▶ **adj.** (of motion) revolving around a center or axis; rotational: *a rotary motion.* ■ (of a thing) acting by means of rotation, esp. (of a machine) operating through the rotation of a part. ▶ **n.** (pl. **-ries**) **1** a rotary machine, engine, or device. **2** a traffic circle. [18th C.: from med. L. *rotarius*, from *rota* 'wheel.']

ro·ta·ry en·gine ▶ **n.** an engine that produces rotary motion or that has rotating parts, in particular: ■ an aircraft engine with a fixed crankshaft around which cylinders and propeller rotate. ■ a Wankel engine.

ro·ta·ry press ▶ **n.** a printing press that prints from a rotating cylindrical surface onto paper.

ro·ta·ry wing ▶ **n.** [usu. as adj.] an airfoil that rotates in an approximately horizontal plane, providing all or most of the lift in a helicopter or autogiro.

ro·tate /ˈrō,tāt/ ▶ **v.** [intrans.] move in a circle around an axis or center: *the wheel continued to rotate* | [as adj.] (**rotating**) *a rotating drum.* ■ [trans.] cause to move around an axis or in a circle. ■ pass to each member of a group in a regularly recurring order. ■ [trans.] grow (different crops) in succession on a particular piece of land to avoid exhausting the soil. ■ [trans.] change the position of (tires) on a motor vehicle to distribute wear. — **ro·tat·a·ble** /ˈrō,tātəbəl; rōˈtā-/ **adj.** **ro·ta·tive** /ˈrō,tātiv/ **adj.** **ro·ta·to·ry** /ˈrōtə,tôrē/ **adj.** [17th C.: from L. *rotat-* 'turned in a circle,' from the v. *rotare*, from *rota* 'wheel.']

ro·ta·tion /rōˈtāshən/ ▶ **n.** the action of rotating around an axis or center: *in the same direction as the earth's rotation.* ■ (also **crop ro·ta·tion**) the action or system of rotating crops. ■ Forestry the cycle of planting, felling, and replanting. ■ the passing of a privilege or responsibility from one member of a group to another in a regularly recurring succession. ■ a tour of duty, esp. by a medical practitioner in training. ■ Math. the conceptual operation of turning a system around an axis. ■ Math. another term for **curl** (sense 2). — **ro·ta·tion·al** /-shənl/ **adj.** **ro·ta·tion·al·ly** /-shənl-ē/ **adv.**

ro·ta·tor /ˈrō,tātər/ ▶ **n.** a thing that rotates or that causes something to rotate. ■ Anat. a muscle whose contraction causes or assists in the rotation of a part of the body.

ro·ta·tor cuff ▶ **n.** Anat. a capsule with fused tendons that supports the arm at the shoulder joint.

ROTC /ˈärōtēˈsē; ˈrätsē/ ▶ **abbr.** (in the US) Reserve Officers' Training Corps.

rote /rōt/ ▶ **n.** mechanical or habitual repetition of something to be learned: *a poem learned by rote.* [ME (also in the sense 'habit, custom'): of unknown origin.]

ro·te·none /ˈrōtn,ōn/ ▶ **n.** Chem. a toxic crystalline substance, $C_{23}H_{22}O_6$, obtained from the roots of derris and related plants, widely used as an insecticide. [1920s: from Japanese *rotenon* (from *roten* 'derris').]

rot·gut /ˈrät,gət/ ▶ **n.** informal poor-quality and potentially harmful alcoholic liquor.

Roth /rôth; räth/, Philip Milton (1933–), US writer. His novels include *Portnoy's Complaint* (1969) and the trilogy *Zuckerman Bound* (1985).

Roth·er·ham /ˈräthərəm/ a town in northern England; pop. 247,000.

Roth IRA /rôth; räth/ ▶ **n.** an individual retirement account allowing a person to set aside after-tax income up to a specified amount each year. [Senator William Victor *Roth* II (1921–) of Delaware.]

Roth·ko /ˈräthkō/, Mark (1903–70), US painter, born in Latvia; born *Marcus Rothkovich.* His series of nine paintings for the Seagram Building in New York City includes *Black on Maroon* (1958).

Roth·schild /ˈrôth(s),chīld; ˈräth(s)-/, Meyer Amschel (1743–1812), German financier. He founded the Rothschild banking house in Frankfurt.

Ro·tif·er·a /rōˈtifərə/ Zool. a small phylum of minute multicellular aquatic animals that have a characteristic wheellike ciliated organ. — **ro·ti·fer** /ˈrōtəfər/ **n.** [mod. L. (pl.), from L. *rota* 'wheel' + *ferre* 'to bear.']

ro·tis·ser·ie /rōˈtisərē/ ▶ **n.** **1** a cooking appliance with a rotating spit for roasting and barbecuing meat. **2** a restaurant serving roasted or barbecued meat. [19th C.: from Fr. *rôtisserie*, from *rôtir* 'to roast.']

ro·to·gra·vure /ˌrōtəgrəˈvyo͝or/ ▶ **n.** a printing system using a rotary press with intaglio cylinders. ■ a sheet or magazine printed with this system, esp. the color magazine of a Sunday newspaper. [20th C.: from Ger. *Rotogravur*, after a printing company.]

ro·tor /ˈrōtər/ ▶ **n.** a rotary part of a machine or vehicle, in particular: ■ a hub with a number of radiating airfoils. ■ the rotating assembly in a turbine. ■ the armature of an electric motor. ■ the rotating part of the distributor of an internal combustion engine. ■ the rotating container in a centrifuge. ■ the rotary winder of a clockwork watch. ■ Meteorol. a large eddy in which the air circulates around a horizontal axis. [20th C.: from **rotator**.]

ro·tor·craft /ˈrōtər,kraft/ ▶ **n.** (pl. same) a rotary-wing aircraft, such as a helicopter or autogiro.

ro·tor wash ▶ **n.** air turbulence caused by a helicopter rotor.

ro·to·scope /ˈrōtə,skōp/ ▶ **n.** a device that projects and enlarges individual frames of filmed live action to permit them to be used to create cartoon animation and composite film sequences. ■ a computer application that combines live action and other images in a film. ▶ **v.** [trans.] transfer (an image from live action film) into another film sequence using a rotoscope. [1950s: perh. from 19th-C. *rotascope*.]

ro·to·till·er /ˈrōtə,tilər/ ▶ **n.** trademark a machine with rotating blades for breaking up or tilling the soil. — **ro·to·till** **v.**

rot·ten /ˈrätn/ ▶ **adj.** (**-ten·er, -ten·est**) suffering from decay: *the supporting beams were rotten.* ■ morally, socially, or politically corrupt. ■ informal very bad: *a rotten cook.* ■ informal extremely unpleasant. ■ [predic.] informal unwell: *she felt rotten.* ▶ **adv.** informal to an extreme degree; very much: *your mother said that I spoiled you rotten.* — **rot·ten·ly** **adv.** **rot·ten·ness** **n.** [ME: from ON *rotinn*.]

rot·ten·stone /ˈrätn,stōn/ ▶ **n.** weathered siliceous limestone used as a powder or paste for polishing metals.

rot·ter /ˈrätər/ ▶ **n.** informal, dated, esp. Brit. a cruel, stingy, or unkind person.

Rot·ter·dam /ˈrätər,dam/ a city in the Netherlands, at the mouth of the Meuse River, 15 miles (25 km) inland from the North Sea; pop. 582,000.

Rottweiler

Rott·wei·ler /ˈrät,wīlər; ˈrôt,vīlər/ ▶ **n.** a large powerful dog of a tall black-and-tan breed. [20th C.: Ger., from *Rottweil*, a town in southwestern Germany.]

ro·tund /rōˈtənd; ˈrō,tənd/ ▶ **adj.** (of a person) plump. ■ round or spherical: *huge stoves held great rotund cauldrons.* ■ fig. (of speech or literary style) indulging in grandiloquent expression. — **ro·tun·di·ty** /-ˈtəndətē/ **n.** **ro·tund·ly** **adv.** [15th C.: from L. *rotundus*, from *rotare* 'rotate.']

ro·tun·da /rōˈtəndə/ ▶ **n.** a round building or room, esp. one with a dome. [17th C.: alt. of Ital. *rotonda (camera)* 'round (chamber),' fem. of *rotondo* 'round' (see **rotund**).]

Rou·ault /roō'ō/, Georges Henri (1871–1958), French painter. Associated with expressionism, he used vivid colors and thick black outlines.

rou·ble ▶ n. var. of RUBLE.

rou·é /roō'ā/ ▶ n. a debauched man, esp. an elderly one. [19th C.: Fr., lit. 'broken on a wheel,' referring to a form of punishment]

rouge /roōzh/ ▶ n. a red powder or cream used as a cosmetic for coloring the cheeks or lips. ▶ v. [trans.] [often as adj.] (**rouged**) color with rouge. [ME: from Fr., from L. *rubeus*.]

rough /rəf/ ▶ adj. **1** having an uneven or irregular surface; not smooth or level. ■ (of ground or terrain) having many bumps or other obstacles; difficult to cross. ■ not soft to the touch: *her skin felt dry and rough.* ■ (of a voice) coming out with difficulty so as to sound harsh and rasping: *his voice was rough with barely suppressed fury.* ■ (of wine or another alcoholic drink) sharp or harsh in taste. **2** (of a person or their behavior) not gentle; violent or boisterous. ■ (of an area or occasion) characterized by or notorious for the occurrence of violent behavior. ■ (of the sea) having large and dangerous waves: *the lifeboat crew braved rough seas to rescue a couple.* ■ (of weather) wild and stormy. ■ informal difficult and unpleasant: *the teachers gave me **a rough time**.* ■ Brit., informal hard; severe: *the first day of a job is **rough on** everyone.* **3** not finished tidily or decoratively; plain and basic: *the customers sat at rough wooden tables.* ■ put together without the proper materials or skill; makeshift: *he had one arm in a rough sling.* ■ (of hair or fur) not well cared for or tidy. ■ lacking sophistication or refinement: *she took care of him in her rough, kindly way.* ■ not worked out or correct in every detail: *a rough draft.* ■ (of stationery) used or designed to be used for making preliminary notes: *rough paper.* ▶ adv. informal in a manner that lacks gentleness; harshly or violently: *treat 'em rough but treat 'em fair.* ▶ n. **1** esp. Brit. a disreputable and violent person. **2** (on a golf course) longer grass around the fairway and the green: *his second shot was **in the rough**.* **3** a preliminary sketch for a design: *I did a rough to work out the scale of the lettering.* **4** an uncut precious stone. ▶ v. [trans.] **1** work or shape (something) in a rough, preliminary fashion: *flat surfaces are **roughed down**.* ■ (**rough something out**) produce a preliminary and unfinished sketch or version of something: *the engineer roughed out a diagram on his notepad.* ■ make uneven or ruffled: ***rough up** the icing with a palette knife.* **2** (**rough it**) live in discomfort with only basic necessities: *she had had to rough it alone in a dive.*

– PHRASES **in the rough** in a natural state; without decoration or other treatment: *a diamond in the rough.* **rough and ready** crude but effective. ■ (of a person or place) unsophisticated or unrefined. **rough around the edges** having a few imperfections. **rough edges** small imperfections in someone or something. **rough justice** treatment that is not scrupulously fair or in accordance with the law. **rough passage** a journey over rough sea. ■ a difficult process of achieving something or of becoming successful. **a rough ride** a difficult time or experience: *rebel shareholders are expected to give officials **a rough ride**.* **rough stuff** boisterous or violent behavior.

– PHRASAL VERBS **rough someone up** informal beat someone up. — **rough·ish** adj. **rough·ness** n. [OE *rūh*, from West Gmc.; akin to Ger. *rauh*.]

rough·age /'rəfij/ ▶ n. fibrous indigestible material in vegetable foodstuffs that aids digestion. ■ Farming coarse, fibrous fodder.

rough and tum·ble (also **rough-and-tum·ble**) ▶ n. a situation without rules or organization; a free-for-all.

rough breath·ing ▶ n. see BREATHING (sense 2).

rough·cast /'rəf,kast/ ▶ n. plaster of lime, cement, and gravel, used on outside walls. ▶ adj. **1** (of a building or part of a building) coated with roughcast. **2** (of a person) lacking refinement. ▶ v. [trans.] (usu. **be roughcast**) coat (a wall) with roughcast: *the walls were to have been roughcast.*

rough cut ▶ n. the first version of a movie after preliminary editing. ▶ v. (**rough-cut**) [trans.] cut (something) rapidly and without particular attention to quality or accuracy.

rough·en /'rəfən/ ▶ v. make or become rough: [trans.] *the wind was roughening the surface of the river.*

rough-hew ▶ v. [trans.] [usu. as adj.] (**rough-hewn**) shape (wood or stone) with a tool such as an ax without smoothing it off afterward: *rough-hewn logs.* ■ [as adj.] (**rough-hewn**) (of a person) uncultivated or uncouth.

rough·house /'rəf,hous; -,houz/ informal ▶ v. [intrans.] act in a boisterous, violent manner. ■ [trans.] handle (someone) roughly or violently. ▶ n. /-,hous/ a violent disturbance or an instance of boisterous play.

rough·ing /'rəfiNG/ ▶ n. Ice Hockey unnecessary or excessive use of force, for which a penalty may be assessed. ■ Football illegal bodily contact with the quarterback or kicker, for which a penalty is assessed.

rough·ly /'rəflē/ ▶ adv. **1** in a manner lacking gentleness; harshly or violently: *the man picked me up roughly.* **2** in a manner lacking refinement and precision. ■ approximately: *this is a walk of roughly 13 miles.*

rough·neck /'rəf,nek/ ▶ n. **1** informal a rough and uncouth person. **2** an oil rig worker. ▶ v. [intrans.] [usu. as n.] (**roughnecking**) work on an oil rig: *his savings from roughnecking are gone.*

rough·rid·er /'rəf'rīdər/ (also **rough rid·er**) ▶ n. a person who breaks in or can ride unbroken horses. ■ a person who rides horses a lot. ■ (**Rough Rider**) a member of the cavalry unit in which Theodore Roosevelt fought during the Spanish-American War.

rough·shod /'rəf,SHäd/ ▶ adj. archaic (of a horse) having shoes with nail-heads projecting to prevent slipping.

– PHRASES **ride roughshod over** see RIDE.

rough trade ▶ n. informal male homosexual prostitution, esp. when involving brutality or sadism. ■ people involved in prostitution of this type.

rough-winged swal·low ▶ n. a brown-backed American swallow (*Stelgidopteryx ruficollis*).

rough·y /'rəfē/ ▶ n. (pl. **rough·ies**) Austral. **1** a marine fish (*Trachichthys* and other genera, family Trachichthyidae) with a deep laterally compressed body and large rough-edged scales that become spiny on the belly. **2** another term for RUFF[2] (sense 1).

rou·ille /'roō-ē; roō'ē(yə)/ ▶ n. a Provençal sauce made from red chilies, garlic, and other ingredients. [Fr., lit. 'rust,' from the color.]

rou·lade /roō'läd/ ▶ n. **1** a dish cooked or served in the form of a roll, typically made from a flat piece of meat, fish, or sponge cake, spread with a soft filling and rolled. **2** a florid passage of runs in classical music for a solo virtuoso, esp. one sung to one syllable. [Fr., from *rouler* 'to roll.']

rou·leau /roō'lō/ ▶ n. (pl. **-leaux** /-'lōz/ or **-leaus**) **1** a cylindrical packet of coins. **2** a coil of ribbon, knitted wool, or other material. [17th C.: French, from obs. Fr. *roule* 'a roll.']

rou·lette /roō'let/ ▶ n. **1** a gambling game in which a ball is dropped onto a revolving wheel (**roulette wheel**) with numbered compartments, the players betting on the number at which the ball comes to rest. **2** a tool or machine with a revolving toothed wheel, used in engraving or for making perforations. ▶ v. [trans.] make slit-shaped perforations in (paper, esp. sheets of postage stamps): *the pages are rouletted.* [18th C.: from Fr., diminutive of *rouelle* 'wheel,' from late L. *rotella*, dimin. of L. *rota* 'wheel.']

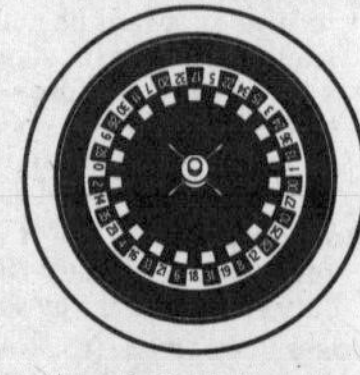

roulette wheel

round /round/ ▶ adj. **1** shaped like or approximately like a circle or cylinder: *she was seated at a round table.* ■ having a curved shape. **2** shaped like or approximately like a sphere. ■ (of a person's body) plump. ■ having a curved surface with no sharp or jagged projections. ■ fig. (of a voice) rich and mellow; not harsh. **3** [attrib.] (of a number) altered for convenience, for example to the nearest whole number or multiple of ten or five: *the size of the fleet in round numbers.* ■ (of a number) convenient for calculation, typically through being a multiple of ten. ▶ n. **1** a circular piece of a particular substance. ■ a thick disk of beef cut from the haunch as a joint. **2** an act of visiting each of a number of people or places: *she **did the rounds** of her family to say goodbye.* ■ a tour of inspection, typically repeated regularly, in which the safety or well-being of those visited is checked: *the doctor is just **making his rounds**.* **3** one of a sequence of sessions or groups of related actions or events: *three rounds of talks.* ■ a division of a contest such as a boxing or wrestling match. ■ an act of playing all the holes in a golf course once. **4** a regularly recurring sequence of activities or functions: *a daily **round** of housework and laundry.* ■ Music a song for three or more unaccompanied voices or parts, each singing the same theme but starting one after another. ■ a set of drinks bought for all the members of a group. **5** a measured quantity or number, in particular: ■ the amount of ammunition needed to fire one shot. ■ Archery a fixed number of arrows shot from a fixed distance. ▶ adv. esp. Brit. variant of AROUND. ▶ prep. esp. Brit. variant of AROUND. ▶ v. [trans.] **1** pass and go around (something) so as to move on in a changed direction: *the ship rounded the cape and sailed north.* **2** alter (a number) to one less exact but more convenient for calculations: *we'll **round** the weight **up** to the nearest pound | the committee **rounded down** the figure.* **3** give a round shape to: *a lathe that rounded chair legs.* ■ [intrans.] become circular in shape: *her eyes rounded in dismay.* ■ Phonet. pronounce (a vowel) with the lips narrowed and protruded.

– PHRASES **in the round 1** (of sculpture) standing free with all sides shown. ■ fig. treated fully and thoroughly; with all aspects shown or considered. **2** (of a theatrical performance) with the audience placed on at least three sides of the stage. **make** (or **go**) **the rounds** (of a story or joke) be passed on from person to person. **round about 1** on all sides or in all directions; surrounding someone or something. **2** at a point or time approximately equal to: *they arrived round about nine.*

– PHRASAL VERBS **round something off** make the edges or corners of something smooth. ■ complete something in a satisfying or suitable way. **round something out** make something more complete. **round somone/something up** drive or collect a number of people or animals together. ■ arrest a number of people. — **round·ish** adj. **round·ness** n. [ME: from OFr. *round-*, from a var. of L. *rotundus* 'rotund.']

round·a·bout /'roundə,bout/ ▶ n. **1** British term for TRAFFIC CIRCLE. **2** British term for MERRY-GO-ROUND. **3** hist. a short, fitted jacket worn by men and boys. ▶ adj. not following a short direct route; circuitous. ■ not saying what is meant clearly and directly.

round dance ▶ n. a folk dance in which the dancers form one large circle. ■ a ballroom dance such as a waltz or polka in which couples move in circles around the ballroom.

round·ed /'roundid/ ▶ adj. **1** having a smooth, curved surface: *rounded gray hills.* ■ having a spherical shape. ■ forming circular or elliptical shapes. ■ Phonet. (of a vowel) pronounced with the lips narrowed and protruded. **2** well developed in all aspects; complete and balanced.

roun·del /'roundl/ ▶ n. **1** a small disk, esp. a decorative medallion. ■ a picture or pattern contained in a circle. ■ Heraldry a plain filled circle as a charge. **2** a short poem consisting of three stanzas of three lines each, rhyming alternately, with the opening words repeated as a refrain after the first and third stanzas. [ME: from OFr. *rondel*, from *ro(u)nd-* (see ROUND).]

roun·de·lay /'roundə,lā/ ▶ **n.** literary a short simple song with a refrain. ■ a circle dance. [ME: from OFr. *rondelet*, from *rondel*; influenced by VIRELAY.]

round·er /'roundər/ ▶ **n.** a person who frequents bars and is often drunk.

round·ers /'roundərz/ ▶ **plural n.** [treated as sing.] a ball game similar to baseball, played chiefly in British schools.

round hand ▶ **n.** a style of handwriting in which the letters have clear rounded shapes.

Round·head /'round,hed/ ▶ **n.** hist. a member or supporter of the Parliamentary party in the English Civil War. [from the short-cropped hairstyle of the Puritans.]

round·heel /'round,hēl/ ▶ **n.** informal a promiscuous woman. — **round·heeled adj.** [1950s: because worn-down heels allow the wearer to lean backwards.]

round·house /'round,hous/ ▶ **n.** **1** a locomotive maintenance shed built around a turntable. **2** informal a blow given with a wide sweep of the arm. ■ a wide turn on a surfboard. **3** esp. hist. a cabin or set of cabins on the after part of the quarterdeck of a sailing ship.

round·ly /'roundlē/ ▶ **adv.** **1** in a vehement or emphatic manner: *the latest attacks have been roundly condemned.* ■ so thoroughly as to leave no doubt: *the army was roundly beaten.* ■ too plainly for politeness; bluntly. **2** so as to form a circular or roughly circular shape.

round rob·in ▶ **n.** **1** [often as adj.] a tournament in which each competitor plays in turn against every other. **2** a petition, esp. one with signatures written in a circle to conceal the order of writing. ■ a letter written by several people in turn, each person adding text before passing the letter on to someone else: [as adj.] *a round-robin letter.* **3** a series or sequence: *round robin of talks in Cairo.*

round-shoul·dered ▶ **adj.** having the shoulders bent forward so that the back is rounded.

rounds·man /'roundzmən/ ▶ **n.** (pl. **-men**) **1** a police officer in charge of a patrol. **2** a person on a regular route delivering and taking orders for milk, bread, etc.

Round Ta·ble n. **1** the table at which King Arthur and his knights sat so that none should have precedence. **2** (**round table**) an assembly for discussion.

round-the-clock ▶ **adj.** lasting all day and all night: *round-the-clock surveillance.*

round trip ▶ **n.** a journey to a place and back again.

round turn ▶ **n.** a complete turn of a rope around another rope or other object.

round·up /'round,əp/ ▶ **n.** a systematic gathering together of people or things. ■ a summary of facts or events: *a news roundup.*

round win·dow ▶ **n.** informal term for *FENESTRA ROTUNDA* (see FENESTRA).

round·worm /'round,wərm/ ▶ **n.** a nematode worm (class Phasmida), esp. a parasitic one found in the intestines of mammals.

roup /ro͞op/ ▶ **n.** an infectious disease of poultry affecting the respiratory tract. — **roup·y adj.** [16th C.: of unknown origin.]

rouse /rouz/ ▶ **v.** [trans.] bring out of sleep; awaken: *she was roused from a deep sleep by a hand on her shoulder.* ■ [intrans.] cease to sleep or to be inactive; wake up. ■ startle out of inactivity; cause to become active: *she'd just stay a few more minutes, then* **rouse herself** *and go back.* ■ startle (game) from a lair or cover. ■ cause to feel angry or excited: *the crowds were* **roused to fever pitch.** ■ cause or give rise to (an emotion or feeling): *his evasiveness roused my curiosity.* — **rous·a·ble adj. rous·er n.** [ME: prob. from Anglo-Norman Fr., referring to a game.]

rous·ing /'rouziNG/ ▶ **adj.** exciting; stirring: *a rousing speech.* — **rous·ing·ly adv.**

Rous·seau¹ /ro͞o'sō/, Henri Julien (1844–1910), French painter; known as **le Douanier** ("customs officer"). He created bold, colorful paintings of fantastic dreams and exotic jungle landscapes.

Rous·seau², Jean-Jacques (1712–78), French philosopher and writer; born in Switzerland. He believed that civilization warps the fundamental goodness of human nature. He wrote *Émile* (1762) and *The Social Contract* (1762).

Rous·seau³, Théodore (1812–67), French painter; full name *Pierre Étienne Théodore Rousseau.* A leading landscapist of the Barbizon School, his works typically depict the forest of Fontainebleau.

roust /roust/ ▶ **v.** [trans.] cause to get up or start moving; rouse: *I rousted him out of his bed.* ■ informal treat roughly; harass. [17th C.: perh. alt. of ROUSE.]

roust·a·bout /'roustə,bout/ ▶ **n.** an unskilled or casual laborer. ■ a laborer on an oil rig. ■ a dock laborer or deckhand. ■ a circus laborer. [19th C.: from ROUST.]

rout¹ /rout/ ▶ **n.** a disorderly retreat of defeated troops: *the retreat degenerated into a rout.* ■ a decisive defeat. ▶ **v.** [trans.] defeat and cause to retreat in disorder: *in a matter of minutes the attackers were routed.*

– PHRASES **put to rout** put to flight; defeat utterly: *I once put a gang to rout.* [ME: ult. based on L. *ruptus* 'broken,' from the v. *rumpere* 'break,' via obs. Fr. *route* and Anglo-Norman Fr. *rute.*]

rout² ▶ **v.** **1** [trans.] cut a groove, or any pattern not extending to the edges, in (a wooden or metal surface). **2** another term for ROOT². ■ find (someone or something), or force them from a place: *Simon routed him from the stable.* [16th C. (sense 2): alt. of the v. ROOT².]

route /ro͞ot; rout/ ▶ **n.** a way or course taken in getting from a starting point to a destination. ■ the line of a road, path, railroad, etc. ■ a circuit traveled in delivering, selling, or collecting goods. ■ a method or process leading to a specified result. ▶ **v.** (**rout·ing**; Brit. also **route·ing**) [trans.] send or direct along a specified course. [ME: from OFr. *rute* 'road,' from L. *rupta (via)* 'broken (way),' fem. past part. of *rumpere.*]

rout·er¹ /'routər/ ▶ **n.** a power tool with a shaped cutter, used in carpentry for making grooves.

rout·er² /'ro͞otər; 'routər/ ▶ **n.** a device that forwards data packets to parts of a computer network.

rou·tine /ro͞o'tēn/ ▶ **n.** a sequence of actions regularly followed; a fixed program: *I settled down into a routine.* ■ a set sequence in a performance such as a dance or comedy act. ■ Comput. a sequence of instructions for performing a task that forms a program or a distinct part of one. ▶ **adj.** performed as part of a regular procedure rather than for a special reason: *a routine annual drill.* ■ monotonous or tedious: *our dull routine existence.* — **rou·tine·ly adv.** [17th C. ('regular course'): from Fr., from *route* 'road' (see ROUTE).]

rou·tin·ize /ro͞o'tē,nīz; 'ro͞otn,īz/ ▶ **v.** [trans.] (usu. **be routinized**) make (something) into a matter of routine; subject to a routing. — **rou·tin·i·za·tion** /-,tēnə'zāsHən; ,ro͞otn-ə-/ **n.**

roux /ro͞o/ ▶ **n.** (pl. same) Cooking a mixture of fat (esp. butter) and flour used in making sauces. [from Fr. *(beurre) roux* 'browned (butter).']

rove¹ /rōv/ ▶ **v.** [intrans., with adverbial of direction] travel constantly without a fixed destination; wander. ■ [trans.] wander over or through (a place) in such a way: *children roving the streets.* ■ [usu. as adj.] (**roving**) travel for one's work, having no fixed base: *he trained as a roving reporter.* ■ (of eyes) look in changing directions in order to see something thoroughly. ▶ **n.** [in sing.] a journey, esp. one with no specific destination; an act of wandering: *a new exhibit will electrify campuses on its national rove.* [15th C. (in archery 'shoot at a casual mark'): perh. from dial. *rave* 'to stray,' prob. of Scand. origin.]

rove² past of REEVE².

rove³ ▶ **n.** a sliver of cotton, wool, or other fiber, drawn out and slightly twisted, esp. preparatory to spinning. ▶ **v.** [trans.] form such into roves. [18th C.: of unknown origin.]

rove⁴ ▶ **n.** a small metal plate or ring for a rivet to pass through and be clenched over, esp. in boatbuilding. [ME: from ON *ró*, with the addition of parasitic *-v-*.]

rove bee·tle ▶ **n.** a long-bodied beetle (family Staphylinidae) with very short wing cases, typically found among decaying matter where it may scavenge or prey on other scavengers.

rov·er¹ /'rōvər/ ▶ **n.** **1** a person who spends their time wandering. **2** (in various sports) a player not restricted to a particular position on the field. **3** a vehicle for driving over rough terrain, esp. one driven by remote control over extraterrestrial terrain. **4** Croquet a ball that has passed all the wickets but not pegged out. ■ a player who has such a ball.

rov·er² ▶ **n.** a person or machine that makes roves of fiber (see ROVE³).

rov·ing /'rōviNG/ ▶ **n.** another term for ROVE³. ■ roves collectively.

rov·ing eye ▶ **n.** [usu. in sing.] a tendency to flirt or be constantly looking to start a new sexual relationship: *if his wife wasn't around, he had a roving eye.*

Ro·vno /'rôvnə/ Russian name for RIVNE.

row¹ /rō/ ▶ **n.** a number of people or things in a more or less straight line: *her villa stood in a row of similar ones.* ■ a line of seats in a theater. ■ a street with a continuous line of houses along one or both of its sides. ■ a horizontal line of entries in a table. ■ a complete line of stitches in knitting or crochet.

– PHRASES **a hard** (or **tough**) **row to hoe** a difficult task. **in a row** forming a line: *four chairs were set in a row.* ■ informal in succession: *we get six days off in a row.* [OE *rāw*, from Gmc.; akin to Ger. *Reihe.*]

row² /rō/ ▶ **v.** [trans.] propel (a boat) with oars: *out in the bay a small figure was rowing a rubber dinghy.* ■ [intrans.] travel by propelling a boat in this way: *we rowed down the river.* ■ convey (a passenger) in a boat by propelling it with oars. ▶ **n.** [in sing.] a period of rowing. — **row·er n.** [OE *rōwan*, of Gmc. origin; rel. to RUDDER; from an Indo-Eur. root shared by L. *remus* 'oar,' Gk. *eretmon* 'oar.']

row³ / rou/ informal, esp. Brit. ▶ **n.** a noisy acrimonious quarrel: *they had a row and she stormed out of the house.* ■ a serious dispute. ■ a loud noise or uproar. ▶ **v.** [intrans.] have a quarrel: *they rowed about who would receive the money from the sale.* [18th C.: of unknown origin.]

row·an /'rōən; 'rouən/ (also **row·an tree**) ▶ **n.** a mountain ash, in particular the European *Sorbus aucuparia.* ■ (also **row·an berry**) the scarlet berry of this tree. [15th C. (Scots, north. Engl.): of Scand. origin; compare Norw. *rogn.*]

row·boat /'rō,bōt/ ▶ **n.** a small boat propelled by oars.

row·dy /'roudē/ ▶ **adj.** (**-di·er**, **-di·est**) noisy and disorderly: *it was a* *rowdy but good-natured crowd.* ▶ **n.** (pl. **-dies**) a noisy and disorderly person. — **row·di·ly** /ˈroudl-ē/ **adv.** **row·di·ness n.** **row·dy·ism** /-ˌizəm/ **n.** [19th C. (US 'lawless backwoodsman') of unknown origin.]

Rowe /rō/, Nicholas (1674–1718), English playwright. He wrote *Tamerlane* (1701).

row·en /ˈrouən/ ▶ **n.** a second growth of grass or hay in one season. [ME: ult. from OFr. *regain* 'an increase.']

row house /rō/ ▶ **n.** any of a row of houses joined by common sidewalls.

row·ing /ˈrō-iNG/ ▶ **n.** the sport or pastime of propelling a boat by means of oars.

row·ing ma·chine ▶ **n.** an exercise machine with a sliding seat, built to exercise the muscles used in rowing.

Rowl·ing /ˈrouliNG/, J.K. (1965–), English writer; full name *Joanne Kathleen Rowling*. Her series of children's books feature the character Harry Potter.

row vec·tor /rō/ ▶ **n.** Math. a vector represented by a matrix consisting of a single row of elements.

Rox·bury /ˈräksˌberē; -bərē/ a district of Boston, Massachusetts.

roy·al /ˈroiəl/ ▶ **adj.** having the status of a king or queen or a member of their family. ■ belonging to or carried out or exercised by a king or queen: *the royal palace.* ■ [attrib.] in the service or under the patronage of a king or queen: *a royal maid.* ▶ **n. 1** informal a member of a royal family, esp. in England. **2** short for ROYAL SAIL or ROYAL MAST. **3** (in full **metric royal**) a paper size, now standardized at 636 × 480 mm. ■ (in full **royal octavo**) a book size, now standardized at 234 × 156 mm. ■ (in full **royal quarto**) a book size, now standardized at 312 × 237 mm.
– PHRASES **royal road to** a way of attaining or reaching something without trouble. — **roy·al·ly adv.** [ME: from OFr. *roial*, from L. *regalis* 'regal.']

Roy·al Air Force (abbr.: **RAF**) the British air force.

roy·al blue ▶ **n.** a deep, vivid blue.

Roy·al Ca·na·di·an Mount·ed Po·lice (abbr.: **RCMP**) the national police force of Canada, founded in 1873. See also MOUNTIE.

roy·al fern ▶ **n.** a large pale green fern (*Osmunda regalis*, family Osmundaceae) that has very long spreading fronds with widely spaced oblong lobes, occurring worldwide in wet habitats.

roy·al flush ▶ **n.** Poker a straight flush including ace, king, queen, jack, and ten all in the same suit, which is the hand of the highest possible value when wild cards are not in use.

Roy·al Gorge (also the **Grand Canyon of the Arkansas**) a steep defile on the Arkansas River in south central Colorado.

roy·al·ist /ˈroiəlist/ ▶ **n.** a person who supports the principle of monarchy or a particular monarchy. ■ **(Royalist)** a supporter of the king against Parliament in the English Civil War. ■ a supporter of the British during the American Revolution; a Tory. ▶ **adj.** giving support to the monarchy. ■ **(Royalist)** (in the English Civil War) supporting the king against Parliament: *the Royalist army.* — **roy·al·ism** /-ˌizəm/ **n.**

roy·al jel·ly ▶ **n.** a substance secreted by honeybee workers and fed by them to larvae that are being raised as potential queen bees.

roy·al mast ▶ **n.** a section of a sailing ship's mast above the topgallant.

Roy·al Na·vy (abbr.: **RN**) the British navy.

Roy·al Oak a city in southeastern Michigan; pop. 65,410.

roy·al palm ▶ **n.** a New World palm (genus *Roystonea*) that is widely cultivated as a roadside tree.

roy·al pur·ple ▶ **n.** a rich deep shade of purple.

roy·al sail ▶ **n.** a sail above a sailing ship's topgallant sail.

Roy·al So·ci·e·ty (in full **Royal Society of London**) the oldest and most prestigious scientific society in Britain. It received its charter from Charles II in 1662.

roy·al·ty /ˈroiəltē/ ▶ **n.** (pl. **-ties**) **1** people of royal blood or status: *diplomats and royalty shared tables at the banquet.* ■ a member of a royal family. ■ the status or power of a king or queen. **2** a sum of money paid to a patentee for the use of a patent or to an author or composer for each copy of a book sold or for each public performance of a work. **3** a royal right (now esp. over minerals) granted by a sovereign to an individual or corporation. ■ a payment made by a producer of minerals, oil, or natural gas to the owner of the site or of the mineral rights over it. [ME: from OFr. *roialte*, from *roial* (see ROYAL).]

roy·al "we" ▶ **n.** the use of "we" instead of "I" by an individual person, as traditionally used by a sovereign.

RP ▶ **abbr.** received pronunciation.

RPG ▶ **abbr.** ■ report program generator, a high-level commercial computer programming language. ■ rocket-propelled grenade. ■ role-playing game.

rpm ▶ **abbr.** ■ resale price maintenance. ■ revolutions per minute.

rps (also **r.p.s.**) ▶ **abbr.** revolutions per second.

rpt ▶ **abbr.** repeat.

RPV ▶ **abbr.** remotely piloted vehicle.

RQ ▶ **abbr.** respiratory quotient.

RR ▶ **abbr.** ■ railroad. ■ rural route.

-rrhea (esp. Brit. **-rrhoea**) ▶ **comb. form** discharge; flow: *diarrhea.* [from Gk. *rhoia* 'flow, flux.']

rRNA ▶ **abbr.** Biochem. ribosomal RNA.

RRR ▶ **abbr.** (of mail) return receipt requested.

RS ▶ **abbr.** ■ (in the US) received standard. ■ (in the UK) Royal Scots.

Rs. ▶ **abbr.** rupee(s).

RSA ▶ **abbr.** ■ Republic of South Africa. ■ Royal Scottish Academy; Royal Scottish Academician.

RSFSR hist. ▶ **abbr.** Russian Soviet Federated Socialist Republic.

RSI ▶ **abbr.** repetitive strain injury.

RSV ▶ **abbr.** Revised Standard Version (of the Bible).

RSVP ▶ **abbr.** répondez s'il vous plaît, or please reply (used at the end of invitations to request a response). [Fr.]

RT ▶ **abbr.** ■ radiotelegraphy. ■ radiotelephony.

rt. ▶ **abbr.** right.

rte. ▶ **abbr.** route.

RTF ▶ **abbr.** rich text format, developed to allow the transfer of graphics and formatted text between different applications and operating systems.

RTFM Comput., informal ▶ **abbr.** read the fucking manual (used esp. in electronic mail in reply to a question whose answer is patently obvious).

Ru ▶ **symb.** the chemical element ruthenium.

RU-486 (also **RU 486**) ▶ **n.** trademark for MIFEPRISTONE.

rub /rəb/ ▶ **v.** (**rubbed, rub·bing**) [trans.] move one's hand or a cloth repeatedly to and fro on the surface of (something) with firm pressure. ■ [trans.] cause (two things) to move to and fro against each other with a certain amount of pressure and friction: ***many insects make noises by rubbing parts of their bodies together.*** ■ [intrans.] move to and fro over something while pressing or grinding against it: ***the ice breaks into small floes that rub against each other.*** ■ [intrans.] (of shoes or other hard items in contact with the skin) cause pain through friction. ■ make dry, clean, or smooth with pressure from a hand, cloth, or other object. ■ [trans.] spread (ointment, polish, etc.) over a surface with repeated movements of one's hand or a cloth: ***she took out her sunblock and rubbed some on her nose.*** ■ (**rub something in/into/through**) work an ingredient into (a mixture) by breaking and blending it with firm movements of one's fingers. ■ reproduce the design of (a gravestone, memorial tablet, etc.) by laying paper on it and rubbing the paper with charcoal, colored chalk, etc. ▶ **n. 1** [usu. in sing.] an act of rubbing: ***she pulled out a towel and gave her head a quick rub.*** ■ an ointment designed to be rubbed on the skin to ease pain: *a muscle rub.* **2** (usu. **the rub**) a difficulty, esp. one of central importance in a situation.
– PHRASES **not have two —— to rub together** informal have none or hardly any of the specified item, esp. money: *she doesn't have two nickels to rub together.* **rub elbows** (or **shoulders**) associate or come into contact (with another person). **rub it in** (or **rub someone's nose in something**) informal emphatically draw someone's attention to an embarrassing or painful fact. **rub noses** rub one's nose against someone else's in greeting (esp. as traditional among Maoris and some other peoples).
– PHRASAL VERBS **rub something down** dry, smooth, or clean something by rubbing. ■ rub the sweat from a horse or one's own body after exercise. **rub off** be transferred by contact or association: ***when parents are having a hard time, their tension can easily rub off on the kids.*** **rub someone out** informal kill someone. [ME (v.): perh. from Low Ger. *rubben*.]

Rub' al Kha·li /ˌro͝ob al ˈkälē; äl ˈKHälē/ a desert in the Arabian peninsula. It is also known as the Great Sandy Desert and the Empty Quarter.

ru·ba·to /ro͞oˈbätō/ Music ▶ **n.** (pl. **-ba·tos** or **-ba·ti** /-ˈbätē/) (also **tem·po ru·ba·to**) the temporary disregarding of strict tempo to allow an expressive quickening or slackening. ▶ **adj.** performed in this way. [Ital., lit. 'robbed.']

rub·ber[1] /ˈrəbər/ ▶ **n.** a tough elastic polymeric substance made from the latex of a tropical plant or synthetically. ■ **(rubbers)** rubber boots; galoshes. ■ Baseball an oblong piece of rubber or similar material embedded in the pitcher's mound, on which the pitcher must keep one foot while delivering the ball. ■ informal a condom. ■ Brit. an eraser for pencil or ink marks. — **rub·ber·i·ness n.** **rub·ber·y adj.** [16th C.: from the v. RUB + -ER[1]; an early use of the substance rubber was to rub out pencil marks.]

rub·ber[2] ▶ **n.** a contest consisting of a series of successive matches (typically three or five) between the same sides or people in tennis, cricket, and other games. ■ (usu. **rubber match** or **rubber game**) a game played to determine the winner of a series. [16th C.: of unknown origin; early use was as a term in lawn bowling.]

rub·ber band ▶ **n.** a loop of stretchy rubber for holding things together.

rub·ber bo·a ▶ **n.** a short snake (*Charina bottae*, family Boidae) with a stout shiny brown body that looks and feels like rubber, found in western North America.

rub·ber ce·ment ▶ **n.** a cement or adhesive containing rubber in a solvent.

rub·ber check ▶ **n.** informal, humorous a check that is returned unpaid. [1920s (orig. US): by association with BOUNCE.]

rub·ber·ize /ˈrəbəˌrīz/ ▶ **v.** [trans.] [usu. as adj.] **(rubberized)** treat or coat (something) with rubber.

rub·ber·neck /ˈrəbərˌnek/ informal ▶ **n.** a person who turns their head to stare foolishly at something. ▶ **v.** [intrans.] stare in such a way: *a passerby rubbernecking at the accident scene.* — **rub·ber·neck·er n.**

rub·ber·oid /ˈrəbəˌroid/ ▶ **adj.** made of or resembling rubber.

rub·ber plant ▶ n. **1** an evergreen tree (*Ficus elastica*) of the mulberry family that has large dark green shiny leaves and is widely cultivated as a houseplant. Native to Southeast Asia, it was formerly grown as a source of rubber. **2** another term for RUBBER TREE.

rub·ber stamp ▶ n. a hand-held device for inking and imprinting a message or design on a surface. ■ fig. a person or organization that approves the decisions of others, not having the power or ability to reject or alter them. ■ an indication of such an approval. ▶ v. (**rub·ber-stamp**) [trans.] approve automatically without proper consideration.

rub·ber tree ▶ n. a tree (*Hevea brasiliensis*) of the spurge family that produces the latex from which rubber is manufactured, native to the Amazonian rain forest and widely cultivated elsewhere. ■ used in names of other trees from which a similar latex can be obtained.

rub·bing /ˈrəbiNG/ ▶ n. **1** the action of rubbing something: *vigorous rubbing could damage the carpet.* **2** an impression of a design on brass or stone, made by rubbing on paper laid over it with pencil, chalk, etc.

rub·bing al·co·hol ▶ n. denatured alcohol, typically perfumed, used as an antiseptic or in massage.

rub·bish /ˈrəbiSH/ ▶ n. waste material; refuse or litter: *an alleyway high with rubbish.* ■ material that is considered unimportant or valueless: *she had to sift through the rubbish in every drawer.* ■ absurd, nonsensical, or worthless talk or ideas. — **rub·bish·y** adj. [ME: from Anglo-Norman Fr. *rubbous*; perh. akin to OFr. *robe* 'spoils.']

rub·ble /ˈrəbəl/ ▶ n. waste or rough fragments of stone, brick, concrete, etc., esp. as the debris from the demolition of buildings. ■ pieces of rough or undressed stone used in building walls, esp. as filling for cavities. — **rub·bly** /ˈrəb(ə)lē/ adj. [ME: perh. ult. from OFr. *robe* 'spoils.']

rub·bled /ˈrəbəld/ ▶ adj. covered in rubble or reduced to rubble.

rub·down /ˈrəbˌdoun/ (also **rub-down**) ▶ n. a massage. ■ an act of drying, smoothing down, or cleaning something by rubbing: *a brisk rubdown with a towel.*

rube /ro͞ob/ ▶ n. informal a country bumpkin. [19th C.: abbrev. of the name *Reuben*.]

ru·bel·la /ro͞oˈbelə/ ▶ n. a contagious viral disease, with symptoms like mild measles. Also called GERMAN MEASLES. [19th C.: mod. L., neut. pl. of L. *rubellus* 'reddish.']

ru·bel·lite /ˈro͞obəˌlīt/ ▶ n. a red variety of tourmaline. [18th C.: from L. *rubellus* 'reddish.']

Ru·bens /ˈro͞obənz/, Sir Peter Paul (1577–1640), Flemish painter. He is best known for his portraits and for his paintings of mythological subjects.

ru·be·o·la /ˌro͞obēˈōlə/ ▶ n. medical term for MEASLES. [17th C.: from med. L., dimin. of L. *rubeus* 'red.']

ru·bes·cent /ro͞oˈbesənt/ ▶ adj. esp. literary reddening; blushing. [18th C.: from L. *rubescent-* 'reddening,' from the v. *rubescere*, from *ruber* 'red.']

Ru·bi·con /ˈro͞obəˌkänˌ/ a stream in northeastern Italy that marked the ancient boundary between Italy and Cisalpine Gaul. ■ [as n.] a point of no return: *on the way to political union we are now **crossing the Rubicon**.*

ru·bi·cund /ˈro͞obəˌkənd/ ▶ adj. (esp. of someone's face) having a ruddy complexion; high-colored. — **ru·bi·cun·di·ty** /ˌro͞obəˈkəndətē/ n. [ME ('red'): from L. *rubicundus*, from *rubere* 'be red.']

ru·bid·i·um /ro͞oˈbidēəm/ ▶ n. the chemical element of atomic number 37, a rare soft silvery reactive metal of the alkali metal group. (Symbol: **Rb**) [19th C.: mod. L., from L. *rubidus* 'red' (from its spectral lines).]

ru·bid·i·um–stron·ti·um dat·ing ▶ n. Geol. a method of dating rocks from the relative proportions of rubidium-87 and its decay product, strontium-87.

ru·big·i·nous /ro͞oˈbijənəs/ ▶ adj. tech. literary rust-colored. [17th C.: from L. *rubigo, rubigin-* 'rust.']

Ru·bik's Cube /ˈro͞obiks/ ▶ n. trademark a puzzle in the form of a plastic cube covered with multicolored squares, which the player attempts to twist and turn so that all the squares on each face are of the same color. [1980s: Erno *Rubik* (1944–), Hungarian inventor.]

Ru·bin·stein /ˈro͞obənˌstīn/, Artur (1888–1982), US pianist; born in Poland. Among his many recordings are the complete works of Chopin.

ru·ble /ˈro͞obəl/ (also **rou·ble**) ▶ n. the basic monetary unit of Russia and some other former republics of the USSR, equal to 100 kopeks. [via Fr. from Russ. *rubl'*.]

ru·bric /ˈro͞obrik/ ▶ n. a heading on a document. ■ a direction in a liturgical book as to how a church service should be conducted. ■ a statement of purpose or function. ■ a category: *party policies on matters falling **under the rubric of** law and order.* — **ru·bri·cal** adj. [ME *rubrish* (orig. referring to text written in red for distinctiveness), from OFr. *rubriche*, from L. *rubrica (terra)* 'red (earth or ocher as writing material).']

Ru·by /ˈro͞obē/, Jack (1911–67), US assassin; born *Jack Rubenstein*. On November 24, 1963, he shot and killed Lee Harvey Oswald, the man accused of murdering President Kennedy.

ru·by /ˈro͞obē/ ▶ n. (pl. **-bies**) a precious stone consisting of corundum in various shades of red. ■ an intense purplish-red color. [ME: from OFr. *rubi*, from med. L. *rubinus*, from the base of L. *rubeus* 'red.']

Ru·by Moun·tains a range in northeastern Nevada.

ru·by port ▶ n. a deep red port, esp. one matured in wood for only a few years and then fined.

ru·by wed·ding (also **ruby wed·ding an·ni·ver·sa·ry**) ▶ n. the fortieth anniversary of a wedding.

ruche /ro͞oSH/ ▶ n. a frill or pleat of fabric as decoration on a garment or home furnishing. — **ruched** adj. **ruch·ing** n. [19th C.: from Fr., from med. L. *rusca* 'tree bark,' of Celtic origin.]

ruck[1] /rək/ ▶ n. a tightly packed crowd of people. ■ (**the ruck**) the mass of ordinary people or things: *education was the key to success, a way out of the ruck.* [ME ('stack of fuel'): prob. of Scand. origin; cf. Norw. *ruke* 'heap of hay.']

ruck[2] ▶ v. [trans.] compress or move (cloth or clothing) so that it forms a number of untidy folds or creases. ■ [intrans.] (of cloth or clothing) form such folds or creases: *Eleanor's dress rucked up at the front.* ▶ n. a crease or wrinkle. [18th C. (n.): from ON *hrukka*.]

Ruck·ey·ser /ˈro͞oˌkīzər/, Muriel (1913–80), US poet and political activist. Her poems reflect her liberal political activism.

ruck·sack /ˈrəkˌsak; ˈro͝ok-/ ▶ n. a bag with shoulder straps that allow it to be carried on someone's back. [19th C.: from Ger., from *rucken* (dial. var. of *Rücken* 'back') + *Sack* 'bag.']

ruck·us /ˈrəkəs/ ▶ n. a disturbance or commotion. [19th C.: perh. akin to RUCTION, RUMPUS.]

ru·co·la /ˈro͞okələ/ ▶ n. another term for ARUGULA.

ruc·tion /ˈrəkSHən/ ▶ n. informal a disturbance or quarrel. ■ (**ructions**) unpleasant reactions to or complaints about something. [19th C.: of unknown origin.]

ru·da·ceous /ˈro͞oˈdāSHəs/ ▶ adj. Geol. (of rock) composed of fragments larger than sand grains. [20th C.: from L. *rudus* 'rubble.']

rud·beck·i·a /ro͞odˈbekēə; ˌrəd-/ ▶ n. a North American plant (genus *Rudbeckia*) of the daisy family, with yellow or orange flowers and a dark conelike center. [mod. L., after Olaf *Rudbeck* (1660–1740), Swedish botanist.]

rudd /rəd/ ▶ n. (pl. same) a freshwater fish (*Scardinius erythrophthalmus*) of the minnow family with a silvery body and red fins. Native to Eurasia, it has isolated populations in the northeastern US. [16th C.: prob. akin to archaic *rud* 'red color.']

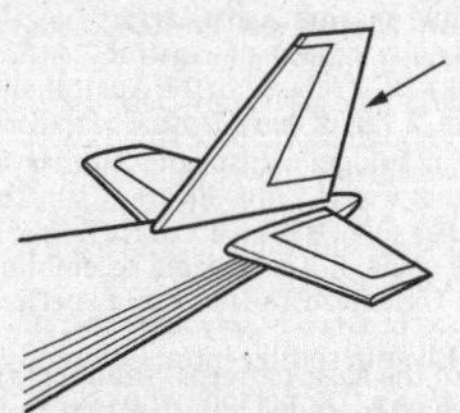

aircraft rudder

rud·der /ˈrədər/ ▶ n. a flat piece hinged vertically near the stern of a boat or ship for steering. ■ a vertical airfoil pivoted from the horizontal stabilizer of an aircraft. ■ application of a rudder in steering a boat, ship, or aircraft. [OE *rōther* 'paddle,' from West Gmc.; akin to Ger. *Ruder*, ROW[2], v.]

rud·der·less /ˈrədərləs/ ▶ adj. lacking a rudder. ■ lacking a clear sense of one's aims or principles.

rud·dy /ˈrədē/ ▶ adj. (**-di·er, -di·est**) (of a person's face) having a healthy red color. ■ having a reddish color: *the ruddy evening light.* ▶ v. (**-dies, -died**) [trans.] make ruddy in color: *a red flash ruddied the belly of a cloud.* — **rud·di·ly** /ˈrədl-ē/ adv. (rare) **rud·di·ness** n. [OE *rudig*, from the base of archaic *rud* 'red color'; akin to RED.]

rud·dy duck ▶ n. a stiff-tailed, broad-billed duck (*Oxyura jamaicensis*) of the New World, the male having mainly deep red-brown plumage and white cheeks.

rude /ro͞od/ ▶ adj. **1** offensively impolite or ill-mannered: *she had **been rude to** her boss.* ■ referring to a taboo subject such as sex in a way considered improper and offensive: *he made a rude gesture.* ■ [attrib.] having a startling abruptness: *the war came as a very **rude awakening**.* **2** roughly made or done; lacking subtlety or sophistication: *a rude coffin.* ■ archaic ignorant and uneducated: *the new religion was first promulgated by rude men.* — **rude·ly** adv. **rude·ness** n. [ME (sense 2): ult. from L. *rudis* 'unwrought'; prob. akin to *rudus* 'broken stone.']

ru·der·al /ˈro͞odərəl/ Bot. ▶ adj. (of a plant) growing on waste ground or among refuse. ▶ n. a plant growing on waste ground or among refuse. [19th C.: from mod. L. *ruderalis*, from L. *rudera*, pl. of *rudus* 'rubble.']

ru·di·ment /ˈro͞odəmənt/ ▶ n. **1** (**the rudiments of**) the first principles of a subject. ■ an elementary or primitive form of something. **2** Biol. an undeveloped or immature part or organ, esp. a structure in an embryo or larva. **3** Music a basic pattern used by drummers. [16th C.: ult. from L. *rudimentum*, from *rudis* 'unwrought.']

ru·di·men·ta·ry /ˌro͞odəˈment(ə)rē/ ▶ adj. involving or limited to basic principles. ■ immature, undeveloped, or basic. — **ru·di·men·ta·ri·ly** /-menˈte(ə)rəlē; -ˈment(ə)rəlē/ adv. **ru·di·men·ta·ri·ness** n.

ru·dist /ˈro͞odist/ (also **ru·dis·tid** /ˈro͞odistid/) ▶ n. a cone-shaped extinct bivalve mollusk (superfamily Rudistacea, order Hippuritoida) that formed colonies resembling reefs in the Cretaceous period. [19th C.: from mod. L. *Rudista*, from L. *rudis* 'rude.']

Ru·dolf, Lake /ˈro͞odälf/ former name (until 1979) for Lake Turkana (see **TURKANA, LAKE**).

Ru·dolph /ˈro͞odôlf; -dälf/, Wilma Glodean (1940–94), US track and field athlete. She was the first woman to win three track and field gold medals in one Olympics (1960).

Ru·dra /ˈro͝odrə/ Hinduism **1** (in the Rig Veda) a Vedic minor god, associated with the storm. **2** one of the names of **SHIVA**.

rue[1] /ro͞o/ ▶ **v.** (**rues, rued, ru·ing** or **rue·ing**) [trans.] bitterly regret (something) and wish it undone: *Christine rued the day she met them.* [OE *hrēow* 'repentance,' *hrēowan* 'affect with contrition,' from Gmc.; akin to Ger. *Reue* 'remorse.']

rue[2] ▶ **n.** a perennial evergreen shrub (*Ruta graveolens*, family Rutaceae) with bitter strong-scented lobed leaves that are used in herbal medicine. ■ used in names of other plants that resemble rue, esp. in leaf shape, e.g., **goat's-rue**. [ME: from OFr., via L. from Gk. *rhutē*.]

rue·ful /ˈro͞ofəl/ ▶ **adj.** expressing sorrow or regret. — **rue·ful·ly adv. rue·ful·ness n.**

ru·fes·cent /ro͞oˈfesənt/ ▶ **adj.** tinged with red. — **ru·fes·cence n.** [19th C.: from L. *rufescent-* 'becoming reddish,' from the v. *rufescere*, from *rufus* 'reddish.']

ruff[1] /rəf/ ▶ **n.** **1** a projecting starched frill worn around the neck. **2** a projecting or conspicuously colored ring of feathers or hair around the neck of a bird or mammal. **3** (pl. same or **ruffs**) a northern Eurasian wading bird (*Philomachus pugnax*) of the sandpiper family, the male of which has a large variously colored ruff and ear tufts in the breeding season, used in display. The female is called a **reeve**. — **ruffed adj.** [16th C.: prob. from **ROUGH**.]

ruff[1] 1

ruff[2] ▶ **n.** **1** an edible marine fish (*Arripis georgianus*, family Arripidae) of Australian inshore waters that is related to the Australian salmon. Also called **ROUGHY** in Australia. **2** var. of **RUFFE**. [19th C.: from **RUFFE**.]

ruff[3] ▶ **v.** [intrans.] (in bridge, whist, and similar card games) play a trump in a trick that was led in a different suit. ■ [trans.] play a trump on (a card in another suit). ▶ **n.** an act of ruffing or opportunity to ruff. [16th C. (orig. the name of a card game resembling whist): from OFr. *rouffle*, a parallel formation to Ital. *ronfa* (perh. an alt. of *trionfo* 'a trump').]

ruff[4] ▶ **n.** Music one of the basic patterns (rudiments) of drumming, consisting of a single note preceded by either two grace notes played with the other stick (**double-stroke ruff** or **drag**) or three grace notes played with alternating sticks (**four-stroke ruff**). [17th C.: prob. imitative.]

ruffe /rəf/ (also **ruff**) ▶ **n.** a freshwater fish (*Gymnocephalus cernua*) of the perch family, with a greenish-brown back and yellow sides and underparts. Native to Eurasia, it has been introduced into Lakes Michigan and Superior. [ME: prob. from a var. of **ROUGH**.]

ruffed grouse ▶ **n.** a North American woodland grouse (*Bonasa umbellus*) that has a black ruff on the sides of the neck.

ruffed le·mur ▶ **n.** a lemur (*Varecia variegata*, family Lemuridae) with a prominent muzzle and dense fur that forms a ruff around the neck, living in the Madagascan rain forest.

ruf·fi·an /ˈrəfēən/ ▶ **n.** a violent person, esp. one involved in crime. — **ruf·fi·an·ism** /-ˌnizəm/ **n. ruf·fi·an·ly adv.** [15th C.: from OFr. *ruffian*, from Ital. *ruffiano*, perh. from dial. *rofia* 'scab, scurf,' of Gmc. origin.]

ruf·fle /ˈrəfəl/ ▶ **v.** [trans.] **1** disorder or disarrange (someone's hair), typically by running one's hands through it: *he ruffled her hair affectionately.* ■ (of a bird) erect (its feathers) in anger or display: *on his departure to the high wires, the starling ruffled his feathers and flirted his wings.* ■ disturb the smoothness or tranquility of: *the evening breeze ruffled the surface of the pond in the yard.* ■ disconcert or upset the composure of (someone): *Brian had been ruffled by her questions.* **2** [usu. as adj.] (**ruffled**) ornament with or gather into a frill: *a blouse with a high ruffled neck.* ▶ **n.** **1** an ornamental gathered or goffered frill of lace or other cloth on a garment, esp. around the wrist or neck. **2** a vibrating drumbeat.

– PHRASES **ruffle someone's feathers** cause someone to become annoyed or upset: *tampering with the traditional approach would ruffle a few feathers.* **smooth someone's ruffled feathers** make someone less angry or irritated by using soothing words. [ME (as a v.): of unknown origin. Current n. senses date from the late 17th C.]

ru·fi·yaa /ˈro͞ofēˌyä/ ▶ **n.** (pl. same) the basic monetary unit of the Maldives, equal to 100 laris. [Maldivian.]

ru·fous /ˈro͞ofəs/ ▶ **adj.** reddish brown in color. ▶ **n.** a reddish-brown color. [18th C.: from L. *rufus* 'red, reddish' + **-OUS**.]

rug /rəg/ ▶ **n.** a floor covering of shaggy or woven material, typically not extending over the entire floor. ■ a small carpet woven in a pattern of colors, typically by hand in a traditional style: *Navajo patterned rugs.* ■ esp. Brit. a thick woolen coverlet or wrap, used esp. when traveling. ■ informal a toupee or wig.

– PHRASES **pull the rug (out) from under someone** abruptly withdraw support (from someone): *the rug was pulled right out from beneath our feet.* [16th C. (denoting a type of coarse woolen cloth): prob. of Scand. origin; rel. to **RAG[1]**.]

rug·by /ˈrəgbē/ (also **rugby football**) ▶ **n.** a team game played with an oval ball that may be kicked, carried, and passed from hand to hand. Points are scored by grounding the ball behind the opponents' goal line (thereby scoring a try) or by kicking it between the two posts and over the crossbar of the opponents' goal. See also **RUGBY LEAGUE** and **RUGBY UNION**. [19th C.: named after *Rugby* School, where the game was first played.]

rug·by league ▶ **n.** a form of rugby played in teams of thirteen, originally by a group of northern English clubs that separated from rugby union in 1895. Besides having somewhat different rules, the game differed from rugby union in always allowing professionalism.

rug·by un·ion ▶ **n.** a form of rugby played in teams of fifteen. Unlike rugby league, the game was originally strictly amateur, being opened to professionalism only in 1995.

rug·e·lach /ˈrəgələкн/ (also **rug·a·lach**) ▶ **n.** a bite-size cookie made with cream-cheese dough rolled around a filling of nuts, poppy seed paste, chocolate, or jam. [Yiddish, literally 'little twists.']

rug·ged /ˈrəgid/ ▶ **adj.** (of ground or terrain) having a broken, rocky, and uneven surface: *a rugged coastline.* ■ (of a machine or other manufactured object) strongly made and capable of withstanding rough handling: *the binoculars are compact, lightweight, and rugged.* ■ having or requiring toughness and determination: *a week of rugged, demanding adventure at an outdoor training center.* ■ (of a man's face or looks) having attractively strong, rough-hewn features: *he was known for his rugged good looks.* — **rug·ged·ly adv. rug·ged·ness n.** [ME (in the sense 'shaggy,' also (of a horse) 'rough-coated'): prob. of Scand. origin; cf. Swed. *rugga* 'roughen,' also with **RUG**.]

rug·ged·ized /ˈrəgidˌīzd/ ▶ **adj.** designed or improved to be hard-wearing or shock-resistant: *ruggedized computers suitable for use on the battlefield.* — **rug·ged·i·za·tion** /ˌrəgidəˈzāsʜən/ **n.**

rug·ger /ˈrəgər/ ▶ **n.** Brit., informal rugby.

ru·go·la /ˈro͞ogələ/ ▶ **n.** another term for **ARUGULA**.

ru·go·sa /ro͞oˈgōsə; -zə/ (also **ru·go·sa rose**) ▶ **n.** a widely cultivated Southeast Asian rose (*Rosa rugosa*) with dark green wrinkled leaves and deep pink flowers. [19th C.: fem. of L. *rugosus* (see **RUGOSE**), used as a specific epithet.]

ru·gose /ˈro͞oˌgōs/ ▶ **adj.** esp. Biol. wrinkled; corrugated: *rugose corals.* — **ru·gos·i·ty** /ro͞oˈgäsətē/ **n.** [ME: from L. *rugosus*, from *ruga* 'wrinkle.']

rug rat (also **rug·rat**) ▶ **n.** informal a child.

Ruhr /ro͝or/ a region of coal mining and heavy industry in North Rhine-Westphalia, in western Germany. It is named after the Ruhr River, which flows through it and meets the Rhine River near Duisburg. The Ruhr was occupied by French troops 1923–24, after Germany defaulted on war reparation payments.

ru·in /ˈro͞oin/ ▶ **n.** the physical destruction or disintegration of something or the state of disintegrating or being destroyed: *a large white house falling into gentle ruin.* ■ the remains of a building, typically an old one, that has suffered much damage or disintegration: *the ruins of the castle* | *the church is a ruin now.* ■ the disastrous disintegration of someone's life: *the ruin and heartbreak wrought by alcohol, divorce, and violence.* ■ the cause of such disintegration: *they don't know how to say no, and that's been their ruin.* ■ the complete loss of one's money and other assets: *the financial cost could mean ruin.* ▶ **v.** **1** [trans.] reduce (a building or place) to a state of decay, collapse, or disintegration: [as adj.] (**ruined**) *a ruined castle.* ■ cause great and usually irreparable damage or harm to; have a disastrous effect on: *a noisy freeway has ruined village life.* ■ reduce to a state of poverty: *they were ruined by the highest interest rates this century.* **2** [intrans.] literary fall headlong or with a crash: *carriages go ruining over the brink from time to time.*

– PHRASES **in ruins** in a state of complete disorder or disintegration: *the economy was in ruins.* [ME (in the sense 'collapse of a building'): from OFr. *ruine*, from L. *ruina*, from *ruere* 'to fall.']

ru·in·a·tion /ˌro͞oəˈnāsʜən/ ▶ **n.** the action or fact of ruining someone or something or of being ruined: *commercial malpractice causes the ruination of thousands of people.* ■ the state of being ruined: *the headquarters fell into ruination.* [17th C.: from obs. *ruinate* + **-ION**.]

ru·in·ous /ˈro͞oənəs/ ▶ **adj.** **1** disastrous or destructive: *a ruinous effect on the environment.* ■ costing far more than can be afforded: *the cost of their ransom might be ruinous.* **2** in ruins; dilapidated: *the castle is ruinous.* — **ru·in·ous·ly adv. ru·in·ous·ness n.** [ME (also in the sense 'falling down'): from L. *ruinosus*, from *ruina* (see **RUIN**).]

Ruis·dael /ˈroisˌdäl/ (also **Ruys·dael**), Jacob van (*c.*1628–82), Dutch landscape painter.

Ru·iz de A·lar·cón y Men·do·za /ro͞oˈēs dä ˌälärˈkōn ē menˈdōsə/, Juan (1580–1639), Spanish playwright, born in Mexico City.

Ruk·ey·ser /ˈro͞oˌkīzər/, Louis (1933–), US economic forecaster and commentator. He hosts the television program "Wall Street Week" (1970–). He also publishes two economic newsletters that he began in 1992 and in 1994.

Rukh /ro͞oкн/ the nationalist movement that established the independence of the Ukraine in 1991. [Ukrainian, 'people's movement.']

rukh /ro͞ok/ ▶ **n.** another term for **ROC**. [from Hindi *rūkh*.]

rule /ro͞ol/ ▶ **n.** **1** one of a set of explicit or understood regulations or principles governing conduct within a particular activity or sphere: *the rules of the game were understood.* ■ a law or principle that operates within a particular sphere of knowledge, describing or prescribing what is possible or allowable: *the rules of grammar.* ■ a code of practice and discipline for a religious order or community: *the Rule of St. Benedict.* ■ control of or dominion over an area or people: *the* *revolution brought an end to British rule.* ■ (**the rule**) the normal or customary state of things: *such accidents are the exception rather than the rule.* **2** a strip of wood or other rigid material used for measuring length or marking straight lines; a ruler. ■ a thin printed line or dash, generally used to separate headings, columns, or sections of text. ■ Law an order made by a judge or court with reference to a particular case only. ▶ **v. 1** [trans.] exercise ultimate power or authority over (an area and its people): *Latin America today is ruled by elected politicians* | [intrans.] *the period in which Spain ruled over Portugal.* ■ (of a feeling) have a powerful and restricting influence on (a person's life): *her whole life seemed to be ruled by fear.* ■ [intrans.] be a dominant or powerful factor or force: [with complement] *the black market rules supreme.* ■ [with clause] pronounce authoritatively and legally to be the case: *a federal court ruled that he was unfairly dismissed from his job.* ■ Astrol. (of a planet) have a particular influence over (a sign of the zodiac, house, aspect of life, etc.). **2** [trans.] make parallel lines across (paper): [as adj.] (**ruled**) *a sheet of ruled paper.* ■ make (a straight line) on paper with a ruler.

– PHRASES **as a rule** usually, but not always. **make it a rule to do something** have it as a habit or general principle to do something: *I make it a rule never to mix business with pleasure.* **rule of law** the restriction of the arbitrary exercise of power by subordinating it to well-defined and established laws. **rule of thumb** a broadly accurate guide or principle, based on experience or practice rather than theory. **rule the roost** be in complete control.

– PHRASAL VERBS **rule something out** (or **in**) exclude (or include) something as a possibility: *the doctor ruled out appendicitis.* — **rule·less** **adj.** [ME: from OFr. *reule* (n.), *reuler* (v.), from late L. *regulare*, from L. *regula* 'straight stick.']

rule of en·gage·ment (abbr.: **ROE**) ▶ **n.** (usu. **rules of engagement**) a directive issued by a military authority specifying the circumstances and limitations under which forces will engage in combat with the enemy.

rule of the road ▶ **n.** (usu. **rules of the road**) a custom or law regulating the direction in which two vehicles (or riders or ships) should move to pass one another on meeting, or which should yield to the other, so as to avoid collision.

rule of three ▶ **n.** Math., dated a method of finding a number in the same ratio to a given number as exists between two other given numbers.

rul·er /ˈro͞olər/ ▶ **n. 1** a person exercising government or dominion. ■ Astrol. another term for RULING PLANET. **2** a straight strip or cylinder of plastic, wood, metal, or other rigid material, typically marked at regular intervals, to draw straight lines or measure distances. — **rul·er·ship** /-ˌSHip/ **n.**

Rules Com·mit·tee ▶ **n.** a legislative committee responsible for expediting the passage of bills. ■ (**rules committee**) the body of people charged with overseeing the rules of an athletic league.

rul·ing /ˈro͞oliNG/ ▶ **n.** an authoritative decision or pronouncement, esp. one made by a judge. ▶ **adj.** currently exercising authority or influence: *the ruling coalition.*

rul·ing eld·er ▶ **n.** a nominated or elected lay official of any of various Christian churches, esp. of a Presbyterian church.

rul·ing pas·sion ▶ **n.** an interest or concern that occupies a large part of someone's time and effort: *football remained their ruling passion.*

rul·ing plan·et ▶ **n.** Astrol. a planet that is held to have a particular influence over a specific sign of the zodiac, house, aspect of life, etc.

rum[1] /rəm/ ▶ **n.** an alcoholic liquor distilled from sugar-cane residues or molasses. ■ intoxicating liquor. [17th C.: perh. an abbrev. of obs. *rumbullion*, in the same sense.]

rum[2] ▶ **adj.** (**rum·mer, rum·mest**) Brit., informal dated odd; peculiar: *it's a rum business, certainly.* — **rum·ly adv. rum·ness n.** [18th C.: of unknown origin.]

Ru·ma·ni·an /ro͞oˈmānēən; -ˈmānyən/ ▶ **adj. & n.** var. of ROMANIAN.

rum·ba /ˈrəmbə; ˈro͝om-; ˈro͞om-/ (also **rhum·ba**) ▶ **n.** a rhythmic dance with Spanish and African elements, originating in Cuba. ■ a piece of music for this dance or in a similar style. ■ a ballroom dance imitative of this dance. ▶ **v.** (**-bas, -baed** /-bəd/, **-ba·ing**) [intrans.] dance the rumba. [1920s: from L. Amer. Sp.]

rum ba·ba /ˈrəm ˈbäbə/ ▶ **n.** see BABA[1].

rum·ble /ˈrəmbəl/ ▶ **v. 1** [intrans.] make a continuous deep, resonant sound: *thunder rumbled, lightning flickered.* ■ [with adverbial of direction] (esp. of a large vehicle) move in the specified direction with such a sound: *heavy trucks rumbled through the streets.* ■ [trans.] utter in a deep, resonant voice: *the man's low voice rumbled an instruction.* ■ (of a person's stomach) make a deep, resonant sound due to hunger. **2** [intrans.] informal take part in a street fight between gangs or large groups: *the five of them rumbled with the men in the other car.* **3** [trans.] Brit., informal discover (an illicit activity or its perpetrator): *it wouldn't need a genius to rumble my little game.* ▶ **n. 1** a continuous deep, resonant sound like distant thunder: *the steady rumble of traffic* | fig. *rumbles of discontent.* **2** informal a street fight between gangs or large groups. [ME: prob. from MDu. *rommelen, rummelen*, of imitative origin. Sense 3 of the **v.** may be a different word.]

rum·bler /ˈrəmb(ə)lər/ ▶ **n.** a person or thing that rumbles. ■ a machine for peeling potatoes. ■ hist. a round bell containing a small hard object placed inside to rattle, formerly used esp. on horses' harnesses.

rum·ble seat ▶ **n.** an uncovered folding seat in the rear of an automobile.

rum·ble strip ▶ **n.** a series of raised strips across a road or along its edge, changing the noise a vehicle's tires make on the surface and so warning drivers of speed restrictions or of the edge of the road.

rum·bling /ˈrəmb(ə)liNG/ ▶ **n.** a continuous deep, resonant sound: *the rumbling of wheels in the distance.* ■ (often **rumblings**) an early indication or rumor of dissatisfaction or incipient change: *there are growing rumblings of discontent.* ▶ **adj.** making or constituting a deep resonant sound: *a rumbling ancient air conditioner* | *a rumbling noise.*

rum·bus·tious /ˌrəmˈbəsCHəs/ ▶ **adj.** informal, esp. Brit. boisterous or unruly. — **rum·bus·tious·ly adv. rum·bus·tious·ness n.** [18th C.: prob. an alt. of archaic *robustious* 'boisterous, robust.']

rum·dum /ˈrəmˌdəm/ ▶ **n.** informal a drunkard, esp. a derelict alcoholic. [19th C.: from RUM[1] + DUMB.]

ru·men /ˈro͞omən/ ▶ **n.** (pl. **-mens** or **-mi·na** /-mənə/) Zool. the first stomach of a ruminant, which receives food or cud from the esophagus, partly digests it with the aid of bacteria, and passes it to the reticulum. [18th C.: from L., lit. 'throat.']

ru·mi·nant /ˈro͞omənənt/ ▶ **n. 1** an even-toed ungulate mammal (suborder Ruminantia, order Artiodactyla) that chews the cud regurgitated from its rumen. The ruminants comprise the cattle, sheep, antelopes, deer, giraffes, and their relatives. **2** a contemplative person; a person given to meditation. ▶ **adj.** of or belonging to ruminants. [17th C.: from L. *ruminant-* 'chewing over again,' from the v. *ruminari*, from *rumen* 'throat' (see RUMEN).]

ru·mi·nate /ˈro͞oməˌnāt/ ▶ **v.** [intrans.] **1** think deeply about something: *we sat **ruminating on** the nature of existence.* **2** (of a ruminant) chew the cud. — **ru·mi·na·tion** /ˌro͞oməˈnāSHən/ **n. ru·mi·na·tive** /-ˌnātiv/ **adj. ru·mi·na·tive·ly** /-ˌnātivlē/ **adv. ru·mi·na·tor** /-ˌnātər/ **n.** [16th C.: from L. *ruminat-* 'chewed over,' from the v. *ruminari.*]

rum·mage /ˈrəmij/ ▶ **v.** [intrans.] search unsystematically and untidily through a mass or receptacle: *he rummaged in his pocket for a handkerchief* | [trans.] *he rummaged the drawer for his false teeth.* ■ [trans.] find (something) by searching in this way: *Mick **rummaged up** his skateboard.* ■ [trans.] (of a customs officer) make a thorough search of (a vessel): *our brief was to rummage as many of the vessels as possible.* ▶ **n.** an unsystematic and untidy search through a mass or receptacle. ■ a thorough search of a vessel by a customs officer. — **rum·mag·er n.** [15th C.: from OFr. *arrumage*, from *arrumer* 'stow (in a hold),' from MDu. *ruim* 'room'; in early use the word referred to the arranging of items in the hold of a ship.]

rum·mage sale ▶ **n.** a sale of miscellaneous secondhand articles, typically held in order to raise money for a charity or a special event.

rum·mer /ˈrəmər/ ▶ **n.** a large drinking glass. [17th C.: of Low Dutch origin; rel. to Du. *roemer*; the original meaning is perh. 'Roman glass.']

rum·my[1] /ˈrəmē/ ▶ **n.** a card game, sometimes played with two decks, in which the players try to form sets and sequences of cards. [20th C.: of unknown origin.]

rum·my[2] ▶ **adj.** (**-mi·er, -mi·est**) another term for RUM[2].

ru·mor /ˈro͞omər/ (Brit. **ru·mour**) ▶ **n.** a currently circulating story or report of uncertain or doubtful truth: *they were investigating rumors of a massacre* | ***rumor has it that** he will take a year off.* ▶ **v.** (**be rumored**) be circulated as an unverified account: [with clause] ***it's rumored that** he lives on a houseboat* | [with infin.] *she is rumored to have gone into hiding.* [ME: from OFr. *rumur*, from L. *rumor* 'noise.']

ru·mor·mon·ger /ˈro͞omərˌmäNGgər; -ˌməNGgər/ ▶ **n.** derog. a person who spreads rumors. — **ru·mor·mon·ger·ing n.**

rump /rəmp/ ▶ **n. 1** the hind part of the body of a mammal or the lower back of a bird. ■ esp. humorous a person's buttocks. **2** a small or unimportant remnant of something originally larger: *once the profitable enterprises have been sold the unprofitable rump will be left.* — **rump·less adj.** [ME: prob. of Scand. origin; cf. Dan. and Norw. *rumpe* 'backside.']

rum·ple /ˈrəmpəl/ ▶ **v.** [trans.] [usu. as adj.] (**rumpled**) give a creased, ruffled, or disheveled appearance to: *a rumpled bed.* ▶ **n.** [in sing.] an untidy state. — **rum·ply** /ˈrəmp(ə)lē/ **adj.** [16th C. (as a n. in the sense 'wrinkle'): from MDu. *rompel.*]

rum·pot /ˈrəmˌpät/ ▶ **n.** informal an alcoholic.

Rump Par·lia·ment the part of the Long Parliament in England that continued to sit after the forced exclusion of Presbyterian members in 1648. It voted for the trial that resulted in the execution of Charles I. [origin uncert.: said to derive from *The Bloody Rump*, the name of a paper written before the trial, the word being popularized after a speech by Major General Brown, given at a public assembly; also said to have been coined by Clem Walker in his *History of Independency* (1648), as a term for those strenuously opposing the king.]

rump·sprung /ˈrəmpˌsprəNG/ ▶ **adj.** informal (of furniture) baggy and worn in the seat: *a rumpsprung armchair.*

rump steak ▶ **n.** a cut of beef from the animal's rump.

rum·pus /ˈrəmpəs/ ▶ **n.** (pl. **-pus·es**) [usu. in sing.] informal a noisy disturbance; a commotion: *he caused a rumpus with his flair for troublemaking.* [18th C.: prob. fanciful.]

rum·pus room ▶ **n.** a room, typically in the basement of a house, used for games and recreation.

Rums·feld /ˈrəmzˌfeld/, Donald Henry (1932–), US secretary of defense

1975–77, 2001–06. His 2006 resignation followed much criticism regarding the orchestration of the War in Iraq.

run /rən/ ▶v. (**run•ning**; past **ran** /ran/; past part. **run**) **1** [intrans.] move at a speed faster than a walk, never having both or all the feet on the ground at the same time: *the dog ran across the road* | *she ran the last few yards* | *he hasn't paid for his drinks—run and catch him.* ■ run as a sport or for exercise: *I run every morning.* ■ (of an athlete or a racehorse) compete in a race: *she ran in the 200 meters.* | [trans.] *Dave has run 42 marathons.* ■ [trans.] enter (a racehorse) for a race. ■ Baseball (of a batter or base runner) attempt to advance to the next base. ■ (of hounds) chase or hunt their quarry. ■ (of a boat) sail directly before the wind, esp. in bad weather. ■ (of a migratory fish) go upriver from the sea in order to spawn. **2** [intrans.] move about in a hurried and hectic way: *I've spent the whole day running around.* ■ (**run to**) have rapid recourse to (someone) for support or help: *don't come running to me for a handout.* **3** pass or cause to pass quickly or smoothly in a particular direction: [no obj., with adverbial of direction] *the rumor ran through the pack of photographers* | [with obj. and adverbial of direction] *Helen ran her fingers through her hair.* ■ move or cause to move somewhere forcefully or with a particular result: [no obj., with adverbial of direction] *the tanker **ran aground** off the Aleutian Islands* | [with obj. and adverbial of direction] *a woman ran a stroller into the back of my legs.* ■ [trans.] informal fail to stop at (a red traffic light). ■ [trans.] navigate (rapids or a waterfall) in a boat. ■ extend or cause to extend in a particular direction: [no obj., with adverbial of direction] *cobbled streets run down to a tiny harbor* | [with obj. and adverbial of direction] *he ran a wire under the carpet.* ■ [intrans.] (**run in**) (of a quality or trait) be common or inherent in members of (a particular family), esp. over several generations: *weight problems run in my family.* ■ [intrans.] pass into or reach a specified state or level: *inflation is **running at** 11 percent* | [with complement] *the decision ran counter to previous government commitments.* **4** [no obj., with adverbial of direction] (of a liquid) flow in a specified direction: *tears were running down her face.* ■ [trans.] cause (a liquid) to flow: [with obj. and adverbial of direction] *she ran cold water into the sink.* ■ [trans.] cause water to flow over (something): *I ran my hands under the faucet.* ■ [trans.] fill (a bath) with water: [with two objs.] *I'll run you a nice hot bath.* ■ [intrans.] (**run with**) be covered or streaming with (a particular liquid): *his face was running with sweat.* ■ [intrans.] emit or exude a liquid: *she was weeping loudly, and her nose was running.* ■ [intrans.] (of a solid substance) melt and become fluid: *it was so hot that the butter ran.* ■ [intrans.] (of the sea, the tide, or a river) rise higher or flow more quickly: *there was still a heavy sea running.* ■ [intrans.] (of dye or color in fabric or paper) dissolve and spread when the fabric or paper becomes wet: *the red dye ran when the socks were washed.* ■ [intrans.] (of a stocking or pair of tights) develop a ravel. **5** [intrans.] (of a bus, train, ferry, or other form of transportation) make a regular journey on a particular route: *buses run into town every half hour.* ■ [trans.] put (a particular form of public transportation) in service: *the group is drawing up plans to run trains on key routes.* ■ [with obj. and adverbial of direction] take (someone) somewhere in a car: *I'll run you home.* **6** [trans.] be in charge of; manage: *Andrea runs her own catering business* | [as adj., in comb.] (**-run**) *an attractive family-run hotel.* ■ [no obj., with adverbial] (of a system, organization, or plan) operate or proceed in a particular way: *everything's running according to plan.* ■ organize and make available for other people: *we decided to run a series of seminars.* ■ carry out (a test or procedure): *he asked the army to run tests on the anti nerve-gas pills.* ■ own, maintain, and use (a vehicle). **7** be in or cause to be in operation; function or cause to function: [intrans.] *the car **runs on** unleaded fuel* | [trans.] *a number of peripherals can be **run off** one SCSI port.* ■ move or cause to move between the spools of a recording machine: [trans.] *I ran the tape back* | [intrans.] *the tape has run out.* **8** [intrans.] continue or be valid or operative for a particular period of time: *the course **ran for** two days* | *this particular debate will **run on and on**.* ■ [with adverbial or complement] happen or arrive at the specified time: *the program was running fifteen minutes late.* ■ (of a play or exhibition) be staged or presented: *the play ran on Broadway last year.* **9** [intrans.] be a candidate in a political election: *he announced that he intended to **run for** President.* ■ [trans.] (esp. of a political party) sponsor (a candidate) in an election: *they ran their first candidate for the school board.* **10** publish or be published in a newspaper or magazine: [trans.] *the tabloids ran the story.* ■ [intrans.] (of a story, argument, or piece of writing) have a specified wording or contents: *"Tapestries slashed!" ran the dramatic headline.* **11** [trans.] bring (goods) into a country illegally and secretly; smuggle: *they run drugs for the cocaine cartels.* **12** [with two objs.] (of an object or act) cost (someone) (a specified amount): *a new photocopier will run us about $1,300.* ▶n. **1** [usu. in sing.] an act or spell of running: *I usually go for a run in the morning* | *a cross-country run.* ■ a running pace: *Bobby set off **at a run**.* ■ an opportunity or attempt to achieve something: *their absence means the Russians will have a **clear run at** the title.* ■ a preliminary test of the efficiency of a procedure or system: *if you are styling your hair yourself, have a practice run.* ■ an attempt to secure election to political office: *his run for the Republican nomination.* ■ an annual mass migration of fish up a river to spawn, or their return migration afterward: *the annual salmon runs.* **2** a journey accomplished or route taken by a vehicle, aircraft, or boat, esp. on a regular basis: *the New York–Washington run.* ■ a short excursion made in a car: *we could take a run out to the country.* ■ the distance covered in a specified period, esp. by a ship: *a record run of 398 miles from noon to noon.* ■ a short flight made by an aircraft on a straight and even course at a constant speed before or while dropping bombs. **3** Baseball a point scored when a base runner reaches home plate after touching the other bases. ■ Cricket a point scored by hitting the ball so that both batsmen are able to run between the wickets, or awarded in some other circumstances. **4** a continuous spell of a particular situation or condition: *he's had a run of bad luck.* ■ a continuous series of performances: *the play had a long run on Broadway.* ■ a quantity or amount of something produced at one time: *a production run of only 150 cars.* ■ a continuous stretch or length of something: *long runs of copper piping.* ■ a rapid series of musical notes forming a scale. ■ a sequence of cards of the same suit. **5** (**a run on**) a widespread and sudden or continuous demand for (a particular currency or commodity): *there's been a big run on nostalgia toys this year.* ■ a sudden demand for repayment from a bank made by a large number of lenders: *growing nervousness among investors led to a run on some banks.* **6** (**the run of**) free and unrestricted use of or access to: *her cats were given the run of the house.* **7** (**the run**) [usu. with adj.] the average or usual type of person or thing: *she stood out from **the general run of** varsity cheerleaders.* **8** an enclosed area in which domestic animals or birds can run freely in the open: *a chicken run.* ■ [usu. with adj.] a track made or regularly used by a particular animal: *a badger run.* ■ a sloping snow-covered course or track used for skiing, bobsledding, or tobogganing: *a ski run.* ■ Austral./NZ a large open stretch of land used for pasture or the raising of stock: *one of the richest cattle runs of the district.* **9** a line of unraveled stitches in stockings or tights. **10** a downward trickle of paint or a similar substance when applied too thickly. **11** a small stream or brook. **12** (**the runs**) informal diarrhea. **13** Naut. the after part of a ship's bottom where it rises and narrows toward the stern.

– PHRASES **be run off one's feet** see FOOT. **come running** be eager to do what someone wants: *he had only to snap his fingers, and she would come running.* **give someone/something a (good) run for their money** provide someone or something with challenging competition or opposition. **have a (good) run for one's money** derive reward or enjoyment in return for one's outlay or efforts. **on the run 1** trying to avoid being captured: *a kidnapper on the run from the FBI.* **2** while running: *he took a pass on the run.* ■ continuously active and busy: *I'm on the run every minute of the day.* **run a blockade** see BLOCKADE. **run afoul** (or **foul**) **of 1** Naut. collide or become entangled with (an obstacle or another vessel): *another ship ran afoul of us.* **2** come into conflict with; go against: *the act may run afoul of consumer protection legislation.* **run dry** (of a well or river) cease to flow or have any water. ■ fig. (esp. of a source of money or information) be completely used up: *municipal relief funds had long since run dry.* **run an errand** carry out an errand, typically on someone else's behalf. (**make a**) **run for it** attempt to escape someone or something by running away. **run the gauntlet** see GAUNTLET[2]. **run high** see HIGH. **run oneself into the ground** see GROUND[1]. **run its course** see COURSE. **run low** (or **short**) become depleted: *supplies had run short.* ■ have too little of something: *we're **running short of** time.* **run a mile** see MILE. **run off at the mouth** informal talk excessively or indiscreetly. **run someone out of town** force someone to leave a place. **run rings around** see RING[1]. **run riot** see RIOT. **run the risk** (or **run risks**) see RISK. **run the show** informal dominate or be in charge of a project, undertaking, or domain. **run a temperature** (or **fever**) be suffering from a fever or high temperature. **run someone/something to earth** (or **ground**) Hunting chase a quarry to its lair. ■ find someone or something, typically after a long search. **run to ruin** archaic fall into disrepair; gradually deteriorate. **run to seed** see SEED. **run wild** see WILD.

– PHRASAL VERBS **run across** meet or find by chance: *I just thought you might have run across him before.* **run after** informal seek to acquire or attain; pursue persistently: *businesses that have spent years running after the boomer market.* ■ seek the company of (someone) with the aim of developing a romantic or sexual relationship with them. **run against** archaic collide with (someone). ■ happen to meet: *I ran against Flanagan the other day.* **run along** [in imper.] informal go away (used typically to address a child): *run along now, there's a good girl.* **run around with** see RUN WITH (sense 2). **run at** rush toward (someone) to attack or as if to attack them. **run away** leave or escape from a place, person, or situation of danger: *children who **run away from** home normally go to big cities.* ■ (also informal **run off**) leave one's home or current partner in order to establish a relationship with someone else: *he **ran off with** his wife's best friend* | *Fran, let's **run away together**.* ■ try to avoid acknowledging or facing up to an unpleasant or difficult situation: *the commissioners are **running away from** their responsibilities.* **run away with 1** (of one's imagination or emotions) work wildly, so as to overwhelm (one): *Susan's imagination was running away with her.* ■ (of a horse) bolt with (its rider). **2** accept (an idea) without thinking it through properly: *a lot of people ran away with the idea that they were Pacifists.* **3** excel in or win (a competition) easily: *the Yankees ran away with the series.* **run something by** (or **past**) tell (someone) about something, esp. in order to ascertain their opinion or reaction. **run someone/something down 1** (of a vehicle or its driver) hit a person or animal and knock them to the ground. ■ (of a boat) collide with another vessel. **2** criticize someone or something unfairly or unkindly. **3** discover someone or something after a search: *she finally ran the professor down.* **4** Baseball (of two or more fielders) try to tag out a base runner who is trapped between two bases, in the process throwing the ball back and forth. **run something down** (or **run down**) reduce (or become reduced) in size, numbers, or resources: *hardwood stocks in some countries are rapidly running down.* ■ lose (or cause to lose) power; stop (or cause to stop) functioning: *the battery has run down.* ■ gradually deteriorate (or cause to deteriorate) in quality or condition: *the property had been allowed to run down.* **run someone in** informal arrest someone. **run into 1** collide with: *he ran into a lamp post.* ■ meet by chance: *I ran into Stasia and Katie on the way home.* ■ experience (a problem or difficult situation): *the bank ran into financial difficulties.* **2** reach (a level or amount): *debts running into millions of dollars.*

3 blend into or appear to coalesce with: *her words ran into each other.* **run off** see RUN AWAY above. **run off with** informal steal: *the treasurer had run off with the pension funds.* **run something off 1** reproduce copies of a piece of writing on a machine. ■ write or recite something quickly and with little effort. **2** drain liquid from a container: *run off the water that has been standing in the pipes.* **run on 1** continue without stopping; go on longer than is expected: *the story ran on for months.* ■ talk incessantly. **2** (also **run upon**) (of a person's mind or a discussion) be preoccupied or concerned with (a particular subject): *my thoughts always ran too much on death.* **3** Print. continue on the same line as the preceding matter. **run out 1** (of a supply of something) be used up: *our food is about to run out.* ■ use up one's supply of something: *we've run out of gasoline.* ■ become no longer valid: *her contract runs out at the end of the year.* **2** (of rope) be paid out: *slowly, he let the cables run out.* **3** [with adverbial of direction] extend; project: *a row of buildings ran out to Cityline Avenue.* **run out on** informal abandon (someone); cease to support or care for. **run over 1** (of a container or its contents) overflow: *the bath's running over.* **2** exceed (an expected limit): *the filming ran over schedule and budget.* **run someone/something over** (of a vehicle or its driver) knock a person or animal down and pass over their body: *I almost ran over that raccoon.* **run through 1** be present in every part of; pervade: *a sense of personal loss runs through many of his lyrics.* **2** use or spend recklessly or rapidly: *her husband had long since run through her money.* **run someone/something through** stab a person or animal so as to kill them. **run through** (or **over**) **something** discuss, read, or repeat something quickly or briefly: *I'll just run through the schedule for the weekend.* ■ rehearse a performance or series of actions: *okay, let's run through Scene 3 again.* **run to 1** extend to or reach (a specified amount or size): *the document ran to almost 100 pages.* ■ be enough to cover (a particular expense); have the financial resources for: *my income doesn't run to luxuries like taxis.* **2** (of a person) show a tendency to or inclination toward: *she was tall and running to fat.* **run something up 1** allow a debt or bill to accumulate quickly: *he ran up debts of $153,000.* ■ achieve a particular score in a game or match: *North Carolina ran up a 62–44 lead.* **2** make something quickly or hurriedly, esp. a piece of clothing: *I'll run up a dress for you.* **3** raise a flag. **run up against** experience or meet (a difficulty or problem): *the proposal has been dropped because it could run up against Federal regulations.* **run with 1** proceed with; accept: *we do lots of tests before we run with a product.* **2** (also **run around with**) informal associate habitually with (someone): *Larry was a good kid until he began running around with the wrong crowd.* — **run·na·ble** adj. [OE *rinnan, irnan* (v.), of Gmc. origin, prob. reinforced in ME by ON *rinna, renna.* The current form with *-u-* in the present tense is first recorded in the 16th C.]

run·a·bout /ˈrənəˌbout/ ▶ n. a small car, motorboat, or light aircraft, esp. one used for short trips.

run·a·round /ˈrənəˌround/ informal ▶ n. difficult or awkward treatment, esp. in which someone is evasive or does not answer one's questions directly: *the times he **got the runaround** looking for work.*

run·a·way /ˈrənəˌwā/ ▶ n. a person who has run away, esp. from their family or an institution. ■ [often as adj.] an animal or vehicle that is running out of control: *a runaway train.* ■ [as adj.] denoting something happening or done quickly, easily, or uncontrollably: *the runaway success of the book.*

run·back /ˈrənˌbak/ ▶ n. Football an act of advancing a ball caught after a kickoff, punt, or interception by running while carrying it.

run·ci·ble spoon /ˈrənsəbəl/ ▶ n. a fork curved like a spoon, with three broad prongs, one of which has a sharpened outer edge for cutting. [19th C.: used by Edward Lear, perh. suggested by late 16th-C. *rouncival,* denoting a large variety of pea.]

run·down ▶ n. /ˈrənˌdoun/ [usu. in sing.] **1** an analysis or summary of something by a knowledgeable person: *he gave his teammates **a rundown on** the opposition.* **2** a reduction in the productivity or activities of a company or institution: *a rundown in the business would be a devastating blow to the local economy.* **3** Baseball an attempt by two or more fielders to tag out a base runner who is trapped between two bases: *he was caught in a rundown and tagged out by the shortstop.* ▶ adj. /ˈrənˈdoun/ (usu. **run-down**) **1** (esp. of a building or area) in a poor or neglected state after having been prosperous: *a run-down, vandalized inner-city area.* ■ (of a company or industry) in a poor economic state. **2** [predic.] tired and somewhat unwell, esp. through overwork: *feeling tired and generally run-down.*

Germanic runes

rune /ro͞on/ ▶ n. a letter of an ancient Germanic alphabet, related to the Roman alphabet. ■ a similar mark of mysterious or magic significance. ■ (**runes**) small stones, pieces of bone, etc., bearing such marks, and used as divinatory symbols. ■ a spell or incantation. ■ a section of an ancient Finnish or Scandinavian poem. — **ru·nic** /ˈro͞onik/ adj. [OE *rūn* 'a secret, mystery'; not recorded between ME and the late 17th C. when it was reintroduced under the influence of ON *rúnir, rúnar* 'magic signs, hidden lore.']

rune stone ▶ n. **1** a large stone carved with runes by ancient Scandinavians or Anglo-Saxons. **2** a small stone, piece of bone, etc., marked with a rune and used in divination.

rung[1] /rəNG/ ▶ n. **1** a horizontal support on a ladder for a person's foot. ■ fig. a level in a hierarchical structure, esp. a class or career structure: *we must ensure that the low-skilled do not get trapped on the bottom rung.* **2** a strengthening crosspiece in the structure of a chair. — **runged** adj. **rung·less** adj. [OE *hrung* (sense 2); rel. to Du. *rong* and Ger. *Runge.*]

rung[2] past participle of RING[2].

run-in ▶ n. **1** informal a disagreement or fight, esp. with someone in an official position: *a run-in with armed police in Rio* | humorous *a run-in with a parking meter.* **2** [usu. in sing.] Brit. the approach to an action or event: *the final run-in to the World Cup.* ■ the home stretch of a racecourse.

run·let /ˈrənlət/ ▶ n. a small stream.

run·nel /ˈrənl/ ▶ n. a narrow channel in the ground for liquid to flow through. ■ a brook or rill. ■ a small stream of a particular liquid: *a **runnel of** sweat.* [16th C. (denoting a brook or rill): var. of dial. *rindle,* influenced by the v. RUN.]

run·ner /ˈrənər/ ▶ n. **1** a person who runs, esp. in a specified way: *a fast runner.* ■ a person who runs competitively as a sport or hobby: *a marathon runner.* ■ a horse that runs in a particular race: *there were only four runners.* ■ a messenger, collector, or agent for a bank, bookmaker, or other organization. ■ Baseball a base runner. ■ a messenger in the army. **2** [in comb.] a person who smuggles specified goods into or out of a country or area: *a drug-runner.* **3** a rod, groove, or blade on which something slides. ■ each of the long pieces on the underside of a sled that forms the contact in sliding. ■ (often **runners**) a roller for moving a heavy article. ■ a ring capable of slipping or sliding along a strap or rod or through which something may be passed or drawn. ■ Naut. a rope run through a block. **4** a shoot, typically leafless, that grows from the base of a plant along the surface of the ground and can take root at points along its length. ■ a plant that spreads by means of such shoots. ■ a twining plant. **5** a long, narrow rug or strip of carpet, esp. for a hall or stairway. **6** (also **run·ner stone**) a revolving millstone. **7** a fast-swimming fish of the jack family, occurring in tropical seas.

run·ner-up ▶ n. (pl. **run·ners-up**) a competitor or team taking second place in a contest: *he was runner-up in the 200 m individual medley.* ■ [with adj.] a competitor finishing behind the winner in the specified position: *third runner-up in last year's election.*

run·ning /ˈrəniNG/ ▶ n. **1** the action or movement of a runner: *he accounted for 31 touchdowns with his running and passing.* ■ the sport of racing on foot: *marathon running.* ■ an act of running a race: *the 122nd running of the Mid-Summer Derby.* **2** the action of managing or operating something: *the day-to-day running of the office.* ▶ adj. **1** [attrib.] denoting something that runs, in particular: ■ (of water) flowing naturally or supplied to a building through pipes and taps: *hot and cold running water.* ■ (of a sore or a part of the body) exuding liquid or pus: *a running sore.* ■ continuous or recurring over a long period: *a running joke.* ■ done while running: *a running jump.* ■ (of a measurement) in a straight line: *today, those same lots are worth $6,000 a running foot.* **2** [postpositive] consecutive; in succession: *he failed to produce an essay for the third week running.*

– PHRASES **in** (or **out of**) **the running** in (or no longer in) contention for an award, victory, or a place on a team: *he is in the running for an Oscar.*

run·ning back ▶ n. Football an offensive player, typically a halfback, who specializes in carrying the ball.

run·ning bat·tle ▶ n. a military engagement that does not occur at a fixed location. ■ a confrontation that has gone on for a long time.

run·ning be·lay ▶ n. Climbing a device attached to a rock face through which a climbing rope runs freely, acting as a pulley if the climber falls.

run·ning board ▶ n. a footboard extending along the side of a vehicle, typically found on some early models of automobiles.

run·ning com·men·ta·ry ▶ n. a verbal description of events, given as they occur.

run·ning dog ▶ n. **1** informal a servile follower, esp. of a political system: *the running dogs of capitalism.* [translating Chin. *zǒugǒu.*] **2** a dog bred to run, esp. for racing or pulling a sled.

run·ning fire ▶ n. successive gunshots from a line of troops. ■ a rapid succession of something: *a running fire of comment in their choicest vernacular.*

run·ning fix ▶ n. a determination of one's position made by taking bearings at different times and allowing for the distance covered in the meantime.

run·ning gear ▶ n. the moving parts of a machine, esp. the wheels, steering, and suspension of a vehicle. ■ the moving rope and tackle used in handling a boat.

run·ning head ▶ n. a heading printed at the top of each page of a book or chapter.

run·ning knot ▶ n. a knot that slips along the rope and changes the size of the loop it forms.

run·ning lights ▶ plural n. small lights on a motor vehicle that remain illuminated while the vehicle is running.

run·ning mate ▶ n. **1** an election candidate for the lesser of two closely associated political offices: *a rationale offered by a presidential candidate for choosing his vice presidential running mate.* **2** a horse entered in a race in order to set the pace for another horse from the same stable, which is intended to win.

run·ning re·pairs ▶ plural n. minor or temporary repairs carried out on machinery while it is in use.

run·ning rig·ging ▶ n. see RIGGING (sense 1).

run·ning stitch ▶ n. a simple needlework stitch consisting of a line of small even stitches that run back and forth through the cloth without overlapping.

run·ning to·tal ▶ n. a total that is continually adjusted to take account of items as they are added.

run·ny /'rənē/ ▶ adj. (**-ni·er, -ni·est**) **1** more liquid than is usual or expected: *the soufflé was hard on top and quite runny underneath.* **2** (of a person's nose) producing or discharging mucus; running.

Run·ny·mede /'rəni,mēd/ a meadow on the southern bank of the Thames River, near Windsor. It is noted for its association with the Magna Carta, which was signed by King John in 1215 here or nearby.

run·off /'rən,ôf; -,äf/ (also **run-off**) ▶ n. **1** a further competition, election, race, etc., after a tie or inconclusive result. **2** the draining away of water (or substances carried in it) from the surface of an area of land, a building or structure, etc. ■ the water or other material that drains freely off the surface of something.

run-of-the-mill ▶ adj. lacking unusual or special aspects; ordinary: *a run-of-the-mill job.*

run-on ▶ adj. **1** [attrib.] denoting a line of verse in which a sentence is continued without a pause beyond the end of a line, couplet, or stanza. **2** (of a sentence) containing two or more independent clauses that are not separated by a colon or semicolon: *his sentences were often run-on or confused.*

run·out /'rən,out/ (also **run-out**) ▶ n. **1** a length of time or stretch of ground over which something gradually ceases or is brought to an end or a halt: *I skied the trail's long runout to the bottom and found the familiar yellow bus waiting.* **2** a slight error in a rotating tool, machine component, etc., such as being off-center or not exactly round.

runt /rənt/ ▶ n. a small pig or other animal, esp. the smallest in a litter. ■ fig. an undersized or weak person. — **runt·y** adj. [16th C. (in the sense 'old or decayed tree stump'): of unknown origin.]

run-through ▶ n. **1** a rehearsal: *a run-through of the whole show.* **2** a brief outline or summary: *the textbooks provide a run-through of research findings.*

run-time Comput. ▶ n. the length of time a program takes to run. ■ the time at which the program is run. ■ a cut-down version of a program that can be run but not changed: *you can distribute the run-time to your colleagues.* ▶ adj. (of software) in a reduced version that can be run but not changed.

run-up ▶ n. **1** a marked rise in the value or level of something: *a sharp run-up of land and stock prices.* **2** the period preceding a notable event: *an acrimonious run-up to legislative elections.* **3** an act of running briefly to gain momentum before performing a jump in track and field or other sports: *high jumper Steve Smith will use his shortened five-stride run-up.* **4** an act of running an engine or turbine to prepare it for use or to test it. **5** Golf a low approach shot that bounces and runs forward.

run·way /'rən,wā/ ▶ n. **1** a strip of hard ground along which aircraft take off and land. **2** a raised aisle extending into the audience from a stage, esp. as used for fashion shows. **3** an animal run, esp. one made by small mammals in grass, under snow, etc. **4** an incline or chute down which something slides or runs.

Run·yon /'rənyən/, Damon (1884–1946), US author and journalist; full name *Alfred Damon Runyon.* His short story collection *Guys and Dolls* (1932) formed the basis for the musical of the same name (1950).

ru·pee /rōō'pē; 'rōō,pē/ ▶ n. the basic monetary unit of India, Pakistan, Sri Lanka, Nepal, Mauritius, and the Seychelles, equal to 100 paisa in India, Pakistan, and Nepal, and 100 cents in Sri Lanka, Mauritius, and the Seychelles. [via Hindi from Sanskrit *rūpya* 'wrought silver.']

Ru·pert, Prince /'rōōpərt/ (1619–82), English general; son of Frederick V (elector of the Palatinate) and nephew of Charles I. The Royalist leader of cavalry, he initially won a series of victories, but was defeated by Parliamentarian forces at Marston Moor in 1644 and Naseby in 1645.

Ru·pert's Land (also **Prince Ru·pert's Land**) a historical region of northern and western Canada, roughly corresponding to what is now Manitoba, Saskatchewan, Yukon, Alberta, and the southern part of the Northwest Territories.

ru·pes·tri·an /rōō'pestrēən/ ▶ adj. (of art) done on rock or cave walls. [18th C.: from mod. Latin *rupestris* 'found on rocks' (from L. *rupes* 'rock') + -AN.]

ru·pi·ah /rōō'pēə/ ▶ n. the basic monetary unit of Indonesia. [Indonesian, from Hindi *rūpyah* (see RUPEE).]

rup·ture /'rəpCHər/ ▶ v. [intrans.] (esp. of a pipe, a vessel, or a bodily part such as an organ or membrane) break or burst suddenly: *if the main artery ruptures he could die.* ■ [trans.] cause to break or burst suddenly and completely: *the impact of the explosion ruptured both fuel tanks.* ■ [trans.] suffer such a bursting of (a bodily part): *it was her first match since rupturing an Achilles tendon.* ■ (**be ruptured** or **rupture oneself**) suffer an abdominal hernia: *one of the boys was ruptured and needed to be fitted with a truss.* ■ [trans.] fig. breach or disturb (a harmonious feeling or situation): *once trust has been ruptured it can be difficult to regain.* ▶ n. an instance of breaking or bursting suddenly and completely: *a small hairline crack could develop into a rupture* | *the patient died after rupture of an aneurysm.* ■ fig. a breach of a harmonious relationship: *the rupture with his father would never be healed.* ■ an abdominal hernia. [ME (as a n.): from OFr. *rupture* or L. *ruptura*, from *rumpere* 'to break.' The v. dates from the mid 18th C.]

ru·ral /'rōōrəl/ ▶ adj. in, relating to, or characteristic of the countryside rather than the town: *remote rural areas.* — **ru·ral·ism** /-,lizəm/ n. **ru·ral·ist** /-list/ n. **ru·ral·i·ty** /rōō'ralitē/ n. **ru·ral·i·za·tion** /,rōōrələ'zāSHən/ n. **ru·ral·ize** /-,līz/ v. **ru·ral·ly** adv. [ME: from OFr., or from late L. *ruralis*, from *rus, rur-* 'country.']

ru·ral route (abbr.: **RR**) ▶ n. a mail delivery route in a rural area.

Ru·rik /'rōōrik/ (also **Ryu·rik**) ▶ n. a member of a dynasty that ruled Muscovy and much of Russia from the 9th century until the death of Fyodor, son of Ivan the Terrible, in 1598. It was reputedly founded by a Varangian chief who settled in Novgorod in 862. ▶ adj. of or relating to the Ruriks.

Ru·ri·ta·ni·a /,rōōri'tānēə/ an imaginary kingdom in central Europe used as a fictional background for the adventure novels of courtly intrigue and romance written by Anthony Hope (1863–1933). — **Ru·ri·ta·ni·an** /-'tānēən/ adj. & n. [from RURAL, on the pattern of *Lusitania.*]

Ruse /'rōōsā/ (also **Rousse**) an industrial city and the principal port of Bulgaria, on the Danube River; pop. 210,000.

ruse /rōōz; rōōs/ ▶ n. an action intended to deceive someone; a trick: *Eleanor tried to think of a ruse to get Paul out of the house.* [ME (as a hunting term): from OFr., from *ruser* 'use trickery,' earlier 'drive back,' perh. based on L. *rursus* 'backward.']

rush[1] /rəSH/ ▶ v. **1** [no obj., with adverbial of direction] move with urgent haste: *Jason rushed after her* | *I rushed outside and hailed a taxi.* ■ (of air or a liquid) flow strongly: *the water rushed in through the great oaken gates.* ■ [intrans.] act with great haste: *as soon as the campaign started, they **rushed into action*** | [with infin.] *shoppers rushed to buy computers.* ■ [trans.] force (someone) to act hastily: *I don't want to **rush you into** something.* ■ [with obj. and adverbial of direction] take (someone) somewhere with great haste: *an ambulance was waiting to rush him to the hospital.* ■ [with two objs.] deliver (something) quickly to (someone): *we'll rush you a copy at once.* ■ (**rush something out**) produce and distribute something, or put something up for sale, very quickly: *a rewritten textbook was rushed out last autumn.* ■ [trans.] deal with (something) hurriedly: *panic measures were **rushed through** Congress* | [as adj.] (**rushed**) *a rushed job.* ■ [trans.] dash toward (someone or something) in an attempt to attack or capture them or it: *he rushed the stronghold.* **2** [trans.] Football advance rapidly toward (an offensive player, esp. the quarterback). ■ [intrans.] gain a specified amount of yardage or score a touchdown or conversion by running from scrimmage with the ball: *he rushed for 100 yards on 22 carries.* **3** [trans.] entertain (a new student) in order to assess their suitability for membership in a college fraternity or sorority. ■ (of a student) visit (a college fraternity or sorority) with a view toward joining it: *he rushed three fraternities.* ▶ n. **1** a sudden quick movement toward something, typically by a number of people: *there was a **rush for** the door.* ■ a flurry of hasty activity: *the pre-Christmas rush* | [as adj.] *a rush job.* ■ a sudden strong demand for a commodity: *there's been a **rush on** the* Tribune *because of the murder.* ■ a sudden flow or flood: *she felt a rush of cold air.* ■ a sudden intense feeling: *Mark felt a rush of anger.* ■ a sudden thrill or feeling of euphoria such as experienced after taking certain drugs: *users experience a rush.* **2** Football a rapid advance by a defensive player or players, esp. toward the quarterback. ■ an act of running from scrimmage with the ball to gain yardage. **3** the process whereby college fraternities or sororities entertain new students in order to assess suitability for membership: *ranking pledges during rush* | [as adj.] *rush week.* **4** (**rushes**) the first prints made of a movie after a period of shooting. — **rush·er** n. **rush·ing·ly** adv. [ME: from an Anglo-Norman Fr. var. of OFr. *ruser* 'drive back,' an early sense of the word in Engl. (see RUSE).]

rush[2] ▶ n. **1** a marsh or waterside plant (genus *Juncus*, family Juncaceae) with slender stemlike pith-filled leaves, widely distributed in temperate areas. Some kinds are used for matting, chair seats, and baskets, and some were formerly used for strewing on floors. ■ used in names of similar plants of wet habitats, e.g., **flowering rush.** ■ a stem of such a plant. ■ such plants used as a material. **2** archaic a thing of no value (used for emphasis): *not one of them is **worth a rush.*** — **rush·like** /-,līk/ adj. **rush·y** adj. [OE *risc, rysc*, of Gmc. origin.]

Rush·die /'rəSHdē/, Salman (1947–), British novelist, born in India; full name *Ahmed Salman Rushdie.* His work includes *The Satanic Verses* (1988), regarded by Muslims as blasphemous, and *Shalimar the Clown* (2005).

rush hour ▶ n. a time during each day when traffic is at its heaviest.

rush·light /'rəSH,līt/ ▶ n. hist. a candle made by dipping the pith of a rush in tallow.

Rush·more, Mount /'rəSH,môr/ a mountain in the Black Hills of South Dakota, noted for its giant busts of four US presidents—George Washington, Thomas Jefferson, Theodore Roosevelt, and Abraham Lincoln—carved 1927–41 under the direction of sculptor Gutzon Borglum (1867–1941).

Russia

Official name: Russian Federation
Location: northern Asia and eastern Europe
Area: 6,594,400 square miles (17,075,200 sq km)
Population: 143,782,000
Capital: Moscow
Languages: Russian (official), many local languages
Currency: Russian ruble

rus in ur·be /ˌro͞os in 'o͝orbe/ ▸ n. literary an illusion of countryside created by a building or garden, within a city. [L., lit. 'country in the city.']

Rusk /rəsk/, Dean (1909–94), US educator and statesman; full name *David Dean Rusk*. As secretary of state 1961–69, he was a strong proponent of US involvement in Vietnam.

rusk /rəsk/ ▸ n. a light, dry biscuit or piece of rebaked bread, esp. one prepared for use as baby food. ■ rebaked bread used as extra filling, for example in sausages, and formerly as rations at sea. [16th C.: from Sp. or Port. *rosca* 'twist, coil, roll of bread,' of unknown ultimate origin.]

Rus·kin /'rəskin/, John (1819–1900), English art and social critic. His prolific writings include attacks on Renaissance art in *The Stones of Venice* (1851–53), capitalism in "The Political Economy of Art" (1857), and utilitarianism in *Unto This Last* (1860).

Rus·sell[1] /'rəsəl/, Bertrand Arthur William, 3rd Earl Russell (1872–1970), British philosopher and mathematician. He expounded logical atomism in *Our Knowledge of the External World* (1914) and neutral monism in *The Analysis of Mind* (1921). Nobel Prize for Literature (1950).

Rus·sell[2], Bill (1934–), US basketball player and coach; full name *William Felton Russell*. A center, he played for the Boston Celtics 1956–69 and also coached them from 1966, becoming the first African-American head coach in the NBA.

Rus·sell[3], John, 1st Earl Russell (1792–1878), British statesman; prime minister 1846–52 and 1865–66.

Rus·sell's par·a·dox a logical paradox stated in terms of set theory, concerning the set of all sets that do not contain themselves as members, namely that the condition for it to contain itself is that it should not contain itself. [1920s: named after Bertrand *Russell* (see **Russell[1]**).]

Rus·sell's vi·per ▸ n. a large viper (*Daboia russelli*) that has a yellow-brown body with black markings. [20th C.: named after Patrick *Russell* (1727–1805), Scottish physician and naturalist.]

Rus·sell·ville /'rəsəlˌvil/ a city in central Arkansas, on the northern shore of the Arkansas River, northwest of Little Rock; pop. 23,682.

rus·set /'rəsət/ ▸ adj. **1** reddish brown in color: *gardens of russet and gold chrysanthemums.* **2** archaic rustic; homely. ▸ n. **1** a reddish-brown color: *the woods in autumn are a riot of russet and gold.* **2** a dessert apple of a variety with a slightly rough greenish-brown skin. **3** hist. a coarse homespun reddish-brown or gray cloth used for simple clothing: *a white blouse and a skirt of russet.* ▸ v. (**-set·ed, -set·ing**) make or become russet in color. ■ (of smooth-skinned fruit) develop a rough reddish-brown or yellowish-brown skin, or patches of such: [trans.] *a week of humid weather has russeted the pears* | [intrans.] *this variety of apple tends not to russet.* — **rus·set·y** adj. [ME: from an Anglo-Norman Fr. var. of OFr. *rousset*, dimin. of *rous* 'red,' from Provençal *ros*, from L. *russus* 'red.']

Rus·sia /'rəsHə/ a country in northern Asia and eastern Europe. *See box.*

Rus·sia leath·er ▸ n. a durable leather made from calfskin and impregnated with birchbark oil, used for bookbinding.

Rus·sian /'rəsHən/ ▸ adj. of or relating to Russia, its people, or their language. ▸ n. **1** a native or national of Russia. ■ a person of Russian descent. ■ hist. (in general use) a national of the former Soviet Union. **2** the East Slavic language of Russia. — **Rus·sian·i·za·tion** /ˌrəsHənə'zāsHən/ n. **Rus·sian·ize** /-ˌnīz/ v. **Rus·sian·ness** n. [16th C.: from med. L. *Russianus*.]

Rus·sian bal·let ▸ n. a style of ballet developed at the Russian Imperial Ballet Academy, popularized in the West by Sergei Diaghilev's Ballets Russes from 1909.

Rus·sian Blue ▸ n. a cat of a breed with short grayish-blue fur, green eyes, and large pointed ears.

Rus·sian boot ▸ n. a boot that loosely encloses the wearer's calf.

Rus·sian Fed·er·a·tion official name for **Russia**.

Rus·sian ol·ive ▸ n. see **oleaster**.

Rus·sian Or·tho·dox Church the national church of Russia. See **Orthodox Church**.

Rus·sian Rev·o·lu·tion the revolution in the Russian empire in 1917, in which the czarist regime was overthrown and replaced by Bolshevik rule under Lenin. There were two phases to the Revolution: the first, in March (Old Style, February, thus **February Revolution**), was sparked by food and fuel shortages during World War I and began with strikes and riots in Petrograd (St. Petersburg). The czar abdicated, and a provisional government was set up. The second phase, in November 1917 (Old Style, October, thus **October Revolution**), was marked by the seizure of power by the Bolsheviks in a coup led by Lenin. After workers' councils or **soviets** took power in major cities, the new Soviet constitution was declared in 1918.

Rus·sian rou·lette ▸ n. the practice of loading a bullet into one chamber of a revolver, spinning the cylinder, and then pulling the trigger while pointing the gun at one's own head. ■ fig. an activity that is potentially very dangerous.

Rus·sian sal·ad ▸ n. Brit. a salad of mixed diced vegetables with mayonnaise.

Rus·sian tea ▸ n. tea laced with rum and typically served with lemon.

Rus·sian this·tle ▸ n. a prickly tumbleweed (*Salsola kali*) of the goosefoot family that is an inland form of saltwort. Native to Eurasia, it was introduced into North America, where it has become a pest. Also called **Russian tumbleweed**.

Rus·si·fy /'rəsəˌfī/ ▸ v. (**-fies, -fied**) [trans.] make Russian in character. — **Rus·si·fi·ca·tion** /ˌrəsəfə'kāsHən/ n.

Russ·ki /'rəskē; 'ro͞oskē/ (also **Russ·ky**) ▶ **n.** (pl. **-kis** or **-kies**) informal, often offens. a Russian. [19th C.: from Russ. *russkiĭ* 'Russian,' or from RUSSIAN, on the pattern of Russian surnames ending in *-skiĭ*.]

Russo- ▶ **comb. form** Russian; Russian and ...: *Russo-Japanese.* ■ relating to Russia.

Rus·so-Jap·an·ese War /'rəsō/ a war between the Russian empire and Japan in 1904–05, caused by territorial disputes in Manchuria and Korea. Russia suffered a series of humiliating defeats, and the peace settlement gave Japan the ascendancy in the disputed region.

Rus·so·phile /'rəsə,fīl/ ▶ **n.** a person who is friendly toward Russia or fond of Russia and Russian things, esp. someone who is sympathetic to the political system and customs of the former Soviet Union. — **Rus·so·phil·i·a** /,rəsə'filēə/ **n.**

Rus·so·phobe /'rəsə,fōb/ ▶ **n.** a person who feels an intense dislike toward Russia and Russian things, esp. the political system or customs of the former Soviet Union. — **Rus·so·pho·bi·a** /,rəsə'fōbēə/ **n.**

rus·su·la /'rəs(y)ələ/ ▶ **n.** a widespread woodland toadstool (genus *Russula*, family Russulaceae) that typically has a brightly colored flattened cap and a white stem and gills. [mod. L., from L. *russus* 'red' (because many, such as the sickener, have a red cap).]

rust /rəst/ ▶ **n. 1** a reddish- or yellowish-brown flaky coating of iron oxide that is formed on iron or steel by oxidation, esp. in the presence of moisture. ■ fig. a state of deterioration or disrepair resulting from neglect or lack of use: *they are here to scrape the rust off the derelict machinery of government.* **2** [usu. with adj.] a disease of plants that results in reddish or brownish patches, caused by a fungus (*Puccinia* and other genera, order Uredinales, class Teliomycetes). **3** a reddish-brown color: [in comb.] *his rust-colored hair.* ▶ **v.** [intrans.] be affected with rust: *the blades had rusted away* | [as adj.] (**rusting**) *rusting machinery.* ■ fig. deteriorate through neglect or lack of use. — **rust·less adj.** [OE *rūst*, of Gmc. origin; rel. to Du. *roest*, Ger. *Rost*, also to RED.]

Rust Belt ▶ **n.** (**the Rust Belt**) informal parts of the northeastern and midwestern US that are characterized by declining industry, aging factories, and a falling population. Steel-producing cities in Pennsylvania and Ohio are at its center: *the smokestacks of the Rust Belt were no longer allowed to blast wastes into the air* | [as adj.] *the state's Rust Belt economy.*

rust buck·et ▶ **n.** informal, often humorous a car, ship, or other vehicle that is old and badly rusted.

rus·tic /'rəstik/ ▶ **adj. 1** having a simplicity and charm that is considered typical of the countryside: *bare plaster walls and a terra-cotta floor give a rustic feel.* ■ lacking the sophistication of the city; backward and provincial: *you are a rustic halfwit.* **2** constructed or made in a plain and simple fashion, in particular: ■ made of untrimmed branches or rough timber: *a rustic oak bench.* ■ Archit. with rough-hewn or roughened surface or with deeply sunk joints: *a rustic bridge.* ■ denoting freely formed lettering, esp. a relatively informal style of handwritten Roman capital letter. ▶ **n.** often derog. an unsophisticated country person. — **rus·ti·cal·ly** /-ik(ə)lē/ **adv. rus·tic·i·ty** /rə'stisətē/ **n.** [ME (in the sense 'rural'): from L. *rusticus*, from *rus* 'the country.']

rus·ti·cate /'rəsti,kāt/ ▶ **v. 1** [intrans.] go to, live in, or spend time in the country. **2** [trans.] fashion (masonry) in large blocks with sunk joints and a roughened surface: [as adj.] (**rusticated**) *the stable block was built of rusticated stone.* **3** [trans.] Brit. suspend (a student) from a university as a punishment (used chiefly at Oxford and Cambridge). — **rus·ti·ca·tion** /,rəsti'kāshən/ **n.** [15th C. (in the sense 'countrify'): from L. *rusticat-* '(having) lived in the country,' from the v. *rusticari*, from *rusticus* (see RUSTIC).]

rus·tle /'rəsəl/ ▶ **v. 1** [intrans.] make a soft, muffled crackling sound like that caused by the movement of dry leaves or paper: *she came closer, her skirt swaying and rustling.* ■ [with adverbial of direction] move with such sound: *a nurse rustled in with a syringe.* ■ [trans.] move (something), causing it to make such a sound: *Dolly rustled the paper irritably.* **2** [trans.] round up and steal (cattle, horses, or sheep). **3** [intrans.] informal move or act quickly or energetically; hustle: *rustle around the kitchen, see what there is.* ▶ **n.** [usu. in sing.] a soft, muffled crackling sound like that made by the movement of dry leaves or paper: *there was a rustle in the undergrowth behind her.*
– PHRASAL VERBS **rustle something up** informal produce something quickly when it is needed: *see if you can rustle up a cup of coffee for Paula and me, please.* — **rus·tler** /'rəs(ə)lər/ **n.** (usu. in sense 2). [ME (as a v.): imitative; cf. Flemish *rijsselen* and Du. *ritselen*. The n. dates from the mid 18th C.]

Rus·ton /'rəstən/ a commercial city in northern Louisiana; pop. 20,546.

rust·proof /'rəst,pro͞of/ ▶ **adj.** (of metal or a metal object) not susceptible to corrosion by rust. ▶ **v.** [trans.] make resistant to corrosion by rust.

rust·y /'rəstē/ ▶ **adj.** (**rust·i·er, rust·i·est**) **1** (of a metal object) affected by rust: *a rusty hinge.* ■ rust-colored: *green grass turning a rusty brown.* **2** (of knowledge or a skill) impaired by lack of recent practice: *my typing is a little rusty.* ■ stiff with age or disuse: *it was my first race for three months and I felt a bit rusty.* ■ (of a voice) croaking: *her voice sounded rusty.* — **rust·i·ly** /'rəstəlē/ **adv. rust·i·ness n.** [OE *rūstig* (see RUST, -Y[1]).]

rust·y dust·y ▶ **n.** black English a person's buttocks. [16th C. (in the sense 'dusty, fusty'): reduplication of RUSTY. The current transferred use dates from the 1950s.]

rut[1] /rət/ ▶ **n.** a long deep track made by the repeated passage of the wheels of vehicles. ■ fig. a habit or pattern of behavior that has become dull and unproductive but is hard to change: *the administration was stuck in a rut and was losing its direction.* — **rut·ted adj. rut·ty adj.** [16th C.: prob. from OFr. *rute* (see ROUTE).]

rut[2] ▶ **n.** (**the rut**) an annual period of sexual activity in deer and some other mammals, during which the males fight each other for access to the females. ▶ **v.** (**rut·ted, rut·ting**) [intrans.] [often as adj.] (**rutting**) engage in such activity: *a rutting stag.* — **rut·tish adj.** [ME: from OFr., from L. *rugitus*, from *rugire* 'to roar.']

ru·ta·ba·ga /'ro͞otə,bāgə; 'ro͝ot-/ ▶ **n. 1** a large, round, yellow-fleshed root that is eaten as a vegetable. **2** the European plant (*Brassica napus*) of the cabbage family that produces this root. [18th C.: from Swed. dial. *rotabagge.*]

Ruth[1] /ro͞oTH/ a book of the Bible telling the story of Ruth, a Moabite woman, who married her deceased husband's kinsman Boaz and bore a son, Obed, who became grandfather to King David.

Ruth[2], Babe (1895–1948), US baseball player; born *George Herman Ruth*; also known as **the Bambino**. Originally a pitcher in Boston, he became a batting legend for the New York Yankees 1919–34, setting a career record of 714 home runs and a single-season record of 60 home runs in 1927.

ruth /ro͞oTH/ ▶ **n.** archaic a feeling of pity, distress, or grief. [ME: from the v. RUE[1], prob. influenced by ON *hrygth.*]

ru·the·ni·um /ro͞o'THēnēəm/ ▶ **n.** the chemical element of atomic number 44, a hard silvery-white metal of the transition series. (Symbol: **Ru**) [19th C.: mod. L., from med. L. *Ruthenia*, so named because it was discovered in ores from the Urals.]

ruth·er /'rəT͟Hər/ ▶ **adv.** nonstandard spelling of RATHER, used in representing dialectal speech: *I'd ruther walk.*

Ruth·er·ford /'rəT͟Hərfərd/, Sir Ernest, 1st Baron Rutherford of Nelson (1871–1937), New Zealand physicist, regarded as the founder of nuclear physics. Nobel Prize for Chemistry (1908).

ruth·er·for·di·um /,rəT͟Hər'fôrdēəm/ ▶ **n.** the chemical element of atomic number 104, a very unstable element made by high-energy atomic collisions. (Symbol: **Rf**) [1960s: mod. L., named after E. *Rutherford* (see RUTHERFORD).]

ruth·less /'ro͞oTHləs/ ▶ **adj.** having or showing no pity or compassion for others: *a ruthless manipulator.* — **ruth·less·ly adv. ruth·less·ness n.** [ME: from RUTH + -LESS.]

ru·ti·lant /'ro͞otl-ənt/ ▶ **adj.** literary glowing or glittering with red or golden light: *rutilant gems.* [ME: from L. *rutilant-* 'glowing red,' from the v. *rutilare*, from *rutilus* 'reddish.']

ru·tile /'ro͞o,tēl/ ▶ **n.** a black or reddish-brown mineral consisting of titanium dioxide, typically occurring as needlelike crystals. [19th C.: from Fr., or from Ger. *Rutil*, from L. *rutilus* 'reddish.']

ru·tin /'ro͞otn/ ▶ **n.** Chem. a compound of the flavonoid class found in common rue, buckwheat, capers, and other plants, and sometimes taken as a dietary supplement. [19th C.: from L. *ruta* 'rue' + -IN[1].]

Rut·land /'rətlənd/ an industrial and commercial city in south central Vermont; pop. 17,292.

Rut·ledge[1] /'rətlij/ a family of US politicians. John (1739–1800), Chief Justice of the US 1795, was governor of South Carolina 1779–82 and a US Supreme Court associate justice 1790–91. His brother Edward (1749–1800), a signer of the Declaration of Independence, was governor of South Carolina 1798–1800.

Rut·ledge[2], Wiley Blount, Jr. (1894–1949), US Supreme Court associate justice.

Ru·wen·zo·ri /,ro͞owən'zôrē/ a mountain range in central Africa, on the Uganda–Democratic Republic of the Congo (formerly Zaire) border between lakes Edward and Albert. It rises to 16,765 feet (5,110 m) at Margherita Peak on Mount Stanley. The range is generally thought to be the "Mountains of the Moon" mentioned by Ptolemy and, as such, the supposed source of the Nile.

Ruys·dael var. of RUISDAEL.

RV ▶ **abbr.** ■ recreational vehicle. ■ a rendezvous point. ■ Revised Version (of the Bible).

Rv. ▶ **abbr.** Bible Revelations.

R-val·ue ▶ **n.** the capacity of an insulating material to resist heat flow. The higher the R-value, the greater the insulating power.

RW ▶ **abbr.** ■ Right Worshipful. ■ Right Worthy.

Rwan·da /ro͞o'ändə; rə'wändə/ a landlocked country in central Africa. *See box on next page.* — **Rwan·dan adj. & n. Rwan·dese** /-dēz; -dēs/ **adj. & n.**

rwy. ▶ **abbr.** Brit. Railway.

Rx ▶ **abbr.** ■ prescription. ■ (in prescriptions) take. ■ tens of rupees.

Ry ▶ **abbr.** Railway.

-ry ▶ **suffix** a shortened form of -ERY (as in *devilry*, *rivalry*).

Ry·an /'rīən/, Nolan (1948–), US baseball player; full name *Lynn Nolan Ryan, Jr.* A pitcher for 27 seasons, he pitched a record seven no-hit games.

Rya·zan /,rēə'zän; ryi-/ an industrial city in western Russia, southeast of Moscow; pop. 522,000.

Ry·binsk /'rib(y)insk/ a city in northwestern Russia, a port on the Volga River; pop. 252,000. It was formerly known as Shcherbakov 1946–57 and as Andropov 1984–89.

Ryd·berg at·om /'rid,bərg/ ▶ **n.** Physics an atom in a highly excited state in which one electron has almost sufficient energy to escape. Atoms, usually hydrogen atoms, in this **Rydberg state** are used in atomic research. [named after J. R. *Rydberg* (see RYDBERG CONSTANT).]

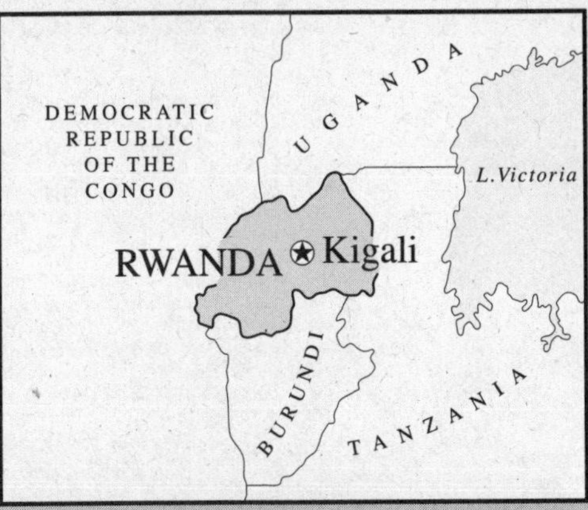

Rwanda

Official name: Republic of Rwanda
Location: central Africa, north of Burundi and south of Uganda
Area: 10,200 square miles (26,300 sq km)
Population: 7,954,000
Capital: Kigali
Languages: Rwanda (a Bantu language), English, and French (all official), Swahili
Currency: Rwandan franc

Ryd·berg con·stant Physics a constant, $1.097 \times 10^7\ m^{-1}$, that appears in the formulae for the wave numbers of lines in atomic spectra and is a function of the rest mass and charge of the electron, the speed of light, and Planck's constant. [20th C.: named after Johannes R. *Rydberg* (1854–1919), Swedish physicist.]

Ry·der[1] /ˈrīdər/, Albert Pinkham (1847–1917), US artist. He is known for seascapes, such as "Toilers of the Sea" (1884), and pastoral landscapes.

Ry·der[2], Jonathan, see LUDLUM.

Ry·der Cup /ˈrīdər/ a golf tournament held every two years and played between teams of male professionals from the US and Europe (originally Great Britain), first held in 1927. [so named because the trophy was donated by Samuel *Ryder* (1859–1936), English seed merchant.]

rye /rī/ ▸n. **1** a wheatlike cereal plant (*Secale cereale*) that tolerates poor soils and low temperatures. ■ grains of this, used mainly for making bread or whiskey and for fodder. **2** (also **rye whis·key**) whiskey in which a significant amount of the grain used in distillation is fermented rye. **3** short for RYE BREAD: *pastrami on rye.* [OE *ryge*, of Gmc. origin; rel. to Du. *rogge* and Ger. *Roggen.*]

rye bread ▸n. bread made with all or part rye flour, typically with caraway seeds added.

rye·grass /ˈrī,gras/ ▸n. a Eurasian grass (genus *Lolium*) that is widely grown as forage. [18th C.: alt. of obs. *ray-grass*, of unknown origin.]

Ryle[1] /rīl/, Gilbert (1900–76), English philosopher. He did much to make Oxford a leading center for philosophical research. In *The Concept of Mind* (1949), he attacked the mind–body dualism of Descartes.

Ryle[2], Sir Martin (1918–84), English astronomer. His demonstration that remote objects appeared to be different from closer ones helped to establish the big bang theory of the universe. Nobel Prize for Physics (1974, shared with Anthony Hewish 1924–).

ryo·kan /rēˈō,kän; -,kan/ ▸n. a traditional Japanese inn. [Japanese.]

ry·ot /ˈrīət/ ▸n. an Indian peasant or tenant farmer. [from Urdu *raiyat*, from Arab. *ra ̔iyya* 'flock, subjects,' from *ra ̔ā* 'to pasture.']

ry·u /rēˈo͞o/ ▸n. (pl. same or **ry·us**) a school or style in Japanese arts, esp. in the martial arts. [Japanese.]

Ryu·kyu Is·lands /rēˈo͞okyo͞o/ a chain of islands in the western Pacific Ocean, stretching about 600 miles (960 km) from the southern tip of the island of Kyushu in Japan to Taiwan. The largest island is Okinawa.

Ryu·rik /rēˈo͝orik; ˈro͝orik/ var. of RURIK.

Ss

S[1] /es/ (also **s**) ▶ **n.** (pl. **Ss** or **S's** /esiz/) **1** the nineteenth letter of the alphabet. ■ denoting the next after R in a set. **2** a shape like that of a capital S: [in comb.] *an S-bend.*

S[2] ▶ **abbr.** ■ (chiefly in Catholic use) Saint: *S Ignatius Loyola.* ■ siemens. ■ small (as a clothes size). ■ South or Southern: *65° S.* ■ Biochem. Svedberg unit(s). ▶ **symb.** ■ the chemical element sulfur. ■ Chem. entropy.

s ▶ **abbr.** ■ second(s). ■ Law section (of an act). ■ shilling(s). ■ Gram. singular. ■ Chem. solid. ■ (in genealogies) son(s). ■ succeeded. ■ Chem. denoting electrons and orbitals possessing zero angular momentum and total symmetry: *s-electrons.* [*s* from *sharp*, orig. applied to lines in atomic spectra.] ▶ **symb.** (in mathematical formulae) distance.

's informal ▶ **contr.** ■ is: *it's raining.* ■ has: *she's gone.* ■ us: *let's go.* ■ does: *what's he do?*

-s[1] ▶ **suffix** denoting the plurals of nouns (as in *apples, wagons*, etc.). Compare with **-ES**[1]. [OE pl. ending *-as.*]

-s[2] ▶ **suffix** forming the third person singular of the present of verbs (as in *sews*). Compare with **-ES**[2]. [OE dial.]

-s[3] ▶ **suffix 1** forming adverbs such as *afterwards, besides.* **2** forming possessive pronouns such as *hers, ours.* [OE *-es*, masc. and neut. genitive sing. ending.]

-'s[1] ▶ **suffix** denoting possession in singular nouns, also in plural nouns not having a final *-s*: *the car's engine.* [OE, masc. and neut. genitive sing. ending.]

-'s[2] ▶ **suffix** denoting the plural of a letter or symbol: *T's* | *9's.*

SA ▶ **abbr.** ■ Salvation Army. ■ South Africa. ■ South America.

s.a. ▶ **abbr.** ■ semiannual. ■ sex appeal. ■ without year or date. [from L. *sine anno.*] ■ subject to approval.

Saa·di var. of **SADI.**

Saa·le[1] /'zälə; 'sä-/ a river in east central Germany. It flows 265 miles (425 km) north to join the Elbe River.

Saa·le[2] ▶ **n.** [usu. as adj.] Geol. the penultimate Pleistocene glaciation in northern Europe, corresponding to the Wolstonian of Britain. ■ the system of deposits laid down at this time. — **Saa·li·an** /'zälēən; 'sä-/ **adj. & n.** [1930s: from **SAALE**[1].]

Saa·me /'sämē/ ▶ **plural n.** var. of **SAMI.**

Saa·mi /'sämē/ ▶ **plural n.** var. of **SAMI.**

Saar /sär; zär/ a river in western Europe. Rising in the Vosges Mountains in eastern France, it flows 150 miles (240 km) north to join the Mosel River in Germany. French name **SARRE.** ■ the Saarland.

Saar·brück·en /sär'brŏŏkən; zär'brʏkən/ a city in western Germany, the capital of Saarland, on the Saar River; pop. 362,000.

Saa·ri·nen /'särənən/, US architects; born in Finland. Eliel (1873–1950) designed the Cranbrook Academy of Art in Michigan 1925. His son Eero (1910–61) designed the Memorial Arch in St. Louis 1948.

Saar·land /'sär,land; 'zär,länt/ a state in western Germany; capital, Saarbrücken. Rich in coal and iron ore, it became the tenth German state in 1957.

Sab. ▶ **abbr.** Sabbath.

Sa·ba /'säbə/ **1** an island in the Netherlands Antilles, in the Caribbean; pop. 1,130. **2** an ancient kingdom in southwestern Arabia, known for its trade in gold and spices; the biblical Sheba.

sab·a·dil·la /,sabə'dilə; -'dēyə/ ▶ **n.** a Mexican plant (*Schoenocaulon officinale*) of the lily family, whose seeds contain veratrine. ■ a preparation of these seeds, used as an agricultural insecticide and in medicines. [19th C.: from Sp. *cebadilla*, dimin. of *cebada* 'barley.']

Sa·bah /'säbä/ a state of Malaysia; capital, Kota Kinabalu.

sa·bal palm /'säbəl/ ▶ **n.** see **PALMETTO.**

sab·ba·tar·i·an /,sabə'te(ə)rēən/ ▶ **n.** a Christian who strictly observes Sunday as the sabbath. ■ a Jew who strictly observes the sabbath. ■ a Christian belonging to a denomination or sect that observes Saturday as the sabbath. ▶ **adj.** relating to or upholding the observance of the sabbath. — **sab·ba·tar·i·an·ism** /-,nizəm/ **n.** [17th C.: from late L. *sabbatarius* (from L. *sabbatum* 'sabbath').]

sab·bath /'sabəTH/ ▶ **n. 1** (often **the Sabbath**) a day of religious observance and abstinence from work, kept by Jews from Friday evening to Saturday evening, and by most Christians on Sunday. **2** (also **witch·es' sab·bath**) a supposed annual midnight meeting of witches with the Devil. [OE, from L. *sabbatum*, via Gk. from Heb. *šabbāṯ*, from *šāḇaṯ* 'to rest.']

sab·bat·i·cal /sə'batikəl/ ▶ **n.** a period of paid leave granted to a college teacher for study or travel, traditionally every seventh year. ▶ **adj.** of or relating to a sabbatical. [16th C.: ult. from Gk. *sabbatikos* 'of the sabbath.']

sab·bat·i·cal year ▶ **n. 1** a year's sabbatical leave. **2** (in biblical times) a year observed every seventh year under the Mosaic law as a "sabbath" during which the land was allowed to rest.

Sa·bel·li·an /sə'belēən/ ▶ **adj.** of or relating to the teachings of Sabellius (*fl.* c.220 in North Africa), who developed a form of the modalist doctrine that the Father, Son, and Holy Spirit are not truly distinct but merely aspects of one divine being. ▶ **n.** a follower of the teachings of Sabellius. — **Sa·bel·li·an·ism** /-,izəm/ **n.**

sa·ber /'sābər/ (Brit. **sa·bre**) ▶ **n.** a heavy cavalry sword with a curved blade and a single cutting edge. ■ a light fencing sword with a tapering blade. ■ the sport of fencing with a saber. ▶ **v.** [trans.] archaic cut down or wound with a saber. [17th C.: from Fr., alt. of obs. *sable*, from Ger. *Sabel* (now *Säbel*), from Hungarian *szablya.*]

cavalry saber

sa·ber·met·rics /,sābər'metriks/ ▶ **n.** Baseball the application of statistical analysis to baseball records, esp. in order to evaluate and compare the performance of individual players. — **sa·ber·me·tri·cian** /,sābərmi'trisHən/ **n.** [1980s: from *SABR*, acronym from Society for American Baseball Research, + **METRICS.**]

sa·ber-rat·tling ▶ **n.** the display or threat of military force.

sa·ber saw ▶ **n.** a portable electric jigsaw.

sa·ber·tooth /'sābər,tōōTH/ ▶ **n. 1** (also **sa·ber-toothed cat** or **sa·ber-toothed ti·ger**) a large extinct carnivorous mammal (genus *Smilodon* of the American Pleistocene and genus *Machairodus* of the Old World Pliocene) of the cat family, with massive, curved upper canine teeth. **2** a large extinct marsupial mammal (genus *Thylacosmilus*, family Borhyaenidae) with similar teeth, of the South American Pliocene.

Sa·bin /'sābin/, Albert Bruce (1906–93), US physician; born in Russia. He developed an oral vaccine against poliomyelitis.

Sa·bine /'sā,bīn; -bin/ ▶ **adj.** of, relating to, or denoting an ancient Oscan-speaking people of the central Apennines in Italy, northeast of Rome, who were incorporated into the Roman state in 290 BC. ▶ **n.** a member of this people. [from L. *Sabinus.*]

Sa·bine Riv·er /sə'bēn/ a river that flows for 360 miles (580 km) from eastern Texas and reaches the Gulf of Mexico at Sabine Pass.

Sa·bin vac·cine /'sābin/ ▶ **n.** a vaccine against poliomyelitis given by mouth. [1950s: Albert B. *Sabin.*]

sab·kha /'sabkə/ ▶ **n.** Geog. an area of coastal flats subject to periodic flooding and evaporation, which result in the accumulation of eolian clays, evaporites, and salts, typically found in North Africa and Arabia. [19th C.: from Arab. *sabḳa* 'salt flat.']

sa·ble[1] /'sābəl/ ▶ **n.** a marten (*Martes zibellina*) with a short tail and dark brown fur, native to Japan and Siberia and valued for its fur. ■ the fur of the sable. [ME: from OFr., in the sense 'sable fur,' from med. L. *sabelum*, of Slavic origin.]

sa·ble[2] ▶ **adj.** literary or Heraldry black. ▶ **n. 1** literary or Heraldry black. ■ (**sables**) archaic mourning garments. **2** (also **sa·ble an·te·lope**) a large African antelope (*Hippotragus niger*) with long curved horns, the male of which has a black coat and the female a russet coat, both having a white belly. [ME: from OFr. (heraldic term), (see **SABLE**[1]).]

sa·ble·fish /'sābəl,fisH/ ▶ **n.** (pl. same or **-fish·es**) a large commercially important fish (*Anoplopoma fimbria*, family Anoplopomatidae) with a slate-blue to black back, occurring throughout the North Pacific.

sab·ot /sa'bō; 'sabō/ ▶ **n. 1** a simple shoe, shaped and hollowed out from a single block of wood. **2** a device that ensures the correct positioning of a bullet or shell in the barrel of a gun. **3** a box from which cards are dealt at casinos in gambling games. Also called **SHOE.** — **sa·boted adj.** (in sense 1). [17th C.: Fr., blend of *savate* 'shoe' and *botte* 'boot.']

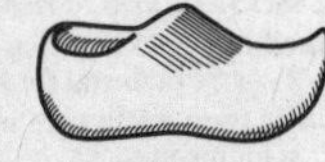

sabot 1

sab·o·tage /'sabə,täzH/ ▶ **v.** [trans.] deliberately destroy, damage, or obstruct (something). ▶ **n.** the action of sabotaging something. [20th C.: from Fr., from *saboter* 'kick with sabots' (see **SABOT**).]

sab·o·teur /,sabə'tər/ ▶ **n.** a person who engages in sabotage. [20th C.: from Fr., from *saboter* (see **SABOTAGE**).]

sa·bra /'säbrə/ ▶ **n.** a Jew born in Israel (or before 1948 in Palestine). [from mod. Heb. *ṣabbār* 'opuntia fruit' (common in coastal regions of Israel).]

sa·bre ▶ **n. & v.** British spelling of SABER.

SAC /sak/ ▶ **abbr.** Strategic Air Command.

Sac ▶ **n.** var. of SAUK.

sac /sak/ ▶ **n.** a hollow, flexible structure resembling a bag or pouch: *a fountain pen with an ink sac.* ■ a cavity enclosed by a membrane within a living organism, containing air, liquid, or solid structures. ■ the membrane surrounding a hernia, cyst, or tumor. [18th C.: from Fr. *sac* or L. *saccus* 'sack, bag.']

Sac·a·ja·we·a /,sakəjə'wēə; -'wäə/ (also **Sacagawea**) (c.1786–1812), Shoshone Indian guide who led the Lewis and Clark expedition across the Rockies 1804–06. Her name means "Bird Woman."

sac·cate /'sa,kit; -āt/ ▶ **adj.** Bot. dilated to form a sac.

sac·cha·ride /'sakə,rīd/ ▶ **n.** Biochem. another term for SUGAR (sense 2). [19th C.: from mod. L. *saccharum* 'sugar.']

sac·cha·rin /'sak(ə)rən/ ▶ **n.** a sweet-tasting synthetic compound, $C_7H_5NO_3S$, used in food and drink as a substitute for sugar. [19th C.: from mod. L. *saccharum* 'sugar.']

sac·cha·rine /'sak(ə)rin; -rēn; -rīn/ ▶ **adj.** [attrib.] excessively sweet or sentimental. ▶ **n.** another term for SACCHARIN. [17th C.: from mod. L. *saccharum*.]

saccharo- ▶ **comb. form** of or relating to sugar. [via L. from Gk. *sakkharon* 'sugar.']

sac·cha·rose /'sakə,rōs/ ▶ **n.** Chem. another term for SUCROSE. [19th C.: from mod. L. *saccharum* 'sugar.']

Sac·co /'sakō/, Nicola (1891–1927), US political radical; born in Italy. In 1921, along with Bartolomeo Vanzetti, he was convicted of murder, and, in 1927, executed in the electric chair. Fifty years later, they were cleared of any crimes.

sac·cule /'sa,kyōōl/ ▶ **n.** Biol. Anat. a small sac. ■ another term for **SACCULUS.** — **sac·cu·lar** /'sakyələr/ **adj.** **sac·cu·lat·ed** /'sakyə,lātid/ **adj.** **sac·cu·la·tion** /,sakyə'lāsʜən/ **n.** [19th C.: Anglicized form of L. *sacculus* (see SACCULUS).]

sac·cu·lus /'sakyələs/ ▶ **n.** Anat. the smaller of the two fluid-filled sacs of the labyrinth of the inner ear. ■ another term for SACCULE. [18th C.: from L., dimin. of *saccus* 'sack.']

sac·er·do·tal /,sasər'dōtl; ,sakər-/ ▶ **adj.** relating to priests or the priesthood; priestly. ■ Theol. relating to a doctrine that ascribes spiritual or supernatural powers to ordained priests. — **sac·er·do·tal·ism** /-,izəm/ **n.** [ME: ult. from L. *sacerdotalis*, from *sacerdos*, *sacerdot-* 'priest.']

sa·chem /'sāchəm/ ▶ **n.** (among some American Indian peoples) a chief or leader. [from Narragansett, 'chief, sagamore.']

sa·chet /sa'shā/ ▶ **n.** a small perfumed bag used to scent clothes. [19th C.: from Fr., dimin. of *sac* 'bag,' from L. *saccus*.]

Sach·sen /'saksən; 'zäk-/ German name for SAXONY.

Sach·sen-An·halt /'änhält/ German name for SAXONY-ANHALT.

sack[1] /sak/ ▶ **n.** **1** a large bag made of a strong material, used for storage and carrying goods. ■ the contents of such a bag or the amount it contains. **2** a loose, unfitted, or shapeless garment. **3** (**the sack**) informal bed, esp. as regarded as a place for sex. **4** (**the sack**) informal dismissal from employment: *he got the sack for swearing.* **5** Baseball, informal a base. **6** Football an act of tackling a quarterback behind the line of scrimmage before he can throw a pass. ▶ **v.** [trans.] **1** informal dismiss from employment. **2** (**sack out**) informal go to sleep or bed. **3** Football tackle (a quarterback) behind the line of scrimmage before he can throw a pass.

– PHRASES **hit the sack** informal go to bed. — **sack·a·ble adj.** **sack·like** /-,līk/ **adj.** [OE *sacc*, from L. *saccus* 'sack, sackcloth,' from Gk. *sakkos*, of Semitic origin.]

sack[2] ▶ **v.** [trans.] (chiefly in historical contexts) plunder and destroy. ▶ **n.** the pillaging of a town or city. [16th C. (n.): from Ital. 'sack, bag,' from L. *saccus*.]

sack[3] ▶ **n.** hist. a dry white wine from Spain. [16th C.: from the phr. *wyne seck*, from Fr. *vin sec* 'dry wine.']

sack·but /'sak,bət/ ▶ **n.** an early form of trombone. [15th C.: from Fr. *saquebute*, from obs. *saqueboute* 'hook for pulling a man off a horse,' from *saquer* 'to pull' + *bouter* 'to hit.']

sack·cloth /'sak,klôth; -,kläth/ ▶ **n.** a very coarse, rough fabric woven from flax or hemp.

– PHRASES **in sackcloth and ashes** in a state of penitence or mourning (Matt 11:21).

sack dress ▶ **n.** a woman's short, loose, unwaisted dress, originally fashionable in the 1950s.

sack·ful /'sak,fōōl/ ▶ **n.** (pl. **-fuls**) the quantity of something held by a sack: *a sackful of rice.*

sack·ing /'sakiNG/ ▶ **n.** **1** an act of sacking someone or something. **2** coarse material for making sacks; sackcloth.

sack race ▶ **n.** a race in which competitors try to jump forward while standing in sacks.

Sack·ville-West /'sak,vil 'west/, Vita (1892–1962), English writer and poet; full name *Victoria Mary Sackville-West*. Her novels include *All Passion Spent* (1931).

sa·cra /'sakrə; 'sā-/ plural form of SACRUM.

sa·cral /'sakrəl; 'sā-/ ▶ **adj.** [attrib.] **1** Anat. of or relating to the sacrum. **2** Anthropol. & Relig. of, for, or relating to sacred rites or symbols: *sacral horns of a Minoan type.* — **sa·cral·i·ty** /sā'kralətē; sə-/ **n.** (in sense 2).

sa·cral·ize /'sakrə,līz; 'sā-/ ▶ **v.** [trans.] imbue with or treat as having a sacred character or quality. — **sa·cral·i·za·tion** /,sakrəli'zāsʜən; ,sā-/ **n.**

sac·ra·ment /'sakrəmənt/ ▶ **n.** a religious ceremony or act of the Christian Church that is regarded as an outward and visible sign of divine grace, in particular: ■ (in the Roman Catholic and many Orthodox Churches) the rites of baptism, confirmation, the Eucharist, penance, anointing of the sick, ordination, and matrimony. ■ (among Protestants) baptism and the Eucharist. ■ (also **the Bless·ed Sac·ra·ment** or **the Ho·ly Sac·ra·ment**) (in Roman Catholic use) the consecrated elements of the Eucharist. ■ a thing of mysterious and sacred significance. [ME: from OFr. *sacrement*, from L. *sacramentum* 'solemn oath,' used in Christian L. as a translation of Gk. *mustērion* 'mystery.']

sac·ra·men·tal /,sakrə'mentl/ ▶ **adj.** relating to or constituting a sacrament or the sacraments. ■ attaching great importance to sacraments. ▶ **n.** an observance analogous to but not reckoned among the sacraments, such as the use of holy water. — **sac·ra·men·tal·ism** /-,izəm/ **n.** **sac·ra·men·tal·i·ty** /,sakrəmən'talitē; -,men-/ **n.** **sac·ra·men·tal·ize** /-,īz/ **v.** **sac·ra·men·tal·ly adv.**

Sac·ra·men·to /,sakrə'mentō/ **1** a river in northern California that flows about 380 miles (611 km) south to San Francisco Bay. **2** the capital of California, northeast of San Francisco; pop. 407,018.

Sac·ra·men·to Moun·tains a range in southern New Mexico and western Texas.

sa·crar·i·um /sə'kre(ə)rēəm/ ▶ **n.** (pl. **-crar·i·a** /-'kre(ə)rēə/) the sanctuary of a church. ■ (in the Roman Catholic Church) a piscina. ■ (in the ancient Roman world) a shrine. [L., from *sacer, sacr-* 'holy.']

sa·cred /'sākrid/ ▶ **adj.** connected with God (or the gods) or dedicated to a religious purpose and so deserving veneration: *sacred rites.* ■ religious rather than secular. ■ (of writing or text) embodying the laws or doctrines of a religion. ■ regarded with great respect and reverence by a particular religion, group, or individual. ■ sacrosanct. — **sa·cred·ly adv.** **sa·cred·ness n.** [ME: past part. of archaic *sacre* 'consecrate,' ult. from L. *sacrare*, from *sacer, sacr-* 'holy.']

sa·cred ba·boon ▶ **n.** another term for HAMADRYAS BABOON.

Sa·cred Col·lege another term for COLLEGE OF CARDINALS.

sa·cred cow ▶ **n.** an idea, custom, or institution held, esp. unreasonably, to be above criticism.

sa·cred i·bis ▶ **n.** a mainly white ibis (*Threskiornis aethiopicus*) with a bare black head and neck and black plumes over the lower back, native to Africa and the Middle East, and venerated by the ancient Egyptians.

sa·cred lo·tus ▶ **n.** see LOTUS (sense 1).

sa·cred scar·ab ▶ **n.** see SCARAB.

sac·ri·fice /'sakrə,fīs/ ▶ **n.** an act of slaughtering an animal or person or surrendering a possession as an offering to God or to a divine or supernatural figure. ■ an animal, person, or object offered in this way. ■ an act of giving up something valued for the sake of something else regarded as more important. ■ Christian Church Christ's offering of himself in the Crucifixion. ■ Christian Church the Eucharist regarded either (in Catholic terms) as a propitiatory offering of the body and blood of Christ or (in Protestant terms) as an act of thanksgiving. ■ (also **sac·ri·fice bunt** or **sac·ri·fice hit**) Baseball a bunted ball that puts the batter out but allows a base runner or runners to advance. ▶ **v.** [trans.] offer or kill as a religious sacrifice. ■ give up (something important or valued) for the sake of other considerations. ■ Baseball advance (a base runner) by a sacrifice. [ME: ult. from L. *sacrificium*; akin to *sacrificus* 'sacrificial,' from *sacer* 'holy.']

sac·ri·fi·cial /,sakrə'fisʜəl/ ▶ **adj.** of, relating to, or constituting a sacrifice: *an altar for sacrificial offerings.* ■ tech. designed to be used up or destroyed. — **sac·ri·fi·cial·ly adv.**

sac·ri·lege /'sakrəlij/ ▶ **n.** violation or misuse of what is regarded as sacred. — **sac·ri·le·gious** /,sakrə'lijəs/ **adj.** **sac·ri·le·gious·ly** /,sakrə'lijəslē/ **adv.** [ME: ult. from L. *sacrilegium*, from *sacrilegus* 'stealer of sacred things,' from *sacer, sacr-* 'sacred' + *legere* 'take possession of.']

sac·ris·tan /'sakristən/ (also **sa·crist** /'sākrist; 'sak-/) ▶ **n.** **1** a person in charge of a sacristy. **2** archaic the sexton of a parish church. [ME: from med. L. *sacristanus*, based on L. *sacer, sacr-* 'sacred.']

sac·ris·ty /'sakristē/ ▶ **n.** (pl. **-ties**) a room in a church where a priest prepares for a service. [ME: ult. from med. L. *sacristia*, based on L. *sacer, sacr-* 'sacred.']

sacro- ▶ **comb. form** of or relating to the sacrum. [from L. *(os) sacrum* 'sacrum.']

sac·ro·il·i·ac /,sakrō'ilē,ak/ ▶ **adj.** Anat. relating to the sacrum and the ilium. ■ denoting the rigid joint at the back of the pelvis.

sac·ro·sanct /'sakrō,saNG(k)t/ ▶ **adj.** (esp. of a principle, place, or routine) regarded as too important or valuable to be interfered with. — **sac·ro·sanc·ti·ty** /,sakrō'saNG(k)titē/ **n.** [15th C.: from L. *sacrosanctus*, from *sacro* 'by a sacred rite' (ablative of *sacrum*) + *sanctus* 'holy.']

sac·rum /'sakrəm; 'sā-/ ▶ **n.** (pl. **sac·ra** /'sakrə; 'sā-/ or **sac·rums**) Anat. a triangular bone in the lower back situated between the two hipbones of the pelvis. [18th C.: from L. *os sacrum*, translation of Gk. *hieron osteon* 'sacred bone.']

SAD ▶ **abbr.** seasonal affective disorder.

sad /sad/ ▶ **adj.** (**sad·der, sad·dest**) **1** feeling or showing sorrow; unhappy: *I was sad and subdued.* ■ causing or characterized by sorrow or regret; unfortunate and regrettable: *a sad day for us all.* **2** informal pathetically inadequate or unfashionable. **3** (of dough) heavy through having failed to rise. — **sad•dish** adj. **sad•ness** n. [OE *sæd* 'sated, weary,' also 'weighty, dense,' of Gmc. origin.]

Sa•dat /sə'dät/, Anwar al- (1918–81), president of Egypt 1970–81; full name *Muhammad Anwar al-Sadat.* He worked to achieve peace in the Middle East. He was assassinated by members of the Islamic Jihad. Nobel Peace Prize (1978, shared with Menachim Begin).

Sad•dam Hus•sein /sə'däm hōō'sān; 'sadəm/ see HUSSEIN³.

sad•den /'sadn/ ▶v. [trans.] (often **be saddened**) cause to feel sorrow; make unhappy: *he was greatly saddened by the death of his only son.*

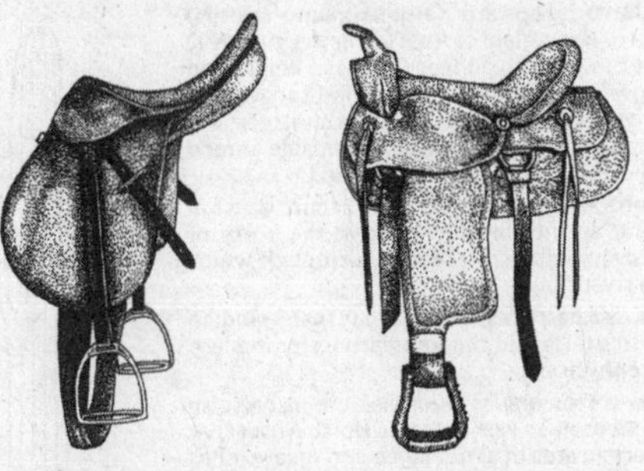

English saddle Western saddle

saddles

sad•dle /'sadl/ ▶n. **1** a leather seat fastened on the back of a horse or other animal for riding. ■ a seat on a bicycle or motorcycle. **2** something resembling a saddle in appearance, function, or position, in particular: ■ a low part of a ridge between two higher points or peaks. ■ Math. a low region of a curve between two high points. ■ a shaped support on which a cable, wire, or pipe rests. **3** a joint of meat consisting of the two loins. ■ the lower part of the back in a mammal or fowl. ▶v. [trans.] put a saddle on (a horse). ■ (usu. **be saddled with**) burden (someone) with an onerous responsibility or task.
– PHRASES **in the saddle** on horseback. ■ fig. in a position of control or responsibility. [OE *sadol*, from Gmc.; akin to Ger. *Sattel*, perh. from Indo-Eur. root shared by L. *sella* 'seat' and SIT.]

sad•dle•back /'sadl,bak/ ▶n. **1** Archit. a tower roof that has two gables connected by a pitched section. **2** a hill with a concave ridge along the top. **3** a black pig with a white stripe across the back. — **sad•dle•backed** adj.

sad•dle•bag /'sadl,bag/ ▶n. each of a pair of bags attached to a horse, bicycle, or motorcycle. ■ (**saddlebags**) excess fat around the hips and thighs.

sad•dle•cloth /'sadl,klôTH; -,kläTH/ ▶n. a cloth laid on a horse's back under the saddle.

sad•dle horse ▶n. **1** a wooden frame or stand on which saddles are cleaned or stored. **2** a horse kept for riding only.

sad•dler /'sadlər/ ▶n. someone who makes, repairs, or deals in saddlery.

sad•dler•y /'sadlərē; -əlrē;/ ▶n. (pl. **-dler•ies**) saddles, bridles, and other equipment for horses. ■ the making or repairing of such equipment. ■ a saddler's business or premises.

sad•dle shoe ▶n. a white oxford shoe with a piece of leather in a contrasting color stitched across the instep.

sad•dle soap ▶n. soft soap containing neat's-foot oil.

sad•dle•sore /'sadl,sôr/ ▶n. a bruise or sore on a horse's back, caused by an ill-fitting saddle. ▶adj. (of a person) chafed from riding on a saddle.

saddle shoe

sad•dle stitch ▶n. a stitch of thread or a wire staple passed through the fold of a magazine or booklet. ■ (in needlework) a decorative stitch made with long stitches on the upper side of the cloth alternated with short stitches on the underside. ▶v. (**saddle-stitch**) [trans.] sew with such a stitch.

sad•dle tree ▶n. a frame around which a saddle is built.

Sad•du•cee /'sajə,sē; 'sadyə-/ ▶n. a member of a Jewish sect that denied the resurrection of the dead, the existence of spirits, and the obligation of oral tradition, emphasizing acceptance of the written Law alone. Compare with PHARISEE. — **Sad•du•ce•an** /,sajə'sēən; ,sadyə-/ adj. [OE *sadducēas* (pl.), ult. from Gk. *Saddoukaios*, from Heb. *ṣĕḏōqī* in the sense 'descendant of Zadok' (2 Sam. 8:17).]

Sade /säd/, Donatien Alphonse François, Comte de (1740–1814), French writer and soldier; known as **the Marquis de Sade**. He was imprisoned periodically for cruelty and debauchery.

sa•dhu /'sädōō/ ▶n. Indian a holy man, sage, or ascetic. [Sanskrit.]

Sa•di /'sädē/ (also **Saa•di**) (*c.*1213–*c.*1291), Persian poet; born *Sheikh Muslih Addin.* His principal works were collected in the *Bustan* (1257) and the *Gulistan* (1258).

sa•dism /'sā,dizəm/ ▶n. the tendency to derive pleasure, esp. sexual gratification, from inflicting pain, suffering, or humiliation on others. ■ (in general use) deliberate cruelty. — **sa•dist** n. **sa•dis•tic** /sə'distik/ adj. **sa•dis•ti•cal•ly** /sə'distik(ə)lē/ adv. [19th C.: from Fr. *sadisme*, after the Marquis de SADE.]

sad•ly /'sadlē/ ▶adv. showing or feeling sadness. ■ [sentence adverb] it is a sad or regrettable fact that; unfortunately: *sadly, the forests of Sulawesi are now under threat.* ■ [as submodifier] to a regrettable extent; regrettably: *his advice is sadly disregarded nowadays.*

sa•do•mas•o•chism /,sādō'masə,kizəm; ,sadō-/ ▶n. psychological tendency or sexual practice characterized by both sadism and masochism. — **sa•do•mas•o•chist** n. **sa•do•mas•o•chis•tic** /,sādō,masə'kistik; ,sadō-/ adj.

sad sack ▶n. informal an inept, blundering person.

sa•fa•ri /sə'färē/ ▶n. (pl. **-ris**) an expedition to observe or hunt animals in their natural habitat. [19th C.: from Kiswahili, from Arab. *safara* 'to travel.']

safe /sāf/ ▶adj. **1** [predic.] protected from or not exposed to danger or risk; not likely to be harmed or lost. ■ Baseball having reached a base without being put out. ■ Baseball allowing the batter to reach base and not involving an error. ■ not likely to cause or lead to harm or injury; not involving danger or risk. ■ (of a place) affording security or protection. ■ often derog. cautious and unenterprising. ■ based on good reasons or evidence and not likely to be proved wrong. **2** uninjured; with no harm done. ▶n. **1** a strong fireproof cabinet with a complex lock, used for the storage of valuables. **2** informal a condom.
– PHRASES **safe in the knowledge that** used to indicate that one can do something without worry on account of a specified fact. **to be on the safe side** in order to have a margin of security against risks. — **safe•ly** adv. **safe•ness** n. [ME (adj.): from OFr. *sauf*, from L. *salvus* 'uninjured.' The n. is from the v. SAVE¹, later assimilated to the adjectival form.]

safe con•duct ▶n. immunity from arrest or harm when passing through an area. ■ a document securing such a privilege.

safe•crack•er /'sāf,krakər/ ▶n. a person who breaks open and robs safes.

safe de•pos•it (also **safe•ty de•pos•it**) ▶n. [usu. as adj.] a strongroom or safe in which valuables may be securely stored, typically within a bank or hotel.

safe•guard /'sāf,gärd/ ▶n. a measure designed to prevent something undesirable. ▶v. [trans.] protect against something undesirable. [ME ('protection'): from OFr. *sauve garde*, from *sauve* 'safe' + *garde* 'guard.']

safe ha•ven ▶n. a place of refuge or security.

safe house ▶n. a house in a secret location, used by spies or criminals in hiding.

safe•keep•ing /'sāf'kēpiNG/ ▶n. preservation in a safe place: *she'd put her wedding ring in her purse for safekeeping.*

safe•light /'sāf,līt/ ▶n. a light with a colored filter that can be used in a darkroom without affecting photosensitive film or paper.

safe sex ▶n. sexual activity in which people take precautions to protect themselves against sexually transmitted diseases such as AIDS.

safe•ty /'sāftē/ ▶n. (pl. **-ties**) **1** the condition of being protected from or unlikely to cause danger, risk, or injury: *they should leave for their own safety.* ■ [as adj.] denoting something designed to prevent injury or damage: *a safety barrier | a safety helmet.* ■ short for SAFETY LOCK. ■ informal a condom. **2** Football a defensive back who normally is positioned well behind the line of scrimmage. ■ a play in which the offense downs the ball in their own end zone, scoring two points for the defense.
– PHRASES **there's safety in numbers** proverb being in a group of people makes you feel more confident about taking action. [ME: from OFr. *sauvete*, from med. L. *salvitas*, from L. *salvus* 'safe.']

safe•ty belt ▶n. another term for SEAT BELT.

safe•ty cage ▶n. a framework of reinforced struts protecting a car's passenger cabin against crash damage.

safe•ty chain ▶n. a chain fitted for security purposes, esp. on a door, watch, or piece of jewelry.

safe•ty cur•tain ▶n. a fireproof curtain that can be lowered between the stage and the main part of a theater.

safe•ty de•pos•it ▶n. another term for SAFE DEPOSIT.

safe•ty fuse ▶n. **1** a protective electric fuse. **2** a fuse that burns at a constant slow rate, used for the controlled firing of a detonator.

safe•ty glass ▶n. **1** glass that has been toughened or laminated so that it is less likely to splinter. **2** (**safety glasses**) toughened glasses or goggles for protecting the eyes.

safe•ty har•ness ▶n. a system of belts or restraints to hold a person to prevent falling or injury.

safe•ty lamp ▶n. a miner's portable lamp with a flame that is protected, typically by wire gauze, to reduce the risk of explosion from ignited methane (firedamp).

safe•ty lock (also **safe•ty catch**) ▶n. a device that prevents a gun from being fired or a machine from being operated accidentally.

safe•ty match ▶n. a match igniting only when struck on a specially prepared surface.

safe·ty net ▶ n. a net placed to catch an acrobat or similar performer in case of a fall. ■ fig. a safeguard against possible adversity.

safe·ty pin ▶ n. a pin with a point that is bent back to the head and is held in a guard when closed. ▶ v. [trans.] **(safety-pin)** fasten with a safety pin.

safe·ty ra·zor ▶ n. a razor with a guard to reduce the risk of cutting the skin.

safe·ty valve ▶ n. a valve opening automatically to relieve excessive pressure, esp. in a boiler. ■ fig. a means of giving harmless vent to feelings of tension or stress.

saf·flow·er /ˈsafˌlouər/ ▶ n. an orange-flowered, thistlelike Eurasian plant (*Carthamus tinctorius*) of the daisy family, with seeds that yield an edible oil and petals that were formerly used to produce a red or yellow dye. ■ **(saf·flow·er oil)** the edible oil obtained from the seeds of this plant. [ME: from Du. *saffloer* or Ger. *Saflor*, via OFr. and Ital. from Arab. *aṣfar* 'yellow'; influenced by SAFFRON and FLOWER.]

saf·fron /ˈsafrən/ ▶ n. **1** an orange-yellow flavoring, food coloring, and dye made from the dried stigmas of a crocus: [as adj.] *saffron buns.* ■ the orange-yellow color of this. **2** (also **saf·fron cro·cus**) an autumn-flowering crocus (*Crocus sativus*) with reddish-purple flowers, native to warmer regions of Eurasia. Enormous numbers of flowers are required to produce a small quantity of the large red stigmas used for the spice. — **saf·fron·y** adj. [ME: from OFr. *safran*, based on Arab. *za farān*.]

sag /sag/ ▶ v. **(sagged, sag·ging)** [intrans.] sink or subside gradually under weight or pressure or through lack of strength: *he sagged against the wall.* ■ hang down loosely or unevenly. ■ have a downward bulge or curve. ■ fig. decline to a lower level, usually temporarily. ▶ n. a downward curve or bulge in a structure caused by weakness or excessive weight or pressure. ■ Geom. the perpendicular distance from the middle of a curve to the straight line between the two supporting points. ■ fig. a decline, esp. a temporary one. — **sag·gy** adj. [ME (v.): prob. rel. to Mid. Low Ger. *sacken*, Du. *zakken* 'subside.']

sa·ga /ˈsägə/ ▶ n. a long story of heroic achievement. ■ a long, involved story, account, or series of incidents. [18th C.: from ON, lit. 'narrative'; akin to SAW[3].]

sa·ga·cious /səˈgāsHəs/ ▶ adj. having or showing keen mental discernment and good judgment; shrewd. — **sa·ga·cious·ly** adv. [17th C.: from L. *sagax, sagac-* 'wise.']

sa·gac·i·ty /səˈgasitē/ ▶ n. the quality of being sagacious: *a man of great political sagacity.*

sag·a·more /ˈsagəˌmôr/ ▶ n. (among some American Indian peoples) a chief; a sachem. [from Eastern Abnaki *sákəmá* 'strong man.']

Sa·gan[1] /ˈsāgən/, Carl Edward (1934-96), US astronomer. He showed that amino acids can be synthesized. He wrote several popular science books and coproduced the television series *Cosmos* (1980).

Sa·gan[2] /säˈgäN/, Françoise (1935–2004), French writer; pen name of *Françoise Quoirez*. She wrote *Bonjour Tristesse* (1954).

sage[1] /sāj/ ▶ n. **1** an aromatic plant (*Salvia officinalis*) of the mint family, with grayish-green leaves that are used as a culinary herb, native to southern Europe and the Mediterranean. **2** (also **white sage**) either of two bushy North American plants with silvery-gray leaves: ■ an aromatic plant (*Artemisia ludoviciana*) of the daisy family, formerly burned by the Cheyenne for its cleansing properties and as an incense. ■ a plant (*Krascheninnikovia lanata*) of the goosefoot family. **3** short for SAGEBRUSH. [ME: from OFr. *sauge*, from L. *salvia* 'healing plant,' from *salvus* 'safe.']

sage[2] ▶ n. a profoundly wise man. ▶ adj. having, showing, or indicating profound wisdom. — **sage·ly** adv. **sage·ness** n. [ME (adj.): from OFr., from L. *sapere* 'be wise.']

sage·brush /ˈsājˌbrəsH/ ▶ n. a shrubby aromatic North American plant (genus *Artemisia*) of the daisy family. ■ scrub that is dominated by such shrubs, occurring chiefly in semiarid regions of western North America.

sage green ▶ n. a grayish-green color like that of sage leaves.

sage grouse ▶ n. a large grouse (*Centrocercus urophasianus*) of western North America, with long pointed tail feathers, noted for the male's courtship display in which air sacs are inflated to make a popping sound.

sag·ger /ˈsagər/ (also **sag·gar**) ▶ n. a protective fireclay box enclosing ceramic ware while it is being fired. [18th C.: prob. a contr. of SAFEGUARD, n.]

Sag Har·bor /sag/ a village in eastern Long Island in New York, a 19th-century whaling port; pop. 2,134.

Sag·i·naw /ˈsagəˌnô/ a city in east central Michigan; pop. 69,512.

Sa·git·ta /səˈjitə/ Astron. a small northern constellation (the Arrow), in the Milky Way north of Aquila. [L.]

sag·it·tal /ˈsajitl/ Anat. ▶ adj. **1** relating to or denoting the front-to-back suture on top of the skull. **2** of or in a plane parallel to this suture. — **sag·it·tal·ly** adv. [ME: from med. L. *sagittalis*, from L. *sagitta* 'arrow.']

Sag·it·tar·i·us /ˌsajiˈte(ə)rēəs/ **1** Astron. a large constellation (the Archer), said to represent a centaur carrying a bow and arrow. **2** Astrol. the ninth sign of the zodiac, which the sun enters about November 22. ■ **(a Sagittarius)** (pl. same) a person born when the sun is in this sign. — **Sag·it·ta·ri·an** /-ˈte(ə)rēən/ n. & adj. (in sense 2). [L.]

sag·it·tate /ˈsajəˌtāt/ ▶ adj. Bot. & Zool. shaped like an arrowhead. [18th C.: from L. *sagitta* 'arrow.']

sa·go /ˈsāgō/ ▶ n. (pl. **-gos**) **1** edible starch that is obtained from a palm and is a staple food in parts of the tropics. ■ (also **sa·go pud·ding**) a sweet dish made from sago and milk. **2** **(sa·go palm)** the palm (*Metroxylon sagu*) from which most sago is obtained, growing in freshwater swamps in Southeast Asia. ■ any of a number of other palms or cycads that yield a similar starch. [16th C.: ult. from Malay *sagu*.]

Sa·gra·da Fa·mi·lia /säˈgrädə fəˈmilyə; -ˈmilēə/ an expiatory temple (not a cathedral) in Barcelona, Spain, begun in 1882 and still unfinished. Antonio Gaudí took over construction of the church in 1883 and in 1891 became its official architect.

sa·gua·ro /səˈ(g)wärō/ (also **sa·gua·ro cac·tus**) ▶ n. (pl. **-ros**) a giant cactus (*Carnegiea gigantea*) that can grow to 66 feet (20 m) in height and whose branches are shaped like candelabra, native to Mexico and the southwestern US. Its reddish-purple fruit is consumable as food and drink. [19th C.: from Mex. Sp.]

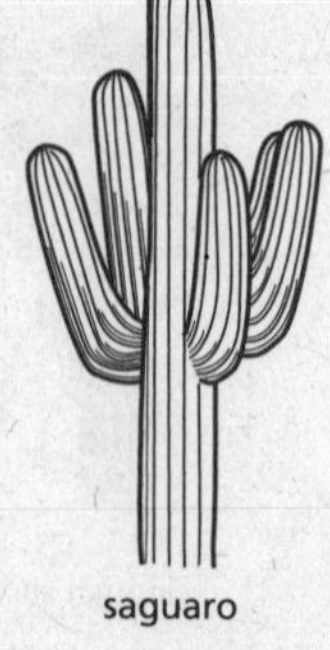
saguaro

Sa·gui·a el Ham·ra /ˈsägēə el ˈhamrə; ˈsägyä el ˈämrä/ an intermittent river in the north of Western Sahara. ■ the region through which this river flows.

Sa·ha /ˈsäˌhä/, Meghnad (1894–1956), Indian physicist. He laid the foundations for modern astrophysics.

Sa·har·a Des·ert /səˈharə; -ˈhe(ə)rə; -ˈhärə/ (also **the Sa·har·a**) a vast desert in North Africa that covers an area of about 3,500,000 square miles (9,065,000 sq km). — **Sa·har·an** adj.

Sa·hel /səˈhāl; -ˈhēl; -ˈhel/ a vast semiarid region of North Africa, south of the Sahara. — **Sa·hel·i·an** /-ēən/ adj. & n.

sa·hib /ˈsä(h)ib/ ▶ n. Indian a polite title or form of address for a man: *the Doctor Sahib.* [Urdu, via Pers. from Arab. *ṣāḥib* 'friend, lord.']

said /sed/ past and past participle of SAY. ▶ adj. used in legal language or humorously to refer to someone or something already mentioned or named.

Sai·da /ˈsīdə/ Arabic name for SIDON.

sai·ga /ˈsīgə/ (also **sai·ga an·te·lope**) ▶ n. an Asian antelope (*Saiga tartarica*) that has a distinctive convex snout with the nostrils opening downward, living in herds on the cold steppes. [19th C.: from Russ.]

Sai·gon /sīˈgän; ˈsīgän/ official name (until 1975) of HO CHI MINH CITY.

sail /sāl/ ▶ n. **1** a piece of material extended on a mast to catch the wind and propel a boat, ship, or other vessel: *all the sails were unfurled.* ■ the use of sailing ships as a means of transport. ■ [in sing.] a voyage or excursion in a ship or boat. **2** something resembling a sail in shape or function, in particular: ■ a wind-catching apparatus, typically one consisting of a set of boards, attached to the arm of a windmill. ■ the broad fin on the back of a sailfish or of some prehistoric reptiles. ■ a structure by which an animal is propelled across the surface of water by the wind. ■ the conning tower of a submarine. ▶ v. [intrans.] **1** travel in a boat with sails. ■ [with adverbial] travel in a ship or boat using sails or engine power. ■ [with adverbial] begin a voyage; leave a harbor. ■ [trans.] travel by ship on or across (a sea) or on (a route): *plastic ships could be sailing the oceans soon.* ■ [trans.] navigate or control (a boat or ship). **2** [with adverbial of direction] move smoothly and rapidly or in a stately or confident manner. ■ **(sail through)** informal succeed easily at (something, esp. a test or examination). ■ **(sail into)** informal attack physically or verbally with force.
– PHRASES **in** (or **under**) **full sail** with all the sails in position or fully spread. **take in sail** furl the sail or sails of a vessel. — **sail·a·ble** adj. **sailed** adj. [in comb.] *a black-sailed ship.* [OE *segel* (n.), *seglian* (v.), Gmc. origin; rel. to Du. *zeil* and Ger. *Segel* (nouns).]

sail·board /ˈsālˌbôrd/ ▶ n. a board with a mast attached to it by a swivel joint, and a sail, used in windsurfing. — **sail·board·er** n. **sail·board·ing** n.

sail·boat /ˈsālˌbōt/ ▶ n. a boat propelled by sails.

sail·cloth /ˈsālˌklôTH; -ˌkläTH/ ▶ n. canvas or other material used for making sails. ■ a canvaslike fabric used for making clothes.

sail·er /ˈsālər/ ▶ n. [usu. with adj.] a sailing ship or boat of specified power or manner of sailing: *the great ships were abominable sailers: sluggish and difficult to maneuver* | *a four-masted motor sailer.*

sail·fin mol·ly /ˈsālˌfin/ ▶ n. a small, brightly colored freshwater fish (genus *Poecilia*, family Poeciliidae), the male of which has a long, high dorsal fin. Native to North and Central America, it is popular in aquariums. [*sailfin* from the dorsal fin + MOLLY.]

sail·fish /ˈsālˌfisH/ ▶ n. (pl. same or **-fish·es**) a fish with a high, saillike dorsal fin, in particular: ■ an edible migratory billfish that is a prized game fish (genus *Istiophorus*, family Istiophoridae, esp. *I. platypterus*). ■ (also **Celebes sailfish**) a small tropical freshwater fish of Sulawesi, popular in aquariums (*Telmatherina ladigesi*, family Atherinidae).

sailfish

sail·ing /ˈsāliNG/ ▶ n. the action of sailing in a ship or boat: [as adj.] *a sailing club.*

sail·ing ship ▶ n. a ship driven by sails.

sail·mak·er /ˈsālˌmākər/ ▶ n. a person who makes, repairs, or alters sails as a profession. — **sail·mak·ing** /-ˌmākiNG/ n.

sail·or /ˈsālər/ ▶ n. a person whose job it is to work as a member of the crew of a commercial or naval ship or boat, esp. one who is below the rank of officer. ■ [usu. with adj.] a person who goes sailing as a sport or recreation. ■ **(a good/bad sailor)** a person who rarely (or often) gets sick at sea in rough weather. — **sail·or·ly** adj. [17th C.: var. of obs. *sailer*.]

sail·or suit ▶ n. a suit of blue and white material resembling the dress uniform of an ordinary seaman.

sail·plane /ˈsālˌplān/ ▶ n. a glider designed for sustained flight.

sain·foin /ˈsānˌfoin/ ▶ n. a pink-flowered plant (*Onobrychis viciifolia*) of the pea family, native to Asia and grown widely for fodder. [17th C.: from obs. Fr. *saintfoin*, from mod. L. *sanum foenum* 'wholesome hay' (from its medicinal properties).]

saint /sānt/ ▶ n. **1** a person acknowledged as holy or virtuous. ■ (in the Catholic and Orthodox Churches) a person formally recognized or canonized by the Church after death, who may be the object of veneration and prayers for intercession. ■ a person who is admired because of their virtue. ■ (in or alluding to biblical use) a Christian believer. ■ **(Saint)** a member of the Church of Jesus Christ of Latter-Day Saints; a Mormon. **2** **(Saint)** (abbr.: **St.** or **S.**) used in titles of religious saints: *the epistles of Saint Paul | St. John's Church.* ■ used in place names or other dedications: *St. Louis.* ▶ v. [trans.] formally recognize as a saint; canonize. ■ [as adj.] **(sainted** /ˈsāntid/**)** worthy of being a saint. — **saint·hood** /-ˌho͝od/ n. **saint·like** /-ˌlīk/ adj. [ME, from OFr. *seint*, from L. *sanctus* 'holy,' past part. of *sancire* 'consecrate.']

St. An·drews a town in eastern Scotland, on the North Sea; pop. 14,000. It is noted for its championship golf courses.

St. An·drew's Cross ▶ n. Heraldry a diagonal or X-shaped cross, esp. white on a blue background (as a national emblem of Scotland). Also called SALTIRE. See illustration at CROSS.

St. An·tho·ny's Cross (also **St. Anthony Cross**) ▶ n. a T-shaped cross.

St. An·tho·ny's Fire ▶ n. **1** another term for ERYSIPELAS. **2** another term for ERGOTISM.

Saint Au·gus·tine a historic city in northeastern Florida, near the Atlantic coast. Founded by the Spanish in 1565, it is the oldest city in the US; pop. 11,692.

St. Bas·il's Ca·the·dral /ˈbazəlz/ a cathedral on the south side of Red Square in Moscow, commissioned by Ivan the Terrible in 1552.

St. Ber·nard /bərˈnärd/ (also **St. Bernard dog**) ▶ n. a large dog of a breed originally kept to rescue travelers by the monks of the Hospice on the Great St. Bernard Pass in the Swiss Alps.

St. Bernard

St. Ber·nard Pass either of two passes across the Alps in southern Europe. The **Great St. Bernard Pass** is on the border between southwestern Switzerland and Italy. The **Little St. Bernard Pass** is on the French–Italian border southeast of Mont Blanc.

Saint Cath·e·rines /ˈkaTH(ə)rənz/ a city in southern Ontario in Canada, on Lake Ontario; pop. 129,300.

Saint Charles a city in east central Missouri, on the Missouri River; pop. 60,321.

St. Chris·to·pher and Ne·vis, Federation of official name of ST. KITTS AND NEVIS.

Saint Clair Riv·er /ˈkle(ə)r/ a short river that forms part of the boundary between Michigan and Ontario.

Saint Cloud a city in east central Minnesota, on the Mississippi River; pop. 59,107.

St. Croix /kroi/ an island in the Caribbean Sea, the largest of the US Virgin Islands; chief town, Christiansted.

Saint Croix Riv·er **1** a river that flows for 75 miles (120 km) from eastern Maine to form the border with New Brunswick in Canada before entering Passamaquoddy Bay. **2** a river that flows for 164 miles (265 km) from northwestern Wisconsin to the Mississippi River.

Saint-Den·is /ˌsaN dəˈnē/ **1** a northern suburb of Paris, France. **2** the capital of the French island of Réunion; pop. 122,000.

Saint Eli·as Moun·tains /iˈlīəs/ a section of the Coast Ranges in southeastern Alaska and Yukon Territory in Canada. Mount Logan, the highest point in Canada, is here, along with other high peaks and numerous glaciers.

St. El·mo's fire /ˈelmōz/ ▶ n. a phenomenon in which a luminous electrical discharge appears on a ship or aircraft during a storm. [*St. Elmo*, patron saint of sailors.]

St.-É·tienne /ˌsaNt āˈtyen/ a city in southeastern central France, southwest of Lyons; pop. 202,000.

St. Eu·sta·ti·us /yo͞oˈstāSH(ē)əs/ a small volcanic island in the Caribbean Sea; pop. 2,000.

Saint-Ex·u·pé·ry /ˌsaNt egˌzypāˈrē/, Antoine Marie Roger de (1900–44), French writer. He wrote *The Little Prince* (1943).

Saint Fran·cis Riv·er a river that flows for 425 miles (685 km) from southeastern Missouri to the Mississippi River.

Saint-Gau·dens /ˈgôdnz/, Augustus (1848–1907), US sculptor; born in Ireland. His gilded bronze statue of General William Tecumseh Sherman on horseback (1892–1903) is in New York's Central Park

Saint George a city in southwestern Utah; pop. 49,663.

St. George's the capital of Grenada, in the southwestern part of the island; pop. 36,000.

St. George's Chan·nel a channel between Wales and Ireland that links the Irish Sea with the Celtic Sea.

St. George's Cross ▶ n. a cross shaped like a plus sign, red on a white background.

St. He·le·na /həˈlēnə/ an island in the South Atlantic, a British dependency; pop. 6,000; capital, Jamestown. The islands of Ascension, Tristan da Cunha, and Gough Island are dependencies of St. Helena. Napoleon died here in 1821. — **St. He·le·ni·an** /-nēən/ adj. & n.

St. Hel·ens /ˈhelənz/ a town in northwestern England; pop. 175,000.

St. Hel·ens, Mount an active volcano in southwestern Washington, in the Cascade Range, that rises to 8,312 feet (2,560 m). A dramatic eruption in May 1980 reduced its height by more than a thousand feet.

St. John **1** an island in the Caribbean Sea, part of the US Virgin Islands. **2** (usu. **Saint John**) a city in New Brunswick, in eastern Canada, a port on the Bay of Fundy; pop. 74,969.

St. John's **1** the capital of Antigua and Barbuda, situated on the northwestern coast of Antigua; pop. 36,000. **2** the capital of Newfoundland, a port on the southeastern coast of the island; pop. 95,770.

St. John's wort (also **St. Johns·wort**) ▶ n. a herbaceous plant or shrub (genus *Hypericum*, family Guttiferae) with distinctive yellow five-petaled flowers and paired oval leaves, used in medicinal preparations to treat various disorders, including depression. [because some species bloom near the feast day of St. John the Baptist (June 24).]

Saint Joseph a city in northwestern Missouri; pop. 73,990.

St. Kitts and Ne·vis /ˈkits an ˈnēvis; ˈnevis/ a country that consists of two adjoining islands in the Leeward Islands in the Caribbean Sea; pop. 44,000; capital, Basseterre.

Saint Lau·rent /ˌsaN lôˈräN/, Yves Mathieu (1936–), French fashion designer; born in Algeria; full name *Yves Henri Donat Mathieu-Saint-Laurent*.

Saint Law·rence Is·land an island in western Alaska, in the Bering Sea.

St. Law·rence Riv·er a river in North America that flows for about 750 miles (1,200 km) from Lake Ontario along the border between Canada and the US to the Gulf of St. Lawrence on the Atlantic coast.

St. Law·rence Sea·way a waterway in North America that flows for 2,342 miles (3,768 km) through the Great Lakes and along the course of the St. Lawrence River to the Atlantic Ocean. It consists of channels connecting the lakes and a number of artificial sections that bypass the rapids in the river.

Saint-Lô /saN ˈlō/ a town in northwestern France, in Normandy; pop. 23,000. It was almost completely destroyed during the Allied invasion of World War II.

St. Lou·is /ˈlo͞o-is; ˈlo͞o-ē/ a city in eastern Missouri, on the Mississippi River just south of its confluence with the Missouri River; pop. 348,189.

Saint Lou·is Park /ˈlo͞oəs/ a city in southeastern Minnesota; pop. 43,787.

St. Lu·cia /ˈlo͞oSHə; lo͞oˈsēə/ a country in the Caribbean Sea, one of the Windward Islands; pop. 164,200; capital, Castries. — **St. Lu·cian** adj. & n.

saint·ly /ˈsāntlē/ ▶ adj. (**-li·er, -li·est**) very holy or virtuous: *a truly saintly woman.* ■ of or relating to a saint: *a crypt for some saintly relic.* — **saint·li·ness** n.

St. Mark's Ca·the·dral the cathedral church of Venice since 1807.

St. Mar·tin /sānt ˈmärtn; ˌsaN märˈtaN/ a small island in the Caribbean, one of the Leeward Islands; pop. 32,000. The southern section of the island forms part of the Netherlands Antilles; the larger northern section is part of the French overseas department of Guadeloupe. Dutch name SINT MAARTEN.

St. Mo·ritz /ˌsānt məˈrits; ˌsaN môˈrēts/ a winter-sports center in southeastern Switzerland.

St. Paul the capital of Minnesota, on the Mississippi River adjacent to Minneapolis with which it forms the Twin Cities metropolitan area; pop. 287,151.

saint·pau·lia /ˌsāntˈpôlēə/ ▶ n. a plant of the genus *Saintpaulia* (family Gesneriaceae), esp. (in gardening) an African violet. [named after Baron W. von *Saint Paul* (1860–1910), the German explorer who discovered it.]

St. Paul's Ca·the·dral a cathedral in London, designed by Sir Christopher Wren and built 1675–1711.

St. Pe·ters /ˈpētərz/ a city in eastern Missouri; pop. 51,381.

St. Pe·ter's Ba·sil·i·ca a Roman Catholic basilica in the Vatican City, built in the 16th century. The supposed site of St. Peter's crucifixion, it is the largest Christian church.

St. Pe·ters·burg /ˈpētərzˌbərg/ **1** a city in northwestern Russia, on the delta of the Neva River; pop. 5,035,000. Founded in 1703 by Peter the Great, St. Petersburg was the capital of Russia from 1712 until the Russian Revolution. Former names **PETROGRAD** (1914-24) and **LENINGRAD** (1924-91). **2** a resort city in western Florida; pop. 248,232.

St. Pierre and Miq·ue·lon /sānt 'pi(ə)r and 'mikə,län; saN 'pyer; mek'lôN/ a group of eight small islands in the North Atlantic Ocean, off the southern coast of Newfoundland; pop. 6,390. The islands are the last remaining French possession in North America.

Saint-Saëns /saN 'säNs/, Charles Camille (1835–1921), French composer. His compositions include *Danse macabre* (1874) and the opera *Samson and Delila* (1877).

saint's day ▶ **n.** a day on which a saint is particularly commemorated in the Christian Church.

Saint-Si·mon[1] /,saN sē'môN/, Claude-Henri de Rouvroy, Comte de (1760–1825), French reformer and philosopher. He argued that society should be given spiritual direction by scientists.

Saint-Si·mon[2], Louis de Rouvroy, Duc de (1675–1755), French writer. His *Mémoires* gave a detailed record of court life between 1694 and 1723.

St. Thom·as an island in the Caribbean Sea, part of the US Virgin Islands, east of Puerto Rico; pop. 48,170; chief town, Charlotte Amalie.

Saint-Tro·pez /,san trō'pā/ a resort on the Mediterranean coast of southern France; pop. 6,000.

St. Vin·cent and the Gren·a·dines an island state in the Windward Islands in the Caribbean Sea that consists of the island of St. Vincent and some of the Grenadine Islands; pop. 108,000; capital, Kingstown.

St. Vi·tus's dance ▶ **n.** old-fashioned term for **SYDENHAM'S CHOREA.** [because a visit to *St. Vitus*'s shrine was believed to alleviate it.]

Sai·pan /sī'pan/ the largest of the Northern Mariana Islands in the western Pacific Ocean.

Sa·kai /'sä'kī/ a city in Japan, south of Osaka; pop. 808,000.

sake[1] /sāk/ ▶ **n.** **1** (**for the sake of something** or **for something's sake**) for the purpose of; in the interest of; in order to achieve or preserve. ■ used in phrases to comment on the speaker's purpose in choosing a particular way of wording a text or presenting an argument: *let us say, for the sake of argument, that the plotter and the assassin are one and the same person.* ■ (**for its own sake** or **something for something's sake** or **for the sake of it**) used to indicate something that is done as an end in itself. **2** (**for the sake of someone** or **for someone's sake**) out of consideration for or in order to help someone. ■ in order to please: *he killed a man for my sake.* **3** (**for God's** or **goodness** etc. **sake**) used to express impatience, annoyance, urgency, or desperation.

– PHRASES **for old times' sake** in memory of former times; in acknowledgment of a shared past. [OE *sacu* 'strife, crime,' from Gmc.; akin to Ger. *Sache*, from Gmc., 'affair, thing.']

sa·ke[2] /'säkē/ (also **sa·ki** or **sa·ké**) ▶ **n.** a Japanese alcoholic drink made from fermented rice, traditionally drunk warm in small porcelain cups. [Japanese.]

sa·ker /'säkər/ ▶ **n.** **1** a large Eurasian falcon (*Falco cherrug*) with a brown back and whitish head, used in falconry. **2** an early form of cannon. [ME: from OFr. *sacre*, from Arab. *ṣaḳr* 'falcon.']

Sa·kha, Republic of /'säkə/ official name for **YAKUTIA.**

Sa·kha·lin /'sakə,lēn; ,səKHəl'yēn/ an island in the Sea of Okhotsk, off the coast of eastern Russia and separated from it by the Tartar Strait; capital, Yuzhno-Sakhalinsk.

Sa·kha·rov /'säKHə,rôf; 'säk-; -,rôv/, Andrei Dmitrievich (1921–89), Russian physicist and civil rights activist. He fought for reform and human rights in the Soviet Union for which he was sentenced to internal exile 1980-86. Nobel Peace Prize (1975).

Sa·ki /'säkē/ (1870–1916), British writer; born in Burma (now Myanmar); pen name of *Hector Hugh Munro*. His stories frequently depict animals as agents seeking revenge on humankind.

sa·ki[1] /'säkē; 'sakē/ ▶ **n.** (pl. **-kis**) a tropical American monkey (genera *Pithecia* and *Chiropotes*, family Cebidae) with coarse fur and a long bushy nonprehensile tail. [18th C.: via Fr. from Tupi *saui*.]

sa·ki[2] ▶ **n.** var. of **SAKE**[2].

sal /sal/ ▶ **n.** a northern Indian tree (*Shorea robusta*, family Dipterocarpaceae) that yields teaklike timber and dammar resin. It is the most commercially important source of timber in India. [18th C.: from Hindi *sāl*.]

sa·laam /sə'läm/ ▶ **exclam.** a common greeting in many Arabic-speaking and Muslim countries. ▶ **n.** a gesture of greeting or respect, consisting of a low bow with the hand or fingers touching the forehead. ■ (**salaams**) respectful compliments. ▶ **v.** [intrans.] make a salaam. [17th C.: from Arab. *(al-)salām (alaikum)* 'peace (be upon you).']

sal·a·ble /'sāləbəl/ (also **sale·a·ble**) ▶ **adj.** fit or able to be sold. — **sal·a·bil·i·ty** /,sālə'bilitē/ **n.**

sa·la·cious /sə'lāSHəs/ ▶ **adj.** (of writing, pictures, or talk) treating sexual matters in an indecent way. ■ lustful; lecherous: *his salacious grin faltered.* — **sa·la·cious·ly** **adv.** **sa·la·cious·ness** **n.** **sa·lac·i·ty** /-'lasitē/ **n.** (dated). [17th C.: from L. *salax, salac-*, from *salire* 'to leap.']

sal·ad /'saləd/ ▶ **n.** a cold dish of various mixtures of raw or cooked vegetables, usually seasoned with oil, vinegar, or other dressing: *a green salad.* ■ [with adj.] a mixture containing a specified ingredient dressed with mayonnaise: *tuna salad.* [ME: from OFr. *salade*, from Provençal *salada*, based on L. *sal* 'salt.']

sal·ad days ▶ **plural n.** (**one's salad days**) the period when one is young and inexperienced. [from Shakespeare's *Antony and Cleopatra*.]

sal·ad dress·ing ▶ **n.** see **DRESSING** (sense 1).

Sal·a·din /'salədn; 'salə,din/ (1137–93), sultan of Egypt and Syria 1174–93; Arabic name *Salah-ad-Din Yusuf ibn-Ayyub*.

sa·lal /sə'lal/ ▶ **n.** a North American plant (*Gaultheria shallon*) of the heath family, with clusters of pink or white flowers and edible purple-black berries. [19th C.: from Chinook Jargon *sallal*.]

Sa·lam /sä'läm/, Abdus (1926–96), Pakistani physicist. He explained electromagnetic interactions and the weak nuclear force. Nobel Prize for Physics (1979, shared with Sheldon Glashown (1932–) and Steven Weinberg (1933–)).

Sal·a·man·ca /,salə'maNGkə; ,sälə'mäNGkə/ a city in western Spain; pop. 186,000.

sal·a·man·der /'salə,mandər/ ▶ **n.** **1** a newtlike amphibian (Salamandridae and other families, order Urodela) that typically has bright markings, and that once was thought to be able to endure fire. **2** a mythical lizardlike creature able to withstand fire. ■ an elemental spirit living in fire. **3** a metal plate heated and placed over food. — **sal·a·man·drine** /,salə'mandrin/ **adj.** [ME (sense 2): from OFr. *salamandre*, via L. from Gk. *salamandra*.]

sa·la·mi /sə'lämē/ ▶ **n.** (pl. same or **-mis**) a type of highly seasoned sausage, originally from Italy. [Ital., pl. of *salame*, from a late L. word meaning 'to salt.']

Sal·a·mis /'saləmis/ an island in the Saronic Gulf in Greece.

sal am·mo·ni·ac /'sal ə'mōnē,ak/ ▶ **n.** old-fashioned term for **AMMONIUM CHLORIDE.** [ME: from L. *sal ammoniacus* 'salt of Ammon' (see **AMMONIACAL**).]

Sa·lang Pass /sä'läNG/ a route across the Hindu Kush in Afghanistan.

sa·lar·i·at /sə'le(ə)rēət/ ▶ **n.** (**the salariat**) salaried white-collar workers. [20th C.: from Fr., from *salaire* 'salary.']

sal·a·ried /'salərēd/ ▶ **adj.** receiving or recompensed by a salary rather than a wage: *salaried employees.*

sal·a·ry /'salərē/ ▶ **n.** (pl. **-ries**) a fixed regular payment, typically paid on a monthly or biweekly basis but often expressed as an annual sum, made by an employer to an employee. Compare with **WAGE.** ▶ **v.** (**-ries, -ried**) [trans.] archaic pay a salary to. [ME: from Anglo-Norman Fr. *salarie*, from L. *salarium*, orig. 'allowance to buy salt,' from *sal* 'salt.']

sal·a·ry·man /'salərēmən/ ▶ **n.** (pl. **-men**) (esp. in Japan) a white-collar worker.

sa·lat /sə'lät/ ▶ **n.** the ritual prayer of Muslims, performed five times daily in a set form. [Arab., pl. of *salāh* 'prayer, worship.']

Sa·la·zar /'salə,zär/, Antonio de Oliveira (1889–1970), prime minister of Portugal 1932–68. He maintained neutrality throughout the Spanish Civil War and World War II.

sal·bu·ta·mol /sal'byōōtə,môl; -,mäl/ ▶ **n.** Med. a synthetic compound used as a bronchodilator. [1960s: from *sal(icylic acid)* + *but(yl)* + *am(ine)*.]

sal·chow /'salkou/ (also **Sal·chow**) ▶ **n.** a jump in figure skating with a backward takeoff from the backward inside edge of one skate to the backward outside edge of the other, with one or more full turns in the air. [20th C.: Ulrich *Salchow* (1877–1949), Swedish skater.]

sale /sāl/ ▶ **n.** **1** the exchange of a commodity for money; the action of selling something. ■ (**sales**) a quantity or amount sold. ■ (**sales**) the activity or business of selling products. **2** an event for the rapid disposal of goods at reduced prices, esp. at the end of a season: *a clearance sale.* ■ [often with adj.] a public or charitable event at which goods are sold. ■ a public auction.

– PHRASES (**up**) **for sale** offered for purchase; to be bought. **on sale** offered for purchase. ■ offered for purchase at a reduced price. [OE *sala*, from ON *sala*, from Gmc.; akin to **SELL.**]

sale·a·ble ▶ **adj.** var. of **SALABLE.**

Sa·lem /'sāləm/ **1** a city in Tamil Nadu in southern India; pop. 364,000. **2** the state capital of Oregon, southwest of Portland; pop. 136,924. **3** a city in northeastern Massachusetts, north of Boston; pop. 38,091. **4** a town in southeastern New Hampshire, southeast of Derry; pop. 28,112.

Sa·ler·no /sə'lərnō; -'le(ə)r-/ a city on the western coast of Italy, on the Gulf of Salerno; pop. 151,000.

sales·clerk /'sālz,klərk/ (also **sales clerk**) ▶ **n.** an assistant who sells goods in a retail store.

sales·girl /'sālz,gərl/ ▶ **n.** a female salesclerk.

sales·la·dy /'sālz,lādē/ ▶ **n.** (pl. **-dies**) a saleswoman, esp. one working as a salesclerk.

sales·man /'sālzmən/ ▶ **n.** (pl. **-men**) a man whose job involves selling or promoting commercial products. — **sales·man·ship** /-,SHip/ **n.**

sales·per·son /'sālz,pərsən/ ▶ **n.** (pl. **-per·sons** or **-peo·ple**) a salesman or saleswoman.

sales·room /'sālz,rōōm; -,rŏŏm/ ▶ **n.** a room in which items are sold at auction. ■ a showroom displaying goods offered for sale.

sales tax ▶ **n.** a tax on sales or on the receipts from sales.

sales·wom·an /'sālz,wŏŏmən/ ▶ **n.** (pl. **-wom·en**) a woman whose job involves selling or promoting commercial products.

Sal·ford /'sôlfərd; 'sal-/ a city in northwestern England; pop. 218,000.

sal·i·cin /'salisin/ ▶ **n.** Chem. a bitter compound present in willow bark. It is a glucoside related to aspirin. [19th C.: from Fr. *salicine*, from L. *salix, salic-* 'willow.']

sal·i·cyl·ic ac·id /ˌsalə'silik/ ▶**n.** Chem. a bitter compound, $C_6H_4(OH)(COOH)$, present in certain plants. It is used as a fungicide and in the manufacture of aspirin and dyestuffs. —**sa·lic·y·late** /sə'lisəˌlāt; -lit/ **n.** [19th C.: from Fr. *salicyle*, radical of the acid.]

sa·li·ent /'sālyənt; -lēənt/ ▶**adj.** **1** most noticeable or important: *the salient points of the case.* ■ prominent; conspicuous. ■ (of an angle) pointing outward. The opposite of REENTRANT. **2** [postpositive] Heraldry (of an animal) standing on its hind legs with the forepaws raised, as if leaping. ▶**n.** a piece of land or section of fortification that juts out to form an angle. ■ an outward bulge in a battle line. —**sa·li·ence n. sa·li·en·cy n. sa·li·ent·ly adv.** [16th C. (heraldic term): from L. *salient-* 'leaping,' from the verb *salire*.]

Sa·li·en·tia /ˌsālē'enCHə/ Zool. another term for ANURA. —**sa·li·en·tian n. & adj.** [mod. L. (pl.), from L. *salire* 'to leap.']

sa·lif·er·ous /sə'lif(ə)rəs/ ▶**adj.** Geol. (of rock or strata) containing much salt. [19th C.: from L. *sal* 'salt.']

Sa·li·na /sə'līnə/ a city in central Kansas; pop. 45,679.

sa·li·na /sə'līnə; -'lē-/ ▶**n.** (chiefly in the Caribbean or South America) a salt pan, salt lake, or salt marsh. [16th C.: from Sp., ult. from L. *salinae* (pl.) 'salt pans.']

Sa·li·nas /sə'lēnəs/ a city in west central California; pop. 108,777.

sa·line /'sāˌlēn; -ˌlīn/ ▶**adj.** containing or impregnated with salt: *saline alluvial soils.* ■ esp. Med. (of a solution) containing sodium chloride and/or a salt of magnesium or other alkali metal. ▶**n.** a solution of salt in water. ■ a saline solution used in medicine. —**sa·lin·i·ty** /sə'linitē/ **n. sal·i·ni·za·tion** /ˌsalənə'zāSHən/ **n. sal·i·nize** /'saləˌnīz/ **v.** [15th C.: from L. *sal* 'salt' + -INE¹.]

Sal·in·ger /'salənjər/, J. D. (1919–), US writer; full name *Jerome David Salinger.* He wrote the novel *The Catcher in the Rye* (1951).

sal·i·nom·e·ter /ˌsalə'nämitər/ ▶**n.** an instrument for measuring the salinity of water.

Salis·bur·y¹ /'sôlzˌberē; 'salz-; -b(ə)rē/ **1** a city in southern England; pop. 35,000. **2** former name (until 1982) of HARARE.

Salis·bur·y² /'sôlzˌberē; 'salz-; -b(ə)rē/, Robert Arthur Talbot Gascoigne-Cecil, 3rd Marquess of (1830–1903), prime minister of Britain 1885–86, 1886–92, 1895–1902.

Sa·lish /'sāliSH/ ▶**n.** (pl. same) **1** a member of a group of American Indian peoples inhabiting areas of the northwestern US and British Columbia. **2** the group of related languages spoken by the Salish. ▶**adj.** of or relating to the Salish or their languages. —**Sa·lish·an** /-ən/ **adj.** [the Flathead name.]

sa·li·va /sə'līvə/ ▶**n.** watery liquid secreted into the mouth by the salivary glands. —**sal·i·var·y** /'saləˌverē/ **adj.** [ME: from L.]

sal·i·vate /'saləˌvāt/ ▶**v.** [intrans.] secrete saliva. ■ fig. display great relish at the sight or prospect of something. —**sal·i·va·tion** /ˌsalə'vāSHən/ **n.**

Salk /sô(l)k/, Jonas Edward (1914–95), US microbiologist. He developed the **Salk vaccine** against polio in the early 1950s.

sal·let /'salit/ ▶**n.** hist. a light helmet with an outward curve extending over the back of the neck. [ME: from Fr. *salade*, based on L. *caelare* 'engrave' (from *caelum* 'chisel').]

sallet

sal·low¹ /'salō/ ▶**adj.** (**-low·er, -low·est**) (of a person's complexion) of an unhealthy yellowish color. ▶**v.** [trans.] rare make sallow. —**sal·low·ish adj. sal·low·ness n.** [OE *salo* 'dusky,' from Gmc.; akin to ON *sǫlr* 'yellow.']

sal·low² ▶**n.** esp. Brit. a willow tree, esp. one of a low-growing or shrubby kind. —**sal·low·y adj.** [OE *salh*, from Gmc.; akin to ON *selja*, and L. *salix* 'willow.']

sal·ly /'salē/ ▶**n.** (pl. **-lies**) a sudden charge out of a besieged place against the enemy; a sortie. ■ a brief journey or sudden start into activity. ■ a witty or lively remark; a retort. ▶**v.** (**-lies, -lied**) [intrans.] make a military sortie: *they sallied out to harass the enemy.* ■ formal or humorous set out from a place to do something. [ME: from Fr. *saillie*, fem. past part. of *saillir* 'come out,' from OFr. *salir* 'to leap,' from L. *salire*.]

Sal·ly Light·foot /'salē 'lītˌfo͝ot/ ▶**n.** (pl. **Sal·ly Light·foots**) a common active crab (*Grapsus grapsus*, family Grapsidae) of rocky shores in the Caribbean, Central America, and the Galapagos Islands.

sal·ma·gun·di /ˌsalmə'gəndē/ ▶**n.** (pl. **-dis**) a dish of chopped meat, anchovies, eggs, onions, and seasoning. ■ a general mixture; a miscellaneous collection. [from Fr. *salmigondis*.]

sal·mi /'salmē/ ▶**n.** (pl. **-mis**) a ragout or casserole of game stewed in a rich sauce: *a pheasant salmi.* [Fr., abbrev. of *salmigondis* (see SALMAGUNDI).]

salm·on /'samən/ ▶**n.** (pl. same or (esp. of types) **-ons**) **1** a large edible game fish that matures in the sea but migrates to freshwater streams to spawn. The **Atlantic salmon** (*Salmo salar*) may return to spawn two or three times, but the five species of Pacific salmon (genus *Oncorhynchus*) always die after spawning. ■ the pink flesh of this fish as food. **2** any of a number of fishes that resemble the true salmons. **3** a pale pinkish orange color. —**salm·on·y adj.** [ME *samoun*, from Anglo-Norman Fr. *saumoun*, from L. *salmo, salmon-*.]

salm·on·ber·ry /'samənˌberē/ ▶**n.** (pl. **-ries**) a North American bramble (genus *Rubus*) that bears pink raspberrylike fruit. ■ the edible fruit of this plant.

sal·mo·nel·la /ˌsalmə'nelə/ ▶**n.** (pl. **-nel·lae** /-'nelē/) a bacterium (genus *Salmonella*) that occurs mainly in the intestine, esp. a serotype causing food poisoning. ■ food poisoning caused by infection with such a bacterium: *an outbreak of salmonella.* —**sal·mo·nel·lo·sis** /-ˌne'lōsis/ **n.** [mod. L., after Daniel E. *Salmon* (1850–1914), American vet-erinary surgeon.]

sal·mo·nid /'sa(l)mənid/ ▶**n.** Zool. a fish of the salmon family (Salmonidae).

sal·mo·noid /'sa(l)məˌnoid/ Zool. ▶**n.** a fish of a group (superfamily Salmonoidea) that includes the salmon family together with the pikes and smelts. ▶**adj.** of or relating to fish of this group.

Salm·on Riv·er a river that flows for 425 miles (685 km) through central Idaho.

salm·on trout ▶**n.** a large trout or troutlike fish, in particular: ■ a lake trout. ■ Brit. a sea trout.

Sa·lo·me /ˌsälə'mā; sə'lōmē/ (in the New Testament) the daughter of Herodias, who danced before her stepfather Herod Antipas. As reward, she asked for the head of St. John the Baptist.

sa·lon /sə'län; sa'lôN/ ▶**n.** **1** an establishment where a hairdresser, beautician, or couturier works. **2** a reception room in a large house. ■ a meeting of intellectuals or other eminent people at the invitation of a celebrity or socialite. [17th C.: from Fr. (see SALOON).]

Sa·lon·i·ca /sə'lônikə; ˌsalə'nēkə/ another name for THESSALONIKI.

sa·loon /sə'lo͞on/ ▶**n.** a public room or building used for a specified purpose: *a billiard saloon.* ■ hist. humorous a place where alcoholic drinks may be bought and drunk. ■ a large public room for use as a lounge on a ship. ■ (also **sa·loon car**) Brit. a luxurious railroad car. [18th C. ('drawing room'): from Fr. *salon*, from Ital. *salone*, augmentative of *sala* 'hall.']

sa·loon·keep·er /sə'lo͞onˌkēpər/ (also **sa·loon keep·er**) ▶**n.** a person who runs a bar; a bartender.

salp /salp/ ▶**n.** a free-swimming marine invertebrate (class Thaliacea) related to the sea squirts with a transparent, barrel-shaped body. [19th C.: from Fr. *salpe*, based on Gk. *salpē* 'fish.']

sal·pi·glos·sis /ˌsalpə'glôsis; -'gläsis/ ▶**n.** a South American plant (genus *Salpiglossis*) of the nightshade family, cultivated for its brightly patterned funnel-shaped flowers. [mod. L., from Gk. *salpinx* 'trumpet' + *glōssa* 'tongue.']

sal·pin·gec·to·my /ˌsalpən'jektəmē/ ▶**n.** (pl. **-mies**) surgical removal of the fallopian tubes.

sal·pin·gi·tis /ˌsalpən'jītis/ ▶**n.** Med. inflammation of the fallopian tubes.

salpingo- (also **salping-** before a vowel) ▶**comb. form** relating to the fallopian tubes: *salpingostomy.* [from Gk. *salpinx, salping-* 'trumpet.']

sal·pin·gos·to·my /ˌsalpən'gästəmē/ ▶**n.** surgical unblocking of a blocked fallopian tube.

sal·sa /'sälsə/ ▶**n.** **1** a type of Latin American dance music incorporating elements of jazz and rock. ■ a dance performed to this music. **2** (esp. in Latin American cooking) a spicy tomato sauce. [Sp., lit. 'sauce.']

sal·si·fy /'salsəfē; -ˌfī/ ▶**n.** an edible European plant (*Tragopogon porrifolius*) of the daisy family, with a long root like that of a parsnip. Also called OYSTER PLANT. ■ the root of this plant used as a vegetable. [17th C.: from Fr. *salsifis*, from obs. Ital. *salsefica*.]

SALT /sôlt/ ▶**abbr.** Strategic Arms Limitation Talks.

salt /sôlt/ ▶**n.** **1** (also **com·mon salt**) sodium chloride (NaCl), a white crystalline substance that gives seawater its characteristic taste and is used for seasoning or preserving food. ■ literary something that adds freshness or piquancy. ■ a saltcellar. ■ table salt mixed with a specified seasoning: *garlic salt.* **2** Chem. any chemical compound formed from the reaction of an acid with a base, with all or part of the hydrogen of the acid replaced by a metal or other cation. **3** (usu. **old salt**) informal an experienced sailor. ▶**adj.** [attrib.] **1** impregnated with, treated with, or tasting of salt: *salt water* | *salt beef.* **2** (of a plant) growing on the coast or in salt marshes. ▶**v.** [trans.] **1** [usu. as adj.] (**salted**) season or preserve with salt: *cook the carrots in boiling salted water.* ■ fig. make (something) piquant or more interesting. ■ sprinkle (a road or path) with salt in order to melt snow or ice. **2** informal fraudulently make (a mine) appear to be a paying one by placing rich ore into it. **3** [as adj.] (**salted**) (of a horse) having developed a resistance to disease by surviving it.

– PHRASES **rub salt into the** (or **someone's**) **wound** make a painful experience even more painful for someone. **the salt of the earth** a person or group of people of great kindness, reliability, or honesty. [with biblical allusion to Matt 5:13.] **take something with a grain** (or **pinch**) **of salt** regard something as exaggerated; believe only part of something. **worth one's salt** good or competent at the job or profession specified.

– PHRASAL VERBS **salt something away** informal secretly store or put by something, esp. money. —**salt·ish adj. salt·less adj.** [OE *sealt* (n.), *sealtan* (v.), of Gmc. origin; rel. to Du. *zout* and Ger. *Salz* (nouns), from an Indo-Eur. root shared by L. *sal*, Gk. *hals* 'salt.']

salt-and-pep·per ▶**adj.** flecked or speckled with intermingled dark and light shades: *his salt-and-pepper hair.*

sal·ta·tion /ˌsôl'tāSHən/ ▶**n.** **1** Biol. abrupt evolutionary change; sudden large-scale mutation. **2** Geol. the movement of hard particles over an uneven surface in a turbulent flow of air or water. —**sal·ta·to·ry** /'saltəˌtôrē; 'sôl-/ **adj.** [17th C. (sense 3): from L. *saltatio(n-)*, from *saltare* 'to dance,' frequentative of *salire* 'to leap.']

sal·ta·to·ri·al /ˌsaltə'tôrēəl; ˌsôl-/ ▶**adj.** esp. Entomol. (esp. of grasshoppers) adapted for leaping.

salt·box /'sôlt,bäks/ ▶n. a frame house having up to three stories at the front and one fewer at the back with a steeply pitched roof.

salt·bush /'sôlt,bo͝osh/ ▶n. a salt-tolerant orache plant sometimes used in the reclamation of saline soils or to provide grazing in areas of salty soil.

salt ce·dar ▶n. a tamarisk (*Tamarix gallica*) with reddish-brown branches and feathery gray foliage.

salt·cel·lar /'sôlt,selər/ ▶n. a container for storing salt, typically a closed container with perforations. [ME: from SALT + obs. *saler*, from OFr. *salier* 'salt-box,' from L. *salarium* (see SALARY).]

salt dome ▶n. a dome-shaped structure in sedimentary rocks, formed where a large mass of salt has been forced upward.

salt·er /'sôltər/ ▶n. hist. a person dealing in or employed in the production of salt. ■ a person whose work involved the preservation of meat or fish in salt.

sal·tern /'sôltərn/ ▶n. a set of pools in which seawater is left to evaporate to make salt. [OE *sealtærn* 'saltworks,' lit. 'salt building.']

salt flats ▶plural n. areas of flat land covered with a layer of salt.

salt grass (also **salt·grass**) ▶n. grass (esp. *Distichlis spicata*) growing in salt marshes or in alkaline regions.

Sal·ti·llo /säl'tēyō/ a city in northern Mexico, capital of the state of Coahuila; pop. 441,000.

sal·tim·boc·ca /,sältim'bōkə/ ▶n. a dish consisting of rolled pieces of veal or poultry cooked with herbs, bacon, and other flavorings. [Ital., lit. 'leap into the mouth.']

sal·tine /sôl'tēn/ ▶n. a thin, crisp, savory cracker sprinkled with salt.

sal·tire /'sal,tī(ə)r; 'sôl-/ ▶n. Heraldry another term for ST. ANDREW'S CROSS. ■ [as adj.] (of a design) incorporating a motif based on such a diagonal cross. — **sal·tire·wise** /-,wīz/ adv. [ME: from OFr. *saultoir* 'stirrup cord,' based on L. *saltare* 'to dance.']

Salt Lake Cit·y the capital of Utah, in the northern part of the state; pop. 181,743. It was founded in 1847 by Brigham Young.

salt lick ▶n. a place where animals go to lick salt from the ground. ■ a block of salt provided for animals to lick.

salt marsh ▶n. an area of coastal grassland that is regularly flooded by seawater.

salt mead·ow ▶n. a meadow that is subject to flooding by seawater; a salt marsh.

Sal·ton Sea /'sôltn/ a salt lake in southeastern California, created by a 1905 diversion of the Colorado River.

salt pan ▶n. a shallow container or depression in the ground in which salt water evaporates to leave a deposit of salt.

salt·pe·ter /sôlt'pētər/ (Brit. **salt·pe·tre**) ▶n. another term for POTASSIUM NITRATE. [ME: from OFr. *salpetre*, from med. L. *salpetra*, prob. from *sal petrae* 'salt of rock' (i.e., encrustation); influenced by SALT.]

salt·wa·ter /'sôlt,wôtər; -,wätər/ ▶adj. [attrib.] of or found in salt water; living in the sea: *saltwater fish.*

salt·wa·ter croc·o·dile ▶n. a large and dangerous crocodile (*Crocodylus porosus*) occurring in estuaries and coastal waters from southwestern India to northern Australia.

salt·wort /'sôltwərt; -'wôrt/ ▶n. a plant (genus *Salsola*) of the goosefoot family that typically grows in salt marshes. It is rich in alkali, and its ashes were formerly used in soap-making.

salt·y /'sôltē/ ▶adj. (**salt·i·er**, **salt·i·est**) tasting of, containing, or preserved with salt. ■ (of language or humor) down-to-earth; coarse. ■ informal tough; aggressive. — **salt·i·ness** n.

sa·lu·bri·ous /sə'lo͞obrēəs/ ▶adj. health-giving; healthy: *salubrious weather.* ■ (of a place) pleasant; not run-down. — **sa·lu·bri·ous·ly** adv. **sa·lu·bri·ous·ness** n. **sa·lu·bri·ty** /-britē/ n. [16th C.: from L. *salubris* from *salus* 'health'.]

sa·lut /sa'lo͞o; sä'ly/ ▶exclam. used to express friendly feelings toward one's companions before drinking. [Fr.]

sal·u·tar·y /'salyə,terē/ ▶adj. (esp. with reference to something unwelcome or unpleasant) producing good effects; beneficial. [ME (n. 'remedy'): ult. from L. *salutaris*, from *salus, salut-* 'health.']

sal·u·ta·tion /,salyə'tāshən/ ▶n. a gesture or utterance made as a greeting or acknowledgment of another's arrival or departure. ■ a standard formula of words used in a letter to address the person being written to. — **sal·u·ta·tion·al** /-shənl/ adj.

sa·lu·ta·to·ri·an /sə,lo͞otə'tôrēən/ ▶n. the student who ranks second highest in a graduating class and delivers the salutatory.

sa·lu·ta·to·ry /sə'lo͞otə,tôrē/ ▶adj. (esp. of an address) relating to or of the nature of a salutation. ▶n. (pl. **-ries**) an address of welcome, esp. one given as an oration by the student ranking second highest in a graduating class at a high school or college.

sa·lute /sə'lo͞ot/ ▶n. a gesture of respect, homage, or polite recognition or acknowledgment, esp. one made to or by a person when arriving or departing. ■ a prescribed movement, typically a raising of a hand to the head, made by a member of a military or similar force as a formal sign of respect or recognition. ■ [often with adj.] the discharge of a gun or guns as a formal or ceremonial sign of respect or celebration. ▶v. [trans.] make a formal salute to. ■ greet. ■ show or express admiration and respect for. — **sa·lut·er** n. [ME (v.): from L. *salutare* 'greet,' from *salus, salut-* 'health, greeting.']

Sal·va·dor /'salvə,dôr; ,salvə'dôr/ a city on the Atlantic coast of eastern Brazil, capital of the state of Bahia; pop. 2,075,000. Former name BAHIA.

Sal·va·dor·ean /,salvə'dôrēən/ ▶adj. of or relating to El Salvador. ▶n. a native or inhabitant of El Salvador.

sal·vage /'salvij/ ▶v. [trans.] rescue (a wrecked or disabled ship or its cargo) from loss at sea. ■ retrieve or preserve (something) from potential loss or adverse circumstances. ▶n. the rescue of a wrecked or disabled ship or its cargo from loss at sea. ■ the cargo saved from a wrecked or sunken ship. ■ the rescue of property or material from potential loss or destruction. — **sal·vage·a·ble** adj. **sal·vag·er** n. [17th C. (payment for saving a ship): from Fr., from med. L. *salvagium*, from L. *salvare* 'to save.']

sal·va·tion /sal'vāshən/ ▶n. Theol. deliverance from sin and its consequences. ■ preservation or deliverance from harm, ruin, or loss. ■ (**one's salvation**) a source or means of being saved in this way: *his only salvation was to outfly the enemy.* [ME: ult. from eccles. L. *salvation-*, from *salvare* 'to save.']

Sal·va·tion Ar·my (abbr.: **SA**) a worldwide Christian evangelical organization on quasi-military lines. Established by William Booth, it is noted for its work with the poor and for its brass bands. — **sal·va·tion·ism** /-,nizəm/ n. **sal·va·tion·ist** /sal'vāshənist/ n.

salve[1] /sav; säv/ ▶n. an ointment used to promote healing of the skin or as protection. ■ fig. something that is soothing or consoling for wounded feelings or an uneasy conscience. ▶v. [trans.] archaic apply salve to. ■ fig. soothe (wounded pride or one's conscience): *charity salves our conscience.* [OE *sealfe* (n.), *sealfian* (v.), of Gmc. origin; rel. to Du. *zalf* and Ger. *Salbe*.]

salve[2] /salv/ ▶v. archaic term for SALVAGE. — **salv·a·ble** /'salvəbəl/ adj. [18th C.: back-form. from the n. SALVAGE.]

sal·ver /'salvər/ ▶n. a tray, typically one made of silver and used in formal circumstances. [17th C.: from Fr. *salve* 'tray for a king,' from Sp. *salva* 'sampling of food,' from *salvar* 'make safe.']

sal·vi·a /'salvēə/ ▶n. a widely distributed plant (genus *Salvia*) of the mint family, esp. (in gardening) a bedding plant cultivated for its spikes of bright flowers. [mod. L., from L. *salvia* 'sage.']

sal·vo /'sal,vō/ ▶n. (pl. **-os** or **-oes**) a simultaneous discharge of artillery or other guns in a battle. ■ a number of weapons released from one or more aircraft in quick succession. ■ fig. a sudden, vigorous, or aggressive act or series of acts. [16th C. (earlier as *salve*): from Fr. *salve*, Ital. *salva* 'salutation.']

sal vo·la·ti·le /,sal və'latl-ē/ ▶n. a scented solution of ammonium carbonate in alcohol, used as smelling salts. [17th C.: mod. L., lit. 'volatile salt.']

sal·vor /'salvər/ ▶n. a person engaged in salvage of a ship or items lost at sea.

Sal·ween /'sal,wēn/ a river in southeastern Asia that rises in Tibet and flows for 1,500 miles (2,400 km) to the Gulf of Martaban, an inlet of the Andaman Sea.

Salz·burg /'sôlz,bərg; 'sälz-; 'zälts,bo͝ork/ a city in western Austria; pop 144,000. It is noted for its annual music festivals.

Salz·git·ter /'zälts,gitər/ a city in Germany, in Lower Saxony; pop. 115,000.

SAM /sam/ ▶abbr. surface-to-air missile.

Sam. ▶abbr. Bible Samuel.

sa·ma·dhi /sə'mädē/ ▶n. (pl. **-dhis**) Hinduism & Buddhism a state of intense concentration achieved through meditation, at which union with the divine is reached. ■ Indian a funerary monument. [from Sanskrit *samādhi* 'contemplation.']

Sa·mar /'sä,mär/ an island in the Philippines, southeast of Luzon. It is the third largest island in the group.

Sam·a·ra /sə'märə/ a city in southwestern central Russia, on the Volga River; pop. 1,258,000. Former name (1935–91) KUIBYSHEV.

sam·a·ra /'samərə; sə'me(ə)rə/ ▶n. Bot. a winged nut or achene containing one seed, as in ash and maple. [16th C.: mod. L., from L., denoting an elm seed.]

Sa·mar·i·a /sə'me(ə)rēə/ **1** an ancient city in central Palestine, founded in the 9th century BC as the capital of the northern Hebrew kingdom of Israel. **2** the region of ancient Palestine around this city, between Galilee in the north and Judaea in the south.

Sam·a·rin·da /,samə'rində/ a city in Indonesia, in eastern Borneo; pop. 265,000.

Sa·mar·i·tan /sə'maritn; -'me(ə)r-/ ▶n. **1** (usu. **good Samaritan**) a charitable or helpful person (with reference to Luke 10:33). **2** a member of a people inhabiting Samaria in biblical times, or of the modern community in the region of Nablus claiming descent from them. **3** the dialect of Aramaic formerly spoken in Samaria. ▶adj. of or relating to Samaria or the Samaritans. — **Sa·mar·i·tan·ism** /-,izəm/ n. [from late L. *Samaritanus*, from Gk. *Samareitēs*, from *Samareia* 'Samaria.']

sa·mar·i·um /sə'me(ə)rēəm/ ▶n. the chemical element of atomic number 62, a hard, silvery-white metal of the lanthanide series. (Symbol: **Sm**) [19th C.: from *samar(skite)*, a mineral in which its spectrum was first observed (named after *Samarsky*, a 19th-cent. Russian official) + -IUM.]

Sam·ar·kand /'samər,kand; səmər'känt/ (also **Sam·ar·qand**) a city in eastern Uzbekistan; pop. 370,000. It was the capital of Tamerlane's Mongol empire in the 14th century.

sam·ba /'sambə; 'säm-/ ▶n. a Brazilian dance of African origin. ■ a piece of music for this dance. ■ a lively modern ballroom dance imitating this dance. ▶v. (**-bas**, **-baed** /-bəd/ or **-ba'd**, **-ba·ing** /-bə,iNG/) [intrans.] dance the samba. [19th C.: from Port., of Afr. origin.]

sam·bar /'sämbər; 'sam-/ ▶ **n.** a dark brown woodland deer (*Cervus unicolor*) with branched antlers, of South Asia and the Philippines. [17th C.: from Hindi *sābar*, from Sanskrit *śambara*.]

Sam·bo /'sambō/ ▶ **n.** (pl. **-bos** or **-boes**) **1** offens. a black person. [18th C.: perh. from Fula *sambo* 'uncle.'] **2** (**sambo**) hist. a person of mixed race, esp. of black and Indian or black and European blood. [18th C.: from Amer. Sp. *zambo*, a kind of monkey.]

Sam Browne belt /sam 'broun/ ▶ **n.** a leather belt with a supporting strap that passes over the right shoulder. [20th C.: Sir *Sam*uel J. *Brown(e)* (1824–1901), British military commander.]

Sa·me /'sāmē/ ▶ **plural n.** var. of **Sami**.

same /sām/ ▶ **adj.** (**the same**) **1** identical; not different; unchanged. ■ (**this/that same**) referring to a person or thing just mentioned: *that same year I went to Boston.* **2** of an identical type: *they all wore the same clothes.* ▶ **pron.** **1** (**the same**) the same thing as something previously mentioned. ■ people or things that are identical or share the same characteristics. **2** (chiefly in formal or legal use) the person or thing just mentioned: *sighted sub, sank same.* ▶ **adv.** similarly; in the same way.
– PHRASES **all** (or **just**) **the same** in spite of this; nevertheless. ■ in any case; anyway. **at the same time 1** simultaneously. **2** on the other hand; nevertheless; yet. **be all the same to** be unimportant to (someone) what happens. **one and the same** the same person or thing (used for emphasis). **same difference** informal used to express the speaker's belief that two or more things are essentially the same, in spite of apparent differences. **same here** informal the same applies to me. (**the**) **same to you!** may you do or have the same thing (a response to a greeting or insult). — **same·ness n.** [ME: from ON *sami*, from an Indo-Eur. root shared by Sanskrit *sama*, Gk. *homos*.]

Sa·mhain /'souən/ ▶ **n.** the first day of November, celebrated by the ancient Celts as a festival marking the beginning of winter and the Celtic new year. [Irish, from Old Irish *samain*.]

Sa·mi /'sāmē/ (also **Saa·mi** /'sä-/, **Sa·me**, or **Saa·me**) ▶ **plural n.** the Lapps of northern Scandinavia. [Lappish, of unknown origin.]

sam·i·sen /'sami,sen/ (also **sham·i·sen** /'sʜam-/) ▶ **n.** a traditional Japanese three-stringed lute with a square body, played with a large plectrum. [17th C.: Japanese, from Chin. *san-hsien*, from *san* 'three' + *hsien* 'string.']

sam·iz·dat /'sämiz,dät; səmyiz'dät/ ▶ **n.** the clandestine copying and distribution of literature banned by the state, esp. formerly in communist countries. [1960s: Russ., lit. 'self-publishing house.']

Sam·nite /'sam,nīt/ ▶ **n.** a member of an Oscan-speaking people of southern Italy in ancient times. ▶ **adj.** of or relating to this people. [from L. *Samnites* (pl.); rel. to *Sabinus* (see **Sabine**).]

Sa·mo·a /sə'mōə/ a group of islands in Polynesia, divided between American Samoa and the nation of Samoa. ■ a country consisting of the western islands of Samoa. *See box.*

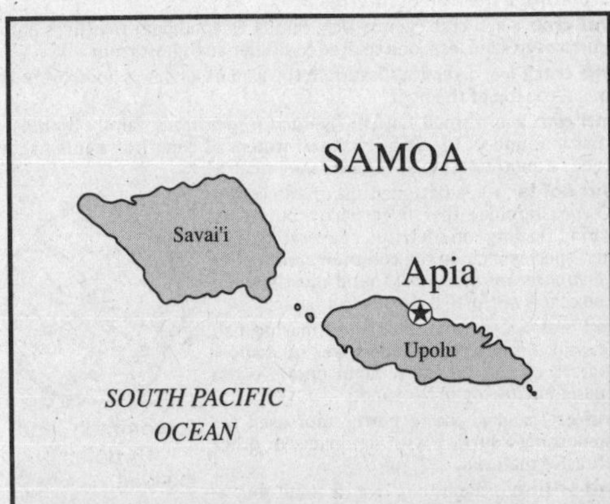

Samoa

Location: South Pacific Ocean, including the western islands of Samoa (the eastern islands are American Samoa)
Area: 1,100 square miles (2,900 sq km)
Population: 177,000
Capital: Apia
Languages: Samoan, English (both official)
Currency: tala

Sa·mo·an /sə'mōən/ ▶ **adj.** of or relating to Samoa, its people, or their language. ▶ **n.** **1** a native or inhabitant of Samoa. **2** the Polynesian language of Samoa, spoken in Samoa, New Zealand, the US, and elsewhere.

Sa·mos /'sāmäs; 'sam-; 'sämôs/ a Greek island in the Aegean Sea.

sa·mo·sa /sə'mōsə/ ▶ **n.** a triangular savory pastry fried in ghee or oil, containing spiced vegetables or meat. [Hindi, from Pers. and Urdu.]

samovar

sam·o·var /'samə,vär/ ▶ **n.** a highly decorated tea urn used in Russia. [Russ., lit. 'self-boiler.']

Sam·o·yed /'samə,yed; sə'moiyid/ ▶ **n.** **1** a member of a group of mainly nomadic peoples of northern Siberia, who traditionally live as reindeer herders. **2** any of several Samoyedic languages of these peoples. ■ another term for **Samoyedic**. **3** a dog of a white Arctic breed. [from Russ. *samoed* 'self-eater,' folk etymology from a Lapp (Sami) phr. 'land of the Sami.']

Sam·o·yed·ic /,samə'yedik/ ▶ **n.** a group of Uralic languages of northern Siberia. ▶ **adj.** of or relating to the Samoyeds or their languages.

sampan

sam·pan /'sam,pan/ ▶ **n.** a small boat of a kind used in the Far East, typically with an oar or oars at the stern. [17th C.: from Chin. *san-ban*, from *san* 'three' + *ban* 'board.']

sam·phire /'sam,fī(ə)r/ ▶ **n.** **1** (also **rock sam·phire**) a European plant (*Crithmum maritimum*) of the parsley family that grows on rocks and cliffs by the sea. Its aromatic, fleshy leaves were formerly much used in pickles. **2** (also **marsh sam·phire**) another term for **glasswort**. [16th C. (as *sampiere*): from Fr. *(herbe de) Saint Pierre* 'St. Peter('s herb).']

sam·ple /'sampəl/ ▶ **n.** a small part or quantity intended to show what the whole is like. ■ a specimen taken for scientific testing or analysis. ■ Stat. a portion drawn from a population, the study of which is intended to lead to statistical estimates of the attributes of the whole population. ■ a small amount of a food or other commodity, esp. one given to a prospective customer. ▶ **v.** [trans.] take a sample or samples of (something) for analysis. ■ try the qualities of (food or drink) by tasting it. ■ get a representative experience of. ■ Electron. ascertain the momentary value of (an analog signal) many times a second so as to convert the signal to digital form. ■ record or extract a small piece of music or sound digitally for reuse. [ME (as a n.): from an Anglo-Norman Fr. var. of OFr. *essample* 'example.' Current senses of the verb date from the mid 18th C.]

sam·pler /'samplər/ ▶ **n.** **1** a piece of embroidery worked in various stitches as a specimen of skill, typically containing the alphabet and some mottoes. **2** a representative collection or example of something. **3** a person or device that takes and analyzes samples. ■ an electronic device for sampling music and sound. [ME (denoting an example to be imitated): from OFr. *essamplaire* 'exemplar.']

sam·pling /'samplinɢ/ ▶ **n.** **1** the taking of a sample or samples. ■ Stat. a sample. **2** the technique of digitally encoding music or sound and reusing it as part of a composition or recording.

Sam·pras /'samprəs/, Peter (1971–), US tennis player. Between 1990 and 2002, he won 14 Grand Slam titles.

sam·sa·ra /səm'särə/ ▶ **n.** Hinduism & Buddhism the cycle of death and rebirth to which life in the material world is bound. — **sam·sa·ric** /-'särik/ **adj.** [from Sanskrit *saṃsāra*.]

sam·ska·ra /səm'skärə/ ▶ **n.** Hinduism a purificatory ceremony or rite marking a major event in one's life. [from Sanskrit *saṃskāra* 'a making perfect.']

Sam·son /'samsən/ (in the Bible) an Israelite leader (probably 11th century BC) famous for his strength. He fell in love with Delilah but she betrayed him to the Philistines, who cut off his hair (his source of strength).

Sam·son post ▸ n. a strong pillar fixed to a ship's deck to act as a support for a tackle or other equipment. [16th C. (denoting a kind of mousetrap): prob. after SAMSON.]

Sam·u·el /'samy(o͞o)əl/ (in the Bible) a Hebrew prophet who became the ruler of the Israelites. ▪ either of two books of the Bible.

Sam·uel·son /'samy(o͞o)əlsən/, Paul Anthony (1915–), US economist. He was a consultant to the Federal Reserve Board and wrote *Economics: An Introductory Analysis* (1948). Nobel Prize in Economics (1970).

sam·u·rai /'samə,rī/ ▸ n. (pl. same) hist. a member of a powerful military caste in feudal Japan, esp. a member of the class of military retainers of the daimyos.

San /sän/ ▸ n. (pl. same) **1** a member of the aboriginal peoples of southern Africa commonly called Bushmen. See BUSHMAN. **2** the group of Khoisan languages spoken by these peoples. ▪ any of these languages. ▸ adj. of or relating to the San or their languages. [from Nama *sān* 'aboriginals.']

Sa·na'a /sä'nä/ (also **Sa·naa**) the capital of Yemen; pop. 500,000.

San An·dre·as fault /,san an'drāəs/ a fault line that extends for about 600 miles (965 km) through the length of coastal California.

San An·ge·lo /san 'anjə,lō/ a city in west central Texas; pop. 84,474.

San An·to·ni·o /,san ən'tōnē,ō/ a city in south central Texas; pop. 1,144,646. It is the site of the Alamo mission.

san·a·to·ri·um /,sanə'tôrēəm/ ▸ n. (pl. **-ri·ums** or **-ri·a** /-rēə/) another term for SANITARIUM. [19th C.: mod. L., based on L. *sanare* 'heal.']

San Ber·nar·di·no /,san ,bərnə(r)'dēnō/ a city in southern California; pop. 164,164.

San·cerre /sän'ser/ ▸ n. a light wine, typically white, produced in the part of France around Sancerre.

San·cho Pan·za /'sänchō 'pänzə/ the squire of Cervantes' Don Quixote, an uneducated peasant.

San Cle·men·te /,san klə'mentē/ a city in southwestern California, on the Pacific Ocean; pop; 41,100.

sanc·ti·fy /'sang(k)tə,fī/ ▸ v. (-fies, -fied) [trans.] set apart as or declare holy; consecrate. ▪ (often **be sanctified**) make legitimate or binding by religious sanction. ▪ free from sin; purify. ▪ (often **be sanctified**) fig. give the appearance of being right or good; legitimize. — **sanc·ti·fi·ca·tion** /-fi'kāshən/ n. **sanc·ti·fi·er** n. [ME: from OFr. *saintifier*, from eccles. Latin *sanctificare*, from L. *sanctus* 'holy.']

sanc·ti·mo·ni·ous /,sang(k)tə'mōnēəs/ ▸ adj. derog. making a show of being morally superior to other people. — **sanc·ti·mo·ni·ous·ly** adv. **sanc·ti·mo·ni·ous·ness** n. **sanc·ti·mo·ny** /'sang(k)tə,mōnē/ n. [17th C. (in the sense 'holy in character'): from L. *sanctimonia* 'sanctity' (from *sanctus* 'holy') + -OUS.]

sanc·tion /'sang(k)shən/ ▸ n. **1** a threatened penalty for disobeying a law or rule. ▪ (**sanctions**) measures taken by a nation to coerce another to conform to an international agreement or norms of conduct. ▪ Ethics a consideration operating to enforce obedience to any rule of conduct. **2** official permission or approval for an action. ▪ official confirmation or ratification of a law. ▪ Law, hist. a law or decree, esp. an ecclesiastical decree. ▸ v. [trans.] **1** (often **be sanctioned**) give official permission or approval for (an action). **2** impose a sanction or penalty on. — **sanc·tion·a·ble** adj. [ME 'eccles. decree': from L. *sanctio(n-)*, from *sancire* 'ratify.']

sanc·ti·tude /'sang(k)tə,t(y)o͞od/ ▸ n. formal the state or quality of being holy, sacred, or saintly. [ME: from L. *sanctitudo*, from *sanctus* 'holy.']

sanc·ti·ty /'sang(k)titē/ ▸ n. (pl. **-ties**) the state or quality of being holy, sacred, or saintly. ▪ ultimate importance and inviolability. [ME ('saintliness'): from OFr. *saincteté*, reinforced by L. *sanctitas*, from *sanctus* 'holy.']

sanc·tu·ar·y /'sang(k)cho͞o,erē/ ▸ n. (pl. **-ar·ies**) **1** a place of refuge or safety. ▪ immunity from arrest. **2** [usu. with adj.] a nature reserve: *a bird sanctuary.* **3** a holy place; a temple or church. ▪ the inmost recess or holiest part of a temple or church. ▪ the part of the chancel of a church containing the high altar. [ME (sense 3): from OFr. *sanctuaire*, from L. *sanctuarium*, from *sanctus* 'holy.']

sanc·tum /'sang(k)təm/ ▸ n. (pl. **-tums**) a sacred place, esp. a shrine within a temple or church. ▪ fig. a private place from which most people are excluded. [16th C.: from L., neut. of *sanctus* 'holy,' from *sancire* 'consecrate.']

sanc·tum sanc·to·rum /'sang(k)təm ,sang(k)'tôrəm/ ▸ n. (pl. **sanc·ta sanc·tor·um** /'sang(k)tə/ or **sanc·tum sanc·to·rums**) the holy of holies in the Jewish temple. ▪ a very private or secret place. [ME: L. *sanctum* (see SANCTUM) + *sanctorum* 'of holy places,' translating Heb. *qōdeš haqqŏdāšîm* 'holy of holies.']

Sanc·tus /'sang(k)təs/ ▸ n. Christian Church a hymn beginning *Sanctus, sanctus, sanctus* (Holy, holy, holy) forming a set part of the Mass. [ME: from L., 'holy.']

Sand /sand; sän(d)/, George (1804–76), French writer; pen name of *Amandine-Aurore Lucille Dupin, Baronne Dudevant*. Her novels include *Lélia* (1833) and *La Mare au diable* (1846).

sand /sand/ ▸ n. a loose granular substance, typically pale yellowish brown, resulting from the erosion of siliceous and other rocks and forming a major constituent of beaches, riverbeds, the seabed, and deserts. ▪ (**sands**) an expanse of sand, typically along a shore. ▪ a stratum of sandstone or compacted sand. ▪ tech. sediment whose particles are larger than silt (typically greater than 0.06 mm). ▪ informal firmness of purpose. ▪ a light yellow-brown color like that of sand. ▸ v. [trans.] **1** smooth or polish with sandpaper or a mechanical sander. **2** sprinkle or overlay with sand, to give better purchase on a surface. [OE, from Gmc.; akin to Ger. *Sand*.]

san·dal[1] /'sandl/ ▸ n. a light shoe with either an openwork upper or straps attaching the sole to the foot. — **san·daled** /'sandld/ (Brit. **san·dalled**) adj. [ME: via L. from Gk. *sandalion*, dimin. of *sandalon* 'wooden shoe,' prob. of Asiatic origin.]

san·dal[2] ▸ n. short for SANDALWOOD.

san·dal·wood /'sandl,wo͝od/ ▸ n. (also **white san·dal·wood**) a widely cultivated Indian tree (*Santalum album*, family Santalaceae) that yields fragrant timber and oil. ▪ a perfume or incense derived from this timber. [16th C.: *sandal* from med. L. *sandalum* (based on Sanskrit *candana*) + WOOD.]

San·dal·wood Is·land another name for SUMBA.

san·da·rac /'sandə,rak/ (also **gum san·da·rac**) ▸ n. a gum resin obtained from the cypress of Spain and North Africa, used in making varnish. [ME (denoting realgar): from L. *sandaraca*, from Gk. *sandarakē*, of Asiatic origin. The current sense dates from the mid 17th C.]

sand·bag /'san(d),bag/ ▸ n. a bag filled with sand, typically used for defensive purposes or as ballast in a boat. ▸ v. (**-bagged, -bag·ging**) [trans.] **1** [usu. as adj.] (**sandbagged**) barricade using sandbags. **2** hit or fell with or as if with a blow from a sandbag. ▪ coerce; bully: *we were sandbagged into staying overnight.* **3** [intrans.] deliberately underperform in a race or competition to gain an unfair advantage. — **sand·bag·ger** n.

sand·bank /'san(d),bangk/ ▸ n. a deposit of sand forming a shallow area in the sea or a river.

sand·bar /'san(d),bär/ ▸ n. a long, narrow sandbank, esp. at the mouth of a river.

sand·blast /'san(d),blast/ ▸ v. [trans.] roughen or clean (a surface) with a jet of sand driven by compressed air or steam. ▸ n. such a jet of sand. — **sand·blast·er** n.

sand·box /'san(d),bäks/ ▸ n. **1** a shallow box or hollow in the ground partly filled with sand for children to play in. **2** (also **sand·box tree**) a tropical American tree (*Hura crepitans*) of the spurge family whose seed cases were formerly used to hold sand for blotting ink. **3** Computing a virtual space in which software or Web sites can be tested, evaluated, or developed before being made generally available.

Sand·burg /'san(d),bərg/, Carl (1878–1967), US poet and writer. His poetry collections include *Chicago Poems* (1915) and *Smoke and Steel* (1920). He is also noted for his six-volume biography of Abraham Lincoln (1926–39).

sand cat ▸ n. a small wild cat (*Felis margarita*) with a plain yellow to grayish coat, a dark-ringed tail, and large eyes, of the deserts of North Africa and southwestern Asia.

sand cher·ry ▸ n. a dwarf North American wild cherry (*Prunus depressa*). ▪ the fruit of this tree.

sand crab ▸ n. a crab (genus *Uca*, family Ocypodidae) that lives on or burrows in sand, esp. one related to fiddler and ghost crabs.

sand crack ▸ n. a vertical fissure in the wall of a horse's hoof, originating at the top of the hoof.

sand dab ▸ n. a small flatfish (genus *Citharichthys*, family Bothidae) that is found in the Pacific coastal waters of America. ▪ this fish as food. ▪ another term for WINDOWPANE (sense 2).

sand dol·lar ▸ n. a flattened sea urchin (order Clypeasteroida) that lives partly buried in sand, feeding on detritus. Several genera and species include the **common sand dollar** (*Echinarachnius parma*) found mostly along the coasts of North America and Japan.

common sand dollar

sand eel ▸ n. a small elongated marine fish (family Ammodytidae) that lives in shallow waters of the northern hemisphere, often found burrowing in the sand.

sand·er /'sandər/ ▸ n. a power tool used for smoothing a surface with sandpaper or other abrasive material.

sand·er·ling /'sandərling/ ▸ n. a small migratory sandpiper (*Calidris alba*) of northern Eurasia and Canada, typically seen running after receding waves on the beach. [17th C.: of unknown origin.]

San·ders /'sandərz/, Lawrence (1920–98), US writer. His novels include *The Dream Lover* (1978) and *Guilty Pleasures* (1998).

sand flea ▸ n. **1** another term for BEACH FLEA. **2** another term for CHIGOE.

sand·fly /'san(d),flī/ ▸ n. (pl. **-flies**) a small, hairy, biting fly (*Phlebotomus* and other genera, family Psychodidae) of tropical and subtropical regions that transmits a number of diseases, including leishmaniasis.

sand·glass /'san(d),glas/ ▸ n. an hourglass measuring a fixed amount of time (not necessarily one hour).

sand·grouse /'san(d),grous/ ▸ n. (pl. same) a seed-eating ground-dwelling bird (genera *Pterocles* and *Syrrhaptes*, family Pteroclididae) with brownish plumage, allied to the pigeons and found in the deserts and arid regions of the Old World.

san·dhi /'sandē; 'sän-/ ▸ n. Phonet. the process whereby the form of a word changes as a result of its position in an utterance (e.g., the change from *a* to *an* before a vowel). [from Sanskrit *saṃdhi* 'putting together.']

sand·hill crane /'san(d),hil/ ▸ n. a chiefly migratory North American crane (*Grus canadensis*, family Gruidae) with grayish plumage and a red crown.

Sand·hills 1 (also **Sand Hills**) a line of low, sandy hills across North and South Carolina and Georgia. **2** a large plains area in west central Nebraska, noted as a ranching district.

sand·hog /ˈsan(d),hôg; -,häg/ ▶ **n.** a person who does construction work underground or under water such as laying foundations or building a tunnel.

sand hop·per /ˈsand,häpər/ ▶ **n.** another term for BEACH FLEA.

San·dia Moun·tains /sanˈdēə/ a range in central New Mexico near Albuquerque.

San Di·e·go /,san dēˈāgō/ a city and naval port on the Pacific coast of southern California, just north of the US-Mexico border; pop. 1,223,400.

San·di·nis·ta /,sandəˈnēstə/ ▶ **n.** a member of a left-wing Nicaraguan political organization, the Sandinista National Liberation Front (FSLN), which came to power in 1979 after overthrowing the dictator Anastasio Somoza; voted out of office in 1990. [after an organization founded by nationalist leader Augusto César *Sandino* (1893–1934).]

S & L ▶ **abbr.** savings and loan.

sand lance ▶ **n.** another term for SAND EEL.

sand liz·ard ▶ **n.** a small, ground-dwelling Old World lizard (genera *Lacerta* and *Pedioplanis*, family Lacertidae), favoring heathland or sandy areas.

sand·lot /ˈsan(d),lät/ ▶ **n.** a piece of unoccupied land used by children for games. ■ [as adj.] denoting or relating to sports played by amateurs: *sandlot baseball.*

S & M ▶ **abbr.** ■ sadomasochism. ■ (in the insurance industry) stock and machinery.

sand·man /ˈsan(d),man/ ▶ **n.** (**the sandman**) a fictional man supposed to make children sleep by sprinkling sand in their eyes.

sand paint·ing ▶ **n.** an American Indian ceremonial art form, important among the Navajo and Pueblo peoples, using colored sands.

sand·pa·per /ˈsan(d),pāpər/ ▶ **n.** paper with sand or another abrasive stuck to it, used for smoothing or polishing woodwork or other surfaces. ■ used to refer to something that feels rough or has a very rough surface. ▶ **v.** [trans.] smooth with sandpaper. — **sand·pa·per·y adj.**

sand·pi·per /ˈsan(d),pīpər/ ▶ **n.** a wading bird (*Calidris, Tringa, Actitis*, and other genera) with a long bill and typically long legs, nesting on the ground near water. Species include the **western sandpiper** (*C. mauri*), which breeds on the seashores of Alaska and winters from the southern US to Peru.

western sandpiper

sand shark ▶ **n.** a voracious, brown-spotted shark (*Odontaspis taurus*, family Odontaspididae) of tropical Atlantic waters. ■ any of a number of mainly harmless rays, dogfish, and sharks found in shallow coastal waters.

sand star·gaz·er ▶ **n.** see STARGAZER (sense 2).

sand·stone /ˈsan(d),stōn/ ▶ **n.** sedimentary rock consisting of sand or quartz grains cemented together, typically red, yellow, or brown in color.

sand·storm /ˈsan(d),stôrm/ ▶ **n.** a strong wind carrying clouds of sand with it, esp. in a desert.

sand wasp ▶ **n.** a digger wasp (*Ammophila* and other genera, family Sphecidae) that excavates its burrow in sandy soil and then catches prey with which to furnish it. Sand wasps typically have an abdomen with a very long and slender "waist."

sand·wich /ˈsan,(d)wicH/ ▶ **n.** an item of food consisting of two pieces of bread with meat, cheese, or other filling between them, eaten as a light meal. ■ something that is constructed like or has the form of a sandwich. ▶ **v.** [trans.] (usu. **be sandwiched between**) insert or squeeze (someone or something) between two other people or things, typically in a restricted space or so as to be uncomfortable. [18th C.: the 4th Earl of *Sandwich* (1718–92), English nobleman.]

sand·wich board ▶ **n.** a pair of advertisement boards connected by straps and hung over a person's shoulders.

sand·wich gen·er·a·tion ▶ **n.** a generation of people, typically in their thirties or forties, responsible for bringing up their own children and for the care of their aging parents.

Sand·wich Is·lands former name for HAWAII.

sand·wich tern ▶ **n.** a large crested tern (*Thalassius sandvicensis*) found in Europe and North and South America. [18th C.: *Sandwich*, town in Kent, England.]

sand·wort /ˈsan(d)wərt; -,wôrt/ ▶ **n.** a widely distributed low-growing plant (*Arenaria* and other genera) of the pink family, typically having small white flowers and growing in dry sandy ground.

Sandy /ˈsandē/ a city in north central Utah, south of Salt Lake City; pop. 88,418.

sand·y /ˈsandē/ ▶ **adj.** (**sand·i·er, sand·i·est**) **1** covered in or consisting mostly of sand. **2** (esp. of hair) light yellowish brown. — **sand·i·ness n. sand·y·ish adj.**

Sandy Hook a peninsula in northeastern New Jersey.

sane /sān/ ▶ **adj.** (of a person) of sound mind; not mad or mentally ill: *hard work kept me sane.* ■ (of an undertaking or manner) reasonable; sensible. — **sane·ly adv. sane·ness n.** [17th C.: from L. *sanus* 'healthy.']

San Fer·nan·do Val·ley /,san fərˈnandō/ (popularly **the Valley**) an irrigated district in California, northwest of downtown Los Angeles.

San·ford /ˈsanfərd/, Edward Terry (1865–1930), US Supreme Court associate justice 1923–30.

San·for·ized /ˈsanfə,rīzd/ ▶ **adj.** trademark (of cotton or other fabrics) preshrunk by a controlled compressive process; meeting certain standards of washing shrinkage. [1930s: *Sanford* L. Cluett (1874–1968), American inventor.]

San Fran·cis·co /,san frənˈsiskō/ a city in western California, on a peninsula between the Pacific Ocean and San Francisco Bay; pop. 776,733. — **San Fran·cis·can** /-kən/ **n. & adj.**

San Fran·cis·co Peaks a mountain group in northern Arizona, north of Flagstaff.

sang /saNG/ past of SING.

San Ga·bri·el Moun·tains a range in southern California, north of Los Angeles. Mount Wilson observatory is here.

san·ga·ree /,saNGgəˈrē/ ▶ **n.** a cold drink of wine mixed with water and spices. [from Sp. *sangría* (see SANGRIA).]

Sang·er[1] /ˈsaNGər/, Frederick (1918–), English biochemist. He determined the complete amino-acid sequence of insulin in 1955 and established the complete nucleotide sequence of a viral DNA in 1977. Nobel Prize for Chemistry (1958, 1980).

Sang·er[2], Margaret Higgins (1883–1966), US nurse. In 1916 she founded the first US birth-control clinic, which eventually became Planned Parenthood.

sang·froid /säNGˈfrwä/ (also **sang-froid**) ▶ **n.** composure or coolness as shown in danger or under trying circumstances. [18th C.: from Fr. *sang-froid*, lit. 'cold blood.']

san·gha /ˈsəNG(g)ə/ ▶ **n.** the Buddhist community of monks, nuns, novices, and laity. [from Sanskrit *saṃgha* 'community.']

san·grail /saNGˈgrāl/ (also **san·greal**) ▶ **n.** another term for GRAIL. [ME: from OFr. *saint graal* 'Holy Grail.']

San·gre de Cris·to Moun·tains /,saNGgrē də ˈkristō/ a range in southern Colorado and northern New Mexico.

san·gri·a /saNGˈgrēə/ ▶ **n.** a Spanish drink of red wine mixed with lemonade, fruit, and spices. [from Sp., lit. 'bleeding.']

san·gui·nar·y /ˈsaNGgwə,nerē/ ▶ **adj.** esp. archaic involving or causing much bloodshed. [ME ('relating to blood'): from L. *sanguinarius*, from *sanguis, sanguin-* 'blood.']

san·guine /ˈsaNGgwin/ ▶ **adj. 1** cheerfully optimistic. ■ (in medieval science and medicine) of or having the constitution associated with the predominance of blood among the bodily humors, supposedly marked by a ruddy complexion and an optimistic disposition. **2** literary & Heraldry blood-red. ▶ **n.** a blood-red color. ■ a deep red-brown crayon or pencil containing iron oxide. ■ Heraldry a blood-red stain used in blazoning. — **san·guine·ly adv. san·guine·ness n.** [ME: from OFr. *sanguin(e)* 'blood-red,' from L. *sanguineus* 'of blood,' from *sanguis, sanguin-* 'blood.']

San·hed·rin /sanˈhedrən; -ˈhēdrin; sän-/ the highest court of justice and the supreme council in ancient Jerusalem. [from late Heb. *sanhedrīn*, from Gk. *sunedrion* 'council,' from *sun-* 'with'+ *hedra* 'seat.']

San·i·bel Is·land /ˈsanəbəl/ a resort island in southwestern Florida, southwest of Fort Myers.

san·i·cle /ˈsanikəl/ ▶ **n.** a plant (genus *Sanicula*) of the parsley family that has burrlike fruit. [ME: ult. from med. L. *sanicula*, perh. from L. *sanus* 'healthy.']

san·i·tar·i·an /,saniˈte(ə)rēən/ ▶ **n.** esp. archaic an official responsible for public health or a person in favor of public health reform.

san·i·tar·i·um /,saniˈte(ə)rēəm/ ▶ **n.** (pl. **-tar·i·ums** or **-tar·i·a** /-ˈte(ə)rēə/) an establishment for the medical treatment of people who are convalescing or have a chronic illness. [19th C.: pseudo-Latin, from L. *sanitas* 'health.']

san·i·tar·y /ˈsani,terē/ ▶ **adj.** of or relating to the conditions that affect hygiene and health, esp. the supply of sewage facilities and clean drinking water. ■ hygienic and clean. — **san·i·tar·i·ly** /-,terəlē/ **adv. san·i·tar·i·ness n.** [19th C.: from Fr. *sanitaire*, from L. *sanitas* 'health,' from *sanus* 'healthy.']

san·i·tar·y nap·kin ▶ **n.** an absorbent pad worn by women to absorb menstrual blood.

san·i·ta·tion /,saniˈtāsHən/ ▶ **n.** conditions relating to public health, esp. the provision of clean drinking water and adequate sewage disposal. [19th C.: from SANITARY.]

san·i·tize /ˈsani,tīz/ ▶ **v.** [trans.] make clean and hygienic: *new chemicals for sanitizing a pool.* ■ (usu. **be sanitized**) derog. alter (something regarded as less acceptable) so as to make it more palatable. — **san·i·ti·za·tion** /,sanətəˈzāsHən/ **n. san·i·tiz·er n.**

san·i·ty /ˈsanitē/ ▶ **n.** the ability to think and behave in a normal and rational manner; sound mental health. ■ reasonable and rational behavior. [ME ('health'): from L. *sanitas* from *sanus* 'healthy.']

San Ja·cin·to Riv·er /,san jəˈsin,tō/ a river in southeastern Texas that flows into Galveston Bay.

San Joa·quin Riv·er /,san wäˈkēn/ a river that flows from south central

California to join the Sacramento River and enter San Francisco Bay.

San Joa·quin Val·ley fe·ver /ˌsan wäˈkēn/ ▶ **n.** informal term for COCCIDIOIDOMYCOSIS.

San Jo·se /ˌsan (h)ōˈzā/ a city in western California, south of San Francisco Bay; pop. 894,943.

San Jo·sé /ˌsan (h)ōˈzā ˌsän hôˈsā/ the capital and chief port of Costa Rica; pop. 319,000.

San Juan /san ˈ(h)wän; sän ˈhwän/ the capital of Puerto Rico, on the northern coast; pop. 437,745.

San Juan Cap·is·tra·no /san ˈwän ˌkapəˈstränō/ a city in southwestern California, the site of a 1776 mission to which migrating swallows return each March 19; pop. 26,183.

San Juan Hill a hill near Santiago de Cuba, in eastern Cuba, the scene of a July 1898 battle during the Spanish-American War.

San Juan Is·lands islands in northwestern Washington, north of Puget Sound and south of the Strait of Georgia.

San Juan Moun·tains a range of the Rocky Mountains in southwestern Colorado and northern New Mexico, the source of the Rio Grande.

sank /saNGk/ past of SINK¹.

San Lu·is Po·to·sí /sän lo͞oˈēs ˌpôtôˈsē/ a state in central Mexico. ■ its capital; pop. 525,000.

San Ma·ri·no /ˌsan məˈrēnō/ a republic in Italy. *See box.*

San Marino

Official name: Republic of San Marino
Location: northeastern Italy, a small enclave near the Adriatic coast
Area: 24 square miles (60 sq km)
Population: 28,000
Capital: San Marino
Language: Italian
Currency: euro

San Mar·tín /ˌsan märˈtēn/, José de (1778–1850), Argentine soldier. He helped to liberate Argentina 1812–13, Chile 1817–18, and Peru 1820–24 from Spanish rule.

San Pe·dro Su·la /sän ˈpedrō ˈso͞olä/ a city in northern Honduras; pop. 325,000.

San Quen·tin /san ˈkwentn/ a site in northwestern California across the Golden Gate from San Francisco, home to a well-known state prison.

sans /sanz/ ▶ **prep.** literary or humorous without. [ME: from OFr. *sanz*, from L. *sine* 'without.']

San Sal·va·dor /san ˈsalvəˌdôr; sän ˌsälväˈdôr/ **1** an island in the southeastern Bahamas, believed to be where Columbus first landed in the New World in 1492; pop. 2,000. **2** the capital of El Salvador; pop. 423,000.

sans-cu·lotte /ˌsanz k(y)o͝oˈlät/ ▶ **n.** a lower-class Parisian republican in the French Revolution. ■ an extreme republican or revolutionary. —**sans-cu·lot·tism** /k(y)əˈlätizəm/ **n.** [Fr., lit. 'without breeches.']

San Se·bas·tián /ˌsan səˈbasCHən; ˌsän sebästˈyän/ a city in northern Spain; pop. 174,000.

san·sei /ˈsänsā/ ▶ **n.** (pl. same) a person born in the US or Canada whose grandparents were immigrants from Japan. Compare with NISEI and ISSEI. [1940s: Japanese, from *san* 'third' + *sei* 'generation.']

san·se·vi·e·ri·a /ˌsansəvēˈi(ə)rēə; -səˈvi(ə)rēə/ (also **san·se·ve·ri·a**) ▶ **n.** a plant of the genus *Sansevieria* in the agave family, certain species of which yield an elastic fiber. [mod. L., after Raimondo di Sangro (1710–71), Prince of *Sanseviero* (now Sansevero), Italy.]

San Sim·e·on /san ˈsimēən/ a community in west central California, site of the Hearst estate.

San·skrit /ˈsanˌskrit/ ▶ **n.** an ancient Indic language of India, in which the Hindu scriptures and classical Indian epic poems are written. ▶ **adj.** of or relating to this language. —**San·skrit·ic** /sanˈskritik/ **adj.** **San·skrit·ist** /ˈsanˌskritist/ **n.** [from Sanskrit *saṃskṛta* 'composed,' from *saṃ* 'together' + *kṛ* 'make' + past part. ending *-ta*.]

sans ser·if /ˌsan(z) ˈserəf/ Print. ▶ **n.** a style of type without serifs. ▶ **adj.** without serifs. [19th C.: appar. from Fr. *sans* 'without' + SERIF.]

San·ta An·a /ˌsäntə ˈänə/ **1** a city in El Salvador, close to the border with Guatemala; pop. 202,340. **2** /ˌsäntə ˈänə/ a volcano in El Salvador, southwest of the city of Santa Ana. **3** /ˌsantə ˈanə/ a city in southern California, southeast of Los Angeles; pop. 337,977.

San·ta An·na /ˌsantə ˈanə/, Antonio López de (1794–1876), Mexican general and leader of Mexico 1833–36, 1844–45, and 1853–55. He engaged in several military actions against the United States, including his victory at the Alamo 1836 and his defeats at San Jacinto 1836 and Buena Vista 1847.

San·ta Bar·ba·ra /ˈsantə ˈbärb(ə)rə/ a city in California, northwest of Los Angeles; pop. 85,571.

San·ta Bar·ba·ra Is·lands (also **Channel Islands**) an island group in southwestern California that includes Santa Catalina.

San·ta Clara /ˌsantə ˈklarə; ˈkle(ə)rə/ a city in north central California; pop. 93,613.

San·ta Clar·i·ta /ˌsantə kləˈrētə/ a city in southwestern California, northwest of Los Angeles; pop. 110,642.

San·ta Claus /ˈsantə ˌklôz/ (also **San·ta**) an imaginary figure said to bring presents for children at Christmas. Also called **Saint Nicholas** or **Saint Nick**. [18th C.: US alt. of Du. dial. *Sante Klaas* 'St. Nicholas.']

San·ta Cruz 1 /ˌsantə ˈkro͞oz; ˌsäntä ˈkro͞os/ a city in central Bolivia; pop. 695,000. **2** /ˌsantə ˈkro͞oz; ˌsäntä ˈkro͞oTH/ the chief city of the island of Tenerife, in the Canary Islands; pop. 192,000. Full name SANTA CRUZ DE TENERIFE. **3** /ˈsantə ˈkro͞oz/ a city in west central California; pop. 49,040.

San·ta Cruz Is·lands an island group in the southeastern Solomon Islands, in the southwestern Pacific Ocean, scene of an October 1942 World War II naval battle between US and Japanese forces.

San·ta Fe /ˈsantə ˌfā; ˌsantə ˈfā/ (also **San·ta Fé** /ˌsäntä ˈfā/) **1** a city in northern Argentina, on the Salado River; pop. 395,000. **2** the capital of New Mexico, in the north central part of the state; pop. 62,302.

San·ta Fé de Bo·go·tá official name for BOGOTÁ.

San·ta Fe Trail a route, established in the 1820s, from St. Louis in Missouri to Santa Fe in New Mexico.

San·ta Lu·cia Range /ˌsantə lo͞oˈsēə/ a range in west central California, part of the Coast Ranges

San·ta Ma·ria /ˌsantə məˈrēə/ a city in southwestern California; pop. 61,284.

San·ta Mon·i·ca /ˈsantə ˈmänikə/ a city on the coast of southwestern California; pop. 86,905.

San·tan·der /ˌsäntänˈder/ a city in northern Spain, north of Madrid; pop. 194,220 (1991).

San·ta Ro·sa /ˌsantə ˈrōzə/ a city in northwestern California, north of San Francisco; pop. 113,313.

San·ta·ya·na /ˌsäntəˈyänä/, George (1863–1952), Spanish philosopher and writer; born *Jorge Augustin Nicolás Ruiz de Santayana*. His works include *The Realms of Being* (1924) and *The Last Puritan* (1935).

San·tee Riv·er /sanˈtē/ a river that flows through eastern South Carolina, to the Atlantic Ocean.

San·te·ri·a /ˌsantəˈrēə/ (also **San·te·rí·a**) ▶ **n.** a pantheistic Afro-Cuban religious cult developed from the beliefs and customs of the Yoruba people and incorporating some elements of the Catholic religion. [Sp., lit. 'holiness.']

San·ti·a·go /ˌsäntēˈägō/ the capital of Chile, in the central part of the country; pop. 5,181,000.

San·ti·a·go de Com·pos·te·la /də ˌkämpəˈstelə/ a city in northwestern Spain; pop. 106,000. The remains of St. James the Great are said to have been brought there after his death.

San·ti·a·go de Cu·ba /də ˈkyo͞obə; de ˈko͞obä/ a port on the coast of southeastern Cuba; pop. 433,000.

san·tim /ˈsäntim/ ▶ **n.** (pl. **-ti·mi** /-təmē/) a monetary unit of Latvia, equal to one hundredth of a lat. [from Latvian *santims*, from Fr. *centime* + Latvian masc. ending *-s*.]

san·to /ˈsantō; ˈsän-/ ▶ **n.** (pl. **-tos**) (in Mexico and Spanish-speaking areas of the southwestern US) a religious symbol, esp. a wooden representation of a saint. [Sp. or Ital.]

San·to Do·min·go /ˈsantōdəˈmiNGgō; ˈsäntōdôˈmiNGgô/ the capital of the Dominican Republic, on the southern coast; pop. 2,055,000. Formerly (1936–61) called **Ciudad Trujillo**.

san·to·li·na /ˌsantəˈlēnə/ ▶ **n.** a plant of the genus *Santolina* in the daisy family, esp. the aromatic *S. chamaecyparissus*, with silvery or greenish foliage and yellow button flowers. [mod. L., perh. alt. of SANTONICA.]

san·ton·i·ca /sanˈtänikə/ ▶ **n.** the dried flowerheads of a wormwood plant (*Artemisia cina*), containing the drug santonin. [17th C.: from L. *Santonica (herba)* '(plant) of the Santoni,' a tribe of Aquitania (now AQUITAINE¹).]

san·to·nin /ˈsantn-in/ ▶ **n.** Chem. a toxic crystalline compound, $C_{15}H_{18}O_3$, present in santonica and related plants, used as an anthelmintic. [19th C.: from SANTONICA + -IN¹.]

San·to·ri·ni /ˌsantəˈrēnē; ˌsäntô-/ another name for THERA.

San·tos /ˈsantōs; ˈsän-/ a city on the coast of Brazil, just southeast of São Paulo; pop. 429,000.

São Fran·cis·co /ˈsoun frənˈsiskō͝o/ a river in eastern Brazil that flows for 1,990 miles (3,200 km) to meet the Atlantic Ocean north of Aracajú.

São Lu·ís /ˈsoun lo͞oˈēs/ a city in northeastern Brazil; pop. 695,000.

Saône /sōn/ a river in eastern France that flows for 298 miles (480 km) to join the Rhône River at Lyons.

São Pau·lo /ˌsou ˈpoulō; ˌsoun ˈpoulo͞o/ a state in southern Brazil. ■ its capital city, the largest city in Brazil; pop. 9,700,000.

São To·mé and Prín·cipe /ˌsou tōˈmä and ˈprinsəpə; ˌsoun to͞oˈmä/ a country in West Africa, in the Gulf of Guinea. *See box.*

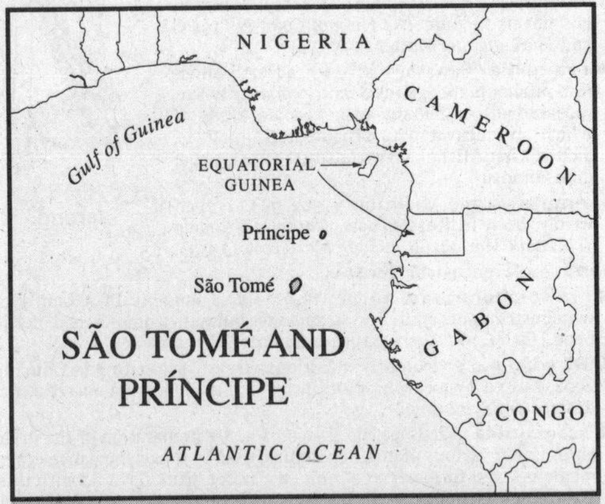

São Tomé and Príncipe

Official name: Democratic Republic of São Tomé and Príncipe
Location: West Africa, in the Gulf of Guinea, including two main islands and several smaller ones
Area: 390 square miles (1,000 sq km)
Population: 181,000
Capital: São Tomé
Languages: Portuguese (official), Portuguese Creole
Currency: dobra

sap[1] /sap/ ▶ **n.** the fluid, chiefly water with dissolved sugars and mineral salts, that circulates in the vascular system of a plant. ■ fig. vigor or energy, esp. sexual vitality. [OE *sæp*, prob. Gmc.]

sap[2] ▶ **n.** hist. a tunnel or trench to conceal an assailant's approach to a fortified place. ▶ **v.** (**sapped, sap·ping**) **1** dig a sap or saps. **2** [trans.] gradually weaken or destroy (a person's strength or power). ■ (**sap someone of**) drain someone of (strength or power). ■ archaic make insecure by removing the foundations of. ■ [often as n.] (**sapping**) Geog. undercut by water or glacial action. [16th C. ('dig a sap or covered trench'): from Fr. *saper*, from Ital. *zappare*, from *zappa* 'spade,' perh. from Arab. *sarab* 'underground passage,' or *sabora* 'burrow, explore.']

sap[3] ▶ **n.** informal a foolish and gullible person. [19th C.: abbrev. of dial. *sapskull* 'person with a head like sapwood.' from SAP[1] 'sapwood.']

sap[4] informal ▶ **n.** a bludgeon or club. ▶ **v.** (**sapped, sap·ping**) [trans.] hit with a bludgeon or club. [19th C. (n.): abbrev. of SAPLING.]

sa·pe·le /səˈpēlē/ ▶ **n.** a large, tropical African hardwood tree (genus *Entandrophragma*, family Meliaceae) with reddish-brown timber that resembles mahogany. [20th C.: after a port on the Benin River, Nigeria.]

sap·id /ˈsapid/ ▶ **adj.** having a strong, pleasant taste. ■ (of talk or writing) pleasant or interesting. — **sa·pid·i·ty** /səˈpiditē/ **n.** [17th C.: from L. *sapidus*, from *sapere* 'to taste.']

sa·pi·ent /ˈsāpēənt/ ▶ **adj.** **1** formal wise, or attempting to appear wise. ■ (chiefly in science fiction) intelligent. **2** of or relating to the human species (*Homo sapiens*). ▶ **n.** a human of the species *Homo sapiens*. — **sa·pi·ence n. sa·pi·ent·ly adv.** [ME: ult. from L. *sapient-* 'being wise,' from the verb *sapere*.]

sap·ling /ˈsapliNG/ ▶ **n.** a young tree, esp. one with a slender trunk. ■ literary a young and slender or inexperienced person. [ME: from the n. SAP[1] + -LING.]

sap·o·dil·la /ˌsapəˈdilə/ ▶ **n.** a large, evergreen, tropical American tree (*Manilkara zapota*, family Sapotaceae) that yields chicle and has edible fruit and hard, durable wood. ■ (also **sap·o·dil·la plum**) the sweet, brownish, bristly fruit of this tree. [17th C.: from Sp. *zapotillo*, dimin. of *zapote*, from Nahuatl *tzápotl*.]

sap·o·na·ceous /ˌsapəˈnāsHəs/ ▶ **adj.** of, like, or containing soap; soapy. [18th C.: from mod. L. *saponaceus* (from L. *sapo, sapon-* 'soap') + -OUS.]

sa·pon·i·fy /səˈpänəˌfī/ ▶ **v.** (**-fies, -fied**) [trans.] Chem. turn (fat or oil) into soap by reaction with an alkali. ■ convert (any ester) into an alcohol and a metal salt by alkaline hydrolysis. — **sa·pon·i·fi·a·ble adj. sa·pon·i·fi·ca·tion** /səˌpänəfiˈkāsHən/ **n.** [19th C.: from Fr. *saponifier*, from L. *sapo, sapon-* 'soap.']

sap·o·nin /ˈsapənən/ ▶ **n.** Chem. a toxic compound that is present in soapwort and makes foam when shaken with water. ■ any of the class of steroid and terpenoid glycosides typified by this, examples of which are used in detergents and foam fire extinguishers. [19th C.: from Fr. *saponine*, from L. *sapo, sapon-* 'soap']

sap·per /ˈsapər/ ▶ **n.** a military engineer who lays or detects and disarms mines. [17th C.: from the verb SAP[2] + -ER[1].]

sap·phic /ˈsafik/ ▶ **adj.** **1** formal or humorous of or relating to lesbians or lesbianism: *sapphic lovers.* **2** (**Sapphic**) of or relating to Sappho or her poetry. ▶ **plural n.** (**sapphics**) verse in a meter associated with Sappho. [16th C. (sense 2): ult. from Gk. *Sapphikos*, from *Sapphō* (see SAPPHO).]

sap·phire /ˈsafˌī(ə)r/ ▶ **n.** a transparent precious stone, typically blue, which is a variety of corundum (aluminum oxide). ■ a bright blue color. — **sap·phir·ine** /ˈsafərin; -ˌrēn; -ˌrīn/ **adj.** [ME: from OFr. *safir*, via L. from Gk. *sappheiros*, prob. denoting lapis lazuli.]

sap·phism /ˈsafizəm/ ▶ **n.** formal humorous lesbianism. [19th C.: from SAPPHO + -ISM.]

Sap·pho /ˈsafō/ (early 7th century BC), Greek lyric poet who lived on Lesbos. She is associated with female homosexuality.

Sap·po·ro /səˈpôrō/ a city in northern Japan, capital of the island of Hokkaido; pop. 1,672,000.

sap·py /ˈsapē/ ▶ **adj.** (**-pi·er, -pi·est**) **1** informal oversentimental; mawkish. **2** (of a plant) containing a lot of sap. — **sap·pi·ly** /-əlē/ **adv. sap·pi·ness n.**

sapro- ▶ **comb. form** Biol. relating to putrefaction or decay: *saprogenic.* [from Gk. *sapros* 'putrid.']

sap·ro·gen·ic /ˌsaprōˈjenik/ ▶ **adj.** Biol. causing or produced by putrefaction or decay.

sap·ro·leg·nia /ˌsaprəˈlegnēə/ ▶ **n.** an aquatic fungus (genus *Saprolegnia*, subdivision Mastigomycotina) that can attack the bodies of fish and other aquatic animals. [mod. L., from SAPRO- 'of decay' + Gk. *legnon* 'border.']

sa·proph·a·gous /səˈpräfəgəs/ ▶ **adj.** Biol. (of an organism) feeding on decaying organic matter. — **sap·ro·phage** /ˈsaprəˌfāj/ **n. sa·proph·a·gy** /-ˈpräfəjē/ **n.**

sap·ro·phyte /ˈsaprəˌfīt/ ▶ **n.** Biol. a plant, fungus, or microorganism that lives on dead or decaying organic matter. — **sap·ro·phyt·ic** /ˌsaprəˈfitik/ **adj. sap·ro·phyt·i·cal·ly** /-ik(ə)lē/ **adv.**

sap·ro·troph /ˈsaprəˌtrōf; -ˌträf/ ▶ **n.** Biol. an organism that feeds on or derives nourishment from decaying organic matter. — **sap·ro·troph·ic** /ˌsaprəˈtrōfik; -ˈträfik/ **adj.** [back-form. from *saprotrophic*.]

sap·suck·er /ˈsapˌsəkər/ ▶ **n.** an American woodpecker (genus *Sphyrapicus varius*) that pecks rows of small holes in trees and visits them for sap and insects.

sap·wood /ˈsapˌwo͝od/ ▶ **n.** the soft outer layers of recently formed wood between the heartwood and the bark, containing the functioning vascular tissue.

sar·a·band /ˈsarəˌband/ (also **sar·a·bande**) ▶ **n.** a slow, stately Spanish dance in triple time. ■ a piece of music written for such a dance. [17th C.: from Fr. *sarabande*, from Sp. and Ital. *zarabanda*.]

Sar·a·cen /ˈsarəsən/ ▶ **n.** an Arab or Muslim, esp. at the time of the Crusades. ■ a nomad of the Syrian and Arabian desert at the time of the Roman Empire. — **Sar·a·cen·ic** /ˌserəˈsenik/ **adj.** [ME, from OFr. *sarrazin*, via late L. from late Gk. *Sarakēnos*, perh. from Arab. *šarḳī* 'eastern.']

Sar·a·gos·sa /ˌsarəˈgäsə/ a city in northern Spain, capital of Aragon, situated on the Ebro River; pop. 614,000. Spanish name ZARAGOZA.

Sar·ah /ˈse(ə)rə/ (in the Bible) the wife of Abraham and mother of Isaac.

Sa·ra·je·vo /ˌsärəˈyāvō; -ˈyēvō/ the capital of Bosnia–Herzegovina; pop. 200,000. It was the scene in June 1914 of the assassination of Archduke Franz Ferdinand (1863–1914), an event that triggered the outbreak of World War I, and of ethnic conflict during the 1990s.

Sa·ran /səˈran/ (also **Sa·ran Wrap**) ▶ **n.** trademark for POLYVINYL CHLORIDE, esp. as plastic wrap. [1940s: of unknown origin.]

Sar·a·nac Lakes /ˈsarəˌnak/ resort lakes in northeastern New York, in Adirondack Park.

Sa·ransk /səˈränsk/ a city in western Russia, capital of Mordvinia, south of Nizhni Novgorod; pop. 316,000.

sa·ra·pe ▶ **n.** var. of SERAPE.

Sar·a·so·ta /ˌsarəˈsōtə/ a city in southwestern Florida, on Sarasota Bay; pop. 50,961.

Sar·a·to·ga, Battle of /ˌsarəˈtōgə/ either of two battles fought in 1777 during the American Revolution, near modern Saratoga Springs, New York. The defeat of the British in both battles is regarded as a turning point for the American side.

Sa·ra·tov /səˈrätəf/ a city in southwestern central Russia, north of Volgograd; pop. 909,000.

Sa·ra·wak /səˈräwək/ a state of Malaysia that occupies the northwestern part of Borneo.

Sar·a·zen /ˈsarəzən/, Gene (1902–99), US golfer; born *Eugene Saraceni*. He was the first player to win all four Grand Slam titles.

sar·casm /ˈsärˌkazəm/ ▶ **n.** the use of irony to mock or convey contempt. [16th C.: ult. from late Greek *sarkasmos*, from Gk. *sarkazein* 'tear flesh,' from *sarx, sark-* 'flesh'.]

sar·cas·tic /särˈkastik/ ▶ **adj.** marked by or given to using irony in order to mock or convey contempt. — **sar·cas·ti·cal·ly** /-ik(ə)lē/ **adv.** [17th C.: from Fr. *sarcastique*, from *sarcasme* (see SARCASM).]

sar·coid /ˈsärˌkoid/ Med. ▶ **adj.** [attrib.] relating to, denoting, or suffering from sarcoidosis. ▶ **n.** a granuloma of the type present in sarcoidosis. ■ the condition and symptoms of sarcoidosis: *tissues affected by sarcoid.* [19th C.: from Gk. *sarx, sark-* 'flesh' + -OID.]

sar·coid·o·sis /ˌsärˌkoiˈdōsis/ ▶ **n.** a chronic disease of unknown cause characterized by the enlargement of lymph nodes in many parts of the body and the widespread appearance of granulomas derived from the reticuloendothelial system.

sar·co·ma /särˈkōmə/ ▶ **n.** (pl. **-mas** or **-ma·ta** /-mətə/) Med. a malignant tumor of connective or other nonepithelial tissue. — **sar·co·ma·to·sis** /särˌkōməˈtōsis/ **n.** **sar·co·ma·tous** /-mətəs/ **adj.** [19th C.: mod. L., from Gk. *sarkōma*, from *sarkoun* 'become fleshy,' from *sarx, sark-* 'flesh.']

sar·coph·a·gus /särˈkäfəgəs/ ▶ **n.** (pl. **-gi** /-ˌjī; -ˌgī/) a stone coffin, typically adorned with a sculpture or inscription and associated with the ancient civilizations of Egypt, Rome, and Greece. [ME: via L. from Gk. *sarkophagos* 'flesh-consuming,' from *sarx, sark-* 'flesh' + *-phagos* '-eating.']

sar·co·plasm /ˈsärkəˌplazəm/ ▶ **n.** Physiol. the cytoplasm of striated muscle cells. — **sar·co·plas·mic** /ˌsärkəˈplazmik/ **adj.** [19th C.: from Gk. *sarx, sark-* 'flesh' + PLASMA.]

sar·co·sine /ˈsärkəˌsēn/ ▶ **n.** Biochem. a crystalline amino acid, CH_3NHCH_2COOH, that occurs in the body as a product of the metabolism of creatine. [19th C.: from Gk. *sarx, sark-* 'flesh' + -INE[4].]

sard /särd/ ▶ **n.** a yellow or brownish-red variety of chalcedony. [ME: from Fr. *sarde* or L. *sarda*, from Gk. *sardios*, prob. from *Sardō* 'Sardinia.']

Sar·de·gna /särˈdenyə/ Italian name for SARDINIA.

sar·dine[1] /särˈdēn/ ▶ **n.** a young pilchard or other young or small herring-like fish. ▶ **v.** [trans.] informal pack closely together.
– PHRASES **packed like sardines** crowded very close together, as sardines are in cans. [ME: from Fr., or from L. *sardina*, from *sarda*, from Gk., prob. from *Sardō* 'Sardinia.']

sar·dine[2] ▶ **n.** another term for SARDIUS. [ME: via late L. from Gk. *sardinos*, var. of *sardios* (see SARDIUS).]

Sar·din·i·a /särˈdinēə/ an Italian island in the Mediterranean Sea, west of Italy; pop. 1,664,000; capital, Cagliari. Italian name SARDEGNA.

Sar·din·i·an /särˈdinēən/ ▶ **adj.** of or relating to Sardinia, its people, or their language. ▶ **n.** **1** a native or inhabitant of Sardinia. **2** the Romance language of Sardinia, which has several distinct dialects.

Sar·dis /ˈsärdis/ an ancient city in Asia Minor, near the western coast of modern Turkey, now in ruins.

sar·di·us /ˈsärdēəs/ ▶ **n.** a red precious stone mentioned in the Bible (e.g., Exod. 28:17) and in classical writings, probably ruby or carnelian. [ME: via late L. from Gk. *sardios*.]

sar·don·ic /särˈdänik/ ▶ **adj.** grimly mocking or cynical. — **sar·don·i·cal·ly** /-ik(ə)lē/ **adv.** **sar·don·i·cism** /-ˈdänəˌsizəm/ **n.** [17th C.: from Fr. *sardonique*, ult. from Gk. *sardonios* 'of Sardinia.']

sar·don·yx /särˈdäniks/ ▶ **n.** onyx in which white layers alternate with sard. [ME: via L. from Gk. *sardonux*, prob. from *sardios* 'sardius' + *onux* 'onyx.']

sa·ree ▶ **n.** var. of SARI.

sar·gas·so /särˈgasō/ (also **sar·gas·so weed**) ▶ **n.** another term for SARGASSUM. [16th C.: from Port. *sargaço*.]

Sar·gas·so Sea /särˈgasō/ a region of the western Atlantic Ocean between the Azores and the Caribbean Sea.

sar·gas·sum /särˈgasəm/ (also **sar·gas·sum weed**) ▶ **n.** a brown seaweed (genus *Sargassum*, class Phaeophyceae) with berrylike air bladders, typically forming large floating masses. [mod. L., from Port. *sargaço* (see SARGASSO).]

sarge /särj/ ▶ **n.** informal sergeant. [19th C.: abbrev.]

Sar·gent /ˈsärjənt/, John Singer (1856–1925), US painter, noted for his portraits, including *Madame Gautreau* (1884).

Sar·go·dha /sərˈgōdə/ a city in north central Pakistan; pop. 294,000.

Sar·gon /ˈsärˌgän/ (2334–2279 BC), the semilegendary founder of the ancient kingdom of Akkad.

Sar·gon II (died 705 BC), king of Assyria 721–705 BC. He conquered cities in Syria and Palestine.

sa·ri /ˈsärē/ (also **sa·ree**) ▶ **n.** (pl. **-ris** or **-rees**) a garment consisting of a length of cotton or silk elaborately draped around the body, traditionally worn by women from the Indian subcontinent. [18th C.: from Hindi *sāṛī*.]

sari

sa·rin /säˈrēn/ ▶ **n.** an organophosphorus nerve gas. [from Ger. *Sarin*, of unknown origin.]

Sar·ma·ti·a /särˈmāsh(ē)ə/ an ancient region that extended from the Ural Mountains to the Don River. — **Sar·ma·ti·an** /-ˈmāsh(ē)ən/ **adj. & n.**

sa·rod /səˈrōd/ ▶ **n.** a lute used in classical northern Indian music, with four main strings. [Urdu, from Pers. *surod* 'song, melody.']

sa·rong /səˈrôNG; -ˈräNG/ ▶ **n.** a garment consisting of a long piece of cloth worn wrapped around the body and tucked at the waist or under the armpits, traditionally worn in Southeast Asia. [19th C.: Malay, lit. 'sheath.']

sarong

Sa·ron·ic Gulf /səˈränik/ an inlet of the Aegean Sea on the coast of southeastern Greece.

sa·ros /ˈse(ə)räs/ ▶ **n.** Astron. a period of about 18 years between repetitions of solar and lunar eclipses. [19th C.: from Gk., from Babylonian *šār(u)* '3,600 (years).']

Sa·roy·an /səˈroi-ən/, William (1908–81), US writer. His novels include *The Human Comedy* (1943) and *The Laughing Matter* (1953).

sar·ra·ce·nia /ˌsarəˈsēnēə; ˌser-/ ▶ **n.** a North American pitcher plant (genus *Sarracenia*, family Sarraceniaceae) of marshy places, some kinds of which are cultivated as ornamentals. [mod. L., named after Michel *Sarrazin* (died 1734), Canadian botanist.]

Sar·raute /säˈrōt/, Nathalie (1902–99), French writer; born in Russia; born *Nathalie Ilyanova Tcherniak*. Her novels include *Martereau* (1953).

Sarre /sär/ French name for SAAR.

sar·ru·so·phone /səˈro͞ozəˌfōn; -ˈrəsə-/ ▶ **n.** a member of a family of wind instruments similar to saxophones but with a double reed like an oboe. [19th C.: W. *Sarrus*, 19th-cent. French bandmaster.]

SARS /särz/ ▶ **n.** a virulently infectious disease originating in China in 2002, caused by a corona virus. [21st C.: acronym from *Severe Acute Respiratory Syndrome*.]

sar·sa·pa·ril·la /ˌsärs(ə)pəˈrilə; ˌsaspə-/ ▶ **n.** **1** a preparation of the dried rhizomes of various plants, esp. smilax, used to flavor some drinks and medicines and formerly as a tonic. ■ a sweet drink flavored with this. **2** the tropical American climbing plant (genus *Smilax*) of the lily family from which these rhizomes are generally obtained, esp. *S. regelii*, which is the chief source of commercial sarsaparilla. [16th C.: from Sp. *zarzaparilla*, from *zarza* 'bramble' + a dimin. of *parra* 'vine.']

sar·sen /ˈsärsən/ (also **sar·sen stone**) ▶ **n.** Geol. a silicified sandstone boulder of a kind that occurs on the chalk downs of southern England. [17th C.: prob. a var. of SARACEN.]

Sar·to /ˈsärtō/, Andrea del (1486–1531), Italian painter; born *Andrea d'Agnolo*. His works include the series of grisailles in the cloister of the Scalzi (1511–26).

Sar·ton /ˈsärtn/, May (1912–95), US writer and poet; born in Belgium; full name *Eleanor May Sarton*. Her novels include *Faithful Are the Wounds* (1955) and *As We Are Now* (1973).

sar·to·ri·al /särˈtôrēəl/ ▶ **adj.** [attrib.] of or relating to tailoring, clothes, or style of dress: *sartorial elegance.* — **sar·to·ri·al·ly** **adv.** [19th C.: from L. *sartor* 'tailor' (from *sarcire* 'to patch') + -IAL.]

sar·to·ri·us /särˈtôrēəs/ (also **sar·to·ri·us mus·cle**) ▶ **n.** Anat. a long, narrow muscle running obliquely across the front of each thigh from the hipbone to the inside of the leg below the knee. [18th C.: mod. L., from L. *sartor* 'tailor' (from the cross-legged position associated with tailors).]

Sar·tre /ˈsärt(rə)/, Jean-Paul (1905–80), French philosopher. A leading existentialist, he dealt with the nature of human life and the structures of consciousness. He refused the Nobel Prize for Literature in 1964.

Sar·um /ˈse(ə)rəm/ an old name for Salisbury, England, still used as the name of its diocese.

sa·rus crane /ˈsärəs/ ▶ **n.** a large, red-headed crane (*Grus antigone*) found from India to the Philippines. [19th C.: *sarus* from Sanskrit *sārasa*.]

SAS ▶ **abbr.** Brit. Special Air Service.

sa·san·qua /səˈsäNGkwə/ ▶ **n.** a Japanese camellia (*Camellia sasanqua*) with fragrant white or pink flowers and seeds that yield tea oil. [19th C.: from Japanese *sasank(w)a*.]

SASE ▶ **abbr.** self-addressed stamped envelope.

sash[1] /sash/ ▶ **n.** a long strip or loop of cloth worn over one shoulder or around the waist. — **sashed** /sasht/ **adj.** **sash·less** **adj.** [16th C.: from Arab. *šāš* 'muslin, turban.']

sash[2] ▶ **n.** a frame holding the glass in a window, typically one of two sliding frames. — **sashed** **adj.** [17th C.: alt. of CHASSIS, interpreted as pl.]

sa·shay /saˈshā/ ▶ **v.** [intrans.] informal **1** [with adverbial of direction] walk in an ostentatious yet casual manner, typically with exaggerated movements of the hips and shoulders. **2** perform the sashay. ▶ **n.** (in American square dancing) a figure in which partners circle each other by taking sideways steps. [19th C. (as a v.): alt. of CHASSÉ.]

sash cord ▶ **n.** a strong cord attaching either of the sash weights of a sash window to a sash.

sa·shi·mi /säˈshēmē/ ▶ **n.** a Japanese dish of bite-sized pieces of raw fish eaten with soy sauce and horseradish paste: *tuna sashimi.*

sash weight ▶ **n.** a weight attached by a cord to each side of a window sash to balance it at any height.

Sask. ▶ **abbr.** Saskatchewan.

Sas·katch·e·wan /sə'skacнəwən; -ə,wän/ **1** a province in central Canada; pop. 994,000; capital, Regina. **2** a river in Canada. Rising in the Rocky Mountains, it flows east to Lake Winnipeg.

Sas·ka·toon /,saskə'to͞on/ a city in south central Saskatchewan in Canada; pop. 186,060.

Sas·quatch /'saskwäcн; -kwacн/ ▶ n. another term for Bigfoot. [20th C.: Salish *sésq əc*.]

sass /sas/ informal ▶ n. impudence; cheek. ▶ v. [trans.] be cheeky or rude to (someone). [19th C.: var. of sauce.]

sas·sa·by /'sasəbē/ ▶ n. an antelope (*Damaliscus lunatus lunatus*) of a race found mainly in southern Africa.

sas·sa·fras /'sasə,fras/ ▶ n. a deciduous North American tree (*Sassafras albidum*, family Lauraceae) with aromatic leaves and bark. The leaves are infused to make tea or ground into filé. ■ an extract of the leaves or bark of this tree, used medicinally or in perfumery. [16th C.: from Sp. *sasafrás*, based on L. *saxifraga* 'saxifrage.']

Sas·se·nach /'sasə,nak/ Scot. Irish, derog. ▶ n. an English person. ▶ adj. English. [18th C. (as a n.): from Scot. Gael. *Sasunnoch*, Irish *Sasanach*, from L. *Saxones* 'Saxons.']

Sas·soon /sə'so͞on; sa-/, Siegfried Lorraine (1886–1967), English poet and writer. His starkly realistic poems were written while serving in World War I.

sas·sy /'sasē/ ▶ adj. (-si·er, -si·est) informal lively, bold, and full of spirit; cheeky. — **sas·si·ly** /-əlē/ adv. **sas·si·ness** n. [19th C.: var. of saucy.]

sas·tru·gi /sə'stro͞ogē; sa'-; 'sastrə-/ ▶ plural n. parallel wavelike ridges caused by winds on the surface of hard snow, esp. in polar regions. [19th C.: from Russ. *zastrugi* 'small ridges.']

SAT /'es ,ā 'tē/ ▶ abbr. ■ trademark Scholastic Assessment Test. ■ (formerly) Scholastic Aptitude Test.

Sat. ▶ abbr. Saturday.

sat /sat/ past and past participle of sit.

Sa·tan /'sātn/ the Devil; Lucifer. [OE, via late L. and Gk. from Heb. *śāṭān*, lit. 'adversary,' from *śāṭān* 'plot against.']

sa·tang /sə'täng/ ▶ n. (pl. same or **-tangs**) a monetary unit of Thailand, equal to one hundredth of a baht. [Thai, from Pali *sata* 'hundred.']

sa·tan·ic /sə'tanik; sā'-/ ▶ adj. of or characteristic of Satan. ■ connected with Satanism. ■ extremely evil or wicked. — **sa·tan·i·cal·ly** /-ik(ə)lē/ adv.

sa·tan·ism /'sātn,izəm/ (also **Sa·tan·ism**) ▶ n. the worship of Satan, typically involving a travesty of Christian symbols and practices. — **sa·tan·ist** n. & adj.

sa·tay /sä'tā; 'sä,tā/ (also **sa·té**) ▶ n. a Southeast Asian dish consisting of small pieces of meat grilled on a skewer and served with spiced sauce. [from Malay *satai*, Indonesian *sate*.]

satch·el /'sacнəl/ ▶ n. a bag carried on the shoulder by a long strap and typically closed by a flap. [ME: from OFr. *sachel*, from L. *saccellus* 'small bag.']

sat·com /'sat,käm/ (also **SATCOM**) ▶ n. satellite communications. [20th C.: blend.]

sate /sāt/ ▶ v. [trans.] satisfy (a desire or an appetite) to the full: *sate your appetite at the restaurant.* ■ supply (someone) with as much as or more of something than is desired or can be managed. ▶ adj. satisfied completely; fulfilled. [17th C.: prob. an alt. of dial. *sade*, from OE *sadian* 'become sated or weary.']

sa·té ▶ n. var. of satay.

sa·teen /sa'tēn/ ▶ n. a cotton fabric woven like satin with a glossy surface. [19th C.: alt. of satin.]

sat·el·lite /'satl,īt/ ▶ n. **1** (also **ar·ti·fi·cial sat·el·lite**) an artificial body placed in orbit around the earth or another planet in order to collect information or for communication. ■ [as adj.] transmitted by satellite; using or relating to satellite technology. ■ satellite television. **2** Astron. a celestial body orbiting the earth or another planet. **3** [usu. as adj.] something that is separated from or on the periphery of something else but is nevertheless dependent on or controlled by it. ■ a small country or state politically or economically dependent on another. **4** Biol. a portion of the DNA of a genome with repeating base sequences and of different density from the main sequence. [16th C. ('follower'): from Fr. *satellite* or L. *satelles, satellit-* 'attendant.']

sat·el·lite dish ▶ n. a bowl-shaped antenna with which signals are transmitted to or received from a communications satellite.

sat·el·lite tel·e·vi·sion ▶ n. television broadcasting using a satellite to relay signals to appropriately equipped customers in a particular area.

Sa·ti /,sə'tē; 'sə,tē/ Hinduism the wife of Shiva, reborn as Parvati. According to some accounts, she died by throwing herself into the sacred fire.

sa·ti ▶ n. var. of suttee.

sa·ti·ate /'sāsнē,āt/ ▶ v. another term for sate. ▶ adj. archaic satisfied to the full; satiated. — **sa·tia·ble** /-sнəbəl/ adj. (archaic) **sa·ti·a·tion** /,sāsнē'āsнən/ n. [ME: from L. *satiatus*, past part. of *satiare*, from *satis* 'enough.']

Sa·tie /sä'tē/, Erik Alfred Leslie (1866–1925), French avant-garde composer, noted for his *Gymnopédies* (1888), a trio of piano compositions.

sa·ti·e·ty /sə'tīətē/ ▶ n. esp. tech. the feeling or state of being sated. [16th C.: from OFr. *saciete*, from L. *satietas*, from *satis* 'enough.']

sat·in /'satn/ ▶ n. a smooth, glossy fabric, typically of silk, produced by a weave in which the threads of the warp are caught and looped by the weft only at certain intervals: [as adj.] *a blue satin dress.* ■ [as adj.] denoting or having a surface or finish resembling this fabric. ▶ adj. smooth like satin: *a luxurious satin look.* — **sat·in·y** adj. [ME: via OFr. from Arab. *zaytūnī* 'of Tsinkiang,' a town in China.]

sat·i·net /,satn'et/ (also **sat·i·nette**) ▶ n. a fabric with a similar finish to satin, made partly or wholly of cotton or synthetic fiber.

sat·in stitch ▶ n. a long straight embroidery stitch, closely placed parallel to similar stitches, giving the appearance of satin.

sat·in wal·nut ▶ n. see sweet gum.

sat·in·wood /'satn,wo͝od/ ▶ n. **1** glossy yellowish timber from a tropical tree, valued for cabinetwork. **2** the tropical hardwood tree of the rue family that produces this timber. Two species: **Ceylon satinwood** (*Chloroxylon swietenia*), native to India and Sri Lanka, and **West Indian** (or **Jamaican**) **satinwood** (*Zanthoxylum flava*), native to the Caribbean, Bermuda, and southern Florida.

sat·ire /'sa,tī(ə)r/ ▶ n. the use of humor, irony, exaggeration, or ridicule to expose and criticize people's stupidity or vices, particularly in the context of contemporary politics and other topical issues. ■ a play, novel, film, or other work that uses satire. ■ a genre of literature characterized by the use of satire. — **sat·i·rist** /'satərist/ n. [16th C.: from Fr., or from L. *satira*, later form of *satura* 'poetic medley.']

sa·tir·i·cal /sə'ti(ə)rikəl/ (also **sa·tir·ic** /-'ti(ə)rik/) ▶ adj. containing or using satire: *a satirical magazine.* ■ (of a person or their behavior) sarcastic, critical, and mocking another's weaknesses. — **sa·tir·i·cal·ly** /-ik(ə)lē/ adv.

sat·i·rize /'satə,rīz/ ▶ v. [trans.] deride and criticize by means of satire. — **sat·i·ri·za·tion** /,satərə'zāsнən/ n.

sat·is·fac·tion /,satis'faksнən/ ▶ n. fulfillment of one's wishes, expectations, or needs, or the pleasure derived from this: *he smiled with satisfaction.* ■ Law the payment of a debt or fulfillment of an obligation or claim. ■ what is felt to be owed or due to one, esp. in reparation of an injustice or wrong. ■ Christian Theol. Christ's atonement for sin. ■ hist. the opportunity to defend one's honor in a duel.
– PHRASES **to one's satisfaction** so that one is satisfied. [ME: from OFr., or from L. *satisfactio(n-)*, from *satisfacere* 'satisfy, content.']

sat·is·fac·to·ry /,satis'fakt(ə)rē/ ▶ adj. fulfilling expectations or needs; acceptable, though not outstanding or perfect. ■ (of a patient in a hospital) not deteriorating or likely to die. ■ Law (of evidence or a verdict) sufficient for the needs of the case. — **sat·is·fac·to·ri·ly** /-t(ə)rəlē/ adv. **sat·is·fac·to·ri·ness** n. [ME: from OFr. *satisfactoire* or med. L. *satisfactorius*, from L. *satisfacere* 'to content.']

sat·is·fied /'satis,fīd/ ▶ adj. contented; pleased.

sat·is·fy /'satis,fī/ ▶ v. (-fies, -fied) [trans.] meet the expectations, needs, or desires of (someone). ■ fulfill (a desire or need). ■ provide (someone) with adequate information or proof so that they are convinced about something. ■ adequately meet or comply with (a condition, obligation, or demand). ■ Math. (of a quantity) make (an equation) true. ■ pay off (a debt or creditor). — **sat·is·fi·a·bil·i·ty** /,satis,fīə'bilitē/ n. **sat·is·fi·a·ble** adj. [ME: from OFr. *satisfier*, formed irregularly from L. *satisfacere* 'to content,' from *satis* 'enough' + *facere* 'make.']

sat·is·fy·ing /'satis,fī-ing/ ▶ adj. giving fulfillment or the pleasure associated with this. — **sat·is·fy·ing·ly** adv.

sa·to·ri /sə'tôrē/ ▶ n. Buddhism sudden enlightenment. [Japanese, 'awakening.']

sa·trap /'sā,trap; 'sa-/ ▶ n. a provincial governor in the ancient Persian empire. ■ any subordinate or local ruler. [ME: ult. from L. *satrapa*, based on Old Pers. *kš athra-pāvan* 'country-protector.']

sa·trap·y /'sātrəpē; 'sa-/ ▶ n. (pl. **-trap·ies**) a province governed by a satrap.

Sat·su·ma /sat'so͞omə; 'satsə,mä/ a former province of southwestern Japan that was located on Kyushu island, also known as the Satsuma Peninsula.

sat·su·ma /sat'so͞omə; 'satsəmə/ ▶ n. **1** a tangerine of a hardy loose-skinned variety, originally grown in Japan. **2** (**Sat·su·ma** or **Sat·su·ma ware**) Japanese pottery from Satsuma [19th C.: Satsuma.]

sat·u·rate ▶ v. /'sacнə,rāt/ [trans.] (usu. **be saturated**) cause (something) to become thoroughly soaked with liquid so that no more can be absorbed. ■ cause (a substance) to combine with, dissolve, or hold the greatest possible quantity of another substance. ■ magnetize or charge (a substance or device) fully. ■ Electron. put (a device) into a state in which no further increase in current is achievable. ■ (usu. **be saturated with**) fig. fill (something or someone) with something until no more can be held or absorbed. ■ supply (a market) beyond the point at which the demand for a product is satisfied. ■ overwhelm (an enemy target area) by concentrated bombing. ▶ n. /-rət/ (usu. **saturates**) a saturated fat. ▶ adj. /-rət/ literary saturated with moisture. — **sat·u·ra·ble** /-əbəl/ adj. (tech.). [ME ('satisfied'): from L. *saturat-* 'filled, glutted,' from the verb *saturare*, from *satur* 'full.']

sat·u·rat·ed /'sacнə,rātid/ ▶ adj. **1** holding as much water or moisture as can be absorbed; thoroughly soaked. ■ Chem. (of a solution) containing the largest possible amount of a particular solute. ■ having or holding as much as can be absorbed of something. **2** Chem. (of an organic molecule) containing the greatest possible number of hydrogen atoms, without carbon–carbon double or triple bonds. ■ denoting fats containing a high proportion of fatty acid molecules without double bonds, considered to be less healthy in the diet than unsaturated fats. **3** (of color) very bright, full, and free from an admixture of white: *intense and saturated color.*

sat·u·ra·tion /ˌsacHəˈrāsHən/ ▶**n.** the state or process that occurs when no more of something can be absorbed, combined with, or added. ■ Chem. the degree or extent to which something is dissolved or absorbed compared with the maximum possible, usually expressed as a percentage. ■ [as adj.] to a very full extent, esp. beyond the point regarded as necessary or desirable. ■ (also **col·or sat·u·ra·tion**) (esp. in photography) the intensity of a color, expressed as the degree to which it differs from white.

sat·u·ra·tion point ▶**n.** [in sing.] Chem. the stage at which no more of a substance can be absorbed into a vapor or dissolved into a solution. ■ fig. the stage beyond which no more of something can be absorbed or accepted.

Sat·ur·day /ˈsatərˌdā; -dē/ ▶**n.** the day of the week before Sunday and following Friday, and (together with Sunday) forming part of the weekend. ▶**adv.** on Saturday: *he made his first appearance Saturday.* ■ **(Saturdays)** on Saturdays; each Saturday. [OE *Sætern(es)dæg*, translation of L. *Saturni dies* 'day of Saturn.']

Sat·ur·day night spe·cial ▶**n.** informal a cheap, low-caliber pistol or revolver, easily obtained.

Sat·urn /ˈsatərn/ **1** Rom. Mythol. an ancient god, regarded as a god of agriculture. Greek equivalent **Cronus**. [from L. *Saturnus*, perh. from Etruscan.] **2** Astron. the sixth planet from the sun in the solar system, circled by a system of broad, flat rings. **3** a series of American space rockets, of which the very large *Saturn V* was used as the launch vehicle for the Apollo missions of 1969–72.

Sat·ur·na·li·a /ˌsatərˈnālēə; -nālyə/ ▶**n.** [treated as sing. or pl.] the ancient Roman festival of Saturn in December, the predecessor of Christmas. ■ **(saturnalia)** an occasion of wild revelry. — **sat·ur·na·li·an** adj. [L., lit. 'matters relating to Saturn,' neut. pl. of *Saturnalis*.]

Sa·tur·ni·an /səˈtərnēən/ ▶**adj.** **1** of or relating to the planet Saturn. **2** another term for **saturnine**.

sa·tur·ni·id /səˈtərnē-id/ ▶**n.** Entomol. a silkworm moth of a family (Saturniidae) that includes the emperor moths and the giant Indian silk moths. They typically have prominent eyespots on the wings. [19th C.: from mod. L. *Saturniidae* (pl.), from the genus name *Saturnia*.]

sat·ur·nine /ˈsatərˌnīn/ ▶**adj.** (of a person or their manner) slow and gloomy: *a saturnine temperament.* ■ (of a person or their features) dark in coloring and moody or mysterious: *his saturnine face and dark, watchful eyes.* ■ (of a place or an occasion) gloomy. — **sat·ur·nine·ly** adv. [ME (as a term in astrology): from OFr. *saturnin*, from med. L. *Saturninus* 'of Saturn.']

sa·tyr /ˈsatər; ˈsātər/ ▶**n.** **1** Gk. Mythol. one of a class of lustful, drunken woodland gods. In Greek art they were represented as a man with a horse's ears and tail, but in Roman representations as a man with a goat's ears, tail, legs, and horns. ■ a man who has strong sexual desires. **2** a satyrid butterfly with chiefly dark brown wings. — **sa·tyr·ic** /səˈtirik/ adj. [ME: from OFr. *satyre*, or via L. from Gk. *saturos*.]

sa·ty·ri·a·sis /ˌsatəˈrīəsis; ˌsā-/ ▶**n.** uncontrollable or excessive sexual desire in a man.

sa·tyr·id /ˈsatərid; ˈsā-/ ▶**n.** Entomol. a butterfly of a group (subfamily Satyrinae, family Nymphalidae) that includes the browns, heaths, ringlets, and related species. They typically have brown wings with small eyespots and many live in woodland and breed on grasses.

sauce /sôs/ ▶**n.** **1** thick liquid served with food, usually savory dishes, to add moistness and flavor. ■ stewed fruit, esp. apples, eaten as dessert or used as a garnish. **2** **(the sauce)** informal alcoholic drink. **3** informal, esp. Brit. impertinence. ▶**v.** [trans.] **1** (usu. **be sauced**) provide a sauce for (something); season with a sauce. ■ fig. make more interesting and exciting. **2** informal be rude or impudent to (someone). — **sauce·less** adj. [ME: from OFr., based on L. *salsus* 'salted,' past part. of *salere* 'to salt,' from *sal* 'salt.' Cf. **salad**.]

sauce·boat /ˈsôsˌbōt/ ▶**n.** a gravy boat.

sauced /sôst/ ▶**adj.** informal drunk.

sauce·pan /ˈsôsˌpan/ ▶**n.** a deep cooking pan, typically round, made of metal, and with one long handle and a lid. — **sauce·pan·ful** /-ˌfo͝ol/ n. (pl. **-fuls**).

sau·cer /ˈsôsər/ ▶**n.** a shallow dish, typically having a circular indentation in the center, on which a cup is placed.
– PHRASES **have eyes like saucers** have one's eyes opened wide in amazement. — **sau·cer·ful** /-ˌfo͝ol/ n. (pl. **-fuls**). **sau·cer·less** adj. [ME: from OFr. *saussier(e)* 'sauceboat.']

sau·cier /sôsˈyā; ˈsôsēər/ ▶**n.** a chef who prepares sauces. [Fr.]

sau·cy /ˈsôsē/ ▶**adj.** (**-ci·er**, **-ci·est**) informal **1** impudent; flippant: *a saucy remark.* **2** bold and lively; smart-looking. **3** sexually suggestive, typically in a way intended to be lighthearted: *saucy songs.* — **sau·ci·ly** /-səlē/ adv. **sau·ci·ness** n. [16th C.: from **sauce** + **-y**[1].]

Sau·di /ˈsoudē; ˈsô-/ ▶**adj.** of or relating to Saudi Arabia or its ruling dynasty. ▶**n.** (pl. **-dis**) a citizen of Saudi Arabia, or a member of its ruling dynasty. [Abdul-Aziz ibn *Saud* (1880–1953), first king of Saudi Arabia.]

Sau·di A·ra·bi·a /ˈsoudē əˈrābēə; ˈsôdē/ a country in the Middle East. *See box.* — **Sau·di A·ra·bi·an** adj. & n.

Saudi Arabia
Official name: Kingdom of Saudi Arabia
Location: Middle East, occupying most of the Arabian peninsula
Area: 757,200 square miles (1,960,600 sq km)
Population: 25,795,000
Capital: Riyadh
Language: Arabic
Currency: Saudi riyal

sau·er·bra·ten /ˈsou(ə)rˌbrätn/ ▶**n.** a German dish consisting of beef marinated in vinegar with peppercorns, onions, and other seasonings before cooking. [from Ger., from *sauer* 'sour' + *Braten* 'roast meat.']

sau·er·kraut /ˈsou(ə)rˌkrout/ ▶**n.** chopped cabbage that has been pickled in brine. [from Ger., from *sauer* 'sour' + *Kraut* 'vegetable.']

sau·ger /ˈsôgər/ ▶**n.** a slender, silver-eyed North American pikeperch (*Stizostedion canadense*), active at twilight and at night. [19th C.: of unknown origin.]

Sauk /sôk/ (also **Sac**) ▶**n.** (pl. same or **Sauks**) **1** a member of an American Indian people inhabiting parts of the central US, formerly in Wisconsin, Illinois, and Iowa, now in Oklahoma and Kansas. **2** the Algonquian language of this people. ▶**adj.** of or relating to this people or their language. [from Canad. Fr. *Saki*, from Ojibwa *osākī* '(people of the) river mouth.']

Saul /sôl/ (in the Bible) the first king of Israel (11th century BC).

Saul of Tar·sus see **Paul, St.**

Sault Sainte Marie /ˈso͞o ˌsānt məˈrē/ each of two North American cities that face each other across the falls of the St. Mary's River, between lakes Superior and Huron. The Canadian port (pop. 72,822) is in Ontario, while the US port (pop. 14,700) is in Michigan.

sau·na /ˈsônə; ˈsou-/ ▶**n.** a small room used as a hot-air or steam bath for cleaning and refreshing the body. ■ a session in such a room. [19th C.: from Finn.]

saun·ter /ˈsôntər/ ▶**v.** [no obj., with adverbial of direction] walk in a slow, relaxed manner, without hurry or effort. ▶**n.** a leisurely stroll: *a quiet saunter down the road.* — **saun·ter·er** n. [ME ('to muse, wonder'): of unknown origin.]

-saur ▶**comb. form** forming names of reptiles, esp. extinct ones: *ichthyosaur | stegosaur.* [mod. L., from Gk. *sauros* 'lizard.']

Sau·ri·a /ˈsôrēə/ Zool. former term for **Lacertilia**. [mod. L. (pl.), from Gk. *sauros* 'lizard.']

sau·ri·an /ˈsôrēən/ ▶**adj.** of or like a lizard. ▶**n.** any large reptile, esp. a dinosaur or other extinct form. [19th C.: from mod. L. *Sauria* (see **Sauria**) + **-an**.]

saur·is·chi·an /sôˈriskēən/ Paleontol. ▶**adj.** of, relating to, or denoting dinosaurs of an order (Saurischia) distinguished by having a pelvic structure resembling that of lizards. Compare with **ornithischian**. ▶**n.** a saurischian dinosaur. [19th C.: from the mod. L. pl. *Saurischia* (from Gk. *sauros* 'lizard' + *iskhion* 'hip joint') + **-an**.]

sau·ro·pod /ˈsôrəˌpäd/ ▶**n.** a very large quadrupedal herbivorous dinosaur (infraorder Sauropoda, suborder Sauropodomorpha, order Saurischia) with a long neck and tail, small head, and massive limbs. [19th C.: from mod. L. *Sauropoda* (pl.), from Gk. *sauros* 'lizard' + *pous*, *pod-* 'foot.']

-saurus ▶**comb. form** forming genus names of reptiles, esp. extinct ones: *stegosaurus.* [mod. L.]

sau·ry /ˈsôrē/ ▶**n.** (pl. **-ries**) a long slender-bodied edible marine fish (family Scomberesocidae) with an elongated snout. Four genera and species include *Scomberesox saurus* of the Atlantic (also called **skipper**[2]). [18th C.: perh. via late L. from Gk. *sauros* 'horse mackerel.']

sau·sage /ˈsôsij/ ▶**n.** a short cylindrical tube of minced pork, beef, or other meat encased in a skin, typically sold raw to be grilled or fried before eating. ■ a cylindrical tube of minced pork, beef, or other meat

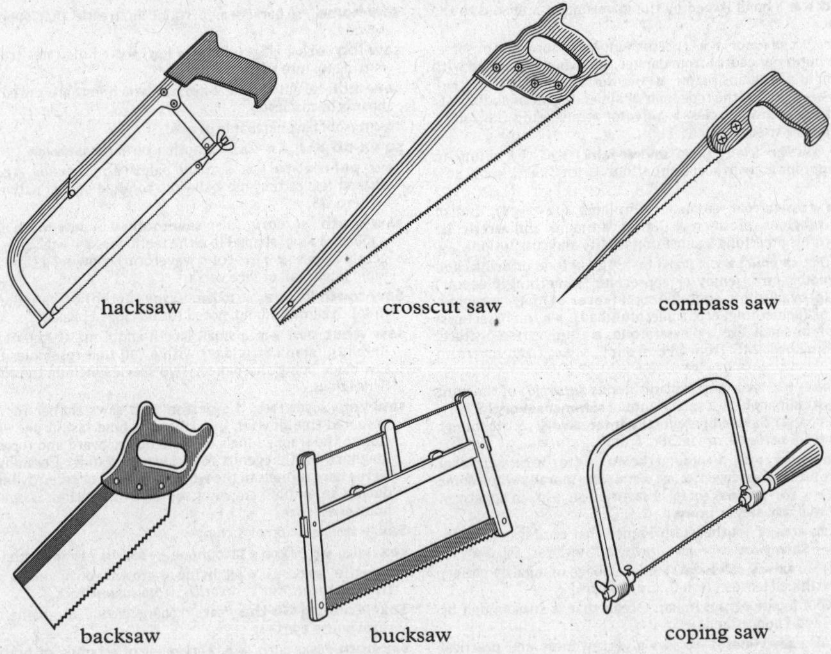

saws

seasoned and cooked or preserved, sold mainly to be eaten cold in slices: *smoked German sausage.* ■ [usu. as adj.] used in references to the characteristic cylindrical shape of sausages: *a sausage shape.* [ME: from Old North. Fr. *saussiche*, from med. L. *salsicia*, from L. *salsus* 'salted' (see SAUCE).]

Saus·sure /sō'sŏŏr; -'syr/, Ferdinand de (1857–1913), Swiss linguist. He was one of the founders of modern linguistics.

sau·té /sô'tā; sō-/ ▶ **adj.** **1** [attrib.] fried quickly in a little hot fat: *sauté potatoes.* **2** Ballet (of a step) performed while jumping. ▶ **n.** a dish cooked in such a way. ▶ **v.** (**-tés, -téed** /-'tād/ or **-téd, -téing** /-'tāiNG/) [trans.] cook in such a way. [19th C.: Fr., lit. 'jumped,' past part. of *sauter*.]

Sau·ternes /sō'tərn; sô-/ ▶ **n.** a sweet white wine from Sauternes in the Bordeaux region of France.

Sau·vi·gnon /,sōvin'yôN; -vē'nyôN/ (also **Sau·vi·gnon Blanc** /'bläN; 'bläNGk/) ▶ **n.** a variety of white wine grape. ■ a white wine made from this grape. [Fr.]

sav·age /'savij/ ▶ **adj.** (of an animal or force of nature) fierce, violent, and uncontrolled: *a savage beast.* ■ cruel and vicious; aggressively hostile. ■ (chiefly in historical or literary contexts) primitive; uncivilized. ■ (of a place) wild-looking and inhospitable; uncultivated. ■ (of something bad or negative) very great; severe. ▶ **n.** (chiefly in historical or literary contexts) a member of a people regarded as primitive and uncivilized. ■ a brutal or vicious person. ▶ **v.** [trans.] (esp. of a dog or wild animal) attack ferociously and maul: *ewes savaged by marauding dogs.* ■ subject to a vicious verbal attack; criticize brutally. — **sav·age·ly adv.** **sav·age·ness n.** **sav·age·ry** /-rē/ **n.** [ME: from OFr. *sauvage* 'wild,' from L. *silvaticus* 'of the woods,' from *silva* 'a wood.']

Sa·vai'i /sə'vī-ē/ (also **Sa·vai·i**) a volcanic island in the southwestern Pacific, part of the Samoan islands.

sa·van·na /sə'vanə/ (also **sa·van·nah**) ▶ **n.** a grassy plain in tropical and subtropical regions, with few trees. [16th C.: from Sp. *sabana*, from Taino *zavana*.]

Sa·van·nah /sə'vanə/ a city in Georgia, on the Savannah River; pop. 131,510.

Sa·vann·ah Riv·er a river that flows along the border of Georgia and South Carolina to reach the Atlantic Ocean near Savannah.

sa·van·nah spar·row /sə'vanə/ ▶ **n.** a small North American sparrow (*Passerculus sandwichensis*) of the bunting family.

sa·vant /sa'vänt; sə-/ ▶ **n.** a learned person, esp. a distinguished scientist. See also IDIOT SAVANT. [18th C.: Fr., lit. 'knowing (person),' pres. part. (used as a n.) of *savoir*.]

sav·a·rin /'savərin/ ▶ **n.** a light ring-shaped cake made with yeast and soaked in liqueur-flavored syrup. [named after Anthelme Brillat-*Savarin* (1755–1826), French gastronome.]

save¹ /sāv/ ▶ **v.** [trans.] **1** keep safe or rescue (someone or something) from harm or danger. ■ prevent (someone) from dying. ■ (in Christian use) preserve (a person's soul) from damnation: *church ladies approach me trying to save my soul* | [intrans.] *Jesus came to save.* ■ keep (someone) in health (used in exclamations and formulaic expressions): *God save the Queen.* **2** keep and store up (something, esp. money) for future use: *she had never been able to save much.* ■ Comput. keep (data) by moving a copy to a storage location. ■ preserve (something) by not expending or using it. ■ [in imper.] (**save it**) informal used to tell someone to stop talking. **3** avoid the need to use up or spend (money, time, or other resources). ■ avoid, lessen, or guard against. **4** prevent an opponent from scoring (a goal or point) in a game or from winning (the game). ■ Baseball (of a relief pitcher in certain game situations) finish (a game) while preserving a winning position gained by another pitcher. ■ Soccer Hockey (of a goalkeeper) stop (a shot) from entering the goal. ■ [intrans.] keep and store up money: ▶ **n.** Baseball an instance of a relief pitcher saving a game. ■ esp. Soccer Hockey an act of preventing an opponent's scoring: *the keeper made a great save.* Bridge another term for SACRIFICE.

– PHRASES **save one's breath** [often in imper.] not bother to say something because it is pointless. **save the day** find or provide a solution to a difficulty or disaster. **save someone's life** prevent someone's dying by taking specific action. ■ (**cannot do something to save one's life**) used to indicate that the person in question is completely incompetent at doing something. — **sav·a·ble** (also **save·a·ble**) **adj.** [ME: from OFr. *sauver*, from late L. *salvare*, from L. *salvus* 'safe.']

save² ▶ **prep. & conj.** formal or literary except; other than. [ME: from OFr. *sauf, sauve*, from L. *salvo, salva* (ablative sing. of *salvus* 'safe'), used in phrs. such as *salvo jure, salva innocentia* 'with no violation of right or innocence.']

sav·er /'sāvər/ ▶ **n.** **1** a person who regularly saves money through a bank or recognized scheme. **2** [in comb.] an object, action, or process that prevents a particular kind of resource from being used up or expended: *a great space-saver.*

sav·in /'savin/ ▶ **n.** **1** a bushy Eurasian juniper (*Juniperus sabina*) that typically has horizontally spreading branches. ■ an extract obtained from this plant, formerly used as an abortifacient. **2** another term for EASTERN RED CEDAR (see RED CEDAR). [OE, from OFr. *savine*, from L. *sabina (herba)* 'Sabine (herb).']

sav·ing /'sāviNG/ ▶ **n.** **1** an economy of or reduction in money, time, or another resource. **2** (usu. **one's savings**) the money one has saved, esp. through a bank or official scheme. **3** Law a reservation; an exception. ▶ **adj.** [in comb.] preventing waste of a particular resource: *an energy-saving light bulb.* ▶ **prep.** **1** with the exception of; except. **2** archaic with due respect to. [ME: from SAVE¹; the prep. prob. from SAVE², on the pattern of *touching*.]

sav·ings ac·count ▶ **n.** a bank account that earns interest.

sav·ings and loan (also **sav·ings and loan as·so·ci·a·tion**) ▶ **n.** an institution that accepts savings at interest and lends money to savers chiefly for home mortgage loans and may offer checking accounts and other services.

sav·ings bank ▶ **n.** a financial institution that receives savings accounts and pays interest to depositors.

sav·ings bond ▶ n. a bond issued by the government and sold to the general public.

sav·ior /'sāvyər/ (Brit. **sav·iour**) ▶ n. a person who saves someone or something (esp. a country or cause) from danger, and who is regarded with the veneration of a religious figure. ■ (**the/our Savior**) (in Christianity) God or Jesus Christ as the redeemer of sin and saver of souls. [ME: from OFr. *sauveour*, from eccles. L. *salvator* (translating Gk. *sōtēr*), from late L. *salvare* 'to save.']

sav·oir faire /,savwär 'fe(ə)r/ (also **sav·oir-faire**) ▶ n. the ability to act or speak appropriately in social situations. [19th C.: Fr., 'know how to do.']

Sav·o·na·ro·la /,savənə'rōlə; sə,vänə-/, Girolamo (1452–98), Italian preacher and religious reformer. A Dominican monk and ascetic, he was popular for his preaching against immorality and corruption.

sa·vor /'sāvər/ (Brit. **sa·vour**) ▶ v. **1** [trans.] taste (good food or drink) and enjoy it completely. ■ fig. enjoy or appreciate (something pleasant) completely, esp. by dwelling on it. **2** [intrans.] (**savor of**) have a suggestion or trace of (something, esp. something bad). ▶ n. a characteristic taste, flavor, or smell, esp. a pleasant one. ■ a suggestion or trace, esp. of something bad. [ME: from OFr., from L. *sapor*, from *sapere* 'to taste.']

sa·vor·y[1] /'sāv(ə)rē/ ▶ n. an aromatic plant (genus *Satureja*) of the mint family, used as a culinary herb, esp. the annual **summer savory** (*S. hortensis*) and the coarser flavored perennial **winter savory** (*S. montana*). [ME: perh. from OE *sætherie*, or via OFr., from L. *satureia*.]

sa·vor·y[2] (Brit. **sa·vour·y**) ▶ adj. **1** (of food) belonging to the category that is salty or spicy rather than sweet. **2** [usu. with negative] morally wholesome or acceptable. ▶ n. (pl. **-vor·ies**) esp. Brit. a savory dish, esp. an appetizer. — **sa·vor·i·ly** /-rəlē/ adv. **sa·vor·i·ness** n.

Sa·voy /sə'voi/ an area of southeastern France that borders on northwestern Italy. — **Sa·voy·ard** /sə'voiərd; ,savoi'ärd; -vwä'yär/ adj. & n.

sa·voy /sə'voi/ (also **sa·voy cab·bage**) ▶ n. a cabbage of a hardy variety with densely wrinkled leaves. [16th C.: from SAVOY.]

Sa·vu Sea /'sävōō/ a part of the Indian Ocean that is surrounded by Sumba, Flores, and Timor islands.

sav·vy /'savē/ (also **sav·vi·ness**) informal ▶ n. shrewdness and practical knowledge, esp. in politics or business. ▶ v. (**-vies, -vied**) know or understand. ▶ adj. (**-vi·er, -vi·est**) shrewd and knowledgeable in the realities of life. [18th C.: orig. black and pidgin Engl. imitating Sp. *sabe usted* 'you know.']

saw[1] /sô/ ▶ n. a hand tool for cutting wood or other materials, typically with a long, thin serrated blade and operated using a backward and forward movement. *See illustration on previous page.* ■ a mechanical power-driven tool for cutting, typically with a toothed rotating disk or moving band. ▶ v. (past part. **sawed** or **sawn** /sôn/) [trans.] cut (something, esp. wood or a tree) using a saw. ■ make or form (something) using a saw. ■ cut (something) as if with a saw, esp. roughly or so as to leave rough or unfinished edges. ■ [intrans.] make rapid sawlike motions in cutting something or in playing a stringed instrument. — **saw·like** /-,līk/ adj. [OE *saga*, of Gmc. origin; rel. to Du. *zaag*.]

saw[2] past of SEE[1].

saw[3] ▶ n. a proverb or maxim. [OE *sagu* 'a saying, speech,' of Gmc. origin; rel. to Ger. *Sage*.]

Sa·watch Range /sə'wäCH/ a range of the Rocky Mountains in central Colorado. Mount Elbert, at 14,433 feet (4,399 m), is the highest peak in the Rocky Mountain system.

saw·bill /'sô,bil/ ▶ n. another term for MERGANSER.

saw·bones /'sô,bōnz/ ▶ n. (pl. same) informal, humorous a doctor, esp. a surgeon.

saw·buck /'sô,bək/ ▶ n. **1** a sawhorse. **2** informal a $10 bill. [by association of the X-shaped ends of a sawhorse with the Roman numeral X (= 10).] [19th C.: from Du. *zaagbok*, from *zaag* 'saw' + *bok* 'vaulting horse.']

saw·dust /'sô,dəst/ ▶ n. powdery particles of wood produced by sawing.

sawed-off /'sôd 'ôf/ (also esp. Brit. **sawn-off**) ▶ adj. [attrib.] (of a gun) having a specially shortened barrel to make handling easier and to give a wider field of fire. ■ informal (of an item of clothing) having been cut short. ■ informal (of a person) short. ▶ n. a sawed-off shotgun.

common sawfish

saw·fish /'sô,fiSH/ ▶ n. (pl. same or **-fish·es**) a large tropical mainly marine fish (family Pristidae) related to the rays, with an elongated flattened snout that bears large blunt teeth along each side. Two genera, in particular *Pristis*, and several species include the **common sawfish** (*P. pectinata*).

saw·fly /'sô,flī/ ▶ n. (pl. **-flies**) an insect (order Hymenoptera) related to the wasps, with a sawlike egg-laying tube used to cut into plant tissue before depositing the eggs. The larvae resemble caterpillars and can be serious pests of crops and foliage.

saw·grass /'sô,gras/ (also **saw grass**) ▶ n. a sedge (genus *Cladium*) with spiny-edged leaves, esp. *C. jamaicensis*, a dominant plant in the Florida Everglades.

saw·horse /'sô,hôrs/ ▶ n. a frame or trestle that supports wood for sawing.

saw·log /'sô,lôg; -,läg/ (also **saw log**) ▶ n. a felled tree trunk suitable for cutting up into timber.

saw·mill /'sô,mil/ ▶ n. a factory in which logs are sawed into planks or boards by machine.

sawn /sôn/ past participle of SAW[1].

sawn-off ▶ adj. & n. esp. Brit. another term for SAWED-OFF.

saw pal·met·to ▶ n. a small palm (esp. *Serenoa repens*) with fan-shaped leaves that have sharply toothed stalks, native to the southeastern US.

saw·tooth /'sô,tōōTH/ (also **saw·toothed** or **saw-tooth** or **saw-toothed** /-,tōōTHt/) ▶ adj. shaped like the teeth of a saw with alternate steep and gentle slopes. ■ Physics (of a waveform) showing a slow linear rise and rapid linear fall or vice versa.

Saw·tooth Range /'sô,tōōTH/ a range of the northern Rocky Mountains in south central Idaho, noted for its jagged peaks.

saw-whet owl ▶ n. a small North and Central American owl (genus *Aegolius*, family Strigidae) with a call that resembles the sound of a saw blade being sharpened. Two species include the North American *A. acadicus*.

saw·yer /'sôyər/ ▶ n. **1** a person who saws timber for a living. **2** an uprooted tree floating in a river but held fast at one end. [with allusion to the trapped log's movement backward and forward.] **3** a large longhorn beetle (genus *Monochamus*, family Cerambycidae) whose larvae bore tunnels in the wood of injured or recently felled trees, producing an audible chewing sound. [ME (earlier as *sawer*): from the noun SAW[1] + -YER.]

Sax. ▶ abbr. ■ Saxon or Saxony.

sax /saks/ ▶ n. informal a saxophone. — **sax·ist** /-ist/ n. [20th C.: abbrev.]

sax·a·tile /'saksə,tīl/ ▶ adj. living or growing on or among rocks. [17th C.: from Fr. *saxatile* or L. *saxatilis*, from *saxum* 'rock.']

Saxe-Co·burg-Go·tha /'saks 'kōbərg 'gōTHə/ the name of the British royal house 1901–17.

sax·horn /'saks,hôrn/ ▶ n. a member of a family of brass instruments with valves and a funnel-shaped mouthpiece, used mainly in military and brass bands. [Charles J. *Sax* (1791–1865) and his son Antoine-Joseph "Adolphe" *Sax* (1814–94), Belgian instrument-makers, + HORN.]

sax·ic·o·line /sak'sikə,līn; -lin/ (also **sax·ic·o·lous** /-'sikələs/) ▶ adj. another term for SAXATILE. [19th C.: from mod. L. *saxicolus* (from *saxum* 'rock' + *colere* 'inhabit') + -INE[1].]

sax·i·frage /'saksə,frij; -,frāj/ ▶ n. a low-growing plant (genus *Saxifraga*, family Saxifragaceae) of poor soils, bearing small white, yellow, or red flowers and forming rosettes of succulent leaves or hummocks of mossy leaves. Many are grown as alpines in rock gardens. [ME: from OFr. *saxifrage* or late L. *saxifraga (herba)*, from L. *saxum* 'rock' + *frangere* 'break.']

Sax·on /'saksən/ ▶ n. **1** a member of an ancient Germanic people, many of whom conquered and settled in southern England in the 5th–6th centuries. ■ a native of modern Saxony in Germany. **2** the language of the Saxons, in particular: ■ (**Old Saxon**) the West Germanic language of the ancient Saxons. ■ another term for OLD ENGLISH. ■ the Low German dialect of modern Saxony. ▶ adj. **1** of or relating to the Anglo-Saxons, their language (Old English), or their period of dominance in England (5th–11th centuries). ■ relating to or denoting the style of early Romanesque architecture preceding the Norman in England. **2** of or relating to Saxony or the continental Saxons or their language. — **Sax·on·ize** /-,nīz/ v. [ME: from OFr., from late L. *Saxones* (pl.), of West Gmc. origin.]

Sax·o·ny /'saksənē/ a large region and former kingdom in Germany. German name SACHSEN. ■ a state in eastern Germany, on the upper reaches of the Elbe River; capital, Dresden.

sax·o·ny /'saksənē/ ▶ n. a fine kind of wool. ■ a fine-quality cloth made from this kind of wool, chiefly used for making coats. [19th C.: from SAXONY.]

Sax·o·ny-An·halt /'änhält/ a state in Germany, on the Elbe and Saale rivers; capital, Magdeburg. German name SACHSEN-ANHALT.

sax·o·phone /'saksə,fōn/ ▶ n. a member of a family of metal wind instruments with a single-reed mouthpiece, used esp. in jazz and dance music. — **sax·o·phon·ic** /,saksə'fänik/ adj. **sax·o·phon·ist** /-,fōnist/ n. [Adolphe *Sax* (see SAXHORN) + -PHONE.]

saxophone

say /sā/ ▶ v. (**says** /sez/; past and past part. **said** /sed/) **1** [reporting verb] utter words so as to convey information, an opinion, a feeling or intention, or an instruction. ■ (of a text or a symbolic representation) convey specified information or instructions. ■ [trans.] enable a listener or reader to learn or understand something by conveying or revealing (information or ideas): fig. *the movie's title says it all.* ■ [trans.] (of a clock or watch) indicate (a specified time). ■ (**be said**) be asserted or reported (often used to avoid committing the speaker or writer to the truth of the assertion). ■ [trans.] (**say something for**) present a consideration in favor of or excusing (someone or something). ■ [trans.] utter the whole of (a speech or other set of words, typically one learned in advance). **2** [with clause] assume something in order to work out what its consequences would be; make a hypoth-

esis: *let's say we pay five thousand dollars.* ■ used parenthetically to indicate that something is being suggested as possible or likely but not certain. ▶ **exclam.** informal used to express surprise or to draw attention to a remark or question. ▶ **n.** [in sing.] an opportunity for stating one's opinion or feelings: *the voters are entitled to have their say.* ■ an opportunity to influence developments and policy.
– PHRASES **have something to say for oneself** contribute a specified amount to a conversation or discussion, esp. as an explanation for one's behavior or actions. **how say you?** Law how do you find? (addressed to the jury when requesting its verdict). **I'll say** informal used to express emphatic agreement. **I wouldn't say no** informal used to indicate that one would like something. **not to say** used to introduce a stronger alternative or addition to something already said. **say no more** informal used to indicate that one understands what someone is trying to imply. **says you!** informal used in spoken English to express disagreement or disbelief. **say when** informal said when helping someone to food or drink to instruct them to indicate when they have enough. **say the word** give permission or instructions to do something. **there is no saying** it is impossible to know. **what do** (or **would**) **you say** used to make a suggestion or offer. **when all is said and done** when everything is taken into account (used to indicate that one is making a generalized judgment about a situation). **you can say that again!** informal used in spoken English to express emphatic agreement. **you don't say!** informal used to express amazement or disbelief. **you said it!** informal used to express the feeling that someone's words are true or appropriate. — **say·a·ble adj. say·er n.** [usu. in comb.] *nay-sayers.* [OE *secgan*, of Gmc. origin; rel. to Du. *zeggen* and Ger. *sagen*.]

Say·ers /'sāərz; se(ə)rz/, Dorothy Leigh (1893–1957), English writer. Her detective novels feature amateur detective Lord Peter Wimsey and include *The Nine Tailors* (1934).

say·ing /'sāiNG/ ▶ **n.** a short, pithy expression that generally contains advice or wisdom. ■ **(sayings)** a collection of such expressions identified with a particular person, esp. a political or religious leader.
– PHRASES **as** (or **so**) **the saying goes** used to introduce or append an expression, drawing attention to its status as a saying or as not part of one's normal language: *I am, as the saying goes, burned out.*

sa·yo·na·ra /,sīə'närə/ ▶ **exclam.** informal goodbye. [Japanese.]

say-so ▶ **n.** [in sing.] informal the power or act of deciding or allowing something. ■ (usu. **on someone's say-so**) a person's arbitrary or unauthorized assertion or instruction.

SB ▶ **abbr.** ■ Bachelor of Science. [L. *Scientiae Baccalaureus*.] ■ simultaneous broadcast. ■ South Britain (England and Wales).

Sb ▶ **symb.** the chemical element antimony. [from L. *stibium*.]

s.b. ▶ **abbr.** Baseball stolen base; stolen bases.

SBA ▶ **abbr.** (in the US) Small Business Administration.

SbE ▶ **abbr.** south by east.

SbW ▶ **abbr.** south by west.

SC ▶ **abbr.** South Carolina (in official postal use).

Sc ▶ **symb.** the chemical element scandium.

sc. ▶ **abbr.** that is to say (used to introduce a word to be supplied or an explanation of an ambiguity). [from SCILICET.]

s.c. ▶ **abbr.** small capitals (used as an instruction for a typesetter).

scab /skab/ ▶ **n. 1** a dry, rough protective crust that forms over a cut or wound during healing. ■ mange or a similar skin disease in animals. ■ [usu. with adj.] any of a number of fungal diseases of plants in which rough patches develop, esp. on apples and potatoes. **2** fig. informal a person or thing regarded with dislike and disgust. ■ derog. a person who refuses to strike or to join a labor union or who takes over the job responsibilities of a striking worker. ▶ **v.** (**scabbed, scab·bing**) [intrans.] **1** [usu. as adj.] (**scabbed**) become encrusted or covered with a scab or scabs: *she rested her scabbed fingers on his arm.* **2** act or work as a scab. — **scab·like** /-,līk/ **adj.** [ME (as a n.): from ON *skabb*; rel. to dial. *shab* (cf. SHABBY). The sense 'contemptible person' (dating from the late 16th C.) was prob. influenced by MDu. *schabbe* 'slut.']

scab·bard /'skabərd/ ▶ **n.** a sheath for the blade of a sword or dagger, typically made of leather or metal. ■ a sheath for a gun or other weapon or tool. [ME: from Anglo-Norman Fr. *escalberc*, from a Gmc. compound of words meaning 'cut' and 'protect.']

scab·by /'skabē/ ▶ **adj.** (**-bi·er, -bi·est**) **1** covered in scabs. **2** informal loathsome; despicable. — **scab·bi·ness n.**

sca·bies /'skābēz/ ▶ **n.** a contagious skin disease marked by itching and small raised red spots, caused by the itch mite. [ME: from L., from *scabere* 'to scratch.']

sca·bi·ous /'skābēəs/ ▶ **n.** a plant (*Scabiosa, Knautia*, and other genera) of the teasel family, with pink, white, or (most commonly) blue pincushion-shaped flowers. ▶ **adj.** affected with mange; scabby. [ME: based on L. *scabiosus* 'rough, scabby'; the noun is from med. L. *scabiosa (herba)* 'rough, scabby (plant),' formerly regarded as a cure for skin disease (see SCABIES).]

scab·lands /'skab,landz/ ▶ **plural n.** Geol. flat elevated land deeply scarred by channels of glacial or fluvioglacial origin and with poor soil and little vegetation.

scab·rous /'skabrəs/ ▶ **adj. 1** rough and covered with, or as if with, scabs. **2** indecent; salacious: *scabrous publications.* — **scab·rous·ly adv. scab·rous·ness n.** [16th C.: from Fr. *scabreux* or late L. *scabrosus*, from L. *scaber* 'rough.']

scads /skadz/ ▶ **plural n.** informal a large number or quantity: *they raised scads of children.* [19th C.: of unknown origin.]

scaf·fold /'skafəld; -,fōld/ ▶ **n. 1** a raised wooden platform used formerly for the public execution of criminals. **2** a structure made using scaffolding. ▶ **v.** [trans.] attach scaffolding to (a building). — **scaf·fold·er n.** [ME: from Anglo-Norman Fr., from OFr. *(e)schaffaut*, from the base of CATAFALQUE.]

scaf·fold·ing /'skafəldiNG; -,fōl-/ ▶ **n.** a temporary structure on the outside of a building, made of wooden planks and metal poles, used by workers while building, repairing, or cleaning the building. ■ the materials used in such a structure.

scag /skag/ ▶ **n. 1** informal an unkempt or despicable person; sleazeball. **2** var. of SKAG.

scal·a·ble /'skāləbəl/ ▶ **adj. 1** able to be scaled or climbed. **2** able to be changed in size or scale: *scalable fonts.* ■ (of a computing process) able to be used or produced in a range of capabilities. **3** tech. able to be measured or graded according to a scale. — **scal·a·bil·i·ty** /,skālə'bilitē/ **n.**

sca·lar /'skālər/ Math. & Physics ▶ **adj.** (of a quantity) having only magnitude, not direction. ▶ **n.** a scalar quantity. Compare with VECTOR (sense 1). [17th C.: from L. *scalaris*, from *scala* 'ladder' (see SCALE[3]).]

sca·lar·i·form /skə'le(ə)rə,fôrm/ ▶ **adj.** Bot. (esp. of the walls of water-conducting cells) having thickened bands arranged like the rungs of a ladder. [19th C.: from L. *scalaris* 'of a ladder' + -IFORM.]

sca·lar prod·uct ▶ **n.** another term for INNER PRODUCT.

scal·a·wag /'skalə,wag/ (also **scal·ly·wag** /'skalē-/) ▶ **n.** informal a person who behaves badly but in an amusingly mischievous rather than harmful way; a rascal. ■ hist. a white Southerner who collaborated with northern Republicans during the Reconstruction, often for personal profit. [19th C.: of unknown origin.]

scald[1] /skôld/ ▶ **v.** [trans.] injure with very hot liquid or steam: *the tea scalded his tongue.* ■ heat (milk or other liquid) to near boiling point. ■ immerse (something) briefly in boiling water for various purposes, such as to facilitate the removal of skin from fruit or to preserve meat. ■ cause to feel a searing sensation like that of boiling water on skin. ▶ **n.** a burn or other injury caused by hot liquid or steam. ■ any of a number of plant diseases that produce a similar effect to that of scalding, esp. a disease of fruit marked by browning and caused by excessive sunlight, bad storage conditions, or atmospheric pollution. See also SUNSCALD. [ME (as a v.): from Anglo-Norman Fr. *escalder*, from late L. *excaldare*, from L. *ex-* 'thoroughly' + *calidus* 'hot.']

scald[2] ▶ **n.** var. of SKALD.

scald·ing /'skôldiNG/ ▶ **adj.** very hot; burning. ■ fig. intense and painful or distressing.

scale[1] /skāl/ ▶ **n. 1** each of the small, thin horny or bony plates protecting the skin of fish and reptiles, typically overlapping one another. **2** something resembling a fish scale in appearance or function, in particular: ■ a thick dry flake of skin. ■ a rudimentary leaf, feather, or bract. ■ each of numerous microscopic tilelike structures covering the wings of butterflies and moths. **3** a flaky deposit, in particular: ■ a white deposit formed in a kettle, boiler, etc., by the evaporation of water containing lime. ■ tartar formed on teeth. ■ a coating of oxide formed on heated metal. ▶ **v. 1** [trans.] remove scale or scales from. ■ remove tartar from (teeth) by scraping them. **2** [intrans.] [often as n.] (**scaling**) (esp. of the skin) form scales: *moisturizers can ease off drying and scaling.* ■ come off in scales or thin pieces; flake off. — **scaled** /skāld/ **adj.** [often in comb.] *a rough-scaled fish.* **scale·less** /'skāl(l)is/ **adj. scal·er n.** [ME: shortening of OFr. *escale*, from the Gmc. base of SCALE[2].]

scale[2] ▶ **n.** (usu. **scales**) an instrument for weighing. ■ (also **scale·pan**) either of the dishes on a simple balance. ■ (**the Scales**) the zodiacal sign or constellation Libra. ▶ **v.** weigh a specified weight. [ME: from ON *skál* 'bowl,' of Gmc. origin; rel. to Du. *schaal*, Ger. *Schale* 'bowl,' also to Engl. dial. *shale* 'dish.']

scale[3] ▶ **n. 1** a graduated range of values forming a standard system for measuring or grading something. ■ a series of marks at regular intervals in a line used in measuring something. ■ a device having such a series of marks. ■ a rule determining the distances between such marks: *a logarithmic scale.* **2** [in sing.] the relative size or extent of something: *the scale of the disaster.* ■ [often as adj.] a ratio of size in a map, model, drawing, or plan: *a one-fifth scale model.* ■ (in full **scale of notation**) Math. a system of numerical notation in which the value of a digit depends upon its position in the number, successive positions representing successive powers of a fixed base. ■ Photog. the range of exposures over which a photographic material will give an acceptable variation in density. **3** Music an arrangement of the notes in any system of music in ascending or descending order of pitch. ▶ **v.** [trans.] **1** climb up or over (something high and steep). **2** represent in proportional dimensions; reduce or increase in size according to a common scale. ■ [intrans.] (of a quantity or property) be variable according to a particular scale. **3** estimate the amount of timber that will be produced from (a log or uncut tree).
– PHRASES **to scale** with a uniform reduction or enlargement: *models built to scale from a drawing.* **in scale** (of a drawing or model) in proportion to the surroundings.
– PHRASAL VERBS **scale something back** reduce something in size, number, or extent. **scale something down** (or **scale down**) reduce something (or be reduced) in size, number or extent. **scale something up** (or **scale up**) increase something (or be increased) in size or

number. — **scal·er** n. [ME: from L. *scala* 'ladder,' from the base of L. *scandere* 'to climb.']

scale in·sect ▶ n. a small insect (suborder Homoptera) with a protective shieldlike scale. It spends most of its life attached by its mouth to a single plant, sometimes occurring in such large numbers that it becomes a serious pest.

sca·lene /skāˈlēn/ ▶ adj. (of a triangle) having sides unequal in length. ▶ n. **1** (also **sca·lene mus·cle**) Anat. another term for SCALENUS. **2** a scalene triangle. [17th C.: via late L. from Gk. *skalēnos* 'unequal'; rel. to *skolios* 'bent.']

sca·le·nus /skāˈlēnəs/ ▶ n. (pl. **-le·ni** /-ˈlēnī/) any of several muscles extending from the neck to the first and second ribs. [18th C.: mod. L., from late L. *scalenus (musculus)* 'unequal (muscle)' (see SCALENE).]

scale of no·ta·tion ▶ n. see SCALE³ (sense 2).

scale·pan /ˈskālˌpan/ ▶ n. see SCALE².

scale·worm /ˈskālˌwərm/ (also **scale worm**) ▶ n. a marine bristle worm (family Aphroditidae) with scales on the upper surface that have a protective function, and in some species are able to luminesce.

Sca·li·a /skəˈlēə/, Antonin (1936–), US Supreme Court associate justice 1986– .

scal·lion /ˈskalyən/ ▶ n. a long-necked onion with a small bulb, in particular a shallot or green onion. [ME: from Anglo-Norman Fr. *scaloun*, based on L. *Ascalonia (caepa)* '(onion) of *Ascalon*,' a port in ancient Palestine.]

scal·lop /ˈskäləp; ˈskal-/ ▶ n. **1** an edible bivalve mollusk (family Pectinidae) with a ribbed fan-shaped shell. Scallops swim by rapidly opening and closing the shell valves. ■ a small pan or dish shaped like a scallop shell and used for baking or serving food. **2** (usu. **scallops**) each of a series of convex rounded projections forming an ornamental edging cut in material or worked in lace or knitting in imitation of the edge of a scallop shell. **3** another term for ESCALOPE. ▶ v. (**-loped, -lop·ing**) **1** [trans.] [usu. as adj.] (**scalloped**) ornament (an edge or material) with scallops. **2** [intrans.] [usu. as n.] (**scalloping**) gather or dredge for scallops. **3** [trans.] bake with milk or a sauce. — **scal·lop·er** n. [ME: shortening of OFr. *escalope*, prob. of Gmc. origin.]

scal·ly·wag /ˈskalēˌwag/ ▶ n. var. of SCALAWAG.

sca·lop·pi·ne /ˌskäləˈpēnē; ˌskal-/ (also **scal·lo·pi·ni**) ▶ plural n. (in Italian cooking) thin, boneless slices of meat, typically veal, sautéed or fried. [Ital., pl. of *scaloppina*, dimin. of *scaloppa* 'envelope.']

scalp /skalp/ ▶ n. the skin covering the head, excluding the face. ■ hist. the scalp with the hair belonging to it cut or torn away from an enemy's head as a battle trophy. ▶ v. [trans.] hist. take the scalp of (an enemy). ■ informal punish severely. ■ informal sell (a ticket) for a popular event at a price higher than the official one. [ME (denoting the skull or cranium): prob. of Scand. origin.]

scal·pel /ˈskalpəl/ ▶ n. a knife with a small, sharp, sometimes detachable blade, as used by a surgeon. [18th C.: from Fr., or from L. *scalpellum*, dimin. of *scalprum* 'chisel,' from *scalpere* 'to scratch.']

scalpel

scalp·er /ˈskalpər/ ▶ n. informal a person who resells shares or tickets at a large or quick profit.

scal·y /ˈskālē/ ▶ adj. (**scal·i·er, scal·i·est**) covered in scales. ■ (of skin) dry and flaking. — **scal·i·ness** n.

scal·y ant·eat·er ▶ n. another term for PANGOLIN.

scam /skam/ ▶ n. informal a dishonest scheme; a fraud. ▶ v. (**scammed, scam·ming**) [trans.] swindle. — **scam·mer** n. [1960s: of unknown origin.]

scam·mo·ny /ˈskamənē/ ▶ n. a plant of the morning glory family, the dried roots of which yield a drastic purgative. Two species: *Convolvulus scammonia* of Asia, and *Ipomoea orizabensis* of Mexico. [OE, from OFr. *escamonie* or L. *scammonia*, from Gk. *skammōnia*.]

scamp /skamp/ ▶ n. informal a person, esp. a child, who is mischievous in a likable or amusing way. ■ a wicked or worthless person; a rogue. — **scamp·ish** adj. [18th C. (denoting a highwayman): from obs. *scamp* 'rob on the highway,' prob. from MDu. *schampen* 'slip away,' from OFr. *eschamper*.]

scamp·er /ˈskampər/ ▶ v. [no obj., with adverbial of direction] (esp. of a small animal or child) run with quick light steps, esp. through fear or excitement. ▶ n. [in sing.] an act of scampering. [17th C.: perh. from SCAMP.]

scam·pi /ˈskampē/ ▶ n. [pl. n.] large shrimp or prawns, esp. when prepared or cooked. ■ a dish of shrimp or prawns, typically sautéed in garlic and butter and often topped with bread crumbs. [Ital.]

scan /skan/ ▶ v. (**scanned, scan·ning**) [trans.] **1** look at all parts of (something) carefully in order to detect some feature. ■ look quickly but not very thoroughly through (a document or other text) in order to identify relevant information. ■ cause (a surface, object, or part of the body) to be traversed by a detector or an electromagnetic beam. ■ [with obj. and adverbial] cause (a beam) to traverse across a surface or object. ■ resolve (a picture) into its elements of light and shade in a prearranged pattern for the purposes of television transmission. ■ convert (a document or picture) into digital form for storage or processing on a computer. **2** analyze the meter of (a line of verse) by reading with the emphasis on its rhythm or by examining the pattern of feet or syllables. ■ [intrans.] (of verse) conform to metrical principles. ▶ n. an act of scanning someone or something. ■ a medical examination using a scanner: *a brain scan.* ■ an image obtained by scanning or with a scanner. — **scan·na·ble** adj. [ME (as a v. in sense 2): from L. *scandere* 'climb.']

scan·dal /ˈskandl/ ▶ n. an action or event regarded as morally or legally wrong and causing general public outrage: *a bribery scandal.* ■ the outrage or anger caused by such an action or event. ■ rumor or malicious gossip about such events or actions. ■ [in sing.] a state of affairs regarded as wrong or reprehensible and causing general public outrage or anger. [ME: from OFr. *scandale*, from eccles. L. *scandalum* 'cause of offense,' from Gk. *skandalon* 'snare, stumbling block.']

scan·dal·ize /ˈskandlˌīz/ ▶ v. [trans.] **1** shock or horrify (someone) by a real or imagined violation of propriety or morality: *their lack of manners scandalized their hosts.* **2** Sailing reduce the area of (a sail) by lowering the head or raising the boom. [19th C.: alt. of obs. *scantelize*, from *scantle* 'make small.'] — **scan·dal·i·za·tion** /ˌskandl-əˈzāsHən/ n. **scan·dal·iz·er** n.

scan·dal·mon·ger /ˈskandlˌməNGgər; -ˌmäNGgər/ ▶ n. a person who stirs up public outrage toward someone or their actions by spreading rumors or malicious gossip.

scan·dal·ous /ˈskandl-əs/ ▶ adj. causing general public outrage by a perceived offense against morality or law: *a series of scandalous liaisons.* ■ (of a state of affairs) disgracefully bad, typically as a result of someone's negligence or irresponsibility. — **scan·dal·ous·ly** adv. **scan·dal·ous·ness** n.

scan·dal sheet ▶ n. derog. a newspaper or magazine giving prominence to scandalous stories or gossip.

Scan·den·tia /skanˈdenCH(ē)ə/ Zool. a small order of mammals that comprises the tree shrews. [mod. L. (pl.), from L. *scandent-* 'climbing,' from the verb *scandere*.]

Scan·di·na·vi·a /ˌskandəˈnāvēə/ a peninsula in northwestern Europe, occupied by Norway and Sweden. ■ a cultural region consisting of the countries of Norway, Sweden, and Denmark and sometimes also of Iceland, Finland, and the Faroe Islands.

Scan·di·na·vi·an /ˌskandəˈnāvēən/ ▶ adj. of or relating to Scandinavia, its people, or their languages. ▶ n. **1** a native or inhabitant of Scandinavia, or a person of Scandinavian descent. **2** the North Germanic languages (Danish, Norwegian, Swedish, Icelandic, Faroese) descended from Old Norse.

scan·di·um /ˈskandēəm/ ▶ n. the chemical element of atomic number 21, a soft silvery-white metal resembling the rare earth elements. (Symbol: **Sc**) [19th C.: mod. L., from *Scandia*, contr. of *Scandinavia*.]

scan·ner /ˈskanər/ ▶ n. a device for examining, reading, or monitoring something, in particular: ■ Med. a machine that examines the body through the use of radiation, ultrasound, or magnetic resonance imaging, as a diagnostic aid. ■ Electron. a device that scans documents and converts them into digital data.

scan·ning e·lec·tron mi·cro·scope (abbr.: **SEM**) ▶ n. an electron microscope in which the surface of a specimen is scanned by a beam of electrons that are reflected to form an image.

scan·ning tun·nel·ing mi·cro·scope (abbr.: **STM**) ▶ n. a high-resolution microscope using neither light nor an electron beam, but with an ultrafine tip able to reveal atomic and molecular details of surfaces.

scan·sion /ˈskansHən/ ▶ n. the action of scanning a line of verse to determine its rhythm. ■ the rhythm of a line of verse. [17th C.: from L. *scansio(n-)*, from *scandere* 'to climb'.]

scant /skant/ ▶ adj. barely sufficient or adequate. ■ [attrib.] barely amounting to a specified number or quantity: *she weighed a scant two pounds.* ▶ v. [trans.] provide grudgingly or in insufficient amounts. ■ deal with inadequately; neglect. — **scant·ly** adv. **scant·ness** n. [ME: from ON *skamt*, neut. of *skammr* 'short.']

scant·ling /ˈskantliNG/ ▶ n. **1** a timber beam of small cross section. ■ the size to which a piece of timber or stone is measured and cut. **2** (often **scantlings**) a set of standard dimensions for parts of a structure, esp. in shipbuilding. [16th C.: alt. of obs. *scantillon* (from OFr. *escantillon* 'sample').]

scant·y /ˈskantē/ ▶ adj. (**scant·i·er, scant·i·est**) small or insufficient in quantity or amount: *scanty wages.* ■ (of clothing) revealing; skimpy. ▶ plural n. (**scanties**) brief underpants. — **scant·i·ly** /ˈskantl-ē/ adv. **scant·i·ness** n. [16th C.: from SCANT + -Y¹.]

Sca·pa Flow /skapə; ˈskä-/ a strait in the Orkney Islands, Scotland.

scape /skāp/ ▶ n. **1** Bot. a long, leafless flower stalk coming directly from a root. **2** Entomol. the basal segment of an insect's antenna, esp. when it is enlarged and lengthened (as in a weevil). [19th C.: via L. from Gk. *skapos* 'rod'; rel. to SCEPTER.].

-scape ▶ comb. form denoting a specified type of scene. [on the pattern of *(land)scape*.]

scape·goat /ˈskāpˌgōt/ ▶ n. (in the Bible) a goat sent into the wilderness after the Jewish chief priest had symbolically laid the sins of the people upon it (Lev. 16). ■ a person who is blamed for the wrongdoings, mistakes, or faults of others, esp. for reasons of expediency. ▶ v. [trans.] make a scapegoat of. — **scape·goat·er** n. **scape·goat·ing** n. **scape·goat·ism** /-ˌizəm/ n. [16th C.: from archaic *scape* 'escape' + GOAT.]

scap·u·la /ˈskapyələ/ ▶ n. (pl. **-lae** /-ˌlē/ or **-las**) Anat. technical term for SHOULDER BLADE. [16th C.: from late L., sing. of L. *scapulae* 'shoulder blades.']

scap·u·lar /ˈskapyələr/ ▶ adj. Anat. & Zool. of or relating to the shoulder or shoulder blade. ▶ n. **1** a short monastic cloak covering the shoulders. ■ a symbol of affiliation to an ecclesiastical order, consisting of two strips of cloth hanging down the breast and back and joined across the shoulders. **2** Med. a bandage passing over and around the shoulders. **3** Ornithol. a feather covering the shoulder, growing above the region where the wing joins the body. [15th C. (sense 1 of the noun): from late L. *scapulare*, from *scapula* 'shoulder.' The adj. (17th C.) and the later senses of the noun are from SCAPULA + -AR[1].]

scap·u·lar·y /'skapyə,lerē/ ▶n. (pl. **-lar·ies**) another term for SCAPULAR (senses 1 and 3). [ME: from an Anglo-Norman Fr. var. of OFr. *eschapeloyre*, based on late L. *scapulare* (see SCAPULAR).]

scar /skär/ ▶n. **1** a mark left on the skin or within body tissue where a wound, burn, or sore has not healed quite completely and fibrous connective tissue has developed: *a faint scar ran the length of his left cheek.* ■ fig. a lasting effect of grief, fear, or other emotion left on a person's character by an unpleasant experience. ■ a mark left on something following damage of some kind. ■ a mark left at the point of separation of a leaf, frond, or other part from a plant. **2** a steep high cliff or rock outcrop, esp. of limestone. [ME: from ON *sker* 'low reef.'] ▶v. (**scarred, scar·ring**) [trans.] (often **be scarred**) mark with a scar or scars. ■ [intrans.] form or be marked with a scar. — **scar·less** adj. [ME: from OFr. *escharre*, via late L. from Gk. *eskhara* 'scab.']

scar·ab /'skarəb/ ▶n. (also **scar·ab bee·tle** or **sa·cred scar·ab**) a large dung beetle (*Scarabaeus sacer*) of the eastern Mediterranean area, regarded as sacred in ancient Egypt. Family Scarabaeidae (the **scarab family**) also includes the smaller dung beetles and chafers, together with some very large tropical kinds such as Hercules, goliath, and rhinoceros beetles. ■ an ancient Egyptian gem cut in the form of this beetle. ■ any scarabaeid beetle. [16th C.: from L. *scarabaeus*, from Gk. *skarabeios*.]

scarab beetle

scar·a·bae·id /,skarə'bē-id/ Entomol. ▶adj. of, pertaining to, or designating the beetle family (Scarabaeidae). ▶n. a beetle of this family, typically having strong spiky forelegs for burrowing. [19th C.: from mod. L. *Scarabaeidae* (pl.), from L. *scarabaeus* (see SCARAB).]

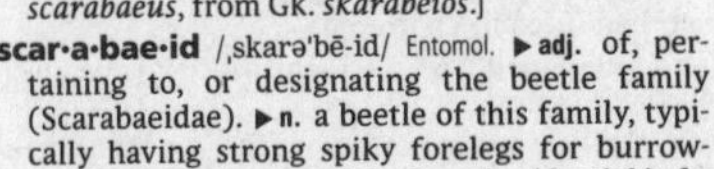

scar·a·bae·oid /,skarə'bē,oid/ ▶n. Entomol. a beetle (superfamily Scarabaeoidea) of a large group that includes the scarabaeids, dor beetles, and stag beetles. Scarabaeoids include the largest known beetles, and are distinguished by having platelike terminal segments to the antennae. Formerly called LAMELLICORN. [19th C.: from mod. L. *Scarabaeoidea* (pl.), from L. *scarabaeus* (see SCARAB).]

scarce /ske(ə)rs/ ▶adj. (esp. of food, money, or some other resource) insufficient for the demand. ■ occurring in small numbers or quantities; rare. ▶adv. archaic scarcely: *a babe scarce two years old.*

– PHRASES **make oneself scarce** informal leave a place, esp. so as to avoid a difficult situation. — **scarce·ness** n. **scar·ci·ty** /'ske(ə)rsitē/ n. [ME: from a shortening of Anglo-Norman *escars*, from a Romance word meaning 'plucked out, selected.']

scarce·ly /'ske(ə)rslē/ ▶adv. only just; almost not. ■ only a very short time before. ■ used to suggest that something is unlikely to be or certainly not the case.

scare /ske(ə)r/ ▶v. [trans.] cause great fear or nervousness in; frighten. ■ [with obj. and adverbial] drive or keep (someone) away by frightening them. ■ [intrans.] become scared. ▶n. a sudden attack of fright. ■ [usu. with modifier] a general feeling of anxiety or alarm about something: *a bomb scare.*

– PHRASAL VERBS **scare something up** informal manage to find or obtain something. — **scar·er** n. [ME: from ON *skirra* 'frighten,' from *skjarr* 'timid.']

scare·crow /'ske(ə)r,krō/ ▶n. an object, usually made to resemble a human figure, set up to scare birds away from a field where crops are growing. ■ informal a person who is very badly dressed, odd-looking, or thin. ■ archaic an object of baseless fear.

scared /ske(ə)rd/ ▶adj. fearful; frightened.

scared·y-cat /'ske(ə)rdē,kat/ ▶n. informal a timid person.

scare·mon·ger /'ske(ə)r,məNGgər; -,mäNGgər/ ▶n. a person who spreads frightening or ominous reports or rumors. — **scare·mon·ger·ing** n. & adj.

scarf[1] /skärf/ ▶n. (pl. **scarves** /skärvz/ or **scarfs** /skärfs/) a length or square of fabric worn around the neck or head. — **scarfed** /skärft/ (also **scarved**) adj. [16th C.: probably based on Old North. Fr. *escarpe*, prob. identical with OFr. *escharpe* 'pilgrim's bag.']

scarf[2] ▶v. [trans.] join the ends of (two pieces of timber or metal) by beveling or notching them so that they fit over or into each other. ▶n. (also **scarf joint**) a joint connecting two pieces of timber or metal in which the ends are beveled or notched so that they fit over or into each other. [ME (as a n.): prob. via OFr. from ON.]

scarf[3] ▶v. [trans.] informal eat or drink (something) hungrily or enthusiastically: *he scarfed down the waffles.* [1960s: var. of SCOFF[2].]

scar·i·fi·er /'skarə,fīər/ ▶n. a tool with spikes or prongs used for breaking up matted vegetation in the surface of a lawn. ■ a machine with spikes used for breaking up the surface of a road.

scar·i·fy[1] /'skarə,fī/ ▶v. (**-fies, -fied**) [trans.] make cuts or scratches in (the surface of something), in particular: ■ break up the surface of (soil or a road or pavement). ■ make shallow incisions in (the skin), esp. as a medical procedure or traditional cosmetic practice. ■ fig. criticize severely and hurtfully. — **scar·i·fi·ca·tion** /-fi'kāSHən/ n. [ME: from OFr. *scarifier*, via late L. from Gk. *skariphasthai* 'scratch an outline,' from *skariphos* 'stylus.']

scar·i·fy[2] /'ske(ə)rə,fī/ ▶v. (**-fies, -fied**) [trans.] [usu. as adj.] (**scarifying**) informal frighten. [18th C.: formed irregularly from SCARE, perh. on the pattern of *terrify*.]

Scar·lat·ti /skär'lätē/ two Italian composers. Alessandro (1660–1725), full name *Pietro Alessandro Gaspare Scarlatti*, composed operas. His son Domenico (1685–1757), full name *Giuseppe Domenico Scarlatti*, wrote sonatas for the harpsichord.

scar·let /'skärlit/ ▶adj. **1** of a brilliant red color. **2** esp. dated (of an offense or sin) wicked; heinous. ■ immoral, esp. promiscuous or unchaste. ▶n. a brilliant red color. ■ clothes or material of this color. [ME: shortening of OFr. *escarlate*, from med. L. *scarlata*, via Arab. and med. Gk. from late L. *sigillatus* 'decorated with small images,' from *sigillum* 'small image.']

scar·let fe·ver ▶n. an infectious bacterial disease affecting esp. children, and causing fever and a scarlet rash.

scar·let pim·per·nel ▶n. a small plant (*Anagallis arvensis* subsp. *arvensis*) of the primrose family, with scarlet flowers that close in rainy or cloudy weather.

scar·let run·ner (also **scar·let run·ner bean**) ▶n. a twining bean plant (*Phaseolus coccineus*) with scarlet flowers and very long flat edible pods. Native to Central and South America, it is widely cultivated in North America. ■ the pod and seed of this plant eaten as food.

scar·let tan·a·ger ▶n. a tanager (*Piranga olivacea*) of eastern North America, the breeding male of which is bright red with black wings and tail.

scarp /skärp/ ▶n. a very steep bank or slope; an escarpment. ■ the inner wall of a ditch in a fortification. Compare with COUNTERSCARP. ▶v. [trans.] cut or erode (a slope or hillside) so that it becomes steep, perpendicular, or precipitous. ■ provide (a ditch in a fortification) with a steep scarp and counterscarp. [16th C. (with ref. to fortification): from Ital. *scarpa*.]

scar·y /'ske(ə)rē/ ▶adj. (**scar·i·er, scar·i·est**) informal frightening; causing fear: *a scary movie.* ■ uncannily striking or surprising. — **scar·i·ly** /-əlē/ adv. **scar·i·ness** n.

scat[1] /skat/ ▶v. (**scat·ted, scat·ting**) [no obj., usu. in imper.] informal go away; leave: *Scat! Leave me alone.* [19th C.: perhaps an abbrev. of SCATTER, or perh. from the sound of a hiss (used to drive an animal away) + *-cat*.]

scat[2] (also **scat sing·ing**) ▶n. improvised jazz singing in which the voice is used in imitation of an instrument. ▶v. (**scat·ted, scat·ting**) [intrans.] sing in such a way. [1920s: prob. imitative.]

scat[3] ▶n. droppings, esp. those of carnivorous mammals. [1950s: from Gk. *skōr, skat-* 'dung.']

scathe /skāTH/ archaic ▶v. [with obj. and usu. with negative] (usu. **be scathed**) harm; injure: *he was barely scathed.* ■ literary damage or destroy by fire or lightning. ▶n. harm; injury. [ME: from ON *skathi* (n.), *skatha* (v.); rel. to Du. and Ger. *schaden* (v.).]

scath·ing /'skāTHiNG/ ▶adj. witheringly scornful; severely critical: *a scathing attack on the governor.* — **scath·ing·ly** adv.

sca·tol·o·gy /skə'täləjē;/ ▶n. an interest in or preoccupation with excrement and excretion. ■ obscene literature that is concerned with excrement and excretion. — **scat·o·log·i·cal** /'skatl'äjikəl/ adj. [19th C.: from Gk. *skōr, skat-* 'dung' + -LOGY.]

scat·ter /'skatər/ ▶v. [trans.] throw in various random directions: *scatter the coconut over the icing.* ■ (**be scattered**) [usu. with adverbial] occur or be found at intervals rather than all together. ■ (of a group of people or animals) separate and move off quickly in different directions. ■ [trans.] cause (a group or people or animals) to act in such a way. ■ (usu. **be scattered with**) cover (a surface) with objects thrown or spread randomly over it. ■ Physics deflect or diffuse (electromagnetic radiation or particles). ▶n. a small, dispersed amount of something. ■ Stat. the degree to which repeated measurements or observations of a quantity differ. ■ Physics the scattering of light, other electromagnetic radiation, or particles. — **scat·ter·a·ble** adj. **scat·ter·a·tion** /,skatə'rāSHən/ n. **scat·ter·er** n. [ME (as a v.): prob. a var. of SHATTER.]

scat·ter·brain /'skatər,brān/ ▶n. a person who tends to be disorganized and lacking in concentration. — **scat·ter·brained** adj.

scat·ter·ing /'skatəriNG/ ▶n. [in sing.] an act of scattering something. ■ a small, dispersed amount of something. ■ Physics the process in which electromagnetic radiation or particles are deflected or diffused.

scat·ter rug ▶n. another term for THROW RUG.

scat·ter·shot /'skatər,SHät/ ▶adj. denoting something that is broad but random and haphazard in its range.

scat·ty /'skatē/ ▶adj. (**-ti·er, -ti·est**) informal absentminded and disorganized. [20th C.: abbrev. of *scatterbrained*.] — **scat·ti·ly** /-əlē/ adv. **scat·ti·ness** n.

scaup /skôp / ▶n. a Eurasian, North American, and New Zealand diving duck (genus *Aythya*), the male of which has a black head with a green or purple gloss. [17th C.: Scots var. of Scots and north. Engl. *scalp* 'mussel bed,' a feeding ground of the duck.]

scav·enge /'skavənj/ ▶v. [trans.] search for and collect (anything usable) from discarded waste. ■ (of an animal) search for (carrion) as food. ■ search for discarded items or food in (a place). ■ remove (combustion products) from an internal combustion engine cylinder on the return stroke of the piston. ■ Chem. combine with and remove (molecules, radicals, etc.) from a particular medium. [17th C. (in the sense 'clean out (dirt)'): back-form. from SCAVENGER.]

scav·eng·er /'skavənjər/ ▶ n. an animal that feeds on carrion, dead plant material, or refuse. ■ a person who searches for and collects discarded items. ■ Chem. a substance that reacts with and removes particular molecules, radicals, etc. [16th C.: alt. of earlier *scavager*, from Anglo-Norman Fr. *scawager*, from Old North. Fr. *escauwer* 'inspect,' from Flemish *scauwen* 'to show.']

scav·eng·er cell ▶ n. another term for PHAGOCYTE.

scav·eng·er hunt ▶ n. a game, typically played in an extensive outdoor area, in which participants have to collect a number of miscellaneous objects.

Sc.B. ▶ abbr. Bachelor of Science. [from L. *Scientiae Baccalaureus*.]

SCC ▶ abbr. Electron. storage connecting circuit.

ScD ▶ abbr. Doctor of Science. [from L. *scientiae doctor*.]

sce·na /'SHānə/ ▶ n. a scene in an opera. ■ an elaborate dramatic solo usually including recitative. [Ital., from L., 'scene.']

sce·nar·i·o /sə'ne(ə)rē,ō; -'när-/ ▶ n. (pl. **-os**) a written outline of a movie, novel, or stage work giving details of the plot and individual scenes. ■ a postulated sequence or development of events. ■ a setting, in particular for a work of art or literature. [19th C.: from Ital., from L. *scena* 'scene.']

sce·nar·ist /sə'ne(ə)rist/ ▶ n. a screenwriter.

scene /sēn/ ▶ n. **1** the place where an incident in real life or fiction occurs or occurred. ■ a place, with the people, objects, and events in it, regarded as having a particular character or making a particular impression: *a scene of carnage.* ■ a landscape. ■ an incident of a specified nature: *some scenes of violence.* ■ a place or representation of an incident: *scenes of 1930s America.* ■ [with modifier] a specified area of activity or interest: *the country music scene.* ■ [usu. in sing.] a public display of emotion or anger. **2** a sequence of continuous action in a play, movie, opera, or book. ■ a subdivision of an act of a play in which the time is continuous and the setting fixed and which does not usually involve a change of characters. ■ [usu. as adj.] the pieces of scenery used in a play or opera: *scene changes.*
– PHRASES **behind the scenes** out of sight of the public at a theater or organization. ■ fig. secretly. **come** (or **appear** or **arrive**) **on the scene** arrive; appear. **not one's scene** informal not something one enjoys or is interested in. **set the scene** describe a place or situation in which something is about to happen. ■ create the conditions for a future event. [16th C.: from L. *scena*, from Gk. *skēnē* 'tent, stage.']

scen·er·y /'sēn(ə)rē/ ▶ n. the natural features of a landscape considered in terms of their appearance, esp. when picturesque. ■ the painted background used to represent natural features or other surroundings on a theater stage or movie set.
– PHRASES **change of scenery** a move to different surroundings. **chew (up) the scenery** (of an actor) overact. [18th C. (earlier as *scenary*): from Ital. *scenario*.]

scene-steal·er ▶ n. an actor who outshines the rest of the cast, esp. unexpectedly. ■ a person or thing that takes more than their fair share of attention.

scene·ster /'sēnstər/ ▶ n. informal a person associated with or immersed in a particular fashionable cultural scene.

sce·nic /'sēnik/ ▶ adj. providing or relating to views of impressive or beautiful natural scenery. ■ [attrib.] of or relating to theatrical scenery. ■ (of a picture) representing an incident. — **sce·ni·cal·ly** /-ik(ə)lē/ adv. [17th C.: via L. from Gk. *skēnikos* 'of the stage,' from *skēnē*.]

sce·nog·ra·phy /sē'nägrəfē/ ▶ n. the design and painting of theatrical scenery. ■ (in painting and drawing) the representation of objects in perspective. — **sce·no·graph·ic** /ˌsēnə'grafik; ˌsenə-/ adj. [17th C.: from Fr. *scénographie*, or via L. from Gk. *skēnographia* 'scene-painting,' from *skēnē*.]

scent /sent/ ▶ n. a distinctive smell, esp. one that is pleasant: *the scent of freshly cut hay.* ■ pleasant-smelling liquid worn on the skin; perfume. ■ a trail indicated by the characteristic smell of an animal and perceptible to hounds or other animals. ■ fig. a trail of evidence or other signs assisting someone in a search or investigation. ▶ v. [trans.] **1** (usu. **be scented with**) impart a pleasant scent to. **2** discern by the sense of smell. ■ fig. sense the presence, existence, or imminence of: *he scented victory.* ■ sniff (the air) for a scent.
– PHRASES **on the scent** in possession of a useful clue in a search or investigation; following a trail that will likely lead to the discovery or acquisition of something. **put** (or **throw**) **someone off the scent** mislead someone in the course of a search or investigation. — **scent·less** adj. [ME: from OFr. *sentir* 'perceive, smell,' from L. *sentire*.]

scent gland ▶ n. an animal gland that secretes an odorous pheromone or defensive substance, esp. one under the tail of a carnivorous mammal such as a civet or skunk.

scent mark ▶ n. (also **scent mark·ing**) an odoriferous substance containing a pheromone that is deposited by a mammal from a scent gland or in the urine or feces, typically on prominent objects in an area. ▶ v. (**scent-mark**) [intrans.] (of a mammal) deposit such a substance.

scep·ter /'septər/ (Brit. **scep·tre**) ▶ n. an ornamented staff carried by rulers on ceremonial occasions as a symbol of sovereignty. — **scep·tered** adj. [ME: from OFr. *ceptre*, via L. from Gk. *skēptron*, from *skēptein* (alt. of *skēptesthai*) 'lean on.']

scepter

sch. ▶ abbr. ■ scholar. ■ school. ■ schooner.

scha·den·freu·de /'SHädən,froidə/ (also **Scha·den·freu·de**) ▶ n. pleasure derived by someone from another person's misfortune. [Ger., from *Schaden* 'harm' + *Freude* 'joy.']

Schaw·low /'SHô,lō/, Arthur Leonard (1921–99), US inventor. With Charles H. Townes, he invented the laser. Nobel Prize in Physics (1981, shared with Nicolaas Bloembergen 1920– and Kai M. Siegbahn 1918–).

sched·ule /'skej(o͞o)əl; -jo͞ol/ ▶ n. **1** a plan for carrying out a process or procedure, giving lists of intended events and times: *we have drawn up an engineering schedule.* ■ (usu. **one's schedule**) one's day-to-day plans or timetable. ■ a timetable. **2** esp. Law an appendix to a formal document or statute, esp. as a list, table, or inventory. **3** (with reference to an income tax system) any of the forms (named "A," "B," etc.) relating to the various classes into which taxable income is divided. ▶ v. [trans.] (often **be scheduled**) arrange or plan (an event) to take place at a particular time. ■ make arrangements for (someone or something) to do something.
– PHRASES **ahead of** (or **behind**) **schedule** earlier (or later) than planned or expected. **on** (or **according to**) **schedule** on time; as planned or expected. — **sched·u·lar** /-ər/ adj. [ME: from OFr. *cedule*, from late L. *schedula* 'slip of paper,' dimin. of *scheda*, from Gk. *skhedē* 'papyrus leaf.']

sched·uled /'skeˌjo͞old; -əld/ ▶ adj. included in or planned according to a schedule. ■ (esp. of an airline or flight) relating to or forming part of a regular service rather than specially chartered.

sched·uled caste (also **Sched·uled Caste**) ▶ n. the official name given in India to the untouchable castes.

sched·ul·er /'skejo͞olər; 'skejələr/ ▶ n. a person or machine that organizes or maintains schedules. ■ Comput. a program that arranges jobs or a computer's operations into an appropriate sequence.

scheel·ite /'SHä,līt/ ▶ n. a fluorescent mineral, white when pure, that consists of calcium tungstate and is an important ore of tungsten. [19th C.: Carl W. *Scheele* (1742–86), Swedish chemist, + -ITE[1].]

schef·fler·a /'SHeflərə; SHef'li(ə)rə/ ▶ n. an evergreen tropical or subtropical shrub or small tree (genus *Schefflera*, family Araliaceae) that is widely grown as a houseplant for its decorative foliage. [mod. L., after J. C. *Scheffler*, 18th-cent. German botanist.]

Sche·her·a·za·de /SHə,herə'zäd; -'zädə/ the character who narrates the *Arabian Nights*.

Scheldt /SHelt; skelt/ (also **Schel·de** /'skeldə; 'SHel-/) a river in northern Europe. Rising in northern France, it flows through Belgium and the Netherlands to the North Sea. French name ESCAUT.

sche·ma /'skēmə/ ▶ n. (pl. **-ma·ta** /-mətə/ or **-mas**) tech. a representation of a plan or theory in the form of an outline or model. ■ Logic a syllogistic figure. ■ (in Kantian philosophy) a conception of what is common to all members of a class; a general or essential type or form. [18th C.: from Gk. *skhēma* 'form, figure.']

sche·mat·ic /skə'matik; skē-/ ▶ adj. (of a diagram or other representation) symbolic and simplified. ■ (of thought, ideas, etc.) simplistic or formulaic in character, usually to an extent inappropriate to the complexities of the subject matter. ▶ n. (in technical contexts) a schematic diagram, in particular of an electric or electronic circuit. — **sche·mat·i·cal·ly** /-ik(ə)lē/ adv.

sche·ma·tism /'skēmə,tizəm/ ▶ n. the arrangement or presentation of something according to a scheme or schema.

sche·ma·tize /'skēmə,tīz/ ▶ v. [trans.] arrange or represent in a schematic form. — **sche·ma·ti·za·tion** /ˌskēməti'zāSHən/ n.

scheme /skēm/ ▶ n. a large-scale systematic plan or arrangement for attaining some particular object or putting a particular idea into effect. ■ a secret or underhanded plan; a plot. ■ a particular ordered system or arrangement: *a classical rhyme scheme.* ▶ v. [intrans.] make plans, esp. in a devious way or with intent to do something illegal or wrong. [16th C.: from L. *schema*, from Gk. (see SCHEMA).]

schem·er /'skēmər/ ▶ n. a person who is involved in making secret or underhanded plans.

schem·ing /'skēmiNG/ ▶ adj. given to or involved in making secret and underhanded plans. ▶ n. the activity or practice of making such plans. — **schem·ing·ly** adv.

Sche·nec·ta·dy /skə'nektədē/ a city in eastern New York, northwest of Albany; pop. 61,821.

scher·zan·do /skərt'sändō/ Music ▶ adv. & adj. (esp. as a direction) in a playful manner. [Ital., lit. 'joking.']

scher·zo /'skertsō/ ▶ n. (pl. **-zos** or **-zi** /-tsē/) Music a vigorous, light, or playful composition, typically comprising a movement in a symphony or sonata. [Ital., lit. 'jest.']

Schia·pa·rel·li /ˌskyäpə'relē; ˌSHäpə-/, Elsa (1896–1973), French fashion designer; born in Italy.

Schil·ler /'SHilər/, Johann Christoph Friedrich von (1759–1805), German playwright, poet, and historian. He was an important figure of the Enlightenment. His plays include *William Tell* (1804).

schil·ling /'SHiliNG/ ▶ n. the basic monetary unit of Austria (until replaced by the euro), equal to 100 groschen. [from Ger. *Schilling*.]

Schin·dler /'SHindlər/, Oskar (1908–74), German industrialist. He saved more than 1,200 Jews from concentration camps by employing them in his factories.

schip·per·ke /'skipərkē/ ▶ **n.** a small black tailless dog of a breed with a ruff of fur around its neck. [19th C.: from Du. dial., lit. 'little boatman,' with ref. to its use as a watchdog on barges.]

schism /'s(k)izəm/ ▶ **n.** a split or division between strongly opposed sections or parties, caused by differences in opinion or belief. ■ the formal separation of a church into two churches or the secession of a group owing to doctrinal and other differences. See also **Great Schism.** [ME: from OFr. *scisme*, via eccles. L. from Gk. *skhisma* 'cleft,' from *skhizein* 'to split.']

schis·mat·ic /s(k)iz'matik/ ▶ **adj.** of, characterized by, or favoring schism. ▶ **n.** esp. hist. (esp. in the Christian Church) a person who promotes schism; an adherent of a schismatic group. — **schis·mat·i·cal·ly** /-ik(ə)lē/ **adv.**

schist /sHist/ ▶ **n.** Geol. a coarse-grained metamorphic rock that consists of layers of different minerals and can be split into thin irregular plates. — **schis·tous** /-təs/ **adj.** [18th C.: from Fr. *schiste*, via L. from Gk. *skhistos* 'split,' from the base of *skhizein* 'cleave.']

schis·to·some /'sHistə,sōm/ ▶ **n.** Zool. & Med. a parasitic flatworm (genus *Schistosoma*) that needs two hosts to complete its life cycle. The immature form infests freshwater snails, and the adult lives in the blood vessels of birds and mammals, causing bilharzia in humans. Also called **blood fluke.** [20th C.: from mod. L. *Schistosoma*, from Gk. *skhistos* 'divided' + *sōma* 'body.']

schis·to·so·mi·a·sis /,sHistōsə'mīəsis/ ▶ **n.** another term for **bilharzia** (the disease).

schiz·o /'skitsō/ informal ▶ **adj.** (of a person or their behavior) schizophrenic. ▶ **n.** (pl. **-os**) a schizophrenic. [1940s: abbrev.]

schizo- ▶ **comb. form** divided; split: *schizocarp.* ■ relating to schizophrenia. [from Gk. *skhizein* 'to split.']

schiz·o·af·fec·tive (also **schiz·o-af·fec·tive**) ▶ **adj.** (of a person or a mental condition) characterized by symptoms of both schizophrenia and manic-depressive psychosis.

schiz·o·carp /'skitsō,kärp/ ▶ **n.** Bot. a dry fruit that splits into single-seeded parts when ripe.

schi·zog·e·nous /ski'zäjənəs; skit'säj-/ ▶ **adj.** Bot. (of an intercellular space in a plant) formed by the splitting of the common wall of contiguous cells. — **schiz·o·gen·ic** /,skizə'jenik; ,skitsə-/ **adj.** **schi·zog·e·ny** /ski'zäjənē; skit'säj-/ **n.**

schi·zog·o·ny /ski'zägənē; skit'säg-/ ▶ **n.** Biol. asexual reproduction by multiple fission, found in some protozoa, esp. parasitic sporozoans. — **schi·zog·o·nous** /-nəs/ **adj.** [19th C.: from **schizo-** 'divided' + Gk. *-gonia* 'production.']

schiz·oid /'skit,soid/ ▶ **adj.** Psychiatry denoting or having a personality type characterized by emotional aloofness and solitary habits. ■ informal (in general use) resembling schizophrenia in having inconsistent or contradictory elements; crazy. ▶ **n.** a schizoid person.

schiz·ont /'skizänt; 'skitsänt/ ▶ **n.** Biol. (in certain sporozoan protozoans) a cell that divides by schizogony to form daughter cells. [20th C.: from **schizo-** 'divided' + **-ont.**]

schiz·o·phre·ni·a /,skitsə'frēnēə; -'frenēə/ ▶ **n.** a long-term mental disorder of a type involving a breakdown in the relation between thought, emotion, and behavior, leading to faulty perception, inappropriate actions and feelings, withdrawal from reality and personal relationships into fantasy and delusion, and a sense of mental fragmentation. ■ (in general use) a mentality or approach characterized by inconsistent or contradictory elements. — **schiz·o·phren·ic** /-'frenik/ **adj. & n.** [20th C.: mod. L., from Gk. *skhizein* 'to split' + *phrēn* 'mind.']

schiz·o·type /'skitsə,tīp/ ▶ **n.** a personality type in which mild symptoms of schizophrenia are present. — **schiz·o·typ·al** /,skitsə'tīpəl/ **adj.** **schiz·o·typ·y** /,skit'sätəpē/ **n.**

Schle·gel /'sHlāgəl/, August Wilhelm von (1767–1845), German poet and critic. He was a founder of art history and comparative philology.

schle·miel /sHlə'mēl/ (also **shle·miel**) ▶ **n.** informal a stupid, awkward, or unlucky person. [19th C.: from Yiddish *shlemiel.*]

schlep /sHlep/ (also **schlepp** or **shlep**) informal ▶ **v.** (**schlepped, schlep·ping**) [trans.] haul or carry (something heavy or awkward). ■ [no obj., with adverbial of direction] (of a person) go or move reluctantly or with effort. ▶ **n.** a tedious or difficult journey. [20th C. (as a v.): from Yiddish *shlepn* 'drag,' from Mid. High Ger. *sleppen.*]

Schles·ing·er /'sHlāziNGər; 'sHlesinjər/ a family of US historians. Arthur Meier (1888–1965) wrote *The Colonial Merchants and the American Revolution, 1763–1776* (1918). His son, Arthur Meier, Jr. (1917–2007), born *Arthur Bancroft Schlesinger*, wrote *A Thousand Days: John F. Kennedy in the White House* (1965).

Schles·wig /'sHleswig; 'sHlāsviKH; -vik/ a former Danish duchy, situated on the Jutland peninsula.

Schles·wig-Hol·stein /'hōl,stīn; -,sHtīn/ a state in northwestern Germany on the Jutland peninsula; capital, Kiel.

Schlie·mann /'sHlē,män/, Heinrich (1822–90), German archaeologist. In 1871, he began excavating in Turkey, discovering the remains of nine cities, one mistakenly identified as Homer's Troy. By 1876, he was excavating at Mycenae.

schlie·ren /'sHli(ə)rən/ ▶ **plural n.** tech. discernible layers in a transparent material that differ from the surrounding material in density or composition. ■ Geol. irregular streaks or masses in igneous rock that differ from the surrounding rock in texture or composition. [19th C.: from Ger. *Schlieren*, pl. of *Schliere* 'streak.']

schlock /sHläk/ (also **shlock**) ▶ **n.** informal cheap or inferior goods or material; trash. — **schlock·y adj.** [20th C.: appar. from Yiddish *shlak* 'an apoplectic stroke,' *shlog* 'wretch.']

schlock·meis·ter /'sHläk,mīstər/ (also **shlock·meis·ter**) ▶ **n.** informal a purveyor of cheap or trashy goods. [20th C.: from **schlock** + Ger. *Meister* 'master.']

schlub /sHləb/ (also **shlub**) ▶ **n.** informal a talentless, unattractive, or boorish person. [1960s: Yiddish *shlub*, perh. from Pol. *żłób.*]

schlump /sHlo͝omp/ (also **shlump**) ▶ **n.** informal a slow, slovenly, or inept person. [1940s: appar. rel. to Yiddish *shlumperdik* 'dowdy' and Ger. *Schlumpe* 'slattern.']

schmaltz /sHmälts; sHmôlts/ (also **schmalz**) ▶ **n.** informal excessive sentimentality, esp. in music or movies. — **schmaltz·y adj.** (**schmaltz·i·er, schmaltz·i·est**). [1930s: from Yiddish *shmaltz*, from Ger. *Schmalz* 'drippings, lard.']

schmat·te /'sHmätə/ (also **shmat·te**) ▶ **n.** informal a rag; a ragged or shabby garment. [1970s: Yiddish *shmatte*, from Pol. *szmata* 'rag.']

schmear /sHmi(ə)r/ (also **schmeer, shmeer,** or **shmear**) informal ▶ **n.** **1** a corrupt or underhanded inducement; a bribe. **2** a smear or spread: *a schmear of cream cheese.* ▶ **v.** [trans.] flatter or ingratiate oneself with (someone).

– PHRASES **the whole schmear** everything possible or available; every aspect of the situation. [1960s: from Yiddish *shmirn* 'flatter, grease.']

schmo /sHmō/ (also **shmo**) ▶ **n.** (pl. **schmoes**) informal a fool or a bore. [1940s: alt. of **schmuck.**]

schmooze /sHmo͞oz/ (also **shmooze**) ▶ **v.** [intrans.] talk intimately and cozily; gossip. ■ [trans.] talk in such a way to (someone), typically in order to manipulate, flatter, or impress them. ▶ **n.** a long and intimate conversation. — **schmooz·er n. schmooz·y adj.** [19th C. (as a v.): from Yiddish *shmuesn* 'converse, chat.']

schmuck /sHmək/ (also **shmuck**) ▶ **n.** informal a foolish or contemptible person. [19th C.: from Yiddish *shmok* 'penis.']

schnapps /sHnäps; sHnaps/ ▶ **n.** a strong alcoholic drink resembling gin and often flavored with fruit. [from Ger. *Schnaps*, 'dram of liquor,' from Low Ger. and Du. *snaps* 'mouthful.']

miniature schnauzer

schnau·zer /'sHnouzər/ ▶ **n.** a medium- or small-sized dog of a German breed with a close wiry coat and heavy whiskers around the muzzle. [20th C.: from Ger., from *Schnauze* 'muzzle, snout.']

schnit·zel /'sHnitsəl/ ▶ **n.** a thin slice of veal or other light meat, coated in breadcrumbs and fried. [from Ger. *Schnitzel*, lit. 'slice.']

schnook /sHno͝ok/ (also **shnook**) ▶ **n.** informal a person easily duped; a fool. [1940s: perh. from Ger. *Schnucke* 'small sheep' or from Yiddish *shnuk* 'snout.']

schnor·rer /'sHnôrər/ (also **shnor·rer**) ▶ **n.** informal a beggar or scrounger; a layabout. [19th C.: from Yiddish *shnorrer*, var. of Ger. *Schnurrer.*]

schnoz /sHnäz/ (also **schnozz** or **schnoz·zo·la** /sHnä'zōlə/) ▶ **n.** informal a person's nose. [1940s: from Yiddish *shnoytz*, from Ger. *Schnauze* 'snout.']

Schoen·berg /'sHə(r)n,bərg; 'sHœn,berk/, Arnold (1874–1951), US composer, born in Austria. He introduced atonality into his second string quartet (1907–08); his works include *Serenade* (1923).

schol·ar /'skälər/ ▶ **n.** a specialist in a particular branch of study, esp. the humanities; a distinguished academic: *a Hebrew scholar.* ■ esp. archaic a person who is highly educated or has an aptitude for study. ■ a student holding a scholarship. ■ archaic a student. [OE *scol(i)ere* 'schoolchild, student,' from late L. *scholaris*, from L. *schola* (see **school**[1]).]

schol·ar·ly /'skälərlē/ ▶ **adj.** involving or relating to serious academic study: *scholarly journals.* ■ having or showing knowledge, learning, or devotion to academic pursuits: *an earnest, scholarly man.* — **schol·ar·li·ness n.**

schol·ar·ship /'skälər,sHip/ ▶ **n.** **1** academic study or achievement; learning of a high level. **2** a grant or payment made to support a student's education, awarded on the basis of academic or other achievement.

scho·las·tic /skə'lastik/ ▶ **adj.** **1** of or concerning schools and education: *scholastic achievement.* ■ of or relating to secondary schools. **2** Philos. & Theol. of, relating to, or characteristic of medieval scholasticism.

■ typical of scholasticism in being pedantic or overly subtle. ▶ n. 1 Philos. & Theol., hist. an adherent of scholasticism; a schoolman. 2 (in the Roman Catholic Church) a member of a religious order, esp. the Society of Jesus, who is between the novitiate and the priesthood. — **scho·las·ti·cal·ly** /-tik(ə)lē/ adv. [16th C.: via L. from Gk. *skholastikos* 'studious,' from *skholazein* 'be at leisure to study,' from *skholē* (see SCHOOL¹).]

scho·las·ti·cism /skəˈlastiˌsizəm/ ▶ n. the system of theology and philosophy taught in medieval European universities, based on Aristotelian logic and the writings of the early Church Fathers and having a strong emphasis on tradition and dogma. ■ narrow-minded insistence on traditional doctrine.

scho·li·ast /ˈskōlēˌast/ ▶ n. hist. a commentator on ancient or classical literature. — **scho·li·as·tic** /ˌskōlēˈastik/ adj. [16th C.: from med. Gk. *skholiastēs*, from *skholiazein* 'write scholia' (see SCHOLIUM).]

scho·li·um /ˈskōlēəm/ ▶ n. (pl. **-li·a** /-lēə/) hist. a marginal note or explanatory comment made by a scholiast. [16th C.: mod. L., from Gk. *skholion*, from *skholē* 'learned discussion.']

school¹ /sko͞ol/ ▶ n. 1 an institution for educating children. ■ the buildings used by such an institution. ■ [treated as pl.] the students and staff of a school. ■ a day's work at school; lessons. ■ [with adj.] fig. used to describe the type of circumstances in which someone was brought up. 2 any institution at which instruction is given in a particular discipline. ■ informal another term for UNIVERSITY. ■ a department or faculty of a college concerned with a particular subject of study. 3 a group of people, particularly writers, artists, or philosophers, sharing the same or similar ideas, methods, or style. ■ [with adj.] a style, approach, or method of a specified character: *the Trump school of deal making.* ▶ v. [trans.] esp. formal send to school; educate. ■ train or discipline (someone) in a particular skill or activity: *he schooled her in horsemanship.*
– PHRASES **leave school** discontinue one's education. **school of thought** a particular way of thinking, typically one disputed by the speaker. [OE *scōl, scolu*, via L. from Gk. *skholē* 'leisure, philosophy, place where lectures are given.']

school² ▶ n. a large group of fish or sea mammals. ▶ v. [intrans.] (of fish or sea mammals) form a large group. [ME: from Mid. Low Ger., MDu. *schōle*, of West Gmc. origin; rel. to OE *scolu* 'troop.']

school age ▶ n. the age range of children normally attending school. — **school-age** or **school-aged** adj.

school board ▶ n. a local board or authority responsible for the provision and maintenance of schools.

school·boy /ˈsko͞olˌboi/ ▶ n. a boy attending school. ■ [as adj.] characteristic of or associated with schoolboys, esp. in being immature: *schoolboy humor.*

school bus ▶ n. a bus that transports students from home to school, school to home, or to school-sponsored events.

school·child /ˈsko͞olˌCHīld/ ▶ n. (pl. **-child·ren**) a child attending school.

school·days /ˈsko͞olˌdāz/ ▶ plural n. the period in someone's life when they attended school.

school dis·trict ▶ n. a geographical unit for the local administration of schools.

schooled /sko͞old/ ▶ adj. [often in comb.] educated or trained in a specified activity or in a particular way.

school·girl /ˈsko͞olˌgərl/ ▶ n. a girl attending school. ■ [as adj.] characteristic of or associated with schoolgirls, esp. in being elementary or immature.

school·house /ˈsko͞olˌhous/ ▶ n. a building used as a school, esp. in a small community or village.

school·ing /ˈsko͞oliNG/ ▶ n. education or training received, esp. at school: *his parents paid for his schooling.*

school·marm /ˈsko͞olˌmä(r)m/ ▶ n. a schoolmistress (typically used with reference to a woman regarded as prim, strict, and brisk in manner). — **school·marm·ish** adj.

school·mas·ter /ˈsko͞olˌmastər/ ▶ n. dated a male teacher in a school. — **school·mas·ter·ly** adj.

school·mate /ˈsko͞olˌmāt/ ▶ n. informal a person who attends or attended the same school as oneself.

school·mis·tress /ˈsko͞olˌmistris/ ▶ n. dated a female teacher in a school.

school·room /ˈsko͞olˌro͞om; -ˌro͝om/ ▶ n. a room in which a class of students is taught. ■ (**the schoolroom**) used to refer to school as an institution.

school·teach·er /ˈsko͞olˌtēCHər/ ▶ n. a person who teaches in a school. — **school·teach·ing** /-ˌtēCHiNG/ n.

school·work /ˈsko͞olˌwərk/ ▶ n. work assigned students by their teachers in school.

school·yard /ˈsko͞olˌyärd/ ▶ n. the grounds of a school, esp. as a place for children to play.

school year ▶ n. another term for ACADEMIC YEAR.

schoon·er /ˈsko͞onər/ ▶ n. 1 a sailing ship with two or more masts, typically with the foremast smaller than the mainmast, and gaff-rigged lower masts. 2 a tall beer glass. [18th C.: of unknown origin.]

Scho·pen·hau·er /ˈSHōpənˌhou-ər/, Arthur (1788–1860), German philosopher. His philosophy is expressed in *The World as Will and Idea* (1818).

schorl /SHôrl/ ▶ n. a black iron-rich variety of tourmaline. [18th C.: from Ger. *Schörl.*]

schot·tische /ˈSHätisH/ ▶ n. a slow polka. [19th C.: from Ger. *der schottische Tanz* 'the Scottish dance.']

schooner

Schrief·fer /ˈSHrēfər/, John Robert, (1931–). See BARDEEN.

Schrö·ding·er /ˈSHrādiNGgər; ˈSHrō-/, Erwin (1887–1961), Austrian physicist. He founded the study of wave mechanics. Nobel Prize for Physics (1933).

schtup ▶ v. var. of SHTUP.

Schu·bert /ˈSHo͞obərt/, Franz (1797–1828), Austrian composer. His large body of work contains elements of both the classical age and the romantic movement.

Schulz /SHo͝olts/, Charles (1922–2000), US cartoonist. He was the creator of the widely syndicated "Peanuts" comic strip, first published in 1950.

Schu·ma·cher /ˈSHo͞oˌmäkHər/, E. F. (1911–77), German economist and conservationist; full name *Ernst Friedrich Schumacher.* He wrote *Small Is Beautiful: Economics As If People Mattered* (1973).

Schu·mann /ˈSHo͞omən; -ˌmän/ a family of German composers and pianists. Robert Alexander (1810–56), was noted as a leading romanticist. His wife, Clara Josephine Wieck (1819–96), is considered the premier female musician of the 19th century.

schuss /SHo͞os; SHo͝os/ ▶ n. a straight downhill run on skis. ▶ v. [intrans.] make a straight downhill run on skis. [1930s: from Ger. *Schuss*, 'shot.']

Schuyl·kill Riv·er /ˈsko͞olˌkil; -kəl/ a river that flows through eastern Pennsylvania to join the Delaware River at Philadelphia.

schwa /SHwä/ ▶ n. Phonet. the unstressed central vowel (as in *a moment ago*), represented by the symbol (ə) in the International Phonetic Alphabet. [19th C.: from Ger., from Heb. *šĕwā'.*]

Schwa·ben /ˈSHväbən/ German name for SWABIA.

Schwann /SHwän; SHfän/, Theodor Ambrose Hubert (1810–82), German physiologist. He discovered the cells that form the myelin sheaths of nerve fibers (Schwann cells).

Schwarz·kopf¹ /ˈSHwôrtsˌkô(p)f; ˈswärtsˌkä(p)f/, Dame Olga Maria Elisabeth Friederike (1915–2006), German opera singer; a British citizen after her marriage. She is noted for roles in works such as Richard Strauss's *Der Rosenkavalier.*

Schwarz·kopf² /ˈSHwôrtsˌkôpf; ˈSHwärts-; -ˌkäpf/, H. Norman, Jr. (1934–), US army officer. Appointed commander in chief of the US Central Command 1988–91, he led the Allied forces against Iraq in the Persian Gulf War 1991.

Schwarz·wald /ˈSHvärtsˌvält/ German name for BLACK FOREST.

Schweit·zer /ˈSHwītsər; ˈSHfī-/, Albert (1875–1965), German missionary and doctor. He established a hospital in Gabon. Nobel Peace Prize (1952).

Schweiz /SHvīts/ German name for SWITZERLAND.

Schwe·rin /SHvāˈrēn/ a city in northeastern Germany, situated on Lake Schwerin; pop. 126,000.

Schwyz /SHvēts/ a canton in northeastern Switzerland.

sci·ae·nid /sīˈēnid/ ▶ n. Zool. a fish of the drum family (Sciaenidae), whose members are mainly marine and important for food or sport. [20th C.: from mod. L. *Sciaenidae* (pl.), from the genus name *Sciaena*, from Gk. *skiaina*, denoting a kind of fish.]

sci·am·a·chy /sīˈaməkē/ ▶ n. archaic sham fighting for exercise or practice. ■ argument or conflict with an imaginary opponent. [17th C.: from Gk. *skiamakhia*, from *skia* 'shadow' + *-makhia* '-fighting.']

sci·at·ic /sīˈatik/ ▶ adj. of or relating to the hip. ■ of or affecting the sciatic nerve. ■ suffering from or liable to sciatica. — **sci·at·i·cal·ly** /-ik(ə)lē/ adv. [16th C.: from Fr. *sciatique*, via late L. from Gk. *iskhiadikos* 'relating to the hips, subject to sciatica,' from *iskhion* 'hip joint.']

sci·at·i·ca /sīˈatikə/ ▶ n. pain affecting the back, hip, and outer side of the leg, caused by compression of a spinal nerve root in the lower back, often owing to degeneration of an intervertebral disk. [ME: from late L. *sciatica (passio)* '(affliction) of sciatica,' fem. of *sciaticus*, from Gk. *iskhiadikos* (see SCIATIC).]

sci·at·ic nerve ▶ n. Anat. a major nerve extending from the lower end of the spinal cord down the back of the thigh, and dividing above the knee joint.

SCID ▶ abbr. severe combined immune deficiency, a rare genetic disorder in which affected children have no resistance to disease and must be kept isolated from infection from birth.

sci·ence /ˈsīəns/ ▶ n. the intellectual and practical activity encompassing the systematic study of the structure and behavior of the physical and natural world through observation and experiment. ■ a particular area of this: *veterinary science.* ■ a systematically organized body of knowledge on a particular subject. [ME: from OFr., from L. *scientia*, from *scire* 'know.']

sci·ence fic·tion (abbr.: **SF** or **Sci Fi**) ▶**n.** fiction based on imagined future scientific or technological advances and major social or environmental changes, frequently portraying space or time travel and life on other planets.

sci·en·tial /sīˈenCHəl/ ▶**adj.** archaic concerning or having knowledge.

sci·en·tif·ic /ˌsīənˈtifik/ ▶**adj.** based on or characterized by the methods and principles of science. ■ relating to or used in science: *scientific instruments.* ■ informal systematic; methodical. — **sci·en·tif·i·cal·ly** /-ik(ə)lē/ **adv.** [16th C.: from Fr. *scientifique* or late L. *scientificus* 'producing knowledge,' from *scientia* (see SCIENCE).]

sci·en·tif·ic meth·od ▶**n.** a method of procedure that has characterized natural science since the 17th century, consisting in systematic observation, measurement, and experiment, and the formulation, testing, and modification of hypotheses.

sci·en·tist /ˈsīəntist/ ▶**n.** a person who is studying or has expert knowledge of one or more of the natural or physical sciences.

Sci·en·tol·o·gy /ˌsīənˈtäləjē/ ▶**n.** trademark a religious system based on the seeking of self-knowledge and spiritual fulfillment through graded courses of study and training. It was founded by American science-fiction writer L. Ron Hubbard (1911–86) in 1955. — **Sci·en·tol·o·gist** /-jist/ **n.** [from L. *scientia* 'knowledge' + -LOGY.]

sci-fi /ˈsī ˈfī/ ▶**n.** informal short for SCIENCE FICTION.

scil·i·cet /ˈsiləˌset/ ▶**adv.** that is to say; namely. [L., from *scire licet* 'one is permitted to know.']

scil·la /ˈsilə/ ▶**n.** a plant (genus *Scilla*) of the lily family that typically bears small blue star- or bell-shaped flowers and glossy straplike leaves, native to Eurasia and temperate Africa. [mod. L., from L. *scilla* 'sea onion,' from Gk. *skilla.*]

Scil·ly Isles /ˈsilē/ (also **Isles of Scil·ly** or **the Scil·lies**) a group of about 140 small islands off the southwestern tip of England; pop. 3,000; capital, Hugh Town (on St. Mary's). — **Scil·lo·ni·an** /səˈlōnēən/ **adj. & n.**

scim·i·tar /ˈsimətər; -ˌtär/ ▶**n.** a short sword with a curved blade that broadens toward the point. [16th C.: from Fr. *cimeterre* or Ital. *scimitarra,* of unknown origin.]

scimitar

scim·i·tar o·ryx (also **scim·i·tar-horned o·ryx**) ▶**n.** an oryx (*Oryx dammah*) with scimitar-shaped horns, now living only along the southern edge of the Sahara.

scin·ti·gram /ˈsintiˌgram/ ▶**n.** Med. an image of an internal part of the body produced by scintigraphy. [1950s: from SCINTILLATION + -GRAM[1].]

scin·tig·ra·phy /sinˈtigrəfē/ ▶**n.** Med. a technique in which a scintillation counter or similar detector is used with a radioactive tracer to obtain an image of a bodily organ or a record of its functioning. — **scin·ti·graph·ic** /ˌsintiˈgrafik/ **adj.** [1950s: from SCINTILLATION + -GRAPHY.]

scin·til·la /sinˈtilə/ ▶**n.** [in sing.] a tiny trace or spark of a specified quality or feeling: ***a scintilla of*** *doubt.* [17th C.: from L.]

scin·til·late /ˈsintlˌāt/ ▶**v.** [intrans.] emit flashes of light; sparkle. ■ Physics fluoresce momentarily when struck by a charged particle or photon. — **scin·til·lant** /-ənt/ **adj. & n.** [17th C.: from L. *scintillat-* 'sparkled,' from the verb *scintillare,* from *scintilla* 'spark.']

scin·til·lat·ing /ˈsintlˌātiNG/ ▶**adj.** sparkling or shining brightly: *the scintillating sun.* ■ brilliantly and excitingly clever or skillful. — **scin·til·lat·ing·ly adv.**

scin·til·la·tion /ˌsintlˈāSHən/ ▶**n.** a flash or sparkle of light. ■ the process or state of emitting flashes of light. ■ Physics a small flash of visible or ultraviolet light emitted by fluorescence in a phosphor when struck by a charged particle or high-energy photon. ■ Astron. the twinkling of the stars, caused by the earth's atmosphere diffracting starlight unevenly.

scin·til·la·tor /ˈsintlˌātər/ ▶**n.** Physics a material that fluoresces when struck by a charged particle or high-energy photon. ■ a detector for charged particles and gamma rays in which scintillations produced in a phosphor are detected and amplified by a photomultiplier, giving an electrical output signal.

scin·ti·scan /ˈsintəˌskan/ ▶**n.** Med. another term for SCINTIGRAM. [1960s: from SCINTILLATION + SCAN.]

sci·on /ˈsīən/ ▶**n. 1** (also **ci·on**) a young shoot or twig of a plant, esp. one cut for grafting or rooting. **2** a descendant of a notable family. [ME: from OFr. *ciun* 'shoot, twig,' of unknown origin.]

Scip·i·o Ae·mil·i·a·nus /ˈsipēˌō iˌmilēˈānəs/ (*c.*185–129 BC), Roman general and politician; full name ***Publius Cornelius Scipio Aemilianus Africanus Minor***; adoptive grandson of Scipio Africanus. He achieved distinction in the siege of Carthage in 146 during the third Punic War and in his campaign in Spain in 133.

Scip·i·o Af·ri·ca·nus /ˈsipēˌōˌafriˈkānəs/ (236–*c.*184 BC), Roman general and politician; full name ***Publius Cornelius Scipio Africanus Major.*** He successfully concluded the second Punic War by victories over the Carthaginians in Spain in 206 and Hannibal in Africa at Zama in 202.

sci·roc·co /SHəˈräkō; sə-/ ▶**n.** var. of SIROCCO.

scir·rhus /ˈs(k)irəs/ ▶**n.** (pl. **scir·rhi** /ˈs(k)irˌī; ˈskirˌē/) Med. a carcinoma that is hard to the touch. — **scir·rhous** /-əs/ **adj.** [ME: mod. L., from Gk. *skirros,* from *skiros* 'hard.']

scis·sile /ˈsisəl; -īl/ ▶**adj.** esp. Biochem. (of a chemical bond) readily undergoing scission. [17th C.: from L. *scissilis,* from *sciss-* 'cut, divided,' from the verb *scindere.*]

scis·sion /ˈsiZHən; ˈsiSH-/ ▶**n.** tech. the action or state of cutting or being cut, in particular: ■ esp. Biochem. breakage of a chemical bond, esp. one in a long chain molecule so that two smaller chains result. ■ a division or split between people or parties; a schism. [ME: from OFr., or from late L. *scissio(n-),* from *scindere* 'cut, cleave.']

scis·sor /ˈsizər/ ▶**v. 1** [with obj. and adverbial] cut (something) with scissors: *pages scissored out of a magazine.* **2** [trans.] move (one's legs) move back and forth in a way resembling the action of scissors. ■ [intrans.] (of a person's legs) move in such a way. ▶**n.** see SCISSORS. [17th C.: from SCISSORS.]

scis·sor hold (also **scis·sors hold**) ▶**n.** Wrestling a hold in which the head or other part of the opponent's body is gripped between the legs, which are then locked at the instep or ankles to apply pressure.

scis·sor jack (also **scis·sors jack**) ▶**n.** a jack for heavy lifting, operated by a horizontal screw that raises or lowers a frame of hinged, lozenge-shaped linkages. See illustration at JACK[1].

scis·sor kick (also **scis·sors kick**) ▶**n.** (in various sports, particularly swimming and soccer) a kick in which the legs make a sharp snapping movement like the blades of a pair of scissors. — **scis·sor-kick v.**

scis·sors /ˈsizərz/ (also **a pair of scis·sors**) ▶**plural n.** an instrument used for cutting cloth, paper, and other material, consisting of two blades laid one on top of the other and fastened in the middle so as to allow them to be opened and closed by a thumb and finger inserted through rings on the end of their handles. ■ (also **scis·sor**) [often as adj.] an action in which two things cross each other or open and close like the blades of a pair of scissors. [ME: from OFr. *cisoires,* from late L. *cisoria,* pl. of *cisorium* 'cutting instrument,' from *cis-,* var. of *caes-,* stem of *caedere* 'to cut.']

scis·sor-tailed fly·catch·er ▶**n.** (also **scis·sor·tail**) a tyrant flycatcher (*Tyrannus forficatus*) with a very long forked tail, found in the southern US and noted for its spectacular aerial display.

scle·ra /ˈskli(ə)rə/ ▶**n.** Anat. the white outer layer of the eyeball, continuous with the cornea at the front. — **scle·ral adj.** [19th C.: mod. L., from Gk. *sklēros* 'hard.']

scle·ren·chy·ma /skliˈreNGkəmə/ ▶**n.** Bot. strengthening tissue in a plant, formed from thick-walled cells. — **scle·ren·chym·a·tous** /ˌsklireNGˈkimətəs/ **adj.** [19th C.: mod. L., from Gk. *sklēros* 'hard' + *enkhuma* 'infusion.']

scle·rite /ˈskli(ə)rīt/ ▶**n.** Zool. a component section of an exoskeleton, esp. each of the plates forming the skeleton of an arthropod. [19th C.: from Gk. *sklēros* 'hard' + -ITE[1].]

scle·ri·tis /skləˈrītis/ ▶**n.** Med. inflammation of the sclera.

sclero- ▶**comb. form** hard; hardened; hardening. [from Gk. *sklēros* 'hard.']

scle·ro·der·ma /ˌskli(ə)rəˈdərmə; ˌskler-/ ▶**n.** Med. a chronic hardening and contraction of the skin and connective tissue, either locally or throughout the body.

scle·roid /ˈskli(ə)rˌoid; ˈskler-/ ▶**adj.** Bot. & Zool. having a hard or hardened texture. [19th C.: from Gk. *sklēros* 'hard.']

scle·ro·pro·tein /ˌskli(ə)rōˈprōtē(ə)n/ ▶**n.** Biochem. an insoluble structural protein such as keratin, collagen, or elastin.

scle·rosed /skliˈrōst; -ˈrōzd; ˈskli(ə)rōst; ˈskler-; -ōzd/ ▶**adj.** Med. (esp. of blood vessels) affected by sclerosis.

scle·ro·sis /skləˈrōsis/ ▶**n.** Med. abnormal hardening of body tissue. ■ see MULTIPLE SCLEROSIS. ■ fig. excessive resistance to change. [ME: via med. L. from Gk. *sklērōsis,* from *sklēroun* 'harden.']

scle·ro·ther·a·py /ˌskli(ə)rəˈTHerəpē/ ▶**n.** Med. the treatment of varicose blood vessels by the injection of an irritant that causes inflammation, coagulation of blood, and narrowing of the blood vessel wall.

scle·rot·ic /skləˈrätik/ ▶**adj. 1** Med. of or having sclerosis. ■ fig. becoming rigid and unresponsive; losing the ability to adapt: *sclerotic management.* **2** Anat. of or relating to the sclera. ▶**n.** another term for SCLERA.

scle·ro·tin /ˈskli(ə)rətn; ˈskler-/ ▶**n.** Biochem. a structural protein that forms the cuticles of insects and is hardened and darkened by a natural tanning process in which protein chains are cross-linked by quinone groups. [1940s: from SCLERO- 'hardened,' on the pattern of such words as *keratin.*]

scle·ro·ti·um /skləˈrōSHēəm/ ▶**n.** (pl. **-ti·a** /-SHēə/) Bot. the hard dark resting body of certain fungi, consisting of a mass of hyphal threads, capable of remaining dormant for long periods. [19th C.: mod. L., from Gk. *sklēros* 'hard.']

scle·ro·tized /ˈskli(ə)rəˌtīzd; ˈskler-/ (also **scle·ro·tised**) ▶**adj.** Entomol. (of an insect's body, or part of one) hardened by conversion into sclerotin. — **scle·ro·ti·za·tion** /ˌskli(ə)rətəˈzāSHən; ˌskler-/ **n.**

scle·ro·tome /ˈskli(ə)rəˌtōm; ˈskler-/ ▶**n.** Embryol. the part of each somite in a vertebrate embryo giving rise to bone or other skeletal tissue. Compare with DERMATOME, MYOTOME.

scle·rous /ˈskli(ə)rəs; ˈskler-/ ▶**adj.** (of tissue) hardened or bony. [19th C.: from Gk. *sklēros* 'hard' + -OUS.]

scoff¹ /skôf; skäf/ ▶ **v.** [intrans.] speak to someone or about something in a scornfully derisive or mocking way: *department officials scoffed at the allegations.* ▶ **n.** an expression of scornful derision. — **scoff·er n. scoff·ing·ly adv.** [ME (first used as a noun in the sense 'mockery, scorn'): perh. of Scand. origin.]

scoff² informal ▶ **v.** [trans.] eat (something) quickly and greedily: *she scoffed down several chops.* ▶ **n.** food. [18th C. (as a v.): orig. a var. of Scots and dial. *scaff*. The noun is from Afrik. *schoff*, representing Du. *schoft* 'quarter of a day,' (by extension) 'meal.']

scoff·law /'skôf,lô; 'skäf-/ ▶ **n.** informal a person who flouts the law, esp. by failing to comply with a law that is difficult to enforce effectively.

scold /skōld/ ▶ **v.** [trans.] remonstrate with or rebuke (someone) angrily. ▶ **n.** archaic a woman who nags or grumbles constantly. — **scold·er n. scold·ing n. & adj.** [ME (n.): prob. from ON *skáld* 'skald.']

sco·li·o·sis /,skōlē'ōsis/ ▶ **n.** Med. abnormal lateral curvature of the spine. — **sco·li·ot·ic** /-'ätik/ **adj.** [18th C.: mod. L., from Gk., from *skolios* 'bent.']

scom·broid /'skäm,broid/ Zool. ▶ **n.** a fish of the mackerel family (Scombridae), or one of a larger group that also includes the barracudas and billfishes. ▶ **adj.** of or relating to fish of this family or group. [19th C.: from mod. L. *Scombroidea*, from Gk. *skombros* 'tuna' or 'mackerel.']

sconce¹ /skäns/ ▶ **n.** **1** a holder of a candle or other light source, attached to a wall with an ornamental bracket. **2** a flaming torch or candle secured in such a holder. [ME ('portable lantern'): shortening of OFr. *esconse* 'lantern,' or from med. L. *sconsa*. from L. *absconsa (laterna)* 'dark (lantern),' from *abscondere* 'to hide.']

sconce¹ 1

sconce² ▶ **n.** archaic a small fort or earthwork. ■ a protective shelter or screen. [ME ('partition,' perh. from SCONCE¹; later senses, the late 16th C.): from Du. *schans* 'brushwood,' from Mid. High Ger. *schanze*.]

scone /skōn; skän/ ▶ **n.** a small unsweetened or lightly sweetened biscuitlike cake. [16th C. (Scots): perh. from MDu. *schoon(broot)* 'fine (bread).']

scooch /skōōCH/ (also **scootch**) ▶ **v.** [intrans.] informal **1** crouch or squat. **2** move in or pass through a restricted space: *waiters kept trying to scooch by.* ■ [trans.] move (something) a short distance or into a restricted space: *scooch your sleeping bags close together.* [19th C.: prob. alt. of SCROOCH; in sense 2 prob. influenced by SCOOT.]

scoop /skōōp/ ▶ **n.** **1** a utensil resembling a spoon, with a long handle and a deep bowl. ■ a short-handled deep shovel. ■ a moving bowl-shaped part of a machine designed to dig or dredge. ■ a long-handled spoonlike surgical instrument. ■ a quantity taken up by a scoop. **2** informal a piece of news published or broadcast in advance of rival media. ■ (**the scoop**) the latest information. ▶ **v.** [trans.] **1** pick up and move (something) with a scoop. ■ create (a hollow or hole) with or as if with a scoop. ■ pick up (someone or something) in a swift, fluid movement. **2** informal publish a news story before (a rival reporter, newspaper, or radio or television station). — **scoop·er n. scoop·ful n.** [ME: from MDu., Mid. Low Ger. *schōpe* 'waterwheel bucket'; from West Gmc. 'draw water'; akin to SHAPE, V.]

scoot /skōōt/ ▶ **v.** [intrans.] informal go or leave quickly.

scootch /skōōCH/ ▶ **v.** var. of SCOOCH.

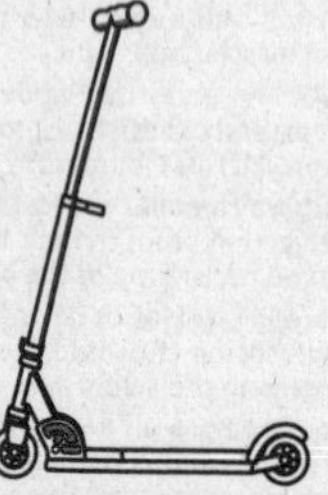
scooter 3

scoot·er /'skōōtər/ ▶ **n.** **1** (also **mo·tor scoot·er**) a light two-wheeled open motor vehicle on which the driver sits with legs together and feet resting on a floorboard. **2** [often with adj.] any small, light, vehicle able to travel quickly across water, ice, or snow. **3** a recreational vehicle consisting of a footboard mounted on two wheels and a long steering handle, propelled by resting one foot on the footboard and pushing the other against the ground. ▶ **v.** [intrans.] travel or ride on a scooter. — **scoot·er·ist** /-ist/ **n.**

sco·pa /'skōpə/ ▶ **n.** (pl. **-pae** /-pē/) Zool. a small brushlike tuft of hairs on some insects, esp. that on which pollen collects on the leg of a bee. [19th C.: from L. *scopae* (pl.) 'twigs, broom.']

scope¹ /skōp/ ▶ **n.** the extent of the area or subject matter that something deals with or to which it is relevant. ■ the opportunity or possibility to do or deal with something. ■ Naut. the length of cable extended when a ship rides at anchor. ■ Ling. & Logic the range of the effect of an operator such as a quantifier or conjunction. [16th C.: from Ital. *scopo* 'aim,' from Gk. *skopos* 'target,' from *skeptesthai* 'look out.']

scope² informal ▶ **n.** a telescope, microscope, or other device having a name ending in *-scope*. ▶ **v.** [trans.] informal look at carefully; scan. ■ assess; weigh up. [17th C. (as a n.): shortened form. The verb dates from the 1970s.]

-scope ▶ **comb. form** denoting an instrument for observing, viewing, or examining: *microscope* | *telescope*. — **-scopic comb. form** in corresponding adjectives. [from mod. L. *-scopium*, from Gk. *skopein* 'look at.']

Scopes Trial /skōps/ (also **Scopes Monkey Trial**) the 1925 trial of John T. Scopes, charged with violating Tennessee state law for teaching evolution in a public school. Prosecuted by a team including William Jennings Bryan and defended by Clarence Darrow, Scopes was pronounced guilty, until the verdict was overturned six months later.

sco·pol·a·mine /skə'pälə,mēn/ ▶ **n.** Chem. a poisonous plant alkaloid, $C_{17}H_{21}NO_4$, used to counter motion sickness and as a preoperative medication for examination of the eye. It is obtained chiefly from plants of the nightshade family (esp. genus *Scopolia*).

scops owl /skäps/ ▶ **n.** a small owl (genus *Otus*, family Strigidae) with distinctive ear tufts, found in Europe, Africa, and Asia. [18th C.: *scops* from mod. L. *Scops* (former genus name), from Gk. *skōps*.]

scop·u·la /skäpyələ/ ▶ **n.** (pl. **scop·u·lae** /'skäpyəlē; 'skäpyə,lī/) Zool. a small brushlike structure, esp. on the legs of spiders. [19th C.: from late L., dimin. of L. *scopa* (see SCOPA).]

-scopy ▶ **comb. form** indicating viewing, observation, or examination, typically with an instrument having a name ending in *-scope*: *endoscopy* | *microscopy*. [from Gk. *skopia* 'observation,' from *skopein* 'examine, look at.']

scor·bu·tic /skôr'byōōtik/ ▶ **adj.** relating to or affected with scurvy. See also ANTISCORBUTIC. [17th C.: from mod. L. *scorbuticus*, from med. L. *scorbutus* 'scurvy,' perh. from Mid. Low Ger. *schorbūk* (from *schoren* 'to break' + *būk* 'belly').]

scorch /skôrCH/ ▶ **v.** **1** [trans.] burn the surface of (something) with flame or heat. ■ [intrans.] become burned when exposed to heat or a flame. ■ [often as adj.] (**scorched**) (of the heat of the sun) cause (vegetation or a place) to become dried out and lifeless. **2** [no obj., with adverbial of direction] informal (of a person or vehicle) move very fast. ▶ **n.** the burning or charring of the surface of something. ■ Bot. a form of plant necrosis, typically of fungal origin, marked by browning of leaf margins. [ME: perh. rel. to ON *skorpna* 'be shriveled.']

scorched earth pol·i·cy ▶ **n.** a military strategy of burning or destroying crops or other resources that might be of use to an invading enemy force. ■ fig. a strategy that involves taking extreme action.

scorch·er /'skôrCHər/ ▶ **n.** [usu. in sing.] informal **1** a day or period of very hot weather. **2** a remarkable or extreme example of something, in particular: ■ a very powerfully struck ball. ■ a sensational book or film. ■ a heated or violent argument.

scorch·ing /'skôrCHiNG/ ▶ **adj.** very hot. ■ (of criticism) harsh; severe. ■ informal very fast. — **scorch·ing·ly adv.**

score /skôr/ ▶ **n.** **1** the number of points, goals, runs, etc., achieved in a game. ■ the number of points, goals, runs, etc., achieved by an individual player or a team in a game. ■ informal an act of gaining a point, goal, or run in a game. ■ a rating or grade, such as a mark achieved in a test. ■ (**the score**) informal the state of affairs; the real facts about the present situation. ■ informal an act of buying illegal drugs. ■ informal the proceeds of a crime. **2** (pl. same) a group or set of twenty or about twenty. ■ (**scores of**) a large amount or number of something. **3** a written representation of a musical composition showing all the vocal and instrumental parts arranged one below the other. ■ the music composed for a movie or play. **4** a notch or line cut or scratched into a surface. ■ hist. a running account kept by marks against a customer's name, typically in a tavern. ▶ **v.** [trans.] **1** gain (a point, goal, run, etc.) in a competitive game: *Penn State scored two touchdowns.* ■ decide on the score to be awarded to (a competitor). ■ gain (a number of points) for a competitor; be worth. ■ decide on the scores to be awarded in (a game or competition). ■ [intrans.] record the score during a game; act as scorer. ■ Baseball cause (a teammate) to score. ■ informal secure (a success or an advantage). ■ [intrans.] informal be successful: [with complement] *his new movie scored big.* ■ informal buy or acquire (something, typically illegal drugs). ■ [intrans.] informal succeed in attracting a sexual partner, typically for a casual encounter. **2** orchestrate or arrange (a piece of music), typically for a specified instrument or instruments. ■ compose the music for (a movie or play). **3** cut or scratch a notch or line on (a surface). ■ hist. record (a total owed) by making marks against a customer's name. ■ Med. & Biol. examine (experimentally treated cells, bacterial colonies, etc.), making a record of the number showing a particular character.
– PHRASES **keep (the) score** register the score of a game as it is made. **know the score** informal be aware of the essential facts about a situation. **on that** (or **this**) **score** so far as that (or this) is concerned. **score points** outdo another person, esp. in an argument. **settle a** (or **the**) **score 1** take revenge on someone for something damaging that they have done in the past. **2** dated pay off a debt or other obligation. — **score·less adj. scor·er n.** [OE *scoru* 'set of twenty,' from Old Norse *skor* 'notch, tally, twenty,' of Gmc. origin; rel. to SHEAR. The verb (ME) is from ON *skora* 'make an incision.']

score·board /'skôr,bôrd/ ▶ **n.** a large board on which the score in a game or match is displayed.

score·card /'skôr,kärd/ (also **score·sheet** or **score·book**) ▶ **n.** (in sports) a card, sheet, or book in which scores are entered.

score·keep·er /'skôr,kēpər/ ▶ **n.** a person who keeps the score of a game.

sco·ri·a /'skôrēə/ ▶ **n.** (pl. **sco·ri·ae** /'skôrē-ē/) basaltic lava ejected as fragments from a volcano, typically with a frothy texture. ■ slag separated from molten metal during smelting. — **sco·ri·a·ceous** /ˌskôrēˈāsHəs/ **adj.** [ME: via L. from Gk. *skōria* 'refuse,' from *skōr* 'dung.']

scorn /skôrn/ ▸ **n.** the feeling or belief that someone or something is worthless or despicable; contempt. ■ [in sing.] archaic a person viewed with such feeling. ■ archaic a statement or gesture indicating such feeling. ▸ **v.** [trans.] feel or express contempt or derision for. ■ reject (something) in a contemptuous way. ■ [no obj., with infin.] refuse to do something because one is too proud: *she scorned to stoop to such tactics.*
– PHRASES **pour** (or **heap**) **scorn on** speak with contempt or mockery of. — **scorn·er n.** (rare). [ME: shortening of OFr. *escarn* (n.), *escharnir* (v.), of Gmc. origin.]

scorn·ful /ˈskôrnfəl/ ▸ **adj.** feeling or expressing contempt or derision. — **scorn·ful·ly adv. scorn·ful·ness n.**

Scor·pi·o /ˈskôrpēˌō/ Astrol. the eighth sign of the zodiac (the Scorpion), which the sun enters about October 23. ■ **(a Scorpio)** (pl. **-os**) a person born when the sun is in this sign. — **Scor·pi·an** /-pēən/ **n. & adj.** [L.]

scor·pi·oid /ˈskôrpēˌoid/ ▸ **adj.** Zool. of, relating to, or resembling a scorpion. ■ Bot. (of a flower cluster) curled up at the end, and uncurling as the flowers develop. [19th C.: from Gk. *skorpioeidēs*, from *skorpios* 'scorpion.']

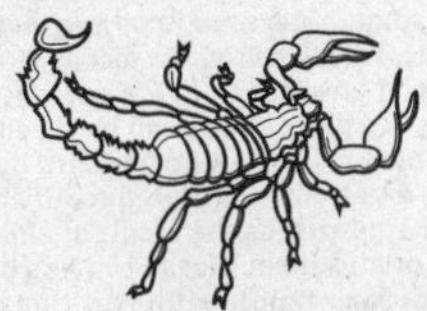

scorpion

scor·pi·on /ˈskôrpēən/ ▸ **n.** a terrestrial arachnid (order Scorpiones) with lobsterlike pincers and a poisonous sting at the end of its jointed tail, which it can hold curved over the back. Most kinds live in tropical and subtropical areas. ■ used in names of other arachnids and insects resembling a scorpion, e.g., **false scorpion, water scorpion.** ■ **(the Scorpion)** the zodiacal sign Scorpio or the constellation Scorpius. ■ **(scorpions)** literary a whip with metal points. [with allusion to 1 Kings 12:11.] [ME: via OFr. from L. *scorpio(n-)*, based on Gk. *skorpios* 'scorpion.']

scor·pi·on·fish /ˈskôrpēənˌfisH/ ▸ **n.** (pl. same or **-fish·es**) a chiefly bottom-dwelling marine fish (family Scorpaenidae) that is typically red in color and has spines on the head that are sometimes venomous.

scor·pi·on·fly /ˈskôrpēənˌflī/ (also **scor·pi·on fly**) ▸ **n.** (pl. **-flies**) a slender predatory insect (Panorpidae and other families, order Mecoptera) with membranous wings, long legs, and a downward-pointing beak. The terminal swollen section of the male's abdomen is carried curved up like a scorpion's stinger.

Scor·pi·us /ˈskôrpēəs/ Astron. a large constellation (the Scorpion). It contains the red giant Antares. [L.]

scor·zo·ne·ra /ˌskôrzəˈni(ə)rə/ ▸ **n.** a plant (*Scorzonera hispanica*) of the daisy family with tapering purple-brown edible roots. ■ the root of this plant used as a vegetable. [17th C.: from Ital., from *scorzone*, from an alt. of med. L. *curtio(n-)* 'venomous snake' (against whose venom the plant may have been regarded as an antidote).]

Scot /skät/ ▸ **n.** a native of Scotland or a person of Scottish descent. ■ a member of a Gaelic people that migrated from Ireland to Scotland around the late 5th century. [OE *Scottas* (pl.), from late L. *Scottus*, of unknown ultimate origin.]

Scot. ▸ **abbr.** Scotland. ■ Scottish.

Scotch /skäcH/ ▸ **adj.** old-fashioned term for SCOTTISH. ▸ **n.** **1** Scotch whisky. **2** [as pl. n.] **(the Scotch)** dated the people of Scotland. **3** dated the form of English spoken in Scotland. — **Scotch·man** (dated) **n.** (pl. **-men**) **Scotch·wom·an** (dated) **n.** (pl. **-wom·en**) [16th C.: contr. of SCOTTISH.]

scotch[1] /skäcH/ ▸ **v. 1** [trans.] decisively put an end to. ■ archaic render (something regarded as dangerous) temporarily harmless. **2** [with obj. and adverbial] wedge (someone or something) somewhere: *he soon scotched himself against a wall.* ▸ **n.** archaic a wedge placed under a wheel or other rolling object to prevent its moving or slipping. [17th C. (as a n.): of unknown origin; perh. rel. to SKATE[1].]

scotch[2] ▸ **v.** [trans.] archaic cut or score the skin or surface of. ▸ **n.** archaic a cut or score in skin or another surface. [ME: of unknown origin.]

Scotch bon·net (also **Scotch bon·net pep·per**) ▸ **n.** another term for HABANERO.

Scotch broth ▸ **n.** a traditional Scottish soup made from beef or mutton stock with pearl barley and vegetables.

Scotch egg ▸ **n.** a hard-boiled egg enclosed in sausage meat, rolled in breadcrumbs, and fried.

Scotch pine ▸ **n.** a long-lived, medium-sized Eurasian pine tree (*Pinus sylvestris*) extensively planted for its timber and other products. It is well established in the northeastern US and the Great Lakes region.

Scotch tape trademark ▸ **n.** transparent adhesive tape. ▸ **v.** **(Scotch-tape)** [with obj. and adverbial] stick with transparent adhesive tape.

Scotch whis·ky (also **Scotch whis·key**) ▸ **n.** whisky distilled in Scotland, esp. from malted barley.

sco·ter /ˈskōtər/ ▸ **n.** (pl. same or **-ters**) a northern diving duck (genus *Melanitta*), esp. of Europe of North America. The male has mainly black plumage. [17th C.: of unknown origin.]

scot-free ▸ **adv.** without suffering any punishment or injury: *they will get off scot-free.* [former *scot*, meaning 'a tax.']

sco·tia /ˈskōsHə/ ▸ **n.** (chiefly in classical architecture) a concave molding, esp. at the base of a column. [16th C.: via L. from Gk. *skotia*, from *skotos* 'darkness,' with ref. to the shadow produced.]

Scot·land /ˈskätlənd/ a country in northern Great Britain, forming part of the United Kingdom; pop. 4,957,300; capital, Edinburgh. See map at UNITED KINGDOM.

Scot·land Yard the headquarters of the London Metropolitan Police. ■ used to allude to the Criminal Investigation Department of the London Metropolitan Police force.

sco·to·ma /skəˈtōmə/ ▸ **n.** (pl. **-mas** or **-ma·ta** /-mətə/) Med. a partial loss of vision or a blind spot in an otherwise normal visual field. — **sco·tom·a·tous** /-mətəs/ **adj.** [16th C.: via late L. from Gk. *skotōma*, from *skotoun* 'darken,' from *skotos* 'darkness.']

sco·top·ic /skəˈtōpik; -ˈtäpik/ ▸ **adj.** Physiol. relating to or denoting vision in dim light, believed to involve chiefly the rods of the retina. Often contrasted with PHOTOPIC. [20th C.: from Gk. *skotos* 'darkness' + -OPIA + -IC.]

Scots /skäts/ ▸ **adj.** another term for SCOTTISH: [northern var., orig. as *Scottis.*] ▸ **n.** the form of English used in Scotland.

Scots·man /ˈskätsmən/ ▸ **n.** (pl. **-men**) a male native or national of Scotland or a man of Scottish descent.

Scots·wom·an /ˈskätsˌwo͝omən/ ▸ **n.** (pl. **-wom·en**) a female native or national of Scotland or a woman of Scottish descent.

Scott[1] /skät/, Dred (*c.* 1795–1858), US slave. He brought suit for his freedom based on the fact that he had lived in free territories for five years, but the US Supreme Court ruled against him in 1857.

Scott[2], Sir Robert Falcon (1868–1912), English explorer. He and four companions arrived at the South Pole in January 1912 to discover that Roald Amundsen had beaten them by a month. Scott and his companions died on the journey back.

Scott[3], Sir Walter (1771–1832), Scottish writer. He established the form of the historical novel in Britain in such works as *Waverley* (1814) and *Ivanhoe* (1819).

Scott[4], Winfield (1786–1866), US general; known as **Old Fuss and Feathers.** A hero of the War of 1812, he became supreme commander of the US Army 1841–61. During the Mexican War, he waged a victorious campaign from Veracruz to Mexico City in 1847.

Scot·ti·cism /ˈskätiˌsizəm/ ▸ **n.** a characteristically Scottish phrase, word, or idiom. [18th C.: from late L. *Scot(t)icus* + -ISM.]

Scot·tie /ˈskätē/ ▸ **n.** informal (also **Scot·tie dog**) a Scottish terrier.

Scot·tish /ˈskätisH/ ▸ **adj.** of or relating to Scotland or its people: *the Scottish Highlands | Scottish dancing.* ▸ **n.** [as pl. n.] **(the Scottish)** the people of Scotland. See also SCOTS. — **Scot·tish·ness n.**

Scot·tish rite ▸ **n.** a ceremonial rite in a Masonic order.

Scot·tish ter·ri·er ▸ **n.** a small terrier of a rough-haired short-legged breed.

Scotts·dale /ˈskätsˌdāl/ a city in south central Arizona, east of Phoenix; pop. 202,705.

scoun·drel /ˈskoundrəl/ ▸ **n.** a dishonest or unscrupulous person; a rogue. — **scoun·drel·ism** /-ˌlizəm/ **n. scoun·drel·ly adj.** [16th C.: of unknown origin.]

scour[1] /skou(ə)r/ ▸ **v.** [trans.] **1** clean or brighten the surface of (something) by rubbing it hard, typically with an abrasive or detergent: *he scoured the bathtub.* ■ remove (dirt or unwanted matter) by rubbing in such a way. ■ (of water or a watercourse) make (a channel or pool) by flowing quickly over something and removing soil or rock. **2** archaic administer a strong purgative to. ▸ **n. 1** the action of scouring or the state of being scoured, esp. by swift-flowing water. ■ [in sing.] an act of rubbing something hard to clean or brighten it. **2** (also **scours**) diarrhea in livestock, esp. cattle and pigs. — **scour·er n.** [ME: from MDu., Mid. Low Ger. *schūren*, from OFr. *escurer*, from late L. *excurare* 'clean (off),' from *ex-* 'away' + *curare* 'to clean.']

scour[2] ▸ **v.** [trans.] subject (a place, text, etc.) to a thorough search in order to locate something. ■ [no obj., with adverbial of direction] move rapidly in a particular direction, esp. in search or pursuit of someone or something: *he scoured up the ladder.* [ME: rel. to obs. *scour* 'moving hastily,' of unknown origin.]

scourge /skərj/ ▸ **n. 1** hist. a whip used as an instrument of punishment. **2** a person or thing that causes great trouble or suffering. ▸ **v.** [trans.] **1** hist. whip (someone) as a punishment. **2** cause great suffering to. — **scourg·er n.** (hist.). [ME: shortening of OFr. *escorge* (n.), *escorgier* (v.), from L. *ex-* 'thoroughly' + *corrigia* 'thong, whip.']

scour·ing rush ▸ **n.** a horsetail (genus *Equisetum*, in particular *E. hyemale*) with a very rough ridged stem, formerly used for scouring and polishing.

scout /skout/ ▸ **n. 1** a soldier or other person sent out ahead of a main force so as to gather information about the enemy's position, strength, or movements. ■ a ship or aircraft employed for reconnaissance, esp. a small fast aircraft. ■ short for TALENT SCOUT. ■ [usu. in sing.] an instance of gathering information, esp. by reconnoitering an area. **2** (also **Scout**) a Boy Scout or Girl Scout. **3** informal, dated a man or boy. ▸ **v.** [intrans.] make a

search for someone or something in various places. ■ (esp. of a soldier) go ahead of a main force so as to gather information about an enemy's position, strength, or movements. ■ [trans.] explore or examine (a place or area of business) so as to gather information about it. ■ look for suitably talented people for recruitment to one's own organization or sports team.
– PHRASES **Scout's honor** the oath taken by a Boy Scout or Girl Scout. ■ informal used to indicate that one has the same honorable standards associated with Scouts and so will stand by a promise or tell the truth. — **scout·er** n. [ME (as a v.): from OFr. *escouter* 'listen,' earlier *ascolter*, from L. *auscultare*.]

scout·ing /'skoutiNG/ ▶ n. 1 the action of gathering information about enemy forces or an area. ■ the activity of a talent scout. 2 (also **Scout·ing**) the characteristic activity and occupation of a Boy Scout or Girl Scout; the Scout movement.

scout·mas·ter /'skout,mastər/ ▶ n. the adult in charge of a group of Boy Scouts.

scow /skou/ ▶ n. a wide-beamed sailing dinghy. ■ a flat-bottomed boat with sloping ends used as a lighter and in other harbor services. [17th C.: from Du. *schouw* 'ferryboat.']

scowl /skoul/ ▶ n. an angry or bad-tempered expression. ▶ v. [intrans.] frown in an angry or bad-tempered way. — **scowl·er** n. [ME: prob. of Scand. origin; cf. Dan. *skule* 'scowl.']

SCPO ▶ abbr. Senior Chief Petty Officer.

scrab·ble /'skrabəl/ ▶ v. [intrans.] scratch or grope around with one's fingers to find, collect, or hold on to something. ■ (of an animal) scratch at something with its claws. ■ [with adverbial of direction] scramble or crawl quickly. ■ make great efforts to get somewhere or achieve something. ▶ n. 1 [in sing.] an act of scratching or scrambling for something. ■ a struggle to get somewhere or achieve something. 2 (**Scrabble**) trademark a board game in which players use lettered tiles to create words in a crossword fashion. — **scrab·bler** n. [16th C.: from MDu. *schrabbelen*, frequentative of *schrabben* 'to scrape.']

scrag /skrag/ ▶ v. (**scragged, scrag·ging**) [trans.] informal, esp. Brit. handle roughly; beat up. ■ dated, informal kill, esp. by strangling or hanging. ▶ n. 1 an unattractively thin person or animal. 2 dated, informal a person's neck. [16th C.: perh. an alt. of Scots and north. Engl. *crag* 'neck.']

scrag·gly /'skraglē/ (also **scrag·gy** /'skragē/) ▶ adj. (**-gli·er, -gli·est**) (of a person or animal) thin and bony. ■ ragged, thin, or untidy in form or appearance. ■ (of a plant, tree, or shrubbery) sparsely foliated or having thin, uneven growth. — **scrag·gi·ly** /-əlē/ adv. **scrag·gli·ness** or **scrag·gi·ness** n.

scram /skram/ informal ▶ v. (**scrammed, scram·ming**) 1 [intrans., usu. in imper.] go away from or get out of somewhere quickly. 2 [trans.] shut down (a nuclear reactor) in an emergency. ▶ n. the emergency shutdown of a nuclear reactor. [20th C.: prob. from the verb SCRAMBLE.]

scram·ble /'skrambəl/ ▶ v. 1 [no obj., with adverbial of direction] make one's way quickly or awkwardly up a steep gradient or over rough ground by using one's hands as well as one's feet. ■ move hurriedly or clumsily from or into a particular place or position. ■ (**scramble into**) put (clothes) on hurriedly. ■ [trans.] informal perform (an action) or achieve (a result) hurriedly, clumsily, or with difficulty. ■ [with infin.] struggle or compete with others for something in an eager or uncontrolled and undignified way. ■ [trans.] (often **be scrambled**) order (a fighter aircraft or its pilot) to take off immediately in an emergency or for action. ■ [intrans.] (of a fighter aircraft or its pilot) take off in such a way. ■ [intrans.] Football (of a quarterback) run around with the ball behind the line of scrimmage while looking for an open receiver. ■ [intrans.] Football run forward with the ball when unable to pass to an open receiver. 2 [trans.] make (something) jumbled or muddled: *alcohol has scrambled his brains.* ■ cook (eggs) by beating them with a little liquid and then cooking and stirring them gently. ■ make (a broadcast transmission, a telephone message, or electronic data) unintelligible unless received by an appropriate decoding device. ▶ n. [usu. in sing.] 1 a difficult or hurried clamber up or over something. ■ a walk up steep terrain involving the use of one's hands. ■ an eager or uncontrolled and undignified struggle with others to obtain or achieve something. ■ an emergency takeoff by fighter aircraft. 2 a disordered mixture of things. — **scram·bling** /-b(ə)liNG/ n. [16th C.: imitative.]

scram·bler /'skramb(ə)lər/ ▶ n. 1 a person or thing that scrambles, esp. a device for scrambling a broadcast transmission, a telephone message, or electronic data. 2 a plant with long slender stems supported by other plants.

Scran·ton /'skrantn/ a city in northeastern Pennsylvania; pop. 76,415.

scrap[1] /skrap/ ▶ n. 1 a small piece or amount of something, esp. one that is left over after the greater part has been used. ■ (**scraps**) bits of uneaten food left after a meal, esp. when fed to animals. ■ used to emphasize the lack or smallness of something: *every scrap of land.* ■ informal a small person or animal, esp. one regarded with affection or sympathy. ■ a particularly small thing of its kind. 2 (also **scrap metal**) discarded metal for reprocessing. ■ [often as adj.] any waste articles or discarded material, esp. that which can be put to another purpose. ▶ v. (**scrapped, scrap·ping**) [trans.] (often **be scrapped**) discard or remove from service (a retired, old, or inoperative vehicle, vessel, or machine), esp. so as to convert it to scrap metal. ■ abolish or cancel (something, esp. a plan, policy, or law) that is now regarded as unnecessary, unwanted, or unsuitable. [ME: from ON *skrap* 'scraps'; rel. to *skrapa* 'to scrape.']

scrap[2] informal ▶ n. a fight or quarrel, esp. a minor or spontaneous one. ▶ v. (**scrapped, scrap·ping**) [intrans.] engage in such a fight or quarrel. ■ compete fiercely. — **scrap·per** n. [17th C.: perh. from the n. SCRAPE.]

scrap·book /'skrap,bo͝ok/ ▶ n. a book of blank pages for sticking clippings, drawings, or pictures in. ▶ v. [intrans.] [usu. as n.] (**scrapbooking**) create a scrapbook as a hobby.

scrape /skrāp/ ▶ v. 1 [trans.] drag or pull a hard or sharp implement across (a surface or object) so as to remove dirt or other matter. ■ [with obj. and adverbial] use a sharp or hard implement to remove (dirt or unwanted matter) from something: *she scraped the mud off her shoes.* ■ [with obj. and adverbial] apply (a hard or sharp implement) in this way: *he scraped the razor across the stubble on his cheek.* ■ make (a hollow) by scraping away soil or rock. 2 rub or cause to rub by accident against a rough or hard surface, causing damage or injury. ■ [trans.] draw or move (something) along or over something else, making a harsh noise: *she scraped back her chair.* ■ [intrans.] move with or make such a sound: *prevent the gate's scraping along the ground.* ■ [intrans.] humorous play a violin or similar stringed instrument tunelessly. ■ [trans.] draw one's hair tightly back off the forehead. 3 [trans.] just manage to achieve; accomplish with great effort or difficulty: *he scraped a living as a tutor.* ■ (**scrape something together/up**) collect or accumulate something with difficulty. ■ [intrans.] try to save as much money as possible; economize. ■ [intrans.] (**scrape by/along**) manage to live with difficulty. ■ [no obj., with adverbial] narrowly pass by or through something: *room to scrape through between the tree and the rock.* ■ [no obj., with adverbial] barely manage to succeed in a particular undertaking. ▶ n. 1 an act or sound of scraping. ■ an injury or mark caused by scraping. ■ a place where soil has been scraped away, esp. a shallow hollow formed in the ground by a bird during a courtship display or for nesting. ■ Med., informal a procedure of dilatation of the cervix and curettage of the uterus, or the result of this. 2 informal an embarrassing or difficult predicament caused by one's own unwise behavior.
– PHRASES **scrape acquaintance with** dated contrive to get to know. **scrape the bottom of the barrel** informal be reduced to using things or people of the poorest quality because there is nothing else available. [OE *scrapian* 'scratch with the fingernails,' of Gmc. origin.]

scrap·er /'skrāpər/ ▶ n. a tool or device used for scraping, esp. for removing dirt, paint, ice, or other unwanted matter from a surface.

scrap heap ▶ n. a pile of discarded materials or articles.

scrap·ie /'skrāpē/ ▶ n. a disease of sheep involving the central nervous system, characterized by a lack of coordination causing affected animals to rub against trees and other objects for support, and thought to be caused by a viruslike agent such as a prion. [20th C.: from the verb SCRAPE + -IE.]

scrap·ing /'skrāpiNG/ ▶ n. the action or sound of something scraping or being scraped. ■ (usu. **scrapings**) a small amount of something that has been obtained by scraping it from a surface.

scrap met·al ▶ n. another term for SCRAP[1] (sense 2).

scrap·ple /'skrapəl/ ▶ n. scraps of pork or other meat stewed with cornmeal and shaped into loaves for slicing and frying. [19th C.: dimin. of the noun SCRAP[1].]

scrap·py /'skrapē/ ▶ adj. (**-pi·er, -pi·est**) 1 consisting of disorganized, untidy, or incomplete parts. [19th C.: deriv. of SCRAP[1].] 2 informal determined, argumentative, or pugnacious. [19th C.: deriv. of SCRAP[2].] — **scrap·pi·ly** /-əlē/ adv. **scrap·pi·ness** n.

scratch /skraCH/ ▶ v. 1 [trans.] score or mark the surface of (something) with a sharp or pointed object. ■ make a long, narrow superficial wound in the skin of. ■ rub (a part of one's body) with one's fingernails to relieve itching. ■ [with obj. and adverbial] make (a mark or hole) by scoring a surface with a sharp or pointed object: *names scratched on the windowpanes.* ■ write (something) hurriedly or awkwardly. ■ [with obj. and adverbial] remove (something) from something else by pulling a sharp implement over it: *he scratched away the plaster.* ■ [intrans.] make a rasping or grating noise by scraping something over a hard surface: *the dog scratched to be let in.* ■ [intrans.] [often as n.] (**scratching**) play a record using the scratch technique (see sense 1 of the n. below.) ■ [intrans.] (of a bird or mammal, esp. a chicken) rake the ground with the beak or claws in search of food. ■ accomplish (something) with great effort or difficulty: *he scratches out a living growing strawberries.* 2 [trans.] cancel or strike out (writing) with a pen or pencil. ■ withdraw (a competitor) from a competition. ■ [intrans.] (of a competitor) withdraw from a competition. ■ cancel or abandon (an undertaking or project): *the schedule has been scratched.* ▶ n. 1 a mark or wound made by scratching. ■ [in sing.] informal a slight or insignificant wound or injury. ■ [in sing.] an act or spell of scratching oneself to relieve itching. ■ a rasping or grating noise produced by something rubbing against a hard surface. ■ a rough hiss, caused by the friction of the stylus in the groove, heard when a record is played. ■ a technique, used esp. in rap music, of stopping a record by hand and moving it back and forth to give a rhythmic scratching effect. 2 the starting point in a handicap for a competitor receiving no odds. [orig. denoting a boundary or starting line for sports competitors.] ■ Golf a handicap of zero, indicating that a player is good enough to achieve par on a course. 3 informal money. ▶ adj. [attrib.] 1 assembled or made from whatever is available, and so unlikely to be of the highest quality: *two vessels set sail with scratch crews.* 2 (of a sports competitor or event) with no handicap given.
– PHRASES **from scratch** from the very beginning, esp. without utilizing or relying on any previous work for assistance. **scratch a —— and find a ——** used to suggest that an investigation of someone or something soon reveals their true nature. **scratch one's head** informal think hard in order to find a solution to something. ■ feel or express bewilderment. **scratch the surface** 1 deal with a matter only in the most superficial

way. **2** initiate the briefest investigation to discover something concealed. **up to scratch** up to the required standard; satisfactory. **you scratch my back and I'll scratch yours** proverb if you do me a favor, I'll return it. — **scratch·er** n. [ME: prob. a blend of the synonymous dial. words *scrat* and *cratch*, both of uncert. origin.]

scratch·pad /ˈskracн,pad/ (also **scratch pad**) ▶ **n.** a notepad. ■ Comput. a small, fast memory for the temporary storage of data.

scratch test ▶ **n.** a test for an allergic reaction in which a possible allergen is applied to a scratched area of skin.

scratch·y /ˈskracнē/ ▶ **adj.** (**scratch·i·er, scratch·i·est**) (esp. of a fabric or garment) having a rough, uncomfortable texture and tending to cause itching or discomfort. ■ (of a voice or sound) rough; grating. ■ (of a record) making a crackling or rough sound because of scratches on the surface. ■ (of writing or a drawing) done with quick and jagged strokes. — **scratch·i·ly** /-əlē/ **adv.** **scratch·i·ness** **n.**

scrawl /skrôl/ ▶ **v.** [trans.] write (something) in a hurried, careless way. ▶ **n.** an example of hurried, careless writing: *reams of handwritten scrawl.* ■ a note or message written in this way. — **scrawl·er** **n.** **scrawl·y** **adj.** [17th C.: appar. an alt. of the verb CRAWL, perh. influenced by obs. *scrawl* 'sprawl.']

scrawn·y /ˈskrônē/ ▶ **adj.** (**scrawn·i·er, scrawn·i·est**) (of a person or animal) unattractively thin and bony. ■ (of vegetation) meager or stunted. — **scrawn·i·ness** **n.** [19th C.: var. of dial. *scranny*; cf. archaic *scrannel* 'weak, feeble.']

scream /skrēm/ ▶ **v.** [intrans.] give a long, loud, piercing cry or cries expressing extreme emotion or pain. ■ [reporting verb] cry something in a high-pitched, frenzied way: *"Help!" he screamed.* ■ urgently and vociferously call attention to one's views or feelings, esp. ones of anger or distress. ■ make a loud, high-pitched sound. ■ [no obj., with adverbial of direction] move very rapidly with or as if with such a sound: *a shell screamed overhead.* ▶ **n.** a long, loud, piercing cry expressing extreme emotion or pain. ■ a high-pitched cry made by an animal. ■ a loud, piercing sound. ■ [in sing.] informal an irresistibly funny person, thing, or situation: *the movie's a scream.* [ME: origin uncert.; perh. from MDu.]

scream·er /ˈskrēmər/ ▶ **n.** **1** a person or thing that makes a screaming sound. **2** informal a thing remarkable for speed or impact. ■ an extremely fast ball or shot. ■ a sensational or very large headline. ■ dated a thing that causes screams of laughter. **3** a large gooselike South American waterbird (family Anhimidae) with a short bill, a sharp bony spur on each wing, and a harsh honking call.

scream·ing·ly /ˈskrēmiNGlē/ ▶ **adv.** [as submodifier] to a very great extent; extremely.

scream·ing meem·ies /ˈmēmēz/ ▶ **plural n.** an attack of panic or anxiety.

scree /skrē/ ▶ **n.** a mass of small loose stones that form or cover a slope on a mountain. ■ a slope covered with such stones. [18th C.: prob. a back-form. from the pl. *screes*, from ON *skritha* 'landslide.']

screech /skrēcн/ ▶ **v.** [intrans.] (of a person or animal) give a loud, harsh, piercing cry: *he screeched with pain.* ■ make a loud, harsh, squealing sound. ■ [no obj., with adverbial of direction] move rapidly with such a sound: *the van screeched around the corner.* ▶ **n.** a loud, harsh, piercing cry. ■ a loud, harsh, squealing sound. — **screech·er** **n.** **screech·y** **adj.** (**screech·i·er, screech·i·est**). [16th C.: alt. of archaic *scritch*, of imitative origin.]

screech owl ▶ **n.** a small American owl (*Otus asio*, family Strigidae) with a screeching call and distinctive ear tufts.

screed /skrēd/ ▶ **n.** **1** a long speech or piece of writing, typically one regarded as tedious. **2** a leveled layer of material (e.g., cement) applied to a floor or other surface. ■ a strip of plaster or other material placed on a surface as a guide to thickness. [ME: prob. a var. of the n. SHRED.]

screen /skrēn/ ▶ **n.** **1** a fixed or movable upright partition used to divide a room, to give shelter from drafts, heat, or light, or to provide concealment or privacy. ■ a thing providing concealment or protection: *parked behind a screen of trees.* ■ Mil. a detachment of troops or ships detailed to cover the movements of the main body. ■ [often with adj.] Archit. a partition of carved wood or stone separating the nave of a church from the chancel, choir, or sanctuary. See also ROOD SCREEN. ■ a frame with fine wire netting used in a window or doorway to keep out mosquitoes and other flying insects. ■ a part of an electrical or other instrument that protects it or prevents it from causing electromagnetic interference. ■ Electron. (also **screen grid**) a grid placed between the control grid and the anode of a valve to reduce the capacitance between these electrodes. **2** the surface of a cathode-ray tube or similar electronic device, esp. that of a television, VDT, or monitor, on which images and data are displayed. ■ a blank, typically white or silver surface on which a photographic image is projected. ■ (**the screen**) movies or television; the motion-picture industry. ■ the data or images displayed on a computer screen: *a help screen.* ■ Photog. a flat piece of ground glass on which the image formed by a camera lens is focused. **3** Print. a transparent, finely ruled plate or film used in halftone reproduction. **4** a large sieve or riddle, esp. one for sorting substances such as grain or coal into different sizes. ▶ **v.** [trans.] **1** conceal, protect, or shelter (someone or something) with a screen or something forming a screen: *a high hedge screened the yard.* ■ (**screen something off**) separate something from something else with or as if with a screen. ■ protect (someone) from something dangerous or unpleasant. ■ prevent from causing or protect from electromagnetic interference. **2** show (a movie or video) or broadcast (a television program). **3** test (a person or substance) for the presence or absence of a disease: *outpatients were screened for cervical cancer.* ■ check on or investigate (someone), typically to ascertain whether they are suitable for or can be trusted in a particular situation or job. ■ evaluate or analyze (something) for its suitability for a particular purpose or application. ■ (**screen someone/something out**) exclude someone or something after such evaluation or investigation. **4** pass (a substance such as grain or coal) through a large sieve or screen, esp. so as to sort it into different sizes. **5** Print. project (a photograph or other image) through a transparent ruled plate so as to be able to reproduce it as a halftone. — **screen·a·ble** **adj.** **screen·er** **n.** **screen·ful** /-,fo͝ol/ **n.** [ME: shortening of Old North. Fr. *escren*, of Gmc. origin.]

screen·ing /ˈskrēniNG/ ▶ **n.** **1** a showing of a movie, video, or television program. **2** the evaluation or investigation of something as part of a methodical survey, to assess suitability for a particular role or purpose. ■ the testing of a person or group of people for the presence of a disease or other condition. **3** (**screenings**) refuse separated by sieving grain.

screen·play /ˈskrēn,plā/ ▶ **n.** the script of a movie, including acting instructions and scene directions.

screen-print ▶ **v.** [trans.] [often as adj.] (**screen-printed**) force ink or metal onto (a surface) through a prepared screen of fine material so as to create a picture or pattern. ▶ **n.** (**screen print**) a picture or design produced by screen-printing.

screen sav·er (also **screen·sav·er**) ▶ **n.** Comput. a program that, after a set time, replaces an unchanging screen display with a moving image to prevent damage to the phosphor.

screen shot (also **screen·shot**) ▶ **n.** Comput. a photograph of the display on a computer screen to demonstrate the operation of a program.

screen test ▶ **n.** a filmed test to ascertain whether an actor is suitable for a film role. ▶ **v.** (**screen-test**) [trans.] give such a test to (an actor).

screen·writ·er /ˈskrēn,rītər/ ▶ **n.** a person who writes a screenplay. — **screen·writ·ing** /-,rītiNG/ **n.**

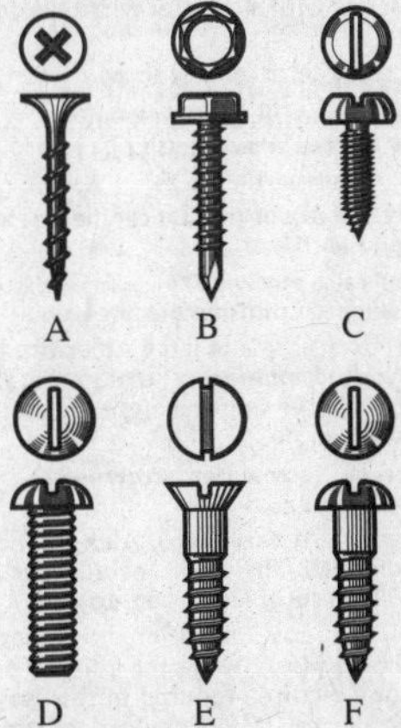

A sheetrock screw, flat head
B self-tapping screw, hex head
C sheet metal screw, pan head
D machine screw, round head
E wood screw, flat head
F wood screw, round head

screws

screw /skro͞o/ ▶ **n.** **1** a short, slender, sharp-pointed metal pin with a raised helical thread running around it and a slotted head, used to join things together by being rotated so that it pierces wood or other material and is held tightly in place. ■ a cylinder with a helical ridge or thread running around the outside (a **male screw**) that can be turned to seal an opening, apply pressure, adjust position, etc., esp. one fitting into a corresponding internal groove or thread (a **female screw**). ■ (**the screws**) hist. an instrument of torture acting in this way. ■ (also **screw pro·pel·ler**) a ship's or aircraft's propeller (considered as acting like a screw in moving through water or air). **2** an act of turning a screw or other object having a thread. **3** informal a prisoner's derogatory term for a prison guard or warden. **4** [in sing.] vulgar slang an act of sexual intercourse. ■ [with adj.] a sexual partner of a specified ability. ▶ **v.** [trans.] **1** fasten or tighten with a screw or screws. ■ rotate (something) so as to fit it into or on to a surface or object by means of a spiral thread. ■ [intrans.] (of an object) be attached or removed by being rotated in this way. ■ (**screw something around**) turn one's head or body around sharply. **2** (usu. **be**

screwed) informal cheat or swindle (someone), esp. by charging them too much for something. ■ (**screw something out of**) extort or force something, esp. money, from (someone). **3** vulgar slang have sexual intercourse with. ■ [intrans.] (of a couple) have sexual intercourse. ■ [in imper.] informal used to express anger or contempt: *Screw him!*
– PHRASES **have a screw loose** informal be slightly eccentric or mentally disturbed. **put the screws on** informal exert strong psychological pressure on (someone) so as to intimidate them into doing something.
– PHRASAL VERBS **screw around 1** vulgar slang have many different sexual partners. **2** informal fool around. **screw up** informal completely mismanage or mishandle a situation. **screw someone up** informal cause someone to be emotionally or mentally disturbed. **screw something up 1** tense the muscles of one's face or around one's eyes, typically so as to register an emotion or because of bright light. **2** informal cause something to fail or go wrong. **3** summon up one's courage. — **screw·a·ble** adj. **screw·er** n. [ME (n.): from OFr. *escroue* 'female screw, nut,' from L. *scrofa* 'sow,' later 'screw.']

screw·ball /'skro͞o,bôl/ ▶ n. **1** Baseball a pitched ball that moves in a direction opposite to that of a curveball. **2** informal a crazy or eccentric person. ▶ adj. informal crazy; absurd.

screw cap ▶ n. a round cap or lid that can be screwed on to a bottle or jar. — **screw-capped** adj.

screw·driv·er /'skro͞o,drīvər/ ▶ n. **1** a tool with a flattened or cross-shaped tip that fits into the head of a screw to turn it. **2** a cocktail made from vodka and orange juice.

screwed /skro͞od/ ▶ adj. **1** (of a bolt or other device) having a helical ridge or thread. **2** informal cheated or swindled. ■ ruined; rendered ineffective.

screwed-up ▶ adj. informal (of a person) emotionally disturbed; neurotic. ■ (of an event or a situation) spoiled by being badly managed or carried out.

screw eye ▶ n. a screw with a loop for passing a cord through, instead of a slotted head.

screw jack ▶ n. another term for JACK SCREW.

screw pine ▶ n. another term for PANDANUS.

screw pro·pel·ler ▶ n. see SCREW (sense 1).

screw thread ▶ n. see THREAD (sense 4).

screw top ▶ n. a round cap or lid that can be screwed on to a bottle or jar. — **screw-topped** adj.

screw·up /'skro͞o,əp/ (also **screw-up**) ▶ n. informal a situation that has been completely mismanaged or mishandled.

screw·worm /'skro͞o,wərm/ ▶ n. a large American blowfly larva (*Cochliomyia* (or **Callitroga**) *hominivorax*) that enters the wounds of mammals, developing under the skin and often causing death. The adult fly is called the **screwworm fly**.

screw·y /'skro͞oē/ ▶ adj. (**screw·i·er, screw·i·est**) informal rather odd or eccentric. — **screw·i·ness** n.

Scria·bin /skrē'äbən/ (also **Skrya·bin**), Aleksandr Nikolaevich (1872–1915), Russian composer. His works include *The Divine Poem* (1903) and *Prometheus: The Poem of Fire* (1909–10).

scrib·ble¹ /'skribəl/ ▶ v. [trans.] write or draw (something) carelessly or hurriedly. ■ [intrans.] informal write for a living or as a hobby. ▶ n. a piece of writing or a picture produced in this way: *illegible scribbles.* — **scrib·bly** /'skrib(ə)lē/ adj. [ME: from med. L. *scribillare*, dimin. of L. *scribere* 'write.']

scrib·ble² ▶ v. [trans.] [often as n.] (**scribbling**) card (wool, cotton, etc.) coarsely. [17th C.: prob. from Low Ger.]

scrib·bler /'skrib(ə)lər/ ▶ n. informal a person who writes for a living or as a hobby.

scribe /skrīb/ ▶ n. **1** hist. a person who copies out documents, esp. one employed to do this before printing was invented. ■ informal, often humorous a writer, esp. a journalist. **2** (also **Scribe**) Jewish History an ancient Jewish record-keeper or, later, a professional theologian and jurist. **3** another term for SCRIBER. ▶ v. [trans.] **1** esp. literary write. **2** mark with a scriber. — **scrib·al** /-bəl/ adj. [ME: from L. *scriba*, from *scribere* 'write.']

scrib·er /'skrībər/ ▶ n. a pointed instrument used for making marks on wood, bricks, etc., to guide a saw or in sign painting.

scrim /skrim/ ▶ n. strong, coarse fabric, chiefly used for heavy-duty lining or upholstery. ■ Theater a piece of gauze cloth that appears opaque until lit from behind, used as a screen or backdrop. ■ a similar heat-proof cloth put over film or television lamps to diffuse the light. ■ a thing that conceals or obscures something: *a thin scrim of fog covered the island.* [18th C.: of unknown origin.]

scrim·mage /'skrimij/ ▶ n. **1** a confused struggle or fight. **2** Football the beginning of each down of play, with the ball placed on the ground with its longest axis at right angles to the goal line. ■ offensive plays begun in this way. ■ esp. Football a session in which teams practice by playing a simulated game. ▶ v. [intrans.] esp. Football engage in a practice scrimmage. — **scrim·mag·er** n. [ME: alt. of dial. *scrimish*, var. of the noun SKIRMISH.]

scrimp /skrimp/ ▶ v. [intrans.] be thrifty or parsimonious; economize: *I have scrimped and saved.* [18th C.: from Scots *scrimp* 'meager'; perh. rel. to SHRIMP.]

scrim·shaw /'skrim,shô/ ▶ v. [trans.] adorn (whalebone, ivory, shells, or other materials) with carved or colored designs. ▶ n. a piece of work done in such a way. ■ the art or technique of producing such work. [19th C.: of unknown origin; perh. influenced by the surname *Scrimshaw*.]

scrip¹ /skrip/ ▶ n. **1** a provisional certificate of money subscribed to a bank or company, entitling the holder to a formal certificate and dividends. ■ such certificates collectively. ■ (also **scrip issue** or **div·i·dend**) Finance an issue of additional shares to shareholders in proportion to the shares already held. **2** (also **land scrip**) a certificate entitling the holder to acquire possession of certain portions of public land. **3** hist. paper money in amounts of less than a dollar. [18th C.: abbrev. of *subscription receipt*.]

scrip² ▶ n. hist. a small bag or pouch, typically one carried by a pilgrim, shepherd, or beggar. [ME: prob. a shortening of OFr. *escrepe* 'purse.']

scrip³ ▶ n. another term for SCRIPT².

Script. ▶ abbr. ■ Scriptural. ■ Scripture.

script¹ /skript/ ▶ n. **1** handwriting as distinct from print; written characters: *her neat, tidy script.* ■ printed type imitating handwriting. ■ [with adj.] writing using a particular alphabet: *Russian script.* **2** the written text of a play, movie, or broadcast. ■ Comput. an automated series of instructions carried out in a specific order. ■ Psychol. the social role or behavior appropriate to particular situations that an individual absorbs through cultural influences and association with others. ▶ v. [trans.] write a script for (a play, movie, or broadcast). [ME: shortening of OFr. *escript*, from L. *scriptum*, neut. past part. (used as a n.) of *scribere* 'write.']

script² ▶ n. informal a doctor's prescription.

scrip·to·ri·um /,skrip'tôrēəm/ ▶ n. (pl. **-to·ri·a** /-'tôrēə/ or **-to·ri·ums**) esp. hist. a room set apart for writing, esp. one in a monastery where manuscripts were copied. [18th C.: from med. L., from L. *script-* 'written,' from the verb *scribere*.]

scrip·tur·al /'skripCHərəl/ ▶ adj. of, from, or relating to the Bible: *scriptural quotations from Genesis.* — **scrip·tur·al·ly** adv.

scrip·ture /'skripCHər/ ▶ n. (often **Scrip·ture** or **Scrip·tures**) the sacred writings of Christianity contained in the Bible: *teachings of the Scriptures.* ■ the sacred writings of another religion. [ME: from L. *scriptura* 'writings,' from *script-* 'written,' from the v. *scribere*.]

script·writ·er /'skript,rītər/ ▶ n. a person who writes a script for a play, movie, or broadcast. — **script·writ·ing** /-,rītiNG/ n.

scriv·e·ner /'skriv(ə)nər/ ▶ n. hist. a clerk, scribe, or notary. [ME: shortening of OFr. *escrivein*, from L. *scriba* (see SCRIBE).]

scrod /skräd/ ▶ n. a young cod, haddock, or similar fish, esp. one prepared for cooking. [19th C.: of unknown origin.]

scrof·u·la /'skrôfyələ/ ▶ n. esp. hist. a disease with glandular swellings, probably a form of tuberculosis. Also formerly called KING'S EVIL. — **scrof·u·lous** /-ləs/ adj. [ME: from med. L., dimin. of L. *scrofa* 'breeding sow' (said to be subject to the disease).]

scroll /skrōl/ ▶ n. **1** a roll of parchment or paper for writing or painting on. ■ an ancient book or document on such a roll. ■ an ornamental design or carving resembling a partly unrolled scroll of parchment, e.g., on the capital of a column, or at the end of a stringed instrument. ■ Art & Heraldry a depiction of a narrow ribbon bearing a motto or inscription. **2** [usu. as adj.] the facility that moves a display on a VDT screen in order to view new material. ▶ v. **1** [no obj., with adverbial] move displayed text or graphics in a particular direction on a computer screen in order to view different parts of them. ■ (of displayed text or graphics) move up, down, or across a computer screen. **2** [trans.] cause to move like paper rolling or unrolling. — **scroll·a·ble** adj. [ME: alt. of obs. *scrow* 'roll,' shortening of ESCROW.]

scroll bar (also **scroll·bar**) ▶ n. a long thin section at the edge of a computer display by which material can be scrolled using a mouse.

scrolled /skrōld/ ▶ adj. having an ornamental design or carving resembling a scroll of parchment.

scroll·er /'skrōlər/ ▶ n. a computer game in which the background scrolls past at a constant rate.

scroll·ing /'skrōliNG/ ▶ n. the action of moving displayed text or graphics up or down on a computer screen in order to view different parts of them. ▶ adj. [attrib.] (of an ornamental design or carving) made to resemble a partly unrolled scroll of parchment.

scroll saw ▶ n. a narrow-bladed saw for cutting decorative spiral lines or patterns.

scroll·work /'skrōl,wərk/ ▶ n. decoration consisting of spiral lines or patterns, esp. as cut by a scroll saw.

scrooch /skro͞oCH/ ▶ v. [intrans.] informal crouch; bend. [19th C.: dial. var. of US *scrouge* 'squeeze, crowd,' perh. reinforced by the verb CROUCH.]

Scrooge /skro͞oj/, Ebenezer, a miserly curmudgeon in Charles Dickens's novel *A Christmas Carol* (1843). ■ [as n.] (**a Scrooge**) a person who is miserly.

scro·tum /'skrōtəm/ ▶ n. (pl. **scro·ta** or **scro·tums**) a pouch of skin containing the testicles. — **scro·tal** /'skrōtl/ adj. [16th C.: from L.]

scrounge /skrounj/ informal ▶ v. [trans.] seek to obtain (something, typically food or money) at the expense or through the generosity of others or by stealth. ▶ n. [in sing.] an act of seeking to obtain something in such a way. — **scroung·er** n. [20th C.: var. of dial. *scrunge* 'steal.']

scrub¹ /skrəb/ ▶ v. (**scrubbed, scrub·bing**) [trans.] rub (someone or something) hard so as to clean them, typically with a brush and water. ■ (**scrub something away/off**) remove dirt by rubbing hard. ■ [intrans.] (**scrub up**) thoroughly clean one's hands and arms, esp. before performing surgery. ■ informal cancel or abandon (something). ■ use water to remove impurities from (gas or vapor). ■ [intrans.] (of a rider) rub the arms and legs urgently on a horse's neck and flanks to urge it to move faster. ▶ n. 1 an act of scrubbing something or someone. 2 a semiabrasive cosmetic lotion applied to the face or body in order to cleanse the skin. 3 (**scrubs**) a hygienic outfit worn by surgeons and other surgical staff while performing or assisting at an operation. — **scrub·ba·ble** adj. [16th C.: prob. from Mid. Low Ger., MDu. *schrobben, schrubben.*]

scrub[2] ▶ n. 1 vegetation consisting mainly of brushwood or stunted forest growth. ■ land covered with such vegetation. 2 [as adj.] denoting a shrubby or small form of a plant. ■ denoting an animal of inferior breed or physique. 3 informal an insignificant or contemptible person. ■ (in sports) a player not among the best or most skilled. — **scrub·by** adj. [ME (in the sense 'stunted tree'): var. of SHRUB[1].]

scrub·ber /'skrəbər/ ▶ n. a brush or other object used to clean something. ■ a person who cleans something. ■ an apparatus using water or a solution for purifying gases or vapors.

scrub jay ▶ n. a jay (*Aphelocoma coerulescens*) with blue and gray plumage and no crest. Found in Mexico and the western US, scrub jays also populate central Florida.

scrub·land /'skrəb,land/ ▶ n. (also **scrublands**) land consisting of scrub vegetation.

scrub nurse ▶ n. a nurse who assists a surgeon by performing certain specialized duties during a surgical operation.

scrub oak ▶ n. a shrubby dwarf oak (genus *Quercus*) that forms thickets.

scrub ty·phus ▶ n. a rickettsial disease transmitted to humans by mites and found in parts of eastern Asia. Also called TSUTSUGAMUSHI DISEASE.

scrub·wo·man /'skrəb,wŏŏmən/ ▶ n. a cleaning woman.

scruff /skrəf/ ▶ n. the back of a person's or animal's neck. [18th C.: alt. of dial. *scuff*, of obscure origin.]

scruff·y /'skrəfē/ ▶ adj. (**scruff·i·er, scruff·i·est**) shabby and untidy or dirty. — **scruff·i·ly** /-əlē/ adv. **scruff·i·ness** n. [17th C.: from *scruff* 'scurf,' var. of SCURF, + -Y[1].]

scrum /skrəm/ ▶ n. Rugby an ordered formation of players in which the forwards of each team push against up against each other with arms interlocked and heads down and the ball is thrown in to restart play. ■ esp. Brit., informal a disorderly crowd of people or things. ▶ v. (**scrummed, scrum·ming**) [intrans.] Rugby form or take part in a scrum. [19th C.: abbrev. of SCRUMMAGE.]

scrum·mage /'skrəmij/ ▶ n. & v. another term for SCRUM.

scrump·tious /'skrəm(p)shəs/ ▶ adj. informal (of food) extremely appetizing or delicious. ■ (of a person) very attractive. — **scrump·tious·ly** adv. **scrump·tious·ness** n. [19th C.: of unknown origin.]

scrunch /skrənch/ ▶ v. [intrans.] make a loud crunching noise. ■ [with obj. and adverbial] crush or squeeze (something) into a compact mass: *Gloria scrunched the handkerchief into a ball.* ■ [no obj., with adverbial] become crushed or squeezed in such a way. ■ [trans.] style (hair) by squeezing or crushing it in the hands to give a tousled look. ▶ n. [in sing.] a loud crunching noise. [18th C.: prob. imitative.]

scrunch·ie /'skrənchē/ ▶ n. a circular band of fabric-covered elastic used for fastening the hair.

scru·ple /'skrōōpəl/ ▶ n. 1 (usu. **scruples**) a feeling of doubt or hesitation with regard to the morality or propriety of a course of action. 2 hist. a unit of weight equal to 20 grains, used by apothecaries. ▶ v. [no obj., with infin.] [usu. with negative] hesitate or be reluctant to do something that one thinks may be wrong. [ME: from Fr. *scrupule* or L. *scrupulus*, from *scrupus*, lit. 'rough pebble,' (figuratively) 'anxiety.']

scru·pu·lous /'skrōōpyələs/ ▶ adj. (of a person or process) diligent, thorough, and extremely attentive to details. ■ very concerned to avoid doing wrong. — **scru·pu·los·i·ty** /,skrōōpyə'läsitē/ n. **scru·pu·lous·ly** adv. **scru·pu·lous·ness** n. [ME: from Fr. *scrupuleux* or L. *scrupulosus*, from *scrupulus.*]

scru·ti·nize /'skrōōtn,īz/ ▶ v. [trans.] examine or inspect closely and thoroughly. — **scru·ti·ni·za·tion** /,skrōōtn-i'zāshən/ n. **scru·ti·niz·er** n.

scru·ti·ny /'skrōōtn-ē/ ▶ n. (pl. **-nies**) critical observation or examination. [ME: from L. *scrutinium*, from *scrutari* 'to search' (orig. 'sort trash,' from *scruta* 'trash').]

scry /skrī/ ▶ v. (**skries, skried**) [intrans.] foretell the future using a crystal ball or other reflective object or surface. — **scry·er** n. [16th C.: shortening of DESCRY.]

SCSI /'skəzē/ Comput. ▶ abbr. small computer system interface, a bus standard for connecting computers and their peripherals.

scu·ba /'skōōbə/ ▶ n. an aqualung. ■ scuba diving. [1950s: from *self-contained underwater breathing apparatus.*]

scu·ba div·ing ▶ n. the sport or pastime of swimming underwater using scuba gear. — **scu·ba dive** (also **scu·ba-dive**) v. **scu·ba div·er** n.

scud /skəd/ ▶ v. (**scud·ded, scud·ding**) [intrans.] move fast in a straight line because or as if driven by the wind: *clouds scudding across the sky.* ▶ n. 1 esp. literary a formation of vapory clouds driven fast by the wind. ■ a mass of windblown spray. ■ a driving shower of rain or snow; a gust. ■ the action of moving fast in a straight line when driven by the wind. 2 (**Scud**) (also **Scud mis·sile**) a type of long-range surface-to-surface guided missile able to be fired from a mobile launcher. [16th C. (v.): perh. an alt. of the noun SCUT[1], reflecting the sense 'race like a hare.']

scu·do /'skōōdō/ ▶ n. (pl. **-di** /-dē/) hist. a coin, typically made of silver, formerly used in various Italian states. [Ital., from L. *scutum* 'shield.']

scuff /skəf/ ▶ v. [trans.] scrape or brush the surface of (a shoe or other object) against something. ■ mark (a surface) by scraping or brushing it, esp. with one's shoes: *the floor was scuffed.* ■ [intrans.] (of an object or surface) become marked by scraping or brushing. ■ drag (one's feet or heels) when walking. ■ [intrans.] walk in such a way. ▶ n. a mark made by scraping or grazing a surface or object. [18th C.: perh. imitative.]

scuf·fle /'skəfəl/ ▶ n. 1 a short, confused fight or struggle at close quarters: *scuffles with police.* 2 an act or sound of moving in a hurried, confused, or shuffling manner: *the scuffle of feet.* ▶ v. [intrans.] 1 engage in a short, confused fight or struggle at close quarters: *two students scuffling.* 2 move in a hurried, confused, or awkward way, making a rustling or shuffling sound. ■ [trans.] (of an animal or person) move (something) in a scrambling or confused manner. [16th C. (v.): prob. of Scand. origin; compare Swed. *skuffa* 'to push'; akin to SHOVE, SHUFFLE.]

scull /skəl/ ▶ n. each of a pair of small oars used by a single rower. ■ an oar placed over the stern of a boat to propel it by a side-to-side motion, reversing the blade at each turn. ■ a light, narrow boat propelled with a scull or a pair of sculls. ■ (**sculls**) a race between boats in which each participant uses a pair of oars. ▶ v. [intrans.] propel a boat with sculls. ■ [trans.] transport (someone) in a boat propelled with sculls. ■ [intrans.] (of an aquatic animal) propel itself with fins or flippers. — **scul·ler** n. [ME: of unknown origin.]

scul·ler·y /'skəl(ə)rē/ ▶ n. (pl. **-ler·ies**) a small kitchen or room at the back of a house used for washing dishes and other dirty household work. [ME: from OFr. *escuelerie*, from *escuele* 'dish,' from L. *scutella* 'salver,' dimin. of *scutra* 'wooden platter.']

scul·lion /'skəlyən/ ▶ n. archaic a servant assigned the most menial kitchen tasks. [15th C.: origin unknown.]

sculp. ▶ abbr. ■ sculptor. ■ sculptural. ■ sculpture.

scul·pin /'skəlpən/ ▶ n. a chiefly marine fish (Cottidae and related families) of the northern hemisphere, with a broad flattened head and spiny scales and fins. Many genera and numerous species include the bullheads. [17th C.: perh. from obs. *scorpene*, via L. from Gk. *skorpaina*, a kind of fish.]

sculpt /skəlpt/ (also **sculp** /skəlp/) ▶ v. [trans.] create or represent (something) by carving, casting, or other shaping techniques. [19th C.: from Fr. *sculpter*, from *sculpteur* 'sculptor.']

Sculp·tor /'skəlptər/ Astron. a faint southern constellation (the Sculptor or Sculptor's Workshop), between Grus and Cetus. [L.]

sculp·tor /'skəlptər/ ▶ n. an artist who makes sculptures. [17th C.: from L., from *sculpt-* 'hollowed out,' from the verb *sculpere.*]

sculp·tress /'skəlptrəs/ ▶ n. a female artist who makes sculptures.

sculp·ture /'skəlpchər/ ▶ n. the art of making two- or three-dimensional representative or abstract forms, esp. by carving stone or wood or by casting metal or plaster. ■ a work of such a kind. ■ Zool. & Bot. raised or sunken patterns or texture on the surface of a shell, pollen grain, cuticle, or other biological specimen. ▶ v. [trans.] make or represent (a form) by carving, casting, or other shaping techniques. ■ form, shape, or mark as if by sculpture, esp. with strong, smooth curves. — **sculp·tur·al** /-chərəl/ adj. **sculp·tur·al·ly** /-ch(ə)rəlē/ adv. [ME: from L. *sculptura*, from *sculpere* 'carve.']

scum /skəm/ ▶ n. a layer of dirt or froth on the surface of a liquid. ■ informal a worthless or contemptible person or group of people. ▶ v. (**scummed, scum·ming**) [intrans.] (of a liquid) become covered with a layer of dirt or froth: *the lagoon scummed over.* ■ [trans.] form a layer of dirt or froth on (a liquid): *litter scummed the surface of the harbor.* — **scum·my** adj. (**-mi·er, -mi·est**). [ME: from Mid. Low Ger., MDu. *schūm*, from Gmc.]

scum·bag /'skəm,bag/ ▶ n. informal a contemptible or objectionable person.

scum·ble /'skəmbəl/ Art ▶ v. [trans.] modify (a painting or color) by applying a very thin coat of opaque paint to give a softer or duller effect. ■ modify (a drawing) in a similar way with light shading in pencil or charcoal. [17th C. (verb): perh. a frequentative of the verb SCUM.]

scun·gil·le /skōōn'jēlā; -lē/ (also **scun·gi·le**) ▶ n. (pl. **-gil·li** /-'jēlē/) a mollusk (esp. with reference to its meat eaten as a delicacy). [from Ital. dial. *scunciglio*, prob. alt. of Ital. *conchiglia* 'seashell.']

scun·ner /'skənər/ esp. Scot. ▶ n. a strong dislike. ▶ v. [intrans.] feel disgust or strong dislike. [ME ('shrink back with fear'): origin unknown.]

scup /skəp/ ▶ n. (pl. same) a common porgy (*Stenotomus chrysops*) with faint dark vertical bars, occurring off the coasts of the northwestern Atlantic. [19th C.: from Narragansett *mishcup*, from *mishe* 'big' + *cuppi* 'close together' (from the shape of the scales).]

scup·per /'skəpər/ ▶ n. (usu. **scuppers**) a hole in a ship's side to carry water overboard from the deck. ■ an outlet in the side of a building for draining water. [ME: perh. ult. from OFr. *escopir* 'to spit'; compare Ger. *Speigatt*, lit. 'spit hole.']

scup·per·nong /'skəpər,näng; -,nông/ ▶ n. a variety of the muscadine grape native to the basin of the Scuppernong River in North Carolina.

scurf /skərf/ ▶ n. flakes on the surface of the skin that form as fresh skin develops below, occurring esp. as dandruff. — **scurf·y** adj. [OE *sceorf*, from the base of *sceorfan* 'gnaw,' *sceorfian* 'cut to shreds.']

scur·ril·ous /'skərələs; 'skə-rə-/ ▶ adj. making or spreading scandalous claims about someone with the intention of damaging their reputation:

a scurrilous attack. ■ humorously insulting. — **scur·ril·i·ty** /skəˈrilitē/ **n.** (pl. **-ties**) **scur·ril·ous·ly adv. scur·ril·ous·ness n.** [16th C.: from Fr. *scurrile* or L. *scurrilus* (from *scurra* 'buffoon') + **-OUS**.]

scur·ry /ˈskərē; ˈskə-rē/ ▶ **v.** (**-ries, -ried**) [intrans.] (of a person or small animal) move hurriedly with short quick steps: *pedestrians scurried for cover.* [19th C.: abbr. of *hurry-scurry*, reduplication of **HURRY**.]

scur·vy /ˈskərvē/ ▶ **n.** a disease caused by a deficiency of vitamin C, characterized by swollen bleeding gums and the opening of previously healed wounds. ▶ **adj.** (**-vi·er, -vi·est**) [attrib.] archaic worthless or contemptible: *a scurvy trick.* — **scur·vi·ly** /-vəlē/ **adv.** [ME ('scurfy'): from **SCURF**.]

scur·vy grass ▶ **n.** a small cresslike plant (genus *Cochlearia*) of the cabbage family, with fleshy tar-flavored leaves, growing near the sea. It is rich in vitamin C and was formerly eaten to prevent scurvy.

scut[1] /skət/ ▶ **n.** the short tail of a hare, rabbit, or deer. [ME: akin to *scut* 'short,' 'shorten.']

scut[2] ▶ **n.** informal, esp. Irish a foolish person. [19th C.: origin unknown.]

scu·ta /ˈsk(y)o͞otə/ plural form of **SCUTUM**.

scu·tage /ˈsk(y)o͞otij/ ▶ **n.** (in a feudal society) money paid by a vassal to his lord in lieu of military service. [ME: from med. L. *scutagium*, from L. *scutum* 'shield.']

Scu·ta·ri /ˈsko͞otərē; -tärē/ a former name for Üsküdar.

scutch /skəCH/ ▶ **v.** [trans.] dress (fibrous material, esp. retted flax) by beating it. — **scutch·er n.** [18th C.: from obs. Fr. *escoucher*, from L. *excutere* 'shake out.']

scutch·eon /ˈskəCHən/ ▶ **n.** archaic spelling of **ESCUTCHEON**.

scute /sk(y)o͞ot/ ▶ **n.** Zool. a thickened horny or bony plate on a turtle's shell or on the back of a crocodile, stegosaurus, etc.

scu·tel·lum /sk(y)o͞oˈteləm/ ▶ **n.** (pl. **-tel·la** /-ˈtelə/) Bot. & Zool. a small shieldlike structure. — **scu·tel·lar** /-ˈtelər/ **adj.** [18th C.: mod. L., dimin. of L. *scutum* 'shield.']

scut·tle[1] /ˈskətl/ ▶ **n.** (in full **coal scut·tle**) a metal container with a sloping hinged lid and a handle, used to fetch and store coal for a domestic fire. [OE *scutel* 'dish, platter,' from ON *skutill*, from L. *scutella* 'dish.']

scut·tle[2] ▶ **v.** [intrans.] run hurriedly or furtively with short quick steps: *a mouse scuttled across the floor.* [15th C.: compare dial. *scuddle*, frequentative of **SCUD**.]

scut·tle[3] ▶ **v.** [trans.] sink (one's own ship) deliberately by holing it or opening its seacocks to let water in. ■ deliberately cause (a scheme) to fail. ▶ **n.** an opening with a lid in a ship's deck or side. [15th C. (n.): perh. from OFr. *escoutille*, from Sp. dimin. *escotilla* 'hatchway.']

scut·tle·butt /ˈskətl,bət/ ▶ **n.** informal rumor; gossip. [19th C.: from *scuttled butt*.]

Scu·tum /ˈsk(y)o͞otəm/ Astron. a small constellation (the Shield) near the celestial equator, lying in the Milky Way between Aquila and Serpens. [L.]

scu·tum /ˈsk(y)o͞otəm/ ▶ **n.** (pl. **-ta** /-tə/) Zool. another term for **SCUTE**. [18th C.: from L., lit. 'oblong shield.']

scut work (also **scut·work**) ▶ **n.** informal tedious, menial work. [1970s: compare **SCUT**[2].]

scuzz /skəz/ ▶ **n.** informal something regarded as disgusting, sordid, or disreputable. ■ a disreputable or unpleasant person. — **scuzz·y adj.** [1960s: prob. a phonetic abbrev. of **DISGUSTING**.]

scuzz·ball /ˈskəz,bôl/ (also **scuzz·bag** /-,bag/) ▶ **n.** informal a despicable or disgusting person.

Scyl·la /ˈsilə/ Gk. Mythol. a female sea monster who devoured sailors when they tried to navigate the narrow channel between her cave and the whirlpool Charybdis. In later legend Scylla was a dangerous rock, situated on the Italian side of the Strait of Messina.
– PHRASES **between Scylla and Charybdis** /kəˈribdis/ used to refer to a situation involving two dangers in which an attempt to avoid one increases the risk from the other.

Scy·pho·zo·a /,sīfəˈzōə/ Zool. a class of marine coelenterates that comprises the jellyfishes. — **scy·pho·zo·an n. & adj.** [mod. L. (pl.), from Gk. *skuphos* 'drinking cup' + *zōion* 'animal.']

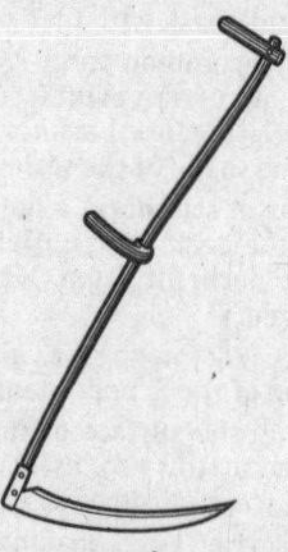
scythe

scythe /sīTH/ ▶ **n.** a tool used for cutting crops such as grass or wheat, with a long curved blade at the end of a long pole attached to one or two short handles. [OE *sīthe*, of Gmc. origin; rel. to Du. *zeis* and Ger. *Sense*.]

Scyth·i·a /ˈsiTHēə/ an ancient region in southeastern Europe and Asia, the center of the Scythian empire 8th–2nd centuries BC. — **Scyth·i·an adj. & n.**

SD ▶ **abbr.** ■ South Dakota (in official postal use).

s.d. ▶ **abbr.** ■ sine die. ■ Stat. standard deviation.

S.Dak. ▶ **abbr.** South Dakota.

SDR ▶ **abbr.** special drawing right (from the International Monetary Fund).

SE ▶ **abbr.** southeast or southeastern.

Se ▶ **symb.** the chemical element selenium.

se- ▶ **prefix** (in words adopted from Latin) apart; without: *secede* | *secure.* [from L. *se-*, from the earlier preposition and adverb *se*.]

sea /sē/ ▶ **n.** (often **the sea**) the expanse of salt water that covers most of the earth's surface and surrounds its landmasses. ■ [often in place names] a roughly definable area of this: *the Black Sea.* ■ [in place names] a large lake: *the Sea of Galilee.* ■ used to refer to waves as opposed to calm sea. ■ (**seas**) large waves. ■ fig. a vast expanse or quantity of something.
– PHRASES **at sea** sailing on the sea. ■ confused or unable to decide what to do. **by sea** by means of a ship or ships. **go to sea** set out on a voyage. ■ become a sailor in a navy or a merchant navy. **put (out) to sea** leave land on a voyage. [OE *sǣ*, of Gmc. origin; rel. to Du. *zee* and Ger. *See*.]

sea an·chor ▶ **n.** an object dragged in the water from the bow of a boat in order to keep the bow pointing into the waves or to lessen leeway.

sea a·nem·o·ne ▶ **n.** a sedentary marine coelenterate (order Actiniaria, class Anthozoa) with a columnar body that bears a ring of stinging tentacles around the mouth.

sea·bag /ˈsē,bag/ ▶ **n.** a sailor's traveling bag or trunk.

giant sea bass

sea bass /bas/ ▶ **n.** any of a number of marine fishes that are related to or resemble the common perch, in particular: ■ a mainly tropical fish of a large family (Serranidae, the **sea bass family**), esp. one of the genus *Centropristis*, including the **giant sea bass** (*C. stiata*). The sea bass family also includes the groupers. ■ (**white sea bass**) a large game fish (*Cynoscion nobilis*) of the drum family, found along the Pacific coast of North America.

sea·bed /ˈsē,bed/ ▶ **n.** the ground under the sea; the ocean floor.

Sea·bee /ˈsē,bē/ ▶ **n.** a member of one of the construction battalions of the Civil Engineer Corps of the US Navy. [from pronunc. of *CB* (from *construction battalion*).]

sea·bird /ˈsē,bərd/ ▶ **n.** a bird that frequents the sea or coast.

sea bis·cuit ▶ **n.** 1 another term for **HARDTACK**. 2 another term for **SAND DOLLAR**.

sea·board /ˈsē,bôrd/ ▶ **n.** a region bordering the sea; the coastline: *the eastern seaboard.*

Sea·borg /ˈsē,bôrg/, Glenn Theodore (1912–99), US chemist. During 1940–58, he helped to produce nine of the transuranic elements (plutonium to nobelium) in a cyclotron. Nobel Prize for Chemistry (1951).

sea·bor·gi·um /sēˈbôrgēəm/ ▶ **n.** the chemical element of atomic number 106, a very unstable element made by high-energy atomic collisions. (Symbol: **Sg**) [mod. L., after G. *Seaborg* (see **SEABORG**).]

sea·borne /ˈsē,bôrn/ ▶ **adj.** transported or traveling by sea: *seaborne trade.*

sea bream ▶ **n.** a deep-bodied marine fish that resembles the freshwater bream, in particular: ■ several genera and species in the family Sparidae (the **sea bream family**), which also includes the porgies. ■ a fish (*Seriolella brama*, family Centrolophidae) of Australasian coastal waters, with a purple back and silver underside.

sea breeze ▶ **n.** a breeze blowing toward the land from the sea, esp. during the day owing to the relative warmth of the land.

sea buck·thorn ▶ **n.** a bushy Eurasian shrub or small tree (*Hippophae rhamnoides*) that typically grows on sandy coasts. It bears orange berries, and some plants are spiny.

sea change ▶ **n.** a profound or notable transformation. [from Shakespeare's *Tempest*.]

sea chest ▶ **n.** a sailor's storage chest.

sea·cock /ˈsē,käk/ ▶ **n.** a valve in an opening through a ship's hull below or near to the waterline (e.g., one connecting a ship's engine-cooling system to the sea).

sea cow ▶ **n.** a sirenian, esp. a manatee.

sea cu·cum·ber ▶ **n.** an echinoderm (class Holothuroidea) that has a thick, wormlike body with tentacles around the mouth. They typically have rows of tube feet along the body.

sea dog ▶ **n.** 1 informal an old or experienced sailor. 2 Heraldry a mythical beast like a dog with fins, webbed feet and a scaly tail.

sea ea·gle ▶ **n.** a large Eurasian fish-eating eagle (genus *Haliaeetus*) that frequents coasts and wetlands. Several species include the widespread **white-tailed sea eagle** (*H. albicilla*), recently reintroduced to Scotland.

sea el·e·phant ▶ **n.** another term for **ELEPHANT SEAL.**

sea fan ▶ **n.** a horny coral (*Gorgonis* and other genera) with a vertical treelike or fanlike skeleton, living chiefly in warmer seas.

sea·far·ing /'sē,fe(ə)riNG/ ▶ **adj.** (of a person) traveling by sea, esp. regularly. ▶ **n.** the practice of traveling by sea, esp. regularly. — **sea·far·er** /-,fe(ə)rər/ **n.**

sea·food /'sē,fo͞od/ ▶ **n.** shellfish and sea fish, served as food.

sea·front /'sē,frənt/ ▶ **n.** another term for **BEACHFRONT.**

sea-girt ▶ **adj.** literary surrounded by sea.

sea·go·ing /'sē,gōiNG/ ▶ **adj.** [attrib.] (of a ship) suitable or designed for voyages on the sea. ■ characterized by or relating to traveling by sea, esp. habitually: *a seagoing life.*

sea goose·ber·ry ▶ **n.** a common comb jelly (*Pleurobrachia pileus*) with a spherical body bearing two long retractile branching tentacles, typically occurring in swarms.

sea·grass /'sē,gras/ ▶ **n.** a grasslike plant that lives in or close to the sea, esp. eelgrass. Numerous genera include *Cymodocea* (family Cymodoceaceae), *Zostera* (family Zosteraceae), and others.

sea-green ▶ **adj.** of a pale bluish green color.

sea·gull /'sē,gəl/ ▶ **n.** a popular name for a gull.

sea hare ▶ **n.** a large sea slug (*Aplysia* and other genera, class Gastropoda) that has a minute internal shell and lateral extensions to the foot. Most species can swim, and many secrete distasteful chemicals to deter predators.

sea hol·ly ▶ **n.** a spiny-leaved plant (*Eryngium maritimum*) of the parsley family, with metallic blue teasellike flowers, growing in sandy places by the sea and native to Europe.

sea·horse /'sē,hôrs/ (also **sea horse**) ▶ **n. 1** a small marine fish (genus *Hippocampus*, family Syngnathidae) with segmented bony armor, an upright posture, and a head and neck suggestive of a horse. Many species, including the American *H. hudsonius.* **2** a mythical creature with a horse's head and fish's tail.

seahorse

Sea Is·lands a chain of islands off the Atlantic coast of northern Florida, Georgia, and South Carolina.

sea krait ▶ **n.** a venomous sea snake (genus *Laticauda*, family Elapidae) with a laterally compressed tail, occurring in tropical coastal waters of the eastern Indian Ocean and western Pacific.

SEAL /sēl/ ▶ **n.** a member of an elite force within the US Navy specializing in guerrilla warfare and counterinsurgency. [acronym from *sea air land (team).*]

seal[1] /sēl/ ▶ **n. 1** a device or substance that is used to join two things together so as to prevent them from coming apart or to prevent anything from passing between them: *worn valve seals.* ■ [in sing.] the state or fact of being joined or rendered impervious by such a substance or device. ■ the water standing in the trap of a drain to prevent foul air from rising, considered in terms of its depth. **2** a piece of wax, lead, or other material with an individual design stamped into it, attached to a document to show that it has come from the person who claims to have issued it. ■ a design embossed in paper for this purpose. ■ an engraved device used for stamping a design that authenticates a document. ■ fig. a thing regarded as a confirmation or guarantee of something: *a seal of approval.* ■ a decorative adhesive stamp. ■ (**the seal**) (also **the seal of confession** or **the seal of the confessional**) the obligation on a priest not to divulge anything said during confession. ▶ **v.** [trans.] fasten or close securely. ■ (**seal something in**) prevent something from escaping by closing a container or opening. ■ (**seal something off**) isolate an area by preventing or monitoring entrance to and exit from it. ■ apply a nonporous coating to (a surface) to make it impervious: *seal the finish with a satin varnish.* ■ fry (food) briefly in hot fat to prevent it from losing too much of its moisture during subsequent cooking. ■ fix a piece of wax or lead stamped with a design to (a document) to authenticate it. ■ conclude, establish, or secure (something) definitively, excluding the possibility of reversal or loss: *seal the deal.* ■ (in the Mormon church) mark (a marriage or adoption) as eternally binding in a formal ceremony.
– PHRASES **under seal** under legal protection of secrecy: *the judge ordered that the tape be kept under seal.* — **seal·a·ble adj.** [ME (sense 2): from OFr. *seel* (n.), *seeler* (v.), from L. *sigillum* 'small picture,' dimin. of *signum* 'a sign.']

seal[2] ▶ **n.** a fish-eating aquatic mammal with a streamlined body and feet developed as flippers, returning to land to breed or rest. Two families: Phocidae (the **true seals**) and Otariidae (the **eared seals**, including the fur seals and sea lions). ■ another term for **SEALSKIN.** ▶ **v.** [intrans.] [usu. as n.] (**sealing**) hunt for seals. [OE *seolh*, of Gmc. origin.]

sea lane ▶ **n.** a route at sea designated for use or regularly used by shipping.

seal·ant /'sēlənt/ ▶ **n.** material used for sealing something so as to make it airtight or watertight.

sea lav·en·der ▶ **n.** a chiefly maritime plant (genus *Limonium*, family Plumbaginaceae) with small pink or lilac funnel-shaped flowers. Several kinds are cultivated and some are used as everlasting flowers.

sealed or·ders ▶ **plural n.** Mil. orders for procedure that are not to be opened before a specified time.

sea legs ▶ **plural n.** (**one's sea legs**) a person's ability to keep their balance and not feel seasick when on board a moving ship.

sea lem·on ▶ **n.** a yellowish sea slug (*Archidoris* and other genera, order Nudibranchia, class Gastropoda).

seal·er[1] /'sēlər / ▶ **n.** [usu. with adj.] a device or substance used to seal something, esp. with a hermetic or an impervious seal.

seal·er[2] ▶ **n.** a ship or person engaged in hunting seals.

sea let·tuce ▶ **n.** an edible seaweed (*Ulva lactuca*) with green fronds that resemble lettuce leaves.

sea lev·el ▶ **n.** the level of the sea's surface, used in reckoning the height of geographical features such as hills and as a barometric standard. Compare with **MEAN SEA LEVEL.**

sea·lift /'sē,lift/ ▶ **n.** a large-scale transportation of troops, supplies, and equipment by sea.

sea lil·y ▶ **n.** a sedentary marine echinoderm (class Crinoidea) that has a small body on a long jointed stalk, with featherlike arms to trap food.

seal·ing wax ▶ **n.** a mixture of shellac and rosin with turpentine and pigment, softened by heating and used to make seals.

sea li·on ▶ **n. 1** an eared seal occurring mainly on Pacific coasts, the large male of which has a mane on the neck and shoulders. **2** Heraldry a mythical beast formed of a lion's head and foreparts and a fish's tail.

sea loch ▶ **n.** see **LOCH.**

seal ring ▶ **n.** esp. hist. a finger ring with a seal for impressing sealing wax.

seal·skin /'sēl,skin/ ▶ **n.** [often as adj.] the skin or prepared fur of a seal, esp. when made into a garment.

seal·stone /'sēl,stōn/ ▶ **n.** a gemstone bearing an engraved device for use as a seal.

seal-top ▶ **adj.** (of a spoon) having a flat design resembling an embossed seal at the end of its handle. ▶ **n.** a spoon with such a handle.

Sea·ly·ham /'sēlēəm; -lē,ham/ (in full **Sea·ly·ham ter·ri·er**) ▶ **n.** a terrier of a wire-haired, short-legged breed. [19th C.: from *Sealyham*, a village in Wales.]

seam /sēm/ ▶ **n. 1** a line where two pieces of fabric are sewn together in a garment or other article. ■ a line where the edges of two pieces of wood, wallpaper, or another material touch each other. ■ a long thin indentation or scar. **2** an underground layer of a mineral such as coal or gold. ▶ **v.** join with a seam. — **seam·er n.** [OE *sēam*, of Gmc. origin; rel. to Du. *zoom* and Ger. *Saum.*]

sea·man /'sēmən/ ▶ **n.** (pl. **-men**) a person who works as a sailor, esp. one below the rank of officer. ■ a sailor of the lowest rank in the US Navy or Coast Guard, ranking below petty officer. — **sea·man·ly adj.**

sea·man·ship /'sēmən,SHip/ ▶ **n.** the skill, techniques, or practice of handling a ship or boat at sea.

sea·mark /'sē,märk/ ▶ **n.** a conspicuous object distinguishable at sea, serving to guide sailors in navigation.

sea mile ▶ **n.** a unit of distance equal to a minute of arc of a great circle and varying between 2,014 yards (1,842 m) at the equator and 2,035 yards (1,861 m) at the pole. Compare with **NAUTICAL MILE.**

seam·less /'sēmlis/ ▶ **adj.** (of a fabric or surface) smooth and without seams or obvious joins. — **seam·less·ly adv. seam·less·ness n.**

sea-moth ▶ **n.** a small fish (family Pegasidae) with bony plates covering the body and large pectoral fins that spread out horizontally like wings. It lives in the warmer waters of the Indo-Pacific. Several genera and species include the widely distributed *Eurypegasus draconis.*

sea·mount /'sē,mount/ ▶ **n.** a submarine mountain.

sea mouse ▶ **n.** a large marine bristle worm (genus *Aphrodite*, class Polychaeta) with a stout, oval body that bears matted, furlike, iridescent chaetae.

seam·stress /'sēmstris/ ▶ **n.** a woman who sews, esp. one who earns her living by sewing. [16th C.: from archaic *seamster, sempster* 'tailor, seamstress' + **-ESS**[1].]

seam·y /'sēmē/ ▶ **adj.** (**seam·i·er, seam·i·est**) sordid and disreputable: *a seamy sex scandal.* — **seam·i·ness n.** [16th C.: from **SEAM** + **-Y**[1]. The sense 'disreputable' (17th C.) arose from the notion of 'having the rough edges of seams visible.']

Sean·ad /'SHônəd; 'SHänəTH/ (also **Sean·ad Eire·ann** /'ārən/) the upper House of Parliament in the Republic of Ireland. [Irish, 'senate (of Ireland).']

se·ance /'sā,äns/ ▶ **n.** a meeting at which people attempt to make contact with the dead, esp. through the agency of a medium. [18th C.: Fr. *séance*, from OFr. *seoir*, from L. *sedere* 'sit.']

sea net·tle ▶ **n.** a large, stinging jellyfish (*Chrysaora* and other genera, class Scyphozoa). Numerous species include the **East Coast sea nettle** (*C. quinquecirrha*). *See illustration on next page.*

sea ot·ter ▶ **n.** an entirely aquatic marine otter (*Enhydra lutris*) of North Pacific coasts, formerly hunted for its dense fur. It is noted for its habit of floating on its back with a stone balanced on the abdomen, in order to crack open bivalve mollusks.

East Coast sea nettle

sea pen ▶**n.** a marine coelenterate (order Pennatulacea, class Anthozoa) related to the corals, forming a feather-shaped colony with a horny or calcareous skeleton.

sea perch ▶**n.** any of a number of marine fishes that typically have a long-based dorsal fin and that are popular as sporting fish, in particular a surfperch.

sea pink ▶**n.** another term for THRIFT (sense 2).

sea·plane /ˈsēˌplān/ ▶**n.** an aircraft with floats instead of wheels, designed to land on and take off from water.

sea·port /ˈsēˌpôrt/ ▶**n.** a town or city with a harbor for seagoing ships.

sea po·ta·to ▶**n.** a yellowish-brown European heart urchin (*Echinocardium cordatum*).

sea pow·er ▶**n.** a country's naval strength, esp. as a weapon of war.

sea·quake /ˈsēˌkwāk/ ▶**n.** a sudden disturbance of the sea caused by a submarine eruption or earthquake.

sear /si(ə)r/ ▶**v.** [trans.] burn or scorch the surface of (something) with a sudden, intense heat. ■ [intrans.] (of pain) be experienced as a sudden, burning sensation. ■ brown (food) quickly at a high temperature so that it will retain its juices in subsequent cooking. ■ archaic cause to wither. ▶**adj.** (also **sere**) literary (esp. of plants) withered. [OE *sēar* (adj.), *sēarian* (v.), of Gmc. origin.]

search /sərCH/ ▶**v.** [intrans.] try to find something by looking or otherwise seeking carefully and thoroughly. ■ [trans.] examine (a place, vehicle, or person) thoroughly in order to find something or someone: *she searched the house.* ■ [as adj.] (**searching**) scrutinizing thoroughly, esp. in a disconcerting way: *searching questions.* ▶**n.** an act of searching for someone or something. ■ (usu. **searches**) Law an investigation of public records to find if a property is subject to any liabilities or encumbrances.
– PHRASES **search me!** informal I do not know (used for emphasis).
— **search·a·ble** adj. **search·er** n. **search·ing·ly** adv. [ME: from OFr. *cerchier* (v.), from late L. *circare* 'go around,' from L. *circus* 'circle.']

search en·gine ▶**n.** Comput. a program for the retrieval of data, files, or documents from a database or network, esp. the Internet.

search·light /ˈsərCHˌlīt/ ▶**n.** a powerful outdoor electric light with a concentrated beam that can be turned in the required direction.

search par·ty ▶**n.** a group of people organized to look for someone or something that is lost.

search war·rant ▶**n.** a legal document authorizing a police officer or other official to enter and search premises.

sear·ing /ˈsi(ə)riNG/ ▶**adj.** extremely hot or intense. ■ severely critical: *a searing indictment.*

sea rob·in ▶**n.** a gurnard (fish), esp. one of warm seas that has winglike pectoral fins that are brightly colored. Family Triglidae includes several genera and many species.

sea room ▶**n.** clear space at sea for a ship to maneuver in.

sea salt ▶**n.** salt produced by the evaporation of seawater.

sea·scape /ˈsēˌskāp/ ▶**n.** a view of an expanse of sea. ■ a picture of such a view.

sea ser·pent ▶**n.** a legendary serpentlike sea monster.

sea·shell /ˈsēˌSHel/ ▶**n.** the shell of a marine mollusk.

sea·shore /ˈsēˌSHôr/ ▶**n.** (usu. **the seashore**) an area of sandy, stony, or rocky land bordering and level with the sea. ■ Law the land between high- and low-water marks.

sea·sick /ˈsēˌsik/ ▶**adj.** suffering from sickness or nausea caused by the motion of a ship at sea. — **sea·sick·ness** n.

sea·side /ˈsēˌsīd/ ▶**n.** (usu. **the seaside**) a place by the sea, esp. a beach area or vacation resort.

sea slat·er ▶**n.** a common shore-dwelling crustacean (*Ligia oceanica*) that is related to the wood louse.

sea slug ▶**n.** a shell-less marine mollusk (order Nudibranchia) that is typically brightly colored, with external gills and a number of appendages on the upper surface.

sea snail ▶**n. 1** a marine mollusk (subclass Prosobranchia, class Gastropoda) esp. one with a spiral shell. **2** another term for SNAILFISH.

sea snake ▶**n.** a venomous marine snake (family Elapidae) with a flattened tail, that lives in the warm coastal waters of the Indian and Pacific oceans and does not come onto land.

sea·son /ˈsēzən/ ▶**n.** each of the four divisions of the year (spring, summer, autumn, and winter) marked by particular weather patterns and daylight hours, resulting from the earth's changing position with regard to the sun. ■ a period of the year characterized by a particular climatic feature or marked by a particular activity, event, or festivity: *the rainy season.* ■ a fixed time in the year when a particular sport is played. ■ the time of year when a particular fruit, vegetable, or other food is plentiful and in good condition: *fruit in season.* ■ an indefinite or unspecified period of time; awhile: *this soul walked with me for a season.* ■ archaic a proper or suitable time: *to everything there is a season.* ▶**v.** [trans.] **1** add salt, herbs, pepper, or other spices to (food). ■ add a quality or feature to (something), esp. so as to make it more lively or exciting. **2** make (wood) suitable for use as timber by adjusting its moisture content to that of the environment in which it will be used: [as adj.] (**seasoned**) *seasoned oak.* ■ [as adj.] (**seasoned**) accustomed to particular conditions; experienced: *a seasoned traveler.* [ME: from OFr. *seson,* from L. *satio(n-)* 'sowing,' from the root of *serere* 'to sow.']

sea·son·a·ble /ˈsēzənəbəl/ ▶**adj. 1** usual for or appropriate to a particular season of the year: *seasonable temperatures.* **2** archaic coming at the right time or meeting the needs of the occasion; opportune. — **sea·son·a·bil·i·ty** /ˌsēzənəˈbilitē/ n. **sea·son·a·ble·ness** n. **sea·son·a·bly** /-blē/ adv.

sea·son·al /ˈsēzənəl/ ▶**adj.** of, relating to, or characteristic of a particular season of the year: *seasonal fresh fruit.* ■ fluctuating or restricted according to the season or time of year: *seasonal rainfall.* — **sea·son·al·i·ty** /ˌsēzəˈnalitē/ n. **sea·son·al·ly** adv.

sea·son·al af·fec·tive dis·or·der ▶**n.** depression associated with late autumn and winter and thought to be caused by a lack of light.

sea·son·ing /ˈsēzəniNG/ ▶**n. 1** salt, herbs, or spices added to food to enhance the flavor. **2** the process of adjusting the moisture content of wood to make it more suitable for use as timber.

sea·son tick·et ▶**n.** a ticket for a period of travel or a series of events that costs less than purchasing several separate tickets.

sea spi·der ▶**n.** a spiderlike marine arachnid (class Pycnogonida) that has a narrow segmented body with a minute abdomen and long legs.

sea squill ▶**n.** see SQUILL (sense 1).

sea squirt ▶**n.** a marine tunicate (class Ascidiacea, subphylum Urochordata) that has a baglike body with orifices through which water flows into and out of a central pharynx.

sea star ▶**n.** a starfish.

seat /sēt/ ▶**n. 1** a thing made or used for sitting on, such as a chair or stool. ■ the roughly horizontal part of a chair, on which one's weight rests directly. ■ a sitting place for a passenger in a vehicle or for a member of an audience. ■ a place in an elected legislative or other body. ■ a site or location of something specified. ■ short for COUNTY SEAT. ■ a part of a machine that supports or guides another part. **2** a person's buttocks. ■ the part of a garment that covers the buttocks. ■ a manner of sitting on a horse. ▶**v.** [trans.] arrange for (someone) to sit somewhere. ■ (**seat oneself** or **be seated**) sit down. ■ (of a place such as a theater or restaurant) have seats for (a specified number of people). ■ [trans.] fit in position: *upper boulders were seated in the interstices below.*
– PHRASES **take one's seat** sit down, typically in a seat assigned to one. [ME (n.): from ON *sæti,* from the Gmc. base of SIT.]

seat belt (also **seat·belt**) ▶**n.** a belt or strap securing a person to prevent injury, esp. in a vehicle or aircraft.

-seater ▶**comb. form** denoting a vehicle, sofa, or building with a specified number of seats: *a six-seater.*

seat·ing /ˈsētiNG/ ▶**n. 1** the seats with which a building or room is provided: *seating for 80.* **2** the act of directing people to seats: *early seatings.*

SEATO /ˈsētō/ ▶**abbr.** Southeast Asia Treaty Organization.

sea trout ▶**n. 1** [with adj.] a troutlike marine fish (genus *Cynoscion*) of the drum family occurring in the western Atlantic. **2** Brit. a European brown trout (*Salmo trutta trutta*) of a salmonlike migratory race.

Se·at·tle /sēˈatl/ a city in the state of Washington, on the eastern shores of Puget Sound; pop. 563,374.

sea tur·tle ▶**n.** see TURTLE (sense 1).

sea ur·chin ▶**n.** a marine echinoderm that has a spherical or flattened shell covered in mobile spines, with a mouth on the underside and calcareous jaws. Several families and genera and numerous species include the **Atlantic purple sea urchin** (*Arbacia punctulata,* family Arbaciidae).

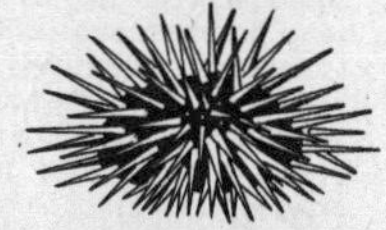

Atlantic purple sea urchin

sea wall ▶**n.** a wall or embankment erected to prevent the sea from encroaching on or eroding an area of land.

sea·ward /ˈsēwərd/ ▶**adv.** toward the sea. ▶**adj.** going or pointing toward the sea. ■ nearer or nearest to the sea. ▶**n.** [in sing.] the side that faces or is nearer to the sea.

sea wasp ▶**n.** a box jellyfish that can inflict a dangerous sting.

sea·wa·ter /ˈsēˌwôtər; -ˌwätər/ ▶**n.** water in or taken from the sea.

sea·way /ˈsēˌwā/ ▶**n. 1** an inland waterway capable of accommodating seagoing ships. ■ a natural channel connecting two areas of sea. ■ a route across the sea used by ships. **2** [in sing.] a stretch of water in which a sea is running.

sea·weed /ˈsē,wēd/ ▶ **n.** large algae growing in the sea or on rocks below the high-water mark.

sea·wor·thy /ˈsē,wərT͟Hē/ ▶ **adj.** (of a vessel) in a good enough condition to sail on the sea. — **sea·wor·thi·ness n.**

se·ba·ceous /səˈbāSHəs/ ▶ **adj.** tech. of or relating to oil or fat. ■ of or relating to a sebaceous gland or its secretion. [18th C.: from L. *sebaceus* (from *sebum* 'tallow') + **-ous**.]

se·ba·ceous cyst ▶ **n.** a swelling in the skin arising in a sebaceous gland, typically filled with yellowish sebum. Also called **wen**[1].

se·ba·ceous gland ▶ **n.** a small gland in the skin which secretes a lubricating oily matter (sebum) into the hair follicles to lubricate the skin and hair.

Se·bas·tian, St. /siˈbasCHən/ (late 3rd century), Roman martyr. According to legend, he was a soldier who confronted the emperor Diocletian and was clubbed to death.

Se·bas·to·pol /səˈbastə,pōl; -,pôl/ a city in Ukraine, near the southern tip of the Crimea; pop. 361,000. Ukrainian and Russian name **Sevastopol**.

Se·bat /səˈbat/ (also **She·bat, She·vat**) ▶ **n.** (in the Jewish calendar) the fifth month of the civil and eleventh of the religious year, usually coinciding with parts of January and February. [from Heb. *šĕḇaṭ*.]

SEbE ▶ **abbr.** southeast by east.

seb·or·rhe·a /,sebəˈrēə/ (Brit. **seb·or·rhoe·a**) ▶ **n.** Med. excessive discharge of sebum from the sebaceous glands. — **seb·or·rhe·ic** /-ˈrē-ik/ **adj.** [19th C.: from **sebum** + **-rrhea**.]

SEbS ▶ **abbr.** southeast by south.

se·bum /ˈsēbəm/ ▶ **n.** an oily secretion of the sebaceous glands. [19th C.: mod. L., from L. *sebum* 'grease.']

SEC ▶ **abbr.** Securities and Exchange Commission, a US governmental agency that monitors trading in securities and company takeovers.

Sec. ▶ **abbr.** secretary.

sec[1] /sek/ ▶ **abbr.** secant.

sec[2] ▶ **n.** **(a sec)** informal a second; a very short space of time: *stay put, I'll be back in a sec.*

sec[3] ▶ **adj.** (of wine) dry. [Fr., from L. *siccus*.]

sec. ▶ **abbr.** second(s).

se·cant /ˈsē,kant; -kənt/ ▶ **n.** **1** (abbr.: **sec**) Math. the ratio of the hypotenuse to the shorter side adjacent to an acute angle (in a right-angled triangle); the reciprocal of a cosine. **2** Geom. a straight line that cuts a curve in two or more parts. [16th C.: from Fr. *sécante*, based on L. *secare* 'to cut.']

sec·a·teurs /ˈsekə,tərz/ ▶ **plural n.** (also **a pair of secateurs**) esp. Brit. a pair of pruning clippers for use with one hand. [19th C.: pl. of Fr. *sécateur* 'cutter,' from L. *secare* 'to cut.']

Sec·chi disc /ˈsekē/ ▶ **n.** an opaque disk, typically white, used to gauge the transparency of water by measuring the depth (**Secchi depth**) at which the disk ceases to be visible from the surface. [20th C.: named after Angelo *Secchi* (1818–78), Italian astronomer.]

sec·co /ˈsekō/ (also **fres·co sec·co**) ▶ **n.** the technique of painting on dry plaster with pigments mixed in water. [19th C.: from Ital., lit. 'dry,' from L. *siccus*.]

se·cede /siˈsēd/ ▶ **v.** [intrans.] withdraw formally from membership in a federal union, an alliance, or a political or religious organization: *the kingdom of Belgium seceded from the Netherlands in 1830.* — **se·ced·er n.** [18th C.: from L. *secedere*, from *se-* 'apart' + *cedere* 'go.']

se·ces·sion /səˈseSHən/ ▶ **n.** the action of withdrawing formally from membership of a federation or body, esp. a political state: *secession from the union.* ■ **(the Secession)** hist. the withdrawal of eleven Southern states from the US Union in 1860, leading to the Civil War. — **se·ces·sion·al** /-SHənl/ **adj.** **se·ces·sion·ism** /-,nizəm/ **n.** **se·ces·sion·ist** /-ist/ **n.** [16th C.: from Fr. *sécession* or L. *secessio(n-)*, from *secedere* 'go apart' (see **secede**).]

Seck·el /ˈsekəl/ ▶ **n.** a pear of a small sweet juicy brownish-red variety, grown chiefly in the US. [19th C.: after an early grower.]

se·clude /siˈklo͞od/ ▶ **v.** [trans.] keep (someone) away from other people: *I secluded myself up here.* [ME ('obstruct access to'): from L. *secludere*, from *se-* 'apart' + *claudere* 'to shut.']

se·clud·ed /siˈklo͞odid/ ▶ **adj.** (of a place) not seen or visited by many people; sheltered and private.

se·clu·sion /siˈklo͞oZHən/ ▶ **n.** the state of being private and away from other people. — **se·clu·sive** /-siv/ **adj.** [17th C.: from med. L. *seclusio(n-)*, from *secludere* (see **seclude**).]

sec·ond[1] /ˈsekənd/ ▶ **ordinal number** **1** constituting number two in a sequence; coming after the first in time or order; 2nd. ■ secondly (used to introduce a second point or reason). ■ alternating; other: *every second week.* ■ Music an interval spanning two consecutive notes in a diatonic scale. ■ the note that is higher by this interval than the tonic of a diatonic scale or root of a chord. ■ the second in a sequence of a vehicle's gears. ■ Baseball second base. ■ the second grade of a school. ■ **(seconds)** informal a second course or second helping of food at a meal. ■ denoting someone or something regarded as comparable to or reminiscent of a better-known predecessor. ■ an act or instance of seconding. **2** subordinate or inferior in position, rank, or importance: *it was second only to Copenhagen.* ■ additional to that already existing, used, or possessed: *a second home.* ■ the second finisher or position in a race or competition: *he finished second.* ■ Music performing a lower or subordinate of two or more parts for the same instrument or voice: *second violins.* ■ **(seconds)** goods of an inferior quality. ■ coarse flour, or bread made from it. **3** an assistant, in particular: ■ an attendant assisting a combatant in a duel or boxing match. ▶ **v.** [trans.] formally support or endorse (a nomination or resolution or its proposer) as a necessary preliminary to adoption or further discussion. ■ express agreement with. — **sec·ond·er n.** [ME: via OFr. from L. *secundus* 'following, second,' from the base of *sequi* 'follow.' The verb dates from the late 16th C.]

sec·ond[2] /ˈsekənd/ ▶ **n.** **1** (abbr.: **s**) a sixtieth of a minute of time, which as the SI unit of time is defined in terms of the natural periodicity of the radiation of a cesium-133 atom. (Symbol: ″) ■ informal a very short time. **2** (also **arc second** or **second of arc**) a sixtieth of a minute of angular distance. (Symbol: ″) [ME: from med. L. *secunda (minuta)* 'second (minute),' fem. of *secundus*, the "second" operation of dividing by sixty.]

se·cond[3] /siˈkänd/ ▶ **v.** [trans.] Brit. transfer (a military officer or other official or worker) temporarily to other employment or another position: *I was seconded to a public relations unit.* — **se·cond·ee** /si,känˈdē/ **n.** [19th C.: from Fr. *en second* 'in the second rank (of officers).']

sec·ond Ad·am ▶ **n.** **(the second Adam)** (in Christian thought) Jesus Christ. [alluding to 1 Cor. 15: 45–47.]

Sec·ond A·dar see **Adar**.

Sec·ond Ad·vent ▶ **n.** another term for **Second Coming**.

sec·ond·ar·y /ˈsekən,derē/ ▶ **adj.** **1** coming after, less important than, or resulting from someone or something else that is primary. ■ [attrib.] of or relating to education for children from the age of eleven to sixteen or eighteen: *a secondary school.* ■ having a reversible chemical reaction and therefore able to store energy. ■ relating to or denoting the output side of a device using electromagnetic induction, esp. in a transformer. **2** **(Secondary)** Geol. former term for **Mesozoic**. **3** Chem. (of an organic compound) having its functional group located on a carbon atom that is bonded to two other carbon atoms. ■ (chiefly of amines) derived from ammonia by replacement of two hydrogen atoms by organic groups. ▶ **n.** (pl. **-ar·ies**) **1** short for: ■ a secondary color. ■ Ornithol. a secondary feather. ■ a secondary coil or winding in an electrical transformer. **2** Football the players in the defensive backfield; the area these players cover. **3** **(the Secondary)** Geol., dated the Secondary or Mesozoic era. — **sec·ond·ar·i·ly** /-,derəlē/ **adv.** **sec·ond·ar·i·ness n.**

sec·ond·ar·y col·or ▶ **n.** a color resulting from the mixing of two primary colors.

sec·ond·ar·y feath·er ▶ **n.** any of the flight feathers growing from the second joint of a bird's wing.

sec·ond·ar·y in·dus·try ▶ **n.** Econ. industry that converts the raw materials provided by primary industry into commodities and products for the consumer; manufacturing industry.

sec·ond·ar·y plan·et ▶ **n.** a satellite of a planet.

sec·ond·ar·y sex·u·al char·ac·ter·is·tics ▶ **plural n.** physical characteristics developed at puberty that distinguish between the sexes but are not involved in reproduction.

sec·ond·ar·y stress ▶ **n.** Phonet. (in a system that postulates three levels of stress) the accent on a syllable of a word or breath group that is weaker than the primary stress but stronger than the lack of stress.

sec·ond·ar·y struc·ture ▶ **n.** Biochem. the local three-dimensional structure of sheets, helices, or other forms adopted by a polynucleotide or polypeptide chain, due to electrostatic attraction between neighboring residues.

sec·ond·ar·y thick·en·ing ▶ **n.** Bot. (in the stem or root of a woody plant) the increase in girth resulting from the formation of new woody tissue by the cambium.

sec·ond best (also **sec·ond-best**) ▶ **adj.** next after the best. ▶ **n.** a less adequate or less desirable alternative: *he would have to settle for second best.*

sec·ond cause ▶ **n.** Logic a cause that is itself caused.

sec·ond cham·ber ▶ **n.** the upper house of a parliament with two chambers.

sec·ond child·hood ▶ **n.** a period in someone's adult life when they act as a child, either for fun or as a consequence of reduced mental capabilities.

sec·ond class ▶ **n.** [in sing.] a set of people or things grouped together as the second best. ■ the second-best accommodations in an aircraft, train, or ship. ▶ **adj. & adv.** of the second-best quality or in the second division: ■ of or relating to the second-best accommodations in an aircraft, train, or ship. ■ of or relating to a class of mail having lower priority than first-class mail. ■ (in North America) denoting a class of mail that includes newspapers and periodicals.

Sec·ond Com·ing ▶ **n.** Christian Theol. the prophesied return of Christ to earth at the Last Judgment.

sec·ond cous·in ▶ **n.** see **cousin**.

sec·ond-de·gree ▶ **adj.** [attrib.] **1** Med. denoting burns that cause blistering but not permanent scars. **2** Law denoting a category of a crime, esp. murder, that is less serious than a first-degree crime.

se·conde /səˈkänd/ ▶ **n.** Fencing the second of eight standard parrying positions. [18th C.: from Fr., fem. of *second* 'second.']

Sec·ond Em·pire the imperial government in France of Napoleon III, 1852–70.

sec·ond-gen·er·a·tion ▶adj. 1 denoting the offspring of parents who have immigrated to a particular country: *a second-generation American.* 2 of a more advanced stage of technology than previous models or systems.

sec·ond growth ▶n. 1 woodland growth that replaces harvested or burned virgin forest. 2 a wine considered to be the second-best in quality compared to the first growth (or PREMIER CRU).

sec·ond-guess ▶v. [trans.] 1 anticipate or predict (someone's actions or thoughts) by guesswork. 2 judge or criticize (someone) with hindsight. — **sec·ond-guess·er** n.

sec·ond·hand /'sekən(d)'hand/ (also **sec·ond-hand**) ▶adj. 1 (of goods) having had a previous owner; not new: *a secondhand car.* ■ [attrib.] denoting a store or shop where such goods can be bought: *a secondhand bookshop.* 2 (of information or experience) accepted on another's authority and not from original investigation. ▶adv. 1 on the basis that something has had a previous owner: *buying secondhand.* 2 on the basis of what others have said; indirectly: *I was discounting anything I heard secondhand.*

sec·ond hand ▶n. an extra hand in some watches and clocks that moves around to indicate the seconds.

sec·ond·hand smoke ▶n. smoke inhaled involuntarily from tobacco being smoked by others.

sec·ond hon·ey·moon ▶n. a romantic vacation taken by a couple who have been married for some time.

sec·ond-in-com·mand ▶n. the officer next in authority to the commanding or chief officer.

sec·ond in·ten·tion ▶n. Med. the healing of a wound in which the edges do not meet, and new epithelium must form across granulation tissue.

sec·ond lieu·ten·ant ▶n. a commissioned officer of the lowest rank in the US Army, Air Force, and Marine Corps ranking above chief warrant officer and below first lieutenant.

sec·ond·ly /'sekən(d)lē/ ▶adv. in the second place (used to introduce a second point or reason).

sec·ond mate ▶n. an assistant mate on a merchant ship.

sec·ond mort·gage ▶n. a mortgage taken out on a property that is already mortgaged.

sec·ond name ▶n. Brit. a surname.

sec·ond na·ture ▶n. a characteristic or habit in someone that appears to be instinctive because that person has behaved in a particular way so often: *deceit was becoming* ***second nature*** *to her.*

se·con·do /sə'kändō; -'kôn-/ ▶n. (pl. **-di** /-dē/) Music the second or lower part in a duet. [Ital.]

sec·ond of·fi·cer ▶n. another term for SECOND MATE.

sec·ond per·son ▶n. see PERSON (sense 2).

sec·ond-rate ▶adj. of mediocre or inferior quality. — **sec·ond-rat·ed·ness** n. **sec·ond-rat·er** n.

sec·ond read·ing ▶n. a second presentation of a bill to a legislative assembly, in the US to debate committee reports and in the UK to approve the bill's general principles.

Sec·ond Reich see REICH.

Sec·ond Re·pub·lic the republican regime in France from the deposition of King Louis Philippe (1848) to the beginning of the Second Empire (1852).

sec·ond sight ▶n. the supposed ability to perceive future or distant events; clairvoyance. — **sec·ond-sight·ed** adj.

sec·ond-stor·y man ▶n. a burglar who enters through an upper-story window.

sec·ond strike ▶n. a retaliatory attack conducted with weapons designed to withstand an initial nuclear attack (a "first strike").

sec·ond string ▶n. 1 (in sports) the players who are available to replace or relieve those who start a game. 2 an alternative resource or course of action in case another one fails. — **sec·ond-string·er** n.

sec·ond thoughts (also **sec·ond thought**) ▶plural n. a change of opinion or resolve reached after considering something again: ***on second thought****, perhaps he was right.*

sec·ond wind /wind/ ▶n. [in sing.] a person's ability to breathe freely during exercise, after having been out of breath. ■ a new strength or energy to continue something that is an effort: *she gained a second wind during the campaign and turned the opinion polls around.*

Sec·ond World ▶n. the former communist block consisting of the Soviet Union and some countries in eastern Europe.

Sec·ond World War another term for WORLD WAR II.

se·cre·cy /'sēkrəsē/ ▶n. the action of keeping something secret or the state of being kept secret. [ME: from SECRET, prob. on the pattern of *privacy.*]

se·cret /'sēkrit/ ▶adj. not known or seen or not meant to be known or seen by others: *a secret plan.* ■ [attrib.] not meant to be known as such by others: *a secret drinker.* ■ fond of or good at keeping things about oneself unknown: *a secret man.* ■ (of information or documents) given the security classification above confidential and below top secret. ▶n. something that is kept or meant to be kept unknown or unseen by others: *a state secret.* ■ something that is not properly understood; a mystery. ■ a valid but not commonly known or recognized method of achieving or maintaining something: *the secret of a happy marriage.* ■ formerly, the name of a prayer said by the priest in a low voice after the offertory in a Roman Catholic Mass.

– PHRASES **in secret** without others knowing. — **se·cret·ly** adv. [ME: from OFr., from L. *secretus* (adj.) 'separate, set apart,' from the verb *secernere*, from *se-* 'apart' + *cernere* 'sift.']

se·cret a·gent ▶n. a spy acting for a country.

sec·re·tar·i·at /ˌsekri'te(ə)rēət/ ▶n. a permanent administrative office or department, esp. a governmental one. ■ [treated as sing. or pl.] the staff working in such an office. [19th C.: from Fr. *secrétariat*, from med. L. *secretariatus*, from *secretarius* (see SECRETARY).]

sec·re·tar·y /'sekriˌterē/ ▶n. (pl. **-tar·ies**) a person employed by an individual or in an office to assist with correspondence, keep records, make appointments, and carry out similar tasks. ■ an official of a society or other organization who conducts its correspondence and keeps its records. ■ an official in charge of a government department. ■ a writing desk with shelves on top of it. — **sec·re·tar·i·al** /-'te(ə)rēəl/ adj. **sec·re·tar·y·ship** /-ˌsHip/ n. [ME (orig. in the sense 'person entrusted with a secret'): from late L. *secretarius* 'confidential officer,' from L. *secretum* 'secret,' neut. of *secretus* (see SECRET).]

sec·re·tar·y bird ▶n. a slender, long-legged African bird of prey (*Sagittarius serpentarius*) that feeds on snakes, having a crest likened to a quill pen stuck behind the ear.

sec·re·tar·y-gen·er·al ▶n. (pl. **sec·re·tar·ies-gen·er·al**) a title given to the principal administrator of some organizations, most notably the United Nations.

sec·re·tar·y of state ▶n. (in the US) the head of the State Department, responsible for foreign affairs.

se·cret bal·lot ▶n. a ballot in which votes are cast in secret.

se·crete[1] /si'krēt/ ▶v. [trans.] (of a cell, gland, or organ) produce and discharge (a substance): *insulin is secreted in response to rising levels of glucose in the blood.* — **se·cre·tor** /-tər/ n. **se·cre·to·ry** /-tərē/ adj. [18th C.: back-form. from SECRETION.]

se·crete[2] ▶v. [trans.] conceal; hide: *the assets had been secreted in Swiss bank accounts.* [18th C.: alt. of the obs. verb *secret* 'keep secret.']

se·cre·tin /si'krētn/ ▶n. Biochem. a hormone released into the bloodstream by the duodenum (esp. in response to acidity) to stimulate secretion by the liver and pancreas. [20th C.: from SECRETION + -IN[1].]

se·cre·tion /si'krēsHən/ ▶n. a process by which substances are produced and discharged from a cell, gland, or organ for a particular function in the organism or for excretion. ■ a substance discharged in such a way. [17th C.: from Fr. *sécrétion* or L. *secretio(n-)* 'separation,' from *secret-* 'moved apart,' from the verb *secernere.*]

se·cre·tive /'sēkritiv/ ▶adj. (of a person or an organization) inclined to conceal feelings and intentions or not to disclose information. ■ (of a state or activity) characterized by the concealment of intentions and information: *secretive deals.* ■ (of a person's expression or manner) having an enigmatic or conspiratorial quality: *a secretive smile.* — **se·cre·tive·ly** adv. **se·cre·tive·ness** n. [19th C.: back-form. from *secretiveness*, suggested by Fr. *secrétivité*, from *secret* 'secret.']

se·cret po·lice ▶n. [treated as pl.] a police force working in secret against a government's political opponents.

se·cret serv·ice ▶n. 1 a government department concerned with espionage. 2 (**Secret Service**) (in the US) a branch of the Treasury Department dealing with counterfeiting and providing protection for the president.

se·cret so·ci·e·ty ▶n. an organization whose members are sworn to secrecy about its activities.

sect /sekt/ ▶n. a group of people with somewhat different religious beliefs (typically regarded as heretical) from those of a larger group to which they belong. ■ often derog. a group that has separated from an established church; a nonconformist church. ■ a philosophical or political group, esp. one regarded as extreme or dangerous. [ME: from OFr. *secte* or L. *secta*, lit. 'following,' hence 'faction, party,' from the stem of *sequi* 'follow.']

sect. ▶abbr. section.

sec·tar·i·an /sek'te(ə)rēən/ ▶adj. denoting or concerning a sect or sects: *sectarian offshoots of Ismailism.* ■ (of an action) carried out on the grounds of membership of a sect, denomination, or other group: *sectarian killings of Catholics.* ■ rigidly following the doctrines of a sect or other group: *sectarian Bolshevism.* ▶n. a member of a sect. ■ a person who rigidly follows the doctrines of a sect or other group. — **sec·tar·i·an·ism** /-ˌnizəm/ n. **sec·tar·i·an·ize** /-ˌnīz/ v.

sec·ta·ry /'sektərē/ ▶n. (pl. **-ries**) a member of a religious or political sect.

sec·tion /'seksHən/ ▶n. 1 any of the more or less distinct parts into which something is or may be divided or from which it is made up: *orange sections.* ■ a relatively distinct part of a book, newspaper, statute, or other document. ■ a measure of land, equal to one square mile. ■ a particular district of a town. 2 a distinct group within a larger body of people or things: *the children's section of the library.* ■ a group of players of a family of instruments within an orchestra: *the brass section.* ■ a small class of students who are part of a larger course but are taught separately. ■ [in names] a specified military unit. ■ a subdivision of an army platoon. ■ Biol. a secondary taxonomic category, esp. a subgenus. 3 the cutting of a solid by or along a plane. ■ the shape resulting from cutting a solid along a plane. ■ a representation of the internal structure of something as if it has been cut through vertically or horizontally. ■ Surg. a separation by cutting. ■ Biol. a thin slice of plant or animal tissue prepared for microscopic examination. ▶ v. [trans.] divide into sections: *section the grapefruit.* ■ **(section something off)** separate an area from a larger one. ■ Biol. cut (animal or plant tissue) into thin slices for microscopic examination. ■ Surg. divide by cutting. — **sec·tioned** adj. [often in comb.] *a square-sectioned iron peg.* [ME (as a n.): from Fr. *section* or L. *sectio(n-)*, from *secare* 'to cut.' The verb dates from the early 19th C.]

sec·tion·al /'seksHənl/ ▶ adj. of or relating to a section or subdivision of a larger whole. ■ of or relating to a section or group within a community: *sectional interests.* ■ of or relating to a view of the structure of an object in section: *sectional drawings.* ■ made or supplied in sections: *sectional sills.* ▶ n. a sofa made in sections that can be used separately as chairs. — **sec·tion·al·ize** /-,īz/ v. **sec·tion·al·ly** adv.

sec·tion·al·ism /'seksHənl,izəm/ ▶ n. restriction of interest to a narrow sphere; undue concern with local interests or petty distinctions at the expense of general well-being. — **sec·tion·al·ist** n. & adj.

sec·tion gang ▶ n. a crew of railroad workers responsible for maintaining a particular section of track.

sec·tion hand ▶ n. a member of a section gang.

sec·tion mark ▶ n. the sign (§) used as a reference mark or to indicate a section of a book.

sec·tor /'sektər/ ▶ n. **1** an area or portion that is distinct from others. ■ a distinct part or branch of a nation's economy or society or of a sphere of activity such as education: *the Muslim sector.* ■ Mil. a subdivision of an area for military operations. ■ Comput. a subdivision of a track on a magnetic disk. **2** the plane figure enclosed by two radii of a circle or ellipse and the arc between them. See illustration at GEOMETRIC. **3** a mathematical instrument consisting of two arms hinged at one end and marked with sines, tangents, etc., for making diagrams. — **sec·tor·al** /-rəl/ adj. [16th C. (in senses 2 and 3): from late L., a technical use of L. *sector* 'cutter,' from *sect-* 'cut off,' from the verb *secare.*]

sec·to·ri·al /sek'tôrēəl/ ▶ adj. **1** of or like a sector. **2** Zool. denoting a carnassial tooth, or a similar cutting tooth in mammals other than carnivores.

sec·u·lar /'sekyələr/ ▶ adj. **1** denoting attitudes, activities, or other things that have no religious or spiritual basis: *secular buildings.* Contrasted with SACRED. **2** Christian Church (of clergy) not subject to or bound by religious rule; not belonging to or living in a monastic or other order. Contrasted with REGULAR. **3** Astron. of or denoting slow changes in the motion of the sun or planets. **4** Econ. (of a fluctuation or trend) occurring or persisting over an indefinitely long period. **5** occurring once every century or similarly long period (used esp. in reference to celebratory games in ancient Rome). ▶ n. a secular priest. — **sec·u·lar·ism** /-,rizəm/ n. **sec·u·lar·ist** /-rist/ n. **sec·u·lar·i·ty** /,sekyə'laritē/ n. **sec·u·lar·i·za·tion** /,sekyələrə'zāsHən/ n. **sec·u·lar·ize** /-,rīz/ v. **sec·u·lar·ly** adv. [ME: senses 1 and 2 from OFr. *seculer*, from L. *saecularis*, from *saeculum* 'generation, age,' used in Christian L. to mean 'the world'; senses 3, 4, and 5 (early 19th C.) from L. *saecularis* 'relating to an age or period.']

sec·u·lar hu·man·ism ▶ n. humanism, with regard in particular to the belief that humanity is capable of morality and self-fulfillment without belief in God. — **sec·u·lar hu·man·ist** n.

se·cund /'sē,kənd; si'kənd/ ▶ adj. Bot. arranged on one side only (such as the flowers of lily of the valley). — **se·cund·ly** adv. [18th C.: from L. *secundus* (see SECOND[1]).]

se·cure /si'kyŏŏr/ ▶ adj. fixed or fastened so as not to give way, become loose, or be lost. ■ not subject to threat; certain to remain or continue safe and unharmed: *their market share remains **secure against** competition.* ■ protected against attack or other criminal activity. ■ (of a place of detention) having provisions against the escape of inmates. ■ feeling safe, stable, and free from fear or anxiety. ■ [predic.] **(secure of)** dated feeling no doubts about attaining; certain to achieve: *she remained secure of admiration.* ▶ v. [trans.] fix or attach (something) firmly so that it cannot be moved or lost. ■ make (a door or container) hard to open; fasten or lock. ■ protect against threats; make safe: *the government will secure the economy **against** too much foreign ownership.* ■ capture (a person or animal). ■ succeed in obtaining (something), esp. with difficulty: *the division secured a major contract.* ■ seek to guarantee repayment of (a loan) by having a right to take possession of an asset in the event of nonpayment: *a loan **secured on** your home.* — **se·cur·a·ble** adj. **se·cure·ly** adv. **se·cure·ment** n. [16th C. (in the sense 'feeling no apprehension'): from L. *securus*, from *se-* 'without' + *cura* 'care.']

se·cu·ri·tize /sə'kyŏŏri,tīz/ ▶ v. [trans.] convert (an asset, esp. a loan) into marketable securities, typically for the purpose of raising cash by selling them to other investors. — **se·cu·ri·ti·za·tion** /-itə'zāsHən/ n.

se·cu·ri·ty /si'kyŏŏritē/ ▶ n. (pl. **-ties**) **1** the state of being free from danger or threat. ■ the safety of a state or organization against criminal activity such as terrorism, theft, or espionage: *national security.* ■ procedures followed or measures taken to ensure such safety. ■ the state of feeling safe, stable, and free from fear or anxiety: *emotional security.* **2** a private police force that guards a building, campus, park, etc. **3** a thing deposited or pledged as a guarantee of the fulfillment of an undertaking or the repayment of a loan, to be forfeited in case of default. **4** (often **securities**) a certificate attesting credit, the ownership of stocks or bonds, or the right to ownership connected with tradable derivatives.

se·cu·ri·ty blan·ket ▶ n. a blanket or other familiar object that is a comfort to someone, typically a child.

Se·cu·ri·ty Coun·cil a permanent body of the United Nations seeking to maintain peace and security. It consists of fifteen members, of which five (China, France, Russia, the UK, and the US) are permanent and have the power of veto. The other members are elected for two-year terms.

secy. (also **sec'y**) ▶ abbr. secretary.

sedan chair

se·dan /si'dan/ ▶ n. **1** (also **sedan chair**) esp. hist. an enclosed chair for conveying one person, carried between horizontal poles by two or more porters. **2** an enclosed automobile for four or more people, having two or four doors. [perh. an alt. of an Ital. dial. word, based on L. *sella* 'saddle,' from *sedere* 'sit.']

Se·dan, Bat·tle of a battle fought in 1870 near Sedan in northeastern France, in which the Prussian army defeated a smaller French army under Napoleon III.

se·date[1] /si'dāt/ ▶ adj. calm, dignified, and unhurried. ■ quiet and rather dull: *sedate suburban domesticity.* — **se·date·ly** adv. **se·date·ness** n. [ME (orig. as a medical term meaning 'not sore or painful,' also 'calm, tranquil'): from L. *sedatus*, past part. of *sedare* 'settle,' from *sedere* 'sit.']

se·date[2] ▶ v. [trans.] calm (someone) or make them sleep by administering a sedative drug: *she was heavily sedated.* [1960s: back-form. from SEDATION.]

se·da·tion /si'dāsHən/ ▶ n. the administering of a sedative drug to produce a state of calm or sleep: *he was distraught with grief and **under sedation.*** [16th C.: from Fr. *sédation* or L. *sedatio(n-)*, from *sedare* 'settle' (see SEDATE[1]).]

sed·a·tive /'sedətiv/ ▶ adj. promoting calm or inducing sleep: *the seeds have a sedative effect.* ▶ n. a drug taken for its calming or sleep-inducing effect.

sed·en·tar·y /'sedn,terē/ ▶ adj. (of a person) tending to spend much time seated; somewhat inactive. ■ (of work or a way of life) characterized by much sitting and little physical exercise. ■ (of a position) sitting; seated. ■ Zool. & Anthropol. inhabiting the same locality throughout life; not migratory or nomadic. ■ Zool. (of an animal) sessile. — **sed·en·tar·i·ly** /-,te(ə)rəlē/ adv. **sed·en·tar·i·ness** n. [16th C. (in the sense 'not migratory'): from Fr. *sédentaire* or L. *sedentarius*, from *sedere* 'sit.']

Se·der /'sādər/ ▶ n. a Jewish ritual service and ceremonial dinner for the first night or first two nights of Passover. [from Heb. *sēḏer* 'order, procedure.']

sedge /sej/ ▶ n. a grasslike plant (*Carex* and other genera, family Cyperaceae) with triangular stems and inconspicuous flowers, widely distributed throughout temperate and cold regions, growing typically in wet ground. — **sedg·y** /'sejē/ adj. [OE *secg*, of Gmc. origin, from an Indo-Eur. root shared by L. *secare* 'to cut.']

sedge war·bler ▶ n. a common migratory Eurasian songbird (*Acrocephalus schoenoboenus*, family Sylviidae) with streaky brown plumage, frequenting marshes and reed beds.

se·dil·i·a /sə'dilēə/ ▶ plural n. (sing. **-di·le** /-'dīlē/) a group of stone seats for clergy in the south chancel wall of a church, usually three in number and often canopied and decorated. [18th C.: from L., 'seat,' from *sedere* 'sit.']

sed·i·ment /'sedəmənt/ ▶ n. matter that settles to the bottom of a liquid; dregs. ■ Geol. particulate matter that is carried by water or wind and deposited on the surface of the land or the seabed, and may in time become consolidated into rock. ▶ v. [intrans.] settle as sediment. ■ (of a liquid) deposit a sediment. ■ [trans.] deposit (something) as a sediment. — **sed·i·men·ta·tion** /,sedəmən'tāsHən/ n. [16th C.: from Fr. *sédiment* or L. *sedimentum* 'settling,' from *sedere* 'sit.']

sed·i·men·ta·ry /,sedə'ment(ə)rē/ ▶ adj. of or relating to sediment. ■ Geol. (of rock) that has formed from sediment deposited by water or air.

se·di·tion /si'disHən/ ▶ n. conduct or speech inciting people to rebel against the authority of a state or monarch. [ME (in the sense 'violent strife'): from OFr., or from L. *seditio(n-)*, from *sed-* 'apart' + *itio(n-)* 'going' (from the verb *ire*).]

se·di·tious /si'disHəs/ ▶ adj. inciting or causing people to rebel against the authority of a state or monarch. — **se·di·tious·ly** adv.

se·duce /si'd(y)ōōs/ ▶ v. [trans.] attract (someone) to a belief or into a course of action that is inadvisable or foolhardy. ■ entice into sexual activity. ■ attract powerfully: *the melody seduces the ear.* — **se·duc·er** n. **se·duc·i·ble** adj. [15th C. (orig. in the sense 'persuade (someone) to abandon their duty'): from L. *seducere*, from *se-* 'away, apart' + *ducere* 'to lead.']

se·duc·tion /si'dəkSHən/ ▶**n.** the action of seducing someone. ■ (often **seductions**) a tempting or attractive thing. [16th C.: from Fr. *séduction* or L. *seductio(n-)*, from *seducere* 'draw aside' (see SEDUCE).]

se·duc·tive /si'dəktiv/ ▶**adj.** tempting and attractive; enticing: *a seductive voice.* — **se·duc·tive·ly adv. se·duc·tive·ness n.**

se·duc·tress /si'dəktris/ ▶**n.** a woman who seduces someone, esp. one who entices a man into sexual activity. [19th C.: from obs. *seductor* 'male seducer,' from *seducere* (see SEDUCE).]

sed·u·lous /'sejələs/ ▶**adj.** (of a person or action) showing dedication and diligence: *he watched himself with the most sedulous care.* — **se·du·li·ty** /sə'jo͞olitē/ **n. sed·u·lous·ly adv. sed·u·lous·ness n.** [16th C.: from L. *sedulus* 'zealous' + -OUS.]

se·dum /'sēdəm/ ▶**n.** a widely distributed fleshy-leaved plant (genus *Sedum*) of the stonecrop family, with small star-shaped yellow, pink, or white flowers, grown as an ornamental.

see[1] /sē/ ▶**v.** (**sees** /sēz/, **see·ing** /sē-iNG/; past **saw** /sô/; past part. **seen** /sēn/) [trans.] **1** perceive with the eyes; discern visually. ■ [with clause] be or become aware of something from observation or from a written or other visual source: *I see that you have asked for training.* ■ be a spectator of (a film, game, or other entertainment); watch. ■ visit (a place) for the first time: *see Alaska in style.* ■ [in imper.] refer to (a specified source) for further information (used as a direction in a text): *(see chapter 11).* ■ experience or witness (an event or situation): *I shall not live to see it.* ■ be the time or setting of (something): *the 1970s saw the beginning of a technological revolution.* ■ observe without being able to affect: *they see their rights being taken away.* ■ (**see something in**) find good or attractive qualities in (someone): *I don't know what I see in you.* **2** discern or deduce mentally after reflection or from information; understand: *she could see what Rhoda meant.* ■ [with clause] ascertain after inquiring, considering, or discovering an outcome: *I'll see if I can get a game.* ■ [trans.] regard in a specified way: *he saw himself as a good teacher.* ■ foresee; view or predict as a possibility: *I can't see him anywhere else.* ■ used to ascertain or express comprehension, agreement, or continued attention, or to emphasize that an earlier prediction was correct: *see, I told you I'd come.* **3** meet (someone one knows) socially or by chance. ■ meet regularly as a boyfriend or girlfriend. ■ consult (a specialist or professional). ■ give an interview or consultation to (someone): *the doctor will see you now.* **4** [trans.] escort or conduct (someone) to a specified place: *don't bother seeing me out.* ■ [intrans.] (**see to**) attend to; provide for the wants of: *I'll see to Dad's lunch.* ■ [intrans.] ensure: *Lucy saw to it that everyone got enough to eat and drink.* **5** (in poker or brag) equal the bet of (an opponent).

– PHRASES **have seen better days** have declined from former prosperity or good condition: *this part of South London has seen better days.* **see one's way clear to do** (or **doing**) **something** find that it is possible or convenient to do something (often used in polite requests). **see sense** (or **reason**) realize that one is wrong and start acting sensibly.

– PHRASAL VERBS **see about** attend to; deal with: *he had gone to see about a job.* **see after** archaic take care of; look after. **see someone off** accompany a person who is leaving to their point of departure. **see through** not be deceived by; detect the true nature of: *he can see through her lies.* **see someone through** support a person for the duration of a difficult time. **see something through** persist with an undertaking until it is completed. — **see·a·ble adj.** [OE *sēon*, of Gmc. origin; rel. to Du. *zien* and Ger. *sehen*, perh. from an Indo-Eur. root shared by L. *sequi* 'follow.']

see[2] ▶**n.** the place in which a cathedral church stands, identified as the seat of authority of a bishop or archbishop. [ME: from Anglo-Norman Fr. *sed*, from L. *sedes* 'seat,' from *sedere* 'sit.']

seed /sēd/ ▶**n. 1** a flowering plant's unit of reproduction, capable of developing into another such plant. ■ a quantity of these: *grass seed.* ■ fig. the cause or latent beginning of a feeling, process, or condition: *seed of doubt.* ■ archaic (chiefly in biblical use) a person's offspring or descendants. ■ a man's semen. ■ (also **seed crystal**) a small crystal introduced into a liquid to act as a nucleus for crystallization. ■ a small container for radioactive material placed in body tissue during radiotherapy. **2** any of a number of stronger competitors in a sports tournament who have been assigned a specified position in an ordered list with the aim of ensuring that they do not play each other in the early rounds. ▶**v. 1** [trans.] sow (land) with seeds: *the shoreline is seeded with a special grass.* ■ sow (a particular kind of seed) on or in the ground. ■ fig. cause (something) to begin to develop or grow: *money to seed their new businesses.* ■ place a crystal or crystalline substance in (something) in order to cause crystallization or condensation (esp. in a cloud to produce rain). **2** [intrans.] (of a plant) produce or drop seeds. ■ (**seed itself**) (of a plant) reproduce itself by means of its own seeds: *feverfew will seed itself readily.* **3** [trans.] remove the seeds from (vegetables or fruit). **4** [trans.] give (a competitor) the status of seed in a tournament.

– PHRASES **go** (or **run**) **to seed** (of a plant) cease flowering as the seeds develop. ■ deteriorate in condition, strength, or efficiency: *he has allowed himself to go to seed.* — **seed·less adj.** [OE *sǣd*, of Gmc. origin; rel. to Du. *zaad*, Ger. *Saat*, also to the verb SOW[1].]

seed·bed /'sēd,bed/ ▶**n.** a bed of fine soil in which seedlings are germinated.

seed cake ▶**n.** cake containing caraway seeds as flavoring.

seed cap·i·tal ▶**n.** see SEED MONEY.

seed coat ▶**n.** Bot. the protective outer coat of a seed.

seed corn ▶**n.** good-quality corn kept for seed.

seed·ed /'sēdid/ ▶**adj. 1** [in comb.] (of a plant or fruit) having a seed or seeds of a specified kind or number: *a single-seeded fruit.* ■ (of land or an area of ground) having been sown with seed. ■ Heraldry (of a flower) having seeds of a specified tincture. **2** (of a fruit or vegetable) having had the seeds removed. **3** given the status of seed in a sports tournament.

seed·er /'sēdər/ ▶**n. 1** a machine for sowing seed mechanically. **2** a plant that produces seeds in a particular way or under particular conditions.

seed fern ▶**n.** another term for PTERIDOSPERM.

seed head ▶**n.** a flowerhead in seed.

seed leaf ▶**n.** Bot. a cotyledon.

seed·ling /'sēdliNG/ ▶**n.** a young plant, esp. one raised from seed and not from a cutting.

seed-lip ▶**n.** esp. hist. a basket for holding seed, used when sowing by hand.

seed mon·ey ▶**n.** money allocated to initiate a project.

seed pearl ▶**n.** a very small pearl.

seed·pod /'sēd,päd/ ▶**n.** see POD[1] (sense 1).

seed po·ta·to ▶**n.** a potato that is planted and used for the production of seeds.

seeds·man /'sēdzmən/ ▶**n.** (pl. **-men**) a person who deals in seeds as a profession.

seed-snipe ▶**n.** a South American bird resembling a small partridge, with mainly brown plumage. Family Thinocoridae includes two genera and four species.

seed time ▶**n.** the sowing season.

seed·y /'sēdē/ ▶**adj.** (**seed·i·er, seed·i·est**) **1** sordid and disreputable: *his seedy affair with a soft-porn starlet.* ■ shabby and squalid: *a seedy apartment building.* **2** dated unwell: *she felt weak and seedy.* — **seed·i·ly** /'sēdl-ē/ **adv. seed·i·ness n.**

See·ger /'sēgər/, Pete (1919–), US singer and songwriter, a prominent figure in the revival of American folk music.

see·ing /'sē-iNG/ ▶**conj.** because; since: **seeing as** *Stuart's an old friend, I thought I might help him out.* ▶**n.** the action of seeing someone or something. ■ Astron. the quality of observed images as determined by atmospheric conditions.

– PHRASES **seeing is believing** proverb you need to see something before you can accept that it really exists or occurs.

See·ing Eye dog ▶**n.** trademark a guide dog trained to lead the blind.

seek /sēk/ ▶**v.** (past **sought** /sôt/) [trans.] attempt to find (something): *they seek shelter.* ■ attempt or desire to obtain or achieve (something): *the new regime sought his extradition.* ■ ask for (something) from someone: *he sought help from the police.* ■ (**seek someone/something out**) search for and find someone or something: *it's his job to seek out new customers.*

– PHRASES **seek one's fortune** travel somewhere in the hope of achieving wealth and success. ■ (**far to seek**) out of reach; a long way off. — **seek·er n.** [often in comb.] *a pleasure-seeker.* [OE *sēcan*, of Gmc. origin; rel. to Du. *zieken* and Ger. *suchen*, from an Indo-Eur. root shared by L. *sagire* 'perceive by scent.']

seel /sēl/ ▶**v.** [trans.] archaic close (a person's eyes); prevent (someone) from seeing. [15th C. 'stitch shut the eyelids of (a hawk)': from Fr. *ciller*, or med. L. *ciliare*, from L. *cilium* 'eyelid.']

seem /sēm/ ▶**v.** [intrans.] give the impression or sensation of being something or having a particular quality: [with complement] *Dawn seemed annoyed.* ■ [with infin.] used to make a statement or description of one's thoughts, feelings, or actions less assertive or forceful: *I seem to remember giving you very precise instructions.* ■ (**cannot seem to do something**) be unable to do something, despite having tried. ■ [with clause] (**it seems** or **it would seem**) used to suggest in a cautious, guarded, or polite way that something is true or a fact. [ME: from ON *sœma* 'to honor,' from *sœmr* 'fitting.']

seem·ing /'sēmiNG/ ▶**adj.** appearing to be real or true, but not necessarily being so; apparent: *Ellen's seeming indifference to the woman's fate.* ■ [in comb.] giving the impression of having a specified quality: *an angry-seeming man.* ▶**n.** literary the outward appearance or aspect of someone or something, esp. when considered as deceptive or as distinguished from reality: *that dissidence between inward reality and outward seeming.*

seem·ing·ly /'sēmiNGlē/ ▶**adv.** so as to give the impression of having a certain quality; apparently: *a seemingly competent and well-organized person.* ■ [sentence adverb] according to the facts as one knows them; as far as one knows.

seem·ly /'sēmlē/ ▶**adj.** conforming to accepted notions of propriety or good taste; decorous. — **seem·li·ness n.** [ME: from ON *sœmiligr*, from *sœmr* 'fitting.']

seen /sēn/ past participle of SEE[1].

See of Rome ▶**n.** another term for HOLY SEE.

seep /sēp/ ▶**v.** [intrans.] (of a liquid) flow or leak slowly through porous material or small holes. ▶**n.** a place where petroleum or water oozes slowly out of the ground. [18th C.: perh. dial. form of OE *sīpian* 'to soak.']

seep·age /'sēpij/ ▶**n.** the slow escape of a liquid or gas through porous material or small holes. ■ the quantity of liquid or gas that seeps out.

se·er[1] /'sēər; si(ə)r/ ▶**n. 1** a person of supposed supernatural insight who sees visions of the future. ■ an expert who provides forecasts of the economic or political future. **2** [usu. in comb.] esp. archaic a person who sees something specified: *a seer of the future* | *ghost-seers.*

seer[2] /si(ə)r/ ▶**n.** (in the Indian subcontinent) a varying unit of weight (about one kilogram) or liquid measure (about one liter). [from Hindi *ser.*]

seer·suck·er /'si(ə)r,səkər/ ▶**n.** a printed cotton or synthetic fabric that has a surface consisting of puckered and flat sections, typically in a striped pattern. [18th C.: from Pers. *širošakar*, lit. 'milk and sugar.']

see·saw /'sē,sô/ (also **see-saw**) ▶**n.** a long plank balanced in the middle on a fixed support, on each end of which children sit and swing up and down by pushing the ground alternately with their feet. ■ fig. a situation characterized by rapid, repeated changes from one state or condition to another. ▶**v.** [intrans.] change rapidly and repeatedly from one position, situation, or condition to another and back again: *the market seesawed.* ■ [trans.] cause (something) to move back and forth or up and down rapidly and repeatedly. [17th C. (orig. used by sawyers as a rhythmical refrain): reduplication of the verb SAW[1] (symbolic of the sawing motion).]

seethe /sēTH/ ▶**v.** [intrans.] (of a liquid) bubble up as a result of being boiled: *the brew foamed and seethed.* ■ (of a river or the sea) foam as if it were boiling; be turbulent. ■ [intrans.] (of a person) be filled with intense but unexpressed anger. ■ (of a place) be crowded with people or things moving about in a rapid or hectic way: *the entire cellar was seething with spiders.* ■ (of a crowd of people) move in a rapid or hectic way. [OE *sēothan* 'make or keep boiling,' of Gmc. origin; rel. to Du. *zieden.*]

see-through ▶**adj.** (esp. of clothing) translucent: *this shirt's a bit see-through when it's wet.*

seg·ment /'segmənt/ ▶**n.** **1** each of the parts into which something is or may be divided. ■ a portion of time allocated to a particular broadcast item on radio or television. ■ a separate broadcast item, typically one of a number that make up a particular program. ■ Phonet. the smallest distinct part of a spoken utterance, in particular the vowels and consonants as opposed to stress and intonation. ■ Zool. each of the series of similar anatomical units of which the body and appendages of some animals are composed, such as the visible rings of an earthworm's body. **2** Geom. a part of a figure cut off by a line or plane intersecting it, in particular: ■ the part of a circle enclosed between an arc and a chord. ■ the part of a line included between two points. ■ the part of a sphere cut off by any plane not passing through the center. ▶**v.** /'seg,ment; seg'ment/ [trans.] divide (something) into separate parts or sections. ■ [intrans.] divide into separate parts or sections. ■ [intrans.] Embryol. (of a cell) undergo cleavage; divide into many cells. — **seg·men·tar·y** /-,terē/ **adj.** **seg·men·ta·tion** /,segmən'tāSHən/ **n.** [16th C.: from L. *segmentum*, from *secare* 'to cut.']

seg·men·tal /seg'mentl/ ▶**adj.** **1** composed of separate parts or sections. **2** Archit. denoting or of the form of an arch the curved part of which forms a shallow arc of a circle, less than a semicircle. — **seg·men·tal·i·za·tion** /-,mentl-i'zāSHən/ **n.** **seg·men·tal·ize** /-,īz/ **v.** **seg·men·tal·ly** **adv.**

seg·men·ta·tion cav·i·ty ▶**n.** another term for BLASTOCOEL.

se·go /'sēgō/ (in full **sego lily**) ▶**n.** (pl. **-gos**) a plant (*Calochortus nuttalli*) of the lily family, with green and white bell-shaped flowers, native to the western US. Closely related to the MARIPOSA LILY. [19th C. Western Shoshone *sikoo.*]

sego

Se·go·vi·a /si'gōvēə/, Andrés (1893–1987), Spanish guitarist and composer. He was largely responsible for the revival of the classical guitar.

seg·re·gate /'segri,gāt/ ▶**v.** [trans.] (usu. **be segregated**) set apart from the rest or from each other; isolate or divide. ■ separate or divide (people, activities, or institutions) along racial, sexual, or religious lines. ■ [intrans.] Genet. (of pairs of alleles) be separated at meiosis and transmitted independently via separate gametes. — **seg·re·ga·ble** /-gəbəl/ **adj.** **seg·re·ga·tive** /-,gātiv/ **adj.** [16th C.: from L. *segregat-* 'separated from the flock,' from the verb *segregare*, from *se-* 'apart' + *grex, greg-* 'flock.']

seg·re·ga·tion /,segri'gāSHən/ ▶**n.** the action or state of setting someone or something apart from other people or things or being set apart. ■ the enforced separation of different racial groups in a country, community, or establishment. ■ Genet. the separation of pairs of alleles at meiosis and their independent transmission via separate gametes. — **seg·re·ga·tion·al** /-SHənl/ **adj.** **seg·re·ga·tion·ist** /-ist/ **adj.** & **n.** (in the racial sense).

se·gue /'segwā; 'sā-/ ▶**v.** (**se·gues, se·gued** /'segwād; 'sā-/, **se·gue·ing** /'segwā-iNG; 'sā-/) [intrans.] (in music and film) move without interruption from one song, melody, or scene to another. ▶**n.** an uninterrupted transition from one piece of music or film scene to another. [Ital., lit. 'follows.']

se·gui·dil·la /,segē'dēə/ ▶**n.** a Spanish dance in triple time. [18th C.: Sp., from *seguida* 'sequence,' from *seguir* 'follow.']

Sehn·sucht /'zān,zo͝okHt/ ▶**n.** literary yearning; wistful longing. [Ger.]

sei·cen·to /sā'CHen,tō/ ▶**n.** [often as adj.] the style of Italian art and literature of the 17th century. — **sei·cen·tist** /-tist/ **n.** [Ital., '600,' shortened from *mille seicento* '1600.']

seiche /sāSH/ ▶**n.** a temporary disturbance or oscillation in the water level of a lake, esp. one caused by changes in atmospheric pressure. [19th C.: from Swiss Fr., perh. from Ger. *Seiche* 'sinking (of water).']

sei·del /'sīdl; 'zīdl/ ▶**n.** dated a beer mug or glass. [20th C.: from Ger. *Seidel*, originally denoting a measure between a third and a half of a liter.]

Seid·litz pow·der /'sedlits/ ▶**n.** a laxative preparation that contains tartaric acid, sodium potassium tartrate, and sodium bicarbonate, and that effervesces when mixed with water. [18th C.: referring to the mineral water of *Seidlitz*, village in Bohemia.]

seif /sāf; sēf/ (in full **seif dune**) ▶**n.** a sand dune in the form of a long narrow ridge. [20th C.: from Arab. *sayf* 'sword' (from the shape).]

sei·gneur /sān'yər/ (also **sei·gnior** /sān'yôr; 'sān,yôr/) ▶**n.** esp. hist. a feudal lord; the lord of a manor. — **sei·gneu·ri·al** /-'yərēəl/ **adj.** [16th C.: from OFr., from L. *senior* 'older, elder.']

seign·ior·age /'sānyərij/ (also **seign·or·age**) ▶**n.** profit made by a government by issuing currency, esp. the difference between the face value of coins and their production costs. ■ hist. a thing claimed by a sovereign or feudal superior as a prerogative.

seign·ior·y /'sānyərē/ (also **seign·eur·y**) ▶**n.** (pl. **-ior·ies**) a feudal lordship; the position, authority, or domain of a feudal lord.

Seine /sān; sen/ a river in northern France that flows northwest to the English Channel.

seine /sān/ ▶**n.** (also **seine net**) a fishing net that hangs vertically in the water with floats at the top and weights at the bottom edge, the ends being drawn together to encircle the fish. — **sein·er** **n.** [OE *segne*, of West Gmc. origin, via L. from Gk. *sagēnē*; reinforced in ME by OFr. *saine.*]

seise /sēz/ ▶**v.** see SEIZE (sense 3).

sei·sin /'sēzən/ (also **sei·zin**) ▶**n.** Law possession of land by freehold. [ME: from OFr. *seisine*, from *saisir* 'seize.']

seis·mic /'sīzmik/ ▶**adj.** of or relating to earthquakes or other vibrations of the earth and its crust. ■ relating to or denoting geological surveying methods involving vibrations produced artificially by explosions. ■ fig. of enormous proportions or effect. — **seis·mi·cal** **adj.** **seis·mi·cal·ly** /-ik(ə)lē/ **adv.** [19th C.: from Gk. *seismos* 'earthquake' (from *seien* 'to shake') + -IC.]

seis·mic·i·ty /sīz'misitē/ ▶**n.** Geol. the occurrence or frequency of earthquakes in a region: *the high seismicity of the area.*

seismo- ▶**comb. form** of an earthquake; relating to earthquakes: *seismograph.* [from Gk. *seismos* 'earthquake.']

seis·mo·gram /'sīzmə,gram/ ▶**n.** a record produced by a seismograph.

seis·mo·graph /'sīzmə,graf/ ▶**n.** an instrument that measures and records details of earthquakes, such as force and duration. — **seis·mo·graph·ic** /,sīzmə'grafik/ **adj.** **seis·mo·graph·i·cal** /,sīzmə'grafikəl/ **adj.**

seis·mol·o·gy /sīz'mäləjē/ ▶**n.** the branch of science concerned with earthquakes and related phenomena. — **seis·mo·log·i·cal** /,sīzmə'läjikəl/ **adj.** **seis·mo·log·i·cal·ly** /,sīzmə'läjik(ə)lē/ **adv.** **seis·mol·o·gist** /-jist/ **n.**

seis·mom·e·ter /sīz'mämitər/ ▶**n.** another term for SEISMOGRAPH.

seis·mo·sau·rus /,sīzmə'sôrəs/ ▶**n.** a huge late Jurassic dinosaur (genus *Seismosaurus*, infraorder Sauropoda) known from only a few bones, probably the longest ever animal with a length of up to 115–150 feet (35–45 m), and one of the heaviest at up to 110 tons. [mod. L., from SEISMO- 'of an earthquake' + *sauros* 'lizard.']

sei whale /sā/ ▶**n.** a small rorqual (*Balaenoptera borealis*) with dark steely-gray skin and white grooves on the belly. [20th C.: from Norw. *sejhval.*]

sei·za /'sāzə/ ▶**n.** [in sing.] an upright kneeling position that is used in Japanese martial arts. [Japanese, from *sei* 'correct' + *za* 'sitting.']

seize /sēz/ ▶**v.** **1** [trans.] take hold of suddenly and forcibly: *she jumped up and seized his arm.* ■ capture (a place) using force. ■ assume (power or control) by force. ■ (of the police or another authority) take possession of (something) by warrant or legal right; confiscate; impound. ■ take (an opportunity or initiative) eagerly and decisively. ■ (of a feeling or pain) affect (someone) suddenly or acutely. ■ strongly appeal to or attract (the imagination or attention). ■ formal understand (something) quickly or clearly: *he always strains to seize the most somber truths.* **2** [intrans.] (of a machine with moving parts or a moving part in a machine) become stuck or jammed: *the engine seized up after only three weeks.* **3** (also **seise**) (**be seized of**) English Law be in legal possession of: *the court is currently seized of custody applications.* ■ hist. have or receive freehold possession of (property): *a person who is seized of land.* ■ be aware or informed of: *the judge was fully seized of the point.* **4** Naut., archaic fasten or attach (someone or something) to something by binding with turns of rope.

– PHRASES **seize the day** make the most of the present moment. [literal translation of CARPE DIEM.]

– PHRASAL VERBS **seize on/upon** take eager advantage of (something); exploit for one's own purposes. — **seiz·a·ble** **adj.** **seiz·er** **n.** [ME: from OFr. *seizir* 'give seisin,' from med. L. *sacire*, in the phr. *ad proprium* *sacire* 'claim as one's own,' from a Gmc. base meaning 'procedure.']

sei·zin ▶ n. var. of SEISIN.

seiz·ing /'sēziNG/ ▶ n. Naut., archaic a length of cord or rope used for fastening or tying.

sei·zure /'sēzHər/ ▶ n. **1** the action of capturing someone or something using force: *the Nazi seizure of power.* ■ the action of confiscating or impounding property by warrant of legal right. **2** a sudden attack of illness, esp. a stroke or an epileptic fit: *the patient had a seizure.*

se·jant /'sējənt/ ▶ adj. [usu. postpositive] Heraldry (of an animal) sitting upright. [15th C.: alt. of OFr. var. of *seant* 'sitting,' from the verb *seoir*, from L. *sedere* 'sit.']

sel. ▶ abbr. ■ select. ■ selected. ■ selection; selections.

se·la·chi·an /sə'lākēən/ Zool. ▶ n. an elasmobranch fish of a group that comprises the sharks and dogfishes. ▶ adj. of or relating to the selachians. [19th C.: from mod. L. *Selachii* (from Gk. *selakhos* 'shark') + -AN.]

se·lag·i·nel·la /sə,lajə'nelə/ ▶ n. a creeping mosslike plant of a genus (*Selaginella*) that includes the lesser club mosses. [mod. L., dimin. of L. *selago* 'club moss.']

se·lah /'sēlə; 'sel-/ ▶ exclam. (in the Bible) occurring frequently at the end of a verse in Psalms and Habakkuk, probably as a musical direction. [from Heb. *selāh*.]

sel·dom /'seldəm/ ▶ adv. not often; rarely. [OE *seldan*, of Gmc. origin; rel. to Du. *zelden* and Ger. *selten*, from a base meaning 'strange, wonderful.']

se·lect /sə'lekt/ ▶ v. [trans.] carefully choose as being the best or most suitable: *students must select courses.* ■ [intrans.] (**select for/against**) Biol. (in terms of evolution) determine whether (a characteristic or organism) will survive. ■ use a mouse or keystrokes to mark (something) on a computer screen for a particular operation. ▶ adj. (of a group of people or things) carefully chosen from a larger number as being the best or most valuable. ■ (of a place or group of people) only used by or consisting of a wealthy or sophisticated elite; exclusive. — **se·lect·a·ble** adj. **se·lect·ness** n. [16th C.: from L. *select-* 'chosen,' from the verb *seligere*, from *se-* 'apart' + *legere* 'choose.']

se·lect·ee /sə,lek'tē/ ▶ n. a person who is selected. ■ a conscript.

se·lec·tion /sə'leksHən/ ▶ n. **1** the action or fact of carefully choosing someone or something as being the best or most suitable. ■ a number of carefully chosen things. ■ a range of things from which a choice may be made: *the restaurant offers a wide selection of hot and cold dishes.* ■ a horse or horses tipped as worth bets in a race or meeting. **2** Biol. a process in which environmental or genetic influences determine which types of organism thrive better than others, regarded as a factor in evolution. See also NATURAL SELECTION.

se·lec·tive /sə'lektiv/ ▶ adj. relating to or involving the selection of the most suitable or best qualified: *the mini-cow is the result of generations of selective breeding.* ■ (of a person) tending to choose carefully. ■ (of a process or agent) affecting some things and not others. ■ esp. Electron. operating at or responding to a particular frequency. — **se·lec·tive·ly** adv.

se·lec·tive·ness /sə'lektivnis/ ▶ n. another term for SELECTIVITY.

se·lec·tive serv·ice ▶ n. service in the armed forces under conscription.

se·lec·tiv·i·ty /səlek'tivitē/ ▶ n. the quality of carefully choosing someone or something as the best or most suitable. ■ the property of affecting some things and not others. ■ Electron. the ability of a device to respond to a particular frequency without interference from others.

se·lect·man /sə'lektmən/ ▶ n. (pl. **-men**) a member of the local government board of a New England town.

se·lec·tor /sə'lektər/ ▶ n. a person or thing that selects something, in particular: ■ a device for selecting a particular gear or other setting of a machine or device.

Se·le·ne /sə'lēnē/ Gk. Mythol. the goddess of the moon who fell in love with Endymion. [from Gk. *selēnē* 'moon.']

se·le·nic ac·id /sə'lenik; -'lē-/ ▶ n. Chem. a crystalline acid, H_2SeO_4, analogous to sulfuric acid, made by oxidizing some selenium compounds. — **sel·e·nate** /'selə,nāt/ n.

sel·e·nite /'selə,nīt/ ▶ n. a form of gypsum occurring as transparent crystals or thin plates. [17th C.: via L. from Gk. *selēnitēs lithos* 'moonstone,' from *selēnē* 'moon' + *lithos* 'stone.']

se·le·ni·um /sə'lēnēəm/ ▶ n. the chemical element of atomic number 34, a gray crystalline nonmetal with semiconducting properties. (Symbol: **Se**) — **sel·e·nide** /'selə,nīd; -nid/ n. [19th C.: mod. L., from Gk. *selēnē* 'moon.']

se·le·ni·um cell ▶ n. a photoelectric device containing a piece of selenium.

seleno- ▶ comb. form of, relating to, or shaped like the moon: *selenography.* [from Gk. *selēnē* 'moon.']

sel·e·nog·ra·phy /,selə'nägrəfē/ ▶ n. the scientific mapping of the moon; lunar geography. — **sel·e·nog·ra·pher** /-fər/ n. **se·le·no·graph·ic** /,selənə'grafik/ adj. **se·le·no·graph·i·cal** /,selənə'grafikəl/ adj.

sel·e·nol·o·gy /,selə'näləjē/ ▶ n. the scientific study of the moon. — **sel·e·nol·o·gist** /-jist/ n.

Sel·es /'seləs/, Monica (1973–), US tennis player; born in Yugoslavia. During 1990–96, she won nine Grand Slam singles titles.

Se·leu·cid /sə'l(y)o͞osid/ ▶ adj. relating to or denoting a dynasty ruling over Syria and a great part of western Asia from 311 to 65 BC. Its capital was at Antioch. ▶ n. a member of this dynasty. [from *Seleucus* Nicator (the name of the founder, one of Alexander the Great's generals) + -ID³.]

self /self/ ▶ n. (pl. **selves** /selvz/) a person's essential being that distinguishes them from others, esp. considered as the object of introspection or reflexive action. ■ [with adj.] a person's particular nature or personality; the qualities that make a person individual or unique: *her usual cheerful self.* ■ one's own interests or pleasure: *the total surrender of self.* ▶ pron. (pl. **selves**) oneself, in particular: ■ [with adj.] (**one's self**) used ironically to refer in specified glowing terms to oneself or someone else. ▶ adj. [attrib.] (of a trimming or cover) of the same material and color as the rest of the item: *a dress with self belt.* ▶ v. [trans.] esp. Bot. self-pollinate; self-fertilize. ■ [usu. as adj.] (**selfed**) Genet. cause (an animal or plant) to breed with or fertilize one of the same hybrid origin or strain. [OE, of Gmc. origin; rel. to Du. *zelf* and Ger. *selbe*. Early use was emphatic, expressing the sense '(I) myself,' '(he) himself,' etc. The verb dates from the early 20th C.]

self- ▶ comb. form of or directed toward oneself or itself: *self-hatred.* ■ by one's own efforts; by its own action: *self-acting.* ■ on, in, for, or relating to oneself or itself: *self-adhesive.*

self-a·ban·don·ment (also **self-a·ban·don**) ▶ n. the action of completely surrendering oneself to a desire or impulse. — **self-a·ban·doned** adj.

self-a·base·ment ▶ n. the belittling or humiliation of oneself.

self-ab·ne·ga·tion ▶ n. the denial or abasement of oneself.

self-ab·sorp·tion ▶ n. **1** preoccupation with one's own emotions, interests, or situation. **2** Physics the absorption by a body of radiation which it has itself emitted. — **self-ab·sorbed** adj.

self-a·buse /ə'byo͞os/ ▶ n. behavior that causes damage or harm to oneself. ■ used euphemistically to refer to masturbation.

self-act·ing ▶ adj. archaic (of a machine or operation) acting without external influence or control; automatic.

self-ac·tu·al·i·za·tion ▶ n. the realization or fulfillment of one's talents and potentialities, esp. considered as a drive or need present in everyone.

self-ad·dressed ▶ adj. (esp. of an envelope) bearing one's own address.

self-ad·he·sive ▶ adj. coated with a sticky substance; adhering without requiring moistening.

self-ad·vance·ment ▶ n. the advancement or promotion of oneself or one's interests.

self-ad·ver·tise·ment ▶ n. the active publicization of oneself. — **self-advertiser** n. **self-advertising** adj.

self-ad·vo·ca·cy ▶ n. the action of representing oneself or one's views or interests.

self-ag·gran·dize·ment ▶ n. the action or process of promoting oneself as being powerful or important. — **self-ag·gran·diz·ing** adj.

self-al·ien·a·tion ▶ n. the process of distancing oneself from one's own feelings or activities, such as may occur in mental illness or as a symptom of emotional distress.

self-a·nal·y·sis ▶ n. the analysis of oneself, in particular one's motives and character. — **self-an·a·lyz·ing** adj.

self-an·ni·hi·la·tion ▶ n. the annihilation or obliteration of self, esp. as a process of mystical contemplation.

self-ap·point·ed ▶ adj. [attrib.] having assumed a position or role without the endorsement of others: *self-appointed experts.*

self-as·ser·tion ▶ n. the confident and forceful expression or promotion of oneself, one's views, or one's desires. — **self-as·sert·ing** adj. (dated) **self-as·ser·tive** adj. **self-as·ser·tive·ness** n.

self-as·sess·ment ▶ n. assessment or evaluation of oneself or one's actions and attitudes, in particular, of one's performance at a job or learning task considered in relation to an objective standard.

self-as·sur·ance ▶ n. confidence in one's own abilities or character. — **self-as·sured** adj. **self-as·sur·ed·ly** adv.

self-a·ware·ness ▶ n. conscious knowledge of one's own character, feelings, motives, and desires. — **self-a·ware** adj.

self-be·tray·al ▶ n. the intentional or inadvertent revelation of the truth about one's actions or thoughts.

self-cen·sor·ship ▶ n. the exercising of control over what one says and does, esp. to avoid castigation.

self-cen·tered ▶ adj. preoccupied with oneself and one's affairs: *he's far too self-centered to care what you do.* — **self-cen·tered·ly** adv. **self-cen·tered·ness** n.

self-col·ored ▶ adj. of a single uniform color: *a self-colored carpet.* ■ of the natural color of something.

self-con·ceit ▶ n. another term for SELF-CONGRATULATION. — **self-con·ceit·ed** adj.

self-con·cept ▶ n. Psychol. an idea of the self constructed from the beliefs one holds about oneself and the responses of others.

self-con·dem·na·tion ▶ n. the blaming of oneself. ■ the inadvertent revelation of one's wrongdoing. — **self-con·demned** adj. **self-con·demn·ing** adj.

self-con·fessed ▶ adj. [attrib.] having openly admitted to being a person with certain characteristics: *a self-confessed chocoholic.* — **self-con·fess·ed·ly** /-'fesidlē/ adv. **self-con·fes·sion** n. **self-con·fes·sion·al** adj.

self-con·fi·dence ▶ n. a feeling of trust in one's abilities, qualities, and judgment. — **self-con·fi·dent** adj. **self-con·fi·dent·ly** adv.

self-con·grat·u·la·tion ▶n. undue complacency or pride regarding one's personal achievements or qualities; self-satisfaction. —**self-con·grat·u·la·to·ry** adj.

self-con·scious ▶adj. feeling undue awareness of oneself, one's appearance, or one's actions. ■ Philos. Psychol. having knowledge of one's own existence, esp. the knowledge of oneself as a conscious being. ■ (esp. of an action or intention) deliberate and with full awareness, esp. affectedly so: *her self-conscious identification with the upper classes.* —**self-con·scious·ly** adv. **self-con·scious·ness** n.

self-con·sis·tent ▶adj. not having parts or aspects that are in conflict or contradiction with each other; consistent. —**self-con·sis·ten·cy** n.

self-con·tained ▶adj. **1** (of a thing) complete, or having all that is needed; in itself. **2** (of a person) quiet and independent; not depending on or influenced by others. —**self-con·tain·ment** n. (in sense 2).

self-con·tra·dic·tion ▶n. inconsistency between aspects or parts of a whole: *a puzzling self-contradiction in masochism.* —**self-con·tra·dict·ing** adj. **self-con·tra·dic·to·ry** adj.

self-con·trol ▶n. the ability to control oneself, in particular one's emotions and desires or the expression of them in one's behavior, esp. in difficult situations. —**self-con·trolled** adj.

self-cor·rect·ing ▶adj. correcting oneself or itself without external help: *a self-correcting optical finder.* —**self-cor·rect** v. **self-cor·rec·tion** n.

self-crit·i·cal ▶adj. critical of oneself, one's abilities, or one's actions in a self-aware or unduly disapproving manner. —**self-crit·i·cism** n.

self-de·ceiv·ing ▶adj. allowing oneself to believe that a false or unvalidated feeling, idea, or situation is true. —**self-de·ceiv·er** n.

self-de·cep·tion ▶n. the action or practice of allowing oneself to believe that a false or unvalidated feeling, idea, or situation is true. —**self-de·cep·tive** adj.

self-de·feat·ing ▶adj. (of an action or policy) unable to achieve the end it is designed to bring about.

self-de·fense ▶n. the defense of one's person or interests, esp. through the use of physical force, which is permitted in certain cases as an answer to a charge of violent crime. —**self-de·fen·sive** adj.

self-def·i·ni·tion ▶n. definition of one's individuality and one's role in life; such definition of a group by its members.

self-de·ni·al ▶n. the denial of one's own interests and needs; self-sacrifice. —**self-de·ny·ing** adj.

self-dep·re·cat·ing ▶adj. modest about or critical of oneself, esp. humorously so: *self-deprecating jokes.* —**self-dep·re·cat·ing·ly** adv. **self-dep·re·ca·tion** n. **self-dep·re·ca·to·ry** adj.

self-de·pre·ci·a·tion ▶n. another term for SELF-DEPRECATION (see SELF-DEPRECATING). —**self-dep·re·ci·a·to·ry** adj.

self-de·struct ▶v. [intrans.] (of a thing) destroy itself by exploding or disintegrating automatically, having been preset to do so. —**self-de·struc·tion** n. **self-de·struc·tive** adj. **self-de·struc·tive·ly** adv.

self-de·ter·mi·na·tion ▶n. the process by which a country determines its own statehood and forms its own allegiances and government. ■ the process by which a person controls their own life.

self-de·vel·op·ment ▶n. the process by which a person's character or abilities are gradually developed.

self-de·vo·tion ▶n. the devotion of oneself to a person or cause.

self-di·rect·ed ▶adj. (of an emotion, statement, or activity) directed at oneself. ■ (of an activity) under one's own control: *self-directed learning.* ■ (of a person) showing initiative and the ability to organize oneself. —**self-di·rec·tion** n.

self-dis·ci·pline ▶n. the ability to control one's feelings and overcome one's weaknesses; the ability to pursue what one thinks is right despite temptations to abandon it. —**self-dis·ci·plined** adj.

self-dis·cov·er·y ▶n. the process of acquiring insight into one's own character.

self-doubt ▶n. lack of confidence in oneself and one's abilities.

self-ed·u·cat·ed ▶adj. educated largely through one's own efforts, rather than by formal instruction. —**self-ed·u·ca·tion** n.

self-ef·fac·ing ▶adj. not claiming attention for oneself; retiring and modest. —**self-ef·face·ment** n. **self-ef·fac·ing·ly** adv.

self-em·ployed ▶adj. working for oneself as a freelancer or the owner of a business rather than for an employer: *a self-employed builder.* —**self-em·ploy·ment** n.

self-en·closed ▶adj. (of a person, community, or system) not choosing to or able to communicate with others or with external systems: *the family is a self-enclosed unit.*

self-es·teem ▶n. confidence in one's own worth or abilities; self-respect.

self-ev·i·dent ▶adj. not needing to be demonstrated or explained; obvious: *self-evident truths.* —**self-ev·i·dence** n. **self-ev·i·dent·ly** adv.

self-ex·am·i·na·tion ▶n. the study of one's own behavior and motivations. ■ the action of examining one's own body for signs of illness.

self-ex·cit·ed ▶adj. Physics relating to or denoting a dynamo-electric machine or analogous system that generates or excites its own magnetic field.

self-ex·ist·ent ▶adj. existing independently of other beings or causes.

self-ex·plan·a·to·ry ▶adj. easily understood; not needing explanation.

self-ex·pres·sion ▶n. the expression of one's feelings, thoughts, or ideas, esp. in writing, art, music, or dance. —**self-ex·pres·sive** adj.

self-feed·er ▶n. **1** a furnace or machine that renews its own fuel or material automatically. **2** a device for supplying food to farm animals automatically. —**self-feed·ing** adj.

self-fer·ti·li·za·tion ▶n. Biol. the fertilization of plants and some invertebrate animals by their own pollen or sperm rather than that of another individual. —**self-fer·ti·lized** adj. **self-fer·ti·liz·ing** adj.

self-fi·nanc·ing ▶adj. (of an organization or enterprise) having or generating enough income to finance itself. —**self-fi·nanced** adj.

self-flag·el·la·tion ▶n. the action of flogging oneself, esp. as a form of religious discipline. ■ fig. excessive criticism of oneself.

self-for·get·ful ▶adj. forgetful of oneself or one's needs. —**self-for·get·ful·ness** n.

self-ful·fill·ing ▶adj. (of an opinion or prediction) bound to be proved correct or to come true as a result of behavior caused by its being expressed.

self-ful·fill·ment (Brit. **self-ful·fil·ment**) ▶n. the fulfillment of one's hopes and ambitions.

self-gen·er·at·ing ▶adj. generated by itself, rather than by some external force: *the strident activity of the industrial scene seems to be self-generating.*

self-gov·ern·ment ▶n. **1** government of a country by its own people, esp. after having been a colony. **2** another term for SELF-CONTROL. —**self-gov·erned** adj. **self-gov·ern·ing** adj.

self-guid·ed ▶adj. (of a walk or visit to a tourist attraction) undertaken without the supervision of a tour guide.

self-heal (also **self·heal**) ▶n. a purple-flowered plant (*Prunella vulgaris*) of the mint family that was formerly widely used for healing wounds. Native to Eurasia, it is now widespread throughout North America.

self-help ▶n. the use of one's own efforts and resources to achieve things without relying on others.

self·hood /ˈselfˌhŏŏd/ ▶n. the quality that constitutes one's individuality; the state of having an individual identity.

self-i·den·ti·fi·ca·tion ▶n. the attribution of certain characteristics or qualities to oneself: *self-identification by the old person as sick or inadequate.*

self-im·age ▶n. the idea one has of one's abilities, appearance, and personality.

self-im·mo·la·tion ▶n. the offering of oneself as a sacrifice, esp. by burning; such suicidal action in the name of a cause or strongly held belief.

self-im·por·tance ▶n. an exaggerated sense of one's own value or importance. —**self-im·por·tant** adj. **self-im·por·tant·ly** adv.

self-im·posed ▶adj. (of a task or circumstance) imposed on oneself, not by an external force: *he went into self-imposed exile.*

self-im·prove·ment ▶n. the improvement of one's knowledge, status, or character by one's own efforts.

self-in·duced ▶adj. brought about by oneself: *self-induced vomiting.*

self-in·dul·gent ▶adj. characterized by doing or tending to do exactly what one wants, esp. when this involves pleasure or idleness. ■ (of a creative work) lacking economy and control. —**self-in·dul·gence** n. **self-in·dul·gent·ly** adv.

self-in·flict·ed ▶adj. (of a wound or other harm) inflicted on oneself.

self-in·sur·ance ▶n. insurance of oneself or one's interests by maintaining a fund to cover possible losses rather than by purchasing an insurance policy.

self-in·ter·est ▶n. one's personal interest or advantage, esp. when pursued without regard for others. —**self-in·ter·est·ed** adj.

self-in·volved ▶adj. wrapped up in oneself or one's own thoughts. —**self-in·volve·ment** n.

self·ish /ˈselfisн/ ▶adj. (of a person, action, or motive) lacking consideration for others; concerned chiefly with one's own personal profit or pleasure. —**self·ish·ly** adv. **self·ish·ness** n.

self-jus·ti·fi·ca·tion ▶n. the justification or excusing of oneself or one's actions. —**self-jus·tif·i·ca·to·ry** adj. **self-jus·ti·fy·ing** adj.

self-knowl·edge ▶n. understanding of oneself or one's own motives or character. —**self-know·ing** adj.

self·less /ˈselfləs/ ▶adj. concerned more with the needs and wishes of others than with one's own; unselfish. —**self·less·ly** adv. **self·less·ness** n.

self-lim·it·ing ▶adj. relating to or denoting something that limits itself, in particular: ■ (also **self-lim·it·ed**) Med. (of a condition) ultimately resolving itself without treatment.

self-liq·ui·dat·ing ▶adj. denoting an asset that earns back its original cost out of income over a fixed period.

self-load·ing ▶adj. (esp. of a gun) loading automatically: *a self-loading pistol.* —**self-load·er** n.

self-love ▶n. regard for one's own well-being and happiness (chiefly considered as a desirable rather than narcissistic characteristic). —**self-lov·ing** adj.

self-made ▶adj. having become successful or rich by one's own efforts:

a self-made millionaire. ■ made by oneself: *a self-made kite.*

self-mas·ter·y ▶ n. self-control.

self-med·i·cate ▶ v. [intrans.] choose and take medicines oneself, rather than by prescription or on expert advice. — **self-med·i·ca·tion** n.

self-mor·ti·fi·ca·tion ▶ n. the subjugation of appetites or desires by self-denial or self-discipline as an aspect of religious devotion.

self-mo·tion ▶ n. movement caused by oneself or itself, not by an external action or agent. — **self-mov·ing** adj.

self-mo·ti·vat·ed ▶ adj. motivated to do or achieve something because of one's own enthusiasm or interest, without needing pressure from others. — **self-mo·ti·vat·ing** adj. **self-mo·ti·va·tion** n.

self-mur·der ▶ n. another term for SUICIDE (sense 1 of the **noun**). — **self-mur·der·er** n.

self-o·pin·ion·at·ed ▶ adj. having an arrogantly high regard for oneself or one's own opinions. — **self-o·pin·ion** n.

self-par·o·dy ▶ n. the intentional or inadvertent parodying or exaggeration of one's usual behavior or speech. — **self-par·o·dy·ing** adj.

self-per·pet·u·at·ing ▶ adj. perpetuating itself or oneself without external agency or intervention: *the self-perpetuating power of the bureaucracy.* — **self-per·pet·u·a·tion** n.

self-pit·y ▶ n. excessive, self-absorbed unhappiness over one's own troubles. — **self-pit·y·ing** adj. **self-pit·y·ing·ly** adv.

self-po·lic·ing ▶ n. the process of keeping order or maintaining control within a community without accountability or reference to an external authority. ▶ adj. (of a community) independently responsible for keeping and maintaining order.

self-pol·li·na·tion ▶ n. Bot. the pollination of a flower by pollen from the same flower or from another flower on the same plant. — **self-pol·li·nat·ed** adj. **self-pol·li·nat·ing** adj. **self-pol·li·na·tor** n.

self-por·trait ▶ n. a portrait that an artist produces of themselves. — **self-por·trai·ture** n.

self-pos·sessed ▶ adj. calm, confident, and in control of one's feelings; composed. — **self-pos·ses·sion** n.

self-pres·er·va·tion ▶ n. the protection of oneself from harm or death, esp. regarded as a basic instinct in human beings and animals.

self-pro·claimed ▶ adj. [attrib.] described as or proclaimed to be such by oneself, without endorsement by others: *self-proclaimed experts.*

self-pro·pelled ▶ adj. moving or able to move without external propulsion or agency: *a self-propelled weapon.* — **self-pro·pel·ling** adj.

self-re·al·i·za·tion ▶ n. fulfillment of one's own potential.

self-ref·er·en·tial ▶ adj. (esp. of a literary or other creative work) making reference to itself, its author or creator, or their other work. — **self-ref·er·en·ti·al·i·ty** n. **self-ref·er·en·tial·ly** adv.

self-re·flex·ive ▶ adj. containing a reflection or image of itself; self-referential: *sociology's self-reflexive critique.*

self-re·gard ▶ n. regard or consideration for oneself; self-respect. ■ conceit; vanity. — **self-re·gard·ing** adj.

self-reg·u·lat·ing ▶ adj. regulating itself without intervention from external bodies.

self-re·li·ance ▶ n. reliance on one's own powers and resources rather than those of others. — **self-re·li·ant** adj. **self-re·li·ant·ly** adv.

self-re·nun·ci·a·tion ▶ n. renunciation of one's own will; self-sacrifice; unselfishness.

self-re·spect ▶ n. pride and confidence in oneself; a feeling that one is behaving with honor and dignity.

self-re·spect·ing ▶ adj. having self-respect: *proud, self-respecting mountain villagers.* ■ [attrib.] often humorous a person who merits a particular role or name: *no self-respecting editor would run such an article.*

self-re·straint ▶ n. restraint imposed by oneself on one's own actions; self-control. — **self-re·strained** adj.

self-re·veal·ing ▶ adj. revealing one's character or motives, esp. inadvertently. — **self-rev·e·la·tion** n. **self-re·vel·a·to·ry** adj.

self-right·eous ▶ adj. having or characterized by a certainty, esp. an unfounded one, that one is totally correct or morally superior: *self-righteous indignation.* — **self-right·eous·ly** adv. **self-right·eous·ness** n.

self-ris·ing flour ▶ n. flour that has a leavening agent already added.

self-rule ▶ n. another term for SELF-GOVERNMENT (sense 1).

self-sac·ri·fice ▶ n. the giving up of one's own interests or wishes in order to help others or to advance a cause. — **self-sac·ri·fi·cial** adj. **self-sac·ri·fic·ing** adj.

self·same /ˈself,sām/ ▶ adj. [attrib.] (usu. **the selfsame**) exactly the same: *he was standing in the selfsame spot.*

self-sat·is·fied ▶ adj. excessively and unwarrantedly satisfied with oneself or one's achievements; smugly complacent: *a self-satisfied smirk.* — **self-sat·is·fac·tion** n.

self-seal·ing ▶ adj. sealing itself without the usual process or procedure, in particular: ■ (of a tire, fuel tank, etc.) able to seal small punctures automatically. ■ (of an envelope) self-adhesive.

self-seek·ing ▶ adj. & n. another term for SELF-SERVING. — **self-seek·er** n.

self-se·lec·tion ▶ n. the action of putting oneself forward for something. — **self-se·lect·ing** adj.

self-serv·ice ▶ adj. denoting a store, restaurant, or service station where customers select goods for themselves or service their car for themselves and pay a cashier: *a self-service cafeteria.* ▶ n. the system whereby customers select goods for themselves or service their car for themselves and pay a cashier: *providing quick self-service.*

self-serv·ing ▶ adj. having concern for one's own welfare and interests before those of others. ▶ n. concern for oneself before others.

self-slaugh·ter ▶ n. poetic/literary term for SUICIDE (sense 1 of the **noun**).

self-sow /ˈsō/ ▶ v. [intrans.] (of a plant) propagate itself by seed.

self-start·er ▶ n. **1** a person who is sufficiently motivated or ambitious to start a new career or business or to pursue further education without the help of others. **2** dated the starter of a motor-vehicle engine. — **self-start·ing** adj.

self-ster·ile ▶ adj. Biol. incapable of self-fertilization. — **self-ste·ril·i·ty** n.

self-stick ▶ adj. coated with an adhesive on one side for ready application to a surface: *peel off self-stick backing.*

self-styled ▶ adj. [attrib.] using a description or title that one has given oneself: *self-styled experts.*

self-suf·fi·cient ▶ adj. needing no outside help in satisfying one's basic needs, esp. with regard to the production of food: *Botswana will never be self-sufficient in food.* ■ emotionally and intellectually independent. — **self-suf·fi·cien·cy** n. **self-suf·fi·cient·ly** adv.

self-sug·ges·tion ▶ n. another term for AUTOSUGGESTION.

self-sup·port·ing ▶ adj. **1** having the resources to be able to survive without outside assistance. **2** staying up or upright without being supported by something else. — **self-sup·port** n.

self-sur·ren·der ▶ n. the surrender of oneself or one's will to an external influence, an emotion, or another person.

self-sus·tain·ing ▶ adj. able to continue in a healthy state without outside assistance: *his puny farms were years from being self-sustaining.* — **self-sus·tained** adj.

self-taught ▶ adj. having acquired knowledge or skill on one's own initiative rather than through formal instruction or training: *a self-taught graphic artist.*

self-tran·scend·ence ▶ n. the overcoming of the limits of the individual self and its desires in spiritual contemplation and realization.

self-un·der·stand·ing ▶ n. awareness of and ability to understand one's own actions and reactions.

self-willed ▶ adj. obstinately doing what one wants in spite of the wishes or orders of others. — **self-will** n.

self-wind·ing /ˈwīndiNG/ ▶ adj. (chiefly of a watch) wound by some automatic means, such as an electric motor or the movement of the wearer, rather than by hand.

self-worth ▶ n. another term for SELF-ESTEEM.

Sel·juk /selˈjo͝ok; ˈsel,jo͞ok/ ▶ n. a member of any of the Turkish dynasties that ruled Asia Minor in the 11th to 13th centuries, successfully invading the Byzantine Empire and defending the Holy Land against the Crusaders. ▶ adj. of or relating to the Seljuks. — **Sel·juk·i·an** /-ˈjo͞okēən/ adj. & n. [from Turk. *seljūq*, the name of the reputed ancestor of the dynasty.]

sell /sel/ ▶ v. (past and past part. **sold** /sōld/) [trans.] **1** give or hand over (something) in exchange for money: *they had sold the car.* ■ have a stock of (something) available for sale: *the store sells electrical goods.* ■ [intrans.] (of a thing) be purchased: *this magazine won't sell.* ■ (of a publication or recording) attain sales of (a specified number of copies): *the album sold 6 million copies.* ■ [intrans.] (**sell for/at**) be available for sale at (a specified price): *these antiques sell for about $375.* ■ [intrans.] (**sell out**) sell all of one's stock of something. ■ [intrans.] (**sell out**) be all sold: *the performances would not sell out.* ■ [intrans.] (**sell through**) (of a product) be purchased by a customer from a retail outlet. ■ [intrans.] (**sell up**) sell all of one's property, possessions, or assets: *Ernest sold up and retired.* ■ (**sell oneself**) have sex in exchange for money. ■ archaic offer (something) dishonorably for money or other reward; make a matter of corrupt bargaining: *do not your lawyers sell all their practice, as your priests their prayers?* ■ (**sell someone out**) betray someone for one's own financial or material benefit. ■ [intrans.] (**sell out**) abandon one's principles for reasons of expedience. **2** persuade someone of the merits of. ■ be the reason for (something) being bought: *what sells CDs to most people is convenience.* ■ cause (someone) to become enthusiastic about: [as adj.] (**sold**) *I'm just not sold on the idea.* **3** archaic trick or deceive (someone): *what we want is to talk this show up, and sell the rest of the town.* ▶ n. informal **1** an act of selling or attempting to sell something: *scientific achievement is too subtle a sell for the public.* **2** a disappointment, typically one arising from being deceived as to the merits of something: *actually, Hawaii's a bit of a sell.*

– PHRASES **sell someone/something short** fail to recognize or state the true value of: *don't sell yourself short.* — **sell·a·ble** adj. [OE *sellan* (v.), of Gmc. origin; rel. to ON *selja* 'give up, sell.' Early use included the sense 'give, hand (something) over voluntarily in response to a request.']

sell·er /ˈselər/ ▶ n. **1** a person who sells something. ■ (**the seller**) the party in a legal transaction who is selling. **2** [with adj.] a product that sells in some specified way: *the biggest seller of the year.*

– PHRASES **seller's** (or **sellers'**) **market** an economic situation in which goods or shares are scarce and sellers can keep prices high.

sell·ing point ▶ n. a feature of a product for sale that makes it attractive to customers.

sell·ing race ▶ n. a horse race after which the winning horse must be auctioned.

sell-off ▶ n. a sale of assets, typically at a low price, carried out in order to dispose of them rather than as normal trade. ■ a sale of shares, bonds, or commodities, esp. one that causes a fall in price.

sell·out /ˈselˌout/ ▶ n. 1 the selling of an entire stock of something, esp. tickets for an entertainment or sports event. ■ an event for which all tickets are sold: *the game is sure to be a sellout.* 2 a sale of a business or company. ■ a betrayal of one's principles for reasons of expedience: *the sellout of socialist economic policy.*

sell-through ▶ n. the ratio of the quantity of goods sold by a retail outlet to the quantity distributed to it wholesale: *the sell-through was amazing, 60 percent.* ■ the retail sale of something, typically a prerecorded videocassette, as opposed to its rental: [as adj.] *the burgeoning sell-through market.*

Sel·ma /ˈselmə/ a city in south central Alabama; site of civil rights demonstrations 1965; pop. 23,755.

selt·zer /ˈseltsər/ (also **selt·zer wa·ter**) ▶ n. soda water. ■ medicinal mineral water from Niederselters in Germany. [18th C.: alt. of Ger. *Selterser*, from *(Nieder)selters* (see above).]

sel·va /ˈselvə/ ▶ n. a tract of land covered by dense equatorial forest, esp. in the Amazon basin. [19th C.: from Sp. or Port., from L. *silva* 'wood.']

sel·vage /ˈselvij/ ▶ n. an edge produced on woven fabric during manufacture that prevents it from unraveling. ■ Geol. a zone of altered rock, esp. volcanic glass, at the edge of a rock mass. [ME: from an alt. of SELF + EDGE, on the pattern of early mod. Du. *selfegghe*. The geological term dates from the 1930s.]

selves /selvz/ plural form of SELF.

Selz·nick /ˈselznik/, David Oliver (1902–65), US movie producer whose classics include *Gone with the Wind* (1939).

SEM ▶ abbr. scanning electron microscope.

Sem. ▶ abbr. ■ seminary. ■ (also **Sem**) Semitic.

sem. ▶ abbr. semicolon.

se·man·tic /səˈmantik/ ▶ adj. relating to meaning in language or logic. — **se·man·ti·cal·ly** /-ik(ə)lē/ adv. [17th C.: from Fr. *sémantique*, from Gk. *sēmantikos* 'significant,' from *sēmainein* 'signify,' from *sēma* 'sign.']

se·man·tics /səˈmantiks/ ▶ plural n. [usu. treated as sing.] the branch of linguistics and logic concerned with meaning. ■ the meaning of a word, phrase, sentence, or text: *such quibbling over semantics may seem petty stuff.* — **se·man·ti·cian** /ˌsēmanˈtisʜən/ n. **se·man·ti·cist** n.

sem·a·phore /ˈseməˌfôr/ ▶ n. 1 a system of sending messages by holding the arms or two flags or poles in certain positions according to an alphabetic code. ■ a signal sent by semaphore. 2 an apparatus for signaling in this way, consisting of an upright with movable parts. ▶ v. [trans.] send (a message) by semaphore or by signals resembling semaphore. — **sem·a·phor·ic** /ˌseməˈfôrik/ adj. **sem·a·phor·i·cal·ly** /ˌseməˈfôrik(ə)lē/ adv. [19th C. (denoting a signaling apparatus): from Fr. *sémaphore*, formed irregularly from Gk. *sēma* 'sign' + -PHORE.]

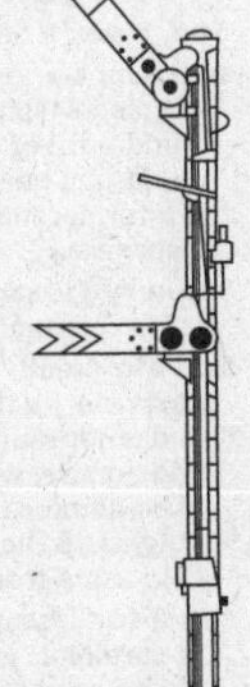
semaphore 2

Se·ma·rang /səˈmäˌräɴɢ/ a city in Indonesia, on the northern coast of Java; pop. 1,249,000.

se·ma·si·ol·o·gy /səˌmāsēˈäləjē; -zē-/ ▶ n. the branch of knowledge that deals with concepts and the terms that represent them. Compare with ONOMASIOLOGY. — **se·ma·si·o·log·i·cal** /-əˈläjikəl/ adj. [19th C.: from Ger. *Semasiologie*, from Gk. *sēmasia* 'meaning,' from *sēmainein* 'signify.']

sem·bla·ble /ˈsembləbəl/ ▶ n. literary a counterpart or equal to someone: *this person is our brother, our semblable, our very self.* [ME (adj.,'like'): from OFr., from *sembler* 'seem.']

sem·blance /ˈsembləns/ ▶ n. the outward appearance or apparent form of something, esp. when the reality is different: *she tried to force her thoughts back into* ***some semblance of order.*** ■ archaic resemblance; similarity. [ME: from OFr., from *sembler* 'seem,' from L. *similare, simulare* 'simulate.']

se·mé /səˈmā/ (also **semée**) ▶ adj. Heraldry covered with small bearings of indefinite number (e.g., stars, fleurs-de-lis) arranged all over the field. [ME: Fr., lit. 'sown,' past part. of *semer*.]

Se·mei /ˈsemā/ (also **Se·mey**) a city in eastern Kazakhstan; pop. 339,000. It was known as Semipalatinsk until 1991.

Sem·e·le /ˈseməlē/ Gk. Mythol. the mother, by Zeus, of Dionysus. The fire of Zeus's thunderbolts killed her but made her child immortal.

se·men /ˈsēmən/ ▶ n. the male reproductive fluid, containing spermatozoa in suspension. [ME: from L., lit. 'seed,' from *serere* 'to sow.']

se·mes·ter /səˈmestər/ ▶ n. a half-year term in a school or university, typically lasting for fifteen to eighteen weeks. [19th C.: from Ger. *Semester*, from L. *semestris* 'six-monthly,' from *sex* 'six' + *mensis* 'month.']

sem·i /ˈsemī/ ▶ n. (pl. **sem·is**) informal 1 a tractor-trailer. 2 a semifinal. [20th C.: abbrev.]

semi- ▶ prefix 1 half: *semicircular.* ■ occurring or appearing twice in a specified period: *semiannual.* 2 partly; in some degree or particular: *semiconscious.* ■ almost: *semidarkness.* [from L.; rel. to Gk. *hemi-*.]

sem·i·an·nu·al /ˌsemēˈanyo͞oəl; ˌsemˌī-/ ▶ adj. occurring twice a year; half-yearly: *their semiannual meetings.* ■ (of a plant) living for half a year only. ▶ n. a semiannual plant. — **sem·i·an·nu·al·ly** adv.

sem·i·a·quat·ic /ˌsemēəˈkwätik; ˌsemˌī-; -ˈkwatik/ ▶ adj. (of an animal) living partly on land and partly in water: *semiaquatic crocodiles.* ■ (of a plant) growing in very wet or waterlogged ground.

sem·i·au·to·mat·ic /ˌsemēˌôtəˈmatik; ˌsemˌī-/ ▶ adj. partially automatic. ■ (of a firearm) having a mechanism for self-loading but not for continuous firing: *semiautomatic rifles.* ▶ n. a semiautomatic firearm.

sem·i·au·ton·o·mous /ˌsemē-ôˈtänəməs; ˌsemˌī-/ ▶ adj. 1 (of a country, state, or community) having a degree of, but not complete, self-government. 2 acting independently to some degree.

sem·i·base·ment /ˈsemēˌbāsmənt; ˈsemˌī-/ ▶ n. a story of a building partly below ground level.

sem·i·bold /ˈsemēˈbōld; ˈsemˌī-/ ▶ adj. Print. printed in a typeface with thick strokes but not as thick as bold.

sem·i·breve /ˈsemēˌbrēv; ˈsemˌī-/ ▶ n. Music, esp. Brit. a whole note.

sem·i·cir·cle /ˈsemēˌsərkəl; ˈsemˌī-/ ▶ n. a half of a circle or of its circumference. — **sem·i·cir·cu·lar** adj.

sem·i·cir·cu·lar ca·nals ▶ plural n. three fluid-filled bony channels in the inner ear. They are situated at right angles to each other and provide information about orientation to the brain to help maintain balance.

sem·i·clas·si·cal /ˌsemēˈklasikəl; ˌsemˌī-/ ▶ adj. 1 (of music) having elements both of classical music and of other more popular genres. 2 Physics (of a theory or method) intermediate between a classical or Newtonian description and one based on quantum mechanics or relativity.

sem·i·co·lon /ˈsemiˌkōlən; ˈsemˌī-/ ▶ n. a punctuation mark (;) indicating a pause, typically between two main clauses, that is more pronounced than that indicated by a comma.

sem·i·con·duc·tor /ˈsemē-kənˌdəktər; ˈsemˌī-/ ▶ n. a solid substance that has a conductivity between that of an insulator and that of most metals, either due to the addition of an impurity or because of temperature effects. Devices made of semiconductors, notably silicon, are essential components of most electronic circuits. — **sem·i·con·duct·ing** adj.

sem·i·con·scious /ˌsemēˈkänsʜəs; ˌsemˌī-/ ▶ adj. (of a person) only partially conscious. ■ (of a feeling or memory) of which the person experiencing it is only vaguely or partially aware.

sem·i·cyl·in·der /ˌsemēˈsiləndər; ˌsemˌī-/ ▶ n. Geom. half of a cylinder cut longitudinally. — **sem·i·cy·lin·dri·cal** /ˌsemēˌsəˈlindrikəl; ˌsemˌī-/ adj.

sem·i·dark·ness /ˌsemēˈdärknəs; ˌsemˌī-/ ▶ n. a light level in which it is possible to see, but not clearly.

sem·i·de·tached /ˌsemēdiˈtacʜt; ˌsemˌī-/ ▶ adj. (of a house) joined to another house on one side only by a common wall.

sem·i·doc·u·men·ta·ry /ˌsemēˌdäkyəˈment(ə)rē; ˌsemˌī-/ ▶ adj. (of a movie) having a factual background and a fictitious story. ▶ n. a semidocumentary movie.

sem·i·dome /ˈsemēˌdōm; ˌsemˌī-/ ▶ n. Archit. a half-dome formed by vertical section.

sem·i·dou·ble /ˌsemēˈdəbəl; ˌsemˌī-/ ▶ adj. (of a flower) intermediate between single and double in having only the outer stamens converted to petals.

sem·i·el·lip·ti·cal /ˌsemē-iˈliptikəl; ˌsemˌī-/ ▶ adj. having the shape of half of an ellipse bisected by one of its diameters, esp. the major axis.

sem·i·fi·nal /ˌsemēˈfīnl; ˌsemˌī-/ ▶ n. a game or round immediately preceding the final, the winner of which goes on to the final. — **sem·i·fi·nal·ist** n.

sem·i·fin·ished /ˌsemēˈfinisʜt; ˌsemˌī-/ ▶ adj. prepared for the final stage of manufacture.

sem·i·fit·ted /ˌsemēˈfitid; ˌsemˌī-/ ▶ adj. (of a garment) shaped to the body but not closely fitted.

sem·i·flu·id /ˌsemēˈflo͞o-id; ˌsemˌī-/ ▶ adj. having a thick consistency between solid and liquid. ▶ n. a semifluid substance.

sem·i·for·mal /ˌsemēˈfôrməl; ˌsemˌī-/ ▶ adj. combining formal and informal elements. ■ used to describe clothing that is neither formal nor casual and that is typically worn for a dance, wedding, or other event. ▶ n. an event at which semiformal attire is expected.

sem·i·gloss /ˈsemēˌgläs; ˈsemˌī-; -ˌglôs/ (also **sem·i-gloss**) ▶ n. a paint that dries to a moderately glossy sheen.

sem·i·in·de·pend·ent ▶ adj. partially free from outside control; not wholly depending on another's authority. ■ (of a country or region) partially self-governing. ■ (of an institution) not wholly supported by public funds.

sem·i·liq·uid /ˌsemēˈlikwid; ˌsemˌī-/ ▶ adj. & n. another term for SEMIFLUID.

sem·i·lit·er·ate /ˌsemēˈlitərit; ˌsemˌī-/ ▶ adj. unable to read or write with ease or fluency; poorly educated. ■ (of a text) poorly written. ▶ n. a person who is poorly educated or unable to read or write with ease or fluency. — **sem·i·lit·er·a·cy** /-əsē/ n.

Sé·mil·lon /sāmē(l)ˈyôɴ/ ▶ n. a variety of white wine grape grown in France and elsewhere. ■ a white wine made from this grape. [Fr. dial., based on L. *semen* 'seed.']

sem·i·lu·nar /ˌsemēˈlo͞onər; ˌsemˌī-/ ▶ adj. esp. Anat. shaped like a half-moon or crescent. [ME: from med. L. *semilunaris* (see SEMI-, LUNAR).]

sem·i·lu·nar valve ▶ n. Anat. each of a pair of valves in the heart, at the bases of the aorta and the pulmonary artery, consisting of three cusps or flaps that prevent the flow of blood back into the heart.

sem·i·ma·jor ax·is /ˈsemēˈmājər; ˈsem,ī-/ ▶ **n.** Geom. either of the halves of the major axis of an ellipse.

sem·i·mi·nor ax·is /ˈsemēˈmīnər; ˈsem,ī-/ ▶ **n.** Geom. either of the halves of the minor axis of an ellipse.

sem·i·month·ly /,semēˈmənTHlē; ,sem,ī-/ ▶ **adj.** occurring or published twice a month: *semimonthly paydays.*

sem·i·nal /ˈsemənl/ ▶ **adj.** **1** (of a work, event, moment, or figure) strongly influencing later developments. **2** of, relating to, or denoting semen. ■ Bot. of, relating to, or derived from the seed of a plant. — **sem·i·nal·ly** adv. [ME (sense 2): from OFr. *seminal* or L. *seminalis*, from *semen* 'seed.' Sense 1 dates from the mid 17th C.]

sem·i·nal ves·i·cle ▶ **n.** Anat. each of a pair of glands that open into the vas deferens near to its junction with the urethra and secrete many of the components of semen.

sem·i·nar /ˈsemə,när/ ▶ **n.** a conference or other meeting for discussion or training. ■ a class at a college or university in which a topic is discussed by a teacher and a small group of students. [19th C.: from Ger. *Seminar*, from L. *seminarium* (see SEMINARY).]

sem·i·nar·y /ˈsemə,nerē/ ▶ **n.** (pl. **-nar·ies**) a college that prepares students to be priests, ministers, or rabbis. ■ archaic, fig. a place or thing in which something is developed or cultivated: *a seminary of sedition.* ■ archaic a private school or college, esp. one for young women. — **sem·i·nar·i·an** /,seməˈne(ə)rēən/ **n.** **sem·i·na·rist** /-nərist/ **n.** [ME (denoting a seed plot): from L. *seminarium* 'seed plot,' neut. of *seminarius* 'of seed,' from *semen* 'seed.']

sem·i·nif·er·ous /,seməˈnif(ə)rəs/ ▶ **adj.** producing or conveying semen. [17th C.: from L. *semen, semin-* 'seed' + -FEROUS.]

Sem·i·nole /ˈsemə,nōl/ ▶ **n.** (pl. same or **-noles**) **1** a member of an American Indian people of the Creek confederacy and their descendants, noted for resistance in the 19th century to encroachment on their land in Georgia and Florida. Many were resettled in Oklahoma. **2** either of the Muskogean languages, usually Creek, spoken by the Seminole. ▶ **adj.** of or relating to the Seminole or their language. [from Creek *simanōli, simalōni*, from Amer. Sp. *cimarrón* 'wild,' (as a n.) 'escaped slave'; cf. MAROON.]

sem·i·of·fi·cial /,semē-əˈfisHəl; ,sem,ī-/ ▶ **adj.** having some, but not full, official authority or recognition. — **sem·i·of·fi·cial·ly** adv.

se·mi·ol·o·gy /,sēmēˈäləjē; ,semē-; ,sē,mī-/ ▶ **n.** another term for SEMIOTICS. — **se·mi·o·log·i·cal** /-əˈläjikəl/ **adj.** **se·mi·ol·o·gist** /-jist/ **n.** [20th C.: from Gk. *sēmeion* 'sign' (from *sēma* 'mark') + -LOGY.]

se·mi·ot·ics /,sēmēˈätiks; ,semē-; ,sē,mī-/ ▶ **plural n.** [treated as sing.] the study of signs and symbols and their use or interpretation. — **se·mi·ot·ic** adj. **se·mi·ot·i·cal·ly** /-ik(ə)lē/ adv. **se·mi·o·ti·cian** /,semēəˈtisHən; ,sēmēə-/ **n.** [19th C.: from Gk. *sēmeiotikos* 'of signs,' from *sēmeioun* 'interpret as a sign.']

sem·i·pal·mat·ed /,semēˈpal,mātid; -ˈpä(l)-; ,sem,ī-/ ▶ **adj.** used in names of wading birds that have toes webbed for part of their length, e.g., **semipalmated sandpiper**.

sem·i·per·ma·nent /,semēˈpərmənənt; ,sem,ī-/ ▶ **adj.** less than permanent, but with some stability or endurance. — **semipermanently** adv.

sem·i·per·me·a·ble /,semēˈpərmēəbəl; ,sem,ī-/ ▶ **adj.** (of a material or membrane) allowing certain substances to pass through it but not others, esp. allowing the passage of a solvent but not of certain solutes.

sem·i·pre·cious /,semēˈpresHəs; ,sem,ī-/ ▶ **adj.** denoting minerals that can be used as gems but are considered to be less valuable than precious stones.

sem·i·pri·vate /,semēˈprīvit; ,sem,ī-/ ▶ **adj.** combining public and private elements. ■ (of a hospital room) accommodating two patients.

sem·i·pro /,semēˈprō; ,semī-/ ▶ **adj.** & **n.** (pl. **-pros**) informal short for SEMIPROFESSIONAL.

sem·i·pro·fes·sion·al /,semē-prəˈfesHənl; ,sem,ī-/ ▶ **adj.** receiving payment for an activity but not relying entirely on it for a living: *a semiprofessional musician.* ■ involving or suitable for people engaged in an activity on such a basis: *training at the semiprofessional level.* ▶ **n.** a person who is engaged in an activity on such a basis.

sem·i·qua·ver /,semēˈkwāvər/ ▶ **n.** Music, esp. Brit. a sixteenth note.

Se·mir·a·mis /səˈmirəməs/ Gk. Mythol. the daughter of an Assyrian goddess who married an Assyrian king. After his death she ruled for many years and became one of the founders of Babylon. She is thought to have been based on the historical queen Sammuramat (c.800 BC).

sem·i·re·tired /,semē-riˈtī(ə)rd; ,semī-/ ▶ **adj.** having retired or withdrawn from employment or an occupation but continuing to work part-time or occasionally. — **sem·i·re·tire·ment** /-ˈtī(ə)rmənt/ **n.**

sem·i·rig·id /,semēˈrijid; ,sem,ī-/ ▶ **adj.** stiff and solid, but not inflexible: *a semirigid polyethylene hose.* ■ (of an airship) having a stiffened keel attached to a flexible gas container.

sem·i·skilled /,semēˈskild; ,sem,ī-/ ▶ **adj.** (of work or a worker) having or needing some, but not extensive, training: *assembly lines of semiskilled workers.*

sem·i·sol·id /,semēˈsälid; ,sem,ī-/ ▶ **adj.** highly viscous; slightly thicker than semifluid.

sem·i·sweet /,semēˈswēt; ,sem,ī-/ ▶ **adj.** (of food) slightly sweetened, but less so than normal. ■ (of wine) neither dry nor sweet; slightly sweeter than medium dry.

sem·i·syn·thet·ic /,semē-sinˈTHetik; ,sem,ī-/ ▶ **adj.** Chem. (of a substance) made by synthesis from a naturally occurring material.

Sem·ite /ˈsemīt/ ▶ **n.** a member of any of the peoples who speak or spoke a Semitic language, including in particular the Jews and Arabs. [from mod. L. *Semita*, via late L. from Gk. *Sēm* 'Shem,' son of Noah in the Bible.]

Se·mit·ic /səˈmitik/ ▶ **adj.** **1** relating to or denoting a family of languages that includes Hebrew, Arabic, and Aramaic and certain ancient languages such as Phoenician and Akkadian, constituting the main subgroup of the Afro-Asiatic family. **2** of or relating to the peoples who speak these languages, esp. Hebrew and Arabic.

sem·i·tone /ˈsemē,tōn; ˈsem,ī-/ ▶ **n.** Music the smallest interval used in classical Western music, equal to a twelfth of an octave or half a tone; a half step.

sem·i·trail·er /ˈsemē,trālər; ˈsem,ī-/ ▶ **n.** a trailer having wheels at the back but supported at the front by a towing vehicle. ■ a tractor-trailer.

sem·i·trop·ics /,semēˈträpiks; ,sem,ī-/ ▶ **plural n.** another term for SUBTROPICS. — **sem·i·trop·i·cal** /-ˈträpikəl/ **adj.**

sem·i·vow·el /ˈsemē,vouəl; ˈsem,ī-/ ▶ **n.** a speech sound intermediate between a vowel and a consonant, e.g., *w* or *y*.

sem·i·week·ly /,semēˈwēklē; ,sem,ī-/ ▶ **adj.** occurring twice a week.

sem·o·li·na /,seməˈlēnə/ ▶ **n.** the hard grains left after the milling of flour, used in puddings and in pasta. [18th C.: from Ital. *semolino*, dimin. of *semola* 'bran,' from L. *simila* 'flour.']

sem·per fi·de·lis /ˈsempər fiˈdālis/ (also **sem·per fi**) ▶ **adj.** always faithful (the motto of the US Marine Corps). [L.]

sem·per·vi·vum /,sempərˈvīvəm/ ▶ **n.** a succulent plant (genus *Sempervivum*) of the stonecrop family, related to the houseleek. [mod. L., from L. *semper* 'always' + *vivus* 'living.']

sem·pi·ter·nal /,sempəˈtərnl/ ▶ **adj.** eternal and unchanging; everlasting. — **sem·pi·ter·nal·ly** adv. **sem·pi·ter·ni·ty** /-ˈtərnitē/ **n.** [ME: from OFr. *sempiternel* or late L. *sempiternalis*, from L. *sempiternus*, from *semper* 'always' + *aeternus* 'eternal.']

sem·pli·ce /ˈsempli,CHā/ ▶ **adv.** Music (as a direction) in a simple style of performance. [Ital., lit. 'simple.']

sem·pre /ˈsem,prā/ ▶ **adv.** Music (in directions) throughout; always: *sempre forte.* [Ital.]

semp·stress /ˈsem(p)stris/ ▶ **n.** another term for SEAMSTRESS.

Sem·tex /ˈsem,teks/ ▶ **n.** a very pliable, odorless plastic explosive. [1980s: prob. a blend of *Semtin* (the name of a village in the Czech Republic near the place of production) and EXPLOSIVE.]

Sen. ▶ **abbr.** ■ Senate. ■ Senator. ■ Senior.

sen /sen/ ▶ **n.** (pl. same) a monetary unit of Brunei, Cambodia, Indonesia, and Malaysia, equal to one hundredth of a dollar in Brunei, one hundredth of a riel in Cambodia, one hundredth of a rupiah in Indonesia, and one hundredth of a ringgit in Malaysia. [representing CENT.] ■ a former monetary unit in Japan, equal to one hundredth of a yen. [Japanese.]

sen·a·ry /ˈsenərē/ ▶ **adj.** rare relating to or based on the number six. [16th C.: from L. *senarius* 'containing six,' based on *sex* 'six.']

sen·ate /ˈsenit/ ▶ **n.** any of various legislative or governing bodies, in particular: ■ the smaller upper assembly in the US, US states, France, and other countries. ■ the state council of the ancient Roman republic and empire, which shared legislative power with the popular assemblies, administration with the magistrates, and judicial power with the knights. ■ the governing body of a university or college. [ME: from OFr. *senat*, from L. *senatus*, from *senex* 'old man.']

sen·a·tor /ˈsenitər/ ▶ **n.** a member of a senate. — **sen·a·to·ri·al** /,senəˈtôrēəl/ **adj.** **sen·a·tor·ship** /-,SHip/ **n.** [ME (denoting a member of the ancient Roman senate): from OFr. *senateur*, from L. *senator* (see SENATE).]

sen·a·tor·i·al cour·tes·y /,senəˈtôrēəl/ ▶ **n.** a custom whereby presidential appointments are confirmed only if there is no objection to them by the senators from the appointee's state, esp. from the senior senator of the president's party from that state.

sen·a·tor·i·al dis·trict ▶ **n.** an electoral division of a state that is represented by a senator in the state's senate.

send /send/ ▶ **v.** (past **sent** /sent/) **1** [trans.] cause to go or be taken to a particular destination; arrange for the delivery of, esp. by mail: *we sent a reminder.* ■ order or instruct to go to a particular destination or in a particular direction: *Clemons sent me to Bangkok.* ■ [intrans.] send a message or letter: *he sent to invite her to supper.* ■ [trans.] cause to move sharply or quickly; propel: *the volcano sent clouds of ash into the air.* ■ (**send someone to**) arrange for someone to go to (an institution) and stay there for a particular purpose. **2** [trans.] informal affect with powerful emotion; put into ecstasy: *it's the spectacle and music that send us, not the words.*

– PHRASES **send someone flying** cause someone to be knocked violently off balance or to the ground. **send word** send a message.

– PHRASAL VERBS **send away for** order or request that (something) be sent to one: *you can send away for the recipe.* **send for** order or instruct (someone) to come to one; summon. ■ order by mail. **send something in** submit material to be considered for a competition or possible publication. **send off for** another way of saying *SEND AWAY FOR* above. **send someone off** instruct someone to go; arrange for someone's departure. **send something off** dispatch something by mail. **send something on** transmit mail or luggage to a further destination or in advance of one's own arrival. **send out for something** order delivery of something. **send something out 1** produce or give out something; emit something.

2 dispatch items to a number of people; distribute something widely. **send someone up** sentence someone to imprisonment. **send someone/something up** informal give an exaggerated imitation of someone or something in order to ridicule them. — **send·a·ble** adj. **send·er** n. [OE *sendan*, of Gmc. origin; rel. to Du. *zenden* and Ger. *senden*.]

Sen·dai /'sen,dī/ a city in Japan, near the northeastern coast of Honshu; pop. 918,000.

Sen·dak /'sen,dak/, Maurice Bernard (1928–), US writer and illustrator. His children's books include *Where the Wild Things Are* (1963).

sen·dal /'sendl/ ▶ n. hist. a fine, rich silk material, chiefly used to make ceremonial robes and banners. [ME: from OFr. *cendal*, ult. from Gk. *sindōn*.]

send-off ▶ n. a celebratory demonstration of goodwill at a person's departure.

send-up /'send,əp/ ▶ n. informal an act of imitating someone or something in order to ridicule them; a parody: *a delicious sendup of a speech given by a trendy academic.*

se·ne /'sānā/ ▶ n. (pl. same or **se·nes**) a monetary unit of Samoa, equal to one hundredth of a tala. [Samoan.]

Sen·e·ca[1] /'senəkə/, Lucius Annaeus (*c.*4 BC–AD 65), Roman writer, philosopher, and playwright; known as **Seneca the Younger**; son of Seneca the Elder. He wrote *Epistulae Morales*.

Sen·e·ca[2], Marcus (or Lucius) Annaeus (*c.*55 BC–*c.*AD39), Roman rhetorician, born in Spain; known as **Seneca the Elder**; father of Seneca the Younger. Only parts of his work on rhetoric survive.

Sen·e·ca[3] ▶ n. (pl. same or **-cas**) 1 a member of an American Indian people that was one of the Five Nations. 2 the Iroquoian language of this people. ▶ adj. of or relating to this people or their language. [via Du. from Algonquian.]

Sen·e·ca Falls a town in west central New York, the site in 1848 of the first women's rights convention in the US; pop. 9,384.

Sen·e·ca Lake the largest of the Finger Lakes in west central New York.

se·ne·cio /sē'nēsē,ō; -SHē,ō/ ▶ n. (pl. **-ci·os**) a plant of the daisy family belong to a genus (*Senecio*) that includes the ragworts and groundsels. Many kinds are cultivated as ornamentals and some are poisonous weeds of grassland. [mod. L., from L., lit. 'old man, groundsel,' from the hairy white fruits.]

Sen·e·gal /'senə,gôl; -,gäl/ a country on the coast of West Africa. *See box.* — **Sen·e·ga·lese** /,senəgə'lēz; -'lēs/ adj. & n.

Senegal

Official name: Republic of Senegal
Location: West Africa, on the Atlantic coast, south of Mauritania
Area: 75,800 square miles (196,200 sq km)
Population: 10,852,000
Capital: Dakar
Languages: French (official), Wolof, Mandinka, and other West African languages
Currency: CFA franc

Sen·e·gal Riv·er (also **Sénégal**) a river in western Africa that flows for 680 miles (1,088 km) from northern Guinea to the Atlantic Ocean in Senegal.

Sen·e·gam·bi·a /,seni'gambēə; -'gäm-/ a region in West Africa that consists of the Senegal and Gambia rivers and the area between them.

se·nes·cence /sə'nesəns/ ▶ n. Biol. the condition or process of deterioration with age. ■ loss of a cell's power of division and growth. — **se·nes·cent** adj.

sen·e·schal /'senəSHəl/ ▶ n. 1 hist. the steward or major-domo of a medieval great house. 2 esp. hist. a governor or other administrative or judicial officer. [ME: from OFr., from med. L. *seniscalus*, from a Gmc. compound of words meaning 'old' and 'servant.']

se·nhor /sēn'yôr; sin-/ ▶ n. (in Portuguese-speaking regions) a man (often used as a title or polite form of address): *Senhor Emilio Sofia Rosa*. [Port., from L. *senior* (see SENIOR).]

se·nho·ra /sēn'yôrə; sin-/ ▶ n. (in Portuguese-speaking regions) a woman, esp. a married woman (often used as a title or polite form of address). [Port., fem. of SENHOR.]

se·nho·ri·ta /,sēnyə'rētə/ ▶ n. (in Portuguese-speaking regions) a young woman, esp. an unmarried one (often used as a title or polite form of address). [Port., dimin. of SENHORA.]

se·nile /'sē,nīl; 'senīl/ ▶ adj. (of a person) having or showing the weaknesses or diseases of old age, esp. a loss of mental faculties: *she couldn't cope with her senile husband.* ■ (of a condition) characteristic of or caused by old age: *senile decay.* ▶ n. a senile person: *you never know where you stand with these so-called seniles.* — **se·nil·i·ty** /si'nilitē/ n. [17th C.: from Fr. *sénile* or L. *senilis*, from *senex* 'old man.']

sen·ior /'sēnyər/ ▶ adj. 1 of a more advanced age: *he is 20 years senior to Leonard.* ■ of the final year of college or high school. ■ relating to or denoting competitors of above a certain age or of the highest status in a particular sport. ■ (often **Senior**) [postpositive] (in names) denoting the elder of two who have the same name in a family, esp. a father as distinct from his son: *Henry James senior.* 2 holding a high and authoritative position. ■ [predic.] (**senior to**) holding a higher position than. ▶ n. a person who is a specified number of years older than someone else: *she was only two years his senior.* ■ an elderly person, esp. one who is retired and living on a pension. ■ a student in the final year of college or high school. ■ a competitor of above a certain age or of the highest status in a particular sport. — **sen·ior·i·ty** /sēn'yôritē; -'yär-/ n. [ME: from L., lit. 'older, older man,' compar. of *senex*, *sen-* 'old man, old.']

sen·ior chief pet·ty of·fi·cer ▶ n. a noncommissioned officer in the US Navy or Coast Guard ranking above chief petty officer and below master chief petty officer.

sen·ior cit·i·zen ▶ n. an elderly person, esp. one who is retired and living on a pension.

sen·ior com·mon room ▶ n. Brit. a room used for social purposes by fellows, lecturers, and other senior members of a college. ■ [treated as sing. or pl.] the senior members of a college regarded collectively.

sen·ior high school ▶ n. a secondary school typically comprising the three highest grades.

sen·ior mas·ter ser·geant ▶ n. a noncommissioned officer in the US Air Force ranking above master sergeant and below chief master sergeant.

sen·ior mo·ment ▶ n. informala temporary mental lapse (humorously attributed to the gradual loss of one's mental faculties as one grows older).

sen·i·ti /'senitē/ ▶ n. (pl. same) a monetary unit of Tonga, equal to one hundredth of a pa'anga.

sen·na /'senə/ ▶ n. the cassia tree. ■ a laxative prepared from the dried pods of this tree. [16th C.: from med. L. *sena*, from Arab. *sanā*.]

Sen·nach·er·ib /sə'nakə,rib/ (died 681 BC) king of Assyria 705–681; son of Sargon II. In 701, he spared Jerusalem from destruction.

sen·net /'senit/ ▶ n. (in the stage directions of Elizabethan plays) a call on a trumpet or cornet to signal the ceremonial entrance or exit of an actor. [16th C.: perh. a var. of SIGNET.]

sen·night /'senīt/ ▶ n. archaic a week. [OE *seofon nihta* 'seven nights.']

sen·nit /'senit/ ▶ n. plaited straw, hemp, or similar fibrous material used in making hats. ■ Naut. braided cordage in flat, round, or square form, used for making mats, lashings, etc. [17th C.: of unknown origin.]

se·ñor /sān'yôr; sen-/ ▶ n. (pl. **se·ño·res** /sān'yôrāz; sen'yôres/ or **se·ñors**) a title or form of address used of or to a Spanish-speaking man, corresponding to *Mr.* or *sir*. [Sp., from L. *senior* (see SENIOR).]

se·ño·ra /sān'yôrə; sen-/ ▶ n. a title or form of address used of or to a Spanish-speaking woman, corresponding to *Mrs.* or *madam*: *Señora Dolores*. [Sp., fem. of SEÑOR.]

se·ño·ri·ta /,sānyə'rētə; ,sen-/ ▶ n. a title or form of address used of or to a Spanish-speaking unmarried woman, corresponding to *Miss*: *a beautiful señorita*. [Sp., dimin. of SEÑORA.]

sen·sate /'sen,sāt/ ▶ adj. literary able to perceive with the senses; sensing: *the infant stretches, sensate.* ■ perceived by the senses: *a sensate world.* [17th C.: from late L. *sensatus* 'having senses,' from *sensus* (see SENSE).]

sen·sa·tion /sen'sāSHən/ ▶ n. 1 a physical feeling or perception resulting from something that happens to or comes into contact with the body. ■ the capacity to have such feelings or perceptions: *they had lost sensation in one or both forearms.* ■ an inexplicable awareness or impression: [with clause] *she had the eerie sensation that she was being watched.* 2 a widespread reaction of interest and excitement: *his arrest for poisoning caused a sensation.* ■ a person, object, or event that arouses such interest and excitement. [17th C.: from med. L. *sensatio(n-)*, from L. *sensus* (see SENSE).]

sen·sa·tion·al /sen'sāSHənl/ ▶ adj. (of an event, a person, or a piece of information) causing great public interest and excitement: *a sensational murder trial.* ■ (of an account or a publication) presenting information in a way that is intended to provoke public interest and excitement, at the expense of accuracy. ■ informal very good indeed; very impressive or attractive.' — **sen·sa·tion·al·ly** adv.

sen·sa·tion·al·ism /sen'sāsHənl,izəm/ ▶ n. 1 (esp. in journalism) the use of exciting or shocking stories or language at the expense of accuracy, in order to provoke public interest or excitement. 2 Philos. another term for PHENOMENALISM. — **sen·sa·tion·al·ist** n. & adj. **sen·sa·tion·al·is·tic** /sen,sāsHənl'istik/ adj.

sen·sa·tion·al·ize /sen'sāsHənl,īz/ ▶ v. [trans.] (esp. of a newspaper) present information about (something) in a way that provokes public interest and excitement, at the expense of accuracy.

sense /sens/ ▶ n. 1 a faculty by which the body perceives an external stimulus; one of the faculties of sight, smell, hearing, taste, and touch: *the bear has a keen sense of smell.* 2 a feeling that something is the case: *she had the sense of being a political outsider.* ■ an awareness or feeling that one is in a specified state: *a sense of well-being.* ■ (**sense of**) a keen intuitive awareness of or sensitivity to the presence or importance of something. 3 a sane and realistic attitude to situations and problems: *he earned respect by the good sense he showed.* ■ a reasonable or comprehensible rationale: *I can't see the sense in leaving all the work to you.* 4 a way in which an expression or a situation can be interpreted; a meaning. 5 esp. Math. Physics a property, e.g., direction of motion, distinguishing a pair of objects, quantities, effects, etc., that differ only in that each is the reverse of the other. ■ [as adj.] Genet. relating to or denoting a coding sequence of nucleotides, complementary to an antisense sequence. ▶ v. [trans.] perceive by a sense or senses: *with the first frost, they could sense a change in the days.* ■ be aware of: *she could sense her father's anger rising.* ■ [with clause] be aware that something is the case without being able to define exactly how one knows: *he could sense that he wasn't liked.* ■ (of a machine or similar device) detect: *an optical fiber senses a current.*

– PHRASES **bring someone to their** (or **come to one's**) **senses** restore someone to (or regain) consciousness. ■ cause someone to (or start to) think and behave reasonably after a period of folly or irrationality. **in one's senses** fully aware and in control of one's thoughts and words; sane. **make sense** be intelligible, justifiable, or practicable. **make sense of** find meaning or coherence in. **out of one's senses** in or into a state of insanity. **a sense of direction** a person's ability to know without explicit guidance the direction in which they are or should be moving. **take leave of one's senses** (in hyperbolic use) go insane. [ME ('meaning'): from L. *sensus* 'faculty of feeling, thought, meaning,' from *sentire* 'feel.']

sense da·tum ▶ n. Philos. an immediate object of perception, which is not a material object; a sense impression.

sen·sei /'sen,sā; sen'sā/ ▶ n. (pl. same) (in martial arts) a teacher: [as title] *Sensei Ritchie began work.* [Japanese, from *sen* 'previous' + *sei* 'birth.']

sense·less /'sensləs/ ▶ adj. 1 [often as complement] (of a person) unconscious. ■ incapable of sensation: *the girl's senseless fingers.* 2 (esp. of violent or wasteful action) without discernible meaning or purpose. ■ lacking common sense; wildly foolish. — **sense·less·ly** adv. **sense·less·ness** n.

sense or·gan ▶ n. an organ of the body that responds to external stimuli by conveying impulses to the sensory nervous system.

sen·si·bil·i·ty /,sensə'bilitē/ ▶ n. (pl. **-ties**) the ability to appreciate and respond to complex emotional or aesthetic influences; sensitivity. ■ (**sensibilities**) a person's delicate sensitivity that makes them readily offended or shocked: *the scale of poverty shocked people's sensibilities.* [ME (denoting the power of sensation): from late L. *sensibilitas*, from *sensibilis* 'that can be perceived by the senses' (see SENSIBLE).]

sen·si·ble /'sensəbəl/ ▶ adj. 1 (of a statement or course of action) chosen in accordance with wisdom or prudence; likely to be of benefit: *a sensible diet.* ■ (of a person) possessing or displaying prudence. ■ (of an object) practical and functional rather than decorative: *sensible shoes.* 2 archaic readily perceived; appreciable. ■ [predic.] (**sensible of/to**) able to notice or appreciate; not unaware of: *we are sensible of the difficulties he faces.* — **sen·si·ble·ness** n. **sen·si·bly** /-blē/ adv. [ME (also in the sense 'perceptible by the senses'): from OFr., or from L. *sensibilis*, from *sensus* (see SENSE).]

sen·si·tive /'sensitiv/ ▶ adj. 1 quick to detect or respond to slight changes, signals, or influences: *spiders are sensitive to vibrations on their web.* ■ easily damaged, injured, or distressed by slight changes. ■ (of photographic materials) prepared so as to respond rapidly to the action of light. ■ (of a market) unstable and liable to quick changes of price because of outside influences. 2 (of a person or a person's behavior) having or displaying a quick and delicate appreciation of others' feelings. ■ easily offended or upset. 3 kept secret or with restrictions on disclosure to avoid endangering security: *sensitive information.* ▶ n. a person who is believed to respond to occult influences. — **sen·si·tive·ly** adv. **sen·si·tive·ness** n. [ME (in the sense 'sensory'): from OFr. *sensitif, -ive* or med. L. *sensitivus*, formed irregularly from L. *sentire* 'feel.']

sen·si·tive plant ▶ n. a tropical American plant (*Mimosa pudica*) of the pea family, whose leaflets fold together and leaves bend down when touched.

sen·si·tiv·i·ty /,sensi'tivitē/ ▶ n. (pl. **-ties**) the quality or condition of being sensitive. ■ (**sensitivities**) a person's feelings which might be easily offended or hurt; sensibilities.

sen·si·tiv·i·ty train·ing ▶ n. training intended to sensitize people to their attitudes and behaviors that may unwittingly cause offense to others, esp. members of various minorities.

sen·si·tize /'sensi,tīz/ ▶ v. [trans.] cause (someone or something) to respond to certain stimuli; make sensitive: *we are sensitized to high prices.* ■ make (photographic film) sensitive to light. ■ (often **be sensitized to**) make (an organism) abnormally sensitive to a foreign substance. — **sen·si·ti·za·tion** /,sensiti'zāsHən/ n. **sen·si·tiz·er** n.

sen·si·tom·e·ter /,sensi'tämitər/ ▶ n. Photog. a device for measuring the sensitivity of photographic equipment to light.

sen·sor /'sensər/ ▶ n. a device that detects or measures a physical property and records, indicates, or otherwise responds to it. [1950s: from SENSORY.]

sen·so·ri·mo·tor /,sensərē'mōtər/ ▶ adj. [attrib.] Physiol. (of nerves or their actions) having or involving both sensory and motor functions or pathways.

sen·so·ri·neu·ral /,sensərē'n(y)o͝orəl/ ▶ adj. Med. (of hearing loss) caused by a lesion or disease of the inner ear or the auditory nerve.

sen·so·ri·um /sen'sôrēəm/ ▶ n. (pl. **-so·ri·a** /-'sôrēə/ or **-so·ri·ums**) the sensory apparatus or faculties considered as a whole: *the human sensorium.* — **sen·so·ri·al** /-'sôrēəl/ adj. **sen·so·ri·al·ly** /-'sôrēəlē/ adv. [17th C.: from late L., from L. *sens-* 'perceived,' from the v. *sentire.*]

sen·so·ry /'sensərē/ ▶ adj. of or relating to sensation or the physical senses; transmitted or perceived by the senses: *sensory input.* — **sen·so·ri·ly** /-rəlē/ adv. [18th C.: from L. *sens-* 'perceived' (from the verb *sentire*) or from the noun SENSE + -ORY².]

sen·su·al /'sensHo͞oəl/ ▶ adj. of or arousing gratification of the senses and physical, esp. sexual, pleasure: *the production of the ballet is sensual and passionate.* — **sen·su·al·ism** /-,lizəm/ n. **sen·su·al·ist** /-ist/ n. **sen·su·al·ize** /-,līz/ v. **sen·su·al·ly** adv. [ME (in the sense 'sensory'): from late L. *sensualis*, from *sensus* (see SENSE).]

sen·su·al·i·ty /,sensHo͞o'alitē/ ▶ n. the enjoyment, expression, or pursuit of physical, esp. sexual, pleasure. ■ the condition of being pleasing or fulfilling to the senses: *life can dazzle with its sensuality, its color.*

sen·sum /'sensəm/ ▶ n. (pl. **-sa** /-sə/) Philos. a sense datum. [19th C.: mod. L., 'something sensed,' neut. past part. of L. *sentire* 'feel.']

sen·su·ous /'sensHo͞oəs/ ▶ adj. 1 relating to or affecting the senses rather than the intellect. 2 attractive or gratifying physically, esp. sexually. — **sen·su·ous·ly** adv. **sen·su·ous·ness** n. [17th C.: from L. *sensus* 'sense' + -OUS.]

sent[1] /sent/ past and past participle of SEND.

sent[2] ▶ n. (pl. **sent·i** /'sentē/) a monetary unit of Estonia, equal to one hundredth of a kroon. [respelling of CENT.]

sen·te /'sen,tē/ ▶ n. (pl. **li·sen·te** /li'sentē/) a monetary unit of Lesotho, equal to one hundredth of a loti. [Sesotho.]

sen·tence /'sentns/ ▶ n. 1 a set of words that is complete in itself, typically containing a subject and predicate, conveying a statement, question, exclamation, or command, and consisting of a main clause and sometimes one or more subordinate clauses. 2 the punishment assigned to a defendant found guilty by a court: *a three-year sentence for fraud.* ■ the punishment fixed by law for a particular offense. ▶ v. [trans.] declare the punishment decided for (an offender): *ten army officers were sentenced to death.*

– PHRASES **under sentence of** having been condemned to: *he was under sentence of death.* [ME (in the senses 'way of thinking, opinion,' 'court's declaration of punishment,' and 'gist (of a piece of writing)'): via OFr. from L. *sententia* 'opinion,' from *sentire* 'feel, be of the opinion.']

sen·tence ad·verb ▶ n. Gram. an adverb or adverbial phrase that expresses a writer's or speaker's attitude to the content of the sentence in which it occurs (such as *frankly, obviously*), or places the sentence in a particular context (such as *technically, politically*).

sen·ten·tious /sen'tencHəs/ ▶ adj. given to moralizing in a pompous or affected manner. — **sen·ten·tious·ly** adv. **sen·ten·tious·ness** n. [ME: from L. *sententiosus*, from *sententia* (see SENTENCE).]

sen·tient /'sencH(ē)ənt/ ▶ adj. able to perceive or feel things: *sentient life forms.* — **sen·tience** n. **sen·tient·ly** adv. [17th C.: from L. *sentient-* 'feeling,' from the v. *sentire.*]

sen·ti·ment /'sentəmənt/ ▶ n. 1 a view of or attitude toward a situation or event; an opinion. ■ general feeling or opinion: *racist sentiment.* 2 a feeling or emotion: *an intense sentiment of horror.* ■ exaggerated and self-indulgent feelings of tenderness, sadness, or nostalgia. [ME: from OFr. *sentement*, from med. L. *sentimentum*, from L. *sentire* 'to feel.']

sen·ti·men·tal /,sentə'mentl/ ▶ adj. of or prompted by feelings of tenderness, sadness, or nostalgia: *she felt a sentimental attachment to the place creep over her.* ■ (of a work of literature, music, or art) dealing with feelings of tenderness, sadness, or nostalgia in an exaggerated and self-indulgent way ■ (of a person) excessively prone to feelings of tenderness, sadness, or nostalgia.

– PHRASES **sentimental value** the value of something to someone because of personal or emotional associations rather than material worth. — **sen·ti·men·tal·ly** adv.

sen·ti·men·tal·ism /,sentə'mentl,izəm/ ▶ n. the excessive expression of feelings of tenderness, sadness, or nostalgia in behavior, writing, or speech. — **sen·ti·men·tal·ist** n.

sen·ti·men·tal·i·ty /,sentəmen'talitē; -mən-/ ▶ n. (pl. **-ties**) excessive tenderness, sadness, or nostalgia.

sen·ti·men·tal·ize /,sentə'mentl,īz/ ▶ v. [trans.] treat (someone or something) with exaggerated and self-indulgent feelings of tenderness, sadness, or nostalgia. — **sen·ti·men·tal·i·za·tion** /-,mentli'zāsHən/ n.

sen·ti·nel /'sentn-əl/ ▶ n. a soldier or guard whose job is to stand and keep watch. ■ fig. something that appears to be standing guard or keeping watch. ■ Med. a thing that acts as an indicator of the presence of disease. ▶ v. (**-neled, -nel·ing**; esp. Brit. **-nelled, -nel·ling**) [trans.] station a soldier or guard by (a place) to keep watch.

– PHRASES **stand sentinel** (of a soldier) keep watch: *soldiers stood sentinel with their muskets* | fig. *a tall round tower standing sentinel over the river.* [16th C.: from Fr. *sentinelle,* from Ital. *sentinella,* of unknown origin.]

sen·try /'sentrē/ ▶ n. (pl. **-tries**) a soldier stationed to keep guard or to control access to a place.

– PHRASES **stand sentry** keep guard or control access to a place. [17th C.: perh. from obs. *centrinel,* var. of SENTINEL.]

sen·try box ▶ n. a structure providing shelter for a standing sentry.

sen·try-go ▶ n. Mil. the duty of being a sentry.

Se·nus·si /sə'nōōsē/ ▶ n. (pl. same or **-sis**) a member of a North African Muslim religious fraternity founded in 1837 by Sidi Muhammad ibn Ali es-Senussi (d.1859).

Seoul /sōl/ the capital of South Korea, located in the northwestern part of the country; pop. 10,628,000.

sep. ▶ abbr. ■ sepal. ■ separable. ■ separate. ■ separated. ■ separation.

se·pal /'sēpəl/ ▶ n. Bot. each of the parts of the calyx of a flower, enclosing the petals and typically green and leaflike. [19th C.: from Fr. *sépale,* mod. L. *sepalum,* from Gk. *skepē* 'covering.']

sep·a·ra·ble /'sep(ə)rəbəl/ ▶ adj. able to be separated or treated separately: *body and soul are not separable.* — **sep·a·ra·bil·i·ty** /ˌsep(ə)rə'bilitē/ n. **sep·a·ra·ble·ness** n. **sep·a·ra·bly** /-blē/ adv. [ME: from L. *separabilis,* from *separare* (see SEPARATE).]

sep·a·rate ▶ adj. /'sep(ə)rit/ forming or viewed as a unit apart or by itself: *two separate issues.* ■ not joined or touching physically: *separate quarters for men and women.* ■ different; distinct: *melt the white and dark chocolate in separate bowls.* ▶ v. /'sepəˌrāt/ **1** [trans.] cause to move or be apart: *they were separated by the war.* ■ form a distinction or boundary between (people, places, or things): *six years separated the two brothers.* ■ [intrans.] become detached or disconnected: *the second stage of the rocket failed to separate.* ■ [intrans.] leave another person's company: *they separated at the corner.* ■ [intrans.] stop living together as a couple: *her parents separated.* ■ (often **be separated**) discharge or dismiss (someone) from service or employment. **2** divide or cause to divide into constituent or distinct elements: [intrans.] *the milk had separated into curds and whey* | [trans.] *separate the eggs and beat the yolks.* ■ [trans.] extract or remove for use or rejection: *the skins are separated from the juice before fermentation* | fig. *we need to separate fact from speculation.* ■ [trans.] distinguish between; consider individually: *we cannot separate his thinking from his activity.* ■ (of a factor or quality) distinguish (someone or something) from others: *his position separates him from those who might share his interests.* ■ [trans.] (**separate something off**) make something form, or view something as, a unit apart or by itself. ▶ n. (**separates**) things forming units by themselves, in particular: ■ individual items of clothing, such as skirts, jackets, or pants, suitable for wearing in different combinations. ■ the self-contained, freestanding components of a sound-reproduction system. ■ portions into which a soil, sediment, etc., can be sorted according to particle size, mineral composition, or other criteria.

– PHRASES **separate but equal** hist. racially segregated but ostensibly ensuring equal opportunities to all races. **separate the sheep from the goats** divide people or things into superior and inferior groups. [with biblical allusion to Matt. 25:33.] — **sep·a·rate·ly** adv. **sep·a·rate·ness** n. [ME: from L. *separat-* 'disjoined, divided,' from the verb *separare,* from *se-* 'apart' + *parare* 'prepare.']

sep·a·ra·tion /ˌsepə'rāsʜən/ ▶ n. **1** the action or state of moving or being moved apart: *the separation of parents and children.* ■ the state in which a husband and wife remain married but live apart: *she and her husband have agreed to a **trial separation**.* **2** the division of something into constituent or distinct elements. ■ the process of distinguishing between two or more things. ■ the process of sorting and then extracting or removing a specified substance for use or rejection.

– PHRASES **separation of powers** an act of vesting the legislative, executive, and judicial powers of government in separate bodies.

sep·a·ra·tion anx·i·e·ty ▶ n. Psychiatry anxiety provoked in a young child by separation or the threat of separation from their mother.

sep·a·ra·tism /'sep(ə)rəˌtizəm/ ▶ n. the advocacy or practice of separation of a certain group of people from a larger body on the basis of ethnicity, religion, or gender: *Kurdish separatism.*

sep·a·ra·tist /'sep(ə)rətist/ ▶ n. a person who supports the separation of a particular group of people from a larger body on the basis of ethnicity, religion, or gender: *religious separatists.* ▶ adj. of or relating to such separation or those supporting it: *a separatist rebellion.*

sep·a·ra·tive /'sep(ə)rətiv/ ▶ adj. tech. tending to cause division into constituent or individual elements.

sep·a·ra·tor /'sepəˌrātər/ ▶ n. a machine or device that separates something into its constituent or distinct elements: *a magnetic separator.* ■ something that keeps two or more things apart.

Se·phar·di /sə'färdē/ ▶ n. (pl. **-phar·dim** /-'färdim; -ˌfär'dēm/) a Jew of Spanish or Portuguese descent. They retain their own distinctive customs, and rituals, preserving Babylonian Jewish traditions rather than the Palestinian ones of the Ashkenazim. Compare with ASHKENAZI. ■ any Jew of the Middle East or North Africa. — **Se·phar·dic** /-dik/ adj. [mod. Heb., from *sĕpāraḏ,* a country mentioned in Obad. 20 and taken to be Spain.]

se·pi·a /'sēpēə/ ▶ n. a reddish-brown color associated particularly with monochrome photographs of the 19th and early 20th centuries. ■ a brown pigment prepared from a black fluid secreted by cuttlefish, used in monochrome drawing and in watercolors. ■ a drawing done with this pigment. ■ a blackish fluid secreted by a cuttlefish as a defensive screen. ▶ adj. of a reddish-brown color: *old sepia photographs.* [ME (cuttlefish): via L. from Gk. *sēpia.*]

se·poy /'sēˌpoi/ ▶ n. hist. an Indian soldier serving under British or other European orders. ■ (in the Indian subcontinent) a police constable. [from Urdu and Pers. *sipāhī* 'soldier,' from *sipāh* 'army.']

Se·poy Mu·ti·ny another term for INDIAN MUTINY.

sep·pu·ku /'sepōōˌkōō; sə'pōōkōō/ ▶ n. another term for HARA-KIRI. [Japanese, from *setsu* 'to cut' + *fuku* 'abdomen.']

seps /seps/ ▶ n. an African lizard (genus *Tetradactylus,* family Gerrhosauridae) with a snakelike body and very short or nonexistent legs. [16th C.: via L. from Gk. *sēps,* from the base of *sēpein* 'make rotten.']

sep·sis /'sepsis/ ▶ n. Med. the presence in tissues of harmful bacteria and their toxins, typically through infection of a wound. [19th C.: mod. L., from Gk. *sēpsis,* from *sēpein* 'make rotten.']

Sept. ▶ abbr. ■ September. ■ Septuagint.

sept /sept/ ▶ n. a clan, originally one in Ireland. [16th C.: prob. an alt. of SECT.]

sept- ▶ comb. form var. of SEPTI- (as in *septcentenary*).

sep·ta /'septə/ plural form of SEPTUM.

sep·tal /'septl/ ▶ adj. relating to or acting as a partition, in particular: ■ Anat. & Biol. relating to a septum or septa.

sep·tate /'sepˌtāt/ ▶ adj. Anat. & Biol. having or partitioned by a septum or septa. — **sep·ta·tion** /sep'tāsʜən/ n.

Sep·tem·ber /sep'tembər/ ▶ n. the ninth month of the year, in the northern hemisphere usually considered the first month of autumn: *sow the plants in early September* | [as adj.] *a warm September evening.* [OE, from L., from *septem* 'seven' (being orig. the seventh month of the Roman year).]

sep·te·nar·i·us /ˌseptə'ne(ə)rēəs/ ▶ n. (pl. **-nar·i·i** /-'ne(ə)rēˌī/) Pros. a Latin verse line of seven feet, esp. a trochaic or iambic tetrameter catalectic, used only in comedy. [19th C.: from L., from *septeni* 'in sevens,' from *septem* 'seven.']

sep·te·nar·y /'septəˌnerē/ ▶ adj. of, relating to, or divided into seven. ▶ n. (pl. **-nar·ies**) a group or set of seven, in particular: ■ a period of seven years. ■ Music the seven notes of the diatonic scale. [ME: from L. *septenarius* (see SEPTENARIUS).]

sep·ten·ni·al /sep'tenēəl/ ▶ adj. recurring every seven years. ■ lasting for or relating to a period of seven years. [17th C.: from late L. *septennis* (from L. *septem* 'seven' + *annus* 'year') + -AL.]

sep·ten·ni·um /sep'tenēəm/ ▶ n. (pl. **-ten·ni·a** /-'tenēə/ or **-ten·ni·ums**) rare a specified period of seven years. [19th C.: from late L., from L. *septem* 'seven' + *annus* 'year.']

sep·tet /sep'tet/ (also **sep·tette**) ▶ n. a group of seven people playing music or singing together. ■ a composition for such a group. [19th C.: from Ger. *Septett,* from L. *septem* 'seven.']

septi- (also **sept-**) ▶ comb. form seven; having seven: *septivalent.* [from L. *septem* 'seven.']

sep·tic /'septik/ ▶ adj. **1** (chiefly of a wound or a part of the body) infected with bacteria. **2** [attrib.] denoting a drainage system incorporating a septic tank. ▶ n. a drainage system incorporating a septic tank. — **sep·ti·cal·ly** /-ik(ə)lē/ adv. **sep·tic·i·ty** /sep'tisitē/ n. [17th C.: via L. from Gk. *sēptikos,* 'rotten.']

sep·ti·ce·mi·a /ˌsepti'sēmēə/ (Brit. **sep·ti·cae·mi·a**) ▶ n. blood poisoning, esp. that caused by bacteria or their toxins. — **sep·ti·ce·mic** /-mik/ adj. [19th C.: mod. L., from Gk. *sēptikos* + *haima* 'blood.']

sep·tic tank ▶ n. a tank, typically underground, in which sewage is collected and allowed to decompose through bacterial activity before draining by means of a leaching field.

sep·til·lion /sep'tilyən/ ▶ cardinal number (pl. **-lions** or (with numeral) same) a thousand raised to the eighth power (10^{24}). ■ dated, esp. Brit. a million raised to the seventh power (10^{42}). [17th C.: from Fr., from *million,* by substitution of the prefix *septi-* 'seven' (from L. *septimus* 'seventh') for the initial letters.]

sep·ti·mal /'septəməl/ ▶ adj. of or relating to the number seven. [19th C.: from L. *septimus* 'seventh' (from *septem* 'seven') + -AL.]

sep·time /'sepˌtēm/ ▶ n. Fencing the seventh of eight standard parrying positions. [19th C.: from L. *septimus* 'seventh.']

sep·to·ria /sep'tôrēə/ ▶ n. a fungus of a genus (*Septoria*) that includes many kinds that cause diseases in plants. ■ leaf spot disease caused by such a fungus. [mod. L., from L. *septum* (see SEPTUM).]

sep·tu·a·ge·nar·i·an /ˌsepcʜōōəjə'ne(ə)rēən/ ▶ n. a person who is from 70 to 79 years old. [18th C.: from L. *septuagenarius* (based on *septuaginta* 'seventy') + -AN.]

Sep·tu·a·ges·i·ma /ˌsepcʜōōə'jesəmə/ (also **Septuagesima Sunday**) n. the Sunday before Sexagesima. [ME: from L., 'seventieth (day),' prob. named by analogy with QUINQUAGESIMA.]

Sep·tu·a·gint /'sepcʜōōəˌjint/ ▶ n. a Greek version of the Hebrew Bible (or Old Testament), including the Apocrypha, made for Greek-speaking Jews in Egypt in the 3rd and 2nd centuries BC and adopted by the early Christian Churches. [16th C. (orig. denoting the translators themselves): from L. *septuaginta* 'seventy,' because of the tradition that it was produced, under divine inspiration, by seventy-two translators working independently.]

sep·tum /'septəm/ ▶ **n.** (pl. **-ta** /-tə/) esp. Anat. & Biol. a partition separating two chambers, such as that between the nostrils or the chambers of the heart. [17th C.: from L. *septum*, from *sepire* 'enclose,' from *sepes* 'hedge.']

sep·tu·ple /'septəpəl; sep't(y)o͞opəl; -'təp-/ rare ▶ **adj.** [attrib.] consisting of seven parts or elements. ■ consisting of seven times as much or as many as usual. ■ (of time in music) having seven beats in a bar. ▶ **v.** [trans.] multiply (something) by seven; increase sevenfold. [17th C. (as a v.): from late L. *septuplus*, from L. *septem* 'seven.']

sep·tup·let /sep'təplit; sep't(y)o͞o-/ ▶ **n. 1** (usu. **septuplets**) each of seven children born at one birth. **2** Music a group of seven notes to be performed in the time of four or six. [19th C.: from L. *septuplus* (see SEPTUPLE), on the pattern of words such as *triplet*.]

sep·ul·cher /'sepəlkər/ (Brit. **sep·ul·chre**) ▶ **n.** a small room or monument, cut in rock or built of stone, in which a dead person is laid or buried. ▶ **v.** [trans.] esp. literary lay or bury in or as if in a sepulcher: *tomes are soon out of print and sepulchered in the dust of libraries.* ■ serve as a burial place for: *when ocean shrouds and sepulchers our dead.* [ME: via OFr. from L. *sepulcrum* 'burial place,' from *sepelire* 'bury.']

se·pul·chral /sə'pəlkrəl/ ▶ **adj.** of or relating to a tomb or interment: *sepulchral monuments.* ■ gloomy; dismal: *a speech delivered in sepulchral tones.* — **se·pul·chral·ly adv.** [17th C.: from Fr. *sépulchral* or L. *sepulchralis*, from *sepulcrum* (see SEPULCHER).]

sep·ul·ture /'sepəlcʜər/ ▶ **n.** archaic burial; interment: *the rites of sepulture.* [ME: via OFr. from L. *sepultura*, from *sepelire* 'bury.']

seq. (also **seqq.**) ▶ **adv.** short for ET SEQ.

se·qua·cious /si'kwāsʜəs/ ▶ **adj.** formal (of a person) lacking independence or originality of thought. — **se·qua·cious·ly adv. se·quac·i·ty** /-'kwasitē/ **n.** [17th C.: from L. *sequax*, *sequac-* 'following' (from *sequi* 'follow') + -IOUS.]

se·quel /'sēkwəl/ ▶ **n.** a published, broadcast, or recorded work that continues the story or develops the theme of an earlier one. ■ something that takes place after or as a result of an earlier event: *this encouragement to grow potatoes had a disastrous sequel some fifty years later.* [ME (in the senses 'body of followers,' 'descendants' and 'consequence'): from OFr. *sequelle* or L. *sequella*, from *sequi* 'follow.']

se·que·la /si'kwelə/ ▶ **n.** (pl. **-que·lae** /-'kwelē; -'kwelī/) (usu. **sequelae**) Med. a condition that is the consequence of a previous disease or injury. [18th C.: from L., from *sequi* 'follow.']

se·quence /'sēkwəns/ ▶ **n. 1** a particular order in which related events, movements, or things follow each other. ■ Music a repetition of a phrase or melody at a higher or lower pitch. ■ Biochem. the order in which amino acid or nucleotide residues are arranged in a protein, DNA, etc. **2** a set of related events, movements, or things that follow each other in a particular order. ■ a set of three or more playing cards of the same suit next to each other in value, for example 10, 9, 8. ■ Math. an infinite ordered series of numerical quantities. **3** a part of a film dealing with one particular event or topic: *the famous underwater sequence.* **4** (in the Eucharist) a hymn said or sung after the Gradual or Alleluia that precedes the Gospel. ▶ **v.** [trans.] arrange in a particular order. ■ Biochem. ascertain the sequence of amino acid or nucleotide residues in (a protein, DNA, etc.).
– PHRASES **in sequence** in a given order. [ME (sense 4): from late L. *sequentia*, from L. *sequent-* 'following,' from the verb *sequi* 'follow.']

se·quence of tens·es ▶ **n.** Gram. the dependence of the tense of a subordinate verb on the tense of the verb in the main clause (e.g., *I think that you* are *wrong*; *I thought that you* were *wrong*).

se·quenc·er /'sēkwənsər/ ▶ **n. 1** a programmable electronic device for storing sequences of musical notes, chords, or rhythms and transmitting them when required to an electronic musical instrument. **2** Biochem. an apparatus for determining the sequence of amino acids or other monomers in a biological polymer.

se·quent /'sēkwənt/ ▶ **adj.** archaic following in a sequence or as a logical conclusion. — **se·quent·ly adv.** [16th C.: from OFr., or from L. *sequent-* 'following' (see SEQUENCE).]

se·quen·tial /si'kwencʜəl/ ▶ **adj.** forming or following in a logical order or sequence: *following a series of sequential steps.* ■ esp. Comput. performed or used in sequence: *sequential processing of data files.* — **se·quen·ti·al·i·ty** /si,kwencʜē'alitē/ **n. se·quen·tial·ly adv.** [19th C. (as a medical term in the sense 'following as a secondary condition'): from SEQUENCE, on the pattern of *consequential*.]

se·quen·tial ac·cess ▶ **n.** access to a computer data file that requires the user to read through the file from the beginning in the order in which it is stored. Compare with DIRECT ACCESS.

se·quen·tial cir·cuit ▶ **n.** Electron. a circuit whose output depends on the order or timing of the inputs.

se·ques·ter /sə'kwestər/ ▶ **v.** [trans.] **1** isolate or hide away (someone or something): *the artist sequestered himself in his studio for two years.* ■ isolate (a jury) from outside influences during a trial. ■ Chem. form a chelate or other stable compound with (an ion, atom, or molecule) so that it is no longer available for reactions. **2** take legal possession of (assets) until a debt has been paid or other claims have been met. ■ take forcible possession of (something); confiscate. ■ legally place (the property of a bankrupt) in the hands of a trustee for division among the creditors. ■ declare (someone) bankrupt. ▶ **n.** a general cut in government spending. [ME: from OFr. *sequestrer* or late L. *sequestrare* 'commit for safekeeping,' from L. *sequester* 'trustee.']

se·ques·tered /sə'kwestərd/ ▶ **adj.** (of a place) isolated and hidden away: *a wild sequestered spot.*

se·ques·trate /'sēkwi,strāt; 'sek-; sə'kwes,trāt/ ▶ **v.** another term for SEQUESTER. — **se·ques·tra·ble** /si'kwestrəbəl/ **adj. se·ques·tra·tor** /'sēkwi,strātər; 'sek-; si'kwes,trātər/ **n.** [ME (in the sense 'separate from general access'): from late L. *sequestrat-* 'given up for safekeeping,' from the verb *sequestrare* (see SEQUESTER).]

se·ques·tra·tion /,sēkwi'strāsʜən; ,sek-/ ▶ **n. 1** the action of taking legal possession of assets until a debt has been paid or other claims have been met. ■ the action of taking forcible possession of something; confiscation. ■ an act of declaring someone bankrupt. ■ the action of making a general cut in government spending. ■ Chem. the action of sequestering a substance. **2** the action of isolating a jury during a trial.

se·quin /'sēkwin/ ▶ **n. 1** a small, shiny disk sewn as one of many onto clothing for decoration. **2** hist. a Venetian gold coin. — **se·quined** (also **se·quinned**) **adj.** [16th C. (sense 2): from Fr., from Ital. *zecchino*, from *zecca* 'a mint,' from Arab. *sikka* 'a die for coining.' Sense 1 dates from the late 19th C.]

se·quoi·a /sə'kwoi-ə/ ▶ **n.** a redwood tree, esp. the California redwood. [from mod. L. *Sequoia* (genus name), from *Sequoya*, the name of the Cherokee Indian who invented the Cherokee syllabary.]

Se·quoi·a Na·tion·al Park a national park in the Sierra Nevada of California, east of Fresno. It was established in 1890 to protect groves of giant sequoia trees.

Se·quoy·a /sə'kwoi-ə/ (also **Sequoyah** or **Sequoia**) (*c.*1770–1843), Cherokee Indian scholar; Cherokee name *Sogwali*; also known as **George Guess** or **Gist**. He invented a writing system 1809–21 for the Cherokee language. The giant sequoia trees of California are named for him.

ser. ▶ **abbr.** ■ serial. ■ series. ■ sermon.

se·ra /'si(ə)rə/ plural form of SERUM.

se·rac /sə'rak/ ▶ **n.** a pinnacle or ridge of ice on the surface of a glacier. [19th C.: from Swiss Fr. *sérac*, orig. the name of a compact white cheese.]

se·ragl·io /sə'rälyō/ ▶ **n.** (pl. **-ios**) **1** the women's apartments (harem) in a Muslim palace. ■ another term for HAREM (sense 2). **2** (**the Seraglio**) hist. a Turkish palace, esp. the Sultan's court and government offices at Constantinople. [16th C.: from Ital. *serraglio*, via Turk. from Pers. *sarāy* 'palace'; cf. SERAI.]

se·ra·i /sə'rī/ ▶ **n.** another term for CARAVANSARY (sense 1).

se·ra·pe /sə'räpē/ (also **sa·ra·pe**) ▶ **n.** a shawl or blanket worn as a cloak in Latin America. [Mex. Sp.]

ser·aph /'serəf/ ▶ **n.** (pl. **ser·a·phim** /'serə,fim/ or **ser·aphs**) an angelic being, regarded in traditional Christian angelology as belonging to the highest order of the ninefold celestial hierarchy, associated with light, ardor, and purity. [OE, back-form. from *seraphim* (pl.), via late L. and Gk. from Heb. *śĕrāpîm*. Cf. CHERUB.]

se·raph·ic /sə'rafik/ ▶ **adj.** characteristic of or resembling a seraph or seraphim: *a seraphic smile.* — **se·raph·i·cal·ly** /-ik(ə)lē/ **adv.** [17th C.: from med. L. *seraphicus*, from late L. *seraphim* (see SERAPH).]

Se·ra·pis /sə'rāpis/ Egyptian Mythol. a god whose cult was developed by Ptolemy I at Memphis as a combination of Apis and Osiris, to unite Greeks and Egyptians in a common worship.

Serb /sərb/ ▶ **n.** a native or national of Serbia. ■ a person of Serbian descent. ▶ **adj.** of or relating to Serbia, the Serbs, or their language. [from Serbo-Croat *Srb*.]

Ser·bi·a /'sərbēə/ a republic in the Balkans; pop. 9,660,000; official language, Serbian; capital, Belgrade.

Ser·bi·an /'sərbēən/ ▶ **n. 1** the dialect of Serbo-Croat used by the Serbs. See SERBO-CROAT. **2** another term for SERB. ▶ **adj.** of or relating to Serbia, the Serbs, or their language.

Serbo- ▶ **comb. form** Serbian; Serbian and ...: *Serbo-Croat.* ■ relating to Serbia.

Ser·bo-Cro·at /'sərbō 'krō,ät; 'krōt/ (also **Ser·bo-Cro·a·tian** /krō'āsʜən/) ▶ **n.** the South Slavic language spoken in Serbia, Croatia, and elsewhere in the former Yugoslavia. Serbo-Croat is generally classed as one language, but comprises two closely similar forms: Serbian, written in the Cyrillic alphabet, and Croat, written in the Roman alphabet. ▶ **adj.** of or relating to this language.

sere[1] /si(ə)r/ ▶ **adj.** var. of SEAR.

sere[2] ▶ **n.** Ecol. a natural succession of plant (or animal) communities, esp. a full series from uncolonized habitat to the appropriate climax vegetation. Compare with SUCCESSION. [20th C.: from L. *serere* 'join in a series.']

ser·e·nade /,serə'nād/ ▶ **n.** a piece of music sung or played in the open air, typically by a man at night under the window of his lover. ■ another term for SERENATA. ▶ **v.** [trans.] entertain (someone) with a serenade. — **ser·e·nad·er n.** [17th C.: from Fr. *sérénade*, from Ital. *serenata*, from *sereno* 'serene.']

ser·e·na·ta /,serə'nätə/ ▶ **n.** Music a cantata with a pastoral subject. ■ a simple form of suite for orchestra or wind band. [Ital., 'serenade' (see SERENADE).]

ser·en·dip·i·ty /,serən'dipitē/ ▶ **n.** the occurrence and development of events by chance in a happy or beneficial way: *a fortunate stroke of serendipity.* — **ser·en·dip·i·tous** /-'dipitəs/ **adj. ser·en·dip·i·tous·ly**

/-'dipətəslē/ **adv.** [1754: coined by Horace Walpole, suggested by *The Three Princes of Serendip*, the title of a fairy tale in which the heroes "were always making discoveries, by accidents and sagacity, of things they were not in quest of."]

se·rene /sə'rēn/ ▶ **adj. 1** calm, peaceful, and untroubled; tranquil: *serene certainty.* **2** (**Serene**) (in a title) used as a term of respect for members of some European royal families: *His Serene Highness.* ▶ **n.** (usu. **the serene**) archaic an expanse of clear sky or calm sea. — **se·rene·ly adv.** [ME (describing the weather or sky as 'clear, fine, and calm'): from L. *serenus.*]

Ser·en·get·i /ˌserən'getē/ a plain in Tanzania, west of the Great Rift Valley. Serengeti National Park is here.

se·ren·i·ty /sə'renitē/ ▶ **n.** (pl. **-ties**) the state of being calm, peaceful, and untroubled: *an oasis of serenity.* ■ (**His**/**Your**, etc., **Serenity**) a title given to a reigning prince or similar dignitary. [ME: from OFr. *serenite*, from L. *serenitas*, from *serenus* 'clear, fair' (see **serene**).]

serf /sərf/ ▶ **n.** an agricultural laborer bound under the feudal system to work on his lord's estate. — **serf·age** /'sərfij/ **n. serf·dom** /-dəm/ **n.** [15th C. (in the sense 'slave'): from OFr., from L. *servus* 'slave.']

serge /sərj/ ▶ **n.** a durable twilled woolen or worsted fabric. ▶ **v.** [trans.] overcast (the edge of a piece of material) to prevent fraying. [ME: from OFr. *sarge*, from a var. of L. *serica (lana)* 'silken (wool),' from *sericus* (see **silk**).]

ser·geant /'särjənt/ ▶ **n.** a noncommissioned officer in the armed forces, in particular (in the US Army or Marine Corps) an NCO ranking above corporal and below staff sergeant, or (in the US Air Force) an NCO ranking above airman and below staff sergeant. ■ Brit. a police officer ranking below an inspector. ■ a police officer ranking below a lieutenant. — **ser·gean·cy** /-jənsē/ **n.** (pl. **-cies**). [ME: from OFr. *sergent*, from L. *servient-* 'serving,' from the verb *servire.*]

Ser·geant Ba·ker ▶ **n.** Austral. a brightly colored edible marine fish (*Aulopus purpurissatus*, family Aulopidae) with two elongated dorsal fin rays, occurring in warm Australian coastal waters. [19th C.: of unknown origin.]

ser·geant first class ▶ **n.** a noncommissioned officer in the US Army of a rank above staff sergeant and below master sergeant.

ser·geant fish ▶ **n.** another term for **cobia**.

ser·geant ma·jor ▶ **n. 1** an noncommissioned officer in the US Army or Marine Corps of the highest rank, above master sergeant and below warrant officer. **2** a warrant officer in the British army. **3** a fish (*Abudefduf saxatilis*, family Pomacentridae) with boldly striped sides that lives in warm seas, typically on coral reefs.

serg·er /'sərjər/ ▶ **n.** a sewing machine used for overcasting to prevent material from fraying at the edge.

Ser·gi·us, St. /'sərjēəs/ (1314–92), Russian reformer and mystic; Russian name *Svyatoi Sergi Radonezhsky.* He inspired the resistance that saved Russia from the Tartars in 1380.

se·ri·al /'si(ə)rēəl/ ▶ **adj. 1** consisting of, forming part of, or taking place in a series: *a serial publication.* ■ Music using transformations of a fixed series of notes. ■ Comput. (of a device) involving the transfer of data as a single sequence of bits. See also **serial port**. ■ Comput. (of a processor) running only a single task, as opposed to multitasking. **2** [attrib.] (of a criminal) repeatedly committing the same offense and typically following a characteristic, predictable behavior pattern: *a suspected serial rapist.* ■ (of a person) repeatedly following the same behavior pattern: *he was a serial adulterer.* ■ denoting an action or behavior pattern that is committed or followed repeatedly: *serial killings* | *serial monogamy.* ▶ **n.** a story or play appearing in regular installments on television or radio or in a magazine or newspaper. ■ (usu. **serials**) (in a library) a periodical. — **se·ri·al·i·ty** /ˌsi(ə)rē'alitē/ **n. se·ri·al·ly adv.** [19th C.: from **series** + **-al**, perh. suggested by Fr. *sérial.*]

se·ri·al·ism /'si(ə)rēəˌlizəm/ ▶ **n.** Music a compositional technique in which a fixed series of notes, esp. the twelve notes of the chromatic scale, are used to generate the harmonic and melodic basis of a piece and are subject to change only in specific ways. The first fully serial movements appeared in 1923 in works by Arnold Schoenberg. See also **twelve-tone**. — **se·ri·al·ist adj. & n.**

se·ri·al·ize /'si(ə)rēəˌlīz/ ▶ **v.** [trans.] **1** publish or broadcast (a story or play) in regular installments. **2** arrange (something) in a series: *each document sent to investors should be individually numbered or serialized.* ■ Music compose according to the techniques of serialism. — **se·ri·al·i·za·tion** /ˌsi(ə)rēələ'zāsʜən/ **n.**

se·ri·al num·ber ▶ **n.** a number showing the position of an item in a series, esp. one printed on paper currency or on a manufactured article for the purposes of identification.

se·ri·al port ▶ **n.** Comput. a connector by which a device that sends data one bit at a time may be connected to a computer.

se·ri·ate /'si(ə)rēˌāt/ tech. ▶ **adj.** arranged or occurring in one or more series. ▶ **v.** [trans.] arrange (items) in a sequence according to prescribed criteria. — **se·ri·a·tion** /ˌsi(ə)rē'āsʜən/ **n.** [19th C.: back-form. from *seriation*, from **series**.]

se·ri·a·tim /ˌsi(ə)rē'ātəm; -'atəm/ ▶ **adv.** formal taking one subject after another in regular order; point by point: *it is proposed to deal with these matters seriatim.* [15th C.: from med. L., from L. *series*, on the pattern of L. *gradatim* and *literatim.*]

ser·i·cul·ture /'seriˌkəlcʜər/ ▶ **n.** the production of silk and the rearing of silkworms for this purpose. — **ser·i·cul·tur·al** /ˌseri'kəlcʜərəl/ **adj. ser·i·cul·tur·ist** /ˌseri'kəlcʜərist/ **n.** [19th C.: abbrev. of French *sériciculture*, from late L. *sericum* 'silk' + Fr. *culture* 'cultivation.']

ser·i·e·ma /ˌserē'ēmə; -'āmə/ ▶ **n.** a large, ground-dwelling South American bird (family Cariamidae) related to the bustards, with a long neck and legs and a crest above the bill. [19th C.: mod. L., from Tupi *siriema* 'crested.']

se·ries /'si(ə)rēz/ ▶ **n.** (pl. same) a number of things, events, or people of a similar kind or related nature coming one after another: ***a series of lectures.*** ■ [usu. with adj.] a set of related television or radio programs, esp. of a specified kind: *a new drama series.* ■ a set of books, maps, periodicals, or other documents published in a common format or under a common title. ■ a set of games played between two teams. See also **World Series**. ■ a line of products, esp. vehicles or machines, sharing features of design or assembly and marketed with a separate number from other lines: [as adj.] *a series III SWB Land Rover.* ■ a set of stamps, banknotes, or coins issued at a particular time or having a common design or theme. ■ [as adj.] denoting electrical circuits or components arranged so that the current passes through each successively. The opposite of **parallel**. ■ Geol. (in chronostratigraphy) a range of strata corresponding to an epoch in time, being a subdivision of a system and itself subdivided into stages. ■ Chem. a set of elements with common properties or of compounds related in composition or structure. ■ Math. a set of quantities constituting a progression or having the several values determined by a common relation. ■ Phonet. a group of speech sounds having at least one phonetic feature in common but distinguished in other respects. ■ Music another term for **tone row**.

– PHRASES **in series** (of a set of batteries or electrical components) arranged so that the current passes through each successively. [17th C.: from L., lit. 'row, chain,' from *serere* 'join, connect.']

ser·if /'serəf/ ▶ **n.** a slight projection finishing off a stroke of a letter, as in T contrasted with T. — **ser·iffed adj.** [19th C.: perh. from Du. *schreef* 'dash, line,' of Gmc. origin.]

ser·i·graph /'seriˌgraf/ ▶ **n.** a printed design produced by means of a silkscreen. — **se·rig·ra·pher** /sə'rigrəfər/ **n. se·rig·ra·phy** /sə'rigrəfē/ **n.** [19th C.: formed irregularly from L. *sericum* 'silk' + **-graph**.]

ser·in /'serən/ ▶ **n.** a small Eurasian and North African finch (genus *Serinus*) related to the canary, with a short bill and typically streaky plumage. [16th C.: from Fr., 'canary.']

ser·ine /'serēn; 'si(ə)r-; -in/ ▶ **n.** Biochem. a hydrophilic amino acid, CH_2O-$HCHNH_2COOH$, that is a constituent of most proteins. [19th C.: from L. *sericum* 'silk' + **-ine**[4].]

se·ri·o·com·ic /ˌsi(ə)rē-ō'kämik/ ▶ **adj.** combining the serious and the comic; serious in intention but jocular in manner or vice versa. — **se·ri·o·com·i·cal·ly** /-ik(ə)lē/ **adv.**

se·ri·ous /'si(ə)rēəs/ ▶ **adj. 1** (of a person) solemn or thoughtful in character or manner. ■ (of a subject, state, or activity) demanding careful consideration or application: *marriage is a serious matter.* ■ (of thought or discussion) careful or profound: *serious consideration.* ■ (of music, literature, or other art forms) requiring deep reflection and inviting a considered response. **2** acting or speaking sincerely and in earnest, rather than in a joking or halfhearted manner. **3** significant or worrying because of possible danger or risk; not slight or negligible: *serious injury.* **4** [attrib.] informal substantial in terms of size, number, or quality: *he suddenly had serious money to spend.* — **se·ri·ous·ness n. se·ri·ous·ly adv.** [ME: from OFr. *serieux* or late L. *seriosus*, from L. *serius* 'earnest, serious.']

ser·jeant-at-law ▶ **n.** (pl. **ser·jeants-at-law**) Brit., hist. a barrister of the highest rank.

ser·jeant·y /'särjəntē/ ▶ **n.** (pl. **-jeant·ies**) Brit., hist. a form of feudal tenure conditional on rendering some specified personal service to the monarch.

ser·mon /'sərmən/ ▶ **n.** a talk on a religious or moral subject, esp. one given during a church service and based on a passage from the Bible. ■ a printed transcript of such a talk. ■ informal a long or tedious piece of admonition or reproof; a lecture. — **ser·mon·ic** /sər'mänik/ **adj.** [ME (also in the sense 'speech, discourse'): from OFr., from L. *sermo(n-)* 'discourse, talk.']

ser·mon·ette /ˌsərmə'net/ ▶ **n.** a short sermon.

ser·mon·ize /'sərməˌnīz/ ▶ **v.** [intrans.] compose or deliver a sermon. ■ deliver an opinionated and dogmatic talk to someone. — **ser·mon·iz·er n.**

Ser·mon on the Mount ▶ **n.** the discourse of Jesus recorded in Matt. 5–7, including the Beatitudes and the Lord's Prayer.

sero- ▶ **comb. form** relating to serum: *serotype.* ■ involving a serous membrane: *serositis.* [representing **serum**.]

se·ro·con·vert /ˌsi(ə)rōkən'vərt/ ▶ **v.** [intrans.] Med. (of a person) undergo a change from a seronegative to a seropositive condition. — **se·ro·con·ver·sion** /-'vərzʜən/ **n.**

se·rol·o·gy /si'räləjē/ ▶ **n.** the scientific study or diagnostic examination of blood serum, esp. with regard to the response of the immune system to pathogens or introduced substances. — **se·ro·log·ic** /ˌsirə'läjik/ **adj. se·ro·log·i·cal** /ˌsirə'läjikəl/ **adj. se·ro·log·i·cal·ly** /ˌsirə'läjik(ə)lē/ **adv. se·rol·o·gist** /-jist/ **n.**

se·ro·neg·a·tive /ˌsi(ə)rō'negətiv/ ▶ **adj.** Med. giving a negative result in a test of blood serum, e.g., for the presence of a virus. — **se·ro·neg·a·tiv·i·ty** /-ˌnegəˈtivitē/ **n.**

se·ro·pos·i·tive /ˌsi(ə)rōˈpäzitiv/ ▶ **adj.** Med. giving a positive result in a test of blood serum, e.g., for the presence of a virus. — **se·ro·pos·i·tiv·i·ty** /-ˌpäziˈtivitē/ **n.**

se·ro·sa /səˈrōsə/ ▶ **n.** Physiol. the tissue of a serous membrane. — **se·ro·sal adj.** [mod. L., fem. of med. L. *serosus* 'serous.']

ser·o·tine /ˈserətin; -ˌtīn/ ▶ **n.** a medium-sized insectivorous bat (family Vespertilionidae), esp. a chiefly Eurasian bat (genus *Eptesicus*) and an African bat (genus *Pipistrellus*). [18th C.: from Fr. *sérotine*, from L. *serotinus* 'of the evening, late,' from *serus* 'late.']

ser·o·to·nin /ˌserəˈtōnən; ˌsi(ə)r-/ ▶ **n.** Biochem. a compound, $C_{10}H_{12}N_2O$, present in blood platelets and serum that constricts the blood vessels and acts as a neurotransmitter. [1940s: from SERUM + TONIC + -IN[1].]

se·ro·type /ˈsi(ə)rəˌtīp; ˈserə-/ Microbiol. ▶ **n.** a serologically distinguishable strain of a microorganism. ▶ **v.** [trans.] assign (a microorganism) to a particular serotype. — **se·ro·typ·ic** /ˌsi(ə)rəˈtipik; ˌserə-/ **adj.**

se·rous /ˈsi(ə)rəs/ ▶ **adj.** Physiol. of, resembling, or producing serum. — **se·ros·i·ty** /siˈräsitē/ **n.** [ME: from Fr. *séreux* or med. L. *serosus*, from *serum* (see SERUM).]

se·rous mem·brane ▶ **n.** a mesothelial tissue that lines certain internal cavities of the body, forming a smooth, transparent, two-layered membrane lubricated by a fluid derived from serum. The peritoneum, pericardium, and pleura are serous membranes.

ser·ow /səˈrō; ˈserō/ ▶ **n.** a goat-antelope (genus *Capricornis*) with short sharp horns, long coarse hair, and a beard, native to forested mountain slopes of Southeast Asia, Taiwan, and Japan. [19th C.: prob. from Lepcha *sā-ro*.]

Ser·pens /ˈsərpənz/ Astron. a large constellation (the Serpent) on the celestial equator, said to represent the snake coiled around Ophiuchus. It is divided into two parts by Ophiuchus, **Serpens Caput** (the "head") and **Serpens Cauda** (the "tail"). [L.]

ser·pent /ˈsərpənt/ ▶ **n. 1** esp. literary a large snake. ■ **(the Serpent)** a biblical name for Satan (see Gen. 3, Rev. 20). ■ a dragon or other mythical snakelike reptile. ■ fig. a sly or treacherous person, esp. one who exploits a position of trust in order to betray it. **2** hist. a bass wind instrument made of leather-covered wood in three U-shaped turns, with a cup-shaped mouthpiece and few keys. It was played in military and church bands from the 17th to 19th centuries. [ME: via OFr. from L. *serpent-* 'creeping,' from the verb *serpere*.]

ser·pen·tine /ˈsərpənˌtēn; -ˌtīn/ ▶ **adj.** of or like a serpent or snake: *serpentine coils.* ■ winding and twisting like a snake. ■ complex, cunning, or treacherous. ▶ **n. 1** a dark green mineral consisting of hydrated magnesium silicate, sometimes mottled or spotted like a snake's skin. **2** a thing in the shape of a winding curve or line, in particular: ■ a riding exercise consisting of a series of half-circles made alternately to right and left. **3** hist. a kind of cannon, used esp. in the 15th and 16th centuries. [ME: via OFr. from late L. *serpentinus* (see SERPENT).]

ser·ra·nid /ˈserənid/ ▶ **n.** Zool. a fish of the sea bass family (Serranidae), whose members are predatory marine fish with a spiny dorsal fin. [20th C.: from mod. L. *Serranidae*, from the genus name *Serranus*, from L. *serra* 'saw.']

ser·ra·no /səˈränō/ ▶ **n.** a small green or red chili pepper of a very hot variety, used esp. in Mexican cooking. [Sp., lit. 'of the mountains, highlander.']

ser·rate /ˈserˌāt; -it/ ▶ **adj.** esp. Bot. serrated. [17th C.: from late L. *serratus*, from L. *serra* 'saw.']

ser·rat·ed /ˈserˌātid; səˈrātid/ ▶ **adj.** having or denoting a jagged edge; sawlike: *a knife with a serrated edge.*

ser·ra·tion /seˈrāsʜən/ ▶ **n.** (usu. **serrations**) a tooth or point of a serrated edge or surface.

ser·ried /ˈserēd/ ▶ **adj.** [attrib.] (of rows of people or things) standing close together: *serried ranks of soldiers.* [17th C.: past part. of *serry* 'press close,' prob. from Fr. *serré* 'close together,' based on L. *sera* 'lock.']

Ser·to·li cell /sərˈtōlē/ ▶ **n.** Anat. a type of somatic cell around which spermatids develop in the tubules of the testis. [19th C.: named after Enrico *Sertoli* (1842–1910), Italian histologist.]

se·rum /ˈsi(ə)rəm/ ▶ **n.** (pl. **se·ra** /ˈsi(ə)rə/ or **se·rums**) an amber-colored, protein-rich liquid that separates out when blood coagulates. ■ the blood serum of an animal, used esp. to provide immunity to a pathogen or toxin by inoculation or as a diagnostic agent. [17th C.: from L., lit. 'whey.']

se·rum hep·a·ti·tis ▶ **n.** a viral form of hepatitis transmitted through infected blood products, causing fever, debility, and jaundice.

serv. ▶ **abbr.** service.

ser·val /ˈsərvəl; sərˈval/ ▶ **n.** a slender African wildcat (*Felis serval*) with long legs, large ears, and a black-spotted orange-brown coat. [18th C.: from Fr., from Port. *cerval* 'deerlike,' from *cervo* 'deer,' from L. *cervus*.]

serv·ant /ˈsərvənt/ ▶ **n.** a person who performs duties for others, esp. a person employed in a house on domestic duties or as a personal attendant. ■ a person employed in the service of a government. See also CIVIL SERVANT, PUBLIC SERVANT. ■ a devoted and helpful follower or supporter: *a tireless servant of God.* — **serv·ant·hood** /-ˌhŏŏd/ **n.** [ME: from OFr., lit. '(person) serving,' pres. part. (used as a n.) of *servir* 'to serve.']

serve /sərv/ ▶ **v.** [trans.] **1** perform duties or services for (another person or an organization). ■ provide (an area or group of people) with a product or service. ■ [intrans.] be employed as a member of the armed forces. ■ spend (a period) in office, in an apprenticeship, or in prison. **2** present (food or drink) to someone: *they serve wine instead of beer.* ■ present (someone) with food or drink: *I'll serve you with coffee and cake.* ■ (of food or drink) be enough for: *the recipe serves four people.* ■ attend to (a customer in a store). ■ supply (goods) to a customer. ■ [intrans.] Christian Church act as a server at the celebration of the Eucharist. ■ [with two objs.] archaic play (a trick) on (someone): *I remember the trick you served me.* **3** Law deliver (a document such as a summons or writ) in a formal manner to the person to whom it is addressed: *a warrant was served on Jack Sherman.* ■ deliver a document to (someone) in such a way: *they were just about to **serve** him **with** a writ.* **4** be of use in achieving or satisfying: *this book will serve a useful purpose.* ■ [intrans.] be of some specified use: *the island's one pub serves as a café by day.* ■ [with obj. and adverbial] function for or treat (someone) in a specified way: *the strategy served him well.* ■ (of a male breeding animal) copulate with (a female). **5** [intrans.] (in tennis and other racket sports) hit the ball or shuttlecock to begin play: *he tossed the ball up to serve* | [trans.] *serve the ball onto the front wall.* ■ [trans.] (in tennis and other racket sports) begin play for each point in (a game). **6** Naut. bind (a rope) with thin cord to protect or strengthen it. **7** Mil. operate (a gun): *before long Lodge was the only man in his section able to serve the guns.* ▶ **n.** (in tennis and other racket sports) an act or turn of hitting the ball or shuttlecock to start play: *he was let down by an erratic serve.*

– PHRASES **serve at table** act as a waiter. **serve someone right** be someone's deserved punishment or misfortune. **serve one's time** (also **serve out one's time**) hold office for the normal period. ■ (also **serve time**) spend time in office, in an apprenticeship, or in prison. **serve two masters** take orders from two superiors or follow two conflicting or opposing principles or policies at the same time. [alluding to Matt. 6:24.]

– PHRASAL VERBS **serve out** Tennis win the final game of a set or match while serving. [ME: from OFr. *servir*, from L. *servire*, from *servus* 'slave.']

serve-and-vol·ley ▶ **adj.** Tennis [attrib.] denoting a style of play in which the server moves close to the net after serving, ready to play an attacking volley off the return. — **serve-and-vol·ley·er n.**

serv·er /ˈsərvər/ ▶ **n.** a person or thing that provides a service or commodity, in particular: ■ a computer or computer program that manages access to a centralized resource or service in a network. ■ (in tennis and other racket sports) the player who serves. ■ a waiter or waitress. ■ Christian Church a person assisting the celebrant at the celebration of the Eucharist. ■ a large utensil for serving food.

serv·ice /ˈsərvis/ ▶ **n. 1** the action of helping or doing work for someone. ■ an act of assistance: *he has done us a great service.* ■ assistance or advice given to customers during and after the sale of goods. ■ short for SERVICE INDUSTRY. ■ work done for a customer other than manufacturing: *goods and services.* ■ the action or process of serving food and drinks to customers. ■ short for SERVICE CHARGE. ■ a period of employment with a company or organization. ■ employment as a servant: *domestic service.* See also *IN SERVICE* below. ■ the use that can be made of a machine: *the computer should provide good service for years.* ■ the provision of the necessary maintenance work for a machine: *they phoned for service on their air conditioning.* ■ a periodic routine inspection and maintenance of a vehicle or other machine. ■ **(the services)** the armed forces. **2** a system supplying a public need such as transport, communications, or utilities such as electricity and water: *a regular bus service.* ■ a public department or organization run by the government: *the US Fish and Wildlife Service.* **3** a ceremony of religious worship according to a prescribed form; the prescribed form for such a ceremony: *a funeral service.* **4** [with adj.] a set of matching dishes and utensils used for serving a particular meal: *a dinner service.* **5** (in tennis and other racket sports) the action or right of serving to begin play. ■ a serve. **6** Law the formal delivery of a document such as a writ or summons. ▶ **v.** [trans.] **1** (usu. **be serviced**) perform routine maintenance or repair work on (a vehicle or machine). ■ supply and maintain systems for public utilities and transportation and communications in (an area): *the town is small but well serviced.* ■ perform a service or services for (someone): *an organization servicing the poor.* ■ pay interest on (a debt). **2** (of a male animal) mate with (a female animal). ■ vulgar slang (of a man) have sexual intercourse with (a woman).

– PHRASES **be at someone's service** be ready to assist someone whenever possible. **be of service** be available to assist someone. **in service 1** in or available for use. **2** dated employed as a servant. **out of service** not available for use. **see service** serve in the armed forces. ■ be used: *the building later saw service as a blacksmith's shop.* [OE, from OFr. *servise* or L. *servitium* 'slavery,' from *servus* 'slave.']

serv·ice·a·ble /ˈsərvəsəbəl/ ▶ **adj.** fulfilling its function adequately; usable. ■ functional and durable rather than attractive. ■ in working order. — **serv·ice·a·bil·i·ty** /ˌsərvəsəˈbilitē/ **n. serv·ice·a·bly** /-blē/ **adv.** [ME (in the sense 'willing to be of service'): from OFr. *servisable*, from *servise* (see SERVICE).]

serv·ice ar·e·a ▶ **n. 1** a roadside area where services are available to motorists. **2** the area transmitted by a broadcasting station.

serv·ice·ber·ry /ˈsərvisˌberē/ ▶ **n. 1** the fruit of the service tree. **2** another term for JUNEBERRY.

serv·ice book ▶ **n.** a book of authorized forms of worship used in a church.

serv·ice cap ▶ **n.** a round, flat-topped cap with a visor that is part of the US Army and US Air Force service uniform.

serv·ice ceil·ing ▶ **n.** the maximum height at which an aircraft can sustain a specified rate of climb dependent on engine type.

serv·ice charge (also **serv·ice fee**) ▶ **n.** an extra charge assessed for a service.

serv·ice club ▶ **n.** an association of business or professional people with the aims of promoting community welfare and goodwill.

serv·ice e·con·o·my ▶ **n.** an economy or the sector of an economy that is based on trade in services.

serv·ice in·dus·try ▶ **n.** a business that does work for a customer, and occasionally provides goods, but is not involved in manufacturing.

serv·ice line ▶ **n.** (in tennis, badminton, and other sports) a line on a court marking the limit of the area into which the ball must be served. ■ (esp. in handball and paddleball) a line on a court marking the boundary of the area in which the server must be standing when serving.

serv·ice·man /ˈsərvəs,mən; -,man/ ▶ **n.** (pl. **-men**) **1** a man serving in the armed forces. **2** a person providing maintenance on machinery, esp. domestic machinery.

serv·ice mark ▶ **n.** a legally registered name or designation used in the manner of a trademark to distinguish an organization's services from those of its competitors.

serv·ice mod·ule ▶ **n.** a detachable compartment of a spacecraft carrying fuel and supplies.

serv·ice road ▶ **n.** another term for FRONTAGE ROAD.

serv·ice sta·tion ▶ **n.** an establishment selling gasoline and oil and typically having the facilities to provide automotive repairs and maintenance.

serv·ice stripe ▶ **n.** Mil. a stripe worn on the left sleeve of an enlisted person's tunic, indicating the number of years in service.

serv·ice tree ▶ **n.** a Eurasian tree (genus *Sorbus*) of the rose family, closely related to the rowan. [16th C.: *service* from an alt. of the pl. of obs. *serve*, from OE *syrfe*, based on L. *sorbus*.]

serv·ice·wom·an /ˈsərvəs,wo͝omən/ ▶ **n.** (pl. **-wom·en**) a woman serving in the armed forces.

ser·vi·ette /,sərvēˈet/ ▶ **n.** Brit. & Canadian a table napkin. [15th C.: from OFr., from *servir* 'to serve.']

ser·vile /ˈsərvəl; -,vīl/ ▶ **adj.** **1** having or showing an excessive willingness to serve or please others. **2** of or characteristic of a slave or slaves. — **ser·vile·ly adv. ser·vil·i·ty** /sərˈvilitē/ **n.** [ME (in the sense 'suitable for a slave or for the working class'): from L. *servilis*, from *servus* 'slave.']

serv·ing /ˈsərviNG/ ▶ **n.** a quantity of food suitable for or served to one person: *a large serving of spaghetti.*

serv·ing·man /ˈsərviNG,man/ ▶ **n.** (pl. **-men**) archaic a male servant or attendant.

serv·ing·wom·an /ˈsərviNG,wo͝omən/ ▶ **n.** (pl. **-wom·en**) archaic a female servant or attendant.

ser·vi·tor /ˈsərvitər; -,tôr/ ▶ **n.** archaic a person who serves or attends on a social superior. — **ser·vi·tor·ship** /-,SHip/ **n.** [ME: via OFr. from late L., from *servit-* 'served,' from the verb *servire* (see SERVE).]

ser·vi·tude /ˈsərvi,t(y)o͞od/ ▶ **n.** the state of being a slave or completely subject to someone more powerful. ■ Law, archaic the subjection of property to an easement. [ME: via OFr. from L. *servitudo*, from *servus* 'slave.']

ser·vo /ˈsərvō/ ▶ **n.** (pl. **-vos**) short for SERVOMECHANISM or SERVOMOTOR. ■ [as adj.] relating to or involving a servomechanism. [19th C.: from L. *servus* 'slave.']

ser·vo·mech·an·ism /ˈsərvō,mekə,nizəm/ ▶ **n.** a powered mechanism producing motion or forces at a higher level of energy than the input level, e.g., in the brakes and steering of large motor vehicles, esp. where feedback is employed to make the control automatic.

ser·vo·mo·tor /ˈsərvō,mōtər/ ▶ **n.** the motive element in a servomechanism.

SES ▶ **abbr.** socioeconomic status.

ses·a·me /ˈsesəmē/ ▶ **n.** a tall annual herbaceous plant (*Sesamum indicum*, family Pedaliaceae) of tropical and subtropical areas of the Old World, cultivated for its oil-rich seeds. ■ (**sesame seed**) the edible seeds of this plant, which are used whole or have the oil extracted. [ME: via L. from Gk. *sēsamon, sēsamē*, prob. of Semitic origin; cf. Arab. *simsim*.]

ses·a·moid /ˈsesə,moid/ (also **sesamoid bone**) ▶ **n.** a small independent bone or bony nodule developed in a tendon where it passes over an angular structure, typically in the hands and feet. The kneecap is a particularly large sesamoid bone. [17th C.: from SESAME (with ref. to the similarity in shape of a sesame seed) + -OID.]

Se·so·tho /səˈso͞oto͞o/ ▶ **n.** the Sotho language of the Basotho people, an official language in Lesotho and South Africa. ▶ **adj.** of or relating to this language. [the name in Sesotho.]

sesqui- ▶ **comb. form** denoting one and a half: *sesquicentenary.* ■ Chem. (of a compound) in which a particular element or group is present in a ratio of 3:2 compared with another: *sesquioxide.* [from L. *semi-* (see SEMI-) + *que* 'and.']

ses·qui·cen·ten·ni·al /,seskwisenˈtenēəl/ ▶ **adj.** of or relating to the one-hundred-and-fiftieth anniversary of a significant event. ▶ **n.** a one-hundred-and-fiftieth anniversary.

ses·qui·pe·da·li·an /,seskwəpəˈdālyən/ ▶ **adj.** formal (of a word) polysyllabic; long: *sesquipedalian surnames.* ■ characterized by long words; long-winded. [17th C.: from L. *sesquipedalis* 'a foot and a half long,' from *sesqui-* (see SESQUI-) + *pes, ped-* 'foot.']

ses·sile /ˈsesəl; -īl/ ▶ **adj.** Biol. (of an organism, e.g., a barnacle) fixed in one place; immobile. ■ Bot. & Zool. (of a plant or animal structure) attached directly by its base without a stalk or peduncle: *sporangia may be stalked or sessile.* [18th C.: from L. *sessilis*, from *sess-* 'seated,' from the verb *sedere*.]

ses·sile oak ▶ **n.** another term for DURMAST OAK.

ses·sion /ˈseSHən/ ▶ **n.** **1** a meeting of a deliberative or judicial body to conduct its business. ■ a period during which such meetings are regularly held. ■ the governing body of a Presbyterian Church. **2** [often with adj.] a period devoted to a particular activity: *a training session.* ■ informal a period of heavy or sustained drinking. ■ a period of recording music in a studio, esp. by a session musician. ■ an academic year. ■ the period during which a school has classes.

– PHRASES **in session** assembled for or proceeding with business. — **ses·sion·al** /-SHənl/ **adj.** [ME: from OFr., or from L. *sessio(n-)*, from *sess-* 'seated' (see SESSILE).]

Ses·sions /ˈseSHənz/, Roger Huntington (1896–1985), US composer. He composed eight symphonies, as well as operas such as *Montezuma* (1959–63).

ses·terce /ˈsestərs/ (also **ses·ter·ti·us** /seˈstərSH(ē)əs/) ▶ **n.** (pl. **ses·terc·es** /ˈsestərsəz/ or **ses·ter·ti·i** /sesˈtərSHē,ī/) an ancient Roman coin and monetary unit equal to one quarter of a denarius. [from L. *sestertius (nummus)* '(coin) that is two and a half (asses).']

ses·tet /sesˈtet/ ▶ **n.** Pros. the last six lines of a sonnet. [19th C.: from Ital. *sestetto*, from *sesto*, from L. *sextus* 'a sixth.']

ses·ti·na /seˈstēnə/ ▶ **n.** Pros. a poem with six stanzas of six lines and a final triplet, all stanzas having the same six words at the line-ends in six different sequences that follow a fixed pattern, and with all six words appearing in the closing three-line envoi. [19th C.: from Ital., from *sesto* (see SESTET).]

Set /set/ var. of SETH.

set[1] /set/ ▶ **v.** (**set·ting**; past **set**) **1** [trans.] put, lay, or stand (something) in a specified place or position: *Dana set the mug of tea down.* ■ (**be set**) be situated or fixed in a specified place or position: *the village was set among olive groves on a hill.* ■ represent (a story, play, movie, or scene) as happening at a specified time or in a specified place: *a spy novel set in Berlin.* ■ mount a precious stone in (something, typically a piece of jewelry): *a bracelet set with emeralds.* ■ mount (a precious stone) in something. ■ Print. arrange (type) as required. ■ Print. arrange the type for (a piece of text): *article headings will be set in Times fourteen point.* ■ prepare (a table) for a meal by placing cutlery, dishes, etc., on it in their proper places. ■ (**set something to**) provide (music) so that a written work can be produced in a musical form: *she set his poem to music.* ■ [intrans.] (of a dancer) acknowledge another dancer, typically one's partner, using the steps prescribed: *the gentleman sets to and turns with the lady on his left hand.* ■ cause (a hen) to sit on eggs. ■ place (eggs) for a hen to sit on. ■ put (a seed or plant) in the ground to grow. ■ give the teeth of (a saw) an alternate outward inclination. ■ Sailing put (a sail) up in position to catch the wind: *a safe distance from shore all sails were set.* See also SET SAIL below. **2** [trans.] put or bring into a specified state: *plunging oil prices set in motion an economic collapse in Houston* | [trans.] *the hostages were set free.* ■ [trans.] cause (someone or something) to start doing something: *the incident set me thinking.* ■ [trans.] instruct (someone) to do something: *he'll set a man to watch you.* ■ give someone (a task): [with two objs.] *the problem we have been set.* ■ devise (a test) and give it to someone to do. ■ establish as (an example) for others to follow, copy, or try to achieve: *the scheme sets a precedent for other companies.* ■ establish (a record): *his time set a national record.* ■ decide on: *they set a date at the end of February.* ■ fix (a price, value, or limit) on something: *the unions had set a limit on the size of the temporary workforce.* **3** [trans.] adjust the hands of (a clock or watch), typically to show the right time. ■ adjust (an alarm clock) to sound at the required time. ■ adjust (a device or its controls) so that it performs a particular operation: *don't set the volume too high.* ■ Electron. cause (a binary device) to enter the state representing the numeral 1. **4** [intrans.] harden into a solid or semisolid state: *cook until the filling has set.* ■ [trans.] arrange (the hair) while damp so that it dries in the required style. ■ [trans.] put parts of (a broken or dislocated bone or limb) into the correct position for healing. ■ [trans.] deal with (a fracture or dislocation) in this way. ■ (of a bone) be restored to its normal condition by knitting together again after being broken: *dogs' bones soon set.* ■ (with reference to a person's face) assume or cause to assume a fixed or rigid expression: [intrans.] *her features never set into a civil parade of attention* | [trans.] *Travis's face was set as he looked up.* ■ (of the eyes) become fixed in position or in the feeling they are expressing. ■ (of a hunting dog) adopt a rigid attitude indicating the presence of game. **5** [intrans.] (of the sun, moon, or another celestial body) appear to move toward and below the earth's horizon as the earth rotates. **6** [intrans.] (of a tide or current) take or have a specified direction or course: *the stream sets to the north.* **7** [trans.] start (a fire). **8** [trans.] (of blossom or a tree) form into or produce (fruit). ■ [intrans.] (of fruit) develop from blossom. ■ (of a plant) produce (seed). **9** informal dialect sit.

– PHRASES **set one's heart** (or **hopes**) **on** have a strong desire for or to do. **set sail** hoist the sails of a vessel. ■ begin a voyage. **set someone straight** inform someone of the truth of a situation.

– PHRASAL VERBS **set about** start doing something with vigor or determination: *set about tackling the problem.* **set someone against** cause

PRONUNCIATION KEY ə *ago, up*; ər *over, fur*; a *hat*; ā *ate*; ä *car*; e *let*; ē *see*; i *fit*; ī *by*; NG *sing*; ō *go*; ô *law, for*; oi *toy*; o͝o *good*; o͞o *goo*; ou *out*; TH *thin*; T̲H̲ *then*; ZH *vision*

someone to be in opposition or conflict with: *his few words had set her against him.* **set something against** offset something against: *allowances can be set against investment income.* **set someone apart** give someone an air of unusual superiority: *his blunt views set him apart.* **set something apart** separate something and keep it for a special purpose: *there were books and rooms set apart as libraries.* **set something aside 1** save or keep something, typically money or time, for a particular purpose. ■ remove land from agricultural production. **2** annul a legal decision or process. **set someone/something back 1** delay or impede the progress of someone or something. **2** informal (of a purchase) cost someone a particular amount of money. **set something by** dated save something for future use. **set someone down** stop and allow someone to alight from a vehicle. **set something down** record something in writing. ■ establish something authoritatively as a rule or principle to be followed. **set forth** begin a journey or trip. **set something forth** state or describe something in writing or speech. **set forward** archaic start on a journey. **set in** (of something unpleasant or unwelcome) begin and seem likely to continue. **set something in** insert something, esp. a sleeve, into a garment. **set off** begin a journey. **set someone off** cause someone to start doing something, esp. laughing or talking. **set something off 1** detonate a bomb. ■ cause an alarm to go off. ■ cause a series of things to occur: *this could set off a chain reaction.* **2** serve as decorative embellishment to: *a pink carnation set off nicely by a cream shirt.* **set something off against** another way of saying SET SOMETHING AGAINST above. **set on** (or **upon**) attack (someone) violently. **set someone/something on** (or **upon**) cause or urge a person or animal to attack: *dogs set upon me.* **set out** begin a journey. ■ aim or intend to do something: *she set out to achieve success.* **set something out** arrange or display something in a particular order or position. ■ present information or ideas in a well-ordered way in writing or speech. **set to** begin doing something vigorously: *she set to with bleach and scouring pads to render the vases spotless.* **set someone up 1** establish someone in a particular capacity or role: *his father set him up in business.* **2** restore or enhance the health of someone. **3** informal make an innocent person appear guilty of something. **set something up 1** place or erect something in position. **2** establish a business, institution, or other organization. ■ make the arrangements necessary for something. **3** begin making a loud sound. **set oneself up as** establish oneself in (a particular occupation): *he set himself up as an attorney in St. Louis.* ■ claim to be or act like a specified kind of person (used to indicate skepticism as to someone's right or ability to do so): *he set himself up as a crusader.* [OE *settan*, of Gmc. origin; rel. to Du. *zetten*, Ger. *setzen*, also to SIT.]

set[2] ▶ **n. 1** a group or collection of things that belong together or resemble one another or are usually found together: *a set of false teeth.* ■ a collection of implements, containers, or other objects customarily used together for a specific purpose: *an electric fondue set.* ■ a group of people with common interests or occupations or of similar social status: *the literary set.* ■ (in tennis, darts, and other games) a group of games counting as a unit toward a match, only the player or side that wins a defined number or proportion of the games being awarded a point toward the final score. ■ (in jazz or popular music) a sequence of songs or pieces performed together and constituting or forming part of a live show or recording. ■ a group of people making up the required number for a square dance or similar country dance. ■ a fixed number of repetitions of a particular bodybuilding exercise. ■ Math. Logic a collection of distinct entities regarded as a unit, being either individually specified or (more usually) satisfying specified conditions. **2** [in sing.] the way in which something is set, disposed, or positioned: *the shape and set of the eyes.* ■ the posture or attitude of a part of the body, typically in relation to the impression this gives of a person's feelings or intentions: *the determined set of her upper torso.* ■ the action of a current or tide of flowing in a particular direction: *the set of the tide.* ■ an arrangement of the hair when damp so that it dries in the required style: *a shampoo and set.* ■ (also **dead set**) a setter's pointing in the presence of game. ■ an alternate outward inclination of the teeth of a saw. ■ a warp or bend in wood, metal, or another material caused by continued strain or pressure. **3** a radio or television receiver: *a TV set.* **4** a collection of scenery, stage furniture, and other articles used for a particular scene in a play or film. ■ the place or area in which filming is taking place or a play is performed: *interviews on set.* **5** a cutting, young plant, or bulb used in the propagation of new plants. ■ a young fruit that has just formed. **6** the last coat of plaster on a wall. **7** Print. the amount of spacing in type controlling the distance between letters. ■ the width of a piece of type. [ME: partly from OFr. *sette*, from L. *secta* 'sect,' partly from SET[1].]

set[3] ▶ **adj. 1** fixed or arranged in advance: *there is no set procedure.* ■ (of a view or habit) unlikely to change: *I'm rather set in my ways.* ■ (of a person's expression) held for an unnaturally long time without changing, typically as a reflection of determination. ■ (of a meal or menu in a restaurant) offered at a fixed price with a limited choice of dishes. ■ having a conventional or predetermined wording; formulaic: *a set speech.* **2** [predic.] ready, prepared, or likely to do something: *"All set for tonight?" he asked.* ■ (**set against**) firmly opposed to. ■ (**set on**) determined to do (something): *he's set on marrying that girl.* [OE, past part. of SET[1].]

set·a·side ▶ **n. 1** the policy of taking land out of production to reduce crop surpluses. ■ land taken out of production in this way: *he has fifty acres of set-aside.* **2** a government contract awarded without competition to a minority-owned business. **3** a portion of funds or other resources reserved for a particular purpose.

set·back /'set,bak/ ▶ **n. 1** a reversal or check in progress: *a serious setback for the peace process.* **2** Archit. a plain, flat offset in a wall. **3** the distance by which a building or part of a building is set back from the property line.

se·ten·ant /sə 'tenənt; sə tə'näN/ ▶ **adj.** Philately (of stamps of different designs) joined together side by side when printed. [20th C.: from Fr., lit. 'holding together.']

Seth /seTH/ (also **Set**) Egyptian Mythol. an evil god who murdered his brother Osiris and wounded Osiris's son Horus. Seth is represented as having the head of an animal with a long pointed snout.

set-in ▶ **adj.** [attrib.] (of a sleeve) made separately and inset into a garment.

set-off ▶ **n. 1** an item or amount that is or may be set off against another in the settlement of accounts. ■ Law a counterbalancing debt pleaded by the defendant in an action to recover money due. ■ dated a compensating circumstance or condition. **2** a step or shoulder at which the thickness of part of a building or machine is reduced. **3** Print. the unwanted transference of ink from one printed sheet or page to another before it has set.

Se·ton /'sētn/, St. Elizabeth Ann Bayley (1774–1821), US religious leader. The first native-born American to be canonized as a saint, she founded the Sisters of Charity, a religious order, in 1813.

set piece ▶ **n.** a thing that has been carefully or elaborately planned or composed, in particular: ■ a self-contained passage or section of a novel, play, film, or piece of music arranged in an elaborate or conventional pattern for maximum effect. ■ a formal and carefully structured speech. ■ a carefully organized and practiced move in a team game by which the ball is returned to play, as at a scrum or a free kick. ■ an arrangement of fireworks forming a picture or design.

set point ▶ **n.** (in tennis and other sports) a point that, if won by one contestant, will also win the set.

set screw ▶ **n.** a screw for adjusting or clamping parts of a machine.

set shot ▶ **n.** Basketball a shot made while standing still.

Sets·wa·na /set'swänə/ ▶ **n.** the Bantu language of the Tswana people, related to the Sotho languages and spoken by over 3 million people in southern Africa. ▶ **adj.** of or relating to this language. [the name in Setswana.]

set·tee /se'tē/ ▶ **n.** a long upholstered seat for more than one person, typically with a back and arms. [18th C.: perh. a fanciful var. of SETTLE[2].]

set·ter /'setər/ ▶ **n. 1** a dog of a large, long-haired breed trained to stand rigid when scenting game. **2** [usu. in comb.] a person or thing that sets something: *trend-setters in Hollywood.*

set the·o·ry ▶ **n.** the branch of mathematics that deals with the formal properties of sets as units (without regard to the nature of their individual constituents) and the expression of other branches of mathematics in terms of sets. — **set-the·o·ret·ic adj. set-the·o·ret·i·cal adj.**

set·ting /'setiNG/ ▶ **n. 1** the place or type of surroundings where something is positioned or where an event takes place: *a peaceful country setting.* ■ the place and time at which a play, novel, or film is represented as happening: *short stories with a contemporary setting.* ■ a piece of metal in which a precious stone or gem is fixed to form a piece of jewelry. ■ a piece of vocal or choral music composed for particular words. ■ short for PLACE SETTING. **2** a speed, height, or temperature at which a machine or device can be adjusted to operate.

set·ting lo·tion ▶ **n.** lotion applied to damp hair before it is set, enabling it to keep its shape longer.

set·tle[1] /'setl/ ▶ **v. 1** [trans.] resolve or reach an agreement about (an argument or problem). ■ end (a legal dispute) by mutual agreement: *the matter was settled out of court* | [intrans.] *he sued for libel and then settled out of court.* ■ determine; decide on: *exactly what goes into the legislation has not been settled* | [intrans.] *they had not yet settled on a date for the wedding.* ■ pay (a debt or account): *his bill was settled by charge card* | [intrans.] *I settled up with your brother for my board and lodging.* ■ (**settle something on**) give money or property to (someone) through a deed of settlement or a will. ■ [intrans.] (**settle for**) accept or agree to (something that one considers to be less than satisfactory): *it was too cold for champagne so they settled for a cup of tea.* ■ dated silence (someone considered a nuisance) by some means: *he told me to hold my tongue or he would find a way to settle me.* **2** [intrans.] adopt a more steady or secure style of life, esp. in a permanent job and home: *one day I will settle down and raise a family.* ■ [with adverbial of place] make one's permanent home somewhere: *in 1863 the family settled in London.* ■ begin to feel comfortable or established in a new home, situation, or job: *she settled in happily with a foster family* | *he had settled into his new job.* ■ [trans.] establish a colony in: *European immigrants settled much of Australia.* ■ (**settle down to**) turn one's attention to; apply oneself to: *Catherine settled down to her studies.* ■ become or make calmer or quieter: [intrans.] *after a few months the controversy settled down* | [trans.] *try to settle your puppy down before going to bed.* **3** [intrans.] sit or come to rest in a comfortable position: *he settled into an armchair.* ■ [trans.] make (someone) comfortable in a particular place or position: *she allowed him to settle her in the taxi.* ■ [trans.] move or adjust (something) so that it rests securely: *she settled her bag on her shoulder.* ■ fall or come down on to a surface: *dust from the mill had settled on the roof.* ■ [intrans.] (of suspended particles) sink slowly in a liquid to form sediment; (of a liquid) become clear or still through this process: *sediment settles near the bottom of the tank* | *he pours a glass and leaves it on the bar to settle.* ■ [intrans.] (of an object or objects) gradually sink down under its or their own weight: *they listened to the soft ticking and creaking as the house settled.* ■ [intrans.] (of a ship or boat) sink gradually.

– PHRASES **settle one's affairs** (or **estate**) make any necessary arrangements, such as writing a will, before one's death. **settle someone's hash** see HASH[1]. — **set·tle·a·ble** adj. **set·tled·ness** n. [OE *setlan* 'to seat, place,' from SETTLE[2].]

set·tle[2] ▶ n. a wooden bench with a high back and arms, typically incorporating a box under the seat. [OE *setl* 'a place to sit,' of Gmc. origin; rel. to Ger. *Sessel* and L. *sella* 'seat,' also to SIT.]

set·tle·ment /'setlmənt/ ▶ n. **1** an official agreement intended to resolve a dispute or conflict: *unions succeeded in reaching a pay settlement* | *the settlement of the Palestinian problem.* ■ a formal arrangement made between the parties to a lawsuit in order to resolve it, esp. out of court. **2** a place, typically one that has hitherto been uninhabited, where people establish a community. ■ the process of settling in such a place: *the early settlement of Plymouth.* ■ the action of allowing or helping people to do this. **3** Law an arrangement whereby property passes to a succession of people as dictated by the settlor. ■ the amount or property given. **4** the action or process of settling an account. **5** subsidence of the ground or a structure built on it: *a boundary wall has cracked due to settlement.*

set·tle·ment house ▶ n. an institution in an inner-city area providing educational, recreational, and other social services to the community.

set·tler /'setl-ər; 'setlər/ ▶ n. a person who settles in an area, typically one with no or few previous inhabitants.

set·tlor /'setl-ər; 'setlər/ ▶ n. Law a person who makes a settlement, esp. of a property.

set-to ▶ n. (pl. **-tos**) informal a fight or argument.

set-top box ▶ n. a device which converts a digital television signal to analog for viewing on a conventional set.

set·up /'set,əp/ ▶ n. [usu. in sing.] informal **1** the way in which something, esp. an organization or equipment, is organized, planned, or arranged. ■ an organization or arrangement. ■ a set of equipment needed for a particular activity or purpose. ■ (in a ball game) a pass or play intended to provide an opportunity for another player to score. **2** a scheme or trick intended to incriminate or deceive someone: *"Listen. He didn't die. It was a setup."* ■ a contest with a prearranged outcome.

Seu·rat /sə'rä/, Georges Pierre (1859–91), French painter. He founded neo-Impressionism.

Seuss /sōōs/, Dr., see GEISEL.

sev /säv; sev/ ▶ n. an Indian snack consisting of long, thin strands of gram flour, deep-fried and spiced. [Hindi.]

Se·vas·to·pol /sə'vastə,pōl; ,sevə'stōpəl/ Ukrainian and Russian name for SEBASTOPOL.

sev·en /'sevən/ ▶ cardinal number equivalent to the sum of three and four; one more than six, or three less than ten; 7 (Roman numeral: **vii**, **VII**). ■ a group or unit of seven people or things: *animals were offered for sacrifice in sevens.* ■ seven years old. ■ seven o'clock. ■ a size of garment or other merchandise denoted by seven. ■ a playing card with seven pips. [OE *seofon*, of Gmc. origin; rel. to Du. *zeven* and Ger. *sieben*, from an Indo-Eur. root shared by L. *septem* and Gk. *hepta*.]

sev·en dead·ly sins ▶ plural n. (**the seven deadly sins**) (in Christian tradition) the sins of pride, covetousness, lust, anger, gluttony, envy, and sloth.

sev·en·fold /'sevən,fōld/ ▶ adj. seven times as great or as numerous: *stock fund sales were up sevenfold.* ■ having seven parts or elements: *the sevenfold purpose.* ▶ adv. by seven times; to seven times the number or amount: *his rent had gone up sevenfold.*

sev·en seas ▶ plural n. (**the seven seas**) all the oceans of the world (conventionally listed as the Arctic, Antarctic, North Pacific, South Pacific, North Atlantic, South Atlantic, and Indian Oceans).

sev·en·teen /,sevən'tēn; 'sevən,tēn/ ▶ cardinal number one more than sixteen, or seven more than ten; 17 (Roman numeral: **xvii**, **XVII**). ■ seventeen years old. ■ a set or team of seventeen individuals. — **sev·en·teenth** /,sevəh'tēnTH; 'sevən,tēnTH/ adj. & n. [OE *seofontīene*, from the Gmc. base of SEVEN.]

sev·en·teen-year lo·cust ▶ n. the nymph of the northern species of the periodical cicada. See PERIODICAL CICADA.

sev·enth /'sevənTH/ ▶ ordinal number constituting number seven in a sequence; 7th: *the seventh of June.* ■ (**a seventh/one seventh**) each of seven equal parts into which something is or may be divided. ■ the seventh finisher or position in a race or competition. ■ seventhly (used to introduce a seventh point or reason). ■ the seventh grade of a school. ■ Music an interval spanning seven consecutive notes in a diatonic scale. ■ Music the note that is higher by this interval than the tonic of a diatonic scale or root of a chord. ■ Music a chord in which the seventh note of the scale forms an important component.

– PHRASES **in seventh heaven** see HEAVEN. — **sev·enth·ly** adv.

Sev·enth-Day Ad·vent·ist ▶ n. a member of a Protestant sect that preaches the imminent return of Christ to Earth (originally expecting the Second Coming in 1844) and observes Saturday as the sabbath. See also ADVENTIST.

sev·en·ty /'sevəntē/ ▶ cardinal number (pl. **-ties**) the number equivalent to the product of seven and ten; ten less than eighty; 70 (Roman numeral: **lxx**, **LXX**). ■ (**seventies**) the numbers from seventy to seventy-nine, esp. the years of a century or of a person's life. ■ seventy years old. ■ seventy miles an hour: *doing about seventy.* — **sev·en·ti·eth** /-tēəTH/ ordinal number **sev·en·ty·fold** /-,fōld/ adj. & adv. [OE *hundseofontig*, from *hund-* (of uncert. origin) + *seofon* 'seven.']

sev·en·ty-eight (usu. **78**) ▶ n. an old phonograph record designed to be played at 78 rpm.

sev·en-up ▶ n. esp. hist. a variety of the card game "all fours" in which the winner is the first to score seven points.

Sev·en Won·ders of the World the seven most spectacular man-made structures of the ancient world. Traditionally they comprise (1) the pyramids of Egypt, especially those at Giza; (2) the Hanging Gardens of Babylon; (3) the Mausoleum of Halicarnassus; (4) the temple of Artemis at Ephesus in Asia Minor; (5) the Colossus of Rhodes; (6) the huge ivory and gold statue of Zeus at Olympia in Peloponnesus, made by Phidias *c.*430 BC; (7) the Pharos of Alexandria (or in some lists, the walls of Babylon).

Sev·en Years' War a war (1756–63) that ranged Britain, Prussia, and Hanover against Austria, France, Russia, Saxony, Sweden, and Spain.

sev·er /'sevər/ ▶ v. [trans.] divide by cutting or slicing, esp. suddenly and forcibly. ■ put an end to (a connection or relationship); break off: *he severed his relations with Lawrence.* — **sev·er·a·ble** adj. [ME: from Anglo-Norman Fr. *severer*, from L. *separare* 'disjoin, divide.']

sev·er·al /'sev(ə)rəl/ ▶ adj. & pron. more than two but not many: [as adj.] *the author of several books* | [as pron.] *Van Gogh was just one of several artists who gathered at Auvers.* ▶ adj. separate or respective: *their several responsibilities.* ■ Law applied or regarded separately. Often contrasted with JOINT. — **sev·er·al·ly** adv. [ME: from Anglo-Norman Fr., from med. L. *separalis*, from L. *separ* 'separate, different.']

sev·er·al·ty /'sev(ə)rəltē/ ▶ n. archaic the condition of being separate. [ME: from Anglo-Norman Fr. *severalte*, from *several* (see SEVERAL).]

sev·er·ance /'sev(ə)rəns/ ▶ n. the action of ending a connection or relationship: *the severance and disestablishment of the Irish Church.* ■ the state of being separated or cut off. ■ dismissal or discharge from employment. ■ short for SEVERANCE PAY. [ME: from Anglo-Norman Fr., based on L. *separare* (see SEVER).]

sev·er·ance pay ▶ n. an amount paid to an employee upon dismissal or discharge from employment.

se·vere /sə'vi(ə)r/ ▶ adj. **1** (of something bad or undesirable) very great; intense: *a severe shortage of technicians.* ■ demanding great ability, skill, or resilience: *a severe test of stamina.* **2** strict or harsh: *a severe sentence.* **3** very plain in style or appearance: *a severe suit.* — **se·vere·ly** adv. **se·ver·i·ty** /-'veritē/ n. [16th C. (sense 2): from Fr. *sévère* or L. *severus*.]

Sev·ern /'sevərn/ a river that flows from central Wales to the Bristol Channel.

Se·ve·rus /sə'vi(ə)rəs/, Septimius (146–211), emperor of Rome 193–211; full name *Lucius Septimius Severus Pertinax.*

sev·er·y /'sev(ə)rē/ ▶ n. (pl. **-er·ies**) Archit. a bay or compartment in a vaulted ceiling. [ME: from OFr. *civoire* 'ciborium' (see CIBORIUM).]

se·vi·che ▶ n. var. of CEVICHE.

Se·vier Riv·er /sə'vi(ə)r/ a river that flows for 325 miles (525 km) through central Utah.

Se·ville /sə'vil/ a city in southern Spain, the capital of Andalusia; pop. 683,000. Spanish name SEVILLA.

Se·ville or·ange ▶ n. a bitter-tasting orange used for marmalade.

Se·vin /'sevin/ ▶ n. trademark for CARBARYL. [1950s: of unknown origin.]

Sè·vres /'sevrə/ ▶ n. a type of fine porcelain characterized by elaborate decoration on backgrounds of intense color, made at Sèvres in the suburbs of Paris.

sev·ru·ga /sə'vrōōgə/ ▶ n. a migratory sturgeon (*Acipenser stellatus*) found only in the basins of the Caspian and Black Seas, much fished for its caviar. ■ caviar obtained from this fish. [16th C.: from Russ. *sevryuga*.]

sew /sō/ ▶ v. (past part. **sewn** /sōn/ or **sewed** /sōd/) [trans.] join, fasten, or repair (something) by making stitches with a needle and thread or a sewing machine: *she sewed the seams* | [intrans.] *I don't even sew very well.* ■ [trans.] attach (something) to something else by sewing: *she could sew the veil on properly in the morning.* ■ make (a garment) by sewing.

– PHRASAL VERBS **sew something up** informal bring something to a favorable conclusion. ■ achieve exclusive control over something. [OE *siwan*, of Gmc. origin, from an Indo-Eur. root shared by L. *suere* and Gk. *suein*.]

sew·age /'sōōij/ ▶ n. waste water and excrement conveyed in sewers. [19th C.: from SEWER[1], by substitution of the suffix -AGE.]

Sew·ard /'sōōərd/, William Henry (1801–72), US secretary of state 1861–69. His negotiated purchase of Alaska from Russia was widely mocked as "Seward's Icebox" and "Seward's Folly."

Sew·ard Pen·in·su·la a region in northwestern Alaska on the Bering Strait and the Chukchi Sea. Nome lies on its southern coast.

sew·er[1] /'sōōər/ ▶ n. an underground conduit for carrying off drainage water and waste matter. [ME (denoting a watercourse to drain marshy land): from Old North. Fr. *seuwiere* 'channel to drain the overflow from a fishpond,' based on L. *ex-* 'out of' + *aqua* 'water.']

sew·er[2] /'sōər/ ▶ n. a person who sews.

sew·er·age /'sōōərij/ ▶ n. the provision of drainage by sewers. ■ another term for SEWAGE.

sew·er rat /ˈsōōər/ ▶ **n.** another term for BROWN RAT.

sew·ing /ˈsō-iNG/ ▶ **n.** the action or activity of sewing. ■ work that is to be or is being sewn.

sew·ing ma·chine ▶ **n.** a machine with a mechanically driven needle for sewing or stitching cloth.

sewn /sōn/ past participle of SEW.

sex /seks/ ▶ **n.** **1** (chiefly with reference to people) sexual activity, including specifically sexual intercourse. ■ [in sing.] a person's genitals (used in novels to avoid more vulgar or anatomically explicit terms). **2** either of the two main categories (male and female) into which humans and most other living things are divided on the basis of their reproductive functions. ■ the fact of belonging to one of these categories. ■ the group of all members of either of these categories: *she improved the social condition of her sex.* ▶ **v.** [trans.] **1** determine the sex of: *sexing chickens.* **2** (**sex someone up**) informal arouse or attempt to arouse someone sexually. [ME (denoting the two categories, male and female): from OFr. *sexe* or L. *sexus*.]

sex- ▶ **comb. form** var. of SEXI-, shortened before a vowel (as in *sexennial*), or shortened before a consonant (as in *sexfoil*).

sex act ▶ **n.** any sexual act. ■ (**the sex act**) the act of sexual intercourse.

sex·a·ge·nar·i·an /ˌseksəjəˈne(ə)rēən/ ▶ **n.** a person who is from 60 to 69 years old. [18th C.: from L. *sexagenarius* (based on *sexaginta* 'sixty') + -AN.]

Sex·a·ges·i·ma /ˌseksəˈjesəmə/ (also **Sexagesima Sunday**) **n.** the Sunday before Quinquagesima. [ME: from eccles. L., lit. 'sixtieth (day),' prob. named by analogy with QUINQUAGESIMA.]

sex·a·ges·i·mal /ˌseksəˈjesəməl/ ▶ **adj.** **1** of, relating to, or reckoning by sixtieths. **2** of or relating to the number sixty. — **sex·a·ges·i·mal·ly adv.** [17th C.: from L. *sexagesimus* 'sixtieth' + -AL.]

sex ap·peal ▶ **n.** the quality of being attractive in a sexual way: *she just oozes sex appeal.*

sex·ca·pade /ˈsekskəˌpād/ ▶ **n.** informal a sexual escapade; an illicit affair. [1960s: blend of SEX and ESCAPADE.]

sex·cen·ten·ar·y /ˌseksenˈtenərē/ ▶ **n.** (pl. **-ar·ies**) the six-hundredth anniversary of a significant event. ▶ **adj.** of or relating to a six-hundredth anniversary.

sex change ▶ **n.** a change in a person's physical sexual characteristics, typically by surgery and hormone treatment.

sex chro·mo·some ▶ **n.** a chromosome involved with determining the sex of an organism, typically one of two kinds. Also called HETEROCHROMOSOME.

sex dis·crim·i·na·tion (also **sex·u·al dis·crim·i·na·tion**) ▶ **n.** discrimination in employment and opportunity against a person (typically a woman) on grounds of sex.

sex drive ▶ **n.** the urge to seek satisfaction of sexual needs.

sexed /sekst/ ▶ **adj.** **1** [with submodifier] having specified sexual appetites: *highly sexed heterosexual males.* **2** [attrib.] having sexual characteristics: *the effects of family and kinship relations on the construction of sexed individuals.*

sex·en·ni·al /sekˈsenēəl/ ▶ **adj.** recurring every six years. ■ lasting for or relating to a period of six years. [17th C.: from L. *sex* 'six' + *annus* 'year' + -AL.]

sex hor·mone ▶ **n.** a hormone, such as estrogen or testosterone, affecting sexual development or reproduction.

sexi- (also **sex-** before a vowel) ▶ **comb. form** six; having six: *sexivalent.* [from L. *sex* 'six.']

sex in·dus·try ▶ **n.** (**the sex industry**) used euphemistically to refer to prostitution.

sex·ism /ˈsekˌsizəm/ ▶ **n.** prejudice, stereotyping, or discrimination, typically against women, on the basis of sex. — **sex·ist adj. & n.**

sex kit·ten ▶ **n.** informal a young woman who asserts or exploits her sexual attractiveness.

sex·less /ˈseksləs/ ▶ **adj.** **1** lacking in sexual desire, interest, activity, or attractiveness: *I've no patience with pious, sexless females.* **2** neither male nor female: *the stylized and sexless falsetto.* — **sex·less·ly adv. sex·less·ness n.**

sex life ▶ **n.** a person's sexual activity and relationships considered as a whole.

sex-linked ▶ **adj.** esp. Biol. tending to be associated with one sex or the other. ■ (of a gene or heritable characteristic) carried by a sex chromosome.

sex ob·ject ▶ **n.** a person regarded by another only in terms of their sexual attractiveness or availability: *we're now in a period when it is permissible for women to make men into sex objects.*

sex·ol·o·gy /sekˈsäləjē/ ▶ **n.** the study of human sexual life or relationships. — **sex·o·log·i·cal** /ˌseksəˈläjikəl/ **adj. sex·ol·o·gist** /-jist/ **n.**

sex·par·tite /seksˈpärˌtīt/ ▶ **adj.** divided or involving division into six parts. [18th C.: from SEXI- 'six' + PARTITE, on the pattern of words such as *bipartite.*]

sex·pert /ˈsekspərt/ ▶ **n.** informal an expert in sexual matters.

sex·ploi·ta·tion /ˌseksploiˈtāsHən/ ▶ **n.** informal the commercial exploitation of sex, esp. in movies. [1940s: blend of SEX and *exploitation* (see EXPLOIT).]

sex·pot /ˈseksˌpät/ ▶ **n.** informal a sexy woman.

sex role ▶ **n.** the role or behavior learned by a person as appropriate to their sex, determined by the prevailing cultural norms.

sex-starved ▶ **adj.** lacking and strongly desiring sexual gratification.

sex sym·bol ▶ **n.** a person widely noted for their sexual attractiveness.

sext /sekst/ ▶ **n.** a service forming part of the Divine Office of the Western Christian Church, traditionally said (or chanted) at the sixth hour of the day (i.e., noon). [ME: from L. *sexta (hora)* 'sixth (hour),' from *sextus* 'sixth.']

Sex·tans /ˈsekstənz/ Astron. a faint constellation (the Sextant), lying on the celestial equator between Leo and Hydra. [L.]

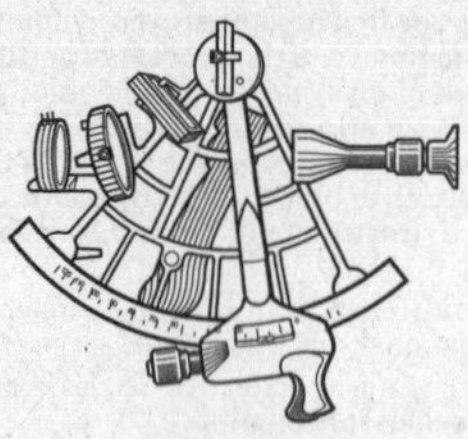

sextant

sex·tant /ˈsekstənt/ ▶ **n.** an instrument with a graduated arc of 60° and a sighting mechanism, used for measuring the angular distances between objects and esp. for taking altitudes in navigation and surveying. [16th C. (denoting the sixth part of a circle): from L. *sextans, sextant-* 'sixth part,' from *sextus* 'sixth.']

sex·tet /sekˈstet/ (also **sex·tette**) ▶ **n.** a group of six people playing music or singing together. ■ a composition for such a group. ■ a set of six people or things. [19th C.: alt. of SESTET, suggested by L. *sex* 'six.']

sex ther·a·py ▶ **n.** counseling or other therapy that addresses a person's psychological or physical sexual problems. — **sex ther·a·pist n.**

sex·tile /ˈsekˌstīl; -stəl/ ▶ **n.** Astrol. an aspect of 60° (one sixth of a circle). [ME: from L. *sextilis*, from *sextus* 'sixth.']

sex·til·lion /sekˈstilyən/ ▶ **cardinal number** (pl. **-lions** or (with numeral) same) a thousand raised to the seventh power (10^{21}). ■ dated, esp. Brit. a million raised to the sixth power (10^{36}). — **sex·til·lionth** /sekˈstilyənTH/ **ordinal number.** [17th C.: from Fr., from *million*, by substitution of the prefix *sexti-* 'six' (from L. *sextus* 'sixth') for the initial letters.]

sex·to·dec·i·mo /ˌsekstəˈdesəˌmō/ (abbr.: **16mo**) ▶ **n.** (pl. **-mos**) a size of book page that results from folding each printed sheet into sixteen leaves (thirty-two pages). ■ a book of this size. [17th C.: from L. *sexto decimo*, ablative of *sextus decimus* 'sixteenth.']

Sex·ton /ˈsekstən/, Anne (1928–74), US poet; born *Anne Harvey.* Her poems are collected in *To Bedlam and Part Way Back* (1960) and *Live or Die* (1966).

sex·ton /ˈsekstən/ ▶ **n.** a person who looks after a church and churchyard, typically acting as bell-ringer and gravedigger. [ME: from Anglo-Norman Fr. *segrestein*, from med. L. *sacristanus* (see SACRISTAN).]

sex tour·ism ▶ **n.** the organization of vacations to take advantage of the lack of restrictions imposed on sex and prostitution by some foreign countries. — **sex tour n. sex tour·ist n.**

sex·tu·ple /sekˈst(y)ōōpəl; -ˈtəpəl/ ▶ **adj.** [attrib.] consisting of six parts or things. ■ six times as much or as many. ▶ **n.** a sixfold number or amount. ▶ **v.** [trans.] multiply by six; increase sixfold. — **sex·tu·ply** /-plē/ **adv.** [17th C.: from med. L. *sextuplus*, formed irregularly from L. *sex* 'six,' on the pattern of late L. *quintuplus* 'quintuple.']

sex·tu·plet /sekˈstəplit; -ˈst(y)ōōplət/ ▶ **n.** **1** each of six children born at one birth. **2** Music a group of six notes to be performed in the time of four. [19th C.: from SEXTUPLE, on the pattern of words such as *triplet.*]

sex typ·ing ▶ **n.** **1** Psychol. & Sociol. the stereotypical categorization of people according to conventional perceptions of what is typical of each sex. **2** Biol. the process of determining the sex of a person or other organism, esp. in difficult cases where special tests are necessary. — **sex-typed adj.**

sex·u·al /ˈseksHōōəl/ ▶ **adj.** **1** relating to the instincts, physiology, and activities connected with physical attraction or intimate contact between individuals. **2** of or relating to the two sexes or to gender. ■ of or characteristic of one sex or the other. ■ Biol. being of one sex or the other; capable of sexual reproduction. — **sex·u·al·ly adv.** [17th C.: from late L. *sexualis*, from L. *sexus* 'sex.']

sex·u·al di·mor·phism ▶ **n.** Zool. distinct difference in size or appearance between the sexes of an animal.

sex·u·al ha·rass·ment ▶ **n.** harassment (typically of a woman) in a workplace, or other professional or social situation, involving the making of unwanted sexual advances or obscene remarks.

sex·u·al in·ter·course ▶ **n.** sexual contact between individuals involving penetration, esp. the insertion of a man's erect penis into a woman's vagina.

sex·u·al in·ver·sion ▶ **n.** see INVERSION (sense 4).

sex·u·al·i·ty /ˌseksHōōˈalitē/ ▶ **n.** (pl. **-ties**) capacity for sexual feelings. ■ a person's sexual orientation or preference. ■ sexual activity.

sex·u·al·ize /ˈseksHōōəˌlīz/ ▶ **v.** [trans.] make sexual; attribute sex or a sex role to. — **sex·u·al·i·za·tion** /ˌseksHōōələˈzāsHən/ **n.**

sex·u·al or·i·en·ta·tion ▸ **n.** a person's sexual identity in relation to the gender to which they are attracted; the fact of being heterosexual, homosexual, or bisexual.

sex·u·al pol·i·tics ▸ **plural n.** [treated as sing.] relations between the sexes regarded in terms of power.

sex·u·al re·la·tions ▸ **n.** sexual behavior between individuals, esp. sexual intercourse.

sex·u·al re·pro·duc·tion ▸ **n.** Biol. the production of new living organisms by combining genetic information from two individuals of different types (sexes).

sex·u·al rev·o·lu·tion ▸ **n.** the liberalization of attitudes toward sex, esp. that occurring in western countries during the 1960s.

sex·u·al se·lec·tion ▸ **n.** Biol. natural selection arising through preference by one sex for certain characteristics in individuals of the other sex.

sex work·er ▸ **n.** used euphemistically to refer to a prostitute.

sex·y /'seksē/ ▸ **adj.** (**sex·i·er, sex·i·est**) sexually attractive or exciting. ■ sexually aroused. ■ informal exciting; appealing: *I've climbed some sexy mountains.* — **sex·i·ly** /-səlē/ **adv.** **sex·i·ness n.**

Sey·chelles /sā'sHel(z)/ (also **the Seychelles**) a country in the Indian Ocean. *See box.* — **Sey·chel·lois** /ˌsāsHel'wä/ **adj. & n.** (pl. same).

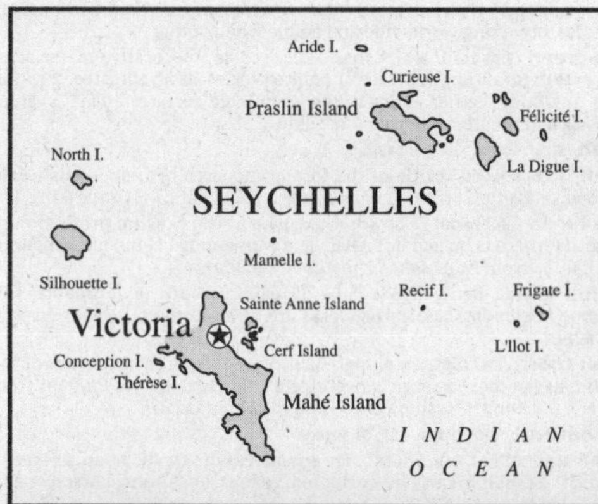

Seychelles

Official name: Republic of Seychelles
Location: Indian Ocean, including about 90 islands, about 600 miles (1000 km) northeast of Madagascar
Area: 180 square miles (460 sq km)
Population: 80,000
Capital: Victoria
Languages: French, English, Creole (all official)
Currency: Seychelles rupee

Sey·fert gal·ax·y /'sēfərt/ ▸ **n.** Astron. a galaxy of a type characterized by a bright compact core that shows strong infrared emission. [named after Carl K. *Seyfert* (1911–60), American astronomer.]

Sey·mour /'sēˌmôr/, Jane (*c.*1509–37), third wife of Henry VIII; mother of Edward VI.

sez /sez/ ▸ **v.** nonstandard spelling of "says," used in representing uneducated speech.

SF ▸ **abbr.** science fiction.

sf Music ▸ **abbr.** sforzando.

SFC ▸ **abbr.** Sergeant First Class.

sfor·zan·do /sfôrt'sändō/ Music ▸ **adv. & adj.** (esp. as a direction) with sudden emphasis. ▸ **n.** (pl. **-dos** or **-di** /-dē/) a sudden or marked emphasis. [Ital., lit. 'using force.']

sfu·ma·to /sfo͞o'mätō/ ▸ **n.** Art the technique of allowing tones and colors to shade gradually into one another, producing softened outlines or hazy forms. [19th C.: Ital., lit. 'shaded off,' past part. of *sfumare.*]

SFX ▸ **abbr.** special effects. [*FX* representing a pronunc. of *effects.*]

sfz Music ▸ **abbr.** sforzando.

SG ▸ **abbr.** ■ Law solicitor general. ■ Physics specific gravity.

Sg ▸ **symb.** the chemical element seaborgium.

sgd ▸ **abbr.** signed.

SGM ▸ **abbr.** sergeant major.

SGML Comput. ▸ **abbr.** Standard Generalized Markup Language, an international standard for defining methods of encoding electronic texts to describe layout, structure, syntax, etc., which can then be used for analysis or to display the text in any desired format.

sgraf·fi·to /zgrä'fētō; skrä-/ ▸ **n.** (pl. **-ti** /-tē/) a form of decoration made by scratching a surface to a lower layer of a contrasting color, typically done in stucco on walls, or in slip on ceramics before firing. [18th C.: Ital., lit. 'scratched away,' past part. of *sgraffiare.*]

's-Gra·ven·ha·ge Dutch name for **Hague**.

Sgt (also **SGT**) ▸ **abbr.** sergeant.

Sgt. Maj. ▸ **abbr.** Sergeant Major.

sh. Brit. ▸ **abbr.** shilling(s).

Shaan·xi /'sHän'sHē/ (also **Shen·si**) a province in central China; capital, Xian.

Sha·ba /'sHäbə/ the name by which the copper-mining region of Katanga in the southeast of the Democratic Republic of the Congo (Zaire) was known between 1972 and 1997.

Sha·ba·ka /'sHabəkə/ (died 698 BC), Egyptian pharaoh; reigned 712–698 BC; founder of the 25th dynasty; known as **Sabacon**.

Shab·bat /sHä'bät/ ▸ **n.** the Jewish Sabbath. [from Heb. *šabbāṯ.*]

Shab·bos /'sHäbəs/ (also **Shab·bas** or **Shab·bes**) ▸ **n.** the Yiddish term for the Jewish Sabbath. [Yiddish, from Heb. *šabbāṯ.*]

shab·by /'sHabē/ ▸ **adj.** (**-bi·er, -bi·est**) in poor condition through long use or lack of care. ■ dressed in old or worn clothes. ■ (of behavior) mean and shameful. ■ inferior in performance or quality. — **shab·bi·ly** /-əlē/ **adv.** **shab·bi·ness n.** [17th C.: from dial. *shab* 'scab' (from a Gmc. base meaning 'itch') + **-y**[1].]

shack /sHak/ ▸ **n.** a roughly built hut or cabin. ▸ **v.** [intrans.] (**shack up**) informal move in or live with someone as a lover. [19th C.: perh. from Mexican *jacal,* Nahuatl *xacatli* 'wooden hut.' The early sense of the verb was 'live in a shack' (orig. a US usage).]

shack·le /'sHakəl/ ▸ **n.** **1** (**shackles**) a pair of fetters connected together by a chain, used to fasten a prisoner's wrists or ankles together. ■ fig. used in reference to something that restrains or impedes: *the shackles of oppression.* **2** a metal link, typically U-shaped, closed by a bolt, used to secure a chain or rope to something. ■ a pivoted link connecting a spring in a vehicle's suspension to the body of the vehicle. ▸ **v.** [trans.] chain with shackles. ■ fig. restrain; limit. [OE *sc(e)acul* 'fetter,' of Gmc. origin; rel. to Du. *schakel* 'link, coupling.']

shack·y /'sHakē/ ▸ **adj.** informal (of a building) dilapidated or ramshackle.

shad /sHad/ ▸ **n.** (pl. same or **shads**) a fish (genera *Alosa* and *Caspialosa*) of the herring family that spends much of its life in the sea, typically entering rivers to spawn. It is an important food fish in many regions. [OE *sceadd,* of unknown origin.]

shad·blow /'sHadˌblō/ ▸ **n.** another term for **juneberry**. [19th C.: from **shad** + **blow**[3] (because its flowering is associated with the presence of shad in the rivers).]

shad·bush /'sHadˌbo͝osH/ (also **shad·blow** /-ˌblō/) ▸ **n.** another term for **juneberry**. [19th C.: so named because it flowers at the same time as shad are found in the rivers.]

shad·chan ▸ **n.** var. of **shadkhan**.

Shad·dai /sHä'dī/ ▸ **n.** one of the names given to God in the Hebrew Bible. [Heb., translated as 'Almighty' in English versions of the Bible, but of uncert. meaning.]

shad·dock /'sHadək/ ▸ **n.** another term for **pomelo**. [17th C.: named after Captain *Shaddock,* who introduced it to the West Indies in the 17th C.]

shadd·up /ˌsHət'əp/ ▸ **exclam.** informal be quiet! [1950s: representing a pronunc. of *shut up.*]

shade /sHād/ ▸ **n.** **1** comparative darkness and coolness caused by shelter from direct sunlight. ■ the darker part of a picture. ■ (usu. **shades**) literary a shadow or area of darkness. ■ fig. a position of relative inferiority or obscurity. ■ hist. a portrait in silhouette. **2** a color, esp. with regard to how light or dark it is or as distinguished from one nearly like it. ■ Art a slight degree of difference between colors. ■ a slightly differing variety of something. ■ [in sing.] a slight amount of something. **3** a lampshade. ■ (often **shades**) a screen or blind on a window. ■ an eyeshade. ■ (**shades**) informal sunglasses. **4** literary a ghost. ■ (**the Shades**) the underworld; Hades. ▸ **v.** [trans.] **1** screen from direct light. ■ cover, moderate, or exclude the light of. **2** darken or color (an illustration or diagram) with parallel pencil lines or a block of color. ■ [intrans.] (of a color or something colored) gradually change into another color. **3** make a slight reduction in the amount, rate, or price of: *banks may shade the margin over base rate they charge customers.*

– PHRASES **a shade ——** a little ——: *he was a shade hung over.* **shades of ——** used to suggest reminiscence of or comparison with someone or something specified: *colleges were conducting campaigns to ban Jewish societies—shades of Nazi Germany.* — **shade·less adj.** **shad·er n.** [OE *sc(e)adu,* of Gmc. origin. Cf. **shadow**.]

shad·ing /'sHādiNG/ ▸ **n.** **1** the darkening or coloring of an illustration or diagram with parallel lines or a block of color. ■ a very slight variation, typically in color or meaning. **2** a layer of paint or material used to provide shade, esp. for plants.

shad·khan ▸ **n.** /'sHätKHən; sHäd'KHän/ (also **shad·chan**) **n.** (pl. same, **shad·kha·nim** /ˌsHädKHä'nēm/, or **shad·khans**) a Jewish professional matchmaker or marriage broker. [from Yiddish *shadkhn,* based on Heb. *šiddēḵ* 'negotiate.']

sha·doof /SHä'do͞of/ ▶ n. a pole with a bucket and counterpoise used esp. in Egypt for raising water. [19th C.: from Egyptian Arab. *šādūf*.]

shadoof

shad·ow /'SHadō/ ▶ n. **1** a dark area or shape produced by a body coming between rays of light and a surface. ■ partial or complete darkness, esp. as produced in this way. ■ the shaded part of a picture. ■ a dark patch or area on a surface: *there are dark shadows beneath your eyes.* ■ a region of opacity on a radiograph: *shadows on his lungs.* ■ short for EYESHADOW. **2** fig. used in reference to proximity, ominous oppressiveness, or sadness and gloom. ■ used in reference to something insubstantial or fleeting: *a freedom more shadow than substance.* ■ used in reference to a position of relative inferiority or obscurity. ■ [with negative] the slightest trace of something: ***without a shadow of a doubt.*** ■ a weak or inferior remnant or version of something: ***a shadow of his former self.*** ■ an expression of perplexity or sadness. **3** an inseparable attendant or companion: *that dog was her faithful shadow.* ■ a person secretly following and observing another. ■ a person who accompanies someone in their daily activities at work in order to gain experience at or insight into a job. ■ [usu. as adj.] Brit. the opposition counterpart of a government minister: *the shadow Chancellor.* ▶ v. [trans.] **1** (often **be shadowed**) envelop in shadow; cast a shadow over. **2** follow and observe (someone) closely and secretly. ■ Brit. (of an opposition politician) be the counterpart of (a government minister or a ministry). ■ accompany (someone) in their daily activities at work in order to gain experience at or insight into a job. — **shad·ow·er** n. **shad·ow·less** adj. [OE *scead(u)we* (n.), oblique case of *sceadu* (see SHADE), *sceadwian* 'screen or shield from attack,' of Gmc. origin.]

shad·ow·box /'SHadō,bäks/ ▶ v. [intrans.] spar with an imaginary opponent as a form of training. ▶ n. (**shadow box**) a case with a protective transparent front, used for displaying jewelry, coins, etc.

shad·ow·graph /'SHadō,graf/ ▶ n. an image formed by the shadow of an object on a surface. ■ an image formed when light shone through a fluid is refracted differently by regions of different density. ■ a radiograph.

shad·ow·land /'SHadō,land/ ▶ n. literary a place in shadow. ■ (usu. **shadowlands**) an indeterminate borderland between places or states, represented as an abode of ghosts and spirits.

shad·ow mask ▶ n. a perforated metal screen situated directly behind the phosphor screen in certain types of color television tubes, having a pattern of precisely located holes through which the electron beams pass so as to strike the correct dots on the phosphor screen.

shad·ow play ▶ n. a display in which the shadows of puppets are cast on a screen that is viewed by the audience from the other side.

shad·ow·y /'SHadōē/ ▶ adj. (**-ow·i·er**, **-ow·i·est**) full of shadows. ■ of uncertain identity or nature: *a shadowy figure.* ■ insubstantial; unreal: *shadowy, ethereal forms.* — **shad·ow·i·ness** n.

shad·y /'SHādē/ ▶ adj. (**shad·i·er**, **shad·i·est**) situated in or full of shade. ■ giving shade from sunlight. ■ informal of doubtful honesty or legality. — **shad·i·ly** adv. **shad·i·ness** n.

shaft /SHaft/ ▶ n. **1** a long, narrow part or section forming the handle of a tool or club or the body of a spear or arrow. ■ an arrow or spear. ■ a column, esp. the main part between the base and capital. ■ a long cylindrical rotating rod for the transmission of motive power in a machine. ■ each of the pair of poles between which a horse is harnessed to a vehicle. ■ a ray of light or bolt of lightning. ■ a sudden flash of a quality or feeling. ■ a remark intended to be witty, wounding, or provoking. ■ vulgar slang a penis. ■ (**the shaft**) informal harsh or unfair treatment. **2** a long, narrow, typically vertical hole that gives access to a mine, accommodates an elevator in a building, or provides ventilation. ▶ v. **1** [intrans.] (of light) shine in beams. **2** [trans.] vulgar slang (of a man) have sexual intercourse with (a woman). ■ informal treat (someone) harshly or unfairly. — **shaft·ed** adj. [in comb.] *a long-shafted harpoon.* [OE *scæft*, *sceaft* 'handle, pole,' of Gmc. origin; rel. to Du. *schaft*, Ger. *Schaft*.]

Shaftes·bur·y /'SHaf(t)s,berē; -b(ə)rē/, Anthony Ashley Cooper, 7th Earl of (1801–85), English philanthropist and social activist. He worked to improve conditions for the working class.

shaft horse·pow·er ▶ n. the power delivered to a propeller or turbine shaft.

shaft·ing /'SHaftiNG/ ▶ n. a system of connected shafts for transmitting motive power in a machine.

shag[1] /SHag/ ▶ n. **1** [usu. as adj.] a carpet or rug with a long, rough pile. ■ [as adj.] (of a pile) long and rough. ■ cloth with a velvet nap on one side. **2** a thick, tangled hairstyle or mass of hair. **3** (also **shag tobacco**) a coarse kind of cut tobacco. [OE *sceacga* 'rough matted hair,' of Gmc. origin; rel. to ON *skegg* 'beard' and SHAW.]

shag[2] ▶ n. a western European and Mediterranean cormorant (*Phalacrocorax aristotelis*) with greenish-black plumage and a long curly crest in the breeding season. [16th C.: perh. a use of SHAG[1], with ref. to the bird's "shaggy" crest.]

shag[3] ▶ n. a dance originating in the US in the 1930s and 1940s, characterized by vigorous hopping from one foot to the other. [of obscure derivation; perh. from obs. *shag* 'waggle.']

shag[4] ▶ v. [trans.] Baseball chase or catch (fly balls) for practice. [20th C.: of unknown origin.]

shag[5] Brit., vulgar slang ▶ v. (**shagged**, **shag·ging**) [trans.] have sexual intercourse with (someone). ▶ n. an act of sexual intercourse. ■ [with adj.] a sexual partner of a specified ability. — **shag·ger** n. [18th C.: of unknown origin.]

shag·bark hick·o·ry /'SHag,bärk/ ▶ n. a North American hickory (*Carya ovata*) with shaggy peeling bark.

shagged /SHagd/ ▶ adj. Brit., informal exhausted. ■ damaged, ruined, or useless.

shag·gy /'SHagē/ ▶ adj. (**-gi·er**, **-gi·est**) (of hair or fur) long, thick, and unkempt. ■ having long, thick, unkempt hair or fur. ■ of or having a covering resembling rough, thick hair.

– PHRASES **shaggy-dog story** a long, rambling story or joke, typically one that is amusing only because it is absurdly inconsequential or pointless. — **shag·gi·ly** /-əlē/ adv. **shag·gi·ness** n.

shag·gy mane ▶ n. a common mushroom (*Coprinus comatus*, family Coprinaceae) that has a tall, narrow white cap covered with shaggy scales, occurring worldwide and edible when young.

sha·green /SHə'grēn/ ▶ n. **1** sharkskin used as a decorative material or, for its natural rough surface of pointed scales, as an abrasive. **2** a kind of untanned leather with a rough granulated surface. [17th C.: var. of CHAGRIN in the literal sense 'rough skin.']

Shah /SHä/, Reza, see PAHLAVI[1].

shah /SHä/ ▶ n. hist. a title of the former monarch of Iran. — **shah·dom** /-dəm/ n. [16th C.: from Persian *šāh*, from Old Pers. *ḵšāyaṯiya* 'king.']

sha·ha·da /SHä'hädə/ (also **sha·ha·dah**) ▶ n. the Muslim profession of faith ("there is no god but Allah, and Muhammad is the messenger of Allah"). [from Arab. *šahāda* 'testimony, evidence.']

Shahn /SHän/, Ben (1898–1989), US painter; born in Lithuania; full name *Benjamin Shahn).* His works are devoted to political and social themes.

shah·toosh /SHä'to͞osh/ ▶ n. high-quality wool from the neck hair of the Himalayan ibex. ■ fabric woven from this. [19th C.: via Punjabi from Pers. *šāh* 'king' + Kashmiri *tośa* 'fine shawl material.']

shaikh /SHēk; SHāk/ ▶ n. var. of SHEIKH.

Shai·tan /SHī'tän/ ▶ n. (in Muslim countries) the Devil, Satan, or an evil spirit. ■ (**shaitan**) an evilly disposed, vicious, or cunning person or animal. [from Arab. *šayṭān*.]

shake /SHāk/ ▶ v. (past **shook** /SHo͝ok/; past part. **shak·en** /'SHākən/) **1** [intrans.] (of a structure or area of land) tremble or vibrate: *buildings shook in Sacramento and tremors were felt in Reno.* ■ [trans.] cause to tremble or vibrate: *earthquakes shook the area.* ■ (of a person, a part of the body, or the voice) tremble uncontrollably from a strong emotion such as fear or anger: ***shaking with rage.*** **2** [trans.] move (an object) up and down or from side to side with rapid, forceful, jerky movements: *she shook her umbrella.* ■ [trans.] remove (an object or substance) from something by movements of this kind: *they shook the sand out of their shoes.* ■ informal get rid of or put an end to (something unwanted): *he was unable to* ***shake off*** *the memories of the trenches.* ■ grasp (someone) and move them roughly to and fro, either in anger or to rouse them from sleep: [trans.] *he shook the driver awake.* ■ brandish in anger or as a warning; make a threatening gesture with: *men shook their fists.* **3** [trans.] upset the composure of; shock or astonish: *rumors of a further loss shook the market.* ■ [trans.] cause a change of mood or attitude by shocking or disturbing (someone): *he shook himself out of his lethargy.* ■ weaken or impair (confidence, a belief, etc.), esp. by shocking or disturbing. ▶ n. **1** an act of shaking. ■ informal an earth tremor. ■ an amount of something that is sprinkled by shaking a container. ■ short for MILK SHAKE. ■ (**the shakes**) informal a fit of trembling or shivering. **2** Music a trill.

– PHRASES **get** (or **give someone**) **a fair shake** informal get (or give someone) just treatment or a fair chance. **in two shakes** (**of a lamb's tail**) informal very quickly: *I'll be back to you in two shakes.* **more —— than one can shake a stick at** informal used to emphasize the largeness of an amount: *more experience than you can shake a stick at.* **no great shakes** informal not very good or significant. **shake a leg** informal make a start; rouse oneself.

– PHRASAL VERBS **shake down** become established in a new situation; settle down. **shake someone down** informal extort money from someone. **shake something down** cause something to fall or settle by shaking. **shake someone off** get away from someone by shaking their grip loose. ■ manage to evade or outmaneuver someone who is following or pestering one. ■ (in sports, esp. a race) outdistance another competitor. **shake something off** successfully deal with or recover from an illness or injury. **shake on** informal confirm (an agreement) by shaking hands. **shake out** eventually prove to happen. **shake something out 1** empty something out by shaking a container. **2** spread or open something such as a cloth or garment by shaking it. ■ restore something crumpled to its natural shape by shaking: *she undid her helmet and shook out her frizzled hair.* ■ Sailing unwind or untie a reef to increase the area of a sail. **shake someone up** rouse someone from lethargy, apathy, or complacency. **shake something up 1** mix ingredients by shaking. **2** make radical changes to the organization or structure of an institution or system. [OE *sc(e)acan* (v.), of Gmc. origin.]

shake•down /ˈsʜāk,doun/ ▶ n. informal **1** a radical change or restructuring, esp. in a hierarchical organization. ■ a thorough search of a person or place. ■ a swindle; a piece of extortion. ■ a test of a new product or model, esp. a vehicle or ship. **2** a makeshift bed.

shak•en /ˈsʜākən/ past participle of SHAKE.

sha•ken ba•by syn•drome ▶ n. injury to a baby caused by being shaken violently and repeatedly, causing swelling of the brain, internal bleeding, detached retinas, blindness, mental retardation, and death.

shake•out /ˈsʜāk,out/ ▶ n. informal an upheaval or reorganization of a business, market, or organization due to competition and typically involving layoffs.

shak•er /ˈsʜākər/ ▶ n. **1** [with adj.] a container used for mixing ingredients by shaking. ■ a container with a pierced top from which a powdered substance such as flour or salt is poured by shaking. **2** (**Shaker**) a member of an American religious sect, the United Society of Believers in Christ's Second Coming, who lived simply in celibate mixed communities. ■ [as adj.] denoting a style of elegantly functional furniture traditionally produced by Shaker communities. — **Shak•er•ism** /-,rizəm/ n. (in sense 2).

Shak•er•ess /ˈsʜāk(ə)ris/ ▶ n. a female Shaker.

Shake•speare /ˈsʜāk,spi(ə)r/, William (1564–1616), English playwright. His plays are written mostly in blank verse and include comedies, historical plays, the Greek and Roman plays, enigmatic comedies, the great tragedies, and the group of tragicomedies with which he ended his career. He also wrote more than 150 sonnets, which were published in 1609, as well as narrative poems. — **Shake•spear•e•an** /sʜākˈspi(ə)rēən/ (also **Shake•spear•i•an**) n. & adj.

Shake•spear•e•an son•net ▶ n. another term for ELIZABETHAN SONNET.

shake-up (also **shake•up**) ▶ n. informal a radical reorganization.

Shakh•ty /ˈsʜäkʜtē/ a coal-mining city in southwestern Russia, in the Donets Basin, northeast of Rostov; pop. 227,000.

shak•o /ˈsʜakō; ˈsʜā-/ ▶ n. (pl. **-os**) a cylindrical or conical military hat with a brim and a plume or pom-pom. [19th C.: via Fr. from Hungarian *csákó (süveg)* 'peaked (cap),' from *csák* 'peak,' from Ger. *Zacken* 'spike.']

shako

Shak•ti /ˈsʜəktē/ ▶ n. Hinduism the female principle of divine energy, esp. when personified as the supreme deity. See also DEVI and PARVATI. [from Sanskrit *śakti* 'power, divine energy.']

shak•y /ˈsʜākē/ ▶ adj. (**shak•i•er, shak•i•est**) shaking or trembling. ■ unstable because of poor construction or heavy use. ■ not safe or reliable. — **shak•i•ly** /-kilē/ adv. **shak•i•ness** n.

shale /sʜāl/ ▶ n. soft, finely stratified sedimentary rock that formed from consolidated mud or clay and can be split easily into fragile plates. — **shal•y** (also **shal•ey**) adj. [18th C.: prob. from Ger. *Schale*; rel. to Engl. dial. *shale* 'dish' (see SCALE[2]).]

shale oil ▶ n. oil obtained from bituminous shale.

shall /sʜal/ ▶ modal verb (3rd sing. pres. **shall**) **1** (in the first person) expressing the future tense: *this time next week I shall be in Scotland.* **2** expressing a strong assertion or intention: *they shall succeed.* **3** expressing an instruction or command: *you shall not steal.* **4** used in questions indicating offers or suggestions: *shall we go?* [OE *sceal*, of Gmc. origin; rel. to Du. *zal* and Ger. *soll*, from a base meaning 'owe.']

shal•lop /ˈsʜaləp/ ▶ n. esp. hist. a light sailboat used mainly for coastal fishing or as a tender. ■ a large heavy boat with one or more masts and carrying fore-and-aft or lug sails and sometimes equipped with guns. [16th C.: from Fr. *chaloupe*, from Du. *sloep* 'sloop.']

shal•lot /sʜəˈlät; ˈsʜalət/ ▶ n. **1** a small bulb that resembles an onion and is used for pickling or as a substitute for onion. **2** the plant (*Allium ascalonicum*) of the lily family that produces these bulbs, each mature bulb producing a cluster of smaller bulbs. [17th C.: shortening of *eschalot*, from Fr. *eschalotte*, alt. of OFr. *eschaloigne* (in Anglo-Norman Fr. *scaloun*: see SCALLION).]

shal•low /ˈsʜalō/ ▶ adj. of little depth. ■ situated at no great depth: *the shallow bed of the North Sea.* ■ varying only slightly from a specified or understood line or direction, esp. the horizontal: *a shallow roof.* ■ not exhibiting, requiring, or capable of serious thought. ■ (of breathing) taking in little air. ▶ n. (**shallows**) an area of the sea, a lake, or a river where the water is not very deep. ▶ v. [intrans.] (of the sea, a lake, or a river) become less deep over time or in a particular place. — **shal•low•ly** adv. **shal•low•ness** n. [ME: obscurely rel. to SHOAL[2].]

sha•lom /sʜäˈlōm; sʜə-/ ▶ exclam. used as salutation by Jews at meeting or parting, meaning "peace." [from Heb. *šālōm*.]

shalt /sʜalt/ archaic second person singular of SHALL.

sham /sʜam/ ▶ n. **1** a thing that is not what it is purported to be. ■ pretense. ■ a person who pretends to be someone or something they are not. **2** short for PILLOW SHAM. ▶ adj. bogus; false. ▶ v. (**shammed, shamming**) [intrans.] falsely present something as the truth: *was he shamming?* ■ [trans.] pretend to be or to be experiencing: *she shams indifference.* — **sham•mer** n. [17th C.: perh. a north. Engl. dial. var. of the noun SHAME.]

sha•man /ˈsʜämən; ˈsʜā-/ ▶ n. (pl. **-mans**) a person having access to, and influence in, the world of spirits, esp. among some peoples of northern Asia and North America. — **sha•man•ic** /sʜəˈmanik/ adj. **sha•man•ism** /-,nizəm/ n. **sha•man•ist** /-nist/ n. & adj. **sha•man•is•tic** /,sʜäməˈnistik; ,sʜā-/ adj. **sha•man•ize** /-,nīz/ v. [17th C.: from Ger. *Schamane* and Russ. *shaman*, from Tungus *šaman*.]

sha•ma•teur /ˈsʜamətər; -,tər; -,cʜŏŏr; -cʜər/ ▶ n. derog. a sports player who makes money from sporting activities though classified as amateur. — **sha•ma•teur•ism** /-,rizəm/ n. [19th C.: blend of SHAM and AMATEUR.]

sham•ble /ˈsʜambəl/ ▶ v. [intrans.] (of a person) move with a slow, shuffling, awkward gait. ▶ n. [in sing.] a slow, shuffling, awkward gait. [16th C.: prob. from dial. *shamble* 'ungainly,' perh. from the phr. *shamble legs*, with ref. to the legs of trestle tables (such as would be used in a meat market: see SHAMBLES).]

sham•bles /ˈsʜambəlz/ ▶ plural n. [treated as sing.] **1** informal a state of total disorder. **2** a butcher's slaughterhouse (archaic except in place names). ■ a scene of carnage. [ME (in the sense 'meat market'): pl. of earlier *shamble* 'stool, stall,' of West Gmc. origin, from L. *scamellum*, dimin. of *scamnum* 'bench.']

sham•bo•lic /sʜamˈbälik/ ▶ adj. informal, esp. Brit. chaotic, disorganized, or mismanaged. [1970s: from SHAMBLES, prob. on the pattern of *symbolic*.]

shame /sʜām/ ▶ n. a painful feeling of humiliation or distress caused by the consciousness of wrong or foolish behavior. ■ a loss of respect or esteem; dishonor. ■ used to reprove someone for something of which they should be ashamed. ■ [in sing.] a regrettable or unfortunate situation or action. ■ a person, action, or situation that brings a loss of respect or honor. ▶ v. [trans.] (of a person, action, or situation) make (someone) feel ashamed: *I shamed him into giving some away.* ■ cause (someone) to feel ashamed or inadequate by surpassing them: *she shames me with her energy.*

– PHRASES **put someone to shame** disgrace or embarrass someone by outdoing or surpassing them. [OE *sc(e)amu* (n.), *sc(e)amian* 'feel shame,' of Gmc. origin; rel. to Du. *schamen* (v.) and Ger. *Scham* (n.), *schämen* (v.).]

shame•faced /ˈsʜām,fāst/ ▶ adj. feeling or expressing shame or embarrassment. — **shame•fac•ed•ly** /-,fāsidlē; -,fāstlē/ adv. **shame•fac•ed•ness** /-,fāsidnis; -,fāst-/ n. [16th C. (in the sense 'modest, shy'): alt. of archaic *shamefast*, by association with FACE.]

shame•ful /ˈsʜāmfəl/ ▶ adj. worthy of or causing shame or disgrace. — **shame•ful•ly** adv. [as submodifier] *record companies are shamefully slow in fulfilling orders.* **shame•ful•ness** n. [OE *sc(e)amful* 'modest, shamefaced' (see SHAME, -FUL).]

shame•less /ˈsʜāmlis/ ▶ adj. (of a person or their conduct) characterized by or showing a lack of shame. — **shame•less•ly** adv. **shame•less•ness** n. [OE *sc(e)amlēas* (see SHAME, -LESS).]

Sha•mir /sʜəˈmi(ə)r/, Yitzhak (1915–), prime minister of Israel 1983–84, 1986–92; born in Poland; Polish name *Yitzhak Jazernicki*.

sham•mes /ˈsʜäməs/ ▶ n. **1** a sexton in a synagogue. **2** the candle that is used to light the others in a menorah for Hanukkah.

sham•my /ˈsʜamē/ (also **sham•my leath•er**) ▶ n. (pl. **-mies**) informal term for CHAMOIS (sense 2). [18th C.: a phonetic spelling.]

sham•poo /sʜamˈpo͞o/ ▶ n. a liquid preparation containing soap for washing the hair. ■ a similar substance for cleaning a carpet or a car. ■ an act of washing or cleaning something, esp. the hair, with shampoo. ▶ v. (**-poos, -pooed** /-ˈpo͞od/) [trans.] wash or clean (something, esp. the hair) with shampoo. ■ (**shampoo something in/out**) wash something in or out of the hair using shampoo. [18th C. (in the sense 'massage (as part of a Turkish bath process)'): from Hindi *cāṃpo!* 'press!,' imper. of *cāṃpnā*.]

sham•rock /ˈsʜam,räk/ ▶ n. a low-growing, cloverlike plant (esp. *Trifolium minus*) of the pea family, with three-lobed leaves, used as the national emblem of Ireland. ■ a spray or leaf of this plant. [16th C.: from Irish *seamróg* 'trefoil' (dimin. of *seamar* 'clover').]

sha•mus /ˈsʜāməs/ ▶ n. informal a private detective. [1920s: of unknown origin.]

Shan /sʜan/ ▶ n. (pl. same or **Shans**) **1** a member of a people living mainly in northern Myanmar (Burma) and adjacent parts of southern China. **2** the Tai language of this people. ▶ adj. of or relating to this people or their language. [Burmese.]

Shan•dong /ˈsʜänˈdôɴɢ/ (also **Shan•tung** /-ˈto͝oɴɢ/) a coastal province in eastern China; capital, Jinan.

shan•dy /ˈsʜandē/ ▶ n. (pl. **-dies**) beer mixed with a nonalcoholic drink (typically lemonade). [19th C.: abbrev. of *shandygaff*, of unknown origin.]

Shang /sʜaɴɢ/ a dynasty that ruled China during the 16th–11th centuries BC, during which were invented Chinese ideographic script and bronze casting.

Shang•hai /ˈsʜaɴɢˈhī/ a city on the eastern coast of China; pop. 7,780,000.

shang•hai /ˈsʜaɴɢ,hī/ ▶ v. (**-hais, -haied** /-,hīd/, **-hai•ing** /-,hī-iɴɢ/) [trans.] hist. force (someone) to join a ship by drugging them. ■ informal coerce or trick (someone) into a position or into doing something. [19th C.: from SHANGHAI.]

Shan•gri-La /ˈsʜaɴɢgri ˈlä/ a Tibetan utopia in James Hilton's novel *Lost Horizon* (1933). ■ [as n.] (**a Shangri-La**) a place regarded as an earthly

PRONUNCIATION KEY ə *ago, up*; ər *over, fur*; a *hat*; ā *ate*; ä *car*; e *let*; ē *see*; i *fit*; ī *by*; ɴɢ *sing*; ō *go*; ô *law, for*; oi *toy*; o͝o *good*; o͞o *goo*; ou *out*; ᴛʜ *thin*; T͟H *then*; ᴢʜ *vision*

paradise, esp. a retreat from modern civilization. [from *Shangri* (an invented name) + Tibetan *la* 'mountain pass.']

shank /SHANGk/ ▶ **n. 1** (often **shanks**) a person's leg, esp. the part from the knee to the ankle. ■ the lower part of an animal's foreleg. ■ this part of an animal's leg as a cut of meat. **2** the shaft or stem of a tool or implement, in particular: ■ a long narrow part of a tool connecting the handle to the operational end. ■ the cylindrical part of a bit by which it is held in a drill. ■ the long stem of a key, spoon, anchor, etc. ■ the straight part of a nail or fishhook. **3** a part or appendage by which something is attached to something else, esp. a wire loop on the back of a button. ■ the band of a ring rather than the setting or gemstone. **4** the narrow middle of the sole of a shoe. **5** informal a dagger made by a prison inmate from available materials. ▶ **v.** [trans.] Golf strike (the ball) with the heel of the club. — **shanked adj.** [usu. in comb.] *a long-shanked hook.* [OE *sceanca*, of West Gmc. origin; rel. to Du. *schenk* 'leg bone' and High Ger. *Schenkel* 'thigh.' The use of the verb as a golfing term dates from the 1920s.]

Shan·kar /'SHANG,kär/, Ravi (1920–), Indian sitar player and composer. He stimulated Western interest in Indian music.

shanks' mare (also **shanks' pony**) ▶ **n.** used to walking. [18th C.: first recorded as *shanks-nag* in R. Fergusson's *Poems* (1785).]

Shan·non /'SHanən/ a river in Ireland that flows from County Leitrim to the Atlantic Ocean. ■ an international airport in the Republic of Ireland, situated on the Shannon River west of Limerick.

shan·ny /'SHanē/ ▶ **n.** (pl. **-nies**) a small, greenish-brown European blenny (*Blennius pholis*) of the shoreline and intertidal waters. [19th C.: of unknown origin; cf. earlier *shan*, in the same sense.]

shan't /SHant/ ▶ **contr.** shall not.

Shan·tou /'SHän'tō/ a city in the province of Guangdong in southeastern China; pop. 860,000.

shan·tung /SHan'təNG/ ▶ **n.** a dress fabric spun from tussore silk with random irregularities in the surface texture. [19th C.: from ***SHANTUNG*** (see **SHANDONG**, where it was orig. made.]

shan·ty¹ /'SHantē/ ▶ **n.** (pl. **-ties**) a small, crudely built shack. [19th C. (orig. a North Amer. usage): perh. from Canad. Fr. *chantier* 'lumberjack's cabin, logging camp.']

shan·ty² ▶ **n.** (pl. **-ties**) var. of **CHANTEY**.

shan·ty·town /'SHantē,toun/ ▶ **n.** a deprived area on the outskirts of a town consisting of large numbers of crude dwellings.

Shan·xi /'SHän'SHē/ (also **Shan·si** /-'sē/) a province in north central China; capital, Taiyuan.

SHAPE /SHāp/ ▶ **abbr.** Supreme Headquarters Allied Powers Europe.

shape /SHāp/ ▶ **n. 1** the external form or appearance of someone or something. ■ a person or thing difficult to see and identify clearly. ■ [usu. with adj.] a specific form or guise assumed by someone or something: *a fiend in human shape.* ■ a piece of material, paper, etc., made or cut in a particular form. **2** [with adj.] the particular condition or state of someone or something: *he was in no shape to drive.* ■ the distinctive nature or qualities of something: *the future shape and direction of the country.* ■ definite or orderly arrangement. ▶ **v.** [trans.] (often **be shaped**) give a particular shape or form to: *shape the dough into two-inch balls.* ■ make (something) fit the form of something else: [with obj. and trans.] *suits have been shaped to fit snugly.* ■ determine the nature of; have a great influence on. ■ [intrans.] develop in a particular way; progress: *the yacht was shaping well in trials.* ■ form or produce (a sound or words).

– PHRASES **get into shape** (or **get someone into shape**) become (or make someone) physically fitter by exercise. **in any (way,) shape or form** in any manner or under any circumstances (used for emphasis). **in (good) shape** in good physical condition. **in the shape of** represented or embodied by: *retribution arrived in the shape of my irate father.* **whip** (or **knock** or **lick**) **someone/something into shape** act forcefully to bring someone or something into a fitter, more efficient, or better organized state. **out of shape 1** (of an object) not having its usual or original shape, esp. after being bent or knocked. **2** (of a person) in poor physical condition; unfit. **shape up or ship out** informal used as an ultimatum to someone to improve their performance or behavior or face being made to leave. **take shape** assume a distinct form; develop into something definite or tangible.

– PHRASAL VERBS **shape up** develop or happen in a particular way: *it was shaping up to be another bleak year.* ■ informal improve performance or behavior: *we have never been afraid to tell our children to shape up.* ■ become physically fit: *I need to shape up.* — **shap·a·ble** (also **shape·a·ble**) **adj. shaped adj.** [usu. in comb.] *egg-shaped* | *X-shaped.* **shap·er n.** [OE *gesceap* 'external form,' also 'creation,' *sceppan* 'create,' of Gmc. origin.]

shaped charge ▶ **n.** an explosive charge with a cavity that causes the blast to be concentrated into a small area.

shape·less /'SHāplis/ ▶ **adj.** (esp. of a garment) lacking a distinctive or attractive shape. — **shape·less·ly adv. shape·less·ness n.**

shape·ly /'SHāplē/ ▶ **adj.** (**-li·er**, **-li·est**) (esp. of a woman) having an attractive or well-proportioned shape. — **shape·li·ness n.**

shape·shift·er /'SHāp,SHiftər/ ▶ **n.** (chiefly in fiction) a person or being with the ability to change their physical form at will. — **shape·shift·ing** /-,SHiftiNG/ **n. & adj.**

Sha·pir·o /SHə'pi(ə)rō/, Karl Jay (1913–2000), US poet. His poems include "Elegy for a Dead Soldier" (1944).

Shap·ley /'SHaplē/, Harlow (1885–1972), US astronomer. He carried out an extensive survey of galaxies.

shard /SHärd/ ▶ **n.** a piece of broken ceramic, metal, glass, or rock, typically having sharp edges: *shards of glass flew in all directions* | fig. *he collected shards of gossip like a crow diving for glinting tin.* [OE *sceard* 'gap, notch, potsherd,' of Gmc. origin: rel. to Du. *schaarde* 'notch,' also to **SHEAR**.]

share¹ /SHe(ə)r/ ▶ **n.** a part of a larger amount that is divided among a number of people, or to which a number of people contribute. ■ one of the equal parts into which a company's capital is divided, entitling the holder to a proportion of the profits. ■ part proprietorship of property held by joint owners. ■ [in sing.] the allotted or due amount of something that a person expects to have or to do. ▶ **v.** [trans.] have a portion of (something) with another or others: *he **shared** the pie **with** her.* ■ [trans.] give a portion of (something) to another or others: *money raised will be shared between the two charities.* ■ use, occupy, or enjoy (something) jointly with another or others: *they once shared a house in the Hamptons* | [intrans.] *there weren't enough plates, so we had to share.* ■ possess (a view or quality) in common with others. ■ [intrans.] (**share in**) (of a number of people or organizations) have a part in (something, esp. an activity): *they would share in the development of a new station.* ■ tell someone about (something), esp. something personal.

– PHRASES **share and share alike** having or receiving an equal share. — **share·a·ble** (also **shar·a·ble**) **adj. shar·er n.** [OE *scearu* 'division, part into which something may be divided,' of Gmc. origin; rel. to Du. *schare* and Ger. *Schar* 'troop, multitude,' also to **SHEAR**. The verb dates from the late 16th C.]

share² ▶ **n.** short for **PLOWSHARE**.

share·crop·per /'SHe(ə)r,kräpər/ ▶ **n.** a tenant farmer who gives a part of each crop as rent. — **share·crop v.** (**-cropped**, **-crop·ping**).

share·hold·er /'SHe(ə)r,hōldər/ ▶ **n.** an owner of shares in a company. — **share·hold·ing** /-,hōldiNG/ **n.**

share·ware /'SHe(ə)r,we(ə)r/ ▶ **n.** Comput. software that is available free of charge and often distributed informally for evaluation, after which a fee may be requested for continued use.

sha·ri·a /SHä'rēə/ (also **sha·ri·ah** or **sha·ri·at** /-ät/) ▶ **n.** Islamic law based on the teachings of the Koran and the traditions of the Prophet (Hadith and Sunna), prescribing both religious and secular duties and sometimes penalties for lawbreaking. [from Arab. *šarī'a*; the var. *shariat* from Urdu and Pers.]

sha·rif /SHə'rēf/ (also **she·reef** or **she·rif**) ▶ **n. 1** a descendant of Muhammad through his daughter Fatima. **2** a Muslim ruler, magistrate, or religious leader. — **sha·rif·i·an adj.** [from Arab. *šarīf* 'noble,' from *šarafa* 'be exalted.']

Shar·jah /'SHärZHə; -jə/ a state of the United Arab Emirates; pop. 400,000. ■ its capital city, on the Persian Gulf; pop. 125,000.

shark¹ /SHärk/ ▶ **n. 1** a long-bodied chiefly marine fish (subclass Elasmobranchii) with a cartilaginous skeleton, a prominent dorsal fin, and toothlike scales. Most sharks are predatory, although the largest kinds feed on plankton. See illustration at **BULL SHARK**. **2** a small Southeast Asian freshwater fish of the minnow family with a sharklike tail, popular in aquariums.

shark² ▶ **n.** informal **1** a person who unscrupulously exploits or swindles others. See also **LOAN SHARK**. **2** an expert in a specified field: *a pool shark.* [16th C.: perh. from Ger. *Schurke* 'worthless rogue,' influenced by **SHARK¹**.]

shark·skin /'SHärk,skin/ ▶ **n.** the rough scaly skin of a shark, sometimes used as shagreen. ■ a stiff, slightly lustrous synthetic fabric.

shark·suck·er /'SHärk,səkər/ ▶ **n.** a remora, esp. *Echeneis naucrates*, the most abundant remora of warm waters.

sharksucker

Shar·on /'SHarən; 'SHe(ə)r-/ a fertile coastal plain in Israel that lies between the Mediterranean Sea and the hills of Samaria.

sharp /SHärp/ ▶ **adj. 1** (of an object) having an edge or point that is able to cut or pierce something. ■ producing a sudden, piercing physical sensation or effect: *a sharp pain in my back.* ■ (of a food, taste, or smell) acidic and intense: *sharp cheese.* ■ (of a sound) sudden and penetrating. ■ (of words or a speaker) intended or intending to criticize or hurt. ■ (of an emotion or experience) felt acutely or intensely; painful. **2** tapering to a point or edge. ■ distinct in outline or detail; clearly defined: *a sharp contrast from her past life.* ■ informal (of clothes or their wearer) neat and stylish. **3** (of an action or change) sudden and marked: *a sharp increase in interest rates.* ■ (of a bend, angle, or turn) making a sudden change of direction. ■ having or showing speed of perception, comprehension, or response. ■ quick to take advantage, esp. in an unscrupulous or dishonest way. **4** (of musical sound) above true or normal pitch. ■ [postpositive, in comb.] (of a note) a semitone higher than a specified note: *the song sits on E and F-sharp.* ■ (of a key) having a sharp or sharps in the key signature. ▶ **adv. 1** precisely (used after an expression of time). **2** in a sudden or abrupt way: *the creek bent sharp left.* **3** above the true or normal pitch of musical sound. ▶ **n. 1** a musical note raised a semitone above natural pitch. ■ the sign (#) indicating this. **2** a long, sharply pointed needle used for general sewing. ■ (usu. **sharps**) a thing with a sharp edge, such as a blade or a fragment of glass. **3** informal a swindler or cheat. See also **CARD SHARP**. ▶ **v.** [trans.] **1** [usu. as adj.] (**sharped**) Music raise the pitch of (a note). **2** archaic cheat or swindle (someone), esp. at cards.

– PHRASES **sharp as a tack** extremely clever or astute. — **sharp·ly adv.**

sharp·ness n. [OE *sc(e)arp*, of Gmc. origin; rel. to Du. *scherp* and Ger. *scharf*.]

Shar-Pei

Shar-Pei /'SHär 'pā/ (also **shar-pei**) ▶n. (pl. **-Peis**) a compact, squarely built dog of a breed of Chinese origin, with a characteristic wrinkly skin and short bristly coat. [1970s: from Chin. *shāpí*, lit. 'sand skin.']

sharp·en /'SHärpən/ ▶v. make or become sharp. ■ improve or cause to improve: [intrans.] *they must sharpen up or risk losing half their business* | [trans.] *students will sharpen up their reading skills.* — **sharp·en·er** n.

sharp·er /'SHärpər/ ▶n. informal a swindler, esp. at cards.

sharp-fea·tured ▶adj. (of a person) having well-defined facial features.

sharp·ie /'SHärpē/ ▶n. (pl. **-ies**) **1** a sharp-prowed, flat-bottomed New England sailboat, with one or two masts each rigged with a triangular sail. **2** informal a dishonest and cunning person, esp. a cheat.

sharp-set ▶adj. dated very hungry.

sharp·shoot·er /'SHärp,SHōōtər/ ▶n. a person who is very skilled in shooting. — **sharp·shoot·ing** /-,SHōōtiNG/ n. & adj.

sharp-tongued ▶adj. (of a person) given to using cutting, harsh, or critical language.

sharp-wit·ted ▶adj. (of a person) quick to notice and understand things. — **sharp-wit·ted·ly** adv. **sharp-wit·ted·ness** n.

shash·lik /'SHäSH,lik; SHäSH'lik/ ▶n. (pl. same or **-liks**) (in Asia and eastern Europe) a mutton kebab. [from Russ. *shashlyk*, based on Turk. *şiş* 'spit, skewer'; cf. SHISH KEBAB.]

Shas·ta, Mount /'SHastə/ a peak in northern California in the Cascade Range.

Shas·ta dai·sy /'SHästə/ ▶n. a tall, widely cultivated plant (*Chrysanthemum superbum*) of the daisy family that bears large white daisylike flowers. [19th C.: named after Mount *Shasta* in California.]

shat /SHat/ past and past participle of SHIT.

Shatt al-A·rab /,SHat al 'arəb; ,SHät äl 'ärəb/ a river in southwestern Asia that is formed by the confluence of the Tigris and Euphrates rivers.

shat·ter /'SHatər/ ▶v. break or cause to break suddenly and violently into pieces. ■ [trans.] damage or destroy (something abstract): *the crisis will shatter their confidence.* ■ [trans.] upset (someone) greatly: *everyone was shattered by the news.* — **shat·ter·er** n. **shat·ter·ing·ly** adv. **shat·ter·proof** /-,prōōf/ adj. [ME (in the sense 'scatter, disperse'): perh. imitative; cf. SCATTER.]

shat·ter cone ▶n. Geol. a fluted conical structure produced in rock by intense mechanical shock, such as that associated with meteoritic impact.

shave /SHāv/ ▶v. **1** [intrans.] cut the hair off one's face with a razor. ■ [trans.] cut the hair off (a part of the body) with a razor. ■ [trans.] cut the hair off the face or another part of the body of (someone) with a razor. ■ cut (hair) off with a razor: *male swimmers shave off their body hair.* **2** [trans.] cut (a thin slice or slices) from the surface of something. ■ reduce by a small amount: *they shaved profit margins.* ■ remove (a small amount) from something: *she **shaved** 0.5 seconds **off** the record.* **3** [trans.] pass or send something close to (something else), missing it narrowly. ▶n. **1** an act of shaving hair from the face or a part of the body. **2** a tool used for shaving very thin slices or layers from wood or other material. [OE *sc(e)afan* 'scrape away the surface of (something) by paring,' of Gmc. origin; rel. to Du. *schaven* and Ger. *schaben*.]

shave·ling /'SHāvliNG/ ▶n. archaic, derog. a man of the church with a tonsured head.

shav·en /'SHāvən/ ▶adj. shaved.

shav·er /'SHāvər/ ▶n. **1** an electric razor. **2** informal a young lad.

shave·tail /'SHāv,tāl/ ▶n. military slang, often derog. a newly commissioned officer, esp. a second lieutenant. ■ informal an inexperienced person. [figuratively, from the early sense 'untrained pack animal' (identified by a shaved tail).]

Sha·vi·an /'SHāvēən/ ▶adj. of, relating to, or in the manner of G. B. Shaw, his writings, or ideas. ▶n. an admirer of Shaw or his work. [from *Shavius* (Latinized form of *Shaw*) + -AN.]

shav·ing /'SHāviNG/ ▶n. **1** a thin strip cut off a surface. **2** the action of shaving.

Sha·vu·oth /SHə'vōō,ōt; ,SHävōō'ōt; SHə'vōōəs/ (also **Sha·vu·ot**) ▶n. a major Jewish festival held on the 6th (and usually the 7th) of Sivan, fifty days after the second day of Passover. Also called PENTECOST, FEAST OF WEEKS. [from Heb. *šābū'ōt* 'weeks,' with ref. to the weeks between Passover and Pentecost.]

Shaw /SHô/, George Bernard (1856–1950), Irish playwright. His plays include *Candida* (1897), *Major Barbara* (1905), and *Pygmalion* (1913). Nobel Prize for Literature (1925).

shaw /SHô/ ▶n. archaic, esp. Scot. a small group of trees; a thicket. [OE *sceaga*, of Gmc. origin; rel. to SHAG[1].]

shawl /SHôl/ ▶n. a piece of fabric worn by women over the shoulders or head or wrapped around a baby. — **shawled** adj. [from Urdu and Pers. *šāl*, prob. from *Shāliāt*, the name of a town in India.]

shawl col·lar ▶n. a rounded turned-down collar, without lapel notches, that extends down the front of a garment.

shawm /SHôm/ ▶n. a medieval and Renaissance wind instrument, forerunner of the oboe, with a double reed. [ME: from OFr. *chalemel*, via L. from Gk. *kalamos* 'reed.']

Shaw·nee[1] /SHô'nē/ a city in northeastern Kansas; pop. 47,996.

Shaw·nee[2] ▶n. (pl. same or **-nees**) **1** a member of an American Indian people living formerly in the eastern US and now chiefly in Oklahoma. **2** the Algonquian language of this people. ▶adj. of or relating to the Shawnee or their language. [Delaware *šáwanōw* (sing.), from the Shawnee self-designation *šáwanōki* (pl.), lit. 'southern people.']

shay /SHā/ ▶n. informal term for CHAISE (sense 1). [18th C.: back-form. from CHAISE, interpreted as pl.]

shaykh /SHāk; SHīk/ ▶n. var. of SHEIKH.

sha·zam /SHə'zam/ ▶exclam. used to introduce an extraordinary deed, story, or transformation. [1940s: an invented word, used by conjurors.]

Shcher·ba·kov /'SHerbə,kôf; -,käf; ,SHCHi(ə)rbə'kôf/ former name (1946–57) of RYBINSK.

she /SHē/ ▶pron. [third person sing.] used to refer to a woman, girl, or female animal previously mentioned or easily identified: *my sister told me that she was not happy.* ■ used to refer to a ship, vehicle, country, or other inanimate thing regarded as female: *I was aboard the St. Roch shortly before she sailed for the Northwest Passage.* ■ used to refer to a person or animal of unspecified sex: *only include your child if you know she won't distract you.* ■ any female person: *she who rocks the cradle rules the world.* ▶n. [in sing.] a female; a woman: *society would label him a slut if he were a she.* ■ [in comb.] female: *a she-bear.* [ME: prob. a phonetic development of the OE fem. personal pronoun *hēo, hīe*.]

s/he /'SHē ər 'hē; 'SHē'hē/ ▶pron. a written representation of "he or she" used as a neutral alternative to indicate someone of either sex.

shea /SHē; SHā/ (also **shea tree**) ▶n. a small tropical African tree (*Vitellaria paradoxa* or *Butyrospermum parkii*) of the sapodilla family that bears oily nuts. [18th C.: from Mande *sye*.]

shea but·ter ▶n. a fatty substance obtained from the nuts of the shea tree, used chiefly in cosmetic skin preparations.

sheaf /SHēf/ ▶n. (pl. **sheaves** /SHēvz/) a bundle of grain stalks laid lengthways and tied together after reaping. ■ a bundle of objects of one kind, esp. papers. ▶v. [trans.] bundle into sheaves. [OE *scēaf*, of Gmc. origin; rel. to Du. *schoof* 'sheaf' and Ger. *Schaub* 'wisp of straw,' also to the verb SHOVE.]

shear /SHi(ə)r/ ▶v. (past part. **shorn** /SHôrn/ or **sheared**) **1** [trans.] cut the wool off (a sheep or other animal). ■ cut off (something such as hair, wool, or grass) with scissors or shears. ■ (**be shorn of**) have something cut off: fig. *the richest man in the US was shorn of nearly $2 billion.* **2** break off or cause to break off, owing to a structural strain: [intrans.] *the derailleur sheared and jammed in the rear wheel* | [trans.] *the left wing had been almost completely **sheared off**.* ▶n. a strain produced by pressure in the structure of a substance, when its layers are laterally shifted in relation to each other. See also WIND SHEAR. — **shear·er** n. [OE *sceran* (orig. in the sense 'cut through with a weapon'), of Gmc. origin; rel. to Du. and Ger. *scheren*, from a base meaning 'divide, shear, shave.']

shear·ling /'SHi(ə)rliNG/ ▶n. a sheep that has been shorn once. ■ wool or fleece from such a sheep. ■ a coat made from or lined with such wool.

shears /SHi(ə)rz/ (also **a pair of shears**) ▶plural n. a cutting instrument in which two blades move past each other, like scissors but typically larger: *garden shears.* [OE *scēara* (pl.) 'scissors, cutting instrument,' of Gmc. origin; rel. to Du. *schaar* and Ger. *Schere*, also to SHEAR.]

shear·wa·ter /'SHi(ə)r,wôtər; -,wätər/ ▶n. **1** a long-winged seabird (*Puffinus* and other genera, family Procellariidae) related to the petrels, often flying low over the surface of the water far from land. **2** North American term for SKIMMER (sense 2).

sheat·fish /'SHēt,fiSH/ ▶n. (pl. same or **-fish·es**) [16th C.: from an alt. of SHEATH + FISH[1].]

sheath /SHēTH/ ▶n. (pl. **sheaths** /SHēTHZ; SHēTHS/) a close-fitting cover for something, esp. something that is elongated in shape, in particular: ■ a cover for the blade of a knife or sword. ■ a structure in living tissue that closely envelops another: *the fatty sheath around nerve fibers.* ■ (also **sheath dress**) a woman's close-fitting dress. ■ a protective covering around an electric cable. ■ a condom. — **sheath·less** adj. [OE *scǣth, scēath* 'scabbard,' of Gmc. origin; rel. to Du. *schede*, Ger. *Scheide*, also to the verb SHED[2].]

sheath·bill /'SHēTH,bil/ ▶n. a mainly white pigeonlike bird (genus *Chionis*, family Chionididae) with a horny sheath around the base of the bill, breeding on the coasts of sub-Antarctic islands and feeding by scavenging.

sheathe /ˈSHēTH/ ▶ **v.** [trans.] put (a weapon such as a knife or sword) into a sheath. ■ (often **be sheathed in**) encase (something) in a close-fitting or protective covering. [ME: from SHEATH.]

sheath·ing /ˈSHēTHiNG/ ▶ **n.** protective casing or covering.

sheath knife ▶ **n.** a short knife similar to a dagger, carried in a sheath.

sheave /SHēv; SHiv/ ▶ **n.** a wheel with a groove for a rope to run on, as in a pulley block. [ME: from a Gmc. base meaning 'wheel, pulley.']

sheaves /SHēvz/ plural form of SHEAF.

She·ba /ˈSHēbə/ the biblical name of Saba in southwestern Arabia.

she·bang /SHəˈbaNG/ ▶ **n.** [in sing.] informal a matter, operation, or set of circumstances: *the Mafia boss who's running the whole shebang.* [19th C.: of unknown origin.]

She·bat /SHəˈbät/ ▶ **n.** var. of SEBAT.

she·been /SHəˈbēn/ ▶ **n.** (esp. in Ireland) an unlicensed establishment or private house selling alcoholic liquor. [18th C.: from Anglo-Irish *síbín*, from *séibe* 'mugful.']

She·boy·gan /SHiˈboigən/ a city in eastern Wisconsin; pop. 50,792.

shed[1] /SHed/ ▶ **n.** a simple roofed structure used as a storage space or a workshop. ■ a larger structure, typically with one or more sides open, for storing or maintaining vehicles or machinery. ▶ **v.** (**shed·ded, shed·ding**) [trans.] (usu. **be shedded**) park (a vehicle) in a depot. [15th C.: appar. a var. of the noun SHADE.]

shed[2] ▶ **v.** (**shed·ding** ; past and past part. **shed**) [trans.] (of a tree or other plant) allow (leaves or fruit) to fall to the ground. ■ (of a reptile, insect, etc.) allow (its skin or shell) to come off, to be replaced by another one that has grown underneath. ■ (of a mammal) lose (hair) as a result of molting, disease, or age. ■ take off (clothes). ■ discard (something undesirable, superfluous, or outdated). ■ have the property of preventing (something) from being absorbed: *latigo leather sheds water, sweat, and salt.* ■ eliminate part of (an electrical power load) by disconnecting circuits.

– PHRASES **shed (someone's) blood** be injured or killed (or kill or injure someone). **shed light on** see LIGHT[1]. **shed tears** weep; cry. [OE *sc(e)ādan* 'separate out (one selected group), divide,' also 'scatter,' of Gmc. origin; rel. to Du. and Ger. *scheiden*. Cf. SHEATH.]

she'd /SHēd/ ▶ **contr.** she had; she would.

she-dev·il ▶ **n.** a malicious or spiteful woman.

sheen /SHēn/ ▶ **n.** [in sing.] a soft luster on a surface. ▶ **v.** literary shine or cause to shine softly. — **sheen·y adj.** [17th C.: from obs. *sheen* 'beautiful, resplendent'; appar. rel. to the verb SHINE.]

sheen·y /ˈSHēnē/ ▶ **n.** derog. a contemptuous term for a Jewish person. [19th C.: origin unknown.]

sheep 1

sheep /SHēp/ ▶ **n.** (pl. same) **1** a domesticated ruminant (*Ovis aries*) of the cattle family with a thick woolly coat and (typically only in the male) curving horns. It is kept in flocks for its wool or meat, and is proverbial for its tendency to follow others in the flock. ■ a wild mammal related to this, such as the argali and bighorn. **2** a person too easily influenced or led.

– PHRASES **count sheep** count imaginary sheep jumping over a fence one by one in an attempt to send oneself to sleep. [OE *scēp, scǣp, scēap*, of West Gmc. origin; rel. to Du. *schaap* and Ger. *Schaf*.]

sheep dip ▶ **n.** a liquid preparation for cleansing sheep of parasites or preserving their wool. ■ a place where sheep are dipped in such a preparation.

sheep·dog /ˈSHēpˌdôg; -ˌdäg/ ▶ **n.** a dog trained to guard and herd sheep. ■ a dog of a breed suitable for this.

sheep·fold /ˈSHēpˌfōld/ ▶ **n.** a sheep pen.

sheep·ish /ˈSHēpiSH/ ▶ **adj.** (of a person or expression) showing embarrassment from shame or a lack of self-confidence: *a sheepish grin.* — **sheep·ish·ly adv. sheep·ish·ness n.**

sheep lau·rel ▶ **n.** a North American kalmia (*Kalmia angustifolia*) that is sometimes cultivated as an ornamental.

sheep·man /ˈSHēpmən/ ▶ **n.** (pl. **-men**) a sheep rancher.

sheep run (also **sheep station**) ▶ **n.** (esp. in Australia) an extensive tract of land on which sheep are pastured.

sheep scab ▶ **n.** an intensely itching skin disease of sheep caused by a parasitic mite (*Psoroptes communis*, family Psoroptidae).

sheep·shank /ˈSHēpˌSHaNGk/ ▶ **n.** a kind of knot used to shorten a rope temporarily.

sheeps·head /ˈSHēpsˌhed/ ▶ **n.** (pl. same) any of a number of boldly marked edible game fishes that live in warm American waters, in particular: ■ a black and silver striped porgy (*Archosargus probatocephalus*) of Atlantic coastal and brackish waters. ■ (**California sheepshead**) a black and red wrasse (*Semicossyphus pulcher*) of Californian coastal waters.

sheep·skin /ˈSHēpˌskin/ ▶ **n.** a sheep's skin with the wool on, esp. when made into a garment or rug. ■ leather from a sheep's skin used in bookbinding. ■ informal a diploma.

sheep sor·rel ▶ **n.** a sorrel (*Rumex acetosella*) that is common on acid soils in north temperate regions.

sheep tick ▶ **n.** a large tick (*Ixodes ricinus*, family Ixodidae) that infests many mammals, including humans, and frequently transmits diseases.

sheer[1] /SHi(ə)r/ ▶ **adj. 1** [attrib.] nothing other than; unmitigated (used for emphasis): *she giggled with sheer delight.* **2** (esp. of a cliff or wall) perpendicular or nearly so: *the sheer ice walls.* **3** (of a fabric) very thin; diaphanous: *sheer white silk chiffon.* ▶ **adv. 1** perpendicularly: *the ridge fell sheer.* **2** archaic completely; right. ▶ **n.** a very fine or diaphanous fabric or article. — **sheer·ly adv. sheer·ness n.** [ME: prob. an alt. of dial. *shire* 'pure, clear,' from the Gmc. base of SHINE.]

sheer[2] ▶ **v.** [intrans.] (typically of a boat or ship) swerve or change course quickly. ■ fig. avoid or move away from an unpleasant topic. ▶ **n.** a sudden deviation from a course, esp. by a boat. [17th C.: perh. from Mid. Low Ger. *scheren* 'to shear.']

sheer[3] ▶ **n.** the upward slope of a ship's lines toward the bow and stern. [17th C.: prob. from the noun SHEAR.]

sheer·legs /ˈSHi(ə)rˌlegz/ ▶ **plural n.** [treated as sing.] a hoisting apparatus made from poles joined at or near the top and separated at the bottom, used for masting ships and lifting heavy objects.

sheesh /SHēSH/ ▶ **exclam.** used to express disbelief or exasperation.

sheet[1] /SHēt/ ▶ **n. 1** a large rectangular piece of cotton or other fabric, used on a bed to cover the mattress and as a layer beneath blankets. ■ used in comparisons to describe the pallor of a person who is ill or has had a shock: *You're as white as a sheet.* ■ a broad flat piece of material such as metal or glass. **2** a rectangular piece of paper, esp. one of a standard size used for writing and printing on. ■ a quantity of text or other information on such a piece of paper: *he produced yet another sheet of figures.* ■ a flat piece of paper as opposed to a reel of continuous paper, the bound pages of a book, or a folded map. ■ all the postage stamps printed on one piece of paper. ■ a map, esp. one part of a series covering a larger area. **3** an extensive unbroken surface area of something: *a sheet of ice.* ■ a broad moving mass of flames or water. ▶ **v. 1** [trans.] cover with or wrap in a sheet or sheets. **2** [intrans.] (of rain) fall in large quantities: *rain sheeted down.* [OE *scēte, scīete*, of Gmc. origin; rel. to the verb SHOOT in its primary sense 'to project.']

sheet[2] Naut. ▶ **n. 1** a rope attached to the lower corner of a sail for securing or extending the sail or for altering its direction. **2** (**sheets**) the space at the bow or stern of an open boat. ▶ **v.** [trans.] (**sheet something in/out**) make a sail more or less taut. ■ (**sheet something home**) extend a sail by tightening the sheets so that the sail is set as flat as possible.

– PHRASES **two** (or **three**) **sheets to the wind** informal drunk. [OE *scēata* 'lower corner of a sail,' of Gmc. origin; rel. to ON *skauti* 'kerchief' (see also SHEET[1]).]

sheet an·chor ▶ **n.** fig. a person or thing that is very dependable and relied upon in the last resort. [15th C. (denoting an additional anchor for use in emergencies): perh. rel. to obs. *shot*, denoting two cables spliced together, later influenced by SHEET[2].]

sheet bend ▶ **n.** a knot used for temporarily fastening one rope through the loop of another.

sheet feed·er ▶ **n.** Comput. a device for feeding paper into a printer a sheet at a time.

sheet·ing /ˈSHētiNG/ ▶ **n.** material formed into or used as a sheet: *a window covered with plastic sheeting.*

sheet light·ning ▶ **n.** lightning with its brightness diffused by reflection within clouds.

sheet met·al ▶ **n.** metal formed into thin sheets, typically by rolling or hammering.

sheet mu·sic ▶ **n.** printed music, as opposed to performed or recorded music. ■ music published in single or interleaved sheets, not bound.

Sheet·rock /ˈSHētˌräk/ ▶ **n.** trademark a plasterboard made of gypsum layered between sheets of heavy paper.

Shef·field /ˈSHefēld/ a city in northern England; pop. 500,000.

sheikh /SHēk; SHāk/ (also **sheik, shaikh,** or **shaykh**) ▶ **n. 1** an Arab leader, in particular the chief or head of an Arab tribe, family, or village. **2** a leader in a Muslim community or organization. — **sheikh·dom** /-dəm/ **n.** [16th C.: based on Arab. *šayḵ* 'old man, sheikh,' from *šāḵa* 'be or grow old.']

shei·tel /ˈSHātl; ˈSHītl/ ▶ **n.** (among Orthodox Ashkenazic Jews) a wig worn by a married woman. [19th C.: from Yiddish *sheytl*, from a Gmc. base meaning 'crown of the head.']

shek·el /ˈSHekəl/ ▶ **n.** the basic monetary unit of modern Israel, equal to 100 agora. ■ hist. a silver coin and unit of weight used in ancient Israel and the Middle East. ■ (**shekels**) informal money; wealth. [from Heb. *šeqel*, from *šāqal* 'weigh.']

She·ki·nah /SHəKHēˈnä; -ˈKHēnə; SHiˈkēnə; -ˈkī-/ (also **She·khi·nah**) ▶ **n.** Jewish & Christian Theol. the glory of the divine presence, conventionally represented as light. [17th C.: from late Heb., from *šākan* 'dwell, rest.']

shel·duck /ˈSHelˌdək/ ▶ **n.** (pl. same or **-ducks**) a large gooselike Old World duck (genus *Tadorna*) with brightly colored plumage, typically showing black and white wings in flight. [18th C.: prob. from dial. *sheld* 'pied' (rel. to MDu. *schillede* 'variegated') + DUCK[1].]

shelf /SHelf/ ▶ n. (pl. **shelves** /SHelvz/) a flat length of wood or rigid material, attached to a wall or forming part of a piece of furniture, that provides a surface for the storage or display of objects. ■ a ledge of rock or protruding strip of land. ■ a submarine bank, or a part of the continental shelf.
– PHRASES **off the shelf** not designed or made to order but taken from existing stock or supplies. **on the shelf** (of people or things) no longer useful or desirable: *an injury that has kept him on the shelf*. — **shelf·ful** /-ˌfo͝ol/ n. (pl. **-fuls**) **shelf·like** /-ˌlīk/ adj. [ME: from Mid. Low Ger. *schelf*; rel. to OE *scylfe* 'partition,' *scylf* 'crag.']

shelf life ▶ n. the length of time for which an item remains usable, fit for consumption, or saleable.

shell /SHel/ ▶ n. **1** the hard protective outer case of a mollusk or crustacean. ■ the thin outer covering of a bird's or reptile's egg. ■ the outer case of a nut kernel or seed. ■ the carapace of a tortoise, turtle, or terrapin. ■ the wing cases of a beetle. ■ the integument of an insect pupa or chrysalis. ■ (**one's shell**) fig. used with reference to a state of shyness or introversion: *she'll soon* ***come out of her shell*** *with the right encouragement.* **2** something resembling or likened to a shell because of its shape or its function as an outer case: *pasta shells.* ■ the walls of an unfinished or gutted building or other structure. ■ fig. an outer form without substance: *he was a shell of the man.* ■ a light racing boat used in the sport of crew. ■ a woman's sleeveless sweater or blouse. ■ the metal framework of a vehicle body. ■ an inner or roughly made coffin. ■ the handguard of a sword. ■ Physics each of a set of orbitals around the nucleus of an atom, occupied or able to be occupied by electrons of similar energies. **3** an explosive artillery projectile or bomb. ■ a hollow metal or paper case used as a container for fireworks, explosives, or cartridges. ■ a cartridge. **4** Comput. short for SHELL PROGRAM. ▶ v. **1** [trans.] bombard with shells. **2** [trans.] remove the shell or pod from (a nut or seed). **3** [intrans.] gather seashells.
– PHRASAL VERBS **shell something out** (or **shell out**) informal pay a specified amount of money, esp. an amount that is resented as being excessive. — **shelled** adj. [in comb.] *a soft-shelled clam.* **shell-less** adj. **shell-like** /-ˌlīk/ adj. **shell·y** /'SHelē/ adj. [OE *scell* (n.), of Gmc. origin; rel. to Du. *schel* 'scale, shell,' also to SCALE[1]. The verb dates from the mid 16th C. in sense 2.]

she'll /SHēl/ ▶ contr. she shall; she will.

shel·lac /SHə'lak/ ▶ n. lac resin melted into thin flakes, used for making varnish. ■ a thin varnish containing this resin. ▶ v. (**-lacked** /-'lakt/, **-lack·ing** /-'lakiNG/) [trans.] **1** [often as adj.] (**shellacked**) varnish (something) with shellac. **2** (usu. **be shellacked**) informal defeat or beat (someone) decisively: *they were shellacked in the election.* [17th C.: from SHELL + LAC[1], translating Fr. *laque en écailles* 'lac in thin plates.']

shell·back /'SHelˌbak/ ▶ n. informal an old or experienced sailor, esp. one who has crossed the equator.

shell com·pa·ny ▶ n. an inactive company used as a vehicle for various financial maneuvers or kept dormant for future use in some other capacity.

Shel·ley /'SHelē/ English literary figures. Percy Bysshe (1792–1822) was a major Romantic poet whose works include *Queen Mab* (1813) and *Prometheus Unbound* (1820). His wife, Mary Wollstonecraft Godwin (1797–1851), daughter of William Godwin and Mary Wollstonecraft, wrote the novel *Frankenstein, or the Modern Prometheus* (1818).

shell·fire /'SHelˌfī(ə)r/ ▶ n. bombardment by artillery shells.

shell·fish /'SHelˌfiSH/ ▶ n. (pl. same) an aquatic shelled mollusk (e.g., an oyster or cockle) or a crustacean (e.g., a crab or shrimp), esp. one that is edible. ■ such mollusks or crustaceans as food.

shell game ▶ n. a game involving sleight of hand, in which three inverted cups or nutshells are moved about, and contestants must spot which is the one with a pea or other object underneath. ■ a deceptive and evasive action or ploy, esp. a political one.

shell jack·et ▶ n. an army officer's tight-fitting undress jacket reaching to the waist.

shell pink ▶ n. a delicate pale pink.

shell pro·gram ▶ n. Comput. a program that provides an interface between the user and the operating system.

shell shock ▶ n. psychological disturbance caused by prolonged exposure to active warfare, esp. being under bombardment. Also called COMBAT FATIGUE. — **shell-shocked** adj. [World War I: with ref. to exposure to shellfire.]

shell·work /'SHelˌwərk/ ▶ n. ornamentation consisting of shells cemented on to a surface.

Shel·ta /'SHeltə/ ▶ n. an ancient secret language used by Irish and Welsh tinkers and gypsies, and based largely on altered Irish or Gaelic words. [19th C.: of unknown origin.]

shel·ter /'SHeltər/ ▶ n. a place giving temporary protection from bad weather or danger. ■ a place providing food and accommodations for the homeless. ■ an animal sanctuary. ■ a shielded or safe condition; protection. ▶ v. [trans.] protect or shield from something harmful, esp. bad weather. ■ [intrans.] find refuge or take cover from bad weather or danger. ■ prevent (someone) from having to do or face something difficult or unpleasant: [as adj.] (**sheltered**) *she led a sheltered life.* ■ protect (income) from taxation: *only your rental income can be sheltered.* — **shel·ter·er** n. **shel·ter·less** adj. [16th C.: perh. an alt. of obs. *sheltron* 'phalanx,' from OE *scieldtruma*, lit. 'shield troop.']

shel·ter belt ▶ n. a line of trees or shrubs planted to protect an area, esp. a field of crops, from fierce weather.

shel·tered work·shop ▶ n. a supervised workplace for physically disabled or mentally handicapped adults.

shel·tie /'SHeltē/ (also **shel·ty**) ▶ n. (pl. **-ties**) a Shetland pony or sheepdog. [17th C.: prob. representing an Orkney pronunc. of ON *Hjalti* 'Shetlander.']

Shel·ton /'SHeltn/ a city in southwestern Connecticut; pop. 35,418.

shelve[1] /SHelv/ ▶ v. [trans.] **1** place or arrange (items, esp. books) on a shelf. ■ fig. decide not to proceed with (a project or plan), either temporarily or permanently: *plans to reopen the school have been shelved.* **2** fit with shelves. — **shelv·er** n. [16th C. (in the sense 'project like a shelf' (Shakespearean usage)): from *shelves*, pl. of SHELF.]

shelve[2] ▶ v. [intrans.] (of ground) slope downward in a specified manner or direction: *the ground shelved gently down to the water.* [ME: origin uncert.; perh. from SHELF.]

shelves /SHelvz/ plural form of SHELF.

shelv·ing /'SHelviNG/ ▶ n. shelves collectively. ■ the action of shelving something.

Shem /SHem/ (in the Bible) a son of Noah, traditional ancestor of the Semites.

She·ma /SHə'mä/ a Hebrew text consisting of three passages from the Pentateuch and beginning "Hear, O Israel, the Lord is our God, the Lord is one." [Heb., lit. 'hear,' the first word of Deut. 6:4.]

she-male (also **she·male**) ▶ n. informal a transvestite. ■ a passive male homosexual. ■ a hermaphrodite.

Shen·an·do·ah /ˌSHenən'dōə/ a river that flows from Virginia to join the Potomac River at Harpers Ferry.

Shen·an·do·ah Na·tion·al Park a national park in the Blue Ridge Mountains of northern Virginia, southeast of the Shenandoah River. It was established in 1935.

she·nan·i·gans /SHə'nanəgənz/ ▶ plural n. informal secret or dishonest activity or maneuvering. ■ silly or high-spirited behavior; mischief. [19th C.: of unknown origin.]

Shen·yang /'SHen'yaNG; 'SHən'yäNG/ a city in northeastern China; pop. 4,500,000. Former name MUKDEN.

Shen·zhen /'SHen'ZHen; -'zen; 'SHən'jən/ a city in southern China; pop. 875,000.

She·ol /'SHēˌōl; SHē'ōl/ the Hebrew underworld, abode of the dead. [Heb.]

Shep·herd /'SHepərd/, Michael, see LUDLUM.

shep·herd /'SHepərd/ ▶ n. a person who tends and rears sheep. ■ fig. a member of the clergy who provides spiritual care and guidance for a congregation. ■ short for GERMAN SHEPHERD. ▶ v. [trans.] [usu. as n.] (**shepherding**) tend (sheep) as a shepherd. ■ guide or direct in a particular direction: *we were shepherded around with great ceremony.* ■ give guidance to (someone), esp. on spiritual matters. [OE *scēaphierde*, from SHEEP + obs. *herd* 'herdsman.']

shep·herd dog ▶ n. a sheepdog.

shep·herd·ess /'SHepərdis/ ▶ n. a female shepherd. ■ an idealized or romanticized rustic maiden in pastoral literature.

shep·herd's crook ▶ n. a staff with a hook at one end used by shepherds.

shep·herd's nee·dle ▶ n. a white-flowered Eurasian plant (*Scandix pecten-veneris*) of the parsley family, with long, needle-shaped fruit.

shep·herd's pie ▶ n. a dish of ground meat under a layer of mashed potato.

shep·herd's plaid (also **shepherd's check**) ▶ n. a small black-and-white check pattern. ■ woolen cloth with this pattern.

shep·herd's purse ▶ n. a widely distributed white-flowered weed (*Capsella bursa-pastoris*) of the cabbage family, with triangular or heart-shaped seedpods.

Sher·a·ton /'SHerətn/ ▶ adj. [attrib.] (of furniture) designed, made by, or in the style of the English furniture maker Thomas Sheraton (1751–1806).

sher·bet /'SHərbit/ ▶ n. a frozen dessert made with fruit juice added to milk or cream, egg white, or gelatin. ■ a frozen fruit juice and sugar mixture served as a dessert or between courses of a meal to cleanse the palate. [17th C.: from Turk. *şerbet*, Pers. *šerbet*, from Arab. *šarba* 'drink,' from *šariba* 'to drink.' Cf. SYRUP.]

sherd /SHərd/ ▶ n. another term for POTSHERD.

she·reef /SHə'rēf/ (also **she·rif**) ▶ n. var. of SHARIF.

Sher·i·dan[1] /'SHeridn/, Philip Henry (1831–88), Union general in the American Civil War. In April 1865, he cut off the Confederate retreat at Appomattox and forced the surrender of General Robert E. Lee.

Sher·i·dan[2], Richard Brinsley (1751–1816), Irish playwright. His plays *The Rivals* (1775) and *The School for Scandal* (1777) epitomize the comedy of manners.

sher·iff /'SHerif/ ▶ n. (in the US) an elected officer in a county who is responsible for keeping the peace. ■ (also **high sheriff**) (in England and Wales) the chief executive officer of the Crown in a county, having various administrative and judicial functions. — **sher·iff·dom** /-dəm/ n.

[OE *scīrgerēfa* (see **SHIRE, REEVE¹**).]

Sher·lock /'SHər,läk/ ▶**n.** informal a person who investigates mysteries or shows great perceptiveness. [20th C.: from *Sherlock* Holmes (see **HOLMES²**).]

Sher·man¹ /'SHərmən/ a city in northeastern Texas; pop. 31,601.

Sher·man², Roger (1721–93), American politician. He signed the Articles of Association 1774, the Declaration of Independence 1776, the Articles of Confederation 1777, and the Constitution 1787.

Sher·man³, William Tecumseh (1820–91), Union general in the American Civil War. In 1864, he set out with 60,000 men on a "March to the Sea" through Georgia, during which he crushed Confederate forces.

Sher·man tank ▶**n.** an American type of medium tank, used in large numbers during World War II.

Sher·pa /'SHərpə/ ▶**n.** (pl. same or **-pas**) a member of a Himalayan people living on the borders of Nepal and Tibet, renowned for their skill in mountaineering. [from Tibetan *sharpa* 'inhabitant of an eastern country.']

Sher·ring·ton /'SHəriNGtən/, Sir Charles Scott (1857–1952), English physiologist. He contributed greatly to the understanding of the nervous system. Nobel Prize for Physiology or Medicine (1932).

sher·ry /'SHerē/ ▶**n.** (pl. **-ries**) a fortified wine originally and mainly from southern Spain, often drunk as an aperitif. [16th C.: alt. of archaic *sherris*, interpreted as pl., from Sp. *(vino de) Xeres* 'Xeres (wine)' (Xeres being the former name of **JEREZ**).]

she's /SHēz/ ▶**contr.** she is; she has.

Shet·land Is·lands /'SHetlənd/ (also **Shet·land** or **the Shet·lands**) a group of about 100 islands off the north coast of Scotland that constitute the administrative region of Shetland; pop. 22,000; chief town, Lerwick. — **Shet·land·er n.**

Shet·land po·ny ▶**n.** a pony of a small, hardy, rough-coated breed.

Shet·land sheep·dog ▶**n.** a small dog of a collielike breed.

Shet·land wool ▶**n.** a type of fine loosely twisted wool from Shetland sheep.

Shev·ard·na·dze /,SHevərd'nädzə/, Eduard Amvrosievich (1928–), president of Georgia 1995–2003. A prominent Soviet Communist, he was Gorbachev's minister of foreign affairs 1985–1990.

She·vat /SHə'vät/ (also **She·bat**) ▶**n.** var. of **SEBAT**.

shew /SHō/ ▶**v.** old-fashioned var. of **SHOW**.

shew·bread /'SHō,bred/ ▶**n.** twelve loaves placed every Sabbath in the Jewish Temple and eaten by the priests at the end of the week. [16th C.: suggested by Ger. *Schaubrot*, representing Heb. *leḥem pānīm*, lit. 'bread of the face (of God).']

shf (also **SHF**) ▶**abbr.** superhigh frequency.

shh /SH/ (also **sh**) ▶**exclam.** used to call for silence: *"Shh! Keep your voice down!"* [19th C.: var. of **HUSH**.]

Shi·a /'SHē,ä/ (also **Shi'a**) ▶**n.** (pl. same or **Shi·as**) one of the two main branches of Islam, followed esp. in Iran, that rejects the first three Sunni caliphs and regards Ali, the fourth caliph, as Muhammad's first true successor. Compare with **SUNNI**. ■ a Muslim who adheres to this branch of Islam. ▶**adj.** of or relating to Shia. [from Arab. *šī'a* 'party (of Ali).']

shi·at·su /SHē'ätsōō/ ▶**n.** a form of therapy of Japanese origin based on the same principles as acupuncture, in which pressure is applied to certain points on the body using the hands. [1960s: Japanese, lit. 'finger pressure.']

shib·bo·leth /'SHibəliTH; -,leTH/ ▶**n.** a custom, principle, or belief distinguishing a class or group of people. [17th C.: from Heb. *šibbōleṯ* 'ear of corn,' used as a test of nationality by its difficult pronunc. (Judg. 12:6).]

shick·er /'SHikər/ (also **shik·ker**) informal ▶**adj.** (also **shick·ered** /-ərd/, **shik·kered**) [predic.] drunk. ▶**n.** a drunk. [19th C.: from Yiddish *shiker*, from Heb. *šikkōr*, from *šākar* 'be drunk.']

shied /SHīd/ past and past participle of **SHY²**.

shield /SHēld/ ▶**n.** **1** a broad piece of metal or another suitable material, held by straps or a handle attached on one side, used as a protection against blows or missiles. **2** something shaped like a shield, in particular: ■ a sports trophy consisting of an engraved metal plate mounted on a piece of wood. ■ a police officer's badge. ■ Heraldry a stylized representation of a shield for displaying a coat of arms. ■ Geol. a large rigid area of the earth's crust, typically of Precambrian rock, unaffected by later orogenic episodes, e.g., the Canadian Shield. **3** a person or thing providing protection. ■ a protective plate or screen on machinery or equipment: *a face shield is sometimes an integral part of a safety helmet.* ■ a device or material that prevents or reduces the emission of light or other radiation: *water is a relatively good shield against cosmic rays.* ■ short for **DRESS SHIELD**. ■ a hard flat or convex part of an animal, esp. a shell. ▶**v.** [trans.] protect (someone or something) from a danger, risk, or unpleasant experience: *detectives last night appealed to anyone shielding the murderer* | [as adj., with submodifier] (**shielded**) *a heavily shielded coaxial cable.* ■ prevent from being seen: *the rocks she sat behind shielded her from the lodge.* ■ enclose or screen (a piece of machinery) to protect the user: *cylindrical ducts shield the propellers.* ■ prevent or reduce the escape of sound, light, or other radiation from (something). — **shield·less adj.** [OE *scild* (n.), *scildan* (v.), from Gmc.; akin to Ger. *Schild*, from base meaning 'to divide.']

shield bug ▶**n.** another term for **STINK BUG**.

shield fern ▶**n.** any of a number of ferns that have circular shield-like scales protecting the spore cases, in particular: ■ a European fern (genus *Polystichum*, family Dryopteridaceae) of damp woodland. ■ a North American evergreen fern (genus *Thelypteris*, family Thelypteridaceae).

shield law ▶**n.** a law that protects witnesses from revealing certain information, esp. in court. ■ a law that protects journalists from having to reveal confidential sources. ■ a law that protects rape victims from having to reveal details of their sexual history.

shield·tail snake /'SHēl(d),tāl/ (also **shield-tailed snake**) ▶**n.** a burrowing snake (*Rhinophis*, *Uropeltis*, and other genera, family Uropeltidae) that has a flat disk formed from an enlarged scale on the upper surface of the tail, native to the rain forests of southern India and Sri Lanka.

shield vol·ca·no ▶**n.** Geol. a broad, domed volcano with gently sloping sides, characteristic of the eruption of fluid, basaltic lava.

shiel·ing /'SHēliNG/ ▶**n.** Scot. a roughly constructed hut used while pasturing animals. ■ an area of pasture. [16th C.: from Scots *shiel* 'hut.']

shift /SHift/ ▶**v.** move or cause to move from one place to another, esp. over a small distance: [trans.] *I shift the weight back to the other leg* | [intrans.] *the roof cracked and shifted.* ■ [intrans.] change the position of one's body, esp. because one is nervous or uncomfortable: *they were shifting from foot to foot.* ■ [trans.] change the emphasis, direction, or focus of: *she's shifting the blame onto me.* ■ [intrans.] change in emphasis, direction, or focus: *the wind had shifted to the east* | *an attempt was made to shift back toward lighter industries.* ■ (**shift oneself**) [in imper.] Brit. informal used to tell someone to move from a place or rouse themselves from a state of inactivity: *shift yourself, Ruby, do something useful and get the plates.* ■ [trans.] Comput. move (data) to the right or left in a register: *the partial remainder is shifted left.* ■ [intrans.] press the shift key on a typewriter or computer keyboard. ■ [trans.] informal sell (something): *product you don't know how to shift.* ■ [intrans.] change gear in a vehicle: *she shifted down to fourth.* ■ [intrans.] archaic be evasive or indirect: *they know not how to shift and rob as the old ones do.* ▶**n.** **1** a slight change in position, direction, or tendency. ■ Astron. the displacement of spectral lines. See also **REDSHIFT**. ■ (also **shift key**) a key on a typewriter or computer keyboard used to switch between two sets of characters or functions, principally between lower- and upper-case letters. ■ the gearshift or gear-changing mechanism in a motor vehicle. ■ Building the positioning of successive rows of bricks so that their ends do not coincide. ■ Comput. a movement of the digits of a word in a register one or more places to left or right, equivalent to multiplying or dividing the corresponding number by a power of whatever number is the base. ■ Football a change of position by two or more players before the ball is put into play. **2** one of two or more recurring periods in which different groups of workers do the same jobs in relay: *they work three shifts—morning, afternoon, and evening.* ■ a group of workers who work in this way. **3** (also **shift dress**) a woman's straight, unwaisted dress. ■ hist. a long, loose-fitting undergarment. **4** archaic an ingenious or devious device or stratagem.

– PHRASES **make shift** do what one wants to do in spite of not having ideal conditions: *they could* **make shift** *with constitutions and parliaments.* **shift for oneself** manage as best one can without help: *the least and the most able were left to shift for themselves.* **shift one's ground** say or write something that contradicts something one has previously written or said. **shifting sands** something constantly changing, esp. unpredictably. — **shift·a·ble** /'SHiftəbəl/ **adj.** [OE *sciftan* 'arrange, divide,' from Gmc.; akin to Ger. *schichten* 'to layer.']

shift·er /'SHiftər/ ▶**n.** [usu. in comb.] a person or thing that shifts something. ■ a gearbox of a motor vehicle or a set of gear levers on a bicycle.

shift·ing cul·ti·va·tion (also **shifting agriculture**) ▶**n.** a form of agriculture, used esp. in tropical Africa, in which an area of ground is cleared of vegetation and cultivated for a few years and then abandoned for a new area until its fertility has been naturally restored.

shift·less /'SHiftlis/ ▶**adj.** (of a person or action) characterized by laziness and a lack of ambition. — **shift·less·ly adv. shift·less·ness n.**

shift reg·is·ter ▶**n.** Comput. a register designed to allow the bits of its contents to be moved to left or right.

shift work ▶**n.** work comprising recurring periods in which groups of workers do the same jobs in rotation.

shift·y /'SHiftē/ ▶**adj.** (**shift·i·er**, **shift·i·est**) informal **1** (of a person or their manner) appearing deceitful or evasive: *he seems so shifty—he won't meet my eyes.* **2** constantly changing; shifting: *it was a close race in a shifty wind on smooth water.* — **shift·i·ly** /-əlē/ **adv. shift·i·ness n.**

shi·gel·la /SHə'gelə/ ▶**n.** a bacterium (genus *Shigella*) that is an intestinal pathogen of humans and other primates, some kinds of which cause dysentery. [mod. L., from Kiyoshi *Shiga* (1870–1957), Japanese bacteriologist.]

Shih Tzu /'SHē 'dzōō/ ▶**n.** a dog of a breed with long, silky, erect hair and short legs. [1920s: from Chin. *shizi* 'lion.']

shi·i·ta·ke /SHē'täkē; SHē-ē'täke/ (also **shiitake mushroom**) ▶**n.** an edible mushroom (*Lentinus edodes*, family Pleurotaceae) that grows on fallen timber, cultivated in Japan and China. [19th C.: from Japanese, from *shii*, a kind of oak, + *take* 'mushroom.']

Shi·ite /'SHē,īt/ (also **Shi'ite**) ▶**n.** an adherent of the Shia branch of Islam. ▶**adj.** of or relating to Shia: *Shiite fundamentalist groups.* — **Shi·ism** /'SHē,izəm/ (also **Shi'ism**) **n.**

Shi·jia·zhuang /'SHœ'jyä'jwäNG/ a city in northeast central China; pop. 1,320,000.

shi·kar /SHi'kär/ ▶**n.** Indian hunting as a sport. [from Urdu and Pers. *šikār*.]

shi·ka·ri /sʜiˈkärē/ ▸ **n.** (pl. **-ris**) Indian **1** a hunter. ■ a guide on hunting expeditions. **2** (also **shi·ka·ra**) (in Kashmir) a light, flat-bottomed boat. [via Urdu from Pers. *šikārī* 'of hunting.']

shik·ker /ˈsʜikər/ ▸ **adj. & n.** var. of SHICKER.

Shi·ko·ku /sʜiˈkō,ko͞o/ the smallest of the four main islands of Japan, an administrative region; pop. 4,195,000; capital, Matsuyama.

shik·ra /ˈsʜikrə/ ▸ **n.** a small, stocky sparrow hawk (esp. *Accipter badius*) found in Africa and Central and South Asia. [19th C.: from Pers. and Urdu *šikara*.]

shik·sa /ˈsʜiksə/ ▸ **n.** often derog. (used esp. by Jews) a gentile girl or woman: *he's got a big blonde on his arm—a shiksa no less* | [as adj.] *your sister has a classic shiksa face.* [19th C.: from Yiddish *shikse*, from Heb. *šiqṣāh* (from *šeqeṣ* 'detested thing').]

shill /sʜil/ informal ▸ **n.** an accomplice of a hawker, gambler, or swindler who acts as an enthusiastic customer to entice or encourage others: *I used to be a shill in a Reno gambling club* | fig. *the agency is a shill for the nuclear power industry.* ▸ **v.** [intrans.] act or work as such a person: *your husband in the crowd could shill for you.* [20th C.: prob. from earlier *shillaber*.]

shil·le·lagh /sʜəˈlālē/ ▸ **n.** a thick stick of blackthorn or oak used in Ireland, typically as a weapon. [18th C.: *Shillelagh*, town in Ireland.]

shil·ling /ˈsʜiliNG/ ▸ **n. 1** a former British coin and monetary unit equal to one twentieth of a pound or twelve pence. **2** the basic monetary unit in Kenya, Tanzania, and Uganda, equal to 100 cents. [OE *scilling*, from Gmc.; akin to Ger. *Schilling*.]

Shil·luk /sʜəˈlo͝ok/ ▸ **n.** (pl. same or **-luks**) **1** a member of a Sudanese people living mainly on the west bank of the Nile. **2** the Nilotic language of this people. ▸ **adj.** of or relating to this people or their language. [Shilluk.]

shil·ly-shal·ly /ˈsʜilē,sʜalē/ ▸ **v.** (**-lies, -lied**) [intrans.] fail to act resolutely or decisively: [as n.] (**shilly-shallying**) *the bungling and shilly-shallying of the past year.* ▸ **n.** indecisive behavior: *a no-nonsense lack of shilly-shally.* ▸ **adj.** vacillating. — **shil·ly-shal·ly·er** /,sʜalēər/ (also **-shal·li·er**) **n.** [18th C.: originally *shill I, shall I*, reduplication of *shall I?*]

Shi·loh /ˈsʜīlō/ a historic site in southwestern Tennessee, site of a major Civil War battle in April 1862.

shim /sʜim/ ▸ **n.** a washer or thin strip of material used to align parts, make them fit, or reduce wear: *an aluminum shim reduces the diameter so that a standard stem will fit.* ▸ **v.** (**shimmed, shim·ming**) [trans.] wedge (something) or fill up (a space) with a shim: *display monitors were shimmed up on cardboard* | *you may have to shim the tube.* [18th C.: origin unknown.]

shim·mer /ˈsʜimər/ ▸ **v.** [intrans.] shine with a soft tremulous light: *a heat haze shimmered above the fields* | [as adj.] (**shimmering**) *shimmering candlelight.* ▸ **n.** [in sing.] a light with such qualities: *a pale shimmer of moonlight.* — **shim·mer·ing·ly adv. shim·mer·y adj.** [OE *scymrian* (v.), from Gmc.; akin to Ger. *schimmern* and SHINE.]

shim·my /ˈsʜimē/ ▸ **n.** (pl. **-mies**) **1** a kind of ragtime dance in which the whole body shakes or sways. ■ shaking, esp. abnormal vibration of the wheels of a motor vehicle. **2** archaic informal term for CHEMISE. ▸ **v.** (**-mies, -mied**) [intrans.] dance the shimmy. ■ shake or vibrate abnormally. ■ move with a graceful swaying motion: *she shimmied down the catwalk.* ■ move swiftly and effortlessly: *he shimmied to the top of the tree.* [20th C.: of unknown origin.]

shin /sʜin/ ▸ **n.** the front of the leg below the knee. ■ a cut of beef from the lower part of a cow's leg. ▸ **v.** (**shinned, shin·ning**) [intrans.] (**shin up/down**) climb quickly up or down by gripping with one's arms and legs: *he shinned up a tree.* [OE *scinu* (n.), prob. from Gmc., 'thin piece'; akin to Ger. *Schiene* 'thin plate.']

Shin Bet /,sʜin ,bet/ (also **Shin Beth**) the principal security service of Israel, concerned primarily with counter-espionage. [mod. Heb., initial letters of the first two words of *šērūṭ biṭṭāhōn kĕlālī* '(general) security service.']

shin·bone /ˈsʜin,bōn/ ▸ **n.** the tibia.

shin·dig /ˈsʜin,dig/ ▸ **n.** informal a large, lively party, esp. one celebrating something: *the glitziest of election night shindigs* | *our album launch shindig.* [19th C.: prob. from nouns SHIN, DIG.]

shin·dy /ˈsʜindē/ ▸ **n.** (pl. **-dies**) informal a noisy disturbance or quarrel. ■ a large, lively party.

shine /sʜīn/ ▸ **v.** (past **shone** /sʜōn/ or **shined**) **1** [intrans.] (of the sun or another source of light) give out a bright light: *the sun shone through the window.* ■ glow or be bright with reflected light: *I could see his eyes shining in the light of the fire.* ■ [trans.] direct (light) somewhere to see something in the dark: *an usher shines his flashlight into the boys' faces.* ■ (of something with a smooth surface) reflect light because clean or polished: *my shoes were polished until they shone like glass.* ■ (of a person's eyes) be bright with the expression of a particular emotion: *his eyes shone with excitement.* ■ [often as adj.] (**shining**) fig. be brilliant or excellent at something: *she shines at comedy.* ■ (**shine through**) fig. (of a quality or skill) be clearly evident: *at Regis his talent shone through.* **2** (past **shined**) [trans.] make (an object made of leather, metal, or wood) bright by rubbing it; polish. ▸ **n.** [in sing.] a quality of brightness, esp. through reflecting light. ■ a high polish or sheen; a luster: *my hair has lost its shine.* ■ an act of rubbing something to give it a shiny surface. ■ derog. a contemptuous term for a black or dark-skinned person.
– PHRASES **take the shine off** spoil the brilliance or excitement of. **take a shine to** informal develop a liking for. — **shin·ing·ly** /-niNGlē/ **adv.** [OE *scīnan*, from Gmc.; akin to Ger. *scheinen*.]

shin·er /ˈsʜīnər/ ▸ **n. 1** a thing that shines or reflects light. ■ [in comb.] a person or thing that polishes something: *shoeshiners.* **2** informal a black eye. **3** a small silvery North American freshwater fish (*Notropis* and other genera) of the minnow family that typically has colorful markings.

shin·gle¹ /ˈsʜiNGgəl/ ▸ **n.** a mass of small rounded pebbles, esp. on a seashore: *a wonderful beach of fine shingle* | [as adj.] *natural features like sand dunes and shingle banks.* — **shin·gly** /-g(ə)lē/ **adj.** [ME: origin unknown.]

shin·gle² ▸ **n. 1** a rectangular wooden, metal, or slate tile used on walls or roofs. **2** dated a woman's short haircut in which the hair tapers from the back of the head to the nape of the neck. **3** a small signboard, esp. one found outside a doctor's or lawyer's office. ▸ **v.** [trans.] **1** roof or clad with shingles. **2** dated cut (a woman's hair) in a shingle.
– PHRASES **hang out one's shingle** begin to practice a profession. [ME: prob. from L. *scindula*, earlier *scandula* 'split piece of wood.']

shin·gle·back /ˈsʜiNGgəl,bak/ (also **shingleback lizard**) ▸ **n.** a slow-moving, heavily built lizard (*Trachydosaurus rugosus*, family Scincidae) with scales resembling those of pine cones, occurring in arid regions of Australia.

shin·gles /ˈsʜiNGgəlz/ ▸ **plural n.** [treated as sing.] Med. an acute, painful inflammation of the nerve ganglia, with a skin eruption often forming a girdle around the middle of the body. It is caused by the same virus as chicken pox. Also called HERPES ZOSTER. [ME: representing med. L. *cingulus*, var. of L. *cingulum* 'girdle,' from *cingere* 'gird.']

shin guard ▸ **n.** a pad worn to protect the shins when playing soccer, hockey, and other sports.

Shin·ing Path a Peruvian Maoist revolutionary movement and terrorist organization, founded in 1970 and led by Abimael Guzmán (1934–) until his capture and imprisonment in 1992. [translating Sp. *Sendero Luminoso*.]

Shin·kan·sen /ˈsʜinkän,sen/ ▸ **n.** (pl. same) (in Japan) a railroad system carrying high-speed passenger trains. ■ (also **shin·kan·sen**) a train operating on such a system: *Shinkansen are fast, regular, and reliable* | *the campus is located northwest of Tokyo, 1 hour and 40 minutes* **by** *Shinkansen.* [Japanese, from *shin* 'new' + *kansen* 'main line.']

shin·ny¹ /ˈsʜinē/ ▸ **v.** (**-nies, -nied**) another term for SHIN. [19th C.: from the noun SHIN + -Y².]

shin·ny² (also **shinny hockey**) ▸ **n.** an informal form of ice hockey played esp. by children, on the street or on ice, often with a ball or other object in place of a puck: *we used to play shinny on the canal with tin cans.* [var. of *shinty*, a game resembling field hockey.]

Shi·no·la /sʜīˈnōlə/ ▸ **n.** trademark a brand of boot polish. ■ informal used as a euphemism for "shit."
– PHRASES **not know shit from Shinola** vulgar slang used to indicate that someone is ignorant or innocent. [20th C.: from SHINE + *-ola* (suffix).]

shin pad ▸ **n.** another term for SHIN GUARD.

shin·plas·ter /ˈsʜin,plastər/ ▸ **n.** hist. informal a piece of paper currency or a promissory note regarded as having little or no value: *"didn't they tell you we don't take no shinplasters here?"* [from the resemblance to a piece of paper used to bandage the shin.]

shin splints ▸ **plural n.** [treated as sing. or pl.] acute pain in the shin and lower leg caused by prolonged running, typically on hard surfaces.

Shin·to /ˈsʜin,tō/ ▸ **n.** a Japanese religion incorporating the worship of ancestors and nature spirits and a belief in sacred power (**kami**) in both animate and inanimate things. It was the state religion of Japan until 1945. See also AMATERASU. — **Shin·to·ism** /-,izəm/ **n. Shin·to·ist** /-ist/ **n.** [Japanese, from Chin. *shen dao* 'way of the gods.']

shin·y /ˈsʜīnē/ ▸ **adj.** (**shin·i·er, shin·i·est**) (of a smooth surface) reflecting light, typically because very clean or polished: *shiny hair* | *shiny black shoes.* ■ (of clothing, esp. the seat of trousers) having the nap worn off. — **shin·i·ly** /-əlē/ **adv. shin·i·ness n.**

ship /sʜip/ ▸ **n.** a vessel larger than a boat for transporting people or goods by sea. ■ a sailing vessel with a bowsprit and three or more square-rigged masts. ■ informal any boat, esp. a racing boat. ■ a spaceship. ■ an aircraft. ▸ **v.** (**shipped, ship·ping**) **1** [trans.] (often **be shipped**) transport (goods or people) on a ship: *the soldiers were shipped home.* ■ transport by some other means: *the freight would be shipped by rail.* ■ [trans.] send (a package) somewhere via the mail service or a private company. ■ deliver (goods) to a forwarding agent for conveyance. ■ [trans.] Electron. make (a product) available for purchase. ■ [intrans.] dated embark on a ship: *passengers ship at Liverpool.* ■ (of a sailor) serve on a ship: *Jack, you shipped with the Admiral once, didn't you?* **2** [trans.] (of a boat) take in (water) over the side: *their craft began to ship water and threatened to founder.* **3** [trans.] take (oars) from the oarlocks and lay them inside a boat. ■ fix (something such as a rudder or mast) in its place on a ship. ■ step (a mast).
– PHRASES **a sinking ship** used to describe a failing organization or endeavor, criticizing someone for leaving it. **ship out** (of a naval force or one of its members) go to sea from a home port: *Bob got sick a week before we shipped out.* **ship something out** send (goods) to a distributor or customer, esp. by ship. **take ship** set off on a voyage by ship; embark. **when someone's ship comes in** when someone's fortune is made. — **ship·less adj. ship·pa·ble adj.** [OE *scip* (n.), OE *scipian* (v.), from Gmc.; akin to Ger. *Schiff*.]

-ship ▶ suffix forming nouns: **1** denoting a quality or condition: *companionship* | *friendship.* **2** denoting status, office, or honor: *ambassadorship* | *citizenship.* ■ denoting a tenure of office: *chairmanship.* **3** denoting a skill in a certain capacity: *entrepreneurship.* **4** denoting the collective individuals of a group: *membership.* [OE *-scipe, -scype*, from Gmc.]

ship·board /ˈSHip,bôrd/ ▶ n. [as adj.] used or occurring on board a ship: *playing in a shipboard jazz orchestra.*

– PHRASES **on shipboard** on board a ship.

ship·build·er /ˈSHip,bildər/ ▶ n. a person or company whose job or business is the design and construction of ships. — **ship·build·ing** /-,bildiNG/ n.

ship ca·nal ▶ n. a canal wide and deep enough for ships to travel along it.

ship chan·dler ▶ n. see CHANDLER.

ship fit·ter ▶ n. a person employed to manufacture or assemble the structural parts of a ship.

ship·lap /ˈSHip,lap/ ▶ v. [trans.] fit (boards) together by halving so that each overlaps the one below. ▶ n. boards fitted together in this way, used for cladding. ■ [usu. as adj.] a joint between boards made by halving.

Ship·ley /ˈSHiplē/, Jenny (1952–), prime minister of New Zealand 1997–99; full name *Jennifer Mary Shipley.*

ship·load /ˈSHip,lōd/ ▶ n. as much cargo or as many people as a ship can carry.

ship·mas·ter /ˈSHip,mastər/ ▶ n. a ship's captain.

ship·mate /ˈSHip,māt/ ▶ n. a fellow member of a ship's crew.

ship·ment /ˈSHipmənt/ ▶ n. the action of shipping goods: *logs waiting for shipment.* ■ a quantity of goods shipped; a consignment.

ship of the des·ert ▶ n. literary a camel.

ship of the line ▶ n. hist. a sailing warship of the largest size, used in the line of battle.

ship·own·er /ˈSHip,ōnər/ ▶ n. a person or company owning a ship or a share in a ship.

ship·per /ˈSHipər/ ▶ n. a person or company that sends or transports goods by sea, land, or air. [OE *scipere* 'sailor.']

ship·ping /ˈSHipiNG/ ▶ n. ships considered collectively, esp. those in a particular area or belonging to a particular country: [as adj.] *the shipping forecast.* ■ the transport of goods by sea or some other means: *the shipping of his works abroad* | *wine shipping* | [as adj.] *a shipping company.* ■ a charge imposed by a retail company to send merchandise to a customer.

ship·ping a·gent ▶ n. a licensed agent in a port who transacts a ship's business, such as insurance or documentation, for the owner.

ship-rigged ▶ adj. (of a sailing ship) square-rigged.

Ship·rock /ˈSHip,räk/ an eroded volcanic feature that stands above the desert in northwestern New Mexico near the Four Corners. Sacred to the Navajo, it serves as a landmark for travelers.

ship's boat ▶ n. a small boat carried on board a ship.

ship's com·pa·ny ▶ n. the crew of a ship.

ship·shape /ˈSHip,SHāp/ ▶ adj. in good order; trim and neat: *there were enough volunteers to keep it operational, though not entirely shipshape.*

ship's pa·pers ▶ plural n. documents establishing the details of a ship, including ownership, nationality, and the nature of the cargo.

ship-to-shore ▶ adj. from a ship to land: *ship-to-shore phone calls.* ▶ n. a radiotelephone connecting a ship to land, or connecting a train or other vehicle to a control center.

ship·way /ˈSHip,wā/ ▶ n. a slope on which a ship is built and down which it slides to be launched.

ship·worm /ˈSHip,wərm/ ▶ n. another term for TEREDO.

ship·wreck /ˈSHip,rek/ ▶ n. the destruction of a ship at sea by sinking or breaking up: *these islands have a history of shipwrecks and smuggling* | fig. *by rejecting conscience, they have made a shipwreck of their faith.* ■ a ship so destroyed. ▶ v. (**be shipwrecked**) (of a person or ship) suffer a shipwreck: *he was shipwrecked off Sardinia* | fig. *her right to a fair trial might be shipwrecked by prosecutorial misconduct* | [as adj.] (**shipwrecked**) *she found herself clinging to the kitchen cabinet like a shipwrecked mariner to a rock.*

ship·wright /ˈSHip,rīt/ ▶ n. a shipbuilder. ■ a ship's carpenter.

ship·yard /ˈSHip,yärd/ ▶ n. a place where ships are built and repaired.

Shi·ras /ˈSHīrəs/, George, Jr. (1832–1924), US Supreme Court associate justice 1892–1903.

Shi·raz[1] /SHiˈräz/ a city in southwest central Iran; pop. 965,000. The city is noted for the school of miniature painting based there between the 14th and 16th centuries, and for the manufacture of carpets.

Shi·raz[2] ▶ n. a variety of black wine grape. ■ a red wine made from this grape. [alt. of Fr. *syrah*, influenced by SHIRAZ[1].]

shire /SHī(ə)r/ ▶ n. Brit. a county, esp. in England. ■ (**the Shires**) used in reference to parts of England regarded as strongholds of traditional rural culture, esp. the rural Midlands. ■ hist. an administrative district in medieval times ruled jointly by an alderman and a sheriff. [OE *scīr* 'care, county,' from Gmc.]

-shire ▶ comb. form forming the names of counties: *Oxfordshire* | *Yorkshire.*

shire horse ▶ n. a heavy powerful horse of a draft breed, originally from the English Midlands.

shirk /SHərk/ ▶ v. [trans.] avoid or neglect (a duty or responsibility): [intrans.] *she is neither shirking nor lying.* — **shirk·er** n. [17th C. ('practice fraud'): from obs. *shirk* 'sponger,' perh. from Ger. *Schurke* 'scoundrel.']

shirr /SHər/ ▶ v. [trans.] **1** gather (an area of fabric or part of a garment) by drawn or elasticized threads in parallel rows: [as adj.] (**shirred**) *a swimsuit with a shirred front.* **2** bake (an egg without its shell). [19th C.: origin unknown.]

shirt /SHərt/ ▶ n. a garment for the upper body made of cloth, with a collar, sleeves, and buttons down the front. ■ [usu. with adj.] a similar garment of stretchable material with few or no buttons, typically worn as casual wear or for sports.

– PHRASES **keep your shirt on** informal don't lose your temper; stay calm. **lose one's shirt** informal lose all one's possessions. **the shirt off one's back** informal one's last remaining possessions. — **shirt·ed** adj. [often in comb.] *the black-shirted balladeer.* **shirt·less** adj. [OE *scyrte*, of Gmc. origin; rel. to SKIRT and SHORT; prob. from a base meaning 'short garment.']

shirt·dress /ˈSHərt,dres/ ▶ n. a dress with a collar and buttons in the style of a shirt, typically cut without a seam at the waist.

shirt·front /ˈSHərt,frənt/ ▶ n. the breast of a shirt, in particular the part that shows when a suit is worn.

shirt·ing /ˈSHərtiNG/ ▶ n. a material for making shirts.

shirt·sleeve /ˈSHərt,slēv/ ▶ n. (usu. **shirtsleeves**) the sleeve of a shirt. ▶ adj. **1** (of weather) warm enough to wear a shirt with no jacket. **2** (of work or an atmosphere) straightforward and unpretentious, with hard work being done.

– PHRASES **in (one's) shirtsleeves** wearing a shirt with nothing over it. — **shirt·sleeved** adj.

shirt·tail /ˈSHərt,tāl/ ▶ n. (also **shirt·tails**) the lower, typically curved, part of a shirt that comes below the waist. ▶ adj. (of relatives) distantly related: *they were shirttail cousins of Curly's parents.*

shirt·waist /ˈSHərt,wāst/ ▶ n. a woman's blouse that resembles a shirt. ■ (also **shirt·waist dress** or **shirt·waist·er**) a woman's dress with a seam at the waist, its bodice incorporating a collar and buttons in the style of a shirt.

shirt·y /ˈSHərtē/ ▶ adj. (**shirt·i·er, shirt·i·est**) informal irritable; querulous: *don't get annoyed or shirty on the phone.* — **shirt·i·ly** /-əlē/ adv. **shirt·i·ness** n.

shish ke·bab /ˈSHiSH kə,bäb/ ▶ n. a dish of pieces of marinated meat and vegetables cooked and served on skewers. [from Turk. *şiş kebap*, from *şiş* 'skewer' + *kebāp* 'roast meat.']

shit /SHit/ vulgar slang ▶ v. (**shit·ting** ; past and past part. **shit·ted** or **shit** or **shat** /SHat/) [intrans.] expel feces from the body. ■ (**shit oneself**) soil one's clothes as a result of expelling feces accidentally. ■ (**shit oneself**) fig. be very frightened. ▶ n. feces. ■ [in sing.] an act of defecating. ■ a contemptible or worthless person. ■ something worthless; garbage; nonsense. ■ unpleasant experiences or treatment. ■ personal belongings; stuff. ■ any psychoactive drug, e.g., marijuana. ▶ exclam. an exclamation of disgust, anger, or annoyance.

– PHRASES **beat the shit out of** see BEAT. **be shitting bricks** be extremely nervous or frightened. **eat shit** an exclamation expressing anger or contempt for, or rejection of, someone. **get one's shit together** organize oneself to be able to deal with or achieve something. **in deep shit** (or **in the shit**) in a difficult situation. **no shit** used to seek confirmation of the truth of a statement or to confirm the truth of a statement. **not give a shit** not care at all. **not know shit** not know anything. **not worth a shit** worthless. **shit for brains** a stupid person. **shit on someone** show contempt or disregard for someone. **be up shit creek** (**without a paddle**) be in an awkward predicament. **when the shit hits the fan** when the disastrous consequences of something become public. [OE *scitte* 'diarrhea,' from Gmc. origin; akin to Ger. *scheissen* (v.).]

shit·bag /ˈSHit,bag/ ▶ n. vulgar slang a contemptible or worthless person.

shite /SHīt/ ▶ n. & exclam. Brit., vulgar slang another term for SHIT.

shit-eat·ing ▶ adj. vulgar slang smug; self-satisfied: *Philip comes strolling in with a shit-eating grin on his face.*

shite·poke /ˈSHīt,pōk/ ▶ n. informal any of a number of birds of the heron family, in particular the green-backed *Butorides striatus.* [18th C.: from SHITE (from its habit of defecating when disturbed) + POKE[1] (n.).]

shit·face /ˈSHit,fās/ ▶ n. vulgar slang an obnoxious person.

shit-faced (also **shit·faced**) ▶ adj. [predic.] vulgar slang drunk or under the influence of drugs.

shit·head /ˈSHit,hed/ ▶ n. vulgar slang a contemptible person.

shit·hole /ˈSHit,hōl/ ▶ n. vulgar slang an extremely dirty, shabby, or otherwise unpleasant place.

shit·house /ˈSHit,hous/ ▶ n. vulgar slang a toilet. ■ fig. an extremely unpleasant place.

– PHRASES **be built like a brick shithouse** **1** (of a person) having a very solid physique. **2** (of a woman) having a very attractive figure.

shit·kick·er /ˈSHit,kikər/ ▶ n. vulgar slang **1** an unsophisticated or oafish person, esp. one from a rural area. **2** a person who listens to or performs country music. **3** (**shitkickers**) substantially made boots with thick soles and typically with reinforced toes. — **shit-kick·ing** /-,kikiNG/ adj.

shit·less /ˈSHitlis/ ▶ adj. (in phrase **be scared** (or **bored**) **shitless**) vulgar slang be extremely frightened (or bored).

shit list (also **shit·list**) ▶ n. vulgar slang a list of those whom one dislikes or plans to harm: *he was unaware of how deeply he had plunged on her shitlist.*

shit-scared ▶ **adj.** vulgar slang terrified.

shit stir·rer ▶ **n.** vulgar slang a person who takes pleasure in causing trouble or discord. — **shit stir·ring n.**

shit·ty /ˈSHitē/ ▶ **adj.** (**-ti·er, -ti·est**) vulgar slang **1** (of a person or action) contemptible; worthless. ■ (of an experience or situation) unpleasant; awful. **2** covered with excrement.

shit·work /ˈSHit,wərk/ ▶ **n.** vulgar slang work considered to be menial or routine.

shi·ur /SHēˈo͝or/ ▶ **n.** (pl. **shi·u·rim** /SHēˈo͝orim; SHē-o͝oˈrēm/) Judaism a Talmudic study session, usually led by a rabbi.

shiv /SHiv/ ▶ **n.** informal a knife or razor used as a weapon. [prob. from Romany *chiv* 'blade.']

Shi·va /ˈSHēvə/ (also **Si·va**) (in Indian religion) a god associated with the powers of reproduction and dissolution. [from Sanskrit *Śiva*, lit. 'the auspicious one.']

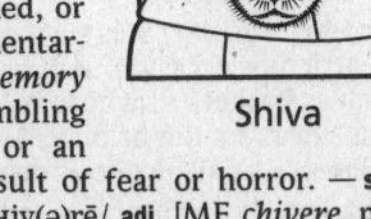
Shiva

shi·va /ˈSHivə/ (also **shi·vah**) ▶ **n.** Judaism a period of seven days' formal mourning for the dead, beginning immediately after the funeral: *she went to her sister's funeral and sat shiva.* [from Heb. *šiḇʿâh* 'seven.']

shiv·a·ree ▶ **n.** var. of **CHARIVARI.**

shiv·er[1] /ˈSHivər/ ▶ **v.** [intrans.] (of a person or animal) shake slightly and uncontrollably as a result of being cold, frightened, or excited. ■ (of a person) tremble momentarily; shudder: *she shivered, a sudden memory seizing her.* ▶ **n.** a momentary trembling movement. ■ (**the shivers**) a spell or an attack of trembling, typically as a result of fear or horror. — **shiv·er·er n. shiv·er·ing·ly adv. shiv·er·y** /ˈSHiv(ə)rē/ **adj.** [ME *chivere*, perh. alt. of dial. *chavele* 'to chatter,' from OE *ceafl* 'jaw.']

shiv·er[2] ▶ **n.** (usu. **shivers**) each of the small fragments into which something such as glass is shattered when broken; a splinter. ▶ **v.** [intrans.] rare break into such splinters or fragments.
– PHRASES **shiver my** (or **me**) **timbers** a mock oath attributed to sailors. [ME: from Gmc., 'to split'; akin to Ger. *Schiefer* 'slate.']

Shi·zu·o·ka /,SHēzo͞oˈōkä/ a port on the southern coast of the island of Honshu in Japan; pop. 472,000.

shlub /SHləb/ ▶ **n.** var. of **SCHLUB.**

shmat·te /ˈSHmätə/ ▶ **n.** var. of **SCHMATTE.**

shmear /SHmi(ə)r/ (also **shmeer**) ▶ **n. & v.** var. of **SCHMEAR.**

shmo /SHmō/ ▶ **n.** (pl. **shmoes**) var. of **SCHMO.**

sho /SHō/ ▶ **adv.** nonstandard spelling of **SURE**, representing its pronunciation in the southern US: *I sho is glad to see ya.*
– PHRASES **sho nuff** nonstandard spelling of ***SURE ENOUGH*** (see **SURE**): *you sho nuff got some foxes in this here town!*

Sho·ah /ˈSHōə; SHōˈä/ ▶ **n.** (**the Shoah**) another term for ***THE HOLOCAUST*** (see **HOLOCAUST** sense 1). [mod. Heb., lit. 'catastrophe.']

shoal[1] /SHōl/ ▶ **n.** a large number of fish swimming together: *a shoal of bream.* Compare with **SCHOOL**[2]. ■ informal a large number of people. ▶ **v.** [intrans.] (of fish) form shoals: *these fish can safely be released to shoal with most adult species.* [16th C.: prob. from MDu. *schōle* 'troop.']

shoal[2] ▶ **n.** an area of shallow water, esp. as a navigational hazard: *we clawed our way out from the Bahamian shoals into the deep waters of the Atlantic.* ■ a submerged sandbank visible at low water. ■ (usu. **shoals**) fig. a hidden danger or difficulty. ▶ **v.** [intrans.] (of water) become shallower: *the water shoals reasonably gently, and the swimming is safe.* ▶ **adj.** (of water) shallow. — **shoal·y adj.** [OE *sceald* (adj.), from Gmc.; akin to **SHALLOW.**]

shoat /SHōt/ (also **shote**) ▶ **n.** a young pig, esp. one that is newly weaned. [ME: compare West Flemish *schote.*]

sho·chet /ˈSHōKHət; -KHit; ˈSHoi-; SHōˈKHet/ ▶ **n.** (pl. **sho·che·tim** /SHōKHˈtēm/) a person officially certified as competent to kill cattle and poultry in the manner prescribed by Jewish law. [19th C.: from Heb. *šōḥēṭ* 'slaughtering.']

sho·chu /ˈSHōCHo͞o/ ▶ **n.** a rough Japanese liquor distilled from any of various ingredients, including sake dregs. [from Japanese *shōchū.*]

shock[1] /SHäk/ ▶ **n.** **1** a sudden upsetting or surprising event or experience. ■ a feeling of disturbed surprise resulting from such an event: *her eyes opened wide in shock.* ■ an acute medical condition associated with a fall in blood pressure, caused by such events as loss of blood, severe burns, bacterial infection, allergic reaction, or sudden emotional stress, and marked by cold, pallid skin, irregular breathing, rapid pulse, and dilated pupils. ■ a disturbance causing instability in an economy. ■ short for **ELECTRIC SHOCK. 2** a violent shaking movement caused by an impact, explosion, or tremor: *earthquake shocks.* ■ short for **SHOCK ABSORBER.** ▶ **v. 1** [trans.] (often **be shocked**) cause (someone) to feel surprised and upset: *she was shocked at his injuries* | [as adj.] (**shocked**) *shocked onlookers watched as detectives broke into the pub.* ■ offend the moral feelings of; outrage: *the revelations shocked the nation.* ■ [intrans.] experience such feelings. ■ (usu. **be shocked**) affect with physiological shock, or with an electric shock: *if a patient is deeply shocked, measurement of blood pressure may be difficult.* **2** [intrans.] archaic collide violently. — **shock·a·bil·i·ty** /SHäk,əˈbilitē/ **n. shock·a·ble adj.** [16th C.: from Fr. *choc* (noun), *choquer*. The original noun sense was 'encounter between charging forces.']

shock[2] ▶ **n.** a group of twelve sheaves of grain placed upright and supporting each other to allow the grain to dry and ripen. ▶ **v.** [trans.] arrange (sheaves of grain) in such a group: *the grain is shocked in the field after it is cut.* [ME: perh. from MDu., Mid. Low Ger. *schok.*]

shock[3] ▶ **n.** an unkempt or thick mass of hair. [17th C.: cf. obs. *shough*, a breed of lapdog.]

shock ab·sorb·er ▶ **n.** a device for absorbing jolts and vibrations, esp. on a motor vehicle: fig. *small firms function as a shock absorber for underemployed workers in a recession.*

shock cord ▶ **n.** heavy elasticized cord; bungee cord.

shock·er /ˈSHäkər/ ▶ **n.** informal something that shocks, esp. through being unacceptable or sensational. ■ a person who behaves badly or acts in a sensational manner.

shock·head·ed /ˈSHäk,hedid/ ▶ **adj.** having thick, shaggy, and unkempt hair.

shock·ing /ˈSHäkiNG/ ▶ **adj.** causing indignation or disgust; offensive. ■ causing a feeling of surprise and dismay. ▶ **adv.** informal to a shocking degree; extremely: *my feet are swollen something shocking.* — **shock·ing·ly adv. shock·ing·ness n.**

shock·ing pink ▶ **n.** a vibrant shade of pink.

shock jock ▶ **n.** a disc jockey on a talk-radio show who expresses opinions in a deliberately offensive or provocative way.

Shock·ley /ˈSHäklē/, William Bradford (1910–89), US physicist. He helped to develop the transistor in 1948. He later became a controversial figure because of his views on race and intelligence. Nobel Prize for Physics (1956, shared with Bardeen and Brattain).

shock·proof /ˈSHäk,pro͞of/ ▶ **adj. 1** designed to resist damage when dropped or knocked. **2** not easily shocked.

shock stall ▶ **n.** a marked increase in drag and a loss of lift and control on an aircraft approaching the speed of sound.

shock tac·tics ▶ **plural n.** a strategy using sudden extreme action to shock someone into doing something: *he was urged to use shock tactics to bring the company back to life.* ■ Mil. a sudden massed charge or attack.

shock ther·a·py (also **shock treatment**) ▶ **n.** treatment of chronic mental conditions by electroconvulsive therapy or by inducing physiological shock. ■ fig. sudden and drastic measures taken to solve an intractable problem: *the economic shock therapy tried by Yeltsin's government.*

shock troops ▶ **plural n.** a group of soldiers trained specially for carrying out a sudden assault: fig. *the miners are the shock troops of the British working class.* ■ a group of people likened to such soldiers.

shock wave ▶ **n.** a sharp change of pressure in a narrow region traveling through a medium, esp. air, caused by explosion or by a body moving faster than sound.

shod /SHäd/ past and past participle of **SHOE.**

shod·dy /ˈSHädē/ ▶ **adj.** (**-di·er, -di·est**) badly made or done. ■ fig. lacking moral principle; sordid. ▶ **n.** an inferior quality yarn or fabric made from the shredded fiber of waste woolen cloth or clippings: *the production of shoddy and mattress stuffing.* ■ inferior cloth made partly from such fiber. — **shod·di·ly** /ˈSHädl-ē/ **adv. shod·di·ness n.** [19th C.: origin unknown.]

shoe /SHo͞o/ ▶ **n. 1** a covering for the foot, typically made of leather, with a sturdy sole and not reaching above the ankle. ■ a horseshoe. **2** something resembling a shoe in shape or use, in particular: ■ a drag for a wheel. ■ short for **BRAKE SHOE.** ■ a socket, esp. on a camera, for fitting a flash unit or other accessory. ■ a metal rim or ferrule, esp. on the runner of a sled. ■ a step for a mast. ■ a box from which cards are dealt in casinos at baccarat or some other card games. ▶ **v.** (**shoes, shoe·ing** /ˈSHo͞oiNG/; past and past part. **shod** /SHäd/) [trans.] (often **be shod**) fit (a horse) with a shoe or shoes. ■ (**be shod**) (of a person) be wearing shoes of a specified kind: *his large feet were shod in sneakers.* ■ protect (the end of an object such as a pole) with a metal shoe. ■ fit a tire to (a wheel).
– PHRASES **be** (or **put oneself**) **in another person's shoes** be (or put oneself) in another person's situation or predicament: *I try to put myself in other people's shoes and imagine their feelings.* **dead men's shoes** property or a position coveted by a prospective successor but available only on a person's death. **the shoe** (or Brit. **boot**) **is on the other foot** the situation, in particular the holding of advantage, has reversed: *putting the shoe on the other foot, turning victims into victimizers and vice versa.* **shoe leather** informal used in reference to the wear on shoes through walking: *you can save on shoe leather by giving us your instructions over the telephone.* **wait for the other shoe to drop** informal be prepared for a further event or complication to occur. — **shoe·less adj.** [OE *scōh* (n.), *scōg(e)an* (v.), from Gmc.; akin to Ger. *Schuh.*]

shoe·bill /ˈSHo͞o,bil/ ▶ **n.** an African stork (*Balaeniceps rex*, the only member of the family Balaenicipitidae) with gray plumage and a very large bill shaped like a wooden shoe.

shoe·black /ˈSHo͞o,blak/ ▶ **n.** dated, esp. Brit. a person who shines the shoes of passersby for payment.

shoe·box /ˈSHo͞o,bäks/ ▶ **n.** a box in which a pair of shoes is delivered or sold. ■ used in references to small or uniform rooms or spaces: [as adj.] *shoebox buildings nestled together like children's blocks.*

shoe·horn /ˈSHo͞o,hôrn/ ▶ **n.** a curved instrument used to ease one's heel into a shoe. ▶ **v.** [trans.] force into an inadequate space.

shoe·lace /ˈsʜo͞o,lās/ ▶ **n.** a cord or leather strip passed through eyelets or hooks on opposite sides of a shoe and pulled tight and fastened.

Shoe·mak·er /ˈsʜo͞o,mākər/, Willie (1931–2003), US jockey; full name *William Lee Shoemaker*. He held the record in horse racing for career wins (8,833) from 1970 until 1999.

shoe·mak·er /ˈsʜo͞o,mākər/ ▶ **n.** a person who makes shoes and other footwear as a profession. — **shoe·mak·ing** /-,mākiɴɢ/ **n.**

Shoe·mak·er–Le·vy 9 /ˈsʜo͞o,mākər ˈlēvē ˈnīn/ a comet discovered in March 1993, when it had just broken up as a result of passing very close to Jupiter. In July 1994 more than twenty separate fragments impacted successively on Jupiter, causing large explosions in its atmosphere. [named after Carolyn (1929–) and Eugene *Shoemaker* (1928–97), US astronomers, and David *Levy* (1948–), Canadian astronomer, discoverers of the comet.]

shoe·pac /ˈsʜo͞o,pak/ (also **shoe·pack**) ▶ **n.** a commercially manufactured oiled leather boot, typically having a rubber sole. [18th C.: alt. of Delaware (Unami) *sippack* 'shoes,' from *č ípahkpo* 'moccasins.']

shoe·shine /ˈsʜo͞o,sʜīn/ ▶ **n.** an act of polishing someone's shoes, esp. for payment: [as adj.] *a shoeshine boy*. — **shoe·shin·er n.**

shoe·string /ˈsʜo͞o,striɴɢ/ ▶ **n. 1** informal a small or inadequate budget. **2** a shoelace. ▶ **adj.** [attrib.] (of a save or tackle in sports) near or around the ankles or feet, or just above the ground.

shoe·string po·ta·toes ▶ **plural n.** potatoes cut into long thin strips and deep-fried.

shoe tree ▶ **n.** a shaped block inserted into a shoe when it is not being worn, to keep the shoe in shape.

sho·far /ˈsʜōfər; sʜōˈfär/ ▶ **n.** (pl. **sho·fars** or **sho·froth** /sʜōˈfrōt; -ˈfrōs/) a ram's-horn trumpet used by Jews in religious ceremonies and as an ancient battle signal. [from Heb. *šōpār*, (pl.) *šōpārōṯ*.]

sho·gun /ˈsʜōgən/ ▶ **n.** a hereditary commander in chief in feudal Japan. Because of his military power and the weakness of the nominal head of state (the mikado or emperor), the shogun was the real ruler of the country until feudalism was abolished in 1867. — **sho·gun·ate** /-gənit; -gə,nāt/ **n.** [Japanese, from Chin. *jiāng jūn* 'general.']

sho·ji /ˈsʜōjē/ (also **sho·ji screen**) ▶ **n.** (pl. same or **-jis**) (in Japan) a sliding outer or inner door made of a latticed screen covered with white paper. [from Japanese *shōji*.]

Sho·lom A·leich·em /ˈsʜōləm əˈlākəm/ (1859–1916), US writer; born in Ukraine; born *Solomon J. Rabinowitz*. His stories formed the basis for the musical *Fiddler on the Roof* (1964).

Sho·na /ˈsʜōnə/ ▶ **n.** (pl. same or **-nas**) **1** a member of a group of peoples inhabiting parts of southern Africa. See also **MASHONA**. **2** any of the Bantu languages spoken by these peoples. ▶ **adj.** of or relating to the Shona or their languages. [local name.]

shone /sʜōn/ past and past participle of **SHINE**.

shoo /sʜo͞o/ ▶ **exclam.** a word said to frighten or drive away a person or animal. ▶ **v.** (**shoos, shooed** /sʜo͞od/) [with trans.] make (a person or animal) go away by waving one's arms at them, saying "shoo," or otherwise acting in a discouraging manner. [ME: natural exclamation.]

shoo-fly pie (also **shoo·fly pie**) ▶ **n.** a rich pie made with molasses and topped with crumbs. [from US interjection *shoo-fly*.]

shoo-in ▶ **n.** a person or thing that is certain to succeed, esp. someone who is certain to win a competition. [1930s: from earlier sense 'winner of a rigged horse race.']

shook[1] /sʜo͝ok/ past of **SHAKE**. ▶ **adj.** [predic.] (**shook up**) informal emotionally or physically disturbed; upset: *she looks pretty shook up from the letter.*

shook[2] ▶ **n.** a set of components ready for assembly into a box or cask. [18th C.: origin unknown.]

shoot /sʜo͞ot/ ▶ **v.** (past **shot** /sʜät/) **1** [trans.] kill or wound (a person or animal) with a bullet or arrow. ■ [intrans.] fire a bullet from a gun or discharge an arrow from a bow: *he shot at me twice* | [trans.] *they shot a volley of arrows into the village.* ■ cause (a gun) to fire. ■ [trans.] damage or remove (something) with a bullet or missile: *Guy, shoot their hats off.* ■ [intrans.] hunt game with a gun: *we go to Scotland to shoot every autumn.* ■ [intrans.] (**shoot over**) shoot game over (an estate or other area of countryside). ■ shoot game in or on (an estate, cover, etc.). **2** [intrans.] move suddenly and rapidly in a particular direction: *the car shot forward.* ■ [trans.] cause to move suddenly and rapidly in a particular direction: *he would have fallen if Marc hadn't shot out a hand to stop him.* ■ [trans.] direct (a glance, question, or remark) at someone: *Luke shot her a quick glance.* ■ [intrans., in imper.] used to invite a comment or question: *"May I just ask you one more question?" "Shoot."* ■ (of a pain) move with a sharp stabbing sensation: *a shaft of pain shot through her chest* | fig. *a pang of regret shot through her.* ■ [trans.] (of a boat) sweep swiftly down or under (rapids, a waterfall, or a bridge). ■ [trans.] informal (of a motor vehicle) pass (a traffic light at red). ■ extend sharply in a particular direction. ■ [trans.] move (a door bolt) to fasten or unfasten a door. **3** [intrans.] (in soccer, hockey, basketball, etc.) kick, hit, or throw the ball or puck in an attempt to score a goal: *Williams twice shot wide* | [trans.] *we went out in the alley to shoot baskets.* ■ [trans.] informal make (a specified score) for a round of golf: *he shot a 65.* ■ [trans.] informal play a game of (pool or dice). **4** [trans.] film or photograph (a scene, film, etc.): *she just shot a video* | [intrans.] *point the camera and just shoot.* **5** [intrans.] (of a plant or seed) send out buds or shoots; germinate. ■ (of a bud or shoot) appear; sprout. **6** [trans.] informal inject oneself or another person with (a narcotic drug): *he shot dope into his arm.* **7** [trans.] plane (the edge of a board) accurately. ▶ **n. 1** a young branch or sucker springing from the main stock of a tree or other plant. **2** an occasion when a group of people hunt and shoot game for sport: *a grouse shoot.* ■ Brit. land used for shooting game. ■ a shooting match or contest. **3** an occasion when a professional photographer takes photographs or when a film or video is being made. **4** var. of **CHUTE**[1]. **5** a rapid in a stream. ▶ **exclam.** informal used as a euphemism for 'shit': *shoot, it was a great day to be alive.*

– PHRASES **have shot one's bolt** see **BOLT**[1]. **shoot the breeze** (or **the bull**) informal have a casual conversation. **shoot from the hip** informal react suddenly or without careful consideration of one's words or actions. **shoot oneself in the foot** informal inadvertently make a situation worse for oneself. **shoot it out** informal engage in a decisive confrontation, typically a gun battle. **shoot one's mouth off** informal talk boastfully or indiscreetly.

– PHRASAL VERBS **shoot someone/something down** kill or wound someone by shooting them, esp. in a ruthless way. ■ bring down an aircraft, missile, or pilot by shooting at it. ■ fig. crush someone or their opinions by forceful criticism or argument. **shoot up 1** (esp. of a child) grow taller rapidly. ■ (of a price or amount) rise suddenly. **2** see ***SHOOT SOMEONE/SOMETHING UP*** (sense 2) below. **shoot someone/something up 1** cause great damage to something by shooting; kill or wound someone by shooting. **2** (also **shoot up**) informal inject a narcotic drug; inject someone with a narcotic drug. — **shoot·a·ble adj.** [OE *scēotan*, from Gmc.; akin to Ger. *schiessen* and **SHEET**[1], **SHOT**[1].]

shoot-'em-up ▶ **n.** informal a fast-moving story or movie, of which gunfire is a dominant feature.

shoot·er /ˈsʜo͞otər/ ▶ **n. 1** a person who uses a gun either regularly or on a particular occasion. ■ informal a gun. **2** a member of a team in games such as basketball whose role is to attempt to score goals. ■ a person who throws a die or dice. **3** a marble used to shoot at other marbles. **4** informal a small alcoholic drink, esp. of distilled liquor.

shoot·ing /ˈsʜo͞otiɴɢ/ ▶ **n.** the action or practice of shooting. ■ the sport or pastime of shooting with a gun. ■ the right of shooting game over an area of land. ■ an estate or other area rented to shoot over. ▶ **adj.** moving or growing quickly: *shooting beams of light played over the sea.* ■ (of a pain) sudden and piercing.

– PHRASES **the whole shooting match** informal everything.

shoot·ing gal·ler·y ▶ **n.** a room or fairground booth used for recreational shooting at targets with guns or air guns. ■ informal a place used for taking drugs, esp. injecting heroin.

shoot·ing i·ron ▶ **n.** informal a firearm.

shoot·ing range ▶ **n.** an area provided with targets for the controlled practice of shooting.

shooting script ▶ **n.** a final movie or television script with scenes arranged in the order in which they will be filmed.

shoot·ing star[1] ▶ **n.** a small, rapidly moving meteor burning up on entering the earth's atmosphere.

shoot·ing star[2] ▶ **n.** a North American plant (genus *Dodecatheon*) of the primrose family, with white, pink, or purple hanging flowers with backward curving petals. The flowers are carried above the leaves on slender stems and turn to face up following fertilization.

shooting star[2]

shoot·ing stick ▶ **n.** a walking stick with a handle that unfolds to form a seat and a sharpened end that can be stuck firmly in the ground.

shoot·ing war ▶ **n.** a war in which there is armed conflict, as opposed to a cold war or war of nerves, for example.

shoot-out ▶ **n.** informal a decisive gun battle. ■ (also **penalty shoot-out**) Soccer a tiebreaker decided by each side taking a specified number of penalty kicks.

shoot-the-chute (also **shoot-the-chutes**) ▶ **n.** another term for **CHUTE-THE-CHUTE**.

shop /sʜäp/ ▶ **n. 1** a building or part of a building where goods or services are sold; a store. **2** [usu. with adj.] a place where things are manufactured or repaired; a workshop. ■ a room or department in a factory where a particular stage of production is carried out: *the machine shop.* ■ short for **SHOP CLASS**. ■ a profession, trade, business, etc., esp. as a subject of conversation: *when mathematicians talk shop, they do it at the blackboard.* ▶ **v.** (**shopped, shop·ping**) **1** [intrans.] go to a store or stores to buy goods. ■ (**shop around**) look for the best available price or rate for something. ■ short for **WINDOW-SHOP**. **2** [trans.] informal, esp. Brit. inform on (someone).

– PHRASES **close** (or **shut**) **up shop** cease business or operation, either temporarily or permanently. ■ informal stop some activity: *rather than close up shop, the team has returned to fighting trim.* **set up shop** establish oneself in a business. [ME: shortening of OFr. *eschoppe* 'lean-to booth,' from West Gmc.; akin to Ger. *Schopf* 'porch.']

shop·a·hol·ic /,sʜäpəˈhôlik; -ˈhälik/ ▶ **n.** informal a compulsive shopper. [1980s: blend of **SHOP** and **ALCOHOLIC**.]

shop class ▶ **n.** a class in which practical skills such as carpentry or engineering are taught.

shop floor ▶ **n.** [in sing.] the part of a workshop or factory where production as distinct from administrative work is carried out: *working conditions on the shop floor.*

shop·keep·er /ˈsʜäp,kēpər/ ▶ **n.** the owner and manager of a shop. — **shop·keep·ing** /-,kēpiɴɢ/ **n.**

shop·lift·ing /'SHäp,liftiNG/ ▶n. the criminal action of stealing goods from a shop while pretending to be a customer. —**shop·lift** v. **shop·lift·er** /-,liftər/ n.

shoppe ▶n. a deliberately archaic spelling of SHOP, used to imply old-fashioned charm or quaintness: *the mishmash of the usual Tourist Gift Shoppe.*

shop·per /'SHäpər/ ▶n. a person who is shopping. ■ a person who is hired to shop for someone else.

shop·ping /'SHäpiNG/ ▶n. [often as adj.] the purchasing of goods from stores. ■ goods bought from stores, esp. food and household goods.

shop·ping cart ▶n. a bag or basket on wheels for carrying shopping purchases, esp. one for the use of supermarket customers.

shop·ping cen·ter ▶n. an area or complex of stores with adjacent parking.

shop·ping list ▶n. a list of purchases to be made. ■ a list of items to be considered or acted on.

shop·ping mall ▶n. see MALL (sense 1).

shop stew·ard ▶n. a person elected by workers to represent them in dealings with management.

shop·talk /'SHäp,tôk/ (also **shop talk**) ▶n. conversation about one's occupation or business at an informal or social occasion.

shop win·dow (also **shop·win·dow**) ▶n. a window of a store, in which goods are displayed.

shop·worn /'SHäp,wôrn/ ▶adj. (of an article) made dirty by being displayed or handled in a store.

shore[1] /SHôr/ ▶n. the land along the edge of a sea, lake, or other large body of water. ■ Law the land between ordinary high- and low-water marks. ■ (usu. **shores**) a country or other geographic area bounded by a coast. —**shore·less** adj. **shore·ward** /-wərd/ adj. & adv. **shore·wards** /-wərdz/ adv. [ME: from MDu., Mid. Low Ger. *schōre*; perh. akin to SHEAR (v.).]

shore[2] ▶n. a prop or beam set obliquely against something as a support. ▶v. [trans.] support or hold up (something) with such props or beams. [ME: from MDu., Mid. Low Ger. *schore* 'prop.']

shore[3] archaic past of SHEAR.

shore-based ▶adj. operating from or based on a shore.

shore·bird /'SHôr,bərd/ ▶n. a wader of the order Charadriiformes, such as a sandpiper. ■ any bird that frequents the shore.

shore crab ▶n. a crab (*Carcinus maenas*, family Carcinidae) that inhabits the seashore and shallow waters.

shore leave ▶n. leisure time spent ashore by a sailor.

shore·line /'SHôr,līn/ ▶n. the line along which a large body of water meets the land.

shore·side /'SHôr,sīd/ ▶n. the edge of a shore.

shor·ing /'SHôriNG/ ▶n. shores or props used to support or hold up something weak or unstable.

shorn /SHôrn/ past participle of SHEAR.

short /SHôrt/ ▶adj. **1** measuring a small distance from end to end: *a short flight of steps | the bed was too short for him.* ■ (of a journey) covering a small distance: *the hotel is a short walk from the sea.* ■ (of a garment or sleeves on a garment) only covering the top part of a person's arms or legs: *a short skirt.* ■ (of a person) small in height. ■ (of a shot in tennis, a ball in cricket, etc.) traveling only a small distance before bouncing: *he uses his opportunities to attack every short ball.* ■ short for SHORTSTOP. **2** lasting or taking a small amount of time. ■ [attrib.] seeming to last less time than is the case; passing quickly: *in 10 short years all this changed.* ■ (of a person's memory) retaining things for only a small amount of time: *he has a short memory for past misdeeds.* ■ Stock Market (of stocks or other securities or commodities) sold in advance of being acquired, with reliance on the price falling so that a profit can be made. ■ Stock Market (of a broker, position in the market, etc.) buying or based on such stocks or other securities or commodities. ■ denoting or having a relatively early date for the maturing of a bill of exchange. **3** relatively small in extent: *he wrote a short book.* ■ [predic.] (**short of/on**) not having enough of (something); lacking or deficient in: *they were short of provisions | I know you're short on cash.* ■ [predic.] in insufficient supply: *food is short.* ■ [predic.] (of a person) terse; uncivil: *he was often sharp and rather short with her.* **4** Phonet. (of a vowel) categorized as short with regard to quality and length (e.g., in standard English the vowel in *good* is short as distinct from the long vowel in *food*). ■ Pros. (of a vowel or syllable) having the lesser of the two recognized durations. **5** (of odds or a chance) reflecting or representing a high level of probability: *they have been backed at short odds to win thousands.* **6** (of pastry) containing a high proportion of fat to flour and therefore crumbly. ■ (of clay) having poor plasticity. ▶adv. (chiefly in sports) at, to, or over a relatively small distance: *you go deep and you go short.* ■ not as far as the point aimed at; not far enough: *all too often you pitch the ball short.* ▶n. **1** Brit., informal a strong alcoholic drink, esp. spirits, served in small measures. **2** a short film as opposed to a feature film. ■ a short sound such as a short signal in Morse code or a short vowel or syllable: *her call was two longs and a short.* ■ a short circuit. **3** Stock Market a person who sells short. ■ (**shorts**) Stock Market short-dated stocks. **4** (**shorts**) a mixture of bran and coarse flour. ▶v. short-circuit or cause to short-circuit: [intrans.] *the electrical circuit had shorted out.* [20th C.: abbr.]

– PHRASES **be caught** (or Brit. **taken**) **short** be put at a disadvantage: *the troubled company has been caught short by price competition in a recession-stricken market.* ■ informal urgently need to urinate or defecate. **two bricks short of a load, an oar short of a pair,** etc. informal (of a person) stupid; crazy: *she's two bricks short of a load.* **bring** (or **pull**) **someone up short** make someone check or pause abruptly: *he was entering the office when he was brought up short by the sight of John.* **come short** fail to reach a goal or standard: *we're so close to getting the job done, but we keep **coming up** short.* ■ S. African get into trouble: *if you try to trick him you'll come short.* **for short** as an abbreviation or nickname: *the File Transfer Protocol, or FTP for short.* **get** (or **have**) **someone by the short hairs** informal have complete control of a person. [from military slang, referring to pubic hair.] **go short** not have enough of something, esp. food: *you won't go short when I die.* **in short** to sum up; briefly: *he was a faithful, orthodox party member; a Stalinist in short.* **in short order** immediately; rapidly. **in the short run** in the near future. **in short supply** scarce. **in the short term** in the near future. **little** (or **nothing**) **short of** almost (or equal to); little (or nothing) less than: *he regarded the cost of living as little short of scandalous.* **make short work of** accomplish, consume, or destroy quickly. **short and sweet** brief and pleasant. **the short end of the stick** an outcome in which one has less advantage than others. **short for** an abbreviation or nickname for: *I'm Robbie—short for Roberta.* **short of** less than: *he died at sixty-one, four years short of his pensionable age.* ■ not reaching as far as: *a rocket failure left a satellite tumbling in an orbit far short of its proper position.* ■ without going so far as (some extreme action): *short of putting out an all-persons alert, there's little else we can do.* **short of breath** panting; short-winded. **short, sharp shock** see SHOCK[1]. **stop short** stop suddenly or abruptly. **stop short of** not go as far as (some extreme action): *the measures stopped short of establishing direct trade links.* —**short·ish** adj. **short·ness** n. [OE *sceort*, of Gmc. origin; rel. to SHIRT and SKIRT.]

short-act·ing ▶adj. (chiefly of a drug) having effects that only last for a short time.

short·age /'SHôrtij/ ▶n. a state or situation in which something needed cannot be obtained in sufficient amounts: *a **shortage of** hard cash | food shortages.*

short·bread /'SHôrt,bred/ ▶n. a crisp, rich, crumbly type of cookie made with butter, flour, and sugar. [19th C.: from SHORT 'easily crumbled.']

short·cake /'SHôrt,kāk/ ▶n. **1** a small cake made of biscuit dough and typically served with fruit and whipped cream as a dessert. ■ a small circular sponge cake used in the same way. **2** a dessert made from shortcake topped with fruit, typically strawberries, and whipped cream. [16th C.: see SHORTBREAD.]

short·change /'SHôrt'CHānj/ (also **short-change**) ▶v. [trans.] cheat by giving insufficient money as change. ■ treat unfairly by withholding something of value.

short cir·cuit ▶n. in a device, an electrical circuit of lower resistance than that of a normal circuit, typically resulting from the unintended contact of components and consequent accidental diversion of the current. ▶v. (**short-cir·cuit**) (of an electrical device) malfunction or fail, or cause to do this, as a result of a short circuit across it. ■ [trans.] fig. shorten (a process or activity) by using a more direct method.

short·com·ing /'SHôrt,kəmiNG/ ▶n. (usu. **shortcomings**) a fault or failure to meet a certain standard, typically in a person's character, a plan, or a system.

short cov·er·ing ▶n. the buying in of stocks or other securities or commodities that have been sold short, typically to avoid loss when prices move upward.

short·cut /'SHôrt,kət/ ▶n. an alternative route that is shorter than the one usually taken. ■ fig. an accelerated way of doing something.

short-dat·ed ▶adj. (of a stock or bond) due for early payment or redemption.

short-day ▶adj. [attrib.] (of a plant) needing a daily period of darkness of more than a certain length to initiate flowering.

short di·vi·sion ▶n. arithmetical division in which the quotient is written directly without a succession of intermediate calculations.

short-eared owl ▶n. a migratory day-flying owl (*Asio flammeus*, family Strigidae) that frequents open country, found in northern Eurasia and North and South America.

short·en /'SHôrtn/ ▶v. make or become shorter. ■ [trans.] Sailing reduce the amount of (sail) exposed to the wind. ■ (of gambling odds) make or become shorter; decrease. ■ [trans.] Pros. & Phonet. make (a vowel or syllable) short.

short·en·ing /'SHôrtniNG; 'SHôrtn-iNG/ ▶n. butter or other fat used for making pastry or bread.

short·fall /'SHôrt,fôl/ ▶n. a deficit of something required or expected.

short-fused ▶adj. informal likely to lose one's temper.

short·hair /'SHôrt,he(ə)r/ ▶n. a cat of a short-haired breed.

short·hand /'SHôrt,hand/ ▶n. a method of rapid writing by means of abbreviations and symbols, used esp. for taking dictation. ■ [in sing.] a short and simple way of expressing or referring to something.

short-hand·ed ▶adj. not having enough or the usual number of staff or crew.

short haul ▶n. a relatively short distance in terms of travel or the transport of goods.

short hop ▶n. Baseball a batted or thrown ball that hits the ground and is caught low just as it bounces. ▶ **v.** [trans.] **(short-hop)** (of a fielder) catch such a ball.

short·horn /'SHôrt,hôrn/ ▶ **n.** an animal of a breed of cattle with short horns.

short hun·dred·weight ▶ **n.** see HUNDREDWEIGHT.

short·ie /'SHôrtē/ ▶ **n.** var. of SHORTY.

short list (also **short-list**) ▶ **n.** a list of selected candidates from which a final choice is made: *a short list of four companies.* ▶ **v.** [trans.] **(short-list)** put (someone or something) on a short list.

short-lived /'livd; 'līvd/ ▶ **adj.** lasting only a short time.

short·ly /'SHôrtlē/ ▶ **adv. 1** in a short time; soon. **2** in a few words; briefly. ■ abruptly, sharply, or curtly.

short or·der ▶ **n.** an order or dish of food that can be quickly prepared and served: *a short order of souvlaki.*
– PHRASES **in short order** see SHORT.

short-range ▶ **adj.** [attrib.] **1** (esp. of a vehicle or missile) only able to be used or be effective over short distances. **2** of or over a short period of future time.

short ribs ▶ **n.** a narrow cut of beef containing the ends of the ribs near to the breastbone.

short-run ▶ **adj.** taken or considered over a short time period; short-term: *the short-run impact appears to be positive.*

shorts /SHôrts/ ▶ **plural n.** short pants that reach only to the knees or thighs: *cycling shorts.* ■ men's underpants.

short-sheet ▶ **v** [trans.] fold and arrange the sheet on (a bed) in such a way that anyone getting into the bed will be unable to stretch their legs out beyond the middle of the bed, as a joke.

short shrift ▶ **n.** rapid and unsympathetic dismissal. ■ archaic little time between condemnation and execution or punishment.

short·sight·ed /'SHôrt'sītid/ (also **short-sight·ed**) ▶ **adj.** British term for NEARSIGHTED. ■ fig. lacking imagination or foresight. —**short·sight·ed·ly adv. short·sight·ed·ness n.**

short-sleeved ▶ **adj.** having sleeves that do not reach below the elbow: *a short-sleeved silk top.*

short·stop /'SHôrt,stäp/ ▶ **n.** Baseball a fielder positioned in the infield between second and third base, or the position itself.

short sto·ry ▶ **n.** a story with a fully developed theme but significantly shorter and less elaborate than a novel.

short sub·ject ▶ **n.** a short movie, typically one shown before the screening of a feature film.

short suit ▶ **n.** (in bridge or whist) a holding of only one or two cards of one suit in a hand.

short-tailed wea·sel ▶ **n.** another term for STOAT.

short tem·per ▶ **n.** a tendency to lose one's temper quickly. —**short-tem·pered adj.**

short-term ▶ **adj.** occurring in or relating to a relatively short period of time.

short-term·ism /'tərmizəm/ ▶ **n.** concentration on short-term projects or objectives for immediate profit at the expense of long-term security.

short-tim·er ▶ **n.** military slang a person nearing the end of their period of military service.

short ti·tle ▶ **n.** an abbreviated form of a title of a book or document.

short ton ▶ **n.** see TON[1].

short waist ▶ **n. 1** a short upper body, with a high waist. **2** archaic a woman's dress with a high waist.

short·wave /'SHôrt'wāv/ ▶ **n.** a radio wave of a wavelength between about 10 and 100 m (and a frequency of about 3 to 30 MHz). ■ broadcasting using radio waves of this wavelength.

short weight ▶ **n.** weight that is less than that declared.

short-wind·ed /'windid/ ▶ **adj.** (of a person) out of breath or quickly becoming so.

short·y /'SHôrtē/ (also **short·ie**) ▶ **n.** (pl. **short·ies**) informal a person shorter than average (often a nickname). ■ [often as adj.] a short garment, esp. a short dress or nightgown.

Sho·sho·ne /SHō'SHōnē/ ▶ **n.** (pl. same or **-nes**) **1** a member of an American Indian people living chiefly in Wyoming, Idaho, and Nevada. **2** the Uto-Aztecan language of this people. ▶ **adj.** of or relating to the Shoshone or their language. [origin unknown.]

Sho·sta·ko·vich /,SHästə'kōviCH; ,SHôstə'kôviCH/, Dmitri Dmitrievich (1906–75), Russian composer. He experimented with atonality and 12-note techniques.

shot[1] /SHät/ ▶ **n. 1** the firing of a gun or cannon. ■ an attempt to hit a target by shooting: *took a shot at a pheasant.* ■ [with adj.] the range of a gun or cannon: *six more desperadoes halted just out of rifle shot.* ■ fig. a critical or aggressive remark: *Paul tried one last shot.* ■ [with adj.] a person with a specified level of ability in shooting: *he was an excellent shot.* **2** a hit, stroke, or kick of the ball in sports such as basketball, tennis, or golf. ■ an attempt to drive a ball into a goal; an attempt to score. ■ informal an attempt to do something: *several of the competitors will have a shot at the title.* **3** (pl. same) a ball of stone or metal used as a missile fired from a large gun or cannon. ■ (also **lead shot**) tiny lead pellets used in quantity in a single charge or cartridge in a shotgun. ■ a heavy ball thrown by a shot-putter. **4** a photograph. ■ a film sequence photographed continuously by one camera: *the movie's opening shot.* ■ the range of a camera's view: *a prop man was standing just out of shot.* **5** informal a small drink, esp. of distilled liquor. ■ an injection of a drug or vaccine. **6** [usu. with adj.] the launch of a space rocket: *a moon shot.*
– PHRASES **give it one's best shot** informal do the best that one can. **like a shot** informal without hesitation; willingly. **a shot across the bows** see BOW[3]. **a shot in the arm** informal an encouraging stimulus. *the movie was a real shot in the arm for our crew.* **a shot in the dark** see DARK. [OE *sc(e)ot, gesc(e)ot*, from Gmc. base of SHOOT (v.); akin to Ger. *Geschoss.*]

shot[2] past and past participle of SHOOT. ▶ **adj. 1** (of colored cloth) woven with a warp and weft of different colors, giving a contrasting iridescent effect: *a dress of shot silk.* ■ interspersed with a different color: *dark hair shot with silver.* **2** informal ruined or worn out: *my nerves are shot.*
– PHRASES **shot through with** suffused with (a particular feature or quality). **shot to pieces** informal ruined.

shote /SHōt/ ▶ **n.** var. of SHOAT.

shot glass ▶ **n.** a small glass used for serving liquor.

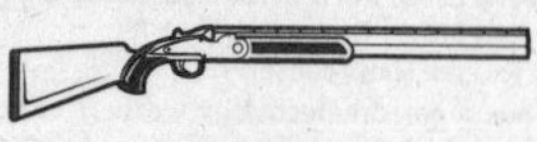

shotgun 1

shot·gun /'SHät,gən/ ▶ **n. 1** a smoothbore gun for firing small shot at short range. **2** (also **shotgun formation**) Football an offensive formation in which the quarterback receives the snap several yards behind the line of scrimmage. ▶ **adj. 1** aimed at a wide range of things; with no specific target. **2** (of a house or other structure) with the rooms lined up one behind another, forming a long narrow whole.
– PHRASES **ride shotgun** see RIDE.

shot·gun mar·riage (also **shot·gun wed·ding**) ▶ **n.** informal an enforced or hurried wedding, esp. because the bride is pregnant.

shot·gun mi·cro·phone ▶ **n.** another term for GUN MICROPHONE.

shot hole ▶ **n. 1** a hole made by the passage of a shot. **2** a hole bored in rock for the insertion of a blasting charge. **3** a small round hole made in a leaf by a fungus or bacterium, esp. in a fruit tree from leaf spot. ■ a small hole made in wood by a boring beetle.

shot·mak·ing /'SHät,mākiNG/ ▶ **n.** the playing of aggressive or decisive strokes in tennis, golf, and other games. —**shot·mak·er** /-,mākər/ **n.**

shot put ▶ **n.** an athletic contest in which a very heavy round ball is thrown as far as possible. —**shot-put·ter n. shot-put·ting n.**

shot·ten her·ring /'SHätn/ ▶ **n.** a herring that has spawned. ■ archaic a weakened or dispirited person. [ME: *shotten*, archaic past part. of SHOOT.]

should /SHo͝od/ ▶ **modal verb** (3rd sing. **should**) **1** used to indicate obligation, duty, or correctness, typically when criticizing someone's actions: *he should have been careful.* ■ indicating a desirable or expected state: *by now students should be able to read.* ■ used to give or ask advice or suggestions: *you should go back to bed.* ■ chiefly Brit., formal **(I should)** used to give advice: *I should hold out if I were you.* **2** used to indicate what is probable: *the bus should arrive in a few minutes.* **3** formal expressing the conditional mood: ■ chiefly Brit. (in the first person) indicating the consequence of an imagined event: *if I were to obey my first impulse, I should spend my days writing letters.* ■ referring to a possible event or situation: *should anyone arrive late, admission is likely to be refused.* **4** used in a clause with "that" after a main clause describing feelings: *it is astonishing that we should find violence here.* **5** used in a clause with "that" expressing purpose: *in order that training should be effective it must be planned systematically.* **6** chiefly Brit. (in the first person) expressing a polite request or acceptance: *we should be grateful for your advice.* **7** chiefly Brit. (in the first person) expressing a conjecture or hope: *he'll have a sore head, I should imagine | "It won't happen again." "I should hope not."* **8** used to emphasize to a listener how striking an event is or was: *you should have seen Marge's face.* ■ **(who/what should —— but)** emphasizing how surprising an event was: *I was in this store when who should I see across the street but Toby.* [OE *sceolde*: past of SHALL.]

shoul·der /'SHōldər/ ▶ **n. 1** the upper joint of each of a person's arms and the part of the body between this and the neck. ■ (in quadrupeds) the joint of the upper forelimb and the adjacent part of the back. ■ the part of a bird or insect at which the wing is attached. ■ a joint of meat from the upper foreleg and shoulder blade of an animal. ■ a part of a garment covering the shoulder. ■ **(shoulders)** the upper part of the back and arms: *a tall youth with broad shoulders.* ■ **(shoulders)** fig. this part of the body regarded as bearing responsibility or hardship or providing strength. **2** a part of something resembling a shoulder in shape, position, or function: *the shoulder of a pulley.* ■ a point at which a steep slope descends from a plateau or highland area: *the shoulder of the hill.* **3** a paved strip alongside a road for stopping on in an emergency. ▶ **v. 1** [trans.] put (something heavy) over one's shoulder or shoulders to carry. ■ fig. take on (a responsibility): *she shouldered the blame for the incident.* **2** [trans.] push (someone or something) out of one's way with one's shoulder: *she shouldered him aside.* ■ [intrans.] move in this way: *he shouldered past a woman with a baby.*
– PHRASES **be looking over one's shoulder** be anxious about a possible danger. **put one's shoulder to the wheel** set to work vigorously. **shoulder arms** hold a rifle against the side of the body, barrel upward. **a shoulder to cry on** someone who listens sympathetically to one's problems. **shoulder to shoulder** side by side. ■ acting together toward a common aim. —**shoul·dered** /'SHōldərd/ **adj.** [in comb.] *broad-shouldered.* [OE *sculdor*, from West Gmc.; akin to Ger. *Schulter.*]

shoul·der bag ▶ **n.** a bag with a long strap that is hung over the shoulder.

shoul·der belt ▶ n. a seat belt that passes over the shoulder and across the chest.

shoul·der blade ▶ n. either of the large, flat, triangular bones that lie against the ribs in the upper back and provide attachments for the bone and muscles of the upper arm. Also called SCAPULA.

should·er har·ness ▶ n. a strap worn around or across the shoulder, specifically: ■ the part of a seat belt that lies diagonally across the chest.

shoul·der-high ▶ adj. & adv. up to or at the height of the shoulders.

shoul·der hol·ster ▶ n. a gun holster worn under the armpit.

shoul·der knot ▶ n. a knot of ribbon, metal, or lace worn as part of ceremonial dress.

shoul·der strap ▶ n. a narrow strip of material going over the shoulder from the front to the back of a garment. ■ a long strap attached to a bag for carrying it over the shoulder. ■ a strip of cloth from shoulder to collar on a military uniform bearing a symbol of rank. ■ a similar strip on a raincoat.

should·n't /'SHŏŏdnt/ ▶ contr. should not.

shout /SHOUT/ ▶ v. [intrans.] (of a person) utter a loud call or cry, typically as an expression of a strong emotion. ■ [reporting verb] say something very loudly; call out: [trans.] *he leaned out of his window and shouted abuse at them.* ■ **(shout at)** speak loudly and angrily to; insult or scold loudly: *he apologized because he had shouted at her.* ■ [trans.] **(shout someone down)** prevent someone from speaking or being heard by shouting: *he was shouted down as he tried to explain the decision.* ■ [trans.] fig. indicate or express (a particular quality) unequivocally: *from crocodile handbag to gold-trimmed shoes she shouted money.* ▶ n. a loud cry expressing a strong emotion or calling attention.
– PHRASES **give someone a shout** informal call for someone's attention. ■ call on or get in touch with someone. — **shout·er** n. **shout·y** adj. (informal). [ME: perh. akin to SHOOT; compare ON *skúta* 'a taunt.']

shout·ing match ▶ n. a loud quarrel.

shove /SHəv/ ▶ v. [trans.] push (someone or something) roughly: *police started **pushing and shoving** people down the street* | [intrans.] *kids pushed, kicked, and shoved.* ■ [intrans.] make one's way by pushing someone or something: *Woody shoved past him.* ■ [trans.] put (something) somewhere carelessly or roughly: *she shoved the books into her briefcase.* ■ **(shove it)** informal used to express angry dismissal of something: *I told him to shove it.* ▶ n. [usu. in sing.] a strong push.
– PHRASAL VERBS **shove off 1** [usu. in imper.] informal go away: *shove off—you're bothering the customers.* **2** push away from the shore or another vessel in a boat. [OE *scūfan* (v.), from Gmc.; akin to Ger. *schieben* SHUFFLE.]

shov·el /'SHəvəl/ ▶ n. a tool with a broad flat blade and typically upturned sides, used for moving coal, earth, snow or other material. ■ a machine or part of a machine having a similar shape or function. ■ an amount of something carried or moved with a shovel: *a few **shovels of earth.*** ▶ v. (**-eled, -el·ing**; Brit. **-elled, -el·ling**) [trans.] move (coal, earth, snow, or similar material) with a shovel: *she shoveled coal on the fire.* ■ [trans.] remove snow from (an area) with a shovel: *I'll shovel the walk.* ■ informal put or push (something, typically food) somewhere quickly and in large quantities. — **shov·el·ful** /-,fŏŏl/ n. (pl. **-fuls**). [OE *scofl*, from Gmc.; akin to Ger. *Schaufel* and SHOVE (v.).]

shov·el·er /'SHəv(ə)lər/ (esp. Brit. **shov·el·ler**) ▶ n. **1** a person or thing that shovels something. **2** a dabbling duck (genus *Anas*) with a long broad bill.

shov·el hat ▶ n. a black felt hat with a low round crown and a broad brim turned up at the sides, formerly worn esp. by clergymen.

shov·el·ler /'SHəv(ə)lər/ ▶ n. British spelling of SHOVELER.

show /SHō/ ▶ v. (past part. **shown** /SHōn/ or **showed**) **1** be or allow or cause to be visible: [intrans.] *wrinkles were starting to show on her face* | [no obj., with complement] *the muscles of her jaws showed white through the skin* | [trans.] *a white blouse will show the blood.* ■ [trans.] offer, exhibit, or produce (something) for scrutiny or inspection: *an alarm salesperson should show an ID card.* ■ put on display in an exhibition or competition: *he ceased early in his career to show his work.* ■ [trans.] present (a movie or television program) on a screen for public viewing. ■ [intrans.] (of a movie) be presented in this way: *a movie showing at the Venice Film Festival.* ■ [trans.] indicate (a particular time, measurement, etc.): *a travel clock showing the time in different cities.* ■ [trans.] represent or depict in art: *a postcard showing the Wicklow Mountains.* ■ **(show oneself)** allow oneself to be seen; appear in public: *he was amazed that she would have the gall to show herself.* ■ [intrans.] informal arrive or turn up for an appointment or at a gathering: *her date failed to show.* ■ [intrans.] finish third or in the first three in a race. ■ [intrans.] informal (of a woman) be visibly pregnant: *Shirley was four months pregnant and just starting to show.* **2** [trans.] display or allow to be perceived (a quality, emotion, or characteristic): *it was Frank's turn to show his frustration.* ■ accord or treat someone with (a specified quality): *he urged his soldiers to fight them and show no mercy* | [with two objs.] *he has learned to show women some respect.* ■ [intrans.] (of an emotion) be noticeable: *he tried not to let his relief show.* **3** [trans.] demonstrate or prove: [with clause] *the figures show that the underlying rate of inflation continues to fall.* ■ **(show oneself)** prove or demonstrate oneself to be: [with infin.] *she showed herself to be a harsh critic.* ■ cause to understand or be capable of doing something by explanation or demonstration: *he showed the boy how to operate the machine.* ■ [with obj. and adverbial of direction] conduct or lead: *show them in, please.* ▶ n. **1** a spectacle or display of something, typically an impressive one: *spectacular shows of bluebells.* **2** a public entertainment, in particular: ■ a play or other stage performance, esp. a musical. ■ a program on television or radio. ■ [usu. with adj.] an event or competition involving the public display or exhibition of animals, plants, or products: *the annual agricultural show.* ■ informal an undertaking, project, or organization: *I man a desk in a little office. I don't run the show.* ■ informal an opportunity for doing something; a chance: *I didn't have a show.* **3** an outward appearance or display of a quality or feeling: *Joanie was frightened of any **show of affection.*** ■ an outward display intended to give a particular, false impression: *Drew **made a show of** looking around for firewood* | *they are all show and no go.* **4** Med. a discharge of blood and mucus from the vagina at the onset of labor or menstruation.
– PHRASES **for show** for the sake of appearance rather than for use. **get** (or **keep**) **the show on the road** informal begin (or succeed in continuing with) an undertaking or enterprise: *"Let's get this show on the road—we're late already."* **good** (or **bad** or **poor**) **show!** Brit., informal dated used to express approval (or disapproval or dissatisfaction). **have something** (or **nothing**) **to show for** have a (or no) visible result of (one's work or experience): *a year later, he had nothing to show for his efforts.* **on show** being exhibited. **show one's cards** another way of saying SHOW ONE'S HAND below. **show cause** Law produce satisfactory grounds for application of (or exemption from) a procedure or penalty. **show someone the door** dismiss or eject someone from a place. **show one's face** appear in public: *she had been up in court and was so ashamed she could hardly show her face.* **show the flag** see FLAG[1]. **show one's hand** (in a card game) reveal one's cards. ■ fig. disclose one's plans: *he needed hard evidence, and to get it he would have to show his hand.* **show of force** a demonstration of the forces at one's command and of one's readiness to use them. **show of hands** the raising of hands among a group of people to indicate a vote for or against something, with numbers typically being estimated rather than counted. **show the way** indicate the direction to be followed to a particular place. ■ indicate what can or should be done by doing it first: *Morgan showed the way by becoming Deputy Governor of Jamaica.*
– PHRASAL VERBS **show something forth** archaic exhibit: *the heavens show forth the glory of God.* **show off** informal make a deliberate or pretentious display of one's abilities or accomplishments. **show someone/something off** display or cause others to take notice of someone or something that is a source of pride: *his jeans were tight-fitting, showing off his compact figure.* **show out** Bridge reveal that one has no cards of a particular suit. **show someone around** act as a guide for someone to points of interest in a place or building. **show through** (of one's real feelings) be revealed inadvertently. **show up 1** be conspicuous or clearly visible. **2** informal arrive or turn up for an appointment or gathering. **show someone/something up** make someone or something conspicuous or clearly visible: *a rising moon showed up the wild seascape.* ■ expose someone or something as being bad or faulty in some way: *it's a pity they haven't **showed up** the authorities **for** what they are.* ■ **(show someone up)** informal embarrass or humiliate someone: *she says I showed her up in front of her friends.* [OE *scēawian* 'look at, inspect,' from a West Gmc. base meaning 'look'; rel. to Du. *schouwen* and Ger. *schauen*.]

show jump·ing ▶ n. the competitive sport of riding horses over a course of fences and other obstacles in an arena, with penalty points for errors. — **show jump** n. **show jumper** n.

show-and-tell ▶ n. a teaching method, used esp. in teaching young children, in which students are encouraged to bring items they have selected to class and describe them to their classmates.

show bill ▶ n. an advertising poster, esp. for a theater performance.

show biz ▶ n. informal term for SHOW BUSINESS. — **show·biz·zy** /'SHō,bizē/ adj.

show·boat /'SHō,bōt/ ▶ n. a river steamboat on which theatrical performances are given. ■ informal a show-off; an exhibitionist. ▶ v. [intrans.] informal show off. — **show·boat·er** n.

show busi·ness ▶ n. the theater, movies, television, and pop music as a profession or industry.

show·case /'SHō,kās/ ▶ n. a glass case used for displaying articles in a store or museum. ■ a place or occasion for presenting something favorably to general attention. ▶ v. [trans.] exhibit; display.

show·down /'SHō,doun/ ▶ n. a final test or confrontation intended to settle a dispute. ■ (in poker) the requirement at the end of a round that the players who remain in must show their cards to determine which is the strongest hand.

show·er /'SHouər/ ▶ n. **1** a brief and usually light fall of rain, hail, sleet, or snow. ■ a mass of small things falling or moving at the same time: ***a shower of** dust.* ■ fig. a large number of things happening or given to someone at the same time. ■ a group of particles produced by a cosmic-ray particle in the earth's atmosphere. **2** an enclosure in which a person stands under a spray of water to wash. ■ the apparatus that produces such a spray of water. ■ an act of washing oneself in a shower. **3** [often with adj.] a party at which presents are given to someone, typically a woman who is about to get married or have a baby. ▶ v. **1** [intrans.] (of a mass of small things) fall or be thrown in a shower: ■ [trans.] cause (a mass of small things) to fall in a shower: *his hooves showered sparks across the concrete floor.* ■ [trans.] **(shower someone with)** throw (a number of small things) all at once toward someone: *hooligans showered him with rotten eggs.* ■ [trans.] **(shower someone with)**

give someone a great number of (things): *he showered her with kisses.* ■ [trans.] (**shower something on/upon**) give a great number of things to (someone). **2** [intrans.] wash oneself in a shower.
– PHRASES **send someone to the showers** informal cause someone to fail early on in a race or contest. [OE *scūr* 'light fall of rain,' from Gmc.; akin to Ger. *Schauer*.]

show·er·proof /'SHouər,prōōf/ ▶ **adj.** (of a garment) resistant to light rain. ▶ **v.** [trans.] make showerproof.

show·er·y /'SHouərē/ ▶ **adj.** (of weather or a period of time) characterized by frequent showers of rain.

show·girl /'SHō,gərl/ ▶ **n.** an actress who sings and dances in musicals, variety acts, and similar shows.

show·ing /'SHō-iNG/ ▶ **n.** the action of showing something or the fact of being shown. ■ a presentation of a movie or television program. ■ [with adj.] a performance of a specified quality: *a strong second-place showing.*

show·man /'SHōmən/ ▶ **n.** (pl. **-men**) a person who produces or presents shows as a profession, esp. the proprietor, manager, or MC of a circus or variety show. ■ a person skilled in dramatic or entertaining presentation, performance, or publicity. — **show·man·ship** /-,SHip/ **n.**

shown /SHōn/ past participle of **SHOW**.

show-off ▶ **n.** informal a person who acts pretentiously or who publicly parades themselves, their possessions, or their accomplishments.

show·piece /'SHō,pēs/ ▶ **n.** something that attracts attention or admiration as an example of its type. ■ something that offers an opportunity for a display of skill. ■ an item of work presented for exhibition or display.

show·place /'SHō,plās/ ▶ **n.** a place of beauty or interest attracting many visitors.

show·room /'SHō,rōōm; -,rōōm/ ▶ **n.** a room used to display goods for sale, such as appliances, cars, or furniture.

show-stop·per ▶ **n.** informal a performance or item receiving prolonged applause. ■ something that is striking or has great popular appeal. — **show-stop·ping adj.**

show tri·al ▶ **n.** a judicial trial held in public with the intention of influencing or satisfying public opinion, rather than of ensuring justice.

show win·dow ▶ **n.** a store window looking on to a street, used for exhibiting goods.

show·y /'SHō-ē/ ▶ **adj.** (**show·i·er, show·i·est**) having a striking appearance or style, typically by being excessively bright, colorful, or ostentatious: *showy flowers.* — **show·i·ly** /-əlē/ **adv. show·i·ness n.**

sho·yu /'SHōyōō/ ▶ **n.** a type of Japanese soy sauce. [from Japanese *shōyu*.]

s.h.p. ▶ **abbr.** shaft horsepower.

shpt. ▶ **abbr.** shipment.

shr. ▶ **abbr.** share; shares.

shrank /SHraNGk/ past of **SHRINK**.

shrap·nel /'SHrapnəl/ ▶ **n.** fragments of a bomb, shell, or other object thrown out by an explosion. [19th C.: General Henry *Shrapnel* (1761–1842), British soldier.]

shred /SHred/ ▶ **n.** (usu. **shreds**) a strip of some material, such as paper, cloth, or food, that has been torn, cut, or scraped from something larger. ■ [often with negative] a very small amount: *there was not a shred of evidence.* ▶ **v.** (**shredded, shredding**) [trans.] tear or cut into shreds: [as adj.] (**shredded**) *shredded cabbage.* [OE *scrēad* 'piece cut off,' *scrēadian* 'to trim,' from West Gmc.; akin to **SHROUD**.]

shred·ded wheat ▶ **n.** a breakfast cereal made of cooked wheat in long brittle shreds that are pressed into compact pieces.

shred·der /'SHredər/ ▶ **n.** **1** a machine or other device for shredding something, esp. documents. **2** informal a snowboarder.

Shreve·port /'SHrēv,pôrt/ a city in northwestern Louisiana, on the Red River; pop. 200,145.

shrew /SHrōō/ ▶ **n.** a small mouselike insectivorous mammal (*Sorex, Crocidura,* and other genera, family Soricidae) with a long pointed snout and tiny eyes. ■ a bad-tempered or aggressively assertive woman. — **shrew·ish adj. shrew·ish·ly adv. shrew·ish·ness n.** [OE *scrēawa, scrǣwa,* from Gmc.; akin to Norw. *skrogg* 'wolf.']

shrewd /SHrōōd/ ▶ **adj.** **1** having or showing sharp powers of judgment; astute. **2** archaic (esp. of weather) piercingly cold: *a shrewd east wind.* ■ (of a blow) severe: *a bayonet's shrewd thrust.* ■ mischievous; malicious. — **shrewd·ly adv. shrewd·ness n.** [ME (in the sense 'evil in nature or character'): from **SHREW** in the sense 'evil person or thing,' or as the past part. of obs. *shrew* 'to curse.']

shrew-mole ▶ **n.** a small shrewlike mole (*Neurotrichus* and other genera) with a long tail, native to Asia and North America.

Shri /SHrē/ ▶ **n.** Indian var. of **SRI**.

shriek /SHrēk/ ▶ **v.** [intrans.] utter a high-pitched piercing sound or words, esp. as an expression of terror, pain, or excitement: *the audience shrieked with laughter* | [trans.] *shrieking abuse at a taxi driver.* ■ (of something inanimate) make a high-pitched screeching sound. ■ fig. be very obvious or strikingly discordant. ▶ **n.** a high-pitched piercing cry or sound; a scream. — **shriek·er n.** [15th C. (v.): imitative; of Scand. origin; compare ON *skrækja*.]

shriev·al /'SHrēvəl/ ▶ **adj.** esp. hist. of or relating to a sheriff. [17th C.: from *shrieve*, obs. var. of **SHERIFF**.]

shriev·al·ty /'SHrēvəltē/ ▶ **n.** (pl. **-ties**) esp. hist. the office, jurisdiction, or tenure of a sheriff.

shrift /SHrift/ ▶ **n.** archaic confession, esp. to a priest: *go to shrift.* See also **SHORT SHRIFT**. ■ absolution by a priest. [OE *scrift*, from **SHRIVE**.]

shrike /SHrīk/ ▶ **n.** a songbird (family Laniidae) with a strong sharply hooked bill, often impaling its prey of small birds, lizards, and insects on thorns. Also called **BUTCHERBIRD**. [16th C.: perh. akin to OE *scrīc* 'thrush,' Mid. Low Ger. *schrīk* 'corn crake,' of imitative origin.]

shrill /SHril/ ▶ **adj.** (of a voice or sound) high-pitched and piercing. ■ derog. (esp. of a complaint or demand) loud and forceful. ▶ **v.** [intrans.] make a shrill noise. ■ speak or cry with a shrill voice. ▶ **n.** [in sing.] a shrill sound or cry. — **shrill·ness n. shril·ly** /'SHri(l)lē/ **adv.** [ME: from Gmc.; akin to Low Ger. *schrell* 'sharp in tone.']

pink shrimp

shrimp /SHrimp/ ▶ **n.** (pl. same or **shrimps**) a small free-swimming crustacean (*Pandalus, Penaeus, Crangon,* and other genera, order Decapoda) with an elongated body, typically marine and frequently harvested for food. Its numerous species include the commercially important **pink shrimp** (*Penaeus duorarum*). ■ informal, derog. a small, physically weak person. ▶ **v.** [intrans.] fish for shrimp: [as adj.] (**shrimping**) *a shrimping net.* — **shrimp·y adj.** [ME: prob. akin to Mid. Low Ger. *schrempen* 'to wrinkle' and **SCRIMP**.]

shrimp·er /'SHrimpər/ ▶ **n.** **1** a boat used for catching shrimp. **2** a person who fishes for shrimp.

shrimp plant ▶ **n.** an evergreen Mexican shrub (*Justicia brandegeana,* family Acanthaceae) with clusters of small flowers in pinkish-brown or pale yellow bracts that are said to resemble shrimp, widely grown as a houseplant.

shrine /SHrīn/ ▶ **n.** a place regarded as holy because of its associations with a divinity or a sacred person or relic, typically marked by a building or other construction. ■ a place associated with or containing memorabilia of a particular revered person or thing. ■ a casket containing sacred relics; a reliquary. ■ a niche or enclosure containing a religious statue or other object. ▶ **v.** [trans.] literary enshrine. [OE *scrīn* 'cabinet,' from Gmc.; akin to Ger. *Schrein*, from L. *scrinium* 'chest for books.']

Shrin·er /'SHrīnər/ ▶ **n.** a member of the Ancient Arabic Order of Nobles of the Mystic Shrine, a charitable society founded in the US in 1872.

shrink /SHriNGk/ ▶ **v.** (past **shrank** /SHraNGk/; past part. **shrunk** /SHrəNGk/ or (esp. as adj.) **shrunk·en** /'SHrəNGkən/) **1** become or make smaller in size or amount; contract or cause to contract. ■ [intrans.] (of clothes or material) become smaller as a result of being immersed in water. ■ [as adj.] (**shrunken**) (esp. of a person's face or other part of the body) withered, wrinkled, or shriveled through old age or illness: *a tiny shrunken face and enormous eyes.* ■ [intrans.] (**shrink into oneself**) become withdrawn. ■ [trans.] (**shrink something on**) slip a metal tire or other fitting onto (something) while it is expanded with heat and allow it to tighten in place. **2** [no obj., with adverbial of direction] move back or away, esp. because of fear or disgust: *he shrank back against the wall.* ■ [often with negative] (**shrink from**) be unwilling to do (something difficult or unappealing). ▶ **n.** informal a clinical psychologist, psychiatrist, or psychotherapist. — **shrink·a·ble adj. shrink·er n. shrink·ing·ly adv.** [OE *scrincan*, from Gmc.; akin to Swed. *skrynka* 'to wrinkle.']

shrink·age /'SHriNGkij/ ▶ **n.** the process, fact, or amount of shrinking. ■ an allowance made for reduction in the earnings of a business due to wastage or theft.

shrink·ing vi·o·let ▶ **n.** informal an exaggeratedly shy person.

shrink-re·sist·ant ▶ **adj.** (of textiles or garments) resistant to shrinkage.

shrink-wrap ▶ **v.** [trans.] package (an article) by enclosing it in clinging transparent plastic film that shrinks tightly onto it. ▶ **n.** clinging transparent plastic film used to enclose an article as packaging.

shrive /SHrīv/ ▶ **v.** (past **shrove** /SHrōv/; past part. **shriv·en** /'SHrivən/) [trans.] archaic (of a priest) hear the confession of, assign penance to, and absolve (someone). ■ (**shrive oneself**) present oneself to a priest for confession, penance, and absolution. [OE *scrīfan*, from Gmc.; akin to Ger. *schreiben* 'write,' from L. *scribere*.]

shriv·el /'SHrivəl/ ▶ **v.** (**-eled, -el·ing** ; Brit. **-elled, -el·ling**) wrinkle and contract or cause to wrinkle and contract, esp. due to loss of moisture. ■ [intrans.] fig. lose momentum, will, or desire; become insignificant or ineffectual. ■ [trans.] fig. cause to feel worthless or insignificant: *she shriveled him with one glance.* [16th C.: perh. of Scand. origin; compare Swed. dial. *skryvla* 'to wrinkle.']

shriv·en /'SHrivən/ past participle of **SHRIVE**.

shroom /SHrōōm/ ▶ **n.** informal a mushroom, esp. one with hallucinogenic properties. — **shroom·er n.** [1970s: shortening of **MUSHROOM**.]

shroud /SHroud/ ▶ **n.** **1** a length of cloth or an enveloping garment in which a dead person is wrapped for burial. ■ fig. a thing that envelops or obscures something: *a shroud of secrecy.* ■ tech. a protective casing or cover. **2** (**shrouds**) a set of ropes forming part of the standing rigging of a sailing vessel and supporting the mast from the sides. ■ (also **shroud line**) each of the lines joining the canopy of a parachute to the harness. ▶ v. [trans.] wrap or dress (a body) in a shroud for burial. ■ fig. cover or envelop so as to conceal from view: *mountains shrouded by cloud.* [OE *scrūd* 'garment,' from Gmc., 'cut'; akin to SHRED.]

shroud-laid ▶ adj. (of rope) made of four strands laid right-handed, typically around a core, used esp. on yachts.

shrove /SHrōv/ past of SHRIVE.

Shrove·tide /'SHrōv,tīd/ ▶ n. Shrove Tuesday and the two days preceding it, when it was formerly customary to attend confession. [ME: from *shrove*, past of SHRIVE + TIDE.]

Shrove Tues·day /SHrōv/ ▶ n. the day before Ash Wednesday. Compare with MARDI GRAS.

shrub[1] /SHrəb/ ▶ n. a woody plant smaller than a tree, with several main stems arising at or near the ground. — **shrub·by** adj. [OE *scrubb, scrybb* 'shrubbery'; compare West Flemish *schrobbe* 'vetch' and SCRUB[2].]

shrub[2] ▶ n. 1 a drink made of sweetened fruit juice and liquor, typically rum or brandy. 2 a slightly acid cordial made from fruit juice and water. [18th C.: from Arab. *šurb, šarāb*, from *šariba* 'to drink.']

shrub·ber·y /'SHrəbərē/ ▶ n. shrubs collectively. ■ (pl. **-ber·ies**) an area planted with shrubs.

shrug /SHrəg/ ▶ v. (**shrugged, shrug·ging**) [trans.] raise (one's shoulders) slightly and momentarily to express doubt, ignorance, or indifference: *Jimmy shrugged his shoulders* | [intrans.] *he just shrugged.* ■ (**shrug something off**) dismiss something as unimportant. ▶ n. an act or instance of shrugging one's shoulders. [ME ('fidget'): origin unknown.]

shrunk /SHrəNGk/ (also **shrunk·en**) past participle of SHRINK.

shtetl /'SHtetl; 'SHtätl/ ▶ n. (pl. **shtet·lach** /'SHtetläKH; 'SHtätläKH/ or **shtetls**) hist. a small Jewish town or village in eastern Europe. [1940s: Yiddish, 'little town.']

shtick /SHtik/ ▶ n. informal an attention-getting or theatrical routine, gimmick, or talent. [1960s: Yiddish, from Ger. *Stück* 'piece.']

shtup /SHto͝op/ (also **schtup**) vulgar slang ▶ v. (**shtupped, shtup·ping**) [trans.] have sexual intercourse with (someone). ▶ n. an act of sexual intercourse. [1960s: Yiddish.]

shuck /SHək/ ▶ n. 1 an outer covering such as a husk or pod, esp. the husk of an ear of corn. ■ the shell of an oyster or clam. ■ the integument of certain insect pupae or larvae. 2 informal a person or thing regarded as worthless or contemptible. ▶ exclam. (**shucks**) informal used to express surprise, regret, irritation, or, in response to praise, self-deprecation. See also AW-SHUCKS. ▶ v. [trans.] 1 remove the shucks from corn or shellfish. ■ informal take off (a garment): *she shucked off her nightdress.* ■ informal abandon; get rid of. 2 informal cause (someone) to believe something that is not true; fool or tease. — **shuck·er** n. [17th C.: origin unknown.]

shud·der /'SHədər/ ▶ v. [intrans.] (of a person) tremble convulsively, typically as a result of fear or repugnance. ■ (esp. of a vehicle, machine, or building) shake or vibrate deeply. ■ [usu. as adj.] (**shuddering**) (of a person's breathing) be unsteady, esp. as a result of emotional disturbance: *he drew a deep, shuddering breath.* ▶ n. an act of shuddering.
– PHRASES **give someone the shudders** informal cause someone to feel repugnance or fear. — **shud·der·ing·ly** adv. **shud·der·y** adj. [ME (v.): from MDu. *schüderen*, from Gmc., 'shake.']

Shu·dra /'so͞odrə/ (also **Su·dra**) ▶ n. a member of the worker caste, lowest of the four Hindu castes. [from Sanskrit *śūdra*.]

shuf·fle /'SHəfəl/ ▶ v. 1 [intrans.] walk by dragging one's feet along or without lifting them fully from the ground: *I stepped into my skis and shuffled to the edge of the steep slope.* ■ shift one's position while sitting or move one's feet while standing, typically because of boredom, nervousness, or embarrassment: *Christine shuffled in her chair* | [trans.] *Ben shuffled his feet in the silence.* 2 [trans.] rearrange (a deck of cards) by sliding the cards over each other quickly. ■ move (people or things) around so as to occupy different positions or to be in a different order: *she shuffled her papers into a neat pile.* ■ [intrans.] (**shuffle through**) sort or look through (a number of things) hurriedly: *he shuffled through the papers on his desk.* 3 [trans.] (**shuffle something into**) put part of one's body into (an item of clothing), typically in a clumsy way. ■ (**shuffle something off**) get out of or avoid a responsibility or obligation: *some hospitals shuffle off their responsibilities by claiming to have no suitable facilities.* ■ [intrans.] archaic behave in a shifty or evasive manner: *Mr. Mills seemed to shuffle about it.* ■ [intrans.] (**shuffle out of**) archaic get out of (a difficult situation) in an underhanded or evasive manner. ▶ n. 1 [in sing.] a shuffling movement, walk, or sound. ■ a quick dragging or scraping movement of the feet in dancing. ■ a dance performed with such steps. ■ a piece of music for or in the style of such a dance. ■ a rhythmic motif based on such a dance step and typical of early jazz, consisting of alternating quarter notes and eighth notes in a triplet pattern. 2 an act of shuffling a deck of cards. ■ a change of order or relative positions; a reshuffle. ■ a facility on a CD player for playing tracks in an arbitrary order. 3 archaic a piece of equivocation or subterfuge.
– PHRASES **be** (or **get**) **lost in the shuffle** informal be overlooked or missed in a confused or crowded situation. **shuffle off this mortal coil** see COIL[2]. — **shuf·fler** /'SHəf(ə)lər/ n. [16th C.: perh. from Low Ger. *schuffeln* 'walk clumsily,' from Gmc.; akin to SHOVE.]

shuf·fle·board /'SHəfəl,bôrd/ ▶ n. a game played by pushing disks with a long-handled cue over a marked surface. [16th C.: alt. of obs. *shove-board*, from SHOVE + BOARD.]

shul /SHo͞ol; SHo͝ol/ ▶ n. a synagogue. [19th C.: Yiddish, from Ger. *Schule* 'school.']

shu·mai /'SHo͞o,mī/ ▶ plural n. small steamed dumplings, typically stuffed with seafood and vegetables. [Japanese, ultimately from Chinese.]

shun /SHən/ ▶ v. (**shunned, shun·ning**) [trans.] persistently avoid, ignore, or reject (someone or something). [OE *scunian* 'abhor, seek safety.']

shunt /SHənt/ ▶ v. 1 [trans.] push or pull (a train or part of a train) from the main line to a siding or from one track to another. ■ (usu. **be shunted**) push or shove (someone or something). ■ direct or divert (someone or something) to a less important place or position. 2 [trans.] provide (an electrical current) with a conductor joining two points of a circuit, through which more or less of the current may be diverted. ▶ n. 1 an act of pushing or shoving something. 2 an electrical conductor joining two points of a circuit, through which more or less of a current may be diverted. ■ Surg. an alternative path for the passage of the blood or other body fluid. — **shunter** n. [ME: perh. from SHUN.]

shu·ra /'SHo͝orə/ ▶ n. Islam the principle of consultation, in particular as applied to government. ■ a consultative council. [from Arab. *šūrā* 'consultation.']

shush /SHo͝oSH; SHəSH/ ▶ exclam. be quiet: *"Shush! Do you want to wake everyone?"* ▶ n. an utterance of "shush." ▶ v. [trans.] tell or signal (someone) to be silent. ■ [intrans.] become or remain silent. [1920s: imitative.]

shut /SHət/ ▶ v. (**shut·ting** ; past **shut**) [trans.] move (something) into position so that it blocks an opening: *shut the window, please.* ■ [intrans.] (of something that can block an opening) move or be moved into position: *the door shut behind him.* ■ block an opening into (something) by moving something into position: *he shut the box.* ■ [trans.] keep (someone or something) in a place by closing something such as a door: *he had accidentally shut his dog outside.* ■ fold or bring together the sides of (something) so as to close it: *he shut his book.* ■ prevent access to or along: *they shut the path to that cliff.* ■ make or become unavailable for business or service, either permanently or until due to be open again; close: [trans.] *we shut the shop for lunch* | [intrans.] *the emergency department will shut.*
– PHRASES **shut the door on** (or **to**) see DOOR. **shut one's eyes to** see EYE. **shut one's mind to** see MIND. **shut up shop** see SHOP. **shut your face** (or **mouth** or **trap**)! informal used as a rude or angry way of telling someone to be quiet.
– PHRASAL VERBS **shut down** (or **shut something down**) cease (or cause something to cease) business or operation. **shut someone/something in** keep someone or something inside a place by closing something such as a door. ■ enclose or surround a place: *the village is shut in by the mountains.* ■ trap something by shutting a door or drawer on it: *you shut your finger in the door.* **shut off** (or **shut something off**) (used esp. in relation to water, electricity, or gas) stop (or cause something to stop) flowing. ■ stop (or cause something to stop) working. ■ (**shut something off**) block the entrances and exits of something. **shut oneself off** isolate oneself from other people. **shut someone/something out** keep someone or something out of a place or situation. ■ prevent an opponent from scoring in a game. ■ screen someone or something from view. ■ prevent something from occurring. ■ block something such as a painful memory from the mind. **shut up** (or **shut someone up**) [often in imper.] informal stop (or cause someone to stop) talking. **shut something up** close all doors and windows of a building or room, typically because it will be unoccupied for some time. [OE *scyttan* 'put (a bolt) in position,' from West Gmc.; akin to Du. *schutten* 'shut up' and SHOOT.]

shut·down /'SHət,doun/ ▶ n. a closure of a factory or system, typically a temporary closure due to a fault or for maintenance. ■ a turning off of a computer or computer system.

Shute /SHo͞ot/, Nevil (1899–1960), English writer; pen name of *Nevil Shute Norway*. His novels include the post-apocalyptic *On the Beach* (1957).

shut-eye ▶ n. informal sleep: *we'd better get some shut-eye.*

shut-in ▶ n. 1 a person confined indoors, esp. as a result of physical or mental disability. 2 a state or period in which an oil or gas well has available but unused capacity. ▶ adj. 1 of or relating to confinement indoors; confined indoors. 2 relating to or denoting available but unused capacity in an oil or gas well.

shut·off (also **shut-off**) ▶ n. [usu. as adj.] a device used for stopping a supply or operation: *a shutoff valve.* ■ the cessation of flow, supply, or activity.

shut·out /'SHət,out/ ▶ n. a competition or game in which the losing side fails to score.

shut·ter /'SHətər/ ▶ n. 1 each of a pair of hinged panels fixed inside or outside a window that can be closed for security or privacy or to keep out light. 2 Photog. a device that opens and closes to expose the film in a camera. ▶ v. [trans.] close the shutters of (a window or building). ■ close (a business). — **shut·ter·less** adj.

shut·ter·bug /'SHətər,bəg/ ▶ n. informal an enthusiastic amateur photographer.

shut·tle /'SHətl/ ▶ n. 1 a form of transportation that travels regularly between two places. ■ short for SPACE SHUTTLE. 2 a wooden device with two pointed ends holding a bobbin, used for carrying the weft thread between the warp threads in weaving. ■ a bobbin carrying the lower thread in a sewing machine. 3 short for SHUTTLECOCK. ▶ v. [intrans.] travel regularly between two or more places. ■ [trans.] transport in a shuttle. [OE *scytel* 'dart,' from Gmc.; akin to ON *skutill* 'harpoon' and SHOOT.]

shuttlecock

shut·tle·cock /'SHətl,käk/ ▶**n.** a cork to which feathers are attached to form a cone shape, or a similar object of plastic, struck with rackets in the games of badminton and battledore.

shut·tle·craft /'SHətl,kraft/ ▶**n.** (in science fiction) a space shuttle, typically one used for traveling between a larger spaceship and a planet or between planets in a solar system.

shut·tle di·plo·ma·cy ▶**n.** negotiations conducted by a mediator who travels between two or more parties that are reluctant to hold direct discussions.

shy[1] /SHī/ ▶**adj.** (**shy·er, shy·est**) **1** having or showing nervousness or timidity in the company of other people: *a shy smile.* ■ [predic.] (**shy about**) slow or reluctant to do (something). ■ [in comb.] having a dislike of or aversion to a specified thing: *camera-shy.* ■ (of a wild mammal or bird) reluctant to remain in sight of humans. **2** [predic.] (**shy of**) informal less than; short of. ■ before: *he left school just shy of his fourteenth birthday.* ▶**v.** (**shies, shied**) [intrans.] (esp. of a horse) start suddenly aside in fright at an object, noise, or movement. ■ (**shy from**) avoid doing or becoming involved in (something) due to nervousness or a lack of confidence. ▶**n.** a sudden startled movement, esp. of a frightened horse. — **shy·er** /'SHīər/ **n. shy·ly adv. shy·ness n.** [OE *scēoh* 'easily frightened,' from Gmc.; akin to Ger. *scheuen* 'shun'; compare ESCHEW.]

shy[2] dated ▶**v.** (**shies, shied**) [trans.] fling or throw (something) at a target. ▶**n.** (pl. **shies**) an act of throwing something at a target. [18th C.: of unknown origin.]

Shy·lock /'SHī,läk/ a Jewish moneylender in Shakespeare's *Merchant of Venice*, who lends money to Antonio but demands in return a pound of Antonio's own flesh should the debt not be repaid on time. ■ [as n.] (**a Shylock**) a moneylender who charges extremely high rates of interest.

shy·ster /'SHīstər/ ▶**n.** informal a person, esp. a lawyer, who uses unscrupulous, fraudulent, or deceptive methods in business. [19th C.: perh. akin to Ger. *Scheisser* 'worthless person,' from *Scheisse* 'excrement.']

SI ▶**abbr.** ■ the international system of units of measurement. [from Fr. *Système International.*]

Si ▶**symb.** the chemical element silicon.

si /sē/ ▶**n.** Music another term for TI. [18th C.: from the initial letters of *Sancte Iohannes*, the closing words of a L. hymn (see SOLMIZATION).]

si·al /'sī,al/ ▶**n.** Geol. the material of the upper part of the earth's crust, characterized as light and rich in silica and alumina. Contrasted with SIMA. [1920s: from initial letters of SILICA, ALUMINA.]

si·al·a·gogue /sī'alə,gäg/ ▶**n.** Med. a drug that promotes the secretion of saliva. [18th C.: from Fr., from Gk. *sialon* 'saliva' + *agōgos* 'leading.']

Si·am /sī'am/ former name (until 1939) of THAILAND.

Si·am, Gulf of former name of the Gulf of Thailand (see THAILAND, GULF OF).

si·a·mang /'sēə,mäNG/ ▶**n.** a large black gibbon (*Hylobates syndactylus*) native to Sumatra and the Malay peninsula. [19th C.: from Malay.]

Si·a·mese /,sīə'mēz/ ▶**n.** (pl. same) **1** dated a native of Siam (now Thailand). **2** old-fashioned term for THAI (the language). **3** (also **Siamese cat**) a cat of a lightly built short-haired breed characterized by slanting blue eyes and typically pale fur with darker points. ▶**adj.** dated of or concerning Siam, its people, or language.

Si·a·mese fight·ing fish ▶**n.** see FIGHTING FISH.

Si·a·mese twins ▶**plural n.** twins that are physically joined at birth, sometimes sharing organs, and sometimes separable by surgery. [after the *Siamese* men Chang and Eng (1811–74), who were joined at the waist.]

sib /sib/ ▶**n. 1** esp. Zool. a brother or sister; a sibling. **2** Anthropol. a group of people recognized by an individual as his or her kindred. [OE, 'rel.']

Si·be·li·us /si'bālēəs/, Jean (1865–1957), Finnish composer; born *Johan Julius Christian Sibelius.* His works include *Finlandia* (1899).

Si·be·ri·a /sī'bi(ə)rēə/ a vast region of Russia that extends from the Ural Mountains to the Pacific Ocean and from the Arctic coast to the northern borders of Kazakhstan, Mongolia, and China. — **Si·be·ri·an adj. & n.**

sib·i·lant /'sibələnt/ ▶**adj.** Phonet. (of a speech sound) sounded with a hissing effect, for example *s, sh.* ■ making or characterized by a hissing sound. ▶**n.** Phonet. a sibilant speech sound. — **sib·i·lance n.** [17th C.: from L. *sibilant-* 'hissing,' from the verb *sibilare.*]

sib·i·late /'sibə,lāt/ ▶**v.** [trans.] utter with a hissing sound. — **sib·i·la·tion** /,sibə'lāSHən/ **n.** [17th C.: from L. *sibilat-* 'hissed, whistled,' from the verb *sibilare.*]

sib·ling /'sibliNG/ ▶**n.** each of two or more children or offspring having one or both parents in common; a brother or sister. [OE, 'relative' (see SIB, -LING).]

sib·yl /'sibəl/ ▶**n.** a woman in ancient times supposed to utter the oracles and prophecies of a god. ■ literary a woman able to foretell the future. — **sib·yl·line** /'sibə,līn; -,lēn/ **adj.** [ult. from med. L. *Sibilla*, via L. from Gk. *Sibulla.*]

Sic. ▶**abbr.** ■ Sicilian. ■ Sicily.

sic[1] /sik/ ▶**adv.** used in brackets after a copied or quoted word that appears odd or erroneous to show that the word is quoted exactly as it stands in the original, as in *a story must hold a child's interest and "enrich his* [sic] *life."* [L., lit. 'so, thus.']

sic[2] (also **sick**) ▶**v.** (**sicced, sic·cing** or **sicked, sick·ing**) [trans.] (**sic something on**) set a dog or other animal on (someone or something). ■ (**sic someone on**) informal set someone to pursue, keep watch on, or accompany (another). [19th C.: dial. var. of SEEK.]

sic·ca·tive /'sikətiv/ ▶**n.** a drying agent used as a component of paint. ▶**adj.** having the property of causing drying. [ME: from late L. *siccativus*, from *siccare* 'to dry.']

Si·chuan /'sicH'wän; 'sœcH-/ (also **Sze·chuan** or **Sze·chwan** /'secH-/) a province in west central China.

Si·ci·lia /si'silyə; sē'cHēlyä/ Italian name for SICILY.

Sic·i·ly /'sisəlē/ a large Italian island in the Mediterranean Sea, off southwestern Italy; capital, Palermo. Italian name SICILIA. — **Si·cil·ian** /si'silyən/ **adj. & n.**

sick[1] /sik/ ▶**adj. 1** affected by physical or mental illness: *we were sick with bronchitis* | [as pl. n.] (**the sick**) *visiting the sick and the elderly.* ■ of or relating to those who are ill: *the company organized a sick fund for its workers.* ■ fig. (of an organization, system, or society) suffering from serious problems, esp. of a financial nature. ■ archaic pining or longing for someone or something: *he was sick for a sight of her.* **2** [predic.] feeling nauseous and wanting to vomit. ■ [attrib.] (of an emotion) so intense as to cause one to feel unwell or nauseous: *he had a sick fear of returning.* ■ informal disappointed, mortified, or miserable: *I feel so sick about losing the game.* **3** [predic.] (**sick of**) intensely annoyed with or bored by (someone or something) as a result of having had too much of them: *Men! I'm sick of them.* **4** informal (esp. of humor) having something unpleasant such as death, illness, or misfortune as its subject and dealing with it in an offensive way: *a sick joke.* ■ (of a person) having abnormal or unnatural tendencies; perverted: *he is a deeply sick man from whom society needs to be protected.* ▶**n.** Brit., informal vomit. ▶**v.** [trans.] (**sick something up**) informal bring something up by vomiting.
– PHRASES **be sick 1** be ill. **2** vomit. **fall** (or **take**) **sick** become ill. **get sick 1** become ill. **2** vomit. **make someone sick** cause someone to vomit or feel nauseous or unwell. ■ cause someone to feel intense annoyance or disgust: *you're so damned self-righteous you make me sick!* — **oneself sick** do something to such an extent that one feels nauseous or unwell (often used for emphasis): *she was worrying herself sick about Mike.* **sick and tired of** informal annoyed about or bored with (something) and unwilling to put up with it any longer. (**as**) **sick as a dog** informal extremely ill. **sick to death of** informal another way of saying SICK AND TIRED OF above. **sick to one's stomach** nauseous. ■ disgusted. **worried sick** extremely worried: *the staff were worried sick about their jobs.* — **sick·ish adj.** [OE *sēoc* 'affected by illness,' from Gmc.; akin to Ger. *siech.*]

sick[2] ▶**v.** variant of SIC[2].

sick·bay /'sik,bā/ (also **sick bay**) ▶**n.** a room or building set aside for the treatment or accommodation of the sick, esp. within a military base or on board a ship.

sick·bed /'sik,bed/ ▶**n.** an invalid's bed (often used to refer to the state or condition of being an invalid): *consecrated bread was taken to baptized believers languishing on a sickbed.*

sick build·ing syn·drome ▶**n.** a condition affecting office workers, typically marked by headaches and respiratory problems, attributed to unhealthy factors in the working environment such as poor ventilation.

sick call ▶**n. 1** a visit to a sick person, typically one made by a doctor or priest. **2** Mil. a summons for those reporting sick to attend for treatment.

sick day ▶**n.** a day taken off from work because of illness.

sick·en /'sikən/ ▶**v. 1** [trans.] (often **be sickened**) make (someone) feel disgusted or appalled: *the stench of blood sickened him.* ■ [intrans.] archaic feel disgust or horror: *he sickened at the thought.* **2** [intrans.] become ill. ■ (**sicken for**) begin to show symptoms of (a particular illness): *I hope I'm not sickening for a cold.*

sick·en·er /'sikənər/ ▶**n. 1** informal something that causes disgust or severe disappointment. **2** (**the sickener**) a poisonous toadstool (genus *Russula*, family Russulaceae) with a red cap and a white or cream-colored stem and gills, found commonly in Eurasia and North America.

sick·en·ing /'sikəniNG/ ▶**adj.** causing or liable to cause a feeling of nausea or disgust: *those who viewed the films found them sickening.* ■ informal causing irritation or annoyance: *it is sickening to think we had done enough to win and then had to leave with nothing.* — **sick·en·ing·ly adv.**

sick head·ache ▶**n.** a headache accompanied by nausea, particularly a migraine.

sick·ie /'sikē/ ▶**n.** informal another term for SICKO.

sick·le /'sikəl/ ▶**n.** a short-handled farming tool with a semicircular blade, used for cutting grain, lopping, or trimming. [OE *sicol, sicel*, from Gmc.; akin to Ger. *Sichel*, based on L. *secula*, from *secare* 'to cut.']

sickle

sick leave ▶**n.** leave of absence granted because of illness.

sick·le cell a·ne·mi·a /'sikəl sel ə'nēmēə/ (also **sick·le cell dis·ease**) ▶**n.** a severe hereditary form of anemia in which a mutated form of hemoglobin distorts the red blood cells into a crescent shape. It is commonest among those of African descent.

sick·le cell trait ▶**n.** a relatively mild condition caused by the presence of a single gene for sickle cell anemia, conferring some resistance to malaria.

sick·le feath·er ▶n. each of the long middle feathers of a rooster's tail.

sick list ▶n. a list, esp. in the army or navy, of people who are ill and unable to work.

sick·ly /'siklē/ ▶adj. (**-li·er, -li·est**) **1** often ill; in poor health. ■ (of a person's complexion or expression) indicative of poor health. ■ literary (of a place, climate, or time) causing or characterized by unhealthiness. **2** (of a flavor, smell, color, or light) so unpleasant as to induce discomfort or nausea: *sickly green.* ■ excessively sentimental or mawkish. ▶adv. in a sick manner; weakly; nauseously: *he stared at the phone sickly | Lisa felt her stomach turn over sickly inside her.* — **sick·li·ness** n.

sick·ness /'siknis/ ▶n. **1** the state of being ill: [as adj.] *a sickness allowance.* ■ [often with adj.] a particular type of illness or disease: *suffering an incurable sickness.* **2** the feeling or fact of being affected with nausea or vomiting: *travel sickness.*

sick·o /'sikō/ ▶n. (pl. **-os**) informal a mentally ill or perverted person, esp. one who is sadistic.

sick·out /'sik,out/ (also **sick-out**) ▶n. informal an organized period of unwarranted sick leave taken as a group protest, usually to avoid a formal strike.

sick·room /'sik,ro͞om/ ▶n. a room in a school or place of work occupied by or set apart for people who are unwell. ■ a room occupied by an ill person.

si·dal·cea /sī'dalshēə/ ▶n. a herbaceous North American plant (genus *Sidalcea*) of the mallow family, several kinds of which are cultivated as ornamentals. [mod. L., from *Sida* + *Alcea*, rel. genera.]

sid·dha /'sidə/ ▶n. Hinduism one who has achieved spiritual realization and supernatural power. [Sanskrit.]

Sid·dhar·tha Gau·ta·ma /si'därtə 'gôtəmə; si'därTHə-/ see **BUDDHA**.

sid·dhi /'sidē/ ▶n. Hinduism & Buddhism **1** complete understanding and enlightenment possessed by a siddha. **2** (pl. **-dhis**) a paranormal power possessed by a siddha. [Sanskrit.]

Sid·dons /'sidnz/, Mrs. Sarah (1755–1831), English actress; sister of John Kemble (1757–1823); born *Sarah Kemble.* She was an acclaimed tragic actress, noted particularly for her role as Lady Macbeth.

side /sīd/ ▶n. **1** a position to the left or right of an object, place, or central point: *a town on the other side of the river | on either side of the entrance was a garden | Rachel tilted her head to one side.* ■ either of the two halves of an object, surface, or place regarded as divided by an imaginary central line: *she lay on her side of the bed | the left side of the brain.* ■ the right or the left part of a person's or animal's body, esp. of the human torso: *he has been paralyzed on his right side since birth.* ■ [in sing.] a place or position closely adjacent to someone: *his wife stood at his side.* ■ either of the lateral halves of the body of a butchered animal, or an animal or fish prepared for eating: *a side of beef.* **2** an upright or sloping surface of a structure or object that is not the top or bottom and generally not the front or back: *a car crashed into the side of the house | line the sides of the cake pan |* [as adj.] *a side entrance.* ■ each of the flat surfaces of a solid object. ■ either of the two surfaces of something flat and thin, such as paper or cloth. ■ the amount of writing needed to fill one side of a sheet of paper: *she told us not to write more than three sides.* ■ either of the two faces of a record or of the two separate tracks on a length of recording tape. **3** a part or region near the edge and away from the middle of something: *a minivan was parked at the side of the road | cabins on the south side of the clearing.* ■ [as adj.] subsidiary to or less important than something: *a side dish of fresh vegetables.* ■ a dish served as subsidiary to the main one: *sides of German potato salad and red cabbage.* ■ each of the lines forming the boundary of a plane rectilinear figure: *the farm buildings formed three sides of a square.* **4** a person or group opposing another or others in a dispute, contest, or debate: *the two sides agreed to resume border trade | whose side are you on?* ■ esp. Brit. a sports team. ■ the position, interests, or attitude of one person or group, esp. when regarded as being in opposition to another or others: *Mrs. Burt hasn't kept her side of the bargain | the conservationists are on the city's side of the case.* ■ a particular aspect of something, esp. a situation or a person's character: *her ability to put up with his disagreeable side.* ■ a person's kinship or line of descent as traced through either their father or mother: *Richard was of French descent on his mother's side.* **5** (also **side·spin**) horizontal spinning motion given to a ball. ■ Billiards another term for **ENGLISH** (sense 3). ▶v. **1** [intrans.] (**side with/against**) support or oppose in a conflict, dispute, or debate: *he felt that Maxwell had betrayed him by siding with Beatrice.* **2** [trans.] provide with a side or sides; form the side of: *the hills that side a long valley.*

– PHRASES **by** (or **at**) **someone's side** close to someone, esp. so as to give them comfort or moral support: *a stepson who stayed by your side when your own son deserted you.* **by the side of** close to: *a house by the side of the road.* **from side to side 1** alternately left and right from a central point: *I shook my head frantically from side to side.* **2** across the entire width; right across: *the fleet stretched four miles from side to side.* **have something on one's side** (or **something is on one's side**) something is operating to one's advantage: *now that he had time on his side, Tom relaxed a little.* **on** (or **to**) **one side** out of one's way; aside. ■ to be dealt with or considered later, esp. because tending to distract one from something more important: *before the kickoff a player has to set his disappointments and frustrations to one side.* **on the —— side** tending toward being ——; rather —— (used to qualify an adjective): *these shoes are a bit on the tight side.* **on the side 1** in addition to one's regular job or as a subsidiary source of income: *no one lived in the property, but the caretaker made a little on the side by renting rooms out.* **2** secretly, esp. with regard to a relationship in addition to one's legal or regular partner: *Brian had a mistress on the side.* **3** served separately from the main dish: *a club sandwich with French fries on the side.* **side by side** (of two or more people or things) close together and facing the same way: *on we jogged, side by side, for a mile.* ■ together: *we have been using both systems, side by side, for two years.* ■ (of people or groups) supporting each other; in cooperation: *the two institutions worked side by side in complete harmony.* **side of the fence** see **FENCE**. **take sides** support one person or cause against another or others in a dispute, conflict, or contest: *I do not want to take sides in this matter.* **take** (or **draw**) **someone to one side** speak to someone in private, esp. so as to advise or warn them about something. **this side of 1** before (a particular time, date, or event): *this side of midnight.* ■ yet to reach (a particular age): *I'm this side of forty-five.* **2** informal used in superlative expressions to denote that something is comparable with a paragon or model of its kind: *the finest coffee this side of Brazil.* — **side·less** adj. [OE *sīde* 'left or right part of the body,' of Gmc. origin; rel. to Du. *zijde* and Ger. *Seite*, prob. from a base meaning 'extending lengthwise.']

side·arm[1] /'sīd,ärm/ ▶adj. [attrib.] (of a throw, pitch, or cast) performed or delivered with a sweeping motion of the arm at or below shoulder level. ■ (of a person, typically a baseball pitcher) using such a sweeping motion of the arm. ▶adv. in a sidearm manner: *I could throw sidearm.* ▶v. [trans.] esp. Baseball throw or pitch a ball to (someone) with such a motion of the arm. ■ throw or pitch (a ball or other object) in this way. — **side·arm·er** n.

side·arm[2] (also **side arm**) ▶n. a weapon worn at a person's side, such as a pistol or other small firearm (or, formerly, a sword or bayonet).

side·band /'sīd,band/ ▶n. Telecom. one of two frequency bands on either side of the carrier wave, containing the modulated signal.

side·bar /'sīd,bär/ ▶n. a short article in a newspaper or magazine, typically boxed, placed alongside a main article, and containing additional material. ■ a secondary, additional, or incidental thing; a side issue: *nut collecting has become a commercial sidebar to most black walnut plantations |* [as adj.] *one of the festival's sidebar series.* ■ (also **sidebar conference**) (in a court of law) a discussion between the lawyers and the judge held out of earshot of the jury.

side bet ▶n. a bet over and above the main bet, esp. on a subsidiary issue: *side bets were made that she would be the next to leave the board.*

side·board /'sīd,bôrd/ ▶n. a flat-topped piece of furniture with cupboards and drawers, used for storing dishes, glasses, and table linen.

side·burn /'sīd,bərn/ ▶n. (usu. **sideburns**) a strip of hair grown by a man down each side of the face in front of his ears: *he kept his small mustache and sideburns neatly trimmed.* [19th C.: from *burnside*, after General *Burnside* (1824–81).]

side·car /'sīd,kär/ ▶n. **1** a small, low vehicle attached to the side of a motorcycle for carrying passengers. **2** a cocktail of brandy and lemon juice with orange liqueur.

side chain ▶n. Chem. a group of atoms attached to the main part of a molecule with a ring or chain structure.

side chair ▶n. an upright wooden chair without arms.

sid·ed /'sīdid/ ▶adj. [in comb.] having sides of a specified number or type: *narrow, steep-sided canyons.* — **sid·ed·ly** adv. [in comb.]. **sid·ed·ness** n.

side dish ▶n. a dish served as subsidiary to the main one: *a side dish of fresh vegetables.*

side drum ▶n. another term for **SNARE DRUM**. [18th C.: because it was suspended from the drummer's side.]

side ef·fect ▶n. a secondary, typically undesirable effect of a drug or medical treatment.

side-glance ▶n. a sideways or brief glance.

side·hill /'sīd,hil/ ▶n. a hillside.

side is·sue ▶n. a point or topic connected to or raised by some other issue, but not as important, esp. one that distracts attention from the more important issue.

side·kick /'sīd,kik/ ▶n. informal a person's close associate, esp. one who has less authority.

side·light /'sīd,līt/ ▶n. a light placed at the side of something: *a designer village with sidelights along the pathways.* ■ (**sidelights**) a ship's port (red) and starboard (green) navigation lights. ■ fig. a piece of incidental information that helps to clarify or enliven a subject: *one has to wade through pages of extraneous material in order to discover these sidelights on the management of an estate.* ■ natural light coming from the side: *through the window blazed the cold light of winter morning; sidelight, the most harsh.*

side·line /'sīd,līn/ ▶n. **1** an activity done in addition to one's main job, esp. to earn extra income: *he founded the fast-food company* **as a sideline to** *his gas station | Frederick is developing* **a sideline in** *composing.* ■ an auxiliary line of goods or business: **a sideline in** *glow-in-the-dark crucifixes.* **2** (usu. **sidelines**) either of the two lines bounding the longer sides of a football field, basketball court, tennis court, or similar playing area. ■ the area immediately outside such lines as a place for nonplayers, substitutes, or spectators. ▶v. [trans.] (often **be sidelined**) cause (a player) to be unable to play on a team or in a game: *an ankle injury has sidelined him for two weeks.* ■ fig. remove from the center of activity or attention: *a respected lawyer will be sidelined by alcohol abuse.*

side·long /'sīd,lôNG/ ▶ **adj. & adv.** directed to or from one side; sideways.

side·man /'sīd,man/ ▶ **n.** (pl. **-men**) a supporting musician in a jazz band or rock group.

side·meat /'sīd,mēt/ ▶ **n.** salt pork or bacon, typically cut from the side of the pig.

side-necked tur·tle ▶ **n.** a freshwater turtle (families Chelidae and Pelomedusidae) with a relatively long head and neck that is retracted sideways into the shell for defense.

side-on ▶ **adv.** with the side of someone or something toward something else. ▶ **adj.** directed from or toward a side. ■ (of a collision) involving the side of a vehicle.

side plate ▶ **n.** a plate smaller than a dinner plate, used for bread or other accompaniments to a meal.

si·de·re·al /sī'di(ə)rēəl/ ▶ **adj.** of or with respect to the stars (i.e., the fixed stars, not the sun or planets). [17th C.: from L. *sidereus*, from *sidus, sider-* 'star.']

si·de·re·al clock ▶ **n.** Astron. a clock measuring sidereal time in terms of 24 equal divisions of a sidereal day.

si·de·re·al day ▶ **n.** Astron. the time between two consecutive transits of the First Point of Aries, almost four minutes shorter than the solar day because of the earth's orbital motion.

si·de·re·al month ▶ **n.** Astron. the time it takes the moon to orbit once around the earth with respect to the stars (approximately 27¼ days).

si·de·re·al pe·ri·od ▶ **n.** Astron. the period of revolution of one body around another with respect to the distant stars.

si·de·re·al time ▶ **n.** Astron. time reckoned from the motion of the earth (or a planet) relative to the distant stars (rather than with respect to the sun).

si·de·re·al year ▶ **n.** Astron. the orbital period of the earth around the sun, about 20 minutes longer than the solar year.

sid·er·ite /'sidə,rīt/ ▶ **n.** **1** a brown mineral consisting of ferrous carbonate, occurring as rhombohedral crystals in mineral veins. **2** a meteorite consisting mainly of nickel and iron. — **sid·er·it·ic** /,sidə'ritik/ **adj.** [16th C.: from Gk. *sidēros* 'iron.']

sidero-[1] ▶ **comb. form** of or relating to the stars: *siderostat.* [from L. *sidus, sider-* 'star.']

sidero-[2] ▶ **comb. form** of or relating to iron: *siderophore.* [from Gk. *sidēros* 'iron.']

sid·er·o·phore /'sidərə,fôr/ ▶ **n.** Biochem. a molecule that binds and transports iron in microorganisms.

sid·er·o·stat /'sidərə,stat/ ▶ **n.** Astron. an instrument used for keeping the image of a celestial object in a fixed position.

side·sad·dle /'sīd,sadl/ (also **side-sad·dle**) ▶ **n.** a saddle in which the rider has both feet on the same side of the horse, used by a woman wearing a skirt. ▶ **adv.** sitting in this position on a horse.

side shoot ▶ **n.** a shoot growing from the side of a plant's stem.

side·show /'sīd,SHō/ ▶ **n.** a small show or stall at an exhibition, fair, or circus. ■ fig. a minor or diverting incident or issue, esp. one that distracts attention from something more important.

side·slip /'sīd,slip/ (also **side-slip**) ▶ **n.** a sideways skid or slip. ■ Aeron. a sideways movement of an aircraft, esp. downward toward the inside of a turn. ■ (in skiing and surfing) an act of traveling down a slope or wave in a direction not in line with one's skis or board. ▶ **v.** [intrans.] skid or slip sideways. ■ Aeron. move in a sideslip: *every so often the machine would lose control and simply sideslip into the ground.* ■ (in skiing and surfing) travel sideways or in any direction not in line with one's skis or board: *he had sideslipped down the sheer drop from the shoulder of the mountain.*

side·spin /'sīd,spin/ ▶ **n.** see **side** (sense 5).

side·split·ting /'sīd,splitiNG/ ▶ **adj.** informal extremely amusing; causing violent laughter.

side·step /'sīd,step/ ▶ **v.** (**-stepped, -step·ping**) [trans.] avoid (someone or something) by stepping sideways. ■ fig. avoid dealing with or discussing (something problematic or disagreeable). ■ [intrans.] Skiing climb or descend by lifting alternate skis while sideways on the slope. ▶ **n.** a step taken sideways, typically to avoid someone or something. — **side·step·per n.**

side·stream smoke /'sīd,strēm/ ▶ **n.** smoke that passes from a cigarette into the surrounding air, rather than into the smoker's lungs: *asthmatics experience a significant decline in lung function when exposed to sidestream smoke.*

side street ▶ **n.** a minor or subsidiary street.

side·stroke /'sīd,strōk/ ▶ **n.** [in sing.] a swimming stroke similar to the breaststroke in which the swimmer lies on their side.

side·swipe /'sīd,swīp/ ▶ **n.** **1** a glancing blow from or on the side of something, esp. a motor vehicle. **2** a passing critical remark about someone or something. ▶ **v.** [trans.] strike (someone or something) with or as if with a glancing blow. *Curtis jerked the wheel hard over and sideswiped the other car.*

side ta·ble ▶ **n.** a table placed at the side of a room or apart from the main table.

side·track /'sīd,trak/ ▶ **v.** [trans.] (usu. **be/get sidetracked**) **1** cause (someone) to be distracted from an immediate or important issue. *he does not let himself get sidetracked by fads and trends.* ■ divert (a project or debate) away from a central issue or previously determined plan. **2** direct (a train) into a branch line or siding. ▶ **n.** a minor path or track. ■ a railroad branch line or siding.

side trip ▶ **n.** a minor excursion during a voyage or trip.

side view ▶ **n.** a view from the side.

side·walk /'sīd,wôk/ ▶ **n.** a raised paved or asphalted path for pedestrians at the side of a road.

side·wall /'sīd,wôl/ ▶ **n.** **1** (often **side wall**) a wall forming the side of a structure or room. **2** the side of a tire, typically untreaded. ■ a tire with distinctively colored sidewalls.

side·ward /'sīdwərd/ ▶ **adj.** another term for **sideways**. ▶ **adv.** (also **side·wards** /-wərdz/) another term for **sideways**.

side·ways /'sīd,wāz/ ▶ **adv. & adj.** to, toward, or from the side. ■ [as adv.] with one side facing forward: *the truck slid sideways across the road.* ■ so as to occupy a job or position at the same level as one previously held rather than be promoted or demoted: [as adj.] *sideways moves for managers.* ■ by an indirect way: [as adv.] *he came into politics sideways, as campaign manager for the president.* ■ [as adj.] from an unconventional or unorthodox viewpoint: *take a sideways look at daily life.*

– PHRASES **knock someone sideways** see **knock**.

side·wheel·er ▶ **n.** a steamboat with paddle wheels on either side. — **side-wheel adj.**

side whisk·ers ▶ **plural n.** whiskers or sideburns on a man's cheeks.

side·wind·er[1] /'sīd,wīndər/ ▶ **n.** a pale-colored, nocturnal, burrowing rattlesnake (*Crotalus cerastes*) that moves sideways over sand by throwing its body into S-shaped curves. It is found in the deserts of North America.

side·wind·er[2] ▶ **n.** a heavy blow with the fist delivered from or on the side.

side·wise /'sīd,wīz/ ▶ **adv. & adj.** another term for **sideways**.

sid·ing /'sīdiNG/ ▶ **n.** **1** a short track at the side of and opening onto a railroad line, used for shunting or stabling trains. ■ a loop line. **2** cladding material for the outside of a building.

si·dle /'sīdl/ ▶ **v.** [intrans.] walk in a furtive or timid manner, esp. obliquely: *I sidled up to her.* ▶ **n.** [in sing.] an instance of walking in this way. [17th C.: back-form. from *sideling* (see **sidelong**).]

Si·don /'sīdn/ a city in Lebanon, on the Mediterranean coast; pop. 38,000. It was a Phoenician seaport and city-state. Arabic name **Saida**.

Sid·ra, Gulf of /'sidrə/ (also **Gulf of Sirte**) a broad inlet of the Mediterranean Sea on the coast of Libya.

SIDS /sidz/ ▶ **abbr.** sudden infant death syndrome.

siege /sēj/ ▶ **n.** a military operation in which enemy forces surround a town or building, cutting off supplies, with the aim of compelling the surrender of those inside. ■ a similar operation by a police or other force to compel the surrender of an armed person. ■ a prolonged period of misfortune.

– PHRASES **lay siege to** conduct a siege of (a place). **under siege** (of a place) undergoing a siege. [ME: from OFr. *sege*, from *asegier* 'besiege.']

siege men·tal·i·ty ▶ **n.** a defensive or paranoid attitude based on the belief that others are hostile toward one.

Sieg·fried /'sēg,frēd/ the hero of the Nibelungenlied. He obtains a hoard of treasure by killing the dragon Fafner, marries Kriemhild, and helps Gunther to win Brunhild before being killed by Hagen.

Sieg·fried Line /'sēg,frēd/ the line of defense constructed by the Germans along the western frontier of Germany before World War II. ■ another term for **Hindenburg Line**.

Sieg Heil /,sēg 'hīl/ ▶ **exclam.** a victory salute used originally by Nazis at political rallies. — **Sieg-Heil·ing adj.** [Ger., lit. 'hail victory!']

Sie·mens /'zēmənz; 'sē-/ a German family of scientists. Ernst Werner (1816–92) was an electrical engineer who developed electroplating and pioneered electrical traction. His brother Karl Wilhelm (1823–83) (also known as *Sir Charles William Siemens*) developed the open-hearth steel furnace. Their brother Friedrich (1826–1904) applied the principles of the open-hearth furnace to glassmaking.

sie·mens /'sēmənz/ (abbr.: **S**) ▶ **n.** Physics the SI unit of conductance, equal to one reciprocal ohm. [1930s: K. W. von **Siemens**.]

Si·e·na /sē'enə/ a city in west central Italy; pop. 58,000. In the 13th and 14th centuries, it was an art center. — **Si·en·ese** /,sēə'nēz; -'nēs/ **adj. & n.**

si·en·na /sē'enə/ ▶ **n.** a kind of ferruginous earth used as a pigment in painting, normally yellowish-brown in color (**raw sienna**) or deep reddish-brown when roasted (**burnt sienna**). ■ the color of this pigment. [18th C.: from Ital. *(terra di) Sienna* '(earth of) Siena.']

Sier·pin·ski tri·an·gle /SHir'pinskē/ (also **Sierpinski gasket**) ▶ **n.** Math. a fractal based on a triangle with four equal triangles inscribed in it. The central triangle is removed and each of the other three treated as the original was, and so on, creating an infinite regression in a finite space. [1970s: named after Waclaw *Sierpiński* (1882–1969), Polish mathematician.]

si·er·ra /sē'erə/ ▶ **n.** **1** a long jagged mountain chain. **2** a code word representing the letter S, used in radio communication. [16th C.: Sp., from L. *serra* 'saw.']

Si·er·ra Le·one /sē,erə lē'ōn/ a country on the coast of West Africa. *See box on next page.* — **Si·er·ra Le·o·ne·an** /lē'ōnēən/ **adj. & n.**

Si·er·ra Ma·dre /'mä,drā/ a mountain system in Mexico.

Si·er·ra Ne·vad·a /nə'vadə/ **1** a mountain range in southern Spain, in Andalusia, southeast of Granada. **2** a mountain range in eastern California.

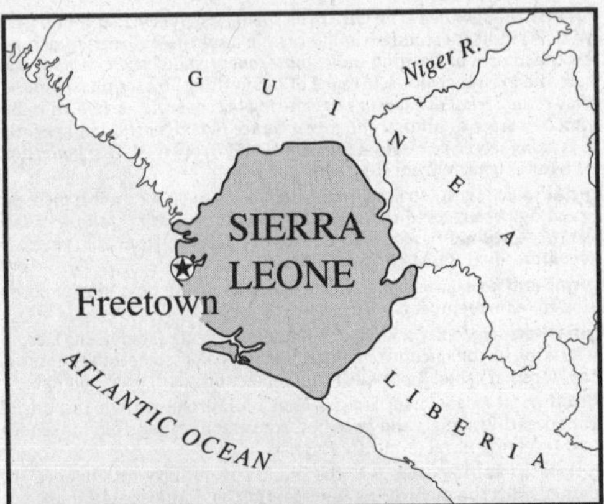

Sierra Leone

Official name: Republic of Sierra Leone
Location: West Africa, on the Atlantic coast, northwest of Liberia
Area: 27,700 square miles (71,700 sq km)
Population: 5,883,000
Capital: Freetown
Languages: English (official), Creole, Temne, and other West African languages
Currency: leone

si·es·ta /sēˈestə/ ▶ n. an afternoon rest or nap, esp. one taken during the hottest hours of the day in a hot climate. [17th C.: Sp., from L. *sexta (hora)* 'sixth hour.']

sieve /siv/ ▶ n. a utensil consisting of a mesh held in a frame, used for straining solids from liquids, for separating coarser from finer particles, or for reducing soft solids to a pulp. ■ used figuratively with reference to the fact that a sieve does not hold all its contents. ▶ v. [trans.] put (a food substance or other material) through a sieve. ■ [intrans.] **(sieve through)** fig. examine in detail. — **sieve·like** /-ˌlīk/ adj. [OE *sife* (n.), from West Gmc.; akin to Ger. *Sieb*.]

sieve plate ▶ n. Bot. an area of relatively large pores in the common end walls of sieve tube elements. ■ Zool. a perforated plate in the integument of an invertebrate, esp. the madreporite of an echinoderm.

sie·vert /ˈsēvərt/ (abbr.: **Sv**) ▶ n. Physics the SI unit of dose equivalent (the biological effect of ionizing radiation), defined as that which delivers a joule of energy per kilogram of recipient mass. [1940s: Rolf M. *Sievert* (1896–1966), Swedish radiologist.]

sieve tube ▶ n. Bot. a series of sieve tube elements placed end to end to form a continuous tube.

si·fa·ka /sнəˈfakə; -ˈfäkə; sə-/ ▶ n. a large gregarious lemur (genus *Propithecus*, family Indriidae) that leaps from tree to tree in an upright position. [19th C.: from Malagasy.]

sift /sift/ ▶ v. [trans.] put (a fine, loose, or powdery substance) through a sieve so as to remove lumps or large particles. ■ fig. examine (something) thoroughly so as to isolate that which is most important or useful: *we sifted the evidence ourselves* | [intrans.] *the fourth stage involves sifting through the data.* ■ **(sift something out)** separate something, esp. something to be discarded, from something else: *he sifted out frivolous applications.* ■ cause to flow or pass as through a sieve: *sifted the sand through her fingers.* ■ [intrans.] (of snow, ash, light, etc.) descend or float down lightly or sparsely as if sprinkled from a sieve. ▶ n. [usu. in sing.] an act of sifting something, esp. so as to isolate that which is most important or useful. ■ an amount of sifted material. — **sift·er** n. [OE *siftan*, from West Gmc.; akin to Du. *ziften* and SIEVE.]

SIG Comput. ▶ abbr. special interest group, a type of newsgroup.

Sig. ▶ abbr. Signor.

sig /sig/ ▶ n. Comput., informal a short personalized message at the end of an e-mail message.

Sig·a·to·ka /ˌsigəˈtōkə/ ▶ n. a disease of banana plants characterized by elongated spots on the leaves, which then rot completely, caused by the fungus *Mycosphaerella musicola*. [1920s: after a district in Fiji.]

sigh /sī/ ▶ v. [intrans.] emit a long, deep, audible breath expressing sadness, relief, or tiredness. ■ fig. (of the wind or something through which the wind blows) make a sound resembling this. *a breeze made the treetops sigh.* ■ **(sigh for)** literary feel a deep yearning for (someone or something lost, unattainable, or distant). ▶ n. a long, deep, audible exhalation expressing sadness, relief, tiredness, or a similar feeling. ■ fig. a gentle sound resembling this, esp. one made by the wind. [ME (v.): prob. back-form. from *sighte*, past of *siche*, *sike*, from OE *sīcan*.]

sight /sīt/ ▶ n. **1** the faculty or power of seeing. ■ the action or fact of seeing someone or something: *the sight of blood.* ■ the area or distance within which someone can see or something can be seen: *he let Rose out of his sight.* ■ dated a person's view or consideration: *equal in the sight of God.* **2** a thing that one sees or that can be seen: *John was a familiar sight in the bar.* ■ **(sights)** places of interest to tourists and visitors in a city, town, or other place. ■ **(a sight)** informal a person or thing having a ridiculous, repulsive, or disheveled appearance. **3** (usu. **sights**) a device on a gun or optical instrument used for assisting a person's precise aim or observation. ■ an observation made with a surveying instrument or aim made through the sight of a weapon: *the navigator gave me a heading after taking a sight from the compass.* ▶ v. **1** [trans.] manage to see or observe (someone or something); catch an initial glimpse of. **2** [intrans.] take aim by looking through the sights of a gun: *she sighted down the barrel.* ■ take a detailed visual measurement of something with or as with a sight. ■ [trans.] adjust the sight of (a firearm or optical instrument). ■ [trans.] provide (a gun, quadrant, etc.) with sights.
– PHRASES **at first sight** on first seeing or meeting someone. ■ after an initial impression (which is then found to be different from what is actually the case). **catch** (or **get a**) **sight of** glimpse for a moment; suddenly notice. **in sight** visible. ■ near at hand; close to being achieved or realized. **in** (or **within**) **sight of** so as to see or be seen from. ■ within reach of; close to attaining. **in** (or **within**) **one's sights** visible, esp. through the sights of one's gun. ■ within the scope of one's ambitions or expectations. **lose sight of** be no longer able to see. ■ fail to consider, be aware of, or remember. **on** (or **at**) **sight** as soon as someone or something has been seen. **out of sight 1** not visible. **2** (also **out·a·sight**) [often as exclam.] informal extremely good; excellent. **out of sight, out of mind** proverb you soon forget people or things that are no longer visible or present. **(get) out of my sight!** go away at once! **raise** (or **lower**) **one's sights** become more (or less) ambitious; increase (or lower) one's expectations. **set one's sights on** have as an ambition; hope strongly to achieve or reach. **a sight for sore eyes** informal a person or thing that one is extremely pleased or relieved to see. **a sight to behold** a person or thing particularly impressive or worth seeing. — **sight·er** n. [OE *(ge)sihth* 'something seen,' from West Gmc.; akin to Ger. *Gesicht* 'sight, face.']

sight·ed /ˈsītid/ ▶ adj. (of a person) having the ability to see; not blind: *a sighted guide is needed* | [as pl. n.] **(the sighted)** *the blind leading the sighted, I thought.* ■ [in comb.] having a specified kind of sight: *the keen-sighted watcher may catch a glimpse.*

sight gag ▶ n. informal a visual joke.

sight glass ▶ n. a transparent tube or window through which the level of liquid in a reservoir or supply line can be checked visually.

sight·ing shot ▶ n. an experimental shot to guide shooters in adjusting their sights.

sight·less /ˈsītlis/ ▶ adj. unable to see; blind. ■ literary invisible. — **sight·less·ly** adv. **sight·less·ness** n.

sight line (also **sight·line**) ▶ n. a hypothetical line from someone's eye to what is seen (used esp. with reference to good or bad visibility).

sight·ly /ˈsītlē/ ▶ adj. pleasing to the eye. — **sight·li·ness** n.

sight-read ▶ v. [trans.] read and perform (music) at sight, without preparation: *by the time he was seven, Mozart could sight-read anything he was given* | [intrans.] *most of us couldn't sight-read.* — **sight-read·er** n. **sight-read·ing** n.

sight rhyme ▶ n. another term for EYE RHYME.

sight·see·ing /ˈsītˌsēiNG/ ▶ n. the activity of visiting places of interest in a particular location: [as adj.] *a sightseeing tour.* — **sight·see** v. **sight·se·er** /ˈsītˌsēər/ n.

sight-sing ▶ v. [trans.] sing (music) at sight, without preparation.

sight un·seen ▶ adv. without the opportunity to look at the object in question beforehand. ■ without being seen.

sig·il /ˈsijəl/ ▶ n. an inscribed or painted symbol considered to have magical power. ■ archaic a seal. ■ literary a sign or symbol. [ME: from late L. *sigillum* 'sign.']

SIGINT /ˈsigint/ ▶ abbr. signals intelligence.

sig·lum /ˈsigləm/ ▶ n. (pl. **sig·la** /ˈsiglə/) a letter (esp. an initial) or other symbol used to denote a word in a book, esp. to refer to a particular text. [18th C.: from late L. *sigla*, perh. from *singula*, neut. pl. of *singulus* 'single.']

sig·ma /ˈsigmə/ ▶ n. the eighteenth letter of the Greek alphabet (Σ, σ), transliterated as 's.' ▶ symb. ■ (Σ) mathematical sum. ■ (σ) standard deviation.

sig·mate /ˈsigmāt; -mit/ ▶ adj. having the shape of a Σ or a letter S.

sig·moid /ˈsigmoid/ ▶ adj. **1** curved like the uncial sigma (C); crescent-shaped. **2** S-shaped. ▶ n. Anat. short for SIGMOID COLON. — **sig·moi·dal** /sigˈmoidəl/ adj.

sig·moid co·lon ▶ n. Anat. the S-shaped last part of the large intestine, leading into the rectum.

sig·moid·os·co·py /ˌsigmoiˈdäskəpē/ ▶ n. examination of the sigmoid colon by means of a flexible tube inserted through the anus. — **sig·moid·o·scope** /sigˈmoidəˌskōp/ n. **sig·moid·o·scop·ic** /sigˌmoidəˈskäpik/ adj.

sign /sīn/ ▶ n. **1** an object, quality, or event whose presence or occurrence indicates the probable presence or occurrence of something else: *flowers are often given as a sign of affection* | [with clause] *the stores are full, which is a sign that the recession is past its worst.* ■ something regarded as an indication or evidence of what is happening or going to happen: ***the signs are*** *that counterfeiting is growing at an alarming rate.* ■ [with negative] used to indicate that someone or something is not present where they should be or are expected to be: *there was still no sign of her.* ■ Med. an indication of a disease detectable by a medical practitioner even if not apparent to the patient. Compare with SYMPTOM. ■ a miracle regarded as evidence of supernatural power (chiefly in biblical and literary use). ■ the trail of a wild animal: *wolverine sign.* **2** a gesture or action used to convey information or instructions: *she gave him the thumbs-up sign.* ■ a notice that is publicly displayed giving information or instructions in a written or symbolic form: *I didn't see the stop sign.* ■ an action or reaction that conveys something about someone's state or experiences: *she gave no sign of having seen him.* ■ a gesture used in a system of sign language. ■ short for SIGN LANGUAGE. ■ a symbol or word used to represent an operation, instruction, concept, or object in algebra, music, or other subjects. ■ a word or gesture given according to prior arrangement as a means of identification; a password. **3** (also **zodiacal sign**) Astrol. each of the twelve equal sections into which the zodiac is divided, named from the constellations formerly situated in each, and associated with successive periods of the year according to the position of the sun on the ecliptic: *a person born* ***under the sign of*** *Virgo.* **4** Math. the positiveness or negativeness of a quantity. ▶v. **1** [trans.] write one's name on (a letter, card, or similar item) to identify oneself as the writer or sender: *the card was signed by the whole class.* ■ indicate agreement with or authorization of the contents of (a document or other written or printed material) by attaching a signature: *the two countries signed a nonaggression treaty.* ■ write (one's name) for purposes of identification or authorization: *she signed her name in the book* | [with obj. and complement] *she* ***signed herself*** *Ingrid* | [intrans.] *he signed on the dotted line.* ■ engage (someone, typically a sports player or a musician) to work for one by signing a contract with them: *the company signed 30 bands.* ■ [intrans.] sign a contract committing oneself to work for a particular person or organization: *Sherman has* ***signed for*** *another two seasons.* **2** [intrans.] use gestures to convey information or instructions: [with infin.] *she signed to her husband to leave the room.* ■ communicate in sign language: *she was learning to sign.* ■ [trans.] express or perform (something) in sign language: [as adj.] (**signed**) *the theater routinely puts on signed performances.* ■ archaic [trans.] mark or consecrate with the sign of the cross.

– PHRASES **sign of the cross** a Christian sign made in blessing or prayer by tracing a cross from the forehead to the chest and to each shoulder, or in the air. **sign of the times** something judged to exemplify or indicate the nature or quality of a particular period, typically something unwelcome or unpleasant: *the theft was a sign of the times.* **signed, sealed, and delivered** (or **signed and sealed**) formally and officially agreed and in effect.

– PHRASAL VERBS **sign something away/over** officially relinquish rights or property by signing a deed: *I have no intention of signing away my inheritance.* **sign for** sign a receipt to confirm that one has received (something delivered or handed over). **sign in** sign a register on arrival, typically in a hotel. **sign someone in** record someone's arrival in a register. **sign off** conclude a letter, broadcast, or other message: *he signed off with a few words of advice.* ■ sign to record that one is leaving work for the day. ■ Bridge indicate by a conventional bid that one is seeking to end the bidding. **sign someone off** record that someone is entitled to miss work, typically because of illness. **sign off on** informal assent or give one's approval to: *it was hard to get celebrities to sign off on those issues.* **sign on 1** commit oneself to employment, membership of a society, or some other undertaking: *I'll sign on with an advertising agency.* **2** begin work, broadcasting, etc., esp. by writing or announcing one's name. **sign someone on** take someone into one's employment. **sign out** sign a register to record one's departure, typically from a hotel. **sign someone out** authorize someone's release or record their departure by signing a register. **sign something out** sign to indicate that one has borrowed or hired something: *I signed out the keys.* **sign up** commit oneself to a period of employment or education or to some other undertaking: *he signed up for a ten-week course.* ■ enlist in the armed forces. ■ (also **sign something up**) conclude a business deal: *the company has already signed up a few orders.* **sign someone up** formally engage someone in employment. — **sign•er** n. [ME: from OFr. *signe* (n.), *signer* (v.), from L. *signum* 'mark, token.']

Si•gnac /sē'nyäk/, Paul (1863–1935), French neo-Impressionist painter. A pointillist, he used a technique characterized by the use of small dashes and patches of pure color rather than dots.

sign•age /'sīnij/ ▶n. signs collectively, esp. commercial or public display signs.

sig•nal¹ /'signəl/ ▶n. **1** a gesture, action, or sound that is used to convey information or instructions, typically by prearrangement between the parties concerned. ■ an indication of a state of affairs: *the markets are waiting for a clear signal about the direction of policy.* ■ an event or statement that provides the impulse or occasion for something specified to happen. ■ an apparatus on a railroad, typically a colored light or a semaphore, giving indications to train engineers of whether or not the line is clear. ■ Bridge a prearranged convention of bidding or play intended to convey information to one's partner. **2** an electrical impulse or radio wave transmitted or received. ▶v. (**-naled, -nal•ing;** esp. Brit. **-nalled, -nal•ling**) [intrans.] transmit information or instructions by means of a gesture, action, or sound. ■ [trans.] instruct (someone) to do something by means of gestures or signs rather than explicit orders: *she signaled Charlotte to be silent.* ■ (of a cyclist, motorist, or vehicle) indicate an intention to turn in a specified direction using an extended arm or flashing indicator: *Stone signaled right.* ■ [trans.] indicate the existence or occurrence of (something) by actions or sounds: *they could signal displeasure by refusing to cooperate.* ■ give an indication of a state of affairs: *she gave a glance that signaled that her father was being secretive.* — **sig•nal•er** n. [ME: ult. from med. L. *signale*, neut. of late L. *signalis*, from L. *signum* (see SIGN).]

sig•nal² ▶adj. [attrib.] striking in extent, seriousness, or importance; outstanding. *he attacked the administration for its signal failure of leadership.* — **sig•nal•ly** adv. [17th C.: from Fr. *signalé*, from Ital. past part. *segnalato* 'distinguished,' from *segnale* 'a signal.']

sig•nal-call•er ▶n. Football a player who signals the next play or formation to team members.

sig•nal•ize /'signə,līz/ ▶v. [trans.] **1** mark or indicate (something), esp. in a striking or conspicuous manner. ■ archaic make (something) noteworthy or remarkable. **2** provide (an intersection) with traffic signals.

sig•nal•man /'signəlmən/ ▶n. (pl. **-men**) a railroad worker responsible for operating signals and switches. ■ a person responsible for sending and receiving naval or military signals.

sig•nals in•tel•li•gence ▶n. the branch of military intelligence concerned with the monitoring, interception, and interpretation of radio signals, radar signals, and telemetry.

sig•na•to•ry /'signə,tôrē/ ▶n. (pl. **-ries**) a party that has signed an agreement, esp. a country that has signed a treaty. [19th C.: from L. *signatorius* 'of sealing,' from *signat-* 'marked,' from the verb *signare.*]

sig•na•ture /'signəCHər; -,CHŏŏr/ ▶n. **1** a person's name written as a form of identification in authorizing a check or document or concluding a letter. ■ the action of signing a document. ■ a distinctive pattern, product, or characteristic by which someone or something can be identified. **2** Music short for KEY SIGNATURE or TIME SIGNATURE. **3** Print. a letter or figure printed at the foot of one or more pages of each sheet of a book as a guide in binding. ■ a printed sheet after being folded to form a group of pages. **4** the part of a medical prescription that gives instructions about the use of the medicine or drug prescribed. [16th C. from med. L. *signatura*, from L. *signare* 'to sign.']

sign•board /'sīn,bôrd/ ▶n. a board displaying the name or logo of a business or product. ■ a board displaying a sign to direct traffic or travelers.

sign•ee /sī'nē; 'sīnē/ ▶n. a person who has signed a contract or other official document.

sig•net /'signit/ ▶n. hist. a small seal, esp. one set in a ring, used to authenticate a document. [ME: from OFr., or from med. L. *signetum*, dimin. of *signum* 'seal.']

sig•net ring ▶n. a ring with letters, usually one's initials, or a design carved into it.

si•gni•fiant /'signə,fīənt/ ▶n. another term for SIGNIFIER.

sig•nif•i•cance /sig'nifikəns/ ▶n. **1** the quality of being worthy of attention; importance. **2** the meaning to be found in words or events. **3** (also **statistical significance**) the extent to which a result deviates from that expected to arise simply from random variation or errors in sampling.

sig•nif•i•cant /sig'nifikənt/ ▶adj. **1** sufficiently great or important to be worthy of attention; noteworthy. **2** having a particular meaning; indicative of something. ■ suggesting a meaning not explicitly stated. **3** Stat. of, relating to, or having significance. — **sig•nif•i•cant•ly** adv. [16th C. (sense 2): from L. *significant-* 'indicating,' from the verb *significare* (see SIGNIFY).]

sig•nif•i•cant fig•ure (also **significant digit**) ▶n. Math. each of the digits of a number that are used to express it to the required degree of accuracy, starting from the first nonzero digit.

sig•nif•i•cant oth•er ▶n. a person with whom someone has an established romantic or sexual relationship.

sig•ni•fi•ca•tion /,signəfi'kāSHən/ ▶n. the representation or conveying of meaning. ■ an exact meaning or sense. [ME: via OFr. from L. *significatio(n-)*, from *significare* 'indicate' (see SIGNIFY).]

sig•nif•i•ca•tive /sig'nifikātiv/ ▶adj. rare being a symbol or sign of something; having a meaning.

sig•ni•fied /'signə,fīd/ ▶n. Ling. the meaning or idea expressed by a sign, as distinct from the physical form in which it is expressed. Compare with SIGNIFIER.

sig•ni•fi•er /'signə,fīər/ ▶n. Ling. a sign's physical form (such as a sound, printed word, or image) as distinct from its meaning. Compare with SIGNIFIED.

sig•ni•fy /'signə,fī/ ▶v. (**-fies, -fied**) [trans.] be an indication of. ■ be a symbol of; have as meaning. ■ (of a person) indicate or declare (a feeling or intention). ■ [intrans.] [with negative] be of importance: *the locked door doesn't necessarily signify.* [ME: from OFr. *signifier*, from L. *significare* 'indicate,' from *signum* 'token.']

sign•ing /'sīniNG/ ▶n. **1** the action of writing one's signature on an official document. ■ the action of recruiting someone, esp. to a professional sports team or record company. ■ an event in a bookstore or other place at which an author signs a number of books to gain publicity and sales. **2** sign language. **3** the provision of signs in a street or other place.

sign lan•guage ▶n. a system of communication using visual gestures and signs, as used by deaf people.

sign-off ▶ n. the conclusion of a letter, broadcast, or other message.

si·gnor /sēn'yôr/ (also **si·gnore**) ▶ n. (pl. **si·gno·ri** /sēn'yôrē/) a title or form of address used of or to an Italian-speaking man, corresponding to *Mr.* or *sir.* [Ital., from L. *senior* (see SENIOR).]

si·gno·ra /sēn'yôrə/ ▶ n. a title or form of address used of or to an Italian-speaking married woman, corresponding to *Mrs.* or *madam.* [Ital., fem. of *signor* (see SIGNOR).]

si·gno·ri·na /ˌsēnyə'rēnə/ ▶ n. a title or form of address used of or to an Italian-speaking unmarried woman, corresponding to *Miss.* [Ital., dimin. of *signora* (see SIGNORA).]

sig·no·ry /'sēnyərē/ ▶ n. (pl. **-ries**) another term for SEIGNIORY.

sign·post /'sīnˌpōst/ ▶ n. a sign giving information such as the direction and distance to a nearby town, typically found at a crossroads. ■ fig. something that acts as guidance or a clue to an unclear or complicated issue.

sign-up ▶ n. [usu. as adj.] the action of enrolling for something or of enrolling or employing someone.

Sig·urd /'sigərd/ (in Norse legend) the Norse equivalent of Siegfried, husband of Gudrun.

Si·ha·nouk /'sēəˌno͝ok/, Norodom (1922–), king of Cambodia 1941–55, 1993–2004.

si·ka /'sēkə/ (also **si·ka deer**) ▶ n. a forest-dwelling deer (*Cervus nippon*) with a grayish winter coat that turns yellowish-brown with white spots in summer. It is native to Japan and Southeast Asia and naturalized elsewhere. [19th C.: from Japanese *shika.*]

Sikh /sēk/ ▶ n. an adherent of Sikhism. ▶ adj. of or relating to Sikhs or Sikhism. [from Punjabi, 'disciple,' from Sanskrit *śiṣya.*]

Sikh·ism /'sēkizəm/ ▶ n. a monotheistic religion founded in Punjab in the 15th century by Guru Nanak.

Si·king /'SHē'jiNG/ former name of **XIAN.**

Sik·kim /'sikim/ a state in northeastern India, in the eastern Himalayas, between Bhutan and Nepal, on the border with Tibet; capital, Gangtok. — **Sik·kim·ese** /ˌsiki'mēz; -'mēs/ adj. & n.

Si·kor·sky /si'kôrskē/, Igor Ivanovich (1889–1972), US aircraft designer; born in Russia. In 1939, he developed the first mass-produced helicopter.

si·lage /'sīlij/ ▶ n. green fodder compacted and stored in airtight conditions, typically in a silo, without being dried, used as animal feed in the winter. [19th C.: alt. of ENSILAGE.]

sil·ane /'silān/ ▶ n. Chem. a colorless gaseous compound, SiH_4, of silicon and hydrogen that has strong reducing properties and is spontaneously flammable in air. ■ any of the large class of hydrides of silicon analogous to the alkanes. [20th C.: from SILICON.]

si·las·tic /si'lastik/ ▶ n. trademark silicone rubber. [1940s: blend of SILICON and ELASTIC.]

Si·lat /si'lat/ ▶ n. the Malay art of self-defense, practiced as a martial art or accompanied by drums as a ceremonial display or dance.

sild /sild/ ▶ n. (pl. same) a small immature herring, esp. one caught in northern European seas. [1920s: from Dan., Norw.]

si·lence /'sīləns/ ▶ n. complete absence of sound. ■ the fact or state of abstaining from speech. ■ the avoidance of mentioning or discussing something. ■ the state of standing still and not speaking as a sign of respect for someone deceased or in an opportunity for prayer. ▶ v. [trans.] (often **be silenced**) cause to become silent; prohibit or prevent from speaking. ■ [usu. as adj.] (**silenced**) fit (a gun or other loud mechanism) with a silencer [ME: ult. from L. *silentium,* from *silere* 'be silent.']

si·lenc·er /'sīlənsər/ ▶ n. a device for reducing the noise emitted by a gun or other loud mechanism. ■ British term for MUFFLER (sense 2).

si·lent /'sīlənt/ ▶ adj. not making or accompanied by any sound. ■ (of a person) not speaking. ■ not expressed aloud: *a silent prayer.* ■ (of a letter) written but not pronounced, e.g., *b* in *doubt.* ■ (of a movie) without an accompanying soundtrack. ■ saying or recording nothing on a particular subject: *the poems are silent on the question of marriage.* ■ (of a person) not prone to speak much; taciturn.
– PHRASES (**as**) **silent as the grave** see GRAVE[1]. **the silent majority** the majority of people, regarded as holding moderate opinions but rarely expressing them. — **si·lent·ly** adv. [15th C.: from L. *silent-* 'being silent,' from the verb *silere.*]

si·lent but·ler ▶ n. a container with a handle and a hinged cover, used for collecting table crumbs or emptying ashtrays.

si·lent part·ner ▶ n. a partner not sharing in the actual work of a firm.

Si·le·nus /sī'lēnəs/ Gk. Mythol. an aged woodland deity who was entrusted with the education of Dionysus. He is depicted either as dignified and musical, or as an old drunkard. ■ [as n.] (**a silenus**) (pl. **-le·ni** /-'lēˌnī/) a woodland spirit, usually depicted as old and having ears like those of a horse.

Si·le·sia /sī'lēZHə; -SHə/ a region of central Europe that is centered on the upper Oder valley, now largely in southwestern Poland. — **Si·le·sian** adj. & n.

si·lex /'sīleks/ ▶ n. silica, esp. quartz or flint. [16th C.: from L., 'flint.']

sil·hou·ette /ˌsilo͞o'et/ ▶ n. the dark shape and outline of someone or something visible against a lighter background, esp. in dim light. ■ a representation of someone or something showing the shape and outline only, typically colored in solid black. ▶ v. [trans.] (usu. **be silhouetted**) cast or show (someone or something) as a dark shape and outline against a lighter background. [18th C.: Étienne de *Silhouette* (1709–67), French author and politician; the reason remains obscure.]

silhouette

sil·i·ca /'silikə/ ▶ n. a hard, unreactive, colorless compound, SiO_2, that occurs as the mineral quartz and as a principal constituent of sandstone and other rocks. — **si·li·ceous** /sə'liSHəs/ (also **si·li·cious**) adj. [19th C.: from L. *silex, silic-* 'flint.']

sil·i·ca gel ▶ n. hydrated silica in a hard granular hygroscopic form used as a desiccant.

sil·i·cate /'siləˌkāt; -kit/ ▶ n. Chem. a salt in which the anion contains both silicon and oxygen, esp. one of the anion $SiO_4 2-$. ■ any of the many minerals consisting of silica combined with metal oxides, forming a major component of the rocks of the earth's crust.

si·lic·ic /sə'lisik/ ▶ adj. Geol. (of rocks) rich in silica.

si·lic·ic ac·id ▶ n. Chem. a weakly acidic colloidal hydrated form of silica made by acidifying solutions of alkali metal silicates.

sil·i·cide /'siləˌsīd/ ▶ n. Chem. a binary compound of silicon with another element or group.

si·lic·i·fy /sə'lisəˌfī/ ▶ v. (**-fies, -fied**) [trans.] (usu. **be silicified**) convert into or impregnate with silica. — **si·lic·i·fi·ca·tion** /səˌlisəfi'kāSHən/ n.

sil·i·con /'siləˌkän; -kən/ ▶ n. the chemical element of atomic number 14, a nonmetal with semiconducting properties, used in making electronic circuits. Pure silicon exists in a shiny dark gray crystalline form and as an amorphous powder. (Symbol: **Si**) [19th C.: alt. of *silicium,* from L. *silex, silic-* 'flint.']

sil·i·con car·bide ▶ n. a hard refractory crystalline compound, SiC, of silicon and carbon; carborundum.

sil·i·con chip ▶ n. a microchip.

sil·i·cone /'siləˌkōn/ ▶ n. a durable synthetic resin with a structure based on chains of alternate silicon and oxygen atoms, with organic groups attached to the silicon atoms.

Sil·i·con Val·ley a name given to an area between San Jose and Palo Alto in California, noted for its computing and electronics industries.

sil·i·co·sis /ˌsilə'kōsis/ ▶ n. Med. lung fibrosis caused by the inhalation of dust containing silica. — **sil·i·cot·ic** /ˌsilə'kätik/ adj.

sil·i·qua /'silikwə/ (also **sil·ique** /sə'lēk/) ▶ n. (pl. **sil·i·quae** /'siləˌkwē/ or **si·liques** /sə'lēks; 'siliks/) Bot. the long, narrow seedpod of many plants of the cabbage family, splitting open when mature. — **sil·i·quose** /-ˌkwōs/ adj. [L., lit. 'pod.']

silk /silk/ ▶ n. a fine, strong, soft, lustrous fiber produced by silkworms in making cocoons and collected to make thread and fabric. ■ a similar fiber spun by some other insect larvae and by most spiders. ■ thread or fabric made from the fiber produced by the silkworm. ■ (**silks**) garments made from such fabric, esp. as worn by a jockey. ■ Riding a cover worn over a riding hat made from a silklike fabric. ■ any silklike threads that grow in plants, such as at the end of an ear of corn or in a milkweed pod. [OE *sioloc, seolec,* from late L. *sericum,* neut. of L. *sericus,* based on Gk. *Sēres* 'people from whom silk was obtained.']

silk cot·ton ▶ n. another term for KAPOK.

silk-cot·ton tree ▶ n. a tree (family Bombacaceae) that produces silk cotton (kapok). Two species: the **Indian silk-cotton tree** (*Bombax ceiba*) and the ceiba.

silk·en /'silkən/ ▶ adj. made of silk: *a silken ribbon.* ■ soft or lustrous like silk: *silken hair.*

silk gland ▶ n. a gland in a silkworm, spider, or other arthropod that secretes the substance that hardens as threads of silk or web.

silk hat ▶ n. a man's tall, cylindrical hat covered with black silk plush.

silk moth ▶ n. see SILKWORM MOTH.

silk oak (also **silk·y oak**) ▶ n. a tall Australian tree (family Proteaceae) that yields silky-textured timber similar to oak.

Silk Road (also **Silk Route**) an ancient caravan route that linked Xian in central China with the eastern Mediterranean.

silk·screen /'silkˌskrēn/ (also **silk screen**) ▶ n. a screen of fine mesh used in screen-printing. ■ a print made by screen-printing. ▶ v. [trans.] print, decorate, or reproduce using a silkscreen.

silk-stock·ing ▶ adj. wealthy; aristocratic.

silk·worm /'silkˌwərm/ ▶ n. the commercially bred caterpillar of the domesticated silkworm moth (*Bombyx mori*), which spins a silk cocoon that is processed to yield silk fiber. ■ [with adj.] a commercial silk-yielding caterpillar of a saturniid moth. See TUSSORE, TUSSORE MOTH.

silk·worm moth ▶ n. a large moth with a caterpillar that spins a protective silken cocoon: ■ (also **the silk moth**) a domesticated Asian moth whose larva is the chief commercial silkworm (*Bombyx mori,* family Bombycidae). ■ (also **giant silk moth**) a saturniid moth.

silk·y /'silkē/ ▶ adj. (**silk·i·er, silk·i·est**) of or resembling silk. ■ (of a person or their speech or manner) smooth, esp. in a way intended to be persuasive. — **silk·i·ly** /'silkəlē/ adv. **silk·i·ness** n.

sill /sil/ ▶ n. a shelf or slab of stone, wood, or metal at the foot of a window or doorway. ■ a strong horizontal member at the base of any structure, e.g., in the frame of a motor or rail vehicle. ■ Geol. a tabular sheet of igneous rock intruded between and parallel with the existing strata. Compare with DIKE[1]. ■ an underwater ridge or rock ledge extending across the bed of a body of water. [OE *syll, sylle* 'horizontal beam,' from Gmc.; akin to Ger. *Schwelle* 'threshold.']

sil·la·bub ▶ n. archaic spelling of SYLLABUB.

Sil·li·toe /'silə,tō/, Alan (1928–), English writer. His novels include *The Loneliness of the Long-Distance Runner* (1959) and *A Man of His Time* (2004).

Sills /silz/, Beverly (1929–), US opera singer; born *Belle Miriam Silverman*. She sang with the New York City Opera 1955–80 and then became its general director 1979–88 and president 1989–90.

sil·ly /'silē/ ▶ adj. (**-li·er, -li·est**) having or showing a lack of common sense or judgment; foolish. ■ ridiculously trivial or frivolous. ■ [as complement] used to convey that an activity or process has been engaged in to such a degree that someone is no longer capable of thinking or acting sensibly: *mother worried herself silly.* ■ archaic (esp. of a woman, child, or animal) helpless; defenseless. ▶ n. (pl. **-lies**) informal a foolish person (often used as a form of address): *Come on, silly.*
– PHRASES **the silly season** high summer, regarded as the season when newspapers often publish trivial material because of a lack of important news. — **sil·li·ly** /'siləlē/ adv. **sil·li·ness** n. [ME ('deserving of pity'): alt. of dial. *seely* 'happy,' from West Gmc., 'luck.']

Sil·ly Put·ty ▶ n. trademark a moldable silicone-based substance, sold chiefly as a toy, with remarkable properties of stretching and bouncing.

silo 1

si·lo /'sīlō/ ▶ n. (pl. **-los**) **1** a tower or pit on a farm used to store grain. ■ a pit or other airtight structure in which green crops are compressed and stored as silage. **2** an underground chamber in which a guided missile is kept ready for firing. [19th C.: from Sp., via L. from Gk. *siros* 'cornpit.']

Si·lo·am /sī'lōəm; si-/ (in the New Testament) a spring and pool of water near Jerusalem.

si·lox·ane /si'läksān/ ▶ n. Chem. a compound having a molecular structure based on a chain of alternate silicon and oxygen atoms, esp. (as in silicone) with organic groups attached to the silicon atoms. [20th C.: blend of SILICON and OXYGEN.]

silt /silt/ ▶ n. fine sand, clay, or other material carried by running water and deposited as a sediment, esp. in a channel or harbor. ■ a bed or layer of such material. ■ tech. sediment whose particles are between clay and sand in size (typically 0.002–0.06 mm). ▶ v. [intrans.] become filled or blocked with silt. ■ [trans.] fill or block with silt. — **sil·ta·tion** /sil'tāsHən/ n. **silt·y** adj. [ME: prob. orig. 'salty deposit,' of Scand. origin, akin to Dan. *sylt* 'salt marsh' and SALT.]

silt·stone /'silt,stōn/ ▶ n. fine-grained sedimentary rock consisting of consolidated silt.

Si·lu·ri·an /si'lo͝orēən; sī-/ ▶ adj. Geol. of, relating to, or denoting the third period of the Paleozoic era, between the Ordovician and Devonian periods. ■ [as n.] (**the Silurian**) the Silurian period or the system of rocks deposited during it. [18th C.: from L. *Silures*, a people of ancient Wales).]

sil·van ▶ adj. var. of SYLVAN.

Sil·va·nus /sil'vānəs/ Rom. Mythol. an Italian woodland deity identified with Pan.

sil·ver /'silvər/ ▶ n. **1** a precious shiny grayish-white transition metal, the chemical element of atomic number 47. (Symbol: **Ag**) **2** a shiny gray-white color or appearance like that of silver. **3** silver dishes, containers, or cutlery. ■ household cutlery of any material. **4** coins made from silver or from a metal that resembles silver. **5** short for SILVER MEDAL. ▶ adj. made wholly or chiefly of silver. ■ colored like silver: *a silver Mercedes.* ■ denoting a twenty-fifth anniversary. ▶ v. [trans.] [often as adj.] (**silvered**) coat or plate with silver. ■ provide (mirror glass) with a backing of a silver-colored material in order to make it reflective. ■ literary (esp. of the moon) give a silvery appearance to: *the brilliant moon silvered the turf.* ■ turn (a person's hair) gray or white. ■ [intrans.] (of a person's hair) turn gray or white.
– PHRASES **be born with a silver spoon in one's mouth** be born into a wealthy family of high social standing. **the silver screen** the movie industry; movies collectively. [OE *seolfor*, from Gmc.; akin to Ger. *Silber*.]

sil·ver age ▶ n. a period regarded as notable but inferior to a golden age.

sil·ver·back /'silvər,bak/ ▶ n. a mature male mountain gorilla, distinguished by an area of silvery hair across the back and the dominant member of its social group.

sil·ver·ber·ry /'silvər,berē/ ▶ n. (pl. **-ries**) a North American shrub (*Elaeagnus commutata*) of the oleaster family, with red-brown stems and silvery leaves, flowers, and berries.

sil·ver birch ▶ n. a European birch (*Betula pendula*) with silver-gray bark, common on poorer soils to the northern limit of tree growth. ■ another term for PAPER BIRCH.

sil·ver bul·let ▶ n. a bullet made of silver, used in fiction as a supposedly magical method of killing werewolves. ■ a simple and seemingly magical solution to a complicated problem.

sil·ver chlo·ride ▶ n. a white insoluble powder that darkens on exposure to light, owing to the production of metallic silver. It is used in making photographic emulsions and papers.

sil·ver·eye /'silvər,ī/ ▶ n. an Australasian songbird (genus *Zosterops*) of the white-eye family, with mainly greenish plumage and a white ring around the eye.

sil·ver fir ▶ n. a fir tree (genus *Abies*) with foliage that appears silvery or bluish because of whitish lines on the undersides of the needles.

sil·ver·fish /'silvər,fisH/ ▶ n. (pl. same or **-fish·es**) **1** a chiefly nocturnal silvery bristletail (*Lepisma saccharina*, family Lepismatidae) that frequents houses and other buildings, feeding on starchy materials. **2** a silver-colored fish, esp. a goldfish of an unpigmented variety.

sil·ver fox ▶ n. a red fox of a North American variety that has black fur with white tips. ■ the fur of this animal.

sil·ver gilt ▶ n. gilded silver. ■ an imitation gilding of yellow lacquer over silver leaf.

sil·ver·ing /'silvəriNG/ ▶ n. silver-colored material used to coat glass in order to make it reflective.

sil·ver i·o·dide ▶ n. a yellow insoluble powder that darkens on exposure to light. It is used in photography and artificial rainmaking.

sil·ver ju·bi·lee ▶ n. the twenty-fifth anniversary of a significant event.

sil·ver leaf ▶ n. **1** a disease of ornamental and fruit trees, esp. plum trees, resulting in silvery discoloration of the leaves, caused by the fungus *Chondrostereum purpureum* (family Stereaceae). **2** silver that has been beaten into a very thin sheet, suitable for applying to surfaces as a decoration.

sil·ver ma·ple ▶ n. a maple (*Acer saccharinum*) of eastern North America with leaves that are silvery underneath.

sil·ver med·al ▶ n. a medal made of or colored silver, awarded for second place in a race or competition.

sil·vern /'silvərn/ ▶ adj. archaic term for SILVER. [OE *seolfren, silfren* (see SILVER, -N[1]).]

sil·ver ni·trate ▶ n. a colorless, water-soluble solid, $AgNO_3$, formerly used in photography.

sil·ver pa·per ▶ n. **1** archaic fine white tissue paper. **2** esp. Brit. foil made of aluminum or other silver-colored metal.

sil·ver plate ▶ n. a thin layer of silver electroplated or otherwise applied as a coating to another metal. ■ objects coated with silver. ■ plates, dishes, etc., made of silver. ▶ v. (**sil·ver-plate**) [trans.] cover (something) with a thin layer of silver.

sil·ver·point /'silvər,point/ ▶ n. the art of drawing with a silver-pointed instrument on paper prepared with a coating of powdered bone or zinc white, creating a fine durable line composed of metal fragments.

sil·ver salm·on ▶ n. another term for COHO.

sil·ver·side /'silvər,sīd/ (also **sil·ver·sides**) ▶ n. a small, slender, chiefly marine fish (family Atherinidae) with a bright silver line along its sides.

sil·ver·smith /'silvər,smiTH/ ▶ n. a person who makes silver articles. — **sil·ver·smith·ing** n.

Sil·ver Spring a city in central Maryland, just north of Washington, DC; pop. 76,046.

sil·ver stand·ard ▶ n. hist. a system by which the value of a currency is defined in terms of silver, for which the currency may be exchanged.

Sil·ver Star ▶ n. a decoration bestowed by the US Army upon a soldier for gallantry in action.

Sil·ver·stein /'silvər,stīn; -,stēn/, Shel (1930?–99), US poet, writer, songwriter, and cartoonist; full name *Sheldon Alan Silverstein*. His children's stories and poetry are collected in *Where the Sidewalk Ends* (1974).

sil·ver·sword /'silvər,sôrd/ ▶ n. a Hawaiian plant (genus *Argyroxiphium*) of the daisy family that has long narrow leaves with silvery hairs and clusters of purplish flowers.

sil·ver thaw ▶ n. a glassy coating of ice formed on the ground or an exposed surface by freezing rain or the refreezing of thawed ice.

sil·ver tongue ▶ n. a tendency to be eloquent and persuasive in speaking. — **sil·ver-tongued** adj.

sil·ver·ware /'silvər,we(ə)r/ ▶ n. dishes, containers, or cutlery made of or coated with silver. ■ eating and serving utensils made of any material.

sil·ver wed·ding (also **silver wedding anniversary**) ▶ n. the twenty-fifth anniversary of a wedding.

sil·ver·weed /'silvər,wēd/ ▶ n. a yellow-flowered herbaceous potentilla (*Potentilla anserina*) with silvery compound leaves, a common grassland weed of north temperate regions.

sil·ver·y /'silvərē/ ▶ adj. like silver in color or appearance; shiny and gray-white. ■ (of a person's hair) gray-white and lustrous. ■ (of a sound) gentle, clear, and melodious. — **sil·ver·i·ness** n.

sil·vi·cul·ture /'silvi,kəlCHər/ ▶ n. the growing and cultivation of trees. — **sil·vi·cul·tur·al** /,silvi'kəlCHərəl/ adj. **sil·vi·cul·tur·ist** /,silvi'kəlCHərist/

n. [19th C.: from Fr. *sylviculture*, from L. *silva* 'wood' + Fr. *culture* 'cultivation.']

s'il vous plaît /ˌsēl vo͞o ˈple/ ▶ **adv.** French for **PLEASE.** [Fr., lit. 'if it pleases you.']

SIM /sim/ (also **SIM card**) ▶ **n.** a smart card inside a cellular phone, carrying an identification number unique to the owner, storing personal data, and preventing operation if removed. [1980s: acronym from *subscriber identification module*.]

sim /sim/ ▶ **n.** informal a video game that simulates an activity such as flying an aircraft or playing a sport. [20th C.: abbrev. of *simulation*.]

si·ma /ˈsīmə/ ▶ **n.** Geol. the material of the lower part of the earth's crust, characterized as heavy and rich in silica and magnesia. Contrasted with **SIAL.** [20th C.: blend of **SILICA** + **MAGNESIUM.**]

sim·cha /ˈsimᴄнə/ ▶ **n.** a Jewish private party or celebration. [from Heb. *śimḥāh* 'rejoicing.']

Si·me·non /ˌsēməˈnôɴ/, Georges Joseph Christian (1903–89), French novelist, born in Belgium. He is best known for his series of detective novels that feature the police inspector Maigret.

Sim·e·on /ˈsimēən/ (in the Bible) a Hebrew patriarch, second son of Jacob and Leah. ■ the tribe of Israel traditionally descended from him.

Sim·fe·ro·pol /s(y)imfiˈrôpəl/ a city in the Crimea, Ukraine; pop. 349,000. Formerly known as Ak-Mechet.

sim·i·an /ˈsimēən/ ▶ **adj.** relating to, resembling, or affecting apes or monkeys. Compare with **PROSIMIAN.** ▶ **n.** an ape or monkey. [17th C.: from L. *simia* 'ape,' perh. via L. from Gk. *simos* 'flat-nosed.']

sim·i·lar /ˈsimələr/ ▶ **adj.** having a resemblance in appearance, character, or quantity, without being identical. ■ Geom. (of figures) having the same shape, with the same angles and proportions, though of different sizes. [ult. from med. L. *similaris*, from L. *similis* 'like.']

sim·i·lar·i·ty /ˌsiməˈlaritē/ ▶ **n.** (pl. **-ties**) the state or fact of being similar. ■ (usu. **similarities**) a similar feature or aspect. — **sim·i·lar·ly adv.**

sim·i·le /ˈsiməlē/ ▶ **n.** a figure of speech involving the comparison of one thing with another thing of a different kind, (e.g., *as brave as a lion*). ■ the use of such a method of comparison. [ME: from L., neut. of *similis* 'like.']

si·mil·i·tude /siˈmiləˌt(y)o͞od/ ▶ **n.** the quality or state of being similar to something. ■ archaic a comparison between two things. [ME: ult. from L. *similitudo*, from *similis* 'like.']

Si·mi Val·ley /ˈsēmē; siˈmē/ a city in southwestern California; pop. 100,217.

SIMM /sim/ Comput. ▶ **abbr.** single in-line memory module, containing RAM chips.

Sim·men·tal /ˈzimənˌtäl/ ▶ **n.** an animal of a red and white breed of cattle farmed for both meat and milk. [1950s: after a valley in Switzerland.]

sim·mer /ˈsimər/ ▶ **v.** [intrans.] (of water or food being heated) stay just below boiling point while bubbling gently. ■ [trans.] keep (something) at such a point when cooking or heating it. ■ be in a state of suppressed anger or excitement. ■ (**simmer down**) become calmer and quieter. ▶ **n.** [in sing.] a state or temperature just below boiling point. [17th C.: alt. of dial. *simper*, perh. imitative.]

sim·nel cake /ˈsimnəl/ ▶ **n.** esp. Brit. a rich fruitcake with a marzipan covering and decoration, eaten esp. at Easter or during Lent. [17th C.: from OFr. *simenel*, based on L. *simila* or Gk. *semidalis* 'fine flour.']

si·mo·le·on /səˈmōlēən/ ▶ **n.** informal a dollar. [19th C.: perh. on the pattern of *napoleon*.]

Si·mon /ˈsīməˌn/ Neil (1927–), US playwright; full name *Marvin Neil Simon*. His plays include *The Odd Couple* (1965) and *Lost in Yonkers* (1991).

Si·mon, St., one of the 12 apostles; known as **Simon the Zealot.**

Si·mon·i·des /sīˈmänəˌdēz/ (*c.*556–468 BC), Greek poet. His poetry celebrates the heroes of the Persian Wars.

si·mon·ize /ˈsīməˌnīz/ ▶ **v.** [trans.] polish (a motor vehicle). [1930s: from proprietary name *Simoniz*.]

si·mon-pure /ˈsīmən ˈpyo͝or/ ▶ **adj.** completely genuine, authentic, or honest. [18th C.: from *(the real) Simon Pure*, character in Centlivre's *Bold Stroke for a Wife* (1717), who is impersonated by another character.]

Si·mon Says /ˈsīmən ˈsez/ ▶ **n.** a children's game in which players obey the leader's instructions if (and only if) they are prefaced with the words "Simon says."

si·mo·ny /ˈsīmənē; ˈsim-/ ▶ **n.** esp. hist. the buying or selling of ecclesiastical privileges. — **si·mo·ni·ac** /sīˈmōnēˌak; si-/ **adj. & n. si·mo·ni·a·cal** /ˌsīməˈnīəkəl; si-/ **adj.** [ME: from OFr. *simonie*, from late L. *simonia*, from *Simon* Magus (Acts 8:18).]

si·moom /siˈmo͞om/ (also **si·moon** /-ˈmo͞on/) ▶ **n.** a hot, dry, dust-laden wind blowing in the desert, esp. in Arabia. [18th C.: from Arab. *samūm*, from *samma* 'to poison.']

simp /simp/ ▶ **n.** informal a silly or foolish person; a simpleton. [20th C.: abbrev. of **SIMPLETON.**]

sim·pa·ti·co /simˈpatiˌkō/ ▶ **adj.** (of a person) likable and easy to get along with. ■ having shared attributes; compatible. [Ital. and Sp.]

sim·per /ˈsimpər/ ▶ **v.** [intrans.] smile in an affectedly coquettish, coy, or ingratiating manner. ▶ **n.** [usu. in sing.] an affectedly coquettish, coy, or ingratiating smile. — **sim·per·ing·ly adv.** [16th C.: compare Ger. *zimpfer* 'elegant.']

sim·ple /ˈsimpəl/ ▶ **adj.** (**-pler, -plest**) **1** easily understood or done; presenting no difficulty. ■ plain, basic, or uncomplicated in form, nature, or design; without much decoration or ornamentation. ■ used to emphasize the fundamental and straightforward nature of something. **2** composed of a single element; not compound. ■ Math. denoting a group that has no proper normal subgroup. ■ Bot. (of a leaf or stem) not divided or branched. ■ (of a lens, microscope, etc.) consisting of a single lens or component. ■ (in English grammar) denoting a tense formed without an auxiliary, for example *sang* as opposed to *was singing*. ■ (of interest) payable on the sum loaned only. Compare with **COMPOUND¹**. **3** of or characteristic of low rank or status; humble and unpretentious. **4** of low or abnormally low intelligence. ▶ **n.** esp. hist. a medicinal herb, or a medicine made from one: *the gatherers of simples*. — **sim·ple·ness n.** [ME (adj.): ult. from L. *simplus*.]

sim·ple eye ▶ **n.** a small eye of an insect or other arthropod that has only one lens, typically present in one or more pairs. Also called **OCELLUS.** Contrasted with **COMPOUND EYE.**

sim·ple frac·ture ▶ **n.** a fracture of the bone only, without damage to the surrounding tissues or breaking of the skin.

sim·ple ma·chine ▶ **n.** Mech. any of the basic mechanical devices for applying a force, such as an inclined plane, wedge, or lever.

sim·ple·mind·ed /ˈsimpəlˈmīndid/ ▶ **adj.** having or showing very little intelligence or judgment. — **sim·ple·mind·ed·ly adv. sim·ple·mind·ed·ness n.**

sim·ple sen·tence ▶ **n.** a sentence consisting of only one clause, with a single subject and predicate.

Sim·ple Si·mon ▶ **n.** a foolish or gullible person. [after a character in various nursery rhymes.]

sim·ple time ▶ **n.** musical rhythm or meter in which each beat in a measure can be subdivided simply into halves or quarters. Compare with **COMPOUND TIME.**

sim·ple·ton /ˈsimpəltən/ ▶ **n.** a foolish or gullible person. [17th C.: from **SIMPLE.**]

sim·plex /ˈsimpleks/ ▶ **adj.** tech. composed of or characterized by a single part or structure. ■ (of a communications system, computer circuit, etc.) only allowing transmission of signals in one direction at a time. ▶ **n.** a simple or uncompounded word. [16th C.: from L., lit. 'single,' var. of *simplus* 'simple.']

sim·plic·i·ty /simˈplisitē/ ▶ **n.** the quality or condition of being easy to understand or do. ■ the quality or condition of being plain or natural. ■ a thing that is plain, natural, or easy to understand. [ME: ult. from L. *simplicitas*, from *simplex* (see **SIMPLEX**).]

sim·pli·fy /ˈsimpləˌfī/ ▶ **v.** (**-fies, -fied**) [trans.] make (something) simpler or easier to do or understand. — **sim·pli·fi·ca·tion** /ˌsimpləfiˈkāsнən/ **n.**

sim·plism /ˈsimplizəm/ ▶ **n.** rare the oversimplification of an issue.

sim·plis·tic /simˈplistik/ ▶ **adj.** treating complex issues and problems as if they were much simpler than they really are: *simplistic solutions*. — **sim·plis·ti·cal·ly adv.**

sim·ply /ˈsimplē/ ▶ **adv. 1** in a straightforward or plain manner. **2** merely; just. ■ absolutely; completely (used for emphasis): *simply furious*. ■ used to introduce a short summary of a situation: *quite simply, some things have to be taught*.

Simp·son, Wallis (1896–1986), wife of Edward, Duke of Windsor (Edward VIII); born *Wallis Warfield*. A divorcée, her relationship with the king forced his abdication in 1936.

sim·u·la·crum /ˌsimyəˈlākrəm; -ˈlak-/ ▶ **n.** (pl. **-la·cra** /-ˈlākrə; -ˈlakrə/ or **-la·crums**) an image or representation of someone or something. ■ an unsatisfactory imitation or substitute. [16th C.: from L., from *simulare* (see **SIMULATE**).]

sim·u·lant /ˈsimyələnt/ ▶ **n.** a thing that simulates or resembles something else: *jade simulants*. [18th C.: from L. *simulant-* 'copying,' from the verb *simulare*.]

sim·u·late /ˈsimyəˌlāt/ ▶ **v.** [trans.] imitate the appearance or character of. ■ pretend to have or feel (an emotion). ■ produce a computer model of. — **sim·u·la·tion** /ˌsimyəˈlāsнən/ **n. sim·u·la·tive** /-ˌlātiv/ **adj.** [17th C.: from L. *simulat-* 'copied,' from the verb *simulare*, from *similis* 'like.']

sim·u·la·tor /ˈsimyəˌlātər/ ▶ **n.** a machine with a similar set of controls designed to provide a realistic imitation of the operation of a vehicle, aircraft, or other complex system, used for training purposes. ■ (also **simulator program**) a program enabling a computer to execute programs written for a different computer.

si·mul·cast /ˈsīməlˌkast/ ▶ **n.** a simultaneous transmission of the same program on radio and television, or on two or more channels. ■ a live closed-circuit transmission of a public celebration or sports event. ▶ **v.** [trans.] broadcast (a program) in such a way. [1940s: blend of **SIMULTANEOUS** and **BROADCAST.**]

si·mul·ta·ne·ous /ˌsīməlˈtānēəs/ ▶ **adj.** occurring, operating, or done at the same time. — **si·mul·ta·ne·i·ty** /ˌsīməltəˈnēitē/ **n. si·mul·ta·ne·ous·ly adv. si·mul·ta·ne·ous·ness n.** [17th C.: based on L. *simul* 'at the same time,' prob. influenced by late L. *momentaneus*.]

si·mul·ta·ne·ous e·qua·tions ▶ **plural n.** equations involving two or more unknowns that are to have the same values in each equation.

sin¹ /sin/ ▶ **n.** an immoral act considered to be a transgression against divine law. ■ an act regarded as a serious or regrettable fault, offense, or omission. ▶ **v.** (**sinned, sin·ning**) [intrans.] commit a sin.

PRONUNCIATION KEY ə *ago, up*; ər *over, fur*; a *hat*; ā *ate*; ä *car*; e *let*; ē *see*; i *fit*; ī *by*; ɴɢ *sing*; ō *go*; ô *law, for*; oi *toy*; o͝o *good*; o͞o *goo*; ou *out*; ᴛʜ *thin*; ᴛʜ *then*; ᴢʜ *vision*

– PHRASES (as) —— **as sin** informal having a particular undesirable quality to a high degree: *as ugly as sin.* **live in sin** informal, dated live together as though married. — **sin·less** adj. **sin·less·ly** adv. **sin·less·ness** n. [OE *synn*; akin to L. *sons, sont-* 'guilty.']

sin² /sīn/ ▶ abbr. sine.

Si·nai /'sī,nī/ an arid mountainous peninsula in northeastern Egypt that extends into the Red Sea between the Gulf of Suez and the Gulf of Aqaba. It was occupied by Israel between 1967 and 1982. In the south is Mount Sinai, where, according to the Bible, Moses received the Ten Commandments (Exod. 19–34).

Si·na·it·ic /,sinē'itik/ ▶ adj. of or relating to Mount Sinai or the Sinai peninsula.

Si·na·lo·a /,sēnə'lōə/ a state in northwestern Mexico.

Si·nan·thro·pus /sin'anTHrəpəs; sī-/ ▶ n. a former genus name applied to some fossilized hominids found in China in 1926. See PEKING MAN. [mod. L., from SINO- + Gk. *anthrōpos* 'man.']

Sin·bad the Sail·or /'sin,bad/ (also **Sind·bad** /'sin(d),bad/) the hero of one of the tales in the *Arabian Nights*, who relates the adventures he meets with in his voyages.

since /sins/ ▶ prep., conj., & adv. **1** in the intervening period between (the time mentioned) and the time under consideration, typically the present: [as prep.] *she has suffered from cystic fibrosis since 1984* | [as conj.] *I've felt better since I've been here* | [as adv.] *she ran away on Friday, and we haven't seen her since.* **2** [conj.] for the reason that: because: *delegates were delighted, since protection of rhino reserves will help protect other rare species.* **3** [adv.] ago: *the settlement had vanished long since.* [ME: contr. of obs. *sithence*, or from dialect *sin* (both from dial. *sithen* 'afterward').]

sin·cere /sin'si(ə)r/ ▶ adj. (**-cer·er, -cer·est**) free from pretense or deceit; proceeding from genuine feelings. ■ (of a person) saying what they genuinely feel or believe; not dishonest or hypocritical. — **sin·cere·ly** /sin'si(ə)rlē/ adv. **sin·cere·ness** n. **sin·cer·i·ty** /sin'seritē/ n. [16th C.: from L. *sincerus* 'clean, pure.']

sin·ci·put /'sinsəpət/ ▶ n. Anat. the front of the skull from the forehead to the crown. — **sin·cip·i·tal** /sin'sipitl/ adj. [16th C.: from L., from *semi-* 'half' + *caput* 'head.']

Sin·clair /sin'kle(ə)r/, Upton Beall (1878–1968), US writer and social reformer. His novels arguing for social justice include *The Jungle* (1906).

Sind /sind/ a province of southeastern Pakistan, crossed by the Indus River; capital, Karachi.

Sind·hi /'sindē/ ▶ n. (pl. **-his**) **1** a native or inhabitant of Sind. **2** the Indic language of Sind, used also in western India. ▶ adj. of or relating to the province of Sind or its people, or the Sindhi language. [from Pers. and Urdu *sindī*, from Sanskrit *sindhu* 'river.']

sine /sīn/ ▶ n. Math. the trigonometric function that is equal to the ratio of the side opposite a given angle (in a right triangle) to the hypotenuse. [16th C.: from L. *sinus* 'curve,' in med. L., translation of Arab. *jayb* 'pocket, sine.']

si·ne·cure /'sīnə,kyo͝or; 'sin-/ ▶ n. a position requiring little or no work but giving the holder status or financial benefit. — **si·ne·cur·ism** /'sīnəkyo͝orizəm; si-/ n. **si·ne·cur·ist** /'sīnə,kyo͝orist; 'sin-/ n. [17th C.: from L. *sine cura* 'without care.']

si·ne curve /sīn/ (also **sine wave**) ▶ n. a curve representing periodic oscillations of constant amplitude as given by a sine function. Also called SINUSOID.

si·ne di·e /'sīnə 'dīē; 'sēnā 'dēā/ ▶ adv. (with reference to business or proceedings that have been adjourned) with no appointed date for resumption: *the case was adjourned sine die.* [L., lit. 'without a day.']

si·ne qua non /,sini ,kwä 'nōn; ,sini ,kwä 'nän/ ▶ n. an essential condition. [L., lit. '(cause) without which not.']

sin·ew /'sinyo͞o/ ▶ n. a piece of tough fibrous tissue uniting muscle to bone or bone to bone; a tendon or ligament. ■ (usu. **sinews**) fig. the parts of a structure, system, or thing that give it strength or bind it together. ▶ v. [trans.] [usu. as adj.] (**sinewed**) literary strengthen with or as if with sinews. — **sin·ew·less** adj. **sin·ew·y** /-yo͞o-ē/ adj. [OE *sin(e)we* 'tendon,' from Gmc.; akin to Ger. *Sehne*.]

sin·fo·ni·a /,sinfə'nēə/ ▶ n. Music a symphony. ■ (in the 17th and 18th centuries) an orchestral piece used as an introduction, interlude, or postlude to an opera, oratorio, cantata, or suite. [Ital.]

sin·fo·ni·a con·cer·tan·te /,sinfə'nēə ,känsər'täntā/ ▶ n. a piece of music for orchestra with more than one soloist, typically from the 18th century. [Ital., lit. 'harmonizing symphony.']

sin·fo·niet·ta /,sinfən'yetə/ ▶ n. Music a short or simple symphony. ■ a small symphony orchestra. [Ital., dimin. of *sinfonia* (see SINFONIA).]

sin·ful /'sinfəl/ ▶ adj. wicked and immoral; committing or characterized by the committing of sins. ■ highly reprehensible. — **sin·ful·ly** adv. **sin·ful·ness** n.

sing /siNG/ ▶ v. (past **sang** /saNG/; past part. **sung** /səNG/) [intrans.] make musical sounds with the voice, esp. words with a set tune: *Bella sang to the baby.* ■ [trans.] perform (a song, words, or tune) in this way: *someone started singing "God Bless America."* ■ (**sing along**) sing in accompaniment to a song or piece of music. ■ (**sing something out**) call something out loudly; shout: *he sang out a greeting.* ■ (of a bird) make characteristic melodious sounds. ■ make a high-pitched whistling or buzzing sound. ■ (of a person's ear) be affected with a continuous buzzing sound, esp. as the aftereffect of a blow or loud noise. ■ informal act as an informer to the police. ■ [trans.] recount or celebrate in a work of literature, esp. poetry: *poetry should sing the variety of the human race* | [intrans.] *these poets sing of the American experience.* ■ archaic compose poetry. ▶ n. [in sing.] informal an act or spell of singing. ■ a meeting for amateur singing.
– PHRASES **sing for one's supper** see SUPPER. **sing the praises of** see PRAISE. **sing someone to sleep** cause someone to fall asleep by singing gently to them. — **sing·a·ble** adj. **sing·ing·ly** adv. [OE *singan* (v.), from Gmc.; akin to Ger. *singen*.]

sing. ▶ abbr. singular.

sing-a·long (also **sing·a·long**) ▶ n. an informal occasion when people sing together in a group. ■ [usu. as adj.] a light popular song or tune to which one can easily sing along in accompaniment.

Sin·ga·pore /'siNGə,pôr/ a country in Southeast Asia. *See box.* — **Sin·ga·po·re·an** /,siNGə'pôrēən/ adj. & n.

Singapore

Official name: Republic of Singapore
Location: Southeast Asia, including the island of Singapore (linked by a causeway to the southern tip of the Malay Peninsula) and about 54 smaller islands
Area: 250 square miles (650 sq km)
Population: 4,353,000
Capital: Singapore
Languages: Chinese, Malay, Tamil, English (all official)
Currency: Singapore dollar

Sin·ga·pore sling ▶ n. a cocktail made from gin and cherry brandy.

singe /sinj/ ▶ v. (**singe·ing**) [trans.] burn (something) superficially or lightly: *the fire had singed his eyebrows* | [as adj.] (**singed**) *a smell of singed feathers.* ■ [intrans.] be burned in this way. ■ burn the bristles or down off (the carcass of a pig or fowl) to prepare it for cooking. ▶ n. a superficial burn. [OE *sencgan*, from West Gmc.; akin to Du. *zengen*.]

Sing·er¹ /'siNGər/, Isaac Bashevis (1904–91), US writer; born in Poland. His works include *The Slave* (1962). Nobel Prize for Literature (1978).

Sing·er², Isaac Merrit (1811–75), US inventor. He designed and built the first commercially successful sewing machine in 1852.

sing·er /'siNGər/ ▶ n. a person who sings, esp. professionally: *a pop singer.*

Sin·gha·lese /,siNGgə'lēz; -'lēs/ ▶ n. & adj. var. of SINHALESE.

sin·gle /'siNGgəl/ ▶ adj. **1** [attrib.] only one; not one of several: *a single red rose.* ■ regarded separately or as distinct from each other or others in a group: *it's our single most popular beach.* ■ [with negative] even one (used for emphasis): *they didn't receive a single reply.* ■ designed or suitable for one person: *a single bed.* ■ archaic not accompanied or supported by others; alone. **2** unmarried or not involved in a stable sexual relationship. **3** [attrib.] consisting of one part: *the studio was a single large room.* ■ Brit. (of a ticket) not valid for the return trip; one-way. ■ (of a flower) having only one whorl of petals. ■ denoting an alcoholic drink that consists of one measure of liquor: *a single whiskey.* **4** archaic free from duplicity or deceit; ingenuous: *a pure and single heart.* ▶ n. **1** an individual person or thing rather than part of a pair or a group. ■ a short record with one song on each side. ■ (**singles**) people who are unmarried or not involved in a stable sexual relationship. ■ Brit. a one-way ticket. ■ a bedroom, esp. in a hotel, that is suitable for one person. ■ a single measure of liquor. ■ informal a one-dollar bill. **2** Baseball a hit that allows the batter to reach first base safely. **3** (**singles**) (esp. in tennis and badminton) a game or competition for individual players, not pairs or teams. ▶ v. [trans.] **1** (**single someone/something out**) choose someone or something from a group for special treatment. **2** [intrans.] Baseball hit a single. ■ (**single in**) [trans.] cause (a run) to be scored by hitting a single. ■ [trans.] advance (a runner) by hitting a single. — **sin·gle·ness** n. **sin·gly** /-glē/ adv. [ME: via OFr. from L. *singulus*, rel. to *simplus* 'simple.']

sin·gle-act·ing ▶ adj. (of an engine) having pressure applied only to one side of the piston.

sin·gle-ac·tion ▶ adj. (of a gun) needing to be cocked by hand before it can be fired.

sin·gle-blind ▶ **adj.** [attrib.] denoting a test or experiment in which information that may bias the results is concealed from either tester or subject.

sin·gle bond ▶ **n.** a chemical bond in which one pair of electrons is shared between two atoms.

sin·gle-breast·ed ▶ **adj.** (of a jacket or coat) showing only one row of buttons at the front when fastened.

sin·gle com·bat ▶ **n.** fighting between two people.

sin·gle-en·try ▶ **adj.** denoting a system of bookkeeping in which each transaction is entered in one account only.

sin·gle file ▶ **n.** [in sing.] a line of people or things arranged one behind another. ▶ **adv.** one behind another.

sin·gle-foot ▶ **v.** [intrans.] (of a horse) walk by moving both legs on each side in alternation, each foot falling separately.

sin·gle-hand·ed (also **sin·gle·hand·ed** /'siNGgəl'handid/) ▶ **adv. & adj.** **1** done without help from anyone else. **2** done or designed to be used with one hand. — **sin·gle-hand·ed·ly** (or **sin·gle·hand·ed·ly**) **adv.** **sin·gle-hand·ed·ness** (or **sin·gle·hand·ed·ness**) **n.**

sin·gle-hand·er ▶ **n.** a boat or other craft that can be sailed single-handed. ■ a person who sails a boat or yacht single-handed.

sin·gle-lens re·flex ▶ **adj.** denoting a reflex camera in which the lens that forms the image on the film also provides the image in the viewfinder.

sin·gle malt (also **sin·gle-malt whiskey**) ▶ **n.** whiskey unblended with any other malt.

sin·gle mar·ket ▶ **n.** an association of countries trading with each other without restrictions or tariffs.

sin·gle-mind·ed (also **sin·gle·mind·ed** /'siNGgəl'mīndid/) ▶ **adj.** having or concentrating on only one aim or purpose: *the single-minded pursuit of profit.* — **sin·gle-mind·ed·ly** (or **sin·gle·mind·ed·ly**) **adv.** **sin·gle-mind·ed·ness** (or **sin·gle·mind·ed·ness**) **n.**

sin·gles bar ▶ **n.** a bar for single people seeking company.

sin·gle seat·er ▶ **n.** a vehicle or aircraft for one person.

sin·gle·stick /'siNGgəl,stik/ (also **sin·gle-stick**) ▶ **n.** Fencing a wooden stick of about a sword's length. ■ fencing with such a stick.

sin·glet /'siNGglit/ ▶ **n.** **1** esp. Brit. a sleeveless garment worn under or instead of a shirt. **2** Physics a single unresolvable line in a spectrum, not part of a multiplet. ■ a state or energy level with zero spin, giving a single value for a particular quantum number. ■ Chem. an atomic or molecular state in which all electron spins are paired. [18th C. ('jacket'): from SINGLE (because the garment was unlined) + -ET[1].]

sin·gle·ton /'siNGgəltən/ ▶ **n.** a single person or thing of the kind under consideration. ■ a child or animal born singly, rather than one of a multiple birth. ■ (in card games, esp. bridge) a card that is the only one of its suit in a hand. [19th C.: from SINGLE.]

sin·gle·tree /'siNGgəl,trē/ ▶ **n.** a crossbar pivoted in the middle, to which the traces are attached in a horse-drawn cart or plow.

sing·song /'siNG,sôNG/ (also **sing-song**) ▶ **adj.** (of a person's voice) having a repeated rising and falling rhythm. ▶ **n.** **1** esp. Brit., informal an informal gathering for singing. **2** [in sing.] a singsong way of speaking. ▶ **v.** (past and past part. **sing·songed**) [intrans.] speak or recite something in a singsong manner.

sing·spiel /'siNG,spēl; 'ziNG,SHpēl/ ▶ **n.** (pl. **sing·spie·le** /-,spēlə; -,SHpēlə/) a form of German light opera, typically with spoken dialogue, popular esp. in the late 18th century. [from Ger. *singen* 'sing' + *Spiel* 'play.']

sin·gu·lar /'siNGgyələr/ ▶ **adj.** **1** exceptionally good or great; remarkable. ■ strange or eccentric in some respect. ■ Math. possessing unique properties. ■ Math. (of a square matrix) having a zero determinant. ■ Math. denoting a point that is a singularity. **2** Gram. (of a word or form) denoting or referring to just one person or thing. **3** single; unique: *she always thought of herself as singular, as his only daughter.* ▶ **n.** (usu. **the singular**) Gram. the singular form of a word: *the first person singular.* — **sin·gu·lar·ly** **adv.** [ME: ult. from L. *singularis*, from *singulus* (see SINGLE).]

sin·gu·lar·i·ty /,siNGgyə'laritē/ ▶ **n.** (pl. **-ties**) **1** the state, fact, quality, or condition of being singular. ■ a peculiarity or odd trait. **2** Physics & Math. a point at which a function takes an infinite value, esp. in space-time when matter is infinitely dense, such as at the center of a black hole.

sin·gu·lar·ize /'siNGgyələ,rīz/ ▶ **v.** [trans.] rare **1** make distinct or conspicuous. **2** give a singular form to (a word). — **sin·gu·lar·i·za·tion** /,siNGgyələrə'zāSHən/ **n.**

Sin·ha·lese /,sinhə'lēz; -'lēs/ (also **Sin·gha·lese** /,siNGgə-/, **Sin·ha·la** /sin-'hälə/) ▶ **n.** (pl. same) **1** a member of a people originally from northern India, now forming the majority of the population of Sri Lanka. **2** the Indic language of this people. ▶ **adj.** of or relating to this people or language. [from Sanskrit *Siṇhala* 'Sri Lanka.']

sin·is·ter /'sinistər/ ▶ **adj.** **1** giving the impression that something harmful or evil is happening or will happen. ■ wicked or criminal. **2** [attrib.] archaic & Heraldry of, on, or toward the left-hand side (in a coat of arms, from the bearer's point of view, i.e., the right as it is depicted). The opposite of DEXTER[1]. — **sin·is·ter·ly** **adv.** **sin·is·ter·ness** **n.** [ME: ult. from L. *sinister* 'left.']

sin·is·tral /'sinəstrəl/ ▶ **adj.** of or on the left side or the left hand (the opposite of DEXTRAL), in particular: ■ left-handed. ■ Zool. (of a spiral mollusk shell) with whorls rising to the left and coiling in a clockwise direction. — **sin·is·tral·i·ty** /,sinə'stralitē/ **n.** **sin·is·tral·ly** **adv.**

sin·is·trorse /'sinə,strôrs/ ▶ **adj.** rising toward the left, esp. of the spiral stem of a plant. [19th C.: from L. *sinistrorsus*, from *sinister* 'left' + *vertere* 'turn.']

Si·nit·ic /si'nitik/ ▶ **adj.** of, relating to, or denoting the division of the Sino-Tibetan language family that includes the many forms of spoken Chinese.

sink[1] /siNGk/ ▶ **v.** (past **sank** /saNGk/ or / **sunk** /səNGk/; past part. **sunk** /səNGk/) **1** [intrans.] go down below the surface of something, esp. of a liquid; become submerged: *the coffin sank below the waves.* ■ (of a ship) go to the bottom of the sea or some other body of water because of damage or a collision. ■ fig. disappear and not be seen or heard of again: *the film sank without trace.* ■ [trans.] cause (a ship) to go to the bottom of the sea or other body of water: *a freak wave sank their boat.* ■ [trans.] fig. cause to fail: *she wishes to sink the company.* ■ [trans.] fig. conceal, keep in the background, or ignore: *they agreed to sink their differences.* **2** [intrans.] descend from a higher to a lower position; drop downward: *the ground sank beneath his feet.* ■ (of a person) lower oneself or drop down gently: *she sank back onto her pillow.* ■ [with adverbial of direction] gradually penetrate into the surface of something: *her feet sank into the carpet.* ■ (**sink in**) fig. (of words or facts) be fully understood or realized. ■ [trans.] (**sink something into**) cause something sharp to penetrate (a surface): *the dog sank its teeth into her arm.* **3** [intrans.] gradually decrease or decline in value, amount, quality, or intensity. ■ lapse or fall into a particular state or condition, typically unpleasant: *he sank into a coma.* ■ be overwhelmed by a darker mood. ■ approach death: *the doctor concluded that Sanders was sinking fast.* **4** [trans.] insert beneath a surface by digging or hollowing out: *the screws were sunk below the surface of the wood.* ■ excavate (a well) or bore (a shaft) vertically downward. ■ pocket (a ball) in billiards. ■ Golf hit the ball into the hole with (a putt or other shot). ■ [trans.] insert into something: *Kelly's hands were sunk deep into her pockets.* ■ [intrans.] (of eyes) appear unusually deep or receded. **5** [trans.] (**sink something into**) put money or energy into (something); invest something in. — **sink·a·ble** **adj.** **sink·age** /'siNGkij/ **n.** [OE *sincan*, from Gmc.; akin to Ger. *sinken*.]

sink[2] ▶ **n.** a fixed basin with a water supply and a drain. ■ short for SINKHOLE. ■ a pool or marsh in which a river's water disappears by evaporation or percolation. ■ tech. a body or process that acts to absorb or remove energy or a particular component from a system; the opposite of SOURCE: *a heat sink.* ■ fig. a place of vice or corruption: *a sink of unnatural vice, pride, and luxury.* [ME: from SINK[1].]

sink·er /'siNGkər/ ▶ **n.** **1** a weight used to sink a fishing line or sounding line. **2** (also **sinker ball**) Baseball a pitch that drops markedly as it nears home plate. **3** a doughnut.

sink·hole /'siNGk,hōl/ ▶ **n.** a cavity in the ground, esp. in a limestone formation, caused by water erosion and providing a route for surface water to disappear underground.

sink·ing fund ▶ **n.** a fund formed by periodically setting aside money for the gradual repayment of a debt or replacement of a wasting asset.

sin·ner /'sinər/ ▶ **n.** a person who transgresses against divine law by committing an immoral act or acts.

sin·net /'sinit/ var. of SENNIT.

Sinn Fein /'SHin 'fān/ a political movement and party seeking a united republican Ireland. — **Sinn Fein·er** **n.** [from Irish *sinn féin* 'we ourselves.']

Sino- /'sīnō/ ▶ **comb. form** Chinese; Chinese and ...: *Sino-American.* ■ relating to China.

si·no·a·tri·al node /,sīnō'ātrēəl/ ▶ **n.** Anat. a small body of specialized muscle tissue in the wall of the right atrium of the heart that acts as a pacemaker by producing a contractile signal at regular intervals. [20th C.: from SINUS + *atrial* (see ATRIUM).]

sin of·fer·ing ▶ **n.** (in traditional or ancient Judaism) an offering made as an atonement for sin.

Si·no-Jap·a·nese Wars two wars (1894–95, 1937–45) fought between China and Japan.

Si·nol·o·gy /sī'näləjē/ ▶ **n.** the study of Chinese language, history, customs, and politics. — **Si·no·log·i·cal** /,sīnl'äjikəl; ,sin-/ **adj.** **Si·nol·o·gist** /-jist/ **n.**

Si·no-Ti·bet·an ▶ **adj.** of, relating to, or denoting a language family of eastern Asia, including Sinitic (Chinese), Tibeto-Burman (Burmese and Tibetan), and, in some classifications, Tai (Thai and Lao). ▶ **n.** this language family.

sin·se·mil·la /,sinsə'mēyə/ ▶ **n.** marijuana of a variety that has a high concentration of psychoactive agents. [1970s: from Amer. Sp., lit. 'without seed.']

sin tax ▶ **n.** informal a tax on items considered undesirable or harmful, such as alcohol or tobacco.

sin·ter /'sintər/ ▶ **n.** **1** Geol. a hard siliceous or calcareous deposit precipitated from mineral springs. **2** solid material that has been sintered, esp. a mixture of iron ore and other materials prepared for smelting. ▶ **v.** [trans.] make (a powdered material) coalesce into a solid or porous mass by heating it (and usually also compressing it) without liquefaction. ■ [intrans.] coalesce in this way. [18th C. (n.): from Ger. *Sinter*; compare CINDER.]

Sint Maar·ten /sint 'märtin/ Dutch name for ST. MARTIN.

sin·u·ate /'sinyo͞oˌāt; -it/ ▶ **adj.** Bot. & Zool. having a wavy or sinuous margin;

with alternate rounded notches and lobes. [17th C.: from L. *sinuatus*, past part. of *sinuare* 'to bend.']

Sin·ui·ju /'sHin'wē'jōō/ a city in North Korea, on the Yalu River; pop. 500,000.

sin·u·os·i·ty /,sinyōō'äsitē/ ▶ **n.** (pl. **-ties**) the ability to curve or bend easily and flexibly. ■ a bend, esp. in a stream or road. [16th C.: ult. from med. L. *sinuositas*, from *sinuosus* (see SINUOUS).]

sin·u·ous /'sinyōōəs/ ▶ **adj.** having many curves and turns. ■ lithe and supple. — **sin·u·ous·ly adv. sin·u·ous·ness n.** [16th C.: ult. from L. *sinuosus*, from *sinus* 'a bend.']

si·nus /'sīnəs/ ▶ **n. 1** (often **sinuses**) Anat. & Zool. a cavity within a bone or other tissue, esp. one in the bones of the face or skull connecting with the nasal cavities. ■ an irregular venous or lymphatic cavity, reservoir, or dilated vessel. ■ Med. an infected tract leading from a deep-seated infection and discharging pus to the surface. ■ Bot. a rounded notch between two lobes on the margin of a leaf or petal. **2** [as adj.] Physiol. relating to or denoting the sinoatrial node of the heart or its function as a pacemaker. [ME: from L., lit. 'a recess, bend.']

si·nus·i·tis /,sīnə'sītis/ ▶ **n.** Med. inflammation of a nasal sinus.

si·nus·oid /'sīnə,soid/ ▶ **n. 1** a curve having the form of a sine wave. **2** Anat. a small irregularly shaped blood vessel found in certain organs, esp. the liver. — **si·nus·oi·dal** /,sīnə'soidl/ **adj. si·nus·oi·dal·ly** /,sīnə'soidəlē/ **adv.** [19th C.: from Fr. *sinusoïde*, from L. *sinus* (see SINUS).]

Sion /'sīən/ ▶ **n.** var. of **ZION**.

-sion ▶ **suffix** forming nouns such as *mansion, persuasion*. [from L. participial stems ending in *-s* + **-ION**.]

Siou·an /'sōōən/ ▶ **n.** a family of North American Indian languages spoken by the Sioux and related peoples, including Crow, Dakota, Hidatsa, Lakota, Mandan, Omaha, and Yankton. ▶ **adj.** of, relating to, or denoting this language family.

Sioux /sōō/ ▶ **n.** (pl. same) another term for the Dakota people or their language. See **DAKOTA**[2]. ▶ **adj.** of or relating to this people or their language. [North Amer. Fr., from *Nadouessioux*, from Ojibwa (Ottawa dial.) *nātowēssiwak*, ult. of Iroquoian origin, prob. lit. 'speaker of a foreign language.']

Sioux Cit·y a city in northwestern Iowa, on the Missouri and Big Sioux rivers; pop. 85,013.

Sioux Falls a city in southeastern South Dakota; pop. 123,975.

sip /sip/ ▶ **v.** (**sipped, sip·ping**) [trans.] drink (something) by taking small mouthfuls: *I sat sipping coffee* | [intrans.] *she sipped at her tea.* ▶ **n.** a small mouthful of liquid. — **sip·per n.** [ME: perh. alt. of **SUP**[1].]

si·phon /'sīfən/ (also **sy·phon**) ▶ **n.** a pipe or tube used to convey liquid upward from a container and then down to a lower level by gravity, the liquid being made to enter the pipe by atmospheric pressure. ■ Zool. a tubular organ in an aquatic animal, esp. a mollusk, through which water is drawn in or expelled. ▶ **v.** [trans.] draw off or convey (liquid) by means of a siphon. ■ fig. draw off or transfer over a period of time, esp. illegally or unfairly. — **si·phon·age** /-nij/ **n. si·phon·al** /-nəl/ **adj.** (Zool.) **si·phon·ic** /sī'fänik/ **adj.** [ME (n.): ult. from Gk. *siphōn* 'pipe.']

Si·pho·noph·o·ra /,sīfə'näfərə/ Zool. an order of colonial marine coelenterates that includes the Portuguese man-of-war, having a float or swimming bell for drifting or swimming on the open sea. — **si·pho·no·phore** /'sīfənə,fôr; sī'fänə-/ **n.** [mod. L. (pl.), from Gk. *siphōn* 'tube' + *pherein* 'to bear.']

si·phon·o·stele /'sīfənə,stēl; sī'fänə,stēl/ ▶ **n.** Bot. a stele consisting of a core of pith surrounded by concentric layers of xylem and phloem.

sip·pet /'sipit/ ▶ **n.** a small piece of bread or toast, used to dip into soup or sauce or as a garnish. [16th C.: prob. a dimin. of **SOP**.]

Sir. ▶ **abbr.** (in biblical references) Sirach (Apocrypha).

sir /sər/ (also **Sir**) ▶ **n.** used as a polite or respectful way of addressing a man, esp. one in a position of authority: *excuse me, sir.* ■ used to address a man at the beginning of a formal or business letter: *Dear Sir.* ■ (in Britain) used as a title before the given name of a knight or baronet. ■ another expression for **SIREE**. [ME: from **SIRE**.]

Si·ra·cu·sa /,sērä'kōōzä/ Italian name for **SYRACUSE** 1.

Sir Dar·yo /sir 'däryə; ,sir där'yä/ a river in central Asia that rises in eastern Uzbekistan and flows to the Aral Sea.

sire /sī(ə)r/ ▶ **n. 1** the male parent of an animal, esp. a stallion or bull kept for breeding. **2** archaic a respectful form of address for someone of high social status, esp. a king. ■ a father or other male forebear. ▶ **v.** [trans.] be the male parent of (an animal). ■ literary (of a person) be the father of. [ME (sense 2): from OFr., from alt. of L. *senior* (see **SENIOR**).]

sir·ee /sə'rē/ (also **sir·ree**) ▶ **exclam.** informal used for emphasis, esp. after *yes* and *no*. [19th C.: from **SIR** + emphatic suffix *-ee*.]

si·ren /'sīrən/ ▶ **n. 1** a device that makes a loud prolonged signal or warning sound. **2** Gk. Mythol. each of a number of women or winged creatures whose singing lured unwary sailors onto rocks. ■ a woman considered to be alluring or fascinating but also dangerous in some way. **3** an eel-like American amphibian (genera *Siren* and *Pseudobranchus*, family Sirenidae) with tiny forelimbs, no hind limbs, small eyes, and external gills, typically living in muddy pools. [ME ('imaginary type of snake'): ult. from late L. *Sirena*, fem. of L. *Siren*, from Gk. *Seirēn*.]

Si·re·ni·a /sī'rēnēə/ Zool. an order (Sirenia) of large aquatic plant-eating mammals that includes the manatees and dugong. — **si·re·ni·an** /-ən/ **n. & adj.** [mod. L. (see **SIREN**).]

Sir Ga·la·had ▶ **n.** see **GALAHAD**.

Sir·i·us /'si(ə)rēəs/ Astron. the brightest star in the sky, south of the celestial equator in the constellation Canis Major. Also called **DOG STAR**. [L., from Gk. *seirios astēr* 'scorching star.']

sir·loin /'sərloin/ ▶ **n.** the choicer part of a loin of beef. [ME: from OFr. (see **SUR-**[1], **LOIN**).]

si·roc·co /sə'räkō/ (also **sci·roc·co** /sHə'räkō; sə-/) ▶ **n.** (pl. **-cos**) a hot wind, often dusty or rainy, blowing from North Africa across the Mediterranean to southern Europe. [17th C.: via Fr. from Ital. *scirocco*, based on Sp. Arab. *Šalūk* 'east wind.']

sir·rah /'sirə/ ▶ **n.** archaic used as a term of address for a man or boy, esp. one younger or of lower status than the speaker. [16th C.: prob. from **SIRE**.]

sir·up ▶ **n.** var. of **SYRUP**.

sir·up·y ▶ **adj.** var. of **SYRUPY**.

sis /sis/ ▶ **n.** informal a person's sister (often used as a form of address): *where are you going, sis?* [17th C.: abbrev.]

si·sal /'sisəl; 'sī-/ ▶ **n.** a Mexican agave (*Agave sisalana*, family Agavaceae) with large fleshy leaves, cultivated for fiber production. ■ the fiber made from this plant, used esp. for ropes or matting. [19th C.: *Sisal*, port in Yucatán, Mexico.]

sis·kin /'siskin/ ▶ **n.** a small finch (genera *Carduelis* and *Serinus*). Its several species include the North American **pine siskin** (*C. pinus*), with dark-streaked plumage, notched tail, and touches of yellow on wings and tail. [16th C.: from MDu. *siseken*, dimin. akin to Ger. *Zeisig*, of Slavic origin.]

Sis·ki·you Moun·tains /'siskē,(y)ōō/ a forested range of the Klamath Mountains, in northwestern California and southwestern Oregon.

sis·sy /'sisē/ informal ▶ **n.** (pl. **-sies**) a person regarded as effeminate or cowardly. ■ usu. offens. an effeminate homosexual. ▶ **adj.** (**-si·er, -si·est**) feeble and cowardly. — **sis·si·fied** /'sisə,fīd/ **adj. sis·si·ness n. sis·sy·ish adj.** [19th C. ('sister'): from **SIS**.]

sis·ter /'sistər/ ▶ **n. 1** a woman or girl in relation to other daughters and sons of her parents. ■ a half-sister, stepsister, or foster sister. ■ a sister-in-law. ■ a close female friend or associate, esp. a female fellow member of a labor union or other organization. ■ (often **Sister**) a member of a religious order or congregation of women. ■ a fellow woman seen in relation to feminist issues. ■ informal a black woman (chiefly used as a term of address by other black people). ■ [usu. as adj.] a thing, esp. an organization, that bears a relationship to another of common origin or allegiance or mutual association: *a sister ship.* **2** (often **Sister**) Brit. a senior female nurse, typically in charge of a ward. — **sis·ter·li·ness n. sis·ter·ly adj.** [OE, from Indo-Eur.; akin to Ger. *Schwester*, L. *soror*.]

sis·ter·hood /'sistər,hŏŏd/ ▶ **n. 1** the relationship between sisters. ■ the feeling of kinship with and closeness to a group of women or all women. **2** (often **Sisterhood**) an association, society, or community of women linked by a common interest, religion, or trade.

sis·ter-in-law ▶ **n.** (pl. **sis·ters-in-law**) the sister of one's wife or husband. ■ the wife of one's brother or brother-in-law.

Sis·tine /'sistēn/ ▶ **adj.** of or relating to any of the popes called Sixtus, esp. Sixtus IV. [from Ital. *Sistino*, from *Sisto* 'Sixtus.']

Sis·tine Chap·el a chapel in the Vatican, built in the late 15th century by Pope Sixtus IV, containing a painted ceiling and fresco of the Last Judgment by Michelangelo and also frescoes by Botticelli.

sis·trum /'sistrəm/ ▶ **n.** (pl. **sis·tra** /'sistrə/ or **sis·trums**) a musical instrument of ancient Egypt consisting of a metal frame with transverse metal rods that rattled when the instrument was shaken. [ME: via L. from Gk. *seistron*, from *seiein* 'to shake.']

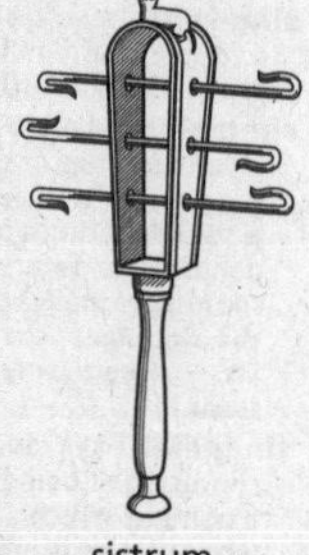

sistrum

Sis·y·phe·an /,sisə'fēən/ ▶ **adj.** (of a task) such that it can never be completed. [16th C.: from L. *Sisypheius* (based on Gk. *Sisuphos*, see **SISYPHUS**.]

Sis·y·phus /'sisəfəs/ Gk. Mythol. the son of Aeolus, punished in Hades by being condemned to the eternal task of rolling a large stone to the top of a hill, from which it always rolled down again.

sit /sit/ ▶ **v.** (**sit·ting** ; past **sat** /sat/) **1** [intrans.] adopt or be in a position in which one's weight is supported by one's buttocks rather than one's feet and one's back is upright: *you'd better sit down.* ■ [trans.] cause to adopt or be in such a position: *sit yourself down and I'll bring you some coffee.* ■ (of an animal) rest with the hind legs bent and the body close to the ground. ■ (of a bird) rest on a branch; perch. ■ (of a bird) remain on its nest to incubate its egg. ■ [trans.] ride or keep one's seat on (a horse). ■ [trans.] not use (a player) in a game: *the manager must decide who to sit in the World Series.* ■ [trans.] (of a table, room, or building) be large enough for (a specified number of seated people): *the cathedral sat about 3,000 people.* ■ (**sit for**) pose, typically in a seated position, for (an artist or photographer). ■ [intrans.] be or remain in a particular position or state: *the fridge was sitting in a pool of water.* ■ [intrans.] (of an item of clothing) fit a person well or badly as specified: *the blue uniform sat well on his big frame.* ■ (**sit with**) be harmonious with. **2** [intrans.] (of a legislature, court of law, etc.) be engaged in its business. ■ serve as a member of a council, jury, or other official body. **3** [trans.] Brit. take (an examination): *pupils are required to sit nine subjects* | [intrans.] *he was about to sit for his Cambridge entrance exam.* **4** [intrans.] live in someone's house while they are away and look after their pet or pets: *Kelly had been cat-sitting for me.* See also **BABYSIT**. ▶ **n.** [in sing.] **1** a period of sitting: *a sit in the shade.* **2** archaic the way in which an item of clothing fits someone: *the sit of her gown.*

– PHRASES **sit on the fence** see FENCE. **sit on one's ass** vulgar slang do nothing; fail to take action. **sit on one's hands** take no action. **sit (heavy) on the stomach** (of food) take a long time to be digested. **sit tight** informal remain firmly in one's place. ■ refrain from taking action or changing one's mind. **sit up (and take notice)** informal suddenly start paying attention or have one's interest aroused.

– PHRASAL VERBS **sit back** relax. ■ take no action; choose not to become involved. *I can't just sit back and let Betsy do all the work.* **sit by** take no action to prevent something undesirable from occurring. **sit down** archaic encamp outside a city in order to besiege it. **sit in 1** (of a group of people) occupy a place as a form of protest. **2** attend a meeting or discussion without taking an active part in it. **sit in for** temporarily carry out the duties of (another person). **sit on** informal **1** fail to deal with. **2** subdue (someone), typically by saying something to discomfit or embarrass them. ■ suppress (something). **sit something out** not take part in a particular event or activity. ■ wait without moving or taking action until a particular unwelcome situation or process is over. **sit through** stay until the end of (a tedious or lengthy meeting or performance). **sit up** (or **sit someone up**) **1** move (or cause someone to move) from a lying or slouching to a sitting position. **2** refrain from going to bed until a later time than usual. [OE *sittan*, from Indo-Eur.; akin to Ger. *sitzen*, L. *sedere*, and Gk. *hezesthai*.]

Si·ta /'sē,tä/ (in the Ramayana) the wife of Rama. She is the Hindu model of the ideal woman, an incarnation of Lakshmi. [from Sanskrit *Sītā*, lit. 'furrow.']

si·tar /si'tär/ ▶ **n.** a large, long-necked Indian lute with movable frets, played with a wire pick. — **si·tar·ist** /-ist/ **n.** [via Urdu from Pers. *sitār*, from *sih* 'three' + *tār* 'string.']

sitar

sit·com /'sit,käm/ ▶ **n.** informal a situation comedy. [1960s: abbrev.]

sit-down ▶ **adj.** [attrib.] (of a meal) eaten sitting at a table. ■ (of a protest) in which demonstrators occupy their workplace or sit down on the ground in a public place, refusing to leave until their demands are met. ▶ **n.** a period of sitting down; a short rest. ■ a sit-down protest.

site /sīt/ ▶ **n.** an area of ground on which a town, building, or monument is constructed: *the proposed site of a hydroelectric dam.* ■ a place where a particular event or activity is occurring or has occurred. ■ short for WEB SITE. ▶ **v.** [trans.] (usu. **be sited**) fix or build (something) in a particular place. [ME (n.): ult. from L. *situs* 'local position.']

sit-in ▶ **n.** a form of protest in which demonstrators occupy a place, refusing to leave until their demands are met.

Sit·ka /'sitkə/ a city in southwestern Alaska; pop. 8,835.

Sit·ka spruce /'sitkə sprōōs/ ▶ **n.** a fast-growing spruce (*Picea sitchensis*) of the northern Pacific coast of North America, widely cultivated in Britain for its strong lightweight timber. [19th C.: *Sitka*, town in Alaska.]

sit·rep /'sit,rep/ ▶ **n.** informal a report on the current military situation in a particular area. [1940s: from *sit(uation) rep(ort)*.]

Sit·tang /'si,täNG/ a river in southern Myanmar (Burma). It flows into the Bay of Bengal.

sit·ter /'sitər/ ▶ **n. 1** a person who sits, esp. for a portrait. ■ a hen sitting on eggs. **2** [usu. in comb.] a person who looks after children, pets, or a house while the parents or owners are away. ■ a person who provides care and companionship for people who are ill.

sit·ting /'sitiNG/ ▶ **n.** a continuous period of being seated, esp. when engaged in a particular activity: *the whole roast was eaten at one sitting.* ■ a period of time spent as a model for an artist or photographer. ■ a scheduled period of time when a group of people are served a meal, esp. in a restaurant. ■ a period of time during which a committee or legislature is engaged in its normal business. ▶ **adj.** [attrib.] **1** denoting a person who has sat down or the position of such a person. ■ (of an animal or bird) not running or flying. **2** (of an elected representative) current; present. **3** (of a hen or other bird) settled on eggs for the purpose of incubating them.

Sit·ting Bull (*c.*1831–90), Sioux Indian chief; Sioux name *Tatanka Iyotake*. He led the Sioux in the fight to retain their lands, resulting in the massacre at Little Bighorn.

sit·ting duck (also **sitting target**) ▶ **n.** informal a person or thing with no protection against an attack or other source of danger.

sit·ting room ▶ **n.** a room in a house or hotel in which people can sit down and relax.

sit·u·ate ▶ **v.** /'sicHōō,āt/ [trans.] (usu. **be situated**) fix or build (something) in a certain place or position: *the pilot light is usually situated at the front of the boiler.* ■ put in context; describe the circumstances surrounding (something). ■ (**be situated**) be in a specified financial or marital position: *Amy is now comfortably situated.* ▶ **adj.** Law or archaic situated. [ME: from med. L. *situat-* 'placed,' from the verb *situare*, from L. *situs* 'site.']

sit·u·a·tion /,sicHōō'āsHən/ ▶ **n. 1** a set of circumstances in which one finds oneself; a state of affairs. **2** the location and surroundings of a place. **3** formal a position of employment; a job. — **sit·u·a·tion·al** /-sHənl/ **adj.** **sit·u·a·tion·al·ly** /-sHənl-ē/ **adv.**

sit·u·a·tion com·e·dy ▶ **n.** a television or radio series in which the same set of characters are involved in various amusing situations.

sit·u·a·tion eth·ics (also **situational ethics**) ▶ **plural n.** [treated as sing.] Philos. the doctrine of flexibility in the application of moral laws according to circumstances.

sit·u·a·tion·ism /,sicHōō'āsHə,nizəm/ ▶ **n.** the theory that human behavior is determined by surrounding circumstances rather than by personal qualities. — **sit·u·a·tion·ist n. & adj.**

sit-up ▶ **n.** a physical exercise designed to strengthen the abdominal muscles, in which a person sits up from a supine position without using the arms for leverage.

si·tus /'sītəs; 'sē-/ ▶ **n.** situation or position, esp. the normal position of an organ or other part of a living thing. ■ Law the place to which, for purposes of legal jurisdiction or taxation, a property belongs.

Sit·well /'sitwəl; -,wel/ English literary family, known for their opposition to the prevailing Georgian style. Dame Edith Louisa (1887–1964) wrote poetry collected in such works as *The Outcasts* (1962). Her brother Sir Osbert (1892–1969) was noted for his fiction and five-volume autobigraphy (1945–50). Their brother Sir Sacheverell (1897–1988), an art critic, also wrote poetry and books on architecture.

sitz bath /sits/ ▶ **n.** a bath in which only the buttocks and hips are immersed in water. [19th C.: partial translation of Ger. *Sitzbad*, from *sitzen* 'sit' + *Bad* 'bath.']

Sitz·fleisch /'sits,flīsH/ (also **sitz·fleisch**) ▶ **n.** informal a person's buttocks. ■ power to endure or to persevere in an activity; staying power. [from Ger., from *sitzen* 'sit' + *Fleisch* 'flesh.']

sitz·krieg /'sits,krēg/ ▶ **n.** a war, or a phase of a war, in which there is little or no active warfare. [1940s: suggested by BLITZKRIEG, from Ger. *sitzen* 'sit.']

sitz·mark /'sits,märk/ ▶ **n.** an impression made in the snow by a skier falling backward. [1930s: from Ger. *sitzen* 'sit' + MARK[1] (n.).]

Si·va /'sHēvə; 'sē-/ var. of SHIVA.

Si·van /'sivən/ ▶ **n.** (in the Jewish calendar) the ninth month of the civil and third of the religious year, usually coinciding with parts of May and June. [from Heb. *sīwān*.]

six /siks/ ▶ **cardinal number** equivalent to the product of two and three; one more than five, or four less than ten; 6. (Roman numeral: **vi, VI.**) ■ a group or unit of six people or things. ■ six years old. ■ six o'clock. ■ a size of garment or other merchandise denoted by six. ■ a playing card or domino with six pips.

– PHRASES **at sixes and sevens** in a state of total confusion or disarray. [OE *siex, six, syx*, from Indo-Eur.; akin to Ger. *sechs*, L. *sex*, Gk. *hex*.]

Six, Les see LES SIX.

six·fold /'siks,fōld/ ▶ **adj.** six times as great or as numerous. ■ having six parts or elements. ▶ **adv.** by six times; to six times the number or amount.

six-gun ▶ **n.** another term for SIX-SHOOTER.

Six Na·tions ▶ **plural n.** (**the Six Nations**) the Five Nations of the original Iroquois confederacy after the Tuscarora joined them in 1722.

six-pack ▶ **n. 1** a pack of six cans of beer or soft drinks typically held together with a plastic fastener. **2** informal a set of well-developed abdominal muscles.

six·pence /'siks,pens; -pəns/ ▶ **n.** Brit. a coin worth six old pence, withdrawn in 1980. ■ the sum of six pence, esp. before decimalization (1971).

six·pen·ny /'siks,penē; -pənē/ ▶ **adj.** [attrib.] Brit. costing or worth six pence, esp. before decimalization (1971).

six-shoot·er ▶ **n.** a revolver with six chambers.

sixte /sikst/ ▶ **n.** Fencing the sixth of eight standard parrying positions. [19th C.: Fr., from L. *sextus* 'sixth.']

six·teen /sik'stēn; 'sik,stēn/ ▶ **cardinal number** equivalent to the product of four and four; one more than fifteen, or six more than ten; 16. (Roman numeral: **xvi, XVI.**) ■ a size of garment or other merchandise denoted by sixteen. ■ sixteen years old. — **six·teenth** /sik'stēnTH; 'sik,stēnTH/ **ordinal number.** [OE *siextīene* (see SIX, -TEEN).]

six·teen·mo /,siks'tēnmō/ ▶ **n.** (pl. **-mos**) another term for SEXTODECIMO.

six·teenth note /,siks'tēnTH/ ▶ **n.** Music a note having the time value of a sixteenth of a whole note or half an eighth note, represented by a large dot with a two-hooked stem. Also called SEMIQUAVER.

sixth /siksTH/ ▶ **ordinal number** constituting number six in a sequence; 6th. ■ (**a sixth/one sixth**) each of six equal parts into which something is or may be divided. ■ the sixth finisher or position in a race or competition. ■ the sixth grade of a school. ■ sixthly (used to introduce a sixth point or reason). ■ Music an interval spanning six consecutive notes in a diatonic major or minor scale, e.g., C to A (**major sixth**) or A to F (**minor sixth**). ■ Music the note that is higher by this interval than the tonic of a scale or root of a chord. — **sixth·ly adv.**

sixth sense ▶ **n.** [in sing.] a supposed intuitive faculty giving awareness not explicable in terms of normal perception: *some sixth sense told him he was not alone.*

six·ty /'sikstē/ ▶ **cardinal number** (pl. **-ties**) the number equivalent to the product of six and ten; ten more than fifty; 60. (Roman numeral:

lx, LX.) ■ **(sixties)** the numbers from sixty to sixty-nine, esp. the years of a century or of a person's life. ■ sixty miles an hour. ■ sixty years old. — **six·ti·eth** /-iTH/ ordinal number. **six·ty·fold** /-'fōld/ adj. & adv. [OE *siextig* (see six, -ty²).]

six·ty-four·mo /,sikstē 'fôrmō/ ▶ n. (pl. **-mos**) a size of book in which each leaf is one sixty-fourth the size of a printing sheet. ■ a book of this size.

six·ty-fourth note ▶ n. Music a note with the time value of half a thirty-second note, represented by a large dot with a four-flagged stem.

six·ty-nine ▶ n. informal sexual activity between two people involving mutual oral stimulation of their genitals. [from the position of the couple.]

siz·a·ble /'sīzəbəl/ (also **size·a·ble**) ▶ adj. fairly large. — **siz·a·bly** /-blē/ adv.

siz·ar /'sīzər/ ▶ n. an undergraduate at Cambridge University or at Trinity College, Dublin, receiving financial help from the college and formerly having certain menial duties. — **siz·ar·ship** /-,SHip/ n. [16th C.: from size¹ 'ration.']

size¹ /sīz/ ▶ n. **1** the relative extent of something; how big something is. ■ extensive dimensions or magnitude. **2** each of the classes, typically numbered, into which garments or other articles are divided according to how large they are. ■ a person or garment corresponding to such a numbered class: *she's a size 10.* ▶ v. [trans.] alter or sort in terms of size or according to size: *some drills are sized in millimeters.* ■ **(size something up)** estimate or measure something's dimensions: *she was trying to size up a room with a tape measure.* ■ **(size someone/something up)** informal form an estimate or rough judgment of someone or something. ▶ adj. [in comb.] having a specified size; sized: *marble-size chunks of hail.*

– PHRASES **of a size** (of two or more people or things) having the same dimensions. **of some size** fairly large. **to size** to the dimensions wanted. — **siz·er** n. [ME: from OFr. *sise*, from *assise* 'ordinance,' or a shortening of ASSIZE.]

size² ▶ n. a gelatinous solution used in gilding paper, stiffening textiles, and preparing plastered walls for decoration. ▶ v. [trans.] treat with size to glaze or stiffen. [ME: perh. same word as SIZE¹.]

size·a·ble ▶ adj. var. of SIZABLE.

sized /sīzd/ ▶ adj. [in comb. or with submodifier] having a specified size: *sparrow-sized birds.*

siz·zle /'sizəl/ ▶ v. [intrans.] (of food) make a hissing sound when frying or cooking. ■ [often as adj.] **(sizzling)** informal be very hot. ■ [often as adj.] **(sizzling)** informal be very exciting or passionate, esp. sexually. ▶ n. [in sing.] a hissing sound, as of food frying or cooking. ■ informal a state or quality of great excitement or passion. — **siz·zler** /'siz(ə)lər/ n. [17th C.: imitative.]

SJ ▶ abbr. Society of Jesus.

Sjæl·land /'SHelän/ Danish name for ZEALAND.

sjam·bok /SHam'bäk; -'bək; 'SHambäk; -bək/ ▶ n. (in South Africa) a long, stiff whip, originally made of rhinoceros hide. ▶ v. [trans.] flog with a sjambok. [from South Afr. Du. *tjambok*, via Malay from Urdu *chābuk*.]

S.J.D. ▶ abbr. Doctor of Juridical Science. [L. *Scientiae Juridicae Doctor*.]

SK ▶ abbr. Saskatchewan (in official postal use).

ska /skä/ ▶ n. a style of fast popular music having a strong offbeat and originating in Jamaica in the 1960s, a forerunner of reggae. [1960s: origin unknown.]

skag /skag/ (also **scag**) ▶ n. informal heroin. [20th C.: origin unknown.]

Skag·er·rak /'skagə,rak; 'skägə,räk/ **(the Skagerrak)** a strait that separates Norway from Denmark.

Skag·way /'skag,wā/ a city in southwestern Alaska; pop. 692. It was a gateway to the 1897–98 Klondike gold rush.

skald /skôld/ (also **scald**) ▶ n. hist. (in ancient Scandinavia) a composer and reciter of poems honoring heroes and their deeds. — **skald·ic** /'skôldik/ adj. [from ON *skáld*.]

Skan·da /'skəndə/ Hinduism the Hindu war god, first son of Shiva and Parvati and brother of Ganesha.

skank /skaNGk/ ▶ n. **1** informal a person perceived to be extremely sleazy or unpleasant. **2** a steady-paced dance performed to reggae music. ■ reggae music suitable for such dancing. ▶ v. [intrans.] [often as adj.] **(skanking)** play reggae music or dance in this style. [1970s: origin unknown.]

skank·y /'skaNGkē/ ▶ adj. informal very unpleasant; revolting. ■ sleazy; sordid.

skat /skat/ ▶ n. a three-handed trick-taking card game with bidding, played with 32 cards. [19th C.: from Ger., from Ital. *scarto* 'a discard,' from *scartare* 'discard.']

skate¹ /skāt/ ▶ n. an ice skate or roller skate. See illustrations at ICE SKATE, IN-LINE SKATE. ■ a device, typically with wheels on the underside, used to move a heavy or unwieldy object. ▶ v. [intrans.] move on ice skates or roller skates in a gliding fashion: *the boys were skating on the ice.* ■ [trans.] perform (a specified figure) on skates. ■ ride on a skateboard. ■ **(skate over/around)** fig. pass over or refer only fleetingly to (a subject or problem). ■ **(skate through)** fig. make quick and easy progress through. — **skat·er** n. [17th C. (as *scates* (pl.)): from Du. *schaats* (sing.), from OFr. *eschasse* 'stilt.']

skate² ▶ n. (pl. same or **skates**) a typically large marine fish of the ray family (Rajidae) with a cartilaginous skeleton and a flattened diamond-shaped body, in particular the commercially valuable *Raja batis*. ■ the flesh of a skate or thornback used as food. [ME: from ON *skata*.]

skate·board /'skāt,bôrd/ ▶ n. a short narrow board with two small wheels fixed to the bottom of either end, on which a person can ride in a standing or crouching position, propelling themselves by pushing one foot against the ground. ▶ v. [intrans.] [often as n.] **(skateboarding)** ride on a skateboard. — **skate·board·er** n.

skat·ing /'skātiNG/ ▶ n. the sport or pastime of skating on ice skates, roller skates, or a skateboard.

skat·ing rink ▶ n. an expanse of ice artificially made for skating, or a floor used for roller skating.

skean dhu /,skē(ə)n 'THōō; 'dōō/ ▶ n. a dagger worn in the stocking as part of Highland dress. [19th C.: from Irish and Scottish Gaelic *sgian* 'knife' + Scot. Gael. *dubh* 'black.']

ske·dad·dle /ski'dadl/ ▶ v. [intrans.] informal depart quickly or hurriedly; run away. ▶ n. a hurried departure or flight. [19th C.: origin unknown.]

skeet /skēt/ (also **skeet shooting**) ▶ n. a shooting sport in which a clay target is thrown from a trap to simulate the flight of a bird. — **skeet shoot·er** n. [1920s: prob. alt. of SHOOT (v.).]

skee·ter /'skētər/ ▶ n. informal a mosquito. [19th C.: shortened form]

skeg /skeg/ ▶ n. a tapering or projecting stern section of a vessel's keel, which protects the propellor and supports the rudder. ■ a fin underneath the rear of a surfboard. [17th C.: from ON *skegg* 'beard,' perh. from Du. *scheg*.]

skein /skān/ ▶ n. a length of thread or yarn, loosely coiled and knotted. ■ a tangled or complicated arrangement, state, or situation. ■ a flock of wild geese or swans in flight, typically in a V-shaped formation. [ME: shortening of OFr. *escaigne*.]

skel·e·tal /'skelətl/ ▶ adj. of, relating to, or functioning as a skeleton. ■ very thin; emaciated. ■ existing only in outline or as a framework of something. — **skel·e·tal·ly** adv.

skel·e·tal mus·cle ▶ n. a muscle that is connected to the skeleton to form part of the mechanical system that moves the limbs and other parts of the body. ■ another term for STRIATED MUSCLE.

skel·e·ton /'skelitn/ ▶ n. an internal or external framework of bone, cartilage, or other rigid material supporting or containing the body of an animal or plant. ■ used in exaggerated reference to a very thin or emaciated person or animal. ■ the remaining part of something after its life or usefulness is gone: *the chapel was stripped to a skeleton of its former self.* ■ the supporting framework, basic structure, or essential part of something. ■ [as adj.] denoting the essential or minimum number of people, things, or parts necessary for something: *a skeleton staff on duty.*

– PHRASES **skeleton in the closet** a discreditable or embarrassing fact that someone wishes to keep secret. — **skel·e·ton·ize** /-,īz/ v. [16th C.: mod. L., from Gk., neut. of *skeletos* 'dried up,' from *skellein* 'dry up.']

skel·e·ton key ▶ n. a key designed to fit many locks by having the interior of the bit hollowed.

skep /skep/ ▶ n. a straw or wicker beehive. ■ archaic a wooden or wicker basket. [OE *sceppe* 'basket,' from ON *skeppa* 'basket, bushel.']

skep·tic /'skeptik/ (Brit. **scep·tic**) ▶ n. **1** a person inclined to question or doubt all accepted opinions. ■ a person who doubts the truth of Christianity and other religions; an atheist or agnostic. **2** Philos. an ancient or modern philosopher who denies the possibility of knowledge, or even rational belief, in some sphere. ▶ adj. another term for SKEPTICAL. — **skep·ti·cism** /'skeptə,sizəm/ (Brit. **scep·ti·cism**) n. [16th C. (sense 2): ult. from Gk. *skeptikos*, from *skepsis* 'inquiry, doubt.']

skep·ti·cal /'skeptikəl/ (Brit. **scep·ti·cal**) ▶ adj. **1** not easily convinced; having doubts or reservations. **2** Philos. relating to the theory that certain knowledge is impossible. — **skep·ti·cal·ly** /-tik(ə)lē/ (Brit. **scep·ti·cal·ly**) adv.

sker·ry /'skerē/ ▶ n. (pl. **-ries**) Scot. a reef or rocky island. [17th C.: Orkney dial., from ON *sker*.]

sketch /skeCH/ ▶ n. **1** a rough drawing or painting, often made to assist in making a more finished picture. ■ a brief account or description of someone or something, giving only basic details. ■ a rough of any creative work. **2** a short humorous play or performance, consisting typically of one scene in a comedy program. **3** informal a comical or amusing person or thing. ▶ v. [trans.] make a rough drawing of: *Modigliani began to sketch her* | [intrans.] *Jeanne sketched whenever she had the time.* ■ give a brief account or general outline of. ■ perform (a gesture) with one's hands or body: *he sketched a graceful bow in her direction.* — **sketch·er** n. [17th C.: from Du. *schets* or Ger. *Skizze*, from Ital. *schizzo*, from *schizzare* 'make a sketch,' based on Gk. *skhedios* 'done extempore.']

sketch·book /'skeCH,bŏŏk/ ▶ n. (also **sketch·pad** /-,pad/) a pad or book of drawing paper for sketching on. ■ a book of drawings or literary sketches.

sketch·y /'skeCHē/ ▶ adj. **(sketch·i·er, sketch·i·est)** not thorough or detailed. ■ (of a picture) resembling a sketch; consisting of outline without much detail. — **sketch·i·ly** /'skeCHəlē/ adv. **sketch·i·ness** n.

skew /skyōō/ ▶ adj. **1** neither parallel nor at right angles to a specified or implied line; askew; crooked. ■ Stat. (of a statistical distribution) not symmetrical. **2** Math. (of a pair of lines) neither parallel nor intersecting. ■ (of a curve) not lying in a plane. ▶ n. an oblique angle; a slant. ■ a bias toward one particular group or subject. ■ Stat. the state of not being symmetrical. ▶ v. [intrans.] suddenly change direction or position: *the car skewed across the track.* ■ twist or turn or cause to do this. ■ [trans.] make biased or distorted in a way that is regarded as inaccurate, unfair, or misleading: *the curriculum is skewed toward the practical subjects.* ■ [trans.] Stat. cause (a distribution) to be asymmetrical. — **skew·ness** n. [ME ('move obliquely'): shortening of Old North. Fr.

eskiuwer, var. of OFr. *eschiver* 'eschew.']

skew arch (also **skew bridge**) ▶ **n.** an arch (or bridge) with the line of the arch not at right angles to the abutment.

skew·back /'skyo͞o,bak/ ▶ **n.** the sloping face of the abutment on which an extremity of an arch rests.

skew·bald /'skyo͞o,bôld/ ▶ **adj.** (of an animal) with irregular patches of white and another color (properly not black). Compare with **PIEBALD**. ▶ **n.** a skewbald animal, esp. a horse. [17th C.: from obs. *skewed* (adj.), of uncert. origin.]

skew·er /'skyo͞oər/ ▶ **n.** a long piece of wood or metal used for holding pieces of food, typically meat, together during cooking. ▶ **v.** [trans.] fasten together or pierce with a pin or skewer. ■ informal criticize (someone) sharply. [ME: origin unknown.]

ski /skē/ ▶ **n.** (pl. **skis**) each of a pair of long narrow pieces of hard flexible material, fastened under the feet for gliding over snow. ■ a similar device attached beneath a vehicle or aircraft. ■ [as adj.] of, relating to, or used for skiing. ■ another term for **WATERSKI**. ▶ **v.** (**skis, skied** /skēd/, **ski·ing** /'skē-iNG/) [intrans.] travel over snow on skis; take part in the sport or recreation of skiing. ■ [trans.] ski on (a particular ski run or type of snow). — **ski·a·ble adj.** [18th C.: from Norw., from ON *skíth* 'stick of wood, snowshoe.']

ski·ag·ra·phy /skī'agrəfē/ ▶ **n.** the use of shading and the projection of shadows to show perspective in architectural or technical drawing. — **ski·a·gram** /'skīə,gram/ **n.** **ski·a·graph** /'skīə,graf/ **n. & v.** **ski·a·graph·ic** /,skīə'grafik/ **adj.** [16th C.: ult. from Gk. *skiagraphia*, from *skia* 'shadow.']

Skia·thos /'skīə,THäs; 'skēə,THôs/ a Greek island in the Aegean Sea, part of the Northern Sporades group.

ski-bob /'skē ,bäb/ ▶ **n.** a device resembling a bicycle with skis instead of wheels, used for sliding down snow-covered slopes. ▶ **v.** (**-bobbed, -bob·bing**) [intrans.] ride a ski-bob. — **ski-bob·ber n.**

skid /skid/ ▶ **v.** (**skid·ded, skid·ding**) **1** [intrans.] (of a vehicle) slide, typically sideways or obliquely, on slippery ground or from stopping or turning too quickly. ■ slip; slide. ■ [trans.] cause to skid. *he skidded his car.* ■ [trans.] move a heavy object on skids. ■ fig. decline; deteriorate. **2** [trans.] fasten a skid to (a wheel) as a brake. ▶ **n. 1** an act of skidding or sliding. **2** a runner attached to the underside of an aircraft for use when landing on snow or grass. ■ each of a set of wooden rollers used for moving a log or other heavy object. **3** a braking device consisting of a wooden or metal shoe preventing a wheel from revolving. **4** a beam or plank used to support a ship under construction or repair.
– PHRASES **hit the skids** informal begin a rapid decline or deterioration. **on the skids** informal (of a person or their career) in a bad state; failing. **put the skids under** informal hasten the decline or failure of. [17th C. ('supporting beam'): perh. akin to ON *skíth* (see **SKI**).]

skid·doo /skə'do͞o/ (also **ski·doo**) ▶ **v.** (**-doos, -dooed**) [intrans.] informal, dated leave somewhere quickly.
– PHRASES **twenty-three skiddoo** a hasty departure. [20th C.: perh. from **SKEDADDLE**.]

skid·pad /'skid,pad/ ▶ **n.** a road surface used for testing the ability of automobiles to withstand lateral acceleration.

skid road ▶ **n.** a road formed of skids along which logs were hauled. ■ hist. a part of a town frequented by loggers. ■ another term for **SKID ROW**.

skid row /rō/ ▶ **n.** informal a run-down part of a town frequented by vagrants, alcoholics, and drug addicts. ■ fig. an unfortunate or difficult situation. [1930s: alt. of **SKID ROAD**.]

ski·er /'skēər/ ▶ **n.** a person who skis.

skiff /skif/ ▶ **n.** a shallow, flat-bottomed open boat with sharp bow and square stern. [15th C.: from Fr. *esquif*, from Ital. *schifo*, from Gmc.; akin to **SHIP**.]

skif·fle /'skifəl/ ▶ **n. 1** (in the US) a style of 1920s and 1930s jazz deriving from blues, ragtime, and folk music, using both improvised and conventional instruments. **2** Brit. a kind of folk music with a blues or jazz flavor popular in the 1950s, played by a small group and incorporating improvised instruments such as washboards. [1920s: perh. imitative.]

ski·ing /'skēiNG/ ▶ **n.** the action of traveling over snow on skis, esp. as a sport or recreation.

ski·jor·ing /,skē'jôriNG; 'skē,jôriNG/ ▶ **n.** the action of being pulled over snow or ice on skis by a horse or dog, as a sport or recreation activity. — **ski·jor·er** /-ər/ **n.** [1920s: from Norw. *skikjøring*, from *ski* 'ski' + *kjøre* 'drive.']

ski jump ▶ **n.** a steep slope leveling off before a vertical drop to a lower slope, used in Nordic skiing to perform jumps. ■ a leap made from such a slope. — **ski jump·er n.** **ski jump·ing n.**

skil·full ▶ **adj.** esp. Brit. var. of **SKILLFUL**.

ski lift ▶ **n.** a system used to transport skiers up a slope to the top of a run, typically consisting of moving seats attached to an overhead cable.

skill /skil/ ▶ **n.** the ability to do something well; expertise. ■ a particular ability. — **skill-less adj.** (archaic). [OE *scele* 'knowledge,' from ON *skil* 'discernment, knowledge.']

skilled /skild/ ▶ **adj.** having or showing the knowledge, ability, or training to perform a certain activity well. ■ based on such training or experience; showing expertise. ■ (of work) requiring special abilities or training.

skil·let /'skilit/ ▶ **n.** a frying pan. ■ hist. a small metal cooking pot with a long handle, typically having legs. [ME: perh. from OFr. *escuelete*, dimin. of *escuele* 'platter,' from late L. *scutella*.]

skill·ful /'skilfəl/ (also esp. Brit. **skil·ful**) ▶ **adj.** having or showing skill. — **skill·ful·ly adv.** **skill·ful·ness n.**

skim /skim/ ▶ **v.** (**skimmed, skim·ming**) **1** [trans.] remove (a substance) from the surface of a liquid. ■ remove a substance from the surface of (a liquid). ■ informal steal or embezzle (money), esp. in small amounts over a period of time. **2** [trans.] go or move quickly and lightly over or on a surface or through the air. ■ [trans.] pass over (a surface), nearly or lightly touching it in the process. ■ [trans.] throw (a flat stone) low over an expanse of water so that it bounces on the surface several times. ■ [trans.] read (something) quickly, noting only the important points: *he sat down and skimmed the report* | [intrans.] *she* ***skimmed through*** *the newspaper.* ■ (**skim over**) deal with or treat (a subject) briefly or superficially. ▶ **n. 1** a thin layer of a substance on the surface of a liquid. **2** an act of reading something quickly or superficially. [ME: back-form. from **SKIMMER**, or from OFr. *escumer*, from *escume* 'scum, foam.']

ski mask ▶ **n.** a protective covering for the head and face, with holes for the eyes, nose, and mouth.

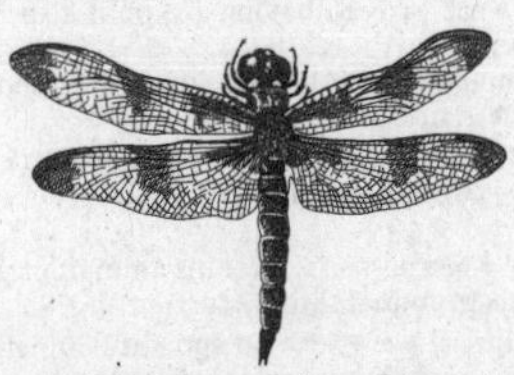
twelve-spotted skimmer

skim·mer /'skimər/ ▶ **n. 1** a person or thing that skims, in particular: ■ a utensil or device for removing a substance from the surface of a liquid. ■ a device or craft designed to collect oil spilled on water. ■ a hydroplane, hydrofoil, hovercraft, or other vessel that has little or no displacement when traveling. **2** a long-winged seabird (genus *Rynchops*) related to the terns, feeding by flying low over the water surface with its knifelike extended lower mandible immersed. **3** a flat, broad-brimmed straw hat. **4** a broad-bodied dragonfly (Libellulidae and related families) commonly found at ponds and swamps. It can rest for long periods on a perch, from which it darts out to grab prey. Several genera and numerous species include the **twelve-spotted skimmer** (*Libellula pulchella*).

skim milk (also **skimmed milk**) ▶ **n.** milk from which the cream has been removed.

ski·mo·bile /'skēmō,bēl/ ▶ **n.** a snowmobile.

skimp /skimp/ ▶ **v.** [intrans.] expend or use less time, money, or material on something than is necessary in an attempt to economize: *don't skimp on insurance.* [18th C.: compare **SCRIMP**.]

skimp·y /'skimpē/ ▶ **adj.** (**skimp·i·er, skimp·i·est**) (of clothes) short and revealing. ■ providing or consisting of less than is needed; meager. — **skimp·i·ly** /'skimpəlē/ **adv.** **skimp·i·ness n.**

skin /skin/ ▶ **n. 1** the thin layer of tissue forming the natural outer covering of the body of a person or animal. ■ the skin of a dead animal with or without the fur, used as material for clothing or other items. ■ a container made from the skin of an animal such as a goat, used for holding liquids. **2** an outer layer or covering, in particular: ■ the peel or outer layer of certain fruits or vegetables. ■ the thin outer covering of a sausage. ■ a thin layer forming on the surface of certain hot liquids, such as milk, as they cool. ■ the outermost layer of a structure such as a building or aircraft. **3** informal a skinhead. **4** (usu. **skins**) informal (esp. in jazz) a drum or drum head. **5** [as adj.] informal relating to or denoting pornographic literature or films: *the skin trade.* ▶ **v.** (**skinned, skin·ning**) **1** [trans.] remove the skin from (an animal or a fruit or vegetable). ■ (in hyperbolic use) punish severely: *Dad would skin me alive if I forgot it.* ■ scratch or scrape the skin off (a part of one's body). ■ informal take money from or swindle (someone). **2** [trans.] archaic cover with skin. ■ [intrans.] (of a wound) form new skin.
– PHRASES **be skin and bones** (of a person or animal) be very thin. **by the skin of one's teeth** by a very narrow margin; barely. **get under someone's skin** informal **1** annoy or irritate someone intensely. **2** fill someone's mind in a compelling and persistent way. **3** reach or display a deep understanding of someone: *movies that get under the skin of our national character.* **give someone (some) skin** black slang shake or slap hands together as a gesture or friendship or solidarity. **have a thick** (or **thin**) **skin** be insensitive (or oversensitive) to criticism or insults. **it's no skin off my nose** (or **off my back**) informal used to indicate that one is not offended or adversely affected by something. **keep** (or **sleep in**) **a whole skin** archaic escape being wounded or injured. **make someone's skin** (or **flesh**) **crawl** (or **creep**) cause someone to feel fear, horror, or disgust. **under the skin** in reality, as opposed to superficial appearances: *he still believes that all women are goddesses under the skin.* — **skin·less adj.** [OE *scinn*, from ON *skinn*; akin to Ger. *schinden* 'to flay.']

skin-deep ▶ **adj.** not deep or lasting; superficial.

skin div·ing ▶ **n.** the action or sport of swimming under water without a diving suit, typically in deep water using an aqualung and flippers. — **skin-dive** v. **skin div·er** n.

skin ef·fect ▶ n. Physics the tendency of a high-frequency alternating current to flow through only the outer layer of a conductor.

skin·flint /ˈskinˌflint/ ▶ n. informal a person who spends as little money as possible; a miser.

skin·ful /ˈskinfo͝ol/ ▶ n. [in sing.] informal enough alcoholic drink to make one drunk.

skin game ▶ n. informal a rigged gambling game; a swindle.

skin graft ▶ n. a surgical operation in which a piece of healthy skin is transplanted to a new site on the body. ■ a piece of skin transferred in this way.

skin·head /ˈskinˌhed/ ▶ n. a young person with close-cropped hair, often perceived as aggressive, violent, and racist.

skink /skiNGk/ ▶ n. a smooth-bodied lizard (family Scincidae) with short or absent limbs, typically burrowing in sandy ground, and occurring throughout tropical and temperate regions. [16th C.: ult. from L. *scincus*, from Gk. *skinkos*.]

skinned /skind/ ▶ adj. [in comb.] having a skin of a specified type: *a fair-skinned woman.*
– PHRASES **be thin-skinned** (or **thick-skinned**) be sensitive (or insensitive) to criticism or insults.

Skin·ner /ˈskinər/, Burrhus Frederic (1904–90), US psychologist. He thought that psychology should predict behavior, and hence be able to control it.

skin·ner /ˈskinər/ ▶ n. a person who skins animals or prepares skins. ■ a person who deals in animal skins; a furrier.

Skin·ner box /ˈskinər/ ▶ n. Psychol. an apparatus for studying conditioning in animals in which the animal is isolated and provided with a lever or switch that it learns to use to obtain a reward, such as a food pellet, or to avoid a punishment. [1940s: named after B. F. SKINNER.]

skin·ny /ˈskinē/ ▶ adj. (**-ni·er, -ni·est**) informal (of a person or part of their body) unattractively thin. ■ (of an article of clothing) tight-fitting. ▶ n. (**the skinny**) confidential information. — **skin·ni·ness** n.

skin·ny-dip ▶ v. [intrans.] informal swim naked. ▶ n. a naked swim.

skin-pop informal ▶ v. [trans.] inject (a drug, typically a narcotic) subcutaneously: *she used her insulin syringes to skin-pop illicit drugs* | [intrans.] *he had been skin-popping, which accounted for the small amount of heroin in his system.* ▶ n. a subcutaneous injection of a drug, typically a narcotic. — **skin-pop·per** n.

skint /skint/ ▶ adj. Brit., informal (of a person) having little or no money available: *I'm a bit skint just now.* [1920s: var. of *skinned*, past part. of SKIN.]

skin test ▶ n. a test to determine whether an immune reaction is elicited when a substance is applied to or injected into the skin. ▶ v. (**skin-test**) [trans.] [usu. as n.] (**skin-testing**) perform such a test on (someone).

skin·tight /ˈskinˈtīt/ (also **skin-tight**) ▶ adj. (of a garment) very close-fitting.

skip[1] /skip/ ▶ v. (**skipped, skip·ping**) [intrans.] move along lightly, stepping from one foot to the other with a hop or bounce. ■ [intrans.] jump over a rope that is held at both ends by oneself or two other people and turned repeatedly over the head and under the feet, as a game or for exercise. ■ [trans.] jump over (a rope) in such a way: *the girls had been skipping rope.* ■ [trans.] jump lightly over: *the children used to skip the puddles.* ■ [trans.] omit (part of a book that one is reading, or a stage in a sequence that one is following): *the video manual allows the viewer to skip sections* | [intrans.] *she* ***skipped over*** *the articles.* ■ [trans.] fail to attend or deal with as appropriate; miss: *try not to skip breakfast.* ■ [intrans.] move quickly and in an unmethodical way from one point or subject to another. ■ [trans.] informal depart quickly and secretly from: *she skipped her home amid rumors of a romance.* ■ [intrans.] informal run away; disappear: *I'm not giving them a chance to* ***skip off*** *again.* ■ (**skip it**) informal abandon an undertaking, conversation, or activity: *after several wrong turns, we decided to skip it.* ■ [trans.] throw (a stone) so that it ricochets off the surface of water: *they skipped stones across the creek.* ▶ n. a light, bouncing step; a skipping movement. ■ Comput. an act of passing over part of a sequence of data or instructions. [ME: prob. of Scand. origin.]

skip[2] ▶ n. the captain or director of a side at lawn bowling or curling. [19th C. (Scots): abbrev. of SKIPPER[1].]

ski pants ▶ plural n. trousers worn for skiing. ■ women's trousers imitating a style of these, made of stretchy fabric with tapering legs and an elastic stirrup under each foot.

skip·jack /ˈskipˌjak/ ▶ n. **1** (also **skipjack tuna**) a small tuna (*Katsuwonus pelamis*) with dark horizontal stripes, widely distributed throughout tropical and temperate seas. **2** another term for CLICK BEETLE. **3** a sloop-rigged sailboat with vertical sides and a flat V-shaped bottom, used chiefly on the east coast of the US. [18th C.: from SKIP[1] (v.) + JACK[1]. Sense 1, from its habit of jumping out of the water.]

ski·plane /ˈskēˌplān/ ▶ n. an airplane having its undercarriage fitted with skis for landing on snow or ice.

ski pole ▶ n. either of two lightweight poles held by a skier to assist in balance or propulsion.

skip·per[1] /ˈskipər/ informal ▶ n. the captain of a ship or boat. ■ the captain of a side in a game or sport. ■ the captain of an aircraft. ▶ v. [trans.] act as captain of. [ME: from MDu., Mid. Low Ger. *schipper*, from *schip* 'ship.']

skip·per[2] ▶ n. **1** a person or thing that skips. ■ used in names of small insects and crustaceans that skip or hop. **2** a small brownish mothlike butterfly (family Hesperiidae) with rapid darting flight. **3** the Atlantic saury (see SAURY).

skirl /skərl/ ▶ n. a shrill sound, esp. that of bagpipes. ▶ v. [intrans.] (of bagpipes) make such a sound. [ME (v.): prob. of Scand. origin; ult. imitative.]

skir·mish /ˈskərmisH/ ▶ n. an episode of irregular or unpremeditated fighting, esp. between small or outlying parts of armies or fleets. ■ a short argument. ▶ v. [intrans.] [often as n.] (**skirmishing**) engage in a skirmish: *reports of skirmishing along the border.* — **skir·mish·er** n. [ME (v.): from OFr. *eskirmiss-*, lengthened stem of *eskirmir*, from Gmc., 'defend.']

skirr /skər/ ▶ v. [intrans.] rare move rapidly, esp. with a whirring sound: *five dark birds rose skirring away.* [16th C.: perh. akin to SCOUR[1] or SCOUR[2].]

skirt /skərt/ ▶ n. a woman's outer garment fastened around the waist and hanging down around the legs. ■ the part of a coat or dress that hangs below the waist. ■ informal women regarded as objects of sexual desire. ■ the curtain that hangs around the base of a hovercraft to contain the air cushion. ■ a small flap on a saddle, covering the bar from which the stirrup leather hangs. ■ archaic an edge, border, or extreme part. ▶ v. [trans.] go around or past the edge of. ■ be situated along or around the edge of: *the fields that skirted the highway were full of cattle.* ■ [intrans.] (**skirt along/around**) go along or around (something) rather than directly through or across it: *the river valley skirts along the northern slopes of the hills.* ■ attempt to ignore; avoid dealing with: *there was a subject she was always skirting* | [intrans.] *the treaty* ***skirted around*** *the question of political cooperation.* — **skirt·ed** adj. [in comb.] *a full-skirted dress.* [ME: from ON *skyrta* 'shirt'; compare OE *scyrte*, SHORT.]

skirt-chas·er ▶ n. informal a man who pursues women amorously and is casual in his affections; a womanizer.

skirt steak ▶ n. a beefsteak cut from the diaphragm muscle.

ski run ▶ n. a track on a slope for skiing.

skit /skit/ ▶ n. a short comedy sketch or piece of humorous writing, esp. a parody. [18th C.: akin to *skit* 'move rapidly,' perh. from ON (compare *skjóta* 'shoot').]

ski tour·ing ▶ n. esp. Brit. cross-country skiing. — **ski tour** n. **ski tour·er** n.

ski tow ▶ n. **1** a type of ski lift, with a moving rope or bars suspended from a moving overhead cable. **2** a tow rope for waterskiers.

skit·ter /ˈskitər/ ▶ v. [intrans.] **1** [intrans.] move lightly and quickly: *the girls skittered up the stairs.* **2** [trans.] draw (bait) jerkily across the surface of the water as a technique in fishing. [19th C.: prob. a frequentative of *skite* 'move rapidly,' perh. of Norse origin.]

skit·ter·y /ˈskitərē/ ▶ adj. restless; skittish.

skit·tish /ˈskitisH/ ▶ adj. lively and unpredictable; playful. ■ (esp. of a horse) nervous; inclined to shy. — **skit·tish·ly** adv. **skit·tish·ness** n. [ME: perh. *skit* 'move rapidly.']

skit·tle /ˈskitl/ ▶ n. **1** (**skittles**) [treated as sing.] a game played, chiefly in Britain, with nine wooden pins set up at the end of an alley to be bowled down with a wooden ball or disk. **2** a pin used in the game of skittles. [17th C.: perh. akin to Dan. *skyttel* 'shuttle, marble.']

skive[1] /skīv/ Brit., informal ▶ v. [intrans.] avoid work or a duty by staying away or leaving early; shirk: *I skived off school* | [trans.] *she used to skive lessons.* — **skiv·er** n. [20th C.: perh. from Fr. *esquiver* 'slink away.']

skive[2] ▶ v. [trans.] tech. pare (the edge of a piece of leather or other material) so as to reduce its thickness. [19th C.: from ON *skífa*.]

skiv·vy /ˈskivē/ ▶ n. (pl. **-vies**) **1** (**skivvies**) trademark underwear, esp. a set consisting of undershirt and underpants, or just the underpants. **2** (also **skiv·vy shirt**) a lightweight high-necked, long-sleeved garment. ■ an undershirt or T-shirt. **3** Brit., informal a low-ranking female domestic servant. ■ a person doing work that is poorly paid and considered menial. [20th C.: origin unknown.]

ski·wear /ˈskēˌwe(ə)r/ ▶ n. clothing designed or suitable for skiing.

skoal /skōl/ (also **skol**) ▶ exclam. used to express friendly feelings toward one's companions before drinking. [17th C. (Scots): from Dan., Norw. *skaal*, Swed. *skål*, from ON *skál* 'bowl.']

Skop·je /ˈskôpye/ the capital of the republic of Macedonia, in the northern part of the country; pop. 440,000.

skort /skôrt/ ▶ n. shorts with full legs and a central flap in front. [blend of SKIRT and *short* (see SHORTS).]

skosh /skōsH/ ▶ n. informal a small amount; a little.
– PHRASES **a skosh** somewhat; slightly. [1950s: from Japanese *sukoshi*.]

Skr. ▶ abbr. Sanskrit.

Skrya·bin /skrēˈäbən/ var. of SCRIABIN.

Skt. ▶ abbr. Sanskrit.

SKU ▶ abbr. stock-keeping unit.

sku·a /ˈskyo͞oə/ ▶ n. a large brownish predatory seabird (family Stercorariidae, genera *Catharacta* and *Stercorarius*) related to the gulls, pursuing other birds to make them disgorge fish they have caught. See also JAEGER. [17th C.: mod. L., from Faroese *skúvur*, from ON *skufr* (prob. imitative).]

skul·dug·ger·y /skəlˈdəgərē/ (also **skull·dug·ger·y**) ▶ n. underhanded or unscrupulous behavior; trickery. [19th C.: alt. of Scots *sculduddery*.]

skulk /skəlk/ ▶ v. [intrans.] keep out of sight, typically with a sinister or cowardly motive. ■ move stealthily or furtively. ■ shirk duty. ▶ n. a group of foxes. — **skulk·er** n. [ME: of Scand. origin; compare Norw. *skulka* 'lurk,' Swed. *skolka* 'shirk.']

skull /skəl/ ▶ n. a bone framework enclosing the brain of a vertebrate;

the skeleton of a person's or animal's head. ■ informal a person's head or brain. ▶ v. [trans.] hit (someone) on the head.
– PHRASES **out of one's skull** informal **1** out of one's mind; crazy. **2** very drunk. **skull and crossbones** a representation of a skull with two thigh bones crossed below it as an emblem of piracy or death. — **skulled** adj. [ME *scolle*; compare ON *skoltr*.]

skull·cap /'skəl,kap/ ▶ n. **1** a small close-fitting cap without a brim. **2** the top part of the skull. **3** a widely distributed plant (genus *Scutellaria*) of the mint family, whose tubular flowers have a helmet-shaped cup at the base.

skullcap 1

skull ses·sion ▶ n. informal a discussion or conference, esp. to discuss policies, tactics, and maneuvers.

skunk /skəNGk/ ▶ n. a cat-sized American mammal (*Mephitis* and other genera) of the weasel family, with distinctive black-and-white-striped fur. When threatened, it squirts a fine spray of foul-smelling irritant liquid from its anal glands toward its attacker. ■ the fur of the skunk. ■ informal a contemptible person. ▶ v. [trans.] informal **1** (often **be skunked**) defeat (someone) overwhelmingly in a game or contest, esp. by preventing them from scoring at all. **2** dated fail to pay (a bill or creditor). [17th C.: from Massachusett *squunck*.]

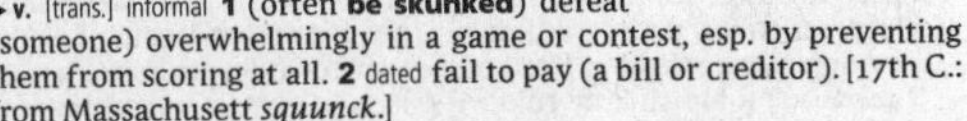

skunk cab·bage ▶ n. a North American plant (genera *Lysichitum* and *Symplocarpus*) of the arum family, the flower of which has a distinctive smell.

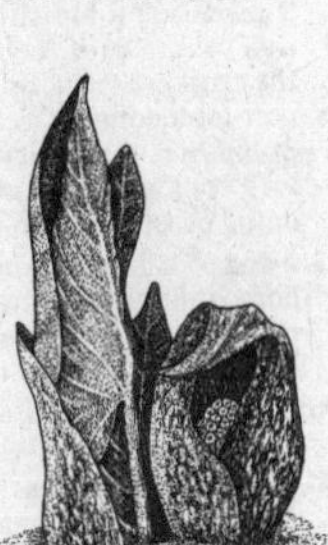
skunk cabbage

skunk·works /'skəNGk,wərks/ (also **skunk works**) ▶ plural n. [usu. treated as sing.] informal an experimental laboratory or department of a company or institution, typically smaller than and independent of its main research division.

sky /skī/ ▶ n. (pl. **skies**) (often **the sky**) the region of the atmosphere and outer space seen from the earth. ■ literary heaven; heavenly power. ▶ v. (**skies, skied**) [trans.] informal hit (a ball) high into the air: *he skied his tee shot.* ■ hang (a picture) very high on a wall, esp. in an exhibition.
– PHRASES **out of a clear blue sky** see BLUE. **the sky's the limit** informal there is practically no limit. **to the skies** very highly; enthusiastically. — **sky·ey** /'skīē/ adj. **sky·less** adj. [ME: from ON *ský* 'cloud.']

sky blue ▶ n. a bright clear blue.

sky·box /'skī,bäks/ ▶ n. a luxurious enclosed seating area high up in a sports arena.

sky·bridge /'skī,brij/ ▶ n. another term for SKYWALK.

sky·cap /'skī,kap/ ▶ n. a porter at an airport.

sky·div·ing /'skī,dīviNG/ ▶ n. the sport of jumping from an aircraft and performing acrobatic maneuvers in the air under free fall before landing by parachute. — **sky·dive** v. **sky·div·er** n.

Skye /skī/ a mountainous island in the Inner Hebrides, linked to Scotland by a bridge; chief town, Portree.

Skye ter·ri·er ▶ n. a small long-haired terrier of a slate-colored or beige-colored Scottish breed.

sky·flow·er /'skī,flouər/ ▶ n. a shrub (*Duranta erecta*) of the verbena family, with clusters of lilac flowers and yellow berries, native to Central and South America.

sky·glow /'skī,glō/ ▶ n. brightness of the night sky in a built-up area as a result of light pollution.

sky-high ▶ adv. & adj. as if reaching the sky; very high. ■ at or to a very high level; very great.

sky·hook /'skī,ho͝ok/ (also **sky hook** or **sky-hook**) ▶ n. **1** dated an imaginary or fanciful device by which something could be suspended in the air. ■ fig. a false hope, or a premise or argument which has no logical grounds. ■ a proposed cable or other structure reaching from the earth's surface to a satellite, which could be used for transporting spacecraft or other items into space. **2** Basketball a very high-arcing hook shot. **3** a helicopter equipped with a steel line and hook for hoisting and transporting heavy objects.

sky·jack /'skī,jak/ ▶ v. [trans.] hijack (an aircraft). ▶ n. an act of skyjacking. — **sky·jack·er** n. [1960s: blend of SKY and HIJACK.]

Sky·lab /'skī,lab/ a US orbiting space laboratory with three manned missions, all launched in 1973.

sky·lark /'skī,lärk/ ▶ n. a common Eurasian and North African lark (genus *Alauda*, family Alaudidae) of farmland and open country, noted for its prolonged song given in hovering flight. ▶ v. [intrans.] pass time by playing tricks or practical jokes; indulge in horseplay: *he was skylarking with a friend when he fell into a pile of boxes.* [17th C. (nautical term): by association with LARK[2] (v.).]

sky·light /'skī,līt/ ▶ n. a window set in the plane of a roof or ceiling. ■ light emanating from the sky. — **sky·light·ed** /'skī,lītid/ adj. **sky·lit** /'skī,lit/ adj.

sky·line /'skī,līn/ ▶ n. an outline of land and buildings defined against the sky: *the skyline of the city.* ■ the line along which the horizon is visible.

sky pi·lot ▶ n. informal a clergyman, esp. a military chaplain.

sky·rock·et /'skī,räkit/ ▶ n. a rocket designed to explode high in the air as a signal or firework. ▶ v. (**-rock·et·ed, -rock·et·ing**) [intrans.] informal (of a price, rate, or amount) increase very steeply or rapidly.

sky·sail /'skī,sāl/ ▶ n. a light sail above the royal.

sky·scrap·er /'skī,skrāpər/ ▶ n. a very tall building of many stories.

sky·surf·ing /'skī,sərfiNG/ ▶ n. the sport of jumping from an aircraft and surfing through the air on a board before landing by parachute.

sky·walk /'skī,wôk/ ▶ n. a covered overhead walkway between buildings.

sky·ward /'skīwərd/ ▶ adv. (also **sky·wards**) toward the sky. ▶ adj. moving or directed toward the sky.

sky·watch /'skī,wäCH/ ▶ v. [intrans.] informal observe or monitor the sky, esp. for heavenly bodies or aircraft. — **sky·watch·er** n.

sky wave ▶ n. a radio wave reflected from the ionosphere.

sky·way /'skī,wā/ ▶ n. **1** a recognized route followed by aircraft. **2** another term for SKYWALK. **3** an elevated highway.

sky·writ·ing /'skī,rītiNG/ ▶ n. words in the form of smoke trails made by an airplane, esp. for advertising. — **sky·writ·er** /-,rītər/ n.

SL ▶ abbr. source language.

s.l. ▶ abbr. ■ salvage loss. ■ (also **sl.**) (in a bibliography) without place (of publication noted).

slab /slab/ ▶ n. a large, thick, flat piece of stone or concrete, typically square or rectangular in shape. ■ a large, thick slice or piece of cake, bread, chocolate, etc. ■ an outer piece of timber sawn from a log. ■ a table used for laying a body on in a morgue. ▶ v. (**slabbed, slab·bing**) [trans.] [often as n.] (**slabbing**) remove slabs from (a log or tree) to prepare it for sawing into planks. — **slabbed** adj. **slab·by** adj. [ME: origin unknown.]

slab·ber /'slabər/ esp. Scot. & Irish ▶ v. [intrans.] dribble at the mouth; slaver: *he was slabbering like a child.* [16th C.: akin to dial. *slab* 'muddy place.']

slack[1] /slak/ ▶ adj. **1** not taut or held tightly in position; loose. **2** (of business) characterized by a lack of work or activity; quiet. ■ slow or sluggish. ■ having or showing laziness or negligence. **3** (of a tide) neither ebbing nor flowing. ▶ n. **1** the part of a rope or line not held taut; the loose or unused part. **2** (**slacks**) casual trousers. **3** informal a spell of inactivity or laziness. ▶ v. [trans.] **1** loosen (something, esp. a rope). ■ reduce the intensity or speed of (something); slacken. ■ [intrans.] (**slack off**) decrease in quantity or intensity: *the flow of blood slacked off.* ■ [intrans.] informal work slowly or lazily: *the girls were slacking.* ■ [intrans.] (**slack up**) slow down. **2** slake (lime). ▶ adv. loosely.
– PHRASES **cut someone some slack** informal allow someone some leeway in their conduct. **take** (or **pick**) **up the slack 1** use up a surplus or improve the use of resources to avoid a lull in business. **2** pull on the loose end or part of a rope in order to make it taut. — **slack·ly** adv. **slack·ness** n. [OE *slæc* 'unhurried,' from Gmc.; akin to L. *laxus* 'loose.']

slack[2] ▶ n. coal dust or small pieces of coal. [ME: prob. from Low Ger. or Du.]

slack·en /'slakən/ ▶ v. make or become slack.

slack·er /'slakər/ ▶ n. informal a person who avoids work or effort. ■ a person who evades military service. ■ a young person of a subculture characterized by apathy and aimlessness.

slack wa·ter ▶ n. the state of the tide when it is turning, esp. at low tide.

slag /slag/ ▶ n. **1** stony waste matter separated from metals during the smelting or refining of ore. ■ similar material produced by a volcano; scoria. **2** Brit., informal derog. a promiscuous woman. ▶ v. (**slagged, slag·ging**) [intrans.] [usu. as n.] (**slagging**) produce deposits of slag. — **slag·gy** adj. (**-gi·er, -gi·est**). [16th C.: from Mid. Low Ger. *slagge*, perh. from *slagen* 'strike.']

slain /slān/ past participle of SLAY.

slake /slāk/ ▶ v. [trans.] **1** quench or satisfy (one's thirst). ■ fig. satisfy (desires). **2** combine (quicklime) with water to produce calcium hydroxide. [OE *slacian* 'become less eager,' 'slacken,' from adj. *slæc* 'slack.']

slaked lime ▶ n. see LIME[1].

sla·lom /'släləm/ ▶ n. a ski race down a winding course marked by flags or poles. ■ a sporting event on water with a winding course marked by obstacles, typically a canoe or sailing race. ▶ v. [intrans.] move or race in a winding path, avoiding obstacles. — **sla·lom·er** n. [1920s: from Norw., lit. 'sloping track.']

slam[1] /slam/ ▶ v. (**slammed, slam·ming**) [trans.] shut (a door, window, or lid) forcefully and loudly. ■ [intrans.] be closed forcefully and loudly. ■ [trans.] push or put somewhere with great force: *Charlie slammed down the phone.* ■ [intrans.] (**slam into**) crash into; collide heavily with. ■ [trans.] informal hit (something) with great force in a particular direction: *he slammed a shot into the net.* ■ put (something) into action suddenly or forcefully: *I slammed on the brakes.* ■ [trans.] move violently or loudly: *he slammed out of the room.* ■ [trans.] (usu. **be slammed**) informal criticize severely. ■ [trans.] informal score points against or gain a victory over (someone) easily. ▶ n. **1** [usu. in sing.] a loud bang caused by the forceful shutting of something such as a door. **2** (usu. **the slam**) informal prison. **3** a poetry contest in which competitors recite their entries and are judged by members of the audience, the winner being elected after several elimination rounds. [17th C.: prob. of Scand. origin; compare ON *slam(b)ra*.]

slam² ▶ **n.** Bridge a grand slam (all thirteen tricks) or small slam (twelve tricks), for which bonus points are scored if bid and made. [17th C. (a card game): perh. from obs. *slampant* 'trickery.']

slam-bang informal ▶ **adj.** exciting and energetic. ■ with no niceties, subtleties, or restraints. ▶ **adv.** suddenly and forcefully or violently.

slam-danc·ing ▶ **n.** a form of dancing to rock music in which the dancers collide with one another. — **slam-dance v. slam danc·er n.**

slam dunk ▶ **n.** Basketball a shot in which a player thrusts the ball emphatically down through the basket. ■ [usu. as adj.] informal something reliable or unfailing. ▶ **v.** (**slam-dunk**) [trans.] thrust (the ball) emphatically down through the basket. ■ informal defeat or dismiss decisively.

slam·mer /'slamər/ ▶ **n.** **1** (usu. **the slammer**) informal prison. **2** a person who deliberately collides with others when slam-dancing.

Slam·min' Sam·my /'slamin 'samē/ see **Snead**.

slan·der /'slandər/ ▶ **n.** Law the action or crime of making a false spoken statement damaging to a person's reputation. Compare with **libel**. ■ a false and malicious spoken statement. ▶ **v.** [trans.] make false and damaging statements about (someone). — **slan·der·er n. slan·der·ous** /-əs/ **adj. slan·der·ous·ly** /-əslē/ **adv.** [ME: from OFr. *esclandre*, alt. of *escandle*, from late L. *scandalum* (see **scandal**).]

slang /slaNG/ ▶ **n.** a type of language that consists of words and phrases that are regarded as very informal, are more common in speech than writing, and are typically restricted to a particular context or group of people. ▶ **v.** [trans.] informal attack (someone) using abusive language. — **slang·y** /'slaNGē/ **adj. slang·i·ly** /'slaNGgəlē/ **adv. slang·i·ness n.** [18th C.: origin unknown.]

slant /slant/ ▶ **v.** [intrans.] slope or lean in a particular direction; diverge from a vertical or horizontal line. ■ (esp. of light or shadow) fall in an oblique direction. ■ [trans.] cause (something) to lean or slope in such a way: *slant your skis as you turn.* ■ [trans.] [often as adj.] (**slanted**) present or view (information) from a particular angle, esp. in a biased or unfair way: *slanted news coverage.* ▶ **n.** **1** [in sing.] a sloping position. **2** a particular point of view from which something is seen or presented: *a new slant on science.* **3** derog. a contemptuous term for an East Asian or Southeast Asian person. ▶ **adj.** [attrib.] sloping: *slant pockets.* [ME: var. of dial. *slent*, of Scand. origin.]

slant·wise /'slant,wīz/ ▶ **adj. & adv.** at an angle or in a sloping direction.

slap /slap/ ▶ **v.** (**slapped, slap·ping**) [trans.] hit (someone or something) with the palm of one's hand or a flat object: *my sister slapped my face.* ■ [intrans.] hit against or into something with the sound of such an action: *water slapped against the boat.* ■ (**slap someone down**) informal reprimand someone forcefully. ■ [trans.] put or apply (something) somewhere quickly, carelessly, or forcefully: *slap on a bit of makeup.* ■ (**slap something on**) informal impose a fine or other penalty on. ▶ **n.** a blow with the palm of the hand or a flat object. ■ a sound made or as if made by such an action. ▶ **adv.** informal suddenly and directly, esp. with great force: *she ran slap into Luke.* ■ exactly; right: *we passed slap through the middle of an enemy armored unit.* [ME (v.): prob. imitative.]

slap and tick·le ▶ **n.** Brit., informal physical amorous play.

slap bass /bās/ ▶ **n.** a style of playing double bass or bass guitar by pulling and releasing the strings sharply against the fingerboard. — **slap bass·ist** /-ist/ **n.**

slap·dash /'slap,dasH/ ▶ **adj.** done too hurriedly and carelessly. ▶ **adv.** dated hurriedly and carelessly.

slap·hap·py /'slap,hapē/ (also **slap-hap·py**) ▶ **adj.** informal **1** casual or flippant in a cheerful and often irresponsible way. ■ (of an action or operation) unmethodical; poorly thought out. **2** dazed or stupefied from happiness or relief.

slap·jack /'slap,jak/ ▶ **n.** a pancake.

slap shot ▶ **n.** Ice Hockey a hard shot made by raising the stick near the waist before striking the puck with a sharp slapping motion.

slap·stick /'slap,stik/ ▶ **n.** comedy based on deliberately clumsy actions and humorously embarrassing events. ■ a device consisting of two flexible pieces of wood joined together at one end, used by clowns and in pantomime to produce a loud slapping noise.

slap-up ▶ **adj.** [attrib.] informal, esp. Brit. (of a meal or celebration) large and sumptuous: *a slap-up dinner.*

slash¹ /slasH/ ▶ **v.** [trans.] cut (something) with a violent sweeping movement, typically using a knife or sword: *vandals slashed a tire on my car* | [intrans.] *the man slashed at him with a sword.* ■ informal reduce (a price, quantity, etc.) greatly. ■ archaic lash, whip, or thrash severely. ■ archaic crack (a whip). ■ archaic criticize (someone or something) severely. ▶ **n.** **1** a cut made with a wide, sweeping stroke. ■ a wound or gash made by such an action. ■ fig. a bright patch or flash of color or light. **2** an oblique stroke (/) in print or writing, used between alternatives (e.g., *and/or*), in fractions (e.g., *3/4*), in ratios (e.g., *miles/day*), or between separate elements of a text. ■ [as adj.] denoting or belonging to a genre of fiction, chiefly published in fanzines, in which any of various male pairings from the popular media is portrayed as having a homosexual relationship. **3** debris resulting from the felling or destruction of trees. [ME: perh. imitative, or from OFr. *esclachier* 'break in pieces.']

slash² ▶ **n.** a tract of swampy ground, esp. in a coastal region.

slash-and-burn ▶ **adj.** [attrib.] of, relating to, or denoting a method of agriculture in which existing vegetation is burned off before seeds are sown, typically used as a method for clearing forest land for farming. ■ fig. aggressive and merciless.

slash·er /'slasHər/ ▶ **n.** informal **1** a person or thing that slashes. **2** (also **slasher film** or **slasher movie**, etc.) a horror movie, esp. one in which victims (typically women or teenagers) are slashed with knives and razors.

slash·ing /'slasHiNG/ ▶ **adj.** [attrib.] informal vigorously incisive or effective: *a slashing magazine attack on her.*

slash pine ▶ **n.** a fast-growing, long-needled pine (*Pinus elliottii*) found in low-lying coastal areas (slashes) of the southeastern US, commonly harvested for timber.

slash pock·et ▶ **n.** a pocket set in a garment with a slit for the opening.

slat /slat/ ▶ **n.** a thin, narrow piece of wood, plastic, or metal, esp. one of a series that overlap or fit into each other, as in a fence or a Venetian blind. — **slat·ted adj.** [ME: shortening of OFr. *esclat* 'splinter,' from *esclater* 'to split.']

slate /slāt/ ▶ **n.** **1** a fine-grained gray, green, or bluish metamorphic rock easily split into smooth, flat plates. ■ a flat plate of such rock used as roofing material. **2** a flat plate of slate used for writing on, typically framed in wood, used in schools. ■ a list of candidates for election to a post or office. ■ a range of something offered: *a $60 million slate of film productions.* ■ a board showing the identifying details of a take of a motion picture, held in front of the camera at its beginning and end. **3** [usu. as adj.] a bluish-gray color. ▶ **v.** [trans.] **1** cover (something, esp. a roof) with slates. **2** Brit., informal criticize severely: *his work was slated by the critics.* **3** (usu. **be slated**) schedule; plan. ■ (usu. **be slated**) nominate (someone) as a candidate for an office or post: *I am being slated for promotion.* **4** identify (a movie take) using a slate.
– PHRASES **wipe the slate clean** see **wipe**. — **slat·y adj.** [ME *sclate*, shortening of OFr. *esclate*, fem., akin to *esclat* (see **slat**).]

Sla·ter /'slātər/, Samuel (1768–1835), US inventor and industrialist; born in England. Often considered the father of the American Industrial Revolution, he built a technologically advanced textile mill from memory in Rhode Island in 1793.

slat·er /'slātər/ ▶ **n.** **1** a person who slates roofs for a living. **2** a wood louse (order Isopoda) or similar isopod crustacean. See also **sea slater**.

slath·er /'slaTHər/ ▶ **n.** (often **slathers**) informal a large amount. ▶ **v.** [trans.] informal spread or smear (a substance) thickly or liberally. [19th C.: origin unknown.]

slat·tern /'slatərn/ ▶ **n.** dated a dirty, untidy woman. — **slat·tern·li·ness n. slat·tern·ly adj.** [17th C.: akin to *slattering* 'slovenly,' from dial. *slatter* 'to spill,' frequentative of *slat* 'strike.']

slaugh·ter /'slôtər/ ▶ **n.** the killing of animals for food. ■ the killing of a large number of people or animals in a violent way; massacre. ■ informal a thorough defeat. ▶ **v.** [trans.] (usu. **be slaughtered**) kill (animals) for food. ■ kill (people or animals) in a cruel or violent way, typically in large numbers. ■ informal defeat (an opponent) thoroughly. — **slaugh·ter·er n. slaugh·ter·ous** /-əs/ **adj.** [ME (n.): from ON *slátr* 'butcher's meat'; akin to **slay**.]

slaugh·ter·house /'slôtər,hous/ ▶ **n.** a place where animals are slaughtered for food.

Slav /släv/ ▶ **n.** a member of a group of peoples in central and eastern Europe speaking Slavic languages. ▶ **adj.** another term for **Slavic**. [from med. L. *Sclavus*, late Gk. *Sklabos*.]

slave /slāv/ ▶ **n.** esp. hist. a person who is the legal property of another and is forced to obey them. ■ a person who works very hard without proper remuneration or appreciation. ■ a person who is excessively dependent upon or controlled by something: *she was no slave to fashion.* ■ a device, or part of one, directly controlled by another: [as adj.] *a slave cassette deck.* Compare with **master¹**. ■ an ant captured by, and made to serve, ants of another species. ▶ **v.** [intrans.] work excessively hard: *slaving away for all those years.* ■ [trans.] subject (a device) to control by another: *the two channels can be slaved together.* [ME: shortening of OFr. *esclave*, akin to med. L. *sclava* (fem.) 'Slavic (captive).']

Slave Coast a part of the west coast of Africa from which slaves were exported in the 16th–19th centuries.

slave driv·er ▶ **n.** a person who oversees and urges on slaves at work. ■ a person who works others very hard. — **slave-drive v.**

slave·hold·er /'slāv,hōldər/ ▶ **n.** an owner of slaves. — **slave·hold·ing n. & adj.**

slave la·bor ▶ **n.** labor that is coerced and inadequately rewarded, or the people who perform such labor.

slave-mak·ing ant (also **slave-mak·er ant**) ▶ **n.** an ant (*Formica*, *Polyergus*, and other genera) that raids the nests of other ant species and steals the pupae, which later become workers in the new colony.

slav·er¹ /'slāvər/ ▶ **n.** esp. hist. a person dealing in or owning slaves. ■ a ship used for transporting slaves.

slav·er² /'slavər/ ▶ **n.** saliva running from the mouth. ■ archaic, fig. excessive or obsequious flattery. ▶ **v.** [intrans.] let saliva run from the mouth. ■ show excessive desire. [ME: prob. from Low Ger.; compare **slobber**.]

slav·er·y /'slāvərē/ ▶ **n.** the state of being a slave. ■ the practice or system of owning slaves. ■ a condition compared to that of a slave in respect of labor or restricted freedom. ■ excessive dependence on or devotion to something.

slave ship ▶ **n.** hist. a ship transporting slaves, esp. one carrying slaves from Africa.

Slave State (also **slave state**) ▶ **n.** hist. any of the Southern states of the

US in which slavery was legal before the Civil War.

slave trade ▶**n.** esp. hist. the procuring, transporting, and selling of human beings as slaves, esp. the former trade in African blacks by European countries and North America. — **slave trad•er n.**

slav•ey /ˈslāvē/ ▶**n.** (pl. **-eys**) Brit., informal dated a maidservant, esp. a hard-worked one.

Slav•ic /ˈslävik/ ▶**adj.** of, relating to, or denoting the branch of the Indo-European language family that includes Russian, Ukrainian, and Belorussian (**East Slavic**), Polish, Czech, Slovak, and Sorbian (**West Slavic**), and Bulgarian, Serbo-Croat, Macedonian, and Slovene (**South Slavic**). ■ of, relating to, or denoting the peoples of central and eastern Europe who speak any of these languages. ▶**n.** the Slavic languages collectively. See also SLAVONIC.

slav•ish /ˈslāvisн/ ▶**adj.** relating to or characteristic of a slave, typically by servility or submissiveness. ■ showing no attempt at originality, constructive interpretation, or development. — **slav•ish•ly adv. slav•ish•ness n.**

Sla•von•ic /sləˈvänik/ ▶**adj. & n.** another term for SLAVIC. See also CHURCH SLAVIC. [from med. L. *S(c)lavonicus*, from *S(c)lavonia* 'country of the Slavs,' from *Sclavus* (see SLAV).]

slaw /slô/ ▶**n.** coleslaw. [18th C.: from Du. *sla*, shortened from *salade* 'salad.']

slay /slā/ ▶**v.** (past **slew** /slo͞o/; past part. **slain** /slān/) [trans.] archaic or literary kill (a person or animal) in a violent way. ■ (usu. **be slain**) murder (someone). ■ informal greatly impress or amuse (someone). — **slay•er n.** [OE *slēan* 'strike, kill,' from Gmc.; akin to Ger. *schlagen*.]

SLBM ▶**abbr.** submarine-launched ballistic missile.

SLCM ▶**abbr.** sea-launched cruise missile.

sld. ▶**abbr.** ■ sailed. ■ sealed.

SLE ▶**abbr.** systemic lupus erythematosus.

sleaze /slēz/ ▶**n.** immoral, sordid, and corrupt behavior or material, esp. in business or politics. ■ informal a sordid, corrupt, or immoral person. ▶**v.** [intrans.] informal behave in an immoral, corrupt, or sordid way. [1960s: back-form. from SLEAZY.]

sleaze•ball /ˈslēz,bôl/ (also **sleaze•bag** /-,bag/) ▶**n.** informal a disreputable, disgusting, or despicable person.

slea•zoid /ˈslē,zoid/ (also **slea•zo** /-,zō/ (pl. **-zos**)) informal ▶**adj.** sleazy, sordid, or despicable: *a sleazoid lawyer.* ▶**n.** a sleazy, sordid, or despicable person.

slea•zy /ˈslēzē/ ▶**adj.** (**-zi•er, -zi•est**) **1** (of a person or situation) sordid, corrupt, or immoral. ■ (of a place) squalid and seedy. **2** dated (of textiles and clothing) flimsy. — **slea•zi•ly** /ˈslēzəlē/ **adv. slea•zi•ness n.** [17th C.: origin unknown.]

sled /sled/ ▶**n.** a vehicle on runners for traveling over snow or ice, either pushed, pulled, drawn by horses or dogs, or allowed to slide downhill. ■ another term for SLEDGE[1]. ▶**v.** (**sled•ded, sled•ding**) [intrans.] ride on a sled. [ME: from Mid. Low Ger. *sledde*; akin to SLIDE (v.).]

sled dog ▶**n.** a dog trained to pull a sled.

sledge[1] /slej/ ▶**n.** a vehicle on runners for conveying loads or passengers esp. over snow or ice, often pulled by draft animals. ■ British term for SLED. ▶**v.** [trans.] carry (a load or passengers) on a sledge. [16th C. (as a n.): from MDu. *sleedse*; rel. to SLED. The v. dates from the early 18th C.]

sledge[2] ▶**n.** a sledgehammer. [OE *slecg*, from Gmc., 'to strike,' akin to SLAY.]

sledge•ham•mer /ˈslej,hamər/ ▶**n.** a large, heavy hammer used for breaking rocks and driving in fence posts. See illustration at HAMMER. ■ [as adj.] powerful; forceful. ■ [as adj.] fig. ruthless or insensitive. ▶**v.** [trans.] hit with a sledgehammer.

sleek /slēk/ ▶**adj.** (of hair, fur, or skin) smooth and glossy: *he was tall, with sleek, dark hair.* ■ (of a person or animal) having smooth, glossy skin, hair, or fur. ■ (of a person) having a wealthy and well-groomed appearance. ■ (of an object) having an elegant, streamlined shape or design: *a sleek black car.* ■ ingratiating; unctuous: *a sleek smile.* ▶**v.** [trans.] make (the hair) smooth and glossy. ▶**adv.** literary in a smooth manner. — **sleek•ly adv. sleek•ness n. sleek•y adj.** [ME: later var. of SLICK (adj., v.).]

sleep /slēp/ ▶**n.** a condition of body and mind such as that which typically recurs for several hours every night, in which the nervous system is inactive, the eyes closed, the postural muscles relaxed, and consciousness practically suspended. ■ esp. literary a state compared to or resembling this, such as death or complete silence. ■ a gummy secretion found in the corners of the eyes after sleep. ▶**v.** (past and past part. **slept** /slept/) [intrans.] rest in such a condition; be asleep. ■ (**sleep through**) fail to be woken by: *he slept through the alarm.* ■ [with adverbial] have sexual intercourse or be involved in a sexual relationship: *I won't sleep with a man who doesn't respect me.* ■ [trans.] (**sleep something off/away**) dispel the effects of or recover from something by going to sleep: *he slept off his hangover.* ■ [trans.] provide (a specified number of people) with beds, rooms, or places to stay the night. ■ fig. be inactive or dormant: *the city that never sleeps.* ■ literary be at peace in death; lie buried.
– PHRASES **get to sleep** manage to fall asleep. **go to sleep** fall asleep. ■ (of a limb) become numb as a result of prolonged pressure. **lose sleep** see LOSE. **put someone to sleep** make someone unconscious by using drugs, alcohol, or an anesthetic. ■ (also **send someone to sleep**) bore someone greatly. **put something to sleep** kill an animal, esp. an old or badly injured one, painlessly (used euphemistically). ■ Comput. put a computer on standby while it is not being used. **sleep easy** see EASY. **sleep like a log** (or **top**) sleep very soundly. **sleep on it** informal delay making a decision on something until the following day so as to have more time to consider it. **the sleep of the just** a deep, untroubled sleep. **sleep rough** see ROUGH. **sleep tight** [usu. in imper.] sleep well (said to someone when parting from them at night).
– PHRASAL VERBS **sleep around** informal have many casual sexual partners. **sleep in** remain asleep or in bed later than usual in the morning. ■ sleep by night at one's place of work. **sleep out** sleep outdoors. **sleep over** spend the night at a place other than one's own home. [OE *slēp, slǣp* (n.), *slēpan, slǣpan* (v.), from Gmc.; akin to Ger. *schlafen*.]

sleep•er /ˈslēpər/ ▶**n.** **1** a person or animal who is asleep. ■ [with adj.] a person with a specified sleep pattern: *he was a light sleeper.* **2** a thing used for or connected with sleeping, in particular: ■ a train carrying sleeping cars. ■ a sleeping car. ■ a berth in a sleeping car. ■ (often **sleepers**) one-piece coverall pajamas for a baby or small child. ■ a sofa or chair that converts into a bed. **3** a movie, book, play, etc., that achieves sudden unexpected success. **4** Brit. a railroad tie. **5** a stocky fish (*Dormitator* and other genera, family Gobiidae (or Eleotridae)) with mottled coloration that occurs widely in warm seas and fresh water.

sleep-in ▶**adj.** [attrib.] (of a domestic employee) resident in an employer's house: *a sleep-in babysitter.* ▶**n.** **1** a person who resides at the premises of their employment. **2** a form of protest in which the participants sleep overnight in premises that they have occupied.

sleep•ing bag ▶**n.** a warm lined padded bag to sleep in, esp. when camping.

sleep•ing car ▶**n.** a railroad car provided with beds or berths.

sleep•ing part•ner ▶**n.** British term for SILENT PARTNER.

sleep•ing pill ▶**n.** a tablet of a drug that helps to induce sleep.

sleep•ing sick•ness ▶**n.** **1** a tropical disease caused by a parasitic protozoan (trypanosome) that is transmitted by the bite of the tsetse fly. It causes fever, chills, pain in the limbs, and anemia, and eventually affects the nervous system causing extreme lethargy and death. See also TRYPANOSOMIASIS. **2** another term for ENCEPHALITIS LETHARGICA.

sleep•less /ˈslēplis/ ▶**adj.** characterized by or experiencing lack of sleep. ■ esp. literary continually active or moving. — **sleep•less•ly adv. sleep•less•ness n.**

sleep mode ▶**n.** Electron. a power-saver in which devices are switched off until needed.

sleep-out ▶**n.** an occasion of sleeping outdoors.

sleep•o•ver /ˈslēp,ōvər/ ▶**n.** an occasion of spending the night away from home, or of having a guest or guests spend the night in one's home, esp. as a party for children.

sleep•walk /ˈslēp,wôk/ ▶**v.** [intrans.] walk around and sometimes perform other actions while asleep. ▶**n.** an instance of such activity. — **sleep•walk•er n. sleep•walk•ing n.**

sleep•wear /ˈslēp,we(ə)r/ ▶**n.** pajamas or other clothing suitable for wearing in bed.

sleep•y /ˈslēpē/ ▶**adj.** (**sleep•i•er, sleep•i•est**) needing or ready for sleep. ■ showing the effects of sleep. ■ inducing sleep; soporific. ■ (of a place) without much activity. ■ (of a business, organization, or industry) lacking the ability or will to respond to change. — **sleep•i•ly** /ˈslēpəlē/ **adv. sleep•i•ness n.**

sleep•y•head /ˈslēpē,hed/ ▶**n.** a sleepy or inattentive person (usually as a form of address).

Sleepy Hollow a town in southeastern New York, associated with the writings of Washington Irving.

sleet /slēt/ ▶**n.** rain containing some ice, as when snow melts as it falls. ■ a thin coating of ice formed by sleet or rain freezing on contact with a cold surface. ▶**v.** [intrans.] (**it sleets, it is sleeting,** etc.) sleet falls. — **sleet•y adj.** [ME: from Gmc.; prob. akin to Mid. Low Ger. *slōten* (pl.) 'hail.']

sleeve /slēv/ ▶**n.** the part of a garment that wholly or partly covers a person's arm. ■ (also **record sleeve** or **album sleeve**) a protective paper or cardboard cover for a record. ■ a protective or connecting tube fitting over or enclosing a rod, spindle, or smaller tube.
– PHRASES **up one's sleeve** (of a strategy, idea, or resource) kept secret and in reserve for use when needed. **wear one's heart on one's sleeve** see HEART. — **sleeved adj. sleeve•less adj.** [OE *slēfe, slīef(e), slӯf*; akin to MDu. *sloove* 'covering.']

sleeve board (also **sleeve•board**) ▶**n.** a small ironing board over which a sleeve is pulled for pressing.

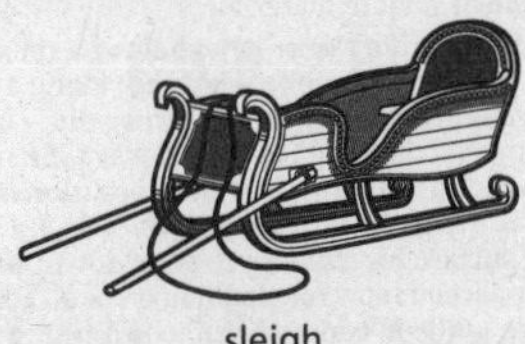

sleigh

sleigh /slā/ ▶**n.** a sled drawn by horses or reindeer, esp. one used for passengers. ▶**v.** [intrans.] [usu. as n.] (**sleighing**) ride on a sleigh. [17th C. (North Amer.): from Du. *slee*; akin to SLED.]

sleigh bed ▶ n. a bed resembling a sleigh, with an outward curving headboard and footboard.

sleigh bell ▶ n. a tinkling bell attached to the harness of a sleigh horse.

sleight /slīt/ ▶ n. literary the use of dexterity or cunning, esp. so as to deceive.
– PHRASES **sleight of hand** manual dexterity, typically in performing tricks. ■ skillful deception. [ME *sleghth* 'cunning, skill,' from ON *slœgth*, from *slœgr* 'sly.']

slen·der /'slendər/ ▶ adj. (**-der·er, -der·est**) **1** (of a person or part of the body) gracefully thin. ■ (esp. of a rod or stem) of small girth or breadth. **2** (of something abstract) barely sufficient in amount or basis: *a slender majority of four.* — **slen·der·ly** adv. **slen·der·ness** n. [ME: origin unknown.]

slen·der·ize /'slendə,rīz/ ▶ v. [trans.] [usu. as adj.] (**slenderizing**) make (a person or a part of their body) appear more slender. ■ [intrans.] (of a person) lose weight; become slim. ■ fig. reduce the size of (something).

slen·der lo·ris ▶ n. see LORIS.

slept /slept/ past and past participle of SLEEP.

sleuth /slo͞oTH/ informal ▶ n. a detective. ▶ v. [intrans.] [often as n.] (**sleuthing**) carry out a search or investigation in the manner of a detective. ■ [trans.] dated investigate (someone or something). [ME ('track,'): from ON *slóth*; compare SLOT².]

sleuth·hound ▶ n. dated a bloodhound. ■ informal an eager investigator; a detective.

slew¹ /slo͞o/ (also **slue**) ▶ v. [intrans.] (of a vehicle or person) turn or slide violently or uncontrollably in a particular direction. ■ [trans.] turn or slide (something, esp. a vehicle) in such a way. ▶ n. [in sing.] a violent or uncontrollable sliding movement. [18th C. (nautical term): origin unknown.]

slew² past of SLAY.

slew³ ▶ n. informal a large number or quantity of something: *he asked me a slew of questions.* [19th C.: from Irish *sluagh*.]

slice /slīs/ ▶ n. **1** a thin, broad piece of food, such as bread, cut from a larger portion. ■ a portion or share of something: *a huge slice of public spending.* **2** Golf a stroke that makes the ball curve away to the right (for a left-handed player, the left), typically inadvertently. **3** a utensil with a broad, flat blade for lifting foods such as cake and fish. ▶ v. [trans.] **1** cut (something, esp. food) into slices. ■ (**slice something off/from**) cut something or a piece of something off or from (something larger). ■ cut with or as if with a sharp implement: *the bomber's wings were slicing the air with some efficiency* | [intrans.] *the blade sliced into his palm.* ■ [intrans.] move easily and quickly: *Senna then sliced past Berger to take third place.* **2** Golf strike (the ball) or play (a stroke) so that the ball curves away to the right (for a left-handed player, the left), typically inadvertently.
– PHRASES **slice and dice 1** divide a quantity of data up into smaller parts, esp. in order to analyze it more closely or in different ways. **2** [as adj.] (**slice-and-dice**) able to be analyzed in a number of different ways; involving the quick rearrangement of elements. **slice of life** a realistic representation of everyday experience in a movie, play, or book. — **slice·a·ble** adj. **slic·er** n. [ME: shortening of OFr. *esclice* 'splinter,' from the verb *esclicier*, from Gmc.; akin to Ger. *schleissen* 'to slice' and SLIT.]

slick /slik/ ▶ adj. **1** (of an action or thing) done or operating in an impressively smooth, efficient, and apparently effortless way. ■ (of a thing) superficially impressive or efficient in presentation. ■ (of a person or their behavior) adroit or clever; glibly assured. **2** (of skin or hair) smooth and glossy. ■ (of a surface) smooth, wet, and slippery. ▶ n. **1** an oil slick. ■ a small smear or patch of a glossy or wet substance, esp. a cosmetic. **2** (usu. **slicks**) a race car or bicycle tire without a tread, for use in dry weather conditions. **3** informal a glossy magazine. ▶ v. **1** [trans.] make (one's hair) flat, smooth, and glossy by applying water, oil, or cream to it. ■ cover with a film of liquid; make wet or slippery. **2** (**slick someone/something up**) make someone or something smart, tidy, or stylish. — **slick·ly** adv. **slick·ness** n. [ME: prob. from OE and akin to ON *slíkr* 'smooth.']

slick·en·side /'slikən,sīd/ ▶ n. (usu. **slickensides**) Geol. a polished and striated rock surface that results from friction along a fault or bedding plane. [18th C.: from dial. var. of SLICK (adj.) + SIDE.]

slick·er /'slikər/ ▶ n. **1** informal a crook or swindler. ■ short for CITY SLICKER. **2** a raincoat made of smooth material.

slide /slīd/ ▶ v. (past **slid** /slid/) [intrans.] move along a smooth surface while in contact with it. ■ [trans.] move (something) along a surface in such a way. ■ move smoothly, quickly, or unobtrusively: *I quickly slid into a seat.* ■ [trans.] move (something) in such a way: *she slid the bottle into her pocket.* ■ change gradually to a worse condition or lower level: *the country slid from recession into depression.* ▶ n. **1** a structure with a smooth sloping surface for children to slide down. ■ a smooth stretch or slope of ice or packed snow for sledding on. ■ an act of moving along a smooth surface while in contact with it. ■ Baseball a sliding approach to a base along the ground. ■ a decline in value or quality. **2** a part of a machine or musical instrument that slides. ■ the place on a machine or instrument where a sliding part operates. ■ slide guitar. **3** (also **microscope slide**) a rectangular piece of glass on which an object is placed for examination under a microscope. ■ a mounted transparency, placed in a projector for viewing on a screen.
– PHRASES **let something slide** negligently allow something to deteriorate. — **slid·a·ble** adj. [OE *slīdan* (v.); akin to SLED, SLEDGE¹.]

slide fas·ten·er ▶ n. dated a zipper.

slide gui·tar ▶ n. a style of guitar playing in which a glissando effect is produced by moving a bottleneck or similar device over the strings, used esp. in blues.

slide pro·jec·tor ▶ n. a piece of equipment used for displaying photographic slides on a screen.

slider 1

slid·er /'slīdər/ ▶ n. **1** a North American freshwater turtle (genus *Trachemys* (or *Pseudemys*), family Emydidae) with a red or yellow patch on the side of the head. Several species include the **red-eared** (or **pond**) **slider** (*T. scripta*). **2** Baseball a pitch that moves laterally as it nears home plate.

slide rule ▶ n. a ruler with a sliding central strip, marked with logarithmic scales and used for making rapid calculations, esp. multiplication and division.

slide show ▶ n. a presentation supplemented by or based on a series of projected photographic slides.

slide valve ▶ n. a piece that opens and closes an aperture by sliding across it.

slid·ing door ▶ n. a door drawn across an aperture on a groove or suspended from a track, rather than turning on hinges.

slid·ing scale ▶ n. a scale of fees, taxes, wages, etc., that varies in accordance with variation of some standard.

slight /slīt/ ▶ adj. **1** small in degree; inconsiderable. ■ (esp. of a creative work) not profound or substantial. **2** (of a person or their build) not sturdy and strongly built. ▶ v. [trans.] **1** insult (someone) by treating or speaking of them without proper respect or attention. **2** archaic raze or destroy (a fortification). ▶ n. an insult caused by a failure to show someone proper respect or attention.
– PHRASES **not in the slightest** not at all. **the slightest ——** [usu. with negative] any —— whatsoever: *I don't have the slightest idea.* — **slight·ing·ly** adv. **slight·ish** adj. **slight·ness** n. [ME; adj. from Old Norse *sléttr* 'smooth,' from Gmc.; akin to Ger. *schlicht* 'simple'; v. from ON *slétta*.]

slight·ly /'slītlē/ ▶ adv. **1** to a small degree; inconsiderably. **2** (with reference to a person's build) in a slender way.

Sli·go /'slīgō/ a county in the Republic of Ireland. ■ its county town; pop. 17,000.

sli·ly ▶ adv. var. of *SLYLY* (see SLY).

slim /slim/ ▶ adj. (**slim·mer, slim·mest**) **1** (of a person or their build) gracefully thin. ■ (of a thing) small in width and typically long and narrow in shape. ■ (of a garment) designed to make the wearer appear slim. ■ (of a business or other organization) reduced to a smaller size in the hope that it will become more efficient. **2** (of something abstract, esp. a chance or margin) very small. ▶ v. (**slimmed, slim·ming**) [intrans.] make oneself thinner by dieting and sometimes exercising. ■ [trans.] make (a person or a bodily part) thinner in such a way: *how can I slim down my hips?* ■ [trans.] reduce (a business or other organization) to a smaller size in the hope of making it more efficient. ▶ n. (also **slim disease**) African term for **AIDS**. — **slim·ly** adv. **slim·ness** n. [17th C.: from Low Ger. or Du. (from a base meaning 'slanting, bad'), from Gmc.]

slime /slīm/ ▶ n. a moist, soft, and slippery substance. ■ informal a slimeball. ▶ v. [trans.] cover with slime: *the grass was slimed over with mud.* [OE *slīm*, from Gmc.; akin to Ger. *Schleim* 'mucus, slime,' L. *limus* 'mud.']

slime·ball /'slīm,bôl/ ▶ n. informal a repulsive or despicable person.

slime mold ▶ n. a simple organism (division Myxomycota or (treated as a protozoan) phylum Gymnomyxa) that consists of an acellular mass of creeping jellylike protoplasm containing nuclei, or a mass of ameboid cells.

slim jim ▶ n. informal a very slim person or thing, in particular: ■ (**slim jims**) a pair of long narrow trousers. ■ (also **Slim Jim**) (trademark) a long thin variety of smoked sausage. ■ a long flexible metal strip with a hooked end, used by car thieves and others for accessing a locked vehicle.

slim·line /'slim,līn/ ▶ adj. (of a person or article) slender in design or build: *a slimline phone.*

slim vol·ume ▶ n. a book, typically of verse, by a little-known author.

slim·y /'slīmē/ ▶ adj. (**slim·i·er, slim·i·est**) covered by or having the consistency of slime. ■ informal disgustingly immoral, dishonest, or obsequious. — **slim·i·ly** /-məlē/ adv. **slim·i·ness** n.

sling¹ /sliNG/ ▶ n. **1** a flexible strap or belt used in the form of a loop to support or raise a hanging weight. ■ a bandage or soft strap looped around the neck to support an injured arm. ■ a pouch or frame for carrying a baby, supported by a strap around the neck or shoulders. **2** a simple weapon in the form of a strap or loop, used to hurl stones or other small missiles. ▶ v. (past **slung** /sləNG/) **1** [trans.] suspend or arrange (something), esp. with a strap or straps, so that it hangs loosely in a particular position: *a hammock was slung between two trees.* ■ carry (something, esp. a garment) loosely and casually: *a jacket slung over one shoulder.* **2** [trans.] informal throw; fling (often used to express the speaker's casual attitude). ■ hurl (a stone or other missile) from a sling or similar weapon. ■ hoist or transfer (something) with a sling.

– PHRASES **put someone's** (or **have one's**) **ass in a sling** vulgar slang cause someone to be (or be) in trouble. **sling hash** informal serve food in a cafe or diner. **slings and arrows** used with reference to adverse factors or circumstances. —**sling·er** n. [ME: prob. from Low German, of symbolic origin; compare Ger. *Schlinge* 'noose.' Verb Sense 2 is from ON *slyngva*.]

sling-back

sling² ▶ n. a sweetened drink of liquor, esp. gin, and water. See also SINGAPORE SLING. [18th C.: origin unknown.]

sling-back (also **sling·back**) ▶ n. a shoe held in place by a strap around the back of the ankle: [as adj.] *a pair of red sling-back pumps.*

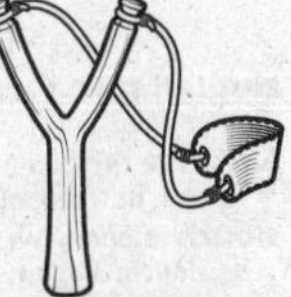
slingshot

sling·shot /ˈslɪNG,SHät/ ▶ n. a forked stick, to which an elastic strap is fastened to the two prongs, used for shooting small stones. ■ [often as adj.] the effect of the gravitational pull of a celestial body in accelerating and changing the course of another body or a spacecraft. ▶ v. (**-shot·ting**; past and past part. **-shot** or **-shot·ted**) forcefully accelerate or cause to accelerate through use of gravity: [intrans.] *the car would hit the first dip, then slingshot off the second rise* | [trans.] *Jupiter's gravity slingshots the fragments toward Earth.*

slink /slɪNGk/ ▶ v. (past **slunk** /sləNGk/) [intrans.] move smoothly and quietly with gliding steps, in a stealthy or sensuous manner. ■ come or go unobtrusively or furtively. ▶ n. [in sing.] an act of moving in this way. [OE *slincan* 'crawl, creep'; compare MDu., Mid. Low Ger. *slinken* 'subside.']

slink·y /ˈslɪNGkē/ ▶ adj. (**slink·i·er, slink·i·est**) informal graceful and sinuous in movement, line, or figure. ▶ n. (**Slinky**) trademark a toy consisting of a flexible helical spring that can be made to somersault down steps. — **slink·i·ly** /ˈslɪNGkəlē/ adv. **slink·i·ness** n.

slip¹ /slip/ ▶ v. (**slipped, slip·ping**) **1** [intrans.] (of a person or animal) slide unintentionally for a short distance, typically losing one's balance or footing. ■ [with adverbial of direction] (of a thing) accidentally slide or move out of position or from someone's grasp: *the envelope slipped through Luke's fingers.* ■ fail to grip or make proper contact with a surface. ■ go or move quietly or quickly, without attracting notice. ■ pass or change to a lower, worse, or different condition, typically in a gradual way. ■ (**be slipping**) informal be behaving in a way that is not up to one's usual level of performance: *you're slipping, Joe—you need a vacation.* ■ (**slip away/by**) (of time) elapse: *the night was slipping away.* ■ [trans.] put (something) in a particular place or position quietly, quickly, or stealthily: *she slipped the map into her pocket.* ■ (**slip into/out of**) put on or take off (a garment) quickly and easily. ■ (**slip something in**) insert a remark smoothly or adroitly into a conversation. **2** [trans.] escape or get loose from (a means of restraint). ■ [intrans.] (**slip out**) (of a remark) be uttered inadvertently. ■ (of a thought or fact) fail to be remembered by (one's mind or memory); elude (one's notice). ■ release (an animal, typically a hunting dog) from restraint. ■ Knitting move (a stitch) to the other needle without knitting it. ■ release (the clutch of a motor vehicle) slightly or for a moment. ■ (of an animal) produce (dead young) prematurely; abort. ▶ n. **1** an act of sliding unintentionally for a short distance. ■ a fall to a lower level or standard. ■ relative movement of an object or surface and a solid surface in contact with it. ■ a reduction in the movement of a pulley or other mechanism due to slipping of the belt, rope, etc. ■ a sideways movement of an aircraft in flight, typically downward toward the center of curvature of a turn. ■ Geol. the extent of relative horizontal displacement of corresponding points on either side of a fault plane. **2** a minor or careless mistake. **3** a woman's loose-fitting, dress- or skirt-length undergarment, suspended by shoulder straps (**full slip**) or by an elasticized waistband (**half slip**): *a silk slip.* **4** a slope built leading into water, used for launching and landing boats and ships or for building and repairing them. ■ a space in which to dock a boat or ship, esp. between two wharves or piers. **5** (also **slip leash**) a leash that enables a dog to be released quickly. **6** Knitting short for SLIP STITCH.

– PHRASES **give someone the slip** informal evade or escape from someone. **let something slip 1** reveal something inadvertently in the course of a conversation. **2** archaic release a hound from the leash to begin the chase. **let something slip through one's fingers** (or **grasp**) lose hold or possession of something. **slip of the pen** (or **the tongue**) a minor mistake in writing (or speech). **there's many a slip 'twixt cup and lip** proverb many things can go wrong between the start of a project and its completion.

– PHRASAL VERBS **slip away** depart without saying goodbye; leave quietly or surreptitiously. ■ slowly disappear; recede or dwindle. ■ die peacefully (used euphemistically). **slip something over on** informal take advantage of (someone) by trickery. **slip up** informal make a careless error. [ME ('move quickly'): prob. from Mid. Low Ger. *slippen* (v.).]

slip² ▶ n. **1** a small piece of paper, typically a form for writing on or one giving printed information. ■ a long, narrow strip of a thin material such as wood. **2** a cutting taken from a plant for grafting or planting; a scion.

– PHRASES **a slip of a ——** used to denote a small, slim person: *you are little more than a slip of a girl.* [ME: prob. from MDu., Mid. Low Ger. *slippe* 'cut, strip.']

slip³ ▶ n. a creamy mixture of clay, water, and typically a pigment, used esp. for decorating earthenware. [17th C.: compare Norw. *slip(a)* 'slime.']

slip·case /ˈslip,kās/ ▶ n. a close-fitting case open at one side or end for an object such as a book.

slip·cov·er /ˈslip,kəvər/ ▶ n. a removable fitted cloth cover for a chair or sofa. ■ a jacket or slipcase for a book.

slip-joint pli·ers ▶ plural n. pliers with a slot in one jaw through which the other jaw slides, permitting a variable span.

slip knot ▶ n. **1** a knot that can be undone by a pull. See illustration at KNOT¹. **2** a running knot.

slip-on ▶ adj. (esp. of shoes or clothes) having no (or few) fasteners and therefore able to be put on and taken off quickly. ▶ n. a shoe or garment that can be easily slipped on and off.

slip·o·ver /ˈslip,ōvər/ ▶ n. a pullover, typically one without sleeves.

slip·page /ˈslipij/ ▶ n. the action or process of something slipping or subsiding; the amount or extent of this. ■ failure to meet a standard or deadline: the extent of this.

slipped /slipt/ ▶ adj. Heraldry (of a flower or leaf) depicted with a stalk.

slipped disk ▶ n. a cartilaginous disk between vertebrae that is displaced or partly protruding, pressing on nearby nerves and causing back pain or sciatica.

slip·per /ˈslipər/ ▶ n. a comfortable slip-on shoe worn indoors. ■ a light slip-on shoe, esp. one used for dancing. — **slip·pered** adj.

slip·per·y /ˈslipərē/ ▶ adj. (of a surface or object) difficult to hold firmly or stand on because it is smooth, wet, or slimy. ■ (of a person) evasive and unpredictable; not to be relied on: *Martin's a slippery customer.* ■ (of a word or concept) elusive in meaning because changing according to one's point of view.

– PHRASES **slippery slope** an idea or course of action that will lead to something unacceptable, wrong, or disastrous. —**slip·per·i·ly** /ˈslipərəlē/ adv. **slip·per·i·ness** n. [15th C.: from dial. *slipper* 'slippery.']

slip·per·y elm ▶ n. a North American elm (*Ulmus rubra* (or *fulva*), family Ulmaceae) with coarsely textured leaves and rough outer bark. ■ the mucilaginous inner bark of this tree, used medicinally.

slip·py /ˈslipē/ ▶ adj. (**slip·pi·er, slip·pi·est**) informal slippery: *the path was slippy with mud* | *slippy tires.* — **slip·pi·ness** n.

slip ring ▶ n. a ring in a dynamo or electric motor that is attached to and rotates with the shaft, passing an electric current to a circuit via a fixed brush pressing against it.

slip·sheet /ˈslip,SHēt/ ▶ n. Print. a sheet of paper placed between newly printed sheets to prevent offset or smudging.

slip·shod /ˈslip,SHäd/ ▶ adj. (typically of a person or method of work) characterized by a lack of care, thought, or organization. ■ archaic (of shoes) worn down at the heel. [16th C. ('wearing slippers'): from SLIP¹ (v.) + SHOD.]

slip stitch ▶ n. **1** (in sewing) a loose stitch joining layers of fabric and not visible externally. **2** [often as adj.] Knitting a type of stitch in which the stitches are moved from one needle to the other without being knitted: *a slip-stitch pattern.* ▶ v. (**slip-stitch**) [trans.] sew or knit with such stitches.

slip·stream /ˈslip,strēm/ ▶ n. a current of air or water driven back by a revolving propeller or jet engine. ■ the partial vacuum created in the wake of a moving vehicle, often used by other vehicles in a race to assist in passing. ■ fig. an assisting force regarded as drawing something along behind something else. ▶ v. [intrans.] (esp. in auto racing) another term for DRAFT (sense 4). ■ [trans.] travel in the slipstream of (someone), esp. in order to overtake them.

slip-up ▶ n. informal a mistake or blunder.

slip·ware /ˈslip,we(ə)r/ ▶ n. pottery decorated with slip (see SLIP³).

slip·way /ˈslip,wā/ ▶ n. another term for SLIP¹ (sense 4).

slit /slit/ ▶ n. a long, narrow cut or opening. ▶ v. (**slit·ting**; past **slit**) [trans.] make a long, narrow cut in (something). ■ cut (something) into strips. ■ (past **slit·ted**) form (one's eyes) into slits; squint. — **slit·ter** n. [OE *slite* (n.); akin to OE *slītan* 'split, rend' (Gmc.).]

slith·er /ˈsli<u>TH</u>ər/ ▶ v. [intrans.] move smoothly over a surface with a twisting motion. ■ slide or slip unsteadily on a loose or slippery surface. ▶ n. [in sing.] a movement in such a manner. — **slith·er·y** adj. [ME: alt. of dial. v. *slidder*, frequentative from base of SLIDE.]

slit trench ▶ n. a narrow trench for a soldier or a small group of soldiers and their equipment.

sliv·er /ˈslivər/ ▶ n. a small, thin, narrow piece of something cut or split off a larger piece. ■ a strip of loose untwisted textile fibers produced by carding. ▶ v. [trans.] [usu. as adj.] (**slivered**) cut or break (something) into small, thin, narrow pieces. ■ convert (textile fibers) into slivers. [ME: from dial. *slive* 'cleave.']

sliv·o·vitz /ˈslivə,vits/ ▶ n. a type of plum brandy made chiefly in eastern Europe. [from Serbo-Croat *šljivovica*, from *šljiva* 'plum.']

Sloan /slōn/, John French (1871–1951), US painter. A member of the Ashcan School, he painted scenes of New York City.

slob /släb/ ▶ n. informal a lazy and slovenly person. — **slob·bish** adj. **slob·by** adj. [18th C.: from Irish *slab* 'mud,' from Anglo-Irish *slab* 'sludge,' prob. of Scand. origin.]

slob·ber /ˈsläbər/ ▶v. [intrans.] have saliva dripping copiously from the mouth. ■ (**slobber over**) fig. be excessively sentimental; show excessive enthusiasm for: *slobbering all over the new baby.* ▶n. saliva dripping copiously from the mouth. —**slob·ber·y** adj. [ME: prob. from MDu. *slobberen* 'walk through mud,' 'feed noisily,' of imitative origin.]

sloe /slō/ ▶n. another term for BLACKTHORN. ■ the small bluish-black fruit of the blackthorn, with a sharp sour taste. [OE *slā(h),* from Gmc.; akin to Ger. *Schlehe,* and prob. L. *livere* 'be blue.']

sloe-eyed ▶adj. having attractive dark, typically almond-shaped eyes.

sloe gin ▶n. a liqueur made by steeping sloes in gin.

slog /släg/ ▶v. (**slogged, slog·ging**) **1** [intrans.] work hard over a period of time. ■ walk or move with difficulty or effort. **2** [intrans.] hit forcefully and typically wildly, esp. in boxing. ■ (**slog it out**) fight or compete at length or fiercely. ▶n. [usu. in sing.] a spell of difficult, tiring work or traveling. —**slog·ger** n. [19th C.: compare with SLUG².]

slo·gan /ˈslōgən/ ▶n. a short and striking or memorable phrase used in advertising. ■ a motto associated with a political party or movement or other group. ■ hist. a Scottish Highland war cry. [16th C.: from Scot. Gael. *sluagh-ghairm,* from *sluagh* 'army' + *gairm* 'shout.']

slo·gan·eer /ˌslōgəˈni(ə)r/ ▶v. [usu. as n.] (**sloganeering**) [intrans.] employ or invent slogans, typically in a political context. ▶n. a person who does this.

slo-mo /ˈslōˈmō/ (also **slo·mo**) ▶n. informal short for SLOW MOTION.

sloop /slo͞op/ ▶n. a one-masted sailboat with a fore-and-aft mainsail and a jib. ■ (also **sloop of war**) hist. a small square-rigged sailing warship with two or three masts. ■ hist. a small antisubmarine warship used for convoy escort in World War II. [17th C.: from Du. *sloep(e).*]

sloop-rigged ▶adj. rigged as a sloop.

slop /släp/ ▶v. (**slopped, slop·ping**) **1** [intrans.] (of a liquid) spill or flow over the edge of a container, typically as a result of careless handling. ■ [trans.] cause (a liquid) to spill or overflow in such a way. ■ [trans.] apply or put (something) somewhere in a casual or careless manner: *slopping on paint.* ■ (**slop through**) wade through (a wet or muddy area). **2** [trans.] feed slops to (an animal, esp. a pig). **3** [intrans.] speak or write in a sentimentally effusive manner; gush. ▶n. **1** (usu. **slops**) waste water from a kitchen, bathroom, or chamber pot that has to be emptied by hand. ■ (usu. **slops**) semiliquid kitchen refuse, often used as animal food. ■ unappetizing weak, semiliquid food. **2** sentimental language or material. [16th C. (v.): prob. akin to SLIP³.]

slope /slōp/ ▶n. **1** a surface of which one end or side is at a higher level than another. ■ a difference in level or sideways position between the two ends or sides of a thing. ■ (often **slopes**) a part of the side of a hill or mountain, esp. as a place for skiing. ■ the gradient of a graph at any point. **2** informal, derog. an Asian person, esp. a Vietnamese or other Southeast Asian. ▶v. [intrans.] (of a surface or line) be inclined from a horizontal or vertical line; slant up or down. ■ [trans.] place or arrange in such a position or inclination: *Poole sloped his shoulders.* [16th C. (v.): from obs. adv. *slope,* shortening of ASLOPE.]

slop·py /ˈsläpē/ ▶adj. (**slop·pi·er, slop·pi·est**) **1** (of semifluid matter) watery and disagreeable or unsatisfactory: *do not make the concrete too sloppy.* **2** careless and unsystematic; excessively casual. ■ (of a garment) casual and loose-fitting. **3** (of literature or behavior) weakly or foolishly sentimental. —**slop·pi·ly** /ˈsläpəlē/ adv. **slop·pi·ness** n.

slop·py joe ▶n. informal a sandwich with a filling of ground beef that has been seasoned with a sauce of tomatoes and spices.

slosh /släsн/ ▶v. [intrans.] (of liquid in a container) move irregularly with a splashing sound. ■ (of a person) move through liquid with a splashing sound. ■ [trans.] pour (liquid) clumsily: *she sloshed coffee into a cracked cup.* ▶n. an act or sound of splashing. [19th C.: var. of SLUSH (n.).]

sloshed /släsнt/ ▶adj. informal drunk.

slosh·y /ˈsläsнē/ ▶adj. (**slosh·i·er, slosh·i·est**) **1** wet and sticky; slushy. **2** excessively sentimental; sloppy: *the program is a sloshy and patronizing affair.*

slot¹ /slät/ ▶n. **1** a long, narrow aperture or slit in a machine for something to be inserted. ■ a groove or channel into which something fits or in which something works, such as one in the head of a screw. **2** an allotted place in a plan such as a broadcasting schedule. ▶v. (**slotted, slotting**) [trans.] place (something) into a long, narrow aperture. ■ [intrans.] be placed or able to be placed into such an aperture. —**slot·ted** adj. [ME ('depression running down the middle of the chest'): from OFr. *esclot.*]

slot² ▶n. (usu. **slots**) the track of a deer, visible as slotted footprints in soft ground. [16th C.: from OFr. *esclot* 'hoofprint,' prob. from ON *slóth* 'trail.']

slot·back /ˈslätˌbak/ ▶n. Football an offensive back who is positioned between the tackle and the split end.

slot car ▶n. an electrically driven miniature race car that travels in a slot in a track.

sloth /slôтн; slätн; slōтн/ ▶n. **1** reluctance to work or make an effort; laziness. **2** a slow-moving tropical American mammal (genera *Bradypus* (**three-toed sloths**) and *Choloepus* (**two-toed sloths**)) that hangs upside down from the branches of trees using its long limbs and hooked claws. [OE: from SLOW.]

sloth bear ▶n. a shaggy-coated nocturnal Indian bear (*Melursus ursinus*) that uses its long curved claws for hanging upside down like a sloth and for opening termite mounds to feed on the insects.

sloth·ful /ˈslôтнfəl; slätн-; ˈslōтн-/ ▶adj. lazy. —**sloth·ful·ly** adv. **sloth·ful·ness** n.

slot ma·chine ▶n. a machine worked by the insertion of a coin, paper currency, or bar-coded credit slip, in particular: ■ a gaming machine that generates random combinations of symbols on a dial or video screen, certain combinations winning varying amounts of money for the player. ■ esp. Brit. a vending machine selling small items.

three-toed sloth

slot·ted spoon ▶n. a large spoon with slots or holes for draining liquid from food.

Slot, the the name given in World War II by US forces to New Georgia Sound, in the central Solomon Islands.

slouch /slouсн/ ▶v. [intrans.] stand, move, or sit in a lazy, drooping way: *he slouched against the wall.* ▶n. [in sing.] **1** a lazy, drooping posture or movement. **2** [usu. with negative] informal an incompetent person: *no slouch at making a buck.* **3** a downward bend of a hat brim. —**slouch·y** adj. [16th C. ('lazy person'): of unknown origin.]

slouch hat ▶n. a hat with a wide flexible brim.

slough¹ /slou; slo͞o/ ▶n. a swamp. ■ fig. a situation characterized by lack of progress or activity. ■ a muddy side channel or inlet. —**slough·y** adj. [OE *slōh, slō(g).*]

slough² /sləf/ ▶v. [trans.] (of an animal, esp. a snake, or a person) cast off or shed (an old or dead skin). ■ [intrans.] (**slough off**) (of dead skin) drop off; be shed. ■ [intrans.] (**slough away/down**) (of soil or rock) collapse or slide into a hole or depression. ▶n. the dropping off of dead tissue from living flesh. —**slough·y** adj. [ME ('a skin'): perh. akin to Low Ger. *slu(we)* 'husk.']

Slough of De·spond (also **slough of despond**) /ˈslou əv dəˈspänd/ ▶n. a state of hopeless depression. [a deep boggy place in John Bunyan's *The Pilgrim's Progress.*]

Slo·vak /ˈslōväk; -vak/ ▶n. **1** a native or national of Slovakia, or a person of Slovak descent. **2** the West Slavic language of Slovakia, closely related to Czech. ▶adj. of or relating to this people or their language. [Slovak, from Slavic root perh. akin to *slovo* 'word.']

Slo·va·ki·a /slōˈväkēə/ a country in central Europe. *See box.* —**Slo·va·ki·an** adj. & n.

Slovakia

Official name: Slovak Republic
Location: central Europe, east of the Czech Republic
Area: 18,900 square miles (48,800 sq km)
Population: 5,432,000
Capital: Bratislava
Languages: Slovak (official), Hungarian
Currency: Slovak koruna

slov·en /ˈsləvən/ ▶n. dated a person who is habitually messy or careless. [15th C.: perh. from Flemish *sloef* 'dirty' or Du. *slof* 'careless.']

Slo·vene /ˈslōvēn/ ▶n. **1** a native or national of Slovenia, or a person of Slovene descent. **2** the South Slavic language of this people. ▶adj. of or relating to Slovenia, its people, or their language. [from Slovene *Slovenec,* from Slavic root shared with SLOVAK (see SLOVAK).]

Slovenia

Official name: Republic of Slovenia
Location: southeastern Europe, south of Austria
Area: 7,800 square miles (20,300 sq km)
Population: 2,011,000
Capital: Ljubljana
Languages: Slovene (official), Serbo-Croatian
Currency: tolar

Slo·ve·ni·a /slō'vēnēə/ a country in southeastern Europe. *See box.*

Slo·ve·ni·an /slō'vēnēən/ ▶ n. & adj. another term for SLOVENE.

slov·en·ly /'sləvənlē; 'slä-/ ▶ adj. (esp. of a person or their appearance) messy and dirty. ■ (esp. of a person or action) careless; excessively casual. — **slov·en·li·ness** n.

slow /slō/ ▶ adj. **1** moving or operating, or designed to do so, only at a low speed. ■ taking a long time to perform a specified action: *a slow reader.* ■ lasting or taking a long time: *a slow process.* | ■ [attrib.] not allowing or intended for fast travel: *the slow lane.* ■ (of a playing field) likely to make the ball bounce or run slowly or to prevent competitors from traveling fast. **2** [predic. or as complement] (of a clock or watch) showing a time earlier than the correct time. **3** not prompt to understand, think, or learn. **4** uneventful and rather dull. ■ (of business) with little activity; slack. **5** Photog. (of a film) needing long exposure. ■ (of a lens) having a small aperture. **6** (of a fire or oven) burning or giving off heat gently. ▶ adv. at a slow pace; slowly. ▶ v. [intrans.] reduce one's speed or the speed of a vehicle or process. ■ (**slow down/up**) live or work less actively or intensely: *I wasn't feeling well and had to slow down.*
– PHRASES **slow but sure** not quick but achieving the required result eventually. — **slow·ish** adj. **slow·ness** n. [OE *slāw* 'slow-witted,' from Gmc.]

slow cook·er ▶ n. a large electric pot used for cooking food, esp. stews, very slowly.

slow·down /'slō,doun/ ▶ n. an act of slowing down. ■ a decline in economic activity.

slow lo·ris ▶ n. see LORIS.

slow match ▶ n. hist. a slow-burning wick or cord for lighting explosives.

slow mo·tion ▶ n. the action of showing film or playing back video more slowly than it was made or recorded, so that the action appears much slower than in real life.

slow·poke /'slō,pōk/ ▶ n. informal a person who acts or moves slowly: *we waited for the slowpokes to catch up.*

slow track ▶ n. a route or method that results in slow progress: *a slow track to economic and monetary union.*

slow-twitch ▶ adj. [attrib.] Physiol. (of a muscle fiber) contracting slowly, providing endurance rather than strength.

slow vi·rus ▶ n. a virus or viruslike organism that multiplies slowly in the host organism and has a long incubation period.

slow-worm ▶ n. a small snakelike Eurasian legless lizard (*Anguis fragilis*, family Anguidae) that is typically brownish or copper-colored and that gives birth to live young. Also called BLINDWORM. [OE *slāwyrm*, from *slā-* (of uncert. origin) + *wyrm* 'snake.']

SLR ▶ abbr. ■ self-loading rifle. ■ single-lens reflex.

slub¹ /sləb/ ▶ n. a lump or thick place in yarn or thread. ■ fabric woven from yarn with such a texture. ▶ adj. [attrib.] (of fabric) having an irregular appearance caused by uneven thickness of the warp. — **slubbed** adj. [19th C.: origin unknown.]

slub² ▶ n. wool that has been slightly twisted in preparation for spinning. ▶ v. (**slubbed, slub·bing**) [trans.] twist (wool) in this way. [19th C.: origin unknown.]

sludge /sləj/ ▶ n. thick, soft, wet mud or a similar viscous mixture of liquid and solid components, esp. the product of an industrial or refining process. ■ dirty oil, esp. in the sump of an internal combustion engine. ■ sea ice newly formed in small pieces. — **sludg·y** adj. [17th C.: compare SLUSH.]

slue ▶ v. & n. var. of SLEW¹.

slug¹ /sləg/ ▶ n. **1** a tough-skinned terrestrial mollusk (order Stylommatophora, class Gastropoda) that typically lacks a shell and secretes a film of mucus for protection. It can be a serious plant pest. See also SEA SLUG. **2** a slow, lazy person; a sluggard. **3** an amount of an alcoholic drink, typically liquor, that is gulped or poured: *he took **a slug of** whiskey.* **4** an elongated, typically rounded piece of metal. ■ a counterfeit coin; a token. ■ a bullet, esp. one of lead. ■ a missile for an air gun. ■ a line of type in Linotype printing. ■ Print. a metal bar used in spacing. ▶ v. (**slugged, slug·ging**) [trans.] drink (something, typically alcohol) in a large draft; swig. [ME (sense 2): prob. of Scand. origin; compare Norw. dial. *slugg* 'large heavy body.']

slug² informal ▶ v. (**slugged, slug·ging**) [trans.] strike (someone) with a hard blow. ■ (**slug it out**) settle a dispute or contest by fighting or competing fiercely. ▶ n. a hard blow. [19th C.: cf. SLOG (v.).]

slug·a·bed /'sləgə,bed/ ▶ n. a lazy person who stays in bed late. [16th C.: from *slug* 'be lazy' + ABED.]

slug·fest /'sləg,fest/ ▶ n. informal a tough and challenging contest, esp. in sports such as boxing and baseball. [20th C.: from SLUG²]

slug·gard /'sləgərd/ ▶ n. a lazy, sluggish person. — **slug·gard·li·ness** n. **slug·gard·ly** adj. [ME: from *slug* 'be lazy.']

slug·ger /'sləgər/ ▶ n. person who throws hard punches. ■ Baseball a player who consistently hits for power, esp. home runs and doubles.

slug·gish /'sləgisH/ ▶ adj. slow-moving or inactive. ■ lacking energy or alertness. ■ slow to respond or make progress. — **slug·gish·ly** adv. **slug·gish·ness** n. [ME: from SLUG¹ (n.) or *slug* (see SLUGGARD).]

sluice /slo͞os/ ▶ n. **1** (also **sluice gate**) a sliding gate or other device for controlling the flow of water, esp. one in a lock gate. ■ (also **sluice·way**) an artificial water channel for carrying off overflow or surplus water. ■ (in gold mining) a channel with grooves into which a current of water is directed to separate gold from the gravel containing it. **2** an act of rinsing or showering with water. ▶ v. [trans.] wash or rinse freely with a stream or shower of water. ■ [intrans.] (of water) pour, flow, or shower freely. [ME (n.): from OFr. *escluse* 'sluice gate,' based on L. *excludere* 'exclude.']

slum /sləm/ ▶ n. a squalid and overcrowded urban street or district inhabited by very poor people. ■ a house or building unfit for human habitation. ▶ v. (**slummed, slum·ming**) [intrans.] informal spend time at a lower social level through curiosity or charity. ■ (**slum it**) put up with conditions that are less comfortable or of a lower quality than one is used to. — **slum·mer** n. **slum·mi·ness** n. **slum·my** adj. [19th C. ('room'): origin unknown.]

slum·ber /'sləmbər/ literary ▶ v. [intrans.] sleep. ▶ n. (often **slumbers**) a sleep. — **slum·ber·er** n. **slum·brous** /-brəs/ (also **slum·ber·ous** /-bərəs/) adj. [ME: alt. of Scots, north. Engl. *sloom*.]

slum·ber·land /'sləmbər,land/ ▶ n. literary or humorous the state of being asleep.

slum·ber par·ty ▶ n. a party, typically for preteen or teenage girls, in which all the guests spend the night at the house where the party is held.

slum·gul·lion /,sləm'gəlyən/ ▶ n. informal cheap or insubstantial stew.

slum·lord /'sləm,lôrd/ ▶ n. informal a landlord of slum property, esp. one who profiteers.

slump /sləmp/ ▶ v. [intrans.] **1** [with adverbial] sit, lean, or fall heavily and limply. **2** undergo a sudden severe or prolonged fall in price, value, or amount. ■ fail or decline substantially. ▶ n. a sudden severe or prolonged fall in the price, value, or amount of something. ■ a prolonged period of abnormally low economic activity, with widespread unemployment. ■ a period of substantial failure or decline. — **slump·y** adj. [17th C.: prob. imitative and akin to Norw. *slumpe* 'to fall.']

slung /sləNG/ past and past participle of SLING¹.

slung shot ▶ n. a hard object, such as a metal ball, attached by a strap or thong to the wrist and used as a weapon.

slunk /sləNGk/ past and past participle of SLINK.

slur /slər/ ▶ v. (**slurred, slur·ring**) [trans.] **1** speak (words) indistinctly so that the sounds run into one another. ■ [intrans.] (of words) be spoken in this way. ■ pass over (a fact or aspect) to conceal or minimize it. **2** Music perform (a group of two or more notes) legato: [as adj.] (**slurred**) *a group of slurred notes.* ■ mark (notes) with a slur. **3** make damaging allegations about. ▶ n. **1** an insinuation or allegation about someone that is likely to insult them or damage their reputation. **2** an act of speaking indistinctly so that sounds or words run into one another or a tendency to speak in such a way: *there was a mean slur in his voice.* **3** Music a curved line used to show that a group of two or more notes are to be sung to one syllable or played or sung legato. [17th C.: from dial. *slur* 'thin mud,' from ME *sloor*.]

slurp /slərp/ ▶ v. [trans.] eat or drink (something) with a loud sucking noise: *she slurped her coffee* | [intrans.] *he slurped noisily from a wine cup.*

▶ n. a loud sucking sound made while eating or drinking. — **slurp·y** adj. [17th C.: from Du. *slurpen*.]

slur·ry /'slərē/ ▶ n. (pl. **-ries**) a semiliquid mixture, typically of fine particles of manure, cement, or coal, and water. [ME: akin to dial. *slur* (see SLUR).]

slush /sləsH/ ▶ n. **1** partially melted snow or ice. ■ watery mud. **2** informal excessive sentiment. ▶ v. [intrans.] make a squelching or splashing sound. [17th C.: prob. imitative; compare SLOSH.]

slush fund ▶ n. a reserve of money used for illicit purposes, esp. political bribery. [19th C.: orig. nautical, 'money collected to buy luxuries, from the sale of *slush*' (refuse fat).]

slush·y /'sləsHē/ ▶ adj. (**slush·i·er, slush·i·est**) **1** resembling, consisting of, or covered with slush: *slushy snow.* **2** informal excessively sentimental: *slushy novels.* — **slush·i·ness** n.

slut /slət/ ▶ n. a slovenly or promiscuous woman. — **slut·tish** adj. **slut·tish·ness** n. [ME: origin unknown.]

sly /slī/ ▶ adj. (**sly·er, sly·est**) having or showing a cunning and deceitful nature. ■ (of a remark, glance, or facial expression) showing in an insinuating way that one has some secret knowledge that may be harmful or embarrassing: *he gave a sly grin.* ■ (of an action) surreptitious.
– PHRASES **on the sly** in a secretive fashion. — **sly·ly** (also **sli·ly**) adv. **sly·ness** n. [ME: from ON *slœgr* 'cunning,' orig. 'able to strike,' from the verb *slá*.]

sly·boots /'slī,bo͞ots/ ▶ n. informal a sly person.

SM ▶ abbr. ■ service mark. ■ sergeant major.

Sm ▶ symb. the chemical element samarium.

S-M (also **s-m, S/M, s/m**) ▶ abbr. ■ (also **S&M**) sadomasochism. ■ sadomasochistic.

sm. ▶ abbr. small.

smack[1] /smak/ ▶ n. a sharp slap or blow, typically one given with the palm of the hand. ■ a loud, sharp sound made by such a blow. ▶ v. [trans.] strike (someone or something), typically with the palm of the hand. ■ [trans.] smash, drive, or put forcefully into or onto something. ■ part (one's lips) noisily in eager anticipation, esp. of food. ▶ adv. informal **1** in a sudden and violent way: *I ran smack into a truck.* **2** exactly; precisely: *smack in the middle.* [16th C.: from MDu. *smacken*, of imitative origin.]

smack[2] ▶ v. [intrans.] (**smack of**) have a flavor of; taste of: *the tea smacked of peppermint.* ■ suggest the presence or effects of (something wrong): *it smacks of a cover-up.* [OE *smæc* 'flavor, smell,' of Gmc. origin; rel. to Ger. *Geschmack*.]

smack[3] ▶ n. a fishing boat, often one equipped with a well for keeping the caught fish alive. [17th C.: from Du. *smak*.]

smack[4] ▶ n. informal heroin.

smack dab ▶ adv. informal exactly; precisely.

smack·down /'smak,doun/ ▶ n. informal **1** a bitter contest or confrontation: *the age-old man versus Nature smackdown.* **2** a decisive or humiliating defeat or setback. [1990s: from SMACK[1].]

smack·er /'smakər/ (also **smack·er·oo** /,smakə'ro͞o/) ▶ n. informal a dollar: *it set me back fifteen smackers.*

small /smôl/ ▶ adj. of a size that is less than normal or usual; little. ■ not great in amount, number, strength, or power: *a small amount.* ■ not fully grown or developed; young: *a small boy.* ■ insignificant; unimportant: *these are small points.* ■ (of a voice) lacking strength and confidence. ■ [attrib.] (of a business or its owner) operating on a modest scale: *a small farmer.* ▶ adv. into small pieces: *the okra cut up small.* ■ in a small size: *you shouldn't write so small.*
– PHRASES **it's a small world** used to express surprise at meeting an acquaintance in a distant place or an unexpected context. **the small of the back** the part of a person's back where the spine curves in at the level of the waist. **small potatoes** informal something insignificant or unimportant. **small wonder** not very surprising. — **small·ish** adj. **small·ness** n. [OE *smæl*, of Gmc. origin; rel. to Du. *smal* and Ger. *schmal*.]

small arms ▶ plural n. portable firearms, esp. rifles, pistols, and light machine guns.

small-bore ▶ adj. denoting a firearm with a narrow bore, generally .22 inch caliber.

small cal·o·rie ▶ n. see CALORIE.

small-cap ▶ adj. [attrib.] Finance denoting or relating to the stock of a company with a small capitalization.

small cap·i·tal ▶ n. a capital letter that is of the same height as a lowercase x in the same typeface, as THIS.

small change ▶ n. coins of low value. ■ fig. a thing that is considered trivial.

small-claims court ▶ n. a local court in which claims for small sums of money can be heard.

small craft ▶ n. a small boat or fishing vessel.

small for·ward ▶ n. Basketball a forward who is typically smaller than a power forward, and is often more agile.

small fry ▶ plural n. young fish, animals, or children. ■ insignificant people or things.

small hours ▶ plural n. (**the small hours**) another way of saying *THE WEE HOURS* (see WEE).

small in·tes·tine ▶ n. the part of the intestine that runs between the stomach and the large intestine; the duodenum, jejunum, and ileum collectively.

small let·ter ▶ n. a lowercase letter, as distinct from a capital letter.

small-mind·ed ▶ adj. having or showing rigid opinions or a narrow outlook; petty. — **small-mind·ed·ly** adv. **small-mind·ed·ness** n.

small·mouth /'smôl,mouTH/ ▶ n. the smallmouth bass. See BLACK BASS.

small·pox /'smôl,päks/ ▶ n. an acute contagious viral disease, with fever and pustules usually leaving permanent scars. It was effectively eradicated through vaccination by 1979. Also called VARIOLA.

small screen ▶ n. (**the small screen**) television as a medium.

small slam ▶ n. Bridge the bidding and winning of twelve of the thirteen tricks.

small-sword ▶ n. esp. hist. a light, tapering thrusting sword used for fencing or dueling.

small talk ▶ n. polite conversation about unimportant or uncontroversial matters, esp. as engaged in on social occasions.

small-time ▶ adj. informal unimportant; minor: *a small-time gangster.* — **small-tim·er** n.

small-town ▶ adj. relating to a small town, esp. as considered to be unsophisticated or petty: *small-town gossip.*

smalt /smôlt/ ▶ n. esp. hist. glass colored blue with cobalt oxide. [16th C.: from Fr., from Ital. *smalto*, of Gmc. origin; rel. to SMELT[1].]

smalt·ite /'smôl,tīt/ ▶ n. a gray metallic mineral consisting chiefly of cobalt arsenide.

smarm /smärm/ informal ▶ v. [intrans.] behave in an ingratiating way in order to gain favor: *I smarmed my way into the air force.* ▶ n. ingratiating behavior: *it takes smarm and confidence.* [19th C. (dial., 'smear'): of unknown origin.]

smarm·y /'smärmē/ ▶ adj. (**smarm·i·er, smarm·i·est**) informal ingratiating and wheedling in a way that is perceived as insincere or excessive; unctuous. — **smarm·i·ly** /-məlē/ adv. **smarm·i·ness** n.

smart /smärt/ ▶ adj. **1** informal having or showing a quick-witted intelligence. ■ (of a device) capable of independent and seemingly intelligent action: *hi-tech smart weapons.* ■ showing impertinence by making clever or sarcastic remarks. **2** (of a person) clean, neat, and well-dressed. ■ (of clothes) attractively neat and stylish: *a smart blue skirt.* ■ (of a person or place) fashionable and upscale: *a smart restaurant.* **3** quick; brisk: *I gave him a smart salute.* ■ painfully severe: *a smart slap.* ▶ v. [intrans.] (of a wound or part of the body) cause a sharp, stinging pain: *the wound was smarting.* ■ (of a person) feel upset and annoyed. ▶ n. **1** (**smarts**) informal intelligence; acumen. **2** sharp stinging pain: *the smart of the wasp sting.* — **smart·ing·ly** adv. **smart·ly** adv. **smart·ness** n. [OE *smeortan*, of West Gmc. origin; rel. to Ger. *schmerzen*; the original sense (late OE) being 'causing sharp pain'.]

smart al·eck (also **smart al·ec**) informal ▶ n. a person considered irritating because they always have a clever answer to a question. ▶ adj. having or showing an irritating, know-it-all attitude: *a smart-aleck answer.* — **smart-al·eck·y** adj. [19th C.: from SMART + *Aleck*, dimin. of the name *Alexander*.]

smart-ass ▶ n. informal another term for SMART ALECK.

smart bomb ▶ n. a radio-controlled or laser-guided bomb, often with a built-in computer.

smart card ▶ n. a plastic card with a built-in microprocessor, used typically for electronic processes such as financial transactions and personal identification.

smart·en /'smärtn/ ▶ v. [trans.] make (something) smarter in appearance: *smarten up the office.* ■ [intrans.] (**smarten up**) acquire more common sense; behave more wisely.

smart mon·ey ▶ n. money invested by people with expert knowledge: *the smart money is in these funds.* ■ knowledgeable people collectively.

smart quotes ▶ plural n. Comput. quotation marks that, although all keyed the same, are automatically interpreted and set as opening or closing marks.

smart·weed /'smärt,wēd/ ▶ n. a plant (genus *Polygonum*) of the dock family, typically having slender leaves and a short spike of tiny compact flowers.

smart·y /'smärtē/ ▶ n. (pl. **smart·ies**) informal a know-it-all or a smart aleck.

smash /smasH/ ▶ v. **1** [trans.] violently break (something). ■ [intrans.] be violently broken into pieces; shatter. ■ violently knock down or crush inward: *soldiers smashed down doors.* ■ crash and severely damage (a vehicle): *my car's been smashed up.* ■ hit or attack (someone) violently. ■ easily or comprehensively beat (a record). ■ completely defeat or destroy something regarded as hostile or dangerous. **2** [intrans.] hit or collide with something with great force and impact. ■ [trans.] (in sports) strike (the ball) or score (a goal, run, etc.) with great force: *Jeter smashed that one into the bleachers.* ■ [trans.] (in tennis, badminton, and similar sports) strike (the ball or shuttlecock) downward with a hard overhand stroke. ▶ n. **1** an act or sound of something smashing. ■ a stroke in tennis, badminton, and similar sports in which the ball is hit downward with a hard overhand volley. **2** (also **smash hit**) informal a very successful song, film, show, or performer: *a box-office smash.* **3** a mixture of liquors (typically brandy) with flavored water and ice. [18th C.: prob. imitative, a blend of words such as *smack, smite* with *bash, mash*, etc.]

smashed /smasHt/ ▶ adj. **1** violently or badly broken or shattered: *a smashed collarbone.* **2** [predic.] informal very drunk.

smash·ing /'smasHiNG/ ▶ adj. informal, esp. Brit. excellent; wonderful: *you look smashing!* — **smash·ing·ly** adv.

smat·ter·ing /ˈsmatəriNG/ (also **smat·ter**) ▶ **n.** a slight superficial knowledge of a language or subject: *a smattering of Spanish.* ■ a small amount of something. [16th C.: from *smatter* 'talk ignorantly, prate', of unknown origin.]

smaze /smāz/ ▶ **n.** a mixture of smoke and haze.

smear /smi(ə)r/ ▶ **v.** [trans.] coat or mark (something) messily or carelessly with a greasy or sticky substance: *his face was smeared with dirt.* ■ [trans.] spread (a greasy, oily, or sticky substance) over something. ■ fig. damage the reputation of (someone) by false accusations; slander. ■ messily blur the outline of (something such as writing or paint); smudge. ▶ **n.** a mark or streak of a greasy or sticky substance. ■ fig. a false accusation intended to damage someone's reputation. ■ a sample of material spread thinly on a microscope slide for examination. — **smear·y adj. smear·er n.** [OE *smierwan, smeoru* 'ointment, grease,' of Gmc. origin; rel. to Ger. *Schmer*.]

smear cam·paign ▶ **n.** a plan to discredit a public figure by making false or dubious accusations.

smec·tic /ˈsmektik/ ▶ **adj.** denoting or involving a state of a liquid crystal in which the molecules are oriented in parallel and arranged in well-defined planes. Compare with NEMATIC. [17th C.: via L. from Gk. *smēktikos* 'cleansing' (from the soaplike consistency).]

smec·tite /ˈsmekˌtīt/ ▶ **n.** a type of clay mineral (e.g., montmorillonite) that undergoes reversible expansion on absorbing water. [19th C.: from Gk. *smēktis* 'fuller's earth' + -ITE[1].]

smeg·ma /ˈsmegmə/ ▶ **n.** a sebaceous secretion in the folds of the skin, esp. under a man's foreskin. [19th C.: via L. from Gk. *smēgma* 'soap,' from *smēkhein* 'cleanse.']

smell /smel/ ▶ **n.** the faculty or power of perceiving odors or scents by means of the organs in the nose. ■ a quality in something that is perceived by this faculty; an odor or scent: *a smell of coffee.* ■ an unpleasant odor. ■ [in sing.] an act of inhaling in order to ascertain an odor or scent: *have a smell of this.* ▶ **v.** (past and past part. **smelled** or **smelt** /smelt/) **1** [trans.] perceive or detect the odor or scent of (something). ■ sniff at (something) in order to perceive or detect its odor or scent. ■ [intrans.] have or use a sense of smell. ■ (**smell something out**) detect or discover something by the faculty of smell. ■ detect or suspect (something) by means of instinct or intuition. **2** [intrans.] emit an odor or scent of a specified kind: *it smelled like cough medicine.* ■ have a strong or unpleasant odor: *it smells in here.* ■ appear in a certain way; be suggestive of something: *it smells like a hoax to me.*
– PHRASES **smell blood** discern weakness or vulnerability in an opponent. **smell a rat** informal suspect trickery or deception. **smell the roses** informal enjoy or appreciate what is often ignored. — **smell·a·ble adj. smell·er n.** [ME: of unknown origin.]

smell·ing salts ▶ **plural n.** esp. hist. a pungent substance sniffed as a restorative in cases of faintness or headache, typically consisting of ammonium carbonate mixed with perfume.

smell·y /ˈsmelē/ ▶ **adj.** (**smell·i·er, smell·i·est**) having a strong or unpleasant smell. — **smell·i·ness n.**

smelt[1] /smelt/ ▶ **v.** [trans.] [often as n.] (**smelting**) extract (metal) from its ore by a process involving heating and melting: *tin smelting.* ■ extract a metal from (ore) in this way. [16th C.: from MDu., Mid. Low Ger. *smelten*; rel. to the verb MELT.]

smelt[2] past and past participle of SMELL.

smelt[3] ▶ **n.** (pl. same or **smelts** /smelts/) a small silvery food fish (family Osmeridae, *Osmerus* and other genera) that lives in both marine and fresh water and is sometimes fished commercially. [OE; obscurely rel. to various European names of fish; cf. SMOLT.]

smelt·er /ˈsmeltər/ ▶ **n.** an installation or factory for smelting a metal from its ore. ■ a person engaged in the business of smelting.

Sme·ta·na /ˈsmetn-ə/, Bedřich (1824–84), Czech composer. His operas include *The Bartered Bride* (1866).

smew /smyo͞o/ ▶ **n.** a small merganser (*Mergus albellus*) of northern Eurasia, the male of which has white plumage with a crest and fine black markings. [17th C.: akin to Du. *smient* 'wigeon' and Ger. *Schmeiente* 'small wild duck.']

smid·gen /ˈsmijin/ (also **smid·geon** or **smid·gin**) ▶ **n.** informal a very small amount of something. [19th C.: perh. from Scots *smitch*.]

smi·lax /ˈsmīlaks/ ▶ **n. 1** a widely distributed climbing shrub (genus *Smilax*) of the lily family. Several South American species yield sarsaparilla from their roots, and some are cultivated as ornamentals. **2** a climbing asparagus (*Asparagus asparagoides*) of the lily family, used by florists. [16th C.: via L. from Gk., lit. 'bindweed.']

smile /smīl/ ▶ **v.** [intrans.] form one's features into a pleased, kind, or amused expression, typically with the corners of the mouth turned up: [as adj.] (**smiling**) *smiling faces.* ■ [trans.] express (a feeling) with such an expression: *he smiled his admiration.* ■ [trans.] give (a smile) of a specified kind: *Linda smiled a grim smile.* ■ (**smile at/on/upon**) regard favorably or indulgently. ▶ **n.** a pleased, kind, or amused facial expression, typically with the corners of the mouth turned up and the front teeth exposed: *he flashed his most winning smile.*
– PHRASES **come up smiling** informal recover from adversity and cheerfully face what is to come. — **smil·er n. smil·ing·ly adv.** [ME: perh. of Scand. origin; rel. to SMIRK.]

Smi·ley /ˈsmīlē/, Jane Graves (1949–), US writer. Her novels include *A Thousand Acres* (1991).

smil·ey /ˈsmīlē/ ▶ **adj.** informal smiling; cheerful. ▶ **n.** a symbol that, when viewed sideways, represents a smiling face, formed by the characters :-) and used in electronic communications to indicate that the writer is pleased or joking.

smirch /smərCH/ ▶ **v.** [trans.] make (something) dirty; soil: *smirched by heat and smoke.* ■ fig. discredit (a person or their reputation); taint. ▶ **n.** a dirty mark or stain. ■ fig. a blot on someone's character; a flaw.

smirk /smərk/ ▶ **v.** [intrans.] smile in an irritatingly smug, conceited, or silly way. ▶ **n.** a smug, conceited, or silly smile: *a self-satisfied smirk.* — **smirk·er n. smirk·i·ly** /-kəlē/ **adv. smirk·ing·ly adv. smirk·y adj.** [OE *sme(a)rcian*, from a base shared by SMILE.]

smite /smīt/ ▶ **v.** (past **smote** /smōt/; past part. **smit·ten** /ˈsmitn/) [trans.] literary strike with a firm blow. ■ archaic defeat or conquer (a people or land). ■ (usu. **be smitten**) fig. (esp. of disease) attack or affect severely: *smitten with flu.* ■ (**be smitten**) be strongly attracted to someone or something. — **smit·er n.** [OE *smītan* 'to smear,' of Gmc. origin; rel. to Du. *smijten* and Ger. *schmeissen* 'to fling.']

Smith[1] /smiTH/, Adam (1723–90), Scottish economist and philosopher. He advocated minimal state interference in economic matters and discredited mercantilism.

Smith[2], Alfred Emanuel (1873–1944), US politician. The governor of New York 1919–20, 1923–28, he was the Democratic presidential candidate in 1928.

Smith[3], Bessie (1894–1937), US singer, noted for her blues singing in the 1920s.

Smith[4], David Roland (1906–65), US sculptor. His works include the *Cubi* series.

Smith[5], Ian Douglas (1919–), prime minister of Rhodesia 1965–79.

Smith[6], John (c.1580–1631), American colonist; born in England. He helped to found the colony of Jamestown in 1607. When captured by Indians he was rescued by Pocahontas.

Smith[7], Joseph (1805–44), US religious leader. He founded the Church of Jesus Christ of Latter-Day Saints (the Mormons) in 1827.

Smith[8], Kate (1909–86), US singer; full name *Kathryn Elizabeth Smith*. In 1938, she introduced Irving Berlin's "God Bless America."

Smith[9], Margaret Chase (1897–1995), US politician. A Republican from Maine, she was a US senator 1949–73.

smith /smiTH/ ▶ **n.** a worker in metal. ■ short for BLACKSMITH. [OE, of Gmc. origin; rel. to Ger. *Schmied*.]

-smith ▶ **comb. form** denoting a person skilled in creating something with a specified material: *goldsmith.*

smith·er·eens /ˌsmiT͟Həˈrēnz/ ▶ **plural n.** informal small pieces: *a grenade blew him to smithereens.*

smith·er·y /ˈsmiTHərē/ ▶ **n.** the work of or goods made by a smith.

Smith·so·ni·an In·sti·tu·tion /ˌsmiTHˈsōnēən/ a foundation for scientific research in Washington, DC, established in 1836, originated with a bequest from English chemist and mineralogist James Smithson (1765–1829).

smith·son·ite /ˈsmiTHsəˌnīt/ ▶ **n.** a yellow, gray, or green mineral consisting of zinc carbonate typically occurring as crusts or rounded masses. [19th C.: from the name *Smithson* (see SMITHSONIAN INSTITUTION) + -ITE[1].]

Smith·town /ˈsmiTHˌtoun/ a town in southeastern New York, on Long Island; pop. 113,406.

smith·y /ˈsmiTHē/ ▶ **n.** (pl. **smith·ies**) a blacksmith's workshop; a forge. ■ a blacksmith.

smit·ten /ˈsmitn/ past participle of SMITE.

smock /smäk/ ▶ **n.** a loose garment worn over one's clothes to protect them: *an artist's smock.* ▶ **v.** [trans.] [usu. as adj.] (**smocked**) decorate (something) with smocking: *smocked dresses.* [OE *smoc*; prob. rel. to OE *smūgan* 'to creep.']

smock·ing /ˈsmäkiNG/ ▶ **n.** decoration on a garment created by gathering a section of the material into tight pleats and holding them together with parallel stitches.

smog /smäg/ ▶ **n.** fog or haze intensified by smoke or other atmospheric pollutants. — **smog·gy adj.** [20th C.: blend of SMOKE and FOG.]

smoke /smōk/ ▶ **n.** a visible suspension of carbon or other particles in air, typically one emitted from a burning substance. ■ an act of smoking tobacco. ■ informal a cigarette or cigar. ▶ **v. 1** [intrans.] emit smoke or visible vapor: *heat the oil until it just smokes* | [as adj.] (**smoking**) *huddled around a smoking fire.* ■ inhale and exhale the smoke of tobacco or a drug: [as n.] (**smoking**) *the effects of smoking.* **2** [trans.] [often as adj.] (**smoked**) cure or preserve (meat or fish) by exposure to smoke: *smoked salmon.* ■ treat (glass) so as to darken it. ■ fumigate, cleanse, or purify by exposure to smoke. ■ subdue (insects, esp. bees) by exposing them to smoke. ■ (**smoke someone/something out**) drive someone or something out of a place by using smoke.
– PHRASES **go up in smoke** informal be destroyed by fire. ■ fig. (of a plan) come to nothing: *a dream about to go up in smoke.* **where there's smoke there's fire** proverb there's always some reason for a rumor. **smoke and mirrors** the obscuring or embellishing of the truth of a situation with misleading or irrelevant information: *the budget is an exercise in smoke and mirrors.* [referring to magic tricks.] — **smok·a·ble** (also **smoke·a·ble**) **adj.** [OE *smoca, smocian*, from the Gmc. base of *smēocan* 'emit smoke'; akin to Ger. *Schmauch*.]

smoke·box /ˈsmōk,bäks/ ▸ n. a device for catching or producing and containing smoke, in particular: ■ an oven for smoking food. ■ the chamber in a steam engine between the flues and the chimney stack.

smoke·bush /ˈsmōk,bŏŏsн/ (also **smoke bush**) ▸ n. another term for SMOKE TREE.

smoke de·tec·tor (also **smoke alarm**) ▸ n. a fire-protection device that automatically detects and gives a warning of the presence of smoke.

smoke·house /ˈsmōk,hous/ ▸ n. a shed or room for curing food by exposure to smoke.

smoke·jump·er /ˈsmōk,jəmpər/ (also **smoke jump·er**) ▸ n. a firefighter who arrives by parachute to extinguish a forest fire.

smoke·less /ˈsmōkləs/ ▸ adj. producing or emitting little or no smoke: *smokeless fuel.*

smoke·less to·bac·co ▸ n. tobacco that is chewed or snuffed rather than smoked by the user.

smok·er /ˈsmōkər/ ▸ n. **1** a person who smokes tobacco. ■ (also **smok·ing car**) a train compartment in which smoking is allowed. **2** a person or device that smokes fish or meat. **3** a device that emits smoke for subduing bees in a hive.

smoke screen (also **smoke·screen**) ▸ n. a cloud of smoke created to conceal military operations. ■ fig. a ruse designed to disguise someone's real intentions or activities.

smoke sig·nal ▸ n. a column of smoke used as a way of conveying a message to a distant person.

smoke·stack /ˈsmōk,stak/ ▸ n. a chimney or funnel for discharging smoke from a locomotive, ship, factory, etc. and helping to induce a draft. ■ [as adj.] pertaining to heavy industry: *America's smokestack cities.*

smoke tree ▸ n. a shrub or small tree (genus *Cotinus*) of the cashew family that bears long feathery plumes of flowers, giving it a smoky appearance.

smok·ing gun ▸ n. fig. a piece of incontrovertible incriminating evidence.

smok·ing jack·et ▸ n. a man's jacket, typically made of velvet, formerly worn while smoking after dinner.

smok·ing room ▸ n. a room set aside for smoking in a hotel or other public building.

smok·y /ˈsmōkē/ ▸ adj. (**smok·i·er, smok·i·est**) filled with or smelling of smoke: *a smoky office.* ■ producing or obscured by a great deal of smoke: *smoky factory chimneys.* ■ having the taste or aroma of smoked food: *smoky bacon.* ■ like smoke in color or appearance: *smoky eyes.* — **smok·i·ly** /-kəlē/ adv. **smok·i·ness** n.

Smok·y Hill Riv·er a river that flows for 540 miles (870 km) from Colorado across Kansas to the Republican River.

smok·y quartz ▸ n. a semiprecious variety of quartz ranging in color from light grayish-brown to nearly black.

smol·der /ˈsmōldər/ ▸ v. [intrans.] burn slowly with smoke but no flame. ■ show or feel barely suppressed anger, hatred, or another powerful emotion: *smoldering with indignation.* ■ exist in a suppressed or concealed state: *the controversy smoldered on* | [as adj.] (**smoldering**) *smoldering rage.* ▸ n. smoke coming from a fire that is burning slowly without a flame. — **smol·der·ing·ly** adv. [ME: rel. to Du. *smeulen.*]

Smo·lensk /smōˈlensk; sməˈlyensk/ a city in western Russia; pop. 346,000.

smolt /smōlt/ ▸ n. a young salmon (or trout) after the parr stage, when it becomes silvery and migrates to the sea for the first time. [ME (orig. Scots and north. Engl.); cf. SMELT[3].]

smooch /smōōcн/ informal ▸ v. [intrans.] kiss and cuddle amorously. ▸ n. a kiss or a spell of amorous kissing and cuddling. — **smooch·er** n. **smooch·y** adj. (**smooch·i·er, smooch·i·est**). [1930s: from dial. *smouch*, imitative.]

smooth /smōōтн/ ▸ adj. **1** even and regular; free from perceptible projections or indentations. ■ (of a person's face or skin) not wrinkled, pitted, or hairy. ■ (of a liquid) with an even consistency; without lumps. ■ (of the sea or another body of water) without heavy waves; calm. ■ (of movement) without jerks: *a smooth ride.* ■ (of an action, event, or process) without problems or difficulties. **2** (of food or drink) without harshness or bitterness: *a smooth, fruity wine.* ■ (of a person or their manner, actions, or words) suavely charming in a way considered to be unctuous: *his voice was infuriatingly smooth.* ▸ v. [trans.] give (something) a flat, regular surface or appearance by running one's hand over it: *she* ***smoothed out*** *the newspaper.* ■ rub off the rough edges of (something): *smooth the wood with sandpaper.* ■ deal successfully with (a problem, difficulty, or perceived fault): *disputes* ***smoothed over.*** ■ free (a course of action) from difficulties or problems: *a conference would be held to smooth the way for the establishment of the provisional government.* ▸ adv. archaic in a way that is without difficulties: *the course of true love never did run smooth.* — **smooth·a·ble** adj. **smooth·er** n. **smooth·ish** adj. **smooth·ly** adv. **smooth·ness** n. [OE *smōth*, prob. of Gmc. origin.]

smooth·bore /ˈsmōōтн,bôr/ ▸ n. [often as adj.] a gun with an unrifled barrel: *smoothbore muskets.*

smooth breath·ing ▸ n. see BREATHING (sense 2).

smooth hound ▸ n. a small European shark (genus *Mustelus*, family Triakidae) that typically lives close to the bottom in shallow waters.

smooth·ie /ˈsmōōтнē/ ▸ n. **1** informal a man with a smooth, suave manner. **2** a thick, smooth drink of fresh fruit puréed with milk, yogurt, or ice cream.

smooth mus·cle ▸ n. Physiol. muscle tissue in which the contractile fibrils are not highly ordered, occurring in the gut and other internal organs and not under voluntary control. Often contrasted with STRIATED MUSCLE.

smooth talk ▸ n. charming or flattering language, esp. when used to persuade someone to do something. ▸ v. (**smooth-talk**) [trans.] use such language to (someone), esp. to persuade them to do something. — **smooth talk·er** n.

smor·gas·bord /ˈsmôrgəs,bôrd/ ▸ n. a buffet offering hot and cold meats, salads, hors d'oeuvres, etc. ■ fig. a wide range of something; a variety: *a smorgasbord of different musical styles.* [Swed., from *smörgås* '(slice of) bread and butter' (from *smör* 'butter' + *gås* 'goose, lump of butter') + *bord* 'table.']

smor·zan·do /smôrtˈsändō/ Music ▸ adv. & adj. (esp. as a direction) dying away. [Ital., lit. 'extinguishing.']

smote /smōt/ past of SMITE.

smoth·er /ˈsməтнər/ ▸ v. [trans.] kill (someone) by covering their nose and mouth so that they suffocate. ■ extinguish (a fire) by covering it. ■ (**smother someone/something in/with**) cover someone or something entirely with: *smothered in cream* | fig. *smothered her with kisses.* ■ make (someone) feel trapped and oppressed by acting in an overly protective manner toward them. ■ suppress (a feeling or an action): *she smothered a sigh.* ■ cook in a covered container: [as adj.] (**smothered**) *smothered onions.* ▸ n. a mass of something that stifles or obscures: *a smother of foam.* — **smoth·er·y** adj. [ME: from the base of OE *smorian* 'suffocate.']

smoul·der /ˈsmōldər/ ▸ v. British spelling of SMOLDER.

SMPTE ▸ abbr. Society of Television and Motion Picture Engineers (used to denote a time coding system for synchronizing video and audiotapes).

smrit·i /ˈsmritē/ ▸ n. (pl. **smrit·is**) a Hindu religious text containing traditional teachings on religion. [from Sanskrit *smṛti* 'remembrance.']

SMS ▸ abbr. short message (or messaging) service, a system that enables cellular phone users to send and receive text messages. ▸ n. a text message that is sent or received using SMS.

smudge[1] /sməj/ ▸ n. a blurred or smeared mark on the surface of something. ▸ v. [trans.] cause (something) to become messily smeared by rubbing it: *don't smudge your makeup.* ■ [intrans.] become smeared when rubbed: *mascaras that smudge.* ■ make blurred or indistinct: *smudged by the photocopier.* — **smudge·less** adj. [ME: of unknown origin.]

smudge[2] ▸ n. a smoky outdoor fire that is lit to keep off insects or protect plants against frost. [18th C.: of unknown origin; rel. to obs. *smudge* 'cure (herring) by smoking,' of obscure origin.]

smudge pot ▸ n. a container for a smudge (see SMUDGE[2]).

smudg·y /ˈsməjē/ ▸ adj. (**smudg·i·er, smudg·i·est**) smeared or blurred from being smudged: *a smudgy photograph.* — **smudg·i·ly** /-jəlē/ adv. **smudg·i·ness** n.

smug /sməg/ ▸ adj. (**smug·ger, smug·gest**) having or showing an excessive pride in oneself or one's achievements. — **smug·ly** adv. **smug·ness** n. [16th C.: from Low Ger. *smuk* 'pretty.']

smug·gle /ˈsməgəl/ ▸ v. [trans.] move (goods) illegally into or out of a country: [as n.] (**smuggling**) *cocaine smuggling.* ■ [trans.] convey (someone or something) somewhere secretly and illicitly. — **smug·gler** /ˈsməg(ə)lər/ n. [17th C.: from Low Ger. *smuggelen*, of unknown ultimate origin.]

smush /sməsн; smŏŏsн/ ▸ v. [trans.] informal crush; smash: *they smushed marshmallows in their mouths.* [19th C.: alt. of MUSH[1].]

smut /smət/ ▸ n. **1** a small flake of soot or other dirt. ■ a mark or smudge made by such a flake. **2** a disease of grains in which parts of the ear change to black powder, caused by a fungus of the order Ustilaginales. **3** obscene or lascivious talk, writing, or pictures. ▸ v. (**smut·ted, smut·ting**) [trans.] [often as adj.] (**smutted**) **1** mark with flakes or soot or other dirt. **2** infect (a plant) with smut: *smutted wheat.* — **smut·ti·ly** /-təlē/ adv. **smut·ti·ness** n. **smut·ty** adj. (**smut·ti·er, smut·ti·est**). [ME (in the sense 'defile, corrupt, make obscene'): rel. to Ger. *schmutzen.*]

Smuts /sməts; smʏts/, Jan Christiaan (1870–1950), prime minister of South Africa 1919–24, 1939–48. He led Boer forces during the Second Boer War.

Smyr·na /ˈsmərnə/ an ancient city on the western coast of Asia Minor, on the site of modern Izmir in Turkey.

Sn ▸ symb. the chemical element tin. [from late L. *stannum* 'tin.']

s.n. ▸ abbr. without name. [from L. *sine nomine.*]

snack /snak/ ▸ n. a small amount of food eaten between meals. ■ a light meal that is eaten in a hurry or in a casual manner. ▸ v. [intrans.] eat a snack. [ME: from MDu. *snac(k)*, from *snacken* 'to bite,' var. of *snappen.*]

snaf·fle /ˈsnafəl/ ▸ n. (also **snaffle bit**) (on a bridle) a simple bit, typically a jointed one, used with a single set of reins. [16th C.: prob. from Low Ger. or Du.; cf. Mid. Low Ger., MDu. *snavel* 'beak, mouth.']

sna·fu /snaˈfōō/ informal ▸ n. a confused or chaotic state; a mess. ▸ adj. in utter confusion or chaos. [1940s: acronym from *situation normal: all fouled (or fucked) up.*]

snag /snag/ ▸ n. **1** an unexpected or hidden obstacle or drawback: *the picture's US release* ***hit a snag.*** **2** a sharp, angular, or jagged projection: *an emery board for nail snags.* ■ a rent or tear in fabric caused by such a projection. **3** a dead tree. ▸ v. (**snagged, snag·ging**) [trans.] catch or tear (something) on a projection: *thorns snagged his sweater.* ■ [intrans.] become caught on a projection: *his clothing* ***snagged on*** *bushes.* ■ informal catch or obtain (someone or something): *they've snagged the star for a photo.* — **snag·gy** adj. (in sense 2). [16th C. (sense 2): prob. of Scand. origin]

snag·gle /'snagəl/ ▶ n. a tangled or knotted mass: fig. *a snaggle of import restrictions.*

snag·gle·tooth /'snagəl,to͞oTH/ ▶ n. **1** (pl. **-teeth** /-,tēTH/) an irregular or projecting tooth. **2** (pl. **-tooths**) a small deep-sea fish (family Astronesthidae) with large fangs at the front of the jaws and a number of light organs on the body. — **snag·gle·toothed** adj.

snail /snāl/ ▶ n. a mollusk (class Gastropoda) with a single spiral shell into which the whole body can be withdrawn. ■ (in metaphorical use) any person or thing that moves exceedingly slowly. — **snail·like** /-,līk/ adj. [OE *snæg(e)l*, of Gmc. origin; rel. to Ger. *Schnecke*.]

snail dart·er ▶ n. a small percoid freshwater fish of a type found in US rivers, now nearly extinct.

snail·fish /'snāl,fiSH/ ▶ n. (pl. same or **-fish·es**) a small fish (*Liparis* and other genera, family Cyclopteridae) of cool or cold seas, with loose jellylike skin and typically a ventral sucker. Also called **SEA SNAIL**.

snail mail ▶ n. informal the ordinary postal system as opposed to electronic mail.

snake /snāk/ ▶ n. **1** a long limbless reptile (suborder Ophidia or Serpentes) that has no eyelids, and jaws that are capable of considerable extension. Some snakes have a venomous bite. ■ (in general use) a limbless lizard or amphibian. **2** (also **snake in the grass**) a treacherous or deceitful person. **3** (in full **plumber's snake**) a long flexible wire for clearing obstacles in pipes. ▶ v. [intrans.] move or extend with the twisting motion of a snake: *a rope snaked down.* — **snake·like** /-,līk/ adj. [OE *snaca*, of Gmc. origin.]

snake·bird /'snāk,bərd/ ▶ n. another term for **ANHINGA**.

snake·bite /'snāk,bīt/ ▶ n. the bite of a snake, esp. a venomous one. ■ the medical condition resulting from a snakebite.

snake charm·er ▶ n. an entertainer who appears to make snakes move by playing music.

snake dance ▶ n. a dance in which the performers handle live snakes or imitate the motions of snakes, in particular a ritual dance of the Hopi Indians.

snake eyes ▶ plural n. [treated as sing.] a throw of two ones with a pair of dice. ■ fig. the worst possible result; a complete lack of success: *his book sadly came up snake eyes.*

snake fence (also **snake-rail fence**) ▶ n. a fence made of roughly split rails or poles joined in a zigzag pattern.

snake fly ▶ n. a slender woodland insect (family Raphidiidae, order Neuroptera) with a long "neck" that allows the head to be raised above the body.

snake·head /snāk,hed/ ▶ n. a freshwater fish (family Channidae) with a long cylindrical body, native to tropical Africa and Asia.

snake mack·er·el ▶ n. another term for **ESCOLAR**.

snake oil ▶ n. informal a substance with no real medicinal value sold as a remedy for all diseases.

snake pit ▶ n. a pit containing poisonous snakes. ■ fig. a scene of vicious behavior or ruthless competition. ■ fig. a place of overcrowded squalor, esp. a poorly run mental hospital. [1946: from the title of a novel by Mary Jane Ward.]

Snake Riv·er a river that flows for 1,038 miles (1,670 km) from Yellowstone National Park in Wyoming through Idaho to the Columbia River in Washington.

snake·root /'snak,ro͞ot; -,ro͝ot/ ▶ n. **1** any of a number of North American plants reputed to contain an antidote to snake poison, in particular: ■ (**Virginia snakeroot**) a birthwort (*Aristolochia serpentaria*) with long heart-shaped leaves and curved tubular flowers. ■ (**white snakeroot**) a poisonous plant (*Eupatorium rugosum*) of the daisy family that causes milk sickness in livestock. **2** any of a number of plants thought to resemble a snake in shape, in particular **Indian snakeroot** (see **RAUWOLFIA**).

snake·skin /'snāk,skin/ ▶ n. [often as adj.] the skin of a snake: *snakeskin boots.*

snake·weed /'snāk,wēd/ ▶ n. **1** another term for **SNAKEROOT**. **2** old-fashioned term for **BISTORT**.

snake·wood /'snāk,wo͝od/ ▶ n. **1** a tree or shrub that has wood from which a snakebite antidote or other medicinal extract is obtained, esp. the tree *Strychnos minor* (family Loganiaceae), of the Indian subcontinent. **2** a tropical American tree (*Brosimum rubescens*) of the mulberry family that has timber with a snakeskin pattern, used for decorative work.

snak·y /'snākē/ ▶ adj. (**snak·i·er**, **snak·i·est**) like a snake in appearance; long and sinuous. ■ of the supposed nature of a snake in showing coldness, venom, or cunning. — **snak·i·ly** /-kəlē/ adv. **snak·i·ness** n.

snap /snap/ ▶ v. (**snapped**, **snap·ping**) **1** break or cause to break suddenly and completely, typically with a sharp cracking sound. ■ [intrans.] emit a sudden, sharp cracking sound. ■ [intrans.] (of an animal) make a sudden audible bite: *a dog was snapping at his heels.* ■ [trans.] cause to move in a specified way with a brisk movement and typically a sharp sound: *she snapped her bag shut.* ■ [intrans.] fig. suddenly lose one's self-control: *she snapped after years of violence.* ■ [reporting verb] say something quickly and irritably to someone: [intrans.] *the clerk snapped at me.* **2** [trans.] take a snapshot of: [intrans.] *photographers were snapping away at her.* **3** [trans.] Football put (the ball) into play by a quick backward movement from the ground. **4** [trans.] fasten with snaps: *she snapped the baby's sweater.* ▶ n. **1** a sudden, sharp cracking sound or movement: *the rope broke with a loud snap.* ■ [in sing.] a hurried, irritable tone or manner: *"I'm still waiting," he said with a snap.* **2** (usu. **snaps**) a small fastener on clothing, engaged by pressing its two halves together. **3** [in sing.] informal an easy task: *a control panel that makes operation a snap.* **4** Football a quick backward movement of the ball from the ground that begins a play. ▶ adj. [attrib.] done or taken on the spur of the moment, unexpectedly, or without notice: *a snap judgment.*

– PHRASES **in a snap** informal in a moment; almost immediately: *ready in a snap.*

– PHRASAL VERBS **snap back** recover quickly and easily from an illness or period of difficulty. **snap out of** [often in imper.] informal get out of (a bad or unhappy mood) by a sudden effort. [15th C.: prob. from MDu. or Mid. Low Ger. *snappen* 'seize'; partly imitative.]

snap-ac·tion ▶ adj. [attrib.] **1** denoting a switch or relay that makes and breaks contact rapidly, whatever the speed of the activating mechanism. **2** denoting a gun whose hinged barrel is secured by a spring catch. ▶ n. (**snap action**) the operation of such a switch, relay, or gun.

snap bean ▶ n. a crisp bean of a variety grown for its edible pods.

snap-brim ▶ adj. (of a hat) with a brim that can be turned up and down at opposite sides.

snap·drag·on /'snap,dragən/ ▶ n. a plant (genus *Antirrhinum*) of the figwort family, bearing spikes of brightly colored two-lobed flowers that gape like a mouth when a bee lands on the curved lip.

snap pea ▶ n. another term for **SUGAR SNAP**.

snap·per /'snapər/ ▶ n. **1** a marine fish of a widespread tropical family (Lutjanidae, the **snapper family**) that snaps its toothed jaws. **2** another term for **SNAPPING TURTLE**.

common snapping turtle

snap·ping tur·tle ▶ n. a large American freshwater turtle (family Chelydridae) with a long neck and strong hooked jaws. Two North American species include the **common snapping turtle** (*Chelydra serpentina*) and the larger **alligator snapping turtle** (*Macroclemys temminckii*).

snap·pish /'snapiSH/ ▶ adj. irritable and curt. — **snap·pish·ly** adv. **snap·pish·ness** n.

snap·py /'snapē/ ▶ adj. (**snap·pi·er**, **snap·pi·est**) informal **1** irritable and inclined to speak sharply; snappish. **2** clever: *snappy slogans.* ■ stylish; elegant: *a snappy dresser.*

– PHRASES **make it snappy** be quick about it. — **snap·pi·ly** /-pəlē/ adv. **snap·pi·ness** n.

snap·shot /'snap,SHät/ ▶ n. an informal photograph taken quickly, typically with a small hand-held camera. ■ a brief look or summary: *a snapshot of a complex industry.*

snare /sne(ə)r/ ▶ n. **1** a trap for catching birds or animals, typically one having a noose of wire or cord. ■ fig. a thing likely to lure or tempt someone into harm or error. ■ Surg. a wire loop for severing polyps or other growths. **2** a length of wire, gut, or hide stretched across a drumhead to produce a rattling sound. ■ short for **SNARE DRUM**. ▶ v. [trans.] catch (a bird or mammal) in a snare. ■ fig. catch or trap (someone): *I snared a passing waiter.* — **snar·er** n. [OE *sneare*, from ON *snara*.]

snare drum ▶ n. a short cylindrical drum with a membrane at each end, the upper one being struck with hard sticks and the lower one fitted with snares. See illustration at **DRUM KIT**. [prob. from Mid. Low Ger., MDu. *snare* 'harp string.']

snark /snärk/ ▶ n. an imaginary animal (used to refer to someone or something that is difficult to track down). [1876: coined by Lewis Carroll.]

snark·y /'snärkē/ ▶ adj. (**snark·i·er**, **snark·i·est**) informal (of a person, words, or a mood) critical; cutting; testy.

snarl[1] /snärl/ ▶ v. [intrans.] (of an animal such as a dog) make an aggressive growl with bared teeth. ■ [reporting verb] (of a person) say something in an angry, bad-tempered voice: *I used to snarl at everyone.* ▶ n. an act or sound of snarling. — **snarl·er** n. **snarl·ing·ly** adv. **snarl·y** adj. [16th C.: from *snar*, of Gmc. origin; rel. to Ger. *schnarren* 'rattle, snarl,' prob. imitative.]

snarl[2] ▶ v. [trans.] **1** entangle or impede something: *snarled up in traffic.* **2** decorate (metalwork) with raised shapes by hammering the underside. ▶ n. a knot or tangle. [ME: from **SNARE**.]

snatch /snaCH/ ▶ v. [trans.] quickly seize (something) in a rude or eager way. ■ informal steal (something) or kidnap (someone), typically by seizing or grabbing suddenly: *someone snatched my handbag.* ■ [intrans.] (**snatch at**) hastily or ineffectually attempt to seize (something): *she snatched at the handle.* ■ quickly secure or obtain (something) when a chance presents itself: *snatch a few hours of sleep.* ▶ **n. 1** an act of snatching or quickly seizing something: *a quick snatch of breath.* ■ a short spell of doing something: *snatches of sleep.* ■ a fragment of song or talk. ■ informal a kidnapping or theft. **2** Weightlifting the rapid raising of a weight from the floor to above the head in one movement. — **snatch·er n.** [ME *sna(c)che* (v.) 'suddenly snap at,' (n.) 'a snare'; perh. rel. to SNACK.]

snaz·zy /'snazē/ ▶ **adj.** (**snaz·zi·er, snaz·zi·est**) informal stylish and attractive: *snazzy little silk dresses.* — **snaz·zi·ly** /-zəlē/ **adv. snaz·zi·ness n.** [1960s: of unknown origin.]

Snead /snēd/, Sam (1912–2002), US golfer; full name *Samuel Jackson Snead.* During 1936–65, he had a record 81 PGA Tour wins.

sneak /snēk/ ▶ **v.** (past **sneaked** or informal **snuck** /'snək/) [intrans.] move or go in a furtive or stealthy manner. ■ [trans.] convey (someone or something) in such a way: *someone sneaked a camera inside.* ■ [trans.] do or obtain (something) in a stealthy or furtive way: *she sneaked a glance at her watch.* ■ (**sneak up on**) creep up on (someone) without being detected. ▶ **n.** informal a furtive person: *branded a prying sneak for eavesdropping.* ▶ **adj.** [attrib.] acting or done surreptitiously, unofficially, or without warning: *a sneak preview.* [16th C.: prob. dial.; perh. rel. to obs. *snike* 'to creep.']

sneak·box /'snēk,bäks/ ▶ **n.** a small, flat boat masked with brush or weeds, used in wildfowl hunting.

sneak·er /'snēkər/ ▶ **n.** a soft shoe with a rubber sole worn for sports or casual occasions.

sneak·ing /'snēkiNG/ ▶ **adj.** [attrib.] (of a feeling) persistent in one's mind but reluctantly held or not fully recognized; nagging.

sneak·y /'snēkē/ ▶ **adj.** (**sneak·i·er, sneak·i·est**) furtive; sly: *sneaky, underhanded tactics.* — **sneak·i·ly** /-kəlē/ **adv. sneak·i·ness n.**

sneer /sni(ə)r/ ▶ **n.** a contemptuous or mocking smile, remark, or tone. ▶ **v.** [intrans.] smile or speak in a contemptuous or mocking manner: *she sneered at my decor.* — **sneer·er n. sneer·ing·ly adv.** [ME: prob. imitative.]

sneeze /snēz/ ▶ **v.** [intrans.] make a sudden involuntary expulsion of air from the nose and mouth due to irritation of one's nostrils. ▶ **n.** an act or the sound of expelling air from the nose in such a way. — **sneez·er n. sneez·y adj.** [ME: appar. an alt. of ME *fnese* due to misreading or misprinting (after initial *fn-* had become unfamiliar).]

sneeze·weed /'snēz,wēd/ ▶ **n.** a yellow-flowered North American plant (genus *Helenium*) of the daisy family. Some kinds are toxic to grazing animals and some are used medicinally, esp. by American Indians.

sneeze·wort /'snēzwərt; -wôrt/ (also **sneezewort yarrow**) ▶ **n.** a Eurasian yarrow (*Achillea ptarmica*), naturalized in North America, whose dried leaves induce sneezing.

snell /snel/ ▶ **n.** a short line (typically of nylon) by which a fishhook is attached to a longer line. ▶ **v.** [trans.] tie or fasten (a hook) to a line: [as adj.] (**snelled**) *a snelled hook.* [19th C.: of unknown origin.]

Snell's law /snelz/ Physics a law stating that the ratio of the sines of the angles of incidence and refraction of a wave are constant when it passes between two given media. [19th C.: named after Willebrord Van Roijen *Snell* (1591–1626), Dutch mathematician.]

snick /snik/ ▶ **v.** [trans.] **1** cut a small notch or incision in (something). **2** cause (something) to make a sharp clicking sound. ■ [intrans.] make such a sound: *the bolt snicked into place.* ▶ **n. 1** a small notch or cut: *he had several shaving snicks.* **2** a sharp click: *the snick of the latch.* [17th C.: prob. from obs. *snick or snee* 'fight with knives.']

snick·er /'snikər/ ▶ **v.** [intrans.] give a smothered or half-suppressed laugh; snigger. ■ (of a horse) whinny. ▶ **n.** a smothered laugh; a snigger. ■ a whinny. — **snick·er·ing·ly adv.** [17th C.: imitative.]

snide /snīd/ ▶ **adj.** derogatory or mocking in an indirect way: *snide remarks.* ■ (of a person) devious and underhanded. — **snide·ly adv. snide·ness n.** [19th C.: of unknown origin.]

sniff /snif/ ▶ **v.** [intrans.] draw in air audibly through the nose: *his dog sniffed at my sleeve.* ■ [trans.] draw in (a scent, substance, or air) through the nose. ■ [usu. with negative] (**sniff at**) show contempt or dislike for: *the price is not to be sniffed at.* ■ (**sniff around**) informal investigate covertly, esp. to find out confidential or incriminating information about someone. ■ [trans.] (**sniff something out**) informal discover something by investigation: *sniffing out tax loopholes.* ▶ **n.** an act or sound of drawing air through the nose: *a sniff of disapproval.* ■ an amount of air or other substance taken up in such a way: *a sniff of amyl nitrite.* ■ [in sing.] informal a trace, hint, or small amount: *the first sniff of trouble.* [ME: imitative.]

sniff·er /'snifər/ ▶ **n. 1** a person who sniffs, esp. one who sniffs a drug or toxic substance: [with adj.] *a glue sniffer.* ■ informal a device for detecting an invisible and dangerous substance, such as gas or radiation. **2** informal a person's nose.

snif·fle /'snifəl/ ▶ **v.** [intrans.] sniff slightly or repeatedly, typically because of a cold or crying. ▶ **n.** an act of sniffing in such a way. ■ a head cold causing a running nose and sniffing: *a slight cough and a sniffle.* — **snif·fler** /'snif(ə)lər/ **n. snif·fly** /'snif(ə)lē/ **adj.** [17th C.: imitative.]

snif·fy /'snifē/ ▶ **adj.** (**snif·fi·er, snif·fi·est**) informal scornful; contemptuous. — **sniff·i·ly** /-fəlē/ **adv. sniff·i·ness n.**

snif·ter /'sniftər/ ▶ **n.** a footed glass that is wide at the bottom and tapers to the top, used for brandy and other drinks.

snig·ger /'snigər/ ▶ **n.** a smothered or half-suppressed laugh. ▶ **v.** [intrans.] give such a laugh: *they snigger at him behind his back.* — **snig·ger·er n. snig·ger·ing·ly adv.** [18th C.: later var. of SNICKER.]

snig·gle /'snigəl/ ▶ **v.** [intrans.] fish for eels by pushing a baited hook into holes in which they are hiding. [17th C.: frequentative, based on earlier *snig* 'small eel,' of unknown origin.]

snip /snip/ ▶ **v.** (**snipped, snip·ping**) [trans.] cut (something) with scissors with small quick strokes. ▶ **n. 1** an act of cutting something in such a way. ■ a small piece of something that has been cut off: *snips of wallpaper.* **2** informal a small or insignificant person. **3** (**snips**) hand shears for cutting metal: *tin snips.* [16th C.: from Low Ger. *snip* 'small piece,' of imitative origin.]

snipe /snīp/ ▶ **n.** (pl. same or **snipes**) a wading bird (*Gallinago* and other genera) of the sandpiper family, living in marshes and wet meadows, with brown camouflaged plumage and a long straight bill. ▶ **v.** [intrans.] shoot at someone from a hiding place, esp. at long range. ■ make a sly or petty verbal attack: *the brothers sniped at each other.* — **snip·er n.** [ME: prob. of Scand. origin; cf. Icelandic *mýrisnípa*; akin to Ger. *Schnepfe.*]

snipe eel ▶ **n.** a slender marine eel (family Nemichthyidae) with a long, thin, beaklike snout, typically occurring in deep water.

snip·pet /'snipit/ ▶ **n.** a small piece or brief extract: *snippets of information.*

snip·py /'snipē/ ▶ **adj.** (**snip·pi·er, snip·pi·est**) informal curt or sharp, esp. in a condescending way. — **snip·pi·ly** /-pəlē/ **adv. snip·pi·ness n.**

snit /snit/ ▶ **n.** informal a fit of irritation; a sulk: *the ambassador had withdrawn in a snit.*

snitch /sniCH/ informal ▶ **v. 1** [trans.] steal. **2** [intrans.] inform on someone. ▶ **n.** an informer. [17th C.: of unknown origin.]

sniv·el /'snivəl/ ▶ **v.** (**sniv·eled, sniv·el·ing**; Brit. **sniv·elled, sniv·el·ling**) [intrans.] cry and sniffle. ■ complain in a whining or tearful way. ▶ **n.** a slight sniff indicating suppressed emotion or crying: *Debra's torrent of howls weakened to a snivel.* — **sniv·el·er n. sniv·el·ing·ly adv.** [OE (in the verbal noun *snyflung* 'mucus'), from *snofl*; cf. SNUFFLE.]

snob /snäb/ ▶ **n.** a person with an exaggerated respect for high social position who dislikes people or activities regarded as lower-class. ■ [with adj.] a person who believes that their tastes in a particular area are superior to those of other people: *a wine snob.* — **snob·ber·y** /-bərē/ **n.** (pl. **-ber·ies**) **snob·bish adj. snob·bism** /-,bizəm/ **n. snob·by adj.** (**-bi·er, -bi·est**). [18th C.: of unknown origin; early senses conveyed a notion of 'lower status or rank,' later denoting a person seeking to imitate those of superior social standing or wealth.]

sno-cone ▶ **n.** var. of SNOW CONE.

snood /sno͝od/ ▶ **n. 1** an ornamental hairnet or fabric bag worn over the hair at the back of a woman's head. ■ hist. a hair ribbon or band worn by unmarried women in Scotland. **2** a wide ring of knitted material worn as a hood or scarf. [OE *snōd*, of unknown origin.]

snook /sno͝ok/ ▶ **n.** a large edible game fish (*Centropomus undecimalis*, family Centropomidae) of the Caribbean that is sometimes found in brackish water. [17th C.: from Du. *snoek* 'pike.']

snook·er /'sno͝okər/ ▶ **n.** a game played with cues on a billiard table in which the players use a cue ball to pocket the other balls in a set order. ▶ **v.** fig. trick, entice, or trap: *they were **snookered into** buying too high.* [19th C.: of unknown origin.]

snoop /sno͞op/ informal ▶ **v.** [intrans.] investigate or look around furtively in an attempt to find out something, esp. information about someone's private affairs. ▶ **n.** a person who snoops. — **snoop·er n. snoop·y adj.** [19th C.: from Du. *snœpen* 'eat on the sly.']

snoop·er·scope /'sno͞opər,skōp/ ▶ **n.** a device that converts infrared radiation into a visible image, used for seeing in the dark.

snoot /sno͞ot/ ▶ **n. 1** informal a person's nose. **2** informal a person who shows contempt for those considered to be of a lower social class; a snob. [19th C.: var. of SNOUT.]

snoot·ful /'sno͞ot,fo͝ol/ ▶ **n.** enough alcoholic drink to make one drunk: *they've **had a snootful**.*

snoot·y /'sno͞otē/ ▶ **adj.** (**snoot·i·er, snoot·i·est**) informal showing disapproval toward others, esp. those considered to be of a lower social class. — **snoot·i·ly** /'sno͞otl-ē/ **adv. snoot·i·ness n.**

snooze /sno͞oz/ informal ▶ **n.** a short, light sleep, esp. during the day; a nap. ■ a boring event or person: *the job's a snooze.* ▶ **v.** [intrans.] have a short, light sleep: *the adults snooze in the sun.* — **snooz·er** /'sno͞ozər/ **n. snooz·y** /'sno͞ozē/ **adj.** (**snooz·i·er, snooz·i·est**). [18th C.: of unknown origin.]

snooze but·ton ▶ **n.** a control on a clock that sets an alarm to repeat after a short interval, allowing time for a little more sleep.

snore /snôr/ ▶ **n.** a snorting or grunting sound in a person's breathing while asleep. ▶ **v.** [intrans.] breathe with a snorting or grunting sound while asleep: [as n.] (**snoring**) *I'm awake all night with your snoring.* — **snor·er n.** [ME: prob. imitative; cf. SNORT.]

snor·kel /'snôrkəl/ ▶ **n.** a short curved tube for a swimmer to breathe through while keeping the face under water. ▶ **v.** (**-keled, -kel·ing**; Brit. **-kel·led, -kel·ling**) [intrans.] [often as n.]

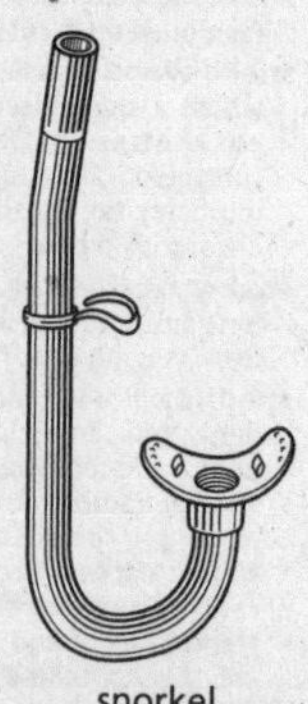
snorkel

(**snorkeling**) swim using a snorkel. — **snor·kel·er** n. [1940s: from Ger. *Schnorchel*.]

Snor·ri Stur·lu·son /'snôrē 'stərləsən/ (1178–1241), Icelandic historian and poet. He wrote the *Heimskringla*, a history of the kings of Norway from mythical times to 1177.

snort /snôrt/ ▶ n. an explosive sound made by the sudden forcing of breath through a person's nose, used to express indignation, derision, or incredulity: *he gave a snort of disgust.* ■ a similar sound made by an animal, typically when excited or frightened. ■ informal an inhaled dose of an illegal powdered drug, esp. cocaine. ■ informal a measure of an alcoholic drink. ▶ v. [intrans.] make a sudden sound through one's nose, esp. to express indignation or derision: *she snorted with laughter.* ■ (of an animal) make such a sound, esp. when excited or frightened. ■ [trans.] informal inhale (an illegal drug). [ME: prob. imitative; cf. SNORE.]

snot /snät/ ▶ n. informal nasal mucus. ■ an obnoxious or disagreeable person. [ME: prob. from MDu., Mid. Low Ger.; rel. to SNOUT.]

snot·ty /'snätē/ ▶ adj. (-ti·er, -ti·est) informal **1** full of or covered with nasal mucus. **2** having or showing a superior or conceited attitude: *a snotty letter.* — **snot·ti·ly** /-tl-ē/ adv. **snot·ti·ness** n.

snout /snout/ ▶ n. the projecting nose and mouth of an animal, esp. a mammal. ■ derog. a person's nose. ■ the projecting front or end of something such as a pistol. — **snout·ed** adj. [often in comb.] *long-snouted baboons.* [ME: from MDu., Mid. Low Ger. *snūt*; rel. to SNOT.]

snout bee·tle ▶ n. another term for WEEVIL.

Snow /snō/, C. P., 1st Baron Snow of Leicester (1905–80), English novelist and scientist; full name *Charles Percy Snow*. His novels deal with moral dilemmas in the academic world.

snow /snō/ ▶ n. **1** atmospheric water vapor frozen into ice crystals and falling in light white flakes or lying on the ground as a white layer. **2** something that resembles snow in color or texture, in particular: ■ a mass of flickering white spots on a television or radar screen, caused by interference or a poor signal. ■ informal cocaine. ▶ v. **1** [intrans.] (**it snows, it is snowing**, etc.) (of snow) to fall: *it's snowing heavily now.* ■ (**be snowed in**) be confined or blocked by a large quantity of snow. **2** [trans.] informal mislead (someone) with elaborate and insincere words: *snow the public into believing that all was well.*
– PHRASAL VERBS **snow someone under** (usu. **be snowed under**) overwhelm someone with a large quantity of something, esp. work. — **snow·less** adj. **snow·like** /-,līk/ adj. [OE *snāw*, of Gmc. origin; rel. to Du. *sneeuw* and Ger. *Schnee*, from an Indo-Eur. root shared by L. *nix, niv-* and Gk. *nipha*.]

snow·ball /'snō,bôl/ ▶ n. a ball of packed snow, esp. one made for throwing at other people for fun. ▶ v. **1** [trans.] throw snowballs at: *the other kids stopped snowballing Karen.* **2** [intrans.] increase rapidly in size, intensity, or importance: *the campaign was snowballing.*
– PHRASES **a snowball's chance (in hell)** informal no chance at all.

snow·bell /'snō,bel/ ▶ n. an Asian tree (*Styrax japonica*) related to the storax, bearing clusters of fragrant white hanging flowers at midsummer, widely cultivated as an ornamental.

snow·ber·ry /'snō,berē/ ▶ n. a North American shrub (*Symphoricarpos albus*) of the honeysuckle family, bearing white berries and often cultivated as an ornamental or for hedging.

snow·bird /'snō,bərd/ ▶ n. **1** informal a northerner who moves to a warmer southern state in the winter. **2** a widespread and variable junco (*Junco hyemalis*) with gray or brown upper parts and a white belly. Also called **northern junco, dark-eyed junco, slate-colored junco.**

snow-blind ▶ adj. temporarily blinded by the glare of light reflected by a large expanse of snow. — **snow blind·ness** n.

snow·blow·er /'snō,blōwər/ ▶ n. a machine that clears fallen snow by blowing it to the side.

snow·board /'snō,bôrd/ ▶ n. a board resembling a short, broad ski, used for sliding downhill on snow. ▶ v. [intrans.] slide downhill on such a board: [as n.] (**snowboarding**) *the thrills of snowboarding.* — **snow·board·er** n.

snow·bound /'snō,bound/ ▶ adj. prevented from traveling or going out by snow or snowy weather: *snowbound in the mountains.*

snow bunt·ing ▶ n. a northern bunting (*Plectrophenax nivalis*) that breeds mainly in the Arctic, the male having white plumage with a black back in the breeding season.

snow·cap /'snō,kap/ ▶ n. a covering of snow on the top of a mountain. — **snow-capped** adj.

snow chains ▶ plural n. a pair or set of meshes of metal chain, fitted around a vehicle's tires to give extra traction in snow.

snow cone (also **sno-cone**) ▶ n. a paper cup of crushed ice flavored with fruit syrup.

snow crab ▶ n. an edible spider crab (*Chionoecetes opilio*) found off the eastern seaboard of Canada.

snow·drift /'snō,drift/ ▶ n. a bank of deep snow heaped up by the wind.

snow·drop /'snō,dräp/ ▶ n. a widely cultivated bulbous European plant (*Galanthus nivalis*) of the lily family that bears drooping white flowers during the late winter.

snow·fall /'snō,fôl/ ▶ n. a fall of snow. ■ the quantity of snow falling within a given area in a given time: *above-average snowfall.*

snow·field /'snō,fēld/ ▶ n. a permanent wide expanse of snow in mountainous or polar regions.

snow·flake /'snō,flāk/ ▶ n. **1** a flake of snow, esp. a feathery ice crystal, typically displaying delicate sixfold symmetry. **2** a white-flowered Eurasian plant (Genus *Leucojum*) related to and resembling the snowdrop, typically blooming in the summer or autumn.

snow goose ▶ n. a gregarious goose (*Anser caerulescens*) that breeds in Arctic Canada and Greenland, typically having white plumage with black wing tips.

snow job ▶ n. informal a deception or concealment of one's real motive in an attempt to flatter or persuade.

snow leop·ard ▶ n. a rare large Asian cat (*Panthera uncia*) that has pale gray fur patterned with dark blotches and rings. Also called OUNCE².

snow line ▶ n. (usu. **the snow line**) the altitude above which some snow remains on the ground in a particular place throughout the year.

snow·man /'snō,man/ ▶ n. (pl. **-men**) a representation of a human figure created with compressed snow.

snow·melt /'snō,melt/ ▶ n. the melting of fallen snow: *heavy rains combine with rapid snowmelt.*

snowmobile

snow·mo·bile /'snōmō,bēl/ ▶ n. a motor vehicle, esp. one with runners in the front and caterpillar tracks in the rear, for traveling over snow. ▶ v. [intrans.] travel by snowmobile: [as n.] (**snowmobiling**) *the resort offers snowmobiling and ice fishing.* — **snow·mo·bil·er** n.

snow pea ▶ n. a pea of a variety with an edible pod, eaten when the pod is young and flat. Compare with SUGAR SNAP.

snow·plow /'snō,plou/ (Brit. **snow·plough**) ▶ n. **1** an implement or vehicle for clearing roads of snow by pushing it aside. **2** Skiing an act of turning the points of one's skis inward in order to slow down or turn. ▶ v. [intrans.] ski with the tips of one's skis pointing inward in order to slow down or turn.

snow·shoe /'snō,sʜo͞o/ ▶ n. a flat device resembling a racket that is attached to the sole of a boot and used for walking on snow. ▶ v. [intrans.] travel wearing snowshoes: *we snowshoed into the next valley.* — **snow·sho·er** /-ər/ n. **snow·shoe·ing** /-iɴɢ/ n.

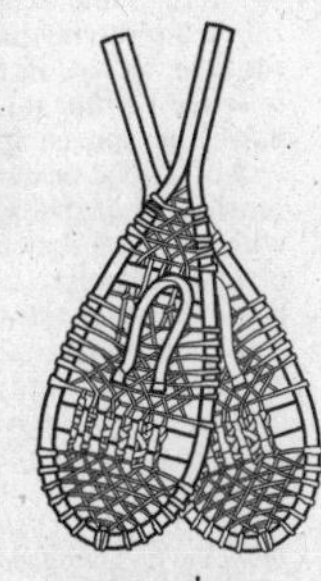
snowshoes

snow·shoe hare (also **snow·shoe rab·bit**) ▶ n. a North American hare (*Lepus americanus*) with large hind feet and a white winter coat.

snow·storm /'snō,stôrm/ ▶ n. a heavy fall of snow, esp. with a high wind. ■ fig. a shower or large quantity of something.

snow·suit /'snō,so͞ot/ ▶ n. a child's one- or two-piece coverall garment with a warm lining for protection against cold.

snow throw·er ▶ n. another term for SNOWBLOWER.

snow tire ▶ n. a tire with a tread that gives extra traction on snow or ice.

snow-white ▶ adj. of a pure white color.

snow·y /'snōē/ ▶ adj. (**snow·i·er, snow·i·est**) covered with snow: *snowy mountains.* ■ (of weather or a period of time) characterized by snowfall. ■ of or like snow, esp. in being pure white: *snowy hair.* — **snow·i·ly** /'snōəlē/ adv. **snow·i·ness** n.

snow·y e·gret ▶ n. a North American egret (*Egretta thula*) with all-white plumage, black legs, and yellow feet.

snow·y owl ▶ n. a large northern owl (*Nyctea scandiaca*) that breeds mainly in the Arctic tundra, the male being entirely white and the female having darker markings.

snow·y plov·er ▶ n. a small white-breasted plover (*Charadrius alexandrinus*) related to the ringed plover, found on most continents.

Snr. ▶ abbr. Senior: *John Hammond Snr.*

snub /snəb/ ▶ v. (**snubbed, snub·bing**) [trans.] **1** rebuff, ignore, or spurn disdainfully: *he snubbed faculty members and students alike.* **2** check the movement of (a horse or boat), esp. by a rope wound around a post: *a horse snubbed to a tree.* ▶ n. an act of showing disdain or a lack of cordiality by rebuffing or ignoring someone or something. ▶ adj. (of a person's or animal's nose) short and turned up at the end: [in comb.] *snub-nosed.* [ME: from ON *snubba* 'chide, check the growth of.']

snuck /snək/ informal past and past participle of SNEAK.

snuff¹ /snəf/ ▶ v. [trans.] extinguish (a candle): *a breeze* ***snuffed out*** *the candle.* ■ informal put an end to (something) in a brutal manner: *his life was snuffed out by a sniper's bullet.* ■ informal kill. ▶ n. the charred part of a candle wick. [ME: of unknown origin.]

snuff² ▶ n. powdered tobacco that is sniffed up the nostril rather than smoked: *a pinch of snuff.* ▶ v. [trans.] inhale or sniff at (something): *they stood* ***snuffing up*** *the keen cold air.*

PRONUNCIATION KEY ə *ago, up*; ər *over, fur*; a *hat*; ā *ate*; ä *car*; e *let*; ē *see*; i *fit*; ī *by*; ɴɢ *sing*; ō *go*; ô *law, for*; oi *toy*; o͝o *good*; o͞o *goo*; ou *out*; ᴛʜ *thin*; T͟H *then*; ᴢʜ *vision*

– PHRASES **up to snuff** informal meeting the required standard: *they need to get their facilities up to snuff.* ■ in good health. [ME: from MDu. *snuffen* 'to snuffle.']

snuff·box /'snəf,bäks/ ▶ n. a small ornamental box for holding snuff.

snuff·er /'snəfər/ (also **can·dle·snuff·er**) ▶ n. a small hollow metal cone on the end of a handle, used to extinguish a candle by smothering the flame. ■ (usu. **snuffers** or **candlesnuffers**) an implement resembling scissors with an inverted metal cup attached to one blade, used to extinguish a candle or trim its wick.

snuff film (also **snuff movie**) ▶ n. informal a pornographic movie of an actual murder.

snuf·fle /'snəfəl/ ▶ v. [intrans.] breathe noisily through the nose due to a cold or crying. ■ (esp. of an animal) make repeated sniffing sounds as though smelling at something. ▶ n. a sniff or sniffing sound. ■ (usu. **the snuffles**) informal a cold or other infection that causes sniffling. — **snuf·fler** n. **snuf·fly** adj. [16th C.: prob. from Low Ger. and Du. *snuffelen*; cf. SNUFF[2] and SNIVEL.]

snuff·y /'snəfē/ ▶ adj. (**snuff·i·er, snuff·i·est**) archaic supercilious or contemptuous: *some snuffy old stockbroker.* ■ easily offended; annoyed.

snug /snəg/ ▶ adj. (**snug·ger, snug·gest**) **1** comfortable, warm, and cozy; well protected from the weather or cold: *a snug cottage.* **2** (esp. of clothing) very tight or close-fitting. ▶ v. [trans.] place (something) safely or cozily: *she snugged the blanket up to his chin.*

– PHRASES **snug as a bug (in a rug)** humorous in an extremely comfortable position or situation. — **snug·ly** adv. **snug·ness** n. [16th C. (from nautical use 'shipshape, prepared for bad weather'): prob. of Low Ger. or Du. origin.]

snug·ger·y /'snəgərē/ ▶ n. (pl. **-ger·ies**) a cozy or comfortable place, esp. someone's private room or den.

snug·gle /'snəgəl/ ▶ v. settle or move into a warm, comfortable position: [intrans.] *I snuggled down into my sleeping bag.*

So. ▶ abbr. South.

s.o. ▶ abbr. ■ seller's option. ■ shipping order.

so[1] /sō/ ▶ adv. **1** [as submodifier] to such a great extent: *the words tumbled out so fast that I could barely hear them.* ■ extremely; very much (used for emphasis): *she looked so pretty | I do love it so.* **2** [as submodifier] [with negative] to the same extent (used in comparisons): *he isn't so bad as you'd think.* **3** referring back to something previously mentioned: ■ that is the case: *"Is it going to rain?" "I think so."* ■ the truth: *I hear that you're a writer—is that so?* ■ similarly; and also: *times have changed and so have I.* ■ expressing agreement: *"It's cold in here." "So it is."* **4** in the way described or demonstrated; thus: *hold your arms so.* ▶ conj. **1** and for this reason; therefore: *it hurt, so I went to see a specialist.* (**so that**) with the result that: *it was overgrown with brambles, so that I had trouble making any progress.* **2** (**so that**) with the aim that; in order that: *whisper so that no one else can hear.* **3** and then; as the next step: *and so to the finals.* **4** introducing a question: *so, what did you do today?* ■ introducing a question following on from what was said previously: *so what did he do about it?* ■ (also **so what?**) informal why should that be considered significant?: *so what if he failed?* **5** introducing a statement that is followed by a defensive comment: *so I like sex—big deal.* **6** introducing a concluding statement: *so that's that.* **7** in the same way; correspondingly: *just as bad money drives out good, so does bad art drive out the good.*

– PHRASES **and so on** (or **forth**) and similar things; et cetera: *these snacks include cheeses, cold meats, and so on.* **just so much** esp. derog. emphasizing a large amount of something: *it's just so much ideological cant.* **only so much** a limited amount: *there is only so much you can do.* **so be it** an expression of acceptance or resignation. **so long!** informal goodbye until we meet again. **so much for 1** indicating that one has finished talking about something: *so much for my love life.* **2** suggesting that something has not been successful or useful: *so much for that idea!* **so to speak** (or **say**) used to highlight the fact that one is describing something in an unusual or metaphorical way: *I looked death in the face, so to speak.* [OE *swā*, of Gmc. origin; rel. to Du. *zo* and Ger. *so*.]

so[2] ▶ n. alternate spelling of SOL[1].

-so ▶ comb. form equivalent to -SOEVER.

soak /sōk/ ▶ v. [trans.] **1** make or allow (something) to become thoroughly wet by immersing it in liquid. ■ [intrans.] be immersed in water or another liquid: *soak in a hot bath.* ■ (of a liquid) cause (something or someone) to become extremely wet: *the rain soaked their hair.* ■ [intrans.] (of a liquid) penetrate or permeate completely: *water was soaking into my shoes.* **2** informal impose heavy charges or taxation on; overcharge. ▶ n. [in sing.] **1** an act of immersing someone or something in liquid for a period of time: *a long soak in the tub.* **2** informal a heavy drinker: *she put the old soak to bed.*

– PHRASAL VERBS **soak something up** absorb a liquid. ■ fig. expose oneself to or experience (something beneficial or enjoyable): *soak up Italian culture.* ■ informal cost or use up money: *the project had soaked up over $1 billion.* — **soak·age** /'sōkij/ n. **soak·er** n. [OE *socian* 'become saturated with a liquid by immersion'; rel. to *sūcan* 'to suck.']

soak·ing /'sōkiNG/ ▶ adj. extremely wet; wet through. ▶ n. an act of wetting something thoroughly: *in spring, give the soil a good soaking.*

so-and-so ▶ n. (pl. **-sos**) a person or thing whose name the speaker does not need to specify or does not know or remember. ■ informal a person who is disliked or is considered to have a particular characteristic, typically an unfavorable one: *nosy old so-and-so!*

soap /sōp/ ▶ n. **1** a substance used with water for washing and cleaning, made of a compound of natural oils or fats with sodium hydroxide or another strong alkali, and typically having perfume and coloring added. **2** informal a soap opera. ▶ v. [trans.] wash with soap: *she soaped her face.* — **soap·less** adj. [OE *sāpe*, of West Gmc. origin; rel. to Du. *zeep* and Ger. *Seife*.]

soap·ber·ry /'sōp,berē/ ▶ n. a tree or shrub with berries that produce a soapy froth when crushed, in particular a plant (genus *Sapindus*, family Sapindaceae) with saponin-rich berries that are used as a soap substitute. ■ the berry of this tree or shrub.

soap·box /'sōp,bäks/ ▶ n. a box or crate used as a makeshift stand by a public speaker. ■ fig. a thing that provides an opportunity for someone to air their views publicly.

soap·box der·by (also **Soap Box Der·by** trademark) ▶ n. a race for children driving motorless, improvised vehicles made from crates and crudely resembling race cars.

soap·fish /'sōp,fisH/ ▶ n. (pl. same or **-fish·es**) a stout-bodied fish (family Grammistidae) of tropical seas that produces large amounts of toxic mucus from the skin.

soap op·er·a ▶ n. a television or radio drama series dealing typically with daily events in the lives of the same group of characters. [1930s: so named because such serials were orig. sponsored by soap manufacturers.]

soap plant ▶ n. a plant (genus *Chlorogalum*) of the lily family, found in dry habitats of California. The fiber-covered bulbs were used as soap by American Indians.

soap·stone /'sōp,stōn/ ▶ n. a soft rock consisting largely of talc. Compare with STEATITE.

soap·wort /'sōpwərt; -,wôrt/ ▶ n. a plant (*Saponaria officinalis*) of the pink family, with fragrant pink or white flowers, and leaves that were formerly used to make soap.

soap·y /'sōpē/ ▶ adj. (**soap·i·er, soap·i·est**) **1** containing or covered with soap: *hot soapy water.* ■ of or like soap: *his hands smelled soapy.* **2** informal characteristic of a soap opera: *soapy little turns of plot.* — **soap·i·ly** /'sōpəlē/ adv. **soap·i·ness** n.

soar /sôr/ ▶ v. [intrans.] fly or rise high in the air: *the bird soared into the air* | fig. *her spirits soared.* ■ maintain height in the air without flapping wings or using engine power: *the gulls soared on the winds.* ■ increase rapidly above the usual level: [as adj.] (**soaring**) *the soaring crime rate.* — **soar·er** n. **soar·ing·ly** adv. [ME: shortening of OFr. *essorer*, based on L. *ex-* 'out of' + *aura* 'breeze.']

SOB ▶ abbr. son of a bitch.

sob /säb/ ▶ v. (**sobbed, sob·bing**) [intrans.] cry noisily, making loud, convulsive gasps. ■ [trans.] say while crying noisily: [with direct speech] *"I thought they'd killed you," he sobbed.* ▶ n. an act or sound of sobbing: *a sob of despair.* — **sob·bing·ly** adv. [ME: perh. of Dutch or Low Ger. origin.]

so·ba /'sōbə/ ▶ n. Japanese noodles made from buckwheat flour.

so·ber /'sōbər/ ▶ adj. (**-ber·er, -ber·est**) not affected by alcohol; not drunk. ■ serious, sensible, and solemn: *a sober view of life.* ■ free from alcoholism; not habitually drinking alcohol. ▶ v. make or become sober after drinking alcohol: [trans.] *that coffee sobered him up.* ■ make or become more serious, sensible, and solemn. — **so·ber·ing·ly** adv. **so·ber·ly** adv. [ME: from OFr. *sobre*, from L. *sobrius*.]

So·bies·ki /sôb'yäskē/, John, see JOHN III.

so·bri·e·ty /sə'brīətē; sō-/ ▶ n. the state of being sober. ■ the quality of being staid or solemn. [ME: from OFr. *sobriete* or L. *sobrietas*, from *sobrius* (see SOBER).]

so·bri·quet /'sōbri,kā; -,ket/ (also **sou·bri·quet** /'sōōbri-/) ▶ n. a person's nickname. [17th C.: Fr., orig. in the sense 'tap under the chin,' of unknown origin.]

sob sis·ter ▶ n. informal a female journalist who writes articles with sentimental appeal or answers readers' problems. ■ an overly sentimental woman.

sob sto·ry ▶ n. informal a story or explanation intended to arouse sympathy for the person relating it.

Soc. ▶ abbr. ■ Socialist. ■ Society.

so·ca /'sōkə/ ▶ n. calypso music with elements of soul, originally from Trinidad. [1970s: blend of SOUL and CALYPSO.]

soc·age /'säkij/ (also **soc·cage**) ▶ n. hist. a feudal tenure of land involving payment of rent or other nonmilitary service to a superior. [ME: from Anglo-Norman Fr., from *soc*, var. of *soke*, a minor administrative district.]

so-called ▶ adj. [attrib.] used to show that something or someone is commonly designated by the name or term specified: *the so-called chaebols or conglomerates.* ■ used to express one's view that such a name or term is inappropriate: *her so-called friends.*

soc·cer /'säkər/ ▶ n. a game played by two teams of eleven players with a round ball that may not be touched with the hands or arms during play except by the goalkeepers. The object is to score goals by kicking or heading the ball into the opponents' goal. [19th C.: from a shortening of 'Association Football' + an extended use of -ER[1].]

So·chi /'sōCHē/ a port and resort in southwestern Russia on the Black Sea coast; pop. 339,000.

so·cia·ble /'sōsHəbəl/ ▶ adj. willing to talk and engage in activities with other people; friendly. ■ (of a place, occasion, or activity) marked by friendliness: *a very sociable little village.* ▶ n. hist. an open carriage with facing side seats. — **so·cia·bil·i·ty** /,sōsHə'bilitē/ n. **so·cia·ble·ness** n. **so·cia·bly** /-blē/ adv. [16th C.: from Fr., or from L. *sociabilis*, from *sociare* 'unite,' from *socius* 'companion.']

so·cial /ˈsōsʜəl/ ▶ **adj.** 1 [attrib.] of or relating to society or its organization: *alcoholism is a major social problem.* ■ of or relating to rank and status in society: *social class in Britain.* ■ needing companionship and therefore best suited to living in communities: *we are social beings.* ■ relating to or designed for activities in which people meet each other for pleasure: *Guy led a full social life.* 2 Zool. (of birds, mammals, insects) living together in organized communities, typically in a hierarchical system. ▶ **n.** an informal social gathering, esp. one organized by the members of a particular group: *a church social.* — **so·ci·al·i·ty** /ˌsōsʜēˈalətē/ **n.** **so·cial·ly** /ˈsōsʜəlē/ **adv.** [ME: from OFr., or from L. *socialis* 'allied,' from *socius* 'friend.']

so·cial climb·er ▶ **n.** derog. a person who is anxious to gain a higher social status. — **so·cial climb·ing n.**

so·cial con·tract (also **social compact**) ▶ **n.** an implicit agreement among the members of a society to cooperate for social benefits.

so·cial Dar·win·ism ▶ **n.** the theory, now largely discredited, that individuals, groups, and peoples are subject to the same Darwinian laws of natural selection as plants and animals.

so·cial de·moc·ra·cy ▶ **n.** a socialist system of government achieved by democratic means. — **so·cial dem·o·crat n.**

so·cial dis·ease ▶ **n.** informal a venereal disease.

so·cial en·gi·neer·ing ▶ **n.** the application of sociological principles to specific social problems. — **so·cial en·gi·neer n.**

so·cial·ism /ˈsōsʜəˌlizəm/ ▶ **n.** a political and economic theory of that advocates that the means of production, distribution, and exchange should be owned or regulated by the community as a whole. ■ (in Marxist theory) a transitional social state between the overthrow of capitalism and the realization of communism. — **so·cial·ist n. & adj.** **so·cial·is·tic** /ˌsōsʜəˈlistik/ **adj.** **so·cial·is·ti·cal·ly** /ˌsōsʜəˈlistik(ə)lē/ **adv.** [19th C.: from Fr. *socialisme*, from *social*.]

so·cial·ist re·al·ism ▶ **n.** the theory of art, literature, and music officially sanctioned by the state in some communist countries (esp. in the Soviet Union under Stalin), by which artistic work was supposed to reflect and promote socialist ideals.

so·cial·ite /ˈsōsʜəˌlīt/ ▶ **n.** a person who is well known in fashionable society and is fond of social activity.

so·cial·ize /ˈsōsʜəˌlīz/ ▶ **v.** 1 [intrans.] mix socially with others. 2 [trans.] make (someone) behave in a way that is acceptable to their society: *newcomers are **socialized into our ways.*** 3 [trans.] organize according to the principles of socialism: [as adj.] (**socialized**) *socialized economies.* — **so·cial·i·za·tion** /ˌsōsʜəliˈzāsʜən/ **n.** (in senses 2 and 3).

so·cial·ized med·i·cine ▶ **n.** the provision of medical and hospital care for all by means of public funds.

so·cial psy·chol·o·gy ▶ **n.** the branch of psychology that deals with social interactions. — **so·cial psy·chol·o·gist n.**

so·cial sci·ence ▶ **n.** the scientific study of human society and social relationships. ■ a subject within this field, such as economics or politics. — **so·cial sci·en·tist n.**

so·cial sec·re·tar·y ▶ **n.** a person who arranges the social activities of a person or organization.

so·cial se·cu·ri·ty ▶ **n.** any government system that provides monetary assistance to people with an inadequate or no income. ■ (**Social Security**) (in the US) a federal insurance program that provides benefits to retired persons, the unemployed, and the disabled.

So·cial Se·cur·i·ty num·ber (abbr.: **SSN**) ▶ **n.** (in the US) a number in the format 000-00-0000, unique for each individual, used to track Social Security benefits and for other identification purposes.

so·cial serv·ice ▶ **n.** (**social services**) government services provided for the benefit of the community, such as education, medical care, and housing.

so·cial stud·ies ▶ **plural n.** [treated as sing.] various aspects or branches of the study of human society, considered as an educational discipline.

so·cial u·nit ▶ **n.** an individual, group, or community, considered as a discrete constituent of a society or larger group.

so·cial work ▶ **n.** work carried out by trained personnel with the aim of alleviating the conditions of those in need of help or welfare. — **so·cial work·er n.**

so·ci·e·tal /səˈsīitl/ ▶ **adj.** of or relating to society or social relations: *societal change.* — **so·ci·e·tal·ly adv.**

so·ci·e·ty /səˈsīətē/ ▶ **n.** (pl. **-ties**) 1 the aggregate of people living together in a more or less ordered community. ■ the community of people living in a particular region and having shared customs, laws, and organizations. ■ [with adj.] a specified section of such a community: *polite society | high society.* ■ a plant or animal community. 2 an organization or club formed for a particular purpose or activity: [in names] *the American Society for the Prevention of Cruelty to Animals.* 3 the situation of being in the company of other people: *she shunned the society of others.* [16th C.: from Fr. *société*, from L. *societas*, from *socius* 'companion.']

So·ci·e·ty Is·lands a group of islands in the South Pacific Ocean, part of French Polynesia.

So·ci·e·ty of Je·sus official name of the Jesuits (see **Jesuit**).

socio- ▶ **comb. form** 1 relating to society; society and ...: *socioeconomic.* 2 relating to sociology; sociology and ...: *sociolinguistics.* [from L. *socius* 'companion.']

so·ci·o·bi·ol·o·gy /ˌsōsēōˌbīˈäləjē/ ▶ **n.** the scientific study of the biological (esp. ecological and evolutionary) aspects of social behavior in animals and humans. — **so·ci·o·bi·o·log·i·cal** /-ˌbīəˈläjikəl/ **adj.** **so·ci·o·bi·o·log·i·cal·ly** /-ˌbīəˈläjik(ə)lē/ **adv.** **so·ci·o·bi·ol·o·gist** /-jist/ **n.**

so·ci·o·cul·tur·al /ˌsōsēōˈkəlcʜərəl/ ▶ **adj.** combining social and cultural factors. — **so·ci·o·cul·tur·al·ly adv.**

so·ci·o·e·col·o·gy /ˌsōsēōˌēˈkäləjē; -eˈkä-/ ▶ **n.** the branch of science that deals with the interactions among the members of a species, and between them and the environment. — **so·ci·o·ec·o·log·i·cal** /-kəˈlsʜjikəl/ **adj.** **so·ci·o·e·col·o·gist** /-jist/ **n.**

so·ci·o·ec·o·nom·ic /ˌsōsēōˌēkəˈnämik; -ˌekə-/ ▶ **adj.** relating to or concerned with the interaction of social and economic factors. — **so·ci·o·ec·o·nom·i·cal·ly adv.**

so·ci·o·lect /ˈsōsēōˌlekt/ ▶ **n.** the dialect of a particular social class. [1970s: from **socio-** + *-lect* as in **dialect**.]

so·ci·o·lin·guis·tics /ˌsōsēōlinɢˈgwistiks/ ▶ **plural n.** [treated as sing.] the study of language in relation to social factors, including differences of regional, class, and occupational dialect. — **so·ci·o·lin·guist** /-ˈlinɢgwist/ **n.** **so·ci·o·lin·guis·tic adj.** **so·ci·o·lin·guis·ti·cal·ly adv.**

so·ci·ol·o·gy /ˌsōsēˈäləjē/ ▶ **n.** the study of the development, structure, and functioning of human society. ■ the study of social problems. — **so·ci·o·log·i·cal** /ˌsōsēōˈläjikəl/ **adj.** **so·ci·o·log·i·cal·ly adv.** **so·ci·ol·o·gist n.**

so·ci·om·e·try /ˌsōsēˈämətrē/ ▶ **n.** the quantitative study and measurement of relationships within a group of people. — **so·ci·o·met·ric** /ˌsōsēōˈmetrik/ **adj.** **so·ci·o·met·ri·cal·ly adv.** **so·ci·om·e·trist** /-trist/ **n.**

so·ci·o·path /ˈsōsēōˌpaᴛʜ/ ▶ **n.** a person with a personality disorder manifesting itself in extreme antisocial attitudes and behavior and a lack of conscience. — **so·ci·o·path·ic** /ˌsōsēōˈpaᴛʜik/ **adj.** **so·ci·op·a·thy** /ˌsōsēˈäpəᴛʜē/ **n.**

so·ci·o·po·lit·i·cal /ˌsōsēˌōpəˈlitikəl/ ▶ **adj.** combining social and political factors.

sock /säk/ ▶ **n.** 1 a garment for the foot and lower part of the leg, typically knitted from wool, cotton, or nylon. ■ a removable inner sole placed inside a shoe or boot for added warmth or to improve the fit. ■ a white marking on the lower part of a horse's leg, not extending as far as the knee or hock. Compare with **stocking**. 2 informal a hard blow: *a sock on the jaw.* ■ force or emphasis: *enough sock in our lineup to score runs.* ▶ **v.** informal [trans.] hit forcefully: *Jess socked his father.* ■ (often **be socked with**) affect disadvantageously: *consumers have been socked with huge price increases.*

– PHRASES **knock** (or **blow**) **someone's socks off** informal amaze or impress someone. **knock the socks off** informal surpass or beat. **—— one's socks off** informal do something with great energy and enthusiasm: *she acted her socks off.* **sock and buskin** archaic the theatrical profession; drama. **sock it to someone** informal attack or make a forceful impression on someone.

– PHRASAL VERBS **sock something away** put money aside as savings: *you'll need to sock away about $900 a month.* **sock something in** (or **sock in**) (of weather) envelop. [OE *socc* 'light shoe,' of Gmc. origin, from L. *soccus* 'comic actor's shoe, light low-heeled slipper,' from Gk. *sukkhos*.]

sock·et /ˈsäkit/ ▶ **n.** 1 a natural or artificial hollow into which something fits or in which something revolves. ■ a hollow, cylindrical part or piece, constructed to receive some part or thing fitting into it. ■ the part of the head of a golf club into which the shaft is fitted. 2 an electrical device receiving a plug or light bulb to make a connection. ▶ **v.** (**-et·ed, -et·ing**) [trans.] place in or fit with a socket. [ME: from an Anglo-Norman Fr. dimin. of OFr. *soc* 'plowshare.']

sock·et wrench ▶ **n.** a ratchet tool with a series of detachable sockets for tightening and loosening nuts of different sizes. See illustration at **wrench**.

sock·eye /ˈsäkˌī/ (also **sock·eye sal·mon**) ▶ **n.** a salmon (*Oncorhynchus nerka*) of the North Pacific and rivers draining into it. Also called **red salmon**. See also **kokanee**. [19th C.: by folk etymology from Salish *sukai*, lit. 'fish of fishes.']

sock hop ▶ **n.** dated a dance for young teenagers at which they may dance in stocking feet.

so·cle /ˈsäkəl/ ▶ **n.** Archit. a plain low block or plinth serving as a support for a column, urn, statue, etc., or as the foundation of a wall. [18th C.: from Fr., from Ital. *zoccolo*, 'wooden shoe,' from L. *socculus*, from *soccus* (see **sock**).]

Soc·ra·tes /ˈsäkrəˌtēz/ (469–399 BC), ancient Athenian philosopher. His disciple Plato wrote about Socrates' attempt to reach understanding and ethical concepts by exposing and dispelling error (the **Socratic method**). — **So·crat·ic adj.**

So·crat·ic i·ro·ny ▶ **n.** a pose of ignorance assumed in order to entice others into making statements that can then be challenged.

sod[1] /säd/ ▶ **n.** (**the sod**) the surface of the ground, with the grass growing on it. ■ a piece of this, usually sold in rolls and used to start a new lawn, athletic field, etc. ▶ **v.** (**sod·ded, sod·ding**) [trans.] cover with sod or pieces of turf: *the stadium has been sodded.* [ME: from MDu., Mid. Low Ger. *sode*.]

sod[2] vulgar slang, esp. Brit. ▶ **n.** an unpleasant or obnoxious person. ■ [with adj.] a person of a specified kind. ■ something that is difficult or causes problems. ▶ **v.** (**sod·ded, sod·ding**) [trans., usu. in imper.] used to express one's anger or annoyance at someone or something. [19th C.: abbrev. of SODOMITE.]

so·da /'sōdə/ ▶ n. 1 (also **soda water** or **club soda**) carbonated water (originally made with sodium bicarbonate). ■ (also **soda pop**) a carbonated soft drink. 2 sodium carbonate, esp. as a natural mineral or as an industrial chemical. ■ sodium in chemical combination: *nitrate of soda.* [ME (sense 2): from med. L., from Arab. *suwwad* 'saltwort.']

so·da ash ▶ n. commercially manufactured anhydrous sodium carbonate.

so·da bread ▶ n. bread leavened with baking soda.

so·da crack·er ▶ n. a thin, crisp cracker leavened with baking soda.

so·da foun·tain ▶ n. a device that dispenses soda water or soft drinks. ■ a shop or counter selling drinks from such a device.

so·da jerk (also **so·da jerk·er**) ▶ n. informal, dated a person who serves soft drinks and ice cream at a soda fountain.

so·da lime ▶ n. a mixture of calcium oxide and sodium hydroxide.

so·da·lite /'sōdl,īt/ ▶ n. a blue mineral consisting mainly of an aluminosilicate and chloride of sodium, occurring chiefly in alkaline igneous rocks.

so·dal·i·ty /sō'dalitē/ ▶ n. (pl. **-ties**) a confraternity or association, esp. a Roman Catholic religious guild. ■ fraternity; friendship. [17th C.: from Fr. *sodalité* or L. *sodalitas*, from *sodalis* 'comrade.']

so·da pop ▶ n. see SODA (sense 1).

so·da wa·ter ▶ n. see SODA (sense 1).

sod·bust·er /'säd,bəstər/ ▶ n. informal a farmer or farm worker who plows the land.

sod·den /'sädn/ ▶ adj. saturated with liquid, esp. water; soaked through: *his clothes were sodden.* ■ [in comb.] having drunk an excessive amount of a particular alcoholic drink: *whiskey-sodden drunk.* — **sod·den·ly** adv. **sod·den·ness** n. [ME: archaic past part. of SEETHE.]

Sod·dy /'sädē/, Frederick (1877–1956), English physicist. He codiscovered helium and coined the word *isotope* in 1913. Nobel Prize for Chemistry (1921).

so·di·um /'sōdēəm/ ▶ n. the chemical element of atomic number 11, a soft silver-white reactive metal of the alkali metal group. (Symbol: **Na**) — **so·dic** /'sōdik/ adj. (Mineral.).

so·di·um am·y·tal ▶ n. see AMYTAL.

so·di·um bi·car·bon·ate ▶ n. a soluble white powder, $NaHCO_3$, used in fire extinguishers and effervescent drinks and as a leavening agent in baking. Also called BAKING SODA.

so·di·um car·bon·ate ▶ n. a white alkaline compound, Na_2CO_3, with many commercial applications including the manufacture of soap and glass.

so·di·um chlo·ride ▶ n. a colorless crystalline compound, NaCl, occurring naturally in seawater and halite; common salt.

so·di·um cy·a·nide ▶ n. a white odorless crystalline soluble compound that has, when damp, an odor of hydrogen cyanide. It is used for extracting gold and silver from their ores and for case-hardening steel.

so·di·um hy·drox·ide ▶ n. a strongly alkaline white deliquescent compound, NaOH, used in many industrial processes, e.g., the manufacture of soap and paper.

so·di·um ni·trate ▶ n. a white powdery compound, $NaNO_3$, used mainly in the manufacture of fertilizers.

so·di·um thi·o·sul·phate /,THīō'səlfāt/ ▶ n. a white soluble compound, $Na_2S_2O_3$, used in photography as a fixer. Also called HYPO[1].

so·di·um-va·por lamp (also **so·di·um lamp**) ▶ n. a lamp in which an electrical discharge in sodium vapor gives a yellow light, typically used in street lighting.

Sod·om /'sädəm/ a town in ancient Palestine, probably south of the Dead Sea. According to Genesis, it was destroyed by fire from heaven, together with Gomorrah, for the wickedness of its inhabitants. ■ [as n.] (**a Sodom**) a wicked or depraved place.

sod·om·ite /'sädə,mīt/ ▶ n. a person who engages in sodomy. — **sod·o·mit·ic** /,sädə'mitik/ adj.

sod·om·y /'sädəmē/ ▶ n. sexual intercourse involving anal or oral copulation. — **sod·om·ize** /'sädə,mīz/ v.

-soever ▶ comb. form of any kind; to any extent: *whatsoever* | *whosoever.*

so·fa /'sōfə/ ▶ n. a long upholstered seat with a back and arms, for two or more people. [17th C.: from Fr., based on Arab. *ṣuffa.*]

so·fa bed ▶ n. a sofa that can be converted into a bed, typically for occasional use.

SOFAR /'sōfär/ (also **sofar**) ▶ n. a system in which the sound waves from an underwater explosion are detected and located. [1940s: from *So(und) f(ixing) a(nd) r(anging).*]

sof·fit /'säfit/ ▶ n. the underside of an architectural structure such as an arch or overhanging eaves. [17th C.: from Fr. *soffite* or Ital. *soffitto*, based on L. *suffixus* 'fastened below.']

So·fi·a /sō'fēə; 'sōfēə/ the capital of Bulgaria, in the western part of the country; pop. 1,221,000.

soft /sôft/ ▶ adj. 1 easy to mold, cut, compress, or fold; not hard or firm to the touch. ■ having a smooth surface or texture that is pleasant to touch; not rough or coarse. ■ rounded; not angular: *soft edges.* 2 having a pleasing quality involving a subtle effect or contrast rather than sharp definition: *soft lighting.* ■ (of a voice or sound) quiet and gentle. ■ (of rain, wind, or other natural force) not strong or violent: *a soft breeze.* ■ (of a consonant) pronounced as a fricative (as *c* in *ice*). ■ (of a market, currency, or commodity) falling or likely to fall in value. 3 sympathetic, lenient, or compassionate, esp. to a degree perceived as excessive; not strict or sufficiently strict: *soft on crime.* ■ (of words or language) not harsh or angry; conciliatory; soothing. ■ not strong or robust: *soft, out-of-shape executives.* ■ informal (of a job or way of life) requiring little effort. ■ (of news or other journalism) regarded more as entertainment than as basic news. ■ willing to compromise in political matters; moderate. ■ informal foolish; silly: *he must be going soft.* ■ [predic.] (**soft on**) informal infatuated with: *was Joe soft on her?* 4 (of a drug) not likely to cause addiction. ■ (of water) free from mineral salts that make lathering difficult. ▶ adv. softly: *I can just speak soft and she'll hear me.*

– PHRASES **have a soft spot for** be fond of or affectionate toward. **soft touch** (also **soft-core**) informal a person who readily gives or does something if asked. — **soft·ish** adj. **soft·ness** n. [OE *sōfte* 'agreeable, calm, gentle,' of West Gmc. origin; rel. to Du. *zacht* and Ger. *sanft.*]

sof·ta /'sôftə/ ▶ n. a Muslim student of sacred law and theology. [Turk., from Pers. *sūḵta* 'burned, on fire.']

soft·ball /'sôft,bôl/ ▶ n. a modified form of baseball played on a smaller field with a larger ball, seven rather than nine innings, and underarm pitching. ■ the ball used in this game.

soft-boiled ▶ adj. (of an egg) boiled for a short time, leaving the yolk soft or liquid. ■ fig. gentle or sentimental.

soft chan·cre /'SHANGkər/ ▶ n. another term for CHANCROID.

soft coal ▶ n. bituminous coal.

soft cop·y ▶ n. Comput. a legible version of a piece of information not printed on a physical medium, esp. as stored or displayed on a computer.

soft cor·al ▶ n. see CORAL (sense 2).

soft-core ▶ adj. (of pornography) suggestive or erotic but not explicit.

soft·cov·er /'sôft,kəvər/ ▶ adj. & n. another term for PAPERBACK.

soft drink ▶ n. a nonalcoholic drink, esp. one that is carbonated.

soft·en /'sôfən/ ▶ v. make or become less hard: [trans.] *lotions to soften the skin.* ■ make or become less severe: [intrans.] *her expression softened.* ■ [trans.] undermine the resistance of (someone): *a tactic to soften them up for eventual surrender.* ■ [trans.] remove mineral salts from (water). — **soft·en·er** n.

soft fo·cus ▶ n. deliberate slight blurring or lack of definition in a photograph or movie.

soft goods ▶ plural n. textiles.

soft-head·ed (also **soft·head·ed**) ▶ adj. lacking wisdom or intelligence. — **soft-head·ed·ness** n.

soft·heart·ed /'sôft'härtid/ ▶ adj. kind and compassionate. — **soft·heart·ed·ness** n.

soft hy·phen ▶ n. a hyphen inserted into a word in word processing, to be displayed or typeset only if it falls at the end of a line of text.

soft·ie /'sôftē/ (also **soft·y**) ▶ n. (pl. **soft·ies**) informal a softhearted, weak, or sentimental person.

soft i·ron ▶ n. iron that has a low carbon content and is easily magnetized and demagnetized, used to make the cores of solenoids and other electrical equipment.

soft land·ing ▶ n. a controlled landing of a spacecraft during which no serious damage is incurred. — **soft-land** v.

soft line ▶ n. a flexible and moderate attitude or policy: *the chancellor is taking a soft line on inflation.*

soft loan ▶ n. a loan, typically one to a developing country, made on terms very favorable to the borrower.

soft·ly /'sôftlē/ ▶ adv. in a quiet voice or manner: *"Can't you sleep?" she asked softly.* ■ with a gentle or slow movement. ■ in a pleasantly subdued manner: *the room was softly lit by a lamp.*

soft mon·ey ▶ n. a contribution to a political party that is not accounted as going to a particular candidate, thus avoiding various legal limitations.

soft-nosed ▶ adj. (of a bullet) expanding on impact.

soft pal·ate /'palit/ ▶ n. the fleshy, flexible part toward the back of the roof of the mouth.

soft-paste ▶ adj. denoting artificial porcelain, typically made with white clay and ground glass and fired at a comparatively low temperature.

soft ped·al ▶ n. a pedal on a piano that can be pressed to make the tone softer. See also UNA CORDA. ▶ v. (**soft-ped·al**) [trans.] Music play with the soft pedal down. ■ refrain from emphasizing the more unpleasant aspects of; play down: *they soft-pedaled the missile program.*

soft rock ▶ n. rock music with a less persistent beat and more emphasis on lyrics and melody than hard rock has.

soft roe ▶ n. see ROE[1].

soft rot ▶ n. any of a number of bacterial and fungal diseases of fruit and vegetables in which the tissue becomes soft and slimy. ■ any of a number of fungal conditions affecting timber, which becomes soft and friable.

soft sell ▶ n. [in sing.] subtly persuasive selling. ▶ v. (**soft-sell**) [trans.] sell (something) by using such a method.

soft-shell clam (also **soft·shell clam**) ▶ n. a marine bivalve mollusk (genus *Mya*, family Myidae, esp. *M. arenaria*) with a thin shell and a long siphon, valued as food on the east coast of North America. Also called **soft clam, steamer.**

soft-shell crab (also **soft•shell crab**) ▶ n. a crab, esp. a blue crab, that has recently molted and has a new shell that is still soft and edible. Also called **soft crab**.

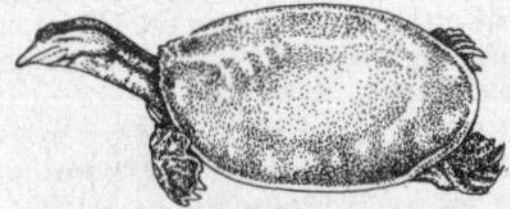

spiny soft-shelled turtle

soft-shelled tur•tle (also **soft-shell tur•tle**) ▶ n. a freshwater turtle (family Trionychidae) with a flattened leathery shell, native to Asia, Africa, and North America. Several genera and many species include the **spiny soft-shelled turtle** (*Apalone* (or *Trionyx*) *spinifera*) of North America.

soft-shoe ▶ n. a kind of tap dance performed in soft-soled shoes. ▶ v. [intrans.] perform a dance of this kind. ■ [no obj., with adverbial of place] move quietly and carefully so as not to draw attention to oneself: fig. *he soft-shoed his way into a safer topic of conversation.*

soft-spo•ken ▶ adj. speaking or said with a gentle, quiet voice.

soft tar•get ▶ n. a person or thing that is relatively unprotected or vulnerable, esp. to military or terrorist attack.

soft•ware /'sôft,we(ə)r/ ▶ n. the programs and other operating information used by a computer. Compare with **HARDWARE**.

soft•wood /'sôft,wo͝od/ ▶ n. the wood from a conifer (such as pine, fir, or spruce) as distinguished from that of broad-leaved trees. ■ a tree producing such wood.

sog•gy /'sägē/ ▶ adj. (**-gi•er, -gi•est**) wet and soft: *the sandbags were soggy.* — **sog•gi•ly** /'sägəlē/ adv. **sog•gi•ness** n. [18th C.: from dial. *sog* 'a swamp' + **-Y**[1].]

so•go sho•sha /'sōgō 'SHōSHə/ ▶ n. (pl. same) a very large Japanese company that trades internationally in a wide range of goods and services. [Japanese, from *sōgō* 'comprehensive' + *shōsha* 'mercantile society.']

Sogwali see **SEQUOYA**.

SOHO /'sō,hō/ ▶ adj. relating to a market for relatively inexpensive consumer electronics used by individuals and small companies. [1990s: acronym from *small office home office*.]

So•Ho /'sō,hō/ a district in southern Manhattan in New York City. Its name is derived from *So*uth of *Ho*uston Street.

soi•gné /swän'yā/ ▶ adj. (fem. **-gnée** pronunc. same) dressed very elegantly; well groomed. [past part. of Fr. *soigner* 'take care of,' from *soin* 'care.']

soil[1] /soil/ ▶ n. the upper layer of earth in which plants grow, a black or dark brown material typically consisting of a mixture of organic remains, clay, and rock particles. ■ the territory of a particular nation: *glad to be on American soil.* — **soil•less** adj. [ME: from Anglo-Norman Fr., perh. from L. *solium* 'seat,' by association with *solum* 'ground.']

soil[2] ▶ v. [trans.] make dirty: *he might soil his suit* | [as adj.] (**soiled**) *a soiled T-shirt.* ■ (esp. of a child, patient, or pet) make (something) dirty by defecating in or on it. ■ fig. bring discredit to; tarnish: *my soiled reputation.* ▶ n. waste matter, esp. sewage containing excrement. See also **NIGHT SOIL**. [ME (as a v.): from OFr. *soiller*, based on L. *sucula*, dimin. of *sus* 'pig.']

soil[3] ▶ v. [trans.] rare feed (cattle) on fresh-cut green fodder (originally for the purpose of purging them). [17th C.: perh. from **SOIL**[2].]

soil me•chan•ics ▶ plural n. [usu. treated as sing.] the branch of science concerned with the properties and behavior of soil as they affect its use in civil engineering.

soil pipe ▶ n. a sewage or waste water pipe.

soil sci•ence ▶ n. the branch of science concerned with the formation, nature, ecology, and classification of soils.

soil stack ▶ n. the pipe that takes all the waste water from the upstairs plumbing system of a building.

soi•rée /swä'rā/ ▶ n. an evening party or gathering, typically in a private house, for conversation or music. [Fr., from *soir* 'evening.']

soi•xante-neuf /,swäsän(t) 'nəf; -zän(t)-/ ▶ n. another term for **SIXTY-NINE**. [Fr., 'sixty-nine,' from the position of the couple.]

so•journ /'sōjərn/ formal ▶ n. a temporary stay. ▶ v. [no obj., with adverbial of place] stay somewhere temporarily: *she had sojourned once in Egypt.* — **so•journ•er** n. [ME: from OFr. *sojourner*, based on L. *sub-* 'under' + late L. *diurnum* 'day.']

So•ka Gak•kai /,sōkə 'gäkī/ a political and lay religious organization founded in Japan in 1930, based on the teachings of the Nichiren Buddhist sect. [Japanese, from *sō* 'create' + *ka* 'value' + *gakkai* '(learned) society.']

SOL ▶ abbr. vulgar slang shit out of luck.

Sol /säl; sōl/ Rom. Mythol. the sun, esp. when personified as a god. [L.]

sol[1] /sōl/ (also **so**) ▶ n. Music (in solmization) the fifth note of a major scale. ■ the note G in the fixed-do system. [ME *sol*: representing the first syllable of *solve*, taken from a L. hymn (see **SOLMIZATION**).]

sol[2] /säl; sôl/ ▶ n. Chem. a fluid suspension of a colloidal solid in a liquid. [19th C.: abbrev. of **SOLUTION**.]

sol[3] /sōl; sôl/ (also **nue•vo sol** /'nwāvō/) ▶ n. (pl. **so•les** /'sōlāz; 'sôles/) the basic monetary unit of Peru, equal to 100 centavos. [Sp., 'sun.']

sol. ▶ abbr. ■ soluble. ■ solution.

-sol ▶ comb. form in nouns denoting different kinds and states of soil: *ultisol* | *vertisol*. [from L. *solum* 'soil.']

so•la[1] /'sōlə/ ▶ n. an Indian swamp plant (*Aeschynomene indica*) of the pea family, with stems that yield the pith that is used to make sola topis. [19th C.: from Bengali *solā*, Hindi *śolā*.]

so•la[2] ▶ n. feminine form of **SOLUS**.

sol•ace /'sälis/ ▶ n. comfort or consolation in a time of distress or sadness: *she sought solace in her religion.* ▶ v. [trans.] give solace to. [ME: from OFr. *solas* (n.), *solacier* (v.), based on L. *solari* 'to console.']

so•lan /'sōlən/ (also **so•lan goose**) ▶ n. the northern gannet. See **GANNET**. [ME: prob. from ON *súla* 'gannet' + *and-* 'duck.']

so•lan•der /sə'landər/ (also **so•lan•der box**) ▶ n. a protective box made in the form of a book, for holding such items as botanical specimens, maps, and color plates. [18th C.: Daniel C. *Solander* (1736–82), Swedish botanist.]

so•la•nine /'sōlə,nēn; -nin/ ▶ n. Chem. a poisonous compound that is present in green potatoes and in related plants. It is a steroid glycoside of the saponin group. [19th C.: from Fr., from the genus name *Solanum* + **-INE**[4].]

so•la•num /sō'lānəm/ ▶ n. a nightshade-family plant of a genus (*Solanum*) that includes the potato and woody nightshade. [L.]

so•lar /'sōlər/ ▶ adj. of, relating to, or determined by the sun: *solar radiation.* ■ relating to or denoting energy derived from the sun's rays: *solar heating.* [ME: from L. *solaris*, from *sol* 'sun.']

so•lar bat•ter•y (also **so•lar cell**) ▶ n. a device converting solar radiation into electricity.

so•lar con•stant n. Physics the rate at which energy reaches the earth's surface from the sun, usually taken to be 1,388 watts per square meter.

so•lar day ▶ n. the time between successive meridian transits of the sun at a particular place.

so•lar e•clipse ▶ n. an eclipse in which the sun is obscured by the moon.

so•lar en•er•gy ▶ n. radiant energy emitted by the sun. ■ another term for **SOLAR POWER**.

so•lar flare ▶ n. Astron. a brief eruption of intense high-energy radiation from the sun's surface.

so•lar•i•um /sə'le(ə)rēəm; sō-/ ▶ n. (pl. **-lar•i•ums** or **-lar•i•a** /-'le(ə)rēə/) a room fitted with extensive areas of glass to admit sunlight. ■ a room equipped with sunlamps or tanning beds that can be used to acquire an artificial suntan. [19th C.: from L. 'sundial, place for sunning oneself,' from *sol* 'sun.']

so•lar•ize /'sōlə,rīz/ ▶ v. [trans.] Photog. change the relative darkness of (a part of an image) by overexposure to light. — **so•lar•i•za•tion** /,sōləri'zāSHən/ n.

so•lar mass ▶ n. Astron. the mass of the sun used as a unit of mass, equal to 1.989 × 1030 kg.

so•lar pan•el ▶ n. a panel designed to absorb the sun's rays for generating electricity or heating.

so•lar plex•us /'pleksəs/ ▶ n. a complex of ganglia and radiating nerves of the sympathetic system at the pit of the stomach. ■ the area of the body near the base of the sternum.

so•lar pow•er ▶ n. power obtained by harnessing the energy of the sun's rays.

so•lar sys•tem ▶ n. Astron. the collection of planets and their moons in orbit around a sun, together with smaller bodies such as asteroids, meteoroids, and comets.

so•lar wind ▶ n. the continuous flow of charged particles from the sun that permeates the solar system.

so•lar year ▶ n. see **YEAR** (sense 1).

SOLAS /'sōləs/ ▶ n. [usu. as adj.] the provisions made during a series of international conventions governing maritime safety. [1960s: acronym from *safety of life at sea*.]

so•la•ti•um /sə'lāSHēəm/ ▶ n. (pl. **-ti•a** /-SHēə/) informal a thing given to someone as a compensation or consolation: *a solatium in the form of an apology was offered.* [19th C.: from L. 'solace.']

sold /sōld/ past and past participle of **SELL**.

sol•der /'sädər/ ▶ n. a low-melting alloy, esp. one based on lead and tin or (for higher temperatures) on brass or silver, used for joining less fusible metals. ▶ v. [trans.] join with solder. — **sol•der•a•ble** adj. **sol•der•er** n. [ME: from OFr. *soudure*, from the verb *souder*, from L. *solidare* 'fasten together,' from *solidus* 'solid.']

sol•der•ing i•ron ▶ n. a tool used for melting solder and applying it to metals that are to be joined.

sol•di /'säldē/ plural form of **SOLDO**.

sol•dier /'sōljər/ ▶ n. **1** a person who serves in an army. ■ (also **common soldier** or **private soldier**) a private in an army. **2** Entomol. a wingless caste of ant or termite with a large specially modified head and jaws, involved chiefly in defense. ▶ v. [intrans.] serve as a soldier. ■ (**soldier on**) informal carry on doggedly; persevere. — **sol•dier•ly** adj. **sol•dier•ship** /-,SHip/ n. (archaic). [ME: from OFr. *soldier*, from *soulde* '(soldier's) pay,' from L. *solidus* (see **SOLIDUS**).]

sol·dier bee·tle ▸ n. an elongated flying beetle (family Cantharidae) with soft downy wing cases, typically found on flowers where it hunts other insects.

sol·dier·fish /'sōljər,fisн/ ▸ n. (pl. same or **-fish·es**) a squirrelfish that is typically bright red in color. Several genera and species are included in the family Holocentridae.

sol·dier fly ▸ n. a bright metallic fly (family Stratiomyidae) with a flattened body that folds its wings flat over its body.

sol·dier of for·tune ▸ n. a person who works as a soldier for any group that will pay them; a mercenary.

sol·dier·y /'sōljərē/ ▸ n. (pl. **-dier·ies**) soldiers collectively. ■ military training or knowledge: *the arts of soldiery.*

sol·do /'säldō/ ▸ n. (pl. **sol·di** /'säldē/) a former Italian coin and monetary unit worth a twentieth of a lira. [Ital., from L. *solidus* (see SOLIDUS).]

sole[1] /sōl/ ▸ n. the undersurface of a person's foot. ■ the section forming the underside of a piece of footwear (typically excluding the heel when this forms a distinct part). ■ the part of the undersurface of a person's foot between the toes and the instep. ■ the undersurface of a tool or implement such as a plane or the head of a golf club. ■ the floor of a ship's cabin or cockpit. ▸ v. [trans.] (usu. **be soled**) put a new sole onto (a shoe). — **soled** adj. [in comb.] *rubber-soled shoes.* [ME: from OFr., from L. *solea* 'sandal, sill,' from *solum* 'bottom, pavement, sole'; cf. Du. *zool* and Ger. *Sohle*.]

sole[2] ▸ n. a marine flatfish of almost worldwide distribution, important as a food fish. Several species are in the families Soleidae, Pleuronectidae, and Bothidae. [ME: from OFr., from Provençal *sola*, from L. *solea* (see SOLE[1]), named from its shape.]

sole[3] ▸ adj. [attrib.] one and only: *my sole aim.* ■ belonging or restricted to one person or group of people: *the health club is for the sole use of our guests.* ■ archaic (esp. of a woman) unmarried. ■ archaic alone, unaccompanied. [ME: from OFr. *soule*, from L. *sola*, fem. of *solus* 'alone.']

sol·e·cism /'sälə,sizəm; 'sō-/ ▸ n. a grammatical mistake in speech or writing. ■ a breach of good manners; a piece of incorrect behavior. — **sol·e·cis·tic** /,sälə'sistik; ,sō-/ adj. [16th C.: from Fr. *solécisme*, or via L. from Gk. *soloikismos*, from *soloikos* 'speaking incorrectly.']

sole·ly /'sōl(l)ē/ ▸ adv. not involving anyone or anything else; only: *appointed solely on the basis of merit.*

sol·emn /'säləm/ ▸ adj. formal and dignified. ■ not cheerful or smiling; serious. ■ characterized by deep sincerity: *he swore a solemn oath.* — **sol·emn·ly** adv. **sol·emn·ness** n. [ME: from OFr. *solemne*, from L. *sollemnis* 'customary, celebrated at a fixed date,' from *sollus* 'entire.']

so·lem·ni·ty /sə'lemnitē/ ▸ n. (pl. **-ties**) the state or quality of being serious and dignified. ■ (usu. **solemnities**) a formal, dignified rite or ceremony: *the solemnities of Epiphany and Ascension.* [ME: from OFr. *solemnite*, from L. *sollemnitas*, from *sollemnis* (see SOLEMN).]

sol·em·nize /'säləm,nīz/ ▸ v. [trans.] duly perform (a ceremony, esp. that of marriage). ■ mark with a formal ceremony. — **sol·em·ni·za·tion** /,sälәmni'zāsнәn/ n. [ME: from OFr. *solemniser*, from med. L. *solemnizare*, from L. *sollemnis* (see SOLEMN).]

Sol·emn Mass ▸ n. another term for HIGH MASS.

so·le·no·don /sə'lēnə,dän; -'lenə-/ ▸ n. a forest-dwelling mammal (family Solenodontidae, genus *Solenodon*) with a long flexible snout and a stiff muscular tail, occurring only in Cuba and Hispaniola. [mod. L., from Gk. *sōlēn* 'channel, pipe' + *odō* (var. of *odous, odont-*) 'tooth.']

so·le·noid /'sōlə,noid/ ▸ n. a cylindrical coil of wire acting as a magnet when carrying electric current. — **so·le·noi·dal** /,sōlə'noidl/ adj. [19th C.: from Fr. *solénoïde*, from Gk. *sōlēn* 'channel, pipe.']

sole·plate /'sōl,plāt/ ▸ n. **1** a metal plate forming the base of an electric iron, machine saw, or other machine. **2** a horizontal timber at the base of a wall frame.

so·le·ra /sə'le(ə)rə/ ▸ n. (also **so·le·ra sys·tem**) a Spanish method of producing wine, esp. sherry and Madeira, whereby small amounts of younger wines stored in an upper tier of casks are systematically blended with the more mature wine in the casks below. [Sp., lit. 'crossbeam, stone base.']

So·leure /sô'lœr/ French name for SOLOTHURN.

so·le·us /'sōlēəs/ (also **so·le·us mus·cle**) ▸ n. Anat. a broad muscle in the lower calf, below the gastrocnemius, that flexes the foot to point the toes downward. [17th C.: mod. L., from L. *solea* 'sole.']

sol-fa /,sōl 'fä/ ▸ n. short for TONIC SOL-FA. ▸ v. (**-fas, -faed** /-'fäd/, **-fa·ing**) [trans.] sing using the sol-fa syllables.

sol·fa·ta·ra /,sälfə'tärə; ,sō-l-/ ▸ n. Geol. a volcanic crater emitting only sulfurous and other gases. [18th C.: from the name of a volcano near Naples, from Ital. *solfo* 'sulfur.']

sol·fège /säl'fezн/ ▸ n. Music **1** solmization. ■ an exercise in singing using solmization syllables. **2** the study of singing and musicianship using solmization syllables. [20th C.: Fr., from Ital. *solfeggio*.]

sol·feg·gio /säl'fejē,ō/ ▸ n. (pl. **-gi** /-jē/) another term for SOLFÈGE, esp. sense 1. [18th C.: Ital.]

so·li /'sōlē/ plural form of SOLO.

so·lic·it /sə'lisit/ ▸ v. (**-it·ed, -it·ing**) [trans.] ask for or try to obtain (something) from someone. ■ ask (someone) for something: *he solicited the critic's opinion.* ■ [intrans.] accost someone and offer one's or someone else's services as a prostitute. — **so·lic·i·ta·tion** /sə,lisə'tāsнən/ n. [ME: from OFr. *solliciter*, from L. *sollicitare* 'agitate,' from *sollicitus* 'anxious,' from *sollus* 'entire' + *citus* (past part. of *ciere* 'set in motion').]

so·lic·i·tor /sə'lisitər/ ▸ n. **1** a person who tries to obtain business orders, advertising, etc.; a canvasser. **2** the chief law officer of a city, town, or government department. [ME: from OFr. *solliciteur*, from *solliciter* (see SOLICIT).]

so·lic·i·tor gen·er·al ▸ n. (pl. **so·lic·i·tors gen·er·al**) the law officer directly below the attorney general in the US Department of Justice, responsible for arguing cases before the US Supreme Court. ■ a similar position in some US states.

so·lic·i·tous /sə'lisitəs/ ▸ adj. characterized by or showing interest or concern: *a solicitous inquiry.* ■ archaic eager or anxious to do something. — **so·lic·i·tous·ly** adv. **so·lic·i·tous·ness** n. [16th C.: from L. *sollicitus* (see SOLICIT) + -OUS.]

so·lic·i·tude /sə'lisi,t(y)o͞od/ ▸ n. care or concern for someone or something: *I was touched by his solicitude.* [ME: from OFr. *sollicitude*, from L. *sollicitudo*, from *sollicitus* (see SOLICITOUS).]

sol·id /'sälid/ ▸ adj. (**-id·er, -id·est**) **1** firm and stable in shape; not liquid or fluid: *frozen solid.* ■ strongly built or made of strong materials; not flimsy or slender: *a solid door.* ■ having three dimensions: *a solid cube.* ■ [attrib.] concerned with objects having three dimensions: *solid geometry.* **2** not hollow or containing spaces or gaps: *solid rock.* ■ consisting of the same substance throughout: *solid silver cutlery.* ■ (of typesetting) without extra space between the lines of characters. ■ (of a line or surface) without spaces; unbroken. ■ (of time) uninterrupted; continuous: *a solid day of meetings.* **3** dependable; reliable: *there is solid evidence of lower inflation.* ■ sound but without any special qualities or flair: *the acting is solid.* ■ unanimous or undivided: *the team received solid support.* ■ financially sound. ■ [predic.] (**solid with**) informal on good terms with: *he put himself in solid with you.* ▸ n. a substance or object that is solid rather than liquid or fluid. ■ (**solids**) food that is not liquid: *she rarely eats solids.* ■ Geom. a body or geometric figure having three dimensions. — **sol·id·ly** adv. **sol·id·ness** n. [ME: from L. *solidus*; rel. to *salvus* 'safe' and *sollus* 'entire.']

sol·i·da·go /,sälə'dāgō/ ▸ n. (pl. **-gos**) a plant of the genus *Solidago* in the daisy family, esp. (in gardening) goldenrod. [mod. L., from a med. L. alt. of late L. *consolida* 'comfrey.']

sol·id an·gle ▸ n. a three-dimensional analog of an angle, such as that subtended by a cone or formed by planes meeting at a point. It is measured in steradians.

sol·i·dar·i·ty /,sälə'de(ə)ritē/ ▸ n. **1** unity or agreement of feeling or action, esp. among individuals with a common interest; mutual support within a group. **2** (**Solidarity**) an independent trade union movement in Poland that developed into a mass campaign for political change and inspired popular opposition to communist regimes across eastern Europe during the 1980s. [translating Pol. *Solidarnoś'c'*.] [19th C.: from Fr. *solidarité*, from *solidaire* 'solidary.']

sol·i·dar·y /'sälə,derē/ ▸ adj. (of a group or community) characterized by solidarity or coincidence of interests. [19th C.: from Fr. *solidaire*, from *solide* 'solid.']

sol·id-bod·y ▸ adj. denoting or relating to an electric guitar without a sound box, the strings being mounted on a solid shaped block forming the guitar body.

sol·id-drawn ▸ adj. (of a tube) pressed or drawn out from a solid bar of metal.

sol·i·di /'säli,dī/ plural form of SOLIDUS.

so·lid·i·fy /sə'lidə,fī/ ▸ v. (**-fies, -fied**) make or become hard or solid: [intrans.] *the magma slowly solidifies.* ■ [trans.] fig. make stronger; reinforce: *social pressures solidified national identities.* — **so·lid·i·fi·ca·tion** /sə,lidəfi'kāsнən/ n. **so·lid·i·fi·er** /-ər/ n.

so·lid·i·ty /sə'liditē/ ▸ n. the quality or state of being firm or strong in structure: *the solidity of Romanesque architecture.* ■ the quality of being substantial or reliable in character.

sol·id so·lu·tion ▸ n. Chem. a solid mixture containing a minor component uniformly distributed within the crystal lattice of the major component.

sol·id state ▸ n. the state of matter in which materials are not fluid but retain their boundaries without support, the atoms or molecules occupying fixed positions with respect to one another and unable to move freely. ▸ adj. (**sol·id-state**) (of a device) making use of the electronic properties of solid semiconductors (as opposed to electron tubes).

sol·i·dus /'sälidəs/ ▸ n. (pl. **-di** /-,dī/) **1** another term for SLASH[1] (sense 2). **2** (also **sol·i·dus curve**) Chem. a curve in a graph of the temperature and composition of a mixture, below which the substance is entirely solid. **3** hist. a gold coin of the later Roman Empire. [from L. *solidus (nummus)*.] [L., lit. 'solid.']

so·li·fluc·tion /,sälə'fləksнən; ,sō-/ ▸ n. Geol. the gradual movement of wet soil or other material down a slope, esp. where frozen subsoil acts as a barrier to the percolation of water. [20th C.: from L. *solum* 'soil' + *fluctio(n-)* 'flowing,' from the verb *fluere*.]

so·lil·o·quy /sə'liləkwē/ ▸ n. (pl. **-quies**) an act of speaking one's thoughts aloud when by oneself or regardless of any hearers, esp. by a character in a play. ■ a part of a play involving such an act. — **so·lil·o·quist** /-kwist/ n. **so·lil·o·quize** /-,kwīz/ v. [ME: from late L. *soliloquium*, from L. *solus* 'alone' + *loqui* 'speak.']

sol·ip·sism /'sälip,sizəm/ ▸ n. the view or theory that the self is all that can be known to exist. — **sol·ip·sist** n. **sol·ip·sis·tic** /,sälip'sistik/ adj. **sol·ip·sis·ti·cal·ly** /,sälip'sistik(ə)lē/ adv. [19th C.: from L. *solus* 'alone' + *ipse* 'self' + -ISM.]

sol·i·taire /'sälə,te(ə)r/ ▸ n. **1** any of various card games played by one person, the object of which is to use up all one's cards by forming particular arrangements and sequences. **2** a diamond or other gem set in a piece of jewelry by itself. ■ a ring set with such a gem. **3** either of two large extinct flightless birds (family Raphidae) related to the dodo, found on two of the Mascarene Islands until they were exterminated in the 18th century. **4** a large American thrush (genus *Myadestes*) with mainly gray plumage and a short bill. [18th C.: from Fr., from L. *solitarius* (see SOLITARY).]

sol·i·tar·y /'säləˌterē/ ▶ **adj.** done or existing alone: *I live a pretty solitary life | tigers are essentially solitary.* ■ (of a place) secluded or isolated. ■ [attrib.] [often with negative] single; only: *not a solitary shred of evidence.* ■ (of a bird, mammal, or insect) living alone or in pairs, esp. in contrast to related social forms. ■ (of a flower or other part) borne singly. ▶ **n.** (pl. **-tar·ies**) **1** a recluse or hermit. **2** informal short for SOLITARY CONFINEMENT. — **sol·i·tar·i·ly** /-rəlē/ **adv. sol·i·tar·i·ness n.** [ME: from L. *solitarius*, from *solus* 'alone.']

sol·i·tar·y con·fine·ment ▶ **n.** the isolation of a prisoner in a separate cell as a punishment.

sol·i·tar·y wave ▶ **n.** another term for SOLITON.

sol·i·ton /'säliˌtän/ ▶ **n.** Physics a quantum or quasiparticle propagated as a traveling nondissipative wave that is neither preceded nor followed by another such disturbance. [1960s: from SOLITARY + -ON.]

sol·i·tude /'säləˌt(y)o͞od/ ▶ **n.** the state or situation of being alone: *a few hours of solitude.* ■ a lonely or uninhabited place. [ME: from OFr., or from L. *solitudo*, from *solus* 'alone.']

sol·mi·za·tion /ˌsälmi'zāsHən; sōl-/ ▶ **n.** Music a system of associating each note of a scale with a particular syllable (typically the sequence *do, re, mi, fa, sol, la, ti*), esp. to teach singing. [18th C.: from Fr. *solmisation*, based on *sol* 'sol' + *mi*.]

soln. ▶ **abbr.** solution.

so·lo /'sōlō/ ▶ **n.** (pl. **-los**) **1** a thing done by one person unaccompanied, in particular: ■ (pl. **so·los** or **so·li** /'sōlē/) a piece of vocal or instrumental music or a dance, or a part or passage in one, for one performer. ■ an unaccompanied flight by a pilot in an aircraft. **2** a card game in which one player plays against the others in an attempt to win a specified number of tricks. ▶ **adj. & adv.** for or done by one person alone; unaccompanied: [as adj.] *a solo album.* ▶ **v.** (**so·loes, so·loed**) [intrans.] perform something unaccompanied, in particular: ■ perform an unaccompanied piece of music or a part or passage in one. ■ fly an aircraft unaccompanied. ■ undertake solo climbing. [17th C. (as a musical term): from Ital., from L. *solus* 'alone.']

so·lo·ist /'sōlōist/ ▶ **n.** a singer or other musician who performs a solo.

Sol·o·mon /'säləmən/, son of David; king of Israel *c.*970–*c.*930 BC. In the Bible he is traditionally associated with the Song of Solomon, Ecclesiastes, and Proverbs. ■ [as n.] (usu. **a Solomon**) a very wise person. — **Sol·o·mon·ic** /ˌsälə'mänik/ **adj.**

Sol·o·mon Is·lands (also **the Sol·o·mons**) a country that consists of a group of islands in the southwestern Pacific. *See box.* — **Sol·o·mon Is·land·er n.**

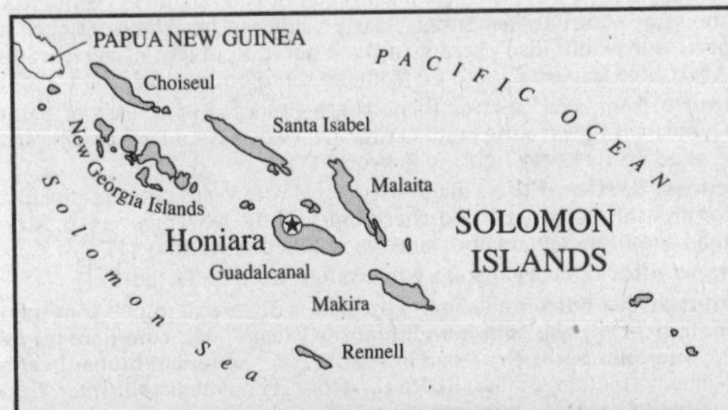

Solomon Islands

Location: southwestern Pacific, to the east of New Guinea
Area: 11,000 square miles (28,500 sq km)
Population: 523,000
Capital: Honiara
Languages: English (official), Pidgin, and Austronesian languages
Currency: Solomon Islands dollar

Sol·o·mon's seal ▶ **n. 1** a figure similar to the Star of David. **2** a widely distributed plant (genus *Polygonatum*) of the lily family, having arching stems that bear a double row of broad leaves with drooping flowers in their axils.

So·lon /'sōlən; 'sōˌlän/ (*c.*630–*c.*560 BC), Athenian statesman and lawgiver. One of the Seven Sages, he revised the code of laws established by Draco.

So·lo·thurn /'zôləˌtərn/ a canton in northwestern Switzerland, in the Jura mountains. French name **SOLEURE**.

sol·stice /'sōlstis/ ▶ **n.** either of the two times in the year, the **summer solstice** and the **winter solstice**, when the sun reaches its highest or lowest point in the sky at noon, marked by the longest and shortest days. — **sol·sti·tial** /sōl'stisHəl/ **adj.** [ME: from OFr., from L. *solstitium*, from *sol* 'sun' + *stit-* 'stopped, stationary' (from the verb *sistere*).]

Sol·ti /'sHōltē/, Sir Georg (1912–97), British conductor; born in Hungary. He was conductor of the Chicago Symphony Orchestra 1969–91 and the London Philharmonic Orchestra 1979–83.

sol·u·bi·lize /'sälyəbəˌlīz/ ▶ **v.** [trans.] tech. make (a substance) soluble or more soluble. — **sol·u·bi·li·za·tion** /ˌsälyəbəli'zāsHən/ **n.**

sol·u·ble /'sälyəbəl/ ▶ **adj. 1** (of a substance) able to be dissolved, esp. in water: *the poison is **soluble in** alcohol.* **2** (of a problem) able to be solved. — **sol·u·bil·i·ty** /ˌsälyə'bilitē/ **n.** [ME: from OFr., from late L. *solubilis*, from *solvere* (see SOLVE).]

sol·u·ble glass ▶ **n.** another term for WATER GLASS (sense 1).

so·lu·nar /sō'lo͞onər/ ▶ **adj.** of or relating to the combined influence or conjunction of the sun and moon. [18th C.: blend of SOL and LUNAR.]

so·lus /'sōləs/ ▶ **adj.** (fem. **so·la** /'sōlə/) alone or unaccompanied (used esp. as a stage direction). [L.]

sol·ute /'sälˌyo͞ot/ ▶ **n.** the minor component in a solution, dissolved in the solvent. [19th C.: from L. *solutum*, neut. of *solutus* 'loosened,' past part. of the verb *solvere*.]

so·lu·tion /sə'lo͞osHən/ ▶ **n. 1** a means of solving a problem or dealing with a difficult situation: *there are no easy solutions to financial and marital problems.* ■ the correct answer to a puzzle. **2** a liquid mixture in which the minor component (the solute) is uniformly distributed within the major component (the solvent). ■ the process or state of being dissolved in a solvent. [ME: from OFr., from L. *solutio(n-)*, from *solvere* 'loosen' (see SOLVE).]

so·lu·tion set ▶ **n.** Math. the set of all the solutions of an equation or condition.

So·lu·tre·an /sə'lo͞otrēən/ ▶ **adj.** Archaeol. of, relating to, or denoting an Upper Paleolithic culture of parts of Europe, dated to about 21,000–18,000 years ago. ■ [as n.] (**the Solutrean**) the Solutrean culture or period. [19th C.: from *Solutré*, the site of a cave in eastern France, where objects from this culture were found, + -AN.]

solv·ate ▶ **v.** /'sälvāt/ [trans.] Chem. (of a solvent) enter into reversible chemical combination with (a dissolved molecule, ion, etc.). ▶ **n.** a more or less loosely bonded complex formed between a solvent and a dissolved species. — **solv·a·tion** /säl'vāsHən/ **n.** [20th C.: formed irregularly from SOLVE + -ATE[1].]

solve /sälv; sôlv/ ▶ **v.** [trans.] find an answer to, explanation for, or means of effectively dealing with (a problem or mystery). — **solv·a·ble adj. solv·er n.** [ME: from L. *solvere* 'loosen, unfasten.']

sol·vent /'sälvənt/ ▶ **adj. 1** having assets in excess of liabilities; able to pay one's debts. **2** [attrib.] able to dissolve other substances: *solvent action.* ▶ **n.** the liquid in which a solute is dissolved to form a solution. ■ a liquid, typically one other than water, used for dissolving other substances. ■ fig. something that acts to weaken or dispel a particular attitude or situation: *an unrivaled solvent of social prejudices.* — **sol·ven·cy n.** (sense 1 of the **adjective**). [17th C.: from L. *solvent-* 'loosening, unfastening, paying,' from the verb *solvere*.]

Sol·way Firth /ˌsôlwā/ an inlet of the Irish Sea that separates northwestern England from Dumfries and Galloway in Scotland.

Sol·zhe·ni·tsyn /ˌsōlzHə'nētsən; ˌsôl-/, Alexander (1918–), Russian writer; Russian name *Aleksandr Isaevich Solzhenitsyn.* His writing, influenced by his eight years in a Soviet labor camp, includes the novel *Cancer Ward* (1968) and the three-volume nonfictional narrative *The Gulag Archipelago* (1973–78). Nobel Prize for Literature (1970).

som /sōm/ ▶ **n.** (pl. same) the basic monetary unit of Kyrgyzstan, equal to 100 tiyin.

so·ma[1] /'sōmə/ ▶ **n.** [usu. in sing.] Biol. the parts of an organism other than the reproductive cells. ■ the body as distinct from the soul, mind, or psyche. [19th C.: from Gk. *sōma* 'body.']

so·ma[2] ▶ **n.** Hinduism an intoxicating drink prepared from a plant and used in Vedic ritual, believed to be the drink of the gods. ■ (also **soma plant**) the plant (*Sarcostemma acidum*, family Asclepiadaceae) from which this drink is prepared. [from Sanskrit *sōma*.]

som·aes·the·tic ▶ **adj.** British spelling of SOMESTHETIC.

So·ma·li /sə'mälē; sō-/ ▶ **n.** (pl. same or **-lis**) a member of a mainly Muslim people of Somalia. ■ the Cushitic language of Somalia. ■ a native or national of Somalia. ▶ **adj.** relating to Somalia, the Somalis, or their language. — **So·ma·li·an** /-lēən/ **adj. & n.** [the name in Somali.]

So·ma·li·a /sə'mälēə; sō'mälyə/ a country in northeastern Africa. *See box on next page.*

So·ma·li Pen·in·su·la another name for HORN OF AFRICA.

so·mat·ic /sə'matik; sō-/ ▶ **adj.** of or relating to the body, esp. as distinct from the mind. ■ Biol. of or relating to the soma. ■ Anat. of or relating to the outer wall of the body, as opposed to the viscera. — **so·mat·i·cal·ly adv.** [18th C.: from Gk. *sōmatikos*, from *sōma* 'body.']

so·mat·ic cell ▶ **n.** Biol. any cell of a living organism other than the reproductive cells.

so·mat·i·za·tion /ˌsəˌmatə'zāsHən; 'sōmə-/ ▶ **n.** Psychiatry the production of recurrent and multiple medical symptoms with no discernible organic cause.

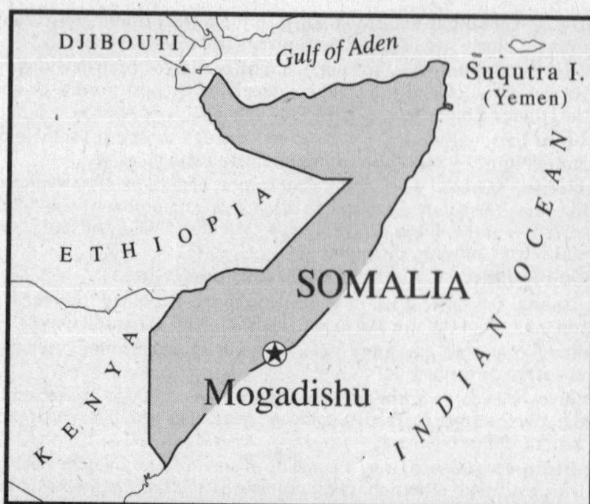

Somalia

Location: northeastern Africa, on the peninsula known as the Horn of Africa
Area: 246,300 square miles (637,700 sq km)
Population: 8,304,000
Capital: Mogadishu
Languages: Somali (official); Arabic, Italian, English
Currency: Somali shilling

somato- ▶ **comb. form** of or relating to the human or animal body: *somatotype.* [from Gk. *sōma, sōmat-* 'body.']

so·mat·o·me·din /sə,matə'mēdn; ,sōmə-/ ▶ **n.** Biochem. a hormone that acts as an intermediate in the stimulation of tissue growth by growth hormone. [1970s: from SOMATO- 'of the body' + *(inter)med(iary)* + -IN[1].]

so·mat·o·pleure /sə'matə,plo͝or; 'sōmətə-/ ▶ **n.** Embryol. a layer of tissue in a vertebrate embryo comprising the ectoderm and the outer layer of mesoderm, and giving rise to the amnion, the chorion, and part of the body wall. Often contrasted with SPLANCHNOPLEURE. [19th C.: from SOMATO- 'of the body' + Gk. *pleura* 'side.']

so·mat·o·sen·so·ry /sə,matə'sensərē; ,sōmətə-/ ▶ **adj.** Physiol. relating to or denoting a sensation (such as pressure, pain, or warmth) that can occur anywhere in the body, in contrast to one localized at a sense organ (such as sight, balance, or taste). Also called SOMESTHETIC.

so·mat·o·stat·in /sə,matə'statn; ,sōmə-/ ▶ **n.** Biochem. a hormone secreted in the pancreas and pituitary gland that inhibits gastric secretion and somatotropin release.

so·mat·o·tro·pin /sə,matə'trōpən/ (also **so·mat·o·tro·phin**) ▶ **n.** Biochem. a growth hormone secreted by the anterior pituitary gland.

so·mat·o·type /sə'matə,tīp; ,sōmə-/ ▶ **n.** a category to which people are assigned according to the extent to which their bodily physique conforms to a basic type (usually endomorphic, mesomorphic, or ectomorphic). — **so·mat·o·typ·ing n.** [1940s: coined by W. H. Sheldon in *Varieties of Human Physique.*]

som·ber /'sämbər/ (Brit. also **som·bre**) ▶ **adj.** dark or dull in color or tone; gloomy. ■ oppressively solemn or sober in mood; grave: *a somber expression.* — **som·ber·ly adv. som·ber·ness n.** [18th C.: from Fr., based on L. *sub* 'under' + *umbra* 'shade.']

som·bre·ro /säm'bre(ə)rō/ ▶ **n.** (pl. **-ros**) a broad-brimmed felt or straw hat, typically worn in Mexico and the southwestern US. [Sp., from *sombra* 'shade' (see SOMBER).]

some /səm/ ▶ **adj. 1** an unspecified amount or number of: *I made some money.* **2** used to refer to someone or something that is unknown or unspecified: *she married some newspaper magnate twice her age.* **3** (used with a number) approximately: *some thirty different languages.* **4** a considerable amount or number of: *for some years now.* **5** at least a small amount or number of: *he liked some music but generally wasn't musical.* **6** expressing admiration of something notable: *that was some goal.* ■ used ironically to express disapproval or disbelief: *Mr. Power gave his stock reply. Some help.* ▶ **pron. 1** an unspecified number or amount of people or things: *if you want whiskey I'll give you some.* **2** at least a small amount or number of people or things: *surely some have noticed.* ▶ **adv.** informal to some extent; somewhat: *the rules change some.*
– PHRASES **and then some** informal and plenty more than that. **some few** see FEW. **some little** a considerable amount of. [OE *sum*, of Gmc. origin, from an Indo-Eur. root shared by Gk. *hamōs* 'somehow' and Sanskrit *sama* 'any, every.']

-some[1] ▶ **suffix** forming adjectives meaning: **1** productive of: *loathsome.* **2** characterized by being: *wholesome.* ■ apt to: *tiresome.* [OE *-sum.*]

-some[2] ▶ **suffix** (forming nouns) denoting a group of a specified number: *foursome.* [OE *sum* 'some.']

-some[3] ▶ **comb. form** denoting a portion of a body, esp. a particle of a cell: *chromosome.* [from Gk. *sōma* 'body.']

some·bod·y /'səm,bädē/ ▶ **pron. 1** some person; someone. **2** a person of importance or authority: *I'd like to be somebody.*

some·day /'səm,dā/ ▶ **adv.** at some time in the future.

some·how /'səm,hou/ ▶ **adv.** in some way; by some means. ■ for a reason that is not known or specified: *he looked different somehow.*

some·one /'səm,wən/ ▶ **pron. 1** an unknown or unspecified person; some person: *there's someone at the door.* **2** a person of importance or authority.

some·place /'səm,plās/ ▶ **adv. & pron.** informal another term for SOMEWHERE.

som·er·sault /'səmər,sôlt/ ▶ **n.** an acrobatic movement in which a person turns head over heels in the air or on the ground and lands or finishes on their feet: fig. *Paula's stomach **turned a somersault.*** ■ fig. a dramatic upset or reversal of policy or opinion. ▶ **v.** [intrans.] perform such an acrobatic feat, or make a similar movement accidentally. [16th C. (as a n.): from OFr. *sombresault*, from Provençal *sobresaut*, from *sobre* 'above' + *saut* 'leap.']

som·es·the·tic /,sōmes'THetik/ (Brit. **som·aes·thet·ic**) ▶ **adj.** another term for SOMATOSENSORY. [19th C.: from Gk. *sōma* 'body' + AESTHETIC.]

some·thing /'səm,THiNG/ ▶ **pron. 1** a thing that is unspecified or unknown: *we stopped for something to eat.* **2** used in various expressions indicating that a description or amount being stated is not exact: *there were **something like** fifty applications.* ▶ **adv.** [as submodifier] informal used for emphasis with a following adjective functioning as an adverb: *my back hurts something terrible.*
– PHRASES **or something** informal added as a reference to an unspecified alternative similar to the thing mentioned. **really** (or **quite**) **something** informal something considered impressive or notable. **something else** informal an exceptional person or thing. **something of** to some degree. **there is something in/to ——** —— is worth considering; there is some truth in ——: *I think there's something in this alien business.* **thirty-something** (**forty-something**, etc.) informal an unspecified age between thirty and forty (forty and fifty, etc.). [OE *sum thing* (see SOME, THING).]

some·time /'səm,tīm/ ▶ **adv.** at some unspecified or unknown time: *come and have supper sometime.* ▶ **adj. 1** former: *the sometime editor of the paper.* **2** occasional: *a sometime contributor.*

some·times /'səm,tīmz/ ▶ **adv.** occasionally, rather than all of the time: *sometimes I want to cry.*

some·way /'səm,wā/ ▶ **adv.** (often **someways**) informal in some way or manner; by some means.

some·what /'səm,(h)wät/ ▶ **adv.** to a moderate extent or by a moderate amount: *matters have improved somewhat.*

some·when /'səm,(h)wen/ ▶ **adv.** informal at some time: *somewhen between 1918 and 1930.*

some·where /'səm,(h)we(ə)r/ ▶ **adv.** in or to some place: *can we go somewhere warm?* ■ used to indicate an approximate amount: ***somewhere around** twenty dollars.* ▶ **pron.** some unspecified place: *somewhere to live.*
– PHRASES **get somewhere** informal make progress; achieve success.

so·mite /'sōmīt/ ▶ **n.** Zool. each of a number of body segments containing the same internal structures, clearly visible in invertebrates such as earthworms but also present in the embryonic stages of vertebrates. Also called METAMERE. [19th C.: from Gk. *sōma* 'body' + -ITE[1].]

Somme /sôm; säm/ a river in northern France. Rising east of Saint-Quentin, it flows to the English Channel northeast of Dieppe. The area around it saw heavy fighting in World War I.

Somme, Battle of the a major battle of World War I between the British and the Germans, in northern France July–November 1916. More than a million men on both sides were killed or wounded.

som·me·lier /,səməl'yā/ ▶ **n.** a wine waiter. [19th C.: Fr. 'butler.']

som·nam·bu·lism /säm'nambyə,lizəm/ ▶ **n.** sleepwalking. — **som·nam·bu·lant** /-lənt/ **adj. som·nam·bu·lant·ly** /-ləntlē/ **adv. som·nam·bu·list n. som·nam·bu·lis·tic** /-,nambyə'listik/ **adj. som·nam·bu·lis·ti·cal·ly** /-,nambyə'listik(ə)lē/ **adv.** [18th C.: from Fr. *somnambulisme*, from L. *somnus* 'sleep' + *ambulare* 'to walk.']

som·nif·er·ous /säm'nifərəs/ ▶ **adj.** tending to induce sleep; soporific. [17th C.: from L. *somnifer* (from *somnium* 'dream') + -OUS.]

som·no·lent /'sämnələnt/ ▶ **adj.** sleepy; drowsy. ■ causing or suggestive of drowsiness. ■ Med. abnormally drowsy. — **som·no·lence n. som·no·len·cy n. som·no·lent·ly adv.** [ME: from OFr. *sompnolent* or L. *somnolentus*, from *somnus* 'sleep.']

So·mo·za /sə'mōsə; -zə/ a family of Nicaraguan presidents. Anastasio (1896–1956), full name *Anastasio Somoza García*, served 1937–47, 1951–56. His son Luis (1922–67), full name *Luis Somoza Debayle*, served 1957–63. Luis's brother Anastasio (1925–80), full name *Anastasio Somoza Debayle*, served 1967–79.

son /sən/ ▶ **n.** a boy or man in relation to either or both of his parents. ■ a male offspring of an animal. ■ a male descendant: *the sons of Adam.* ■ (**the Son**) (in Christian belief) the second person of the Trinity; Christ. ■ a man considered in relation to his native country or area. ■ a man regarded as the product of a particular person, influence, or environment: *sons of the French Revolution.* ■ (also **my son**) used by an elder person as a form of address for a boy or young man.
– PHRASES **son of a bitch** (pl. **sons of bitch·es**) used as a general term of contempt or abuse. **son of a gun** (pl. **sons of guns**) informal a jocular or affectionate way of addressing or referring to someone: *he's a cranky son of a gun.* [with ref. to the guns carried aboard ships: the epithet is said to have been applied orig. to babies born at sea to women allowed to accompany their husbands.] — **son·ship** /'sən,SHip/ **n.** [OE *sunu*, of

Gmc. origin; rel. to Du. *zoon* and Ger. *Sohn*, from an Indo-Eur. root shared by Gk. *huios*.]

so·nar /'sō,när/ ▶ **n.** a system for the detection of objects under water and for measuring the water's depth by emitting sound pulses and detecting or measuring their return after being reflected. ■ an apparatus used in this system. ■ the method of echolocation used in air or water by animals such as whales and bats. [1940s: from *so(und) na(vigation and) r(anging)*, on the pattern of *radar*.]

so·na·ta /sə'nätə/ ▶ **n.** a classical composition for an instrumental soloist, often with a piano accompaniment. [17th C.: Ital. 'sounded' (orig. as distinct from 'sung'), fem. past part. of *sonare*.]

son·a·ti·na /,sänə'tēnə; ,sōnə-/ ▶ **n.** a simple or short sonata. [18th C.: Ital., dimin. of SONATA.]

sonde /sänd/ ▶ **n.** an instrument probe that automatically transmits information about its surroundings underground, under water, in the atmosphere, etc. [20th C.: from Fr. 'sounding (line).']

Sond·heim /'sänd,hīm/, Stephen Joshua (1930–), US composer and lyricist. He wrote the lyrics for *West Side Story* (1957) and composed the musicals *A Little Night Music* (1973) and *Sweeney Todd* (1979).

sone /sōn/ ▶ **n.** a unit of subjective loudness, equal to 40 phons. [1930s: from L. *sonus* 'a sound.']

son et lu·mière /'sôN nāloo͞m'yer; lY'myer/ ▶ **n.** an entertainment held by night at a historic monument or building, telling its history by the use of lighting effects and recorded sound. [Fr. 'sound and light.']

Song var. of SUNG.

song /sôNG/ ▶ **n.** a short poem or other set of words set to music or meant to be sung. ■ singing or vocal music: *the young men* ***broke into song***. ■ a musical composition suggestive of a song. ■ the musical phrases uttered by some birds, whales, and insects, typically forming a recognizable and repeated sequence and used chiefly for territorial defense or for attracting mates. ■ a poem, esp. one in rhymed stanzas: *The Song of Hiawatha*. ■ archaic poetry.
– PHRASES **for a song** informal very cheaply. **a song and dance** informal a long explanation that is pointless or deliberately evasive. ■ esp. Brit. a fuss or commotion. [OE *sang*, of Gmc. origin.]

song·bird /'sôNG,bərd/ ▶ **n.** 1 a bird with a musical song. 2 Ornithol. a perching bird of the suborder Oscines, distinguished by having the muscles of the syrinx attached to the bronchial semirings; an oscine passerine. 3 fig. a woman singer.

song·book /'sôNG,bo͝ok/ ▶ **n.** a book containing a collection of songs with music.

song cy·cle ▶ **n.** a set of related songs, often on a romantic theme, intended to form a single musical entity.

song form ▶ **n.** a form used in the composition of a song, in particular a simple melody and accompaniment or a three-part work in which the third part is a repetition of the first.

Son·ghai /säNG'gī/ ▶ **n.** (pl. same or **-ghais**) 1 a member of a people living mainly in Niger and Mali. 2 ■ the Nilo-Saharan language of this people. ▶ **adj.** of or relating to this people or their language. [the name in Songhai.]

Song Hong Vietnamese name for RED RIVER (sense 1).

Song·nam /'səNG'näm/ a city in northwestern South Korea, southeast of Seoul; pop. 869,000.

Song of Songs (also **Song of Sol·o·mon**) a book of the Bible containing an anthology of Hebrew love poems traditionally ascribed to Solomon but in fact dating from a much later period.

song·smith /'sôNG,smiTH/ ▶ **n.** informal a person who writes popular songs.

song spar·row ▶ **n.** a sparrowlike North American bird (*Melospiza melodia*) of the bunting family, noted for its constant and characteristic song.

song·ster /'sôNGstər/ ▶ **n.** a person who sings, esp. fluently and skillfully. ■ a person who writes songs or verse. ■ a songbird. [OE *sangestre* (see SONG, -STER).]

song·stress /'sôNGstris/ ▶ **n.** a female songster.

song thrush ▶ **n.** a common European and central Asian thrush (*Turdus philomelos*) with a buff spotted breast, having a loud song in which each phrase is repeated two or three times.

song·writ·er /'sôNG,rītər/ ▶ **n.** a person who writes popular songs or the music for them. — **song·writ·ing n.**

son·ic /'sänik/ ▶ **adj.** relating to or using sound waves. ■ denoting or having a speed equal to that of sound. — **son·i·cal·ly** /-ik(ə)lē/ **adv.** [1920s: from L. *sonus* 'sound' + -IC.]

son·i·cate /'sänikāt/ Biochem. ▶ **v.** [trans.] (usu. **be sonicated**) subject (a biological sample) to ultrasonic vibration so as to fragment the cells, macromolecules, and membranes. ▶ **n.** a biological sample that has been subjected to such treatment. [1950s: from SONIC + -ATE².]

son·ic bar·ri·er ▶ **n.** another term for SOUND BARRIER.

son·ic boom ▶ **n.** a loud explosive noise caused by the shock wave from an aircraft traveling faster than the speed of sound.

son·ics /'säniks/ ▶ **plural n.** musical sounds artificially produced or reproduced.

So·nin·ke /sä'nēNGkā/ ▶ **n.** (pl. same or **-kes**) 1 a member of a people living in Mali and Senegal. 2 the Mande language of this people. ▶ **adj.** of or relating to this people or their language. [the name in Soninke.]

son-in-law ▶ **n.** (pl. **sons-in-law**) the husband of one's daughter.

son·net /'sänit/ ▶ **n.** a poem of fourteen lines using any of a number of formal rhyme schemes, in English typically having ten syllables per line. [16th C.: from Fr., or from Ital. *sonetto*, dimin. of *suono* 'a sound.']

son·net·eer /,säni'ti(ə)r/ ▶ **n.** a writer of sonnets.

son·ny /'sənē/ ▶ **n.** informal used by an older person as a familiar form of address to a young boy.

sono- ▶ **comb. form** of or relating to sound: *sonometer*. [from L. *sonus* 'sound.']

son·o·bu·oy /'sänə,bo͞oē; -,boi/ ▶ **n.** a buoy equipped to detect underwater sounds and transmit them by radio.

son·o·gram /'sänə,gram/ ▶ **n.** 1 a graph representing a sound, showing the distribution of energy at different frequencies. 2 a visual image produced from an ultrasound examination.

so·nog·ra·phy /sə'nägrəfē/ ▶ **n.** 1 the analysis of sound using an instrument that produces a graphical representation of its component frequencies. 2 another term for ULTRASONOGRAPHY. — **son·o·graph** /'sänə,graf/ **n.** **son·o·graph·ic** /,sänə'grafik/ **adj.**

son·o·lu·mi·nes·cence /,sänō,loo͞mə'nesəns/ ▶ **n.** Physics luminescence excited in a substance by the passage of sound waves through it. — **son·o·lu·mi·nes·cent adj.**

So·no·ma Coun·ty a county in northwestern California, known for its wineries; pop. 388,222.

So·no·ra /sə'nôrə/ a state of northwestern Mexico, on the Gulf of California; capital, Hermosillo.

So·no·ra Des·ert an arid region in North America, in southeastern California and southwestern Arizona in the US and much of Baja California and the western part of Sonora in Mexico.

So·no·ran /sə'nôrən/ ▶ **adj.** relating to, denoting, or characteristic of a biogeographical region including desert areas of the southwestern US and central Mexico. [19th C.: from SONORA + -AN.]

so·no·rant /'sänərənt/ ▶ **n.** Phonet. a sound produced with the vocal cords so positioned that spontaneous voicing is possible; a vowel, a glide, or a liquid or nasal consonant. [1930s: from SONOROUS + -ANT.]

so·nor·i·ty /sə'nôritē/ ▶ **n.** the quality or fact of being sonorous. ■ Phonet. the relative loudness of a speech sound.

so·no·rous /'sänərəs/ ▶ **adj.** (of a person's voice or other sound) imposingly deep and full. ■ capable of producing a deep or ringing sound. ■ (of a speech or style) using imposing language. ■ having a pleasing sound. — **so·no·rous·ly adv.** **so·no·rous·ness n.** [17th C.: from L. *sonorus* (from *sonor* 'sound') + -OUS.]

Son·tag /'sän,tag/, Susan (1933–2004), US writer and critic. Her works include *Against Interpretation* (essays, 1966) and the novel *In America* (1999).

sook /so͝ok; sək/ ▶ **n.** a female crab. [1950s: of unknown origin.]

soon /so͞on/ ▶ **adv.** 1 in or after a short time: *he'll be home soon*. ■ early: *it was too soon to know*. 2 used to indicate one's preference in a particular matter: ***I'd just as soon*** *Tim did it*.
– PHRASES **no sooner —— than** used to convey that the second event mentioned happens immediately after the first. **sooner or later** at some future time; eventually. — **soon·ish adv.** [OE *sōna* 'immediately,' of West Gmc. origin.]

Soon·er State /'so͞onər/ a nickname for the state of OKLAHOMA.

soot /so͝ot/ ▶ **n.** a black powdery or flaky substance consisting largely of amorphous carbon, produced by the incomplete burning of organic matter. ▶ **v.** [trans.] cover or clog (something) with soot. [OE *sōt*, of Gmc. origin; rel. to Ger. dial. *Sott*, from an Indo-Eur. root shared by the verb SIT.]

sooth /so͞oTH/ ▶ **n.** archaic truth.
– PHRASES **in sooth** in truth; really. [OE *sōth*, of Gmc. origin.]

soothe /so͞oTH/ ▶ **v.** [trans.] gently calm (a person or their feelings). ■ reduce pain or discomfort in (a part of the body). ■ relieve or ease (pain). — **sooth·er n.** **sooth·ing·ly adv.** [OE *sōthian* 'verify, show to be true,' from *sōth* 'true' (see SOOTH).]

sooth·say·er /'so͞oTH,sāər/ ▶ **n.** a person supposed to be able to foresee the future. — **sooth·say·ing n.** [ME: see SOOTH.]

soot·y /'so͝otē/ ▶ **adj.** (**soot·i·er**, **soot·i·est**) covered with or colored like soot. ■ used in names of birds and other animals that are mainly blackish or brownish black, e.g., **sooty tern**. — **soot·i·ly** /'so͝otl-ē/ **adv.** **soot·i·ness n.**

soot·y mold ▶ **n.** a black velvety mold (family Capnodiaceae, subdivision Ascomycotina) that grows on the surfaces of leaves and stems affected by honeydew.

soot·y tern ▶ **n.** a large oceanic tern (*Sterna fuscata*) that is blackish above and white below, and breeds throughout the tropical oceans.

SOP ▶ **abbr.** ■ Standard Operating Procedure. ■ Standing Operating Procedure.

sop /säp/ ▶ **n.** 1 a thing given or done as a concession of no great value to appease someone whose main concerns or demands are not being met. 2 a piece of bread dipped in gravy, soup, or sauce. ▶ **v.** (**sopped**, **sop·ping**) [trans.] (**sop something up**) soak up liquid using an absorbent substance. [OE *soppian* 'dip (bread) in liquid,' *sopp* (n.), prob. from the base of OE *sūpan* 'sup.']

sop. ▶ abbr. soprano.

so·pai·pil·la /ˌsōpīˈpēyə/ (also **so·pa·pil·la** /ˌsōpə-/) ▶ n. (esp. in New Mexico) a deep-fried pastry, typically square, eaten with honey or sugar or as a bread. [Amer. Sp.]

soph. ▶ abbr. sophomore.

soph·ism /ˈsäfizəm/ ▶ n. a fallacious argument, esp. one used deliberately to deceive. [ME: from OFr. *sophime*, via L. from Gk. *sophisma* 'clever device,' from *sophizesthai* 'become wise' (see SOPHIST).]

soph·ist /ˈsäfist/ ▶ n. a paid teacher of philosophy and rhetoric in ancient Greece, associated in popular thought with moral skepticism and specious reasoning. ■ a person who reasons with clever but fallacious arguments. — **so·phis·tic** /səˈfistik/ adj. **so·phis·ti·cal** /səˈfistikəl/ adj. **so·phis·ti·cal·ly** /səˈfistik(ə)lē/ adv. [16th C.: via L. from Gk. *sophistēs*, from *sophizesthai* 'devise, become wise,' from *sophos* 'wise.']

so·phis·ti·cate ▶ v. /səˈfistəˌkāt/ [trans.] cause (a person or their thoughts, attitudes, and expectations) to become less simple or straightforward through education or experience. ■ develop (something such as a piece of equipment or a technique) into a more complex form. ▶ adj. /səˈfistəˌkāt; -kit/ archaic sophisticated. ▶ n. /səˈfistəˌkāt; -kit/ a person with much worldly experience and knowledge of fashion and culture: *jokes made by New York sophisticates.* — **so·phis·ti·ca·tion** /səˌfistiˈkāsHən/ n. [ME: from med. L. *sophisticatus* 'tampered with,' past part. of the verb *sophisticare*, from *sophisticus* 'sophistic.']

so·phis·ti·cat·ed /səˈfistiˌkātid/ ▶ adj. (of a machine, system, or technique) developed to a high degree of complexity. ■ (of a person or their thoughts, reactions, and understanding) aware of and able to interpret complex issues; subtle: *a sophisticated response to a text.* ■ having, revealing, or proceeding from a great deal of worldly experience and knowledge of fashion and culture: *a chic, sophisticated woman.* ■ appealing to people with such knowledge of experience. — **so·phis·ti·cat·ed·ly** adv.

soph·ist·ry /ˈsäfəstrē/ ▶ n. (pl. **-ries**) the use of fallacious arguments, esp. with the intention of deceiving. ■ a fallacious argument.

Soph·o·cles /ˈsäfəˌklēz/ (c.496–406 BC), Greek playwright. His seven surviving plays include *Antigone* and *Oedipus Rex* (also called *Oedipus Tyrannus*).

soph·o·more /ˈsäf(ə)ˌmôr/ ▶ n. a second-year university or high school student. [17th C.: perh. from earlier *sophumer*, from *sophum, sophom* (obs. vars. of SOPHISM) + -ER[1].]

soph·o·mor·ic /ˌsäf(ə)ˈmôrik/ ▶ adj. of, relating to, or characteristic of a sophomore. ■ pretentious or juvenile.

So·phy /ˈsōfē; ˈsä-/ ▶ n. (pl. **-phies**) hist. a former title for the ruler of Persia. [from Arab. *Ṣafī-al-dīn* 'pure of religion.']

sop·o·rif·ic /ˌsäpəˈrifik/ ▶ adj. tending to induce drowsiness or sleep. ■ sleepy or drowsy. ■ tediously boring or monotonous. ▶ n. a drug or other agent of this kind. — **sop·o·rif·i·cal·ly** /-ik(ə)lē/ adv. [17th C.: from L. *sopor* 'sleep' + -IFIC.]

sop·ping /ˈsäpiNG/ ▶ adj. saturated with liquid; wet through: [as submodifier] *the handkerchief was sopping wet.* [19th C.: pres. part. of SOP.]

sop·py /ˈsäpē/ ▶ adj. (**-pi·er, -pi·est**) informal self-indulgently sentimental. — **sop·pi·ly** /ˈsäpəlē/ adv. **sop·pi·ness** n. [19th C.: from SOP + -Y[1].]

so·pra·ni·no /ˌsäprəˈnēnō/ ▶ n. Music (pl. **-ni·nos**) an instrument, esp. a recorder or saxophone, higher than soprano. [20th C.: Ital., dimin. of SOPRANO.]

so·pran·o /səˈpranō/ ▶ n. (pl. **-pran·os**) the highest of the four standard singing voices. ■ a female or boy singer with such a voice. ■ a part written for such a voice. ■ [usu. as adj.] an instrument of a high or the highest pitch in its family: *a soprano saxophone.* [18th C.: Ital., from *sopra* 'above,' from L. *supra*.]

so·pran·o clef /klef/ ▶ n. Music an obsolete clef placing middle C on the lowest line of the staff.

so·pran·o re·cord·er ▶ n. Music the most common size of recorder, with a range of two octaves from the C above middle C upward.

so·ra /ˈsôrə/ (also **so·ra crake** or **rail**) ▶ n. a common small brown and gray American rail (*Porzana carolina*), frequenting marshes. [18th C.: prob. from an Amer. Ind. language.]

Sorb /sôrb/ ▶ n. a member of a Slavic people living in parts of southeastern Brandenburg and eastern Saxony. Also called WEND. [from Ger. *Sorbe*.]

sorb /sôrb/ ▶ n. the fruit of the true service tree. [16th C.: from Fr. *sorbe* or L. *sorbus* 'service tree,' *sorbum* 'serviceberry.']

sor·bent /ˈsôrbənt/ ▶ n. Chem. a substance that has the property of collecting molecules of another substance by sorption. [20th C.: from *sorb* 'take up by sorption,' on the pattern of *absorbent*.]

sor·bet /sôrˈbā; ˈsôrbit/ ▶ n. a dessert consisting of frozen fruit juice or flavored water and sugar. [16th C.: from Fr., from Ital. *sorbetto*, from Turk. *şerbet*, based on Arab. *šariba* 'to drink'; cf. SHERBET.]

Sorb·i·an /ˈsôrbēən/ ▶ adj. of or relating to the Sorbs or their language. ▶ n. the West Slavic language of the Sorbs, which has been revived from near extinction and has around 70,000 speakers. Also called WENDISH or LUSATIAN.

sor·bi·tan /ˈsôrbəˌtan/ ▶ n. [usu. as adj.] Chem. any of a group of compounds that are cyclic ethers derived from sorbitol or its derivatives. [1930s: blend of SORBITOL and ANHYDRIDE.]

sor·bi·tol /ˈsôrbiˌtôl; -ˌtäl/ ▶ n. Chem. a sweet-tasting crystalline compound, $CH_2OH(CHOH)_4CH_2OH$, found in some fruit, used in industry and as a food additive. [19th C.: from SORB + -ITE[1] + -OL.]

Sor·bonne /sôrˈbən/ the seat of the faculties of science and literature of the University of Paris. [orig. a theological college founded by Robert de *Sorbon*, chaplain to Louis IX, c.1257.]

sor·cer·er /ˈsôrsərər/ ▶ n. a person who has magic powers; a wizard. [ME: from *sorser* (from OFr. *sorcier*, based on L. *sors, sort-* 'lot') + -ER[1].]

sor·cer·er's ap·pren·tice ▶ n. a person who instigates a process or project which they are then unable to control. [translating Fr. *l'apprenti sorcier*, a symphonic poem (1897) by Paul Dukas, suggested by Ger. *der Zauberlehrling* (1797), a poem by Goethe.]

sor·cer·ess /ˈsôrsəris/ ▶ n. a female sorcerer; a witch. ■ informal literary a seductive or captivating woman.

sor·cer·y /ˈsôrsərē/ ▶ n. the use of magic, esp. black magic. — **sor·cer·ous** /-rəs/ adj.

sor·did /ˈsôrdid/ ▶ adj. involving ignoble actions and motives; arousing moral distaste and contempt. ■ dirty or squalid. — **sor·did·ly** adv. **sor·did·ness** n. [ME: from Fr. *sordide* or L. *sordidus*, from *sordere* 'be dirty.']

sor·di·no /sôrˈdēnō/ ▶ n. (pl. **-ni** /-nē/) Music a mute. ■ (**sordini**) (on a piano) the dampers. [16th C.: from Ital., from *sordo* 'mute,' from L. *surdus*.]

sor·dor /ˈsôrdər/ ▶ n. esp. literary physical or moral sordidness. [19th C.: from SORDID.]

sore /sôr/ ▶ adj. (of a part of one's body) painful or aching. ■ [predic.] suffering pain from a part of one's body: *he was sore from the long ride.* ■ [predic.] informal upset and angry: *I didn't even know they were sore at us.* ■ [attrib.] severe; urgent. ▶ n. a raw or painful place on the body. ■ a cause or source of distress or annoyance. ▶ adv. archaic extremely; severely: *they were sore afraid.*

– PHRASES **sore point** a subject or issue about which someone feels distressed or annoyed. **stand** (or **stick**) **out like a sore thumb** be obviously different from the surrounding people or things. — **sore·ness** n. [OE *sār* (n. and adj.), *sāre* (adv.), of Gmc. origin; rel. to Du. *zeer* 'sore' and Ger. *sehr* 'very.']

sore·head /ˈsôrˌhed/ ▶ n. informal a person who is in a bad temper or easily irritated.

sore·ly /ˈsôrlē/ ▶ adv. to a very high degree or level of intensity (esp. of an unwelcome or unpleasant state or emotion): *help was sorely needed.* [OE *sārlīce* (see SORE, -LY[2]).]

sor·ghum /ˈsôrgəm/ ▶ n. a widely cultivated cereal (genus *Sorghum*) native to warm regions of the Old World. It is a major source of grain and of feed for livestock. ■ a syrupy sweetener made from a type of this cereal. [16th C.: mod. L., from Ital. *sorgo*, perh. based on a var. of L. *syricum* 'Syrian.']

so·ri /ˈsôˌrī/ plural form of SORUS.

so·ro·ral /səˈrôrəl/ ▶ adj. formal of or like a sister or sisters. [17th C.: from L. *soror* 'sister' + -AL.]

so·ror·i·ty /səˈrôritē; -ˈrä-/ ▶ n. (pl. **-ties**) a society for female students in a university or college, typically for social purposes. [16th C.: from med. L. *sororitas*, or from L. *soror* 'sister.']

so·ro·sis /səˈrōsis/ ▶ n. (pl. **-ses** /-ˌsēz/) Bot. a fleshy multiple fruit, e.g., a pineapple or mulberry, derived from the ovaries of several flowers. [19th C.: mod. L., from Gk. *sōros* 'heap.']

sorp·tion /ˈsôrpsHən/ ▶ n. Chem. absorption and adsorption considered as a single process. [20th C.: back-form. from ABSORPTION and *ADSORPTION* (see ADSORB).]

sor·rel[1] /ˈsôrəl; ˈsär-/ ▶ n. a European plant (genus *Rumex*) of the dock family, with arrow-shaped leaves that are used in salads and cooking for their acidic flavor. See also WOOD SORREL. [ME: from OFr. *sorele*, of Gmc. origin; rel. to SOUR.]

sor·rel[2] ▶ n. a horse with a light reddish-brown coat. ■ [usu. as adj.] a light reddish-brown color: *a sorrel mare.* [ME: from OFr. *sorel*, from *sor* 'yellowish,' from a Gmc. adj. meaning 'dry.']

sor·rel tree ▶ n. another term for SOURWOOD.

sor·row /ˈsärō; ˈsôr-/ ▶ n. a feeling of deep distress caused by loss, disappointment, or other misfortune suffered by oneself or others. ■ an event or circumstance that causes such a feeling: *their separation was a great sorrow to her.* ■ the outward expression of grief; lamentation. ▶ v. [intrans.] feel or display deep distress. [OE *sorh, sorg* (n.), *sorgian* (v.), of Gmc. origin; rel. to Du. *zorg* and Ger. *Sorge*.]

sor·row·ful /ˈsärəfəl; ˈsôr-/ ▶ adj. feeling or showing grief: *sorrowful eyes.* ■ causing grief: *sorrowful news.* — **sor·row·ful·ly** adv. **sor·row·ful·ness** n. [OE *sorhful* (see SORROW, -FUL).]

sor·ry /ˈsärē; ˈsôr-/ ▶ adj. (**-ri·er, -ri·est**) **1** [predic.] feeling distress, esp. through sympathy with someone else's misfortune. ■ (**sorry for**) filled with compassion for. ■ feeling regret or penitence: *I'm sorry if I was a bit brusque.* ■ used as an expression of apology: *sorry—I didn't mean it.* ■ used as a polite request that someone should repeat something that one has failed to hear or understand. **2** [attrib.] in a poor or pitiful state or condition: *a sorry sight.* ■ unpleasant and regrettable, esp. on account of incompetence or misbehavior: *the whole sorry business.*

– PHRASES **sorry for oneself** sad and self-pitying. — **sor·ri·ly** /ˈsärəlē; ˈsôr-/ adv. **sor·ri·ness** n. [OE *sārig* 'pained, distressed,' of West Gmc. origin, from the base of the n. SORE.]

sort /sôrt/ ▶ n. **1** a category of things or people having some common feature; a type: *a radical change poses all sorts of questions.* ■ [with adj.] informal a person of a specified character or nature: *a genuinely friendly sort.* **2** Comput. the arrangement of data in a prescribed sequence. **3** Print.

a letter or piece in a font of type. ▶ **v.** [trans.] **1** arrange systematically in groups; separate according to type, class, etc.: *she sorted out the clothes.* ■ (**sort through**) look at (a group of things) one after another in order to classify them or make a selection: *she sorted through her mail.* **2** resolve (a problem or difficulty). ■ resolve the problems or difficulties of (someone): *time to sort myself out.*

– PHRASES **after a sort** dated after a fashion. **in some sort** to a certain extent. **nothing of the sort** used as an emphatic way of denying permission or refuting an earlier statement or assumption. **of a sort** (or **of sorts**) informal of an atypical and typically inferior type. **out of sorts** slightly unwell. ■ in low spirits; irritable. **sort of** informal to some extent; in some way or other (used to convey inexactness or vagueness). **the —— sort** the kind of person likely to do or be involved with the thing specified: *the marrying sort.*

– PHRASAL VERBS **sort someone out** informal deal with someone who is causing trouble, typically by restraining, reprimanding, or punishing them. **sort something out 1** separate something from a mixed group. **2** arrange; prepare. —**sort·a·ble adj. sort·er n.** [ME: from OFr. *sorte,* from an alt. of L. *sors, sort-* 'lot, condition.']

sor·tal /'sôrtl/ Ling. & Philos. ▶ **adj.** denoting or relating to a term representing a semantic feature that applies to an entity, classifying it as being of a particular kind. ▶ **n.** a term of this kind, for example *human* as opposed to *engineer.*

sor·tes /'sôr,tēz; -,tāz/ ▶ **plural n.** [treated as sing.] divination, or the seeking of guidance, by chance selection of a passage in the Bible or another text regarded as authoritative. [L., 'chance selections (of the Bible).']

sort·ie /,sôr'tē; 'sôrtē/ ▶ **n.** an attack made by troops coming out from a position of defense. ■ an operational flight by a single military aircraft. ■ a short trip or journey: *a shopping sortie.* ▶ **v.** (**-ies, -ied, -ie·ing**) [intrans.] come out from a defensive position to make an attack. [18th C.: from Fr., fem. past part. of *sortir* 'go out.']

sor·ti·lege /'sôrtl-ij/ ▶ **n.** esp. hist. the practice of foretelling the future from a card or other item drawn at random from a collection. [ME: via OFr. from med. L. *sortilegium* 'sorcery,' from L. *sortilegus* 'sorcerer,' from *sors, sort-* 'lot, chance' + *legere* 'choose.']

sor·ti·tion /sôr'tisʜən/ ▶ **n.** the action of selecting or determining something by the casting or drawing of lots. [16th C.: from L. *sortitio(n-),* from *sortire* 'divide or obtain by lot.']

so·rus /'sôrəs/ ▶ **n.** (pl. **so·ri** /'sôrī/) Bot. a cluster of spore-producing receptacles on the underside of a fern frond. ■ a gamete-producing or fruiting body in certain algae and fungi. [19th C.: mod. L., from Gk. *sōros* 'heap.']

SOS ▶ **n.** (pl. **SOSs**) an international code signal of extreme distress, used esp. by ships at sea. ■ an urgent appeal for help. [20th C.: letters chosen as being easily transmitted and recognized in Morse code; by folk etymology an abbr. of *save our souls.*]

so-so ▶ **adj.** neither very good nor very bad.

sos·te·nu·to /,sästə'nōōtō/ Music ▶ **adj.** (of a passage of music) to be played in a sustained or prolonged manner. ▶ **n.** (pl. **-tos**) a passage to be played in a sustained and prolonged manner. ■ performance in this manner. [Ital., 'sustained.']

sot /sät/ ▶ **n.** a habitual drunkard. —**sot·tish adj.** [OE *sott* 'foolish person,' from med. L. *sottus,* reinforced by OFr. *sot* 'foolish.']

so·te·ri·ol·o·gy /sə,ti(ə)rē'äləjē/ ▶ **n.** Theol. the doctrine of salvation. —**so·te·ri·o·log·i·cal** /-ēə'läjikəl/ **adj.** [19th C.: from Gk. *sōtēria* 'salvation' + **-LOGY**.]

So·thic /'sōᴛʜik; 'sä-/ ▶ **adj.** of or relating to Sirius (the Dog Star), esp. with reference to the ancient Egyptian year fixed by its heliacal rising. [19th C.: from Gk. *Sōthis* (from an Egyptian name of the Dog Star) + **-IC**.]

So·tho /'sōtō/ ▶ **n.** (pl. same or **-thos**) **1** a member of a group of peoples living chiefly in Botswana, Lesotho, and northern South Africa. **2** the group of Bantu languages spoken by these peoples. ▶ **adj.** of or relating to this people or their languages. [the stem of **BASOTHO** and **SESOTHO**.]

so·tol /'sō,tōl/ ▶ **n.** a North American desert plant (genus *Dasylirion*) of the agave family, with spiny-edged leaves and small white flowers. ■ an alcoholic drink made from the sap of this plant. [19th C.: via Amer. Sp. from Nahuatl *tzotolli.*]

sot·to vo·ce /'sätō 'vōcʜē/ ▶ **adv. & adj.** (of singing or a spoken remark) in a quiet voice, as if not to be overheard. [from Ital. *sotto* 'under' + *voce* 'voice.']

sou /sōō/ ▶ **n.** hist. a former French coin of low value. ■ [usu. with negative] informal a very small amount of money: *he didn't have a sou.* [Fr., orig. as *sous* (pl.), from OFr. *sout,* from L. *solidus* (see **SOLIDUS**).]

sou·bise /sōō'bēz/ ▶ **n.** a thick white sauce made with onion purée and often served with fish or eggs. [Charles de Rohan *Soubise* (1715–87), French general and courtier.]

sou·brette /sōō'bret/ ▶ **n.** a minor female role in a comedy, typically that of a pert maidservant. [18th C.: Fr., from Provençal *soubreto,* fem. of *soubret* 'coy,' from *sobrar,* from L. *superare* 'be above.']

sou·bri·quet ▶ **n.** var. of **SOBRIQUET**.

sou·chong /'sōō'cʜông; 'sʜông/ ▶ **n.** a fine black variety of China tea. [18th C.: from Chin. *siú* 'small' + *chúng* 'sort.']

souf·fle /'sōōfəl/ ▶ **n.** Med. a low murmuring or blowing sound heard through a stethoscope. [19th C.: from Fr., from *souffler* 'to blow,' from L. *sufflare.*]

souf·flé /sōō'flā/ ▶ **n.** a light, spongy baked dish made typically by adding flavored egg yolks to stiffly beaten egg whites. ■ any of various light dishes made with beaten egg whites. [Fr. 'blown,' past part. of *souffler* (see **SOUFFLE**).]

Sou·fri·ère /sōō'frɪer/ **1** a dormant volcano on Guadeloupe in the Caribbean. Rising to 4,813 feet (1,468 m), it is the highest peak in the Lesser Antilles. **2** an active volcanic peak on St. Vincent in the Caribbean. It rises to a height of 4,006 feet (1,234 m).

sough /səf; sou/ ▶ **v.** [intrans.] (of the wind in trees, the sea, etc.) make a moaning, whistling, or rushing sound. ▶ **n.** [in sing.] a sound of this type. [OE *swōgan,* of Gmc. origin.]

sought /sôt/ past and past participle of **SEEK**.

sought af·ter ▶ **adj.** in demand; generally desired.

souk /sōōk/ (also **suk, sukh,** or **suq**) ▶ **n.** an Arab market or marketplace; a bazaar. [from Arab. *sūḳ*]

soul /sōl/ ▶ **n. 1** the spiritual or immaterial part of a human being or animal, regarded as immortal. ■ a person's moral or emotional nature or sense of identity. ■ the essence of something: *integrity is the soul of intellectual life.* ■ emotional or intellectual energy or intensity, esp. as revealed in a work of art or an artistic performance. **2** a person regarded as the embodiment of a specified quality. ■ an individual person: *I'll never tell a soul.* ■ a person regarded with affection or pity. **3** African-American culture or ethnic pride. ■ short for **SOUL MUSIC**.

– PHRASES **lost soul** a soul that is damned. ■ esp. humorous a person who seems unable to cope with everyday life. **upon my soul** dated an exclamation of surprise. —**souled adj.** [in comb.] *she was a great-souled character.* [OE *sāwol, sāw(e)l,* of Gmc. origin; rel. to Du. *ziel* and Ger. *Seele.*]

soul food ▶ **n.** traditional southern African-American food.

soul·ful /'sōlfəl/ ▶ **adj.** expressing or appearing to express deep and often sorrowful feeling. —**soul·ful·ly adv. soul·ful·ness n.**

soul kiss ▶ **n.** another term for **FRENCH KISS**.

soul·less /'sōl,lis/ ▶ **adj.** (of a building, room, or other place) lacking character and individuality. ■ (of an activity) tedious and uninspiring. ■ lacking or suggesting the lack of human feelings and qualities. —**soul·less·ly adv. soul·less·ness n.**

soul mate (also **soul·mate**) ▶ **n.** a person ideally suited to another as a close friend or romantic partner.

soul mu·sic ▶ **n.** a kind of music incorporating elements of rhythm and blues and gospel music, popularized by African-Americans.

soul-search·ing ▶ **n.** deep and anxious consideration of one's emotions and motives or of the correctness of a course of action. ▶ **adj.** involving or expressing such consideration: *long, soul-searching conversations.*

soul·ster /'sōlstər/ ▶ **n.** informal a singer of soul music.

sound[1] /sound/ ▶ **n.** vibrations that travel through the air or another medium and can be heard when they reach a person's or animal's ear. ■ a group of vibrations of this kind; a thing that can be heard: *the sound of voices.* ■ the area or distance within which something can be heard: *within sound of the train whistles.* ■ the ideas or impressions conveyed by words: *you've had a hard day, by the sound of it.* ■ (also **musical sound**) sound produced by continuous and regular vibrations, as opposed to noise. ■ music, speech, and sound effects when recorded, used to accompany a film or video production, or broadcast. ■ broadcasting by radio as distinct from television. ■ the distinctive quality of the music of a particular composer or performer or of the sound produced by a particular musical instrument. ■ (**sounds**) informal music, esp. popular music: *sounds of the sixties.* ▶ **v.** [intrans.] emit sound. ■ [trans.] cause (something) to emit sound: *she sounded the horn.* ■ [trans.] give an audible signal to warn of or indicate (something): *a different bell begins to sound midnight.* ■ [trans.] say (something); utter: *he sounded a warning.* ■ convey a specified impression when heard. ■ (of something or someone that has been described to one) convey a specified impression: [with complement] *the house sounds lovely.* ■ [trans.] test (the lungs or another body cavity) by noting the sound they produce: *the doctor sounded her chest.*

– PHRASAL VERBS **sound off** express one's opinions in a loud or forceful manner. —**sound·less adj. sound·less·ly adv. sound·less·ness n.** [ME *soun,* from Anglo-Norman Fr. *soun* (n.), *suner* (v.), from L. *sonus.*]

sound[2] ▶ **adj. 1** in good condition; not damaged, injured, or diseased: *he was not of sound mind.* ■ based on reason, sense, or judgment: *sound advice for healthy living.* ■ competent, reliable, or holding acceptable views. ■ financially secure: *business on a sound footing.* **2** (of sleep) deep and undisturbed. ■ (of a person) tending to sleep deeply. **3** severe: *a sound thrashing.* ▶ **adv.** soundly.

– PHRASES **(as) sound as a bell** in perfect condition. —**sound·ly adv. sound·ness n.** [ME: from OE *gesund,* of West Gmc. origin.]

sound[3] ▶ **v. 1** [trans.] ascertain (the depth of water), typically by means of a line or pole or using sound echoes. ■ Med. examine (a person's bladder or other internal cavity) with a long surgical probe. **2** [trans.] question (someone), typically in a cautious or discreet way, as to their opinions or feelings on a subject. ■ inquire into (someone's opinions of feelings) in this way: *officials arrived to sound out public opinion.* **3** [intrans.] (esp. of a whale) dive down steeply to a great depth. ▶ **n.** a long surgical probe, typically with a curved, blunt end. —**sound·er n.** [ME: from OFr. *sonder,* based on L. *sub-* 'below' + *unda* 'wave.']

sound[4] ▶ **n.** a narrow stretch of water forming an inlet or connecting two wider areas of water such as two seas or a sea and a lake. [ME: from ON *sund* 'swimming, strait'; rel. to **SWIM**.]

Sound, the another name for **ØRESUND**.

sound·a·like /'soundə,līk/ ▶ **n.** a person or thing that closely resembles another in sound.

sound bar·ri·er ▶ **n.** (**the sound barrier**) the increased drag, reduced controllability, and other effects that occur when an aircraft approaches the speed of sound, formerly regarded as an obstacle to supersonic flight.

sound bite ▶ **n.** a short extract from a recorded interview, chosen for its pungency or appropriateness.

sound·board /'sound,bôrd/ (also **sound·ing board**) ▶ **n.** a thin sheet of wood over which the strings of a piano or similar instrument are positioned to increase the sound produced.

sound box (also **sound·box** /'sound,bäks/) ▶ **n.** the hollow chamber that forms the body of a stringed musical instrument and provides resonance.

sound card ▶ **n.** a device that can be slotted into a computer to allow the use of audio components for multimedia applications.

sound check (also **sound·check** /'sound,CHek/) ▶ **n.** a test of sound equipment before a musical performance or recording to check that the desired sound is being produced.

sound ef·fect ▶ **n.** a sound other than speech or music made artificially for use in a play, movie, or other broadcast production.

sound en·gi·neer ▶ **n.** a technician dealing with acoustics for a broadcast or musical performance.

Sound·ex /'soundeks/ ▶ **n.** Comput. a phonetic coding system intended to suppress spelling variations, used esp. to encode surnames for the linkage of medical and other records. [1950s: from **SOUND**[1] + the arbitrary ending *-ex*.]

sound·ing[1] /'soundiNG/ ▶ **n.** the action or process of measuring the depth of the sea or other body of water. ■ a measurement taken by sounding. ■ the determination of any physical property at a depth in the sea or at a height in the atmosphere. ■ (**soundings**) fig. information or evidence ascertained as a preliminary step before deciding on a course of action.

sound·ing[2] ▶ **adj.** [attrib.] archaic giving forth sound, esp. loud or resonant sound. ■ having an imposing sound but little substance: *the orator speaks in sounding commonplaces.*

sound·ing board ▶ **n. 1** a board or screen placed over or behind a pulpit or stage to reflect a speaker's voice forward. ■ another term for **SOUNDBOARD**. **2** a person or group whose reactions to suggested ideas are used as a test of their validity or likely success before they are made public. ■ a channel through which ideas are disseminated.

sound·ing line ▶ **n.** a weighted line with distances marked off at regular intervals, used to measure the depth of water under a boat.

sound·ing rod ▶ **n.** a rod used to measure the depth of water under a boat or in a ship's hold or other container.

sound pres·sure ▶ **n.** Physics the difference between the instantaneous pressure at a point in the presence of a sound wave and the static pressure of the medium.

sound·proof /'sound,proof/ ▶ **adj.** preventing, or constructed of material that prevents, the passage of sound. ▶ **v.** [trans.] make (a room or building) resistant to the passage of sound. — **sound·proof·ing n.**

sound·scape /'sound,skāp/ ▶ **n.** a piece of music considered in terms of its component sounds. ■ the sounds heard in a particular location, considered as a whole.

sound spec·tro·graph ▶ **n.** an instrument for analyzing sound into its frequency components.

sound·stage /'sound,stāj/ (also **sound stage**) ▶ **n.** an area of a movie studio with acoustic properties suitable for the recording of sound, typically used to record dialogue.

sound sym·bol·ism ▶ **n.** the partial representation of the sense of a word by its sound, as in *bang, fizz,* and *slide.* See also **ONOMATOPOEIA**.

sound sys·tem ▶ **n.** a set of equipment for the reproduction and amplification of sound.

sound·track /'sound,trak/ ▶ **n.** a recording of the musical accompaniment to a movie. ■ a strip on the edge of a film on which the sound component is recorded. ▶ **v.** [trans.] provide (a movie) with a soundtrack.

sound wave ▶ **n.** Physics a wave of compression and rarefaction, by which sound is propagated in an elastic medium such as air.

soup /soop/ ▶ **n. 1** a liquid dish, typically made by boiling meat, fish, or vegetables, etc., in stock or water. ■ fig. a substance or mixture perceived to resemble soup in appearance or consistency. **2** informal nitroglycerine or gelignite, esp. as used for safecracking. **3** informal the chemicals in which film is developed.

– PHRASES **from soup to nuts** informal from beginning to end; completely. [from the courses of a dinner.] **in the soup** informal in trouble.

– PHRASAL VERBS **soup something up** informal increase the power and efficiency of an engine or other machine. ■ make something more elaborate or impressive. [1930s, perh. influenced by **SUPER-**.] — **soup·like adj.** [ME: from OFr. *soupe* 'sop, broth (poured on slices of bread),' from late L. *suppa*, of Gmc. origin.]

soup·çon /soop'sôN/ ▶ **n.** [in sing.] a very small quantity of something. [18th C.: Fr., from OFr. *souspeçon*, from med. L. *suspectio* (see **SUSPICION**).]

soup kitch·en ▶ **n.** a place where free food is served to those who are homeless or destitute.

soup·spoon /'soop,spoon/ (also **soup spoon**) ▶ **n.** a large spoon with a round bowl, used for eating soup.

soup·y /'soopē/ ▶ **adj.** (**soup·i·er, soup·i·est**) having the appearance or consistency of soup. ■ (of the air or climate) humid. ■ informal mawkishly sentimental. — **soup·i·ly** /'soopəlē/ **adv. soup·i·ness n.**

sour /'sou(ə)r/ ▶ **adj.** having an acid taste like lemon or vinegar. ■ (of food, esp. milk) spoiled because of fermentation. ■ having a rancid smell: *sour breath.* ■ fig. feeling or expressing resentment, disappointment, or anger. ■ (of soil) deficient in lime and usually dank. ■ (of petroleum or natural gas) containing a relatively high sulfur content. ▶ **n.** [with adj.] a drink made by mixing an alcoholic beverage with lemon juice or lime juice: *a rum sour.* ▶ **v.** make or become sour. ■ make or become unpleasant, acrimonious, or difficult.

– PHRASES **go** (or **turn**) **sour** become less pleasant or attractive; turn out badly. **sour grapes** an attitude in which someone disparages or affects to despise something because they cannot have it themselves. [with allusion to Aesop's fable *The Fox and the Grapes*.] — **sour·ish adj. sour·ly adv. sour·ness n.** [OE *sūr*, of Gmc.]

sour ball ▶ **n.** a jawbreaker candy with a sour flavor.

source /sôrs/ ▶ **n.** a place, person, or thing from which something comes or can be obtained. ■ a spring or fountainhead from which a river or stream issues. ■ a person who provides information. ■ a book or document used to provide evidence in research. ■ tech. a body or process by which energy or a particular component enters a system. The opposite of **SINK**[2]. ■ Electron. a part of a field-effect transistor from which carriers flow into the interelectrode channel. ▶ **v.** [trans.] (often **be sourced**) obtain from a particular source: *each type of coffee is sourced from one country.* ■ find out where (something) can be obtained. — **source·less adj.** [ME: from OFr. *sours(e)*, past part. of *sourdre* 'to rise,' from L. *surgere*.]

source·book /'sôrs,book/ ▶ **n.** a collection of writings and articles on a particular subject, esp. one used as a basic introduction to that subject.

source code ▶ **n.** Comput. a text listing of commands to be compiled or assembled into an executable computer program.

source pro·gram ▶ **n.** Comput. a program written in a language other than machine code, typically a high-level language.

source rock ▶ **n.** Geol. a rock from which later sediments are derived or in which a particular mineral originates. ■ a sediment containing sufficient organic matter to be a future source of hydrocarbons.

sour cher·ry ▶ **n.** another term for **MORELLO**.

sour cream ▶ **n.** cream that has been deliberately fermented by the addition of certain bacteria.

sour·dough /'sou(ə)r,dō/ ▶ **n. 1** leaven for making bread, consisting of fermenting dough, typically that left over from a previous batch. ■ bread made using such leaven. **2** an experienced prospector in the western US or Canada; an old-timer.

sour·gum /'sou(ə)r,gəm/ (also **sour gum**) ▶ **n.** a tupelo (*Nyssa sylvatica*) of eastern North America, with dark bark that has a deeply checkered pattern. Also called **BLACK GUM, BLACK TUPELO, PEPPERIDGE**.

sour mash ▶ **n.** a mash used in distilling certain malt whiskeys. ■ whiskey distilled from this.

sour·puss /'sou(ə)r,poos/ ▶ **n.** informal a bad-tempered or habitually sullen person. [1930s (orig. US): from **SOUR** + **PUSS**[2].]

sour·sop /'sou(ə)r,säp/ ▶ **n. 1** a large acidic fruit with white fibrous flesh. **2** the evergreen tropical American tree (*Annona muricata*) of the custard apple family that bears this fruit.

sour·wood /'sou(ə)r,wood/ ▶ **n.** a North American tree (*Oxydendrum arboreum*) of the heath family with sour-tasting leaves, most common in the southeastern US.

sous- ▶ **prefix** (in words adopted from French) subordinate: *sous-chef.* [from Fr. *sous* 'under.']

Sou·sa /'soozə/, John Philip (1854–1932), US composer; known as the **March King**. His works include *The Stars and Stripes Forever* (1896).

sou·sa·phone /'soozə,fōn/ ▶ **n.** a form of tuba with a wide bell pointing forward above the player's head and circular coils resting on the player's left shoulder and right hip, used in marching bands. — **sou·sa·phon·ist** /-ist/ **n.** [1920s: J. P. **SOUSA**, on the pattern of *saxophone*.]

souse /sous/ ▶ **v.** [trans.] soak in or drench with liquid: *souse the quilts in warm suds.* ■ [often as adj.] (**soused**) put (gherkins, fish, etc.) in a pickling solution or a marinade. ■ [as adj.] (**soused**) informal drunk. ▶ **n. 1** liquid, typically salted, used for pickling. ■ pickled food, esp. a pig's head. **2** informal a drunkard. ■ dated a drinking bout. [ME: from OFr. *sous* 'pickle,' of Gmc. origin.]

sous·lik /'sooslik/ (also **sus·lik** /'səs,lik/) ▶ **n.** a short-tailed ground squirrel (genus *Spermophilus*) native to Eurasia and the Arctic. [18th C.: from Russ.]

sous vide /soo 'vēd/ ▶ **n.** a method of treating food by partial cooking followed by vacuum-sealing and chilling. ▶ **adj. & adv.** (of food or cooking) involving such preparation. [Fr., 'under vacuum.']

sou·tache /soo'tasH/ ▶ **n.** a narrow, flat, ornamental braid used to trim garments. [19th C.: from Fr., from Hungarian *sujtás*.]

sou·tane /soo'tän/ ▶ **n.** a type of cassock worn by Roman Catholic priests. [19th C.: from Fr., from Ital. *sottana*, from *sotto* 'under,' from L. *subtus*.]

Sou·ter /ˈso͞otər/, David Hackett (1939–), US Supreme Court associate justice 1990– .

south /south/ ▶**n.** (usu. **the south**) **1** the direction toward the point of the horizon 90° clockwise from east, or the point on the horizon itself. ■ the compass point corresponding to this. **2** the southern part of the world or of a specified country, region, or town: *the south of France.* ■ (usu. **the South**) the southern states of the United States. **3** [as name] (**South**) Bridge the player sitting opposite and partnering North. ▶**adj.** [attrib.] **1** lying toward, near, or facing the south: *the south coast.* ■ (of a wind) blowing from the south. **2** of or denoting the southern part of a specified area, city, or country or its inhabitants. ▶**adv.** to or toward the south: *they journeyed south.* ▶**v.** [intrans.] move toward the south: *the wind southed a point or two.* ■ (of a celestial body) cross the meridian. [OE *sūth*, of Gmc. origin; rel. to Low Ger. *sud.*]

South Af·ri·ca a country that occupies the most southern part of Africa. *See box.* — **South Af·ri·can adj. & n.**

South Af·ri·can Dutch ▶**n.** the Afrikaans language from the 17th to the 19th centuries, during its development from Dutch.

South A·mer·i·ca a continent that comprises the southern half of the American landmass, connected to North America by the Isthmus of Panama. (See also AMERICA.) *See box on next page.* — **South A·mer·i·can adj. & n.**

South·amp·ton /southˈ(h)amptən/ **1** a city on the southern coast of England; pop. 194,000. **2** a town in southeastern New York, on Long Island; pop. 44,976.

South At·lan·tic O·cean see ATLANTIC OCEAN.

South Aus·tral·ia a state in south central Australia; capital, Adelaide.

South Bend a city in northern Indiana; pop. 107,789. The University of Notre Dame is nearby.

south·bound /ˈsouth,bound/ ▶**adj.** traveling or leading toward the south: *southbound traffic.*

South Car·o·li·na /,karəˈlīnə/ a state in the southeastern US, on the coast of the Atlantic Ocean; pop. 4,012,012; capital, Columbia; statehood, May 23, 1788 (8). — **South Car·o·lin·i·an n. & adj.**

South Chi·na Sea see CHINA SEA.

South Da·ko·ta a state in the northern central US; pop. 754,844; capital, Pierre; statehood, Nov. 2, 1889 (40). — **South Da·ko·tan n. & adj.**

south·east /,southˈēst/ ▶**n. 1** (usu. **the southeast**) the direction toward the point of the horizon midway between south and east, or the point on the horizon itself: *a ship was coming in from the southeast.* ■ the compass point corresponding to this. **2** (also **the Southeast**) the southeastern part of a country, region, or town. ▶**adj.** [attrib.] **1** lying toward, near, or facing the southeast. ■ (of a wind) blowing from the southeast. **2** of or denoting the southeastern part of a specified country, region, or town or its inhabitants: *Southeast Asia.* ▶**adv.** to or toward the southeast. — **south·east·ern** /-ərn/ **adj.**

South·east A·sia an area in southeastern Asia that includes the countries of Cambodia, Indonesia, Laos, Malaysia, Myanmar, Philippines, Singapore, Thailand, and Vietnam.

South·east A·sia Trea·ty Or·gan·i·za·tion (abbr.: **SEATO**) a defense alliance that existed between 1954 and 1977 for countries of Southeast Asia and part of the southwestern Pacific, to further a US policy of containing communism. Its members were Australia, Britain, France, New Zealand, Pakistan, the Philippines, Thailand, and the US.

south·east·er /,southˈēstər/ ▶**n.** a wind blowing from the southeast.

south·east·er·ly /,southˈēstərlē/ ▶**adj. & adv.** another term for SOUTHEAST: [as adj.] *southeasterly winds.* ▶**n.** another term for SOUTHEASTER.

south·east·ward /,southˈēstwərd/ ▶**adv.** (also **south·east·wards**) toward the southeast: *he walked southeastward.* ▶**adj.** situated in, directed toward, or facing the southeast.

South E·qua·to·ri·al Cur·rent an ocean current that flows west across the Pacific Ocean just south of the equator.

south·er·ly /ˈsə<u>th</u>ərlē/ ▶**adj. & adv.** in a southward position or direction. ■ (of a wind) blowing from the south. ▶**n.** (often **southerlies**) a wind blowing from the south.

south·ern /ˈsə<u>th</u>ərn/ ▶**adj. 1** [attrib.] situated in the south or directed toward or facing the south. ■ (of a wind) blowing from the south. **2** living in or originating from the south. ■ of, relating to, or characteristic of the south or its inhabitants. — **south·ern·most** /-,mōst/ **adj.**

South·ern Alps a mountain range on the South Island, New Zealand. Aoraki-Mount Cook, its highest peak, rises to 12,349 feet (3,764 m).

South·ern Bap·tist ▶**n.** a member of a large convention of Baptist churches established in the US in 1845, typically having a fundamentalist and evangelistic approach to Christianity.

South·ern blot ▶**n.** Biol. a procedure for identifying specific sequences of DNA, in which fragments separated on a gel are transferred directly to a second medium on which detection by hybridization may be carried out. [20th C.: Edwin M. *Southern* (born 1938), British biochemist.]

South·ern Cone ▶**n.** the region of South America comprising the countries of Brazil, Paraguay, Uruguay, Argentina, and Chile.

South·ern Cross Astron. the smallest constellation (the Crux or Cross), but the most familiar one to observers in the southern hemisphere.

South·ern·er /ˈsə<u>th</u>ərnər/ (also **south·ern·er**) ▶**n.** a native or inhabitant of the south, esp. of the southern US.

South Africa

Official name: Republic of South Africa
Location: southernmost Africa, bordering Namibia, Botswana, Zimbabwe, Mozambique, and Swaziland, and enclosing Lesotho
Area: 471,100 square miles (1,219,900 sq km)
Population: 42,718,000
Capital: Pretoria (administrative), Cape Town (legislative), Bloemfontein (judicial)
Languages: official languages include Afrikaans, English, Xhosa, Zulu, and others
Currency: rand

South Korea

Official name: Republic of Korea
Location: eastern Asia, occupying the southern part of the peninsula of Korea
Area: 38, 000 square miles (98,500 sq km)
Population: 48,598,000
Capital: Seoul
Languages: Korean (official), English
Currency: South Korean won

south·ern-fried ▶**adj.** (of food, esp. chicken) coated in flour, egg, and breadcrumbs and then deep-fried.

south·ern hem·i·sphere the half of the earth that is south of the equator.

south·ern lights another name for the aurora australis. See AURORA.

South·ern O·cean the sea surrounding Antarctica.

South·ern Rho·de·sia see ZIMBABWE.

Sou·they /ˈsou<u>th</u>ē; ˈsə<u>th</u>ē/, Robert (1774–1843), English poet, associated with the Lake Poets. His poems include "Battle of Blenheim" (1798). He was made England's poet laureate in 1813.

South Geor·gia a barren island in the South Atlantic Ocean, 700 miles (1,120 km) east of the Falkland Islands, of which it is a dependency.

south·ing /ˈsouTHiNG/ ▶n. distance traveled or measured southward, esp. at sea. ■ a figure or line representing southward distance on a map. ■ Astron. the transit of a celestial object, esp. the sun, across the meridian due south of the observer. ■ Astron. the angular distance of a star or other object south of the celestial equator.

South Is·land the larger and more southern of the two main islands of New Zealand, separated from North Island by Cook Strait.

South Ko·re·a a country in eastern Asia, occupying the southern part of the peninsula of Korea. *See box on previous page.* — **South Ko·re·an** adj. & n.

South Ork·ney Is·lands a group of uninhabited islands in the South Atlantic Ocean. Discovered in 1821, they are administered as part of the British Antarctic Territory.

South Os·se·tia an autonomous region of Georgia, situated in the Caucasus on the border with Russia; capital, Tskhinvali. (See also OSSETIA.)

south·paw /'souTH,pô/ ▶ n. a left-handed person, esp. a boxer who leads with the right hand or a baseball pitcher. [19th C.: the usage in baseball is perh. from the orientation of early baseball fields to the same points of the compass, such that the pitcher's left arm was on the "south" side of his body.]

South Platte Riv·er a river that flows from the Rocky Mountains across Colorado to Nebraska, where it joins the North Platte River to form the Platte River.

South Pole ▶ n. see POLE².

South Sand·wich Is·lands a group of uninhabited volcanic islands in the South Atlantic Ocean. They are administered from the Falkland Islands.

South Sea (also **South Seas**) archaic the southern Pacific Ocean.

South Sea Bub·ble a speculative boom in the shares of the South Sea Company in 1720 that ended with the failure of the company and a general financial collapse.

South Shet·land Is·lands a group of uninhabited islands in the South Atlantic Ocean. Discovered in 1819, they are administered as part of the British Antarctic Territory.

south-south·east ▶ n. the compass point or direction midway between south and southeast.

south-south·west ▶ n. the compass point or direction midway between south and southwest.

South, the in the US, a term with several definitions, most commonly the 11 states of the 1861–65 Confederacy: Alabama, Arkansas, Florida, Georgia, Louisiana, Mississippi, North Carolina, South Carolina, Tennessee, Texas, and Virginia. — **South·ern adj.**

south·ward /'souTHwərd/ Naut. ▶ adj. in a southerly direction: *a southward drift.* ▶ adv. (also **south·wards**) toward the south. ▶ n. (**the southward**) the direction or region to the south. — **south·ward·ly adv.**

south·west /,souTH'west/ ▶ n. **1** (usu. **the southwest**) the direction toward the point of the horizon midway between south and west, or the point of the horizon itself. ■ the compass point corresponding to this. **2** the southwestern part of a country, region, or town. ■ (usu. **the Southwest**) the southwestern part of the United States. ▶ adj. [attrib.] **1** lying toward, near, or facing the southwest. ■ (of a wind) blowing from the southwest. **2** of or denoting the southwestern part of a specified country, region, or town or its inhabitants. ▶ adv. to or toward the southwest. — **south·west·ern** /-ərn/ **adj.**

South West Af·ri·ca former name of NAMIBIA.

south·west·er /,souTH'westər/ ▶ n. a wind blowing from the southwest.

south·west·er·ly /,souTH'westərlē/ ▶ adj. & adv. another term for SOUTHWEST. ▶ n. another term for SOUTHWESTER.

south·west·ward /,souTH'westwərd/ ▶ adv. (also **south·west·wards**) toward the southwest. ▶ adj. situated in, directed toward, or facing the southwest.

Sou·tine /soo'tēn/, Chaim (1893–1943), French painter; born in Lithuania. He was a major exponent of expressionism.

sou·ve·nir /,soovə'ni(ə)r/ ▶ n. a thing that is kept as a reminder of a person, place, or event. ▶ v. [trans.] informal take as a memento: *many parts of the aircraft have been souvenired.* [18th C.: from Fr., from *souvenir* 'remember,' from L. *subvenire* 'occur to the mind.']

souv·la·ki /soov'läkē/ ▶ n. (pl. **-la·kia** /-'läkyä/ or **-la·kis**) a Greek dish of pieces of meat grilled on a skewer. [mod. Gk.]

sou'·west·er /,sou'westər/ ▶ n. a waterproof hat with a broad flap covering the neck.

sou'wester

sov·er·eign /'säv(ə)rən/ ▶ n. **1** a supreme ruler, esp. a monarch. **2** a former British gold coin worth one pound sterling, now only minted for commemorative purposes. ▶ adj. possessing supreme or ultimate power: *the people's will is in theory sovereign.* ■ [attrib.] (of a nation or state) fully independent and determining its own affairs. ■ [attrib.] (of affairs) subject to a specified state's control without outside interference. ■ [attrib.] archaic literary possessing royal power and status: *our most sovereign lord the King.* ■ [attrib.] dated very good or effective: *a sovereign remedy.* — **sov·er·eign·ly adv.** [ME: from OFr. *soverain*, based on L. *super* 'above.']

sov·er·eign pon·tiff ▶ n. see PONTIFF.

sov·er·eign·ty /'säv(ə)rəntē/ ▶ n. (pl. **-ties**) supreme power or authority. ■ the authority of a state to govern itself or another state. ■ a self-governing state. [ME: from OFr. *sovereinete*, from *soverain* (see SOVEREIGN).]

so·vi·et /'sōvēit; -,et/ ▶ n. **1** an elected local, district, or national council in the former USSR. ■ a revolutionary council of workers or peasants in Russia before 1917. **2** (**So·vi·et**) a citizen of the former USSR. ▶ adj. (**So·vi·et**) of or concerning the former Soviet Union. — **So·vi·et·i·za·tion** /,sōvēiti'zāsHən/ **n.** **So·vi·et·ize** /-,tīz/ **v.** [20th C.: from Russ. *sovet* 'council.']

So·vi·et·ol·o·gist /,sōvēi'täləjist/ ▶ n. a person who studies the former Soviet Union. — **So·vi·et·o·log·i·cal** /-tə'läjikəl/ **adj.** **So·vi·et·ol·o·gy**/-jē/ **n.**

So·vi·et Un·ion a former federation of communist republics that occupied the northern half of Asia and part of eastern Europe; capital, Moscow. Created from the Russian empire in the aftermath of the 1917 Russian Revolution, the Soviet Union was the largest country in the world. After decades of repression and economic failure, the Soviet Union was formally dissolved in 1991. Full name UNION OF SOVIET SOCIALIST REPUBLICS.

sov·khoz /'säv,kôz/ ▶ n. (pl. same, **-khoz·es**, or **-kho·zy** /-,kôzē/) a state-owned farm in the former USSR. [Russ., from *sov(etskoe) khoz(yaĭstvo)* 'Soviet farm.']

sow¹ /sō/ ▶ v. (past **sowed**; past part. **sown** /sōn/ or **sowed**) [trans.] plant (seed) by scattering it on or in the earth. ■ plant the seeds of (a plant or crop). ■ plant (a piece of land) with seed: *the field was sown with oats.* ■ (**be sown with**) be thickly covered with: *a valley sown with boulders.* ■ cause to appear or spread: *the new policy has sown confusion.*
– PHRASES **sow the seeds** (or **seed**) **of** do something that will eventually bring about (a particular result, esp. a disastrous one). — **sow·er n.** [OE *sāwan*, of Gmc. origin; rel. to Du. *zaaien* and Ger. *säen*.]

sow² /sou/ ▶ n. **1** an adult female pig, esp. one that has farrowed. ■ the female of certain other mammals, e.g., the guinea pig. **2** a large block of metal (larger than a "pig") made by smelting. [OE *sugu*; rel. to Du. *zeug*, Ger. *Sau*, from an Indo-Eur. root shared by L. *sus* and Gk. *hus* 'pig.']

sow·back /'sou,bak/ ▶ n. a low ridge of sand.

sow·bug /'sou,bəg/ (also **sow bug**) ▶ n. another term for WOOD LOUSE.

So·we·to /sə'wetō; -'wātō/ a large urban area, consisting of several townships, in South Africa, southwest of Johannesburg. — **So·we·tan** /-'wetn; -'wātn/ **n. & adj.**

sown /sōn/ past participle of SOW¹.

sow this·tle /'sou 'THisəl/ (also **sow-this·tle**) ▶ n. a Eurasian plant (genus *Sonchus*) of the daisy family, with yellow flowers, thistlelike leaves, and milky sap.

sox /säks/ ▶ n. nonstandard plural spelling of SOCK (sense 1).

Soxh·let /'säkslət/ ▶ n. [as adj.] Chem. denoting a form of condensing apparatus used for the continuous solvent extraction of a solid. [19th C.: Franz *Soxhlet* (1848–1926), Belgian chemist.]

soy /soi/ ▶ n. another term for SOYBEAN. [from Japanese *shō-yu*, from Chin. *shi-yu*, from *shi* 'salted beans' + *yu* 'oil.']

soy·a /'soiə/ (also **soy·a bean**) ▶ n. British term for SOY or SOYBEAN. [17th C.: from Du. *soja*, from Malay *soi* (see SOY).]

soy·bean /'soi,bēn/ ▶ n. a leguminous plant native to Asia, *Glycine max*, widely cultivated for its edible seeds. ■ the fruit of this plant, used in a variety of foods and fodder, esp. as a replacement for animal protein.

So·yin·ka /soi'iNGkə/, Wole (1934–), Nigerian writer; full name *Akinwande Oluwole Soyinka*. His works include the play *The Lion and the Jewel* (1959) and the novel *The Interpreters* (1965). Nobel Prize for Literature (1986).

soy milk (also **soy·bean milk**) ▶ n. the liquid obtained by suspending soybean flour in water, used as a fat-free substitute for milk.

soy sauce (also esp. Brit. **soya sauce**) ▶ n. a sauce made with fermented soybeans, used in Chinese and Japanese cooking.

So·yuz /'sô,yooz/ a series of manned Soviet orbiting spacecraft, used to investigate the operation of orbiting space stations. [from Russ. *Soyúz*, 'union.']

soz·zled /'säzəld/ ▶ adj. informal very drunk. [19th C.: past part. of dial. *sozzle* 'mix sloppily,' prob. imitative.]

SP ▶ abbr. starting price.

s.p. ▶ abbr. without issue; childless. [from L. *sine prole*.]

Sp. ▶ abbr. ■ Spain. ■ Spaniard. ■ (also **Sp**) Spanish.

sp. ▶ abbr. species (usually singular).

spa /spä/ ▶ n. a mineral spring considered to have health-giving properties. ■ a place or resort with such a spring. ■ a commercial establishment offering health and beauty treatment through such means as steam baths, exercise equipment, and massage. ■ a bath or small pool containing hot aerated water. [17th C.: from Spa, a town in Belgium with mineral springs considered curative.]

Spaatz /späts/, Carl (1891–1974), US air force officer; born *Carl Spatz*. He directed the US bombing force in Germany in 1944 and in Japan in 1945, including the dropping of atomic bombs on Hiroshima and Nagasaki.

space /spās/ ▶ n. **1** a continuous area or expanse that is free, available, or unoccupied: *he backed out of the parking space.* ■ an area of land that is not occupied by buildings: *open spaces.* ■ an empty area left between one-, two-, or three-dimensional points or objects. ■ a blank between printed, typed, or written words, characters, numbers, etc. ■ Music each of the four gaps between the five lines of a staff. ■ an interval of time (often used to suggest that the time is short, considering what has happened or been achieved in it): *five cars stolen in the space of three days.* ■ pages in a newspaper, or time between television or radio programs, available for advertising. ■ (also **commercial space**) an area rented or sold as business premises. ■ the amount of paper used or needed to write about a subject. ■ the freedom and scope to live, think, and develop in a way that suits one: *she needs her own space.* ■ Telecom. one

of two possible states of a signal in certain systems. The opposite of MARK[1] (sense 2). **2** the dimensions of height, depth, and width within which all things exist and move: *a journey in space and time.* ■ (also **outer space**) the physical universe beyond the earth's atmosphere. ■ the near-vacuum extending between the planets and stars, containing small amounts of gas and dust. ■ Math. a mathematical concept generally regarded as a set of points having some specified structure. ▶ **v. 1** [trans.] (usu. **be spaced**) position (two or more items) at a distance from one another: *the houses are spaced out.* ■ (in printing or writing) put blanks between (words, letters, or lines). **2** (usu. **be spaced out** or **space out**) informal be or become distracted, euphoric, or disoriented, esp. from taking drugs; cease to be aware of one's surroundings: *I began to feel totally spaced out.*
– PHRASES **watch this space** informal further developments are expected and more information will be given later. — **spac·er** n. [ME: shortening of OFr. *espace*, from L. *spatium*.]

space age ▶ n. (**the space age** or **the Space Age**) the era starting when the exploration of space became possible. ▶ adj. (**space-age**) very modern; technologically advanced: *a space-age control room.*

space bar ▶ n. a long key on a typewriter or computer keyboard for making a space between words.

space ca·det ▶ n. a trainee astronaut. ■ an enthusiast for space travel, typically a young person. ■ informal a person perceived as out of touch with reality, as though high on drugs.

space cap·sule ▶ n. a small spacecraft or the part of a larger one that contains the instruments or crew.

space charge ▶ n. Physics a collection of particles with a net electric charge occupying a region, either in free space or in a device.

space·craft /ˈspās,kraft/ ▶ n. (pl. same or **-crafts**) a vehicle used for traveling in space.

space den·si·ty ▶ n. Astron. the frequency of occurrence of stars, particles, or other heavenly bodies, per specified volume of space.

space·far·ing /ˈspās,fe(ə)riNG/ ▶ n. the action or activity of traveling in space. — **space·far·er** /-rer/ n.

space flight ▶ n. a journey through space. ■ space travel: *the stresses involved in space flight.*

space frame ▶ n. a three-dimensional structural framework that is designed to behave as an integral unit and to withstand loads applied at any point.

space heat·er ▶ n. a self-contained appliance, usually electric, for heating an enclosed room. — **space-heat·ed** adj. **space heat·ing** n.

space lat·tice /ˈlatis/ ▶ n. Crystallog. a regular, indefinitely repeated array of points in three dimensions in which the points lie at the intersections of three sets of parallel equidistant planes.

space·man /ˈspās,man; -mən/ ▶ n. (pl. **-men**) a male astronaut.

space op·er·a ▶ n. informal a novel, movie, or television program set in outer space, typically of a simplistic and melodramatic nature.

space·plane /ˈspās,plān/ ▶ n. an aircraft that takes off and lands conventionally but is capable of entry into orbit or travel through space.

space·port /ˈspās,pôrt/ ▶ n. a base from which spacecraft are launched.

space probe ▶ n. see PROBE.

space race ▶ n. (**the space race**) the competition between nations regarding achievements in the field of space exploration.

space rock·et ▶ n. a rocket designed to travel through space or to launch a spacecraft.

space·ship /ˈspās,SHip/ ▶ n. a spacecraft, esp. one controlled by a crew.

Space·ship Earth ▶ n. [in sing.] the world considered as possessing finite resources common to all humankind. [1966: popularized as the title of a work by Barbara Ward (1914–81).]

space shot ▶ n. the launch of a spacecraft and its subsequent progress in space.

space shut·tle ▶ n. a rocket-launched spacecraft, able to land like an unpowered aircraft, used to make repeated journeys between the earth and earth orbit.

space sta·tion ▶ n. a large artificial satellite used as a long-term base for manned operations in space.

space·suit /ˈspās,so͞ot/ ▶ n. a garment designed to allow an astronaut to survive in space.

space tel·e·scope ▶ n. an astronomical telescope that operates in space by remote control, to avoid interference by the earth's atmosphere.

space-time ▶ n. Physics the concepts of time and three-dimensional space regarded as fused in a four-dimensional continuum.

space ve·hi·cle ▶ n. a spacecraft.

space·walk /ˈspās,wôk/ ▶ n. a period of physical activity engaged in by an astronaut in space outside a spacecraft. — **space·walk·er** n.

space warp ▶ n. an imaginary or hypothetical distortion of space-time that enables space travelers to travel faster than light.

space·wom·an /ˈspās,wo͝omən/ ▶ n. (pl. **-wom·en**) a female astronaut.

spac·ey /ˈspāsē/ (also **spac·y**) ▶ adj. (**spac·i·er, spac·i·est**) informal out of touch with reality, as though high on drugs. ■ (of popular, esp. electronic music) drifting and ethereal.

spa·cial ▶ adj. var. of SPATIAL.

spa·cious /ˈspāSHəs/ ▶ adj. (esp. of a room or building) having ample space. — **spa·cious·ly** adv. **spa·cious·ness** n. [ME: from OFr. *spacios* or L. *spatiosus*, from *spatium* (see SPACE).]

spack·le /ˈspakəl/ ▶ n. (**spackle**) trademark a compound used to fill cracks in plaster or drywall and produce a smooth surface. ▶ v. [trans.] repair (a surface) or fill (a hole or crack) with Spackle. [1920s: perh. a blend of SPARKLE and Ger. *Spachtel* 'putty knife, mastic.']

spade[1] /spād/ ▶ n. a tool with a sharp-edged, typically rectangular, metal blade and a long handle, used for digging or cutting earth, sand, turf, etc. ■ a tool of a similar shape for another purpose, esp. one for removing the blubber from a whale. ■ the part of the trail of a gun carriage that digs into the earth to brace the gun during recoil. ▶ v. [trans.] dig in (ground) with a spade. ■ [with obj. and adverbial of direction] move (soil) with a spade: *earth is spaded into the grave.*
– PHRASES **call a spade a spade** speak plainly without avoiding unpleasant or embarrassing issues. — **spade·ful** /-,fo͝ol/ n. (pl. **-fuls**). [OE *spadu, spada*, of Gmc. origin; rel. to Du. *spade* and Ger. *Spaten*.]

spade[2] ▶ n. **1** (**spades**) one of the four suits in a conventional deck of playing cards, denoted by a black inverted heart-shaped figure with a small stalk. ■ (**a spade**) a card of this suit. **2** informal, derog. a black person.
– PHRASES **in spades** informal to a very high degree. [16th C.: from Ital. *spade*, pl. of *spada* 'sword,' via L. from Gk. *spathē*; cf. SPADE[1].]

spade·fish /ˈspād,fiSH/ ▶ n. (pl. same or **-fish·es**) a marine fish (*Chaetodipterus* and other genera, family Ephippidae) with an almost disk-shaped body. It lives in tropical inshore waters, where it often forms schools.

spade·foot toad /ˈspād,fo͝ot/ ▶ n. a short-legged burrowing toad (family Pelobatidae) with a prominent sharp-edged tubercle on the hind feet, native to North America and Europe. Several genera include *Scaphiophus* (of America) and *Pelobates* (of Europe), and several species, in particular *P. fuscus*.

spade·work /ˈspād,wərk/ ▶ n. routine or difficult preparatory work.

spa·dille /spəˈdil/ ▶ n. (in the card games ombre and quadrille) the ace of spades. [17th C.: from Fr., from Sp. *espadilla*, dimin. of *espada* 'sword' (see SPADE[2]).]

spa·dix /ˈspādiks/ ▶ n. (pl. **-di·ces** /-dəsēz/) **1** Bot. a spike of minute flowers closely arranged around a fleshy axis and typically enclosed in a spathe, characteristic of the arums. **2** Zool. (in certain invertebrates) a part or organ that is more or less conical in shape, e.g., a group of connected tentacles in a nautiloid. [18th C.: via L. from Gk., 'palm branch.']

spaetz·le /ˈSHpetslə; -səl; -slē/ (also **spätz·le**) ▶ plural n. [treated as sing. or pl.] small dumplings of a type made in southern Germany and Alsace, consisting of seasoned dough poached in boiling water. [from Ger. dial. *Spätzle* 'little sparrows.']

spa·ghet·ti /spəˈgetē/ ▶ n. pasta made in long, slender, solid strings. ■ an Italian dish consisting largely of this, typically with a sauce. ■ fig. a tangle of stringlike objects, resembling a plate of cooked spaghetti. ■ Electron. a type of narrow tubing that encases and insulates wire. [Ital., pl. of the dimin. of *spago* 'string.']

spa·ghet·ti bo·lo·gnese /,bōlənˈyēz; -ˈyāz/ ▶ n. spaghetti served with a sauce of ground beef, tomato, onion, and herbs. [Ital., 'spaghetti of Bologna.']

spa·ghet·ti·ni /,spagəˈtēnē/ ▶ n. pasta in the form of strings of thin spaghetti. [Ital., dimin. of *spaghetti* 'little strings' (see SPAGHETTI).]

spa·ghet·ti squash ▶ n. an edible squash of a variety with slightly stringy flesh which when cooked has a texture and appearance like that of spaghetti. Also called VEGETABLE SPAGHETTI.

spa·ghet·ti strap ▶ n. a thin shoulder strap on an item of women's clothing.

spa·ghet·ti west·ern ▶ n. informal a western movie made cheaply in Europe by an Italian director.

spa·hi /ˈspähē/ ▶ n. hist. **1** a member of the Turkish irregular cavalry. **2** a member of the Algerian cavalry in French service. [16th C.: from Turk. *sipahi*, from Pers. *sipāhī* (see SEPOY).]

Spahn /spän/, Warren Edward (1921–2003), US baseball player. He holds the record for the most games won (363) by a left-handed pitcher.

Spain /spān/ a country in southwestern Europe. Spanish name **España**. *See box on next page.*

spake /spāk/ archaic or literary past of SPEAK.

spall /spôl/ ▶ v. [trans.] break (ore, rock, stone, or concrete) into smaller pieces, esp. in preparation for sorting. ■ [intrans.] (of ore, rock, or stone) break off in fragments: *cracks below the surface cause slabs to spall off.* ▶ n. a splinter or chip, esp. of rock. [ME (as a n.): of unknown origin. The verb dates from the 18th C.]

spall·a·tion /spôˈlāSHən/ ▶ n. **1** Physics the breakup of a bombarded nucleus into several parts. **2** Geol. separation of fragments from the surface of a rock, esp. by interaction with a compression wave.

spal·peen /spalˈpēn/ ▶ n. Irish a rascal. [18th C.: from Irish *spailpín*, of unknown origin.]

spalt·ed /ˈspôltid/ ▶ adj. (of wood) containing blackish irregular lines as a result of fungal decay, and sometimes used to produce a decorative surface. [1970s: from dial. *spalt* 'to split, splinter' + -ED[1].]

spam /spam/ ▶ n. **1** (**Spam**) trademark a canned meat product made mainly from ham. **2** irrelevant or inappropriate messages sent on the Internet to a large number of recipients. ▶ v. [trans.] send the same message indiscriminately to (large numbers of recipients) on the Internet. — **spam·mer** n. [1930s: appar. from *sp(iced h)am*.]

span[1] /span/ ▶ n. the full extent of something from end to end; the amount of space that something covers. ■ the length of time for which something lasts: *a short concentration span.* ■ the wingspan of an aircraft or a bird. ■ an arch or part of a bridge between piers or supports. ■ the maximum distance between the tips of the thumb and little finger, taken as the basis of a measurement equal to 9 inches. ■ archaic a short distance or time. ▶ v. (**spanned, span·ning**) [trans.] (of a bridge, arch, etc.) extend from side to side of: *spanned by a narrow bridge.* ■ extend across (a period of time or a range of subjects). ■ cover or enclose with the length of one's hand: *a waist slender enough to span with his hands.* [OE, 'distance between the tips of the thumb and little finger,' of Gmc. origin; reinforced in ME by OFr. *espan.*]

Spain

Official name: Kingdom of Spain
Location: southwestern Europe, occupying the greater part of the Iberian peninsula
Area: 194,900 square miles (504,800 sq km)
Population: 40,280,000
Capital: Madrid
Languages: Castilian Spanish (official), Catalan, Galician, Basque
Currency: euro

span[2] ▶ n. **1** Naut. a rope with its ends fastened at different points to a spar or other object in order to provide a purchase. **2** a team of people or animals, in particular: ■ a matched pair of horses, mules, or oxen. [16th C. (as a verb meaning 'harness or yoke (an animal)'): from Du. or Low Ger. *spannen.*]

span[3] ▶ adj. see SPICK-AND-SPAN.

span[4] esp. archaic past of SPIN.

Span. ▶ abbr. ■ Spaniard. ■ Spanish.

spa·na·ko·pi·ta /ˌspanəˈkäpitə; ˌspänäˈkôpētä/ ▶ n. (in Greek cooking) a phyllo pastry stuffed with spinach and feta cheese. [mod. Gk., 'spinach pie.']

span·dex /ˈspandeks/ ▶ n. a type of stretchy polyurethane fabric. [1950s: an arbitrary formation from EXPAND.]

spandrel

span·drel /ˈspandrəl/ ▶ n. Archit. the almost triangular space between one side of the outer curve of an arch and the rectangle formed by the moldings enclosing it. ■ the space between the shoulders of adjoining arches and the ceiling or molding above. [ME: perh. from Anglo-Norman Fr. *spaund(e)re,* or from *espaundre* 'expand.']

span·drel wall ▶ n. a wall built on the curve of an arch, filling in the spandrel.

spang /spaNG/ ▶ adv. informal directly; completely. [19th C.: of unknown origin.]

span·gle /ˈspaNGgəl/ ▶ n. a small thin piece of glittering material, typically used in quantity to ornament a dress; a sequin. ■ a small sparkling object; a spot of bright color or light. ▶ v. [trans.] [usu. as adj.] (**spangled**) cover with spangles or other small sparkling objects. — **span·gly** adj. [ME: dimin. from obs. *spang* 'glittering ornament,' from MDu. *spange* 'buckle.']

Spang·lish /ˈspaNGgliSH/ ▶ n. a hybrid language combining words and idioms from both Spanish and English, esp. Spanish speech that uses many English words and expressions.

span·iel /ˈspanyəl/ ▶ n. a dog of a breed with a long silky coat and drooping ears. ■ used in similes and metaphors as a symbol of devotion or obsequiousness: *I followed as faithfully as any spaniel.* [ME: from OFr. *espaigneul* 'Spanish (dog),' from L. *Hispaniolus* 'Sp.']

Span·ish /ˈspaniSH/ ▶ adj. of or relating to Spain, its people, or its language. ▶ n. **1** [as pl. n.] (**the Spanish**) the people of Spain. **2** the Romance language of most of Spain and of much of Central and South America and several other countries. — **Span·ish·ness** n. [ME: from SPAIN + -ISH[1], with later shortening of the first vowel.]

Span·ish A·mer·i·ca the parts of America once colonized by Spaniards and in which Spanish is still generally spoken. This includes most of Central and South America (except Brazil) and part of the Caribbean.

Span·ish-A·mer·i·can War a war between Spain and the United States in the Caribbean and the Philippines in 1898.

Span·ish Ar·ma·da see ARMADA.

Span·ish bay·o·net (also **Span·ish dag·ger**) ▶ n. a yucca (genus *Yucca*) native to the southern US and the American tropics. Its several species include *Y. aloifolia.*

Span·ish chest·nut ▶ n. see CHESTNUT (sense 2).

Span·ish Civ·il War the conflict (1936–39) between Nationalist forces (including monarchists and members of the Falange Party) and Republicans (including socialists, communists, and Catalan and Basque separatists) in Spain.

Span·ish-Co·lo·ni·al ▶ adj. denoting a style of architecture characteristic of Spanish America.

Span·ish flu (also **Spanish influenza**) ▶ n. influenza caused by an influenza virus of type A, in particular that of the pandemic that began in 1918.

Span·ish fly ▶ n. a bright green European blister beetle (*Lytta vesicatoria*) with a mousy smell. ■ a toxic preparation of the dried bodies of these beetles, formerly used in medicine as a counterirritant and sometimes taken as an aphrodisiac.

Span·ish gui·tar ▶ n. the standard six-stringed acoustic guitar, used esp. for classical and folk music.

Span·ish i·bex (also **Spanish goat**) ▶ n. see IBEX.

Span·ish In·qui·si·tion /ˌiNGkwiˈziSHən/ an ecclesiastical court established in Roman Catholic Spain in 1478 and directed originally against converts from Judaism and Islam but later also against Protestants.

Span·ish mack·er·el ▶ n. a large edible game fish (genus *Scomberomorus*) of the mackerel family.

Span·ish Main /mān/ the former name for the northwestern coast of South America between the Orinoco River and Panama and adjoining parts of the Caribbean Sea when they were under Spanish control.

Span·ish moss ▶ n. a tropical American plant (*Tillandsia usneoides,* family Bromeliaceae) that grows as silvery-green festoons on trees, obtaining water and nutrients directly through its surface. See also AIR PLANT.

Span·ish om·e·let ▶ n. an omelet containing chopped vegetables, often served open rather than folded.

Span·ish on·ion ▶ n. a large cultivated onion with a mild flavor.

Span·ish rice ▶ n. a dish of rice with onions, peppers, tomatoes, and other vegetables, often colored and flavored with saffron.

Span·ish Sa·har·a former name (1958–75) of WESTERN SAHARA.

Span·ish Suc·ces·sion, War of the a European war (1701–14), provoked by the death of the Spanish king Charles II without issue. The Grand Alliance of Britain, the Netherlands, and the Holy Roman Emperor prevented Spain and France from being united under one crown.

Span·ish Town a town in Jamaica, west of Kingston, the second largest town in Jamaica, a former capital; pop. 110,000.

Span·ish wind·lass ▶ n. a device for tightening a rope or cable by twisting it using a stick as a lever.

spank /spaNGk/ ▶ v. [trans.] slap with one's open hand or a flat object, esp. on the buttocks as a punishment. ▶ n. a slap of this type. [18th C.: perh. imitative.]

spank·er /ˈspaNGkər/ ▶ n. **1** a fore-and-aft sail set on the after side of a ship's mast, esp. the mizzenmast. **2** informal, dated a very fine person or thing.

spank·ing /ˈspaNGkiNG/ ▶ adj. **1** (esp. of a horse or its gait) lively; brisk: *a spanking trot.* **2** informal very good: *we had a spanking time.* ■ fine and impressive: *a spanking white Rolls Royce.* ▶ n. [in sing.] an act of slapping, esp. on the buttocks as a punishment for children.

span·ner /ˈspanər/ ▶ n. esp. Brit. a wrench. [18th C.: from Ger. *spannen* 'draw tight' + -ER[1].]

span·sule /ˈspansoo͝l/ ▶ n. trademark a capsule that when swallowed releases one or more medicinal drugs over a set period. [20th C.: blend of the noun SPAN[1] and CAPSULE.]

span·worm /ˈspanˌwərm/ ▶ n. another term for INCHWORM.

spar[1] /spär/ ▶ n. a thick, strong pole such as is used for a mast or yard on a ship. ■ the main longitudinal beam of an airplane wing. [ME: shortening of OFr. *esparre,* or from ON *sperra.*]

spar[2] ▶ v. (**sparred, spar·ring**) [intrans.] make the motions of boxing

PRONUNCIATION KEY ə *ago, up;* ər *over, fur;* a *hat;* ā *ate;* ä *car;* e *let;* ē *see;* i *fit;* ī *by;* NG *sing;* ō *go;* ô *law, for;* oi *toy;* o͝o *good;* o͞o *goo;* ou *out;* TH *thin;* T͟H *then;* ZH *vision*

without landing heavy blows, as a form of training: *broke his nose while sparring.* ■ engage in argument, typically of a kind that is prolonged or repeated but not violent. ■ (of a gamecock) fight with the feet or spurs. ▶ n. a period or bout of sparring. [OE *sperran, spyrran* 'strike out,' of unknown origin.]

spar[3] ▶ n. [usu. in comb. or with adj.] a crystalline, easily cleavable, light-colored mineral.'— **spar·ry** adj. [16th C.: from Mid. Low Ger.; rel. to OE *spærstān* 'gypsum.']

spar·a·ble /'sparəbəl/ ▶ n. a headless nail used for the soles and heels of shoes. [17th C.: contr. of *sparrow-bill,* in the same sense.]

spar bu·oy ▶ n. a buoy made of a spar with one end moored so that the other stands up.

spar deck ▶ n. an upper deck of a ship or other vessel.

spare /spe(ə)r/ ▶ adj. **1** additional to what is required for ordinary use: *few people had spare cash.* ■ not currently in use or occupied: *the spare bedroom.* **2** with no excess fat; thin: *a spare, bearded figure.* ■ elegantly simple. ■ meager; nearly inadequate. ▶ n. **1** an item kept in case another item of the same type is lost, broken, or worn out. ■ a spare tire: *the spare is in the trunk.* **2** (in tenpin bowling) an act of knocking down all the pins with two consecutive rolls of the ball. ▶ v. **1** [with two objs.] give (something of which one has enough) to (someone); afford to give to: *she asked if I could spare her a dollar or two.* ■ make free or available. **2** [trans.] refrain from killing, injuring, or distressing. ■ [with two objs.] refrain from inflicting (something) on (someone): *the country had been spared the violence occurring elsewhere.* ■ (**spare oneself**) [with negative] try to ensure or satisfy one's own comfort or needs: *she has never spared herself.*
– PHRASES **spare no expense** (or **no expense spared**) be prepared to pay any amount (used to indicate the importance of achieving something). **spare a thought for** esp. Brit. remember: *spare a thought for our volunteer group at Christmas.* **to spare** left over: *plenty for all with some to spare.* — **spare·ly** adv. **spare·ness** n. **spar·er** n. (rare). [OE *spær* 'not plentiful, meager,' *sparian* 'refrain from injuring,' 'refrain from using,' of Gmc. origin.]

spare part ▶ n. a duplicate part to replace a lost or damaged part of a machine.

spare·ribs /'spe(ə)r,ribz/ (also **spare ribs**) ▶ plural n. closely trimmed ribs of pork or sometimes beef. [16th C.: probably from Mid. Low Ger. *ribbesper* (by transposition of the syllables), and associated with the adjective SPARE.]

spare tire ▶ n. an extra tire carried in a motor vehicle for emergencies. ■ informal a roll of fat around a person's waist.

sparge /spärj/ esp. tech. ▶ v. [trans.] moisten by sprinkling, esp. with water in brewing. ▶ n. the action of sprinkling or splashing. ■ a spray of hot water, esp. water sprinkled over malt when brewing. — **sparg·er** n. [16th C.: appar. from L. *spargere* 'to sprinkle.']

spar·ing /'spe(ə)riNG/ ▶ adj. moderate; economical. — **spar·ing·ly** adv. **spar·ing·ness** n.

Spark /spärk/, Dame Muriel (1918–2006), Scottish writer. Her works include *The Prime of Miss Jean Brodie* (1961) and *Symposium* (1990).

spark[1] /spärk/ ▶ n. a small fiery particle thrown off from a fire, alight in ashes, or produced by striking together two hard surfaces such as stone or metal. ■ a light produced by a sudden disruptive electrical discharge through the air. ■ a discharge such as this serving to ignite the explosive mixture in an internal combustion engine. ■ a small bright object or point: *a spark of light.* ■ a trace of a specified quality or intense feeling: *a tiny spark of anger.* ■ a sense of liveliness and excitement: *a spark between them.* ▶ v. **1** [intrans.] emit sparks of fire or electricity. ■ produce sparks at the point where an electric circuit is interrupted. **2** [trans.] ignite: *the explosion sparked a fire.* ■ fig. provide the stimulus for (a dramatic event or process): *the plan sparked off street protests.*
– PHRASES **sparks fly** an encounter becomes heated or lively. — **spark·er** n. **spark·less** adj. **spark·y** adj. [OE *spærca, spearca,* of unknown origin.]

spark[2] archaic ▶ n. a lively young fellow. ▶ v. [intrans.] engage in courtship. — **spark·ish** adj. [16th C.: prob. a figurative use of SPARK[1].]

spark gap ▶ n. a space between electrical terminals across which a transient discharge passes.

spar·kle /'spärkəl/ ▶ v. [intrans.] shine brightly with flashes of light. ■ be vivacious and witty. ■ [as adj.] (**sparkling**) (of wine and similar drinks) effervescent. ▶ n. a glittering flash of light. ■ vivacity and wit. — **spar·kling·ly** adv. **spar·kly** adj. [ME: frequentative (v.) or dimin. (n.) of SPARK[1].]

spar·kler /'spärk(ə)lər/ ▶ n. **1** a thing that sparkles, in particular: ■ a hand-held firework that emits sparks. ■ informal a gemstone, esp. a diamond. ■ informal a sparkling wine. **2** a nozzle attached to the spout on a beer pump to give the beer a frothy head.

spark plug ▶ n. a device for firing the explosive mixture in an internal combustion engine.

spar·ling /'spärliNG/ ▶ n. an edible European smelt (*Osmerus eperlanus*) that migrates into fresh water to spawn. [ME: shortening of OFr. *esperlinge,* of Gmc. origin.]

spar·ring part·ner ▶ n. a boxer employed to engage in sparring with another as training. ■ a person with whom one continually argues or contends.

spar·row /'sparō/ ▶ n. **1** a small finchlike Old World bird (*Passer* and other genera, family Passeridae or Ploceidae) related to the weaverbirds, typically with brown and gray plumage. **2** any of a number of birds that resemble true sparrows in size or color, including an American bunting and a waxbill. [OE *spearwa,* of Gmc. origin.]

spar·row·grass /'sparō,gras/ ▶ n. dialect term for ASPARAGUS. [17th C.: corruption (by folk etymology) of obs. *sparagus* 'asparagus.']

spar·row hawk ▶ n. a small Old World woodland hawk (genus *Accipiter*) that preys on small birds. ■ the American kestrel (see KESTREL).

sparse /spärs/ ▶ adj. thinly dispersed or scattered. ■ austere; meager. — **sparse·ly** adv. **sparse·ness** n. **spar·si·ty** /'spärsitē/ n. [18th C.: from L. *sparsus,* past part. of *spargere* 'scatter.']

Spar·ta /'spärtə/ a city in the southern Peloponnese in Greece, capital of Laconia; pop. 13,000. It was a powerful city-state in the 5th century BC.

Spar·ta·cus /'spärtəkəs/ (died *c.*71 BC), Thracian slave and gladiator. He led a revolt against Rome in 73, but was defeated by Crassus in 71 and probably killed in battle.

Spar·tan /'spärtn/ ▶ adj. of or relating to Sparta in ancient Greece. ■ showing the indifference to comfort or luxury traditionally associated with ancient Sparta. ▶ n. a citizen of Sparta.

spar·ti·na /'spärtn-ə/ (also **spar·ti·na grass**) ▶ n. a grass of the genus *Spartina,* which comprises the cordgrasses. [mod. L., from Gk. *spartinē* 'rope.']

spar tree ▶ n. Forestry a tree or other tall structure to which cables are attached for hauling logs.

spasm /'spazəm/ ▶ n. a sudden involuntary muscular contraction or convulsive movement. ■ a sudden and brief spell of an activity or sensation: *a spasm of coughing.* ■ prolonged involuntary muscle contraction: *airways in the lungs go into spasm.* [ME: from OFr. *spasme,* or via L. from Gk. *spasmos, spasma,* from *span* 'pull.']

spas·mod·ic /spaz'mädik/ ▶ adj. occurring or done in brief, irregular bursts: *spasmodic fighting continued.* ■ caused by, subject to, or in the nature of a spasm or spasms: *a spasmodic cough.* — **spas·mod·i·cal·ly** /-ik(ə)lē/ adv.

spas·mo·lyt·ic /,spazmə'litik/ Med. ▶ adj. (of a drug or treatment) able to relieve spasm of smooth muscle. ▶ n. a drug of this kind.

spas·mo·phil·i·a /,spazmə'filēə/ ▶ n. Med. undue tendency of the muscles to contract, caused by ionic imbalance in the blood, or associated with anxiety disorders. — **spas·mo·phile** /'spazmə,fīl/ n.

Spas·sky /'spaskē; 'späs-/, Boris Vasilevich (1937–), Russian chess player; world champion 1969–72.

spas·tic /'spastik/ ▶ adj. relating to or affected by muscle spasm. ■ relating to or denoting a form of muscular weakness (**spastic paralysis**) typical of cerebral palsy, caused by damage to the brain or spinal cord and involving reflex resistance to passive movement of the limbs and difficulty in initiating and controlling muscular movement. ■ (of a person) suffering from cerebral palsy. ■ informal, offens. incompetent or uncoordinated. ▶ n. a person suffering from cerebral palsy. ■ informal, offens. an incompetent or uncoordinated person. — **spas·ti·cal·ly** adv. **spas·tic·i·ty** /spa'stisitē/ n. [18th C.: via L. from Gk. *spastikos* 'pulling,' from *span* 'pull.']

spat[1] /spat/ past and past participle of SPIT[1].

spat[2] ▶ n. **1** (usu. **spats**) hist. a short cloth gaiter covering the instep and ankle. **2** a cover for the upper part of an aircraft wheel. [19th C.: abbrev. of SPATTERDASH.]

spat[2] 1

spat[3] informal ▶ n. a petty quarrel. ▶ v. (**spat·ted, spat·ting**) [intrans.] quarrel pettily. ■ slap lightly. [19th C. (orig. a US colloq. usage): prob. imitative.]

spat[4] ▶ n. the spawn or larvae of shellfish, esp. oysters. [17th C.: from Anglo-Norman Fr., of unknown ultimate origin.]

spatch·cock /'spach,käk/ ▶ n. a chicken or game bird split open and grilled. ▶ v. [trans.] split open (a poultry or game bird) to prepare it for grilling. [18th C. (orig. an Irish usage): perh. rel. to the noun DISPATCH + COCK[1].]

spate /spāt/ ▶ n. **1** [usu. in sing.] a large number of similar things or events appearing or occurring in quick succession: *a spate of attacks on travelers.* **2** esp. Brit. a sudden flood in a river, esp. one caused by heavy rains or melting snow.
– PHRASES **in (full) spate** (of a river) overflowing due to a sudden flood. ■ fig. (of a person or action) at the height of activity: *work was in full spate.* [ME (orig. Scots and north. Engl. in the sense 'flood, inundation'): of unknown origin.]

spathe /spāTH/ ▶ n. Bot. a large sheathing bract enclosing the flower cluster of certain plants, esp. the spadix of arums and palms. [18th C.: via L. from Gk. *spathē* 'broad blade.']

spath·u·late /'spaTHyəlit; -,lāt/ ▶ adj. Bot. & Zool. var. of SPATULATE.

spa·tial /'spāSHəl/ (also **spa·cial**) ▶ adj. of or relating to space: *the spatial distribution of population.* — **spa·ti·al·i·ty** /,spāSHē'alitē/ n. **spa·tial·i·za·tion** /,spāSHələ'zāSHən/ n. **spa·tial·ize** /'spāSHə,līz/ v. **spa·tial·ly** adv. [19th C.: from L. *spatium* 'space' + -AL.]

spa·ti·o·tem·po·ral /,spāSHēō'tempərəl/ ▶ adj. Physics & Philos. belonging to both space and time or to space-time. — **spa·ti·o·tem·po·ral·ly** adv.

spat·ter /'spatər/ ▶ v. [trans.] cover with drops or spots of something: *spattered his shoes with mud.* ■ scatter or splash (liquid, mud, etc.) over a surface. ■ [intrans.] fall so as to be scattered over an area. ▶ n. a spray or splash of something. ■ a sprinkling. ■ a short outburst of sound. [16th C.: frequentative, from a base shared by Du., Low Ger. *spatten* 'burst, spout.']

spat·ter·dash /'spatər,dasH/ ▶ n. (usu. **spatterdashes**) hist. a long gaiter or legging worn to keep stockings or pants clean, esp. when riding.

spat·ter·dock /ˈspatər,däk/ ▶ **n.** a yellow-flowered water lily (genus *Nuphar*).

spat·ter·ware /ˈspatər,we(ə)r/ ▶ **n.** pottery decorated by sponging with color; sponged ware.

spat·u·la /ˈspachələ/ ▶ **n.** an implement with a broad, flat, blunt blade, used for mixing and spreading things, esp. in cooking and painting. [16th C.: from L., var. of *spathula*, dimin. of *spatha* (see SPATHE).]

spat·u·late /ˈspachələt/ ▶ **adj.** having a broad, rounded end: *his thick, spatulate fingers.* ■ (also **spath·u·late**) Bot. & Zool. broad at the apex and tapered to the base: *large spatulate leaves.*

spätz·le ▶ **plural n.** var. of SPAETZLE.

spav·in /ˈspavin/ ▶ **n.** a disorder of a horse's hock. See BONE SPAVIN. — **spav·ined adj.** [ME: shortening of OFr. *espavin*, var. of *esparvain*, of Gmc. origin.]

spawn /spôn/ ▶ **v.** [intrans.] (of a fish, frog, mollusk, crustacean, etc.) release or deposit eggs. ■ (**be spawned**) (of a fish, frog, etc.) be laid as eggs. ■ [trans.] (of a person) produce (offspring, typically offspring regarded as undesirable): *who could spawn a boy like that?* ■ [trans.] produce or generate, esp. in large numbers. ▶ **n.** the eggs of fish, frogs, etc. ■ the process of producing such eggs. ■ the product or offspring of a person or place (used to express distaste or disgust): *the spawn of chaos: demons and sorcerers.* ■ the mycelium of a fungus, esp. a cultivated mushroom. — **spawn·er n.** [ME: shortening of Anglo-Norman Fr. *espaundre* 'to shed roe,' var. of OFr. *espandre* 'pour out,' from L. *expandere* 'expand.']

spay /spā/ ▶ **v.** [trans.] (usu. **be spayed**) sterilize (a female animal) by removing the ovaries. [ME: shortening of OFr. *espeer* 'cut with a sword,' from *espee* 'sword,' from L. *spatha* (see SPATHE).]

spaz /spaz/ (also **spazz**) informal ▶ **n.** (pl. **spaz·zes**) offens. short for SPASTIC. ▶ **v.** [intrans.] (**spaz out**) lose physical or emotional control. [1960s: abbrev. of SPASTIC.]

SPCA ▶ **abbr.** Society for the Prevention of Cruelty to Animals.

SPCC ▶ **abbr.** Society for the Prevention of Cruelty to Children.

speak /spēk/ ▶ **v.** (past **spoke** /spōk/; past part. **spo·ken** /ˈspōkən/) [intrans.] **1** say something in order to convey information, an opinion, or a feeling. ■ have a conversation: *I'll speak to him if he calls.* ■ [trans.] utter (a word, message, speech, etc.). ■ [trans.] communicate in or be able to communicate in (a specified language). ■ make a speech before an audience, or make a contribution to a debate. ■ (**speak for**) express the views or position of (another person or group). ■ convey one's views or position indirectly: *speaking through his attorney, he refused to join the debate.* ■ (**speak of**) mention or discuss in speech or writing. ■ (of behavior, a quality, an event, etc.) serve as evidence for something: *her harping on him spoke strongly of a crush.* ■ (of an object that typically makes a sound when it functions) make a characteristic sound: *the gun spoke again.* ■ (of an organ pipe or other musical instrument) make a sound. ■ (of a dog) bark. **2** (**speak to**) talk to in order to reprove or advise. ■ talk to in order to give or extract information: *he had spoken to the police.* ■ discuss or comment on formally. ■ appeal or relate to.
– PHRASES **not to speak of** used in introducing a further factor to be considered. **nothing** (or **no** —— or **none**) **to speak of** used to indicate that there is some but very little of something: *I've no capital—well, none to speak of.* **something speaks for itself** something's implications are so clear that it needs no supporting evidence or comments. **speak for oneself** give one's own opinions. ■ [in imper.] used to tell someone that what they have said may apply to them but does not apply to others. **speaking of** used to introduce a statement or question about a topic recently alluded to. **speak one's mind** express one's feelings or opinions frankly. **speak volumes** (of a gesture, circumstance, or object) convey a great deal. ■ be good evidence for: *his record speaks volumes for his determination.* **speak well** (or **ill**) **of** praise (or criticize).
– PHRASAL VERBS **speak out** (or **up**) express one's feelings or opinions frankly and publicly. **speak up** speak more loudly. **speak up for** speak in defense or support of. — **speak·a·ble adj.** [OE *sprecan*, later *specan*, of West Gmc. origin.]

-speak ▶ **comb. form** forming nouns denoting a manner of speaking, characteristic of a specified field or group: *technospeak.* [on the pattern of *(New)speak*.]

speak·eas·y /ˈspēk,ēzē/ ▶ **n.** (pl. **-eas·ies**) informal (during Prohibition) an illicit liquor store or nightclub.

speak·er /ˈspēkər/ ▶ **n. 1** a person who speaks. ■ a person who delivers a speech or lecture. ■ [usu. with adj. or in comb.] a person who speaks a specified language. **2** (**Speaker**) the presiding officer in a legislative assembly, esp. the House of Representatives. **3** short for LOUDSPEAKER. — **speak·er·ship** /-,ship/ **n.** (sense 2).

speak·er·phone /ˈspēkər,fōn/ ▶ **n.** a telephone with a loudspeaker and microphone, allowing it to be used without picking up the handset.

speak·ing /ˈspēking/ ▶ **n.** the action of conveying information or expressing one's thoughts and feelings in spoken language. ■ the activity of delivering speeches or lectures. ▶ **adj.** [attrib.] used for or engaged in speech: *a clear speaking voice.* ■ conveying meaning as though in words: *a speaking look.* ■ (of a portrait) so like the subject as to seem to be alive and capable of speech. ■ [in comb.] able to communicate in a specified language: *an English-speaking guide.*
– PHRASES **on speaking terms 1** slightly acquainted. **2** sufficiently friendly to talk to each other. —— **speaking** used to indicate the degree of accuracy intended in a statement or the point of view from which it is made: *broadly speaking.* **speaking in tongues** another term for GLOSSOLALIA.

speak·ing tube ▶ **n.** a pipe for conveying a person's voice from one room or building to another.

spear /spi(ə)r/ ▶ **n.** a weapon with a long shaft and a pointed tip, typically of metal, used for thrusting or throwing. ■ a similar barbed instrument used for catching fish. ■ a plant shoot, esp. a pointed stem of asparagus or broccoli. ▶ **v.** [trans.] pierce or strike with a spear or other pointed object: *she speared a French fry with her fork.* ■ quickly extend the arm to catch (a fast-moving ball or other object). [OE *spere*, of Gmc. origin; cf. Du. *speer* and Ger. *Speer*.]

spear car·ri·er (also **spear-car·rier**) ▶ **n.** an actor with a walk-on part. ■ an unimportant participant in something.

spear·fish /ˈspi(ə)r,fish/ ▶ **n.** (pl. same or **-fish·es**) a billfish (genus *Tetrapturus*) that resembles the marlin. ▶ **v.** [intrans.] fish using a spear.

spear grass (also **spear·grass**) ▶ **n.** any of a number of grasses (*Heteropogon*, *Stipa*, and other genera) with hard pointed seed heads, some of which are sharp enough to harm livestock.

spear·gun /ˈspi(ə)r,gən/ ▶ **n.** a gun used to propel a spear in underwater fishing.

spear·head /ˈspi(ə)r,hed/ ▶ **n.** the point of a spear. ■ an individual or group chosen to lead an attack or movement. ▶ **v.** [trans.] lead (an attack or movement): *he's spearheading the campaign.*

spear·man /ˈspi(ə)rmən/ ▶ **n.** (pl. **-men**) esp. hist. a man, esp. a soldier, who uses a spear.

spear·mint /ˈspi(ə)r,mint/ ▶ **n.** the common garden mint (*Mentha spicata*), used as a culinary herb and to flavor candy, chewing gum, etc.

spear side ▶ **n.** the male side or members of a family. The opposite of DISTAFF SIDE.

spear·wort /ˈspi(ə)rwərt; -,wôrt/ ▶ **n.** a plant of the buttercup family (genus *Ranunculus*) that grows in marshes and ditches, with thick hollow stems and long narrow spear-shaped leaves.

spec[1] /spek/ ▶ **n.** (in phrase **on spec**) informal in the hope of success but without any specific commission or instructions. [18th C.: abbr. of *SPECULATION* (see SPECULATE).]

spec[2] ▶ **n.** informal a detailed working description: *I'll have to look at the specs on the equipment.* [1950s: abbr. of SPECIFICATION.]

spe·cial /ˈspeshəl/ ▶ **adj.** better, greater, or otherwise different from what is usual: *a special effort.* ■ exceptionally good or precious. ■ belonging specifically to a particular person or place. ■ designed or organized for a particular person, purpose, or occasion: *travel by special coaches.* ■ (of a subject) studied in particular depth. ■ used to denote education for children with particular needs, esp. those with learning difficulties. ■ Math. denoting a group consisting of matrices of unit determinant. ▶ **n.** a thing, such as an event, product, or broadcast, that is designed or organized for a particular occasion or purpose: *television's election night specials.* ■ a dish not on the regular menu at a restaurant but served on a particular day. ■ informal a product or service offered at a temporarily reduced price.
– PHRASES **on special** available for sale at a reduced price. — **spe·cial·ness n.** [ME: shortening of OFr. *especial* 'especial' or L. *specialis*, from *species* 'appearance' (see SPECIES).]

spe·cial case ▶ **n. 1** a situation or person that has unusual qualities or needs. **2** Law a written statement of fact presented by litigants to a court.

spe·cial cor·re·spond·ent ▶ **n.** a journalist writing for a newspaper on special events or a special area of interest.

spe·cial de·liv·er·y ▶ **n.** a former express mail service of the United States Postal Service that involved expedited delivery of mail, often by special courier. ■ any mail service that involves special handling or expedited delivery. ■ a letter or parcel sent by a special-delivery service.

spe·cial e·di·tion ▶ **n.** an edition of a newspaper, magazine, television program, etc., that differs from the usual format, esp. in concentrating on one particularly important story.

spe·cial ef·fects (also **spe·cial FX**) ▶ **plural n.** illusions created for movies and television by props, camerawork, computer graphics, etc.

Spe·cial For·ces ▶ **n.** an elite force within the US Army specializing in guerrilla warfare and counterinsurgency.

spe·cial in·ter·est (also **special interest group**) ▶ **n.** a group of people or an organization seeking or receiving special advantages, typically through political lobbying.

spe·cial·ist /ˈspeshəlist/ ▶ **n.** a person who concentrates primarily on a particular subject or activity; a person highly skilled in a specific and restricted field. ■ a person highly trained in a particular branch of medicine. ■ (in the US Army) an enlisted person of one of four grades who has technical or administrative duties but does not exercise command. ▶ **adj.** possessing or involving detailed knowledge or study of a restricted topic. ■ [attrib.] concentrating on a restricted field, market, or area of activity: *a specialist electrical shop.* — **spe·cial·ism** /-,lizəm/ **n.**

spe·ci·al·i·ty /,speshēˈalitē/ ▶ **n.** (pl. **-ties**) British term for SPECIALTY.

spe·cial·ize /ˈspeshə,līz/ ▶ **v.** [intrans.] concentrate on and become expert in a particular subject or skill: *he could specialize in tropical medicine.*

■ confine oneself to providing a particular product or service. ■ make a habit of engaging in a particular activity. ■ [trans.] (often **be specialized**) Biol. adapt or set apart (an organ or part) to serve a special function or to suit a particular way of life: *zooids specialized for different functions.* — **spe·cial·i·za·tion** /ˌspeshəliˈzāshən/ **n.**

spe·cial·ized /ˈspeshəˌlīzd/ ▶ **adj.** requiring or involving detailed and specific knowledge or training. ■ concentrating on a small area of a subject. ■ designed for a particular purpose: *specialized software.*

spe·cial·ly /ˈspeshəlē/ ▶ **adv.** for a special purpose: *fabricated specially* | [as submodifier] *a specially commissioned report.*

spe·cial needs ▶ **plural n.** (in the context of children at school) particular educational requirements resulting from learning difficulties, physical disability, or emotional and behavioral difficulties.

Spe·cial O·lym·pics ▶ **n.** an international competition, modeled on the Olympic Games, in which mentally and physically handicapped athletes compete.

spe·cial plead·ing ▶ **n.** argument in which the speaker deliberately ignores aspects that are unfavorable to their point of view. ■ appeals to give a particular interest group special treatment: *special pleading for his constituency.*

spe·cial team ▶ **n.** Football a squad that is used for kickoffs, punts, or other special plays.

spe·cial·ty /ˈspeshəltē/ (Brit. also **spe·ci·al·i·ty** /ˌspeshēˈalitē/) ▶ **n.** (pl. **-ties**) **1** a pursuit, area of study, or skill to which someone has devoted much time and effort and in which they are expert: *his specialty was watercolors.* ■ a particular branch of medicine or surgery. ■ a product, esp. a type of food, that a person or region is famous for making well. ■ [as adj.] meeting particular tastes or needs: *specialty potatoes for salads.* **2** Law a contract under seal. [ME: shortening of OFr. *especialte*, from *especial* (see SPECIAL).]

spe·cial ver·dict ▶ **n.** Law a verdict that requires an answer to a specific detailed question. ■ a verdict that an accused is not guilty by reason of insanity.

spe·ci·a·tion /ˌspēshēˈāshən; ˌspēsē-/ ▶ **n.** Biol. the formation of new and distinct species in the course of evolution. — **spe·ci·ate** /ˈspēshēˌāt; ˈspēsē-/ **v.**

spe·cie /ˈspēshē; -sē/ ▶ **n.** money in the form of coins rather than notes.
– PHRASES **in specie 1** in coin. **2** Law in the real, precise, or actual form specified. [16th C. (sense 2): from L., ablative of *species* 'form, kind,' in the phr. *in specie* 'in the actual form.']

spe·cies /ˈspēshēz; -sēz/ ▶ **n.** (pl. same) **1** (abbr.: **sp., spp.**) Biol. a group of living organisms consisting of similar individuals capable of exchanging genes or interbreeding. The species is the principal natural taxonomic unit, ranking below a genus and denoted by a Latin binomial, e.g., *Homo sapiens.* ■ Logic a group subordinate to a genus and containing individuals agreeing in some common attributes and called by a common name. ■ a kind or sort: *a species of invective.* ■ used humorously to refer to people who share a characteristic or occupation. ■ Chem. & Physics a particular kind of atom, molecule, ion, or particle: *a new molecular species.* **2** Christian Church the visible form of each of the elements of consecrated bread and wine in the Eucharist. [ME: from L., lit. 'appearance, form, beauty,' from *specere* 'to look.']

spe·cies·ism /ˈspēshēˌzizəm; spēsē-/ ▶ **n.** the assumption of human superiority leading to the exploitation of animals. — **spe·cies·ist adj. & n.**

spe·cies rose ▶ **n.** a rose belonging to a distinct species and not to one of the many varieties produced by hybridization.

specif. ▶ **abbr.** ■ specific; specifically.

spe·cif·ic /spəˈsifik/ ▶ **adj. 1** clearly defined or identified. ■ precise and clear in making statements or issuing instructions: *when ordering goods be specific.* ■ belonging or relating uniquely to a particular subject. **2** Biol. of, relating to, or connected with species or a species. **3** (of a duty or a tax) levied at a fixed rate per physical unit of the thing taxed, regardless of its price. **4** Physics of or denoting a number equal to the ratio of the value of some property of a given substance to the value of the same property of some other substance used as a reference, such as water, or of a vacuum, under equivalent conditions. ■ of or denoting a physical quantity expressed in terms of a unit mass, volume, or other measure, in order to give a value independent of the properties or scale of the particular system studied. ▶ **n. 1** dated a medicine or remedy effective in treating a particular disease or part of the body. **2** (usu. **specifics**) a precise detail: *the specifics of the contract.* — **spe·cif·i·cal·ly adv. spec·i·fic·i·ty** /ˌspesəˈfisitē/ **n.** [17th C.: from late L. *specificus*, from L. *species* (see SPECIES).]

spe·cif·ic ac·tiv·i·ty ▶ **n.** Physics the activity of a given radioisotope per unit mass.

spec·i·fi·ca·tion /ˌspesəfiˈkāshən/ ▶ **n.** an act of describing or identifying something precisely or of stating a precise requirement. ■ (usu. **specifications**) a detailed description of the design and materials used to make something. ■ a standard of workmanship, materials, etc., required to be met in a piece of work: *built to a higher specification.* ■ a description of an invention accompanying an application for a patent.

spe·cif·ic charge ▶ **n.** Physics the ratio of the charge of an ion or subatomic particle to its mass.

spe·cif·ic dis·ease ▶ **n.** a disease caused by a particular and characteristic organism.

spe·cif·ic ep·i·thet /spəˈsifik ˈepəˌthet/ ▶ **n.** esp. Bot. & Microbiol. the second element in the Latin binomial name of a species, which follows the generic name and distinguishes the species from others in the same genus. Compare with SPECIFIC NAME, TRIVIAL NAME.

spe·cif·ic grav·i·ty ▶ **n.** Chem. the ratio of the density of a substance to the density of a standard, usually water for a liquid or solid, and air for a gas.

spe·cif·ic heat ▶ **n.** Physics the heat required to raise the temperature of the unit mass of a given substance by a given amount (usually one degree).

spe·cif·ic name ▶ **n.** esp. Bot. & Microbiol. the Latin binomial name of a species, consisting of the generic name followed by the specific epithet. ■ esp. Zool. another term for SPECIFIC EPITHET.

spec·i·fy /ˈspesəˌfī/ ▶ **v.** (**-fies, -fied**) [trans.] identify clearly and definitely: *he did not specify a date.* ■ [with clause] state a fact or requirement clearly and precisely: *the agency failed to specify that the workers were not their employees.* ■ include in an architect's or engineer's specifications. — **spec·i·fi·a·ble** /ˌspesəˈfīəbəl/ **adj. spec·i·fi·er n.** [ME: from OFr. *specifier* or late L. *specificare* (see SPECIFIC).]

spec·i·men /ˈspesəmən/ ▶ **n.** an individual animal, plant, piece of a mineral, etc., used as an example of its species or type for scientific study or display. ■ an example of something such as a product or piece of work, regarded as typical of its class or group. ■ a sample for medical testing, esp. of urine. ■ informal used to refer humorously to a person or animal: *a sorry specimen of manhood.* [17th C.: from L., from *specere* 'to look.']

spec·i·men plant ▶ **n.** an unusual or impressive plant grown as a focus of interest in a garden.

spe·cious /ˈspēshəs/ ▶ **adj.** superficially plausible, but actually wrong: *a specious argument.* ■ misleading in appearance, esp. misleadingly attractive: *a specious appearance of novelty.* — **spe·cious·ly adv. spe·cious·ness n.** [ME: from L. *speciosus* 'fair,' from *species* (see SPECIES).]

speck /spek/ ▶ **n.** a tiny spot: *the figure had become a mere speck.* ■ a small particle of a substance: *specks of dust.* ▶ **v.** [trans.] (usu. **be specked**) mark with small spots: *their skin was specked with goose pimples.* — **speck·less adj.** [OE *specca.*]

speck·le /ˈspekəl/ ▶ **n.** (usu. **speckles**) a small spot or patch of color. ▶ **v.** [trans.] [often as adj.] (**speckled**) mark with a large number of small spots or patches of color. [ME: from MDu. *spekkel.*]

speck·led trout ▶ **n.** the brook trout. see CHAR[3].

speck·led wood ▶ **n.** a brown Eurasian butterfly (*Pararge aegeria*, family Nymphalidae) with cream or orange markings, favoring light woodland habitats.

specs /ˈspeks/ ▶ **plural n.** informal **1** a pair of spectacles. **2** plural form of SPEC[2]. [19th C.: abbrev.]

spect /spekt/ ▶ **v.** nonstandard form of EXPECT: *I spect they've been to a party.*

spec·ta·cle /ˈspektəkəl/ ▶ **n.** a visually striking performance or display: *the show is pure spectacle.* ■ an event or scene regarded in terms of its visual impact: *the spectacle of a city's mass grief.*
– PHRASES **make a spectacle of oneself** draw attention to oneself by publicly behaving in a ridiculous way. [ME: via OFr. from L. *spectaculum* 'public show,' from *spectare*, frequentative of *specere* 'to look.']

spec·ta·cled /ˈspektəkəld/ ▶ **adj.** wearing spectacles. ■ used in names of animals with markings that resemble spectacles.

spec·ta·cled bear ▶ **n.** an endangered South American bear (*Tremarctos ornatus*) with a black or dark brown coat and white markings around the eyes.

spec·ta·cled cai·man /ˈkāmən/ ▶ **n.** a small South American caiman (*Caiman sclerops*) with a bony ridge between the eyes that gives the appearance of spectacles.

spectacled cobra

spec·ta·cled co·bra ▶ **n.** an Asian cobra (*Naja naja*) with a marking on the hood that resembles spectacles. Also called **Asian cobra, Indian cobra.**

spec·ta·cles /ˈspektəkəlz/ ▶ **plural n.** another term for GLASSES.

spec·tac·u·lar /spekˈtakyələr/ ▶ **adj.** beautiful in a dramatic and eye-catching way: *spectacular scenery.* ■ strikingly large or obvious: *a spectacular loss.* ▶ **n.** an event such as a pageant or musical, produced on a large scale and with striking effects. — **spec·tac·u·lar·ly adv.** [17th C.: from SPECTACLE, on the pattern of words such as *oracular.*]

spec·tate /spekˈtāt/ ▶ **v.** [intrans.] be a spectator, esp. at a sporting event. [18th C.: back-form. from SPECTATOR.]

spec·ta·tor /ˈspekˌtātər/ ▶ **n.** a person who watches at a show, game, or other event. — **spec·ta·to·ri·al** /ˌspektəˈtôrēəl/ **adj.** (rare). [16th C.: from Fr. *spectateur* or L. *spectator*, from *spectare* 'gaze at, observe' (see SPECTACLE).]

spec·ta·tor sport ▶ **n.** a sport that many people find entertaining to watch.

spec·ter /ˈspektər/ (Brit. **spec·tre**) ▶ **n.** a ghost. ■ something widely feared as a possible unpleasant or dangerous occurrence. [17th C.: from Fr. *spectre* or L. *spectrum* (see SPECTRUM).]

spec·ti·no·my·cin /ˌspektənəˈmīsin/ ▶ **n.** Med. an antibiotic obtained from the bacterium *Streptomyces spectabilis*, used as an alternative to penicillin. [1960s: from the specific epithet *spectabilis* (see above), lit. 'visible, remarkable' + -MYCIN.]

spec·tra /ˈspektrə/ plural form of SPECTRUM.

spec·tral /ˈspektrəl/ ▶ **adj.** **1** of or like a ghost. [18th C.: from SPECTER + -AL.] **2** of or concerning spectra or the spectrum. [19th C.: from SPECTRUM + -AL.] — **spec·tral·ly adv.**

spec·tral in·dex ▶ **n.** an exponential factor relating the flux density of a radio source to its frequency.

spec·tral tar·si·er /ˈtärsēər/ ▶ **n.** a tarsier (*Tarsius spectrum*) that has a tail with a long bushy tuft and a scaly base, native to Sulawesi.

spec·tral type (also **spectral class**) ▶ **n.** Astron. the group in which a star is classified according to its spectrum, esp. using the Harvard classification. See also HARVARD CLASSIFICATION.

spec·tre ▶ **n.** British spelling of SPECTER.

spectro- ▶ **comb. form** representing SPECTRUM.

spec·tro·gram /ˈspektrəˌgram/ ▶ **n.** a photographic or other visual or electronic representation of a spectrum.

spec·tro·graph /ˈspektrəˌgraf/ ▶ **n.** an apparatus for photographing or otherwise recording spectra. — **spec·tro·graph·ic** /ˌspektrəˈgrafik/ **adj.** **spec·tro·graph·i·cal·ly** /ˌspektrəˈgrafik(ə)lē/ **adv.** **spec·trog·ra·phy** /spekˈträgrəfē/ **n.**

spec·tro·he·li·o·graph /ˌspektrōˈhēlēəˌgraf/ ▶ **n.** an instrument for taking photographs of the sun in light of one wavelength only.

spec·tro·he·li·o·scope /ˌspektrōˈhēlēəˌskōp/ ▶ **n.** a device similar to a spectroheliograph that produces a directly observable monochromatic image of the sun.

spec·trom·e·ter /spekˈträmitər/ ▶ **n.** an apparatus used for recording and measuring spectra, esp. as a method of analysis. — **spec·tro·met·ric** /ˌspektrəˈmetrik/ **adj.** **spec·trom·e·try** /spekˈträmətrē/ **n.**

spec·tro·pho·tom·e·ter /ˌspektrōfōˈtämitər/ ▶ **n.** an apparatus for measuring the intensity of light in a part of the spectrum, esp. as transmitted or emitted by particular substances. — **spec·tro·pho·to·met·ric** /ˌspektrəˌfōtəˈmetrik/ **adj.** **spec·tro·pho·to·met·ri·cal·ly** /ˌspektrəˌfōtəˈmetrik(ə)lē/ **adv.** **spec·tro·pho·tom·e·try** /-mətrē/ **n.**

spec·tro·scope /ˈspektrəˌskōp/ ▶ **n.** an apparatus for producing and recording spectra for examination.

spec·tros·co·py /spekˈträskəpē/ ▶ **n.** the branch of science concerned with the investigation and measurement of spectra produced when matter interacts with or emits electromagnetic radiation. — **spec·tro·scop·ic** /ˌspektrəˈskäpik/ **adj.** **spec·tro·scop·i·cal·ly** /ˌspektrəˈskäpik(ə)lē/ **adv.** **spec·tros·co·pist** /-pist/ **n.**

spec·trum /ˈspektrəm/ ▶ **n.** (pl. **-tra** /-trə/) **1** a band of colors, as seen in a rainbow, produced by separation of the components of light by their different degrees of refraction according to wavelength. ■ (**the spectrum**) the entire range of wavelengths of electromagnetic radiation. ■ an image or distribution of components of any electromagnetic radiation arranged in a progressive series according to wavelength. ■ a similar image or distribution of components of sound, particles, etc., arranged according to such characteristics as frequency, charge, and energy. **2** used to classify something, or suggest that it can be classified, in terms of its position on a scale between two extreme or opposite points: *the left or the right of the political spectrum.* ■ a wide range. [17th C.: from L., 'image, apparition,' from *specere* 'to look.']

spec·trum an·a·lyz·er ▶ **n.** a device for analyzing a system of oscillations, esp. sound, into its separate components.

spec·u·la /ˈspəkyələ/ plural form of SPECULUM.

spec·u·lar /ˈspekyələr/ ▶ **adj.** of, relating to, or having the properties of a mirror. [16th C. (in *specular stone*, a substance formerly used as glass): from L. *specularis*, from *speculum* (see SPECULUM).]

spec·u·late /ˈspekyəˌlāt/ ▶ **v.** [intrans.] **1** form a theory or conjecture about a subject without firm evidence. **2** invest in stocks, property, or other ventures in the hope of gain but with the risk of loss. — **spec·u·la·tion** /ˌspekyəˈlāsʜən/ **n.** **spec·u·la·tor** /-ˌlātər/ **n.** [16th C.: from L. *speculat-* 'observed from a vantage point,' from the verb *speculari*, from *specula* 'watchtower,' from *specere* 'to look.']

spec·u·la·tive /ˈspekyəˌlātiv; -lətiv/ ▶ **adj.** **1** engaged in, expressing, or based on conjecture rather than knowledge. **2** (of an investment) involving a high risk of loss. ■ (of a business venture) undertaken on the chance of success, without a preexisting contract. — **spec·u·la·tive·ly adv.** **spec·u·la·tive·ness n.**

spec·u·lum /ˈspekyələm/ ▶ **n.** (pl. **-la** /-lə/) **1** Med. a metal or plastic instrument that is used to dilate an orifice or canal in the body to allow inspection. **2** Ornithol. a bright patch of plumage on the wings of certain birds, esp. a strip of metallic sheen on the secondary flight feathers of many ducks. **3** a mirror or reflector of glass or metal, esp. (formerly) a metallic mirror in a reflecting telescope. ■ short for SPECULUM METAL. [ME: from L., 'mirror,' from *specere* 'to look.']

spec·u·lum met·al ▶ **n.** an alloy of copper and tin used to make mirrors, esp. formerly for telescopes.

sped /sped/ past and past participle of SPEED.

speech /spēcʜ/ ▶ **n.** **1** the expression of or the ability to express thoughts and feelings by articulate sounds. ■ a person's style of speaking. ■ the language of a nation, region, or group. **2** a formal address or discourse delivered to an audience. ■ a sequence of lines written for one character in a play. [OE *sprǣc*, *sprēc*, later *spēc*, of West Gmc. origin.]

speech cen·ter (also **speech area**) ▶ **n.** a region of the brain involved in the comprehension or production of speech.

speech·i·fy /ˈspēcʜəˌfī/ ▶ **v.** (**-fies, -fied**) [intrans.] deliver a speech, esp. in a tedious or pompous way: [as n.] (**speechifying**) *the after-dinner speechifying begins.* — **speech·i·fi·ca·tion** /ˌspēcʜəfiˈkāsʜən/ **n.** **speech·i·fi·er n.**

speech·less /ˈspēcʜlis/ ▶ **adj.** unable to speak, esp. as the temporary result of shock or some strong emotion. ■ unable to be expressed in words: *speechless passion.* — **speech·less·ly adv.** **speech·less·ness n.** [OE *spǣclēas* (see SPEECH, -LESS).]

speech pa·thol·o·gy /pəˈᴛʜäləjē/ ▶ **n.** another term for SPEECH THERAPY. — **speech pa·thol·o·gist** /-jist/ **n.**

speech syn·the·siz·er /ˈsinᴛʜəˌsīzər/ ▶ **n.** a machine that generates spoken language on the basis of written input. — **speech syn·the·sis** /ˈsinᴛʜəsis/ **n.**

speech ther·a·py ▶ **n.** training to help people with speech and language problems to speak more clearly. — **speech ther·a·pist n.**

speech·writ·er /ˈspēcʜˌrītər/ ▶ **n.** a person employed to write speeches for others to deliver.

speed /spēd/ ▶ **n.** **1** rapidity of movement or action: *excessive speed* | fig. *the speed of events.* ■ the rate at which someone or something is able to move or operate. ■ each of the possible gear ratios of a bicycle or motor vehicle. ■ the sensitivity of photographic film to light. ■ the light-gathering power or f-number of a camera lens. ■ the duration of a photographic exposure. **2** informal an amphetamine drug, esp. methamphetamine. **3** informal something that matches one's tastes or inclinations: *oak tables and chairs are more his speed.* **4** archaic success; prosperity: *wish me good speed.* ▶ **v.** (past **sped** /sped/ or **speed·ed**) **1** [no obj., with adverbial of direction] move quickly: *I got into the car and home we sped.* ■ [intrans.] (of a motorist) travel at a speed that is greater than the legal limit: *the car that crashed was speeding.* ■ (**speed up**) move or work more quickly. ■ [trans.] cause to move, act, or happen more quickly: *speed up decision-making.* **2** [trans.] archaic make prosperous or successful: *may God speed you.* **3** [intrans.] informal take or be under the influence of an amphetamine drug.

– PHRASES **at speed** quickly. **up to speed** operating at full speed. ■ (of a person or company) performing at an anticipated rate or level. ■ (of a person) fully informed or up to date. — **speed·er n.** [OE. *spēd* (n.), *spēdan* (v.), from the Gmc. base of OE *spōwan* 'prosper, succeed,' a sense reflected in early usage.]

speed bag ▶ **n.** a small punching bag used by boxers for practicing quick punches.

speed·ball /ˈspēdˌbôl/ ▶ **n.** informal a mixture of cocaine and heroin.

speed·boat /ˈspēdˌbōt/ ▶ **n.** a motorboat designed for high speed. — **speed·boat·ing n.**

speed bump ▶ **n.** a ridge set in a road surface, typically at intervals, to control the speed of vehicles.

speed dat·ing (also trademark **Speed Dating**) ▶ **n.** a social activity in which equal complements of potential partners spend a few minutes in short interviews with all other participants in order to determine whether there is interest.

speed di·al ▶ **n.** a function on some telephones that allows numbers to be entered into a memory and dialed using fewer buttons. ▶ **v.** (**speed-dial**) [trans.] dial (a telephone number) by using the speed dial function.

speed lim·it ▶ **n.** the maximum speed at which a vehicle may legally travel on a particular stretch of road.

speed mer·chant ▶ **n.** informal **1** a motorist who enjoys driving fast. **2** Baseball a player noted for speed, such as a very fast base runner or a fastball pitcher.

speed·o /ˈspēdō/ ▶ **n.** (pl. **-os**) **1** informal short for SPEEDOMETER. **2** (**Speedo**) trademark a bathing suit, typically in a form-fitting style.

speed·om·e·ter /spiˈdämitər/ ▶ **n.** an instrument on a vehicle's dashboard indicating its speed.

speed-read /rēd/ ▶ **v.** [trans.] read rapidly by assimilating several phrases or sentences at once. — **speed-read·er n.**

speed skat·ing ▶ **n.** the sport of competitive racing on specially designed skates, typically around an oval track.

speed·ster /ˈspēdstər/ ▶ **n.** informal a person who drives or runs fast. ■ a thing that operates well at high speed, for example a fast car.

speed trap ▶ **n.** an area of road in which hidden police detect vehicles exceeding a speed limit, typically by radar.

speed-up ▶ **n.** an increase in speed, esp. in a person's or machine's rate of working.

speed·way /ˈspēdˌwā/ ▶ **n.** a stadium or track used for automobile or motorcycle racing. ■ a highway for fast motor traffic.

speed·well /'spēd,wel/ ▸ **n.** a small creeping herbaceous plant (genus *Veronica*) of the figwort family, with small blue or pink flowers, found in north temperate regions.

speed·writ·ing /'spēd,rītiNG/ ▸ **n.** trademark a form of shorthand using the letters of the alphabet. — **speed·writ·er** /-tər/ **n.**

speed·y /'spēdē/ ▸ **adj.** (**speed·i·er, speed·i·est**) **1** done or occurring quickly: *a speedy recovery.* **2** moving quickly: *a speedy center fielder.* — **speed·i·ly** /'spēdl-ē/ **adv. speed·i·ness n.**

Speer /spi(ə)r/, Albert (1905–81), German architect and Nazi government official. He was minister for armaments and munitions. Following the Nuremberg trials, he served 20 years in Spandau prison.

speiss /spīs/ ▸ **n.** a mixture of impure arsenides and antimonides of nickel, cobalt, iron, and other metals, produced in the smelting of cobalt and other ores. [18th C.: from Ger. *Speise* 'food, amalgam.']

Speke /spēk/, John Hanning (1827–64), English explorer. With Sir Richard Burton, he was the first European to visit Lake Tanganyika (1858). He named Lake Victoria in honor of the queen.

spe·le·ol·o·gy /,spēlē'äləjē/ ▸ **n.** the study or exploration of caves. — **spe·le·o·log·i·cal** /,spēlēə'läjikəl/ **adj. spe·le·ol·o·gist** /-jist/ **n.** [19th C.: from Fr. *spéléologie*, via L. from Gk. *spēlaion* 'cave.']

spe·le·o·them /'spēlēə,THem/ ▸ **n.** Geol. a structure formed in a cave by the deposition of minerals from water, e.g., a stalactite or stalagmite. [1950s: from Gk. *spēlaion* 'cave' + *thema* 'deposit.']

spell[1] /spel/ ▸ **v.** (past and past part. **spelled** /speld/ or esp. Brit. **spelt** /spelt/) [trans.] write or name the letters that form (a word) in correct sequence. ■ (of letters) make up or form (a word). ■ be recognizable as a sign or characteristic of: *she had the chic look that spells Milan.* ■ lead to: *the plans would spell disaster.*
– PHRASAL VERBS **spell something out** speak the letters that form a word in sequence. ■ explain something in detail. [ME: shortening of OFr. *espeller*, from the Gmc. base of SPELL[2].]

spell[2] ▸ **n.** a form of words used as a magical charm or incantation. ■ a state of enchantment caused by such a form of words. ■ an ability to control or influence people as though one had magical power over them.
– PHRASES **under a spell** not fully in control of one's thoughts and actions, as though in a state of enchantment. **under someone's spell** so devoted to someone that they seem to have magic power over one. [OE *spel(l)* 'narration,' of Gmc. origin.]

spell[3] ▸ **n.** a short period. ■ a period spent in an activity: *a spell of greenhouse work.* ■ a period of a specified kind of weather. ■ a period of suffering from a specified kind of illness: *a spell of amnesia.* ▸ **v.** [trans.] allow (someone) to rest briefly by taking their place in some activity: *I needed her to spell me for a while at the wheel.* [16th C.: var. of dial. *spele* 'take the place of,' of unknown origin.]

spell·bind /'spel,bīnd/ ▸ **v.** (past and past part. **-bound**) [trans.] hold the complete attention of (someone) as though by magic; fascinate: [as adj.] (**spellbinding**) *she told the spellbinding story of her life.* — **spell·bind·er n. spell·bind·ing·ly adv.**

spell-check (also **spell check**) Comput. ▸ **v.** [trans.] check the spelling in (a text) using a spell-checker. ▸ **n.** a check of the spelling in a file of text using a spell-checker. ■ a spell-checker.

spell-check·er (also **spell checker**) ▸ **n.** a computer program that checks the spelling of words in files of text, typically by comparison with a stored list of words.

spell·er /'spelər/ ▸ **n.** [with adj.] a person who spells with a specified ability: *a very weak speller.* ■ a book for teaching spelling. ■ another term for SPELL-CHECKER.

spell·ing /'speliNG/ ▸ **n.** the process or activity of writing or naming the letters of a word. ■ the way a word is spelled. ■ a person's ability to spell words. ■ a school subject.

spell·ing bee ▸ **n.** a spelling competition.

spell·ing check·er ▸ **n.** another term for SPELL-CHECKER.

spelt[1] past and past participle of SPELL[1].

spelt[2] /spelt/ ▸ **n.** an old kind of wheat (*Triticum spelta*) with bearded ears and spikelets that each contain two narrow grains, not widely grown but favored as a health food. Compare with EINKORN, EMMER. [OE, from Old Saxon *spelta*.]

spel·ter /'speltər/ ▸ **n.** commercial crude smelted zinc. ■ a solder or other alloy in which zinc is the main constituent. [17th C.: cf. OFr. *espeautre*, MDu. *speauter*; rel. to PEWTER.]

spe·lunk·ing /spi'ləNGkiNG/ ▸ **n.** the exploration of caves, esp. as a hobby. — **spe·lunk·er** /-kər/ **n.** [1940s: from obs. *spelunk* 'cave' (from L. *spelunca*) + -ING[1].]

Spen·cer /'spensər/, Herbert (1820–1903), English philosopher and sociologist. He developed social Darwinism and coined the phrase the "survival of the fittest" in 1864.

spen·cer[1] /'spensər/ ▸ **n.** a short, close-fitting jacket, worn by women and children in the early 19th century. ■ a thin woolen vest, worn by women for extra warmth in winter. [prob. for the second Earl *Spencer* (1758–1834), English politician.]

spen·cer[2] ▸ **n.** Sailing a boomless gaff sail on a square-rigged ship's foremast or mainmast (replaced in the mid 19th cent. by staysails). [19th C.: of unknown origin.]

Spen·ce·ri·an /spen'si(ə)rēən/ ▸ **adj.** of or relating to a style of sloping handwriting widely taught in American schools from around 1850. [19th C.: for US calligrapher Platt Rogers *Spencer* (1800–64) who developed it.]

spend /spend/ ▸ **v.** (past and past part. **spent** /spent/) [trans.] pay out (money) in buying or hiring goods or services: *they spent $100,000 **on** hardware and software.* ■ pay out (money) for a particular person's benefit or for the improvement of something. ■ used to show the activity in which someone is engaged or the place where they are living over a period of time: *she spent a lot of time traveling.* ■ use or give out the whole of; exhaust: *she had already spent her money.* ▸ **n.** informal an amount of money paid for a particular purpose or over a particular period of time. — **spend·a·ble adj. spend·er n.** [OE *spendan*, from L. *expendere* 'pay out'; partly also a shortening of obs. *dispend*, from L. *dispendere* 'pay out.']

Spen·der /'spendər/, Sir Stephen (1909–95), English poet and critic. He wrote *The Destructive Element* (1935).

spend·ing mon·ey ▸ **n.** money available to be spent on pleasures and entertainment.

spend·thrift /'spen(d),THrift/ ▸ **n.** a person who spends money in an extravagant, irresponsible way.

Speng·ler /'speNGglər; 'SHpeNG-/, Oswald (1880–1936), German philosopher. He wrote *The Decline of the West* (1918–22).

Spen·ser /'spensər/, Edmund (c.1552–99), English poet. He wrote the *Faerie Queene* (1590; 1596), an allegorical romance that celebrated Queen Elizabeth I. — **Spen·se·ri·an** /spen'si(ə)rēən/ **adj.**

Spen·se·ri·an stan·za /spen'sirēən/ ▸ **n.** the stanza used by Spenser in the *Faerie Queene*, consisting of eight iambic pentameters and an alexandrine, with the rhyming scheme *ababbcbcc*.

spent /spent/ past and past participle of SPEND. ▸ **adj.** having been used and unable to be used again: *a spent matchstick.* ■ having no power or energy left: *a spent force.*

sperm /spərm/ ▸ **n.** (pl. same or **sperms**) **1** short for SPERMATOZOON. ■ informal semen. **2** short for SPERM WHALE. ■ short for SPERMACETI or SPERM OIL. [ME: via late L. from Gk. *sperma* 'seed,' from *speirein* 'to sow.']

sper·ma·cet·i /,spərmə'setē/ ▸ **n.** a white waxy substance produced by the sperm whale, formerly used in candles and ointments. It is present in a rounded organ in the head, where it focuses acoustic signals and aids in the control of buoyancy. [15th C.: from med. L., from late L. *sperma* 'sperm' + *ceti* 'of a whale' (genitive of *cetus*, from Gk. *kētos* 'whale'), from the belief that it was whale spawn.]

sper·ma·the·ca /,spərmə'THēkə/ ▸ **n.** (pl. **-cae** /-kē/) Zool. (in a female or hermaphrodite invertebrate) a receptacle in which sperm is stored after mating. [19th C.: from late L. *sperma* 'sperm' + THECA.]

sper·mat·ic /spər'matik/ ▸ **adj.** [attrib.] of or relating to sperm or semen. — **sper·mat·i·cal·ly adv.**

sper·mat·ic cord ▸ **n.** a bundle of nerves, ducts, and blood vessels connecting the testicles to the abdominal cavity.

sper·ma·tid /'spərmə,tid/ ▸ **n.** Biol. an immature male sex cell formed from a spermatocyte that can develop into a spermatozoon without further division. — **sper·ma·ti·dal** /,spərmə'tīdl/ **adj.**

spermato- ▸ **comb. form** Biol. relating to sperm or seeds: *spermatozoid.* [from Gk. *sperma, spermat-* 'sperm.']

sper·mat·o·cyte /spər'matə,sīt/ ▸ **n.** Biol. a cell produced at the second stage in the formation of spermatozoa, formed from a spermatogonium and dividing by meiosis into spermatids.

sper·mat·o·gen·e·sis /,spərmətə'jenəsis; spər,ma-/ ▸ **n.** Biol. the production or development of mature spermatozoa.

sper·mat·o·go·ni·um /spər,matə'gōnēəm; ,spərmə-/ ▸ **n.** (pl. **-go·ni·a** /-'gōnēə/) Biol. a cell produced at an early stage in the formation of spermatozoa, formed in the wall of a seminiferous tubule and giving rise by mitosis to spermatocytes. — **sper·mat·o·go·ni·al** /-nēəl/ **adj.** [19th C.: from SPERM + mod. L. *gonium* (from Gk. *gonos* 'offspring, seed').]

sper·mat·o·phore /spər'matə,fôr/ ▸ **n.** Zool. a protein capsule containing a mass of spermatozoa, transferred during mating in various insects, arthropods, cephalopods, etc.

sper·mat·o·phyte /spər'matə,fīt/ ▸ **n.** Bot. a plant of a large division (Spermatophyta) that comprises those that bear seeds, including the gymnosperms and angiosperms.

sper·ma·to·zo·id /,spərmətə'zoid; spər,mat-/ ▸ **n.** Bot. a motile male gamete produced by a lower plant or a gymnosperm. Also called ANTHEROZOID.

sper·ma·to·zo·on /,spərmətə'zōən; spər,mat-/ ▸ **n.** (pl. **-zo·a** /-'zōə/) Biol. the mature motile male sex cell of an animal, by which the ovum is fertilized, typically having a compact head and one or more long flagella for swimming. — **sper·ma·to·zo·al** /-zōəl/ **adj. sper·ma·to·zo·an** /-'zōən/ **adj.** [19th C.: from Gk. *sperma, spermat-* 'seed' + *zōion* 'animal.']

sperm bank ▸ **n.** a place where semen is kept in cold storage for use in artificial insemination.

sperm count ▸ **n.** a measure of the number of spermatozoa per ejaculation or per measured amount of semen, used as an indication of a man's fertility.

sper·mi·cide /'spərmə,sīd/ ▸ **n.** a substance that kills spermatozoa, used as a contraceptive. — **sper·mi·cid·al** /,spərmə'sīdl/ **adj.**

sper·mi·dine /'spərmə,dēn/ ▸ **n.** Biochem. a colorless compound, $H_2N(CH_2)_3NH(CH_2)_4NH_2$, with a similar distribution and effect to spermine. [1920s: from SPERM + -IDE + -INE[4].]

sper·mine /'spər,mēn/ ▸ **n.** Biochem. a deliquescent compound, $(H_2N(CH_2)_3NH(CH_2)_2)_2$, that acts to stabilize various components of living cells and is widely distributed in living and decaying tissues. [so called because first found in sperm.]

spermo- ▸ **comb. form** equivalent to SPERMATO-.

sperm oil ▶ **n.** an oil found with spermaceti in the head of the sperm whale, used formerly as a lubricant.

sperm whale ▶ **n.** a toothed whale of the family Physeteridae (esp. the very large *Physeter macrocephalus*), with a massive head, typically feeding at great depths on squid, formerly valued for the spermaceti and sperm oil in its head and the ambergris in its intestines. [19th C.: *sperm*, abbrev. of SPERMACETI.]

spes·sart·ine /ˈspesərˌtēn/ ▶ **n.** a form of garnet containing manganese and aluminum, occurring as orange-red to dark brown crystals. [19th C.: from Fr., from *Spessart*, a district in northwestern Bavaria, Germany, + -INE[4].]

spew /spyo͞o/ ▶ **v.** [trans.] expel large quantities of (something) rapidly and forcibly. ■ [no obj., with adverbial of direction] be poured or forced out in large quantities: *oil spewed out of the damaged tanker.* ■ [intrans.] informal vomit. — **spew·er n.** [OE *spīwan, spēowan*, of Gmc. origin; rel. to Ger. *speien*.]

Spey /spā/ a river in east central Scotland. Rising in the Grampian Mountains, it flows northeast to the North Sea.

SPF ▶ **abbr.** sun protection factor (indicating the effectiveness of protective skin preparations).

sphag·num /ˈsfagnəm; ˈspag-/ ▶ **n.** a plant of the family Sphagnaceae belonging to the genus *Sphagnum*, which comprises the peat mosses. [18th C.: mod. L., from Gk. *sphagnos*, denoting a kind of moss.]

sphal·er·ite /ˈsfaləˌrīt/ ▶ **n.** a shiny mineral, yellow to dark brown or black in color, consisting of zinc sulfide. [19th C.: from Gk. *sphaleros* 'deceptive' + -ITE[1].]

sphene /sfēn/ ▶ **n.** a greenish-yellow or brown mineral consisting of a silicate of calcium and titanium, occurring in granitic and metamorphic rocks in wedge-shaped crystals. [19th C.: from Fr. *sphène*, from Gk. *sphēn* 'wedge.']

sphe·noid /ˈsfēnoid/ Anat. ▶ **n.** (also **sphe·noid bone**) a compound bone that forms the base of the cranium, behind the eye and below the front part of the brain. It contains two air-filled sinuses. ▶ **adj.** of or relating to this bone. — **sphe·noi·dal** /sfēˈnoidl/ **adj.** [18th C.: from mod. L. *sphenoides*, from Gk. *sphēnoeidēs*, from *sphēn* 'wedge.']

Sphe·nop·si·da /sfiˈnäpsidə/ Bot. a class of pteridophyte plants that comprises the horsetails and their extinct relatives. — **sphe·nop·sid** /-sid/ **n. & adj.** [mod. L. (pl.), from Gk. *sphēn* 'wedge' + *opsis* 'appearance.']

sphere /sfi(ə)r/ ▶ **n. 1** a round solid figure, or its surface, with every point on its surface equidistant from its center. See illustration at GEOMETRIC. ■ an object having this shape; a ball or globe. ■ a globe representing the earth. ■ esp. literary a celestial body. ■ literary the sky perceived as a vault upon or in which celestial bodies are represented as lying. ■ each of a series of revolving concentrically arranged spherical shells in which celestial bodies were formerly thought to be set in a fixed relationship. **2** an area of activity, interest, or expertise. ■ a section of society or an aspect of life distinguished and unified by a particular characteristic.
– PHRASES **music** (or **harmony**) **of the spheres** the natural harmonic tones supposedly produced by the movement of the celestial spheres or the bodies fixed in them. **sphere of influence** (or **interest**) a country or area in which another country has power to affect developments although it has no formal authority. ■ a field or area in which an individual or organization has power to affect events and developments. [ME: from OFr. *espere*, from late L. *sphera*, earlier *sphaera*, from Gk. *sphaira* 'ball.']

-sphere ▶ **comb. form** denoting a structure or region of spherical form, esp. a region round the earth: *ionosphere.* [from SPHERE, on the pattern of *(atmo)sphere.*]

spher·ic /ˈsfi(ə)rik; ˈsfer-/ ▶ **adj.** spherical. — **sphe·ric·i·ty** /sfiˈrisitē/ **n.**

spher·i·cal /ˈsfi(ə)rikəl; ˈsfer-/ ▶ **adj.** shaped like a sphere. ■ of or relating to the properties of spheres. ■ formed inside or on the surface of a sphere. — **spher·i·cal·ly adv.** [15th C.: via late L. from Gk. *sphairikos*, from *sphaira* (see SPHERE).]

spher·i·cal ab·er·ra·tion /ˌabəˈrāsʜən/ ▶ **n.** a loss of definition in the image arising from the surface geometry of a spherical mirror or lens.

sphe·roid /ˈsfi(ə)rˌoid/ ▶ **n.** a spherelike but not perfectly spherical body. ■ a solid generated by a half-revolution of an ellipse about its major axis (**prolate spheroid**) or minor axis (**oblate spheroid**). — **sphe·roi·dal** /sfiˈroidl/ **adj.** **sphe·roi·dic·i·ty** /ˌsfi(ə)roiˈdisitē/ **n.**

sphe·ro·plast /ˈsfi(ə)rəˌplast; ˈsfer-/ ▶ **n.** Biol. a bacterium or plant cell bound by its plasma membrane, the cell wall being deficient or lacking and the whole having a spherical form.

spher·ule /ˈsfi(ə)r(y)o͞ol; ˈsfer-/ ▶ **n.** a small sphere. — **spher·u·lar** /-yo͞olər/ **adj.** [17th C.: from late L. *sphaerula*, dimin. of L. *sphaera* (see SPHERE).]

spher·u·lite /ˈsfi(ə)r(y)əˌlīt; ˈsfer-/ ▶ **n.** esp. Geol. a small spheroidal mass of crystals (esp. of a mineral) grouped radially around a point. — **spher·u·lit·ic** /ˌsfi(ə)r(y)əˈlitik; ˌsfer-/ **adj.** [19th C.: from SPHERULE + -ITE[1].]

sphinc·ter /ˈsfiNGktər/ ▶ **n.** Anat. a ring of muscle surrounding and serving to guard or close an opening or tube, such as the anus or the openings of the stomach. — **sphinc·ter·al** /-əl/ **adj.** **sphinc·ter·ic** /ˌsfiNGkˈterik/ **adj.** [16th C.: via L. from Gk. *sphinktēr*, from *sphingein* 'bind tight.']

sphin·gid /ˈsfinjid/ ▶ **n.** Entomol. a moth of the hawk moth family (Sphingidae). [20th C.: from mod. L. *Sphingidae* (pl.), from Gk. *Sphinx* (see SPHINX).]

sphingo- ▶ **comb. form** used in the names of various related compounds isolated from the brain and nervous tissue: *sphingomyelin.* [from Gk. *Sphinx, Sphing-* 'Sphinx,' orig. in *sphingosine*, with ref. to the enigmatic nature of the compound.]

sphin·go·lip·id /ˌsfiNGgōˈlipid/ ▶ **n.** Biochem. any of a class of compounds that are fatty acid derivatives of sphingosine and occur chiefly in the cell membranes of the brain and nervous tissue.

sphin·go·my·e·lin /ˌsfiNGgōˈmīəlin/ ▶ **n.** Biochem. a substance that occurs widely in brain and nervous tissue, consisting of complex phosphoryl derivatives of sphingosine and choline.

sphin·go·sine /ˈsfiNGgəˌsēn/ ▶ **n.** Biochem. a basic compound, $C_{18}H_{37}NO_2$, that is a constituent of a number of substances important in the metabolism of nerve cells, esp. sphingomyelins.

sphinx /sfiNGks/ ▶ **n. 1** (**Sphinx**) Gk. Mythol. a winged monster of Thebes, having a woman's head and a lion's body. It asked a riddle, killing those who failed to solve it, until Oedipus was successful, whereupon the Sphinx committed suicide. ■ an ancient Egyptian stone figure having a lion's body and a human or animal head, esp. the huge statue near the Pyramids at Giza. ■ an enigmatic or inscrutable person. **2** (also **sphinx moth**) another term for HAWK MOTH. [ME: via L. from Gk. *Sphinx*, appar. from *sphingein* 'draw tight.']

sp ht ▶ **abbr.** specific heat.

sphygmo- ▶ **comb. form** Physiol. of or relating to the pulse or pulsation: *sphygmograph.* [from Gk. *sphugmos* 'pulse.']

sphyg·mo·graph /ˈsfigməˌgraf/ ▶ **n.** an instrument that produces a line recording the strength and rate of a person's pulse.

sphyg·mo·ma·nom·e·ter /ˌsfigmōməˈnämitər/ ▶ **n.** an instrument for measuring blood pressure, typically consisting of an inflatable rubber cuff that is applied to the arm and connected to a column of mercury next to a graduated scale. — **sphyg·mo·ma·nom·e·try** /-ˈnämətrē/ **n.**

Sphynx /sfiNGks/ ▶ **n.** a cat of a hairless breed, originally from North America.

spic /spik/ ▶ **n.** informal, derog. a contemptuous term for a Spanish-speaking person from Central or South America or the Caribbean. [20th C.: abbrev. of US slang *spiggoty*, in the same sense, of uncert. origin: perh. an alt. of *speak the* in 'no speak the English.']

Spi·ca /ˈspīkə/ Astron. the brightest star in the constellation Virgo. [L., 'ear of wheat (in the hand of the goddess).']

spi·ca /ˈspīkə/ ▶ **n.** Med. a bandage folded into a spiral arrangement resembling an ear of wheat or barley. [17th C.: from L., 'spike, ear of corn'; rel. to *spina* 'spine.']

spic-and-span ▶ **adj.** var. of SPICK-AND-SPAN.

spic·ca·to /spiˈkätō/ Music ▶ **n.** a style of staccato playing on stringed instruments involving bouncing the bow on the strings. ▶ **adj. & adv.** to be performed in this style. [Ital., 'detailed, distinct.']

spice /spīs/ ▶ **n. 1** an aromatic or pungent vegetable substance used to flavor food, e.g., cloves, pepper, or mace: *enjoy the taste and aroma of freshly ground spices.* ■ an element providing interest and excitement. **2** a russet color. ▶ **v.** [trans.] [often as adj.] (**spiced**) flavor with spice. ■ add an interesting or piquant quality to; make more exciting: *adding details to spice up the story.* [ME: shortening of OFr. *espice*, from L. *species* 'sort, kind,' in late L. 'wares.']

spice·bush /ˈspīsˌbo͝osʜ/ ▶ **n.** a North American shrub (*Lindera benzoin*, family Lauraceae) with aromatic leaves, bark, and fruit. The leaves were formerly used for a tea and the fruit as an allspice substitute.

Spice Is·lands former name of MOLUCCA ISLANDS.

spick-and-span /ˈspik ən ˈspan/ (also **spic-and-span**) ▶ **adj.** spotlessly clean and well looked after. [16th C.: from *spick and span new*, emphatic extension of dial. *span new*, from ON *spán-nýr*, from *spánn* 'chip' + *nýr* 'new'; *spick* influenced by Du. *spiksplinternieuw*, 'splinter new.']

spic·ule /ˈspikˌyo͞ol/ ▶ **n. 1** tech. a minute sharp-pointed object or structure that is typically present in large numbers, such as a fine particle of ice. ■ Zool. each of the small needlelike or sharp-pointed structures of calcite or silica that make up the skeleton of a sponge. **2** Astron. a short-lived, relatively small radial jet of gas in the chromosphere or lower corona of the sun. — **spic·u·lar** /-yələr/ **adj.** **spic·u·late** /-yəlit; -yəˌlāt/ **adj.** **spic·u·la·tion n.** [18th C.: from mod. L. *spicula, spiculum*, diminutives of *spica* 'ear of grain.']

spic·y /ˈspīsē/ ▶ **adj.** (**spic·i·er, spic·i·est**) flavored with or fragrant with spice: *pasta in a spicy tomato sauce.* ■ exciting or entertaining, esp. through being mildly indecent: *spicy jokes and suggestive songs.* — **spic·i·ly** /ˈspīsəlē/ **adv.** **spic·i·ness n.**

spi·der /ˈspīdər/ ▶ **n.** an eight-legged predatory arachnid (order Araneae, class Arachnida) with an unsegmented body consisting of a fused head and thorax and a rounded abdomen. Spiders have fangs that inject poison into their prey, and most kinds spin webs in which to capture insects. ■ used in names of similar or related arachnids, e.g., **sea spider.** ■ any object resembling a spider, esp. one having numerous or prominent legs or radiating spokes. ■ a cast-iron iron frying pan, originally made with legs for cooking on coals in a hearth. ▶ **v.** [intrans.] move in a scuttling manner suggestive of a spider: *a nuthatch spidered head first down the tree trunk.* ■ form a pattern suggestive of a spider or its web. — **spi·der·ish adj.** [OE *spīthra*, from *spinnan* (see SPIN).]

spi·der crab ▶ **n.** a crab (*Macropodia* and other genera, Majidae and other families) with long thin legs and a compact pear-shaped body, which is camouflaged in some kinds by attached sponges and seaweed.

spi·der flow·er ▶ n. a plant with clusters of flowers that have long protruding stamens or styles, giving the flowerhead a spiderlike appearance, in particular a South American plant (genus *Cleome*, family Capparidaceae).

spi·der mite ▶ n. an active plant-eating mite (family Tetranychidae) that resembles a minute spider and is frequently a serious garden and greenhouse pest, in particular the **red spider mite** (*Tetranychus urticae*).

spi·der mon·key ▶ n. a South American monkey (genus *Brachyteles*, family Cebidae) with very long limbs and a long prehensile tail.

spi·der ne·vus /ˈnēvəs/ ▶ n. a cluster of minute red blood vessels visible under the skin.

spi·der plant ▶ n. a plant (*Chlorophytum comosum*) of the lily family that has long narrow leaves with a central yellow or white stripe, native to southern Africa and popular as a houseplant.

spider plant

spi·der veins ▶ plural n. dilated capillaries on the skin, resembling spider legs, and common among children and pregnant women.

spi·der·web /ˈspīdərweb/ ▶ n. a web made by a spider. ■ a thing resembling such a web. ■ a type of turquoise crisscrossed with fine dark lines. ▶ v. (**-webbed, -web·bing**) [trans.] cover with a pattern resembling a spiderweb: *a glass block spiderwebbed with cracks.*

spi·der·wort /ˈspīdərwərt; -wôrt/ ▶ n. an American plant (genus *Tradescantia*, family Commelinaceae) whose flowers bear long hairy stamens.

spi·der·y /ˈspīdərē/ ▶ adj. resembling a spider, esp. having long, thin, angular lines like a spider's legs.

spie·gel·ei·sen /ˈspēgəˌlīzən/ ▶ n. an alloy of iron and manganese, used in steelmaking. [19th C.: from Ger., from *Spiegel* 'mirror' + *Eisen* 'iron.']

spiel /spēl; SHpēl/ informal ▶ n. a long or fast speech or story, typically one intended as a means of persuasion or as an excuse but regarded with skepticism or contempt by those who hear it. ▶ v. [trans.] reel off; recite: *he solemnly spieled all he knew.* ■ [intrans.] speak glibly or at length. [19th C.: from Ger. *Spiel* 'a game.']

Spiel·berg /ˈspēlˌbərg/, Steven Allan (1947–), US filmmaker. His movies include *ET: The Extra-Terrestrial* (1982) and *Munich* (2005).

spiel·er /ˈspēlər/ informal ▶ n. **1** a glib or voluble speaker. **2** esp. Brit. a gambling club. [19th C.: from Ger. *Spieler* 'player' (see SPIEL).]

spiff /spif/ ▶ v. [trans.] (**spiff someone/something up**) informal make someone or something attractive, tidy, or stylish: *he arrived all spiffed up in a dinner jacket.* [19th C.: perh. from dial. *spiff* 'well-dressed.']

spif·fing /ˈspifiNG/ ▶ adj. Brit., informal dated excellent; splendid: *how spiffing you look!* [19th C.: of unknown origin.]

spif·fli·cate /ˈspifliˌkāt/ (also **spif·li·cate**) ▶ v. [trans.] informal, humorous treat roughly or severely; destroy. —**spif·fli·ca·tion** /ˌspifliˈkāSHən/ n. [18th C.: a fanciful formation.]

spiff·y /ˈspifē/ ▶ adj. (**spiff·i·er, spiff·i·est**) informal smart in appearance: *a spiffy new outfit.* —**spif·fi·ly** /ˈspifəlē/ adv. [19th C.: of unknown origin.]

spig·ot /ˈspigət/ ▶ n. **1** a small peg or plug, esp. for insertion into the vent of a cask. **2** a faucet. ■ a device for controlling the flow of liquid in a tap. **3** the plain end of a section of a pipe fitting into the socket of the next one. [ME: perh. an alt. of Provençal *espigou(n)*, from L. *spiculum*, dimin. of *spicum*, var. of *spica* (see SPICA).]

spike[1] /spīk/ ▶ n. **1** a thin, pointed piece of metal, wood, or another rigid material. ■ a large stout nail, esp. one used to fasten a rail to a railroad tie. ■ each of several metal points set into the sole of an athletic shoe to prevent slipping. ■ (**spikes**) a pair of athletic shoes with such metal points. ■ short for SPIKE HEEL. ■ informal a hypodermic needle. **2** a sharp increase in the magnitude or concentration of something: *the oil price spike.* ■ Electron. a pulse of very short duration in which a rapid increase in voltage is followed by a rapid decrease. ▶ v. [trans.] **1** impale on or pierce with a sharp point. ■ Baseball injure (a player) with the spikes on one's shoes. ■ (of a newspaper editor) reject (a story) by or as if by filing it on a spike: *the editors deemed the article in bad taste and spiked it.* ■ stop the progress of (a plan or undertaking); put an end to. ■ hist. render (a gun) useless by plugging up the vent with a spike. **2** form into or cover with sharp points. ■ [intrans.] take on a sharp, pointed shape: *lightning spiked across the sky.* ■ [intrans.] increase and then decrease sharply; reach a peak. **3** informal add alcohol or a drug to contaminate (drink or food) surreptitiously: *orange juice spiked with vodka.* ■ add sharp or pungent flavoring to (food or drink). ■ enrich (a nuclear reactor or its fuel) with a particular isotope. **4** (in volleyball) hit (the ball) forcefully from a position near the net so that it moves downward into the opposite court. ■ Football fling (the ball) forcefully to the ground, typically in celebration of a touchdown. [ME: perh. from Mid. Low Ger., MDu. *spiker*, rel. to SPOKE[1].]

spike[2] ▶ n. Bot. a flower cluster formed of many flowerheads attached directly to a long stem. Compare with CYME, RACEME. [ME: from L. *spica* (see SPICA).]

spike heel ▶ n. a high tapering heel on a woman's shoe.

spike·let /ˈspīklit/ ▶ n. Bot. the basic unit of a grass flower, consisting of two glumes or outer bracts at the base and one or more florets above.

spike·nard /ˈspīkˌnärd/ ▶ n. **1** hist. a costly perfumed ointment much valued in ancient times. **2** the Himalayan plant (*Nardostachys grandiflora*) of the valerian family that produces the rhizome from which this ointment was prepared. ■ a plant resembling spikenard in fragrance. [ME: from med. L. *spica nardi* (see SPIKE[2], NARD), translating Gk. *nardostakhus*.]

spik·y /ˈspīkē/ ▶ adj. (**spik·i·er, spik·i·est**) like a spike or spikes or having many spikes. ■ informal easily offended or annoyed. —**spik·i·ly** /-kəlē/ adv. **spik·i·ness** n.

spile /spīl/ ▶ n. **1** a small wooden peg or spigot for stopping a cask. ■ a small wooden or metal spout for tapping the sap from a sugar maple. **2** a large, heavy timber driven into the ground to support a superstructure. ▶ v. [trans.] broach (a cask) with a peg in order to draw off liquid. [16th C.: from MDu., Mid. Low Ger., 'wooden peg.']

spi·lite /ˈspīˌlīt/ ▶ n. Geol. an altered form of basalt, rich in albite and commonly amygdaloidal in texture, typical of basaltic lava solidified under water. —**spi·lit·ic** /spīˈlitik/ adj. [19th C.: from Fr. *spillite*, from Gk. *spilos* 'spot, stain.']

spill[1] /spil/ ▶ v. (past **spilled** or **spilt** /spilt/) [trans.] cause or allow (liquid) to flow over the edge of its container, esp. unintentionally: fig. *azaleas spilled cascades of flowers over the pathways.* ■ [intrans.] (of liquid) flow over the edge of its container: *some of the wine spilled onto the floor.* ■ [intrans.] (of the contents of something) be emptied out onto a surface. ■ cause or allow (the contents of something) to be emptied out. ■ [no obj., with adverbial of direction] (of a number of people) move out of somewhere quickly: *students began to spill out of the building.* ■ informal reveal (confidential information) to someone. ■ cause (someone) to fall off a horse or bicycle. ■ Sailing let (wind) out of a sail, typically by slackening the sheets. ▶ n. **1** a quantity of liquid that has spilled or been spilled: *wipe up spills immediately.* ■ an instance of a liquid spilling or being spilled. **2** a fall from a horse or bicycle.

– PHRASES **spill the beans** informal reveal secret information unintentionally or indiscreetly. **spill (someone's) blood** kill or wound people. **spill one's guts** informal reveal copious information to someone in an uninhibited way. —**spill·er** n. [OE *spillan* 'kill, destroy, waste, shed (blood)'; of unknown origin.]

spill[2] ▶ n. a thin strip of wood or paper used for lighting a fire, candle, pipe, etc. [ME: obscurely rel. to SPILE.]

spill·age /ˈspilij/ ▶ n. the action of causing or allowing a liquid to spill, or liquid spilled in this way.

Spil·lane /spəˈlān/, Mickey (1918–2006), US writer; pen name of *Frank Morrison Spillane*. His detective novels often feature private detective Mike Hammer and include *Kiss Me Deadly* (1955).

spil·li·kin /ˈspilikin/ ▶ n. **1** (**spillikins**) another term for JACKSTRAW. **2** a splinter or fragment. [18th C.: from SPILL[2] + -KIN.]

spill·o·ver /ˈspilˌōvər/ ▶ n. an instance of overflowing or spreading into another area. ■ a thing that spreads or has spread into another area. ■ [usu. as adj.] an unexpected consequence, repercussion, or by-product: *the spillover effect of the quarrel.*

spill·way /ˈspilˌwā/ ▶ n. a passage for surplus water from a dam. ■ a natural drainage channel cut by water from melting glaciers or ice fields.

spilt /spilt/ past and past participle of SPILL[1].

spilth /spilTH/ ▶ n. archaic the action of spilling; material that is spilled.

spin /spin/ ▶ v. (**spin·ning**; past and past part. **spun** /spən/) **1** turn or cause to turn or whirl around quickly: *the rear wheels spun violently.* ■ [intrans.] (of a person's head) give a sensation of dizziness: *it makes her head spin.* ■ [trans.] esp. Cricket impart a revolving motion to (a ball) when bowling. ■ [intrans.] (of a ball) move through the air with such a revolving motion. ■ [trans.] give (a news story) a favorable emphasis or slant. ■ [trans.] shape (sheet metal) by pressure applied during rotation on a lathe: [as adj.] (**spun**) *spun metal components.* **2** [trans.] draw out (wool, cotton, or other material) and convert it into threads, either by hand or with machinery: *they spin wool into the yarn for weaving.* ■ make (threads) in this way. ■ (of a spider or a silkworm or other insect) produce (gossamer or silk) or construct (a web or cocoon) by extruding a fine viscous thread from a special gland. ▶ n. **1** a rapid turning or whirling motion. ■ revolving motion imparted to a ball in a game such as baseball, cricket, tennis, or billiards: *this racket enables the player to impart more spin to the ball* ■ [in sing.] a favorable bias or slant in a news story. ■ [usu. in sing.] a fast revolving motion of an aircraft as it descends rapidly. ■ Physics the intrinsic angular momentum of a subatomic particle. **2** [in sing.] informal a brief trip in a vehicle for pleasure.

– PHRASES **spin one's wheels** informal waste one's time or efforts. **spin a yarn** tell a long, far-fetched story.

– PHRASAL VERBS **spin something off** (of a parent company) turn a subsidiary into a new and separate company. **spin out** (of a driver or car) lose control, esp. in a skid. **spin something out** make something last as long as possible. ■ spend or occupy time aimlessly or without profit: *played games to spin out the afternoon.* [OE *spinnan* 'draw out and twist (fiber)'; rel. to Ger. *spinnen*.]

spi·na bif·i·da /ˈspīnə ˈbifidə/ ▶ n. a congenital defect of the spine in which part of the spinal cord and its meninges are exposed through a gap in the backbone. It often causes paralysis of the lower limbs, and sometimes mental handicap. [18th C.: mod. L. (see SPINE, BIFID).]

spin·ach /ˈspiniCH/ ▶ n. a widely cultivated edible Asian plant (*Spinacia oleracea*) of the goosefoot family, with large, dark green leaves that are eaten raw or cooked as a vegetable. —**spin·ach·y** adj. [ME: prob. from OFr. *espinache*, via Arab. from Pers. *aspānāk*.]

spi·nal /ˈspīnl/ ▶ **adj.** of or relating to the spine. ■ relating to or forming the central axis or backbone of something: *the building of a new spinal road.* — **spi·nal·ly adv.** [16th C.: from late L. *spinalis*, from L. *spina* (see **SPINE**).]

spi·nal ca·nal ▶ **n.** a cavity that runs successively through each of the vertebrae and contains the spinal cord.

spi·nal col·umn ▶ **n.** the spine; the backbone.

spi·nal cord ▶ **n.** the cylindrical bundle of nerve fibers and associated tissue that is enclosed in the spine and connects nearly all parts of the body to the brain, with which it forms the central nervous system.

spin·dle /ˈspindl/ ▶ **n. 1** a slender rounded rod with tapered ends used in hand spinning to twist and wind thread from a mass of wool or flax held on a distaff. ■ a pin or rod used on a spinning wheel to twist and wind the thread. ■ a pin bearing the bobbin of a spinning machine. ■ a measure of length for yarn, equal to 15,120 yards (13,826 m) for cotton or 14,400 yards (13,167 m) for linen. ■ a pointed metal rod on a base, used to impale paper items for temporary filing. ■ a turned piece of wood used as a banister or chair leg. **2** a rod or pin serving as an axis that revolves or on which something revolves. ■ the vertical rod at the center of a record turntable that keeps the record in place during play. **3** Biol. a slender mass of microtubules formed when a cell divides. At metaphase, the chromosomes become attached to it by their centromeres before being pulled toward its ends. **4** (also **spindle tree**) a shrub or small tree (genus *Euonymus*, family Celastraceae) with slender toothed leaves and pink capsules containing bright orange seeds. The hard timber was formerly used for making spindles. ▶ **v.** [trans.] impale (a piece of paper) on a metal spindle for temporary filing purposes. [OE *spinel*, from the base of the verb **SPIN**.]

spin·dle cell ▶ **n.** a narrow, elongated cell, in particular: ■ Med. a cell of this shape indicating the presence of a type of sarcoma. ■ Zool. a cell of this shape present in the blood of most nonmammalian vertebrates, functioning as a platelet.

spin·dle legs (also **spin·dle·shanks** /ˈspindl,SHANGks/) ▶ **plural n.** long thin legs. ■ [treated as sing.] a person with long thin legs. — **spin·dle-leg·ged adj.**

spin·dle-shaped ▶ **adj.** having a circular cross section and tapering toward each end.

spin·dle tree ▶ **n.** see **SPINDLE** (sense 4).

spin·dly /ˈspindlē/ ▶ **adj.** (of a person or limb) long or tall and thin: *spindly arms and legs.* ■ (of a thing) thin and weak or insubstantial in construction: *spindly chairs.*

spin doc·tor ▶ **n.** informal a spokesperson employed to give a favorable interpretation of events to the media, esp. on behalf of a political party.

spin-down ▶ **n.** a decrease in the speed of rotation of a spinning object, in particular a heavenly body or a computer disk.

spin·drift /ˈspin,drift/ ▶ **n.** spray blown from the crests of waves by the wind. ■ driving snow or sand. [17th C. (orig. Scots): var. of *spoondrift*, from archaic *spoon* 'run before wind or sea' + the noun **DRIFT**.]

spin dry·er ▶ **n.** a machine for drying wet clothes by spinning them in a revolving perforated drum. — **spin-dry v.**

spine /spīn/ ▶ **n. 1** a series of vertebrae extending from the skull to the small of the back, enclosing the spinal cord and providing support for the thorax and abdomen; the backbone. ■ fig. a thing's central feature or main source of strength: *these players form the spine of our team.* ■ fig. resolution or strength of character. ■ the part of a book's jacket or cover that encloses the inner edges of the pages, facing outward when the book is on a shelf and typically bearing the title and the author's name. **2** Zool. & Bot. any hard pointed defensive projection or structure, such as a prickle of a hedgehog, a spikelike projection on a sea urchin, a sharp ray in a fish's fin, or a spike on the stem of a plant. ■ Geol. a tall mass of viscous lava extruded from a volcano. — **spined adj.** [in comb.] *broken-spined paperbacks.* [ME: shortening of OFr. *espine*, or from L. *spina* 'thorn, prickle, backbone.']

spine-chill·er ▶ **n.** a story or movie that inspires terror and excitement.

spine-chill·ing ▶ **adj.** inspiring terror or terrified excitement: *a spine-chilling silence.*

spi·nel /spiˈnel/ ▶ **n.** a hard glassy mineral occurring as octahedral crystals of variable color and consisting chiefly of magnesium and aluminum oxides. ■ Chem. any of a class of oxides including this, containing aluminum and another metal and having the general formula MAl_2O_4. [16th C.: from Fr. *spinelle*, from Ital. *spinella*, dimin. of *spina* 'thorn.']

spine·less /ˈspīnlis/ ▶ **adj. 1** having no spine or backbone; invertebrate. ■ fig. (of a person) lacking resolution; weak and purposeless. **2** (of an animal or plant) lacking spines: *spineless forms of prickly pear.* — **spine·less·ly adv. spine·less·ness n.**

spi·nel ru·by ▶ **n.** a deep red variety of spinel, often of gem quality.

spin·et /ˈspinit/ ▶ **n. 1** hist. a small harpsichord with the strings set obliquely to the keyboard, popular in the 18th century. **2** a type of small upright piano. [17th C.: shortening of obs. Fr. *espinette*, from Ital. *spinetta* 'virginal, spinet,' dimin. of *spina* 'thorn' (see **SPINE**), the strings being plucked by quills.]

spine-tin·gling ▶ **adj.** informal thrilling or pleasurably frightening.

Spin·garn /ˈspin,gärn/, Joel Elias (1875–1939), US writer and social reformer. A prominent early officer of the NAACP, he was a co-founder of the publishing house Harcourt, Brace & Co. in 1919.

spin·na·ker /ˈspinəkər/ ▶ **n.** a large three-cornered sail, typically bulging when full, set forward of the mainsail of a yacht when running before

spinnaker

the wind. [19th C.: appar. a fanciful formation from *Sphinx*, the yacht first using it, perh. influenced by **SPANKER**.]

spin·ner /ˈspinər/ ▶ **n. 1** a person occupied in making thread by spinning. **2** a person or thing that spins. **3** (also **spin·ner·bait**) Fishing a lure designed to revolve when pulled through the water. ■ a type of fishing fly, used chiefly for trout. **4** a metal fairing that is attached to and revolves with the propeller boss of an aircraft in order to streamline it.

spin·ner dol·phin ▶ **n.** a dolphin (genus *Stenella*) of warm seas that has a long slender beak and is noted for rotating several times while leaping into the air.

spin·ner·et /,spinəˈret/ ▶ **n.** Zool. any of a number of different organs through which the silk, gossamer, or thread of spiders, silkworms, and certain other insects is produced. ■ (in the production of man-made fibers) a cap or plate with a number of small holes through which a fiber-forming solution is forced.

spin·ney /ˈspinē/ ▶ **n.** (pl. **-neys**) Brit. a small area of trees and bushes. [16th C.: shortening of OFr. *espinei*, from an alt. of L. *spinetum* 'thicket,' from *spina* 'thorn.']

spin·ning /ˈspiniNG/ ▶ **n.** the action or process of converting fibers into thread or yarn.

spin·ning jen·ny ▶ **n.** hist. a machine for spinning with more than one spindle at a time, patented by James Hargreaves in 1770.

spin·ning mule ▶ **n.** see **MULE**[1] (sense 3).

spin·ning top ▶ **n.** see **TOP**[2].

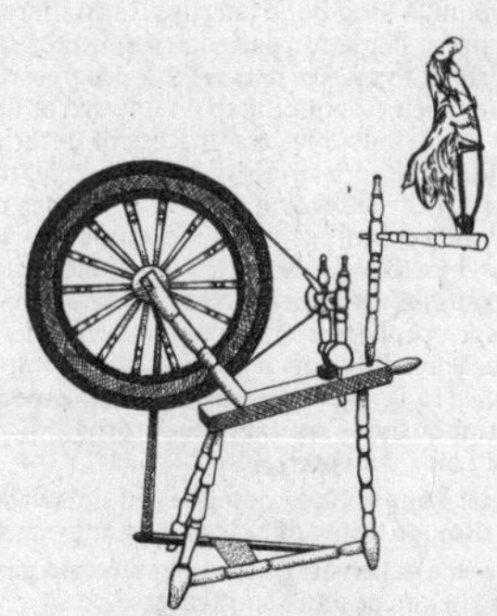

spinning wheel

spin·ning wheel ▶ **n.** an apparatus for spinning yarn or thread, with a spindle driven by a wheel attached to a crank or treadle.

spin-off (also **spin·off**) ▶ **n.** a byproduct or incidental result of a larger project. ■ a product marketed by its association with a popular television program, movie, personality, etc. ■ a business or organization developed out of or by members of another organization, in particular a subsidiary of a parent company that has been sold off, creating a new company.

Spi·no·ne /spiˈnōnē/ ▶ **n.** (pl. **-no·ni** pronunc. same) a wire-haired gun dog of an Italian breed, typically white with brown markings, drooping ears, and a docked tail. [1940s: Ital.]

spi·nose /ˈspīnōs/ (also **spi·nous** /-nəs/) ▶ **adj.** esp. Bot. & Zool. having spines; spiny.

spin-out ▶ **n.** informal **1** another term for **SPIN-OFF**. **2** a skidding spin by a vehicle out of control.

Spi·no·za /spiˈnōzə/, Baruch (or Benedict) de (1632–77), Dutch philosopher. Spinoza espoused a pantheistic system, seeing "God or nature" as a single infinite substance. — **Spi·no·zism** /-,zizəm/ **n. Spi·no·zist** /-zist/ **n. & adj. Spi·no·zis·tic** /,spinəˈzistik/ **adj.**

spin-sta·bi·lized ▶ **adj.** (of a satellite or spacecraft) stabilized in a desired orientation by being made to rotate about an axis. — **spin-sta·bi·li·za·tion n.**

PRONUNCIATION KEY ə *ago, up*; ər *over, fur*; a *hat*; ā *ate*; ä *car*; e *let*; ē *see*; i *fit*; ī *by*; NG *sing*; ō *go*; ô *law, for*; oi *toy*; o͝o *good*; o͞o *goo*; ou *out*; TH *thin*; T͟H *then*; ZH *vision*

spin·ster /'spinstər/ ▶ n. an unmarried woman, typically an older woman beyond the usual age for marriage. — **spin·ster·hood** /-,ho͝od/ n. **spin·ster·ish** adj. [ME (in the sense 'woman who spins'): from the verb SPIN + -STER; in early use the term was appended to names of women to denote their occupation.]

spin·thar·i·scope /spin'THarə,skōp/ ▶ n. Physics an instrument that shows the incidence of alpha particles by flashes on a fluorescent screen. [20th C.: formed irregularly from Gk. *spintharis* 'spark' + -SCOPE.]

spin-the-bot·tle ▶ n. a party game in which players take turns spinning a bottle lying flat, and then kiss the person to whom the bottle neck points on stopping.

spin·to /'spintō/ ▶ n. (pl. **-tos**) a lyric soprano or tenor voice of powerful dramatic quality. ■ a singer with such a voice. [1950s: Ital., 'pushed,' past part. of *spingere* 'push.']

spin·u·lose /'spīnyə,lōs/ ▶ adj. Bot. & Zool. having small spines. [19th C.: from mod. L. *spinulosus*, from *spinula*, dimin. of *spina* 'thorn, spine.']

spin·y /'spīnē/ ▶ adj. (**spin·i·er, spin·i·est**) full of or covered with prickles: *a spiny cactus.* ■ informal difficult to understand or handle. — **spin·i·ness** n.

spin·y ant·eat·er ▶ n. another term for ECHIDNA.

spin·y dog·fish ▶ n. a large white-spotted gray dogfish (*Squalus acanthias*, family Squalidae) with venomous spines in front of the dorsal fins. It occurs in the North Atlantic and the Mediterranean, often in large shoals.

spin·y lob·ster ▶ n. a large edible crustacean (*Palinuris* and other genera, family Palinuridae) with a spiny shell and long heavy antennae, but lacking the large claws of true lobsters.

spin·y mouse ▶ n. a mouse (genus *Acomys*) that has spines mixed with the hair on its back, native to Africa and southwestern Asia.

spi·ra·cle /'spirəkəl; 'spī-/ ▶ n. Zool. an external respiratory opening, esp. each of a number of pores on the body of an insect, or each of a pair of vestigial gill slits behind the eye of a cartilaginous fish. — **spi·rac·u·lar** /spī'rakyələr; spī-/ adj. [18th C.: from L. *spiraculum*, from *spirare* 'breathe.']

spi·rae·a ▶ n. var. of SPIREA.

spi·ral /'spīrəl/ ▶ adj. winding in a continuous and gradually widening (or tightening) curve, either around a central point on a flat plane or about an axis so as to form a cone: *a spiral pattern.* ■ winding in a continuous curve of constant diameter about a central axis, as though along a cylinder; helical. ■ (of a staircase) constantly turning in one direction as it rises, around a solid or open center. ■ Med. (of a fracture) curving around a long bone lengthwise. ■ short for SPIRAL-BOUND. ▶ n. **1** a spiral curve, shape, or pattern: *a spiral of smoke.* ■ a spiral spring. ■ Astron. short for SPIRAL GALAXY. **2** a progressive rise or fall of prices, wages, etc., each responding to an upward or downward stimulus provided by a previous one. ■ a process of deterioration through the continuous increase or decrease of a specified feature: *a downward spiral of sex and drink.* **3** Football a pass or kick that moves smoothly through the air while spinning on its long axis. ▶ v. (**-raled, -ral·ing**; Brit. **-ralled, -ral·ling**) **1** [no obj., with adverbial of direction] move in a spiral course: *a wisp of smoke spiraled up from the trees.* ■ [with obj. and adverbial] cause to have a spiral shape or follow a spiral course: *spiral the bandage around the injured limb.* **2** [intrans.] show a continuous and dramatic increase: *inflation continued to spiral.* ■ (**spiral down/downward**) decrease or deteriorate continuously. — **spi·ral·ly** adv. [16th C.: from med. L. *spiralis*, from L. *spira* 'coil' (see SPIRE[2]).]

spi·ral-bound ▶ adj. (of a book or notepad) bound with a wire or plastic spiral threaded through a row of holes along one edge.

spi·ral gal·ax·y ▶ n. a galaxy in which the stars and gas clouds are concentrated mainly in one or more spiral arms.

spi·rant /'spīrənt/ ▶ adj. Phonet. (of a consonant) uttered with a continuous expulsion of breath. ▶ n. such a consonant; a fricative. — **spi·rant·i·za·tion** /,spīrəntə'zāSHən/ n. **spi·rant·ize** /-,tīz/ v. [19th C.: from L. *spirant-* 'breathing,' from the verb *spirare.*]

spire[1] /spī(ə)r/ ▶ n. a tapering conical or pyramidal structure on the top of a building, typically a church tower. ■ the continuation of a tree trunk above the point where branching begins, esp. in a tree of a tapering form. ■ a long tapering object: *spires of delphiniums.* — **spired** adj. **spir·y** adj. [OE *spīr* 'tall slender stem of a plant'; rel. to Ger. *Spier* 'tip of a blade of grass.']

spire[1]

spire[2] ▶ n. Zool. the upper tapering part of the spiral shell of a gastropod mollusk, comprising all but the whorl containing the body. [16th C.: from Fr., or via L. from Gk. *speira* 'a coil.']

spi·re·a /spī'rēə/ (also **spi·rae·a**) ▶ n. a shrub (genus *Spiraea*) of the rose family, with clusters of small white or pink flowers. [mod. L., from Gk. *speiraia*, from *speira* 'a coil.']

spire shell ▶ n. a marine or freshwater mollusk (Hydrobiidae and related families) with a long conical spiral shell.

spi·ril·lum /spī'riləm/ ▶ n. (pl. **-la** /-lə/) a bacterium (genus *Spirillum*) with a rigid spiral structure, found in stagnant water and sometimes causing disease. [mod. L., irregular dimin. of L. *spira* 'a coil.']

spir·it /'spirit/ ▶ n. **1** the nonphysical part of a person that is the seat of emotions and character; the soul. ■ such a part regarded as a person's true self and as capable of surviving physical death or separation. ■ such a part manifested as an apparition after their death; a ghost. ■ a supernatural being: *shrines to nature spirits.* ■ (**the Spirit**) short for HOLY SPIRIT. **2** [in sing.] those qualities regarded as forming the definitive or typical elements in the character of a person, nation, or group or in the thought and attitudes of a particular period. ■ [with adj.] a person identified with their most prominent mental or moral characteristics or with their role in a group or movement: *he was a leading spirit in the conference.* ■ a specified emotion or mood, esp. one prevailing at a particular time: *a spirit of confidence.* ■ (**spirits**) a person's mood. ■ the quality of courage, energy, and determination or assertiveness: *his visitors admired his spirit.* ■ the attitude or intentions with which someone undertakes or regards something. ■ the real meaning or the intention behind something as opposed to its strict verbal interpretation. **3** (usu. **spirits**) strong distilled liquor such as brandy, whiskey, gin, or rum. ■ [with adj.] a volatile liquid, esp. a fuel, prepared by distillation: *aviation spirit.* ■ archaic a solution of volatile components extracted from something, typically by distillation or by solution in alcohol: *spirits of turpentine.* ▶ v. (**-it·ed, -it·ing**) [with obj. and adverbial of direction] convey rapidly and secretly: *stolen cows were spirited away.*

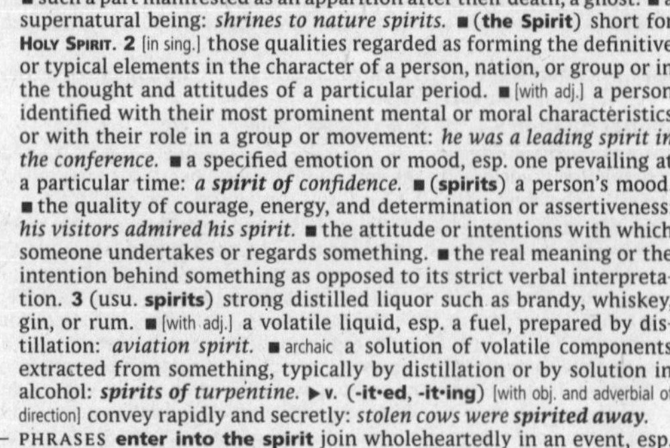

– PHRASES **enter into the spirit** join wholeheartedly in an event, esp. one of celebration and festivity. **in** (or **in the**) **spirit** in thought or intention though not physically. **out of spirits** sad; discouraged. **the spirit is willing but the flesh is weak** proverb someone has good intentions but fails to live up to them. [with biblical allusion to Matt. 26:41.] **when the spirit moves someone** when someone feels inclined to do something. [a phr. orig. in Quaker use, with ref. to the Holy Spirit.] **the spirit world** (in animistic and occult belief) the nonphysical realm in which disembodied spirits have their existence. [ME: from Anglo-Norman Fr., from L. *spiritus* 'breath, spirit,' from *spirare* 'breathe.']

spir·it·ed /'spiritid/ ▶ adj. **1** full of energy, enthusiasm, and determination: *a spirited campaigner.* **2** [in comb.] having a specified character, outlook on life, or mood: *he was a generous-spirited man.* — **spir·it·ed·ly** adv. **spir·it·ed·ness** n.

spir·it gum ▶ n. a quick-drying solution of gum, chiefly used by actors to attach false hair to their faces.

spir·it·ism /'spiri,tizəm/ ▶ n. another term for SPIRITUALISM (sense 1). — **spir·it·ist** /'spiritist/ adj. & n. **spir·it·is·tic** /,spiri'tistik/ adj.

spir·it lamp ▶ n. a lamp burning volatile spirits, esp. methylated spirits, instead of oil.

spir·it·less /'spiritlis/ ▶ adj. lacking courage, vigor, or vivacity: *a spiritless game of Scrabble.* — **spir·it·less·ly** adv. **spir·it·less·ness** n.

spir·it lev·el ▶ n. a device consisting of a sealed glass tube partially filled with alcohol or other liquid, containing an air bubble whose position reveals whether a surface is perfectly level. Also called LEVEL.

spir·it of harts·horn /'härts,hôrn/ ▶ n. see HARTSHORN.

spir·i·tous /'spiritəs/ ▶ adj. another term for SPIRITUOUS.

spir·it·u·al /'spiriCHo͞oəl/ ▶ adj. **1** of, relating to, or affecting the human spirit or soul as opposed to material or physical things. ■ (of a person) not concerned with material values or pursuits. **2** of or relating to religion or religious belief: *Iran's spiritual leader.* ▶ n. (also **Negro spiritual**) a religious song of a kind associated with black Christians of the southern US, and thought to derive from the combination of European hymns and African musical elements by black slaves.

– PHRASES **one's spiritual home** a place in which one feels a profound sense of belonging. — **spir·it·u·al·i·ty** /,spiriCHo͞o'alitē/ n. **spir·it·u·al·ly** adv. [ME: from OFr. *spirituel*, from L. *spiritualis*, from *spiritus* (see SPIRIT).]

spir·it·u·al·ism /'spiriCHo͞oə,lizəm/ ▶ n. **1** a system of belief or religious practice based on supposed communication with the spirits of the dead, esp. through mediums. **2** Philos. the doctrine that the spirit exists as distinct from matter, or that spirit is the only reality. — **spir·it·u·al·ist** n. **spir·it·u·al·is·tic** /,spiriCHo͞oə'listik/ adj.

spir·it·u·al·ize /'spiriCHo͞oə,līz/ ▶ v. [trans.] elevate to a spiritual level. — **spir·it·u·al·i·za·tion** /,spiriCHo͞oələ'zāSHən/ n.

spir·it·u·ous /'spiriCHo͞oəs/ ▶ adj. formal archaic containing much alcohol; distilled: *spirituous beverages.* [16th C. (in the sense 'spirited, lively'): from L. *spiritus* 'spirit' + -OUS, or from Fr. *spiritueux.*]

spir·i·tus /'spiritəs/ ▶ n. Latin term for BREATH, often used figuratively to mean spirit.

spir·i·tus rec·tor /'spiritus 'rektər/ ▶ n. a ruling or directing spirit. [L.]

spiro-[1] ▶ comb. form **1** spiral; in a spiral: *spirochaete.* **2** Chem. denoting a molecule with two rings with one atom common to both: *spironolactone.* [from L. *spira*, Gk. *speira* 'a coil.']

spiro-[2] ▶ comb. form relating to breathing: *spirometer.* [formed irregularly from L. *spirare* 'breathe.']

spi·ro·chete /'spīrə,kēt/ (Brit. **spi·ro·chaete**) ▶ n. a flexible spirally twisted bacterium (*Treponema* and other genera, order Spirochaetales), esp. one that causes syphilis. [19th C.: from SPIRO-[1] 'in a spiral' + Gk. *khaitē* 'long hair.']

spi·ro·graph /'spīrə,graf/ ▶ n. an instrument for recording breathing movements. — **spi·ro·graph·ic** /,spīrə'grafik/ adj. (in sense 1).

spi·ro·gy·ra /,spīrə'jīrə/ ▶ n. Bot. a filamentous freshwater green alga (genus *Spirogyra*, division Chlorophyta) containing spiral bands of chloroplasts. [mod. L., from SPIRO-[1] 'spiral' + Gk. *guros*, *gura* 'round.']

spi·rom·e·ter /spī'rämitər/ ▶ n. an instrument for measuring the air capacity of the lungs. — **spi·rom·e·try** /-mitrē/ n.

spi·ro·no·lac·tone /,spīrənō'laktōn/ ▶ n. Med. a steroid drug that promotes sodium excretion and is used in the treatment of certain types of edema and hypertension. [1960s: from SPIRO-[1] (sense 2 + LACTONE, with the insertion of -ONE.]

spirt /spərt/ ▶v. & n. old-fashioned spelling of SPURT.

spi·ru·li·na /ˌspīrə'līnə/ ▶n. filamentous cyanobacteria (genus *Spirulina*) that form tangled masses in warm alkaline lakes in Africa and Central and South America. ■ (usu. **Spirulina**) the substance of such growths dried and prepared as a food or food additive, which is a rich source of many vitamins and minerals. [mod. L., from *spirula* 'small spiral (shell).']

spit[1] /spit/ ▶v. (**spit·ting**; past and past part. **spit** or **spat** /spat/) [intrans.] eject saliva forcibly from one's mouth, sometimes as a gesture of contempt or anger. ■ [trans.] forcibly eject (food or liquid) from one's mouth: fig. *teller machines that spit out $20 bills.* ■ (**spit up**) (esp. of a baby) vomit or regurgitate food. ■ [trans.] utter in a hostile or aggressive way: *she spat abuse at the jury.* ■ be extremely angry or frustrated: *spitting with sudden fury.* ■ (of a fire or something being cooked) emit small bursts of sparks or hot fat with a series of short, explosive noises. ■ (of a cat) make a hissing noise as a sign of anger or hostility. ▶n. **1** saliva, typically that which has been ejected from a person's mouth. ■ short for CUCKOO SPIT. **2** an act of spitting.
– PHRASES **spit in the eye** (or **face**) **of** show contempt or scorn for. **spit it out** informal used to urge someone to say or confess something quickly. [OE *spittan*, of imitative origin.]

spit[2] ▶n. **1** a long, thin metal rod pushed through meat in order to hold and turn it while it is roasted over an open fire: *chicken cooked on a spit.* **2** a narrow point of land projecting into the sea. ▶v. (**spit·ted, spit·ting**) [trans.] put a spit through (meat) in order to roast it over an open fire. [OE *spitu*, of West Gmc. origin; rel. to Du. *spit* and Ger. *Spiess*.]

spit[3] ▶n. (pl. same or **spits**) a layer of earth whose depth is equal to the length of the blade of a spade. [16th C.: from MDu. and Mid. Low Ger.; prob. rel. to SPIT[2].]

spit and pol·ish ▶n. thorough or exaggerated cleaning and polishing, esp. by a soldier.

spit·ball /'spitˌbôl/ ▶n. **1** a piece of paper that has been chewed and shaped into a ball for use as a missile. **2** Baseball an illegal pitch made with a ball moistened with saliva or another substance to make it move erratically. ▶v. [trans.] informal throw out (a suggestion) for discussion. — **spit·ball·er** n.

spitch·cock /'spicHˌkäk/ ▶n. an eel that has been split and grilled or fried. ▶v. [intrans.] prepare (an eel or other fish) in this way. [15th C.: of unknown origin.]

spit curl ▶n. a small curl of hair trained to lie flat on the forehead, at the nape of the neck, or in front of the ear.

spite /spīt/ ▶n. a desire to hurt, annoy, or offend someone: *he'd think I was saying it out of spite.* ▶v. [trans.] deliberately hurt, annoy, or offend (someone).
– PHRASES **in spite of** without being affected by the particular factor mentioned. **in spite of oneself** although one did not want or expect to do so. [ME: shortening of OFr. *despit* 'contempt,' *despiter* 'show contempt for.']

spite·ful /'spītfəl/ ▶adj. showing or caused by malice. — **spite·ful·ly** adv. **spite·ful·ness** n.

spit·fire /'spitˌfī(ə)r/ ▶n. a person with a fierce temper.

Spit·head /ˌspit'hed/ a channel between the northeastern coast of the Isle of Wight and the mainland of southern England.

spit-roast ▶v. [trans.] [usu. as adj.] (**spit-roasted**) cook (a piece of meat) on a spit: *spit-roasted lamb.*

Spits·ber·gen /'spitsˌbərgən/ a Norwegian island in the Arctic Ocean north of Norway; principal settlement, Longyearbyen.

spit·ter /'spitər/ ▶n. **1** a person who spits. **2** another term for SPITBALL (sense 2).

spit·ting co·bra ▶n. an African cobra (genera *Naja* and *Hemachatus*) that defends itself by spitting venom from the fangs, typically at the aggressor's eyes.

spit·ting im·age ▶n. (**the spitting image of**) informal the exact double of (another person or thing).

spit·tle /'spitl/ ▶n. saliva, esp. as ejected from the mouth. — **spit·tly** adj. [15th C.: alt. of dial. *spattle*.]

spit·tle·bug /'spitlˌbəg/ ▶n. another term for FROGHOPPER.

spit·toon /spi'to͞on/ ▶n. a metal or earthenware pot typically having a funnel-shaped top, used for spitting into.

Spitz /spits/, Mark Andrew (1950–), US swimmer. He won a record seven gold medals in the 1972 Olympic Games.

spitz /spits/ ▶n. a dog of a small breed with a pointed muzzle, esp. a Pomeranian. [19th C.: from Ger. *Spitz(hund)*, from *spitz* 'pointed' + *Hund* 'dog.']

splake /splāk/ ▶n. a hybrid trout of North American lakes, produced by crossing the speckled trout (*S. fontinalis*) with the lake trout (*Salvelinus namaycush*). [1950s: blend of *speckled* and LAKE[1].]

splanch·nic /'splaNGknik/ ▶adj. of or relating to the viscera or internal organs, esp. those of the abdomen. [17th C.: from mod. L. *splanchnicus*, from Gk. *splankhnikos*, from *splankhna* 'entrails.']

splanch·no·pleure /'splaNGknəˌplo͝or/ ▶n. Embryol. a layer of tissue in a vertebrate embryo comprising the endoderm and the inner layer of mesoderm, and giving rise to the gut, lungs, and yolk sac. Often contrasted with SOMATOPLEURE. [19th C.: from Gk. *splankhna* 'entrails' + *pleura* 'side.']

splash /splasH/ ▶n. a sound made by something striking or falling into liquid: *we hit the water with a splash.* ■ a spell of moving about in water energetically: *a splash in the pool.* ■ a small quantity of liquid that has fallen or been dashed against a surface: ***a splash of gravy.*** ■ a small quantity of liquid added to a drink: ***a splash of gin.*** ■ a bright patch of color. ■ informal a prominent or sensational news feature or story. ■ informal a striking, ostentatious, or exciting effect or event. ▶v. [with obj. and adverbial of direction] cause (liquid) to strike or fall on something in irregular drops. ■ [trans.] make wet by doing this: *they splashed each other with water.* ■ [no obj., with adverbial of direction] (of a liquid) fall or be scattered in irregular drops: *a tear splashed onto the pillow.* ■ [no obj., with adverbial] strike or move around in a body of water, causing it to fly about noisily: *some stones splashed into the water.* ■ (**be splashed with**) be decorated with scattered patches of. ■ [trans.] print (a story or photograph, esp. a sensational one) in a prominent place in a newspaper or magazine.
– PHRASES **make a splash** informal attract a great deal of attention.
– PHRASAL VERBS **splash down** (of a spacecraft) land on water. [18th C. (as a verb): alt. of PLASH.]

splash·board /'splasHˌbôrd/ ▶n. a screen designed to protect the passengers of a vehicle or boat from splashes.

splash·down /'splasHˌdoun/ ▶n. the alighting of a returning spacecraft on the sea, with the assistance of parachutes.

splash·y /'splasHē/ ▶adj. (**splash·i·er, splash·i·est**) **1** characterized by water flying about noisily in irregular drops: *a splashy waterfall.* ■ characterized by irregular patches of bright color. **2** informal attracting a great deal of attention; elaborately or ostentatiously impressive: *splashy Hollywood parties.*

splat[1] /splat/ ▶n. a piece of thin wood in the center of a chair back. [19th C.: from obs. *splat* 'split up'; rel. to SPLIT.]

splat[2] informal ▶n. a sound of something soft and wet or heavy striking a surface. ▶adv. with a sound of this type: *he lands splat on his head.* ▶v. (**splat·ted, splat·ting**) [trans.] crush or squash (something) with a sound of this type: *he was splatting a bug.* ■ [intrans.] land or be squashed with a sound of this type. [19th C.: abbr. of SPLATTER.]

splat·ter /'splatər/ ▶v. [trans.] splash with a sticky or viscous liquid: *a passing cart splattered him with mud.* ■ splash (such a liquid) over a surface or object. ■ [no obj., with adverbial] (of such a liquid) splash: *rain splatters onto the windshield.* ■ informal prominently or sensationally publish (a story) in a newspaper. ▶n. **1** a spot or trail of a sticky or viscous liquid splashed over a surface or object. **2** [as adj.] informal denoting or referring to films featuring many violent and gruesome deaths. [18th C.: imitative.]

splat·ter·punk /'splatərˌpəNGk/ ▶n. informal a literary genre characterized by the explicit description of horrific, violent, or pornographic scenes.

splay /splā/ ▶v. [trans.] thrust or spread (things, esp. limbs or fingers) out and apart: *her hands were splayed across his broad shoulders.* ■ [intrans.] (esp. of limbs or fingers) be thrust or spread out and apart: ***his legs splayed out in front of him.*** ■ [intrans.] (of a thing) diverge in shape or position; become wider or more separated. ■ [usu. as adj.] (**splayed**) construct (a window, doorway, or aperture) so that it diverges or is wider at one side of the wall than the other. ▶n. **1** a widening or outward tapering of something, in particular: ■ a tapered widening of a road at an intersection to increase visibility. ■ a splayed window aperture or other opening. **2** a surface making an oblique angle with another, such as the splayed side of a window or embrasure. ■ the degree of bevel or slant of a surface. ▶adj. [usu. in comb.] turned outward or widened: *the girls were sitting splay-legged.* [ME (in the sense 'unfold to view, display'): shortening of the verb DISPLAY.]

splay·foot ▶n. a broad flat foot turned outward. — **splay·foot·ed** adj.

spleen /splēn/ ▶n. **1** Anat. an abdominal organ involved in the production and removal of blood cells in most vertebrates and forming part of the immune system. **2** bad temper; spite: *he could vent his spleen on the institutions that had duped him.* [from the earlier belief that the spleen was the seat of such emotions.] — **spleen·ful** /-fəl/ adj. (in sense 2). [ME: shortening of OFr. *esplen*, via L. from Gk. *splēn*.]

spleen·wort /'splēnwərt; -ˌwôrt/ ▶n. a small fern (genus *Asplenium*, family Aspleniaceae) that grows in rosettes on rocks and walls, typically with rounded or triangular lobes on a slender stem and formerly used as a remedy for disorders of the spleen.

splen- ▶comb. form Anat. of or relating to the spleen: *splenectomy.* [from Gk. *splēn* 'spleen.']

splen·did /'splendid/ ▶adj. magnificent; very impressive: *a splendid view of Windsor Castle.* ■ informal excellent; very good.
– PHRASES **splendid isolation** used to emphasize the isolation of a person or thing. [1896: first applied to the period from 1890 to 1907 when Britain pursued a policy of diplomatic and commercial noninvolvement.] — **splen·did·ly** adv. [as submodifier] *a splendidly ornate style.* **splen·did·ness** n. [17th C.: from Fr. *splendide* or L. *splendidus*, from *splendere* 'shine, be bright.']

splen·dif·er·ous /splen'difərəs/ ▶adj. informal, humorous splendid: *a splendiferous Sunday dinner.* — **splen·dif·er·ous·ly** adv. **splen·dif·er·ous·ness** n. [19th C.: formed irregularly from SPLENDOR.]

splen·dor /'splendər/ ▶n. magnificent and splendid appearance; grandeur. ■ (**splendors**) magnificent features or qualities. [ME: from

PRONUNCIATION KEY ə *ago, up*; ər *over, fur*; a *hat*; ā *ate*; ä *car*; e *let*; ē *see*; i *fit*; ī *by*; NG *sing*; ō *go*; ô *law, for*; oi *toy*; o͝o *good*; o͞o *goo*; ou *out*; TH *thin*; T͟H *then*; ZH *vision*

Anglo-Norman Fr. *splendur* or L. *splendor*, from *splendere* 'shine, be bright.']

sple·nec·to·my /splə'nektəmē/ ▶ **n.** (pl. **-mies**) a surgical operation involving removal of the spleen.

sple·net·ic /splə'netik/ ▶ **adj. 1** bad-tempered; spiteful. **2** archaic term for SPLENIC. — **sple·net·i·cal·ly adv.** (in sense 1). [ME: from late L. *splene-ticus*, from Gk. *splēn* (see SPLEEN).]

splen·ic /'splēnik; 'sple-/ ▶ **adj.** of or relating to the spleen: *the splenic artery.* [17th C.: from Fr. *splénique*, or via L. from Gk. *splēnikos*, from *splēn* (see SPLEEN).]

sple·ni·tis /splē'nītis; sple-/ ▶ **n.** Med. inflammation of the spleen.

sple·ni·um /'splēnēəm/ ▶ **n.** Anat. the thick posterior part of the corpus callosum of the brain. — **sple·ni·al** /'splēnēəl/ **adj.** [19th C.: from L.]

sple·ni·us /'splēnēəs/ (also **sple·ni·us mus·cle**) ▶ **n.** (pl. **-ni·i** /-nē,ī/) Anat. any of two pairs of muscles attached to the vertebrae in the neck and upper back that draw back the head. [18th C.: mod. L., from Gk. *splēnion* 'bandage.']

sple·no·meg·a·ly /,splēnə'megəlē; ,sple-/ ▶ **n.** abnormal enlargement of the spleen. [20th C.: from SPLEN- 'spleen' + Gk. *megas, megal-* 'great.']

rope splices

splice /splīs/ ▶ **v.** [trans.] join or connect (a rope or ropes) by interweaving the strands. ■ join (pieces of timber, film, or tape) at the ends: *I was splicing together footage.* ■ Genet. join or insert (a gene or gene fragment). ▶ **n.** a union of two ropes, pieces of timber, or similar materials spliced together at the ends. — **splic·er n.** [16th C.: prob. from MDu. *splissen*, of unknown origin.]

spline /splīn/ ▶ **n. 1** a rectangular key fitting into grooves in the hub and shaft of a wheel, esp. one formed integrally with the shaft that allows movement of the wheel on the shaft. ■ a corresponding groove in a hub along which the key may slide. **2** a slat. ■ a flexible wood or rubber strip used esp. in drawing large curves. **3** (also **spline curve**) Math. a continuous curve constructed so as to pass through a given set of points and have a certain number of continuous derivatives. ▶ **v.** [trans.] secure (a part) by means of a spline. ■ [usu. as adj.] (**splined**) fit with a spline. [18th C.: perh. rel. to SPLINTER.]

splint /splint/ ▶ **n. 1** a strip of rigid material used for supporting and immobilizing a broken bone when it has been set: *she had to wear splints on her legs.* **2** a long, thin strip of wood used to light a fire. ■ a rigid or flexible strip, esp. of wood, used in basketwork. **3** a bony enlargement on the inside of a horse's leg, on the splint bone. ▶ **v.** [trans.] secure (a broken limb) with a splint or splints. [ME: from MDu., Mid. Low Ger. *splinte* 'metal plate or pin'; rel. to SPLINTER.]

splint bone ▶ **n.** either of two small bones in the foreleg of a horse or other large quadruped, lying behind and close to the cannon bone.

splin·ter /'splintər/ ▶ **n.** a small, thin, sharp piece of wood, glass, or similar material broken off from a larger piece: *a splinter of ice.* ▶ **v.** break or cause to break into small sharp fragments: [trans.] *the crash splintered the wooden barricade.* — **splin·ter·y adj.** [ME: from MDu. *splinter, splenter*; rel. to SPLINT.]

splin·ter group (also **splinter party**) ▶ **n.** a small organization, typically a political party, that has broken away from a larger one.

splin·ter-proof ▶ **adj. 1** capable of withstanding splinters from bursting shells or bombs. **2** not producing splinters when broken.

split /split/ ▶ **v.** (**split·ting**; past and past part. **split**) **1** break or cause to break forcibly into parts, esp. into halves or along the grain. ■ remove or be removed by breaking, separating, or dividing: [intrans.] *an incentive for regions to split away from countries.* ■ divide or cause to divide into parts or elements: [trans.] *splitting water into oxygen and hydrogen.* ■ [trans.] divide and share (something, esp. resources or responsibilities). ■ [trans.] cause the fission of (an atom). ■ [trans.] issue new shares of (stock) to existing stockholders in proportion to their current holdings. **2** (with reference to a group of people) divide into two or more groups. ■ [intrans.] end a marriage or an emotional or working relationship. ■ [trans.] (often **be split**) (of an issue) cause (a group) to be divided because of opposing views: *the party was split over its future direction.* **3** [intrans.] informal (of one's head) suffer great pain from a headache: *my head is splitting.* **4** [intrans.] informal leave a place, esp. suddenly. ▶ **n. 1** a tear, crack, or fissure in something, esp. down the middle or along the grain. ■ an instance or act of splitting or being split; a division: *the split between the rich and the poor.* ■ a separation into parties or within a party; a schism. ■ an ending of a marriage or an emotional or working relationship. ■ short for STOCK SPLIT. **2** (**a split** or **the splits**) (in gymnastics and dance) an act of leaping in the air or sitting down with the legs straight and at right angles to the upright body, one in front and the other behind, or one at each side. **3** a thing that is divided or split, in particular: ■ a bun, roll, or cake that is split or cut in half. ■ a split osier used in basketwork. ■ each strip of steel or cane that makes up the reed in a loom. ■ half a bottle or glass of champagne or other liquor. ■ a single thickness of split hide. ■ (in bowling) a formation of standing pins after the first ball in which there is a gap between two pins or groups of pins, making a spare unlikely. ■ a drawn game or series. ■ a split-level house. **4** the time taken to complete a recognized part of a race, or the point in the race where such a time is measured.
– PHRASES **split the difference** take the average of two proposed amounts. **split one's sides** (also **split a gut**) informal be convulsed with laughter. **split the ticket** (or **one's vote**) vote for candidates of more than one party. **split the vote** (of a candidate or minority party) attract votes from another candidate or party with the result that both are defeated by a third. [16th C.: from MDu. *splitten*, of unknown ultimate origin.]

split-brain ▶ **adj.** [attrib.] Psychiatry (of a person or animal) having the corpus callosum severed or absent, so as to eliminate the main connection between the two hemispheres of the brain.

split de·ci·sion ▶ **n.** a decision based on a majority verdict rather than on a unanimous one, esp. on a court panel or among referees judging the winner of a boxing match.

split end ▶ **n. 1** (usu. **split ends**) a tip of a person's hair that has split from dryness or ill-treatment. **2** Football an offensive end positioned on the line of scrimmage but several yards away from the other linemen.

split-half ▶ **adj.** [attrib.] Stat. relating to or denoting a technique of splitting a body of supposedly homogeneous data into two halves and calculating the results separately for each to assess their reliability.

split im·age ▶ **n.** an image in a rangefinder or camera focusing system that has been bisected by optical means, the halves being aligned only when the system is in focus.

split in·fin·i·tive ▶ **n.** a construction consisting of an infinitive with an adverb or other word inserted between *to* and the verb, e.g., *she seems to really like it.*

split-lev·el ▶ **adj.** (of a building) having a room or rooms higher than others by less than a whole story. ■ (of a room) having its floor on two levels. ▶ **n.** a split-level building.

split pea ▶ **n.** a pea dried and split in half for cooking.

split per·son·al·i·ty ▶ **n.** less common term for MULTIPLE PERSONALITY. ■ archaic term for SCHIZOPHRENIA.

split-phase ▶ **adj.** denoting or relating to an induction motor or other device utilizing two or more voltages at different phases produced from a single-phase supply.

split-rail ▶ **adj.** denoting a fence or enclosure made from pieces of wood split lengthwise from a log.

split run ▶ **n.** a print run of a newspaper during which some articles or advertisements are changed so as to produce different editions.

split screen ▶ **n.** a movie, television, or computer screen on which two or more separate images are displayed.

split sec·ond ▶ **n.** a very brief moment of time. ▶ **adj.** very rapid or accurate: *split-second timing is crucial.*

split shift ▶ **n.** a working shift comprising two or more separate periods of duty in a day.

split shot ▶ **n. 1** (also **split-shot**) small pellets used to weight a fishing line. **2** Croquet a stroke driving two touching balls in different directions.

splits·ville /'splits,vil/ ▶ **n.** informal the termination of a relationship, esp. a romantic one: *it's splitsville for Steve and Nikki.* [1980s: from SPLIT + *-s-* + -VILLE.]

split·ter /'splitər/ ▶ **n.** a person or thing occupied in or designed for splitting something: *a log splitter.* ■ a person, esp. a taxonomist, who attaches more importance to differences than to similarities in classification. Contrasted with LUMPER.

split·tism /'splitizəm/ ▶ **n.** (among communists, or in communist countries) the pursuance of factional interests in opposition to official Communist Party policy. — **split·tist n.**

splosh /spläsн/ informal ▶ **v.** [no obj., with adverbial of direction] make a soft splashing sound as one moves. ▶ **n.** a soft splashing sound: *a quiet splosh.* ■ a splash of liquid: *sploshes of wine.* [19th C.: imitative.]

splotch /spläcн/ informal ▶ **n.** a daub, blot, or smear of something, typically a liquid. ▶ **v.** [trans.] (usu. **be splotched**) make such a daub, blot, or smear on: *a rag splotched with grease.* — **splotch·y adj.** [17th C.: perh. a blend of SPOT and obs. *plotch* 'blotch.']

splurge /splərj/ informal ▶ **n.** an act of spending money freely or extravagantly: *the pre-Christmas splurge.* ■ a large or excessive amount of something. ▶ v. [trans.] spend (money) freely or extravagantly: [intrans.] *we splurged on T-bone steaks.* [19th C. (orig. US): prob. imitative.]

splurt /splərt/ informal ▶ n. a sudden gush, esp. of saliva. ■ a sudden brief outburst of something. ▶ v. [trans.] push out with force; spit out. [18th C.: imitative.]

splut·ter /ˈsplətər/ ▶ v. [intrans.] make a series of short explosive spitting or choking sounds. ■ [reporting verb] say something rapidly, indistinctly, and with a spitting sound, as a result of anger, embarrassment, or another strong emotion. ■ [trans.] spit (something) out from one's mouth noisily and in small splashes. ▶ n. a short explosive spitting or choking noise. —**splut·ter·er** n. **splut·ter·ing·ly** adv. [17th C.: imitative; cf. SPUTTER.]

Spock /späk/, Benjamin McLane (1903–98), US pediatrician; known as **Dr. Spock**. He wrote *The Common Sense Book of Baby and Child Care* (1946).

Spode /ˈspōd/ ▶ n. trademark fine pottery or porcelain made at the factories of the English potter Josiah Spode (1755–1827) or his successors.

spod·o·sol /ˈspädəˌsäl; -ˌsôl/ ▶ n. Soil Science a soil of an order rich in aluminum oxide and organic matter. [1960s: from Gk. *spodos* 'ashes, embers' + -SOL + L. *solum* 'soil.']

spod·u·mene /ˈspäjo͞oˌmēn/ ▶ n. an aluminosilicate mineral that is an important source of lithium. [19th C.: from Fr. *spodumène*, from Gk. *spodoumenos* 'burning to ashes,' pres. part. of *spodousthai*, from *spodos* 'ashes.']

spoil /spoil/ ▶ v. (past and past part. **spoiled** or esp. Brit. **spoilt** /spoilt/) [trans.] **1** diminish or destroy the value or quality of: *I wouldn't want to spoil your fun.* ■ prevent someone from enjoying (an occasion or event). ■ [intrans.] (of food) become unfit for eating: *I've got some ham that'll spoil.* **2** harm the character of (a child) by being too lenient or indulgent: *the last thing I want to do is spoil Thomas.* ■ treat with great or excessive kindness, consideration, or generosity: *breakfast in bed—you're spoiling me!* **3** [intrans.] (**be spoiling for**) be extremely or aggressively eager for: *Cooper was spoiling for a fight.* ▶ n. **1** (usu. **spoils**) goods stolen or taken forcibly. **2** waste material brought up during the course of an excavation or a dredging or mining operation. [ME (in the sense 'to plunder'): shortening of OFr. *espoille* (n.), *espoillier* (v.), from L. *spoliare*, from *spolium* 'plunder, skin stripped from an animal,' or a shortening of DESPOIL.]

spoil·age /ˈspoilij/ ▶ n. **1** the action of spoiling. **2** waste produced by material being spoiled, esp. paper that is spoiled.

spoil·er /ˈspoilər/ ▶ n. **1** a person or thing that spoils. ■ (esp. in a political context) a person who obstructs an opponent's success while having no chance of winning themselves. ■ an electronic device for preventing unauthorized copying of sound recordings by means of a disruptive signal inaudible on the original. **2** a flap on an aircraft or glider that can create drag and so reduce speed. ■ a similar device on a motor vehicle intended to prevent it from being lifted off the road when traveling at very high speeds.

spoils·man /ˈspoilzmən/ ▶ n. (pl. **-men**) a person who seeks to profit by the spoils system; a person who supports this system.

spoil·sport /ˈspoilˌspôrt/ ▶ n. a person who behaves in a way that spoils others' pleasure.

spoils sys·tem ▶ n. the practice of a successful political party giving public office to its supporters.

spoilt /spoilt/ esp. Brit. past and past participle of SPOIL.

Spo·kane /spōˈkan/ a city in eastern Washington, at the falls of the Spokane River; pop. 195,629.

spoke[1] /spōk/ ▶ n. each of the bars or wire rods connecting the center of a wheel to its outer edge. ■ each of a set of radial handles projecting from a ship's wheel. ■ each of the metal rods in an umbrella. —**spoked** adj. [OE *spāca*, of West Gmc. origin; rel. to Du. *speek*, Ger. *Speiche*, from the base of SPIKE[1].]

spoke[2] past of SPEAK.

spo·ken /ˈspōkən/ past participle of SPEAK. ▶ adj. [in comb.] speaking in a specified way: *a blunt-spoken man.*

– PHRASES **be spoken for** be already claimed or reserved. ■ (of a person) already have a romantic commitment: *he knows Claudine is spoken for.*

spoke·shave /ˈspōkˌshāv/ ▶ n. a small plane with handles, used for shaping curved surfaces. ▶ v. [trans.] shape with a plane of this type.

spokes·man /ˈspōksmən/ ▶ n. (pl. **-men**) a person, esp. a man, who speaks for another individual or a group. [16th C.: formed irregularly from SPOKE[2], on the pattern of words such as *craftsman*.]

spokes·per·son /ˈspōksˌpərsən/ ▶ n. (pl. **-per·sons** or **-peo·ple** /-ˌpēpəl/) a spokesman or spokeswoman.

spokes·wom·an /ˈspōksˌwo͝omən/ ▶ n. (pl. **-wom·en**) a woman who speaks for another individual or a group.

spo·li·a·tion /ˌspōlēˈāshən/ ▶ n. **1** the action of ruining or destroying something. **2** the action of taking goods or property from somewhere by illegal or unethical means. —**spo·li·a·tor** /ˈspōlēˌātər/ n. [ME (denoting pillaging): from L. *spoliatio(n-)*, from the verb *spoliare* 'strip, deprive' (see SPOIL).]

spon·dee /ˈspändē/ ▶ n. Pros. a foot consisting of two long (or stressed) syllables. [ME: from OFr., or via L. from Gk. *spondeios (pous)* '(foot) of a libation,' from *spondē* 'libation' (being characteristic of music accompanying libations).]

sponge /spənj/ ▶ n. **1** a primitive sedentary aquatic invertebrate (phylum Porifera) with a soft porous body that is typically supported by a framework of fibers or calcareous or glassy spicules. Sponges draw in a current of water to extract nutrients and oxygen. **2** a piece of a soft, light, porous substance originally consisting of the fibrous skeleton of such an invertebrate but now usually made of synthetic material. Sponges absorb liquid and are used for washing and cleaning. ■ [in sing.] an act of wiping or cleaning with a sponge: *they gave him a quick sponge down.* ■ such a substance used as padding or insulating material: *the headguard is padded with sponge.* ■ a piece of such a substance impregnated with spermicide and inserted into a woman's vagina as a form of barrier contraceptive. ■ informal a heavy drinker. ■ [with adj.] metal in a porous form, typically prepared by reduction without fusion or by electrolysis: *platinum sponge.* **3** (also **sponge pudding**) a steamed or baked pudding of fat, flour, and eggs. **4** informal a person who lives at someone else's expense. ▶ v. (**spong·ing** or **sponge·ing**) **1** [trans.] wipe, rub, or clean with a wet sponge or cloth: *she sponged him down in an attempt to cool his fever.* ■ remove or wipe away (liquid or a mark) in such a way: *I'll go and sponge this orange juice off my dress.* ■ give a decorative mottled or textured effect to (a painted wall or surface) by applying a different shade of paint with a sponge. **2** [intrans.] informal obtain or accept money or food from other people without doing or intending to do anything in return: *they found they could earn a perfectly good living by sponging off others.* ■ [trans.] obtain (something) in such a way: *he edged closer, clearly intending to sponge money from her.* —**sponge·a·ble** adj. **sponge·like** /ˈspənjˌlīk/ adj. [OE (sense 2 of the n.), via L. from Gk. *spongia*, later form of *spongos*, reinforced in ME by OFr. *esponge*.]

sponge bath ▶ n. an all-over washing with a wet sponge or washcloth rather than in a tub or shower.

spong·er /ˈspənjər/ ▶ n. **1** informal a person who lives at others' expense. **2** a person who applies paint to pottery using a sponge.

sponge rub·ber ▶ n. rubber latex processed into a spongelike substance.

sponge tree ▶ n. another term for HUISACHE.

spon·gi·form /ˈspənjiˌfôrm/ ▶ adj. esp. Vet. Med. having or denoting a porous structure.

spon·gin /ˈspənjin/ ▶ n. Biochem. the horny or fibrous substance found in the skeleton of many sponges.

spon·gy /ˈspənjē/ ▶ adj. (**-gi·er, -gi·est**) like a sponge: *a soft, spongy blanket of moss.* ■ (of metal) having an open, porous structure. —**spon·gi·ly** /ˈspənjəlē/ adv. **spon·gi·ness** n.

spon·son /ˈspänsən/ ▶ n. a projection on the side of a boat, ship, or seaplane. [19th C.: of unknown origin.]

spon·sor /ˈspänsər/ ▶ n. **1** a person or organization that provides funds or support for a project or activity carried out by another, in particular: ■ an individual or organization that pays some or all of the costs involved in return for advertising. ■ a person who pledges to donate a certain amount of money to another person after they have participated in a fund-raising event. **2** a person who supports a proposal for legislation. ■ a person taking official responsibility for the actions of another. ■ a godparent at a child's baptism. ■ (esp. in the Roman Catholic Church) a person presenting a candidate for confirmation. ▶ v. [trans.] **1** provide funds for (a project or activity or the person carrying it out). ■ pay some or all of the costs involved in staging (a sporting or artistic event) in return for advertising. ■ pledge to donate a certain sum of money to (someone) after they have participated in a fund-raising event. ■ [often as adj.] (**sponsored**) pledge to donate money because someone is taking part in (an event): *a sponsored walk.* **2** introduce (a proposal) in a legislative assembly. ■ propose and organize (negotiations or talks) between other people or groups. —**spon·sor·ship** /-ˌship/ n. [17th C. (as a n.): from L., from *spondere* 'promise solemnly'. The verb dates from the late 19th C.]

spon·ta·ne·ous /spänˈtānēəs/ ▶ adj. performed or occurring without premeditation or external stimulus: *spontaneous applause.* ■ (of a person) having a natural, and uninhibited manner. ■ (of a process or event) occurring without apparent external cause. ■ Biol. (of movement or activity in an organism) instinctive or involuntary. —**spon·ta·ne·i·ty** /ˌspäntəˈnēitē; -ˈnā-/ n. **spon·ta·ne·ous·ly** adv. [17th C.: from late L. *spontaneus* (from *(sua) sponte* 'of (one's) own accord') + -OUS.]

spon·ta·ne·ous com·bus·tion ▶ n. the ignition of organic matter without apparent cause, typically through heat generated internally by rapid oxidation.

spon·ta·ne·ous gen·er·a·tion ▶ n. hist. the supposed production of living organisms from nonliving matter.

spoof /spo͞of/ informal ▶ n. **1** a humorous imitation of something: *a Robin Hood spoof.* **2** a trick played on someone as a joke. ▶ v. [trans.] **1** imitate (something) while exaggerating its characteristic features for comic effect: *"Scary Movie" spoofs horror movies.* **2** hoax or trick (someone). ■ interfere with (radio or radar signals) so as to make them useless. —**spoof·er** n. **spoof·er·y** /ˈspo͞ofərē/ n. [19th C.: coined by Arthur Roberts (1852–1933), English comedian.]

spook /spo͝ok/ informal ▶ n. **1** a ghost. **2** a spy: *a CIA spook.* **3** dated, derog. a contemptuous term for a black person. ▶ v. [trans.] frighten; unnerve. ■ [intrans.] (esp. of an animal) take fright suddenly. [19th C.: from Du., of unknown origin.]

spook·y /ˈspo͝okē/ ▶ adj. (**spook·i·er, spook·i·est**) informal **1** sinister or ghostly in a way that causes fear. **2** (of a person or animal) easily frightened; nervous. — **spook·i·ly** /ˈspo͝okəlē/ **adv. spook·i·ness n.**

spool /spo͞ol/ ▶ **n.** a cylindrical device on which something can be wound; a reel: *spools of electrical cable.* ■ a cylindrical device attached to a fishing rod and used for winding and unwinding the line as required. ■ [as adj.] denoting furniture ornamented with a series of small knobs resembling spools. ▶ **v. 1** [trans.] wind (magnetic tape or thread) on to a spool: *he was trying to spool his tapes.* ■ [intrans.] be wound on or off a spool. **2** [trans.] Comput. send (data intended for printing or processing on a peripheral device) to an intermediate store. [acronym from *simultaneous peripheral operation online.*] **3** [intrans.] (of an engine) increase its speed of rotation. [ME: shortening of OFr. *espole* or from Mid. Low Ger. *spōle*, of West Gmc. origin.]

spoon /spo͞on/ ▶ **n. 1** an implement consisting of a small, shallow oval or round bowl on a long handle. ■ the contents of such an implement: *three spoons of sugar.* ■ (**spoons**) a pair of spoons beaten together rhythmically. **2** a thing resembling a spoon in shape, in particular: ■ (also **spoon bait**) a fishing lure designed to wobble when pulled through the water. ■ an oar with a broad curved blade. ▶ **v. 1** [trans.] convey (food) somewhere by using a spoon: *Rosie spooned sugar into her mug.* ■ hit (a ball) up into the air with a soft or weak stroke: *he spooned his shot high over the bar.* **2** [intrans.] informal dated (of two people) behave in an amorous way; kiss and cuddle: *I saw them spooning.* — **spoon·er n.** (in sense 2 of the verb) **spoon·ful** /-ˌfo͝ol/ **n.** (pl. **-fuls** /-ˌfo͝olz/). [OE *spōn* 'chip of wood,' of Gmc. origin; rel. to Ger. *Span* 'shaving.' Sense 1 is of Scand. origin.]

spoon·bill /ˈspo͞onˌbil/ ▶ **n.** a tall mainly white or pinkish wading bird (genera *Platalea* and *Ajaia*) of the ibis family, having a long bill with a very broad flat tip.

spoon bread ▶ **n.** soft cornbread served with a spoon.

spoon·er·ism /ˈspo͞onəˌrizəm/ ▶ **n.** a verbal error in which a speaker accidentally transposes the initial sounds or letters of two or more words, often to humorous effect. [20th C.: for the Rev. W. A. *Spooner* (1844–1930), an English scholar who reputedly made such errors in speaking.]

spoon-feed ▶ **v.** [trans.] feed with a spoon. ■ fig. provide (someone) with so much help that they do not need to think for themselves.

spoon·worm /ˈspo͞onˌwərm/ ▶ **n.** an unsegmented wormlike marine invertebrate (phylum Echiura) that lives in burrows, crevices, or discarded shells. They typically have a sausage-shaped body with a long proboscis that can be extended over the seabed.

spoon·y /ˈspo͞onē/ informal ▶ **adj.** (**spoon·i·er, spoon·i·est**) dated sentimentally or foolishly amorous. ▶ **n.** (pl. **spoon·ies**) archaic a simple, silly, or foolish person. — **spoon·i·ly** /ˈspo͞onəlē/ **adv. spoon·i·ness n.**

spoor /spo͝or; spôr/ ▶ **n.** the track or scent of an animal: *the trail is marked by wolf spoor.* ▶ **v.** [trans.] follow the track or scent of. — **spoor·er n.** [19th C.: from Afrik., from MDu. *spor*, of Gmc. origin.]

Spor·a·des /ˈspôrəˌdēz/ two groups of Greek islands in the Aegean Sea. The **Northern Sporades** include the islands of Euboea, Skiros, Skiathos, and Skopelos. The **Southern Sporades** include Rhodes and the other islands of the Dodecanese.

spo·rad·ic /spəˈradik/ ▶ **adj.** occurring at irregular intervals or only in a few places; scattered or isolated. — **spo·rad·i·cal·ly** /-ik(ə)lē/ **adv.** [17th C.: via med. L. from Gk. *sporadikos*, from *sporas, sporad-* 'scattered'; rel. to *speirein* 'to sow.']

spo·ran·gi·um /spəˈranjēəm/ ▶ **n.** (pl. **-gi·a** /-jēə/) Bot. (in ferns and lower plants) a receptacle in which asexual spores are formed. — **spo·ran·gi·al** /-jēəl/ **adj.** [19th C.: mod. L., from Gk. *spora* 'spore' + *angeion* 'vessel.']

spore /spôr/ ▶ **n.** Biol. a minute, typically one-celled, reproductive unit capable of giving rise to a new individual without sexual fusion. ■ Bot. (in a plant exhibiting alternation of generations) a haploid reproductive cell that gives rise to a gametophyte. [19th C.: from mod. L. *spora*, from Gk. *spora* 'sowing, seed,' from *speirein* 'to sow.']

sporo- ▶ **comb. form** Biol. of or relating to spores. [from Gk. *spora* 'spore.']

spo·ro·cyst /ˈspôrəˌsist/ ▶ **n.** Zool. a parasitic fluke in the initial stage of infection in a snail host, developed from a miracidium. ■ (in parasitic sporozoans) an encysted zygote in an invertebrate host.

spo·ro·gen·e·sis /ˌspôrəˈjenəsis/ ▶ **n.** esp. Bot. the process of spore formation.

spo·rog·o·ny /spəˈrägənē/ ▶ **n.** Zool. the asexual process of spore formation in parasitic sporozoans.

spo·ro·phore /ˈspôrəˌfôr/ ▶ **n.** Bot. the spore-bearing structure of a fungus.

spo·ro·phyte /ˈspôrəˌfīt/ ▶ **n.** Bot. (in the life cycle of plants with alternating generations) the asexual and usually diploid phase, producing spores from which the gametophyte arises. — **spo·ro·phyt·ic** /ˌspôrəˈfitik/ **adj.**

spo·ro·tri·cho·sis /ˌspôrətriˈkōsis/ ▶ **n.** Med. a chronic infection producing nodules and ulcers in the lymph nodes and skin, caused by the fungus *Sporothrix schenckii.*

spo·ro·zo·ite /ˌspôrəˈzōˌīt/ ▶ **n.** Zool. & Med. a motile sporelike stage in the life cycle of some parasitic sporozoans (e.g., the malaria organism) that is typically the infective agent introduced into a host. [19th C.: from **SPORO-** 'relating to spores' + Gk. *zōion* 'animal' + **-ITE**[1].]

spor·ran /ˈspärən/ ▶ **n.** a small waist pouch as part of men's Scottish Highland dress. [18th C.: from Scot. Gael. *sporan.*]

sport /spôrt/ ▶ **n. 1** an activity involving physical exertion and skill in which an individual or team competes against another or others. ■ dated entertainment; fun. **2** informal a person who behaves in a specified way in response to teasing, defeat, or a similarly trying situation. **3** Biol. an animal or plant showing abnormal or striking variation from the parent type, esp. in form or color, as a result of spontaneous mutation. ▶ **v. 1** [trans.] wear or display: *sporting a mustache.* **2** [intrans.] amuse oneself or play in a lively way.

– PHRASES **make sport of** dated make fun of. **the sport of kings** horse racing. — **sport·er n.** [ME (in the sense 'pastime, entertainment'): shortening of **DISPORT**.]

sport coat (also **sports coat** or **sport jack·et** or **sports jack·et**) ▶ **n.** a man's jacket for informal wear.

spor·tif /spôrˈtēf/ ▶ **adj.** (of a person) active or interested in athletic sports: *he was sportif.* ■ (of an action or event) intended in fun or as a joke. ■ (of a garment or style of dress) casual. ▶ **n.** a person who is active or interested in sport. [Fr.]

sport·ing /ˈspôrtiNG/ ▶ **adj. 1** [attrib.] connected with or interested in sports: *a major sporting event.* **2** fair and generous in one's behavior or treatment of others, esp. in a game or contest. — **sport·ing·ly adv.** (in sense 2).

sport·ing chance ▶ **n.** [in sing.] a reasonable chance of winning or succeeding: *I'll give you a sporting chance.*

spor·tive /ˈspôrtiv/ ▶ **adj.** playful; lighthearted. — **spor·tive·ly adv. spor·tive·ness n.**

sports bar ▶ **n.** a bar where televised sporting events are shown continuously.

sports car ▶ **n.** a low-built car designed for performance at high speeds.

sports·cast /ˈspôrtsˌkast/ ▶ **n.** a broadcast of sports news or a sports event. — **sports·cast·er n. sports·cast·ing n.**

sports·man /ˈspôrtsmən/ ▶ **n.** (pl. **-men**) a man who takes part in a sport, esp. as a professional. ■ a person who behaves sportingly. ■ dated a man who hunts or shoots wild animals as a pastime. — **sports·man·like** /-ˌlīk/ **adj. sports·man·ship** /-ˌSHip/ **n.**

sport·ster /ˈspôrtstər/ ▶ **n.** informal a sports car.

sports·wear /ˈspôrtsˌwe(ə)r/ ▶ **n.** clothes worn for casual outdoor use or for such sports activities as jogging, cycling, tennis, sailing, etc.

sports·wom·an /ˈspôrtsˌwo͝omən/ ▶ **n.** (pl. **-wom·en**) a woman who takes part in sports, esp. professionally. — **sports·wom·an·ship** /-ˌSHip/ **n.**

sports·writ·er /ˈspôrtsˌrītər/ ▶ **n.** a journalist who writes about sports. — **sports·writ·ing** /-ˌrītiNG/ **n.**

sport u·til·i·ty ve·hi·cle (abbr.: **SUV**) ▶ **n.** a high-performance four-wheel-drive vehicle.

sport·y /ˈspôrtē/ ▶ **adj.** (**sport·i·er, sport·i·est**) informal flashy or showy in dress or behavior. ■ (of clothing) casual yet attractively stylish: *a sporty outfit.* ■ (of a car) compact and with fast acceleration: *a sporty red coupe.* ■ fond of or good at sports. — **sport·i·ly** /ˈspôrt-l-ē/ **adv. sport·i·ness n.**

spor·u·late /ˈspôryəˌlāt/ ▶ **v.** [intrans.] Biol. produce or form a spore or spores. — **spor·u·la·tion** /ˌspôryəˈlāSHən/ **n.**

spor·ule /ˈspôryo͞ol/ ▶ **n.** Biol. a small spore. — **spor·u·lar** /-yələr/ **adj.**

s'pose /s(ə)ˈpōz/ ▶ **v.** nonstandard spelling of **SUPPOSE**, representing informal speech.

spot /spät/ ▶ **n. 1** a small round or roundish mark, differing in color or texture from the surface around it: *ladybugs have black spots on their red wing covers.* ■ a small mark or stain: *a spot of mildew on the wall.* ■ a pimple. ■ archaic a moral blemish or stain. ■ a pip on a domino, playing card, or die. ■ [in comb.] informal a banknote of a specified value: *a ten-spot.* **2** a particular place or point: *an ideal picnic spot.* ■ [with adj.] a small feature or part of something with a particular quality: *there was one bright spot in a night of dismal failure.* ■ a position within a listing; a ranking: *the runner-up spot.* ■ Sports an advantage allowed to a player as a handicap. ■ a place for an individual item within a show: *she couldn't do her usual singing spot in the club.* **3** informal, esp. Brit. a small amount of something: *a spot of rain.* **4** [as adj.] denoting a system of trading in which commodities or currencies are delivered and paid for immediately after a sale: *trading in the spot markets | the current spot price.* **5** short for **SPOTLIGHT**. ▶ **v.** (**spot·ted, spot·ting**) **1** [trans.] see, notice, or recognize (someone or something) that is difficult to detect or that one is searching for: *Andrew spotted the ad in the paper | the men were spotted by police.* ■ (usu. **be spotted**) recognize that (someone) has a particular talent, esp. for sports or show business: *we were spotted by a talent scout.* ■ [intrans.] Mil. locate an enemy's position, typically from the air: *they were spotting for enemy aircraft.* **2** [trans.] (usu. **be spotted**) mark with spots: *the velvet was spotted with stains.* ■ [intrans.] become marked with spots: *a damp atmosphere causes the flowers to spot.* ■ cover (a surface or area) thinly: *thorn trees spotted the land.* ■ archaic stain or sully the moral character or qualities of. **3** [trans.] place (a billiard ball or football) on its designated starting point. **4** [with two objs.] informal give or lend (money) to (someone): *I'll spot you $300.* ■ allow (an advantage) to (someone) in a game or sport: *the higher-rated team spots the lower-rated team the difference in their handicaps.* **5** [trans.] observe or assist (a gymnast) during a performance in order to minimize the chance of injury to the gymnast.

– PHRASES **hit the spot** informal be exactly what is required. **in a spot** informal in a difficult situation. **on the spot 1** without any delay; immediately: *he offered me the job on the spot.* **2** at the scene of an action or event: *journalists on the spot reported no progress.* **put someone on the spot** informal force someone into a situation in which they must make a difficult decision or answer a difficult question. [ME: perh. from MDu. *spotte*. The sense 'notice, recognize' arose from the early 19th-cent. slang use 'note as a suspect or criminal.']

spot check ▶ n. a test made without warning on a randomly selected subject. ▶ v. (**spot-check**) [trans.] subject (someone or something) to such a test.

spot·less /'spätlis/ ▶ adj. absolutely clean or pure; immaculate: *a spotless white apron.* — **spot·less·ly** adv. **spot·less·ness** n.

spot·light /'spät,līt/ ▶ n. a lamp projecting a narrow, intense beam of light directly onto a place or person, esp. a performer on stage. ■ a beam of light from a lamp of this kind: *the knife flashed in the spotlight.* ■ (**the spotlight**) fig. intense scrutiny or public attention: *she was constantly in the media spotlight.* ▶ v. (past and past part. **-light·ed** or **-lit** /-lit/) [trans.] illuminate with a spotlight. ■ fig. direct attention to (a particular problem or situation): *the protest spotlighted the overcrowding in federal prisons.*

spot news ▶ n. news reported of events as they occur.

spot·ted /'spätid/ ▶ adj. marked or decorated with spots. — **spot·ted·ness** n.

spot·ted ca·vy ▶ n. another term for PACA.

spot·ted deer ▶ n. another term for AXIS DEER.

spot·ted fe·ver ▶ n. any of a number of diseases characterized by fever and skin spots: ■ cerebrospinal meningitis. ■ typhus. ■ see ROCKY MOUNTAIN SPOTTED FEVER.

spotted hyena

spot·ted hy·e·na /hī'ēnə/ ▶ n. a southern African hyena (*Crocuta crocuta*) that has a grayish-yellow to reddish coat with irregular dark spots, and a wide range of vocalizations. Also called LAUGHING HYENA.

spotted turtle

spot·ted tur·tle ▶ n. a North American freshwater turtle (*Clemmys guttata*, family Emydidae) with few or numerous yellow spots on the carapace. Once abundant, esp. along the east coast of the US, the spotted turtle is protected in many areas.

spot·ter /'spätər/ ▶ n. informal a person employed by a company or business to keep watch on employees or customers. ■ an aviator or aircraft employed in locating or observing enemy positions: [as adj.] *spotter planes.* ■ a person who observes or assists a gymnast during a performance in order to minimize the chance of injury to the gymnast.

spot·ty /'spätē/ ▶ adj. (**-ti·er**, **-ti·est**) marked with spots: *a spotty purple flower.* ■ of uneven quality; patchy: *his spotty record on the environment.* — **spot·ti·ly** /'spätl-ē/ adv. **spot·ti·ness** n.

spot-weld ▶ v. [trans.] join by welding at a number of separate points: *the wire was spot-welded in place.* ▶ n. (**spot weld**) each of the welds so made. — **spot weld·er** n. **spot weld·ing** n.

spous·al /'spouzəl/ ▶ adj. [attrib.] Law of or relating to marriage or to a husband or wife: *the spousal benefits of married couples.*

spouse /spous/ ▶ n. a husband or wife, considered in relation to their partner. [ME: from OFr. *spous(e)*, var. of *espous(e)*, from L. *sponsus* (masc.), *sponsa* (fem.), past participles of *spondere* 'betroth.']

spout /spout/ ▶ n. **1** a tube or lip projecting from a container, through which liquid can be poured: *a teapot with a chipped spout.* ■ a pipe or trough through which water may be carried away or from which it can flow out. ■ a sloping trough for conveying something to a lower level; a chute. ■ hist. a lift in a pawnshop used to convey pawned items up for storage. **2** a stream of liquid issuing from somewhere with great force: *the tall spouts of geysers.* ■ the plume of water vapor ejected from the blowhole of a whale: *the spout of an occasional whale.* ▶ v. [trans.] **1** send out (liquid) forcibly in a stream: *volcanoes spouted ash and lava.* ■ [no obj., with adverbial] (of a liquid) flow out of somewhere in such a way: *blood was spouting from the cuts on my hand.* ■ (of a whale or dolphin) eject (water vapor and air) through its blowhole. **2** express (one's views or ideas) in a lengthy, declamatory, and unreflecting way: *he was spouting platitudes about animal rights* | [intrans.] *they like to spout off at each other.* — **spout·ed** adj. **spout·er** n. **spout·less** adj. [ME (as a verb): from MDu. *spouten*, from an imitative base shared by ON *spýta* 'to spit.']

spp. ▶ abbr. species (plural).

SPQR ▶ abbr. ■ hist. the Senate and people of Rome. [from L. *Senatus Populusque Romanus*.]

spr. ▶ abbr. spring.

Sprach·ge·fühl /'SHpräkgə,fo͝ol/ ▶ n. intuitive feeling for the natural idiom of a language. [Ger., from *Sprache* 'speech, a language' + *Gefühl* 'feeling.']

sprad·dle /'spradl/ ▶ v. [trans.] [usu. as adj.] (**spraddled**) spread (one's legs) far apart. [17th C. (in the sense 'sprawl'): prob. from *sprad*, dial. past part. of SPREAD.]

sprag /sprag/ ▶ n. **1** a simple brake on a vehicle. ■ a one-way clutch to prevent rolling backwards. **2** Mining a prop used to support a roof, wall, or seam. [19th C.: of unknown origin.]

sprain /sprān/ ▶ v. [trans.] wrench or twist the ligaments of (an ankle, wrist, or other joint) violently. ▶ n. the result of such a wrench or twist of a joint. [17th C.: of unknown origin.]

sprang /spraNG/ past of SPRING.

sprat /sprat/ ▶ n. a small marine fish (*Sprattus* and other genera) of the herring family, widely caught for food and fish products.

sprawl /sprôl/ ▶ v. [no obj., with adverbial] sit, lie, or fall with one's arms and legs spread out in an ungainly or awkward way: *she lay sprawled on the bed.* ■ spread out over a large area in an untidy way. ▶ n. [usu. in sing.] an ungainly or carelessly relaxed position in which one's arms and legs are spread out. ■ a group or mass of something that has spread out in an untidy or irregular way. ■ the expansion of an urban or industrial area into the adjoining countryside in a way perceived to be disorganized and unattractive: *urban sprawl.* ■ such an area. — **sprawl·ing·ly** adv. [OE *spreawlian* 'move the limbs convulsively'; rel. to Dan. *sprælle* 'kick or splash around.' The noun dates from the early 18th C.]

spray[1] /sprā/ ▶ n. liquid that is blown or driven through the air in the form of tiny drops: *a spray of mud.* ■ a liquid preparation that can be forced out of a can or other container in such a form. ■ a can or container holding such a preparation. ■ an act of applying such a preparation. ▶ v. [trans.] apply (liquid) to someone or something in the form of a shower of tiny drops. ■ [trans.] sprinkle or cover (someone or something) with a shower of tiny drops of liquid. ■ [intrans.] (of liquid) be driven through the air or forced out of something in such a form. ■ [trans.] treat (a plant) with insecticide or herbicide in such a way. ■ scatter (something) somewhere with great force. ■ [trans.] fire a rapid succession of bullets at. ■ [trans.] (of a male cat) direct a stream of urine over (an object or area) to mark a territory. — **spray·a·ble** adj. **spray·er** n. [17th C. (earlier as *spry*): rel. to MDu. *spra(e)yen* 'sprinkle.']

spray[2] ▶ n. a stem or small branch of a tree or plant. ■ a bunch of cut flowers arranged in an attractive way. [ME: representing late OE *(e)sprei*, recorded in personal and place names, of unknown origin.]

spray gun ▶ n. a device resembling a gun that is used to spray a liquid such as paint or pesticide under pressure.

spray-paint ▶ v. [trans.] (often **be spray-painted**) paint (an image or message) onto a surface with a spray. ■ paint (a surface) with a spray. ▶ n. (**spray paint**) paint in an aerosol can.

spread /spred/ ▶ v. (past and past part. **spread**) **1** [trans.] open out (something) so as to extend its surface area. ■ stretch out (arms, legs, hands, fingers, or wings). **2** [intrans.] extend over a large or increasing area. ■ (**spread out**) (of a group of people) move apart so as to cover a wider area. ■ [trans.] distribute or disperse (something) over a certain area. ■ gradually reach or cause to reach a larger and larger area or more and more people: [intrans.] *the violence spread.* ■ (of people, animals, or plants) become distributed over a large or larger area. ■ [trans.] distribute (something) in a specified way: ***spread** the payments **over** time.* **3** [trans.] apply (a substance) to an object or surface in an even layer. ■ cover (a surface) with a substance in such a way. ■ [intrans.] be able to be applied in such a way. ▶ n. **1** the fact or process of spreading over an area. **2** the extent, width, or area covered by something. ■ the wingspan of a bird. ■ an expanse or amount of something. ■ a large farm or ranch. **3** the range or variety of something: *a spread of ages.* ■ the difference between two rates or prices. ■ short for POINT SPREAD. **4** a soft paste that can be applied in a layer. **5** an article or advertisement covering several columns or pages of a newspaper or magazine. ■ a bedspread. **6** informal a large and impressively elaborate meal.

– PHRASES **spread like wildfire** see WILDFIRE. **spread oneself too thin** be involved in so many different activities or projects that one's time and energy are not used to good effect. **spread one's wings** see WING.

— **spread·a·ble** adj. (usu. in sense 3). [OE *-sprǣdan* (used in combinations), of West Gmc. origin; rel. to Du. *spreiden* and Ger. *spreiten*.]

spread-ea·gle ▶ v. [trans.] (usu. **be spread-eagled**) stretch out with arms and legs extended. ■ [intrans.] Skating perform a spread eagle. ▶ n. (**spread ea·gle**) an emblematic representation of an eagle with its legs and wings extended. ■ Figure Skating a straight glide made with feet in line, heels touching, and arms stretched out to either side. ▶ adj. stretched out with one's arms and legs extended.

spread·er /'spredər/ ▶ n. a device used for spreading or scattering a substance over a wide area. ■ a person who spreads or disseminates something. ■ [often in comb.] a device that spreads apart one thing from another. ■ a bar attached to the mast of a yacht in order to spread the angle of the upper shrouds.

spread·sheet /ˈspred,SHēt/ ▶ n. a computer program used chiefly for accounting, in which figures are arranged in the rows and columns of a grid. ▶ v. [intrans.] [usu. as n.] (**spreadsheeting**) use such a computer program.

spree /sprē/ ▶ n. a spell or sustained period of unrestrained activity of a particular kind: *a shopping spree.* ■ a spell of unrestrained drinking. [18th C.: of unknown origin.]

sprig /sprig/ ▶ n. a small stem bearing leaves or flowers, taken from a bush or plant: *a sprig of holly.* ■ a descendant or younger member of a family or social class: *a sprig of nobility.* ■ a small molded decoration applied to a piece of pottery before firing. ▶ v. decorate (pottery) with separately molded designs. [ME: from or rel. to Low Ger. *sprick.*]

sprigged /sprigd/ ▶ adj. (chiefly of fabric or paper) decorated with a design of sprigs of leaves or flowers.

spright·ly /ˈsprītlē/ (also **sprite·ly**) ▶ adj. (**-li·er**, **-li·est**) lively; full of energy. — **spright·li·ness** n. [16th C.: from *spright* (rare var. of SPRITE) + -LY[1].]

spring 2

spring /spriNG/ ▶ v. (past **sprang** /spraNG/ or **sprung** /sprəNG/; past part. **sprung**) **1** [intrans.] move or jump suddenly upward or forward. ■ [intrans.] move rapidly or suddenly from a constrained position by or as if by the action of a spring. ■ [trans.] operate or cause to operate by means of a mechanism. ■ [trans.] informal bring about the escape or release of (a prisoner): *spring the hostages.* **2** [intrans.] (**spring from**) originate or arise from. ■ appear suddenly or unexpectedly from. ■ (**spring up**) suddenly develop or appear. ■ [trans.] (**spring something on**) present or propose something suddenly or unexpectedly to (someone). **3** [trans.] [usu. as adj.] (**sprung**) cushion or fit (a vehicle or item of furniture) with springs. **4** [intrans.] (esp. of wood) become warped or split. ■ [trans.] (of a boat) suffer splitting of (a mast or other part). **5** [intrans.] (**spring for**) informal pay for. ▶ n. **1** the season after winter and before summer. ■ Astron. the period from the vernal equinox to the summer solstice. ■ short for SPRING TIDE. **2** a resilient device, typically a helical metal coil, that can be pressed or pulled but returns to its former shape when released. ■ elasticity: *the mattress has lost its spring.* **3** [in sing.] a sudden jump upward or forward. ■ informal, dated an escape or release from prison. **4** a place where water or oil wells up from an underground source, or the basin or flow formed in such a way: [as adj.] *spring water.* ■ fig. the origin or a source of something. **5** an upward curvature of a ship's deck planking from the horizontal. ■ a split in a wooden plank or spar under strain.

– PHRASES **spring a leak** (of a boat or container) develop a leak. [orig. a phr. in nautical use, referring to timbers springing out of position.] — **spring·less** adj. **spring·like** /-,līk/ adj. [OE *spring* (n.), *springan* (v.), of Gmc. origin; rel. to Du. and Ger. *springen.*]

spring beau·ty ▶ n. a spring-flowering succulent plant (genus *Claytonia*) of the purslane family.

spring·board /ˈspriNG,bôrd/ ▶ n. a strong, flexible board from which someone can jump in order to gain added impetus. ■ fig. a thing that lends impetus or assistance to.

spring·bok /ˈspriNG,bäk/ ▶ n. a gazelle (*Antidorcas marsupialis*) with a characteristic habit of leaping when disturbed. Springboks form large herds on arid plains in southern Africa. [18th C.: from Afrik., from Du. *springen* 'to spring' + *bok* 'antelope.']

spring chick·en ▶ n. **1** informal a young person. **2** a young chicken for eating.

spring clean·ing ▶ n. a thorough cleaning of a house or room, typically undertaken in spring. ▶ v. (**spring-clean**) [trans.] clean thoroughly.

springe /sprinj/ ▶ n. a noose or snare for catching small game. [ME: from the base of SPRING.]

spring e·qui·nox ▶ n. another term for VERNAL EQUINOX.

spring·er /ˈspriNGər/ ▶ n. **1** (usu. **spring·er span·iel**) a small spaniel of a breed originally used to spring game. There are two main breeds, the **English springer spaniel** and the **Welsh springer spaniel**. **2** Archit. the lowest stone in an arch, where the curve begins. **3** a cow or heifer near to calving.

spring fe·ver ▶ n. a feeling of restlessness and excitement felt at the beginning of spring.

Spring·field /ˈspriNG,fēld/ **1** the state capital of Illinois, in the central part of the state; pop. 111,454. **2** a city in southwestern Massachusetts; pop. 152,082. **3** a city in southwestern Missouri; pop. 151,580.

spring·form pan /ˈspriNG,fôrm/ ▶ n. a round cake pan with a removable bottom that is held in place by a sprung collar forming the sides.

spring·hare /ˈspriNG,he(ə)r/ (also **spring·haas** /ˈspriNG,häs/) ▶ n. (pl. **-hares** also **-haas**) a large nocturnal burrowing rodent (*Pedetes capensis*, family Pedetidae) resembling a miniature kangaroo, with a rabbitlike head, a long bushy tail, and long hind limbs, native to southern Africa.

spring line ▶ n. a hawser laid out diagonally aft from a ship's bow or forward from a ship's stern and secured to a fixed point.

spring-load·ed ▶ adj. containing a compressed or stretched spring pressing one part against another.

spring lock ▶ n. a type of lock with a spring-loaded bolt that requires a key to open it.

spring peep·er ▶ n. see PEEPER[2].

spring roll ▶ n. an Asian snack of rice paper filled with minced vegetables and meat and rolled.

spring·tail /ˈspriNG,tāl/ ▶ n. a minute primitive wingless insect (order Collembola) that has a springlike organ under the abdomen that enables it to leap when disturbed. Springtails are abundant in the soil and leaf litter.

spring·tide ▶ n. literary term for SPRINGTIME.

spring tide /ˈspriNG ,tīd/ ▶ n. a tide just after a new or full moon.

spring·time /ˈspriNG,tīm/ ▶ n. the season of spring: *the sounds of lambing in springtime.* ■ fig. literary the early part or first stage of: *the springtime of their marriage.*

spring·y /ˈspriNGē/ ▶ adj. (**spring·i·er**, **spring·i·est**) springing back quickly when squeezed or stretched. ■ (of movements) light and confident: *a springy step.* — **spring·i·ly** /ˈspriNGəlē/ adv. **spring·i·ness** n.

sprin·kle /ˈspriNGkəl/ ▶ v. **1** [with obj. and adverbial] scatter or pour small drops or particles of a substance over. ■ scatter or pour (small drops or particles of a substance) over an object or surface. ■ fig. distribute or disperse something randomly or irregularly throughout. ■ fig. place or attach (a number of things) at irregularly spaced intervals. **2** [intrans.] (**it sprinkles, it is sprinkling**, etc.) rain very lightly. ▶ n. **1** a small quantity or amount of something scattered over an object or surface: *a generous sprinkle.* **2** [in sing.] a light rain. **3** (**sprinkles**) tiny sugar shapes. [ME: perh. from MDu. *sprenkelen.*]

sprin·kler /ˈspriNGk(ə)lər/ ▶ n. a device that sprays water. ■ a device used for watering lawns. ■ an automatic fire extinguisher installed in the ceilings of a building.

sprin·kling /ˈspriNGk(ə)liNG/ ▶ n. a small thinly distributed amount of something: *a sprinkling of gray.*

sprint /sprint/ ▶ v. [intrans.] run at full speed over a short distance. ▶ n. an act or short spell of running at full speed. ■ a short, fast race in which the competitors run a distance of 400 meters or less: *the 100 meters sprint.* ■ a short, fast race or exercise. — **sprint·er** n. [18th C. (as a dial. term meaning 'a bound or spring'): rel. to Swed. *spritta.*]

sprint·ing /ˈsprintiNG/ ▶ n. the competitive athletic sport of running distances of 400 meters or less.

sprit /sprit/ ▶ n. Sailing a small spar reaching diagonally from low on a mast to the upper outer corner of a sail. [OE *sprēot* '(punting) pole'; rel. to SPROUT.]

sprite /sprīt/ ▶ n. **1** an elf or fairy. **2** a computer graphic that may be moved on-screen and otherwise manipulated as a single entity. **3** a faint flash, typically red, sometimes emitted in the upper atmosphere over a thunderstorm. [ME: alt. of *sprit*, a contr. of SPIRIT.]

sprite·ly ▶ adj. var. of SPRIGHTLY.

sprit·sail /ˈsprit,sāl; -səl/ ▶ n. a sail extended by a sprit.

spritz /sprits/ ▶ v. [trans.] squirt or spray something at or onto (something) in quick short bursts. ▶ n. an act of squirting or spraying in quick short bursts. [20th C.: from Ger. *spritzen* 'to squirt.']

spritz·er /ˈspritsər/ ▶ n. wine and soda water mixed. [1960s: from Ger. *Spritzer* 'a splash.']

sprock·et /ˈspräkit/ ▶ n. each of several projections on the rim of a wheel that engage with the links of a chain or with holes in film, tape, or paper. ■ (also **sprocket wheel**) a wheel with teeth. [16th C. (denoting a triangular piece of timber used in a roof): of unknown origin.]

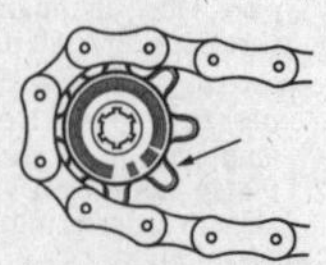
sprocket

sprout /sprout/ ▶ v. [intrans.] (of a plant) put forth shoots: *the weeds begin to sprout.* ■ [trans.] grow (plant shoots or hair). ■ [intrans.] (of a plant, flower, or hair) start to grow; spring up. ▶ n. **1** a shoot of a plant. ■ (**sprouts**) young shoots eaten as a vegetable. **2** short for BRUSSELS SPROUT. [ME: of West Gmc. origin; rel. to Du. *spruiten* and Ger. *spriessen.*]

spruce[1] /sproo͞s/ ▶ n. a widespread coniferous tree (genus *Picea*) of the pine family that has a distinctive conical shape and hanging cones, widely grown for timber, pulp, and Christmas trees. [ME (denoting Prussia or something originating in Prussia): alt. of obs. *Pruce* 'Prussia.' The application to the tree dates from the early 17th C.]

spruce[2] ▶ adj. neat in dress and appearance. ▶ v. [trans.] (**spruce someone/something up**) make a person or place smarter or tidier. — **spruce·ly** adv. **spruce·ness** n. [16th C.: perh. from SPRUCE[1] in the obs. sense 'Prussian,' in the phr. *spruce (leather) jerkin.*]

spruce bud·worm ▶ n. the brown caterpillar (*Choristoneura fumiferana*, family Tortricidae) of a small North American moth that is a serious pest of spruce and other conifers.

sprue[1] /sproo͞/ ▶ n. a channel through which metal or plastic is poured into a mold. ■ metal or plastic that has solidified in a sprue. [19th C.: of unknown origin.]

sprue[2] ▶ n. disease of the small intestine causing malabsorption of food, in particular: ■ (also **tropical sprue**) a disease characterized by ulceration of the mouth and chronic enteritis. ■ (also **nontropical sprue**) another term for CELIAC DISEASE. [19th C.: from Du. *spruw* 'thrush'; perh. rel. to Flemish *spruwen* 'sprinkle.']

sprung /sprəNG/ past and past participle of SPRING.

sprung rhythm ▶ **n.** a poetic meter approximating speech, each foot having one stressed syllable followed by a varying number of unstressed ones. [19th C.: coined by G. M. Hopkins, who used the meter.]

spry /sprī/ ▶ **adj.** (**spry·er, spry·est** or **spri·er, spri·est**) active; lively. — **spry·ly adv. spry·ness n.** [18th C.: of unknown origin.]

spud /spəd/ ▶ **n.** **1** informal a potato. **2** a small, narrow spade for cutting the roots of plants. **3** [often as adj.] a short length of pipe that is used to connect two components or that projects from a fitting so a pipe may be attached. **4** a chisellike tool. ▶ **v.** (**spud·ded, spud·ding**) [trans.] **1** dig up or cut (plants, esp. weeds) with a spud. **2** make the initial drilling for (an oil well). [ME (denoting a short knife): of unknown origin. The sense 'potato' (dating from the mid 19th C.) was orig. slang and dial.]

spud wrench ▶ **n.** a long bar with a socket on the end.

spu·man·te /sp(y)ə'mäntē/ ▶ **n.** an Italian sparkling white wine. [Ital., lit. 'sparkling.']

spume /spyo͞om/ literary ▶ **n.** froth or foam. ▶ **v.** [intrans.] form or produce a mass of froth or foam. — **spu·mous** /-məs/ **adj. spum·y adj.** [ME: from OFr. *(e)spume* or L. *spuma.*]

spu·mo·ni /spo͝o'mōnē/ (also **spu·mo·ne**) ▶ **n.** a kind of ice cream with different colors and flavors in layers. [from Ital. *spumone*, from *spuma* 'foam.']

spun /spən/ past and past participle of SPIN.

spunk /spəNGk/ ▶ **n.** **1** informal courage and determination. **2** tinder; touchwood. [16th C. (in the sense 'a spark, vestige'): of unknown origin; perh. a blend of SPARK[1] and obs. *funk* 'spark.']

spunk·y /'spəNGkē/ ▶ **adj.** (**spunk·i·er, spunk·i·est**) informal courageous and determined: *a spunky performance.* — **spunk·i·ly** /'spəNGkəlē/ **adv. spunk·i·ness n.**

spun silk ▶ **n.** yarn made of short-fibered and waste silk. ■ fabric made from this yarn.

spun sug·ar ▶ **n.** hardened sugar syrup drawn out into long filaments and used to make cotton candy.

spun yarn ▶ **n.** Naut. cord made by twisting together from two to four untwisted yarns of tarred hemp.

spur /spər/ ▶ **n.** **1** a device with a small spike or a spiked wheel that is worn on a rider's heel. ■ fig. an incentive. ■ a hard spike on the back of the leg of a cock or male game bird, used in fighting. ■ a steel point fastened to the leg of a gamecock. **2** a thing that projects or branches off from a main body, in particular: ■ a projection from a mountain or mountain range. ■ a short branch road or rail line. ■ Bot. a slender tubular projection from the base of a flower, typically containing nectar. ■ a short fruit-bearing side shoot. ▶ **v.** (**spurred, spur·ring**) [trans.] urge (a horse) forward by digging one's spurs into its sides. ■ give an incentive or encouragement to (someone). ■ cause or promote the development of; stimulate.

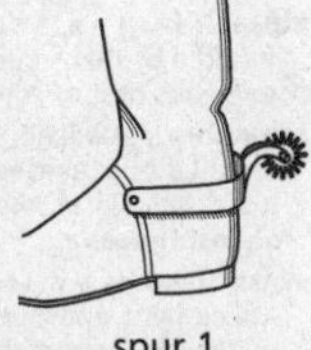
spur 1

– PHRASES **on the spur of the moment** on a momentary impulse; without premeditation. — **spur·less adj. spurred adj.** [OE *spora, spura*, of Gmc. origin; rel. to Du. *spoor* and Ger. *Sporn*, also to SPURN.]

spurge /spərj/ ▶ **n.** a herbaceous plant or shrub (genus *Euphorbia*, family Euphorbiaceae) with milky latex and very small typically greenish flowers. Many kinds are cultivated as ornamentals and some are of commercial importance. [ME: shortening of OFr. *espurge*, from *espurgier*, from L. *expurgare* 'cleanse' (because of the purgative properties of the milky latex).]

spur gear ▶ **n.** a gearwheel with teeth projecting parallel to the wheel's axis.

spurge lau·rel ▶ **n.** a low-growing evergreen Eurasian shrub (*Daphne laureola*, family Thymelaeaceae) with leathery leaves, small green flowers, and black poisonous berries.

spu·ri·ous /'spyo͝orēəs/ ▶ **adj.** not being what it purports to be; false or fake: *spurious claims.* ■ (of a line of reasoning) apparently but not actually valid: *this spurious reasoning results in nonsense.* — **spu·ri·ous·ly adv. spu·ri·ous·ness n.** [16th C. (in the sense 'born out of wedlock'): from L. *spurius* 'false' + -OUS.]

spurn /spərn/ ▶ **v.** [trans.] reject with disdain. — **spurn·er n.** [OE *spurnan, spornan*; rel. to L. *spernere* 'to scorn'; cf. SPUR.]

spur·rey /'spərē; 'spə-rē/ (also **spur·ry**) ▶ **n.** (pl. **-reys** or **-ries**) a small widely distributed plant (genera *Spergula* and *Spergularia*) of the pink family, with pink or white flowers. [16th C.: from Du. *spurrie*; prob. rel. to med. L. *spergula.*]

spur·ri·er /'spərēər/ ▶ **n.** rare a person who makes spurs.

spurt /spərt/ ▶ **v.** [intrans.] gush out in a sudden and forceful stream: *blood spurted out.* ■ [trans.] cause to gush out suddenly. ■ move with a sudden burst of speed. ▶ **n.** a sudden gushing stream: *a sudden spurt of water.* ■ a sudden marked burst or increase of activity: *late in the race he put on a spurt and reached second place.* [16th C.: of unknown origin.]

Sput·nik /'spətnik; 'spo͝ot-/ ▶ **n.** each of a series of Soviet artificial satellites, the first of which was the first satellite to be placed in orbit (October 4, 1957). [Russ., 'fellow-traveler.']

sput·ter /'spətər/ ▶ **v.** **1** [intrans.] make a series of soft explosive sounds: *the engine sputtered and stopped.* ■ [reporting verb] speak in a series of incoherent bursts as a result of a strong emotion: [with direct speech] *"But ... but ..." she sputtered.* ■ [trans.] emit with a spitting sound: *sputtering fat.* ■ [with adverbial] fig. proceed or develop in a spasmodic and feeble way. **2** [trans.] Physics deposit (metal) on a surface by using fast ions to eject particles of it from a target. ■ cover (a surface) with metal by this method. ▶ **n.** a series of soft explosive sounds. — **sput·ter·er n.** [16th C. (as a v.): from Du. *sputteren*, of imitative origin.]

spu·tum /'spyo͞otəm/ ▶ **n.** a mixture of saliva and mucus coughed up from the respiratory tract. [17th C.: from L., neut. past part. of *spuere* 'to spit.']

spy /spī/ ▶ **n.** (pl. **spies**) a person who secretly collects and reports information about an enemy or competitor. ■ a person who keeps watch on others secretly. ▶ **v.** (**spies, spied, spy·ing**) [intrans.] work for an organization by secretly collecting information about enemies or competitors. ■ (**spy on**) observe (someone) furtively. ■ [trans.] discern or make out: *spy a figure in the distance.* [ME: shortening of OFr. *espie* 'espying,' *espier* 'espy,' of Gmc. origin.]

spyglass

spy·glass /'spī,glas/ ▶ **n.** a small hand-held telescope.

spy·ware /'spī,we(ə)r/ ▶ **n.** software that self-installs on a computer, enabling information to be gathered covertly about a person's Internet use, passwords, etc.

sq ▶ **abbr.** square: *51,100 sq km.*

SQL Comput. ▶ **abbr.** Structured Query Language, an international standard for database manipulation.

squab /skwäb/ ▶ **n.** **1** a young unfledged pigeon. ■ the flesh of such a bird as food: *roast squab.* **2** a thick stuffed cushion. [17th C. (in the sense 'inexperienced person'): of unknown origin; cf. obs. *quab* 'shapeless thing' and Swed. dial. *skvabba* 'fat woman.']

squab·ble /'skwäbəl/ ▶ **n.** a noisy petty quarrel. ▶ **v.** [intrans.] quarrel noisily over a trivial matter. — **squab·bler** /'skwäb(ə)lər/ **n.** [17th C.: prob. imitative; cf. Swed. dial. *skvabbel* 'a dispute.']

squad /skwäd/ ▶ **n.** [treated as sing. or pl.] a small group of people having a particular task. ■ a small number of soldiers assembled for drill or assigned to some special task. ■ a group of sports players or competitors from which a team is chosen. ■ a division of a police force dealing with a particular crime or type of crime. [17th C.: shortening of Fr. *escouade*, var. of *escadre*, from Ital. *squadra* 'square.']

squad car ▶ **n.** a police patrol car.

squad·ron /'skwädrən/ ▶ **n.** an operational unit in an air force consisting of two or more flights of aircraft and the personnel required to fly them. ■ a principal division of an armored or cavalry regiment, consisting of two or more troops. ■ a group of warships detached on a particular duty or under the command of a flag officer. ■ informal a large group of people or things: *a squadron of architects.* [16th C.: from Ital. *squadrone*, from *squadra* 'square.']

squa·lene /'skwālēn/ ▶ **n.** Biochem. an oily liquid hydrocarbon, $C_{30}H_{50}$, that occurs in shark liver oil and human sebum, and is a metabolic precursor of sterols. [20th C.: from L. *squalus* (denoting a kind of marine fish and used as a rare term in English for 'shark') + -ENE.]

squal·id /'skwälid/ ▶ **adj.** (of a place) extremely dirty and unpleasant, esp. as a result of poverty or neglect: ■ showing a contemptible lack of moral standards. — **squal·id·ly adv. squal·id·ness n.** [16th C.: from L. *squalidus*, from *squalere* 'be rough or dirty.']

squall /skwôl/ ▶ **n.** a sudden violent gust of wind or a localized storm, esp. one bringing rain, snow, or sleet. ■ a loud cry: *he emitted a short mournful squall.* ▶ **v.** [intrans.] (of a baby or small child) cry noisily and continuously. — **squal·ly adj.** [17th C.: prob. an alt. of SQUEAL, influenced by BAWL.]

squall line ▶ **n.** Meteorol. a narrow band of high winds and storms associated with a cold front.

squal·or /'skwälər/ ▶ **n.** a state of being extremely dirty. [17th C.: from L., from *squalere* 'be dirty.']

Squa·ma·ta /skwä'mätə/ Zool. an order of reptiles that comprises snakes, lizards, and worm lizards. — **squa·mate** /'skwāmāt/ **adj. & n.** [mod. L. (pl.), from L. *squama* 'scale.']

squa·mo·sal /skwə'mōsəl/ ▶ **n.** Zool. the squamous portion of the temporal bone. [19th C.: from L. *squamosus* (from *squama* 'scale') + -AL.]

squa·mous /'skwāməs/ (also **squa·mose**) ▶ **adj.** covered with or characterized by scales. ■ Anat. consisting of or denoting a layer of epithelium that consists of very thin flattened cells. ■ [attrib.] Anat. denoting the flat portion of the temporal bone that forms part of the side of the skull. [ME: from L. *squamosus*, from *squama* 'scale.']

squan·der /'skwändər/ ▶ **v.** [trans.] waste (something, esp. money or time) in a reckless and foolish manner: *entrepreneurs squander their profits on expensive cars.* ■ allow (an opportunity) to pass or be lost. — **squand·er·er n.** [16th C.: of unknown origin.]

Squan·to /'skwäntō/ (*c.*1585–1622), Pawtuxet Indian. He befriended the

Pilgrims in Plymouth Colony in 1621 and acted as their interpreter and adviser on planting and fishing.

square /skwe(ə)r/ ▶n. **1** a plane figure with four equal straight sides and four right angles. ■ a thing having such a shape. ■ a thing having the shape or approximate shape of a cube. ■ an open (typically four-sided) area surrounded by buildings. ■ an open area at the meeting of streets. ■ a small square area on the board used in a game. ■ a block of buildings bounded by four streets. ■ a unit of 100 square ft. used as a measure of flooring, roofing, etc. **2** the product of a number multiplied by itself. **3** an L-shaped or T-shaped instrument used for obtaining or testing right angles: *a carpenter's square.* ■ Astrol. an aspect of 90° (one quarter of a circle). **4** informal a person considered to be old-fashioned. **5** informal a square meal: *three squares a day.* ▶adj. **1** having the shape of a square. ■ having the shape or approximate shape of a cube. ■ having or in the form of two right angles: *wood with square ends.* ■ having an outline resembling two corners of a square: *his square jaw.* ■ broad and solid in shape: *he was short and square.* **2** denoting a unit of measurement equal to the area of a square whose side is of the unit specified: *30,000 square feet of new gallery space.* ■ [postpositive] denoting the length of each side of a square shape or object: *the office was fifteen feet square.* **3** at right angles; perpendicular: *these lines must be* ***square*** *to the top.* ■ Astrol. having or denoting an aspect of 90°. **4** level or parallel: *they are exactly square.* ■ properly arranged; in good order: *we should get everything square.* ■ compatible or in agreement: *he wanted to make sure we were* ***square with*** *the court's decision and not subject to a lawsuit.* ■ fair and honest: *she'd been square with him.* **5** (of two people) owing nothing to each other: *an acknowledgment that we are square.* ■ with both players or sides having equal scores in a game: *the goal brought the match* ***all square*** *once again.* **6** informal old-fashioned or boringly conventional: *Elvis was anything but square.* **7** (of rhythm) simple and straightforward. ▶adv. directly; straight: *it hit me square in the forehead.* ■ informal fairly; honestly: *I'd acted square and on the level.* ▶v. [trans.] **1** make square or rectangular; give a square or rectangular cross section to: *you can* ***square off*** *the other edge.* ■ [usu. as adj.] (**squared**) mark out in squares. **2** multiply (a number) by itself: *5 squared equals 25.* ■ [usu. as postpositive adj.] (**squared**) convert (a linear unit of measurement) to a unit of area equal to a square whose side is of the unit specified: *there were only three people per kilometer squared.* **3** make compatible; reconcile: *I'm able to* ***square*** *my profession* ***with*** *my religious beliefs.* ■ [intrans.] be compatible: ***square with*** *the facts.* **4** balance (an account): *they need to square their books before the audit.* ■ make the score of (a match or game) even. ■ informal secure the help, acquiescence, or silence of (someone), esp. by offering an inducement: *trying to square the press.* **5** bring (one's shoulders) into a position in which they appear square and broad, typically to prepare oneself for a difficult task or event: *chin up, shoulders squared, she stepped into the room.* ■ (**square oneself**) adopt a posture of defense. **6** Sailing set (a yard or other part of a ship) approximately at right angles to the keel or other point of reference. **7** Astrol. (of a planet) have a square aspect with (another planet or position): *Saturn squares the Sun on the 17th.*

– PHRASES **back to** (or **at**) **square one** informal back to where one started, with no progress having been made. **on the square 1** informal honest; straightforward. **2** informal honestly; fairly. **3** at right angles. **out of square** not at right angles. **square the circle** construct a square equal in area to a given circle (a problem incapable of a purely geometric solution). ■ do something that is considered to be impossible.

– PHRASAL VERBS **square something away** arrange or deal with in a satisfactory way: *don't you worry, we'll get things squared away.* **square off** assume the attitude of a person about to fight: *the two men squared off.* **square up** settle or pay an account: *would you square up the bill?* ■ settle a dispute or misunderstanding: *I want to square up whatever's wrong between us.* — **square·ness** n. **squar·er** n. **squar·ish** adj. [ME: shortening of OFr. *esquare* (n.), *esquarre* (past part., used as an adj.), *esquarrer* (v.), based on L. *quadra* 'square.']

square brack·et ▶plural n. see BRACKET (sense 1).

square dance ▶n. a country dance that starts with four couples facing one another in a square, with the steps and movements shouted out by a caller. ▶v. (**square dance**) [intrans.] [often as n.] (**square dancing**) participate in a square dance. — **square danc·er** n.

square deal ▶n. [usu. in sing.] a fair bargain or treatment: *the workers feel they are not getting a square deal.*

square·head /ˈskwe(ə)rˌhed/ ▶n. informal **1** a stupid or inept person. **2** offens. a person of German, Dutch, or Scandinavian, esp. Swedish, origin.

square knot ▶n. a type of double knot that is made symmetrically to hold securely and to be easy to untie. See illustration at KNOT[1].

square law ▶n. Physics a law relating two variables, one of which varies (directly or inversely) as the square of the other.

square·ly /ˈskwe(ə)rlē/ ▶adv. directly, without deviating to one side: *Ashley looked at him squarely.* ■ in a direct and uncompromising manner; without equivocation: *they placed the blame squarely on the president.*

square meal ▶n. a substantial, satisfying, and balanced meal: *three square meals a day.* [said to derive from nautical use, with ref. to the square platters on which meals were served on board ship.]

square meas·ure ▶n. a unit of measurement relating to area.

square-rigged ▶adj. (of a sailing ship) having the principal sails at right angles to the length of the ship, supported by horizontal yards attached to the mast or masts.

square-rig·ger ▶n. a square-rigged sailing ship.

square rod ▶n. see ROD (sense 3).

square root ▶n. a number that produces a specified quantity when multiplied by itself: *7 is a square root of 49.*

square sail ▶n. a four-cornered sail supported by a yard attached to a mast.

square-should·ered ▶adj. (of a person) having broad shoulders that do not slope.

square·tail /ˈskwe(ə)rˌtāl/ ▶n. a fish (genus *Tetragonurus*, family Tetragonuridae) of warm seas that has a slender cylindrical body and long tail, the base of which is square in cross section.

square-toed ▶adj. (of shoes or boots) having broad, square toes. ■ archaic old-fashioned or formal.

square wave ▶n. Electron. a periodic wave that varies abruptly in amplitude between two fixed values, spending equal times at each.

squark /skwärk/ ▶n. Physics the supersymmetric counterpart of a quark, with spin 0 instead of 1/2. [1980s: from *s(uper)* + QUARK.]

squash[1] /skwäsн; skwôsн/ ▶v. [trans.] crush or squeeze (something) with force so that it becomes flat, soft, or out of shape: *wash and squash the cans for the recycling bin* | [as adj.] (**squashed**) *a squashed banana.* ■ [with obj. and trans.] squeeze or force (someone or something) into a small or restricted space: *she squashed some of her clothes inside the bag.* ■ [no obj., with intrans.] make one's way into a small or restricted space: *I squashed into the middle of the crowd.* ■ suppress, stifle, or subdue (a feeling, conjecture, or action): *the mournful sound did nothing to squash her high spirits.* ■ firmly reject (an idea or suggestion): *the proposal was immediately squashed by the Historical Society.* ▶n. **1** [in sing.] a state of being squeezed or forced into a small or restricted space: *it was a tight squash but he didn't seem to mind.* **2** esp. Brit. a concentrated liquid made from fruit juice and sugar, which is diluted to make a drink: *orange squash.* **3** (also **squash racquets**) a game in which two players use rackets to hit a small, soft rubber ball against the walls of a closed court. See illustration at RACKET[1]. [16th C. (as a v.): alt. of QUASH.]

squash[2] ▶n. (pl. same or **squash·es**) **1** an edible gourd, the flesh of which may be cooked and eaten as a vegetable. **2** the trailing plant (genus *Cucurbita*) of the gourd family that produces this fruit. [17th C.: abbr. of Narragansett *asquutasquash*.]

squash·ber·ry /ˈskwäsнˌberē; ˈskwôsн-/ ▶n. (pl. **-ries**) a North American viburnum (*Viburnum edule*) which bears edible berries.

squash blos·som ▶n. [as adj.] denoting a type of silver jewelry made by Navajos characterized by designs resembling the flower of the squash plant.

squash bug ▶n. a dark-colored bug (family Coreidae) with forewings marked by many veins, in particular the North American *Anasa tristis*, a serious pest of squashes and similar fruit.

squash·y /ˈskwäsнē; ˈskwôsнē/ ▶adj. (**squash·i·er**, **squash·i·est**) easily crushed or squeezed into a different shape; having a soft consistency: *a big, squashy leather chair.* — **squash·i·ly** /ˈskwäsнəlē; ˈskwôsнəlē/ adv. **squash·i·ness** n.

squat /skwät/ ▶v. (**squat·ted**, **squat·ting**) **1** [intrans.] crouch or sit with knees bent and heels close to or touching the buttocks or the back of thighs: *I squatted down in front of him.* ■ [trans.] Weightlifting crouch down in such a way and rise again while holding (a specified weight) at one's shoulders: *he can squat 850 pounds.* **2** [intrans.] unlawfully occupy an uninhabited building or settle on a piece of land: *eight families are squatting in the house.* ■ [trans.] occupy (an uninhabited building) in such a way. ▶adj. (**squat·ter**, **squat·test**) short and thickset; disproportionately broad or wide: *he was muscular and squat* | *a squat gray house.* ▶n. **1** [in sing.] a position in which knees are bent and heels are close to or touching buttocks or the back of thighs. ■ Weightlifting an exercise in which a person squats down and rises again while holding a barbell at shoulder level. ■ (in gymnastics) an exercise involving a squatting movement or action. **2** informal short for DIDDLY-SQUAT: *I didn't know squat about writing plays.* **3** an unlawful occupation of an uninhabited building. — **squat·ly** adv. **squat·ness** n. [ME (in the sense 'thrust down with force'): from OFr. *esquatir* 'flatten,' based on L. *coactus*, past part. of *cogere* 'compel' (see COGENT). The current sense of the adjective dates from the mid 17th C.]

squat·ter /ˈskwätər/ ▶n. a person who unlawfully occupies an uninhabited building or unused land.

squat thrust ▶n. an exercise in which the legs are thrust backward to their full extent from a squatting position with the hands on the floor.

squaw /skwô/ ▶n. offens. an American Indian woman or wife. ■ a woman or wife. [17th C.: from Narragansett *squaws* 'woman,' with rel. forms in many Algonquian dialects.]

squaw·fish /ˈskwôˌfisн/ ▶n. (pl. same or **-fish·es**) a large predatory freshwater fish (genus *Ptychocheilus*) of the minnow family, with a slender body and large mouth, found in western North America. [19th C.: the word derives from the former importance to Amer. Indians of such fish, as food.]

squawk /skwôk/ ▶v. [intrans.] (of a bird) make a loud, harsh noise: *the geese flew upriver, squawking.* ■ [with direct speech] say something in a loud, discordant tone. ■ complain or protest about something. ▶n. a loud, harsh or discordant noise made by a bird or a person. ■ a complaint or protest. — **squawk·er** n. [19th C.: imitative.]

squawk box ▶n. informal a loudspeaker, esp. one that is part of an intercom system.

squaw man ▶n. offens. a white or black man married to an American Indian woman.

squaw·root /ˈskwôˌro͞ot/ ▶n. either of two North American plants: ■ a yellow-brown parasitic plant (*Conopholis americana*, family Orobanchaceae) related to the broomrape. ■ the blue cohosh. See COHOSH.

Squaw Val·ley /ˈskwô/ a resort in northeastern California, site of the 1960 Winter Olympic games.

squeak /skwēk/ ▶n. a short, high-pitched sound or cry: *the door opened with a slight squeak.* ■ [with negative] a single remark, statement, or communication: *I didn't hear a squeak from him for months.* ▶v. [intrans.] **1** make a high-pitched sound or cry: *he oiled the hinges to stop them from squeaking.* ■ [with direct speech] say something in a nervous or excited high-pitched tone: *"You're scaring me," she squeaked.* ■ informal inform on someone. **2** [with adverbial] informal succeed in achieving something by a very narrow margin: *the bill squeaked through with just six votes to spare.* ■ (**squeak by**) make or have just enough money for basic necessities: *she was squeaking by on her minimum-wage job.* [ME (as a v.): imitative; cf. Swed. *skväka* 'croak,' also with SQUEAL and SHRIEK. The noun dates from the early 17th C.]

squeak·er /ˈskwēkər/ ▶n. a person or thing that squeaks. ■ informal a competition or election won or likely to be won by a narrow margin.

squeak·y /ˈskwēkē/ ▶adj. (**squeak·i·er**, **squeak·i·est**) having or making a high-pitched sound or cry: *a high, squeaky voice.* — **squeak·i·ly** /-kəlē/ adv. **squeak·i·ness** n.

squeak·y-clean (also **squeak·y clean**) ▶adj. informal completely clean: *squeaky-clean restrooms.* ■ beyond reproach; without vice: *politicians who are less than squeaky clean.*

squeal /skwēl/ ▶n. a long, high-pitched cry or noise: *we heard a splash and a squeal.* ▶v. [intrans.] **1** make such a cry or noise: *the girls squealed with delight.* ■ [with direct speech] say something in a high-pitched, excited tone: *"Don't you dare!" she squealed.* ■ complain or protest about something: *the bookies only squealed because we beat them.* **2** informal inform on someone to the police or a person in authority: *she feared they would victimize her for* ***squealing on*** *their pals.* — **squeal·er** n. (esp. in sense 2). [ME (as a v.): imitative. The noun dates from the mid 18th C.]

squeam·ish /ˈskwēmisн/ ▶adj. (of a person) easily made to feel sick, faint, or disgusted. ■ (of a person) having strong moral views; scrupulous. — **squeam·ish·ly** adv. **squeam·ish·ness** n. [ME: alt. of dial. *squeamous*, from Anglo-Norman Fr. *escoymos*, of unknown origin.]

squee·gee /ˈskwēˌjē/ ▶n. a scraping implement with a rubber-edged blade set on a handle, typically used for cleaning windows. ■ a similar small instrument or roller used esp. in photography for squeezing water out of prints. ■ [usu. as adj.] informal a person who cleans the windshield of a car stopped in traffic and then demands payment from the driver: *squeegee guys at every corner* | *the squeegees wait at busy intersections.* ▶v. (**-gees**, **-geed**, **-gee·ing**) [trans.] clean or scrape (something) with a squeegee: *squeegee the shower doors while the surfaces are still wet.* [19th C.: from archaic *squeege* 'to press,' strengthened form of SQUEEZE.]

squeeze /skwēz/ ▶v. **1** [trans.] firmly press (something soft or yielding), typically with one's fingers: *Kate squeezed his hand affectionately* | [intrans.] *he squeezed with all his strength.* ■ [trans.] extract (liquid or a soft substance) from something by compressing or twisting it firmly: ***squeeze out*** *as much juice as you can* | [as adj., with submodifier] (**squeezed**) *freshly squeezed orange juice.* ■ [trans.] obtain (something) from someone with difficulty: *a governor who wants to* ***squeeze*** *as much money* ***out of*** *taxpayers as he can.* ■ informal pressure (someone) in order to obtain something from them: *squeeze him for information.* ■ (esp. in a financial or commercial context) have a damaging or restricting effect on: *the economy is being squeezed by foreign debt repayments.* ■ (**squeeze off**) informal shoot a round or shot from a gun: *squeeze off a few well-aimed shots.* **2** [intrans.] manage to get into or through a narrow or restricted space: *Sarah squeezed in beside her* | *he found a hole in the hedge and* ***squeezed his way*** *through.* ■ [trans.] manage to force into or through such a space: *she squeezed herself into her tightest pair of jeans.* ■ [intrans.] (**squeeze up**) move closer to someone or something so that one is pressed tightly against them or it: *squeeze up and make room.* ■ [trans.] (**squeeze someone/something in**) manage to find time for someone or something: *the doctor can squeeze you in at noon.* ■ [trans.] (**squeeze someone/something out**) force someone or something out of a domain or activity: *workers have been squeezed out of their jobs.* ▶n. **1** an act of pressing something with one's fingers: *a gentle squeeze of the trigger.* ■ a hug. ■ a state of forcing oneself or being forced into a small or restricted space: *it was a* ***tight squeeze*** *in the tiny hall.* ■ dated a crowded social gathering. ■ a small amount of liquid extracted from something by pressing it firmly with one's fingers: *a* ***squeeze of*** *lemon juice.* ■ a strong financial demand or pressure, typically a restriction on borrowing, spending, or investment in a financial crisis: *industry faced higher costs and a* ***squeeze on*** *profits.* ■ a molding or cast of an object, or an impression or copy of a design, obtained by pressing a pliable substance around or over it. ■ informal money illegally extorted or exacted from someone: *he was out to extract some squeeze from her.* ■ Bridge a tactic that forces an opponent to discard an important card. ■ (also **squeeze play** or **suicide squeeze**) Baseball an act of bunting a ball in order to enable a runner on third base to start for home as soon as the ball is pitched. **2** informal a person's girlfriend or boyfriend: *the poor guy just lost his* ***main squeeze.***
– PHRASES **put the squeeze on** informal coerce or pressure (someone). — **squeez·a·ble** adj. **squeez·er** n. [16th C.: from earlier *squise*, from obs. *queise*, of unknown origin.]

squeeze bot·tle ▶n. a container made of flexible plastic that is squeezed to extract the contents.

squeeze·box /ˈskwēzˌbäks/ (also **squeeze box**) ▶n. informal an accordion or concertina.

squelch /skwelcн/ ▶v. [intrans.] make a soft sucking sound such as that made by walking heavily through mud: *bedraggled guests squelched across the lawn to seek shelter.* ■ informal forcefully silence or suppress: *property developers tried to squelch public protest.* ▶n. **1** a soft sucking sound made when pressure is applied to liquid or mud: *the squelch of their feet.* **2** (also **squelch circuit**) Electron. a circuit that suppresses the output of a radio receiver if the signal strength falls below a certain level. — **squelch·er** n. **squelch·y** adj. [17th C. (orig. denoting a heavy crushing fall on to something soft): imitative.]

squib /skwib/ ▶n. **1** a small firework that burns with a hissing sound before exploding. ■ a short piece of satirical writing. ■ a short news item or filler in a newspaper. **2** a small, slight, or weak person, esp. a child. **3** Football a short kick on a kickoff. ■ Baseball (also **squib·ber**) a blooper or infield grounder that becomes a base hit. ▶v. (**squibbed**, **squib·bing**) [trans.] Football kick (the ball) a comparatively short distance on a kickoff; execute (a kick) in this way. ■ Baseball hit (the ball) with little force, usually with the end of the bat, the typical result being a blooper or infield grounder. [16th C. (sense 1): of unknown origin; perh. imitative of a small explosion.]

SQUID /skwid/ ▶n. Physics a device used in particular in sensitive magnetometers, which consists of a superconducting ring containing one or more Josephson junctions. A change by one flux quantum in the ring's magnetic flux linkage produces a sharp change in its impedance. [1960s: acronym from *superconducting quantum interference device*.]

squid

squid /skwid/ ▶n. (pl. same or **squids**) an elongated, fast-swimming cephalopod (*Loligo* and other genera, orders Teuthoidea and Vampyromorpha) with ten arms (technically, eight arms and two long tentacles), typically able to change color. ■ this mollusk used as food. [16th C.: of unknown origin.]

squiffed /skwift/ ▶adj. informal slightly drunk. [19th C.: of unknown origin.]

squig·gle /ˈskwigəl/ ▶n. a short line that curls and loops in an irregular way: *some prescriptions are a series of meaningless squiggles.* ▶v. [intrans.] wriggle; squirm: *a worm that squiggled in his palm.* ■ [trans.] squeeze so as to make irregular, curly lines. — **squig·gly** /ˈskwig(ə)lē/ adj. [19th C.: perh. a blend of SQUIRM and WIGGLE or WRIGGLE.]

squill /skwil/ ▶n. **1** (also **sea squill**) a coastal Mediterranean plant (*Drimia maritima*) of the lily family, with broad leaves, white flowers, and a very large bulb. ■ (also **squills**) an extract of the bulb of this plant, which is poisonous and has medicinal and other uses. **2** [usu. with adj.] a small plant (*Scilla*, *Puschkinia*, and other genera) of the lily family that resembles a hyacinth and has small clusters of violet-blue or blue-striped flowers. [ME: via L. from Gk. *skilla*.]

squinch[1] /skwincн/ ▶n. a straight or arched structure across an interior angle of a square tower to carry a superstructure such as a dome. [15th C.: alt. of obs. *scunch*, ult. from OFr. *escoinson* 'inside of a door jamb or window frame.']

squinch[2] ▶v. [trans.] tense up the muscles of (one's eyes or face): *Gina* ***squinched*** *her face* ***up.*** ■ [intrans.] (of a person's eyes) narrow so as to be almost closed, typically in reaction to strong light: *he flicked on the light, which made my eyes* ***squinch up.*** ■ [intrans.] crouch down in order to make oneself seem smaller or to occupy less space: *I squinched down under the sheet.* [19th C.: perh. a blend of the verbs SQUEEZE and PINCH.]

squint /skwint/ ▶v. [intrans.] look at someone or something with one or both eyes partly closed in an attempt to see more clearly or as a reaction to strong light: *the bright sun made them squint.* ■ [trans.] partly close (one's eyes). ▶n. **1** [in sing.] a permanent deviation in the direction of the gaze of one eye: *I had a bad squint.* **2** [in sing.] informal a quick or casual look: *let me have a squint.* **3** an oblique opening through a wall in a church permitting a view of the altar from an aisle or side chapel. — **squint·er** n. **squint·y** adj. [often in comb.] *squinty-eyed.* [16th C. (in the sense 'squinting,' as in SQUINT-EYED): shortening of ASQUINT.]

squint-eyed ▶adj. derog. (of a person) having a squint.

squire /ˈskwī(ə)r/ ▶n. **1** a man of high social standing who owns and lives on an estate in a rural area, esp. the chief landowner in such an area: *the squire of Radbourne Hall.* **2** hist. a young nobleman acting as an attendant to a knight before becoming a knight himself. ▶v. [trans.] (of a man) accompany or escort (a woman): *she was squired around Rome by a reporter.* — **squire·dom** /-dəm/ n. **squire·ship** /-ˌsнip/ n. [ME (sense 2): shortening of OFr. *esquier* 'esquire.']

squire·ar·chy /ˈskwī(ə)rärkē/ ▶n. (pl. **-chies**) landowners collectively, esp. when considered as a class having political or social influence. [18th C.: from SQUIRE, on the pattern of words such as *hierarchy*.]

squirl /skwərl/ ▶n. informal an ornamental flourish or curve, esp. in handwriting. [19th C.: perh. a blend of SQUIGGLE and TWIRL or WHIRL.]

squirm /skwərm/ ▶ v. [intrans.] wriggle or twist the body from side to side, esp. as a result of nervousness or discomfort: *all my efforts to squirm out of his grasp were useless.* ■ show or feel embarrassment or shame. ▶ n. [in sing.] a wriggling movement. — **squirm·er** n. **squirm·y** adj. [17th C.: symbolic of writhing movement; prob. associated with WORM.]

squir·rel /'skwər(ə)l/ ▶ n. an agile tree-dwelling rodent (*Sciurus* and other genera, family Sciuridae) with a bushy tail, typically feeding on nuts and seeds. ■ a related rodent of this family (see GROUND SQUIRREL, FLYING SQUIRREL). ■ the fur of the squirrel. ▶ v. (**-reled, -rel·ing**) **1** [trans.] (**squirrel something away**) hide money or something of value in a safe place: *the money was squirreled away in foreign bank accounts.* **2** [intrans.] move in an inquisitive and restless manner: *they were squirreling around in the woods in search of something.* [ME: shortening of OFr. *esquireul*, from a dimin. of L. *sciurus*, from Gk. *skiouros*, from *skia* 'shade' + *oura* 'tail.' Current verb senses date from the early 20th C.]

squir·rel cage ▶ n. a rotating cylindrical cage in which a small captive animal can exercise as on a treadmill. ■ a monotonous or repetitive activity or way of life: *running madly about in a squirrel cage of activity.* ■ a form of rotor used in small electric motors, resembling a cylindrical cage.

squir·rel·fish /'skwər(ə)l,fisʜ/ ▶ n. (pl. same or **-fish·es**) a chiefly nocturnal large-eyed marine fish (family Holocentridae) that is typically brightly colored and lives around rocks or coral reefs in warm seas.

squir·rel·ly /'skwər(ə)lē/ ▶ adj. **1** resembling a squirrel. **2** informal restless, nervous, or unpredictable. ■ eccentric or insane.

squir·rel mon·key ▶ n. a small South American monkey (genus *Saimiri*, family Cebidae) with a nonprehensile tail, typically moving through trees by leaping.

squirt /skwərt/ ▶ v. [with obj. and adverbial of direction] cause (a liquid) to be ejected from a small opening in something in a thin, fast stream or jet: *she squirted soda into a glass.* ■ cause (a container of liquid) to eject its contents in this way: *some youngsters squirted a water pistol in her face.* ■ [trans.] wet (someone or something) with a jet or stream of liquid in this way: *she squirted me with the juice from her lemon wedge.* ■ [intrans.] (of a liquid) be ejected from something in this way. ■ [intrans.] (of an object) move suddenly and unpredictably: *he got his glove on the ball but it squirted away.* ▶ n. **1** a thin stream or small quantity of liquid ejected from something: ***a quick squirt of perfume.*** ■ a small device from which a liquid may be ejected in a thin, fast stream. ■ a compressed radio signal transmitted at high speed. **2** informal a person perceived to be insignificant, impudent, or presumptuous: *this patronizing little squirt.* — **squirt·er** n. [ME (first recorded as a verb): imitative.]

squirt gun ▶ n. a water pistol.

squish /skwisʜ/ ▶ v. [intrans.] make a soft squelching sound when walked on or in: *the mud squished under my shoes.* ■ yield easily to pressure when squeezed or squashed: *strawberries so ripe that they squished if picked too firmly.* ■ [trans.] informal squash (something): *Naomi was furiously squishing her ice cream in her bowl.* ■ [trans.] squeeze oneself into somewhere: *she squished in among them on the couch.* ▶ n. [in sing.] a soft squelching sound. — **squish·y** adj. (**squish·i·er, squish·i·est**). [17th C.: imitative.]

Sr. ▶ abbr. ■ senior (in names): *E. T. Krebs, Sr.* ■ Señor. ■ Signor. ■ Sister (in a religious order): [as a title] *Sr Agatha.* ▶ symb. the chemical element strontium.

sr ▶ abbr. steradian(s).

Sra. ▶ abbr. ■ Senhora. ■ Señora.

SRAM ▶ n. Electron. a type of memory chip that is faster and requires less power than dynamic memory. [acronym from *static random-access memory*.]

Sri /srē/ (also **Shri**) ▶ n. Indian a title of respect used before the name of a man, a god, or a sacred book: *Sri Chaudhuri.* [from Sanskrit *Śrī* 'beauty, fortune,' used as an honorific title.]

Sri Lan·ka /,srē 'läɴɢkə; ,sʜrē; 'laɴɢkə/ an island country off the southeastern coast of India. *See box.* Former name (until 1972) CEYLON. — **Sri Lan·kan** adj. & n.

Sri·na·gar /srē'nəgər; sʜrē-/ a city in northwestern India, on the Jhelum River; pop. 595,000.

SRN ▶ abbr. State Registered Nurse.

sRNA ▶ abbr. soluble RNA.

Srta. ▶ abbr. ■ Senhorita. ■ Señorita.

SS[1] ▶ abbr. ■ Saints: *the Church of SS Peter and Paul.* ■ Baseball shortstop. ■ social security. ■ (in prescriptions) in the strict sense. [from L. *sensu stricto*.] ■ steamship: *the SS Canberra.* ■ Sunday School.

SS[2] the Nazi special police force. [abbr. of Ger. *Schutzstaffel* 'defense squadron.']

ss. ▶ abbr. ■ Law to wit; that is to say; namely (used on legal documents). [from L. *scilicet*.] ■ sections. ■ Baseball shortstop.

s/s ▶ abbr. same size.

SSA ▶ abbr. ■ Social Security Act. ■ Social Security Administration.

SSB ▶ abbr. single sideband transmission.

SSC ▶ abbr. ■ Physics superconducting super collider.

SSE ▶ abbr. south-south-east.

S.Sgt. (or **SSGT**) ▶ abbr. staff sergeant.

SSI ▶ abbr. ■ Electron. small-scale integration; the process of concentrating semiconductor devices in a single integrated circuit. ■ Supplemental Security Income.

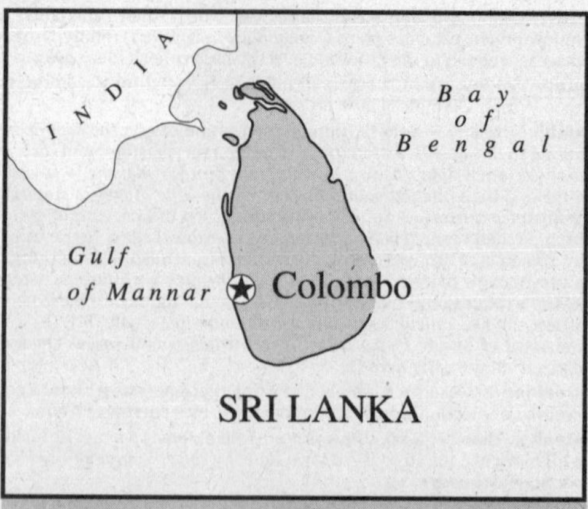

Sri Lanka

Official name: Democratic Socialist Republic of Sri Lanka
Location: off the southeastern coast of India
Area: 25,300 square miles (65,600 sq km)
Population: 19,905,000
Capital: Colombo
Languages: Sinhala (official), Tamil, English
Currency: Sri Lankan rupee

SSN ▶ abbr. Social Security Number.

ssp. ▶ abbr. subspecies (usually singular).

sspp. ▶ abbr. subspecies (plural).

SSR hist. ▶ abbr. Soviet Socialist Republic.

SSRI ▶ abbr. selective serotonin reuptake inhibitor, the designation for a class of antidepressants that work by increasing levels of serotonin in the brain.

SSS ▶ abbr. Selective Service System.

SST ▶ abbr. supersonic transport.

SSW ▶ abbr. south-southwest.

St ▶ abbr. ■ Saint: *St. George.* ■ Physics stokes.

-st ▶ suffix var. of -EST[2].

Sta. ▶ abbr. station.

stab /stab/ ▶ v. (**stabbed, stab·bing**) [trans.] (of a person) thrust a knife or other pointed weapon into (someone) so as to wound or kill: *he stabbed him.* ■ [intrans.] make a thrusting gesture or movement at something with a pointed object: *she stabbed at the earth with the fork* | [trans.] *she stabbed the air with her forefinger.* ■ [intrans.] (**stab into/through**) (of a sharp or pointed object) violently pierce: *a sharp end of wicker stabbed into his sole.* ■ [intrans.] (**stab at**) (of a pain or painful thing) cause a sudden sharp sensation: [as adj.] (**stabbing**) *I felt a stabbing pain in my chest.* ▶ n. **1** a thrust with a knife or other pointed weapon: [as adj.] *multiple stab wounds.* ■ a wound made in such a way: *she had a deep stab in the back.* ■ a thrusting movement with a finger or other pointed object: ***impatient stabs of his finger.*** ■ Tennis a shot made with a thrusting motion. ■ a sudden sharp feeling or pain: *she felt a stab of jealousy.* **2** (**stab at**) informal an attempt to do (something): *Meredith made a feeble stab at joining in.*

– PHRASES **a stab in the back** a treacherous act or statement. **stab someone in the back** betray someone. **a stab in the dark** see DARK. — **stab·ber** n. [ME: of unknown origin.]

Sta·bat Ma·ter /'stäbät 'mätər; 'stābat 'mātər/ ▶ n. a medieval Latin hymn on the suffering of the Virgin Mary at the Crucifixion. [from the opening words *Stabat mater dolorosa* 'Stood the mother, full of grief.']

sta·bi·la·tor /'stābə,lātər/ ▶ n. a combined stabilizer and elevator at the tail of an aircraft.

sta·bile /'stā,bēl/ ▶ n. Art a freestanding abstract sculpture or structure, typically of wire or sheet metal, in the style of a mobile but rigid and stationary. [1940s: from L. *stabilis* 'stable,' influenced by MOBILE.]

sta·bil·i·ty /stə'bilitē/ ▶ n. the state of being stable. [ME: from OFr. *stablete*, from L. *stabilitas*, from *stabilis* 'stable.']

sta·bi·lize /'stābə,līz/ ▶ v. [trans.] make or become stable: [intrans.] *his condition appears to have stabilized* | [trans.] *an emergency program designed to stabilize the economy.* ■ [trans.] cause (an object or structure) to be unlikely to overturn: *the craft was stabilized.* — **sta·bi·li·za·tion** /,stābəli'zāsʜən/ n.

sta·bi·liz·er /'stābə,līzər/ ▶ n. a thing used to keep something steady or stable, in particular: ■ a gyroscopically controlled system used to reduce the rolling of a ship. ■ a substance that prevents the breakdown of emulsions, especially in foods and paints. ■ a financial mechanism that prevents unsettling fluctuation in an economic system.

sta·ble[1] /'stābəl/ ▶ adj. (**-bler, -blest**) not likely to change or fail; firmly established: *a stable relationship* | *prices have remained relatively stable.*

■ (of a patient or a medical condition) not deteriorating in health after an injury or operation: *he is now in a stable condition in the hospital.* ■ (of a person) sane and sensible; not easily upset or disturbed: *the officer concerned is mentally and emotionally stable.* ■ (of an object or structure) not likely to give way or overturn; firmly fixed: *specially designed dinghies that are very stable.* ■ not liable to undergo chemical decomposition, radioactive decay, or other physical change. — **sta·bly** /-b(ə)lē/ **adv.** [ME: from Anglo-Norman Fr., from L. *stabilis*, from the base of *stare* 'to stand.']

sta·ble² ▶ **n.** a building set apart and adapted for keeping horses. ■ an establishment where racehorses are kept and trained. ■ the racehorses of a particular training establishment. ■ an organization or establishment providing the same background or training for its members: *the player comes from the same stable as Agassi.* ■ a group of people trained by the same person or under one management: *the agent looked after a big stable of European golfers.* ▶ **v.** [trans.] put or keep (a horse) in a specially adapted building. ■ put or base (a train) in a depot. — **sta·ble·ful** /'stābəl,fo͝ol/ **n.** (pl. **-fuls**). [ME: shortening of OFr. *estable* 'stable, pigpen,' from L. *stabulum*, from the base of *stare* 'to stand.']

sta·ble e·qui·lib·ri·um ▶ **n.** a state in which a body tends to return to its original position after being disturbed.

sta·ble fly ▶ **n.** a bloodsucking fly (*Stomoxis calcitrans*, family Muscidae) related to the housefly, biting large mammals including humans.

sta·ble·mate /'stābəl,māt/ ▶ **n.** a horse, esp. a racehorse, from the same establishment as another. ■ a person or product from the same organization or background as another: *it is a marketing challenge for Fiat and its stablemate, Alfa Romeo.*

sta·bling /'stāb(ə)liNG/ ▶ **n.** accommodations for horses.

stac·ca·to /stə'kätō/ esp. Music ▶ **adv. & adj.** with each sound or note sharply detached or separated from the others: [as adj.] *a staccato rhythm.* Compare with LEGATO, MARCATO. ▶ **n.** (pl. **-tos**) performance in this manner. ■ a noise or speech resembling a series of short, detached musical notes: *her heels made a rapid staccato on the polished boards.* [Ital., lit. 'detached.']

stack /stak/ ▶ **n. 1** a pile of objects, typically one that is neatly arranged: *a stack of boxes.* ■ **(a stack of/stacks of)** informal a large quantity of something: *there's stacks of work for me now.* ■ a rectangular or cylindrical pile of hay or straw or of grain in sheaf. ■ a vertical arrangement of stereo or guitar amplification equipment. ■ a number of aircraft flying in circles at different altitudes around the same point while waiting for permission to land at an airport. ■ a pyramidal group of rifles. ■ **(the stacks)** units of shelving in part of a library, used to store books compactly. ■ Comput. a set of storage locations that store data in such a way that the most recently stored item is the first to be retrieved. **2** a chimney, esp. one on a factory, or a vertical exhaust pipe on a vehicle. ■ a column of rock standing in the sea, remaining after erosion of cliffs. ▶ **v.** [trans.] **1** arrange (a number of things) in a pile, typically a neat one: *the books had been **stacked up** in three piles | she stood up, beginning to stack the plates.* ■ fill or cover (a place or surface) with piles of things, typically neat ones: *he spent most of the time stacking shelves.* ■ cause (an aircraft) to fly in circles while waiting for permission to land at an airport: *I hope we aren't stacked for hours over Kennedy.* **2** shuffle or arrange (a deck of cards) dishonestly so as to gain an unfair advantage. ■ **(be stacked against/in favor of)** used to refer to a situation in which an unfavorable or a favorable outcome is overwhelmingly likely: *the odds were stacked against Fiji in the World Cup | they found the courts stacked in favor of timber interests.* **3** [intrans.] (in snowboarding) fall over.
– PHRASAL VERBS **stack up** (also **sea stack**) **1** build up. **2** informal measure up; compare. ■ [usu. with negative] make sense; correspond to reality: *to blame all urban crime on the poor doesn't stack up.* — **stack·a·ble adj. stack·er n.** [ME: from ON *stakkr* 'haystack,' of Gmc. origin.]

stacked /stakt/ ▶ **adj. 1** (of a number of things) put or arranged in a stack or stacks: *the stacked chairs.* ■ (of a place or surface) filled or covered with goods: *the stacked shelves.* ■ (of a machine) having sections that are arranged vertically: *full-sized washer/dryers are replacing stacked units.* ■ (of a heel) made from thin layers of wood, plastic, or another material glued one on top of the other. **2** (of a deck of cards) shuffled or arranged dishonestly so as to gain an unfair advantage. **3** informal (of a woman) having large breasts. **4** Comput. (of a task) placed in a queue for subsequent processing. ■ (of a stream of data) stored in such a way that the most recently stored item is the first to be retrieved.

stad·dle /'stadl/ ▶ **n.** a platform or framework supporting a stack or rick. ■ (also **staddle stone**) a stone, esp. one resembling a mushroom in shape, supporting a framework. [OE *stathol* 'base, support,' of Gmc. origin; rel. to the verb STAND.]

sta·di·a rod /'stādēə/ ▶ **n.** another term for LEVELING ROD.

sta·di·um /'stādēəm/ ▶ **n.** (pl. **-di·ums** or **-di·a** /-dēə/) **1** a sports arena with tiers of seats for spectators. ■ (in ancient Rome or Greece) a track for a foot race or chariot race. **2** (pl. **-di·a**) an ancient Roman or Greek measure of length, about 185 meters. [orig. denoting the length of a stadium.] [ME (sense 2): via L. from Gk. *stadion*. Sense 1 dates from the mid 19th C.]

stadt·hold·er /'stat,hōldər/ (also **stad·hold·er**) ▶ **n.** (15th century–late 18th century) the chief magistrate of the United Provinces of the Netherlands. — **stadt·hold·er·ship** /-,SHip/ **n.** [16th C.: from Du. *stadhouder* 'deputy,' from *stad* 'place' + *houder* 'holder,' translating med. L. *locum tenens*.]

Staël /stäl/, Mme de, see DE STAËL.

staff¹ /staf/ ▶ **n. 1** [treated as sing. or pl.] all the people employed by a particular organization: *a staff of 600.* ■ the teachers in a school or college: [as adj.] *a staff meeting.* **2** [treated as sing. or pl.] a group of officers assisting an officer in command of an army formation or administration headquarters. ■ (usu. **Staff**) short for STAFF SERGEANT. **3** a long stick used as a support when walking or climbing or as a weapon. ■ a rod or scepter held as a sign of office or authority. ■ short for FLAGSTAFF. ■ Surveying a rod for measuring distances or heights. **4** (pl. **staves** /stāvz/) (also **stave**) Music a set of five parallel lines and the spaces between them, on which notes are written to indicate their pitch. ▶ **v.** [trans.] (usu. **be staffed**) provide (an organization, business, etc.) with staff: *legal advice centers are staffed by volunteer lawyers* | [as adj., with submodifier] **(staffed)** *all units are fully staffed.*
– PHRASES **the staff of life** a staple food, esp. bread. [OE *stæf* (sense 3), of Gmc. origin; rel. to Du. *staf* and Ger. *Stab*.]

staff² ▶ **n.** a mixture of plaster of Paris, cement, or a similar material, used for temporary building work. [19th C.: of unknown origin.]

staff·er /'stafər/ ▶ **n.** a member of the staff of an organization, esp. of a newspaper.

staff no·ta·tion ▶ **n.** Music notation by means of a stave, esp. as distinct from the tonic sol-fa.

staff of·fi·cer ▶ **n.** Mil. an officer serving on the staff of a military headquarters or government department.

Staf·ford·shire bull ter·ri·er /'stafərd,SHi(ə)r/ ▶ **n.** a dog of a small stocky breed of short-haired terrier, with a short, broad head and wide-set forelegs.

staff ser·geant ▶ **n.** a noncommissioned officer in the armed forces.

stag /stag/ ▶ **n.** a male deer. ■ [usu. as adj.] a social gathering attended by men only. ▶ **adv.** without a partner at a social gathering: *a lot of boys went stag.* [ME (as a n.): rel. to ON *steggr* 'male bird,' Icelandic *steggi* 'tomcat.']

stag bee·tle ▶ **n.** a large dark beetle (family Lucanidae), the male of which has large branched jaws that resemble a stag's antlers.

stage /stāj/ ▶ **n. 1** a point, period, or step in a process or development: *there is no need at this stage to give explicit details | I was in the early stages of pregnancy.* ■ a section of a journey or race: *the final stage of the journey is made by taxi.* ■ each of two or more sections of a rocket or spacecraft that have their own engines and are jettisoned in turn when their propellant is exhausted. ■ [with adj.] Electron. a specified part of a circuit, typically one consisting of a single amplifying transistor or valve with the associated equipment. **2** a raised floor or platform, typically in a theater, on which actors, entertainers, or speakers perform: *there are only two characters **on stage**.* ■ **(the stage)** the acting or theatrical profession: *I've always wanted to **go on the stage**.* ■ [in sing.] a scene of action or forum of debate, esp. in a particular political context: *Argentina is playing a leading role on the international stage.* **3** a floor or level of a building or structure. ■ (on a microscope) a raised and usually movable plate on which a slide or object is placed for examination. **4** Geol. (in chronostratigraphy) a range of strata corresponding to an age in time, forming a subdivision of a series. ■ (in paleoclimatology) a period of time marked by a characteristic climate: *the Boreal stage.* **5** archaic term for STAGECOACH. ▶ **v.** [trans.] **1** present a performance of (a play or other show): *the show is being staged at the Goodspeed Opera House.* ■ (of a person or group) organize and participate in (a public event): *UDF supporters staged a demonstration in Sofia.* ■ cause (something dramatic or unexpected) to happen: *the president's attempt to stage a comeback | the dollar staged a partial recovery.* **2** Med. diagnose or classify (a disease or patient) as having reached a particular stage in the expected progression of the disease.
– PHRASES **hold the stage** dominate a scene of action or forum of debate. **set the stage for** prepare the conditions for (the occurrence or beginning of something): *these churchmen helped to set the stage for popular reform.* **stage left** (or **right**) on the left (or right) side of a stage when facing the audience. — **stage·a·bil·i·ty** /,stājə'bilitē/ **n. stage·a·ble adj.** [ME (denoting a floor of a building, a platform, or a stopping place): shortening of OFr. *estage* 'dwelling,' based on L. *stare* 'to stand.' Current senses of the verb date from the early 17th C.]

stagecoach

stage·coach /'stāj,kōCH/ ▶ **n.** a large, closed horse-drawn vehicle formerly used to carry passengers and often mail along a regular route between two places.

stage·craft /'stāj,kraft/ ▶ **n.** skill or experience in writing or staging plays.

stage di·rec·tion ▶ **n.** an instruction in the text of a play.

stage door ▶ **n.** an actors' and workers' entrance from the street to the area of a theater behind the stage.

stage ef·fect ▶ n. an effect produced by the lighting, sound, or scenery in a play, movie, etc.

stage fright ▶ n. nervousness before or during an appearance before an audience.

stage·hand /ˈstāj,hand/ ▶ n. a person who moves scenery or props before, during, or after the performance of a play.

stage-man·age ▶ v. [trans.] be responsible for the lighting and other technical arrangements for (a stage play). ■ arrange and control (something) carefully in order to create a certain effect: *he stage-managed his image with astounding success.* — **stage man·age·ment** n.

stage man·ag·er ▶ n. the person responsible for the lighting and other technical arrangements for a stage play.

stage name ▶ n. a name assumed for professional purposes by an actor or other performer.

stage pres·ence ▶ n. the ability to command the attention of a theater audience by the impressiveness of one's manner or appearance.

stage-struck ▶ adj. having a passionate desire to become an actor.

stage whis·per ▶ n. a loud whisper uttered by an actor on stage, intended to be heard by the audience but supposedly unheard by other characters in the play. ■ any loud whisper intended to be overheard.

stage·y ▶ adj. var. of STAGY.

stag·fla·tion /,stagˈflāsHən/ ▶ n. Econ. persistent high inflation combined with high unemployment and stagnant demand in a country's economy. [1960s: blend of *stagnation* (see STAGNATE) and INFLATION.]

stag·ger /ˈstagər/ ▶ v. **1** [intrans.] walk or move unsteadily, as if about to fall: *he staggered to his feet, swaying a little.* ■ [trans.] fig. continue in existence or operation uncertainly or precariously: *the council staggered from one crisis to the next.* ■ archaic waver in purpose; hesitate. ■ archaic (of a blow) cause (someone) to walk or move unsteadily, as if about to fall: *the collision staggered her and she fell.* **2** [trans.] astonish or deeply shock: *I was staggered to find it was six o'clock* | [as adj.] (**staggering**) *the staggering bills for maintenance and repair.* **3** [trans.] arrange (events, payments, hours, etc.) so that they do not occur at the same time; spread over a period of time: *meetings are staggered throughout the day.* ■ arrange (objects or parts of an object) in a zigzag order or so that they are not in line: *stagger the screws at each joint.* ▶ n. [in sing.] **1** an unsteady walk or movement: *she walked with a stagger.* **2** an arrangement of things in a zigzag order or so that they are not in line. — **stag·ger·er** n. **stag·ger·ing·ly** adv. [ME (as a v.): alt. of dial. *stacker*, from ON *stakra*, frequentative of *staka* 'push, stagger.' The noun dates from the late 16th C.]

stag·horn cor·al /ˈstag,hôrn/ ▶ n. a large stony coral (genus *Acropora*, order Scleractinia) with antlerlike branches.

stag·horn fern ▶ n. a fern (genus *Platycerium*, family Polypodiaceae) with fronds that resemble antlers, occurring in tropical rain forests where it typically grows as an epiphyte.

stag·horn su·mac ▶ n. see SUMAC.

stag·hound /ˈstag,hound/ ▶ n. a large dog of a breed used for hunting deer by sight or scent.

stag·ing /ˈstājiNG/ ▶ n. **1** an instance or method of presenting a play or other dramatic performance: *one of the better stagings of* Hamlet. ■ an instance of organizing a public event or protest: *the fourteenth staging of the championships.* **2** a stage or set of stages or temporary platforms arranged as a support for performers or between different levels of scaffolding. **3** Med. diagnosis or classification of the particular stage reached by a progressive disease. **4** the arrangement of stages in a rocket or spacecraft. ■ the separation and jettisoning of a stage from the remainder of a rocket when its propellant is spent.

stag·ing ar·e·a (also **staging point** or **staging post**) ▶ n. a stopping place or assembly point en route to a destination: *a vast staging area for guerrilla attacks* | *the geese's major staging area on the St. Lawrence River.*

stag·nant /ˈstagnənt/ ▶ adj. (of a body of water or the atmosphere of a confined space) having no current or flow and often having an unpleasant smell as a consequence: *a stagnant ditch.* ■ fig. showing no activity; dull and sluggish: *a stagnant economy.* — **stag·nan·cy** /-nənsē/ n. **stag·nant·ly** adv. [17th C.: from L. *stagnant-* 'forming a pool of standing water,' from the verb *stagnare*, from *stagnum* 'pool.']

stag·nate /ˈstag,nāt/ ▶ v. [intrans.] (of water or air) cease to flow or move; become stagnant. ■ fig. cease developing; become inactive or dull. — **stag·na·tion** /stagˈnāsHən/ n. [17th C.: from L. *stagnat-* 'settled as a still pool,' from the verb *stagnare*, from *stagnum* 'pool.']

stag par·ty ▶ n. a celebration held for a man shortly before his wedding, attended by his male friends only. ■ any party attended by men only.

stag·y /ˈstājē/ (also **stag·ey**) ▶ adj. (**stag·i·er**, **stag·i·est**) excessively theatrical; exaggerated: *a stagy melodramatic voice.* — **stag·i·ly** /-jilē/ adv. **stag·i·ness** n.

staid /stād/ ▶ adj. sedate, respectable, and unadventurous: *staid law firms.* — **staid·ly** adv. **staid·ness** n. [16th C.: archaic past part. of STAY[1].]

stain /stān/ ▶ v. [trans.] **1** mark (something) with colored patches or dirty marks that are not easily removed: *her clothing was stained with blood* | [as adj.] (**stained**) *a stained placemat* | [intrans.] *red ink can stain.* ■ [intrans.] be marked or be liable to be marked with such patches. ■ fig. damage or bring disgrace to (the reputation or image of someone or something): *the awful events would unfairly stain the city's reputation.* **2** color (a material or object) by applying a penetrative dye or chemical: *wood can always be stained to a darker shade.* ▶ n. **1** a colored patch or dirty mark that is difficult to remove: *there were mud stains on my shoes.* ■ a thing that damages or brings disgrace to someone or something's reputation: *he regarded his time in jail as a* **stain on** *his character.* ■ a patch of brighter or deeper color that suffuses something: *the sun left a red stain behind as it retreated.* **2** a penetrative dye or chemical used in coloring a material or object. ■ Biol. a special dye used to color organic tissue so as to make the structure visible for microscopic examination. ■ Heraldry any of the minor colors used in blazoning and liveries, esp. tenné and sanguine. — **stain·a·ble** adj. **stain·er** n. (both in sense 2 of the verb). [ME (as a v.): shortening of archaic *distain*, from OFr. *desteindre* 'tinge with a color different from the natural one.' The noun was first recorded (mid 16th C.) in the sense 'defilement, disgrace.']

stained glass ▶ n. colored glass used to form decorative or pictorial designs, notably for church windows, both by painting and esp. by setting contrasting pieces in a lead framework like a mosaic.

stain·less /ˈstānlis/ ▶ adj. unmarked by or resistant to stains or discoloration. ■ fig. (of a person or their reputation) free from wrongdoing or disgrace: *her supposedly stainless past.*

stain·less steel ▶ n. a form of steel containing chromium, resistant to tarnishing and rust.

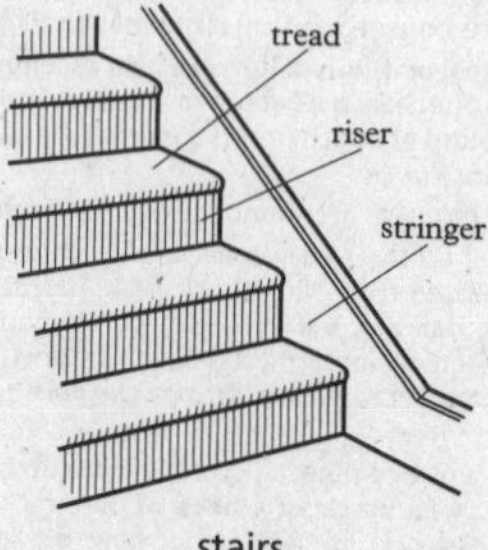

stairs

stair /ste(ə)r/ ▶ n. (usu. **stairs**) a set of steps leading from one floor of a building to another, typically inside the building: *he came up the stairs.* ■ single step in such a set: *the bottom stair.* [OE *stǣger*, of Gmc. origin; rel. to Du. *steiger* 'scaffolding,' from a base meaning 'climb.']

stair·case /ˈste(ə)r,kās/ ▶ n. a set of stairs and its surrounding walls or structure.

stair·lift /ˈste(ə)r,lift/ ▶ n. a lift in the form of a chair that can be raised or lowered at the edge of a domestic staircase, used for carrying a person who is unable to go up or down the stairs.

stair·way /ˈste(ə)r,wā/ ▶ n. a set of steps or stairs and its surrounding walls or structure.

stair·well /ˈste(ə)r,wel/ ▶ n. a shaft in a building in which a staircase is built.

stake[1] /stāk/ ▶ n. **1** a strong wooden or metal post with a point at one end, driven into the ground to support a tree, form part of a fence, act as a boundary mark, etc. ■ a long vertical rod used in basket-making. ■ a metalworker's small anvil, typically with a projection for fitting into a socket on a bench. **2** (**the stake**) hist. a wooden post to which a person was tied before being burned alive as a punishment. **3** a territorial division of the Mormon Church under the jurisdiction of a president. ▶ v. [trans.] **1** support (a tree or plant) with a stake or stakes. **2** (**stake something out**) mark an area with stakes so as to claim ownership of it: *the boundary between the two ranches was properly staked out* | fig. *the local dog staked out his territory.* ■ be assertive in defining and defending a position or policy: *Elena was staking out a role for herself as a formidable political force.*

– PHRASES **pull up stakes** move or go to live elsewhere. **stake a claim** assert one's right to something.

– PHRASAL VERBS **stake someone/something out** informal continuously watch a place or person in secret: *they'd staked out Culley's house for half a day.* [OE *staca*, of West Gmc. origin; rel. to Du. *staak*, also to STICK[2].]

stake[2] ▶ n. (usu. **stakes**) a sum of money or something else of value gambled on the outcome of a risky game or venture: *playing dice for high stakes* | fig. *the mayor* **raised the stakes** *in the battle for power.* ■ a share or interest in a business, situation, or system: *GM acquired a 50 percent stake in Saab.* ■ (**stakes**) prize money, esp. in horse racing. ■ [in names] (**stakes**) a horse race in which all the owners of the racehorses running contribute to the prize money: *the horse is to run in the Lexington Stakes.* ■ [with adj.] (**stakes**) a situation involving competition in a specified area: *we will keep you one step ahead in the fashion stakes.* ▶ v. [trans.] **1** gamble (money or something else of value) on the outcome of a game or race. **2** informal give financial or other support to: *he staked him to an education at the École des Beaux-Arts.*

– PHRASES **at stake 1** to be won or lost; at risk: *people's lives could be at stake.* **2** at issue or in question: *there's more at stake than logic.* [ME: perh. a specialized usage of STAKE[1], from the notion of an object being placed as a wager on a post or stake.]

stake bod·y ▶ n. a body for a truck having a flat open platform with removable posts along the sides.

stake·hold·er /ˈstāk,hōldər/ ▶ n. **1** (in gambling) an independent party with whom each of those who make a wager deposits the money or counters wagered. **2** a person with an interest or concern in something, esp. a business.

stake·out /'stāk,out/ ▶ **n.** informal a period of secret surveillance of a building or an area by police in order to observe someone's activities.

Sta·kha·nov·ite /stə'kānə,vīt/ ▶ **n.** a hardworking and productive laborer in the former USSR. ■ an exceptionally hardworking or zealous person. — **Sta·kha·nov·ism** /-,vizəm/ **n.** **Sta·kha·nov·ist** /-vist/ **n. & adj.** [1930s: from the name of Aleksei Grigorevich *Stakhanov* (1906–1977), Russian coal miner.]

sta·lac·tite /stə'lak,tīt/ ▶ **n.** a tapering structure hanging like an icicle from the roof of a cave, formed of calcium salts deposited by dripping water. Compare with STALAGMITE. — **sta·lac·tit·ic** /,staləkˈtitik/ **adj.** [17th C.: from mod. L. *stalactites*, from Gk. *stalaktos* 'dripping,' based on *stalassein* 'to drip.']

stalactites and stalagmites

Sta·lag /'stä,läg/ (also **sta·lag**) ▶ **n.** (in World War II) a German prison camp, esp. for noncommissioned officers and privates. [Ger., contr. of *Stammlager*, from *Stamm* 'base, main stock' + *Lager* 'camp.']

sta·lag·mite /stə'lag,mīt/ ▶ **n.** a mound or tapering column rising from the floor of a cave, formed of calcium salts deposited by dripping water and often uniting with a stalactite. — **stal·ag·mit·ic** /,staləg'mitik/ **adj.** [17th C.: from mod. L. *stalagmites*, from Gk. *stalagma* 'a drop,' based on *stalassein* (see STALACTITE).]

stale[1] /stāl/ ▶ **adj.** (**stal·er, stal·est**) (of food) no longer fresh and pleasant to eat; hard, musty, or dry: *stale bread.* ■ no longer new and interesting or exciting: *their marriage had gone stale.* ■ [predic.] (of a person) no longer able to perform well or creatively because of having done something for too long. ▶ **v.** make or become stale. — **stale·ly** /'stāl(l)ē/ **adv.** **stale·ness n.** [ME (describing beer in the sense 'clear from long standing, strong'): prob. from Anglo-Norman Fr. and OFr., from *estaler* 'to halt'; cf. the verb STALL.]

stale[2] ▶ **v.** [intrans.] (of an animal, esp. a horse) urinate. [ME: perh. from OFr. *estaler* 'come to a stop, halt' (cf. STALE[1]).]

stale·mate /'stāl,māt/ ▶ **n.** Chess a position counting as a draw, in which a player is not in check but cannot move except into check. ■ a situation in which further action or progress by opposing or competing parties seems impossible: *the war had again reached stalemate.* ▶ **v.** [trans.] bring to or cause to reach stalemate: [as adj.] (**stalemated**) *the currently stalemated peace talks.* [18th C.: from obs. *stale* (from Anglo-Norman Fr. *estale* 'position,' from *estaler* 'be placed') + MATE[2].]

Sta·lin /'stälin/, Joseph (1879–1953), Communist leader; general secretary of the Communist Party of the Soviet Union 1922–53; born *Iosif Vissarionovich Dzhugashvili.*

Sta·lin·a·bad /,stälənə'bäd/ former name (1929–61) for DUSHANBE.

Sta·lin·grad /'stälən,grad; -,gräd/ former name (1925–61) of VOLGOGRAD.

Sta·lin·ism /'stälə,nizəm/ ▶ **n.** the ideology and policies adopted by Stalin. ■ any rigid centralized authoritarian form of communism. — **Sta·lin·ist n. & adj.**

Sta·lin Peak former name (1933-1962) of COMMUNISM PEAK.

stalk[1] /stôk/ ▶ **n.** the main stem of a herbaceous plant: *he chewed a stalk of grass.* ■ the slender attachment or support of a leaf, flower, or fruit: *the acorns grow on stalks.* ■ a similar support for a sessile animal, or for an organ in an animal. ■ a slender support or stem of something: *drinking glasses with long stalks.* — **stalked adj.** [in comb.] *rough-stalked meadow grass* **stalk·less adj.** **stalk·like** /-,līk/ **adj.** **stalk·y adj.** [ME: prob. a dimin. of dial. *stale* 'rung of a ladder, long handle.']

stalk[2] ▶ **v.** **1** [trans.] pursue or approach stealthily: *a cat stalking a bird.* ■ harass or persecute (someone) with unwanted and obsessive attention: *the fan stalked the actor.* ■ esp. literary move silently or threateningly through (a place). **2** [intrans.] stride somewhere in a proud, stiff, or angry manner. ▶ **n.** **1** a stealthy pursuit of someone or something. **2** a stiff, striding gait. [OE -*stealcian* (in *bistealcian* 'walk cautiously or stealthily'), of Gmc. origin; rel. to STEAL.]

stalk·er /'stôkər/ ▶ **n.** a person who stealthily hunts or pursues an animal or another person. ■ a person who harasses or persecutes someone with unwanted and obsessive attention.

stalk-eyed ▶ **adj.** (of a crustacean) having eyes mounted on stalks.

stalk·ing horse ▶ **n.** a horse-shaped screen behind which a hunter can stay concealed when stalking prey. ■ a false pretext concealing someone's real intentions. ■ a political candidate who runs only in order to provoke the election and thus allow a stronger candidate to come forward. [16th C.: from the former practice of using a horse trained to allow a fowler to hide behind it, or under its coverings, until within easy range of prey.]

stall /stôl/ ▶ **n.** **1** a stand, booth, or compartment for the sale of goods in a market or large covered area: *fruit and vegetable stalls.* **2** an individual compartment for an animal in a stable or barn, enclosed on three sides. ■ a stable. ■ a marked-out parking space for a vehicle. ■ a compartment for one person in a restroom. **3** a fixed seat in the choir or chancel of a church, more or less enclosed at the back and sides and often canopied, typically reserved for a particular member of the clergy. **4** (**stalls**) Brit. the seats on the ground floor in a theater. **5** an instance of an engine, vehicle, aircraft, or boat stalling: *speed must be maintained to avoid a stall and loss of control.* ▶ **v.** **1** [intrans.] (of a motor vehicle or its engine) stop running, typically because of an overload on the engine: *her car stalled at the crossroads.* ■ (of an aircraft or its pilot) reach a condition where the speed is too low to allow effective operation of the controls. ■ Sailing have insufficient wind power in the sails to give controlled motion. ■ [trans.] cause (an engine, vehicle, aircraft, or boat) to stall. **2** [intrans.] (of a situation or process) stop making progress: *his career had stalled, hers taken off.* ■ [trans.] delay, obstruct, or block the progress of (something): *the government has stalled the much-needed project.* ■ speak or act in a deliberately vague way in order to gain more time to deal with a question or issue; prevaricate: *she was stalling for time.* ■ [trans.] delay or divert (someone) by acting in such a way: *stall him until I've had time to take a look.* **3** [trans.] put or keep (an animal) in a stall, esp. in order to fatten it. [OE *steall* 'stable or cattle shed,' of Gmc. origin; rel. to Du. *stal*, also to STAND.]

stal·lion /'stalyən/ ▶ **n.** an uncastrated adult male horse. [ME: from an Anglo-Norman Fr. var. of OFr. *estalon*, from a deriv. of a Gmc. base shared by STALL.]

stal·wart /'stôlwərt/ ▶ **adj.** loyal, reliable, and hardworking: *he remained a stalwart supporter of the cause.* ■ dated strongly built and sturdy: *he was of stalwart build.* ▶ **n.** a loyal, reliable, and hardworking supporter or participant in an organization or team: *the stalwarts of the Ladies' Auxiliary.* — **stal·wart·ly adv.** **stal·wart·ness n.** [ME: Scots var. of obs. *stalworth*, from OE *stǣl* 'place' + *weorth* 'worth.']

Stam·boul /stam'bo͞ol; stäm-/ archaic name for ISTANBUL.

sta·men /'stāmin/ ▶ **n.** Bot. the male fertilizing organ of a flower, typically consisting of a pollen-containing anther and a filament. [17th C.: from L., 'warp in an upright loom, thread.']

Stam·ford /'stamfərd/ a city in southwestern Connecticut; pop. 117,083.

stam·i·na /'stamənə/ ▶ **n.** the ability to sustain prolonged physical or mental effort. [17th C.: from L., pl. of STAMEN in the sense 'threads spun by the Fates.']

stam·i·nate /'stamə,nāt/ ▶ **adj.** Bot. (of a plant or flower) having stamens but no pistils. Compare with PISTILLATE.

stam·i·node /'stamə,nōd/ ▶ **n.** Bot. a sterile or abortive stamen, frequently resembling a stamen without its anther.

stam·mer /'stamər/ ▶ **v.** [intrans.] speak with sudden involuntary pauses and a tendency to repeat the initial letters of words. ■ [trans.] utter (words) in such a way: *I stammered out my history* | [with direct speech] *"I ... I can't," Isabel stammered.* ▶ **n.** [in sing.] a tendency to stammer. — **stam·mer·er n.** **stam·mer·ing·ly adv.** [OE *stamerian*, of West Gmc. origin; rel. to STUMBLE.]

stamp /stamp/ ▶ **v.** [trans.] **1** bring down (one's foot) heavily on the ground or on something on the ground. ■ [trans.] crush, flatten, or remove with a heavy blow from one's feet: *he stamped out the flames before they could grow.* ■ (**stamp something out**) suppress or put an end to something by taking decisive action: *urgent action is required to stamp out corruption.* ■ [intrans.] walk with heavy, forceful steps: *John stamped off, muttering.* **2** impress a pattern or mark, esp. an official one, on (a surface, object, or document) using an engraved or inked block or die or other instrument: *the woman stamped my passport.* ■ impress (a pattern or mark) on something in such a way: *a key with a number stamped on the shaft* | fig. *he must be able to stamp his authority on his team.* ■ make (something) by cutting it out with a die or mold: *the knives are stamped out from a flat strip of steel.* ■ fig. reveal or mark out as having a particular character, quality, or ability: *his style stamps him as a player to watch.* **3** affix a postage stamp or stamps onto (a letter or package): *Annie stamped the envelope for her.* **4** crush or pulverize (ore). ▶ **n.** **1** an instrument for stamping a pattern or mark. ■ a mark or pattern made by such an instrument, esp. one indicating official validation or certification: *passports with visa stamps* | fig. *the emperor gave them his stamp of approval.* ■ fig. a characteristic or distinctive impression or quality: *the whole project has the stamp of authority.* ■ a particular class or type or person or thing: *empiricism of this stamp has been influential in British philosophy.* **2** a small adhesive piece of paper stuck to something to show that money has been paid. **3** an act or sound of stamping with the foot: *the stamp of boots on the bare floor.* **4** a block for crushing ore in a stamp mill. — **stamp·er n.** [ME: of Gmc. origin; rel. to Ger. *stampfen* 'stamp with the foot'; reinforced by OFr. *estamper* 'to stamp.' Cf. STOMP.]

Stamp Act ▶ **n.** an act of the British Parliament in 1756 that exacted revenue from the American colonies by imposing a stamp duty on newspapers and legal and commercial documents.

stam·pede /stam'pēd/ ▶ **n.** a sudden panicked rush of a number of horses, cattle, or other animals. ■ a sudden rapid movement or reaction of a mass of people in response to a particular circumstance or stimulus: *a stampede of bargain hunters.* ■ [often in titles] a rodeo: *the Calgary Stampede.* ▶ **v.** [intrans.] (of horses, cattle, or other animals) rush wildly in a sudden mass panic: *the nearby sheep stampeded as if they sensed impending danger.* ■ [intrans.] (of people) move rapidly in a mass: *the children stampeded through the kitchen* ■ [trans.] cause (people or animals) to move in such a way: fig. *don't let them stampede us into anything.* — **stam·ped·er n.** [19th C.: Mex. Sp. use of Sp. *estampida* 'crash, uproar,' of Gmc. origin; rel. to the verb STAMP.]

stamp·ing ground ▶ n. another term for STOMPING GROUND.

stamp mill ▶ n. a mill for crushing ore.

stance /stans/ ▶ n. **1** the way in which someone stands, esp. when deliberately adopted (as in baseball, golf, and other sports); a person's posture: *she altered her stance, resting all her weight on one leg.* ■ the attitude of a person or organization toward something; a standpoint: *its* ***stance on*** *the draft.* **2** Climbing a ledge or foothold on which a belay can be secured. [ME: from Fr., from Ital. *stanza.*]

stanch[1] /stônch; stänch/ (also **staunch**) ▶ v. [trans.] stop or restrict (a flow of blood) from a wound. ■ stop the flow of blood from (a wound). [ME: from OFr. *estanchier*, from the base of STAUNCH[1].]

stanch[2] ▶ adj. var. of STAUNCH[1] (sense 2).

stan·chion /'stanchən/ ▶ n. an upright bar, post, or frame forming a support or barrier. — **stan·chioned** adj. [ME: from Anglo-Norman Fr. *stanchon*, from OFr. *estanchon*, from *estance* 'a support,' prob. based on L. *stant-* 'standing,' from the verb *stare.*]

stand /stand/ ▶ v. (past **stood** /stŏŏd/) **1** [no obj., usu. with adverbial of place] have or maintain an upright position, supported by one's feet: *Lionel stood in the doorway | she stood still, heart hammering.* ■ rise to one's feet: *the two men* ***stood up*** *and shook hands.* ■ [intrans.] move to and remain in a specified position: *she stood aside to let them enter.* ■ [intrans.] place or set in an upright or specified position: *don't stand the plant in direct sunlight.* ■ [trans.] Bell-ringing bring (a bell) to rest in the mouth upward position ready for ringing. **2** [trans.] (of an object, building, or settlement) be situated in a particular place or position. ■ (of a building or other vertical structure) remain upright and entire rather than fall into ruin or be destroyed: *after the heavy storms, only one house was left standing.* ■ remain valid or unaltered: *my decision stands.* ■ (esp. of a vehicle) remain stationary: *the train now standing on track 3.* ■ (of a liquid) collect and remain motionless: *avoid planting in soil where water stands in winter.* ■ (of food, a mixture, or liquid) rest without disturbance, typically so as to infuse or marinate: *pour boiling water over the fruit and leave it to stand for 5 minutes.* ■ [intrans.] (of a ship) remain on a specified course: *the ship was standing north.* **3** [intrans.] be in a specified state or condition: *since mother's death, the house had stood empty | sorry, darling—I stand corrected.* ■ adopt a particular attitude toward a matter or issue: *take a stand on this issue.* ■ be of a specified height: *Sampson was a small man, standing 5 ft. 4 in. tall.* ■ (**stand at**) be at (a particular level or value): *the budget stood at $14 million per annum.* ■ [intrans.] be in a situation where one is likely to do something: *investors stood to lose heavily.* ■ act in a specified capacity as: *he stood watch all night.* ■ (also **stand at stud**) [intrans.] (of a stallion) be available for breeding. **4** [trans.] withstand (an experience or test) without being damaged: *small boats that could stand the punishment of heavy seas.* ■ [usu. with negative] informal be able to endure or tolerate: *I can't stand the way Mom talks to him.* ■ [with modal and negative] informal strongly dislike: *I can't stand brandy.* **5** [intrans.] Brit. be a candidate in an election. **6** [usu. with two objs.] provide (food or drink) for someone at one's own expense: *somebody in the bar would stand him a beer.* ▶ n. **1** [usu. in sing.] an attitude toward a particular issue; a position taken in an argument: *the party's tough stand on welfare | his traditionalist stand.* ■ a determined effort to resist or fight for something: *we have to* ***take a stand against*** *racism.* ■ an act of holding one's ground against or halting to resist an opposing force: *Custer's legendary last stand.* **2** a place where, or an object on which, someone or something stands, sits, or rests, in particular: ■ a large raised tiered structure for spectators, typically at a sports arena: *her parents watched from the stands.* ■ a rack, base, or piece of furniture for holding, supporting, or displaying something: *a microphone stand.* ■ a small stall or booth in a street, market, or public building from which goods are sold: *a hot-dog stand.* ■ a raised platform for a band, orchestra, or speaker. ■ (**the stand**) (also **witness stand**) a witness box: *Sergeant Harris took the stand.* ■ the place where someone typically stands or sits: *she took her stand in front of the desks.* ■ a place where vehicles, typically taxicabs, wait for passengers. **3** [usu. in sing.] a cessation from motion or progress: *the train drew to a stand by the signal box.* ■ each halt made on a touring theatrical production to give one or more performances. **4** a group of growing plants of a specified kind, esp. trees: *a stand of poplars.*

— PHRASES **as it stands** in its present condition: *there are no merits in the proposal as it stands.* ■ (also **as things stand**) in the present circumstances. **stand one's ground** maintain one's position, typically in the face of opposition: *she stood her ground, refusing to let him intimidate her.* **stand on one's own (two) feet** be or become self-reliant or independent. **stand trial** be tried in a court of law. **stand up and be counted** state publicly one's support for someone or something. **will the real —— please stand up** informal used rhetorically to indicate that the specified person should clarify their position or reveal their true character.

— PHRASAL VERBS **stand alone** be unequaled: *when it came to fun, Julia stood alone.* **stand aside** take no action to prevent, or not involve oneself in, something that is happening: *the army had stood aside as the monarchy fell.* ■ another way of saying STAND DOWN (sense 1) below. **stand back** withdraw from a situation emotionally in order to view it more objectively. ■ another way of saying STAND ASIDE above. **stand by 1** be present while something bad is happening but fail to take any action to stop it: *he was beaten to the ground as onlookers stood by.* **2** support or remain loyal to (someone), typically in a time of need: *she had stood by him during his years in prison.* ■ adhere to or abide by (something promised, stated, or decided): *the government must stand by its pledges.* **3** be ready to deal or assist with something: *two battalions were on their way, and a third was standing by.* **stand down 1** withdraw or resign from a position or office. **2** (**stand down** or **stand someone down**) relax or cause to relax after a state of readiness: *if something doesn't happen soon, I guess they'll stand us down.* **3** (of a witness) leave the witness stand after giving evidence. **stand for 1** be an abbreviation of or symbol for. **2** [with negative] informal refuse to endure or tolerate. **3** support (a cause or principle). **stand in 1** deputize: *Brown stood in for the injured Simpson.* **2** Naut. sail closer to the shore. **stand off** move or keep away: *the women stood off at a slight distance.* ■ Naut. sail further away from the shore. **stand someone off** keep someone away: repel someone. **stand on 1** be scrupulous in the observance of: *let's not stand on formality.* **2** Naut. continue on the same course. **stand out 1** project from a surface: *the veins in his neck stood out.* ■ be easily noticeable: *he was one of those men who stood out in a crowd.* ■ be clearly better or more significant than someone or something: *four issues stand out as being of crucial importance.* **2** persist in opposition or support of something. **stand over** stand close to (someone) so as to watch, supervise, or intimidate them. **stand to** [often in imper.] Mil. stand ready for an attack, esp. one before dawn or after dark. **stand up** (of an argument, claim, evidence, etc.) remain valid after close scrutiny or analysis: *but will your story stand up in court?* **stand someone up** informal fail to keep an appointment with a boyfriend or girlfriend. **stand up for** speak or act in support of: *she learned to* ***stand up for herself.*** ■ act as best man for in a wedding. **stand up to 1** make a spirited defense against: *giving workers the confidence to stand up to their employers.* **2** be resistant to the harmful effects of (prolonged wear or use). — **stand·er** n. [OE *standan* (v.), *stand* (n.), of Gmc. origin, from an Indo-Eur. root shared by L. *stare* and Gk. *histanai*, also by the noun STEAD.]

stand-a·lone (also **stand·a·lone** /'standə,lōn/) ▶ adj. (of computer hardware or software) able to operate independently of other hardware or software.

stand·ard /'standərd/ ▶ n. **1** a level of quality or attainment: *their restaurant offers a high standard of service | the governor's ambition to raise standards in schools.* ■ a required or agreed level of quality or attainment: *half of the beaches fail to comply with EPA standards | their tap water was not* ***up to standard.*** **2** an idea or thing used as a measure, norm, or model in comparative evaluations: *the wages are low by today's standards | the system had become an industry standard.* ■ (**standards**) principles of conduct informed by notions of honor and decency: *a decline in moral standards.* ■ a form of language that is widely accepted as the correct form. ■ the prescribed weight of fine metal in gold or silver coins: *the sterling standard for silver.* ■ a system by which the value of a currency is defined in terms of gold or silver or both. **3** an object that is supported in an upright position, in particular: ■ a military or ceremonial flag carried on a pole or hoisted on a rope. ■ a tree or shrub that grows on an erect stem of full height. ■ a shrub grafted on an erect stem and trained in tree form. ■ Bot. the large frequently erect uppermost petal of a papilionaceous flower. Also called VEXILLUM. ■ Bot. one of the inner petals of an iris flower, frequently erect. ■ an upright water or gas pipe. **4** a tune or song of established popularity. ▶ adj. **1** used or accepted as normal or average: *the standard rate of income tax | it is standard practice in museums to register objects as they are acquired.* ■ (of a size, measure, design, etc.) such as is regularly used or produced; not special or exceptional: *all these doors come in a range of standard sizes.* ■ (of a work, repertoire, or writer) viewed as authoritative or of permanent value and so widely read or performed: *his essays on the interpretation of reality became a standard text.* ■ denoting or relating to the spoken or written form of a language widely accepted as usual and correct: *speakers of standard English.* **2** [attrib.] (of a tree or shrub) growing on an erect stem of full height. ■ (of a shrub) grafted on an erect stem and trained in tree form: *standard roses.*

— PHRASES **raise one's** (or **the**) **standard** esp. fig. take up arms: *he is the only one who has dared raise his standard against her.* — **stand·ard·ly** adv. [ME: shortening of OFr. *estendart*, from *estendre* 'extend.']

stand·ard-bear·er ▶ n. a soldier responsible for carrying the distinctive flag of a unit, regiment, or army. ■ a leading figure in a cause or movement: *the announcement made her a standard-bearer for gay rights.*

Stand·ard·bred /'standərd,bred/ (also **stand·ard·bred**) ▶ n. a horse of a breed able to attain a specified speed, developed esp. for trotting.

stand·ard de·vi·a·tion ▶ n. Stat. a quantity calculated to indicate the extent of deviation for a group as a whole.

stand·ard er·ror ▶ n. Stat. a measure of the statistical accuracy of an estimate, equal to the standard deviation of the theoretical distribution of a large population of such estimates.

stand·ard gauge ▶ n. a railroad gauge of 56.5 inches (1.435 m), standard in the US, Britain, and many other parts of the world.

stand·ard·ize /'standər,dīz/ ▶ v. [trans.] cause (something) to conform to a standard: *Jones's effort to standardize oriental spelling.* ■ [intrans.] (**standardize on**) adopt (something) as one's standard: *we could standardize on US equipment.* ■ determine the properties of by comparison with a standard. — **stand·ard·iz·a·ble** adj. **stand·ard·i·za·tion** /,standərdi'zāshən/ n. **stand·ard·iz·er** n.

stand·ard mod·el ▶ n. (**the standard model**) Physics a mathematical description of the elementary particles of matter and the electromagnetic, weak, and strong forces by which they interact.

stand·ard of liv·ing ▶ n. the degree of wealth and material comfort available to a person or community.

stand·ard time ▶ n. a uniform time for places in approximately the same longitude.

stand·by /'stand,bī/ ▶ n. (pl. **-bys**) readiness for duty or immediate deployment: *buses were placed* ***on standby*** *for the trip to Washington.* ■ the state of waiting to secure an unreserved place for a journey or performance, allocated on the basis of earliest availability: *passengers were obliged to go* ***on standby.*** ■ a person waiting to secure such a place. ■ a person or thing ready to be deployed immediately, esp. if needed as backup in an emergency: *a generator was kept as a standby* | [as adj.] *a standby rescue vessel.* ■ an operational mode of an electrical appliance in which the power is switched on but the appliance is not actually functioning.

stand-down ▶ n. esp. Mil. a period of relaxation after a state of alert. ■ an off-duty period.

stand·ee /stan'dē/ ▶ n. a person who stands, esp. in a passenger vehicle when all the seats are occupied or at a performance or sporting event.

stand-in ▶ n. a person who stands in for another.

stand·ing /'standiNG/ ▶ n. **1** position, status, or reputation: *their standing in the community* | *a man of high social standing.* ■ (**standings**) the table of scores indicating the relative positions of competitors in a sporting contest: *she heads the world championship standings.* **2** used to specify the length of time that something has lasted or that someone has fulfilled a particular role: *an interdepartmental squabble* ***of long standing.*** ▶ adj. [attrib.] **1** (of a jump or a start in a running race) performed from rest or an upright position, without a run-up or the use of starting blocks. **2** remaining in force or use; permanent: *he has a standing invitation to visit them* | *a standing army.* **3** (of water) stagnant or still. **4** (of grain) not yet reaped and so still erect. **5** Print. (of metal type) kept set up after use.

– PHRASES **in good standing** in favor or on good terms with someone. **leave someone/something standing** informal be much better or make much faster progress than someone or something else.

stand·ing com·mit·tee ▶ n. a permanent committee that meets regularly.

stand·ing count (also **standing eight count**) ▶ n. Boxing a count of eight taken on a boxer who has not been knocked down but who appears unfit to continue.

stand·ing crop ▶ n. a growing crop, esp. of a grain. ■ Ecol. the total biomass of an ecosystem or any of its components at a given time.

stand·ing joke ▶ n. something that regularly causes amusement or provokes ridicule.

stand·ing or·der ▶ n. **1** an order or ruling governing the procedures of a society, council, or other deliberative body. **2** a military order or ruling that is retained irrespective of changing conditions.

stand·ing o·va·tion ▶ n. a period of prolonged applause from an audience on their feet.

stand·ing part ▶ n. the end of a rope in a ship's rigging that is made fast, as distinct from the end to be hauled on. ■ (in knot-tying) the main part of the rope as opposed to the free end.

stand·ing rig·ging ▶ n. see RIGGING (sense 1).

stand·ing room ▶ n. space available for people to stand rather than sit in a vehicle, building, or stadium.

stand·ing wave ▶ n. Physics a vibration of a system in which some particular points remain fixed while others between them vibrate with the maximum amplitude. Compare with TRAVELING WAVE.

Stan·dish /'standiSH/, Miles (*c.*1584–1656), American colonist; born in England. He accompanied the Pilgrims to America in 1620 and became the military leader of Plymouth Colony.

stand·ish /'standiSH/ ▶ n. esp. hist. a stand for holding pens, ink, and other writing equipment. [ME: commonly held to be from the verb STAND + DISH, but evidence of such a use of *dish* is lacking.]

stand·off /'stand,ôf; -,äf/ ▶ n. a stalemate or deadlock between two equally matched opponents.

stand·off·ish /,stand'ôfiSH; -'äfiSH/ ▶ adj. informal distant and cold in manner; unfriendly. — **stand·off·ish·ly** adv. **stand·off·ish·ness** n.

stand·out /'stand,out/ informal ▶ n. a person or thing of exceptional ability or high quality. ▶ adj. [attrib.] exceptionally good: *he became a standout quarterback in the NFL.*

stand·pipe /'stand,pīp/ ▶ n. a vertical pipe extending from a water supply, esp. one connecting a temporary tap to the main.

stand·point /'stand,point/ ▶ n. an attitude to or outlook on issues: ***from the standpoint of*** *a believer.* ■ the position from which someone is able to view a scene or an object.

stand·still /'stand,stil/ ▶ n. [in sing.] a situation or condition in which there is no movement or activity at all: *the traffic* ***came to a standstill.***

stand·still a·gree·ment ▶ n. Finance an agreement between two countries in which a debt owed by one to the other is held in abeyance for a specified period. ■ an agreement between a company and a bidder for the company in which the bidder agrees to buy no more shares for a specified period.

stand-to ▶ n. Mil. the state of readiness for action or attack. ■ the formal start to a day of military operations.

stand-up (also **stand·up** /'stand,əp/) ▶ adj. [attrib.] **1** involving, done by, or engaged in by people standing up: *a stand-up party.* ■ such that people have to stand rather than sit: *a stand-up bar.* ■ (of a comedian) performing by standing in front of an audience and telling jokes. ■ (of comedy) performed in such a way: *his stand-up routine depends on improvised observations.* **2** informal courageous and loyal in a combative way: *he was a stand-up kind of guy.* **3** designed to stay upright or erect. ▶ n. a comedian who performs by standing in front of an audience and telling jokes. ■ comedy performed in such a way: *he began doing stand-up when he was fifteen.* ■ a brief monologue by a television news reporter.

Stan·ford-Bi·net test /'stanfərd bə'nā/ ▶ n. an intelligence test based on the Binet-Simon scale.

stan·hope /'stan,hōp; 'stanəp/ ▶ n. hist. a light open horse-drawn carriage for one person, with two or four wheels. [19th C.: named after Fitzroy *Stanhope* (1787–1864), an English clergyman for whom the first one was made.]

Stan·is·laus, St. /'stanə,slôs; -,släs/ (1030–79), patron saint of Poland; Polish name *Stanisław*; known as **St. Stanislaus of Cracow.** As bishop of Cracow 1072–79, he excommunicated King Boleslaus II.

Stan·i·slav·sky /,stanə'släfskē/, Konstantin (Sergeevich) (1863–1938), Russian theater director, actor, and teacher; born *Konstantin Sergeevich Alekseev*. His theory and teaching technique were later developed into method acting.

stank /staNGk/ past of STINK.

Stan·ley, Sir Henry Morton (1841–1904), Welsh explorer; born *John Rowlands*. In 1871, he found David Livingstone (1813–73) in Africa.

Stan·ley, Mount a mountain in the Ruwenzori range in central Africa. African name NGALIEMA, MOUNT.

Stan·ley Cup a trophy awarded annually to the ice hockey team that wins the championship in the National Hockey League. [for Lord *Stanley* of Preston (1841–1908), the governor general of Canada who donated the trophy in 1893.]

stan·nic /'stanik/ ▶ adj. Chem. of tin with a valence of four; of tin(IV). Compare with STANNOUS. [18th C.: from late L. *stannum* 'tin' + -IC.]

stan·nous /'stanəs/ ▶ adj. Chem. of tin with a valence of two; of tin(II). Compare with STANNIC. [19th C.: from late L. *stannum* 'tin' + -OUS.]

Stan·ton[1] /'stantən/, Edwin McMasters (1814–69), US public official. As secretary of war 1862–67 and briefly during 1868, he played a pivotal role in the impeachment proceedings against President Andrew Johnson.

Stan·ton[2], Elizabeth Cady (1815–1902), US reformer. From 1852, she led the women's rights movement with Susan B. Anthony. She was president of the National Woman Suffrage Association 1869–90.

stan·za /'stanzə/ ▶ n. a group of lines forming the basic recurring metrical unit in a poem; a verse. ■ a group of four lines in some Greek and Latin meters. — **stan·zaed** (also **stan·za'd**) adj. **stan·za·ic** /stan'zā-ik/ adj. [16th C.: from Ital., 'standing place,' also 'stanza.']

sta·pe·di·al /stə'pēdēəl/ ▶ adj. [attrib.] Anat. Zool. of or relating to the stapes. [19th C.: from mod. L. *stapedius* (denoting the muscle attached to the neck of the stapes) + -AL.]

sta·pe·li·a /stə'pēlyə/ ▶ n. a succulent African plant (genus *Stapelia*, family Asclepiadaceae) with large star-shaped fleshy flowers that have bold markings and a fetid carrionlike smell that attracts pollinating flies. [mod. L., named after Jan Bode von *Stapel* (died 1636), Dutch botanist.]

sta·pes /'stāpēz/ ▶ n. (pl. same) Anat. a small stirrup-shaped bone in the middle ear, transmitting vibrations from the incus to the inner ear. Also called STIRRUP. [17th C.: mod. L., from med. L. *stapes* 'stirrup.']

staph /staf/ ▶ n. informal **1** Med. short for STAPHYLOCOCCUS. **2** Entomol. short for STAPHYLINID.

staph·y·lin·id /,stafə'linid/ ▶ n. Entomol. a beetle of a family (Staphylinidae) that comprises the rove beetles. [19th C.: from mod. L. *Staphylinidae* (pl.), from the genus name *Staphylinus*, from Gk. *staphulinos*, denoting a kind of insect.]

staph·y·lo·coc·cus /,stafəlō'käkəs/ ▶ n. (pl. **-coc·ci** /-'käk,sī; -,sē/) a bacterium of a genus (*Staphylococcus*) that includes many pathogenic kinds that cause pus formation, esp. in the skin and mucous membranes. — **staph·y·lo·coc·cal** /-'käkəl/ adj. [mod. L., from Gk. *staphulē* 'bunch of grapes' + *kokkos* 'berry.']

sta·ple[1] /'stāpəl/ ▶ n. a piece of bent metal or wire pushed through something or clipped over it as a fastening, in particular: ■ a piece of thin bracket-shaped wire that is driven by a stapler through papers to fasten them together. ■ a small U-shaped metal bar with pointed ends for driving into wood to hold attachments such as electric wires, battens, or sheets of cloth in place. ▶ v. [trans.] attach or secure with a staple or staples: *Mark stapled the papers together.* [OE *stapol*, of Gmc. origin; rel. to Du. *stapel* 'pillar' (a sense reflected in Engl. in early use).]

sta·ple[2] ▶ n. **1** a main or important element of something, esp. of a diet: *bread, milk, and other staples.* ■ a main item of trade or production: *rubber became the staple of the Malayan economy.* **2** the fiber of cotton or wool considered with regard to its length and degree of fineness. **3** [often with adj.] hist. a center of trade, esp. in a specified commodity: *a wool staple at Pisa.* ▶ adj. [attrib.] main or important, esp. in terms of consumption: *the staple foods of the poor.* ■ most important in terms of trade or production. ▶ v. sort or classify (wool, etc.) according to fiber. — **stapled** adj. [ME (sense 3): from OFr. *estaple* 'market,' from Mid. Low Ger., MDu. *stapel* 'pillar, emporium'; rel. to STAPLE[1].]

sta·ple gun ▶ n. a hand-held mechanical tool for driving staples into a hard surface.

sta·pler /'stāp(ə)lər/ ▶ n. a device for fastening together sheets of paper with a staple or staples.

star /stär/ ▶ n. **1** a fixed luminous point in the night sky that is a large, remote incandescent body like the sun. **2** a conventional or stylized representation of a star, typically one having five or more points. ■ a symbol of this shape used to indicate a category of excellence: *the hotel has three stars* ■ an asterisk. ■ a white patch on the forehead of a horse or other animal. ■ (also **star network**) [usu. as adj.] a data or communication network in which all nodes are independently connected to one central unit: *computers in a star layout.* **3** a famous or exceptionally talented performer in the world of entertainment or sports: *a pop star* | [as adj.] *singers of* ***star quality.*** ■ an outstandingly good or successful person or thing in a group: *a* ***rising star*** *in the party* | [as adj.] *Ellen was a star pupil.* **4** Astrol. a planet, constellation, or configuration regarded as influencing someone's fortunes. ■ (**stars**) a horoscope published in a newspaper or magazine: *what do my stars say?* ▶ **v.** (**starred, star·ring**) [trans.] **1** (of a movie, play, or other show) have (someone) as a principal performer: *a film starring Liza Minnelli.* ■ [intrans.] (of a performer) have a principal role in a movie, play, or other show. ■ [intrans.] (of a person) perform brilliantly or prominently in a particular endeavor or event: *Vitt starred at third base for the Detroit Tigers.* **2** decorate or cover with star-shaped marks or objects: *thick grass* ***starred with*** *flowers.* ■ mark (something) for special notice or recommendation with an asterisk or other star-shaped symbol: *the activities listed below are starred according to their fitness ratings* | [as adj., in comb.] (**-starred**) *Michelin-starred restaurants.*

– PHRASES **my stars!** informal, dated an expression of astonishment. **reach for the stars** have high or ambitious aims. **see stars** see flashes of light, esp. after being hit on the head. **stars in one's eyes** used to describe someone who is idealistically hopeful or enthusiastic about their future. — **star·less adj. star·like** /-ˌlīk/ **adj.** [OE *steorra,* of Gmc. origin; rel. to Du. *ster,* Ger. *Stern,* from an Indo-Eur. root shared by L. *stella* and Gk. *astēr.*]

star an·ise ▶ **n.** see ANISE (sense 2).

star ap·ple ▶ **n.** an edible purple fruit with a star-shaped cross section. It is produced by an evergreen tropical American tree *Chrysophyllum cainito* of the sapodilla family.

star·board /ˈstärˌbôrd/ ▶ **n.** the side of a ship or aircraft that is on the right when one is facing forward. The opposite of PORT[3]. ▶ **v.** [trans.] turn (a ship or its helm) to starboard. [OE *stēorbord* 'rudder side' (see STEER[1], BOARD), because early Teutonic sailing vessels were steered with a paddle over the right side.]

star·board watch ▶ **n.** see WATCH (sense 2).

star·burst /ˈstärˌbərst/ ▶ **n.** a pattern of lines or rays radiating from a central object or source of light: [as adj.] *a starburst pattern.* ■ an explosion producing such an effect. ■ a camera lens attachment that produces a pattern of rays around the image of a source of light. ■ a period of intense activity in a galaxy involving the formation of stars.

starch /stärCH/ ▶ **n.** an odorless tasteless white substance occurring widely in plant tissue and obtained chiefly from cereals and potatoes. It is a polysaccharide that functions as a carbohydrate store and is an important constituent of the human diet. ■ food containing this substance. ■ powder or spray made from this substance and used before ironing to stiffen fabric or clothing. ■ fig. stiffness of manner or character: *the starch in her voice.* ▶ **v.** [trans.] stiffen (fabric or clothing) with starch: [as adj.] (**starched**) *his immaculately starched shirt.* ■ informal (of a boxer) defeat (an opponent) by a knockout: *Domenge starched Geddami in the first.*

– PHRASES **take the starch out of someone** deflate or humiliate someone. — **starch·er n.** [OE (recorded only in the past part. *sterced* 'stiffened'), of Gmc. origin; rel. to Du. *sterken,* Ger. *stärken* 'strengthen,' also to STARK.]

starch·y /ˈstärCHē/ ▶ **adj.** (**starch·i·er, starch·i·est**) **1** (of food or diet) containing a relatively high amount of starch. **2** (of clothing) stiff with starch. ■ informal very stiff, formal, or prim in manner or character: *the manager is usually a bit starchy.* — **starch·i·ly** /-CHəlē/ **adv. starch·i·ness n.**

star-crossed ▶ **adj.** literary (of a person or a plan) thwarted by bad luck.

star·dom /ˈstärdəm/ ▶ **n.** the state or status of being a famous or exceptionally talented performer in the world of entertainment or sports.

star·dust /ˈstärˌdəst/ ▶ **n.** (esp. in the context of success in the world of entertainment or sports) a magical or charismatic quality or feeling.

stare /ste(ə)r/ ▶ **v.** [intrans.] look fixedly or vacantly at someone or something with one's eyes wide open. ■ (of a person's eyes) be wide open, with a fixed or vacant expression: *her gray eyes stared back at him.* ■ [intrans.] (of a thing) be unpleasantly prominent or striking: *the obituaries stared out at us.* ■ [trans.] (**stare someone into**) reduce someone to (a specified condition) by looking fixedly at them. ▶ **n.** a long fixed or vacant look: *she gave him a cold stare.*

– PHRASES **be staring something in the face** be on the verge of something inevitable or inescapable. **stare someone in the eye** (or **face**) look fixedly or boldly at someone. **stare someone in the face** be glaringly apparent or obvious.

– PHRASAL VERBS **stare someone down** look fixedly at someone until they feel forced to lower their eyes or turn away. — **star·er n.** [OE *starian,* of Gmc. origin, from a base meaning 'be rigid.']

sta·re de·ci·sis /ˈste(ə)rē diˈsīsis/ ▶ **n.** Law the legal principle of determining points in litigation according to precedent. [L., lit. 'stand by things decided.']

star·fish /ˈstärˌfiSH/ ▶ **n.** (pl. same or **-fish·es**) a marine echinoderm (class Asteroidea) with five or more radiating arms. The undersides of the arms bear tube feet for locomotion and, in predatory species, for opening the shells of mollusks.

star·flow·er /ˈstärˌflouər/ ▶ **n.** a plant with starlike flowers, in particular: ■ a small North American woodland plant (*Trientalis borealis*) of the primrose family. ■ a star-of-Bethlehem.

star fruit (also **star·fruit**) ▶ **n.** another term for CARAMBOLA.

star·gaz·er /ˈstärˌgāzər/ ▶ **n.** **1** informal an astronomer or astrologer. ■ a daydreamer. **2** a fish (families Uranoscopidae and Dactyloscopidae) of warm seas that normally lies buried in the sand with only its eyes, which are on top of the head, protruding. — **star·gaze v.**

stark /stärk/ ▶ **adj.** **1** severe or bare in appearance or outline: *a stark silhouette against the sky.* ■ unpleasantly or sharply clear; impossible to avoid: *his position on civil rights is* ***in stark contrast to*** *that of his liberal opponent.* **2** [attrib.] complete; sheer: *in stark terror.* ■ rare completely naked.

– PHRASES **stark naked** completely naked. **stark raving mad** informal completely crazy. — **stark·ly adv.** [as submodifier] *the reality is starkly different.* **stark·ness n.** [OE *stearc* 'unyielding, severe,' of Gmc. origin; rel. to Du. *sterk* and Ger. *stark* 'strong.']

Stark ef·fect /stärk/ ▶ **n.** Physics the splitting of a spectrum line into several components by the application of an electric field. [20th C.: for Johannes *Stark* (1874–1957), German physicist.]

star·let /ˈstärlit/ ▶ **n.** informal a young actress with aspirations to become a star: *a Hollywood starlet.*

star·light /ˈstärˌlīt/ ▶ **n.** the light that comes from the stars.

Star·ling /ˈstärliNG/, Ernest Henry (1866–1927), English physiologist, founder of the science of endocrinology.

star·ling /ˈstärliNG/ ▶ **n.** a gregarious Old World songbird (*Sturnus* and other genera) with a straight bill, typically with dark lustrous or iridescent plumage but sometimes brightly colored. The **starling family** also includes the mynahs, grackles, and (usually) the oxpeckers. [OE *stærlinc,* from *stær* 'starling' (of Gmc. origin) + -LING.]

star·lit /ˈstärˌlit/ ▶ **adj.** lit or made brighter by stars.

star net·work ▶ **n.** another term for STAR (sense 2).

star-nosed mole ▶ **n.** a mole (*Condylura cristata*) with a number of fleshy radiating tentacles around its nostrils, native to northeastern North America.

Star of Beth·le·hem ▶ **n.** a resplendent star that is said to have guided the Magi to the birthplace of the infant Jesus.

star-of-Beth·le·hem ▶ **n.** a plant (genera *Ornithogalum* and *Gagea*) of the lily family with star-shaped flowers that typically have green stripes on the outer surface, native to the temperate regions of the Old World.

Star of Da·vid ▶ **n.** a six-pointed figure consisting of two interlaced equilateral triangles, used as a Jewish and Israeli symbol. Also called MAGEN DAVID.

Star of David

star route ▶ **n.** a postal delivery route served by a private contractor. [from the use of a star or asterisk to mark the routes in postal records.]

star ru·by ▶ **n.** a cabochon ruby reflecting an opalescent starlike image owing to its regular internal structure.

star·ry /ˈstärē/ ▶ **adj.** (**-ri·er, -ri·est**) full of or lit by stars: *a starry sky.* ■ resembling a star in brightness or shape: *tiny white starry flowers.* — **star·ri·ness n.**

star·ry-eyed ▶ **adj.** naively enthusiastic or idealistic; failing to recognize the practical realities of a situation.

Stars and Bars ▶ **plural n.** [treated as sing.] hist. the flag of the Confederate States of America.

Stars and Stripes ▶ **plural n.** [treated as sing.] the national flag of the US. It has 13 horizontal red and white stripes for the original Thirteen Colonies. In the upper left corner is a field of blue with 50 white stars for the 50 states.

star sap·phire ▶ **n.** a cabochon sapphire that reflects a starlike image resulting from its regular internal structure.

star shell ▶ **n.** an explosive projectile designed to burst in the air and light up an enemy's position.

star·ship /ˈstärˌSHip/ ▶ **n.** (in science fiction) a large manned spaceship used for interstellar travel.

star-span·gled ▶ **adj.** literary covered, glittering, or decorated with stars: *the star-spangled horizon.* ■ fig. glitteringly successful: *a star-spangled career.* ■ used humorously with reference to the US national flag and a perceived American identity: *star-spangled decency.*

Star-Span·gled Ban·ner the US national anthem, officially adopted in 1931. The words were written in 1814 by Francis Scott Key as a poem originally titled "Defence of Fort M'Henry" and were later put to a tune adapted from a popular English song, "To Anacreon in Heaven."

star stream ▶ **n.** Astron. a systematic drift of stars in the same general direction within a galaxy.

star-struck ▶ **adj.** fascinated or greatly impressed by famous people, esp. those connected with the entertainment industry: *I was a star-struck teenager.*

star-stud·ded ▶ **adj.** **1** (of the night sky) filled with stars. **2** informal featuring a number of famous people, esp. actors or sports players: *a star-studded cast.*

star sys·tem ▶ **n.** **1** a large number of stars with a perceptible structure; a galaxy. **2** the practice of promoting or otherwise favoring individuals who have become famous and popular.

START /stärt/ ▶**abbr.** Strategic Arms Reduction Talks.

start /stärt/ ▶**v. 1** [intrans.] come into being; begin or be reckoned from a particular point in time or space. ■ [with infin. or pres. part.] embark on a continuing action or a new venture. ■ use a particular point, action, or circumstance as an opening for a course of action: *the teacher can* ***start by*** *capitalizing on children's curiosity* | *I shall* ***start with*** *the case you mention first.* ■ [intrans.] begin to move or travel: *we started out into the snow.* | ■ [trans.] begin to attend (an educational establishment) or engage in (an occupation, esp. a profession): *he started work at a travel agency.* ■ begin one's working life: *she* ***started off*** *as a general practitioner.* ■ [trans.] begin to live through (a period distinguished by a specified characteristic): *they started their married life.* ■ cost at least a specified amount: *fees* ***start at*** *around $300.* **2** [trans.] cause (an event or process) to happen: *two men started the blaze that caused the explosion.* ■ bring (a project or an institution) into being; cause to take effect or begin to work or operate: *I'm starting a campaign to get the law changed.* ■ cause (a machine) to begin to work: *we had trouble starting the car* | *he* ***starts up*** *his van.* ■ [intrans.] (of a machine or device) begin operating or being used: *the noise of a tractor* ***starting up*** | *there was a moment of silence before the organ started.* ■ cause or enable (someone or something) to begin doing or pursuing something: *his father* ***started him off*** *in business.* ■ give a signal to (competitors) to start in a race. **3** [intrans.] give a small jump or make a sudden jerking movement from surprise or alarm. ■ [intrans.] literary move or appear suddenly: *she had seen Meg start suddenly from a thicket.* ■ (of eyes) bulge so as to appear to burst out of their sockets: *his eyes* ***started out of*** *his head like a hare's.* ■ [trans.] rouse (game) from its lair. ▶**n.** [in sing.] **1** the point in time or space at which something has its origin; the beginning of something: *he takes over as chief executive at the start of next year* | *the event was a shambles from start to finish* | *his bicycle was found close to the start of a forest trail.* ■ the point or moment at which a race begins. ■ an act of beginning to do or deal with something: *I can* ***make a start on*** *cleaning up* | *an early start enabled us to avoid the traffic.* ■ used to indicate that a useful initial contribution has been made but that more remains to be done: *if he would tell her the truth, it would be a start.* ■ a person's position or circumstances at the beginning of their life, esp. a position of advantage: *the best* ***start in life.*** ■ an advantage consisting in having set out in a race or on journey earlier than one's rivals or opponents: *a ninety-minute* ***start on*** *them.* **2** a sudden movement of surprise or alarm: *she awoke* ***with a start*** | *the woman* ***gave*** *a nervous* ***start.***

– PHRASES **don't start** (or **don't you start**) informal used to tell someone not to grumble or criticize. **for a start** informal used to introduce or emphasize the first or most important of a number of considerations. **get the start of** dated gain an advantage over. **start a family** conceive one's first child. **start something** informal cause trouble. **to start with** at the beginning of a series of events or period of time. ■ as the first thing to be taken into account: *to start with, I was feeling down.*

– PHRASAL VERBS **start in** informal begin doing something, esp. talking: *people groan when she starts in about her acting ambitions.* ■ (**start in on**) begin to do or deal with: *you vacuum the stairs and I'll start in on the laundry.* ■ (**start in on**) attack verbally; begin to criticize: *before you start in on me, let me explain.* **start off** (or **start someone/something off**) begin (or cause someone or something to begin) working, operating, or dealing with something: *start off with attention to diet.* ■ (**start off**) begin a meal: *she* ***started off with*** *soup.* **start on 1** begin to work on or deal with. **2** informal begin to talk to someone, esp. in a critical or hostile way: *she started on about my not having nice furniture.* **start over** make a new beginning. **start out** (or **up**) embark on a venture or undertaking, esp. a commercial one: *the company will start out with a hundred employees.* [OE *styrtan* 'to caper, leap,' of Gmc. origin.]

start·er /'stärtər/ ▶**n.** a person or thing that starts an event, activity, or process, in particular: ■ esp. Brit. the first course of a meal; an appetizer. ■ an automatic device for starting a machine, esp. the engine of a vehicle. ■ a person who gives the signal for the start of a race. ■ [with adj.] a horse, competitor, or player taking part in a race or game at the start. ■ Baseball the pitcher who starts the game. ■ Baseball a pitcher who normally starts games, and seldom is used as a relief pitcher. ■ [with adj.] a person or thing that starts in a specified way, esp. with reference to time or speed: *he was a* ***late starter*** *in photography.* ■ a topic, question, or other item with which to start a group discussion or course of study: *material to act as a* ***starter for*** *discussion.* ■ (also **starter culture**) a bacterial culture used to initiate souring in making yogurt, cheese, or butter. ■ a preparation of chemicals to initiate the breakdown of vegetable matter in making compost.

– PHRASES **for starters** informal first of all; to start with.

start·er home ▶**n.** a relatively small, economical house or condominium; a first home.

start·ing block ▶**n.** (usu. **starting blocks**) a shaped rigid block for bracing the feet of a runner at the start of a race.

start·ing gate ▶**n.** (usu. **the starting gate**) a restraining structure incorporating a barrier that is raised at the start of a race, typically in horse racing and skiing, to ensure a simultaneous start.

start·ing pis·tol ▶**n.** a pistol used to give the signal for the start of a race.

star·tle /'stärtl/ ▶**v.** [trans.] cause (a person or animal) to feel sudden shock or alarm: *a sudden sound in the doorway startled her* | [with infin.] *he was startled to see a column of smoke.* — **star·tler** **n.** [OE *steartlian* 'kick, struggle,' from the base of START.]

star·tling /'stärtl-iNG/ ▶**adj.** very surprising, astonishing, or remarkable: *she had startling blue eyes.* — **star·tling·ly** **adv.** [as submodifier] *a startlingly good memory.*

start-up (also **start·up** /'stärt,əp/) ▶**n.** the action or process of setting something in motion: *the start-up of marketing in Europe* | [as adj.] *start-up costs.* ■ a newly established business: *problems facing start-ups and small firms in rural areas.*

starve /stärv/ ▶**v.** [intrans.] (of a person or animal) suffer severely or die from hunger. ■ [trans.] cause (a person or animal) to suffer severely or die from hunger: *for a while she had considered starving herself.* ■ (**be starving** or **starved**) informal feel very hungry: *I don't know about you, but I'm starving.* ■ (**starve someone out** or **into**) force someone out of a place or into a specified state by stopping supplies of food. ■ [trans.] (usu. **be starved of** or **for**) deprive of something necessary: *starved of funds.* — **star·va·tion** /-'vāsHən/ **n.** [OE *steorfan* 'to die,' of Gmc. origin, prob. from a base meaning 'be rigid' (cf. STARE); rel. to Du. *sterven* and Ger. *sterben.*]

starve·ling /'stärvliNG/ archaic ▶**n.** an undernourished or emaciated person or animal. ▶**adj.** (of a person or animal) lacking enough food; emaciated: *a starveling child.*

stash /stasH/ informal ▶**v.** [trans.] store (something) safely and secretly in a specified place: *their wealth had been* ***stashed away*** *in Swiss banks.* ▶**n. 1** a secret store of something: *a* ***stash of*** *money.* ■ a quantity of an illegal drug, esp. one kept for personal use: *one prisoner tried to swallow his stash.* **2** dated a hiding place or hideout. [18th C.: of unknown origin.]

sta·sis /'stāsis/ ▶**n.** formal tech. a period or state of inactivity or equilibrium. ■ Med. a stoppage of flow of a body fluid. [18th C.: mod. L., from Gk., lit. 'standing, stoppage,' from *sta-*, base of *histanai* 'to stand.']

-stasis ▶**comb. form** (pl. **-stas·es**) Physiol. slowing down; stopping: *hemostasis.* — **-static** **comb. form** in corresponding adjectives. [from Gk. *stasis* 'standing, stoppage.']

stat[1] /stat/ informal ▶**abbr.** ■ photostat. ■ statistic. ■ statistics: [as adj.] *a stat sheet.* ■ thermostat.

stat[2] ▶**adv.** (in a medical direction or prescription) immediately. [19th C.: abbrev. of L. *statim.*]

stat. ▶**abbr.** ■ (in prescriptions) immediately. [from L. *statim.*] ■ statuary. ■ statue. ■ statute.

-stat ▶**comb. form** denoting instruments, substances, etc., maintaining a controlled state: *thermostat* | *hemostat.* [partly from *(helio)stat*, partly a back-form. from STATIC.]

state /stāt/ ▶**n. 1** the particular condition that someone or something is in at a specific time: *the state of the company's finances* | *we're worried about her state of mind.* ■ a physical condition as regards internal or molecular form or structure: *water in a liquid state.* ■ [in sing.] (**a state**) informal an agitated or anxious condition: *don't* ***get into a state.*** ■ [in sing.] informal a dirty or untidy condition: *look at the state of you—what a mess!* ■ Physics short for QUANTUM STATE. **2** a nation or territory considered as an organized political community under one government: *the state of Israel.* ■ an organized political community or area forming part of a federal republic: *the German state of Bavaria.* ■ (**the States**) informal term for UNITED STATES. **3** the civil government of a country: ***affairs of state.*** **4** pomp and ceremony associated with monarchy or high levels of government: *he was* ***buried in state.*** ▶**adj.** [attrib.] **1** of, provided by, or concerned with the civil government of a country: *the future of state education.* **2** used or done on ceremonial occasions; involving the ceremony associated with a head of state: *a state visit to Hungary by Queen Elizabeth.* ▶**v. 1** [reporting verb] express something definitely or clearly in speech or writing: [with clause] *the report stated that more than 51 percent of voters failed to participate* | [trans.] *people will be invited to state their views.* ■ [trans.] esp. Law specify the facts of (a case) for consideration: *both sides must state their case.* **2** [trans.] Music present or introduce (a theme or melody) in a composition.

– PHRASES **state of affairs** (or **things**) a situation or set of circumstances. **state of the art** the most recent stage in the development of a product, incorporating the newest ideas and the most up-to-date features. ■ [as adj.] incorporating the newest ideas and the most up-to-date features: *a new state-of-the-art hospital.* **state of emergency** a situation of national danger or disaster in which a government suspends normal constitutional procedures in order to regain control. **state of grace** a condition of being free from sin. **state of life** (in religious contexts) a person's occupation, calling, or status. **state of war** a situation when war has been declared or is in progress. — **stat·a·ble** **adj.** [ME (as a n.): partly a shortening of ESTATE, partly from L. *status* 'manner of standing, condition' (see STATUS).]

state cap·i·tal·ism ▶**n.** a political system in which the state has control of production and the use of capital.

State De·part·ment the department in the US government dealing with foreign affairs.

state·hood /'stāt,ho͝od/ ▶**n.** the status of being a recognized independent nation: *the Jewish struggle for statehood.* ■ the status of being a state of the US: *a proposed referendum on statehood for Puerto Rico.*

state house (also **state·house**) ▶**n.** the building where a state legislature meets.

state·less /'stātlis/ ▶**adj.** (of a person) not recognized as a citizen of any country. — **state·less·ness** /'stātlisnis/ **n.**

state·ly /'stātlē/ ▶**adj.** (**-li·er, -li·est**) having a dignified, unhurried, and grand manner; majestic in manner and appearance: *a stately procession* | *his tall and stately wife.* — **state·li·ness** n.

state·ment /'stātmənt/ ▶ n. a definite or clear expression of something in speech or writing: *do you agree with this statement?* | *this is correct as a statement of fact.* ■ an official account of facts, views, or plans, esp. one for release to the media: *the officials issued a joint statement calling for negotiations.* ■ a formal account of events given by a witness, defendant, or other party to the police or in a court of law: *she made a statement to the police.* ■ a document setting out items of debit and credit between a bank or other organization and a customer. ■ the expression of an idea or opinion through something other than words: *their humorous kitschiness makes a statement of serious wealth.* ■ Music the occurrence of a musical idea or motive within a composition: *a carefully structured musical and dramatic progression from the first statement of this theme.*

Stat·en Is·land /'statn/ an island borough of southwestern New York City; pop. 378,977.

State of the Un·ion mes·sage (also **State of the Union address**) ▶ n. a yearly address on the state of the nation delivered in January by the president of the US to Congress.

stat·er /'stātər/ ▶ n. hist. an ancient Greek gold or silver coin. [via late L. from Gk. *statēr*, from a base meaning 'weigh.']

state·room /'stāt,ro͞om; -,ro͝om/ ▶ n. a private compartment on a ship. ■ a captain's or superior officer's room on a ship. ■ a private compartment on a train. ■ a large room in a palace or public building, for formal use.

state's at·tor·ney ▶ n. a lawyer representing a state in court.

state school ▶ n. another term for STATE UNIVERSITY.

state se·cret ▶ n. a sensitive issue or piece of information that is kept secret by the government, usually to protect the public. ■ humorous a piece of information, usually of a trivial or personal nature, that is closely guarded and desired to be kept private: *she thought her affair with the boss was a state secret, but we all knew about it.*

state's ev·i·dence ▶ n. Law evidence for the prosecution given by a participant in or accomplice to the crime being tried.
– PHRASES **turn state's evidence** give such evidence: *persuading one-time gang members to turn state's evidence.*

States-Gen·er·al ▶ n. 1 the bicameral legislative body in the Netherlands. 2 (also **Es·tates Gen·er·al**) hist. the legislative body in France until 1789, representing the clergy, the nobility, and the commons.

state·side /'stāt,sīd/ ▶ adj. & adv. informal of, in, or toward the US (used in reference to the US from elsewhere or from Alaska and Hawaii): [as adj.] *stateside police departments* | [as adv.] *they were headed stateside.*

states·man /'stātsmən/ ▶ n. (pl. **-men**) a skilled, experienced, and respected political leader or figure. — **states·man·like** /-,līk/ adj. **states·man·ship** /-,ship/ n. [16th C.: from *state's man*, translating Fr. *homme d'état.*]

state so·cial·ism ▶ n. a political system in which the state has control of industries and services.

states' rights ▶ plural n. the rights and powers held by individual US states rather than by the federal government.

states·wom·an /'stāts,wo͝omən/ ▶ n. (pl. **-wom·en**) a skilled, experienced, and respected female political leader.

state u·ni·ver·si·ty ▶ n. a university managed by the public authorities of a particular US state.

state vis·it ▶ n. a ceremonial visit to a foreign country by a head of state.

state·wide /'stāt'wīd/ ▶ adj. & adv. extending throughout a particular US state: [as adj.] *a statewide health system.*

stat·ic /'statik/ ▶ adj. 1 lacking in movement, action, or change, esp. in a way viewed as undesirable or uninteresting: *demand has grown in what was a fairly static market* | *the whole ballet appeared too static.* ■ Computing (of a process or variable) not able to be changed during a set period. 2 Physics concerned with bodies at rest or forces in equilibrium. Often contrasted with DYNAMIC. ■ (of an electric charge) having gathered on or in an object that cannot conduct a current. ■ acting as weight but not moving. ■ of statics. 3 Computing (of a memory or store) not needing to be periodically refreshed by an applied voltage. ▶ n. crackling or hissing noises on a telephone, radio, or other telecommunications system. ■ short for STATIC ELECTRICITY. ■ informal angry or critical talk or behavior: *the reception was going sour, breaking up into static.* — **stat·i·cal·ly** /-ik(ə)lē/ adv. **stat·ick·y** /-ikē/ adj. [16th C.: via mod. L. from Gk. *statikē (tekhnē)* 'science of weighing'; the adjective from mod. L. *staticus*, from Gk. *statikos* 'causing to stand,' from the verb *histanai.*]

stat·ic cling ▶ n. the adhering of a garment to the wearer's body or to another garment, caused by a buildup of static electricity.

stat·ice /'statisē; 'statis/ ▶ n. another term for SEA LAVENDER, esp. when cultivated as a garden plant. [18th C.: from mod. L. *statice* (former genus name), based on Gk., fem. of *statikos* 'causing to stand still' (with ref. to medicinal use of the plant to stanch blood).]

stat·ic e·lec·tric·i·ty ▶ n. a stationary electric charge, typically produced by friction, that causes sparks or crackling or the attraction of dust or hair.

stat·ic pres·sure ▶ n. Physics the pressure of a fluid on a body when the body is at rest relative to the fluid.

stat·ics /'statiks/ ▶ plural n. 1 [usu. treated as sing.] the branch of mechanics concerned with bodies at rest and forces in equilibrium. Compare with DYNAMICS (sense 1). 2 another term for STATIC.

sta·tion /'stāshən/ ▶ n. 1 a regular stopping place on a public transportation route, esp. one on a railroad line with a platform and often one or more buildings. 2 [usu. with adj.] a place or building where a specified activity or service is based: *a research station.* ■ a small military base, esp. of a specified kind: *a naval station.* ■ a police station. ■ a subsidiary post office. 3 [with adj.] a company involved in broadcasting of a specified kind: *a radio station.* 4 the place where someone or something stands or is placed on military or other duty: *the lookout resumed his station in the bow.* ■ dated one's social rank or position: *Karen was getting ideas above her station.* 5 Bot. a particular site at which an interesting or rare plant grows. 6 short for STATION OF THE CROSS. ▶ v. [trans.] put in or assign to a specified place for a particular purpose, esp. a military one: *troops were stationed in the town* | *a young girl had stationed herself by the door.* [ME (as a n.): via OFr. from L. *statio(n-)*, from *stare* 'to stand.']

sta·tion·ar·y /'stāshə,nerē/ ▶ adj. not moving or not intended to be moved: *a car collided with a stationary vehicle.* ■ Astron. (of a planet) having no apparent motion in longitude. ■ not changing in quantity or condition: *a stationary population.* [ME: from L. *stationarius* (orig. in the sense 'belonging to a military station'), from *station-* 'standing' (see STATION).]
– USAGE Be careful to distinguish **stationary** ('not moving, fixed') from **stationery** ('writing paper and other supplies').

sta·tion break ▶ n. a pause between broadcast programs for an announcement of the identity of the station transmitting them, also for commercials.

sta·tion·er /'stāsh(ə)nər/ ▶ n. a person or store selling paper, pens, and other writing and office materials. [ME (in the sense 'bookseller'): from med. L. *stationarius* 'tradesman (at a fixed location, i.e., not itinerant).' Cf. STATIONARY.]

sta·tion·er·y /'stāshə,nerē/ ▶ n. writing paper, esp. with matching envelopes. ■ writing and other office materials.

sta·tion house ▶ n. a police or fire station.

sta·tion·mas·ter /'stāshən,mastər/ ▶ n. an official in charge of a railroad station.

Sta·tion of the Cross ▶ n. (usu. **Stations of the Cross**) one of a series of fourteen pictures or carvings representing successive incidents leading to and during Jesus' progress from Pilate's house to his crucifixion.

sta·tion wag·on ▶ n. a car with a long body, incorporating a large carrying area behind the seats and having a rear door for easy loading.

stat·ism /'stāt,izəm/ ▶ n. a political system in which the state has substantial centralized control over social and economic affairs: *the rise of authoritarian statism.* — **stat·ist** n. & adj.

sta·tis·tic /stə'tistik/ ▶ n. a fact or piece of data from a study of a large quantity of numerical data: *the statistics show that the crime rate has increased.* ■ an event or person regarded as no more than such a piece of data (used to suggest an inappropriately impersonal approach): *he was just another statistic.* ▶ adj. another term for STATISTICAL. [18th C.: from Ger. *statistisch* (adj.), *Statistik* (n.).]

sta·tis·ti·cal /stə'tistikəl/ ▶ adj. of or relating to the use of statistics: *a statistical comparison.* — **sta·tis·ti·cal·ly** /-tik(ə)lē/ adv. [sentence adverb] *these differences were not statistically significant.*

sta·tis·ti·cal me·chan·ics ▶ plural n. [treated as sing.] the description of physical phenomena in terms of a statistical treatment of the behavior of large numbers of atoms or molecules, esp. with regard to the distribution of energy among them.

sta·tis·ti·cal sig·nif·i·cance ▶ n. see SIGNIFICANCE.

stat·is·ti·cian /,stati'stishən/ ▶ n. an expert in the preparation and analysis of statistics.

sta·tis·tics /stə'tistiks/ ▶ plural n. [treated as sing.] the practice or science of collecting and analyzing numerical data in large quantities.

Sta·ti·us /'stāsh(ē)əs/, Publius Papinius (*c.* AD45–96), Roman poet. He is best known for the *Silvae*, a miscellany of poems addressed to friends.

sta·tive /'stātiv/ Ling. ▶ adj. (of a verb) expressing a state or condition rather than an activity or event, such as *be* or *know*, as opposed to *run* or *grow*. Contrasted with DYNAMIC. ▶ n. a stative verb. [17th C.: from L. *stativus*, from *stat-* 'stopped, standing,' from the verb *stare.*]

stato- ▶ comb. form relating to statics: *statocyst.* [from Gk. *statos* 'standing.']

stat·o·blast /'statə,blast/ ▶ n. Zool. (in bryozoans) a resistant reproductive body produced asexually.

stat·o·cyst /'statə,sist/ ▶ n. Zool. a small organ of balance and orientation in some aquatic invertebrates, consisting of a sensory vesicle or cell containing statoliths. Also called OTOCYST.

stat·o·lith /'statl-ith/ ▶ n. Zool. a calcareous particle in the statocysts of invertebrates that stimulates sensory receptors in response to gravity, so enabling balance and orientation. ■ another term for OTOLITH.

sta·tor /'stātər/ ▶ n. the stationary portion of an electric generator or motor, esp. of an induction motor. ■ a row of small stationary airfoils attached to the casing of an axial-flow turbine, positioned between the rotors. [19th C.: from STATIONARY, on the pattern of *rotor.*]

stat·o·scope /'statə,skōp/ ▶ n. a form of aneroid barometer for measuring minute variations of pressure, used esp. to indicate the altitude of an aircraft. [20th C.: from Gk. *statos* 'standing' + -SCOPE.]

stats /stats/ ▶ plural n. informal short for STATISTICS.

stat·u·ar·y /'stachoo͞,erē/ ▶ n. statues collectively. [16th C.: from L. *statuarius*, from *statua* (see STATUE).]

stat·ue /ˈstacHo͞o/ ▸ **n.** a carved or cast figure of a person or animal, esp. one that is life-size or larger. — **stat·ued** adj. [ME: from OFr., from L. *statua*, from *stare* 'to stand.']

Stat·ue of Lib·er·ty a statue at the entrance to New York Harbor, a symbol of welcome to immigrants. It was a gift from France in 1886.

stat·u·esque /ˌstacHo͞oˈesk/ ▸ **adj.** (esp. of a woman) attractively tall and dignified: *her statuesque beauty.* — **stat·u·esque·ly** adv. **stat·u·esque·ness** n. [18th C.: from STATUE, on the pattern of *picturesque*.]

stat·u·ette /ˌstacHo͞oˈet/ ▸ **n.** a small statue or figurine. [19th C.: from Fr., dimin. of *statue*.]

stat·ure /ˈstacHər/ ▸ **n.** a person's natural height: *she was small in stature.* ■ importance or reputation gained by ability or achievement: *an architect of international stature.* — **stat·ured** adj. [ME: via OFr. from L. *statura*, from *stare* 'to stand.']

sta·tus /ˈstātəs; ˈstatəs/ ▸ **n. 1** the relative social, professional, or other standing of someone or something: *an improvement in the status of women.* ■ high rank or social standing. ■ the official classification given to a person, country, or organization, determining their rights or responsibilities: *the duchy had been elevated to the status of a principality.* **2** the position of affairs at a particular time, esp. in political or commercial contexts: *an update on the status of the bill.* [18th C.: from L., 'standing,' from *stare* 'to stand.']

sta·tus bar ▸ **n.** Comput. a horizontal bar, typically at the bottom of the screen or window, showing information about a document being edited or a program running.

sta·tus quo /ˈstātəs ˈkwō; ˈstatəs/ ▸ **n.** (usu. **the status quo**) the existing state of affairs, esp. regarding social or political issues: *they have a vested interest in maintaining the status quo.* [L., lit. 'the state in which.']

sta·tus sym·bol ▸ **n.** a possession that is taken to indicate a person's wealth or high social or professional status.

stat·ute /ˈstacHo͞ot/ ▸ **n.** a written law passed by a legislative body: *violation of the hate crimes statute | the tax is not specifically disallowed by statute.* ■ a rule of an organization or institution: *the appointment will be subject to the statutes of the university.* ■ archaic (in biblical use) a law or decree made by a sovereign, or by God. [ME: from OFr. *statut*, from late L. *statutum*, neut. past part. of L. *statuere* 'set up,' from *status* 'standing' (see STATUS).]

stat·ute book ▸ **n.** a book in which laws are written.

stat·ute mile ▸ **n.** see MILE.

stat·ute of lim·i·ta·tions ▸ **n.** Law a statute prescribing a period of limitation for the bringing of certain kinds of legal action.

stat·u·to·ry /ˈstacHəˌtôrē/ ▸ **adj.** required, permitted, or enacted by statute: *the courts did award statutory damages to each of the plaintiffs.* ■ (of a criminal offense) carrying a penalty prescribed by statute: *statutory theft.* ■ of or relating to statutes: *constitutional and statutory interpretation.* — **stat·u·to·ri·ly** /-ˌtôrəlē/ adv.

stat·u·to·ry law ▸ **n.** the rules of law laid down in statutes. Compare with COMMON LAW, CASE LAW.

stat·u·to·ry rape ▸ **n.** Law sexual intercourse with a minor.

staunch[1] /stôncH; stäncH/ ▸ **adj. 1** loyal and committed in attitude: *a staunch supporter of the antinuclear lobby | a staunch Catholic.* **2** (of a wall) of strong or firm construction. ■ (also **stanch**) archaic (of a ship) watertight. — **staunch·ly** adv. **staunch·ness** n. [ME (in the sense 'watertight'): from OFr. *estanche*, fem. of *estanc*, from a Romance base meaning 'dried up, weary.']

staunch[2] ▸ **v.** var. of STANCH[1].

stau·ro·lite /ˈstôrəˌlīt/ ▸ **n.** a brown glassy mineral that occurs as hexagonal prisms often twinned in the shape of a cross. It consists of a silicate of aluminum and iron. [19th C.: from Gk. *stauros* 'cross' + -LITE.]

stave /stāv/ ▸ **n. 1** a vertical wooden post or plank in a building or other structure. ■ any of the lengths of wood attached side by side to make a barrel, bucket, or other container. ■ a strong wooden stick or iron pole used as a weapon. **2** Music another term for STAFF[1] (sense 4). **3** a verse or stanza of a poem. ▸ **v.** [trans.] **1** (past and past part. **staved** or **stove** /stōv/) (**stave something in**) break something by forcing it inward or piercing it roughly: *the door was staved in.* **2** (past and past part. **staved**) (**stave something off**) avert or delay something bad or dangerous: *a reassuring presence can stave off a panic attack.* [ME: back-form. from *staves*.]

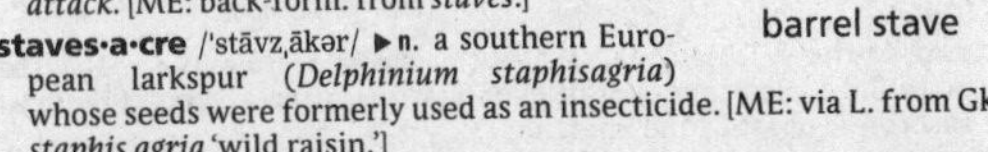

barrel stave

staves·a·cre /ˈstāvzˌākər/ ▸ **n.** a southern European larkspur (*Delphinium staphisagria*) whose seeds were formerly used as an insecticide. [ME: via L. from Gk. *staphis agria* 'wild raisin.']

Stav·ro·pol /ˈstävrəpəl; stavˈrōpəl/ **1** an administrative territory in southern Russia. ■ its capital city; pop. 324,000. **2** former name (until 1964) for TOGLIATTI.

stay[1] /stā/ ▸ **v. 1** [intrans.] remain in the same place: *you stay here and I'll be back soon | Jenny decided to stay at home with their young child | he stayed with the firm as a consultant.* ■ (**stay for/to**) delay leaving so as to join in (an activity): *why not stay for lunch?* ■ (**stay down**) (of food) remain in the stomach, rather than be thrown up as vomit. ■ (**stay with**) remain in the mind or memory of (someone): *Gary's words stayed with her all evening.* **2** [intrans.] remain in a specified state or position: *her ability to stay calm | tactics used to stay in power | I managed to stay out of trouble.* ■ (**stay with**) continue or persevere with (an activity or task): *the incentive needed to stay with a healthy diet.* ■ (**stay with**) (of a competitor or player) keep up with (another) during a race or match. **3** [intrans.] (of a person) live somewhere temporarily as a visitor or guest: *the girls had gone to stay with friends | Minton invited him to stay the night.* **4** [trans.] stop, delay, or prevent (something), in particular suspend or postpone (judicial proceedings) or refrain from pressing (charges). ■ assuage (hunger) for a short time: *I grabbed something to stay the pangs of hunger.* ■ literary curb; check: *he tries to stay the destructive course of barbarism.* ■ [no obj., in imper.] archaic wait a moment in order to allow someone time to think or speak: *stay, stand apart, I know not which is which.* **5** [trans.] (usu. **be stayed**) literary support or prop up. ▸ **n. 1** a period of staying somewhere, in particular of living somewhere temporarily as a visitor or guest: *an overnight stay at a luxury hotel.* **2** literary a curb or check: *a good public library as a stay against boredom.* ■ Law a suspension or postponement of judicial proceedings: *a stay of prosecution.* **3** a device used as a brace or support. ■ (**stays**) hist. a corset made of two pieces laced together and stiffened by strips of whalebone. **4** archaic power of endurance.

– PHRASES **be here** (or **have come**) **to stay** informal be permanent or widely accepted: *the Internet is here to stay.* **stay the course** (or **distance**) keep going strongly to the end of a race or contest. ■ pursue a difficult task or activity to the end. **a stay of execution** a delay in carrying out a court order. **stay put** (of a person or object) remain somewhere without moving or being moved.

– PHRASAL VERBS **stay on** continue to study, work, or be somewhere after others have left: *75 percent of sixteen-year-olds stay on in full-time education.* **stay over** (of a guest or visitor) sleep somewhere, esp. at someone's home, for the night. **stay up** not go to bed: *they stayed up all night.* [ME (as a verb): from Anglo-Norman Fr. *estai-*, stem of OFr. *ester*, from L. *stare* 'to stand'; in the sense 'support,' partly from OFr. *estaye* (n.), *estayer* (v.), of Gmc. origin.]

stay[2] ▸ **n.** a large rope, wire, or rod used to support a ship's mast, leading from the masthead to another mast or spar or down to the deck. ■ a guy or rope supporting a flagpole or other upright pole. ■ a supporting wire or cable on an aircraft. ▸ **v.** [trans.] secure or steady (a mast) by means of stays. [OE *stæg*, of Gmc. origin; rel. to Du. *stag*, from a base meaning 'be firm.']

stay-at-home informal ▸ **adj.** [attrib.] preferring to be at home rather than to travel, socialize, or go out to work: *a stay-at-home family man.* ▸ **n.** a person who lives in such a way.

stay·er /ˈstāər/ ▸ **n. 1** a tenacious person or thing, esp. a horse able to hold out to the end of a race. **2** a person who lives somewhere temporarily as a visitor or guest.

stay·ing pow·er ▸ **n.** informal the ability to maintain an activity or commitment despite fatigue or difficulty; stamina: *do you have the staying power to study alone at home?* ■ long-term popularity of a product or trend: *hip-hop has a remarkable staying power.*

stay-in strike ▸ **n.** Brit. a sit-down strike.

Stay·man /ˈstāmən/ (also **Stay·man Wine·sap** /ˈwīnˌsap/) ▸ **n.** an apple of a deep red variety with a mildly tart flavor, originating in the US.

stay·sail /ˈstāsəl; -ˌsāl/ ▸ **n.** a triangular fore-and-aft sail extended on a stay.

stbd. ▸ **abbr.** starboard.

STD ▸ **abbr.** ■ Doctor of Sacred Theology. [from L. *Sanctae Theologiae Doctor*.] ■ sexually transmitted disease.

std. ▸ **abbr.** standard.

Ste. ▸ **abbr.** Saint (referring to a woman). [from Fr. *Sainte*.]

stead /sted/ ▸ **n.** the place or role that someone or something should have or fill (used in referring to a substitute): *to be appointed in his stead.*

– PHRASES **stand someone in good stead** be advantageous or useful to someone over time or in the future: *his early training stood him in good stead.* [OE *stede* 'place,' of Gmc. origin; rel. to Du. *stad* 'town,' Ger. *Statt* 'place,' *Stadt* 'town,' from an Indo-Eur. root shared by the verb STAND.]

stead·fast /ˈstedˌfast/ ▸ **adj.** resolutely or dutifully firm and unwavering: *steadfast loyalty.* — **stead·fast·ly** adv. **stead·fast·ness** n. [OE *stedefæst* 'standing firm' (see STEAD, FAST[1]).]

stead·y /ˈstedē/ ▸ **adj.** (**stead·i·er, stead·i·est**) **1** firmly fixed, supported, or balanced; not shaking or moving: *the lighter the camera, the harder it is to hold steady | he refilled her glass with a steady hand.* ■ not faltering or wavering; controlled: *a steady gaze | she tried to keep her voice steady.* ■ (of a person) sensible, reliable, and self-restrained: *a solid, steady young man.* **2** regular, even, and continuous in development, frequency, or intensity: *a steady decline in the national birth rate | sales remain steady.* ■ not changing; regular and established: *I thought I'd better get a steady job | a steady boyfriend.* ■ (of a ship) moving without deviation from its course. ▸ **v.** (**stead·ies, stead·ied**) make or become steady: [trans.] *I took a deep breath to steady my nerves* | [as adj.] (**steadying**) *she's the one steadying influence in his life.* ▸ **exclam.** used as a warning to someone to keep calm or take care: *Steady now! Don't hurt yourself.* ▸ **n.** (pl. **stead·ies**) informal a person's regular boyfriend or girlfriend: *his steady chucked him two weeks ago.*

– PHRASES **go steady** informal have a regular romantic or sexual relationship with a particular person. — **stead·i·er** n. **stead·i·ly** /'stedl-ē/ adv. **stead·i·ness** n. [ME: from STEAD + -Y[1].]

stead·y state ▶ n. an unvarying condition in a physical process, esp. as in the theory that the universe is eternal and maintained by constant creation of matter. The theory has now largely been abandoned in favor of the big bang theory and an evolving universe.

steak /stāk/ ▶ n. high-quality beef taken from the hindquarters of the animal, typically cut into thick slices that are cooked by broiling or frying: *he liked his steak rare.* ■ a thick slice of such beef or other high-quality meat or fish: *a salmon steak.* ■ poorer-quality beef that is cubed or ground and cooked more slowly by braising or stewing. [ME: from ON *steik*; rel. to *steikja* 'roast on a spit' and *stikna* 'be roasted.']

steak au poivre /ō 'pwävrə; 'pwäv/ ▶ n. steak coated liberally with crushed peppercorns before cooking. [Fr., lit. 'steak with pepper.']

steak·house /'stāk,hous/ ▶ n. a restaurant that specializes in serving steaks.

steak knife ▶ n. a knife with a serrated blade for use when eating steak.

steak tar·tare /tär'tär/ ▶ n. a dish consisting of raw ground steak mixed with raw egg, onion, and seasonings.

steal /stēl/ ▶ v. (past **stole** /stōl/; past part. **sto·len** /'stōlən/) **1** [trans.] take (another person's property) without permission or legal right and without intending to return it: *thieves stole her bicycle* | [intrans.] *she was found guilty of stealing from her employers* | [as adj.] (**stolen**) *stolen goods.* ■ dishonestly pass off (another person's ideas) as one's own: *accusations that one group had stolen ideas from the other were soon flying.* ■ take the opportunity to give or share (a kiss) when it is not expected or when people are not watching: *he was allowed to steal a kiss in the darkness.* ■ (in various sports) gain (an advantage, a run, or possession of the ball) unexpectedly or by exploiting the temporary distraction of an opponent. ■ Baseball (of a base runner) advance safely to (the next base) by running to it as the pitcher begins the delivery: *Rickey stole third base.* ■ attract the most notice in (a scene or a theatrical production) while not being the featured performer: *the jester steals the scene.* **2** [intrans.] move somewhere quietly or surreptitiously: *he stole down to the kitchen* | fig. *a delicious languor was stealing over her.* ■ [trans.] direct (a look) quickly and unobtrusively: *he stole a furtive glance at her.* ▶ n. [in sing.] **1** informal a bargain: *for $5 it was a steal.* **2** an act of stealing something: *New York's biggest art steal.* ■ an idea taken from another work. ■ Baseball an act of stealing a base.

– PHRASES **steal a march on** gain an advantage over (someone), typically by acting before they do. **steal someone's heart** win someone's love. **steal the show** attract the most attention and praise. **steal someone's thunder** win praise for oneself by preempting someone else's attempt to impress. — **steal·er** n. [in comb.] *a sheep-stealer.* [OE *stelan* (v.), of Gmc. origin; rel. to Du. *stelen* and Ger. *stehlen.*]

stealth /stelTH/ ▶ n. cautious and surreptitious action or movement: *the silence and stealth of a hungry cat* | *why did you slip away by stealth like this?* ▶ adj. (chiefly of aircraft) designed to make detection by radar or sonar difficult: *a stealth bomber.* ■ secretive; trying to avoid notice: *she has been ducking the press as befits a stealth candidate.* [ME (in the sense 'theft'): prob. representing an OE word rel. to STEAL, + -TH[2].]

stealth·y /'stelTHē/ ▶ adj. (**stealth·i·er**, **stealth·i·est**) behaving, done, or made in a cautious and surreptitious manner, so as not to be seen or heard: *stealthy footsteps.* — **stealth·i·ly** /-THələ/ adv. **stealth·i·ness** n.

steam /stēm/ ▶ n. the vapor into which water is converted when heated, forming a white mist of minute water droplets in the air. ■ the invisible gaseous form of water, formed by boiling, from which this vapor condenses. ■ the expansive force of this vapor used as a source of power for machines: *the equipment was originally powered by steam* | [as adj.] *a steam train.* ■ locomotives and railroad systems powered in this way: *the last years of steam.* ■ fig. energy and momentum or impetus: *the anticorruption drive gathered steam.* ▶ v. **1** [intrans.] give off or produce steam: *a mug of coffee was steaming at her elbow.* ■ (**steam up** or **steam something up**) become or cause to become covered or misted over with steam: [intrans.] *the glass keeps steaming up* | [trans.] *the warm air had begun to steam up the windows.* ■ (often **be/get steamed up**) informal be or become extremely agitated or angry: *you got all steamed up over nothing!* **2** [trans.] cook (food) by heating it in steam from boiling water: *steam the vegetables until just tender.* ■ [intrans.] (of food) cook in this way: *add the mussels and leave them to steam.* ■ clean or otherwise treat with steam: *he steamed his shirts in the bathroom to remove the wrinkles.* ■ [trans.] apply steam to (something fixed with adhesive) so as to open or loosen it: *he'd steamed the letter open and then resealed it.* ■ operate (a steam locomotive). **3** [intrans.] (of a ship or train) travel somewhere under steam power: *the 11:54 steamed into the station.* ■ informal come, go, or move somewhere rapidly or in a forceful way: *Jerry steamed in ten minutes late* | fig. *the company has steamed ahead with its investment program.*

– PHRASES **pick up** (or **get up**) **steam 1** generate enough pressure to drive a steam engine. **2** (of a project in its early stages) gradually gain more impetus and driving force: *his campaign steadily picked up steam.* **have steam coming out of one's ears** informal be extremely angry or irritated. **in steam** (of a steam locomotive) ready for work, with steam in the boiler. **let** (or **blow**) **off steam** informal (of a person) get rid of pent-up energy or strong emotion. **run out of** (or **lose**) **steam** informal lose impetus or enthusiasm. **under one's own steam** (with reference to travel) without assistance from others. **under steam** (of a machine) being operated by steam. [OE *stēam* 'vapor,' *stēman* 'emit a scent, be exhaled,' of Gmc. origin; rel. to Du. *stoom* 'steam.']

steam bath ▶ n. a room that is filled with hot steam for the purpose of cleaning and refreshing the body and for relaxation. ■ a session in such a bath.

steam·boat /'stēm,bōt/ ▶ n. a boat that is propelled by a steam engine, esp. a paddle-wheel craft of a type used widely on rivers in the 19th century.

steam boil·er ▶ n. a container such as that in a steam engine in which water is boiled to generate steam.

steam dis·til·la·tion ▶ n. Chem. distillation of a liquid in a current of steam, used esp. to purify liquids that are not very volatile and are immiscible with water.

steamed /stēmd/ ▶ adj. **1** having been cooked by steaming: *a cornucopia of steamed dumplings.* **2** [predic.] informal extremely angry: *you're simply steamed about some editor's bad treatment of you.*

steam en·gine ▶ n. an engine that uses the expansion or rapid condensation of steam to generate power. ■ a steam locomotive.

steam·er /'stēmər/ ▶ n. **1** a ship or boat powered by steam. ■ informal a steam locomotive. **2** a type of saucepan in which food can be steamed. ■ a device used to direct a jet of hot steam onto a garment in order to remove creases. **3** (in full **steamer clam**) another term for SOFT-SHELL CLAM. **4** informal a wetsuit.

steam·er rug ▶ n. a lap robe, esp. for use on board a passenger ship for keeping warm on deck.

steam gauge ▶ n. a pressure gauge attached to a steam boiler.

steam heat ▶ n. heat produced by steam, esp. by a central heating system in a building or on a train or ship that uses steam. ▶ v. [trans.] (**steam-heat**) heat (something) by passing hot steam through it, esp. at high pressure.

steam·ing /'stēmiNG/ ▶ adj. **1** giving off steam: *a basin of steaming water.* **2** informal very angry. ▶ adv. [as submodifier] (**steaming hot**) extremely hot.

steam i·ron ▶ n. an electric iron that emits steam from holes in its flat surface.

steam·roll·er /'stēm,rōlər/ ▶ n. a heavy, slow-moving vehicle with a roller, used to flatten the surfaces of roads during construction. ■ fig. an oppressive and relentless power or force: *victims of an ideological steamroller.* ▶ v. (also **steam·roll**) [trans.] (of a government or other authority) forcibly pass (a measure) by restricting debate or otherwise overriding opposition: *they would have to work together to steamroller the necessary bills past the smaller parties.* ■ force (someone) into doing or accepting something: *an attempt to steamroller the country into political reforms.* ■ [intrans.] proceed forcefully and seemingly invincibly: *they steamrolled through the playoffs undefeated.*

steam·ship /'stēm,SHip/ ▶ n. a ship that is propelled by a steam engine.

steam shov·el ▶ n. an excavator that is powered by steam.

steam ta·ble ▶ n. (in a cafeteria or restaurant) a table with slots to hold food containers that are kept hot by steam circulating beneath them.

steam·tight /'stēm,tīt/ ▶ adj. not allowing steam to pass through: *steam-tight joints.*

steam tur·bine ▶ n. a turbine in which a high-velocity jet of steam rotates a bladed disk or drum.

steam·y /'stēmē/ ▶ adj. (**steam·i·er**, **steam·i·est**) producing, filled with, or clouded with steam: *a small steamy kitchen.* ■ (of a place or its atmosphere) hot and humid: *the hot, steamy jungle.* ■ informal depicting or involving erotic sexual activity: *steamy sex scenes* | *a steamy affair.* — **steam·i·ly** /-məlē/ adv. **steam·i·ness** /-mēnis/ n.

ste·ar·ic ac·id /stē'arik; 'sti(ə)r-/ ▶ n. Chem. a solid saturated fatty acid, $CH_3(CH_2)_{16}COOH$, obtained from animal or vegetable fats. — **ste·a·rate** /'stē-ə,rāt; 'sti(ə)r,āt/ n. [19th C.: *stearic* from Fr. *stéarique*, from Gk. *stear* 'tallow.']

ste·a·rin /'sti(ə)rin/ ▶ n. a white crystalline substance that is the main constituent of tallow and suet. It is a glyceryl ester of stearic acid. ■ a mixture of fatty acids used in candlemaking. [19th C.: from Fr. *stéarine*, from Gk. *stear* 'tallow.']

ste·a·tite /'stēə,tīt/ ▶ n. the mineral talc occurring in consolidated form, esp. as soapstone. — **ste·a·tit·ic** /,stēə'titik/ adj. [18th C.: via L. from Gk. *steatitēs*, from *stear, steat-* 'tallow.']

steato- ▶ comb. form relating to fatty matter or tissue: *steatosis.* [from Gk. *stear, steat-* 'tallow, fat.']

ste·at·o·py·gi·a /,stēətə'pijēə; stē,atə-/ ▶ n. accumulation of large amounts of fat on the buttocks. — **ste·at·o·py·gous** /,stēətə'pīgəs; ,stēə'täpəgəs/ adj. [19th C.: mod. L., from Gk. *stear, steat-* 'tallow' + *pugē* 'rump.']

ste·at·or·rhe·a /,stēətə'rēə; stē,atə-/ (Brit. **ste·at·or·rhoe·a**) ▶ n. Med. the excretion of abnormal quantities of fat with the feces owing to reduced absorption of fat by the intestine.

ste·a·to·sis /,stēə'tōsis/ ▶ n. Med. infiltration of liver cells with fat, associated with disturbance of the metabolism by, for example, alcoholism, malnutrition, pregnancy, or drug therapy.

steed /stēd/ ▶ n. archaic literary a riding horse. [OE *stēda* 'stallion'; rel. to STUD[2].]

steel /stēl/ ▶ n. a hard, strong, gray or bluish-gray alloy of iron with carbon and usually other elements, used extensively as a structural and fabricating material. ■ used as a symbol or embodiment of strength and firmness: *nerves of steel* | [as adj.] *a steel will.* ■ a rod of roughened steel on which knives are sharpened. ▶ v. [trans.] mentally prepare (oneself) to do or face something difficult: *I speak quickly, steeling myself for a mean reply.* [OE *stȳle, stēli*, of Gmc. origin; rel. to Du. *staal*, Ger. *Stahl*, also to STAY².]

steel band ▶ n. a band that plays music on steel drums.

steel blue ▶ n. a dark bluish-gray color.

steel drum ▶ n. a percussion instrument originating in Trinidad, made out of an oil drum with one end beaten down and divided by grooves into sections to give different notes. Also called PAN¹ (esp. by players).

Steele /stēl/, Sir Richard (1672–1729), Irish writer and playwright. He founded and wrote for the magazines *Tatler* (1709–11) and *The Spectator* (1711–12).

steel en·grav·ing ▶ n. the process or action of engraving a design into a steel plate. ■ a print made from an engraved steel plate.

steel gray ▶ n. a dark purplish-gray color: [as adj.] *the steel-gray November sky.*

steel·head /ˈstēlˌhed/ (also **steel·head trout**) ▶ n. a rainbow trout of a large migratory variety.

steel wool ▶ n. fine strands of steel matted together into a mass, used as an abrasive.

steel·work /ˈstēlˌwərk/ ▶ n. articles of steel.

steel·works /ˈstēlˌwərks/ ▶ plural n. [usu. treated as sing.] a factory where steel is manufactured. — **steel·work·er** /-ˌwərkər/ n.

steel·y /ˈstēlē/ ▶ adj. (**steel·i·er, steel·i·est**) resembling steel in color, brightness, or strength: *a steely blue.* ■ fig. coldly determined; hard: *there was a steely edge to his questions.* — **steel·i·ness** n.

steel·yard /ˈstēlˌyärd/ ▶ n. an apparatus for weighing that has a short arm taking the item to be weighed and a long graduated arm along which a weight is moved until it balances.

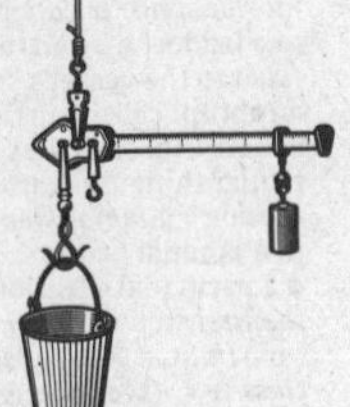

steelyard

steen·bok /ˈstēnˌbäk/ (also **stein·bok** or **steen·buck**) ▶ n. a small African antelope (*Raphiceros campestris*) with large ears, a small tail, and smooth upright horns. [18th C.: from Du., from *steen* 'stone' + *bok* 'buck.']

steep¹ /stēp/ ▶ adj. **1** (of a slope, flight of stairs, angle, ascent, etc.) rising or falling sharply; nearly perpendicular: *she pushed the bike up the steep hill.* ■ (of a rise or fall in an amount) large or rapid: *the steep rise in unemployment.* **2** informal (of a price or demand) not reasonable; excessive: *a steep membership fee.* ■ dated (of a claim or account) exaggerated or incredible: *this is a rather steep statement.* ▶ n. esp. Skiing or literary a steep mountain slope: *hair-raising steeps.* — **steep·ish** adj. **steep·ly** adv. **steep·ness** n. [OE *stēap* 'extending to a great height,' of West Gmc. origin; rel. to STEEPLE and STOOP¹.]

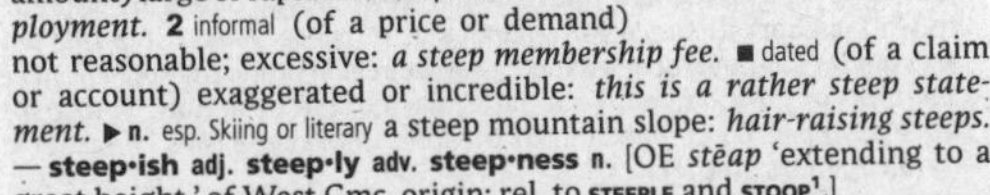

steep² ▶ v. [trans.] soak (food or tea) in water or other liquid so as to extract its flavor or to soften it: *the chilies are steeped in olive oil* | [intrans.] *the noodles should be left to steep for 3–4 minutes.* ■ soak or saturate (cloth) in water or other liquid. ■ (usu. **be steeped in**) fig. surround or fill with a quality or influence: *a city steeped in history.* [ME: of Gmc. origin; rel. to STOUP.]

steep·en /ˈstēpən/ ▶ v. become or cause to become steeper: [intrans.] *the snow improved as the slope steepened.*

stee·ple /ˈstēpəl/ ▶ n. a church tower and spire. ■ a spire on the top of a church tower or roof. ■ archaic a tall tower of a church or other building. — **stee·pled** adj. [OE *stēpel*, of Gmc. origin; rel. to STEEP¹.]

stee·ple·chase /ˈstēpəlˌCHās/ ▶ n. a horse race run on a racecourse having ditches and hedges as jumps. ■ a running race in which runners must clear hurdles and water jumps. — **stee·ple·chas·er** n. **stee·ple·chas·ing** n. [18th C.: from STEEPLE (because orig. a steeple marked the finishing point across country) + CHASE¹.]

stee·ple·jack /ˈstēpəlˌjak/ ▶ n. a person who climbs tall structures such as chimneys and steeples in order to carry out repairs.

steer¹ /sti(ə)r/ ▶ v. [trans.] (of a person) guide or control the movement of (a vehicle, vessel, or aircraft). ■ [intrans.] (of a vehicle, vessel, or aircraft) be guided in a specified direction in such a way: *the ship steered into port.* ■ [trans.] follow (a course) in a specified direction: *the fishermen were steering a direct course for Kodiak* | [intrans.] fig. *try to steer away from foods based on sugar.* ■ [trans.] guide the movement or course of (someone or something): *he had steered her to a chair* | fig. *he made an attempt to steer the conversation back to Heather.* ▶ n. informal a piece of advice or information concerning the development of a situation: *the need for the school to be given a clear steer as to its future direction.*

– PHRASES **steer clear of** take care to avoid or keep away from: *his program steers clear of prickly local issues.* — **steer·a·ble** /ˈsti(ə)rəbəl/ adj. [OE *stīeran*, of Gmc. origin; rel. to Du. *sturen* and Ger. *steuern*.]

steer² ▶ n. a male domestic bovine animal that has been castrated and is raised for beef. [OE *stēor*, of Gmc. origin; rel. to Du. *stier* and Ger. *Stier*.]

steer·age /ˈsti(ə)rij/ ▶ n. hist. the part of a ship providing accommodations for passengers with the cheapest tickets: *poor emigrants in steerage* | [as adj.] *steerage passengers.* ▶ adv. hist. in the part of a ship providing the cheapest accommodation: *his grandparents had come over from Ireland traveling steerage* | *he was sent steerage to Canada to work on a farm.*

steer·age·way /ˈsti(ə)rijˌwā/ (also **steer·age-way**) ▶ n. (of a vessel) the minimum speed required for proper response to the helm.

steer·ing col·umn ▶ n. a shaft that connects the steering wheel of a vehicle to the rest of the steering mechanism.

steer·ing com·mit·tee (Brit. also **steer·ing group**) ▶ n. a committee that decides on the priorities or order of business of an organization and manages the general course of its operations.

steer·ing wheel ▶ n. a wheel that a driver rotates in order to steer a vehicle.

steers·man /ˈsti(ə)rzmən/ ▶ n. (pl. **-men**) a person who is steering a boat or ship.

steeve /stēv/ ▶ n. (in a sailing ship) the angle of the bowsprit in relation to a horizontal plane. ▶ v. [trans.] (usu. **be steeved**) give (the bowsprit) a specified inclination. [17th C.: of unknown origin.]

Stef·fens /ˈstefənz/, Lincoln (1866–1936) US journalist; full name *Joseph Lincoln Steffens.* He was a leader of the muckraking movement.

Steg·ner /ˈstegnər/, Wallace Earle (1909–93), US writer. His novels include *The Big Rock Candy Mountain* (1943) and *Angle of Repose* (1971).

steg·o·saur /ˈstegəˌsôr/ (also **steg·o·sau·rus** /ˌstegəˈsôrəs/) ▶ n. a small-headed quadrupedal herbivorous dinosaur (*Stegosaurus* and other genera, order Ornithischia) of the Jurassic and early Cretaceous periods, with a double row of large bony plates or spines along the back. See illustration at DINOSAUR. [mod. L., from Gk. *stegē* 'covering' + *sauros* 'lizard.']

Stei·chen /ˈstīkən/, Edward Jean (1879–1973), US photographer; born in Luxembourg. He is credited with transforming photography to an art form.

Stein /stīn/, Gertrude (1874–1946), US writer. She developed an esoteric stream-of-consciousness style, notably in *The Autobiography of Alice B. Toklas* (1933).

stein /stīn/ ▶ n. a large earthenware beer mug. [19th C.: from Ger. *Stein*, 'stone.']

Stein·beck /ˈstīnˌbek/, John Ernst (1902–68), US writer. His novels include *Of Mice and Men* (1937) and *The Grapes of Wrath* (1939). Nobel Prize for Literature (1962).

stein·bok /ˈstīnˌbäk/ ▶ n. var. of STEENBOK.

Stein·em /ˈstīnəm/, Gloria (1934–), US social activist and journalist. She cofounded the National Women's Political Caucus in 1971 and *Ms.* magazine in 1972.

ste·la /ˈstēlə/ ▶ n. (pl. **-lae** /-ˌlē/) Archaeol. an upright stone slab or column typically bearing a commemorative inscription or relief design, often serving as a gravestone. [18th C.: via L. from Gk. (see STELE).]

ste·le /stēl; ˈstēlē/ ▶ n. **1** Bot. the central core of the stem and root of a vascular plant, consisting of the vascular tissue (xylem and phloem) and associated supporting tissue. Also called VASCULAR CYLINDER. **2** Archaeol. another term for STELA. — **ste·lar** /ˈstēlər/ adj. (sense 1). [19th C.: from Gk. *stēlē* 'standing block.']

Stel·la /ˈstelə/, Frank Philip (1936–), US painter. An important figure in minimalism, he is known for his series of all-black paintings.

Stel·la Mar·is /ˈstelə ˈmaris/ ▶ n. esp. literary a female protector or guiding spirit at sea (a title sometimes given to the Virgin Mary). [L., 'star of the sea.']

stel·lar /ˈstelər/ ▶ adj. of or relating to a star or stars: *stellar structure and evolution.* ■ informal featuring or having the quality of a star performer or performers: *a stellar cast had been assembled.* ■ informal exceptionally good; outstanding: *his restaurant has received stellar ratings in the guides.* — **stel·li·form** /ˈsteləˌfôrm/ adj. [17th C.: from late L. *stellaris*, from L. *stella* 'star.']

stel·lar·a·tor /ˈsteləˌrātər/ ▶ n. Physics a toroidal apparatus for producing controlled fusion reactions in hot plasma, where all the controlling magnetic fields inside it are produced by external windings. [1950s: from STELLAR (with ref. to the fusion processes in stars), on the pattern of *generator*.]

stel·lar wind /wind/ ▶ n. Astron. a continuous flow of charged particles from a star.

stel·late /ˈstelit; -ˌāt/ ▶ adj. tech. arranged in a radiating pattern like that of a star. — **stel·lat·ed** adj. [17th C.: from L. *stellatus*, from *stella* 'star.']

Stel·ler's jay ▶ n. a blue jay (*Cyanocitta stelleri*) with a dark crest, found in western North America.

Stel·ler's sea cow ▶ n. a very large relative of the dugong (*Hydrodamalis gigas*) that was formerly found in the area of the Bering Sea and Kamchatka Peninsula, discovered and exterminated in the 18th century.

stem¹ /stem/ ▶ n. **1** the main body or stalk of a plant or shrub, typically rising above ground but occasionally subterranean. ■ the stalk supporting a fruit, flower, or leaf, and attaching it to a larger branch, twig, or stalk. **2** a long and thin supportive or main section of something: *the main stem of the wing feathers.* ■ the slender part of a wineglass between the base and the bowl. ■ the tube of a tobacco pipe. ■ a rod or cylinder in a mechanism, for example the sliding shaft of a bolt or the winding pin of a watch. ■ a vertical stroke in a letter or musical note. **3** Gram. the root or main part of a noun, adjective, or other word, to which inflections or formative elements are added; the part that appears unchanged throughout the cases and derivatives of a noun,

persons of a tense, etc. ■ archaic literary the main line of descent of a family or nation: *the Hellenic tribes were derived from the Aryan stem.* **4** the main upright timber or metal piece at the bow of a ship, to which the ship's sides are joined: *the spines and bow stems of abandoned hulks.* ■ the prow, bows, or whole front section of a vessel: *the quay was packed with freighters moored* **stem to stem** | [as adj.] *the stem rail of a ferry.* See also FROM STEM TO STERN below. **5** informal a pipe used for smoking crack or opium. ▶v. (**stemmed, stem·ming**) **1** [intrans.] (**stem from**) originate in or be caused by: *many of the universities' problems stem from rapid expansion.* **2** [trans.] remove the stems from (fruit or tobacco leaves): *her aunt and her mother were stemming currants on the side porch.* **3** [trans.] (of a boat) make headway against (the tide or current).
– PHRASES **from stem to stern** from the front to the back, esp. of a ship. ■ along the entire length of something; throughout: *the album is a joy from stem to stern.* — **stem·less** adj. **stem·like** /-ˌlīk/ adj. [OE *stemn, stefn*, of Gmc. origin; related to Du. *stam* and Ger. *Stamm*. Sense 4 is rel. to Du. *steven*, Ger. *Steven*.]

stem² ▶v. (**stemmed, stem·ming**) **1** [trans.] stop or restrict (the flow of something): *stem the bleeding.* **2** [intrans.] Skiing slide the tail of one ski or both skis outward in order to turn or slow down. [ME: from ON *stemma*, of Gmc. origin. The skiing term (early 20th C.) is from the Ger. verb *stemmen*.]

stem cell ▶n. Biol. an undifferentiated cell of a multicellular organism that is capable of giving rise to indefinitely more cells of the same type, and from which certain other kinds of cell arise by differentiation.

stem·ma /ˈstemə/ ▶n. (pl. **-ma·ta**) a family tree. ■ a diagram showing the relationship between a text and its various manuscript versions. [17th C.: via L. from Gk. *stemma* 'wreath,' from *stephein* 'wreathe, crown.']

stemmed /stemd/ ▶adj. [attrib.] **1** [in comb.] having a stem of a specified length or kind: *red-stemmed alder bushes.* **2** (of a glass, cup, or dish) having a slender supportive section between the base and bowl: *a stemmed goblet.* **3** (of fruit or leaves) having had the stems removed.

stem turn ▶n. Skiing a turn made by stemming with the upper ski and lifting the lower one parallel to it toward the end of the turn.

stem·ware /ˈstemˌwe(ə)r/ ▶n. goblets and stemmed glasses regarded collectively.

stem-wind·er /ˌwīndər/ (also **stem·wind·er**) ▶n. **1** informal an entertaining and rousing speech: *the speech was a classic stem-winder in the best southern tradition.* **2** dated a watch wound by turning a knob on the end of a stem. [sense 1 from the notion of "winding up" or causing a lively reaction from those listening.]

sten. ▶abbr. ■ stenographer. ■ stenography.

stench /stenCH/ ▶n. a strong and very unpleasant smell: *the stench of rotting fish.* [OE *stenc* 'smell,' of Gmc. origin; rel. to Du. *stank*, Ger. *Gestank*, also to the verb STINK.]

STENCIL

stenciled lettering

sten·cil /ˈstensəl/ ▶n. a thin sheet of cardboard, plastic, or metal with a pattern or letters cut out of it, used to produce the cut design on the surface below by the application of ink or paint through the holes. ■ a design produced by such a sheet: *a floral stencil around the top of the room.* ▶v. (**-ciled, -cil·ing**; Brit. **-cilled, -cil·ling**) [trans.] decorate (a surface) with such a design: *the walls had been* **stenciled with** *designs* | [as n.] (**stenciling**) *the art of stenciling.* ■ produce (a design) with a stencil: *stencil a border around the door* | [as adj.] (**stenciled**) *the stenciled letters.* [18th C.: from earlier *stansel* 'ornament with various colors' (based on L. *scintilla* 'spark').]

Sten·dhal /stenˈdäl; steN-/ (1783–1842), French writer; pen name of *Marie Henri Beyle*. His novels include *Le Rouge et le noir* (1830).

Sten·gel /ˈsteNGgəl/, Casey (1890–1975), US baseball player and manager; born *Charles Dillon Stengel*. As a manager 1934–65, mostly with the New York Yankees, he was famed for his championship seasons and his sarcastic wit.

Sten gun /ˈsten/ ▶n. a type of lightweight British submachine gun. [1940s: from the initials of the inventors' surnames, *S*hepherd and *T*urpin, suggested by BREN.]

sten·o /ˈstenō/ ▶n. (pl. **-os**) informal a stenographer: *it was written by the steno herself.* ■ [as adj.] short for STENOGRAPHY: *the steno pool* | *I carry a steno pad and two pens.*

ste·nog·ra·phy /stəˈnägrəfē/ ▶n. the action or process of writing in shorthand or taking dictation. — **ste·nog·ra·pher** /-fər/ n. **sten·o·graph·ic** /ˌstenəˈgrafik/ adj. [17th C.: from Gk. *stenos* 'narrow' + -GRAPHY.]

ste·no·ha·line /ˌstenəˈhālīn; -halīn/ ▶adj. Ecol. (of an aquatic organism) able to tolerate only a narrow range of salinity. Often contrasted with EURYHALINE. [1930s: from Gk. *stenos* 'narrow' + *halinos* 'of salt.']

ste·no·sis /stəˈnōsis/ ▶n. (pl. **-ses** /-ˌsēz/) Med. the abnormal narrowing of a passage in the body. — **ste·nosed** /stəˈnōst; -nōzd/ adj. **ste·nos·ing** /-ˈnōsiNG; -ˈnōz-/ adj. **ste·not·ic** /stəˈnätik/ adj. [19th C.: mod. L., from Gk. *stenōsis* 'narrowing,' from *stenoun* 'make narrow,' from *stenos* 'narrow.']

sten·o·ther·mal /ˌstenəˈTHərməl/ ▶adj. Ecol. (of an organism) able to tolerate only a small range of temperature. Often contrasted with EURYTHERMAL. [19th C.: from Gk. *stenos* 'narrow' + THERMAL.]

sten·o·top·ic /ˌstenəˈtäpik/ ▶adj. Ecol. (of an organism) able to tolerate only a restricted range of habitats or ecological conditions. Often contrasted with EURYTOPIC. [1940s: from Gk. *stenos* 'narrow' + *topos* 'place' + -IC.]

sten·o·type /ˈstenəˌtīp/ ▶n. a machine resembling a typewriter that is used for recording speech in syllables or phonemes. — **sten·o·typ·ist** /-ˌtīpist/ n. **sten·o·typ·y** /-ˌtīpē/ n. [19th C.: from STENOGRAPHY + TYPE.]

stent /stent/ ▶n. Med. a tubular support placed temporarily inside a blood vessel, canal, or duct to aid healing or relieve an obstruction. ■ an impression or cast of a part or body cavity, used to maintain pressure so as to promote healing, esp. of a skin graft. [19th C.: from the name of Charles T. *Stent* (1807–85), English dentist. The sense 'tubular support' dates from the 1960s.]

sten·tor /ˈstenˌtôr; ˈstentər/ ▶n. **1** literary a person with a powerful voice. **2** Zool. a sedentary trumpet-shaped single-celled animal (genus *Stentor*, phylum Ciliophora) that is widespread in fresh water. [17th C.: from Gk. *Stentōr*, the name of a herald in the Trojan War.]

sten·to·ri·an /stenˈtôrēən/ ▶adj. (of a person's voice) loud and powerful: *he introduced me to the staff with a stentorian announcement.*

step /step/ ▶n. **1** an act or movement of putting one leg in front of the other in walking or running: *Ron took a step back* | *she turned and retraced her steps.* ■ the distance covered by such a movement: *Richard came a couple of steps nearer.* ■ [usu. in sing.] a person's particular way of walking: *she left the room with a springy step.* ■ one of the sequences of movement of the feet that make up a dance. ■ a short or easily walked distance: *the market is only a short step from the end of the lake.* **2** a flat surface, esp. one in a series, on which to place one's foot when moving from one level to another: *the bottom step of the staircase* | *a flight of marble steps.* ■ a doorstep: *there was a pint of milk on the step.* ■ a rung of a ladder. ■ Climbing a foothold cut in a slope of ice. ■ a block, typically fixed to the vessel's keel, on which the base of a mast is seated. ■ Physics an abrupt change in the value of a quantity, esp. voltage. **3** a measure or action, esp. one of a series taken in order to deal with or achieve a particular thing: *the government must* **take steps** *to discourage age discrimination* | *a major step forward in the fight against terrorism.* ■ a stage in a gradual process: *sales are up, which is a step in the right direction.* ■ a particular position or grade on an ascending or hierarchical scale: *the first step on the managerial ladder.* **4** Music an interval in a scale; a tone (whole step) or semitone (half step). **5** step aerobics: [as adj.] *a step class.* ▶v. (**stepped, step·ping**) **1** [intrans.] lift and set down one's foot or one foot after the other in order to walk somewhere or move to a new position: *Claudia tried to step back* | *I accidentally stepped on his foot.* ■ [as imper.] used as a polite or deferential way of asking someone to walk a short distance for a particular purpose: *please step this way.* ■ (**step it**) dated perform a dance: *they stepped it down the room between the lines of dancers.* ■ take a particular course of action: *young men have temporarily stepped out of the labor market.* **2** [trans.] Naut. set up (a mast) in its step.
– PHRASES **break step** stop walking or marching in step with others. **fall into step** change the way one is walking so that one is walking in step with another person. **in** (or **out of**) **step** putting (or not putting) one's feet forward alternately in the same rhythm as the people one is walking, marching, or dancing with. ■ fig. conforming (or not conforming) to what others are doing or thinking: *the party is clearly* **out of step with** *voters.* ■ Physics (of two or more oscillations or other cyclic phenomena) having (or not having) the same frequency and always in the same phase. **keep step** remain walking, marching, or dancing in step. **one step ahead** managing to avoid competition or danger from someone or something: *I try to keep one step ahead of the rest of the staff.* **step by step** so as to progress gradually and carefully from one stage to the next: *I'll explain it to you step by step* | [as adj.] *a step-by-step guide.* **step into someone's shoes** take control of a task or job from another person. **step on it** (or **step on the gas**) informal go faster, typically in a motor vehicle. **step** (or **tread**) **on someone's toes** offend someone by encroaching on their area of responsibility. **step out of line** behave inappropriately or disobediently.
– PHRASAL VERBS **step aside** another way of saying STEP DOWN below. **step back** mentally withdraw from a situation in order to consider it objectively. **step down** withdraw or resign from an important position or office. **step forward** offer one's help or services: *a company has stepped forward to sponsor the team.* **step in** become involved in a difficult or problematic situation, esp. in order to help or prevent something from happening. ■ act as a substitute for someone: *Lucy stepped in at very short notice to take Joan's place.* **step out 1** leave a room or building, typically for a short time. **2** informal go out with: *he was* **stepping out with** *a redheaded waitress.* **3** walk with long or vigorous steps: *she enjoyed the outing, stepping out manfully.* **step something up** increase the amount, speed, or intensity of something. ■ increase voltage using a transformer. — **step·like** /-ˌlīk/ adj. [OE *stæpe, stepe* (n.), *stæppan, steppan* (v.), of Gmc. origin; rel. to Du. *steppen* and Ger. *stapfen*.]

step- ▶comb. form denoting a relationship resulting from a remarriage: *stepmother.* [OE *stēop-*, from a Gmc. base meaning 'bereaved, orphaned.']

step·broth·er /ˈstepˌbrəTHər/ ▶n. a son of one's stepparent, by a marriage other than that with one's own father or mother.

step·child /ˈstepˌCHīld/ ▶n. (pl. **-chil·dren**) a child of one's husband or wife by a previous marriage. [OE *stēopcild* (see STEP-, CHILD).]

step·daugh·ter /ˈstepˌdôtər; ˈstepˌdätər/ ▶n. a daughter of one's husband or wife by a previous marriage.

step·fam·i·ly /ˈstepˌfam(ə)lē/ ▶n. (pl. **-lies**) a family that is formed on the remarriage of a divorced or widowed person and that includes one or more children.

step·fa·ther /ˈstepˌfäT͟Hər/ ▶ **n.** a man who is married to one's mother after the divorce of one's parents or the death of one's father.

step func·tion ▶ **n.** Math. & Electron. a function that increases or decreases abruptly from one constant value to another.

steph·a·no·tis /ˌstefəˈnōtis/ ▶ **n.** a Madagascan climbing plant (genus *Stephanotis*, family Asclepiadaceae) that is cultivated for its fragrant waxy white flowers. [mod. L., from Gk., 'fit for a wreath,' from *stephanos* 'wreath.']

Ste·phen /ˈstēvən/ (*c.* 1097–1154), king of England 1135–54, grandson of William the Conqueror.

Ste·phen, St.[1] (died *c.* 35), the first Christian martyr. He was one of the original seven deacons in Jerusalem appointed by the Apostles.

Ste·phen, St.[2] (*c.* 977–1038), king and patron saint of Hungary; reigned 1000–38. He was the first king of Hungary.

Ste·phen·son /ˈstēvənsən/, George (1781–1848), British engineer; a pioneer of steam locomotives and railways. With his son Robert (1803–59) he built the *Rocket* (1829), the prototype for all future steam locomotives.

step-in ▶ **adj.** [attrib.] denoting a garment or pair of shoes without fasteners that is put on by being stepped into. ▶ **n.** **(step-ins)** a pair of such shoes; slip-ons.

step·lad·der /ˈstepˌladər/ ▶ **n.** a short folding ladder with flat steps and a small platform.

step·moth·er /ˈstepˌməT͟Hər/ ▶ **n.** a woman who is married to one's father after the divorce of one's parents or the death of one's mother.

step·par·ent /ˈstepˌparənt; -ˌpe(ə)r-/ ▶ **n.** a stepfather or stepmother.

steppe /step/ ▶ **n.** (often **steppes**) a large area of flat unforested grassland in southeastern Europe or Siberia. [17th C.: from Russ. *step'*.]

stepped /stept/ ▶ **adj.** having or formed into a step or series of steps: *a building with stepped access.* ■ carried out or occurring in stages or with pauses rather than continuously: *a stepped scale of discounts.*

step·per /ˈstepər/ ▶ **n.** **1** an electric motor or other device that moves or rotates in a series of small discrete steps. **2** a portable block used in step aerobics. **3** dated a horse with a brisk, attractive walking gait: *choosing a showy gray stepper for May's brougham.* ■ a person who steps, esp. a dancer.

step·ping·stone /ˈstepiNGˌstōn/ ▶ **n.** a raised stone used singly or in a series as a place on which to step when crossing a stream or muddy area. ■ fig. an undertaking or event that helps one to make progress toward a specified goal: *the school championships are a steppingstone to international competition.*

step re·sponse ▶ **n.** Electron. the output of a device in response to an abrupt change in voltage.

step·sis·ter /ˈstepˌsistər/ ▶ **n.** a daughter of one's stepparent by a marriage other than with one's own father or mother.

step·son /ˈstepˌsən/ ▶ **n.** a son of one's husband or wife by a previous marriage. [OE *stēopsunu* (see STEP-, SON).]

step·wise /ˈstepˌwīz/ ▶ **adv. & adj.** **1** in a series of distinct stages; not continuously: [as adv.] *concentrations of the acid tend to decrease stepwise.* **2** Music (of melodic motion) moving by adjacent scale steps rather than leaps: *crackling solos and juicy, stepwise guitar counterpoints.*

-ster ▶ **suffix** **1** denoting a person engaged in or associated with a particular activity or thing: *gangster* | *songster.* **2** denoting a person with a particular quality: *youngster.* [OE *-estre, -istre*, etc., of Gmc. origin.]

ste·ra·di·an /stəˈrādēən/ (abbr.: **sr**) ▶ **n.** the SI unit of solid angle, equal to the angle at the center of a sphere subtended by a part of the surface equal in area to the square of the radius. [19th C.: from Gk. *stereos* 'solid' + RADIAN.]

ster·ane /ˈsterˌān; ˈsti(ə)r-/ ▶ **n.** Chem. any of a class of saturated polycyclic hydrocarbons that are found in crude oils and are derived from the sterols of ancient organisms. [1950s: from STEROID + -ANE[2].]

ster·co·ra·ceous /ˌstərkəˈrāSHəs/ ▶ **adj.** tech. consisting of or resembling dung or feces. ■ (of an insect) living in dung. [18th C.: from L. *stercus, stercor-* 'dung' + -ACEOUS.]

stere /sti(ə)r/ ▶ **n.** a unit of volume equal to one cubic meter. [18th C.: from Fr. *stère*, from Gk. *stereos* 'solid.']

ster·e·o /ˈsterēˌō; ˈsti(ə)r-/ ▶ **n.** (pl. **-os**) **1** sound that is directed through two or more speakers so that it seems to surround the listener and to come from more than one source; stereophonic sound. ■ a sound system, typically including a CD, tape, or record player, that has two or more speakers and produces stereo sound. **2** Photog. another term for STEREOSCOPE. **3** Print. short for STEREOTYPE. ▶ **adj.** **1** short for STEREOPHONIC: *stereo equipment* | *stereo sound.* **2** Photog. short for STEREOSCOPIC (see STEREOSCOPE).

stereo- ▶ **comb. form** relating to solid forms having three dimensions: *stereography.* ■ relating to a three-dimensional effect, arrangement, etc.: *stereochemistry* | *stereophonic* | *stereoscope.* [from Gk. *stereos* 'solid.']

ster·e·o·bate /ˈsterēəˌbāt; ˈsti(ə)r-/ ▶ **n.** Archit. a solid mass of masonry serving as a foundation for a wall or row of columns. [19th C.: from Fr. *stéréobate*, via L. from Gk. *stereobatēs*, from *stereos* 'solid' + *batēs* 'base' (from *bainein* 'to walk').]

ster·e·o·chem·is·try /ˌsterēōˈkeməstrē; ˌsti(ə)r-/ ▶ **n.** the branch of chemistry concerned with the three-dimensional arrangement of atoms and molecules and the effect of this on chemical reactions. — **ster·e·o·chem·i·cal** /-ˈkemikəl/ **adj.** **ster·e·o·chem·i·cal·ly** /-ˈkemik(ə)lē/ **adv.**

ster·e·o·gram /ˈsterēəˌgram; ˈsti(ə)r-/ ▶ **n.** **1** a diagram or computer-generated image giving a three-dimensional representation of a solid object or surface. **2** another term for STEREOGRAPH (see STEREOGRAPHY).

ster·e·og·ra·phy /ˌsterēˈägrəfē; ˌsti(ə)r-/ ▶ **n.** the depiction or representation of three-dimensional things by projection onto a two-dimensional surface, e.g., in cartography. — **ster·e·o·graph** /ˈsterēəˌgraf; ˈsti(ə)r-/ **n.** **ster·e·o·graph·ic** /ˌsterēəˈgrafik; ˌsti(ə)r-/ **adj.**

ster·e·o·i·so·mer /ˌsterēōˈīsəmər; ˌsti(ə)r-/ ▶ **n.** Chem. each of two or more compounds differing only in the spatial arrangement of their atoms. — **ster·e·o·i·so·mer·ic** /-ˌīsəˈmerik/ **adj.** **ster·e·o·i·som·er·ism** /-īˈsäməˌrizəm/ **n.**

ster·e·om·e·try /ˌsterēˈämitrē; ˌsti(ə)r-/ ▶ **n.** Geom. the measurement of solid bodies.

ster·e·o·phon·ic /ˌsterēəˈfänik; ˌsti(ə)r-/ ▶ **adj.** (of sound recording and reproduction) using two or more channels of transmission and reproduction so that the reproduced sound seems to surround the listener and to come from more than one source. — **ster·e·o·phon·i·cal·ly** /-ik(ə)lē/ **adv.** **ster·e·oph·o·ny** /-ˈäfənē/ **n.**

ster·e·op·sis /ˌsterēˈäpsis; ˌsti(ə)r-/ ▶ **n.** the perception of depth produced by the reception in the brain of visual stimuli from both eyes in combination; binocular vision. — **ster·e·op·tic** /-ˈäptik/ **adj.** [20th C.: from STEREO- 'three-dimensional' + Gk. *opsis* 'sight.']

ster·e·op·ti·con /ˌsterēˈäptiˌkän; ˌsti(ə)r-/ ▶ **n.** a slide projector that combines two images to create a three-dimensional effect, or makes one image dissolve into another. [19th C.: from STEREO- 'three-dimensional' + Gk. *optikon*, neut. of *optikos* 'relating to vision.']

ster·e·o·scope /ˈsterēəˌskōp; ˈsti(ə)r-/ ▶ **n.** a device by which two photographs of the same object taken at slightly different angles are viewed together, creating an impression of depth and solidity. — **ster·e·o·scop·ic** /ˌsterēəˈskäpik; ˌsti(ə)r-/ **adj.** **ster·e·o·scop·i·cal·ly** /ˌsterēˈäskəpē; ˌsti(ə)r-/ **adv.** **ster·e·os·co·py** /ˌsterēˈäskəpē/ **n.**

ster·e·o sep·a·ra·tion ▶ **n.** see SEPARATION (sense 2).

ster·e·o·spe·cif·ic /ˌsterēōspəˈsifik; ˌsti(ə)r-/ ▶ **adj.** Chem. (of a reaction) preferentially producing a particular stereoisomeric form of the product, irrespective of the configuration of the reactant. — **ster·e·o·spe·cif·i·cal·ly** /-ik(ə)lē/ **adv.** **ster·e·o·spec·i·fic·i·ty** /-ˌspesəˈfisitē/ **n.**

ster·e·o·spon·dyl /ˌsterēəˈspändl; ˌsti(ə)r-/ ▶ **n.** an extinct amphibian (suborder Stereospondyli, order Temnospondyli) with a broad flat head, occurring in the Permian and Triassic periods. [20th C.: from mod. L. *Stereospondyli* (pl.), from Gk. *stereos* 'solid' + *spondulos* 'vertebra.']

ster·e·o·type /ˈsterēəˌtīp; ˈsti(ə)r-/ ▶ **n.** **1** a widely held but fixed and oversimplified image or idea of a particular type of person or thing: *sexual and racial stereotypes.* ■ a person or thing that conforms to such an image. **2** a relief printing plate cast in a mold made from composed type or an original plate. ▶ **v.** [trans.] view or represent as a stereotype: [as adj.] **(stereotyped)** *the film is weakened by its stereotyped characters.* — **ster·e·o·typ·ic** /ˌsterēəˈtipik; ˌsti(ə)r-/ **adj.** **ster·e·o·typ·i·cal** /ˌsterēəˈtipikəl; ˌsti(ə)r-/ **adj.** **ster·e·o·typ·i·cal·ly** /ˌsterēəˈtipik(ə)lē; ˌsti(ə)r-/ **adv.** [18th C.: from Fr. *stéréotype* (adj.).]

ster·e·o·typ·y /ˈsterēəˌtīpē; ˈsti(ə)r-/ ▶ **n.** the persistent repetition of an act, esp. by an animal, for no obvious purpose.

ster·ic /ˈsterik; ˈsti(ə)r-/ ▶ **adj.** Chem. of or relating to the spatial arrangement of atoms in a molecule, esp. as it affects chemical reactions. — **ster·i·cal·ly** /ik(ə)lē/ **adv.** [19th C.: formed irregularly from Gk. *stereos* 'solid' + -IC.]

ste·rig·ma /stəˈrigmə/ ▶ **n.** (pl. **-ma·ta** /-mətə/) Bot. (in some fungi) a spore-bearing projection from a cell. [19th C.: mod. L., from Gk. *stērigma* 'a support,' from *stērizein* 'to support.']

ster·i·lant /ˈsterələnt/ ▶ **n.** an agent used to destroy microorganisms; a disinfectant. ■ a chemical agent used to destroy pests and diseases in the soil, esp. fungi and nematodes.

ster·ile /ˈsterəl/ ▶ **adj.** **1** not able to produce children or young: *the disease had made him sterile.* ■ (of a plant) not able to produce fruit or seeds. ■ (of land or soil) too poor in quality to produce crops. ■ lacking in imagination, creativity, or excitement; uninspiring or unproductive: *he found the fraternity's teachings sterile.* **2** free from bacteria or other living microorganisms; totally clean: *a sterile needle and syringes.* — **ster·ile·ly** /ˈsterə(l)lē/ **adv.** **ste·ril·i·ty** /stəˈrilitē/ **n.** [ME: from OFr., or from L. *sterilis*; rel. to Gk. *steira* 'barren cow.']

ster·i·lize /ˈsterəˌlīz/ ▶ **v.** [trans.] **1** make (something) free from bacteria or other living microorganisms: *babies' feeding equipment can be cleaned and sterilized* | [as adj.] **(sterilized)** *sterilized jars.* **2** (usu. **be sterilized**) deprive (a person or animal) of the ability to produce offspring, typically by removing or blocking the sex organs. ■ make (land or water) unable to produce crops or support life. — **ster·i·liz·a·ble** **adj.** **ster·i·li·za·tion** /ˌsterələˈzāSHən/ **n.** **ster·i·liz·er** **n.**

ster·let /ˈstərlit/ ▶ **n.** a small sturgeon (*Acipenser ruthenus*) of the Danube basin and Caspian Sea area, farmed and commercially fished for its flesh and caviar. [16th C.: from Russ. *sterlyad'*.]

ster·ling /ˈstərliNG/ ▶ **n.** British money. ■ short for STERLING SILVER: [as adj.] *a sterling spoon.* ▶ **adj.** (of a person or their work, efforts, or qualities) excellent or valuable: *this organization does sterling work for youngsters.* [ME: prob. from *steorra* 'star' + -LING (because some early Norman pennies bore a small star).]

ster·ling sil·ver ▶ **n.** silver of 92¼ percent purity.

Stern /stərn/, Isaac (1920–2001), US violinist; born in Russia. He made his New York debut in 1937 at Carnegie Hall.

stern[1] /stərn/ ▶ **adj.** (of a person or their manner) serious and unrelenting, esp. in the assertion of authority and exercise of discipline: *a smile transformed his stern face | Mama looked stern.* ■ (of an act or statement) strict and severe; using extreme measures or terms: *stern measures to restrict growth of traffic.* ■ (of competition or opposition) putting someone or something under extreme pressure: *the past year has been a stern test of the ability of local industry.*
– PHRASES **be made of sterner stuff** have a stronger character and be more able to overcome problems than others. [from Shakespeare's *Julius Caesar* (III. 2. 93).] **the sterner sex** archaic men regarded collectively and in contrast to women. — **stern·ly adv. stern·ness n.** [OE *styrne*, prob. from the West Gmc. base of the verb STARE.]

stern[2] ▶ **n.** the rearmost part of a ship or boat. ■ humorous a person's bottom. — **sterned** /stərnd/ **adj.** [in comb.] *a square-sterned vessel* **stern·most** /-ˌmōst/ **adj. stern·ward** /-wərd/ **adv.** [ME: prob. from ON *stjórn* 'steering,' from *stýra* 'to steer.']

ster·nal /ˈstərnl/ ▶ **adj.** of or relating to the sternum.

stern·drive /ˈstərnˌdrīv/ ▶ **n.** an inboard engine connected to an outboard drive unit at the rear of a powerboat.

Stern Gang /ˈstərn/ a militant Zionist group that campaigned in Palestine during the 1940s for the creation of a Jewish state.

ster·nite /ˈstərˌnīt/ ▶ **n.** Entomol. (in an insect) a sclerotized plate forming the sternum of a segment. Compare with TERGITE.

Ster·no /ˈstərnō/ ▶ **n.** trademark flammable hydrocarbon jelly supplied in cans for use as fuel. [20th C.: from *Sternau* and Co., New York, + **-o**.]

ster·no·clei·do·mas·toid /ˌstərnōˌklīdəˈmastoid/ (also **sternocleidomastoid muscle**) ▶ **n.** Anat. each of a pair of long muscles that connect the sternum, clavicle, and mastoid process of the temporal bone and serve to turn and nod the head.

stern·post /ˈstərnˌpōst/ ▶ **n.** the central upright structure at the stern of a vessel, typically bearing the rudder.

stern·sheets /ˈstərnˌsʜēts/ ▶ **plural n.** the flooring planks or seating in a boat's after section.

ster·num /ˈstərnəm/ ▶ **n.** (pl. **-nums** or **-na** /-nə/) the breastbone. ■ Zool. a thickened ventral plate on each segment of the body of an arthropod. [17th C.: mod. L., from Gk. *sternon* 'chest.']

ster·nu·ta·tion /ˌstərnyəˈtāsʜən/ ▶ **n.** formal the action of sneezing. [ME: from L. *sternutatio(n-)*, from the verb *sternutare*, frequentative of *sternuere* 'to sneeze.']

ster·nu·ta·tor /ˈstərnyəˌtātər/ ▶ **n.** tech. an agent that causes sneezing. ■ an agent used in chemical warfare that causes irritation to the nose and eyes, chest pain, and nausea. — **ster·nu·ta·to·ry** /stərˈnyōōtəˌtôrē/ **adj. & n.** (pl. **-ries**).

stern·way /ˈstərnˌwā/ ▶ **n.** backward movement of a ship: *we begin making sternway toward the shoal.*

stern·wheel·er /ˈstərnˌ(h)wēlər/ ▶ **n.** a steamer propelled by a paddle wheel positioned at the stern.

ste·roid /ˈsterˌoid; ˈsti(ə)r-/ ▶ **n.** Biochem. any of a large class of organic compounds with a characteristic molecular structure containing four rings of carbon atoms (three six-membered and one five). ■ short for ANABOLIC STEROID. — **ste·roi·dal** /steˈroidl; sti-/ **adj.** [1930s: from STEROL + -OID.]

ste·rol /ˈsterôl; -äl; ˈsti(ə)r-/ ▶ **n.** Biochem. any of a group of naturally occurring unsaturated steroid alcohols. [20th C.: independent usage of the ending of words such as CHOLESTEROL and ERGOSTEROL.]

ster·to·rous /ˈstərtərəs/ ▶ **adj.** (of breathing) noisy and labored. — **ster·to·rous·ly adv.** [19th C.: from mod. L. *stertor* 'snoring sound' (from L. *stertere* 'to snore') + -OUS.]

stet /stet/ ▶ **v.** (**stet·ted, stet·ting**) [intrans.] let it stand (used as an instruction on a printed proof to indicate that a correction or alteration should be ignored). ■ [trans.] write such an instruction against (something corrected or deleted). ▶ **n.** such an instruction made on a printed proof. [L., 'let it stand,' from *stare* 'to stand.']

steth·o·scope /ˈsteTHəˌskōp/ ▶ **n.** a medical instrument for listening to the action of someone's heart or breathing, typically having a small disk-shaped resonator that is placed against the chest and two tubes connected to earpieces. — **steth·o·scop·ic** /ˌsteTHəˈskäpik/ **adj.** [19th C.: from Fr. *stéthoscope*, from Gk. *stēthos* 'breast' + *skopein* 'look at.']

stethoscope

Stet·son /ˈstetsən/ ▶ **n.** trademark a hat with a high crown and a wide brim, traditionally worn by cowboys. [19th C.: for John B. *Stetson* (1830–1906), American hat manufacturer.]

Stet·tin /sʜteˈtēn/ German name for SZCZECIN.

Steu·ben /ˈsʜtoibən; ˈst(y)ōōbən/, Friedrich Wilhelm Ludolf Gerhard Augustin von (1730–94), American army officer; born in Prussia. Appointed inspector general of the Continental Army in 1778, he is credited with creating the models of discipline, organization, and tactical strategies that are still fundamental to the modern US Army.

ste·ve·dore /ˈstēvəˌdôr/ ▶ **n.** a person employed, or a contractor engaged, at a dock to load and unload cargo from ships. [18th C.: from Sp. *estivador*, from *estivar* 'stow a cargo,' from L. *stipare*.]

Ste·ven·graph /ˈstēvənˌgraf/ ▶ **n.** a type of small picture made from brightly colored woven silk, produced during the late 19th century. [named after Thomas *Stevens* (1828–88), English weaver, whose firm made them.]

Ste·vens[1] /ˈstēvənz/, John Paul (1920–), US Supreme Court associate justice 1975– .

Ste·vens[2], Wallace (1879–1955), US poet. His *Collected Poems* (1954) won a Pulitzer Prize.

Ste·ven·son[1] /ˈstēvənsən/, Adlai Ewing (1900–1965), US politician. The governor of Illinois 1949–53, he was twice (1952, 1956) the unsuccessful Democratic candidate for the presidency.

Ste·ven·son[2], Robert Louis Balfour (1850–94), Scottish writer. He wrote *Treasure Island* (1883) and *Kidnapped* (1886).

ste·vi·a /ˈstēvēə; ˈstev-/ ▶ **n.** a sweet compound of the glycoside class obtained from the leaves of a South American shrub (*Stevia rebaudiana*) of the daisy family and used as a food sweetener. [1930s: after P. J. *Esteve* (died 1566), Spanish botanist.]

stew[1] /st(y)ōō/ ▶ **n.** **1** a dish of meat and vegetables cooked slowly in liquid in a closed dish or pan: *lamb stew | add to casseroles, stews, and sauces.* **2** [in sing.] informal a state of great anxiety or agitation: *I suppose he's all in a stew.* ▶ **v.** [trans.] cook (meat, fruit, or other food) slowly in liquid in a closed dish or pan: *a new way to stew rhubarb.* ■ [intrans.] (of meat, fruit, or other food) be cooked in such a way. ■ [intrans.] informal remain in a heated or stifling atmosphere: *sweaty clothes left to stew in a plastic bag.* ■ [intrans.] informal worry about something, esp. on one's own: *James will be expecting us, so we will let him stew a bit.* ■ [intrans.] Brit. (of tea) become strong and bitter with prolonged brewing. ■ (**be stewed in**) literary be steeped in or imbued with: *politics there are stewed in sexual prejudice and privilege.*
– PHRASES **stew in one's own juice** informal suffer anxiety or the unpleasant consequences of one's own actions without the consoling intervention of others. [ME: from OFr. *estuve* (rel. to *estuver* 'heat in steam'), prob. based on Gk. *tuphos* 'smoke, steam.']

stew[2] ▶ **n.** informal an air steward or stewardess. [1970s: abbr.]

stew·ard /ˈst(y)ōōərd/ ▶ **n.** **1** a person who looks after the passengers on a ship, aircraft, or train and brings them meals. ■ a person responsible for supplies of food to a college, club, or other institution. **2** an official appointed to supervise arrangements or keep order at a large public event, for example a sporting event. ■ short for SHOP STEWARD. **3** a person employed to manage another's property, esp. a large house or estate. ■ a person who takes care of something. ▶ **v.** [trans.] **1** (of an official) supervise arrangements or keep order at (a large public event): *the event was organized and stewarded properly.* **2** manage or look after (another's property). — **stew·ard·ship n.** [OE *stiweard*, from *stig* (prob. in the sense 'house, hall') + *weard* 'ward.']

stew·ard·ess /ˈst(y)ōōərdis/ ▶ **n.** a woman who is employed to look after the passengers on a ship or aircraft.

Stew·art[1] ▶ **adj. & n.** var. of STUART[5].

Stew·art[2], Potter (1915–85), US Supreme Court associate justice 1958–81.

stewed /st(y)ōōd/ ▶ **adj.** (of food) cooked slowly in liquid in a closed dish or pan: *stewed apples.* ■ [predic.] informal drunk: *we got stewed at their party.* ■ Brit. (of tea) tasting strong and bitter because of prolonged brewing.

stew·ing /ˈst(y)ōōiɴɢ/ ▶ **adj.** [attrib.] (of meat or other food) suitable for stewing: *a stewing chicken.*

stew·pot /ˈst(y)ōōˌpät/ ▶ **n.** a large pot in which stews are cooked.

St. Ex. ▶ **abbr.** Stock Exchange.

stg ▶ **abbr.** sterling.

stge. ▶ **abbr.** storage.

Sth ▶ **abbr.** south.

sthen·ic /ˈsTHenik/ ▶ **adj.** Med., dated of or having a high or excessive level of strength and energy. [18th C.: from Gk. *sthenos* 'strength,' on the pattern of *asthenic*.]

stib·nite /ˈstibnīt/ ▶ **n.** a lead-gray mineral, typically occurring as striated prismatic crystals, that consists of antimony sulfide and is the chief ore of antimony. [19th C.: from L. *stibium* 'black antimony' + -INE[4] + -ITE[1].]

sti·cho·myth·i·a /ˌstikəˈmiTHēə/ ▶ **n.** dialogue in which two characters speak alternate lines of verse, used as a stylistic device in ancient Greek drama. [19th C.: mod. L., from Gk. *stikhomuthia*, from *stikhos* 'row, line of verse' + *muthos* 'speech, talk.']

stick[1] /stik/ ▶ **n.** **1** a thin piece of wood that has fallen or been cut from a tree. **2** a thin piece of wood that has been trimmed for a particular purpose, in particular: ■ a long piece of wood used for support in walking or as a weapon with which to hit someone or something. ■ (in hockey, polo, and other games) a long implement, typically made of wood, with a head or blade of varying form that is used to hit or direct the ball or puck. ■ [usu. with adj.] a short piece of wood used to impale food: *Popsicle sticks.* ■ fig. a piece of basic furniture: *every stick of furniture just vanished.* ■ (**sticks**) (in field hockey) the foul play of raising the stick above the shoulder. ■ Naut. archaic a mast or spar. ■ (**the sticks**) Brit., informal goalposts. **3** something resembling or likened to a stick, in particular: ■ a long, thin piece of something: *a stick of dynamite | cinnamon sticks.* ■ a quarter-pound rectangular block of butter or margarine. ■ a conductor's baton. ■ a gear or control lever. ■ (in extended and metaphorical use) a very thin person or limb: *the girl was a stick | her arms* *were like sticks.* ■ a number of bombs or paratroopers dropped rapidly from an aircraft. ■ a small group of soldiers assigned to a particular duty: *a stick of heavily armed guards.* ■ informal a marijuana cigarette. **4** a threat of punishment or unwelcome measures (often contrasted with the offer of reward as a means of persuasion): *training that relies more on the carrot than on the stick.* ■ Brit., informal severe criticism or treatment: *I took a lot of stick from the press.* **5** **(the sticks)** informal derog. rural areas far from cities: *a small, dusty town out in the sticks.* **6** [with adj.] informal dated a person of a specified kind: *Janet's not such a bad old stick sometimes.* — **stick·like** /-ˌlīk/ **adj.** [OE *sticca* 'peg, stick, spoon,' of West Gmc. origin; rel. to Du. *stek* 'cutting from a plant' and Ger. *Stecken* 'staff, stick.']

stick[2] ▶ **v.** (past **stuck** /stək/) **1** [trans.] **(stick something in/into/through)** push a sharp or pointed object into or through (something): *he stuck his fork into the sausage | the candle was stuck in a straw-covered bottle.* ■ **(stick something on)** fix something on (a point or pointed object): *stick the balls of wool on knitting needles.* ■ [intrans.] **(stick in/into/through)** (of a pointed object) be or remain fixed with its point embedded in (something): *there was a slim rod sticking into the ground beside me.* ■ [trans.] insert, thrust, or push: *a youth with a cigarette stuck behind one ear | she stuck out her tongue at him.* ■ [intrans.] protrude or extend in a certain direction: *his front teeth stick out | Sue's hair was sticking up at all angles.* ■ [trans.] put somewhere, typically in a quick or careless way: *just stick that sandwich on my desk.* ■ informal used to express angry dismissal of a particular thing: *he told them they could stick the job—he didn't want it anyway.* ■ informal cause to incur an expense or loss: *she stuck me for all of last month's rent.* ■ stab or pierce with a sharp object: [as adj.] **(stuck)** *he screamed like a stuck pig.* **2** [intrans.] adhere or cling to a substance or surface: *the plastic seats stuck to my skin.* ■ [trans.] fasten or cause to adhere to an object or surface: *she stuck the stamp on the envelope.* ■ be or become fixed or jammed in one place as a result of an obstruction: *he drove into a bog, where his wheels stuck fast.* ■ remain in a static condition; fail to progress: *he lost a lot of weight but had stuck at 210 pounds.* ■ (of a feeling or thought) remain persistently in one's mind: *one particular incident sticks in my mind.* ■ informal be or become convincing, established, or regarded as valid: *the authorities couldn't make the charges stick | the name stuck and Anastasia she remained.* ■ (in blackjack and similar card games) decline to add to one's hand. **3** **(be stuck)** be fixed in a particular position or unable to move or be moved: *Sara tried to open the window but it was stuck | the cat's stuck up a tree.* ■ be unable to progress with a task or find the answer or solution to something: *I'm doing the crossword and I've gotten stuck.* ■ [with adverbial of place] informal be or remain in a specified place or situation, typically one perceived as tedious or unpleasant: *I don't want to be stuck in an office all my life.* ■ **(be stuck for)** be at a loss for or in need of. ■ **(be stuck with)** informal be unable to get rid of or escape from. ■ **(be stuck on)** informal be infatuated with.

– PHRASES **get stuck in** (or **into**) Brit., informal start doing (something) enthusiastically or with determination: *we got stuck into the decorating.* **stick at nothing** allow nothing to deter one from achieving one's aim, however wrong or dishonest: *he would stick at nothing to preserve his privileges.* **stick 'em up!** informal hands up! (spoken typically by a person threatening someone else with a gun). **stick in one's throat** (or **craw**) be difficult or impossible to accept; be a source of continuing annoyance. ■ (of words) be difficult or impossible to say. **stick it out** informal put up with or persevere with something difficult or disagreeable. **stick it to** informal treat (someone) harshly or severely. **stick one's neck out** informal risk incurring criticism or anger by acting or speaking boldly. **stick to one's ribs** (of food) be filling and nourishing.

– PHRASAL VERBS **stick around** informal remain in or near a place. **stick at** informal persevere with (a task or endeavor) in a steady and determined way. **stick by 1** continue to support or be loyal to (someone), typically during difficult times. **2** another way of saying STICK TO in sense 2 below. **stick something on** informal place the blame for a mistake or wrongdoing on (someone). **stick out** be extremely noticeable. **stick out for** refuse to accept less than (what one has asked for); persist in demanding (something). **stick to 1** continue or confine oneself to doing or using (a particular thing). ■ not move or digress from (a path or a subject). **2** adhere to (a commitment, belief, or rule). **stick together** informal remain united or mutually loyal. **stick someone/something up** informal rob someone at gunpoint. **stick up for** support or defend (a person or cause). **stick with** informal **1** persevere or continue with. **2** another way of saying STICK BY above. [OE *stician*, of Gmc. origin; rel. to Ger. *sticken* 'embroider,' from an Indo-Eur. root shared by Gk. *stizein* 'to prick,' *stigma* 'a mark' and L. *instigare* 'spur on.']

stick·a·bil·i·ty /ˌstikəˈbilitē/ ▶ **n.** informal a person's ability to persevere with something; staying power: *the secret of success is stickability.*

stick·ball /ˈstikˌbôl/ ▶ **n.** an informal game resembling baseball, played with a stick and a (usually rubber) ball.

stick·er /ˈstikər/ ▶ **n.** an adhesive label or notice, generally printed or illustrated. ■ short for STICKER PRICE.

stick·er price ▶ **n.** the advertised retail price of an item, esp. the price listed on a sticker attached to the window of a new automobile.

stick·er shock ▶ **n.** informal shock or dismay experienced by the potential buyers of a particular product on discovering its high or increased price: *drugstore consumers are feeling the pain of sticker shock as never before.*

stick·ie /ˈstikē/ ▶ **n.** (pl. **-ies**) informal term for POST-IT.

stick·ing plas·ter ▶ **n.** esp. Brit. an adhesive bandage, available in a roll or as individual patches.

stick·ing point ▶ **n.** a point at which an obstacle arises in progress toward an agreement or goal: *Jerusalem emerged as a key sticking point in Israeli–Palestinian negotiations.*

stick in·sect ▶ **n.** another term for WALKING STICK (sense 2).

stick-in-the-mud ▶ **n.** informal a person who is dull and unadventurous and who resists change.

three-spined stickleback

stick·le·back /ˈstikəlˌbak/ ▶ **n.** a small fish (family Gasterosteidae) with sharp spines along its back, able to live in both salt and fresh water and found in both Eurasia and North America. Its several species include the common and widespread **three-spined stickleback** (*Gasterosteus aculeatus*). [ME: from OE *sticel* 'thorn, sting' + *bæc* 'back.']

stick·ler /ˈstik(ə)lər/ ▶ **n. 1** a person who insists on a certain quality or type of behavior: *a stickler for accuracy | a stickler when it comes to timekeeping.* **2** a difficult problem; a conundrum. [16th C.: from obsolete *stickle* 'be umpire,' alt. of obs. *stightle* 'to control,' frequentative of OE *stiht(i)an* 'set in order.']

stick-nest rat ▶ **n.** a fluffy-haired gregarious Australian rat (genus *Leporillus*) that builds nests of interwoven sticks.

stick·pin /ˈstikˌpin/ ▶ **n.** a straight pin with an ornamental head, worn to keep a tie in place or as a brooch.

stick·seed /ˈstikˌsēd/ ▶ **n.** a plant (genera *Hackelia* and *Lappula*) of the borage family that bears small barbed seeds.

stick shift ▶ **n.** a manual transmission.

stick-to-it·ive·ness /stik ˈto͞oitivnis/ ▶ **n.** informal perseverance; persistence.

stick·um /ˈstikəm/ ▶ **n.** informal a sticky or adhesive substance; gum or paste. [20th C.: from the verb STICK[2] + *-um* (representing the pronoun *them*).]

stick·up /ˈstikˌəp/ ▶ **n.** informal an armed robbery in which a gun is used to threaten people.

stick·weed /ˈstikˌwēd/ ▶ **n.** any of a number of North American plants with hooked or barbed seeds, e.g., ragweed.

stick·y /ˈstikē/ ▶ **adj.** **(stick·i·er, stick·i·est) 1** tending or designed to stick to things on contact or covered with something that sticks: *her sticky bubblegum | sticky tape.* ■ (of a substance) glutinous; viscous: *the dough should be moist but not sticky.* ■ (of prices, interest rates, or wages) slow to change or react to change. **2** (of the weather) hot and damp; muggy. ■ damp with sweat: *she felt hot and sticky and changed her clothes.* **3** informal involving problems; difficult or awkward: *the relationship is going through a sticky patch.*

– PHRASES **sticky fingers** informal a propensity to steal. — **stick·i·ly** /ˈstikīlē/ **adv.** **stick·i·ness** **n.**

stick·y end ▶ **n.** Biochem. an end of a DNA double helix at which a few unpaired nucleotides of one strand extend beyond the other.

stick·y-fin·gered ▶ **adj.** informal given to stealing: *a sticky-fingered con artist.*

stic·tion /ˈstikshən/ ▶ **n.** Physics the friction that tends to prevent stationary surfaces from being set in motion.

Stieg·litz /ˈstēglits/, Alfred (1864–1946), US photographer; husband of Georgia O'Keeffe. He pioneered the establishment of photography as a fine art.

stiff /stif/ ▶ **adj. 1** not easily bent or changed in shape; rigid: *stiff cardboard.* ■ not moving as freely as is usual or desirable; difficult to turn or operate: *the shower tap is a little stiff.* ■ (of a person or part of the body) unable to move easily and without pain: *a stiff back.* ■ (of a person or their manner) not relaxed or friendly; constrained: *she greeted him with stiff politeness.* ■ viscous; thick: *add wheat until the mixture is quite stiff.* **2** severe or strong: *a stiff increase in taxes.* ■ (of a wind) blowing strongly: *a stiff breeze stirring the lake.* ■ requiring strength or effort; difficult: *a long stiff climb up the bare hillside.* ■ (of an alcoholic drink) strong: *a stiff measure of brandy.* **3** [predic.] **(stiff with)** informal full of: *the place is stiff with alarm systems.* **4** (— **stiff**) informal having a specified unpleasant feeling to an extreme extent: *I was bored stiff with my project.* **5** Bridge a card that is the only one of its suit in a hand: *two red aces and a stiff club.* ▶ **n.** informal **1** a dead body. **2** a boring, conventional person: *ordinary working stiffs in respectable offices.* ■ informal a fellow: *the lucky stiff!* ▶ **v.** [trans.] informal **1** (often **be stiffed**) cheat (someone) out of something, esp. money: *several workers were stiffed out of their pay.* ■ fail to leave (someone) a tip. **2** ignore deliberately; snub. ■ fail to appear for a promised engagement or appointment: *he stiffed us and didn't show up.* **3** kill: *I want to get those pigs who stiffed your doctor.* ■ [intrans.] be unsuccessful: *as soon as he began singing about the wife and kids, his albums stiffed.*

– PHRASES **stiff as a board** informal (of a person or part of the body) extremely stiff. **a stiff upper lip** a quality of uncomplaining stoicism. — **stiff·ish** **adj.** **stiff·ly** **adv.** **stiff·ness** **n.** [OE *stīf*, of Gmc. origin; rel. to Du. *stijf*.]

stiff-arm ▶ **v.** [trans.] tackle or fend off (a person) by extending an arm rigidly.

stiff·en /ˈstifən/ ▶v. make or become stiff or rigid. ■ [trans.] support or strengthen (a garment or fabric), typically by adding tape or an adhesive layer. ■ fig. make or become stronger or more steadfast: [trans.] *outrage over the murders stiffened the government's resolve to confront the Mafia* | [intrans.] *the regime's resistance stiffened.* — **stiff·en·er** /ˈstif(ə)nər/ n.

stiff·en·ing /ˈstif(ə)niNG/ ▶n. material used to stiffen a garment, fabric, or other object.

stiff-necked ▶adj. (of a person or their behavior) haughty and stubborn.

stif·fy /ˈstifē/ (also **stif·fie**) ▶n. (pl. **-fies**) vulgar slang an erection of a man's penis.

sti·fle[1] /ˈstīfəl/ ▶v. [trans.] **1** make (someone) unable to breathe properly; suffocate: *those in the streets were stifled by the fumes* | [as adj.] (**stifling**) *stifling heat.* **2** restrain (a reaction) or stop oneself acting on (an emotion): *she stifled a giggle.* ■ prevent or constrain (an activity or idea): *high taxes were stifling private enterprise.* — **sti·fler** /-f(ə)lər/ n. **sti·fling·ly** /-f(ə)liNGlē/ adv. [as submodifier] *a stiflingly hot day.* [ME: perh. from a frequentative of OFr. *estouffer* 'smother, stifle.']

sti·fle[2] (also **sti·fle joint**) ▶n. a joint in the legs of horses, dogs, and other animals, equivalent to the knee in humans. [ME: of unknown origin.]

sti·fle bone ▶n. the bone in front of a stifle.

stig·ma /ˈstigmə/ ▶n. (pl. **stig·mas** or esp. in sense 2 **stig·ma·ta** /stigˈmätə; ˈstigmətə/) **1** a mark of disgrace associated with a particular circumstance, quality, or person: *the stigma of mental disorder* | *to be a nonreader carries a social stigma.* **2** (**stigmata**) (in Christian tradition) marks corresponding to those left on Jesus' body by the Crucifixion, said to have been impressed by divine favor on the bodies of St. Francis of Assisi and others. **3** Med. a visible sign or characteristic of a disease. ■ a mark or spot on the skin. **4** Bot. (in a flower) the part of a pistil that receives the pollen during pollination. [16th C.: via L. from Gk. *stigma* 'a mark made by a pointed instrument, a dot'; rel. to STICK[1].]

stig·mar·i·a /stigˈme(ə)rēə/ ▶n. (pl. **-mar·i·ae** /-ˈme(ə)rē-ē/) Paleontol. a fossilized root of a giant lycopod (*Lepidodendron*, *Sigillaria*, and other genera), common in Carboniferous coal measures. — **stig·mar·i·an** adj. [19th C.: mod. L., from Gk. *stigma*, with ref. to the scars where rootlets were attached, covering the fossils.]

stig·mat·ic /stigˈmatik/ ▶adj. **1** of or relating to a stigma or stigmas, in particular constituting or conveying a mark of disgrace. **2** another term for ANASTIGMATIC. ▶n. a person bearing stigmata. — **stig·mat·i·cal·ly** /-ik(ə)lē/ adv. [16th C. (in the sense '(person) marked with a blemish or deformity'): from L. *stigma, stigmat-* + -IC.]

stig·ma·tize /ˈstigməˌtīz/ ▶v. [trans.] **1** (usu. **be stigmatized**) describe or regard as worthy of disgrace or great disapproval: *the institution was stigmatized as a last resort for the destitute.* **2** mark with stigmata. — **stig·ma·ti·za·tion** /ˌstigmətiˈzāSHən/ n. [16th C.: from Fr. *stigmatiser* or med. L. *stigmatizare*, from Gk. *stigmatizein*, from *stigma* (see STIGMA).]

Stijl /stīl/ see DE STIJL.

stil·bene /ˈstilˌbēn/ ▶n. Chem. a synthetic aromatic hydrocarbon ($C_6H_5CH{=}CHC_6H_5$) that forms phosphorescent crystals and is used in dye manufacture. [19th C.: from Gk. *stilbein* 'to glitter' + -ENE.]

stil·bes·trol /stilˈbesˌtrôl; -ˌträl/ (Brit. **stil·boes·trol**) ▶n. Biochem. a powerful synthetic estrogen used in hormone therapy, as a post-coital contraceptive, and as a growth-promoting agent for livestock. [1930s: from STILBENE + ESTRUS + -OL.]

stile[1] /stīl/ ▶n. an arrangement of steps that allows people but not animals to climb over a fence or wall. [OE *stigel*, from a Gmc. root meaning 'to climb.']

stile[2] ▶n. a vertical piece in the frame of a paneled door or sash window. Compare with RAIL[1] (sense 3). [17th C.: prob. from Du. *stijl* 'pillar, doorpost.']

sti·let·to /stəˈletō/ ▶n. (pl. **-tos**) **1** a short dagger with a tapering blade. ■ a sharp-pointed tool for making eyelet holes. **2** (also **sti·let·to heel**) a thin, high, tapering heel on a woman's shoe. ■ a shoe with such a heel. [17th C.: from Ital., dimin. of *stilo* 'dagger.']

still[1] /stil/ ▶adj. not moving or making a sound: *the still body of the young man.* ■ (of air or water) undisturbed by wind, sound, or current; calm and tranquil: *her voice carried on the still air* | *a still autumn day.* ■ (of a drink such as wine) not effervescent. ▶n. **1** deep silence and calm; stillness: *the still of the night.* **2** an ordinary static photograph as opposed to a motion picture, esp. a single shot from a movie. ▶adv. **1** without moving: *the sheriff commanded him to stand still and drop the gun.* **2** up to and including the present or the time mentioned; even now (or then) as formerly: *he still lives with his mother* | *it was still raining.* ■ referring to something that will or may happen in the future: *we could still win.* **3** nevertheless; all the same: *I'm afraid he's crazy. Still, he's harmless.* **4** even (used with comparatives for emphasis): *write, or better still, type, captions for the pictures* | *Hank, already sweltering, began to sweat still more profusely.* ▶v. make or become still: [trans.] *she raised her hand, stilling Erica's protests* | [intrans.] *the din in the hall stilled.*

– PHRASES **still and all** informal nevertheless; even so. **still small voice** the voice of one's conscience (with reference to 1 Kings 19:12). **still waters run deep** proverb a quiet or placid manner may conceal a more passionate nature. — **still·ness** n. [OE *stille* (adj. and adv.), *stillan* (v.), of West Gmc. origin, from a base meaning 'be fixed, stand.']

still[2] ▶n. an apparatus for distilling alcoholic beverages such as whiskey. [16th C.: from the rare verb *still* 'extract by distillation,' shortening of DISTILL.]

still·birth /ˈstilˌbərTH/ ▶n. the birth of an infant that has died in the womb after having survived through at least the first 28 weeks of pregnancy.

still·born /ˈstilˌbôrn/ ▶adj. (of an infant) born dead. ■ fig. (of a proposal or plan) having failed to develop or succeed; unrealized: *the proposed wealth tax was stillborn.*

still-hunt ▶v. [intrans.] [often as n.] (**still-hunting**) hunt game stealthily; stalk. ▶n. (**still hunt**) a stealthy hunt for game.

still life ▶n. (pl. **still lifes** /ˌlīfs/) a painting or drawing of an arrangement of objects. ■ this type or genre of painting or drawing.

Still·son /ˈstilsən/ (also **Still·son wrench**) ▶n. a large wrench with jaws that tighten as pressure is increased. [20th C.: for Daniel C. *Stillson* (1830–99), its American inventor.]

stil·ly /ˈstil-lē/ literary ▶adv. quietly and with little movement: *the birds rested stilly.* ▶adj. still and quiet: *the stilly night.*

stilt /stilt/ ▶n. **1** either of a pair of upright poles with supports for the feet enabling the user to walk at a distance above the ground. ■ each of a set of posts or piles supporting a building above the ground. ■ a small, flat, three-pointed support for ceramic ware in a kiln. **2** a long-billed wading bird (*Himantopus* and other genera, family Recurvirostridae) with predominantly black and white plumage and long slender reddish legs.

– PHRASES **on stilts 1** supported by stilts. **2** (of language) bombastic or stilted: *he is talking nonsense on stilts, and he knows it.* [ME: of Gmc. origin; rel. to Du. *stelt* and Ger. *Stelze*.]

stilt bug ▶n. a plant bug (family Berytidae) with very long slender legs.

stilt·ed /ˈstiltid/ ▶adj. **1** (of a manner of talking or writing) stiff and self-conscious or unnatural: *we made stilted conversation.* **2** standing on stilts: *villages of stilted houses.* ■ Archit. (of an arch) with pieces of upright masonry between the imposts and the springers. — **stilt·ed·ly** adv. **stilt·ed·ness** n.

Stil·ton /ˈstiltn/ ▶n. trademark a kind of strong rich cheese, often with blue veins, originally made at various places in Leicestershire, England. [so named because it was formerly sold to travelers at a coaching inn in Stilton, England.]

Stil·well /ˈstilˌwel/, Joseph Warren (1883–1946), US general; known as **Uncle Joe** or **Vinegar Joe**. He commanded US troops in the China-Burma-India theater 1942–44.

Stim·son /ˈstimsən/, Henry Lewis (1867–1950), US secretary of war 1911–13, 1940–45, and secretary of state 1929–33. His re-appointment as war secretary at the onset of World War II was due largely to his aggressive position against Hitler's Nazi regime.

stim·u·lant /ˈstimyələnt/ ▶n. a substance that raises levels of physiological or nervous activity in the body. ■ something that increases activity, interest, or enthusiasm in a specified field: *population growth is a major stimulant to industrial development.* ▶adj. raising levels of physiological or nervous activity in the body: *caffeine has stimulant effects on the heart.* [18th C.: from L. *stimulant-* 'urging, goading,' from the verb *stimulare*.]

stim·u·late /ˈstimyəˌlāt/ ▶v. [trans.] raise levels of physiological or nervous activity in (the body or any biological system): *the women are given fertility drugs to stimulate their ovaries.* ■ encourage interest or activity in (a person or animal): *the reader could not fail to be stimulated by the ideas presented* | [as adj.] (**stimulating**) *a rich and stimulating working environment.* ■ encourage development of or increased activity in (a state or process): *the courses stimulate a passion for learning* | *tax changes designed to stimulate economic growth.* — **stim·u·la·ble** /-ləbəl/ adj. **stim·u·lat·ing·ly** adv. **stim·u·la·tion** /ˌstimyəˈlāSHən/ n. **stim·u·la·tive** /-ˌlātiv; -lətiv/ adj. **stim·u·la·tor** /-ˌlātər/ n. **stim·u·la·to·ry** /-ləˌtôrē/ adj. [16th C.: from L. *stimulat-* 'urged, goaded,' from the verb *stimulare*.]

stim·u·lus /ˈstimyələs/ ▶n. (pl. **-li** /-ˌlī/) a thing or event that evokes a specific functional reaction in an organ or tissue: *areas of the brain which respond to auditory stimuli.* ■ a thing that rouses activity or energy in someone or something; a spur or incentive: *if the tax were abolished, it would act as a stimulus to exports.* ■ an interesting and exciting quality: *she loved the stimulus of the job.* [17th C.: from L., 'goad, spur, incentive.']

sting /stiNG/ ▶n. **1** a small sharp-pointed organ at the end of the abdomen of bees, wasps, ants, and scorpions, capable of inflicting a painful or dangerous wound by injecting poison. ■ any of a number of minute hairs or other organs of plants, jellyfishes, etc., that inject a poisonous or irritating fluid when touched. ■ a wound from such an animal or plant organ: *a wasp or bee sting.* ■ a sharp tingling or burning pain or sensation: *I felt the sting of the cold, bitter air.* ■ [in sing.] fig. a hurtful quality or effect: *she smiled to take the sting out of her words.* **2** informal a carefully planned operation, typically one involving deception: *five blackmailers were jailed last week after they were snared in a police sting.* ▶v. (past and past part. **stung** /stəNG/) **1** [trans.] wound or pierce with a sting: *he was stung by a jellyfish* | [intrans.] *a nettle stings if you brush it lightly.* **2** feel or cause to feel a sharp tingling or burning pain or sensation: [intrans.] *her eyes stung* | [trans.] *the brandy stung his throat* | [as adj.] (**stinging**) *a stinging pain.* ■ [trans.] fig. (typically of something said) hurt or upset (someone): *stung by her mockery, Frank hung his head.* ■ (**sting someone into**) provoke someone to do (something) by causing annoyance or offense: *he was stung into action by an article in the paper.* **3** [trans.] informal swindle or exorbitantly overcharge (someone): *an elaborate fraud that stung a bank for thousands.*

– PHRASES **sting in the tail** an unexpected, typically unpleasant or problematic end to something. — **sting·ing·ly** adv. **sting·less** adj. [OE *sting* (n.), *stingan* (v.), of Gmc. origin.]

sting·a·ree /ˌstiNGəˈrē/ ▸ n. a cinnamon-brown short-tailed stingray (*Urolophus testaceus*) occurring on sand flats in shallow Australian waters. ▪ informal any stingray. [19th C.: alt. of STINGRAY.]

stinge /stinj/ ▸ n. informal a mean or ungenerous person. [20th C.: back-form. from STINGY.]

sting·er /ˈstiNGər/ ▸ n. **1** an insect or animal that stings, such as a bee or jellyfish. ▪ the part of an insect or animal that holds a sting. ▪ informal a painful blow: *he suffered a stinger on his right shoulder.* **2** a cocktail including crème de menthe and brandy. **3** (**Stinger**) a heat-seeking ground-to-air missile that is launched from the shoulder.

sting·ing net·tle ▸ n. a nettle (esp. *Urtica dioica*) covered in minute hairs that inject irritants when they are touched.

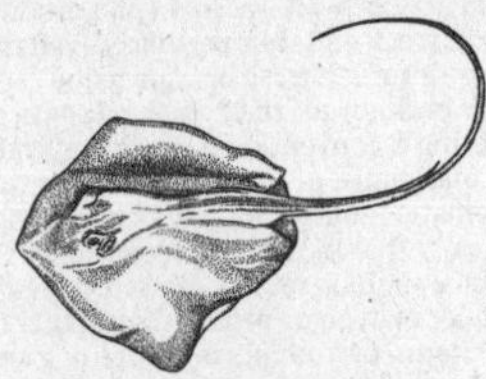

common stingray

sting·ray /ˈstiNG,rā/ ▸ n. a marine ray (families Dasyatidae and Urolophidae) with a flattened diamond-shaped body and a long poisonous serrated spine at the base of the tail. Several species, including the **common stingray** (*D. centrourus*).

stin·gy /ˈstinjē/ ▸ adj. (**-gi·er**, **-gi·est**) unwilling to give or spend; ungenerous: *his employer is stingy and idle.* ▪ insufficient in quantity; scanty: *the crabmeat is stingy and the black bean soup is not quite hot enough.* — **stin·gi·ly** /-lē/ adv. **stin·gi·ness** n. [17th C.: perh. a dial. var. of the noun STING + -Y[1].]

stink /stiNGk/ ▸ v. (past **stank** /staNGk/ or **stunk** /stəNGk/; past part. **stunk**) [intrans.] **1** have a strong unpleasant smell: *the place stank like a sewer* | *his breath* **stank of** *drink.* ▪ [trans.] (**stink a place up**) fill a place with such a smell. **2** informal be very unpleasant, contemptible, or scandalous: *the industry's reputation stinks.* ▪ (**stink of**) be highly suggestive of (something regarded with disapproval): *the whole affair stinks of a setup.* ▪ (**stink of**) have or appear to have a scandalously large amount of (something, esp. money): *the whole place was luxurious and stank of money.* ▸ n. [in sing.] **1** a strong unpleasant smell; a stench: *the stink of the place hit me as I went in.* **2** informal a commotion or fuss: *Brad made a big stink about getting a fountainside table.* [OE *stincan*, of West Gmc. origin; rel. to Du. and Ger. *stinken*, also to STENCH.]

stink·ard /ˈstiNGkərd/ ▸ n. a member of a lower social order in some American Indian communities.

stink bomb ▸ n. a small bomb that emits a strong and unpleasant smell when exploded.

stink bug ▸ n. a broad shield-shaped bug (Pentatomidae and other families) that is typically brightly colored or boldly marked. It emits a foul smell when handled or molested.

stink·er /ˈstiNGkər/ ▸ n. informal a person or thing that smells very bad. ▪ a very bad or unpleasant person or thing: *have those little stinkers been bullying you?* ▪ a difficult task: *Tackled the crossword yet? It's a stinker.*

stink·horn /ˈstiNGk,hôrn/ ▸ n. a widely distributed fungus (family Phallaceae, class Gasteromycetes) that has a tall whitish stem with a rounded greenish-brown gelatinous head that turns into a foul-smelling slime containing the spores.

stink·ing /ˈstiNGkiNG/ ▸ adj. foul-smelling: *he was locked in a stinking cell.* ▪ informal very bad or unpleasant: *a stinking cold.* ▸ adv. [as submodifier] informal extremely: *she is obviously stinking rich* | *I want to get stinking drunk and forget.* — **stink·ing·ly** adv.

stink·ing ce·dar ▸ n. a tree (*Torreya taxifolia*) of the yew family found only in Florida, with fetid leaves, branches, and timber.

stink·ing smut ▸ n. another term for BUNT[2].

stink·o /ˈstiNGkō/ ▸ adj. informal **1** extremely drunk: *they took three-hour lunches and came back stinko.* **2** worthless or contemptible: *the plot and cast of characters are just plain stinko.*

stink·pot /ˈstiNGk,pät/ ▸ n. informal an unpleasant person (used as a term of abuse). ▪ a vehicle that emits foul-smelling exhaust fumes, esp. a motorboat as opposed to a sailboat.

stink·weed /ˈstiNGk,wēd/ ▸ n. any of a number of plants with a strong or fetid smell, e.g., jimson weed.

stink·wood /ˈstiNGk,wo͝od/ ▸ n. any of a number of trees that yield timber with an unpleasant odor, in particular the South African **black stinkwood** (*Ocotea bullata*, family Lauraceae).

stink·y /ˈstiNGkē/ ▸ adj. (**stink·i·er**, **stink·i·est**) informal having a strong or unpleasant smell: *stinky cigarette smoke.* ▪ very disagreeable and unpleasant: *a stinky job.*

stint[1] /stint/ ▸ v. [trans.] [often with negative] supply an ungenerous or inadequate amount of (something): *stowage room hasn't been stinted.* ▪ [intrans.] be economical or frugal about spending or providing something: *he doesn't* **stint on** *wining and dining.* ▪ restrict (someone) in the amount of something (esp. money) given or permitted: *to avoid having to stint yourself, budget in advance.* ▸ n. **1** a person's fixed or allotted period of work: *his varied career included a stint as a magician.* **2** limitation of supply or effort: *a collector with an eye for quality and the means to indulge it* **without stint**. [OE *styntan* 'make blunt,' of Gmc. origin; rel. to STUNT[1].]

stint[2] ▸ n. a small short-legged sandpiper (genus *Calidris*) of northern Eurasia and Alaska, with a brownish back and white underparts. [ME: of unknown origin.]

stip. ▸ abbr. ▪ stipend. ▪ stipulation.

stipe /stīp/ ▸ n. Bot. a stalk or stem, esp. the stem of a seaweed or fungus or the stalk of a fern frond. [18th C.: from Fr., from L. *stipes* (see STIPES).]

sti·pend /ˈstī,pend; -pənd/ ▸ n. a fixed regular sum paid as a salary or allowance. [ME: from OFr. *stipendie* or L. *stipendium*, from *stips* 'wages' + *pendere* 'to pay.']

sti·pen·di·ar·y /stīˈpendē,erē/ ▸ adj. receiving a stipend: *stipendiary clergy.* ▪ of, relating to, or of the nature of a stipend: *stipendiary obligations.* ▸ n. (pl. **-ar·ies**) a person receiving a stipend. [ME (as a n.): from L. *stipendiarius*, from *stipendium* (see STIPEND).]

sti·pes /ˈstī,pēz/ ▸ n. (pl. **sti·pi·tes** /ˈstipə,tēz/) Zool. a part or organ resembling a stalk, esp. the second joint of the maxilla of an insect. ▪ Bot. more technical term for STIPE. [18th C.: from L., lit. 'log, tree trunk.']

stip·i·tate /ˈstipi,tāt/ ▸ adj. esp. Bot. (esp. of a fungus) having a stipe or a stipes.

stip·ple /ˈstipəl/ ▸ v. [trans.] (in drawing, painting, and engraving) mark (a surface) with numerous small dots or specks: [as n.] (**stippling**) *the miniaturist's use of stippling.* ▪ produce a decorative effect on (paint or other material) by roughening its surface when it is wet. ▸ n. the process or technique of stippling a surface, or the effect so created. — **stip·pler** /ˈstip(ə)lər/ n. [17th C.: from Du. *stippelen*, frequentative of *stippen* 'to prick,' from *stip* 'a point.']

stip·u·late[1] /ˈstipyə,lāt/ ▸ v. [trans.] demand or specify (a requirement), typically as part of a bargain or agreement: *he stipulated certain conditions before their marriage* | [as adj.] (**stipulated**) *the stipulated time has elapsed.* — **stip·u·la·tion** /,stipyəˈlāSHən/ n. **stip·u·la·tor** /-,lātər/ n. [17th C.: from L. *stipulat-* 'demanded as a formal promise,' from the verb *stipulari*.]

stip·u·late[2] ▸ adj. Bot. (of a leaf or plant) having stipules. [18th C.: from L. *stipula* (see STIPULE) + -ATE[2].]

stip·ule /ˈstipyo͞ol/ ▸ n. Bot. a small leaflike appendage to a leaf, typically borne in pairs at the base of the leaf stalk. — **stip·u·lar** /-yələr/ adj. [18th C.: from Fr. *stipule* or L. *stipula* 'straw.']

stir[1] /stər/ ▸ v. (**stirred**, **stir·ring**) **1** [trans.] move a spoon or other implement around in (a liquid or other substance) in order to mix it thoroughly: *stir the batter until it is just combined.* ▪ (**stir something in/into**) add an ingredient to (a liquid or other substance) in such a way: *stir in the flour and cook gently for two minutes.* **2** [intrans.] move or begin to move slightly: *nothing stirred except the wind.* ▪ [trans.] cause to move or be disturbed slightly: *a gentle breeze stirred the leaves* | *cloudiness is caused by the fish* **stirring up** *mud.* ▪ (of a person or animal) rise or wake from sleep. ▪ (**stir from**) (of a person) leave or go out of (a place): *as he grew older, he seldom stirred from his apartment.* ▪ begin or cause to begin to be active or to develop: [intrans.] *the 1960s, when the civil rights movement stirred* | [trans.] *a voice* **stirred** *her* **from** *her reverie.* **3** [trans.] arouse strong feelings in (someone); move or excite: *they will be* **stirred to** *action by what is written.* ▪ arouse or prompt (a feeling or memory) or inspire (the imagination): *the story stirred many memories of my childhood.* ▸ n. [in sing.] **1** a slight physical movement: *I stood, straining eyes and ears for the faintest stir.* ▪ a commotion: *the event caused quite a stir.* ▪ an initial sign of a specified feeling: *Caroline felt a stir of anger deep within her breast.* **2** an act of mixing food or drink with a spoon or other implement: *he gives his chocolate milk a stir.*

– PHRASES **stir someone's blood** make someone excited or enthusiastic.

– PHRASAL VERBS **stir something up** cause or provoke trouble or bad feeling. [OE *styrian*, of Gmc. origin; rel. to Ger. *stören* 'disturb.']

stir[2] ▸ n. informal prison: *I've spent twenty-eight years* **in stir**. [19th C.: perh. from Romany *sturbin* 'jail.']

stir-cra·zy ▸ adj. informal psychologically disturbed, esp. as a result of being confined or imprisoned.

stir-fry ▸ v. [trans.] fry (meat, fish, or vegetables) rapidly over a high heat while stirring briskly: [as adj.] (**stir-fried**) *stir-fried beef.* ▸ n. a dish cooked by such a method.

stirk /stərk/ ▸ n. Brit. a yearling bullock or heifer. [OE *stirc*, perh. from *stēor* 'steer' + *-oc* (see -OCK).]

Stir·ling en·gine /ˈstərliNG/ ▸ n. a machine used to provide power or refrigeration, operating on a closed cycle in which a working fluid is cyclically compressed and expanded at different temperatures.

stir·rer /ˈstərər/ ▸ n. an object or mechanical device used for stirring something.

stir·ring /ˈstəriNG/ ▸ adj. causing great excitement or strong emotion;

rousing: *stirring songs.* ▶n. an initial sign of activity, movement, or emotion: *the first stirrings of anger.* — **stir•ring•ly** adv.

stir•rup /ˈstərəp; ˈstə-rəp; ˈstir-/ ▶n. **1** each of a pair of devices attached to each side of a horse's saddle, in the form of a loop with a flat base to support the rider's foot. **2** (**stir•rups**) a pair of metal supports in which a woman's heels may be placed during gynecological examinations and childbirth, to hold her legs in a position that will facilitate medical examination or intervention. **3** (also **stir•rup bone**) another term for STAPES. **4** (**stirrups**) short for STIRRUP PANTS. [OE *stigrāp*, from the Gmc. base of obs. *sty* 'climb' + ROPE.]

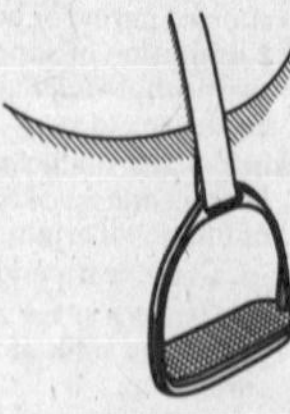

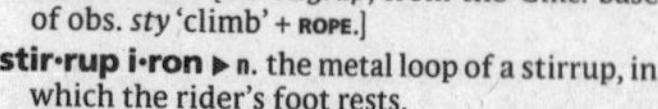

stirrup 1

stir•rup i•ron ▶n. the metal loop of a stirrup, in which the rider's foot rests.

stir•rup pants ▶plural n. a pair of women's or girls' stretch pants with a band of elastic at the bottom of each leg that passes under the arch of the foot.

stir•rup pump ▶n. esp. hist. a portable hand-operated water pump with a footrest resembling a stirrup, used to extinguish small fires.

stish•ov•ite /ˈstisHə,vīt/ ▶n. a mineral that is a dense polymorph of silica and is formed at very high pressures, esp. in meteorite craters. [1960s: from Sergei M. *Stishov*, 20th-cent. Russian chemist, + -ITE[1].]

stitch /sticH/ ▶n. **1** a loop of thread or yarn resulting from a single pass or movement of the needle in sewing, knitting, or crocheting. ■ a loop of thread used to join the edges of a wound or surgical incision: *a neck wound requiring forty stitches.* ■ [usu. with adj.] a method of sewing, knitting, or crocheting producing a particular pattern or design: *basic embroidery stitches.* ■ [in sing., usu. with negative] informal the smallest item of clothing: *a man answered the door without a stitch on.* **2** a sudden sharp pain in the side of the body, caused by strenuous exercise: *she ran with a stitch in her side.* ▶v. [trans.] make, mend, or join (something) with stitches: *stitch a plain seam with right sides together* | *they stitched the cut on her face* | [as adj.], [in comb.] (**stitched**) *hand-stitched English dresses.*
– PHRASES **in stitches** informal laughing uncontrollably: *his unique brand of droll self-mockery had his audiences in stitches.* **a stitch in time saves nine** proverb if you sort out a problem immediately it may save a lot of extra work later. — **stitch•er** n. **stitch•er•y** n. [OE *stice* 'a puncture, stabbing pain,' of Gmc. origin; rel. to Ger. *Stich* 'a sting, prick,' also to STICK[2].]

stitch•bird /ˈsticH,bərd/ ▶n. a rare New Zealand honeyeater (*Notiomystis cincta*) with mainly dark brown or blackish plumage and a sharp call that resembles the word "stitch."

stitch•ing /ˈsticHiNG/ ▶n. a row of stitches sewn onto cloth: *the gloves were white with black stitching.* ■ the action or work of stitching or sewing: *one of the mares cut her leg and it required stitching.*

stitch•wort /ˈsticHwərt; -,wôrt/ ▶n. a straggling plant (genus *Stellaria*) of the pink family with a slender stem and white starry flowers. It was formerly thought to cure a stitch in the side.

sti•ver /ˈstīvər/ ▶n. a small coin formerly used in the Netherlands, equal to one twentieth of a guilder. ■ archaic any coin of low value. ■ [with negative] archaic a very small or insignificant amount: *they didn't care a stiver.* [from Du. *stuiver*, denoting a small coin; prob. rel. to the noun STUB.]

STM ▶abbr. scanning tunnelling microscope.

sto•a /ˈstōə/ ▶n. a classical portico or roofed colonnade. ■ (**the Stoa**) a great hall in Athens. [Gk.]

stoat /stōt/ ▶n. a small carnivorous mammal (*Mustela erminea*) of the weasel family that has chestnut fur with white underparts and a black-tipped tail. It is native to both Eurasia and North America, and in northern areas the coat turns white in winter. Also called SHORT-TAILED WEASEL. Compare with ERMINE. [ME: of unknown origin.]

stob /stäb/ ▶n. dialect a broken branch or a stump. ■ a stake used for fencing. [ME: var. of STUB.]

sto•chas•tic /stəˈkastik/ ▶adj. randomly determined; having a random probability distribution or pattern that may be analyzed statistically but may not be predicted precisely. — **sto•chas•ti•cal•ly** /-tik(ə)lē/ adv. [17th C.: from Gk. *stokhastikos*, from *stokhazesthai* 'aim at, guess,' from *stokhos* 'aim.']

stock /stäk/ ▶n. **1** the goods or merchandise kept on the premises of a business or warehouse and available for sale or distribution. ■ a supply or quantity of something accumulated or available for future use: *my stock of wine.* ■ farm animals such as cattle, pigs, and sheep, bred and kept for their meat or milk; livestock. ■ short for ROLLING STOCK. ■ (also **film stock**) photographic film that has not been exposed or processed. ■ the undealt cards of the deck, left on the table to be drawn from in some card games. **2** the capital raised by a business or corporation through the issue and subscription of shares: *the company's stock rose by 86%.* ■ (also **stocks**) a portion of this as held by an individual or group as an investment. ■ (also **stocks**) the shares of a particular company, type of company, or industry: *blue-chip stocks.* ■ securities issued by the government in fixed units with a fixed rate of interest. ■ fig. a person's reputation or popularity. **3** liquid made by cooking bones, meat, fish, or vegetables slowly in water, used as a basis for the preparation of soup, gravy, or sauces. ■ [with adj.] the raw material from which a specified commodity can be manufactured. **4** [usu. with adj.] a person's ancestry or line of descent: *her mother was of French stock.* ■ a breed, variety, or population of an animal or plant. **5** the trunk or woody stem of a living tree or shrub, esp. one into which a graft (scion) is inserted. ■ the perennial part of a herbaceous plant, esp. a rhizome. **6** a herbaceous European plant (genus *Matthiola*) of the cabbage family, widely cultivated for its fragrant flowers, which are typically lilac, pink, or white. **7** (**the stocks**) [treated as sing. or pl.] hist. an instrument of punishment consisting of an adjustable wooden structure with holes for securing a person's feet and hands, in which criminals were locked and exposed to public ridicule or assault. **8** the part of a rifle or other firearm to which the barrel and firing mechanism are attached, held against one's shoulder when firing the gun. ■ the crosspiece of an anchor. ■ the handle of something such as a whip or fishing rod. ■ short for HEADSTOCK (sense 1). ■ short for TAILSTOCK. **9** a band of white material tied like a cravat and worn as a part of formal horse-riding dress. ■ a piece of black material worn under a clerical collar. **10** (**stocks**) a frame used to support a ship or boat out of water, esp. when under construction. ▶adj. [attrib.] **1** (of a product or type of product) usually kept in stock and thus regularly available for sale: *25 percent off stock items.* **2** (of a phrase or expression) so regularly used as to be automatic or hackneyed: *their stock response was "We can't take everyone."* ■ denoting a conventional character type or situation that recurs in a particular genre of literature, theater, or film. ■ denoting or relating to cinematic footage that can be regularly used in different productions, typically that of outdoor scenes used to add realism to a production shot in an indoor set. ▶v. [trans.] **1** have or keep a supply of (a particular product or type or product) available for sale. ■ provide or fill with goods, items, or a supply of something. ■ [intrans.] (**stock up**) amass supplies of something, typically for a particular occasion or purpose. **2** fit (a rifle or other firearm) with a stock.
– PHRASES **in** (or **out of**) **stock** (of goods) available (or unavailable) for immediate sale in a store. **put stock in** [often with negative] have a specified amount of belief or faith in: *I don't put much stock in modern medicine.* **take stock** review or make an overall assessment of a particular situation, typically as a prelude to making a decision. [OE *stoc(c)* 'trunk, block of wood, post,' of Gmc. origin; rel. to Du. *stok* and Ger. *Stock* 'stick.']

stock•ade /stäˈkād/ ▶n. a barrier formed from upright wooden posts or stakes, esp. as a defense against attack or as a means of confining animals. ■ an enclosure bound by such a barrier: *we got ashore and into the stockade.* ■ a military prison. ▶v. [trans.] [usu. as adj.] (**stockaded**) enclose (an area) by erecting such a barrier. [17th C.: shortening of obs. Fr. *estocade*, alt. of *estacade*, from Sp. *estacada*, from the Gmc. base of the noun STAKE[1].]

stock•breed•er /ˈstäk,brēdər/ ▶n. a farmer who breeds livestock. — **stock•breed•ing** /-,brēdiNG/ n.

stock•brok•er /ˈstäk,brōkər/ ▶n. a broker who buys and sells securities on a stock exchange on behalf of clients. — **stock•brok•er•age** /-,brōk(ə)rij/ n. **stock•brok•ing** /-,brōkiNG/ n.

stock car ▶n. **1** an ordinary car that has been modified for racing. **2** a railroad car for transporting livestock.

stock com•pa•ny ▶n. a repertory company that is largely based in one theater.

stock dove /dəv/ ▶n. a gray Eurasian and North African pigeon (*Columba oenas*) that resembles a small wood pigeon and nests in holes in trees.

stock ex•change ▶n. a market in which securities are bought and sold: *the company was floated on the Stock Exchange.* ■ (**the Stock Exchange**) the level of prices in such a market: *a plunge in the Stock Exchange during the election campaign.*

stock•fish /ˈstäk,fisH/ ▶n. (pl. same or **-fish•es**) **1** cod or a similar fish split and dried in the open air without salt. **2** a commercially valuable hake (*Merluccius capensis*) of coastal waters of southern Africa. [ME (sense 1): from Mid. Low Ger., MDu. *stokvisch*, of unknown origin; sense 2 (early 19th C.) from South Afr. Du.]

stock•hold•er /ˈstäk,hōldər/ ▶n. a shareholder. — **stock•hold•ing** /-,hōldiNG/ n.

Stock•holm /ˈstäk,hō(l)m/ the capital of Sweden, a seaport on the eastern coast; pop. 674,000.

Stock•holm syn•drome ▶n. feelings of trust or affection felt in many cases of kidnapping or hostage-taking by a victim toward a captor. [1970s: with ref. to a bank robbery in Stockholm, Sweden.]

stock horse ▶n. a horse that is trained to herd livestock.

stock•i•nette /,stäkəˈnet/ (also **stock•i•net**) ▶n. **1** a soft, loosely knitted stretch fabric. **2** (also **stockinette stitch**) a knitting stitch consisting of alternate rows of knit (plain) and purl stitch. [18th C.: prob. an alt. of *stocking-net.*]

stock•ing /ˈstäkiNG/ ▶n. a women's garment, typically made of translucent nylon or silk, that fits closely over the foot and leg. ■ short for CHRISTMAS STOCKING. ■ a long sock worn by men. ■ [usu. with adj.] a cylindrical bandage or other medical covering for the leg resembling a stocking, esp. an elasticized support used in the treatment of disorders of the veins. ■ a white marking of the lower part of a horse's leg, extending as far as, or just beyond, the knee or hock.
– PHRASES **in** (**one's**) **stocking feet** without shoes: *she stood five feet ten in her stocking feet.* — **stock•inged** /ˈstäkiNGd/ adj. [in comb.] *her black-stockinged legs* **stock•ing•less** adj. [16th C.: from STOCK in the dial. sense 'stocking' + -ING[1].]

stock•ing cap ▶n. a knitted conical hat with a long tapered end, often bearing a tassel, that hangs down.

stock•ing mask ▶n. a nylon stocking pulled over the face to disguise the features, used by criminals.

stock·ing stuff·er ▶ n. a small present suitable for putting in a Christmas stocking.

stock-in-trade ▶ n. the typical subject or commodity a person, company, or profession uses or deals in: *information is our stock-in-trade.* ■ qualities, ideas, or behavior characteristic of a person or their work: *flippancy is his stock-in-trade.* ■ the goods kept on hand by a business for the purposes of its trade.

stock·man /'stäkmən; -,man/ ▶ n. (pl. **-men**) **1** a person who looks after livestock. ■ an owner of livestock. **2** a person who looks after a stockroom or warehouse.

stock mar·ket ▶ n. (usu. **the stock market**) a stock exchange.

stock op·tion ▶ n. a benefit in the form of an option given by a company to an employee to buy stock in the company at a discount or at a stated fixed price.

stock·pile /'stäk,pīl/ ▶ n. a large accumulated stock of goods or materials, esp. one held in reserve for use at a time of shortage or other emergency. ▶ v. [trans.] accumulate a large stock of (goods or materials): *he claimed that the weapons were being stockpiled.* — **stock·pil·er** n.

Stock·port /'stäk,pôrt/ a city in northwestern England; pop. 130,000.

stock·pot /'stäk,pät/ ▶ n. a pot in which stock for soup is prepared by long, slow cooking.

stock·room /'stäk,ro͞om; -,ro͝om/ ▶ n. a room in which quantities of goods are stored.

stock split ▶ n. an issue of new shares in a company to existing shareholders in proportion to their current holdings.

stock·tak·ing /'stäk,tākiNG/ ▶ n. the action or process of recording the amount of stock held by a business: *the store is closed for stocktaking.* ■ the action of reviewing and assessing one's situation and options: *she had some mental stocktaking to do.* — **stock·take** n. **stock·tak·er** /-,tākər/ n.

Stock·ton /'stäktən/ a city in north central California, a port on the San Joaquin River; pop. 243,771.

stock whip ▶ n. a whip used for driving cattle.

stock·y /'stäkē/ ▶ adj. (**stock·i·er, stock·i·est**) (of a person) broad and sturdily built. — **stock·i·ly** /'stäkəlē/ adv. **stock·i·ness** n.

stock·yard /'stäk,yärd/ ▶ n. a large yard containing pens and sheds, typically adjacent to a slaughterhouse, in which livestock is kept and sorted.

stodg·y /'stäjē/ ▶ adj. (**stodg·i·er, stodg·i·est**) **1** dull and uninspired. **2** Brit. (of food) heavy, filling, and high in carbohydrates. ■ bulky or heavy in appearance: *this stodgy three-story building.* — **stodg·i·ly** /'stäjəlē/ adv. **stodg·i·ness** n.

sto·gie /'stōgē/ (also **sto·gy**) ▶ n. (pl. **-gies**) a long, thin, inexpensive cigar. [19th C. (orig. as *stoga*): from *Conestoga*, because the cigars are thought to have been smoked by the drivers of Conestoga wagons.]

sto·ic /'stō-ik/ ▶ n. **1** a person who can endure pain or hardship without showing their feelings or complaining. **2** (**Stoic**) a member of the ancient philosophical school of Stoicism. ▶ adj. **1** another term for STOICAL. **2** (**Stoic**) of or belonging to the Stoics or their school of philosophy. [ME: via L. from Gk. *stōikos*, from STOA (with ref. to Zeno's teaching in the *Stoa Poikilē* or Painted Porch, at Athens).]

sto·i·cal /'stō-ikəl/ ▶ adj. enduring pain and hardship without showing one's feelings or complaining: *he taught a stoical acceptance of suffering.* — **sto·i·cal·ly** /-ik(ə)lē/ adv.

stoi·chi·om·e·try /,stoikē'ämitrē/ ▶ n. Chem. the relationship between the relative quantities of substances taking part in a reaction or forming a compound, typically a ratio of whole integers. — **stoi·chi·o·met·ric** /,stoikē-ō'metrik/ adj. **stoi·chi·o·met·ri·cal·ly** /-ik(ə)lē/ adv. [19th C.: from Gk. *stoikheion* 'element' + -METRY.]

sto·i·cism /'stō-i,sizəm/ ▶ n. **1** the endurance of pain or hardship without a display of feelings and without complaint. **2** (**Stoicism**) an ancient Greek school of philosophy founded at Athens by Zeno of Citium.

stoke /stōk/ ▶ v. [trans.] add coal or other solid fuel to (a fire, furnace, or boiler). ■ encourage or incite (a strong emotion or tendency): *his composure had the effect of stoking her anger.* ■ [often as adj.] (**stoked**) informal excite or thrill: *when they told me I was on the team, I was stoked.* ■ [intrans.] informal consume a large quantity of food or drink to give one energy: *Carol was at the coffee machine, stoking up for the day.* [17th C.: back-form. from STOKER.]

stoke·hold /'stōk,hōld/ ▶ n. a compartment in a steamship from which the boiler fires are stoked.

stoke·hole /'stōk,hōl/ ▶ n. a space in front of a furnace in which a stoker works.

Stoke-on-Trent /'stōk än 'trent; ôn/ a city in west central England; pop. 245,000.

Stok·er /'stōkər/, Bram (1847–1912), Irish writer; full name *Abraham Stoker*. He wrote the vampire story *Dracula* (1897).

stok·er /'stōkər/ ▶ n. a person who tends the furnace on a steamship or steam locomotive. ■ a mechanical device for supplying fuel to a firebox or furnace, esp. on a steam locomotive. [17th C.: from Du., from *stoken* 'stoke (a furnace),' from MDu. *stoken* 'push, poke'; rel. to STICK[1].]

Stokes' law /stōks/ Physics **1** a law stating that in fluorescence the wavelength of the emitted radiation is longer than that of the radiation causing it. **2** an expression describing the resisting force on a particle moving through a viscous fluid and showing that a maximum velocity is reached in such cases, e.g., for an object falling under gravity through a fluid. [19th C.: for Sir George *Stokes* (1819–1903), British physicist.]

Sto·kow·ski /stə'kôfskē; -'kou-/, Leopold (1882–1977), US conductor; born in Britain; born *Antoni Stanislaw Boleslawowicz*. He led various orchestras, including the Philadelphia Orchestra (1912–38), and conducted the music for Walt Disney's movie *Fantasia* (1940).

STOL /'estôl; stôl/ Aeron. ▶ abbr. short takeoff and landing.

stole[1] /stōl/ ▶ n. a woman's long scarf or shawl, esp. fur or similar material, worn loosely over the shoulders. ■ a strip of fabric used as an ecclesiastical vestment, worn over the shoulders and hanging down to the knee or below. [OE, via L. from Gk. *stolē* 'clothing,' from *stellein* 'array.']

ecclesiastical stole

stole[2] past of STEAL.

sto·len /'stōlən/ past participle of STEAL.

stol·id /'stälid/ ▶ adj. (of a person) calm, dependable, and showing little emotion or animation. — **sto·lid·i·ty** /stə'liditē/ n. **stol·id·ly** adv. **stol·id·ness** n. [16th C.: from obs. Fr. *stolide* or L. *stolidus*.]

stol·len /'stōlən; 'sHtô-/ ▶ n. a rich German fruit and nut loaf. [from Ger. *Stollen*.]

sto·lon /'stōlən/ ▶ n. **1** Bot. a creeping horizontal plant stem or runner that takes root at points along its length to form new plants. ■ an arching stem of a plant that roots at the tip to form a new plant, as in the bramble. **2** Zool. the branched stemlike structure of some colonial hydroid coelenterates, attaching the colony to the substrate. — **sto·lon·ate** /-nit; -,nāt/ adj. **sto·lo·nif·er·ous** /,stōlə'nif(ə)rəs/ adj. [17th C.: from L. *stolo, stolon-* 'shoot, scion.']

sto·ma /'stōmə/ ▶ n. (pl. **sto·mas** or **sto·ma·ta** /-mətə; ,stō'mätə/) Bot. any of the minute pores in the epidermis of the leaf or stem of a plant, forming a slit of variable width that allows movement of gases in and out of the intercellular spaces. Also called STOMATE. ■ Zool. a small mouthlike opening in some lower animals. ■ Med. an artificial opening made into a hollow organ, esp. one on the surface of the body leading to the gut or trachea. — **sto·mal** adj. (Med.) **stom·a·tal** /'stōmətl; 'stäm-/ adj. [17th C.: mod. L., from Gk. *stoma* 'mouth.']

stom·ach /'stəmək/ ▶ n. **1** the internal organ in which the first part of digestion occurs, being (in humans and many mammals) a pear-shaped enlargement of the alimentary canal linking the esophagus to the small intestine. ■ each of four such organs in a ruminant (the rumen, reticulum, omasum, and abomasum). ■ any of a number of analogous organs in lower animals. ■ the front part of the body between the chest and thighs; the belly: *Blake hit him in the stomach.* ■ [in sing.] the stomach viewed as the seat of hunger, nausea, anxiety, or other unsettling feelings: *Virginia had a sick feeling in her stomach.* **2** [in sing.] [usu. with negative] an appetite for food or drink: *she doesn't have the stomach to eat anything.* ■ a desire or inclination for something involving conflict, difficulty, or unpleasantness: *the teams proved to have no stomach for a fight.* ▶ v. [trans.] (usu. **cannot stomach**) consume (food or drink) without feeling or being sick: *if you cannot stomach orange juice, try apple juice.* ■ endure or accept (an obnoxious thing or person): *I can't stomach the self-righteous attitude of some managers.*

– PHRASES **on a full** (or **an empty**) **stomach** after having eaten (or having not eaten): *I think better on a full stomach.* **a strong stomach** an ability to see or do unpleasant things without feeling sick or squeamish. — **stom·ach·ful** /-,fo͝ol/ n. (pl. **-fuls**). [ME: from OFr. *estomac, stomaque*, via L. from Gk. *stomakhos* 'gullet,' from *stoma* 'mouth.']

stom·ach·ache /'stəmək,āk/ ▶ n. a pain in the belly.

stom·ach·er /'stəməkər/ ▶ n. hist. a V-shaped piece of decorative cloth, worn over the chest and stomach in the 16th century. [ME: prob. a shortening of OFr. *estomachier*, from *estomac* (see STOMACH).]

stom·ach flu ▶ n. a short-lived stomach disorder of unknown cause, popularly attributed to a virus.

sto·mach·ic /stə'makik/ dated ▶ adj. promoting the appetite or assisting digestion. ■ of or relating to the stomach. ▶ n. a medicine or tonic that promotes the appetite or assists digestion.

sto·ma·ta /'stōmətə; stō'mätə/ plural form of STOMA.

sto·mate /'stō,māt/ ▶ n. Bot. another term for STOMA. [19th C.: appar. an Engl. sing. of STOMATA.]

sto·ma·ti·tis /,stōmə'tītis/ ▶ n. Med. inflammation of the mucous membrane of the mouth. [19th C.: mod. L., from *stoma, stomat-* 'mouth' + -ITIS.]

stomp /stämp; stômp/ ▶ v. [intrans.] tread heavily and noisily, typically in order to show anger. ■ [intrans.] (**stomp on**) tread heavily or stamp on. ■ [trans.] deliberately trample or tread heavily on. ■ [trans.] stamp (one's feet). ■ [intrans.] dance with heavy stamping steps. ▶ n. informal (in jazz or popular music) a tune or song with a fast tempo and a heavy beat. ■ a lively dance performed to such music, involving heavy stamping.

— **stomp·er** n. **stomp·y** adj. [19th C. (orig. US dial.): var. of the verb STAMP.]

stomp·ing /ˈstämpiNG; ˈstôm-/ ▶ adj. (of music) having a lively stamping rhythm.

stomp·ing ground (also **stamp·ing ground**) ▶ n. a place where someone regularly spends time; a favorite haunt.

Stone[1] /stōn/, Edward Durell (1902–78), US architect. His designs include the John F. Kennedy Center for the Performing Arts in Washington, DC 1964–69.

Stone[2], Harlan Fiske (1872–1946), Chief Justice of the US 1941–46. He served as a US Supreme Court associate justice 1925–41 before his appointment to chief justice by President Franklin D. Roosevelt.

Stone[3], Lucy (1818–93), US feminist and abolitionist. In 1869, she founded the American Woman Suffrage Association.

stone /stōn/ ▶ n. **1** the hard, solid, nonmetallic mineral matter of which rock is made, esp. as a building material. ■ a small piece of rock found on the ground. ■ (in metaphorical use) weight or lack of feeling, expression, or movement: *Isabel stood as if **turned to stone**.* ■ Astron. a meteorite made of rock, as opposed to metal. ■ Med. a calculus; a gallstone or kidney stone. **2** a piece of stone shaped for a purpose, esp. one of commemoration, ceremony, or demarcation: *a memorial stone | boundary stones.* ■ a gem or jewel. ■ short for CURLING STONE. ■ a round piece or counter, originally made of stone, used in various board games such as backgammon. ■ a large flat table or sheet, originally made of stone and later usually of metal, on which pages of type were made up. **3** a hard seed in a cherry, plum, peach, and some other fruits. **4** (pl. same) Brit. a unit of weight equal to 14 pounds (6.35 kg): *I weighed 10 stone.* **5** a natural shade of whitish-gray or brownish-gray: [as adj.] *stone stretch trousers.* ▶ v. [trans.] **1** throw stones at: *policemen were stoned by the crowd.* ■ esp. hist. execute (someone) by throwing stones at them: *Stephen **was stoned to death** in Jerusalem.* **2** remove the stone from (a fruit): *halve, stone, and peel the avocados.* **3** build, face, or pave with stone.

– PHRASES **be written** (or **engraved** or **set**) **in stone** used to emphasize that something is fixed and unchangeable: *anything can change—nothing is written in stone.* **cast** (or **throw**) **the first stone** be the first to make an accusation. [John 8:7.] **leave no stone unturned** try every possible course of action in order to achieve something. **a stone's throw** a short distance: *wild whales blowing a stone's throw from the boat.* — **stone·less** adj. [OE *stān* (n.), of Gmc. origin; rel. to Du. *steen* and Ger. *Stein*. The verb dates from ME.]

Stone Age a prehistoric period preceding the Bronze Age, when weapons and tools were made mostly of stone. The Stone Age covers a period of about 2.5 million years and is subdivided into the Paleolithic, Mesolithic, and Neolithic periods.

stone-broke ▶ adj. informal entirely without money.

stone·chat /ˈstōn,CHat/ ▶ n. a small Old World songbird (genus *Saxicola*) of the thrush family, having bold markings and a call that sounds like two stones being knocked together.

stone chi·na ▶ n. a kind of very hard earthenware resembling porcelain.

stone cold ▶ adj. completely cold. ▶ adv. **(stone-cold)** [as submodifier] completely: *stone-cold sober.*

stone crab ▶ n. a large, heavy, edible crab (*Menippe mercenaria*, family Xanthidae) of the Gulf of Mexico and Caribbean area.

stone·crop /ˈstōn,kräp/ ▶ n. a small fleshy-leaved plant (genus *Sedum*, family Crassulaceae) that typically has star-shaped yellow or white flowers and grows among rocks or on walls.

stone·cut·ter /ˈstōn,kətər/ ▶ n. a person who cuts stone from a quarry or who shapes and carves it for use.

stoned /stōnd/ ▶ adj. informal under the influence of drugs, esp. marijuana: *he was up in the deck chair **getting stoned**.* ■ very drunk.

stone deaf ▶ adj. completely deaf.

stone face ▶ n. informal a face that reveals no emotions. — **stone-faced** adj.

stone·fish /ˈstōn,fiSH/ ▶ n. (pl. same or **-fish·es**) a chiefly marine fish (*Synanceia* and other genera, family Synanceiidae) of bizarre appearance that lives in the tropical Indo-Pacific. It rests motionless in the sand with its venomous dorsal spines projecting and is a frequent cause of injury to swimmers.

stone·fly /ˈstōn,flī/ ▶ n. (pl. **-flies**) a slender insect (order Plecoptera) with transparent membranous wings, the larvae of which live in clean running water. The adults are used as bait by fly fishermen.

stone·ground /ˈstōnˈground/ ▶ adj. (of flour) ground with millstones.

Stone·henge /ˈstōn,henj/ a megalithic monument on Salisbury Plain in Wiltshire, England. Completed in several constructional phases from *c.* 2950 BC, it was probably used for ritual purposes. [from OE *stān* 'stone' + an element rel. to *hengan* 'to hang.']

stone lil·y ▶ n. (pl. **-lil·ies**) dated a fossilized sea lily.

stone mar·ten ▶ n. a Eurasian marten (*Martes foina*) that has chocolate-brown fur with a white throat.

stone·ma·son /ˈstōn,māsən/ ▶ n. a person who cuts, prepares, and builds with stone. — **stone·ma·son·ry** /-,māsənrē/ n.

Stone Moun·tain a granite mass east of Atlanta in Georgia, site of the Confederate National Monument (1917–67).

ston·er /ˈstōnər/ ▶ n. **1** informal a person who regularly takes drugs, esp. marijuana. **2** [in comb.] Brit. a person or thing that weighs a specified number of stone: *a couple of 16-stoners.*

stone·roll·er ▶ n. a small freshwater fish (genus *Campostoma*) of the minnow family that uses the hard ridge on its lower jaw to scrape food, esp. algae, from rocks.

stone·wall /ˈstōn,wôl/ ▶ v. [trans.] delay or block (a request, process, or person) by refusing to answer questions or by giving evasive replies, esp. in politics. — **stone·wall·er** n.

Stone·wall Jack·son see JACKSON[7].

stoneware /ˈstōn,we(ə)r/ ▶ n. a type of pottery that is impermeable and partly vitrified but opaque.

stone·washed /ˈstōn,wôSHt; -,wäSHt/ (also **stone·wash**) ▶ adj. (of a garment or fabric, esp. denim) washed with abrasives to produce a worn or faded appearance.

stone·work /ˈstōn,wərk/ ▶ n. the parts of a building that are made of stone. ■ the work of a mason: *a masterpiece of clever stonework.* — **stone·work·er** n.

stone·wort /ˈstōnwərt; -,wôrt/ ▶ n. a freshwater plant (*Chara* and other genera, class Charophyceae) with whorls of slender leaves, related to green algae. Many kinds become encrusted with chalky deposits, giving them a stony feel.

stonk /stäNGk/ military slang ▶ n. a concentrated artillery bombardment. ▶ v. [trans.] bombard with concentrated artillery fire. [1940s: said to be formed from elements of the artillery term *Standard Regimental Concentration*.]

ston·y /ˈstōnē/ ▶ adj. **(ston·i·er, ston·i·est)** covered with or full of small pieces of rock: *rough stony paths.* ■ made of or resembling stone: *stony steps.* ■ not having or showing feeling or sympathy: *Lorenzo's hard, stony eyes.* ■ Astron. (of a meteorite) consisting mostly of rock, as opposed to metal. — **ston·i·ly** /-nl-ē/ adv. **ston·i·ness** n. [OE *stānig* (see STONE, -Y[1]).]

ston·y-heart·ed ▶ adj. cruel or unfeeling.

stood /stŏŏd/ past and past participle of STAND.

stooge /stōōj/ ▶ n. **1** derog. a person who serves merely to support or assist others, particularly in doing unpleasant work: *you let her make you a stooge.* ■ a person who is employed to assume a particular role while keeping their true identity hidden: *a police stooge.* **2** a performer whose act involves being the butt of a comedian's jokes. ▶ v. [intrans.] **1** move around aimlessly; drift or cruise: *she **stooged around** in the bathroom for a while.* **2** perform a role that involves being the butt of a comedian's jokes. [20th C.: of unknown origin.]

stool /stōōl/ ▶ n. **1** a seat without a back or arms. ■ a support on which to stand in order to reach high objects. ■ short for FOOTSTOOL. **2** a piece of feces. **3** a root or stump of a tree or plant from which shoots spring. **4** a decoy bird in hunting. ▶ v. [intrans.] (of a plant) throw up shoots from the root. ■ [trans.] cut back (a plant) to or near ground level in order to induce new growth.

– PHRASES **at stool** Med. when defecating. [OE, of Gmc. origin; rel. to Du. *stoel*, Ger. *Stuhl*, also to STAND.]

stool·ie /ˈstōōlē/ ▶ n. informal short for STOOL PIGEON.

stool pi·geon ▶ n. a police informer. ■ a person acting as a decoy. [19th C.: so named from the original use of a pigeon fixed to a stool as a decoy.]

stoop[1] /stōōp/ ▶ v. [intrans.] **1** bend one's head or body forward and downward: *he **stooped down**.* ■ have the head and shoulders habitually bent forward: *he tends to stoop when he walks.* ■ (of a bird of prey) swoop down on a quarry. **2** lower one's moral standards so far as to do something reprehensible: *Craig wouldn't **stoop to** thieving | she was unwilling to believe that anyone could **stoop so low as** to steal from a dead woman.* ■ [with infin.] condescend to do something. ▶ n. **1** [in sing.] a posture in which the head and shoulders are habitually bent forward: *a tall, thin man with a stoop.* **2** the downward swoop of a bird of prey. [OE *stūpian* (v.), of Gmc. origin; rel. to the adj. STEEP[1].]

stoop[2] ▶ n. a porch with steps in front of a house or other building. [18th C.: from Du. *stoep*.]

stoop ball ▶ n. a ball game resembling baseball in which the ball is thrown against a building or the steps of a stoop rather than to a batter.

stooped /stōōpt/ ▶ adj. (of a person) having the head and shoulders habitually bent forward: *a thin, stooped figure.* ■ (of the shoulders or another part of the body) habitually bent forward: *the man was slight, with stooped shoulders.*

stoop la·bor ▶ n. agricultural labor performed in a stooping or squatting position.

stop /stäp/ ▶ v. **(stopped, stop·ping) 1** [intrans.] (of an event, action, or process) come to an end; cease. ■ [with pres. part.] cease to perform a specified action or have a specified experience: *she stopped giggling* | [trans.] *he stopped work for tea.* ■ [with pres. part.] abandon a specified practice or habit: *I've stopped eating meat.* ■ stop moving or operating: *he stopped to look at the view | my watch has stopped.* ■ (of a bus or train) call at a designated place to pick up or let off passengers: *main-line trains stop at platform 7.* **2** [trans.] cause (an action, process, or event) to come to an end: *this harassment has got to be stopped.* ■ prevent (an action or event) from happening: *a security guard was killed trying to stop a raid.* ■ prevent or dissuade (someone) from continuing in an activity or achieving an aim: *a campaign is under way to stop the bombers.* ■ [trans.] prevent (someone or something) from performing a specified action or undergoing a specified experience: *you can't **stop** me **from** getting what*

I want. ■ cause or order to cease moving or operating: *he stopped his car by the house* | *police were given powers to stop and search suspects.* ■ informal be hit by (a bullet). ■ instruct a bank to withhold payment on (a check). ■ refuse to supply as usual; withhold or deduct: *the union has threatened to stop the supply of minerals.* ■ Boxing defeat (an opponent) by a knockout: *he was stopped in the sixth by Tyson.* **3** [trans.] block or close up (a hole or leak). ■ block the mouth of (a fox's earth) prior to a hunt. ■ plug the upper end of (an organ pipe), giving a note an octave lower. ■ obtain the required pitch from (the string of a violin or similar instrument) by pressing at the appropriate point with the finger. ■ make (a rope) fast with a stopper. ▶**n.** **1** a cessation of movement or operation. ■ a break or halt during a journey: *allow an hour or so for driving and as long as you like for stops* | *the flight landed for a refueling stop.* ■ a place designated for a bus or train to halt and pick up or drop off passengers: *the bus was pulling up at her stop.* ■ an object or part of a mechanism that is used to prevent something from moving: *the shelves have special stops to prevent them from being pulled out too far.* ■ used in telegrams to indicate a period. ■ Phonet. a consonant produced with complete closure of the vocal tract. ■ Bridge a high card that prevents the opponents from establishing a particular suit; a control. ■ Naut. a short length of cord used to secure something. **2** a set of organ pipes of a particular tone and range of pitch. ■ (also **stop knob**) a knob, lever, or similar device in an organ or harpsichord that brings into play a set of pipes or strings of a particular tone and range of pitch. **3** Photog. the effective diameter of a lens.

– PHRASES **pull out all the stops** make a very great effort to achieve something. ■ do something very elaborately or on a grand scale. [referring to organ stops.] **put a stop to** cause (an activity) to end. **stop at nothing** be utterly ruthless or determined in one's attempt to achieve something. **stop dead** (or **short**) suddenly cease moving, speaking, or acting. **stop one's ears** put one's fingers in one's ears to avoid hearing something. **stop someone's mouth** induce someone to keep silent about something. **stop payment** instruct a bank to withhold payment on a check. **stop the show** (of a performer) provoke prolonged applause or laughter, causing an interruption.

– PHRASAL VERBS **stop by** (or **in**) call briefly and informally as a visitor. **stop off** (or **over**) pay a short visit en route to one's ultimate destination when traveling. — **stop·pa·ble** adj. [OE *(for)stoppian* 'block up (an aperture),' of West Gmc. origin; rel. to Ger. *stopfen*, from late L. *stuppare* 'to stuff.']

stop-and-go ▶**n.** [usu. as adj.] alternate stopping and restarting of progress: *stop-and-go driving.*

stop·band /'stäp,band/ ▶**n.** Electron. a band of frequencies that are attenuated by a filter.

stop bath ▶**n.** Photog. a bath for stopping the action of a preceding bath by neutralizing any of its chemical still present.

stop·cock /'stäp,käk/ ▶**n.** an externally operated valve regulating the flow of a liquid or gas through a pipe.

stope /stōp/ ▶**n.** (usu. **stopes**) a steplike part of a mine where minerals are being extracted. ▶**v.** [intrans.] [usu. as n.] (**stoping**) (in mining) excavate a series of steps or layers in (the ground or rock). ■ [as n.] (**stoping**) Geol. the process by which country rock is broken up and removed by the upward movement of magma. [18th C.: appar. rel. to the noun STEP.]

stop·gap /'stäp,gap/ ▶**n.** a temporary way of dealing with a problem or satisfying a need: *transplants are only a stopgap until more sophisticated alternatives can work.*

stop·light /'stäp,līt/ ▶**n.** another term for TRAFFIC LIGHT. ■ a red traffic light.

stop list ▶**n.** a list of words automatically omitted from a computer-generated concordance or index, typically the most frequent words, which would slow down processing unacceptably.

stop-mo·tion ▶**n.** [usu. as adj.] a cinematographic technique whereby the camera is repeatedly stopped and started, for example to give animated figures the impression of movement.

stop-off ▶**n.** another term for STOPOVER.

stop·o·ver /'stäp,ōvər/ ▶**n.** a break in a journey: *the one-day stopover in Honolulu.* ■ a place where a journey is broken: *an inviting stopover between Quebec City and Montreal.*

stop·page /'stäpij/ ▶**n.** an instance of movement, activity, or supply stopping or being stopped: *the result of the air raid was complete stoppage of production.* ■ a blockage in a narrow passage, such as the barrel of a gun. ■ a cessation of work by employees protesting the terms set by their employers. ■ Boxing a knockout.

Stop·pard /'stäpərd; 'stäp,ärd/, Sir Tom (1937–), British playwright, born in Czechoslovakia; born *Tomás Straussler*. He wrote *Rosencrantz and Guildenstern Are Dead* (1966) and *Rock 'n' Roll* (2006).

stop·per /'stäpər/ ▶**n.** **1** a plug for sealing a hole, esp. in the neck of a bottle or other container. **2** a person or thing that halts or obstructs a specified thing: [in comb.] *a crime-stopper.* ■ (in soccer and other sports) a player whose function is to block attacks on goal from the middle of the field. ■ Baseball a starting pitcher depended on to win a game or stop a losing streak, or a relief pitcher used to prevent the opposing team from scoring. ■ (in sailing or climbing) a rope or clamp for preventing a rope or cable from running out. ■ Bridge another term for CONTROL. ▶**v.** [usu. as adj.] (**stoppered**) use a stopper to seal (a bottle or other container): *a small stoppered jar.*

– PHRASES **put a** (or **the**) **stopper on** informal prevent from happening or continuing.

stop·ping point ▶**n.** a point or place at which it is convenient to stop during a journey or activity.

stop·ple /'stäpəl/ ▶**n.** a stopper or plug. ▶**v.** [trans.] seal with a stopper. [ME: partly a shortening of OFr. *estouppail* 'bung,' reinforced by the verb STOP.]

stop time ▶**n.** (in jazz) a rhythmic device whereby a chord or accent is played only on the first beat of every bar or every other bar, typically accompanying a solo.

stop valve ▶**n.** a valve used to stop the flow of liquid in a pipe.

stop·watch /'stäp,wäCH/ ▶**n.** a special watch used to time races.

stor·age /'stôrij/ ▶**n.** the action or method of storing something for future use: *the chair can be folded flat for easy storage* | [as adj.] *the room lacked storage space.* ■ the retention of retrievable data on a computer or other electronic system; memory. ■ space available for storing something. ■ the cost of storing something in a warehouse.

stor·age bat·ter·y (also **stor·age cell**) ▶**n.** a battery (or cell) used for storing electrical energy.

stor·age de·vice ▶**n.** a piece of computer equipment on which information can be stored.

stor·age ring ▶**n.** Physics an approximately circular accelerator in which particles can be effectively stored by being made to circulate continuously at high energy.

sto·rax /'stô,raks/ (also **sty·rax** /'stī-/) ▶**n.** **1** a rare fragrant gum resin obtained from an eastern Mediterranean tree, sometimes used in medicine, perfumery, and incense. ■ (**liquid storax**) a liquid balsam obtained from the Asian liquidambar tree. **2** a tropical or subtropical tree or shrub (genus *Styrax*, family Styracaceae) with showy white flowers in drooping clusters. [ME: from L., from a var. of Gk. *sturax*.]

store /stôr/ ▶**n.** **1** a retail establishment selling items to the public: *a health-food store.* ■ [as adj.] store-bought: *there's a loaf of store bread.* **2** a quantity or supply of something kept for use as needed: *the squirrel has a store of food* | fig. *her vast store of knowledge.* ■ a place where things are kept for future use or sale: *a grain store.* ■ (**stores**) supplies of equipment and food kept for use. ▶**v.** [trans.] keep or accumulate (something) for future use: *a small room used for storing furniture.* ■ retain or enter (information) for future electronic retrieval: *the data is stored on disk.* ■ (**be stored with**) have a supply of (something useful): *a mind well stored with esoteric knowledge.* ■ [intrans.] remain fresh while being stored: *they do not ship or store well.*

– PHRASES **in store** **1** in a safe place while not being used or displayed: *items held in store.* **2** coming in the future; about to happen: *he did not yet know what lay in store for him.* **set** (or **lay** or **put**) **store by** (or **on**) consider (something) to be of a particular degree of importance or value. — **stor·a·ble** adj. **stor·er** n. [ME: shortening of OFr. *estore* (n.), *estorer* (v.), from L. *instaurare* 'renew'; cf. RESTORE.]

store-and-for·ward ▶**adj.** [attrib.] Telecom. relating to or denoting a data network in which messages are routed to one or more intermediate stations where they may be stored before being forwarded to their destinations.

store-bought ▶**adj.** bought ready-made from a store; not homemade.

store·front /'stôr,frənt/ ▶**n.** **1** the facade of a store. **2** a room or set of rooms facing the street on the ground floor of a commercial building, typically used as a store: [as adj.] *a bright storefront eatery.*

store·house /'stôr,hous/ ▶**n.** a storage building. ■ a large supply of something: *storehouse of facts.*

store·keep·er /'stôr,kēpər/ ▶**n.** **1** a person who owns or runs a store. **2** a person responsible for stored goods.

store·room /'stôr,ro͞om; -,ro͝om/ ▶**n.** a room in which items are stored.

sto·rey /'stôrē/ ▶**n.** esp. Brit. var. of STORY[2].

sto·ried /'stôrēd/ ▶**adj.** [attrib.] literary celebrated in or associated with stories or legends: *the island's storied past.*

stork /stôrk/ ▶**n.** a tall long-legged wading bird (family Ciconiidae) with a long heavy bill and typically with white and black plumage, esp. the European **white stork** (*Ciconia ciconia*), which often nests on tall buildings. ■ the white stork as the pretended bringer of babies. [OE *storc*, of Gmc. origin; prob. rel. to STARK (because of its rigid stance).]

storm /stôrm/ ▶**n.** **1** a violent disturbance of the atmosphere with strong winds and usually rain, thunder, lightning, or snow. ■ (also **storm system**) an intense low-pressure weather system; a cyclone. ■ a wind of force 10 on the Beaufort scale (48–55 knots or 55-63 mph). ■ a heavy discharge of missiles or blows: *two men were taken by a storm of bullets.* **2** [usu. in sing.] a tumultuous reaction; an uproar. ■ a violent or noisy outburst of a specified feeling or reaction: *the disclosure raised a storm of protest.* **3** (**storms**) storm windows. **4** a direct assault by troops on a fortified place. ▶**v.** **1** [intrans.] move angrily or forcefully in a specified direction: *she stormed off.* ■ [with direct speech] shout (something) angrily; rage. ■ move forcefully and decisively to a specified position in a game or contest: *he barged past and stormed to the checkered flag.* **2** [trans.] (of troops) suddenly attack and capture (a building or other place) by means of force. **3** [intrans.] (of the weather) be violent, with strong winds and usually rain, thunder, lightning, or snow.

– PHRASES **the calm** (or **lull**) **before the storm** a period of unusual tranquility or stability that seems likely to presage difficult times. **storm and stress** another term for STURM UND DRANG. **take something by storm** (of troops) capture a place by a sudden and violent attack. ■ have great and rapid success in a particular place or with a particular group of people: *his first collection took the fashion world by storm.* — **up a storm** perform the specified action with great enthusiasm and energy: *the band could really play up a storm.* — **storm·proof** /-ˌpro͞of/ **adj.** [OE, of Gmc. origin; rel. to Du. *storm* and Ger. *Sturm.*]

storm cen·ter ▶ **n.** the point to which the wind blows spirally inward in a cyclonic storm. ■ the central point around which controversy or trouble happens.

storm cloud ▶ **n.** a heavy, dark rain cloud. ■ (**storm clouds**) used in reference to a threatening or ominous state of affairs.

storm cuff ▶ **n.** a tight-fitting inner cuff, typically an elasticized one, that prevents rain or wind from getting inside a coat.

storm door ▶ **n.** an additional outer door for protection in bad weather or winter.

storm flap ▶ **n.** a piece of material designed to protect an opening or fastener on a tent or coat from the effects of rain.

storm glass ▶ **n.** a sealed tube containing a solution whose clarity is thought to change when storms approach.

Storm·in' Nor·man /ˈstôrmin/ see SCHWARZKOPF[2].

storm pet·rel ▶ **n.** a small seabird (*Hydrobates* and other genera, family Hydrobatidae) of the open ocean, typically having blackish plumage and a white rump, and formerly believed to be a harbinger of bad weather.

storm surge ▶ **n.** a rising of the sea as a result of atmospheric pressure changes and wind associated with a storm.

storm troops ▶ **plural n.** another term for SHOCK TROOPS. ■ (**Storm Troops**) hist. the Nazi political militia. — **storm troop·er n.**

storm win·dow ▶ **n.** a window fixed outside a normal window for protection and insulation in bad weather or winter.

storm·y /ˈstôrmē/ ▶ **adj.** (**storm·i·er, storm·i·est**) (of weather) characterized by strong winds and usually rain, thunder, lightning, or snow: *a dark and stormy night.* ■ (of the sea or sky) having large waves or dark clouds because of windy or rainy conditions. ■ full of angry or violent outbursts of feeling. — **storm·i·ly** /ˈstôrməlē/ **adv. storm·i·ness n.**

storm·y pet·rel ▶ **n.** another term for STORM PETREL.

Stor·y /ˈstôrē/, Joseph (1779–1845), US Supreme Court associate justice (1811–45).

sto·ry[1] /ˈstôrē/ ▶ **n.** (pl. **-ries**) **1** an account of imaginary or real people and events told for entertainment: *an adventure story.* ■ a plot or story line: *the novel has a good story.* ■ a report of an item of news in a newspaper, magazine, or news broadcast: *stories in the local papers.* ■ a piece of gossip; a rumor: *there have been lots of stories going around, as you can imagine.* ■ informal a false statement or explanation; a lie: *Ellie never told stories—she believed in the truth.* **2** an account of past events in someone's life or in the evolution of something: *the story of modern farming.* ■ a particular person's representation of the facts of a matter, esp. as given in self-defense: *during police interviews, Harper changed his story.* ■ [in sing.] a situation viewed in terms of the information known about it or its similarity to another: *it is not the whole story.*

– PHRASES **but that's another story** informal used after raising a matter to indicate that one does not want to expand on it for now. **end of story** informal used to emphasize that there is nothing to add on a matter just mentioned. **it's a long story** informal used to indicate that, for now, one does not want to talk about something that is too involved or painful. **it's** (or **that's**) **the story of one's life** informal used to lament the fact that a particular misfortune has happened too often in one's experience. **the same old story** used to indicate that a particular bad situation is tediously familiar. **the story goes** it is said or rumored. **to make** (or Brit. **cut**) **a long story short** used to end an account of events quickly. [ME: shortening of Anglo-Norman Fr. *estorie*, from L. *historia* (see HISTORY).]

sto·ry[2] (Brit. also **sto·rey**) ▶ **n.** a part of a building comprising all the rooms that are on the same level: [in comb.] *a three-story building.* — **sto·ried** (Brit. also **sto·reyed**) **adj.** [in comb.] *four-storied houses.* [ME: shortening of Latin *historia* 'history, story,' a special use in Anglo-L., perh. orig. denoting a tier of painted windows or sculptures on the front of a building (representing a historical subject).]

sto·ry·board /ˈstôrēˌbôrd/ ▶ **n.** a sequence of drawings, typically with some directions and dialogue, representing the shots planned for a movie or television production.

sto·ry·book /ˈstôrēˌbo͝ok/ ▶ **n.** a book containing a story or collection of stories intended for children. ■ [as adj.] denoting something that is as idyllically perfect as things typically are in storybooks.

sto·ry ed·i·tor ▶ **n.** an editor who advises on the content and form of movie or television scripts.

sto·ry line ▶ **n.** the plot of a novel, play, movie, or other narrative form.

sto·ry·tell·er /ˈstôrēˌtelər/ ▶ **n.** a person who tells stories. — **sto·ry·tell·ing** /-ˌteliNG/ **n. & adj.**

sto·tin /stäˈtēn/ ▶ **n.** a monetary unit of Slovenia, equal to one hundredth of a tolar. [Slovene.]

sto·tin·ka /stōˈtiNGkə/ ▶ **n.** (pl. **-ki** /-kē/) a monetary unit of Bulgaria, equal to one hundredth of a lev. [Bulgarian, 'one hundredth.']

stoup /sto͞op/ ▶ **n.** a basin for holy water, esp. on the wall near the door of a Roman Catholic church for worshipers to dip their fingers in before crossing themselves. ■ archaic a flagon or beaker for drink. [ME: from ON *staup*, of Gmc. origin; rel. to the verb STEEP[2].]

Stout /stout/, Rex Todhunter (1886–1975), US writer. He created Nero Wolfe, a detective who appeared in many of his novels.

stout /stout/ ▶ **adj. 1** (of a person) somewhat fat or of heavy build. ■ (of an object) strong and thick: *stout walking boots.* **2** (of an act, quality, or person) brave and determined: *he put up a stout defense in court.* ▶ **n.** a kind of strong, dark beer brewed with roasted malt or barley. — **stout·ish adj.** (in sense 1) **stout·ly adv. stout·ness n.** (in sense 1). [ME: from Anglo-Norman Fr. and OFr. dial., of West Gmc. origin; perh. rel. to STILT. The noun (17th C.) orig. denoted any strong beer and is prob. elliptical for *stout ale.*]

stout·heart·ed /ˈstoutˈhärtid/ ▶ **adj.** courageous or determined. — **stout·heart·ed·ly adv. stout·heart·ed·ness n.**

stove[1] /stōv/ ▶ **n.** an apparatus for cooking or heating that operates by burning fuel or using electricity. ▶ **v.** [trans.] treat (an object) by heating it in a stove in order to apply a desired surface coating. [ME: from MDu. or Mid. Low Ger. *stove*; perh. rel. to STEW[1].]

stove[2] past and past participle of STAVE.

stove·pipe /ˈstōvˌpīp/ ▶ **n.** the pipe taking the smoke and gases from a stove up through a roof or to a chimney.

stove·pipe hat ▶ **n.** a silk hat resembling a top hat but much taller.

stove·top /ˈstōvˌtäp/ ▶ **n.** the upper surface of a cooking stove, including the burners. ▶ **adj.** of or related to a stovetop: *healthy, no-oil stovetop grillpan.* ■ designed to be prepared on a stovetop, rather than in an oven: *beef noodle stovetop casserole.*

stow /stō/ ▶ **v.** [trans.] pack or store (an object) carefully and neatly in a particular place.

– PHRASES **stow it!** informal used as a way of urging someone to be quiet or to stop doing something.

– PHRASAL VERBS **stow away** conceal oneself on a ship, aircraft, or other passenger vehicle in order to travel secretly or without paying the fare. [ME: shortening of BESTOW.]

stow·age /ˈstōij/ ▶ **n.** the action or manner of stowing something. ■ space for stowing something in: *there is plenty of stowage beneath the berth.*

stow·a·way /ˈstōəˌwā/ ▶ **n.** a person who stows away.

Stowe /stō/, Harriet Elizabeth Beecher (1811–96), US writer. She wrote *Uncle Tom's Cabin* (1852), which strengthened the contemporary abolitionist cause.

STP ▶ **abbr.** ■ Physiol. short-term potentiation. ■ Chem. standard temperature and pressure. ■ Professor of Sacred Theology. [from L. *Sanctae Theologiae Professor.*]

STR ▶ **abbr.** synchronous transmitter receiver.

str. ▶ **abbr.** ■ strait. ■ Rowing stroke.

stra·bis·mus /strəˈbizməs/ ▶ **n.** abnormal alignment of the eyes; the condition of having a squint. — **stra·bis·mic** /-mik/ **adj.** [17th C.: mod. L., from Gk. *strabismos*, from *strabizein* 'to squint,' from *strabos* 'squinting.']

Stra·bo /ˈsträbō/ (*c.*63 BC–*c.*AD 23), historian and geographer. His *Geographica* provides a detailed physical and historical geography of the ancient world during the reign of Augustus.

Stra·chey /ˈsträCHē/, Lytton (1880–1932), English writer; full name *Giles Lytton Strachey.* He wrote *Eminent Victorians* (1918).

strad·dle /ˈstradl/ ▶ **v.** [trans.] sit or stand with one leg on either side of: *he straddled the chair.* ■ place (one's legs) wide apart. ■ extend across or be situated on both sides of: *a mountain range straddling the Franco-Swiss border.* ■ take up or maintain an equivocal position with regard to (a political issue): *a man who had straddled the issue of taxes.* ▶ **n. 1** an act of sitting or standing with one's legs wide apart. **2** Stock Market a simultaneous purchase of options to buy and to sell a security or commodity at a fixed price. — **strad·dler n.** [16th C.: alt. of dialect *striddle*, back-form. from dial. *striddling* 'astride,' from STRIDE + the adverbial suffix *-ling.*]

Strad·i·var·i·us /ˌstradəˈve(ə)rēəs/ ▶ **n.** a violin or other stringed instrument made by Antonio Stradivari (1644–1737) or his followers. [19th C.: Latinized form of *Stradivari.*]

strafe /strāf/ ▶ **v.** [trans.] attack repeatedly with bombs or machine-gun fire from low-flying aircraft: *military aircraft strafed the village.* ▶ **n.** an attack from low-flying aircraft. [20th C.: humorous adaptation of the German World War I catchphrase *Gott strafe England* 'may God punish England.']

strag·gle /ˈstragəl/ ▶ **v.** [intrans.] move along slowly, typically in a small irregular group, so as to remain some distance behind the person or people in front. ■ grow, spread, or be laid out in an irregular way. ▶ **n.** an untidy or irregularly arranged mass or group of something: *a straggle of cottages.* — **strag·gler** /ˈstrag(ə)lər/ **n. strag·gly** /ˈstrag(ə)lē/ **adj.** [ME: perh. from dial. *strake* 'go.']

straight /strāt/ ▶ **adj. 1** extending or moving uniformly in one direction only; without a curve or bend: *a long, straight road.* ■ Geom. (of a line) lying on the shortest path between any two of its points. ■ (of an aim, blow, or course) going direct to the intended target: *a straight punch to the face.* ■ (of hair) not curly or wavy. ■ (of a garment) not flared or fitted closely to the body: *a straight skirt.* ■ (of an arch) flat-topped. **2** properly positioned so as to be level, upright, or symmetrical: *he made sure his tie was straight.* ■ [predic.] in proper order or condition: *it'll take a long time to get the place straight.* **3** not evasive; honest: *a straight answer | thank you for being straight with me.* ■ simple; straightforward. ■ (of a look) bold and steady: *he gave her a straight, no-nonsense look.* ■ (of thinking) clear, logical, and unemotional. ■ not addicted to drugs. **4** [attrib.] in continuous succession: *he scored his fourth straight win.* ■ supporting all the principles and candidates of one political party: *he generally voted a straight ticket.* **5** (of an alcoholic drink) undiluted; neat: *straight brandy.* **6** (esp. of drama) serious as opposed to comic or musical; employing the conventional techniques of its art form: *a straight play.* ■ informal (of a person) conventional or respectable: *she looked pretty straight in her school clothes.* ■ informal heterosexual. ▶ **adv. 1** in a straight line; directly: *he was gazing straight at her* | *keep* ***straight on.*** ■ with no delay or diversion; directly or immediately. **2** in or into a level, even, or upright position: *he pulled his clothes straight* | *sit up straight!* **3** correctly; clearly: *I'm so tired I can hardly think straight.* ■ honestly and directly; in a straightforward manner. **4** without a break; continuously: *he remembered working sixteen hours straight.* ▶ **n. 1** a part of something that is not curved or bent. **2** Poker a continuous sequence of five cards. **3** informal a conventional person. ■ a heterosexual.

– PHRASES **get something straight** make a situation clear, esp. by reaching an understanding. **go straight** live an honest life after being a criminal. **a straight face** a blank or serious facial expression, esp. when trying not to laugh. **the straight and narrow** the honest and morally acceptable way of living. **straight out** (or **off**) informal without hesitation or deliberation. **straight up** informal unmixed; unadulterated: *a dry Martini served straight up.* — **straight·ish adj. straight·ly adv. straight·ness n.** [ME (as an adj. and adv.): archaic past part. of STRETCH.]

straight-a·head ▶ **adj.** (esp. of popular music) straightforward, simple, or unadorned.

straight an·gle ▶ **n.** Math. an angle of 180°.

straight-arm ▶ **v.** [trans.] informal ward off (an opponent) or remove (an obstacle) with the arm unflexed: *I straight-armed the woman leaning in on her.*

straight ar·row ▶ **n.** informal an honest, morally upright person.

straight·a·way /ˈstrātəˌwā/ ▶ **adv.** immediately. ▶ **adj.** extending or moving in a straight line. ▶ **n.** a straight section of a road or racetrack.

straight chain ▶ **n.** Chem. a chain of atoms in a molecule, usually carbon atoms, that is neither branched nor formed into a ring.

straight chair ▶ **n.** a straight-backed side chair.

straight·en /ˈstrātn/ ▶ **v.** make or become straight. ■ [trans.] make tidy or put in order again. ■ [intrans.] stand or sit erect after bending: *he straightened up.* ■ (**straighten up**) (of a vehicle, ship, or aircraft) stop turning and move in a straight line. — **straight·en·er n.**

straight-faced ▶ **adj.** with a blank or serious facial expression.

straight flush ▶ **n.** (in poker or brag) a hand of cards all of one suit and in a continuous sequence (for example, the seven, eight, nine, ten, and jack of spades).

straight·for·ward /ˌstrātˈfôrwərd/ ▶ **adj.** uncomplicated and easy to do or understand: *in a straightforward case no fees will be charged.* ■ (of a person) honest and frank. — **straight·for·ward·ly adv. straight·for·ward·ness n.**

straight·jack·et ▶ **n. & v.** var. of STRAITJACKET.

straight-laced ▶ **adj.** var. of STRAIT-LACED.

straight-line ▶ **adj.** containing, characterized by, or relating to straight lines or motion in a straight line: *the Porsche's straight-line stability.* ■ Finance of or relating to a method of depreciation allocating a given percentage of the cost of an asset each year for a fixed period,

straight man ▶ **n.** the person in a comedy duo who speaks lines that give a comedian the opportunity to make jokes.

straight pool ▶ **n.** a form of pool in which the players specify the ball they plan to pocket and which pocket the ball will drop into before taking a shot.

straight ra·zor ▶ **n.** a razor having a long blade set in a handle, usually folding like a penknife.

straight shoot·er ▶ **n.** informal an honest and forthright person. — **straight-shoot·ing adj.**

straight stitch ▶ **n.** a single, short, separate embroidery stitch.

straight time ▶ **n.** normal working hours, paid at a regular rate.

straight-up ▶ **adj.** informal honest; trustworthy: *you sounded like a straight-up guy.*

strain¹ /strān/ ▶ **v. 1** [trans.] force (a part of one's body or oneself) to make a strenuous or unusually great effort: *I stopped and listened, straining my ears for any sound.* ■ injure (a limb, muscle, or organ) by overexerting it or twisting it awkwardly: *glare from the screen can strain your eyes.* ■ [intrans.] make a strenuous and continuous effort: *his voice was so quiet that I had to strain to hear it.* ■ make severe or excessive demands on: *he strained her tolerance to the limit.* ■ [intrans.] pull or push forcibly at something: *the bear* ***strained at*** *the chain around its neck.* ■ stretch (something) tightly: *the barbed wire fence was strained to posts six feet high.* **2** [trans.] pour (a mainly liquid substance) through a porous or perforated device or material in order to separate out any solid matter: *strain the custard into a bowl.* ■ cause liquid to drain off (food that has been boiled, soaked, or canned) by using such a device. ■ drain off (liquid) in this way: ***strain off*** *the surplus fat.* ▶ **n. 1** a force tending to pull or stretch something to an extreme or damaging degree: *the usual type of chair puts an enormous strain on the spine* | *aluminum may bend under strain.* ■ Physics the magnitude of a deformation, equal to the change in the dimension of a deformed object divided by its original dimension. ■ an injury to a part of the body caused by overexertion or twisting a muscle awkwardly: *he has a slight groin strain.* **2** a severe or excessive demand on the strength, resources, or abilities of someone or something: *she's obviously* ***under*** *considerable* ***strain.*** ■ a state of tension or exhaustion resulting from this: *the telltale signs of nervous strain.* **3** (usu. **strains**) the sound of a piece of music as it is played or performed: *the strains of a hurdy-gurdy playing in the street.* — **strain·a·ble adj.** [ME (as a v.): from OFr. *estreindre,* from L. *stringere* 'draw tight.']

strain² ▶ **n. 1** a breed, stock, or variety of an animal or plant developed by breeding. ■ a natural or cultured variety of a microorganism with a distinct form, biochemistry, or virulence. **2** a particular tendency as part of a person's character: *there was a powerful strain of insanity on her mother's side of the family.* ■ a variety of a particular abstract thing: *a strain of feminist thought.* [OE *strīon* 'acquisition, gain,' of Gmc. origin; rel. to L. *struere* 'to build up.']

strained /strānd/ ▶ **adj. 1** (of an atmosphere, situation, or relationship) not relaxed or comfortable; tense or uneasy: *there was a strained silence.* ■ (of a person) showing signs of tiredness or nervous tension: *Jean's pale, strained face.* ■ (of an appearance or performance) produced by deliberate effort rather than natural impulse; artificial or forced: *I put on my strained smile for the next customer.* ■ (of a statement or representation) labored or far-fetched: *my example may seem a little strained and artificial.* **2** (of a limb or muscle) injured by overexertion or twisting. **3** (of a mainly liquid substance) having been strained to separate out any solid matter.

strain·er /ˈstrānər/ ▶ **n.** a device having holes punched in it or made of crossed wires for separating solid matter from a liquid: *a tea strainer.*

strait /strāt/ ▶ **n. 1** (also **straits**) a narrow passage of water connecting two seas or two large areas of water: [in place names] *the Strait of Gibraltar.* **2** (**straits**) used in reference to a situation characterized by a specified degree of trouble or difficulty. — **strait·ly adv. strait·ness n.** [ME: shortening of OFr. *estreit* 'tight, narrow,' from L. *strictus* 'drawn tight' (see STRICT).]

strait·ened /ˈstrātnd/ ▶ **adj. 1** characterized by poverty: *they lived in straitened circumstances.* **2** restricted in range or scope: *their straitened horizons.*

strait·jack·et /ˈstrātˌjakət/ (also **straight·jack·et**) ▶ **n.** a strong garment with long sleeves that can be tied together to confine the arms of a violent prisoner or mental patient. ■ used in reference to something that restricts freedom of action, development, or expression: *the government is operating in an economic straitjacket.* ▶ **v.** (**-jack·eted, -jack·eting**) [trans.] restrain with a straitjacket. ■ impose severely restrictive measures on (a person or activity): *the treaty should not be used as a tool to straitjacket international trade.*

strait-laced (also **straight-laced**) ▶ **adj.** having or showing very strict moral attitudes.

strake /strāk/ ▶ **n. 1** a continuous line of planking or plates from the stem to the stern of a ship or boat. **2** a protruding ridge fitted to an aircraft or other structure to improve aerodynamic stability. [ME: from Anglo-L. *stracus, straca;* prob. from the Gmc. base of the verb STRETCH.]

stra·mo·ni·um /strəˈmōnēəm/ ▶ **n.** a preparation of the dried leaves or poisonous seeds of the jimson weed, with medical and other uses. [17th C.: mod. L. (part of the plant's binomial), perh. an alt. of Tartar *turman* 'horse medicine.']

strand¹ /strand/ ▶ **v.** [trans.] drive or leave (a boat, sailor, or sea creature) aground on a shore: *the ships were stranded in shallow water* | [as adj.] (**stranded**) *a stranded whale.* ■ leave (someone) without the means to move from somewhere: *they were stranded in St. Louis by the blizzard.* ▶ **n.** literary the shore of a sea, lake, or large river: *a heron glided to rest on a pebbly strand.* [OE (as a n.), of unknown origin.]

strand² ▶ **n.** a single thin length of something such as thread, fiber, or wire, esp. as twisted together with others: *a strand of cotton* | *strands of grass.* ■ a string of beads or pearls. ■ an element that forms part of a complex whole: *Marxist theories evolved from different strands of social analysis.* [15th C.: of unknown origin.]

strand·ed /ˈstrandid/ ▶ **adj.** [attrib.] (of thread, rope, or similar) arranged in single thin lengths twisted together: *stranded cotton* | [in comb.] fig. *the many-stranded passions of the country.*

strand·wolf /ˈstrandˌwo͝olf/ ▶ **n.** S. African the brown hyena (*Hyaena brunnea*), which often frequents the shore, where it scavenges dead fish and birds. [18th C.: from South Afr. Du., from *strand* 'beach' + *wolf* 'wolf.']

strange /strānj/ ▶ **adj. 1** unusual or surprising in a way that is unsettling or hard to understand. **2** not previously visited, seen, or encountered; unfamiliar or alien: *she found herself in bed in a strange place.* ■ [predic.] (**strange to/at/in**) archaic unaccustomed to or unfamiliar with: *I am strange to the work.*

– PHRASES **strange to say** (or literary **tell**) it is surprising or unusual that. — **strange·ly adv.** [ME: shortening of OFr. *estrange,* from L. *extraneus* 'external, strange.']

strange·ness /ˈstrānjnis/ ▶ **n. 1** the state or fact of being strange. **2** Physics one of six flavors of quark.

stran·ger /ˈstrānjər/ ▶ **n.** a person whom one does not know or with whom one is not familiar: *she remained* ***a stranger to*** *him.* ■ a person who does not know, or is not known in, a particular place or community: *I'm* ***a stranger in*** *these parts.* ■ (**stranger to**) a person entirely unaccustomed to (a feeling, experience, or situation).

– PHRASES **hello, stranger!** humorous used to greet someone whom one has not seen for some time. [ME: shortening of OFr. *estrangier,* from L. *extraneus* (see STRANGE).]

PRONUNCIATION KEY ə *ago, up;* ər *over, fur;* a *hat;* ā *ate;* ä *car;* e *let;* ē *see;* i *fit;* ī *by;* NG *sing;* ō *go;* ô *law, for;* oi *toy;* o͝o *good;* o͞o *goo;* ou *out;* TH *thin;* T͟H *then;* ZH *vision*

stran·gle /'straNGgəl/ ▶v. [trans.] squeeze or constrict the neck of (a person or animal), esp. so as to cause death: *the victim was strangled with a scarf.* ■ [as adj.] (**strangled**) sounding as though the speaker's throat is constricted: *a series of strangled gasps.* ■ suppress (an impulse, action, or sound): *she strangled a sob.* ■ hamper or hinder the development or activity of: *overrestrictive policies that strangle growth.* —**stran·gler** /'straNGg(ə)lər/ n. [ME: shortening of OFr. *estrangler*, from L. *strangulare*, from Gk. *strangalan*, from *strangalē* 'halter,' rel. to *strangos* 'twisted.']

stran·gle·hold /'straNGgəl,hōld/ ▶n. [in sing.] a grip around the neck of another person that can kill by asphyxiation if held for long enough. ■ complete or overwhelming control: *he broke the union that held a stranglehold on bus service.*

stran·gles /'straNGgəlz/ ▶plural n. [usu. treated as sing.] an infection of the upper respiratory tract of horses, caused by the bacterium *Streptococcus equi* and resulting in enlargement of the lymph nodes in the throat, which may impair breathing. [17th C.: pl. of obs. *strangle* 'strangulation,' from STRANGLE.]

stran·gu·late /'straNGgyə,lāt/ ▶v. [trans.] [often as adj.] (**strangulated**) **1** Med. prevent circulation of the blood supply through (a part of the body, esp. a hernia) by constriction: *a strangulated hernia.* **2** informal strangle; throttle. ■ [as adj.] (**strangulated**) sounding as though the speaker's throat is constricted: *a strangulated cry.* [17th C. (in the sense 'suffocate'): from L. *strangulat-* 'choked,' from the verb *strangulare* (see STRANGLE).]

stran·gu·la·tion /,straNGgyə'lāsHən/ ▶n. **1** the action or state of strangling or being strangled: *death due to strangulation.* ■ the process or state of severely restricting the activities or supplies of an area or community or of undergoing such restrictions: *economic strangulation.* **2** Med. the condition in which circulation of blood to a part of the body (esp. a hernia) is cut off by constriction.

stran·gu·ry /'straNGgyərē/ ▶n. a condition caused by blockage or irritation at the base of the bladder, resulting in severe pain and a strong desire to urinate. —**stran·gu·ri·ous** /-'gyo͝orēəs/ adj. [ME: via L. from Gk. *strangouria*, from *stranx, strang-* 'drop squeezed out' + *ouron* 'urine.']

strap /strap/ ▶n. a strip of leather, cloth, or other flexible material, often with a buckle, used to fasten, secure, or carry something or to hold on to something. ■ a strip of metal, often hinged, used to fasten or secure something. ■ (**the strap**) punishment by beating with a strip of leather. ■ var. of STROP. ▶v. (**strapped, strap·ping**) **1** [trans.] fasten or secure in a specified place or position with a strap or seat belt. **2** [trans.] beat (someone) with a strip of leather: *I expected when my dad walked in that he'd strap him.* [16th C. (denoting a trap for birds, also a piece of timber fastening two objects together): dial. form of STROP.]

strap·hang·er /'strap,haNGər/ ▶n. informal a standing passenger in a bus or train. ■ a person who commutes to work by public transportation. —**strap-hang** v.

strap hinge ▶n. a hinge with long leaves or flaps for screwing onto the surface of a door or gate.

strap·less /'strapləs/ ▶adj. (esp. of a dress or bra) without shoulder straps.

strap·pa·do /strə'pādō; -'pä-/ ▶n. (pl. **-dos**) (usu. **the strappado**) hist. a form of punishment or torture in which the victim was secured to a rope and made to fall from a height almost to the ground before being stopped with an abrupt jerk. ■ the instrument used for inflicting this punishment or torture. [16th C.: from Fr. *(e)strapade*, from Ital. *strappata*, from *strappare* 'to snatch.']

strapped /strapt/ ▶adj. informal short of money: *I'm constantly strapped for cash.*

strap·ping[1] /'strapiNG/ ▶adj. big and strong: *they had three strapping sons.*

strap·ping[2] ▶n. **1** adhesive plaster for binding injured parts of the body. **2** strips of leather or pliable metal used to hold, strengthen, or fasten something.

Stras·berg /'stras,bərg; 'sträs-/, Lee (1901–82), US drama teacher, born in Austria; born *Israel Strassberg.* He was a leading figure in the development of method acting.

Stras·bourg /'sträs,bo͝org; 'sträz-; -,bərg/ a city in northeastern France; pop. 256,000.

stra·ta /'strātə; 'stratə/ plural form of STRATUM.

strat·a·gem /'stratəjəm/ ▶n. a plan or scheme, esp. one used to outwit an opponent or achieve an end: *a series of devious stratagems.* ■ archaic skill in devising such plans or schemes; cunning. [15th C. (orig. denoting a military ploy): from Fr. *stratagème*, via L. from Gk. *stratēgēma*, from *stratēgein* 'be a general,' from *stratēgos*, from *stratos* 'army' + *agein* 'to lead.']

stra·tal /'strātl/ ▶adj. relating or belonging to strata or a stratum.

stra·te·gic /strə'tējik/ ▶adj. relating to the identification of long-term or overall aims and interests and the means of achieving them: *strategic planning.* ■ carefully designed or planned to serve a particular purpose or advantage: *alarms are positioned at strategic points around the prison.* ■ relating to the gaining of overall or long-term military advantage. ■ (of human or material resources) essential in fighting a war: *the strategic forces on Russian territory.* ■ (of bombing or weapons) done or for use against industrial areas and communication centers of enemy territory as a long-term military objective: *strategic nuclear missiles.* Often contrasted with TACTICAL. —**stra·te·gi·cal** adj. **stra·te·gi·cal·ly** /-ik(ə)lē/ adv. [as submodifier] *a strategically placed mirror.* [19th C.: from Fr. *stratégique*, from Gk. *stratēgikos*, from *stratēgos* (see STRATAGEM).]

Stra·te·gic Arms Lim·i·ta·tion Talks (abbr. **SALT**) a series of negotiations between the US and the Soviet Union (1968–83) aimed at the limitation or reduction of nuclear armaments.

Stra·te·gic Arms Re·duc·tion Talks (abbr.: **START**) a series of arms-reduction negotiations between the US and the Soviet Union begun in 1983.

strat·e·gist /'stratəjist/ ▶n. a person skilled in planning action or policy, esp. in war or politics.

strat·e·gize /'stratə,jīz/ ▶v. [intrans.] devise a strategy or strategies.

strat·e·gy /'stratəjē/ ▶n. (pl. **-gies**) a plan of action or policy designed to achieve a major or overall aim. ■ the art of planning and directing overall military operations and movements in a war or battle. Often contrasted with TACTICS (see TACTIC). ■ a plan for such military operations and movements: *nonprovocative defense strategies.* [19th C.: from Fr. *stratégie*, from Gk. *stratēgia* 'generalship,' from *stratēgos* (see STRATAGEM).]

Strat·ford-up·on-A·von /'stratfərd ə,pän 'āvən; ə,pôn; 'ā,vän/ a town in central England, the birth and burial place of William Shakespeare; pop. 20,000. —**Strat·for·di·an** /strat'fôrdēən/ n.

strath·spey /straTH'spā/ ▶n. a slow Scottish dance. ■ a piece of music for such a dance, typically in four-four time. [18th C.: from *Strathspey*, the name of the valley of the Spey River in Scotland.]

strat·i·form /'stratə,fôrm/ ▶adj. tech. arranged in layers: *stratiform clouds.* ■ Geol. (of a mineral deposit) formed parallel to the bedding planes of the surrounding rock.

strat·i·fy /'stratə,fī/ ▶v. (**-fies, -fied**) [trans.] [usu. as adj.] (**stratified**) form or arrange into strata: *socially stratified cities* | [intrans.] *the residues have begun to stratify.* ■ arrange or classify: *stratifying patients into well-defined risk groups.* ■ place (seeds) close together in layers in moist sand or peat to preserve them or to help them germinate. ■ [intrans.] (of seeds) be germinated by this method. —**strat·i·fi·ca·tion** /,stratəfi'kāsHən/ n.

stra·tig·ra·phy /strə'tigrəfē/ ▶n. the branch of geology concerned with the order and relative position of strata and their relationship to the geological time scale. —**stra·tig·ra·pher** /-fər/ n. **strat·i·graph·ic** /,stratə'grafik/ adj. **strat·i·graph·i·cal** /,stratə'grafikəl/ adj. [19th C.: from STRATUM + -GRAPHY.]

stra·toc·ra·cy /strə'täkrəsē/ ▶n. (pl. **-cies**) rare government by military forces. ■ a military government.

stra·to·cu·mu·lus /,stratō'kyo͞omyələs; ,strā-/ ▶n. cloud forming a low layer of clumped or broken gray masses.

stra·to·pause /'stratə,pôz/ ▶n. the interface between the stratosphere and the ionosphere. [1950s: from STRATOSPHERE, suggested by TROPOPAUSE.]

strat·o·sphere /'stratə,sfi(ə)r/ ▶n. the layer of the earth's atmosphere above the troposphere, extending to about 50 km above the earth's surface (the lower boundary of the mesosphere). ■ fig. the very highest levels of a profession or other sphere, or of prices or other quantities: *her next big campaign launched her into the fashion stratosphere.* —**strat·o·spher·ic** /,stratə'sfi(ə)rik; -'sferik/ adj.

strat·o·vol·ca·no /,stratōväl'kānō; ,strā-/ ▶n. (pl. **-noes**) a volcano built up of alternate layers of lava and ash.

Strat·ton /'stratn/, Charles S. see THUMB.

stra·tum /'strātəm; 'strat-/ ▶n. (pl. **stra·ta** /'strātə; 'strat-/) **1** a layer or a series of layers of rock in the ground: *a stratum of flint.* ■ a thin layer within any structure: *thin strata of air.* **2** a level or class to which people are assigned according to their social status, education, or income. ■ Stat. a group into which members of a population are divided in stratified sampling. [16th C.: mod. L., from L., 'something spread or laid down,' neut. past part. of *sternere* 'strew.']

stra·tum cor·ne·um /'strātəm ,kôrnēəm; 'stra-/ ▶n. Anat. the horny outer layer of the skin. [L., lit. 'horny layer.']

stra·tus /'strātəs; 'strat-/ ▶n. cloud forming a continuous horizontal gray sheet, often with rain or snow. [19th C.: mod. L., from L., 'strewn,' past part. of *sternere*.]

Strauss[1] /strous; sHtrous/ a family of Austrian composers. Johann (1804–49), known as **Strauss the Elder**, composed waltzes. His son Johann (1825–99), known as **Strauss the Younger** and **the Waltz King**, also composed many famous waltzes, such as *The Blue Danube* (1867).

Strauss[2] /strous/, Levi (c.1829–1902), US manufacturer; born in Germany. He established Levi Strauss & Company in 1850 to sell the work pants that became known as blue jeans.

Strauss[3] /strous; sHtrous/, Richard (1864–1949), German composer. His operas include *Der Rosenkavalier* (1911).

Stra·vin·sky /strə'vinskē/, Igor Fyodorovich (1882–1971), Russian composer. His compositions for ballet include *The Firebird* (1910) and *The Rite of Spring* (1913).

straw /strô/ ▶n. **1** dried stalks of grain, used esp. as fodder or as material for thatching, packing, or weaving: [as adj.] *a straw hat.* ■ a pale yellow color like that of straw: [as adj.] *a dull straw color.* ■ used in reference to something insubstantial or worthless: *it seemed as if the words were merely straw.* ■ [with negative] anything or at all (used to emphasize how little something is valued): *if he finds you here, my life won't be worth a straw.* **2** a single dried stalk of grain: *the tramp sat chewing a straw.* ■ a stalk of grain or something similar used in drawing lots: *we had to*

draw straws for the food we had. **3** a thin hollow tube of paper or plastic for sucking drink from a glass or bottle.
– PHRASES **grasp** (or **clutch** or **catch**) **at straws** (or **a straw**) be in such a desperate situation as to resort to even the most unlikely means of salvation. **draw the short straw** be the unluckiest of a group of people. **the last** (or **final**) **straw** a further difficulty or annoyance that makes a situation unbearable. **a straw in the wind** a slight hint of future developments. — **straw·y** adj. [OE *strēaw*, of Gmc. origin; rel. to Du. *stroo* and Ger. *Stroh*, also to STREW.]

straw·ber·ry /ˈstrô,berē; -b(ə)rē/ ▶ n. **1** a sweet soft red fruit with a seed-studded surface. **2** the low-growing plant (genus *Fragaria*) of the rose family that produces this fruit, having white flowers, lobed leaves, and runners, and found throughout north temperate regions. **3** a deep pinkish-red color. [OE *strēa(w)berige, strēowberige* (see STRAW, BERRY).]

straw·ber·ry blond (also **strawberry blonde**) ▶ adj. (of hair) of a light reddish-blond color. ■ (of a person) having hair of such a color. ▶ n. a light reddish-blond hair color. ■ a person who has hair of such a color.

straw·ber·ry mark ▶ n. a soft red birthmark.

straw·ber·ry roan ▶ adj. denoting an animal's coat that is chestnut mixed with white or gray. ▶ n. a strawberry roan animal.

straw·ber·ry tree ▶ n. a small evergreen tree (*Arbutus unedo*) of the heath family that bears clusters of whitish flowers late in the year, often at the same time as the strawberrylike fruit from the previous season's flowers.

straw·board /ˈstrô,bôrd/ ▶ n. board made of straw pulp, used in building (faced with paper) and in book covers.

straw boss ▶ n. informal a junior supervisor, esp. a worker who has some responsibility but little authority.

straw·flow·er /ˈstrô,flou(ə)r/ ▶ n. an everlasting flower (*Helichrysum, Helipterum*, and other genera) of the daisy family.

straw man ▶ n. a person compared to a straw image; a sham. ■ a sham argument set up to be defeated.

straw poll (also **straw vote**) ▶ n. an unofficial ballot conducted as a test of opinion: *I took a straw poll among my immediate colleagues.*

stray /strā/ ▶ v. [intrans.] move without a specific purpose or by mistake, esp. so as to get lost or arrive somewhere where one should not be: *I strayed a few blocks.* ■ move so as to escape from control or leave the place where one should be: *dog owners are urged not to allow their dogs to stray* | fig. *I appear to have strayed a long way from our original topic.* ■ [intrans.] (of the eyes or a hand) move idly or casually in a specified direction: *her eyes strayed to the telephone.* ■ (of a person who is married or in a long-term relationship) be unfaithful. ■ [intrans.] literary wander or roam in a specified direction: *over these mounds the Kurdish shepherd strays.* ▶ adj. [attrib.] **1** not in the right place; not where it should be or where other items of the same kind are: *he pushed a few stray hairs from her face.* ■ appearing somewhere by chance or accident; not part of a general pattern or plan: *she was killed by a stray bullet.* ■ (of a domestic animal) having no home or having wandered away from home: *stray dogs.* **2** Physics (of a physical quantity) arising as a consequence of the laws of physics, not by deliberate design, and usually having a detrimental effect on the operation or efficiency of equipment: *stray capacitance.* ▶ n. **1** a stray person or thing, esp. a domestic animal. **2** (**strays**) electrical phenomena interfering with radio reception. — **stray·er** n. [ME: shortening of Anglo-Norman Fr. and OFr. *estrayer* (v.), Anglo-Norman Fr. *strey* (n.), partly from ASTRAY.]

streak /strēk/ ▶ n. **1** a long, thin line or mark of a different substance or color from its surroundings: *a streak of oil.* ■ Microbiol. a narrow line of bacteria smeared on the surface of a solid culture medium. **2** an element of a specified kind in someone's character: *Lucy had a ruthless streak.* ■ [usu. with adj.] a continuous period of specified success or luck: *the theater is **on a winning streak** | the team's 11-game **losing streak**.* ▶ v. **1** [trans.] cover (a surface) with streaks: *tears streaking her face, Cynthia looked up.* ■ dye (hair) with long, thin lines of a different, typically lighter color than one's natural hair color. ■ Microbiol. smear (a needle, swab, etc.) over the surface of a solid culture medium to initiate a culture. **2** [intrans.] move very fast in a specified direction: *the cat leaped free and streaked across the street.* **3** [intrans.] informal run naked in a public place so as to shock or amuse others.
– PHRASES **like a streak** informal very fast: *he is off like a streak.* **streak of lightning** a flash of lightning. — **streak·er** n. (in sense 3 of the **verb**). [OE *strica*, of Gmc. origin; rel. to Du. *streek* and Ger. *Strich*, also to STRIKE. The sense 'run naked' was orig. US slang.]

streak·ing /ˈstrēkiNG/ ▶ n. long, thin lines of a different color from their surroundings, esp. on dyed hair.

streak·y /ˈstrēkē/ ▶ adj. (**streak·i·er, streak·i·est**) having streaks of different colors or textures: *streaky blond hair.* ■ informal variable in quality; not predictable or reliable: *King has always been a famously streaky hitter.* — **streak·i·ly** /-lē/ adv. **streak·i·ness** n.

stream /strēm/ ▶ n. **1** a small, narrow river. **2** a continuous flow of liquid, air, or gas. ■ (**a stream/streams of**) a mass of people or things moving continuously in the same direction: *there is a steady stream of visitors.* ■ (**a stream/streams of**) a large number of things that happen or come one after the other: *a woman shouted a stream of abuse.* ■ Comput. a continuous flow of data or instructions, typically one having a constant or predictable rate. ▶ v. **1** [intrans.] (of liquid) run or flow in a continuous current in a specified direction. ■ (of a mass of people or things) move in a continuous flow in a specified direction: *he was watching the taxis streaming past.* **2** [intrans.] (usu. **be streaming**) (of a person or part of the body) produce a continuous flow of liquid; run with liquid: *my eyes were streaming.* **3** [intrans.] (of hair, clothing, etc.) float or wave at full extent in the wind: *her cloak **streamed behind** her.*
– PHRASES **against** (or **with**) **the stream** against (or with) the prevailing view or tendency. **on stream** in or into operation or existence; available: *more jobs are **coming on stream**.* — **stream·let** /-lit/ n. [OE *strēam* (n.), of Gmc. origin; rel. to Du. *stroom*, Ger. *Strom*, from an Indo-Eur. root shared by Gk. *rhein* 'to flow.']

stream·er /ˈstrēmər/ ▶ n. a long, narrow strip of material used as a decoration or symbol: *plastic party streamers* | fig. *a streamer of smoke.* ■ [usu. as adj.] a banner headline in a newspaper: *his appearance was announced with a streamer headline.* ■ Astron. an elongated mass of luminous matter, e.g., in auroras or the sun's corona.

stream·ing /ˈstrēmiNG/ ▶ adj. [attrib.] Comput. relating to or making use of a form of tape transport, used mainly to provide backup storage, in which data may be transferred in bulk while the tape is in motion. ▶ n. a method of relaying data (esp. video and audio material) over a computer network as a steady continuous stream.

stream·line /ˈstrēm,līn/ ▶ v. [trans.] [usu. as adj.] (**streamlined**) design or provide with a form that presents very little resistance to a flow of air or water, increasing speed and ease of movement: *streamlined passenger trains.* ■ fig. make (an organization or system) more efficient and effective by employing faster or simpler working methods: *the company streamlined its operations by removing whole layers of management.* ▶ n. a line along which the flow of a moving fluid is least turbulent. ▶ adj. **1** (of fluid flow) free from turbulence. **2** dated having a streamlined shape: *a streamline airplane.*

stream of con·scious·ness ▶ n. Psychol. a person's thoughts and conscious reactions to events, perceived as a continuous flow. ■ a literary style in which one's thoughts and feelings are depicted in a continuous and uninterrupted flow.

street /strēt/ ▶ n. a public road in a city or town, typically with houses and buildings on one or both sides: | [in place names] *45 Lake Street.* ■ (**the street**) used to refer to the financial markets and activities on Wall Street. ■ (**the street/streets**) the roads or public areas of a city or town: *every week, fans stop me in the street.* ■ [as adj.] of or relating to the outlook, values, or lifestyle of those young people who are perceived as composing a fashionable urban subculture: *New York City street culture.* ■ [as adj.] denoting someone who is homeless: *he ministered to street people in storefront missions.* ■ [as adj.] performing or being performed on the street: *street theater.*
– PHRASES **on the streets 1** homeless. **2** working as a prostitute. [OE *strǣt*, of West Gmc. origin, from late L. *strāta (via)* 'paved (way),' fem. past part. of *sternere* 'lay down.']

street Ar·ab ▶ n. archaic a raggedly dressed homeless child wandering the streets.

street·car /ˈstrēt,kär/ ▶ n. another term for TROLLEY CAR.

street clothes ▶ n. clothes suitable for everyday wear in public.

street cred·i·bil·i·ty (also informal **street cred**) ▶ n. acceptability among young black urban residents.

street hock·ey ▶ n. a form of hockey played on a paved surface using in-line skates.

street-leg·al ▶ adj. (of a vehicle) meeting all legal requirements for use on ordinary roads.

street·light /ˈstrēt,līt/ (also **street·lamp**) ▶ n. a light illuminating a road, typically mounted on a tall post.

street-smart ▶ adj. informal having the skills and knowledge necessary for dealing with modern urban life, esp. the difficult or criminal aspects of it: *a street-smart hustler on a motorcycle.* ▶ n. (**street smarts**) these skills and knowledge.

street val·ue ▶ n. the price a commodity, esp. an amount of drugs, would fetch if sold illicitly: *detectives seized drugs with a street value of $300,000.*

street·walk·er /ˈstrēt,wôkər/ ▶ n. a prostitute who seeks customers in the street. — **street·walk·ing** /-,wôkiNG/ n. & adj.

street·wise /ˈstrēt,wīz/ ▶ adj. another term for STREET-SMART. ■ reflective of modern urban life, esp. that of urban youth: *streetwise fashion.*

strength /streNG(k)TH; strenTH/ ▶ n. **1** the quality or state of being strong, in particular: ■ physical power and energy: *cycling can help you build up your strength.* ■ the emotional or mental qualities necessary in dealing with situations or events that are distressing or difficult: *many people find strength in religion.* ■ the capacity of an object or substance to withstand great force or pressure: *they were taking no chances with the strength of the retaining wall.* ■ the influence or power possessed by a person, organization, or country: *the political and military strength of European governments.* ■ the degree of intensity of a feeling or belief: *street protests demonstrated the strength of feeling against the president.* ■ the cogency of an argument or case: *the strength of the argument for property taxation.* ■ the potency, intensity, or speed of a force or natural agency: *the wind had markedly increased in strength.* ■ the potency or degree of concentration of a drug, chemical, or drink: *it's double the strength of your average beer.* **2** a good or beneficial quality or attribute of a person or thing: *his strength was his obsessive single-mindedness.* ■ literary a person or thing perceived as a source of mental or emotional support: *he was my closest friend, my* *strength and shield.* **3** the number of people comprising a group, typically a team or army: *the peacetime strength of the army was 415,000.* ■ a number of people required to make such a group complete: *we are now 100 officers **below strength**.*

– PHRASES **from strength** from a secure or advantageous position. **go from strength to strength** develop or progress with increasing success. **in strength** in large numbers. **on the strength of** on the basis or with the justification of. **tower** (or **pillar**) **of strength** a person who can be relied upon to give a great deal of support and comfort to others. — **strength·less** adj. [OE *strengthu*, from the Gmc. base of STRONG.]

strength·en /ˈstreNG(k)THən; ˈstrenTHən/ ▶v. make or become stronger: *strengthen the teeth.*

– PHRASES **strengthen someone's hand** (or **hands**) enable or encourage a person to act more vigorously or effectively. — **strength·en·er** n.

stren·u·ous /ˈstrenyo͞oəs/ ▶adj. requiring or using great exertion: *Beijing's strenuous efforts to join the World Trade Organization.* — **stren·u·ous·ly** adv. **stren·u·ous·ness** n. [17th C.: from L. *strenuus* 'brisk' + -OUS.]

strep /strep/ ▶n. Med., informal short for STREPTOCOCCUS.

Strep·sip·ter·a /strepˈsiptərə/ Entomol. an order of minute parasitic insects that comprises the stylopids. — **strep·sip·ter·an** n. & adj. [mod. L. (pl.), from Gk. *strepsi-* (combining form of *strephein* 'to turn') + *pteron* 'wing.']

strepto- ▶comb. form twisted; in the form of a twisted chain: *streptomycete.* ■ associated with streptococci or streptomycetes: *streptokinase.* [from Gk. *streptos* 'twisted,' from *strephein* 'to turn.']

strep·to·coc·cus /ˌstreptəˈkäkəs/ ▶n. (pl. **-coc·ci** /-ˈkäksī; -sē/) a bacterium of a genus (*Streptococcus*) that includes the agents of souring of milk and dental decay, and hemolytic pathogens causing various infections such as scarlet fever and pneumonia. — **strep·to·coc·cal** /-ˈkäkəl/ adj.

strep·to·ki·nase /ˌstreptəˈkīnās; -ˈkinās; -nāz/ ▶n. Biochem. an enzyme produced by some streptococci that is involved in breaking down red blood cells. It is used to treat inflammation and blood clots.

strep·to·my·cete /ˌstreptəˈmīsēt/ ▶n. a bacterium (*Streptomyces* and related genera, order Actinomycetales) that occurs chiefly in soil as aerobic saprophytes resembling molds, several of which are important sources of antibiotics. [1950s: Anglicized sing. of mod. L. *Streptomyces*, from STREPTO- 'twisted' + Gk. *mukēs, mukēt-* 'fungus.']

strep·to·my·cin /ˌstreptəˈmīsin/ ▶n. Med. an antibiotic produced by the bacterium *Streptomyces griseus*. It was the first drug to be successful against tuberculosis but is now chiefly used with other drugs because of its toxic side effects.

stress /stres/ ▶n. **1** pressure or tension exerted on a material object: *the distribution of stress is uniform across the bar.* ■ the degree of this measured in units of force per unit area. **2** a state of mental or emotional strain or tension resulting from adverse or very demanding circumstances: *he's obviously **under a lot of stress*** | [in comb.] *stress-related illnesses.* ■ something that causes such a state: *the stresses and strains of public life.* **3** particular emphasis or importance: *he has started to lay greater stress on the government's role in industry.* ■ emphasis given to a particular syllable or word in speech, typically through a combination of relatively greater loudness, higher pitch, and longer duration: *normally, the stress falls on the first syllable.* ▶v. **1** [reporting verb] give particular emphasis or importance to in speech or writing. ■ [trans.] give emphasis to (a syllable or word) when pronouncing it. **2** subject to pressure or tension: *this type of workout does stress the shoulder and knee joints.* **3** [trans.] cause mental or emotional strain or tension in. ■ [intrans.] informal become tense or anxious; worry. — **stress·less** adj. **stres·sor** /ˈstresər/ n. (in senses 2 and 3 of the verb). [ME: shortening of DISTRESS, or partly from OFr. *estresse* 'narrowness, oppression,' based on L. *strictus* 'drawn tight' (see STRICT).]

stress frac·ture ▶n. a fracture of a bone caused by repeated (rather than sudden) mechanical stress.

stress·ful /ˈstresfəl/ ▶adj. causing mental or emotional stress: *corporate finance work can be stressful.* — **stress·ful·ly** adv. **stress·ful·ness** n.

stress in·con·ti·nence ▶n. a condition (found chiefly in women) in which there is involuntary emission of urine when pressure within the abdomen increases suddenly, as in coughing or jumping.

stress-timed ▶adj. (of a language) characterized by a rhythm in which primary stresses occur at roughly equal intervals, irrespective of the number of unstressed syllables in between. English is a stress-timed language.

stretch /strecH/ ▶v. [intrans.] **1** (of something soft or elastic) be made or be capable of being made longer or wider without tearing or breaking: *rubber will stretch easily when pulled.* ■ [trans.] cause to do this: *stretch the elastic.* ■ [trans.] pull (something) tightly from one point to another or across a space: *canvas was stretched over the bamboo frame.* ■ last or cause to last longer than expected: [intrans.] *her nap had stretched to two hours.* ■ [trans.] make great demands on the capacity or resources of: *the cost had **stretched** their finances **to the limit**.* ■ [trans.] cause (someone) to make maximum use of their talents or abilities: *it's too easy—it doesn't stretch me.* ■ [trans.] adapt or extend the scope of (something) in a way that exceeds a reasonable or acceptable limit: *to describe her as sweet would be stretching it a bit.* **2** straighten or extend one's body or a part of one's body to its full length, typically so as to tighten one's muscles or in order to reach something: *the cat yawned and stretched.* **3** [trans.] extend or spread over an area or period of time: *the beach stretches for over four miles.* ▶n. **1** an act of stretching one's limbs or body. ■ the fact or condition of a muscle being stretched. ■ Baseball a phase of a pitcher's delivery, during which the arms are raised above and behind the head. ■ Baseball a shortened form of a pitcher's windup, typically used to prevent base runners from stealing or gaining a long lead. ■ [usu. as adj.] the capacity of a material or garment to stretch or be stretched; elasticity: *stretch jeans.* ■ a difficult or demanding task: *it was a stretch for me sometimes to come up with the rent.* **2** a continuous area or expanse of land or water: *a treacherous stretch of road.* ■ a continuous period of time: *long stretches of time.* ■ informal a period of time spent in prison: *a four-year stretch for tax fraud.* ■ a straight part of a racetrack, typically the homestretch: *he made a promising start, but faded down the stretch.* ■ Sailing the distance covered on one tack. **3** [usu. as adj.] informal a motor vehicle or aircraft modified so as to have extended seating or storage capacity: *a black stretch limo.*

– PHRASES **at a stretch** in one continuous period. **by no** (or **not by any**) **stretch of the imagination** used to emphasize that something is definitely not the case. **stretch one's legs** go for a short walk, typically after sitting in one place for some time. — **stretch·a·bil·i·ty** /-əˈbilitē/ n. **stretch·a·ble** adj. [OE *streccan*, of West Gmc. origin; rel. to Du. *strekken* and Ger. *strecken*.]

stretch·er /ˈstrecHər/ ▶n. **1** a framework of two poles with a long piece of canvas slung between them, used for carrying sick, injured, or dead people. **2** a thing that stretches something, in particular: ■ a wooden frame over which a canvas is spread and tautened ready for painting. **3** a rod or bar joining and supporting chair legs. ■ a crosspiece in the bottom of a boat on which a rower's feet are braced. **4** a brick or stone laid with its long side along the face of a wall. Compare with HEADER (sense 3).

stretch·er-bear·er ▶n. a person who helps to carry the sick or injured on stretchers.

stretch marks ▶plural n. streaks or stripes on the skin, esp. on the abdomen, caused by distension of the skin from obesity or during pregnancy.

stretch re·cep·tor ▶n. Physiol. a sensory receptor that responds to the stretching of surrounding muscle tissue and so contributes to the coordination of muscle activity.

stretch·y /ˈstrecHē/ ▶adj. (**stretch·i·er**, **stretch·i·est**) (esp. of material or a garment) able to stretch or be stretched easily. — **stretch·i·ness** n.

stret·to /ˈstretō/ Music ▶n. (pl. **stret·ti** /ˈstretē/) a section at the end of a fugue in which successive introductions of the theme follow at shorter intervals than before, increasing the sense of excitement. ■ (also **stret·ta**) a passage, esp. at the end of an aria or movement, to be performed in quicker time. ▶adv. (as a direction) in quicker time. [Ital., 'narrow.']

streu·sel /ˈstro͞ozəl; ˈstroi-/ ▶n. a crumbly topping or filling made from fat, flour, sugar, and often cinnamon. ■ a cake or pastry with such a topping. [from Ger. *Streusel*, from *streuen* 'sprinkle.']

strew /stro͞o/ ▶v. (past part. **strewn** /stro͞on/ or **strewed**) [trans.] (usu. **be strewn**) scatter or spread (things) untidily over a surface or area. ■ (usu. **be strewn with**) cover (a surface or area) with untidily scattered things. ■ be scattered or spread untidily over (a surface or area): *leaves strewed the path.* — **strew·er** n. [OE *stre(o)wian*, of Gmc. origin; rel. to Du. *strooien*, Ger. *streuen*, from an Indo-Eur. root shared by L. *sternere* 'lay flat.']

strewn field ▶n. Geol. a region of the earth's surface over which tektites of a similar age and presumed origin are found.

stri·a /ˈstrīə/ ▶n. (pl. **stri·ae** /ˈstrī-ē/) tech. a linear mark, slight ridge, or groove on a surface, often one of a number of similar parallel features. ■ Anat. any of a number of longitudinal collections of nerve fibers in the brain. [17th C.: from L., 'furrow.']

stri·ate /ˈstrīˌāt/ tech. ▶adj. marked with striae. ▶v. [trans.] [usu. as adj.] (**stri·at·ed**) mark with striae. — **stri·a·tion** /strīˈāsHən/ n.

stri·at·ed mus·cle ▶n. Physiol. muscle tissue in which the contractile fibrils in the cells are aligned in parallel bundles, so that their different regions form stripes visible in a microscope. Also called SKELETAL MUSCLE. Often contrasted with SMOOTH MUSCLE.

stri·a·tum /strīˈātəm/ ▶n. (pl. **-a·ta** /-ˈātə/) Anat. short for CORPUS STRIATUM. — **stri·a·tal** /-ˈātl/ adj.

strick·en /ˈstrikən/ past participle of STRIKE. ▶adj. seriously affected by an undesirable condition or unpleasant feeling. ■ (of a face or look) showing great distress.

strick·le /ˈstrikəl/ ▶n. **1** a rod used to level off a heaped measure. **2** a whetting tool. [OE *stricel* (sense 1); rel. to STRIKE.]

strict /strikt/ ▶adj. demanding that rules concerning behavior are obeyed and observed. ■ (of a rule or discipline) demanding total obedience or observance; rigidly enforced. ■ (of a person) following rules or beliefs exactly. ■ exact in correspondence or adherence to something; not allowing or admitting deviation or relaxation. — **strict·ness** n. [ME: from L. *strictus*, past part. of *stringere* 'tighten, draw tight.']

strict·ly /ˈstriktlē/ ▶adv. **1** in a way that involves rigid enforcement or that demands obedience. **2** used to indicate that one is applying words or rules exactly or rigidly: [sentence adverb] ***strictly speaking**, ham is a cured, cooked leg of pork.* ■ with no exceptions; completely or absolutely. ■ no more than; purely.

stric·ture /ˈstrikcHər/ ▶n. **1** a restriction on a person or activity: *religious strictures on everyday life.* **2** a sternly critical or censorious remark or instruction. **3** Med. abnormal narrowing of a canal or duct in the body: *a colonic stricture.* — **stric·tured** adj.

stride /strīd/ ▶v. (past **strode** /strōd/; past part. **strid·den** /ˈstridn/) **1** [no obj., with adverbial of direction] walk with long, decisive steps in a specified direction:

he strode across the road. ■ [trans.] walk about or along (a street or other place) in this way: *a woman striding the cobbled streets.* **2** [intrans.] (**stride across/over**) cross (an obstacle) with one long step. ■ [trans.] literary bestride. ▶**n. 1** a long, decisive step. ■ [in sing.] the length of a step or manner of taking steps in walking or running: *the horse shortened its stride.* **2** (usu. **strides**) a step or stage in progress toward an aim. ■ (**one's stride**) a good or regular rate of progress, esp. after a slow or hesitant start: *he seems to have hit his stride.* **3** [as adj.] denoting or relating to a rhythmic style of jazz piano playing in which the left hand alternately plays single bass notes on the downbeat and chords an octave higher on the upbeat.

– PHRASES **break (one's) stride** slow or interrupt the pace at which one walks or moves. **match someone stride for stride** manage to keep up with a competitor. **take something in (one's) stride** deal with something difficult or unpleasant in a calm and accepting way. — **strid•er n.** [OE *stride* (n.) 'single long step,' *strīdan* (v.) 'stand or walk with the legs wide apart,' prob. from a Gmc. base meaning 'strive, quarrel'; rel. to Du. *strijden* 'fight' and Ger. *streiten* 'quarrel.']

stri•dent /'strīdnt/ ▶**adj.** loud and harsh; grating. ■ presenting a point of view, esp. a controversial one, in an excessively and unpleasantly forceful way. ■ Phonet. another term for SIBILANT. — **stri•den•cy n. stri•dent•ly adv.** [17th C.: from L. *strident-* 'creaking,' from the verb *stridere.*]

stri•dor /'strīdər/ ▶**n.** a harsh or grating sound. ■ Med. a harsh vibrating noise when breathing, caused by obstruction of the windpipe or larynx. [17th C.: from L., from *stridere* 'to creak.']

strid•u•late /'strijə,lāt/ ▶**v.** [intrans.] (of an insect, esp. a male cricket or grasshopper) make a shrill sound by rubbing the legs, wings, or other parts of the body together. —**strid•u•lant** /-lənt/ **adj. strid•u•la•tion** /,strijə'lāSHən/ **n. strid•u•la•to•ry** /-lə,tôrē/ **adj.** [19th C.: from Fr. *striduler*, from L. *stridulus* 'creaking,' from the verb *stridere*.]

strife /strīf/ ▶**n.** angry or bitter disagreement over fundamental issues; conflict. [ME: shortening of Old Fr. *estrif* (rel. to OFr. *estriver* 'strive').]

strig•il /'strijəl/ ▶**n.** an instrument with a curved blade used, esp. by ancient Greeks and Romans, to scrape sweat and dirt from the skin in a hot-air bath or after exercise; a scraper. ■ Entomol. a comblike structure on the forelegs of some insects, used chiefly for grooming. [from L. *strigilis*, from *stringere* 'touch lightly.']

stri•gose /'strī,gōs/ ▶**adj.** Bot. covered with short stiff adpressed hairs. ■ Entomol. finely grooved or furrowed. [18th C.: from L. *striga* 'swath, furrow' + -OSE[1].]

strike /strīk/ ▶**v.** (past **struck** /strək/) **1** [trans.] hit forcibly and deliberately with one's hand or a weapon or other implement. ■ inflict (a blow): [with two objs.] *he struck her two blows.* ■ accidentally hit (a part of one's body) against something. ■ come into forcible contact or collision with. ■ (of a beam or ray of light or heat) fall on (an object or surface): *the light struck her diamond.* ■ (in sporting contexts) hit or kick (a ball) so as to score a run, point, or goal. ■ [intrans.] (of a clock) indicate the time by sounding a chime or stroke. ■ ignite (a match) by rubbing it briskly against an abrasive surface. ■ produce (fire or a spark) as a result of friction. ■ bring (an electric arc) into being. ■ produce (a musical note) by pressing or hitting a key. **2** [trans.] (of a disaster, disease, or other unwelcome phenomenon) occur suddenly and have harmful or damaging effects on: *an earthquake struck the island.* ■ [intrans.] carry out an aggressive or violent action, typically without warning: *the murderer struck again.* ■ (usu. **be struck down**) kill or seriously incapacitate (someone). ■ (**strike something into**) cause or create a particular strong emotion in (someone): *drugs strike fear into parents' hearts.* ■ [with obj. and complement] cause (someone) to be in a specified state. **3** [trans.] (of a thought or idea) come into the mind of (someone) suddenly or unexpectedly. ■ cause (someone) to have a particular impression: *the idea struck her as odd.* ■ (**be struck by/with**) find particularly interesting, noticeable, or impressive. **4** [intrans.] (of employees) refuse to work as a form of organized protest, typically in an attempt to obtain a particular concession or concessions from their employer. ■ [trans.] undertake such action against (an employer). **5** [trans.] cancel, remove, or cross out with or as if with a pen. ■ (**strike someone off**) officially remove someone from membership of a professional group. ■ (**strike something down**) abolish a law or regulation. **6** [trans.] make (a coin or medal) by stamping metal. ■ (in cinematography) make (another print) of a film. ■ reach, achieve, or agree to (something involving agreement, balance, or compromise): *you have to strike a happy medium.* ■ (in financial contexts) reach (a figure) by balancing an account. **7** [trans.] discover (gold, minerals, or oil) by drilling or mining. ■ [intrans.] (**strike on/upon**) discover or think of, esp. unexpectedly or by chance. ■ come to or reach: *we struck the main trail.* **8** [no obj., with adverbial of direction] move or proceed vigorously or purposefully: *she struck out into the lake with a practiced crawl.* ■ (**strike out**) start out on a new or independent course or endeavor. **9** [trans.] take down (a tent or the tents of an encampment). ■ dismantle (theatrical scenery): *start striking the set.* ■ lower or take down (a flag or sail), esp. as a salute or to signify surrender. **10** [trans.] insert (a cutting of a plant) in soil to take root. ■ [intrans.] (of a plant or cutting) develop roots: *small conifers will strike from cuttings.* ■ [intrans.] (of a young oyster) attach itself to a bed. ▶**n. 1** a refusal to work organized by a body of employees as a form of protest, typically in an attempt to gain a concession or concessions from their employer: *local workers went on strike.* ■ [with adj.] a refusal to do something expected or required, typically by a body of people, with a similar aim: *a rent strike.* **2** a sudden attack, typically a military one. ■ (in bowling) an act of knocking down all the pins with one's first ball. **3** a discovery of gold, minerals, or oil by drilling or mining. **4** Baseball a pitch that is counted against the batter, in particular one that the batter swings at and misses, or that passes through the strike zone without the batter swinging, or that the batter hits foul (unless two strikes have already been called). A batter accumulating three strikes is out. ■ a pitch that passes through the strike zone and is not hit. ■ something to one's discredit. **5** the horizontal or compass direction of a stratum, fault, or other geological feature.

– PHRASES **strike a blow for** (or **at/against**) do something to help (or hinder) a cause, belief, or principle. **strike hands** archaic (of two people) clasp hands to seal a deal or agreement. **strike it rich** informal acquire a great deal of money, typically in a sudden or unexpected way. **strike a pose** (or **attitude**) hold one's body in a particular position to create an impression. **strike while the iron is hot** make use of an opportunity immediately. [with ref. to smithing.]

– PHRASAL VERBS **strike back 1** retaliate. **2** (of a gas burner) burn from an internal point before the gas has become mixed with air. **strike someone out** (or **strike out**) Baseball put a batter out (or be put out) from play as a batter by means of three strikes. ■ (**strike out**) informal fail or be unsuccessful. **strike up** (or **strike something up**) (of a band or orchestra) begin to play a piece of music. ■ (**strike something up**) begin a friendship or conversation with someone, typically in a casual way. [OE *strīcan* 'go, flow' and 'rub lightly,' of West Gmc. origin; rel. to Ger. *streichen* 'to stroke,' also to STROKE.]

strike•break•er /'strīk,brākər/ ▶**n.** a person who works or is employed in place of others who are on strike, thereby making the strike ineffectual. — **strike•break v. strike•break•ing** /-,brākiNG/ **n.**

strike force ▶**n.** [treated as sing. or pl.] a military force equipped and organized for sudden attack.

strike•out /'strīk,out/ ▶**n.** Baseball an out called when a batter accumulates three strikes. ▶**adj.** Comput. (of text) having a horizontal line through the middle; crossed out.

strike pay ▶**n.** money paid to strikers by their trade union.

strike price ▶**n.** Finance **1** the price fixed by the seller of a security after receiving bids in a tender offer, typically for a sale of bonds or a new stock market issue. **2** the price at which a put or call option can be exercised.

strik•er /'strīkər/ ▶**n. 1** an employee on strike. **2** the player who is to strike the ball in a game; a player considered in terms of ability to strike the ball. ■ (chiefly in soccer) a forward or attacker.

strik•er plate ▶**n.** a metal plate attached to a doorjamb or lidded container, against which the end of a spring-lock bolt strikes when the door or lid is closed.

strike-slip fault ▶**n.** Geol. a fault in which rock strata are displaced mainly in a horizontal direction, parallel to the line of the fault.

strike zone ▶**n.** Baseball an area over home plate extending approximately from the armpits to the knees of a batter when in the batting position. The ball must be pitched through this area in order for a strike to be called.

strik•ing /'strīkiNG/ ▶**adj. 1** attracting attention by reason of being unusual, extreme, or prominent. ■ dramatically good-looking or beautiful. **2** [attrib.] (of an employee) on strike. ▶**n.** the action of striking. — **strik•ing•ly adv.** [as submodifier] *a strikingly beautiful girl.*

strik•ing price ▶**n.** another term for STRIKE PRICE.

Strind•berg /'strin(d),bərg/, Johan August (1849–1912), Swedish playwright and novelist. His plays include *Miss Julie* (1888).

Strine /strīn/ (also **strine**) informal ▶**n.** the English language as spoken by Australians; the Australian accent, esp. when considered striking or uneducated. ■ an Australian. ▶**adj.** of or relating to Australians or Australian English. [1960s: representing the pronunc. of *Australian* in Strine.]

string /striNG/ ▶**n. 1** material consisting of threads of cotton, hemp, or other material twisted together to form a thin length. ■ a piece of such material used to tie around or attach to something. ■ a piece of catgut or similar material interwoven with others to form the head of a sports racket. ■ a length of catgut or wire on a musical instrument, producing a note by vibration. ■ (**strings**) the stringed instruments in an orchestra. ■ [as adj.] of, relating to, or consisting of stringed instruments. **2** a set of things tied or threaded together on a thin cord: *she wore a string of agates.* ■ a sequence of similar items or events. ■ Comput. a linear sequence of characters, words, or other data. ■ a group of racehorses trained at one stable. ■ a team or player holding a specified position in an order of preference. **3** a tough piece of fiber in vegetables, meat, or other food, such as a tough elongated piece connecting the two halves of a bean pod. **4** short for STRINGBOARD. **5** a hypothetical one-dimensional subatomic particle having the dynamical properties of a flexible loop. ■ (also **cosmic string**) (in cosmology) a hypothetical threadlike concentration of energy within the structure of space-time. ▶**v.** (past **strung** /strəNG/) **1** [with obj. and adverbial] hang (something) so that it stretches in a long line. ■ thread (a series of small objects) on a string. ■ (**be strung**) be arranged in a long line. ■ (**string something together**) add items to one another to form a series or coherent whole. **2** [trans.] fit a string or strings to (a musical instrument, a racket, or a bow). **3** [trans.] remove the strings from (a bean).

– PHRASES **no strings attached** informal used to show that an offer or opportunity carries no special conditions or restrictions. **on a string** under one's control or influence.

– PHRASAL VERBS **string along** informal stay with or accompany a person or group casually or as long as it is convenient. **string someone along** informal mislead someone deliberately over a length of time, esp. about one's intentions. **string something out** cause something to stretch out; prolong something. ■ **(string out)** stretch out into a long line. ■ **(be strung out)** be nervous or tense. ■ **(be strung out)** be under the influence of alcohol or drugs. **string someone/something up** hang something up on strings. ■ kill someone by hanging. — **string·less** adj. **string·like** /-ˌlīk/ adj. [OE *streng* (n.), of Gmc. origin; rel. to Ger. *Strang*, also to STRONG. The verb (dating from ME) is first recorded in the senses 'arrange in a row' and 'fit with a string.']

string bass /bās/ ▶ n. (esp. among jazz musicians) a double bass.

string bean ▶ n. **1** any of various beans eaten in their fibrous pods, such as scarlet runners. **2** informal a tall thin person.

string bi·ki·ni ▶ n. a scant bikini with straps of thin cord.

string·board /ˈstriNG,bôrd/ ▶ n. a board with which the ends of the steps in a staircase are covered.

string·course /ˈstriNG,kôrs/ ▶ n. a raised horizontal band or course of bricks on a building. Also called CORDON.

stringed /striNGd/ ▶ adj. (of a musical instrument) having strings.

strin·gen·do /strēnˈjendō; strin-/ Music ▶ adv. & adj. (esp. as a direction) with increasing speed. ▶ n. (pl. **-gen·dos** or **-gen·di** /-ˈjendē/) a passage marked to be performed in this way. [Ital., 'squeezing, binding together.']

strin·gent /ˈstrinjənt/ ▶ adj. (of regulations, requirements, or conditions) strict, precise, and exacting. — **strin·gen·cy** n. **strin·gent·ly** adv. [17th C.: from L. *stringent-* 'drawing tight,' from the verb *stringere*.]

string·er /ˈstriNGər/ ▶ n. **1** a longitudinal structural piece in a framework, esp. that of a ship or aircraft. **2** informal a newspaper correspondent not on the regular staff of a newspaper, esp. one retained on a part-time basis to report on events in a particular place. **3** a side of a staircase, which supports the treads and risers. *See illustration at* STAIR. **4** [in comb.] a sports player holding a specified position in an order of preference.

string·halt /ˈstriNG,hôlt/ ▶ n. a condition affecting one or both of a horse's hind legs, causing exaggerated bending of the hock.

string or·ches·tra ▶ n. an orchestra consisting only of bowed string instruments of the violin family.

string·piece /ˈstriNG,pēs/ ▶ n. a long piece supporting and connecting the parts of a wooden framework.

string quar·tet ▶ n. a chamber music ensemble consisting of first and second violins, viola, and cello. ■ a piece of music for such an ensemble.

string the·o·ry ▶ n. a cosmological theory based on the existence of cosmic strings. See also STRING (sense 5).

string tie ▶ n. a very narrow necktie.

string·y /ˈstriNGē/ ▶ adj. (**string·i·er**, **string·i·est**) (esp. of hair) resembling string; long, thin, and lusterless. ■ (of a person) tall, wiry, and thin. ■ (of food) containing tough fibers and so hard to eat. ■ (of a liquid) viscous; forming strings. — **string·i·ly** /-əlē/ adv. **string·i·ness** n.

strip[1] /strip/ ▶ v. (**stripped, strip·ping**) [trans.] **1** remove all coverings from. ■ remove the clothes from (someone). ■ [intrans.] take off one's clothes: *she stripped down to her underwear.* ■ pull or tear off (a garment or covering). ■ remove bark and branches from (a tree). ■ remove paint from (a surface) with solvent. ■ remove (paint) in this way. ■ remove the stems from (tobacco). ■ milk (a cow) to the last drop. **2** leave bare of accessories or fittings. ■ remove the accessory fittings of or take apart (a machine, motor vehicle, etc.) to inspect or adjust it/ **3** (**strip someone of**) deprive someone of (rank, power, or property). **4** sell off (the assets of a company) for profit. ■ Finance divest (a bond) of its interest coupons so that it and they may be sold separately. **5** tear the thread or teeth from (a screw, gearwheel, etc.). ■ [intrans.] (of a screw, gearwheel, etc.) lose its thread or teeth. **6** [intrans.] (of a bullet) be fired from a rifled gun without spin owing to a loss of surface. ▶ n. an act of undressing, esp. in a striptease. ■ [as adj.] used for or involving the performance of stripteases. [ME: of Gmc. origin; rel. to Du. *stropen*.]

strip[2] ▶ n. **1** a long, narrow piece of cloth, paper, plastic, or some other material. ■ a long, narrow area of land. ■ a main road in or leading out of a town, lined with shops, restaurants, and other facilities. ■ steel or other metal in the form of narrow flat bars. **2** a comic strip. [ME: from or rel. to Mid. Low Ger. *strippe* 'strap, thong,' prob. also to STRIPE.]

strip crop·ping ▶ n. cultivation in which different crops are sown in alternate strips to prevent soil erosion.

stripe /strīp/ ▶ n. **1** a long narrow band or strip, typically of the same width throughout its length, differing in color or texture from the surface on either side of it. ■ archaic a blow with a scourge or lash. **2** a chevron sewn onto a uniform to denote military rank. ■ a type or category: *entrepreneurs of all stripes are joining in the offensive.* ▶ v. [trans.] (usu. **be striped**) mark with stripes. [ME: perh. a back-form. from STRIPED, of Du. or Low Ger. origin.]

striped /strīpt/ ▶ adj. marked with or having stripes.

striped bass ▶ n. a large bass (*Morone saxatilis*, family Perchichthyidae) of North American coastal waters, with dark horizontal stripes along the upper sides, migrating up streams to breed.

striped hy·e·na ▶ n. a hyena (*Hyaena hyaena*) with numerous black stripes on the body and legs, living in steppe and desert areas from northeastern Africa to India.

striped ma·ple ▶ n. a compact North American maple (*Acer pennsylvanicum*) with large leaves and vertically striped bark.

striped pole·cat ▶ n. another term for ZORILLA.

strip·ey /ˈstrīpē/ ▶ adj. var. of STRIPY.

strip·ling /ˈstripliNG/ ▶ n. humorous a young man. [ME: prob. from STRIP[2] (from the notion of "narrowness," i.e., slimness) + -LING.]

strip mall ▶ n. a shopping mall consisting of stores and restaurants typically in one-story buildings located on a busy main road.

strip-mine ▶ v. [trans.] obtain (ore or coal) by open-pit mining. ■ subject (an area of land) to open-pit mining. ▶ n. (**strip mine**) a mine worked by this method.

stripped-down ▶ adj. [attrib.] reduced to essentials. ■ (of a machine, motor vehicle, etc.) having had all internal parts removed; dismantled.

strip·per /ˈstripər/ ▶ n. **1** a device used for stripping something. ■ solvent for removing paint. **2** a striptease performer.

strip pok·er ▶ n. a form of poker in which a player with a losing hand takes off an item of clothing as a forfeit.

strip-search ▶ v. [trans.] search (someone) for concealed items, typically drugs or weapons, in a way that involves the removal of all their clothes. ▶ n. (**strip search**) an act of searching someone in such a way.

strip·tease /ˈstrip,tēz/ ▶ n. a form of entertainment in which a performer gradually undresses to music in a way intended to be sexually exciting. — **strip·teas·er** n.

strip·y /ˈstrīpē/ (also **strip·ey**) ▶ adj. striped.

strive /strīv/ ▶ v. (past **strove** /strōv/ or **strived**; past part. **striv·en** /strivən/ or **strived**) [intrans.] make great efforts to achieve or obtain something. ■ struggle or fight vigorously: *scholars must strive against bias.* — **striv·er** n. [ME: shortening of OFr. *estriver*; rel. to *estrif* 'strife.']

strobe /strōb/ informal ▶ n. **1** a stroboscope. ■ a stroboscopic lamp. **2** an electronic flash for a camera. ▶ v. [intrans.] **1** flash intermittently. ■ [trans.] light as if with a stroboscope. **2** exhibit or give rise to strobing. [1940s: abbrev. of *stroboscopic* (see STROBOSCOPE).]

stro·bi·la /strəˈbīlə/ ▶ n. (pl. **-lae** /-lē/) Zool. a form of an invertebrate that can divide to form a series of individual organisms. ■ the segmented part of the body of a tapeworm that consists of a long chain of proglottids. ■ a stack of immature larval jellyfish formed on a sessile polyplike form by sequential budding. — **strob·i·la·tion** /ˌstrōbəˈlāSHən/ n. [19th C.: mod. L., from Gk. *strobilē* 'twisted plug of lint,' from *strephein* 'to twist.']

stro·bi·lus /ˈstrōbələs/ ▶ n. (pl. **-li** /-ˌlī/) Bot. the cone of a pine, fir, or other conifer. ■ a conelike structure, such as the flower of the hop. [18th C.: from late L., from Gk. *strobilos*, from *strephein* 'to twist.']

strob·ing /ˈstrōbiNG/ ▶ n. **1** irregular movement and loss of continuity sometimes seen in lines and stripes in a television picture. **2** jerkiness in what should be a smooth movement of an image on a screen.

stro·bo·scope /ˈstrōbə,skōp/ ▶ n. Physics an instrument for studying periodic motion or determining speeds of rotation by shining a momentary bright light at intervals so that a moving object appears stationary. ■ a lamp made to flash intermittently, esp. for this purpose. — **stro·bo·scop·ic** /ˌstrōbəˈskäpik/ adj. **stro·bo·scop·i·cal·ly** /ˌstrōbəˈskäpik(ə)lē/ adv. [19th C.: from Gk. *strobos* 'whirling' + -SCOPE.]

strode /strōd/ past of STRIDE.

stro·ga·noff /ˈstrôgə,nôf; ˈstrō-/ ▶ n. a dish in which the central ingredient, typically strips of beef, is cooked in a sauce containing sour cream. [for Count Pavel *Stroganov* (1772–1817), Russian diplomat.]

stroke /strōk/ ▶ n. **1** an act of hitting or striking someone or something; a blow. ■ a method of striking the ball in sports or games. ■ Golf an act of hitting the ball with a club, as a unit of scoring. ■ the sound made by a striking clock. **2** an act of moving one's hand or an object across a surface, applying gentle pressure. ■ a mark made by drawing a pen, pencil, or paintbrush in one direction across paper or canvas: *careful, regular strokes.* ■ a line forming part of a written or printed character. ■ a short printed or written diagonal line typically separating characters or figures. **3** a movement, esp. one of a series, in which something moves out of its position and back into it; a beat: *the ray swam with effortless strokes of its huge wings.* ■ the whole motion of a piston in either direction. ■ the rhythm to which a series of repeated movements is performed. ■ a movement of the arms and legs forming one of a series in swimming. ■ style of moving the arms and legs in swimming. ■ (in rowing) the mode or action of moving the oar. ■ (also **stroke oar**) the oar or oarsman nearest the stern of a boat, setting the timing for the other rowers. **4** a sudden disabling attack or loss of consciousness caused by an interruption in the flow of blood to the brain, esp. through thrombosis. ▶ v. [trans.] **1** move one's hand with gentle pressure over (a surface, esp. hair, fur, or skin), typically repeatedly; caress. ■ [with obj. and adverbial of place] apply (something) to a surface using a gentle movement: *she strokes blue eyeshadow on her eyelids.* ■ informal reassure or flatter (someone), esp. in order to gain their cooperation. **2** act as the stroke of (a boat or crew). **3** hit or kick (a ball) smoothly and deliberately. ■ score (a run or point) in such a manner: *the senior stroked a two-run single.*

– PHRASES **at a** (or **one**) **stroke** by a single action having immediate effect. **not** (or **never**) **do a stroke of work** do no work at all. **on the stroke of ——** precisely at the specified time. **put someone off their stroke** disconcert someone so that they do not work or perform as well as they might; break the pattern or rhythm of someone's work. **stroke**

of genius an outstandingly brilliant and original idea. **stroke of luck** (or **good luck**) a fortunate occurrence that could not have been predicted or expected. [OE *strācian* 'caress lightly,' of Gmc. origin; rel. to Du. *streek* 'a stroke,' Ger. *streichen* 'to stroke,' also to STRIKE.]

stroke play ▶ n. a game of golf in which the score is reckoned by counting the number of strokes taken overall, as opposed to the number of holes won.

stroll /strōl/ ▶ v. [no obj., with adverbial of direction] walk in a leisurely way: *I strolled around the city.* ▶ n. a short leisurely walk. ■ fig. a victory or objective that is easily achieved. [17th C.: prob. from Ger. *strollen, strolchen*, from *Strolch* 'vagabond,' of unknown ultimate origin.]

stroll·er /'strōlər/ ▶ n. **1** a chair on wheels, typically folding, in which a baby or young child can be pushed along. **2** a person taking a leisurely walk.

stroll·ing play·ers ▶ plural n. hist. a troupe of itinerant actors.

stro·ma /'strōmə/ ▶ n. (pl. **-ma·ta** /-mətə/) **1** Anat. & Biol. the supportive tissue of an epithelial organ, tumor, gonad, etc., consisting of connective tissues and blood vessels. ■ the spongy framework of protein fibers in a red blood cell or platelet. ■ Bot. the matrix of a chloroplast, in which the grana are embedded. **2** Bot. a cushionlike mass of fungal tissue, having spore-bearing structures either embedded in it or on its surface. — **stro·mal** adj. (esp. Anat.) **stro·mat·ic** /strō'matik/ adj. (esp. Bot.). [19th C.: mod. L., via late L. from Gk. *strōma* 'coverlet.']

Strom·bo·li /'strämbəlē/ a volcanic island in the Mediterranean Sea, one of the Lipari Islands.

Strom·bo·li·an /sträm'bōlēən/ ▶ adj. Geol. denoting volcanic activity of the kind typified by Stromboli, with continual mild eruptions in which lava fragments are ejected.

Strong /strông; sträng/, William (1808–95), US Supreme Court associate justice 1870–80.

strong /strông/ ▶ adj. (**strong·er** /'strông(g)ər/, **strong·est** /'strông(g)ist/) **1** having the power to move heavy weights or perform other physically demanding tasks. ■ [attrib.] able to perform a specified action well and powerfully: *he was not a strong swimmer.* ■ exerting great force. ■ (of an argument or case) likely to succeed because of sound reasoning or convincing evidence. ■ possessing skills and qualities that create a likelihood of success. ■ powerfully affecting the mind, senses, or emotions. ■ used after a number to indicate the size of a group: *a crowd several thousand strong.* **2** able to withstand great force or pressure. ■ (of a person's constitution) not easily affected by disease or hardship. ■ (of a person's nervous or emotional state) not easily disturbed or upset. ■ (of a person's character) showing determination, self-control, and good judgment. ■ in a secure financial position. ■ (of a market) having steadily high or rising prices. ■ offering security and advantage: *the company was in a strong position to negotiate a deal.* ■ (of a belief or feeling) intense and firmly held. ■ (of a relationship) lasting and remaining warm despite difficulties. **3** (of light) very intense. ■ (of something seen or heard) not soft or muted; clear or prominent: *strong colors.* ■ (of food or its flavor) distinctive and pungent. ■ (of a solution or drink) containing a large proportion of a particular substance; concentrated. ■ (of language or actions) forceful and extreme, esp. excessively or unacceptably so. ■ Chem. (of an acid or base) fully ionized into cations and anions in solution; having (respectively) a very low or a very high pH. **4** Gram. denoting a class of verbs in Germanic languages that form the past tense and past participle by a change of vowel within the stem rather than by addition of a suffix (e.g., *swim, swam, swum*). **5** Physics of, relating to, or denoting the strongest of the known kinds of force between particles, which acts between nucleons and other hadrons when closer than about 10–13 cm.
– PHRASES **come on strong** informal **1** behave aggressively or assertively, esp. in making sexual advances to someone. **2** improve one's position considerably. **going strong** informal continuing to be healthy, vigorous, or successful. **strong on** good at. ■ possessing large quantities of: *our pizza wasn't strong on pepperoni.* **one's strong point** something at which one excels. — **strong·ish** adj. **strong·ly** adv. [OE, of Gmc. origin; rel. to Du. and Ger. *streng*, also to STRING.]

strong-arm ▶ adj. [attrib.] using or characterized by force or violence. ▶ v. [trans.] use force or violence against.

strong·box /'strông,bäks/ ▶ n. a small lockable box, typically made of metal, in which valuables may be kept.

strong drink ▶ n. alcohol, esp. liquor.

strong·hold /'strông,hōld/ ▶ n. a place that has been fortified so as to protect it against attack. ■ a place where a particular cause or belief is strongly defended or upheld.

strong in·ter·ac·tion ▶ n. interaction at short distances between certain subatomic particles mediated by the strong force. See STRONG (sense 5).

strong·man /'strông,man/ ▶ n. (pl. **-men**) a man of great physical strength, esp. one who performs feats of strength as a form of entertainment. ■ a leader who rules by the exercise of threats, force, or violence.

strong-mind·ed ▶ adj. not easily influenced by others; resolute and determined. — **strong-mind·ed·ness** n.

strong·point /'strông,point/ ▶ n. a specially fortified defensive position.

strong·room /'strông,ro͞om; -,ro͝om/ ▶ n. a room, typically one in a bank, designed to protect valuable items against fire and theft.

strong safe·ty ▶ n. Football a defensive back positioned opposite the offensive team's stronger side, who often covers the tight end.

strong side ▶ n. Sports (on teams with an odd number of players) the half of an offensive or defensive alignment that has one player more.

strong suit ▶ n. (in bridge) a holding of a number of high cards of one suit in a hand. ■ a desirable quality that is particularly prominent in someone's character or an activity at which they excel.

stron·gyle /'strän,jīl/ ▶ n. a nematode worm (family Strongylidae, class Phasmida) of a group that includes several common disease-causing parasites of mammals and birds. [19th C.: from mod. L. *Strongylus*, from Gk. *strongulos* 'round.']

stron·gy·loi·di·a·sis /,stränjəloi'dīəsis/ ▶ n. infestation with threadworms of a type (genus *Strongyloides*, class Phasmida) found in tropical and subtropical regions, chiefly affecting the small intestine and causing ulceration and diarrhea.

stron·ti·a /'stränsh(ē)ə/ ▶ n. Chem. strontium oxide, SrO, a white solid resembling quicklime. [19th C.: from earlier *strontian*, denoting native strontium carbonate from *Strontian*, in Scotland, where it was discovered.]

stron·ti·an·ite /'stränsh(ē)ə,nīt/ ▶ n. a rare pale greenish-yellow or white mineral consisting of strontium carbonate. [18th C.: from *strontian* (see STRONTIA) + -ITE[1].]

stron·ti·um /'strănchēəm; -tēəm/ ▶ n. the chemical element of atomic number 38, a soft, silver-white metal of the alkaline earth series. Its salts are used in fireworks and flares because they give a brilliant red light. (Symbol: **Sr**) [19th C.: from STRONTIA + -IUM.]

strop /sträp/ ▶ n. a device, typically a strip of leather, for sharpening straight razors. ■ (also **strap**) Naut. a rope sling for handling cargo. ▶ v. (**stropped, strop·ping**) [trans.] sharpen on or with a strop. [ME: prob. a West Gmc. adoption of L. *stroppus* 'thong.']

stro·phan·thin /strō'fanthən/ ▶ n. Med. a poisonous substance of the glycoside class, obtained from certain African trees (genera *Strophanthus* and *Acokanthera*) of the dogbane family and used as a heart stimulant. [19th C.: from mod. L. *strophanthus* (from Gk. *strophos* 'twisted cord' + *anthos* 'flower,' referring to the long segments of the corolla) + -IN[1].]

stro·phe /'strōfē/ ▶ n. the first section of an ancient Greek choral ode or of one division of it. Compare with ANTISTROPHE and EPODE (sense 2). ■ a structural division of a poem containing stanzas of varying line-length, especially an ode or free verse poem. — **stroph·ic** /sträfik; 'strō-/ adj. [17th C.: from Gk. *strophē*, 'turning,' from *strephein* 'to turn'; the term orig. denoted a movement from right to left made by a Greek chorus, or lines of choral song recited during this.]

stroud /stroud/ ▶ n. coarse woolen fabric, formerly used in the manufacture of blankets for sale to North American Indians.

strove /strōv/ past of STRIVE.

struck /strək/ past and past participle of STRIKE.

struck joint ▶ n. a masonry joint in which the mortar between two courses of bricks is sloped inward so as to be flush with the surface of one but below that of the other.

struc·tur·al /'strəkchərəl/ ▶ adj. of, relating to, or forming part of the structure of a building or other item. ■ of or relating to the arrangement of and relations between the parts or elements of a complex whole. — **struc·tur·al·ly** adv.

struc·tur·al en·gi·neer·ing ▶ n. the branch of civil engineering that deals with large modern buildings and similar structures. — **struc·tur·al en·gi·neer** n.

struc·tur·al·ism /'strəkchərə,lizəm/ ▶ n. a method of interpretation and analysis of aspects of human cognition, behavior, culture, and experience that focuses on relationships of contrast between elements in a conceptual system that reflect patterns underlying a superficial diversity. ■ the doctrine that structure is more important than function. — **struc·tur·al·ist** n. & adj.

struc·tur·al lin·guis·tics ▶ plural n. [treated as sing.] the branch of linguistics that deals with language as a system of interrelated structures, in particular the theories and methods of Leonard Bloomfield, emphasizing the accurate identification of syntactic and lexical form as opposed to meaning and historical development.

struc·tur·a·tion /,strəkchə'rāshən/ ▶ n. the state or process of organization in a structured form.

struc·ture /'strəkchər/ ▶ n. the arrangement of and relations between the parts or elements of something complex. ■ the organization of a society or other group and the relations between its members, determining its working. ■ a building or other object constructed from several parts. ■ the quality of being organized: *we want to give some structure to the discussion.* ▶ v. [trans.] (often **be structured**) construct or arrange according to a plan; give a pattern or organization to. — **struc·ture·less** adj. [ME: from OFr., or from L. *structura*, from *struere* 'to build.']

stru·del /'stro͞odl/ ▶ n. a confection of thin pastry rolled up around a fruit filling and baked. [from Ger. *Strudel* 'whirlpool.']

strug·gle /'strəgəl/ ▶ v. [intrans.] make forceful or violent efforts to get free of restraint or constriction. ■ strive to achieve or attain something in the face of difficulty or resistance. ■ (**struggle with**) have difficulty handling or coping with. ■ engage in conflict. ■ [no obj., with adverbial of direction] make one's way with difficulty: *he struggled to the summit.* ■ have difficulty in gaining recognition or a living. ▶ n. a forceful or violent effort to get free of restraint or resist attack. ■ a conflict or contest. ■ a great physical effort. ■ a determined effort under difficulties. ■ a very difficult task.

– PHRASES **the struggle for existence** (or **life**) the competition between organisms, esp. as an element in natural selection, or between people seeking a livelihood. — **strug·gler** /'strəg(ə)lər/ n. [ME: frequentative, perh. of imitative origin.]

strum /strəm/ ▶ v. (**strummed, strum·ming**) [trans.] play (a guitar or similar instrument) by sweeping the thumb or a plectrum up or down the strings. ■ play (a tune) in such a way. ■ [intrans.] play casually or unskillfully on a stringed or keyboard instrument. ▶ n. [in sing.] the sound made by strumming. ■ an instance or spell of strumming. — **strum·mer** n. [18th C.: imitative; cf. THRUM[1].]

stru·ma /'strōōmə/ ▶ n. (pl. **-mae** /-mē;/) Med. a swelling of the thyroid gland; a goiter. [16th C. (in the L. sense): mod. L., from L., 'scrofulous tumor.']

stru·mous /'strōōməs/ ▶ adj. archaic scrofulous. [16th C.: from L. *strumosus*, from *struma* (see STRUMA).]

strum·pet /'strəmpət/ ▶ n. dated a female prostitute or a promiscuous woman. [ME: of unknown origin.]

strung /strəNG/ past and past participle of STRING.

strut /strət/ ▶ n. **1** a rod or bar forming part of a framework and designed to resist compression. **2** [in sing.] a stiff, erect, and apparently arrogant or conceited gait. ▶ v. (**strut·ted, strut·ting**) **1** [no obj., with adverbial] walk with a stiff, erect, and apparently arrogant or conceited gait. **2** [trans.] brace (something) with a strut or struts.

– PHRASES **strut one's stuff** informal dance or behave in a confident and expressive way. — **strut·ter** n. **strut·ting·ly** adv. [OE *strūtian* 'protrude stiffly,' of Gmc. origin.]

Stru·ve /'SHtrōōvə/, Otto (1897–1963), US astronomer, born in Russia. In 1938, he discovered the presence of ionized hydrogen in interstellar space.

strych·nine /'strik,nīn; -,nēn/ ▶ n. a bitter and highly poisonous compound obtained from nux vomica and related plants. An alkaloid, it has occasionally been used as a stimulant. [19th C.: from Fr., via L. from Gk. *strukhnos*, denoting a kind of nightshade.]

Sts. ▶ abbr. Saints.

Stu·art[1] /'st(y)ōōərt/, Charles Edward (1720–88), son of James Stuart; pretender to the British throne; known as **the Young Pretender** or **Bonnie Prince Charlie**.

Stu·art[2], Gilbert Charles (1755–1828), US artist. He is best known for his portraits of the first five presidents, painted between 1817 and 1821.

Stu·art[3], James Francis Edward (1688–1766), son of James II (James VII of Scotland); pretender to the British throne; known as **the Old Pretender**.

Stu·art[4], Jeb (1833–64), US military officer; full name *James Ewell Brown Stuart*. He joined the Confederate army in 1861. The raid he led to surround McClellan's Union army in 1862 is praised as superb military strategy.

Stu·art[5], Mary, see MARY, QUEEN OF SCOTS.

Stu·art[6] (also **Stew·art**) adj. of or relating to the royal family ruling Scotland 1371–1714 and Britain 1603–1649 and 1660–1714. ▶ n. a member of this family.

stub /stəb/ ▶ n. **1** the truncated remnant of a pencil, cigarette, or similar-shaped object after use. ■ a truncated or unusually short thing. ■ [as adj.] denoting a projection or hole that goes only part of the way through a surface. **2** the part of a check, receipt, ticket, or other document torn off and kept as a record. ▶ v. (**stubbed, stub·bing**) [trans.] **1** accidentally strike (one's toe) against something. **2** extinguish (a lighted cigarette) by pressing the lighted end against something. **3** dig up (a plant) by the roots. [OE *stub(b)* 'stump of a tree,' of Gmc. origin.]

stub ax·le ▶ n. an axle supporting only one wheel of a pair on opposite sides of a vehicle.

stub·ble /'stəbəl/ ▶ n. the cut stalks of grain plants left sticking out of the ground after the grain is harvested. ■ short, stiff hairs growing on a man's face when he has not shaved for a while. — **stub·bled** adj. **stub·bly** /'stəb(ə)lē/ adj. [ME: from Anglo-Norman Fr. *stuble*, from L. *stupla*, *stupula*, vars. of *stipula* 'straw.']

stub·born /'stəbərn/ ▶ adj. having or showing dogged determination not to change one's attitude or position on something, esp. in spite of good arguments or reasons to do so. ■ difficult to move, remove, or cure. — **stub·born·ly** adv. **stub·born·ness** n. [ME: of unknown origin.]

stub·by /'stəbē/ ▶ adj. (**-bi·er, -bi·est**) short and thick. — **stub·bi·ly** /-əlē/ adv. **stub·bi·ness** n.

stuc·co /'stəkō/ ▶ n. fine plaster used for coating wall surfaces or molding into architectural decorations. ▶ v. (**-coes, -coed**) [trans.] [usu. as adj.] (**stuccoed**) coat or decorate with such plaster. [16th C.: from Ital., of Gmc. origin.]

stuck /stək/ past and past participle of STICK[2].

stuck-up ▶ adj. informal staying aloof from others because one thinks one is superior.

stud[1] /stəd/ ▶ n. **1** a large-headed piece of metal that pierces and projects from a surface, esp. for decoration. ■ a small, simple piece of jewelry for wearing in pierced ears or nostrils. ■ a fastener consisting of two buttons joined with a bar, used in formal wear to fasten a shirtfront or to fasten a collar to a shirt. ■ (usu. **studs**) a small projection fixed to the base of footwear, esp. athletic shoes, to allow the wearer to grip the ground. ■ (usu. **studs**) a small metal piece set into the tire of a motor vehicle to improve roadholding in slippery conditions. **2** an upright support in the wall of a building to which laths and plasterboard are attached. ■ the height of a room as indicated by the length of this. **3** a rivet or crosspiece in each link of a chain cable. ▶ v. (**stud·ded, stud·ding**) [trans.] (usu. **be studded**) decorate or augment (something) with many studs or similar small objects. ■ strew or cover (something) with a scattering of small objects or features: *the sky was studded with stars.* [OE *studu, stuthu* 'post, upright prop'; rel. to Ger. *stützen* 'to prop.' The sense 'ornamental metal knob' arose in ME.]

stud[2] ▶ n. **1** an establishment where horses or other domesticated animals are kept for breeding: [as adj.] *a stud farm.* ■ a collection of horses or other domesticated animals belonging to one person. ■ (also **stud horse**) a stallion. ■ informal a young man thought to be very active sexually or regarded as a good sexual partner. **2** (also **stud poker**) a form of poker in which the first card of a player's hand is dealt face down and the others face up, with betting after each round of the deal. [OE *stōd*, of Gmc. origin; rel. to Ger. *Stute* 'mare,' also to STAND.]

stud. ▶ abbr. student.

stud book ▶ n. a book containing the pedigrees of horses.

stud·ding /'stədiNG/ ▶ n. studs collectively. See STUD[1] (sense 2).

stud·ding·sail /'stədiNG,sāl; 'stənsəl/ ▶ n. (on a square-rigged sailing ship) an additional sail set at the end of a yard in light winds. [16th C.: *studding* perh. from Mid. Low Ger., MDu. *stōtinge* 'a thrusting.']

stu·dent /'st(y)ōōdnt/ ▶ n. a person who is studying at a school or college. ■ [as adj.] denoting someone who is studying in order to enter a particular profession: *student nurses.* ■ a person who takes an interest in a particular subject. [ME: from L. *student-* 'applying oneself to,' from the verb *studere*, rel. to *studium* 'painstaking application.']

stud horse ▶ n. see STUD[2].

stud·ied /'stədēd/ ▶ adj. (of a quality or result) achieved or maintained by careful and deliberate effort: *studied politeness.* — **stud·ied·ly** adv. **stud·ied·ness** n.

stu·di·o /'st(y)ōōdē,ō/ ▶ n. (pl. **-os**) **1** a room where an artist, photographer, sculptor, etc., works. ■ a place where performers, esp. dancers, practice and exercise. ■ a room where musical or sound recordings can be made. ■ a room from which television or radio programs are broadcast, or in which they are recorded. ■ a place where movies are made or produced. **2** a film or television production company. **3** a studio apartment. [19th C.: from Ital., from L. *studium* (see STUDY).]

stu·di·o a·part·ment ▶ n. an apartment containing one main room.

stu·di·o the·a·ter ▶ n. a small theater where experimental and innovative productions are staged.

stu·di·ous /'st(y)ōōdēəs/ ▶ adj. spending a lot of time studying or reading. ■ done deliberately or with a purpose in mind. ■ showing great care or attention. — **stu·di·ous·ly** adv. **stu·di·ous·ness** n. [ME: from L. *studiosus*, from *studium* 'painstaking application.']

stud·muf·fin /'stəd,məfin/ ▶ n. informal a man perceived as sexually attractive, typically one with well-developed muscles.

stud pok·er ▶ n. see STUD[2] (sense 2).

stud·y /'stədē/ ▶ n. (pl. **stud·ies**) **1** the devotion of time and attention to acquiring knowledge on an academic subject, esp. by means of books. ■ (**studies**) activity of this type as pursued by one person. ■ an academic book or article on a particular topic. ■ (**studies**) used in the title of an academic subject: *a major in East Asian studies.* **2** a detailed investigation and analysis of a subject or situation. ■ a portrayal in literature or another art form of an aspect of behavior or character: *a study of thwarted ambition.* ■ [with adj.] a person who learns a skill or acquires knowledge at a specified speed: *I'm a quick study.* [orig. theatrical slang, referring to an actor who memorizes a role.] **3** a room used or designed for reading, writing, or academic work. **4** a piece of work, esp. a drawing, done for practice or as an experiment. ■ a musical composition designed to develop a player's technical skill. **5** (**a study in**) a thing or person that is an embodiment or good example of something: *a study in confusion and misery.* ■ informal an amusing or remarkable thing or person. ▶ v. (**stud·ies, stud·ied**) [trans.] **1** devote time and attention to acquiring knowledge on (an academic subject), esp. by means of books. ■ investigate and analyze (a subject or situation) in detail. ■ [intrans.] apply oneself to study: *he didn't spend his time studying.* ■ [intrans.] acquire academic knowledge at an educational establishment. ■ [intrans.] (**study up**) learn intensively about something, esp. in preparation for a test of knowledge. ■ (of an actor) try to learn (the words of one's role). **2** look at closely in order to observe or read. [ME: shortening of OFr. *estudie* (n.), *estudier* (v.), both based on L. *studium* 'zeal, painstaking application.']

stud·y hall ▶ n. the period of time in a school curriculum set aside for the preparation of schoolwork. ■ a schoolroom used for such work.

stuff /stəf/ ▶ n. **1** matter, material, articles, or activities of a specified or indeterminate kind that are being referred to, indicated, or implied. ■ a person's belongings, equipment, or baggage. ■ Brit., informal dated worthless or foolish ideas, speech, or writing; [as exclam.] *stuff and nonsense!* ■ informal drink or drugs. ■ (**one's stuff**) things in which one is knowledgeable and experienced; one's area of expertise. **2** the basic constituents or characteristics of something or someone: *Healey was made of sterner stuff.* **3** (in sports) spin given to a ball to make it vary its course. ■ Baseball a pitcher's ability to produce such spin or control the speed of delivery of a pitch. ▶ v. [trans.] fill (a receptacle or space) tightly with something. ■ informal force or cram (something) tightly into a receptacle or space. ■ informal hastily or clumsily push (something) into a space. ■ fill (the cavity of an item of food) with a savory

or sweet mixture, esp. before cooking. ■ (**be stuffed up**) (of a person) have one's nose blocked up with mucus as a result of a cold. ■ informal fill (oneself) with large amounts of food. ■ fill out the skin of (a dead animal or bird) with material to restore the original shape and appearance. ■ informal fill (envelopes) with identical copies of printed matter. ■ place bogus votes in (a ballot box).
– PHRASES **and stuff** informal said in vague reference to additional things of a similar nature to those specified. **get stuffed** [usu. in imper.] vulgar slang said in anger to tell someone to go away or as an expression of contempt. **stuff it** informal said to express indifference, resignation, or rejection. **that's the stuff** informal said in approval of what has just been done or said. — **stuff·er** n. [in comb.] *a sausage-stuffer.* [ME: shortening of OFr. *estoffe* 'material, furniture,' *estoffer* 'equip, furnish,' from Gk. *stuphein* 'draw together.']

stuffed shirt ▶ n. informal a conservative, pompous person.

stuff·ing /'stəfiNG/ ▶ n. **1** a mixture used to stuff another food, traditionally poultry, before cooking. **2** padding used to stuff cushions, furniture, or soft toys.
– PHRASES **knock** (or **take**) **the stuffing out of** informal severely impair the confidence or strength of (someone).

stuff·ing box ▶ n. a casing in which material such as greased wool is compressed around a shaft or axle to form a seal against gas or liquid.

stuff sack ▶ n. a bag into which a sleeping bag, clothing, and other items can be stuffed or packed.

stuff·y /'stəfē/ ▶ adj. (**stuff·i·er, stuff·i·est**) (of a place) lacking fresh air or ventilation. ■ (of a person's nose) blocked up and making breathing difficult, typically as a result of illness. ■ (of a person) not receptive to new or unusual ideas and behavior; conventional and narrow-minded. — **stuff·i·ly** /'stəfəlē/ adv. **stuff·i·ness** n.

stul·ti·fy /'stəltəˌfī/ ▶ v. (**-fies, -fied**) [trans.] **1** [usu. as adj.] (**stultifying**) cause to lose enthusiasm and initiative, esp. as a result of a tedious or restrictive routine. **2** cause (someone) to appear foolish or absurd. — **stul·ti·fi·ca·tion** /ˌstəltəfi'kāSHən/ n. **stul·ti·fi·er** n. [18th C.: from late L. *stultificare*, from L. *stultus* 'foolish.']

stum /stəm/ ▶ n. unfermented grape juice. ▶ v. (**stummed, stum·ming**) [trans.] **1** prevent or stop the fermentation of (wine) by fumigating a cask with burning sulfur. **2** renew the fermentation of (wine) by adding stum. [17th C.: from Du. *stom* (n.), *stommen* (v.), from *stom* 'dumb.']

stum·ble /'stəmbəl/ ▶ v. [intrans.] trip or momentarily lose one's balance; almost fall. ■ [with adverbial of direction] trip repeatedly as one walks. ■ make a mistake or repeated mistakes in speaking. ■ (**stumble across/on/upon**) find or encounter by chance. ▶ n. an act of stumbling. ■ a stumbling walk. — **stum·bler** /-b(ə)lər/ n. **stum·bling·ly** /-b(ə)liNGlē/ adv. [ME: from ON, from the Gmc. base of STAMMER.]

stum·ble·bum /'stəmbəlˌbəm/ ▶ n. informal a clumsy or inept person.

stum·bling block ▶ n. a circumstance that causes difficulty or hesitation.

stump /stəmp/ ▶ n. **1** the bottom part of a tree left projecting from the ground after most of the trunk has fallen or been cut down. ■ the small projecting remnant of something that has been cut or broken off or worn away. **2** Art a cylinder with conical ends made of rolled paper or other soft material, used for softening or blending marks made with a crayon or pencil. **3** [as adj.] engaged in or involving political campaigning. [referring to the use of a tree stump, from which an orator would speak.] ▶ v. [trans.] **1** (usu. **be stumped**) (of a question or problem) be too hard for; baffle. ■ (**be stumped**) be at a loss; be unable to work out what to do or say. **2** [no obj., with adverbial of direction] walk stiffly and noisily. **3** travel around (a district) making political speeches. **4** use a stump on (a drawing, line, etc.).
– PHRASES **on the stump** informal engaged in political campaigning. **up a stump** informal in a situation too difficult for one to manage. [ME: from Mid. Low Ger. *stump(e)* or MDu. *stomp*.]

stump·er /'stəmpər/ ▶ n. informal a puzzling question.

stump·y /'stəmpē/ ▶ adj. (**stump·i·er, stump·i·est**) short and thick; squat: *weak stumpy legs.* — **stump·i·ly** /-pəlē/ adv. **stump·i·ness** n.

stun /stən/ ▶ v. (**stunned, stun·ning**) [trans.] knock unconscious or into a dazed or semiconscious state. ■ (usu. **be stunned**) astonish or shock (someone) so that they are temporarily unable to react. ■ (of a sound) deafen temporarily. [ME: shortening of OFr. *estoner* 'astonish.']

stung /stəNG/ past and past participle of STING.

stun gun ▶ n. a device used to immobilize an attacker without causing serious injury, typically by administering an electric shock.

stunk /stəNGk/ past and past participle of STINK.

stun·ner /'stənər/ ▶ n. informal a strikingly beautiful or impressive person or thing: *the girl was a stunner.* ■ an amazing turn of events.

stun·ning /'stəniNG/ ▶ adj. extremely impressive or attractive: *she looked stunning.* — **stun·ning·ly** adv.

stunt¹ /stənt/ ▶ v. [trans.] [often as adj.] (**stunted**) retard the growth or development of. ■ frustrate and spoil: *the stunted lives of those around her.* [16th C.: from dial. *stunt* 'foolish, stubborn,' of Gmc. origin; perh. rel. to STUMP.]

stunt² ▶ n. an action displaying spectacular skill and daring. ■ something unusual done to attract attention. ▶ v. [intrans.] perform stunts, esp. aerobatics. [19th C. (orig. US college slang): of unknown origin.]

stunt·man /'stəntˌman/ ▶ n. (pl. **-men**) a man employed to take an actor's place in performing dangerous stunts.

stunt·wom·an /'stəntˌwo͝omən/ ▶ n. (pl. **-wom·en**) a woman employed to take an actor's place in performing dangerous stunts.

stu·pa /'sto͞opə/ ▶ n. a dome-shaped structure erected as a Buddhist shrine. [from Sanskrit *stūpa*.]

stupe ▶ n. informal a stupid person. [18th C.: abbr. of STUPID.]

stu·pe·fa·cient /ˌst(y)o͞opə'fāSHənt/ Med. ▶ adj. (chiefly of a drug) causing semiconsciousness. ▶ n. a drug of this type. [17th C.: from L. *stupefacient-* 'stupefying,' from the verb *stupefacere*.]

stu·pe·fy /'st(y)o͞opəˌfī/ ▶ v. (**-fies, -fied**) [trans.] make (someone) unable to think or feel properly. ■ astonish and shock. — **stu·pe·fac·tion** /ˌst(y)o͞opə'fakSHən/ n. **stu·pe·fi·er** n. **stu·pe·fy·ing·ly** adv. [ME: from Fr. *stupéfier*, from L. *stupefacere*, from *stupere* 'be struck senseless.']

stu·pen·dous /st(y)o͞o'pendəs/ ▶ adj. informal extremely impressive: *a stupendous display of technique.* — **stu·pen·dous·ly** adv. **stu·pen·dous·ness** n. [16th C.: from L. *stupendus* 'to be wondered at' (gerundive of *stupere*) + -OUS.]

stu·pid /'st(y)o͞opid/ ▶ adj. (**-pid·er, -pid·est**) lacking intelligence or common sense. ■ dazed and unable to think clearly. ■ informal used to express exasperation or boredom. ▶ n. informal a stupid person (often used as a term of address): *you're not a coward, stupid!* — **stu·pid·i·ty** /st(y)o͞o'piditē/ n. **stu·pid·ly** adv. [16th C.: from Fr. *stupide* or L. *stupidus*, from *stupere* 'be amazed or stunned.']

stu·por /'st(y)o͞opər/ ▶ n. [in sing.] a state of near-unconsciousness or insensibility: *a drunken stupor.* — **stu·por·ous** /-rəs/ adj. [ME: from L., from *stupere* 'be amazed or stunned.']

stur·dy /'stərdē/ ▶ adj. (**-di·er, -di·est**) (of a person or their body) strongly and solidly built. ■ strong enough to withstand rough work or treatment. ■ showing confidence and determination. ▶ n. vertigo in sheep caused by a tapeworm larva encysted in the brain. — **stur·died** adj. (from the noun) **stur·di·ly** /-dl-ē/ adv. **stur·di·ness** n. [ME: shortening of OFr. *esturdi* 'stunned, dazed.']

stur·geon /'stərjən/ ▶ n. a very large primitive fish (family Acipenseridae) with bony plates on the body. It occurs in temperate seas and rivers of the northern hemisphere, esp. central Eurasia, and is of commercial importance for its caviar and flesh. [ME: from Anglo-Norman Fr., of Gmc. origin; rel. to Du. *steur* and Ger. *Stör*.]

Sturm und Drang /'SHto͝orm o͝on(d) 'dräNG/ ▶ n. a literary and artistic movement in Germany in the late 18th century, influenced by Jean-Jacques Rousseau and characterized by the expression of emotional unrest and a rejection of neoclassical literary norms. [Ger., 'storm and stress.']

stut·ter /'stətər/ ▶ v. [intrans.] talk with continued involuntary repetition of sounds, esp. initial consonants. ■ [trans.] utter in such a way. ■ (of a machine or gun) produce a series of short, sharp sounds. ▶ n. a tendency to stutter while speaking. ■ a series of short, sharp sounds produced by a machine or gun. — **stut·ter·er** n. **stut·ter·ing·ly** adv. [16th C.: frequentative of dial. *stut*, of Gmc. origin; rel. to Ger. *stossen* 'strike against.']

Stutt·gart /'SHto͝otˌgärt; 'sto͝ot-; 'stət-/ a city in western Germany, on the Neckar River; pop. 592,000.

Stuy·ves·ant /'stīvəsənt/, Peter (c.1610–72), Dutch colonial administrator in North America. He was colonial governor of New Netherland 1647–64.

sty¹ /stī/ ▶ n. a pigpen. [OE *stī-*, prob. identical with *stig* 'hall,' of Gmc. origin.]

sty² (also **stye**) ▶ n. (pl. **sties** /stīz/ or **styes**) an inflamed swelling on the edge of an eyelid, caused by bacterial infection. [17th C.: from dial. *styany*, from *styan* (from OE *stīgend* 'riser') + EYE.]

Styg·i·an /'stijēən/ ▶ adj. of or relating to the Styx River. ■ literary very dark: *the Stygian crypt.*

sty·lar /'stīlər/ ▶ adj. Bot. of or relating to the style or styles of a flower.

style /stīl/ ▶ n. **1** a manner of doing something. ■ a way of painting, writing, composing, building, etc., characteristic of a particular period, place, person, or movement. ■ a way of using language. ■ [usu. with negative] a way of behaving or approaching a situation that is characteristic of or favored by a particular person: *backing out isn't my style.* **2** a distinctive appearance, typically determined by the principles according to which something is designed. ■ a particular design of clothing. ■ a way of arranging the hair. **3** elegance and sophistication. **4** a rodlike object or part, in particular: ■ Bot. (in a flower) a narrow, typically elongated extension of the ovary, bearing the stigma. ■ Zool. (in an invertebrate) a small slender pointed appendage; a stylet. ▶ v. [trans.] **1** design or make in a particular form. ■ arrange (hair) in a particular way. **2** [with obj. and complement] designate with a particular name, description, or title. — **style·less** /'stīl(l)is/ adj. **style·less·ness** /'stīl(l)isnis/ n. **styl·er** n. [ME: from OFr. *stile*, from L. *stilus*.]

-style ▶ suffix (forming adjectives and adverbs) in a manner characteristic of: *family-style* | *church-style.*

style sheet ▶ n. Comput. a type of template file consisting of font and layout settings to give a standardized look to certain documents.

sty·let /stī'let; 'stīlit/ ▶ n. **1** Med. a slender probe. ■ a wire or piece of plastic run through a catheter or cannula in order to stiffen it or to clear it. **2** Zool. (in an invertebrate) a small style, esp. a piercing mouthpart of an insect. [17th C.: from Fr. *stilet*, from Ital. *stiletto* (see STILETTO).]

sty·li /'stīlī/ plural form of STYLUS.

PRONUNCIATION KEY ə *ago, up*; ər *over, fur*; a *hat*; ā *ate*; ä *car*; e *let*; ē *see*; i *fit*; ī *by*; NG *sing*; ō *go*; ô *law, for*; oi *toy*; o͝o *good*; o͞o *goo*; ou *out*; TH *thin*; T͟H *then*; ZH *vision*

sty·lish /'stīlisн/ ▶ **adj.** having or displaying a good sense of style: *these are elegant and stylish performances.* ■ fashionably elegant. — **styl·ish·ly adv. styl·ish·ness n.**

styl·ist /'stīlist/ ▶ **n. 1** a person who works creatively in the fashion and beauty industry, in particular: ■ a designer of fashionable styles of clothing. ■ a hairdresser. **2** a person noted for elegant work or performance, in particular: ■ a writer noted for taking great pains over the style in which he or she writes. ■ (in sports or music) a person who performs with style.

sty·lis·tic /stī'listik/ ▶ **adj.** of or concerning style, esp. literary style: *the stylistic conventions of magazine stories.* — **styl·is·ti·cal·ly** /-ik(ə)lē/ **adv.**

sty·lite /'stī,līt/ ▶ **n.** hist. an ascetic living on top of a pillar, esp. in ancient or medieval Syria, Turkey, and Greece in the 5th century AD. [17th C.: from eccles. Gk. *stulitēs*, from *stulos* 'pillar.']

styl·ize /'stī,līz/ ▶ **v.** [trans.] [usu. as adj.] (**stylized**) depict or treat in a mannered and nonrealistic style. — **styl·i·za·tion** /,stīli'zāsнən/ **n.**

sty·lo·bate /'stīlə,bāt/ ▶ **n.** a continuous base supporting a row of columns in classical Greek architecture. [17th C.: via L. from Gk. *stulobatēs*, from *stulos* 'pillar' + *batēs* 'base' (from *bainein* 'to walk').]

sty·loid /'stī,loid/ ▶ **adj.** tech. resembling a stylus or pen. ▶ **n.** short for STYLOID PROCESS.

sty·loid proc·ess ▶ **n.** Anat. a slender projection of bone, such as that from the lower surface of the temporal bone of the skull, or those at the lower ends of the ulna and radius.

sty·lo·lite /'stīlə,līt/ ▶ **n.** Geol. an irregular surface or seam within a limestone or other sedimentary rock, characterized by irregular interlocking pegs and sockets and a concentration of insoluble minerals. ■ a grooved peg forming part of such a seam. [19th C.: from Gk. *stulos* 'column' + -LITE.]

sty·lops /'stī,läps/ ▶ **n.** (pl. same) a minute insect (order Strepsiptera) that spends part or all of its life as an internal parasite of other insects, esp. bees or wasps. The males are winged and the females typically retain a grublike form and remain parasitic. — **sty·lo·pid** /-lə,pid/ **n. & adj.** [19th C.: mod. L., from Gk. *stulos* 'column' + *ōps* 'eye, face.']

sty·lus /'stīləs/ ▶ **n.** (pl. **-li** /-,lī/ or **-lus·es**) **1** a hard point, typically of diamond or sapphire, following a groove in a phonograph record and transmitting the recorded sound for reproduction. ■ a similar point producing such a groove when recording sound. **2** an ancient writing implement, consisting of a small rod with a pointed end for scratching letters on wax-covered tablets, and a blunt end for obliterating them. ■ an implement of similar shape used esp. for engraving and tracing. ■ Comput. a penlike device used to input handwritten text or drawings directly into a computer or for input on a touch-senstitive monitor. [18th C.: erroneous spelling of L. *stilus*.]

sty·mie /'stīmē/ ▶ **v.** (**-mies, -mied, -my·ing** or **-mie·ing**) [trans.] informal prevent or hinder the progress of. [19th C.: of unknown origin.]

styp·tic /'stiptik/ Med. ▶ **adj.** (of a substance) capable of causing bleeding to stop when it is applied to a wound. ▶ **n.** a substance of this kind. [ME: via L. from Gk. *stuptikos*, from *stuphein* 'to contract.']

sty·rax /'stī,raks/ ▶ **n.** variant of STORAX.

sty·rene /'stī,rēn/ ▶ **n.** Chem. an unsaturated liquid hydrocarbon, $C_6H_5CH{=}CH_2$, obtained as a petroleum byproduct. It is easily polymerized and is used to make plastics and resins. [19th C.: from STYRAX + -ENE.]

sty·ro·foam /'stīrə,fōm/ ▶ **n.** (trademark) a kind of expanded polystyrene. [1950s: from POLYSTYRENE + FOAM.]

Sty·ron /'stīrən/, William Clark, Jr. (1925–2006), US writer. His novels include *The Confessions of Nat Turner* (1967) and *Sophie's Choice* (1979).

Styx /stiks/ Gk. Mythol. a river in the underworld, over which Charon ferried the souls of the dead. [from Gk. *Stux*, from *stugnos* 'hateful, gloomy.']

sua·sion /'swāzнən/ ▶ **n.** formal persuasion as opposed to force or compulsion. [ME: from OFr., or from L. *suasio(n-)*, from *suadere* 'to urge.']

sua·sive /'swāsiv/ ▶ **adj.** serving to persuade. ■ Gram. denoting a class of English verbs, for example *insist*, whose meaning includes the notion of persuading.

suave /swäv/ ▶ **adj.** (**suav·er, suav·est**) (esp. of a man) charming, confident, and elegant. — **suave·ly adv. suav·i·ty** /-itē/ **n.** [ME: from OFr., or from L. *suavis* 'agreeable.']

sub /səb/ informal ▶ **n. 1** a submarine. ■ short for SUBMARINE SANDWICH. **2** a substitute. ▶ **v.** (**subbed, sub·bing**) [intrans.] act as a substitute for someone: *he subbed for Scott as weatherman.*

sub. ▶ **abbr.** ■ subordinated. ■ subscription. ■ substitute. ■ suburb. ■ suburban. ■ subway.

sub- ▶ **prefix 1** at, to, or from a lower level or position. ■ lower in rank. ■ of a smaller size; of a subordinate nature: *subculture.* ■ of lesser quality; inferior: *substandard* **2** somewhat; nearly; more or less: *subantarctic.* **3** denoting a later or secondary action of the same kind: *sublet* | *subdivision* | *subsequent.* **4** denoting support. **5** Chem. in names of compounds containing a relatively small proportion of a component: *suboxide.* [from L. *sub* 'under, close to.']

sub·a·cute /,səbə'kyo͞ot/ ▶ **adj. 1** Med. (of a condition) between acute and chronic. **2** moderately acute in shape or angle.

sub·aer·i·al /,səb'e(ə)rēəl/ ▶ **adj.** Geol. existing, occurring, or formed in the open air or on the earth's surface, not underwater or underground. — **sub·aer·i·al·ly adv.**

sub·al·pine /,səb'alpīn/ ▶ **adj.** of or situated on the higher slopes of mountains just below the treeline.

sub·al·tern /səb'ôltərn/ ▶ **n.** an officer in the British army below the rank of captain. ▶ **adj.** /səb'ôltərn/ of lower status. [16th C.: from late L. *subalternus*, from L. *sub-* 'below' + *alternus* 'every other.']

sub·ant·arc·tic /,səbant'ärktik; -'ärtik/ ▶ **adj.** of or relating to the region immediately north of the Antarctic Circle.

sub·a·quat·ic /,səbə'kwätik; -'kwat-/ ▶ **adj.** underwater: *a narrow, subaquatic microclimate.*

sub·a·que·ous /,səb'ākwēəs; -'ak-/ ▶ **adj.** existing, formed, or taking place underwater. ■ fig. lacking in substance or strength.

sub·a·rach·noid /,səbə'raknoid/ ▶ **adj.** Anat. denoting or occurring in the fluid-filled space around the brain between the arachnoid membrane and the pia mater, through which major blood vessels pass.

sub·arc·tic /,səb'ärktik; -'ärtik/ ▶ **adj.** of or relating to the region immediately south of the Arctic Circle.

sub·as·sem·bly /,səbə'semblē/ ▶ **n.** (pl. **-blies**) a unit assembled separately but designed to be incorporated with other units into a larger manufactured product.

sub·a·tom·ic /,səbə'tämik/ ▶ **adj.** smaller than or occurring within an atom.

sub·au·di·tion /,səbô'disнən/ ▶ **n.** a thing that is not stated, only implied or inferred. [18th C.: from late L. *subauditio(n-)*, from *subaudire* 'understand.']

sub·branch ▶ **n.** a secondary or subordinate branch.

sub·cat·e·go·ry /'səb,katə,gôrē/ ▶ **n.** (pl. **-ries**) a secondary or subordinate category. — **sub·cat·e·go·ri·za·tion** /,səb,katəgəri'zāsнən/ **n. sub·cat·e·go·rize** /,səb'katəgə,rīz/ **v.**

sub·class /'səb,klas/ ▶ **n.** a secondary or subordinate class. ■ Biol. a taxonomic category that ranks below class and above order.

sub·cla·vi·an /,səb'klāvēən/ ▶ **adj.** Anat. relating to or denoting an artery or vein that serves the neck and arm on the left or right side of the body. [17th C.: from mod. L. *subclavius*, from *sub* 'under' + *clavis* 'key' (see CLAVICLE), + -IAN.]

sub·clin·i·cal /,səb'klinikəl/ ▶ **adj.** Med. relating to or denoting a disease that is not severe enough to present definite or readily observable symptoms.

sub·com·mit·tee /'səbkə,mitē/ ▶ **n.** a committee composed of some members of a larger committee, board, or other body and reporting to it.

sub·com·pact /,səb'kämpakt/ ▶ **n.** a motor vehicle that is smaller than a compact.

sub·con·scious /,səb'känsнəs/ ▶ **adj.** of or concerning the part of the mind of which one is not fully aware but which influences one's actions and feelings. ▶ **n.** (**one's/the subconscious**) this part of the mind (not in technical use in psychoanalysis, where *unconscious* is preferred). — **sub·con·scious·ly adv. sub·con·scious·ness n.**

sub·con·ti·nent /,səb'käntənənt/ ▶ **n.** a large, distinguishable part of a continent, such as North America or southern Africa. See also INDIAN SUBCONTINENT. — **sub·con·ti·nen·tal** /-,käntə'nen(t)l/ **adj.**

sub·con·tract ▶ **v.** /,səbkən'trakt/ [trans.] employ a business or person outside one's company to do (work) as part of a larger project. ■ [intrans.] (of a business or person) carry out work for a company as part of a larger project. ▶ **n.** /,səb'käntrakt/ a contract for a company or person to do work for another company as part of a larger project.

sub·con·trac·tor /,səb'kän,traktər/ ▶ **n.** a business or person that carries out work for a company as part of a larger project.

sub·cor·ti·cal /,səb'kôrtikəl/ ▶ **adj.** below the cortex. ■ Anat. relating to or denoting the region of the brain below the cortex.

sub·cos·tal /,səb'kôstl; -'kästl/ ▶ **adj.** Anat. beneath a rib; below the ribs.

sub·crit·i·cal /,səb'kritikəl/ ▶ **adj.** Physics below a critical threshold, in particular: ■ (in nuclear physics) containing or involving less than the critical mass. ■ (of a flow of fluid) slower than the speed at which waves travel in the fluid.

sub·cul·ture /'səb,kəlcнər/ ▶ **n.** a cultural group within a larger culture, often having beliefs or interests at variance with those of the larger culture. — **sub·cul·tur·al** /,səb'kəlcнərəl/ **adj.**

sub·cu·ta·ne·ous /,səbkyo͞o'tānēəs/ ▶ **adj.** Anat. & Med. situated or applied under the skin: *subcutaneous fat.* — **sub·cu·ta·ne·ous·ly adv.**

sub·di·vide /'səbdə,vīd/ ▶ **v.** [trans.] divide (something that has already been divided or that is a separate unit).

sub·di·vi·sion /'səbdə,vizнən/ ▶ **n.** the action of subdividing or being subdivided. ■ a secondary or subordinate division. ■ an area of land divided into plots for sale; an area of housing. ■ Biol. any taxonomic subcategory, esp. (in botany) one that ranks below division and above class.

sub·dom·i·nant /,səb'dämənənt/ ▶ **n.** Music the fourth note of the diatonic scale of any key.

sub·duc·tion /səb'dəksнən/ ▶ **n.** Geol. the sideways and downward movement of the edge of a plate of the earth's crust into the mantle beneath another plate. — **sub·duct** /-'dəkt/ **v.** [1970s: via Fr. from L. *subductio(n-)*, from *subduct-* 'drawn from below,' from the verb *subducere*.]

sub·due /səb'd(y)o͞o/ ▶ **v.** (**-dues, -dued, -du·ing**) [trans.] overcome or bring under control (a feeling or person). ■ bring (a country or people) under control by force. — **sub·du·a·ble adj.** [ME: from Anglo-Norman Fr. *suduire*, from L. *subducere*, 'draw from below.']

sub·dued /səb'd(y)o͞od/ ▶ **adj.** **1** (of a person or their manner) quiet and rather reflective or depressed. **2** (of color or lighting) soft and restrained.

sub·du·ral /səb'd(y)o͝orəl/ ▶ **adj.** Anat. situated or occurring between the dura mater and the arachnoid membrane of the brain and spinal cord.

su·ber·in /'so͞obərən/ ▶ **n.** Bot. an inert impermeable waxy substance present in the cell walls of corky tissues. [19th C.: from L. *suber* 'cork' + -IN[1].]

sub·fam·i·ly /'səb,fam(ə)lē/ ▶ **n.** (pl. **-lies**) a subdivision of a group. ■ Biol. a taxonomic category that ranks below family and above tribe or genus, usually ending in *-inae* (in zoology) or *-oideae* (in botany).

sub·floor /'səb,flôr/ ▶ **n.** the foundation for a floor in a building.

sub·fusc /,səb'fəsk/ ▶ **adj.** literary dull; gloomy. [18th C.: from L. *subfuscus*, from *sub-* 'somewhat' + *fuscus* 'dark brown.']

sub·ge·nus /'səb,jēnəs/ ▶ **n.** (pl. **-gen·er·a** /-,jenərə/) Biol. a taxonomic category that ranks below genus and above species. — **sub·ge·ner·ic** /,səbjə'nerik/ **adj.**

sub·gla·cial /,səb'glāshəl/ ▶ **adj.** Geol. situated or occurring underneath a glacier or ice sheet.

sub·group /'səb,gro͞op/ ▶ **n.** a subdivision of a group. ■ Math. a group whose members are all members of another group, both being subject to the same operations.

sub·head·ing /'səb,hediNG/ (also **sub·head**) ▶ **n.** a heading given to a subsection of a piece of writing.

sub·hu·man /,səb'(h)yo͞omən/ ▶ **adj.** of a lower order of being than the human. ■ Zool. (of a primate) closely related to humans. ■ derog. (of people or their behavior) not worthy of a human being; debased or depraved. ▶ **n.** a subhuman creature or person.

Su·bic Bay /'so͞obik/ an inlet of the South China Sea in the Philippines, off central Luzon Island.

subj. ▶ **abbr.** ■ subject. ■ subjective. ■ subjunctive.

sub·ja·cent /,səb'jāsənt/ ▶ **adj.** tech. situated below something else. — **sub·ja·cen·cy** **n.** [16th C.: from L. *subjacent-* 'lying underneath,' from *sub-* 'under' + *jacere* 'to lie.']

sub·ject ▶ **n.** /'səbjəkt/ **1** a person or thing that is being discussed, described, or dealt with. ■ a person or circumstance giving rise to a specified feeling, response, or action. ■ Gram. a noun phrase functioning as one of the main components of a clause, being the element about which the rest of the clause is predicated. ■ Logic the part of a proposition about which a statement is made. ■ Music a theme of a fugue or of a piece in sonata form; a leading phrase or motif. ■ a person who is the focus of scientific or medical attention or experiment. **2** a branch of knowledge studied or taught in a school, college, or university. **3** a citizen or member of a state other than its ruler. **4** Philos. a thinking or feeling entity; the conscious mind; the ego, esp. as opposed to anything external to the mind. ■ the central substance or core of a thing as opposed to its attributes. ▶ **adj.** /'səbjəkt/ [predic.] (**subject to**) **1** likely or prone to be affected by (a particular condition or occurrence, typically an unwelcome or unpleasant one). **2** dependent or conditional upon. **3** under the authority of. ■ [attrib.] under the control or domination of (another ruler, country, or government). ▶ **adv.** /'səbjəkt/ (**subject to**) conditionally upon. ▶ **v.** /səb'jekt/ [trans.] **1** (**subject someone/something to**) cause or force to undergo (a particular experience of form of treatment). **2** bring (a person or country) under one's control or jurisdiction, typically by using force: — **sub·jec·tion** /səb'jekshən/ **n.** **sub·ject·less** /'səbjəktləs/ **adj.** [ME: from OFr. *suget*, from L. *subjectus* 'brought under,' past part. of *subicere*, from *sub-* 'under' + *jacere* 'throw.']

sub·jec·tive /səb'jektiv/ ▶ **adj.** **1** based on or influenced by personal feelings, tastes, or opinions. Contrasted with OBJECTIVE. ■ dependent on the mind or on an individual's perception for its existence. **2** Gram. of, relating to, or denoting a case of nouns and pronouns used for the subject of a sentence. ▶ **n.** (**the subjective**) Gram. the subjective case. — **sub·jec·tive·ly** **adv.** **sub·jec·tive·ness** **n.** **sub·jec·tiv·i·ty** /,səbjek'tivitē/ **n.**

sub·jec·tiv·ism /səb'jektə,vizəm/ ▶ **n.** Philos. the doctrine that knowledge is merely subjective and that there is no external or objective truth. — **sub·jec·tiv·ist** **n. & adj.**

sub·ject mat·ter ▶ **n.** the topic dealt with or the subject represented in a debate, exposition, or work of art.

sub·join /səb'join/ ▶ **v.** [trans.] formal add (comments or supplementary information) at the end of a speech or text. [16th C.: from obs. Fr. *subjoindre*, from L. *subjungere*, from *sub-* 'in addition' + *jungere* 'to join.']

sub ju·di·ce /,so͞ob 'yo͞odi,kā; ,səb 'jo͞odi,sē/ ▶ **adj.** Law under judicial consideration and therefore prohibited from public discussion elsewhere. [L., 'under a judge.']

sub·ju·gate /'səbjə,gāt/ ▶ **v.** [trans.] bring under domination or control, esp. by conquest. ■ (**subjugate someone/something to**) make someone or something subordinate to. — **sub·ju·ga·tion** /,səbjə'gāshən/ **n.** **sub·ju·ga·tor** /-,gātər/ **n.** [ME: from late L. *subjugat-* 'brought under a yoke,' from the verb *subjugare*, based on *jugum* 'yoke.']

sub·junc·tive /səb'jəNG(k)tiv/ Gram. ▶ **adj.** relating to or denoting a mood of verbs expressing what is imagined or wished or possible. Compare with INDICATIVE. ▶ **n.** a verb in the subjunctive mood. ■ (**the subjunctive**) the subjunctive mood. — **sub·junc·tive·ly** **adv.** [16th C.: from Fr. *subjonctif, -ive* or late L. *subjunctivus*, from *subjungere* (see SUBJOIN), rendering Gk. *hupotaktikos* 'subjoined.']

sub·king·dom /'səb,kiNGdəm/ ▶ **n.** Biol. a taxonomic category that ranks below kingdom and above phylum or division.

sub·late /sə'blāt/ ▶ **v.** [trans.] Philos. assimilate (a smaller entity) into a larger one. — **sub·la·tion** /-'blāshən/ **n.** [19th C.: from L. *sublat-* 'taken away,' from *sub-* 'from below' + *lat-* (from the stem of *tollere* 'take away').]

sub·lat·er·al /'səb,latərəl/ ▶ **n.** a side shoot developing from a lateral shoot or branch of a plant.

sub·lease ▶ **n.** /'səb,lēs/ a lease of a property by a tenant to a subtenant. ▶ **v.** /səb'lēs/ another term for SUBLET.

sub·let ▶ **v.** /,səb'let/ (**-let·ting**; past and past part. **-let**) [trans.] lease (a property) to a subtenant. ▶ **n.** /'səb,let/ another term for SUBLEASE. ■ informal a property that has been subleased.

sub·le·thal /,səb'lēTHəl/ ▶ **adj.** having an effect less than lethal.

sub·li·mate ▶ **v.** /'səblə,māt/ **1** [trans.] (esp. in psychoanalytic theory) divert or modify (an instinctual impulse) into a culturally higher or socially more acceptable activity. **2** Chem. another term for SUBLIME. ▶ **n.** /-,mit; -,māt/ Chem. a solid deposit of a substance that has sublimed. — **sub·li·ma·tion** /,səblə'māshən/ **n.** [ME: from L. *sublimat-* 'raised up,' from the verb *sublimare*.]

sub·lime /sə'blīm/ ▶ **adj.** (**-lim·er**, **-lim·est**) of such excellence, grandeur, or beauty as to inspire great admiration or awe: [as n.] (**the sublime**) *ranging from the sublime to the ridiculous.* ■ used to denote the extreme or unparalleled nature of a person's attitude or behavior. ▶ **v.** [intrans.] Chem. (of a solid substance) change directly into vapor when heated, typically forming a solid deposit again on cooling. ■ [trans.] cause (a substance) to do this. — **sub·lime·ly** **adv.** **sub·lim·i·ty** /-'blimitē/ **n.** [16th C.: from L. *sublimis*, from *sub-* 'up to' + a second element perh. rel. to *limen* 'threshold,' *limus* 'oblique.']

Sub·lime Porte /sə'blīm 'pôrt/ ▶ **n.** see PORTE.

sub·lim·i·nal /sə'bliminəl/ ▶ **adj.** Psychol. (of a stimulus or mental process) below the threshold of sensation or consciousness; perceived by or affecting someone's mind without their being aware of it. — **sub·lim·i·nal·ly** **adv.** [19th C.: from SUB- 'below' + L. *limen, limin-* 'threshold' + -AL.]

sub·lit·to·ral /,səb'litərəl/ esp. Ecol. ▶ **adj.** (of a marine animal, plant, or deposit) living, growing, or accumulating near to or just below the shore. ■ relating to or denoting a biogeographic zone extending (in the sea) from the average line of low tide to the edge of the continental shelf or (in a large lake) beyond the littoral zone but still well lit. ▶ **n.** (**the sublittoral**) the sublittoral zone.

sub·lu·nar /,səb'lo͞onər/ ▶ **adj.** Astron. within the moon's orbit and subject to its influence.

sub·lu·nar·y /,səb'lo͞onərē/ ▶ **adj.** literary belonging to this world as contrasted with a better or more spiritual one: *the concept was irrational to sublunary minds.* [16th C.: from mod. L. *sublunaris*.]

sub·lux·a·tion /,səblək'sāshən/ ▶ **n.** Med. a partial dislocation. ■ a slight misalignment of the vertebrae.

sub·ma·chine gun /,səbmə'shēn/ ▶ **n.** a hand-held, lightweight machine gun.

sub·mar·gin·al /,səb'märjənl/ ▶ **adj.** (of land) not allowing profitable farming or cultivation.

sub·ma·rine /,səbmə'rēn; 'səbmə,rēn/ ▶ **n.** a warship with a streamlined hull designed to operate completely submerged in the sea for long periods, equipped with an internal store of air and a periscope and typically armed with torpedoes and/or missiles. ■ a submersible craft of any kind. ■ a submarine sandwich. ▶ **adj.** existing, occurring, done, or used under the surface of the sea: *submarine volcanic activity.* — **sub·ma·rin·er** /,səb'marənər; -mə'rēnər/ **n.**

sub·ma·rine sand·wich ▶ **n.** a sandwich made of a long roll typically filled with meat, cheese, and vegetables such as lettuce, tomato, and onions.

sub·me·di·ant /,səb'mēdēənt/ ▶ **n.** Music the sixth note of the diatonic scale of any key.

sub·merge /səb'mərj/ ▶ **v.** [trans.] (usu. **be submerged**) cause to be under water. ■ [intrans.] descend below the surface of an area of water. ■ completely cover or obscure. — **sub·mer·gence** /-jəns/ **n.** **sub·mer·gi·ble** /-jəbəl/ **adj.** [17th C.: from L. *submergere*, from *sub-* 'under' + *mergere* 'to dip.']

sub·merse /səb'mərs/ ▶ **v.** [trans.] submerge. ▶ **adj.** (**submersed**) Bot. denoting or characteristic of a plant growing entirely underwater. Contrasted with EMERSED. — **sub·mer·sion** /-'mərZHən; -SHən/ **n.** [ME: from L. *submers-* 'plunged below,' from the verb *submergere* (see SUBMERGE).]

sub·mers·i·ble /səb'mərsəbəl/ ▶ **adj.** designed to function while completely submerged. ▶ **n.** a small boat or other craft of this kind, esp. one designed for research and exploration.

sub·mi·cro·scop·ic /,səb,mīkrə'skäpik/ ▶ **adj.** too small to be seen by an ordinary light microscope.

sub·min·i·a·ture /səb'min(ē)əCHər; -,CHo͝or/ ▶ **adj.** of greatly reduced size. ■ (of a camera) very small and using 16-mm film.

sub·mis·sion /səb'miSHən/ ▶ **n.** **1** the action or fact of accepting or yielding to a superior force or to the will or authority of another person. ■ Wrestling an act of surrendering to a hold by one's opponent. **2** the action of presenting a proposal, application, or other document for consideration or judgment. ■ a proposal, application, or other document presented in this way. ■ Law a proposition or argument presented by a lawyer to a judge or jury. [ME: from OFr., or from L. *submissio(n-)*, from the verb *submittere* (see SUBMIT).]

sub·mis·sive /səb'misiv/ ▶ **adj.** ready to conform to the authority or will of others; meekly obedient or passive. — **sub·mis·sive·ly adv. sub·mis·sive·ness n.**

sub·mit /səb'mit/ ▶ **v.** (**-mit·ted, -mit·ting**) **1** [intrans.] accept or yield to a superior force or to the authority or will of another person. ■ (**submit oneself**) consent to undergo a certain treatment: *he submitted himself to a body search.* ■ [trans.] subject to a particular process, treatment, or condition: *samples submitted to low pressure.* ■ agree to refer a matter to a third party for decision or adjudication. **2** [trans.] present (a proposal, application, or other document) to a person or body for consideration or judgment. ■ [with clause] (esp. in judicial contexts) suggest; argue. — **sub·mit·ter n.** [ME: from L. *submittere*, from *sub-* 'under' + *mittere* 'send, put.']

sub·mod·i·fi·er /ˌsəb'mädəˌfīər/ ▶ **n.** Gram. an adverb used in front of an adjective or another adverb to modify its meaning, for example *very* in *very cold* or *unusually* in *an unusually large house.* — **sub·mod·i·fi·ca·tion** /ˌsəbˌmädəfi'kāsHən/ **n. sub·mod·i·fy** /-ˌfī/ **v.**

sub·mon·tane /ˌsəb'mänˌtān/ ▶ **adj.** passing under or through mountains. ■ situated in the foothills or lower slopes of a mountain range.

sub·mul·ti·ple /ˌsəb'məltəpəl/ ▶ **n.** a number that can be divided exactly into a specified number. ▶ **adj.** of or pertaining to such a number.

sub·nor·mal /ˌsəb'nôrməl/ ▶ **adj.** not meeting standards or reaching a level regarded as usual, esp. with respect to intelligence or development. — **sub·nor·mal·i·ty** /ˌsəbnôr'malitē/ **n.**

sub·nu·cle·ar /ˌsəb'n(y)o͞oklēər/ ▶ **adj.** Physics occurring in or smaller than an atomic nucleus.

sub·or·bit·al /ˌsəb'ôrbitl/ ▶ **adj. 1** situated below or behind the orbit of the eye. **2** of, relating to, or denoting a trajectory that does not complete a full orbit of the earth or other celestial body.

sub·or·der /'səbˌôrdər/ ▶ **n.** Biol. a taxonomic category that ranks below order and above family.

sub·or·di·nar·y /ˌsəb'ôrdnˌerē/ ▶ **n.** (pl. **-nar·ies**) Heraldry a simple device or bearing that is less common than the ordinaries (e.g., roundel, orle, lozenge).

sub·or·di·nate ▶ **adj.** /sə'bôrdn-it/ lower in rank or position: *his subordinate officers.* ■ of less or secondary importance. ▶ **n.** a person under the authority or control of another within an organization. ▶ **v.** /-ˌāt/ [trans.] treat or regard as of lesser importance than something else. ■ make subservient to or dependent on something else. — **sub·or·di·nate·ly adv. sub·or·di·na·tion** /-ˌbôrdn'āsHən/ **n. sub·or·di·na·tive** /-ətiv/ **adj.** [ME: from med. L. *subordinatus* 'placed in an inferior rank,' from L. *sub-* 'below' + *ordinare* 'ordain.']

sub·or·di·nate clause ▶ **n.** a clause, typically introduced by a conjunction, that forms part of and is dependent on a main clause (e.g., "when it rang" in "she answered the phone when it rang").

sub·or·di·nat·ing con·junc·tion /sə'bôrdnˌātiNG/ ▶ **n.** a conjunction that introduces a subordinate clause, e.g., *although, because.* Contrasted with COORDINATING CONJUNCTION.

sub·orn /sə'bôrn/ ▶ **v.** [trans.] bribe or otherwise induce (someone) to commit an unlawful act such as perjury. — **sub·or·na·tion** /ˌsəbôr'nāsHən/ **n. sub·orn·er n.** [16th C.: from L. *subornare* 'incite secretly,' from *sub-* 'secretly' + *ornare* 'equip.']

sub·os·cine /ˌsəb'äsin; -īn/ Ornithol. ▶ **adj.** of, relating to, or denoting passerine birds of a division (suborder Deutero-Oscines, order Passeriformes) that includes those other than songbirds, found chiefly in America. Compare with OSCINE. ▶ **n.** a bird of this division.

sub·ox·ide /ˌsəb'äkˌsīd/ ▶ **n.** Chem. an oxide containing the lowest or an unusually small proportion of oxygen.

sub·par /ˌsəb'pär/ ▶ **adj.** below an average level.

sub·phy·lum /'səbˌfīləm/ ▶ **n.** (pl. **-phy·la** /-ˌfīlə/) Zool. a taxonomic category that ranks below phylum and above class.

sub·plot /'səbˌplät/ ▶ **n.** a subordinate plot in a play, novel, or similar work.

sub·poe·na /sə'pēnə/ Law ▶ **n.** (in full **subpoena ad testificandum**) a writ ordering a person to attend a court: *they were all under subpoena to appear.* ▶ **v.** (**-nas, -naed** /-nəd/, **-na·ing**) [trans.] summon (someone) with a subpoena. ■ require (a document or other evidence) to be submitted to a court of law. [ME: from L. *sub poena* 'under penalty' (the first words of the writ).]

sub·re·gion /'səbˌrējən/ ▶ **n.** a division of a region. — **sub·re·gion·al** /ˌsəb'rēj(ə)nəl/ **adj.**

sub·ro·ga·tion /ˌsəbrə'gāsHən/ ▶ **n.** Law the substitution of one person or group by another in respect of a debt or insurance claim, accompanied by the transfer of any associated rights and duties. — **sub·ro·gate** /'səbrəˌgāt/ **v.** [ME: from late L. *subrogatio(n-)*, from *subrogare* 'choose as substitute,' from *sub-* 'in place of another' + *rogare* 'ask.']

sub ro·sa /ˌsəb 'rōzə/ ▶ **adj. & adv.** formal happening or done in secret. [L., lit. 'under the rose,' as an emblem of secrecy.]

sub·rou·tine /'səbro͞oˌtēn/ ▶ **n.** Comput. a set of instructions designed to perform a frequently used operation within a program.

sub-Sa·har·an ▶ **adj.** [attrib.] from or forming part of the African regions south of the Sahara desert.

sub·sam·ple /'səbˌsampəl/ ▶ **n.** a sample drawn from a larger sample. ▶ **v.** /ˌsəb'sampəl/ [trans.] take such a sample from.

sub·scribe /səb'skrīb/ ▶ **v. 1** [intrans.] arrange to receive something regularly, typically a publication, by paying in advance. ■ esp. Brit. contribute or undertake to contribute a certain sum of money to a particular fund, project, or charitable cause, typically on a regular basis. ■ (**subscribe to**) fig. express or feel agreement with (an idea or proposal): *we prefer to subscribe to an alternative explanation.* ■ [trans.] apply to participate in. ■ apply for or undertake to pay for an offering of shares of stock. ■ [trans.] (of a bookseller) agree before publication to take (a certain number of copies of a book). **2** [trans.] formal sign (a will, contract, or other document): *he subscribed the will as a witness.* ■ sign (one's name) on such a document. — **sub·scrib·er n.** [ME: from L. *subscribere*, from *sub-* 'under' + *scribere* 'write.']

sub·script /'səbˌskript/ ▶ **adj.** (of a letter, figure, or symbol) written or printed below the line. ▶ **n.** a subscript letter, figure, or symbol. ■ Comput. a symbol (notionally written as a subscript but in practice usually not) used in a program, alone or with others, to specify one of the elements of an array. [18th C.: from L. *subscript-* 'written below,' from the verb *subscribere* (see SUBSCRIBE).]

sub·scrip·tion /səb'skripsHən/ ▶ **n. 1** the action of making or agreeing to make an advance payment in order to receive or participate in something. ■ esp. Brit. a payment of such a type. ■ a system in which the production of a book is wholly or partly financed by advance orders. **2** formal a signature or short piece of writing at the end of a document. ■ archaic a signed declaration or agreement.

sub·sec·tion /'səbˌseksHən/ ▶ **n.** a division of a section.

sub·se·quence[1] /'səbsəkwəns/ ▶ **n.** formal the state of following something, esp. as a result or effect.

sub·se·quence[2] /'səbˌsēkwəns/ ▶ **n.** a sequence contained in or forming part of another sequence. ■ Math. a sequence derived from another by the omission of a number of terms.

sub·se·quent /'səbsəkwənt/ ▶ **adj.** coming after something in time; following. ■ Geol. (of a stream or valley) having a direction or character determined by the resistance to erosion of the underlying rock, and typically following the strike of the strata. — **sub·se·quent·ly adv.** [ME: from OFr., or from L. *subsequent-* 'following after' (from the verb *subsequi*).]

sub·serve /səb'sərv/ ▶ **v.** [trans.] help to further or promote. [17th C.: from L. *subservire* (see SUB-, SERVE).]

sub·ser·vi·ent /səb'sərvēənt/ ▶ **adj.** prepared to obey others unquestioningly. ■ less important; subordinate. ■ serving as a means to an end. — **sub·ser·vi·ence n. sub·ser·vi·en·cy n. sub·ser·vi·ent·ly adv.** [17th C.: from L. *subservient-* 'subjecting to, complying with,' from the verb *subservire* (see SUBSERVE).]

sub·set /'səbˌset/ ▶ **n.** a part of a larger group of related things. ■ Math. a set of which all the elements are contained in another set.

sub·side /səb'sīd/ ▶ **v.** [intrans.] **1** become less intense, violent, or severe: *I'll wait until the storm subsides.* ■ lapse into silence or inactivity. **2** (of water) go down to a lower or the normal level. ■ (of the ground) cave in; sink: *the island is subsiding.* ■ (of a swelling) reduce until gone. [17th C.: from L. *subsidere*, from *sub-* 'below' + *sidere* 'settle' (rel. to *sedere* 'sit').]

sub·sid·ence /səb'sīdns; 'səbsidns/ ▶ **n.** the gradual caving in or sinking of an area of land. [17th C.: from L. *subsidentia* 'sediment,' from the verb *subsidere* (see SUBSIDE).]

sub·sid·i·ar·y /səb'sidēˌerē/ ▶ **adj.** less important than but related or supplementary to. ■ [attrib.] (of a company) controlled by a holding or parent company. ▶ **n.** (pl. **-ar·ies**) a company controlled by a holding company. — **sub·sid·i·ar·i·ly** /-ˌsidē'e(ə)rəlē/ **adv.** (rare). [16th C.: from L. *subsidiarius*, from *subsidium* 'support, assistance' (see SUBSIDY).]

sub·si·dize /'səbsəˌdīz/ ▶ **v.** [trans.] support (an organization or activity) financially. ■ pay part of the cost of producing (something) to reduce prices for the buyer. — **sub·si·di·za·tion** /ˌsəbsədi'zāsHən/ **n. sub·si·diz·er n.**

sub·si·dy /'səbsidē/ ▶ **n.** (pl. **-dies**) **1** a sum of money granted by the government or a public body to assist an industry or business so that the price of a commodity or service may remain low or competitive. ■ a sum of money granted to support an arts organization or other undertaking held to be in the public interest. ■ a sum of money paid by one government to another for the preservation of neutrality, the promotion of war, or to repay military aid. ■ a grant or contribution of money. **2** hist. a parliamentary grant to the sovereign for state needs. ■ a tax levied on a particular occasion. [ME: from Anglo-Norman Fr. *subsidie*, from L. *subsidium* 'assistance.']

sub·sist /səb'sist/ ▶ **v.** [intrans.] **1** maintain or support oneself, esp. at a minimal level. **2** esp. Law remain in being, force, or effect. ■ (**subsist in**) be attributable to. — **sub·sist·ent** /-ənt/ **adj.** [16th C.: from L. *subsistere* 'stand firm,' from *sub-* 'from below' + *sistere* 'set, stand.']

sub·sist·ence /səb'sistəns/ ▶ **n. 1** the action or fact of maintaining or supporting oneself at a minimum level. ■ the means of doing this. ■ [as adj.] denoting or relating to production at a level sufficient only for one's own use or consumption, without any surplus for trade: *subsistence agriculture.* **2** esp. Law the state of remaining in force or effect.

sub·sist·ence lev·el (also **subsistence wage**) ▶ **n.** a standard of living (or wage) that provides only the bare necessities of life.

sub·soil /'səbˌsoil/ ▶ **n.** the soil lying immediately under the surface soil. ▶ **v.** [trans.] [usu. as n.] (**subsoiling**) plow (land) so as to cut into the subsoil.

sub·son·ic /ˌsəb'sänik/ ▶ **adj.** relating to or flying at a speed or speeds less than that of sound. — **sub·son·i·cal·ly** /-ik(ə)lē/ **adv.**

sub·space /'səbˌspās/ ▶ **n. 1** Math. a space that is wholly contained in another space, or whose points or elements are all in another space.

2 (in science fiction) a hypothetical space-time continuum used for communication at a speed faster than that of light.

sub·spe·cies /ˈsəbˌspēsHēz; -sēz/ (abbr.: **subsp.** or **ssp.**) ▶ **n.** (pl. same) Biol. a taxonomic category that ranks below species, usually a fairly permanent geographically isolated race. Subspecies are designated by a Latin trinomial, e.g., (in zoology) *Ursus arctos horribilis* or (in botany) *Beta vulgaris* subsp. *crassa*. Compare with FORM (sense 3) and VARIETY (sense 2). — **sub·spe·cif·ic** /ˌsəbspəˈsifik/ **adj.**

subst. ▶ **abbr.** ■ substantive. ■ substitute.

sub·stage /ˈsəbˌstāj/ ▶ **n.** [usu. as adj.] an apparatus fixed beneath the ordinary stage of a compound microscope to support mirrors and other accessories.

sub·stance /ˈsəbstəns/ ▶ **n.** **1** a particular kind of matter with uniform properties: *a waxy substance.* ■ an intoxicating, stimulating, or narcotic chemical or drug, esp. an illegal one. **2** the real physical matter of which a person or thing consists and which has a tangible, solid presence. ■ the quality of having a solid basis in reality or fact. ■ the quality of being dependable or stable. **3** the quality of being important, valid, or significant. ■ the most important or essential part of something; the real or essential meaning. ■ the subject matter of a text, speech, or work of art, esp. as contrasted with the form or style in which it is presented. ■ wealth and possessions. ■ Philos. the essential nature underlying phenomena, which is subject to changes and accidents. [ME: from OFr., from L. *substantia* 'being, essence,' from *substant-* 'standing firm,' from the verb *substare.*]

sub·stance a·buse ▶ **n.** overindulgence in or dependence on an addictive substance, esp. alcohol or drugs.

sub·stand·ard /ˌsəbˈstandərd/ ▶ **adj.** **1** below the usual or required standard: *sub-standard housing.* **2** another term for NONSTANDARD.

sub·stan·tial /səbˈstancHəl/ ▶ **adj.** **1** of considerable importance, size, or worth: *a substantial amount of cash.* ■ strongly built or made. ■ (of a meal) large and filling. ■ important in material or social terms; wealthy. **2** concerning the essentials of something. **3** real and tangible rather than imaginary. — **sub·stan·ti·al·i·ty** /-ˌstancHēˈalitē/ **n.**

sub·stan·tial·ize /səbˈstancHəˌlīz/ ▶ **v.** [trans.] give (something) substance or actual existence.

sub·stan·tial·ly /səbˈstancHəlē/ ▶ **adv.** **1** to a great or significant extent: *profits grew substantially.* **2** for the most part; essentially.

sub·stan·ti·ate /səbˈstancHēˌāt/ ▶ **v.** [trans.] provide evidence to support or prove the truth of. — **sub·stan·ti·a·tion** /-ˌstancHēˈāsHən/ **n.**

sub·stan·tive /ˈsəbstəntiv/ ▶ **adj.** **1** having a firm basis in reality and therefore important, meaningful, or considerable. **2** having a separate and independent existence. ■ (of a dye) not needing a mordant. **3** (of law) defining rights and duties as opposed to giving the rules by which such things are established. ▶ **n.** Gram. a noun. — **sub·stan·ti·val** /ˌsəbstənˈtīvəl/ **adj.** **sub·stan·tive·ly** **adv.** [ME: ult. from late L. *substantivus*, from *substantia* 'essence.']

sub·sta·tion /ˈsəbˌstāsHən/ ▶ **n.** **1** a set of equipment reducing the high voltage of electrical power transmission to that suitable for supply to consumers. **2** a subordinate station for the police or fire department. ■ a small post office.

sub·stit·u·ent /səbˈsticHo͞oənt/ ▶ **n.** Chem. an atom or group of atoms taking the place of another atom or group or occupying a specified position in a molecule. [19th C.: from L. *substituent-* 'standing in place of,' from *substituere.*]

sub·sti·tute /ˈsəbstiˌt(y)o͞ot/ ▶ **n.** a person or thing acting or serving in place of another. ■ a sports player nominated as eligible to replace another after a game has begun. ■ Psychol. a person or thing that becomes the object of love or other emotion deprived of its natural outlet: *a father substitute.* ▶ **v.** [trans.] use or add in place of. ■ [intrans.] act or serve as a substitute. ■ replace (someone or something) with another. ■ replace (a sports player) with a substitute during a contest. ■ Chem. replace (an atom or group in a molecule, esp. a hydrogen atom) with another. ■ [as adj.] (**substituted**) Chem. (of a compound) in which one or more hydrogen atoms have been replaced by other atoms or groups: *a substituted alkaloid.* — **sub·sti·tut·a·bil·i·ty** /ˌsəbstəˌt(y)o͞otəˈbilitē/ **n.** **sub·sti·tut·a·ble** **adj.** **sub·sti·tu·tive** /-ˌt(y)o͞otiv/ **adj.** [ME: from L. *substitutus* 'put in place of,' past part. of *substituere*, based on *statuere* 'set up.']

sub·sti·tu·tion /ˌsəbstiˈt(y)o͞osHən/ ▶ **n.** the action of replacing someone or something with another person or thing. — **sub·sti·tu·tion·al** /-sHənl/ **adj.** **sub·sti·tu·tion·ar·y** /-ˌnerē/ **adj.**

sub·strate /ˈsəbˌstrāt/ ▶ **n.** a substance or layer that underlies something, or on which some process occurs, in particular: ■ the surface or material on or from which an organism lives, grows, or obtains its nourishment. ■ the substance on which an enzyme acts. ■ a material that provides the surface on which something is deposited or inscribed, for example the silicon wafer used to manufacture integrated circuits. [19th C.: Anglicized form of SUBSTRATUM.]

sub·stra·tum /ˈsəbˌstrātəm; -ˌstra-/ ▶ **n.** (pl. **-ta** /-tə/) an underlying layer or substance, in particular a layer of rock or soil beneath the surface of the ground. ■ a foundation or basis of something. [17th C.: mod. L., neut. past part. (used as a n.) of L. *substernere*, from *sub-* 'below' + *sternere* 'strew.']

sub·sume /səbˈso͞om/ ▶ **v.** [trans.] (often **be subsumed**) include or absorb (something) in something else. — **sub·sum·a·ble** **adj.** **sub·sump·tion** /-ˈsəm(p)sHən/ **n.** [16th C.: from med. L. *subsumere*, from *sub-* 'from below' + *sumere* 'take.']

sub·sur·face /ˈsəbˌsərfəs/ ▶ **n.** the stratum or strata below the earth's surface.

sub·ten·ant /ˌsəbˈtenənt/ ▶ **n.** a person who leases property from a tenant. — **sub·ten·an·cy** /-ˈtenənsē/ **n.**

sub·tend /səbˈtend/ ▶ **v.** [trans.] **1** (of a line, arc, or figure) form (an angle) at a particular point when straight lines from its extremities are joined at that point. ■ (of an angle or chord) have bounding lines or points that meet or coincide with those of (a line or arc). **2** Bot. (of a bract) extend under (a flower) so as to support or enfold it. [16th C.: from L. *subtendere*, from *sub-* 'under' + *tendere* 'stretch.']

sub·ter·fuge /ˈsəbtərˌfyo͞oj/ ▶ **n.** deceit used in order to achieve one's goal. ■ a statement or action resorted to in order to deceive. [16th C.: from Fr., or from late L. *subterfugium*, from L. *subterfugere* 'escape secretly,' from *subter-* 'beneath' + *fugere* 'flee.']

sub·ter·ra·ne·an /ˌsəbtəˈrānēən/ ▶ **adj.** existing, occurring, or done under the earth's surface. ■ secret; concealed. — **sub·ter·ra·ne·ous·ly** /-ˈrānēəslē/ **adv.** [17th C.: from L. *subterraneus* (from *sub-* 'below' + *terra* 'earth') + -AN.]

sub·text /ˈsəbˌtekst/ ▶ **n.** an underlying and often distinct theme in a piece of writing or conversation.

sub·ti·tle /ˈsəbˌtītl/ ▶ **n.** **1** (**subtitles**) captions displayed at the bottom of a movie or television screen that translate or transcribe the dialogue or narrative. **2** a subordinate title of a published work or article. ▶ **v.** [trans.] (usu. **be subtitled**) **1** provide (a movie or program) with subtitles. **2** provide (a published work or article) with a subtitle.

sub·tle /ˈsətl/ ▶ **adj.** (**-tler, -tlest**) (esp. of a change or distinction) so delicate or precise as to be difficult to analyze or describe. ■ (of a mixture or effect) delicately complex and understated. ■ making use of clever and indirect methods to achieve something. ■ capable of making fine distinctions. ■ arranged in an ingenious and elaborate way. ■ archaic crafty; cunning. — **sub·tle·ness** **n.** **sub·tly** **adv.** [ME: from OFr. *sotil*, from L. *subtilis* 'fine, delicate.']

sub·tle·ty /ˈsətltē/ ▶ **n.** (pl. **-ties**) the quality or state of being subtle. ■ a subtle distinction, feature, or argument.

sub·ton·ic /səbˈtänik/ ▶ **n.** Music the note below the tonic, the seventh note of the diatonic scale of any key.

sub·to·tal /ˈsəbˌtōtl/ ▶ **n.** the total of one set of a larger group of figures to be added. ▶ **v.** (**-taled, -tal·ing**; Brit. **-talled, -tal·ling**) [trans.] add (numbers) so as to obtain a subtotal. ▶ **adj.** Med. (of an injury or a surgical operation) partial; not total.

sub·tract /səbˈtrakt/ ▶ **v.** [trans.] take away (a number or amount) from another to calculate the difference. ■ take away (something) from something else so as to decrease the size, number, or amount. — **sub·tract·er** **n.** **sub·trac·tive** /-tiv/ **adj.** [16th C.: from L. *subtract-* 'drawn away,' from *sub-* 'from below' + *trahere* 'to draw.']

sub·trac·tion /səbˈtraksHən/ ▶ **n.** the process or skill of taking one number or amount away from another. ■ Math. the process of taking a matrix, vector, or other quantity away from another under specific rules to obtain the difference.

sub·trop·ics /ˌsəbˈträpiks/ ▶ **plural n.** (**the subtropics**) the regions adjacent to or bordering on the tropics. — **sub·trop·i·cal** /-ˈträpikəl/ **adj.**

su·bu·late /ˈsəbyəlit; -ˌlāt/ ▶ **adj.** Bot. & Zool. (of a part) slender and tapering to a point; awl-shaped. [18th C.: from L. *subula* 'awl' + -ATE[2].]

sub·u·nit /ˈsəbˌyo͞onit/ ▶ **n.** a distinct component of something: *chemical subunits of human DNA.*

sub·urb /ˈsəbərb/ ▶ **n.** an outlying district of a city, esp. a residential one. [ME: from OFr. *suburbe* or L. *suburbium*, from *sub-* 'near to' + *urbs, urb-* 'city.']

sub·ur·ban /səˈbərbən/ ▶ **adj.** of or characteristic of a suburb: *suburban life.* ■ contemptibly dull and ordinary. — **sub·ur·ban·ite** /-ˌnīt/ **n.** **sub·ur·ban·i·za·tion** /səˌbərbənəˈzāsHən/ **n.** **sub·ur·ban·ize** /-ˌnīz/ **v.**

sub·ur·bi·a /səˈbərbēə/ ▶ **n.** the suburbs or their inhabitants viewed collectively.

sub·ver·sive /səbˈvərsiv/ ▶ **adj.** seeking or intended to subvert an established system or institution. ▶ **n.** a person with such aims. — **sub·ver·sive·ly** **adv.** **sub·ver·sive·ness** **n.** [17th C.: from med. L. *subversivus*, from the verb *subvertere* (see SUBVERT).]

sub·vert /səbˈvərt/ ▶ **v.** [trans.] undermine the power and authority of (an established system or institution). — **sub·ver·sion** /-ˈvərzHən; -sHən/ **n.** **sub·vert·er** **n.** [ME: ult. from L. *subvertere*, from *sub-* 'from below' + *vertere* 'to turn.']

sub·way /ˈsəbˌwā/ ▶ **n.** **1** an underground electric railroad. **2** Brit. a tunnel under a road for use by pedestrians.

sub·woof·er /ˈsəbˌwo͝ofər/ ▶ **n.** a loudspeaker component designed to reproduce very low bass frequencies.

sub·ze·ro /ˌsəbˈzi(ə)rō/ ▶ **adj.** (of temperature) lower than zero; below freezing.

suc- ▶ **prefix** var. of SUB- assimilated before *c* (as in *succeed, succussion*).

suc·cah /so͞oˈkä; ˈso͝okə/ (also **suk·kah**) ▶ **n.** a booth in which a practicing Jew spends part of the Feast of Tabernacles. [19th C.: from Heb. *sukkāh* 'hut.']

suc·ceed /səkˈsēd/ ▶ **v.** **1** [intrans.] achieve what one aims or wants to: *he succeeded in winning a pardon.* ■ (of a plan, request, or undertaking) lead to the desired result. **2** [trans.] take over a throne, inheritance, office, or other position from. ■ [intrans.] become the new rightful holder of an inheritance, office, title, or property. ■ come after and take the place of.

– PHRASES **nothing succeeds like success** proverb success leads to opportunities for further and greater successes. —**suc·ceed·er** n. (archaic). [ME: ult. from L. *succedere* 'come close after,' from *sub-* 'close to' + *cedere* 'go.']

suc·cess /sək'ses/ ▶ n. the accomplishment of an aim or purpose. ■ the attainment of popularity or profit. ■ a person or thing that achieves desired aims or attains prosperity. ■ archaic the outcome of an undertaking, specified as achieving or failing to achieve its aims. [16th C.: from L. *successus*, from the verb *succedere* 'come close after' (see SUCCEED).]

suc·cess·ful /sək'sesfəl/ ▶ adj. accomplishing an aim or purpose: *a successful attack on the town.* ■ having achieved popularity, profit, or distinction. — **suc·cess·ful·ly** adv.

suc·ces·sion /sək'sesHən/ ▶ n. **1** a number of people or things sharing a specified characteristic and following one after the other. ■ Geol. a group of strata representing a single chronological sequence. **2** the action or process of inheriting a title, office, property, etc. ■ the right or sequence of inheriting a position, title, etc. ■ Ecol. the process by which a plant or animal community successively gives way to another until a stable climax is reached. Compare with SERE[2].

– PHRASES **in quick** (or **rapid**) **succession** following one another at short intervals. **in succession** following one after the other without interruption. — **suc·ces·sion·al** /-SHənl/ adj. [ME: from OFr., or from L. *successio(n-)*, from the verb *succedere* (see SUCCEED).]

suc·ces·sive /sək'sesiv/ ▶ adj. [attrib.] following one another or following others: *their fifth successive win.* — **suc·ces·sive·ly** adv. **suc·ces·sive·ness** n.

suc·ces·sor /sək'sesər/ ▶ n. a person or thing that succeeds another.

suc·cinct /sək'siNGkt/ ▶ adj. (esp. of something written or spoken) briefly and clearly expressed. — **suc·cinct·ly** adv. **suc·cinct·ness** n. [ME: from L. *succinctus* 'tucked up,' past part. of *succingere*, from *sub-* 'from below' + *cingere* 'gird.']

suc·cin·ic ac·id /sək,sinik/ ▶ n. Biochem. a crystalline organic acid, $HOOC(CH_2)_2COOH$, which occurs in living tissue as an intermediate in glucose metabolism. — **suc·ci·nate** /'səksə,nāt/ n. [18th C.: *succinic* from Fr. *succinique*, from L. *succinum* 'amber.']

suc·ci·nyl·cho·line chlo·ride /'səksənl'kōlēn/ ▶ n. Med. a synthetic compound used as a short-acting muscle relaxant and local anesthetic.

suc·cor /'səkər/ ▶ n. assistance and support in times of hardship and distress. ▶ v. [trans.] give assistance or aid to. — **suc·cor·less** adj. [ME: via OFr. from med. L. *succursus*, from L. *succurrere* 'run to the help of,' from *sub-* 'from below' + *currere* 'run.']

suc·co·tash /'səkə,tasH/ ▶ n. a dish of corn and lima beans cooked together. [18th C.: from Narragansett *msíquatash* (pl.).]

Suc·coth /sōō'kōt; 'sŏŏkəs/ ▶ n. a major Jewish festival held in the autumn to commemorate the sheltering of the Israelites in the wilderness. It is marked by the erection of small booths covered in natural materials. Also called FEAST OF TABERNACLES. [from Heb. *sukkōt*, pl. of *sukkāh* 'thicket, hut.']

suc·cu·bus /'səkyəbəs/ ▶ n. (pl. **-bi** /-,bī/) a female demon believed to have sexual intercourse with sleeping men. [ME: from med. L. *succubus* 'prostitute,' from *succubare*, from *sub-* 'under' + *cubare* 'to lie.']

suc·cu·lent /'səkyələnt/ ▶ adj. (of food) tender, juicy, and tasty. ■ Bot. (of a plant, esp. a xerophyte) having thick fleshy leaves or stems adapted to storing water. ▶ n. Bot. a succulent plant. — **suc·cu·lence** n. **suc·cu·lent·ly** adv. [17th C.: from L. *succulentus*, from *succus* 'juice.']

suc·cumb /sə'kəm/ ▶ v. [intrans.] fail to resist (pressure, temptation, or some other negative force). ■ die from the effect of a disease or injury. [15th C.: from OFr. *succomber* or L. *succumbere*, from *sub-* 'under' + a verb rel. to *cubare* 'to lie.']

suc·cuss /sə'kəs/ ▶ v. [trans.] (in preparing homeopathic remedies) shake (a solution) vigorously. — **suc·cus·sion** /-'kəsHən/ n. [19th C.: from L. *succuss-* 'shaken,' from the verb *succutere*, from *sub-* 'away' + *quatere* 'to shake.']

such /səcH/ ▶ adj., predeterminer, & pron. **1** of the type previously mentioned: [as adj.] *I have been involved in many such courses* | [as predeterminer] *I longed to find a kindred spirit, and in him I thought I had found such a person* | [as pron.] *second-class citizens and treated us as such.* **2** (**such —— as/that**) of the type about to be mentioned: [as adj.] *no such thing as a free lunch* | [as predeterminer] *organized in such a way that it can be run by two adults* | [as pron.] *the wound was such that I needed stitches.* **3** to so high a degree; so great (often used to emphasize a quality): [as adj.] *this material is of **such** importance **that** it has a powerful bearing on the case* | [as predeterminer] *autumn's such a beautiful season* | [as pron.] ***such** is the elegance of his typeface **that** it is still the designer's favorite.*

– PHRASES **and such** and similar things. **as such** [often with negative] in the exact sense of the word. **such and such** (or **such-and-such**) used to refer vaguely to a person or thing that does not need to be specified. **such as 1** for example: *wildflowers such as daisies and red clover.* **2** of a kind that; like: *an event such as we've shared.* **such as it is** (or **they are**) what little there is; for what it's worth. **such a one** such a person or thing. **such that** to the extent that. [OE *swilc, swylc*; rel. to Du. *zulk*, Ger. *solch*, from the Gmc. bases of SO[1] and ALIKE.]

such·like /'səcH,līk/ ▶ pron. things of the type mentioned: *carpets, old chairs, tables, and suchlike.* ▶ adj. of the type mentioned.

suck /sək/ ▶ v. **1** [trans.] draw into the mouth by contracting the muscles of the lip and mouth to make a partial vacuum: *they suck mint juleps through straws.* ■ hold (something) in the mouth and draw at it by contracting the lip and cheek muscles. ■ draw milk, juice, or other fluid from (something) into the mouth or by suction. ■ [with obj. and adverbial of direction] draw in a specified direction by creating a vacuum: *he was sucked under the surface of the river.* ■ fig. involve (someone) in something without their choosing. ■ [intrans.] (of a pump) make a gurgling sound as a result of drawing air. **2** [intrans.] informal be very bad, disagreeable, or disgusting. ▶ n. an act of sucking something. ■ the sound made by water retreating and drawing at something.

– PHRASES **give suck** archaic give milk from the breast or teat; suckle. **suck someone dry** exhaust someone's physical, material, or emotional resources. **suck someone in** cheat or deceive someone. **suck someone off** vulgar slang perform fellatio on (someone). **suck it up** informal accept a hardship.

– PHRASAL VERBS **suck up** informal behave obsequiously, esp. for one's own advantage. [OE *sūcan* (v.), from an Indo-Eur. imitative root; rel. to SOAK.]

suck·er /'səkər/ ▶ n. **1** a person or thing that sucks, in particular: ■ a flat or concave organ enabling an animal to cling to a surface by suction. ■ the piston of a suction pump. ■ a pipe through which liquid is drawn by suction. **2** informal a gullible or easily deceived person. ■ (**a sucker for**) a person especially susceptible to or fond of a specified thing. **3** informal a thing or person not specified by name. **4** Bot. a shoot springing from the base of a tree or other plant, esp. one arising from the root below ground level at some distance from the main stem or trunk. ■ a side shoot from an axillary bud, as in tomato plants. **5** a freshwater fish (family Catostomidae) with thick lips that are used to suck up food from the bottom, native to North America and Asia. **6** informal a lollipop. ▶ v. **1** [intrans.] Bot. (of a plant) produce suckers. **2** [trans.] informal fool or trick (someone).

suck·er·fish /'səkər,fisH/ ▶ n. (pl. same or **-fish·es**) another term for REMORA.

suck·er punch ▶ n. an unexpected punch or blow. ▶ v. (**suck·er-punch**) [trans.] hit (someone) with such a punch or blow.

suck·le /'səkəl/ ▶ v. [trans.] feed (a baby or young animal) from the breast or teat. ■ [intrans.] (of a baby or young animal) feed by sucking the breast or teat: *the infant's biological need to suckle.* [ME: prob. a back-form. from SUCKLING.]

suck·ler /'sək(ə)lər/ ▶ n. an unweaned animal, esp. a calf. ■ a cow used to breed and suckle calves for beef.

suck·ling /'səkliNG/ ▶ n. an unweaned child or animal. [ME: from the verb SUCK + -LING.]

suck-up ▶ n. informal a person who behaves obsequiously, esp. to earn approval or favoritism.

suck·y /'səkē/ ▶ adj. (**suck·i·er, suck·i·est**) informal disagreeable; unpleasant: *her sucky job.*

su·crase /'sōō,krās; -,krāz/ ▶ n. another term for INVERTASE.

Su·cre[1] /'sōōkrā/ the judicial capital of Bolivia; pop. 131,000. It was named Chuquisaca by the Spanish in 1539. It was renamed in 1825 in honor of Antonio José de Sucre.

Su·cre[2] /'sōō,krā/, Antonio José de (1795–1830), president of Bolivia 1826–28; born in Venezuela.

su·cre /'sōō,krā/ ▶ n. the basic monetary unit of Ecuador, equal to 100 centavos. [for A. J. de *Sucre* (see SUCRE[2]).]

su·crose /'sōō,krōs/ ▶ n. Chem. a compound, $C_{12}H_{22}O_{11}$, that is the chief component of cane or beet sugar. [19th C.: from Fr. *sucre* 'sugar' + -OSE[2].]

suc·tion /'səksHən/ ▶ n. the production of a partial vacuum by the removal of air in order to force fluid into a vacant space or procure adhesion. ▶ v. [with obj. and adverbial of direction] remove (something) using suction. [17th C.: from late L. *suctio(n-)*, from L. *sugere* 'suck.']

suc·to·ri·al /,sək'tôrēəl/ ▶ adj. esp. Zool. adapted for sucking (descriptive, for example, of the mouthparts of some insects). ■ (of an animal) having a sucker for feeding or adhering to something. — **suc·to·ri·al·ly** adv. [19th C.: from mod. L. *suctorius* (from L. *sugere* 'suck') + -AL.]

Su·dan /sōō'dan/ (also **the Sudan**) **1** a country in northeastern Africa. *See box on next page.* **2** a vast region in North Africa that extends across the width of the continent from the southern edge of the Sahara to the tropical equatorial zone in the south. — **Su·da·nese** /,sōōdn'ēz; -'ēs/ adj. & n.

su·dan grass /sōō'dan/ ▶ n. a Sudanese sorghum (*Sorghum sudanense*) cultivated for fodder in dry regions of the US.

sud·den /'sədn/ ▶ adj. occurring or done quickly and unexpectedly or without warning: *a sudden bright flash.*

– PHRASES **all of a sudden** suddenly. [ME: from Anglo-Norman Fr. *sudein*, from an alt. of L. *subitaneus*, from *subitus* 'sudden.']

sud·den death ▶ n. informal a means of deciding the winner in a tied contest, in which play continues and the winner is the first side or player to score.

sud·den in·fant death syn·drome (abbr.: **SIDS**) ▶ n. the death of a seemingly healthy baby in its sleep, due to an apparent spontaneous cessation of breathing.

sud·den·ly /'sədn-lē/ ▶ adv. quickly and unexpectedly.

Su·de·ten·land /sōō'dātn,land; -,länt/ an area in the northwestern Czech Republic, on the border with Germany. Czech name SUDETY.

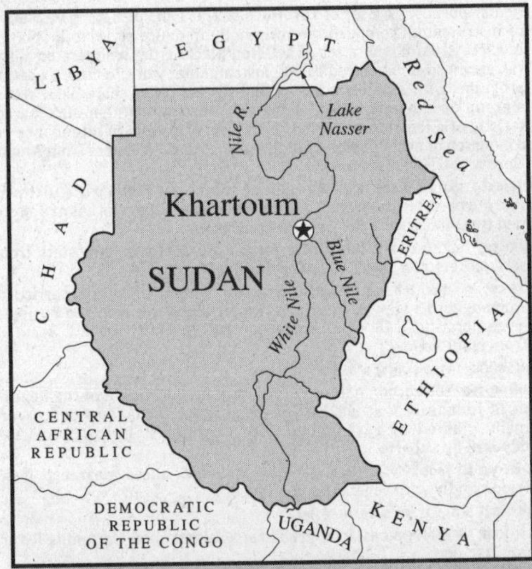

Sudan

Official name: Republic of Sudan
Location: northeastern Africa, south of Egypt, with a coastline on the Red Sea
Area: 967,700 square miles (2,505,800 sq km)
Population: 39,148,000
Capital: Khartoum
Languages: Arabic (official), English, Dinka, Hausa, and others
Currency: Sudanese dinar

su·do·ku /so͞o'dōko͞o/ ▶ n. a logic puzzle consisting of a grid containing nine squares, each subdivided into a further nine squares, which contain some of the numbers from 1 to 9; the grid has to be completed so that each square, vertical column, and horizontal row in the grid contains the numbers from 1 to 9. [21st C.: from Japanese *Sūdoku*, from *sū-* (in *sūji* 'number') + *-doku* (in *dokushin* 'single status'), elements of the puzzle's former name.]

su·dor·if·er·ous /ˌso͞odə'rif(ə)rəs/ ▶ adj. (of a gland) secreting sweat. [16th C.: from late L. *sudorifer* (from L. *sudor* 'sweat') + **-ous**.]

su·dor·if·ic /ˌso͞odə'rifik/ Med. ▶ adj. relating to or causing sweating. ▶ n. a drug that induces sweating. [17th C.: from mod. L. *sudorificus*, from L. *sudor* 'sweat.']

suds /sədz/ ▶ plural n. (also **soapsuds**) froth made from soap and water. ■ informal beer. ▶ v. [trans.] lather, cover, or wash in soapy water. ■ [intrans.] form suds. — **suds·y** adj. [19th C.: cf. MDu. *sudse* 'marsh, bog'; prob. rel. to **seethe**.]

suds·er /'sədzər/ ▶ n. informal a soap opera.

sue /so͞o/ ▶ v. (**sues, sued, su·ing**) **1** [trans.] institute legal proceedings against (a person or institution), typically for redress. **2** [intrans.] formal appeal formally to a person for something. — **su·er** /'so͞oər/ n. [ME: from Anglo-Norman Fr. *suer*, based on L. *sequi* 'follow.']

suede /swād/ ▶ n. leather, esp. kidskin, with the flesh side rubbed to make a velvety nap. [17th C.: from Fr. *(gants de) Suède* '(gloves of) Sweden.']

su·et /'so͞oit/ ▶ n. the hard white fat on the kidneys and loins of cattle, sheep, and other animals, used to make foods including puddings, pastry, and mincemeat. — **su·et·y** adj. [ME: from Anglo-Norman Fr., from the synonymous word *su*, from L. *sebum* 'tallow.']

Sue·to·ni·us /so͞oə'tōnēəs; swē'tō-/ (*c.*69–*c.*150), Roman writer and historian; full name *Gaius Suetonius Tranquillus*. His works include *Lives of the Caesars*.

Su·ez, Isthmus of /so͞o'ez; 'so͞oˌez/ an isthmus between the Mediterranean and the Red seas that connects Egypt and Africa to the Sinai Peninsula and Asia.

Su·ez Ca·nal a shipping canal that connects the Mediterranean Sea at Port Said with the Red Sea. It was constructed 1859–69.

suf. ▶ abbr. suffix.

suf- ▶ prefix var. of **sub-** assimilated before *f* (as in *suffocate, suffuse*).

suff. ▶ abbr. ■ sufficient. ■ suffix.

suf·fer /'səfər/ ▶ v. [trans.] **1** experience or be subjected to (something bad or unpleasant). ■ [intrans.] (**suffer from**) be affected by or subject to (an illness or ailment). ■ [intrans.] become or appear worse in quality. **2** dated tolerate. ■ [with obj. and infin.] allow (someone) to do something.
– PHRASES **not suffer fools gladly** be impatient or intolerant toward people one regards as foolish or unintelligent. [with biblical allusion to 2 Cor. 11–19.] — **suf·fer·a·ble** /'səf(ə)rəbəl/ adj. **suf·fer·er** /'səf(ə)rər/ n. (in sense 1). [ME: from Anglo-Norman Fr. *suffrir*, from L. *sufferre*, from *sub-* 'from below' + *ferre* 'to bear.']

suf·fer·ance /'səf(ə)rəns/ ▶ n. **1** absence of objection rather than genuine approval; toleration. ■ Law the condition of the holder of an estate who continues to hold it after the title has ceased, without the express permission of the owner: *an estate at sufferance*. ■ archaic patient endurance. **2** archaic the suffering or undergoing of something bad or unpleasant.

suf·fice /sə'fīs/ ▶ v. [intrans.] be enough or adequate. ■ [trans.] meet the needs of.
– PHRASES **suffice (it) to say** used to indicate that one is saying enough to make one's meaning clear while withholding something for reasons of discretion or brevity. [ME: from OFr. *suffis-*, stem of *suffire*, from L. *sufficere* 'put under, meet the need of,' from *sub-* 'under' + *facere* 'make.']

suf·fi·cien·cy /sə'fisʜənsē/ ▶ n. (pl. **-cies**) the condition or quality of being adequate or sufficient. ■ [in sing.] an adequate amount of something, esp. of something essential: ***a sufficiency of good food***.

suf·fi·cient /sə'fisʜənt/ ▶ adj. enough; adequate. — **suf·fi·cient·ly** adv. [ME: from OFr., or from L. *sufficient-* 'meeting the need of' (see **suffice**).]

suf·fix ▶ n. /'səfiks/ a morpheme added at the end of a word to form a derivative, e.g., *-ation, -fy, -ing, -itis*. ▶ v. /'səfiks; sə'fiks/ [trans.] append, esp. as a suffix. — **suf·fix·a·tion** /ˌsəfik'sāsʜən/ n. [18th C.: from mod. L. *suffixum*, neut. past part. (used as a n.) of L. *suffigere*, from *sub-* 'subordinately' + *figere* 'fasten.']

suf·fo·cate /'səfəˌkāt/ ▶ v. die or cause to die from lack of air or inability to breathe. ■ have or cause to have difficulty in breathing. ■ fig. feel or cause to feel trapped and oppressed. — **suf·fo·cat·ing·ly** adv. **suf·fo·ca·tion** /ˌsəfə'kāsʜən/ n. [15th C.: from L. *suffocat-* 'stifled,' from the verb *suffocare*, from *sub-* 'below' + *fauces* 'throat.']

Suf·folk /'səfək/ a county in eastern England, on the coast of East Anglia; county town, Ipswich.

suf·frage /'səfrij/ ▶ n. **1** the right to vote in political elections. **2** (usu. **suffrages**) a series of intercessory prayers or petitions. [ME: from L. *suffragium*, reinforced by Fr. *suffrage*.]

suf·fra·gette /ˌsəfrə'jet/ ▶ n. hist. a woman seeking the right to vote through organized protest.

suf·fra·gist /'səfrəjist/ ▶ n. esp. hist. a person advocating the extension of suffrage, esp. to women. — **suf·fra·gism** /-ˌjizəm/ n.

suf·fuse /sə'fyo͞oz/ ▶ v. [trans.] gradually spread through or over: *her cheeks were suffused with color*. — **suf·fu·sion** /-'fyo͞ozʜən/ n. **suf·fu·sive** /-'fyo͞osiv/ adj. [16th C.: from L. *suffus-* 'poured into,' from *sub-* 'below, from below' + *fundere* 'pour.']

Su·fi /'so͞ofē/ ▶ n. (pl. **-fis**) a Muslim ascetic and mystic. — **Su·fic** /-fik/ adj. [17th C.: from Arab. *ṣūfī*, perh. from *ṣūf* 'wool.']

sug- ▶ prefix var. of **sub-** assimilated before *g* (as in *suggest*).

sug·ar /'sʜo͝ogər/ ▶ n. **1** a sweet crystalline substance obtained from various plants, esp. sugar cane and sugar beet, consisting essentially of sucrose, and used as a sweetener in food and drink. ■ a lump or teaspoonful of this, used to sweeten tea or coffee. ■ informal used as a term of endearment or an affectionate form of address. ■ [as exclam.] informal used as a euphemism for "shit." ■ informal a psychoactive drug in the form of white powder, esp. heroin or cocaine. **2** Biochem. any of the class of soluble, crystalline, typically sweet-tasting carbohydrates found in living tissues and exemplified by glucose and sucrose. ▶ v. [trans.] sweeten, sprinkle, or coat with sugar. ■ fig. make more agreeable or palatable. — **sug·ar·less** adj. [ME: from OFr. *sukere*, from Ital. *zucchero*, prob. via med. L. from Arab. *sukkar*.]

sug·ar ap·ple ▶ n. another term for **sweetsop**.

sug·ar beet ▶ n. beet of a variety from which sugar is extracted.

sug·ar·bird /'sʜo͝ogərˌbərd/ (also **sug·ar bird**) ▶ n. **1** a southern African songbird (genus *Promerops*, family Promeropidae or Meliphagidae) with a long fine bill and very long tail, feeding on nectar and insects. **2** another term for **bananaquit**.

sug·ar bush (also **sug·ar·bush** /'sʜo͝ogərˌbo͝osʜ/) ▶ n. a plantation of sugar maples.

sug·ar cane (also **sug·arcane** /'sʜo͝ogərˌkān/) ▶ n. a perennial tropical grass (genus *Saccharum*) with tall stout jointed stems from which sugar is extracted. The fibrous residue can be used as fuel, in fiberboard, and for a number of other purposes.

sug·ar·coat /'sʜo͝ogərˌkōt/ ▶ v. [trans.] coat (an item of food) with sugar. ■ make superficially attractive or acceptable. ■ make excessively sentimental.

sug·ar dad·dy ▶ n. informal a rich older man who lavishes gifts on a young woman in return for her company or sexual favors.

sug·ar glid·er ▶ n. a flying phalanger (*Petaurus breviceps*) that feeds on wattle gum and eucalyptus sap, native to Australia, New Guinea, and Tasmania.

sug·ar·ing /'sʜo͝ogəriɴɢ/ ▶ n. (also **sug·ar·ing off**) the boiling down of maple sap until it thickens into syrup or crystallizes into sugar.

sug·ar·loaf /'sʜo͝ogərˌlōf/ ▶ n. a conical molded mass of sugar (now used chiefly in similes and metaphors to describe the shape of other objects).

Sug·ar Loaf Moun·tain a rocky peak in Brazil, northeast of Rio de Janeiro's Copacabana Beach.

sug·ar ma·ple ▶ n. see MAPLE.

sug·ar of lead /led/ ▶ n. Chem., dated lead acetate, $Pb(CH_3CO_2)_2$, a soluble white crystalline salt.

sug·ar pine ▶ n. a tall pine tree (*Pinus lambertiana*), the heartwood of which exudes a sweet substance, hence its name. Found primarily in California and Oregon, sugar pines have very long cones, some reaching 26 inches in length.

sug·ar·plum /ˈsʜo͝ogər,pləm/ ▶ n. a small round candy of flavored boiled sugar.

sug·ar snap (also **sug·ar snap pea**) ▶ n. a snow pea, esp. of a variety with distinctively thick and rounded pods.

sug·ar·y /ˈsʜo͝ogərē/ ▶ adj. containing much sugar. ■ resembling or coated in sugar. ■ excessively sentimental. — **sug·ar·i·ness** n.

sug·gest /sə(g)ˈjest/ ▶ v. [reporting verb] put forward for consideration: [with clause] *I suggest that we wait a day or two.* ■ [trans.] cause one to think that (something) exists or is the case. ■ state or express indirectly: [with clause] *are you suggesting that I should ignore her?* ■ [trans.] evoke: *the theatrical interpretation of weather and water almost suggests El Greco.* ■ (**suggest itself**) (of an idea) come into one's mind. — **sug·gest·er** n. [16th C.: from L. *suggest-* 'suggested, prompted,' from the verb *suggerere*, from *sub-* 'from below' + *gerere* 'bring.']

sug·gest·i·ble /sə(g)ˈjestəbəl/ ▶ adj. open to suggestion; easily swayed: *a suggestible client would comply.* — **sug·gest·i·bil·i·ty** /-ˌjestəˈbilitē/ n.

sug·ges·tion /sə(g)ˈjescʜən/ ▶ n. an idea or plan put forward for consideration. ■ the action of doing this. ■ something that implies or indicates a certain fact or situation. ■ a slight trace or indication of something: *a suggestion of a smile.* ■ the action or process of calling up an idea or thought in someone's mind by associating it with other things. ■ Psychol. the influencing of a person to accept an idea, belief, or impulse uncritically, esp. as a technique in hypnosis or other therapies. ■ Psychol. a belief or impulse of this type. [ME: via OFr. from L. *suggestio(n-)*, from the verb *suggerere* (see SUGGEST).]

sug·ges·tive /sə(g)ˈjestiv/ ▶ adj. tending to suggest an idea. ■ indicative or evocative. ■ making someone think of sex and sexual relationships. — **sug·ges·tive·ly** adv. **sug·ges·tive·ness** n.

Su·har·to /so͞oˈhärtō/, Raden (1921–), president of Indonesia 1967–98. He overthrew Sukarno on an anticommunist pretext and established his own military government, which was marked by corruption.

Sui /swē/ a dynasty that ruled in China AD 581–618 and reunified the country.

su·i·cid·al /ˌso͞oiˈsīdl/ ▶ adj. deeply unhappy or depressed and likely to commit suicide. ■ relating to or likely to lead to suicide. ■ likely to have a disastrously damaging effect on oneself or one's interests: *a suicidal career move.* — **su·i·cid·al·ly** adv.

su·i·cide /ˈso͞oiˌsīd/ ▶ n. the action of killing oneself intentionally: *he committed suicide at the age of forty.* ■ a person who does this. ■ a course of action that is disastrously damaging to oneself or one's own interests. ■ [as adj.] relating to or denoting a military operation carried out by people who do not expect to survive it: *a suicide bomber.* ▶ v. [intrans.] intentionally kill oneself. [17th C.: from mod. L. *suicida* 'act of suicide,' *suicidium* 'person who commits suicide,' from L. *sui* 'of oneself' + *caedere* 'kill.']

su·i ge·ne·ris /ˌso͞oˌī ˈjenərəs; ˌso͞oē/ ▶ adj. unique. [L., 'of its own kind.']

su·i ju·ris /ˌso͞oˌī ˈjo͞oris; ˌso͞oē/ ▶ adj. Law of age; independent: *the beneficiaries are all sui juris.* [L., lit. 'of one's own right.']

su·int /ˈso͞oənt; swint/ ▶ n. the natural grease in sheep's wool, from which lanolin is obtained. [18th C.: from Fr., from *suer* 'sweat.']

Suisse /swēs/ French name for SWITZERLAND.

suit /so͞ot/ ▶ n. **1** a set of outer clothes made of the same fabric and designed to be worn together, typically consisting of a jacket and trousers or a jacket and skirt. ■ a set of clothes to be worn for a particular occasion or activity. ■ a complete set of pieces of armor for covering the whole body. ■ a complete set of sails required for a ship or for a set of spars. ■ (usu. **suits**) informal a high-ranking executive in a business or organization, typically one regarded as exercising influence in an impersonal way. **2** any of the sets distinguished by their pictorial symbols into which a deck of playing cards is divided, in conventional decks comprising spades, hearts, diamonds, and clubs. **3** short for LAWSUIT. ■ the process of trying to win a woman's affection, typically with a view to marriage. ■ literary a petition or entreaty made to a person in authority. ▶ v. **1** [trans.] be convenient for or acceptable to. ■ (**suit oneself**) [often in imper.] act entirely according to one's own wishes (often used to express the speaker's annoyance). ■ go well with or enhance the features, figure, or character of (someone). **2** [intrans.] put on clothes, typically for a particular activity: *I suited up and entered the water.* [ME: from Anglo-Norman Fr. *siwte*, from a fem. past part. of a Romance verb based on L. *sequi* 'follow.']

suit·a·ble /ˈso͞otəbəl/ ▶ adj. right or appropriate for a particular person, purpose, or situation. — **suit·a·bil·i·ty** /ˌso͞otəˈbilitē/ n. **suit·a·ble·ness** n. **suit·a·bly** /-blē/ adv.

suit·case /ˈso͞otˌkās/ ▶ n. a case with a handle and a hinged lid, used for carrying clothes and other personal possessions. — **suit·case·ful** /-ˌfo͝ol/ n. (pl. **-fuls**).

suite /swēt/ ▶ n. **1** a set of things belonging together, in particular: ■ a set of rooms designated for one person's or family's use or for a particular purpose. ■ a set of furniture of the same design. ■ Music a set of instrumental compositions, originally in dance style, to be played in succession. ■ Music a set of selected pieces from an opera or musical, arranged to be played as one instrumental work. ■ Comput. a set of programs with a uniform design and the ability to share data. ■ Geol. a group of minerals, rocks, or fossils occurring together and characteristic of a location or period. **2** a group of people in attendance on a monarch or other person of high rank. [17th C.: from Fr., from Anglo-Norman Fr. *siwte* (see SUIT).]

suit·ed /ˈso͞otid/ ▶ adj. **1** [predic.] right or appropriate for a particular person, purpose, or situation. **2** [in comb.] wearing a suit of clothes of a specified type, fabric, or color: *a dark-suited man.*

suit·ing /ˈso͞otiɴɢ/ ▶ n. fabric of a suitable quality for making suits, trousers, jackets, and skirts. ■ suits collectively.

suit·or /ˈso͞otər/ ▶ n. a man who pursues a relationship with a particular woman, with a view to marriage. ■ a prospective buyer of a business or corporation. [ME: from Anglo-Norman Fr. *seutor*, from L. *secutor*, from *sequi* 'follow.']

suk /so͞ok/ (also **sukh**) ▶ n. var. of SOUK.

Su·kar·no /so͞oˈkärnō/, Achmad (1901–70), first president of the Republic of Indonesia 1945–68. He led the struggle for independence, formally granted in 1949. Allied with Communist interests, he was deposed by Suharto.

su·ki·ya·ki /so͞okēˈyäkē/ ▶ n. a Japanese dish of sliced meat, esp. beef, fried rapidly with vegetables and sauce.

suk·kah ▶ n. var. of SUCCAH.

Suk·kur /ˈso͞okər/ a city in southeastern Pakistan, on the Indus River; pop. 350,000.

Su·la·we·si /ˌso͞oləˈwāsē/ an island in Indonesia, east of Borneo. Former name CELEBES.

sul·cate /ˈsəlˌkāt/ ▶ adj. Bot. & Zool. marked with parallel grooves. [18th C.: from L. *sulcatus* 'furrowed,' past part. of *sulcare*.]

sul·cus /ˈsəlkəs/ ▶ n. (pl. **sul·ci** /ˈsəlˌsī; -ˌsē/) Anat. a groove or furrow, esp. one on the surface of the brain. [17th C.: from L., 'furrow, wrinkle.']

Su·lei·man I /ˌso͞olāˈmän/ (also **Soliman** or **Solyman**) (*c.*1494–1566), sultan of the Ottoman Empire 1520–66; also known as **Suleiman the Magnificent** or **Suleiman the Lawgiver**.

sul·fa /ˈsəlfə/ (esp. Brit. also **sul·pha**) ▶ n. [usu. as adj.] the sulfonamide family of drugs. [1940s: abbr.]

sulfa- (esp. Brit. also **sulph-**) ▶ comb. form in names of drugs derived from sulfanilamide.

sul·fa·di·a·zine /ˌsəlfəˈdīəˌzēn/ (esp. Brit. also **sul·pha·di·a·zine**) ▶ n. Med. a sulfonamide antibiotic used to treat meningococcal meningitis.

sul·fa·mic ac·id /səlˈfamik/ (esp. Brit. also **sul·pham·ic ac·id**) ▶ n. Chem. a strongly acid crystalline, $HOSO_2NH_2$, compound used in cleaning agents and to make weed killers. — **sul·fa·mate** /ˈsəlfəˌmāt/ n. [19th C.: *sulfamic* from SULFUR + AMIDE + -IC.]

sul·fa·nil·a·mide /ˌsəlfəˈniləˌmīd/ (esp. Brit. also **sul·pha·nil·a·mide**) ▶ n. Med. a synthetic compound, $(H_2N)C_6H_4(SO_2NH_2)$, with antibacterial properties that is the basis of the sulfonamide drugs. [1930s: from *sulfanilic* (from SULFUR + ANILINE + -IC) + AMIDE.]

sul·fate /ˈsəlˌfāt/ (esp. Brit. also **sul·phate**) ▶ n. Chem. a salt or ester of sulfuric acid, containing the anion $SO_4 2-$ or the divalent group $-OSO_2O-$. [18th C.: Fr., from L. *sulfur*.]

sul·fide /ˈsəlˌfīd/ (esp. Brit. also **sul·phide**) ▶ n. Chem. a binary compound of sulfur with another element or group.

sul·fite /ˈsəlˌfīt/ (esp. Brit. also **sul·phite**) ▶ n. Chem. a salt of sulfurous acid, containing the anion $SO_3 2-$. [18th C.: Fr., alt. of *sulfate*.]

sul·fon·a·mide /səlˈfänəˌmīd/ (esp. Brit. also **sul·phon·a·mide**) ▶ n. Med. any of a class of synthetic drugs, derived from sulfanilamide, that are able to prevent the multiplication of some pathogenic bacteria. [19th C.: from SULFONE + AMIDE.]

sul·fo·nate /ˈsəlfəˌnāt/ (esp. Brit. also **sul·pho·nate**) Chem. ▶ n. a salt or ester of a sulfonic acid. ▶ v. [trans.] convert (a compound) into a sulfonate, typically by reaction with sulfuric acid. — **sul·fo·na·tion** /ˌsəlfəˈnāsʜən/ n.

sul·fone /ˈsəlˌfōn/ (esp. Brit. also **sul·phone**) ▶ n. Chem. an organic compound containing a sulfonyl group linking two organic groups. [19th C.: from Ger. *Sulfon*, from *Sulfur*.]

sul·fon·ic ac·id /səlˈfänik/ (esp. Brit. also **sul·phon·ic**) ▶ n. Chem. an organic acid containing the group $-SO_2OH$.

sul·fo·nyl /ˈsəlfənil/ (esp. Brit. also **sul·pho·nyl**) ▶ n. [as adj.] Chem. of or denoting a divalent radical, $-SO_2-$, derived from a sulfonic acid group.

sul·fur /ˈsəlfər/ (also esp. Brit. **sul·phur**) ▶ n. **1** the chemical element of atomic number 16, a yellow combustible nonmetal. It occurs uncombined in volcanic and sedimentary deposits, as well as being a constituent of many minerals and petroleum. It is normally a bright yellow crystalline solid, but several other allotropic forms can be made. (Symbol: **S**) ■ the material of which hellfire and lightning were believed to consist. ■ a pale greenish-yellow color: [as adj.] *the bird's sulfur-yellow throat.* **2** an American butterfly (*Colias*, *Phoebis*, and other genera, family Pieridae) with predominantly yellow wings that may bear darker patches. ▶ v. [trans.] disinfect or fumigate with sulfur. — **sul·fur·y** adj. [ME: from Anglo-Norman Fr. *sulfre*, from L. *sulfur*, *sulphur*.]

sul·fu·rate /ˈsəlf(y)əˌrāt/ (esp. Brit. also **sul·phu·rate**) ▶ v. impregnate, fumigate, or treat with sulfur, esp. in bleaching. — **sul·fu·ra·tion** /ˌsəlf(y)əˈrāsʜən/ n. **sul·fu·ra·tor** /-ˌrātər/ n.

sul·fur di·ox·ide ▶ n. Chem. a colorless pungent toxic gas, SO_2, formed by burning sulfur in air.

sul·fu·re·ous /səl'fyo͝orēəs/ (esp. Brit. also **sul·phu·re·ous**) ▶ adj. of, like, or containing sulfur.

sul·fu·ric /səl'fyo͝orik/ (esp. Brit. also **sul·phu·ric**) ▶ adj. containing sulfur or sulfuric acid.

sul·fu·ric ac·id ▶ n. a strong acid made by oxidizing solutions of sulfur dioxide, H_2SO_4, and used in large quantities as an industrial and laboratory reagent. The concentrated form is an oily, dense, corrosive liquid.

sul·fu·rize /'səlf(y)ə,rīz/ (also esp. Brit. also **sul·phu·rize**) ▶ v. another term for SULFURATE. — **sul·fu·ri·za·tion** /,səlf(y)ərə'zāsʜən/ n.

sul·fur·ous /'səlfərəs/ (esp. Brit. also **sul·phur·ous**) ▶ adj. (chiefly of vapor or smoke) containing or derived from sulfur. ■ sulfureous. ■ like sulfur in color; pale yellow. ■ marked by bad temper, anger, or profanity.

sul·fur·ous ac·id ▶ n. Chem. an unstable weak acid, H_2SO_3, formed when sulfur dioxide dissolves in water. It is used as a reducing and bleaching agent.

sulk /səlk/ ▶ v. [intrans.] be silent, morose, and bad-tempered out of annoyance or disappointment. ▶ n. a period of gloomy and bad-tempered silence stemming from annoyance and resentment. — **sulk·er** n. [18th C.: perh. a back-form. from SULKY.]

sulky

sulk·y /'səlkē/ ▶ adj. (**sulk·i·er, sulk·i·est**) morose, bad-tempered, and resentful; refusing to be cooperative or cheerful: *disappointment was making her sulky.* ■ expressing or suggesting gloom and bad temper. ■ fig. not quick to work or respond: *a sulky fire.* ▶ n. (pl. **sulk·ies**) a light two-wheeled horse-drawn vehicle for one person, used chiefly in harness racing. — **sulk·i·ly** /-kəlē/ adv. **sulk·i·ness** n. [18th C.: perh. from obs. *sulke* 'hard to dispose of,' of unknown origin.]

Sul·la /'sələ/ (138–78 BC), Roman general and politician; full name *Lucius Cornelius Sulla Felix.* Sulla invaded Italy in 83 and was elected dictator in 82.

sul·lage /'səlij/ ▶ n. waste from household sinks, showers, and baths, but not toilets. ■ archaic refuse, esp. sewage. [16th C.: perh. from Anglo-Norman Fr. *suillage,* from *suiller* 'to soil.']

sul·len /'sələn/ ▶ adj. bad-tempered and sulky; gloomy. ■ (esp. of water) slow-moving: *rivers in sullen flood.* — **sul·len·ly** adv. **sul·len·ness** n. [ME: from Anglo-Norman Fr. *sulein,* from *sol* 'sole.']

Sul·li·van[1] /'sələvən/, Sir Arthur Seymour (1842–1900), English composer. He wrote 14 light operas in collaboration with librettist W. S. Gilbert.

Sul·li·van[2], John Lawrence (1858–1918), US boxer. He was the world heavyweight champion in 1882.

Sul·li·van[3], Louis Henry (1856–1924), US architect. He developed modern functionalism in architecture by designing skyscrapers.

Sul·ly /'səlē/, Thomas (1783–1872), US painter; born in England. His work includes portraits of Queen Victoria, Thomas Jefferson, and James Monroe.

sul·ly /'səlē/ ▶ v. (**-lies, -lied**) [trans.] literary or ironic damage the purity or integrity of; defile. ■ make dirty: *she wondered if she dared sully the gleaming sink.* [16th C.: perh. from Fr. *souiller* 'to soil.']

sulpha- ▶ comb. form chiefly British spelling of SULFA-.

sul·phur, etc. ▶ n. chiefly British spelling of SULFUR, etc.

sul·tan /'səltn/ ▶ n. a Muslim sovereign. ■ (**the Sultan**) hist. the sultan of Turkey. — **sul·tan·ate** /-,āt/ n. [16th C.: from Fr., or from med. L. *sultanus,* from Arab. *sulṭān* 'power, ruler.']

sul·tan·a /səl'tanə/ ▶ n. **1** a small, light brown, seedless raisin used in foods such as puddings and cakes. **2** a wife or concubine of a sultan. ■ any other woman in a sultan's family. [16th C.: from Ital., fem. of *sultano* (see SULTAN).]

sul·try /'səltrē/ ▶ adj. (**-tri·er, -tri·est**) **1** (of the air or weather) hot and humid. **2** (of a person, esp. a woman) attractive in a way that suggests a passionate nature. — **sul·tri·ly** /-trəlē/ adv. **sul·tri·ness** n. [16th C.: from obs. *sulter* 'swelter.']

su·lu /'so͞olo͞o/ ▶ n. (pl. **-lus**) a length of cotton or other light fabric wrapped about the body as a sarong, worn from the waist by men and full-length by women from the Melanesian Islands. [Fijian.]

Su·lu Sea /'so͞olo͞o/ a sea in the Malay Archipelago, surrounded by Borneo and the Philippines.

sum /səm/ ▶ n. **1** a particular amount of money. **2** (**the sum of**) the total amount resulting from the addition of two or more numbers, amounts, or items. ■ the total amount of something that exists. **3** an arithmetical problem, esp. at an elementary level. ▶ v. (**summed, sum·ming**) [trans.] tech. find the sum of (two or more amounts). ■ [intrans.] (**sum to**) (of two or more amounts) add up to a specified total.

– PHRASES **in sum** to sum up; in summary.

– PHRASAL VERBS **sum up** give a brief summary of something. ■ Law (of a judge) review the evidence at the end of a case, and direct the jury regarding points of law. **sum someone/something up** express a concise idea of the nature or character of a person or thing. [ME: via OFr. from L. *summa* 'main part, sum total,' fem. of *summus* 'highest.']

su·mac /'so͞omak; 'sʜo͞o-/ (also **su·mach**) ▶ n. a shrub or small tree (genera *Rhus* and *Cotinus*) with compound leaves, fruits in conical clusters, and bright autumn colors. Its several species include the North American **staghorn sumac** (*R. typhina*), with reddish hairy fruits, and **poison sumac** (*R. vernix*), with greenish-white fruits. [ME: from OFr. *sumac* or med. L. *sumac(h),* from Arab. *summāḳ.*]

Su·ma·tra /sə'mätrə/ a large island in Indonesia, southwest of the Malay Peninsula. — **Su·ma·tran** adj. & n.

Su·ma·tran rhi·noc·er·os /sə'mätrən/ ▶ n. a rare hairy two-horned rhinoceros (*Dicerorhinus sumatrensis*) found in montane rain forests from Malaysia to Borneo.

Sum·ba /'so͞ombə/ an island in Indonesia; chief town, Waingapu. Also called SANDALWOOD ISLAND.

Sum·ba·wa /so͞om'bäwə/ an island in Indonesia.

Su·mer /'so͞omər/ an ancient region in southwestern Asia, in present-day Iraq, comprising the southern part of Mesopotamia.

Su·me·ri·an /sə'merēən; -'mi(ə)r-/ ▶ adj. of or relating to Sumer, its ancient language, or the early, non-Semitic element it contributed to Babylonian civilization. ▶ n. **1** a member of the indigenous non-Semitic people of ancient Babylonia. **2** the Sumerian language.

Sum·ga·it /,so͞omgä'ēt/ Russian name for SUMQAYIT.

su·mi /'so͞omē/ ▶ n. a type of black Japanese ink prepared in solid sticks and used for painting and writing. [20th C.: Japanese, 'ink, blacking.']

sum·ma cum lau·de /'so͞omə ,ko͞om 'loudə; 'loudē/ ▶ adv. & adj. with the highest distinction: [as adv.] *he graduated summa cum laude.* [L., 'with highest praise.']

sum·ma·rize /'səmə,rīz/ ▶ v. [trans.] give a brief statement of the main points of (something). — **sum·ma·ri·za·tion** /,səməri'zāsʜən/ n. **sum·ma·riz·er** n.

sum·ma·ry /'səmərē/ ▶ n. (pl. **-ries**) a brief statement or account of the main points of something. ▶ adj. **1** dispensing with needless details or formalities; brief: *summary financial statements.* **2** Law (of a judicial process) conducted without the customary legal formalities: *summary arrest.* ■ (of a conviction) made by a judge or magistrate without a jury.

– PHRASES **in summary** in short. — **sum·mar·i·ly** /sə'me(ə)rəlē; 'səmərəlē/ adv. **sum·mar·i·ness** /sə'me(ə)rēnis/ n. [ME (as an adj.): from L. *summarius,* from *summa* 'sum total' (see SUM).]

sum·ma·tion /sə'māsʜən/ ▶ n. **1** the process of adding things together. ■ a sum total of things added together. **2** the process of summing something up. ■ a summary. ■ Law an attorney's closing speech at the conclusion of the giving of evidence. — **sum·ma·tion·al** /-sʜənl/ adj. **sum·ma·tive** /'səmətiv/ adj.

sum·mer[1] /'səmər/ ▶ n. the warmest season of the year, in the northern hemisphere from June to August and in the southern hemisphere from December to February: [as adj.] *summer holidays.* ■ Astron. the period from the summer solstice to the autumnal equinox. ■ (**summers**) literary years, esp. of a person's age: *a girl of sixteen summers.* ▶ v. [no obj., with adverbial of place] spend the summer in a particular place. ■ [trans.] pasture (cattle) for the summer. — **sum·mer·y** adj. [OE *sumor,* of Gmc. origin; rel. to Du. *zomer,* Ger. *Sommer,* also to Sanskrit *samā* 'year.']

sum·mer[2] (also **sum·mer·tree** /'səmər,trē/) ▶ n. a horizontal bearing beam, esp. one supporting joists or rafters. ■ a capstone that supports an arch or lintel. ■ a lintel. [ME: from OFr. *somier* 'packhorse,' from late L. *sagmarius,* from Gk. *sagma* 'packsaddle.']

sum·mer cy·press ▶ n. another term for KOCHIA.

sum·mer·house /'səmər,hous/ (also **sum·mer house**) ▶ n. a small, typically rustic building in a garden or park, used for sitting in during the summer. ■ (usu. **summer house**) a cottage or house use as a second residence, esp. during the summer.

Sum·mer Pal·ace a palace (now in ruins) of the former Chinese emperors near Beijing.

sum·mer·sault ▶ n. & v. archaic spelling of SOMERSAULT.

sum·mer sau·sage ▶ n. a type of hard dried and smoked sausage that is similar to salami in preparation and can be kept without refrigeration.

sum·mer school ▶ n. courses held during school summer vacations, taken for remedial purposes, as part of an academic program, or for professional or personal purposes.

sum·mer sol·stice ▶ n. the solstice that marks the onset of summer, at the time of the longest day, about June 21 in the northern hemisphere and December 22 in the southern hemisphere. ■ Astron. the solstice in June.

sum·mer squash ▶ n. a squash (*Cucurbita pepo* var. *melopepo*) that is eaten before the seeds and rind have hardened. Unlike winter squash, summer squash does not keep well.

sum·mer stock ▶ n. theatrical productions by a repertory company organized for the summer season, esp. at vacation resorts or in a suburban area.

sum·mer tan·a·ger ▶n. a tanager (*Piranga rubra*), the adult male of which is rosy red, and which is a common summer visitor in the central and southern US.

sum·mer·time /ˈsəmər,tīm/ ▶n. the season or period of summer: *in summertime trains run every ten minutes.*

sum·mer·tree /ˈsəmər,trē/ ▶n. see SUMMER².

sum·mer-weight ▶adj. (of clothes) made of light fabric and therefore cool to wear.

sum·ming-up ▶n. a restatement of the main points of an argument, case, etc.

sum·mit /ˈsəmit/ ▶n. **1** the highest point of a hill or mountain. ■ fig. the highest attainable level of achievement. **2** a meeting between heads of government. [ME: from OFr. *somete*, from *som* 'top,' from L. *summum*, neut. of *summus* 'highest.']

sum·mit·eer /,səmiˈti(ə)r/ ▶n. a participant in a meeting between heads of government.

sum·mon /ˈsəmən/ ▶v. [trans.] authoritatively or urgently call on (someone) to be present, esp. as a defendant or witness in a law court. ■ urgently demand (help). ■ call people to attend (a meeting). ■ bring to the surface (a particular quality or reaction) from within oneself. ■ (**summon something up**) call an image to mind. — **sum·mon·a·ble** adj. **sum·mon·er** n. [ME: from OFr. *somondre*, from L. *summonere* 'give a hint,' later 'call, summon,' from *sub-* 'secretly' + *monere* 'warn.']

sum·mons /ˈsəmənz/ ▶n. (pl. **-mons·es**) an order to appear before a judge or magistrate, or the writ containing it: *a summons for nonpayment of a parking ticket.* ■ an authoritative or urgent call to someone to be present or to do something. ▶v. [trans.] esp. Law serve (someone) with a summons. [ME: from OFr. *sumunse*, from an alt. of L. *summonita*, fem. past part. of *summonere* (see SUMMON).]

su·mo /ˈsōōmō/ ▶n. (pl. **-mos**) a Japanese form of heavyweight wrestling, in which a wrestler wins a bout by forcing his opponent outside a marked circle or by making him touch the ground with any part of his body except the soles of his feet. ■ a sumo wrestler. [from Japanese *sūmo*.]

sump /səmp/ ▶n. a pit or hollow in which liquid collects, in particular: ■ the base of an internal combustion engine, which serves as a reservoir of oil for the lubrication system. ■ a depression in the floor of a mine or basement in which water collects. ■ a cesspool. [ME: from MDu. or Low Ger. *sump*; rel. to SWAMP.]

sump·tu·ar·y /ˈsəm(p)CHōō,erē/ ▶adj. [attrib.] esp. hist. relating to or denoting laws that limit private expenditure on food and personal items. [17th C.: from L. *sumptuarius*, from *sumptus* 'cost, expenditure,' from *sumere* 'take.']

sump·tu·ous /ˈsəm(p)CHōōəs/ ▶adj. splendid and expensive-looking. — **sump·tu·os·i·ty** /,səm(p)CHōōˈäsitē/ n. **sump·tu·ous·ly** adv. **sump·tu·ous·ness** n. [ME: from OFr. *somptueux*, from L. *sumptuosus*, from *sumptus* 'expenditure' (see SUMPTUARY).]

Sum·qay·it /,sōōmgäˈ(y)ēt/ a city in eastern Azerbaijan; pop. 235,000 (1990). Russian name **SUMGAIT**.

sum to·tal ▶n. another term for SUM (sense 2).

Su·my /ˈsōōmē/ a city in northeastern Ukraine; pop. 296,000.

Sun. ▶abbr. Sunday.

sun /sən/ ▶n. **1** (also **Sun**) the star around which the earth orbits. The sun is the central body of the solar system. It provides the light and energy that sustains life on earth, and its changing position relative to the earth's axis determines the terrestrial seasons. ■ any similar star in the universe, with or without planets. **2** (usu. **the sun**) the light or warmth received from the earth's sun: *we sat outside in the sun.* ■ literary a person or thing regarded as a source of glory or inspiration or understanding. ■ literary used with reference to someone's success or prosperity. **3** literary a day or a year. ▶v. (**sunned, sun·ning**) (**sun oneself**) sit or lie in the sun. ■ [trans.] expose (something) to the sun, esp. to warm or dry it.

— PHRASES **on which the sun never sets** (of an empire) worldwide. [applied in the 17th C. to the Spanish dominions, later to the British Empire.] **under the sun** on earth; in existence (used in expressions emphasizing the large number of something). — **sun·less** adj. **sun·less·ness** n. **sun·like** /-,līk/ adj. **sun·ward** /-wərd/ adj. & adv. **sun·wards** /-wərdz/ adv. [OE *sunne*, of Gmc. origin; rel. to Du. *zon* and Ger. *Sonne*, from an Indo-Eur. root shared by Gk. *hēlios* and L. *sol*.]

sun-baked ▶adj. (esp. of the ground) exposed to the heat of the sun and therefore dry and hard.

sun·bath /ˈsən,baTH/ ▶n. a period of sunbathing.

sun·bathe /ˈsən,bāTH/ ▶v. [intrans.] sit or lie in the sun, esp. to tan the skin. — **sun·bath·er** n.

sun·beam /ˈsən,bēm/ ▶n. a ray of sunlight.

sun bear ▶n. a small mainly nocturnal bear (*Helarctos malayanus*) that has a brownish-black coat with a light-colored mark on the chest, native to Southeast Asia. Also called **Malayan sun bear**.

sun·belt /ˈsən,belt/ (also **sun belt**) ▶n. a strip of territory receiving a high amount of sunshine, esp.: ■ (**Sunbelt** or **Sun Belt**) the southern US from California to Florida.

sun·bird /ˈsən,bərd/ ▶n. a small, brightly colored Old World songbird (*Nectarinia* and other genera, family Nectariniidae) with a long downcurved bill, feeding on nectar and resembling a hummingbird (but not able to hover).

sun·bit·tern /ˈsən,bitərn/ (also **sun bit·tern**) ▶n. a tropical American wading bird (*Eurypyga helias*, family Eurypygidae) with a long bill, neck, and legs, having mainly grayish plumage but showing chestnut and orange on the wings when they are spread in display.

sun·block /ˈsən,bläk/ ▶n. a cream or lotion for protecting the skin from the sun and preventing sunburn.

sun·bon·net /ˈsən,bänit/ ▶n. a close-fitting brimmed cotton hat that protects the head and neck from the sun, worn esp. by infants and formerly by women.

sun·burn /ˈsən,bərn/ ▶n. reddening, inflammation, and, in severe cases, blistering and peeling of the skin caused by overexposure to the ultraviolet rays of the sun. ▶v. (past and past part. **-burned** or **-burnt**) (**be sunburned**) (of a person or bodily part) suffer from sunburn. ■ [usu. as adj.] (**sunburned** or **sunburnt**) ruddy from exposure to the sun: *a handsome sunburned face.* ■ [intrans.] suffer from sunburn.

sun·burst /ˈsən,bərst/ ▶n. a sudden brief appearance of the full sun from behind clouds. ■ a decoration or ornament resembling the sun and its rays. ■ a pattern of irregular concentric bands of color with the brightest at the center.

sun·dae /ˈsən,dā/ ▶n. a dish of ice cream with added ingredients such as fruit, nuts, syrup, and whipped cream. [19th C. (orig. US): perh. an alt. of SUNDAY.]

Sun·da Is·lands /ˈsəndə; ˈsōōn-/ a chain of islands in the southwestern part of the Malay Archipelago. The **Greater Sunda Islands** include Sumatra, Java, Borneo, and Sulawesi, and the **Lesser Sunda Islands** include Bali, Sumbawa, Flores, Sumba, and Timor.

sun dance ▶n. a dance performed by North American Plains Indians in honor of the sun.

Sun·da·nese /,səndəˈnēz; -ˈnēs/ ▶n. (pl. same) **1** a member of a mainly Muslim people of western Java. **2** the Indonesian language of this people. ▶adj. of or relating to the Sundanese or their language. [from Sundanese *Sunda*, the western part of Java, + -ESE.]

Sun·day /ˈsəndā; -dē/ ▶n. the day of the week before Monday and following Saturday, observed by Christians as a day of rest and religious worship. ▶adv. on Sunday: *the concert will be held Sunday.* ■ (**Sundays**) on Sundays; each Sunday. [OE *Sunnandæg* 'day of the sun.']

Sun·day best ▶n. a person's best clothes, worn to church or on special occasions.

Sun·day driv·er ▶n. a person perceived as driving in an inexperienced or unskillful way, esp. one who drives slowly.

Sun·day-go-to-meet·ing ▶adj. (of a hat, clothes, etc.) suitable for going to church in.

Sun·day school ▶n. a class held on Sundays to teach children about their religion.

sun deck ▶n. **1** the deck, or part of a deck, of a yacht or cruise ship that is open to the sky. **2** a terrace or balcony positioned to catch the sun.

sun·der /ˈsəndər/ ▶v. [trans.] literary split apart. [OE *sundrian*; rel. to Ger. *sondern*.]

Sun·der·land /ˈsəndərlənd/ a city in northeastern England; pop. 287,000.

sun·dew /ˈsən,d(y)ōō/ ▶n. a small carnivorous plant (genus *Drosera*, family Droseraceae) of boggy places, with rosettes of leaves that bear sticky glandular hairs. These trap insects, which are then digested.

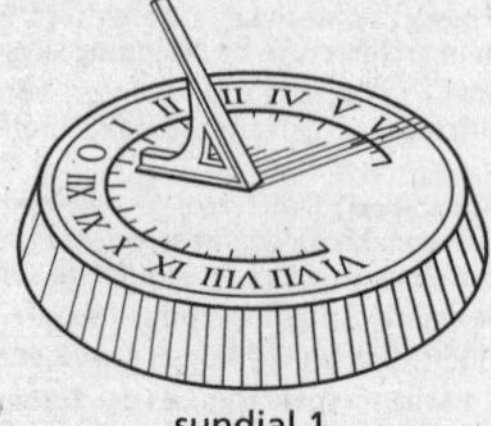

sundial 1

sun·di·al /ˈsən,dīl/ ▶n. **1** an instrument showing the time by the shadow of a pointer cast by the sun onto a plate marked with the hours of the day. **2** (also **sundial shell**) a mollusk (family Architectonicidae) with a flattened spiral shell that is typically patterned in shades of brown, living in tropical and subtropical seas.

sun dog (also **sun·dog** /ˈsən,dôg/) ▶n. another term for PARHELION.

sun·down /ˈsən,doun/ ▶n. [in sing.] the time in the evening when the sun disappears or daylight fades.

sun·dress /ˈsən,dres/ ▶n. a light, loose, sleeveless dress, typically having a wide neckline and thin shoulder straps.

sun·drops /ˈsən,dräps/ ▶n. a day-flowering North American plant (genera *Oenothera* and *Calylophus*, family Onagraceae) with yellow flowers, related to the evening primrose.

sun·dry /ˈsəndrē/ ▶adj. [attrib.] of various kinds; several. ▶n. (pl. **-ies**) (**sundries**) various items not important enough to be mentioned individually. [OE *syndrig* 'distinct, separate'; rel. to SUNDER.]

sun-dry ▶v. [trans.] [usu. as adj.] (**sun-dried**) dry (something, esp. food) in the sun, as opposed to using artificial heat: *sun-dried tomatoes.*

sun·fast /ˈsən,fast/ ▶adj. (of a dye or fabric) not prone to fade in sunlight.

sun·fish /ˈsənˌfisн/ ▶**n.** (pl. same or **-fish·es**) **1** a large deep-bodied marine fish (family Molidae) of warm seas, with tall dorsal and anal fins near the rear of the body and a very short tail. Its several species include the very large **ocean sunfish** (*Mola mola*), also known as **mola mola**. **2** a nest-building freshwater fish native to North America and popular in aquariums. The **freshwater sunfish family** (Centrarchidae) also includes sport fish such as the black basses, rock bass, bluegill, and crappies.

ocean sunfish

sun·flow·er /ˈsənˌflouər/ ▶**n.** a tall North American plant (*Helianthus annus*) of the daisy family, with very large golden-rayed flowers. Sunflowers are cultivated for their edible seeds, which are an important source of oil for cooking and margarine.

sunflower

Sung /so͝onɢ/ (also **Song**) a dynasty that ruled in China AD 960–1279.

sung /sənɢ/ past participle of **SING**.

sun·glass·es /ˈsənˌglasiz/ ▶**plural n.** glasses tinted to protect the eyes from sunlight or glare.

sunk /sənɢk/ past and past participle of **SINK**[1].

sunk·en /ˈsənɢkən/ ▶**adj.** **1** [attrib.] having sunk or been submerged in water: *the wreck of a sunken ship.* **2** having sunk below the usual or expected level. ■ [attrib.] at a lower level than the surrounding area: *a sunken garden.* ■ (of a person's eyes or cheeks) deeply recessed, esp. as a result of illness, hunger, or stress. [ME: past part. of **SINK**[1].]

Sun King the nickname of Louis XIV of France (see **LOUIS**[1]).

sun-kissed ▶**adj.** made warm or brown by the sun.

sun·lamp /ˈsənˌlamp/ ▶**n.** **1** a lamp emitting ultraviolet rays used as a substitute for sunlight, typically to produce an artificial suntan or in therapy. **2** a large lamp with a parabolic reflector used in filmmaking.

sun·light /ˈsənˌlīt/ ▶**n.** light from the sun.

sun·lit /ˈsənˌlit/ ▶**adj.** illuminated by direct light from the sun: *clear sunlit waters.*

Sun·na /ˈsənə/ ▶**n.** the traditional portion of Muslim law based on Muhammad's words or acts, accepted (together with the Koran) as authoritative by Muslims and followed particularly by Sunni Muslims. [Arab., 'form, way, course, rule.']

Sun·ni /ˈso͝onē/ ▶**n.** (pl. same or **-nis**) one of the two main branches of Islam, commonly described as orthodox, and differing from Shia in its understanding of the Sunna and in its acceptance of the first three caliphs. Compare with **SHIA**. ■ a Muslim who adheres to this branch of Islam. — **Sun·nite** /so͝onīt/ **adj. & n.** [Arab., 'custom, normative rule.']

sun·ny /ˈsənē/ ▶**adj.** (**-ni·er**, **-ni·est**) bright with sunlight: *a sunny day.* ■ (of a place) receiving much sunlight. ■ (of a person or their temperament) cheery and bright. ■ suggestive of the warmth or brightness of the sun. — **sun·ni·ly** /ˈsənl-ē/ **adv.** **sun·ni·ness** **n.**

sun·ny side ▶**n.** the side of something that receives the sun for longest: *the sunny side of the island.* ■ the more cheerful or pleasant aspect of a state of affairs: *he was fond of the sunny side of life.*
– PHRASES **sunny side up** (of an egg) fried on one side only.

Sun·ny·vale /ˈsənēˌvāl/ a city in north central California, part of Silicon Valley; pop. 117,229.

sun porch (also **sun·porch** /ˈsənˌpôrcн/) ▶**n.** another term for **SUNROOM**.

sun·rise /ˈsənˌrīz/ ▶**n.** [in sing.] the time in the morning when the sun appears or full daylight arrives. ■ the colors and light visible in the sky on an occasion of the sun's first appearance in the morning, considered as a view or spectacle.

sun·rise in·dus·try ▶**n.** a new and growing industry, esp. in electronics or telecommunications.

sun·roof /ˈsənˌro͞of; -ˌro͝of/ ▶**n.** a panel in the roof of a car that can be opened for extra ventilation.

sun·room /ˈsənˌro͞om; -ˌro͝om/ ▶**n.** a room with large windows and sometimes a glass roof, designed to allow in a lot of sunlight.

sun·scald /ˈsənˌskôld/ (also **sun scald**) ▶**n.** damage to plant tissue, esp. bark or fruit, caused by exposure to excessive sunlight.

sun·screen /ˈsənˌskrēn/ ▶**n.** a cream or lotion rubbed onto the skin to protect it from the sun. ■ an active ingredient of creams and lotions of this kind and other preparations for the skin.

sun·set /ˈsənˌset/ ▶**n.** [in sing.] the time in the evening when the sun disappears or daylight fades. ■ the colors and light visible in the sky on an occasion of the sun's disappearance in the evening, considered as a view or spectacle. ■ fig. a period of decline, esp. the last years of a person's life.

sun·set in·dus·try ▶**n.** an old and declining industry.

sun·set pro·vi·sion ▶**n.** a stipulation that an agency or program be disbanded or terminated at the end of a fixed period unless it is formally renewed.

sun·shade /ˈsənˌsнād/ ▶**n.** a parasol, awning, or other device giving protection from the sun.

sun·shine /ˈsənˌsнīn/ ▶**n.** direct sunlight unbroken by cloud, esp. over a comparatively large area. ■ fig. cheerfulness; happiness. — **sun·shin·y** **adj.**

sun·shine law ▶**n.** a law requiring certain proceedings of government agencies to be open or available to the public.

sun·spot /ˈsənˌspät/ ▶**n.** Astron. a spot or patch appearing from time to time on the sun's surface, appearing dark by contrast with its surroundings.

sun·star /ˈsənˌstär/ ▶**n.** a widely distributed starfish (genus *Solaster*) with a large number of arms.

sun·stroke /ˈsənˌstrōk/ ▶**n.** heatstroke brought about by excessive exposure to the sun.

sun·suit /ˈsənˌso͞ot/ ▶**n.** a child's one- or two-piece suit of clothes, typically consisting of shorts and sleeveless top, worn in hot sunny weather.

sun·tan /ˈsənˌtan/ ▶**n.** a browning of skin caused by exposure to the sun: *he had acquired quite a suntan.* ■ a light or medium brownish color. ▶**v.** [trans.] [usu. as adj.] (**suntanned**) expose to the sun in order to achieve such a brown color.

sun·up /ˈsənˌəp/ ▶**n.** [in sing.] the time in the morning when the sun appears or full daylight arrives.

Sun Yat-sen /ˈso͝on ˈyät ˈsen/ (also **Sun Yi·xian** /ˈyēsнēˈän/) (1866–1925), president of the Southern Chinese Republic 1923–25. He organized the Kuomintang force and established a secessionist government at Guangzhou.

Suo·mi /ˈso͞o-ōmē; ˈswômē/ Finnish name for **FINLAND**.

sup[1] /səp/ ▶**v.** (**supped**, **sup·ping**) [trans.] dated or dialect take (drink or liquid food) by sips or spoonfuls: *she supped up her soup delightedly.* ▶**n.** a sip of liquid: *he took another sup of wine.* [OE *sūpan* (v.), *sūpa* (n.), of Gmc. origin; rel. to Du. *zuipen*, Ger. *saufen* 'to drink.']

sup[2] ▶**v.** (**supped**, **sup·ping**) [intrans.] dated eat supper. [ME: from OFr. *super*, of Gmc. origin; rel. to **SUP**[1].]

sup. ▶**abbr.** ■ superior. ■ superlative. ■ supine. ■ supplement. ■ supplementary. ■ supply. ■ supra.

sup- ▶**prefix** var. of **SUB-** assimilated before *p* (as in *suppurate*).

Sup. Ct. ▶**abbr.** ■ Superior Court. ■ Supreme Court.

su·per /ˈso͞opər/ ▶**adj.** **1** informal very good or pleasant; excellent: *Julie was a super girl.* **2** (of a manufactured product) superfine. ▶**adv.** [as submodifier] informal especially; particularly. ▶**n.** informal **1** a superintendent. **2** superphosphate. **3** superfine fabric or manufacture. [19th C.: abbr.]

super. ▶**abbr.** ■ superintendent. ■ superior.

super- ▶**comb. form** above; over; beyond: *superstructure.* ■ to a great or extreme degree: *supercool.* ■ extra large of its kind: *supercontinent.* ■ having greater influence, capacity, etc., than another of its kind: *superpower.* ■ of a higher kind (esp. in names of classificatory divisions): *superfamily.* [from L. *super-*, from *super* 'above, beyond.']

su·per·a·ble /ˈso͞opər-əbəl/ ▶**adj.** able to be overcome. [17th C.: from L. *superabilis*, from *superare* 'overcome.']

su·per·a·bun·dant /ˌso͞opər-əˈbəndənt/ ▶**adj.** excessive in quantity; more than sufficient; overabundant. — **su·per·a·bun·dance** **n.** **su·per·a·bun·dant·ly** **adv.** [ME: from late L. *superabundant-* 'abounding to excess,' from the verb *superabundare*.]

su·per·al·loy /ˈso͞opərˌaloi/ ▶**n.** an alloy capable of withstanding high temperatures, high stresses, and often highly oxidizing atmospheres.

su·per·an·nu·ate /ˌso͞opərˈanyo͞oˌāt/ ▶**v.** [trans.] (usu. **be superannuated**) retire (someone) with a pension. ■ [as adj.] (**superannuated**) (of a post or employee) belonging to a superannuation scheme. ■ [usu. as adj.] (**superannuated**) cause to become obsolete through age or new technological or intellectual developments. — **su·per·an·nu·a·ble** /-ˈanyo͞oəbəl/ **adj.** [17th C.: back-form. from *superannuated*, from med. L. *superannuatus*, from L. *super-* 'over' + *annus* 'year.']

su·per·an·nu·a·tion /ˌso͞opərˌanyo͞oˈāsнən/ ▶**n.** [usu. as adj.] regular payment made into a fund by an employee toward a future pension. ■ a pension of this type paid to a retired person. ■ the process of superannuating an employee.

su·perb /so͞oˈpərb; sə-/ ▶**adj.** **1** excellent. **2** impressively splendid: *a superb statue of Osiris.* — **su·perb·ly** **adv.** **su·perb·ness** **n.** [16th C. (sense 2): from L. *superbus* 'proud, magnificent.']

Su·per Bowl ▶**n.** the National Football League championship game, played annually between the champions of the National and the American Football Conferences.

su·per·bug /ˈso͞opərˌbəg/ ▶**n.** **1** a bacterium that is useful in biotechnology, typically one that has been genetically engineered to enhance its usefulness for a particular purpose. **2** a strain of bacteria that has become resistant to antibiotic drugs. ■ an insect that is difficult to control or eradicate, esp. because it has become immune to insecticides.

su·per·cal·en·der /ˈso͞opərˌkaləndər/ ▶**v.** [trans.] give a highly glazed finish to (paper) by calendering it more than normally calendered paper.

su·per·car·go /ˈso͞opərˌkärgō/ ▶**n.** (pl. **-goes** or **-gos**) a representative of the ship's owner on board a merchant ship, responsible for overseeing the cargo and its sale. [17th C.: alt. of earlier *supracargo*, from Sp. *sobrecargo*, from *sobre* 'over' + *cargo* 'cargo.']

su·per·cede ▶**v.** var. of **SUPERSEDE**.

su·per·charge /ˈso͞opərˌcнärj/ ▶**v.** [trans.] fit or design (an internal combustion engine) with a supercharger. ■ [usu. as adj.] (**supercharged**) supply with extra energy or power. ■ [as adj.] (**supercharged**) having powerful emotional overtones or associations.

su·per·charg·er /ˈso͞opər,CHärjər/ ▶n. a device that increases the pressure of the fuel-air mixture in an internal combustion engine, used in order to achieve greater efficiency.

su·per·cil·i·ar·y /,so͞opərˈsilē,erē/ ▶adj. [attrib.] Anat. of or relating to the eyebrow or the region over the eye. [18th C.: from L. *supercilium* 'eyebrow' (from *super-* 'above' + *cilium* 'eyelid') + -ARY[1].]

su·per·cil·i·ous /,so͞opərˈsilēəs/ ▶adj. behaving or looking as though one thinks one is superior to others. — **su·per·cil·i·ous·ly** adv. **su·per·cil·i·ous·ness** n. [16th C.: from L. *superciliosus* 'haughty,' from *supercilium* 'eyebrow.']

su·per·class /ˈso͞opər,klas/ ▶n. Biol. a taxonomic category that ranks above class and below phylum.

su·per·clus·ter /ˈso͞opər,kləstər/ ▶n. Astron. a cluster of galaxies which themselves occur as clusters.

su·per·coil /ˈso͞opər,koil/ Biochem. ▶n. another term for SUPERHELIX. ▶v. [trans.] form (a substance) into a superhelix.

su·per·col·lid·er /ˈso͞opər-kə,līdər/ ▶n. Physics a collider in which superconducting magnets are used to accelerate particles to energies of millions of megavolts.

su·per·com·put·er /ˈso͞opər-kəm,pyo͞otər/ ▶n. a particularly powerful mainframe computer. — **su·per·com·put·ing** /-,pyo͞otiNG/ n.

su·per·con·duc·tiv·i·ty /,so͞opər,kän,dəkˈtivitē/ ▶n. Physics the property of zero electrical resistance in some substances at very low absolute temperatures. — **su·per·con·duct** /-kənˈdəkt/ v. **su·per·con·duct·ing** /-kənˈdəktiNG/ adj. **su·per·con·duc·tive** /-kənˈdəktiv/ adj.

su·per·con·duc·tor /ˈso͞opər-kən,dəktər/ ▶n. Physics a substance capable of becoming superconducting at sufficiently low temperatures. ■ a substance in the superconducting state.

su·per·con·scious /,so͞opərˈkänSHəs/ ▶adj. transcending human or normal consciousness. — **su·per·con·scious·ly** adv. **su·per·con·scious·ness** n.

su·per·con·ti·nent /ˈso͞opər,käntn-ənt/ ▶n. each of several large landmasses thought to have divided to form the present continents in the geological past.

su·per·cool /,so͞opərˈko͞ol/ ▶v. [trans.] Chem. cool (a liquid) below its freezing point without solidification or crystallization. ■ [intrans.] Biol. (of a living organism) survive body temperatures below the freezing point of water. ▶adj. informal extremely attractive, impressive, or calm.

su·per·crit·i·cal /,so͞opərˈkritikəl/ ▶adj. Physics above a critical threshold, in particular: ■ (in nuclear physics) containing or involving more than the critical mass. ■ (of a flow of fluid) faster than the speed at which waves travel in the fluid. ■ denoting an airfoil or aircraft wing designed to tolerate shock-wave formation at transonic speeds. ■ of, relating to, or denoting a fluid at a temperature and pressure greater than its critical temperature and pressure.

su·per-du·per /ˈso͞opər ˈdo͞opər/ ▶adj. humorous very good; marvelous: *this new line of toys is super-duper.* ■ tremendous or colossal in size or degree.

su·per·e·go /,so͞opərˈēgō/ ▶n. (pl. **-gos**) Psychoanal. the part of a person's mind that acts as a self-critical conscience, reflecting social standards learned from parents and teachers. Compare with EGO and ID.

su·per·er·o·ga·tion /,so͞opər,erəˈgāSHən/ ▶n. the performance of more work than duty requires. — **su·per·e·rog·a·to·ry** /-əˈrägə,tôrē/ adj. [16th C.: from late L. *supererogatio(n-)*, from *supererogare* 'pay in addition,' from *super-* 'over' + *erogare* 'pay out.']

su·per·ette /,so͞opərˈet/ ▶n. a small supermarket. [1930s: from SUPERMARKET + -ETTE.]

su·per·fam·i·ly /ˈso͞opər,fam(ə)lē/ ▶n. (pl. **-lies**) Biol. a taxonomic category that ranks above family and below order. ■ Ling. another term for PHYLUM.

su·per·fe·cun·da·tion /,so͞opər,fekənˈdāSHən/ ▶n. Med. & Zool. another term for SUPERFETATION.

su·per·fe·ta·tion /,so͞opər,fēˈtāSHən/ ▶n. Med. & Zool. the occurrence of a second conception during pregnancy, giving rise to embryos of different ages in the uterus. ■ fig. the accretion of one thing on another. [17th C.: from Fr. *superfétation* or mod. L. *superfetatio(n-)*, from L. *superfetare*, from *super-* 'above' + *fetus* 'fetus.']

su·per·fi·cial /,so͞opərˈfiSHəl/ ▶adj. existing or occurring at or on the surface: *superficial damage.* ■ situated or occurring on the skin or immediately beneath it. ■ appearing to be true or real only until examined more closely. ■ not thorough, deep, or complete; cursory: *only a superficial knowledge of foreign countries.* ■ not having or showing any depth of character or understanding. — **su·per·fi·ci·al·i·ty** /-,fiSHēˈalitē/ n. (pl. **-ties**) **su·per·fi·cial·ly** adv. **su·per·fi·cial·ness** n. [ME: from late L. *superficialis*, from L. *superficies*.]

su·per·fine /,so͞opərˈfīn/ ▶adj. **1** of especially high quality: *superfine upholstery.* **2** (of fibers or an instrument) very thin. ■ consisting of especially small particles.

su·per·flu·id·i·ty /,so͞opər,flo͞oˈiditē/ ▶n. Physics the property of flowing without friction or viscosity, as in liquid helium below about 2.18 kelvins. — **su·per·flu·id** /ˈso͞opər,flo͞o-id/ n. & adj.

su·per·flu·i·ty /,so͞opərˈflo͞o-itē/ ▶n. (pl. **-ties**) [in sing.] an unnecessarily or excessively large amount or number of something: *a superfluity of unoccupied time.* ■ an unnecessary thing. ■ the state of being superfluous. [ME: from OFr. *superfluite*, from late L. *superfluitas*, from L. *superfluus* 'running over' (see SUPERFLUOUS).]

su·per·flu·ous /so͞oˈpərflo͞oəs/ ▶adj. unnecessary, esp. through being more than enough. — **su·per·flu·ous·ly** adv. **su·per·flu·ous·ness** n. [ME: from L. *superfluus*, from *super-* 'over' + *fluere* 'to flow.']

su·per·fund /ˈso͞opər,fənd/ ▶n. a fund established to finance a long-term, expensive project. ■ (**Superfund**) a US federal government program designed to fund the cleanup of toxic wastes.

su·per·gal·ax·y /ˈso͞opər,galəksē/ ▶n. (pl. **-ax·ies**) another term for SUPERCLUSTER.

su·per·gene ▶n. Genet. a group of closely linked genes, typically having related functions.

su·per·gi·ant /ˈso͞opər,jīənt/ ▶n. Astron. a very large star that is even brighter than a giant, often despite being relatively cool.

su·per·glue /ˈso͞opər,glo͞o/ ▶n. a very strong quick-setting adhesive, based on cyanoacrylates or similar polymers. ▶v. (**-glues, -glued, -glu·ing** or **-glue·ing**) [trans.] stick with superglue: *he superglued his hands together.*

su·per·grav·i·ty /,so͞opərˈgravitē/ ▶n. Physics gravity as described or predicted by a supersymmetric quantum field theory.

su·per·group /ˈso͞opər,gro͞op/ ▶n. an exceptionally successful rock group, in particular one formed by musicians already famous from playing in other groups.

su·per·heat /,so͞opərˈhēt/ Physics ▶v. [trans.] heat (a liquid) under pressure above its boiling point without vaporization. ■ heat (a vapor) above its temperature of saturation. ■ heat to a very high temperature. ▶n. the excess of temperature of a vapor above its temperature of saturation. — **su·per·heat·er** n.

su·per·he·lix /ˈso͞opər,hēliks/ ▶n. (pl. **-hel·i·ces** /-,heləˌsēz; -,hēlə,sēz/ or **-he·lix·es**) Biochem. a helical structure formed from a number of protein or nucleic acid chains that are individually helical. — **su·per·hel·i·cal** /,so͞opərˈhelikəl; -ˈhēli-/ adj.

su·per·he·ro /ˈso͞opər,hi(ə)rō/ ▶n. (pl. **-roes**) a benevolent fictional character with superhuman powers, such as Superman.

su·per·high·way /ˈso͞opər,hīwā; ,so͞opərˈhī,wā/ ▶n. **1** an expressway. **2** (also **information superhighway**) an extensive electronic network such as the Internet, used for the rapid transfer of information such as sound, video, and graphics in digital form.

su·per·hu·man /,so͞opərˈ(h)yo͞omən/ ▶adj. having or showing exceptional ability or powers. — **su·per·hu·man·ly** adv. [17th C.: from late L. *superhumanus* (see SUPER-, HUMAN).]

su·per·im·pose /,so͞opər-imˈpōz/ ▶v. [trans.] place or lay (one thing) over another, typically so that both are still evident. — **su·per·im·pos·a·ble** adj. **su·per·im·po·si·tion** /-,impəˈziSHən/ n.

su·per·in·cum·bent /,so͞opər-inˈkəmbənt; -iNGˈkəm-/ ▶adj. literary lying on something else.

su·per·in·duce /,so͞opər-inˈd(y)o͞os/ ▶v. [trans.] introduce or induce in addition. [16th C.: from L. *superinducere* 'cover over, bring from outside' (see SUPER-, INDUCE).]

su·per·in·fec·tion /,so͞opər-inˈfekSHən/ ▶n. Med. infection occurring after or on top of an earlier infection, esp. following treatment with broad-spectrum antibiotics.

su·per·in·tend /,so͞opər-inˈtend/ ▶v. [trans.] be responsible for the management or arrangement of (an activity or organization); oversee. — **su·per·in·tend·ence** /-dəns/ n. **su·per·in·tend·en·cy** /-dənsē/ n. [17th C.: from eccles. L. *superintendere*, translating Gk. *episkopein*.]

su·per·in·tend·ent /,so͞opər-inˈtendənt/ ▶n. a person who manages or superintends an organization or activity: *the construction superintendent.* ■ a high-ranking official, esp. the head of a large urban police department. ■ the caretaker of a building.

su·pe·ri·or /səˈpi(ə)rēər/ ▶adj. **1** higher in rank, status, or quality: *a superior officer.* ■ of high standard or quality: *superior malt whiskeys.* ■ greater in size or power: *deploying superior force.* ■ [predic.] (**superior to**) above yielding to or being influenced by. ■ having or showing an overly high opinion of oneself; supercilious. **2** esp. Anat. further above or out; higher in position. ■ (of a letter, figure, or symbol) written or printed above the line. ■ Astron. (of a planet) having an orbit further from the sun than the earth's. ■ Bot. (of the ovary of a flower) situated above the sepals and petals. ▶n. **1** a person or thing superior to another in rank, status, or quality, esp. a colleague in a higher position. ■ the head of a monastery or other religious institution. **2** Print. a superior letter, figure, or symbol. — **su·pe·ri·or·ly** adv. [ME: from OFr. *superiour*, from L. *superior*, compar. of *superus* 'that is above,' from *super* 'above.']

Su·pe·ri·or, Lake the largest of the five Great Lakes of North America, on the border between Canada and the US. It is the largest freshwater lake in the world.

su·pe·ri·or court ▶n. Law **1** (in many states of the US) a court of appeals or a court of general jurisdiction. **2** a court with general jurisdiction over other courts; a higher court.

su·pe·ri·or·i·ty /sə,pi(ə)rēˈôritē; -ˈäritē/ ▶n. the state of being superior: *the allies have achieved air superiority.* ■ a supercilious manner or attitude.

su·pe·ri·or·i·ty com·plex ▶n. an attitude of superiority that conceals actual feelings of inferiority and failure.

su·per·ja·cent /,so͞opərˈjāsənt/ ▶adj. tech. lying over or above something else; overlying. [16th C.: from L. *superjacent-*, from *super-* 'over' + *jacere* 'to lie.']

su·per·la·tive /səˈpərlətiv/ ▶adj. **1** of the highest quality or degree: *a* *superlative piece of skill.* **2** Gram. (of an adjective or adverb) expressing the highest or a very high degree of a quality (e.g., *bravest, most fiercely*). Contrasted with POSITIVE and COMPARATIVE. ▶ **n. 1** Gram. a superlative adjective or adverb. ■ **(the superlative)** the highest degree of comparison. **2** (usu. **superlatives**) an exaggerated or hyperbolical expression of praise: *the critics ran out of superlatives.* **3** something or someone embodying excellence. — **su·per·la·tive·ly adv. su·per·la·tive·ness n.** [ME: from OFr. *superlatif, -ive*, from late L. *superlativus*, from L. *superlatus* 'carried beyond,' past part. of *superferre*.]

su·per·lu·mi·nal /ˌso͞opərˈlo͞omənl/ ▶ **adj.** Physics denoting or having a speed greater than that of light. [1950s: from SUPER- 'above' + L. *lumen, lumin-* 'a light' + -AL.]

su·per·lu·na·ry /ˌso͞opərˈlo͞onərē/ ▶ **adj.** belonging to a higher world; celestial. [17th C.: from med. L. *superlunaris* (see SUPER-, LUNAR).]

su·per·ma·jor·i·ty /ˈso͞opər-məˌjôritē; -ˌjär-/ ▶ **n.** (pl. **-ties**) a number that is much more than half of a total, esp. in a vote.

su·per·man /ˈso͞opərˌman/ ▶ **n.** (pl. **-men**) **1** esp. Philos. the ideal superior man of the future. See ÜBERMENSCH. **2** **(a superman)** informal a man with exceptional physical or mental ability. [20th C.: from SUPER- 'exceptional' + MAN, coined by G. B. Shaw in imitation of Ger. *Übermensch* (used by Nietzsche).]

su·per·mar·ket /ˈso͞opərˌmärkit/ ▶ **n.** a large self-service store selling foods and household goods.

su·per·min·i /ˈso͞opərˌminē/ (also **su·per·min·i·com·put·er**) ▶ **n.** (pl. **-min·is**) a microcomputer with the speed, power, and capabilities of a mainframe.

su·per·mod·el /ˈso͞opərˌmädl/ ▶ **n.** a successful fashion model who has reached the status of a celebrity.

su·per·nal /səˈpərnl/ ▶ **adj.** esp. literary of or relating to the sky or the heavens; celestial. ■ of exceptional quality or extent. — **su·per·nal·ly adv.** [ME: from OFr., or from med. L. *supernalis*, from L. *supernus*, from *super* 'above.']

su·per·na·tant /ˌso͞opərˈnātnt/ tech. ▶ **adj.** denoting the liquid lying above a solid residue after crystallization, precipitation, centrifugation, or other process. ▶ **n.** a volume of supernatant liquid.

su·per·nat·u·ral /ˌso͞opərˈnacн(ə)rəl/ ▶ **adj.** (of a manifestation or event) attributed to some force beyond scientific understanding or the laws of nature. ■ unnaturally or extraordinarily great. ▶ **n.** **(the supernatural)** manifestations or events considered to be of supernatural origin, such as ghosts. — **su·per·nat·u·ral·ism** /-ˌlizəm/ **n. su·per·nat·u·ral·ist n. su·per·nat·u·ral·ly adv.** [as submodifier] *the monster was supernaturally strong.*

su·per·no·va /ˈso͞opərˌnōvə/ ▶ **n.** (pl. **-no·vae** /-ˌnōvē/ or **-no·vas**) Astron. a star that suddenly increases greatly in brightness because of a catastrophic explosion that ejects most of its mass.

su·per·nu·mer·ar·y /ˌso͞opərˈn(y)o͞oməˌrerē/ ▶ **adj.** present in excess of the normal or requisite number, in particular: ■ (of a person) not belonging to a regular staff but engaged for extra work. ■ not wanted or needed; redundant. ■ Bot. & Zool. denoting a structure or organ occurring in addition to the normal ones. ■ (of an actor) appearing on stage but not speaking. ▶ **n.** (pl. **-ar·ies**) a supernumerary person or thing. [17th C.: from late L. *supernumerarius* '(soldier) added to a legion after it is complete,' from L. *super numerum* 'beyond the number.']

su·per·or·der /ˈso͞opərˌôrdər/ ▶ **n.** Biol. a taxonomic category that ranks above order and below class.

su·per·or·di·nate /ˌso͞opərˈôrdn-ət/ ▶ **n.** a thing that represents a superior order or category within a system of classification. ■ a person who has authority over or control of another within an organization. ▶ **adj.** superior in status: *senior staff's superordinate position.* [17th C.: from SUPER-.]

su·per·ox·ide /ˌso͞opərˈäkˌsīd/ ▶ **n.** Chem. an oxide containing the anion O_2^-.

su·per·plas·tic /ˈso͞opərˌplastik/ Metallurgy ▶ **adj.** (of a metal or alloy) capable of extreme plastic extension under load. ▶ **n.** a metal or alloy having this property. — **su·per·plas·tic·i·ty** /ˌso͞opərplasˈtisitē/ **n.**

su·per·pose /ˌso͞opərˈpōz/ ▶ **v.** [trans.] place (something) on or above something else, esp. so that they coincide: [as adj.] **(superposed)** *superposed triangles.* — **su·per·pos·a·ble adj. su·per·po·si·tion** /-pəˈzisнən/ **n.** [19th C.: from Fr. *superposer*, from *super-* 'above' + *poser* 'to place.']

su·per·pow·er /ˈso͞opərˌpouər/ ▶ **n.** a very powerful and influential nation (used esp. with reference to the US and the former USSR when these were perceived as the two most powerful nations in the world). ■ a dominant or preeminent individual or organization, esp. in a particular field.

su·per·sat·u·rate /ˌso͞opərˈsacнəˌrāt/ ▶ **v.** [trans.] Chem. increase the concentration of (a solution) beyond saturation point. — **su·per·sat·u·ra·tion** /-ˌsacнəˈrāsнən/ **n.**

su·per·scribe /ˌso͞opərˈskrīb/ ▶ **v.** [trans.] write or print (an inscription) at the top of or on the outside of a document. ■ write or print an inscription at the top of or on the outside of (a document). ■ write or print (a letter, word, symbol, or line of writing or printing) above an existing letter, word, or line. — **su·per·scrip·tion** /-ˈskripsнən/ **n.** [15th C.: from L. *superscribere*, from *super-* 'over' + *scribere* 'write.']

su·per·script /ˈso͞opərˌskript/ ▶ **adj.** (of a letter, figure, or symbol) written or printed above the line. ▶ **n.** a superscript letter, figure, or symbol. [19th C.: from L. *superscriptus* 'written above,' past part. of *superscribere*.]

su·per·sede /ˌso͞opərˈsēd/ ▶ **v.** [trans.] take the place of (a person or thing previously in authority or use); supplant: *the older models have now been superseded.* — **su·per·ses·sion** /-ˈsesнən/ **n.** [15th C.: from OFr. *superseder*, from L. *supersedere* 'be superior to,' from *super-* 'above' + *sedere* 'sit.']

su·per·size /ˈso͞opərˌsīz/ ▶ **v.** [trans.] [often as adj.] **(supersized)** produce or serve (something) in a larger size: *supersized suitcases on wheels.* ▶ **adj.** larger than average or standard sizes; very large.

su·per·son·ic /ˌso͞opərˈsänik/ ▶ **adj.** involving or denoting a speed greater than that of sound. — **su·per·son·i·cal·ly** /-ik(ə)lē/ **adv.**

su·per·son·ic trans·port (abbr.: **SST**) ▶ **n.** a commercial jet capable of exceeding the speed of sound.

su·per·space /ˈso͞opərˌspās/ ▶ **n.** Physics a concept of space-time in which points are defined by more than four coordinates. ■ a space of infinitely many dimensions postulated to contain actual space-time and all possible spaces.

su·per·star /ˈso͞opərˌstär/ ▶ **n.** a high-profile and extremely successful performer or athlete. — **su·per·star·dom** /-dəm/ **n.**

su·per·state /ˈso͞opərˌstāt/ ▶ **n.** a large and powerful state or union formed from a federation of nations.

su·per·sti·tion /ˌso͞opərˈstisнən/ ▶ **n.** excessively credulous belief in and reverence for supernatural beings. ■ a widely held but unjustified belief in supernatural causation leading to certain consequences of an action or event, or a practice based on such a belief. — **su·per·sti·tious** /-ˈstisнəs/ **adj. su·per·sti·tious·ly** /-ˈstisнəslē/ **adv. su·per·sti·tious·ness** /-ˈstisнəsnəs/ **n.** [ME: from OFr., or from L. *superstitio(n-)*, from *super-* 'over' + *stare* 'to stand.']

su·per·store /ˈso͞opərˌstôr/ ▶ **n.** a retail store, as a grocery store or bookstore, with more than the average amount of space and variety of stock.

su·per·string /ˈso͞opərˌstriNG/ ▶ **n.** Physics a subatomic particle in a version of string theory that incorporates supersymmetry.

su·per·struc·ture /ˈso͞opərˌstrəkcнər/ ▶ **n.** a structure built on top of something else. ■ the parts of a ship, other than masts and rigging, built above its hull and main deck. ■ the part of a building above its foundations. ■ a concept or idea based on others. ■ (in Marxist theory) the institutions and culture considered to result from or reflect the economic system underlying a society. — **su·per·struc·tur·al** /ˌso͞opərˈstrəkcнərəl/ **adj.**

su·per·sym·me·try /ˈso͞opərˌsimitrē/ ▶ **n.** Physics a very general type of mathematical symmetry that relates fermions and bosons. — **su·per·sym·met·ric** /-siˈmetrik/ **adj.**

su·per·tank·er /ˈso͞opərˌtaNGkər/ ▶ **n.** a very large oil tanker, specifically one whose dead-weight capacity exceeds 75,000 tons.

su·per·ti·tle /ˈso͞opərˌtītl/ ▶ **n.** (usu. **supertitles**) a caption projected on a screen above the stage in an opera, translating the text being sung. ▶ **v.** [trans.] provide (an opera) with supertitles.

su·per·ton·ic /ˈso͞opərˌtänik/ ▶ **n.** Music the second note of the diatonic scale of any key; the note above the tonic.

Su·per Tues·day ▶ **n.** informal a day on which several US states hold primary elections.

su·per·vene /ˌso͞opərˈvēn/ ▶ **v.** [intrans.] occur later than a specified or implied event or action, typically in such a way as to change the situation. ■ Philos. (of a fact or property) be entailed by or consequent on the existence or establishment of another. — **su·per·ven·ient** /-ˈvēnyənt/ **adj. su·per·ven·tion** /-ˈvencнən/ **n.** [17th C.: from L. *supervenire*, from *super-* 'in addition' + *venire* 'come.']

su·per·vise /ˈso͞opərˌvīz/ ▶ **v.** [trans.] observe and direct the execution of (a task, project, or activity). ■ observe and direct the work of (someone). ■ keep watch over (someone) in the interest of their or others' security. — **su·per·vi·sion** /ˌso͞opərˈvizнən/ **n. su·per·vi·sor** /-ˌvīzər/ **n. su·per·vi·so·ry** /ˌso͞opərˈvīzərē/ **adj.** [15th C.: from med. L. *supervis-* 'surveyed, supervised,' from *supervidere*, from *super-* 'over' + *videre* 'to see.']

su·per·wom·an /ˈso͞opərˌwo͝omən/ ▶ **n.** (pl. **-wom·en**) informal a woman with exceptional physical or mental ability, esp. one who successfully manages a home, brings up children, and has a full-time job.

su·pi·nate /ˈso͞opəˌnāt/ ▶ **v.** [trans.] tech. put or hold (a hand, foot, or limb) with the palm or sole turned upward. Compare with PRONATE. — **su·pi·na·tion** /ˌso͞opəˈnāsнən/ **n.** [19th C.: back-form. from *supination*, from L. *supinatio(n-)*, from *supinare* 'lay backward,' from *supinus* (see SUPINE).]

su·pine /ˈso͞oˌpīn/ ▶ **adj. 1** (of a person) lying face upward. ■ tech. having the front or ventral part upward. ■ (of the hand) with the palm upward. **2** failing to act or protest as a result of moral weakness or indolence: *supine in the face of racial injustice.* ▶ **n.** a Latin verbal noun used only in the accusative and ablative cases, esp. to denote purpose (e.g., *dictu* in *mirabile dictu* "wonderful to relate"). — **su·pine·ly adv. su·pine·ness n.** [ME: the adj. from L. *supinus* 'bent backward' (rel. to *super* 'above'); the noun from late L. *supinum*, neut. of *supinus*.]

supp. ▶ **abbr.** ■ supplement. ■ supplementary.

sup·per /ˈsəpər/ ▶ **n.** an evening meal, typically a light or informal one: *we had a delicious cold supper.* ■ a late-night dinner. ■ an evening social event at which food is served.

– PHRASES **sing for one's supper** earn a favor or benefit by providing a service in return. — **sup·per·less** adj. [ME: from OFr. *super* 'to sup' (used as a noun) (see SUP²).]

suppl. ▶ abbr. ■ supplement. ■ supplementary.

sup·plant /sə'plant/ ▶ v. [trans.] supersede and replace. — **sup·plant·er** n. [ME: from OFr. *supplanter* or L. *supplantare* 'trip up,' from *sub-* 'from below' + *planta* 'sole.']

sup·ple /'səpəl/ ▶ adj. (**-pler, -plest**) bending and moving easily and gracefully; flexible. ■ not stiff or hard; easily manipulated. ▶ v. [trans.] make more flexible. — **sup·ple·ly** /'səp(ə)lē/ (also **sup·ply**) adv. **sup·ple·ness** n. [ME: from OFr. *souple*, from L. *supplex, supplic-* 'submissive,' from *sub-* 'under' + *placere* 'propitiate.']

sup·ple·jack /'səpəl,jak/ ▶ n. either of two New World twining plants: ■ a tall North American climber (*Berchemia scandens*) of the buckthorn family. ■ a tropical American plant (*Paullinia plumieri*) of the soapberry family.

sup·ple·ment ▶ n. /'səpləmənt/ **1** something that completes or enhances something else when added to it. ■ a substance taken to remedy the deficiencies in a person's diet. ■ a part added to a book to provide further or corrected information but separate from the main body of the text. ■ a separate section, esp. a color magazine, added to a newspaper or periodical. **2** Geom. the amount by which an angle is less than 180°. ▶ v. /'səplə,ment; -mənt/ [trans.] add an extra element or amount to: *she tried to supplement her husband's income.* — **sup·ple·men·tal** /,səplə'mentl/ adj. **sup·ple·men·tal·ly** /,səplə'mentl-ē/ adv. **sup·ple·men·ta·tion** /,səplə,men'tāshən/ n. [ME: from L. *supplementum*, from *supplere* 'fill up, complete' (see SUPPLY¹).]

sup·ple·men·ta·ry /,səplə'ment(ə)rē/ ▶ adj. completing or enhancing something. ▶ n. a supplementary person or thing. — **sup·ple·men·tar·i·ly** /-,men'te(ə)rəlē/ adv.

sup·ple·men·ta·ry an·gle ▶ n. Math. either of two angles whose sum is 180°.

sup·pli·ant /'səplēənt/ ▶ n. a person making a humble plea to someone in power or authority. ▶ adj. making or expressing a plea, esp. to someone in power or authority: *their faces were suppliant.* — **sup·pli·ant·ly** adv. [ME: from Fr., 'beseeching,' pres. part. of *supplier*, from L. *supplicare* (see SUPPLICATE).]

sup·pli·cate /'səpli,kāt/ ▶ v. [intrans.] ask or beg for something earnestly or humbly. — **sup·pli·cant** /-kənt/ adj. & n. **sup·pli·ca·tion** /,səpli'kāshən/ n. **sup·pli·ca·to·ry** /-kə,tôrē/ adj. [ME: from L. *supplicat-* 'implored,' from the verb *supplicare*, from *sub-* 'from below' + *placere* 'propitiate.']

sup·ply¹ /sə'plī/ ▶ v. (**-plies, -plied**) [trans.] make (something needed or wanted) available to someone; provide: *the farm supplies apples to cider makers.* ■ provide (someone) with something needed or wanted. ■ be a source of (something needed). ■ be adequate to satisfy (a requirement or demand). ▶ n. (pl. **-plies**) a stock of a resource from which a person or place can be provided with the necessary amount of that resource. ■ the action of providing what is needed or wanted. ■ Econ. the amount of a good or service offered for sale. ■ (**supplies**) the provisions and equipment necessary for an army or for people engaged in a particular project or expedition. ■ [usu. as adj.] a person acting as a temporary substitute for another. ■ [as adj.] providing necessary goods and equipment.

– PHRASES **in short supply** not easily obtainable; scarce. **supply and demand** the amount of a good or service available and the desire of buyers for it, considered as factors regulating its price. — **sup·pli·er** n. [ME: from OFr. *soupleer*, from L. *supplere* 'fill up,' from *sub-* 'from below' + *plere* 'fill.']

sup·ply² /'səp(ə)lē/ ▶ adv. var. of *SUPPLELY* (see SUPPLE).

sup·ply-side ▶ adj. [attrib.] Econ. denoting or relating to a policy designed to increase output and employment by changing the conditions under which goods and services are supplied, esp. by measures that reduce government involvement in the economy and allow the free market to operate. — **sup·ply-sid·er** n.

sup·port /sə'pôrt/ ▶ v. [trans.] **1** bear all or part of the weight of; hold up. ■ produce enough food and water for; be capable of sustaining. ■ be capable of fulfilling (a role) adequately. ■ endure; tolerate. **2** give assistance to, esp. financially; enable to function or act. ■ provide with a home and the necessities of life. ■ give comfort and emotional help to. ■ approve of and encourage. ■ suggest the truth of; corroborate. ■ be actively interested in and concerned for the success of (a particular sports team). ■ [as adj.] (**supporting**) (of an actor or a role) important in a play or film but subordinate to the leading parts. ■ (of a pop or rock group or performer) function as a secondary act to (another) at a concert. **3** Comput. (of a computer or operating system) allow the use or operation of (a program, language, or device). ▶ n. **1** a thing that bears the weight of something or keeps it upright: *the best support for a camera is a tripod.* ■ the action or state of bearing the weight of something or someone or of being so supported. **2** material assistance: *military support.* ■ comfort and emotional help offered to someone in distress. ■ approval and encouragement. ■ a secondary act at a pop or rock concert. ■ technical help given to the user of a computer or other product.

– PHRASES **in support of** giving assistance to. ■ showing approval of. ■ attempting to promote or obtain. — **sup·port·a·bil·i·ty** /sə,pôrtə'bilitē/ n. **sup·port·a·ble** adj. [ME: from OFr. *supporter*, from L. *supportare*, from *sub-* 'from below' + *portare* 'carry.']

sup·port·er /sə'pôrtər/ ▶ n. **1** a person who approves of and encourages someone or something (typically a public figure, a movement or party, or a policy). ■ a person who is actively interested in and wishes success for a particular sports team. **2** Heraldry a representation of an animal or other figure, typically one of a pair, holding up or standing beside an escutcheon. **3** (in full **athletic supporter**) another term for JOCKSTRAP.

sup·port·ive /sə'pôrtiv/ ▶ adj. providing encouragement or emotional help. — **sup·port·ive·ly** adv. **sup·port·ive·ness** n.

sup·port sys·tem ▶ n. **1** a group of people who are available to support one another emotionally, socially, and sometimes financially: *a support group for gay teens.* **2** a system implemented with the aim of providing support for an enterprise, product line, or project.

sup·pose /sə'pōz/ ▶ v. **1** [with clause] assume that something is the case on the basis of evidence or probability but without proof or certain knowledge. ■ used to make a reluctant or hesitant admission. ■ used to introduce a hypothesis and trace or ask about what follows from it. ■ [in imper.] used to introduce a suggestion. ■ (of a theory or argument) assume or require that something is the case as a precondition. ■ [trans.] believe to exist or to possess a specified characteristic: *he supposed the girl to be about twelve.* **2** (**be supposed to do something**) be required to do something because of the position one is in or an agreement one has made: *I'm supposed to be meeting someone.* ■ [with negative] be forbidden to do something: *I'm not supposed to go in there.*

– PHRASES **I suppose so** used to express hesitant or reluctant agreement. — **sup·pos·a·ble** adj. [ME: from OFr. *supposer*, from L. *supponere* (from *sub-* 'from below' + *ponere* 'to place').]

sup·pos·ed·ly /sə'pōzidlē/ ▶ adv. [sentence adverb] according to what is generally assumed or believed (often used to indicate that the speaker doubts the truth of the statement).

sup·po·si·tion /,səpə'zishən/ ▶ n. an uncertain belief. — **sup·po·si·tion·al** /-shənl/ adj.

sup·po·si·tious /,səpə'zishəs/ ▶ adj. **1** based on assumption rather than fact. **2** supposititious. — **sup·po·si·tious·ly** adv. **sup·po·si·tious·ness** n.

sup·pos·i·ti·tious /sə,päzə'tishəs/ ▶ adj. **1** substituted for the real thing; not genuine. **2** suppositious. — **sup·pos·i·ti·tious·ly** adv. **sup·pos·i·ti·tious·ness** n. [17th C.: from L. *supposititius* (from *supponere* 'to substitute') + -OUS.]

sup·pos·i·to·ry /sə'päzə,tôrē/ ▶ n. (pl. **-ries**) a solid medical preparation in a roughly conical or cylindrical shape, designed to be inserted into the rectum or vagina to dissolve. [ME: from med. L. *suppositorium*, neut. (used as a n.) of late L. *suppositorius* 'placed underneath.']

sup·press /sə'pres/ ▶ v. [trans.] forcibly put an end to. ■ prevent the development, action, or expression of (a feeling, impulse, idea, etc.); restrain. ■ prevent the dissemination of (information). ■ prevent or inhibit (a process or reaction): *the drug suppressed the immune response.* ■ partly or wholly eliminate (electrical interference). ■ Psychoanal. consciously inhibit (an unpleasant idea or memory) to avoid considering it. — **sup·press·i·ble** adj. **sup·pres·sive** /-siv/ adj. **sup·pres·sor** /-sər/ n. [ME: from L. *suppress-* 'pressed down,' from the verb *supprimere*, from *sub-* 'down' + *premere* 'to press.']

sup·pres·sant /sə'presənt/ ▶ n. a drug or other substance that acts to suppress or restrain something.

sup·pres·sion /sə'preshən/ ▶ n. the action of suppressing something such as an activity or publication. ■ Med. stoppage or reduction of a discharge or secretion. ■ Biol. the absence or nondevelopment of a part or organ that is normally present. ■ Genet. the canceling of the effect of one mutation by a second mutation. ■ Psychol. the restraint or repression of an idea, activity, or reaction by something more powerful. ■ Psychoanal. the conscious inhibition of unacceptable memories, impulses, or desires. ■ prevention of electrical interference.

sup·pu·rate /'səpyə,rāt/ ▶ v. [intrans.] undergo the formation of pus; fester. — **sup·pu·ra·tion** /,səpyə'rāshən/ n. **sup·pu·ra·tive** /-,rātiv/ adj. [ME: based on L. *sub-* 'below' + *pus, pur-* 'pus.']

supr. ▶ abbr. ■ superior. ■ supreme.

su·pra /'so͞oprə/ ▶ adv. formal used in academic or legal texts to refer to someone or something mentioned above or earlier. [L.]

supra- ▶ prefix **1** beyond; transcending: *supranational.* **2** above: *suprarenal.* [from L. *supra* 'above, beyond, before in time.']

su·pra·mo·lec·u·lar /,so͞oprəmə'lekyələr/ ▶ adj. Biochem. relating to or denoting structures composed of several or many molecules.

su·pra·na·tion·al /,so͞oprə'nashənl/ ▶ adj. having power or influence that transcends national boundaries or governments: *supranational law.* — **su·pra·na·tion·al·ism** /-,izəm/ n. **su·pra·na·tion·al·i·ty** /-,nashə'nalitē/ n.

su·pra·or·bit·al /,so͞oprə'ôrbitl/ ▶ adj. Anat. situated above the orbit of the eye.

su·pra·re·nal /,so͞oprə'rēnl/ ▶ adj. Anat. another term for ADRENAL.

su·prem·a·cist /sə'preməsist; so͞o-/ ▶ n. an advocate of the supremacy of a particular group, esp. one determined by race or sex: *a white supremacist.* ▶ adj. relating to or advocating such supremacy. — **su·prem·a·cism** /-,sizəm/ n.

su·prem·a·cy /sə'preməsē; so͞o-/ ▶ n. the state or condition of being superior to all others in authority, power, or status: *the supremacy of the king.*

su·preme /sə'prēm; so͞o-/ ▶ adj. (of authority or an office, or someone holding it) superior to all others. ■ strongest, most important, or most powerful. ■ very great or intense; extreme. ■ (of a penalty or sacrifice) involving death. ■ [postpositive] used to indicate that someone or something is very good at or well known for a specified activity.

▶ n. (also **su·prême**) a rich cream sauce. ■ a dish served in such a sauce: *chicken supreme.*
– PHRASES **the Supreme Being** a name for God. — **su·preme·ly** adv. [15th C.: from L. *supremus*, superlative of *superus* 'that is above,' from *super* 'above.']

Su·preme Court ▶ n. the highest judicial court in most US states. ■ (in full **US Supreme Court**) the highest federal court in the US, consisting of nine justices and taking judicial precedence over all other courts in the nation.

Su·preme So·vi·et ▶ n. the governing council of the former USSR or one of its constituent republics.

Supt. ▶ abbr. Superintendent.

supvr. ▶ abbr. supervisor.

suq ▶ n. var. of SOUK.

sur. ▶ abbr. ■ surface. ■ surplus.

sur-[1] ▶ prefix equivalent to SUPER- (as in *surcharge, surmount*). [from Fr.]

sur-[2] ▶ prefix var. of SUB- assimilated before *r* (as in *surrogate*).

su·ra /ˈsŏŏrə/ (also **su·rah**) ▶ n. a chapter or section of the Koran. [from Arab. *sūra*.]

Su·ra·ba·ya /ˌsŏŏrəˈbīə/ a city in Indonesia, on Java; pop. 2,473,000.

su·rah /ˈsŏŏrə/ ▶ n. a soft twilled silk fabric used in dressmaking. [19th C.: from SURAT, where it was orig. made.]

su·ral /ˈsŏŏrəl/ ▶ adj. Anat. of or relating to the calf of the leg. [17th C.: from mod. L. *suralis*, from L. *sura* 'calf.']

Su·rat /ˈsŏŏrˌat; sŏŏˈrat/ a city in western India, on the Tapti River; pop. 1,497,000.

sur·cease /sərˈsēs/ ▶ n. cessation. ■ relief or consolation. [ME: from Old Fr. *sursis*, past part. of OFr. *surseoir* 'refrain, delay,' from L. *supersedere* (see SUPERSEDE).]

sur·charge /ˈsərˌCHärj/ ▶ n. **1** an additional charge or payment: *no surcharges will be added to the cost.* ■ a charge made by assessors as a penalty for false returns of taxable property. ■ the showing of an omission in an account for which credit should have been given. **2** a mark printed on a postage stamp changing its value. ▶ v. [trans.] **1** exact an additional charge or payment from. **2** mark (a postage stamp) with a surcharge. [ME: from OFr. *surcharger* (see SUR-[1], CHARGE).]

sur·cin·gle /ˈsərˌsiNGgəl/ ▶ n. a wide strap that runs over the back and under the belly of a horse, used to keep a blanket or other equipment in place. [ME: from OFr. *surcengle*, based on *cengle* 'girth,' from L. *cingula*, from *cingere* 'gird.']

sur·cu·lose /ˈsərkyəˌlōs; -ˌlōz/ ▶ adj. Bot. producing suckers. [19th C.: from L. *surculosus*, from *surculus* 'twig.']

surd /sərd/ ▶ adj. **1** Math. (of a number) irrational. **2** Phonet. (of a speech sound) uttered with the breath and not the voice (e.g., *f, k, p, s, t*). ▶ n. **1** Math. a surd number, esp. the irrational root of an integer. **2** Phonet. a surd consonant. [16th C.: from L. *surdus* 'deaf, mute.']

sure /SHŏŏr/ ▶ adj. [predic.] [often with clause] confident in what one thinks or knows; having no doubt that one is right: *I'm sure I've seen that dress before.* ■ (**sure of**) having a certain prospect or confident anticipation of. ■ [with infin.] certain to do something: *it's sure to rain before morning.* ■ true beyond any doubt. ■ [attrib.] able to be relied on or trusted. ■ confident; assured. ▶ adv. informal certainly (used for emphasis). ■ [as an exclam.] used to show assent.
– PHRASES **be sure** [usu. in imper.] do not fail (used to emphasize an invitation or instruction). **for sure** informal without doubt. **make sure** [usu. with clause] establish that something is definitely so; confirm. ■ ensure that something is done or happens. **sure enough** informal used to introduce a statement that confirms something previously predicted. **sure of oneself** very confident of one's own abilities or views. **sure thing** informal a certainty. ■ [as exclam.] certainly; of course. **to be sure** used to concede the truth of something that conflicts with another point that one wishes to make. ■ used for emphasis. — **sure·ness** n. [ME: from OFr. *sur*, from L. *securus* 'free from care.']

sure-fire ▶ adj. [attrib.] informal certain to succeed.

sure-foot·ed (also **sure·foot·ed**) ▶ adj. unlikely to stumble or slip: *tough, sure-footed ponies.* ■ confident and competent. — **sure-foot·ed·ly** adv. **sure-foot·ed·ness** n.

sure·ly /ˈSHŏŏrlē/ ▶ adv. **1** [sentence adverb] used to emphasize the speaker's firm belief that what they are saying is true and often their surprise that there is any doubt of this. ■ without doubt; certainly. ■ [as exclam.] informal of course; yes. **2** with assurance or confidence.

sur·e·ty /ˈSHŏŏritē/ ▶ n. (pl. **-ties**) a person who takes responsibility for another's performance of an undertaking, for example their appearing in court or the payment of a debt. ■ money given to support an undertaking that someone will perform a duty, pay their debts, etc.; a guarantee. ■ the state of being sure or certain of something. — **sur·e·ty·ship** /-ˌSHip/ n. [ME: from OFr. *surte*, from L. *securitas* (see SECURITY).]

surf /sərf/ ▶ n. the mass or line of foam formed by waves breaking on a seashore or reef: *the roar of the surf.* ■ [in sing.] a spell of surfing: *he went for an early surf.* ▶ v. [intrans.] ride on the crest of a wave, typically toward the shore while riding on a surfboard: *learning to surf.* ■ [trans.] ride (a wave) toward the shore in such a way. ■ informal ride on the roof or outside of a fast-moving vehicle, typically a train, for excitement. ■ (also **channel surf**) browse television broadcasts by frequently or continuously changing channels, esp. by using a remote control. ■ [trans.] move from site to site on (the Internet). — **surf·er** n. **surf·y** adj. [17th C.: appar. from obs. *suff*, of unknown origin.]

sur·face /ˈsərfis/ ▶ n. **1** the outside part or uppermost layer of something (often used when describing its texture, form, or extent): *the earth's surface.* ■ the level top of something: *a floured surface.* ■ (also **surface area**) the area of such an outer part or uppermost layer: *the surface area of a cube.* ■ [in sing.] the upper limit of a body of liquid: *the surface of the water.* ■ [in sing.] what is apparent on a casual view or consideration of someone or something, esp. as distinct from feelings or qualities that are not immediately obvious. **2** Geom. a set of points that has length and breadth but no thickness. ▶ adj. [attrib.] of, relating to, or occurring on the upper or outer part of something: *surface workers at the copper mines.* ■ denoting ships that travel on the surface of the water as distinct from submarines. ■ carried by or denoting transportation by sea or overland as contrasted with by air. ▶ v. **1** [intrans.] rise or come up to the surface of the water or the ground: *he surfaced from his dive.* ■ come to people's attention; become apparent. ■ informal (of a person) appear after having been asleep: *it was noon before Anthony surfaced.* **2** [trans.] (usu. **be surfaced**) provide (something, esp. a road) with a particular upper or outer layer. — **sur·faced** adj. **sur·fac·er** n. [17th C.: from Fr. (see SUR-[1], FACE), suggested by L. *superficies*.]

sur·face-ac·tive ▶ adj. (of a substance, such as a detergent) tending to reduce the surface tension of a liquid in which it is dissolved.

sur·face noise ▶ n. extraneous noise in playing a phonograph record, caused by imperfections in the grooves or in the pickup system.

sur·face ten·sion ▶ n. the tension of the surface film of a liquid caused by the attraction of the particles in the surface layer by the bulk of the liquid, which tends to minimize surface area.

sur·face-to-air ▶ adj. [attrib.] (of a missile) designed to be fired from the ground or a vessel at an aircraft.

sur·face-to-sur·face ▶ adj. [attrib.] (of a missile) designed to be fired from one point on the ground or a vessel at another such point or vessel.

sur·face wa·ter ▶ n. **1** water that collects on the surface of the ground. **2** (also **surface waters**) the top layer of a body of water: *the surface water of a pond or lake.*

sur·fac·tant /sərˈfaktənt/ ▶ n. a substance that tends to reduce the surface tension of a liquid in which it is dissolved. [1950s: from *surf(ace)-act(ive)* + -ANT.]

surf·bird /ˈsərfˌbərd/ ▶ n. a small migratory wader (*Aphriza virgata*) of the sandpiper family, with mainly dark gray plumage and a short bill and legs, breeding in Alaska.

surf·board /ˈsərfˌbôrd/ ▶ n. a long, narrow streamlined board used in surfing.

surf·cast·ing /ˈsərfˌkastiNG/ (also **surf cast·ing** or **surf-cast·ing**) ▶ n. fishing by casting a line into the sea from the shore or near the shore. — **surf·cast·er** /-ˌkastər/ n.

sur·feit /ˈsərfət/ ▶ n. [usu. in sing.] an excessive amount of something: *a surfeit of food and drink.* ▶ v. (**-feit·ed, -feit·ing**) [trans.] (usu. **be surfeited with**) cause (someone) to desire no more of something as a result of having consumed or done it to excess. [ME: from OFr. *surfeit*, based on L. *super-* 'above, in excess' + *facere* 'do.']

sur·fi·cial /sərˈfiSHəl/ ▶ adj. Geol. of or relating to the earth's surface: *surficial deposits.* — **sur·fi·cial·ly** adv. [19th C.: from SURFACE.]

surf·ing /ˈsərfiNG/ ▶ n. the sport or pastime of being carried to the shore on the crest of large waves while standing or lying on a surfboard.

surf 'n' turf /ˈsərf ən ˈtərf/ (also **surf and turf**) ▶ n. a dish containing both seafood and meat, typically shellfish and steak.

surf·perch /ˈsərfˌpərCH/ ▶ n. (pl. same or **-perch·es**) a deep-bodied live-bearing fish (family Embiotocidae) of the North Pacific, living chiefly in coastal waters.

surg. ▶ abbr. ■ surgeon. ■ surgery. ■ surgical.

surge /sərj/ ▶ n. a sudden powerful forward or upward movement, esp. by a crowd or by a natural force such as the waves or tide: *flooding caused by tidal surges.* ■ a sudden large increase, typically a brief one that happens during an otherwise stable or quiescent period. ■ a powerful rush of an emotion or feeling. ■ a sudden marked increase in voltage or current in an electric circuit. ▶ v. [no obj., usu. with adverbial] (of a crowd or a natural force) move suddenly and powerfully forward or upward: *the journalists surged forward.* ■ increase suddenly and powerfully, typically during an otherwise stable or quiescent period. ■ (of an emotion or feeling) affect someone powerfully and suddenly. ■ (of an electric voltage or current) increase suddenly. ■ Naut. (of a rope, chain, or windlass) slip back with a jerk. [15th C.: the noun (in early use) from Old Fr. *sourgeon*; the verb partly from the OFr. stem *sourge-*, based on L. *surgere* 'to rise.']

sur·geon /ˈsərjən/ ▶ n. a medical practitioner qualified to practice surgery. [ME: from Anglo-Norman Fr. *surgien*, contr. of OFr. *serurgien*, based on L. *chirurgia*, from Gk. *kheirourgia* 'handiwork, surgery,' from *kheir* 'hand' + *ergon* 'work.']

sur·geon·fish /ˈsərjənˌfiSH/ ▶ n. (pl. same or **-fish·es**) a deep-bodied and typically brightly colored tropical marine fish (family Acanthuridae) with a scalpellike spine on each side of the tail.

sur·geon gen·er·al ▶ n. (pl. **sur·geons gen·er·al**) the head of a public health service or of an armed forces medical service.

sur·ger·y /ˈsərjərē/ ▶ n. (pl. **-ger·ies**) the branch of medicine concerned with treatment of injuries or disorders of the body by incision or manipulation, esp. with instruments: *cardiac surgery.* ■ such treatment, as performed by a surgeon. [ME: from OFr. *surgerie,* contr. of *serurgerie,* from *serurgien* (see SURGEON).]

sur·gi·cal /ˈsərjikəl/ ▶ **adj.** of, relating to, or used in surgery: *a surgical dressing | a surgical mask.* ■ (of a special garment or appliance) worn to correct or relieve an injury, illness, or deformity. ■ fig. denoting something done with great precision, esp. a swift and highly accurate military attack from the air. — **sur·gi·cal·ly** /-ik(ə)lē/ **adv.** [18th C.: from Fr. *cirurgical,* from OFr. *sirurgie* (see SURGERY).]

surgical mask

Su·ri·ba·chi, Mount /ˌsŏŏrəˈbächē/ a small dormant volcano on Iwo Jima, in the Pacific Ocean, site of a February 1945 flag-raising by US Marines.

su·ri·cate /ˈsŏŏriˌkāt/ ▶ **n.** a gregarious burrowing meerkat (*Suricata suricatta*) with dark bands on the back and a black-tipped tail, native to southern Africa. [18th C.: via Fr. from a local African word.]

suricate

Su·ri·na·me /ˌsŏŏrəˈnämə; ˈsŏŏrəˌnäm; -ˌnam/ (also **Su·ri·nam** /ˈsŏŏrəˌnäm; -ˌnam/) a country on the northeastern coast of South America. *See box.* Former name (until 1948) DUTCH GUIANA. — **Su·ri·nam·er** /ˌsŏŏrəˈnämər/ **n.** **Su·ri·na·mese** /ˌsŏŏrənəˈmēz; -ˈmēs/ **adj. & n.**

Su·ri·nam toad /ˈsŏŏrəˌnam/ ▶ **n.** an aquatic South American toad (*Pipa pipa,* family Pipidae) with a flat body and long webbed feet, the female of which carries the eggs and tadpoles in pockets on her back.

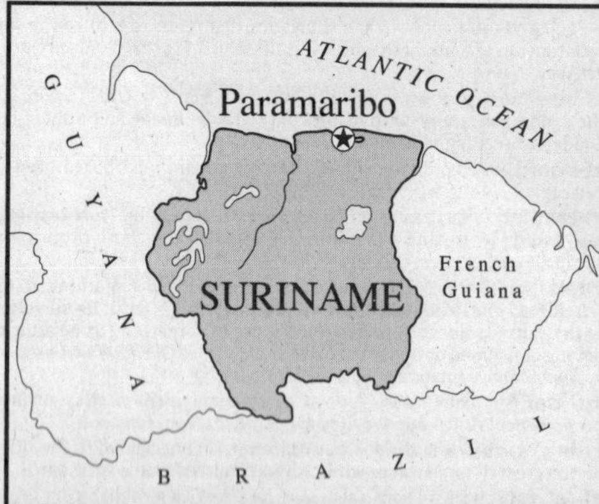

Suriname

Official name: Republic of Suriname
Location: South America, on the northeastern coast
Area: 63,100 square miles (163,300 sq km)
Population: 437,000
Capital: Paramaribo
Languages: Dutch (official), English, Hindustani, Javanese
Currency: Surinamese guilder

sur·ly /ˈsərlē/ ▶ **adj.** (**-li·er, -li·est**) bad-tempered and unfriendly: *he left with a surly expression.* — **sur·li·ly** /-ləlē/ **adv.** **sur·li·ness** **n.** [16th C.: alt. of obs. *sirly* (see SIR, -LY[1]).]

sur·mise /sərˈmīz/ ▶ **v.** [intrans.] [usu. with clause] suppose that something is true without having evidence to confirm it: *he surmised that something must be wrong.* ▶ **n.** /sərˈmīz; ˈsərˌmīz/ a supposition that something may be true, even though there is no evidence to confirm it: *all these observations remain surmise.* [ME (in the senses 'formal allegation' and 'allege formally'): from Anglo-Norman Fr. and OFr. *surmise,* fem. past part. of *surmettre* 'accuse,' from late L. *supermittere* 'put in afterwards.']

sur·mount /sərˈmount/ ▶ **v.** [trans.] **1** overcome (a difficulty or obstacle). **2** (usu. **be surmounted**) stand or be placed on top of. — **sur·mount·a·ble** **adj.** [ME: from OFr. *surmonter* (see SUR-[1], MOUNT[1]).]

sur·mul·let /sərˈmələt/ ▶ **n.** a goatfish (*Pseudupeneus fraterculus*) that is widely distributed in the tropical Indo-Pacific. [17th C.: from Fr. *surmulet,* from OFr. *sor* 'red' + *mulet* 'mullet.']

sur·name /ˈsərˌnām/ ▶ **n.** a hereditary name common to all members of a family, as distinct from a given name. ▶ **v.** [trans.] (usu. **be surnamed**) give a surname to. [ME: partial translation of Anglo-Norman Fr. *surnoun,* suggested by med. L. *supernomen.*]

sur·pass /sərˈpas/ ▶ **v.** [trans.] exceed; be greater than. ■ be better than: *he continued to surpass me at all games.* ■ (**surpass oneself**) do or be better than ever before. ■ [as adj.] (**surpassing**) dated literary incomparable or outstanding: *a picture of surpassing beauty.* — **sur·pass·a·ble** **adj.** **sur·pass·ing·ly** **adv.** [16th C.: from Fr. *surpasser,* from *sur-* 'above' + *passer* 'to pass.']

sur·plice /ˈsərplis/ ▶ **n.** a loose white linen vestment varying from hip-length to calf-length, worn over a cassock by clergy, acolytes, and choristers at Christian church services. — **sur·pliced** **adj.** [ME: from OFr. *sourpelis,* from med. L. *superpellicium,* from *super-* 'above' + *pellicia* 'fur garment.']

surplice

sur·plus /ˈsərpləs/ ▶ **n.** an amount of something left over when requirements have been met; an excess of production or supply over demand. ■ an excess of income or assets over expenditure or liabilities in a given period, typically a fiscal year. ■ the excess value of a company's assets over the face value of its stock. ▶ **adj.** more than what is needed or used; excess. ■ denoting a store selling excess or out-of-date military equipment or clothing: *an army surplus store.* [ME: from OFr. *sourplus,* from med. L. *superplus,* from *super-* 'in addition' + *plus* 'more.']

sur·plus val·ue ▶ **n.** Econ. (in Marxist theory) the excess of value produced by the labor of workers over the wages they are paid.

sur·prise /sə(r)ˈprīz/ ▶ **n.** **1** an unexpected or astonishing event, fact, or thing. ■ a feeling of mild astonishment or shock caused by something unexpected. ■ [as adj.] denoting something made, done, or happening unexpectedly. **2** [as adj.] Bell-ringing denoting a class of complex methods of change-ringing: *surprise major.* ▶ **v.** [trans.] (often **be surprised**) (of something unexpected) cause (someone) to feel mild astonishment or shock. ■ capture, attack, or discover suddenly and unexpectedly; catch unawares.

– PHRASES **surprise, surprise** informal said when giving someone a surprise. ■ said ironically when one believes that something was entirely predictable: *surprise, surprise, here you are drinking again.* **take someone/something by surprise** attack or capture someone or something unexpectedly. ■ (**take someone by surprise**) happen when someone is not prepared or is expecting something different. — **sur·pris·ed·ly** /-z(i)dlē/ **adv.** **sur·pris·ing·ly** **adv.** **sur·pris·ing·ness** **n.** [ME: from OFr., fem. past part. of *surprendre,* from med. L. *superprehendere* 'seize.']

surr. ▶ **abbr.** surrender.

sur·ra /ˈsŏŏrə; ˈsərə/ ▶ **n.** a parasitic disease of camels and other mammals caused by trypanosomes, transmitted by biting flies and occurring chiefly in North Africa and Asia. [19th C.: from Marathi *sūra* 'air breathed through the nostrils.']

sur·re·al /səˈrēəl/ ▶ **adj.** having the qualities of surrealism; bizarre: *a surreal mix of fact and fantasy.* — **sur·re·al·i·ty** /ˌsərēˈalitē/ **n.** **sur·re·al·ly** **adv.** [1930s: back-form. from SURREALISM.]

sur·re·al·ism /səˈrēəˌlizəm/ ▶ **n.** a 20th-century avant-garde movement in art and literature that sought to release the creative potential of the unconscious mind. — **sur·re·al·ist** **n. & adj.** **sur·re·al·is·tic** /səˌrēəˈlistik/ **adj.** **sur·re·al·is·ti·cal·ly** /səˌrēəˈlistik(ə)lē/ **adv.** [20th C.: from Fr. *surréalisme* (see SUR-[1], REALISM).]

sur·ren·der /səˈrendər/ ▶ **v.** [intrans.] cease resistance to an enemy or opponent and submit to their authority. ■ [trans.] give up or hand over (a person, right, or possession), typically on compulsion or demand. ■ [trans.] (in a sporting context) lose (a point, game, or advantage). ■ (**surrender to**) abandon oneself entirely to (a powerful emotion or influence); give in to: *he surrendered himself to the mood of the hills.* ■ [trans.] (of an insured person) cancel (a life insurance policy) and receive back a proportion of the premiums paid. ▶ **n.** the action of surrendering. ■ the action of surrendering a life insurance policy. [ME: from Anglo-Norman Fr. (see SUR-[1], RENDER).]

sur·ren·der val·ue ▶ **n.** the amount payable to a person who surrenders a life insurance policy.

sur·rep·ti·tious /ˌsərəpˈtisHəs/ ▶ **adj.** kept secret, esp. because it would not be approved of. — **sur·rep·ti·tious·ly** **adv.** **sur·rep·ti·tious·ness** **n.** [ME: from L. *surreptitius* (from the verb *surripere,* from *sub-* 'secretly' + *rapere* 'seize') + -OUS.]

Sur·rey /ˈsərē/ a county in southeastern England.

surrey

sur·rey /ˈsərē/ ▶ **n.** (pl. **-reys**) hist. a light four-wheeled carriage with two seats facing forward. [19th C.: orig. denoting a *Surrey cart,* first made in SURREY.]

sur·ro·ga·cy /ˈsərəgəsē/ ▶n. the action or state of being a surrogate. ■ the process of giving birth as a surrogate mother or of arranging such a birth.

sur·ro·gate /ˈsərəgit; -ˌgāt/ ▶n. a substitute, esp. a person deputizing for another in a specific role or office. ■ (in the Christian Church) a bishop's deputy who grants marriage licenses. ■ a judge in charge of probate, inheritance, and guardianship. [17th C.: from L. *surrogatus*, past part. of *surrogare* 'elect as a substitute,' from *super-* 'over' + *rogare* 'ask.']

sur·ro·gate moth·er ▶n. **1** a person, animal, or thing that takes on all or part of the role of mother to another person or animal. **2** a woman who bears a child on behalf of another woman, either from her own egg fertilized by the other woman's partner, or from the implantation in her uterus of a fertilized egg from the other woman.

sur·round /səˈround/ ▶v. [trans.] (usu. **be surrounded**) be all around (someone or something): *the hotel is surrounded by its own gardens.* ■ (of troops, police, etc.) encircle (someone or something) so as to cut off communication or escape. ■ be associated with: *surrounded by controversy.* ▶n. a thing that forms a border or edging around an object: *an oak fireplace surround.* ■ (usu. **surrounds**) the area encircling something; surroundings. [ME: from OFr. *souronder*, from late L. *superundare*, from *super-* 'over' + *undare* 'to flow' (from *unda* 'a wave').]

sur·round·ings /səˈroundiNGz/ ▶plural n. the things and conditions around a person or thing.

sur·round sound ▶n. a system of stereophonic sound involving three or more speakers surrounding the listener so as to create a more realistic effect.

sur·tax /ˈsərˌtaks/ ▶n. an additional tax on something already taxed, such as a higher rate of tax on incomes above a certain level. [19th C.: from Fr. *surtaxe* (see SUR-[1], TAX).]

sur·veil·lance /sərˈvāləns/ ▶n. close observation, esp. of a suspected spy or criminal. [19th C.: from Fr., from *sur-* 'over' + *veiller* 'watch' (from L. *vigilare* 'keep watch').]

sur·vey ▶v. /sərˈvā/ [trans.] **1** (of a person or their eyes) look carefully and thoroughly at (someone or something), esp. so as to appraise them. ■ investigate the opinions or experience of (a group of people) by asking them questions. ■ investigate (behavior or opinions) by questioning a group of people. **2** examine and record the area and features of (an area of land) so as to construct a map, plan, or description. ▶n. /ˈsərˌvā/ **1** a general view, examination, or description of someone or something. ■ an investigation of the opinions or experience of a group of people, based on a series of questions. **2** an act of surveying an area of land. ■ a map, plan, or detailed description obtained in such a way. ■ a department carrying out the surveying of land: *the US Geological Survey.* [ME: from Anglo-Norman Fr. *surveier*, from med. L. *supervidere*, from *super-* 'over' + *videre* 'to see.']

sur·vey·or /sərˈvāər/ ▶n. a person who surveys, esp. one whose profession is the surveying of land. ■ a person who investigates or examines something, esp. boats for seaworthiness: *a marine surveyor.* —**sur·vey·or·ship** /-ˌSHip/ n.

sur·viv·a·ble /sərˈvīvəbəl/ ▶adj. (of an accident or ordeal) able to be survived; not fatal.

sur·viv·al /sərˈvīvəl/ ▶n. the state or fact of continuing to live or exist, typically in spite of an accident, ordeal, or difficult circumstances. ■ an object or practice that has continued to exist from an earlier time: *a survival from his army days.*

– PHRASES **survival of the fittest** Biol. the continued existence of organisms that are best adapted to their environment, with the extinction of others, as a concept in the Darwinian theory of evolution. Compare with NATURAL SELECTION.

sur·viv·al·ism /sərˈvīvəˌlizəm/ ▶n. **1** the policy of trying to ensure one's own survival or that of one's social or national group. **2** the practicing of outdoor survival skills as a sport or hobby. —**sur·viv·al·ist** n. & adj.

sur·vive /sərˈvīv/ ▶v. [intrans.] continue to live or exist, esp. in spite of danger or hardship. ■ [trans.] continue to live or exist in spite of (an accident or ordeal). ■ [trans.] remain alive after the death of (a particular person). ■ [intrans.] manage to keep going in difficult circumstances: *she had to survive on two hours sleep.* [ME: from OFr. *sourvivre*, from L. *supervivere*, from *super-* 'in addition' + *vivere* 'live.']

sur·vi·vor /sərˈvīvər/ ▶n. a person who survives, esp. a person remaining alive after an event in which others have died: *the sole survivor of the massacre.* ■ the remainder of a group of people or things. ■ a person who copes well with difficulties in their life. ■ Law a joint tenant who has the right to the whole estate on the other's death.

sur·vi·vor·ship /sərˈvīvərˌSHip/ ▶n. the state or condition of being a survivor; survival. ■ Law a right depending on survival, esp. the right of a survivor of people with a joint interest to take the whole on the death of the others.

sus- ▶prefix var. of SUB- before *c, p, t* (as in *susceptible, suspend, sustain.*)

Su·sa /ˈsoōzə; -sə/ an ancient city in southwestern Asia, capital of the Persian Achaemenid dynasty.

sus·cep·ti·bil·i·ty /səˌseptəˈbilitē/ ▶n. (pl. **-ties**) **1** the state or fact of being likely or liable to be influenced or harmed by a particular thing. ■ (**susceptibilities**) a person's feelings, typically considered as being easily hurt. **2** Physics the ratio of magnetization to a magnetizing force.

sus·cep·ti·ble /səˈseptəbəl/ ▶adj. **1** likely or liable to be influenced or harmed by a particular thing. ■ (of a person) easily influenced by feelings or emotions; sensitive. **2** [predic.] (**susceptible of**) capable or admitting of. —**sus·cep·ti·bly** /-blē/ adv. [17th C.: from late L. *susceptibilis*, from L. *suscipere* 'take up, sustain,' from *sub-* 'from below' + *capere* 'take.']

su·shi /ˈsoōSHē/ ▶n. a Japanese dish consisting of small balls or rolls of vinegar-flavored cold cooked rice served with a garnish of vegetables, egg, or raw seafood.

sus·lik /ˈsəsˌlik/ ▶n. var. of SOUSLIK.

sus·pect ▶v. /səˈspekt/ [trans.] **1** have an idea or impression of the existence, presence, or truth of (something) without certain proof. ■ believe or feel that (someone) is guilty of an illegal, dishonest, or unpleasant act, without certain proof. **2** doubt the genuineness or truth of. ▶n. /ˈsəsˌpekt/ a person thought to be guilty of a crime or offense: *the police have arrested a suspect.* ▶adj. /ˈsəsˌpekt/ not to be relied on or trusted; possibly dangerous or false: *a suspect package was found.* [ME: from L. *suspectus* 'mistrusted,' past part. of *suspicere*, from *sub-* 'from below' + *specere* 'to look.']

sus·pend /səˈspend/ ▶v. [trans.] (usu. **be suspended**) **1** temporarily prevent from continuing or being in force or effect: *work on the dam was suspended.* ■ officially prohibit (someone) from holding their usual post or carrying out their usual role for a particular length of time. ■ defer or delay (an action, event, or judgment). ■ Law (of a judge or court) cause (an imposed sentence) to be unenforced as long as no further offense is committed within a specified period. **2** hang (something) from somewhere. **3** (**be suspended**) (of solid particles) be dispersed throughout the bulk of a fluid.

– PHRASES **suspend disbelief** temporarily allow oneself to believe something that isn't true, esp. in order to enjoy a work of fiction. **suspend payment** (of a company) cease to meet its financial obligations as a result of insolvency or insufficient funds. [ME: from OFr. *suspendre* or L. *suspendere*, from *sub-* 'from below' + *pendere* 'hang.']

sus·pend·ed an·i·ma·tion ▶n. the temporary cessation of most vital functions without death, as in a dormant seed or a hibernating animal.

sus·pend·ers /səˈspendərz/ ▶n. a pair of straps that pass over the shoulders and fasten to the waistband of a pair of trousers or a skirt at the front and back to hold it up.

sus·pense /səˈspens/ ▶n. **1** a state or feeling of excited or anxious uncertainty about what may happen. ■ a quality in a work of fiction that arouses excited expectation or uncertainty about what may happen. **2** esp. Law the temporary cessation or suspension of something. —**sus·pense·ful** /-fəl/ adj. [ME: from OFr. *suspens* 'abeyance,' based on L. *suspensus* 'suspended, hovering, doubtful,' past part. of *suspendere*.]

sus·pen·sion /səˈspenSHən/ ▶n. **1** the action of suspending someone or something or the condition of being suspended, in particular: ■ the temporary prevention of something from continuing or being in force or effect. ■ the official prohibition of someone from holding their usual post or carrying out their usual role for a particular length of time. ■ Music a discord made by prolonging a note of a chord into the following chord. **2** the system of springs and shock absorbers by which a vehicle is cushioned from road conditions. **3** a mixture in which particles are dispersed throughout the bulk of a fluid. ■ the state of being dispersed in such a way. [ME: from Fr., or from L. *suspensio(n-)*, from the verb *suspendere*.]

sus·pen·sion bridge ▶n. a bridge in which the weight of the deck is supported by vertical cables suspended from further cables that run between towers and are anchored in abutments at each end. See illustration at BRIDGE[1].

sus·pen·sive /səˈspensiv/ ▶adj. **1** of or relating to the deferral or suspension of an event, action, or legal obligation. **2** causing suspense. —**sus·pen·sive·ly** adv. **sus·pen·sive·ness** n.

sus·pen·so·ry /səˈspensərē/ ▶adj. **1** holding and supporting an organ or part: *a suspensory ligament.* **2** of or relating to the deferral or suspension of an event, action, or legal obligation. [ME: from med. L. *suspensorius* 'used for hanging something up,' from L. *suspendere* (see SUSPEND).]

sus·pi·cion /səˈspiSHən/ ▶n. **1** a feeling or thought that something is possible, likely, or true. ■ a feeling or belief that someone is guilty of an illegal, dishonest, or unpleasant action. ■ cautious distrust. **2** a very slight trace of something.

– PHRASES **above suspicion** too obviously good or honest to be thought capable of wrongdoing. **under suspicion** thought to be guilty of wrongdoing. [ME: from Anglo-Norman Fr. *suspeciun*, from med. L. *suspectio(n-)*, from *suspicere* 'mistrust.']

sus·pi·cious /səˈspiSHəs/ ▶adj. having or showing a cautious distrust of someone or something. ■ causing one to have the idea or impression that something or someone is of questionable, dishonest, or dangerous character or condition. ■ having the belief or impression that someone is involved in an illegal or dishonest activity. —**sus·pi·cious·ly** adv. **sus·pi·cious·ness** n.

sus·pire /səˈspī(ə)r/ ▶v. [intrans.] literary breathe. —**sus·pi·ra·tion** /ˌsəspəˈrāSHən/ n. [ME: from L. *suspirare*, from *sub-* 'from below' + *spirare* 'breathe.']

Sus·que·han·na /ˌsəskwəˈhanə/ a river in the northeastern US. Its two headstreams meet in central Pennsylvania. The river then flows south to Chesapeake Bay.

sus·tain /səˈstān/ ▶v. [trans.] **1** strengthen or support physically or mentally. ■ cause to continue or be prolonged for an extended period or without interruption. ■ (of a performer) represent (a part or character) convincingly: *he sustained the role with burly resilience.* ■ bear (the weight of an object) without breaking or falling. **2** undergo or suffer (something unpleasant, esp. an injury): *he died after sustaining severe head injuries.* **3** uphold, affirm, or confirm the justice or validity of. ▶ **n.** Music an effect or facility on a keyboard or electronic instrument whereby a note can be sustained after the key is released. — **sus·tain·ed·ly** /-nidlē/ **adv.** **sus·tain·er n.** **sus·tain·ment n.** [ME: from OFr. *soustenir*, from L. *sustinere*, from *sub-* 'from below' + *tenere* 'hold.']

sus·tain·a·ble /sə'stānəbəl/ ▶ **adj.** able to be maintained at a certain rate or level. ■ Ecol. (esp. of development, exploitation, or agriculture) conserving an ecological balance by avoiding depletion of natural resources. ■ able to be upheld or defended. — **sus·tain·a·bil·i·ty** /sə,stānə'bilitē/ **n.** (Ecol.) **sus·tain·a·bly** /-blē/ **adv.** (Ecol.).

sus·tained yield ▶ **n.** a level of exploitation or crop production that is maintained by restricting the quantity harvested to avoid long-term depletion.

sus·te·nance /'səstənəns/ ▶ **n.** food and drink regarded as a source of strength; nourishment. ■ the maintaining of someone or something in life or existence: *the sustenance of democracy.* [ME: from OFr. *soustenance*, from the verb *soustenir* (see **SUSTAIN**).]

sus·ten·ta·tion /,səst(ə)n'tāSHən/ ▶ **n.** formal the support or maintenance of someone or something, esp. through the provision of money. [ME: from OFr., or from L. *sustentatio(n-)*, from *sustentare* 'uphold, sustain,' frequentative of *sustinere* (see **SUSTAIN**).]

Su·su /'so͞o,so͞o/ ▶ **n.** (pl. same) **1** a member of a people of northwestern Sierra Leone and the southern coast of Guinea. **2** the Mande language of this people. ▶ **adj.** of or relating to this people or their language. [the name in Susu.]

su·sur·rus /so͞o'sərəs/ (also **su·sur·ra·tion** /,so͞osə'rāSHən/) ▶ **n.** literary whispering, murmuring, or rustling: *the susurrus of the stream.* — **su·sur·rant** /so͞o'sərənt/ **adj.** **su·sur·rate** /'so͞osə,rāt; so͞o'sər,āt/ **v.** **su·sur·rous** /so͞o'sərəs/ **adj.** [ME: from late L. *susurratio(n-)*, from L. *susurrare* 'to murmur, hum.']

Suth·er·land[1] /'səTHərlənd/, George (1862–1942), US Supreme Court associate justice 1922–38.

Suth·er·land[2], Dame Joan (1926–), Australian opera singer. She is noted for her dramatic coloratura roles.

Sut·lej /'sətlij/ a river that rises in southwestern Tibet and flows for 900 miles (1,450 km) through India into Pakistan, where it joins the Chenab River.

su·tra /'so͞otrə/ ▶ **n.** a rule or aphorism in Sanskrit literature, or a set of these on a technical subject. See also **KAMA SUTRA.** ■ a Buddhist or Jain scripture. [from Sanskrit *sūtra* 'thread, rule,' from *siv* 'sew.']

sut·tee /,sə'tē; 'sə,tē/ (also **sa·ti** pronunc. same) ▶ **n.** (pl. **sut·tees;** also **sa·tis** /,sə'tēz; 'sə,tēz/) the former Hindu practice of a widow immolating herself on her husband's funeral pyre. ■ a widow who committed such an act. [Hindi, from Sanskrit *satī* 'faithful wife,' from *sat* 'good.']

su·ture /'so͞oCHər/ ▶ **n.** **1** a stitch or row of stitches holding together the edges of a wound or surgical incision. ■ a thread or wire used for this. ■ the action of stitching together the edges of a wound or incision. **2** a seamlike immovable junction between two bones, such as those of the skull. ■ Zool. a similar junction, such as between the sclerites of an insect's body. ■ Geol. a line of junction formed by two crustal plates that have collided. ▶ **v.** [trans.] stitch up (a wound or incision) with a suture. — **su·tur·al** /-CHərəl/ **adj.** [ME: from Fr., or from L. *sutura*, from *suere* 'sew.']

SUV ▶ **abbr.** sport utility vehicle.

Su·va /'so͞ovə/ the capital of Fiji, on the southeastern coast of the island of Viti Levu; pop. 72,000.

Su·wan·nee /'swänē; sə'wänē/ (also **Swa·nee** /'swä-/) a river in southeastern US that flows from southeastern Georgia through northern Florida to the Gulf of Mexico.

su·ze·rain /'so͞ozərən; -,rān/ ▶ **n.** a sovereign or state having some control over another state that is internally autonomous. ■ hist. a feudal overlord. — **su·ze·rain·ty** /-rəntē; -,rāntē/ **n.** [19th C.: from Fr., appar. from *sus* 'above' (from L. *su(r)sum* 'upward').]

Su·zu·ki /sə'zo͞okē/ ▶ **adj.** relating to or denoting a method of teaching the violin, typically to very young children in large groups, developed by Shin'ichi Suzuki (1898–1998), Japanese violin teacher.

Sv ▶ **abbr.** sievert(s).

s.v. ▶ **abbr.** used in textual references before a word or heading to indicate that a specified item can be found under it. [from L. *sub voce* or *sub verbo*, 'under the word or voice.']

Sval·bard /'sväl,bär(d)/ a group of islands in the Arctic Ocean about 400 miles (640 km) north of Norway.

svelte /svelt; sfelt/ ▶ **adj.** (of a person) slender and elegant. [19th C.: from Fr., from Ital. *svelto*.]

Sven·ga·li /sven'gälē; sfen-/ a musician in George du Maurier's novel *Trilby* (1894) who trains Trilby's voice and controls her stage singing hypnotically. ■ [as n.] (**a Svengali**) a person who exercises a controlling or mesmeric influence on another, esp. for a sinister purpose.

Sverd·lovsk /sverd'lôfsk; svərd-/ former name (1924–91) of **EKATERINBURG.**

Sve·ri·ge /'svaryə/ Swedish name for **SWEDEN.**

SVGA ▶ **abbr.** super video graphics array, a high-resolution standard for monitors and screens.

svgs. ▶ **abbr.** savings.

S-VHS ▶ **abbr.** super video home system, an improved version of VHS using the same tape cassettes as the standard version.

Sviz·ze·ra /'zvētsə,rä/ Italian name for **SWITZERLAND.**

SW ▶ **abbr.** ■ southwest. ■ southwestern.

Sw. (also **Swed**) ▶ **abbr.** ■ Sweden. ■ Swedish.

sw. ▶ **abbr.** switch.

swab /swäb/ ▶ **n.** **1** an absorbent pad or piece of material used in surgery and medicine for cleaning wounds, applying medication, or taking specimens. ■ a specimen of a secretion taken with a swab for examination. ■ a piece of absorbent material used for cleaning the bore of a firearm. **2** a mop or other absorbent device for cleaning or mopping up a floor or other surface. **3** another term for **SWABBIE.** ▶ **v.** (**swabbed, swab·bing**) [trans.] clean (a wound or surface) with a swab: *swabbing down the decks.* ■ [with adverbial] absorb or clear (moisture) with a swab: *the blood was swabbed away.* [17th C.: back-form. from *swabber* 'sailor detailed to swab decks,' from early mod. Du. *zwabber*, from a Gmc. base meaning 'splash' or 'sway.']

swab·bie /'swäbē/ (also **swab·by**) ▶ **n.** (pl. **-bies**) Nautical slang a member of the navy, typically one of low rank.

Swa·bi·a /'swābēə/ a former duchy of medieval Germany. German name **SCHWABEN.** — **Swa·bi·an adj. & n.**

swacked /swakt/ ▶ **adj.** informal drunk. [1930s: past part. of Scots *swack* 'fling, strike heavily.']

swad·dle /'swädl/ ▶ **v.** [trans.] wrap (someone, esp. a baby) in garments or cloth: *she swaddled the baby tightly.* [ME: frequentative of **SWATHE.**]

swad·dling clothes /'swädliNG/ ▶ **plural n.** narrow bands of cloth formerly wrapped around a newborn child to restrain its movements and quiet it.

swag /swag/ ▶ **n.** **1** an ornamental festoon of flowers, fruit, and greenery: *ribbon-tied swags of flowers.* ■ a carved or painted representation of such a festoon: *fine plaster swags.* ■ a curtain or piece of fabric fastened so as to hang in a drooping curve. **2** informal money or goods taken by a thief or burglar. ■ goods given away for promotional purposes: *my bag was full to bursting with free swag.* **3** Austral./NZ a traveler's or miner's bundle of personal belongings. ▶ **v.** (**swagged, swag·ging**) [trans.] **1** arrange in or decorate with a swag or swags of fabric. **2** Austral./NZ travel with one's personal belongings in a bundle: *swagging it in Queensland.* **3** [intrans.] esp. literary hang heavily. ■ sway from side to side. [ME: prob. of Scand. origin.]

swage /swāj/ ▶ **n.** **1** a shaped tool or die for giving a desired form to metal by hammering or pressure. **2** a groove, ridge, or other molding on an object. ▶ **v.** [trans.] shape (metal) using a swage, esp. in order to reduce its cross section. ■ [with adverbial] join (metal pieces) together by this process. [ME (sense 2): from OFr. *souage* 'decorative groove,' of unknown origin.]

swag·ger /'swagər/ ▶ **v.** [no obj., with adverbial of direction] walk or behave in a very confident and typically arrogant or aggressive way: *he swaggered along the corridor.* ▶ **n.** [in sing.] a very confident and typically arrogant or aggressive gait or manner. ▶ **adj.** [attrib.] denoting a coat or jacket cut with a loose flare from the shoulders. — **swag·ger·er** /'swagərər/ **n.** **swag·ger·ing·ly** /'swagəriNGlē/ **adv.** [16th C.: appar. a frequentative of the verb **SWAG.**]

swag·ger stick ▶ **n.** a short cane carried by a military officer.

Swa·hi·li /swä'hēlē/ ▶ **n.** (pl. same) **1** a Bantu language widely used as a lingua franca in East Africa and having official status in several countries. Also called **KISWAHILI.** **2** a member of a people of Zanzibar and nearby coastal regions, descendants of the original speakers of Swahili. ▶ **adj.** of or relating to this language or to the people who are its native speakers. [from Arab. *sawāḥil*, pl. of *sāḥil* 'coast.']

swain /swān/ ▶ **n.** archaic a country youth. ■ literary a young lover or suitor. [OE, from ON *sveinn* 'lad.']

Swain·son's hawk /'swānsənz/ ▶ **n.** a dark-colored, narrow-winged buteo (*Buteo swainsoni*) of western North America. [19th C.: for William *Swainson* (1789–1855), English naturalist.]

SWAK ▶ **abbr.** sealed with a kiss (written on the flap of an envelope).

swale /swāl/ ▶ **n.** a low or hollow place, esp. a marshy depression between ridges. [16th C.: British, of unknown origin.]

swal·low[1] /'swälō/ ▶ **v.** [trans.] cause or allow (something, esp. food or drink) to pass down the throat. ■ [intrans.] perform the muscular movement of the esophagus required to do this, esp. through fear or nervousness. ■ put up with or meekly accept (something insulting or unwelcome). ■ believe unquestioningly (a lie or unlikely assertion). ■ resist expressing (a feeling) or uttering (words). ■ take in and cause to disappear; engulf. ■ completely use up (money or resources). ▶ **n.** an act of swallowing something, esp. food or drink. ■ an amount of something swallowed in one action. — **swal·low·a·ble adj.** **swal·low·er n.** [OE *swelgan*, of Gmc. origin; rel. to Du. *zwelgen* and Ger. *schwelgen*.]

swal·low[2] ▶ **n.** a migratory swift-flying songbird (*Hirundo* and other genera, family Hirundinidae) with a forked tail and long pointed wings, feeding on insects in flight. Its numerous species include the widespread **barn swallow** (*H. rustica*). [OE *swealwe*, of Gmc. origin; rel. to Du. *zwaluw* and Ger. *Schwalbe*.]

swal·low·tail /'swälō,tāl/ ▶ **n.** (also **swallowtail butterfly**) a large brightly colored butterfly (family Papilionidae) with taillike projections (suggestive of a swallow's tail) on the hind wings. Many genera and species include the **eastern tiger swallowtail** (*Papilio glaucus*) of eastern North America.

barn swallow

eastern tiger swallowtail

swal·low·wort /ˈswälōwərt; -ˌwôrt/ ▶ **n.** **1** a plant (*Cynanchum* and other genera) of the milkweed family, the follicles of which suggest a swallow with outstretched wings, often becoming a weed. **2** esp. Brit. the greater celandine, formerly believed to be used by swallows to restore their sight.

swam /swam/ past of SWIM.

swa·mi /ˈswämē/ ▶ **n.** (pl. **-mis**) a Hindu male religious teacher: [as title] *Swami Satchidananda.* [from Hindi *swāmī* 'master, prince,' from Sanskrit *svāmin.*]

swamp /swämp/ ▶ **n.** an area of low-lying, uncultivated ground where water collects; a bog or marsh. ■ used to emphasize the degree to which a piece of ground is waterlogged. ▶ **v.** [trans.] overwhelm or flood with water. ■ fig. overwhelm with an excessive amount of something; inundate. ■ [intrans.] (of a boat) become overwhelmed with water and sink. — **swamp·y** **adj.** [17th C.: prob. ult. from a Gmc. base meaning 'sponge' or 'fungus.']

swamp·er /ˈswämpər/ ▶ **n.** informal, dated **1** a laborer, esp. one employed as a general assistant to a riverboat captain. ■ a worker who trims felled trees and clears a road for lumberers in a forest. **2** a native or inhabitant of a swampy region.

swamp fe·ver ▶ **n.** **1** a contagious viral disease of horses that causes anemia and emaciation and is usually fatal. **2** dated malaria.

Swamp Fox see MARION.

swamp gas ▶ **n.** another term for MARSH GAS.

swamp·land /ˈswämpˌland/ ▶ **n.** (also **swamplands**) land consisting of swamps.

swan /swän/ ▶ **n.** a large waterbird (genera *Cygnus* and *Coscoroba*, family Anatidae) with a long flexible neck, short legs, webbed feet, a broad bill, and typically all-white plumage. See illustration at MUTE SWAN. ▶ **v.** (**swanned, swan·ning**) [intrans.] informal move about or go somewhere in a casual, relaxed way, typically perceived as irresponsible or ostentatious by others. — **swan·like** /-ˌlīk/ **adj.** [OE, of Gmc. origin; rel. to Du. *zwaan* and Ger. *Schwan.*]

swan dive ▶ **n.** a dive performed with one's arms outspread until close to the water. ▶ **v.** [intrans.] (**swan-dive**) perform a swan drive.

swank /swaNGk/ informal ▶ **v.** [intrans.] display one's wealth, knowledge, or achievements in a way that is intended to impress others. ▶ **n.** behavior, talk, or display intended to impress others. ▶ **adj.** another term for SWANKY. [19th C.: of unknown origin.]

swank·y /ˈswaNGkē/ ▶ **adj.** (**swank·i·er, swank·i·est**) informal stylishly luxurious and expensive. ■ using one's wealth, knowledge, or achievements to try to impress others. — **swank·i·ly** /-kəlē/ **adv.** **swank·i·ness** **n.**

swan neck ▶ **n.** a curved structure shaped like a swan's neck: [as adj.] *a small swan-neck dispenser.* ■ another term for GOOSENECK. — **swan-necked** **adj.**

swan·ner·y /ˈswänərē/ ▶ **n.** (pl. **-ner·ies**) a place set aside for swans to breed.

swans·down /ˈswänzˌdoun/ (also **swan's down**) ▶ **n.** **1** the fine down of a swan, used for trimmings and powder puffs. **2** a thick cotton fabric with a soft nap on one side, used esp. for baby clothes. ■ a soft, thick fabric made from wool mixed with a little silk or cotton.

Swan·sea /ˈswänzē/ a city in southern Wales; pop. 182,000. Welsh name ABERTAWE.

swan song ▶ **n.** a person's final public performance or professional activity before retirement. [19th C.: from the tradition that a dying swan sings a beautiful song.]

swap /swäp/ (also **swop**) ▶ **v.** (**swapped, swap·ping**) [trans.] take part in an exchange of. ■ give (one thing) and receive something else in exchange. ■ substitute (one thing) for another. ▶ **n.** an act of exchanging one thing for another. ■ a thing that has been or may be given in exchange for something else. ■ Finance an exchange of liabilities between two borrowers, either so that each acquires access to funds in a currency they need or so that a fixed interest rate is exchanged for a floating rate. — **swap·pa·ble** **adj.** **swap·per** **n.** [ME: prob. imitative of a resounding blow.]

swap·file /ˈswäpˌfīl/ ▶ **n.** Comput. a file on a hard disk used to provide space for programs that have been transferred from the processor's memory.

swap meet ▶ **n.** a gathering at which enthusiasts or collectors trade or exchange items of common interest. ■ a flea market.

SWAPO /ˈswäpō/ (also **Swapo**) ▶ **abbr.** South West Africa People's Organization.

swap shop ▶ **n.** informal an agency that provides a communication channel for people with articles to exchange or trade. ■ an event to which people are invited to bring articles for exchange or trade.

sward /swôrd/ ▶ **n.** an expanse of short grass. ■ Farming the upper layer of soil, esp. when covered with grass. — **sward·ed** **adj.** [OE *sweard* 'skin.']

swarm /swôrm/ ▶ **n.** a large or dense group of insects, esp. flying ones. ■ a large number of honeybees that leave a hive en masse with a newly fertilized queen in order to establish a new colony. ■ (**a swarm/swarms of**) a large number of people or things. ■ a series of similar-sized earthquakes occurring together, typically near a volcano. ■ Astron. a large number of minor celestial objects occurring together in space, esp. a dense shower of meteors. ▶ **v.** **1** [intrans.] (of insects) move in or form a swarm: [as adj.] (**swarming**) *swarming locusts.* ■ (of honeybees, ants, or termites) issue from the nest in large numbers with a newly fertilized queen in order to found new colonies. **2** [no obj., with adverbial] move somewhere in large numbers: *protesters were swarming into the building.* ■ (**swarm with**) (of a place) be crowded or overrun with (moving people or things).

– PHRASAL VERBS **swarm up** climb (something) rapidly by gripping it with one's hands and feet, alternately hauling and pushing oneself upward: [OE *swearm* (n.), of Gmc. origin; rel. to Ger. *Schwarm.*]

swarm·er /ˈswôrmər/ (also **swarm·er cell**) ▶ **n.** Biol. another term for ZOOSPORE.

swarth·y /ˈswôrT͟Hē/ ▶ **adj.** (**swarth·i·er, swarth·i·est**) dark-skinned. — **swarth·i·ly** /ˈswôrT͟Hәlē/ **adv.** **swarth·i·ness** **n.** [16th C.: alt. of obs. *swarty*, from OE.]

swash[1] /swôsн; swäsн/ ▶ **v.** [intrans.] **1** (of water or an object in water) move with a splashing sound. **2** archaic (of a person) flamboyantly swagger about or wield a sword. ▶ **n.** the rush of seawater up the beach after the breaking of a wave. [16th C.: imitative.]

swash[2] ▶ **adj.** Print. denoting an ornamental written or printed character, typically a capital letter. [17th C.: of unknown origin.]

swash·buck·le /ˈswôsнˌbəkəl; ˈswäsн-/ ▶ **v.** [intrans.] [usu. as adj.] (**swashbuckling**) engage in daring and romantic adventures with ostentatious bravado or flamboyance: *a crew of swashbuckling buccaneers.* [19th C.: back-form. from SWASHBUCKLER.]

swash·buck·ler /ˈswôsнˌbəklər; ˈswäsн-/ ▶ **n.** a swashbuckling person. [16th C.: from SWASH[1] + BUCKLER.]

swas·ti·ka /ˈswästikə/ ▶ **n.** an ancient symbol in the form of an equal-armed cross with each arm continued at a right angle, used (in clockwise form) as the emblem of the German Nazi Party. [19th C.: from Sanskrit *svastika*, from *svasti* 'well-being,' from *su* 'good' + *asti* 'being.']

swastika

swat /swät/ ▶ **v.** (**swat·ted, swat·ting**) [trans.] hit or crush (something, esp. an insect) with a sharp blow from a flat object. ■ hit (someone) with a sharp blow. ▶ **n.** such a sharp blow: *a sideways swat.* [17th C.: north. Engl. dial. and US var. of SQUAT.]

swatch /swäcн/ ▶ **n.** a sample, esp. of fabric. ■ a collection of such samples, esp. in the form of a book. ■ a patch or area of a material or surface. [16th C.: of unknown origin.]

swath /swätн; swôтн/ (also **swathe** /swäT͟H; swôT͟H; swāT͟H/) ▶ **n.** (pl. **swaths** /swätнs; swôтнs/ or **swathes** /swäT͟Hz/) **1** a row or line of grass, grain, or other crop as it lies when mown or reaped. ■ a strip left clear by the passage of a mowing machine or scythe. **2** a broad strip or area of something.

– PHRASES **cut a swath through** pass through (something) causing great damage, destruction, or change. **cut a wide swath** attract a great deal of attention by trying to impress others. [OE *swæth, swathu* 'track, trace,' of West Gmc. origin.]

swathe /swäT͟H; swāT͟H/ ▶ **v.** [trans.] (usu. **be swathed in**) wrap in several layers of fabric. ▶ **n.** a piece or strip of material in which something is wrapped. [OE *swath-* (n.), *swathian* (v.); cf. SWADDLE.]

sway /swā/ ▶ **v.** move or cause to move slowly or rhythmically backward and forward or from side to side. ■ [trans.] control or influence (a person or course of action). ■ literary rule; govern. ▶ **n.** **1** a rhythmical movement from side to side. **2** rule; control: *the area under Russia's sway.*

– PHRASES **hold sway** have great power or influence over a particular person, place, or domain. [ME: corresponding in sense to Low Ger. *swājen* 'be blown to and fro' and Du. *zwaaien* 'swing, walk totteringly.']

sway·back /ˈswāˌbak/ ▶ **n.** an abnormally hollowed back, esp. in a horse; lordosis. — **sway-backed** **adj.**

Swayne /swān/, Noah Haynes (1804–84), US Supreme Court associate justice 1862–81.

Swa·zi /ˈswäzē/ ▶ **n.** (pl. same or **-zis**) **1** a member of a people inhabiting Swaziland and parts of eastern Transvaal. ■ a native or national of Swaziland. **2** the Nguni language of this people, an official language in Swaziland and South Africa. ▶**adj.** of or relating to Swaziland, the Swazis, or their language. [after *Mswati*, a 19th-cent. king of the Swazis.]

Swa·zi·land /ˈswäzēˌland/ a small landlocked kingdom in southern Africa. *See box.*

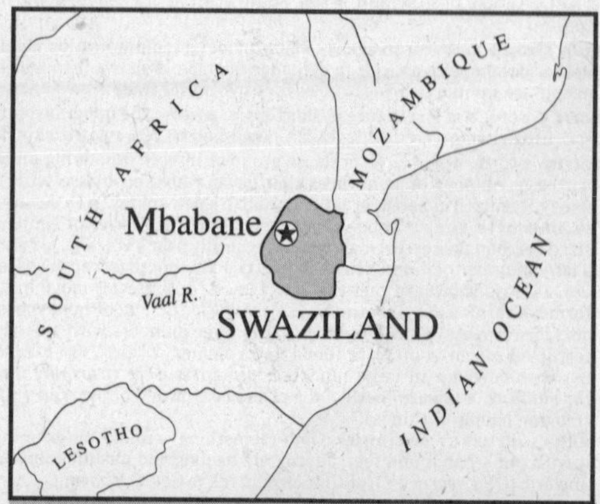

Swaziland

Official name: Kingdom of Swaziland
Location: southern Africa, bounded by South Africa and Mozambique
Area: 6,700 square miles (17,400 sq km)
Population: 1,169,000
Capital: Mbabane
Languages: English and Swazi (both official)
Currency: lilangeni

SWbS ▶**abbr.** southwest by south.

SWbW ▶**abbr.** southwest by west.

swear /swe(ə)r/ ▶**v.** (past **swore** /swôr/; past part. **sworn** /swôrn/) **1** [reporting verb] make a solemn statement or promise undertaking to do something or affirming that something is the case: [with infin.] *he swore to obey the rules.* ■ [trans.] take (an oath). ■ [trans.] take a solemn oath as to the truth of (a statement). ■ [trans.] (**swear someone in**) admit someone to a particular office or position by directing them to take a formal oath. ■ [trans.] make (someone) promise to observe a certain course of action: *I've been sworn to secrecy.* ■ [no obj., usu. with negative] (**swear to**) express one's assurance that something is the case. ■ [intrans.] (**swear off**) informal promise to abstain from. ■ [intrans.] (**swear by**) informal have or express great confidence in the use, value, or effectiveness of: *Iris swears by her yoga.* **2** [intrans.] use offensive language, esp. as an expression of anger.
– PHRASES **swear up and down** informal affirm something emphatically.
– PHRASAL VERBS **swear something out** Law obtain the issue of (a warrant for arrest) by making a charge on oath. — **swear·er** n. [OE *swerian*, of Gmc. origin.]

swear word ▶**n.** an offensive word, used esp. as an expression of anger.

sweat /swet/ ▶**n.** **1** moisture exuded through the pores of the skin, typically in profuse quantities as a reaction to heat, physical exertion, fever, or fear. ■ an instance of exuding moisture in this way over a period of time. ■ informal a state of flustered anxiety or distress. ■ informal hard work; effort. **2** (**sweats**) informal term for SWEATSUIT or SWEATPANTS. ■ [as adj.] denoting loose casual garments made of thick, fleecy cotton: *sweat tops and bottoms.* ▶**v.** (past **sweat·ed** or **sweat**) **1** [intrans.] exude sweat: *he was sweating profusely.* ■ [trans.] (**sweat something out/off**) get rid of (something) from the body by exuding sweat. ■ [trans.] cause (a person or animal) to exude sweat by exercise or exertion. ■ (of food or an object) ooze or exude beads of moisture onto its surface. ■ (of a person) exert a great deal of strenuous effort: *I've sweated over this for six months.* ■ (of a person) be or remain in a state of extreme anxiety, typically for a prolonged period. ■ [trans.] informal worry about (something): *sweat the details.* **2** [trans.] heat (chopped vegetables) slowly in a pan with a small amount of fat, so that they cook in their own juices. ■ [intrans.] (of chopped vegetables) be cooked in this way: *let the chopped onion sweat gently for five minutes.* **3** [with obj. and adverbial] subject (metal) to surface melting, esp. to fasten or join by solder without a soldering iron.
– PHRASES **break a sweat** informal exert oneself physically. **by the sweat of one's brow** by one's own hard work, typically manual labor. **don't sweat it** used to urge someone not to worry. **no sweat** informal used to convey that one perceives no difficulty or problem with something. **sweat blood** informal make an extraordinarily strenuous effort to do something. ■ be extremely anxious. **sweat buckets** informal sweat profusely. **sweat bullets** informal be extremely anxious or nervous. **sweat it out** informal endure an unpleasant experience, typically one involving physical exertion in great heat. ■ wait in a state of extreme anxiety for something to happen or be resolved. **sweat the small stuff** worry about trivial things. [OE *swāt* (n.), *swǣtan* (v.), of Gmc. origin.]

sweat·band /ˈswetˌband/ ▶**n.** a band of absorbent material worn around the head or wrist to soak up sweat, esp. by participants in sports. ■ a band of absorbent material lining a hat.

sweat eq·ui·ty ▶**n.** informal an interest or increased value in a property earned from labor toward upkeep or restoration.

sweat·er /ˈswetər/ ▶**n.** **1** a knitted garment, typically with long sleeves, worn over the upper body. **2** dated an employer who works employees hard in poor conditions for low pay.

sweat·er set ▶**n.** another term for TWINSET.

sweat gland ▶**n.** a small gland that secretes sweat, situated in the dermis of the skin. Such glands are found over most of the body and have a simple coiled tubular structure.

sweat lodge ▶**n.** a hut, typically dome-shaped and made with natural materials, used by North American Indians for ritual steam baths as a means of purification.

sweat·pants /ˈswetˌpants/ ▶**plural n.** loose, warm trousers with an elasticized or drawstring waist, worn when exercising or as leisurewear.

sweat·shirt /ˈswetˌsʜərt/ ▶**n.** a loose, heavy shirt, typically made of cotton, worn when exercising or as leisurewear.

sweat·shop /ˈswetˌsʜäp/ ▶**n.** a factory or workshop, esp. in the clothing industry, where manual workers are employed at very low wages for long hours and under poor conditions.

sweat·suit /ˈswetˌso͞ot/ ▶**n.** a suit consisting of a sweatshirt and sweatpants, worn when exercising or as leisurewear.

sweat·y /ˈswetē/ ▶**adj.** (**sweat·i·er**, **sweat·i·est**) exuding, soaked in, or inducing sweat: *my feet got so sweaty.* — **sweat·i·ly** /ˈswetl-ē/ **adv.** **sweat·i·ness** **n.**

Swede /swēd/ ▶**n.** a native or national of Sweden, or a person of Swedish descent. [from Mid. Low Ger. and MDu. *Swēde*, prob. from ON *Svíthjóth*, from *Svíar* 'Swedes' + *thjóth* 'people.']

Swe·den /ˈswēdn/ a country in northern Europe, on the Scandinavian peninsula. *See box.* Swedish name SVERIGE.

Sweden

Official name: Kingdom of Sweden
Location: northern Europe, occupying the eastern part of the Scandinavian peninsula
Area: 173,800 square miles (450,000 sq km)
Population: 8,986,000
Capital: Stockholm
Language: Swedish
Currency: Swedish krona

Swe·den·borg /ˈswēdnˌbôrg/, Emanuel (1688–1772), Swedish scientist, philosopher, and mystic. His spiritual beliefs blended Christianity with pantheism and theosophy. — **Swe·den·bor·gi·an** /ˌswēdənˈbôrgēən/ **adj. & n.**

Swed·ish /ˈswēdisн/ ▶ **adj.** of or relating to Sweden, its people, or their language. ▶ **n.** the North Germanic language of Sweden, also spoken in parts of Finland.

Swed·ish mas·sage ▶ **n.** a popular general-purpose system of massage, devised in Sweden.

sweep /swēp/ ▶ **v.** (past **swept** /swept/) **1** [trans.] clean (an area) by brushing away dirt or litter. ■ [with obj. and adverbial of direction] move or remove (dirt or litter) in such a way. ■ [with obj. and adverbial of direction] move or push (someone or something) with great force. ■ [with obj. and adverbial of direction] brush (hair) back from one's face or upward. ■ search (an area) for something. ■ examine (a place or thing) for electronic listening devices. ■ cover (an entire area) with a gun. **2** [no obj., with adverbial of direction] move swiftly and smoothly: fig. *a wave of sympathy swept over him.* ■ [with obj. and adverbial of direction] cause to move swiftly and smoothly. ■ (of a person) move in a confident and stately manner. ■ (of a geographical or natural feature) extend continuously in a particular direction, esp. in a curve. ■ [trans.] look swiftly over. ■ affect (an area or place) swiftly and widely: *violence swept the country.* ■ [trans.] win all the games in (a series); take each of the winning or main places in (a contest or event). ▶ **n. 1** an act of sweeping something with a brush. ■ short for CHIMNEY SWEEP. **2** a long, swift, curving movement. ■ a comprehensive search or survey of a place or area. ■ Electron. the movement of a beam across the screen of a cathode-ray tube. ■ (often **sweeps**) a survey of the ratings of broadcast stations, carried out at regular intervals to determine advertising rates. **3** a long, typically curved stretch of road, river, country, etc.: *a sweep of country perhaps a hundred miles across.* ■ a curved part of a drive in front of a building. ■ fig. the range or scope of something. **4** informal a sweepstake. **5** an instance of winning every event, award, or place in a contest: *a World Series sweep.* **6** a long heavy oar used to row a barge or other vessel. **7** a sail of a windmill. **8** a long pole mounted as a lever for raising buckets from a well.
– PHRASES **sweep the board** (or **boards**) win every event or prize in a contest. **sweep something under the rug** (or **carpet**) conceal or ignore a problem or difficulty in the hope that it will be forgotten.
– PHRASAL VERBS **sweep something away** (or **aside**) remove, dispel, or abolish something in a swift and sudden way. [OE *swāpan* (v.), of Gmc. origin; rel. to Ger. *schweifen* 'sweep in a curve.']

sweep·back /ˈswēpˌbak/ ▶ **n.** the angle at which an aircraft's wing is set back from a right angle to the body.

sweep·er /ˈswēpər/ ▶ **n. 1** a person or device that cleans a floor or road by sweeping. **2** a small nocturnal shoaling fish (family Pempheridae) of reefs and coastal waters, occurring chiefly in the tropical Indo-Pacific.

sweep·ing /ˈswēpiNG/ ▶ **adj.** wide in range or effect. ■ extending or performed in a long, continuous curve. ■ (of a statement) taking no account of particular cases or exceptions; too general: *a sweeping assertion.* ▶ **n.** (**sweepings**) dirt or refuse collected by sweeping. — **sweep·ing·ly adv. sweep·ing·ness n.**

sweep·stake /ˈswēpˌstāk/ ▶ **n.** (also **sweepstakes**) a form of gambling, esp. on horse races, in which all the stakes are divided among the winners. ■ a race on which money is bet in this way. ■ a prize or prizes won in a sweepstake.

sweet /swēt/ ▶ **adj. 1** having the pleasant taste characteristic of sugar or honey; not salty, sour, or bitter. ■ (of sausage) mild rather than hot. ■ (of air, water, or food) fresh, pure, and untainted. ■ [often in comb.] smelling pleasant like flowers or perfume; fragrant: *sweet-smelling flowers.* **2** pleasing in general; delightful: *the sweet life.* ■ highly satisfying or gratifying. ■ [often as exclam.] informal used in expressions of assent or approval. ■ working, moving, or done smoothly or easily. ■ (of sound) melodious or harmonious. ■ denoting music, esp. jazz, played at a steady tempo without improvisation. **3** (of a person or action) pleasant and kind or thoughtful. ■ (esp. of a person or animal) charming and endearing. ■ [predic.] (**sweet on**) informal dated infatuated or in love with. ■ dear; beloved. **4** used for emphasis in various phrases and exclamations: *What had happened? Sweet nothing.* ■ (**one's own sweet ——**) used to emphasize the unpredictable individuality of someone's actions. ▶ **n. 1** used as an affectionate form of address to a person one is very fond of: *hello, my sweet.* **2** (**the sweet**) archaic literary the sweet part or element of something: *first the bitter, now the sweet.* ■ (**sweets**) the pleasures or delights found in something.
– PHRASES **sweet dreams** used to express good wishes to a person going to bed. — **sweet·ish adj. sweet·ly adv.** [OE *swēte*, of Gmc. origin; from an Indo-Eur. root shared by L. *suavis* and Gk. *hēdus*.]

sweet-and-sour ▶ **adj.** [attrib.] (esp. of Chinese-style food) cooked in a sauce containing sugar and either vinegar or lemon.

sweet birch ▶ **n.** a North American birch (*Betula lenta*), esp. of Appalachian forests, with brown or black bark. Its broken twigs smell of wintergreen. The leaves and sap yield oil of wintergreen. Also called BLACK BIRCH.

sweet·bread /ˈswētˌbred/ ▶ **n.** the thymus gland (or, rarely, the pancreas) of an animal, esp. as used for food.

sweet·bri·er /ˈswētˌbrīər/ (also **sweet·bri·ar**) ▶ **n.** a Eurasian wild rose (*Rosa eleganteria*) with fragrant leaves and flowers.

sweet cher·ry ▶ **n.** another term for MAZZARD.

sweet chest·nut ▶ **n.** see CHESTNUT.

sweet clov·er ▶ **n.** another term for MELILOT.

sweet corn ▶ **n.** corn of a variety with kernels that have a high sugar content. ■ the kernels of this plant eaten as a vegetable.

sweet·en /ˈswētn/ ▶ **v.** make or become sweet or sweeter, esp. in taste. ■ [trans.] make more agreeable or acceptable. ■ [trans.] informal induce (someone) to be well disposed or helpful to oneself: *I'm sweetening him up.*
– PHRASES **sweeten the pot** add to the total sum of bets made in poker. ■ add an inducement, typically in the form of money or a concession.

sweet·en·er /ˈswētn-ər; ˈswētnər/ ▶ **n.** a substance used to sweeten food or drink, esp. one other than sugar. ■ informal, an inducement, typically in the form of money or a concession.

sweet fen·nel ▶ **n.** see FENNEL.

sweet flag (also **sweet-flag**) ▶ **n.** an Old World waterside plant (*Acorus calamus*) of the arum family, with leaves that resemble those of the iris. It is used medicinally and as a flavoring. Also called CALAMUS.

sweet gale ▶ **n.** a deciduous shrub (*Myrica gale*, family Myricaceae) of boggy places, with short upright catkins and aromatic gray-green leaves. It has insecticidal properties. [17th C.: *gale* from OE *gagel, gagelle*, of Gmc. origin; rel. to Du. *gagel*, Ger. *Gagel*.]

sweet·grass /ˈswētˌgras/ ▶ **n.** any of a number of grasses (*Glyceria, Hierochloe*, and other genera) that possess a sweet flavor, making them attractive to livestock, or a sweet smell, resulting in their former use as herbs for strewing or burning.

sweet gum ▶ **n.** the North American liquidambar (*Liquidambar styraciflua*), which yields a balsam and decorative heartwood that is marketed as satin walnut.

sweet·heart /ˈswētˌhärt/ ▶ **n.** used as a term of endearment or affectionate form of address. ■ a person that one is in love with. ■ a particularly lovable or pleasing person or thing. ■ [as adj.] informal denoting an arrangement reached privately by two sides, esp. an employer and a trade union, in their own interests: *a sweetheart agreement.*

sweet·heart neck·line ▶ **n.** a neckline on a dress or blouse that is low at the front and shaped like the top of a stylized heart.

sweet·heart rose ▶ **n.** a rose with small pink, white, or yellow flowers that are particularly attractive as buds.

sweet·ie /ˈswētē/ informal ▶ **n. 1** (also **sweet·ie pie**) used as a term of endearment (esp. as a form of address). **2** a green-skinned grapefruit of a variety noted for its sweet taste.

sweet·ing /ˈswētiNG/ ▶ **n.** an apple of a sweet-flavored variety.

sweet·lips /ˈswētˌlips/ (also **sweet·lip**) ▶ **n.** (pl. same) a patterned grunt (*Plectorhynchus* and other genera, family Pomadasyidae) that changes its color and markings with age, occurring in the Indo-Pacific and sometimes kept in aquariums.

sweet·meat /ˈswētˌmēt/ ▶ **n.** archaic an item of confectionery or sweet food.

sweet·ness /ˈswētnis/ ▶ **n.** the quality of being sweet. ■ used as an affectionate form of address, though often ironically: *I've just got to go, sweetness.*
– PHRASES **sweetness and light** social or political harmony. ■ a reasonable and peaceable person.

sweet pea ▶ **n.** a climbing plant (genus *Lathyrus*) of the pea family, widely cultivated for its colorful fragrant flowers.

sweet pep·per ▶ **n.** a large green, yellow, orange, or red variety of capsicum (*Capsicum annuum* var. *annuum*) that has a mild or sweet flavor and is often eaten raw.

sweet po·ta·to ▶ **n. 1** an edible tropical tuber with pinkish orange, slightly sweet flesh. **2** the widely cultivated Central American climbing plant (*Ipomoea batatas*) of the morning glory family that yields this tuber. **3** informal another term for OCARINA.

sweet·sop /ˈswētˌsäp/ ▶ **n. 1** a round or heart-shaped custard apple that has a green scaly rind and a sweet pulp. Also called SUGAR APPLE. **2** the tropical American evergreen shrub (*Annona squamosa*) that yields this fruit.

sweet spot ▶ **n.** informal the point or area on a bat, club, or racket at which it makes most effective contact with the ball.

sweet talk informal ▶ **v.** (**sweet-talk**) [trans.] insincerely praise (someone) in order to persuade them to do something. ▶ **n.** insincere praise used to persuade someone to do something.

sweet tooth ▶ **n.** [usu. in sing.] (pl. **sweet tooths**) a great liking for sweet-tasting foods. — **sweet-toothed adj.**

sweet vi·o·let ▶ **n.** a sweet-scented Old World violet (*Viola odorata*) with heart-shaped leaves, used in perfumery and as a flavoring.

sweet wil·liam (also **sweet Wil·liam**) ▶ **n.** a fragrant garden plant (*Dianthus barbatus*) of the pink family, with flattened clusters of vivid red, pink, or white flowers.

swell /swel/ ▶ **v.** (past part. **swol·len** /ˈswōlən/ or **swelled**) [intrans.] (esp. of a part of the body) become larger or rounder in size, typically as a result of an accumulation of fluid. ■ become or make greater in intensity, number, amount, or volume. ■ be intensely affected or filled with a particular emotion. ▶ **n. 1** [in sing.] a full or gently rounded shape or form. ■ a gradual increase in sound, amount, or intensity. ■ a welling up of a feeling. **2** [usu. in sing.] a slow, regular movement of the sea in rolling waves that do not break: *there was a heavy swell.* **3** a mechanism for producing a crescendo or diminuendo in an organ or harmonium. **4** informal, dated a person of wealth or high social position, typically one perceived as fashionable or stylish. ▶ **adj.** informal, dated excellent; very good. ▶ **adv.** informal, dated excellently; very well.

– PHRASES **someone's head swells** someone becomes conceited. [OE *swellan* (v.), of Gmc. origin; rel. to Ger. *schwellen*.]

swell box ▶ **n.** a part of a large organ in which some of the pipes are enclosed, with a movable shutter for controlling the sound level.

swell·ing /'sweliNG/ ▶ **n.** an abnormal enlargement of a part of the body, typically as a result of an accumulation of fluid. ■ a natural rounded protuberance.

swel·ter /'sweltər/ ▶ **v.** [intrans.] (of a person or the atmosphere at a particular time or place) be uncomfortably hot. ▶ **n.** [in sing.] an uncomfortably hot atmosphere. — **swel·ter·ing·ly adv.** [ME: from the base of dial. *swelt* 'perish,' of Gmc. origin.]

swept /swept/ past and past participle of SWEEP.

swept-back ▶ **adj.** [attrib.] (of an aircraft wing) positioned to point somewhat backward.

swept-up ▶ **adj.** another term for UPSWEPT.

swept-wing ▶ **adj.** [attrib.] (of an aircraft) having swept-back wings.

swerve /swərv/ ▶ **v.** change or cause to change direction abruptly. ▶ **n.** an abrupt change of direction. — **swerv·er n.** [OE *sweorfan* 'depart, leave, turn aside,' of Gmc. origin; rel. to MDu. *swerven* 'to stray.']

Sweyn I /sven; svān/ (also **Sven** /sven/) (died 1014), king of Denmark *c.*985–1014; known as **Sweyn Forkbeard**. In 1013, Sweyn became king of England by conquest but died five weeks later.

swid·den /'swidn/ ▶ **n.** an area of land cleared for cultivation by slashing and burning vegetation. ■ the method of clearing land in this way. [18th C.: var. of dial. *swithen* 'to burn.']

Swift /swift/, Jonathan (1667–1745), Irish satirist; known as **Dean Swift**. He wrote *Gulliver's Travels* (1726).

swift /swift/ ▶ **adj.** happening quickly or promptly. ■ moving or capable of moving at high speed. ▶ **adv.** literary except in combination swiftly. ▶ **n. 1** a swift-flying insectivorous bird (family Apodidae) with long slender wings and a superficial resemblance to a swallow, spending most of its life on the wing. See illustration at CHIMNEY SWIFT. **2** (also **swift moth**) a moth (*Hepialus* and other genera, family Hepialidae), typically yellow-brown in color, with fast darting flight. The eggs are scattered in flight and the larvae live underground feeding on roots, where they can be a serious pest. **3** a light, adjustable reel for holding a skein of silk or wool. — **swift·ly adv. swift·ness n.** [OE (as an adj.), from the Gmc. base of OE *swīfan* 'move in a course, sweep.']

swift·let /'swif(t)lit/ ▶ **n.** a small swift (genera *Aerodramus* and *Collocalia*) found in South Asia and Australasia.

swig /swig/ informal ▶ **v.** (**swigged** /swigd/, **swig·ging**) [trans.] drink in large gulps: *Dave swigged the wine.* ▶ **n.** a large draft of drink: *he took a swig of tea.* — **swig·ger n.** [16th C.: of unknown origin.]

swill /swil/ ▶ **v. 1** [trans.] Brit. wash or rinse out (an area or container) by pouring large amounts of water or other liquid over or into it: *I swilled out the mug.* ■ cause (liquid) to swirl around in a container or cavity. ■ [no obj., with adverbial] (of a liquid) move or splash about over a surface. **2** [trans.] drink (something) greedily or in large quantities: [as adj.] (**swilling**) *his beer-swilling pals.* ■ accompany (food) with large quantities of drink. ▶ **n. 1** kitchen refuse and scraps of waste food mixed with water for feeding to pigs. ■ alcohol of inferior quality: *the beer was just warm swill.* **2** a large mouthful of a drink: *a swill of ale.* — **swill·er n.** [OE *swillan, swilian* (v.), of unknown origin.]

swim /swim/ ▶ **v.** (**swim·ming**; past **swam** /swam/; past part. **swum** /swəm/) **1** [intrans.] propel the body through water by using the limbs, or (in the case of a fish or other aquatic animal) by using fins, tail, or other bodily movement: *they swam ashore.* ■ [trans.] cross (a particular stretch of water) in this way. ■ float on or at the surface of a liquid. ■ [trans.] cause to float or move across water. **2** [intrans.] be immersed in or covered with liquid. **3** [intrans.] appear to reel or whirl before one's eyes. ■ experience a dizzily confusing sensation in one's head. ▶ **n.** an act or period of swimming: *a swim in the river.*

– PHRASES **in the swim** involved in or aware of current affairs or events. **swim with** (or **against**) **the tide** act in accordance with (or against) the prevailing opinion or tendency. — **swim·ma·ble adj. swim·mer n.** [OE *swimman* (v.), of Gmc. origin; rel. to Du. *zwemmen* and Ger. *schwimmen*.]

swim blad·der ▶ **n.** Zool. a gas-filled sac present in the body of many bony fishes, used to maintain and control buoyancy.

swim·mer·et /,swimə'ret/ ▶ **n.** another term for PLEOPOD.

swim·ming /'swimiNG/ ▶ **n.** the sport or activity of propelling oneself through water using the limbs.

swim·ming crab ▶ **n.** a coastal crab (family Portunidae) that has paddlelike rear legs for swimming.

swim·ming hole ▶ **n.** a deep place for swimming in a stream or river.

swim·ming·ly /'swimiNGlē/ ▶ **adv.** smoothly and satisfactorily: *things are going swimmingly.*

swim·ming pool ▶ **n.** an artificial pool for swimming in.

swim·suit /'swim,so͞ot/ ▶ **n.** an item of clothing worn for swimming by women. — **swim·suit·ed adj.**

swim trunks (also **swim·ming trunks**) ▶ **plural n.** shorts worn by men for swimming.

swim·wear /'swim,we(ə)r/ ▶ **n.** clothing worn for swimming.

Swin·burne /'swin,bərn/, Algernon Charles (1837–1909), English poet and critic. Associated with the Pre-Raphaelites, he also contributed to the revival of interest in Elizabethan and Jacobean drama.

swin·dle /'swindl/ ▶ **v.** [trans.] use deception to deprive (someone) of money or possessions. ■ obtain (money) fraudulently. ▶ **n.** a fraudulent scheme or action. — **swin·dler n.** [18th C.: back-form. from *swindler*, from Ger. *Schwindler* 'swindler,' from *schwindeln* 'be giddy,' also 'tell lies.']

swine /swīn/ ▶ **n.** (pl. same) **1** a pig. **2** (pl. same or **swines**) informal a person regarded by the speaker with contempt and disgust. — **swin·ish adj. swin·ish·ly adv. swin·ish·ness n.** [OE *swīn*, of Gmc. origin; rel. to Ger. *Schwein* and to SOW[2].]

swine fe·ver ▶ **n.** an intestinal viral disease of pigs.

swine·herd /'swīn,hərd/ ▶ **n.** esp. hist. a person who tends pigs. [OE, from SWINE + obs. *herd* 'herdsman.']

swing /swiNG/ ▶ **v.** (past **swung** /swəNG/) **1** move or cause to move back and forth or from side to side while or as if suspended. ■ [often with adverbial or complement] move or cause to move in alternate directions or in either direction on an axis. ■ [trans.] turn (a ship or aircraft) to all compass points in succession, in order to test compass error. ■ informal be executed by hanging. **2** [no obj., with adverbial of direction] move by grasping a support from below and leaping. ■ move quickly around to the opposite direction. ■ move with a rhythmic swaying gait. **3** [with adverbial of direction] move or cause to move in a smooth, curving line: [trans.] *he swung her bag up onto the rack.* ■ [trans.] bring down (something held) with a curving movement, typically in order to hit an object. ■ [intrans.] (**swing at**) attempt to hit or punch, typically with a wide curving movement of the arm. ■ throw (a punch) with such a movement. **4** shift or cause to shift from one opinion, mood, or state of affairs to another: [intrans.] *opinion swung in the chancellor's favor.* ■ [trans.] have a decisive influence on (something, esp. a vote or election). ■ [trans.] informal succeed in bringing about: *we might be able to swing something.* **5** [intrans.] play music with an easy flowing but vigorous rhythm. ■ (of music) be played with such a rhythm. **6** [intrans.] informal (of an event, place, or way of life) be lively, exciting, or fashionable. **7** [intrans.] informal be promiscuous, typically by engaging in group sex or swapping sexual partners. ▶ **n. 1** a seat suspended by ropes or chains, on which someone may sit and swing back and forth. ■ a spell of swinging on such an apparatus. **2** an act of swinging. ■ the manner in which a golf club or a bat is swung. ■ the motion of swinging. ■ [in sing.] a smooth flowing rhythm or action. **3** a discernible change in opinion. **4** a style of jazz or dance music with an easy flowing but vigorous rhythm. ■ the rhythmic feeling or drive of such music. **5** a swift tour involving a number of stops, esp. one undertaken as part of a political campaign.

– PHRASES **get (back) into the swing of things** informal get used to (or return to) being easy and relaxed about an activity or routine one is engaged in. **in full swing** at the height of activity. **swing into action** quickly begin acting or operating. — **swing·er n.** [OE *swingan* 'to beat, whip,' also 'rush,' *geswing* 'a stroke with a weapon,' of Gmc. origin; rel. to Ger. *schwingen* 'brandish.']

swing bridge ▶ **n.** a bridge over water that can be rotated horizontally to allow ships through.

swing·by /'swiNG,bī/ ▶ **n.** a change in the flight path of a spacecraft using the gravitational pull of a celestial body. Compare with SLINGSHOT.

swinge /swinj/ ▶ **v.** (**swinge·ing**) [trans.] literary strike hard; beat. [OE *swengan* 'shake, shatter, move violently,' of Gmc. origin.]

swing·ing /'swiNGiNG/ ▶ **adj.** informal (of a person, place, or way of life) lively, exciting, and fashionable. ■ sexually liberated or promiscuous. — **swing·ing·ly adv.**

swin·gle /'swiNGgəl/ ▶ **n. 1** a wooden tool for beating flax and removing the woody parts from it. **2** the swinging part of a flail. ▶ **v.** [trans.] beat (flax) with such a tool. [ME: from MDu. *swinghel*, from the base of the verb SWING.]

swing shift ▶ **n.** a work shift from mid-afternoon to around midnight.

swing vote ▶ **n.** a vote that has a decisive influence on the result of an election. — **swing vot·er n.**

swipe /swīp/ informal ▶ **v.** [trans.] **1** hit or try to hit with a swinging blow: *she swiped me right across the nose.* **2** steal: *someone swiped one of his sausages.* **3** pass (a card with a magnetic strip) through the electronic device that reads it. ▶ **n.** a sweeping blow: *he missed the ball with his first swipe.* ■ an attack or criticism: *he took a swipe at his critics.* — **swip·er n.** [18th C.: perh. a var. of SWEEP.]

swipe card ▶ **n.** a plastic card such as a credit card or ID card bearing magnetically encoded information that is read when the edge of the card is slid through an electronic device.

swirl /swərl/ ▶ **v.** [intrans.] move in a twisting or spiraling pattern: *the smoke was swirling around him.* ■ [trans.] cause to move in such a pattern. ▶ **n.** a quantity of something moving in such a pattern. ■ a twisting or spiraling movement or pattern. — **swirl·y adj.** [ME: perh. of Low Ger. or Du. origin; cf. Du. *zwirrelen* 'to whirl.']

swish /swiSH/ ▶ **v.** [no obj., with adverbial of direction] move with a hissing or rushing sound: *a car swished by.* ■ [trans.] cause to move with such a sound. ■ aim a swinging blow at something. ■ [trans.] Basketball sink (a shot) without the ball touching the backboard or rim. ▶ **n. 1** a hissing or rustling sound: *the swish of a distant car.* ■ a rapid swinging movement: *the cow gave a swish of its tail.* ■ Basketball, informal a shot that goes through the basket without touching the backboard or rim. **2** informal offens. an effeminate male homosexual. ▶ **adj.** informal offens. effeminate. [18th C.: imitative.]

swish·y /'swiSHē/ ▶ **adj. 1** making a swishing sound or movement. **2** informal effeminate.

Swiss /swis/ ▶ **adj.** of or relating to Switzerland or its people. ■ [as pl. n.] **(the Swiss)** the people of Switzerland. ▶ **n.** (pl. same) a native or national of Switzerland, or a person of Swiss descent. [16th C.: from Fr. *Suisse*, from Mid. High Ger. *Swīz* 'Switzerland.']

Swiss chard ▶ **n.** see CHARD.

Swiss cheese ▶ **n.** cheese of a style originating in Switzerland, typically containing large holes. ■ used figuratively to refer something that is full of holes, gaps, or defects: *the team has Swiss cheese for a defense.*

Swiss Con·fed·er·a·tion the confederation of cantons that form Switzerland.

Swiss guard ▶ **n.** [often treated as pl.] Swiss mercenaries employed as a special guard, esp. at the Vatican.

switch /swiCH/ ▶ **n. 1** a device for making and breaking the connection in an electric circuit. ■ Comput. a program variable that activates or deactivates a certain function of a program. **2** an act of adopting one policy or way of life, or choosing one type of item, in place of another; a change, esp. a radical one. **3** a slender flexible shoot cut from a tree. **4** a junction of two railroad tracks, with a pair of linked tapering rails that can be moved laterally to allow a train to pass from one line to the other. **5** a tress of false or detached hair tied at one end, used in hairdressing to supplement natural hair. ▶ **v.** [trans.] change the position, direction, or focus of. ■ adopt (something different) in place of something else; change. ■ [intrans.] adopt a new policy, position, way of life, etc. ■ substitute (two items) for each other; exchange.
– PHRASAL VERBS **switch something off** turn off an electrical device. ■ **(switch off)** informal cease to pay attention. **switch something on** turn on an electrical device. — **switch·a·ble adj.** [16th C.: prob. from Low Ger.]

switch·back /'swiCH,bak/ ▶ **n.** a 180° bend in a road or path, esp. one leading up the side of a mountain. ▶ **v.** [intrans.] (of a road or vehicle) make a series of switchback turns: *a road that switchbacked up distant hills.*

switch·blade /'swiCH,blād/ ▶ **n.** a knife with a blade that springs out from the handle when a button is pressed.

switch·board /'swiCH,bôrd/ ▶ **n.** an installation for the manual control of telephone connections in an office, hotel, or other large building. ■ an apparatus for varying connections between electric circuits in other applications.

switch·er /'swiCHər/ ▶ **n. 1** a shunting engine. **2** a piece of electronic equipment used to select or combine different video and audio signals.

switch·er·oo /,swiCHə'ro͞o/ ▶ **n.** informal a change, reversal, or exchange, esp. a surprising or deceptive one. [20th C.: from the noun SWITCH + *-eroo* in the sense 'unexpected.']

switch·grass /'swiCH,gras/ ▶ **n.** a tall North American panic grass (*Panicum virgatum*) that forms large clumps.

switch-hit·ter ▶ **n.** Baseball a batter who can hit from either side of home plate. ■ informal a bisexual. — **switch-hit v. switch-hit·ting adj.**

switch·o·ver (also **switch·o·ver**) ▶ **n.** an instance of adopting a new policy, position, way of life, etc.

Swith·in, St. /'swiT͟Hən/ (also **Swithun**) (died 862), English ecclesiastic; bishop of Winchester 852–862.

Switz·er·land /'switsərlənd/ a country in central Europe. *See box.* French name SUISSE, German name SCHWEIZ, Italian name SVIZZERA; also called by its Latin name HELVETIA.

swive /swīv/ ▶ **v.** [trans.] archaic, humorous have sexual intercourse with. [ME: appar. from the OE v. *swīfan* 'move (along a course), sweep.']

swiv·el /'swivəl/ ▶ **n.** a coupling between two parts enabling one to revolve without turning the other. ▶ **v.** (**-eled, -el·ing**; Brit. **-elled, -el·ling**) [often with adverbial] turn around a point or axis or on a swivel: [intrans.] *he swiveled in the chair.* [ME, from the base of OE *swīfan* 'to move (along a course), sweep.']

swiv·el chair ▶ **n.** a chair with a seat able to be turned on its base to face in any direction.

swiv·et /'swivit/ ▶ **n.** [in sing.] a fluster or panic. [19th C.: of unknown origin.]

swiz·zle /'swizəl/ ▶ **n.** a mixed alcoholic drink, esp. a frothy one of rum or gin and bitters. ▶ **v.** [trans.] stir (a drink) with a swizzle stick. [19th C.: of unknown origin.]

swiz·zle stick ▶ **n.** a stick used for stirring still drinks or taking the fizz out of sparkling ones.

swol·len /'swōlən/ past participle of SWELL.

swoon /swo͞on/ ▶ **v.** [intrans.] faint from extreme emotion: *I don't want a nurse who swoons at the sight of blood.* ■ be emotionally affected by someone or something that one admires; become ecstatic. ▶ **n.** an occurrence of fainting: *she fell into a swoon.* [ME: the verb from obs. *swown* 'fainting,' the noun from *aswoon* 'in a faint,' both from OE *geswōgen* 'overcome.']

swoop /swo͞op/ ▶ **v. 1** [no obj., with adverbial of direction] (esp. of a bird) move rapidly downward through the air: *the aircraft swooped in to land.* ■ carry out a sudden attack, esp. in order to make a capture or arrest. **2** [trans.] informal seize with a sweeping motion. ▶ **n.** a swooping or snatching movement or action.
– PHRASES **at** (or **in**) **one fell swoop** see FELL[4]. [16th C.: perh. a dial. var. of OE *swāpan* (see SWEEP).]

swoosh /swo͝osH; swo͞osH/ ▶ **n.** the sound produced by a sudden rush of air or liquid: *the swoosh of surf.* ▶ **v.** [no obj., with adverbial of direction] move with such a sound: *swooshing down beautiful ski slopes.* [19th C.: imitative.]

Switzerland

Official name: Swiss Confederation
Location: central Europe, north of Italy
Area: 15,900 square miles (41,300 sq km)
Population: 7,450,000
Capital: Berne
Languages: German, French, and Italian (all official), Romansh
Currency: Swiss franc

swop /swäp/ ▶ **v. & n.** var. of SWAP.

sword /sôrd/ ▶ **n.** a weapon with a long metal blade and a hilt with a handguard, used for thrusting or striking and now typically worn as part of ceremonial dress. ■ **(the sword)** literary military power, violence, or destruction: *not many perished by the sword.* ■ **(swords)** one of the suits in a tarot pack.
– PHRASES **beat** (or **turn**) **swords into ploughshares** devote resources to peaceful rather than warlike ends. [with biblical allusion to Is. 2:4 and Mic. 4:3.] **put to the sword** kill, esp. in war. — **sword·like** /-,līk/ **adj.** [OE *sw(e)ord*, of Gmc. origin; rel. to Du. *zwaard* and Ger. *Schwert.*]

sword-and-sor·cer·y ▶ **n.** a genre of fiction characterized by heroic adventures and elements of fantasy.

sword-bear·er ▶ **n.** an official who carries a sword for a sovereign or other dignitary on formal occasions.

sword dance ▶ **n.** a dance in which the performers brandish swords or step around swords laid on the ground, originally as a tribal preparation for war or as a victory celebration.

sword fern ▶ **n.** a fern (genera *Polystichum* and *Nephrolepis*, family Dryopteridaceae) with long slender fronds.

swordfish

sword·fish /'sôrd,fisH/ ▶ **n.** (pl. same or **-fish·es**) a large edible marine fish (*Xiphias gladius*, family Xiphiidae) with a streamlined body and a long flattened swordlike snout, related to the billfishes and popular as a game fish.

sword knot ▶ **n.** a ribbon or tassel attached to a sword hilt, originally for securing it to the wrist.

sword of Dam·o·cles ▶ **n.** see DAMOCLES.

sword·play /'sôrd,plā/ ▶ **n.** the activity or skill of fencing with swords or foils. ■ fig. repartee; skillful debate: *intellectual swordplay.*

swords·man /'sôrdzmən/ ▶ **n.** (pl. **-men**) a man who fights with a sword (typically with his level of skill specified): *an expert swordsman.* — **swords·man·ship** /-,sHip/ **n.**

sword swal·low·er ▶ **n.** a person who passes (or pretends to pass) a sword blade down the throat and gullet as entertainment.

sword·tail /'sôrd,tāl/ ▶ **n.** a livebearing freshwater fish (*Xiphophorus helleri*, family Poeciliidae) of Central America, popular in aquariums. The lower edge of the tail is elongated and brightly marked in the male.

swore /swôr/ past of SWEAR.

sworn /swôrn/ past participle of SWEAR. ▶ **adj.** [attrib.] **1** (of testimony or evidence) given under oath: *he made a sworn statement.* **2** determined to remain in the role or condition specified: *they were sworn enemies.*

swum /swəm/ past participle of SWIM.

swung /swəNG/ past and past participle of SWING.

swung dash ▶ **n.** a dash (~) in the form of a reverse *s* on its side.

SY ▶ **abbr.** steam yacht: *the SY Morning.*

-sy ▶ **suffix** forming diminutive nouns and adjectives such as *folksy, mopsy*, also nicknames or hypocoristics such as *Patsy*. [var. of -Y².]

syb·a·rite /'sibə,rīt/ ▶ **n.** a person who is self-indulgent in their fondness for sensuous luxury. — **syb·a·rit·ism** /-rīt,izəm/ **n.** [16th C.: via L. from Gk. *Subaritēs*.]

syb·a·rit·ic /,sibə'ritik/ ▶ **adj.** fond of sensuous luxury or pleasure; self-indulgent: *their sybaritic lifestyle.*

syc·a·more /'sikə,môr/ ▶ **n. 1** an American plane tree, esp. *P. occidentalis*, the largest deciduous tree in the US. **2** (in full **sycamore maple**) a large Eurasian maple (*Acer pseudoplatanus*), native to central and southern Europe. [ME: from OFr. *sic(h)amor*, via L. from Gk. *sukomoros*, from *sukon* 'fig' + *moron* 'mulberry.']

sy·con /'sī,kän/ ▶ **n.** Zool. a sponge of intermediate structure, showing some folding of the body wall with choanocytes lining only radial canals. Compare with ASCON and LEUCON. — **sy·co·noid** /-kə,noid/ **adj.** [19th C.: adopted as a genus name from Gk. *sukon* 'fig.']

sy·co·ni·um /sī'kōnēəm/ ▶ **n.** (pl. **-ni·a** /-nēə/) Bot. a fleshy hollow receptacle that develops into a multiple fruit, as in the fig. [19th C.: mod. L., from Gk. *sukon* 'fig.']

syc·o·phant /'sikəfənt; -,fant/ ▶ **n.** a person who acts obsequiously toward someone in order to gain advantage; a servile flatterer. — **syc·o·phan·cy** /-fənsē; -,fansē/ **n.** **syc·o·phan·tic** /,sikə'fantik/ **adj.** **syc·o·phan·ti·cal·ly** /,sikə'fantik(ə)lē/ **adv.** [16th C.: from Fr. *sycophante*, or via L. from Gk. *sukophantēs* 'informer,' from *sukon* 'fig' + *phainein* 'to show.']

sy·co·sis /sī'kōsis/ ▶ **n.** inflammation of the hair follicles in the bearded part of the face, caused by bacterial infection. [16th C.: mod. L., from Gk. *sukōsis*, from *sukon* 'fig.']

Sy·den·ham /'sidn-əm; 'sidnəm/, Thomas (*c.*1624–89), English physician; known as **the English Hippocrates**.

Sy·den·ham's cho·rea /'sidn-əmz kô'rēə/ ▶ **n.** a form of chorea chiefly affecting children, associated with rheumatic fever. Formerly called ST. VITUS'S DANCE.

Syd·ney /'sidnē/ a city in southeastern Australia, the country's largest; pop. 3,098,000.

sy·e·nite /'sīə,nīt/ ▶ **n.** Geol. a coarse-grained gray igneous rock composed mainly of alkali feldspar and ferromagnesian minerals such as hornblende. — **sy·e·nit·ic** /,sīə'nitik/ **adj.** [18th C.: from Fr. *syénite*, from L. *Syenites (lapis)* '(stone) of *Syene*' (from Gk. *Suēnē* 'Aswan,' a town in Egypt).]

syl. ▶ **abbr.** syllable.

syl- ▶ **prefix** var. of SYN- assimilated before *l* (as in *syllogism*).

syll. ▶ **abbr.** ■ syllable. ■ syllabus.

syl·la·bar·y /'silə,berē/ ▶ **n.** (pl. **-bar·ies**) a set of written characters representing syllables and (in some languages or stages of writing) serving the purpose of an alphabet. [19th C.: from mod. L. *syllabarium*, from L. *syllaba* (see SYLLABLE).]

syl·la·bi /'silə,bī/ plural form of SYLLABUS.

syl·lab·ic /sə'labik/ ▶ **adj.** of, relating to, or based on syllables: *a system of syllabic symbols.* ■ Pros. based on the number of syllables in a line. ■ (of a consonant, esp. a nasal or other continuant) constituting a whole syllable, such as the *m* in *Mbabane* or the *l* in *bottle*. ■ articulated in syllables: *syllabic singing.* ▶ **n.** a written character that represents a syllable. — **syl·lab·i·cal·ly** /-ik(ə)lē/ **adv.** **syl·la·bic·i·ty** /,silə'bisitē/ **n.** [18th C.: ult. from Gk. *sullabikos*, from *sullabē* 'syllable.']

syl·lab·i·fi·ca·tion /sə,labəfi'kāSHən/ (also **syl·lab·i·ca·tion** /sə'labi'kāSHən/) ▶ **n.** the division of words into syllables, either in speech or in writing. — **syl·lab·i·fy** /sə'labə,fī/ **v.** (**-fies, -fied**).

syl·la·bize /'silə,bīz/ ▶ **v.** [trans.] divide into or articulate by syllables.

syl·la·ble /'siləbəl/ ▶ **n.** a unit of pronunciation having one vowel sound, with or without surrounding consonants, forming the whole or a part of a word; e.g., there are two syllables in *water* and three in *inferno*. ■ a character or characters representing a syllable. ■ [usu. with negative] the least amount of speech or writing; the least mention of something. ▶ **v.** [trans.] pronounce (a word or phrase) clearly, syllable by syllable. — **syl·la·bled adj.** [usu. in comb.] *poems of few-syllabled lines.* [ME: ult. from OFr. *sillabe*, via L. from Gk. *sullabē*, from *sun-* 'together' + *lambanein* 'take.']

syl·la·bub /'silə,bəb/ ▶ **n.** a whipped cream dessert, typically flavored with white wine or sherry. [of unknown origin.]

syl·la·bus /'siləbəs/ ▶ **n.** (pl. **-bus·es** or **-bi** /-,bī/) **1** an outline of the subjects in a course of study or teaching: *there isn't time to cover the syllabus.* **2** (in the Roman Catholic Church) a summary of points decided by papal decree regarding heretical doctrines or practices. [17th C.: mod. L., orig. a misreading of L. *sittybas*, accusative pl. of *sittyba*, from Gk. *sittuba* 'title slip, label.']

syl·lep·sis /sə'lepsis/ ▶ **n.** (pl. **-ses** /-sēz/) a figure of speech in which a word is applied to two others in different senses (e.g., *caught the train and a bad cold*) or to two others of which it grammatically suits only one (e.g., *neither they nor it is working*). Compare with ZEUGMA. — **syl·lep·tic** /-tik/ **adj.** [ME: via late L. from Gk. *sullēpsis* 'taking together.']

syl·lo·gism /'silə,jizəm/ ▶ **n.** an instance of a form of reasoning in which a conclusion is drawn from two given or assumed propositions (premises); a common or middle term is present in the two premises but not in the conclusion, which may be invalid (e.g., *all dogs are animals; all animals have four legs; therefore all dogs have four legs*). ■ deductive reasoning as distinct from induction. — **syl·lo·gis·tic** /,silə'jistik/ **adj.** **syl·lo·gis·ti·cal·ly** /,silə'jistik(ə)lē/ **adv.** [ME: via OFr. or L. from Gk. *sullogismos*, from *sullogizesthai*, from *sun-* 'with' + *logizesthai* 'to reason' (from *logos* 'reasoning').]

syl·lo·gize /'silə,jīz/ ▶ **v.** [intrans.] use syllogisms. ■ [trans.] put (facts or an argument) in the form of syllogism.

sylph /silf/ ▶ **n.** an imaginary spirit of the air. ■ a slender woman or girl. [17th C.: from mod. L. *sylphes, sylphi* and the Ger. pl. *Sylphen*, perh. based on L. *sylvestris* 'of the woods' + *nympha* 'nymph.']

syl·van /'silvən/ (also **sil·van**) ▶ **adj.** esp. literary consisting of or associated with woods; wooded. ■ pleasantly rural or pastoral: *vistas of sylvan charm.* [16th C.: from Fr. *sylvain* or L. *Silvanus* 'woodland deity,' from *silva* 'a wood.']

syl·vat·ic /sil'vatik/ ▶ **adj.** Vet. Med. relating to or denoting certain diseases when contracted by wild animals, and the pathogens causing them. [1930s: from L. *silvaticus*, from *silva* 'wood.']

syl·vite /'sil,vīt/ ▶ **n.** a colorless or white mineral consisting of potassium chloride, occurring typically as cubic crystals. Also called **sylvine**. [19th C.: from mod. L. *(sal digestivus) Sylvii*, the old name of this salt, + -ITE¹.]

sym. ▶ **abbr.** ■ symbol. ■ Chem. symmetrical. ■ symphony. ■ symptom.

sym- ▶ **prefix** var. of SYN- assimilated before *b, m, p* (as in *symbiosis, symmetry, symphysis*).

sym·bi·ont /'simbē,änt; -bī-/ ▶ **n.** Biol. either of two organisms that live in symbiosis with one another. [19th C.: from Gk. *sumbiōn* 'living together,' from *sumbioun*.]

sym·bi·o·sis /,simbē'ōsis; -bī-/ ▶ **n.** (pl. **-ses** /-,sēz/) Biol. interaction between two different organisms living in close physical association, typically to the advantage of both. Compare with ANTIBIOSIS. ■ a mutually beneficial relationship between different people or groups. — **sym·bi·ot·ic** /-'ätik/ **adj.** **sym·bi·ot·i·cal·ly** /-'ätik(ə)lē/ **adv.** [19th C.: mod. L., from Gk. *sumbiōsis* 'a living together,' from *sumbioun* 'live together,' from *sumbios* 'companion.']

sym·bol /'simbəl/ ▶ **n.** a thing that represents or stands for something else, esp. a material object representing something abstract. ■ a mark or character used as a conventional representation of an object, function, or process, e.g., the letter or letters standing for a chemical element or a character in musical notation. ■ a shape or sign used to represent something such as an organization, e.g., a red cross or a Star of David. [ME: from L. *symbolum* 'symbol, Creed,' from Gk. *sumbolon* 'mark, token,' from *sun-* 'with' + *ballein* 'to throw.']

sym·bol·ic /sim'bälik/ ▶ **adj. 1** serving as a symbol. ■ significant purely in terms of what is being represented or implied: *an important symbolic gesture.* **2** involving the use of symbols or symbolism. — **sym·bol·i·cal adj.** **sym·bol·i·cal·ly** /-ik(ə)lē/ **adv.**

sym·bol·ic log·ic ▶ **n.** the use of symbols to denote propositions, terms, and relations in order to assist reasoning.

sym·bol·ism /'simbə,lizəm/ ▶ **n.** the use of symbols to represent ideas or qualities. ■ symbolic meaning attributed to natural objects or facts. ■ (also **Symbolism**) an artistic and poetic movement or style using symbolic images and indirect suggestion to express mystical ideas and emotions. It originated in late 19th century France and Belgium. — **sym·bol·ist n. & adj.**

sym·bol·ize /'simbə,līz/ ▶ **v.** [trans.] be a symbol of. ■ represent by means of symbols. — **sym·bol·i·za·tion** /,simbəli'zāSHən/ **n.**

sym·bol·o·gy /sim'bäləjē/ ▶ **n.** the study or use of symbols. ■ symbols collectively: *the use of religious symbology.*

sym·met·ri·cal /sə'metrikəl/ ▶ **adj.** made up of exactly similar parts facing each other or around an axis; showing symmetry. — **sym·met·ric adj.** **sym·met·ri·cal·ly** /-rik(ə)lē/ **adv.**

sym·me·try /'simitrē/ ▶ **n.** (pl. **-tries**) the quality of being made up of exactly similar parts facing each other or around an axis. ■ correct or pleasing proportion of the parts of a thing. ■ similarity or exact correspondence between different things. ■ Physics & Math. a law or operation where a physical property or process has an equivalence in two or more directions. — **sym·me·trize** /-,trīz/ **v.** [16th C.: from Fr. *symétrie* or L. *symmetria*, from Gk., from *sun-* 'with' + *metron* 'measure.']

sym·path·ec·to·my /,simpə'THektəmē/ ▶ **n.** the surgical cutting of a sympathetic nerve or removal of a ganglion to relieve a condition affected by its stimulation.

sym·pa·thet·ic /,simpə'THetik/ ▶ **adj. 1** feeling, showing, or expressing sympathy. ■ [predic.] showing approval of or favor toward an idea or action: *he was sympathetic to evolutionary ideas.* **2** pleasant or agreeable, in particular: ■ (of a person) attracting the liking of others. ■ (of a structure) designed in a sensitive or fitting way. **3** relating to or denoting the part of the autonomic nervous system consisting of nerves arising from ganglia near the middle part of the spinal cord, supplying the internal organs, blood vessels, and glands, and balancing the action of the parasympathetic nerves. **4** relating to, producing, or denoting an effect that arises in response to a similar action elsewhere. — **sym·pa·thet·i·cal·ly** /-ik(ə)lē/ **adv.** [17th C.: from SYMPATHY, on the pattern of *pathetic*.]

sym·pa·thet·ic string ▶ **n.** each of a group of additional wire strings fitted to certain stringed instruments to give extra resonance.

sym·pa·thize /ˈsimpə,THīz/ ▶v. [intrans.] **1** feel or express sympathy. **2** agree with a sentiment or opinion. — **sym·pa·thiz·er** n.

sym·pa·thy /ˈsimpəTHē/ ▶n. (pl. **-thies**) **1** feelings of pity and sorrow for someone else's misfortune. ■ (**one's sympathies**) formal expression of such feelings; condolences. **2** understanding between people; common feeling. ■ (**sympathies**) support in the form of shared feelings or opinions. ■ agreement with or approval of an opinion or aim; a favorable attitude. ■ (**in sympathy**) relating harmoniously to something else; in keeping. ■ the state or fact of responding in a way similar or corresponding to an action elsewhere. [16th C. (sense 2): via L. from Gk. *sumpatheia*, from *sumpathēs*, from *sun-* 'with' + *pathos* 'feeling.']

sym·pat·ric /simˈpatrik/ ▶adj. Biol. (of animals or plants, esp. of related species or populations) occurring within the same geographical area; overlapping in distribution. Compare with ALLOPATRIC. ■ (of speciation) taking place without geographical separation. — **sym·pa·try** /ˈsim,patrē; -pətrē/ n. [20th C.: from SYM- 'with, together' + Gk. *patra* 'fatherland' + -IC.]

sym·phon·ic /simˈfänik/ ▶adj. (of music) relating to or having the form or character of a symphony. ■ relating to or written for a symphony orchestra. — **sym·phon·i·cal·ly** /-ik(ə)lē/ adv.

sym·phon·ic po·em ▶n. another term for TONE POEM.

sym·pho·nist /ˈsimfənist/ ▶n. a composer of symphonies.

sym·pho·ny /ˈsimfənē/ ▶n. (pl. **-nies**) an elaborate musical composition for full orchestra, typically in four movements, at least one of which is traditionally in sonata form. ■ esp. hist. an orchestral interlude in a large-scale vocal work. ■ something regarded, typically favorably, as a composition of different elements. ■ (esp. in names of orchestras) short for SYMPHONY ORCHESTRA. ■ a concert performed by a symphony orchestra. [ME: ult. from Gk. *sumphōnia*, from *sumphōnos* 'harmonious,' from *sun-* 'together' + *phōnē* 'sound.']

sym·pho·ny or·ches·tra ▶n. a large classical orchestra, including string, wind, brass, and percussion instruments.

Sym·phy·la /ˈsimfələ/ Zool. a small class of myriapod invertebrates that resemble the centipedes. — **sym·phy·lan** n. & adj. [mod. L. (pl.), from SYM- 'together' + Gk. *phulē*, *phulon* 'tribe.']

sym·phy·sis /ˈsimfəsis/ ▶n. (pl. **-ses** /-,sēz/) **1** the process of growing together. **2** a place where two bones are closely joined, either forming an immovable joint (as between the pubic bones in the center of the pelvis) or completely fused (as at the midline of the lower jaw). — **sym·phys·e·al** /simˈfizēəl/ adj. **sym·phys·i·al** /simˈfizēəl/ adj. [16th C.: mod. L., from Gk. *sumphusis*, from *sun-* 'together' + *phusis* 'growth.']

sym·po·di·um /simˈpōdēəm/ ▶n. (pl. **-di·a** /-dēə/) Bot. the apparent main axis or stem of a plant, made up of successive secondary axes due to the death of each season's terminal bud, as in the vine. — **sym·po·di·al** /-dēəl/ adj. [19th C.: mod. L., from Gk. *syn-* 'together' + *pous, pod-* 'foot.']

sym·po·si·ast /simˈpōzēəst/ ▶n. a participant in a symposium.

sym·po·si·um /simˈpōzēəm/ ▶n. (pl. **-si·a** /-zēə/ or **-si·ums**) a conference or meeting to discuss a particular subject. ■ a collection of essays or papers on a particular subject by a number of contributors. ■ a drinking party or convivial discussion, esp. as held in ancient Greece after a banquet. [16th C.: via L. from Gk. *sumposion*, from *sumpotēs* 'fellow drinker,' from *sun-* 'together' + *potēs* 'drinker.']

symp·tom /ˈsim(p)təm/ ▶n. Med. a physical or mental feature that is regarded as indicating a condition of disease, particularly such a feature that is apparent to the patient: Compare with SIGN (sense 1). ■ a sign of the existence of something, esp. of an undesirable situation. — **symp·tom·less** adj. [ME *synthoma*, from med. L., based on Gk. *sumptōma* 'chance, symptom,' from *sumpiptein* 'happen.']

symp·to·mat·ic /,sim(p)təˈmatik/ ▶adj. serving as a symptom or sign, esp. of something undesirable. ■ exhibiting or involving symptoms. — **symp·to·mat·i·cal·ly** /-ik(ə)lē/ adv.

symp·tom·a·tol·o·gy /,sim(p)təməˈtäləjē/ ▶n. the set of symptoms characteristic of a medical condition or exhibited by a patient.

syn. ▶abbr. ■ synonym. ■ synonymous. ■ synonymy.

syn- ▶prefix united; acting or considered together: *synchrony* | *syncarpous*. [from Gk. *sun* 'with.']

syn·a·gogue /ˈsinə,gäg/ ▶n. the building where a Jewish assembly or congregation meets for religious observance and instruction. ■ such a Jewish assembly or congregation. — **syn·a·gog·al** /,sinəˈgägəl; -ˈgôgəl/ adj. **syn·a·gog·i·cal** /,sinəˈgäjikəl/ adj. [ME: ult. from Gk. *sunagōgē* 'meeting,' from *sun-* 'together' + *agein* 'bring.']

syn·apse /ˈsin,aps/ ▶n. a junction between two nerve cells, consisting of a minute gap across which impulses pass by diffusion of a neurotransmitter. [19th C.: from Gk. *sunapsis*, from *sun-* 'together' + *hapsis* 'joining,' from *haptein* 'to join.']

syn·ap·sis /səˈnapsis/ ▶n. Biol. the fusion of chromosome pairs at the start of meiosis. [19th C.: mod. L., from Gk. *sunapsis* 'connection, junction.']

syn·ap·tic /səˈnaptik/ ▶adj. Anat. of or relating to a synapse or synapses between nerve cells. — **syn·ap·ti·cal·ly** /-tik(ə)lē/ adv.

syn·ar·thro·sis /,sinärˈTHrōsis/ ▶n. (pl. **-ses** /-,sēz/) Anat. an immovably fixed joint between bones connected by fibrous tissue (for example, the sutures of the skull). [16th C.: from mod. L., from Gk. *sunarthrōsis*, from *sun-* 'together' + *arthrōsis* 'jointing' (from *arthron* 'joint').]

sync /siNGk/ (also **synch**) informal ▶n. synchronization. ▶v. [trans.] synchronize.

– PHRASES **in** (or **out of**) **sync** working well (or badly) together; in (or out of) agreement. [1920s: abbr.]

syn·car·pous /sinˈkärpəs/ ▶adj. Bot. (of a flower, fruit, or ovary) having the carpels united. Often contrasted with APOCARPOUS. [19th C.: from SYN- 'together' + Gk. *karpos* 'fruit' + -OUS.]

syn·chon·dro·sis /,siNGkənˈdrōsis/ ▶n. (pl. **-ses** /-,sēz/) Anat. an almost immovable joint between bones bound by a layer of cartilage, as in the vertebrae. [16th C.: from mod. L., from Gk. *sunkhondrōsis*, from *sun-* 'together' + *khondros* 'cartilage.']

syn·chro /ˈsiNGkrō/ ▶n. **1** short for SYNCHROMESH. **2** synchronized or synchronization.

synchro- ▶comb. form synchronous: *synchrotron*.

syn·chro·cy·clo·tron /,siNGkrōˈsīklə,trän/ ▶n. Physics a cyclotron able to achieve higher energies by decreasing the frequency of the accelerating electric field as the particles increase in energy and mass.

syn·chro·mesh /ˈsiNGkrō,mesH/ ▶n. a system of gear changing, esp. in motor vehicles, in which the driving and driven gearwheels are made to revolve at the same speed during engagement by means of a set of friction clutches, thereby easing the change. [1920s: contr. of *synchronized mesh*.]

syn·chron·ic /siNGˈkränik/ ▶adj. concerned with something, esp. a language, as it exists at one point in time. Often contrasted with DIACHRONIC. — **syn·chron·i·cal·ly** /-ik(ə)lē/ adv.

syn·chro·nic·i·ty /,siNGkrəˈnisitē/ ▶n. **1** the simultaneous occurrence of events that appear significantly related but have no discernible causal connection. **2** another term for SYNCHRONY (sense 1).

syn·chro·nism /ˈsiNGkrə,nizəm/ ▶n. another term for SYNCHRONY. — **syn·chro·nis·tic** /,siNGkrəˈnistik/ adj. **syn·chro·nis·ti·cal·ly** /,siNGkrəˈnistik(ə)lē/ adv.

syn·chro·nize /ˈsiNGkrə,nīz/ ▶v. [trans.] cause to occur or operate at the same time or rate. ■ [intrans.] occur at the same time or rate. ■ adjust (a clock or watch) to show the same time as another. ■ [intrans.] tally; agree. ■ coordinate; combine. — **syn·chro·ni·za·tion** /,siNGkrənəˈzāSHən/ n. **syn·chro·niz·er** n.

syn·chro·nous /ˈsiNGkrənəs/ ▶adj. **1** existing or occurring at the same time. **2** (of a satellite or its orbit) making or denoting an orbit around the earth or another celestial body in which one revolution is completed in the period taken for the body to rotate about its axis. — **syn·chro·nous·ly** adv. [17th C.: from late L. *synchronus* (from Gk. *sunkhronos*, from *sun-* 'together' + *khronos* 'time') + -OUS.]

syn·chro·ny /ˈsiNGkrənē/ ▶n. **1** simultaneous action, development, or occurrence. ■ the state of operating or developing according to the same time scale as something else. **2** synchronic treatment or study.

syn·chro·tron /ˈsiNGkrə,trän/ ▶n. Physics a cyclotron in which the magnetic field strength increases with the energy of the particles to keep their orbital radius constant.

syn·cline /ˈsin,klīn/ ▶n. Geol. a trough or fold of stratified rock in which the strata slope upward from the axis. Compare with ANTICLINE. — **syn·cli·nal** /sinˈklīnl/ adj. [19th C.: from SYN- 'together' + Gk. *klinein* 'to lean.']

syn·co·pate /ˈsiNGkə,pāt/ ▶v. [trans.] **1** [usu. as adj.] (**syncopated**) displace the beats or accents in (music or a rhythm) so that strong beats become weak and vice versa: *syncopated dance music*. **2** shorten (a word) by dropping sounds or letters in the middle, as in *symbology* for *symbology*. — **syn·co·pa·tion** /,siNGkəˈpāSHən/ n. **syn·co·pa·tor** /-,pātər/ n.

syn·co·pe /ˈsiNGkəpē/ ▶n. **1** Med. temporary loss of consciousness caused by a fall in blood pressure. **2** Gram. the omission of sounds or letters from within a word, e.g., when *probably* is pronounced /ˈpräblē/. — **syn·co·pal** /-pəl/ adj. [ME: via late L. from Gk. *sunkopē*, from *sun-* 'together' + *koptein* 'strike, cut off.']

syn·cre·tism /ˈsiNGkrə,tizəm/ ▶n. **1** the amalgamation or attempted amalgamation of different religions, cultures, or schools of thought. **2** Ling. the merging of different inflectional varieties of a word during the development of a language. — **syn·cret·ic** /siNGˈkretik/ adj. **syn·cre·tist** n. & adj. **syn·cre·tis·tic** /,siNGkrəˈtistik/ adj. [17th C.: ult. from Gk. *sunkrētismos*, from *sunkrētizein* 'unite against a third party,' from *sun-* 'together' + *krēs* 'Cretan.']

syn·cre·tize /ˈsiNGkri,tīz/ ▶v. [trans.] attempt to amalgamate or reconcile (differing things, esp. religious beliefs, cultural elements, or schools of thought). — **syn·cre·ti·za·tion** /,siNGkritəˈzāSHən/ n.

syn·cy·tium /sinˈsisHəm/ ▶n. (pl. **-cy·tia** /-ˈsisHə/) Biol. a single cell or cytoplasmic mass containing several nuclei, formed by fusion of cells or by division of nuclei. ■ Embryol. material of this kind forming the outermost layer of the trophoblast. — **syn·cy·tial** /-SHəl/ adj. [19th C.: from SYN- 'together' + -CYTE 'cell' + -IUM.]

synd. ▶abbr. ■ syndicate. ■ syndicated.

syn·dac·tyl·y /sinˈdaktl-ē/ ▶n. Med. & Zool. the condition of having some or all of the fingers or toes wholly or partly united, either naturally (as in web-footed animals) or as a malformation. [19th C.: from SYN- 'united' + Gk. *daktulos* 'finger' + -Y[3].]

syn·des·mo·sis /,sin,dezˈmōsis/ ▶n. (pl. **-ses** /-,sēz/) Anat. an immovable joint in which bones are joined by connective tissue (e.g., between the fibula and tibia at the ankle). [16th C.: mod. L., from Gk. *sundesmos* 'binding, fastening.']

syn·det·ic /sinˈdetik/ ▶adj. Gram. of or using conjunctions. [17th C.: from Gk. *sundetikos*, from *sundein* 'bind together.']

PRONUNCIATION KEY ə *ago, up*; ər *over, fur*; a *hat*; ā *ate*; ä *car*; e *let*; ē *see*; i *fit*; ī *by*; NG *sing*; ō *go*; ô *law, for*; oi *toy*; o͝o *good*; o͞o *goo*; ou *out*; TH *thin*; T͟H *then*; ZH *vision*

syn·dic /ˈsindik/ ▶n. **1** a government official in various countries. **2** (in the UK) a business agent of certain universities and corporations. —**syn·di·cal** adj. [17th C.: from Fr., via late L. from Gk. *sundikos*, from *sun-* 'together' + *dikē* 'justice.']

syn·di·cal·ism /ˈsindəkəˌlizəm/ ▶n. hist. a movement, at its most vigorous between 1900 and 1914, for transferring the ownership and control of the means of production and distribution to workers' unions. —**syn·di·cal·ist** n. & adj. [20th C.: from Fr. *syndicalisme*, from *syndical*, from *syndic* 'a delegate' (see SYNDIC).]

syn·di·cate ▶n. /ˈsindikit/ a group of individuals or organizations combined to promote some common interest: *a crime syndicate.* ■ an association or agency supplying material simultaneously to a number of newspapers or periodicals. ■ a committee of syndics. ▶v. /ˈsindiˌkāt/ [trans.] (usu. **be syndicated**) control or manage by a syndicate. ■ publish or broadcast (material) simultaneously in a number of newspapers, television stations, etc. ■ sell (a horse) to a syndicate. —**syn·di·ca·tion** /ˌsindiˈkāsʜən/ n. **syn·di·ca·tor** /-ˌkātər/ n. [17th C.: from Fr. *syndicat*, from med. L. *syndicatus*, from late L. *syndicus* 'delegate of a corporation' (see SYNDIC).]

syn·drome /ˈsinˌdrōm/ ▶n. a group of symptoms that consistently occur together or a condition characterized by a set of associated symptoms. ■ a characteristic combination of opinions, emotions, or behavior: *the "Not In My Back Yard" syndrome.* —**syn·drom·ic** /sinˈdrämik/ adj. [16th C.: mod. L., from Gk. *sundromē*, from *sun-* 'together' + *dramein* 'to run.']

syne /sīn/ ▶adv. Scot. ago. See also AULD LANG SYNE, LANG SYNE. [ME: contr. of dial. *sithen* 'ever since.']

syn·ec·do·che /siˈnekdəkē/ ▶n. a figure of speech in which a part is made to represent the whole or vice versa, as in *Cleveland won by six runs* (meaning "Cleveland's baseball team"). —**syn·ec·doch·ic** /ˌsinekˈdäkik/ adj. **syn·ec·doch·i·cal** /ˌsinekˈdäkikəl/ adj. **syn·ec·doch·i·cal·ly** /-ˈdäkik(ə)lē/ adv. [ME: via L. from Gk. *sunekdokhē*, from *sun-* 'together' + *ekdekhesthai* 'take up.']

syn·e·col·o·gy /ˌsiniˈkäləjē/ ▶n. the ecological study of whole plant or animal communities. Contrasted with AUTECOLOGY. —**syn·ec·o·log·i·cal** /sinˌekəˈläjikəl; -ˌēkə-/ adj. **syn·e·col·o·gist** /-jist/ n.

syn·er·e·sis /səˈnerəsis/ ▶n. (pl. **-ses** /-ˌsēz/) **1** the contraction of two vowels into a diphthong or single vowel. **2** Chem. the contraction of a gel accompanied by the separating out of liquid. [16th C.: via late L. from Gk. *sunairesis*, based on *sun-* 'together' + *hairein* 'take.']

syn·er·gist /ˈsinərjist/ ▶n. a substance, organ, or other agent that participates in an effect of synergy. —**syn·er·gis·tic** /ˌsinərˈjistik/ adj. **syn·er·gis·ti·cal·ly** /ˌsinərˈjistik(ə)lē/ adv.

syn·er·gy /ˈsinərjē/ (also **syn·er·gism** /-jizəm/) ▶n. the interaction or cooperation of two or more organizations, substances, or other agents to produce a combined effect greater than the sum of their separate effects: *the synergy between artist and record company.* —**syn·er·get·ic** /ˌsinərˈjetik/ adj. **syn·er·gic** /səˈnərjik/ adj. [19th C.: from Gk. *sunergos* 'working together,' from *sun-* 'together' + *ergon* 'work.']

syn·es·the·sia /ˌsinəsˈᴛʜēzʜə/ (Brit. **syn·aes·the·sia**) ▶n. Physiol. & Psychol. the production of a sense impression relating to one sense or part of the body by stimulation of another sense or part of the body. ■ the poetic description of a sense impression in terms of another sense, as in "a loud perfume." —**syn·es·thete** /ˈsinisˌᴛʜēt/ n. **syn·es·thet·ic** /-ˈᴛʜetik/ adj. [19th C.: mod. L., from SYN- 'with,' on the pattern of *anesthesia*.]

syn·fu·el /ˈsinˌfyo͞oəl/ ▶n. fuel made from coal, corn, etc., as a substitute for a petroleum product.

syn·ga·my /ˈsiɴɢgəmē/ ▶n. Biol. the fusion of two cells, or of their nuclei, in reproduction. [20th C.: from SYN- 'with' + Gk. *gamos* 'marriage.']

Synge /siɴɢ/, J. M. (1871–1909), Irish playwright; full name *Edmund John Millington Synge.* He wrote *The Playboy of the Western World* (1907).

syn·od /ˈsinəd/ ▶n. **1** an assembly of the clergy and sometimes also the laity in a diocese or other division of a particular church. **2** a Presbyterian ecclesiastical court above the presbyteries and subject to the General Assembly. [ME: via late L. from Gk. *sunodos* 'meeting,' from *sun-* 'together' + *hodos* 'way.']

syn·od·ic /səˈnädik/ ▶adj. Astron. relating to or involving the conjunction of stars, planets, or other celestial objects.

syn·od·i·cal /səˈnädikəl/ ▶adj. **1** Christian Church of, relating to, or constituted as a synod: *synodical government.* **2** Astron. another term for SYNODIC. —**syn·od·al** /ˈsinədl/ adj. (in sense 1).

syn·od·ic month ▶n. Astron. another term for LUNAR MONTH.

syn·o·nym /ˈsinəˌnim/ ▶n. a word or phrase that means exactly or nearly the same as another word or phrase in the same language, for example *shut* is a synonym of *close.* ■ a person or thing so closely associated with a particular quality or idea that the mention of their name calls it to mind. ■ Biol. a taxonomic name that has the same application as another, esp. one that has been superseded and is no longer valid. —**syn·o·nym·ic** /ˌsinəˈnimik/ adj. **syn·o·nym·i·ty** /ˌsinəˈnimitē/ n. [ME: via L. from Gk. *sunōnumon*, neut. (used as a n.) of the adjective *sunōnumos*, from *sun-* 'with' + *onoma* 'name.']

syn·on·y·mous /səˈnänəməs/ ▶adj. (of a word or phrase) having the same meaning as another word or phrase in the same language. ■ closely associated with or suggestive of something: *his deeds had made his name synonymous with victory.* —**syn·on·y·mous·ly** adv. **syn·on·y·mous·ness** n.

syn·on·y·my /səˈnänəmē/ ▶n. the state of being synonymous.

syn·op·sis /səˈnäpsis/ ▶n. (pl. **-ses** /-ˌsēz/) a brief summary or general survey of something. ■ an outline of the plot of a play, film, or book. —**syn·op·size** /-ˌsīz/ v. [17th C.: via late L. from Gk., from *sun-* 'together' + *opsis* 'seeing.']

syn·op·tic /səˈnäptik/ ▶adj. **1** of or forming a general summary or synopsis: *a synoptic outline of the contents.* ■ taking or involving a comprehensive mental view. **2** of or relating to the Synoptic Gospels. ▶n. (**Synoptics**) the Synoptic Gospels. —**syn·op·ti·cal** adj. **syn·op·ti·cal·ly** /-tik(ə)lē/ adv. [17th C.: from Gk. *sunoptikos*, from *sunopsis* (see SYNOPSIS).]

Syn·op·tic Gos·pels ▶plural n. the Gospels of Matthew, Mark, and Luke, which describe events from a similar point of view, as contrasted with that of John.

syn·o·vi·al /səˈnōvēəl/ ▶adj. relating to or denoting a type of joint that is surrounded by a thick flexible membrane forming a sac into which is secreted a viscous fluid that lubricates the joint. [18th C.: from mod. L. *synovia.*]

syn·o·vi·tis /ˌsinəˈvītis/ ▶n. Med. inflammation of a synovial membrane.

syn·tac·tic /sinˈtaktik/ ▶adj. of or according to syntax. —**syn·tac·ti·cal** adj. **syn·tac·ti·cal·ly** /-tik(ə)lē/ adv. [19th C.: from Gk. *suntaktikos*, from *suntassein* 'arrange together' (see SYNTAX).]

syn·tax /ˈsinˌtaks/ ▶n. the arrangement of words and phrases to create well-formed sentences in a language. ■ a set of rules for or an analysis of this: *generative syntax.* ■ the branch of linguistics that deals with this. [16th C.: ult. from Gk. *suntaxis*, from *sun-* 'together' + *tassein* 'arrange.']

synth /sinᴛʜ/ ▶n. informal short for SYNTHESIZER.

syn·the·sis /ˈsinᴛʜəsis/ ▶n. (pl. **-ses** /-ˌsēz/) combination or composition, in particular: ■ the combination of ideas to form a theory or system. Often contrasted with ANALYSIS. ■ the production of chemical compounds by reaction from simpler materials. ■ (in Hegelian philosophy) the final stage in the process of dialectical reasoning, in which a new idea resolves the conflict between thesis and antithesis. ■ Gram. the process of making compound and derivative words. ■ Ling. the use of inflected forms rather than word order to express grammatical structure. —**syn·the·sist** n. [17th C.: via L. from Gk. *sunthesis*, from *suntithenai* 'place together.']

syn·the·size /ˈsinᴛʜiˌsīz/ (also **syn·the·tize** /-ˌtīz/) ▶v. [trans.] make (something) by synthesis, esp. chemically. ■ combine (a number of things) into a coherent whole. ■ produce (sound) electronically.

syn·the·siz·er /ˈsinᴛʜəˌsīzər/ ▶n. an electronic musical instrument, typically operated by a keyboard, producing a wide variety of sounds by generating and combining signals of different frequencies.

syn·thet·ic /sinˈᴛʜetik/ ▶adj. relating to or using synthesis. ■ (of a substance) made by chemical synthesis, esp. to imitate a natural product. ■ (of an emotion or action) not genuine; insincere. ■ Logic (of a proposition) having truth or falsity determinable by recourse to experience. Compare with ANALYTIC. ■ Ling. (of a language) characterized by the use of inflections rather than word order to express grammatical structure. Contrasted with AGGLUTINATIVE and ANALYTIC. ▶n. (usu. **synthetics**) a synthetic material or chemical, esp. a textile fiber. —**syn·thet·i·cal** adj. **syn·thet·i·cal·ly** /-ik(ə)lē/ adv. [17th C.: ult. from Gk. *sunthetikos*, based on *suntithenai* 'place together.']

syn·thet·ic res·in ▶n. see RESIN.

syn·ton·ic /sinˈtänik/ ▶adj. Psychol. (of a person) responsive to and in harmony with their environment so that affect is appropriate to the given situation. ■ [in comb.] (of a psychiatric condition or psychological process) consistent with other aspects of an individual's personality and belief system: *this phobia was ego-syntonic.* ■ hist. relating to or denoting the lively and responsive type of temperament that was considered liable to manic-depressive psychosis. See also CYCLOTHYMIA. —**syn·tone** /ˈsinˌtōn/ n. [19th C.: from Ger. *Syntonie* 'state of being syntonic' + -IC.]

syn·type /ˈsinˌtīp/ ▶n. Bot. & Zool. each of a set of type specimens of equal status, upon which the description and name of a new species is based. Compare with HOLOTYPE.

syph·i·lis /ˈsifəlis/ ▶n. a chronic bacterial disease caused by the spirochete *Treponema pallidum.* It is contracted chiefly by infection during sexual intercourse, but also congenitally by infection of a developing fetus. —**syph·i·lit·ic** /ˌsifəˈlitik/ adj. & n. [18th C.: mod. L., from *Syphilis, sive Morbus Gallicus*, a Latin poem (1530), after the character *Syphilus*, the supposed first sufferer of the disease.]

sy·phon ▶n. & v. var. of SIPHON.

Syr·a·cuse /ˈsirəˌkyo͞os; -ˌkyo͞oz/ **1** a city on eastern Sicily; pop. 125,000. Italian name **SIRACUSA**. **2** a city in New York, southeast of Lake Ontario; pop. 147,306.

syr·ette /siˈret/ ▶n. Med., trademark a disposable injection unit comprising a collapsible tube with an attached hypodermic needle and a single dose of a drug, commonly morphine. [1940s: from SYRINGE + -ETTE.]

Syr·i·a /ˈsi(ə)rēə/ a country in the Middle East. *See box.* —**Syr·i·an** adj. & n.

Syr·i·ac /ˈsi(ə)rēˌak/ ▶n. the language of ancient Syria, still used by Syrian Christians as a liturgical language. ▶adj. of or relating to this language.

sy·rin·ga /səˈriɴɢgə/ ▶n. **1** a plant of a genus (*Syringa*) in the olive family that includes the lilac. **2** informal another term for MOCK ORANGE. [mod. L., from Gk. *surinx, suring-* 'tube.']

sy·ringe /səˈrinj; ˈsirinj/ ▶n. Med. a tube with a nozzle and piston or bulb for sucking in and ejecting liquid in a thin stream, used for cleaning

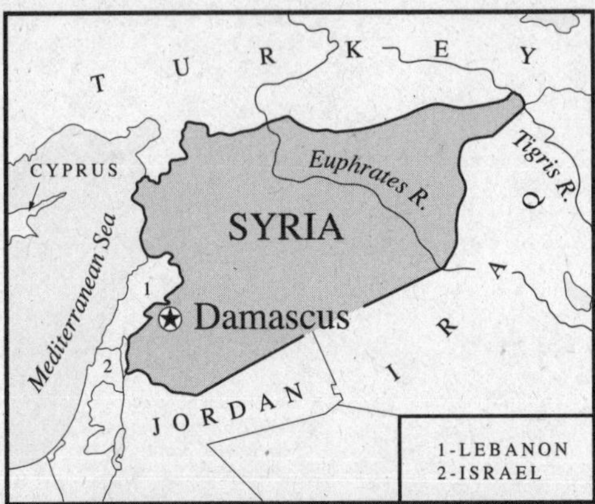

Syria

Official name: Syrian Arab Republic
Location: Middle East, south of Turkey
Area: 71,500 square miles (185,200 sq km)
Population: 18,016,000
Capital: Damascus
Languages: Arabic (official), Kurdish, Armenian, Aramaic, Circassian
Currency: Syrian pound

wounds or body cavities, or fitted with a hollow needle for injecting or withdrawing fluids. ■ any similar device used in gardening or cooking. ▶ v. (**-ring·ing**) [trans.] spray liquid into (the ear or a wound) with a syringe. ■ spray liquid over (plants) with a syringe. [ME: from med. L. *syringa*, from *syrinx* (see SYRINX).]

medical syringe

sy·rin·go·my·e·li·a /sə,riNGgōmī'ēlēə; -'ēlyə/ ▶ n. Med. a chronic progressive disease in which longitudinal cavities form in the cervical region of the spinal cord. [19th C.: mod. L., from Gk. *surinx*, *suring-* 'tube, channel' + *muelos* 'marrow.']

syr·inx /'siriNGks/ ▶ n. (pl. **-inx·es**) **1** a set of panpipes. **2** Ornithol. the lower larynx or voice organ in birds. [17th C.: via L. from Gk. *surinx* 'pipe, channel.']

Syro- ▶ comb. form Syrian; Syrian and ...: *Syro-Palestinian.* ■ relating to Syria.

syr·up /'sirəp; 'sər-/ (also **sirup**) ▶ n. a thick sweet liquid made by dissolving sugar in boiling water, often used for preserving fruit. ■ a thick sweet liquid containing medicine or used as a drink. ■ a thick sticky liquid derived from a sugar-rich plant, esp. sugar cane, corn, and maple. ■ fig. excessive sweetness or sentimentality of style or manner. [ME: from OFr. *sirop* or med. L. *siropus*, from Arab. *šarāb* 'beverage.']

syr·up·y /'sirəpē; 'sər-/ (also **sir·up·y**) ▶ adj. having the consistency or sweetness of syrup: *syrupy desserts.* ■ fig. excessively sentimental.

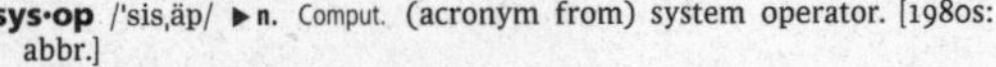

sys·op /'sis,äp/ ▶ n. Comput. (acronym from) system operator. [1980s: abbr.]

syst. ▶ abbr. system.

sys·tem /'sistəm/ ▶ n. **1** a set of connected things or parts forming a complex whole, in particular: ■ a set of things working together as parts of a mechanism or an interconnecting network. ■ Physiol. a set of organs in the body with a common structure or function. ■ the human or animal body as a whole. ■ Comput. a group of related hardware units or programs or both, esp. when dedicated to a single application. ■ Geol. (in chronostratigraphy) a major range of strata that corresponds to a period in time, subdivided into series. ■ Astron. a group of celestial objects connected by their mutual attractive forces, esp. moving in orbits about a center. ■ short for CRYSTAL SYSTEM. **2** a set of principles or procedures according to which something is done; an organized scheme or method. ■ orderliness; method. ■ a method of choosing one's procedure in gambling. ■ a set of rules used in measurement or classification. ■ (**the system**) the prevailing political or social order, esp. when regarded as oppressive and intransigent. **3** Music a set of staves in a musical score joined by a brace.
– PHRASES **get something out of one's system** informal get rid of a preoccupation or anxiety. [17th C.: from Fr. *système* or late L. *systema*, from Gk. *sustēma*, from *sun-* 'with' + *histanai* 'set up.']

sys·tem·at·ic /,sistə'matik/ ▶ adj. done or acting according to a fixed plan or system; methodical. —**sys·tem·at·i·cal·ly** adv. **sys·tem·a·tist** /'sistəmə,tist/ n.

sys·tem·at·ics /,sistə'matiks/ ▶ plural n. [treated as sing.] the branch of biology that deals with classification and nomenclature; taxonomy.

sys·tem·a·tize /'sistəmə,tīz/ ▶ v. [trans.] arrange according to an organized system; make systematic. —**sys·tem·a·ti·za·tion** /,sistəməti'zāsHən/ n. **sys·tem·a·tiz·er** n.

sys·tem·ic /si'stemik/ ▶ adj. **1** of or relating to a system, esp. as opposed to a particular part. ■ (of an insecticide, fungicide, or similar substance) entering the plant via the roots or shoots and passing through the tissues. **2** Physiol. denoting the part of the circulatory system concerned with the transportation of oxygen to and carbon dioxide from the body in general, esp. as distinct from the pulmonary part concerned with the transportation of oxygen from and carbon dioxide to the lungs. —**sys·tem·i·cal·ly** adv.

sys·tem·ize /'sistə,mīz/ ▶ v. another term for SYSTEMATIZE. —**sys·tem·i·za·tion** /,sistəmi'zāsHən/ n. **sys·tem·iz·er** n.

sys·tem op·er·a·tor (also **sys·tems op·er·a·tor**) ▶ n. Comput. a person who manages the operation of a computer system, such as an electronic bulletin board.

sys·tems an·a·lyst ▶ n. a person who analyzes a complex process or operation in order to improve its efficiency, esp. by applying a computer system. —**sys·tems a·nal·y·sis** n.

sys·to·le /'sistəlē/ ▶ n. Physiol. the phase of the heartbeat when the heart muscle contracts and pumps blood from the chambers into the arteries. Often contrasted with DIASTOLE. —**sys·tol·ic** /si'stälik/ adj. [16th C.: via late L. from Gk. *sustolē*, from *sustellein* 'to contract.']

syz·y·gy /'sizijē/ ▶ n. (pl. **-gies**) Astron. a conjunction or opposition, esp. of the moon with the sun. ■ a pair of connected or corresponding things. [17th C.: via late L. from Gk. *suzugia*, from *suzugos* 'yoked, paired,' from *sun-* 'with, together' + the stem of *zeugnunai* 'to yoke.']

Szcze·cin /'sHcHecHēn/ a city in northwestern Poland; pop. 413,000. German name STETTIN.

Sze·chuan /'secH'wän/ (also **Sze·chwan**) variant of SICHUAN.

Sze·ged /'seged/ a city in southern Hungary, a port on the Tisza River; pop. 178,000.

Szi·lard /'zilärd; 'sil-; -ərd/, Leo (1898–1964), US physicist and biologist; born in Hungary. He was a central figure in the Manhattan Project, which developed the atom bomb.

PRONUNCIATION KEY ə *ago, up*; ər *over, fur*; a *hat*; ā *ate*; ä *car*; e *let*; ē *see*; i *fit*; ī *by*; NG *sing*; ō *go*; ô *law, for*; oi *toy*; o͝o *good*; o͞o *goo*; ou *out*; TH *thin*; T͟H *then*; ZH *vision*

Tt

T[1] /tē/ (also **t**) ▸ **n.** (pl. **Ts** or **T's**) **1** the twentieth letter of the alphabet. ■ denoting the next after S in a set of items, categories, etc. **2** (**T**) (also **tee**) a shape like that of a capital T: [in comb.] *make a T-shaped cut.* See also **T-SQUARE**, etc.
– PHRASES **cross the T** hist. (of a naval force) cross in front of an enemy force approximately at right angles, securing a tactical advantage for gunnery. **to a T** informal exactly; to perfection.

T[2] ▸ **abbr.** ■ [in comb.] (in units of measurement) tera- (1012): *12 Tbytes of data storage.* ■ tesla. ▸ **symb.** ■ temperature. ■ Chem. the hydrogen isotope tritium.

t ▸ **abbr.** long or metric ton(s). ▸ **symb.** (*t*) Stat. a number characterizing the distribution of a sample taken from a population with a normal distribution.

't /t/ ▸ **contr.** the word "it," attached to the end of a verb, esp. in the transcription of regional spoken use: *I'll never do't again.*

-t[1] ▸ **suffix** equivalent to **-ED**[2] (as in *crept, sent, slept*).

-t[2] ▸ **suffix** equivalent to **-EST**[2] (as in *shalt*).

T-1 ▸ **n.** (also **T-3**) Comput. a high-speed data transmission line.

Ta ▸ **symb.** the chemical element tantalum.

ta /tä/ ▸ **exclam.** Brit., informal thank you. [18th C.: a child's word.]

tab[1] /tab/ ▸ **n. 1** a small flap of material on something, used to hold or manipulate it, or for identification and information. ■ a similar piece of material forming part of a garment: [as adj.] *tab collars.* ■ a strip or ring of metal attached to the top of a canned drink and pulled to open the can. **2** informal a restaurant or bar bill. **3** Aeron. a part of a control surface, typically hinged, that modifies the action or response of the surface. ▸ **v.** (**tabbed, tab·bing**) [trans.] mark or identify with a projecting piece of material: *a page tabbed by a bookmark.* ■ fig. identify as being of a specified type or suitable for a specified position: *he was tabbed as the next chairman.*
– PHRASES **keep tabs** (or **a tab**) **on** informal monitor the activities or development of; keep under observation. **pick up the tab** informal pay for something. — **tabbed adj.** [ME: perh. rel. to **TAG**[1].]

tab[2] ▸ **n.** a facility in a word-processing program, or a device on a typewriter, used for advancing to a sequence of set positions in tabular work. ▸ **v.** (**tabbed, tab·bing**) **1** short for **TABULATE. 2** activate the tab feature on a word processor or typewriter.

tab[3] ▸ **n.** informal a tablet containing a dose of a drug.

tab[4] ▸ **n.** informal a tabloid.

tab. ▸ **abbr.** ■ tables. ■ (in prescriptions) tablet. [from L. *tabella.*]

tab·ard /'tabərd/ ▸ **n.** a sleeveless jerkin consisting only of front and back pieces with a hole for the head. ■ hist. a coarse garment of this kind as the outer dress of medieval peasants and clerics, or worn as a surcoat over armor. ■ a herald's official coat emblazoned with the arms of the sovereign. [ME: from OFr. *tabart.*]

Ta·bas·co[1] /tə'baskō; -'bäs-/ a state in southeastern Mexico, on the Gulf of Mexico.

Ta·bas·co[2] /tə'baskō/ (also **Ta·bas·co sauce**) ▸ **n.** trademark a pungent sauce made from the fruit of a capsicum pepper (*Capsicum frutescens*). [19th C.: see **TABASCO**[1].]

tab·bou·leh /tə'bo͞olē/ (also **ta·bou·li**) ▸ **n.** an Arab salad of cracked wheat mixed with finely chopped ingredients such as tomatoes, onions, and parsley. [from Arab. *tabbūla.*]

tab·by /'tabē/ ▸ **n.** (pl. **-bies**) **1** (also **tab·by cat**) a cat whose fur is mottled or streaked with dark stripes. [17th C. (as *tabby cat*): said to be so named from its striped coloring.] ■ informal any domestic cat. **2** a fabric with a watered pattern, typically silk. **3** a plain weave. **4** a type of concrete made of lime, shells, gravel, and stones that dries very hard. ▸ **adj.** (of a cat) gray or brownish in color and streaked with dark stripes. [16th C. ('a kind of taffeta'): from Fr. *tabis*, based on Arab. *al-Attābiyya*, a quarter of Baghdad.]

tab·er·nac·le /'tabər,nakəl/ ▸ **n. 1** (in biblical use) a habitation, typically of light construction. ■ a tent used as a sanctuary for the Ark of the Covenant by the Israelites. **2** a meeting place for worship used by some Protestants or Mormons. **3** an ornamented receptacle or cabinet in which a pyx or ciborium containing the reserved sacrament may be placed in Catholic churches. ■ archaic a canopied niche or recess in the wall of a church. — **tab·er·nac·led adj.** [ME: via Fr. from L. *tabernaculum* 'tent,' dimin. of *taberna* 'hut, tavern.']

ta·bes /'tābēz/ ▸ **n.** Med. emaciation. See also **TABES DORSALIS**. — **ta·bet·ic** /tə'betik/ **adj.** [16th C.: from L., lit. 'wasting away.']

ta·bes·cent /tə'besənt/ ▸ **adj.** wasting away. [19th C.: from L. *tabescent-* 'beginning to waste away,' from the verb *tabescere*, from *tabere* 'waste away.']

ta·bes dor·sal·is /'tābēz dôr'salis; -'sālis/ ▸ **n.** Med. loss of coordination of movement, esp. as a result of syphilitic infection of the spinal cord. Also called **LOCOMOTOR ATAXIA**. [mod. L., lit. 'wasting of the back.']

ta·bla /'täblə/ ▸ **n.** a pair of small hand drums attached together, used in Indian music. [from Pers. and Urdu *tablah*, Hindi *tablā*, from Arab. *ṭabl* 'drum.']

tab·la·ture /'tabləCHər; -,CHo͝or/ ▸ **n.** esp. hist. a form of musical notation indicating fingering rather than the pitch of notes. [16th C.: from Fr., prob. from Ital. *tavolatura*, from *tavolare* 'set to music.']

ta·ble /'tābəl/ ▸ **n. 1** a piece of furniture with a flat top and one or more legs, providing a level surface on which objects may be placed. ■ [in sing.] food provided in a restaurant or household: *the finest French table of the time.* ■ a group seated at a table for a meal: *the whole table was laughing.* ■ (**the table**) a meeting place for formal discussions held to settle an issue or dispute: *the negotiating table.* **2** a set of facts or figures systematically displayed, esp. in columns. *a table of contents.* ■ Comput. a collection of data stored in memory as a series of records, each defined by a unique key stored with it. **3** a flat surface, in particular: ■ Archit. a flat, typically rectangular, vertical surface. ■ a horizontal molding, esp. a cornice. ■ a slab of wood or stone bearing an inscription. ■ a flat surface of a gem. ■ a cut gem with two flat faces. ■ each half or quarter of a folding board for backgammon. ▸ **v.** [trans.] **1** postpone consideration of: *I'd like the issue to be tabled for the next few months.* **2** Brit. present formally for discussion or consideration at a meeting: *an MP tabled an amendment to the bill.*
– PHRASES **at table** seated at a table eating a meal. **lay something on the table 1** make something known so that it can be freely and sensibly discussed. **2** postpone something indefinitely. **on the table** offered for discussion. **turn the tables** reverse one's position relative to someone else, esp. by turning a position of disadvantage into one of advantage. **under the table 1** informal very drunk. **2** (esp. of making a payment) secretly or covertly. ■ another term for **UNDER THE COUNTER** (see **COUNTER**[1]). — **ta·ble·ful** /-,fo͝ol/ **n.** (pl. **-fuls**). [OE *tabule* 'flat slab, inscribed tablet,' from L. *tabula* 'plank, tablet, list.']

tab·leau /ta'blō/ ▸ **n.** (pl. **tab·leaux** /ta'blōz/) a group of models or motionless figures representing a scene from a story or from history; a tableau vivant. [17th C. from Fr., lit. 'picture,' dimin. of *table* (see **TABLE**).]

tab·leau vi·vant /tä'blō vē'väN; -'vänt/ ▸ **n.** (pl. **tab·leaux vi·vants** pronunc. same) esp. hist. a silent and motionless group of people arranged to represent a scene or incident. [Fr., lit. 'living picture.']

ta·ble·cloth /'tābəl,klôTH; -,kläTH/ ▸ **n.** a cloth spread over a table, esp. during meals.

ta·ble d'hôte /,täbəl 'dōt; ,täblə; ,tabəl/ ▸ **n.** a restaurant meal offered at a fixed price and with few if any choices. [17th C.: Fr., lit. 'host's table.']

ta·ble·land /'tābəl,land/ ▸ **n.** a broad, high, level region; a plateau.

ta·ble lin·en ▸ **n.** fabric items used at mealtimes, such as tablecloths and napkins, collectively.

Ta·ble Moun·tain a flat-topped mountain near the southwestern tip of South Africa.

ta·ble salt ▸ **n.** salt suitable for sprinkling on food at meals.

table saw

ta·ble saw ▸ **n.** a circular saw mounted under a table or bench so that the blade projects up through a slot.

ta·ble·spoon /'tābəl,spo͞on/ ▸ **n.** a large spoon for serving food. ■ (abbr.: **tbsp.** or **tbs.** or **T**) a measurement in cooking, equivalent to 1/2 fluid ounce, three teaspoons, or 15 ml. — **ta·ble·spoon·ful** /-,fo͝ol/ **n.** (pl. **-fuls**).

tab·let /'tablit/ ▸ **n.** a flat slab of stone, clay, or wood, used esp. for an inscription. ■ a small disk or cylinder of a compressed solid substance, typically of a medicine or drug; a pill. ■ a writing pad. ■ Archit. another term for TABLE (sense 3). [ME: from OFr. *tablete*, from a dimin. of L. *tabula* (see TABLE).]

ta·ble talk ▶ n. informal conversation carried on at meals.

ta·ble ten·nis ▶ n. an indoor game based on tennis, played with small paddles and a ball bounced on a table divided by a net.

ta·ble·top /ˈtābəlˌtäp/ ▶ n. the horizontal top part of a table. ■ [as adj.] small or portable enough to be placed or used on a table.

ta·ble·ware /ˈtābəlˌwe(ə)r/ ▶ n. dishes, utensils, and glassware used for serving and eating meals at a table.

ta·ble wine ▶ n. wine of moderate quality considered suitable for drinking with a meal.

tab·loid /ˈtabloid/ ▶ n. a newspaper having pages half the size of those of a standard newspaper, typically popular in style and dominated by headlines, photographs, and sensational stories. ■ [as adj.] sensational in a lurid or vulgar way. [19th C.: from TABLET + -OID.]

tab·loid·i·za·tion /ˌtabloidəˈzāsʜən/ ▶ n. a change in emphasis from the factual to the sensational, esp. in television news.

ta·boo /təˈbo͞o; ta-/ (also **ta·bu**) ▶ n. (pl. **-boos** also **-bus** /-ˈbo͞oz/) a custom prohibiting or restricting a particular practice or forbidding association with a particular person, place, or thing. ▶ adj. prohibited or restricted by custom. ■ designated as sacred and prohibited. ▶ v. (**-boos, -booed** /-ˈbo͞od/ or **-bus, -bued**) [trans.] place under such prohibition. [18th C.: from Tongan *tabu* 'set apart, forbidden'; introduced into English by Captain Cook.]

ta·bor /ˈtābər/ ▶ n. hist. a small drum, esp. one used simultaneously by the player of a simple pipe. [ME: from OFr. *tabour* 'drum'; perh. rel. to Pers. *tabīra* 'drum.']

tab·o·ret /tabəˈret; ˈtabərit/ (**tab·ou·ret**) ▶ n. a low stool or small table. [17th C.: from Fr., 'stool,' dimin. of *tabour* 'drum' (see TABOR).]

ta·bou·li ▶ n. var. of TABBOULEH.

Ta·briz /təˈbrēz/ a city in northwestern Iran, high above sea level.

Ta·briz rug ▶ n. a rug made in Tabriz, the older styles of which typically have a rich decorative medallion pattern.

tab·u·lar /ˈtabyələr/ ▶ adj. **1** (of data) consisting of or presented in columns or tables. **2** broad and flat like the top of a table: *a huge tabular iceberg.* ■ (of a crystal) relatively broad and thin, with two well-developed parallel faces. — **tab·u·lar·ly** adv. [17th C. (sense 2): from L. *tabularis*, from *tabula* (see TABLE).]

ta·bu·la ra·sa /ˈtäbyo͝olə ˈräsə; ˈräzə/ ▶ n. (pl. **ta·bu·lae ra·sae** /ˈtäbyo͝olē ˈräsē; ˈräzē/) an absence of preconceived ideas or predetermined goals; a clean slate. ■ the human mind, esp. at birth, viewed as having no innate ideas. [L., lit. 'scraped tablet.']

tab·u·late /ˈtabyəˌlāt/ ▶ v. [trans.] arrange (data) in tabular form: [as adj.] (**tabulated**) *tabulated results.* — **tab·u·la·tion** /ˌtabyəˈlāsʜən/ n.

tab·u·la·tor /ˈtabyəlātər/ ▶ n. **1** a person or thing that arranges data in tabular form. **2** another term for TAB[2].

ta·bun /ˈtäbo͝on/ ▶ n. an organophosphorus nerve gas, developed in Germany during World War II. [Ger., of unknown origin.]

TAC ▶ abbr. Tactical Air Command.

tac·a·ma·hac /ˈtakəməˌhak/ ▶ n. another term for BALSAM POPLAR. [16th C.: from obs. Sp. *tacamahaca*, from Aztec *tecomahiyac*.]

tac·an /ˈtakən/ ▶ n. an electronic ultrahigh-frequency navigational aid system for aircraft that measures bearing and distance from a ground beacon. [1950s: from *tac(tical) a(ir) n(avigation).*]

ta·cet /ˈtāsit; ˈtas-; ˈtäket/ ▶ v. [intrans.] Music (as a direction) indicating that a voice or instrument is silent. [L., 'is silent,' from *tacere* 'be silent.']

tach /tak/ ▶ n. informal short for TACHOMETER.

tach·ism /ˈtasʜizəm/ (also **tach·isme**) ▶ n. a style of painting adopted by some French artists from the 1940s, involving the use of dabs or splotches of color, similar in aims to abstract expressionism. [1950s: from Fr. *tachisme*, from *tache* 'a stain.']

tacho- ▶ comb. form relating to speed: *tachometer.* [from Gk. *takhos* 'speed.']

ta·chom·e·ter /taˈkämitər; tə-/ ▶ n. an instrument that measures the working speed of an engine (esp. in a road vehicle), typically in revolutions per minute.

tachy- ▶ comb. form rapid: *tachycardia.* [from Gk. *takhus* 'swift.']

tach·y·car·di·a /ˌtakiˈkärdēə/ ▶ n. an abnormally rapid heart rate. [19th C.: from TACHY- 'swift' + Gk. *kardia* 'heart.']

ta·chyg·ra·phy /taˈkigrəfē; tə-/ ▶ n. stenography or shorthand, esp. that of ancient or medieval scribes. — **tach·y·graph·ic** /ˌtakiˈgrafik/ adj.

tach·y·on /ˈtakēˌän/ ▶ n. Physics a hypothetical particle that travels faster than light.

tach·yp·ne·a /ˌtakə(p)ˈnēə/ (Brit. **tach·yp·noe·a**) ▶ n. Med. abnormally rapid breathing. [19th C.: from TACHY- 'swift' + Gk. *pnoē* 'breathing.']

tac·it /ˈtasit/ ▶ adj. understood or implied without being stated. — **tac·it·ly** adv. [17th C.: from L. *tacitus*, past part. of *tacere* 'be silent.']

tac·i·turn /ˈtasiˌtərn/ ▶ adj. (of a person) reserved or uncommunicative in speech; saying little. — **tac·i·tur·ni·ty** /ˌtasiˈtərnitē/ n. **tac·i·turn·ly** adv. [18th C.: from L. *taciturnus*, from *tacitus* (see TACIT).]

Tac·i·tus /ˈtasitəs/ (*c.* 56–120), Roman historian who wrote major accounts of the Roman Empire; full name *Publius*, or *Gaius*, *Cornelius Tacitus*.

tack[1] /tak/ ▶ n. **1** a small, sharp, broad-headed nail. ■ a thumbtack. **2** a long stitch used to fasten fabrics together temporarily, prior to permanent sewing. **3** Sailing an act of changing course by turning a vessel's head into and through the wind, so as to bring the wind on the opposite side. ■ a boat's course relative to the direction of the wind: *the brig bowled past **on the opposite tack**.* ■ a distance sailed between such changes of course. ■ fig. a method of dealing with a situation or problem: *try another tack.* **4** Sailing a rope for securing the weather clew of a course. ■ the weather clew of a course, or the lower forward corner of a fore-and-aft sail. **5** the quality of being sticky. ▶ v. **1** [trans.] fasten or fix in place with tacks. ■ fasten (pieces of cloth) together temporarily with long stitches. ■ (**tack something on**) add or append something to something already existing. **2** [intrans.] Sailing change course by turning a boat's head into and through the wind. Compare with WEAR[2]. ■ [trans.] alter the course of (a boat) in such a way. ■ make a series of such changes of course while sailing: *she spent the entire night tacking back and forth.* ■ fig. make a change in one's conduct, policy, or direction of attention: *she had tacked and was on a new tangent.* — **tack·er** n. [ME: prob. rel. to OFr. *tache* 'clasp, large nail.']

tack[2] ▶ n. equipment used in horse riding, including the saddle and bridle. ▶ v. [trans.] (usu. **tack up**) put tack on (a horse). [18th C.: shortening of TACKLE. The noun sense dates from the 1920s.]

tack·le /ˈtakəl/ ▶ n. **1** the equipment required for a task or sport: *fishing tackle.* **2** a mechanism consisting of ropes, pulley blocks, hooks, or other things for lifting heavy objects. ■ the running rigging and gear used to work a boat's sails. **3** Football & Rugby an act of seizing and stopping a player in possession of the ball by knocking them to the ground. ■ (in soccer and other games) an act of taking the ball, or attempting to take the ball, from an opponent. **4** Football a player who lines up inside the end along the line of scrimmage. ▶ v. [trans.] make determined efforts to deal with (a problem or difficult task): *tackling crime.* ■ Football & Rugby stop the forward progress of (the ball carrier) by seizing them and knocking them to the ground. ■ esp. Soccer try to take the ball from (an opponent) by intercepting them. — **tack·ler** n. [ME: prob. from Mid. Low Ger. *takel*, from *taken* 'lay hold of.']

tack·le block ▶ n. a pulley over which a rope runs.

tack room ▶ n. a room in a stable building where saddles, bridles, and other equipment are kept.

tack·y[1] /ˈtakē/ ▶ adj. (**tack·i·er, tack·i·est**) (of glue, paint, etc.) retaining a slightly sticky feel; not fully dry. — **tack·i·ness** n.

tack·y[2] ▶ adj. (**tack·i·er, tack·i·est**) informal showing poor taste and quality: *his tacky decor.* — **tack·i·ly** adv. **tack·i·ness** n. [19th C.: of unknown origin. Early use was as a noun denoting a horse of little value, later applied to a poor white in some Southern states, hence 'shabby, cheap, in bad taste'.]

ta·co /ˈtäkō/ ▶ n. (pl. **-cos**) a Mexican dish consisting of a fried folded tortilla, filled with various mixtures, such as seasoned meat, beans, lettuce, and tomatoes. [Mex. Sp., from Sp., lit. 'plug, wad.']

ta·co chip ▶ n. a fried fragment of a taco, flavored with spices and eaten as a snack.

Ta·co·ma /təˈkōmə/ a city in west central Washington, on Puget Sound; pop. 193,556.

Ta·con·ic Moun·tains /təˈkänik/ (also **the Taconics**) a range of the Appalachian system, along the eastern border of New York.

tac·o·nite /ˈtakəˌnīt/ ▶ n. a low-grade iron ore consisting largely of chert, occurring chiefly around Lake Superior. [20th C.: from the name of the *Taconic* Mountains (in southeastern New York State, western Massachusetts, and southwestern Vermont) + -ITE[1].]

tac·rine /ˈtakrēn/ ▶ n. Med. a synthetic drug, $C_{13}H_{15}N_2Cl$, used in Alzheimer's disease to inhibit the breakdown of acetylcholine by cholinesterase and thereby enhance neurological function. [1960s: from *t(etra-) + acr(id)ine.*]

tact /takt/ ▶ n. adroitness and sensitivity in dealing with others or with difficult issues. — **tact·ful** adj. **tact·ful·ly** adv. **tact·ful·ness** n. [17th C.: via Fr. from L. *tactus* 'touch,' from *tangere* 'to touch.']

tac·tic /ˈtaktik/ ▶ n. an action or strategy carefully planned to achieve a specific end. ■ (**tactics**) [also treated as sing.] the art of disposing armed forces in order of battle and of organizing operations, esp. during contact with an enemy. Often contrasted with STRATEGY. — **tac·ti·cian** /takˈtisʜən/ n. [18th C.: from mod. L. *tactica*, from Gk. *taktikē (tekhnē)* '(art) of tactics,' fem. of *taktikos*, from *taktos* 'ordered, arranged.']

tac·ti·cal /ˈtaktikəl/ ▶ adj. of, relating to, or constituting tactics. ■ (of bombing or weapons) done or for use in immediate support of military or naval operations. Often contrasted with STRATEGIC. ■ (of a person or their actions) showing adroit planning; aiming at an end beyond the immediate action. — **tac·ti·cal·ly** adv.

tac·tile /ˈtaktl; ˈtaktīl/ ▶ adj. of or connected with the sense of touch. ■ perceptible by touch or apparently so; tangible: *an almost tactile memory.* ■ designed to be perceived by touch: *tactile exhibits of modern sculpture.* ■ (of a person) given to touching others, esp. as an unselfconscious expression of sympathy or affection. — **tac·til·i·ty** /takˈtilitē/ n. [17th C.: from L. *tactilis*, from *tangere* 'to touch.']

tact·less /ˈtaktlis/ ▶ adj. having or showing a lack of tact. — **tact·less·ly** adv. **tact·less·ness** n.

tac·tu·al /ˈtakcʜo͞oəl/ ▶ adj. another term for TACTILE.

tad /tad/ informal ▶ adv. (**a tad**) to a small extent; somewhat: *a tad amused.* ▶ n. [in sing.] a small amount of something. [19th C.: perh. from TADPOLE.]

ta-da /tä ˈdä/ (also **ta-dah**) ▶ exclam. an imitation of a fanfare, used typically to call attention to an impressive entrance or a dramatic announcement. [20th C.: imitative.]

Ta·djik ▶ n. & adj. var. of TAJIK.

tad·pole /'tad,pōl/ ▶ n. the tailed aquatic larva of an amphibian, breathing through gills and lacking legs until its later stages of development. [15th C.: from OE *tāda* 'toad' + POLL.]

Ta·dzhik ▶ n. & adj. var. of TAJIK.

tae-bo /'tī 'bō/ ▶ n. trademark an exercise system combining elements of aerobics and kick-boxing. [1990s: from Korean *t'ae* 'foot' + *bo*, short for *boxing*.]

Tae·gu /'tagōō/ a city in southeastern South Korea; pop. 2,229,000.

Tae·jon /'ta'jən; -'jôn/ a city in central South Korea; pop. 1,062,000.

tae kwon do /'tī 'kwän 'dō/ ▶ n. a modern Korean martial art similar to karate. [Kor., from *tae* 'kick' + *kwon* 'fist' + *do* 'art, method.']

tael /tāl/ ▶ n. a weight used in China and the Far East, about 38 grams (113 oz.). ■ a former Chinese monetary unit based on the value of this weight of standard silver. [from Malay *tahil* 'weight.']

tae·ni·a /'tēnēə/ (also **te·ni·a**) ▶ n. (pl. **-ni·ae** /-nē,ē; -nē,ī/ or **-ni·as**) **1** Anat. a flat ribbonlike structure in the body. ■ (**tae·ni·ae co·li** /'kōlī/) the smooth longitudinal muscles of the colon. **2** Archit. a fillet between a Doric architrave and frieze. **3** (in ancient Greece) a band or ribbon worn around a person's head. **4** a large tapeworm (genus *Taenia*) that parasitizes mammals. — **tae·ni·oid** /-nē,oid/ adj. [16th C. (sense 2): via L. from Gk. *tainia* 'band, ribbon.']

taen·ite /'tēnīt/ ▶ n. a nickel-iron alloy occurring as lamellae and strips in meteorites. [19th C.: from TAENIA + -ITE[1].]

taf·fe·ta /'tafitə/ ▶ n. a fine lustrous silk or similar synthetic fabric with a crisp texture. [ME: from OFr. *taffetas* or med. L. *taffata*, based on Pers. *tāftan* 'to shine.']

taff·rail /'taf,rāl; -rəl/ ▶ n. a rail and ornamentation around a ship's stern. [19th C.: alt. of obs. *tafferel* 'panel,' from Du. *tafereel*.]

taf·fy /'tafē/ ▶ n. (pl. **-ies**) **1** a candy similar to toffee, made from sugar or molasses, boiled with butter and pulled until glossy. **2** informal insincere flattery. [19th C.: earlier form of TOFFEE.]

Taft /taft/ a family of US politicians from Ohio, prominent in the Republican Party. William Howard (1857–1930) was 27th president of the US 1909–13 and Chief Justice of the US 1921–30. His administration is remembered for its use of dollar diplomacy, enforcement of antitrust laws, and enactment of tariff laws. His son Robert Alphonso (1889–1953) was a US senator 1939–53. Robert's son Robert, Jr. (1917–1993) was a US representative 1963–65 and a US senator 1971–76.

tag[1] /tag/ ▶ n. **1** a label attached to someone or something for identification or other information. ■ an electronic device that can be attached to someone or something for monitoring purposes, e.g., to deter shoplifters. ■ a nickname or description popularly given to someone or something. ■ a license plate of a motor vehicle. ■ Comput. a character or set of characters appended to an item of data to identify it. **2** a small piece or part attached to a main body. ■ a ragged lock of wool on a sheep. ■ the tip of an animal's tail when it is distinctively colored. ■ a loose or spare end of something; a leftover. ■ a metal or plastic point at the end of a shoelace that stiffens it, making it easier to insert through an eyelet. **3** a frequently repeated quotation or stock phrase. ■ Theater a closing speech addressed to the audience. ■ the refrain of a song. ■ a musical phrase added to the end of a piece. ■ Gram. a short phrase or clause added to an already complete sentence, as in *I like it, I do*. See also TAG QUESTION. ▶ v. (**tagged, tag·ging**) [trans.] **1** attach a label to. ■ give a specified name or description to: *he didn't want to be tagged as a soap star.* ■ attach an electronic tag to. ■ Comput. add a character or set of characters to (an item of data) in order to identify it for later retrieval. ■ Biol. & Chem. label (something) with a radioactive isotope, fluorescent dye, or other marker. **2** add to something, esp. as an afterthought or with no real connection: *I tried to tag a question on at the end.* ■ [intrans.] follow or accompany someone, esp. without invitation: *must he tag along?* **3** shear away ragged locks of wool from (sheep). [ME: of unknown origin.]

tag[2] ▶ n. a children's game in which one chases the rest, and anyone who is touched then becomes the pursuer. ■ Baseball the action of tagging out a runner or tagging a base: *a nice tag by the first baseman.* ■ [as adj.] denoting a form of wrestling involving tag teams. See TAG TEAM. ▶ v. (**tagged, tag·ging**) [trans.] touch (someone being chased) in a game of tag. ■ (**tag out**) Baseball put out (a runner) offbase by touching them with the ball or with the glove holding the ball. ■ Baseball (of a base runner, or a fielder with the ball) touch (a base) with the foot. ■ (usu. **tag up**) ■ Baseball (of a base runner) touch the base one has occupied after a fly ball is caught, before running to the next base.

Ta·ga·log /tə'gäləg; -,lôg/ ▶ n. **1** a member of a people originally of central Luzon in the Philippine Islands. **2** the Austronesian language of this people. ▶ adj. of or relating to this people or their language. [the name in Tagalog, from *tagá* 'native' + *ilog* 'river.']

Tag·a·met /'tagə,met/ ▶ n. trademark for CIMETIDINE.

tag·board /'tag,bôrd/ ▶ n. a kind of sturdy cardboard used esp. for making luggage labels and posters.

tag line ▶ n. informal a catchphrase or slogan, esp. as used in advertising, or the punchline of a joke.

Ta·gore /tə'gôr/, Rabindranath (1861–1941), Indian poet whose work pioneered the use of colloquial Bengali. Nobel Prize for Literature (1913).

tag ques·tion ▶ n. Gram. a question converted from a statement by an appended interrogative formula, e.g., *it's nice out, isn't it?*

tag sale ▶ n. a rummage sale or garage sale.

tag team ▶ n. a pair of wrestlers who fight as a team, taking the ring alternately. ■ informal a pair of people working together.

ta·gua nut /'tägwə/ ▶ n. another term for IVORY NUT. [19th C.: *tagua*, via Sp. from Quechua *tawa*.]

Ta·gus /'tāgəs/ a river in southwestern Europe that flows from eastern Spain to the Atlantic Ocean near Lisbon, Portugal. Spanish name TAJO, Portuguese name TEJO.

ta·hi·ni /tə'hēnē/ (also **ta·hi·na** /-nə/) ▶ n. a Middle Eastern paste made from ground sesame seeds. [from mod. Gk. *takhini*, based on Arab. *ṭaḥana* 'to crush.']

Ta·hi·ti /tə'hētē; tä-/ an island in the central South Pacific Ocean, one of the Society Islands that forms part of French Polynesia; pop. 116,000; capital, Papeete.

Ta·hi·tian /tə'hēsнən/ ▶ n. **1** a native or national of Tahiti, or a person of Tahitian descent. **2** the Polynesian language of Tahiti. ▶ adj. of or relating to Tahiti, its people, or their language.

Ta·hoe, Lake /'tähō/ a mountain lake on the border of north central California and Nevada.

Tai /tī/ ▶ adj. of, relating to, or denoting a family of Southeast Asian languages, of uncertain affinity but sometimes linked with Sino-Tibetan.

Tai·'an /'tī'än/ a city in northeastern China, in Shandong province; pop. 1,370,000.

t'ai chi ch'uan /'tī ,CHē 'CHwän; jē/ (also **t'ai chi** /'tī 'CHē/) ▶ n. a Chinese martial art and system of calisthenics, consisting of sequences of very slow controlled movements. [Chin., from *tài* 'extreme' + *jí* 'limit' + *quán* 'fist, boxing.']

Tai·chung /'tī'CHŏŏNG/ a city in west central Taiwan; pop. 774,000.

Ta·'if /'tä-if/ a city in western Saudi Arabia, southeast of Mecca; pop. 205,000.

tai·ga /'tīgə/ ▶ n. (often **the taiga**) the swampy coniferous forest of high northern latitudes, esp. that between the tundra and steppes of Siberia and North America. [19th C.: from Russ. *taĭga*, from Mongolian.]

tai·ko /'tīkō/ ▶ n. (pl. same or **-kos**) a Japanese barrel-shaped drum.

tail[1] /tāl/ ▶ n. **1** the hindmost part of an animal, esp. when prolonged beyond the rest of the body. ■ a thing resembling an animal's tail in its shape or position, typically extending downward or outward at the end of something: *the trailed tail of a capital* Q. ■ the rear part of an airplane, with the rudder and horizontal stabilizer. ■ the lower or hanging part of a garment, esp. the back of a shirt or coat. ■ (**tails**) informal a tailcoat; a man's formal evening suit with such a coat. ■ the luminous trail of particles following a comet. ■ the lower end of a pool or stream. ■ the exposed end of a slate or tile in a roof. **2** the end of a long train or line of people or vehicles. ■ [in sing.] the final, more distant, or weaker part of something: *the forecast says we're in for the tail of a hurricane.* ■ informal a person secretly following another to observe their movements. **3** informal a person's buttocks. ■ vulgar slang a woman's genitals. ■ informal women collectively regarded as a means of sexual gratification: *just another guy chasing tail.* **4** (**tails**) the reverse side of a coin (used when tossing a coin). ▶ v. [trans.] **1** informal follow and observe (someone) closely, esp. in secret. ■ [intrans.] follow: *Bill and Sally tailed along.* **2** [intrans.] (of an object in flight) drift or curve in a particular direction: *it tailed in on me at the last second.*

– PHRASES **chase one's (own) tail** informal rush around ineffectually. **on someone's tail** following someone closely. **a piece of tail** see PIECE. **with one's tail between one's legs** informal in a state of dejection or humiliation.

– PHRASAL VERBS **tail something in** (or **into**) insert the end of a beam, stone, or brick, into (a wall). **tail off** (or **away**) gradually diminish in amount, strength, or intensity. — **tailed** adj. [in comb.] *a white-tailed deer.* **tail·less** adj. **tail·less·ness** n. [OE *tæg(e)l*, from a Gmc. base meaning 'hair, hairy tail'; rel. to Mid. Low Ger. *tagel* 'twisted whip, rope's end.']

tail[2] ▶ n. Law, esp. hist. limitation of ownership, esp. of an estate or title limited to a person and their heirs: *the land was held in tail general.* See also FEE TAIL. [ME (denoting a tallage): from OFr. *taille* 'notch, tax,' from *taillier* 'to cut,' based on L. *talea* 'twig, cutting.']

tail·back /'tāl,bak/ ▶ n. Football (in some offensive formations) the back who is positioned farthest from the line of scrimmage.

tail·bone /'tāl,bōn/ ▶ n. less technical term for COCCYX.

tail·coat /'tāl,kōt/ ▶ n. a man's formal morning or evening coat, with a long skirt divided at the back into tails and cut away in front.

tail cov·ert ▶ n. (in a bird's tail) each of the smaller feathers covering the bases of the main feathers.

tail end ▶ n. [in sing.] the last or hindmost part of something: *the tail end of the 19th century.* — **tail-end·er** n. (Cricket).

tail fin ▶ n. Zool. a fin at the rear of a fish's body, typically continuous with the tail. Also called CAUDAL FIN. ■ Aeron. a projecting vertical surface on the tail of an aircraft, providing stability. ■ an upswept projection on each rear corner of an automobile, popular in the 1950s.

tail·gate /'tāl,gāt/ ▶ n. a hinged flap at the back of a truck that can be lowered or removed when loading or unloading the vehicle. ■ the door at the back of a station wagon. ■ [as adj.] relating to or denoting an informal meal served from the back of a parked vehicle, typically in the parking lot of a sports stadium: *a tailgate party.* ■ [as adj.] denoting a style of jazz trombone playing characterized by improvisation in the manner of the early New Orleans musicians. ▶**v.** informal drive too closely behind another vehicle: [trans.] *he started tailgating the car in front* | [intrans.] *drivers who tailgate at 90 mph.* ■ eat a meal served from the back of a parked vehicle. — **tail·gat·er** *n.*

tail·ing /ˈtāliNG/ ▶**n.** **1** (**tailings**) the residue of something, esp. ore. **2** the part of a beam or projecting brick or stone embedded in a wall.

taille /tāl; ˈtäyə/ ▶**n.** (pl. same) (in France before 1789) a tax levied on the common people by the king or an overlord. [Fr.]

tail·leur /täˈyər/ ▶**n.** (pl. same) dated formal a woman's tailor-made suit. [Fr.]

tail·light /ˈtālˌlīt/ ▶**n.** a red light at the rear of a motor vehicle, train, or bicycle.

tai·lor /ˈtālər/ ▶**n.** a person whose occupation is making fitted clothes for individual customers. ▶**v.** [trans.] (usu. **be tailored**) (of a tailor) make (clothes) to fit individual customers. ■ make or adapt for a particular purpose or person: *arrangements tailored to your needs.* [ME: from Anglo-Norman Fr. *taillour*, lit. 'cutter,' based on late L. *taliare* 'to cut.']

tai·lor·bird /ˈtālərˌbərd/ ▶**n.** a small South Asian warbler (genus *Orthotomus*, family Sylviidae) that makes a row of holes in one or two large leaves and stitches them together with cottony fibers or silk to form a container for the nest.

tai·lored /ˈtālərd/ ▶**adj.** (of clothes) smart, fitted, and well cut. ■ (of clothes) cut in a particular way: *a poorly tailored suit.*

tai·lor·ing /ˈtāləriNG/ ▶**n.** the activity or trade of a tailor. ■ the style or cut of a garment or garments.

tai·lor-made ▶**adj.** (of clothes) made by a tailor for a particular customer. ■ made, adapted, or suited for a particular purpose or person: *he was tailor-made for the job.* ▶**n.** a garment specially made for a particular customer: *wear your red tailor-made.*

tail·piece /ˈtālˌpēs/ ▶**n.** a final or end part of something, in particular: ■ a part added to the end of a piece of writing. ■ a small decorative design at the foot of a page or the end of a chapter or book. ■ the piece at the base of a violin or other stringed instrument to which the strings are attached.

tail·pipe /ˈtālˌpīp/ ▶**n.** the rear section of the exhaust system of a motor vehicle.

tail·race /ˈtālˌrās/ ▶**n.** a fast-flowing stretch of a river or stream below a dam or water mill.

tail·spin /ˈtālˌspin/ ▶**n.** an aircraft's diving descent combined with rotation. ■ a state or situation of chaos, panic, or loss of control. ▶**v.** (**-spin·ning**; past and past part. **-spun**) [intrans.] become out of control.

tail·stock /ˈtālˌstäk/ ▶**n.** the adjustable part of a lathe holding the fixed spindle.

tail·wa·ter /ˈtālˌwôtər; -ˌwätər/ ▶**n.** the water in a tailrace.

tail·wind /ˈtālˌwind/ ▶**n.** a wind blowing in the direction of travel of a vehicle or aircraft; a wind blowing from behind.

Tai·myr Pen·in·su·la /tīˈmi(ə)r/ (also **Tay·myr**) a peninsula on the northern coast of central Russia; the northernmost point in Asia.

Tai·no /ˈtīnō/ ▶**n.** **1** a member of an extinct Arawak people formerly inhabiting the Greater Antilles and the Bahamas. **2** the extinct Arawakan language of this people. [from Taino *taino* 'noble, lord.']

taint /tānt/ ▶**n.** a trace of a bad or undesirable quality or substance: *the taint of corruption.* ■ a thing whose influence or effect is perceived as contaminating or undesirable: *the taint that stains the company.* ■ an unpleasant smell: *the taint of creosote.* ▶**v.** [trans.] (often **be tainted**) contaminate or pollute (something). ■ affect with a bad or undesirable quality: *his administration was tainted by scandal.* ■ [intrans.] archaic (of food or water) become contaminated or polluted. [ME: partly from OFr. *teint* 'tinged,' based on L. *tingere* 'to dye, tinge'; partly a shortening of ATTAINT.]

tai·pan[1] /ˈtīˌpan/ ▶**n.** a foreigner who is head of a business in China or Hong Kong. [19th C.: from Chin. (Cantonese dial.) *daaihbāan*.]

tai·pan[2] ▶**n.** a large, brown, highly venomous Australian snake (genus *Oxyuranus*, family Elapidae). [1930s: from Wik Munkan *dhayban*.]

Tai·pei /ˌtīˈpā; -ˈbā/ the capital of Taiwan, in the northern part of the country; pop. 2,718,000.

Tai·wan /ˌtīˈwän/ an island country off the southeastern coast of China. *See box.* Former name **FORMOSA**. — **Tai·wan·ese** /ˌtīwəˈnēz; -ˈnēs; -wä-/ **adj.** & **n.**

Tai·yuan /ˈtīˈyōōˈän/ a city in northern China, capital of Shanxi province; pop. 1,900,000.

Ta·'iz /täˈēz/ a city in southwestern Yemen; pop. 290,000.

Ta·jik /täˈjik/ (also **Ta·djik** or **Ta·dzhik**) ▶**n.** **1** a member of a mainly Muslim people inhabiting Tajikistan and parts of neighboring countries. ■ a native or national of the republic of Tajikistan. **2** (also **Ta·ji·ki** /-ˈjikē/) the Iranian language of the Tajiks. ▶**adj.** of or relating to Tajikistan, the Tajiks, or their language. [from Pers. *tājīk* 'someone who is neither an Arab nor a Turk.']

Ta·jik·i·stan /təˈjēkəˌstan; -ˌstän; -ˈjikə; tä-/ (also **Ta·dzhi·ki·stan**) a republic in central Asia. *See box.*

Taj Ma·hal /ˈtäzH məˈhäl; ˈtäj/ a mausoleum at Agra, India, completed *c.*1649, built by the Mogul emperor Shah Jahan (1592–1666) in memory of his favorite wife. [perh. a corruption of Pers. *Mumtaz Mahal*, from *mumtāz* 'chosen one' and *mahal* 'abode.']

Ta·jo /ˈtähō/ Spanish name for **TAGUS**.

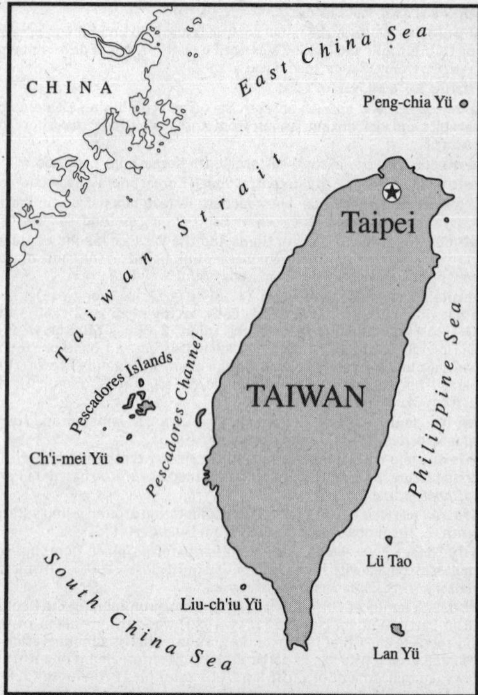

Taiwan

Official name: Republic of China
Location: Pacific Ocean, off the southeastern coast of China
Area: 13,900 square miles (36,000 sq km)
Population: 22,700,000
Capital: Taipei
Languages: Mandarin Chinese (official), Min, Hakka dialects
Currency: New Taiwan dollar

Tajikistan

Official name: Republic of Tajikistan
Location: central Asia, north of Afghanistan
Area: 55,300 square miles (143,100 sq km)
Population: 7,011,000
Capital: Dushanbe
Languages: Tajik (official), Russian
Currency: somoni

ta·ka /ˈtäkə/ ▶**n.** (pl. same) the basic monetary unit of Bangladesh, equal to 100 poisha.

take /tāk/ ▶ **v.** (past **took**; past part. **tak•en**) [trans.] **1** lay hold of (something) with one's hands; reach for and hold. ■ remove (someone or something) from a particular place: *the police took him away.* ■ consume as food, drink, medicine, or drugs. ■ capture or gain possession of by force or military means: *the French took Ghent.* ■ (in bridge, hearts, and similar card games) win (a trick). ■ Chess capture (an opposing piece or pawn). ■ dispossess someone of (something); steal or illicitly remove: *when was the cash taken?* ■ cheat (someone) of something: *can I get taken by buying mutual funds?* ■ subtract: *take two* ***from*** *ten.* ■ occupy (a place or position): *all the seats were taken.* ■ buy or rent (a house). ■ agree to buy (an item): *I'll take the one on the end.* ■ gain or acquire (possession or ownership of something): *he took possession of a ceramic piece.* ■ (**be taken**) humorous (of a person) already be married or in an emotional relationship. ■ [in imper.] use or have ready to use: *take half the marzipan and roll out.* ■ [usu. in imper.] use as an instance or example in support of an argument: *let's take Napoleon, for instance.* ■ regularly buy or subscribe to (a particular newspaper or periodical). ■ ascertain by measurement or observation: *the nurse takes my blood pressure.* ■ write down: *taking notes.* ■ make (a photograph) with a camera. ■ (usu. **be taken**) (esp. of illness) suddenly strike or afflict (someone): *he was taken with the flu.* ■ have sexual intercourse with. **2** carry or bring with one; convey: *he took along a portfolio of drawings.* ■ accompany or guide (someone) to a specified place: *take me to my room.* ■ bring into a specified state: *the invasion took Europe to the brink of war.* ■ use as a route or a means of transportation: *take 95 north to Baltimore.* **3** accept or receive (someone or something): *they don't take children.* ■ understand or accept as valid: *I take your point.* ■ acquire or assume (a position, state, or form): *he took office in September.* ■ achieve or attain (a victory or result): *John Martin took the men's title.* ■ act on (an opportunity): *he took his chance to get out while the house was quiet.* ■ experience or be affected by: *the boy took a savage beating.* ■ react to or regard (news or an event) in a specified way: *she took the news well.* ■ deal with (a physical obstacle or course) in a specified way: *he took the corner recklessly.* ■ Baseball (of a batter) allow a pitch to go by without attempting to hit the ball. ■ regard or view in a specified way: *he somehow* ***took it as*** *a personal insult.* ■ (**be taken by/with**) be attracted or charmed by: *Billie was very taken with him.* ■ submit to, tolerate, or endure: *they refused to take it any more.* ■ (**take it**) assume: *I take it that someone is coming to meet you.* **4** make, undertake, or perform (an action or task): *Lucy took a deep breath* | *he took the oath of office.* ■ be taught or examined in (a subject): *some degrees require a student to take a secondary subject.* ■ Brit. obtain (an academic degree) after fulfilling the required conditions. **5** require or use up (a specified amount of time): *the jury took an hour to find her guilty.* ■ (of a task or situation) need or call for (a particular person or thing): *it will take an electronics expert to dismantle it.* ■ hold; accommodate: *an exclusive inn that takes twenty guests.* ■ wear or require (a particular size of garment or type of complementary article): *he takes size 5 boots.* **6** [intrans.] (of a plant or seed) take root or begin to grow; germinate: *the fuchsia cuttings had taken.* ■ (of an added substance) become successfully established. **7** Gram. have or require as part of the appropriate construction: *a verb that takes a finite clause as its object.* ▶ **n.** **1** a scene or sequence of sound or vision photographed or recorded continuously at one time: *we completed the scene in two takes.* ■ a particular version of or approach to something: *his* ***take on*** *life.* **2** an amount of something gained or acquired from one source or in one session: *the take from commodity taxation.* ■ the money received at a theater, arena, etc., for seats. **3** Print. an amount of copy set up at one time or by one compositor.

– PHRASES **be on the take** informal take bribes. **be taken ill** become ill suddenly. **have what it takes** informal have the necessary qualities for success. **take advantage of, take advice,** etc. see ADVANTAGE, ADVICE, etc. **take the cake** informal (of a person or incident) be the most remarkable or foolish of their kind. **take five** (or **ten**) take a five (or ten) minute break before resuming work or another activity. **take a lot of** (or **some**) —— be difficult to do or effect in the specified way: *he might take some convincing.* **take someone in hand** undertake to control or reform someone. **take something in hand** start doing or dealing with a task. **take the heat** informal accept blame or withstand disapproval. **take it from me** I can assure you. **take it on one** (or **oneself**) **to do something** decide to do something without asking for permission or advice. **take it or leave it** [usu. in imper.] said to express that the offer one has made is not negotiable and that one is indifferent to another's reaction to it. **take it out of** exhaust the strength of (someone): *parties can take it out of you.* **take the stand** testify at a trial. **take someone out of themselves** make a person forget their worries. **take that!** exclaimed when hitting someone or taking decisive action against them. **take one's time** not hurry.

– PHRASAL VERBS **take after** resemble (a parent or ancestor). **take something apart** dismantle something. ■ (**take someone/something apart**) informal attack, criticize, or defeat someone or something in a vigorous or forceful way. **take away from** detract from: *that shouldn't take away from her fine career.* **take someone back** strongly remind someone of a past time. **take something back 1** retract a statement. **2** return unsatisfactory goods to a store. ■ (of a store) accept such goods. **3** Print. transfer text to the previous line. **take something down 1** write down spoken words: *I took down the address.* **2** dismantle and remove a structure. **take from** another way of saying TAKE AWAY FROM. **take someone in 1** accommodate someone as a lodger or because they are homeless or in difficulties. **2** cheat, fool, or deceive someone. **take something in 1** undertake work at home: *she took in laundry on weekends.* **2** make a garment tighter by altering its seams. ■ Sailing furl a sail. **3** receive a specified amount of money as payment or earnings. **4** include or encompass something: *a view that takes in Otsego Lake.* ■ fully understand or absorb something heard or seen: *he hasn't taken it all in.* **5** visit or attend a place or event in a casual way or on the way to another: *he'd maybe take in a movie, or just relax.* **take off 1** (of an aircraft or bird) become airborne. ■ (of an enterprise) become successful or popular: *iPods have taken off.* **2** depart hastily: *the officer took off after his men.* **take something off 1** remove clothing from one's or another's body. **2** deduct part of an amount. **3** choose to have a period away from work: *I took the day off.* **take someone on 1** hire an employee. **2** be willing or ready to meet an adversary or opponent, esp. a stronger one. **take something on 1** undertake a task or responsibility, esp. a difficult one. **2** acquire a particular meaning or quality: *art has taken on a new purpose for me.* **take someone/something out** informal kill, destroy, or disable someone or something. **take something out 1** obtain an official document or service: *I'll take out a loan.* ■ get a license or summons issued. **2** buy food at a cafe or restaurant for eating elsewhere. **take something out on** relieve frustration or anger by attacking or mistreating (a person or thing not responsible for such feelings). **take something over 1** (also **take over**) assume control of something: *British troops had taken over the German trenches.* ■ (of a company) buy out another. ■ become responsible for a task in succession to another: *she took over as CEO.* **2** Print. transfer text to the next line. **take to 1** begin or fall into the habit of: *he took to hiding food.* **2** form a liking for: *Mrs. Brady never took to Moran.* ■ develop an ability for (something), esp. quickly or easily: *I took to pole-vaulting right away.* **3** go to (a place) to escape danger or an enemy: *they took to the hills.* **take something up 1** become interested or engaged in a pursuit: *she took up tennis at the age of 11.* ■ begin to hold or fulfill a position or post. ■ accept an offer or challenge. **2** occupy time, space, or attention: *I don't want to take up any more of your time.* **3** pursue a matter later or further: *he'll have to* ***take it up with*** *the bishop.* ■ (also **take up**) resume speaking after an interruption: *I took up where I had left off.* **4** shorten a garment by turning up the hem. **take someone up on 1** accept (an offer or challenge) from someone. **2** challenge or question a speaker on (a particular point): *the interviewer did not take him up on his quotation.* **take up with** begin to associate with (someone), esp. in a way disapproved of by the speaker: *he's taken up with druggies.* — **tak•a•ble** /'tākəbəl/ (also **take•a•ble**) **adj.** [OE *tacan* 'get (esp. by force), capture,' from ON *taka* 'grasp, lay hold of.']

take•a•way /'tākə,wā/ ▶ **n.** **1** Sports (in football and hockey) an act of regaining the ball or puck from the opposing team. **2** Brit. a takeout restaurant. ■ a meal or dish of such food.

take•down /'tāk,doun/ ▶ **n.** **1** a wrestling maneuver in which an opponent is swiftly brought to the mat from a standing position. **2** informal a police raid or arrest. **3** [as adj.] denoting a firearm with the capacity to have the barrel and magazine detached from the stock.

take-home pay ▶ **n.** the pay received by an employee after the deduction of taxes and other obligations.

take•off /'tāk,ôf; -,äf/ (also **take-off**) ▶ **n.** **1** the action of becoming airborne. **2** an act of mimicking someone or something: *a* ***takeoff on*** *Bush.*

take•out /'tāk,out/ (also **take-out**) ▶ **n.** food cooked and sold by a restaurant or store to be eaten elsewhere.

take•o•ver /'tāk,ōvər/ ▶ **n.** assuming control of something, esp. the buying out of one company by another.

tak•er /'tākər/ ▶ **n.** **1** [in comb.] a person who takes a specified thing: *a drug-taker* | *a risk-taker.* **2** a person who takes a bet or accepts an offer or challenge: *any takers?*

Tak•e•shi•ta /,tākə'sнētə/, Noboru (1924–2000) prime minister of Japan 1987–89.

take-up ▶ **n.** **1** a device for taking up slack or excess. **2** the action of taking something up: *the take-up of the thread.*

tak•ing /'tākiNG/ ▶ **n.** (**takings**) the amount of money earned by a business from the sale of goods or services: *box-office takings were scant.*

– PHRASES **for the taking** ready or available for someone to take advantage of: *it's yours for the taking.* — **tak•ing•ly adv.**

Ta•kli•ma•kan Des•ert /,tākləmə'kän/ (also **Tak•la Ma•kan**) a desert in the Xinjiang autonomous region of northwestern China.

Ta•ko•ra•di /,täkə'rädē/ a city in western Ghana, on the Gulf of Guinea; pop. 615,000.

ta•la[1] /'tälə/ ▶ **n.** a traditional rhythmic pattern in classical Indian music. [from Sanskrit *tāla* 'handclapping.']

ta•la[2] ▶ **n.** (pl. same or **ta•las** /'täləz/) the basic monetary unit of Western Samoa, equal to 100 sene. [from Samoan *tālā*.]

ta•lar•i•a /tə'le(ə)rēə/ ▶ **plural n.** (in Roman mythology) winged sandals as worn by certain gods and goddesses, esp. Mercury. [L., neut. pl. of *talaris*, from *talus* 'ankle.']

tal•bot /'talbət; 'tôl-/ ▶ **n.** a dog of an extinct light-colored breed of hound with large ears and heavy jaws. [ME: prob. from the family name *Talbot*.]

talc /talk/ ▶ **n.** talcum powder. ■ a white, gray, or pale green soft mineral with a greasy feel, occurring as translucent masses or laminae and consisting of magnesium hydroxyl silicate. ▶ **v.** (**talced, talc•ing**) [trans.]

powder or treat (something) with talc. — **talc·ose** /ˈtalkōs/ **adj.** (Geol.). **talcy** /ˈtalkē/ **adj.** [16th C.: from med. L. *talcum* (see TALCUM).]

tal·cum /ˈtalkəm/ (also **tal·cum pow·der**) ▶ **n.** a cosmetic or toilet preparation consisting of the mineral talc in powdered form, typically perfumed. ▶ **v.** (**-cumed, -cum·ing**) [trans.] powder (something) with this substance. [16th C.: from med. L., from Arab. *ṭalḳ*, from Pers.]

tale /tāl/ ▶ **n.** a fictitious or true narrative or story, esp. an imaginative one. ■ a lie.
– PHRASES **tell tales** see TELL[1]. [OE *talu* 'telling, something told,' of Gmc. origin; rel. to Ger. *Zahl* 'number,' also to TELL[1].]

ta·leg·gio /təˈlejē,ō/ ▶ **n.** a type of soft Italian cheese made from cows' milk. [the *Taleggio* valley in Lombardy.]

tal·ent /ˈtalənt/ ▶ **n. 1** natural aptitude or skill. ■ a person or people possessing such aptitude or skill: *the talent in their Toledo clubhouse.* ■ informal people regarded as sexually attractive or as prospective sexual partners: *let's hunt for some new talent.* **2** a former weight and unit of currency, used esp. by the ancient Romans and Greeks. — **tal·ent·less adj.** [OE *talente, talentan* (as a unit of weight), from L. *talenta*, pl. of *talentum* 'weight, sum of money,' from Gk. *talanton*.]

tal·ent·ed /ˈtaləntid/ ▶ **adj.** having a natural aptitude or skill for something: *a talented young musician.*

tal·ent scout ▶ **n.** a person whose job is to search for talented performers who can be employed or promoted, esp. in sports and entertainment.

tales /tālz; ˈtālēz/ ▶ **n.** Law a writ for summoning substitute jurors when the original jury has become deficient in number. [from L. *tales (de circumstantibus)* 'such (of the bystanders).']

tales·man /ˈtālzmən/ ▶ **n.** (pl. **-men**) Law a person summoned by a tales.

tale-tell·er ▶ **n.** a person who tells stories. ■ a person who spreads gossip or reveals secrets. — **tale-tell·ing n.**

ta·li /ˈtālī/ plural form of TALUS[1].

Tal·i·ban /ˈtali,ban/ a fundamentalist Muslim movement whose militia took control of much of Afghanistan from early 1995, and in 1996 took Kabul and set up an Islamic state. The Taliban government was unseated in 2001 by the military action of an American-led coalition. [from Pashto or Dari, from Pers., lit. 'students.']

tal·i·pes /ˈtalə,pēz/ ▶ **n.** Med. technical term for CLUB FOOT. [19th C.: mod. L., from L. *talus* 'ankle' + *pes* 'foot.']

tal·i·pot /ˈtalə,pät/ ▶ **n.** a tall Indian palm (*Corypha umbraculifera*) with very large fan-shaped leaves that are used as sunshades and for thatching. [17th C.: from Malayalam *tālipat*, from Sanskrit *tālīpatra*, from *tālī* 'palm' + *patra* 'leaf.']

tal·is·man /ˈtalismən; -iz-/ ▶ **n.** (pl. **-mans**) an object, typically an inscribed ring or stone, thought to have magic powers and to bring good luck. — **tal·is·man·ic** /,talizˈmanik/ **adj.** [17th C.: based on Arab. *ṭilsam*, appar. from late Gk. *telesma* 'completion, religious rite,' from *telos* 'result, end.']

talk /tôk/ ▶ **v.** [intrans.] speak in order to give information or express ideas or feelings; converse or communicate by spoken words: *the two men talked | it was no use talking to Anthony* | [trans.] *you're talking rubbish.* ■ have the power of speech: *he can talk as well as you or I can.* ■ discuss personal or intimate feelings: *we need to talk, Maggie.* ■ have formal dealings or discussions; negotiate: *they won't talk to the regime.* ■ (**talk something over/through**) discuss something thoroughly. ■ (**talk at**) address (someone) in a hectoring or self-important way without listening to their replies: *he never talked at you.* ■ (**talk to**) reprimand or scold (someone): *someone will have to talk to Lily.* ■ [trans.] (**be talking**) informal used to emphasize the seriousness, importance, or extent of the thing one is mentioning: *we're talking big money.* ■ [trans.] use (a particular language) in speech: *we were talking German.* ■ [trans.] persuade or cause (someone) to do something by talking: *don't try to talk me into acting as a go-between.* ■ reveal secret or confidential information; betray secrets. ■ gossip: *you'll have the whole school talking.* ▶ **n.** conversation; discussion: *a lull in the talk.* ■ a period of conversation or discussion, esp. a relatively serious one: *my mother had a talk with Louis.* ■ an informal address or lecture. ■ rumor, gossip, or speculation: *there is talk of an armistice.* ■ empty promises or boasting: *he's all talk.* ■ (**the talk of**) a current subject of widespread gossip or speculation in (a particular place). ■ (**talks**) formal discussions or negotiations over a period: *peace talks.*
– PHRASES **you should** (or **shouldn't**) **talk** informal used to convey that a criticism made applies equally well to the person who has made it: *"He'd chase anything in a skirt!" "You should talk!"* **don't talk to me about ——** informal said in protest when someone introduces a subject of which the speaker has had bitter personal experience. **know what one is talking about** be expert or authoritative on a specified subject. **look who's talking** another way of saying **you should talk**. **now you're talking** see NOW. **talk a blue streak** see BLUE. **talk about ——!** informal used to emphasize that something is an extreme or striking example of a particular situation or experience: *talk about hangovers!* **talk big** informal talk boastfully or overconfidently. **talk dirty** see DIRTY. **talk sense into** persuade (someone) to behave more sensibly. **talk shop** see SHOP. **talk through one's hat** (or **ass** or **backside**) informal talk foolishly, wildly, or ignorantly. **talk turkey** see TURKEY.
– PHRASAL VERBS **talk back** reply defiantly or insolently. **talk down to** speak patronizingly or condescendingly to. **talk someone around** bring someone to a particular point of view by talking. **talk someone through** enable someone to perform (a task) by giving them continuous instruction. **talk someone/something up** (or **down**) discuss someone or something in a way that makes them seem more (or less) interesting or attractive. — **talk·er n.** [ME: frequentative v. from the Gmc. base of TALE or TELL[1].]

talk·a·tive /ˈtôkətiv/ ▶ **adj.** fond of or given to talking. — **talk·a·tive·ly adv. talk·a·tive·ness n.**

talk·back /ˈtôk,bak/ ▶ **n.** a system of two-way communication by loudspeaker.

talk·ie /ˈtôkē/ ▶ **n.** informal short for TALKING PICTURE. [20th C.: from TALK.]

talk·ing /ˈtôkiNG/ ▶ **adj.** [attrib.] engaging in speech. ■ (of an animal or object) able to make sounds similar to those of speech: *Pepe, the talking crow.* ■ silently expressive: *he has talking eyes.* ▶ **n.** the action of talking; speech or discussion: *I'll do the talking.*

talk·ing blues ▶ **plural n.** a style of blues music in which the lyrics are more or less spoken rather than sung.

talk·ing book ▶ **n.** a recorded reading of a book, originally designed for use by the blind.

talk·ing cure ▶ **n.** a form of psychotherapy that relies on verbal interaction, esp. psychoanalysis.

talk·ing drum ▶ **n.** one of a set of West African drums, each having a different pitch, that are beaten to transmit a tonal language.

talk·ing head ▶ **n.** informal a presenter or reporter on television who addresses the camera and is viewed in close-up.

talk·ing pic·ture ▶ **n.** dated a movie with a soundtrack, as distinct from a silent film.

talk·ing-to ▶ **n.** [in sing.] informal a sharp reprimand in which someone is told that they have done wrong.

talk ra·di·o ▶ **n.** a type of radio broadcast in which the presenter talks about topical issues and encourages listeners to call in to air their opinions.

talk show ▶ **n.** a television or radio show in which various topics are discussed informally and listeners, viewers, or the studio audience are invited to participate in the discussion.

talk time ▶ **n.** the time during which a mobile telephone is in use to handle calls, esp. as a measure of the duration of the telephone's battery.

tall /tôl/ ▶ **adj. 1** of great or more than average height, esp. (with reference to an object) relative to width. ■ (after a measurement and in questions) measuring a specified distance from top to bottom: *he was six feet tall.* ■ [as adv.] used in reference to proud and confident movement or behavior: *stop moping and **walk tall**!* **2** [attrib.] informal (of an account) fanciful and difficult to believe; unlikely: ***a tall tale**.*
– PHRASES **a tall order** an unreasonable or difficult demand. — **tall·ish adj. tall·ness n.** [ME: prob. from OE *getæl* 'swift, prompt.']

tal·lage /ˈtalij/ ▶ **n.** hist. a form of arbitrary taxation levied by kings on the towns and lands of the Crown. ■ a tax levied on feudal dependents by their superiors. [ME: from OFr. *taillage*, from *tailler* 'to cut' (see TAIL[2]).]

Tal·la·has·see /,taləˈhasē/ the capital of Florida, in the northwestern part of the state; pop. 150,624.

tall·boy /ˈtôl,boi/ ▶ **n.** esp. Brit. a tall chest of drawers, typically one mounted on legs and in two sections, one standing on the other. Compare with HIGHBOY.

Tal·ley·rand /ˈtali,rand; ,tālēˈräN/, Charles Maurice de (1754–1838), French statesman; full surname *Talleyrand-Périgord*. He became head of the new government after the fall of Napoleon in 1814.

tall hat ▶ **n.** another term for TOP HAT.

Tal·linn /ˈtälin; ˈtal-/ the capital of Estonia, a port on the Gulf of Finland; pop. 505,000.

tal·lith /ˈtälis; täˈlēt/ (also **tal·lis**) ▶ **n.** a fringed shawl traditionally worn by Jewish men at prayer. [from Rabbinical Heb. *ṭallīt*, from biblical Heb. *ṭillēl* 'to cover.']

tal·low /ˈtalō/ ▶ **n.** a hard fatty substance made from rendered animal fat, used in making candles and soap. — **tal·low·y adj.** [ME: perh. from Mid. Low Ger.; rel. to Du. *talk* and Ger. *Talg*.]

tall ship ▶ **n.** a sailing ship with high masts.

tall tim·ber ▶ **n.** dense and uninhabited forest. ■ (usu. **tall timbers**) informal a remote or unknown place.

tal·ly /ˈtalē/ ▶ **n.** (pl. **-lies**) a current score or amount. ■ a record of a score or amount: *I **kept a running tally** of David's debt.* ■ a particular number taken as a group or unit to facilitate counting. ■ a mark registering such a number. ■ (also **tal·ly stick**) hist. a piece of wood scored across with notches for the items of an account and then split into halves, each party keeping one. ■ an account kept in such a way. ■ archaic a counterpart or duplicate of something. ▶ **v.** (**-lies, -lied**) **1** [intrans.] agree or correspond: *signatures should tally with the names.* **2** [trans.] calculate the total number of: *tally the votes.* — **tal·li·er n.** [ME: from Anglo-Norman Fr. *tallie*, from L. *talea* 'twig, cutting.']

tal·ly-ho /ˈtalēˈhō/ (also **tal·ly-ho**) ▶ **exclam.** a huntsman's cry to the hounds on sighting a fox. ▶ **n.** (pl. **-hos**) **1** an utterance of this. **2** hist. a fast horse-drawn coach. ▶ **v.** (**-hoes, -hoed**) [intrans.] utter a cry of "tallyho." [18th C.: appar. an alt. of Fr. *taïaut*, of unknown origin.]

Tal·mud /ˈtälmo͝od; ˈtalməd/ ▶ **n.** (**the Talmud**) the body of Jewish civil and ceremonial law and legend comprising the Mishnah (text) and the Gemara (commentary). — **Tal·mud·ic** /talˈm(y)o͞odik; -ˈmo͝odik/ **adj. Tal·mud·i·cal** /talˈm(y)o͞odikəl; -ˈmo͝od-/ **adj. Tal·mud·ist n.** [from late Heb. *talmūḏ* 'instruction,' from Heb. *lāmaḏ* 'learn.']

tal·on /ˈtalən/ ▶ **n. 1** a claw, esp. one belonging to a bird of prey. **2** the shoulder of a bolt against which the key presses to slide it in a lock. **3** (in various card games) the cards remaining undealt. — **tal·oned adj.** [ME (denoting any heellike part or object): from OFr., lit. 'heel,' from

L. *talus* 'anklebone, heel.']

ta·lus¹ /'tāləs/ ▶ **n.** (pl. **ta·li** /'tālī/) Anat. the large bone in the ankle that articulates with the tibia of the leg and the calcaneum and navicular bone of the foot. Also called ASTRAGALUS. [16th C.: from L., lit. 'ankle, heel.']

ta·lus² ▶ **n.** (pl. **ta·lus·es**) a sloping mass of rock fragments at the foot of a cliff. ■ the sloping side of an earthwork, or of a wall that tapers to the top. [17th C.: from Fr., of unknown origin.]

tam /tam/ ▶ **n.** a tam-o'-shanter. [19th C.: abbrev.]

ta·ma·got·chi /ˌtäməˈgōCHē; -ˈgäCHē; ˌtam-/ ▶ **n.** an electronic toy displaying a digital image of a creature, which has to be looked after and responded to by the "owner" as if it were a pet. [Japanese.]

ta·ma·le /təˈmälē/ ▶ **n.** a Mexican dish of seasoned meat wrapped in cornmeal dough and steamed or baked in corn husks. [from Mex. Sp. *tamal*, pl. *tamales*, from Nahuatl *tamalli*.]

ta·man·du·a /təˈmandōōə/ ▶ **n.** a small nocturnal arboreal anteater (genus *Tamandua*, family Myrmecophagidae) with a naked prehensile tail, native to tropical America. [17th C.: via Port. from Tupi *tamanduá*, from *taly* 'ant' + *monduar* 'hunter.']

tam·a·rack /ˈtaməˌrak/ ▶ **n.** a slender North American larch (*Larix laricina*). [19th C.: from Canad. Fr. *tamarac*, prob. of Algonquian origin.]

ta·ma·ri /təˈmärē/ (also **ta·ma·ri sauce**) ▶ **n.** a variety of rich, naturally fermented soy sauce. [Japanese.]

ta·ma·ril·lo /ˌtaməˈrilō; -ˈrē-ō/ ▶ **n.** (pl. **-los**) a tropical South American plant (*Cyphomandra betacea*) of the nightshade family that bears edible egg-shaped red fruits. ■ the fruit of this plant. [1960s: invented name.]

tam·a·rin /ˈtamərin; -ˌran/ ▶ **n.** a small forest-dwelling South American monkey (genera *Saguinus* and *Leontopithecus*) of the marmoset family, typically brightly colored and with tufts and crests of hair around the face and neck. See illustration at LION TAMARIN. [18th C.: from Fr., from Galibi.]

tam·a·rind /ˈtaməˌrind/ ▶ **n.** **1** sticky brown acidic pulp from the pod of a tree of the pea family, widely used as a flavoring in Asian cooking. ■ the pod from which this pulp is extracted. **2** the tropical African tree (*Tamarindus indica*) that yields these pods, cultivated throughout the tropics and also grown as an ornamental and shade tree. [ME: from med. L. *tamarindus*, from Arab. *tamr hindī* 'Indian date.']

tam·a·risk /ˈtaməˌrisk/ ▶ **n.** an Old World shrub or small tree (genus *Tamarix*, family Tamaricaceae) with tiny scalelike leaves borne on slender branches, giving it a feathery appearance. [ME: from late L. *tamariscus*, var. of L. *tamarix*, of unknown origin.]

Ta·mau·li·pas /ˌtämouˈlēpäs/ a state in northeastern Mexico; capital, Ciudad Victoria.

tam·ba·la /tämˈbälə/ ▶ **n.** (pl. same or **-las**) a monetary unit of Malawi, equal to one hundredth of a kwacha. [from Nyanja, lit. 'cockerel.']

tam·bour /ˈtambŏŏr/ ▶ **n.** **1** hist. a small drum. **2** something resembling a drum in shape or construction, in particular: ■ a circular frame for holding fabric taut while it is being embroidered. ■ Archit. a wall of circular plan, such as one supporting a dome or surrounded by a colonnade. ■ Archit. each of a sequence of cylindrical stones forming the shaft of a column. ■ a sloping buttress or projection in a court tennis or fives court. ■ [usu. as adj.] a sliding flexible shutter or door on a piece of furniture, made of strips of wood attached to a backing of canvas: *a tambour door.* ▶ **v.** [trans.] [often as adj.] (**tamboured**) decorate or embroider on a tambour: *a tamboured waistcoat.* [15th C.: from Fr. *tambour* 'drum'; perh. rel. to Pers. *tabīra* 'drum.']

tam·bou·ra /tamˈbŏŏrə/ (also **tam·bu·ra**) ▶ **n.** **1** a large four-stringed lute used in Indian music as a drone accompaniment. **2** a long-necked lute or mandolin of Balkan countries. [16th C.: from Arab. *ṭanbūr* or Pers. *tunbūra*, both from Pers. *dunbara*, lit. 'lamb's tail.']

tam·bou·rin /ˈtambŏŏrin; taNbōōˈraN/ ▶ **n.** a long narrow drum used in Provence. ■ a dance accompanied by such a drum. [Fr., dimin. of *tambour* (see TAMBOUR).]

tam·bou·rine /ˌtambəˈrēn/ ▶ **n.** a percussion instrument resembling a shallow drum with small metal disks in slots around the edge, played by being shaken or hit with the hand. —**tam·bou·rin·ist** **n.** [16th C.: from Fr. *tambourin* (see TAMBOURIN).]

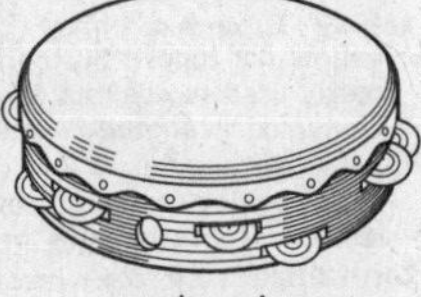
tambourine

tam·bu·ra ▶ **n.** var. of TAMBOURA.

tam·bu·rit·za /tamˈbŏŏritsə; ˌtambəˈritsə/ ▶ **n.** a kind of long-necked mandolin played in Croatia and neighboring countries. [Serbo-Croat, dimin. of *tambura* TAMBOURA.]

tame /tām/ ▶ **adj.** **1** (of an animal) not dangerous or frightened of people; domesticated. ■ not exciting, adventurous, or controversial: *network TV is pretty tame.* ■ informal (of a person) willing to cooperate. **2** (of a plant) produced by cultivation. ■ (of land) cultivated. ▶ **v.** [trans.] (often **be tamed**) domesticate (an animal). ■ make less powerful and easier to control: *the battle to tame inflation.* ■ cultivate (land or wilderness). —**tam·a·ble** (also **tame·a·ble**) **adj.** **tame·ly** **adv.** **tame·ness** **n.** **tam·er** **n.** [OE *tam* (adj.), *temmian* (v.), rel. to Ger. *zahm*, L. *domare*, and Gk. *daman* 'tame, subdue.']

Tam·er·lane /ˈtamərˌlān-/ (also **Tam·bur·laine** /ˈtambər-/) (1336–1405), Mongol ruler of Samarkand 1369–1405; Tartar name *Timur Lenk* ("lame Timur"). He conquered Persia, northern India, and Syria.

Tam·il /ˈtaməl/ ▶ **n.** **1** a member of a people inhabiting parts of southern India and Sri Lanka. **2** the Dravidian language of the Tamils. ▶ **adj.** of or relating to this people or their language. —**Tam·il·i·an** /təˈmilēən/ **adj.** & **n.** [the name in Tamil.]

Tam·il Na·du /ˈtaməl ˈnädōō/ a state in southeastern India; capital, Madras. Former name (until 1968) MADRAS.

Tam·il Ti·gers a Sri Lankan guerrilla organization founded in 1972 that seeks the establishment of an independent state (Eelam) in the northeast of the country for the Tamil community. Also called LIBERATION TIGERS OF TAMIL EELAM.

Tam·ma·ny /ˈtamənē/ (also **Tam·ma·ny Hall**) a powerful organization within the Democratic Party that was widely associated with corruption. It dominated political life in New York City in the 19th and early 20th centuries. ■ [as n.] (**a Tammany**) a corrupt political organization or group. —**Tam·ma·ny·ite** /-nēˌīt/ **n.** [after an American Indian chief of the late 17th C.]

Tam·muz¹ /ˈtämōōz; ˈtaməz/ Near Eastern Mythol. a Mesopotamian god, lover of Ishtar and similar in some respects to the Greek Adonis. [from Ezek. 8:14, from Akkadian *Dumuzi*.]

Tam·muz² var. of THAMMUZ.

tam-o'-shan·ter /ˈtam ə ˌSHantər/ ▶ **n.** a round cap of Scottish origin, with a pom-pom in the center. [19th C.: named after the hero of Burns's poem *Tam o' Shanter* (1790).]

tam-o'-shanter

ta·mox·i·fen /təˈmäksəfən/ ▶ **n.** Med. a synthetic drug used to treat breast cancer and infertility in women. It acts as an estrogen antagonist. [1970s: based on TRANS-, AMINE, OXY-², PHENOL.]

tamp /tamp/ ▶ **v.** [trans.] pack (a blast hole) full of clay or sand to concentrate the force of the explosion. ■ ram or pack (a substance) down or into something firmly: *he tamped down the tobacco with his thumb.* [19th C.: prob. a back-form. from *tampin*, var. of TAMPION.]

Tam·pa /ˈtampə/ a city in western Florida; pop. 303,447.

Tam·pa Bay an inlet of the Gulf of Mexico, in southwestern Florida.

tam·per /ˈtampər/ ▶ **v.** [intrans.] **1** (**tamper with**) interfere with (something) to cause damage or make unauthorized alterations. **2** exert a secret or corrupt influence upon; bribe. ▶ **n.** a person or thing that tamps something down, esp. a machine or tool for tamping down earth or ballast. —**tam·per·er** **n.** [16th C.: alt. of the verb TEMPER.]

tam·per-ev·i·dent ▶ **adj.** (of packaging) designed to reveal any interference with the contents.

tam·per-proof ▶ **adj.** made so that it cannot be interfered with or changed.

Tam·pi·co /tamˈpēkō; täm-/ a city in Mexico, on the Gulf of Mexico; pop. 272,000.

tam·pi·on /ˈtampēən/ (also **tom·pi·on** /ˈtämpēən/) ▶ **n.** a wooden stopper for the muzzle of a gun. ■ a plug for the top of an organ pipe. [ME: from Fr. *tampon* 'tampon.']

tam·pon /ˈtampän/ ▶ **n.** a plug of soft material inserted into the vagina to absorb menstrual blood. ■ Med. a plug of material used to stop a wound or block an opening in the body and absorb blood or secretions. ▶ **v.** (**-poned**, **-pon·ing**) plug with a tampon. [19th C.: from Fr., nasalized var. of *tapon* 'plug, stopper,' ult. of Gmc. origin and rel. to TAP¹.]

tam·pon·ade /ˌtampəˈnād/ ▶ **n.** Med. **1** (in full **cardiac tamponade**) compression of the heart by an accumulation of fluid in the pericardial sac. **2** the surgical use of a plug of absorbent material.

tam-tam /ˈtəm ˌtəm; ˈtam ˌtam/ ▶ **n.** a large metal gong with indefinite pitch. [19th C.: perh. from Hindi *ṭam-ṭam* (see TOM-TOM).]

Tan /tan/, Amy (1952–), US writer. Her works include *The Joy Luck Club* (1989).

tan¹ /tan/ ▶ **n.** **1** a yellowish-brown color. ■ a golden-brown shade of skin developed by pale-skinned people after exposure to the sun. **2** (also **tan·bark** /ˈtanˌbärk/) bark of oak or other trees, used as a source of tannin for converting hides into leather. ▶ **v.** (**tanned**, **tan·ning**) **1** [intrans.] (of a pale-skinned person or their skin) become brown or browner after exposure to the sun. ■ [trans.] [usu. as adj.] (**tanned**) (of the sun) cause (a pale-skinned person or their skin) to become brown or browner: *he looked tanned and fit.* **2** [trans.] convert (animal skin) into leather by soaking in a liquid containing tannic acid, or by the use of other chemicals. **3** [trans.] informal, dated beat (someone) repeatedly, esp. as a punishment: *I'll tan his hide!* ▶ **adj.** of a yellowish-brown color. ■ (of a pale-skinned person) having golden-brown skin after exposure to the sun. —**tan·na·ble** **adj.** **tan·nish** **adj.** [OE *tannian* 'convert into leather,' prob. from med. L. *tannare*.]

tan² ▶ **abbr.** tangent.

Ta·na, Lake /ˈtänə/ a lake in northern Ethiopia, the source of the Blue Nile.

tan·a·ger /ˈtanəjər/ ▶ **n.** a small American songbird (*Tangara* and other genera) of the bunting family, the male of which typically has brightly colored plumage. [17th C.: from Tupi *tangará*.]

Ta·na·na·rive /ˌtanənəˈrēv; təˌnanə-/ former name (until 1975) of ANTANANARIVO.

Tan·a·na Riv·er /ˈtanə,nô/ a river that flows from Yukon Territory to the Yukon River in Alaska.

tan·bark /ˈtan,bärk/ ▶ **n.** see TAN[1] (sense 2).

T & A ▶ **abbr.** tits and ass.

tan·dem /ˈtandəm/ ▶ **n.** (also **tan·dem bicycle**) a bicycle with seats and pedals for two riders, one behind the other. ■ a carriage driven by two animals harnessed one in front of the other. ■ a group of two people or machines working together. ■ a truck with two rear drive axles. ▶ **adv.** with two or more horses harnessed one behind another: *I rode tandem to Paris.* ■ alongside each other; together. ▶ **adj.** having two things arranged one in front of the other: *tandem trailers.*
– PHRASES **in tandem** alongside each other; together. ■ one behind another. [18th C.: humorously from L., lit. 'at length.']

tan·door /tanˈdo͝or; tän-/ ▶ **n.** a clay oven of a type used originally in northern India and Pakistan. [from Urdu *tandūr*, from Pers. *tanūr*, based on Arab. *tannūr* 'oven.']

tan·door·i /tanˈdo͝orē; tän-/ ▶ **adj.** denoting or relating to a style of Indian cooking based on the use of a tandoor: *tandoori chicken.* ▶ **n.** food or cooking of this type. ■ a restaurant serving such food. [from Urdu and Pers. *tandūrī*, from *tandūr* (see TANDOOR).]

Tan·ey /ˈtônē/, Roger Brooke (1777–1864), Chief Justice of the US 1836–64. He was US attorney general 1831–33.

Tang /tang/ a dynasty ruling China 618–*c.*906, noted for territorial conquest and great wealth and regarded as the golden age of Chinese poetry and art.

tang[1] /tang/ ▶ **n.** **1** [in sing.] a strong taste, flavor, or smell. ■ a characteristic quality: *the tang of finality.* **2** the projection on the blade of a tool such as a knife, by which the blade is held firmly in the handle. [ME: from ON *tangi* 'point, tang of a knife.']

tang[2] ▶ **v.** [intrans.] make a loud ringing or clanging sound. ▶ **n.** a tanging sound. [16th C.: imitative.]

tang[3] ▶ **n.** a surgeonfish (genus *Acanthurus*) that occurs around reefs and rocky areas, where it browses on algae. Its several species include the **blue tang** (*A. coeruleus*) of the western Atlantic. [18th C.: from TANG[1].]

Tan·gan·yi·ka, Lake /,tan-gənˈyēkə; ,tang-/ a lake in East Africa; the deepest lake in Africa and the longest freshwater lake in the world.

tan·ge·lo /ˈtanjə,lō/ ▶ **n.** (pl. **-los**) a hybrid of the tangerine and grapefruit. [20th C.: blend of TANGERINE and POMELO.]

tan·gent /ˈtanjənt/ ▶ **n.** **1** a straight line or plane that touches a curve or curved surface at a point, but if extended does not cross it at that point. ■ fig. a completely different line of thought or action: *she went off on a tangent about gas prices.* **2** Math. the trigonometric function that is equal to the ratio of the sides (other than the hypotenuse) opposite and adjacent to an angle in a right triangle. ▶ **adj.** (of a line or plane) touching, but not intersecting, a curve or curved surface. — **tan·gen·cy** /-jənsē/ **n.** [16th C.: from L. *tangent-* 'touching,' from the verb *tangere.*]

tangent 1

tan·gen·tial /tanˈjenchəl/ ▶ **adj.** of, relating to, or along a tangent: *a tangential line.* ■ diverging from a previous course or line; erratic: *tangential thoughts.* ■ hardly touching a matter; peripheral: *tax reform was tangential to the main objective.* — **tan·gen·tial·ly adv.**

tan·ge·rine /,tanjəˈrēn/ ▶ **n.** **1** a small citrus fruit with a loose skin, esp. one of a variety with deep orange-red skin. ■ a deep orange-red color. **2** the tree (*Citrus reticulata*) that bears this fruit. [19th C.: from *Tanger* (TANGIER) + -INE[1].]

tan·gi·ble /ˈtanjəbəl/ ▶ **adj.** perceptible by touch. ■ clear and definite; real: *tangible results.* ▶ **n.** (usu. **tangibles**) a thing that is perceptible by touch. — **tan·gi·bil·i·ty** /,tanjəˈbilitē/ **n.** **tan·gi·ble·ness n.** **tan·gi·bly adv.** [16th C.: from Fr., or from late L. *tangibilis*, from *tangere* 'to touch.']

Tan·gier /tanˈji(ə)r/ a city on the northern coast of Morocco, on the Strait of Gibraltar; pop. 307,000.

tan·gle /ˈtanggəl/ ▶ **v.** [trans.] (usu. **be tangled**) twist together into a confused mass. ■ [intrans.] (**tangle with**) informal become involved in a conflict or fight with: *there'll be trouble if I tangle with him.* ▶ **n.** a confused mass of something twisted together: *a tangle of hair.* ■ a confused or complicated state; a muddle. ■ informal a fight, argument, or disagreement. — **tan·gly adj.** [ME: prob. of Scand. origin and rel. to Swed. dial. *taggla* 'disarrange.']

tan·gle·foot /ˈtanggəl,fo͝ot/ ▶ **n.** **1** trademark material applied to a tree trunk as a grease band, esp. to prevent infestation by insects. **2** informal intoxicating liquor, esp. cheap whiskey.

tan·go /ˈtanggō/ ▶ **n.** (pl. **-gos**) **1** a ballroom dance originating in Buenos Aires, characterized by marked rhythms and postures and abrupt pauses. ■ a piece of music written for or in the style of this dance, typically in a slow dotted duple rhythm. **2** a code word representing the letter T, used in radio communication. ▶ **v.** (**-goes, -goed**) [intrans.] dance the tango. [19th C.: from L. Amer. Sp., perh. of Afr. origin.]

tan·gram /ˈtanggrəm/ ▶ **n.** a Chinese geometric puzzle consisting of a square cut into seven pieces that can be arranged to make various other shapes. [19th C.: of unknown origin.]

Tang·shan /ˈtängˈshän/ a city in northeastern China, in Hebei province; pop. 1,500,000.

tang·y /ˈtangē/ ▶ **adj.** (**tang·i·er, tang·i·est**) having a strong, piquant flavor or smell: *a tangy salad.* — **tang·i·ness n.**

Tan·jung·ka·rang /,tänjo͝ongˈkäräng/ see BANDAR LAMPUNG.

tank 2

tank /tangk/ ▶ **n.** **1** a large receptacle or storage chamber, esp. for liquid or gas. ■ the container holding the fuel supply in a motor vehicle. ■ a receptacle with transparent sides in which to keep fish; an aquarium. **2** a heavy armored fighting vehicle carrying guns and moving on a continuous articulated metal track. **3** informal a cell in a police station or jail. ▶ **v.** **1** [intrans.] fill the tank of a vehicle with fuel: *the cars stopped to tank up.* ■ (**be/get tanked up**) informal drink heavily; become drunk. **2** [intrans.] informal fail completely, esp. at great financial cost. ■ [trans.] informal (in sports) deliberately lose or fail to finish (a game). — **tank·ful** /ˈtangk,fo͝ol/ **n.** (pl. **-fuls**). **tank·less adj.** [17th C.: perh. from Gujarati *tānku-* or Marathi *tānke-* 'underground cistern.']

tan·ka /ˈtängkə/ ▶ **n.** (pl. same or **-kas**) a Japanese poem consisting of five lines, the first and third of which have five syllables and the others seven. [Japanese, from *tan* 'short' + *ka* 'song.']

tank·age /ˈtangkij/ ▶ **n.** **1** the storage capacity of a tank. ■ the storage of something in a tank or a charge made for such storage. **2** a fertilizer or animal feed obtained from the residue from tanks in which animal carcasses have been rendered.

tan·kard /ˈtangkərd/ ▶ **n.** a tall beer mug, typically made of silver or pewter, with a handle and sometimes a hinged lid. ■ the contents of or an amount held by such a mug. [ME: perh. rel. to Du. *tanckaert.*]

tank·er /ˈtangkər/ ▶ **n.** a ship, road vehicle, or aircraft for carrying liquids, esp. petroleum, in bulk.

tank·i·ni /tangˈkēnē/ ▶ **n.** a two-piece bathing suit consisting of a tank top and a bikini bottom.

tank kill·er ▶ **n.** an aircraft, vehicle, or missile effective against tanks.

tank top ▶ **n.** a close-fitting sleeveless top.

tank town ▶ **n.** a small unimportant town (used originally of a town at which trains stopped to take on water).

tan·ner /ˈtanər/ ▶ **n.** **1** a person who is employed to tan animal hides. **2** a lotion or cream designed to promote the development of a suntan or produce a similar skin color artificially.

tan·ner·y /ˈtanərē/ ▶ **n.** (pl. **-ner·ies**) a place where animal hides are tanned; the workshop of a tanner.

Tann·häu·ser /ˈtän,hoizər/ (*c.*1200–*c.*1270), German poet. In reality a minnesinger whose works included lyrics and love poetry, he became a legendary figure as a knight who visited Venus's grotto.

tan·nic /ˈtanik/ ▶ **adj.** of or related to tannin. [19th C.: from Fr. *tannique*, from *tanin* (see TANNIN).]

tan·nic ac·id ▶ **n.** another term for TANNIN. — **tan·nate** /ˈtanāt/ **n.**

tan·nin /ˈtanin/ ▶ **n.** a yellowish or brownish bitter-tasting organic substance present in some galls and barks, consisting of derivatives of gallic acid, used in leather production and ink manufacture. [19th C.: from Fr. *tanin*, from *tan* 'tanbark' (rel. to TAN[1]) + -IN[1].]

tan·ning bed ▶ **n.** an apparatus used for tanning, consisting of a bank of sunlamp tubes, typically horizontal for lying on, with another above.

Tan·nu-Tu·va /ˈtäno͞o ˈto͞ovə/ former name for TUVA.

Ta·no·an /ˈtänōən/ ▶ **n.** a small language family comprising a number of Pueblo Indian languages, including Tewa and Tiwa, and related to Kiowa. ▶ **adj.** of or relating to this language family. [from Sp. *Tano* + -AN.]

tan·sy /ˈtanzē/ ▶ **n.** a plant (genus *Tanacetum*) of the daisy family with yellow flat-topped buttonlike flowerheads and aromatic leaves, formerly used in cooking and medicine. [ME: from OFr. *tanesie*, prob. from med. L. *athanasia* 'immortality,' from Gk.]

tan·ta·lite /ˈtantl,īt/ ▶ **n.** a rare, dense, black mineral consisting of a mixed oxide of tantalum, of which it is the principal source, and iron. [19th C.: from TANTALUM + -ITE[1].]

tan·ta·lize /ˈtantl,īz/ ▶ **v.** [trans.] torment or tease (someone) with the sight or promise of something unobtainable. ■ excite the senses or desires of (someone). — **tan·ta·li·za·tion** /,tantl-iˈzāshən/ **n.** **tan·ta·liz·er n.** **tan·ta·liz·ing·ly adv.** [16th C.: from TANTALUS + -IZE.]

tan·ta·lum /ˈtantl-əm/ ▶ **n.** the chemical element of atomic number 73, a hard silver-gray metal of the transition series. (Symbol: **Ta**) — **tan·tal·ic** /tanˈtalik/ **adj.** [19th C.: from TANTALUS.]

Tan·ta·lus /ˈtantl-əs/ Gk. Mythol. a Lydian king, son of Zeus and father of Pelops. As punishment for his crimes, he was forced to remain in chin-deep water with fruit-laden branches over his head, both of which receded when he reached for them.

tan·ta·mount /ˈtantə,mount/ ▶ **adj.** [predic.] (**tantamount to**) equivalent in seriousness to; virtually the same as: *the resignations were tantamount to an admission of guilt.* [17th C.: from *tantamount* 'amount to as much,' from Ital. *tanto montare.*]

tant mieux /ˈtän ˈmyə/ ▶ **exclam.** so much the better. [Fr.]

tan·to /'täntō/ ▶ n. (pl. **-tos**) a Japanese short sword or dagger.

tant pis /'täN 'pē/ ▶ exclam. so much the worse; the situation is regrettable but now beyond retrieval. [Fr.]

tan·tra /'təntrə; 'tan-/ ▶ n. a Hindu or Buddhist mystical or ritual text. ■ adherence to the doctrines of the tantras, involving mantras, meditation, yoga, and ritual. — **tan·tric** adj. **tan·trism** n. **tan·trist** n. [Sanskrit, lit. 'loom, groundwork, doctrine,' from *tan* 'stretch.']

tan·trum /'tantrəm/ ▶ n. an uncontrolled outburst of anger and frustration, typically in a young child. [18th C.: of unknown origin.]

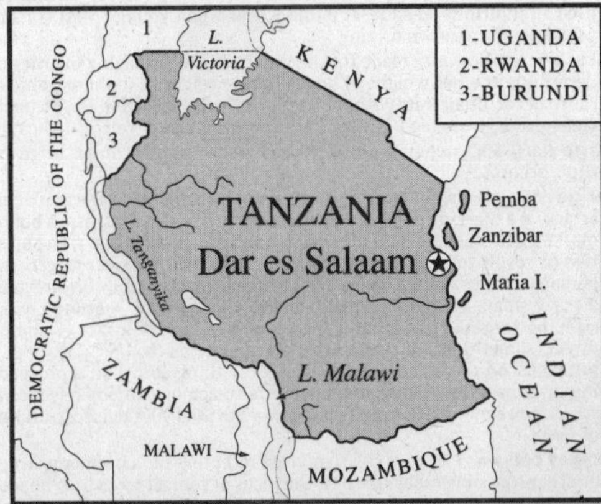

Tanzania
Official name: United Republic of Tanzania
Location: East Africa, on the Indian Ocean
Area: 365,000 square miles (945,100 sq km)
Population: 36,580,000
Capital: Dar es Salaam (legislative offices in Dodoma)
Languages: Kiswahili or Swahili, Kiunguju (name for Swahili in Zanzibar), English (all official), Arabic, many local languages
Currency: Tanzanian shilling

Tan·za·ni·a /,tanzə'nēə/ a country in East Africa. *See box.* — **Tan·za·ni·an** adj. & n.

tan·za·nite /'tanzə,nīt/ ▶ n. a blue or violet gem variety of zoisite, containing vanadium. [1960s: from TANZANIA + -ITE[1].]

Tao /dou; tou/ ▶ n. (in Chinese philosophy) the absolute principle underlying the universe, combining within itself the principles of yin and yang and signifying the way, in harmony with the natural order. [Chin., lit. '(right) way.']

Tao·ism /'douizəm; 'tou-/ ▶ n. a Chinese philosophy based on the writings of Lao-tzu (*fl.* 6th century BC), advocating humility and religious piety. — **Tao·ist** n. & adj. **Tao·is·tic** /tou'istik/ adj.

Taos /tous; 'tä-ōs/ ▶ n. (pl. same) a North American people native to New Mexico. ■ a member of this people. ■ the language of this people.

Tao-te-Ching /'dou də 'jiNG/ ▶ n. the central Taoist text, ascribed to Lao-tzu. [Chin., lit. 'the Book of the Way and its Power.']

tap[1] /tap/ ▶ n. **1** a device by which a flow of liquid or gas from a pipe or container can be controlled. ■ a device connected to a telephone used for listening secretly to someone's conversations. ■ an act of listening secretly to someone's telephone conversation. ■ (also **tap·ping**) an electrical connection made to some point between the end terminals of a transformer coil or other component. **2** an instrument for cutting a threaded hole in a material. ▶ v. (**tapped, tap·ping**) [trans.] **1** draw liquid through the tap or spout of (a cask, barrel, or other container). ■ draw (liquid) from a cask, barrel, or other container. ■ (often **be tapped**) connect a device to (a telephone) so that conversation can be listened to secretly. ■ informal obtain money or information from (someone): *he considered whom he could **tap for** information.* ■ exploit or draw a supply from (a resource): *clients seeking to tap our expertise* | [intrans.] *these magazines have **tapped into** a target market of consumers.* ■ draw sap from (a tree) by cutting into it. **2** cut a thread in (something) to accept a screw.
– PHRASES **on tap** ready to be poured from a tap. ■ informal freely available whenever needed. ■ informal on schedule to occur. — **tap·pa·ble** adj. [OE *tæppa* 'peg,' *tæppian* 'provide with a stopper,' of Gmc. origin; rel. to Ger. *Zapfen* (n.).]

tap[2] ▶ v. (**tapped, tap·ping**) [trans.] **1** strike (someone or something) with a quick light blow or blows. ■ strike (something) against something else with a quick light blow or blows: *tapping her feet in time to the music.* ■ (**tap something out**) produce (a rhythm) with a series of quick light blows on a surface. ■ write or enter (something) using a keyboard or keypad: *he **tapped out** a few words.* **2** (usu. **be tapped**) informal designate or select (someone) for a task or honor, esp. membership in an organization or committee: *he had been tapped to serve in Costa Rica.* ▶ n. **1** a quick light blow or the sound of such a blow. **2** tap dancing. ■ a piece of metal attached to the toe and heel of a tap dancer's shoe to make a tapping sound. **3** (**taps**) [treated as sing. or pl.] a bugle call for lights to be put out in army quarters. ■ a similar call sounded at a military funeral. — **tap·per** n. [ME: from OFr. *taper*, or of imitative origin.]

ta·pa /'täpə/ ▶ n. the bark of the paper mulberry tree. ■ (also **ta·pa cloth**) cloth made from such bark, used in the Pacific islands. [19th C.: of Polynesian origin.]

ta·pas /'täpəs/ ▶ plural n. small Spanish savory dishes, typically served with drinks at a bar. [Sp., lit. 'cover, lid.']

tap dance ▶ n. a dance performed wearing shoes fitted with metal taps, characterized by rhythmical tapping of the toes and heels. ▶ v. [intrans.] (**tap-dance**) perform such a dance. — **tap danc·er** n. **tap danc·ing** n.

tape /tāp/ ▶ n. a narrow strip of material, typically used to hold or fasten something. ■ [often with adj.] long narrow flexible material with magnetic properties, used for recording sound, pictures, or computer data. ■ a cassette or reel containing such material. ■ a recording on such a cassette or reel. ■ (also **adhesive tape**) a strip of paper or plastic coated with adhesive, used to stick things together. ■ a strip of material stretched across the finish line of a race, to be broken by the winner. ■ a strip of white material at the top of a tennis net. ■ a strip of material used to mark off an area. ■ a tape measure. ▶ v. [trans.] **1** record (sound or pictures) on audiotape or videotape. **2** fasten or attach (something) with adhesive tape. **3** (**tape something off**) seal or mark off an area or thing with tape.
– PHRASES **on tape** recorded on magnetic tape. [OE *tæppa, tæppe*; perh. rel. to Mid. Low Ger. *teppen* 'pluck, tear.']

tape deck ▶ n. a piece of equipment for playing audiotapes, esp. as part of a stereo system.

tape grass ▶ n. a submerged aquatic plant (genus *Vallisneria*) of the frog's-bit family, with narrow grasslike leaves. Also called EELGRASS and RIBBON GRASS.

tape meas·ure ▶ n. a length of tape or thin flexible metal, marked at graded intervals for measuring.

ta·pe·nade /,täpə'näd/ ▶ n. a Provençal paste or dip, made from black olives, capers, and anchovies. [Fr., from Provençal.]

ta·per /'tāpər/ ▶ n. a slender candle. ■ a wick coated with wax, used for conveying a flame. ■ a gradual narrowing. ▶ v. diminish or reduce or cause to diminish or reduce in thickness toward one end: [intrans.] *the tail tapers to a rounded tip* | [trans.] *a tailor can taper his trousers.* ■ gradually lessen: *the rain is **tapering off**.* [OE, dissimilated form of L. *papyrus* (see PAPYRUS.]

tape re·cord·er ▶ n. an apparatus for recording sounds on magnetic tape and later reproducing them. — **tape-re·cord** v. **tape re·cord·ing** n.

tap·es·try /'tapistrē/ ▶ n. (pl. **-tries**) a piece of thick textile fabric with pictures or designs formed by weaving colored weft threads or by embroidering on canvas, used as a wall hanging or furniture covering. ■ fig. used in reference to an intricate combination of things or sequence of events: *a tapestry of cultures.* — **tap·es·tried** adj. [ME: from OFr. *tapisserie*, from *tapissier* 'tapestry worker' or *tapisser* 'to carpet,' from *tapis* 'carpet, tapis.']

ta·pe·tum /tə'pētəm/ ▶ n. Zool. a reflective layer of the choroid in the eyes of many animals, causing them to shine in the dark. [18th C.: from late L., from L. *tapete* 'carpet.']

tape·worm /'tāp,wərm/ ▶ n. a parasitic flatworm (class Cestoda), the adult of which lives in the intestine of humans and other vertebrates. It has a long ribbonlike body with many segments that can become independent, and a small head bearing hooks and suckers.

ta·phon·o·my /tə'fänəmē/ ▶ n. the branch of paleontology that deals with the processes of fossilization. — **taph·o·nom·ic** /,tafə'nämik/ adj. **ta·phon·o·mist** n. [1940s: from Gk. *taphos* 'grave' + -NOMY.]

tap-in ▶ n. esp. Golf, Soccer, & Basketball an easy, close-range putt, shot, or tap of the ball into the goal or hole.

tap·i·o·ca /,tapē'ōkə/ ▶ n. a starchy substance in the form of hard white grains, obtained from cassava and used in cooking puddings and other dishes. [18th C.: from Tupi-Guarani *tipioca*, from *tipi* 'dregs' + *og, ok* 'squeeze out.']

mountain tapir

ta·pir /'tāpər/ ▶ n. a nocturnal hoofed mammal (family Tapiridae, genus *Tapirus*) with a stout body, sturdy limbs, and a short flexible proboscis, native to the forests of tropical America and Malaysia. Four species, including the reddish-brown or black **mountain tapir**

(*T. pinchaque*), which is the smallest tapir. [18th C.: via Sp. and Port. from Tupi *tapyra*.]

tap·is /'tapē; 'tapis; tä'pē/ ▶ **n.** (pl. same) archaic a tapestry or richly decorated cloth, used as a hanging or a covering for something. [Fr., from OFr. *tapiz*, via late L. from Gk. *tapētion*, dimin. of *tapēs* 'tapestry.']

ta·pote·ment /tə'pōtmənt/ ▶ **n.** rapid and repeated striking of the body as a technique in massage. [19th C.: Fr., from *tapoter* 'to tap.']

tap pants ▶ **plural n.** a pair of brief lingerie shorts, usually worn with a camisole top.

Tap·pan Zee /'tapən ˌzē/ a broadening of the Hudson River in southeastern New York.

tap·pet /'tapit/ ▶ **n.** a lever or projecting part on a machine that intermittently makes contact with a cam or other part so as to give or receive motion. [18th C.: appar. dimin. of TAP².]

tap·ping /'tapiNG/ ▶ **n.** the action of a person or things that taps. ■ a sound made by this.

tap·room /'tapˌro͞om; -ˌro͝om/ ▶ **n.** a room in which alcoholic drinks, esp. beer, are available on tap.

tap·root /'tapˌro͞ot; -ˌro͝ot/ ▶ **n.** a straight tapering root growing vertically downward and forming the center from which subsidiary rootlets spring.

tap shoe ▶ **n.** a shoe with a specially hardened sole or attached metal plates at toe and heel to make a tapping sound in tap dancing.

tap wa·ter ▶ **n.** water from a piped supply.

ta·que·ri·a /ˌtäkə'rēə; ˌtak-/ ▶ **n.** a Mexican restaurant specializing in tacos.

tar¹ /tär/ ▶ **n.** a dark, thick, flammable liquid distilled from wood or coal, consisting of hydrocarbons, resins, and alcohols, and used in roadmaking and for coating and preserving timber. ■ a similar substance formed by burning tobacco or other material. ▶ **v.** (**tarred, tar·ring**) [trans.] [usu. as adj.] (**tarred**) cover (something) with tar: *a newly tarred road.*
– PHRASES **beat the tar out of** informal beat or thrash severely. **tar and feather** smear with tar and then cover with feathers as a punishment. **tar people with the same brush** consider specified people to have the same faults. [OE *teru, teoru*, of Gmc. origin; rel. to Du. *teer*, Ger. *Teer*, and perh. ult. to TREE.]

tar² ▶ **n.** informal, dated a sailor. [17th C.: perh. an abbrev. of TARPAULIN.]

Ta·rab·u·lus Al-Gharb /tə'räbələs al 'gärb/ Arabic name for TRIPOLI (sense 1).

Ta·rab·u·lus Ash-Sham /tə'räbələs aSH 'SHam/ Arabic name for TRIPOLI (sense 2).

tar·a·did·dle /'tarəˌdidl/ (also **tar·ra·did·dle**) ▶ **n.** informal, esp. Brit. a petty lie. ■ pretentious nonsense. [18th C.: perh. rel. to DIDDLE.]

Ta·ra·hu·ma·ra /ˌtärəho͞o'märə/ ▶ **n.** (pl. same) **1** a member of a native people of northwestern Mexico. **2** the Uto-Aztecan language of this people. ▶ **adj.** of or relating to this people or their language. [Sp., from Tarahumara *rarámuri*.]

ta·ra·ma·sa·la·ta /ˌtärəmə-sə'lätə/ (also **ta·ra·ma** /ˌtärə'mä/) ▶ **n.** a pinkish paste or dip made from the roe of certain fish, mixed with olive oil and seasoning. [from mod. Gk. *taramas* 'roe' (from Turk. *tarama*, denoting a preparation of soft roe or red caviar) + *salata* 'salad.']

tar·an·tel·la /ˌtarən'telə/ (also **tar·an·telle** /-'tel/) ▶ **n.** a rapid whirling dance originating in southern Italy. ■ a piece of music written in fast 6/8 time in the style of this dance. [18th C.: Ital., after TARANTO.]

tar·ant·ism /'tarənˌtizəm/ ▶ **n.** a psychological illness characterized by an impulse to dance, prevalent in southern Italy from the 15th to the 17th century, believed at the time to have been caused by the bite of a tarantula. [17th C.: from Ital. *tarantismo*, after TARANTO.]

Ta·ran·to /'tärənˌtō; tə'räntō/ a city and port in southeastern Italy; pop. 244,000.

ta·ran·tu·la /tə'ranCHələ/ ▶ **n.** **1** a large hairy spider (family Theraphosidae, numerous species) found chiefly in tropical and subtropical America, some kinds of which are able to catch small lizards, frogs, and birds. **2** a large black wolf spider (*Lycosa tarentula*) of southern Europe whose bite was formerly believed to cause tarantism. [16th C.: from med. L., from Old Ital. *tarantola* 'tarantula,' after TARANTO.]

tarantula 1

Ta·ra·wa /tə'räwə; 'tarəˌwä/ an atoll in Kiribati, in the South Pacific; pop. 28,000.

ta·rax·a·cum /tə'raksəkəm/ ▶ **n.** any plant of the genus *Taraxacum* (daisy family), including the dandelion. ■ a preparation of the dried roots of this, used medicinally. [18th C.: from med. L. *altaraxacon*, via Arab. from Pers. *talk* 'bitter' + *čakūk* 'purslane.']

tar ba·by ▶ **n.** informal a difficult problem that is only aggravated by attempts to solve it. [with allusion to the doll smeared with tar as a trap for Brer Rabbit, in J. C. Harris's *Uncle Remus*.]

Tar·bell /'tärbəl/, Ida Minerva (1857–1944), US writer. A leader of the muckraking movement, she wrote the exposé *The History of the Standard Oil Company* (1904).

tar·boosh /tär'bo͞osH/ ▶ **n.** a man's cap similar to a fez, typically of red felt with a tassel at the top. [18th C.: from Egyptian Arab. *ṭarbūš*, based on Pers. *sarpūš*, from *sar* 'head' + *pūš* 'cover.']

Tar·di·gra·da /tär'digrədə/ Zool. a small phylum that comprises the water bears. — **tar·di·grade** /'tärdəˌgrād/ **n.** [mod. L. (pl.), from L. *tardigradus*, from *tardus* 'slow' + *gradi* 'to walk.']

tar·dive dys·ki·ne·sia /ˌtärdiv ˌdiskə'nēZH(ē)ə/ ▶ **n.** Med. a neurological disorder characterized by involuntary movements of the face and jaw. [1960s: *tardive* from Fr. *tardif, tardive* (see TARDY).]

tar·dy /'tärdē/ ▶ **adj.** (**-di·er, -di·est**) delaying or delayed beyond the right or expected time; late. ■ slow in action or response; sluggish. — **tar·di·ly adv. tar·di·ness n.** [16th C.: from Fr. *tardif, -ive*, from L. *tardus* 'slow.']

tare¹ /te(ə)r/ ▶ **n.** **1** a vetch, esp. the common vetch. **2** (**tares**) (in biblical use) an injurious weed resembling wheat when young (Matt. 13:24–30). [ME: of unknown origin.]

tare² ▶ **n.** an allowance made for the weight of the packaging in order to determine the net weight of goods. ■ the weight of a motor vehicle, railroad car, or aircraft without its fuel or load. [ME: from Fr., lit. 'deficiency, tare,' from med. L. *tara*, based on Arab. *ṭaraḥa* 'reject, deduct.']

targe /tärj/ ▶ **n.** archaic term for TARGET (sense 2). [OE *targa, targe*, of Gmc. origin.]

tar·get /'tärgit/ ▶ **n.** **1** a person, object, or place selected as the aim of an attack. ■ a mark or point at which someone fires or aims, esp. a board marked with concentric circles used in archery or shooting. ■ an objective or result toward which efforts are directed: *our sales target.* ■ a person or thing against whom criticism or abuse is or may be directed. **2** hist. a small, round shield or buckler. ▶ **v.** (**-get·ed, -get·ing**) [trans.] (usu. **be targeted**) select as an object of attention or attack. ■ aim or direct (something): *nuclear capability targeted on the US.*
– PHRASES **on target** accurately hitting the thing aimed at. ■ proceeding or improving at a good enough rate to achieve an objective: *construction remains on target.* — **tar·get·a·ble adj.** [ME (sense 2): dimin. of TARGE.]

tar·get cell ▶ **n.** **1** Physiol. a cell that bears receptors for a hormone, drug, or other signaling molecule, or is the focus of contact by a virus, phagocyte, nerve fiber, etc. **2** Med. an abnormal form of red blood cell that appears as a dark ring surrounding a dark central spot, typical of certain kinds of anemia.

tar·get lan·guage ▶ **n.** the language into which a text, document, or speech is translated. ■ a foreign language which a person intends to learn.

Tar·gum /'tärgo͝om; -go͞om/ ▶ **n.** an ancient Aramaic paraphrase or interpretation of the Hebrew Bible. [from Aramaic *targūm* 'interpretation.']

tar·iff /'tarif/ ▶ **n.** a tax or duty to be paid on a particular class of imports or exports. ■ a list of these taxes. ■ a table of the fixed charges made by a business, esp. in a hotel or restaurant. ▶ **v.** [trans.] fix the price of (something) according to a tariff. [16th C.: via Fr. from Ital. *tariffa*, based on Arab. *arrafa* 'notify.']

Ta·rim /'tä'rēm/ a river in northwestern China, in Xinjiang autonomous region. For much of its course the river follows no clearly defined bed and is subject to much evaporation.

Tar·king·ton /'tärkiNGtən/, Booth (1869–1946), US writer; full name *Newton Booth Tarkington*. His novels include *Penrod* (1914) and *The Magnificent Ambersons* (1918).

tar·la·tan /'tärlətn/ ▶ **n.** a thin, starched, open-weave muslin fabric, used for stiffening evening gowns. [18th C.: from Fr. *tarlatane*, prob. of Ind. origin.]

Tar·mac /'tärmak/ ▶ **n.** (usu. **tarmac**) (trademark) material used for surfacing roads or other outdoor areas, consisting of broken stone mixed with tar. ■ (**the tarmac**) a runway or other area surfaced with such material.

tar·mac·ad·am /'tärməˌkadəm/ ▶ **n.** esp. Brit. another term for TARMAC. — **tar·mac·ad·amed adj.** [19th C.: from TAR¹ + MACADAM.]

Tarn /tärn/ a river in southern France that empties into the Garonne River northwest of Toulouse.

tarn /tärn/ ▶ **n.** a small mountain lake. [ME: from ON *tjǫrn*.]

tar·na·tion /tär'nāSHən/ ▶ **n. & exclam.** used as a euphemism for "damnation." [18th C.: alt.]

tar·nish /'tärnisH/ ▶ **v.** lose or cause to lose luster, esp. as a result of exposure to air or moisture: [intrans.] *silver tarnishes easily* | [trans.] *lemon juice will tarnish the spoon.* ■ fig. make or become less valuable or respected: [trans.] *his office was tarnished by scandal.* ▶ **n.** dullness of color; loss of brightness. ■ a film or stain formed on an exposed surface of a mineral or metal. ■ fig. damage or harm done to something. — **tar·nish·a·ble adj.** [ME (as a v.): from Fr. *terniss-*, lengthened stem of *ternir*, from *terne* 'dark, dull.']

ta·ro /'tarō; 'te(ə)rō/ ▶ **n.** a tropical Asian plant (*Colocasia esculenta* var. *esculenta*) of the arum family that has edible starchy corms and fleshy leaves, esp. a variety with a large central corm grown as a staple in the Pacific. Also called DASHEEN. Compare with EDDO. ■ the corm of this plant. [18th C.: of Polynesian origin.]

ta·rot /'tarō; 'te(ə)rō; ta'rō/ ▶ **n.** (**the Tarot**) playing cards, traditionally a deck of 78 with five suits, used for fortune-telling and (esp. in Europe) in certain games. [16th C.: from Fr., from Ital. *tarocchi*, of unknown origin.]

tarp /tärp/ ▶ **n.** informal a tarpaulin sheet or cover. [20th C.: abbr.]

tar·pan /'tärpan/ ▶ **n.** a grayish wild horse (*Equus caballus gomelini*) that was formerly common in eastern Europe and western Asia, exterminated in 1919. [Kyrgyz.]

tar·pa·per /'tärˌpāpər/ ▶ **n.** a heavy paper coated with tar and used as a waterproofing material in building.

tar·pau·lin /tär'pôlən; 'tärpə-/ ▶ n. 1 heavy-duty waterproof cloth, originally of tarred canvas. 2 hist. a sailor's tarred or oilskin hat. ■ archaic a sailor. [17th C.: prob. from TAR[1] + PALL[1] + -ING[1].]

Tar·pe·ia /tär'pēə/ a Vestal Virgin who betrayed the citadel to the Sabines, who killed her by throwing their shields onto her.

tar pit ▶ n. a hollow in which natural tar accumulates by seepage. ■ fig. a complicated or difficult situation or problem: *the tar pit of municipal poverty.*

tar·pon /'tärpən/ ▶ n. a large tropical marine fish (family Megalopidae) of herringlike appearance. Two species: *Tarpon atlanticus*, a prized Atlantic game fish, and *Megalops cyprinoides* of the Indo-Pacific. [17th C.: prob. from Du. *tarpoen*.]

Tar·quin·i·us /tär'kwinēəs/ the name of two semilegendary Etruscan kings of ancient Rome; anglicized name *Tarquin*: ■ Tarquinius Priscus, reigned *c.*616–*c.*578 BC; full name *Lucius Tarquinius Priscus*. ■ Tarquinius Superbus, reigned *c.*534–*c.*510 BC; full name *Lucius Tarquinius Superbus*; known as **Tarquin the Proud**.

tar·ra·did·dle /'tarə,didl/ ▶ n. var. of TARADIDDLE.

tar·ra·gon /'tarə,gän; -gən/ ▶ n. a perennial plant (*Artemisia dracunculus*) of the daisy family, with narrow aromatic leaves that are used as a culinary herb. [16th C.: representing med. L. *tragonia* and *tarchon*, perh. from an Arab. alt. of Gk. *drakōn* 'dragon.']

tar·ry[1] /'tärē/ ▶ adj. (-ri·er, -ri·est) of, like, or covered with tar: *a length of tarry rope.* — **tar·ri·ness** n.

tar·ry[2] /'tarē/ ▶ v. (-ries, -ried) [intrans.] dated stay longer than intended; delay leaving a place: *I shall not tarry.* — **tar·ri·er** n. (rare). [ME: of unknown origin.]

tar·sal /'tärsəl/ Anat. & Zool. ▶ adj. of or relating to the tarsus. ▶ n. a bone of the tarsus. [19th C.: from TARSUS + -AL.]

tar sand ▶ n. (often **tar sands**) Geol. a deposit of sand impregnated with bitumen.

tar·si /'tärsī; -sē/ plural form of TARSUS.

tar·si·er /'tärsēər/ ▶ n. a small insectivorous, tree-dwelling, nocturnal primate (genus *Tarsius*, family Tarsiidae) with large eyes, a long tufted tail, and long hind limbs, native to the islands of Southeast Asia. [18th C.: from Fr., from *tarse* 'tarsus.']

tar·so·met·a·tar·sus /'tärsō,metə'tärsəs/ ▶ n. (pl. **-tar·si** /-'tärsī; -sē/) Zool. a long bone in the lower leg of birds and some reptiles, formed by fusion of tarsal and metatarsal structures. — **tar·so·met·a·tar·sal** /-'tärsəl/ adj.

Tar·sus /'tärsəs/ an ancient city in southern Turkey; the birthplace of St. Paul.

tar·sus /'tärsəs/ ▶ n. (pl. **tar·si** /'tärsī; -sē/) Anat. a group of small bones between the main part of the hind limb and the metatarsus in terrestrial vertebrates. The seven bones of the human tarsus form the ankle and upper part of the foot. ■ Zool. the shank or tarsometatarsus of the leg of a bird or reptile. ■ Zool. the foot or fifth joint of the leg of an insect or other arthropod. [ME: mod. L., from Gk. *tarsos* 'flat of the foot, the eyelid.']

tart[1] /tärt/ ▶ n. an open pastry case containing a filling. — **tart·let** /-lit/ n. [ME (denoting a savory pie): from OFr. *tarte* or med. L. *tarta*, of unknown origin.]

tart[2] ▶ n. informal, derog. a prostitute or a promiscuous woman. [19th C.: prob. an abbr. of SWEETHEART.] ▶ v. [trans.] (**tart oneself up**) informal, esp. Brit. dress or make oneself up in order to look attractive. ■ (**tart something up**) decorate or improve the appearance of something: *page layouts tarted up with cartoons.*

tart[3] ▶ adj. sharp or acid in taste: *a tart apple.* ■ (of a remark or tone of voice) cutting, bitter, or sarcastic. — **tart·ly** adv. **tart·ness** n. [OE *teart* 'harsh, severe,' of unknown origin.]

tar·tan[1] /'tärtn/ ▶ n. a woolen cloth woven in one of several patterns of plaid, esp. of a design associated with a particular Scottish clan. ▶ adj. used allusively in reference to Scotland or the Scots. [15th C.: perh. from OFr. *tertaine*, denoting a kind of cloth.]

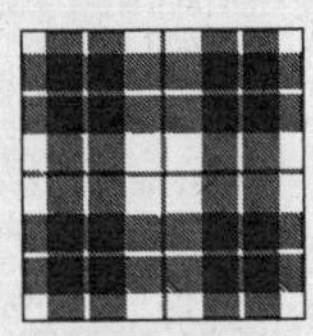

tartan[1]

tar·tan[2] ▶ n. hist. a lateen-rigged, single-masted ship used in the Mediterranean. [17th C.: from Fr. *tartane*, from Ital. *tartana*, perh. from Arab. *ṭarida*.]

Tar·tar /'tärtər/ ▶ n. hist. a member of the combined forces of central Asian peoples, who under Genghis Khan conquered much of Asia and eastern Europe and under Tamerlane established an empire with its capital at Samarkand. See also TATAR. ■ (**tar·tar**) a harsh, fierce, or intractable person. — **Tar·tar·i·an** /tär'te(ə)rēən/ adj. [from OFr. *Tartare* or med. L. *Tartarus*, alt. of TATAR.]

tar·tar /'tärtər/ ▶ n. a hard calcified deposit that forms on the teeth and contributes to their decay. ■ a deposit of impure potassium hydrogen tartrate formed during the fermentation of wine. See also CREAM OF TARTAR. — **tar·tar·ic** /tär'tarik/ adj. [ME: via med. L. from med. Gk. *tartaron*, of unknown origin.]

tar·tare /tär'tär; 'tärtər/ ▶ adj. [postpositive] (of fish) served raw, typically seasoned and shaped into small cakes. See also STEAK TARTARE. [Fr., lit. 'Tartar.']

tar·tar e·met·ic ▶ n. a toxic compound, $K(SbO)C_4H_4O_6$, used in treating protozoal disease in animals, as a mordant in dyeing, and formerly as an emetic.

tar·tar·ic ac·id ▶ n. Chem. a crystalline organic acid, $COOH(CHOH)_2COOH$, that is present esp. in unripe grapes and is used in baking powders and as a food additive. [18th C.: *tartaric* from obs. Fr. *tartarique*, from med. L. *tartarum* (see TARTAR).]

tar·tar sauce (also **tar·tare sauce**) ▶ n. a cold sauce, typically eaten with fish, consisting of mayonnaise mixed with chopped pickles, capers, etc.

Tar·ta·rus /'tärtərəs/ Gk. Mythol. 1 a primeval god, offspring of Chaos. 2 a part of the underworld where the wicked suffered punishment for their misdeeds. — **Tar·tar·e·an** /tär'te(ə)rēən/ adj.

Tar·ta·ry /'tärtərē/ a historical region of Asia and eastern Europe, esp. that which formed part of the Tartar empire in the Middle Ages.

tar·trate /'tärtrāt/ ▶ n. Chem. a salt or ester of tartaric acid. [18th C.: from Fr., from *tartre* 'tartar' + -ATE[1].]

Tar·tuffe /tär'to͝of/ ▶ n. literary or humorous a religious hypocrite, or a hypocritical pretender to excellence of any kind. — **Tar·tuf·fer·ie** /-'to͝ofərē/ (also **Tar·tuf·fer·y**) n. [after the principal character in Molière's *Tartuffe* (1664).]

tar·tu·fo /tär'to͞ofō/ ▶ n. 1 an edible fungus, esp. the white truffle. 2 an Italian dessert, containing chocolate, of a creamy mousselike consistency. [Ital., lit. 'truffle.']

Tar·zan /'tärzan; -zən/ a fictitious character created by Edgar Rice Burroughs. Orphaned in infancy in West Africa, Tarzan is reared by apes and becomes a heroic figure of jungle adventure. ■ [as n.] (**a Tarzan**) a man of great agility and powerful physique.

Ta·ser /'tāzər/ (also **ta·ser**) ▶ n. trademark a weapon firing barbs attached by wires to batteries, causing temporary paralysis.

Tash·kent /tasʜ'kent; täsʜ-/ the capital of Uzbekistan, in the northeastern part of the country, in the western Tien Shan mountains; pop. 2,094,000.

task /task/ ▶ n. a piece of work to be done or undertaken. ▶ v. [trans.] (usu. **be tasked**) assign such a piece of work to: *these troops are tasked with peacemaking.* ■ make great demands on (someone's resources or abilities): *it tasked his diplomatic skills.*

– PHRASES **take someone to task** reprimand or criticize someone severely for a fault or mistake. [ME: from an Old North. Fr. var. of OFr. *tasche*, from med. L. *tasca*, alt. of *taxa*, from L. *taxare* 'censure, charge' (see TAX).]

task force ▶ n. an armed force organized for a special operation. ■ a unit specially organized for a task.

task·mas·ter /'task,mastər/ ▶ n. a person who imposes a harsh or onerous workload on someone.

Tas·man /'tazmən/, Abel Janszoon (1603–*c.*1659), Dutch navigator. He explored Tasmania, New Zealand, Tonga, and Fiji.

Tas·ma·ni·a /taz'mānēə; -'mānyə/ a state in Australia that consists of the mountainous island of Tasmania itself and several smaller islands; pop. 458,000; capital, Hobart. — **Tas·ma·ni·an** adj. & n.

Tas·ma·ni·an dev·il /taz'mānēən; -'mānyən/ ▶ n. a heavily built marsupial (*Sarcophilus harrisii*, family Dasyuridae) with a large head, powerful jaws, and mainly black fur, found only in Tasmania. It is slow-moving and aggressive, feeding mainly on carrion.

Tas·ma·ni·an wolf (also **Tas·ma·ni·an ti·ger**) ▶ n. another term for THYLACINE.

Tas·man Sea /'tazmən/ an arm of the South Pacific Ocean that lies between Australia and New Zealand.

Tass /täs; tas/ the official news agency of the former Soviet Union, renamed ITAR-Tass in 1992.

tas·sel /'tasəl/ ▶ n. a tuft of loosely hanging threads, cords, or other material knotted at one end and attached for decoration to home furnishings, clothing, or other items. ■ the tufted head of some plants, esp. a flowerhead with prominent stamens at the top of a cornstalk. ▶ v. (**-seled, -sel·ing**; Brit. **-selled, -sel·ling**) 1 [trans.] [usu. as adj.] (**tasseled**) provide with a tassel or tassels: *a tasseled tablecloth.* 2 [intrans.] (of corn or other plants) form tassels. [ME: from OFr. *tassel* 'clasp.']

tas·so /'tasō; 'ta-/ ▶ n. N. Amer. spicy cured pork cut into strips. [perh. from Sp. *tasajo* 'slice of dried meat.']

taste /tāst/ ▶ n. 1 the sensation of flavor perceived in the mouth and throat on contact with a substance. ■ the faculty of perceiving this quality: *a highly developed sense of taste.* ■ a small portion of food or drink taken as a sample. ■ a brief experience of something, conveying its basic character: *his first taste of real fun.* 2 a person's liking for particular flavors: *this pudding is too sweet for my taste.* ■ a person's tendency to like and dislike certain things: *the competitiveness was not to his taste.* ■ (**taste for**) a liking for or interest in (something): *a taste for adventure.* ■ the ability to discern what is of good quality or of a high aesthetic standard: *she has awful taste in literature.* ■ conformity or failure to conform with generally held views concerning what is offensive or acceptable: *a joke in bad taste.* ▶ v. [trans.] perceive or experience the flavor of. ■ [intrans.] have a specified flavor: [with complement] *the spinach tastes delicious.* ■ sample or test the flavor of (food or drink) by taking it into the mouth. ■ eat or drink a small portion of. ■ have experience of: *the team has not yet tasted victory at home.*

– PHRASES **a bad** (or **bitter**) **taste in someone's mouth** informal a feeling of distress or disgust following an experience. **taste blood** see BLOOD.

to taste in the amount needed to give a flavor pleasing to someone eating a dish: *add salt and pepper to taste.* [ME: from OFr. *tast* (n.), *taster* (v.) 'touch, try, taste,' perh. based on a blend of L. *tangere* 'to touch' and *gustare* 'to taste.']

taste bud ▶ n. (usu. **taste buds**) any of the clusters of bulbous nerve endings on the tongue and in the lining of the mouth that provide the sense of taste.

taste·ful /'tāstfəl/ ▶ adj. showing good aesthetic judgment or appropriate behavior: *tasteful decor.* — **taste·ful·ly** adv. **taste·ful·ness** n.

taste·less /'tāstlis/ ▶ adj. **1** lacking flavor. **2** considered to be lacking in aesthetic judgment or to offend against what is regarded as appropriate behavior: *a tasteless joke.* — **taste·less·ly** adv. **taste·less·ness** n.

taste·mak·er /'tāst,mākər/ ▶ n. a person who decides or influences what is or will become fashionable.

tast·er /'tāstər/ ▶ n. a person employed to test food or drink for quality by tasting it: *experienced tasters can tell which plantation coffee beans are from.*

tast·ing /'tāstiNG/ ▶ n. a gathering at which people sample, compare, and evaluate different wines, or other drinks or food: *we did a tasting of over forty of the cheaper champagnes.* See also WINE TASTING.

tast·y /'tāstē/ ▶ adj. (**tast·i·er, tast·i·est**) (of food) having a pleasant, distinct flavor: *a tasty snack.* ■ informal, esp. Brit. attractive; very appealing: *some tasty acoustic piano licks.* — **tast·i·ly** adv. **tast·i·ness** n.

tat[1] /tat/ ▶ v. (**tat·ted, tat·ting**) [trans.] make (a decorative mat or edging) by tying knots in thread and using a small shuttle to form lace. [19th C.: back-form. from TATTING.]

tat[2] ▶ n. (in phrase **tit for tat**) see TIT[3].

tat[3] ▶ n. Brit., informal tasteless or shoddy clothes, jewelry, or ornaments. [19th C.: prob. a back-form. from TATTY.]

ta-ta /tä 'tä/ ▶ exclam. informal, esp. Brit. goodbye. [19th C.: of unknown origin.]

ta·ta·mi /tə'tämē/ (also **ta·ta·mi mat**) ▶ n. (pl. same or **-mis**) a rush-covered straw mat forming a traditional Japanese floor covering.

Ta·tar /'tätər/ ▶ n. **1** a member of a Turkic people living in Tatarstan and various other parts of Russia and Ukraine. They are the descendants of the Tartars who ruled central Asia in the 14th century. **2** the Turkic language of this people. ▶ adj. of or relating to this people or their language. [the Turkic name of a Tartar tribe.]

Ta·tar·stan /'tätər,stan; -,stän/ an autonomous republic in western Russia; pop. 3,658,000; capital, Kazan.

Tate /tāt/, Nahum (1652–1715), Irish poet. He was appointed England's poet laureate in 1692.

ta·ter /'tātər/ ▶ n. informal a potato. [18th C.: alt.]

Ta·tha·ga·ta /tə'tägətə/ ▶ n. an honorific title of a buddha. [from Pali *Tathāgata*, from *tathā* 'in that manner' + *gata* 'gone.']

ta·tha·ta /'tətə,tä/ ▶ n. Buddhism the ultimate inexpressible nature of all things. [Pali, lit. 'true state of things.']

Ta·tra Moun·tains /'tätrə/ (also **the Ta·tras**) the highest range in the Carpathian Mountains of eastern Europe.

tat·tered /'tatərd/ ▶ adj. torn, old, and in generally poor condition; in tatters: *an old woman in tattered clothes.* ■ fig. virtually destroyed; ruined: *the tattered remnants of her dreams.* [ME: appar. from *tatter* 'scrap of cloth.']

tat·ters /'tatərz/ ▶ plural n. irregularly torn pieces of cloth, paper, or other material.
– PHRASES **in tatters** informal torn in many places; in shreds: *wallpaper hung in tatters.* ■ fig. destroyed; ruined: *the cease-fire was in tatters within hours.* [ME: from ON *tǫtrar* 'rags.']

tat·ter·sall /'tatər,sôl/ (also **tat·ter·sall check**) ▶ n. a woolen fabric with a pattern of colored checks and intersecting lines, resembling a tartan. [19th C.: Tattersalls, English firm of horse auctioneers.]

tat·ting /'tatiNG/ ▶ n. a kind of knotted lace made by hand with a small shuttle, used chiefly for trimming. ■ the process of making such lace. [19th C.: of unknown origin.]

tat·tle /'tatl/ ▶ v. [intrans.] report another's wrongdoing: *he never tattled or told tales | I would tattle on her whenever I had hard evidence.* ■ gossip idly. ▶ n. gossip; idle talk. [15th C.: from Middle Flemish *tatelen, tateren.*]

tat·tler /'tatl-ər; 'tatlər/ ▶ n. **1** a person who tattles. **2** a migratory sandpiper (genus *Heteroscelus*) with mainly gray plumage, breeding in northwestern Canada or eastern Siberia.

tat·tle·tale /'tatl,tāl/ ▶ n. a person, esp. a child, who reveals secrets or informs on others; a telltale.

tat·too[1] /ta'to͞o/ ▶ n. (pl. **-toos**) an evening drum or bugle signal recalling soldiers to their quarters. ■ an entertainment consisting of music, marching, and the performance of displays and exercises by military personnel. ■ a rhythmic tapping or drumming. [17th C.: from Du. *taptoe!*, lit. 'close the tap (of the cask)!']

tat·too[2] ▶ v. (**-toos, -tooed** /-'to͞od/) [trans.] mark (a person or a part of the body) with an indelible design by inserting pigment into punctures in the skin: *his cheek was tattooed with a winged fist.* ■ make (a design) in such a way: *he has a heart tattooed on his left hand.* ▶ n. (pl. **-toos**) a design made in such a way. — **tat·too·er** n. **tat·too·ist** n. [18th C.: from Tahitian, Tongan, and Samoan *ta-tau* or Marquesan *ta-tu.*]

tat·ty /'tatē/ ▶ adj. (**-ti·er, -ti·est**) informal worn and shabby; in poor condition: *the room was furnished in slightly tatty upholstered furniture.* ■ of poor quality: *his gap-toothed smile and tatty haircut.* — **tat·ti·ly** adv. **tat·ti·ness** n. [16th C.: appar. rel. to OE *tættec* 'rag,' of Gmc. origin.]

tau /tou; tô/ ▶ n. the nineteenth letter of the Greek alphabet (Υ, τ), transliterated as 't.' ■ (in full **tau particle** or **tau lepton**) Physics an unstable subatomic particle of the lepton class, with a charge of −1 and a mass roughly 3,500 times that of the electron.

tau cross ▶ n. a T-shaped cross. See illustration at CROSS.

taught /tôt/ past and past participle of TEACH.

tau neu·tri·no ▶ n. Physics a neutrino of the type associated with the tau particle.

taunt /tônt/ ▶ n. a remark made in order to anger, wound, or provoke someone. ▶ v. [trans.] provoke or challenge (someone) with insulting remarks: *students began taunting her about her weight.* ■ reproach (someone) with something in a contemptuous way: *she had taunted him with going to another man.* — **taunt·er** n. **taunt·ing·ly** adv. [16th C.: from Fr. *tant pour tant* 'like for like, tit for tat,' from *tant* 'so much,' from L. *tantum*, neut. of *tantus.*]

tau par·ti·cle ▶ n. see TAU.

taupe /tōp/ ▶ n. gray with a tinge of brown: [as adj.] *a taupe overcoat.* [20th C.: from Fr., lit. 'mole, moleskin,' from L. *talpa.*]

Tau·po, Lake /'toupō/ the largest lake of New Zealand, in the center of North Island. Maori name TAUPOMOANA.

tau·rine[1] /'tôrēn/ ▶ n. Biochem. a sulfur-containing amino acid, $NH_2CH_2CH_2SO_3H$, important in the metabolism of fats. [19th C.: from Gk. *tauros* 'bull.']

tau·rine[2] /'tôrīn/ ▶ adj. of or like a bull. ■ of or relating to bullfighting: *taurine skill.* [17th C.: from L. *taurinus*, from *taurus* 'bull.']

Tau·rus /'tôrəs/ **1** Astron. a constellation (the Bull), said to represent a bull with brazen feet that was tamed by Jason. Its many bright stars include Aldebaran (the bull's eye), and it contains the Crab Nebula and the star clusters of the Hyades and the Pleiades. **2** Astrol. the second sign of the zodiac, which the sun enters on about April 21. ■ (**a Taurus**) (pl. same) a person born when the sun is in this sign. — **Tau·re·an** /'tôrēən; tô 'rēən/ n. & adj. (in sense 2).

Tau·rus Moun·tains a range of mountains in southern Turkey, parallel to the Mediterranean coast.

taut /tôt/ ▶ adj. stretched or pulled tight; not slack: *the fabric stays taut without adhesive.* ■ (esp. of muscles or nerves) tense; not relaxed. ■ fig. (of writing, music, etc.) concise and controlled: *a taut text of only a hundred and twenty pages.* ■ (of a ship) having a disciplined and efficient crew. — **taut·en** /'tôtn/ v. **taut·ly** adv. **taut·ness** n. [ME *tought* 'distended,' perh. a var. of TOUGH.]

tauto- ▶ comb. form same: *tautology.* [from Gk. *tauto*, contr. of *to auto* 'the same.']

tau·tog /tô'tôg; tô'täg/ ▶ n. a grayish-olive edible wrasse (*Tautoga onitis*) that occurs off the Atlantic coast of North America. [17th C.: from Narragansett *tautauog*, pl. of *taut.*]

tau·tol·o·gy /tô'täləjē/ ▶ n. (pl. **-gies**) the saying of the same thing twice in different words, generally considered to be a fault of style (e.g., *they arrived one after the other in succession*). ■ a phrase or expression in which the same thing is said twice in different words. ■ Logic a statement that is true by necessity or by virtue of its logical form. — **tau·to·log·i·cal** /,tôtl'äjikəl/ adj. **tau·to·log·i·cal·ly** /,tôtl'äjik(ə)lē/ adv. **tau·tol·o·gist** n. **tau·tol·o·gize** /-,jīz/ v. **tau·tol·o·gous** /-gəs/ adj.

tau·to·mer /'tôtəmər/ ▶ n. Chem. each of two or more isomers of a compound that exist together in equilibrium, and are readily interchanged by migration of an atom or group within the molecule. — **tau·to·mer·ic** /,tôtə'merik/ adj. **tau·tom·er·ism** /tô'tämə,rizəm/ n. [20th C.: blend of TAUTO- 'same' and ISOMER.]

tau·to·nym /'tôtə,nim/ ▶ n. Bot. & Zool. a scientific name in which the same word is used for both genus and species, for example *Vulpes vulpes* (the red fox). ■ Ling. a word that designates different objects or concepts in different dialects (e.g., *corn* is *maize* in American English, *wheat* in England, and *oats* in Scotland). — **tau·ton·y·my** /tô'tänəmē/ n.

tav·ern /'tavərn/ ▶ n. an establishment for the sale of beer and other drinks to be consumed on the premises, sometimes also serving food. [ME: from OFr. *taverne*, from L. *taberna* 'hut, tavern.']

taw[1] /tô/ ▶ v. [trans.] make (hide) into leather without the use of tannin, esp. by soaking it in a solution of alum and salt. — **taw·er** n. [OE *tawian* 'prepare raw material,' of Gmc. origin; rel. to TOOL.]

taw[2] ▶ n. a large marble. ■ a game of marbles. ■ a line from which players throw marbles. [18th C.: of unknown origin.]

taw·dry /'tôdrē/ ▶ adj. (**-dri·er, -dri·est**) showy but cheap and of poor quality: *tawdry jewelry.* ■ sordid or unpleasant: *the tawdry business of politics.* ▶ n. archaic cheap and gaudy finery. — **taw·dri·ly** adv. **taw·dri·ness** n. [17th C.: short for *tawdry lace*, a lace or ribbon, contr. of *St. Audrey's lace*, from *Etheldrida* (died 679), patron saint of Ely, England.]

taw·ny /'tônē/ ▶ adj. (**-ni·er, -ni·est**) of an orange-brown or yellowish-brown color: *tawny eyes.* ▶ n. an orange-brown or yellowish-brown color. — **taw·ni·ness** n. [ME: from OFr. *tane*, from *tan* 'tanbark'; rel. to TAN[1].]

taw·ny owl ▶ n. a common Eurasian owl (*Strix aluco*, family Strigidae) with either reddish-brown or gray plumage and a quavering hoot.

taw·ny port ▶ n. a port wine made from a blend of several vintages matured in wood.

tawse /tôz/ (also **taws**) ▶ n. Scot. a thong with a slit end, formerly used in schools for punishing children. [16th C.: appar. the pl. of obs. *taw* 'tawed leather,' from TAW[1].]

tax /taks/ ▶ **n.** a compulsory contribution to state revenue, levied by the government on workers' income and business profits or added to the cost of some goods, services, and transactions. ■ [in sing.] fig. a strain or heavy demand: *a heavy tax on the reader's attention.* ▶ **v.** [trans.] **1** impose a tax on (someone or something): *hardware and software is taxed at 7.5 percent.* ■ fig. make heavy demands on (someone's powers or resources): *an ordeal that taxed all her strength.* **2** confront (someone) with a fault or wrongdoing: *why are you taxing me with these preposterous allegations?* **3** Law examine and assess (the costs of a case). — **tax·a·ble adj. tax·er n.** [ME: from OFr. *taxer*, from L. *taxare* 'to censure, charge, compute,' perh. from Gk. *tassein* 'fix.']

tax·a /'taksə/ plural form of TAXON.

tax·a·tion /tak'sāsнən/ ▶ **n.** the levying of tax. ■ money paid as tax.

tax brack·et ▶ **n.** Econ. a range of incomes taxed at a given rate.

tax break ▶ **n.** informal a tax concession or advantage allowed by a government.

tax cred·it ▶ **n.** an amount of money that can be offset against a tax liability.

tax-de·duct·i·ble ▶ **adj.** able to be deducted from taxable income or the amount of tax to be paid.

tax e·va·sion ▶ **n.** the illegal nonpayment or underpayment of tax.

tax ex·ile ▶ **n.** a person with a high income or considerable wealth who chooses to live in a country or area with low tax rates.

tax-free ▶ **adj. & adv.** (of goods, income, etc.) exempt from tax: [as adj.] *a tax-free lump sum* | [as adv.] *your return is paid to you tax-free.*

tax ha·ven ▶ **n.** a country or independent area where taxes are levied at a low rate.

tax·i /'taksē/ ▶ **n.** (pl. **tax·is**) short for TAXICAB. ■ a boat or other means of transportation used to convey passengers in return for payment of a fare. ▶ **v.** (**tax·is, tax·ied, tax·i·ing** or **tax·y·ing**) [intrans.] **1** (of an aircraft) move slowly along the ground before takeoff or after landing: *the plane taxis up to a waiting limousine.* ■ [trans.] (of a pilot) cause (an aircraft) to move in such a way: *he taxied it to the very end of the airstrip.* **2** take a taxi as a means of transport. [20th C.: abbr. of *taxicab* or *taximeter cab* (see TAXIMETER).]

tax·i·cab /'taksē,kab/ ▶ **n.** a car licensed to transport passengers in return for payment of a fare, usually fitted with a taximeter. [20th C.: shortened form of *taximeter cab.*]

tax·i danc·er ▶ **n.** a dancing partner available for a fee.

tax·i·der·my /'taksə,dərmē/ ▶ **n.** the art of preparing, stuffing, and mounting the skins of animals with lifelike effect. — **tax·i·der·mal** /,taksə'dərməl/ **adj. tax·i·der·mic** /,taksə'dərmik/ **adj. tax·i·der·mi·cal·ly** /,taksə'dərmik(ə)lē/ **adv. tax·i·der·mist n.** [19th C.: from Gk. *taxis* 'arrangement' + *derma* 'skin.']

tax·i·me·ter /'taksē,mētər/ ▶ **n.** a device used in taxicabs that automatically records the distance traveled and the fare payable. [19th C.: from Fr. *taximètre*, from *taxe* 'tariff,' from the verb *taxer* 'to tax' + *-mètre* '(instrument) measuring.']

tax·ing /'taksiнg/ ▶ **adj.** physically or mentally demanding: *they find the work too taxing.*

tax·is /'taksis/ ▶ **n.** (pl. **tax·es** /'taksēz/) **1** Surg. the restoration of displaced bones or organs by manual pressure alone. **2** Biol. a motion or orientation of a cell, organism, or part in response to an external stimulus. Compare with KINESIS. **3** Ling. the systematic arrangement of linguistic units (phonemes, morphemes, words, phrases, or clauses) in linear sequence. [18th C. (sense 1): from Gk., lit. 'arrangement,' from *tassein* 'arrange.']

tax·i squad ▶ **n.** Football a group of players who take part in practices and may be called on as reserves for the team.

tax·i stand (Brit. **tax·i rank**) ▶ **n.** a place where taxicabs park while waiting to be engaged.

tax·i·way /'taksē,wā/ ▶ **n.** a route along which an aircraft can taxi when moving to or from a runway.

tax loss ▶ **n.** Econ. a loss that can be offset against taxable profit earned elsewhere or in a different period.

Tax·ol /'taksôl; -säl/ (also **tax·ol**) ▶ **n.** Med., trademark a compound, originally obtained from the bark of the Pacific yew tree, that has been found to inhibit the growth of certain cancers.

tax·on /'taksän/ ▶ **n.** (pl. **tax·a** /'taksə/) Biol. a taxonomic group of any rank, such as a species, family, or class. [1920s: back-form. from TAXONOMY.]

tax·on·o·my /tak'sänəmē/ ▶ **n.** esp. Biol. the branch of science concerned with classification, esp. of organisms; systematics. ■ the classification of something, esp. organisms: *the taxonomy of these fossils.* ■ a scheme of classification: *a taxonomy of smells.* — **tax·o·nom·ic** /,taksə'nämik/ **adj. tax·o·nom·i·cal** /,taksə'nämikəl/ **adj. tax·o·nom·i·cal·ly** /,taksə'nämik(ə)lē/ **adv. tax·on·o·mist n.** [19th C.: coined in Fr. from Gk. *taxis* 'arrangement' + *-nomia* 'distribution.']

tax·pay·er /'taks,pāər/ ▶ **n.** a person who pays taxes.

tax re·turn ▶ **n.** a form on which a taxpayer makes an annual statement of income and personal circumstances, used by the tax authorities to assess liability for tax.

tax shel·ter ▶ **n.** a financial arrangement made to avoid or minimize taxes.

Tay /tā/ the longest river in Scotland. It flows 120 miles (192 km) to the North Sea.

Tay·lor /'tālər/ Zachary (1784–1850), 12th president of the US 1849–50. A celebrated general in the war with Mexico 1846–48, he was the last Whig president. He died before resolving his conflict with Congress over his desire to admit California to the Union as a free state.

Tay·lor·ism /'tālə,rizəm/ ▶ **n.** the principles or practice of scientific management. — **Tay·lor·ist n. & adj.** [19th C.: Frederick W. *Taylor* (1856–1915), American engineer.]

Tay·lor se·ries ▶ **n.** Math. an infinite sum giving the value of a function *f(z)* in the neighborhood of a point *a* in terms of the derivatives of the function evaluated at *a.* [19th C.: named after Brook *Taylor* (1685–1731), English mathematician.]

tay·ra /'tīrə/ ▶ **n.** a large, agile, tree-dwelling mammal (*Eira barbara*) of the weasel family, with a short dark coat, native to Central and South America. [19th C.: from Tupi *taira.*]

Tay-Sachs dis·ease /'tā ,saks/ ▶ **n.** an inherited metabolic disorder in which certain lipids accumulate in the brain, causing spasticity and death in childhood. [20th C.: Warren *Tay* (1843–1927), English ophthalmologist, and Bernard *Sachs* (1858–1944), American neurologist.]

TB ▶ **abbr.** ■ terabyte(s). ■ (also **t.b.**) tubercle bacillus. ■ (also **t.b.**) tuberculosis.

Tb ▶ **abbr.** ■ terabyte(s). ■ Bible Tobit. ▶ **symb.** the chemical element terbium.

t.b.a. ▶ **abbr.** to be announced (in notices about events): *7 p.m. party with live band t.b.a.*

T-back ▶ **n.** a high-cut undergarment or swimsuit having only a thin strip of material passing between the buttocks. ■ a style of back on a bra or bikini top in which the shoulder straps meet a supporting lateral strap below the shoulder blades.

T-bar ▶ **n. 1** a beam or bar shaped like the letter T. ■ (also **T-bar lift**) a type of ski lift in the form of a series of inverted T-shaped bars for towing two skiers at a time uphill. **2** the horizontal line of the letter *T.*

Tbi·li·si /təbə'lēsē/ the capital of Georgia; pop. 1,267,000. From 1845 until 1936, its name was Tiflis.

T-bill ▶ **n.** informal short for TREASURY BILL.

T-bone ▶ **n.** (also **T-bone steak**) a large choice piece of loin steak containing a T-shaped bone. ▶ **v.** [trans.] crash head-on into the side of another vehicle.

tbsp (also **tbs.**) (pl. same or **tbsps.**) ▶ **abbr.** tablespoonful.

Tc ▶ **symb.** the chemical element technetium.

T cell (also **T-cell**) ▶ **n.** Physiol. a lymphocyte of a type produced or processed by the thymus gland and actively participating in the immune response. Also called T LYMPHOCYTE. Compare with B CELL. [1970s: from *T* for *thymus.*]

Tchai·kov·sky /cнī'kôfskē/, Pyotr Ilich (1840–93), Russian composer. His works include the ballets *Swan Lake* (1877) and *The Nutcracker* (1892) and the overture *1812* (1880).

tchotch·ke /'cнäcнkə/ (also **tsats·ke**) ▶ **n.** informal **1** a small object that is decorative rather than strictly functional; a trinket. **2** a pretty girl or woman. [1960s: Yiddish.]

TCP/IP trademark ▶ **abbr.** transmission control protocol/Internet protocol, used to govern the connection of computer systems to the Internet.

TD ▶ **abbr.** ■ technical drawing. ■ Football touchdown. ■ Treasury Department.

TDD ▶ **abbr.** telecommunications device for the deaf.

TDN (also **t.d.n.**) ▶ **abbr.** totally digestible nutrients.

TDY ▶ **abbr.** temporary duty.

Te ▶ **symb.** the chemical element tellurium.

tea /tē/ ▶ **n. 1** a hot drink made by infusing the dried, crushed leaves of the tea plant in boiling water. ■ the dried leaves used to make such a drink. ■ (also **iced tea**) such a drink served cold with ice cubes. ■ [usu. with adj.] a hot drink made from the infused leaves, fruits, or flowers of other plants: *herbal tea* | *fruit teas.* **2** (also **tea plant**) the evergreen shrub or small tree (*Camellia sinensis*, family Theaceae) that produces these leaves, native to South and eastern Asia and grown as a major cash crop. **3** esp. Brit. a light afternoon meal consisting typically of tea to drink, sandwiches, and cakes. ■ Brit. a cooked evening meal. See also HIGH TEA. **4** informal another term for MARIJUANA.

– PHRASES **not for all the tea in China** informal there is nothing at all that could induce one to do something: *I wouldn't do that girl's job—not for all the tea in China.* **tea and sympathy** informal kind and attentive behavior toward someone who is upset or in trouble. [17th C.: prob. via Malay from Chin. (Min dial.) *te.*]

tea bag ▶ **n.** a small porous bag containing tea leaves or powdered tea, onto which boiling water is poured in order to make a drink of tea.

tea ball ▶ **n.** a hollow ball of perforated metal to hold tea leaves, over which boiling water is poured in order to make a drink of tea.

tea cad·dy ▶ **n.** a small container in which tea is kept for daily use.

tea·cake /'tē,kāk/ ▶ **n.** Brit. a light yeast-raised sweet bun with dried fruit, typically served toasted and buttered.

tea cer·e·mo·ny ▶ **n.** an elaborate Japanese ritual of serving and drinking tea, as an expression of Zen Buddhist philosophy.

Teach /tēcн/, Edward, see BLACKBEARD.

teach /tēcн/ ▶ **v.** (past **taught**) [trans.] show or explain to (someone) how to do something: *she taught him to read.* ■ give information about or instruction in (a subject or skill): *he came one day each week to teach painting* | [with two objs.] *she teaches me French.* ■ [intrans.] give such instruction professionally: *she teaches at the high school.* ■ [trans.] encourage someone to accept (something) as a fact or principle: *the philosophy teaches self-control.* ■ cause (someone) to learn or understand something: *she'd been taught to be passive.* ■ induce (someone) by example or punishment to do or not to do something: *my upbringing taught me respect.* ■ informal make (someone) less inclined to do something: *"I'll teach you to mess with girls!"* ▶ n. informal a teacher.

– PHRASES **teach someone a lesson** see LESSON. **teach school** be a schoolteacher. [OE *tǣcan* 'show, present, point out,' rel. to TOKEN, from an Indo-Eur. root shared by Gk. *deiknunai* 'show,' and L. *dicere* 'say.']

teach·a·ble /'tēCHəbəl/ ▶ adj. **1** (of a person) able to learn by being taught. **2** (of a subject) able to be taught. — **teach·a·bil·i·ty** /,tēCHə'bilitē/ n. **teach·a·ble·ness** n.

teach·er /'tēCHər/ ▶ n. a person who teaches, esp. in a school. — **teach·er·ly** adj.

teach·ers col·lege (also **Teach·ers Col·lege**) ▶ n. a four-year college with a special curriculum for training primary and secondary schoolteachers.

tea chest ▶ n. a light metal-lined wooden box in which tea is transported.

teach-in ▶ n. informal an informal lecture and discussion or series of lectures on a subject of public interest.

teach·ing /'tēCHiNG/ ▶ n. **1** the occupation, profession, or work of a teacher. **2** (**teachings**) ideas or principles taught by an authority: *the teachings of the Koran.*

teach·ing fel·low ▶ n. a postgraduate student who carries out teaching or laboratory duties in return for accommodations, tuition, or expenses.

teach·ing hos·pi·tal ▶ n. a hospital that is affiliated with a medical school, in which medical students receive practical training.

teach·ing ma·chine ▶ n. a machine or computer that gives instruction to a student according to a program, reacting to their responses.

tea co·zy ▶ n. a thick or padded cover placed over a teapot to keep the tea hot.

tea·cup /'tē,kəp/ ▶ n. a cup from which tea is drunk. ■ an amount held by this, about 150 ml. — **tea·cup·ful** /-,fo͝ol/ n. (pl. **-fuls**).

tea gar·den ▶ n. **1** a garden in which tea and other refreshments are served to the public. **2** a tea plantation.

teak /tēk/ ▶ n. **1** hard durable timber used in shipbuilding and for making furniture. **2** the large deciduous tree (*Tectona grandis*, family Verbenaceae) native to India and Southeast Asia that yields this timber. [17th C.: from Port. *teca*, from Tamil and Malayalam *tēkku*.]

tea·ket·tle /'tē,ketl/ ▶ n. a container with a lid, spout, and handle, used for boiling water.

teal /tēl/ ▶ n. (pl. same or **teals**) a small freshwater duck (genus *Anas*), typically with a greenish band on the wing that is most prominent in flight. ■ (**green-winged**) a dark greenish-blue color. [ME: rel. to Du. *teling*.]

tea leaf ▶ n. a dried leaf of tea. ■ (**tea leaves**) dried leaves of tea after they have been used to make tea or as dregs.

team /tēm/ ▶ n. [treated as sing. or pl.] a group of players forming one side in a competitive game or sport. ■ two or more people working together: ***a team of researchers*** | [as adj.] *a team effort.* ■ two or more animals, esp. horses, harnessed together to pull a vehicle. ▶ v. **1** [intrans.] (**team up**) come together as a team to achieve a common goal: ***he teamed up with the band.*** **2** [trans.] (usu. **team something with**) match or coordinate a garment with (another). **3** [trans.] harness (animals, esp. horses) together to pull a vehicle: *the horses are teamed in pairs.* [OE *tēam* 'team of draft animals,' rel. to Ger. *Zaum* 'bridle,' also to TEEM¹, from an Indo-Eur. root shared by L. *ducere* 'to lead.']

team·mate /'tēm,māt/ ▶ n. a fellow member of a team.

team play·er ▶ n. a person who plays or works well as a member of a team or group.

team·ster /'tēmstər/ ▶ n. **1** a truck driver. ■ a member of the Teamsters Union, including truck drivers, chauffeurs, and warehouse workers. **2** a driver of a team of animals.

team teach·ing ▶ n. coordinated teaching by a team of teachers working together.

team·work /'tēm,wərk/ ▶ n. the combined action of a group of people, esp. when effective and efficient.

tea oil ▶ n. an oil resembling olive oil obtained from the seeds of the sasanqua and related plants, used chiefly in China and Japan.

tea par·ty ▶ n. a social gathering in the afternoon at which tea, cakes, and other light refreshments are served.

tea·pot /'tē,pät/ ▶ n. a pot with a handle, spout, and lid, in which tea is brewed and from which it is poured. ■ a teakettle.

Tea·pot Dome an oil field in southeastern Wyoming that was the focus of a 1920s corruption scandal.

tea·poy /'tē,poi/ ▶ n. a small three-legged table or stand, esp. one that holds a tea caddy. [19th C.: from Hindi *tī-* 'three' + Urdu and Pers. *pāī* 'foot.']

tear¹ /te(ə)r/ ▶ v. (past **tore**; past part. **torn**) **1** [trans.] pull or rip (something) apart or to pieces with force: *I **tore up** the letter.* ■ remove by pulling or ripping forcefully: *he tore up the floorboards* | *he **tore off** his belt* | *Joe **tore** the sack **from** her hand.* ■ (**be torn between**) fig. have great difficulty in choosing between: *he was torn between his duty and his better instincts.* ■ make a hole or split in (something) by ripping or pulling at it: *she was always tearing her clothes.* ■ make (a hole or split) in something by force: *the blast tore a hole in the wall.* ■ [intrans.] come apart; rip: *the material wouldn't tear.* ■ damage (a muscle or ligament) by overstretching it: *he tore a ligament playing squash.* **2** [intrans.] informal move very quickly, typically in a reckless or excited manner: *she tore down the road.* ▶ n. **1** a hole or split in something caused by it having been pulled apart forcefully. **2** informal a spell of great success or excellence in performance: *he went **on a tear**, winning every hand.* ■ a brief spell of erratic behavior; a binge or spree: *every so often she goes **on a tear**.*

– PHRASES **tear one's hair out** informal act with or show extreme desperation. **tear someone/something to shreds** (or **pieces**) informal criticize someone or something forcefully or aggressively: *a defense counsel would tear his evidence to shreds.*

– PHRASAL VERBS **tear someone/something apart 1** destroy something, esp. good relations between people: *a bloody civil war had torn the country apart.* **2** upset someone greatly. **3** search a place thoroughly: *we'll tear the house apart if we have to.* **4** criticize someone or something harshly. **tear oneself away** [often with negative] leave despite a strong desire to stay. **tear someone/something down 1** demolish something, esp. a building. **2** informal criticize or punish someone severely. **tear into 1** attack verbally. **2** make an energetic or enthusiastic start on: *a jazz trio tearing into the tune.* — **tear·a·ble** adj. **tear·er** n. [OE *teran*, rel. to Ger. *zehren*, from an Indo-Eur. root shared by Gk. *derein* 'flay.']

tear² /ti(ə)r/ ▶ n. a drop of clear salty liquid secreted from glands in a person's eye when they cry or when the eye is irritated. ■ a drop of such liquid secreted continuously to lubricate the surface of the eyeball under the eyelid. ■ (**tears**) the state or action of crying: *he was nearly **in tears*** | *it moved Jack **to tears**.* ▶ v. [intrans.] (of the eye) produce tears. — **tear·like** adj. [OE *tēar*, rel. to Ger. *Zähre*, from an Indo-Eur. root shared by L. *lacrima* and Gk. *dakru*.]

tear·drop /'ti(ə)r,dräp/ ▶ n. a single tear. ■ [as adj.] shaped like a single tear: *teardrop handles.*

tear duct /ti(ə)r/ ▶ n. a passage through which tears pass from the lachrymal glands to the eye or from the eye to the nose.

tear·ful /'ti(ə)rfəl/ ▶ adj. crying or inclined to cry. ■ causing tears; sad or emotional: *a tearful farewell.* — **tear·ful·ly** adv. **tear·ful·ness** n.

tear gas /ti(ə)r/ ▶ n. gas that causes severe irritation to the eyes, used in riot control to force crowds to disperse. ▶ v. (**tear-gas**) [trans.] (usu. **be tear-gassed**) attack with tear gas.

tear·ing /'te(ə)riNG/ ▶ adj. [attrib.] violent; extreme: *he did seem to be in a tearing hurry* | *the tearing wind.*

tear·jerk·er /'ti(ə)r,jərkər/ ▶ n. informal a sentimental story, movie, or song that evokes sadness or sympathy. — **tear·jerk·ing** /-,jərkiNG/ n. & adj.

tear·less /'ti(ə)rlis/ ▶ adj. not crying: *his tearless widow.* — **tear·less·ly** adv. **tear·less·ness** n.

tear-off /te(ə)r/ ▶ adj. denoting something that is removed by being torn off, typically along a perforated line.

tea·room /'tē,ro͞om; -,ro͝om/ (also **tea room**) ▶ n. **1** a small restaurant or café where tea and other light refreshments are served. **2** informal a public restroom used as a meeting place for homosexual encounters.

tea rose ▶ n. a garden rose (numerous cultivars of the Chinese hybrid *Rosa* × *odorata*) with flowers that have a delicate scent said to resemble that of tea.

tear sheet /te(ə)r/ ▶ n. a page that can be or has been removed from a newspaper, magazine, or book for use separately.

tear-stained /ti(ə)r/ ▶ adj. wet with tears: *I looked at the man's tear-stained face.*

Teas·dale /'tēz,dāl/, Sara (1884–1933), US poet; born *Sarah Trevor*. Her poetry collections include *Helen of Troy and Other Poetry* (1911) and *Strange Victory* (1933).

tease /tēz/ ▶ v. [trans.] **1** make fun of or attempt to provoke (a person or animal) in a playful way: *he teased Jill about her dress* | [intrans.] *she was just teasing.* ■ tempt (someone) sexually with no intention of satisfying the desire aroused. **2** gently pull or comb (something tangled, esp. wool or hair) into separate strands: *she teased out the curls.* ■ fig. find something out from a mass of irrelevant information: *a historian who tries to **tease out** the truth.* ■ comb (hair) in the reverse direction of its natural growth in order to make it appear fuller. ■ archaic comb (the surface of woven cloth) to raise a nap. ▶ n. informal a person who makes fun of someone playfully or unkindly. ■ a person who tempts someone sexually with no intention of satisfying the desire aroused. ■ [in sing.] an act of making fun of or tempting someone. — **teas·ing·ly** adv. [OE *tǣsan* (sense 2), of West Gmc. origin; rel. to TEASEL.]

tea·sel /'tēzəl/ (also **tea·zle** or **tea·zel**) ▶ n. a tall prickly Eurasian plant (genus *Dipsacus*, family Dipsacaceae) with spiny purple flowerheads. Its several species include **fuller's teasel**. ■ a large, dried, spiny head from such a plant, or a device serving as a substitute for one of these, used in the textile industry to raise a nap on woven cloth. [OE *tǣsl*, *tǣsel*, of West Gmc. origin; rel. to TEASE.]

teas·er /'tēzər/ ▶ n. **1** informal a difficult or tricky question or task. **2** a person who makes fun of or provokes others in a playful or unkind way. ■ a person who tempts someone sexually with no intention of satisfying the desire aroused. ■ a short introductory advertisement for a product, esp. one that does not mention the name of the thing being advertised.

tea set (also **tea serv·ice**) ▶ n. a set of dishes, typically of china or silver, used for serving tea.

tea shop ▶ n. another term for TEAROOM (sense 1).

tea·spoon /'tē,spo͞on/ ▶ n. a small spoon used typically for adding sugar to and stirring hot drinks or for eating some soft foods. ■ (abbr.: **tsp** or **t**) a measurement used in cooking, equivalent to 16 fluid ounce, .13 tablespoon, or 4.9 ml. — **tea·spoon·ful** /-,fo͝ol/ n. (pl. **-fuls**).

tea strain·er ▶ n. a small device incorporating a fine mesh for straining tea.

teat /tēt/ ▶ n. a nipple of the mammary gland of a female mammal, from which the milk is sucked by the young. [ME: from OFr. *tete*, prob. of Gmc. origin.]

tea·time /'tē,tīm/ ▶ n. esp. Brit. the time in the afternoon when tea is traditionally served.

tea tow·el ▶ n. chiefly British term for DISH TOWEL.

tea tray ▶ n. a tray from which tea is served.

tea tree ▶ n. an Australasian flowering shrub or small tree (genus *Leptospermum*) of the myrtle family, having leaves used for tea and yielding an essential oil used medicinally.

tea·zle (also **tea·zel**) ▶ n. var. of TEASEL.

Te·bet /'tāvās; -vāt; te'vet/ (also **Te·vet**) ▶ n. (in the Jewish calendar) the fourth month of the civil and tenth of the religious year, usually coinciding with parts of December and January. [from Heb. *ṭēḇēṯ*.]

tec. ▶ abbr. ■ technical. ■ technician.

tech /tek/ (Brit. also **tec**) ▶ n. informal technology. See also HIGH-TECH, LOW-TECH. ■ a technician. ■ Basketball a technical foul. ▶ adj. technical: *I was in tech school then.*

tech. ▶ abbr. ■ technic. ■ technical. ■ technology.

tech·ie /'tekē/ (also **tek·kie** or **tech·y**) ▶ n. (pl. **-ies**) informal a person who is expert in or enthusiastic about technology, esp. computing. [1960s: from TECH + -IE.]

tech·ne·ti·um /tek'nēsн(ē)əm/ ▶ n. the chemical element of atomic number 43, a radioactive metal. Technetium was the first element to be created artificially, in 1937, by bombarding molybdenum with deuterons. (Symbol: **Tc**) [1940s: mod. L., from Gk. *tekhnētos* 'artificial,' from *tekhnasthai* 'make by art,' from *tekhnē* 'art.']

tech·nic /'teknik/ ▶ n. **1** technique. **2** (**technics**) [treated as sing. or pl.] technical terms, details, and methods; technology. — **tech·ni·cist** /-nisist/ n. [17th C.: from L. *technicus*, from Gk. *tekhnikos*, from *tekhnē* 'art.']

tech·ni·cal /'teknikəl/ ▶ adj. **1** of or relating to a particular subject, art, or craft, or its techniques: *technical terms* | *a test of an artist's technical skill.* ■ (esp. of a book or article) requiring special knowledge to be understood: *a technical report.* **2** of, involving, or concerned with applied and industrial sciences: *an important technical achievement.* **3** resulting from mechanical failure: *a technical fault.* **4** according to a strict application or interpretation of the law or rules: *a technical violation of the treaty.* ▶ n. Basketball short for TECHNICAL FOUL.

tech·ni·cal col·lege ▶ n. a college providing courses in a range of practical subjects, such as information technology, applied sciences, engineering, agriculture, and secretarial skills.

tech·ni·cal draw·ing ▶ n. the practice or skill of delineating objects in a precise way using certain techniques of draftsmanship, as employed in architecture or engineering. ■ a drawing produced in such a way.

tech·ni·cal foul ▶ n. Basketball a violation of certain rules of the game, not usually involving physical contact, but often involving unsportsmanlike actions.

tech·ni·cal·i·ty /,tekni'kalitē/ ▶ n. (pl. **-ties**) a point of law or a small detail of a set of rules: *their convictions were overturned* **on a technicality**. ■ (**technicalities**) the specific details or terms belonging to a particular field: *technicalities of the game.* ■ the state of being technical; the use of technical terms or methods: *the technicality of her speech.*

tech·ni·cal knock·out (abbr.: **TKO**) ▶ n. Boxing the ending of a fight by the referee on the grounds of one contestant's inability to continue, the opponent being declared the winner.

tech·ni·cal·ly /'teknik(ə)lē/ ▶ adv. **1** [usu. sentence adverb] according to the facts or exact meaning of something; strictly: *technically, a nut is a single-seeded fruit.* **2** with reference to the technique displayed: *a technically brilliant boxing contest.* **3** involving or regarding the technology available: *technically advanced tools.*

tech·ni·cal ser·geant ▶ n. a noncommissioned officer in the US Air Force ranking above staff sergeant and below master sergeant.

tech·ni·cal sup·port ▶ n. Comput. a service provided by a hardware or software company that provides registered users with help and advice about their products. ■ a department within an organization that maintains and repairs computers and computer networks.

tech·ni·cian /tek'nisнən/ ▶ n. a person employed to look after technical equipment or do practical work in a laboratory. ■ an expert in the practical application of a science. ■ a person skilled in the technique of an art or craft.

Tech·ni·col·or /'tekni,kələr/ ▶ n. trademark a process of color cinematography using synchronized monochrome films, each of a different color, to produce a movie in color. ■ (**technicolor**) informal vivid color: [as adj.] *a technicolor bruise.* — **tech·ni·col·ored** adj.

tech·nique /tek'nēk/ ▶ n. a way of carrying out a particular task, esp. the execution or performance of an artistic work or a scientific procedure. ■ skill or ability in a particular field: *he has excellent technique* | [in sing.] *an athlete with a good technique.* ■ a skillful or efficient way of doing or achieving something: *a good technique for evaluation.* [19th C.: from Fr., from L. *technicus* (see TECHNIC).]

tech·no /'teknō/ ▶ n. a style of fast, heavy electronic dance music, typically with few or no vocals. [1980s: abbr. of TECHNOLOGICAL.]

techno- ▶ comb. form relating to technology or its use: *technophobe.* [from Gk. *tekhnē* 'art, craft.']

tech·no·bab·ble /'teknō,babəl/ ▶ n. informal incomprehensible technical jargon.

tech·noc·ra·cy /tek'näkrəsē/ ▶ n. (pl. **-cies**) the government or control of society or industry by an elite of technical experts. ■ an instance or application of this. ■ an elite of technical experts. [20th C.: from Gk. *tekhnē* 'art, craft' + -CRACY.]

tech·no·crat /'teknə,krat/ ▶ n. an exponent or advocate of technocracy. ■ a member of a technically skilled elite. — **tech·no·crat·ic** /,teknə'kratik/ adj. **tech·no·crat·i·cal·ly** /,teknə'kratik(ə)lē/ adv.

technol. ▶ abbr. technology.

tech·no·log·i·cal /,teknə'läjikəl/ ▶ adj. of, relating to, or using technology. — **tech·no·log·i·cal·ly** adv.

tech·nol·o·gy /tek'näləjē/ ▶ n. (pl. **-gies**) the application of scientific knowledge for practical purposes, esp. in industry: *computer technology* | *recycling technologies.* ■ machinery and equipment developed from such scientific knowledge. ■ the branch of knowledge dealing with engineering or applied sciences. — **tech·nol·o·gist** n. **tech·nol·o·gize** /-,jīz/ v.

tech·nol·o·gy park ▶ n. a science park.

tech·nol·o·gy trans·fer ▶ n. the transfer of new technology from the originator to a secondary user, esp. from developed to less developed countries in an attempt to boost their economies.

tech·no·phile /'teknə,fīl/ ▶ n. a person who is enthusiastic about new technology. — **tech·no·phil·i·a** /,teknə'filēə/ n. **tech·no·phil·ic** /,teknə'filik/ adj.

tech·no·phobe /'teknə,fōb/ ▶ n. a person who fears, dislikes, or avoids new technology. — **tech·no·pho·bi·a** /,teknə'fōbēə/ n. **tech·no·pho·bic** /,teknə'fōbik/ adj.

tech·no·speak /'teknō,spēk/ ▶ n. another term for TECHNOBABBLE.

tech·no·stress /'teknō,stres/ ▶ n. informal stress or psychosomatic illness caused by working with computer technology on a daily basis.

tech·no·struc·ture /'teknō,strəkcнər/ ▶ n. [treated as sing. or pl.] a group of technologists or technical experts having considerable control over the workings of industry or government.

tech·no-thril·ler /'teknō 'T͟Hrilər/ ▶ n. a novel or movie in which the excitement of the plot depends in large part upon the descriptions of computers, weapons, software, military vehicles, or other machines.

tech·y /'tecнē/ ▶ n. var. of TECHIE.

tec·ton·ic /tek'tänik/ ▶ adj. **1** Geol. of or relating to the structure of the earth's crust and the large-scale processes that take place within it. **2** of or relating to building or construction. — **tec·ton·i·cal·ly** adv. [17th C. (sense 2): via late L. from Gk. *tektonikos*, from *tektōn* 'carpenter, builder.']

tec·ton·ics /tek'täniks/ ▶ plural n. [treated as sing. or pl.] Geol. large-scale processes affecting the structure of the earth's crust.

tec·to·no·phys·ics /tek,tänō'fiziks; ,tektənō-/ ▶ plural n. [treated as sing.] the branch of geophysics that deals with the forces that cause movement and deformation in the earth's crust. — **tec·to·no·phys·i·cist** /-'fizəsist/ n. [1950s: from TECTONICS + PHYSICS.]

tec·to·ri·al /tek'tôrēəl/ ▶ adj. Anat. forming a covering. ■ denoting the membrane covering the organ of Corti in the inner ear. [19th C.: from L. *tectorium* 'covering, a cover' (from *tegere* 'to cover') + -AL.]

tec·trix /'tektriks/ ▶ n. (Pl. **tec·tri·ces** /'tektrisēz/) Ornithol. a covert of a bird. [19th C.: mod. L., from L. *tect-* 'covered,' from the verb *tegere*.]

tec·tum /'tektəm/ ▶ n. Anat. the uppermost part of the midbrain, lying to the rear of the cerebral aqueduct. ■ (in full **optic tectum**) a rounded swelling (colliculus) forming part of this and containing cells involved in the visual system. [20th C.: from L., 'roof.']

Te·cum·seh /tə'kəmsə/ (1768–1813) Shawnee Indian chief; also *Tecumtha.* His plan to organize tribes to resist US encroachment was thwarted by the defeat of his brother, Tenskwatawa (c.1768–1834) (also called *the Prophet*), at Tippecanoe 1811.

ted /ted/ ▶ v. (**tedded, tedding**) [trans.] [often as n.] (**tedding**) turn over and spread out (grass, hay, or straw) to dry or for bedding. — **ted·der** n. [ME: from ON *tethja* 'spread manure' (past tense *tadda*), rel. to *tad* 'dung.']

ted·dy /'tedē/ ▶ n. (pl. **-dies**) **1** (also **ted·dy bear**) a soft toy bear. **2** a woman's all-in-one undergarment. [20th C.: from *Teddy*, nickname for *Theodore*: in sense 1 alluding to *Theodore* ROOSEVELT[3].]

Ted·dy boy ▶ n. Brit. (in the 1950s) a young man of a subculture characterized by a style of dress based on Edwardian fashion and a liking for rock and roll music. [from *Teddy*, nickname for *Edward*.]

Te De·um /tā 'dāəm; tē 'dēəm/ ▶ n. a hymn beginning *Te Deum laudamus*, "We praise Thee, O God." ■ a musical setting of this. ■ an expression of thanksgiving or exultation. [L.]

te·di·ous /'tēdēəs/ ▶ adj. too long, slow, or dull: tiresome or monotonous: *a tedious journey.* — **te·di·ous·ly** adv. **te·di·ous·ness** n. [ME: from OFr. *tedieus* or late L. *taediosus*, from L. *taedium* (see TEDIUM).]

te·di·um /'tēdēəm/ ▶ n. the state of being tedious: *the tedium of winter* *nights.* [17th C.: from L. *taedium*, from *taedere* 'be weary of.']

tee[1] /tē/ ▶ **n.** see **T**[1] (sense 2).

tee[2] ▶ **n.** **1** a cleared space on a golf course, from which the ball is struck at the beginning of play for each hole. ■ a small peg with a concave head that can be placed in the ground to support a golf ball before it is struck from such an area. ■ Football a small stand on which the ball is placed for a placekick. ■ a waist-high or higher stand used in tee-ball to hold a baseball before it is hit with a bat. [17th C.: of unknown origin.] **2** a mark aimed at in lawn bowling, quoits, curling, and other similar games. [18th C.: perh. the same word as TEE[1].] ▶ **v.** (**tees, teed, tee·ing**) [intrans.] (usu. **tee up**) Golf place the ball on a tee ready to make the first stroke of the round or hole: *he teed up for the last hole* | [trans.] *she fished in her pocket for a ball and teed it.* ■ [trans.] place (something) in position, esp. to be struck: *they intend to tee up the smaller companies for a takeover.*
– PHRASAL VERBS **tee off** Golf play the ball from a tee; begin a round or hole of golf. ■ informal make a start on something. **tee someone off** (usu. **be teed off**) informal make someone angry or annoyed: *he was teed off at Ernie.*

tee[3] ▶ **n.** informal a T-shirt.

tee-ball (also **t-ball**) ▶ **n.** a game for young children, played by the rules of baseball, in which the ball is not pitched but hit from a stationary tee.

tee-hee /ˌtē'hē/ ▶ **n.** a giggle or titter. ▶ **v.** (**-hees, -heed, -hee·ing**) [intrans.] titter or giggle in such a way. [ME (as a v.): imitative.]

teem[1] /tēm/ ▶ **v.** [intrans.] (**teem with**) be full of or swarming with: *every garden is teeming with wildlife.* [OE *tēman, tīeman*, of Gmc. origin; rel. to TEAM.]

teem[2] ▶ **v.** [intrans.] (of water, esp. rain) pour down; fall heavily: *rain teeming down at the manor.* [ME: from ON *tœma* 'to empty,' from *tómr* 'empty.']

teen /tēn/ informal ▶ **adj.** [attrib.] of or relating to teenagers: *a teen idol.* ▶ **n.** a teenager. [19th C. (as a n.): abbr.]

-teen ▶ **suffix** forming the names of numerals from 13 to 19: *fourteen* | *eighteen.* [OE, inflected form of TEN.]

teen·age /'tēnˌāj/ ▶ **adj.** [attrib.] denoting a person between 13 and 19 years old: *a teenage girl.* ■ relating to or characteristic of people of this age. — **teen·aged adj.**

teen·ag·er /'tēnˌājər/ ▶ **n.** a person aged from 13 to 19 years.

teens /tēnz/ ▶ **plural n.** the years of a person's age from 13 to 19: *they were both in their late teens.* [17th C.: from -TEEN.]

teen·sy /'tēnsē/ ▶ **adj.** (**-si·er, -si·est**) informal tiny: *the dress just needs to be altered a teensy bit.* [19th C. (orig. dial.): prob. an extension of TEENY.]

teen·sy-ween·sy /'wēnsē/ ▶ **adj.** informal tiny.

tee·ny /'tēnē/ ▶ **adj.** (**-ni·er, -ni·est**) informal tiny. [19th C.: var. of TINY.]

tee·ny·bop·per /'tēnēˌbäpər/ ▶ **n.** informal a young teenager, esp. a girl, who keenly follows the latest fashions in clothes and pop music. — **tee·ny·bop adj.**

tee·ny-wee·ny /'wēnē/ ▶ **adj.** informal tiny.

tee·pee ▶ **n.** var. of TEPEE.

Tees /tēz/ a river in northeastern England that flows to the North Sea.

tee shirt ▶ **n.** var. of T-SHIRT.

tee·ter /'tētər/ ▶ **v.** [intrans.] move or balance unsteadily; sway back and forth. ■ (often **teeter between**) fig. be unable to decide between different courses; waver: *she teetered between tears and anger.*
– PHRASES **teeter on the brink** (or **edge**) be very close to a difficult or dangerous situation: *the country teetered on the brink of civil war.* [19th C.: var. of dial. *titter*, from ON *titra* 'shake, shiver.']

tee·ter-tot·ter /'tētər ˌtätər/ ▶ **n.** a seesaw. ▶ **v.** [intrans.] teeter; waver. [19th C.: reduplication of TEETER or TOTTER.]

teeth /tēᴛʜ/ plural form of TOOTH.

teethe /tē<u>ᴛʜ</u>/ ▶ **v.** [intrans.] grow or cut teeth, esp. milk teeth. — **teeth·ing** /'tē<u>ᴛʜ</u>ɪɴɢ/ **n.** [ME: from TEETH.]

teeth·ing ring ▶ **n.** a small ring for an infant to bite on while teething.

tee·to·tal /'tēˌtōtl/ ▶ **adj.** choosing or characterized by abstinence from alcohol: *a teetotal lifestyle.* — **tee·to·tal·ism n.** [19th C.: from TOTAL.]

tee·to·tal·er /'tēˌtōtl-ər/ (Brit. **tee·to·tal·ler**) ▶ **n.** a person who never drinks alcohol.

tee·to·tum /tē'tōtəm/ ▶ **n.** a small spinning top spun with the fingers, esp. one with four sides lettered to determine whether the spinner has won or lost. [18th C.: from *T (totum)* + L. *totum* 'the whole' (stake).]

tee·vee /tē'vē/ ▶ **n.** nonstandard spelling of **TV**.

te·fil·lin /tə'fīlin; -fē'lēn/ ▶ **plural n.** collective term for Jewish phylacteries. [from Aramaic *tĕpillīn* 'prayers.']

TEFL /'tefəl/ ▶ **abbr.** teaching of English as a foreign language.

Tef·lon /'teflän/ ▶ **n.** trademark for POLYTETRAFLUOROETHYLENE. ▶ **adj.** able to withstand criticism or attack with no apparent effect: *a crime boss known as the Teflon Don because of his many acquittals.* [1940s: from TETRA- 'four' + FLUORO- + *-on.*]

teg /teg/ ▶ **n.** a sheep in its second year. [16th C.: perh. rel. to Swed. *tacka* 'ewe.']

teg·men /'tegmən/ ▶ **n.** (pl. **-mi·na** /-mənə/) Biol. a covering structure or roof of an organ, in particular: ■ Entomol. a sclerotized forewing serving to cover the hind wing in grasshoppers and related insects. ■ Bot. the delicate inner protective layer of a seed. ■ (also **tegmen tympani**) Anat. a plate of thin bone forming the roof of the middle ear, a part of the temporal bone. [19th C.: from L., 'covering,' from *tegere* 'to cover.']

teg·men·tum /teg'mentəm/ ▶ **n.** (pl. **-men·ta** /-'mentə/) Anat. a region of gray matter on either side of the cerebral aqueduct in the midbrain. — **teg·men·tal** /teg'mentl/ **adj.** [19th C.: from L., var. of *tegumentum* 'tegument.']

te·gu /ti'go͞o/ ▶ **n.** (pl. same or **-gus**) a large stocky lizard (genus *Tupinambis*, family Teiidae) that has dark skin with pale bands of small spots, native to the tropical forests of South America. [1950s: abbr. of *teguexin*, from Aztec *tecoixin* 'lizard.']

Te·gu·ci·gal·pa /təˌgo͞osə'galpə; -sē'gäl-/ the capital of Honduras; pop. 670,000.

teg·u·la /'tegyələ/ ▶ **n.** (pl. **-lae** /-lē/) **1** Entomol. a small scalelike sclerite covering the base of the forewing in many insects. **2** Archaeol. a flat roof tile, used esp. in Roman roofs. [19th C.: from L., lit. 'tile,' from *tegere* 'to cover.']

teg·u·ment /'tegyəmənt/ ▶ **n.** esp. Zool. the integument of an organism, esp. a parasitic flatworm. — **teg·u·men·tal** /ˌtegyə'mentl/ **adj.** **teg·u·men·ta·ry** /ˌtegyə'men(t)ərē/ **adj.** [ME: from L. *tegumentum*, from *tegere* 'to cover.']

Te·hach·a·pi Moun·tains /tə'hacʜəˌpē/ a range that is sometimes considered the divider between north and south California.

Teh·ran /ˌte(ə)'ran; -'rän/ (also **Tehe·ran**) the capital of Iran; pop. 6,750,000.

te·in /'tā-in/ ▶ **n.** (pl. same or **-ins**) a monetary unit of Kazakhstan, equal to one hundredth of a tenge.

Te·ja·no /tə'hänō/ ▶ **n.** (pl. **-nos**) a Mexican-American inhabitant of southern Texas. ■ a style of folk or popular music originating among such people, with elements from Mexican-Spanish vocal traditions and Czech and German dance tunes and rhythms, traditionally played by small groups featuring accordion and guitar. [Amer. Sp., alt. of *Texano* 'Texan.']

Te·jo /'tāzʜo͞o/ Portuguese name for **TAGUS**.

tek·kie ▶ **n.** var. of TECHIE.

tek·tite /'tektīt/ ▶ **n.** Geol. a small black glassy object, many of which are found over certain areas of the earth's surface, believed to have been formed as molten debris in meteorite impacts. [20th C.: coined in Ger. from Gk. *tēktos* 'molten' (from *tēkein* 'melt') + -ITE[1].]

tel. (also **Tel.**) ▶ **abbr.** telephone.

tel·a·mon /'teləˌmän/ ▶ **n.** (pl. **tel·a·mo·nes** /ˌtelə'mōnēz/) Archit. a male figure used as a pillar to support an entablature or other structure. [17th C.: via L. from Gk. *telamōnes*, pl. of *Telamōn*, the name of a mythical hero.]

tel·an·gi·ec·ta·sia /telˌanjē-ek'tāzʜə/ (also **tel·an·gi·ec·ta·sis** /-'ektəsis/) ▶ **n.** Med. a condition characterized by dilation of the capillaries, which causes them to appear as small red or purple clusters, often spidery in appearance, on the skin or the surface of an organ. — **tel·an·gi·ec·tat·ic** /-'tatik/ **adj.** [19th C.: mod. L., from Gk. *telos* 'end' + *angeion* 'vessel' + *ektasis* 'dilatation.']

Tel A·viv /ˌtel ə'vēv/ (also **Tel A·viv-Jaf·fa**) a city on the coast of Israel; pop. 355,000 (with Jaffa).

tel·co /'telkō/ ▶ **n.** (pl. **-cos**) a telecommunications company. [20th C.: abbr.]

tele- ▶ **comb. form** **1** to or at a distance: *telekinesis.* ■ used in names of instruments for operating over long distances: *telemeter.* [from Gk. *tēle-* 'far off.'] **2** relating to television: *telecine.* **3** done by means of the telephone: *telemarketing.*

tel·e·cast /'teləˌkast/ ▶ **n.** a television broadcast. ▶ **v.** [trans.] (usu. **be telecast**) transmit by television. — **tel·e·cast·er n.**

tel·e·cin·e /'teləˌsinē/ ▶ **n.** the broadcasting of a movie on television. ■ equipment used in such broadcasting.

tel·e·com /'teləˌkäm/ (Brit. also **tel·e·coms**) ▶ **plural n.** [treated as sing.] telecommunications. [1960s: abbr.]

tel·e·com·mu·ni·ca·tion /ˌteləkəˌmyo͞oni'kāsʜən/ ▶ **n.** communication over a distance by cable, telegraph, telephone, or broadcasting. ■ (**telecommunications**) [treated as sing.] the branch of technology concerned with such communication. ■ formal a message sent by such means.

tel·e·com·mute /ˌteləkə'myo͞ot/ ▶ **v.** [intrans.] [usu. as n.] (**telecommuting**) work from home, communicating with the workplace using equipment such as telephones, fax machines, and modems. — **tel·e·com·mut·er n.**

tel·e·com·put·er /ˌteləkəm'pyo͞otər/ ▶ **n.** a device that combines the capabilities of a computer with those of a television and a telephone, particularly for multimedia applications. — **tel·e·com·put·ing n.**

tel·e·con·fer·ence /'teləˌkänf(ə)rəns/ ▶ **n.** a conference with participants in different locations linked by telecommunications devices. ▶ **v.** [intrans.] participate in a teleconference. — **tel·e·con·fer·enc·ing n.**

tel·e·con·nec·tion /ˌteləkə'neksʜən/ ▶ **n.** a causal connection or correlation between meteorological or other environmental phenomena that occur a long distance apart.

tel·e·con·vert·er /ˌteləkən'vərtər/ ▶ **n.** Photog. a camera lens designed to be fitted in front of a standard lens to increase its effective focal length.

Tel·e·cop·i·er /'teləˌkäpēər/ ▶ **n.** trademark a device that transmits and reproduces facsimile copies over a telephone line.

tel·e·fac·sim·i·le /ˌteləfak'siməlē/ ▶ **n.** another term for FAX.

tel·e·fax /'teləˌfaks/ trademark ▶ **n.** the transmission of documents by fax: *contact us by telefax.* ■ a document sent in such a way. ■ a fax machine. ▶ **v.** [trans.] [usu. as adj.] (**telefaxed**) send (a message) by fax: *telefaxed bills* *of lading.* [1940s: abbr. of TELEFACSIMILE.]

tel·e·film /'telə,film/ ▶ **n.** a movie made for or broadcast on television.

teleg. ▶ **abbr.** ■ telegram. ■ telegraph. ■ telegraphy.

tel·e·gen·ic /,telə'jenik/ ▶ **adj.** having an appearance or manner that is appealing on television. — **tel·e·gen·i·cal·ly adv.**

tel·e·gram /'telə,gram/ ▶ **n.** a message sent by telegraph and then delivered in written or printed form.

tel·e·graph /'telə,graf/ ▶ **n.** a system for transmitting messages from a distance along a wire, esp. one creating signals by making and breaking an electrical connection: *news came from the outside world by telegraph.* ■ a device for transmitting messages in such a way. ▶ **v.** [trans.] send (someone) a message by telegraph. ■ send (a message) by telegraph. ■ convey (an intentional or unconscious message), esp. with facial expression or body language: *a tiny movement of her arm telegraphed her intention to strike.* — **te·leg·ra·pher** /tə'legrəfər/ **n.**

tel·e·graph·ic /,telə'grafik/ ▶ **adj. 1** of or by telegraphs or telegrams: *the telegraphic transfer of the funds.* **2** (esp. of speech) omitting inessential words; concise. — **tel·e·graph·i·cal·ly adv.**

te·leg·ra·phist /tə'legrəfist/ ▶ **n.** a person skilled or employed in telegraphy. ■ a person whose job is to operate telegraph equipment.

tel·e·graph key ▶ **n.** a button that is pressed to produce a signal when transmitting Morse code.

tel·e·graph plant ▶ **n.** a tropical Asian plant (*Codariocalyx motorius*) of the pea family whose leaves have a spontaneous jerking motion.

te·leg·ra·phy /tə'legrəfē/ ▶ **n.** the science or practice of using or constructing communications systems for the transmission or reproduction of information.

Tel·e·gu ▶ **n.** var. of TELUGU.

tel·e·ki·ne·sis /,teləki'nēsis/ ▶ **n.** the supposed ability to move objects at a distance by mental power or other nonphysical means. — **tel·e·ki·net·ic** /-'netik/ **adj.** [19th C.: from TELE- 'at a distance' + Gk. *kinēsis* 'motion' (from *kinein* 'to move').]

Te·lem·a·chus /tə'leməkəs/ Gk. Mythol. the son of Odysseus and Penelope.

Te·le·mann /'tālə,män; 'tel-/, Georg Philipp (1681–1767), German composer and organist.

tel·e·mark /'telə,märk/ Skiing ▶ **n.** a turn or a landing style in ski jumping with one ski advanced and the knees bent. ▶ **v.** [intrans.] perform such a turn while skiing. [20th C.: *Telemark*, a district in Norway.]

tel·e·mar·ket·ing /'telə,märkitiNG/ ▶ **n.** the marketing of goods or services by means of telephone calls, typically unsolicited, to potential customers. — **tel·e·mar·ket·er n.**

tel·e·mat·ics /,telə'matiks/ ▶ **plural n.** [treated as sing.] the branch of information technology that deals with the long-distance transmission of computerized information. — **tel·e·mat·ic adj.** [1970s: blend of TELECOMMUNICATION and INFORMATICS.]

tel·e·med·i·cine /'telə,medisin/ ▶ **n.** the remote diagnosis and treatment of patients by means of telecommunications technology.

te·lem·e·ter /tə'lemitər; 'telə,mētər/ ▶ **n.** an apparatus for recording the readings of an instrument and transmitting them by radio. ▶ **v.** /'telə,mētər/ [trans.] transmit (readings) to a distant receiving set or station. — **tel·e·met·ric** /,telə'metrik/ **adj.** **te·lem·e·try** /tə'lemitrē/ **n.**

tel·en·ceph·a·lon /,telən'sefəlän; -lən/ ▶ **n.** Anat. the most highly developed and anterior part of the forebrain, consisting chiefly of the cerebral hemispheres. Compare with DIENCEPHALON. [19th C.: from TELE- 'far' + ENCEPHALON.]

tel·e·no·vel·a /,telənō'velə/ ▶ **n.** (in Latin America) a television soap opera.

tel·e·o·log·i·cal ar·gu·ment /,telēə'läjikəl; ,tēlē-/ ▶ **n.** Philos. the argument for the existence of God from the evidence of order, and hence design, in nature. Compare with COSMOLOGICAL ARGUMENT and ONTOLOGICAL ARGUMENT.

tel·e·ol·o·gy /,telē'äləjē; ,tēlē-/ ▶ **n.** (pl. **-gies**) Philos. the explanation of phenomena by the purpose they serve rather than by postulated causes. ■ Theol. the doctrine of design and purpose in the material world. — **tel·e·o·log·ic** /-ə'läjik/ **adj.** **tel·e·o·log·i·cal** /-ə'läjikəl/ **adj.** **tel·e·o·log·i·cal·ly** /-ə'läjik(ə)lē/ **adv.** **tel·e·ol·o·gism n.** **tel·e·ol·o·gist n.** [18th C.: from mod. L. *teleologia*, from Gk. *telos* 'end' + *-logia* (see -LOGY).]

tel·e·op·er·a·tion /,telə,äpə'rāsHən/ ▶ **n.** the electronic remote control of machines. — **tel·e·op·er·ate** /-'äpə,rāt/ **v.**

tel·e·op·er·a·tor /,telə'äpə,rātər/ ▶ **n.** a machine operated by remote control so as to imitate the movements of its operator.

tel·e·ost /'telē,äst; 'tēlē-/ ▶ **n.** Zool. a fish (division Teleostei, subclass Actinopterygii) of a large group that comprises all ray-finned fishes apart from the primitive sturgeons, paddlefishes, freshwater garfishes, and bowfins. [19th C.: from Gk. *teleos* 'complete' + *osteon* 'bone.']

tel·e·path /'telə,paTH/ ▶ **n.** a person with the ability to communicate using telepathy. [19th C.: back-form. from TELEPATHY.]

te·lep·a·thy /tə'lepəTHē/ ▶ **n.** the supposed communication of thoughts or ideas by means other than the known senses. — **tel·e·path·ic** /,telə'paTHik/ **adj.** **tel·e·path·i·cal·ly** /,telə'paTHik(ə)lē/ **adv.** **te·lep·a·thist n.**

tel·e·phone /'telə,fōn/ ▶ **n.** a system that converts acoustic vibrations to electrical signals in order to transmit sound, typically voices, over a distance using wire or radio. ■ an instrument used as part of such a system, typically a single unit including a handset with a transmitting microphone and a set of numbered buttons by which a connection can be made to another such instrument. ▶ **v.** [trans.] call or speak to (someone) using the telephone: *he had just finished telephoning his wife.* ■ [intrans.] make a telephone call: *she telephoned for help.* ■ send (a message) by telephone. — **tel·e·phon·er n.** **tel·e·phon·ic** /,telə'fänik/ **adj.** **tel·e·phon·i·cal·ly** /,telə'fänik(ə)lē/ **adv.**

tel·e·phone book ▶ **n.** a telephone directory.

tel·e·phone booth (Brit. also **tel·e·phone box**) ▶ **n.** a public booth or enclosure housing a pay phone.

tel·e·phone card ▶ **n.** another term for CALLING CARD (sense 2).

tel·e·phone di·rec·to·ry ▶ **n.** a book listing the names, addresses, and telephone numbers of the people in a particular area.

tel·e·phone ex·change ▶ **n.** a set of equipment that connects telephone lines during a call.

tel·e·phone num·ber ▶ **n.** a number assigned to a particular telephone and used in making connections to it.

tel·e·phone op·er·a·tor ▶ **n.** a person who works at the switchboard of a telephone exchange.

tel·e·phone pole ▶ **n.** a tall pole used to carry telephone wires and electric cables.

tel·e·phone tag ▶ **n.** informal the action of two people continually trying unsuccessfully to reach each other by telephone.

te·leph·o·ny /tə'lefənē; 'telə,fōnē/ ▶ **n.** the working or use of telephones.

tel·e·pho·to /'telə,fōtō/ (also **tel·e·pho·to lens**) ▶ **n.** (pl. **-tos**) a lens with a longer focal length than standard, giving a narrow field of view and a magnified image.

tel·e·play /'telə,plā/ ▶ **n.** a play written or adapted for television.

tel·e·port /'telə,pôrt/ ▶ **v.** (esp. in science fiction) transport or be transported across space and distance instantly. ▶ **n. 1** a center providing interconnections between different forms of telecommunications, esp. one that links satellites to ground-based communications. [1980s: orig. the name of such a center in New York.] **2** an act of teleporting. — **tel·e·por·ta·tion** /,teləpôr'tāsHən/ **n.** [1950s: back-form. from *teleportation*, from TELE- + a shortened form of TRANSPORTATION.]

tel·e·pres·ence /'telə,prezəns/ ▶ **n.** the use of virtual reality technology, esp. for remote control of machinery or for apparent participation in distant events. ■ a sensation of being elsewhere, created in such a way.

tel·e·print·er /'telə,printər/ ▶ **n.** a device for transmitting telegraph messages as they are keyed, and for printing messages received.

Tel·e·Promp·Ter /'telə,prämptər/ ▶ **n.** trademark a device used in television and moviemaking to project a speaker's script out of sight of the audience.

tel·e·sales /'telə,sālz/ ▶ **plural n.** the selling of goods or services over the telephone.

telescope

tel·e·scope /'telə,skōp/ ▶ **n.** an optical instrument designed to make distant objects appear nearer, containing an arrangement of lenses, or of curved mirrors and lenses, by which rays of light are collected and focused and the resulting image magnified. ■ short for RADIO TELESCOPE. ▶ **v.** [trans.] cause (an object made of concentric tubular parts) to slide into itself, so that it becomes smaller. ■ [intrans.] be capable of sliding together in this way. ■ crush (a vehicle) by the force of an impact. ■ fig. condense or conflate so as to occupy less space or time: *telescoping many events into a relatively brief period.*

tel·e·scop·ic /,telə'skäpik/ ▶ **adj. 1** of, relating to, or made with a telescope. ■ capable of viewing and magnifying distant objects. ■ Astron. visible only through a telescope. **2** having or consisting of concentric tubular sections designed to slide into one another: *a telescopic umbrella.* — **tel·e·scop·i·cal·ly adv.**

tel·e·scop·ic sight ▶ **n.** a small telescope used for sighting, typically mounted on a rifle.

tel·e·shop·ping /'telə,sHäpiNG/ ▶ **n.** the ordering of goods by customers using a telephone or computer.

tel·e·the·sia /,teləs'THēZH(ē)ə/ (Brit. **tel·aes·the·sia**) ▶ **n.** the supposed perception of distant occurrences or objects otherwise than by the recognized senses. — **tel·es·thet·ic** /-'THetik/ **adj.** [19th C.: from TELE- + Gk. *aisthēsis* 'perception.']

tel·e·text /ˈteləˌtekst/ ▶**n.** a news and information service in the form of text and graphics, transmitted using the spare capacity of existing television channels to televisions with appropriate receivers.

tel·e·thon /ˈteləˌTHän/ ▶**n.** a very long television program, esp. one to raise money for a charity. [1940s (orig. US): from TELE- 'at a distance' + *-thon* on the pattern of *marathon*.]

Tel·e·type /ˈteləˌtīp/ (often **tel·e·type**) ▶**n.** trademark a kind of teleprinter. ■ a message received and printed by a teleprinter. ▶**v.** [with obj. and usu. with adverbial of direction] send (a message) by means of a teleprinter.

tel·e·type·writ·er /ˌteləˈtīpˌrītər/ ▶**n.** a teleprinter.

tel·e·van·ge·list /ˌteləˈvanjəlist/ ▶**n.** an evangelical preacher who appears regularly on television to preach and appeal for funds. — **tel·e·van·gel·i·cal** /ˌteləvanˈjelikəl/ **adj.** **tel·e·van·ge·lism n.**

tel·e·view·er /ˈteləˌvyo͞oər/ ▶**v.** a person who watches television. — **tel·e·view·ing n. & adj.**

tel·e·vise /ˈteləˌvīz/ ▶**v.** [trans.] [usu. as adj.] (**televised**) transmit by television: *a live televised debate.* — **tel·e·vis·a·ble adj.** [1920s: back-form. from TELEVISION.]

tel·e·vi·sion /ˈteləˌviZHən/ ▶**n. 1** a system for transmitting visual images and sound that are reproduced on screens, chiefly used to broadcast programs for entertainment, information, and education. ■ the activity, profession, or medium of broadcasting on television: *my children showed no inclination to follow me into television* | [as adj.] *television news.* ■ television programs: *watching television.* **2** (also **tel·e·vi·sion set**) a box-shaped device that receives and reproduces television signals.
– PHRASES **on (the) television** being broadcast by television; appearing in a television program.

tel·e·vi·sion sta·tion ▶**n.** an organization transmitting television programs.

tel·e·vis·u·al /ˌteləˈviZHo͞oəl/ ▶**adj.** relating to or suitable for television: *the world of televisual images.* — **tel·e·vi·su·al·ly adv.**

tel·e·work /ˈteləˌwərk/ ▶**v.** another term for TELECOMMUTE. ▶**n.** work performed primarily on computers linked to other locations, esp. from home or a remote location. — **tel·e·work·er n. tel·e·work·ing n.**

tel·ex /ˈteleks/ ▶**n.** an international system of telegraphy with printed messages transmitted and received by teleprinters using the public telecommunications network. ■ a device used for this. ■ a message sent by this system. ▶**v.** [trans.] communicate with (someone) by telex. ■ send (a message) by telex. [1930s: blend of TELEPRINTER and EXCHANGE.]

tel·ic /ˈtelik; ˈtē-/ ▶**adj.** (of an action or attitude) directed or tending to a definite end. ■ Ling. (of a verb, conjunction, or clause) expressing goal, result, or purpose. — **te·lic·i·ty** /təˈlisitē/ **n.** [19th C.: from Gk. *telikos* 'final,' from *telos* 'end.']

Tell /tel/, William, a legendary hero of the liberation of Switzerland from Austrian oppression in the 14th century. He is noted for having hit with an arrow an apple placed on his son's head.

tell[1] /tel/ ▶**v.** [trans.] (past **told**) **1** communicate information, facts, or news to someone in spoken or written words: *I told her you were coming* | *"We have nothing in common," she told him* | *he's telling the truth.* ■ order, instruct, or advise someone to do something: *tell him to go away.* ■ narrate or relate (a tale or story). ■ reveal information to (someone) in a nonverbal way: *the figures tell a different story.* ■ [intrans.] divulge confidential or private information: *I won't tell.* ■ [intrans.] (**tell on**) informal inform someone of the misdemeanors of: *friends don't tell on each other.* **2** decide or determine correctly or with certainty: *you can tell they're in love.* ■ distinguish one person or thing from another; perceive the difference between one person or thing and another: *I can't tell the difference between margarine and butter.* **3** [intrans.] (of an experience or period of time) have a noticeable, typically harmful, effect on someone: *the strain was beginning to tell on him.* ■ (of a particular factor) play a part in the success or otherwise of someone or something: *lack of fitness told against him on his first run of the season.*
– PHRASES **as far as one can tell** judging from the available information. **I tell you** (or **I can tell you**) used to emphasize a statement: *that took me by surprise, I can tell you!* **I** (or **I'll**) **tell you what** used to introduce a suggestion: *I tell you what, why don't we meet for lunch tomorrow?* **I told you** (**so**) used as a way of pointing out that one's warnings, although ignored, have been proved to be well founded. **tell someone's fortune** see FORTUNE. **tell it like it is** informal describe the facts of a situation no matter how unpleasant they may be. **tell me about it** informal used as an ironic acknowledgment of one's familiarity with a difficult or unpleasant situation or experience described by someone else. **tell me another** informal used as an expression of disbelief or incredulity. **tell tales** make known or gossip about another person's secrets, wrongdoings, or faults. **tell it to the marines** see MARINE. **tell time** be able to ascertain the time from reading the face of a clock or watch. **tell someone where to get off** (or **where they get off**) informal angrily dismiss or rebuke someone. **tell someone where to put** (or **what to do with**) **something** informal angrily or emphatically reject something: *I told him what he could do with his diamond.* **there is no telling** used to convey the impossibility of knowing what has happened or will happen: *there's no telling how she will react.* **to tell (you) the truth** used as a preface to a confession or admission of something. **you're telling me!** informal used to emphasize that one is already well aware of something or in complete agreement with a statement.
– PHRASAL VERBS **tell someone off** informal reprimand or scold someone. — **tell·a·ble adj.** [OE *tellan* 'relate, count, estimate,' of Gmc. origin; rel. to Ger. *zählen* 'reckon, count,' also to TALE.]

tell[2] ▶**n.** Archaeol. (in the Middle East) an artificial mound formed by the accumulated remains of ancient settlements. [19th C.: from Arab. *tall* 'hillock.']

tell-all ▶**adj.** revealing private or salacious details: *a tell-all article in the tabloids.* ▶**n.** a biography or memoir that reveals intimate details about its subject.

Tell·er /ˈtelər/, Edward, (1908–2003), US physicist, born in Hungary. Work under his guidance led to the detonation of the first hydrogen bomb in 1952.

tell·er /ˈtelər/ ▶**n. 1** a person employed to deal with customers' transactions in a bank. **2** a person who tells something: *a teller of lies.* **3** a person appointed to count votes, esp. in a legislature. — **tell·er·ship n.** (esp. hist.) (in sense 1).

tell·ing /ˈteliNG/ ▶**adj.** having a striking or revealing effect; significant: *a telling argument against this theory.* — **tell·ing·ly adv.**

tell·tale /ˈtelˌtāl/ ▶**adj.** [attrib.] revealing, indicating, or betraying something: *the telltale bulge of a weapon.* ▶**n. 1** a person, esp. a child, who reports others' wrongdoings or reveals their secrets. **2** a device or object that automatically gives a visual indication of the state or presence of something. ■ (on a sailboat) a piece of string or fabric that shows the direction and force of the wind.

tel·lu·ri·an /təˈlo͝orēən/ formal literary ▶**adj.** of or inhabiting the earth. ▶**n.** an inhabitant of the earth. [19th C.: from L. *tellus, tellur-* 'earth' + -IAN.]

tel·lu·ric /təˈlo͝orik/ ▶**adj.** of the earth as a planet. ■ of the soil. [19th C.: from L. *tellus, tellur-* 'earth' + -IC.]

tel·lu·ric ac·id ▶**n.** Chem. a crystalline acid, $Te(OH)_6$, made by oxidizing tellurium dioxide. — **tel·lu·rate** /ˈtelyəˌrāt/ **n.**

tel·lu·rite /ˈtelyəˌrīt/ ▶**n.** Chem. a salt of the anion $TeO_3 2-$.

tel·lu·ri·um /təˈlo͝orēəm/ ▶**n.** the chemical element of atomic number 52, a brittle, shiny, silvery-white semimetal resembling selenium and occurring mainly in small amounts in metallic sulfide ores. It is a semiconductor and is used in some electrical devices and in specialized alloys. (Symbol: **Te**) — **tel·lu·ride** /ˈtelyəˌrīd/ **n.** [19th C.: mod. L., from L. *tellus, tellur-* 'earth.']

tel·ly /ˈtelē/ ▶**n.** (pl. **-lies**) Brit. informal term for TELEVISION.

tel·net /ˈtelˌnet/ Comput. ▶**n.** a network protocol that allows a user on one computer to log on to another computer that is part of the same network. ■ a program that establishes a connection from one computer to another by means of such a protocol. ■ a link established in such a way. ▶**v.** (**-net·ted, -net·ting**) [intrans.] informal log on to a remote computer using a telnet program. — **tel·net·ta·ble adj.** [1970s: blend of TELECOMMUNICATION and NETWORK.]

tel·o·lec·i·thal /ˌtelōˈlesiTHəl; ˌtēlō-/ ▶**adj.** Zool. (of an egg or egg cell) having a large yolk situated at or near one end. [19th C.: from Gk. *telos* 'end' + *lekithos* 'egg yolk' + -AL.]

tel·o·mer·ase /təˈläməˌrās; -ˌrāz; təˈlō-/ ▶**n.** an enzyme that adds nucleotides to telomeres, especially in cancer cells.

tel·o·mere /ˈteləˌmi(ə)r; ˈtēlə-/ ▶**n.** Genet. a compound structure at the end of a chromosome. — **tel·o·mer·ic** /ˌteləˈmerik; ˌtēlə-/ **adj.** [1940s: from Gk. *telos* 'end' + *meros* 'part.']

tel·o·phase /ˈteləˌfāz; ˈtēlə-/ ▶**n.** Biol. the final phase of cell division, between anaphase and interphase, in which the chromatids or chromosomes move to opposite ends of the cell and two nuclei are formed. [19th C.: from Gk. *telos* 'end' + PHASE.]

te·los /ˈteläs; ˈtē-/ ▶**n.** (pl. **te·loi** /ˈteloi; ˈtēloi/) esp. Philos. or literary an ultimate object or aim. [Gk., lit. 'end.']

tel·son /ˈtelsən/ ▶**n.** Zool. the last segment in the abdomen, or a terminal appendage to it, in crustaceans, chelicerates, and embryonic insects. [19th C.: from Gk., lit. 'limit.']

Tel·star /ˈtelˌstär/ the first of the active communications satellites (i.e., both receiving and retransmitting signals, not merely reflecting signals from the earth). It was launched by the US in 1962 and used in the transmission of television broadcasting and telephone communication.

Tel·u·gu /ˈteləˌgo͞o/ (also **Tel·e·gu**) ▶**n.** (pl. same or **-gus**) **1** a member of a people of southeastern India. **2** the Dravidian language of this people, spoken mainly in the state of Andhra Pradesh. ▶**adj.** of or relating to this people or their language. [from the name in Telugu, *telugu*.]

tem·blor /ˈtemblər; -blôr/ ▶**n.** an earthquake. [19th C.: from Amer. Sp.]

tem·er·ar·i·ous /ˌteməˈre(ə)rēəs/ ▶**adj.** literary reckless; rash. [16th C.: from L. *temerarius* (from *temere* 'rashly') + -OUS.]

te·mer·i·ty /təˈméritē/ ▶**n.** excessive confidence or boldness; audacity: *no one had the temerity to question his conclusions.* [ME: from L. *temeritas*, from *temere* 'rashly.']

Tem·es·vár /ˈtemesHˌvär/ Hungarian name for TIMIŞOARA.

Tem·ne /ˈtemnē/ ▶**n.** (pl. same or **-nes**) **1** a member of a people of Sierra Leone. **2** the Niger–Congo language of this people, the main language of Sierra Leone. ▶**adj.** of or relating to this people or their language. [the name in Temne.]

tem·no·spon·dyl /ˌtemnōˈspändl/ ▶**n.** an extinct amphibian of a large group (order Temnospondyli) that was dominant from the Carboniferous to the Triassic. [20th C.: from mod. L. *Temnospondyli* (pl.), from Gk. *temnein* 'to cut' + *spondulos* 'vertebra.']

temp[1] /temp/ informal ▶**n.** a temporary employee, typically an office worker who finds employment through an agency. ▶**v.** [intrans.] work as a temporary employee.

temp² ▶ abbr. temperature.

temp. ▶ abbr. in or from the time of: *a Roman aqueduct temp. Augustus.* [from L. *tempore*, ablative of *tempus* 'time.']

Tem·pe /'tempē/ a city in south central Arizona, east of Phoenix; pop. 158,625.

tem·peh /'tempā/ ▶ n. an Indonesian dish made by deep-frying fermented soybeans. [from Indonesian *tempe*.]

tem·per /'tempər/ ▶ n. **1** [in sing.] a person's state of mind seen in terms of their being angry or calm. ■ a tendency to become angry easily: *my temper gets the better of me.* ■ an angry state of mind: *Drew walked out in a temper* | *I said it in a fit of temper.* ■ a character or mode of thought: *the temper of the sixties.* **2** the degree of hardness and elasticity in steel or other metal: *when it heats up, the metal loses its temper.* ▶ v. [trans.] **1** improve the hardness and elasticity of (steel or other metal) by reheating and then cooling it. ■ improve the consistency or resiliency of (a substance) by heating it or adding particular substances to it. **2** (often **be tempered with**) serve as a neutralizing or counterbalancing force to (something): *their idealism is tempered with realism.* **3** tune (a piano or other instrument) so as to adjust the note intervals correctly.
– PHRASES **keep** (or **lose**) **one's temper** refrain (or fail to refrain) from becoming angry. **out of temper** in an irritable mood. — **tem·per·er** n. [OE *temprian* 'to moderate,' from L. *temperare* 'mingle, restrain oneself.']

tem·per·a /'tempərə/ ▶ n. a method of painting with pigments dispersed in an emulsion miscible with water, typically egg yolk. The method was used in Europe for fine painting, mainly on wood panels, from the 12th or early 13th century until the 15th, when it began to give way to oils. ■ emulsion used in this method of painting. [19th C.: from Ital., in *pingere a tempera* 'paint in distemper.']

tem·per·a·ment /'temp(ə)rəmənt/ ▶ n. **1** a person's or animal's nature, esp. as it permanently affects their behavior: *she had an artistic temperament.* ■ the tendency to behave angrily or emotionally. **2** the adjustment of intervals in tuning a piano or other musical instrument so as to fit the scale for use in different keys; in **equal temperament**, the octave consists of twelve equal semitones. [ME: from L. *temperamentum* 'correct mixture,' from *temperare* 'mingle.']

tem·per·a·men·tal /,temp(ə)rə'mentl/ ▶ adj. **1** (of a person) liable to unreasonable changes of mood. **2** of or relating to a person's temperament: *they were firm friends in spite of temperamental differences.* — **tem·per·a·men·tal·ly** adv.

tem·per·ance /'temp(ə)rəns/ ▶ n. abstinence from alcoholic drink: [as adj.] *the temperance movement.* ■ moderation or self-restraint, esp. in eating and drinking.

tem·per·ate /'temp(ə)rit/ ▶ adj. **1** of, relating to, or denoting a region or climate characterized by mild temperatures. **2** showing moderation or self-restraint: *Charles was temperate in his consumption of both food and drink.* — **tem·per·ate·ly** adv. **tem·per·ate·ness** n.

tem·per·ate zone (also **Tem·per·ate Zone**) ▶ n. each of the two belts of latitude between the torrid zone and the northern and southern frigid zones.

tem·per·a·ture /'temp(ə)rəCHər; -,CHŏŏr/ ▶ n. the degree or intensity of heat present in a substance or object, esp. as expressed according to a comparative scale and shown by a thermometer or perceived by touch. ■ Med. the degree of internal heat of a person's body: *I'll take her temperature.* ■ informal a body temperature above the normal; fever: *he was running a temperature.* ■ the degree of excitement or tension in a discussion or confrontation. [ME: from Fr. *température* or L. *temperatura*, from *temperare* 'restrain.']

tem·per·a·ture in·ver·sion ▶ n. see INVERSION (sense 2).

-tempered ▶ comb. form having a specified temper or disposition: *ill-tempered.* — **-temperedly** comb. form in corresponding adverbs. **-temperedness** comb. form in corresponding nouns.

tem·pest /'tempist/ ▶ n. a violent windy storm.
– PHRASES **a tempest in a teapot** great anger or excitement about a trivial matter. [ME: from OFr. *tempeste*, from L. *tempestas* 'season, weather, storm,' from *tempus* 'time, season.']

tem·pes·tu·ous /tem'pesCHōōəs/ ▶ adj. **1** characterized by strong and turbulent or conflicting emotion. **2** very stormy: *a tempestuous wind.* — **tem·pes·tu·ous·ly** adv. **tem·pes·tu·ous·ness** n. [ME: from late L. *tempestuosus*, from L. *tempestas* (see TEMPEST).]

tem·pi /'tempē/ plural form of TEMPO.

tem·plate /'templit/ ▶ n. **1** a shaped piece of metal, wood, card, plastic, or other material used as a pattern for processes such as cutting out, shaping, or drilling. ■ fig. something that serves as a model for others to copy: *a template for change.* ■ Comput. a preset format for a document or file, used so that the format does not have to be recreated each time it is used: *a memo template.* ■ Comput. a guide that fits over all or part of a computer keyboard to describe the functions of each key for a particular software application. ■ Biochem. a nucleic acid molecule that acts as a pattern for the sequence of assembly of a protein, nucleic acid, or other large molecule. **2** a timber or plate used to distribute the weight in a wall or under a support. [17th C.: prob. from TEMPLE³ + -ET¹.]

Tem·ple, Shirley (1928–), US actress and diplomat; married name *Shirley Temple Black.* As a child star, her movies included *Rebecca of Sunnybrook Farm* (1938). She later represented the US as a UN ambassador.

tem·ple¹ /'tempəl/ ▶ n. a building devoted to the worship, or regarded as the dwelling place, of a god or gods or other objects of religious reverence. [OE *templ, tempel*, from L. *templum* 'open or consecrated space.']

tem·ple² ▶ n. the flat part of either side of the head between the forehead and the ear. [ME: from OFr., from an alt. of L. *tempora*, pl. of *tempus* 'temple of the head.']

tem·ple³ ▶ n. a device in a loom for keeping the cloth stretched. [ME: from OFr., perh. the same word as TEMPLE².]

tem·ple block ▶ n. a percussion instrument consisting of a hollow block of wood that is struck with a stick.

tem·plet ▶ n. rare spelling of TEMPLATE.

tem·po /'tempō/ ▶ n. (pl. **-pos** or **-pi** /-pē/) **1** Music the speed at which a passage of music is or should be played. **2** the rate or speed of motion or activity; pace. [17th C.: from Ital., from L. *tempus* 'time.']

tem·po·ral¹ /'temp(ə)rəl/ ▶ adj. **1** relating to worldly as opposed to spiritual affairs; secular. **2** of or relating to time. ■ Gram. relating to or denoting time or tense. — **tem·po·ral·ly** adv. [ME: from OFr. *temporel* or L. *temporalis*, from *tempus, tempor-* 'time.']

tem·po·ral² ▶ adj. Anat. of or situated in the temples of the head. [ME: from late L. *temporalis*, from *tempora* 'the temples' (see TEMPLE²).]

tem·po·ral bone ▶ n. Anat. either of a pair of bones that form part of the side of the skull on each side and enclose the middle and inner ear.

tem·po·ral·is /,tempə'ralis; -'rālis/ ▶ n. Anat. a fan-shaped muscle that runs from the side of the skull to the back of the lower jaw and is involved in closing the mouth and chewing.

tem·po·ral·i·ty /,tempə'ralitē/ ▶ n. (pl. **-ties**) **1** the state of existing within or having some relationship with time. **2** (usu. **temporalities**) a secular possession, esp. the properties and revenues of a religious body or a member of the clergy.

tem·po·ral lobe ▶ n. each of the paired lobes of the brain lying beneath the temples, including areas concerned with the understanding of speech.

tem·po·ral pow·er ▶ n. the power of a bishop or cleric, esp. the pope, in secular matters.

tem·po·rar·y /'tempə,rerē/ ▶ adj. lasting for only a limited period of time; not permanent: *a temporary job.* ▶ n. (pl. **-rar·ies**) a person employed on a temporary basis, typically an office worker who finds employment through an agency. See also TEMP¹. — **tem·po·rar·i·ly** /,tempə're(ə)rəlē/ adv. **tem·po·rar·i·ness** n. [16th C.: from L. *temporarius*, from *tempus, tempor-* 'time.']

tem·po·rize /'tempə,rīz/ ▶ v. **1** [intrans.] avoid making a decision or committing oneself in order to gain time: *opportunity was missed because the mayor temporized.* **2** temporarily adopt a particular course in order to conform to the circumstances: *their unwillingness to temporize had driven the country into conflict.* — **tem·po·ri·za·tion** /,tempəri'zāSHən/ n. **tem·po·riz·er** n. [16th C.: from Fr. *temporiser* 'bide one's time,' from med. L. *temporizare* 'to delay,' from L. *tempus, tempor-* 'time.']

tem·po·ro·man·dib·u·lar joint /,tempə,rō-man'dibyələr/ (abbr.: **TMJ**) ▶ n. Anat. the hinge joint between the temporal bone and the lower jaw.

tem·po ru·ba·to /rōō'bätō/ ▶ n. fuller term for RUBATO.

Tem·pra·ni·llo /,temprə'nē(l)yō/ ▶ n. a variety of wine grape grown in Spain, used to make Rioja wine. ■ a red wine made from this grape. [named after a village in northern Spain.]

tempt /tempt/ ▶ v. [trans.] entice or attempt to entice (someone) to do or acquire something that they find attractive but know to be wrong or not beneficial: *it could tempt you into crime* | *tempted by the money.* ■ (**be tempted to do something**) have an urge or inclination to do something: *I was tempted to look at my watch.* ■ attract; allure: *he was tempted out of retirement.*
– PHRASES **tempt fate** (or **providence**) do something that is risky or dangerous. — **tempt·a·bil·i·ty** /,tem(p)tə'bilitē/ n. **tempt·a·ble** adj. [ME: from OFr. *tempter* 'to test,' from L. *temptare* 'handle, test, try.']

temp·ta·tion /temp'tāSHən/ ▶ n. a desire to do something, esp. something wrong or unwise: *he resisted the temptation to call Celia* | *we gave in to temptation.* ■ a thing or course of action that attracts or tempts someone: *the temptations of life in New York.* ■ (**the Temptation**) the tempting of Jesus by the Devil.

tempt·er /'temptər/ ▶ n. a person or thing that tempts. ■ (**the Tempter**) the Devil.

tempt·ing /'temptiNG/ ▶ adj. appealing to or attracting someone, even if wrong or inadvisable: *a tempting offer* | *it is tempting to act rashly.* — **tempt·ing·ly** adv.

tempt·ress /'temptris/ ▶ n. a woman who tempts someone to do something, typically a sexually attractive woman who sets out to allure or seduce someone.

tem·pu·ra /tem'pŏŏrə/ ▶ n. a Japanese dish of fish, shellfish, or vegetables, fried in batter. [Japanese, prob. from Port. *tempêro* 'seasoning.']

ten /ten/ ▶ cardinal number equivalent to the product of five and two; one more than nine; 10. (Roman numeral: **x, X**) ■ a group or unit of ten people or things: *count in tens.* ■ ten years old. ■ ten o'clock: *about ten at night.* ■ a size of garment or other merchandise denoted by ten. ■ a ten-dollar bill. ■ a playing card with ten pips. ■ (**a ten**) used to indicate that someone has done something well; the highest mark on a scale of one to ten.
– PHRASES **ten to one** very probably: *ten to one you'll never find out who*

did this. [OE *tēn, tien*, rel. to Ger. *zehn*, from an Indo-Eur. root shared by Gk. *deka* and L. *decem*.]

ten. Music ▶ **abbr.** tenuto.

ten·a·ble /ˈtenəbəl/ ▶ **adj.** **1** able to be maintained or defended against attack or objection. **2** (of an office, position, scholarship, etc.) able to be held or used: *the post is tenable for three years.* — **ten·a·bil·i·ty** /ˌtenəˈbilitē/ **n.** [16th C.: from Fr., from *tenir* 'to hold,' from L. *tenere*.]

ten·ace /ˈtenās; ˈtenis/ ▶ **n.** (in bridge, whist, and similar card games) a pair of cards in one hand that rank immediately above and below a card held by an opponent, e.g., the ace and queen in a suit of which an opponent holds the king. [17th C.: from Fr., from Sp. *tenaza*, lit. 'pincers.']

te·na·cious /təˈnāsHəs/ ▶ **adj.** not readily letting go of, giving up, or separated from an object that one holds, a position, or a principle: *a tenacious grip.* ■ not easily dispelled or discouraged; persisting in existence or in a course of action: *a tenacious legend.* — **te·na·cious·ly adv. te·na·cious·ness n. te·nac·i·ty** /-ˈnasitē/ **n.** [17th C.: from L. *tenax, tenac-* (from *tenere* 'to hold') + **-IOUS**.]

te·nac·u·lum /təˈnakyələm/ ▶ **n.** (pl. **-u·la** /-yələ/) a surgical clamp with sharp hooks at the end, used to hold or pick up small pieces of tissue such as the ends of arteries. [17th C.: from L., lit. 'holder,' from *tenere* 'to hold.']

ten·an·cy /ˈtenənsē/ ▶ **n.** (pl. **-cies**) possession of land or property as a tenant: *I took over the tenancy of the farm.*

ten·an·cy in com·mon ▶ **n.** Law a shared tenancy in which each holder has a distinct, separately transferable interest.

ten·ant /ˈtenənt/ ▶ **n.** a person who occupies land or property rented from a landlord. ■ Law a person holding real property by private ownership. ▶ **v.** [trans.] (usu. **be tenanted**) occupy (property) as a tenant. — **ten·ant·a·ble adj.** (formal) **ten·ant·less adj.** [ME: from OFr., lit. 'holding,' pres. part. of *tenir*, from L. *tenere*.]

ten·ant at will ▶ **n.** (pl. **ten·ants at will**) Law a tenant that can be evicted without notice.

ten·ant farm·er ▶ **n.** a person who farms rented land.

ten·ant·ry /ˈtenəntrē/ ▶ **n.** **1** [treated as sing. or pl.] the tenants of an estate. **2** tenancy.

Ten·cel /ˈtensel/ ▶ **n.** trademark a cellulosic fiber obtained from wood pulp using recyclable solvents. ■ a fabric made from this.

tench /tencH/ ▶ **n.** (pl. same) a European freshwater fish (*Tinca tinca*) of the minnow family, popular with anglers and widely introduced elsewhere, including several US states. [ME: from OFr. *tenche*, from late L. *tinca*.]

Ten Com·mand·ments (in the Bible) the divine rules of conduct given by God to Moses on Mount Sinai.

tend[1] /tend/ ▶ **v.** [intrans.] regularly or frequently behave in a particular way or have a certain characteristic: *written language tends to be formal.* ■ [intrans.] (**tend to/toward**) be liable to possess or display (a particular characteristic): *Walter tended toward corpulence.* ■ [no obj., with adverbial] go or move in a particular direction: *the road tends west around small mountains.* ■ Math. approach (a quantity or limit): *the Fourier coefficients tend to zero.* [ME: from OFr. *tendre* 'stretch, tend,' from L. *tendere*.]

tend[2] ▶ **v.** [trans.] care for or look after; give one's attention to: *Viola tended plants on the roof* | [intrans.] *for two or three months he tended to business.* ■ direct or manage; work in: *tending bar at the airport.* — **tend·ance** /ˈtendəns/ **n.** (archaic). [ME: shortening of **ATTEND**.]

ten·den·cy /ˈtendənsē/ ▶ **n.** (pl. **-cies**) an inclination toward a particular characteristic or type of behavior: *her tendency to socialize* | *criminal tendencies.* ■ a group within a larger political party or movement: *the dominant tendency in the party remained right-wing.* [17th C.: from med. L. *tendentia*, from *tendere* 'to stretch' (see **TEND**[1]).]

ten·den·tious /tenˈdensHəs/ ▶ **adj.** expressing or intending to promote a particular cause or point of view, esp. a controversial one: *a tendentious reading of history.* — **ten·den·tious·ly adv. ten·den·tious·ness n.**

ten·der[1] /ˈtendər/ ▶ **adj.** (**-der·er, -der·est**) **1** showing gentleness and concern or sympathy: *he was being so kind and tender.* ■ [predic.] (**tender of**) archaic solicitous of; concerned for: *be tender of a lady's reputation.* **2** (of food) easy to cut or chew; not tough. ■ (of a plant) easily injured by severe weather and therefore needing protection. ■ (of a part of the body) sensitive to pain. ■ young, immature, and vulnerable: *at the tender age of five.* ■ requiring tact or careful handling: *the issue was a particularly tender one.* ■ Naut. (of a ship) leaning or readily inclined to roll in response to the wind.

– PHRASES **tender mercies** used ironically to imply that someone cannot be trusted to look after or treat someone else kindly or well: *they have abandoned their children to the tender mercies of the social services.* — **ten·der·ly adv. ten·der·ness n.** [ME: from OFr. *tendre*, from L. *tener* 'tender, delicate.']

ten·der[2] ▶ **v.** [trans.] offer or present (something) formally: *he tendered his resignation as leader.* ■ offer (money) as payment: *she tendered her fare.* ■ [intrans.] make a formal written offer to carry out work, supply goods, or buy land, shares, or another asset for a stated fixed price: *decorators have been tendering for the work.* ■ [trans.] make such an offer giving (a stated fixed price): *what price should we tender?* ▶ **n.** an offer to carry out work, supply goods, or buy land, shares, or another asset at a stated fixed price.

– PHRASES **put something out to tender** seek offers to carry out work or supply goods at a stated fixed price. — **ten·der·er n.** [16th C.: from OFr. *tendre*, from L. *tendere* 'to stretch, hold forth' (see **TEND**[1]).]

ten·der[3] ▶ **n.** **1** a person who looks after someone else or a machine or place: *the engine tenders.* **2** a boat used to ferry people and supplies to and from a ship. **3** a trailing vehicle closely coupled to a steam locomotive to carry fuel and water. [ME: from **TEND**[2] or shortening of *attender* (see **ATTEND**).]

ten·der·foot /ˈtendərˌfo͝ot/ ▶ **n.** (pl. **-foots** or **-feet**) **1** a newcomer or novice, esp. a person unaccustomed to hardships. **2** a Boy Scout of the lowest rank.

ten·der·heart·ed /ˈtendərˈhärtid/ ▶ **adj.** having a kind, gentle, or sentimental nature. — **ten·der·heart·ed·ness n.**

ten·der·ize /ˈtendəˌrīz/ ▶ **v.** make (meat) more tender by beating or slow cooking.

ten·der·iz·er /ˈtendəˌrīzər/ ▶ **n.** a thing used to make meat tender, in particular: ■ a substance such as papain that is rubbed onto meat or used as a marinade to soften the fibers. ■ a small hammer with teeth on the head, used to beat meat.

ten·der·loin /ˈtendərˌloin/ ▶ **n.** **1** the tenderest part of a loin of beef, pork, etc., taken from under the short ribs in the hindquarters. ■ the undercut of a sirloin. **2** informal a district of a city where vice and corruption are prominent.

ten·di·ni·tis /ˌtendəˈnītis/ (also **ten·do·ni·tis**) ▶ **n.** inflammation of a tendon, most commonly from overuse but also from infection or rheumatic disease.

ten·don /ˈtendən/ ▶ **n.** a flexible but inelastic cord of strong fibrous collagen tissue attaching a muscle to a bone. ■ the hamstring of a quadruped. — **ten·di·nous** /-dənəs/ **adj.** [ME: from Fr. or med. L. *tendo(n-)*, from *teinein* 'to stretch.']

ten·don or·gan ▶ **n.** Anat. a sensory receptor within a tendon that responds to tension and relays impulses to the central nervous system.

ten·dril /ˈtendrəl/ ▶ **n.** a slender threadlike appendage of a climbing plant, often growing in a spiral form, that stretches out and twines around any suitable support. ■ something resembling a plant tendril, esp. a slender curl or ringlet of hair. [16th C.: prob. a dimin. of OFr. *tendron* 'young shoot,' from L. *tener* 'tender.']

ten·du /tänˈdo͞o; tänˈdY/ ▶ **adj.** [postpositive] Ballet (of a position) stretched out or held tautly: *battement tendu.* [Fr.]

ten·du leaf ▶ **n.** the leaves of an Asian ebony tree (*Diospyros melanoxylon*), gathered in India as a cheap tobacco substitute. [Hindi *tendu*.]

Ten·e·brae /ˈtenəˌbrā; -ˌbrē/ ▶ **plural n.** hist. (in the Roman Catholic Church) matins and lauds for the last three days of Holy Week, at which candles were successively extinguished. [L., 'darkness.']

ten·e·brous /ˈtenəbrəs/ ▶ **adj.** literary dark; shadowy or obscure. [ME: via OFr. from L. *tenebrosus*, from *tenebrae* 'darkness.']

ten·e·ment /ˈtenəmənt/ ▶ **n.** **1** a room or a set of rooms forming a separate residence within a house or block of apartments. ■ (also **ten·e·ment house**) a house divided into and rented in such separate residences, esp. one that is run-down and overcrowded. **2** a piece of land held by an owner. ■ Law any kind of permanent property, e.g., lands or rents, held from a superior. [ME: via OFr. from med. L. *tenementum*, from *tenere* 'to hold.']

Ten·er·ife /ˌtenəˈrēf; -ˈrif; -ˈrēfā/ a volcanic island, the largest of the Canary Islands; pop. 771,000; capital, Santa Cruz.

te·nes·mus /təˈnezməs/ ▶ **n.** Med. a continual or recurrent inclination to evacuate the bowels, caused by disorder of the rectum or other illness. [16th C.: via med. L. from Gk. *teinesmos* 'straining,' from *teinein* 'stretch, strain.']

ten·et /ˈtenit/ ▶ **n.** a principle or belief, esp. one of the main principles of a religion or philosophy. [16th C.: from L., lit. 'he holds,' from the verb *tenere*.]

ten·fold /ˈtenˌfōld/ ▶ **adj.** ten times as great or as numerous: *a tenfold increase in the use of insecticides.* ■ having ten parts or elements. ▶ **adv.** by ten times; to ten times the number or amount.

ten-gal·lon hat ▶ **n.** a large, broad-brimmed hat, traditionally worn by cowboys.

ten·ge /ˈteNGgā/ ▶ **n.** (pl. same or **-ges**) **1** the basic monetary unit of Kazakhstan, equal to 100 teins. **2** a monetary unit of Turkmenistan, equal to one hundredth of a manat.

te·ni·a ▶ **n.** var. of **TAENIA**.

Ten·iers /ˈtenyərz; təˈni(ə)rs/, David (1610–90), Flemish painter; known as **David Teniers the Younger**.

Ten Lost Tribes of Is·ra·el see **LOST TRIBES**.

Tenn. ▶ **abbr.** Tennessee.

ten·nant·ite /ˈtenənˌtīt/ ▶ **n.** a gray-black mineral consisting of a sulfide of copper, iron, and arsenic. It is an important ore of copper. [19th C.: Smithson *Tennant* (1761–1815), English chemist.]

ten·né /ˈtenē/ (also **ten·ny**) Heraldry ▶ **n.** orange-brown, as a stain used in blazoning. ▶ **adj.** [usu. postpositive] of this color. [16th C.: obs. Fr., var. of OFr. *tane* (see **TAWNY**).]

Ten·nes·see /ˌtenəˈsē/ **1** a river in the southeastern US, flowing in a great loop for about 875 miles (1,400 km) to join the Ohio River in western Kentucky. **2** a state in the central southeastern US; pop. 5,689,283; capital, Nashville; statehood, June 1, 1796 (16). — **Ten·nes·see·an** /-ˈsēən/ **n. & adj.**

Ten·nes·see Val·ley Au·thor·i·ty (abbr.: **TVA**) an independent federal government agency in the US, created in 1933. It provides one of the world's greatest irrigation and hydroelectric power systems.

Ten·nes·see Walk·ing Horse ▶n. a powerful riding horse of a breed with a characteristic fast walking pace.

ten·nies /'tenēz/ ▶plural n. informal tennis shoes.

ten·nis /'tenis/ ▶n. a game in which two or four players strike a ball with rackets over a net stretched across a court. The usual form (originally called **lawn tennis**) is played with a felt-covered hollow rubber ball on a grass, clay, or artificial surface. See also COURT TENNIS. See illustration at RACKET[1]. [ME *tenetz, tenes* 'court tennis,' appar. from OFr. *tenez* 'take, receive,' imper. of *tenir*.]

ten·nis brace·let ▶n. a bracelet containing many small gems, usually diamonds, linked together in a narrow chain.

ten·nis el·bow ▶n. inflammation of the tendons of the elbow caused by overuse of the muscles of the forearm.

ten·nis shoe ▶n. a light canvas or leather soft-soled shoe suitable for tennis or casual wear.

Ten·no /'tenō/ ▶n. (pl. **-nos**) the Emperor of Japan.

ten·ny /'tenē/ ▶n. & adj. var. of TENNÉ.

Ten·ny·son /'tenəsən/, Alfred, 1st Baron Tennyson of Aldworth and Freshwater (1809–92), English poet. His works include "The Charge of the Light Brigade" (1854) and *Idylls of the King* (1859). He was England's poet laureate from 1850.

Te·noch·ti·tlán /tə,nôCHtēt'län/ the ancient capital of the Aztec empire, founded *c.*1320. In 1521, the Spanish conquistador Cortés destroyed it and established Mexico City on its site.

ten·on /'tenən/ ▶n. a projecting piece of wood made for insertion into a mortise in another piece. See illustration at DOVETAIL. ▶v. [trans.] (usu. **be tenoned**) join by means of a tenon. ■ cut as a tenon. — **ten·on·er** n. [ME: from Fr., from *tenir* 'to hold,' from L. *tenere*.]

ten·or[1] /'tenər/ ▶n. a singing voice between baritone and alto or countertenor, the highest of the ordinary adult male range. ■ a singer with such a voice. ■ a part written for such a voice. ■ [usu. as adj.] an instrument, esp. a saxophone, trombone, tuba, or viol, of the lowest pitch but one in its family: *a tenor sax.* [ME: via OFr. from med. L., based on *tenere* 'to hold.']

ten·or[2] ▶n. **1** [in sing.] the general meaning, sense, or content of something: *the tenor of the debate.* ■ the subject to which a metaphor refers, e.g., "a large, difficult challenge" conveyed by *bear* in *this one is going to be a bear.* Often contrasted with VEHICLE (sense 2). **2** [in sing.] a settled or prevailing character or direction, esp. the course of a person's life or habits: *the even tenor of life on the island.* **3** Law the actual wording of a document. **4** Finance the time that must elapse before a bill of exchange or promissory note becomes due for payment. [ME: from OFr. *tenour*, from L. *tenor* 'course,' from *tenere* 'to hold.']

ten·or clef ▶n. Music a clef placing middle C on the second-highest line of the stave, used chiefly for cello and bassoon music.

te·no·ri·no /,tenə'rēnō/ ▶n. (pl. **-ri·ni** /-'rēnē/) a high tenor. [Ital., dimin. of *tenore* 'tenor.']

ten·o·syn·o·vi·tis /,tenō,sinə'vītis/ ▶n. Med. inflammation and swelling of a tendon, typically in the wrist, often caused by repetitive movements. [19th C.: from Gk. *tenōn* 'tendon' + SYNOVITIS.]

te·not·o·my /tə'nätəmē/ ▶n. the surgical cutting of a tendon, esp. as a remedy for club foot. [19th C.: coined in Fr. from Gk. *tenōn* 'tendon' + *-tomia* (see -TOMY).]

ten·pin /'ten,pin/ ▶n. a wooden pin used in tenpin bowling. ■ **(tenpins)** [treated as sing.] tenpin bowling.

ten·pin bowl·ing ▶n. a game in which ten wooden pins are set up at the end of a track (typically one of several in a large, automated alley) and bowled down with hard rubber or plastic balls.

ten·pound·er /'ten'poundər/ ▶n. a large, silvery-blue, herringlike fish (*Elops saurus*, family Elopidae) of tropical seas that is popular as a game fish. Also called LADYFISH.

ten·rec /'ten,rek/ ▶n. a small, insectivorous mammal (family Tenrecidae) native to Madagascar, different kinds of which resemble hedgehogs, shrews, or small otters. The **common** (or **tailless**) **tenrec** (*Tenrec ecaudatus*) is also found in the Comoro islands. [18th C.: from Fr. *tanrec*, from Malagasy *tàndraka*.]

TENS /tenz/ ▶abbr. transcutaneous electrical nerve stimulation, a technique intended to provide pain relief by applying electrodes to the skin to block impulses in underlying nerves.

tense[1] /tens/ ▶adj. (esp. of a muscle or someone's body) stretched tight or rigid. ■ (of a person) unable to relax because of nervousness, anxiety, or stimulation: *tense with excitement.* ■ (of a situation, event, etc.) causing or showing anxiety and nervousness: *relations had been tense in recent years.* ■ Phonet. (of a speech sound, esp. a vowel) pronounced with the vocal muscles stretched tight. The opposite of LAX. ▶v. [intrans.] become tense, typically through anxiety or nervousness: *her body tensed up.* ■ [trans.] make (a muscle or one's body) tight or rigid. — **tense·ly** adv. **tense·ness** n. **ten·si·ty** /'tensitē/ n. (dated). [17th C.: from L. *tensus* 'stretched,' from the verb *tendere*.]

tense[2] ▶n. Gram. a set of forms taken by a verb to indicate the time (and sometimes also the continuance or completeness) of the action in relation to the time of the utterance: *the past tense.* — **tense·less** adj. [ME: from OFr. *tens*, from L. *tempus* 'time.']

ten·seg·ri·ty /ten'segritē/ ▶n. Archit. the characteristic property of a stable three-dimensional structure consisting of members under tension that are contiguous and members under compression that are not. [1950s: from *tensional integrity*.]

ten·sile /'tensəl; -sīl/ ▶adj. **1** of or relating to tension. **2** capable of being drawn out or stretched. — **ten·sil·i·ty** /ten'silitē/ n. [17th C. (sense 2): from med. L. *tensilis*, from L. *tendere* 'to stretch.']

ten·sile strength ▶n. the resistance of a material to breaking under tension. Compare with COMPRESSIVE STRENGTH.

ten·sion /'tensHən/ ▶n. **1** the state of being stretched tight: *the parachute keeps the cable under tension as it drops.* ■ the state of having the muscles stretched tight, esp. as causing strain or discomfort: *the elimination of neck tension can relieve headaches.* ■ a strained state or condition resulting from forces acting in opposition to each other. ■ the degree of tightness of stitches in knitting and machine sewing. ■ electromotive force. **2** mental or emotional strain. ■ a strained political or social state or relationship: *racial tensions.* ■ a relationship between ideas or qualities with conflicting demands or implications: *the basic tension between freedom and control.* ▶v. [trans.] apply a force to (something) that tends to stretch it. — **ten·sion·al** /-sHənl/ adj. **ten·sion·al·ly** /-sHənl-ē/ adv. **ten·sion·er** n. **ten·sion·less** adj. [16th C. (as a medical term denoting a condition or feeling of being physically stretched or strained): from Fr., or from L. *tensio(n-)*, from *tendere* 'stretch.']

ten·sive /'tensiv/ ▶adj. causing of expressing tension.

Tens·kwa·ta·wa /ten'skwätə,wä/ see TECUMSEH.

ten·sor /'tensər; 'tensôr/ ▶n. **1** Math. a mathematical object analogous to but more general than a vector, represented by an array of components that are functions of the coordinates of a space. **2** Anat. a muscle that tightens or stretches a part of the body. — **ten·so·ri·al** /ten'sôrēəl/ adj. [18th C.: mod. L., from L. *tendere* 'to stretch.']

tent /tent/ ▶n. a portable shelter made of cloth, supported by one or more poles and stretched tight by cords or loops attached to pegs driven into the ground. ▶v. **1** [trans.] cover with or as if with a tent. ■ arrange in a shape that looks like a tent: *Tim tented his fingers.* ■ [as adj.] **(tented)** composed of or provided with tents: *they were living in large tented camps.* **2** [intrans.] (esp. of traveling circus people) live in a tent. [ME: from OFr. *tente*, based on L. *tent-* 'stretched,' from the verb *tendere*.]

ten·ta·cle /'tentəkəl/ ▶n. a slender flexible limb or appendage in an animal, esp. around the mouth of an invertebrate, used for grasping, moving about, or bearing sense organs. ■ (in a plant) a tendril or a sensitive glandular hair. ■ something resembling a tentacle in shape or flexibility: *trailing tentacles of vapor.* ■ (usu. **tentacles**) fig. an insidious spread of influence and control: *the Party's tentacles reached into everyone's lives.* — **ten·ta·cled** adj. **ten·tac·u·lar** /ten'takyələr/ adj. **ten·tac·u·late** /ten'takyəlit/ adj. [18th C.: Anglicized from mod. L. *tentaculum*, from L. *tentare, temptare* 'to feel, try.']

ten·ta·tive /'tentətiv/ ▶adj. not certain or fixed; provisional: *a tentative conclusion.* ■ done without confidence; hesitant: *tentative steps.* — **ten·ta·tive·ly** adv. **ten·ta·tive·ness** n. [16th C.: from med. L. *tentativus*, from *tentare*, var. of *temptare* 'handle, try.']

tent cat·er·pil·lar ▶n. a chiefly American moth caterpillar (family Lasiocampidae) that lives in groups inside communal silken webs in a tree, which it often defoliates. Its several species include the common *Malacosoma americana.*

tent dress ▶n. a full, loose-fitting dress that is narrow at the shoulders and very wide at the hem, having no waistline or darts.

ten·ter /'tentər/ ▶n. a framework on which fabric can be held taut for drying or other treatment during manufacture. [ME: from med. L. *tentorium*, from *tent-* 'stretched,' from the verb *tendere*.]

ten·ter·hook /'tentər,ho͝ok/ ▶n. hist. a hook used to fasten cloth on a drying frame or tenter.

– PHRASES **on tenterhooks** in a state of suspense or agitation because of uncertainty about a future event.

tenth /tenTH/ ▶n. constituting number ten in a sequence; 10th. ■ **(a tenth/one tenth)** each of ten equal parts into which something is or may be divided. ■ the tenth grade of a school. ■ Music an interval or chord spanning an octave and a third in the diatonic scale, or a note separated from another by this interval. — **tenth·ly** adv.

tenth-rate ▶adj. informal of extremely poor quality.

ten·to·ri·um /ten'tôrēəm/ ▶n. (pl. **-to·ria** /-'tôrēə/) **1** Anat. a fold of the dura mater forming a partition between the cerebrum and cerebellum. **2** Entomol. an internal skeletal framework in the head of an insect. [19th C.: from L., 'tent.']

tent peg ▶n. see PEG (sense 1).

tent stitch ▶n. a series of parallel diagonal stitches.

te·nu·i·ty /te'n(y)o͞oitē; tə-/ ▶n. lack of solidity or substance; thinness. [ME: from L. *tenuitas*, from *tenuis* 'thin.']

ten·u·ous /'tenyo͞oəs/ ▶adj. very weak or slight: *the tenuous link between interest rates and investment.* ■ very slender or fine; insubstantial: *a tenuous cloud.* — **ten·u·ous·ly** adv. **ten·u·ous·ness** n. [16th C.: formed irregularly from L. *tenuis* 'thin' + -OUS.]

ten·ure /'tenyər; -yo͝or/ ▶n. **1** the conditions under which land or buildings are held or occupied. **2** the holding of an office: *his tenure of the premiership.* ■ a period for which an office is held. **3** guaranteed permanent employment, esp. as a teacher or professor, after a probationary period. ▶v. [trans.] give (someone) a permanent post, esp. as a teacher or professor. ■ [as adj.] **(tenured)** having or denoting such a post. [ME: from OFr., from *tenir* 'to hold,' from L. *tenere*.]

ten·ure track ▶n. [usu. as adj.] an employment structure whereby the holder of a post, typically an academic one, is guaranteed consideration for eventual tenure: *a tenure-track position.*

te·nu·to /te'nōōtō/ Music ▶ **adv. & adj.** (of a note) held for its full time value or slightly more. ▶ **n.** (pl. **-nu·tos** or **-nu·ti** /-'nōōtē/) a note or chord performed in this way. [Ital., lit. 'held,' past part. of *tenere.*]

Ten·zing Nor·gay /'tenziNG 'nôrgā/ (1914–86), Sherpa mountaineer. In 1953, he and Sir Edmund Hillary were the first to reach the summit of Mount Everest.

te·o·cal·li /,tē-ō'kälē; ,tā-/ ▶ **n.** (pl. **-lis**) a temple of the Aztecs or other Mexican peoples, typically standing on a truncated pyramid. [Amer. Sp., from Nahuatl *teo:kalli*, from *teo:tl* 'god' + *kalli* 'house.']

te·o·sin·te /,tē-ō'sintē; ,tā-/ ▶ **n.** a Mexican grass (*Zea mays* subsp. *mexicana*) that is grown as fodder and is considered to be one of the parent plants of modern corn. [19th C.: from Fr. *téosinté*, from Nahuatl *teocintli*, appar. from *teo:tl* 'god' + *cintli* 'dried ear of maize.']

Te·o·ti·hua·c·án /,tēə,tēwä'kän/ the largest city in pre-Columbian America, 25 miles (40 km) northeast of Mexico City.

te·pa·che /tə'päCHē/ ▶ **n.** a Mexican drink, typically made with pineapple, water, and brown sugar and partially fermented.

te·pal /'tēpəl; 'tepəl/ ▶ **n.** Bot. a segment of the outer whorl in a flower that has no differentiation between petals and sepals. [19th C.: from Fr. *tépale*, blend of *pétale* 'petal' and *sépal* 'sepal.']

tep·a·ry bean /'tepərē/ ▶ **n.** a bean plant (*Phaseolus acutifolius*) native to the southwestern US, cultivated in Mexico and Arizona for its drought-resistant qualities. [20th C.: from Sp. *tepari*, from Pima.]

te·pee /'tēpē/ (also **tee·pee** or **ti·pi**) ▶ **n.** a portable conical tent made of skins, cloth, or canvas on a frame of poles, used by American Indians of the Plains and Great Lakes regions. [18th C.: from Sioux *tīpī* 'dwelling.']

tepee

teph·ra /'tefrə/ ▶ **n.** Geol. rock fragments and particles ejected by a volcanic eruption. [1940s: from Gk., 'ash, ashes.']

tep·id /'tepid/ ▶ **adj.** (esp. of a liquid) only slightly warm; lukewarm. ■ fig. showing little enthusiasm: *tepid applause.* — **te·pid·i·ty** /tə'piditē/ **n.** **tep·id·ly adv. tep·id·ness n.** [ME: from L. *tepidus*, from *tepere* 'be warm.']

TEPP ▶ **abbr.** Chem. tetraethyl pyrophosphate.

tep·pan·ya·ki /'tepän 'yäkē/ ▶ **n.** a Japanese dish of meat, fish, or both, fried with vegetables on a hot steel plate forming the center of the dining table. [Japanese, from *teppan* 'steel plate' + *yaki* 'to fry.']

te·qui·la /tə'kēlə/ ▶ **n.** a Mexican liquor made from an agave. [Mex. Sp., after the town of *Tequila* in Mexico.]

te·qui·la sun·rise ▶ **n.** a cocktail containing tequila, orange juice, and grenadine.

ter. ▶ **abbr.** ■ (in prescriptions) rub. [from L. *tere.*] ■ terrace. ■ territorial. ■ territory.

ter- ▶ **comb. form** three; having three: *tercentenary.* [from L. *ter* 'thrice.']

tera- ▶ **comb. form** used in units of measurement: **1** denoting a factor of 1012: *terawatt.* **2** Comput. denoting a factor of 240. [from Gk. *teras* 'monster.']

ter·a·byte /'terə,bīt/ (abbr.: **Tb** or **TB**) ▶ **n.** Comput. a unit of information equal to one million million (1012) or strictly, 240 bytes.

ter·a·flop /'terə,fläp/ ▶ **n.** Comput. a unit of computing speed equal to one million million floating-point operations per second.

te·rai /tə'rī/ (also **te·rai hat**) ▶ **n.** a wide-brimmed felt hat, typically with a double crown, worn chiefly by travelers in subtropical regions. [19th C.: from *Terai*, a belt of jungle, from Hindi *tarāī* 'marshy lowlands.']

ter·a·phim /'terə,fim/ ▶ **plural n.** [also treated as sing.] small images or cult objects used as domestic deities or oracles by ancient Semitic peoples. [ME: via late L. from Gk. *theraphin*, from Heb. *tĕrāpīm*.]

terato- ▶ **comb. form** relating to monsters or abnormal forms: *teratology.* [from Gk. *teras, terat-* 'monster.']

te·rat·o·car·ci·no·ma /,terətō,kärsə'nōmə/ ▶ **n.** (pl. **-ma·ta** /-mətə/ or **-mas**) Med. a form of malignant teratoma occurring esp. in the testis.

te·rat·o·gen /te'ratəjən; -,jen; 'terətəjən/ ▶ **n.** an agent or factor that causes malformation of an embryo. — **te·rat·o·gen·ic** /tə,ratə'jenik; ,terətə-/ **adj.** **te·rat·o·ge·nic·i·ty** /tə,ratəjə'nisitē; ,terə,tō-/ **n.**

te·rat·o·gen·e·sis /,terətō'jenəsis; tə,ratō-/ ▶ **n.** the process by which congenital malformations are produced in an embryo or fetus.

ter·a·tol·o·gy /,terə'täləjē/ ▶ **n.** **1** Med. & Biol. the scientific study of congenital abnormalities and abnormal formations. **2** mythology relating to fantastic creatures and monsters. — **ter·a·to·log·i·cal** /,terətə'läjikəl/ **adj.** **ter·a·tol·o·gist** /-jist/ **n.**

ter·a·to·ma /,terə'tōmə/ ▶ **n.** (pl. **-mas** or **-ma·ta** /-mətə/) Med. a tumor composed of tissues not normally present at the site (the site being typically in the gonads).

ter·a·watt /'terə,wät/ ▶ **n.** a unit of power equal to 1012 watts or a million megawatts.

ter·bi·um /'tərbēəm/ ▶ **n.** the chemical element of atomic number 65, a silvery-white metal of the lanthanide series. The main use of terbium is in making semiconductors. (Symbol: **Tb**) [19th C.: mod. L., from *Ytterby*, a village in Sweden.]

ter·bu·ta·line /tər'byōōtl,ēn/ ▶ **n.** Med. a synthetic compound, $C_{12}H_{19}NO_3$, with bronchodilator properties, used esp. in the treatment of asthma. [1960s: from TER- + BUTYL.]

terce /tərs/ ▶ **n.** a service forming part of the Divine Office of the Western Christian Church, traditionally said (or chanted) at the third hour of the day (i.e., 9 a.m.). [ME: from OFr., from L. *tertia*, fem. of *tertius* 'third.']

ter·cel /'tərsəl/ ▶ **n.** var. of TIERCEL.

ter·cen·ten·ar·y /,tərsen'tenərē; tər'sentn,erē/ ▶ **adj. & n.** (pl. **-ar·ies**) another term for TRICENTENNIAL.

ter·cen·ten·ni·al /,tərsen'tenēəl/ ▶ **adj. & n.** another term for TRICENTENNIAL.

ter·cet /'tərsit/ ▶ **n.** Pros. a set or group of three lines of verse rhyming together or connected by rhyme with an adjacent tercet. [16th C.: from Fr., from Ital. *terzetto*, dimin. of *terzo* 'third,' from L. *tertius.*]

ter·e·binth /'terə,binTH/ ▶ **n.** a small southern European tree (*Pistacia terebinthus*) of the cashew family that was formerly a source of turpentine. [ME: from OFr. *therebinte*, or via L. from Gk. *terebinthos.*]

te·re·do /tə'rēdō/ ▶ **n.** Zool. (pl. **-dos**) a wormlike bivalve mollusk (genus *Teredo*, family Teredinidae) with reduced shells that it uses to drill into wood. It can cause substantial damage to wooden structures and (formerly) ships. Also called SHIPWORM. [ME: via L. from Gk. *terēdōn*; rel. to *teirein* 'rub hard, wear away.']

Ter·ence /'terəns/ (*c.*190–159 BC), Roman playwright; Latin name *Publius Terentius Afer.* His six surviving comedies are based on Greek New Comedy.

ter·eph·thal·ic ac·id /'teref,THalik/ ▶ **n.** Chem. a crystalline organic acid, $C_6H_4(COOH)_2$, used in making polyester resins and other polymers. — **ter·eph·thal·ate** /,terəf'THalāt/ **n.** [19th C.: blend of *terebic* 'of or from turpentine' (from TEREBINTH) and PHTHALIC ACID.]

te·res /'ti(ə)rēz; 'terēz/ ▶ **n.** Anat. either of two muscles passing below the shoulder joint from the scapula to the upper part of the humerus, one (**teres major**) drawing the arm toward the body and rotating it inward, the other (**teres minor**) rotating it outward. [18th C.: mod. L., from L., 'rounded.']

Te·re·sa, Moth·er /tə'rēsə; -'rāsə/ (also **The·re·sa**) (1910–97), Roman Catholic nun and missionary; born in what is now the Republic of Macedonia; born *Agnes Gonxha Bojaxhiu.* She founded the Order of Missionaries of Charity, noted for its work among the poor in Calcutta. Nobel Peace Prize (1979).

Te·resh·ko·va /,terəsH'kôvə/, Valentina Vladimirovna (1937–), Russian cosmonaut. In June 1963, she was the first woman to go into space.

te·rete /tə'rēt; 'terēt/ ▶ **adj.** esp. Bot. cylindrical or slightly tapering, and without substantial furrows or ridges. [17th C.: from L. *teres, teret-* 'rounded off.']

ter·gal /'tərgəl/ ▶ **adj.** Zool. of or relating to a tergum of an arthropod. [19th C.: from L. *tergum* 'back' + -AL.]

ter·gite /'tərjīt/ ▶ **n.** Entomol. (in an insect) a sclerotized plate forming the tergum of a segment. Compare with STERNITE. [19th C.: from TERGUM + -ITE[1].]

ter·gi·ver·sate /tər'jivər,sāt; 'tərjivər-/ ▶ **v.** [intrans.] **1** make conflicting or evasive statements; equivocate: *the more she tergiversated, the greater grew the media interest.* **2** change one's loyalties; be apostate. — **ter·gi·ver·sa·tion** /,tərjivər'sāsHən/ **n.** **ter·gi·ver·sa·tor** /-,sātər/ **n.** [17th C.: from L. *tergiversat-* 'with one's back turned,' from the verb *tergiversari*, from *tergum* 'back' + *vertere* 'to turn.']

ter·gum /'tərgəm/ ▶ **n.** (pl. **-ga** /-gə/) Zool. a thickened dorsal plate on each segment of the body of an arthropod. [19th C.: from L., 'back.']

Ter·hune /tər'hyōōn/, Albert Payson (1872–1942), US writer. His fiction for young readers about dogs includes *Lad: A Dog* (1919).

-teria ▶ **suffix** denoting self-service establishments: *washeteria.* [on the pattern of *(cafe)teria.*]

ter·i·ya·ki /,terē'yäkē/ ▶ **n.** a Japanese dish consisting of fish or meat marinated in soy sauce and grilled. ■ (also **ter·i·ya·ki sauce**) a mixture of soy sauce, sake, ginger, and other flavorings, used in Japanese cooking as a marinade or glaze for such dishes.

Ter·kel /'tərkəl/, Studs (1912–), US writer; full name *Louis Terkel.* His journalistic works include *Working* (1974) and *The Good War* (1984).

term /tərm/ ▶ **n.** **1** a word or phrase used to describe a thing or to express a concept, esp. in a particular kind of language or branch of study: *a term of abuse.* ■ (**terms**) language used on a particular occasion; a way of expressing oneself: *a protest in the strongest possible terms.* ■ Logic a word or words that may be the subject or predicate of a proposition. **2** a fixed or limited period for which something, e.g., office, imprisonment, or investment, lasts or is intended to last: *the president is elected for a four-year term.* ■ (also **full term**) the completion of a normal length of pregnancy: *the pregnancy went to full term | low birthweight at term.* ■ (also **term for years** or Brit. **term of years**) Law a tenancy of a fixed period. **3** each of the periods in the year, alternating with holidays or vacations, during which instruction is given in a school, college, or university, or during which a law court holds sessions: *the summer term.* **4** (**terms**) conditions under which an action may be undertaken or agreement reached; stipulated or agreed-upon requirements: *the contract's terms | he would be dealt with on his own terms.* ■ conditions with regard to payment for something; stated charges: *favorable terms.* ■ agreed conditions under which a war or other dispute is brought to an end: *a deal that could force the Serbs to come to terms.* **5** Math. each of the quantities in a ratio, series, or mathematical expression. **6** Archit. another term for TERMINUS. ▶ **v.** [trans.] give a descriptive name to; call by a specified name: *he has been termed the father of theology.*

– PHRASES **come to terms with** come to accept (a new and painful or difficult event or situation); reconcile oneself to. **in terms of** (or **in —— terms**) with regard to the particular aspect or subject specified: *it is difficult to justify in terms of cost | sales are down by nearly 7 percent in real terms.* **the long/short term** used to refer to a time that is a specified way into the future. **on —— terms** in a specified relation or on a specified footing: *on friendly terms.* [ME: from OFr. *terme*, from L. *terminus* 'end, boundary, limit.']

term. ▶ abbr. ■ terminal. ■ termination.

ter·ma·gant /'tərməgənt/ ▶ n. **1** a harsh-tempered or overbearing woman. **2** (**Termagant**) hist. an imaginary deity of violent and turbulent character, often appearing in morality plays. [ME (sense 2): via OFr. from Ital. *Trivigante*, taken to be from L. *tri-* 'three' + *vagant-* 'wandering.']

ter·mi·na·ble /'tərmənəbəl/ ▶ adj. **1** able to be terminated. **2** coming to an end after a certain time.

ter·mi·nal /'tərmənl/ ▶ adj. **1** [attrib.] of, forming, or situated at the end or extremity of something: *a terminal date | the terminal tip of the probe.* ■ of or forming a transportation terminal: *terminal platforms.* ■ Zool. situated at, forming, or denoting the end of a part or series of parts furthest from the center of the body. ■ Bot. (of a flower, inflorescence, etc.) borne at the end of a stem or branch. Often contrasted with AXILLARY. **2** (of a disease) predicted to lead to death, esp. slowly; incurable: *terminal cancer.* ■ [attrib.] suffering from or relating to such a disease: *a hospice for terminal cases.* ■ [attrib.] (of a condition) forming the last stage of such a disease. ■ informal extreme and usually beyond cure or alteration (used to emphasize the extent of something regarded as bad or unfortunate): *making a terminal ass of yourself.* ▶ n. **1** an end or extremity of something, in particular: ■ the end of a railroad or other transport route, or a station at such a point. ■ a departure and arrival building for air passengers at an airport. ■ an installation where oil or gas is stored at the end of a pipeline or at a port. **2** a point of connection for closing an electric circuit. **3** a device at which a user enters data or commands for a computer system and that displays the received output. **4** (also **terminal figure**) another term for TERMINUS (sense 3). — **ter·mi·nal·ly** adv. (in sense 2 of the **adjective**) [as submodifier] *a terminally ill woman.* [19th C.: from L. *terminalis*, from *terminus* 'end, boundary.']

ter·mi·nal mo·raine ▶ n. Geol. a moraine deposited at the point of furthest advance of a glacier or ice sheet.

ter·mi·nal ve·loc·i·ty ▶ n. Physics the constant speed that a freely falling object eventually reaches when the resistance of the medium through which it is falling prevents further acceleration.

ter·mi·nate /'tərmə,nāt/ ▶ v. [trans.] bring to an end: *he was advised to terminate the contract.* ■ [intrans.] (**terminate in**) (of a thing) have its end at (a specified place) or of (a specified form): *the chain terminated in a ball covered with spikes.* ■ [intrans.] (of a train, bus, or boat service) end its journey. ■ end (a pregnancy) before term by artificial means. ■ end the employment of (someone); dismiss. ■ assassinate (someone, esp. an intelligence agent). ■ archaic form the physical end or extremity of (an area).

ter·mi·na·tion /,tərmə'nāsHən/ ▶ n. **1** the action of bringing something or coming to an end: *the termination of a contract.* ■ an act of dismissing someone from employment. ■ an induced abortion. ■ an assassination, esp. of an intelligence agent. **2** an ending or final point of something, in particular: ■ the final letter or letters or syllable of a word, esp. when constituting an element in inflection or derivation. — **ter·mi·na·tion·al** /-sHənl/ adj.

ter·mi·na·tor /'tərmə,nātər/ ▶ n. a person or thing that terminates something. ■ Astron. the dividing line between the light and dark part of a planetary body. ■ Biochem. a sequence of polynucleotides that causes transcription to end and the newly synthesized nucleic acid to be released from the template molecule.

ter·mi·ner /'tərmənər/ ▶ n. see OYER AND TERMINER.

ter·mi·ni /'tərmə,nī/ plural form of TERMINUS.

ter·mi·nol·o·gy /,tərmə'näləjē/ ▶ n. (pl. **-gies**) the body of terms used with a particular technical application in a subject of study, theory, profession, etc. — **ter·mi·no·log·i·cal** /-nl'äjikəl/ adj. **ter·mi·no·log·i·cal·ly** /-nl'äjik(ə)lē/ adv. **ter·mi·nol·o·gist** n. [19th C.: from Ger. *Terminologie*, from med. L. *terminus* 'term.']

ter·mi·nus /'tərmənəs/ ▶ n. (pl. **-ni** /-,nī/ or **-nus·es**) **1** a final point in space or time; an end or extremity: *the exhibition's terminus is 1962.* ■ Biochem. the end of a polypeptide or polynucleotide chain or similar long molecule. **2** the end of a railroad or other transportation route, or a station at such a point; a terminal. ■ an oil or gas terminal. **3** Archit. a figure of a human bust or an animal ending in a square pillar from which it appears to spring, originally used as a boundary marker in ancient Rome. [16th C.: from L., 'end, limit, boundary.']

ter·mi·nus ad quem /'tərmənəs äd 'kwem/ ▶ n. the point at which something ends or finishes. ■ an aim or goal. [L., 'end to which.']

ter·mi·nus an·te quem /'tərmənəs 'antē 'kwem/ ▶ n. the latest possible date for something. [L., 'end before which.']

ter·mi·nus a quo /'tərmənəs ä 'kwō/ ▶ n. the earliest possible date for something. ■ a starting point or initial impulse. [L., 'end from which.']

ter·mi·nus post quem /'tərmənəs 'pōst 'kwem/ ▶ n. the earliest possible date for something. [L., 'end after which.']

ter·mi·tar·i·um /,tərmi'te(ə)rēəm/ ▶ n. (pl. **-tar·i·a** /-'te(ə)rēə/) a colony of termites, typically within a mound of cemented earth. [19th C.: mod. L., from L. *termes, termit-* 'termite.']

ter·mi·ta·ry /'tərmi,terē/ ▶ n. (pl. **-ries**) another term for TERMITARIUM.

termite

ter·mite /'tərmīt/ ▶ n. a small, pale soft-bodied insect (order Isoptera) that lives in large colonies with several different castes, typically within a mound of cemented earth. Many kinds feed on wood and can be highly destructive to trees and timber. Also called WHITE ANT. [18th C.: from L. *termes, termit-* 'woodworm,' alt. of L. *tarmes.*]

term pa·per ▶ n. a student's lengthy essay on a subject drawn from the work done during a school or college term.

terms of trade ▶ plural n. Econ. the ratio of an index of a country's export prices to an index of its import prices.

tern /tərn/ ▶ n. a seabird (*Sterna* and other genera, family Sternidae, or Laridae) related to the gulls, typically smaller and more slender, with long pointed wings and a forked tail. [17th C.: of Scand. origin; rel. to Dan. *terne.*]

ter·na·ry /'tərnərē/ ▶ adj. composed of three parts. ■ Math. using three as a base. [ME: from L. *ternarius*, from *terni* 'three at once.']

ter·na·ry form ▶ n. Music the form of a movement in which the first subject is repeated after an interposed second subject in a related key.

terne /tərn/ ▶ n. (also **terne metal**) a lead alloy containing about 20 percent tin and often some antimony. ■ (also **terne·plate**) thin sheet iron or steel coated with this. [19th C.: prob. from Fr. *terne* 'dull, tarnished.']

ter·pene /'tərpēn/ ▶ n. Chem. any of a large group of volatile unsaturated hydrocarbons found in the essential oils of plants, esp. conifers and citrus trees, and based on a cyclic molecule with the formula $C_{10}H_{16}$. [19th C.: from Ger. *Terpentin* 'turpentine' + -ENE.]

ter·pe·noid /'tərpə,noid/ Chem. ▶ n. any of a large class of organic compounds including terpenes, diterpenes, and sesquiterpenes. They have unsaturated molecules composed of linked isoprene units, generally having the formula $(C_5H_8)n$. ▶ adj. denoting such a compound.

ter·pol·y·mer /tər'päləmər/ ▶ n. Chem. a polymer synthesized from three different monomers.

Terp·sich·o·re /,tərp'sikərē/ Greek & Rom. Mythol. the Muse of lyric poetry and dance. [Gk., lit. 'delighting in dancing.']

terp·si·cho·re·an /,tərpsikə'rēən; -'kôrēən/ formal or humorous ▶ adj. of or relating to dancing: *"the twist" was a revolutionary terpsichorean innovation.* ▶ n. a dancer. [19th C.: from *Terpsichore.*]

terr. ▶ abbr. ■ terrace. ■ territorial. ■ territory.

ter·ra /'terə/ ▶ n. **1** (also **Ter·ra**) (in science fiction) the planet earth. **2** [usu. with adj.] land or territory. [L., 'earth.']

ter·ra al·ba /'terə 'albə/ ▶ n. pulverized gypsum, esp. as an ingredient of medicines. [L., 'white earth.']

ter·race /'teris/ ▶ n. **1** a level paved area or platform next to a building; a patio or veranda. ■ each of a series of flat areas made on a slope, used for cultivation. ■ Geol. a natural horizontal shelflike formation, such as a raised beach. **2** esp. Brit. a block of row houses. ■ a row house. ▶ v. [trans.] make or form (sloping land) into a number of level flat areas resembling a series of steps. [16th C.: from OFr., lit. 'rubble, platform,' based on L. *terra* 'earth.']

ter·raced /'terist/ ▶ adj. **1** (of land) having been formed into a number of level areas resembling a series of steps. **2** esp. Brit. (of a house) in the style of a row house.

ter·ra cot·ta /'terə 'kätə/ (also **ter·ra·cot·ta**) ▶ n. unglazed, typically brownish-red earthenware, used as an ornamental building material and in modeling. ■ a statuette or other object made of such earthenware. ■ a strong brownish-red or brownish-orange color. [18th C.: from Ital. *terra cotta* 'baked earth,' from L. *terra cocta.*]

ter·ra fir·ma /'terə 'fərmə/ ▶ n. dry land; the ground as distinct from the sea or air. [17th C.: from L., 'firm land.']

ter·ra·form /'terə,fôrm/ ▶ v. [trans.] (esp. in science fiction) transform (a planet) so as to resemble the earth, esp. so that it can support human life. — **ter·ra·form·er** n. [1940s: from L. *terra* 'earth' + the verb FORM.]

ter·rain /tə'rān/ ▶ n. **1** a stretch of land, esp. with regard to its physical features: *rough terrain.* **2** Geol. var. of TERRANE. [18th C.: from Fr., from a pop. L. var. of L. *terrenum*, neut. of *terrenus* (see TERRENE).]

ter·ra in·cog·ni·ta /'terə ,inkäg'nētə; in'kägnitə/ ▶ n. unknown or unexplored territory. [L., 'unknown land.']

Ter·ran /'terən/ ▶ n. (in science fiction) an inhabitant of the planet Earth. ▶ adj. (in science fiction) of or relating to the planet Earth or its inhabitants.

ter·rane /tə'rān; 'terān/ (also **ter·rain**) ▶ n. Geol. a fault-bounded area or region with a distinctive stratigraphy, structure, and geological history. [19th C.: from pop. L. *terranum.*]

ter·ra·pin /'terə,pin/ ▶ n. **1** (also **diamondback terrapin**) a small edible turtle (*Malaclemys terrapin*, family Emydidae) with lozenge-shaped markings on its shell, found in coastal marshes of the eastern US. **2** a freshwater turtle (Emydidae and other families), esp. one of the smaller kinds of the Old World. [17th C.: of Algonquian origin.]

diamondback terrapin

ter·ra·que·ous /ter'ākwēəs; -'ak-/ ▶ **adj.** consisting of, or formed of, land and water. [17th C.: from L. *terra* 'land' + AQUEOUS.]

ter·rar·i·um /tə're(ə)rēəm/ ▶ **n.** (pl. **-rar·i·ums** or **-rar·i·a** /-'re(ə)rēə/) a vivarium for smaller land animals, esp. reptiles, amphibians, or terrestrial invertebrates, typically in the form of a glass-fronted case. ■ a sealed transparent globe or similar container in which plants are grown. [19th C.: mod. L., from L. *terra* 'earth,' on the pattern of *aquarium*.]

ter·rasse /te'räs/ ▶ **n.** (pl. same) (in France) a flat, paved area outside a cafe where patrons may sit. [Fr., lit. 'terrace.']

ter·raz·zo /tə'räzō; ti'rätsō/ ▶ **n.** flooring material consisting of chips of marble or granite set in concrete and polished to give a smooth surface. [20th C.: Ital., lit. 'terrace,' based on L. *terra* 'earth.']

Ter·re Haute /,terə 'hōt/ a city in western Indiana, on the Wabash River; pop. 59,614.

ter·rene /tə'rēn; 'terēn/ ▶ **adj.** archaic of or like earth; earthy. ■ occurring on or inhabiting dry land. ■ of the world; secular rather than spiritual. [ME: from Anglo-Norman Fr., from L. *terrenus*, from *terra* 'earth.']

terre·plein /'terə,plān/ ▶ **n.** esp. hist. a level space where a battery of guns is mounted. [16th C.: from Fr. *terre-plein*, from Ital. *terrapieno*, from *terrapienare* 'fill with earth.']

ter·res·tri·al /tə'restrēəl/ ▶ **adj.** of, on, or relating to the earth: *terrestrial ecosystems.* ■ denoting television broadcast using equipment situated on the ground rather than by satellite. ■ of or on dry land: *a submarine eruption will be more explosive than its terrestrial counterpart.* ■ (of an animal) living on or in the ground; not aquatic, arboreal, or aerial. ■ (of a plant) growing on land or in the soil; not aquatic or epiphytic. ■ Astron. (of a planet) similar in size or composition to the earth, esp. being one of the four inner planets. ■ archaic of or relating to the earth as opposed to heaven. ▶ **n.** an inhabitant of the earth. — **ter·res·tri·al·ly** **adv.** [ME: from L. *terrestris* (from *terra* 'earth') + -AL.]

ter·res·tri·al globe ▶ **n.** a spherical representation of the earth with a map on the surface.

ter·res·tri·al mag·net·ism ▶ **n.** the magnetic properties of the earth as a whole.

ter·res·tri·al tel·e·scope ▶ **n.** a telescope that is used for observing terrestrial objects and gives an uninverted image.

ter·ret /'terit/ ▶ **n.** each of the loops or rings on a harness pad for the driving reins to pass through. See illustration at HARNESS. [15th C.: from OFr. *touret*, dimin. of *tour* 'a turn.']

terre verte /'ter 'vert/ ▶ **n.** a grayish-green pigment made from a kind of clay (glauconite) and used esp. for watercolors and tempera. Also called GREEN EARTH. [17th C.: Fr., lit. 'green earth.']

ter·ri·bi·li·tà /,terə,bilē'tä/ ▶ **n.** awesomeness or emotional intensity of conception and execution in an artist or work of art, originally as a quality attributed to Michelangelo by his contemporaries. [Ital.]

ter·ri·ble /'terəbəl/ ▶ **adj.** extremely and shockingly or distressingly bad or serious: *a terrible crime.* ■ causing or likely to cause terror; sinister: *a terrible smile.* ■ of extremely poor quality: *terrible living conditions.* ■ [attrib.] informal used to emphasize the extent of something unpleasant or bad: *a terrible mess.* ■ extremely incompetent or unskillful: *she is* ***terrible at*** *managing money.* ■ [as complement] feeling or looking extremely unwell: *I felt terrible for two solid days.* ■ [as complement] (of a person or their feelings) troubled or guilty: *Maria felt terrible because she had forgotten the woman's name.* — **ter·ri·ble·ness** **n.** [ME: via Fr. from L. *terribilis*, from *terrere* 'frighten.']

ter·ri·bly /'terəblē/ ▶ **adv.** **1** [usu. as submodifier] very; extremely: *I'm terribly sorry.* **2** very badly or unpleasantly: *they beat me terribly.* ■ very greatly (used to emphasize something bad, distressing, or unpleasant): *Father misses you terribly.*

ter·ric·o·lous /te'rikələs/ ▶ **adj.** Zool. (of an animal such as an earthworm) living on the ground or in the soil. ■ Bot. (of a plant, esp. a lichen) growing on soil or on the ground. [19th C.: from L. *terricola* 'earth dweller' (from *terra* 'earth' + *colere* 'inhabit') + -OUS.]

ter·ri·er /'terēər/ ▶ **n.** a small dog of a breed originally used for turning out foxes and other burrowing animals from their lairs. ■ used in similes to emphasize tenacity or eagerness: *she would fight like a terrier for every penny.* [ME: from OFr. *(chien) terrier* 'earth (dog),' from med. L. *terrarius*, from L. *terra* 'earth.']

ter·rif·ic /tə'rifik/ ▶ **adj.** **1** of great size, amount, or intensity: *there was a terrific bang.* ■ informal extremely good; excellent: *you look terrific.* **2** archaic causing terror. — **ter·rif·i·cal·ly** **adv.** [as submodifier] *she's been terrifically busy lately.* [17th C. (sense 2): from L. *terrificus*, from *terrere* 'frighten.']

ter·ri·fy /'terə,fī/ ▶ **v.** (**-fies, -fied**) [trans.] cause to feel extreme fear: *the thought terrifies me* | *he is* ***terrified of*** *spiders* | [with clause] *she was terrified he would drop her* | [as adj.] (**terrifying**) *terrifying events.* — **ter·ri·fi·er** **n.** **ter·ri·fy·ing·ly** /'terə,fī-iNGlē/ **adv.** [as submodifier] *the bombs are terrifyingly accurate.* [16th C.: from L. *terrificare*, from *terrificus*.]

ter·rig·e·nous /te'rijənəs/ ▶ **adj.** Geol. (of a marine deposit) made of material eroded from the land. [17th C.: from L. *terrigenus* (from *terra* 'earth' + *-genus* 'born') + -OUS.]

ter·rine /tə'rēn/ ▶ **n.** a meat, fish, or vegetable mixture that has been cooked or otherwise prepared in advance and allowed to cool or set in its container, typically served in slices. ■ a container used for such a dish, typically of an oblong shape and made of earthenware. [18th C.: from Fr., lit. 'large earthenware pot,' from *terrin* 'earthen.']

ter·ri·to·ri·al /,teri'tôrēəl/ ▶ **adj.** **1** of or relating to the ownership of an area of land or sea: *territorial disputes.* ■ Zool. (of an animal or species) defending a territory. ■ of or relating to an animal's territory or its defense: *territorial growls.* **2** of or relating to a particular territory, district, or locality: *a bizarre territorial rite.* ■ (usu. **Territorial**) of or relating to a Territory, in the US or Canada. — **ter·ri·to·ri·al·i·ty** /-,tôrē'alitē/ **n.** **ter·ri·to·ri·al·ly** **adv.**

ter·ri·to·ri·al im·per·a·tive ▶ **n.** [usu. in sing.] Zool. & Psychol. the need to claim and defend a territory.

ter·ri·to·ri·al wa·ters ▶ **plural n.** the waters under the jurisdiction of a state, esp. the part of the sea within a stated distance of the shore (traditionally three miles from low-water mark).

ter·ri·to·ry /'terə,tôrē/ ▶ **n.** (pl. **-ries**) **1** an area of land under the jurisdiction of a ruler or state: *enemy territory.* ■ Zool. an area defended by an animal or group of animals against others of the same sex or species. Compare with HOME RANGE. ■ an area defended by a team or player in a game or sport. ■ an area in which one has certain rights or for which one has responsibility with regard to a particular type of activity: *a sales rep for a large territory.* ■ fig. an area of knowledge, activity, or experience: *the way she felt now—she was in unknown territory.* ■ [with adj.] land with a specified characteristic: *woodland territory.* **2** (**Territory**) (esp. in the US, Canada, or Australia) an organized division of a country that is not yet admitted to the full rights of a state.
– PHRASES **go** (or **come**) **with the territory** be an unavoidable result of a particular situation. [ME: from L. *territorium*, from *terra* 'land.']

ter·ror /'terər/ ▶ **n.** **1** extreme fear: *people fled* ***in terror*** | [in sing.] *a terror of darkness.* ■ the use of such fear to intimidate people, esp. for political reasons: *weapons of terror.* ■ [in sing.] a person or thing that causes extreme fear: *he became* ***the terror of*** *the Chicago mob.* ■ (**the Terror**) the period of the French Revolution between mid 1793 and July 1794 when the ruling Jacobins, dominated by Robespierre, ruthlessly executed anyone considered a threat to their regime. Also called REIGN OF TERROR. **2** (also **holy terror**) informal a person, esp. a child, who causes trouble or annoyance. [ME: from OFr. *terrour*, from L. *terror*, from *terrere* 'frighten.']

ter·ror·ism /'terə,rizəm/ ▶ **n.** the use of violence and intimidation in the pursuit of political aims.

ter·ror·ist /'terərist/ ▶ **n.** a person who uses terrorism in the pursuit of political aims. — **ter·ror·is·tic** /,terə'ristik/ **adj.** **ter·ror·is·ti·cal·ly** /,terə'ristik(ə)lē/ **adv.** [18th C.: from Fr. *terroriste*, from L. *terror* (see TERROR).]

ter·ror·ize /'terə,rīz/ ▶ **v.** [trans.] create and maintain a state of extreme fear and distress in (someone); fill with terror: *he used his army to terrorize the population.* — **ter·ror·i·za·tion** /,terərə'zāSHən/ **n.** **ter·ror·iz·er** **n.**

ter·ror-strick·en (also **terror-struck**) ▶ **adj.** feeling or expressing extreme fear.

ter·ry /'terē/ (also **terry cloth**) ▶ **n.** (pl. **-ies**) a fabric with raised uncut loops of thread covering both surfaces, used esp. for towels. [18th C.: of unknown origin.]

terse /tərs/ ▶ **adj.** (**ters·er, ters·est**) sparing in the use of words; abrupt: *a terse statement.* — **terse·ly** **adv.** **terse·ness** **n.** [17th C.: from L. *tersus* 'wiped, polished,' from the verb *tergere*.]

ter·tian /'tərSHən/ ▶ **adj.** [attrib.] Med. denoting a form of malaria causing a fever that recurs every second day. The common benign tertian malaria is caused by infection with *Plasmodium vivax* or *P. ovale*, and malignant tertian malaria is caused by *P. falciparum*. [ME *(fever) terciane*, from L. *(febris) tertiana*, from *tertius* 'third.']

ter·ti·ar·y /'tərSHē,erē; -SHərē/ ▶ **adj.** **1** third in order or level: *the tertiary stage of the disease.* ■ esp. Brit. relating to or denoting education at a level beyond that provided by schools, esp. that provided by a college or university. ■ relating to or denoting the medical treatment provided at a specialist institution. **2** (**Tertiary**) Geol. of, relating to, or denoting the first period of the Cenozoic era, between the Cretaceous and Quaternary periods, and comprising the Paleogene and Neogene subperiods. **3** Chem. (of an organic compound) having its functional group located on a carbon atom that is itself bonded to three other carbon atoms. ■ Chem. (chiefly of amines) derived from ammonia by replacement of three hydrogen atoms by organic groups. ▶ **n.** **1** (**the Tertiary**) Geol. the Tertiary period or the system of rocks deposited during it, lasting from about 65 million to 1.6 million years ago. The mammals diversified following the demise of the dinosaurs and became dominant, as did the flowering plants. **2** a lay associate of certain Christian monastic organizations: *a Franciscan tertiary.* [16th C.: from L. *tertiarius* 'of the third part or rank,' from *tertius* 'third.']

ter·ti·ar·y struc·ture ▶ **n.** Biochem. the overall three-dimensional structure resulting from folding and covalent cross-linking of a protein or polynucleotide molecule.

ter·ti·um quid /'tərsHēəm 'kwid; 'tərtēəm/ ▶ **n.** a third thing that is indefinite and undefined but is related to two definite or known things. [18th C.: from late L., 'some third thing.']

Ter·tul·li·an /tər'təlēən; -'təlyən/ (*c.*160–*c.*240), early Christian theologian; Latin name *Quintus Septimius Florens Tertullianus.* His writings include Christian apologetics and attacks on paganism and Gnosticism.

ter·va·lent /tər'vālənt/ ▶ **adj.** Chem. another term for TRIVALENT.

ter·za ri·ma /,tertsə 'rēmə/ ▶ **n.** Pros. an arrangement of triplets, esp. in iambs, that rhyme *aba bcb cdc*, etc., as in Dante's *Divine Comedy*. [Ital., lit. 'third rhyme.']

TESL /'tesəl/ ▶ **abbr.** teaching of English as a second language.

Tes·la /'teslə/, Nikola (1856–1943), US engineer and inventor; born in what is now Croatia. He developed the first alternating-current induction motor, the Tesla coil, and a wireless guidance system for ships.

tes·la /'teslə/ (abbr.: **T**) ▶ **n.** Physics the SI unit of magnetic flux density. [1960s: named after N. TESLA.]

Tes·la coil ▶ **n.** a form of induction coil for producing high-frequency alternating currents.

TESOL /'te,säl; -,sôl; 'tesəl/ ▶ **abbr.** teaching of English to speakers of other languages.

tes·sel·late /'tesə,lāt/ (also **tes·se·late**) ▶ **v.** [trans.] decorate (a floor) with mosaics. ■ Math. cover (a plane surface) by repeated use of a single shape, without gaps or overlapping. — **tes·sel·la·tion** /,tesə'lāsHən/ (also **tes·se·la·tion**) **n.** [18th C.: from late L. *tessellat-*, from the verb *tessellare*, from *tessella*, dimin. of *tessera* (see TESSERA).]

tes·ser·a /'tesərə/ ▶ **n.** (pl. **tes·se·rae** /'tesərē/) a small block of stone, tile, glass, or other material used in the construction of a mosaic. ■ (in ancient Greece and Rome) a small tablet of wood or bone used as a token. — **tes·ser·al** /-rəl/ **adj.** [17th C.: via L. from Gk., neut. of *tesseres*, var. of *tessares* 'four.']

Tes·sin /te'saN; -'sēn/ French and German name for TICINO.

tes·si·tu·ra /,tesi'to͝orə/ ▶ **n.** Music the range within which most notes of a vocal part fall. [Ital., lit. 'texture,' from L. *textura* (see TEXTURE).]

Test. ▶ **abbr.** Testament.

test¹ /test/ ▶ **n. 1** a procedure intended to establish the quality, performance, or reliability of something, esp. before it is taken into widespread use. ■ a short written or spoken examination of a person's proficiency or knowledge: *a spelling test.* ■ an event or situation that reveals the strength or quality of someone or something by putting them under strain: *the first serious test of the agreement.* ■ an examination of part of the body for medical purposes, esp. by means of a chemical or mechanical procedure rather than simple inspection: *a blood test for HIV.* ■ Chem. a procedure employed to identify a substance or to reveal the presence or absence of a constituent within a substance. ■ the result of a medical examination or analytical procedure: *a positive test for protein.* ■ a means of establishing whether an action, item, or situation is an instance of a specified quality, esp. one held to be undesirable: *a statutory test of obscenity.* **2** Metallurgy a movable hearth in a reverberating furnace, used for separating gold or silver from lead. ▶ **v.** [trans.] take measures to check the quality, performance, or reliability of (something), esp. before putting it into widespread use or practice: *not tested on animals* | [as n.] (**testing**) *the testing of prototypes* | fig. *a useful way to test out ideas.* ■ reveal the strengths or capabilities of (someone or something) by putting them under strain: *such behavior would test any marriage* ■ give (someone) a short written or oral examination of their proficiency or knowledge: *all children are tested at age ten.* ■ judge or measure (someone's proficiency or knowledge) by means of such an examination. ■ carry out a medical test on (a person, a part of the body, or a body fluid). ■ [intrans.] produce a specified result in a medical test, esp. a drug test or AIDS test: *he tested positive for steroids during the race.* ■ Chem. examine (a substance) by means of a reagent. ■ touch or taste (something) to check that it is acceptable before proceeding further: *test the water with your elbow.*

– PHRASES **put someone/something to the test** find out how useful, strong, or effective someone or something is. **stand the test of time** last or remain popular for a long time. **test the water** judge people's feelings or opinions before taking further action. — **test·a·bil·i·ty** /,testə'bilitē/ **n.** **test·a·ble adj.** **test·ee** /tes'tē/ **n.** [ME: via OFr. from L. *testu, testum* 'earthen pot,' var. of *testa* 'jug, shell.']

test² ▶ **n.** Zool. the shell or integument of some invertebrates and protozoans, esp. the chalky shell of a foraminiferan or the tough outer layer of a tunicate. [19th C.: from L. *testa* 'tile, jug, shell.']

test. ▶ **abbr.** ■ testator. ■ testimony.

tes·ta /'testə/ ▶ **n.** (pl. **-tae** /-tē/) Bot. the protective outer covering of a seed; the seed coat. [18th C.: from L., 'tile, shell.']

tes·ta·ceous /te'stāsHəs/ ▶ **adj.** esp. Entomol. of a dull brick-red color. [17th C.: from L. *testaceus* (from *testa* 'tile') + **-ous**.]

tes·ta·ment /'testəmənt/ ▶ **n. 1** a person's will, esp. the part relating to personal property. **2** something that serves as a sign or evidence of a specified fact, event, or quality: ***a testament to my love.*** **3** (in biblical use) a covenant or dispensation. ■ (**Testament**) a division of the Bible. See also OLD TESTAMENT, NEW TESTAMENT. ■ (**Testament**) a copy of the New Testament. [ME: from L. *testamentum* 'a will' (from *testari* 'testify').]

tes·ta·men·ta·ry /,testə'men(t)ərē/ ▶ **adj.** of, relating to, or bequeathed or appointed through a will.

tes·tate /'testāt/ ▶ **adj.** [predic.] having made a valid will before one dies. ▶ **n.** a person who has died leaving such a will. [ME: from L. *testatus* 'testified, witnessed,' past part. of *testari*, from *testis* 'a witness.']

tes·ta·tion /te'stāsHən/ ▶ **n.** Law the disposal of property by will.

tes·ta·tor /'testātər/ ▶ **n.** Law a person who has made a will or given a legacy.

tes·ta·trix /te'stātriks/ ▶ **n.** (pl. **-tri·ces** /-trisēz/ or **-trix·es**) dated, Law a woman who has made a will or given a legacy. [16th C.: from late L., fem. of *testator*.]

Test-Ban Trea·ty an international agreement not to test nuclear weapons in the atmosphere, in space, or underwater, signed in 1963 by the US, the UK, and the USSR, and later by more than 100 governments.

test bed ▶ **n.** a piece of equipment used for testing new machinery, esp. aircraft engines.

test case ▶ **n.** Law a case that sets a precedent for other cases involving the same question of law.

test drive ▶ **n.** an act of driving a motor vehicle that one is considering buying in order to determine its quality. ■ fig. a test of a product before purchase or release. ▶ **v.** (**test-drive**) [trans.] drive (a vehicle) to determine its qualities with a view to buying it. ■ fig. test (a product) before purchase or release.

test·er¹ /'testər/ ▶ **n.** a person who tests something, esp. a new product. ■ a person who tests another's proficiency. ■ a device that tests the functioning of something: *a cake tester.* ■ a sample of a product provided so that customers can try it before buying it.

test·er² ▶ **n.** a canopy over a four-poster bed. [ME: from med. L. *testerium, testrum*, from a Romance word meaning 'head,' based on L. *testa* 'tile.']

tes·tes /'testēz/ plural form of TESTIS.

test flight ▶ **n.** a flight during which the performance of an aircraft or its equipment is tested. — **test-fly v.**

tes·ti·cle /'testikəl/ ▶ **n.** either of the two oval organs that produce sperm in men and other male mammals, enclosed in the scrotum behind the penis. Also called TESTIS. — **tes·tic·u·lar** /te'stikyələr/ **adj.** [ME: from L. *testiculus*, dimin. of *testis* 'a witness' (i.e., to virility).]

tes·tic·u·lar fem·i·ni·za·tion /te'stikyələr ,femənі'zāsHən/ ▶ **n.** a condition produced in genetically male people by the failure of tissue to respond to male sex hormones, resulting in normal female anatomy but with testes in place of ovaries.

tes·tic·u·late /te'stikyəlit/ ▶ **adj.** Bot. (esp. of the twin tubers of some orchids) shaped like a pair of testicles. [18th C.: from late L. *testiculatus*, from *testiculus*.]

tes·ti·fy /'testə,fī/ ▶ **v.** (**-fies, -fied**) [intrans.] give evidence as a witness in a court of law: *he testified against his son* | [with clause] *he testified that he had sold crack.* ■ serve as evidence or proof of something's existing or being the case: *the bleak lines testify to inner torment.* — **tes·ti·fi·er n.** [ME: from L. *testificari*, from *testis* 'a witness.']

tes·ti·mo·ni·al /,testə'mōnēəl/ ▶ **n.** a formal statement testifying to someone's character and qualifications. ■ a public tribute to someone and to their achievements. ■ [often as adj.] (in sports) a game or event held in honor of a player, who typically receives part of the income generated: *a testimonial day for Gehrig.*

tes·ti·mo·ny /'testə,mōnē/ ▶ **n.** (pl. **-nies**) a formal written or spoken statement, esp. one given in a court of law. ■ evidence or proof provided by the existence or appearance of something: *his black eye was testimony to the fact that he'd been fighting.* ■ a public recounting of a religious conversion or experience. [ME: from L. *testimonium*, from *testis* 'a witness.']

test·ing ground ▶ **n.** an area or field of activity used for the testing of a product or an idea, esp. a military site used for the testing of weapons.

tes·tis /'testis/ ▶ **n.** (pl. **-tes** /-tēz/) Anat. & Zool. an organ that produces spermatozoa (male reproductive cells). Compare with TESTICLE. [18th C.: from L., lit. 'a witness.']

test match ▶ **n.** an international cricket or rugby match.

test meal ▶ **n.** Med. a portion of food of specified quantity and composition, eaten to stimulate digestive secretions which can then be analyzed.

tes·tos·ter·one /te'stästə,rōn/ ▶ **n.** a steroid hormone that stimulates development of male secondary sexual characteristics, produced mainly in the testes, but also in the ovaries and adrenal cortex. [1930s: from TESTIS + *sterone* (blend of STEROL and KETONE).]

test pa·per ▶ **n.** Chem. a paper impregnated with an indicator that changes color under known conditions, used esp. to test for acidity.

test pat·tern ▶ **n.** a geometric design broadcast by a television station so that viewers can adjust the quality of their reception.

test pi·lot ▶ **n.** a pilot who flies an aircraft to test its performance.

test strip ▶ **n.** a strip of material used in testing, esp. (in photography) a strip of sensitized material, sections of which are exposed for varying lengths of time to assess its response.

test tube ▶ **n.** a thin glass tube closed at one end, used to hold small amounts of material for laboratory testing or experiments. ■ [as adj.] denoting things produced or processes performed in a laboratory: *new forms of test-tube life.*

test-tube ba·by ▶ **n.** informal a baby conceived by in vitro fertilization.

Tes·tu·di·nes /te'st(y)o͞odn,ēz/ Zool. an order of reptiles that comprises the turtles, terrapins, and tortoises. They are distinguished by having a shell of bony plates covered with horny scales, and many kinds are aquatic. Also called, esp. formerly, CHELONIA. [mod. L. (pl.), based on L. *testa* 'shell.']

tes·tu·do /te'st(y)o͞odō/ ▶ **n.** (pl. **-dos** or **-di·nes** /-dn,ēz/) (in ancient Rome) a screen on wheels and with an arched roof, used to protect besieging troops. ■ a protective screen formed by a body of troops holding their shields above their heads in such a way that the shields overlap. [ME: from L., lit. 'tortoise,' from *testa* 'tile, shell.']

tes·ty /'testē/ ▶ **adj.** easily irritated; impatient and somewhat bad-tempered. — **tes·ti·ly adv. tes·ti·ness n.** [ME: from Anglo-Norman Fr. *testif*, from OFr. *teste* 'head,' from L. *testa* 'shell.']

te·tan·ic /te'tanik/ ▶ **adj.** relating to or characteristic of tetanus, esp. in connection with tonic muscle spasm. — **te·tan·i·cal·ly adv.**

tet·a·nus /'tetn-əs/ ▶ **n. 1** a disease marked by rigidity and spasms of the voluntary muscles, caused by the bacterium *Clostridium tetani*. See also TRISMUS. **2** Physiol. the prolonged contraction of a muscle caused by rapidly repeated stimuli. — **tet·a·nize v. tet·a·noid adj.** [ME: from L., from Gk. *tetanos* 'muscular spasm,' from *teinein* 'to stretch.']

tet·a·ny /'tetn-ē/ ▶ **n.** a condition marked by intermittent muscular spasms, caused by malfunction of the parathyroid glands and a consequent deficiency of calcium. [19th C.: from Fr. *tétanie*, from L. *tetanus* (see TETANUS).]

tetch·y /'tecHē/ (also **tech·y**) ▶ **adj.** bad-tempered and irritable. — **tetch·i·ly adv. tetch·i·ness n.** [16th C.: prob. from a var. of Scots *tache* 'blotch, fault,' from OFr. *teche*.]

tête-à-tête /'tāt ə 'tāt; 'tet ə 'tet/ ▶ **n. 1** a private conversation between two people. **2** an S-shaped sofa on which two people can sit face to face. ▶ **adj. & adv.** involving or happening between two people in private: [as adj.] *a tête-à-tête meal* | [as adv.] *his business was conducted tête-à-tête.* [17th C.: Fr., lit. 'head-to-head.']

tête-bêche /tet 'besH/ ▶ **adj.** (of a postage stamp) printed upside down or sideways relative to another. [Fr., from *tête* 'head' and *bêche*, contr. of obs. *béchevet* 'placed with the head of one against the foot of the other.']

teth·er /'teTHər/ ▶ **n.** a rope or chain with which an animal is tied to restrict its movement. ▶ **v.** [trans.] tie (an animal) with a rope or chain so as to restrict its movement: *the horse is tethered to a post.*
– PHRASES **the end of one's tether** see END. [ME: from ON *tjóthr*, from a Gmc. base meaning 'fasten.']

teth·er·ball /'teTHər,bôl/ ▶ **n.** a game in which two people use their hands or paddles to hit a ball suspended on a cord from an upright post, the winner being the first person to wind the cord completely around the post.

Te·thys /'tēTHis/ **1** Gk. Mythol. a goddess of the sea, daughter of Uranus (Heaven) and Gaia (Earth). **2** Astron. a satellite of Saturn, the ninth closest to the planet, discovered by Cassini in 1684. It is probably composed mainly of ice and has a diameter of 659 miles (1,060 km). **3** Geol. an ocean formerly separating the supercontinents of Gondwana and Laurasia, the forerunner of the present-day Mediterranean.

Tet Of·fen·sive /tet/ an offensive in January–February 1968 by the Vietcong and North Vietnamese armies against South Vietnam, begun with a surprise attack on the first day of Tet (Vietnamese New Year).

Te·ton /'tētän/ (also **Te·ton Sioux**) ▶ **n.** another term for LAKOTA. [based on Lakota *thíthu-wa-*, possibly meaning 'dwellers on the prairie.']

Té·touan /tā'twän/ a city in northern Morocco; pop. 272,000.

tet·ra /'tetrə/ ▶ **n.** a small tropical freshwater fish (family Characidae) that is typically brightly colored. Native to Africa and America, many tetras are popular in aquariums. [20th C.: abbr. of mod. L. *Tetragonopterus*, lit. 'tetragonal-finned.']

tetra- (also **tetr-** before a vowel) ▶ **comb. form 1** four; having four: *tetramerous* | *tetragram* | *tetrode*. **2** Chem. (in names of compounds) containing four atoms or groups of a specified kind: *tetracycline*. [from Gk., from *tettares* 'four.']

tet·ra·chord /'tetrə,kôrd/ ▶ **n.** Music a scale of four notes, the interval between the first and last being a perfect fourth. ■ hist. a musical instrument with four strings.

tet·ra·cy·cline /,tetrə'sīklēn; -klin/ ▶ **n.** Med. any of a large group of antibiotics (often obtained from bacteria of the genus *Streptomyces*) with a molecular structure containing four rings. [1950s: from TETRA- + CYCLIC + -INE[4].]

tet·rad /'tetrad/ ▶ **n.** tech. a group or set of four. [17th C.: from Gk. *tetras*, *tetrad-* 'four, a group of four.']

tet·ra·dac·tyl /,tetrə'daktl/ ▶ **adj.** Zool. (of a vertebrate limb) having four toes or fingers.

tet·ra·eth·yl lead /,tetrə'eTHəl 'led/ ▶ **n.** Chem. a toxic colorless oily liquid, $Pb(C_2H_5)_4$, made synthetically and used as an antiknock agent in leaded gasoline.

tet·ra·fluo·ro·eth·yl·ene /,tetrə,flo͝orō'eTHə,lēn/ ▶ **n.** Chem. a dense colorless gas, $F_2C{=}CF_2$, that is polymerized to make plastics such as polytetrafluoroethylene.

te·trag·o·nal /te'tragənl/ ▶ **adj.** of or denoting a crystal system or three-dimensional geometric arrangement having three axes at right angles, two of them equal. — **te·trag·o·nal·ly adv.** [16th C.: via late L. from Gk. *tetragōnon* (neut. of *tetragōnos* 'four-angled') + -AL.]

tet·ra·gram /'tetrə,gram/ ▶ **n.** a word consisting of four letters or characters.

Tet·ra·gram·ma·ton /,tetrə'graməˌtän/ ▶ **n.** the Hebrew name of God transliterated in four letters as *YHWH* or *JHVH* and articulated as *Yahweh* or *Jehovah*. [Gk., neut. of *tetragrammatos* 'having four letters,' from *tetra-* 'four' + *gramma*, *grammat-* 'letter.']

tet·ra·he·drite /,tetrə'hēdrīt/ ▶ **n.** a gray mineral consisting of a sulfide of antimony, iron, and copper, typically occurring as tetrahedral crystals.

tet·ra·he·dron /,tetrə'hēdrən/ ▶ **n.** (pl. **-dra** /-drə/ or **-drons**) a solid having four plane triangular faces; a triangular pyramid. — **tet·ra·he·dral** /-drəl/ **adj.** [16th C.: from late Gk. *tetraedron*, neut. of *tetraedros* 'four-sided.']

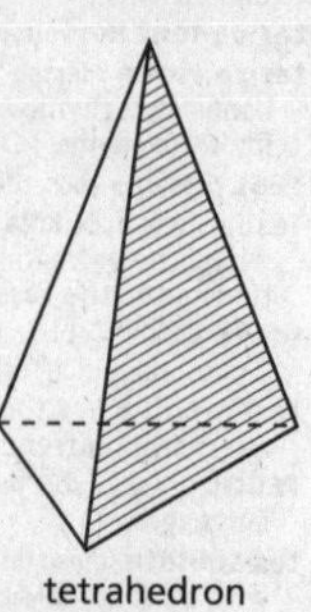

tetrahedron

tet·ra·hy·dro·can·nab·i·nol /,tetrə,hīdrəkə'nabə,nôl; -,näl/ ▶ **n.** Chem. a crystalline compound, $C_{21}H_{30}O_2$, that is the main active ingredient of cannabis.

tet·ra·hy·dro·fu·ran /,tetrə,hīdrō'fyo͝oran/ ▶ **n.** Chem. a colorless liquid (C_4H_8O) used chiefly as a solvent for plastics and as an intermediate in organic syntheses.

te·tral·o·gy /te'träləjē/ ▶ **n.** (pl. **-gies**) **1** a group of four related literary or operatic works. ■ a series of four ancient Greek dramas, three tragedies and one satyr play, originally presented together. **2** Med. a set of four related symptoms or abnormalities frequently occurring together.

tet·ra·mer /'tetrəmər/ ▶ **n.** Chem. a polymer comprising four monomer units. — **tet·ra·mer·ic** /,tetrə'merik/ **adj.**

te·tram·er·ous /te'tramərəs/ ▶ **adj.** Bot. & Zool. having parts arranged in groups of four. ■ consisting of four joints or parts.

te·tram·e·ter /te'tramitər/ ▶ **n.** Pros. a verse of four measures.

tet·ra·ple·gi·a /,tetrə'plēj(ē)ə/ ▶ **n.** another term for QUADRIPLEGIA. — **tet·ra·ple·gic** /-'plējik/ **adj. & n.** [20th C.: from TETRA- 'four' + PARAPLEGIA.]

tet·ra·ploid /'tetrə,ploid/ Biol. ▶ **adj.** (of a cell or nucleus) containing four homologous sets of chromosomes. ■ (of an organism or species) composed of such cells. ▶ **n.** an organism, variety, or species of this type. — **tet·ra·ploi·dy n.**

tet·ra·pod /'tetrə,päd/ ▶ **n.** Zool. a four-footed animal (superclass Tetrapoda), esp. a member of a group that includes all vertebrates higher than fishes. ■ an object or structure with four feet, legs, or supports. [19th C.: from mod. L. *tetrapodus*, from Gk. *tetrapous*, *tetrapod-* 'four-footed,' from *tetra-* 'four' + *pous* 'foot.']

te·trap·ter·ous /te'traptərəs/ ▶ **adj.** Entomol. (of an insect) having two pairs of wings. [19th C.: from mod. L. *tetrapterus* (from Gk. *tetrapteros*, from *tetra-* 'four' + *pteron* 'wing') + -OUS.]

te·trarch /'teträrk/ ▶ **n.** (in the Roman Empire) the governor of one of four divisions of a country or province. ■ one of four joint rulers. ■ archaic a subordinate ruler. — **te·trar·chy n.** (pl. **-chies**). [OE, from late L. *tetrarcha*, from L. *tetrarches*, from Gk. *tetrarkhēs*, from *tetra-* 'four' + *arkhein* 'to rule.']

tet·ra·spore /'tetrə,spôr/ ▶ **n.** Bot. a spore occurring in groups of four, in particular (in a red alga) each of four spores produced together, two of which produce male plants and two female.

tet·ra·stich /'tetrə,stik/ ▶ **n.** Pros. a group of four lines of verse. [16th C.: via L. from Gk. *tetrastikhon* 'having four rows,' from *tetra-* 'four' + *stikhon* 'row, line of verse.']

tet·ra·tom·ic /,tetrə'tämik/ ▶ **adj.** Chem. consisting of four atoms.

tet·ra·va·lent /,tetrə'vālənt/ ▶ **adj.** Chem. having a valence of four.

tet·ra·zole /'tetrə,zōl/ ▶ **n.** Chem. an acidic crystalline compound, CH_2N_4, whose molecule is a five-membered ring of one carbon and four nitrogen atoms. [19th C.: from TETRA- 'four' + AZO- + -OLE.]

tet·ra·zo·li·um /,tetrə'zōlēəm/ ▶ **n.** [as adj.] Chem. a cation derived from tetrazole or one of its derivatives, esp. the triphenyl derivative. ■ (also **ni·tro·blue tet·ra·zo·li·um**) a yellow dye used as a test for viability in biological material.

tet·raz·zi·ni /,tetrə'zēnē/ ▶ **adj.** [postpositive] served over pasta with mushrooms and almonds in a cream sauce, sprinkled with cheese, and baked in the oven: *turkey tetrazzini.* [20th C.: named after Luisa *Tetrazzini* (1871–1940), Ital. operatic soprano.]

tet·rode /'tetrōd/ ▶ **n.** a thermionic tube having four electrodes. [20th C.: from TETRA- 'four' + Gk. *hodos* 'way.']

te·tro·do·tox·in /te,trōdə'täksin/ ▶ **n.** a poisonous compound present in the ovaries of certain pufferfishes. It is a powerful neurotoxin. [20th C.: from mod. L. *Tetrodon* from Gk. *tetra-* 'fourfold' + *odous*, *odont-* 'tooth').]

tet·rose /'tetrōs; -trōz/ ▶ **n.** Chem. any of a group of monosaccharide sugars whose molecules contain four carbon atoms.

te·trox·ide /te'träksīd/ ▶ **n.** Chem. an oxide containing four atoms of oxygen in its molecule or empirical formula.

tet·ter /'tetər/ ▶ **n.** esp. archaic a skin disease in humans or animals causing itchy or pustular patches, such as eczema or ringworm. [OE *teter*, from an Indo-Eur. root shared by Sanskrit *dadru* 'skin disease.']

Teut. ▶ **abbr.** ■ Teuton. ■ Teutonic.

Teu·ton /ˈt(y)o͞otn/ ▶ **n.** a member of a people who lived in Jutland in the 4th century BC and fought the Romans in France in the 2nd century BC. ■ often derog. a German. [from L. *Teutones, Teutoni* (pl.), from an Indo-Eur. root meaning 'people' or 'country.']

Teu·ton·ic /t(y)o͞oˈtänik/ ▶ **adj.** **1** of or relating to the Teutons. ■ informal, often derog. displaying characteristics popularly attributed to Germans. *your Teutonic strictness.* **2** archaic denoting the Germanic branch of the Indo-European language family. ▶ **n.** archaic the language of the Teutons. — **Teu·ton·i·cism** /-ˈtänəˌsizəm/ **n.**

Teu·ton·ic Knights a military and religious order of German knights, priests, and lay brothers, originally enrolled *c.*1191 as the Teutonic Knights of St. Mary of Jerusalem.

Te·ve·re /ˈtāvəˌrā/ Italian name for TIBER.

Te·vet ▶ **n.** var. of TEBET.

Te·wa /ˈtāwə; ˈtē-/ ▶ **n.** (pl. same or **-was**) **1** a member of a Pueblo Indian people of the Rio Grande area in the southwestern US. **2** the Tanoan language of this people. Do not confuse with TIWA. ▶ **adj.** of or relating to this people or their language. [based on the Tewa self-designation *téwa.*]

Tex. ▶ **abbr.** Texas.

Tex·ar·kana /ˌteksärˈkanə/ twin cities on the Texas-Arkansas border. The Texas city is in the northeastern part of the state; pop. 31,656. The Arkansas city is in the southwestern part of the state; pop. 26,448.

Tex·as /ˈteksəs/ a state in the southern US, on the border with Mexico, with a coastline on the Gulf of Mexico; pop. 20,851,820; capital, Austin; statehood, Dec. 29, 1845 (28). The area was part of Mexico until 1836, when it declared independence, became a republic, and began to work for admittance to the US as a state. — **Tex·an** /ˈteksən/ **adj. & n.**

Tex·as fe·ver ▶ **n.** the disease babesiosis in cattle.

Tex·as hold 'em /ˈhōldəm/ ▶ **n.** a poker game in which players compose their hands from cards dealt to them combined with community cards dealt face up and shared among them.

Tex·as lea·guer ▶ **n.** Baseball a pop fly that falls to the ground between the infield and the outfield and results in a base hit.

Tex·as Rang·er ▶ **n.** a member of the Texas State police force (formerly, of certain locally mustered regiments in the federal service during the Mexican War).

Tex-Mex /ˈteks ˈmeks/ ▶ **adj.** (esp. of cooking and music) having a blend of Mexican and southern American features originally characteristic of the border regions of Texas and Mexico. ▶ **n.** **1** music or cooking of such a type. **2** a variety of Mexican Spanish spoken in Texas. [1940s: blend of *Texan* and *Mexican.*]

text /tekst/ ▶ **n.** **1** a book or other written or printed work, regarded in terms of its content rather than its physical form: *a text which explores pain and grief.* ■ a piece of written or printed material regarded as conveying the authentic or primary form of a particular work: *the text of the lecture.* ■ written or printed words, typically forming a connected piece of work: *stylistic features of journalistic text.* ■ Comput. data in written form, esp. when stored, processed, or displayed in a word processor. ■ [in sing.] the main body of a book or other piece of writing, as distinct from other material such as notes, appendices, and illustrations: *the pictures relate well to the text.* ■ a script or libretto. ■ a written work chosen or assigned as a subject of study: *a secondary text for religion courses.* ■ a textbook. ■ a passage from the Bible or other religious work, esp. when used as the subject of a sermon. ■ a subject or theme for a discussion or exposition: *he took as his text the fact that Australia is paradise.* **2** (also **text-hand**) fine, large handwriting, used esp. for manuscripts. **3** a text message. ▶ **v.** [trans.] send a text message to (someone). ■ send (a text message). — **text·less adj.** [ME: from Old North. Fr. *texte,* from L. *textus* 'tissue,' from *text-* 'woven,' from the verb *texere.*]

text·book /ˈteks(t)ˌbo͝ok/ ▶ **n.** a book used as a standard work for the study of a particular subject. ▶ **adj.** [attrib.] conforming to or corresponding to a standard or type that is prescribed or widely held by theorists: *a textbook emergency response.* — **text·book·ish adj.**

text ed·i·tor ▶ **n.** Comput. a system or program that allows a user to edit text.

tex·tile /ˈtekstīl/ ▶ **n.** **1** (usu. **textiles**) a type of cloth or woven fabric. ■ (**textiles**) the branch of industry involved in the manufacture of cloth. **2** informal used by nudists to describe someone wearing clothes, esp. on a beach. ▶ **adj.** **1** [attrib.] of or relating to fabric or weaving: *the textile industry.* **2** informal used by nudists to describe something relating to or restricted to people wearing clothes. [17th C.: from L. *textilis,* from *text-* 'woven,' from the verb *texere.*]

text mes·sage ▶ **n.** an electronic communication sent and received by cellular phone. — **text mes·sag·ing n.**

text proc·ess·ing ▶ **n.** Comput. the manipulation of text, esp. the transformation of text from one format to another.

tex·tu·al /ˈteksCHo͞oəl/ ▶ **adj.** of or relating to a text or texts: *textual analysis.* — **tex·tu·al·ly adv.** [ME: from med. L. *textualis,* from L. *textus* (see TEXT).]

tex·tu·al crit·i·cism ▶ **n.** the process of attempting to ascertain the original wording of a text.

tex·tu·al·ist /ˈteksCHo͞oəlist/ ▶ **n.** a person who adheres strictly to a text, esp. that of the scriptures. — **tex·tu·al·ism n.**

tex·tu·al·i·ty /ˌteksCHo͞oˈalitē/ ▶ **n.** **1** the quality or use of language characteristic of written works as opposed to spoken usage. **2** strict adherence to a text; textualism.

tex·ture /ˈteksCHər/ ▶ **n.** the feel, appearance, or consistency of a surface or a substance: *skin texture | the cheese is firm in texture | the textures of bark.* ■ the character or appearance of a textile fabric as determined by the arrangement and thickness of its threads: *a shirt of rough texture.* ■ Art the tactile quality of the surface of a work of art. ■ the quality created by the combination of the different elements in a work of music or literature: *the symphonic texture.* ▶ **v.** [trans.] [usu. as adj.] (**textured**) give (a surface, esp. of a fabric or wall covering) a rough or raised texture: *wallcoverings which create a textured finish.* — **tex·tur·al** /-CHərəl/ **adj.** **tex·tur·al·ly** /-CHərəlē/ **adv.** **tex·ture·less adj.** [ME: from L. *textura* 'weaving,' from *text-* 'woven,' from the verb *texere.*]

tex·tured veg·e·ta·ble pro·tein ▶ **n.** a type of protein obtained from soybeans and made to resemble minced meat.

tex·ture map·ping ▶ **n.** Comput. the application of patterns or images to three-dimensional graphics to enhance the realism of their surfaces.

tex·tur·ing /ˈteksCHəriNG/ ▶ **n.** the representation or use of texture, esp. in music, fine art, and interior design.

tex·tur·ize /ˈteksCHəˌrīz/ ▶ **v.** [trans.] impart a particular texture to (a product, esp. a fabric or foodstuff) in order to make it more attractive. ■ cut (hair) in such a way as to remove its weight and create extra fullness.

text wrap ▶ **n.** (in word processing) a facility allowing text to surround embedded features such as pictures.

T-for·ma·tion ▶ **n.** Football a T-shaped offensive formation, with the halfbacks and fullback positioned in a line parallel to the line of scrimmage.

TFT ▶ **abbr.** Electron. thin-film transistor, denoting a technology used to make flat color display screens, usually for high-end portable computers.

TG ▶ **abbr.** ■ transformational grammar or transformational-generative grammar.

t.g. ▶ **abbr.** Biol. type genus.

TGIF ▶ **abbr.** informal thank God it's Friday.

T-group ▶ **n.** Psychol. a group of people undergoing therapy or training in which they observe and seek to improve their own interpersonal relationships or communication skills. [1950s: *T* for *training.*]

tgt. ▶ **abbr.** target.

TGV ▶ **n.** a French high-speed electric passenger train. [abbrev. of Fr. *train à grande vitesse.*]

Th ▶ **symb.** the chemical element thorium.

Th. ▶ **abbr.** Thursday.

-th[1] (also **-eth**) ▶ **suffix** forming ordinal and fractional numbers from *four* onwards: *fifth | sixty-sixth.* [OE *-(o)tha, -(o)the.*]

-th[2] ▶ **suffix** forming nouns: **1** (from verbs) denoting an action or process: *birth | growth.* **2** (from adjectives) denoting a state: *filth | width.* [OE *-thu, -tho, -th.*]

-th[3] ▶ **suffix** var. of -ETH[2] (as in *doth*).

Thack·er·ay /ˈTHak(ə)rē; -əˌrā/, William Makepeace (1811–63), British writer; born in India. His novels include the satirical *Vanity Fair* (1847–48).

Thad·dae·us /ˈTHadēəs/ an apostle named in St. Matthew's gospel, traditionally identified with St. Jude.

Thai /tī/ ▶ **adj.** of or relating to Thailand, its people, or their language. ▶ **n.** (pl. same or **Thais**) **1** a native or national of Thailand. ■ a member of the largest ethnic group in Thailand. ■ a person of Thai descent. **2** the Tai language that is the official language of Thailand. [Thai, lit. 'free.']

Thai·land /ˈtīˌland/ a country in Southeast Asia. *See box on next page.* Former name (until 1939) SIAM.

Thai·land, Gulf of an inlet of the South China Sea between the Malay Peninsula on the west and Thailand and Cambodia on the east. Formerly called Gulf of Siam.

Thai stick ▶ **n.** strong cannabis in leaf form, twisted into a small, tightly packed cylinder ready for smoking.

thal·a·mus /ˈTHaləməs/ ▶ **n.** (pl. **-mi** /-ˌmī/) Anat. either of two masses of gray matter lying between the cerebral hemispheres on either side of the third ventricle, relaying sensory information and acting as a center for pain perception. — **tha·lam·ic** /THəˈlamik/ **adj.** [17th C.: via L. from Gk. *thalamos.*]

thal·as·se·mi·a /ˌTHaləˈsēmēə/ (Brit. **thal·as·sae·mi·a**) ▶ **n.** Med. any of a group of hereditary hemolytic diseases caused by faulty hemoglobin synthesis, widespread in Mediterranean, African, and Asian countries. [1930s: from Gk. *thalassa* 'sea.']

tha·las·sic /THəˈlasik/ ▶ **adj.** literary or tech. of or relating to the sea. [19th C.: from Fr. *thalassique,* from Gk. *thalassa* 'sea.']

tha·las·so·ther·a·py /THəˌlasōˈTHerəpē; ˌTHalasō-/ ▶ **n.** the use of seawater in cosmetic and health treatment. [19th C.: from Gk. *thalassa* 'sea' + THERAPY.]

tha·ler /ˈtälər/ ▶ **n.** hist. a German silver coin. [Ger., earlier form of *Taler* (see DOLLAR).]

Tha·les /ˈTHālēz/ (*c.*624–*c.*545 BC), Greek philosopher, mathematician, and astronomer. Judged by Aristotle to be the founder of physical science, he is also credited with founding geometry. He proposed that water was the primary substance from which all things were derived.

Tha·li·a /ˈTHālēə/ **1** Greek & Rom. Mythol. the Muse of comedy. **2** Gk. Mythol. one of the Graces.

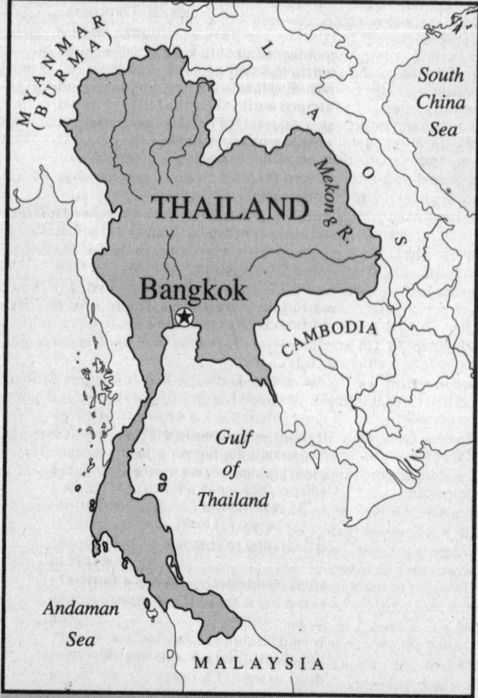

Thailand

Official name: Kingdom of Thailand
Location: Southeast Asia, on the Gulf of Thailand, west of Laos
Area: 198,500 square miles (514,000 sq km)
Population: 64,865,000
Capital: Bangkok
Languages: Thai (official), English, ethnic and regional dialects
Currency: baht

tha·lid·o·mide /THəˈlidə,mīd/ ▶ **n.** a drug formerly used as a sedative, but withdrawn in the early 1960s after it was found to cause congenital malformation or absence of limbs in children whose mothers took the drug during early pregnancy. It has more recently been used in the treatment of certain diseases, including cancer. [1950s: from *(ph)thal(ic acid)* + *(im)ido* + *(i)mide*.]

thal·li /ˈTHalī/ plural form of THALLUS.

thal·li·um /ˈTHalēəm/ ▶ **n.** the chemical element of atomic number 81, a soft silvery-white metal that occurs naturally in small amounts in iron pyrites, sphalerite, and other ores. Its compounds are very poisonous. (Symbol: **Tl**) [19th C.: mod. L., from Gk. *thallos* 'green shoot.']

thal·lo·phyte /ˈTHalə,fīt/ ▶ **n.** Bot. a plant that consists of a thallus. — **thal·lo·phyt·ic** /-ˈfitik/ **adj.** [19th C.: from mod. L. *Thallophyta*, from Gk. *thallos* (see THALLUS).]

thal·lus /ˈTHaləs/ ▶ **n.** (pl. **thal·li** /ˈTHalī/) Bot. a plant body that is not differentiated into stem and leaves and lacks true roots and a vascular system. Thalli are typical of algae, fungi, lichens, and some liverworts. — **thal·loid adj.** [19th C.: from Gk. *thallos* 'green shoot,' from *thallein* 'to bloom.']

thal·weg /ˈtäl,veg/ ▶ **n.** Geol. a line connecting the lowest points of successive cross-sections along the course of a valley or river. [19th C.: from Ger., from obs. *Thal* 'valley, dale' + *Weg* 'way.']

Thames 1 /temz/ a river that flows for 160 miles (260 km) across southern Ontario in Canada. **2** /temz/ a river in southern England that flows 210 miles (338 km) from the Cotswolds to the North Sea. **3** /THāmz; tāmz; temz/ a river in southeastern Connecticut that flows to Long Island Sound.

Tham·muz /ˈtämo͝oz; täˈmo͞oz/ (also **Tam·muz** pronunc. same) ▶ **n.** (in the Jewish calendar) the tenth month of the civil and fourth of the religious year, usually coinciding with parts of June and July. [from Heb. *tammūz*.]

than /T͟Han; T͟Hən/ ▶ **conj. & prep. 1** introducing the second element in a comparison: [as prep.] *he was smaller than his son* | [as conj.] *Jack knows more than I do.* **2** used in expressions introducing an exception or contrast: [as prep.] *he claims not to own anything* ***other than*** *his home* | [as conj.] *they observe* ***rather than*** *act.* **3** [conj.] used in expressions indicating one thing happening immediately after another: ***scarcely*** *was the work completed* ***than*** *it was abandoned.* [OE *than(ne), thon(ne), thænne*, orig. the same word as THEN.]

than·age /ˈTHānij/ ▶ **n.** hist. the tenure, land, and rank granted to a thane.

than·a·tol·o·gy /,THanəˈtäləjē/ ▶ **n.** the scientific study of death and the practices associated with it, including the study of the needs of the terminally ill and their families. — **than·a·to·log·i·cal** /-ətəˈläjikəl/ **adj.** **than·a·tol·o·gist n.** [19th C.: from Gk. *thanatos* 'death' + -LOGY.]

Than·a·tos /ˈTHanə,tōs; -,täs/ (in Freudian theory) the death instinct. Often contrasted with EROS. [from Gk. *thanatos* 'death.']

thane /THān/ ▶ **n.** hist. (in Anglo-Saxon England) a man who held land granted by the king or by a military nobleman, ranking between an ordinary freeman and a hereditary noble. ■ (in Scotland) a man, often the chief of a clan, who held land from a Scottish king and ranked with an earl's son. — **thane·dom** /-dəm/ **n.** [OE *theg(e)n* 'servant, soldier,' of Gmc. origin; rel. to Ger. *Degen* 'warrior,' from an Indo-Eur. root shared by Gk. *teknon* 'child,' *tokeus* 'parent.']

thang /THaNG/ ▶ **n.** informal nonstandard spelling of THING representing Southern US pronunciation, and typically used to denote a feeling or tendency: *I'm doing the wild thang now.*

thank /THaNGk/ ▶ **v.** [trans.] express gratitude to (someone), esp. by saying "Thank you": *Mac* ***thanked*** *her* ***for*** *the meal and left.* ■ used ironically to assign blame or responsibility for something: *you have yourself to thank for this mess.*

– PHRASES **I will thank you to do something** used to make a request or command and implying a reproach or annoyance: *I'll thank you not to interrupt me again.* **thank goodness** (or **God** or **heavens**) an expression of relief: *thank goodness no one was badly injured.* **thank one's lucky stars** feel grateful for one's good fortune. [OE *thancian*, of Gmc. origin; rel. to Ger. *danken*.]

thank·ful /ˈTHaNGkfəl/ ▶ **adj.** pleased and relieved: [with clause] *they were thankful that the war was finally over* | [with infin.] *I was very thankful to be alive.* ■ expressing gratitude and relief: *a thankful prayer.* — **thank·ful·ness n.**

thank·ful·ly /ˈTHaNGkfəlē/ ▶ **adv.** in a thankful manner: *she thankfully accepted the armchair she was offered.* ■ [sentence adverb] used to express pleasure or relief at the situation or outcome that one is reporting; fortunately: *thankfully, everything went smoothly.*

thank·less /ˈTHaNGklis/ ▶ **adj.** (of a job or task) difficult or unpleasant and not likely to bring one pleasure or the appreciation of others. ■ (of a person) not expressing or feeling gratitude. — **thank·less·ly adv.** **thank·less·ness n.**

thank-of·fer·ing ▶ **n.** an offering made as an act of thanksgiving.

thanks /THaNGks/ ▶ **plural n.** an expression of gratitude: *we give thanks for the harvest* | *a letter of thanks.* ■ a feeling of gratitude: *they expressed their thanks and wished her well.* ■ another way of saying THANK YOU: *thanks for being so helpful* | *many thanks.*

– PHRASES **no thanks to** used to imply that someone has failed to contribute to, or has hindered, a successful outcome: *we've won, but no thanks to you.* **thanks a million** informal thank you very much. **thanks to** as a result of; due to: *it's thanks to you that he's in this mess.* [OE *thancas*, pl. of *thanc* '(kindly) thought, gratitude,' of Gmc. origin; rel. to Du. *dank* and Ger. *Dank*, also to THINK.]

thanks·giv·ing /,THaNGksˈgiviNG; ˈTHaNGks-/ ▶ **n. 1** the expression of gratitude, esp. to God: *he offered prayers* ***in thanksgiving for*** *his safe arrival.* **2** (**Thanksgiving** or **Thanksgiving Day**) a US holiday held on the fourth Thursday in November, commemorating a harvest festival celebrated by the Pilgrims in 1621. A similar holiday is held in Canada, usually on the second Monday in October.

thank you ▶ **exclam.** a polite expression used when acknowledging a gift, service, or compliment, or accepting or refusing an offer: *thank you for your letter* | *no thank you, I don't believe I will.* ▶ **n.** an instance or means of expressing thanks: *the party was a thank you to the nurses* | [as adj.] *a thank-you note.*

Thant /THänt; THant/, U (1909–74), Burmese statesman. He served as UN secretary-general 1961–71.

Thar Des·ert /tär/ a desert region in northwestern India and southeastern Pakistan. Also called GREAT INDIAN DESERT.

Tharp /THärp/, Twyla (1941–), US dancer and choreographer. She directed a modern dance troupe 1965–88 and choreographed dances for several movies, including *Hair* (1979), and *Amadeus* (1984).

that /T͟Hat; T͟Hət/ ▶ **pron.** (pl. **those** /T͟Hōz/) **1** used to identify a specific person or thing observed by the speaker: *that's his wife over there.* ■ referring to the more distant of two things near to the speaker (the other, if specified, being identified by "this"): *this is stronger than that.* **2** referring to a specific thing previously mentioned, known, or understood: *that's my idea* | *what about that?* **3** [often with clause] used in singling out someone or something and ascribing a distinctive feature to them: *attracted to* ***that which*** *is aesthetically pleasing* | *her appearance* ***was that of*** *a man.* **4** (pl. **that**) [relative pron.] used to introduce a defining or restrictive clause, esp. one essential to identification: ■ instead of "which," "who," or "whom": *the book that I've just written.* ■ instead of "when" after an expression of time: *the year that Anna was born.* ▶ **adj.** (pl. **those**) **1** used to identify a specific person or thing observed or heard by the speaker: *look at that man.* ■ referring to the more distant of two things near to the speaker (the other, if specified, being identified by "this"). **2** referring to a specific thing previously mentioned, known, or understood: *he lived in Mysore at that time.* **3** [usu. with clause] used in singling out someone or something and ascribing a distinctive feature to them: *I envy those who make their own bread.* **4** referring to a specific person or thing assumed as understood or familiar to the person being addressed: *where is that son of yours?* | *Dad got that look.* ▶**adv.** [as submodifier] to such a degree; so: *I would not go that far.* ■ used with a gesture to indicate size: *it was that big.* ■ [with negative] informal very: *he wasn't that far away.* ▶**conj. 1** introducing a subordinate clause expressing a statement or hypothesis: *she said that she was satisfied.* ■ expressing a reason or cause: *he seemed pleased that I wanted to continue.* ■ expressing a result: *she was* **so** *tired* **that** *she couldn't think.* ■ [usu. with modal] expressing a purpose, hope, or intention: *we pray that the coming year may be a year of peace.* **2** [usu. with modal] literary expressing a wish or regret: *oh that he could be restored to health.*

– PHRASES **and all that** informal and that sort of thing; and so on: *other people depend on them for food and all that.* **at that** see AT[1]. **like that 1** of that nature or in that manner: *don't talk like that.* **2** informal with no preparation or introduction; instantly or effortlessly: *he can't just leave like that.* **not all that —** not very —: *it was not all that long ago.* **that is** (or **that is to say**) a formula introducing or following an explanation or further clarification of a preceding word or words: *androcentric—that is to say, male-dominated—concepts.* **that said** even so (introducing a concessive statement): *It's just a gimmick. That said, I'd love to do it.* **that's it** see IT. **that's that** there is nothing more to do or say about the matter. **that will do** no more is needed or desirable. [OE *thæt*, nominative and accusative sing. neut. of *se* 'the,' of Gmc. origin; rel. to Du. *dat* and Ger. *das*.]

that·a·way /'THatə,wā/ ▶**adv.** informal **1** in that direction. **2** in that way; like that.

thatch /THACH/ ▶**n.** a roof covering of straw, reeds, palm leaves, or a similar material. ■ straw or a similar material used for such a covering. ■ informal the hair on a person's head, esp. if thick or unruly. ■ a matted layer of dead stalks, moss, and other material in a lawn. ▶**v.** [trans.] cover (a roof or a building) with straw or a similar material: [as adj.] **(thatched)** *thatched cottages* — **thatch·er n.** [OE *theccan* 'cover,' of Gmc. origin; rel. to Du. *dekken* and Ger. *decken*.]

Thatch·er /'THACHər/, Margaret Hilda, Baroness Thatcher of Kesteven (1925–), prime minister of Britain 1979–90. — **Thatch·er·ism n. Thatch·er·ite** /-ə,rīt/ **n. & adj.**

thau·ma·tin /'THômə,tēn; -mətn/ ▶**n.** a sweet-tasting protein isolated from a West African fruit, used as a sweetener in food. [1970s: *thaumat-* from mod. L. *Thaumatococcus daniellii*, from Gk. *thauma, thaumat-* 'marvel' + -IN[1].]

thau·ma·turge /'THômə,tərj/ ▶**n.** a worker of wonders and performer of miracles; a magician. — **thau·ma·tur·gic** /,THômə'tərjik/ **adj. thau·ma·tur·gi·cal** /,THômə'tərjikəl/ **adj. thau·ma·tur·gist n. thau·ma·tur·gy n.** [18th C. (as *thaumaturg*): via med. L. from Gk. *thaumatourgos*, from *thauma* 'marvel' + *-ergos* '-working.']

thaw /THô/ ▶**v.** [intrans.] (of ice, snow, or another frozen substance, such as food) become liquid or soft as a result of warming: *the river thawed* | [as n.] **(thawing)** *catastrophic floods caused by thawing.* ■ **(it thaws, it is thawing**, etc.) the weather becomes warmer and melts snow and ice. ■ [trans.] make (something) warm enough to become liquid or soft: *exporters thawed their beef before unloading.* ■ (of a part of the body) become warm enough to stop feeling numb: *Ryan felt his toes thaw out.* ■ become friendlier or more cordial: *she* **thawed out** *sufficiently to allow a smile to appear.* ■ [trans.] make friendlier or more cordial: *the cast thawed the audience.* ▶**n.** a period of warmer weather that thaws ice and snow: *the thaw came yesterday afternoon.* ■ an increase in friendliness or cordiality: *a thaw in relations between the USA and Iran.* [OE *thawian* (v.), of West Gmc. origin; rel. to Du. *dooien*.]

Th.B. ▶**abbr.** Bachelor of Theology. [mod. L. *Theologicae Baccalaureus*.]

THC ▶**abbr.** tetrahydrocannabinol.

Th.D. ▶**abbr.** Doctor of Theology. [mod. L. *Theologicae Doctor*.]

the /THē; THə/ [called the definite article] ▶**adj. 1** denoting one or more people or things already mentioned or assumed to be common knowledge: *what's the matter?* | *call the doctor* | *the phone rang.* Compare with A. ■ used to refer to a person, place, or thing that is unique: *the Queen* | *the Mona Lisa* | *the Nile.* ■ informal denoting a disease or affliction: *I've got the flu.* ■ (with a unit of time) the present; the current: *dish of the day* | *man of the moment.* ■ informal used instead of a possessive to refer to someone with whom the speaker or person addressed is associated: *I'm meeting the boss* | *how's the family?* ■ used with a surname to refer to a family or married couple: *the Johnsons were not wealthy.* ■ used before the surname of the chief of a Scottish or Irish clan: *the O'Donoghue.* **2** used to point forward to a following qualifying or defining clause or phrase: *the fuss that he made of her.* ■ (chiefly with rulers and family members with the same name) used after a name to qualify it: *George the Sixth* | *Jack the Ripper.* **3** used to make a generalized reference to something rather than identifying a particular instance: *he taught himself to play the violin* | *worry about the future.* ■ used with a singular noun to indicate that it represents a whole species or class: *the African elephant is endangered.* ■ used with an adjective to refer to those people who are of the type described: *the unemployed.* ■ used with an adjective to refer to something of the class or quality described: *trying to accomplish the impossible.* ■ used with the name of a unit to state a rate: *120 miles* **to the** *gallon.* **4** enough of (a particular thing): *he hoped to publish monthly, if only he could find the money.* **5** (pronounced stressing "the") used to indicate that someone or something is the best known or most important of that name or type: *he was* **the** *hot prospect.* **6** used adverbially with comparatives to indicate how one amount or degree of something varies in relation to another: **the** *more you give,* **the** *more you get.* ■ (usu. **all the —**) used to emphasize the amount or degree to which something is affected: *commodities made all the more desirable by their rarity.* [OE *se, sēo, thæt*, ult. superseded by forms from Northumbrian and North Mercian *thē*, of Gmc. origin; rel. to Du. *de, dat*, and Ger. *der, die, das*.]

the·an·throp·ic /,THēən'THräpik/ ▶**adj.** embodying deity in a human form; both divine and human. [17th C.: from eccles. Gk. *theanthrōpos* 'god-man' (from *theos* 'god' + *anthrōpos* 'human being') + -IC.]

the·ar·chy /'THē,ärkē/ ▶**n.** (pl. **-chies**) archaic rule by a god or gods. [17th C.: from eccles. Gk. *thearkhia* 'godhead,' from *theos* 'god' + *arkhein* 'to rule.']

theat. ▶**abbr.** ■ theater. ■ theatrical.

the·a·ter /'THēətər/ (also **the·a·tre**) ▶**n.** a building or outdoor area in which plays and other dramatic performances are given. ■ (often **the theater**) the activity or profession of acting in, producing, directing, or writing plays: *what made you go into theater?* ■ a play or other activity or presentation considered in terms of its dramatic quality: *this is intense theater.* ■ a movie theater. ■ a room or hall for lectures, etc., with seats in tiers. ■ the area in which something happens: *a new theater of war.* ■ [as adj.] denoting weapons for use in a particular region between tactical and strategic: *theater defense missiles.* [ME, from OFr. *theatre*, or from L. *theatrum*, from Gk. *theatron*, from *theasthai* 'behold.']

the·a·ter-in-the-round ▶**n.** a form of theatrical presentation in which the audience is seated in a circle around the stage or on at least three of its sides.

The·a·ter of the Ab·surd ▶**n.** **(the Theater of the Absurd)** drama using the abandonment of conventional dramatic form to portray the futility of human struggle in a senseless world.

the·at·ric /THē'atrik/ ▶**adj.** another term for THEATRICAL.

the·at·ri·cal /THē'atrikəl/ ▶**adj.** of, for, or relating to acting, actors, or the theater: *theatrical productions.* ■ exaggerated and excessively dramatic: *Henry looked over his shoulder with theatrical caution.* — **the·at·ri·cal·ism n. the·at·ri·cal·i·ty** /-,atri'kalitē/ **n. the·at·ri·cal·i·za·tion** /-,atrikəli'zāSHən/ **n. the·at·ri·cal·ize v. the·at·ri·cal·ly adv.**

the·at·ri·cals /THē'atrikəlz/ ▶**plural n.** dramatic performances: *amateur theatricals.*

the·at·rics /THē'atriks/ ▶**plural n.** excessively emotional and dramatic behavior: *stop your theatrics.* ■ another term for THEATRICALS.

the·be /'tebe/ ▶**n.** (pl. same) a monetary unit of Botswana, equal to one hundredth of a pula. [Setswana, lit. 'shield.']

Thebes /THēbz/ **1** the Greek name for an ancient city in Upper Egypt. It is the site of the major temples of Luxor and Karnak. **2** a city in Greece. A major military power, it was destroyed by Alexander the Great in 336 BC. Greek name **THÍVAI**. — **The·ban** /'THēbən/ **adj. & n.**

the·ca /'THēkə/ ▶**n.** (pl. **the·cae** /'THēsē/) a receptacle, sheath, or cell enclosing an organ, part, or structure, in particular: ■ Anat. the loose sheath enclosing the spinal cord. ■ Zool. a cuplike or tubular structure containing a coral polyp. ■ Bot. either of the lobes of an anther, each containing two pollen sacs. ■ (also **the·ca fol·lic·u·li** /fə'likyə,lī/) Anat. the outer layer of cells of a Graafian follicle. — **the·cal adj. the·cate** /-kāt/ **adj.** [17th C.: via L. from Gk. *thēkē* 'case.']

the·co·dont /'THēkə,dänt/ ▶**n.** a fossil quadrupedal or partly bipedal reptile (order Thecodontia, subdivision Archosauria) of the Triassic period, having teeth fixed in sockets in the jaw. Thecodonts are ancestral to the dinosaurs and other archosaurs. [19th C.: from mod. L. *Thecodontia*, from Gk. *thēkē* 'case' + *odous, odont-* 'tooth.']

thee /THē/ ▶**pron.** [second person sing.] archaic or dialect form of YOU, as the singular object of a verb or preposition: *we beseech thee O lord.* Compare with THOU[1]. [OE *thē*, accusative and dative case of *thū* 'thou.']

theft /THeft/ ▶**n.** the action or crime of stealing: *he was convicted of theft* | *the latest theft happened at a garage.* [OE *thīefth, thēofth*, of Gmc. origin; rel. to THIEF.]

thegn /THān/ ▶**n.** hist. an English thane. [19th C.: from OE *theg(e)n*.]

the·ine /'THē-ēn; -in/ ▶**n.** caffeine, esp. when it occurs in tea. [19th C.: from mod. L. *Thea*, from Du. *thee*) + -INE[4].]

their /THe(ə)r/ ▶**possessive adj. 1** belonging to or associated with the people or things previously mentioned or easily identified: *her taunts had lost their power to touch him.* ■ belonging to or associated with a person of unspecified sex: *she heard someone blow their nose loudly.* **2 (Their)** used in titles: *a double portrait of Their Majesties.* [ME: from ON *their(r)a* 'of them,' genitive pl. of the demonstrative *sá*; rel. to THEM and THEY.]

theirs /THe(ə)rz/ ▶**possessive pron.** used to refer to a thing or things belonging to or associated with two or more people or things previously mentioned: *they think everything is theirs* | *a favorite game of theirs.* [ME: from THEIR + -'S[1].]

their·selves /THe(ə)r'selvz/ ▶**pron.** [third person pl.] dialect form of THEMSELVES.

the·ism /'THēizəm/ ▶**n.** belief in the existence of a god or gods, esp. belief in one god as creator of the universe, intervening in it and sustaining a personal relation to his creatures. Compare with DEISM. — **the·ist n. the·is·tic** /THē'istik/ **adj.** [17th C.: from Gk. *theos* 'god' + -ISM.]

The·lon River /ˈTHēlän/ a river in the Northwest Territories in Canada that flows to Hudson Bay.

them /THem; THəm/ ▶ **pron.** [third person pl.] **1** used as the object of a verb or preposition to refer to two or more people or things previously mentioned or easily identified: *I bathed the kids and read them stories* | *rows of doors, most of* **them** *locked.* Compare with THEY. ■ used after the verb "to be" and after "than" or "as": *you think that's them?* | *we're better than them.* ■ [sing.] referring to a person of unspecified sex: *how well do you have to know someone before you call them?* **2** archaic themselves. ▶ **adj.** informal dialect those: *look at them eyes.* [ME: from ON *theim* 'to those, to them,' dative pl. of *sá*; rel. to THEIR and THEM.]

the·mat·ic /THiˈmatik/ ▶ **adj.** **1** having or relating to subjects or a particular subject: *the orientation of this anthology is essentially thematic.* ■ Ling. belonging to, relating to, or denoting the theme of a sentence. ■ Music of, relating to, or containing melodic subjects: *the repetition of thematic fragments.* ■ Philately British term for TOPICAL. **2** Ling. of or relating to the theme of an inflected word. ■ (of a vowel) connecting the theme of a word to its inflections. ■ (of a word) having a vowel connecting its theme to its inflections. ▶ **n.** **1** (**thematics**) [treated as sing. or pl.] a body of topics for study or discussion. **2** Philately British term for TOPICAL. — **the·mat·i·cal·ly** adv. [17th C.: from Gk. *thematikos*, from *thema* (see THEME).]

The·mat·ic Ap·per·cep·tion Test ▶ **n.** Psychol. a projective test designed to reveal a person's social drives or needs by their interpretation of a series of pictures of emotionally ambiguous situations.

the·ma·tize /ˈTHēməˌtīz/ ▶ **v.** [trans.] present or select (a subject) as a theme. ■ Ling. place (a word or phrase) at the start of a sentence in order to focus attention on it. — **the·mat·i·za·tion** /ˌTHēmətiˈzāSHən/ **n.**

theme /THēm/ ▶ **n.** **1** the subject of a talk, a piece of writing, a person's thoughts, or an exhibition; a topic: *the theme of the sermon was reverence.* ■ Ling. the first major constituent of a clause, indicating the subject-matter, typically being the subject but optionally other constituents, as in "*poor* he is not." ■ an idea that recurs in or pervades a work of art or literature. ■ Music a prominent or frequently recurring melody or group of notes in a composition. ■ [as adj.] (of music) frequently recurring in or accompanying the beginning and end of a film, play, or musical: *a theme song.* ■ a setting or ambience given to a leisure venue or activity: *a family fun park with a western theme.* ■ [as adj.] denoting a restaurant or bar in which the decor and the food and drink served are intended to suggest a particular foreign country, historical period, or other ambience: *a New Deal theme restaurant.* ■ an essay written by a student on an assigned subject. **2** Ling. the stem of a noun or verb; the part to which inflections are added, esp. one composed of the root and an added vowel. **3** hist. any of the twenty-nine provinces in the Byzantine empire. ▶ **v.** [trans.] give a particular setting or ambience to (a venue or activity): [as adj.] (**themed**) *themed menus.* [ME: via OFr. from L. *thema*, from Gk., lit. 'proposition'; rel. to *tithenai* 'to set or place.']

theme park ▶ **n.** an amusement park with a unifying setting or idea.

The·mis /ˈTHēmis/ Gk. Mythol. a goddess, daughter of Uranus (Heaven) and Gaia (Earth). In Homer she was the personification of order and justice, who convened the assembly of the gods.

The·mis·to·cles /THəˈmistəˌklēz/ (*c.*528–462 BC), Athenian statesman. He helped build up the Athenian fleet and defeated the Persian fleet at Salamis in 480.

them·self /THəmˈself; THem-/ ▶ **pron.** [third person sing.] used instead of "himself" or "herself" to refer to a person of unspecified sex: *the casual observer might easily think themself back in 1945.*

them·selves /THəmˈselvz; THem-/ ▶ **pron.** [third person pl.] **1** [reflexive] used as the object of a verb or preposition to refer to a group of people or things previously mentioned as the subject of the clause: *countries unable to look after themselves.* **2** [emphatic] used to emphasize a particular group of people or things mentioned: *excellent at organizing others, they may well be disorganized themselves.* **3** [sing.] used instead of "himself" or "herself" to refer to a person of unspecified sex: *anyone who fancies themselves as a racing driver.*

– PHRASES (**not**) **be themselves** see BE ONESELF, NOT BE ONESELF at BE. **by themselves** see BY ONESELF at BY.

then /THen/ ▶ **adv.** **1** at that time; at the time in question: *I was living in Cairo then* | [after prep.] *by then I was exhausted* | [as adj.] *Adams, the then president.* **2** after that; next; afterward: *she won the first and then the second game.* ■ also; in addition: *the job is fun, and then there's the money.* **3** in that case; therefore: *well, that's okay then.* ■ used at the end of a sentence to emphasize an inference being drawn: *so you're still here, then.* ■ used to finish off a conversation: *see you in an hour, then.*

– PHRASES **but then** (**again**) after all; on the other hand (introducing a contrasting comment): *it couldn't help, but then again, it probably couldn't hurt.* **then and there** immediately: *she made up her mind then and there.* [OE *thænne, thanne, thonne*, of Gmc. origin; rel. to Du. *dan* and Ger. *dann*, also to THAT and THE.]

the·nar /ˈTHēnär/ Anat. ▶ **adj.** of or relating to the rounded fleshy part of the hand at the base of the thumb (the ball of the thumb). ▶ **n.** this part of the hand. [17th C.: from Gk., 'palm of the hand, sole of the foot.']

the·nard·ite /THəˈnärdīt; tə-/ ▶ **n.** a white to brownish translucent crystalline mineral occurring in evaporated salt lakes, consisting of anhydrous sodium sulfate. [19th C.: Baron Louis-Jacques *Thénard* (1777–1857), French chemist, + -ITE[1].]

thence /THens/ (also **from thence**) ▶ **adv.** formal from a place or source previously mentioned: *they intended to cycle on into France and thence home via Belgium.* ■ as a consequence: *we believed, and thence we prayed.* ■ from that time: *four months thence I stood there again.* [ME *thennes*, from earlier *thenne* (from OE *thanon*, of West Gmc. origin) + -s[3].]

thence·forth /ˌTHensˈfôrTH/ (also **from thence·forth**) ▶ **adv.** archaic, literary from that time, place, or point onward: *thenceforth he made his life in England.*

thence·for·ward /ˌTHensˈfôrwərd/ ▶ **adv.** another term for THENCEFORTH.

theo- ▶ **comb. form** relating to God or deities: *theocentric* | *theocracy.* [from Gk. *theos* 'god.']

the·o·bro·mine /ˌTHēəˈbrōmēn; -min/ ▶ **n.** Chem. a bitter, volatile compound, $C_7H_8N_4O_2$, obtained from cacao seeds. It is an alkaloid resembling caffeine in its physiological effects. [19th C.: from mod. L. *Theobroma* (genus name, from Gk. *theos* 'god' and *brōma* 'food') + -INE[4].]

the·o·cen·tric /ˌTHēōˈsentrik/ ▶ **adj.** having God as a central focus: *a theocentric civilization.*

the·oc·ra·cy /THēˈäkrəsē/ ▶ **n.** (pl. **-cies**) a system of government in which priests rule in the name of God or a god. — **the·o·crat** /ˈTHēəˌkrat/ **n.** **the·o·crat·ic** /ˌTHēəˈkratik/ **adj.** **the·o·crat·i·cal·ly** /ˌTHēəˈkratik(ə)lē/ **adv.** [17th C.: from Gk. *theokratia* (see THEO-, -CRACY).]

The·oc·ri·tus /THēˈäkritəs/ (*c.*310–*c.*250 BC), Greek poet; born in Sicily. He is chiefly known for *Idylls*.

the·od·i·cy /THēˈädəsē/ ▶ **n.** (pl. **-cies**) the vindication of divine goodness and providence in view of the existence of evil. — **the·od·i·ce·an** /-ˌädəˈsēən/ **adj.** [18th C.: from Fr. *Théodicée*, from Gk. *theos* 'god' + *dikē* 'justice.']

the·od·o·lite /THēˈädəˌlīt/ ▶ **n.** a surveying instrument with a rotating telescope for measuring horizontal and vertical angles. — **the·od·o·lit·ic** /-ˌädəˈlitik/ **adj.** [16th C.: from mod. L. *theodelitus*.]

The·o·do·ra /ˌTHēəˈdôrə/ (*c.*500–548), Byzantine empress; wife of Justinian.

The·o·dore Roo·se·velt National Park /ˈTHēəˌdôr/ a preserve in western North Dakota that incorporates Roosevelt's ranch home.

The·od·o·ric /THēˈädərik/ (*c.*454–526), king of the Ostrogoths 471–526; known as **Theodoric the Great**.

The·o·do·si·us I /ˌTHēəˈdōSH(ē)əs/ (*c.*346–395), Roman emperor 379–395; full name *Flavius Theodosius*; known as **Theodosius the Great**.

the·og·o·ny /THēˈägənē/ ▶ **n.** (pl. **-nies**) the genealogy of a group or system of gods. [17th C.: from Gk. *theogonia*, from *theos* 'god' + *-gonia* '-begetting.']

theol. ▶ **abbr.** ■ theologian. ■ theological. ■ theology.

the·o·lo·gian /ˌTHēəˈlōjən/ ▶ **n.** a person who engages or is an expert in theology. [15th C.: from Fr. *théologien*, from *théologie* or L. *theologia* (see THEOLOGY).]

the·o·log·i·cal /ˌTHēəˈläjikəl/ ▶ **adj.** of or relating to the study of theology. — **the·o·log·i·cal·ly** **adv.** [sentence adverb].

the·o·log·i·cal vir·tue ▶ **n.** each of the three virtues of faith, hope, and charity as defined by St. Paul. Often contrasted with CARDINAL VIRTUE.

the·ol·o·gize /THēˈäləˌjīz/ ▶ **v.** **1** [intrans.] engage in theological reasoning or speculation. **2** [trans.] treat (a person or subject) in theological terms: *he even theologizes writing problems.*

the·ol·o·gy /THēˈäləjē/ ▶ **n.** (pl. **-gies**) the study of the nature of God and religious belief. ■ religious beliefs and theory when systematically developed: *Christian theology.* — **the·ol·o·gist** **n.** [ME: from Fr. *théologie*, from L. *theologia*, from Gk., from *theos* 'god' + *-logia* (see -LOGY).]

the·om·a·chy /THēˈäməkē/ ▶ **n.** (pl. **-chies**) a war or struggle against God or among or against the gods. [16th C.: from Gk. *theomakhia*, from *theos* 'god' + *-makhia* 'fighting.']

the·oph·a·ny /THēˈäfənē/ ▶ **n.** (pl. **-nies**) a visible manifestation to humankind of God or a god. [OE, via eccles. L. from Gk. *theophaneia*, from *theos* 'god' + *phainein* 'to show.']

the·o·phor·ic /THēəˈfôrik/ (also **the·o·phor·ous** /THēəˈfôrəs/) ▶ **adj.** bearing the name of a god.

The·o·phras·tus /ˌTHēəˈfrastəs/ (*c.*370–*c.*287 BC), Greek philosopher and scientist. He was a pupil and successor of Aristotle.

the·o·phyl·line /THēˈäfəlin; ˌTHēəˈfilēn/ ▶ **n.** Chem. a bitter crystalline compound present in small quantities in tea leaves, isomeric with theobromine. [19th C.: from mod. L. *Thea* (former genus name of the tea plant, from Du. *thee*) + Gk. *phullon* 'leaf' + -INE[4].]

the·or·bo /THēˈôrbō/ ▶ **n.** (pl. **-bos**) a large lute with the neck extended to carry several long bass strings, used for accompaniment in 17th- and early 18th-century music. [17th C.: from Ital. *tiorba*, of unknown origin.]

the·o·rem /ˈTHēərəm; ˈTHi(ə)r-/ ▶ **n.** Physics Math. a general proposition not self-evident but proved by a chain of reasoning; a truth established by means of accepted truths. ■ a rule in algebra or other branches of mathematics expressed by symbols or formulae. — **the·o·re·mat·ic** /ˌTHēərəˈmatik; ˌTHi(ə)rə-/ **adj.** [16th C.: from Fr. *théorème*, or via late L. from Gk. *theōrēma* 'speculation, proposition,' from *theōrein* 'look at,' from *theōros* 'spectator.']

the·o·ret·ic /THēəˈretik/ ▶ **adj.** another term for THEORETICAL. [17th C. (in the sense 'conjectural'): via late L. from Gk. *theōrētikos*, from *theōrētos* 'that may be seen,' from *theōrein* (see THEOREM).]

the·o·ret·i·cal /THēəˈretikəl/ ▶ **adj.** concerned with or involving the theory of a subject or area of study rather than its practical application: *a theoretical physicist.* ■ based on or calculated through theory rather than experience or practice: *a theoretical reformer of opinions.*

— **the·o·ret·i·cal·ly** adv. [sentence adverb] *theoretically we might expect this to be true.*

the·o·re·ti·cian /ˌᴛʜēərəˈtisʜən; ˌᴛʜi(ə)rə-/ ▶ n. a person who forms, develops, or studies the theoretical framework of a subject.

the·o·rist /ˈᴛʜēərist; ˈᴛʜi(ə)r-/ ▶ n. a person concerned with the theoretical aspects of a subject; a theoretician.

the·o·rize /ˈᴛʜēəˌrīz; ˈᴛʜi(ə)rˌīz/ ▶ v. [intrans.] form a theory or set of theories about something: [as n.] (**theorizing**) *they are more interested in political theorizing.* ■ [trans.] create a theoretical premise or framework for (something): *live feminism, don't theorize it.* — **the·o·ri·za·tion** /ˌᴛʜēərəˈzāsʜən; ˌᴛʜi(ə)r-/ n. **the·o·riz·er** n.

the·o·ry /ˈᴛʜēərē; ˈᴛʜi(ə)rē/ ▶ n. (pl. **-ries**) a supposition or a system of ideas intended to explain something, esp. one based on general principles independent of the thing to be explained: *Darwin's theory of evolution.* ■ a set of principles on which the practice of an activity is based: *a theory of education* | *music theory.* ■ an idea used to account for a situation or justify a course of action: *my theory would be that the place has been seriously mismanaged.* ■ Math. a collection of propositions to illustrate the principles of a subject.
– PHRASES **in theory** used in describing what is supposed to happen or be possible, usually with the implication that it does not in fact happen: *in theory, things can get better; in practice, they may get worse.* [16th C.: via late L. from Gk. *theōria* 'contemplation, speculation,' from *theōros* 'spectator.']

the·o·ry-lad·en ▶ adj. denoting a term, concept, or statement that has meaning only as part of some theory, so that its use implies the acceptance of that theory.

the·o·ry of games ▶ n. another term for GAME THEORY.

the·os·o·phy /ᴛʜēˈäsəfē/ ▶ n. any of a number of philosophies maintaining that a knowledge of God may be achieved through spiritual ecstasy, direct intuition, or special individual relations. — **the·os·o·pher** n. **the·o·soph·ic** /ˌᴛʜēəˈsäfik/ adj. **the·o·soph·i·cal** /ˌᴛʜēəˈsäfikəl/ adj. **the·o·soph·i·cal·ly** /ˌᴛʜēəˈsäfik(ə)lē/ adv. **the·os·o·phist** n. [17th C.: from med. L. *theosophia*, from late Gk., from *theosophos* 'wise concerning God,' from *theos* 'god' + *sophos* 'wise.']

The·o·to·kos /ˌᴛʜēˈəˈtäkəs/ ▶ n. (**the Theotokos**) Mother of God (used in the Eastern Orthodox Church as a title of the Virgin Mary). [from eccles. Gk., from *theos* 'god' + *-tokos* 'bringing forth.']

The·ra /ˈᴛʜi(ə)rə/ a Greek island in the southern Cyclades. Remains of an ancient Minoan civilization were preserved after a violent volcanic eruption in about 1500 BC. Also called SANTORINI. Greek name THÍRA.

therap. ▶ abbr. therapeutic; therapeutics.

ther·a·peu·tic /ˌᴛʜerəˈpyo͞otik/ ▶ adj. of or relating to the healing of disease: *therapeutic facilities.* ■ administered or applied for reasons of health: *a therapeutic shampoo.* ■ having a good effect on the body or mind; contributing to a sense of well-being. — **ther·a·peu·ti·cal** adj. **ther·a·peu·ti·cal·ly** adv. **ther·a·peu·tist** n. (archaic) [17th C.: via mod. L. from Gk. *therapeutikos*, from *therapeuein* 'minister to, treat medically.']

ther·a·peu·tics /ˌᴛʜerəˈpyo͞otiks/ ▶ plural n. [treated as sing.] the branch of medicine concerned with the treatment of disease and the action of remedial agents.

ther·a·pize /ˈᴛʜerəˌpīz/ ▶ v. [trans.] subject to psychological therapy: *you don't need to therapize or fix each other.*

the·rap·sid /ᴛʜəˈrapsid/ ▶ n. an extinct reptile (order Therapsida, subclass Synapsida) of a Permian and Triassic order, the members of which are related to the ancestors of mammals. [20th C.: from mod. L. *Therapsida*, from Gk. *thēr* 'beast' + *hapsis, hapsid-* 'arch.']

ther·a·py /ˈᴛʜerəpē/ ▶ n. (pl. **-pies**) treatment intended to relieve or heal a disorder: *cancer therapies.* ■ the treatment of mental or psychological disorders by psychological means: *he is currently* ***in therapy*** | [as adj.] *therapy sessions.* — **ther·a·pist** n. [19th C.: from mod. L. *therapia*, from Gk. *therapeia* 'healing,' from *therapeuein* 'minister to, treat medically.']

Ther·a·va·da /ˌᴛʜerəˈvädə/ (also **Ther·a·va·da Bud·dhism**) ▶ n. the more conservative of the two major traditions of Buddhism (the other being Mahayana), and a school of Hinayana Buddhism. It is practiced mainly in Sri Lanka, Myanmar (Burma), Thailand, Cambodia, and Laos. [from Pali *theravāda*, lit. 'doctrine of the elders,' from *thera* 'elder, old' + *vāda* 'speech, doctrine.']

there /ᴛʜe(ə)r/ ▶ adv. **1** in, at, or to that place or position: *we stayed there eleven days* | [after prep.] *I'm going in there* | fig. *the opportunity is right there.* ■ used when pointing or gesturing to indicate the place in mind: *there on the right* | *if anyone wants out,* ***there's the door!*** ■ at that point (in speech, performance, writing, etc.): *"I'm quite—" There she stopped.* ■ in that respect; on that issue: *I don't agree with you there.* ■ [with infin.] used to indicate one's role in a particular situation: *we are there to make money.* **2** used in attracting someone's attention or calling attention to someone or something: *hello there!* **3** (usu. **there is/are**) used to indicate the fact or existence of something: *there's a restaurant around the corner.* ▶ exclam. **1** used to focus attention on something and express satisfaction or annoyance at it: *there, I told you!* **2** used to comfort someone: *there, there, don't cry.*
– PHRASES **been there, done that** informal used to express past experience of or familiarity with something, esp. something now regarded as boring or unwelcome. **be there for someone** be available to provide support or comfort for someone, esp. at a time of adversity. **have been there before** informal know all about a situation from experience. **here and there** see HERE. **not all there** (of a person) not fully alert and functioning. **so there!** informal used to express one's defiance or awareness that someone will not like what one has decided or is saying. **there and then** immediately. **there goes ——** used to express the destruction or failure of something: *there goes my career.* **there it is** that is the situation: *pretty ridiculous, I know, but there it is.* **there or thereabouts** in or very near a particular place or position. ■ approximately: *forty years, there or thereabouts, had elapsed.* **there you are** (or **go**) informal **1** this is what you wanted: *there you are—that'll be $3.80.* **2** expressing confirmation, triumph, or resignation: *sometimes it is hard, but there you go.* **there you go again** used to criticize someone for behaving in a way that is typical of them. **there you have it** used to emphasize or draw attention to a particular fact: *so there you have it—the ultimate grand unified theory.* ■ used to draw attention to the simplicity of a process or action: *simply turn the handle three times and there you have it.* [OE *thǣr, thēr*, of Gmc. origin; rel. to Du. *daar* and Ger. *da*, also to THAT and THE.]

there·a·bouts /ˈᴛʜe(ə)rəˌbouts/ (also **there·a·bout**) ▶ adv. near that place: *the land is dry in places thereabouts.* ■ used to indicate that a date or figure is approximate: *the notes were written in 1860 or thereabouts.*

there·af·ter /ˌᴛʜe(ə)rˈaftər/ ▶ adv. formal after that time: *thereafter their fortunes suffered a steep decline.*

there·at /ˌᴛʜe(ə)rˈat/ ▶ adv. archaic, formal **1** at that place. **2** on account of or after that.

there·by /ˌᴛʜe(ə)rˈbī/ ▶ adv. by that means; as a result of that: *children listen to their parents and thereby learn from them.*
– PHRASES **thereby hangs a tale** used to indicate that there is more to say about something.

there·for /ˌᴛʜe(ə)rˈfôr/ ▶ adv. archaic for that object or purpose.

there·fore /ˈᴛʜe(ə)rˌfôr/ ▶ adv. for that reason; consequently: *he was injured and therefore unable to play.*

there·from /ˌᴛʜe(ə)rˈfrəm/ ▶ adv. archaic or formal from that or that place.

there·in /ˌᴛʜe(ə)rˈin/ ▶ adv. archaic or formal in that place, document, or respect: *the facts therein contained.*

there·in·af·ter /ˌᴛʜe(ə)rinˈaftər/ ▶ adv. archaic or formal in a later part of that document.

there·in·be·fore /ˌᴛʜe(ə)rinbiˈfôr/ ▶ adv. archaic or formal in an earlier part of that document.

there·in·to /ˌᴛʜe(ə)rˈinto͞o/ ▶ adv. archaic or formal into that place.

ther·e·min /ˈᴛʜerəˌmin/ ▶ n. an electronic musical instrument in which the tone is generated by two high-frequency oscillators and the pitch controlled by the movement of the performer's hand. [20th C.: named after Lev *Theremin* (1896–1993), its Russian inventor.]

there·of /ˌᴛʜe(ə)rˈəv/ ▶ adv. formal of the thing just mentioned; of that: *the member state or a part thereof.*

there·on /ˌᴛʜe(ə)rˈän; -ˈôn/ ▶ adv. formal on or following from the thing just mentioned: *the order of the court and the taxation consequent thereon.*

there·out /ˌᴛʜe(ə)rˈout/ ▶ adv. archaic out of that; from that source.

there's /ᴛʜe(ə)rz/ ▶ contr. there is: *there's nothing there.*

The·re·sa, Moth·er see TERESA, MOTHER.

there·to /ˌᴛʜe(ə)rˈto͞o/ ▶ adv. archaic or formal to that or that place: *the third party assents thereto.*

there·to·fore /ˌᴛʜe(ə)rtəˈfôr/ ▶ adv. archaic or formal before that time.

there·un·der /ˌᴛʜe(ə)rˈəndər/ ▶ adv. archaic or formal in accordance with the thing mentioned.

there·un·to /ˌᴛʜe(ə)rˌənˈto͞o/ ▶ adv. archaic or formal to that: *his agent thereunto lawfully authorized in writing or by will.*

there·up·on /ˈᴛʜe(ə)rəˌpän/ ▶ adv. formal immediately or shortly after that: *he thereupon returned to Moscow.*

there·with /ˌᴛʜe(ə)rˈwiᴛʜ; -ˈwiᴛʜ/ ▶ adv. archaic or formal **1** with or in the thing mentioned: *documents lodged therewith.* **2** soon or immediately after that; forthwith.

there·with·al /ˈᴛʜe(ə)r-wiᴛʜˌôl; -wiᴛʜ-/ ▶ adv. archaic together with that; besides: *he was to make a voyage and his fortune therewithal.*

The·ri·a /ˈᴛʜi(ə)rēə/ Zool. a major group of mammals (subclass Theria) that comprises the marsupials and placentals. Compare with PROTOTHERIA. — **the·ri·an** n. & adj. [mod. L. (pl.), from Gk. *thēria* 'wild animals.']

the·ri·an·throp·ic /ˌᴛʜi(ə)rēanˈᴛʜräpik/ ▶ adj. (esp. of a deity) combining the form of an animal with that of a man. [19th C.: from Gk. *thērion* 'wild animal' + *anthrōpos* 'human being' + -IC.]

the·ri·o·mor·phic /ˌᴛʜi(ə)rēəˈmôrfik/ ▶ adj. (esp. of a deity) having an animal form. [19th C.: from Gk. *thērion* 'wild beast' + -MORPH + -IC.]

therm /ᴛʜərm/ ▶ n. a unit of heat equivalent to 100,000 British thermal units or 1.055 × 108 joules. [1920s: from Gk. *thermē* 'heat.']

therm. ▶ abbr. thermometer.

ther·mal /ˈᴛʜərməl/ ▶ adj. of or relating to heat. ■ another term for GEOTHERMAL. ■ (of a garment) made of a fabric that provides exceptional insulation to keep the body warm: *thermal underwear.* ▶ n. **1** an upward current of warm air, used by gliders, balloons, and birds to gain height. **2** (usu. **thermals**) a thermal garment, esp. underwear. — **ther·mal·ly** adv. [18th C. (in the sense 'relating to hot springs'): from Fr., from Gk. *thermē* 'heat.']

ther·mal ef·fi·cien·cy ▶ n. the efficiency of a heat engine measured by the ratio of the work done by it to the heat supplied to it.

ther·mal im·ag·ing ▶ n. the technique of using the heat given off by an object to produce an image of it or locate it.

ther·mal in·ver·sion ▶ n. see INVERSION (sense 2).

ther·mal·ize /ˈTHərməˌlīz/ ▶ v. attain or cause to attain thermal equilibrium with the environment. — **ther·mal·i·za·tion** /ˌTHərməliˈzāSHən/ n.

ther·mal noise ▶ n. Electron. electrical fluctuations arising from the random thermal motion of electrons.

ther·mal pa·per ▶ n. heat-sensitive paper used in thermal printers.

ther·mal print·er ▶ n. a printer in which fine heated pins form characters on heat-sensitive paper.

ther·mal re·ac·tor ▶ n. a nuclear reactor using thermal neutrons.

ther·mal spring ▶ n. a spring of naturally hot water.

ther·mal u·nit ▶ n. a unit for measuring heat.

ther·mic /ˈTHərmik/ ▶ adj. of or relating to heat. [19th C.: from Gk. *thermē* 'heat' + -IC.]

therm·i·on /ˈTHərmˌīən/ ▶ n. an ion or electron emitted by a substance at high temperature. [20th C.: from THERMO- 'of heat' + ION.]

therm·i·on·ic /ˌTHərmīˈänik/ ▶ adj. of or relating to electrons emitted from a substance at very high temperature.

therm·i·on·ic e·mis·sion ▶ n. the emission of electrons from a heated source.

therm·i·on·ics /ˌTHərmīˈäniks/ ▶ plural n. [treated as sing.] the branch of science and technology concerned with thermionic emission.

therm·i·on·ic tube ▶ n. Electron. a device giving a flow of thermionic electrons in one direction, used esp. in the rectification of a current and in radio reception.

therm·is·tor /ˈTHərmistər/ ▶ n. an electrical resistor whose resistance is greatly reduced by heating, used for measurement and control. [1940s: contr. of *thermal resistor*.]

ther·mite /ˈTHərmīt/ (also trademark **Thermit** /-mit/) ▶ n. a mixture of finely powdered aluminum and iron oxide that produces a very high temperature on combustion, used in welding and for incendiary bombs. [20th C.: coined in Ger. from THERMO- 'of heat' + -ITE¹.]

thermo- ▶ comb. form relating to heat: *thermoelectric*. [from Gk. *thermos* 'hot,' *thermē* 'heat.']

ther·mo·chem·is·try /ˌTHərmōˈkemistrē/ ▶ n. the branch of chemistry concerned with the quantities of heat evolved or absorbed during chemical reactions. — **ther·mo·chem·i·cal** /-ˈkemikəl/ adj.

ther·mo·cline /ˈTHərmōˌklīn/ ▶ n. an abrupt temperature gradient in a body of water such as a lake, marked by a layer above and below which the water is at different temperatures.

ther·mo·cou·ple /ˈTHərmōˌkəpəl/ ▶ n. a thermoelectric device for measuring temperature, consisting of two wires of different metals connected at two points, a voltage being developed between the two junctions in proportion to the temperature difference.

ther·mo·dy·nam·ics /ˌTHərmōdīˈnamiks/ ▶ plural n. [treated as sing.] the branch of physical science that deals with the relations between heat and other forms of energy (such as mechanical, electrical, or chemical energy), and, by extension, of the relationships and interconvertibility of all forms of energy. — **ther·mo·dy·nam·ic** adj. **ther·mo·dy·nam·i·cal** adj. **ther·mo·dy·nam·i·cal·ly** adv. **ther·mo·dy·nam·i·cist** /-isist/ n.

ther·mo·e·las·tic /ˌTHərmō-iˈlastik/ ▶ adj. of or relating to elasticity in connection with heat.

ther·mo·e·lec·tric /ˌTHərmō-iˈlektrik/ ▶ adj. producing electricity by a difference of temperatures. — **ther·mo·e·lec·tri·cal·ly** adv. **ther·mo·e·lec·tric·i·ty** /-ilekˈtrisitē; -ˌēlek-/ n.

ther·mo·form·ing /ˈTHərməˌfôrmiNG/ ▶ n. the process of heating a thermoplastic material and shaping it in a mold.

ther·mo·gen·e·sis /ˌTHərmōˈjenəsis/ ▶ n. the production of heat, esp. in a human or animal body. — **ther·mo·gen·ic** /-məˈjenik/ adj.

ther·mo·gram /ˈTHərməˌgram/ ▶ n. a record made by a thermograph.

ther·mo·graph /ˈTHərməˌgraf/ ▶ n. an instrument that produces a trace or image representing a record of the varying temperature or infrared radiation over an area or during a period of time.

ther·mog·ra·phy /THərˈmägrəfē/ ▶ n. **1** the use of thermograms to study heat distribution in structures or regions, for example in detecting tumors. **2** a printing technique in which a wet ink image is fused by heat or infrared radiation with a resinous powder to produce a raised impression. — **ther·mo·graph·ic** /ˌTHərməˈgrafik/ adj.

ther·mo·karst /ˈTHərməˌkärst/ ▶ n. Geol. a form of periglacial topography resembling karst, with hollows produced by the selective melting of permafrost.

ther·mo·la·bile /ˌTHərmōˈlābīl; -bəl/ ▶ adj. esp. Biochem. (of a substance) readily destroyed or deactivated by heat.

ther·mo·lu·mi·nes·cence /ˌTHərmōˌlo͞oməˈnesəns/ ▶ n. the property of some materials that have accumulated energy over a long period of becoming luminescent when pretreated and subjected to high temperatures, used as a means of dating ancient ceramics and other artifacts. — **ther·mo·lu·mi·nes·cent** adj.

ther·mol·y·sis /THərˈmäləsis/ ▶ n. Chem. the breakdown of molecules by the action of heat. — **ther·mo·lyt·ic** /ˌTHərməˈlitik/ adj.

ther·mom·e·ter /THərˈmämitər/ ▶ n. an instrument for measuring and indicating temperature, typically one consisting of a narrow, hermetically sealed glass tube marked with graduations and having at one end a bulb containing mercury or alcohol, which extends along the tube as it expands. — **ther·mo·met·ric** /ˌTHərməˈmetrik/ adj. **ther·mo·met·ri·cal** /ˌTHərməˈmetrikəl/ adj. **ther·mom·e·try** n. [17th C.: from Fr. *thermomètre* or mod. L. *thermometrum*, from THERMO- 'of heat' + *-metrum* 'measure.']

ther·mo·nu·cle·ar /ˌTHərmōˈn(y)o͞oklēər/ ▶ adj. relating to or using nuclear reactions that occur only at very high temperatures. ■ of, relating to, or involving weapons in which explosive force is produced by thermonuclear reactions.

ther·mo·phile /ˈTHərməˌfīl/ ▶ n. Microbiol. a bacterium or other microorganism that grows best at higher than normal temperatures. — **ther·mo·phil·ic** /ˌTHərməˈfilik/ adj.

ther·mo·pile /ˈTHərməˌpīl/ ▶ n. a set of thermocouples arranged for measuring small quantities of radiant heat.

ther·mo·plas·tic /ˌTHərməˈplastik/ Chem. ▶ adj. denoting substances (esp. synthetic resins) that become plastic on heating and harden on cooling and are able to repeat these processes. Often contrasted with THERMOSETTING. ▶ n. (usu. **thermoplastics**) a substance of this kind.

Ther·mop·y·lae /THərˈmäpəˌlē; -ˌlī/ a pass between the mountains and the sea in Greece. In 480 BC it was defended against the Persian army of Xerxes I by 6,000 Greeks; among them were 300 Spartans, all of whom were killed.

ther·mo·reg·u·late /ˌTHərmōˈregyəˌlāt/ ▶ v. [intrans.] regulate temperature, esp. one's own body temperature. — **ther·mo·reg·u·la·tion** /-ˌregyəˈlāSHən/ n. **ther·mo·reg·u·la·to·ry** /-ləˌtôrē/ adj.

ther·mos /ˈTHərməs/ (also **ther·mos bot·tle**) ▶ n. a container that keeps a drink or other fluid hot or cold by means of a double wall enclosing a vacuum. [20th C.: from Gk., lit. 'hot.']

ther·mo·set·ting /ˈTHərmōˌsetiNG/ ▶ adj. Chem. denoting substances (esp. synthetic resins) that set permanently when heated. Often contrasted with THERMOPLASTIC. — **ther·mo·set** adj. & n.

ther·mo·sphere /ˈTHərmōˌsfi(ə)r/ ▶ n. the region of the atmosphere above the mesosphere and below the height at which the atmosphere ceases to have the properties of a continuous medium. The thermosphere is characterized throughout by an increase in temperature with height.

ther·mo·sta·ble /ˈTHərmōˌstābəl/ ▶ adj. esp. Biochem. (of a substance) not readily destroyed or deactivated by heat.

ther·mo·stat /ˈTHərməˌstat/ ▶ n. a device that automatically regulates temperature, or that activates a device when the temperature reaches a certain point. — **ther·mo·stat·ic** /ˌTHərməˈstatik/ adj. **ther·mo·stat·i·cal·ly** /ˌTHərməˈstatik(ə)lē/ adv.

ther·mot·ro·pism /THərˈmätrəˌpizəm/ ▶ n. Biol. the turning or bending of a plant or other organism in response to a directional source of heat. — **ther·mo·trop·ic** /ˌTHərməˈtrōpik; -ˈträpik/ adj.

the·ro·pod /ˈTHi(ə)rəˌpäd/ ▶ n. a carnivorous dinosaur (suborder Theropoda, order Saurischia) of a group whose members are typically bipedal and range from small and delicately built to very large. [1930s: from Gk. *thēr* 'beast' + *pous, pod-* 'foot.']

The·roux /THəˈro͞o/, Paul (1941–), US writer. His works include the novel *The Mosquito Coast* (1982) and the traveloque *Dark Star Safari* (2002).

the·sau·rus /THəˈsôrəs/ ▶ n. (pl. **-sau·ri** /-ˈsôrī/ or **-sau·rus·es**) a book that lists words in groups of synonyms and related concepts. ■ archaic a dictionary or encyclopedia. [16th C.: via L. from Gk. *thēsauros* 'storehouse, treasure.']

these /T͟Hēz/ plural form of THIS.

The·se·us /ˈTHēsēəs; -syo͞os/ Gk. Mythol. The legendary hero of Athens, son of Poseidon (or, in another account, of Aegeus, king of Athens) and husband of Phaedra. He slew the Cretan Minotaur with the help of Ariadne.

the·sis /ˈTHēsis/ ▶ n. (pl. **-ses** /-sēz/) **1** a statement or theory that is put forward as a premise to be maintained or proved: *can you support your thesis?* ■ (in Hegelian philosophy) a proposition forming the first stage in the process of dialectical reasoning. Compare with ANTITHESIS, SYNTHESIS. **2** a long essay or dissertation involving personal research, written by a candidate for a college degree. **3** Pros. an unstressed syllable or part of a metrical foot in Greek or Latin verse. Often contrasted with ARSIS. [ME (sense 3): via late L. from Gk., lit. 'placing, a proposition,' from the root of *tithenai* 'to place.']

thesp informal ▶ abbr. thespian.

thes·pi·an /ˈTHespēən/ formal humorous ▶ adj. of or relating to drama and the theater: *thespian talents*. ▶ n. an actor or actress: *an aging thespian* | *an unemployed thespian lodger*. [17th C.: from the name THESPIS + -IAN.]

Thes·pis /ˈTHespis/ (6th century BC), Greek dramatic poet. He is regarded as the founder of Greek tragedy.

Thess. ▶ abbr. Bible Thessalonians.

Thes·sa·lo·ni·ans /ˌTHesəˈlōnēənz/ either of two books of the New Testament, epistles of St. Paul to the new church at Thessalonica.

Thes·sa·lo·ní·ki /ˌTHesəlōˈnēkē/ a seaport in northeastern Greece, the second largest city in Greece; pop. 378,000. Also called SALONICA; Latin name THESSALONICA.

Thes·sa·ly /ˈTHesəlē/ a region of northeastern Greece. Greek name THESSALÍA. — **Thes·sa·li·an** /THeˈsālēən; -ˈsālyən/ adj. & n.

the·ta /ˈTHātə; ˈTHē-/ ▶ n. the eighth letter of the Greek alphabet (Ρ, ρ), transliterated as 'th.' ■ [as adj.] Chem. denoting a temperature at which a polymer solution behaves ideally as regards its osmotic pressure. ■ [as adj.] denoting electrical activity observed in the brain under certain conditions, consisting of oscillations having a frequency of 4 to 7 hertz: *theta rhythm*. ▶ symb. ■ (ρ) temperature (esp. in degrees Celsius). ■ (ρ) a plane angle. ■ (ρ) a polar coordinate.

The·tis /ˈTHētis/ Gk. Mythol. a sea nymph, mother of Achilles.

the·ur·gy /ˈTHēərjē/ ▶ **n.** the operation or effect of a supernatural or divine agency in human affairs. ■ a system of white magic practiced by the early Neoplatonists. — **the·ur·gic** /THēˈərjik/ **adj.** **the·ur·gi·cal** /THēˈərjikəl/ **adj.** **the·ur·gist n.** [16th C.: via late L. from Gk. *theourgia* 'sorcery,' from *theos* 'god' + *-ergos* 'working.']

thew /TH(y)o͞o/ ▶ **n.** literary muscular strength. ■ (**thews**) muscles and tendons perceived as generating such strength. — **thew·y adj.** [OE *thēaw* 'usage, custom.']

they /T͟Hā/ ▶ **pron.** [third person pl.] **1** used to refer to two or more people or things previously mentioned or easily identified: *the two men could get life sentences if they are convicted.* ■ people in general: *the rest, as they say, is history.* ■ informal a group of people in authority regarded collectively: *they cut my water off.* **2** [sing.] used to refer to a person of unspecified sex: *ask a friend if they could help.* [ME: from ON *their*, nominative pl. masc. of *sá*; rel. to THEM and THEIR, also to THAT and THE.]

they'd /T͟Hād/ ▶ **contr.** ■ they had. ■ they would.

they'll /T͟Hāl/ ▶ **contr.** they shall; they will.

they're /T͟He(ə)r/ ▶ **contr.** they are.

they've /T͟Hāv/ ▶ **contr.** they have.

THI ▶ **abbr.** temperature–humidity index.

thi·a·ben·da·zole /ˌTHīəˈbendəˌzōl/ ▶ **n.** Med. a synthetic compound with anthelmintic properties, derived from thiazole and used chiefly to treat infestation with intestinal nematodes. [1960s: from elements from THIAZOLE + BENZENE + IMIDAZOLE.]

thi·a·mine /ˈTHīəmin; -mēn/ (also **thi·a·min** /-min/) ▶ **n.** Biochem. a vitamin of the B complex, found in unrefined grains, beans, and liver, a deficiency of which causes beriberi. Also called VITAMIN B_1.

thi·a·zide /ˈTHīəˌzīd/ ▶ **n.** Med. any of a class of sulfur-containing drugs that are used as diuretics and to lower blood pressure. [1950s: from elements of THIO- + AZINE + OXIDE.]

thi·a·zole /ˈTHīəˌzōl/ ▶ **n.** Chem. a synthetic foul-smelling liquid, C_3H_3NS, whose molecule is a ring of one nitrogen, one sulfur, and three carbon atoms.

thick /THik/ ▶ **adj.** **1** with opposite sides or surfaces that are a great or relatively great distance apart: *thick slices of bread* | *the walls are 5 feet thick.* ■ (of a garment or other knitted or woven item) made of heavy material for warmth or comfort. ■ of large diameter: *thick cables.* ■ (of script or type) consisting of broad lines: *thick black type.* **2** made up of a large number of things or people close together: *his hair was long and thick* | *thick forest.* ■ [predic.] (**thick with**) densely filled or covered with: *a room thick with smoke* | fig. *the air was thick with rumors.* ■ (of air, the atmosphere, or an odor carried by them) heavy or dense: *a thick odor of perfume.* ■ (of darkness or a substance in the air) so black or dense as to be impossible or difficult to see through: *thick fog.* **3** (of a liquid or a semiliquid substance) relatively firm in consistency; not flowing freely: *thick mud.* **4** informal of low intelligence; stupid: *he's a bit thick.* **5** (of a voice) not clear or distinct; hoarse or husky. ■ (of an accent) very marked and difficult to understand. **6** [predic.] informal having a very close, friendly relationship: ***he's thick with the new boss.*** ▶ **n.** (**the thick**) rare the busiest or most crowded part of something; the middle of something: *the thick of battle.* ▶ **adv.** in or with deep, dense, or heavy mass: *bread spread thick with butter.*
– PHRASES **have a thick skin** see SKIN. **(as) thick as thieves** informal (of two or more people) very close or friendly; sharing secrets. **through thick and thin** under all circumstances, no matter how difficult: *they stuck together through thick and thin.* — **thick·ish adj.** **thick·ly adv.** [as submodifier] *thickly carpeted corridors.* [OE *thicce*, of Gmc. origin; rel. to Du. *dik* and Ger. *dick.*]

thick·en /ˈTHikən/ ▶ **v.** make or become thick or thicker: [trans.] *thicken the sauce with flour* | [intrans.] *the fog had thickened.*
– PHRASES **the plot thickens** used when a situation is becoming more and more complicated and puzzling. — **thick·en·er n.**

thick·en·ing /ˈTHikəniNG/ ▶ **n.** **1** the process or result of becoming broader, deeper, or denser. ■ a broader, deeper, or denser area of animal or plant tissue. **2** a thickener. ▶ **adj.** becoming broader, deeper, or denser: *a hazardous journey through thickening fog.*

thick·et /ˈTHikit/ ▶ **n.** a dense group of bushes or trees. [OE *thiccet* (see THICK, -ET[1]).]

thick·head /ˈTHikˌhed/ ▶ **n.** informal a stupid person. — **thick·head·ed adj.** **thick·head·ed·ness n.**

thick·ness /ˈTHiknis/ ▶ **n.** **1** the distance between opposite sides of something: *the gateway is several feet in thickness* | *paving slabs in varying thicknesses.* ■ the quality of being broad or deep: *the immense thickness of the walls.* ■ a layer of a specified material: *the framework has to support two thicknesses of plasterboard.* ■ [in sing.] a broad or deep part of a specified thing: *the beams were set into the thickness of the wall.* **2** the quality of being dense: *the thickness of the fog.* ■ the state or quality of being made up of many closely packed parts: *the thickness of his hair.* [OE *thicness* (see THICK, -NESS).]

thick·set /ˈTHikˌset/ ▶ **adj.** (of a person or animal) heavily or solidly built; stocky.

thick-wit·ted ▶ **adj.** dull and stupid.

thief /THēf/ ▶ **n.** (pl. **thieves** /THēvz/) a person who steals another person's property, esp. by stealth and without using force or violence. [OE *thīof*, *thēof*, of Gmc. origin; rel. to Du. *dief* and Ger. *Dieb*, also to THEFT.]

thieve /THēv/ ▶ **v.** [intrans.] be a thief; steal something: *they began thieving again* | [as adj.] (**thieving**) *get lost, you thieving swine.* [OE *thēofian*, from *thēof* 'thief.' Transitive uses began in the late 17th C.]

thiev·er·y /ˈTHēv(ə)rē/ ▶ **n.** the action of stealing another person's property.

thieves /THēvz/ plural form of THIEF.

thiev·ish /ˈTHēvisH/ ▶ **adj.** of, relating to, or given to stealing. — **thiev·ish·ly adv.** **thiev·ish·ness n.**

thigh /THī/ ▶ **n.** the part of the human leg between the hip and the knee. ■ the corresponding part in other animals. — **thighed adj.** [in comb.]. [OE *thēh*, *thēoh*, *thīoh*, of Gmc. origin; rel. to Du. *dij.*]

thigh bone ▶ **n.** the femur.

thigh-high ▶ **adj.** (of an item of clothing) reaching as far as a person's thigh. ■ at or reaching to the level of a person's thigh: *he waded into the thigh-high river.* ▶ **n.** an item of clothing, esp. a garterless stocking, that reaches to a person's thigh.

thigh-slap·per ▶ **n.** informal a joke or anecdote considered to be exceptionally funny. — **thigh-slap·ping adj.**

thig·mo·tax·is /ˌTHigməˈtaksis/ ▶ **n.** Biol. the motion or orientation of an organism in response to a touch stimulus. — **thig·mo·tac·tic** /-ˈtaktik/ **adj.** [20th C.: from Gk. *thigma* 'touch' + TAXIS.]

thig·mot·ro·pism /THigˈmätrəˌpizəm/ ▶ **n.** Biol. the turning or bending of a plant or other organism in response to a touch stimulus. — **thig·mo·trop·ic** /ˌTHigməˈtrōpik; -ˈträpik/ **adj.** [20th C.: from Gk. *thigma* 'touch' + TROPISM.]

thill /THil/ ▶ **n.** hist. a shaft, esp. one of a pair, used to attach a cart or carriage to the animal drawing it. [ME: of unknown origin.]

thim·ble /ˈTHimbəl/ ▶ **n.** a metal or plastic cap with a closed end, worn to protect the finger and push the needle in sewing. ■ a short metal tube or ferrule. ■ Naut. a metal ring, concave on the outside, around which a loop of rope is spliced. [OE *thȳmel* 'finger stall' (see THUMB, -LE[1]).]

thim·ble·ber·ry /ˈTHimbəlˌberē/ ▶ **n.** (pl. **-ries**) a North American blackberry or raspberry (genus *Rubus*) with thimble-shaped fruit.

thim·ble·ful /ˈTHimbəlˌfo͝ol/ ▶ **n.** (pl. **-fuls**) a small quantity of liquid, esp. alcohol.

thim·ble·rig /ˈTHimbəlˌrig/ ▶ **n.** another term for SHELL GAME. — **thim·ble·rig·ger n.** [19th C.: from THIMBLE + RIG[2] in the sense 'trick, dodge.']

thimerosal /THīˈmerəsəl/ ▶ **n.** a local antiseptic, $C_9H_9HgNaO_2S$, for abrasions and minor cuts.

Thim·phu /timˈpo͞o; THim-/ (also **Thim·bu** /-ˈbo͞o/) the capital of Bhutan, in the Himalaya Mountains at an altitude of 8,000 feet (2,450 m); pop. 30,000.

thin /THin/ ▶ **adj.** (**thin·ner, thin·nest**) **1** having opposite surfaces or sides close together; of little thickness or depth: *thin slices of bread.* ■ (of a person) having little, or too little, flesh or fat on their body. ■ (of a garment or other knitted or woven item) made of light material for coolness or elegance. ■ (of a garment) having had a considerable amount of fabric worn away. ■ (of script or type) consisting of narrow lines: *tall, thin lettering.* **2** having few parts or members relative to the area covered or filled; sparse: *a depressingly thin crowd* | *his hair was going thin.* ■ not dense: *the thin cold air of the mountains.* ■ containing much liquid and not much solid substance: *thin soup.* ■ Climbing denoting a route on which the holds are small or scarce. **3** (of a sound) faint and high-pitched: *a thin voice.* ■ (of a smile) weak and forced. ■ too weak to justify a result or effect; inadequate: *the evidence is rather thin.* ▶ **adv.** [often in comb.] with little thickness or depth: *thin-sliced ham* | *cut it as thin as possible.* ▶ **v.** (**thinned, thin·ning**) **1** make or become less dense, crowded, or numerous: [trans.] ***the remorseless fire of archers thinned their ranks*** | [intrans.] ***the trees began to thin out*** | [as adj.] (**thinning**) *thinning hair.* ■ [trans.] remove some plants from (a row or area) to allow the others more room to grow: ***thin out the peas.*** ■ make or become weaker or more watery: [trans.] ***add water to thin it down*** | [intrans.] *the blood thins.* **2** make or become smaller in width or thickness: [trans.] *thinning the ozone layer* | [intrans.] *have I thinned?* **3** [trans.] Golf hit (a ball) above its center.
– PHRASES **on thin ice** see ICE. **thin air** used to refer to the state of being invisible or nonexistent: *she just vanished **into thin air*** | *they pluck numbers **out of thin air.*** **the thin blue line** informal used to refer to the police, typically in the context of situations of civil unrest. **thin on top** informal balding. — **thin·ly adv.** **thin·ness n.** **thin·nish adj.** [OE *thynne*, of Gmc. origin; rel. to Du. *dun* and Ger. *dünn*, from an Indo-Eur. root shared by L. *tenuis.*]

-thin ▶ **comb. form** denoting a specified degree of thinness: *gossamer-thin* | *wafer-thin.*

thine /T͟Hīn/ ▶ **possessive pron.** archaic form of YOURS; the thing or things belonging to or associated with thee: *his spirit will take courage from thine.* ▶ **possessive adj.** form of THY used before a vowel: *inquire into thine own heart.* [OE *thīn*, of Gmc. origin; rel. to Ger. *dein*, also to THOU[1].]

thin-film ▶ **adj.** (of a process or device) using or involving a very thin solid or liquid film. ■ Electron. denoting a miniature circuit or device consisting of a thin layer of metal or semiconductor on a ceramic or glass substrate.

thing /THiNG/ ▶ **n.** **1** an object that one need not, cannot, or does not wish to give a specific name to: *that metal thing* | *things I'd like to buy.* ■ (**things**) personal belongings or clothing: *unpack your things.* ■ [with adj.] (**things**) objects, equipment, or utensils used for a particular purpose: *they cleared away the last few lunch things.* ■ [with negative] (**a thing**) anything (used for emphasis): *she couldn't find a thing to wear.* ■ used to express one's disapproval or contempt for something: *I won't smoke those filthy things.* ■ [with postpositive adj.] (**things**) all that can be described in the specified way: *all things Italian.* **2** an inanimate material object as distinct from a living sentient being: *I'm not a thing, not a work of art.* ■ [with adj.] a living creature or plant: *all living things on earth.* ■ [with adj.] used to express and give a reason for one's pity, affection, approval, or contempt for a person or animal: *have a nice trip, you lucky thing!* | *the lamb was a puny little thing.* **3** an action, activity, event, thought, or utterance: *the only thing I could do well was cook.* ■ (**things**) circumstances, conditions, or matters that are unspecified: *how are things with you?* ■ an abstract entity or concept: *mourning and depression are not the same thing.* ■ a quality or attribute: *they had one thing in common—they were men of action.* ■ a specimen or type of something: *the latest thing in family fun.* ■ (**one's thing**) informal one's special interest or concern: *reading isn't my thing.* ■ [with adj.] (**a thing**) informal a situation or activity of a specified type or quality: *your being here is just a friendship thing, OK?* **4** (**the thing**) informal what is needed or required: *you need a tonic—and here's just the thing.* ■ what is socially acceptable or fashionable: *it wouldn't be quite the thing to go to a garden party in boots.* ■ used to introduce or draw attention to an important fact or consideration: *the thing is, I'm leaving.*

– PHRASES **be all things to all men** (or **people**) please everyone, typically by regularly altering one's behavior or opinions in order to conform to those of others. ■ be able to be interpreted or used differently by different people to their own satisfaction. **be hearing** (or **seeing**) **things** imagine that one can hear (or see) something that is not in fact there. **do one's own thing** informal follow one's own interests or inclinations regardless of others. **do the —— thing** informal engage in the kind of behavior typically associated with someone or something: *he does the bad-guy thing.* **do things to** informal have a powerful emotional effect on: *it does things to me when we kiss.* **for one thing** used to introduce one of two or more possible reasons for something, the remainder of which may or may not be stated: *Why hadn't he arranged to see her at the house? For one thing, it would have been warmer.* **have a thing about** informal have an obsessive interest in or dislike of: *she had a thing about men who wore glasses.* **—— is one thing, —— is another** used to indicate that the second item mentioned is much more serious or important than the first, and cannot be compared to it: *physical attraction was one thing, love was quite another.* **make a (big) thing of** (or **about**) informal make (something) seem more important than it actually is. **of all things** out of all conceivable possibilities (used to express surprise): *he bought a cat, of all things.* **(just) one of those things** informal used to indicate that one wishes to pass over an unfortunate event or experience by regarding it as unavoidable or to be accepted. **one thing leads to another** used to suggest that the exact sequence of events is too obvious to need recounting, the listener or reader being able to guess easily what happened. **a thing of the past** a thing that no longer happens or exists. **a thing or two** informal used to refer to useful information that can be imparted or learned: *Teddy taught me a thing or two about wine.* **things that go bump in the night** informal, humorous unexplained and frightening noises at night. [OE, of Gmc. origin; rel. to Ger. *Ding.* Early senses included 'meeting' and 'matter, concern' as well as 'inanimate object.']

thing·a·ma·jig /ˈTHiNGəməˌjig/ (also **thing·u·ma·jig**; **thing·a·ma·bob** or **thing·um·a·bob** /-ˌbäb/) ▶ **n.** informal used to refer to a thing whose name one has forgotten, does not know, or does not wish to mention. [19th C.: arbitrary extension of earlier *thingum* (from THING + a meaningless suffix). *Thingumabob* dates from the 18th C.]

thing·y /ˈTHiNGē/ ▶ **n.** (pl. **thing·ies**) another term for THINGAMAJIG.

think /THiNGk/ ▶ **v.** (past and past part. **thought**) **1** [with clause] have a particular opinion, belief, or idea about someone or something: *she thought that nothing would be the same again* | [intrans.] *what would John think of her?* | (**be thought**) *it's thought he may have collapsed from shock* | [with infin.] *up to 300 people were thought to have died.* ■ used in questions to express anger or surprise: *What do you think you're doing?* ■ (**I think**) used in speech to reduce the force of a statement or opinion, or to politely suggest or refuse something: *I thought we could go out for a meal.* **2** [intrans.] direct one's mind toward someone or something; use one's mind actively to form connected ideas: *he was thinking about Colin* | [trans.] *thinking deep thoughts.* ■ (**think of/about**) take into account or consideration when deciding on a possible action: *there are the children to think about.* ■ (**think of/about**) consider the possibility or advantages of (a course of action): *he was thinking of becoming a zoologist.* ■ have a particular mental attitude or approach: *he thought like a general* | [with complement] *always think positive.* ■ (**think of**) have a particular opinion of: *I think of him as a friend.* ■ call something to mind; remember: *thyme is a natural with any chicken dish you can think of* | [with infin.] *I hadn't thought to warn Rachel.* ■ imagine (an actual or possible situation): *think of being paid to hunt big game!* ■ [usu. with clause] expect: *I never thought we'd raise so much money* | [with infin.] *something he'd never thought to have heard said again.* ■ (**think oneself into**) concentrate on imagining what it would be like to be in (a position or role): *she tried to think herself into the part of Peter's fiancée.* ▶ **n.** [in sing.] informal an act of thinking: *I had a think.*

– PHRASES **have (got) another think coming** informal used to express the speaker's disagreement with or unwillingness to do something suggested by someone else: *if they think I'm going, they've got another think coming.* **think again** reconsider something, typically so as to alter one's intentions or ideas. **think out loud** express one's thoughts as soon as they occur. **think better of** decide not to do (something) after reconsideration. **think big** see BIG. **think for oneself** have an independent mind or attitude. **think nothing** (or **little**) **of** consider (an activity others regard as odd, wrong, or difficult) as straightforward or normal. **think nothing of it** see NOTHING. **think on one's feet** see FOOT. **think twice** consider a course of action carefully before embarking on it. **think the world of** see WORLD.

– PHRASAL VERBS **think back** recall a past event or time. **think on** think of or about. **think something out** consider something in all its aspects before taking action. **think something over** consider something carefully. **think something through** consider all the possible effects or implications of something. **think something up** informal use one's ingenuity to invent or devise something. — **think·a·ble adj.** [OE *thencan*, of Gmc. origin; rel. to Du. and Ger. *denken.*]

think·er /ˈTHiNGkər/ ▶ **n.** a person who thinks deeply and seriously. ■ a person with a highly developed intellect, esp. one whose profession involves intellectual activity.

think·ing /ˈTHiNGkiNG/ ▶ **adj.** [attrib.] using thought or rational judgment; intelligent: *a thinking man.* ▶ **n.** the process of using one's mind to consider or reason about something: *they have done some thinking about welfare reform.* ■ a person's ideas or opinions: *his thinking is progressive.* ■ (**thinkings**) archaic thoughts; meditations.

– PHRASES **good** (or **nice**) **thinking** used as an expression of approval for an ingenious plan, explanation, or observation. **put on one's thinking cap** informal meditate on a problem.

think piece ▶ **n.** an article in a newspaper, magazine, or journal presenting personal opinions, analysis, or discussion, rather than bare facts.

think tank ▶ **n.** a body of experts providing advice and ideas on specific political or economic problems. — **think tank·er n.**

thin-lay·er chro·ma·tog·ra·phy ▶ **n.** Chem. chromatography in which compounds are separated on a thin layer of adsorbent material, typically a coating of silica gel on a glass plate or plastic sheet.

thin·ner /ˈTHinər/ ▶ **n.** a volatile solvent used to make paint or other solutions less viscous.

thio- ▶ **comb. form** Chem. denoting replacement of oxygen by sulfur in a compound: *thiosulphate.* [from Gk. *theion* 'sulfur.']

thi·o·cy·a·nate /ˌTHī-ōˈsīəˌnāt/ ▶ **n.** Chem. a salt containing the anion SCN–.

thi·ol /ˈTHīōl; -äl/ ▶ **n.** Chem. an organic compound containing the group –SH, i.e., a sulfur-containing analog of an alcohol.

thi·o·nyl /ˈTHīəˌnil/ ▶ **n.** [as adj.] Chem. of or denoting the divalent radical =SO. [1857: so named by Hugo Schiff (1834–1915), German chemist.]

thi·o·pen·tal /ˌTHī-ōˈpental; -tôl/ ▶ **n.** Med. a sulfur-containing barbiturate drug used as a general anesthetic and hypnotic, and (reputedly) as a truth serum. [1940s: from THIO- + a contr. of PENTOBARBITAL.]

thi·o·rid·a·zine /ˌTHīəˈridəˌzēn; -zin/ ▶ **n.** Med. a synthetic compound derived from phenothiazine, used as a tranquilizer, chiefly in the treatment of mental illness. [1950s: from THIO- + *(pipe)rid(ine)* + AZINE.]

thi·o·sul·fate /ˌTHī-ōˈsəlfāt/ ▶ **n.** Chem. a salt containing the anion $S_2O_3 2-$, i.e., a sulfate with one oxygen atom replaced by sulfur.

thi·o·u·re·a /ˌTHī-ō-yəˈrēə/ ▶ **n.** Chem. a synthetic crystalline compound, $SC(NH_2)_2$, used in photography and the manufacture of synthetic resins.

Thí·ra /ˈTHi(ə)rə/ Greek name for THERA.

thi·ram /ˈTHīram/ ▶ **n.** Chem. a synthetic sulfur-containing compound, $(CH_3)_2NCSS_2SCN(CH_3)_2$, used as a fungicide and seed protectant. [1950s: from THIO-, *(u)r(ea)*, and *am(ine)*, elements of the systematic name.]

third /THərd/ ▶ **ordinal number** constituting number three in a sequence; 3rd: *the third century* | *Edward the Third.* ■ (**a third/one third**) each of three equal parts into which something is or may be divided: *a third of a mile.* ■ the third finisher or position in a race or competition. ■ the third in a sequence of a vehicle's gears. ■ Baseball third base. ■ the third grade of a school. ■ thirdly (used to introduce a third point or reason): *second, they are lightly regulated; and third, they do business with nonresident clients.* ■ Music an interval spanning three consecutive notes in a diatonic scale, e.g., C to E (**major third**, equal to two tones) or A to C (**minor third**, equal to a tone and a semitone). ■ Music the note that is higher by this interval than the tonic of a diatonic scale or root of a chord.

– PHRASES **third time is a charm** used to express the hope that, after twice failing to accomplish something, one may succeed in the third attempt. [OE *thridda*, of Gmc. origin; rel. to Du. *derde* and Ger. *dritte*, also to THREE.]

third class ▶ **n.** [in sing.] a group of people or things considered together as third best. ■ a cheap class of mail for the handling of advertising and other printed material that weighs less than 16 ounces and is unsealed. ■ esp. hist. the cheapest and least comfortable accommodations in a train or ship. ▶ **adj. & adv.** of the third-best quality or of lower status: [as adj.] *third-class citizens.* ■ of or relating to a cheap class of mail including advertising and other printed material weighing less than 16 ounces. ■ esp. hist. of or relating to the cheapest and least comfortable accommodations in a train or ship.

third cous·in ▶ **n.** see COUSIN.

third-de·gree ▶ **adj.** [attrib.] **1** denoting burns of the most severe kind, affecting tissue below the skin. **2** Law denoting the least serious category of a crime, esp. murder. ▶ **n.** (**the third degree**) long and harsh questioning, esp. by police, to obtain information or a confession.

third es·tate ▶ **n.** [treated as sing. or pl.] the commons. [the first two estates were formerly represented by the clergy, and the barons and knights; later the Lords spiritual and the Lords temporal.] ■ (**the Third Estate**) the French bourgeoisie and working class before the French Revolution. [translating Fr. *le tiers état.*]

third eye ▶ **n.** **1** Hinduism the locus of occult power and wisdom in the forehead of a deity, esp. the god Shiva. ■ the "eye of insight" located in the forehead, which can be activated through the practice of yoga. **2** informal term for PINEAL EYE.

third eye·lid ▶ **n.** informal term for NICTITATING MEMBRANE.

third force ▶ **n.** [in sing.] a political group or party acting as a check on conflict between two extreme or opposing groups.

third-hand (also **third·hand**) ▶ **adj.** **1** (of goods) having had two previous owners: *a thirdhand dinner suit.* **2** (of information) acquired from or via several intermediate sources and consequently not authoritative or reliable: *the story is thirdhand, told long after the event.* ▶ **adv.** from or via several intermediate sources.

Third In·ter·na·tion·al see INTERNATIONAL.

third·ly /'THərdlē/ ▶ **adv.** in the third place (used to introduce a third point or reason).

third mar·ket ▶ **n.** Finance used to refer to over-the-counter trading in listed stocks outside the stock exchange.

third par·ty ▶ **n.** a person or group besides the two primarily involved in a situation, esp. a dispute. ■ a political party organized as an alternative to the major parties in a two-party system. ▶ **adj.** [attrib.] of or relating to a person or group besides the two primarily involved in a situation.

third per·son ▶ **n.** **1** a third party. **2** see PERSON (sense 2).

third rail ▶ **n.** an additional rail supplying electric current, used in some electric railroad systems. ■ Informal a subject, esp. Social Security, considered by politicians too dangerous to modify or discuss.

third-rate ▶ **adj.** of inferior or very poor quality. — **third-rat·er n.**

Third Reich the Nazi regime, 1933–45.

Third Re·pub·lic the republican regime in France between the fall of Napoleon III in 1870 and the German occupation of 1940.

third ven·tri·cle ▶ **n.** Anat. the central cavity of the brain, lying between the thalamus and hypothalamus of the two cerebral hemispheres.

third way (also **Third Way**) ▶ **n.** an option regarded as an alternative to two extremes, esp. a political agenda that is consensus-based rather than left- or right-wing.

Third World ▶ **n.** (usu. **the Third World**) the developing countries of Asia, Africa, and Latin America. [first applied in the 1950s by French commentators who used *tiers monde* to distinguish the developing countries from the capitalist and communist blocs.]

thirst /THərst/ ▶ **n.** a feeling of needing or wanting to drink something. ■ lack of the liquid needed to sustain life: *dying of thirst.* ■ (usu. **thirst for**) literary a strong desire for something: *a thirst for knowledge.* ▶ **v.** [intrans.] archaic (of a person or animal) feel a need to drink something. ■ (usu. **thirst for/after**) literary have a strong desire for something: *an opponent thirsting for revenge.* [OE *thurst* (n.), *thyrstan* (v.), of Gmc. origin; rel. to Du. *dorst, dorsten* and Ger. *Durst, dürsten.*]

thirst·y /'THərstē/ ▶ **adj.** (**thirst·i·er, thirst·i·est**) feeling a need to drink something. ■ (of land, plants, or skin) in need of water: dry or parched. ■ (of an engine, plant, or crop) consuming a lot of fuel or water. ■ having or showing a strong desire for something: *thirsty for scandal.* ■ [attrib.] informal (of activity, weather, or a time) causing the feeling of a need to drink something: *modeling is thirsty work.* — **thirst·i·ly adv.** **thirst·i·ness n.**

thir·teen /THər'tēn; 'THər,tēn/ ▶ **cardinal number** equivalent to the sum of six and seven; one more than twelve, or seven less than twenty; 13: *thirteen miles away.* (Roman numeral: **xiii, XIII.**) ■ a size of garment or other merchandise denoted by thirteen. ■ thirteen years old: *two boys aged eleven and thirteen.* — **thir·teenth** /THər'tēnTH; 'THər,tēnTH/ **ordinal number.** [OE *thrēotīene* (see THREE, -TEEN). The spelling with initial *thi-* is recorded in ME.]

Thir·teen Col·o·nies the 13 British colonies (Virginia, Massachusetts, Maryland, Connecticut, Rhode Island, North Carolina, South Carolina, New York, New Jersey, Delaware, New Hampshire, Pennsylvania, Georgia) that ratified the Declaration of Independence in 1776.

thir·ty /'THərtē/ ▶ **cardinal number** (pl. **-ties**) the number equivalent to the product of three and ten; ten less than forty; 30: *thirty years ago.* (Roman numeral: **xxx, XXX.**) ■ (**thirties**) the numbers from thirty to thirty-nine, esp. the years of a century or of a person's life: *a woman in her thirties | she was famous in the thirties.* ■ thirty years old. ■ thirty miles an hour: *doing about thirty.* — **thir·ti·eth** /-iTH/ **ordinal number** **thir·ty·fold adj. & adv.** [OE *thrītig* (see THREE, -TY²). The spelling with initial *thi-* is recorded in literature in the 15th cent., and has been the prevalent form since the 16th C.]

thir·ty-eight ▶ **n.** a revolver of .38 caliber.

thir·ty-sec·ond note ▶ **n.** Music a note having the time value of half a sixteenth note, represented by a large dot with a three-hooked stem.

thir·ty-two-mo /'THərtē 'to͞o mō/ ▶ **n.** (pl. **-mos**) a size of book page that results from folding each printed sheet into thirty-two leaves (sixty-four pages). ■ a book of this size.

Thir·ty Years War a European war of 1618–48 that broke out between the Catholic Holy Roman Emperor and some of his German Protestant states and developed into a struggle for continental hegemony with France, Sweden, Spain, and the Holy Roman Empire as the major protagonists. It was ended by the Treaty of Westphalia.

this /T͟His/ ▶ **pron.** (pl. **these**) **1** used to identify a specific person or thing close at hand or being indicated or experienced: *is this your bag?* ■ used to introduce someone or something: *listen to this.* ■ referring to the nearer of two things close to the speaker (the other, if specified, being identified by "that"): *this is different from that.* **2** referring to a specific thing or situation just mentioned: *he was alive, and this was all that mattered.* ▶ **adj.** (pl. **these**) **1** used to identify a specific person or thing close at hand or being indicated or experienced: *don't listen to this guy | these croissants are delicious.* ■ referring to the nearer of two things close to the speaker (the other, if specified, being identified by "that"): *this one or that one?* **2** referring to a specific thing or situation just mentioned: *there was a court case resulting from this incident.* **3** used with periods of time related to the present: *I thought you were busy all this week.* ■ referring to a period of time that has just passed: *I haven't left my bed these three days.* **4** informal used (chiefly in narrative) to refer to a person or thing previously unspecified: *I've got this problem and I need help.* ▶ **adv.** [as submodifier] to the degree or extent indicated: *they can't handle a job this big.*

– PHRASES **this and that** (or **this, that, and the other**) informal various unspecified things: *chatting about this and that.* **this here** informal used to draw attention emphatically to someone or something: *I sleep in this here bed.* [OE, neut. of *thes*, of West Gmc. origin; rel. to THAT and THE.]

This·be /'THizbē/ Rom. Mythol. a Babylonian girl, lover of Pyramus.

this·tle /'THisəl/ ▶ **n.** **1** a widely distributed herbaceous plant (*Carlina, Cirsium, Carduus,* and other genera) of the daisy family, which typically has a prickly stem and leaves and rounded heads of purple flowers. Its numerous species include the **bull thistle** (*Cirsium vulgare*). **2** a plant of this type as the Scottish national emblem, esp. the **Scotch thistle** (*Onopordum acanthium.* — **this·tly adj.** [OE *thistel*, of Gmc. origin; rel. to Du. *distel* and Ger. *Distel.*]

bull thistle

this·tle·down /'THisəl,doun/ ▶ **n.** light fluffy down attached to thistle seeds, eventually wind-borne.

thith·er /'THiT͟Hər/ ▶ **adv.** esp. archaic literary to or toward that place: *trickery that attracted him thither.* [OE *thider*, alt. (by association with HITHER) of *thæder*, of Gmc. origin; rel. to THAT and THE.]

Thí·vai /'THēve/ Greek name for THEBES 2.

thix·ot·ro·py /THik'sätrəpē/ ▶ **n.** Chem. the property of becoming less viscous when subjected to an applied stress, shown for example by some gels that become temporarily fluid when shaken or stirred. — **thix·o·trop·ic** /,THiksə'träpik; -'trōpik/ **adj.** [1920s: from Gk. *thixis* 'touching' + *tropē* 'turning.']

Th.M. ▶ **abbr.** Master of Theology.

tho /T͟Hō/ (also **tho'**) ▶ **conj. & adv.** informal spelling of THOUGH.

thole /THōl/ ▶ **v.** [trans.] Scot. or archaic endure (something) without complaint or resistance; tolerate. [OE *tholian*, of Gmc. origin.]

thole pin ▶ **n.** a pin, typically one of a pair, fitted to the gunwale of a rowboat to act as the fulcrum for an oar. [OE, of Gmc. origin; rel. to Du. *dol.*]

Thom·as¹ /'täməs/, Clarence (1948–), US Supreme Court associate justice 1991– .

Thom·as², Dylan Marlais (1914–53), Welsh poet and writer. His works include the play *Under Milk Wood* (completed 1953).

Thom·as³, Norman Mattoon (1884–1968), US social reformer and politician. He was a Socialist Party presidential candidate six times between 1928 and 1948.

Thom·as, St. one of the 12 apostles; known as **Doubting Thomas**.

Thom·as à Kem·pis /ə 'kempəs/ (c.1380–1471), German theologian; born *Thomas Hemerken. On the Imitation of Christ* (c.1415–24) is attributed to him.

Thom·as A·qui·nas, St. /ə'kwīnəs/, see AQUINAS, ST. THOMAS.

Thom·as More, St. see MORE.

Tho·mism /'tōmizəm/ ▶ **n.** the theology of Thomas Aquinas or of his followers. — **Tho·mist n. & adj. Tho·mis·tic** /tə'mistik/ **adj.**

Thomp·son¹ /'tämpsən/, Francis (1859–1907), English poet. His works include "The Hound of Heaven" (1893).

Thomp·son², Smith (1768–1843), US Supreme Court associate justice 1823–43.

thong /THôNG; THäNG/ ▶ **n.** **1** a narrow strip of leather or other material, used esp. as a fastening or as the lash of a whip. **2** an item of clothing fastened by or including such a narrow strip, in particular: ■ a skimpy bathing suit or pair of underpants like a G-string. ■ another term for FLIP-FLOP (sense 1). ▶ **v.** [trans.] archaic flog or lash (someone) with a whip. — **thonged adj. thong·y adj.** [OE *thwang, thwong*, of Gmc. origin; rel. to Ger. *Zwang* 'compulsion.' Cf. WHANG.]

Thor /THôr/ Scand. Mythol. the god of thunder, the weather, agriculture, and the home, the son of Odin and Freya (Frigga). Thursday is named after him.

thor·a·ces /'THôra,sēz/ ▶ **n. pl.** plural form of THORAX.

tho·rac·ic /THəˈrasik/ ▶ **adj.** Anat. & Zool. of or relating to the thorax.

tho·rac·ic duct ▶ **n.** Anat. the main vessel of the lymphatic system, passing upward in front of the spine and draining into the left innominate vein near the base of the neck.

tho·rac·ic ver·te·bra ▶ **n.** Anat. each of the twelve bones of the backbone to which the ribs are attached.

tho·ra·co·lum·bar /ˌTHôrəkəˈləmbər/ ▶ **adj.** Anat. of or relating to the thoracic and lumbar regions of the spine. ■ denoting the sympathetic nervous system.

tho·ra·cot·o·my /ˌTHôrəˈkätəmē/ ▶ **n.** surgical incision into the chest wall. [19th C.: from Gk. *thōrax, thorāc-* 'chest' + -TOMY.]

tho·rax /ˈTHôraks/ ▶ **n.** (pl. **tho·rax·es** or **tho·ra·ces** /ˈTHôrəˌsēz/) Anat. & Zool. the part of the body of a mammal between the neck and the abdomen, including the cavity enclosed by the ribs, breastbone, and dorsal vertebrae, and containing the chief organs of circulation and respiration; the chest. ■ Zool. the corresponding part of a bird, reptile, amphibian, or fish. ■ Entomol. the middle section of the body of an insect, between the head and the abdomen, bearing the legs and wings. [ME: via L. from Gk. *thōrax.*]

Tho·ra·zine /ˈTHôrəˌzēn/ ▶ **n.** trademark for CHLORPROMAZINE. [1950s: formed from elements of the systematic name.]

Tho·reau /THəˈrō; THô-; ˈTHôrō/, Henry David (1817–62), US essayist and poet. A key proponent of transcendentalism, he is best known for *Walden, or Life in the Woods* (1854).

tho·ri·a /ˈTHôrēə/ ▶ **n.** Chem. thorium dioxide, ThO_2, a white refractory solid used in making gas mantles and other materials for high-temperature applications. [19th C.: from THORIUM, on the pattern of words such as *alumina* and *magnesia.*]

tho·ri·um /ˈTHôrēəm/ ▶ **n.** the chemical element of atomic number 90, a white radioactive metal of the actinide series. (Symbol: **Th**) [19th C.: named after the god THOR.]

Thorn /tôrn/ German name for TORUŃ.

thorn /THôrn/ ▶ **n. 1** a stiff, sharp-pointed, straight or curved woody projection on the stem or other part of a plant. ■ fig. a source of discomfort, annoyance, or difficulty; an irritation or an obstacle. See also *A THORN IN SOMEONE'S SIDE* below. **2** (also **thorn bush** or **thorn tree**) a thorny bush, shrub, or tree, esp. a hawthorn. **3** an Old English and Icelandic runic letter, Þ or þ, representing the dental fricatives /TH/ and /TH/. In English it was eventually superseded by the digraph *th.* Compare with ETH. [so named from the word of which it was the first letter.]
– PHRASES **a thorn in someone's side** (or **flesh**) a source of continual annoyance or trouble. — **thorn·less adj.** (in sense 1). [OE, of Gmc. origin; rel. to Du. *doorn* and Ger. *Dorn.*]

thorn ap·ple ▶ **n.** another term for JIMSON WEED.

thorn·y /ˈTHôrnē/ ▶ **adj.** (**thorn·i·er, thorn·i·est**) having many thorns or thorn bushes. ■ fig. causing distress, difficulty, or trouble: *a thorny problem for our team to solve.* — **thorn·i·ly adv. thorn·i·ness n.**

thor·ough /ˈTHərō; ˈTHə-rō/ ▶ **adj.** complete with regard to every detail; not superficial or partial: *planners need a thorough understanding of the subject.* ■ performed or written with great care and completeness: *a thorough examination of the wreckage.* ■ taking pains to do something carefully and completely: *the Canadian authorities are very thorough.* ■ [attrib.] absolute (used to emphasize the degree of something, typically something unwelcome or unpleasant): *the child is being a thorough nuisance.* — **thor·ough·ly adv. thor·ough·ness n.** [OE *thuruh,* alt. of *thurh* 'through'; orig. used as an adv. and prep., in senses of *through;* this sense survives in *thoroughfare.*]

thor·ough·bred /ˈTHərəˌbred; ˈTHə-rə-/ ▶ **adj.** (of a horse) of pure breed, esp. of a breed originating from English mares and Arab stallions and widely used as racehorses. ■ informal of outstanding quality: *a thoroughbred car.* ▶ **n.** a horse of a thoroughbred breed. ■ informal an outstanding or first-class person or thing: *this is a real thoroughbred of a record.*

thor·ough·fare /ˈTHərəˌfe(ə)r; ˈTHə-rə-/ ▶ **n.** a road or path forming a route between two places. ■ a main road in a town.

thor·ough·go·ing /ˈTHərəˌgōiNG; ˈTHə-rə-/ ▶ **adj.** involving or attending to every detail or aspect of something: *a thoroughgoing reform of the whole economy.* ■ [attrib.] exemplifying a specified characteristic fully; absolute: *a thoroughgoing chocoholic.*

thor·ough-paced ▶ **adj.** archaic highly skilled or trained. ■ absolute (used to emphasize the degree to which someone or something exemplifies a characteristic).

thor·ough·pin /ˈTHərəˌpin; ˈTHə-rə-/ ▶ **n.** a swelling of the tendon sheath above the hock of a horse, which may be pressed from inside to outside and vice versa.

thorp /THôrp/ (also **thorpe**) ▶ **n.** [in place names] a village or hamlet: *Scunthorpe.* [OE *thorp, throp,* of Gmc. origin; rel. to Du. *dorp* and Ger. *Dorf.*]

Thorpe /THôrp/, Jim, (1888–1953) US track and field athlete; full name *James Francis Thorpe.* He won Olympic gold medals in the pentathlon and decathlon 1912.

Thor·vald·sen /ˈtŏŏrˌvälsən/ (also **Thor·wald·sen**), Bertel (*c.*1770–1844), Danish sculptor.

Thos ▶ **abbr.** Thomas.

those /THōz/ plural form of THAT.

Thoth /THōTH; tōt/ Egyptian Mythol. a moon god, the god of wisdom, justice, and writing, patron of the sciences, and messenger of Ra.

thou[1] /THou/ ▶ **pron.** [second person sing.] archaic or dialect form of YOU, as the singular subject of a verb: *thou art fair, o my beloved.* Compare with THEE. [OE *thu,* of Gmc. origin; rel. to Ger. *du,* from an Indo-Eur. root shared by L. *tu.*]

thou[2] /THou/ ▶ **n.** (pl. same or **thous**) informal a thousand. ■ one thousandth of an inch. [19th C.: abbr.]

though /THō/ ▶ **conj.** despite the fact that; although: *though they were whispering, Philip could hear them.* ■ [with modal] even if (introducing a possibility): *you will be informed of its progress, slow though that may be.* ■ however; but (introducing something opposed to or qualifying what has just been said): *her first name was Rose, though no one called her that.* ▶ **adv.** however (indicating that a factor qualifies or imposes restrictions on what was said previously): *I was hunting for work. Jobs were scarce though.*
– PHRASES **as though** see AS[1]. **even though** see EVEN[1]. [OE *thēah,* of Gmc. origin; rel. to Du. and Ger. *doch;* superseded in ME by forms from ON *thó, thau.*]

thought[1] /THôt/ ▶ **n. 1** an idea or opinion produced by thinking or occurring suddenly in the mind: *Mrs. Oliver's first thought was to get help.* ■ an idea or mental picture, imagined and contemplated: *the mere thought of Peter made her see red.* ■ (**one's thoughts**) one's mind or attention: *you are in our thoughts.* ■ an act of considering or remembering someone or something: *she hadn't given a thought to Max.* ■ (usu. **thought of**) an intention, hope, or idea of doing or receiving something: *he gave up any thought of college.* **2** the action or process of thinking: *deep in thought.* ■ the formation of opinions, esp. as a philosophy or system of ideas, or the opinions so formed: *the traditions of Western thought.* ■ careful consideration or attention: *I haven't given it much thought.* ■ concern for another's well-being or convenience: *he is carrying on, with no thought for me.*
– PHRASES **don't give it another thought** informal used to tell someone not to worry when they have apologized for something. **it's the thought that counts** informal used to indicate that it is the kindness behind an act that matters, however imperfect or insignificant the act may be. **a second thought** [with negative] more than the slightest consideration: *not one of them gave a second thought to the risks involved.* **that's a thought!** informal used to express approval of a comment or suggestion. [OE *thōht,* of Gmc. origin; rel. to Du. *gedachte,* also to THINK.]

thought[2] past and past participle of THINK.

thought con·trol ▶ **n.** the attempt to restrict ideas and impose opinions through censorship and the control of school curricula.

thought·crime /ˈTHôtˌkrīm/ (also **thought-crime**) ▶ **n.** an instance of unorthodox or controversial thinking, considered as a criminal offense or as socially unacceptable.

thought dis·or·der ▶ **n.** Psychiatry a disorder of cognitive organization, characteristic of psychotic mental illness, in which thoughts and conversation appear illogical and lacking in sequence and may be delusional or bizarre in content.

thought ex·per·i·ment ▶ **n.** an experiment carried out only in the imagination.

thought form ▶ **n.** (often **thought forms**) (esp. in Christian theology) a combination of presuppositions, imagery, and vocabulary current at a particular time or place and forming the context for thinking on a subject.

thought·ful /ˈTHôtfəl/ ▶ **adj.** absorbed in or involving thought: *brows drawn together in thoughtful consideration.* ■ showing consideration for the needs of other people: *how thoughtful of you!* ■ showing careful consideration or attention: *her work is thoughtful and provocative.* — **thought·ful·ly adv. thought·ful·ness n.**

thought·less /ˈTHôtlis/ ▶ **adj.** (of a person or their behavior) not showing consideration for the needs of other people: *it was thoughtless of her to walk out.* ■ without consideration of the possible consequences: *a few minutes of thoughtless pleasure ended in tragedy.* — **thought·less·ly adv. thought·less·ness n.**

thought pat·tern ▶ **n.** a habit of thinking in a particular way, using particular assumptions. ■ a quality characterizing someone's thought processes as expressed in language: *thought patterns such as overgeneralization and illogicality.* ■ another term for THOUGHT FORM.

thought-pro·vok·ing ▶ **adj.** stimulating careful consideration or attention: *thought-provoking questions.*

thought re·form ▶ **n.** the systematic alteration of a person's mode of thinking, esp. (in communist China) a process of individual political indoctrination.

thought trans·fer·ence ▶ **n.** another term for TELEPATHY.

thought wave ▶ **n.** a supposed pattern of energy by which it is claimed that thoughts are transferred from one person to another.

thou·sand /ˈTHouzənd/ ▶ **cardinal number** (pl. **-sands** or (with numeral or quantifying word) same) (**a/one thousand**) the number equivalent to the product of a hundred and ten; 1,000: *two thousand acres.* (Roman numeral: **m, M**). ■ (**thousands**) the numbers from one thousand to 9,999: *the cost of repairs could be in the thousands.* ■ (usu. **thousands**) informal an unspecified large number: *you'll meet thousands of girls.* — **thou·sand·fold adj. & adv. thou·sandth** /-zən(t)TH/ **ordinal number.** [OE *thūsend,* of Gmc. origin; rel. to Du. *duizend* and Ger. *Tausend.*]

Thou·sand and One Nights another name for ARABIAN NIGHTS.

Thou·sand Is·land dress·ing ▶ **n.** a dressing made with mayonnaise, ketchup, and chopped gherkins.

Thou·sand Is·lands 1 a group of about 1,500 US and Canadian islands in a widening of the St. Lawrence River, just below Kingston, Ontario, Canada. **2** a group of about 100 small islands off the northern coast of Java. Indonesian name PULAU SERIBU.

Thou·sand Oaks an industrial city in southwestern California, northwest of Los Angeles; pop. 104,352.

thp (also **t.hp.**) ▶ abbr. thrust horsepower.

Thrace /THrās/ an ancient country that was west of the Black Sea and north of the Aegean Sea. — **Thra·cian** /'THrāSHən/ adj. & n.

thrall /THrôl/ ▶ n. literary the state of being in someone's power or having great power over someone: *she was **in thrall to** her abusive husband.* ■ hist. a slave, servant, or captive. — **thrall·dom** /-dəm/ (also **thral·dom**) n. [OE *thrǣl* 'slave,' from ON *thrǽll*.]

thrash /THrasH/ ▶ v. [trans.] beat (a person or animal) repeatedly and violently with a stick or whip. ■ hit (something) hard and repeatedly: *the mast thrashed the deck.* ■ [intrans.] make a repeated crashing by or as if by hitting something: *the surf thrashed and thundered.* ■ [intrans.] move in a violent and convulsive way: *he lay **thrashing around** in pain* | [trans.] *she thrashed her arms, attempting to swim.* ■ [intrans.] (**thrash around**) struggle in a wild or desperate way to do something: *two months of thrashing around on my own.* ■ informal defeat (someone) heavily in a contest or match. ■ [intrans.] move with brute determination or violent movements: *I wrench the steering wheel back and thrash on up the hill.* ■ rare term for THRESH (sense 1). ▶ n. **1** [usu. in sing.] a violent or noisy movement, typically involving hitting something repeatedly: *the thrash of the waves.* **2** (also **thrash metal**) a style of fast, loud, harsh-sounding rock music, combining elements of punk and heavy metal. ■ a short, fast, loud piece or passage of rock music.

– PHRASAL VERBS **thrash something out** discuss something thoroughly and honestly. ■ produce a conclusion by such discussion. [OE, var. of THRESH (an early sense). Current senses of the noun date from the mid 19th C.]

thrash·er[1] /'THrasHər/ ▶ n. **1** a person or thing that thrashes. **2** archaic spelling of THRESHER (sense 1).

thrash·er[2] ▶ n. a thrushlike American songbird (*Toxostoma* and other genera) of the mockingbird family, with mainly brown or gray plumage, a long tail, and a down-curved bill. [19th C.: perh. from Engl. dial. *thrusher, thresher* 'thrush.']

thread /THred/ ▶ n. **1** a long, thin strand of cotton, nylon, or other fibers used in sewing or weaving. ■ cotton, nylon, or other fibers spun into long, thin strands and used for sewing. ■ (**threads**) informal clothes. **2** a thing resembling a thread in length or thinness, in particular: ■ esp. literary a long, thin line or piece of something: *the river was a thread of silver.* ■ [in sing.] something abstract or intangible, regarded as weak or fragile: *the tenuous thread of life.* ■ a theme or characteristic, typically forming one of several, running throughout a situation or piece of writing: *a common thread running through the scandals was the failure to conduct audits.* **3** Comput. a group of linked messages posted on the Internet that share a common subject or theme. ■ a programming structure or process formed by linking a number of separate elements or subroutines. **4** (also **screw thread**) a helical ridge on the outside of a screw, bolt, etc., or on the inside of a cylindrical hole, to allow two parts to be screwed together. ▶ v. [trans.] **1** pass a thread through the eye of (a needle) or through the needle and guides of (a sewing machine). ■ pass (a long, thin object or piece of material) through something and into the required position for use: *he threaded the rope through a pulley.* ■ [intrans.] move carefully or skillfully in and out of obstacles: *she **threaded her way** through the tables.* ■ interweave or intersperse as if with threads: *his hair was **threaded with** gray.* ■ put (beads, chunks of food, or other small objects) together or singly on a thread, chain, or skewer that runs through the center of each one. **2** [usu. as adj.] (**threaded**) cut a screw thread in or on (a hole, screw, or other object).

– PHRASES **hang by a thread** be in a highly precarious state. **lose the** (or **one's**) **thread** be unable to follow what someone is saying or remember what one is going to say next. — **thread·like** adj. [OE *thrǣd* (n.), of Gmc. origin; rel. to Du. *draad* and Ger. *Draht*, also to the verb THROW. The verb dates from ME.]

thread·bare /'THred,be(ə)r/ ▶ adj. (of cloth, clothing, or soft furnishings) becoming thin and tattered with age: *threadbare carpets* | fig. *threadbare clichés.* ■ (of a person, building, or room) poor or shabby in appearance.

thread·er /'THredər/ ▶ n. **1** a device for passing a thread through the needle and guides of a sewing machine. ■ a factory worker who attaches spools of yarn to a loom. **2** a device for cutting a spiral ridge on the outside of a screw or the inside of a hole.

thread·fin /'THred,fin/ ▶ n. a tropical marine fish (family Polynemidae) that has long streamers or rays arising from its pectoral fins, locally important as a food fish.

thread·worm /'THred,wərm/ ▶ n. a very slender parasitic nematode, esp. a pinworm.

thread·y /'THredē/ ▶ adj. (**thread·i·er, thread·i·est**) **1** of, relating to, or resembling a thread. **2** (of a sound, esp. the voice) scarcely audible: *he managed a thready whisper.* ■ Med. (of a person's pulse) scarcely perceptible.

threat /THret/ ▶ n. **1** a statement of an intention to inflict pain, injury, damage, or other hostile action on someone in retribution for something done or not done: *the family has received **death threats**.* ■ Law a menace of bodily harm, such as may restrain a person's freedom of action. **2** a person or thing likely to cause damage or danger: *hurricanes pose a **threat to** coastal communities.* ■ [in sing.] the possibility of trouble, danger, or ruin: *the threat of bankruptcy* | *our jobs came **under threat**.* [OE *thrēat* 'oppression,' of Gmc. origin; rel. to Du. *verdrieten* 'grieve,' Ger. *verdriessen* 'irritate.']

threat·en /'THretn/ ▶ v. [reporting verb] state one's intention to take hostile action against someone in retribution for something done or not done: [trans.] *the unions threatened a strike* | [with infin.] *Tom threatened to leave* | [with direct speech] *"I'll sue," he threatened.* ■ [trans.] express one's intention to harm or kill (someone): *the men **threatened** the customers **with** a handgun.* ■ [trans.] cause (someone or something) to be vulnerable or at risk; endanger: *a broken finger threatened his career* | *hospitals **threatened with** closure.* ■ [with infin.] (of a situation or weather conditions) seem likely to produce an unpleasant or unwelcome result: *the dispute threatened to spread to other cities* | [trans.] *the sky threatened rain.* ■ [intrans.] (of something undesirable) seem likely to occur: *when war threatens, policies change.* — **threat·en·er** n. [OE *thrēatnian* 'urge or induce, esp. by using threats,' from *thrēat* (see THREAT).]

threat·en·ing /'THretn-iNG/ ▶ adj. having a hostile or deliberately frightening quality or manner. ■ Law (of behavior) showing an intention to cause bodily harm. ■ (of a person or situation) causing someone to feel vulnerable or at risk. ■ (of weather conditions) indicating that bad weather is likely. — **threat·en·ing·ly** adv.

three /THrē/ ▶ cardinal number equivalent to the sum of one and two; one more than two; 3: *her three children* | *a three-bedroom house.* (Roman numeral: **iii, III**) ■ a group or unit of three people or things: *clustered in threes.* ■ three years old: *she is only three.* ■ three o'clock: *I'll come at three.* ■ a size of garment or other merchandise denoted by three. ■ a playing card or domino with three pips. [OE *thrīe* (masc.), *thrīo, thrēo* (fem.), of Gmc. origin; rel. to Du. *drie* and Ger. *drei*, from an Indo-Eur. root shared by L. *tres* and Gk. *treis*.]

three-card mon·te ▶ n. a game traditionally associated with con men, in which the dealer shows the player three cards then moves them around facedown, the player being obliged to pick the specified card from among the three.

three cheers ▶ plural n. see CHEER.

three-col·or proc·ess ▶ n. Photog. a means of reproducing natural colors by combining photographic images in the three primary colors.

three-cor·nered ▶ adj. triangular. ■ (esp. of a contest) between three people or groups.

three-deck·er ▶ n. a thing with three levels or layers: [as adj.] *three-decker sandwiches.* ■ hist. a sailing warship with three gun decks.

three-di·men·sion·al ▶ adj. having or appearing to have length, breadth, and depth. ■ fig. (of a literary or dramatic work) sufficiently full in characterization and representation of events to be believable. — **three-di·men·sion·al·i·ty** n. **three-di·men·sion·al·ly** adv.

three·fold /'THrē,fōld/ ▶ adj. three times as great or as numerous: *a threefold increase in taxes.* ■ having three parts or elements: *the differences are threefold.* ▶ adv. by three times; to three times the number or amount: *the aftershocks intensify threefold each time.*

3G ▶ adj. (of telephone technology) third-generation.

Three Grac·es see GRACE.

three-leg·ged race /'legid/ ▶ n. a race run by pairs of people, one member of each pair having their left leg tied to the right leg of the other.

Three Mile Is·land an island in the Susquehanna River near Harrisburg, Pennsylvania, site of a nuclear power station. In 1979, an accident caused damage to the reactor core.

three-mile lim·it ▶ n. Law the outer border of the area extending 3 miles (4.8 km) out to sea from the coast of a state or country, considered to be within its jurisdiction.

three-peat (also **three·peat**) ▶ v. [intrans.] win a particular sports championship three times, esp. consecutively: *the Bulls rate as the favorite to three-peat.* ▶ n. [in sing.] a third win of a particular sports championship, esp. the third of three consecutive wins. [1980s: from THREE + a shortened form of REPEAT.]

three·pence /'THrepəns; 'THrəp-; 'THrē,pens/ ▶ n. Brit. the sum of three pence, esp. before decimalization (1971).

three·pen·ny /'THrip(ə)nē; 'THrəp-; 'THrē,penē/ ▶ adj. [attrib.] Brit. costing or worth three pence, esp. before decimalization (1971). ■ trifling or paltry; of little worth: *a threepenny show.*

three-phase ▶ adj. (of an electric generator, motor, or other device) designed to supply or use simultaneously three separate alternating currents of the same voltage, but with phases differing by a third of a period.

three-piece ▶ adj. [attrib.] consisting of three separate and complementary items, in particular: ■ (of a set of furniture) consisting of a sofa and two armchairs. ■ (of a set of clothes) consisting of slacks or a skirt with a vest and jacket. ▶ n. a set of three separate and complementary items.

three-ply ▶ adj. (of material) having three layers or strands. ▶ n. **1** knitting wool made of three strands. **2** plywood made by gluing together three layers with the grain in different directions.

three-point land·ing ▶ n. a landing of an aircraft on the two main wheels and the tailwheel or skid simultaneously.

three-point turn ▶ n. a method of turning a vehicle around in a narrow space by moving forward, backward, and forward again in a sequence of arcs.

three-quar·ter ▶ adj. [attrib.] consisting of three quarters of something (used esp. with reference to size or length): *a three-quarter length* *cashmere coat.* ■ (of a view or depiction of a person's face) at an angle between full face and profile.

three-ring cir·cus ▶ n. a circus with three rings for simultaneous performances. ■ a public spectacle, esp. one with little substance.

three·score /ˈTHrēˈskôr/ ▶ **cardinal number** literary sixty.

three·some /ˈTHrēsəm/ ▶ n. a group of three people engaged in the same activity. ■ a game or activity for three people.

three-star ▶ adj. (esp. of a hotel or restaurant) given three stars in a grading system, typically one in which this denotes a high or average class or quality (four- or five-star denoting the highest standard). ■ (in the US armed services) having or denoting the rank of lieutenant general, distinguished by three stars on the uniform.

three strikes ▶ n. [usu. as adj.] legislation providing that an offender's third felony is punishable by life imprisonment or another severe sentence. [1990s: from the phr. *three strikes and you're out* (with allusion to baseball).]

three-way ▶ adj. involving three directions, processes, or participants: *a three-way race for the presidency.*

three-wheel·er ▶ n. a vehicle with three wheels, esp. a child's tricycle.

Three Wise Men another name for **MAGI**.

threm·ma·tol·o·gy /ˌTHreməˈtäləjē/ ▶ n. the science of breeding animals and plants. [19th C.: from Gk. *thremma, thremmat-* 'nursling' + -LOGY.]

thren·o·dy /ˈTHrenədē/ ▶ n. (pl. **-dies**) a lament. — **thre·no·di·al** /THrəˈnōdēəl/ adj. **thre·nod·ic** /THrəˈnädik/ adj. **thren·o·dist** n. [17th C.: from Gk. *thrēnōidia*, from *thrēnos* 'wailing' + *ōidē* 'song.']

thre·o·nine /ˈTHrēəˌnēn; -nin/ ▶ n. Biochem. a hydrophilic amino acid, $CH_3CH(OH)CH(NH_2)COOH$, that is a constituent of most proteins. It is an essential nutrient in the diet of vertebrates. [1930s: from *threose* (the name of a tetrose sugar) + -INE[4].]

thresh /THresH/ ▶ v. [trans.] **1** separate grain from (a plant), typically with a flail or by the action of a revolving mechanism: *machinery that threshes corn* | [as n.] (**threshing**) *the afternoon's threshing.* **2** var. of **THRASH** (in the sense of violent movement). [OE *therscan*, later *threscan*, of Gmc. origin; rel. to Du. *dorsen* and Ger. *dreschen*. Cf. **THRASH**.]

thresh·er /ˈTHresHər/ ▶ n. **1** a person or machine that separates grain from the plants by beating. **2** (also **thresher shark**) a surface-living shark (*Alopias vulpinus*, family Alopidae) with a long upper lobe to the tail. Threshers often hunt in pairs, lashing the water with their tails to herd fish into a tightly packed shoal.

thresh·ing floor ▶ n. a hard, level surface on which grain is threshed with a flail.

thresh·ing ma·chine ▶ n. a power-driven machine for separating the grain from the plants.

thresh·old /ˈTHresHˌ(h)ōld/ ▶ n. **1** a strip of wood, metal, or stone forming the bottom of a doorway and crossed in entering a house or room. ■ [in sing.] a point of entry or beginning: ***on the threshold** of a dazzling career.* ■ the beginning of an airport runway on which an aircraft is attempting to land. **2** the magnitude or intensity that must be exceeded for a certain reaction, phenomenon, result, or condition to occur or be manifested. ■ the maximum level of radiation or a concentration of a substance considered to be acceptable or safe: *the safety threshold of 50 mg of nitrates per liter.* ■ Physiol. & Psychol. a limit below which a stimulus causes no reaction: *everyone has a different pain threshold.* [OE *therscold, threscold*; related to Ger. dial. *Drischaufel*; the first element is rel. to **THRESH** (in a Gmc. sense 'tread'), but the origin of the second element is unknown.]

threw /THrōō/ past of **THROW**.

thrice /THrīs/ ▶ adv. chiefly formal or literary three times: *a dose of 25 mg thrice daily* | *thrice married.* ■ [as submodifier] extremely; very: *I was thrice blessed.* [ME *thries*, from earlier *thrie* (from OE *thrīga*, rel. to **THREE**) + -s[3] (later respelled *-ce* to denote the unvoiced sound); cf. **ONCE**.]

thrift /THrift/ ▶ n. **1** the quality of using money and other resources carefully and not wastefully. ■ another term for **SAVINGS AND LOAN**. **2** a European plant (*Armeria maritima*, family Plumbaginaceae) that forms low-growing tufts of slender leaves with rounded pink flowerheads, growing chiefly on sea cliffs and mountains. [ME (in the sense 'prosperity, acquired wealth, success'): from ON, from *thrífa* 'grasp, get hold of.' Cf. **THRIVE**.]

thrift·less /ˈTHriftlis/ ▶ adj. (of a person or their behavior) spending money in an extravagant and wasteful way. — **thrift·less·ly** adv. **thrift·less·ness** n.

thrift shop (also **thrift store**) ▶ n. a store selling secondhand clothes and other household goods, typically to raise funds for a charitable institution.

thrift·y /ˈTHriftē/ ▶ adj. (**thrift·i·er, thrift·i·est**) (of a person or their behavior) using money and other resources carefully and not wastefully: *he had been brought up to be thrifty and careful* | *a thrifty housewife.* — **thrift·i·ly** adv. **thrift·i·ness** n.

thrill /THril/ ▶ n. a sudden feeling of excitement and pleasure: *the thrill of jumping out of an airplane.* ■ an experience that produces such a feeling. ■ a wave or nervous tremor of emotion or sensation. ■ archaic a throb or pulsation. ■ Med. a vibratory movement or resonance heard through a stethoscope. ▶ v. **1** [trans.] cause (someone) to have a sudden feeling of excitement and pleasure: *his kiss thrilled her* | *they were **thrilled to pieces*** | [as adj.] (**thrilling**) *a thrilling ride.* ■ [intrans.] experience such feeling: ***thrill to** the magic.* **2** [intrans.] (of an emotion or sensation) pass with a nervous tremor. ■ [intrans.] literary quiver or throb.

– PHRASES **thrills and chills** the excitement of dangerous sports or entertainments, as experienced by spectators. — **thrill·ing·ly** adv. [ME (as a v. in the sense 'pierce or penetrate'): alt. of dial. *thirl* 'pierce, bore.']

thrill·er /ˈTHrilər/ ▶ n. a novel, play, or movie with an exciting plot, typically involving crime or espionage. ■ a person, thing, or experience that thrills.

thrips /THrips/ (also **thrip**) ▶ n. (pl. same) a minute black winged insect (order Thysanoptera) that sucks plant sap and can be a serious pest of ornamental and food plants when present in large numbers. [18th C.: via L. from Gk., lit. 'woodworm.']

thrive /THrīv/ ▶ v. (past **throve** or **thrived**; past part. **thriven** /ˈTHrivən/ or **thrived**) [intrans.] (of a child, animal, or plant) grow or develop well or vigorously: *the new baby thrived.* ■ prosper; flourish: *education groups **thrive on** organization* | [as adj.] (**thriving**) *a thriving economy.* [ME (orig. in the sense 'grow, increase'): from ON *thrífask*, reflexive of *thrífa* 'grasp, get hold of.' Cf. **THRIFT**.]

thro' /THrōō/ (or **thro**) ▶ prep., adv., & adj. poetic/literary spelling of **THROUGH**.

throat /THrōt/ ▶ n. the passage that leads from the back of the mouth of a person or animal. ■ the front part of a person's or animal's neck, behind which the esophagus, trachea, and blood vessels serving the head are situated. ■ literary a voice of a person or a songbird: *from a hundred throats came the cry "Vive l'Empereur!"* ■ a thing compared to a throat, esp. a narrow passage, entrance, or exit. ■ Sailing the forward upper corner of a quadrilateral fore-and-aft sail.

– PHRASES **be at each other's throats** (of people or organizations) quarrel or fight persistently. **cut one's own throat** bring about one's own downfall by one's actions. **force** (or **shove** or **ram**) **something down someone's throat** force ideas or material on a person's attention by repeatedly putting them forward. **grab** (or **take**) **someone by the throat** put one's hands around someone's throat, typically in an attempt to throttle them. ■ attract someone's undivided attention: *the movie grabs you by the throat.* **jump down someone's throat** see **JUMP**. **stick in one's throat** see **STICK**[2]. — **throat·ed** adj. [in comb.] *a full-throated baritone* | *a ruby-throated hummingbird.* [OE *throte, throtu*, of Gmc. origin; rel. to Ger. *Drossel*. Cf. **THROTTLE**.]

throat·latch /ˈTHrōtˌlacH/ (also **throat·lash** /-ˌlasH/) ▶ n. a strap passing under a horse's throat to help keep the bridle in position. See illustration at **HARNESS**.

throat·y /ˈTHrōtē/ ▶ adj. (**throat·i·er, throat·i·est**) (of a sound such as a person's voice or the noise of an engine) deep and rasping: *rich, throaty laughter.* — **throat·i·ly** adv. **throat·i·ness** n.

throb /THräb/ ▶ v. (**throbbed, throb·bing**) [intrans.] beat or sound with a strong, regular rhythm; pulsate steadily: *the war drums throbbed* | fig. *the crowded streets **throbbed with** life.* ■ feel pain in a series of regular beats: *her foot **throbbed with** pain* | [as adj.] (**throbbing**) *a throbbing headache.* ▶ n. [usu. in sing.] a strong, regular beat or sound; a steady pulsation: *the throb of the ship's engines.* ■ a feeling of pain in a series of regular beats. [ME: prob. imitative.]

throes /THrōz/ ▶ plural n. intense or violent pain and struggle, esp. accompanying birth, death, or great change: *he convulsed in his **death throes**.*

– PHRASES **in the throes of** in the middle of doing or dealing with something very difficult or painful. [ME *throwe* (sing.); perh. rel. to OE *thrēa, thrawu* 'calamity,' influenced by *thrōwian* 'suffer.']

throm·bi /ˈTHrämbī/ plural form of **THROMBUS**.

throm·bin /ˈTHrämbin/ ▶ n. Biochem. an enzyme in blood plasma that causes the clotting of blood by converting fibrinogen to fibrin. [19th C.: from Gk. *thrombos* 'blood clot' + -IN[1].]

thrombo- ▶ comb. form relating to the clotting of blood. [from Gk. *thrombos* 'blood clot.']

throm·bo·cyte /ˈTHrämbəˌsīt/ ▶ n. another term for **PLATELET**.

throm·bo·cy·to·pe·ni·a /ˌTHrämbōˌsītəˈpēnēə/ ▶ n. Med. deficiency of platelets in the blood. This causes bleeding into the tissues, bruising, and slow blood clotting after injury. [1920s: from **THROMBOCYTE** + Gk. *penia* 'poverty.']

throm·bo·em·bo·lism /ˌTHrämbōˈembəˌlizəm/ ▶ n. Med. obstruction of a blood vessel by a blood clot that has become dislodged from another site in the circulation. — **throm·bo·em·bol·ic** /-ˌemˈbälik/ adj.

throm·bo·phle·bi·tis /ˌTHrämbōfləˈbītis/ ▶ n. Med. inflammation of the wall of a vein with associated thrombosis, often occurring in the legs during pregnancy.

throm·bo·plas·tin /ˌTHrämbōˈplastin/ ▶ n. Biochem. an enzyme released from damaged cells, esp. platelets, that converts prothrombin to thrombin during the early stages of blood coagulation.

throm·bo·sis /THrämˈbōsis/ ▶ n. (pl. **-ses** /-sēz/) local coagulation or clotting of the blood in a part of the circulatory system. — **throm·bot·ic** /-ˈbätik/ adj. [18th C.: mod. L., from Gk. *thrombōsis* 'curdling,' from *thrombos* 'blood clot.']

throm·box·ane /THrämˈbäksān/ ▶ n. Biochem. a hormone of the prostacyclin type released from blood platelets. It induces platelet aggregation and arterial constriction.

throm·bus /ˈTHrämbəs/ ▶ n. (pl. **-bi** /-bī/) a blood clot formed in situ within the vascular system of the body and impeding blood flow. [19th C.: mod. L., from Gk. *thrombos* 'lump, blood clot.']

throne /THrōn/ ▶ n. a ceremonial chair for a sovereign, bishop, or similar figure. ■ (**the throne**) used to signify sovereign power: *the heir to the throne.* ■ humorous a toilet. ■ (**thrones**) (in traditional Christian angelology) the third-highest order of the ninefold celestial hierarchy. ▶ v. [trans.] (usu. **be throned**) literary place (someone) on a throne: *the king was throned on a rock.* [ME: from OFr. *trone*, via L. from Gk. *thronos* 'elevated seat.']

throng /THrông; THräng/ ▶ n. a large, densely packed crowd of people or animals: *he pushed his way through the throng* | *a throng of birds.* ▶ v. [trans.] (of a crowd) fill or be present in (a place or area): *a crowd thronged the station.* ■ [intrans.] flock or be present in great numbers: *tourists thronged to the village.* [OE *(ge)thrang* 'crowd, tumult,' of Gmc. origin. The early sense of the verb (ME) was 'press violently, force one's way.']

thros•tle /'THrôsəl/ ▶ n. **1** Brit. old-fashioned term for SONG THRUSH. **2** (also **thros•tle frame**) hist. a machine for continuously spinning wool or cotton. [OE, of Gmc. origin, from an Indo-Eur. root shared by L. *turdus* 'thrush.' Sense 2 dates from the early 19th C. and was appar. named from the humming sound of the machine.]

throt•tle /'THrätl/ ▶ n. **1** a device controlling the flow of fuel or power to an engine: *engines at full throttle.* **2** archaic a throat, gullet, or windpipe. ▶ v. [trans.] **1** attack or kill (someone) by choking or strangling them. **2** control (an engine or vehicle) with a throttle. ■ (**throttle back** or **down**) reduce the power of an engine or vehicle by use of the throttle. —**throt•tler** n. [ME (as a v.): perhaps a frequentative, from THROAT; the noun (dating from the mid 16th C. in sense 2) is perh. a dimin. of THROAT, but the history of the word is not clear.]

throt•tle•hold /'THrätl,hōld/ ▶ n. another term for STRANGLEHOLD.

through /THrōō/ ▶ prep. & adv. **1** moving in one side and out of the other side of (an opening, channel, or location): [as prep.] *stepping through the doorway* | [as adv.] *we opened the gate, and they came streaming through.* ■ so as to make a hole or opening in (a physical object): [as prep.] *the truck smashed through a wall* | [as adv.] *cut it, but not all the way through.* ■ moving around or from one side to the other within (a crowd or group): [as prep.] *making my way through the guests.* ■ so as to be perceived from the other side of (an intervening obstacle): [as prep.] *the sun streaming in through the window* | [as adv.] *moonlight streamed through.* ■ [prep.] expressing the position or location of something beyond or at the far end of (an opening or an obstacle): *the path is through a gate.* ■ expressing the extent of turning from one orientation to another: [as prep.] *each joint can move through an angle within fixed limits.* **2** continuing in time toward completion of (a process or period): [as prep.] *he showed up halfway through the second act* | [as adv.] *to struggle through until payday.* ■ so as to complete (a particular stage or trial) successfully: [as prep.] *she had come through her sternest test* | [as adv.] *I will struggle through alone.* ■ from beginning to end of (an experience or activity, typically a tedious or stressful one): [as prep.] *we sat through boring speeches* | [as adv.] *Karl will see you through, Ingrid.* **3** so as to inspect all or part of (a collection, inventory, or publication): [as prep.] *flipping through the pages of a notebook* | [as adv.] *she read the letter through carefully.* **4** [prep.] up to and including (a particular point in an ordered sequence): *from March 24 through May 7.* **5** [prep.] by means of (a process or intermediate stage): *dioxins get into mothers' milk through contaminated food.* ■ by means of (an intermediary or agent): *seeking justice through the proper channels.* **6** [adv.] so as to be connected by telephone: *he put a call through to the senator.* ▶ adj. **1** [attrib.] (of a means of public transportation or a ticket) continuing or valid to the final destination: *a through train from Boston.* **2** [attrib.] denoting traffic that passes from one side of a place to another in the course of a longer journey. ■ denoting a road that is open at both ends, allowing traffic free passage from one end to the other. **3** [attrib.] (of a room) running the whole length of a building. **4** [predic.] informal having no prospect of any future relationship, dealings, or success: *you and I are through.*

– PHRASES **through and through** in every aspect; thoroughly or completely. [OE *thurh* (prep. and adv.), of Gmc. origin; rel. to Du. *door* and Ger. *durch*. The spelling change to *thr-* appears *c.*1300, becoming standard from Caxton onward.]

through•out /THrōō'out/ ▶ prep. & adv. all the way through, in particular: ■ in every part of (a place or object): [as prep.] *it had repercussions throughout Europe* | [as adv.] *the house is in good order throughout.* ■ from beginning to end of (an event or period of time): [as prep.] *she was a faithful member throughout her life* | [as adv.] *both sets of parents retained a smiling dignity throughout.*

through•put /'THrōō,pŏŏt/ ▶ n. the amount of material or items passing through a system or process.

through•way ▶ n. another spelling of THRUWAY.

throve /THrōv/ past of THRIVE.

throw /THrō/ ▶ v. [trans.] (past **threw**; past part. **thrown** /THrōn/) **1** propel (something) with force through the air by a movement of the arm and hand. ■ push or force (someone or something) violently and suddenly into a particular physical position or state. ■ put in place or erect quickly: *the stewards had thrown a cordon across the fairway.* ■ move (a part of the body) quickly or suddenly in a particular direction: *she threw her head back.* ■ project or cast (light or shadow) in a particular direction: *a chandelier threw its bright light over the walls.* ■ deliver (a punch). ■ direct a particular kind of look or facial expression: *she threw a withering glance at him.* ■ project (one's voice) so that it appears to come from someone or something else, as in ventriloquism. ■ (**throw something off/on**) put on or take off (a garment) hastily: *I threw on my housecoat.* ■ move (a switch or lever) so as to operate a device. ■ roll (dice). ■ obtain (a specified number) by rolling dice. ■ informal lose (a race or contest) intentionally, esp. in return for a bribe. **2** cause to enter suddenly a particular state or condition: *the bond market was thrown into confusion.* ■ put (someone) in a particular place or state, esp. in a rough, abrupt, or summary fashion: *these guys should be thrown in jail.* ■ [trans.] disconcert; confuse: *she frowned, thrown by this apparent change of tack.* **3** send (one's opponent) to the ground in wrestling, judo, or similar activity. ■ (of a horse) unseat (its rider). ■ (of a horse) lose (a shoe). ■ (of an animal) give birth to (young, of a specified kind). **4** form (ceramic ware) on a potter's wheel. ■ turn (wood or other material) on a lathe. ■ twist (silk or other fabrics) into thread or yarn. **5** have (a fit or tantrum). **6** give or hold (a party). ▶ n. **1** an act of throwing something: *Jeter's throw to first.* ■ an act of throwing one's opponent in wrestling, judo, or similar sport: *a shoulder throw.* **2** a light cover for furniture. ■ short for THROW RUG. **3** short for *THROW OF THE DICE* (see DICE). **4** Geol. the extent of vertical displacement in a fault. **5** [usu. in sing.] the action or motion of a slide valve or of a crank, eccentric wheel, or cam. ■ the extent of such motion. ■ the distance moved by the pointer of an instrument. **6** (**a throw**) informal used to indicate how much a single item, turn, or attempt costs: *portraits at $25 a throw.*

– PHRASES **throw away the key** used to suggest that someone who has been put in prison should or will never be released. **throw good money after bad** incur further loss in a hopeless attempt to recoup a previous loss. **throw one's hand in** withdraw from a card game, poker, because one has a poor hand. ■ withdraw from a contest or activity; give up. **throw in the towel** (of boxers or their seconds) throw a towel (or sponge) into the ring as a token of defeat. ■ abandon a struggle; admit defeat. **throw oneself on** (or **upon**) **someone's mercy** abjectly ask someone for help, forgiveness, or leniency. **throw up one's hands** raise both hands in the air as an indication of one's exasperation.

– PHRASAL VERBS **throw money around** spend money freely and ostentatiously. **throw oneself at** appear too eager to become the sexual partner of. **throw something away 1** discard something as useless or unwanted. ■ waste or fail to make use of an opportunity or advantage. ■ discard a playing card in a game. **2** (of an actor) deliver a line with deliberate underemphasis for increased dramatic effect. **throw something in 1** include something, typically at no extra cost, with something that is being sold or offered: *they cut the price and threw in an AC adaptor.* **2** make a remark casually as an interjection in a conversation: *he threw in a sensible remark about funding.* **throw oneself into** start to do (something) with enthusiasm and vigor: *Eve threw herself into her work.* **throw something off 1** rid oneself of something: *struggling to throw off a virus.* **2** write or utter in an offhand manner: *Thomas threw off the question.* **throw oneself on** (or **upon**) attack someone vigorously. **throw something open** make something accessible: *the market was thrown open.* ■ invite general discussion of or participation in a subject or a debate or other event: *the debate will be thrown open to the audience.* **throw someone out 1** expel someone unceremoniously from a place, organization, or activity. **2** Baseball put out a runner by a throw to the base being approached followed by a tag. **throw something out 1** discard something as unwanted. **2** (of a court, legislature, or other body) dismiss or reject something brought before it: *the charges were thrown out by the judge.* **3** put forward a suggestion tentatively. **4** cause numbers or calculations to become inaccurate: *an undisclosed stock option throws out all your figures.* **5** emit or radiate something: *a big range fire that threw out heat like a furnace.* **6** (of a plant) rapidly develop a side shoot, bud, etc. **throw someone over** abandon or reject someone as a lover. **throw people together** bring people into contact, esp. by chance. **throw something together** make or produce something hastily, without careful planning or arrangement. **throw up** vomit. **throw something up 1** informal vomit something one has eaten or drunk. **2** produce something and bring it to notice: *a fruitful tradition that threw up new ideas.* **3** erect a building or structure hastily. —**throw•a•ble** adj. **throw•er** n. [OE *thrāwan* 'to twist, turn,' of West Gmc. origin.]

throw•a•way /'THrōə,wā/ ▶ adj. **1** denoting or relating to products that are intended to be discarded after being used once or a few times: *a throwaway camera.* **2** (of a remark) expressed in a casual or understated way: *some people overreacted to a few throwaway lines.* ▶ n. a thing intended or destined to be discarded after brief use or appeal. ■ a casual or understated remark or idea.

throw•back /'THrō,bak/ ▶ n. a reversion to an earlier ancestral characteristic. ■ a person or thing having the characteristics of a former time: *a lot of his work is a throwback to the fifties.*

throw•down /'THrō,doun/ ▶ n. informal a performance by or competition between rappers, breakdancers, etc.: *a funky hip-hop throwdown.*

throw-in ▶ n. something or someone that is included as part of an arrangement or transaction, with no additional cost or obligation to the recipient. ■ Soccer the act of throwing the ball from the sideline to restart play after the ball has gone out of bounds.

throw pil•low ▶ n. a small decorative pillow placed on a chair or couch.

throw rug ▶ n. a small decorative rug designed to be placed with a casual effect and moved as required.

throw•ster /'THrōstər/ ▶ n. a person who twists silk fibers into thread.

thru /THrōō/ ▶ prep., adv., & adj. informal spelling of THROUGH.

thrum[1] /THrəm/ ▶ v. (**thrummed, thrum•ming**) [intrans.] make a continuous

PRONUNCIATION KEY ə *ago, up*; ər *over, fur*; a *hat*; ā *ate*; ä *car*; e *let*; ē *see*; i *fit*; ī *by*; NG *sing*; ō *go*; ô *law, for*; oi *toy*; ŏŏ *good*; ōō *goo*; ou *out*; TH *thin*; TH *then*; ZH *vision*

rhythmic humming sound. ■ [trans.] strum (the strings of a musical instrument) in a rhythmic way. ▶ n. [usu. in sing.] a continuous rhythmic humming sound: *the steady thrum of rain on the windows.* [16th C. (as a v.): imitative.]

thrum² ▶ n. (in weaving) an unwoven end of a warp thread, or a fringe of such ends, left in the loom when the finished cloth is cut away. ■ any short loose thread. ▶ v. (**thrummed, thrum·ming**) [trans.] cover or adorn (cloth or clothing) with ends of thread. — **thrum·mer** n. **thrum·my** adj. [OE *thrum* (only in *tungethrum* 'ligament of the tongue'): of Gmc. origin; rel. to Du. *dreum* 'thrum' and Ger. *Trumm* 'endpiece.' The current sense dates from ME.]

thrush¹ /THrəsH/ ▶ n. a small or medium-sized songbird (*Turdus* and other genera), typically having a brown back, spotted breast, and loud song. The **thrush family** (subfamily Turdinae, family Muscicapidae) includes the chats, robins, bluebirds, blackbirds, nightingales, redstarts, and wheatears. See illustration at HERMIT THRUSH. [OE *thrysce*, of Gmc. origin; rel. to THROSTLE.]

thrush² ▶ n. **1** infection of the mouth and throat, producing whitish patches, caused by a yeastlike fungus (genus *Candida*), esp. *C. albicans.* ■ infection of the female genitals with the same fungus. **2** a chronic condition affecting the frog of a horse's foot, causing the accumulation of a dark, foul-smelling substance. Also called CANKER. [17th C.: origin uncert.; sense 1 possibly rel. to Swed. *torsk* and Dan. *troske*; sense 2 perhaps from dial. *frush* in the same sense, perh. from OFr. *fourchette* 'frog of a horse's hoof.']

thrust /THrəst/ ▶ v. (past **thrust**) [trans.] push (something or someone) suddenly or violently in the specified direction: *she thrust her hands into her pockets* | fig. *thrust into the limelight* | [intrans.] *he thrust at his opponent with his sword.* ■ [intrans.] (of a person) move or advance forcibly: *she thrust through the brambles.* ■ [intrans.] (of a thing) extend so as to project conspicuously: *a jetty thrust out into the water.* ■ (**thrust something on/upon**) force (someone) to accept or deal with something: *fame had been thrust upon him.* ■ [intrans.] (of a man) penetrate the vagina or anus of a sexual partner with forceful movements of the penis. ▶ n. **1** a sudden or violent lunge with a pointed weapon or a bodily part: *one powerful thrust.* ■ a forceful attack or effort: *a new thrust in business development.* ■ [in sing.] the principal purpose or theme of a course of action or line of reasoning: *anti-Americanism became the main thrust of their policy.* **2** the propulsive force of a jet or rocket engine. ■ the lateral pressure exerted by an arch or other support in a building. **3** (also **thrust fault**) Geol. a reverse fault of low angle, with older strata displaced horizontally over newer.
– PHRASES **cut and thrust** see CUT. [ME (as a v.): from ON *thrýsta*; perh. rel. to L. *trudere* 'to thrust.' The noun is first recorded (early 16th C.) in the sense 'act of pressing.']

thrust·er /'THrəstər/ ▶ n. a person or thing that thrusts, in particular: ■ a small rocket engine on a spacecraft, used to make alterations in its flight path or altitude. ■ a secondary jet or propeller on a ship or offshore rig, used for accurate maneuvering and maintenance of position.

thrust·ing /'THrəstiNG/ ▶ n. the motion of pushing or lunging suddenly or violently. ■ Geol. the pushing upward of the earth's crust.

thrust stage ▶ n. a stage that extends into the auditorium so that the audience is seated around three sides.

thru·way /'THrōō,wā/ (also **through·way**) ▶ n. a major road or highway.

Thu·cyd·i·des /THōō'sidi,dēz/ (*c.*455–*c.*400 BC), Greek historian and author of *History of the Peloponnesian War.*

thud /THəd/ ▶ n. a dull, heavy sound, such as that made by an object falling to the ground. ▶ v. (**thud·ded, thud·ding**) [intrans.] move, fall, or strike something with a dull, heavy sound. [ME (orig. Scots): prob. from OE *thyddan* 'to push.']

thug /THəg/ ▶ n. **1** a violent person, esp. a criminal. [19th C.: extension of sense 2.] **2** (**Thug**) hist. a member of a religious organization of robbers and assassins in India, suppressed by the British in the 1830s. — **thug·ger·y** n. **thug·gish** adj. **thug·gish·ly** adv. **thug·gish·ness** n. [19th C. (sense 2): from Hindi *ṭhag* 'swindler, thief,' based on Sanskrit *sthagati* 'he covers or conceals.']

thu·ja /'THōōjə/ (also **thu·ya** /'THōōyə/) ▶ n. a North American and eastern Asian cedar of a genus (*Thuja*) that includes the arbor vitaes. ■ the wood from this tree. [mod. L. (genus name), from Gk. *thuia*, denoting an African tree formerly included in the genus.]

Thu·le 1 /'THōōlē; THōōl/ a country described by the ancient Greek explorer Pytheas (*c.*310 BC) as being six days' sail north of Britain, most plausibly identified with Norway. **2** /'tōōlē/ an Eskimo culture existing from Alaska to Greenland *c.*AD 500–1400. **3** /'tōōlē/ a settlement on the northwestern coast of Greenland.

thu·li·um /'TH(y)ōōlēəm/ ▶ n. the chemical element of atomic number 69, a soft silvery-white metal of the lanthanide series. (Symbol: **Tm**) [19th C.: mod. L., from L. *Thule* THULE (sense 1), from Gk. *Thoulē*, of unknown origin.]

Thumb /THəm/, General Tom, (1838–83) US circus entertainer; born *Charles S. Stratton.* A 40-inch-tall man, he was a sideshow attraction for P. T. Barnum.

thumb /THəm/ ▶ n. the short, thick first digit of the human hand, set lower and apart from the other four and opposable to them. ■ the corresponding digit of primates or other mammals. ■ the part of a glove intended to cover the thumb. ▶ v. [trans.] press, move, or touch (something) with one's thumb: *she thumbed the button, to open the door.* ■ turn over (pages) with or as if with one's thumb: [intrans.] *thumbing through that magazine.* ■ (usu. **be thumbed**) wear or soil (a book's pages) by repeated handling. ■ hitchhike by signaling with one's thumb: *I tried to **thumb a ride*** | [intrans.] *he **thumbed his way** across France.*
– PHRASES **be all thumbs** informal be clumsy or awkward in one's actions. **thumb one's nose at** informal show disdain or contempt for. **thumbs up** (or **down**) informal an indication of satisfaction or approval (or of rejection or failure): *plans to build a house have been given the thumbs down.* **under someone's thumb** completely under someone's influence or control. — **thumbed** adj. **thumb·less** adj. [OE *thūma*, of West Gmc. origin.]

thumb in·dex ▶ n. a set of lettered grooves cut down the side of a book, esp. a diary or dictionary, for easy reference. — **thumb-in·dexed** adj.

thumb·nail /'THəm,nāl/ ▶ n. **1** the nail of the thumb. **2** [usu. as adj.] a very small or concise description, representation, or summary: *a thumbnail sketch.* ■ Comput. a small picture of an image or page layout.

thumb pi·an·o ▶ n. any of various musical instruments, mainly of African origin, made from strips of metal fastened to a resonator and played by plucking with the fingers and thumbs. Also called KALIMBA, MBIRA.

thumb·print /'THəm,print/ ▶ n. an impression or mark made on a surface by the inner part of the top joint of the thumb, esp. as used for identifying individuals from the unique pattern of whorls and lines. ■ fig. a distinctive identifying characteristic: *it has an individuality and thumbprint of its own.*

thumb·screw /'THəm,skrōō/ ▶ n. **1** a screw with a protruding winged or flattened head for turning with the thumb and forefinger. **2** (usu. **thumbscrews**) an instrument of torture for crushing the thumbs.

thumb·suck·er /'THəm,səkər/ (also **thumb-suck·er**) ▶ n. informal, often derog. a serious piece of journalism that concentrates on the background and interpretation of events rather than on the news or action; a think piece. ■ a journalist who writes in this style.

thumb·tack /'THəm,tak/ ▶ n. a short flat-headed pin, used for fastening paper to a wall or other surface.

thumb·wheel /'THəm,(h)wēl/ ▶ n. a control device for electrical or mechanical equipment in the form of a wheel operated with the thumb.

Thum·mim ▶ n. see URIM AND THUMMIM.

thump /THəmp/ ▶ v. [trans.] hit (someone or something) heavily, esp. with the fist or a blunt implement: *he thumped the desk with his hand* | [intrans.] *thump on the door.* ■ move (something) forcefully, noisily, or decisively: *she thumped down the cup.* ■ [intrans.] move or do something with a heavy deadened sound: *Phil thumped down on the sofa.* ■ [intrans.] (of a person's heart or pulse) beat or pulsate strongly, typically because of fear or excitement. ■ informal defeat heavily: *Tampa Bay thumped Toronto 8–0.* ▶ n. a heavy dull blow with a person's fist or a blunt implement: *I felt a thump on my back.* ■ a loud deadened sound. ■ a strong heartbeat, esp. one caused by fear or excitement. — **thump·er** n. [16th C.: imitative.]

thump·ing /'THəmpiNG/ ▶ adj. [attrib.] **1** pounding; throbbing: *the thumping beat of her heart.* **2** informal of an impressive size, extent, or amount: *a thumping 64 percent majority.*

thun·der /'THəndər/ ▶ n. a loud rumbling or crashing noise heard after a lightning flash due to the expansion of rapidly heated air. ■ a resounding loud deep noise: *the thunder of the falls in the distance.* ■ used in similes and comparisons to refer to an angry facial expression or tone of voice: *he spoke in a voice like thunder.* ■ [as exclam.] dated used to express anger, annoyance, or incredulity: ***by thunder**, I intend to have my own way.* ▶ v. [intrans.] (**it thunders, it is thundering**, etc.) thunder sounds: *it began to thunder.* ■ make a loud, deep resounding noise: *the train thundered through the night.* ■ [trans.] strike powerfully: *McGwire thundered that one out of the stadium.* ■ speak loudly and forcefully or angrily, esp. to denounce or criticize: ***he thundered against** the ruling* | [with direct speech] *"Sit down!" thundered Morse.*
– PHRASES **steal someone's thunder** see STEAL. — **thun·der·er** n. **thun·der·y** adj. [OE *thunor* (n.), *thunrian* (v.), of Gmc. origin; rel. to Du. *donder* and Ger. *Donner*, from an Indo-Eur. root shared by L. *tonare* 'to thunder.']

Thun·der Bay a city on a large bay of Lake Superior in western Ontario, Canada; pop. 113,946.

thun·der·bird /'THəndər,bərd/ ▶ n. a mythical bird thought by some North American Indians to bring thunder.

thun·der·bolt /'THəndər,bōlt/ ▶ n. literary a flash of lightning with a simultaneous crash of thunder. ■ a supposed bolt or shaft believed to be the destructive agent in a lightning flash, esp. as an attribute of a god such as Jupiter or Thor. ■ used in similes and comparisons to refer to a very sudden or unexpected event or item of news, esp. of an unpleasant nature: *it hit her like a thunderbolt.* ■ informal a very fast and powerful shot, throw, or stroke.

thun·der·clap /'THəndər,klap/ ▶ n. a crash of thunder (often used to refer to something startling or unexpected): *the door opened like a thunderclap.*

thun·der·cloud /'THəndər,kloud/ ▶ n. a cumulus cloud with a towering or spreading top, charged with electricity and producing thunder and lightning.

thun·der·head /'THəndər,hed/ ▶ n. a rounded, projecting head of a cumulus cloud, which portends a thunderstorm.

thun·der·ing /'THənd(ə)riNG/ ▶ adj. [attrib.] making a resounding, loud, deep noise: *thundering waterfalls.* ■ informal extremely great, severe, or impressive. — **thun·der·ing·ly** adv. [as submodifier] *it was so thunderingly dull.*

thun·der·ous /'THənd(ə)rəs/ ▶ adj. of, relating to, or giving warning of thunder: *a thunderous gray cloud.* ■ very loud: *thunderous applause.* ■ very powerful or intense: *thunderous adventures.* — **thun·der·ous·ly** adv. **thun·der·ous·ness** n.

thun·der·storm /'THəndər,stôrm/ ▶ n. a storm with thunder and lightning and typically also heavy rain or hail.

thun·der·struck /'THəndər,strək/ ▶ adj. extremely surprised or shocked.

thun·der thighs ▶ n. informal large thighs, especially those with a great deal of cellulite.

thunk[1] /THəNGk/ ▶ n. & v. informal term for THUD.

thunk[2] informal or humorous past and past participle of THINK: *who woulda thunk it?*

Thur. ▶ abbr. Thursday.

Thur·ber /'THərbər/, James Grover (1894–1961), US humorist and cartoonist. His works include *My World—And Welcome to It* (1942), which contains the story "The Secret Life of Walter Mitty."

thu·ri·ble /'THo͝orəbəl/ ▶ n. a censer. [ME: from OFr., or from L. *thuribulum*, from *thus, thur-* 'incense' (see THURIFER).]

thu·ri·fer /'THo͝orəfər/ ▶ n. an acolyte carrying a censer. [19th C.: from late L., from L. *thus, thur-* 'incense' (from Gk. *thuos* 'sacrifice') + *-fer* '-bearing.']

Thu·rin·gi·a /THo͝o'rinj(ē)ə/ a densely forested state of central Germany. German name **THÜRINGEN.**

Thur·mond /'THərmənd/, Strom (1902–2003), US politician; full name *James Strom Thurmond.* He was a member of the US Senate from South Carolina 1954–2003.

Thurs. ▶ abbr. Thursday.

Thurs·day /'THərzdā; -dē/ ▶ n. the day of the week before Friday and following Wednesday. ▶ adv. on Thursday: *he called her up Thursday.* ■ (**Thursdays**) on Thursdays; each Thursday: *the column is published Thursdays.* [OE *Thu(n)resdæg* 'day of thunder,' translation of late L. *Jovis dies* 'day of Jupiter' (god associated with thunder): cf. Du. *donderdag* and Ger. *Donnerstag.*]

thus /T͟Həs/ ▶ adv. literary or formal **1** as a result or consequence of this; therefore. **2** in the manner now being indicated or exemplified; in this way: *she phoned Susan, and while she was thus engaged, Charles summoned the doctor.* **3** to this point; so: *he has not been a burden thus far.* [OE, of unknown origin.]

thus·ly /'T͟Həslē/ ▶ adv. informal another term for THUS (sense 2): *the review was conducted thusly.*

thu·ya /'THo͞oyə/ ▶ n. var. of THUJA.

thwack /THwak/ ▶ v. [trans.] strike forcefully with a sharp blow: *she thwacked the back of their knees.* ▶ n. a sharp blow: *he hit it with a hefty thwack.* [ME: imitative.]

thwart /THwôrt/ ▶ v. [trans.] prevent (someone) from accomplishing something: *he never did anything to thwart his father* | *he was thwarted in his plans.* ■ oppose (a plan, attempt, or ambition) successfully: *they thwarted all attempts to form opposition parties.* ▶ n. a structural crosspiece forming a seat for a rower in a boat. ▶ prep. & adv. archaic or literary from one side to another side of; across: [as prep.] *a cloud spread thwart the shore.* [ME *thwerte,* from the adjective *thwert* 'perverse, obstinate, adverse,' from ON *thvert,* neut. of *thverr* 'transverse,' from an Indo-Eur. root shared by L. *torquere* 'to twist.']

thy /T͟Hī/ (also **thine** before a vowel) ▶ possessive adj. archaic or dialect form of YOUR: *honor thy father.* [ME *thi* (orig. before words beginning with any consonant except *h*), reduced from *thin,* from OE *thīn* (see THINE).]

Thy·es·tes /THī'estēz/ Gk. Mythol. the brother of Atreus and father of Aegisthus. — **Thy·es·te·an** /-tēən/ adj.

thy·la·cine /'THīlə,sīn; -sin/ ▶ n. a doglike carnivorous marsupial (*Thylacinus cynocephalus,* family Thylacinidae) with stripes across the rump, found only in Tasmania. There have been no confirmed sightings since one was captured in 1933, and it may now be extinct. Also called TASMANIAN WOLF. [19th C.: from mod. L. *Thylacinus* (genus name), from Gk. *thulakos* 'pouch.']

thy·la·koid /'THīlə,koid/ ▶ n. Bot. each of a number of flattened sacs inside a chloroplast, bounded by pigmented membranes on which the light reactions of photosynthesis take place, and arranged in stacks or grana. [1960s: from Ger. *Thylakoid,* from Gk. *thulakoidēs* 'pouchlike,' from *thulakos* 'pouch.']

thyme /tīm/ ▶ n. a low-growing aromatic plant (genus *Thymus*) of the mint family. The small leaves are used as a culinary herb, and the plant yields a medicinal oil. — **thym·y** adj. [ME: from OFr. *thym,* via L. from Gk. *thumon,* from *thuein* 'burn, sacrifice.']

thy·mec·to·my /THī'mektəmē/ ▶ n. (pl. **-mies**) surgical removal of the thymus gland.

thy·mi /'THīmī/ plural form of THYMUS.

thy·mic /'THīmik/ ▶ adj. Physiol. of or relating to the thymus gland or its functions.

thy·mi·dine /'THīmə,dēn/ ▶ n. Biochem. a crystalline nucleoside present in DNA, consisting of thymine linked to deoxyribose. [20th C.: from THYMINE + -IDE + -INE[4].]

thy·mine /'THīmēn; -min/ ▶ n. Biochem. a compound, $C_5H_6N_2O_2$, that is one of the four constituent bases of nucleic acids. A pyrimidine derivative, it is paired with adenine in double-stranded DNA. [19th C.: from THYMUS + -INE[4].]

thy·mo·cyte /'THīmə,sīt/ ▶ n. Physiol. a lymphocyte within the thymus gland. [1920s: from THYMUS + -CYTE.]

thy·mol /'THīmôl; -mōl/ ▶ n. Chem. a white crystalline compound, $C_{10}H_{13}OH$, present in oil of thyme and used as a flavoring and preservative. [19th C.: from Gk. *thumon* 'thyme' + -OL.]

thy·mo·ma /THī'mōmə/ ▶ n. (pl. **-mas** or **-ma·ta** /-mətə/) Med. a rare, usually benign tumor arising from thymus tissue and sometimes associated with myasthenia gravis. [20th C.: from THYMUS + -OMA.]

thy·mus /'THīməs/ (also **thy·mus gland**) ▶ n. (pl. **-mus·es** or **-mi** /-mī/) a lymphoid organ situated in the neck of vertebrates that produces T cells for the immune system. The human thymus becomes much smaller at the approach of puberty. [16th C. (denoting a growth or tumor resembling a bud): from Gk. *thumos* 'excrescence like a thyme bud, thymus gland.']

thy·ris·tor /THī'ristər/ ▶ n. Electron. a four-layered semiconductor rectifier in which the flow of current between two electrodes is triggered by a signal at a third electrode. [1950s: blend of *thyratron,* denoting a kind of thermionic tube (from Gk. *thura* 'gate') and TRANSISTOR.]

thyro- ▶ comb. form representing THYROID.

thy·ro·cal·ci·to·nin /,THīrō,kalsi'tōnin/ ▶ n. another term for CALCITONIN, believed until the late 1960s to denote a different hormone.

thy·ro·glob·u·lin /,THīrō'gläbyəlin/ ▶ n. Biochem. a protein present in the thyroid gland, from which thyroid hormones are synthesized.

thy·roid /'THīroid/ ▶ n. **1** (also **thyroid gland**) a large ductless gland in the neck that secretes hormones regulating growth and development through the rate of metabolism. ■ an extract prepared from the thyroid gland of animals and used in treating deficiency of thyroid hormones. **2** (also **thyroid cartilage**) a large cartilage of the larynx, a projection of which forms the Adam's apple in humans. [18th C. (as an adj.): from Gk. *(khondros) thureoeidēs* 'shield-shaped (cartilage),' from *thureos* 'oblong shield.']

thy·roid·i·tis /,THīroi'dītis/ ▶ n. inflammation of the thyroid.

thy·roid-stim·u·lat·ing hor·mone ▶ n. another term for THYROTROPIN.

thy·ro·tox·i·co·sis /,THīrō,täksi'kōsis/ ▶ n. another term for HYPERTHYROIDISM.

thy·ro·tro·pin /,THīrō'trōpin; THī'rätrə-/ (also **thy·ro·tro·phin** /-fin/) ▶ n. Biochem. a hormone secreted by the pituitary gland that regulates the production of thyroid hormones.

thy·ro·tro·pin-re·leas·ing hor·mone (also **thyrotropin-releasing factor**) ▶ n. Biochem. a hormone secreted by the hypothalamus which stimulates release of thyrotropin.

thy·rox·ine /THī'räksēn; -sin/ (also **thy·rox·in** /-'räksin/) ▶ n. Biochem. the main hormone, $C_{15}H_{11}NO_4I_4$, produced by the thyroid gland, acting to increase metabolic rate and so regulating growth and development. [20th C.: from THYROID + OX- 'oxygen' + *in* from INDOLE (because of an early misunderstanding of its chemical structure), alt. by substitution of -INE[4].]

thyr·sus /'THərsəs/ ▶ n. (pl. **-si** /-sī/) (in ancient Greece and Rome) a staff or spear tipped with an ornament like a pine cone, carried by Dionysus and his followers. [L., from Gk. *thursos* 'plant stalk, Bacchic staff.']

Thy·sa·nop·ter·a /,THīsə'näptərə; ,THis-/ Entomol. an order of insects that comprises the thrips. ■ [as pl. n.] (**thysanoptera**) insects of this order; thrips. — **thy·sa·nop·ter·an** n. & adj. [mod. L. (pl.), from Gk. *thusanos* 'tassel' + *pteron* 'wing.']

Thy·sa·nu·ra /,THīsə'n(y)o͝orə/ Entomol. an order of insects that comprises the true, or three-pronged, bristletails. ■ [as pl. n.] (**thysanura**) insects of this order; bristletails. — **thy·sa·nu·ran** n. & adj. [mod. L. (pl.), from Gk. *thusanos* 'tassel' + *oura* 'tail.']

thy·self /,T͟Hī'self/ ▶ pron. [second person sing.] archaic or dialect form of YOURSELF, corresponding to the subject THOU[1]: *thou shalt love thy neighbor as thyself.*

Thz ▶ abbr. terahertz.

Ti ▶ symb. the chemical element titanium.

ti /tē/ ▶ n. (in solmization) the seventh note of a major scale. ■ the note B in the fixed-do system. [19th C.: alt. of SI, adopted to avoid having two notes (*sol* and *si*) beginning with the same letter (see SOLMIZATION).]

TIA Med. ▶ abbr. transient ischemic attack.

tian /tyan/ ▶ n. (pl. same) a dish of finely chopped vegetables cooked in olive oil and then baked au gratin. ■ a large oval earthenware cooking pot traditionally used in Provence. [Provençal, based on Gk. *tēganon* 'frying pan.']

Tian·an·men Square /'tyän'än,men; tē'enə(n)-/ a square in the center of Beijing adjacent to the Forbidden City. In 1989, government troops opened fire there on unarmed pro-democracy protesters, killing more than 2,000. [Chin., lit. 'gate of heavenly peace.']

Tian·jin /'tyen'jin/ (also **Tien·tsin** pronunc. same or /'tyent'sin/) a port in northeastern China, in Hubei province; pop. 5,700,000.

ti·ar·a /tē'ärə; -'arə; -'e(ə)rə/ ▶ n. **1** a jeweled ornamental band worn on the front of a woman's hair. **2** a high diadem encircled with three crowns and worn by a pope. ■ hist. a turban worn by ancient Persian kings. [16th cent. (denoting the Pers. royal headdress): via L. from Gk.,

PRONUNCIATION KEY ə *ago, up*; ər *over, fur*; a *hat*; ā *ate*; ä *car*; e *let*; ē *see*; i *fit*; ī *by*; NG *sing*; ō *go*; ô *law, for*; oi *toy*; o͝o *good*; o͞o *goo*; ou *out*; TH *thin*; T͟H *then*; ZH *vision*

partly via Ital. Sense 1 dates from the early 18th C.]

Ti·ber /'tībər/ a river in central Italy that rises in the Tuscan Apennines and flows through Rome to the Tyrrhenian Sea at Ostia. Italian name **Tevere.**

Ti·be·ri·as, Lake /tī'bi(ə)rēəs/ another name for Sea of Galilee (see **Galilee, Sea of**).

Ti·be·ri·us /tī'bi(ə)rēəs/ (42 BC–AD 37), Roman emperor AD 14–37; full name *Tiberius Julius Caesar Augustus.*

Ti·bes·ti Moun·tains /ti'bestē/ a mountain range in north central Africa, in Chad and Libya.

Ti·bet /ti'bet/ a mountainous region in Asia on the northern side of the Himalayas, since 1965 forming an autonomous region in the west of China; pop. 2,196,000; official languages, Tibetan and Chinese; capital, Lhasa. Chinese name **Xizang.**

Ti·bet·an /ti'betn/ ▶ **n. 1** a native of Tibet or a person of Tibetan descent. **2** the Tibeto-Burman language of Tibet, also spoken in neighboring areas of China, India, and Nepal. ▶ **adj.** of or relating to Tibet, its people, or its language.

Ti·bet·an Bud·dhism ▶ **n.** the religion of Tibet, a form of Mahayana Buddhism. It was formed in the 8th century AD from a combination of Buddhism and the indigenous Tibetan religion. The head of the religion is the Dalai Lama.

Ti·bet·an mas·tiff ▶ **n.** an animal of a breed of large black-and-tan dog with a thick coat and drop ears.

Ti·bet·an span·iel ▶ **n.** an animal of a breed of small white, brown, or black dog with a silky coat of medium length.

Ti·bet·an ter·ri·er ▶ **n.** an animal of a breed of gray, black, cream, or particolored terrier with a thick shaggy coat.

Ti·bet·o-Bur·man /ti'betō 'bərmən/ ▶ **adj.** of, relating to, or denoting a division of the Sino-Tibetan language family that includes Tibetan, Burmese, and a number of other languages spoken in mountainous regions of central southern Asia.

tib·i·a /'tibēə/ ▶ **n.** (pl. **tib·i·ae** /'tibē,ē/ or **tib·i·as**) Anat. the inner and typically larger of the two bones between the knee and the ankle (or the equivalent joints in other terrestrial vertebrates), parallel with the fibula. ■ Zool. the tibiotarsus of a bird. ■ Entomol. the fourth segment of the leg of an insect, between the femur and the tarsus. — **tib·i·al adj.** [ME: from L., 'shin bone.']

tib·i·a·lis /,tibē'alis; -'ālis/ ▶ **n.** Anat. any of several muscles and tendons in the calf of the leg concerned with movements of the foot. [19th C.: from L., 'relating to the shin bone.']

tib·i·o·tar·sus /,tibēō'tärsəs/ ▶ **n.** (pl. **-si** /-sī/) Zool. the bone in a bird's leg corresponding to the tibia, fused at the lower end with some bones of the tarsus. [19th C.: blend of **tibia** and **tarsus.**]

tic /tik/ ▶ **n.** a habitual spasmodic contraction of the muscles, most often in the face. ■ a characteristic or recurrent behavioral trait; idiosyncrasy: *generalization is his tic as a writer.* [19th C.: from Fr., from Ital. *ticchio.*]

tic dou·lou·reux /'tik ,do͞olə'ro͞o/ ▶ **n.** another term for **trigeminal neuralgia.** [19th C.: Fr., lit. 'painful tic.']

Ti·ci·no /ti'chēnō/ a predominantly Italian-speaking canton in southern Switzerland, on the Italian border. French name **Tessin,** German name **Tessin.**

tick[1] /tik/ ▶ **n. 1** a regular short, sharp sound, esp. that made every second by a clock or watch. ■ Brit., informal a moment: *I'll be with you in a tick.* **2** a check mark. **3** Stock Market the smallest recognized amount by which a price of the security or future may fluctuate. ▶ **v. 1** [intrans.] (of a clock or other mechanical device) make regular short sharp sounds, typically for every second of time passing: *I could hear the clock ticking.* ■ (**tick away/by/past**) (of time) pass (used esp. when someone is pressed for time or keenly awaiting an event): *the minutes were ticking away.* ■ [trans.] (**tick something away**) (of a clock or watch) mark the passing of time with regular short sharp sounds: *the clock ticked the minutes away.* ■ proceed or progress: *her book was ticking along nicely.* **2** [trans.] mark (an item) with a check mark, typically to show that it has been chosen, checked, or approved. ■ (**tick something off**) list items one by one in one's mind or during a speech.

– PHRASES **what makes someone tick** informal what motivates someone: *what makes these men tick?*

– PHRASAL VERBS **tick someone off 1** informal make someone annoyed or angry. **2** Brit., informal reprimand or rebuke someone: [as n.] (**ticking off**) *he got a ticking off from the boss.* [ME (as a verb in the sense 'pat, touch'): prob. of Gmc. origin and rel. to Du. *tik* (n.), *tikken* (v.) 'pat, touch.']

tick[2] ▶ **n.** a parasitic arachnid (suborder Ixodida, order Acarina) that attaches itself to the skin of a terrestrial vertebrate from which it sucks blood, leaving the host when sated. Some species transmit diseases, including tularemia and Lyme disease. See illustration at **wood tick.** ■ informal a parasitic louse fly. [OE *ticia,* of Gmc. origin; rel. to Du. *teek* and Ger. *Zecke.*]

tick[3] ▶ **n.** a fabric case stuffed with feathers or other material to form a mattress or pillow. ■ short for **ticking.** [ME: prob. Mid. Low Ger., Middle Du. *tēke,* or MDu. *tīke,* via West Gmc. from L. *theca* 'case,' from Gk. *thēkē.*]

tick-borne ▶ **adj.** transmitted or carried by ticks.

tick·er /'tikər/ ▶ **n. 1** informal a watch. ■ a person's heart. **2** a telegraphic or electronic machine that prints out data on a strip of paper, esp. stock market information or news reports.

tick·er tape ▶ **n.** a paper strip on which messages are recorded in a telegraphic tape machine. ■ [as adj.] denoting a parade or other event in which this or similar material is thrown from windows.

tick·et /'tikit/ ▶ **n. 1** a piece of paper or small card that gives the holder a certain right, esp. to enter a place, travel by public transport, or participate in an event. ■ (**ticket to/out of**) a method of getting into or out of (a specified state or situation): *drugs are seen as the only ticket out of poverty | companies that appeared to have a* ***one-way ticket to*** *profitability.* **2** a certificate or warrant, in particular: ■ an official notice of a traffic offense. ■ a certificate of qualification as a ship's master, pilot, or other crew member. **3** a label attached to a retail product, giving its price, size, and other details. **4** [in sing.] a list of candidates put forward by a party in an election: *his presence on the Republican ticket.* ■ a set of principles or policies supported by a party in an election: *a strong right-wing, no-nonsense ticket.* **5** (**the ticket**) informal dated the desirable or correct thing: *a wet day would be* ***just the ticket*** *for the garden.* ▶ **v.** (**-et·ed, -et·ing**) [trans.] **1** issue (someone) with an official notice of a traffic or other offense. **2** (**be ticketed**) (of a passenger) be issued with a travel ticket: *passengers can now get electronically ticketed.* ■ be destined or heading for a specified state or position: *Downing was ticketed for greatness.* **3** (**be ticketed**) (of a retail product) be marked with a label giving its price, size, and other details.

– PHRASES **write one's (own) ticket** informal dictate one's own terms. — **tick·et·less adj.** [16th C.: shortening of obs. Fr. *étiquet,* from OFr. *estiquet(te),* from *estiquier* 'to fix,' from MDu. *steken.* Cf. **etiquette.**]

tick·et of·fice ▶ **n.** an office or kiosk where tickets are sold, esp. for entertainment events or travel accommodations.

tick fe·ver ▶ **n.** any bacterial or rickettsial fever transmitted by the bite of a tick.

tick·ing /'tiking/ ▶ **n.** a strong, durable material, typically striped, used to cover mattresses and pillows. [17th C.: from **tick**[3] + **-ing**[1].]

tick·le /'tikəl/ ▶ **v.** [trans.] **1** lightly touch or prod (a person or a part of the body) in a way that causes itching and often laughter: *she tickled me under the chin.* ■ [intrans.] (of a part of the body) give a sensation of mild discomfort similar to that caused by being touched in this way: *his throat had stopped tickling.* ■ touch with light finger movements: *tickling the safe open took nearly ninety minutes.* **2** appeal to (someone's taste, sense of humor, curiosity, etc.): *anecdotes that might* ***tickle your fancy.*** ■ (usu. **be tickled**) cause (someone) amusement or pleasure: *he is tickled by the idea.* ▶ **n.** [in sing.] an act of tickling someone: *a little tickle.* ■ a sensation like that of being lightly touched or prodded: *I had a tickle between my shoulder blades.*

– PHRASES **be tickled pink** (or **to death**) informal be extremely amused or pleased. **tickle the ivories** informal play the piano. [ME: perh. a frequentative of **tick**[1], or an alt. of Scots and dial. *kittle* 'to tickle.']

tick·ler /'tik(ə)lər/ ▶ **n.** a thing that tickles. ■ a memorandum.

tick·lish /'tik(ə)lish/ ▶ **adj. 1** sensitive to being tickled. ■ (of a cough) characterized by persistent irritation in the throat. **2** (of a situation or problem) difficult to deal with; requiring careful handling: *ticklish questions.* ■ (of a person) easily upset. — **tick·lish·ly adv. tick·lish·ness n.**

tick·ly /'tik(ə)lē/ ▶ **adj.** another term for **ticklish.**

tick·seed /'tik,sēd/ ▶ **n.** another term for **coreopsis.** [16th C.: so named because of the resemblance of the seed to a parasitic tick.]

tick-tack-toe ▶ **n.** var. of **tic-tac-toe.**

tick-tock /'tik ,täk/ ▶ **n.** [in sing.] the sound of a large clock ticking. ▶ **v.** [intrans.] make a ticking sound. [19th C.: imitative; cf. **tick**[1].]

tick tre·foil ▶ **n.** a tall, spindly leguminous North American plant (genus *Desmodium*), the pods of which break up into one-seeded joints that adhere to clothing, animals' fur, etc.

tick·y-tack·y /'tikē ,takē/ informal ▶ **n.** inferior or cheap material, esp. as used in suburban building. ▶ **adj.** (esp. of a building or housing development) made of inferior material; cheap or in poor taste: *ticky-tacky little houses.* [1960s: prob. a reduplication of **tacky**[2].]

tic-tac-toe /'tik ,tak 'tō/ (also **tick-tack-toe**) ▶ **n.** a game in which two players seek to complete a row of either three O's or three X's drawn alternately in the spaces of a grid of nine squares. [1960s: imitative; from *tick-tack,* used earlier to denote games in which the pieces made clicking sounds.]

t.i.d. ▶ **abbr.** (in prescriptions) three times a day. [from L. *ter in die.*]

tid·al /'tīdl/ ▶ **adj.** of, relating to, or affected by tides. — **tid·al·ly adv.**

tid·al ba·sin ▶ **n.** a basin for boats that is accessible or navigable only at high tide.

tid·al bore ▶ **n.** a large wave or bore caused by the constriction of the spring tide as it enters a long, narrow, shallow inlet.

tid·al wave ▶ **n.** a nontechnical term for **tsunami.** ■ fig. a widespread or overwhelming manifestation of an emotion or phenomenon: *a tidal wave of crime.*

tid·bit /'tid,bit/ (also esp. Brit. **tit·bit** /'tit-/) ▶ **n.** a small piece of tasty food. ■ a small and particularly interesting item of gossip or information. [17th C. (as *tyd bit, tid-bit*): from dial. *tid* 'tender' (of unknown origin) + **bit**[1].]

tid·dle·dy·wink /'tidl-dē,wingk/ ▶ **n.** var. of **tiddlywink.**

tid·dly /'tidlē/ ▶ **adj.** (**-dli·er, -dli·est**) informal, esp. Brit. slightly drunk. [19th cent. (as a noun denoting an alcoholic drink, particularly of spirits): perh. from slang *tiddlywink,* denoting an unlicensed bar. The current sense dates from the 20th C.]

tid·dly·wink /'tidlē,wingk/ (also **tid·dle·dy·wink** /'tidl-dē-/) ▶ **n. 1** (**tiddlywinks**) a game in which small plastic counters are flicked into a central receptacle by being pressed on the edge with a larger counter. **2** a counter used in such a game. [19th cent.: of unknown origin; perh. rel. to TIDDLY. The word orig. denoted an unlicensed bar, also a game of dominoes. Current senses date from the late 19th C.]

tide /tīd/ ▶ **n.** the alternate rising and falling of the sea, usually twice in each lunar day at a particular place, due to the attraction of the moon and sun. ■ the water as affected by this: *the rising tide covered the wharf.* ■ fig. a powerful surge of feeling or trend of events: *he drifted into sleep on a tide of euphoria* | *the growing tide of racism.* ▶ **v.** [intrans.] archaic drift with or as if with the tide. ■ (of a ship) float or drift in or out of a harbor by taking advantage of favoring tides.
– PHRASES **turn the tide** reverse the trend of events.
– PHRASAL VERBS **tide someone over** help someone through a difficult period, esp. with financial assistance. — **tide·less adj.** [OE *tīd* 'time, period, era,' of Gmc. origin; rel. to Du. *tijd* and Ger. *Zeit*, also to TIME. The sense relating to the sea dates from ME.]

-tide ▶ **comb. form** literary denoting a specified time or season: *springtide.* ■ denoting a festival of the Christian Church: *Shrovetide.*

tide·land /'tīd,land/ ▶ **n.** (also **tidelands**) land that is submerged at high tide.

tide·line /'tīd,līn/ (also **tide line**) ▶ **n.** a line left or reached by the sea on a shore at the highest point of a tide.

tide·mark /'tīd,märk/ ▶ **n.** a mark left or reached by the sea on a shore at the highest or lowest point of a tide.

tide rip ▶ **n.** an area of rough water typically caused by opposing tides or by a rapid current passing over an uneven bottom.

tide ta·ble ▶ **n.** a table indicating the times of high and low tides at a particular place.

tide·wait·er /'tīd,wātər/ ▶ **n.** hist. a customs officer who boarded ships on their arrival to enforce the customs regulations.

tide·wa·ter /'tīd,wôtər; -,wätər/ ▶ **n.** water brought or affected by tides. ■ an area that is affected by tides.

Tide·wa·ter, the coastal regions of eastern Virginia where tidal water flows up the Potomac, Rappahannock, York, James, and smaller rivers.

tide·way /'tīd,wā/ ▶ **n.** a channel in which a tide runs, esp. the tidal part of a river.

ti·dings /'tīdiNGz/ ▶ **plural n.** literary news; information: *the bearer of glad tidings.* [late OE *tīdung* 'announcement, piece of news,' prob. from ON *títhindi* 'news of events,' from *títhr* 'occurring.']

ti·dy /'tīdē/ ▶ **adj.** (**-di·er**, **-di·est**) **1** arranged neatly and in order: *his scrupulously tidy apartment.* ■ (of a person) inclined to keep things or one's appearance neat and in order. ■ not messy; neat and controlled: *he wrote down her replies in a small, tidy hand.* **2** [attrib.] informal (of an amount, esp. of money) considerable: *the book will bring in a tidy sum.* ▶ **n.** (pl. **-dies**) **1** [usu. with adj.] a receptacle for holding small objects or waste scraps: *a desk tidy.* **2** another term for ANTIMACASSAR. ▶ **v.** (**-dies**, **-died**) [trans.] (often **tidy someone/something up**) bring order to; arrange neatly: *I'd better try to tidy my desk up a bit* | [intrans.] *I'll just go and tidy up.* — **ti·di·ly adv. ti·di·ness n.** [ME: from the n. TIDE + -Y[1].]

tie /tī/ ▶ **v.** (**ty·ing**) **1** [trans.] attach or fasten (someone or something) with string or similar cord: *they tied Max to a chair.* ■ fasten (something) to or around someone or something by means of its strings or by forming the ends into a knot or bow: *Lewis tied on his apron.* ■ form (a string, ribbon, or lace) into a knot or bow. ■ form (a knot or bow) in this way. ■ [intrans.] be fastened with a knot or bow: *a sarong that ties at the waist.* ■ (often **be tied**) restrict or limit (someone) to a particular situation, occupation, or place: *she didn't want to be like her mother, tied to a feckless man.* **2** [trans.] (often **be tied**) connect; link: *good health is tied to good sleep.* ■ hold together by a crosspiece or tie: *ceiling joists tie the rafter feet.* ■ Music unite (written notes) by a tie. ■ Music perform (two notes) as one unbroken note. **3** [intrans.] achieve the same score or ranking as another competitor or team: *he tied for second in the league* | [trans.] *Toronto tied the score in the fourth inning.* ▶ **n.** (pl. **ties**) **1** a piece of string, cord, or the like used for fastening or tying something. ■ (usu. **ties**) fig. a thing that unites or links people: *family ties.* ■ (usu. **ties**) fig. a thing that restricts someone's freedom of action: *freed from feudal ties.* ■ a rod or beam holding parts of a structure together. ■ a wooden or concrete beam laid transversely under a railroad track to support it. ■ Music a curved line above or below two notes of the same pitch indicating that they are to be played for the combined duration of their time values. ■ a shoe tied with a lace. **2** a strip of material worn around the collar and tied in a knot at the front with the ends hanging down, typically forming part of a man's business or formal outfit. **3** a result in a game or other competitive situation in which two or more competitors or teams have the same score or ranking; a draw: *there was a tie for first place.*
– PHRASES **fit to be tied** see FIT[1]. **tie someone (up) in knots** see KNOT[1]. **tie the knot** see KNOT[1]. **tie one on** informal get drunk.
– PHRASAL VERBS **tie someone down** restrict someone to a particular situation or place. **tie something in** (or **tie in**) cause something to fit or harmonize with something else: *ideas that don't necessarily tie in with mine.* **tie someone up** bind someone's legs and arms together or bind someone to something so that they cannot move or escape. ■ (usu. **be tied up**) informal occupy someone to the exclusion of any other activity. **tie something up 1** bind or fasten something securely with rope, cord, or string. ■ moor a vessel. ■ (often **be tied up**) invest or reserve capital so that it is not immediately available for use. **2** bring something to a satisfactory conclusion; settle: *he said he had a business deal to tie up.* — **tie·less adj.** [OE *tīgan* (v.), *tēah* (n.), of Gmc. origin.]

tie-back (also **tie·back**) ▶ **n.** a decorative strip of fabric or cord, typically used for holding an open curtain back from the window.

tie beam ▶ **n.** a horizontal beam connecting two rafters in a roof or roof truss.

tie·break·er /'tī,brākər/ ▶ **n.** a means of deciding a winner from competitors who have tied, in particular (in tennis) a special game to decide the winner of a set when the score is six games all.

tie clasp (also **tie clip**) ▶ **n.** an ornamental clip for holding a necktie in place.

tie-down ▶ **n.** rope, cord, straps, or chains used to attach or secure an item. ■ a stationary ring, post, or the like to which items are secured with tie-downs.

tie-dye ▶ **n.** [often as adj.] a method of producing textile patterns by tying parts of the fabric to shield it from the dye: *tie-dye T-shirts.* ▶ **v.** [trans.] dye (a garment or piece of cloth) by such a process.

tie-in ▶ **n.** a connection or association: *there's a tie-in to another case I'm working on.* ■ a book, movie, or other product produced to take advantage of a related work in another medium. ■ [as adj.] denoting sales made conditional on the purchase of an additional item or items from the same supplier.

tie line ▶ **n.** a transmission line connecting parts of a system, esp. a telephone line connecting two private branch exchanges.

Tien Shan /'tyen 'SHän/ (also **Tian Shan**) a mountain range in the Xinjiang autonomous region of China and eastern Kyrgyzstan.

tier /ti(ə)r/ ▶ **n.** a row or level of a structure, typically one of a series of rows placed one above the other and successively receding or diminishing in size: *a tier of seats* | [in comb.] *three-tier metal bunks.* ■ one of a number of successively overlapping ruffles or flounces on a garment. ■ a level or grade within the hierarchy of an organization or system. — **tiered adj.** [15th C.: from Fr. *tire* 'sequence, order,' from *tirer* 'elongate, draw.']

tierce /ti(ə)rs/ ▶ **n. 1** another term for TERCE. **2** Music an organ stop sounding two octaves and a major third above the pitch of the diapason. **3** (in piquet) a sequence of three cards of the same suit. **4** Fencing the third of eight standard parrying positions. **5** a former measure of wine equal to one third of a pipe, usually equivalent to 35 gallons (about 156 liters). ■ archaic a cask containing a certain quantity of provisions, the amount varying with the goods. [ME: var. of TERCE.]

tier·cel /'ti(ə)rsəl/ (also **ter·cel**) ▶ **n.** Falconry the male of a hawk, esp. a peregrine or a goshawk. Compare with FALCON. [ME: from OFr., based on L. *tertius* 'third.']

tie rod ▶ **n.** a rod acting as a tie in a building or other structure. ■ a rod in the steering gear of a motor vehicle.

Tier·ra del Fue·go /tē'erə del 'fwāgō/ an island off the southern tip of South America. It is divided between Argentina and Chile.

tie tack (also **tie tac**) ▶ **n.** a short pin with an ornamental head, used to attach the ends of a necktie to a shirt front.

tie-up ▶ **n. 1** a link or connection, esp. one between commercial companies: *marketing tie-ups.* ■ a telecommunications link or network. **2** a building where cattle are tied up for the night. ■ a place for mooring a boat. **3** a traffic holdup.

TIFF /tif/ Comput. ▶ **abbr.** tagged image file format, widely used in desktop publishing.

tiff /tif/ ▶ **n.** informal a petty quarrel, esp. one between friends or lovers. [18th C. (denoting a slight outburst of temper): prob. of dial. origin.]

Tif·fa·ny /'tifənē/, Louis Comfort (1848–1933), US glassmaker and interior decorator. He was a leading exponent of art nouveau in the US.

tif·fa·ny /'tifənē/ ▶ **n.** thin gauze muslin. [17th C.: from OFr. *tifanie*, via eccles. L. from Gk. *theophaneia* 'epiphany.']

tif·fin /'tifin/ ▶ **n.** dated or Indian a light meal, esp. lunch. [19th C.: appar. from dial. *tiffing* 'sipping,' of unknown origin.]

Tif·lis /'tiflis; tə'flēs/ official Russian name (1845–1936) for TBILISI.

tiger

ti·ger /'tīgər/ ▶ **n.** a very large solitary cat (*Panthera tigris*) with a yellow-brown coat striped with black, native to the forests of Asia but becoming increasingly rare. ■ used to refer to someone fierce, determined, or ambitious: *despite his wound, he still fought like a tiger* | *one of the sport's young tigers.* ■ (also **tiger economy**) a dynamic economy of one of the smaller eastern Asian countries, esp. that of Singapore, Taiwan, or South Korea.
– PHRASES **have a tiger by the tail** have embarked on a course of action that proves unexpectedly difficult but that cannot easily or safely be abandoned. [ME: from OFr. *tigre*, from L. *tigris*, from Gk.]

ti·ger bee·tle ▶ **n.** a fast-running predatory beetle (*Cicindela* and other genera, family Cicindelidae) that has spotted or striped wing cases and flies in sunshine. The larvae live in tunnels from which they snatch passing insect prey.

ti·ger cat ▶ n. a small forest cat (*Felis tigrina*) that has a light brown coat with dark stripes and blotches, native to Central and South America. ■ any moderate-sized striped cat, such as the ocelot, serval, or margay. ■ a domestic cat with markings like a tiger's.

ti·ger e·con·o·my ▶ n. see TIGER.

ti·ger·ish /'tīgəriSH/ ▶ adj. resembling or likened to a tiger, esp. in being fierce and determined. — **ti·ger·ish·ly** adv.

ti·ger lil·y ▶ n. a tall lily (*Lilium lancifolium*, or *L. tigrinum*) that has orange flowers spotted with black or purple.

ti·ger moth ▶ n. a stout moth (*Arctia* and other genera, family Arctiidae) that has boldly spotted and streaked wings.

ti·ger sal·a·man·der ▶ n. a large North American salamander (*Ambystoma tigrinum*, family Ambystomatidae) that is blackish with yellow patches or stripes.

ti·ger's eye (also **ti·ger eye**) ▶ n. a yellowish-brown semiprecious variety of quartz with a silky or chatoyant luster, formed by replacement of crocidolite with chalcedony.

ti·ger shark ▶ n. an aggressive shark (*Galeocerdo cuvieri*, family Carcharhinidae) of warm seas, with dark vertical stripes on the body.

ti·ger shrimp ▶ n. a large edible shrimp (genus *Penaeus*, class Malacostraca) marked with dark bands, found in the Indian and Pacific oceans, in particular the widely farmed *P. monodon*.

tight /tīt/ ▶ adj. **1** fixed, fastened, or closed firmly; hard to move, undo, or open. ■ (of clothes or shoes) close-fitting, esp. uncomfortably so. ■ (of a grip) very firm so as not to let go: fig. ***presidential advisers keep a tight grip on domestic policy.*** ■ (of a ship, building, or object) well sealed against something such as water or air: [in comb.] *a light-tight container.* ■ (of a formation or a group of people or things) closely or densely packed together: *a tight knot of clerical wives.* ■ (of a community or other group of people) having close relations; secretive. **2** (of a rope, fabric, or surface) stretched so as to leave no slack; not loose. ■ (of a part of the body or a bodily sensation) feeling painful and constricted, as a result of anxiety or illness: *there was a tight feeling in his gut.* ■ (of appearance or manner) tense, irritated, or angry. ■ (of a rule, policy, or form of control) strictly imposed: *security was tight.* ■ (of a game or contest) with evenly matched competitors; very close. ■ (of a written work or form) concise, condensed, or well structured. ■ (of an organization or group of people) disciplined or professional; well coordinated. **3** (of an area or space) having or allowing little room for maneuver. ■ (of a bend, turn, or angle) changing direction sharply; having a short radius. ■ (of money or time) limited or restricted. ■ informal (of a person) not willing to spend or give much money; stingy. **4** [predic.] informal drunk: *he got tight on brandy.* ▶ adv. very firmly, closely, or tensely: *hold on tight.*
– PHRASES **run a tight ship** be very strict in managing an organization or operation. **a tight corner** (or **spot**) a difficult situation, — **tight·ly** adv. **tight·ness** n. [ME (in the sense 'healthy, vigorous,' later 'firm, solid'): prob. an alt. of *thight* 'firm, solid,' later 'close-packed, dense,' of Gmc. origin; rel. to Ger. *dicht* 'dense, close.']

tight-ass ▶ n. informal an inhibited, repressed, or excessively conventional person. — **tight-assed** adj.

tight·en /'tītn/ ▶ v. make or become tight or tighter: [trans.] *tighten the bolts* | [intrans.] *the revenue laws were tightening up.*
– PHRASES **tighten one's belt** see BELT. **tighten the screw** see SCREW.

tight end ▶ n. Football an offensive end who lines up close to the tackle.

tight·fist·ed /'tīt'fistid/ (also **tight-fist·ed**) ▶ adj. informal not willing to spend or give much money; miserly.

tight-fit·ting ▶ adj. (of a garment) fitting close to and showing the contours of the body. ■ (of a lid or cover) forming a tight seal when placed on a container.

tight-knit (also **tight·ly knit**) ▶ adj. (of a group of people) united or bound together by strong relationships and common interests: *tight-knit mining communities.*

tight-lipped ▶ adj. with the lips firmly closed, esp. as a sign of suppressed emotion or determined reticence.

tight·rope /'tīt,rōp/ ▶ n. a rope or wire stretched tightly high above the ground, on which acrobats perform feats of balancing: fig. ***he continues to walk a tightrope between success and failure.*** ▶ v. [intrans.] walk or perform on such a rope.

tights /tīts/ ▶ plural n. a woman's thin, close-fitting garment, typically made of nylon, cotton, or wool, covering the lower half of the body. ■ a similar garment worn by a dancer or acrobat.

tight·wad /'tīt,wäd/ ▶ n. informal a mean or miserly person.

tigh·ty-whi·ties /'tītē '(h)wītēz/ ▶ n. informal men's white cotton briefs.

ti·gnon /'tēyôN; tē'yôN/ ▶ n. a piece of cloth worn as a turban headdress by Creole women from Louisiana. [Louisana French, from Fr. *tigne*, dial. var. of *teigne* 'moth.']

ti·gon /'tīgən/ (also **ti·glon** /-glən/) ▶ n. the hybrid offspring of a male tiger and a lioness. [1920s: portmanteau word from TIGER and LION.]

Ti·gray /tə'grā/ (also **Ti·gre**) a province of Ethiopia, in the north of the country, bordering Eritrea. — **Ti·gray·an** /-'grāən/ (also **Ti·gre·an**) adj. & n.

Ti·gre /'tēgrā/ ▶ n. a Semitic language spoken in Eritrea and adjoining parts of Sudan. It is not the language of Tigray, which is Tigrinya. [the name in Tigre.]

ti·gress /'tīgris/ ▶ n. a female tiger. ■ fig. a fierce or passionate woman.

Ti·grin·ya /ti'grēnyə/ ▶ n. a Semitic language spoken in Tigray. Compare with TIGRE. [the name in Tigrinya.]

Ti·gris /'tīgris/ a river in southwestern Asia. It rises in Turkey and flows southeast for 1,150 miles (1,850 km) through Iraq to join the Euphrates River to form the Shatt al-Arab, which flows into the Persian Gulf.

Ti·hwa /'dē'hwä/ former name (until 1954) for URUMQI.

Ti·jua·na /,tēə'wänə; tē'hwänə/ a town in northwestern Mexico, just south of the US border; pop. 743,000.

tike ▶ n. var. of TYKE.

til·ak /'tilək/ ▶ n. a mark worn by a Hindu on the forehead to indicate caste, status, or sect, or as an ornament. [from Sanskrit *tilaka*.]

ti·la·pi·a /tə'läpēə/ ▶ n. an African freshwater cichlid (*Tilapia* and related genera) that has been widely introduced to many areas for food. [mod. L., of unknown origin.]

Til·burg /'til,bərg/ an industrial city in the southern Netherlands; pop. 159,000.

til·bur·y /'til,berē; -bərē/ ▶ n. (pl. **-bur·ies**) hist. a light, open two-wheeled carriage. [19th C.: named after its inventor.]

til·de /'tildə/ ▶ n. an accent (~) placed over Spanish *n* when pronounced *ny* (as in *señor*) or Portuguese *a* or *o* when nasalized (as in *São Paulo*), or over a vowel in phonetic transcription, indicating nasalization. ■ a similar symbol used in mathematics to indicate similarity, and in logic to indicate negation. [19th C.: from Sp., based on L. *titulus* (see TITLE).]

Til·den /'tildən/, Bill (1893–1953), US tennis player; full name *William Tatem Tilden II*. He led the US to seven straight Davis Cup victories 1920–26.

tile /tīl/ ▶ n. a thin rectangular slab of baked clay, concrete, or other material, used in overlapping rows for covering roofs. ■ a thin square slab of glazed pottery, cork, linoleum, or other material for covering floors, walls, or other surfaces. ■ a thin, flat piece used in Scrabble, mah-jongg, and certain other games. ■ Math. a plane shape used in tiling. ▶ v. [trans.] (usu. **be tiled**) cover (something) with tiles. ■ Comput. arrange (two or more windows) on a computer screen so that they do not overlap. [OE *tigele*, from L. *tegula*, from an Indo-Eur. root meaning 'cover.']

tile·fish /'tīl,fiSH/ ▶ n. (pl. same or **-fish·es**) a long, slender bottom-dwelling fish (Malacanthidae, or Branchiostegidae) of warm seas, in particular the large and edible *Lopholatilus chamaeleonticeps* of the Atlantic coast of North America.

til·er /'tīlər/ ▶ n. **1** a person who lays tiles: *a roof tiler.* **2** the doorkeeper of a Masonic lodge, who prevents outsiders from entering.

til·ing /'tīliNG/ ▶ n. the action of laying tiles. ■ a surface covered by tiles: *an area of plain tiling.* ■ tiles collectively, when used to cover a roof, floor, etc. ■ a technique for displaying several nonoverlapping windows on a computer screen. ■ Math. a way of arranging identical plane shapes so that they completely cover an area without overlapping.

till[1] /til/ ▶ prep. & conj. less formal way of saying UNTIL. [OE *til*, of Gmc. origin; rel. to ON *til* 'to,' also ult. to TILL[3].]

till[2] ▶ n. a cash register or drawer for money in a store, bank, or restaurant.
– PHRASES **have** (or **with**) **one's fingers** (or **hand**) **in the till** used in reference to theft from one's place of work. [ME (in the general sense 'drawer or compartment for valuables'): of unknown origin.]

till[3] ▶ v. [trans.] prepare and cultivate (land) for crops. — **till·a·ble** adj. [OE *tilian* 'strive for, obtain by effort,' of Gmc. origin; rel. to Du. *telen* 'produce, cultivate' and Ger. *zielen* 'aim, strive,' also ult. to TILL[1]. The current sense dates from ME.]

till[4] ▶ n. Geol. boulder clay or other unstratified sediment deposited by melting glaciers or ice sheets. [17th C. (orig. Scots, denoting shale): of unknown origin.]

till·age /'tilij/ ▶ n. the preparation of land for growing crops. ■ land under cultivation: *forty acres of tillage.*

till·er[1] /'tilər/ ▶ n. a horizontal bar fitted to the head of a boat's rudder post and used for steering. [ME: from Anglo-Norman Fr. *telier* 'weaver's beam, stock of a crossbow,' from med. L. *telarium*, from L. *tela* 'web.']

till·er[2] ▶ n. an implement or machine for breaking up soil; a plow or cultivator.

till·er[3] ▶ n. a lateral shoot from the base of the stem, esp. in a grass or cereal. ▶ v. [intrans.] [usu. as n.] (**tillering**) develop tillers. [17th C. (denoting a sapling arising from the stool of a felled tree): appar. based on OE *telga* 'bough,' of Gmc. origin.]

Til·lich /'tilik/, Paul Johannes (1886–1965), US theologian and philosopher; born in Germany. He proposed a reconciliation of religion and secular society.

till·ite /'tilīt/ ▶ n. Geol. sedimentary rock composed of compacted glacial till.

Til·sit /'tilsit; -zit/ ▶ n. a semihard mildly flavored cheese. [named after the town in East Prussia (now Sovetsk, Russia) where it was first produced.]

tilt /tilt/ ▶ v. **1** move or cause to move into a sloping position: [intrans.] *the floor tilted slightly* | fig. *the balance of industrial power tilted toward the workers* | [trans.] *he tilted his head to one side.* ■ fig. incline or cause to incline toward a particular opinion: [intrans.] *he is tilting toward a new economic course.* ■ [trans.] move (a camera) in a vertical plane. **2** [intrans.] (**tilt at**) hist. (in jousting) thrust at with a lance or other weapon: *he tilts at his prey* | fig. *the lonely hero tilting at the system.* ■ (**tilt with**) archaic engage in a contest with. ▶ n. **1** a sloping position or movement. ■ an upward or downward pivoting movement of a camera. ■ an inclination or bias: *the paper's tilt toward the Republicans.* ▪ short for TILT HAMMER. **2** hist. a combat for exercise or sport between two men on horseback with lances; a joust. ▪ an attempt at winning (something) or defeating (someone), esp. in sports: *a tilt at the championship.*

– PHRASES **(at) full tilt** with maximum energy or force; at top speed. **tilt at windmills** attack imaginary enemies or evils. [with allusion to the story of Don Quixote tilting at windmills, believing they were giants.] — **tilt·er** n. [ME (in the sense 'fall or cause to fall, topple)': perhaps related to OE *tealt* 'unsteady,' or perh. of Scand. origin and rel. to Norw. *tylten* 'unsteady' and Swed. *tulta* 'totter.']

tilth /tilTH/ ▶n. cultivation of land; tillage. ▪ [in sing.] the condition of tilled soil, esp. in respect to suitability for sowing seeds: *he could determine whether the soil was of the right tilth.* ▪ prepared surface soil. [OE *tilth, tilthe,* from *tilian* (see TILL³).]

tilt ham·mer ▶n. a heavy pivoted hammer used in forging, raised mechanically and allowed to drop on the metal being worked.

tilt yard ▶n. hist. a place where jousts took place.

Tim. ▶abbr. Bible Timothy.

tim·bal /'timbəl/ (also **tym·bal**) ▶n. **1** archaic a kettledrum. **2** a membrane that forms part of the sound-producing organ in various insects, as the cicada. [17th C.: from Fr. *timbale,* alt. (influenced by *cymbale* 'cymbal') of obs. *tamballe,* from Sp. *atabal,* from Arab. *aṭ-ṭabl* 'the drum.']

tim·bale /'timbəl; tim'bäl/ ▶n. **1** a dish of finely minced meat or fish cooked with other ingredients in a pastry shell or in a mold. **2** (**timbales**) paired cylindrical drums played with sticks in Latin American dance music. [Fr., 'drum' (in sense 1 with ref. to the shape of the prepared dish; in sense 2 short for *timbales cubains* or *timbales creoles* 'Cuban' or 'Creole drums').]

tim·ber /'timbər/ ▶n. wood prepared for use in building and carpentry. ▪ trees grown for such wood: *contracts to cut timber.* ▪ (usu. **timbers**) a wooden beam or board used in building a house or ship. ▪ [as exclam.] used to warn that a tree is about to fall after being cut. ▪ [usu. with adj.] personal qualities or character, esp. as seen as suitable for a particular role: *she is frequently hailed as presidential timber.* [OE in the sense 'a building,' also 'building material,' of Gmc. origin; rel. to Ger. *Zimmer* 'room,' from an Indo-Eur. root meaning 'build.']

tim·bered /'timbərd/ ▶adj. **1** (of a building) made wholly or partly of timber. ▪ (of the walls or other surface of a room) covered with wooden panels: *the timbered banqueting hall.* **2** having many trees; wooded.

tim·ber hitch ▶n. a knot used to attach a rope to a log or spar. See illustration at KNOT¹. — **tim·ber-hitch** v.

tim·ber·ing /'timb(ə)riNG/ ▶n. the action of building with wood. ▪ wood as a building material, or finished work built from wood.

tim·ber·land /'timbər,land/ ▶n. (also **timberlands**) land covered with forest suitable or managed for timber.

tim·ber·line /'timbər,līn/ ▶n. (on a mountain) the line or altitude above which no trees grow. Also called TREE LINE. ▪ (in high northern (or southern) latitudes) the line north (or south) of which no trees grow.

tim·ber wolf ▶n. a wolf of a large variety found mainly in northern North America, with gray brindled fur. Also called GRAY WOLF.

tim·bre /'tambər; 'tänbrə/ ▶n. the character or quality of a musical sound or voice as distinct from its pitch and intensity. [19th C.: from Fr., from med. Greek *timbanon,* from Gk. *tumpanon* 'drum.']

tim·brel /'timbrəl/ ▶n. archaic a tambourine or similar instrument. [16th C.: perh. a dimin. of obs. *timbre,* in the same sense, from OFr. (see TIMBRE).]

Tim·buk·tu /,timbək'tōō/ (also **Tim·buc·too**) a town in northern Mali; pop. 20,000. French name TOMBOUCTOU. ▪ used in reference to a remote or distant place.

time /tīm/ ▶n. **1** the indefinite continued progress of existence and events in the past, present, and future regarded as a whole. ▪ the progress of this as affecting people and things: *things were getting better as time passed.* ▪ time or an amount of time as reckoned by a conventional standard: *it's eight o'clock Eastern Standard Time.* ▪ (**Time** or **Father Time**) the personification of time, typically as an old man with a scythe and hourglass. **2** a point of time as measured in hours and minutes past midnight or noon: *the time is 9:30.* ▪ a moment or definite portion of time allotted, used, or suitable for a purpose: *should we set a time for the meeting?* ▪ (often **time for/to do something**) the favorable or appropriate time to do something; the right moment: *it's time for bed.* ▪ (**a time**) an indefinite period: *traveling always distorts one's feelings for a time.* ▪ (also **times**) a more or less definite portion of time in history or characterized by particular events or circumstances: *Victorian times | the park is beautiful at this time of year.* ▪ (also **times**) the conditions of life during a particular period: *times have changed.* ▪ (**the Times**) used in names of newspapers. ▪ (**one's time**) one's lifetime: *I've known a lot of women in my time.* ▪ (**one's time**) the successful, fortunate, or influential part of a person's life or career: *in my time that was unheard of.* ▪ (**one's time**) the appropriate or expected time for something, in particular childbirth or death: *he seemed old before his time.* ▪ an apprenticeship: *all of our foremen served their time on the loading dock.* ▪ dated a period of menstruation or pregnancy. ▪ the normal rate of pay for time spent working: *they are paid time and a half.* ▪ the length of time taken to run a race or complete an event or journey: *his time for the mile was 3:49.31.* ▪ (in sports) a moment at which play is stopped temporarily within a game, or the act of calling for this. ▪ Soccer the end of the game. **3** time as allotted, available, or used: *we need more time.* ▪ informal a prison sentence: *doing time for fraud.* **4** an instance of something happening or being done; an occasion: *the nurse came in four times a day.* ▪ an event, occasion, or period experienced in a particular way: *a good time | having a rough time of it.* **5** (**times**) (following a number) expressing multiplication: *five goes into fifteen three times.* **6** the rhythmic pattern of a piece of music, as expressed by a time signature: *tunes in waltz time.* ▪ the tempo at which a piece of music is played or marked to be played. ▶v. **1** [trans.] plan, schedule, or arrange when (something) should happen or be done: *the first race is timed for 11:15.* ▪ perform (an action) at a particular moment: *Williams timed his pass perfectly from about thirty yards.* **2** [trans.] measure the time taken by (a process or activity, or a person doing it). **3** [trans.] (**time something out**) Comput. (of a computer or a program) cancel an operation automatically because a predefined interval of time has passed without a certain event happening.

– PHRASES **about time** used to convey that something now happening or about to happen should have happened earlier: *it's about time I admitted it.* **against time** with utmost speed, so as to finish by a specified time: *working against time.* **ahead of time** earlier than expected or required. **ahead of one's time** having ideas too enlightened or advanced to be accepted by one's contemporaries. **all the time** at all times. ▪ very frequently or regularly. **at one time** in or during a known but unspecified past period: *she was a nurse at one time.* **at the same time 1** simultaneously; at once. **2** nevertheless (used to introduce a fact that should be taken into account): *I can't really explain it, but at the same time I'm not convinced.* **at times** sometimes; on occasions. **before time** before the due or expected time. **behind time** late. **behind the times** not aware of or using the latest ideas or techniques; out of date. **for the time being** for the present; until some other arrangement is made. **give someone the time of day** [usu. with negative] be pleasantly polite or friendly to someone: *I wouldn't give him the time of day if I could help it.* **have no time for** be unable or unwilling to spend time on. ▪ dislike or disapprove of. **have the time 1** be able to spend the time needed to do something. **2** know from having a watch what time it is. **in (less than) no time** very quickly or very soon. **in one's own time 1** (also **in one's own good time**) at a time and a rate decided by oneself. **2** (also **on one's own time**) outside working hours; without being paid. **in time 1** not late; punctual. **2** eventually. **3** in accordance with the appropriate musical rhythm or tempo. **keep time** play or rhythmically accompany music in time. **lose no time** do a specified thing immediately or as soon as possible. **no time** a very short interval or period: *the renovations were done in no time.* **on time** punctual; punctually. **out of time 1** at the wrong time or period: *I felt that I was born out of time.* ▪ not following or maintaining the correct rhythm (of music). **2** with no time remaining to continue or complete something, esp. a task for which a specific amount of time had been allowed. **pass the time of day** exchange greetings or casual remarks. **time after time** (also **time and again** or **time and time again**) on very many occasions; repeatedly. **time immemorial** used to refer to a point of time in the past that was so long ago that people have no knowledge or memory of it. **the time of one's life** a period or occasion of exceptional enjoyment. **time out of mind** another way of saying TIME IMMEMORIAL. **time was** there was a time when: *time was, each street had its own specialized trade.* **(only) time will tell** the truth or correctness of something will (only) be established at some time in the future. [OE *tīma,* of Gmc. origin; rel. to TIDE, which it superseded in temporal senses. The earliest of the current verb senses (dating from ME) is 'do at a particular moment.']

time-and-mo·tion stud·y ▶n. a procedure in which the efficiency of an industrial or other operation is evaluated.

time base ▶n. Electron. a signal for uniformly and repeatedly deflecting the electron beam of a cathode-ray tube. ▪ a line on the display produced in this way and serving as a time axis.

time bomb ▶n. a bomb designed to explode at a preset time. ▪ fig. a process or procedure causing a problematic situation that will eventually become dangerous if not addressed: *an environmental time bomb.*

time cap·sule ▶n. a container storing a selection of objects chosen as being typical of the present time, buried for discovery in the future.

time·card /'tīm,kärd/ ▶n. a card used to record an employee's starting and quitting times, usually stamped by a time clock.

time clock ▶n. a clock with a device for recording employees' times of arrival and departure.

time con·stant ▶n. Physics a time that represents the speed with which a particular system can respond to change, typically equal to the time taken for a specified parameter to vary by a factor of $1 - 1/e$ (approximately 0.6321).

time-con·sum·ing ▶adj. taking a lot of or too much time: *an extremely time-consuming process.*

time de·pos·it ▶n. a deposit in a bank account that cannot be withdrawn before a set date or for which notice of withdrawal is required.

time di·vi·sion mul·ti·plex·ing ▶n. Telecom. a technique for transmitting two or more signals over the same telephone line, radio channel, or other medium.

time do·main ▶n. Physics time considered as an independent variable in the analysis or measurement of time-dependent phenomena.

time ex·po·sure ▶n. the exposure of photographic film for longer than the maximum normal shutter setting.

time frame ▶ **n.** a period of time, esp. a specified period in which something occurs or is planned to take place.

time-hon·ored ▶ **adj.** [attrib.] (of a custom or tradition) respected or valued because it has existed for a long time.

time·keep·er /'tīm,kēpər/ ▶ **n. 1** a person who measures or records the amount of time taken, esp. in a sports competition. **2** [usu. with adj.] a person regarded as being punctual or not punctual: *we were good timekeepers.* ▪ a watch or clock regarded as recording time accurately or inaccurately. ▪ archaic a clock. — **time·keep·ing n.**

time lag ▶ **n.** see LAG[1] (sense 1).

time-lapse ▶ **adj.** denoting the photographic technique of taking a sequence of frames at set intervals to record changes that take place slowly over time. When the frames are shown at normal speed, or in quick succession, the action seems much faster.

time·less /'tīmlis/ ▶ **adj.** not affected by the passage of time or changes in fashion: *timeless designs.* — **time·less·ly adv. time·less·ness n.**

time lim·it ▶ **n.** a limit of time within which something must be done.

time·line /'tīm,līn/ (also **time line**) ▶ **n.** a graphic representation of the passage of time as a line.

time lock ▶ **n.** a lock fitted with a device that prevents it from being unlocked until a set time. ▪ a device built into a computer program to stop it operating after a certain time. ▶ **v.** **(time-lock)** [trans.] secure (a door or other locking mechanism) with a time lock. ▪ link (something) inextricably to a certain period of time.

time·ly /'tīmlē/ ▶ **adj.** done or occurring at a favorable or useful time; opportune: *a timely warning.* — **time·li·ness n.**

time ma·chine ▶ **n.** (in science fiction) a machine capable of transporting a person backward or forward in time.

time off ▶ **n.** time for rest or recreation away from one's usual work or studies: *we're too busy to take time off.*

time out ▶ **n. 1** time for rest or recreation away from one's usual work or studies. ▪ (usu. **timeout** or **time-out**) a brief break in play in a game or sport. ▪ (also **timeout** or **time-out**) an imposed temporary suspension of activities, esp. the separation of a misbehaving child from one or more playmates as a disciplinary measure. **2** (usu. **timeout**) Comput. a cancellation or cessation that automatically occurs when a predefined interval of time has passed without a certain event occurring.

time·piece /'tīm,pēs/ ▶ **n.** an instrument, such as a clock or watch, for measuring time.

tim·er /'tīmər/ ▶ **n. 1** an automatic mechanism for activating a device at a preset time: *a video timer.* ▪ a person or device that measures or records the amount of time taken by a process or activity. **2** [in comb.] used to indicate how many times someone has done something: *we're first-timers.*

time-re·lease ▶ **adj.** denoting something, esp. a drug preparation, that releases an active substance gradually.

times /tīmz/ ▶ **prep.** multiplied by: *11 times 4 is 44.* [see TIME sense 5 of the **n.**]

time·sav·ing /'tīm,sāviNG/ ▶ **adj.** (of a device, method, etc.) reducing the time spent or required through greater efficiency or a shorter route. — **time·sav·er n.**

time se·ries ▶ **n.** Stat. a series of values of a quantity obtained at successive times, often with equal intervals between them.

time-serv·er ▶ **n. 1** a person who changes their views to suit the prevailing circumstances or fashion. **2** a person who makes very little effort at work because they are waiting to leave or retire. — **time-serv·ing adj.**

time·share /'tīm,SHe(ə)r/ ▶ **n.** the arrangement whereby several joint owners have the right to use a property as a vacation home under a time-sharing scheme. ▪ a property owned in such a way.

time-shar·ing ▶ **n. 1** the operation of a computer system by several users for different operations at the same time. **2** the use of a property as a vacation home at specified times by several joint owners.

time sheet (also **time·sheet** /'tīm,SHēt/) ▶ **n.** a piece of paper for recording the number of hours worked.

time-shift ▶ **v. 1** [intrans.] move from one period in time to another. **2** [trans.] record (a television program) for later viewing. ▶ **n.** **(time shift)** a movement from one period in time to another, esp. in a play or movie.

time sig·na·ture ▶ **n.** Music an indication of rhythm following a clef, generally expressed as a fraction with the denominator defining the beat as a division of a whole note and the numerator giving the number of beats in each bar.

time slice ▶ **n.** Comput. a short interval of time during which a computer or its central processor deals uninterruptedly with one user or program, before switching to another.

times ta·ble ▶ **n.** informal term for MULTIPLICATION TABLE.

time·ta·ble /'tīm,tābəl/ ▶ **n.** a chart showing the departure and arrival times of trains, buses, or planes. ▪ a plan of times at which events are scheduled to take place, esp. toward a particular end. ▶ **v.** [trans.] schedule (something) to take place at a particular time: *weigh-ins are timetabled for Mondays.*

time trav·el ▶ **n.** (in science fiction) the action of traveling through time into the past or the future. — **time-trav·el v. time trav·el·er n.**

time tri·al ▶ **n.** (in various sports) a test of a competitor's individual speed over a set distance, esp. a cycling race in which competitors are separately timed.

time warp ▶ **n.** (esp. in science fiction) an imaginary distortion of space in relation to time whereby people or objects of one period can be moved to another.

time·worn /'tīm,wôrn/ (also **time-worn**) ▶ **adj.** damaged or impaired, or made less striking or attractive, as a result of age or much use.

time zone ▶ **n.** see ZONE (sense 1).

tim·id /'timid/ ▶ **adj.** (**-id·er, -id·est**) showing a lack of courage or confidence; easily frightened. — **ti·mid·i·ty** /ti'miditē/ **n. tim·id·ly adv. tim·id·ness n.** [16th C.: from L. *timidus*, from *timere* 'to fear.']

tim·ing /'tīmiNG/ ▶ **n.** the choice, judgment, or control of when something should be done: *one of the secrets of golf is good timing.* ▪ a particular point or period of time when something happens. ▪ (in an internal combustion engine) the times when the valves open and close, and the time of the ignition spark, in relation to the movement of the piston in the cylinder.

tim·ing belt ▶ **n.** a metal chain or reinforced rubber belt that drives the camshaft of an internal-combustion engine. Also called **timing chain.**

Ti·mi·şoa·ra /,tēmēSH'wärə/ a city in western Romania; pop. 325,000. Hungarian name TEMESVÁR.

ti·moc·ra·cy /tə'mäkrəsē/ ▶ **n.** (pl. **-cies**) esp. Philos. **1** a form of government in which possession of property is required in order to hold office. **2** a form of government in which rulers are motivated by ambition or love of honor. — **ti·mo·crat·ic** /,timə'kratik/ **adj.** [15th C.: from OFr. *timocracie*, via med. L. from Gk. *timokratia*, from *timē* 'honor, worth' + *-kratia* 'power.' Sense 1 reflects Aristotle's usage, sense 2 Plato's.]

Ti·mor /'tēmôr/ the largest of the Lesser Sunda Islands, in the southern Malay Archipelago; pop. 3,383,000. — **Ti·mo·rese** /,tēmə'rēz; -'rēs/ **adj. & n.**

tim·or·ous /'timərəs/ ▶ **adj.** showing or suffering from nervousness, fear, or a lack of confidence: *a timorous voice.* — **tim·or·ous·ly adv. tim·or·ous·ness n.** [ME (in the sense 'feeling fear'): from OFr. *temoreus*, from med. L. *timorosus*, from L. *timor* 'fear,' from *timere* 'to fear.']

Ti·mor Sea an arm of the Indian Ocean between Timor and northwestern Australia.

Tim·o·thy /'timəTHē/ either of two books of the New Testament, epistles of St. Paul addressed to St. Timothy.

tim·o·thy /'timəTHē/ (also **tim·o·thy grass**) ▶ **n.** a Eurasian grass (*Phleum pratense*) that is widely grown for grazing and hay. It is naturalized in North America, where many cultivars have been developed. [18th C.: named after *Timothy* Hanson, the American farmer who introduced it to Carolina from New York (*c.*1720).]

Tim·o·thy, St. (1st century AD), disciple of St. Paul.

tim·pa·ni /'timpənē/ (also **tym·pa·ni**) ▶ **plural n.** kettledrums, esp. when played by one musician in an orchestra. — **tim·pa·nist n.** [19th C.: from Ital., pl. of *timpano* 'kettledrum,' from L. *tympanum* 'drum' (see TYMPANUM).]

tin /tin/ ▶ **n. 1** a silvery-white metal, the chemical element of atomic number 50. It is used in various alloys, notably bronze, and for electroplating iron or steel sheets to make tinplate. (Symbol: **Sn**) ▪ short for TINPLATE. **2** a metal container, in particular: ▪ esp. Brit. an airtight sealed container for preserving food, made of tinplate or aluminum; a can. ▪ a lidded airtight container made of tinplate or aluminum: *a cookie tin.* ▶ **v.** (**tinned** /tind/, **tin·ning**) [trans.] cover with a thin layer of tin.
– PHRASES **have a tin ear** be tone-deaf. [OE, of Gmc. origin; rel. to Du. *tin* and Ger. *Zinn*.]

tin·a·mou /'tinə,mōō/ ▶ **n.** a ground-dwelling tropical American bird (family Tinamidae) that looks somewhat like a grouse. [18th C.: via Fr. from Galibi *tinamu*.]

Tin·ber·gen[1] /'tin,bergən/, Jan (1903–94), Dutch economist; brother of Nikolaas Tinbergen. He pioneered in econometrics. Nobel Prize for Economics (1969, shared with Ragnar Frisch).

Tin·ber·gen[2], Nikolaas (1907–88), Dutch zoologist; brother of Jan Tinbergen. He introduced the concept of displacement activity. Nobel Prize for Physiology or Medicine (1973, shared with Lorentz and Karl von Frisch).

tin can ▶ **n.** a tinplate or aluminum container for preserving food, esp. an empty one. ▪ Nautical slang a destroyer or a submarine.

tinct. ▶ **abbr.** tincture.

tinc·to·ri·al /tiNGk'tôrēəl/ ▶ **adj.** tech. of or relating to dyeing, coloring, or staining properties. [17th C.: from L. *tinctorius* (from *tinctor* 'dyer,' from *tingere* 'to dye or color') + -AL.]

tinc·ture /'tiNGkCHər/ ▶ **n. 1** a medicine made by dissolving a drug in alcohol. **2** a slight trace of something: ***a tincture of bitterness.*** **3** Heraldry any of the conventional colors (including the metals and stains, and often the furs) used in coats of arms. ▶ **v.** **(be tinctured)** be tinged, flavored, or imbued with a slight amount of. [ME (denoting a dye or pigment): from L. *tinctura* 'dyeing,' from *tingere* 'to dye or color.' Sense 2 (early 17th C.) comes from the obs. sense 'imparted quality,' likened to a tint imparted by a dye.]

tin·der /'tindər/ ▶ **n.** dry, flammable material, such as wood or paper, used for lighting a fire. — **tin·der·y adj.** [OE *tynder, tyndre*, of Gmc. origin; rel. to Du. *tonder* and Ger. *Zunder*.]

tin·der·box /'tindər,bäks/ ▶ **n.** hist. a box containing tinder, flint, a steel, and other items for kindling fires. ▪ fig. a thing that is readily ignited. ▪ fig. a volatile situation, or a person who is readily aroused, esp. to anger.

tine /tīn/ ▶ **n.** a prong or sharp point, such as that on a fork or antler. — **tined adj.** [OE *tind*, of Gmc. origin; rel. to Ger. *Zinne* 'pinnacle.']

tin·e·a /'tinēə/ ▶ **n.** technical term for RINGWORM. [ME: from L., 'worm.']

tin·foil /ˈtinˌfoil/ (also **tin foil**) ▶ **n.** foil made of aluminum or a similar silvery-gray metal, used esp. for covering or wrapping food.

ting /tiNG/ ▶ **n.** a sharp, clear ringing sound, such as when a glass is struck by a metal object. ▶ **v.** [intrans.] emit such a sound. [ME (as a verb): imitative. The noun dates from the 17th C.]

tinge /tinj/ ▶ **v.** (**ting·ing** or **tinge·ing**) [trans.] (often **be tinged**) color slightly. ■ fig. have a slight influence on: *this visit will be tinged with sadness.* ▶ **n.** a tendency toward or trace of some color: *there was a faint pink tinge to the sky.* ■ fig. a slight trace of a feeling or quality. [15th cent.: from L. *tingere* 'to dip or color.' The noun dates from the 18th C.]

tin·gle /ˈtiNGgəl/ ▶ **v.** [intrans.] (of a person or a part of their body) experience a slight prickling or stinging sensation. ■ [trans.] cause to experience such a sensation. ■ [intrans.] (of such a sensation) be experienced in a part of one's body. ▶ **n.** a slight prickling or stinging sensation. [ME: perhaps a var. of TINKLE. The original notion was perh. 'ring in response to a loud noise,' but the term was very early applied to the result of hearing something shocking.]

tin·gly /ˈtiNG(g)əlē/ ▶ **adj.** (**-gli·er**, **-gli·est**) causing or experiencing a slight prickling or stinging sensation.

tin god ▶ **n.** a person, esp. a minor official, who is pompous and self-important. ■ an object of unjustified veneration or respect.

tin·horn /ˈtinˌhôrn/ ▶ **n.** informal a contemptible person, esp. one pretending to have money, influence, or ability.

tin·ker /ˈtiNGkər/ ▶ **n.** **1** (esp. in former times) a person who travels from place to place mending pans, kettles, and other metal utensils as a way of making a living. ■ a person who makes minor mechanical repairs, esp. on a variety of appliances and apparatuses, usually for a living. **2** an act of attempting to repair something. ▶ **v.** [intrans.] attempt to repair or improve something in a casual or desultory way, often to no useful effect.
– PHRASES **not give a tinker's damn** informal not care at all. — **tin·ker·er n.** [ME (first recorded in Anglo-L. as a surname): of unknown origin.]

Tin·ker·toy /ˈtiNGkərˌtoi/ ▶ **n.** trademark a children's building toy consisting of pieces held together by pegs in holes.

tin·kle /ˈtiNGkəl/ ▶ **v.** **1** make or cause to make a light, clear ringing sound: [intrans.] *cool water tinkled in the stone fountains* | [trans.] *the maid tinkled a bell.* **2** [intrans.] informal urinate. ▶ **n.** **1** a light, clear ringing sound. ■ Brit., informal a telephone call: *I'll give them a tinkle.* **2** informal an act of urinating. — **tin·kly adj.** [ME (also in the sense 'tingle'): frequentative of obs. *tink* 'to chink or clink,' of imitative origin.]

Tin Liz·zie /ˈlizē/ (also **tin liz·zie**) ▶ **n.** informal, dated a cheap, old, or rundown automobile (originally used as a nickname for early Ford cars, esp. the Model T). [20th C.: *Lizzie*, a nickname for the given name *Elizabeth*.]

tinned /tind/ ▶ **adj.** **1** [attrib.] covered or coated in tin or a tin alloy. **2** esp. Brit. (of food) preserved in a sealed airtight container made of tinplate or aluminum: *tinned fruit.*

tin·ner /ˈtinər/ ▶ **n.** a tin miner or tinsmith.

tin·ni·tus /ˈtinitəs; tiˈnī-/ ▶ **n.** Med. ringing or buzzing in the ears. [19th C.: from L., from *tinnire* 'to ring, tinkle,' of imitative origin.]

tin·ny /ˈtinē/ ▶ **adj.** (**-ni·er**, **-ni·est**) having a displeasingly thin, metallic sound. ■ (of an object) made of thin or poor-quality metal. ■ having an unpleasantly metallic taste. — **tin·ni·ly adv. tin·ni·ness n.**

Tin Pan Al·ley the name given to a district in New York City around 28th Street, between 5th Avenue and Broadway, where many music publishers were formerly based. ■ [as n.] [usu. as adj.] the world of composers and publishers of popular music.

tin·plate /ˈtinˌplāt/ (also **tin plate**) ▶ **n.** sheet steel or iron coated with tin. ▶ **v.** [trans.] [often as adj.] (**tinplated** or **tin-plated**) coat (an object) with tin.

tin·pot /ˈtinˌpät/ (also **tin-pot**) ▶ **adj.** [attrib.] informal (esp. of a country or its leader) having or showing poor leadership or organization: *a tin-pot dictator.*

tin·sel /ˈtinsəl/ ▶ **n.** a form of decoration consisting of thin strips of shiny metal foil. ■ showy or superficial attractiveness or glamour. — **tin·sel·ly adj.** [ME (denoting fabric either interwoven with metallic thread or spangled): from OFr. *estincele* 'spark,' or *estinceler* 'to sparkle,' based on L. *scintilla* 'a spark.']

tin·seled /ˈtinsəld/ (also esp. Brit. **tin·selled**) ▶ **adj.** decorated or adorned with tinsel. ■ showily or superficially attractive or glamorous.

Tin·sel·town /ˈtinsəlˌtoun/ ▶ **n.** informal Hollywood, or the superficially glamorous world it represents.

tin·smith /ˈtinˌsmiTH/ ▶ **n.** a person who makes or repairs articles of tin or tinplate.

tin snips (also **tin·snips**) ▶ **plural n.** a pair of clippers for cutting sheet metal.

tin sol·dier ▶ **n.** a toy soldier made of metal.

tin·stone /ˈtinˌstōn/ ▶ **n.** another term for CASSITERITE.

tint /tint/ ▶ **n.** **1** a shade or variety of color. ■ Print. an area of faint even color printed as a halftone, used for highlighting overprinted text. ■ a set of parallel engraved lines to give uniform shading. ■ a trace of something: *a tint of glamour.* **2** an artificial dye for coloring the hair. ■ an application of such a substance. ▶ **v.** [trans.] (usu. **be tinted**) color (something) slightly; tinge: [as adj.] (**tinted**) *a black car with tinted windows.* ■ dye (someone's hair) with a tint. — **tint·er n.** [18th C.: alt. (perh. influenced by Ital. *tinta*) of obs. *tinct* 'to color, tint,' from L. *tinctus* 'dyeing,' from *tingere* 'to dye or color.']

tin·tin·nab·u·la·tion /ˌtintəˌnabyəˈlāSHən/ ▶ **n.** a ringing or tinkling sound. [19th C.: from L. *tintinnabulum* 'tinkling bell' (from *tintinnare*, reduplication of *tinnire* 'to ring, tinkle') + -ATION.]

Tin·to·ret·to /ˌtintəˈretō/ (1518–94), Italian painter; born *Jacopo Robusti*. His work is in a mannerist style.

tin·type /ˈtinˌtīp/ ▶ **n.** hist. a photograph taken as a positive on a thin tin plate.

tin·ware /ˈtinˌwe(ə)r/ ▶ **n.** kitchen utensils or other articles made of tin or tinplate.

tin whis·tle ▶ **n.** a small flutelike instrument made from a thin metal tube, with six finger holes of varying size on top and no thumb holes.

ti·ny /ˈtīnē/ ▶ **adj.** (**-ni·er**, **-ni·est**) very small. — **ti·ni·ly adv. ti·ni·ness n.** [16th C.: extension of obs. *tine* 'small, dimin.,' of unknown origin.]

-tion ▶ **suffix** forming nouns of action, condition, etc., such as *completion, relation.* [from L. participial stems ending in *-t* + -ION.]

tip¹ /tip/ ▶ **n.** the pointed or rounded end or extremity of something slender or tapering. ■ a small piece or part fitted to the end of an object: *the rubber tip of the walking stick.* ▶ **v.** (**tipped**, **tip·ping**) [trans.] **1** [usu. as adj.] (**tipped**) attach to or cover the end or extremity of: *mountains tipped with snow* | [in comb.] *steel-tipped spears.* ■ color (something) at its end or edge. **2** (**tip a page in**) (in bookbinding) paste a single page, typically an illustration, to the neighboring page of a book by a thin line of paste down its inner margin.
– PHRASES **on the tip of one's tongue** used to indicate that someone is almost but not quite able to bring a particular word or name to mind. **the tip of the iceberg** see ICEBERG. [ME: from ON *typpi* (n.), *typpa* (v.), *typptr* 'tipped'; rel. to TOP¹.]

tip² ▶ **v.** (**tipped**, **tip·ping**) **1** overbalance or cause to overbalance so as to fall or turn over: [intrans.] *the hay caught fire when the candle tipped over* | [trans.] *a youth sprinted past, tipping over her glass.* ■ be or cause to be in a sloping position with one end or side higher than the other: [trans.] *I tipped my seat back* | [intrans.] *the car tipped to one side.* **2** [trans.] strike or touch lightly. ■ cause (an object) to move somewhere by striking or touching it in this way. **3** [intrans.] (**tip off**) Basketball put the ball in play by throwing it up between two opponents. ▶ **n.** Brit. a place where trash is deposited; a dump.
– PHRASES **tip one's hand** informal reveal one's intentions inadvertently. **tip one's hat** (or **cap**) raise or touch one's hat or cap as a way of greeting or acknowledging someone. **tip the scales** (or **balance**) (of a circumstance or event) be the deciding factor; make the critical difference. **tip the scales at** have a weight of (a specified amount). [ME: perh. of Scand. origin, influenced later by TIP¹ in the sense 'touch with a tip or point.' Current senses of the noun date from the mid 19th C.]

tip³ ▶ **n.** **1** a sum of money given to someone as a way of rewarding them for their services. **2** a small but useful piece of practical advice. ■ a prediction or piece of expert information about the likely winner of a race or contest. ▶ **v.** (**tipped**, **tip·ping**) give (someone) a sum of money as a way of rewarding them for their services: [trans.] *I tipped her five dollars* | [intrans.] *that sort of person never tips.*
– PHRASES **tip someone off** informal give someone information about something, typically in a discreet or confidential way. [17th C. (in the sense 'give, hand, pass'): prob. from TIP¹.]

tip·cat /ˈtipˌkat/ ▶ **n.** esp. hist. a game in which a piece of wood tapered at both ends is struck at one end with a stick so as to spring up and is then knocked away by the same player. ■ a tapered piece of wood of this kind.

ti·pi ▶ **n.** var. of TEPEE.

tip-in ▶ **n.** Basketball a score made by tipping a rebound into the basket.

tip-off (also **tip·off**) ▶ **n.** **1** informal a piece of information, typically one given in a discreet or confidential way. **2** (usu. **tipoff**) a jump ball that begins each period in a basketball game (used esp. in reference to the first tipoff of the game).

Tip·pe·ca·noe Riv·er /ˌtipikəˈnoo/ a river that flows through Indiana to join the Wabash River.

tip·per /ˈtipər/ ▶ **n.** [usu. with adj.] a person who leaves a specified sort of tip as a reward for services they have received: *he's a big tipper.*

Tip·per·ar·y /ˌtipəˈre(ə)rē/ a county in the Republic of Ireland, in the central part of the country.

tip·pet /ˈtipit/ ▶ **n.** a woman's long cape or scarf, typically of fur or similar material. ■ a similar ceremonial garment worn esp. by the clergy. ■ hist. a long, narrow strip of cloth forming part of or attached to a hood or sleeve. [ME: prob. from an Anglo-Norman deriv. of the noun TIP¹.]

tip·ping point ▶ **n.** the point at which the buildup of minor changes or incidents reaches a level that triggers a more significant change or makes someone do something they had formerly resisted.

tip·ple¹ /ˈtipəl/ ▶ **v.** [intrans.] drink alcohol, esp. habitually: *those who liked to tipple and gamble.* ▶ **n.** informal an alcoholic drink. [15th C. (in the sense 'sell (alcoholic drink) at retail'): back-form. from TIPPLER¹.]

tip·ple² ▶ **n.** a revolving frame or cage in which a truck or freight car is inverted to discharge its load. ■ a place where such loads, esp. from a coal mine, are dumped. [19th C.: from dial. *tipple* 'tumble over.']

tip·pler¹ /ˈtip(ə)lər/ ▶ **n.** a habitual drinker of alcohol. [ME (denoting a retailer of alcoholic liquor): of unknown origin.]

tip·pler² ▶ **n.** a person who operates or works at a tipple, esp. at a mine.

tip·py /ˈtipē/ ▶ **adj.** inclined to tilt or overturn; unsteady.

tip·py-toe ▶ **v.** [intrans.] informal walk on the tips of one's toes; tiptoe: *he tippy-toed around the house.*
– PHRASES **on tippy-toe** (or **tippy-toes**) on the tips of one's toes; on tiptoe. [19th C.: alt. of TIPTOE.]

tip·staff /ˈtip,staf/ ▶ **n.** a sheriff's officer; a bailiff. [16th C. (first denoting a metal-tipped staff): contr. of *tipped staff* (carried by a bailiff).]

tip·ster /ˈtipstər/ ▶ **n.** a person who gives tips, esp. about the likely winner of a race or contest, and esp. for a fee.

tip·sy /ˈtipsē/ ▶ **adj.** (**-si·er**, **-si·est**) slightly drunk. — **tip·si·ly** **adv.** **tip·si·ness** **n.** [16th C.: from the verb TIP[2] + -SY.]

tip·toe /ˈtip,tō/ ▶ **v.** (**-toes**, **-toed**, **-toe·ing**) [intrans.] walk quietly and carefully with one's heels raised and one's weight on the balls of the feet.
– PHRASES **on tiptoe** (or **tiptoes**) (also **on one's tiptoes**) with one's heels raised and one's weight on the balls of the feet, esp. in order to move quietly or make oneself taller.

tip-top (also **tip·top**) ▶ **adj.** of the very best class or quality; excellent: *an athlete in tip-top condition.* ▶ **n.** the highest part or point of excellence.

tip-up ▶ **n.** a device used in ice fishing in which a wire attached to the rod is tripped, raising a signal flag, when a fish takes the bait.

ti·rade /ˈtīrād; tīˈrād/ ▶ **n.** a long, angry speech of criticism or accusation: *a tirade of abuse.* [19th C.: from Fr., lit. 'long speech,' from Ital. *tirata* 'volley,' from *tirare* 'to pull.']

tir·a·mi·su /,tirəmēˈsōō; -ˈmēsōō/ (also **tir·a·mi·sù**) ▶ **n.** an Italian dessert consisting of layers of sponge cake soaked in coffee and brandy or liqueur with powdered chocolate and mascarpone cheese. [Ital., from the phr. *tira mi sù* 'pick me up.']

Ti·ra·na /tiˈränə/ (also **Ti·ra·në**) the capital of Albania, in the central part of the country, on the Ishm River; pop. 210,000.

tire[1] /tī(ə)r/ ▶ **v.** [intrans.] become in need of rest or sleep; grow weary. ■ [trans.] cause to feel in need of rest or sleep; weary. ■ (**tire of**) lose interest in; become bored with. ■ [trans.] exhaust the patience or interest of; bore. [OE *tēorian* 'fail, come to an end,' also 'become physically exhausted,' of unknown origin.]

tire[2] ▶ **n.** a rubber covering, typically inflated or surrounding an inflated inner tube, placed around a wheel to form a soft contact with the road. ■ a strengthening band of metal fitted around the rim of a wheel, esp. of a railroad vehicle. [15th C. (denoting the curved pieces of iron plate with which carriage wheels were formerly shod): perh. a shortening of ATTIRE (because the tire was the "clothing" of the wheel).]

tired /tī(ə)rd/ ▶ **adj.** in need of sleep or rest; weary. ■ (**tired of**) bored with. ■ (of a thing) no longer fresh or in good condition. ■ (esp. of a statement or idea) boring or uninteresting because overfamiliar. — **tired·ly** **adv.** **tired·ness** **n.**

tire gauge ▶ **n.** a portable pressure gauge for measuring the air pressure in a tire.

tire i·ron ▶ **n.** a steel lever for removing tires from wheel rims.

tire·less /ˈtī(ə)rlis/ ▶ **adj.** having or showing great effort or energy: *a tireless campaigner.* — **tire·less·ly** **adv.** **tire·less·ness** **n.**

Ti·re·si·as /tiˈrēsēəs/ (also **Tei·re·si·as**) Gk. Mythol. a blind Theban prophet, so wise that even his ghost had its wits and was not a mere phantom.

tire·some /ˈtī(ə)rsəm/ ▶ **adj.** causing one to feel bored or annoyed: *weeding is a tiresome but essential job.* — **tire·some·ly** **adv.** [as submodifier] *a tiresomely predictable attitude.* **tire·some·ness** **n.**

Ti·rich Mir /ˈtiricH ˈmir/ the highest peak in the Hindu Kush, in Pakistan. It rises to 25,230 feet (7,690 m).

ti·ro ▶ **n.** var. of TYRO.

Tir·ol /təˈrōl; tīˈrōl; ˈtīrōl/ German name for TYROL.

Tir·u·chi·ra·pal·li /,tirəcHəˈräpəlē/ a city in southern India; pop. 387,000. Also called TRICHINOPOLY.

'tis /tiz/ esp. literary ▶ **contr.** it is.

Ti·sa /ˈtēsä/ Serbian name for TISZA.

ti·sane /tiˈzan; -ˈzän/ ▶ **n.** an herbal tea, consumed esp. for its medicinal properties. [1930s: from Fr.]

Tish·ri /ˈtisHrē; -rā/ (also **Tis·ri** /ˈtiz-/) ▶ **n.** (in the Jewish calendar) the first month of the civil and seventh of the religious year, usually coinciding with parts of September and October. [from Heb. *tišrī*.]

Ti·siph·o·ne /tiˈsifənē/ Gk. Mythol. one of the Furies. [Gk., lit. 'the avenger of blood.']

tis·sue /ˈtisHōō/ ▶ **n.** **1** any of the distinct types of material of which animals or plants are made, consisting of specialized cells and their products. **2** tissue paper. ■ a disposable piece of absorbent paper, used esp. as a handkerchief or for cleaning the skin. ■ rich or fine material of a delicate or gauzy texture. **3** [in sing.] an intricate structure or network made from a number of connected items: *such scandalous stories are a tissue of lies.* — **tis·su·ey** **adj.** (in sense 2). [ME: from OFr. *tissu* 'woven,' past part. of *tistre*, from L. *texere* 'to weave.']

tis·sue cul·ture ▶ **n.** Biol. & Med. the growth in an artificial medium of cells derived from living tissue. ■ a cell culture of this kind.

tis·sue flu·id ▶ **n.** Physiol. extracellular fluid that bathes the cells of most tissues, arriving via blood capillaries and being removed via the lymphatic vessels.

tis·sue pa·per ▶ **n.** thin, soft paper, typically used for wrapping or protecting fragile or delicate articles.

Ti·sza /ˈtisä/ a river in southeastern Europe, the longest tributary of the Danube River. It rises in Ukraine and flows into Hungary and then joins the Danube River in Serbia. Serbian name TISA.

Tit. ▶ **abbr.** Bible Titus.

tit[1] /tit/ ▶ **n.** a titmouse, or a similar or related bird. [16th cent.: prob. of Scand. origin and rel. to Icelandic *titlingur* 'sparrow'; cf. TITMOUSE. Earlier senses were 'small horse' and 'girl'; the current sense dates from the early 18th C.]

tit[2] ▶ **n.** vulgar slang a woman's breast or nipple.
– PHRASES **tits and ass** vulgar slang used in reference to the use of crudely sexual images of women. [OE *tit* 'teat, nipple,' of Gmc. origin; rel. to Du. *tit* and Ger. *Zitze*. The vulgar slang use was orig. US and dates from the early 20th C.]

tit[3] ▶ **n.** (in phrase **tit for tat**) the infliction of an injury or insult in return for one that one has suffered. [16th C.: var. of obs. *tip for tap*.]

Ti·tan /ˈtītn/ **1** Gk. Mythol. any of the older gods who preceded the Olympians and were the children of Uranus (Heaven) and Gaia (Earth). Led by Cronus, they overthrew Uranus; Cronus' son, Zeus, eventually defeated the Titans. ■ [as n.] (usu. **a titan**) a person or thing of very great strength, intellect, or importance: *a titan of industry.* **2** Astron. the largest satellite of Saturn, the fifteenth closest to the planet, discovered by C. Huygens in 1655, and having a diameter of 3,200 miles (5,150 km). It is unique in having a hazy atmosphere of nitrogen, methane, and oily hydrocarbons.

ti·tan·ate /ˈtītn,āt/ ▶ **n.** Chem. a salt in which the anion contains both titanium and oxygen, in particular one of the anion $TiO_3 2-$. [19th C.: from TITANIUM + -ATE[1].]

Ti·tan·ess /ˈtītn-is/ ▶ **n.** a female Titan. ■ (**titaness**) a female person of very great strength, intellect, or importance.

Ti·ta·ni·a /tiˈtānēə/ Astron. the largest satellite of Uranus, the fourteenth closest to the planet, discovered by W. Herschel in 1787. It has an icy surface and a diameter 1,000 miles (1,610 km). [the name of the queen of the fairies in Shakespeare's *A Midsummer Night's Dream*.]

Ti·tan·ic /tīˈtanik/ a large British passenger liner that struck an iceberg in the North Atlantic on its maiden voyage in April 1912 and sank with the loss of 1,490 lives.

ti·tan·ic[1] /tīˈtanik/ ▶ **adj.** of exceptional strength, size, or power: *a series of titanic explosions.* — **ti·tan·i·cal·ly** **adv.** [17th C. (in the sense 'relating to the sun'): from Gk. *titanikos*, from *Titan* (see TITAN).]

ti·tan·ic[2] ▶ **adj.** Chem. of titanium with a valence of four; of titanium(IV). Compare with TITANOUS. [19th C.: from TITANIUM + -IC.]

ti·tan·if·er·ous /,tītnˈifərəs/ ▶ **adj.** (of rocks and minerals) containing or yielding titanium.

ti·tan·ite /ˈtītn,īt/ ▶ **n.** another term for SPHENE. [18th C.: from TITANIUM + -ITE[1].]

ti·ta·ni·um /tīˈtānēəm/ ▶ **n.** the chemical element of atomic number 22, a hard silver-gray metal of the transition series, used in strong, light, corrosion-resistant alloys, and as a white pigment in paper, paint, etc. (Symbol: **Ti**) [18th C.: from TITAN, on the pattern of *uranium*.]

ti·ta·ni·um di·ox·ide (also **ti·ta·ni·um ox·ide**) ▶ **n.** a white unreactive solid, TiO_2, that occurs naturally as the mineral rutile and is used extensively as a white pigment.

ti·ta·ni·um white ▶ **n.** a white pigment consisting chiefly or wholly of titanium dioxide.

ti·tan·ous /tīˈtanəs/ ▶ **adj.** Chem. of titanium with a lower valence, usually three. Compare with TITANIC[2]. [19th C.: from TITANIUM, on the pattern of words such as *ferrous*.]

tit·bit /ˈtit,bit/ ▶ **n.** chiefly British spelling of TIDBIT.

ti·ter /ˈtītər/ (Brit. **ti·tre**) ▶ **n.** Chem. the concentration of a solution as determined by titration. ■ Med. the concentration of an antibody, as determined by finding the highest dilution at which it is still able to cause agglutination of the antigen. [19th C.: from Fr. *titre*, from *titrer* (see TITRATE).]

tithe /tīTH/ ▶ **n.** one tenth of annual produce or earnings, formerly taken as a tax for the support of the church and clergy. ■ (in certain religious denominations) a tenth of an individual's income pledged to the church. ▶ **v.** [trans.] pay or give as a tithe. ■ hist. subject to a tax of one tenth of income or produce. — **tith·a·ble** **adj.** [OE *tēotha* (adj. in the ordinal sense 'tenth,' used in a specialized sense as a n.), *tēothian* (v.).]

tith·ing /ˈtīTHiNG/ ▶ **n.** **1** the practice of taking or paying a tithe. **2** hist. (in England) a group of ten householders who lived close together and were collectively responsible for each other's behavior. [OE *tēothung* (see TITHE, -ING[1]).]

Ti·tho·nus /tīˈTHōnəs/ Gk. Mythol. a Trojan prince with whom the goddess Aurora fell in love. She asked Zeus to make him immortal but omitted to ask for eternal youth, and he became very old and decrepit although he talked perpetually. Tithonus begged her to remove him from this world, and she changed him into a grasshopper, which chirps ceaselessly.

ti·ti[1] /ˈtēˈtē/ (also **ti·ti mon·key**) ▶ **n.** (pl. **-tis**) a small forest-dwelling monkey (genus *Callicebus*, family Cebidae) of South America. [18th C.: from Aymara.]

ti·ti[2] /ˈtī,tī; ˈtē,tē/ ▶ **n.** (pl. **-tis**) a shrub or small tree (family Cyrillaceae) with leathery leaves, esp. *Cyrilla racemiflora* (**leatherwood**) and *Cliftonia monophylla* (**buckwheat tree**), both of the coastal southeastern US. [19th C.: perh. of Amer. Ind. origin.]

Ti·tian[1] /ˈtisHən/ (*c.*1488–1576), Italian painter; real name *Tiziano Vecellio*. He was the most important painter of the Venetian school.

Ti·tian[2] (also **ti·tian**) ▶ **adj.** (of hair) bright golden auburn: *a mass of Titian curls.* [19th C.: from TITIAN[1], by association with the bright auburn hair portrayed in many of his works.]

Ti·ti·ca·ca, Lake /ˌtitēˈkäkə/ a lake in the Andes, on the border of Peru and Bolivia. At an altitude of 12,497 feet (3,809 m), it is the highest large lake in the world.

tit·il·late /ˈtitlˌāt/ ▶ **v.** [trans.] stimulate or excite (someone), esp. in a sexual way. — **tit·il·lat·ing adj. tit·il·lat·ing·ly adv. tit·il·la·tion** /ˌtitlˈāsʜən/ **n.** [17th C.: from L. *titillat-* 'tickled,' from the verb *titillare*.]

tit·i·vate /ˈtitəˌvāt/ ▶ **v.** [trans.] informal make small enhancing alterations to (something): *she slapped on her warpaint and titivated her hair.* ■ **(titivate oneself)** make oneself look attractive. — **tit·i·va·tion** /ˌtitəˈvāsʜən/ **n.** [19th C. (in early use, also as *tidivate*): perh. from **TIDY**, on the pattern of *cultivate*.]

tit·lark /ˈtitˌlärk/ ▶ **n.** dialect a pipit.

ti·tle /ˈtītl/ ▶ **n.** **1** the name of a book, composition, or other artistic work: *the author and title of the book.* ■ (usu. as **titles**) a caption or credit in a movie or broadcast. ■ a book, magazine, or newspaper considered as a publication. **2** a name that describes someone's position or job: *Leese assumed the title of director general.* ■ a word such as *Lord* or *Dame* that is used before someone's name, or a form that is used instead of someone's name, to indicate high social or official rank. ■ a word such as *Mrs.* or *Dr.* that is used before someone's name to indicate their profession or marital status. ■ a descriptive or distinctive name that is earned or chosen: *Nata's deserved the title of Best Restaurant of the Year.* **3** the position of being the champion of a major sports competition: *Davis won the world title in 1981.* **4** Law a right or claim to the ownership of property or to a rank or throne. **5** (in church use) a fixed sphere of work and source of income as a condition for ordination. ■ a parish church in Rome under a cardinal. ▶ **v.** [trans.] (usu. **be titled**) give a name to (a book, composition, or other work): *a song titled "Blue Moon."* [OE *titul*, reinforced by OFr. *title*, both from L. *titulus* 'inscription, title.']

ti·tle bar ▶ **n.** Comput. a horizontal bar at the top of a window, bearing the name of the program and typically the name of the currently active document.

ti·tled /ˈtītld/ ▶ **adj.** (of a person) having a title indicating high social or official rank.

ti·tle deed ▶ **n.** a legal deed or document constituting evidence of a right, esp. to ownership of property.

ti·tle·hold·er /ˈtītlˌhōldər/ (also **ti·tle hold·er**) ▶ **n.** a person who holds a title, esp. a sports champion.

ti·tle page ▶ **n.** a page at the beginning of a book giving its title, the names of the author and publisher, and other publication information.

ti·tle role ▶ **n.** the part in a play, movie, television show, etc., from which the work's title is taken.

tit·mouse /ˈtitˌmous/ ▶ **n.** (pl. **-mice**) a small songbird (*Parus* and other genera, familyParidae) that searches acrobatically for insects among foliage and branches. Its numerous species include the chickadees and the **tufted titmouse** (*P. bicolor*). [ME: from **TIT**[1] + obs. *mose* 'titmouse.' The change in the ending in the 16th C. was due to association with **MOUSE**, prob. because of the bird's size and quick movements.]

Ti·to /ˈtētō/ (1892–1980), president of Yugoslava 1953–80; born *Josip Broz*. He established Yugoslavia as a nonaligned communist state with a federal constitution.

Ti·to·grad /ˈtētōˌgrad; -ˌgräd/ former name (1946–93) for **PODGORICA**.

ti·trate /ˈtīˌtrāt/ ▶ **v.** [trans.] Chem. ascertain the amount of a constituent in (a solution) by measuring the volume of a known concentration of reagent required to complete a reaction with it, typically using an indicator. ■ Med. continuously measure and adjust the balance of (a physiological function or drug dosage). — **ti·tra·ta·ble adj. ti·tra·tion** /tīˈtrāsʜən/ **n.** [19th C.: from Fr. *titrer* (from *titre* in the sense 'fineness of alloyed gold or silver') + **-ATE**[3].]

ti·tre ▶ **n.** British spelling of **TITER**.

tit·ter /ˈtitər/ ▶ **v.** [intrans.] give a short, half-suppressed laugh; giggle: *her stutter caused the children to titter.* ▶ **n.** a short, half-suppressed laugh. — **tit·ter·er n. tit·ter·ing·ly adv.** [17th C.: imitative.]

tit·ti·vate ▶ **v.** archaic spelling of **TITIVATE**.

tit·tle /ˈtitl/ ▶ **n.** [in sing.] a tiny amount or part of something. ■ archaic a small written or printed stroke or dot, indicating omitted letters in a word. [ME: from L. *titulus* (see **TITLE**), in med. L. 'small stroke, accent'; the phr. *jot or tittle* is from Matt. 5:18.]

tit·tle-tat·tle ▶ **n.** idle talk; gossip. ▶ **v.** [intrans.] engage in such talk. [16th C.: reduplication of **TATTLE**.]

tit·ty /ˈtitē/ (also **tit·tie**) ▶ **n.** (pl. **-ties**) another term for **TIT**[2].

tit·u·ba·tion /ˌticʜəˈbāsʜən/ ▶ **n.** Med. nodding movement of the head or body, esp. as caused by a nervous disorder. [17th C.: from L. *titubatio(n-)*, from *titubare* 'to totter.']

tit·u·lar /ˈticʜələr/ ▶ **adj.** **1** holding or constituting a purely formal position or title without any real authority: *the queen is titular head of the Church of England.* ■ [attrib.] (of a cleric) nominally appointed to serve a diocese, abbey, or other foundation no longer in existence, and typically in fact having authority in another capacity. **2** denoting a person or thing from whom or which the name of an artistic work or similar is taken: *the work's titular song.* ■ [attrib.] denoting any of the parish churches in Rome to which cardinals are formally appointed. [16th C. (in the sense 'existing only in name'): from Fr. *titulaire* or mod. L. *titularis*, from *titulus* (see **TITLE**).]

tit·u·lar·ly /ˈticʜələrlē/ ▶ **adv.** in name or in name only.

Ti·tus[1] /ˈtītəs/ (AD 39–81), Roman emperor 79–81; full name *Titus Vespasianus Augustus*; born *Titus Flavius Vespasianus*; son of Vespasian. In 70, he ended a revolt in Judaea with the conquest of Jerusalem.

Ti·tus[2] a book of the New Testament, an epistle of St. Paul addressed to St. Titus.

Ti·tus, St. (1st century AD), Greek churchman. A convert, he was St. Paul's helper.

Ti·tus·ville /ˈtītəsˌvil/ a historic city in northwestern Pennsylvania, site of the first operative oil well (1859); pop. 6,434.

Tiv /tiv/ ▶ **n.** (pl. same or **Tivs**) **1** a member of a people of southeastern Nigeria. **2** the Benue-Congo language of this people. ▶ **adj.** of or relating to this people or their language. [the name in Tiv.]

Ti·wa /ˈtēwə/ ▶ **n.** (pl. same or **-was**) **1** a member of a Pueblo Indian people living mainly in northern New Mexico. **2** the Tanoan language of this people. Do not confuse with **TEWA**. ▶ **adj.** of or relating to this people or their language. [from Sp. *Tigua*, from a Tanoan name like the Southern Tiwa self-designation *tiwáde*.]

ti·yin /tēˈ(y)in/ ▶ **n.** (pl. same or **-yins**) a monetary unit of Kyrgyzstan, equal to one hundredth of a som.

tiz·zy /ˈtizē/ ▶ **n.** (pl. **-zies**) [in sing.] informal a state of nervous excitement or agitation: *he got into a tizzy.* [1930s (orig. US): of unknown origin.]

TKO ▶ **abbr.** Boxing technical knockout.

tkt. ▶ **abbr.** ticket.

Tl ▶ **symb.** the chemical element thallium.

TLA ▶ **abbr.** three-letter acronym.

Tlax·ca·la /tläˈskälə/ a state in eastern central Mexico.

TLC ▶ **abbr.** informal tender loving care.

Tlin·git /ˈtlɪnɢ(g)it/ ▶ **n.** (pl. same or **-gits**) **1** a member of an American Indian people of the coasts and islands of southeastern Alaska and adjacent British Columbia. **2** the Na-Dene language of this people. ▶ **adj.** of or relating to this people or their language. [the name in Tlingit.]

T lym·pho·cyte (also **T-lym·pho·cyte**) ▶ **n.** another term for **T CELL**.

TM ▶ **abbr.** trademark. Transcendental Meditation.

Tm ▶ **symb.** the chemical element thulium.

t.m. ▶ **abbr.** true mean.

tme·sis /təˈmēsis/ ▶ **n.** (pl. **-ses** /-sēz/) the separation of parts of a compound word by an intervening word or words, heard mainly in informal speech (e.g., *shove it back any-old-where in the pile*). [16th C.: from Gk. *tmēsis* 'cutting,' from *temnein* 'to cut.']

TMJ ▶ **abbr.** temporomandibular joint.

TN ▶ **abbr.** Tennessee (in official postal use).

tn ▶ **abbr.** ■ ton(s). ■ town. ■ train.

tng. ▶ **abbr.** training.

tnpk. ▶ **abbr.** turnpike.

TNT ▶ **n.** a high explosive, $C_7H_5(NO_2)_3$, formed from toluene by substitution of three hydrogen atoms with nitro groups. It is relatively insensitive to shock and can be conveniently melted. [an abbr. of its full name, *trinitrotoluene*.]

to /to͞o/ ▶ **prep.** **1** expressing motion in the direction of (a particular location): *my first visit to Africa.* ■ expressing location, typically in relation to a specified point of reference: *forty miles to the south of the site.* ■ expressing a point reached at the end of a range or after a period of time: *from 1938 to 1945.* ■ (in telling the time) before (the hour specified): *it's five to ten.* ■ approaching or reaching (a particular condition): *she was close to tears.* ■ expressing the result of a process or action: *smashed to smithereens.* **2** identifying the person or thing affected: *you were terribly unkind to her.* ■ identifying the recipient or intended recipient of something: *I am deeply grateful to my parents.* **3** identifying a particular relationship between one person and another: *he is married to Jan's cousin.* ■ in various phrases indicating how something is related to something else (often followed by a noun without a determiner): *made to order.* ■ indicating a rate of return on something, e.g., the distance traveled in exchange for fuel used, or an exchange rate that can be obtained in one currency for another: *ten miles to the gallon.* ■ **(to the)** Math. indicating the power (exponent) to which a number is raised: *ten to the minus thirty-three.* **4** indicating that two things are attached: *he had left his bike chained to a fence.* **5** concerning or likely to concern (something, esp. something abstract): *a threat to world peace.* **6** governing a phrase expressing someone's reaction to something: *to her astonishment, he smiled.* **7** used to introduce the second element in a comparison: *it's nothing to what it once was.* ▶ **infinitive marker** **1** used with the base form of a verb to indicate that the verb is in the infinitive, in particular: ■ expressing purpose or intention: *we tried to help.* ■ expressing an outcome, result, or consequence: *he managed to escape.* ■ expressing a cause: *I'm sorry to hear that.* ■ indicating a desired or advisable action: *we asked her to explain.* ■ indicating a proposition that is known, believed, or reported about a specified person or thing: *a house that people believed to be haunted.* ■ **(about to)** forming a future tense with reference to the immediate future: *he was about to sing.* ■ after a noun, indicating its function or purpose: *something to eat.* ■ after a phrase containing an ordinal number: *the first person to arrive.* **2** used without a verb following when the missing verb is clearly understood: *he asked her to come but she said she didn't want to.* ▶ **adv.** so as to be closed or nearly closed: *he pulled the* *door to behind him.* [OE tō (adv. and prep.), of West Gmc. origin; rel. to Du. *toe* and Ger. *zu*.]

t.o. ▸ abbr. ▪ turnover. ▪ turn over.

toad /tōd/ ▸ n. **1** a tailless amphibian (Bufonidae and other families, order Anura) with a short stout body and short legs, typically having dry warty skin that can exude poison. **2** a contemptible or detestable person (used as a general term of abuse): *you're an arrogant little toad.* — **toad·ish** adj. [OE *tādde*, *tāda*, abbr. of *tādige*, of unknown origin.]

toad·fish /'tōd,fish/ ▸ n. (pl. same or **-fish·es**) any of a number of fishes with a wide flattened head, esp. a chiefly bottom-dwelling large-mouthed fish (family Batrachoididae) of warm seas that can produce loud grunts

toad·flax /'tōd,flaks/ ▸ n. a Eurasian plant (*Linaria* and related genera) of the figwort family, typically having yellow or purplish snapdragon-like flowers and slender leaves. Its several species include **butter-and-eggs** (*L. vulgaris*), with yellow and orange flowers and found widely as a naturalized North American weed.

toad·stone /'tōd,stōn/ ▸ n. a gem, fossil tooth, or other stone formerly supposed to have been formed in the body of a toad, and credited with therapeutic or protective properties.

toad·stool /'tōd,stōōl/ ▸ n. the spore-bearing fruiting body of a fungus, typically in the form of a rounded cap on a stalk, esp. one that is believed to be inedible or poisonous. See also MUSHROOM. [ME: a fanciful name.]

toad·y /'tōdē/ ▸ n. (pl. **toad·ies**) a person who behaves obsequiously to someone important. ▸ v. (**toad·ies, toad·ied**) [intrans.] act in an obsequious way. — **toad·y·ish** adj. **toad·y·ism** n. [19th C.: said to be a contr. of *toad-eater*, a charlatan's assistant who ate toads; toads were regarded as poisonous, and the assistant's survival was thought to be due to the efficacy of the charlatan's remedy.]

to and fro (also **to-and-fro**) ▸ adv. in a constant movement backward and forward or from side to side. ▸ v. [intrans.] (**be toing and froing**) move constantly backward and forward: *the ducks were toing and froing.* ▪ repeatedly discuss or think about something without making any progress. ▸ n. [in sing.] constant movement backward and forward. ▪ constant change in action, attitude, or focus.

toast[1] /tōst/ ▸ n. **1** sliced bread browned on both sides by exposure to radiant heat. **2** a call to a gathering of people to raise their glasses and drink together in honor of a person or thing, or an instance of drinking in this way. ▪ [in sing.] a person or thing that is very popular or held in high regard by a particular group of people: *he found himself the toast of the baseball world.* ▸ v. [trans.] **1** cook or brown (food, esp. bread or cheese) by exposure to a grill, fire, or other source of radiant heat. ▪ [intrans.] (of food) cook or become brown in this way. ▪ warm (oneself or part of one's body) in front of a fire or other source or heat. **2** drink to the health or in honor of (someone or something) by raising one's glass together with others.
– PHRASES **be toast** informal be or be likely to become finished, defunct, or dead: *one mistake and you're toast.* [ME (as a verb in the sense 'burn as the sun does, parch'): from OFr. *toster* 'roast,' from L. *torrere* 'parch.']

toast[2] ▸ v. [intrans.] [usu. as n.] (**toasting**) (of a DJ) accompany a reggae backing track or music with improvised rhythmic speech. — **toast·er** n. [20th C.: perh. the same word as TOAST[1].]

toast·er /'tōstər/ ▸ n. an electrical device for making toast.

toast·mas·ter /'tōst,mastər/ ▸ n. an official responsible for proposing toasts, introducing speakers, and making other formal announcements at a large social event.

toast·mis·tress /'tōst,mistris/ ▸ n. a female toastmaster.

toast·y /'tōstē/ ▸ adj. of or resembling toast. ▪ comfortably warm.

Tob. ▸ abbr. (in biblical references) Tobit (Apocrypha).

to·bac·co /tə'bakō/ ▸ n. (pl. **-cos**) **1** a preparation of the nicotine-rich leaves of an American plant, which are cured by a process of drying and fermentation for smoking or chewing. **2** (also **tobacco plant**) the plant (*Nicotiana tabacum*) of the nightshade family that yields these leaves, native to tropical America. It is widely cultivated in warm regions, esp. in the US and China. [16th C.: from Sp. *tabaco*; said to be from a Carib word denoting a tobacco pipe or from a Taino word for a primitive cigar, but perh. from Arab.]

to·bac·co mo·sa·ic vi·rus ▸ n. a virus that causes mosaic disease in tobacco, much used in biochemical research.

to·bac·co·nist /tə'bakənist/ ▸ n. a dealer in cigarettes, tobacco, cigars, and other items used by smokers.

To·ba·go /tə'bāgō/ see TRINIDAD AND TOBAGO.

To·bit /'tōbit/ a pious Israelite living during the Babylonian Captivity, described in the Apocrypha. ▪ a book of the Apocrypha telling the story of Tobit.

toboggan

to·bog·gan /tə'bägən/ ▸ n. a long narrow sled used for the sport of coasting downhill over snow or ice. It typically is made of a lightweight board that is curved upward and backward at the front. ▸ v. [intrans.] ride on a toboggan. — **to·bog·gan·er** n. **to·bog·gan·ist** n. [19th C.: from Canad. Fr. *tabaganne*, from Micmac *topăgan* 'sled.']

To·bruk /tə'brōōk; 'tōbrōōk/ a port on the coast of Libya; pop. 94,000. It was the scene of fierce fighting during the North African campaign in World War II.

To·by jug /'tōbē/ (also **to·by jug**) ▸ n. a beer jug or mug in the form of a stout old man wearing a three-cornered hat. [19th C.: nickname for the given name *Tobias*, and said to come from an 18th-cent. poem about *Toby Philpot* (with a pun on *fill pot*), a soldier who liked to drink.]

To·can·tins /,tōkən'tēns/ a river in South America that rises in central Brazil and flows 1,640 miles (2,640 km) north, joining the Pará River.

toc·ca·ta /tə'kätə/ ▸ n. a musical composition for a keyboard instrument designed to exhibit the performer's touch and technique. [18th C.: from Ital., fem. past part. of *toccare* 'to touch.']

To·char·i·an /tō'ke(ə)rēən; -'kär-/ ▸ n. **1** a member of a central Asian people who inhabited the Tarim Basin in the 1st millennium AD. **2** ▪ either of two extinct languages (**Tocharian A** and **Tocharian B**) spoken by this people, the most easterly of known ancient Indo-European languages, surviving in a few documents and inscriptions and showing affinities to Celtic and Italic languages. ▸ adj. of or relating to this people or their language. [from Fr. *tocharien*, via L. from Gk. *Tokharoi*, the name of a Scythian tribe (almost certainly unrelated to the Tocharians).]

to·co /'tōkō/ (also **to·co tou·can**) ▸ n. (pl. **-cos**) the largest and most familiar South American toucan (*Ramphastos toco*), with mainly black plumage, a white throat and breast, and a massive black-tipped orange bill. [18th C.: via Port. from Tupi; cf. TOUCAN.]

to·coph·er·ol /tə'käfə,rôl; -,räl/ ▸ n. Biochem. any of several closely related compounds, found in wheat germ oil, egg yolk, and leafy vegetables, that collectively constitute vitamin E. [1930s: from Gk. *tokos* 'offspring' + *pherein* 'to bear' + -OL.]

Tocque·ville /'tōk,vil/, Alexis de (1805–59) French politician and historian; full name *Alexis Charles Henri Maurice Clérel de Tocqueville*. He wrote *Democracy in America* (1835–40).

toc·sin /'täksin/ ▸ n. an alarm bell or signal. [16th C.: from OFr. *toquassen*, from Provençal *tocasenh*, from *tocar* 'to touch' + *senh* 'signal bell.']

tod /täd/ ▸ n. a bushy mass of foliage, esp. ivy.

to·day /tə'dā/ ▸ adv. on or in the course of this present day: *she's thirty today.* ▪ at the present period of time; nowadays. ▸ n. this present day: *today is a day of rest.* ▪ the present period of time: *today's society.* [OE *tō dæg* 'on (this) day.' Cf. TOMORROW and TONIGHT.]

Todd /täd/, Thomas (1765–1826) US Supreme Court associate justice 1807–26.

tod·dle /'tädl/ ▸ v. [intrans.] (of a young child) move with short unsteady steps while learning to walk. ▪ informal walk or go somewhere in a casual or leisurely way: *they would toddle off home.* ▸ n. [in sing.] a young child's unsteady walk. [16th C.: of unknown origin.]

tod·dler /'tädlər/ ▸ n. a young child who is just beginning to walk. — **tod·dler·hood** n.

tod·dy /'tädē/ ▸ n. (pl. **-dies**) **1** a drink made of alcoholic liquor with hot water, sugar, and sometimes spices. **2** the sap of some kinds of palm, fermented to produce arrack. [17th C. (sense 2): from Marathi *tāḍī*, Hindi *tāṛī*, from Sanskrit *tāḍī* 'palmyra.']

to-do /tə 'dōō/ ▸ n. [in sing.] informal a commotion or fuss. [16th C.: from *to do* as in *much to do*, orig. meaning 'much needing to be done' but later interpreted as the adjective *much* and a noun; cf. ADO.]

to·dy /'tōdē/ ▸ n. (pl. **-dies**) a small insectivorous Caribbean bird (family Todidae and genus *Todus*: five species) related to the motmots, with a large head, long bill, bright green upper parts, and a red throat. [18th C.: from Fr. *todier*, from L. *todus*, the name of a small bird.]

toe /tō/ ▸ n. **1** any of the five digits at the end of the human foot: *he cut his big toe on a sharp stone.* ▪ any of the digits of the foot of a quadruped or bird. ▪ the part of an item of footwear that covers a person's toes. **2** the lower end, tip, or point of something, in particular: ▪ the tip of the head of a golf club, furthest from the shaft. ▪ the foot or base of a cliff, slope, or embankment. ▪ a flattish portion at the foot of an otherwise steep curve on a graph. ▪ a section of a rhizome or similar fleshy root from which a new plant may be propagated. ▸ v. (**toes, toed, toe·ing**) **1** [trans.] push, touch, or kick (something) with one's toe: *he toed off his shoes and flexed his feet.* ▪ Golf strike (the ball) with the toe of the club. **2** [intrans.] (**toe in/out**) walk with the toes pointed in (or out): *he toes out when he walks.* ▪ (of a pair of wheels) converge (or diverge) slightly at the front: *on a turn, the inner wheel toes out more.*
– PHRASES **on one's toes** ready for any eventuality; alert. **toe the line** accept the authority, principles, or policies of a particular group, esp. under pressure. [from the literal sense 'stand with the tips of the toes exactly touching a line.'] **toe to toe** (of two people) standing directly in front of one another, esp. in order to fight or argue. — **toed** adj. [in comb.] *three-toed feet.* **toe·less** adj. [OE *tā*, of Gmc. origin; rel. to Du. *tee* and Ger. *Zeh, Zehe*. Current senses of the verb date from the mid 19th C.]

toe·a /'toi-ə/ ▸ n. (pl. same) a monetary unit of Papua New Guinea, equal to one hundredth of a kina. [Motu, a Melanesian language, lit. 'cone-shaped shell.']

toe cap (also **toe·cap**) ▸ n. a piece of steel or leather constituting or fitted over the front part of a boot or shoe as protection or reinforcement.

toe clip ▸ n. a clip on a bicycle pedal to prevent the foot from slipping.

toe·hold /'tō,hōld/ ▸ n. a small place where a person's foot can be lodged to support them, esp. while climbing. ▪ a relatively insignificant position from which further progress may be made. ▪ Wrestling a hold in which the opponent's toe is seized and the leg forced backward.

toe-in ▶ **n.** a slight forward convergence of a pair of wheels so that they are closer together in front than behind.

toe loop ▶ **n.** Figure Skating a jump, initiated with the help of the supporting foot, in which the skater makes a full turn in the air, taking off from and landing on the outside edge of the same foot.

toe·nail /ˈtōˌnāl/ ▶ **n.** **1** the nail at the tip of each toe. **2** a nail driven obliquely through a piece of wood to secure it. ▶ **v.** [trans.] fasten (a piece of wood) in this way.

toe-out ▶ **n.** a slight forward divergence of a pair of wheels so that they are closer together behind than in front.

toe-tap·ping ▶ **adj.** informal (of music) making one want to tap one's feet; lively.

toff /täf/ Brit., informal ▶ **n.** derog. a rich or upper-class person. [19th C.: perh. an alt. of **tuft**, used to denote a gold tassel worn on the cap by titled undergraduates at Oxford and Cambridge.]

tof·fee /ˈtôfē; ˈtäfē/ ▶ **n.** (pl. **-fees**) a kind of firm or hard candy that softens when sucked or chewed, made by boiling together sugar and butter, often with other ingredients or flavorings added. ■ a small shaped piece of such candy. [19th C.: alt. of **taffy**.]

tof·fee-nosed ▶ **adj.** informal, esp. Brit. pretentiously superior; snobbish. — **tof·fee nose n.**

Toff·ler /ˈtôflər/ US writers and social analysts. Alvin (1928–) and his wife, Heidi (1929–), collaborated on such works as *Future Shock* (1970) and *Revolutionary Wealth* (2006).

to·fu /ˈtōfo͞o/ ▶ **n.** curd made from mashed soybeans, used chiefly in Asian and vegetarian cooking. [from Japanese *tōfu*, from Chin. *dòufu*, from *dòu* 'beans' + *fǔ* 'rot, turn sour.']

tog /täg/ informal ▶ **n.** (**togs**) clothes: *running togs.* ▶ **v.** (**togged, tog·ging**) (**be/get togged up/out**) be or get dressed for a particular occasion or activity. [18th C. (as a slang term for a coat or outer garment): appar. an abbr. of obs. criminals' slang *togeman(s)* 'a light cloak,' from Fr. *toge* or L. *toga* (see **toga**).]

to·ga /ˈtōgə/ ▶ **n.** a loose flowing outer garment worn by the citizens of ancient Rome, made of a single piece of cloth and covering the whole body apart from the right arm. ■ a robe of office; a mantle of responsibility, etc. [L.; rel. to *tegere* 'to cover.']

toga

to·geth·er /təˈgeT͟Hər/ ▶ **adv.** **1** with or in proximity to another person or people: *they stood together.* ■ so as to touch or combine: *pieces of wood nailed together.* ■ in combination; collectively: *taken together, these measures would improve chances of surviving.* ■ into companionship or close association: *the experience has brought us together.* ■ (of two people) married or in a sexual relationship with each other: *they split up after ten years together.* ■ so as to be united or in agreement: *he could not bring the two sides together.* **2** at the same time: *they both spoke together.* **3** without interruption; continuously: *she sits for hours together in the lotus position.* ▶ **adj.** informal self-confident, level-headed, or well organized: *she seems a very together young woman.* [OE *tōgædere*, based on the prep. **to** + a West Gmc. word rel. to **gather**. The adj. dates from the 1960s.]

to·geth·er·ness /təˈgeT͟Hərnis/ ▶ **n.** the state of being close to another person or other people.

tog·ger·y /ˈtägərē/ ▶ **n.** informal, humorous clothes.

tog·gle /ˈtägəl/ ▶ **n.** **1** a short rod of wood or plastic sewn to one side of a coat or other garment, pushed through a hole or loop on the other side and twisted so as to act as a fastener. ■ a pin or other crosspiece put through the eye of a rope or a link of a chain to keep it in place. ■ (also **toggle bolt**) a kind of wall fastener for use on hollow walls, having a part that springs open or turns through 90° after it is inserted so as to prevent withdrawal. See illustration at **bolt**[1]. ■ a movable pivoted crosspiece acting as a barb on a harpoon. **2** (also **toggle switch** or **toggle key**) Comput. a key or command that is operated the same way but with opposite effect on successive occasions. ▶ **v.** **1** [intrans.] Comput. switch from one effect, feature, or state to another by using a toggle. **2** [trans.] provide or fasten with a toggle or toggles. [18th C. (orig. in nautical use): of unknown origin.]

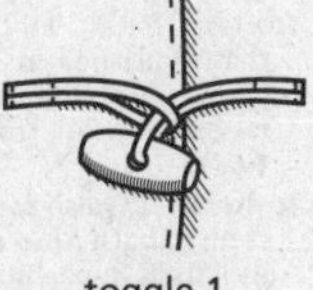

toggle 1

tog·gle switch ▶ **n.** **1** an electric switch operated by means of a projecting lever that is moved up and down. **2** Comput. another term for **toggle**.

To·gliat·ti /tôlˈyätē; täl-/ a city in southwestern Russia; pop. 642,000. Former name (until 1964) **Stavropol**. Russian name **Tolyatti**.

To·go /ˈtōgō/ a country in West Africa. *See box.* — **To·go·lese** /ˌtōgōˈlēz; -ˈlēs; ˌtōgə-/ **adj. & n.**

toil /toil/ ▶ **v.** [intrans.] work extremely hard or incessantly. ■ move slowly and with difficulty. ▶ **n.** exhausting physical labor: *a life of toil.* — **toil·er n.** [ME: from Anglo-Norman Fr. *toiler* 'strive, dispute,' *toil* 'confusion,' from L. *tudiculare* 'stir around,' from *tudicula* 'machine for crushing olives,' rel. to *tundere* 'crush.']

toile /twäl/ ▶ **n.** **1** an early version of a finished garment made up in cheap material so that the design can be tested and perfected. **2** a translucent linen or cotton fabric, used for making clothes. ■ short for **toile de Jouy**. [ME (denoting cloth or canvas for painting on): from Fr. *toile* 'cloth, web,' from L. *tela* 'web.']

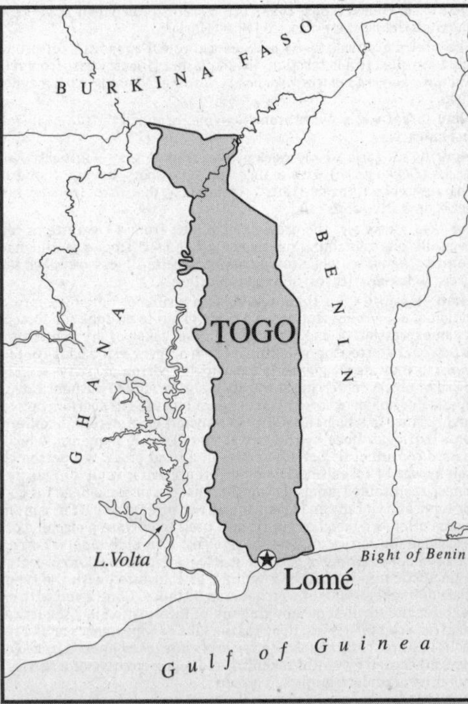

Togo

Official name: Togolese Republic
Location: West Africa, between Ghana and Benin, with a short coastline on the Gulf of Guinea
Area: 21,900 square miles (56,800 sq km)
Population: 5,556,000
Capital: Lome
Languages: French (official), West African languages
Currency: CFA franc

toile de Jouy /ˌtwäl də ˈZHwē/ ▶ **n.** a type of printed calico with a characteristic floral, figure, or landscape design on a light background, typically used for upholstery or curtains. [orig. made at *Jouy*-en-Josas, near Paris.]

toi·let /ˈtoilit/ ▶ **n.** **1** a large bowl for urinating or defecating into, typically plumbed into a sewage system and with a flushing mechanism. ■ a room, building, or cubicle containing one or more of these. **2** [in sing.] the process of washing oneself, dressing, and attending to one's appearance. ■ [as adj.] denoting articles used in this process. ■ the cleansing of part of a person's body as a medical procedure. ▶ **v.** (**-let·ed, -let·ing**) [trans.] [usu. as n.] (**toileting**) assist or supervise (someone, esp. an infant or invalid) in using a toilet. [16th C.: from Fr. *toilette* 'cloth, wrapper,' dimin. of *toile* (see **toile**).]

toi·let pa·per ▶ **n.** paper in sheets or on a roll for wiping oneself clean after urination or defecation. ▶ **v.** [trans.] drape or wind toilet paper around something as a prank.

toi·let·ries /ˈtoilitrēz/ ▶ **plural n.** articles used in washing and taking care of one's body, such as soap, shampoo, and toothpaste.

toi·lette /twäˈlet/ ▶ **n.** [in sing.] dated the process of washing oneself, dressing, and attending to one's appearance: *Emily got up to begin her morning toilette.* [17th C.: Fr. (see **toilet**).]

toi·let tis·sue ▶ **n.** another term for **toilet paper**.

toi·let-train ▶ **v.** [trans.] teach (a young child) to use the toilet.

toi·let wa·ter ▶ **n.** a dilute form of perfume. Also called **eau de toilette**.

toils /toilz/ ▶ **plural n.** literary used in reference to a situation regarded as a trap: *Henry had become caught in the toils of his own deviousness.* [16th C. (denoting a net into which a hunted quarry is driven): pl. of *toil*, from OFr. *toile* 'net, trap' (see **toile**).]

toil·some /ˈtoilsəm/ ▶ **adj.** archaic or literary involving hard or tedious work. — **toil·some·ly adv. toil·some·ness n.**

toil·worn /ˈtoilˌwôrn/ ▶ **adj.** literary exhausted by hard physical labor.

To·jo /'tō'jō/, Hideki (1884–1948), prime minister of Japan 1941–44. He initiated the Japanese attack on Pearl Harbor.

to·ka·mak /'tōkə,mak; 'tä-/ ▶ **n.** Physics a toroidal apparatus for producing controlled fusion reactions in hot plasma. [1960s: Russ., from *toroidal'naya kamera s magnitnym polem* 'toroidal chamber with magnetic field.']

To·kay /tō'kā/ ▶ **n.** a sweet aromatic wine, originally made near Tokaj in Hungary.

to·kay /tō'kā/ (also **to·kay geck·o**) ▶ **n.** a large gray Southeast Asian gecko (*Gekko gecko*) with orange and blue spots, having a loud call that resembles its name. [18th C.: from Malay dial. *toke'*, from Javanese *tekèk*, imitative of its call.]

toke /tōk/ informal ▶ **n.** the drawing of a puff from a cigarette or pipe, typically one containing marijuana. ▶ **v.** [intrans.] smoke marijuana or tobacco: *he muses while **toking** on a cigarette* | [trans.] *we toked some grass.* — **tok·er n.** [1950s: of unknown origin.]

to·ken /'tōkən/ ▶ **n.** **1** a thing serving as a visible or tangible representation of something abstract. ■ a thing given to or done for someone as an expression of one's feelings: *a small token of my appreciation.* ■ archaic a characteristic or distinctive sign or mark, esp. a badge or favor worn to indicate allegiance to a particular person or party. ■ archaic a word or object conferring authority on or serving to authenticate the speaker or holder. ■ Comput. a sequence of bits used in a certain network architecture in which the ability to transmit information is conferred on a particular node by the arrival there of this sequence, which is passed continuously between nodes in a fixed order. ■ a person chosen by way of tokenism as a nominal representative of a minority or under-represented group. **2** a voucher that can be exchanged for goods or services, typically one given as a gift or offered as part of a promotional offer. ■ a metal or plastic disk used to operate a machine or in exchange for particular goods or services. **3** an individual occurrence of a symbol or string, in particular: ■ Ling. an individual occurrence of a linguistic unit in speech or writing, as contrasted with the type or class of linguistic unit of which it is an instance. Contrasted with **TYPE**. ■ Comput. the smallest meaningful unit of information in a sequence of data for a compiler. ▶ **adj.** done for the sake of appearances or as a symbolic gesture: *cases like these often bring just token fines.* ■ [attrib.] (of a person) chosen by way of tokenism as a representative of a particular minority or underrepresented group.
– PHRASES **by the same token** in the same way or for the same reason. [OE *tāc(e)n*, of Gmc. origin; rel. to Du. *teken* and Ger. *Zeichen*, also to **TEACH**.]

to·ken·ism /'tōkə,nizəm/ ▶ **n.** the practice of making only a perfunctory or symbolic effort to do a particular thing, esp. by recruiting a small number of people from underrepresented groups in order to give the appearance of sexual or racial equality within a workforce. — **to·ken·is·tic** /,tōkə'nistik/ **adj.**

to·ken ring ▶ **n.** Comput. a local area network in which a node can transmit only when in possession of a sequence of bits (called the token) that is passed to each node in turn.

Tok·las /'tōkləs/, Alice Babette, (1877–1967) US writer. A companion to Gertrude Stein, her letters are collected in *Staying on Alone* (1973).

to·ko·no·ma /,tōkə'nōmə/ ▶ **n.** (in a Japanese house) a recess or alcove, typically a few inches above floor level, for displaying flowers, pictures, and ornaments. [Japanese.]

Tok Pis·in /,täk 'pisin/ ▶ **n.** an English-based Creole used as a commercial and administrative language by over 2 million people in Papua New Guinea. Also called **Neo-Melanesian**. [the name in Tok Pisin, lit. 'pidgin talk.']

To·ku·ga·wa /,tōkōō'gäwə/ the last shogunate in Japan (1603–1867), founded by Tokugawa Ieyasu (1543–1616). The shogunate was followed by the restoration of imperial power under Meiji Tenno.

To·ky·o /'tōkē,ō/ the capital of Japan, on southeastern Honshu; pop. 8,163,000. Formerly called Edo, it was renamed Tokyo in 1868 and replaced Kyoto as the imperial capital.

to·lar /'tälär/ ▶ **n.** the basic monetary unit of Slovenia, equal to 100 stotins. [Slovene; cf. **THALER**.]

Tol·bu·khin /tôl'bōōkin; -KHin/ former name (1949–91) of **DOBRICH**.

tol·bu·ta·mide /täl'byōōtə,mīd/ ▶ **n.** Med. a synthetic compound ($C_{12}H_{18}N_2O_3S$) used to lower blood sugar levels in the treatment of diabetes. Also called **1-butyl-3-tosylurea**. [1950s: from *tol(uene)* + *but(yl)* + **AMIDE**.]

told /tōld/ past and past participle of **TELL**[1].

tole /tōl/ (also **tôle**) ▶ **n.** painted, enameled, or lacquered tin plate used to make decorative domestic objects. — **tole·ware** /-,we(ə)r/ **n.** [1940s: Fr. *tôle* 'sheet iron,' from dial. *taule* 'table,' from L. *tabula* 'flat board.']

To·le·do 1 /tə'lādō; -'lē-/ a city in central Spain on the Tagus River, capital of Castilla-La Mancha region; pop. 64,000. **2** /tə'lēdō/ a city in northwestern Ohio; pop. 313,619. — **To·le·dan** /tə'lēdn/ **adj. & n.**

tol·er·a·ble /'tälərəbəl/ ▶ **adj.** able to be endured. ■ fairly good; mediocre: *he had a tolerable voice.* — **tol·er·a·bil·i·ty** /,täl(ə)rə'bilitē/ **n.** **tol·er·a·bly adv.** [as submodifier] *the welfare state works tolerably well.* [ME: via OFr. from L. *tolerabilis*, from *tolerare* (see **TOLERATE**).]

tol·er·ance /'tälərəns/ ▶ **n.** **1** the ability or willingness to tolerate something, in particular the existence of opinions or behavior that one does not necessarily agree with: *religious tolerance.* ■ the capacity to endure continued subjection to something, esp. a drug, transplant, antigen, or environmental conditions, without adverse reaction. ■ diminution in the body's response to a drug after continued use. **2** an allowable amount of variation of a specified quantity, esp. in the dimensions of a machine or part. [ME (denoting the action of bearing hardship, or the ability to bear pain and hardship): via OFr. from L. *tolerantia*, from *tolerare* (see **TOLERATE**).]

tol·er·ant /'tälərənt/ ▶ **adj.** **1** showing willingness to allow the existence of opinions or behavior that one does not necessarily agree with. **2** (of a plant, animal, or machine) able to endure (specified conditions or treatment). — **tol·er·ant·ly adv.** (in sense 1). [18th C.: from Fr. *tolérant*, pres. part. of *tolérer*, from L. *tolerare* (see **TOLERATE**). Cf. earlier **INTOLERANT**.]

tol·er·ate /'tälə,rāt/ ▶ **v.** [trans.] allow the existence, occurrence, or practice of (something that one does not necessarily like or agree with) without interference. ■ accept or endure (someone or something unpleasant or disliked) with forbearance. ■ be capable of continued subjection to (a drug, toxin, or environmental condition) without adverse reaction. — **tol·er·a·tor** /-,rātər/ **n.** [16th C. (in the sense 'endure (pain)'): from L. *tolerat-* 'endured,' from the verb *tolerare*.]

tol·er·a·tion /,tälə'rāSHən/ ▶ **n.** the practice of tolerating something, in particular differences of opinion or behavior. [15th C. (denoting the granting of permission by authority): from Fr. *tolération*, from L. *toleratio(n-)*, from *tolerare* (see **TOLERATE**).]

Tol·kien /'tōlkēn; 'täl-/, J. R. R. (1892–1973), British writer; born in South Africa; full name *John Ronald Reuel Tolkien*. He wrote *The Hobbit* (1937) and *The Lord of the Rings* (1954–55).

toll[1] /tōl/ ▶ **n.** **1** a charge payable for permission to use a particular bridge or road. ■ a charge for a long-distance telephone call. **2** [in sing.] the number of deaths, casualties, or injuries arising from particular circumstances, such as a natural disaster, conflict, or accident. ■ the cost or damage resulting from something. ▶ **v.** [trans.] [usu. as n.] (**tolling**) charge a toll for the use of (a bridge or road).
– PHRASES **take its toll** (or **take a heavy toll**) have an adverse effect, esp. so as to cause damage, suffering, or death. [OE (denoting a charge, tax, or duty), from med. L. *toloneum*, alt. of late L. *teloneum*, from Gk. *telōnion* 'tollhouse,' from *telos* 'tax.']

toll[2] ▶ **v.** [intrans.] (of a bell) sound with a slow, uniform succession of strokes, as a signal or announcement. ■ [trans.] cause (a bell) to make such a sound. ■ (of a bell) announce or mark (the time, a service, or a person's death). ▶ **n.** [in sing.] a single ring of a bell. [ME: prob. a special use of dial. *toll* 'drag, pull.']

toll·booth /'tōl,bōōTH/ ▶ **n.** a booth where drivers must pay to use a bridge or road.

toll bridge ▶ **n.** a bridge where drivers or pedestrians must pay to cross.

toll·gate /'tōl,gāt/ ▶ **n.** a barrier across a road where drivers or pedestrians must pay to go further.

toll·house /'tōl,hous/ ▶ **n.** a small house by a tollgate or toll bridge where money is collected from road users.

toll·house cook·ie ▶ **n.** a cookie made with flour, brown sugar, chocolate chips, and usually chopped nuts. [named after the *Toll House* in Whitman, Massachusetts, source of the original recipe.]

toll pla·za ▶ **n.** a row of tollbooths on a toll road.

toll road ▶ **n.** a road that drivers must pay to use.

toll·way /'tōl,wā/ ▶ **n.** a highway for the use of which a charge is made.

Tol·stoy /'tôlstoi; 'tōl-/, Count Leo (1828–1910), Russian writer; Russian name *Lev Nikolaevich Tolstoi*. His novels include *War and Peace* (1863–69) and *Anna Karenina* (1873–77).

Tol·tec /'tōltek; 'täl-/ ▶ **n.** a member of an American Indian people that flourished in Mexico before the Aztecs. ■ the language of this people. ▶ **adj.** of or relating to this people. — **Tol·tec·an** /tōl'tekən; täl-/ **adj.** [via Sp. from Nahuatl *toltecatl*, lit. 'a person from *Tula*' (see **TULA**).]

to·lu /tə'lōō/ (also **to·lu bal·sam**) ▶ **n.** a fragrant brown balsam obtained from a South American tree (esp. *Myroxylon balsamum* of the pea family), used in perfumery and medicine. [17th C.: named after *Santiago de Tolú* in Colombia, from where it was exported.]

To·lu·ca /tə'lōōkə/ a city in central Mexico, pop. 488,000. Full name **TOLUCA DE LERDO**.

tol·u·ene /'tälyōō,ēn/ ▶ **n.** Chem. a colorless liquid hydrocarbon ($C_6H_5CH_3$) present in coal tar and petroleum and used as a solvent and in organic synthesis. Also called **methylbenzene**. [19th C.: from **TOLU** + **-ENE**.]

to·lu·i·dine blue /tə'lōōə,dēn/ ▶ **n.** a synthetic blue dye ($C_{15}H_{16}ClN_3S$) used chiefly as a stain in biology. [19th C.: *toluidine* from **TOLUENE** + **-IDE** + **-INE**[4].]

To·lyat·ti /tôl'yätē; täl-/ Russian name for **TOGLIATTI**.

tom /täm/ ▶ **n.** **1** the male of various animals, esp. a turkey or domestic cat. **2** (**Tom**) informal short for **UNCLE TOM**. ▶ **v.** (**Tom**) (**Tommed, Tom·ming**) [intrans.] informal, derog. (of a black person) behave in an excessively obedient or servile way. [ME (denoting an ordinary man, surviving in *tomfool*, *tomboy*, and the phr. *Tom, Dick, and Harry*): abbr. of the given name *Thomas*. Sense 1 dates from the mid 18th C.]

tom·a·hawk /'tämə,hôk/ ▶ **n.** a light ax used as a tool or weapon by American Indians.

tomahawk

▶ v. [trans.] strike or cut with or as if with a tomahawk. [17th C.: from a Virginia Algonquian language.]

tom·al·ley /'täm,alē/ ▶ n. the digestive gland of a lobster, which turns green when cooked. It is sometimes considered a delicacy. [17th C.: from Fr. *taumalin*, from Carib *taumali*.]

Tom and Jer·ry /'täm and 'jerē/ ▶ n. (pl. **-ries**) a kind of hot spiced rum cocktail, made with eggs.

to·ma·til·lo /,tōmə'tē(y)ō/ ▶ n. (pl. **-los**) **1** a small edible fruit that is purplish or yellow when ripe, but is most often used when green for salsas and preserves. **2** the Mexican plant (*Physalis philadelphica*) of the nightshade family that bears this fruit. [20th C.: from Sp., dimin. of *tomate* 'tomato.']

to·ma·to /tə'mātō; -'mätō/ ▶ n. (pl. **-toes**) **1** a glossy red, or occasionally yellow, pulpy edible fruit that is typically eaten as a vegetable or in salad. ■ the bright red color of a ripe tomato. **2** the widely cultivated South American plant (*Lycopersicon esculentum*) of the nightshade family that produces this fruit. — **to·ma·to·ey** adj. [17th C.: from Fr., Sp., or Port. *tomate*, from Nahuatl *tomatl*.]

tomb /tōōm/ ▶ n. a large vault, typically an underground one, for burying the dead. ■ an enclosure for a corpse cut in the earth or in rock. ■ a monument to the memory of a dead person, erected over their burial place. ■ used in similes and metaphors to refer to a place or situation that is extremely cold, quiet, or dark, or that forms a confining enclosure: *the house was as quiet as a tomb.* ■ **(the tomb)** literary death: *none escape the tomb.* [ME: from OFr. *tombe*, from late L. *tumba*, from Gk. *tumbos*.]

Tom·baugh /'tämbô/, Clyde William (1906–97), US astronomer. He discovered the dwarf planet Pluto in 1930.

Tom·big·bee Riv·er /täm'bigbē/ a river that flows from northeastern Mississippi through Alabama to the Alabama River.

tom·bo·lo /'tämbə,lō/ ▶ n. (pl. **-los**) a bar of sand or shingle joining an island to the mainland. [19th C.: from Ital., lit. 'sand dune.']

Tom·bouc·tou /,tôNbōōk'tōō; ,tämbək-/ French name for TIMBUKTU.

tom·boy /'täm,boi/ ▶ n. a girl who enjoys rough, noisy activities traditionally associated with boys. — **tom·boy·ish** adj. **tom·boy·ish·ness** n.

Tomb·stone /'tōōm,stōn/ a frontier town in southeastern Arizona, the site of the 1881 gunfight at the O.K. Corral; pop. 1,220.

tomb·stone /'tōōm,stōn/ ▶ n. a large, flat inscribed stone standing or laid over a grave.

tom·cat /'täm,kat/ ▶ n. a male domestic cat. ■ informal a sexually aggressive man; a womanizer. ▶ v. **(-cat·ted, -cat·ting)** [intrans.] informal pursue women promiscuously for sexual gratification.

tom·cod /'täm,käd/ ▶ n. (pl. same or **-cods**) a small edible greenish-brown North American fish (genus *Microgradus*) of the cod family, popular with anglers.

Tom Col·lins /täm 'kälinz/ ▶ n. a cocktail made from gin mixed with soda water, sugar, and lemon or lime juice. [sometimes said to have been named after a 19th-cent. London bartender.]

Tom, Dick, and Har·ry /'täm 'dik and 'harē/ (also **Tom, Dick, or Harry**) ▶ n. used to refer to ordinary people in general.

tome /tōm/ ▶ n. esp. humorous a book, esp. a large, heavy, scholarly one: *a weighty tome.* [16th C. (denoting one volume of a larger work): from Fr., via L. from Gk. *tomos* 'section, roll of papyrus, volume'; rel. to *temnein* 'to cut.']

-tome ▶ comb. form **1** denoting an instrument for cutting: *microtome.* **2** denoting a section or segment: *myotome.* [sense 1 from Greek *-tomon* (neut.) 'that cuts'; sense 2 from Gk. *tomē* 'a cutting,' both from *temnein* 'to cut.']

to·men·tum /tō'mentəm/ ▶ n. (pl. **-ta** /-tə/) Bot. a layer of matted woolly down on the surface of a plant. — **to·men·tose** /tō'mentōs; 'tōmən,tōs/ adj. **to·men·tous** /-təs/ adj. [17th C.: from L., lit. 'cushion stuffing.']

tom·fool /'täm'fōōl/ ▶ n. dated a foolish person.

tom·fool·er·y /,täm'fōōl(ə)rē/ ▶ n. foolish or silly behavior.

To·mis /'tōmis/ ancient name for CONSTANȚA.

Tom·my /'tämē/ (also **tom·my**) ▶ n. (pl. **-mies**) informal a British private soldier. [nickname for the given name *Thomas*; from a use of the name *Thomas Atkins* in specimens of completed official forms in the British army during the 19th C.]

tom·my gun /'tämē/ ▶ n. informal a type of submachine gun. [1920s: contr. of *Thompson gun*, named by its designer after John T. *Thompson* (1860–1940), the US army officer who conceived the idea for it.]

tom·my·rot /'tämē,rät/ ▶ n. informal, dated nonsense; rubbish: *did you ever hear such awful tommyrot?*

to·mo·gram /'tōmə,gram/ ▶ n. a record obtained by tomography.

to·mog·ra·phy /tə'mägrəfē/ ▶ n. a technique for displaying a representation of a cross section through a human body or other solid object using X-rays or ultrasound. — **to·mo·graph·ic** /,tōmə'grafik/ adj. [1930s: from Gk. *tomos* 'slice, section' + -GRAPHY.]

to·mor·row /tə'môrō; -'märō/ ▶ adv. on the day after today: *the show opens tomorrow.* ■ in the future, esp. the near future: *East Germany will not disappear tomorrow.* ▶ n. the day after today. ■ the future, esp. the near future: *today's engineers are tomorrow's buyers.*

– PHRASES **as if there was** (or **as though there were**) **no tomorrow** with no regard for the future consequences. [ME (as two words): from the prep. TO + MORROW. Cf. TODAY and TONIGHT.]

tom·pi·on /'tämpēən/ ▶ n. var. of TAMPION.

Tomsk /tämsk; tômsk/ a city in southern Siberia in Russia; pop. 506,000.

Tom Thumb n. [usu. as adj.] a dwarf variety of a cultivated flower or vegetable: *Tom Thumb lettuce.* [19th C.: from the name of the hero of a children's story, a plowman's son who was only as tall as his father's thumb.]

tom·tit /'täm,tit/ ▶ n. a popular name for any of a number of small active songbirds, esp. a tit or a chickadee.

tom-tom ▶ n. a medium-sized cylindrical drum beaten with the hands and used in jazz bands, etc. See illustration at DRUM KIT. ■ an early drum, of Native American or Asian origin, typically played with the hands. [17th C.: from Hindi *ṭam ṭam*, Telugu *ṭamaṭama*, of imitative origin.]

-tomy ▶ comb. form cutting, esp. as part of a surgical process: *episiotomy.* [from Gk. *-tomia* 'cutting,' from *temnein* 'to cut.']

ton[1] /tən/ (abbr.: **t** also **tn**) ▶ n. **1** (also **short ton**) a unit of weight equal to 2,000 pounds avoirdupois (907.19 kg). ■ (also **long ton**) a unit of weight equal to 2,240 pounds avoirdupois (1016.05 kg). ■ short for METRIC TON. ■ (also **displacement ton**) a unit of measurement of a ship's weight representing the weight of water it displaces with the load line just immersed, equal to 2,240 pounds or 35 cubic feet (0.99 cu m). ■ (also **freight ton**) a unit of weight or volume of sea cargo, equal to a metric ton 40 cubic feet (1,000 kg). ■ (also **gross ton**) a unit of gross internal capacity, equal to 100 cubic feet (2.83 cu m). ■ (also **net** or **register ton**) an equivalent unit of net internal capacity. ■ a unit of refrigerating power able to freeze 2,000 pounds of water at 0°C in 24 hours. ■ a measure of capacity for various materials, esp. 40 cubic feet of timber. **2** (usu. **a ton of/tons of**) informal a large number or amount. [ME: var. of TUN, both spellings being used for the container and the weight. The senses were differentiated in the late 17th C.]

ton[2] /tôN/ ▶ n. fashionable style or distinction. ■ **(the ton)** [treated as sing. or pl.] fashionable society. [Fr., from L. *tonus* (see TONE).]

ton·al /'tōnl/ ▶ adj. of or relating to the tone of music, color, or writing. ■ of or relating to music written using conventional keys and harmony. ■ Phonet. (of a language) expressing semantic differences by varying the intonation given to words or syllables of a similar sound. — **ton·al·ly** adv. [18th C. (designating church music in plainsong mode): from med. L. *tonalis*, from L. *tonus* (see TONE).]

to·nal·i·ty /tō'nalitē/ ▶ n. (pl. **-ties**) **1** the character of a piece of music as determined by the key in which it is played or the relations between the notes of a scale or key. ■ the harmonic effect of being in a particular key: *a tonality of C major.* ■ the use of conventional keys and harmony as the basis of musical composition. **2** the color scheme or range of tones used in a picture.

ton·do /'tändō/ ▶ n. (pl. **-di** /-dē/) a circular painting or relief. [19th C.: from Ital., lit. 'round object,' from *rotondo* 'round,' from L. *rotundus*.]

tone /tōn/ ▶ n. **1** the overall quality of a musical or vocal sound: *the piano tone is lacking in warmth.* ■ a modulation of the voice expressing a particular feeling or mood: *a firm tone of voice.* ■ a manner of expression in writing: *a general tone of glee.* **2** the general character of a group of people or a place or event. ■ informal an atmosphere of respectability or class. **3** a musical sound, esp. one of a definite pitch and character. ■ a musical note, warble, or other sound used as a particular signal on a telephone or answering machine. ■ Phonet. (in some languages, such as Chinese) a particular pitch pattern on a syllable used to make semantic distinctions. ■ Phonet. (in some languages, such as English) intonation on a word or phrase used to add functional meaning. **4** (also **whole tone**) a basic interval in classical Western music, equal to two semitones and separating, for example, the first and second notes of an ordinary scale (such as C and D, or E and F sharp); a major second or whole step. **5** the particular quality of brightness, deepness, or hue of a tint or shade of a color: *vivid tones of red and blue.* ■ the general effect of color or of light and shade in a picture. ■ a slight degree of difference in the intensity of a color. **6** (also **muscle tone**) the normal level of firmness or slight contraction in a resting muscle. ■ Physiol. the normal level of activity in a nerve fiber. ▶ v. [trans.] **1** give greater strength or firmness to (the body or a part of it): *exercise tones up the muscles.* ■ [intrans.] **(tone up)** (of a muscle or bodily part) became stronger or firmer. **2** [intrans.] **(tone with)** harmonize with (something) in terms of color. **3** Photog. give (a monochrome picture) an altered color in finishing by means of a chemical solution.

– PHRASAL VERBS **tone something down** make something less harsh in sound or color. ■ make something less extreme or intense: *she saw the need to tone down her protests.* — **toned** adj. **tone·less** adj. **tone·less·ly** adv. [ME: from OFr. *ton*, from L. *tonus*, from Gk. *tonos* 'tension, tone,' from *teinein* 'to stretch.']

tone arm (also **tone·arm** /'tōn,ärm/) ▶ n. the movable arm supporting the pickup of a record player.

tone clus·ter ▶ n. another term for NOTE CLUSTER.

tone col·or ▶ n. Music another term for TIMBRE.

tone-deaf ▶ adj. (of a person) unable to perceive differences of musical pitch accurately. — **tone-deaf·ness** n.

tone lan·guage ▶ n. Ling. a language in which variations in pitch distinguish different words.

ton·eme /'tōnēm/ ▶ n. Phonet. a phoneme distinguished from another only by its tone. — **to·ne·mic** /tō'nēmik/ adj. [1920s: from TONE, on the pattern of *phoneme*.]

tone po·em ▶n. a piece of orchestral music, typically in one movement, on a descriptive or rhapsodic theme.

ton·er /'tōnər/ ▶n. **1** an astringent liquid applied to the skin to reduce oiliness and improve its condition. ■ [with adj.] a device or exercise for making a specified part of the body firmer and stronger: *a tummy toner.* **2** a black or colored powder used in xerographic copying processes. ■ a chemical bath for changing the color or shade of a photographic print, esp. as specified.

tone row ▶n. a particular sequence of the twelve notes of the chromatic scale used as a basis for twelve-tone (serial) music.

tong[1] /tông; täng/ ▶n. a Chinese association or secret society in the US, frequently associated with underworld criminal activity. [19th C.: from Chin. (Cantonese dial.) *t'ong*, lit. 'meeting place.']

tong[2] ▶v. [trans.] collect, lift, or handle (items such as logs or oysters) using tongs.

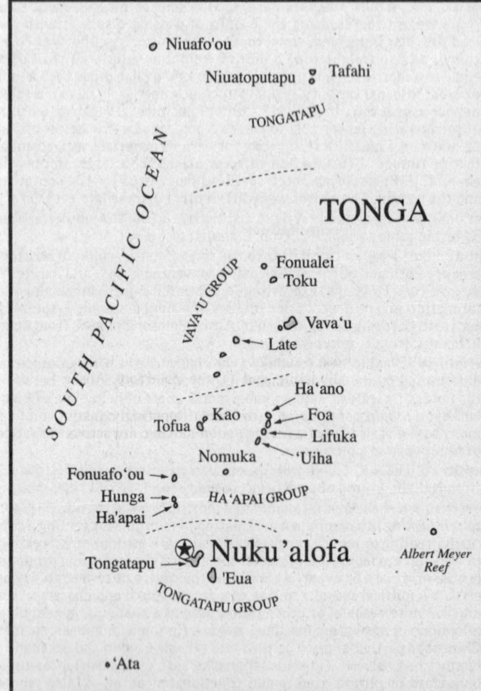

Tonga

Official name: Kingdom of Tonga

Location: South Pacific Ocean, consisting of an island group southeast of Fiji

Area: 290 square miles (750 sq km)

Population: 110,000

Capital: Nuku'alofa

Languages: Tongan, English (both official)

Currency: pa'anga

Ton·ga /'täNGgə/ a country in the South Pacific Ocean. *See box.*

ton·ga /'täNGgə/ ▶n. a light horse-drawn two-wheeled vehicle used in India. [from Hindi *tā-gā*.]

Ton·gan /'täNGgən/ ▶adj. of or relating to Tonga or its people or language. ▶n. **1** a native or national of Tonga. **2** the Polynesian language spoken in Tonga.

tongs /tôNGz; täNGz/ ▶plural n. (also **a pair of tongs**) an instrument with two movable arms that are joined at one end, used for picking up and holding things: *ice tongs.* [OE *tang(e)* (sing.), of Gmc. origin; rel. to Du. *tang* and Ger. *Zange*.]

Tong·shan /'toŏNG'sHän/ former name (1912–45) of XUZHOU.

tongue /təNG/ ▶n. **1** the fleshy muscular organ in the mouth of a mammal, used for tasting, licking, swallowing, and (in humans) articulating speech. ■ the equivalent organ in other vertebrates, sometimes used (in snakes) as a scent organ or (in chameleons) for catching food. ■ an analogous organ in insects, formed from some of the mouthparts and used in feeding. ■ the tongue of a hoofed mammal, in particular an ox or lamb, as food. ■ used in reference to a person's style or manner of speaking: *a caustic tongue.* ■ a particular language: *the prioress chatted in a strange tongue.* ■ (**tongues**) see *THE GIFT OF TONGUES* below. **2** a thing resembling or likened to a tongue, in particular: ■ a long, low promontory of land. ■ a strip of leather or fabric under the laces in a shoe, attached only at the front end. ■ the pin of a buckle. ■ a projecting strip on a wooden board fitting into a groove on another. ■ the vibrating reed of a musical instrument or organ pipe. ■ a jet of flame. ▶v. (**tongues, ton·gued, ton·guing**) [trans.] **1** Music sound (a note) distinctly on a wind instrument by interrupting the air flow with the tongue. **2** lick or caress with the tongue.
– PHRASES **find** (or **lose**) **one's tongue** be able (or unable) to express oneself after a shock. **the gift of tongues** the power of speaking in unknown languages, regarded as one of the gifts of the Holy Spirit (Acts 2). **give tongue** (of hounds) bark, esp. on finding a scent. ■ express one's feelings or opinions freely, sometimes objectionably so. **keep a civil tongue in one's head** speak politely. **speak in tongues** speak in an unknown language during religious worship. **someone's tongue is hanging out** someone is very eager for something. — **tongue·less** adj. [OE *tunge*, of Gmc. origin; rel. to Du. *tong*, Ger. *Zunge* and L. *lingua*.]

tongue and groove ▶n. wooden planking in which adjacent boards are joined by means of interlocking ridges and hollows down their sides. — **tongued-and-grooved** adj.

tongued /təNGd/ ▶adj. **1** [in comb.] having a specified kind of tongue: *the blue-tongued lizard.* ■ (in carpentry) constructed using a tongue. **2** (of a note) played by tonguing.

tongue de·pres·sor ▶n. an instrument, typically a small flat piece of wood, used by health practitioners to press down the tongue in order to allow inspection of the mouth or throat.

tongue-in-cheek ▶adj. & adv. with ironic or flippant intent: [as adj.] *tongue-in-cheek humor* | [as adv.] *"I swear there's a conspiracy!" he complained, tongue-in-cheek.*

tongue-lash·ing ▶n. [in sing.] a loud or severe scolding. — **tongue-lash** v.

tongue-tie ▶n. a malformation that restricts the movement of the tongue and causes a speech impediment.

tongue-tied ▶adj. **1** too shy or embarrassed to speak. **2** having a malformation restricting the movement of the tongue.

tongue-twist·er ▶n. a sequence of words or sounds, typically alliterative, that are difficult to pronounce quickly, as, for example, *tie twine to three tree twigs.* — **tongue-twist·ing** adj.

ton·ic /'tänik/ ▶n. **1** a medicinal substance taken to give a feeling of vigor or well-being. ■ something with an invigorating effect. **2** short for TONIC WATER. **3** Music the first note in a scale that, in conventional harmony, provides the keynote of a piece of music. ▶adj. **1** giving a feeling of vigor or well-being; invigorating. **2** Music relating to or denoting the first degree of a scale. **3** Phonet. denoting or relating to the syllable within a tone group that has greatest prominence, because it carries the main change of pitch. **4** relating to or restoring normal tone to muscles or other organs. ■ Physiol. relating to, denoting, or producing continuous muscular contraction. — **ton·i·cal·ly** adv. [17th C.: from Fr. *tonique*, from Gk. *tonikos* 'of or for stretching,' from *tonos* (see TONE).]

to·nic·i·ty /tō'nisitē/ ▶n. **1** muscle tone. **2** Ling. the pattern of tones or stress in speech. **3** Biol. the state of a solution in respect of osmotic pressure: *the tonicity of the fluid.*

ton·ic sol-fa /ˌsōl 'fä/ ▶n. a system of naming the notes of the scale (usually **do, re, mi, fa, sol, la, ti**) developed in England and used esp. to teach singing, with do as the keynote of all major keys and la as the keynote of all minor keys. See SOLMIZATION.

ton·ic wa·ter ▶n. a bitter-flavored carbonated soft drink made with quinine, used esp. as a mixer with gin or other liquors (originally used as a stimulant of appetite and digestion).

ton·i·fy /'tōnəˌfī; 'tä-/ ▶v. (**-fies, -fied**) [trans.] impart tone to (the body or a part of it). ■ (of acupuncture or herbal medicine) increase the available energy of (an organ, part, or system of the body). — **ton·i·fi·ca·tion** /ˌtōnəfi'kāsHən/ n.

to·night /tə'nīt/ ▶adv. on the present or approaching evening or night: *are you doing anything tonight?* ▶n. the evening or night of the present day. [OE *tō niht*, from the prep. TO + NIGHT. Cf. TODAY and TOMORROW.]

ton·ka bean /'täNGkə/ ▶n. the vanilla-scented black seed of a South American tree (*Dipteryx odorata*) of the pea family. The dried beans are cured in rum or other alcohol and then used in perfumery and for scenting and flavoring tobacco, ice cream, and other products. [18th C.: *tonka*, a local word in Guyana.]

Ton·kin /'täNGkin; 'tän'kin/ a mountainous region in northern Vietnam, centered on the Red River delta.

Ton·kin, Gulf of an arm of the South China Sea, bounded by southern China and northern Vietnam.

Ton·lé Sap /tôn'lā'sap/ a lake in central Cambodia, linked to the Mekong River by the Tonlé Sap River. Site of the ruins of the ancient city Angkor.

ton-mile /'tən 'mīl/ ▶n. one ton of freight carried one mile, as a unit of traffic.

ton·nage /'tənij/ ▶n. weight in tons, esp. of cargo or freight: *road convoys carry more tonnage.* ■ the size or carrying capacity of a ship measured in tons. ■ shipping considered in terms of total carrying capacity: *the port's total tonnage.* [17th C. (denoting a charge per ton on cargo): from TON[1] + -AGE.]

tonne /tən/ ▶n. another term for METRIC TON. [19th C.: from Fr.; cf. TON[1].]

ton·neau /tə'nō; 'tänō/ ▶n. (pl. **ton·neaus** or **ton·neaux** /tə'nōz; 'tänōz/) the part of an automobile, typically an open car, occupied by the back seats. ■ short for TONNEAU COVER.

ton·neau cov·er ▶ **n.** a protective cover for the seats in an open car or cabin cruiser when they are not in use.

to·nom·e·ter /tō'nämitər/ ▶ **n.** **1** a tuning fork or other instrument for measuring the pitch of musical tones. **2** an instrument for measuring the pressure in a part of the body, such as the eyeball (to test for glaucoma) or a blood vessel. [18th C.: from Gk. *tonos* (see TONE) + -METER.]

ton·sil /'tänsəl/ ▶ **n.** either of two small masses of lymphoid tissue in the throat, one on each side of the root of the tongue. — **ton·sil·lar** /-sələr/ **adj.** [16th C.: from Fr. *tonsilles* or L. *tonsillae* (pl.).]

ton·sil·lec·to·my /,tänsə'lektəmē/ ▶ **n.** (pl. **-mies**) a surgical operation to remove the tonsils.

ton·sil·li·tis /,tänsə'lītis/ ▶ **n.** inflammation of the tonsils.

ton·so·ri·al /tän'sôrēəl/ ▶ **adj.** formal or humorous of or relating to hairdressing: *she'd had her customary go at me over sartorial sloppiness and tonsorial neglect.* [19th C.: from L. *tonsorius* (from *tonsor* 'barber,' from *tondere* 'shear, clip') + -AL.]

ton·sure /'tänSHər/ ▶ **n.** a part of a monk's or priest's head left bare on top by shaving off the hair. ■ [in sing.] an act of shaving the top of a monk's or priest's head as a preparation for entering a religious order. ▶ **v.** [trans.] [often as adj.] (**tonsured**) shave the hair on the crown of. [ME: from OFr., or from L. *tonsura*, from *tondere* 'shear, clip.']

ton·tine /'täntēn; tän'tēn/ ▶ **n.** an annuity shared by subscribers to a loan or common fund, the shares increasing as subscribers die until the last survivor enjoys the whole income. [18th C.: from Fr., named after Lorenzo *Tonti* (1630–95), a Neapolitan banker who started such a program to raise government loans in France (*c.*1653).]

to·nus /'tōnəs/ ▶ **n.** the constant low-level activity of a body tissue, esp. muscle tone. [19th C.: from L., from Gk. *tonos* 'tension.']

Ton·y /'tōnē/ ▶ **n.** (pl. **Ton·ys**) any of a number of awards given annually in the US for outstanding achievement in the theater in various categories. [from the nickname of Antoinette Perry (1888–1946), US actress and director.]

ton·y /'tōnē/ ▶ **adj.** (**ton·i·er, ton·i·est**) informal fashionable among wealthy or stylish people: *a tony restaurant.* [19th C.: from the noun TONE + -Y[1].]

too /to͞o/ ▶ **adv.** **1** [as submodifier] to a higher degree than is desirable, permissible, or possible; excessively: *he was driving too fast* | *he wore suits a size too small for him.* ■ informal very: *you're too kind.* **2** in addition; also: *is he coming, too?* ■ moreover (used when adding a further point): *she is a grown woman, and a strong one too.*

– PHRASES **all too ——** used to emphasize that something is the case to an extreme or unwelcome extent: *failures are all too common.* **none too ——** far from; not very: *her sight's none too good.* [OE, stressed form of TO, spelled *too* from the 16th C.]

too·dle-oo /,to͞odl 'o͞o/ ▶ **exclam.** informal, dated goodbye. [20th C.: perh. an alt. of Fr. *à tout à l'heure* 'see you soon.']

took /to͝ok/ past of TAKE.

tool /to͞ol/ ▶ **n.** **1** a device or implement, esp. one held in the hand, used to carry out a particular function. ■ a thing used in an occupation or pursuit: *the computer is an essential tool.* ■ a person used or exploited by another. ■ Comput. a piece of software that carries out a particular function, typically creating or modifying another program. **2** a distinct design in the tooling of a book. ■ a small stamp or roller used to make such a design. **3** vulgar slang a man's penis. ■ informal derog. a dull, slow-witted, or socially inept person. ▶ **v.** **1** [trans.] (usu. **be tooled**) impress a design on (leather, esp. a leather book cover). ■ dress (stone) with a chisel. **2** equip or be equipped with tools for industrial production: [intrans.] *they were tooling up for production.* **3** [intrans.] informal drive or ride in a casual or leisurely manner. — **tool·er** **n.** [OE *tōl*, from a Gmc. base meaning 'prepare'; cf. TAW[1]. The verb dates from the early 19th C.]

tool·bar /'to͞ol,bär/ ▶ **n.** Comput. (in a program with a graphical user interface) a strip of icons used to perform certain functions.

tool·box /'to͞ol,bäks/ ▶ **n.** a box or container for keeping tools in. ■ Comput. a set of software tools. ■ Comput. the set of programs or functions accessible from a single menu.

tool·ing /'to͞oliNG/ ▶ **n.** **1** assorted tools, esp. ones required for a mechanized process. ■ the process of making or working something with tools. **2** the ornamentation of a leather book cover with designs impressed by heated tools.

tool kit ▶ **n.** a set of tools, esp. one kept in a bag or box and used for a particular purpose. ■ Comput. a set of software tools.

tool·mak·er /'to͞ol,mākər/ ▶ **n.** a maker of tools, esp. a person who makes and maintains tools for use in a manufacturing process. — **tool·mak·ing** **n.**

tool push·er (also **tool·push·er**) ▶ **n.** a person who directs the drilling on an oil rig.

tool·shed /'to͞ol,SHed/ (also **tool shed**) ▶ **n.** a one-story structure, typically in a backyard, used for storing tools.

toon /to͞on/ ▶ **n.** informal a cartoon film. ■ a character in such a film. [1930s: shortening of CARTOON.]

toot /to͞ot/ ▶ **n.** **1** a short, sharp sound made by a horn, trumpet, or similar instrument. **2** informal a snort of a drug, esp. cocaine. ■ cocaine. **3** informal a spell of drinking and lively enjoyment; a spree: *a sales manager on a toot.* ▶ **v.** [trans.] **1** sound (a horn or similar) with a short, sharp sound: *behind us an impatient driver tooted a horn.* ■ [intrans.] make such a sound: *a car tooted at us.* **2** informal snort (cocaine). — **toot·er** **n.** [16th C.: prob. from Mid. Low Ger. *tūten*, but possibly an independent imitative formation.]

tooth /to͞oTH/ ▶ **n.** (pl. **teeth**) **1** each of a set of hard, bony enamel-coated structures in the jaws of most vertebrates, used for biting and chewing. ■ a similar hard, pointed structure in invertebrate animals, typically functioning in the mechanical breakdown of food. ■ an appetite or liking for a particular thing. ■ roughness given to a surface to allow color or glue to adhere. ■ (**teeth**) fig. genuine force or effectiveness of a body or in a law or agreement. **2** a projecting part on a tool or other instrument, esp. one of a series that function or engage together, such as a cog on a gearwheel or a point on a saw or comb. ■ a projecting part on an animal or plant, esp. one of a jagged or dentate row on the margin of a leaf or shell.

– PHRASES **get** (or **sink**) **one's teeth into** work energetically and productively on (a task). — **toothed** **adj.** **tooth·like** **adj.** [OE *tōth* (pl. *tēth*), of Gmc. origin; rel. to Du. *tand* and Ger. *Zahn*, from an Indo-Eur. root shared by L. *dent-*, Gk. *odont-*.]

tooth·ache /'to͞oTH,āk/ ▶ **n.** a pain in a tooth or teeth: *he has a toothache.*

tooth·ache tree ▶ **n.** another term for NORTHERN PRICKLY-ASH (see PRICKLY-ASH).

tooth·brush /'to͞oTH,brəSH/ ▶ **n.** a small brush with a long handle, used for cleaning the teeth.

toothed whale ▶ **n.** a predatory whale (suborder Odontoceti, order Cetacea) having teeth rather than baleen plates. Toothed whales include sperm whales, killer whales, beaked whales, narwhals, dolphins, and porpoises.

tooth fair·y ▶ **n.** a fairy said to leave a gift, esp. a coin, under a child's pillow in exchange for a baby tooth that has fallen out and been put under the pillow.

tooth·less /'to͞oTHlis/ ▶ **adj.** having no teeth, typically through old age: *a toothless old man.* ■ fig. lacking genuine force or effectiveness. — **tooth·less·ly** **adv.** **tooth·less·ness** **n.**

tooth·paste /'to͞oTH,pāst/ ▶ **n.** a thick, soft, moist substance used on a toothbrush for cleaning the teeth.

tooth·pick /'to͞oTH,pik/ ▶ **n.** a short pointed piece of wood or plastic used for removing bits of food lodged between the teeth.

tooth pow·der ▶ **n.** powder used for cleaning the teeth.

tooth shell ▶ **n.** a burrowing mollusk (*Dentalium* and other genera, class Scaphopoda) with a slender tusk-shaped shell, which is open at both ends and typically white, and a three-lobed foot. Also called TUSK SHELL.

tooth·some /'to͞oTHsəm/ ▶ **adj.** (of food) temptingly tasty: *a toothsome morsel.* ■ informal (of a person) good-looking; attractive. — **tooth·some·ly** **adv.** **tooth·some·ness** **n.**

tooth·y /'to͞oTHē/ ▶ **adj.** (**tooth·i·er, tooth·i·est**) having or showing large, numerous, or prominent teeth. — **tooth·i·ly** **adv.**

toot·in' /'to͞otn/ ▶ **adj.** informal used for emphasis: *he said he was damned tootin' he was right.*

too·tle /'to͞otl/ ▶ **v.** **1** [intrans.] casually make a series of sounds on a horn, trumpet, or similar instrument. ■ [trans.] play (an instrument) or make (a sound or tune) in such a way: *the video games tootled their tunes.* **2** [intrans.] informal go or travel in a leisurely way: *tootling along the coast.* ▶ **n.** [usu. in sing.] **1** an act or sound of casual playing on an instrument such as a horn or trumpet. **2** informal a leisurely journey. [19th C.: frequentative of TOOT.]

too-too ▶ **adv. & adj.** informal, used affectedly to convey that one finds something excessively annoying or fatiguing: [as adv.] *it had become too-too tiring* | [as adj.] *it is all just too-too.* [19th C.: reduplication of TOO.]

toot·sie /'to͞otsē/ (also **toot·sy**) ▶ **n.** (pl. **-sies**) informal **1** a person's foot. **2** a young woman, esp. one perceived as being sexually available. [19th C.: humorous dimin. of FOOT.]

toot sweet ▶ **adv.** informal immediately. [20th C.: Anglicized form of Fr. *tout de suite*.]

top[1] /täp/ ▶ **n.** **1** [usu. in sing.] the highest or uppermost point, part, or surface of something. ■ (usu. **tops**) the leaves, stems, and shoots of a plant, esp. those of a vegetable grown for its root. ■ esp. Brit. the end of something that is furthest from the speaker or a point of reference: *the top of the road.* **2** a thing or part placed on, fitted to, or covering the upper part of something, in particular: ■ a garment covering the upper part of the body and worn with a skirt, pants, or shorts. ■ a lid, cover, or cap for something. ■ a platform at the head of a ship's mast, esp. (in a sailing ship) a platform around the head of each of the lower masts, serving to extend the topmast shrouds. **3** (**the top**) the highest or most important rank, level, or position: *her talent will take her right to the top.* ■ a person or thing occupying such a position: *North Korea was top of the agenda.* ■ (**tops**) informal a person or thing regarded as particularly good or pleasant. ■ the utmost degree or the highest level: *she shouted at the top of her voice.* ■ the high-frequency component of reproduced sound. **4** Baseball the first half of an inning: *the top of the eighth.* **5** short for TOPSPIN. **6** (usu. **tops**) a bundle of long wool fibers prepared for spinning. **7** Physics one of six flavors of quark. **8** informal a male who takes the active role in homosexual intercourse, esp. anal intercourse. ▶ **adj.** [attrib.] highest in position, rank, or degree. ▶ **v.** (**topped, top·ping**) [trans.] **1** exceed (an amount, level, or number); be more than: *losses are expected to top $100 million this year.* ■ be at the highest place or rank in (a list, poll, chart, or league). ■ be taller than: *he topped her by several inches.* ■ surpass (a person or previous

PRONUNCIATION KEY ə *ago, up*; ər *over, fur*; a *hat*; ā *ate*; ä *car*; e *let*; ē *see*; i *fit*; ī *by*; NG *sing*; ō *go*; ô *law, for*; oi *toy*; o͝o *good*; o͞o *goo*; ou *out*; TH *thin*; TH *then*; ZH *vision*

achievement or action); outdo. ■ appear as the chief performer or attraction at: *Hopper topped a great night of boxing.* ■ reach the top of (a hill or other stretch of rising ground). **2** (usu. **be topped**) provide with a top or topping. ■ complete (an outfit) with an upper garment, hat, or item of jewelry. ■ remove the top of (a vegetable or fruit) in preparation for cooking. **3** Golf mishit (the ball or a stroke) by hitting above the center of the ball. ▶ **adv.** (**tops**) informal at the most: *he makes $28,000, tops.*

– PHRASES **at the top of one's lungs** as loudly as possible. **from top to bottom** completely; thoroughly. **from the top** informal from the beginning. **on top of the world** informal happy and elated. **over the top 1** informal to an excessive or exaggerated degree, in particular so as to go beyond reasonable or acceptable limits. **2** esp. hist. over the parapet of a trench and into battle. **top dollar** informal a very high price: *I pay top dollar for my materials.* **to top it all** as a culminating, typically unpleasant, event or action in a series: *her father had a fatal heart attack, and to top it all her mother disowned her.*

– PHRASAL VERBS **top something off 1** (often **be topped off**) finish something in a memorable or notable way. **2** informal fill up a nearly full tank with fuel. **top out** reach an upper limit. — **top·most adj. topped adj.** [late OE *topp* (n.), of Gmc. origin; rel. to Du. *top* 'summit, crest.']

top[2] ▶ **n.** (also **spinning top**) a conical, spherical, or pear-shaped toy that with a quick or vigorous twist may be set to spin. [late OE, of unknown origin.]

to·paz /'tōpaz/ ▶ **n. 1** a precious stone, typically colorless, yellow, or pale blue, consisting of a fluorine-containing aluminum silicate. ■ a dark yellow color. **2** a large tropical American hummingbird (genus *Topaza*) with a yellowish throat and a long tail. [ME (denoting a yellow sapphire): from OFr. *topace*, via L. from Gk. *topazos*.]

to·paz·o·lite /tō'pazə,līt/ ▶ **n.** a yellowish-green variety of andradite (garnet). [19th C.: from TOPAZ + -LITE.]

top boot ▶ **n.** esp. hist. a high boot with a broad band of a different material or color at the top.

top brass ▶ **n.** see BRASS.

top·coat /'täp,kōt/ ▶ **n. 1** an overcoat. **2** an outer coat of paint.

top dog ▶ **n.** informal a person who is successful or dominant in their field: *he was a top dog in the City.*

top-down ▶ **adj. 1** denoting a system of government or management in which actions and policies are initiated at the highest level; hierarchical. **2** proceeding from the general to the particular. ■ Comput. working from the top or root of a treelike system toward the branches.

top draw·er ▶ **n.** the uppermost drawer in a chest or desk. ■ (**the top drawer**) informal high social position or class. ▶ **adj.** (**top-draw·er**) informal of the highest quality or social class: *a top-drawer performance.*

top-dress·ing (also **top dres·sing**) ▶ **n.** an application of manure or fertilizer to the surface layer of soil or a lawn. — **top-dress v.**

tope[1] /tōp/ ▶ **v.** [intrans.] archaic literary drink alcohol to excess, esp. on a regular basis. — **top·er n.** [17th C.: perhaps an alt. of obs. *top* 'overbalance'; perh. from Du. *toppen* 'slant or tilt a ship's yard.']

tope[2] ▶ **n.** another term for STUPA. [from Punjabi *thūp*, *thop* 'barrow, mound,' appar. rel. to Sanskrit *stūpa*.]

tope[3] ▶ **n.** a small grayish slender-bodied shark (genus *Galeorhinus*, family Carcharhinidae), occurring chiefly in inshore waters. Species include the eastern Atlantic *G. galeus*, and the commercially important *G. australis* of Australia. [17th C.: perh. of Cornish origin.]

To·pe·ka /tə'pēkə/ the capital of Kansas, in the east central part of the state; pop. 122,377.

top fer·men·ta·tion ▶ **n.** the process by which ale-type beers are fermented, proceeding for a relatively short period at high temperature with the yeast rising to the top.

top flight ▶ **n.** (**the top flight**) the highest rank or level. ▶ **adj.** [attrib.] of the highest rank or level.

Top 40 ▶ **plural n.** the forty most popular songs of a given time period. ▶ **adj.** made up of, or broadcasting the Top 40.

top·gal·lant /täp'galənt; tə'gal-/ ▶ **n.** (also **topgallant mast**) the section of a square-rigged sailing ship's mast immediately above the topmast. ■ (also **topgallant sail**) a sail set on such a mast.

top-ham·per ▶ **n.** Sailing sails, rigging, or other things above decks creating top-heavy weight or wind-resistant surfaces.

top hat ▶ **n.** a man's formal hat with a high cylindrical crown.

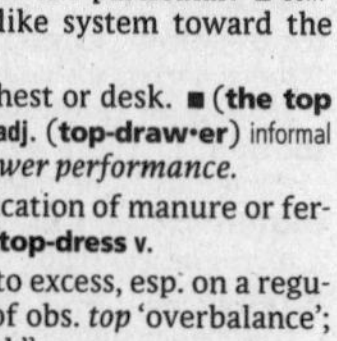

top hat

top-heav·y ▶ **adj.** disproportionately heavy at the top so as to be in danger of toppling. ■ (of an organization) having a disproportionately large number of people in senior administrative positions. ■ informal (of a woman) having a disproportionately large bust. — **top-heav·i·ly adv. top-heav·i·ness n.**

To·phet /'tōfet/ ▶ **n.** a term for hell. [ME: from Heb. *tōpeṯ*, the name of a place in the Valley of Hinnom near Jerusalem used for idolatrous worship, including the sacrifice of children (see Jeremiah 19:6), and later for burning refuse.]

top-hole ▶ **adj.** Brit., informal dated excellent; first-rate.

to·phus /'tōfəs/ ▶ **n.** (pl. **-phi** /-fī/) Med. a deposit of crystalline uric acid and other substances at the surface of joints or in skin or cartilage, typically as a feature of gout. [17th C.: from L., denoting loose porous stones of various kinds.]

to·pi·ar·y /'tōpē,erē/ ▶ **n.** (pl. **-ar·ies**) the art or practice of clipping shrubs or trees into ornamental shapes. ■ shrubs or trees clipped into ornamental shapes in such a way. — **to·pi·ar·i·an** /,tōpē'e(ə)rēən/ **adj. to·pi·a·rist** /-ərist/ **n.** [16th C.: from Fr. *topiaire*, from L. *topiarius* 'ornamental gardener,' from *topia opera* 'fancy gardening,' from a dimin. of Gk. *topos* 'place.']

topiary

top·ic /'täpik/ ▶ **n.** a matter dealt with in a text, discourse, or conversation; a subject. ■ Ling. that part of a sentence about which something is said, typically the first major constituent. [15th C. (orig. denoting a set or book of general rules or ideas): from L. *topica*, from Gk. *ta topika*, lit. 'matters concerning commonplaces' (the title of a treatise by Aristotle), from *topos* 'a place.']

top·i·cal /'täpikəl/ ▶ **adj. 1** (of a subject) of immediate relevance, interest, or importance owing to its relation to current events. ■ relating to a particular subject; classified according to subject. ■ Philately relating to the collecting of postage stamps with designs connected with the same subject. **2** esp. Med. relating or applied directly to a part of the body. ▶ **n.** Philately a postage stamp forming part of a set or collection with designs connected with the same subject. — **top·i·cal·i·ty** /,täpi'kalitē/ **n. top·i·cal·ly adv.** [16th C.: from Gk. *topikos* + -AL. Early use was as a term in logic and rhetoric describing a rule or argument as 'applicable in most but not all cases.']

top·i·cal·ize /'täpikə,līz/ ▶ **v.** [trans.] Ling. cause (a subject, word, or phrase) to be the topic of a sentence or discourse, typically by placing it first. — **top·i·cal·i·za·tion** /,täpəkəli'zāsʜən/ **n.**

top·ic sen·tence ▶ **n.** a sentence that expresses the main idea of the paragraph in which it occurs.

top·knot /'täp,nät/ ▶ **n.** a knot of hair arranged on the top of the head. ■ a decorative knot or bow of ribbon worn on the top of the head, popular in the 18th century. ■ (in an animal or bird) a tuft or crest of hair or feathers.

top·less /'täplis/ ▶ **adj.** (of a woman or a woman's item of clothing) having or leaving the breasts uncovered. ■ (of a place such as a bar or beach) where there are women wearing such clothes. — **top·less·ness n.**

top-lev·el ▶ **adj.** of the highest level of importance or prestige: *top-level talks.*

top·loft·y /'täp,lôftē; -,läftē/ ▶ **adj.** informal haughty and arrogant.

top·mast /'täp,mast; -məst/ ▶ **n.** the second section of a square-rigged sailing ship's mast, immediately above the lower mast.

top·min·now /'täp,minō/ ▶ **n.** a small surface-swimming fish (genus *Fundulus*, family Fundulidae) related to the killifishes, found in fresh, brackish, and salt water throughout North America.

top-notch ▶ **adj.** informal of the highest quality; excellent. — **top-notch·er n.**

top·o /'täpō/ ▶ **n.** (pl. **top·os**) informal a topographic map. ■ Climbing a diagram of a mountain with details of routes to the top marked on it. ▶ **adj.** short for TOPOGRAPHICAL. [1970s: abbr. of *topographic* (see TOPOGRAPHICAL).]

topog. ▶ **abbr.** ■ topographical. ■ topography.

top·o·graph·i·cal /,täpə'grafikəl/ ▶ **adj.** of or relating to the arrangement or accurate representation of the physical features of an area. ■ (of a work of art or an artist) dealing with or depicting places (esp. towns), buildings, and natural prospects in a realistic and detailed manner. ■ Anat. & Biol. relating to or representing the physical distribution of parts or features on the surface of or within an organ or organism. — **top·o·graph·ic adj. top·o·graph·i·cal·ly adv.**

to·pog·ra·phy /tə'pägrəfē/ ▶ **n.** the arrangement of the natural and artificial physical features of an area. ■ a detailed description or representation on a map of such features. ■ Anat. & Biol. the distribution of parts or features on the surface of or within an organ or organism. — **to·pog·ra·pher n.** [ME: via late L. from Gk. *topographia*, from *topos* 'place' + *-graphia* (see -GRAPHY).]

to·poi /'tōpoi/ plural form of TOPOS.

to·pol·o·gy /tə'päləjē/ ▶ **n. 1** Math. the study of geometric properties and spatial relations unaffected by the continuous change of shape or size of figures. ■ a family of open subsets of an abstract space such that the union and the intersection of any two of them are members of the family, and that includes the space itself and the empty set. **2** the way in which constituent parts are interrelated or arranged: *the topology of a computer network.* — **top·o·log·i·cal** /,täpə'läjikəl/ **adj. top·o·log·i·cal·ly** /,täpə'läjik(ə)lē/ **adv. to·pol·o·gist n.** [19th C.: via Ger. from Gk. *topos* 'place' + -LOGY.]

top·o·nym /'täpə,nim/ ▶ **n.** a place name, esp. one derived from a topographical feature. [1930s: from Gk. *topos* 'place' + *onuma* 'a name.']

to·pon·y·my /tə'pänəmē/ ▶ **n.** the study of place names. — **top·o·nym·ic** /,täpə'nimik/ **adj.** [19th C.: from Gk. *topos* 'place' + *onuma* 'name.']

to·pos /'tōpōs/ ▶ **n.** (pl. **-poi** /-poi/) a traditional theme or formula in literature. [1940s: from Gk., lit. 'place.']

top·per /'täpər/ ▶ **n. 1** something that goes on top of something else: *decorative cake toppers.* **2** something that culminates a situation; a clincher. **3** a hard protective lightweight cover or shell mounted on the back or bed of a pickup truck. ■ a type of camper mounted on a truck bed. **4** informal a top hat. **5** Brit. informal dated an exceptionally good person or thing. **6** a woman's loose, short coat.

top·ping /'täpiɴɢ/ ▶ **n.** a layer of food poured or spread over a base of a different type of food to add flavor. ▶ **adj.** Brit., informal, dated excellent.

top·ple /'täpəl/ ▶ **v.** [intrans.] overbalance or become unsteady and fall slowly. ■ [trans.] cause to fall in such a way: fig. *disagreement had threatened to topple the government.* [16th C. (in the sense 'roll around'): frequentative of TOP[1].]

top quark (abbr.: **t**) ▶ **n.** a hypothetical quark with a mass of 360,000 times that of an electron and a charge of +23.

top rope Climbing ▶ **n.** a rope lowered from above to the lead climber in a group, typically to give assistance at a difficult part of a climb. ▶ **v.** (**top-rope**) [trans.] climb (a route or part of one) using a top rope.

top round ▶ **n.** a cut of meat taken from an inner section of a round of beef.

top·sail /'täpsəl; -ˌsāl/ ▶ **n.** a sail set on a ship's topmast. ■ a fore-and-aft sail set above the gaff.

top se·cret ▶ **adj.** of the highest secrecy; highly confidential: *a top-secret mission.* ■ (of information or documents) given the highest security classification, above secret.

top-shelf ▶ **adj. 1** of a high quality; excellent: *top-shelf vocal talent.* **2** Brit. (of a magazine or other publication) pornographic.

top·side /'täpˌsīd/ ▶ **n.** (often **topsides**) the upper part of a ship's side, above the waterline. ▶ **adv.** on or toward the upper decks of a ship.

Top-Sid·er ▶ **n.** trademark a casual shoe, typically made of leather or canvas with a rubber sole, designed to be worn on boats.

top·soil /'täpˌsoil/ ▶ **n.** the top layer of soil.

top·spin /'täpˌspin/ ▶ **n.** a fast forward spinning motion imparted to a ball when throwing or hitting it, often resulting in a curved path or a strong forward motion on rebounding. — **top·spin·ner n.**

top·stitch /'täpˌsticн/ ▶ **v.** [intrans.] make a row of continuous stitches on the top or right side of a garment or other article as a decorative feature.

top·sy-tur·vy /'täpsē 'tərvē/ ▶ **adj. & adv.** upside down. ■ in a state of confusion. — **top·sy-tur·vi·ly adv. top·sy-tur·vi·ness n.** [16th C.: a jingle appar. based on TOP[1] and obs. *terve* 'overturn.']

top·wa·ter /'täpˌwôtər; -ˌwätər/ ▶ **adj.** Fishing (of a bait) floating on or near the top of the water.

toque /tōk/ ▶ **n.** a woman's small hat, typically having a narrow, closely turned-up brim. ■ hist. a small cap or bonnet of such a type worn by a man or woman. ■ a tall white hat with a full pouched crown, worn by chefs. [16th C.: from Fr., of unknown origin.]

to·qui·lla /tō'kē(y)ə/ ▶ **n.** a palmlike tree, *Carludovica palmata*, native to South America. ■ the fiber obtained from this plant, used esp. to make hats. [19th C.: from an Amer. Sp. use of Sp. *toquilla* 'small gauze headdress,' dimin. of *toca* 'toque.']

tor /tôr/ ▶ **n.** a hill or rocky peak. [OE *torr*, perh. of Celtic origin and rel. to Welsh *tor* 'belly' and Scot. Gael. *tòrr* 'bulging hill.']

To·rah /'tōrə; 'tôr-; tō'rä/ ▶ **n.** (usu. **the Torah**) (in Judaism) the law of God as revealed to Moses and recorded in the first five books of the Hebrew scriptures (the Pentateuch). ■ a scroll containing this. [from Heb. *tōrāh* 'instruction, doctrine, law,' from *yārāh* 'show, direct, instruct.']

torc /tôrk/ (also **torque**) ▶ **n.** hist. a neck ornament consisting of a band of twisted metal, worn esp. by the ancient Gauls and Britons. [19th C.: from Fr. *torque*, from L. *torques* (see TORCH).]

torch /tôrcн/ ▶ **n.** esp. hist. a portable means of illumination such as a piece of wood or cloth soaked in tallow or an oil lamp on a pole, sometimes carried ceremonially. ■ (usu. **the torch**) fig. used to refer to a valuable quality, principle, or cause that needs to be protected and maintained: *the torch of independence.* ■ a blowtorch. ■ informal an arsonist. ■ British term for FLASHLIGHT. ▶ **v.** [trans.] informal set fire to.
– PHRASES **carry a torch for** suffer from unrequited love for. [ME: from OFr. *torche*, from L. *torqua*, var. of *torques* 'necklace, wreath,' from *torquere* 'to twist.' The current verb sense was orig. US slang and dates from the 1930s.]

torch·bear·er /'tôrcнˌbe(ə)rər/ ▶ **n.** a person who carries a ceremonial torch. ■ fig. a person who leads or inspires others in working toward a valued goal.

tor·chère /tôr'sнe(ə)r/ ▶ **n.** a tall ornamental flat-topped stand, traditionally used as a stand for a candlestick. [20th C.: Fr., from *torche* (see TORCH).]

torch·light /'tôrcнˌlīt/ ▶ **n.** the light of a torch or torches. — **torch·lit** /-lit/ **adj.**

tor·chon lace /'tôrsнän; tôr'sнôn/ ▶ **n.** coarse bobbin lace with geometric designs. [19th C.: from Fr., lit. 'duster, dishcloth,' from *torcher* 'to wipe.']

torch song ▶ **n.** a sad or sentimental song of unrequited love. — **torch sing·er n.** [1920s: *torch* from the phr. 'carry a torch for' (see TORCH).]

tore[1] /tôr/ past of TEAR[1].

tore[2] ▶ **n.** archaic term for TORUS. [17th C.: from Fr.]

tor·e·a·dor /'tôrēəˌdôr/ ▶ **n.** a bullfighter. [Sp., from *torear* 'fight bulls,' from *toro* 'bull.']

tor·e·a·dor pants ▶ **plural n.** women's tight-fitting calf-length trousers.

to·re·ro /tə're(ə)rō/ ▶ **n.** (pl. **-ros**) a bullfighter. [Sp., from *toro* 'bull' (see TOREADOR).]

to·reu·tics /tə'rōōtiks/ ▶ **plural n.** [treated as sing.] the art of making designs in relief or intaglio, esp. by chasing, carving, and embossing in metal. — **to·reu·tic adj.** [19th C.: from Gk. *toreutikos*, from *toreuein* 'to work in relief.']

to·ri /'tôrī/ plural form of TORUS.

tor·ic /'tôrik/ ▶ **adj.** Geom. having the form of a torus or part of a torus. ■ (of a contact lens) having two different curves instead of one, used to correct both astigmatism and near- or farsightedness.

to·ri·i /'tôrēˌē/ ▶ **n.** (pl. same) the gateway of a Shinto shrine, with two uprights and two crosspieces. [Japanese, from *tori* 'bird' + *i* 'sit, perch.']

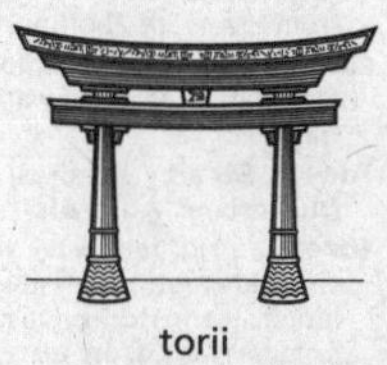

torii

To·ri·no /tə'rēnō/ Italian name for TURIN.

tor·ment ▶ **n.** /'tôrment/ severe physical or mental suffering: *their deaths have left both families in torment.* ■ a cause of such suffering. ▶ **v.** /tôr'ment/ [trans.] cause to experience severe mental or physical suffering: *he was tormented by jealousy.* ■ annoy or provoke in a deliberately unkind way. — **tor·ment·ed·ly adv. tor·ment·ing·ly adv. tor·men·tor n.** [ME (as both noun and verb referring to the infliction or suffering of torture): from OFr. *torment* (n.), *tormenter* (v.), from L. *tormentum* 'instrument of torture,' from *torquere* 'to twist.']

tor·men·til /'tôrmənˌtil/ ▶ **n.** a low-growing Eurasian plant (*Potentilla erecta*) of the rose family, with bright yellow flowers. The root is used in herbal medicine to treat diarrhea. [ME: from Fr. *tormentille*, from med. L. *tormentilla*, of unknown origin.]

torn /tôrn/ past participle of TEAR[1].

tor·na·do /tôr'nādō/ ▶ **n.** (pl. **-does** or **-dos**) a mobile, destructive vortex of violently rotating winds having the appearance of a funnel-shaped cloud and advancing beneath a large storm system. ■ fig. a person or thing characterized by violent or devastating action or emotion. — **tor·nad·ic** /-'nādik; -'nadik/ **adj.** [16th C. (denoting a violent thunderstorm of the tropical Atlantic Ocean): perh. an alt. of Spanish *tronada* 'thunderstorm' (from *tronar* 'to thunder') by association with Sp. *tornar* 'to turn.']

to·roid /'tôroid/ ▶ **n.** Geom. a figure with a shape resembling a torus. ■ Electron. a coil shaped like a torus or doughnut. — **to·roi·dal** /tô'roidl/ **adj. to·roi·dal·ly adv.**

To·ron·to /tə'räntō/ a city in Canada, capital of Ontario, on the northern shore of Lake Ontario; pop. 653,734.

tor·pe·do /tôr'pēdō/ ▶ **n.** (pl. **-does**) **1** a cigar-shaped self-propelled underwater missile designed to be fired from a ship or submarine or dropped into the water from an aircraft and to explode on reaching a target. ■ a signal placed on a railroad track, exploding as the train passes over it. ■ a firework exploding on impact with a hard surface. ■ informal a submarine sandwich. ■ informal a gangster hired to commit a murder or other violent act. ■ an explosive device lowered into oil wells to clear obstructions. **2** (also **tor·pe·do ray**) an electric ray. ▶ **v.** (**-does, -doed**) [trans.] attack or sink (a ship) with a torpedo or torpedoes. ■ fig. destroy or ruin (a plan or project). — **tor·pe·do·like adj.** [16th cent. (sense 2): from L., lit. 'stiffness, numbness,' by extension 'electric ray' (which gives a shock causing numbness), from *torpere* 'be numb or sluggish.' Sense 1 dates from the late 18th C. and first described a timed explosive device for detonation under water.]

tor·pe·do boat ▶ **n.** a small, fast, light warship armed with torpedoes.

tor·pe·do net ▶ **n.** hist. a net made of steel wire, hung in the water around an anchored ship to intercept torpedoes.

tor·pe·do tube ▶ **n.** a tube in a submarine or other ship from which torpedoes are fired by the use of compressed air or an explosive charge.

tor·pe·fy /'tôrpəˌfī/ ▶ **v.** (**-fies, -fied**) [trans.] formal make (someone or something) numb, paralyzed, or lifeless. [19th C.: from L. *torpefacere*, from *torpere* 'be numb or sluggish.']

tor·pid /'tôrpid/ ▶ **adj.** mentally or physically inactive; lethargic: *we sat around in a torpid state.* ■ (of an animal) dormant, esp. during hibernation. — **tor·pid·i·ty** /tôr'piditē/ **n. tor·pid·ly adv.** [ME: from L. *torpidus*, from *torpere* 'be numb or sluggish.']

tor·por /'tôrpər/ ▶ **n.** a state of physical or mental inactivity; lethargy. [ME: from L., from *torpere* 'be numb or sluggish.']

torque /tôrk/ ▶ **n. 1** Mech. a twisting force that tends to cause rotation. **2** var. of TORC. ▶ **v.** [trans.] apply torque or a twisting force to (an object). — **tor·quey adj.** [19th C.: from L. *torquere* 'to twist.']

torque con·vert·er ▶ **n.** a device that transmits or multiplies torque generated by an engine.

Tor·que·ma·da /ˌtôrkə'mädə; ˌtôrkä'mäтнä/, Tomás de (*c.*1420–98), Spanish cleric and Grand Inquisitor. A Dominican monk, he was the prime mover behind the Inquisition in 1478.

torque wrench ▶ **n.** a tool for setting and adjusting the tightness of nuts and bolts to a desired value.

torr /tôr/ ▶ **n.** (pl. same) a unit of pressure used in measuring partial vacuums, equal to 133.32 pascals. [1940s: named after the Italian physicist E. *Torricelli* (1608–47).]

Tor·rance /'tôrəns; 'tär-/ a city in southwestern California, south of Los Angeles; pop. 133,107.

Tor·rens sys·tem /'tôrənz; 'tär-/ ▶ **n.** Law a system of land title registration, adopted originally in Australia and later in some states of the US. [19th C.: named after Sir Robert *Torrens* (1814-84), first premier of South Australia.]

tor·rent /'tôrənt; 'tär-/ ▶ n. a strong and fast-moving stream of water or other liquid. ■ (**a torrent of** or **torrents of**) a sudden, violent, and copious outpouring of (something, typically words or feelings): *she was subjected to a torrent of abuse.* [16th C.: from Fr., from Ital. *torrente,* from L. *torrent-* 'boiling, roaring,' from *torrere* 'parch, scorch.']

tor·ren·tial /tô'renCHəl; tə-/ ▶ adj. (of rain) falling rapidly and in copious quantities. ■ (of water) flowing rapidly and with force. — **tor·ren·tial·ly** adv.

Tor·res Strait /'tôrez; -əs/ a channel that separates the northern tip of Queensland, Australia, from the island of New Guinea.

tor·rid /'tôrid; 'tär-/ ▶ adj. very hot and dry. ■ full of passionate or highly charged emotions arising from sexual love. ■ full of difficulty or tribulation. — **tor·rid·i·ty** /tə'riditē/ n. **tor·rid·ly** adv. [16th C.: from Fr. *torride* or L. *torridus,* from *torrere* 'parch, scorch.']

tor·rid zone (also **Tor·rid Zone**) ▶ n. the hot central belt of the earth bounded by the tropics of Cancer and Capricorn.

tor·sade /tôr'säd; -'säd/ ▶ n. a decorative twisted braid, ribbon, or other strand used as trimming. ■ an artificial plait of hair. [19th C.: from Fr., from L. *tors-* 'twisted,' from *torquere* 'to twist.']

tor·sade de poin·tes /də 'pwänt/ ▶ n. Med. a form of tachycardia in which the electrical pulse in the heart undergoes a cyclical variation in strength, giving a characteristic electrocardiogram resembling a twisted fringe of spikes. [1960s: Fr., lit. 'twist of spikes.']

torse /tôrs/ ▶ n. Heraldry a wreath. [16th C.: from obs. Fr., from L. *torta,* fem. past part. of *torquere* 'twist.']

tor·sion /'tôrSHən/ ▶ n. the action of twisting or the state of being twisted, esp. of one end of an object relative to the other. ■ Math. the extent to which a curve departs from being planar. ■ Zool. (in a gastropod mollusk) the spontaneous twisting of the visceral hump through 180° during larval development. — **tor·sion·al** /-SHənl/ adj. **tor·sion·al·ly** /-SHənl-ē/ adv. **tor·sion·less** adj. [ME: via OFr. from late L. *torsio(n-),* var. of *tortio(n-)* 'twisting, torture,' from L. *torquere* 'to twist.']

tor·sion bal·ance ▶ n. an instrument for measuring very weak forces by their effect on a system of fine twisted wire.

tor·sion bar ▶ n. a bar forming part of a vehicle suspension, twisting in response to the motion of the wheels and absorbing their vertical movement.

tor·sion pen·du·lum ▶ n. a pendulum that rotates rather than swings.

tor·so /'tôrsō/ ▶ n. (pl. **-sos** or **-si** /-sē/) the trunk of the human body. ■ the trunk of a statue without, or considered independently of, the head and limbs. ■ fig. an unfinished or mutilated thing, esp. a work of art or literature: *the Requiem torso was preceded by the cantata.* [18th C.: from Ital., lit. 'stalk, stump,' from L. *thyrsus* (see THYRSUS).]

tort /tôrt/ ▶ n. Law a wrongful act or an infringement of a right (other than under contract) leading to legal liability. [ME (in the general sense 'wrong, injury'): from OFr., from med. L. *tortum* 'wrong, injustice,' neut. past part. of L. *torquere* 'to twist.']

torte /tôrt; 'tôrtə/ ▶ n. (pl. **tortes** or German **tor·ten** /'tôrtn/) a sweet cake or tart. [from Ger. *Torte,* via Ital. from late L. *torta* 'round loaf, cake.' Cf. TORTILLA.]

tor·tel·li /tôr'telē/ ▶ n. small pasta parcels stuffed with a cheese, meat, or vegetable mixture. [Ital., pl. of *tortello* 'small cake, fritter.']

tor·tel·li·ni /,tôrtl'ēnē/ ▶ n. tortelli that has been rolled and formed into small rings. See illustration at PASTA. [Ital., pl. of *tortellino,* dimin. of *tortello* 'small cake, fritter.']

tort·fea·sor /'tôrt,fēzər; -zôr/ ▶ n. Law a person who commits a tort. [17th C.: from OFr. *tort-fesor,* from *tort* 'wrong' and *fesor* 'doer.']

tor·ti·col·lis /,tôrti'kälis/ ▶ n. Med. a condition in which the head becomes persistently turned to one side, often associated with painful muscle spasms. Also called WRYNECK. [19th C.: mod. L., from L. *tortus* 'crooked, twisted' + *collum* 'neck.']

tor·til·la /tôr'tē(y)ə/ ▶ n. (in Mexican cooking) a thin, flat cornmeal pancake, eaten hot or cold, typically with a savory filling. ■ (in Spanish cooking) a thick omelet containing potato and other vegetables, typically served cut into wedges. [Sp., dimin. of *torta* 'cake.']

tor·tious /'tôrSHəs/ ▶ adj. Law constituting a tort; wrongful. — **tor·tious·ly** adv. [ME: from Anglo-Norman Fr. *torcious,* from the stem of *torcion* 'extortion, violence,' from late L. *tortio(n-)* (see TORSION). The original sense was 'injurious.']

tor·toise /'tôrtəs/ ▶ n. **1** a turtle, typically a herbivorous one that lives on land. ■ informal anything exceptionally slow-moving. **2** another term for TESTUDO. — **tor·toise·like** adj. & adv. [ME *tortu, tortuce*: from OFr. *tortue* and Sp. *tortuga,* both from med. L. *tortuca,* of uncert. origin. The current spelling dates from the mid 16th C.]

tor·toise bee·tle ▶ n. a small flattened leaf beetle (*Cassida* and other genera, family Chrysomelidae) with an enlarged thorax, having wing cases that cover the entire insect and provide camouflage and protection. The larva carries a construction of feces and molted skins for camouflage.

tor·toise·shell /'tôrtəs,SHel/ ▶ n. **1** the semitransparent mottled yellow and brown shell of certain turtles, typically used to make jewelry or ornaments. ■ a synthetic substance made in imitation of this. **2** (in full **tortoiseshell cat**) a domestic cat with markings resembling a tortoiseshell.

Tor·to·la /tôr'tōlə/ the principal island of the British Virgin Islands in the Caribbean Sea.

tor·trix /'tôrtriks/ (also **tor·trix moth**) ▶ n. (pl. **-tri·ces** /-trisēz/) a small moth (family Tortricidae) with typically green caterpillars that live inside rolled leaves and can be a serious pest of fruit and other trees. — **tor·tri·cid** /-trisid/ n. & adj. [18th C.: mod. L., fem. of L. *tortor* 'twister,' from *torquere* 'to twist.']

tor·tu·ous /'tôrCHōōəs/ ▶ adj. full of twists and turns. ■ excessively lengthy and complex: *a tortuous argument.* — **tor·tu·os·i·ty** /,tôrCHōō'äsitē/ n. (pl. **-ties**) **tor·tu·ous·ly** adv. **tor·tu·ous·ness** n. [ME: via OFr. from L. *tortuosus,* from *tortus* 'twisting, a twist,' from L. *torquere* 'to twist.']

tor·ture /'tôrCHər/ ▶ n. the action or practice of inflicting severe pain on someone as a punishment or in order to force them to do or say something. ■ great physical or mental suffering or anxiety. ■ a cause of such suffering or anxiety. ▶ v. [trans.] inflict severe pain on. ■ cause great mental suffering or anxiety to. — **tor·tur·er** n. [ME (in the sense 'distortion, twisting,' or a physical disorder characterized by this): via Fr. from late L. *tortura* 'twisting, torment,' from L. *torquere* 'to twist.']

tor·tur·ous /'tôrCHərəs/ ▶ adj. characterized by, involving, or causing excruciating pain or suffering. — **tor·tur·ous·ly** adv. [15th C.: from Anglo-Norman Fr., from *torture* 'torture.']

tor·u·la /'tôr(y)ələ/ ▶ n. (pl. **-lae** /-lē; -lī/) **1** (also **tor·u·la yeast**) a yeast (*Candida utilis*) cultured for use in medicine and as a food additive, esp. as a source of vitamins and protein. **2** a yeastlike fungus (genus *Torula,* subdivision Deuteromycotina) composed of chains of rounded cells, several kinds growing on dead vegetation and some causing infections, in particular *T. herbarum,* which grows on dead grasses. [mod. L. (genus name), dimin. of L. *torus* 'swelling, bolster.']

To·ruń /'tôrōōn(yə)/ a city in northern Poland, on the Vistula River; pop. 201,000. German name THORN.

to·rus /'tôrəs/ ▶ n. (pl. **to·ri** /'tôrī/ or **to·rus·es**) **1** Geom. a surface or solid formed by rotating a closed curve, esp. a circle, around a line that lies in the same plane but does not intersect it (e.g., like a ring-shaped doughnut). ■ a thing of this shape, esp. a large ring-shaped chamber used in physical research. **2** Archit. a large convex molding, typically semicircular in cross section, esp. as the lowest part of the base of a column. **3** Anat. a ridge of bone or muscle: *the maxillary torus.* **4** Bot. the receptacle of a flower. [16th C. (sense 2): from L., lit. 'swelling, bolster, round molding.' The other senses date from the 19th C.]

To·ry /'tôrē/ ▶ n. (pl. **-ries**) **1** an American colonist who supported the British during the American Revolution. **2** (in the UK) a member or supporter of the Conservative Party. ■ a member of the English political party opposing the exclusion of James II from the succession. It remained the name for members of the English, later British, parliamentary party supporting the established religious and political order until the emergence of the Conservative Party in the 1830s. Compare with WHIG (sense 1). ▶ adj. of or relating to the British Conservative Party or its supporters: *Tory voters.* — **To·ry·ism** n. [17th C.: prob. from Irish *toraidhe* 'outlaw, highwayman,' from *tóir* 'pursue.' The word was used of Irish peasants dispossessed by English settlers and living as robbers, and extended to other marauders esp. in the Scottish Highlands. It was then adopted *c.*1679 as an abusive nickname for supporters of the Catholic James II.]

to·sa /'tōsə/ ▶ n. a dog of a breed of mastiff originally kept for dogfighting. [1940s: from *Tosa,* the name of a former province in Japan.]

Tos·ca·na /tô'skänä/ Italian name for TUSCANY.

Tos·ca·ni·ni /,täskə'nēnē/, Arturo (1867–1957), Italian conductor. He was a conductor at the Metropolitan Opera 1908–21 and the New York Philharmonic Orchestra 1928–38.

tosh /täSH/ ▶ n. Brit., informal rubbish; nonsense. [19th C.: of unknown origin.]

toss /tôs; täs/ ▶ v. **1** [trans.] throw (something) somewhere lightly, easily, or casually: [with two objs.] *she tossed me a box of matches.* ■ (of a horse) throw (a rider) off its back. ■ throw (a coin) into the air in order to make a decision between two alternatives, based on which side of the coin faces up when it lands. ■ settle a matter with (someone) by doing this: ***I'll toss you for it.*** ■ move or cause to move from side to side or back and forth: [intrans.] *the tops of the olive trees swayed and tossed* | [trans.] *the yachts were tossed around in the harbor.* ■ jerk (one's head or hair) sharply backward. ■ shake or turn (food) in a liquid, so as to coat it lightly. **2** [trans.] informal search (a place): *I could toss her office.* ▶ n. an action or instance of tossing something. ■ (**the toss**) the action of tossing a coin as a method of deciding which team has the right to make a particular decision at the beginning of a game.

– PHRASES **toss one's cookies** informal vomit. — **toss·er** n. [16th C.: of unknown origin.]

toss·pot /'tôs,pät; 'täs-/ ▶ n. informal a habitual drinker (also used as a general term of abuse).

toss-up ▶ n. informal the tossing of a coin to make a decision between two alternatives. ■ a situation in which all outcomes or options are equally possible or equally attractive.

tos·ta·da /tō'städə/ (also **tos·ta·do** /-dō/) ▶ n. (pl. **-das** also **-dos**) a Mexican deep-fried corn-flour pancake topped with a seasoned mixture of beans, ground meat, and vegetables. [Sp., lit. 'toasted,' past part. of *tostar.*]

tos·to·ne /tōs'tōnā; täs-/ ▶ n. a Mexican dish of fried plantains, typically served with a dip. [Sp.]

tot[1] /tät/ ▶ n. **1** a very young child. **2** esp. Brit. a small amount of a strong alcoholic drink such as whiskey or brandy: ***a tot of brandy.*** [18th C. (orig. dial.): of unknown origin.]

tot[2] ▶ v. (**tot·ted, tot·ting**) [trans.] esp. Brit. (**tot something up**) add up numbers or amounts. ■ accumulate something over a period of time: *he has already totted up 89 victories.* [18th C.: from archaic *tot* 'set of figures to be added up,' abbr. of TOTAL or of L. *totum* 'the whole.']

to·tal /'tōtl/ ▶ **adj.** **1** [attrib.] comprising the whole number or amount: *a total cost of $4,000.* **2** complete; absolute: *a total stranger.* ▶ **n.** the whole number or amount of something. ▶ **v.** [trans.] (**-taled**, **-tal·ing** ; Brit. **-talled**, **-tal·ling**) **1** amount in number to: *with debts totaling $6,260.* ■ add up the full number or amount of. **2** informal damage (something, typically a vehicle) beyond repair; wreck. [ME: via OFr. from med. L. *totalis*, from *totum* 'the whole,' neut. of L. *totus* 'whole, entire.' The verb, at first in the sense 'add up,' dates from the 16th C.]

to·tal de·prav·i·ty ▶ **n.** Christian Theol. the Calvinist doctrine that human nature is thoroughly corrupt and sinful as a result of the Fall.

to·tal e·clipse ▶ **n.** an eclipse in which the whole of the disk of the sun or moon is obscured.

to·tal heat ▶ **n.** another term for ENTHALPY.

to·tal·i·tar·i·an /tō,tali'te(ə)rēən/ ▶ **adj.** of or relating to a system of government that is centralized and dictatorial and requires complete subservience to the state. ▶ **n.** a person advocating such a system of government. — **to·tal·i·tar·i·an·ism** **n.**

to·tal·i·ty /tō'talitē/ ▶ **n.** the whole of something: *the totality of their current policies.* ■ Astron. the moment or duration of total obscuration of the sun or moon during an eclipse.

– PHRASES **in its totality** as a whole.

to·tal·i·za·tor /'tōtl-ə,zātər/ ▶ **n.** a device showing the number and amount of bets staked on a race, to facilitate the division of the total among those backing the winner.

to·tal·ize /'tōtl,īz/ ▶ **v.** [trans.] [usu. as adj.] (**totalizing**) comprehend in an all-encompassing way. — **to·tal·i·za·tion** /,tōtl-ə'zāsHən/ **n.**

to·tal·iz·er /'tōtl,īzər/ ▶ **n.** another term for TOTALIZATOR.

to·tal·ly /'tōtl-ē/ ▶ **adv.** completely; absolutely.

To·tal Qual·i·ty Man·age·ment ▶ **n.** a system of management based on the principle that every staff member must be committed to maintaining high standards of work in every aspect of a company's operations.

to·tal re·call ▶ **n.** the ability to remember with clarity every detail of the events of one's life or of a particular event, object, or experience.

to·tal war ▶ **n.** a war that is unrestricted in terms of the weapons used, the territory or combatants involved, or the objectives pursued, esp. one in which the laws of war are disregarded.

tote[1] /tōt/ ▶ **v.** [trans.] informal carry, wield, or convey (something heavy or substantial): *help him tote the books* | [as adj., in comb.] (**-toting**) *a gun-toting loner.* ▶ **n.** short for TOTE BAG. — **tot·er** **n.** [in comb.] *a gun-toter.* [17th C.: prob. of dial. origin.]

tote[2] ▶ **n.** (**the tote**) informal a system of betting based on the use of the totalizator, in which dividends are calculated according to the amount staked rather than odds offered. [19th C.: abbr.]

tote bag ▶ **n.** a large bag used for carrying a number of items.

to·tem /'tōtəm/ ▶ **n.** a natural object or animal believed by a particular society to have spiritual significance and adopted by it as an emblem. — **to·tem·ic** /tō'temik/ **adj.** **to·tem·ism** **n.** **to·tem·ist** **n.** **to·tem·is·tic** /,tōtə'mistik/ **adj.** [18th C.: from Ojibwa *nindoodem* 'my totem.']

to·tem pole ▶ **n.** a pole on which totems are hung or on which the images of totems are carved. ■ fig. a hierarchy: *the social totem pole.*

totem pole

t'oth·er /'təTHər/ (also **toth·er**) ▶ **adj. & pron.** dialect or humorous the other: [as adj.] *I was talking about it t'other day* | [as pron.] *we were talking of this, that, and t'other.* [ME *the tother*, wrong division of *thet other* 'the other' (*thet*, from OE *thaet*, the obs. neut. form of *the*).]

to·tip·o·tent /tō'tipətənt/ ▶ **adj.** Biol. (of an immature or stem cell) capable of giving rise to any cell type or (of a blastomere) a complete embryo. [20th C.: from L. *totus* 'whole' + POTENT.]

tot·ter /'tätər/ ▶ **v.** [intrans.] move in a feeble or unsteady way. ■ [usu. as adj.] (**tottering**) (of a building) shake or rock as if about to collapse. ■ fig. be insecure or about to collapse. ▶ **n.** [in sing.] a feeble or unsteady gait. — **tot·ter·er** **n.** **tot·ter·y** **adj.** [ME: from MDu. *touteren* 'to swing' (the original sense in Engl.).]

tou·can /'tōōkan; -kän/ ▶ **n.** a tropical American fruit-eating bird (genera *Ramphastos* and *Andigena*, family Ramphastidae) with a massive bill and typically brightly colored plumage. [16th C.: via Fr. and Port. from Tupi *tucan*, imitative of its call.]

touch /təcH/ ▶ **v.** [trans.] **1** come so close to (an object) as to be or come into contact with it. ■ bring one's hand or another part of one's body into contact with: *he touched a strand of her hair.* ■ (**touch something to**) move a part of one's body to bring it into contact with: *he gently touched his lips to her cheek.* ■ lightly press or strike (a button or key on a device or instrument) to operate or play it. ■ [intrans.] (of two people or two or more things, typically ones of the same kind) come into contact with each other. ■ cause (two or more things, typically ones of the same kind) to come into contact. ■ Geom. be tangent to (a curve or surface) at a certain point. ■ informal reach (a specified level or amount): *sales touched twenty grand last year.* ■ [usu. with negative] informal be comparable to in quality or excellence: *there's no one who can touch him at lightweight judo.* **2** handle in order to manipulate, alter, or otherwise affect, esp. in an adverse way: *I didn't touch her stuff.* ■ cause harm to (someone). ■ take some of (a store, esp. of money) for use: *I haven't touched a cent of the money.* ■ [usu. with negative] consume a small amount of (food or drink): *the beer was hardly touched.* ■ [with negative] used to indicate that something is avoided or rejected: *jobs that nobody else would touch.* ■ (**touch someone for**) informal ask someone for (money or some other commodity) as a loan or gift. **3** have an effect on; make a difference to. ■ be relevant to. ■ (usu. **be touched**) (of a quality or feature) be visible or apparent in the appearance or character of (something): *trees touched by the colors of autumn.* ■ reach and affect the appearance of: *a wry smile touched his lips.* ■ (**touch something in**) esp. Art lightly mark in features or other details with a brush or pencil. ■ (often **be touched**) produce feelings of affection, gratitude, or sympathy in. ■ [as adj.] (**touched**) informal slightly insane. ▶ **n.** **1** an act of bringing a part of one's body, typically one's hand, into contact with someone or something: *her touch on his shoulder.* ■ [in sing.] an act of lightly pressing or striking something in order to move or operate it. ■ the faculty of perception through physical contact, esp. with the fingers: *reading by touch.* ■ a musician's manner of playing keys or strings. ■ the manner in which a musical instrument's keys or strings respond to being played. ■ a light stroke with a pen, pencil, etc. ■ [in sing.] informal, dated an act of asking for and getting money or some other commodity from someone as a loan or gift. **2** a small amount; a trace: *add a touch of vinegar.* ■ a detail or feature, typically one that gives something a distinctive character. ■ [in sing.] a distinctive manner or method of dealing with something: *later he showed a surer political touch.* ■ [in sing.] an ability to deal with something successfully: *we're losing our touch.* **3** Bell-ringing a series of changes shorter than a peal. **4** short for TOUCH FOOTBALL.

– PHRASES **a touch** to a slight degree; a little: *the water was a touch too chilly.* **in touch** **1** in or into communication: *she said that you kept in touch.* **2** possessing up-to-date knowledge. ■ having an intuitive or empathetic awareness: *you need to be in touch with your feelings.* **lose touch** **1** cease to correspond or be in communication. **2** cease to be aware or informed. **out of touch** lacking knowledge or information concerning current events and developments. ■ lacking in awareness or sympathy. **to the touch** used to describe the qualities of something perceived by touching it or the sensations felt by someone who is touched: *the silk was slightly rough to the touch.*

– PHRASAL VERBS **touch down** (of an aircraft or spacecraft) make contact with the ground in landing. **touch something off** cause something to ignite or explode by touching it with a match. ■ cause something to happen, esp. suddenly. **touch on** (or **upon**) **1** deal briefly with (a subject) in written or spoken discussion. **2** come near to being: *a self-confident manner touching on the arrogant.* **touch something up** make small improvements to something. — **touch·a·ble** **adj.** **touch·er** **n.** [ME: the verb from Old Fr. *tochier*, prob. from a Romance word of imitative origin; the noun orig. from OFr. *touche*, later (in certain senses) directly from the verb.]

touch and go (also **touch-and-go**) ▶ **adj.** (of an outcome, esp. one that is desired) possible but very uncertain. ▶ **n.** (**touch-and-go**) (pl. **touch-and-goes**) a maneuver in which an aircraft touches the ground as in landing, and immediately takes off again.

touch·back /'təcH,bak/ ▶ **n.** Football a ball one downs deliberately behind one's own goal line or that is kicked through one's end zone. It is taken to the 20-yard line to resume play.

touch·down /'təcH,doun/ ▶ **n.** **1** the moment at which an aircraft's wheels or part of a spacecraft make contact with the ground during landing. **2** Football a six-point score made by carrying or passing the ball into the end zone of the opposing side, or by recovering it there following a fumble or blocked kick. ■ Rugby an act of touching the ground with the ball behind the opponents' goal line, scoring a try.

tou·ché /tōō'sHā/ ▶ **exclam.** (in fencing) used as an acknowledgment of a hit by one's opponent. ■ used as an acknowledgment during a discussion of a good or clever point made at one's expense by another person. [Fr., lit. 'touched,' past part. of *toucher*.]

touch foot·ball ▶ **n.** a form of football in which a ball carrier is downed by touching instead of tackling.

touch·hole /'təcH,hōl/ ▶ **n.** a small hole in early firearms through which the charge is ignited.

touch·ing /'təcHiNG/ ▶ **adj.** arousing strong feelings of sympathy, appreciation, or gratitude. [16th C.: from TOUCH + -ING[2].] ▶ **prep.** concerning; about: *evidence touching the facts of Roger's case.* [ME: from Fr. *touchant*, pres. part. of *toucher* 'to touch.'] — **touch·ing·ly** **adv.** **touch·ing·ness** **n.**

touch·line /'təcH,līn/ ▶ **n.** Rugby & Soccer the boundary line on each side of the field.

touch-me-not ▶ **n.** a plant (genus *Impatiens*) of the balsam family whose ripe seed capsules burst when touched, scattering seeds over some distance. Also called **jewelweed**.

touch·pad /'təcH,pad/ ▶ **n.** a computer input device in the form of a small panel containing different touch-sensitive areas.

touch screen (also **touch·screen**) ▶ **n.** a display device that allows a user to interact with a computer by touching areas on the screen.

touch·stone /'təcH,stōn/ ▶ **n.** a piece of fine-grained dark schist or jasper formerly used for testing alloys of gold by observing the color of the mark that they made on it. ■ a standard or criterion by which something is judged or recognized.

touch-tone (also **Touch-Tone**) ▶ **adj.** (of a telephone) having push buttons and generating tones to dial rather than pulses. ■ (of a service) accessed or controlled by the tones generated by these telephones. ▶ **n.** trademark a telephone of this type. ■ one of the set of tones generated by these telephones.

touch-type ▶ **v.** [intrans.] type using all one's fingers and without looking at the keys. — **touch-typ•ist n.**

touch-up ▶ **n.** a quick restoration or improvement made to the appearance or state of something.

touch•wood /ˈtəCH,wo͝od/ ▶ **n.** archaic readily flammable wood used as tinder, esp. when made soft by fungi.

touch•y /ˈtəCHē/ ▶ **adj.** (**touch•i•er, touch•i•est**) (of a person) oversensitive and irritable. ■ (of an issue or situation) requiring careful handling; delicate: *the monarchy has become a touchy topic.* — **touch•i•ly adv. touch•i•ness n.** [17th C.: perh. an alt. of TETCHY, influenced by TOUCH.]

touch•y-feel•y /ˈfēlē/ ▶ **adj.** informal, often derog. openly expressing affection or other emotions, esp. through physical contact. ■ characteristic of or relating to such behavior.

tough /təf/ ▶ **adj. 1** (of a substance or object) strong enough to withstand adverse conditions or rough or careless handling: *tough backpacks for climbers.* ■ (of a person or animal) able to endure hardship or pain; physically robust. ■ able to protect one's own interests or maintain one's own opinions without being intimidated by opposition; confident and determined. ■ demonstrating a strict and uncompromising attitude or approach: *tough new laws on tobacco advertising.* ■ (of a person) strong and prone to violence. ■ (of an area) notorious for violence and crime. ■ (of food, esp. meat) difficult to cut or chew. **2** involving considerable difficulty or hardship; requiring great determination or effort: *the training is tough.* ■ used to express sympathy with someone in an unpleasant or difficult situation: *It's tough on her.* ■ [often as exclam.] used to express a lack of sympathy with someone: *if you don't like it, tough.* ▶ **n.** a tough person, esp. a gangster or criminal.

– PHRASES **tough it out** informal endure a period of hardship or difficulty. **tough shit** (or **titty**) vulgar slang used to express a lack of sympathy with someone. — **tough•ish adj. tough•ly adv. tough•ness n.** [OE *tōh*, of Gmc. origin; rel. to Du. *taai* and Ger. *zäh*.]

tough•en /ˈtəfən/ ▶ **v.** make or become tougher: [trans.] *he tried to toughen his son up* | [intrans.] *if removed from the oven too soon meringues shrink and toughen.* ■ [trans.] make (rules or a policy) stricter and more harsh: *new congressional efforts to toughen the laws.* — **tough•en•er n.**

tough•ie /ˈtəfē/ ▶ **n.** informal **1** a person who is tough, determined, and not easily daunted. **2** a difficult problem or question.

tough love ▶ **n.** promotion of a person's welfare, esp. that of an addict, child, or criminal, by enforcing certain constraints on them, or requiring them to take responsibility for their actions. ■ a political policy designed to encourage self-help by restricting state benefits.

tough-mind•ed ▶ **adj.** strong, determined, and able to face up to reality. — **tough-mind•ed•ness n.**

Tou•lon /to͞oˈlôN/ a port on the Mediterranean coast of southern France; pop. 170,000.

Tou•louse /to͞oˈlo͞oz/ a city in southwestern France on the Garonne River; pop. 366,000.

Tou•louse-Lau•trec /to͞oˈlo͞oz lōˈtrek/, Henri Marie Raymond de (1864–1901), French painter. His color lithographs depict actors, music-hall singers, prostitutes, and waitresses from the 1890s.

tou•pee /to͞oˈpā/ ▶ **n.** a small wig or artificial hairpiece worn to cover a bald spot. [18th C. (denoting a curl or lock of artificial hair): alt. of Fr. *toupet* 'hair tuft,' dimin. of OFr. *toup* 'tuft,' ult. of Gmc. origin and rel. to TOP[1].]

tour /to͝or/ ▶ **n. 1** a journey for pleasure in which several different places are visited. ■ a short trip to or through a place in order to view or inspect something: *a tour of the White House.* **2** a journey made by performers or an athletic team, in which they perform or play in several different places. ■ (**the tour**) (in golf, tennis, and other sports) the annual round of events in which top professionals compete. **3** (also **tour of duty**) a period of duty on military or diplomatic service. ▶ **v.** [trans.] make a tour of (an area): *he decided to tour France* | [intrans.] *they had toured in a little minivan.* ■ take (a performer, production, etc.) on tour. [ME (sense 3; also denoting a circular movement): from OFr., 'turn,' via L. from Gk. *tornos* 'lathe.' Sense 1 dates from the mid 17th C.]

tou•ra•co /ˈto͝orə,kō/ (also **tu•ra•co**) ▶ **n.** (pl. **-cos**) a fruit-eating African bird (*Musophaga* and other genera) with brightly colored plumage, a prominent crest, and a long tail. [18th C.: Fr., from a West Afr. word.]

Tou•rane /to͞oˈrän/ former name of DA NANG.

tour de force /ˈto͝or də ˈfôrs/ ▶ **n.** (pl. **tours de force** pronunc. same or /ˈto͝orz/) an impressive performance or achievement that has been accomplished or managed with great skill: *his novel is a tour de force.* [Fr., lit. 'feat of strength.']

Tour de France /ˈto͝or də ˈfrans/ a French race for professional cyclists held annually since 1903, covering approximately 3,000 miles (4,800 km) of roads in about three weeks, renowned for its mountain stages.

tour d'ho•ri•zon /ˈto͝or dôrēˈzôN/ ▶ **n.** (pl. **tours d'ho•ri•zon** pronunc. same) a broad general survey or summary of an argument or event. [Fr., lit. 'tour of the horizon.']

tour en l'air /ˈto͝or än ˈle(ə)r/ ▶ **n.** (pl. **tours en l'air** /ˈto͝orz/) Ballet a movement in which a dancer jumps straight upward and completes at least one full revolution in the air before landing. [Fr., lit. 'turn in the air.']

Tou•rette's syn•drome /to͞oˈrets/ ▶ **n.** Med. a neurological disorder characterized by involuntary tics and vocalizations and often the compulsive utterance of obscenities. [19th C.: named after Gilles de la *Tourette* (1857–1904), French neurologist.]

tour•ing car ▶ **n.** a car designed with room for passengers and luggage. ■ a car of this type used in auto racing, as distinct from a specially designed race car.

tour•ism /ˈto͝orizəm/ ▶ **n.** the commercial organization and operation of vacations and visits to places of interest.

tour•ist /ˈto͝orist/ ▶ **n. 1** a person who is traveling or visiting a place for pleasure. **2** short for TOURIST CLASS. — **tour•is•tic** /to͞oˈristik/ **adj. tour•is•ti•cal•ly** /to͞oˈristik(ə)lē/ **adv.**

tour•ist class ▶ **n.** the cheapest accommodations or seating for passengers in a ship, aircraft, or hotel. ▶ **adj. & adv.** of, relating to, or by such accommodations or seating: [as adj.] *a tourist-class hotel* | [as adv.] *they had come tourist class from Cairo.*

tour•ist•y /ˈto͝oristē/ ▶ **adj.** informal relating to, appealing to, or visited by tourists (often used to suggest tawdriness or lack of authenticity): *a touristy shopping street.*

tour•ma•line /ˈto͝ormәlin; -,lēn/ ▶ **n.** a brittle gray or black mineral that occurs as prismatic crystals in granitic and other rocks. It consists of a boron aluminosilicate and has pyroelectric and polarizing properties, and is used in electrical and optical instruments and as a gemstone. [18th C.: from Fr., based on Sinhalese *tōramalli* 'carnelian.']

tour•na•ment /ˈtərnəmənt; ˈto͝or-/ ▶ **n. 1** (in a sport or game) a series of contests between a number of competitors, who compete for an overall prize. **2** (in the Middle Ages) a sporting event in which two knights (or two groups of knights) jousted on horseback with blunted weapons, each trying to knock the other off, the winner receiving a prize. [ME (sense 2): from Anglo-Norman Fr. vars. of OFr. *torneiement*, from *torneier* 'take part in a tourney' (see TOURNEY).]

tour•ne•dos /ˈto͝ornə,dō/ ▶ **n.** (pl. same) a small round thick cut from a fillet of beef. [Fr., from *tourner* 'to turn' + *dos* 'back.']

tour•ney /ˈtərnē; ˈto͝or-/ ▶ **n.** (pl. **-neys**) a tournament. ▶ **v.** (**-neys, -neyed**) [intrans.] take part in a tournament. [ME: from OFr. *tornei* (n.), *torneier* (v.), based on L. *tornus* 'a turn.']

tour•ni•quet /ˈtərnikit; ˈto͝or-/ ▶ **n.** a device for stopping the flow of blood through an artery, typically by compressing a limb with a cord or tight bandage. [17th C.: from Fr., prob. from OFr. *tournicle* 'coat of mail,' influenced by *tourner* 'to turn.']

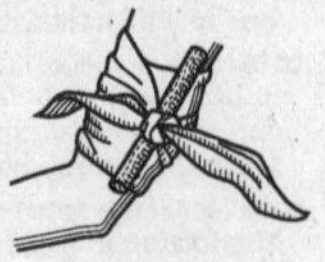
tourniquet

Tours /to͝or/ a city in western central France; pop. 133,000.

tou•sle /ˈtouzəl/ ▶ **v.** [trans.] [usu. as adj.] (**tousled**) make (something, esp. a person's hair) untidy. ▶ **n.** an act of tousling something, esp. hair. ■ a tousled mass, esp. of hair. [ME (in the sense 'handle roughly or rudely'): frequentative of dial. *touse* 'handle roughly,' of Gmc. origin and rel. to Ger. *zausen*. Cf. TUSSLE.]

Tous•saint L'Ou•ver•ture /to͞oˈsaN ,lo͞overˈtyr/, Pierre Dominique (*c.*1743–1803), Haitian revolutionary. He was one of the leaders of a rebellion that emancipated the island's slaves in 1791.

tout[1] /tout/ ▶ **v. 1** [trans.] attempt to sell (something), typically by pestering people in an aggressive or bold manner: *Jim was touting his wares.* ■ (often **be touted**) attempt to persuade people of the merits of (someone or something). ■ Brit. scalp (a ticket). **2** [intrans.] offer racing tips for a share of any resulting winnings. ■ [trans.] spy out the movements and condition of (a racehorse in training) in order to gain information to be used when betting. ▶ **n. 1** a person soliciting custom or business, typically in an aggressive or bold manner. ■ Brit. a person who buys tickets for an event to resell them at a profit; a scalper. **2** a person who offers racing tips for a share of any resulting winnings. — **tout•er n.** [ME *tute* 'look out,' of Gmc. origin.]

tout[2] /to͞o/ ▶ **adj.** (often **le tout**) used before the name of a city to refer to its high society or people of importance: *le tout Washington adored him.* [Fr., suggested by *le tout Paris* 'all (of) Paris,' used to refer to Parisian high society.]

tout court /,to͞o ˈko͝or/ ▶ **adv.** with no addition or qualification; simply: *he saw it as an illusion, tout court.* [Fr., lit. 'very short.']

tout de suite /,to͞ot ˈswēt/ ▶ **adv.** immediately; at once. [Fr., lit. 'quite in sequence.']

tout le monde /,to͞o lə ˈmônd/ ▶ **n.** [treated as sing. or pl.] everyone: *he shouted "Bon appetit, tout le monde!"* [Fr.]

to•va•rish /təˈvärisH/ (also **to•va•rich**) ▶ **n.** (in the former USSR) a comrade (often used as a form of address). [from Russ. *tovarishch*, from Turkic.]

TOW /tō/ ▶ **abbr.** tube-launched, optically guided, wire-guided (missile).

tow[1] /tō/ ▶ **v.** [trans.] (of a motor vehicle or boat) pull (another vehicle or boat) along with a rope, chain, or tow bar. ■ (of a person) pull (someone or something) along behind one. ▶ **n.** [in sing.] an act of towing a vehicle or boat. ■ a rope or line used to tow a vehicle or boat.

– PHRASES **in tow 1** being towed by another vehicle or boat. **2** accompanying or following someone: *with three children in tow.* — **tow•a•ble adj.** [OE *togian* 'draw, drag,' of Gmc. origin; rel. to TUG. The noun dates from the early 17th C.]

tow[2] ▶ **n.** the coarse and broken part of flax or hemp prepared for spinning. ■ a bundle of untwisted natural or man-made fibers. — **tow•y adj.** [OE (recorded in *towcræft* 'spinning'), of Gmc. origin.]

tow·age /'tō-ij/ ▶ **n.** **1** [usu. as adj.] the action or process of towing. **2** a charge for towing a boat or vehicle.

to·ward /tôrd; t(ə)'wôrd/ ▶ **prep.** (also **to·wards**) **1** in the direction of. ▪ getting closer to achieving (a goal): *move toward freedom.* ▪ close or closer to (a particular time): *toward the end of April.* **2** as regards; in relation to: *our attitude toward death.* ▪ paying homage to, esp. in a superficial or insincere way: *he gave a nod toward the work done by the fund.* **3** contributing to the cost of (something): *the council provided a grant toward the cost of new buses.* ▶ **adj.** [predic.] archaic going on; in progress. [OE *tōweard* (see TO, -WARD).]

tow bar ▶ **n.** a bar fitted to the back of a vehicle, used in towing a trailer.

tow-col·ored ▶ **adj.** (of hair) very light blonde.

tow·el /'touəl/ ▶ **n.** a piece of thick absorbent cloth or paper used for drying oneself or wiping things dry. ▶ **v.** (**-eled**, **-el·ing**; Brit. **-elled**, **-el·ling**) [trans.] wipe or dry (a person or thing) with a towel: *she toweled her hair dry* | [intrans.] *towel off and dress for dinner.*
– PHRASES **throw in the towel** see THROW. [ME: from OFr. *toaille*, of Gmc. origin. The verb, orig. meaning 'beat or thrash,' dates from the 18th cent. The sense 'wipe with a towel' arose in the 19th C.]

tow·el·ette /tou(ə)'let/ ▶ **n.** a small paper or cloth towel, usually premoistened in a sealed package, used for cleansing.

tow·el·ing /'tou(ə)liNG/ (Brit. **tow·el·ling**) ▶ **n.** thick absorbent cloth, typically cotton with uncut loops, used for towels and robes.

tow·er /'touər/ ▶ **n.** **1** a tall narrow building, either freestanding or forming part of a building such as a church or castle. ▪ [with adj.] a tall structure that houses machinery, operators, etc. ▪ [with adj.] a tall structure used as a receptacle or for storage: *a CD tower.* ▪ a tall pile or mass of something: *a titanic tower of garbage.* **2** a place of defense; a protection. ▶ **v.** [intrans.] **1** rise to or reach a great height: *he seemed to tower over everyone else.* **2** (of a bird) soar to a great height, esp. (of a falcon) so as to be able to swoop down on the quarry.
– PHRASES **tower of strength** see STRENGTH. — **tow·ered adj.** (esp. literary). [OE *torr*, reinforced in ME by OFr. *tour*, from L. *turris*, from Gk.]

tow·er·ing /'touəriNG/ ▶ **adj.** [attrib.] extremely tall, esp. in comparison with the surroundings. ▪ of exceptional importance or influence. ▪ of great intensity: *his towering anger.*

Tow·er of Ba·bel /'babəl; 'bā-/ (in the Bible) a tower built in an attempt to reach heaven, which God frustrated by confusing the languages of its builders so that they could not understand one another. [*Babel* from Heb. *Bāḇel* 'Babylon,' from Akkadian *bāb ili* 'gate of god.']

Tow·er of Lon·don a fortress by the Thames River in London. The oldest part was begun in 1078. Later used as a state prison, it is now a repository of ancient armor, weapons, and the Crown jewels.

tow·head /'tō,hed/ ▶ **n.** a head of tow-colored or very blond hair. ▪ a person with such hair. — **tow·head·ed adj.**

tow·hee /'tō,hē; 'tou-/ ▶ **n.** a North American songbird (genera *Pipilo* and *Chlorurus*) of the bunting family, typically with brownish plumage but sometimes black and rufous. [18th C.: imitative of the call of *Pipilo erythrophthalmus*.]

tow·line /'tō,līn/ ▶ **n.** a rope, cable, or other line used in towing.

town /toun/ ▶ **n.** an urban area that has a name, defined boundaries, and local government, and that is larger than a village and generally smaller than a city. ▪ the particular town under consideration, esp. one's own town: *Carson was in town.* ▪ the central part of a neighborhood, with its business or shopping area. ▪ Brit., dated the chief city or town of a region. ▪ a densely populated area, esp. as contrasted with the country or suburbs. ▪ [in sing.] a town's community: *the whole town is talking about it.* ▪ the permanent residents of a college town as distinct from the members of the college. Often contrasted with GOWN. ▪ another term for TOWNSHIP (sense 3).
– PHRASES **go to town** informal do something thoroughly, enthusiastically, or extravagantly. **on the town** informal enjoying the entertainments, esp. the nightlife, of a city or town. — **town·ish adj.** **town·let** /-lit/ **n.** **town·ward** /-wərd/ **adj. & adv.** **town·wards** /-wərdz/ **adv.** [OE *tūn* 'enclosed piece of land, homestead, village,' of Gmc. origin; rel. to Du. *tuin* 'garden' and Ger. *Zaun* 'fence.']

town car ▶ **n.** a limousine.

town clerk ▶ **n.** a public official in charge of the records of a town.

town coun·cil ▶ **n.** an elected governing body in a municipality. — **town coun·ci·lor n.**

town cri·er ▶ **n.** hist. a person employed to make public announcements in the streets or marketplace of a town.

Townes /tounz/, Charles Hard (1915–), US physicist. He invented the maser in 1954. Nobel Prize for Physics (1964, shared with Nicolaye Basov 1922– and Aleksandr Prokhorov 1916–).

town hall ▶ **n.** a building used for the administration of local government.

town·house /'toun,hous/ (also **town house**) ▶ **n.** **1** a tall, narrow, traditional row house, generally having three or more floors. ▪ a modern two- or three-story house built as one of a group of similar houses. **2** a house in a town or city belonging to someone who has another property in the country.

town·ie /'tounē/ ▶ **n.** a person who lives in a town (used esp. with reference to their supposed lack of familiarity with rural affairs). ▪ a resident in a university town, rather than a student.

town meet·ing ▶ **n.** a meeting of the voters of a town for the transaction of public business.

towns·folk /'tounz,fōk/ ▶ **plural n.** another term for TOWNSPEOPLE.

town·ship /'toun,SHip/ ▶ **n.** **1** a division of a county with some corporate powers. ▪ a district six miles square. **2** (in South Africa) a suburb or city of predominantly black occupation, formerly officially designated for black occupation by apartheid legislation. **3** Brit., hist. a manor or parish as a territorial division. ▪ a small town or village forming part of a large parish. [OE *tūnscipe* 'the inhabitants of a village' (see TOWN, -SHIP).]

towns·man /'tounzmən/ ▶ **n.** (pl. **-men**) a man living in a particular town or city.

towns·peo·ple /'tounz,pēpəl/ (also **towns·folk** /-,fōk/) ▶ **plural n.** the people living in a particular town or city.

towns·wom·an /'tounz,wo͝omən/ ▶ **n.** (pl. **-wom·en**) a woman living in a particular town or city.

tow·path /'tō,paTH/ ▶ **n.** a path beside a river or canal, originally used as a pathway for horses towing barges.

tow·plane /'tō,plān/ ▶ **n.** an aircraft that tows gliders.

tow rope ▶ **n.** another term for TOWLINE.

tow truck ▶ **n.** a truck used to tow or pick up damaged or disabled vehicles.

tox·a·phene /'täksə,fēn/ ▶ **n.** a synthetic amber waxy solid with an odor of chlorine and camphor, used as an insecticide. It is a chlorinated terpene. [1940s: from TOXIN + *(cam)phene*, a rel. terpene.]

tox·e·mi·a /täk'sēmēə/ (Brit. **tox·ae·mi·a**) ▶ **n.** blood poisoning by toxins from a local bacterial infection. ▪ (also **toxemia of pregnancy**) another term for PREECLAMPSIA. — **tox·e·mic adj.** [19th C.: from TOXI- + -EMIA.]

toxi- ▶ **comb. form** representing TOXIC or TOXIN.

tox·ic /'täksik/ ▶ **adj.** poisonous. ▪ of or relating to poison. ▪ caused by poison. ▶ **n.** (**toxics**) poisonous substances. — **tox·i·cal·ly adv.** **tox·ic·i·ty** /täk'sisitē/ **n.** [17th C.: from med. L. *toxicus* 'poisoned,' from L. *toxicum* 'poison,' from Gk. *toxikon (pharmakon)* '(poison for) arrows,' from *toxon* 'bow.']

tox·i·cant /'täksikənt/ ▶ **n.** a toxic substance introduced into the environment, e.g., a pesticide. [19th C.: var. of INTOXICANT, differentiated in sense.]

toxico- ▶ **comb. form** equivalent to TOXI-. [from Gk. *toxicon* 'poison.']

tox·i·col·o·gy /,täksi'käləjē/ ▶ **n.** the branch of science concerned with the nature, effects, and detection of poisons. — **tox·i·co·log·ic** /-kə'läjik/ **adj.** **tox·i·co·log·i·cal** /-kə'läjikəl/ **adj.** **tox·i·co·log·i·cal·ly** /-kə'läjik(ə)lē/ **adv.** **tox·i·col·o·gist n.**

tox·ic shock syn·drome (abbr.: **TSS**) ▶ **n.** acute septicemia in women, typically caused by bacterial infection from a retained tampon or IUD.

tox·i·gen·ic /,täksi'jenik/ ▶ **adj.** (esp. of a bacterium) producing a toxin or toxic effect. — **tox·i·ge·nic·i·ty** /-jə'nisitē/ **n.**

tox·in /'täksin/ ▶ **n.** an antigenic poison or venom of plant or animal origin, esp. one produced by or derived from microorganisms and causing disease when present at low concentration in the body. [19th C.: from TOXIC + -IN[1].]

toxo- ▶ **comb. form** equivalent to TOXI-.

tox·oid /'täksoid/ ▶ **n.** Med. a chemically modified toxin from a pathogenic microorganism, that is no longer toxic but is still antigenic and can be used as a vaccine.

tox·oph·i·lite /täk'säfə,līt/ rare ▶ **n.** a student or lover of archery. ▶ **adj.** of or relating to archers and archery. — **tox·oph·i·ly** /-'säfəlē/ **n.** [18th C.: from *Toxophilus* (a name invented by Ascham, used as the title of his treatise on archery (1545), from Gk. *toxon* 'bow' + *-philos* 'loving') + -ITE[1].]

tox·o·plas·ma /,täksə'plazmə/ ▶ **n.** a parasitic spore-forming protozoan (genus *Toxoplasma*, phylum Sporozoa) that can sometimes cause disease in humans.

tox·o·plas·mo·sis /,täksōplaz'mōsis/ ▶ **n.** a disease caused by toxoplasmas, transmitted chiefly through undercooked meat, soil, or in cat feces. Symptoms generally pass unremarked in adults, but infection can be dangerous to unborn children.

toy /toi/ ▶ **n.** **1** an object for a child to play with, typically a model or miniature replica of something. ▪ an object, esp. a gadget or machine, regarded as providing amusement for an adult: *in 1914 the car was still a rich man's toy.* ▪ a person treated by another as a source of pleasure or amusement rather than with due seriousness: *a man needed a friend, not a toy.* **2** [as adj.] denoting a diminutive breed or variety of dog.
– PHRASAL VERBS **toy with 1** consider (an idea, movement, or proposal) casually or indecisively. ▪ treat (someone) without due seriousness, esp. in a superficially amorous way. **2** move or handle (an object) absentmindedly or nervously. ▪ eat or drink in an unenthusiastic or restrained way. — **toy·like adj.** [ME: of unknown origin. The word orig. denoted a funny story or remark, later an antic or trick, or a frivolous entertainment. The verb dates from the early 16th C.]

toy boy ▶ **n.** Brit., informal a male lover who is much younger than his partner.

Toyn·bee /'toinbē/ English historians. Arnold (1852–83), an economics historian, wrote *Lectures on the Industrial Revolution in England* (1884). His nephew Arnold Joseph (1889–1975) wrote the 12-volume

A Study of History (1934–61).

to·yon /ˈtoi-än/ ▶ **n.** an evergreen Californian shrub (*Heteromeles arbutifolia*) of the rose family, the fruiting branches of which are used for Christmas decorations. [19th C.: from Mex. Sp. *tollón*.]

tp. ▶ **abbr.** ■ township. ■ troop.

t.p. ▶ **abbr.** ■ title page. ■ toilet paper. ■ (in surveying) turning point. ▶ **v.** (also **TP**) short for TOILET PAPER.

TPA ▶ **abbr.** tissue plasminogen activator.

tpk. ▶ **abbr.** turnpike.

TQM ▶ **abbr.** Total Quality Management.

tr. ▶ **abbr.** ■ tare. ■ tincture. ■ trace. ■ train. ■ transaction. ■ transitive. ■ translated. ■ translation. ■ translator. ■ transpose. ■ transposition. ■ treasurer. ■ Music trill. ■ troop. ■ trust. ■ trustee.

tra·be·a·tion /ˌtrābēˈāsʜən/ ▶ **n.** the use of beams in architectural construction, rather than arches or vaulting. — **tra·be·at·ed** /ˈtrābēˌātid/ **adj.** [16th C. (denoting a horizontal beam): formed irregularly from L. *trabs, trab-* 'beam, timber' + -ATION.]

tra·bec·u·la /trəˈbekyələ/ ▶ **n.** (usu. in pl. **-lae** /-lē/) **1** Anat. each of a series or group of partitions formed by bands or columns of connective tissue, esp. a plate of the calcareous tissue forming cancellous bone. **2** Bot. any of a number of rodlike structures in plants, e.g., a strand of sterile tissue dividing the cavity in a sporangium. — **tra·bec·u·lar adj. tra·bec·u·late** /-lit/ **adj.** [19th C.: from L., dimin. of *trabs* 'beam, timber.']

Trâ·blous /ˈtrablo͞os/ Arabic name for TRIPOLI (sense 2).

trace¹ /trās/ ▶ **v.** [trans.] **1** find or discover by investigation: *police are trying to trace a white van seen in the area.* ■ find or describe the origin or development of. ■ follow or mark the course or position of (something) with one's eye, mind, or finger. ■ take (a particular path or route): *a tear traced a lonely path down her cheek.* **2** copy (a drawing, map, or design) by drawing over its lines on a superimposed piece of transparent paper. ■ draw (a pattern or line), esp. with one's finger or toe. ■ give an outline of: *the article traces out the connections between education and the labor market.* ▶ **n. 1** a mark, object, or other indication of the existence or passing of something: *remove all traces of the gum.* ■ a beaten path or small road; a track. ■ a physical change in the brain presumed to be caused by a process of learning or memory. ■ a procedure to investigate the source of something, such as the place from which a telephone call was made, or the origin of an error in a computer program. **2** a very small quantity, esp. one too small to be accurately measured. ■ a slight indication or barely discernible hint of something: *just a trace of a smile.* **3** a line or pattern displayed by an instrument using a moving pen or a luminous spot on a screen to show the existence or nature of something that is being investigated. ■ a line that represents the projection of a curve or surface on a plane or the intersection of a curve or surface with a plane. **4** Math. the sum of the elements in the principle diagonal of a square matrix. — **trace·a·bil·i·ty** /ˌtrāsəˈbilitē/ **n. trace·a·ble adj. trace·less adj.** [ME (first recorded as a noun in the sense 'path that someone or something takes'): from OFr. *trace* (n.), *tracier* (v.), based on L. *tractus* (see TRACT¹).]

trace² ▶ **n.** each of the two side straps, chains, or ropes by which a horse is attached to a vehicle that it is pulling. See illustration at HARNESS. [ME (denoting a pair of traces): from OFr. *trais*, pl. of *trait* (see TRAIT).]

trace el·e·ment ▶ **n.** a chemical element present only in minute amounts in a particular sample or environment. ■ a chemical element required only in minute amounts by living organisms for normal growth.

trace fos·sil ▶ **n.** Geol. a fossil of a footprint, trail, burrow, or other trace of an animal rather than of the animal itself.

trac·er /ˈtrāsər/ ▶ **n.** a person or thing that traces something or by which something may be traced, in particular: ■ a bullet or shell whose course is made visible in flight by a trail of flames or smoke, used to assist in aiming. ■ a substance introduced into a biological organism or other system so that its subsequent distribution can be readily followed from its color, fluorescence, radioactivity, or other distinctive property. ■ a device that transmits a signal and so can be located when attached to a moving vehicle or other object.

trac·er·y /ˈtrāsərē/ ▶ **n.** (pl. **-er·ies**) Archit. ornamental stone openwork, typically in the upper part of a Gothic window. ■ a delicate branching pattern: *a tracery of red veins.* — **trac·er·ied adj.**

tra·che·a /ˈtrākēə/ ▶ **n.** (pl. **-che·ae** /-kēˌē/ or **-che·as**) Anat. a large membranous tube reinforced by rings of cartilage, extending from the larynx to the bronchial tubes and conveying air to and from the lungs; the windpipe. ■ Entomol. each of a number of fine chitinous tubes in the body of an insect, conveying air directly to the tissues. ■ Bot. any duct or vessel in a plant, providing support and conveying water and salts. — **tra·che·al adj. tra·che·ate** /-it; -ˌāt/ **adj.** [ME: from med. L., from late L. *trachia*, from Gk. *trakheia (artēria)* 'rough (artery),' from *trakhus* 'rough.']

tra·che·id /ˈtrākēid/ ▶ **n.** Bot. a type of water-conducting cell in the xylem that lacks perforations in the cell wall. [19th C.: from Ger. *Tracheïde*, from med. L. *trachea* (see TRACHEA).]

tra·che·i·tis /ˌtrākēˈītis/ ▶ **n.** Med. inflammation of the trachea, usually secondary to a nose or throat infection.

tracheo- ▶ **comb. form** relating to the trachea: *tracheotomy.*

tra·che·ot·o·my /ˌtrākēˈätəmē/ (also **tra·che·os·to·my** /-ˈästəmē/) ▶ **n.** (pl. **-mies**) Med. an incision in the windpipe made to relieve an obstruction to breathing.

tra·cho·ma /trəˈkōmə/ ▶ **n.** a contagious bacterial infection of the eye (caused by the chlamydial organism *Chlamydia trichomatis*) in which there is inflamed granulation on the inner surface of the lids. — **tra·chom·a·tous** /-mətəs/ **adj.** [17th C.: from Gk. *trakhōma* 'roughness,' from *trakhus* 'rough.']

tra·chyte /ˈtrakīt; ˈtrā-/ ▶ **n.** Geol. a gray fine-grained volcanic rock consisting largely of alkali feldspar. [19th C. (denoting a volcanic rock with a rough or gritty surface): from Gk. *trakhus* 'rough' or *trakhutēs* 'roughness.']

tra·chyt·ic /trəˈkitik/ ▶ **adj.** Geol. relating to or denoting a rock texture (characteristic of trachyte) in which crystals show parallel alignment due to flow in the magma.

trac·ing /ˈtrāsiNG/ ▶ **n.** a copy of a drawing, map, or design made by tracing it. ■ a faint or delicate mark or pattern: *tracings of apple blossoms against the deep greens of pines.* ■ another term for TRACE¹ (sense 3). ■ Figure Skating the marking out of a figure on the ice when skating.

trac·ing pa·per ▶ **n.** transparent paper used for tracing maps, drawings, or designs.

track¹ /trak/ ▶ **n. 1** a rough path or minor road, typically one beaten by use rather than constructed. ■ a prepared course or circuit for athletes, horses, motor vehicles, bicycles, or dogs to race on. ■ the sport of running on such a track. ■ (usu. **tracks**) a mark or line of marks left by a person, animal, or vehicle in passing. ■ the course or route followed by someone or something (used esp. in talking about their pursuit by others). ■ fig. a course of action; a way of proceeding: *our plan follows a different track.* **2** a continuous line of rails on a railroad. ■ a metal or plastic strip or rail from which a curtain or spotlight may be hung or fitted. ■ a continuous articulated metal band around the wheels of a heavy vehicle such as a tank or bulldozer, intended to facilitate movement over rough or soft ground. ■ Electron. a continuous line of conductive material on a printed circuit board, used to connect parts of a circuit. ■ Sailing a strip on the mast, boom, or deck of a yacht along which a slide attached to a sail can be moved, used to adjust the position of the sail. **3** a section of a record, compact disc, or cassette tape containing one song or piece of music. [orig. denoting a groove on a phonograph record.] ■ a lengthwise strip of magnetic tape containing one sequence of signals. ■ the soundtrack of a film or video. **4** the transverse distance between a vehicle's wheels. **5** a group in which schoolchildren of the same age and ability are taught: ▶ **v. 1** [trans.] follow the course or trail of (someone or something), typically in order to find them or note their location at various points. ■ fig. follow and note the course or progress of: *tracking the girth of stars.* ■ [intrans.] follow a particular course: *the storm was tracking across the ground at 30 mph.* ■ (of a stylus) follow (a groove in a record). ■ [intrans.] (of a film or television camera) move in relation to the subject being filmed. [with ref. to early filming when a camera was mobile by means of a track.] ■ (**track something up**) leave a trail of dirty footprints on a surface. ■ (**track something in**) leave a trail of dirt, debris, or snow from one's feet: *the road salt I'd tracked in from the street.* **2** [intrans.] (of wheels) run so that the back ones are exactly in the track of the front ones. **3** [intrans.] Electron. (of a tunable circuit or component) vary in frequency in the same way as another circuit or component, so that the frequency difference between them remains constant. **4** [trans.] assign (a pupil) to a course of study according to ability.

– PHRASES **in one's tracks** informal where one or something is at that moment; suddenly. **keep** (or **lose**) **track of** keep (or fail to keep) fully aware of or informed about. **make tracks** (**for**) informal leave hurriedly (for a place). **off the beaten track** see BEATEN. **off the track** departing from the right course of thinking or behavior. **on the right** (or **wrong**) **track** acting or thinking in a way that is likely to result in success (or failure). **on track** acting or thinking in a way that is likely to achieve what is required. **the wrong** (or **right**) **side of the tracks** informal a poor, less prestigious (or wealthy, prestigious) part of town.

– PHRASAL VERBS **track someone/something down** find someone or something after a thorough or difficult search. **track up** (of a horse at the trot) create sufficient impulsion in its hindquarters to cause the hind feet to step on to or slightly ahead of the former position of the forefeet. [15th C.: the noun from OFr. *trac*, perh. from Low Ger. or Du. *trek* 'drawing, pull'; the verb from Fr. *traquer* or directly from the noun.]

track² ▶ **v.** [trans.] tow (a boat) along a waterway from the bank. [18th C.: appar. from Du. *trekken* 'to draw, pull, or travel.' The change in the vowel was due to association with TRACK¹.]

track·age /ˈtrakij/ ▶ **n.** the tracks or lines of a railroad system.

track and field ▶ **n.** athletic events that take place on a running track and a nearby field; track events and field events.

track·ball /ˈtrakˌbôl/ ▶ **n.** a small ball set in a holder that can be rotated by hand to move a cursor on a computer screen.

track·bed /ˈtrakˌbed/ ▶ **n.** a roadbed for a railroad.

track·er /ˈtrakər/ ▶ **n. 1** a person who tracks someone or something by following their trail. **2** Music a connecting rod in the mechanism of some organs.

track e·vents ▶ **plural n.** track-and-field contests that take place on a running track, as opposed to those involving throwing or other activities. Compare with FIELD EVENTS.

track·ing /ˈtrakiNG/ ▶ **n. 1** the action of tracking someone or something. ■ Electron. the maintenance of a constant difference in frequency between two or more connected circuits or components. ■ the alignment of the wheels of a vehicle. ■ the formation of a conducting path for an electric current over the surface of an insulating material. ■ a control in a videocassette recorder that electronically adjusts the manner in which the head receives signals from the videotape, providing a clearer playback. **2** the practice of putting schoolchildren in groups of the same age and ability to be taught together.

track·ing sta·tion ▶ n. a place from which the movements of missiles, aircraft, or satellites are tracked by radar or radio.

track·lay·er /ˈtrakˌlāər/ ▶ n. **1** a tractor or other vehicle equipped with continuous tracks. **2** another term for TRACKMAN (sense 1).

track·less /ˈtraklis/ ▶ adj. **1** (of land) having no paths or tracks on it: *leading travelers into trackless wastelands.* ■ literary not leaving a track or trace. **2** (of a vehicle or component) not running on a track or tracks.

track light·ing ▶ n. a lighting system in which the lights are fitted on tracks, allowing variable positioning. — **track lights** n.

track·man /ˈtrakmən; -ˌman/ **1** n. (pl. **-men**) a person employed in laying and maintaining railroad track. **2** an athlete in track events.

track rec·ord ▶ n. the best recorded performance in a particular track-and-field event at a particular track. ■ the past achievements or performance of a person, organization, or product.

track shoe ▶ n. a running shoe.

track·side /ˈtrakˌsīd/ ▶ n. **1** the area alongside a railroad track. **2** the area alongside a playing field or a racetrack.

track suit ▶ n. a loose, warm set of clothes consisting of a sweatshirt or light jacket and pants with an elastic or drawstring waist, worn when exercising or as casual wear.

tract[1] /trakt/ ▶ n. **1** an area of indefinite extent, typically a large one: *large tracts of natural forest.* ■ literary an indefinitely large extent of something. **2** a major passage in the body, large bundle of nerve fibers, or other continuous elongated anatomical structure or region: *the digestive tract.* [ME (in the sense 'duration or course (of time)'): from L. *tractus* 'drawing, dragging,' from *trahere* 'draw, pull.']

tract[2] ▶ n. a short treatise in pamphlet form, typically on a religious subject. [ME (denoting a written work treating a particular topic), appar. an abbr. of L. *tractatus* (see TRACTATE). The current sense dates from the early 19th C.]

trac·ta·ble /ˈtraktəbəl/ ▶ adj. (of a person or animal) easy to control or influence. ■ (of a situation or problem) easy to deal with. — **trac·ta·bil·i·ty** /ˌtraktəˈbilitē/ n. **trac·ta·bly** adv. [16th C.: from L. *tractabilis*, from *tractare* 'to handle' (see TRACTATE).]

Trac·tar·i·an·ism /trakˈte(ə)rēəˌnizəm/ ▶ n. another name for OXFORD MOVEMENT. — **Trac·tar·i·an** adj. & n. [19th C.: from *Tracts for the Times*, the title of a series of pamphlets on theological topics started by J. H. Newman and published in Oxford 1833–41, which set out the doctrines on which the movement was based.]

trac·tate /ˈtraktāt/ ▶ n. formal a treatise. ■ a book of the Talmud. [15th C.: from L. *tractatus*, from *tractare* 'to handle,' frequentative of *trahere* 'draw.']

trac·tion /ˈtrakSHən/ ▶ n. **1** the action of drawing or pulling a thing over a surface, esp. a road or track. ■ motive power provided for such movement, esp. on a railroad: *the changeover to diesel and electric traction.* ■ locomotives collectively. **2** Med. the application of a sustained pull on a limb or muscle, esp. in order to maintain the position of a fractured bone or to correct a deformity. **3** the grip of a tire on a road or a wheel on a rail. **4** the degree to which progress can be made; the ability to make progress: *so far no initiative has gained much traction.* [ME (denoting contraction, such as that of a muscle): from Fr., or from med. L. *traction-*, from L. *trahere* 'draw, pull.' Current senses date from the early 19th C.]

trac·tive /ˈtraktiv/ ▶ adj. [attrib.] relating to or denoting the power exerted in pulling, esp. by a vehicle or other machine.

trac·tor /ˈtraktər/ ▶ n. a powerful motor vehicle with large rear wheels, used chiefly on farms for hauling equipment and trailers. ■ a short truck consisting of the driver's cab, designed to pull a large trailer. [18th C. (in the general sense 'someone or something that pulls'): from L., from *tract-* 'pulled,' from the verb *trahere*.]

trac·tor beam ▶ n. (in science fiction) a hypothetical beam of energy that can be used to move objects such as space ships or hold them stationary.

trac·tor-trail·er ▶ n. a vehicle consisting of a tractor or cab with an engine and a separate, attached trailer in which goods can be transported.

trac·tot·o·my /trakˈtätəmē/ ▶ n. the surgical severing of nerve tracts esp. in the medulla of the brain, typically to relieve intractable pain or mental illness, or in research.

trac·trix /ˈtraktriks/ ▶ n. (pl. **trac·tri·ces** /ˌtrakˈtrīsēz; ˈtraktrəˌsēz/) Geom. a curve whose tangents all intercept the *x*-axis at the same distance from the point of contact, being the involute of a catenary. ■ one of a class of curves similarly traced by one end of a rigid rod, whose other end moves along a fixed line or curve. [18th C.: mod. L., fem. of late L. *tractor* 'that which pulls' (see TRACTOR).]

trad /trad/ informal ▶ adj. (esp. of music) traditional: *trad jazz.* ▶ n. traditional jazz or folk music. [1950s: abbr.]

trade /trād/ ▶ n. **1** the action of buying and selling goods and services. ■ dated, esp. derog. the practice of making one's living in business, as opposed to in a profession or from unearned income: *contemptuous of those in trade.* ■ (in sports) a transfer; an exchange. **2** a skilled job, typically one requiring manual skills and special training: *a carpenter by trade.* ■ (**the trade**) [treated as sing. or pl.] the people engaged in a particular area of business. ■ (**the trade**) [treated as sing. or pl.] Brit. people licensed to sell alcoholic drink. ■ informal a person in gay male sexual encounters who is not penetrated sexually and usually considers himself to be heterosexual. **3** (usu. **trades**) a trade wind: *the north-east trades.* ▶ v. [intrans.] buy and sell goods and services. ■ [trans.] buy or sell (a particular item or product). ■ [intrans.] (esp. of shares or currency) be bought and sold at a specified price. ■ [trans.] exchange (something) for something else, typically as a commercial transaction. ■ fig. give and receive (typically insults or blows). ■ [trans.] transfer (a player) to another club or team.

– PHRASAL VERBS **trade down** (or **up**) sell something in order to buy something similar but less (or more) expensive. **trade something in** exchange a used article in part payment for another. **trade something off** exchange something of value, esp. as part of a compromise. **trade on** take advantage of (something), esp. in an unfair way: *the government is trading on fears of inflation.* — **trad·a·ble** (or **trade·a·ble**) adj. [ME (as a n.): from Mid. Low Ger., lit. 'track,' of West Gmc. origin; rel. to TREAD. Early senses included 'course, way of life,' which gave rise in the 16th cent. to 'habitual practice of an occupation,' 'skilled handicraft.' The current verb senses date from the late 16th C.]

trade book ▶ n. a book published by a commercial publisher and intended for general readership.

trade def·i·cit ▶ n. the amount by which the cost of a country's imports exceeds the value of its exports.

trade dis·count ▶ n. a discount on the retail price of something allowed or agreed between traders or to a retailer by a wholesaler.

trade e·di·tion ▶ n. an edition of a book intended for general sale rather than for book clubs or specialist suppliers.

trade-in ▶ n. a used article accepted by a retailer in partial payment for another.

trade jour·nal (also **trade magazine**) ▶ n. a periodical containing news and items of interest concerning a particular trade.

trade·mark /ˈtrādˌmärk/ ▶ n. a symbol, word, or words legally registered or established by use as representing a company or product. ■ fig. a distinctive characteristic or object. ▶ v. [trans.] provide with a trademark. ■ fig. identify (a habit, quality, or way of life) as typical of someone: *his trademarked grandiose style.*

trade name ▶ n. **1** a name that has the status of a trademark. **2** a name by which something is known in a particular trade or profession.

trade-off ▶ n. a balance achieved between two desirable but incompatible features; a compromise.

trade pa·per ▶ n. another term for TRADE JOURNAL.

trad·er /ˈtrādər/ ▶ n. a person who buys and sells goods, currency, or stocks. ■ a merchant ship.

trad·es·can·tia /ˌtradəˈskanCH(ē)ə; -tēə/ ▶ n. an American plant (genus *Tradescantia*, family Commelinaceae) with triangular three-petaled flowers, esp. a tender kind widely grown as a houseplant for its trailing, typically variegated, foliage. [mod. L., named in honor of the English botanist John *Tradescant* (1570–1638).]

trade se·cret ▶ n. a secret device or technique used by a company in manufacturing its products.

trades·man /ˈtrādzmən/ ▶ n. (pl. **-men**) a person engaged in trading or a trade, typically on a relatively small scale.

trades·peo·ple /ˈtrādzˌpēpəl/ ▶ plural n. people engaged in trade.

trade sur·plus ▶ n. the amount by which the value of a country's exports exceeds the cost of its imports.

trade un·ion (Brit. also **trades un·ion**) ▶ n. a labor union of workers in a particular trade. — **trade un·ion·ism** n. **trade un·ion·ist** n.

trade-up ▶ n. a sale of an article in order to buy something similar but more expensive and of higher quality.

trade war ▶ n. a situation in which countries try to damage each other's trade, typically by the imposition of tariffs or quota restrictions.

trade wind /wind/ ▶ n. a wind blowing steadily toward the equator from the northeast in the northern hemisphere or the southeast in the southern hemisphere, esp. at sea. [17th C.: from the phr. *blow trade* 'blow steadily in the same direction.' Because of the importance of these winds to navigation, 18th-cent. etymologists were led erroneously to connect the word *trade* with "commerce."]

trad·ing /ˈtrādiNG/ ▶ n. the action of engaging in trade.

trad·ing card ▶ n. one of a set of cards, such as those depicting professional athletes, that are collected and traded, esp. by children.

trad·ing floor ▶ n. an area within an exchange or a bank or securities house where dealers trade in stocks or other securities.

trad·ing post ▶ n. a store or small settlement established for trading, typically in a remote place.

trad·ing stamp ▶ n. a stamp given by some stores to a customer according to the amount spent, and exchangeable in the appropriate number for various articles.

tra·di·tion /trəˈdiSHən/ ▶ n. **1** the transmission of customs or beliefs from generation to generation, or the fact of being passed on in this way. ■ a long-established custom or belief that has been passed on in this way. ■ [in sing.] an artistic or literary method or style established by an artist, writer, or movement, and subsequently followed by others: *visionary works in the tradition of William Blake.* **2** Theol. a doctrine believed to have divine authority though not in the scriptures, in particular: ■ (in Christianity) doctrine not explicit in the Bible but held to derive from the oral teaching of Jesus and the Apostles. ■ (in Judaism) an ordinance of the oral law not in the Torah but held to have been given by God to Moses. ■ (in Islam) a saying or act ascribed to the Prophet but not recorded in the Koran. See HADITH. — **tra·di·tion·ar·y** /-əˌnerē/ adj. **tra·di·tion·ist** n. **tra·di·tion·less** adj. [ME: from OFr. *tradicion*, or from L. *traditio(n-)*, from *tradere* 'deliver, betray,' from *trans-* 'across' + *dare* 'give.']

tra·di·tion·al /trəˈdisHənl/ ▶ adj. existing in or as part of a tradition; long-established. ■ produced, done, or used in accordance with tradition. ■ habitually done, used, or found. ■ (of a person or group) adhering to tradition, or to a particular tradition: *traditional Elgarians.* ■ (of jazz) in the style of the early 20th century. — **tra·di·tion·al·ly** adv.

tra·di·tion·al·ism /trəˈdisHənlˌizəm/ ▶ n. the upholding or maintenance of tradition, esp. so as to resist change. ■ esp. hist. the theory that all moral and religious truth comes from divine revelation passed on by tradition, human reason being incapable of attaining it. — **tra·di·tion·al·ist** n. & adj. **tra·di·tion·al·is·tic** /trəˌdisHənlˈistik/ adj.

tra·duce /trəˈd(y)o͞os/ ▶ v. [trans.] speak badly of or tell lies about (someone) so as to damage their reputation. — **tra·duce·ment** n. **tra·duc·er** n. [16th C. (in the sense 'transport, transmit'): from L. *traducere* 'lead in front of others, expose to ridicule,' from *trans-* 'over, across' + *ducere* 'to lead.']

Tra·fal·gar, Bat·tle of /trəˈfalgər/ a naval battle (October 21, 1805), off the cape of Trafalgar on the south coast of Spain, in which Napoleon's fleet was defeated by the British fleet under Horatio Nelson.

traf·fic /ˈtrafik/ ▶ n. **1** vehicles moving on a public highway: *a stream of heavy traffic.* ■ a large number of such vehicles. ■ the movement of other forms of transportation or of pedestrians. ■ the transportation of goods or passengers. ■ the messages or signals transmitted through a communications system. **2** the action of dealing or trading in something illegal. **3** archaic dealings or communication between people. ▶ v. (**-ficked, -fick·ing**) [intrans.] deal or trade in something illegal: *individuals who traffic in drugs.* — **traf·fick·er** n. **traf·fic·less** adj. [16th C. (denoting commercial transportation of merchandise or passengers): from Fr. *traffique*, Sp. *tráfico*, or Ital. *traffico*, of unknown origin. Sense 1 dates from the 19th C.]

traf·fic cir·cle ▶ n. a road junction at which traffic moves in one direction around a central island.

traf·fic is·land ▶ n. a small raised area in the middle of a road that provides a safe place for pedestrians to stand and marks a division between two opposing streams of traffic.

traf·fic jam ▶ n. road traffic at or near a standstill because of road construction, an accident, or heavy congestion.

traf·fic light (also **traf·fic sig·nal**) ▶ n. a set of automatically operated colored lights, typically red, amber, and green, for controlling traffic at road junctions crosswalks.

traf·fic pat·tern ▶ n. a pattern in the air above an airport of permitted lanes for aircraft to follow after takeoff or prior to landing. ■ the characteristic distribution of traffic on a route: *the filming had screwed up the traffic patterns in town.*

trag·a·canth /ˈtragəˌkanTH; ˈtraj-/ (also **gum tragacanth**) ▶ n. a white or reddish gum used in the food, textile, and pharmaceutical industries. It is obtained from plants of the pea family belonging to the genus *Astragalus.* [16th C.: from Fr. *tragacante*, via L. from Gk. *tragakantha* 'goat's thorn,' from *tragos* 'goat' (because it is browsed by goats) + *akantha* 'thorn' (referring to the shrub's spines).]

tra·ge·di·an /trəˈjēdēən/ ▶ n. an actor who specializes in tragic roles. ■ a writer of tragedies. [ME (denoting a writer of tragedies): from OFr. *tragediane*, from *tragedie* (see TRAGEDY).]

tra·ge·di·enne /trəˌjēdēˈen/ ▶ n. an actress who specializes in tragic roles. [19th C.: from Fr. *tragédienne*, fem. of *tragédien*.]

trag·e·dy /ˈtrajidē/ ▶ n. (pl. **-dies**) **1** an event causing great suffering, destruction, and distress, such as a serious accident, crime, or natural catastrophe. **2** a play dealing with tragic events and having an unhappy ending, esp. one concerning the downfall of the main character. ■ the dramatic genre represented by such plays: *Greek tragedy.* Compare with COMEDY. [ME: from OFr. *tragedie*, via L. from Gk. *tragōidia*, appar. from *tragos* 'goat' (the reason remains unexplained) + *ōidē* 'song, ode.' Cf. TRAGIC.]

tra·ghet·to /träˈgetō/ ▶ n. (pl. **-ghet·ti** /-ˈgetē/) (in Venice) a landing place or jetty for gondolas. ■ a gondola ferry. [Ital.]

trag·ic /ˈtrajik/ ▶ adj. causing or characterized by extreme distress or sorrow. ■ suffering extreme distress or sorrow. ■ of or relating to tragedy in a literary work. — **trag·i·cal** adj. **trag·i·cal·ly** adv. [16th C.: from Fr. *tragique*, via L. from Gk. *tragikos*, from *tragos* 'goat,' but associated with *tragōidia* (see TRAGEDY).]

trag·ic flaw ▶ n. less technical term for HAMARTIA.

trag·ic i·ro·ny ▶ n. see IRONY[1].

trag·i·com·e·dy /ˌtrajəˈkämidē/ ▶ n. (pl. **-dies**) a play or novel containing elements of both comedy and tragedy. ■ such works as a genre. — **trag·i·com·ic** adj. **trag·i·com·i·cal·ly** adv. [16th C.: from Fr. *tragicomédie* or Ital. *tragicomedia*, based on L. *tragicocomoedia*, from *tragicus* (see TRAGIC) + *comoedia* (see COMEDY).]

trag·o·pan /ˈtragəˌpan/ ▶ n. an Asian pheasant (genus *Tragopan*, family Phasianidae) of highland forests, the male of which has brightly colored plumage used in courtship. [mod. L., from Gk., the name of a horned bird, from *tragos* 'goat' + the name *Pan* (see PAN).]

tra·gus /ˈtrāgəs/ ▶ n. (pl. **-gi** /-jī; -gī/) Anat. & Zool. a prominence on the inner side of the external ear, in front of and partly closing the passage to the organs of hearing. [17th C.: from late L., via L. from Gk. *tragos* 'goat' (with ref. to the characteristic tuft of hair that is often present, likened to a goat's beard).]

tra·hi·son des clercs /trä-ēˈzôN dā ˈkler/ ▶ n. literary a betrayal of intellectual, artistic, or moral standards by writers, academics, or artists. [Fr., lit. 'treason of the scholars,' the title of a book by Julien Benda (1927).]

trail /trāl/ ▶ n. **1** a mark or a series of signs or objects left behind by the passage of someone or something. ■ a track or scent used in following someone or hunting an animal. ■ a part, typically long and thin, stretching behind or hanging down from someone or something: *trails of ivy.* ■ a line of people or things following behind each other: *a trail of ants.* **2** a beaten path through rough country such as a forest or moor. ■ a route planned or followed for a particular purpose: *on the campaign trail* ■ (also **ski trail**) a downhill ski run or cross-country ski route. **3** short for TRAILER (sense 2). **4** the rear end of a gun carriage, resting or sliding on the ground when the gun is unlimbered. ▶ v. **1** draw or be drawn along the ground or other surface behind someone or something: [trans.] *he trailed a hand through the water* | [intrans.] *her robe trailed along the ground.* ■ [intrans.] (typically of a plant) grow or hang over the edge of something or along the ground. ■ [trans.] follow (a person or animal), typically by using marks, signs, or scent left behind. ■ [intrans.] be losing to an opponent in a game or contest. **2** [intrans.] walk or move slowly or wearily. ■ (of the voice or a speaker) fade gradually before stopping: *her voice trailed away.* **3** [trans.] advertise (something, esp. a film or program) in advance by broadcasting extracts or details. **4** [trans.] apply (slip) through a nozzle or spout to decorate ceramic ware. [ME (as a v.): from OFr. *traillier* 'to tow,' or Mid. Low Ger. *treilen* 'haul (a boat),' based on L. *tragula* 'dragnet,' from *trahere* 'to pull.']

trail bike ▶ n. a light motorcycle for use in rough terrain.

trail·blaz·er /ˈtrālˌblāzər/ ▶ n. a person who makes a new track through wild country. ■ a pioneer; an innovator. — **trail·blaz·ing** n. & adj.

trail boss ▶ n. a foreman in charge of a cattle drive.

trail·er /ˈtrālər/ ▶ n. **1** an unpowered vehicle towed by another, in particular: ■ the rear section of a tractor-trailer. ■ an open cart. ■ a platform for transporting a boat. ■ an unpowered vehicle equipped for living in, typically used during vacations. **2** an excerpt or series of excerpts from a movie or program used to advertise it in advance; a preview. **3** a thing that trails, esp. a trailing plant. ▶ v. [trans.] **1** advertise (a movie or program) in advance by broadcasting excerpts or details. **2** transport (something) by trailer.

trail·er park (also **trail·er court**) ▶ n. an area with special amenities where trailers are parked and used for recreation or as permanent homes. ■ [as adj.] lacking refinement, taste, or quality; coarse.

trail·er truck ▶ n. a tractor-trailer.

trail·head /ˈtrālˌhed/ ▶ n. the place where a trail begins.

trail·ing ar·bu·tus ▶ n. see ARBUTUS.

trail·ing edge ▶ n. the rear edge of a moving body, esp. an aircraft wing or propeller blade. ■ Electron. the part of a pulse in which the amplitude diminishes.

trail mix ▶ n. a mixture of dried fruit and nuts eaten as a snack food, originally by hikers and campers.

train /trān/ ▶ v. **1** [trans.] teach (a person or animal) a particular skill or type of behavior through practice and instruction over a period of time. ■ [intrans.] be taught in such a way: *he trained as a classicist.* ■ [usu. as adj.] (**trained**) cause (a mental or physical faculty) to be sharp, discerning, or developed as a result of instruction or practice: *an alert mind and trained eye.* ■ cause (a plant) to grow in a particular direction or into a required shape. ■ [intrans.] undertake a course of exercise and diet in order to reach or maintain a high level of physical fitness, typically in preparation for participating in a specific sport or event. ■ cause to undertake such a course of exercise: *the horse was trained in Paris.* ■ [intrans.] (**train down**) reduce one's weight through diet and exercise in order to be fit for a particular event. **2** [trans.] (**train something on**) point or aim something, typically a gun or camera, at. **3** [intrans.] dated go by train. **4** [trans.] archaic entice (someone) by offering pleasure or a reward. ▶ n. **1** a series of railroad cars moved as a unit by a locomotive or by integral motors. **2** a succession of vehicles or pack animals traveling in the same direction: *a camel train.* ■ a retinue of attendants accompanying an important person. ■ a series of connected events: *a train of events that will cause harm.* ■ a series of gears or other connected parts in machinery. **3** a long piece of material attached to the back of a formal dress or robe that trails along the ground. **4** a trail of gunpowder for firing an explosive charge.

– PHRASES **train of thought** the way in which someone reaches a conclusion; a line of reasoning. — **train·a·bil·i·ty** /ˌtrānəˈbilitē/ n. **train·a·ble** adj. [ME (as a n. in the sense 'delay'): from OFr. *train* (masc.), *traine* (fem.), from *trahiner* (v.), from L. *trahere* 'pull, draw.']

train·band /ˈtrānˌband/ ▶ n. hist. a division of civilian soldiers in London and other areas of England, in particular in the Stuart period.

train·ee /trāˈnē/ ▶ n. a person undergoing training for a particular job or profession. — **train·ee·ship** n.

train·er /ˈtrānər/ ▶ n. **1** a person who trains people or animals. ■ informal an aircraft or simulator used to train pilots. **2** a person whose job is to provide medical assistance to athletes. **3** Brit. a soft shoe, suitable for sports or casual wear.

train·ing /ˈtrāniNG/ ▶ n. the action of teaching a person or animal a particular skill or type of behavior. ■ the action of undertaking a course of

exercise and diet in preparation for a sporting event.
– PHRASES **in** (or **out of**) **training** undergoing (or no longer undergoing) physical training for a sporting event. ■ physically fit (or unfit) as a result of the amount of training one has undertaken.

train·ing ship ▶ n. a ship on which people are taught sailing and related skills.

train·ing ta·ble ▶ n. a table in a dining hall where athletes in training are served specially prepared meals.

train·ing wheels ▶ plural n. a pair of small supporting wheels fitted on either side of the rear wheel of a child's bicycle.

train·load /'trān,lōd/ ▶ n. a number of people or a quantity of a commodity transported by train.

train·man /'trānmən; -,man/ ▶ n. (pl. **-men**) a railroad employee who works on trains.

train oil ▶ n. esp. hist. oil obtained from the blubber of a whale (and formerly of other sea creatures), esp. the right whale. [16th C.: from obs. *train* 'train oil,' from Mid. Low Ger. *trān*, MDu. *traen*, lit. 'tear' (because it was extracted in droplets).]

traipse /trāps/ ▶ v. [intrans.] walk or move wearily or reluctantly. ■ walk about casually or needlessly. ▶ n. **1** [in sing.] a tedious or tiring journey on foot. **2** archaic a slovenly woman. [16th C. (as a v.): of unknown origin. The noun is first recorded in sense 2 in the late 17th C.]

trait /trāt/ ▶ n. a distinguishing quality or characteristic, typically one belonging to a person. ■ a genetically determined characteristic. [16th C.: from Fr., from L. *tractus* 'drawing, pulling' (see TRACT[1]).]

trai·tor /'trātər/ ▶ n. a person who betrays a friend, country, principle, etc.
– PHRASAL VERBS **turn traitor** betray a group or person. — **trai·tor·ous** /-tərəs/ adj. **trai·tor·ous·ly** /-rəslē/ adv. [ME: from OFr. *traitour*, from L. *traditor*, from *tradere* 'hand over.']

Tra·jan /'trājən/ (c.53–117), Roman emperor 98–117; Latin name *Marcus Ulpius Traianus*.

tra·jec·to·ry /trə'jektərē/ ▶ n. (pl. **-ries**) **1** the path described by a projectile flying or an object moving under the action of given forces. **2** Geom. a curve or surface cutting a family of curves or surfaces at a constant angle. [17th C.: from mod. L. *trajectoria* (fem.), from L. *traject-* 'thrown across,' from the verb *traicere*, from *trans-* 'across' + *jacere* 'to throw.']

Tra·keh·ner /trä'kānər/ ▶ n. **1** a saddle horse of a light breed first developed at the Trakehnen stud farm near Kaliningrad in Russia. **2** a type of fence used in horse trials, consisting of a ditch spanned by center rails. [20th C.: from Ger.]

tra la /trä 'lä/ (also **tra-la** or **tra-la-la**) ▶ exclam. esp. ironic expressing joy or gaiety: *off to his life and wife, tra la.* [19th C.: imitative of a fanfare or of the refrain of a song.]

Tra·lee /trə'lē/ a city on the southwestern coast of the Republic of Ireland; pop. 17,200.

tram /tram/ (also **tram·car**) ▶ n. **1** Brit. a trolley car. **2** a cable car. **3** hist. a low four-wheeled cart or barrow used in coal mines. [16th C. (denoting a shaft of a barrow; also in sense 3): from Mid. Low Ger. and MDu. *trame* 'beam, barrow shaft.']

Tra·mi·ner /trə'mēnər/ ▶ n. a variety of white wine grape grown chiefly in Germany and Alsace. ■ a white wine with a perfumed bouquet made from this grape. [named after the Italian village *Termeno*.]

tram·mel /'traməl/ ▶ n. **1** (usu. **trammels**) literary a restriction or impediment to someone's freedom of action: *free from the trammels of materialism.* **2** (also **tram·mel net**) a set-net consisting of three layers of netting, designed so that a fish entering through one of the large-meshed outer sections will push part of the finer-meshed central section through the large meshes on the further side, forming a pocket in which the fish is trapped. **3** an instrument consisting of a board with two grooves intersecting at right angles, in which the two ends of a beam compass can slide to draw an ellipse. [18th C.: so named because the motion of the beam is 'restricted' by the grooves.] ■ a beam compass. **4** a hook in a fireplace for a kettle. ▶ v. (**-meled, -mel·ing**; Brit. **-melled, -mel·ling**) [trans.] deprive of freedom of action. [ME (sense 2): from OFr. *tramail*, from a med. L. var. of *trimaculum*, perh. from L. *tri-* 'three' + *macula* 'mesh.']

tra·mon·ta·na /,trämən'tänə/ ▶ n. a cold north wind blowing in Italy or the adjoining regions of the Adriatic and Mediterranean. [Ital., 'north wind, North Star' (see TRAMONTANE).]

tra·mon·tane /trə'mäntān; 'tramən,tān/ ▶ adj. rare traveling to, situated on, or living on the other side of mountains. ■ archaic (esp. from the Italian point of view) foreign; barbarous. ▶ n. **1** another term for TRAMONTANA. **2** archaic a person who lives on the other side of mountains (used in particular by Italians to refer to people beyond the Alps). [ME (as a n. denoting the Pole Star): from Ital. *tramontana* 'North Star, north wind,' *tramontani* 'people living beyond the Alps,' from L. *transmontanus* 'beyond the mountains,' from *trans-* 'across' + *mons, mont-* 'mountain.']

tramp /tramp/ ▶ v. [intrans.] walk heavily or noisily. ■ walk through or over a place wearily or reluctantly and for long distances. ■ [trans.] tread or stamp on. ▶ n. **1** a person who travels from place to place on foot in search of work or as a vagrant or beggar. **2** [in sing.] the sound of heavy steps, typically of several people: *the tramp of marching feet.* **3** [in sing.] a long walk, typically a tiring one. **4** [usu. as adj.] a cargo vessel that carries goods among many different ports rather than sailing a fixed route: *a tramp steamer.* **5** informal a promiscuous woman. **6** a metal plate protecting the sole of a boot. ■ the top of the blade of a spade. — **tramp·er** n. **tramp·ish** adj. [ME (as a v.): prob. of Low Ger. origin. The noun dates from the mid 17th C.]

tram·ple /'trampəl/ ▶ v. [trans.] tread on and crush: *the fence had been trampled down* | [intrans.] *her dog trampled on his tulips.* ■ [intrans.] (**trample on/over**) fig. treat with contempt. ▶ n. literary an act or the sound of trampling. — **tram·pler** n. [ME (in the sense 'tread heavily'): frequentative of TRAMP.]

tram·po·line /'trampə,lēn/ ▶ n. a strong fabric sheet connected by springs to a frame, used as a springboard and landing area in doing acrobatic or gymnastic exercises. ▶ v. [intrans.] do acrobatic or gymnastic exercises on a trampoline as a recreation or sport. ■ leap or rebound from something with a springy base. — **tram·po·lin·er** n. **tram·po·lin·ist** n. [18th C.: from Ital. *trampolino*, from *trampoli* 'stilts.']

tram road ▶ n. hist. a road with wooden, stone, or metal tracks for wheels, used by wagons in mining districts.

tram·way /'tram,wā/ ▶ n. **1** Brit. a set of rails that forms the route for a streetcar. ■ a streetcar system. **2** another term for CABLE CAR. **3** hist. another term for TRAM ROAD.

trance /trans/ ▶ n. a half-conscious state characterized by an absence of response to external stimuli, typically as induced by hypnosis or entered by a medium. ■ a state of abstraction. ■ (also **trance music**) a type of electronic dance music characterized by hypnotic rhythms and sounds. ▶ v. [trans.] literary put into a trance: *she's been tranced.* — **tranced·ly** /'transtlē; 'transid-/ adv. **trance·like** adj. [ME (orig. as a v. in the sense 'be in a trance'): from OFr. *transir* 'depart, fall into trance,' from L. *transire* 'go across.']

tranche /tränsh/ ▶ n. a portion of something, esp. money: *they released the first* **tranche** *of the loan.* [15th C.: from OFr., lit. 'slice.']

trank /trangk/ (also **tranq**) ▶ n. informal term for TRANQUILIZER. — **tranked** adj.

tran·nie /'tranē/ (also **tran·ny**) ▶ n. informal **1** a transvestite. **2** the transmission in a motor vehicle. **3** a photographic transparency. **4** esp. Brit. a transistor radio. [1960s: abbr.]

tran·quil /'trangkwəl/ ▶ adj. free from disturbance; calm: *her tranquil gaze* | *the sea was tranquil.* — **tran·quil·i·ty** /trang'kwilitē/ (also **tran·quil·li·ty**) n. **tran·quil·ly** adv. [ME: from Fr. *tranquille* or L. *tranquillus*.]

tran·quil·ize /'trangkwə,līz/ (Brit. **tran·quil·lize**) ▶ v. [trans.] [usu. as adj.] (**tranquilizing**) (of a drug) have a calming or sedative effect on. ■ administer such a drug to (a person or animal). ■ literary make tranquil: *joys that tranquilize the mind.*

tran·quil·iz·er /'trangkwə,līzər/ (Brit. **tran·quil·liz·er**) ▶ n. a medicinal drug taken to reduce tension or anxiety.

trans /tranz; trans/ ▶ adj. Chem. denoting or relating to a molecular structure in which two particular atoms or groups lie on opposite sides of a given plane in the molecule, in particular denoting an isomer in which substituents at opposite ends of a carbon–carbon double bond are also on opposite sides of the bond: *the trans isomer of stilbene.* Compare with CIS. [independent usage of TRANS-.]

trans. ▶ abbr. ■ transaction; transactions. ■ transfer. ■ transferred. ■ transformer. ■ transit. ■ transitive. ■ translated. ■ translation. ■ translator. ■ transparent. ■ transportation. ■ transpose. ■ transverse.

trans- ▶ prefix **1** across; beyond: *transcontinental.* ■ on or to the other side of: *transatlantic* | *transalpine.* Often contrasted with CIS-. **2** through: *transonic.* ■ into another state or place: *transform.* ■ surpassing; transcending: *transfinite.* **3** Chem. (usu. *trans-*) denoting molecules with trans arrangements of substituents: trans-*1, 2-dichloroethylene.* ■ Genet. denoting alleles on different chromosomes. [from L. *trans* 'across.']

trans·act /tran'sakt; -'zakt/ ▶ v. [trans.] conduct or carry out (business). — **trans·ac·tor** /-'aktər/ n. [16th C.: from L. *transact-* 'driven through,' from the verb *transigere*, from *trans-* 'through' + *agere* 'do, lead.']

trans·ac·tion /tran'sakshən; -'zak-/ ▶ n. an instance of buying or selling something; a business deal. ■ the action of conducting business. ■ an exchange or interaction between people. ■ (**transactions**) published reports of proceedings at the meetings of a learned society. ■ an input message to a computer system that must be dealt with as a single unit of work. — **trans·ac·tion·al** /-shənl/ adj. **trans·ac·tion·al·ly** /-shənl-ē/ adv. [ME (as a term in Roman law): from late L. *transactio(n-)*, from *transigere* 'drive through' (see TRANSACT).]

trans·ac·tion·al a·nal·y·sis ▶ n. a system of popular psychology based on the idea that one's behavior and social relationships reflect an interchange between parental (critical and nurturing), adult (rational), and childlike (intuitive and dependent) aspects of personality established early in life.

trans·ac·ti·va·tion /,trans,aktə'vāshən; -,tranz-/ ▶ n. Biochem. activation of a gene at one locus by the presence of a particular gene at another locus, typically following infection by a virus.

Trans-Alaska Pipeline /'transə'laskə; 'tranz-/ an oil pipeline in Alaska that extends for 800 miles (1,300 km) from Prudhoe Bay to Prince William Sound.

trans·al·pine /trans'alpīn; tranz-/ ▶ adj. of, related to, or situated in the area beyond the Alps, in particular as viewed from Italy. See also GAUL[1]. ■ crossing the Alps: *transalpine road freight.* [16th C.: from L. *transalpinus*, from *trans-* 'across' + *alpinus* (see ALPINE).]

trans·am·i·nase /trans'amə,nās; -,nāz; tranz-/ ▶ **n.** Biochem. an enzyme that catalyzes a particular transamination reaction.

trans·am·i·na·tion /trans,amə'nāsHən; tranz-/ ▶ **n.** Biochem. the transfer of an amino group from one molecule to another, esp. from an amino acid to a keto acid. — **trans·am·i·nate** /-,nāt/ **v.**

trans·at·lan·tic /,trans-ət'lantik; ,tranz-/ ▶ **adj.** crossing the Atlantic: *a transatlantic flight.* ■ concerning countries on both sides of the Atlantic: *the transatlantic relationship.* ■ of, relating to, or situated on the other side of the Atlantic; British or European (from an American point of view). — **trans·at·lan·ti·cal·ly** adv.

trans·ax·le /,trans'aksəl; ,tranz-/ ▶ **n.** an integral driving axle and differential gear in a motor vehicle.

Trans-Canada Highway /,trans'kanədə; ,tranz-/ a route, 4,860 miles (7,820 km) long, between Victoria in British Columbia and Saint John's in Newfoundland.

Trans·cau·ca·sia /,trans,kô'kāzHə; ,tranz-/ a region that lies to the south of the Caucasus Mountains, between the Black Sea and the Caspian Sea, and that comprises the present-day republics of Georgia, Armenia, and Azerbaijan. — **Trans·cau·ca·sian** adj.

trans·ceiv·er /tran'sēvər/ ▶ **n.** a device that can both transmit and receive communications, in particular a combined radio transmitter and receiver. [1930s: blend of TRANSMITTER and RECEIVER.]

tran·scend /tran'send/ ▶ **v.** [trans.] be or go beyond the range or limits of (something abstract, typically a conceptual field or division). ■ surpass (a person or an achievement). [ME: from OFr. *transcendre* or L. *transcendere*, from *trans-* 'across' + *scandere* 'climb.']

tran·scend·ent /tran'sendənt/ ▶ **adj.** beyond or above the range of normal or merely physical human experience: *a transcendent level of knowledge.* ■ surpassing the ordinary; exceptional. ■ (of God) existing apart from and not subject to the limitations of the material universe. ■ (in scholastic philosophy) higher than or not included in any of Aristotle's ten categories. ■ (in Kantian philosophy) not realizable in experience. — **tran·scend·ence** n. **tran·scend·en·cy** n. **tran·scend·ent·ly** adv. [ME: from L. *transcendent-* 'climbing over,' from the verb *transcendere* (see TRANSCEND).]

tran·scen·den·tal /,transen'dentl; -sən-/ ▶ **adj.** **1** of or relating to a spiritual or nonphysical realm. ■ (in Kantian philosophy) presupposed in and necessary to experience; a priori. ■ relating to or denoting Transcendentalism. **2** Math. (of a number, e.g., *e* or π) real but not a root of an algebraic equation with rational roots. ■ (of a function) not capable of being produced by the algebraical operations of addition, multiplication, and involution, or the inverse operations. — **tran·scen·den·tal·ize** v. **tran·scen·den·tal·ly** adv. [17th C.: from med. L. *transcendentalis* (see TRANSCENDENT).]

tran·scen·den·tal·ism /,transen'dentl,izəm/ ▶ **n.** **1** (**Transcendentalism**) a 19th-century idealistic philosophical and social movement that taught that divinity pervades all nature and humanity. **2** a system developed by Immanuel Kant, based on the idea that, in order to understand the nature of reality, one must first examine and analyze the reasoning process that governs the nature of experience. — **tran·scen·den·tal·ist** (also **Tran·scen·den·tal·ist**) n. & adj.

Tran·scen·den·tal Med·i·ta·tion (abbr.: **TM**) ▶ **n.** trademark a technique for detaching oneself from anxiety and promoting harmony and self-realization by meditation and repetition of a mantra.

trans·code /,trans'kōd; ,tranz-/ ▶ **v.** [trans.] convert (language or information) from one form of coded representation to another.

trans·con·duct·ance /,trans-kən'dəktəns; ,tranz-/ ▶ **n.** Electron. the ratio of the change in current at the output terminal to the change in the voltage at the input terminal of an active device.

trans·con·ti·nen·tal /,trans-käntə'nentl; ,tranz-/ ▶ **adj.** (esp. of a railroad line) crossing a continent. ■ extending across or relating to two or more continents: *a transcontinental radio audience.* ▶ **n.** Canadian a transcontinental railroad or train. — **trans·con·ti·nen·tal·ly** adv.

trans·cor·ti·cal /,trans'kôrtikəl; ,tranz-/ ▶ **adj.** Physiol. of or relating to nerve pathways that cross the cerebral cortex of the brain.

tran·scribe /tran'skrīb/ ▶ **v.** [trans.] put (thoughts, speech, or data) into written or printed form. ■ transliterate (foreign characters) or write or type out (shorthand, notes, or other abbreviated forms) into ordinary characters or full sentences. ■ arrange (a piece of music) for a different instrument, voice, or group of these. ■ Biochem. synthesize (a nucleic acid, typically RNA) using an existing nucleic acid, typically DNA, as a template, thus copying the genetic information in the latter. — **tran·scrib·er** n. [16th C. (in the sense 'make a copy in writing'): from L. *transcribere*, from *trans-* 'across' + *scribere* 'write.']

tran·script /'tran,skript/ ▶ **n.** a written or printed version of material originally presented in another medium. ■ Biochem. a length of RNA or DNA that has been transcribed respectively from a DNA or RNA template. ■ an official record of a student's work, showing courses taken and grades achieved. — **tran·scrip·tive** /tran'skriptiv/ adj. [ME: from OFr. *transcrit*, from L. *transcriptum*, neut. past part. of *transcribere* (see TRANSCRIBE). The spelling change in the 15th C. was due to association with the Latin.]

tran·scrip·tase /tran'skriptās; -tāz/ ▶ **n.** Biochem. an enzyme that catalyzes the formation of RNA from a DNA template during transcription. Also called **RNA polymerase**.

tran·scrip·tion /tran'skripsHən/ ▶ **n.** a written or printed representation of something. ■ the action or process of transcribing something. ■ an arrangement of a piece of music for a different instrument, voice, or number of these. ■ a form in which a speech sound or a foreign character is represented. ■ Biochem. the process by which genetic information represented by a sequence of DNA nucleotides is copied into newly synthesized molecules of RNA, with the DNA serving as a template. — **tran·scrip·tion·al** /-sHənl/ adj. **tran·scrip·tion·al·ly** /-sHənl-ē/ adv. **tran·scrip·tion·ist** n. [16th C.: from Fr., or from L. *transcriptio(n-)*, from the verb *transcribere* (see TRANSCRIBE).]

trans·cul·tur·al /,trans'kəlcHərəl; ,tranz-/ ▶ **adj.** relating to or involving more than one culture; cross-cultural: *the possibility of transcultural understanding.*

trans·cu·ta·ne·ous /,trans-kyo͞o'tānēəs; ,tranz-/ ▶ **adj.** existing, applied, or measured across the depth of the skin.

trans·der·mal /,trans'dərməl; ,tranz-/ ▶ **adj.** relating to or denoting the application of a medicine or drug through the skin, typically by using an adhesive patch, so that it is absorbed slowly into the body.

trans·duc·er /trans'd(y)o͞osər; tranz-/ ▶ **n.** a device that converts variations in a physical quantity, such as pressure or brightness, into an electrical signal, or vice versa. — **trans·duce** v. **trans·duc·tion** /-'dəksHən/ n. [1920s: from L. *transducere* 'lead across' (from *trans-* 'across' + *ducere* 'lead') + -ER[1].]

tran·sect /tran'sekt/ tech. ▶ **v.** [trans.] cut across or make a transverse section in. ▶ **n.** a straight line or narrow section through an object or natural feature or across the earth's surface, along which observations are made or measurements taken. — **tran·sec·tion** /-'seksHən/ n. [17th C. (as a verb): from TRANS- 'through' + L. *sect-* 'divided by cutting' (from the verb *secare*).]

tran·sept /'transept/ ▶ **n.** (in a cross-shaped church) either of the two parts forming the arms of the cross shape, projecting at right angles from the nave: *the north transept.* — **tran·sep·tal** /tran'septl/ adj. [16th C.: from mod. L. *transeptum* (see TRANS-, SEPTUM).]

trans-fat ▶ **n.** another term for TRANS-FATTY ACID.

trans-fat·ty ac·id ▶ **n.** an unsaturated fatty acid with a trans arrangement of the carbon atoms adjacent to its double bonds. Such acids occur esp. in margarines and cooking oils as a result of the hydrogenation process.

trans·fect /trans'fekt/ ▶ **v.** [trans.] Microbiol. infect (a cell) with free nucleic acid. ■ introduce (genetic material) in this way. — **trans·fec·tant** /-ənt/ n. **trans·fec·tion** /trans'feksHən/ n. [1960s: from TRANS- 'across' + INFECT, or a blend of TRANSFER and INFECT.]

trans·fer ▶ **v.** /trans'fər; 'transfər/ (**-ferred, -fer·ring**) [trans.] move (someone or something) from one place to another. ■ move or cause to move to another group, occupation, or service: [intrans.] *she transferred to the Physics Department* | [trans.] *employees have been transferred to the installation team.* ■ enroll in a different school or college. ■ (in professional sports) move or cause to move to another team: [intrans.] *he transferred to the Dodgers* | [trans.] *when a player is transferred to the minors.* ■ [intrans.] change to another place, route, or means of transportation during a journey. ■ make over the possession of (property, a right, or a responsibility) to someone else. ■ convey (a drawing or design) from one surface to another. ■ [usu. as adj.] (**transferred**) change (the sense of a word or phrase) by extension or metaphor. ■ redirect (a telephone call) to another line or extension. ▶ **n.** /'transfər/ an act of moving something or someone to another place. ■ a change of employment, typically within an organization or field. ■ a student who has enrolled in a different school or college: [as adj.] *transfer students.* ■ a conveyance of property, esp. stocks, from one person to another. ■ a small colored picture or design on paper that can be transferred to another surface by being pressed or heated. ■ a ticket allowing a passenger to change from one public transportation vehicle to another as part of a single journey. — **trans·fer·ee** /,transfə'rē/ n. **trans·fer·or** /trans'fərər; 'transfərər/ n. (esp. Law) **trans·fer·rer** n. [ME (as a v.): from Fr. *transférer* or L. *transferre*, from *trans-* 'across' + *ferre* 'to bear.' The earliest use of the noun (late 17th C.) was as a legal term in the sense 'conveyance of property.']

trans·fer·a·ble /trans'fərəbəl; 'transfərə-/ ▶ **adj.** (typically of financial assets, liabilities, or legal rights) able to be transferred or made over to the possession of another person. — **trans·fer·a·bil·i·ty** /,transfərə'bilitē/ n.

trans·fer·ase /'transfə,rās; -,rāz/ ▶ **n.** Biochem. an enzyme that catalyzes the transfer of a particular group from one molecule to another.

trans·fer·ence /trans'fərəns; 'transfər-/ ▶ **n.** the action of transferring something or the process of being transferred: *education involves the transference of knowledge.* ■ Psychoanal. the redirection to a substitute, usually a therapist, of emotions that were originally felt in childhood (in a phase of analysis called **transference neurosis**).

trans·fer or·bit ▶ **n.** a trajectory by which a spacecraft can pass from one orbit to another at a higher altitude, esp. a geostationary orbit.

trans·fer pay·ment ▶ **n.** Econ. a payment made or income received in which no goods or services are being paid for, such as a benefit payment or subsidy.

trans·fer·ral /trans'fərəl/ ▶ **n.** an act of transferring someone or something.

trans·fer·rin /trans'ferin/ ▶ **n.** Biochem. a protein of the beta globulin group that binds and transports iron in blood serum. [1940s: from TRANS- 'across' + L. *ferrum* 'iron' + -IN[1].]

trans·fer RNA ▶ **n.** Biochem. RNA consisting of folded molecules that transport amino acids from the cytoplasm of a cell to a ribosome.

trans·fig·u·ra·tion /,transfigyə'rāsHən/ ▶ **n.** a complete change of form or appearance into a more beautiful or spiritual state. ■ (**the Transfiguration**) Christ's appearance in radiant glory to three of his disciples (Matthew 17:2, Mark 9:2–3, Luke 9:28–36). ■ the church festival commemorating this, held on August 6. [ME (with biblical ref.): from OFr., or from L. *transfiguratio(n-)*, from the verb *transfigurare* (see TRANSFIGURE).]

trans·fig·ure /trans'figyər/ ▶ v. [trans.] (usu. **be transfigured**) transform into something more beautiful or elevated: *the world is made luminous and is transfigured.* [ME: from OFr. *transfigurer* or L. *transfigurare*, from *trans-* 'across' + *figura* 'figure.']

trans·fi·nite /trans'fīnīt/ ▶ adj. **1** Math. relating to or denoting a number corresponding to an infinite set in the way that a natural number denotes or counts members of a finite set. **2** beyond or surpassing the finite.

trans·fix /trans'fiks/ ▶ v. [trans.] **1** (usu. **be transfixed**) cause (someone) to become motionless with horror, wonder, or astonishment. **2** pierce with a sharp implement or weapon. — **trans·fix·ion** /-'fiksHən/ n. [16th C. (in sense 2): from L. *transfix-* 'pierced through,' from the verb *transfigere*, from *trans-* 'across' + *figere* 'fix, fasten.']

trans·form /trans'fôrm/ ▶ v. [trans.] make a thorough or dramatic change in the form, appearance, or character of. ■ [intrans.] undergo such a change: *an automobile that transformed into a boat.* ■ change the voltage of (an electric current). ■ Math. change (a mathematical entity) by transformation. ▶ n. Math. & Ling. the product of a transformation. ■ a rule for making a transformation. — **trans·form·a·ble** adj. **trans·form·a·tive** /-'fôrmətiv/ adj. [ME (as a v.): from OFr. *transformer* or L. *transformare* (see TRANS-, FORM).]

trans·for·ma·tion /,transfər'māsHən/ ▶ n. a thorough or dramatic change in form or appearance. ■ a metamorphosis during the life cycle of an animal. ■ Physics the induced or spontaneous change of one element into another by a nuclear process. ■ Math. & Logic a process by which one figure, expression, or function is converted into another that is equivalent in some important respect but is differently expressed or represented. ■ Ling. a process by which an element in the underlying deep structure of a sentence is converted to an element in the surface structure. ■ Biol. the genetic alteration of a cell by introduction of extraneous DNA, esp. by a plasmid. ■ Biol. the heritable modification of a cell from its normal state to a malignant state. [ME: from OFr., or from late L. *transformatio(n-)*, from the verb *transformare* (see TRANSFORM).]

trans·for·ma·tion·al /,transfər'māsHənl/ ▶ adj. relating to or involving transformation or transformations. ■ of or relating to transformational grammar. — **trans·for·ma·tion·al·ly** adv.

trans·for·ma·tion·al gram·mar ▶ n. Ling. a type of grammar that describes a language in terms of transformations applied to an underlying deep structure in order to generate the surface structure of sentences that can actually occur. See also GENERATIVE GRAMMAR.

trans·form·er /trans'fôrmər/ ▶ n. **1** an apparatus for reducing or increasing the voltage of an alternating current. **2** a person or thing that transforms something.

trans·form fault ▶ n. Geol. a strike-slip fault occurring at the boundary between two plates of the earth's crust.

trans·fuse /trans'fyo͞oz/ ▶ v. [trans.] **1** Med. transfer (blood or its components) from one person or animal to another. ■ inject (liquid) into a blood vessel to replace lost fluid. **2** cause (something or someone) to be permeated or infused by something: *we became transfused by a radiance of joy.* [ME (in the sense 'cause to pass from one person to another'): from L. *transfus-* 'poured from one container to another,' from the verb *transfundere*, from *trans-* 'across' + *fundere* 'pour.']

trans·fu·sion /trans'fyo͞ozHən/ ▶ n. an act of transfusing donated blood, blood products, or other fluid into the circulatory system of a person or animal.

trans·gen·der /tranz'jendər; trans-/ (also **trans·gen·dered**) ▶ adj. identified with a gender other than the biological one.

trans·gen·ic /trans'jenik; tranz-/ ▶ adj. Biol. of, relating to, or denoting an organism that contains genetic material into which DNA from an unrelated organism has been artificially introduced. [1980s: from TRANS- 'across' + GENE + -IC.]

trans·gen·ics /trans'jeniks; tranz-/ ▶ plural n. [usu. treated as sing.] the branch of biology concerned with transgenic organisms.

trans·glob·al /trans'glōbəl; tranz-/ ▶ adj. (of an expedition, enterprise, search, or network) moving or extending across or around the world.

trans·gress /trans'gres; tranz-/ ▶ v. [trans.] infringe or go beyond the bounds of (a moral principle or other established standard of behavior): *she had transgressed an unwritten social law* | [intrans.] *they must control the impulses that lead them to transgress.* ■ Geol. (of the sea) spread over (an area of land). — **trans·gres·sion** /-'gresHən/ n. **trans·gres·sor** /-'gresər/ n. [15th C.: from OFr. *transgresser* or L. *transgress-* 'stepped across,' from the verb *transgredi*, from *trans-* 'across' + *gradi* 'go.']

trans·gres·sive /trans'gresiv; tranz-/ ▶ adj. involving a violation of accepted or imposed boundaries, esp. those of social acceptability. ■ of or relating to fiction, cinematography, or art in which orthodox cultural, moral, and artistic boundaries are challenged by the representation of unconventional behavior and the use of experimental forms. ■ Geol. (of a stratum) overlapping others unconformably, esp. as a result of marine transgression.

tran·ship ▶ v. var. of TRANSSHIP.

trans·his·tor·i·cal /,trans-hi'stôrikəl; -'stär; ,tranz-/ ▶ adj. transcending historical boundaries; eternal: *femininity may not be a transhistorical absolute.*

trans·hu·mance /trans'(h)yo͞oməns; tranz-/ ▶ n. the action or practice of moving livestock from one grazing ground to another in a seasonal cycle, typically to lowlands in winter and highlands in summer. — **trans·hu·mant** /-mənt/ adj. [20th C.: from Fr., from the verb *transhumer*, based on L. *trans-* 'across' + *humus* 'ground.']

tran·sient /'transHənt; -zHənt; -zēənt/ ▶ adj. lasting only for a short time; impermanent. ■ staying or working in a place for only a short time. ▶ n. **1** a person who is staying or working in a place for only a short time. **2** a momentary variation in current, voltage, or frequency. — **tran·sience** n. **tran·sien·cy** n. **tran·sient·ly** adv. [16th C.: from L. *transient-* 'going across,' from the verb *transire*, from *trans-* 'across' + *ire* 'go.']

tran·si·ent is·che·mic at·tack (abbr.: **TIA**) ▶ n. technical term for MINISTROKE.

trans·il·lu·mi·nate /,trans-ə'lo͞omə,nāt; ,tranz-/ ▶ v. [trans.] pass strong light through (an organ or part of the body) in order to detect disease or abnormality. — **trans·il·lu·mi·na·tion** /-ə,lo͞omə'nāsHən/ n.

tran·sis·tor /tran'zistər/ ▶ n. a semiconductor device with three connections, capable of amplification in addition to rectification. ■ (also **transistor radio**) a portable radio using circuits containing transistors rather than vacuum tubes. [1940s: from TRANSCONDUCTANCE, on the pattern of words such as *varistor*.]

tran·sis·tor·ize /tran'zistə,rīz/ ▶ v. [trans.] [usu. as adj.] (**transistorized**) design or make with transistors rather than vacuum tubes: *a transistorized tape recorder.* — **tran·sis·tor·i·za·tion** /-,zistəri'zāsHən/ n.

tran·sit /'tranzit/ ▶ n. **1** the carrying of people, goods, or materials from one place to another: *a painting was damaged in transit.* ■ an act of passing through or across a place. ■ the conveyance of passengers on public transportation. ■ Astron. the passage of an inferior planet across the face of the sun, or of a moon or its shadow across the face of a planet. ■ Astron. the apparent passage of a celestial body across the meridian of a place. ■ Astrol. the passage of a celestial body through a specified sign, house, or area of a chart. **2** informal (in full **transit theodolite**) a tool used by surveyors to measure horizontal angles. ▶ v. (**-sit·ed, -sit·ing**) [trans.] pass across or through (an area): *ships too big to transit the canal.* ■ Astron. (of a planet or other celestial body) pass across (a meridian or the face of another body). ■ Astrol. (of a celestial body) pass across (a specified sign, house, or area of a chart). [ME (denoting passage from one place to another): from L. *transitus*, from *transire* 'go across.']

tran·si·tion /tran'zisHən; -'sisHən/ ▶ n. the process or a period of changing from one state or condition to another. ■ a passage in a piece of writing that smoothly connects two topics or sections to each other. ■ Music a momentary modulation from one key to another. ■ Physics a change of an atom, nucleus, electron, etc., from one quantum state to another, with emission or absorption of radiation. ▶ v. undergo or cause to undergo a process or period of transition: [intrans.] *we had to transition to a new set of products* | [trans.] *members discussed how to transition the industry to Linux.* — **tran·si·tion·al** /-sHənl/ adj. **tran·si·tion·a·ry** /-sHə,nerē/ adj. [16th C.: from Fr., or from L. *transitio(n-)*, from *transire* 'go across.']

tran·si·tion met·al (also **tran·si·tion el·e·ment**) ▶ n. Chem. any of the set of metallic elements occupying a central block (Groups IVB–VIII, IB, and IIB, or 4–12) in the periodic table, e.g., iron, manganese, and copper.

tran·si·tive /'transitiv; -zi-/ ▶ adj. **1** Gram. (of a verb or a sense or use of a verb) able to take a direct object (expressed or implied), e.g., *saw* in *he saw the donkey.* The opposite of INTRANSITIVE. **2** Logic Math. (of a relation) such that, if it applies between successive members of a sequence, it must also apply between any two members taken in order. For instance, if A is larger than B, and B is larger than C, then A is larger than C. ▶ n. a transitive verb. — **tran·si·tive·ly** adv. **tran·si·tive·ness** n. **tran·si·tiv·i·ty** /,transi'tivitē; -zi-/ n. [16th C. (in the sense 'transitory'): from late L. *transitivus*, from *transit-* 'gone across' (see TRANSIT).]

tran·si·to·ry /'transi,tôrē; -zi-/ ▶ adj. not permanent: *transitory periods of medieval greatness.* — **tran·si·to·ri·ly** /-'tôrəlē/ adv. **tran·si·to·ri·ness** n. [ME: from OFr. *transitoire*, from Christian L. *transitorius*, from *transit-* 'gone across' (see TRANSIT).]

tran·sit vi·sa ▶ n. a visa allowing its holder to pass through a country but not to stay there.

Trans·jor·dan /,trans'jôrdn; ,tranz-/ former name (until 1949) of what is now the main part of Jordan. — **Trans·jor·da·ni·an** /,trans-jôr'dānēən; ,tranz-/ adj.

Trans·kei /tran'skī; -'skā/ a former homeland established in South Africa for the Xhosa people, now part of the province of Eastern Cape.

trans·late /trans'lāt; tranz-; 'translāt; 'tranz-/ ▶ v. [trans.] **1** express the sense of (words or text) in another language. ■ [intrans.] be expressed or be capable of being expressed in another language: *shiatsu literally translates as "finger pressure."* ■ (**translate something into/translate into**) convert or be converted into (another form or medium): [trans.] *few of Shakespeare's other works have been translated into ballets.* **2** move from one place or condition to another. ■ formal move (a bishop) to another see or pastoral charge. ■ formal remove (a saint's relics) to another place. ■ literary convey (someone, typically still alive) to heaven. ■ Biol. convert (a sequence of nucleotides in messenger RNA) to an amino-acid sequence in a protein or polypeptide during synthesis. **3** Physics cause (a body) to move so that all its parts travel in the same direction, without rotation or change of shape. ■ Math. transform (a geometric figure) in an analogous way. —**trans·lat·a·bil·i·ty** /,translātəˈbilətē; ,tranz-/ **n.** **trans·lat·a·ble adj.** [ME: from L. *translatus* 'carried across,' past part. of *transferre* (see TRANSFER).]

trans·la·tion /transˈlāsHən; tranz-/ ▶**n.** **1** the process of translating words or text from one language into another: *Constantine's translation of Arabic texts into Latin.* ■ a written or spoken rendering of the meaning of a word, speech, book, or other text, in another language. ■ the conversion of something from one form or medium into another. ■ Biol. the process by which a sequence of nucleotide triplets in a messenger RNA molecule gives rise to a specific sequence of amino acids during synthesis of a polypeptide or protein. **2** formal tech. the process of moving something from one place to another. ■ Math. movement of a body from one point of space to another such that every point of the body moves in the same direction and over the same distance, without any rotation, reflection, or change in size. —**trans·la·tion·al** /-sHənl/ **adj.** **trans·la·tion·al·ly** /-sHənl-ē/ **adv.** [ME: from OFr., or from L. *translatio(n-)*, from *translat-* 'carried across' (see TRANSLATE).]

trans·la·tor /ˈtranslātər; ˈtranz-/ ▶**n.** a person who translates from one language into another, esp. as a profession. ■ a program that translates from one programming language into another.

trans·lit·er·ate /transˈlitə,rāt; tranz-/ ▶**v.** [trans.] (usu. **be transliterated**) write or print (a letter or word) using the closest corresponding letters of a different alphabet or language. —**trans·lit·er·a·tion** /trans,litəˈrāsHən; tranz-/ **n.** **trans·lit·er·a·tor** /-ə,rātər/ **n.** [19th C.: from TRANS- 'across' + L. *littera* 'letter' + -ATE[3].]

trans·lo·cate /,transˈlōkāt; ,tranz-/ ▶**v.** [trans.] esp. tech. move from one place to another: *translocating rhinos to other reserves* | [intrans.] *the cell bodies translocate into the other side of the brain.* ■ [trans.] Physiol. & Biochem. transport (a dissolved substance) within an organism, esp. in the phloem of a plant, or actively across a cell membrane. ■ [trans.] Genet. move (a portion of a chromosome) to a new position on the same or another chromosome. —**trans·lo·ca·tion** /,translōˈkāsHən; ,tranz-/ **n.**

trans·lu·cent /transˈlo͞osnt; tranz-/ ▶**adj.** (of a substance) allowing light, but not detailed images, to pass through; semitransparent. —**trans·lu·cence n.** **trans·lu·cen·cy n.** **trans·lu·cent·ly adv.** [16th C. (in the L. sense): from L. *translucent-* 'shining through,' from the verb *translucere*, from *trans-* 'through' + *lucere* 'to shine.']

trans·lu·nar /transˈlo͞onər; tranz-/ ▶**adj.** of, relating to, or denoting the trajectory of a spacecraft traveling between the earth and the moon.

trans·ma·rine /,transməˈrēn; ,tranz-/ ▶**adj.** dated situated or originating on the other side of the sea. ■ of or involving crossing the sea. [16th C.: from L. *transmarinus*, from *trans-* 'across' + *marinus* 'marine, of the sea.']

trans·mem·brane /transˈmembrān; tranz-/ ▶**adj.** Biol. existing or occurring across a cell membrane.

trans·mi·grant /transˈmīgrənt; tranz-/ ▶**n.** rare a person passing through a country or region in the course of emigrating to another region. [17th C.: from L. *transmigrant-* 'migrating across,' from the verb *transmigrare* (see TRANSMIGRATE).]

trans·mi·grate /transˈmīgrāt; tranz-/ ▶**v.** [intrans.] **1** (of the soul) pass into a different body after death. **2** rare migrate. —**trans·mi·gra·tion** /,transmīˈgrāsHən; ,tranz-/ **n.** **trans·mi·gra·tor** /-grātər/ **n.** **trans·mi·gra·to·ry** /-grə,tôrē/ **adj.** [ME (as an adj. in the sense 'transferred'): from L. *transmigrat-* 'removed from one place to another,' from the verb *transmigrare* (see TRANS-, MIGRATE).]

trans·mis·sion /transˈmisHən; tranz-/ ▶**n.** **1** the action or process of transmitting something or the state of being transmitted: *the transmission of the HIV virus.* ■ a program or signal that is broadcast or sent out. **2** the mechanism by which power is transmitted from an engine to the axle in a motor vehicle. [17th C.: from L. *transmissio* (see TRANS-, MISSION).]

trans·mis·sion line ▶**n.** a conductor or conductors designed to carry electricity or an electrical signal over large distances with minimum losses and distortion.

trans·mis·siv·i·ty /,trans-miˈsivitē; ,tranz-/ ▶**n.** (pl. **-ties**) the degree to which a medium allows something, in particular electromagnetic radiation, to pass through it.

trans·mit /tranzˈmit; trans-/ ▶**v.** (**-mit·ted, -mit·ting**) [trans.] cause (something) to pass on from one place or person to another. ■ broadcast or send out (an electrical signal or a radio or television program). ■ pass on (a disease or trait) to another. ■ allow (heat, light, sound, electricity, or other energy) to pass through a medium. ■ communicate or be a medium for (an idea or emotion). —**trans·mis·si·bil·i·ty** /-,misəˈbilitē/ **n.** (esp. Med.). **trans·mis·si·ble** /-ˈmisəbəl/ **adj.** (esp. Med.). **trans·mis·sive** /-ˈmisiv/ **adj.** **trans·mit·ta·ble adj.** **trans·mit·tal** /-ˈmitl/ **n.** [ME: from L. *transmittere*, from *trans-* 'across' + *mittere* 'send.']

trans·mit·tance /transˈmitns; tranz-/ ▶**n.** Physics the ratio of the light energy falling on a body to that transmitted through it.

trans·mit·ter /transˈmitər; tranz-/ ▶**n.** a set of equipment used to generate and transmit electromagnetic waves carrying messages or signals, esp. those of radio or television. ■ a person or thing that transmits something. ■ short for NEUROTRANSMITTER.

trans·mog·ri·fy /transˈmägrə,fī; tranz-/ ▶**v.** (**-fies, -fied**) [trans.] (often **be transmogrified**) usu. humorous transform, esp. in a surprising or magical manner. —**trans·mog·ri·fi·ca·tion** /-,mägrəfiˈkāsHən/ **n.** [17th C.: of unknown origin.]

trans·mon·tane /transˈmäntān; tranz-/ ▶**adj.** another term for TRAMONTANE.

trans·mu·ral /transˈmyo͝orəl; tranz-/ ▶**adj.** Med. existing or occurring across the entire wall of an organ or blood vessel.

trans·mu·ta·tion /,transmyo͞oˈtāsHən; ,tranz-/ ▶**n.** the action of changing or the state of being changed into another form: *the transmutation of the economy.* ■ Physics the changing of one element into another by radioactive decay, nuclear bombardment, or similar processes. ■ Biol., esp. hist. the conversion or transformation of one species into another. ■ the supposed alchemical process of changing base metals into gold. —**trans·mu·ta·tion·al** /-sHənl/ **adj.** **trans·mu·ta·tion·ist n.**

trans·mute /transˈmyo͞ot; tranz-/ ▶**v.** change in form, nature, or substance: [trans.] *his experience was transmuted into stories* | [intrans.] *elements can transmute by radioactivity.* ■ [trans.] subject (base metals) to alchemical transmutation: *the quest to transmute lead into gold.* —**trans·mut·a·bil·i·ty** /-,myo͞otəˈbilitē/ **n.** **trans·mut·a·ble adj.** **trans·mut·a·tive** /-ˈmyo͞otətiv/ **adj.** **trans·mut·er n.** [ME: from L. *transmutare*, from *trans-* 'across' + *mutare* 'to change.']

trans·na·tion·al /,transˈnasHənl; ,tranz-/ ▶**adj.** extending or operating across national boundaries. ▶**n.** a large company operating internationally; a multinational. —**trans·na·tion·al·ism n.** **trans·na·tion·al·ly adv.**

trans·o·ce·an·ic /,trans-ōsHēˈanik; ,tranz-/ ▶**adj.** crossing an ocean: *the transoceanic cable system.* ■ coming from or situated beyond an ocean.

tran·som /ˈtransəm/ ▶**n.** the flat surface forming the stern of a vessel. ■ a horizontal beam reinforcing the stern of a vessel. ■ a strengthening crossbar, in particular one set above a window or door. Compare with MULLION. ■ short for TRANSOM WINDOW.

– PHRASES **over the transom** informal offered or sent without prior agreement; unsolicited. —**tran·somed adj.** [ME (earlier as *traversayn*): from OFr. *traversin*, from the verb *traverser* 'to cross' (see TRAVERSE).]

tran·som win·dow ▶**n.** a window set above the transom of a door or larger window; a fanlight. See illustration at FANLIGHT.

tran·son·ic /tranˈsänik/ (also **trans·son·ic**) ▶**adj.** denoting or relating to speeds close to that of sound. [1940s: from TRANS- 'through, across' + SONIC, on the pattern of words such as *supersonic*.]

trans·pa·cif·ic /,trans-pəˈsifik; ,tranz-/ ▶**adj.** crossing the Pacific. ■ of or relating to an area beyond the Pacific.

trans·par·ence /transˈpe(ə)rəns; -ˈpar-/ ▶**n.** rare term for TRANSPARENCY (sense 1).

trans·par·en·cy /transˈpe(ə)rənsē; -ˈpar-/ ▶**n.** (pl. **-cies**) **1** the condition of being transparent. **2** an image, text, or positive transparent photograph printed on transparent plastic or glass, able to be viewed using a projector. [16th C. (as a general term denoting a transparent object): from med. L. *transparentia*, from *transparent-* 'shining through' (see TRANSPARENT).]

trans·par·ent /transˈpe(ə)rənt; -ˈpar-/ ▶**adj.** (of a material or article) allowing light to pass through so that objects behind can be distinctly seen. ■ easy to perceive or detect. ■ having thoughts, feelings, or motives that are easily perceived. ■ Physics transmitting heat or other electromagnetic rays without distortion. ■ Comput. (of a process or interface) functioning without the user being aware of its presence. —**trans·par·ent·ly adv.** [ME: from OFr., from med. L. *transparent-* 'shining through,' from L. *transparere*, from *trans-* 'through' + *parere* 'appear.']

trans·per·son·al /transˈpərsənl; tranz-/ ▶**adj.** of, denoting, or dealing with states or areas of consciousness beyond the limits of personal identity.

tran·spic·u·ous /tranˈspikyo͞oəs/ ▶**adj.** rare transparent. ■ easily understood, lucid. [17th C.: from mod. L. *transpicuus* (from L. *transpicere* 'look through') + -OUS.]

trans·pierce /transˈpi(ə)rs/ ▶**v.** [trans.] literary pierce through (someone or something).

tran·spire /tranˈspī(ə)r/ ▶**v.** [intrans.] **1** occur; happen. ■ prove to be the case: *as it transpired, he was right.* ■ (usu. **it transpires**) (of a secret or something unknown) come to be known; be revealed: *Yaddo, it transpired, had been under FBI surveillance.* **2** Bot. (of a plant or leaf) give off water vapor through the stomata. —**tran·spi·ra·tion** /-spəˈrāsHən/ **n.** (in sense 2). [ME: from Fr. *transpirer* or med. L. *transpirare*, from L. *trans-* 'through' + *spirare* 'breathe.']

trans·plant ▶**v.** /transˈplant/ [trans.] move or transfer (something) to another place or situation, typically with some effort or upheaval. ■ replant (a plant) in another place. ■ remove (living tissue or an organ) and implant it in another part of the body or in another body. ▶**n.** /ˈtrans,plant/ an operation in which an organ or tissue is transplanted. ■ an organ or tissue that is transplanted. ■ a plant that has been or is to be transplanted. ■ a person or thing that has been moved to a new place or situation. —**trans·plant·a·ble** /transˈplantəbəl/ **adj.** **trans·plan·ta·tion** /,transplanˈtāsHən/ **n.** **trans·plant·er n.** [ME: from late L. *transplantare*, from L. *trans-* 'across' + *plantare* 'to plant.']

tran·spon·der /tranˈspändər/ ▶**n.** a device for receiving a radio signal and automatically transmitting a different signal. [1940s: blend of TRANSMIT and RESPOND, + -ER[1].]

trans·pon·tine /transˈpäntīn/ ▶**adj.** dated **1** on or from the other side of an ocean, in particular the Atlantic. [19th C.: from TRANS- 'across' + L. *pontus* 'sea' + -INE[1].] **2** on or from the other side of a bridge. [19th C.: from TRANS- 'across' + L. *pons, pont-* 'bridge' + -INE[1].]

trans·port ▶**v.** /transˈpôrt/ [trans.] take or carry (people or goods) from one place to another by means of a vehicle, aircraft, or ship. ■ fig. cause (someone) to feel that they are in another place or time. ■ (usu. **be transported**) overwhelm (someone) with a strong emotion, esp. joy.

■ hist. send (a convict) to a penal colony. ▶ n. /'trans,pôrt/ **1** a system or means of conveying people or goods from place to place by means of a vehicle, aircraft, or ship. ■ the action of transporting something or the state of being transported. ■ a large vehicle, ship, or aircraft used to carry troops or stores. ■ hist. a convict who was transported to a penal colony. **2** (usu. **transports**) an overwhelmingly strong emotion: *art can send people into* ***transports of delight.*** [ME: from OFr. *transporter* or L. *transportare*, from *trans-* 'across' + *portare* 'carry.']

trans·port·a·ble /trans'pôrtəbəl/ ▶ adj. **1** able to be carried or moved: *the first transportable phones.* **2** hist. (of an offender or an offense) punishable by transportation. ▶ n. a large portable computer or telephone. — **trans·port·a·bil·i·ty** /trans,pôrtə'bilitē/ n.

trans·por·ta·tion /,transpər'tāsʜən/ ▶ n. **1** the action of transporting someone or something or the process of being transported. ■ a system or means of transporting people or goods. **2** hist. the action or practice of transporting convicts to a penal colony.

trans·port·er /trans'pôrtər/ ▶ n. a person or thing that transports something, in particular: ■ a large vehicle used to carry heavy objects, e.g., cars. ■ (in science fiction) a device that conveys people or things instantaneously from one place to another.

trans·pose /trans'pōz/ ▶ v. [trans.] **1** cause (two or more things) to change places with each other. **2** transfer to a different place or context. ■ write or play (music) in a different key from the original. ■ Math. transfer (a term), with its sign changed, to the other side of an equation. ■ change into a new form. ▶ n. Math. a matrix obtained from a given matrix by interchanging each row and the corresponding column. — **trans·pos·a·ble** adj. **trans·pos·al** /-'pōzəl/ n. **trans·pos·er** n. [ME (also in the sense 'transform, convert'): from OFr. *transposer*, from *trans-* 'across' + *poser* 'to place.']

trans·po·si·tion /,transpə'zisʜən/ ▶ n. the action of transposing something. ■ a thing that has been produced by transposing something: *the dragon is a transposition of the serpent.* — **trans·po·si·tion·al** /-'zisʜənl/ adj. [16th C.: from late L. *transpositio(n-)* (see TRANS-, POSITION).]

trans·po·son /trans'pōzän/ ▶ n. Genet. a chromosomal segment that can undergo transposition, esp. a segment of bacterial DNA that can be translocated as a whole between chromosomal, phage, and plasmid DNA in the absence of a complementary sequence in the host DNA. Also called JUMPING GENE. [1970s: from TRANSPOSITION + -ON.]

trans·put·er /trans'pyo͞otər/ ▶ n. a microprocessor with integral memory designed for parallel processing. [1970s: blend of TRANSISTOR and COMPUTER.]

trans·ra·cial /tranz'rāsʜəl; trans-/ ▶ adj. across or crossing racial boundaries.

trans·sex·u·al /tran(s)'seksʜo͞oəl/ ▶ n. a person born with the physical characteristics of one sex who emotionally and psychologically feels that they belong to the opposite sex. ■ a person who has undergone surgery and hormone treatment in order to acquire the physical characteristics of the opposite sex. ▶ adj. of or relating to such a person. — **trans·sex·u·al·ism** n. **trans·sex·u·al·i·ty** /-,seksʜo͞o'alitē/ n.

trans·ship /,tran(s)'sʜip/ (also **tran·ship**) ▶ v. (**-shipped, -ship·ping**) [trans.] transfer (cargo) from one ship or other form of transport to another. — **trans·ship·ment** n.

trans·son·ic ▶ adj. var. of TRANSONIC.

trans·syn·ap·tic /,tran(s)sə'naptik; ,tranz-/ ▶ adj. Physiol. occurring or existing across a nerve synapse.

tran·sub·stan·ti·ate /,transəb'stancʜē,āt/ ▶ v. [trans.] (usu. **be transubstantiated**) Christian Theol. convert (the substance of the Eucharistic elements) into the body and blood of Christ. ■ formal change the form or substance of (something) into something different. [ME: from med. L. *transubstantiat-* 'changed in substance,' from the verb *transubstantiare*, from L. *trans-* 'across' + *substantia* 'substance.']

tran·sub·stan·ti·a·tion /,transəb,stancʜē'āsʜən/ ▶ n. Christian Theol. (esp. in the Roman Catholic Church) the conversion of the substance of the Eucharistic elements into the body and blood of Christ at consecration, only the appearances of bread and wine still remaining. ■ formal a change in the form or substance of something.

tran·sude /tran'so͞od/ ▶ v. [trans.] archaic discharge (a fluid) gradually through pores in a membrane, esp. within the body. ■ [intrans.] (of a fluid) be discharged in such a way. — **tran·su·date** /'transo͞o,dāt/ n. **tran·su·da·tion** /,transo͞o'dāsʜən/ n. [17th C.: from Fr. *transsuder* (in OFr. *tressuer*), from L. *trans-* 'across' + *sudare* 'to sweat.']

trans·u·ran·ic /,trans-yə'ranik; tranz-/ ▶ adj. Chem. (of an element) having a higher atomic number than uranium (92).

trans·u·re·thral /,trans-yo͝o'rēᴛʜrəl; ,tranz-/ ▶ adj. (of a medical procedure) performed via the urethra.

Trans·vaal /trans'väl; tranz-; -'fäl/ (also **the Trans·vaal**) a former province in northeastern South Africa, north of the Vaal River.

trans·val·ue /trans'valyo͞o; tranz-/ ▶ v. (**-val·ues, -val·ued, -val·u·ing**) [trans.] (often **be transvalued**) represent (something, typically an idea, custom, or quality) in a different way, altering people's judgment of or reaction to it. — **trans·val·u·a·tion** /,trans-valyo͞o'āsʜən; ,tranz-/ n.

trans·ver·sal /trans'vərsəl; tranz-/ Geom. ▶ adj. (of a line) intersecting a system of lines. ▶ n. a transversal line. — **trans·ver·sal·i·ty** /,transvər'salitē; ,tranz-/ n. **trans·ver·sal·ly** adv. [ME (as a synonym of TRANSVERSE): from med. L. *transversalis*, from L. *transversus* 'lying across.']

trans·verse /trans'vərs; tranz-/ ▶ adj. situated or extending across something: *a transverse beam.* — **transversely** adv. [ME: from L. *transversus* 'turned across,' past part. of *transvertere*, from *trans-* 'across' + *vertere* 'to turn.']

trans·verse co·lon ▶ n. Anat. the middle part of the large intestine, passing across the abdomen from right to left below the stomach.

trans·verse flute ▶ n. a flute that is held horizontally when played, e.g., the modern flute as opposed to the recorder.

trans·verse mag·net ▶ n. a magnet with poles at the sides and not the ends.

trans·verse proc·ess ▶ n. Anat. a lateral process of a vertebra.

trans·verse wave ▶ n. Physics a wave vibrating at right angles to the direction of its propagation.

trans·ves·tite /trans'vestīt; tranz-/ ▶ n. a person, typically a man, who derives pleasure from dressing in clothes appropriate to the opposite sex. — **trans·ves·tism** n. **trans·ves·tist** n. (dated). **trans·ves·ti·tism** /-ti,tizəm/ n. [1920s: from Ger. *Transvestit*, from L. *trans-* 'across' + *vestire* 'clothe.']

Tran·syl·va·nia /,transəl'vānyə; -'vānēə/ **1** a large tableland region of northwestern Romania, separated from the rest of the country by the Carpathian Mountains and the Transylvanian Alps. **2** (in US history) an unrecognized fourteenth colony that was proposed in the 1770s in what is now central Kentucky and neighboring Tennessee. — **Tran·syl·va·ni·an** adj.

trap¹ /trap/ ▶ n. **1** a device or enclosure designed to catch and retain animals, typically by allowing entry but not exit or by catching hold of a part of the body. ■ a curve in the waste pipe from a bathtub, sink, or toilet that is always full of liquid and prevents gases from coming up the pipe into the building. ■ [with adj.] a container or device used to collect a specified thing: *a water trap.* ■ a bunker or other hollow on a golf course. ■ the compartment from which a greyhound is released at the start of a race. ■ fig. a trick by which someone is misled into giving themselves away or otherwise acting contrary to their interests or intentions: *I was* ***walking into a trap.*** ■ fig. an unpleasant situation from which it is hard to escape: ***they fell into the trap of*** *relying too little on equity financing.* **2** a device for hurling an object such as a clay pigeon into the air to be shot at. ■ (in the game of trapball) the shoe-shaped device that is hit with a bat to send the ball into the air. **3** esp. hist. a light, two-wheeled carriage pulled by a horse or pony. **4** short for TRAPDOOR. **5** informal a person's mouth (used in expressions to do with speaking): *keep your trap shut!* **6** (usu. **traps**) informal percussion instruments, typically in a jazz band. **7** Baseball & Football an act of trapping the ball. ▶ v. (**trapped, trap·ping**) [trans.] catch (an animal) in a trap. ■ (often **be trapped**) prevent (someone) from escaping from a place. ■ have (something, typically a part of the body) held tightly by something so that it cannot move or be freed. ■ induce (someone), by means of trickery or deception, to do something they would not otherwise want to do: *I hoped to* ***trap*** *him* ***into*** *an admission.* ■ Baseball & Football catch (the ball) after it has briefly touched the ground. ■ Soccer bring (the ball) under control with the feet or other part of the body on receiving it. — **trap·like** /-,līk/ adj. [OE *træppe* (in *coltetræppe* 'Christ's thorn'); rel. to MDu. *trappe* and med. L. *trappa*, of uncert. origin. The verb dates from ME.]

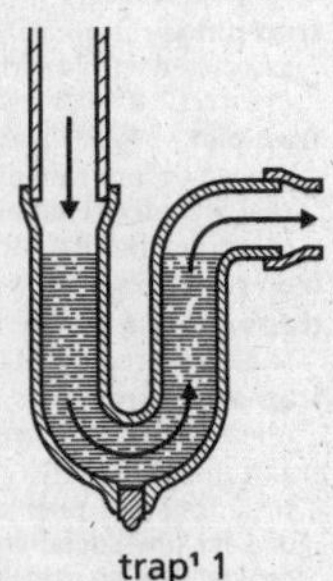
trap¹ 1

trap² ▶ v. (**trapped, trap·ping**) [trans.] [usu. as adj.] (**trapped**) archaic put trappings on (a horse, etc.). [ME: from the obs. noun *trap* 'trappings,' from OFr. *drap* 'drape.']

trap³ (also **trap·rock**) ▶ n. basalt or a similar dark, fine-grained igneous rock. [18th C.: from Swed. *trapp*, from *trappa* 'stair' (because of the often stairlike appearance of its outcroppings).]

trap·door /'trap,dôr/ (also **trap door**) ▶ n. a hinged or removable panel in a floor, ceiling, or roof. ■ a feature or defect of a computer system that allows surreptitious unauthorized access to data belonging to other users.

trapes ▶ v. & n. archaic spelling of TRAIPSE.

tra·peze /trə'pēz; tra-/ ▶ n. **1** (also **flying trapeze**) a horizontal bar hanging by two ropes (usually high in the air) and free to swing, used by acrobats in a circus. **2** Sailing a harness attached by a cable to a dinghy's mast, enabling a sailor to balance the boat by leaning backward out over the windward side. [19th C.: from Fr. *trapèze*, from late L. *trapezium* (see TRAPEZIUM).]

Tra·pe·zi·um /trə'pēzēəm/ (**the Trapezium**) Astron. the multiple star Theta Orionis, which lies within the Great Nebula of Orion and illuminates it. Four stars are visible in a small telescope and two more with a larger telescope.

tra·pe·zi·um /trə'pēzēəm/ ▶ n. (pl. **-zi·a** /-zēə/ or **-zi·ums**) **1** Geom. a type of quadrilateral: ■ a quadrilateral with no sides parallel. Compare with TRAPEZOID. ■ Brit. a quadrilateral with one pair of sides parallel. **2** (also **os trapezium**) Anat. a bone in the wrist below the base of the thumb. [16th C.: via late L. from Gk. *trapezion*, from *trapeza*

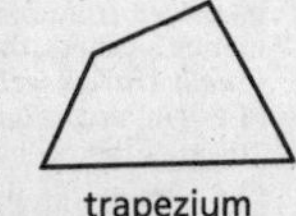
trapezium

PRONUNCIATION KEY ə *ago, up*; ər *over, fur*; a *hat*; ā *ate*; ä *car*; e *let*; ē *see*; i *fit*; ī *by*; ɴɢ *sing*; ō *go*; ô *law, for*; oi *toy*; o͝o *good*; o͞o *goo*; ou *out*; ᴛʜ *thin*; T̲H̲ *then*; ᴢʜ *vision* 'table.' The term has been used in anatomy since the mid 19th C.]

tra·pe·zi·us /trə'pēzēəs/ (also **trapezius muscle**) ▶ **n.** (pl. **-zi·i** /-zē,ī/ or **-zi·us·es**) Anat. either of a pair of large triangular muscles extending over the back of the neck and shoulders and moving the head and shoulder blade. [18th C.: from mod. L., from Gk. *trapezion* 'trapezium' (because of the shape formed by the muscles).]

tra·pe·zo·he·dron /trə,pēzō'hēdrən; ,trapizō-/ ▶ **n.** (pl. **-dra** /-drə/ or **-drons**) a solid figure whose faces are trapeziums or trapezoids. — **tra·pe·zo·he·dral** /-drəl/ **adj.** [19th C.: from TRAPEZIUM + -HEDRON, on the pattern of words such as *polyhedron.*]

trap·e·zoid /'trapi,zoid/ ▶ **n.** **1** Geom. a type of quadrilateral: ■ N. Amer. a quadrilateral with only one pair of parallel sides. ■ Brit. a quadrilateral with no sides parallel. Compare with TRAPEZIUM. **2** (also **trapezoid bone**) Anat. a small carpal bone in the base of the hand, articulating with the metacarpal of the index finger. — **trap·e·zoi·dal** /,trapi'zoidl/ **adj.** [18th C.: from mod. L. *trapezoides*, from late Gk. *trapezoeidēs*, from *trapeza* 'table' (see TRAPEZIUM).]

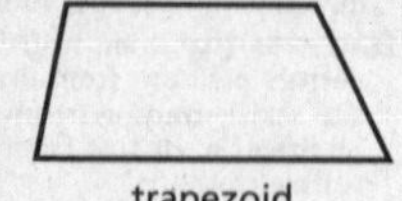
trapezoid

trap·line /'trap,līn/ ▶ **n.** a series of traps for game.

trap·per /'trapər/ ▶ **n.** a person who traps wild animals, esp. for their fur.

trap·pings /'trapiNGz/ ▶ **plural n.** the outward signs, features, or objects associated with a particular situation, role, or thing: *I had the trappings of success.* ■ a horse's ornamental harness. [ME: deriv. of TRAP².]

Trap·pist /'trapist/ ▶ **adj.** of, relating to, or denoting a branch of the Cistercian order of monks founded in 1664 and noted for an austere rule that includes remaining silent for much of the time. ▶ **n.** a member of this order. [19th C.: from Fr. *trappiste*, from *La Trappe* in Normandy.]

trap·rock /'trap,räk/ ▶ **n.** see TRAP³.

traps /traps/ ▶ **plural n.** informal personal belongings; baggage: *I was ready to pack my traps and leave.* [19th C.: perh. a contr. of TRAPPINGS.]

trap·shoot·ing /'trap,SHōōtiNG/ ▶ **n.** the sport of shooting at clay pigeons released from a spring trap. — **trap·shoot·er** /-,SHōōtər/ **n.**

trash /trasH/ ▶ **n.** discarded matter; refuse. ■ writing, art, or other cultural items of poor quality. ■ a person or people regarded as being of very low social standing. ■ nonsense. ▶ **v.** [trans.] informal **1** damage or wreck. ■ discard. ■ Comput. kill (a file or process) or wipe (a disk). ■ criticize severely. ■ [as adj.] (**trashed**) intoxicated with alcohol or drugs. **2** strip (sugar cane) of its outer leaves to ripen it faster. [ME: of unknown origin. The verb is first recorded (18th cent.) in sense 2; the other senses have arisen in the 20th C.]

trash talk (also **trash talk·ing**) informal ▶ **n.** insulting or boastful speech intended to demoralize, intimidate, or humiliate someone. ▶ **v.** [intrans.] (**trash-talk**) use insulting or boastful speech for such a purpose. — **trash talk·er** (also **trash-talk·er**) **n.**

trash·y /'trasHē/ ▶ **adj.** (**trash·i·er, trash·i·est**) (esp. of items of popular culture) of poor quality. — **trash·i·ly** /'trasHəlē/ **adv.** **trash·i·ness** **n.**

trass /tras/ ▶ **n.** a light-colored variety of volcanic ash resembling pozzolana, used in making water-resistant cement. [18th C.: from Du. *tras*, Ger. *Trass*, based on L. *terra* 'earth.']

trat·to·ri·a /,trätə'rēə/ ▶ **n.** an Italian restaurant serving simple food. [Ital.]

trau·ma /'troumə; 'trô-/ ▶ **n.** (pl. **-mas** or **-ma·ta** /-mətə/) a deeply distressing or disturbing experience. ■ emotional shock following a stressful event or a physical injury, which may be associated with physical shock and sometimes leads to long-term neurosis. ■ Med. physical injury. [17th C.: from Gk., lit. 'wound.']

trau·mat·ic /trə'matik; trou-; trô-/ ▶ **adj.** emotionally disturbing or distressing. ■ relating to or causing psychological trauma. ■ Med. relating to or denoting physical injury. — **trau·mat·i·cal·ly** /-ik(ə)lē/ **adv.** [19th C.: via late L. from Gk. *traumatikos*, from *trauma* (see TRAUMA).]

trau·ma·tism /'troumə,tizəm/ ▶ **n.** esp. tech. a traumatic effect or condition.

trau·ma·tize /'troumə,tīz; 'trô-/ ▶ **v.** [trans.] subject to lasting shock as a result of an emotionally disturbing experience or physical injury. ■ Med. cause physical injury to. — **trau·ma·ti·za·tion** /,troumәti'zāsHən; ,trô-/ **n.**

trav. ▶ **abbr.** ■ traveler. ■ travels.

tra·vail /trə'vāl; 'trav,āl/ literary ▶ **n.** (also **travails**) painful or laborious effort. ■ labor pains: *a woman in travail.* ▶ **v.** [intrans.] engage in painful or laborious effort. ■ (of a woman) be in labor. [ME: via OFr. from med. L. *trepalium* 'instrument of torture,' from L. *tres* 'three' + *palus* 'stake.']

trav·el /'travəl/ ▶ **v.** (**-eled, -el·ing** ; also esp. Brit. **-elled, -el·ling**) **1** [intrans.] make a journey, typically of some length or abroad. ■ [trans.] journey along (a road) or through (a region). ■ [usu. as adj.] (**traveling**) go or be moved from place to place: *a traveling exhibition.* ■ informal resist motion sickness, damage, or some other impairment on a journey: *he usually travels well.* ■ be enjoyed or successful away from the place of origin: *accordion music travels well.* ■ dated go from place to place as a sales representative. ■ (of an object or radiation) move, typically in a constant or predictable way. ■ informal (esp. of a vehicle) move quickly. **2** [intrans.] Basketball take more than the allowed number of steps (typically two) while holding the ball without dribbling it. ▶ **n.** the action of traveling, typically abroad. ■ (**travels**) journeys, esp. long or exotic ones. ■ [as adj.] (of a device) designed so as to be sufficiently compact for use on a journey: *a travel iron.* ■ the range, rate, or mode of motion of a part of a machine. [ME: var. of TRAVAIL and orig. in the same sense.]

trav·el a·gen·cy (also **travel bureau**) ▶ **n.** an agency that makes the necessary arrangements for travelers, esp. the booking of airline tickets and hotel rooms. — **trav·el a·gent** **n.**

trav·el·a·tor /'travə,lātər/ (also **trav·o·la·tor**) ▶ **n.** a moving walkway, typically at an airport. [1950s: from TRAVEL, suggested by ESCALATOR.]

trav·el card ▶ **n.** a prepaid card allowing unlimited travel on buses or trains for a specified period of time.

trav·eled /'travəld/ ▶ **adj.** **1** having traveled to many places: *he was widely traveled.* **2** used by people traveling: *a less well-traveled route.*

trav·el·er /'trav(ə)lər/ (Brit. **trav·el·ler**) ▶ **n.** a person who is traveling or who often travels.

trav·el·er's check ▶ **n.** a check for a fixed amount that can be cashed or used in payment after endorsement with the holder's signature.

trav·el·er's tale ▶ **n.** a story about the unusual characteristics or customs of a foreign country, regarded as probably exaggerated or untrue.

trav·el·ing sales·man ▶ **n.** a representative of a company who visits stores and other businesses to show samples and gain orders.

trav·el·ing wave ▶ **n.** Physics a wave in which the medium moves in the direction of propagation.

trav·e·logue /'travə,lôg; -,läg/ ▶ **n.** a movie, book, or illustrated lecture about the places visited and experiences encountered by a traveler. [20th C.: from TRAVEL, on the pattern of *monologue.*]

trav·ers /'travərs; trə'vərs/ (also **trav·erse**) ▶ **n.** a movement performed in dressage, in which the horse moves parallel to the side of the arena, with its shoulders carried closer to the wall than its hindquarters and its body curved toward the center. [Fr., from *pied de travers* 'foot askew.']

tra·verse /trə'vərs/ ▶ **v.** [trans.] **1** travel across or through: *he traversed the forest.* ■ extend across or through. ■ [intrans.] cross a hill or mountain by means of a series of sideways movements. ■ ski diagonally across (a slope), with only a slight descent. ■ fig. consider or discuss the whole extent of (a subject): *he would traverse a number of subjects.* **2** move (something) back and forth or sideways: *a probe is traversed along the tunnel.* ■ turn (a large gun or other device on a pivot) to face a different direction. ■ [intrans.] (of such a gun or device) be turned in this way. **3** Law deny (an allegation) in pleading. ■ archaic oppose or thwart (a plan). ▶ **n.** **1** an act of traversing something. ■ a sideways movement, or a series of such movements, across a rock face from one line of ascent or descent to another. ■ a place where a movement of this type is necessary: *a narrow traverse made lethal by ice.* ■ a movement following a diagonal course made by a skier descending a slope. ■ a zigzag course followed by a ship because winds or currents prevent it from sailing directly toward its destination. **2** a part of a structure that extends or is fixed across something. ■ a gallery extending from side to side of a church or other building. **3** a mechanism enabling a large gun to be turned to face a different direction. ■ the sideways movement of a part in a machine. **4** a single line of survey, usually plotted from compass bearings and chained or paced distances between angular points. ■ a tract surveyed in this way. **5** Mil. a pair of right-angled bends incorporated in a trench to avoid enfilading fire. **6** var. of TRAVERS. ▶ **adj.** (of a curtain rod) allowing the curtain to be opened and closed by sliding it along the rod. — **tra·vers·a·ble** **adj.** **tra·vers·al** /-'vərsəl/ **n.** **tra·vers·er** **n.** [ME (sense 3 of the v.): from Old Fr. *traverser*, from late L. *traversare*; the noun is from OFr. *travers* (masc.), *traverse* (fem.), partly based on *traverser.*]

trav·er·tine /'travər,tēn; -tin/ ▶ **n.** white or light-colored calcareous rock deposited from mineral springs, used in building. [18th C.: from Ital. *travertino, tivertino*, from L. *tiburtinus* 'of Tibur' (now Tivoli, a district near Rome).]

trav·es·ty /'travistē/ ▶ **n.** (pl. **-ties**) a false, absurd, or distorted representation of something. ▶ **v.** (**-ties, -tied**) [trans.] represent in such a way. [17th C. (as an adj. in the sense 'dressed to appear ridiculous'): from Fr. *travesti* 'disguised,' past part. of *travestir*, from Ital. *travestire*, from *trans-* 'across' + *vestire* 'clothe.']

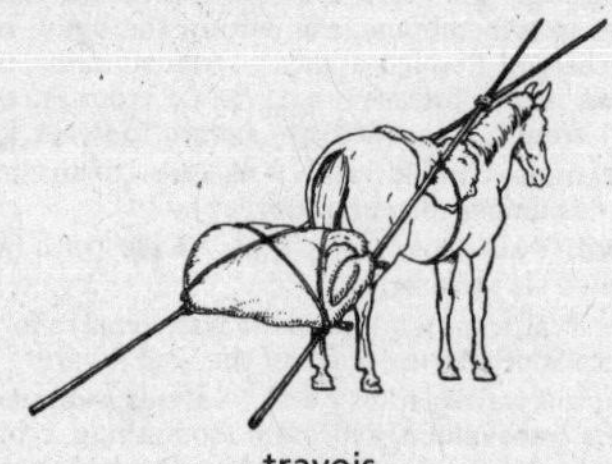
travois

tra·vois /trə'voi; 'trav,oi/ ▶ **n.** (pl. same) a type of sled formerly used by North American Indians to carry goods, consisting of two joined poles dragged by a horse. [19th C.: alt. of synonymous *travail*, from Fr.]

trav·ol·a·tor ▶ **n.** var. of TRAVELATOR.

trawl /trôl/ ▶ **v.** [intrans.] fish with a trawl net or seine. ■ [trans.] catch with a trawl net. ■ sift through as part of a search: *they trawled through the confidential files* | [trans.] *he trawled his memory.* ■ [trans.] drag or trail (something) through water or other liquid. ▶n. **1** an act of fishing with a trawl net. ■ an act of sifting through something as part of a search. **2** (also **trawl net**) a large wide-mouthed fishing net dragged by a vessel along the bottom of the sea or a lake. **3** (also **trawl line**) a long fishing line with many short side lines bearing baited hooks, set on the sea bottom and lifted periodically to remove caught fish. [16th C. (as a v.): prob. from MDu. *traghelen* 'to drag' (rel. to *traghel* 'dragnet'), perh. from L. *tragula* 'dragnet.']

trawl·er /'trôlər/ ▶n. a fishing boat used for trawling.

tray /trā/ ▶n. a flat, shallow container with a raised rim, typically used for carrying food and drink, or for holding small items. —**tray·ful** /-,fo͝ol/ n. (pl. **-fuls**). [OE *trīg*, from the Gmc. base of TREE; the primary sense may have been 'wooden container.']

trayf /trāf/ (also **treyf** or **trey·fa** /'trāfə/) ▶adj. (of food) not satisfying the requirements of Jewish law. [19th C.: from Heb. *ṭĕrēpāh* 'the flesh of an animal torn or mauled,' from *ṭārap* 'rend.']

treach·er·ous /'treCHərəs/ ▶adj. guilty of or involving betrayal or deception. ■ (of ground, water, conditions, etc.) hazardous because of presenting hidden or unpredictable dangers. —**treach·er·ous·ly** adv. **treach·er·ous·ness** n.

treach·er·y /'treCHərē/ ▶n. (pl. **-er·ies**) betrayal of trust; deceptive action or nature. [ME: from OFr. *trecherie*, from *trechier* 'to cheat.']

trea·cle /'trēkəl/ ▶n. British term for MOLASSES. ■ fig. cloying sentimentality or flattery. —**trea·cly** /'trēk(ə)lē/ adj. [ME: from OFr. *triacle*, via L. from Gk. *thēriakē* 'antidote against venom,' fem. of *thēriakos* (adj.), from *thērion* 'wild beast.']

tread /tred/ ▶v. (past **trod** /träd träd/; past part. **trod·den** /'trädn/ or **trod**) [intrans.] walk in a specified way. ■ (**tread on**) set one's foot down on top of. ■ [trans.] walk on or along. ■ [trans.] press down into the ground or another surface with the feet. ■ [trans.] crush or flatten something with the feet. ▶n. **1** [in sing.] a manner or the sound of someone walking. **2** the top surface of a step or stair. See illustration at STAIR. **3** the molded part of a vehicle tire that grips the road. ■ the part of a wheel that touches the ground or rail. ■ the upper surface of a railroad track, in contact with the wheels. ■ the part of the sole of a shoe that rests on the ground.

– PHRASES **tread water** (past **tread·ed**) maintain an upright position in deep water by moving the feet with a walking movement and the hands with a downward circular motion. ■ fig. fail to advance or make progress. —**tread·er** n. [OE *tredan* (as a v.), of West Gmc. origin; rel. to Du. *treden* and Ger. *treten*.]

trea·dle /'tredl/ ▶n. a lever worked by the foot that imparts motion to a machine. ▶v. [trans.] operate (a machine) using a treadle. [OE *tredel* 'stair, step' (see TREAD).]

tread·mill /'tred,mil/ ▶n. a device formerly used for driving machinery, consisting of a large wheel with steps fitted into its inner surface. It was turned by the weight of people or animals treading the steps. ■ an exercise machine, typically with a continuous belt, that allows one to walk or run in place. ■ fig. a job or situation that is tiring, boring, or unpleasant and from which it is hard to escape.

treas. ▶abbr. ■ treasurer. ■ (also **Treas.**) Treasury.

trea·son /'trēzən/ ▶n. (also **high treason**) the crime of betraying one's country, esp. by attempting to kill the sovereign or overthrow the government. ■ the action of betraying someone or something. ■ (**petty treason**) hist. the crime of murdering someone to whom the murderer owed allegiance, such as a master or husband. —**trea·son·a·ble** /'trēzənəbəl/ adj. **trea·son·a·bly** /-blē/ adv. **trea·son·ous** /'trēzənəs/ adj. [ME: from Anglo-Norman Fr. *treisoun*, from L. *traditio(n-)* 'handing over,' from the verb *tradere*.]

treas·ure /'trezHər/ ▶n. a quantity of precious metals, gems, or other valuable objects. ■ a very valuable object. ■ informal a person whom the speaker loves or who is valued for the assistance they can give. ▶v. [trans.] keep carefully (a valuable or valued item). ■ value highly. [ME: from OFr. *tresor*, based on Gk. *thēsauros* (see THESAURUS).]

treas·ur·er /'trezHərər/ ▶n. a person appointed to administer or manage the financial assets and liabilities of a society, company, local authority, or other body. —**treas·ur·er·ship** /-,SHip/ n.

treas·ure trove ▶n. valuables of unknown ownership that are found hidden, in some cases declared the property of the finder. ■ a hidden store of valuable or delightful things. [ME: from Anglo-Norman Fr. *tresor trové*, lit. 'found treasure.']

treas·ur·y /'trezHərē/ ▶n. (pl. **-ur·ies**) **1** the funds or revenue of a government, corporation, or institution. ■ (**Treasury**) (in some countries) the government department responsible for budgeting for and controlling public expenditure, management of the national debt, and the overall management of the economy. **2** a place or building where treasure is stored. ■ a collection of valuable or delightful things. [ME: from OFr. *tresorie* (see TREASURE).]

Treas·ur·y bill ▶n. a short-dated government security, yielding no interest but issued at a discount on its redemption price.

Treas·ur·y bond ▶n. a government bond issued by the US Treasury.

Treas·ur·y note ▶n. a note issued by the US Treasury for use as currency.

treat /trēt/ ▶v. [trans.] **1** behave toward or deal with in a certain way: *she had been brutally treated.* ■ (**treat something as**) regard something as being of a specified nature with implications for one's actions concerning it: *treated as classified information.* ■ give medical care or attention to; try to heal or cure: *they were treated for cuts.* ■ apply a process or a substance to (something) to protect or preserve it or to give it particular properties. ■ present or discuss (a subject): *the level at which subjects are treated.* **2** (**treat someone to**) provide someone with (food, drink, or entertainment) at one's own expense. ■ give someone (something) as a favor. ■ (**treat oneself**) do or have something that gives one great pleasure. **3** [intrans.] negotiate terms with someone, esp. an opponent: *he was treating with the enemy.* ▶n. an event or item that is out of the ordinary and gives great pleasure. ■ used with a possessive adjective to indicate that the person specified is paying for food, entertainment, etc., for someone else. —**treat·a·ble** adj. **treat·er** n. [ME: from OFr. *traitier*, from L. *tractare* 'handle,' frequentative of *trahere* 'draw, pull.']

trea·tise /'trētis/ ▶n. a written work dealing formally and systematically with a subject. [ME: from Anglo-Norman Fr. *tretis*, from OFr. *traitier* (see TREAT).]

treat·ment /'trētmənt/ ▶n. the manner in which someone behaves toward or deals with someone or something. ■ medical care given to a patient for an illness or injury. ■ a session of medical care or the administration of a dose of medicine. ■ the use of a chemical, physical, or biological agent to preserve or give particular properties to something. ■ the presentation or discussion of a subject. ■ (**the full treatment**) informal used to indicate that something is done enthusiastically, vigorously, or to an extreme degree.

trea·ty /'trētē/ ▶n. (pl. **-ties**) a formally concluded and ratified agreement between countries. [ME: from OFr. *traite*, from L. *tractatus* 'treatise' (see TRACTATE).]

Treb·bia·no /treb'yänō/ ▶n. a variety of wine grape widely cultivated in Italy and elsewhere. ■ a wine made from this grape. [Ital., after the *Trebbia* River, in Italy.]

tre·ble[1] /'trebəl/ ▶adj. [attrib.] consisting of three parts; threefold. ■ multiplied or occurring three times. ▶predeterminer three times as much or as many. ▶n. a threefold quantity or thing, in particular: ■ (in show jumping) a fence consisting of three elements. ■ a crochet stitch made with three loops of wool on the hook at a time. ■ a drink of liquor of three times the standard measure. ▶pron. a number or amount that is three times as large as a contrasting or usual number or amount. ▶v. make or become three times as large or numerous. [ME: via OFr. from L. *triplus* (see TRIPLE).]

tre·ble[2] ▶n. a high-pitched voice, esp. a boy's singing voice. ■ a boy or girl with such a singing voice. ■ a part written for a high voice or an instrument of a high pitch. ■ [as adj.] denoting a relatively high-pitched member of a family of similar instruments. ■ (also **treble bell**) the smallest and highest-pitched bell of a set. ■ the high-frequency output of an audio system or radio, corresponding to the treble in music. [ME: from TREBLE[1].]

tre·ble clef ▶n. a clef placing G above middle C on the second-lowest line of the staff.

Tre·blin·ka /trə'bliNGkə; tre-/ a Nazi concentration camp in Poland during World War II, where a great many of the Jews of the Warsaw ghetto were murdered.

tre·bly /'treblē/ ▶adj. (of sound, esp. recorded music) having much or excessive treble. ▶adv. [as submodifier] three times as much: *trebly impressive.*

treb·u·chet /,trebyə'SHet/ ▶n. a machine used in medieval siege warfare for hurling large stones or other missiles. [ME: from OFr., from *trebucher* 'overthrow.']

tre·cen·to /trā'CHentō/ ▶n. (**the trecento**) the 14th century as a period of Italian art, architecture, or literature. [Ital., lit. '300,' shortened from *milletrecento* '1300.']

tree /trē/ ▶n. **1** a woody perennial plant, typically having a single trunk growing to a considerable height and bearing lateral branches at some distance from the ground. Compare with SHRUB[1]. ■ (in general use) any bush, shrub, or herbaceous plant with a tall erect stem, e.g., a banana plant. **2** a wooden structure or part of a structure. ■ archaic or literary the cross on which Christ was crucified. **3** a thing that has a branching structure resembling that of a tree. ■ (also **tree diagram**) a diagram with a structure of branching connecting lines, representing different processes and relationships. ▶v. (**trees, treed, tree·ing**) [trans.] force (a hunted animal) to take refuge in a tree. ■ informal force (someone) into a difficult situation.

– PHRASES **out of one's tree** informal completely stupid; insane. **up a tree** informal in a difficult situation without escape; cornered. [OE *trēow, trēo*: from a Gmc. var. of an Indo-Eur. root shared by Gk. *doru* 'wood, spear,' *drus* 'oak.']

tree duck ▶n. another term for WHISTLING DUCK.

tree fern ▶n. a large palmlike fern (Cyatheaceae and related families, class Filicopsida) with a trunklike stem bearing a crown of large fronds, sometimes reaching a height of 24 m and occurring chiefly in the tropics, particularly the southern hemisphere.

tree frog ▶n. an arboreal frog (families Hylidae, of Eurasia, America, and Australia; and Rhacophoridae of Africa and Asia) that has long toes with adhesive disks and is typically small and brightly colored. The numerous species include the common **green tree frog** (*Hyla arborea*) of southern Europe

tree·hop·per /'trē,häpər/ ▶n. a tree-dwelling jumping bug (family Membracidae, suborder Homoptera) that lives chiefly in the tropics.

tree house (also **tree·house**) ▶ n. a structure built in the branches of a tree for children to play in.

tree kan·ga·roo ▶ n. an agile tree-climbing kangaroo (genus *Dendrolagus*, family Macropodidae) with a long furred tail, and fore- and hind limbs that are of almost equal length, found in the rain forests of Australia and New Guinea.

tree line ▶ n. another term for TIMBERLINE.

tree·nail /ˈtrēˌnāl; ˈtrenl/ ▶ n. a trunnel.

tree of heav·en (also **tree-of-heav·en**) ▶ n. a fast-growing Chinese ailanthus (*Ailanthus altissima*) that is widely cultivated as an ornamental.

tree of know·ledge (also **tree of the knowledge of good and evil**) ▶ n. (in the Bible) the tree in the Garden of Eden bearing the forbidden fruit that Adam and Eve disobediently ate (Gen. 2:9, 3).

tree of life ▶ n. **1** (**Tree of Life**) (in the Bible) a tree in the Garden of Eden whose fruit imparts eternal life (Gen. 3:22–24). ■ an imaginary branching, treelike structure representing the evolutionary divergence of all living creatures. ■ (in cabalism) a diagram in the form of a tree bearing spheres that represent the sephiroth. **2** the thuja or arbor vitae.

tree pip·it ▶ n. a widespread Old World pipit (*Anthus trivialis*) that inhabits open country with scattered trees.

tree ring ▶ n. each of the concentric rings in the cross section of a tree trunk, representing a year's growth.

tree shrew ▶ n. a small squirrellike insectivorous mammal (family Tupaiidae and order Scandentia) with a pointed snout, native to Southeast Asia, esp. Borneo.

tree snake ▶ n. a harmless arboreal snake (family Colubridae), typically very slender and able to mimic a twig.

tree spar·row ▶ n. **1** a Eurasian sparrow (*Passer montanus*) with a chocolate-brown cap in both sexes, inhabiting agricultural land. **2** a migratory sparrowlike songbird (*Spizella arborea*) of the bunting family, breeding on the edge of the North American tundra.

tree squir·rel ▶ n. an arboreal squirrel (*Sciurus* and other genera) that is typically active in daylight and does not hibernate.

tree struc·ture ▶ n. Comput. a structure that has successive branchings or subdivisions.

tree sur·geon ▶ n. a person who prunes and treats old or damaged trees in order to preserve them. — **tree sur·ger·y** n.

tree swal·low ▶ n. a North American swallow (*Tachycineta bicolor*) that nests in trees.

tree toad ▶ n. another term for TREE FROG.

tree to·ma·to ▶ n. another term for TAMARILLO.

tree·top /ˈtrēˌtäp/ ▶ n. (usu. **treetops**) the uppermost part of a tree.

tre·foil /ˈtrēˌfoil; ˈtrefoil/ ▶ n. a small plant (genera *Trifolium* and *Lotus*) of the pea family with yellow flowers and three-lobed cloverlike leaves. ■ a similar or related plant with three-lobed leaves. ■ an ornamental design of three rounded lobes like a clover leaf, used typically in architectural tracery. ■ a thing having three parts; a set of three. ■ [as adj.] denoting something shaped in the form of a trefoil leaf. — **tre·foiled** adj. [ME: from Anglo-Norman Fr. *trifoil*, from L. *trifolium*, from *tri-* 'three' + *folium* 'leaf.']

trefoil design

trek /trek/ ▶ n. a long arduous journey, esp. one made on foot. ▶ v. (**trekked, trek·king**) [intrans.] go on a long arduous journey, typically on foot. — **trek·ker** n. [19th C.: from South Afr. Du. *trek* (n.), *trekken* (v.) 'pull, travel.']

Trek·kie /ˈtrekē/ ▶ n. (pl. **-kies**) informal a fan of the US science-fiction television program *Star Trek*.

trel·lis /ˈtrelis/ ▶ n. a framework of light wooden or metal bars, chiefly used as a support for fruit trees or climbing plants. ▶ v. (**-lised, -lis·ing**) [trans.] [usu. as adj.] (**trellised**) provide with or enclose in a trellis. ■ support (a climbing plant) with a trellis. [ME (denoting any latticed screen): from OFr. *trelis*, from L. *trilix* 'three-ply,' from *tri-* 'three' + *licium* 'warp thread.']

trem /trem/ (also **trem arm**) ▶ n. informal a tremolo arm.

trem·ble /ˈtrembəl/ ▶ v. [intrans.] shake involuntarily, typically as a result of anxiety, excitement, or frailty. ■ be in a state of extreme apprehension: [with infin.] *I tremble to think that we could ever return to conditions like these.* ■ [usu. as adj.] (**trembling**) (of a person's voice) sound unsteady or hesitant. ■ shake or quiver slightly. ▶ n. **1** a trembling feeling, movement, or sound. **2** (**the trembles**) informal a physical or emotional condition marked by trembling. ■ another term for MILK SICKNESS. — **trem·bling·ly** /-b(ə)liNGlē/ adv. [ME (as a v.): from OFr. *trembler*, from med. L. *tremulare*, from L. *tremulus* (see TREMULOUS).]

trem·bler /ˈtremb(ə)lər/ ▶ n. **1** informal an earthquake. **2** a songbird (genera *Cinclocerthia* and *Ramphocinclus*) of the mockingbird family, found in the Lesser Antilles and named from its habit of violent shaking.

trem·blor /ˈtremblər; -ˌblôr/ ▶ n. an earth tremor. [20th C.: alt. of Sp. *temblor* 'shudder,' influenced by TREMBLER.]

trem·bly /ˈtremb(ə)lē/ ▶ adj. (**-bli·er, -bli·est**) informal shaking or quivering involuntarily.

tre·men·dous /trəˈmendəs/ ▶ adj. very great in amount, scale, or intensity. ■ informal extremely good or impressive; excellent. — **tre·men·dous·ly** adv. **tre·men·dous·ness** n. [17th C.: from L. *tremendus* (gerundive of *tremere* 'tremble') + -OUS.]

trem·o·lite /ˈtreməˌlīt/ ▶ n. a white to gray amphibole mineral that occurs widely in igneous rocks. [18th C.: from *Tremola* Valley, Switzerland, + -ITE[1].]

trem·o·lo /ˈtreməˌlō/ ▶ n. (pl. **-los**) Music a wavering effect in a musical tone, produced by rapid reiteration of a note, by rapid repeated variation in the pitch of a note, or by sounding two notes of slightly different pitches to produce prominent overtones. Compare with VIBRATO. ■ a mechanism in an organ producing such an effect. ■ (also **tremolo arm**) a lever on an electric guitar, used to produce such an effect. [18th C.: from Ital.]

trem·or /ˈtremər/ ▶ n. an involuntary quivering movement. ■ (also **earth tremor**) a slight earthquake. ■ a sudden feeling of fear or excitement. ■ a tremble or quaver in a person's voice. [17th C.: from L. *tremor*, from *tremere* 'to tremble.']

trem·u·lous /ˈtremyələs/ ▶ adj. shaking or quivering slightly. ■ timid; nervous. — **trem·u·lous·ly** adv. **trem·u·lous·ness** n. [17th C.: from L. *tremulus* (from *tremere* 'tremble') + -OUS.]

trench /trenCH/ ▶ n. a long, narrow ditch. ■ such a ditch dug by troops to provide a place of shelter from enemy fire. ■ (**trenches**) a connected system of such ditches forming an army's line. ■ (**the trenches**) the battlefields of northern France and Belgium in World War I. ■ (also **ocean trench**) a long, narrow, deep depression in the ocean bed. ▶ v. [trans.] dig a trench or trenches in (the ground): *she trenched the terrace to a depth of 6 feet.* ■ turn over the earth of (a field or garden) by digging a succession of adjoining ditches. [ME: from OFr. *trenche* (n.), *trenchier* (v.), based on L. *truncare* (see TRUNCATE).]

trench·ant /ˈtrenCHənt/ ▶ adj. vigorous or incisive in expression or style. — **trench·an·cy** /-CHənsē/ n. **trench·ant·ly** adv. [ME: from OFr., lit. 'cutting,' pres. part. of *trenchier* (see TRENCH).]

trench coat ▶ n. a loose, belted, double-breasted raincoat in a military style. ■ a lined or padded waterproof coat worn by soldiers.

trench·er[1] /ˈtrenCHər/ ▶ n. **1** hist. a wooden plate or platter for food. ■ a thick slice of bread used as a plate or platter. **2** old-fashioned term for MORTARBOARD (sense 1). [ME: from Anglo-Norman Fr. *trenchour*, from OFr. *trenchier* 'to cut' (see TRENCH).]

trench·er[2] ▶ n. a machine or attachment used in digging trenches.

trench·er·man /ˈtrenCHərmən/ ▶ n. (pl. **-men**) [usu. with adj.] humorous a person who eats in a specified manner, typically heartily.

trench fe·ver ▶ n. a highly contagious rickettsial disease transmitted by lice, that infected soldiers in the trenches in World War I.

trench foot ▶ n. a painful condition of the feet caused by long immersion in cold water or mud and marked by blackening and death of surface tissue.

trench mor·tar ▶ n. a light simple mortar designed to propel a bomb into enemy trenches.

trench mouth ▶ n. ulcerative gingivitis.

trench war·fare ▶ n. a type of combat in which opposing troops fight from trenches facing each other.

trend /trend/ ▶ n. a general direction in which something is developing or changing. ■ a fashion. ▶ v. [intrans.] (esp. of geographical features) bend or turn away in a specified direction. ■ change or develop in a general direction. [OE *trendan* 'revolve, rotate,' of Gmc. origin.]

trend·i·fy /ˈtrendəˌfī/ ▶ v. [trans.] informal, esp. derog. make (something or someone) very fashionable or up to date in style or influence.

trend·oid /ˈtrendoid/ informal ▶ n. a person who follows fashion blindly or excessively. ▶ adj. following fashion blindly or extravagantly.

trend·set·ter /ˈtren(d)ˌsetər/ ▶ n. a person who leads the way in fashion or ideas. — **trend·set·ting** /-ˌsetiNG/ adj.

trend·y /ˈtrendē/ informal ▶ adj. (**trend·i·er, trend·i·est**) very fashionable or up to date in style or influence. ▶ n. (pl. **trend·ies**) a person who is very fashionable. — **trend·i·ly** /-dəlē/ adv. **trend·i·ness** n.

Trent /trent/ a river in central England.

Trent, Coun·cil of an ecumenical council of the Roman Catholic Church, held in three sessions between 1545 and 1563 in Trento, Italy. Prompted by the opposition of the Reformation, the council clarified and redefined the church's doctrine, abolished many ecclesiastical abuses, and strengthened the authority of the papacy.

Tren·ton /ˈtrentn/ the capital of New Jersey, in the west central part of the state; pop. 85,403.

tre·pan /trəˈpan/ ▶ n. esp. hist. a trephine (hole saw) used by surgeons for perforating the skull. ▶ v. (**-panned, -pan·ning**) [trans.] perforate (a person's skull) with a trepan. — **trep·a·na·tion** /ˌtrepəˈnāSHən/ n. [ME: the noun via med. L. from Gk. *trupanon*, from *trupan* 'to bore,' from *trupē* 'hole.']

tre·pang /trəˈpaNG/ ▶ n. another term for BÊCHE-DE-MER (sense 1). [18th C.: from Malay *teripang*.]

tre·phine /triˈfīn/ ▶ n. a hole saw used in surgery to remove a circle of tissue or bone. ▶ v. [trans.] operate on with a trephine. — **treph·i·na·tion** /ˌtrefəˈnāSHən/ n. [17th C.: from L. *tres fines* 'three ends,' appar. influenced by TREPAN.]

trep·i·da·tion /ˌtrepiˈdāSHən/ ▶ n. **1** a feeling of fear or agitation about something that may happen. **2** archaic trembling motion. [15th C.: from L. *trepidatio(n-)*, from *trepidare* 'be agitated, tremble,' from *trepidus* 'alarmed.']

trep·o·ne·me /ˈtrepəˌnēm/ (also **trep·o·ne·ma** /ˌtrepəˈnēmə/) ▶ n. a spirochete bacterium (genus *Treponema*, order Spirochaetales) that is parasitic or pathogenic in humans and warm-blooded animals, including the causal agents of syphilis and yaws. — **trep·o·ne·mal** /-'nēməl/ **adj.** [20th C.: from mod. L. *Treponema*, from Gk. *trepein* 'to turn' + *nēma* 'thread.']

très /trā/ ▶ **adv.** (usually with reference to a fashionable quality) very: *très macho, très chic.* [Fr.]

tres·pass /'trespəs; -ˌpas/ ▶ **v.** [intrans.] **1** enter the owner's land or property without permission. ■ **(tresspass on)** make unfair claims on or take advantage of (something). **2** **(trespass against)** archaic literary commit an offense against (a person or a set of rules). ▶ **n.** **1** Law a voluntary wrongful act against the person or property of another, esp. unlawful entry to a person's land or property without their permission. **2** archaic literary a sin; an offense. — **tres·pass·er n.** [ME (sense 2): from OFr. *trespasser* 'pass over, trespass,' *trespas* 'passing across,' from med. L. *transpassare* (see TRANS-, PASS[1]).]

tress /tres/ ▶ **n.** (usu. **tresses**) a long lock of a woman's hair. ▶ **v.** [trans.] archaic arrange (a person's hair) into long locks. — **tressed adj.** [often in comb.] *a blonde-tressed sex symbol.* **tress·y adj.** [ME: from OFr. *tresse*, perh. based on Gk. *trikha* 'threefold.']

tres·sure /'tresHər/ ▶ **n.** Heraldry a thin border inset from the edge of a shield, narrower than an orle and usually borne double. ■ an ornamental enclosure containing a figure or distinctive device, formerly found on various gold and silver coins. [ME (denoting a ribbon or band for the hair): from OFr. *tressour* (see TRESS).]

tres·tle /'tresəl/ ▶ **n.** a framework consisting of a horizontal beam supported by two pairs of sloping legs, used in pairs to support a flat surface. ■ (also **tres·tle·work**) an open braced framework used to support an elevated structure such as a bridge. ■ short for TRESTLE TABLE. ■ (also **tres·tle·tree**) each of a pair of horizontal pieces on a sailing ship's lower mast supporting the topmast. [ME: from OFr. *trestel*, based on L. *transtrum* 'beam.']

tres·tle ta·ble ▶ **n.** a table consisting of a board or boards laid on trestles.

tret /tret/ ▶ **n.** hist. an allowance of extra weight made to purchasers of certain goods to compensate for waste during transportation. [15th C.: from an OFr. var. of *trait* 'act of dragging' (see TRAIT).]

tre·tin·o·in /trə'tinō-in/ ▶ **n.** a drug related to retinol (Vitamin A), used as a topical ointment in the treatment of acne and other disorders of the skin.

Tre·vi Foun·tain /'trevē/ the largest and most famous of the fountains of Rome, situated at the intersection of three roads, built in 1735.

Tre·vi·no /trə'vēnō/, Lee Buck (1939–), US golfer. In 1971, he won the Canadian, US, and British open championships.

trey /trā/ ▶ **n.** (pl. **treys**) a thing having three of something, in particular: ■ (in basketball) a shot scoring three points. ■ a playing card or die with three spots. [ME: from OFr. *trei* 'three,' from L. *tres.*]

trey·fa /'trāfə/ (also **treyf**) /'trāf/ ▶ **adj.** another term for TRAYF.

TRH ▶ **abbr.** ■ Their Royal Highnesses. ■ Biochem. thyrotropin-releasing hormone.

tri- ▶ **comb. form** three; having three: *triathlon.* ■ Chem. (in names of compounds) containing three atoms or groups of a specified kind: *trichloroethane.* [from L. and Gk., from L. *tres*, Gk. *treis* 'three.']

tri·a·ble /'trīəbəl/ ▶ **adj.** Law (of an offense) liable to a judicial trial. ■ (of a case or issue) able to be investigated and decided judicially. [ME: from Anglo-Norman Fr., from OFr. *trier* 'sift' (see TRY).]

tri·ac /'trīak/ ▶ **n.** Electron. a three-electrode semiconductor device that will conduct in either direction when triggered by a positive or negative signal at the gate electrode. [1960s: from TRIODE + **AC** (short for *alternating current*).]

tri·ac·e·tate /trī'asiˌtāt/ (also **cellulose triacetate**) ▶ **n.** a form of cellulose acetate containing three acetate groups per glucose monomer, used as a basis for man-made fibers.

tri·ad /'trīˌad/ ▶ **n.** a group or set of three connected people or things. ■ a chord of three musical notes, consisting of a given note with the third and fifth above it. — **tri·ad·ic** /trī'adik/ **adj.** [16th C.: from Fr. *triade*, or via late L. from Gk. *trias, triad-*, from *treis* 'three.']

tri·age /trē'äzH; 'trēˌäzH/ ▶ **n.** **1** the action of sorting according to quality. **2** (in medical use) the assignment of degrees of urgency to wounds or illnesses to decide the order of treatment of a large number of patients or casualties. ▶ **v.** [trans.] assign degrees of urgency to (wounded or ill patients). [18th C.: from Fr., from *trier* 'separate out.']

tri·al /'trī(ə)l/ ▶ **n.** **1** a formal examination of evidence by a judge, typically before a jury, in order to decide guilt in a case of criminal or civil proceedings. **2** a test of the performance, qualities, or suitability of someone or something. ■ an athletic contest to test the ability of players eligible for selection to a team. ■ **(trials)** an event in which horses, dogs, or other animals compete or perform. **3** a person, thing, or situation that tests a person's endurance or forbearance. ▶ **v.** (**tri·aled, tri·al·ing**; Brit. **tri·alled, tri·al·ling**) **1** [trans.] test (something, esp. a new product) to assess its suitability or performance. **2** [intrans.] (of a horse, dog, or other animal) compete in trials.

– PHRASES **on trial** being tried in a court of law. **trial and error** the process of experimenting with various methods of doing something until one finds the most successful. [ME: from Anglo-Norman Fr., or from med. L. *triallum.*]

tri·al bal·ance ▶ **n.** a statement of all debits and credits in a double-entry account book, with any disagreement indicating an error.

tri·al bal·loon ▶ **n.** a tentative measure taken or statement made to see how a new policy will be received.

tri·al·ist /'trīəlist/ ▶ **n.** a person who participates in a trial, in particular: ■ a person who takes part in a sports trial or motorcycle trial. ■ a person who takes part in a clinical or market test of a new product.

tri·a·logue /'trīəˌlôg; -ˌläg/ ▶ **n.** a dialogue between three people. [16th C.: from TRI- 'three' + DIALOGUE.]

tri·al run ▶ **n.** a preliminary test of how a new system or product works.

tri·an·gle /'trīˌaNGgəl/ ▶ **n.** a plane figure with three straight sides and three angles. See illustration at GEOMETRIC. ■ a thing shaped like such a figure. ■ a situation involving three people or things, esp. an emotional relationship. ■ a musical instrument consisting of a steel rod bent into a triangle and sounded by being struck with a small steel rod. ■ a frame used to position the balls in pool and snooker. ■ a drawing instrument in the form of a right triangle. ■ **(triangles)** hist. a frame of three halberds joined at the top to which a soldier was bound for flogging. [ME: from OFr. *triangle* or L. *triangulum*, neut. of *triangulus* 'three-cornered' (see TRI-, ANGLE[1]).]

tri·an·gu·lar /trī'aNGgyələr/ ▶ **adj.** shaped like a triangle; having three sides and three corners. ■ involving three people or parties. ■ (of a pyramid) having a three-sided base. — **tri·an·gu·lar·i·ty** /trīˌaNGgyə'laritē/ **n.** **tri·an·gu·lar·ly adv.**

tri·an·gu·late ▶ **v.** /trī'aNGgyəˌlāt/ **1** [trans.] divide (an area) into triangles for surveying purposes. ■ measure and map (an area) by the use of triangles with a known base length and base angles. ■ determine (a height, distance, or location) in this way. **2** [trans.] form into a triangle or triangles.

tri·an·gu·la·tion /ˌtrīˌaNGgyə'lāsHən/ ▶ **n.** **1** (in surveying) the tracing and measurement of a series or network of triangles in order to determine the distances and relative positions of points spread over a territory or region. **2** formation of or division into triangles.

Tri·an·gu·lum /trī'aNGgyələm/ Astron. a small northern constellation (the Triangle), between Andromeda and Aries.

Tri·an·gu·lum Aus·tra·le /ô'strālē/ Astron. a small southern constellation (the Southern Triangle), lying in the Milky Way near the south celestial pole.

Tri·a·non /'trēəˌnän/ either of two small palaces in the great park at Versailles in France. The larger was built by Louis XIV in 1687; the smaller was built by Louis XV 1762–68.

Tri·as·sic /trī'asik/ ▶ **adj.** Geol. of, relating to, or denoting the earliest period of the Mesozoic era (between the Permian and Jurassic periods, about 245 million to 208 million years ago), a time when the first dinosaurs, ammonites, and primitive mammals appeared. ■ [as n.] (**the Triassic** or **the Trias**) the Triassic period or the system of rocks deposited during it. [19th C.: from late L. *trias* (see TRIAD).]

tri·ath·lon /trī'aTHlən; -ˌlän/ ▶ **n.** an athletic contest consisting of three different events, typically swimming, cycling, and long-distance running. — **tri·ath·lete** /-ˌlēt/ **n.** [1970s: from TRI- 'three,' on the pattern of *decathlon.*]

tri·a·tom·ic /ˌtrīə'tämik/ ▶ **adj.** Chem. consisting of three atoms.

tri·ax·i·al /trī'aksēəl/ ▶ **adj.** having or relating to three axes, esp. in mechanical or astronomical contexts.

tri·a·zine /'trīəˌzēn/ ▶ **n.** Chem. any of a group of compounds whose molecules contain an unsaturated ring of three carbon and three nitrogen atoms.

tri·a·zole /'trīəˌzōl; trī'azôl/ ▶ **n.** a compound, $C_2H_3N_3$, whose molecule contains a ring of three nitrogen and two carbon atoms, in particular each of five isomeric compounds containing such a ring with two double bonds.

trib. ▶ **abbr.** tributary.

trib·ade /'tribəd/ ▶ **n.** a lesbian. — **trib·a·dism** /-ˌdizəm/ **n.** [17th C.: from Fr. *tribade*, or via L. from Gk. *tribas*, from *tribein* 'to rub.']

trib·al /'trībəl/ ▶ **adj.** of or characteristic of a tribe or tribes. ■ esp. derog. characterized by a tendency to form groups or by strong group loyalty. ▶ **n.** (**tribals**) members of tribal communities, esp. in the Indian subcontinent. — **trib·al·ly adv.**

trib·al·ism /'trībəˌlizəm/ ▶ **n.** the state or fact of being organized in a tribe or tribes. ■ esp. derog. the behavior and attitudes that stem from strong loyalty to one's own tribe or social group. — **trib·al·ist** /'trībəlist/ **n.** **tri·bal·is·tic** /ˌtrībə'listik/ **adj.**

tri·ba·sic /trī'bāsik/ ▶ **adj.** Chem. (of an acid) having three replaceable hydrogen atoms.

tribe /trīb/ ▶ **n.** **1** a social division in a traditional society consisting of families or communities linked by social, economic, religious, or blood ties, with a common culture and dialect, typically having a leader. ■ (in ancient Rome) each of several political divisions, originally three, later thirty, ultimately thirty-five. ■ informal family. ■ derog. a distinctive close-knit social or political group. ■ derog. a group or class of people or things. ■ (often **tribes**) informal large numbers of people or animals. **2** Biol. a taxonomic category that ranks above genus and below family or subfamily, usually ending in *-ini* (in zoology) or *-eae* (in botany). [ME: from OFr. *tribu* or L. *tribus* (sing. and pl.); perh. rel. to *tri-* 'three.']

Tri·Be·Ca /trī'bekə/ a residential and commercial section of southern Manhattan in New York City.

tribes·man /'trībzmən/ ▸ **n.** (pl. **-men**) a man belonging to a tribe in a traditional society or group.

Tribes of Is·ra·el the twelve divisions of ancient Israel, each traditionally descended from one of the twelve sons of Jacob. Also called **Twelve Tribes of Israel**.

tribes·peo·ple /'trībz,pēpəl/ ▸ **plural n.** people belonging to a tribe in a traditional society or group.

tribes·wom·an /'trībz,wo͝omən/ ▸ **n.** (pl. **-wom·en**) a woman belonging to a tribe in a traditional society or group.

tribo- ▸ **comb. form** relating to friction: *triboelectricity.* [from Gk. *tribos* 'rubbing.']

tri·bo·e·lec·tric·i·ty /,trībō-ilək'trisitē; -,ēlek-/ ▸ **n.** electric charge generated by friction.

tri·bol·o·gy /trī'bäləjē/ ▸ **n.** the study of friction, wear, lubrication, and the design of bearings; the science of interacting surfaces in relative motion. — **tri·bo·log·i·cal** /-bə'läjikəl/ **adj. tri·bol·o·gist** /-jist/ **n.**

tri·bo·lu·mi·nes·cence /,trībō,lo͞omə'nesəns/ ▸ **n.** the emission of light from a substance caused by rubbing, scratching, or similar frictional contact. — **tri·bo·lu·mi·nes·cent adj.**

tri·bom·e·ter /trī'bämitər/ ▸ **n.** an instrument for measuring friction in sliding.

tri·brach /'trī,brak/ ▸ **n.** Pros. a metrical foot of three short or unstressed syllables. — **tri·brach·ic** /trī'brakik/ **adj.** [16th C.: via L. from Gk. *tribrakhus*, from *tri-* 'three' + *brakhus* 'short.']

trib·u·la·tion /,tribyə'lāsHən/ ▸ **n.** (usu. **tribulations**) a cause of great trouble or suffering. ■ a state of great trouble or suffering. ■ (**the tribulation** or **the Great Tribulation**) Christian Theol. a period of great suffering expected during the end times. [ME: via OFr. from eccles. Latin *tribulatio(n-)*, from L. *tribulare* 'press, oppress,' from *tribulum* 'threshing board (constructed of sharp points),' based on *terere* 'rub.']

tri·bu·nal /trī'byo͞onl; trə-/ ▸ **n.** a court of justice. ■ a seat or bench for a judge or judges. [ME (denoting a seat for judges): from OFr., or from L. *tribunal* 'raised platform provided for magistrates' seats,' from *tribunus* (see **tribune[1]**).]

trib·une[1] /'tribyo͞on; tri'byo͞on/ ▸ **n.** (also **tribune of the people**) an official in ancient Rome chosen by the plebeians to protect their interests. ■ (also **military tribune**) a Roman legionary officer. ■ fig. a popular leader; a champion of the people. ■ used in names of newspapers. — **trib·u·nate** /'tribyənit; trī'byo͞onit; -,nāt/ **n. trib·une·ship** /-,sHip/ **n.** [ME: from L. *tribunus*, lit. 'head of a tribe,' from *tribus* 'tribe.']

trib·une[2] ▸ **n.** **1** an apse in a basilica. **2** a dais or rostrum, esp. in a church. ■ a raised area or gallery with seats, esp. in a church. [17th C.: via Fr. from Ital., from med. L. *tribuna*, alt. of L. *tribunal* (see **tribunal**).]

trib·u·tar·y /'tribyə,terē/ ▸ **n.** (pl. **-tar·ies**) **1** a river or stream flowing into a larger river or lake. **2** hist. a person or state that pays tribute to another state or ruler. [ME (sense 2): from L. *tributarius*, from *tributum* (see **tribute**).]

trib·ute /'tribyo͞ot/ ▸ **n.** **1** an act, statement, or gift that is intended to show gratitude, respect, or admiration. ■ [in sing.] something resulting from something else and indicating its worth. **2** hist. payment made periodically by one state or ruler to another, esp. as a sign of dependence. **3** hist. a proportion of ore or its equivalent, paid to a miner for his work, or to the owner or lessor of a mine. [ME: from L. *tributum*, neut. past part. of *tribuere* 'assign,' from *tribus* 'tribe.']

tri·cam·er·al /trī'kamərəl/ ▸ **adj.** of or relating to the parliamentary system operating in South Africa between 1983 and 1994, in which the legislature consisted of three ethnically based houses.

tri·car·box·yl·ic ac·id cy·cle /,trīkärbäk'silik/ ▸ **n.** another term for **Krebs cycle.**

trice /trīs/ ▸ **n.** (in phrase **in a trice**) in a moment; very quickly. [ME *trice* 'a tug,' from MDu. *trisen* 'pull sharply.']

tri·cen·ten·ar·y /trī'sentn,erē; ,trīsen'tenərē/ ▸ **n.** (pl. **-ar·ies**) another term for **tricentennial.**

tri·cen·ten·ni·al /,trīsen'tenēəl/ ▸ **n.** the three-hundredth anniversary of a significant event. ▸ **adj.** of or relating to a three-hundredth anniversary.

tri·ceps /'trī,seps/ ▸ **n.** (pl. same or **-ceps·es**) Anat. any of several muscles having three points of attachment at one end, particularly (also **tri·ceps bra·chi·i** /'brākē,ī; -kē,ē; 'brak-/) the large muscle at the back of the upper arm. [16th C.: from L., lit. 'three-headed,' from *tri-* 'three' + *-ceps* (from *caput* 'head').]

tri·cer·a·tops /trī'serə,täps/ ▸ **n.** a large quadrupedal herbivorous dinosaur (genus *Triceratops*, infraorder Ceratopsia, order Ornithischia) living at the end of the Cretaceous period, having a massive head with two large horns, a smaller horn on the beaked snout, and a bony frill above the neck. See illustration at **dinosaur.** [mod. L., from Gk. *trikeratos* 'three-horned' + *ōps* 'face.']

tri·chi·a·sis /tri'kīəsis/ ▸ **n.** Med. ingrowth or introversion of the eyelashes. [17th C.: via late L. from Gk. *trikhiasis*, from *trikhian* 'be hairy.']

tri·chi·na /tri'kīnə/ ▸ **n.** (pl. **-nae** /-nē/) a parasitic nematode (genus *Trichinella*, class Aphasmida) of humans and other mammals, the adults of which live in the small intestine. The larvae form hard cysts in the muscles, where they remain until eaten by the next host. [19th C.: from mod. L. (former genus name), from Gk. *trikhinos* 'of hair.']

Trich·i·nop·o·ly /,trikə'näpəlē; ,tricH-/ another name for **Tiruchirapalli.**

trich·i·no·sis /,trikə'nōsis/ ▸ **n.** a disease caused by trichinae (usually *Trichinella spiralis*), typically from infected meat, esp. pork, characterized by digestive disturbance, fever, and muscular rigidity.

tri·chlo·ro·a·ce·tic ac·id /trī,klôrōə'sētik/ (also **tri·chlor·a·ce·tic acid** /-,klôrə'setik/) ▸ **n.** Chem. a toxic deliquescent crystalline solid, CCl_3COOH, used as a solvent, analgesic, and anesthetic. — **tri·chlo·ro·ac·e·tate** /-'asi,tāt/ **n.**

tri·chlo·ro·eth·ane /trī,klôrō'eTHān/ ▸ **n.** Chem. a colorless, nonflammable volatile liquid, CCl_3CH_3, used as a solvent and cleaner. Also called **1,1,1-trichloroethane.**

tri·chlo·ro·eth·yl·ene /trī,klôrō'eTHə,lēn/ ▸ **n.** Chem. a colorless volatile liquid, $CCl_2{=}CHCl$, used as a solvent and formerly as an anesthetic.

tri·chlo·ro·phe·nol /trī,klôrō'fēnôl; -nōl/ ▸ **n.** Chem. a synthetic crystalline compound ($C_6H_2Cl_3(OH)$; six isomers) used as an insecticide and preservative and in the synthesis of pesticides.

tricho- ▸ **comb. form** of or relating to hair: *trichology.* [from Gk. *thrix, trikhos* 'hair.']

trich·o·cyst /'trikə,sist/ ▸ **n.** Biol. any of numerous minute, rodlike structures, each containing a protrusible filament, found near the surface of ciliates and dinoflagellates.

tri·chol·o·gy /tri'käləjē/ ▸ **n.** the branch of medical and cosmetic study and practice concerned with the hair and scalp. — **trich·o·log·i·cal** /,trikə'läjikəl/ **adj. tri·chol·o·gist** /-jist/ **n.**

trich·ome /'trī,kōm; 'trikōm/ ▸ **n.** Bot. a small hair or other outgrowth from the epidermis of a plant, typically unicellular and glandular. [19th C.: from Gk. *trikhōma*, from *trikhoun* 'cover with hair.']

trich·o·mon·ad /,trikə'mänad; -'mō-/ ▸ **n.** Zool. & Med. a parasitic protozoan (order Trichomonadida, phylum Parabasilia, kingdom Protista) with four to six flagella and an undulating membrane, infesting the urogenital or digestive system. — **trich·o·mon·al** /-'mänl; -'mōnl/ **adj.** [19th C.: from mod. L. *Trichomonadida* (pl.), from Gk. *thrix, trikh-* 'hair' + *monas, monad-* 'unit.']

trich·o·mo·ni·a·sis /,trikəmə'nīəsis/ ▸ **n.** Med. an infection caused by parasitic trichomonads (genus *Trichomonas*), chiefly affecting the urinary tract, vagina, or digestive system.

Tri·chop·ter·a /trī'käptərə/ Entomol. an order of insects that comprises the caddisflies. ■ [as pl. n.] (**trichoptera**) insects of this order. — **tri·chop·ter·an n. & adj.** [mod. L. (pl.), from **tricho-** 'hair' + Gk. *pteron* 'wing.']

tri·chot·o·my /trī'kätəmē/ ▸ **n.** (pl. **-mies**) a division into three categories. ■ the division of the human person into body, soul, and spirit. — **tri·chot·o·mous** /-məs/ **adj.** [17th C.: from Gk. *trikha* 'threefold,' from *treis* 'three,' on the pattern of *dichotomy*.]

tri·chro·ic /trī'krōik/ ▸ **adj.** Crystallog. (of a crystal) appearing with different colors when viewed along the three crystallographic directions. — **tri·chro·ism** /'trīkrō,izəm/ **n.** [19th C.: from Gk. *trikhroos* (from *tri-* 'three' + *khrōs* 'color') + **-ic.**]

tri·chro·mat·ic /,trīkrō'matik/ ▸ **adj.** having or using three colors. ■ having normal color vision, which is sensitive to all three primary colors. — **tri·chro·ma·tism** /-'krōmə,tizəm/ **n.**

tri·chrome /'trī,krōm/ ▸ **adj.** Biol. denoting a stain or method of histological staining in which different tissues are stained, each in one of three different colors. [20th C.: from **tri-** 'three' + Gk. *khrōma* 'color.']

trick /trik/ ▸ **n.** **1** a cunning or skillful act or scheme intended to deceive or outwit someone. ■ a mischievous practical joke. ■ a skillful act performed for entertainment or amusement. ■ an illusion. ■ a clever or particular way of doing something. **2** a peculiar or characteristic habit or mannerism. **3** (in bridge, whist, and similar card games) a sequence of cards forming a single round of play. One card is laid down by each player, the highest card being the winner. **4** informal a prostitute's client. **5** a sailor's turn at the helm, usually lasting for two or four hours. ▸ **v.** [trans.] **1** (often **be tricked**) deceive or outwit (someone) by being cunning or skillful. ■ (**trick someone into**) use deception to make someone do (something). ■ (**trick someone out of**) use deception to deprive someone of (something). **2** Heraldry sketch (a coat of arms) in outline, with the colors indicated by letters or signs. ▸ **adj.** [attrib.] **1** intended or used to deceive or mystify, or to create an illusion. **2** liable to fail; defective: *a trick knee.*

– PHRASES **do the trick** informal achieve the required result. **every trick in the book** informal every available method of achieving what one wants. **how's tricks?** informal used as a friendly greeting. **not miss a trick** see **miss[1]**. **the oldest trick in the book** a ruse so hackneyed that it should no longer deceive anyone. **trick or treat** a children's custom of calling at houses at Halloween with the threat of pranks if they are not given a small gift (often used as a greeting by children doing this). **tricks of the trade** special ingenious techniques used in a profession or craft, esp. those that are little known by outsiders. **turn a trick** informal (of a prostitute) have a session with a client. **up to one's (old) tricks** informal misbehaving in a characteristic way.

– PHRASAL VERBS **trick someone/something out** (or **up**) (usu. **be tricked out**) dress or decorate someone or something in an elaborate or showy way. — **trick·er n. trick·ish adj.** (dated). [ME (as a n.): from an OFr. dial. var. of *triche*, from *trichier* 'deceive.']

trick·er·y /'trikərē/ ▸ **n.** (pl. **-er·ies**) the practice of deception.

trick·le /'trikəl/ ▸ **v.** [intrans.] (of a liquid) flow in a small stream. ■ [trans.] cause (a liquid) to flow in a small stream. ■ come or go slowly or gradually. ▸ **n.** a small flow of liquid. ■ a small group or number of people or things moving slowly. [ME (as a v.): imitative.]

trick·le-down ▸ **adj.** (of an economic system) in which the poorest gradually benefit as a result of the increasing wealth of the richest.

trick·ster /'trikstər/ ▶ n. a person who cheats or deceives people.

trick·y /'trikē/ ▶ adj. (**trick·i·er, trick·i·est**) (of a task, problem, or situation) requiring care and skill because difficult or awkward. ■ (of a person or act) deceitful, crafty, or skillful. — **trick·i·ly** /'trikəlē/ adv. **trick·i·ness** n.

tri·clad /'trī,klad/ ▶ n. Zool. a free-living flatworm of an order (Tricladida, class Turbellaria) characterized by having a gut with three branches, including the planarians. [19th C.: from mod. L. *Tricladida*, from TRI- 'three' + Gk. *klados* 'branch.']

tri·clin·ic /trī'klinik/ ▶ adj. of or denoting a crystal system or three-dimensional geometric arrangement having three unequal oblique axes. [19th C.: from Gk. TRI- 'three' + *-clinic*, on the pattern of *monoclinic*.]

tri·clin·i·um /trī'klinēəm/ ▶ n. (pl. **-clin·i·a** /-'klinēə/) a dining table with couches along three sides used in ancient Rome. ■ a room containing such a table. [L., from Gk. *triklinion*, from *tri-* 'three' + *klinē* 'couch.']

tri·col·or /'trī,kələr/ (Brit. **tri·col·our**) ▶ n. a flag with three bands or blocks of different colors, esp. the French national flag with equal upright bands of blue, white, and red. ▶ adj. (also **tri·col·ored**) having three colors.

tri·corne /'trī,kôrn/ (also **tri·corn**) ▶ adj. [attrib.] (of a hat) having a brim turned up on three sides. ▶ n. a hat of this kind. [19th C.: from Fr. *tricorne* or L. *tricornis*, from *tri-* 'three' + *cornu* 'horn.']

tri·cot /'trēkō/ ▶ n. a fine knitted fabric made of a natural or man-made fiber. [18th C.: from Fr., lit. 'knitting,' from *tricoter* 'to knit,' of unknown origin.]

tric-trac /'trik ,trak/ ▶ n. hist. a form of backgammon. [17th C.: from Fr., imitative.]

tri·cus·pid /trī'kəspid/ ▶ adj. **1** having three cusps or points, in particular: ■ denoting a tooth with three cusps or points. ■ denoting a valve formed of three triangular segments, particularly that between the right atrium and ventricle of the heart. **2** [attrib.] of or relating to the tricuspid valve. [17th C.: from TRI- 'three' + L. *cuspis, cuspid-* 'cusp.']

tri·cy·cle /'trīsikəl; -,sikəl/ ▶ n. a vehicle similar to a bicycle, but having three wheels, two at the back and one at the front. ▶ v. [intrans.] [often as n.] (**tricycling**) ride on a tricycle. — **tri·cy·clist** /-ist/ n.

tri·cy·clic /trī'sīklik; -'sik-/ ▶ adj. Chem. (of a compound) having three rings of atoms in its molecule. ▶ n. (usu. **tricyclics**) Med. any of a class of antidepressant drugs having molecules with three fused rings.

tri·dac·tyl /trī'daktl/ ▶ adj. Zool. (of a vertebrate limb) having three toes or fingers. [19th C.: from TRI- 'three' + Gk. *daktulos* 'finger.']

tri·dent /'trīdnt/ ▶ n. a three-pronged spear, esp. as an attribute of Poseidon (Neptune) or Britannia. ■ (**Trident**) a US design of submarine-launched long-range ballistic missile. [ME: from L. *trident-*, from *tri-* 'three' + *dens, dent-* 'tooth.']

Tri·den·tine /trī'den,tēn; -,tīn/ ▶ adj. of or relating to the Council of Trent, esp. as the basis of Roman Catholic doctrine. [from med. L. *Tridentinus*, from *Tridentum* 'Trent.']

Tri·den·tine mass ▶ n. the Latin Eucharistic liturgy used by the Roman Catholic Church from 1570 to 1964.

tried /trīd/ past and past participle of TRY. ▶ adj. [attrib.] used in various phrases to describe something that has proved effective or reliable before.
– PHRASES **the tried and true** something that has proved effective or reliable before.

trident

tri·ene /'trī,ēn/ ▶ n. Chem. an unsaturated hydrocarbon containing three double bonds between carbon atoms.

tri·en·ni·al /trī'enēəl/ ▶ adj. recurring every three years. ■ lasting for or relating to a period of three years. ▶ n. a visitation of an Anglican diocese by its bishop every three years. — **tri·en·ni·al·ly** adv.

tri·en·ni·um /trī'enēəm/ ▶ n. (pl. **-en·ni·a** /-'enēə/ or **-en·ni·ums**) a specified period of three years. [19th C.: from L., from *tri-* 'three' + *annus* 'year.']

tri·er /'trīər/ ▶ n. **1** a person who always makes an effort, however unsuccessful they may be. **2** a person or body responsible for investigating and deciding a case judicially.

Tri·este /trē'est; -'estā/ a city in northeastern Italy, on the Adriatic Sea; pop. 231,000.

tri·fa·cial nerve /trī'fāshəl/ ▶ n. another term for TRIGEMINAL NERVE.

tri·fect·a /trī'fektə/ ▶ n. a bet in which the person betting forecasts the first three finishers in a race in the correct order. ■ [in sing.] a run of three wins or grand events. [1970s: from TRI- 'three' + PERFECTA.]

tri·fid /'trīfid/ ▶ adj. esp. Biol. partly or wholly split into three divisions or lobes. [18th C.: from L. *trifidus*, from *tri-* 'three' + *fid-* 'split, divided' (from the verb *findere*).]

tri·fle /'trīfəl/ ▶ n. **1** a thing of little value or importance. ■ [in sing.] a small amount of something. **2** Brit. a cold dessert of sponge cake and fruit covered with layers of custard, jelly, and cream. ▶ v. [intrans.] (**trifle with**) treat (someone or something) without seriousness or respect.
– PHRASES **a trifle** a little; somewhat. — **tri·fler** /-f(ə)lər/ n. [ME: from OFr. *trufle*, by-form of *trufe* 'deceit.']

tri·fling /'trīf(ə)liNG/ ▶ adj. unimportant or trivial. — **tri·fling·ly** adv.

tri·fo·cal /'trī,fōkəl/ ▶ adj. (of a pair of glasses) having lenses with three parts with different focal lengths. ▶ n. (**trifocals**) a pair of glasses with such lenses.

tri·fo·li·ate /trī'fōlē-it; -,āt/ ▶ adj. (of a compound leaf) having three leaflets. ■ (of a plant) having such leaves. ■ (of an object or design) having the form of such a leaf. ▶ n. a plant with such leaves.

tri·fo·ri·um /trī'fôrēəm/ ▶ n. (pl. **-for·i·a** /-'fôrēə/) a gallery or arcade above the arches of the nave, choir, and transepts of a church. [18th C.: from Anglo-L., of unknown origin.]

tri·form /'trī,fôrm/ ▶ adj. tech. composed of three parts.

tri·fur·cate ▶ v. /'trīfər,kāt/ [intrans.] divide into three branches or forks. ▶ adj. (also **tri·fur·cat·ed**) divided into three branches or forks. — **tri·fur·ca·tion** /,trīfər'kāSHən/ n. [19th C.: from L. *trifurcus* 'three-forked' (from *tri-* 'three' + *furca* 'fork') + -ATE².]

trig¹ /trig/ ▶ n. informal trigonometry.

trig² ▶ adj. neat and smart in appearance. ▶ v. (**trigged, trig·ging**) [trans.] make neat and smart in appearance. [ME: from ON *tryggr*; rel. to TRUE.]

trig. ▶ abbr. ■ trigonometric. ■ trigonometrical. ■ trigonometry.

trig·a·mous /'trigəməs/ ▶ adj. having three wives or husbands at the same time. — **trig·a·mist** /-mist/ n. **trig·a·my** /-mē/ n. [19th C.: from Gk. *trigamos* (from *tri-* 'three' + *gamos* 'marriage') + -OUS.]

tri·gem·i·nal nerve /trī'jemənl/ ▶ n. Anat. each of the fifth and largest pair of cranial nerves, supplying the front part of the head and dividing into the ophthalmic, maxillary, and mandibular nerves.

tri·gem·i·nal neu·ral·gia ▶ n. Med. neuralgia involving one or more of the branches of the trigeminal nerves, and often causing severe pain.

tri·gem·i·nus /trī'jemənəs/ ▶ n. (pl. **-ni** /-,nī/) Anat. the trigeminal nerve. [19th C.: from L., lit. 'three born at the same birth.']

trig·ger /'trigər/ ▶ n. a small device that releases a spring or catch and so sets off a mechanism, esp. in order to fire a gun. ■ an event or thing that causes something to happen. ▶ v. [trans.] (often **be triggered**) cause (an event or situation) to happen or exist. ■ cause (a device) to function.
– PHRASES **quick on the trigger** quick to respond. — **trig·gered** adj. [17th C.: from dial. *tricker*, from Du. *trekker*, from *trekken* 'to pull.']

trig·ger fin·ger ▶ n. **1** the forefinger of the hand, as that with which the trigger of a gun is typically pulled. **2** Med. a defect in a tendon causing a finger to jerk or snap straight when the hand is extended.

trig·ger·fish /'trigər,fiSH/ ▶ n. (pl. same or **-fish·es**) a marine fish (family Balistidae: numerous genera and species) occurring chiefly in tropical inshore waters. It has a large, stout dorsal spine that can be erected and locked into place, allowing the fish to wedge itself into crevices.

trig·ger hair ▶ n. a hairlike structure that triggers a rapid movement when touched, in particular: ■ Zool. (in a coelenterate) a filament at the mouth of a nematocyst, triggering the emission of the stinging hair. ■ Bot. a bristle on the leaf of a Venus flytrap, triggering the closure of the leaf around an insect.

trig·ger-hap·py ▶ adj. ready to react violently, esp. by shooting, on the slightest provocation.

trig·ger point ▶ n. a particular circumstance or situation that causes an event to occur. ■ Physiol. & Med. a sensitive area of the body, stimulation or irritation of which causes a specific effect in another part, esp. a tender area in a muscle that causes generalized musculoskeletal pain when overstimulated.

Tri·glav /'trē,gläf; -,gläv/ a mountain in the Julian Alps, in northwestern Slovenia, near the Italian border.

tri·glyc·er·ide /trī'glisə,rīd/ ▶ n. Chem. an ester formed from glycerol and three fatty acid groups. Triglycerides are the main constituents of natural fats and oils.

tri·glyph /'trī,glif/ ▶ n. Archit. a tablet in a Doric frieze with three vertical grooves. Triglyphs alternate with metopes. — **tri·glyph·ic** /trī'glifik/ adj. [16th C.: via L. from Gk. *trigluphos*, from *tri-* 'three' + *gluphē* 'carving.']

tri·gon /'trī,gän/ ▶ n. archaic term for TRIANGLE. ■ an ancient triangular lyre or harp. ■ a triangular cutting region formed by three cusps on an upper molar tooth. [17th C. (in the sense 'triangle'): via L. from Gk. *trigōnon*, neut. of *trigōnos* 'three-cornered.']

trigon. ▶ abbr. ■ trigonometric. ■ trigonometrical. ■ trigonometry.

trig·o·nal /'trigənl/ ▶ adj. triangular. ■ esp. Biol. triangular in cross section. ■ of or denoting a crystal system or three-dimensional geometric arrangement having three equal axes separated by equal angles that are not right angles. — **trig·o·nal·ly** adv.

trig·o·no·met·ric func·tion ▶ n. Math. a function of an angle, or of an abstract quantity, used in trigonometry. The sine, tangent, and secant, for example, are trigonometric functions. Also called CIRCULAR FUNCTION.

trig·o·nom·e·try /,trigə'nämitrē/ ▶ n. the branch of mathematics dealing with the relations of the sides and angles of triangles and with the relevant functions of any angles. — **trig·o·no·met·ric** /-nə'metrik/ adj. **trig·o·no·met·ri·cal** /-nə'metrikəl/ adj. [17th C.: from mod. L. *trigonometria* (see TRIGON, -METRY).]

tri·gram /'trī,gram/ ▶ n. **1** another term for TRIGRAPH. **2** each of the eight figures formed of three parallel lines, each either whole or broken, combined to form the sixty-four hexagrams of the *I Ching*.

tri·graph /'trī,graf/ ▶ n. a group of three letters representing one sound, for example German *sch-*.

tri·he·dral /trī'hēdrəl/ ▶ **adj.** (of a solid figure or body) having three sides or faces (in addition to the base or ends); triangular in cross section. ▶ **n.** a trihedral figure. [18th C.: from Gk. *tri-* 'three' + *hedra* 'base' + -AL.]

tri·he·dron /trī'hēdrən/ ▶ **n.** (pl. **-drons** or **-dra** /-drə/) a solid figure having three sides or faces (in addition to the base or ends).

tri·i·o·do·meth·ane /,trī-īōdō'meTHān; -,ädō-/ ▶ **n.** another term for IODOFORM.

tri·i·o·do·thy·ro·nine /,trī-ī,ōdō'THīrə,nēn; -ī,ädō-/ ▶ **n.** Biochem. a thyroid hormone similar to thyroxine but having greater potency.

tri·jet /'trī,jet/ ▶ **n.** an aircraft powered by three jet engines.

trike /trīk/ informal ▶ **n.** a tricycle. [19th C.: abbr.]

tri·lat·er·al /trī'latərəl/ ▶ **adj.** shared by or involving three parties. ■ Geom. of, on, or with three sides. ▶ **n.** a triangle.

tril·by /'trilbē/ ▶ **n.** (pl. **-bies**) esp. Brit. a soft felt hat with a narrow brim and indented crown. — **tril·bied adj.** [19th C.: from the name of the heroine in G. du Maurier's novel *Trilby* (1894).]

tri·lin·e·ar /trī'linēar/ ▶ **adj.** Math. of or having three lines.

tri·lin·gual /trī'liNGgwəl/ ▶ **adj.** (of a person) speaking three languages fluently. ■ (of a text or an activity) written or conducted in three languages. — **tri·lin·gual·ism** /-gwə,lizəm/ **n.** [19th C.: from TRI- 'three' + L. *lingua* 'tongue' + -AL.]

trill /tril/ ▶ **n.** a quavering or vibratory sound, esp. a rapid alternation of sung or played notes. ■ the pronunciation of a consonant, esp. *r*, with rapid vibration of the tongue against the hard or soft palate or the uvula. ▶ **v.** [intrans.] produce a quavering or warbling sound. ■ [trans.] sing (a note or song) with a warbling or quavering sound. ■ [trans.] pronounce (a consonant) by rapid vibration of the tongue against the hard or soft palate or the uvula. [17th C.: from Ital. *trillo* (n.), *trillare* (v.).]

trill·er /'trilər/ ▶ **n.** an Australasian and Southeast Asian songbird (genera *Lalage* and *Chlamydochaera*, family Campephagidae) with mainly black and white plumage.

Tril·lin /'trilən/, Calvin (1935–), US writer. He wrote *Remembering Denny* (1993).

tril·lion /'trilyən/ ▶ **cardinal number** (pl. **-lions** or [with numeral] same) a million million (1,000,000,000,000 or 10^{12}). ■ (**trillions**) informal a very large number or amount: *trillions of voices.* ■ dated, esp. Brit. a million million million (1,000,000,000,000,000,000 or 10^{18}). — **tril·lionth** /-yənTH/ **ordinal number.** [17th C.: from Fr., from *million*, by substitution of the prefix *tri-* 'three' for the initial letters.]

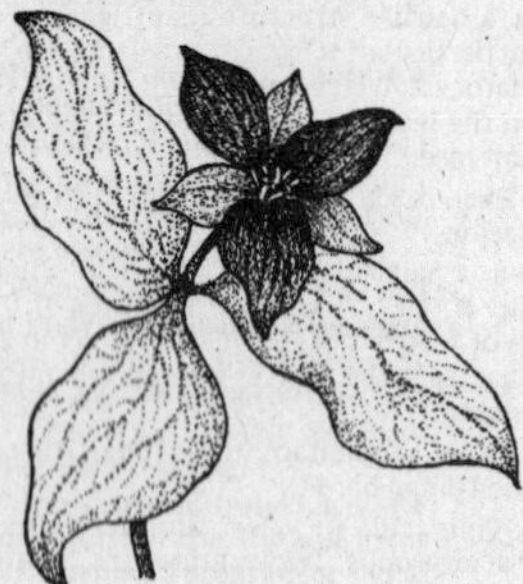

red trillium

tril·li·um /'trilēəm/ ▶ **n.** a plant (genus *Trillium*) of the lily family with a solitary three-petaled flower above a whorl of three leaves, native to North America and Asia. Its several species include the **red** (or **purple**) **trillium** (*T. erectum*). [mod. L., appar. an alt. of Swed. *trilling* 'triplet.']

tri·lo·bite /'trīlə,bīt/ ▶ **n.** an extinct marine arthropod (subphylum Trilobita) that occurred abundantly during the Paleozoic era, with a carapace over the forepart, and a segmented hindpart divided longitudinally into three lobes. [19th C.: from mod. L. *Trilobites*, from Gk. *tri-* 'three' + *lobos* 'lobe.']

tril·o·gy /'triləjē/ ▶ **n.** (pl. **-gies**) a group of three related novels, plays, films, operas, or albums. ■ (in ancient Greece) a series of three tragedies performed one after the other. ■ fig. a group or series of three related things: *a trilogy of cases reflected this development.*

trim /trim/ ▶ **v.** (**trimmed, trimming**) [trans.] **1** make (something) neat or of the required size or form by cutting away irregular or unwanted parts. ■ cut off (irregular or unwanted parts). ■ fig. reduce the size, amount, or number of (something, typically expenditure or costs). ■ [intrans.] (**trim down**) (of a person) lose weight; become slimmer. ■ firm up or lose weight from (a part of one's body). **2** (usu. **be trimmed**) decorate (something), typically with contrasting items or pieces of material. **3** adjust (sails) to take best advantage of the wind. ■ adjust the forward and after drafts of (a vessel) by changing the distribution of weight on board, esp. cargo and ballast. ■ stow (a bulk cargo) properly in a ship's hold by use of manual labor or machinery. ■ keep or adjust the degree to which (an aircraft) can be maintained at a constant altitude without any control forces being present. ■ [intrans.] adapt one's views to the prevailing political trends for personal advancement. **4** informal, dated get the better of (someone), typically by cheating them out of money. **5** informal, dated rebuke (someone) angrily. ▶ **n. 1** additional decoration, typically along the edges of something and in contrasting color or material. ■ decorative additions to a vehicle, typically the upholstery or interior lining of a car. **2** [in sing.] an act of cutting off part of something in order to neaten it: *his hair needs a trim.* ■ a short piece of film cut out during the final editing stage. **3** the state of being in good order or condition: *no one had been there for months—everything was out of trim.* **4** the degree to which an aircraft can be maintained at a constant altitude without any control forces being present. **5** the difference between a vessel's forward and after drafts, esp. as it affects its navigability. ▶ **adj.** (**trimmer, trimmest**) neat and smart in appearance; in good order. ■ (of a person or their body) slim and fit.
– PHRASES **in trim** slim and fit. ■ Naut. in good order. — **trim·ly adv. trim·ness n.** [OE *trymman, trymian* 'make firm, arrange.']

tri·ma·ran /'trīmə,ran/ ▶ **n.** a yacht with three hulls in parallel. [1940s: from TRI- + CATAMARAN.]

Trim·ble /'trimbəl/, Robert (1776–1828), US Supreme Court associate justice 1826–28.

tri·mer /'trīmər/ ▶ **n.** Chem. a polymer comprising three monomer units. — **tri·mer·ic** /trī'merik/ **adj.**

trim·er·ous /'trimərəs/ ▶ **adj.** Bot. & Zool. having parts arranged in groups of three. ■ consisting of three joints or parts.

tri·mes·ter /trī'mestər; 'trī,mes-/ ▶ **n.** a period of three months, esp. as a division of the duration of pregnancy. ■ each of the three terms in an academic year. — **tri·mes·tral** /trī'mestrəl/ **adj.** **tri·mes·tri·al** /trī'mestrēəl/ **adj.** [19th C.: from Fr. *trimestre*, from L. *trimestris*, from *tri-* 'three' + *mensis* 'month.']

trim·e·ter /'trimitər/ ▶ **n.** Pros. a line of verse consisting of three metrical feet. — **tri·met·ric** /trī'metrik/ **adj.** **tri·met·ri·cal** /trī'metrikəl/ **adj.** [16th C.: via L. from Gk. *trimetros*, from *tri-* 'three' + *metron* 'measure.']

tri·meth·o·prim /trī'meTHə,prim/ ▶ **n.** Med. a synthetic antibiotic used to treat malaria and respiratory and urinary infections (usually in conjunction with a sulfonamide). [1960s: from *trimeth(yl)* + *o(xy-)* + *p(y)rim(idine)*.]

trim·mer /'trimər/ ▶ **n. 1** an implement used for trimming off unwanted or untidy parts. **2** a person who adapts their views to the prevailing political trends for personal advancement. **3** a person who decorates something: *window trimmers.* **4** (also **trimmer joist**) Archit. a crosspiece fixed between full-length joists (and often across the end of truncated joists) to form part of the frame of an opening in a floor or roof. **5** a person responsible for trimming the sails of a yacht. ■ a person employed to arrange cargo or fuel in a ship's hold. **6** a small capacitor or other component used to tune a circuit such as a radio set.

trim·ming /'trimiNG/ ▶ **n. 1** the action of cutting off the unwanted or untidy parts of something. ■ (**trimmings**) small pieces cut off in such a way. **2** decoration, esp. for clothing: *lace trimming.* ■ (**the trimmings**) informal the traditional accompaniments to something, esp. a meal or special occasion.

Tri·mon·ti·um /trī'mäntēəm/ Roman name for PLOVDIV.

trim·pot /'trim,pät/ ▶ **n.** a small potentiometer used to make small adjustments to the value of resistance or voltage in an electronic circuit.

trim tab (also **trim·ming tab**) ▶ **n.** Aeron. an adjustable tab or airfoil attached to a control surface, used to trim an aircraft in flight.

Tri·mur·ti /tri'mŏŏrtē/ Hinduism the trinity of Brahma the creator, Vishnu the preserver, and Shiva the destroyer. [from Sanskrit *tri* 'three' + *mūrti* 'form.']

trine /trīn/ Astrol. ▶ **n.** an aspect of 120° (one third of a circle): *Venus in trine to Mars* | [as adj.] *a trine aspect.* ▶ **v.** [trans.] (of a planet) be in a trine aspect with (another planet or position): *Jupiter trines Pluto all month.* [ME: from OFr. *trin(e)*, from L. *trinus* 'threefold,' from *tres* 'three.']

Trin·i /'trinē/ ▶ **n.** W. Indian a Trinidadian.

Trin·i·dad and To·ba·go /'trinə,dad and tə'bāgō/ a country in the West Indies. *See box on next page.* — **Trin·i·da·di·an** /,trinə'dadēən; -'dādē-/ **adj.** & **n.** **To·ba·gan** /tə'bāgən/ **adj.** & **n.** **To·ba·go·ni·an** /,tōbə'gōnēən/ **adj.** & **n.**

Trin·i·tar·i·an /,trinə'te(ə)rēən/ ▶ **adj.** of or relating to belief in the doctrine of the Trinity. ▶ **n.** a person who believes in the doctrine of the Trinity. — **Trin·i·tar·i·an·ism** /-,nizəm/ **n.**

tri·ni·tro·tol·u·ene /trī,nītrō'tälyə,wēn/ ▶ **n.** see TNT.

trin·i·ty /'trinitē/ ▶ **n.** (pl. **-ties**) (also **the Trin·i·ty** or **the Ho·ly Trin·i·ty**) the Christian Godhead as one God in three persons: Father, Son, and Holy Spirit. ■ a group of three people or things. ■ the state of being three: *God is said to be trinity in unity.* [ME: from OFr. *trinite*, from L. *trinitas* 'triad,' from *trinus* 'threefold' (see TRINE).]

Trin·i·ty Sun·day ▶ **n.** the next Sunday after Pentecost, observed in the Western Christian Church as a feast in honor of the Holy Trinity.

trin·ket /'triNGkit/ ▶ **n.** a small ornament or item of jewelry that is of little value. — **trin·ket·ry** /-trē/ **n.** [16th C.: of unknown origin.]

tri·no·mi·al /trī'nōmēəl/ ▶ **adj. 1** (of an algebraic expression) consisting of three terms. **2** Biol. (of a taxonomic name) consisting of three terms of which the first is the name of the genus, the second that of the species, and the third that of the subspecies or variety. ▶ **n. 1** an algebraic expression of three terms. **2** Biol. a trinomial taxonomic name. [17th C.: from TRI- 'three,' on the pattern of *binomial*.]

tri·o /'trē-ō/ ▶ **n.** (pl. **-os**) a set or group of three people or things: *the hotel was run by a trio of brothers.* ■ a group of three musicians: *a jazz trio.* ■ a composition written for three musicians: *Chopin's G minor Trio.* ■ the central, typically contrastive, section of a minuet, scherzo, or march. ■ (in piquet) a set of three aces, kings, queens, jacks, or tens held in one hand. [18th C.: from Ital., from L. *tres* 'three,' on the pattern of *duo*.]

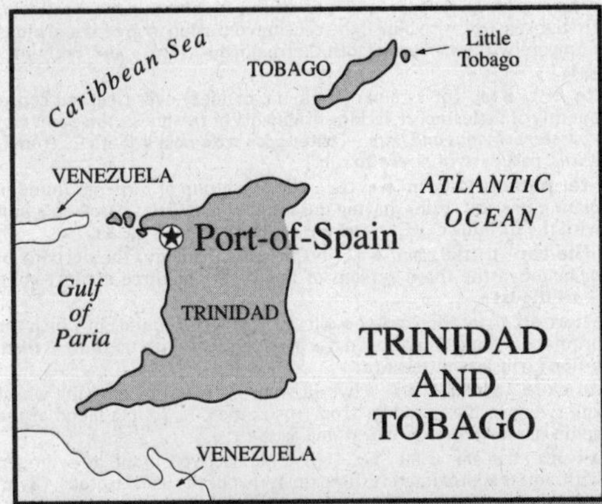

Trinidad and Tobago

Official name: Republic of Trinidad and Tobago
Location: West Indies, comprising two main islands off the northeastern coast of Venezuela
Area: 2,000 square miles (5100 sq km)
Population: 1,400,000
Capital: Port-of-Spain
Languages: English (official), Hindi, French, Spanish, Chinese
Currency: Trinidad and Tobago dollar

tri·ode /'trīˌōd/ ▶ **n.** a vacuum tube having three electrodes. ■ a semiconductor rectifier having three connections. [20th C.: from TRI- 'three' + ELECTRODE.]

tri·o·let /'trēəlit; 'trī-; ˌtrēə'lā/ ▶ **n.** a poem of eight lines, typically of eight syllables each, rhyming *abaaabab* and so structured that the first line recurs as the fourth and seventh and the second as the eighth. [17th C.: from Fr.]

tri·ose /'trīˌōs/ ▶ **n.** Chem. any of a group of monosaccharide sugars whose molecules contain three carbon atoms.

tri·o so·na·ta ▶ **n.** a baroque composition written in three parts, two upper parts and one bass, and usually performed with a keyboard continuo.

tri·ox·ide /trī'äkˌsīd/ ▶ **n.** Chem. an oxide containing three atoms of oxygen in its molecule or empirical formula.

trip /trip/ ▶ **v.** (**tripped, trip·ping**) **1** [intrans.] catch one's foot on something and stumble or fall. ■ [trans.] cause (someone) to do this: *he tripped me!* ■ (**trip up**) make a mistake. ■ [trans.] (**trip someone up**) detect or expose someone in an error, blunder, or inconsistency. **2** [intrans.] walk, run, or dance with quick light steps: *they tripped up the terrace steps.* ■ (of words) flow lightly and easily: *a name that trips off the tongue.* **3** [trans.] activate (a mechanism), esp. by contact with a switch, catch, or other electrical device. ■ [intrans.] (of part of an electric circuit) disconnect automatically as a safety measure. **4** [trans.] Naut. release and raise (an anchor) from the seabed by means of a buoyed line attached to the anchor's crown. ■ turn (a yard or other object) from a horizontal to a vertical position for lowering. **5** [intrans.] informal experience hallucinations induced by taking a psychedelic drug, esp. LSD. **6** [intrans.] go on a short journey: *tripping through the Yukon.* ▶ **n. 1** a journey or excursion, esp. for pleasure. ■ an act of going to a place and returning: *a quick trip to the store.* **2** a stumble or fall due to catching one's foot on something. ■ archaic a mistake. **3** informal a hallucinatory experience caused by taking a psychedelic drug, esp. LSD. ■ an exciting or stimulating experience: *it was a trip seeing him again.* ■ a self-indulgent attitude or activity: *politics was a sixties trip.* **4** a device that activates or disconnects a mechanism, circuit, etc. ■ an instance of a device deactivating or the power supply disconnecting as a safety measure. **5** archaic a light, lively movement of a person's feet.
– PHRASES **trip the light fantastic** humorous dance, in particular engage in ballroom dancing. [ME: from OFr. *triper*, from MDu. *trippen* 'to skip, hop.']

tri·par·tite /trī'pärˌtīt/ ▶ **adj.** consisting of three parts: *a tripartite classification.* ■ shared by or involving three parties: *a tripartite coalition government.* — **tri·par·tite·ly adv. tri·par·ti·tion** /ˌtrīpär'tisHən/ **n.** [ME: from L. *tripartitus*, from *tri-* 'three' + *partitus* 'divided' (past part. of *partiri*).]

tripe /trīp/ ▶ **n. 1** the first or second stomach of a cow or other ruminant used as food. **2** informal nonsense; rubbish: *you do talk tripe sometimes.* [ME: from OFr., of unknown origin.]

trip ham·mer ▶ **n.** a large, heavy pivoted hammer used in forging, raised by a cam or lever and allowed to drop on the metal being worked.

trip-hop ▶ **n.** a style of dance music, usually slow in tempo, that combines elements of hip-hop and dub reggae with softer, more ambient sounds.

triph·thong /'trifˌTHôNG; 'trip-/ ▶ **n.** a union of three vowels (letters or sounds) pronounced in one syllable (as in some pronunciations of *our*). Contrasted with DIPHTHONG, MONOPHTHONG. ■ a vowel trigraph (as in *beau*). — **triph·thong·al** /trif'THôNG(g)əl; trip-; -'THäNG(g)əl/ **adj.** [16th C.: from Fr. *triphtongue*, from *tri-* 'three,' on the pattern of *diphthong*.]

Tri·pit·a·ka /tri'pitikə/ ▶ **n.** (**the Tripitaka**) the sacred canon of Theravada Buddhism, written in the Pali language. [from Sanskrit *tripiṭaka*, lit. 'the three baskets or collections.']

tri·plane /'trīˌplān/ ▶ **n.** an early type of airplane with three pairs of wings, one above the other.

tri·ple /'tripəl/ ▶ **adj.** [attrib.] consisting of or involving three parts, things, or people: *a triple murder.* ■ having three times the usual size, quality, or strength: *a triple rum.* ■ (of a person or animal) having done or won something three times: *a triple champion.* ▶ **predeterminer** three times as much or as many: *the copper energy cells had triple the efficiency of silicon cells.* ▶ **n. 1** a set of three things or parts. ■ an amount that is three times as large as another. ■ Bowling three consecutive strikes. **2** (**triples**) a sporting contest in which each side has three players. **3** (**Triples**) Bell-ringing a system of change ringing using seven bells, with three pairs changing places each time. **4** (**Triple**) [sing.] Baseball a hit that enables the batter to reach third base. **5** another term for TRIFECTA. ▶ **v.** [intrans.] **1** become three times as much or as many. ■ [trans.] multiply (something) by three. **2** Baseball hit a triple: *he tripled into right field.* — **trip·ly** /'triplē/ **adv.** [ME (as an adj. and adv.): from OFr., or from L. *triplus*, from Gk. *triplous*.]

tri·ple A (also **AAA**) ▶ **n. 1** [usu. as adj.] Finance the highest grading available from credit rating agencies. **2** the highest competitive level in minor league baseball. **3** a 1.5 volt dry cell battery size.

Tri·ple Al·li·ance ▶ **n.** a union or association between three powers or states, in particular that made in 1668 between England, the Netherlands, and Sweden against France, and that in 1882 between Germany, Austria-Hungary, and Italy against France and Russia.

tri·ple bond ▶ **n.** Chem. a chemical bond in which three pairs of electrons are shared between two atoms.

tri·ple crown ▶ **n. 1** (**Triple Crown**) an award or honor for winning a group of three important events in a sport, in particular victory by one horse in the Kentucky Derby, the Preakness, and the Belmont Stakes. **2** the papal tiara.

Tri·ple En·tente /än'tänt/ an early 20th-century alliance between Great Britain, France, and Russia. It formed the basis of the Allied powers in World War I.

tri·ple jump ▶ **n. 1** (**the triple jump**) a track and field event in which competitors attempt to jump as far as possible by performing a hop, a step, and a jump from a running start. **2** Skating a jump in which the skater makes three full turns while in the air. ▶ **v.** (**tri·ple-jump**) [intrans.] (of an athlete) perform a triple jump. — **tri·ple jump·er n.**

tri·ple play ▶ **n.** Baseball a defensive play in which three runners are put out.

tri·ple point ▶ **n.** Chem. the temperature and pressure at which the solid, liquid, and vapor phases of a pure substance can coexist in equilibrium.

tri·ple rhyme ▶ **n.** a rhyme involving three syllables.

tri·plet /'triplit/ ▶ **n. 1** (usu. **triplets**) one of three children or animals born at the same birth. **2** a set or succession of three similar things. ■ Music a group of three equal notes to be performed in the time of two or four. ■ a set of three rhyming lines of verse. **3** Physics & Chem. an atomic or molecular state characterized by two unpaired electrons with parallel spins. ■ a group of three associated lines close together in a spectrum or electrophoretic gel. [17th C.: from TRIPLE, on the pattern of *doublet*.]

tri·plet code ▶ **n.** Biol. the standard version of the genetic code, in which a sequence of three nucleotides in a DNA or RNA molecule codes for a specific amino acid in protein synthesis.

tri·ple time ▶ **n.** musical time with three beats to the bar.

tri·ple tongu·ing ▶ **n.** Music a technique in which alternate movements of the tongue are made (typically as in sounding *ttk*) to facilitate rapid playing of a wind instrument.

tri·plex /'tripleks; 'trī-/ ▶ **n. 1** a building divided into three self-contained residences. ■ a movie theater with three separate screening rooms. **2** Biochem. a triple-stranded polynucleotide molecule. ▶ **adj.** having three parts, in particular: ■ (of a residence) on three floors: *his vast triplex apartment.* ▶ **v.** (**be triplexed**) (of electrical equipment or systems) be provided or fitted in triplicate so as to ensure reliability. [17th C.: from L., 'threefold,' from *tri-* 'three' + *plicare* 'to fold.']

trip·li·cate ▶ **adj.** /'triplikit/ [attrib.] existing in three copies or examples: *triplicate measurements.* ▶ **n.** /'triplikit/ archaic a thing that is part of a set of three copies or corresponding parts. ▶ **v.** /-ˌkāt/ [trans.] make three copies of (something); multiply by three.
– PHRASES **in triplicate** three times in exactly the same way. ■ existing as a set of three exact copies. — **trip·li·ca·tion** /ˌtriplə'kāsHən/ **n.** [ME: from L. *triplicat-* 'made three,' from the verb *triplicare*, from *triplex*,

triplic- 'threefold' (see TRIPLEX).]

tri·plic·i·ty /tri'plisitē/ ▶ **n.** (pl. **-ties**) rare a group of three people or things. ■ archaic the state of being triple.

trip·lo·blas·tic /ˌtriplō'blastik/ ▶ **adj.** Zool. having a body derived from three embryonic cell layers (ectoderm, mesoderm, and endoderm), as in all multicellular animals except sponges and coelenterates. [19th C.: from Gk. *triploos* 'threefold' + -BLAST + -IC.]

trip·loid /'triploid/ Genet. ▶ **adj.** (of a cell or nucleus) containing three homologous sets of chromosomes. ■ (of an organism or species) composed of triploid cells. ▶ **n.** a triploid organism, variety, or species. — **trip·loi·dy** /'triˌploidē/ **n.**

trip·me·ter /'tripˌmētər/ ▶ **n.** a vehicle instrument that can be set to record the distance of individual journeys.

tri·pod /'trīpäd/ ▶ **n.** **1** a three-legged stand for supporting a camera or other apparatus. **2** archaic a stool, table, or cauldron resting on three legs. ■ hist. the bronze altar at Delphi on which a priestess sat to utter oracles. — **trip·o·dal** /trī'pōdl/ **adj.** [17th C.: via L. from Gk. *tripous, tripod-*, from *tri-* 'three' + *pous, pod-* 'foot.']

Trip·o·li /'tripəlē/ **1** the capital of Libya, on the Mediterranean coast in the northwestern part of the country; pop. 991,000. Its ancient name was *Oea*. Arabic name **TARABULUS AL-GHARB**, 'western Tripoli'. **2** a port in northwestern Lebanon; pop. 160,000.

trip·o·li /'tripəlē/ ▶ **n.** another term for ROTTENSTONE. [17th C.: from Fr., from TRIPOLI.]

Tri·pol·i·tan Wars /tri'pälitn/ another name for the **BARBARY WARS**.

trip·pant /'tripənt/ ▶ **adj.** [usu. postpositive] Heraldry (of a stag or deer) represented as walking. Compare with PASSANT. [17th C.: from OFr., lit. 'walking or springing lightly,' pres. part. of *tripper*.]

trip·per /'tripər/ ▶ **n.** informal **1** a person who goes on a pleasure trip or excursion. **2** a device that triggers a signal or other operating device.

trip·py /'tripē/ ▶ **adj.** (**-pi·er, -pi·est**) informal resembling or inducing the hallucinatory effect produced by taking a psychedelic drug: *trippy house music.*

trip·tych /'triptik/ ▶ **n.** a picture or relief carving on three panels, typically hinged together vertically and used as an altarpiece. ■ a set of three associated artistic, literary, or musical works intended to be appreciated together. [18th C.: from TRI- 'three,' on the pattern of *diptych*.]

trip·tyque /trip'tēk; 'triptik/ ▶ **n.** dated a customs permit serving as a passport for a motor vehicle. [20th C.: from Fr., lit. 'triptych.']

trip·wire /'tripˌwī(ə)r/ ▶ **n.** a wire stretched close to the ground, working a trap, explosion, or alarm when disturbed and serving to detect or prevent people or animals from entering an area. ■ a comparatively weak military force employed as a first line of defense, engagement with which will trigger the intervention of strong forces.

tri·que·tra /trī'kwētrə; -'kwetrə/ ▶ **n.** (pl. **-trae** /-trē/) a symmetrical triangular ornament of three interlaced arcs used on metalwork and stone crosses. [16th C. (orig. denoting a triangle): from L., fem. of *triquetrus* 'three-cornered.']

tri·que·tral /trī'kwētrəl; -'kwetrəl/ (also **tri·que·tral bone**) ▶ **n.** Anat. a carpal bone on the outside of the wrist, articulating with the lunate, hamate, and pisiform bones.

tri·reme /'trīˌrēm/ ▶ **n.** an ancient Greek or Roman war galley with three banks of oars. The rowers are believed to have sat in threes on angled benches, rather than in three superimposed banks. [from L. *triremis*, from *tri-* 'three' + *remus* 'oar.']

tri·sac·cha·ride /trī'sakəˌrīd/ ▶ **n.** Chem. any of the class of sugars whose molecules contain three monosaccharide molecules.

Tris·a·gi·on /trē'sagēən; -'säyôn/ ▶ **n.** a hymn, esp. in the Orthodox Church, with a triple invocation of God as holy. [ME: from Gk., neut. of *trisagios*, from *tris* 'three times' + *hagios* 'holy.']

tri·sect /trī'sekt/ ▶ **v.** [trans.] divide (something) into three parts, typically three equal parts. — **tri·sec·tion** /-'sekshən/ **n.** **tri·sec·tor** /-tər/ **n.** [17th C.: from TRI- 'three' + L. *sect-* 'divided, cut' (from the verb *secare*).]

tri·shaw /'trīˌshô/ ▶ **n.** a light three-wheeled vehicle with pedals used in the Far East. [1940s: from TRI- 'three' + RICKSHA.]

tris·kai·dek·a·pho·bi·a /ˌtriskīˌdekə'fōbēə; ˌtriskə-/ ▶ **n.** extreme superstition regarding the number thirteen. [20th C.: from Gk. *treiskaideka* 'thirteen' + -PHOBIA.]

tris·kel·i·on /trī'skelēən; tri-/ ▶ **n.** a Celtic symbol consisting of three legs or lines radiating from a center. [19th C.: from TRI- 'three' + Gk. *skelos* 'leg.']

tris·mus /'trizməs/ ▶ **n.** Med. spasm of the jaw muscles, causing the mouth to remain tightly closed, typically as a symptom of tetanus. Also called LOCKJAW. [17th C.: from mod. L., from Gk. *trismos* 'a scream, grinding.']

tri·so·my /trī'sōmē; 'trīsō-/ ▶ **n.** Med. a condition in which an extra copy of a chromosome is present in the cell nuclei, causing developmental abnormalities. [1930s: from TRI- 'three' + -SOME[3].]

tri·so·my-21 ▶ **n.** Med. the most common form of Down syndrome, caused by an extra copy of chromosome number 21.

Tris·tan /'trisˌtän; -tən/ var. of TRISTRAM.

tris·tesse /trē'stes/ ▶ **n.** literary a state of melancholy sadness. [Fr.]

Tris·tram /'tristrəm/ (also **Tris·tan** /'trisˌtän; -tən/) (in medieval legend) a knight who was the lover of Iseult.

tri·syl·la·ble /trī'siləbəl/ ▶ **n.** a word or metrical foot of three syllables. — **tri·syl·lab·ic** /ˌtrīsə'labik/ **adj.**

tri·tag·o·nist /trī'tagənist/ ▶ **n.** the person who is third in importance, after the protagonist and deuteragonist, in an ancient Greek drama. [19th C.: from Gk. *tritagōnistēs*, from *tritos* 'third' + *agōnistēs* 'actor.']

trit·an·ope /'trītnˌōp/ ▶ **n.** a person suffering from tritanopia.

trit·an·o·pi·a /ˌtrītn'ōpēə/ ▶ **n.** a rare form of color-blindness resulting from insensitivity to blue light, causing confusion of greens and blues. Compare with PROTANOPIA. [20th C.: from TRITO- 'third' + AN-[1] 'without' + -OPIA.]

trite /trīt/ ▶ **adj.** (of a remark, opinion, or idea) overused and consequently of little import; lacking originality or freshness: *this point may now seem obvious and trite.* — **trite·ly** **adv.** **trite·ness** **n.** [16th C.: from L. *tritus*, past part. of *terere* 'to rub.']

tri·ter·pene /trī'tərpēn/ ▶ **n.** Chem. any of a group of terpenes found in plant gums and resins, having unsaturated molecules based on a unit with the formula $C_{30}H_{48}$. — **tri·ter·pe·noid** /-pəˌnoid/ **adj.** & **n.**

tri·the·ism /trī'THēˌizəm/ ▶ **n.** (in Christian theology) the doctrine of or belief in the three persons of the Trinity as three distinct gods. — **tri·the·ist** **n.**

tri·ti·at·ed /'tritēˌātid; 'trisH-/ ▶ **adj.** Chem. (of a compound) in which the ordinary isotope of hydrogen has been replaced with tritium. — **tri·ti·a·tion** /ˌtritē'āsHən; ˌtrisH-/ **n.**

trit·i·ca·le /ˌtriti'kālē/ ▶ **n.** a hybrid grain produced by crossing wheat and rye, grown as a fodder crop. [1950s: mod. L., from a blend of the genus names *Triticum* 'wheat' and *Secale* 'rye.']

trit·i·um /'tritēəm; 'trisH-/ ▶ **n.** Chem. a radioactive isotope of hydrogen with a mass approximately three times that of the usual isotope. (Symbol: **T**) [1930s: from mod. L., from Gk. *tritos* 'third.']

trito- ▶ **comb. form** third: *tritocerebrum.* [from Gk. *tritos* 'third.']

tri·to·cer·e·brum /ˌtrītōsə'rēbrəm; -'serə-/ ▶ **n.** (pl. **-bra** /-brə/) Entomol. the third and hindmost segment of an insect's brain.

Tri·ton /'trītn/ **1** Gk. Mythol. a minor sea god usually represented as a man with a fish's tail and carrying a trident and shell trumpet. **2** Astron. the largest satellite of Neptune, the seventh closest to the planet, discovered in 1846. It has a retrograde orbit, a thin nitrogen atmosphere, and a diameter of 1,678 miles (2,700 km).

tri·ton[1] /'trītn/ ▶ **n.** a large mollusk (genus *Charonia*, family Cymatiidae) that has a tall spiral shell with a large aperture, living in tropical and subtropical seas. [18th C.: from TRITON.]

tri·ton[2] ▶ **n.** a nucleus of a tritium atom, consisting of a proton and two neutrons. [1940s: from TRITIUM + -ON.]

tri·tone /'trīˌtōn/ ▶ **n.** Music an interval of three whole tones (an augmented fourth), as between C and F sharp.

trit·u·rate /'tricHəˌrāt/ ▶ **v.** [trans.] tech. grind to a fine powder. ■ chew or grind (food) thoroughly. — **trit·u·ra·tion** /ˌtricHə'rāsHən/ **n.** **trit·u·ra·tor** /-ˌrātər/ **n.** [18th C.: from L. *triturat-* '(of corn) threshed,' from *tritura* 'rubbing' (from the verb *terere*).]

tri·umph /'trīəmf/ ▶ **n.** **1** a great victory or achievement. ■ the state of being victorious or successful: *we returned in triumph.* ■ joy or satisfaction resulting from a success or victory: *Helen's voice rose in triumph.* ■ a highly successful example of something. **2** the processional entry of a victorious general into ancient Rome. ▶ **v.** [intrans.] **1** achieve a victory; be successful: *capitalism seems to have triumphed over socialism.* ■ rejoice or exult at a victory or success: *"There!" triumphed Alima.* **2** (of a Roman general) ride into ancient Rome after a victory. [ME: from OFr. *triumphe* (n.), from L. *triump(h)us*, prob. from Gk. *thriambos* 'hymn to Bacchus.']

tri·um·phal /trī'əmfəl/ ▶ **adj.** made, carried out, or used in celebration of a great victory or achievement.

tri·um·phal·ism /trī'əmfəˌlizəm/ ▶ **n.** excessive exultation over one's success or achievements (used esp. in a political context). — **tri·um·phal·ist** **adj.** & **n.**

tri·um·phant /trī'əmfənt/ ▶ **adj.** having won a battle or contest; victorious. ■ feeling or expressing jubilation after having won a victory or mastered a difficulty. — **tri·um·phant·ly** **adv.**

tri·um·vir /trī'əmvər/ ▶ **n.** (pl. **-virs** or **-vi·ri** /-vəˌrī/) (in ancient Rome) each of three public officers jointly responsible for overseeing any of the administrative departments. — **tri·um·vi·ral** /-rəl/ **adj.** [L., orig. as *triumviri* (pl.), back-form. from *trium virorum* 'of three men,' genitive of *tres viri*.]

tri·um·vi·rate /trī'əmvərit; -ˌrāt/ ▶ **n.** **1** (in ancient Rome) a group of three men holding power, in particular (**the First Triumvirate**) the unofficial coalition of Julius Caesar, Pompey, and Crassus in 60 BC and (**the Second Triumvirate**) a coalition formed by Antony, Lepidus, and Octavian in 43 BC. ■ a group of three powerful or notable people or things existing in relation to each other. **2** the office of triumvir in ancient Rome.

tri·une /'trīˌ(y)o͞on/ ▶ **adj.** consisting of three in one (used esp. with reference to the Trinity). — **tri·u·ni·ty** /trī'yo͞onitē/ **n.** (pl. **-ties**). [17th C.: from TRI- 'three' + L. *unus* 'one.']

tri·va·lent /trī'vālənt/ ▶ **adj.** Chem. having a valence of three.

triv·et /'trivit/ ▶ **n.** an iron tripod placed over a fire for a cooking pot or kettle to stand on. ■ an iron bracket designed to hook onto bars of a grate for a similar purpose. ■ a small plate placed under a hot serving dish to protect a table. [ME: appar. from L. *tripes, triped-* 'three-legged,' from *tri-* 'three' + *pes, ped-* 'foot.']

triv·i·a /'trivēə/ ▶ **plural n.** details, considerations, or pieces of information of little importance or value. [20th C.: from mod. L., pl. of *trivium* 'place where three roads meet,' influenced in sense by TRIVIAL.]

triv·i·al /'trivēəl/ ▶ **adj.** of little value or importance. ■ (of a person) concerned only with trifling or unimportant things. ■ Math. denoting a subgroup that either contains only the identity element or is identical with the given group. — **triv·i·al·i·ty** /ˌtrivēˈalitē/ **n.** (pl. **-ties**) **triv·i·al·ly adv.** [ME (in the sense 'belonging to the trivium'): from med. L. *trivialis*, from L. *trivium* (see TRIVIUM).]

triv·i·al·ize /ˈtrivēəˌlīz/ ▶ **v.** [trans.] make (something) seem less important, significant, or complex than it really is. — **triv·i·al·i·za·tion** /ˌtrivēəliˈzāsʜən/ **n.**

triv·i·al name ▶ **n.** esp. Chem. a name that is in general use although not part of systematic nomenclature. ■ esp. Zool. another term for SPECIFIC EPITHET.

triv·i·um /ˈtrivēəm/ ▶ **n.** hist. an introductory curriculum at a medieval university involving the study of grammar, rhetoric, and logic. Compare with QUADRIVIUM. [19th C.: from L., lit. 'place where three roads meet,' from *tri-* 'three' + *via* 'road.']

-trix ▶ **suffix** (pl. **-trices** or **-trixes**) (chiefly in legal terms) forming feminine agent nouns corresponding to masculine nouns ending in *-tor* (such as *executrix* corresponding to *executor*). [from L.]

tRNA Biol. ▶ **abbr.** transfer RNA.

Tro·ad /ˈtrōˌad/ an ancient region in Asia Minor. Troy was its chief city.

Tro·bri·and Is·lands /ˈtrōbrēˌand; -ˌänd/ a small group of islands in the southwestern Pacific Ocean, in Papua New Guinea.

tro·car /ˈtrōˌkär/ ▶ **n.** a surgical instrument with a three-sided cutting point enclosed in a tube, used for withdrawing fluid from a body cavity. [18th C.: from Fr. *trocart*, *trois-quarts*, from *trois* 'three' + *carre* 'side, face of an instrument.']

tro·cha·ic /trōˈkā-ik/ Pros. ▶ **adj.** consisting of or featuring trochees. ▶ **n.** (usu. **trochaics**) a type of verse that consists of or features trochees. [16th C.: via L. from Gk. *trokhaikos*, from *trokhaios* (see TROCHEE).]

tro·chal disk /ˈtrōkal/ ▶ **n.** Zool. each of two projections below the neck of the femur (thigh bone) to which muscles are attached. [19th C.: *trochal* from Gk. *trokhos* 'wheel' + -AL.]

tro·chan·ter /trōˈkantər/ ▶ **n.** **1** Anat. any of two bony protuberances by which muscles are attached to the upper part of the thigh bone. **2** Entomol. the small second segment of the leg of an insect, between the coxa and the femur. [17th C.: from Fr., from Gk. *trokhantēr*, from *trekhein* 'to run.']

tro·chee /ˈtrōkē/ ▶ **n.** Pros. a foot consisting of one long or stressed syllable followed by one short or unstressed syllable. [16th C.: via L. from Gk. *trokhaios (pous)* 'running (foot),' from *trekhein* 'to run.']

troch·le·a /ˈträklēə/ ▶ **n.** (pl. **-le·ae** /-lēˌē/) Anat. a structure resembling or acting like a pulley, such as the groove at the lower end of the humerus forming part of the elbow joint. — **troch·le·ar adj.** [17th C.: L., 'pulley.']

troch·le·ar nerve ▶ **n.** Anat. each of the fourth pair of cranial nerves, supplying the superior oblique muscle of the eyeball.

tro·choid /ˈtrōˌkoid/ ▶ **adj.** **1** Anat. denoting a joint in which one element rotates on its own axis (e.g., the atlas vertebra). **2** Geom. denoting a curve traced by a point on a radius of a circle rotating along a straight line or another circle (a cycloid, epicycloid, or hypocycloid). **3** Zool. having or denoting a form of mollusk shell that is conical with a flat base, like a top shell. ▶ **n.** **1** a trochoid curve. **2** a trochoid joint. — **tro·choi·dal** /trōˈkoidl/ **adj.** [18th C.: from Gk. *trokhoeidēs* 'wheellike,' from *trokhos* 'wheel.']

troch·o·phore /ˈträkəˌfôr/ ▶ **n.** Zool. the planktonic larva of certain invertebrates, including some mollusks and polychaete worms, having a roughly spherical body, a band of cilia, and a spinning motion. [19th C.: from Gk. *trokhos* 'wheel' + -PHORE.]

troc·to·lite /ˈträktəˌlīt/ ▶ **n.** Geol. gabbro made up mainly of olivine and calcic plagioclase, often having a spotted appearance likened to a trout's back. [19th C.: from Ger. *Troklotit*, from Gk. *trōktēs*, a marine fish (taken to be 'trout').]

trod /träd/ past and past participle of TREAD.

trod·den /ˈträdn/ past participle of TREAD.

trog·lo·dyte /ˈträgləˌdīt/ ▶ **n.** (esp. in prehistoric times) a person who lived in a cave. ■ a hermit. ■ a person who is regarded as being deliberately ignorant or old-fashioned. — **trog·lo·dyt·ic** /ˌträgləˈditik/ **adj.** **trog·lo·dyt·ism** /-dīˌtizəm/ **n.** [15th C.: via L. from Gk. *trōglodutēs*, alt. of the name of an Ethiopian people, influenced by *trōglē* 'hole.']

tro·gon /ˈtrōˌgän/ ▶ **n.** a bird (*Trogon* and other genera, family Trogonidae) of tropical American forests, with a long tail and brilliantly colored plumage. [18th C.: from mod. L., from Gk. *trōgōn*, from *trōgein* 'gnaw.']

troi·ka /ˈtroikə/ ▶ **n.** **1** a Russian vehicle pulled by a team of three horses abreast. ■ a team of three horses for such a vehicle. **2** a group of three people working together, esp. in an administrative or managerial capacity. [Russ., from *troe* 'set of three.']

troil·ism /ˈtroiˌlizəm/ ▶ **n.** sexual activity involving three participants. [1950s: perh. based on Fr. *trois* 'three.']

Troi·lus /ˈtroiləs/ Gk. Mythol. a Trojan prince, the son of Priam and Hecuba, killed by Achilles. In medieval legends of the Trojan war he is portrayed as the forsaken lover of Cressida.

Tro·jan /ˈtrōjən/ ▶ **adj.** of or relating to ancient Troy in Asia Minor: *Trojan legends.* ▶ **n.** a native or inhabitant of ancient Troy.
– PHRASES **work like a Trojan** (or **Trojans**) work extremely hard. [ME: from L. *Troianus*, from *Troia* 'Troy.']

Tro·jan Horse ▶ **n.** Greek mythology a hollow wooden statue of a horse in which the Greeks concealed themselves in order to enter Troy. ■ (also **Trojan horse**) fig. a person or thing intended secretly to undermine or bring about the downfall of an enemy or opponent. ■ (also **Trojan horse**) Comput. a program designed to breach the security of a computer system while ostensibly performing some innocuous function.

Tro·jan War the legendary ten-year siege of Troy by a coalition of Greeks, described in Homer's *Iliad*.

troll[1] /trōl/ ▶ **n.** a mythical, cave-dwelling being depicted in folklore as either a giant or a dwarf, typically having a very ugly appearance. [from ON and Swed. *troll*, Dan. *trold*; adopted into Engl. from Scand. in the mid 19th C.]

troll[2] ▶ **v.** [intrans.] **1** fish by trailing a baited line along behind a boat: *we trolled for mackerel.* ■ search for something. **2** [trans.] sing (something) in a happy and carefree way. **3** Comput., informal send (an e-mail message or posting on the Internet) intended to provoke a response from the reader by containing errors. **4** [intrans.] esp. Brit. walk; stroll. ▶ **n.** **1** the action of trolling for fish. ■ a line or bait used in such fishing. **2** Comput., informal an e-mail message or posting on the Internet intended to provoke a response in the reader by containing errors. — **troll·er n.** [ME: compare Mid. High Ger. *trollen* 'stroll.']

trol·ley /ˈträlē/ ▶ **n.** (pl. **-leys**) **1** short for TROLLEY CAR or TROLLEY BUS. **2** (also **trolley wheel**) a wheel attached to a pole, used for collecting current from an overhead electric wire to drive a streetcar. **3** a large metal basket or frame on wheels, resembling a shopping cart and used for transporting luggage at an airport or railroad station; a luggage cart. ■ Brit. a shopping cart. ■ Brit. a small table on wheels or casters, typically used to convey food and drink. **4** esp. Brit. a low truck, usually without sides or ends, running on a railroad or a track in a factory.
– PHRASES **off one's trolley** informal mad; insane. [19th C.: of dial. origin, perh. from TROLL[2].]

trol·ley bus ▶ **n.** a bus powered by electricity obtained from an overhead cable by means of a trolley wheel.

trol·ley car ▶ **n.** a passenger vehicle powered by electricity obtained from an overhead cable by means of a trolley wheel. Also called STREETCAR.

trol·lop /ˈträləp/ ▶ **n.** dated or humorous a woman perceived as sexually disreputable or promiscuous. [17th C.: perh. rel. to TRULL.]

Trol·lope /ˈträləp/, Anthony (1815–82), English writer. He is noted for his six "Barsetshire" novels, including *Barchester Towers* (1857), and for his six "Palliser" novels.

trombone

trom·bone /trämˈbōn; trəm-/ ▶ **n.** a large brass wind instrument with straight tubing in three sections, ending in a bell over the player's left shoulder, different fundamental notes being made using a forward-pointing extendable slide. ■ an organ stop with the quality of such an instrument. — **trom·bon·ist** /-ˈbōnist/ **n.** [18th C.: from Fr. or Italian, from Ital. *tromba* 'trumpet.']

trom·mel /ˈträməl/ ▶ **n.** Mining a rotating cylindrical sieve or screen used for washing and sorting pieces of ore or coal. [19th C.: from Ger., lit. 'drum.']

trompe l'oeil /ˌtrômp ˈloi/ ▶ **n.** (pl. **trompe l'oeils** pronunc. same) visual illusion in art, esp. as used to trick the eye into perceiving a painted detail as a three-dimensional object. ■ a painting or design intended to create such an illusion. [Fr., lit. 'deceives the eye.']

-tron ▶ **suffix** Physics **1** denoting a subatomic particle: *positron.* **2** denoting a particle accelerator: *cyclotron.* [from *(elec)tron.*]

tro·na /ˈtrōnə/ ▶ **n.** a gray mineral that occurs as an evaporite in salt deposits and consists of a hydrated carbonate and bicarbonate of sodium. [18th C.: from Swed., from Arab. *naṭrūn* (see NATRON).]

Trond·heim /ˈtränˌhām; ˈtrôn-/ a city in western central Norway; pop. 138,000.

troop /tro͞op/ ▶ **n.** **1** a group of soldiers, esp. a cavalry unit commanded by a captain, or an airborne unit. ■ (**troops**) soldiers or armed forces. ■ a unit of Girl or Boy Scouts organized under a troop leader. **2** a group of people or animals of a particular kind. ▶ **v.** [intrans.] (of a group of people) come or go together or in large numbers: *the girls trooped in for dinner.* ■ (of a lone person) walk at a slow or steady pace. [16th C.: from Fr. *troupe*, back-form. from *troupeau*, dimin. of med. L. *troppus* 'flock,' prob. of Gmc. origin.]

troop car·ri·er ▶ **n.** a large aircraft or armored vehicle designed for transporting troops.

troop·er /ˈtro͞opər/ ▶ **n.** **1** a state police officer. ■ a mounted police officer. **2** a private soldier in a cavalry, armored, or airborne unit. ■ a cavalry horse. ■ esp. Brit. a ship used for transporting troops.
– PHRASES **swear like a trooper** swear a great deal.

troop·ship /ˈtro͞opˌsʜip/ ▶ **n.** a ship designed or used for transporting troops.

trop. ▶ **abbr.** ■ tropic. ■ tropical.

trope /trōp/ ▶ **n.** a figurative or metaphorical use of a word or expression.

■ a conventional idea or phrase. ▶ v. [intrans.] create a trope. [16th C.: via L. from Gk. *tropos* 'turn, way, trope,' from *trepein* 'to turn.']

troph·al·lax·is /ˌträfəˈlaksis; ˌtrō-/ ▶ n. Entomol. the mutual exchange of regurgitated liquids between adult social insects or between them and their larvae. [20th C.: from TROPHO- 'nourishment' + Gk. *allaxis* 'exchange.']

troph·ec·to·derm /träfˈektəˌdərm; trōf-/ ▶ n. another term for TROPHOBLAST.

troph·ic /ˈtrōfik; ˈträf-/ ▶ adj. Ecol. of or relating to feeding and nutrition. ■ Physiol. (of a hormone or its effect) stimulating the activity of another endocrine gland. [19th C.: from Gk. *trophikos*, from *trophē* 'nourishment,' from *trephein* 'nourish.']

-trophic ▶ comb. form **1** relating to nutrition: *oligotrophic*. **2** relating to maintenance or regulation of a bodily organ or function, esp. by a hormone: *gonadotrophic*. — **-trophism** comb. form in corresponding nouns **-trophy** comb. form in corresponding nouns. [from Gk. *trophikos*, from *trophē* 'nourishment.']

troph·ic lev·el ▶ n. Ecol. each of several hierarchical levels in an ecosystem, consisting of organisms sharing the same function in the food chain and the same nutritional relationship to the primary sources of energy.

tropho- ▶ comb. form relating to nourishment: *trophoblast*. [from Gk. *trophē* 'nourishment.']

troph·o·blast /ˈträfəˌblast; ˈtrō-/ ▶ n. Embryol. a layer of tissue on the outside of a mammalian blastula, supplying the embryo with nourishment and later forming the major part of the placenta. — **troph·o·blas·tic** /ˌträfəˈblastik/ adj.

troph·o·zo·ite /ˌträfəˈzōˌīt; ˌtrō-/ ▶ n. Zool. & Med. a growing stage in the life cycle of some sporozoan parasites, when they are absorbing nutrients from the host.

tro·phy /ˈtrōfē/ ▶ n. (pl. **-phies**) **1** a cup or other decorative object awarded as a prize for a victory or success. ■ a souvenir of an achievement, esp. a part of an animal taken when hunting. **2** (in ancient Greece or Rome) the weapons and other spoils of a defeated army set up as a memorial of victory. ■ a representation of such a memorial; an ornamental group of symbolic objects arranged for display. [15th C. (sense 2, denoting a display of weapons): from Fr. *trophée*, via L. from Gk. *tropaion*, from *tropē* 'a rout,' from *trepein* 'to turn.']

tro·phy wife ▶ n. informal, derog. a young, attractive wife regarded as a status symbol for an older man.

trop·ic[1] /ˈträpik/ ▶ n. the parallel of latitude 23°27′ north (**tropic of Cancer**) or south (**tropic of Capricorn**) of the equator. ■ Astron. each of two corresponding circles on the celestial sphere where the sun appears to turn after reaching its greatest declination, marking the northern and southern limits of the ecliptic. ■ (**the tropics**) the region between the tropics of Cancer and Capricorn. ▶ adj. another term for TROPICAL (sense 1). [ME: via L. from Gk. *tropikos*, from *trepein* 'to turn.']

trop·ic[2] ▶ adj. **1** Biol. relating to, consisting of, or exhibiting tropism. **2** Physiol. var. of TROPHIC.

-tropic ▶ comb. form **1** turning toward: *heliotropic*. **2** affecting: *psychotropic*. **3** (esp. in names of hormones) equivalent to -TROPHIC. [from Gk. *tropē* 'turn, turning.']

trop·i·cal /ˈträpikəl/ ▶ adj. **1** of, typical of, or peculiar to the tropics: *tropical countries | a tropical rain forest*. ■ resembling the tropics, esp. in being very hot and humid: *last year's tropical summer heat*. **2** archaic of or involving a trope; figurative. — **trop·i·cal·ly** /-ik(ə)lē/ adv.

trop·i·cal storm (also **trop·i·cal cy·clone**) ▶ n. a localized, very intense low-pressure wind system, forming over tropical oceans and with winds of hurricane force.

trop·i·cal year ▶ n. see YEAR (sense 1).

trop·ic of Can·cer ▶ n. see TROPIC[1].

trop·ic of Cap·ri·corn ▶ n. see TROPIC[1].

tro·pism /ˈtrōˌpizəm/ ▶ n. Biol. the turning of all or part of an organism in a particular direction in response to an external stimulus. [19th C.: from Gk. *tropos* 'turning' (from *trepein* 'to turn') + -ISM.]

tro·pol·o·gy /trəˈpäləjē/ ▶ n. the figurative use of language. ■ Christian Theol. the figurative interpretation of the scriptures as a source of moral guidance. — **trop·o·log·i·cal** /ˌträpəˈläjikəl/ adj. [ME: via late L. from Gk. *tropologia*, from *tropos* (see TROPE).]

trop·o·lone /ˈträpəˌlōn; ˈtrō-/ ▶ n. Chem. an organic compound, $C_7H_6O_2$, present in various plants, with a molecule based on a seven-membered carbon ring. [1940s: from *tropilidine* (a liquid hydrocarbon) + -OL + -ONE.]

trop·o·my·o·sin /ˌträpōˈmīəsən; ˌtrō-/ ▶ n. Biochem. a protein involved in muscle contraction. It is related to myosin and occurs together with troponin in the thin filaments of muscle tissue. [1940s: from Gk. *tropos* 'turning' + MYOSIN.]

tro·po·nin /ˈträpənən; ˈtrō-/ ▶ n. Biochem. a globular protein complex involved in muscle contraction. It occurs with tropomyosin in the thin filaments of muscle tissue. [1960s: from TROPOMYOSIN + *-n-* + -IN[1].]

trop·o·pause /ˈträpəˌpôz; ˈtrō-/ ▶ n. the interface between the troposphere and the stratosphere. [20th C.: from Gk. *tropos* 'turning' + PAUSE.]

trop·o·sphere /ˈträpəˌsfi(ə)r; ˈtrō-/ ▶ n. the lowest region of the atmosphere, extending from the earth's surface to a height of about 6–10 km (the lower boundary of the stratosphere). — **trop·o·spher·ic** /ˌträpəˈsfi(ə)rik; -ˈsferik; ˌtrō-/ adj. [20th C.: from Gk. *tropos* 'turning' + SPHERE.]

trop·po[1] /ˈträpō; ˈtrôpō/ ▶ adv. [usu. with negative] Music (in directions) too much; excessively.

– PHRASES **ma non troppo** /mä ˌnôn ˈtrôpō/ (as a direction) but not too much (used to suggest moderate application of another direction): *allegro ma non troppo*. [Ital.]

trop·po[2] /ˈträpō/ ▶ adj. Austral./NZ, informal mentally disturbed, supposedly as a result of spending too much time in a tropical climate: *have you gone troppo?* [1940s: from TROPIC[1] + -O.]

trot /trät/ ▶ v. (**trotted, trotting**) (of a horse or other quadruped) proceed at a pace faster than a walk, lifting each diagonal pair of legs alternately. ■ [trans.] cause (a horse) to move at such a pace. ■ [intrans.] (of a person) run at a moderate pace, typically with short steps. ■ [intrans.] informal go or walk briskly. ▶ n. **1** a trotting pace: *our horses slowed to a trot*. **2** (**the trots**) informal diarrhea. **3** informal a literal translation of a foreign language text for use by students, esp. in a surreptitious way: *adult readers who can turn to translations without being penalized for depending on trots*. [ME: from OFr. *trot* (n.), *troter* (v.), from med. L. *trottare*, of Gmc. origin.]

troth /trôTH; trōTH/ ▶ n. **1** archaic formal faith or loyalty when pledged in a solemn agreement or undertaking. **2** archaic truth.

– PHRASES **pledge** (or **plight**) **one's troth** make a solemn pledge of commitment, esp. in marriage. [ME: var. of TRUTH.]

Trot·sky /ˈträtskē/, Leon (1879–1940), Russian revolutionary; born *Lev Davidovich Bronshtein*. He helped to organize the October Revolution with Lenin and was later murdered by a Stalinist assassin.

Trot·sky·ism /ˈträtskēˌizəm/ ▶ n. the political or economic principles of Leon Trotsky, esp. the theory that socialism should be established throughout the world by continuing revolution. — **Trot·sky·ist** n. & adj. **Trot·sky·ite** /-ˌīt/ n. & adj. (derog.).

trot·ter /ˈträtər/ ▶ n. **1** a horse bred or trained for the sport of harness racing. **2** a pig's foot used as food. ■ humorous a human foot.

trot·ting /ˈträtiNG/ ▶ n. another term for HARNESS RACING.

trou·ba·dour /ˈtro͞obəˌdôr; -ˌdo͝or/ ▶ n. a French medieval lyric poet composing and singing in Provençal in the 11th to 13th centuries, esp. on the theme of courtly love. ■ a poet who writes verse to music. [Fr., from Provençal *trobador*, from *trobar* 'find, invent, compose in verse.']

trou·ble /ˈtrəbəl/ ▶ n. **1** difficulty or problems. ■ the malfunction of something such as a machine or a part of the body. ■ effort or exertion made to do something, esp. when inconvenient: *he's gone to a lot of trouble to help you*. ■ a cause of worry or inconvenience: *the kid had been no trouble up to now*. ■ a particular aspect or quality of something regarded as unsatisfactory or as a source of difficulty: *that's the trouble with capitalism*. ■ a situation in which one is liable to incur punishment or blame: *he's been in trouble with the police*. ■ informal dated used to refer to the condition of a pregnant unmarried woman. **2** public unrest or disorder. ▶ v. [trans.] **1** (often **be troubled**) cause distress or anxiety to: *he was not troubled by doubts*. ■ [intrans.] (**trouble about/over/with**) be distressed or anxious about. ■ cause (someone) pain: *my legs trouble me*. ■ cause (someone) inconvenience (typically used as a polite way of asking someone to do or provide something): *sorry to trouble you*. ■ make the effort required to do something: *oh, don't trouble to answer*. **2** disturb or agitate (the surface in a pool or other body of water): *the waters were troubled*.

– PHRASES **ask for trouble** informal act in a way that is likely to incur problems or difficulties: *hitching a lift is asking for trouble*. **look for trouble** informal behave in a way that is likely to provoke an argument or fight. — **trou·bler** /-b(ə)lər/ n. [ME: from OFr. *truble* (n.), *trubler* (v.), based on L. *turbidus* (see TURBID).]

trou·bled /ˈtrəbəld/ ▶ adj. beset by problems or conflict. ■ showing distress or anxiety: *his troubled face*.

– PHRASES **troubled waters** a difficult situation or time.

trou·ble·mak·er /ˈtrəbəlˌmākər/ ▶ n. a person who habitually causes difficulty or problems, esp. by inciting others to defy those in authority. — **trou·ble·mak·ing** /-ˌmākiNG/ n. & adj.

trou·ble·shoot /ˈtrəbəlˌSHo͞ot/ ▶ v. [intrans.] [usu. as n.] (**troubleshooting**) solve serious problems for a company or other organization. ■ trace and correct faults in a mechanical or electronic system. — **trou·ble·shoot·er** n.

trou·ble·some /ˈtrəbəlsəm/ ▶ adj. causing difficulty or annoyance: *a troublesome knee injury*. — **trou·ble·some·ly** adv. **trou·ble·some·ness** n.

trou·ble spot ▶ n. a place where difficulties regularly occur, esp. a country or area where there is a continuous cycle of violence.

trou·blous /ˈtrəbləs/ ▶ adj. archaic or literary full of difficulty or agitation: *those were troublous times*.

trough /trôf/ ▶ n. a long, narrow open container for animals to eat or drink out of: *a water trough*. ■ a container of a similar shape used for a purpose such as growing plants or mixing chemicals. ■ a channel used to convey a liquid. ■ a long hollow in the earth's surface: *a vast glacial trough*. ■ an elongated region of low atmospheric pressure. ■ a hollow between two wave crests in the sea. ■ a low level of economic activity. ■ Math. a region around the minimum on a curve of variation of a quantity. ■ a point of low achievement or satisfaction. [OE *trog*, of Gmc. origin; rel. to Du. *trog* and Ger. *Trog*, also to TREE.]

trounce /trouns/ ▶ v. [trans.] defeat heavily in a contest. ■ rebuke or punish severely. — **trounc·er** n. [16th C. (also in the sense 'afflict'): of unknown origin.]

troupe /tro͞op/ ▶ n. a group of dancers, actors, or other entertainers who tour to different venues. [19th C.: from Fr., lit. 'troop.']

troup·er /'troōpər/ ▶ n. an actor or other entertainer, typically one with long experience. ■ a reliable and uncomplaining person.

troup·i·al /'troōpēəl/ ▶ n. a gregarious songbird (esp. *Icterus icterus*) of the American oriole family, typically having orange and black plumage and yellow eyes. [19th C.: from Fr. *troupiale*, alt. of Amer. Sp. *turpial*, of unknown origin.]

trou·ser /'trouzər/ ▶ n. [as adj.] relating to trousers: *his trouser pocket | a trouser press.* ■ a trouser leg: *his trouser was torn.*

trou·sers /'trouzərz/ (also **a pair of trousers**) ▶ plural n. an outer garment covering the body from the waist to the ankles, with a separate part for each leg. — **trou·sered** /-zərd/ adj. [17th C.: from archaic *trouse* (sing.), from Irish *triús* and Scot. Gael. *triubhas*, on the pattern of *drawers*.]

trous·seau /'troō,sō; ,troō'sō/ ▶ n. (pl. **-seaux** pronunc. same, or **-seaus**) the clothes, household linen, and other belongings collected by a bride for her marriage. [19th C.: from Fr., dimin. of *trousse* 'bundle.']

trout /trout/ ▶ n. (pl. same or **trouts**) a chiefly freshwater fish (genera *Salmo* and *Salvelinus*) of the salmon family, found in Eurasia and North America and highly valued as food and game. [late OE *truht*, from late L. *tructa*, based on Gk. *trōgein* 'gnaw.']

trout lil·y ▶ n. a North American dogtooth violet (*Erythronium americanum*) with yellow flowers, so called from its mottled leaves. Also called ADDER'S TONGUE.

trou·vaille /troō'vī/ ▶ n. a lucky find: *one of numerous trouvailles to be gleaned from his book.* [Fr., from *trouver* 'find.']

trou·vère /troō'ver/ ▶ n. a medieval epic poet in northern France in the 11th–14th centuries. [from OFr. *trovere*, from *trover* 'to find'; cf. TROUBADOUR.]

trove /trōv/ ▶ n. a store of valuable or delightful things. [19th C.: from TREASURE TROVE.]

tro·ver /'trōvər/ ▶ n. Law common-law action to recover the value of personal property that has been wrongfully disposed of by another person. [16th C.: from an Anglo-Norman Fr. noun use of OFr. *trover* 'to find.']

trow /trō/ ▶ v. [trans.] archaic think or believe. [OE *trūwian*, *trēowian* 'to trust'; rel. to TRUCE.]

trow·el /'trouəl/ ▶ n. **1** a small hand-held tool with a flat, pointed blade, used to apply and spread mortar or plaster. **2** a small hand-held tool with a curved scoop for lifting plants or earth. ▶ v. (**-eled**, **-el·ing**; Brit. **-elled**, **-el·ling**) [trans.] apply or spread with or as if with a trowel. [ME (as a n.): from OFr. *truele*, from med. L. *truella*, alt. of L. *trulla* 'scoop,' dimin. of *trua* 'skimmer.']

Troy /troi/ **1** (in Homeric legend) the city of King Priam, besieged for ten years by the Greeks during the Trojan War. It was thought to be a purely legendary city until Heinrich Schliemann identified the site of Troy in Turkey. Also called ILIUM. **2** a city in southeastern Michigan; pop. 80,959. **3** a city in eastern New York, northeast of Albany; pop. 49,170.

troy /troi/ (in full **troy weight**) ▶ n. a system of weights used mainly for precious metals and gems, with a pound of 12 ounces or 5,760 grains. Compare with AVOIRDUPOIS. [ME: from a weight used at the fair of *Troyes*.]

Troyes /trwä/, Chrétien de, see CHRÉTIEN DE TROYES.

tru·ant /'troōənt/ ▶ n. a student who stays away from school without leave or explanation. ▶ adj. (of a student) being a truant: *truant children.* ■ wandering; straying: *her truant husband.* ▶ v. [intrans.] another way of saying *PLAY TRUANT* below.

– PHRASES **play truant** stay away from school or work without permission or explanation; play hooky. — **tru·an·cy** /-ənsē/ n. [ME: from OFr., prob. of Celtic origin; compare Welsh *truan*, 'wretched.']

truce /troōs/ ▶ n. an agreement between enemies or opponents to stop fighting or arguing for a certain time: *the guerrillas called a three-day truce.* [ME *trewes*, *trues* (plural), from OE *trēowa*, pl. of *trēow* 'belief, trust,' of Gmc. origin; rel. to Du. *trouw* and Ger. *Treue*, also to TRUE.]

Tru·cial States /'troōsHəl/ former name (until 1971) of UNITED ARAB EMIRATES.

truck[1] /trək/ ▶ n. **1** a wheeled vehicle, in particular: ■ a large, heavy motor vehicle, used for transporting goods, materials, or troops. ■ Brit. a railroad vehicle for carrying freight, esp. a small open one. ■ a low flat-topped cart used for moving heavy items. **2** an undercarriage with four or six wheels pivoted beneath the end of a railroad vehicle. ■ each of two axle units on a skateboard, to which the wheels are attached. **3** a wooden disk at the top of a ship's mast or flagstaff, with sheaves for signal halyards. ▶ v. [trans.] convey by truck. ■ [intrans.] drive a truck. ■ [intrans.] informal go or proceed, esp. in a casual or leisurely way: *he walked confidently behind them and trucked on through!* — **truck·age** /-ij/ n. [ME: perh. short for TRUCKLE[1] in the sense 'wheel, pulley.']

truck[2] ▶ n. **1** archaic barter. ■ esp. hist. the payment of workers in kind or with vouchers rather than money. **2** esp. archaic small wares. ■ informal odds and ends. **3** market-garden produce, esp. vegetables. ▶ v. [trans.] archaic barter or exchange.

– PHRASES **have** (or **want**) **no truck with** avoid or wish to avoid dealings or being associated with. [ME (as a v.): prob. from OFr.]

truck·er /'trəkər/ ▶ n. a long-distance truck driver.

truck farm ▶ n. a farm that produces vegetables for the market.

truck·le[1] /'trəkəl/ ▶ n. a small barrel-shaped cheese, esp. cheddar. [ME: from Anglo-Norman Fr. *trocle*, from L. *trochlea* 'sheave of a pulley.']

truck·le[2] ▶ v. [intrans.] submit or behave obsequiously: *she despised her husband, who truckled to her.* — **truck·ler** /'trək(ə)lər/ n. [17th C.: from TRUCKLE BED.]

truck·le bed ▶ n. esp. Brit. a trundle bed. [ME: from TRUCKLE[1] in the sense 'wheel' + BED.]

truck·load /'trək,lōd/ ▶ n. a quantity of goods that can be transported in a truck: *a truckload of chemicals.* ■ (**a truckload/truckloads of**) informal a large quantity or number of something.

truck stop ▶ n. a large roadside service station and restaurant for truck drivers on interstate highways.

truc·u·lent /'trəkyələnt/ ▶ adj. eager or quick to argue or fight; aggressively defiant. — **truc·u·lence** n. **truc·u·lent·ly** adv. [16th C.: from L. *truculentus*, from *trux*, *truc-* 'fierce.']

Tru·deau /troō'dō/, Pierre Elliott (1919–2000), prime minister of Canada 1968–79 and 1980–84.

trudge /trəj/ ▶ v. [intrans.] walk slowly and with heavy steps, typically because of exhaustion or harsh conditions. ▶ n. a difficult or laborious walk: *the long trudge back.* — **trudg·er** n. [16th C. (as a v.): of unknown origin.]

trudg·en /'trəjən/ ▶ n. [in sing.] a swimming stroke like the crawl with a scissors movement of the legs. [19th C.: named after John *Trudgen* (1852–1902), English swimmer.]

true /troō/ ▶ adj. (**tru·er**, **tru·est**) **1** in accordance with fact or reality: *a true story | of course it's true.* ■ [attrib.] rightly or strictly so called; genuine: *we believe in true love.* ■ [attrib.] real or actual: *my true intentions.* ■ said when conceding a point in argument or discussion: *true, it faced north, but you got used to that.* **2** accurate or exact: *it was a true depiction.* ■ (of a note) exactly in tune. ■ (of a compass bearing) measured relative to true north: *steer 085 degrees true.* ■ correctly positioned, balanced, or aligned; upright or level. **3** loyal or faithful: *he was a true friend.* ■ [predic.] (**true to**) accurately conforming to (a standard or expectation); faithful to. **4** esp. archaic honest: *all good men and true.* ▶ adv. **1** esp. literary truly: *he spoke truer than he knew.* **2** accurately or without variation. ▶ v. (**trues, trued, tru·ing** or **true·ing**) [trans.] bring (an object, wheel, or other construction) into the exact shape, alignment, or position required.

– PHRASES **come true** actually happen or become the case: *dreams can come true.* **out of true** not in the correct or exact shape or alignment. **true to form** (or **type**) being or behaving as expected. — **true·ness** n. [OE *trēowe*, *trȳwe* 'steadfast, loyal'; rel. to Du. *getrouw*, Ger. *treu*, also to TRUCE.]

true bill ▶ n. Law a bill of indictment found by a grand jury to be supported by sufficient evidence to justify the hearing of a case.

true-blue ▶ adj. extremely loyal or orthodox.

true-born ▶ adj. [attrib.] of a specified kind by birth; genuine: *a true-born criminal.*

true bug ▶ n. see BUG (sense 2).

true-false test ▶ n. a test consisting of statements that must be marked as either true or false.

true·heart·ed /'troō'härtəd/ ▶ adj. literary loyal or faithful: *a truehearted paladin.*

true leaf ▶ n. Bot. a foliage leaf of a plant, as opposed to a seed leaf or cotyledon.

true-life ▶ adj. true to life; realistic.

true-love knot (also **true-lov·er's knot**) ▶ n. a kind of knot with interlacing bows on each side, symbolizing the bonds of love.

true north ▶ n. north according to the earth's axis, not magnetic north.

true rib ▶ n. a rib that is attached directly to the breastbone. Compare with FLOATING RIB.

Truf·faut /troō'fō/, François (1932–84), French movie director. He directed *The 400 Blows* (1959) and *Jules et Jim* (1961).

truf·fle /'trəfəl/ ▶ n. **1** a strong-smelling underground fungus (*Tuber* and other genera, family Tuberaceae) that resembles an irregular, rough-skinned potato, growing chiefly in broad-leaved woodland on calcareous soils. It is considered a culinary delicacy and found, esp. in France, with the aid of trained dogs or pigs. **2** a soft candy made of a chocolate mixture, typically flavored with rum and covered with cocoa. [16th C.: prob. via Du. from obs. Fr. *truffle*, perh. based on L. *tubera*, pl. of *tuber* 'hump, swelling.']

truf·fled /'trəfəld/ ▶ adj. (of food) cooked, garnished, or stuffed with truffles: *a truffled turkey.*

truf·fling /'trəf(ə)liNG/ ▶ n. the activity of hunting or rooting for truffles.

trug /trəg/ (also **trug basket**) ▶ n. Brit. a shallow oblong basket made of strips of wood, traditionally used for carrying garden flowers and produce. [ME (denoting a basin): perh. a dial. var. of TROUGH.]

tru·ism /'troō,izəm/ ▶ n. a statement that is obviously true and says nothing new or interesting. ■ Logic a proposition that states nothing beyond what is implied by any of its terms. — **tru·is·tic** /troō'istik/ adj.

Tru·ji·llo[1] /troō'hēyō/ a city on the coast of northwestern Peru; pop. 509,000.

Tru·ji·llo[2], Rafael (1891–1961), president of the Dominican Republic 1930–38 and 1942–52; born *Rafael Leónidas Trujillo Molina*; known as **Generalissimo**.

trull /trəl/ ▶ n. archaic a prostitute. [16th C.: from Ger. *Trulle*.]

tru·ly /'tro͞olē/ ▶**adv.** **1** in a truthful way: *he speaks truly.* ■ used to emphasize emotional sincerity or seriousness: *it is truly a privilege to be here.* **2** to the fullest degree; genuinely or properly: *a truly free press.* ■ absolutely or completely (used to emphasize a description): *a truly dreadful song.* **3** in fact or without doubt; really: *this is truly a miracle.* **4** archaic loyally or faithfully: *why cannot all masters be served truly?*
– PHRASES **yours truly** used as a formula for ending a letter. ■ humorous used to refer to oneself: *the demos will be organized by yours truly.* [OE *trēowlīce* 'faithfully' (see TRUE, -LY²).]

Tru·man /'tro͞omən/, Harry S (1884–1972), 33rd president of the US 1945–53. A Democrat, he served in the US Senate 1934–45 and as vice president 1945, succeeding to the presidency upon the death of Franklin D. Roosevelt. As president, he authorized the atomic bombing of Hiroshima and Nagasaki 1945, initiated the Truman Doctrine 1947, introduced the Marshall Plan 1948, and helped to establish NATO 1949. He later involved the US in the Korean War.

Tru·man Doc·trine the principle, first expressed in 1947 by US President Truman, that the US should give support to countries or peoples threatened by Soviet forces or communist insurrection.

Trum·bull, John (1756–1843), US artist. He created paintings for the rotunda of the Capitol building in Washington, DC, and several portraits of George Washington.

tru·meau /tro͞o'mō/ ▶**n.** (pl. **-meaux** /-'mōz; -'mō/) a section of wall or a pillar between two openings, esp. a pillar dividing a large doorway in a church. [19th C.: from Fr., lit. 'calf of the leg.']

trump¹ /trəmp/ ▶**n.** (in bridge, whist, and similar card games) a playing card of the suit chosen to rank above the others, which can win a trick where a card of a different suit has been led. ■ (**trumps**) the suit having this rank in a particular hand: *the ace of trumps.* ■ (in a tarot pack) any of a special suit of 22 cards depicting symbolic and typical figures and scenes. ■ (also **trump card**) fig. a valuable resource that may be used, esp. as a surprise, in order to gain an advantage. ■ informal, dated a helpful or admirable person. ▶**v.** [trans.] (in bridge, whist, and similar card games) play a trump on (a card of another suit), having no cards of the suit led. ■ fig. beat (someone or something) by saying or doing something better.
– PHRASAL VERBS **trump something up** invent a false accusation or excuse: *they've trumped up charges against her.* [16th C.: alt. of TRIUMPH.]

trump² ▶**n.** archaic a trumpet or a trumpet blast. [ME: from OFr. *trompe*, of Gmc. origin; prob. imitative.]

trump·er·y /'trəmpərē/ archaic ▶**n.** (pl. **-er·ies**) attractive articles of little value or use. ■ practices or beliefs that are superficially or visually appealing but have little real value or worth. ▶**adj.** showy but worthless: *trumpery jewelry.* ■ delusive or shallow: *our trumpery hope.* [ME (denoting trickery): from OFr. *tromperie*, from *tromper* 'deceive.']

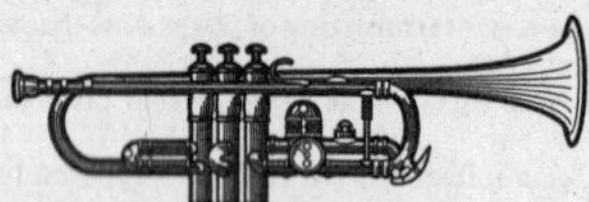
trumpet 1

trum·pet /'trəmpit/ ▶**n.** **1** a brass musical instrument with a flared bell and a bright, penetrating tone. The modern instrument has the tubing looped to form a straight-sided coil, with three valves. ■ an organ reed stop with a quality resembling that of a trumpet. ■ something shaped like a trumpet, esp. the tubular corona of a daffodil flower. ■ a sound resembling that of a trumpet, esp. the loud cry of an elephant. **2** (**trumpets**) a North American pitcher plant (genus *Sarracenia*, family Sarraceniaceae). ▶**v.** (**-pet·ed, -pet·ing**) **1** [intrans.] play a trumpet: [as adj.] (**trumpeting**) *figures of two trumpeting angels.* ■ make a loud, penetrating sound resembling that of a trumpet: *wild elephants trumpeting in the bush.* **2** [trans.] proclaim widely or loudly: *the press trumpeted another defeat for the government.* [ME: from OFr. *trompette*, dimin. of *trompe* (see TRUMP²).]

trum·pet creep·er ▶**n.** another term for TRUMPET VINE.

trum·pet·er /'trəmpitər/ ▶**n.** **1** a person who plays a trumpet. **2** a large gregarious ground-dwelling bird (genus *Psophia*, family Psophiidae) of tropical South American forests, with mainly black plumage and loud trumpeting and booming calls. **3** a pigeon of a domestic breed that makes a trumpetlike sound. **4** an edible marine fish (family Latridae) with a spiny dorsal fin, found chiefly in cool Australasian waters and said to make a grunting or trumpeting sound when taken out of the water.

trum·pet·er swan ▶**n.** a large migratory swan (*Cygnus buccinator*) with a black and yellow bill and a honking call, breeding in northern North America.

trum·pet ma·jor ▶**n.** the chief trumpeter of a cavalry regiment, typically a principal musician in a regimental band.

trum·pet vine (also **trumpet creeper**) ▶**n.** a climbing shrub (genus *Campsis*, family Bignoniaceae) with orange or red trumpet-shaped flowers, cultivated as an ornamental. Two species include the North American *C. radicans* and the Chinese *C. grandiflora*.

North American trumpet vine

trun·cal /'trəNGkəl/ ▶**adj.** Med. of or affecting the trunk of the body, or of a nerve.

trun·cate ▶**v.** /'trəNG,kāt/ [trans.] [often as adj.] (**truncated**) shorten (something) by cutting off the top or the end: *a truncated cone shape.* ■ Crystallog. replace (an edge or an angle) by a plane, typically so as to make equal angles with the adjacent faces. ▶**adj.** Bot. & Zool. (of a leaf, feather, or other part) ending abruptly as if cut off across the base or tip. — **trun·ca·tion** /,trəNG'kāSHən/ **n.** [15th C. (as a verb): from L. *truncat-* 'maimed,' from the verb *truncare*.]

trun·cheon /'trənCHən/ ▶**n.** esp. Brit. a short, thick stick carried as a weapon by a police officer. ■ a staff or baton acting as a symbol of authority. [ME: from OFr. *tronchon* 'stump,' based on L. *truncus* 'trunk.']

trun·dle /'trəndl/ ▶**v.** [intrans.] (of a wheeled vehicle or its occupants) move slowly and heavily, typically in a noisy or uneven way: *ten cars trundled past.* ■ (of a person) move in a similar way. ■ [trans.] cause (something, typically a wheeled vehicle) to roll or move in such a way: *we trundled a wheelbarrow down to the river.* ▶**n.** [in sing.] an act of moving in such a way. [16th C. (denoting a small wheel or roller): a parallel formation to obs. or dial. *trendle, trindle* '(cause to) revolve'; rel. to TREND.]

trun·dle bed ▶**n.** a low bed on wheels that can be stored under a larger bed.

trunk /trəNGk/ ▶**n.** **1** the main woody stem of a tree as distinct from its branches and roots. ■ the main part of an artery, nerve, or other anatomical structure from which smaller branches arise. ■ short for TRUNK LINE. ■ an enclosed shaft or conduit for cables or ventilation. **2** a person's or animal's body apart from the limbs and head. **3** the elongated, prehensile nose of an elephant. **4** a large box with a hinged lid for storing or transporting clothes and other articles. ■ the space at the back of a car for carrying luggage and other goods. — **trunk·ful** /-,fo͝ol/ **n.** (pl. **-fuls**) **trunk·less adj.** [ME: from OFr. *tronc*, from L. *truncus*.]

trunk call ▶**n.** dated, esp. Brit. a long-distance telephone call made within the same country.

trunk·fish /'trəNGk,fiSH/ ▶**n.** (pl. same or **-fish·es**) another term for BOXFISH.

trunk line ▶**n.** a main line of a railroad, telephone system, or other network.

trunks /trəNGks/ ▶**plural n.** men's shorts, worn esp. for swimming or boxing. [19th C.: pl. of TRUNKS.]

trun·nel /'trənl/ ▶**n.** a hard wooden pin used for fastening timbers together.

trun·nion /'trənyən/ ▶**n.** a pin or pivot forming one of a pair on which something is supported. ■ a supporting cylindrical projection on each side of a cannon or mortar. [17th C.: from Fr. *trognon* 'core, tree trunk,' of unknown origin.]

truss 1

truss /trəs/ ▶**n.** **1** a framework, typically consisting of rafters, posts, and struts, supporting a roof, bridge, or other structure: *roof trusses.* ■ a surgical appliance worn to support a hernia, typically a padded belt. ■ a large projection of stone or timber, typically one supporting a cornice. **2** Brit., esp. hist. a bundle of old hay (56 lb), new hay (60 lb), or straw (36 lb). **3** a compact cluster of flowers or fruit growing on one stalk. **4** Sailing a heavy metal ring securing the lower yards to a mast. ▶**v.** [trans.] **1** tie up the wings and legs of (a chicken or other bird) before cooking. ■ tie up (someone) with their arms at their sides. **2** [usu. as adj.] (**trussed**) support (a roof, bridge, or other structure) with a truss or trusses. — **truss·er n.** [ME: from OFr. *trusse* (n.), *trusser* 'pack up, bind in,' based on late L. *tors-* 'twisted,' from the verb *torquere*.]

trust /trəst/ ▶**n.** **1** firm belief in the reliability, truth, ability, or strength of someone or something. ■ acceptance of the truth of a statement without evidence or investigation: *I was taking nothing on trust.* ■ the state of being responsible for someone or something: *a man in a position of trust.* ■ literary a person or duty for which one has responsibility. ■ literary a hope or expectation. **2** Law confidence placed in a person by making that person the nominal owner of property to be held or used for the benefit of one or more others. ■ an arrangement whereby property is held in such a way: *a trust was set up* | *property held in trust.* **3** a body of trustees. ■ an organization or company managed by trustees. ■ dated a large company that has or attempts to gain monopolistic control of a market. ▶**v.** [trans.] **1** believe in the reliability, truth, ability, or strength of. ■ (**trust someone with**) allow someone to have, use, or

look after (someone or something of importance or value) with confidence: *I'd trust you with my life.* ■ (**trust someone/something to**) commit (someone or something) to the safekeeping of. ■ have confidence; hope (used as a polite formula in conversation): *I trust that you have enjoyed this book.* ■ [intrans.] have faith or confidence: *she trusted in God.* ■ [intrans.] (**trust to**) place reliance on (luck, fate, or something else over which one has little control): *trusting to the cover of night, I ventured out.* **2** esp. archaic allow credit to (a customer).
– PHRASES **trust someone to ——** it is characteristic or predictable for someone to act in the specified way: *trust Sam to have all the inside information.* — **trust·a·ble** adj. **trust·er** n. [ME: from ON *traust*, from *traustr* 'strong'; the verb from ON *treysta*, assimilated to the noun.]

trust·bust·er /'trəst,bəstər/ ▸ n. informal a person or agency employed to enforce antitrust legislation.

trust com·pa·ny ▸ n. a company formed to act as a trustee or to deal with trusts.

trust deed ▸ n. Law a deed of conveyance creating and setting out the conditions of a trust.

trust·ee /trə'stē/ ▸ n. Law an individual person or member of a board given control or powers of administration of property in trust with a legal obligation to administer it solely for the purposes specified. ■ a state made responsible for the government of a trust territory by the United Nations. — **trust·ee·ship** /-,SHip/ n.

trust·ful /'trəstfəl/ ▸ adj. having or marked by a total belief in the reliability, truth, ability, or strength of someone. — **trust·ful·ly** adv. **trust·ful·ness** n.

trust fund ▸ n. a fund consisting of assets belonging to a trust, held by the trustees for the beneficiaries.

trust·ing /'trəstiNG/ ▸ adj. showing or tending to have a belief in a person's honesty or sincerity; not suspicious. — **trust·ing·ly** adv. **trust·ing·ness** n.

trust ter·ri·to·ry ▸ n. a territory under the trusteeship of the United Nations or of a country designated by it.

trust·wor·thy /'trəst,wərT͟Hē/ ▸ adj. able to be relied on as honest or truthful: *leave a spare key with a trustworthy neighbor.* — **trust·wor·thi·ly** /-T͟Həlē/ adv. **trust·wor·thi·ness** n.

trust·y /'trəstē/ ▸ adj. (**trust·i·er, trust·i·est**) [attrib.] archaic or humorous having served for a long time and regarded as reliable or faithful: *his trusty Corona typewriter.* ▸ n. (pl. **trust·ies**) a prisoner who is given special privileges or responsibilities in return for good behavior. — **trust·i·ly** /-tl-ē/ adv. **trust·i·ness** n.

Truth /tro͞oTH/, Sojourner (*c.*1797–1883), US evangelist and reformer; previously *Isabella Van Wagener*. A former slave, she preached in favor of black rights and women's suffrage.

truth /tro͞oTH/ ▸ n. (pl. **truths** /tro͞oT͟HZ; tro͞oTHS/) the quality or state of being true: *the truth of her accusation.* ■ (also **the truth**) that which is true or in accordance with fact or reality: *tell me the truth.* ■ a fact or belief that is accepted as true: *scientific truths.*
– PHRASES **in truth** really; in fact: *in truth, she was more than a little unhappy.* **of a truth** archaic certainly. **to tell the truth** (or **truth to tell** or **if truth be told**) to be frank (used esp. when making an admission or when expressing an unwelcome or controversial opinion). [OE *trīewth, trēowth* 'faithfulness, constancy' (see TRUE, -TH[2]).]

truth con·di·tion ▸ n. Logic the condition under which a given proposition is true. ■ a statement of this condition, sometimes taken to be the meaning of the proposition.

truth·ful /'tro͞oTHfəl/ ▸ adj. (of a person or statement) telling or expressing the truth; honest. ■ (of artistic or literary representation) characterized by accuracy or realism; true to life. — **truth·ful·ly** adv. **truth·ful·ness** n.

truth se·rum (also **truth drug**) ▸ n. a drug supposedly able to induce a state in which a person answers questions truthfully.

truth ta·ble ▸ n. Logic a diagram in rows and columns showing how the truth or falsity of a proposition varies with that of its components. ■ Electron. a similar diagram of the outputs from all possible combinations of input.

truth val·ue ▸ n. Logic the attribute assigned to a proposition in respect of its truth or falsehood, which in classical logic has only two possible values (true or false).

try /trī/ ▸ v. (**tries, tried**) **1** [intrans.] make an attempt or effort to do something: *he tried to regain his breath* | *none of them tried very hard* | [trans.] *he tried the maneuver.* ■ (**try for**) attempt to achieve or attain. ■ [trans.] use, test, or do (something new or different) in order to see if it is suitable, effective, or pleasant. ■ (**try out for**) compete or audition in order to join (a team) or be given (a position). ■ [trans.] go to (a place) or attempt to contact (someone), typically in order to obtain something: *I've tried the apartment, but the number is busy.* ■ [trans.] push or pull (a door or window) to determine whether it is locked: *I tried the doors.* ■ [trans.] make severe demands on (a person or a quality, typically patience). **2** [trans.] (usu. **be tried**) subject (someone) to trial. ■ investigate and decide (a case or issue) in a formal trial. **3** [trans.] smooth (roughly planed wood) with a plane to give an accurately flat surface. **4** [trans.] extract (oil or fat) by heating. ▸ n. (pl. **tries**) **1** an effort to accomplish something; an attempt: *Mitterrand was elected president on his third try.* ■ an act of doing, using, or testing something new or different to see if it is suitable, effective, or pleasant: *she agreed that they should give the idea a try.* **2** Rugby an act of touching the ball down behind the opposing goal line, scoring points and entitling the scoring side to a goal kick.
– PHRASES **I, he,** etc., **will try anything once** used to indicate willingness to do or experience something new. **try something on for size** assess whether something is suitable. **try one's hand at** attempt to do (something) for the first time, typically in order to find out if one is good at it. **try me** used to suggest that one may be willing to do something unexpected or unlikely: *"You won't use a gun up here." "Try me."*
– PHRASAL VERBS **try something on** put on an item of clothing to see if it fits or suits one. **try someone/something out** test someone or something new or different to assess their suitability or effectiveness: *I try out new recipes on my daughter.* [ME: from OFr. *trier* 'sift.']

try·ing /'trī-iNG/ ▸ adj. difficult or annoying; hard to endure: *it had been a very trying day.* — **try·ing·ly** adv.

try·ing plane ▸ n. a long, heavy plane used in smoothing roughly planed wood.

try·out /'trī,out/ ▸ n. a test of the potential of someone or something, esp. in the context of entertainment or sports: *she would be too distraught to compete in cheerleader tryouts.*

try·pan·o·some /trə'panə,sōm; 'tripənə-/ ▸ n. Med. & Zool. a single-celled parasitic protozoan (genus *Trypanosoma*, phylum Kinetoplastida) with a trailing flagellum, infesting the blood. [20th C.: from Gk. *trupanon* 'borer' + -SOME[3].]

try·pan·o·so·mi·a·sis /trə,panəsō'mīəsis; 'tripənə-/ ▸ n. Med. any tropical disease caused by trypanosomes and typically transmitted by biting insects, esp. sleeping sickness and Chagas' disease.

tryp·sin /'tripsin/ ▸ n. Biochem. a digestive enzyme that breaks down proteins in the small intestine. It is secreted by the pancreas in an inactive form, trypsinogen. — **tryp·tic** /-tik/ adj. [19th C.: from Gk. *tripsis* 'friction,' from *tribein* 'to rub.']

tryp·sin·o·gen /trip'sinəjən; -,jen/ ▸ n. Biochem. an inactive substance secreted by the pancreas, from which the digestive enzyme trypsin is formed in the duodenum.

tryp·ta·mine /'triptə,mēn/ ▸ n. Biochem. a compound, $C_8H_6NCH_2CH_2NH$, of which serotonin is a derivative, produced from tryptophan by decarboxylation.

tryp·to·phan /'triptə,fan/ ▸ n. Biochem. an amino acid, $C_8H_6NCH_2CH(NH_2)COOH$, that is a constituent of most proteins. It is an essential nutrient in the diet of vertebrates. [19th C.: from *tryptic* 'relating to trypsin' + Gk. *phainein* 'appear.']

try·sail /'trīsəl; -,sāl/ ▸ n. a small, strong fore-and-aft sail set on the mast of a sailing vessel in heavy weather.

try square ▸ n. an implement used to check and mark right angles in construction work.

tryst /trist/ literary ▸ n. a private, romantic rendezvous between lovers: *a moonlight tryst.* ▸ v. [intrans.] keep a rendezvous of this kind. — **trys·ter** n. [ME (orig. Scots): var. of obs. *trist* 'an appointed place in hunting,' from Fr. *triste* or med. L. *trista*.]

Tsao-chuang /'jou jo͞o'äNG/ variant of ZAOZHUANG.

tsar, etc. ▸ n. var. of CZAR, etc.

Tsa·ri·tsyn /(t)sä'rētsin/ former name (until 1925) of VOLGOGRAD.

tsats·ke /'tsätskə/ ▸ n. var. of TCHOTCHKE.

tsetse

tset·se /'(t)sētsē; '(t)set-/ (also **tset·se fly**) ▸ n. an African bloodsucking fly (genus *Glossina*, family Tabanidae) that bites humans and other mammals, transmitting sleeping sickness and nagana. [19th C.: from Setswana.]

TSgt ▸ abbr. technical sergeant.

TSH ▸ abbr. thyroid-stimulating hormone.

T-shirt (also **tee shirt**) ▸ n. a short-sleeved casual top, generally made of cotton, having the shape of a T when spread out flat.

tsim·mes /'tsimis/ (also **tzim·mes** or **tzim·mis**) ▸ n. (pl. same) a Jewish stew of sweetened vegetables or vegetables and fruit, sometimes with meat. ■ fig. a fuss or muddle. [Yiddish.]

Tsim·shi·an /'CHimSHēən; 'tsim-/ ▸ n. (pl. same) **1** a member of an American Indian people of coastal British Columbia. **2** the Penutian language of this people. ▸ adj. of or relating to this people or their language. [from the Tsimshian self-designation *c'msyan*, lit. 'inside the Skeena River.']

Tsi·nan /'jē'nän/ variant of JINAN.

Tsing·hai /'tsiNG'hī; 'CHiNG/ variant of QINGHAI.

tsk tsk /tisk tisk/ ▸ exclam. expressing disapproval or annoyance: *you of all people, Goldie—tsk, tsk.* ▸ v. (**tsk-tsk**) [intrans.] make such an exclamation.

[1940s: imitative.]

tsp ▶ **abbr.** (pl. same or **tsps.**) teaspoonful.

T-square (also **T square**) ▶ **n.** a T-shaped instrument for drawing or testing right angles.

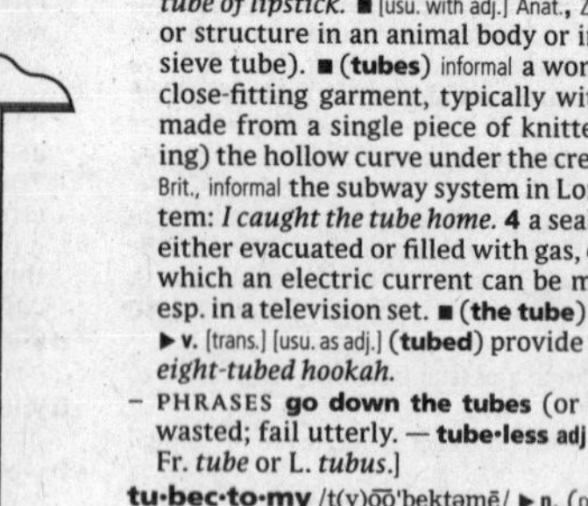
T-square

TSR Comput. ▶ **abbr.** terminate and stay resident, denoting a type of program that remains in the memory of a microcomputer after it has finished running and which can be quickly reactivated.

TSS ▶ **abbr.** toxic shock syndrome.

T-storm ▶ **n.** informal short for THUNDERSTORM.

tsu·ba /'tso͞obə/ ▶ **n.** (pl. same or **-bas**) a Japanese sword guard, typically elaborately decorated and made of iron or leather.

tsu·bo /'tso͞obō/ ▶ **n.** (pl. same or **-bos**) **1** a Japanese unit of area equal to approximately 3.31 square miles (3.95 sq m). **2** (in complementary medicine) a point on the face or body to which pressure or other stimulation is applied during treatment.

tsu·na·mi /(t)so͞o'nämē/ ▶ **n.** (pl. same or **-mis**) a long high sea wave caused by an earthquake or other disturbance. [19th C.: from Japanese, from *tsu* 'harbor' + *nami* 'wave.']

tsu·ris /'tso͝oris; 'tsər/ ▶ **n.** Informal trouble or woe; aggravation. [20th C.: from Heb.]

Tsu·shi·ma /(t)so͞o'shēmə/ a Japanese island in Korea Strait, between South Korea and Japan.

tsu·tsu·ga·mu·shi dis·ease /,(t)so͞otsəgə'mo͞oshē/ ▶ **n.** another term for SCRUB TYPHUS. [20th C.: *tsutsugamushi*, from the Japanese name of the mite that transmits the disease.]

Tswa·na /'(t)swänə/ ▶ **n.** (pl. same, **Tswa·nas**, or **Ba·tswa·na** /bät'swänə/) **1** a member of a people living in Botswana, South Africa, and neighboring areas. **2** the Bantu language of this people, also called Setswana. ▶ **adj.** of or relating to the Tswana or their language. [stem of Setswana *moTswana*, pl. *baTswana*.]

TTL ▶ **n.** Electron. a widely used technology for making integrated circuits. [abbr. of *transistor transistor logic*.] ▶ **adj.** Photog. (of a camera focusing system) through-the-lens.

T-top ▶ **n.** a car roof with removable panels.

TTY ▶ **abbr.** teletypewriter.

TU ▶ **abbr.** trade union.

Tu. ▶ **abbr.** Tuesday.

Tu·a·mo·tu Ar·chi·pel·a·go /,to͞oə'mōto͞o/ a group of about 80 coral islands that form part of French Polynesia, in the South Pacific Ocean; pop. 12,000.

Tua·reg /'twä,reg/ ▶ **n.** (pl. same or **-regs**) a member of a Berber people of the western and central Sahara, living mainly in Algeria, Mali, Niger, and western Libya, traditionally as nomadic pastoralists. ▶ **adj.** of or relating to this people. [from Arab. *ṭawāriq*.]

tu·a·ta·ra /,to͞oə'tärə/ ▶ **n.** a nocturnal burrowing lizardlike reptile (*Sphenodon punctatum*, order Rhynchocephalia) with a crest of soft spines along its back, now confined to some small islands off New Zealand. [19th C.: from Maori, from *tua* 'on the back' + *tara* 'spine.']

tub /təb/ ▶ **n.** **1** a wide, open, deep, typically round container with a flat bottom used for holding liquids, growing plants, etc. ■ a similar small plastic or cardboard container in which food is bought or stored. ■ the contents of such a container or the amount it can contain: *she ate a tub of yogurt.* ■ a washtub. ■ informal a bathtub. ■ Mining a container for conveying ore, coal, etc. **2** informal an old, awkward, or run-down vessel. ▶ **v.** (**tubbed, tub·bing**) [trans.] **1** [usu. as adj.] (**tubbed**) plant in a tub: *tubbed fruit trees.* **2** dated wash or bathe (someone or something) in or as in a tub or bath. ■ [intrans.] Brit., informal have a bath. — **tub·ba·ble adj.** (informal) (sense 2 of the verb) **tub·ful** /-,fo͝ol/ **n.** (pl. **-fuls**). [ME: prob. of Low Ger. or Du. origin; compare MDu. *tubbe*.]

tu·ba /'t(y)o͞obə/ ▶ **n.** a large brass wind instrument of bass pitch, with three to six valves and a broad bell typically facing upward. ■ a powerful reed stop on an organ with the quality of a tuba. [19th C.: via Ital. from L., 'trumpet.']

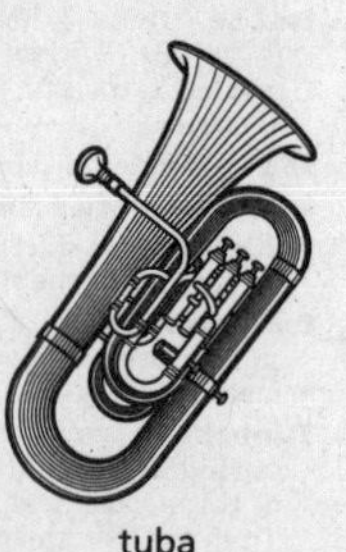
tuba

tub·al /'t(y)o͞obəl/ ▶ **adj.** of, relating to, or occurring in a tube, esp. the fallopian tubes.

tub·al li·ga·tion ▶ **n.** a surgical procedure for female sterilization that involves severing and tying the fallopian tubes.

tub·al preg·nan·cy ▶ **n.** Med. an ectopic pregnancy in which the fetus develops in a fallopian tube.

tub·by /'təbē/ ▶ **adj.** (**-bi·er, -bi·est**) **1** informal (of a person) short and rather fat. **2** (of a sound) lacking resonance; dull. — **tub·bi·ness n.**

tub chair ▶ **n.** a chair with solid arms continuous with a semicircular back.

tube /t(y)o͞ob/ ▶ **n.** **1** a long, hollow cylinder of metal, plastic, glass, etc., for holding or transporting something, chiefly liquids or gases. ■ the inner tube of a bicycle tire. ■ material in such a cylindrical form; tubing. **2** a thing in the form of or resembling such a cylinder, in particular: ■ a flexible metal or plastic container sealed at one end and having a screw cap at the other, for holding a semiliquid substance ready for use: *a tube of toothpaste.* ■ a rigid cylindrical container: *a tube of lipstick.* ■ [usu. with adj.] Anat., Zool., & Bot. a hollow cylindrical organ or structure in an animal body or in a plant (e.g., a Eustachian tube, a sieve tube). ■ (**tubes**) informal a woman's Fallopian tubes. ■ a woman's close-fitting garment, typically without darts or other tailoring and made from a single piece of knitted or elasticized fabric. ■ (in surfing) the hollow curve under the crest of a breaking wave. **3** (**the tube**) Brit., informal the subway system in London. ■ a train running on this system: *I caught the tube home.* **4** a sealed container, typically of glass and either evacuated or filled with gas, containing two electrodes between which an electric current can be made to flow. ■ a cathode-ray tube, esp. in a television set. ■ (**the tube**) informal television. ■ a vacuum tube. ▶ **v.** [trans.] [usu. as adj.] (**tubed**) provide with a tube or tubes: [in comb.] *a giant eight-tubed hookah.*
— PHRASES **go down the tubes** (or **tube**) informal be completely lost or wasted; fail utterly. — **tube·less adj. tube·like** /-,līk/ **adj.** [17th C.: from Fr. *tube* or L. *tubus*.]

tu·bec·to·my /t(y)o͞o'bektəmē/ ▶ **n.** (pl. **-mies**) another term for SALPINGECTOMY.

tube foot ▶ **n.** (usu. **tube feet**) Zool. (in an echinoderm) each of a large number of small, flexible, hollow appendages protruding through the ambulacra, used either for locomotion or for collecting food and operated by hydraulic pressure within the water-vascular system.

tube pan ▶ **n.** a round cake pan with a hollow, cone-shaped center, used for baking ring-shaped cakes.

tu·ber /'t(y)o͞obər/ ▶ **n.** **1** a much thickened underground part of a stem or rhizome, e.g., in the potato, serving as a food reserve and bearing buds from which new plants arise. ■ a tuberous root, e.g., of the dahlia. **2** Anat. a rounded swelling or protuberant part. [17th C.: from L., lit. 'hump, swelling.']

tu·ber ci·ne·re·um /si'ne(ə)rēəm/ ▶ **n.** Anat. the part of the hypothalamus to which the pituitary gland is attached. [L. *cinereum*, neut. of *cinereus* 'ash-colored.']

tu·ber·cle /'t(y)o͞obərkəl/ ▶ **n.** **1** Anat., Zool., & Bot. a small rounded projection or protuberance, esp. on a bone or on the surface of an animal or plant. **2** Med. a small nodular lesion in the lungs or other tissues, characteristic of tuberculosis. — **tu·ber·cu·late** /t(y)o͞o'bərkyə,lāt; -lit/ **adj.** (in sense 1). [16th C.: from L. *tuberculum*, dimin. of *tuber* (see TUBER).]

tu·ber·cle ba·cil·lus ▶ **n.** a bacterium that causes tuberculosis.

tu·ber·cu·lar /tə'bərkyələr/ ▶ **adj.** Med. of, relating to, or affected with tuberculosis: *a tubercular kidney.* ■ Biol. & Med. having or covered with tubercles. ▶ **n.** a person with tuberculosis.

tu·ber·cu·la·tion /t(y)o͞o,bərkyə'lāshən/ ▶ **n.** esp. Biol. the formation or presence of tubercles, esp. of a specified type.

tu·ber·cu·lin /t(y)o͞o'bərkyəlin/ ▶ **n.** a sterile protein extract from cultures of tubercle bacillus, used in a test by hypodermic injection for infection with or immunity to tuberculosis, and also formerly in the treatment of the disease. [19th C.: from L. *tuberculum* (see TUBERCLE) + -IN[1].]

tu·ber·cu·loid /t(y)o͞o'bərkyə,loid/ ▶ **adj.** Med. resembling tuberculosis or its symptoms, in particular: ■ relating to or denoting the milder of the two principal forms of leprosy, marked by few, well-defined lesions similar to those of tuberculosis, often with loss of feeling in the affected areas. Compare with LEPROMATOUS.

tu·ber·cu·lo·sis /tə,bərkyə'lōsis; t(y)o͞o-/ (abbr.: **TB**) ▶ **n.** an infectious disease characterized by the growth of nodules (tubercles) in the tissues, esp. the lungs, caused chiefly by the bacterium *Mycobacterium tuberculosis*. [19th C.: mod. L., from L. *tuberculum* (see TUBERCLE) + -OSIS.]

tu·ber·cu·lous /tə'bərkyələs; t(y)o͞o-/ ▶ **adj.** another term for TUBERCULAR.

tube·rose /'t(y)o͞ob(ə),rōz/ ▶ **n.** **1** a Mexican plant (*Polianthes tuberosa*) of the agave family, with heavily scented white waxy flowers and a bulblike base. Unknown in the wild, it was formerly cultivated as a flavoring for chocolate; the flower oil is used in perfumery. **2** var. of TUBEROUS. [17th C.: sense 1 from L. *tuberosa*, fem. of *tuberosus* 'with protuberances'; sense 2 from L. *tuberosus*.]

tu·ber·ous /'t(y)o͞obərəs/ (also **tu·ber·ose** /-bə,rōs/) ▶ **adj.** **1** Bot. of the nature of a tuber. See TUBEROUS ROOT. ■ (of a plant) having tubers or a tuberous root. **2** Med. characterized by or affected by rounded swellings: *tuberous sclerosis.* — **tu·ber·os·i·ty** /,t(y)o͞obə'räsitē/ **n.**

tu·ber·ous root ▶ **n.** a thick and fleshy root like a tuber but without buds, as in the dahlia.

tube sock ▶ **n.** a sock without a shaped heel.

tube top ▶ **n.** a tight-fitting strapless top made of stretchy material and worn by women or girls.

tube worm ▶ **n.** a marine bristle worm (families Serpulidae and Sabellidae, phylum Polychaeta) that lives in a tube made from sand particles or in a calcareous tube that it secretes. ■ a pogonophoran or vestimentiferan worm.

tu·bic·o·lous /t(y)o͞o'bikələs/ ▶ **adj.** Zool. (of a marine worm) living in a tube.

tu·bi·fex /'t(y)o͞obə,feks/ ▶ **n.** a small red annelid (genus *Tubifex*, family Tubificidae) that lives in fresh water, partly buried in the mud. [mod. L., from L. *tubus* 'tube' + *-fex* from *facere* 'make.']

tub·ing /'t(y)o͞obiNG/ ▶ **n.** **1** a length or lengths of metal, plastic, glass, etc., in tubular form. **2** the leisure activity of riding on water or snow on a large inflated inner tube.

Tub·man /'təbmən/, Harriet Ross (*c.*1820–1913), US abolitionist; born

Araminta Ross; known as the *Moses of Her People*. She escaped slavery via the Underground Railroad in 1849 and then returned to lead about 300 slaves to safety in the North.

tub-thump·ing informal, derog. ▶ **adj.** [attrib.] expressing opinions in a loud and violent or dramatic manner. ▶ **n.** the expression of opinions in such a way. — **tub-thump·er n.**

tu·bu·lar /ˈt(y)o͞obyələr/ ▶ **adj.** **1** long, round, and hollow like a tube: *tubular flowers of deep crimson.* ■ made from a tube or tubes: *tubular steel chairs.* ■ Surfing (of a wave) hollow and well curved. **2** Med. of or involving tubules or other tube-shaped structures. ▶ **n. 1** short for TUBULAR TIRE. **2** (**tubulars**) oil-drilling equipment made from tubes.

tu·bu·lar bells ▶ **plural n.** an orchestral instrument consisting of a row of vertically suspended metal tubes struck with a mallet.

tu·bu·lar tire ▶ **n.** a completely enclosed tire cemented onto the wheel rim, used on racing bicycles.

tu·bule /ˈt(y)o͞oˌbyo͞ol/ ▶ **n.** a minute tube, esp. as an anatomical structure: *kidney tubules.* [17th C.: from L. *tubulus*, dimin. of *tubus* 'tube.']

Tu·bu·li·den·ta·ta /ˌt(y)o͞obyəlidenˈtätə/ Zool. an order of mammals that comprises only the aardvark. [mod. L. (pl.), from TUBULE + Gk. *odous, odont-* 'tooth.']

tu·bu·lin /ˈt(y)o͞obyəlin/ ▶ **n.** Biochem. a protein that is the main constituent of the microtubules of living cells. [1960s: from TUBULE + -IN[1].]

Tu·can·a /t(y)o͞oˈkänə; -ˈkanə/ Astron. a southern constellation (the Toucan), south of Grus and Phoenix. It contains the Small Magellanic Cloud.

Tuch·man /ˈtəkmən/, Barbara (1912–89), US historian and writer. Her many works include *The Guns of August* (1962) and *A Distant Mirror* (1978).

tuck /tək/ ▶ **v. 1** [trans.] push, fold, or turn (the edges or ends of something, esp. a garment or bedclothes) so as to hide them or hold them in place: *he tucked his shirt into his trousers.* ■ (**tuck someone in**) make someone, esp. a child, comfortable in bed by pulling the edges of the bedclothes firmly under the mattress. ■ draw (something, esp. part of one's body) together into a small space: *she tucked her legs under her.* ■ (often **be tucked**) put (something) away in a specified place or way so as to be hidden, safe, comfortable, or tidy. **2** [trans.] make a flattened, stitched fold in (a garment or material), typically so as to shorten or tighten it, or for decoration. ▶ **n. 1** a flattened, stitched fold in a garment or material, typically one of several parallel folds put in a garment for shortening, tightening, or decoration. ■ [usu. with adj.] informal a surgical operation to reduce surplus flesh or fat: *a tummy tuck.* **2** Brit., informal food, typically cakes and candy, eaten by children at school as a snack. **3** (also **tuck position**) (in diving, gymnastics, downhill skiing, etc.) a position with the knees bent and held close to the chest, often with the hands clasped around the shins.
– PHRASAL VERBS **tuck something away 1** store something in a secure place. ■ (usu. **be tucked away**) put or keep someone or something in an inconspicuous or concealed place. **2** esp. Brit. informal eat a lot of food. **tuck in** (or **into**) esp. Brit. informal eat food heartily. [OE *tūcian* 'to punish, ill-treat': of West Gmc. origin; rel. to TUG.]

tuck·a·hoe /ˈtəkəˌhō/ ▶ **n.** a root or other underground plant part formerly eaten by North American Indians, in particular: ■ the starchy rhizome of an arum (*Peltandra virginica*) that grows chiefly in marshland. ■ the underground sclerotium of a bracket fungus (*Poria cocos*). [17th C.: from Virginia Algonquian *tockawhoughe*.]

tuck·er /ˈtəkər/ ▶ **n.** hist. a piece of lace or linen worn in or around the top of a bodice or as an insert at the front of a low-cut dress. See also *ONE'S BEST BIB AND TUCKER* at BIB[1]. ▶ **v.** [trans.] (usu. **be tuckered out**) informal exhaust; wear out.

tuck·et /ˈtəkit/ ▶ **n.** archaic a flourish on a trumpet. [16th C.: from obs. *tuck* 'beat (a drum),' from Old North. Fr. *toquer*, from the base of TOUCH.]

tuck·ing /təkiNG/ ▶ **n.** a series of stitched tucks in a garment.

tuck-point ▶ **v.** [trans.] point (brickwork) with colored mortar so as to have a narrow groove that is filled with fine white lime putty allowed to project slightly.

tuck po·si·tion ▶ **n.** see TUCK (sense 3).

Tuc·son /ˈto͞oˌsän; to͞oˈsän/ a city in southeastern Arizona; pop. 486,699.

'tude /t(y)o͞od/ ▶ **n.** informal short for ATTITUDE: *the song bristles with lotsa 'tude.*

-tude ▶ **suffix** forming abstract nouns such as *beatitude, solitude*. [from Fr. *-tude*, from L. *-tudo*.]

Tu·deh /ˈto͞odā/ (also **Tu·deh Par·ty**) the Communist Party of Iran. [Pers., lit. 'mass.']

Tu·dor[1] /ˈt(y)o͞odər/ **adj.** of or relating to the English royal dynasty that held the throne from the accession of Henry VII in 1485 until the death of Elizabeth I in 1603. ■ of, denoting, or relating to the prevalent architectural style of the Tudor period, characterized esp. by half-timbering. **n.** a member of this dynasty.

Tu·dor[2], Henry, Henry VII of England (see HENRY[1]).

Tu·dor[3], Mary, Mary I of England (see MARY[2]).

Tu·dor rose ▶ **n.** a conventionalized, typically five-lobed figure of a rose used in architectural and other decoration in the Tudor period, in particular a combination of the red and white roses of Lancaster or York adopted as a badge by Henry VII.

Tues. (also **Tue.**) ▶ **abbr.** Tuesday.

Tues·day /ˈt(y)o͞ozˌdā; -dē/ ▶ **n.** the day of the week before Wednesday and following Monday. ▶ **adv.** on Tuesday: *they're all leaving Tuesday.* ■ (**Tuesdays**) on Tuesdays; each Tuesday. [OE *Tīwesdæg*, named after the Gmc. god *Tīw*.]

tu·fa /ˈt(y)o͞ofə/ ▶ **n.** a porous rock composed of calcium carbonate and formed by precipitation from water, e.g., around mineral springs. ■ another term for TUFF. — **tu·fa·ceous** /t(y)o͞oˈfāSHəs/ **adj.** [18th C.: from Ital., var. of *tufo* (see TUFF).]

tuff /təf/ ▶ **n.** a light, porous rock formed by consolidation of volcanic ash. — **tuff·a·ceous** /təˈfāSHəs/ **adj.** [16th C.: via Fr. from Ital. *tufo*, from late L. *tofus*, L. *tophus* (see TOPHUS).]

tuf·fet /ˈtəfit/ ▶ **n. 1** a tuft or clump of something. **2** a footstool or low seat. [16th C.: alt. of TUFT.]

tuft /təft/ ▶ **n.** a bunch or collection of something, typically threads, grass, or hair, held or growing together at the base: *scrubby tufts of grass.* ■ Anat. & Zool. a bunch of small blood vessels, respiratory tentacles, or other small anatomical structures. ▶ **v.** [trans.] **1** (usu. **be tufted**) provide (something) with a tuft or tufts. **2** Needlework make depressions at regular intervals in (a mattress or cushion) by passing a thread through it. — **tuft·y adj.** [ME: prob. from OFr. *tofe*.]

tuft·ed /ˈtəftid/ ▶ **adj.** having or growing in a tuft or tufts: *tufted grass.*

tug /təg/ ▶ **v.** (**tugged, tug·ging**) [trans.] pull (something) hard or suddenly: *she tugged off her boots* | [intrans.] *he tugged at Tom's coat sleeve.* ▶ **n. 1** a hard or sudden pull. **2** short for TUGBOAT. ■ an aircraft towing a glider. **3** a loop from a horse's saddle that supports a shaft or trace. — **tug·ger n.** [ME: from the base of TOW[1].]

tugboat

tug·boat ▶ **n.** a small, powerful boat used for towing larger boats and ships, esp. in harbor.

tug of war ▶ **n.** a contest in which two teams pull at opposite ends of a rope until one drags the other over a central line. ■ fig. a situation in which two evenly matched people or factions are striving to keep or obtain the same thing.

tu·grik /ˈto͞ogrik/ ▶ **n.** (pl. same or **-griks**) the basic monetary unit of Mongolia, equal to 100 mongos. [Mongolian.]

tu·i /ˈto͞oē/ ▶ **n.** a large New Zealand honeyeater (*Prosthemadura novaeseelandiae*) with glossy blackish plumage and two white tufts at the throat. [19th C.: from Maori.]

tuile /twē/ ▶ **n.** (pl. same) a thin curved cookie, typically made with almonds. [Fr., lit. 'tile.']

Tu·i·nal /ˈto͞oəˌnôl; -ˌnal/ ▶ **n.** Med., trademark a sedative and hypnotic drug consisting of a combination of two barbiturates.

tu·i·tion /t(y)o͞oˈiSHən/ ▶ **n.** a sum of money charged for teaching or instruction by a school, college, or university: *I'm not paying next year's tuition.* ■ teaching or instruction, esp. of individual pupils or small groups: *private tuition in French.* — **tu·i·tion·al** /-SHənl/ **adj.** [ME: via OFr. from L. *tuitio(n-)*, from *tueri* 'to watch, guard.']

tuk-tuk /ˈto͝ok ˌto͝ok/ ▶ **n.** (in Thailand) a three-wheeled motorized vehicle used as a taxi. [imitative.]

Tu·la /ˈto͞olə/ **1** a city in western Russia; pop. 543,000. **2** the ancient capital city of the Toltecs, usually identified with a site near the town of Tula in Hidalgo State, in central Mexico.

tu·la·re·mi·a /ˌt(y)o͞oləˈrēmēə/ (Brit. **tu·la·rae·mi·a**) ▶ **n.** a severe infectious disease of animals transmissible to humans, caused by the bacterium *Francisella tularensis* and characterized by ulcers at the site of infection, fever, and loss of weight. — **tu·la·re·mic** /ˈrēmik/ **adj.** [1920s: mod. L., from *Tulare*, the county in California.]

tu·le /ˈto͞olē/ ▶ **n.** a large bulrush that is abundant in marshy areas of California. Two species: *Scirpus acutus* and *S. validus*. [19th C.: via Sp. from Nahuatl *tullin*.]

tu·lip /ˈt(y)o͞oləp/ ▶ **n.** a bulbous spring-flowering plant (genus *Tulipa*) of the lily family, with boldly colored cup-shaped flowers. [16th C.: from Fr. *tulipe*, via Turk. from Pers. *dulband* 'turban.']

tu·lip tree (also **tu·lip·tree**) ▶ **n.** a deciduous North American tree (*Liriodendron tulipifera*) of the magnolia family, with large distinctively lobed leaves and insignificant tuliplike flowers. Also called YELLOW POPLAR.

tu·lip·wood /ˈt(y)o͞oləpˌwo͝od/ ▶ **n. 1** the pale timber of the tulip tree. **2** an Australian tree (*Harpullia pendula*) of the soapberry family, with heavy black and yellow timber.

Tull /təl/, Jethro (1674–1741), English agriculturalist. In 1701, he invented the seed drill.

tulle /to͞ol/ ▶ **n.** a soft, fine silk, cotton, or nylon material like net, used for making veils and dresses. [19th C.: *Tulle*, a town in France.]

Tul·sa /ˈtəlsə/ a city in northeastern Oklahoma; pop. 393,049.

tum /təm/ ▶ **n.** informal a person's stomach or abdomen. [19th C.: abbr. of TUMMY.]

tum·ble /ˈtəmbəl/ ▶v. **1** [intrans.] (typically of a person) fall suddenly, clumsily, or headlong. ■ move or rush in a headlong or uncontrolled way. ■ (of something abstract) fall rapidly in amount or value: *property prices tumbled.* ■ [trans.] rumple; disarrange: [as adj.] (**tumbled**) *his tumbled bedclothes.* ■ [trans.] informal have sexual intercourse with (someone). **2** [intrans.] (**tumble to**) informal understand the meaning or hidden implication of (a situation): *she tumbled to our scam.* **3** [intrans.] perform acrobatic or gymnastic exercises, typically handsprings and somersaults in the air. ■ (of a breed of pigeon) repeatedly turn over backward in flight. **4** [trans.] clean (castings, gemstones, etc.) in a tumbling barrel. ▶n. **1** a sudden or headlong fall: *I took a tumble.* ■ a rapid fall in amount or value. ■ an untidy or confused arrangement or state. ■ informal an act of sexual intercourse. ■ a handspring, somersault in the air, or other acrobatic feat. **2** informal a friendly sign of recognition, acknowledgment, or interest: *not a soul gave him a tumble.* [ME (as a v., also in the sense 'dance with contortions'): from Mid. Low Ger. *tummelen*; cf. OE *tumbian* 'to dance.']

tum·ble·bug /ˈtəmbəl,bəg/ ▶n. a dung beetle that rolls balls of dung along the ground.

tum·ble·down /ˈtəmbəl,doun/ ▶adj. (of a building or structure) falling or fallen into ruin; dilapidated.

tum·ble dry ▶v. (**dries, dried**) [intrans.] dry washed clothes by spinning them in hot air inside a dryer.

tum·ble·home /ˈtəmbəl,hōm/ ▶n. the inward slope of the upper part of the sides of a boat or ship.

tum·bler /ˈtəmblər/ ▶n. **1** a drinking glass with straight sides and no handle or stem. **2** an acrobat or gymnast, esp. one who performs somersaults. ■ a pigeon of a breed that repeatedly turns over backward in flight. **3** a pivoted piece in a lock that holds the bolt until lifted by a key. ■ a notched pivoted plate in a gunlock. **4** another term for TUMBLING BARREL. —**tum·bler·ful** /-,fo͝ol/ n. (pl. **-fuls**).

tum·ble·weed /ˈtəmbəl,wēd/ ▶n. a plant of arid regions that breaks off near the ground in late summer, forming light globular masses that are tumbled about by the wind. Its two genera are *Salsola* of the goosefoot family and *Amaranthus* of the amaranth family.

tum·bling bar·rel /ˈtəmb(ə)liNG/ (also **tum·bling box**) ▶n. a revolving device containing an abrasive substance, in which castings, gemstones, or other hard objects can be cleaned by friction.

tum·bril /ˈtəmbrəl/ (also **tum·brel**) ▶n. hist. an open cart that tilted backward to empty out its load, in particular one used to convey condemned prisoners to the guillotine during the French Revolution. ■ a two-wheeled covered cart that carried tools or ammunition for an army. [ME: from OFr. *tomberel*, from *tomber* 'to fall.']

tu·me·fy /ˈt(y)o͞omə,fī/ ▶v. (**-fies, -fied**) [intrans.] become swollen. —**tu·me·fac·tion** /,t(y)o͞oməˈfakSHən/ n. [16th C. (in the sense 'cause to swell'): from Fr. *tuméfier*, from L. *tumefacere*, from *tumere* 'to swell.']

tu·mes·cent /t(y)o͞oˈmesənt/ ▶adj. swollen or becoming swollen, esp. as a response to sexual arousal. ■ fig. (esp. of language or literary style) pompous or pretentious; tumid. —**tu·mes·cence** n. **tu·mes·cent·ly** adv. [19th C.: from L. *tumescent-* 'beginning to swell,' from the verb *tumescere*, from *tumere* 'to swell.']

tu·mid /ˈt(y)o͞omid/ ▶adj. (esp. of a part of the body) swollen: *a tumid belly.* ■ fig. (esp. of language or literary style) pompous or bombastic: *tumid oratory.* —**tu·mid·i·ty** /t(y)o͞oˈmiditē/ n. **tu·mid·ly** adv. [16th C.: from L. *tumidus*, from *tumere* 'to swell.']

tumm·ler /ˈto͝omlər/ ▶n. a person who makes things happen, in particular a professional entertainer whose function is to encourage an audience, guests at a resort, etc., to participate in the entertainments or activities. ■ a professional comedian. [1960s: Yiddish, from Ger. *tummeln* 'to stir.']

tum·my /ˈtəmē/ ▶n. (pl. **-mies**) informal a person's stomach or abdomen. [19th C.: child's pronunc. of STOMACH.]

tum·my tuck ▶n. informal a surgical operation involving the removal of excess flesh from the abdomen, for cosmetic purposes.

tu·mor /ˈt(y)o͞omər/ (Brit. **tu·mour**) ▶n. a swelling of a part of the body, generally without inflammation, caused by an abnormal growth of tissue, whether benign or malignant. ■ archaic a swelling of any kind. —**tu·mor·ous** /-mərəs/ adj. [ME: from L. *tumor*, from *tumere* 'to swell.']

tu·mor·i·gen·e·sis /,t(y)o͞oməraˈjenəsis/ ▶n. the production or formation of a tumor or tumors.

tu·mor·i·gen·ic /,t(y)o͞oməraˈjenik/ ▶adj. capable of forming or tending to form tumors. —**tu·mor·i·ge·nic·i·ty** /-jəˈnisitē/ n.

tump /təmp/ ▶n. Brit., esp. dialect [often in place names] **1** a small rounded hill or mound; a tumulus. **2** a clump of trees, shrubs, or grass. [16th C.: of unknown origin.]

tump·line /ˈtəmp,līn/ ▶n. a sling for carrying a load on the back, with a strap that passes around the forehead. ■ a strap of this kind. [18th C.: based on Algonquian *(mat)tump* + the noun LINE[1].]

tu·mult /ˈt(y)o͞o,məlt/ ▶n. [usu. in sing.] a loud, confused noise, esp. one caused by a large mass of people. ■ confusion or disorder. [ME: from OFr. *tumulte* or L. *tumultus*.]

tu·mul·tu·ous /t(y)o͞oˈməlCHo͞oəs; tə-/ ▶adj. making a loud, confused noise; uproarious: *tumultuous applause.* ■ excited, confused, or disorderly. —**tu·mul·tu·ous·ly** adv. **tu·mul·tu·ous·ness** n.

tu·mu·lus /ˈt(y)o͞omyələs/ ▶n. (pl. **-li** /-,lī/) an ancient burial mound; a barrow. [ME: from L.; rel. to *tumere* 'swell.']

tun /tən/ ▶n. **1** a large beer or wine cask. ■ a brewer's fermenting vat. **2** an imperial measure of capacity, equal to 4 hogsheads. ▶v. (**tunned, tun·ning**) [trans.] archaic store (wine or other alcoholic drinks) in a tun. [OE *tunne*, from med. L. *tunna*, prob. of Gaulish origin.]

tu·na[1] /ˈt(y)o͞onə/ ▶n. (pl. same or **-nas**) a large and active predatory schooling fish (*Thunnus* and other genera) of the mackerel family. Found in warm seas, it is extensively fished commercially and is popular as a game fish. See illustration at ALBACORE. ■ (also **tuna fish**) the flesh of this fish as food, usually canned. [19th C.: from Amer. Sp., from Sp. *atún* 'tunny.']

tu·na[2] ▶n. **1** the edible fruit of a prickly pear cactus. **2** a cactus that produces such fruit, in particular *Opuntia tuna* of Central America and the Caribbean. [16th C.: via Sp. from Taino.]

tun·dra /ˈtəndrə/ ▶n. a vast, flat, treeless Arctic region of Europe, Asia, and North America in which the subsoil is permanently frozen. [16th C.: from Lappish.]

tun·dra swan ▶n. an Arctic-breeding migratory swan (*Cygnus columbianus*) with a yellow and black bill often known by the names of its constituent races, e.g., whistling swan.

tune /t(y)o͞on/ ▶n. a melody, esp. one that characterizes a certain piece of music: *she left the theater humming a cheerful tune.* ▶v. [trans.] adjust (a musical instrument) to the correct or uniform pitch: *he tuned the harp for me.* ■ adjust (a receiver circuit such as a radio or television) to the frequency of the required signal: *the radio was tuned to WFAN* | [intrans.] *they tuned in to watch the game.* ■ (often **tune up**) adjust (an engine) or balance (mechanical parts) so that a vehicle runs smoothly and efficiently. ■ (usu. **be tuned**) fig. adjust or adapt (something) to a particular purpose or situation: *the animals are finely tuned to life in the desert.* ■ [intrans.] (**tune into**) fig. become sensitive to: *you must tune into the needs of loved ones.*

– PHRASES **be tuned in** informal be aware of, sensitive to, or able to understand something. **in** (or **out of**) **tune** with correct (or incorrect) pitch or intonation. ■ (of an engine or other machine) properly (or poorly) adjusted. ■ fig. in (or not in) agreement or harmony: *he was out of tune with conventional belief.* **to the tune of** informal amounting to or involving (a specified considerable sum): *he was in debt to the tune of forty thousand dollars.*

– PHRASAL VERBS **tune out** informal stop listening or paying attention. **tune up** (of a musician) adjust one's instrument to the correct or uniform pitch. —**tun·a·ble** (also **tune·a·ble**) adj. **tun·ing** n. [ME: alt. of TONE.]

tune·ful /ˈt(y)o͞onfəl/ ▶adj. having a pleasing tune; melodious. —**tune·ful·ly** adv. **tune·ful·ness** n.

tune·less /ˈt(y)o͞onləs/ ▶adj. not pleasing to listen to; unmelodious. —**tune·less·ly** adv. **tune·less·ness** n.

tun·er /ˈt(y)o͞onər/ ▶n. a person who tunes musical instruments, esp. pianos. ■ an electronic device for tuning a guitar or other instrument. ■ an electronic device for varying the frequency to which a radio or television is tuned. ■ a separate unit for detecting and preamplifying a program signal and supplying it to an audio amplifier.

tune·smith /ˈt(y)o͞on,smiTH/ ▶n. informal a composer of popular music.

tune-up (also **tune·up**) ▶n. an act of tuning something up: *take your car in for a tune-up if it's an older model.* ■ a sporting event that serves as a practice for a subsequent event: *a tune-up for the college's fall league.*

tung oil ▶n. an oil used as a drying agent in inks, paints, and varnishes. This oil is obtained from the seeds of certain trees (genus *Aleurites*) of the spurge family. [19th C.: *tung*, from Chin.]

tung·state /ˈtəNG,stāt/ ▶n. Chem. a salt in which the anion contains both tungsten and oxygen, esp. one of the anion WO_42-. [19th C.: from TUNGSTEN + -ATE[1].]

tung·sten /ˈtəNGstən/ ▶n. the chemical element of atomic number 74, a hard steel-gray metal of the transition series. It has a very high melting point (3410°C) and is used to make electric light filaments. (Symbol: **W**) [18th C.: from Swed., from *tung* 'heavy' + *sten* 'stone.']

tung·sten car·bide ▶n. a very hard gray compound, WC (or W_2C), made by reaction of tungsten and carbon at high temperatures, used in making engineering dies, cutting and drilling tools, etc.

tung·stite /ˈtəNG,stīt/ ▶n. a yellow mineral consisting of hydrated tungsten oxide, typically occurring as a powdery coating on tungsten ores. [19th C.: from TUNGSTEN + -ITE[1].]

Tun·gus /,to͝oNGˈgo͞oz; ,təNG-/ ▶n. (pl. same) a member of the northern Evenki people of Siberia. ■ older term for EVENKI (the language). [Russ., from a Turkic language.]

Tun·gus·ic /,to͝oNGˈgo͞ozik; ,təNG-/ ▶adj. of, relating to, or denoting a small family of Altaic languages of Siberia and northern China. ▶n. this family of languages collectively.

Tun·gu·ska /,to͝oNGˈgo͞oskə; ,təNG-/ two rivers in Siberia in Russia, the **Lower Tunguska** and the **Stony Tunguska**, that flow to the Yenisei River.

tu·nic /ˈt(y)o͞onik/ ▶n. **1** a loose garment, typically sleeveless and reaching to the wearer's knees, as worn in ancient Greece and Rome. ■ a loose, thigh-length garment, worn typically by women over a skirt or trousers. **2** a close-fitting short coat as part of a uniform, esp. a police or military uniform. **3** Biol. & Anat. an integument or membrane enclosing or lining an organ or part. ■ Bot. any of the concentric layers of a plant bulb, e.g., an onion. ■ Zool. the rubbery outer coat of a sea squirt. [OE, from OFr. *tunique* or L. *tunica*.]

tu·ni·ca /ˈt(y)o͞onikə/ ▶n. (pl. **-ni·cae** /-nəkē; -sē/) **1** Anat. a membranous sheath enveloping or lining an organ. **2** Bot. the outer layer or layers of cells in an apical meristem, which contribute to surface growth.

[17th C.: from L., lit. 'tunic.']

tu·ni·cate /'t(y)o͞oni,kāt/ ▶ **n.** Zool. a marine invertebrate of a group (subphylum Urochordata) that includes the sea squirts and salps. They have a rubbery or hard outer coat and two siphons to draw water into and out of the body. ▶ **adj.** (usu. **tunicated**) Bot. (of a plant bulb, e.g., an onion) having concentric layers.

tu·ni·cle /'t(y)o͞onikəl/ ▶ **n.** a short liturgical vestment that is traditionally worn over the alb by a subdeacon at celebrations of the Mass. [ME: from OFr. *tunicle* or L. *tunicula*, dimin. of *tunica* (see TUNICA).]

tuning fork

tun·ing fork ▶ **n.** a two-pronged steel device used by musicians, which vibrates when struck to give a note of specific pitch.

Tu·nis /'t(y)o͞onəs/ the capital of Tunisia, a port on the Mediterranean coast of North Africa; pop. 597,000.

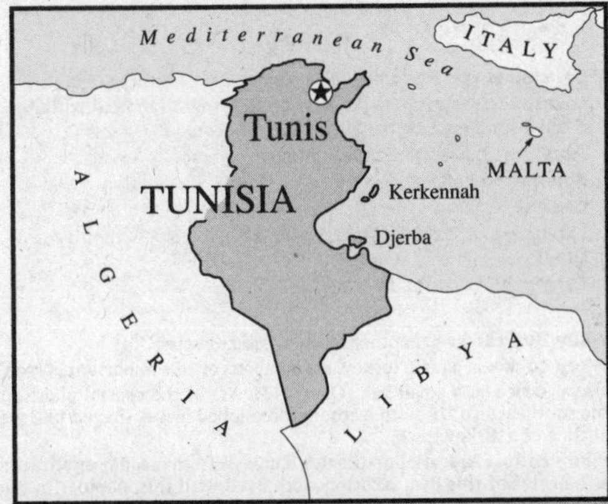

Tunisia

Official name: Republic of Tunisia
Location: North Africa, on the Mediterranean Sea and extending south into the Sahara Desert
Area: 63,200 square miles (163,600 sq km)
Population: 9,974,000
Capital: Tunis
Languages: Arabic (official), French
Currency: Tunisian dinar

Tu·ni·sia /t(y)o͞o'nēzhə/ a country in North Africa. *See box.* — **Tu·ni·sian adj. & n.**

tun·nel /'tənl/ ▶ **n.** an artificial underground passage, esp. one built through a hill or under a building, road, or river. ■ an underground passage dug by a burrowing animal. ■ [in sing.] a passage in a sports stadium by which players enter or leave the field. ▶ **v.** (**-neled, -nel·ing**; Brit. **-nelled, -nel·ling**) **1** [intrans.] dig or force a passage underground or through something. **2** [intrans.] Physics (of a particle) pass through a potential barrier.
– PHRASES **light at the end of the tunnel** see LIGHT[1]. — **tun·nel·er n.** [ME: from OFr. *tonel*, dimin. of *tonne* 'cask.']

tun·nel di·ode ▶ **n.** Electron. a two-terminal semiconductor diode using tunneling electrons to perform high-speed switching operations.

tun·nel of love ▶ **n.** a fairground amusement for couples involving a train or boat ride through a darkened tunnel.

tun·nel vi·sion ▶ **n.** defective sight in which objects cannot be properly seen if not close to the center of the field of view. ■ informal the tendency to focus exclusively on a single or limited goal or point of view.

Tun·ney /'tənē/, Gene (1898–1978), US boxer; born *James Joseph Tunney*. He became world heavyweight champion in 1926 by defeating Jack Dempsey.

tun·ny /'tənē/ (also **tun·ny fish**) ▶ **n.** esp. Brit. (pl. same or **-nies**) a tuna, esp. the bluefin. ■ tuna as food. [16th C.: from Fr. *thon*, via L. from Gk. *thunnos*.]

tup /təp/ ▶ **n.** esp. Brit. a ram. ▶ **v.** (**tupped, tup·ping**) [trans.] [often as n.] (**tupping**) esp. Brit. (of a ram) copulate with (a ewe). ■ vulgar slang (of a man) have sexual intercourse with (a woman). [ME: of unknown origin.]

Tu·pe·lo /'t(y)o͞opə,lō/ a city in northeastern Mississippi; pop. 34,211. It is also the birthplace of Elvis Presley.

tu·pe·lo /'t(y)o͞opə,lō/ ▶ **n.** (pl. **-los**) a North American or Asian tree (genus *Nyssa*, family Nyssaceae) of damp and swampy habitats that yields useful timber. Its several species include the **water tupelo** (*N. aquatica*), which grows in the coastal-plain swamps of the southeastern US. [18th C.: from Creek, from *ito* 'tree' + *opilwa* 'swamp.']

Tu·pi /'to͞opē; to͞o'pē/ ▶ **n.** (pl. same or **-pis**) **1** a member of a group of American Indian peoples living in scattered areas throughout the Amazon basin. **2** any of the languages of these peoples, a branch of the Tupi-Guarani language family. ▶ **adj.** of or relating to these peoples or their languages. — **Tu·pi·an** /-pēən/ **adj.** [a local name.]

Tu·pi-Gua·ra·ni /to͞o'pē ,gwärə'nē/ ▶ **n.** a South American Indian language family whose principal members are Guarani and the Tupian languages. ▶ **adj.** of, relating to, or denoting these languages.

tup·pence ▶ **n.** Brit. var. of TWOPENCE.

tup·pen·ny /'təp(ə)nē/ ▶ **adj.** Brit. var. of TWOPENNY.

Tup·per·ware /'təpər,we(ə)r/ ▶ **n.** trademark a range of plastic containers used chiefly for storing food.

tuque /t(y)o͞ok/ ▶ **n.** Canadian a close-fitting knitted stocking cap. [Canad. Fr. form of TOQUE.]

tu·ra·co ▶ **n.** var. of TOURACO.

Tu·ra·ni·an /t(y)o͝o'rānēən/ ▶ **adj.** dated of, relating to, or denoting the languages of central Asia, particularly those of the Uralic and Altaic families, or the peoples that speak them. [18th C.: from Pers. *Tūrān*, the region beyond the Oxus, + -IAN.]

tur·ban /'tərbən/ ▶ **n.** a man's headdress, consisting of a long length of cotton or silk wound around a cap or the head, worn esp. by Muslims and Sikhs. — **tur·baned adj.** [16th C.: via Fr. from Turk. *tülbent*, from Pers. *dulband*.]

tur·bid /'tərbid/ ▶ **adj.** (of a liquid) cloudy, opaque, or thick with suspended matter: *the turbid estuary.* — **tur·bid·i·ty** /tər'biditē/ **n.** **tur·bid·ly adv.** **tur·bid·ness n.** [ME: from L. *turbidus*, from *turba* 'a crowd, a disturbance.']

tur·bi·dim·e·ter /,tərbi'dimitər/ ▶ **n.** an instrument for measuring the turbidity of a liquid suspension, usually as a means of determining the surface area of the suspended particles. — **tur·bi·di·met·ric** /-də'metrik/ **adj.** **tur·bi·dim·e·try** /-trē/ **n.**

tur·bi·dite /'tərbi,dīt/ ▶ **n.** Geol. a sediment or rock deposited by a turbidity current. — **turbiditic** /,tərbi'ditik/ **adj.**

tur·bid·i·ty cur·rent /tər'biditē/ ▶ **n.** an underwater current flowing swiftly downslope owing to the weight of sediment it carries.

tur·bi·nal /'tərbənl/ ▶ **n.** (usu. **turbinals**) Anat. & Zool. each of three thin curved shelves of bone in the sides of the nasal cavity in humans and other warm-blooded vertebrates, covered in mucous membrane. [16th C.: from L. *turbo, turbin-* 'spinning top' + -AL.]

tur·bi·nate /'tərbənit; -,nāt/ ▶ **adj.** esp. Zool. (esp. of a shell) shaped like a spinning top or inverted cone. ■ Anat. relating to or denoting the turbinals. ▶ **n.** (also **turbinate bone**) Anat. another term for TURBINAL.

tur·bine /'tər,bīn; -bin/ ▶ **n.** a machine for producing continuous power in which a wheel or rotor, typically fitted with vanes, is made to revolve by a fast-moving flow of water, steam, gas, air, or other fluid. [19th C.: from Fr., from L. *turbo, turbin-* 'spinning top, whirl.']

tur·bit /'tərbit/ ▶ **n.** a stoutly built pigeon of a domestic breed with a neck frill and short beak. [17th C.: appar. from L. *turbo* 'spinning top,' from its shape.]

tur·bo /'tərbō/ ▶ **n.** (pl. **-bos**) short for TURBOCHARGER. ■ a motor vehicle equipped with a turbocharger. ■ a computer program, machine, or other object equipped to operate at high speed.

turbo- ▶ **comb. form** having or driven by a turbine: *turboshaft.* [from TURBINE.]

tur·bo·boost /'tərbō,bo͞ost/ ▶ **n.** the increase in speed or power produced by turbocharging a car's engine or, specifically, when the turbocharger becomes activated.

tur·bo·charge /'tərbō,CHärj/ ▶ **v.** [trans.] [often as adj.] (**turbocharged**) equip (an engine or vehicle) with a turbocharger. ■ add speed or energy to (something): *Asia's turbocharged economies.*

tur·bo·charg·er /'tərbō,CHärjər/ ▶ **n.** a supercharger driven by a turbine powered by the engine's exhaust gases.

tur·bo die·sel ▶ **n.** a turbocharged diesel engine. ■ a vehicle equipped with such an engine.

tur·bo·fan /'tərbō,fan/ ▶ **n.** a jet engine in which a turbine-driven fan provides additional thrust. ■ an aircraft powered by such an engine.

tur·bo·gen·er·a·tor /,tərbō'jenə,rātər/ ▶ **n.** a large electricity generator driven by a steam turbine.

tur·bo·jet /'tərbō,jet/ ▶ **n.** a jet engine in which the jet gases also operate a turbine-driven compressor for compressing the air drawn into the engine. ■ an aircraft powered by such an engine.

tur·bo·prop /'tərbō,präp/ ▶ **n.** a jet engine in which a turbine is used to drive a propeller. ■ an aircraft powered by such an engine.

tur·bo·shaft /'tərbō,SHaft/ ▶ **n.** a gas turbine engine in which the turbine drives a shaft other than a propeller shaft.

tur·bo·su·per·charg·er /,tərbō'so͞opər,CHärjər/ ▶ **n.** another term for TURBOCHARGER.

tur·bot /'tərbət/ ▶ **n.** (pl. same or **-bots**) a European flatfish (*Scophthalmus maximus*, family Scophthalmidae) of inshore waters that has large bony tubercles on the body and is prized as food. ■ used in names of similar flatfishes. [ME: from OFr., of Scand. origin.]

tur·bu·lence /'tərbyələns/ ▶ **n.** violent or unsteady movement of air or water, or of some other fluid. ■ fig. conflict; confusion: *political turbulence.*

tur·bu·lent /'tərbyələnt/ ▶ **adj.** characterized by conflict, disorder, or confusion; not controlled or calm. ■ (of air or water) moving unsteadily or violently. ■ tech. of, relating to, or denoting flow of a fluid in which the velocity at any point fluctuates irregularly and there is continual mixing rather than a steady or laminar flow pattern. — **tur·bu·lent·ly adv.** [ME: from L. *turbulentus* 'full of commotion,' from *turba* 'crowd.']

Tur·co /'tərkō/ ▶ **n.** (pl. **-cos**) hist. an Algerian soldier in the French army. [19th C.: from Sp., Port., and Ital., lit. 'Turk.']

Turco- (also **Turko-**) ▶ **comb. form** Turkish; Turkish and ...: *Turco-Tartar.* ■ relating to Turkey.

Tur·co·man ▶ **n.** var. of TURKOMAN.

turd /tərd/ ▶ **n.** vulgar slang a lump of excrement. ■ a person regarded as obnoxious or contemptible. [OE *tord*, of Gmc. origin.]

tu·reen /t(y)ŏŏ'rēn/ ▶ **n.** a deep covered dish from which soup is served. [18th C.: alt. of earlier *terrine*, from Fr. *terrine* (see TERRINE), fem. of OFr. *terrin* 'earthen,' based on L. *terra* 'earth.']

turf /tərf/ ▶ **n.** (pl. **turfs** or **turves** /tərvz/) **1** grass and the surface layer of earth held together by its roots. ■ Brit. a piece of such grass and earth cut from the ground. ■ peat used for fuel. **2** (**the turf**) horse racing or racecourses generally. **3** informal an area regarded as someone's personal territory; one's home ground. ■ a person's sphere of influence or activity. ▶ **v. 1** [trans.] informal, esp. Brit. force (someone) to leave somewhere: *they were turfed off the bus.* **2** [trans.] cover (a patch of ground) with turf. [OE, rel. to Ger. *Torf*, from an Indo-Eur. root shared by Sanskrit *darbha* 'tuft of grass.']

turf·man /'tərfmən/ ▶ **n.** (pl. **-men**) a devotee of horse racing, esp. one who owns or trains horses.

turf war (also **turf battle**) ▶ **n.** informal an acrimonious dispute between rival groups over territory or a particular sphere of influence.

turf·y /'tərfē/ ▶ **adj.** (**turf·i·er, turf·i·est**) covered with or consisting of turf; grassy: *a turfy plain.* ■ of or like peat; peaty: *I inhaled the turfy air.*

Tur·ge·nev /tŏŏr'gānyəf/, Ivan Sergeevich (1818–83), Russian writer. His novels include *Fathers and Sons* (1862).

tur·ges·cent /tər'jesənt/ ▶ **adj.** esp. tech. becoming or seeming swollen or distended. — **tur·ges·cence n.** [18th C.: from L. *turgescent-* 'beginning to swell,' from the verb *turgescere*, from *turgere* 'to swell.']

tur·gid /'tərjid/ ▶ **adj.** swollen and distended or congested: *a turgid and fast-moving river.* ■ (of language or style) tediously pompous or bombastic: *some turgid verses on the death of Prince Albert.* — **tur·gid·i·ty** /tər'jiditē/ **n.** **tur·gid·ly adv.** [17th C.: from L. *turgidus*, from *turgere* 'to swell.']

tur·gor /'tərgər/ ▶ **n.** esp. Bot. the state of turgidity and resulting rigidity of cells (or tissues), typically due to the absorption of fluid. [19th C.: from late L., from *turgere* 'to swell.']

Tu·rin /'t(y)ŏŏrən; t(y)ŏŏ'rin/ a city in northwestern Italy on the Po River; pop. 992,000. Italian name TORINO.

Tu·rin, Shroud of a relic, preserved at Turin since 1578, venerated as the winding sheet in which Christ's body was wrapped for burial. Scientific tests carried out in 1988 dated the shroud to the 13th–14th centuries.

Tu·ring /'t(y)ŏŏriNG/, Alan Mathison (1912–54), English mathematician. He developed the concept of a theoretical computing machine and investigated artificial intelligence.

Tu·ring ma·chine ▶ **n.** a mathematical model of a hypothetical computing machine that can use a predefined set of rules to determine a result from a set of input variables.

Tu·ring test ▶ **n.** a series of questions used as a test for intelligence in a computer.

tu·ri·on /'t(y)ŏŏrē,än/ ▶ **n.** Bot. (in some aquatic plants) a wintering bud that becomes detached and remains dormant at the bottom of the water. [18th C.: from Fr., from L. *turio(n-)* 'a shoot.']

tu·ris·ta /tŏŏ'rēstə/ ▶ **n.** informal diarrhea as suffered by travelers when visiting certain foreign countries. [Sp., lit. 'tourist.']

Turk /tərk/ ▶ **n. 1** a native or national of Turkey, or a person of Turkish descent. **2** hist. a member of any of the ancient central Asian peoples who spoke Turkic languages, including the Seljuks and Ottomans. **3** archaic a member of the ruling Muslim population of the Ottoman Empire. [ME: via OFr. from Turk. *türk*.]

Tur·ka·na /tər'känə/ ▶ **n.** (pl. same) **1** a member of an East African people living between Lake Turkana and the Nile. **2** the Nilotic language of the Turkana, spoken by about 250,000 people. ▶ **adj.** of or relating to the Turkana or their language. [a local name.]

Tur·ka·na, Lake /tər'kanə; -'känə/ a salt lake in northwestern Kenya, with no outlet.

Tur·ke·stan /'tərkə,stan; -,stän/ (also **Tur·ki·stan**) a region in central Asia between the Caspian Sea and the Gobi Desert, inhabited mainly by Turkic peoples.

Tur·key /'tərkē/ a country in western Asia and southeastern Europe. *See box.*

tur·key /'tərkē/ ▶ **n.** (pl. **-keys**) **1** a large mainly domesticated game bird (*Meleagris gallopavo*, family Meleagridae) native to North America, having a bald head and (in the male) red wattles. It is prized as food, esp. on festive occasions such as Thanksgiving and Christmas. ■ the flesh of the turkey as food. **2** informal something that is extremely or completely unsuccessful, esp. a play or movie. ■ a stupid or inept person.

– PHRASES **talk turkey** informal discuss something frankly and straightforwardly. [16th C.: short for TURKEY COCK or *turkey hen*, orig. the guinea fowl.]

Turkey

Official name: Republic of Turkey
Location: western Asia, mostly on the Anatolian peninsula, with a small enclave in southeastern Europe
Area: 301,500 square miles (780,600 sq km)
Population: 68,893,000
Capital: Ankara
Languages: Turkish (official), Kurdish, Arabic, Armenian, Greek
Currency: Turkish lira

tur·key buz·zard ▶ **n.** another term for TURKEY VULTURE.

tur·key cock ▶ **n.** a male turkey. ■ a pompous or self-important person.

tur·key oak ▶ **n.** a small oak (*Quercus laevis*) of the coastal plains of the southeastern US, with leathery three-lobed leaves shaped like the outline of a turkey track.

Tur·key red ▶ **n.** a scarlet textile dye obtained from madder or alizarin. ■ the color of this dye. ■ cotton cloth dyed with this, popular in the 19th century.

tur·key shoot ▶ **n.** informal a situation, typically in a war, in which the aggressor has an overwhelming advantage.

tur·key trot ▶ **n.** a kind of ballroom dance to ragtime music that was popular in the early 20th century.

tur·key vul·ture ▶ **n.** a common American vulture (*Cathartes aura*) with black plumage and a bare red head.

Tur·kic /'tərkik/ ▶ **adj.** of, relating to, or denoting a large group of closely related Altaic languages of western and central Asia, including Turkish, Azerbaijani, Kazakh, Kyrgyz, Uighur, Uzbek, and Tatar. ▶ **n.** the Turkic languages collectively.

Turk·ish /'tərkiSH/ ▶ **adj.** of or relating to Turkey or to the Turks or their language. ■ hist. relating to or associated with the Ottoman Empire. ▶ **n.** the Turkic language that is the official language of Turkey.

Turk·ish bath ▶ **n.** a cleansing or relaxing treatment that involves a period of time spent sitting in a room filled with very hot air or steam, generally followed by washing and massage. ■ a building or room where such a treatment is available.

Turk·ish cof·fee ▶ **n.** very strong black coffee served with the fine grounds in it.

Turk·ish de·light ▶ **n.** a dessert consisting of flavored gelatin coated in powdered sugar.

Turk·ish slip·per ▶ **n.** a soft heelless slipper with a turned-up toe.

Turk·ish tow·el ▶ **n.** a towel made of cotton terry toweling.

Turk·ish Van (in full **Turkish Van cat**) ▶ **n.** a cat of a long-haired breed, with a white body, auburn markings on the head and tail, and light orange eyes. [1960s: named after the town of *Van*, Turkey.]

Tur·ki·stan var. of TURKESTAN.

Turk·men /'tərkmen; -mən/ ▶ **n.** (pl. same or **-mens**) **1** a member of a group of Turkic peoples inhabiting the region east of the Caspian Sea and south of the Aral Sea, now comprising Turkmenistan and parts of Iran and Afghanistan. **2** the Turkic language of these peoples. ▶ **adj.** of or relating to the Turkmens, their language, or the region that they inhabit. [from Pers. *turkmān*, from Turk. *türkmen*.]

Turk·me·ni·stan /tərk'menə,stan; -,stän/ a republic in central Asia. *See box on next page.* Also called TURKMENIA.

Turko- ▶ **comb. form** var. of TURCO-.

Tur·ko·man /'tərkəmən/ (also **Tur·co·man**) ▶ **n.** (pl. **-mans**) another term for TURKMEN. [17th C.: from med. L. *Turcomannus*, Fr. *turcoman*, from Pers. *turkmān* (see TURKMEN).]

Turks and Cai·cos Is·lands /'tərks and 'kākəs; 'kākōs/ a British dependency in the Caribbean Sea that is composed of two island groups; pop. 12,000; capital, Cockburn Town.

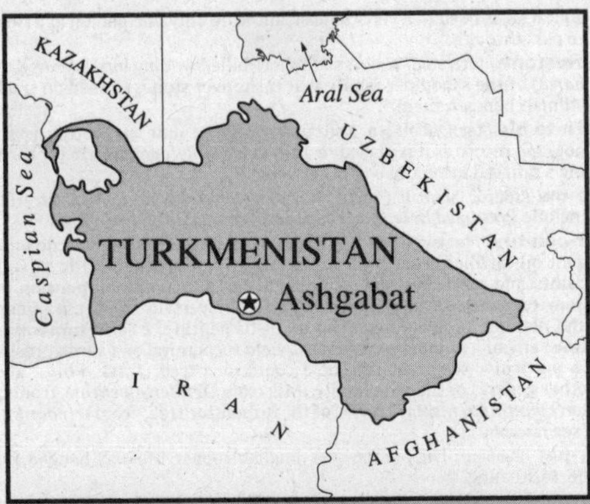

Turkmenistan

Location: central Asia, on the Caspian Sea, north of Iran
Area: 188,500 square miles (488,100 sq km)
Population: 3,861,000
Capital: Ashgabat
Languages: Turkmen (official), Russian, Uzbek
Currency: Turkmen manat

Turk's-cap lil·y ▶ n. a lily (*Lilium superbum*) with orange flowers that resemble turbans due to the almost completely reflexed petals.

Turk's-cap lily

Turk's head ▶ n. an ornamental knot resembling a turban in shape, made in the end of a rope to form a stopper.

Tur·ku /'to͝orko͞o/ a city in southwestern Finland; pop. 159,000. Swedish name **Åbo**.

tur·mer·ic /'tərmərik/ ▶ n. **1** a bright yellow aromatic powder obtained from the rhizome of a plant of the ginger family, used for flavoring and coloring in Asian cooking and formerly as a fabric dye. **2** the Asian plant (*Curcuma longa*) from which this rhizome is obtained. [ME: perh. from Fr. *terre mérite* and mod. L. *terra merita*, lit. 'deserving earth.']

tur·moil /'tər,moil/ ▶ n. a state of great disturbance, confusion, or uncertainty. [16th C.: of unknown origin.]

turn /tərn/ ▶ v. **1** move or cause to move in a circular direction wholly or partly around an axis or point: [intrans.] *the big wheel was turning* | [trans.] *I turned the key.* ■ [trans.] move (something) so that it is in a different position in relation to its surroundings or its previous position: *turn the cards over.* ■ [trans.] move (a page) over so that it is flat against the previous or next page: *she turned a page noisily* | [intrans.] *turn to page five.* ■ change or cause to change direction: [intrans.] *we turned around.* ■ [trans.] aim, point, or direct (something): *she turned her head toward me.* ■ [intrans.] change the position of one's body so that one is facing in a different direction. ■ [intrans.] (of the tide) change from flood to ebb or vice versa. ■ [trans.] pass around (the flank or defensive lines of an army) so as to attack it from the side or rear. ■ [trans.] perform (a somersault or cartwheel). ■ [trans.] twist or sprain (an ankle). ■ [trans.] fold or unfold (fabric or a piece of a garment) in the specified way: *he turned up the collar of his coat.* ■ [trans.] remake (a garment or a sheet), putting the worn outer side on the inside. ■ [trans.] [usu. as adj.] (**turned**) Print. set or print (a type or letter) upside down. ■ [trans.] archaic bend back (the edge of a blade) so as to make it blunt. **2** [intrans.] change in nature, state, form, or color; become: *Emmeline turned pale.* ■ [trans.] cause to change in such a way; cause to become: *potatoes are covered to keep the light from turning them green.* ■ [intrans.] (of leaves) change color in the autumn. ■ [trans.] pass the age or time of: *I've just turned forty.* ■ (with reference to milk) make or become sour. ■ (with reference to the stomach) make or become nauseated. ■ [trans.] send or put into a specified place or condition: *the dogs were turned loose on the crowd.* **3** [intrans.] (**turn to**) start doing or becoming involved with: *in 1939 he turned to films in earnest.* ■ go on to consider next: *we can now turn to another aspect of the problem.* ■ go to for help, advice, or information: *who can she turn to?* ■ have recourse to (something, esp. something dangerous or unhealthy): *he turned to drink.* **4** [trans.] shape (something) on a lathe. ■ give a graceful or elegant form to: [as adj.] (**turned**) *many finely turned words.* ■ make (a profit). ▶ n. **1** an act of moving something in a circular direction around an axis or point: *four turns of the key.* ■ a change of direction when moving: *they made a left turn.* ■ a development or change in circumstances or a course of events: *life has taken a turn for the better.* ■ a time when one specified period of time ends and another begins: *the turn of the century.* ■ a bend or curve in a road, path, river, etc. ■ a place where a road meets or branches off another. ■ (**the turn**) the beginning of the second nine holes of a round of golf: *he made the turn in one under par.* ■ a change of the tide from ebb to flow or vice versa. ■ one round in a coil of rope or other material. **2** an opportunity or obligation to do something that comes successively to each of a number of people: *it was his turn to speak.* ■ a short performance, esp. one of a number given by different performers in succession: *a comic turn.* ■ a performer giving such a performance. **3** a short walk or ride: *take a turn around the garden.* **4** informal a shock: *you gave us quite a turn!* ■ a brief feeling or experience of illness. **5** the difference between the buying and selling price of stocks or other financial products. ■ a profit made from such a difference. **6** Music a melodic ornament consisting of the principal note with those above and below it.

– PHRASES **at every turn** on every occasion; continually. **by turns** one after the other; alternately. **do someone a good** (or **bad**) **turn** do something that is helpful (or unhelpful) for someone. **in turn** in succession; one after the other. **on the turn** at a turning point; in a state of change. **out of turn** at a time when it is not one's turn. **speak** (or **talk**) **out of turn** speak in a tactless or foolish way. **take turns** (of two or more people) do something alternately or in succession. **to a turn** to exactly the right degree (used esp. in relation to cooking). **turn the corner** pass the critical point and start to improve. **turn over a new leaf** start to act or behave in a better or more responsible way. **turn tail** informal turn around and run away.

– PHRASAL VERBS **turn against** (or **turn someone against**) become (or cause someone to become) hostile toward: *public opinion turned against him.* **turn around** move so as to face in the opposite direction: *Alice turned around and walked down the corridor.* **turn something around 1** prepare a ship or aircraft for its return journey. **2** reverse the previously poor performance of something, esp. a company, and make it successful. **turn someone away** refuse to allow someone to enter or pass through a place. **turn back** (or **turn someone/something back**) go (or cause to go) back in the direction in which one has come: *they turned back before reaching the church.* **turn someone down** reject an offer or application made by someone: *the Air Force turned him down.* **turn something down 1** reject something offered or proposed. **2** adjust a control on a device to reduce the volume, heat, etc. **turn in** informal go to bed in the evening. **turn someone in** hand someone over to the authorities. **turn something in** give something to someone in authority: *I've turned in my resignation.* ■ produce or achieve a particular score or a performance of a specified quality. **turn off** leave one road in order to join another. **turn someone off** informal induce a feeling of boredom or disgust in someone. **turn something off** stop the operation or flow of something by means of a valve, switch, or button. ■ operate a valve or switch in order to do this. **turn on 1** suddenly attack (someone) physically or verbally: *he turned on her with cold savagery.* **2** have as the main topic or point of interest: *for most businessmen, the central questions will turn on taxation.* **turn someone on** informal excite or stimulate the interest of someone, esp. sexually. **turn something on** start the flow or operation of something by means of a valve, switch, or button. ■ operate a valve or switch in order to do this. **turn someone on to** informal cause someone to become interested or involved in (something, esp. drugs). **turn out 1** prove to be the case: *the job turned out to be beyond his abilities.* **2** go somewhere in order to do something, esp. to attend a meeting, to play a game, or to vote: *75 percent of the electorate turned out to vote.* **turn someone out 1** eject or expel someone from a place. **2** Mil. call a guard from the guardroom. **3** (**be turned out**) be dressed in the manner specified: *she was smartly turned out and as well groomed as always.* **turn something out 1** extinguish a light. **2** produce something: *the plant takes 53 hours to turn out each car.* **3** empty something, esp. one's pockets. **4** tip prepared food from a mold or other container. **turn over** (of an engine) start or continue to run properly. **turn someone over to** deliver someone to the care or custody of (another person or body, esp. one in authority): *they turned him over to the police.* **turn something over 1** cause an engine to run. **2** transfer control or management of something to someone else. **3** change the function or use of something: *the factory was turned over to the production of aircraft parts.* **4** informal rob a place. **5** (of a business) have a turnover of a specified amount: *last year the company turned over $12 million.* **turn up 1** be found, esp. by chance, after being lost. **2** put in an appearance; arrive. **turn something up 1** increase the volume or strength of sound, heat, etc., by turning a knob or switch on a device. **2** reveal or discover something. **3** shorten a garment by raising the hem. [OE *tyrnan, turnian* (v.), from L. *tornare*, from *tornus* 'lathe,' from Gk. *tornos* 'lathe, circular movement.']

turn·a·bout /'tərnə,bout/ ▶ n. a sudden and complete change or reversal of policy, opinion, or of a situation.

turn·a·round /'tərnə,round/ ▶ n. **1** an abrupt or unexpected change, esp. one that results in a more favorable situation. **2** the process of completing or the time needed to complete a task, esp. one involving receiving something, processing it, and sending it out again. ■ the process of or time taken for unloading and reloading a ship, aircraft, or vehicle. **3** a space for vehicles to turn around in, esp. one at the end of a driveway or dead end street.

turn-back /'tərn,bak/ ▶ n. a part of a garment that is folded back: [as adj.] *the jacket has turn-back cuffs.*

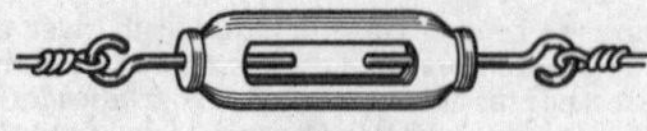
turnbuckle

turn·buck·le /ˈtərnˌbəkəl/ ▶ n. a coupling with internal screw threads used to connect two rods, lengths of boat's rigging, etc., lengthwise and to regulate their length or tension.

turn·coat /ˈtərnˌkōt/ ▶ n. a person who deserts one party or cause in order to join an opposing one.

turn·cock /ˈtərnˌkäk/ ▶ n. hist. a waterworks official responsible for turning on water at the mains.

turn·down /ˈtərnˌdoun/ ▶ n. **1** a rejection or refusal. **2** a decline in something; a downturn. ▶ adj. **1** (of a collar) turned down. **2** denoting a hotel service in which the sheets are turned back in preparation for sleeping.

Tur·ner[1] /ˈtərnər/, Frederick Jackson (1861–1932), US historian and writer. He revolutionized the study of the American frontier with his paper "The Significance of the Frontier in American History" (1893).

Turn·er[2], J. M. W. (1775–1851), English painter; full name *Joseph Mallord William Turner*. He painted landscapes and stormy seascapes.

Tur·ner[3], Nat (1800–1831), US slave leader. He was hanged for organizing a slave uprising in Southampton, Virginia, in August 1831.

turn·er /ˈtərnər/ ▶ n. **1** a person who is skilled in turning wood on a lathe. **2** an implement that can be used to turn or flip something over: *a pancake turner.*

Turn·er's syn·drome ▶ n. Med. a genetic defect in which affected women have only one X chromosome, causing developmental abnormalities and infertility. [named after Henry Hubert *Turner* (1892–1970), the American physician who described it.]

turn·er·y /ˈtərnərē/ ▶ n. the action or skill of making objects on a lathe. ■ objects made on a lathe.

turn·ing /ˈtərniNG/ ▶ n. **1** a place where a road branches off another: *take the first turning on the right.* **2** the action or skill of using a lathe. ■ (**turnings**) shavings of wood or metal resulting from turning something on a lathe.

turn·ing point ▶ n. a time at which a decisive change in a situation occurs, esp. one with beneficial results.

tur·nip /ˈtərnəp/ ▶ n. **1** a round root with white or cream flesh that is eaten as a vegetable and also has edible leaves. ■ a similar or related root, esp. a rutabaga. **2** the European plant (*Brassica rapa*) of the cabbage family that produces this root. **3** informal a large, thick, old-fashioned pocket watch. [16th C.: first element of unknown origin + NEEP.]

turn·key /ˈtərnˌkē/ ▶ n. (pl. **-keys**) archaic a jailer. ▶ adj. of or involving the provision of a complete product or service that is ready for immediate use.

turn·off /ˈtərnˌôf/ (also **turn-off**) ▶ n. **1** a junction at which a road branches off from a main road. **2** [usu. in sing.] informal a person or thing that causes someone to feel bored, disgusted, or sexually repelled. **3** an instance of turning or switching something off.

turn·on ▶ n. **1** [usu. in sing.] informal a person or thing that causes someone to feel excited or sexually aroused. **2** an instance of turning or switching something on.

turn·out /ˈtərnˌout/ ▶ n. **1** [usu. in sing.] the number of people attending or taking part in an event, esp. the number of people voting in an election. **2** a turn in a road. ■ a point at which a railroad track diverges. ■ a widened place in a road for cars to pass each other or park temporarily. **3** a carriage or other horse-drawn vehicle with its horse or horses. **4** [in sing.] the way in which a person or thing is equipped or dressed: *his turnout was exceedingly elegant.* **5** Ballet the ability to rotate the legs outward at the hips.

turn·o·ver /ˈtərnˌōvər/ ▶ n. **1** the amount of money taken by a business in a particular period. ■ Stock Market the volume of shares traded during a particular period, as a percentage of total shares listed. **2** the rate at which employees leave a workforce and are replaced. ■ the rate at which goods are sold and replaced in a shop. **3** a small pie made by folding a piece of pastry over on itself to enclose a sweet filling: *an apple turnover.* **4** (in a game) a loss of possession of the ball to the opposing team.

turn·pike /ˈtərnˌpīk/ ▶ n. **1** an expressway, esp. one on which a toll is charged. ■ hist. a toll gate. ■ (also **turnpike road**) hist. a road on which a toll was collected at such a gate. **2** hist. a spiked barrier fixed in or across a road or passage as a defense against sudden attack.

turn sig·nal ▶ n. a flashing light on a vehicle to show that it is about to change lanes or turn.

turn·sole /ˈtərnˌsōl/ ▶ n. a Mediterranean plant (*Chrozophora tinctoria*) of the spurge family, whose flowers are said to turn with the sun. [ME: from OFr. *tournesole*, based on L. *tornare* (see TURN) + *sol* 'sun.']

turn·spit /ˈtərnˌspit/ ▶ n. hist. a servant whose job was to turn a spit on which meat was roasting. ■ a dog kept to perform this task by running on a treadmill connected to the spit.

turns ra·tio ▶ n. the ratio of the number of turns on the primary coil of an electrical transformer to the number on the secondary, or vice versa.

turn·stile /ˈtərnˌstīl/ ▶ n. a mechanical gate consisting of revolving horizontal arms fixed to a vertical post, allowing only one person at a time to pass through.

turn·stone /ˈtərnˌstōn/ ▶ n. a small, short-billed wading bird (genus *Arenaria*) of the sandpiper family that turns over stones to feed on small animals beneath them.

turn·ta·ble /ˈtərnˌtābəl/ ▶ n. a circular revolving plate supporting a phonograph record as it is played. ■ a circular revolving platform for turning a railroad locomotive or other vehicle.

Tur·ow /ˈto͝orō/, Scott F. (1949–), US lawyer and writer. His mysteries include *Presumed Innocent* (1987) and *Personal Injuries* (1999).

tur·pen·tine /ˈtərpənˌtīn/ ▶ n. **1** (also **oil of turpentine**) a volatile pungent oil distilled from gum turpentine or pine wood, used in mixing paints and varnishes and in liniment. ■ (also **crude turpentine** or **gum turpentine**) an oleoresin secreted by certain trees, esp. pines, and distilled to make rosin and oil of turpentine. **2** (also **turpentine tree**) any of a number of trees that yield turpentine or a similar resin, in particular the terebinth, or a coniferous tree (*Larix, Pinus*, and other genera) of the pine family. [ME: from OFr. *ter(e)bentine*, from L. *ter(e)binthina (resina)* '(resin) of the turpentine tree,' from *terebinthus* (see TEREBINTH).]

Tur·pin /ˈtərpən/, Dick (1706–39), English robber. He was hanged for horse-stealing.

tur·pi·tude /ˈtərpiˌt(y)o͞od/ ▶ n. formal depravity; wickedness: *acts of moral turpitude.* [15th C.: from Fr., or from L. *turpitudo*, from *turpis* 'disgraceful, base.']

turps /tərps/ ▶ n. informal turpentine. [19th C.: abbr.]

tur·quoise /ˈtərˌk(w)oiz/ ▶ n. **1** a semiprecious stone, typically opaque and of a greenish-blue or sky-blue color, consisting of a hydrated hydroxyl phosphate of copper and aluminum. **2** a greenish-blue color like that of this stone. [ME: from OFr. *turqueise* 'Turk. (stone).']

turret

tur·ret /ˈtərit/ ▶ n. a small tower on top of a larger tower or at the corner of a building or wall, typically of a castle. ■ a low, flat armored tower, typically one that revolves, for a gun and gunners in a ship, aircraft, fort, or tank. ■ a rotating holder for tools, esp. on a lathe. — **tur·ret·ed** adj. [ME: from OFr. *tourete*, dimin. of *tour* 'tower.']

tur·tle /ˈtərtl/ ▶ n. **1** a slow-moving reptile (family Testudinidae) of warm climates, enclosed in a scaly or leathery domed shell into which it can retract its head and thick legs. **2** (also **sea turtle**) a large marine reptile (families Cheloniidae and Dermochelyidae) with a bony or leathery shell and flippers, coming ashore annually on sandy beaches to lay eggs. ■ the flesh of a sea turtle, esp. the green turtle, used chiefly for soup. **3** a freshwater reptile (Emydidae and other families) related to the turtles, typically having a flattened shell. Called TERRAPIN in South Africa and India and TORTOISE in Australia. ■ any reptile of this order, including the terrapins and tortoises. **4** Comput. a directional cursor in a computer graphics system that can be instructed to move around a screen. **5** short for TURTLENECK.

– PHRASES **turn turtle** (chiefly of a boat) capsize. [16th C.: appar. an alt. of Fr. *tortue* (see TORTOISE).]

tur·tle·dove /ˈtərtlˌdəv/ ▶ n. a small Old World dove (genus *Streptopelia*) with a soft purring call, noted for the apparent affection shown for its mate.

tur·tle·head /ˈtərtlˌhed/ ▶ n. a North American plant (genus *Chelone*) of the figwort family that produces spikes of pink or white flowers that are said to resemble the head of a turtle.

tur·tle·neck /ˈtərtlˌnek/ ▶ n. a high, close-fitting, turned-over collar on a garment, typically a shirt or sweater: [as adj.] *a turtleneck sweater.* ■ a shirt or sweater with a neck of this type.

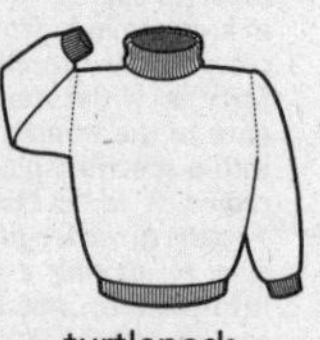
turtleneck

tur·tle·shell /ˈtərtlˌsHel/ ▶ n. another term for TORTOISESHELL.

turves /tərvz/ plural form of TURF.

Tus·ca·loo·sa /ˌtəskəˈlo͞osə/ a city in west central Alabama, home to the University of Alabama; pop. 77,906.

Tus·can /ˈtəskən/ ▶ adj. **1** of or relating to Tuscany, its inhabitants, or the form of Italian spoken there, which is the standard variety taught to foreign learners. **2** relating to or denoting a classical order of architecture resembling the Doric but lacking all ornamentation. ▶ n. **1** a native or inhabitant of Tuscany. **2** the form of Italian spoken in Tuscany. **3** the Tuscan order of architecture. [ME (as a n. denoting an Etruscan): via Fr. from L. *Tuscanus*, from *Tuscus* 'an Etruscan.']

Tus·ca·ny /ˈtəskənē/ a region in west central Italy; capital, Florence. Italian name **Toscana**.

Tus·ca·ro·ra /ˌtəskəˈrôrə/ ▶ **n.** (pl. same or **-ras**) **1** an American Indian people forming part of the Six Nations, originally inhabiting the Carolinas and later New York. **2** the Iroquoian language of this people. ▶ **adj.** of or relating to the Tuscarora or their language. [from an Iroquoian name, perh. from Catawba (a Siouan language) *taskarudē*.]

tusch·e /ˈto͝osH(ə)/ ▶ **n.** a greasy black composition, in liquid form or to be mixed with liquids, used as ink for making lithographic drawings. [20th C.: from Ger. *tuschen*, from Fr. *toucher* 'to touch'.]

tush¹ /təsH/ ▶ **exclam.** archaic or humorous expressing disapproval, impatience, or dismissal. [natural utterance: first recorded in ME.]

tush² /təsH/ ▶ **n.** a long pointed tooth, in particular a canine tooth of a male horse. ■ a stunted tusk of some Indian elephants. [OE *tusc* (see **tusk**).]

tush³ /to͝osH/ ▶ **n.** informal a person's buttocks. [1960s (as *tushie*): from Yiddish *tokhes*, from Heb. *taḥaṯ* 'beneath.']

tush·y /ˈto͝osHē/ ▶ **n.** (pl. **tush·ies**) another term for **tush³**.

tusk /təsk/ ▶ **n.** a long, pointed tooth, esp. one specially developed so as to protrude from the closed mouth, as in the elephant, walrus, or wild boar. ■ a long, tapering object or projection resembling such a tooth. — **tusked adj. tusk·y adj.** (literary). [OE *tux*, var. of *tusc* (see **tush²**).]

Tus·ke·gee Air·men /təˈskēgē/ popular name for the first cadre of African-American pilots in the US military. Based in Tuskegee, Alabama, and formed as a fighter squadron of the US Army Air Corps in 1941, they served with distinction in World War II.

tusk·er /ˈtəskər/ ▶ **n.** an elephant or wild boar with well-developed tusks.

tusk shell ▶ **n.** another term for **tooth shell**.

tus·sah /ˈtəsə; -sô/ ▶ **n.** var. of **tussore**.

tus·sive /ˈtəsiv/ ▶ **adj.** Med. relating to coughing. [19th C.: from L. *tussis* 'a cough' + **-ive**.]

tus·sle /ˈtəsəl/ ▶ **n.** a vigorous struggle or scuffle, typically in order to obtain or achieve something. ▶ **v.** [intrans.] engage in such a struggle or scuffle: *the demonstrators tussled with police.* [ME: perh. a dimin. of dial. *touse* 'handle roughly' (see **tousle**).]

tus·sock /ˈtəsək/ ▶ **n. 1** a small area of grass that is thicker or longer than the grass growing around it. **2** (also **tussock moth**) a woodland moth (family Lymantriidae) whose adults and brightly colored caterpillars both bear tufts of irritant hairs. The caterpillars can be a pest of trees, damaging fruit and stripping leaves. — **tus·sock·y adj.** [16th C.: perh. an alt. of dial. *tusk* 'tuft,' of unknown origin.]

tus·sore /ˈtəsôr/ (also **tus·sah** /ˈtəsə; -sô/) ▶ **n.** (also **tussore silk**) coarse silk from the larvae of the tussore moth and related species. [16th C.: from Hindi *tasar*, from Sanskrit *tasara* 'shuttle.']

tus·sore moth ▶ **n.** a silkworm moth (*Antheraea mylitta*, family Saturniidae) that is sometimes kept in India and China, with caterpillars (**tussore silkworms**) that yield a strong but coarse brown silk.

tut /tət/ ▶ **exclam., n., & v.** short for **tut-tut**.

Tut·ankh·a·men /ˌto͞oˌtaNGˈkämən; ˌto͞oˌtäNG-/ (also **Tut·ankh·a·mun**) (died *c.*1352 BC), Egyptian pharaoh of the 18th dynasty; reigned *c.*1361–*c.*1352 BC; know as **King Tut**. His tomb, was discovered virtually intact by English archaeologist Howard Carter in 1922.

tu·tee /t(y)o͞oˈtē/ ▶ **n.** a student or pupil of a tutor.

tu·te·lage /ˈt(y)o͞otl-ij/ ▶ **n.** protection of or authority over someone or something; guardianship. ■ instruction; tuition. [17th C.: from L. *tutela* 'keeping' (from *tut-* 'watched,' from the verb *tueri*) + **-age**.]

tu·te·lar·y /ˈt(y)o͞otl,erē/ (also **tu·te·lar** /-tl-ər/) ▶ **adj.** serving as a protector, guardian, or patron. ■ of or relating to protection or a guardian.

tu·tor /ˈt(y)o͞otər/ ▶ **n.** a private teacher, typically one who teaches a single student or a very small group. ■ esp. Brit. a university or college teacher responsible for the teaching and supervision of assigned students. ■ an assistant lecturer in a college or university. ▶ **v.** [trans.] act as a tutor to (a single pupil or a very small group): *his children were privately tutored.* ■ [intrans.] work as a tutor. — **tu·tor·age** /-tərij/ **n. tu·tor·ship** /-ˌsHip/ **n.** [ME: from OFr. *tutour* or L. *tutor*, from *tueri* 'to watch, guard.']

tu·to·ri·al /t(y)o͞oˈtôrēəl/ ▶ **adj.** of or relating to a tutor or a tutor's instruction: *tutorial sessions.* ▶ **n.** a period of instruction given by a university or college tutor to an individual or very small group. ■ an account or explanation of a subject, printed or on a computer screen, intended for private study.

Tut·si /ˈto͞otsē/ ▶ **n.** (pl. same or **-sis**) a member of a people forming a minority of the population of Rwanda and Burundi, who formerly dominated the Hutu majority. Historical antagonism between the peoples led in 1994 to large-scale ethnic violence, esp. in Rwanda. ▶ **adj.** of or relating to this people. [a local name. See also **Watusi**.]

tut·ti /ˈto͞otē/ Music ▶ **adv. & adj.** (esp. as a direction after a solo section) with all voices or instruments together. ▶ **n.** (pl. **-tis**) a passage to be performed in this way. [Ital., pl. of *tutto* 'all,' from L. *totus*.]

tut·ti-frut·ti /ˈto͞otē ˈfro͞otē/ ▶ **n.** (pl. **-frut·tis**) a type of ice cream containing or flavored with mixed fruits and sometimes nuts. [Ital., lit. 'all fruits.']

tut-tut /ˈtət ˈtət/ (also **tut**) ▶ **exclam.** expressing disapproval or annoyance: *tut-tut, Robin, you disappoint me.* ▶ **n.** such an exclamation: *tut-tuts of disapproval.* ▶ **v.** (**tut-tut·ted, tut-tut·ting**) [intrans.] make such an exclamation: *Aunt Mary tut-tutted at all the goings-on.* [natural utterance: early 16th C.]

Tu·tu /ˈto͞o,to͞o/, Desmond Mpilo (1931–), South African clergyman. He was a leading voice in the struggle against apartheid. Nobel Peace Prize (1984).

tu·tu /ˈto͞o,to͞o/ ▶ **n.** a female ballet dancer's costume consisting of a bodice and an attached skirt incorporating numerous layers of fabric, this being either short and stiff and projecting horizontally from the waist (the **classical tutu**) or long, soft, and bell-shaped (the **romantic tutu**). [20th C.: from Fr., child's alt. of *cucu*, informal dimin. of *cul* 'buttocks.']

classical tutu

Tu·va /ˈto͞ovə/ an autonomous republic in south central Russia; pop. 314,000. Former name **Tannu-Tuva**.

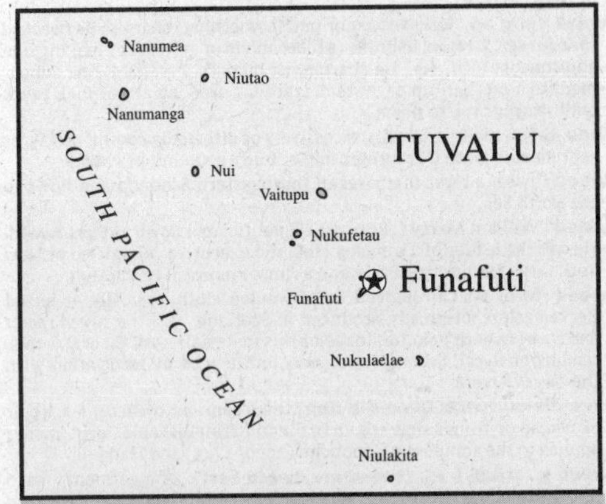

Tuvalu

Location: southwestern Pacific Ocean, consisting of a group of nine main islands
Area: 10 square miles (26 sq km)
Population: 11,400
Capital: Funafuti
Languages: Tuvaluan, English
Currency: Australian dollar

Tu·va·lu /to͞oˈvälo͞o/ a country in the southwestern Pacific Ocean. *See box.* — **Tu·va·lu·an** /-lo͞oən/ **adj. & n.**

tu-whit tu-whoo /to͞o ˈ(h)wit tə ˈ(h)wo͞o/ ▶ **n.** a stylized representation of the cry of the tawny owl.

tux /təks/ ▶ **n.** informal a tuxedo.

tux·e·do /təkˈsēdō/ ▶ **n.** (pl. **-dos** or **-does**) a man's dinner jacket. ■ a suit of formal evening clothes including such a jacket. — **tux·e·doed adj.** [19th C.: from *Tuxedo* Park, the site of a country club in New York.]

Tux·tla Gu·tiér·rez /ˈto͞ostlä go͞oˈtyeres/ a city in southeastern Mexico, capital of Chiapas; pop. 296,000.

tu·yère /to͞oˈyer; twē-/ ▶ **n.** a nozzle through which air is forced into a smelter, furnace, or forge. [18th C.: Fr., from *tuyau* 'pipe.']

TV ▶ **abbr.** ■ television (the system or a set): *anything good on TV tonight?* ■ transvestite.

TVA ▶ **abbr.** Tennessee Valley Authority.

TV din·ner ▶ **n.** a prepared prepackaged meal that only requires heating before it is ready to eat.

Tver /tver/ a city in western Russia; pop. 454,000. It was known as Kalinin 1931–91.

TVP trademark ▶ **abbr.** textured vegetable protein.

Twa /twä/ ▶ **n.** (pl. same or **Twas**) a member of a pygmy people inhabiting parts of Burundi, Rwanda, and the Democratic Republic of the Congo (formerly Zaire). ▶ **adj.** of or relating to the Twa. [a local word meaning 'foreigner, outsider.']

twad·dle /ˈtwädl/ informal ▶ **n.** trivial or foolish speech or writing; nonsense. ▶ **v.** [intrans.] archaic talk or write in a trivial or foolish way. — **twad·dler** /ˈtwädlər; ˈtwädl-ər/ **n.** [18th C.: alt. of earlier *twattle*, of unknown origin.]

Twain /twān/, Mark (1835–1910), US writer; pen name of *Samuel Langhorne Clemens*. His novels include *The Adventures of Tom Sawyer* (1876) and *The Adventures of Huckleberry Finn* (1885).

twain /twān/ ▶ **cardinal number** archaic term for **two**: *he split it in twain.*

– PHRASES **never the twain shall meet** used to suggest that two things are too different to exist alongside each other. [OE *twegen*, masc. of *twā* (see TWO).]

twang /twaNG/ ▶ **n.** a strong ringing sound such as that made by the plucked string of a musical instrument or a released bowstring. ■ a nasal or other distinctive manner of pronunciation or intonation characteristic of the speech of an individual, area, or country: *an American twang.* ▶ **v.** make or cause to make such a sound. ■ [trans.] play (an instrument) in such a way as to produce such sounds: *some old men were twanging banjos.* ■ [trans.] utter (something) with a nasal twang. — **twang·y** adj. [16th C.: imitative.]

'twas /twəz; twäz/ archaic or literary ▶ **contr.** it was.

twat /twät/ ▶ **n.** vulgar slang a woman's genitals. ■ a person regarded as stupid or obnoxious. [17th C.: of unknown origin.]

tway·blade /ˈtwā,blād/ ▶ **n.** an orchid (genera *Listera* and *Liparis*) with a slender spike of greenish or mauvish flowers and a single pair of broad leaves near the base or midway up the stem. [16th C.: from *tway* (var. of TWAIN) + BLADE.]

tweak /twēk/ ▶ **v.** [trans.] **1** twist or pull (something) sharply: *he tweaked the boy's ear.* **2** informal improve (a mechanism or system) by making fine adjustments to it. ▶ **n. 1** a sharp twist or pull. **2** informal a fine adjustment to a mechanism or system. [17th C.: prob. an alt. of dial. *twick* 'pull sharply'; rel. to TWITCH.]

twee /twē/ ▶ **adj.** Brit., esp. derog. excessively or affectedly quaint, pretty, or sentimental. [20th C.: representing a child's pronunc. of SWEET.]

Tweed[1] /twēd/ a river that rises in southeastern Scotland and flows to the North Sea.

Tweed[2], William Marcy (1823–78) US politician; known as **Boss Tweed**. He was the leader of Tammany Hall, the executive committee of New York City's Democratic Party and a ring of political corruption.

tweed /twēd/ ▶ **n.** a rough-surfaced woolen cloth, typically of mixed flecked colors, originally produced in Scotland: [as adj.] *a tweed sports jacket.* ■ (**tweeds**) clothes made of this material. [19th C.: orig. a misreading of *tweel*, Scots form of TWILL, influenced by association with the *Tweed* River.]

Twee·dle·dum and Twee·dle·dee /,twēdlˈdəm and ,twēdlˈdē/ ▶ **n.** a pair of people or things that are virtually indistinguishable. [orig. names applied to the composers Bononcini (1670–1747) and Handel.]

tweed·y /ˈtwēdē/ ▶ **adj.** (**tweed·i·er, tweed·i·est**) (of a garment) made of tweed cloth: *a tweedy suit.* ■ informal (of a person) habitually wearing tweed clothes: *a stout, tweedy woman.* ■ informal of a refined, traditional, upscale character: *the tweedy world of books.* — **tweed·i·ly** /ˈtwēdl-ē/ adv. **tweed·i·ness** n.

'tween /twēn/ archaic literary ▶ **contr.** between.

'tween decks ▶ **plural n.** Naut. the space between the decks of a ship, esp. that above the lowest deck and below the upper deck.

tween·y /ˈtwēnē/ ▶ **n.** (pl. **tween·ies**) archaic, informal a maid who assisted two other members of a domestic staff. [19th C.: from *between-maid*, a servant assisting two others.]

tweet /twēt/ (also **tweet tweet**) ▶ **n.** the chirp of a small or young bird. ▶ **v.** [intrans.] make a chirping noise. [19th C.: imitative.]

tweet·er /ˈtwētər/ ▶ **n.** a loudspeaker designed to reproduce high frequencies.

tweeze /twēz/ ▶ **v.** [trans.] pluck, grasp, or pull with or as if with tweezers. [1930s: back-form. from *tweezer* (see TWEEZERS).]

tweez·ers /ˈtwēzərz/ ▶ **plural n.** (also **a pair of tweezers**) a small instrument like a pair of pincers for plucking out hairs and picking up small objects. [17th C.: extended form of obs. *tweeze* 'case of surgical instruments,' shortening of *etweese*, pl. of ETUI.]

twelfth /twelfTH/ ▶ **ordinal number** constituting number twelve in a sequence; 12th. ■ (**a twelfth/one twelfth**) each of twelve equal parts into which something is or may be divided. ■ the twelfth grade of a school. ■ Music an interval or chord spanning an octave and a fifth in the diatonic scale, or a note separated from another by this interval. ■ (**the Twelfth**) July 12, celebrated by upholders of Protestant supremacy in Ireland as the anniversary of William III's victory over James II at the Battle of the Boyne. — **twelfth·ly** adv. **twelve·fold** /ˈtwel(v),fōld/ adj. & adv.

Twelfth Day ▶ **n.** archaic term for TWELFTH NIGHT.

Twelfth Night n. January 6, the feast of the Epiphany. ■ strictly, the evening of January 5, the eve of the Epiphany and formerly the twelfth and last day of Christmas festivities.

twelve /twelv/ ▶ **cardinal number** equivalent to the product of three and four; two more than ten; 12. (Roman numeral: **xii, XII.**) ■ a group or unit of twelve people or things. ■ twelve years old. ■ twelve o'clock. ■ a size of garment or other merchandise denoted by twelve. ■ (**the Twelve**) the twelve Apostles. [OE *twelf(e)*, from the base of TWO + a second element (prob. 'left over'); of Gmc. origin.]

twelve-bar ▶ **adj.** denoting or relating to a musical structure based on a sequence lasting twelve bars and typically consisting of three chords, the basic unit of much blues and rock and roll music. ▶ **n.** a song or piece of music having such a structure.

twelve-bore ▶ **n.** British term for TWELVE-GAUGE.

twelve-gauge ▶ **n.** a shotgun with a gauge corresponding to the diameter of a round bullet of which twelve constitute a pound in weight.

twelve·mo /ˈtwelv,mō/ ▶ **n.** another term for DUODECIMO.

twelve·month /ˈtwelv,mənTH/ ▶ **n.** archaic a year.

twelve step ▶ **adj.** denoting or relating to a process of recovery from addiction by following a twelve-stage program, esp. one modeled on that of Alcoholics Anonymous. ▶ **v.** (often as noun **twelve-stepping**) (of an addict) undergo such a program.

Twelve Ta·bles a set of laws drawn up in ancient Rome in 451 and 450 BC, embodying the most important rules of Roman law.

twelve-tone (also **twelve-note**) ▶ **adj.** denoting a system of musical composition using the twelve chromatic notes of the octave on an equal basis without dependence on a key system. Developed by Arnold Schoenberg, the technique is central to serialism and involves the transposition and inversion of a fixed sequence of pitches.

Twelve Tribes of Is·ra·el see TRIBES OF ISRAEL.

twen·ty /ˈtwentē/ ▶ **cardinal number** (pl. **-ties**) the number equivalent to the product of two and ten; ten less than thirty; 20. (Roman numeral: **xx, XX.**) ■ (**twenties**) the numbers from twenty to twenty-nine, esp. the years of a century or of a person's life: *he's in his late twenties.* ■ twenty years old. ■ twenty miles an hour. ■ a size of garment or other merchandise denoted by twenty. ■ a twenty-dollar bill. — **twen·ti·eth** /-tēiTH/ **ordinal number twen·ty·fold** /-,fōld/ adj. & adv. [OE *twentig*, from the base of TWO + -TY[2].]

twen·ty-four-hour clock (also **24-hour clock**) ▶ **n.** a method of measuring the time based on the full twenty-four hours of the day, rather than dividing it into two units of twelve hours.

24/7 /ˈtwentē,fôr ˈsevən/ (also **24-7**) ▶ **adv.** informal twenty-four hours a day, seven days a week; all the time.

twen·ty-one ▶ **n.** the card game blackjack.

twen·ty-twen·ty (also **20/20**) ▶ **adj.** denoting vision of normal acuity.

'twere /twər/ archaic or literary ▶ **contr.** it were.

twerp /twərp/ (also **twirp**) ▶ **n.** informal a silly or annoying person. [19th C.: of unknown origin.]

Twi /twē/ ▶ **n.** (pl. same or **Twis**) **1** a member of an Akan-speaking people of Ghana. **2** another term for AKAN (the language). ▶ **adj.** or or relating to this people or their language. [the name in Akan.]

twi·bill /ˈtwī,bil/ ▶ **n.** archaic a double-bladed battle-ax. [OE *twibile* 'ax with two cutting edges,' from *twi-* 'double' + BILL[3].]

twice /twīs/ ▶ **adv.** two times; on two occasions. ■ double in degree or quantity: *I'm twice your age.* [OE *twiges*, from the base of TWO + -S[3].]

twice-born ▶ **adj.** having undergone a renewal of faith or life, in particular: ■ (of a Hindu) belonging to one of the three highest castes, esp. as an initiated Brahman. ■ (of a Christian) born-again.

twid·dle /ˈtwidl/ ▶ **v.** [trans.] twist, move, or fiddle with (something), typically in a purposeless or nervous way. ■ [intrans.] archaic turn or move in a twirling way. ▶ **n.** an act of twisting or fiddling with something.

– PHRASES **twiddle one's thumbs** rotate one's thumbs around each other with the fingers linked together. ■ be bored or idle because one has nothing to do. — **twid·dler** /ˈtwidlər; ˈtwidl-ər/ n. **twid·dly** /ˈtwidlē; ˈtwidl-ē/ adj. [16th C.: appar. imitative.]

twig[1] /twig/ ▶ **n.** a slender woody shoot growing from a branch or stem of a tree or shrub. ■ Anat. a small branch of a blood vessel or nerve. — **twigged** adj. **twig·gy** adj. [OE *twigge*, of Gmc. origin; rel. to Ger. *Zweig*, also to TWAIN.]

twig[2] ▶ **v.** (**twigged, twig·ging**) [intrans.] Brit., informal understand or realize something. ■ [trans.] archaic perceive; observe. [18th C.: of unknown origin.]

twig fur·ni·ture ▶ **n.** a rustic style of furniture in which the natural state of the wood is retained as an aesthetic feature.

twi·light /ˈtwī,līt/ ▶ **n.** the soft glowing light from the sky when the sun is below the horizon, caused by the reflection of the sun's rays from the atmosphere. ■ the period of the evening during which this takes place, between daylight and darkness. ■ [in sing.] fig. a period or state of obscurity, ambiguity, or gradual decline: *he was in the twilight of his career.* [ME: from OE *twi-* 'two'.]

twi·light of the gods Scandinavian & Germanic Mythol. the destruction of the gods and the world in a final conflict with the powers of evil. Also called GÖTTERDÄMMERUNG, RAGNARÖK.

twi·light sleep ▶ **n.** Med. a state of partial narcosis or stupor without total loss of consciousness, in particular a state induced by an injection of morphine and scopolamine, formerly popular for use during childbirth.

twi·light zone ▶ **n. 1** a conceptual area that is undefined or intermediate. ■ a sphere of experience that appears sinister or dangerous because of its uncertainty, unpredictability, or ambiguity. **2** the lowest level of the ocean to which light can penetrate.

twi·lit /ˈtwī,lit/ ▶ **adj.** dimly illuminated by or as if by twilight: *the deserted twilit street.* ■ relating to or denoting the period of twilight. [19th C.: past part. of the literary verb *twilight*.]

twill /twil/ ▶ **n.** a fabric so woven as to have a surface of diagonal parallel ridges. ▶ **v.** [trans.] [usu. as adj.] (**twilled**) weave (fabric) in this way: *twilled cotton.* [ME: from a Scots and north. Engl. var. of obs. *twilly*, from OE *twi-* 'two.']

'twill /twil/ archaic or literary ▶ **contr.** it will: *I am only afraid 'twill not be believ'd.*

twin /twin/ ▶ **n. 1** one of two children or animals born at the same birth. ■ a person or thing that is exactly like another. ■ (**the Twins**) the zodiacal sign or constellation Gemini. **2** something containing or consisting of two matching or corresponding parts, in particular: ■ a twin-bedded room. ■ a twin-engined aircraft. ■ a twinned crystal. ▶ **adj.** [attrib.] forming, or being one of, a pair born at one birth: *her twin sister.* ■ forming a matching, complementary, or closely connected pair: *the twin problems of economic failure and social disintegration.* ■ Bot. growing in pairs: *twin seed leaves.* ■ (of a bedroom) containing two single beds. ■ (of a crystal) twinned. ▶ **v.** (**twinned, twin·ning**) [trans.] (usu. **be twinned**) link; combine. [OE *twinn* 'double,' from *twi-* 'two'; rel. to ON *tvinnr.*]

twin bed ▶ **n.** a bed designed or suitable for one person; a single bed, esp. one of a pair of matching single beds. — **twin-bed·ded adj.**

twin-cam ▶ **adj.** denoting an engine having two camshafts.

twin cit·y ▶ **n.** either of two neighboring cities lying close together. ■ (**the Twin Cities**) Minneapolis and St. Paul in Minnesota.

twine /twīn/ ▶ **n.** strong thread or string consisting of two or more strands of hemp, cotton, or nylon twisted together. ▶ **v.** [trans.] cause to wind or spiral round something. ■ [intrans.] (of a plant) grow so as to spiral around a support. ■ interlace. — **twin·er n.** [OE *twīn* 'thread, linen,' from the Gmc. base of *twi-* 'two'; rel. to Du. *twijn.*]

twin-en·gined (also **twin-en·gine**) ▶ **adj.** (chiefly of an aircraft) having two engines.

twin·flow·er /'twin,flou(-ə)r/ ▶ **n.** a slender evergreen trailing plant (*Linnaea borealis*) of the honeysuckle family, with pairs of very small trumpet-shaped pink flowers in the leaf axils, native to coniferous woodlands in northern latitudes.

twinge /twinj/ ▶ **n.** a sudden, sharp localized pain. ■ a brief experience of an emotion, typically an unpleasant one: *Kate felt a twinge of guilt.* ▶ **v.** (**twinge·ing** or **twing·ing**) [intrans.] (of a part of the body) suffer a sudden, sharp localized pain. [OE *twengan* 'pinch, wring,' of Gmc. origin.]

Twin·kie /'twiNGkē/ ▶ **n.** (pl. **-kies**) **1** trademark a small finger-shaped sponge cake with a white synthetic cream filling. **2** (also **twinkie**) informal, offens. a gay or effeminate man. ■ a young gay male who is meticulous about his dress, hair, weight, and other aspects of his personal appearance.

twin·kle /'twiNGkəl/ ▶ **v.** [intrans.] (of a star or light, or a shiny object) shine with a gleam that varies repeatedly between bright and faint. ■ (of a person's eyes) sparkle, esp. with amusement. ■ smile so that one's eyes sparkle. ■ (of a person's feet) move lightly and rapidly. ▶ **n.** a sparkle or gleam in a person's eyes. ■ a light that appears continually to grow brighter and fainter: *the distant twinkle of the lights.*
– PHRASES **in a twinkling** (or **the twinkling of an eye**) in an instant; very quickly. — **twin·kler** /-k(ə)lər/ **n.** **twin·kly** /-k(ə)lē/ **adj.** [OE *twinclian* (v.), of Gmc. origin.]

twin·kle·toes /'twiNGkəl,tōz/ ▶ **n.** informal a person who is nimble and quick on their feet.

twin-lens ▶ **adj.** (of a camera) having two identical sets of lenses, either for taking stereoscopic pictures, or with one forming an image for viewing and the other an image to be photographed (**twin-lens reflex**).

twinned /twind/ ▶ **adj.** (of a crystal) that is a composite consisting of two (or sometimes more) parts that are reversed in orientation with respect to each other (typically by reflection in a particular plane).

twin·ning /'twiniNG/ ▶ **n.** the bearing of twins: *the study showed an increased level of twinning in cattle.* ■ the occurrence or formation of twinned crystals.

twin par·a·dox n. Physics the apparent paradox arising from relativity theory that if one of a pair of twins makes a long journey at near the speed of light and then returns, he or she will have aged less than the twin who remains behind.

twin-screw ▶ **adj.** (of a ship) having two propellers on separate shafts that rotate in opposite directions.

twin·set /'twin,set/ ▶ **n.** a woman's matching cardigan and pullover sweater.

twirl /twərl/ ▶ **v.** [intrans.] spin quickly and lightly around, esp. repeatedly. ■ [trans.] cause to rotate: *she twirled her fork in the pasta.* ■ [trans.] Baseball pitch (the ball). ▶ **n.** an act of spinning: *Kate did a twirl.* ■ a spiraling or swirling shape, esp. a flourish made with a pen. — **twirl·er n.** **twirl·y adj.** [16th C.: prob. an alt. (by association with WHIRL) of *tirl*, a var. of archaic *trill* 'twiddle, spin.']

twirp ▶ **n.** var. of TWERP.

twist /twist/ ▶ **v.** [trans.] **1** form into a bent, curling, or distorted shape. ■ form (something) into a particular shape by taking hold of one or both ends and turning them: *she twisted her handkerchief into a knot.* ■ turn or bend into a specified position or in a specified direction: *she twisted his arm behind his back.* ■ (**twist something off**) remove something by pulling and rotating it. ■ [intrans.] move one's body so that the shoulders and hips are facing in different directions: *she twisted in her seat.* ■ [intrans.] move in a wriggling or writhing fashion: *he twisted himself free.* ■ injure (a joint) by wrenching it. ■ distort or misrepresent the meaning of (words). ■ [as adj.] (**twisted**) (of a personality or a way of thinking) unpleasantly or unhealthily abnormal: *a twisted mind.* **2** cause to rotate around something that remains stationary; turn: *she twisted her ring around on her finger.* ■ wind around or through something: *she twisted a lock of hair around her finger.* ■ move or cause to move around each other; interlace. ■ make (something) by interlacing or winding strands together. ■ [intrans.] take or have a winding course: *the road twisted through a dozen tiny villages.* **3** [intrans.] dance the twist. **4** Brit., informal cheat; defraud. ▶ **n.** **1** an act of turning something so that it moves in relation to something that remains stationary. ■ an act of turning one's body or part of one's body. ■ (**the twist**) a dance with a twisting movement of the body, popular in the 1960s. ■ the extent of twisting of a rod or other object. ■ force producing twisting; torque. ■ forward motion combined with rotation about an axis. ■ the rifling in the bore of a gun. **2** a thing with a spiral shape: *a licorice twist.* ■ a curled piece of lemon peel used to flavor a drink. **3** a distorted shape: *he had a cruel twist to his mouth.* ■ an unusual feature of a person's personality, typically an unhealthy one. **4** a point at which something turns or bends: *the twists and turns of the mountain road.* ■ an unexpected development of events: *the next twist of fate in his career.* ■ a new treatment or outlook; a variation. **5** a fine strong thread consisting of twisted strands of cotton or silk. **6** Brit. a drink consisting of two ingredients mixed together. **7** a carpet with a tightly curled pile.
– PHRASES **twist someone's arm** informal persuade someone to do something that they are or might be reluctant to do. **twist in the wind** be left in a state of suspense or uncertainty. **twists and turns** intricate or convoluted dealings or circumstances. — **twist·y adj.** [OE (as a n.), of Gmc. origin; prob. from the base of TWIN.]

twist drill ▶ **n.** a drill with a twisted body like that of an auger.

twist·ed pair ▶ **n.** Electron. a cable consisting of two wires twisted around each other, used esp. for telephone or computer applications.

twist·er /'twistər/ ▶ **n.** a tornado.

twist-grip ▶ **n.** a control operated manually by twisting, esp. one serving as a handgrip for operating the throttle on a motorcycle or for changing gear on a bicycle.

twist-lock ▶ **n.** a locking device for securing freight containers to the trailers on which they are transported.

twist·or /'twistər/ ▶ **n.** Physics a complex variable used in some descriptions of space-time.

twist tie ▶ **n.** a small piece of paper- or plastic-covered wire, to be twisted around the neck of a plastic bag as a closure.

twit[1] /twit/ ▶ **n.** informal, a silly or foolish person. — **twit·tish adj.** [1930s: perh. from TWIT[2].]

twit[2] ▶ **v.** (**twit·ted, twit·ting**) [trans.] dated tease or taunt (someone), esp. in a good-humored way. ▶ **n.** [in sing.] a state of nervous excitement: *we're in a twit about your visit.* [OE *ætwītan* 'reproach with,' from *æt* 'at' + *wītan* 'to blame.']

twitch /twiCH/ ▶ **v.** **1** give or cause to give a short, sudden jerking or convulsive movement. ■ [trans.] cause to move in a specified direction by giving a sharp pull: *he twitched a cigarette out of a packet.* **2** [trans.] apply a sudden pull or jerk to (a horse). ▶ **n.** **1** a short, sudden jerking or convulsive movement. ■ a sudden pull or jerk: *he gave a twitch at his mustache.* ■ a sudden sharp sensation; a pang: *he felt a twitch of annoyance.* **2** a stick with a small noose attached to one end. The noose may be twisted around the upper lip or the ear of a horse to subdue it, esp. during veterinary procedures. [ME: of Gmc. origin; rel. to OE *twiccian* 'to pluck, pull sharply.']

twitch·er /'twiCHər/ ▶ **n.** a person or thing that twitches. ■ Brit. informal a birdwatcher whose main aim is to collect sightings of rare birds.

twitch grass ▶ **n.** another term for COUCH GRASS. [16th C.: *twitch*, alt. of QUITCH.]

twitch·y /'twiCHē/ ▶ **adj.** (**twitch·i·er, twitch·i·est**) informal nervous; anxious. ■ given to twitching: *a mouse with a twitchy nose.*

twit·ter /'twitər/ ▶ **v.** [intrans.] (of a bird) give a call consisting of repeated light tremulous sounds. ■ talk in a light, high-pitched voice. ■ talk rapidly and at length in an idle or trivial way: *he twittered on about buying a new workshop.* ▶ **n.** a series of short, high-pitched calls or sounds. ■ idle or ignorant talk: *drawing-room twitter.*
– PHRASES **in** (or **of**) **a twitter** informal in a state of agitation or excitement. — **twit·ter·er n.** **twit·ter·y adj.** [ME (as a v.): imitative.]

'twixt /twikst/ ▶ **contr.** betwixt.

two /tōō/ ▶ **cardinal number** equivalent to the sum of one and one; one less than three; 2. (Roman numeral: **ii, II.**) ■ a group or unit of two people or things: *they would straggle home in ones and twos.* ■ two years old. ■ two o'clock. ■ a size of garment or other merchandise denoted by two. ■ a playing card or domino with two pips.
– PHRASES **a —— or two** (or **two or three ——**) used to denote a small but unspecified number: *a minute or two had passed.* **in two** in or into two halves or pieces. **put two and two together** draw an obvious conclusion from what is known or evident. **that makes two of us** one is in the same position or holds the same opinion as the previous speaker: *"I haven't a clue!" "That makes two of us."* **two by two** side by side in pairs. [OE *twā* (fem. and neut.), rel. to Ger. *zwei*, from an Indo-Eur. root shared by L. and Gk. *duo.*]

two-bit ▶ **adj.** [attrib.] informal insignificant, cheap, or worthless: *some two-bit town.*

two-by-four ▶ **n.** a piece of lumber with a rectangular cross section nominally two inches by four inches. ■ [usu. as adj.] a small or insignificant thing, typically a building: *they lived in a two-by-four shack.*

two-cy·cle ▶ **adj.** another term for TWO-STROKE.

two-di·men·sion·al ▶ **adj.** having or appearing to have length and breadth but no depth. ■ lacking depth or substance; superficial. — **two-di·men·sion·al·i·ty n.** **two-di·men·sion·al·ly adv.**

two-edged ▶ **adj.** double-edged.

two-faced ▶ **adj.** insincere and deceitful.

two·fer /'tōōfər/ ▶ **n.** informal an item or offer that comprises two items

PRONUNCIATION KEY ə *ago, up*; ər *over, fur*; a *hat*; ā *ate*; ä *car*; e *let*; ē *see*; i *fit*; ī *by*; NG *sing*; ō *go*; ô *law, for*; oi *toy*; o͝o *good*; o͞o *goo*; ou *out*; TH *thin*; TH *then*; ZH *vision*

but is sold for the price of one. [20th C.: representing a pronunc. of *two for* in 'two for the price of one.']

two fin·gers ▶ plural n. [often treated as sing.] Brit. another term for V-SIGN (chiefly in sense 2).

two-fist·ed ▶ adj. strong, virile, and straightforward.

two·fold /'to͞o,fōld/ ▶ adj. twice as great or as numerous: *a twofold increase in the risk.* ■ having two parts or elements. ▶ adv. so as to double; to twice the number or amount.

two-hand·ed ▶ adj. & adv. having, using, or requiring the use of two hands. — **two-hand·ed·ly** adv.

two-hand·er ▶ n. **1** a play for two actors. **2** Tennis a shot taken with both hands on the racket.

two·ness /'to͞onəs/ ▶ n. the fact or state of being two; duality.

two·pence /'təpəns/ ▶ n. Brit. the sum of two pence, esp. before decimalization (1971).

two·pen·ny /'təp(ə)nē; 'to͞o,penē/ ▶ adj. [attrib.] Brit. costing or worth two pence, esp. before decimalization (1971).

two-phase ▶ adj. (of an electric generator, motor, or other device) designed to supply or use simultaneously two separate alternating currents of the same voltage, but with phases differing by half a period.

two-piece ▶ adj. denoting something consisting of two matching items: *a two-piece suit.* ▶ n. a thing consisting of two matching parts, esp. a suit or swimsuit.

two-ply ▶ adj. (of a material or yarn) consisting of two layers or strands. ▶ n. **1** a yarn consisting of two strands. **2** plywood made by gluing together two layers with the grain in different directions.

two-seat·er ▶ n. a vehicle or piece of furniture with seating for two people.

two shot ▶ n. a movie or television shot of two people together.

two-sid·ed ▶ adj. having two sides: *a colorful two-sided leaflet.* ■ having two aspects: *the two-sided nature of the debate.*

two·some /'to͞osəm/ ▶ n. a pair of people considered together. ■ a game or dance for or involving two people.

two-star ▶ adj. given two stars in a grading system, typically one in which this denotes a low middle standard (four- or five-star denoting the highest standard). ■ (in the US armed forces) having or denoting the rank of major general, distinguished by two stars on the uniform.

two-step ▶ n. a round dance with a sliding step in march or polka time.

two-stroke ▶ adj. denoting an internal combustion engine having its power cycle completed in one up-and-down movement of the piston. ■ denoting a vehicle having such an engine. ▶ n. a two-stroke engine or vehicle.

two-time ▶ v. [trans.] informal deceive or be unfaithful to (a lover or spouse): *he was two-timing a fiancé.* ▶ adj. [attrib.] denoting someone who has done or experienced something twice: *a two-time winner of the event.* — **two-tim·er** n.

two-tone (also **two-toned**) ▶ adj. having two different shades or colors: *a two-tone jacket.* ■ emitting or consisting of two different sounds, typically alternately and at intervals: *a two-tone pulse signal.*

'twould /two͝od/ archaic ▶ contr. it would.

two-way ▶ adj. allowing or involving movement or communication in opposite directions: *a two-way radio.* ■ involving two participants: *a two-way presidential race.* ■ (of a switch) permitting a current to be switched on or off from either of two points.
– PHRASES **two-way street** a situation or relationship involving mutual or reciprocal action or obligation.

two-way mir·ror ▶ n. a panel of glass that can be seen through from one side and is a mirror on the other.

2WD ▶ abbr. two-wheel drive.

two-wheel drive ▶ n. a transmission system in a motor vehicle, providing power to either the front or the rear wheels only.

two-wheel·er ▶ n. a bicycle or motorcycle.

twp. ▶ abbr. township.

TWX ▶ abbr. teletypewriter exchange.

TX ▶ abbr. Texas (in official postal use).

-ty[1] ▶ suffix forming nouns denoting quality or condition such as *beauty, royalty.* [via OFr. from L. *-tas, -tat-*.]

-ty[2] ▶ suffix denoting specified groups of ten: *forty* | *ninety.* [OE *-tig*.]

ty·chism /'tī,kizəm/ ▶ n. Philos. the doctrine that account must be taken of the element of chance in reasoning or explanation of the universe. [19th C.: from Gk. *tukhē* 'chance' + -ISM.]

ty·coon /tī'ko͞on/ ▶ n. **1** a wealthy, powerful person in business or industry: *a newspaper tycoon.* **2** a title applied by foreigners to the shogun of Japan in power between 1857 and 1868. [19th C.: from Japanese *taikun* 'great lord.']

ty·ing /'tī-iNG/ present participle of TIE.

ty·ing-up ▶ n. another term for AZOTURIA in horses.

tyke /tīk/ (also **tike**) ▶ n. **1** [usu. with adj.] informal a small child: *is the little tyke up to his tricks again?* **2** Brit. a dog, esp. a mongrel. [ME (in senses 2 and 3): from ON *tík* 'bitch.']

Ty·le·nol /'tīlə,nôl; -,näl/ ▶ n. trademark for ACETAMINOPHEN.

Tyl·er[1] /'tīlər/, Anne (1941–), US writer. Her novels include *The Accidental Tourist* (1986) and *Digging to America* (2006).

Ty·ler[2], John (1790–1862), 10th president of the US 1841–45. A Virginia Whig who advocated states' rights, he served as US representative 1817–21, governor of Virginia 1825–27, US senator 1827–36, and US vice president 1841. He succeeded to the presidency upon the death of President William H. Harrison. He is noted for securing the annexation of Texas (1845).

Ty·ler[3], Wat (died 1381), English leader of the Peasants' Revolt of 1381.

tym·bal ▶ n. var. of TIMBAL.

tym·pan /'timpən/ ▶ n. **1** (in letterpress printing) a layer of packing, typically of paper, placed between the platen and the paper to be printed to equalize the pressure over the whole form. **2** Archit. another term for TYMPANUM. [16th C. (sense 1): from Fr. *tympan* or L. *tympanum* (see TYMPANUM).]

tym·pa·na /'timpənə/ plural form of TYMPANUM.

tym·pa·ni ▶ plural n. var. of TIMPANI.

tym·pan·ic /tim'panik/ ▶ adj. **1** Anat. of, relating to, or having a tympanum. **2** resembling or acting like a drumhead.

tym·pan·ic bone ▶ n. Zool. a small bone supporting the tympanic membrane in some vertebrates.

tym·pan·ic mem·brane ▶ n. a membrane forming part of the organ of hearing, which vibrates in response to sound waves. In humans and other higher vertebrates it forms the eardrum, between the outer and middle ear.

tym·pa·ni·tes /,timpə'nītēz/ ▶ n. Med. swelling of the abdomen with air or gas. — **tym·pa·nit·ic** /-'nitik/ adj. [ME: via late L. from Gk. *tumpanitēs*, from *tumpanon* (see TYMPANUM).]

tym·pa·num /'timpənəm/ ▶ n. (pl. **-nums** or **-na** /-nə/) **1** Anat. & Zool. the tympanic membrane or eardrum. ■ Entomol. a membrane covering the hearing organ on the leg or body of some insects, sometimes adapted (as in cicadas) for producing sound. ■ archaic a drum. **2** Archit. a vertical recessed triangular space forming the center of a pediment, typically decorated. ■ a similar space over a door between the lintel and the arch. [17th C.: via L. from Gk. *tumpanon* 'drum,' based on *tuptein* 'to strike.']

tym·pa·ny /'timpənē/ ▶ n. another term for TYMPANITES (used esp. in veterinary medicine). [16th C.: from Gk. *tumpanias*, from *tumpanon* (see TYMPANUM).]

Tyn·dall /'tindəl/, John (1820–93), Irish physicist. He is best known for his work on heat.

Tyne /tīn/ a river in northeastern England, formed by the confluence of two headstreams, the North Tyne and the South Tyne.

typ. ▶ abbr. ■ typographer. ■ typographic. ■ typographical. ■ typography.

a **a** *a*

roman boldface italic

type 3

type /tīp/ ▶ n. **1** a category of people or things having common characteristics: *blood types.* ■ a person, thing, or event considered as a representative of such a category: *I'm an adventurous type.* ■ [with adj.] informal a person of a specified character or nature: ***professor types in tweed.*** ■ (**one's type**) informal the sort of person one likes or finds attractive: *she's not really my type.* ■ Ling. an abstract category or class of linguistic item or unit, as distinct from actual occurrences in speech or writing. Contrasted with TOKEN. **2** a person or thing symbolizing or exemplifying the ideal or defining characteristics of something. ■ an object, conception, or work of art serving as a model for subsequent artists. ■ Bot. & Zool. an organism or taxon chosen as having the essential characteristics of its group. ■ short for TYPE SPECIMEN. **3** printed characters or letters: *bold or italic type.* ■ a piece of metal with a raised letter or character on its upper surface, for use in letterpress printing. ■ such pieces collectively. **4** a design on either side of a medal or coin. **5** Theol. a foreshadowing in the Old Testament of a person or event of the Christian tradition. ▶ v. [trans.] **1** write (something) on a typewriter or computer by pressing the keys: ***he typed out the second draft*** | [intrans.] *I am learning how to type.* **2** Med. determine the type to which (a person or their blood or tissue) belongs: *the kidney was typed.* **3** short for TYPECAST.
– PHRASES **in type** Print. composed and ready for printing. — **typ·al** /-pəl/ adj. (rare). [15th C.: from Fr., or from L. *typus*, from Gk. *tupos* 'impression, figure, type,' from *tuptein* 'to strike.']

-type ▶ suffix (forming adjectives) resembling or having the characteristics of a specified thing: *the dish-type radio telescope* | *a champagne-type fizzy wine.*

Type A ▶ n. a personality type characterized by ambition, high energy, and competitiveness, and thought to be susceptible to stress and heart disease.

Type B ▶ n. a personality type characterized as easygoing and thought to have low susceptibility to stress.

type·cast /'tīp,kast/ ▶ v. (past and past part. **-cast**) [trans.] (usu. **be typecast**) assign (an actor or actress) repeatedly to the same type of role, as a result of the appropriateness of their appearance or previous success in such roles. ■ represent or regard (a person or their role) as a stereotype: *typecast by their accents.*

type·face /'tīp,fās/ ▶ n. Print. a particular design of type.

type found·er ▶ n. Print. a designer and maker of metal type. — **type found·ry** n.

type lo·cal·i·ty ▶ n. **1** Bot. & Zool. the place in which a type specimen was found. **2** Geol. a place where deposits regarded as defining the characteristics of a particular geological formation or period occur.

type met·al ▶ n. Print. an alloy of lead, tin, and antimony, used for casting type.

type·script /'tīp,skript/ ▶ n. a typed copy of a text.

type·set /'tīp,set/ ▶ v. (**-set·ting**; past and past part. **-set**) [trans.] arrange or generate the type for (a piece of text to be printed). — **type·set·ting** n.

type·set·ter /'tīp,setər/ ▶ n. Print. a person who typesets text. ■ a typesetting machine.

type spe·cies ▶ n. Bot. & Zool. the particular species on which the description of a genus is based and with which the genus name remains associated during any taxonomic revision.

type spec·i·men ▶ n. Bot. & Zool. the specimen, or each of a set of specimens, on which the description and name of a new species is based. See also HOLOTYPE, SYNTYPE.

type·writ·er /'tīp,rītər/ ▶ n. an electric, electronic, or manual machine with keys for producing printlike characters one at a time on paper inserted around a roller. — **type·writ·ing** /-,rītiNG/ n. **type·writ·ten** /-,ritn/ adj.

typh·li·tis /tif'lītis/ ▶ n. Med. inflammation of the cecum. — **typh·lit·ic** /-'litik/ adj. [19th C.: mod. L., from Gk. *tuphlon* 'cecum or blind gut' (from *tuphlos* 'blind') + -ITIS.]

ty·phoid /'tī,foid/ (also **ty·phoid fe·ver**) ▶ n. an infectious fever with an eruption of red spots on the chest and abdomen and severe intestinal irritation, caused by the bacterium *Salmonella typhi*. — **ty·phoi·dal** /tī'foidl/ adj. [19th C.: from TYPHUS + -OID.]

Ty·phoid Mar·y ▶ n. (pl. **Ty·phoid Mar·ys**) informal a transmitter of undesirable opinions, sentiments, or attitudes. [the nickname of *Mary* Mallon (c.1870–1938), an Irish-born cook who transmitted typhoid fever in the US.]

ty·phoon /tī'foon/ ▶ n. a tropical storm in the region of the Indian or western Pacific oceans. — **ty·phon·ic** /-'fänik/ adj. [16th C.: partly via Port. from Arab. *ṭūfān* (perh. from Gk. *tuphōn* 'whirlwind'); reinforced by Chin. dial. *tai fung* 'big wind.']

ty·phus /'tīfəs/ ▶ n. an infectious disease caused by rickettsiae, characterized by a purple rash, headaches, fever, and usually delirium, and historically a cause of high mortality during wars and famines. There are several forms, transmitted by vectors such as lice, ticks, mites, and rat fleas. Also called SPOTTED FEVER. — **ty·phous** /-fəs/ adj. [17th C.: mod. L., from Gk. *tuphos* 'smoke, stupor,' from *tuphein* 'to smoke.']

typ·i·cal /'tipikəl/ ▶ adj. having the distinctive qualities of a particular type of person or thing: *a typical day.* ■ characteristic of a particular person or thing: *his typical good humor.* ■ informal showing the characteristics expected of or popularly associated with a particular person, situation, or thing: *"Typical woman!"* ■ representative as a symbol; symbolic. — **typ·i·cal·i·ty** /,tipi'kalitē/ n. **typ·i·cal·ly** /-ik(ə)lē/ adv. [17th C.: from med. L. *typicalis*, via L. from Gk. *tupikos*, from *tupos* (see TYPE).]

typ·i·fy /'tipə,fī/ ▶ v. (**-fies, -fied**) [trans.] be characteristic of or a representative example of: *tough, low-lying vegetation typifies this arctic area.* ■ represent; symbolize: *the sun typified the Greeks.* — **typ·i·fi·ca·tion** /,tipəfi'kāSHən/ n. **typ·i·fi·er** n.

typ·ing /'tīpiNG/ ▶ n. the action or skill of writing something by means of a typewriter or computer. ■ writing produced in such a way: *five pages of typing.*

typ·ist /'tīpist/ ▶ n. a person who is skilled in using a typewriter or computer keyboard, esp. one who is employed for this purpose.

ty·po /'tīpō/ ▶ n. (pl. **-pos**) informal a typographical error.

typo. ▶ abbr. ■ typographer. ■ typographic. ■ typographical. ■ typography.

ty·pog·ra·phy /tī'pägrəfē/ ▶ n. the art or process of setting and arranging types and printing from them. ■ the style and appearance of printed matter. — **ty·pog·ra·pher** /-fər/ n. **ty·po·graph·ic** /,tīpə'grafik/ adj. **ty·po·graph·i·cal** /,tīpə'grafikəl/ adj. **ty·po·graph·i·cal·ly** /,tīpə'grafik(ə)lē/ adv. [17th C.: from Fr. *typographie* or mod. L. *typographia* (see TYPE, -GRAPHY).]

ty·pol·o·gy /tī'päləjē/ ▶ n. (pl. **-gies**) **1** a classification according to general type, esp. in archaeology, psychology, or the social sciences. ■ study or analysis using such classification. **2** the study and interpretation of types and symbols, originally esp. in the Bible. — **ty·po·log·i·cal** /,tīpə'läjikəl/ adj. **ty·pol·o·gist** /-jist/ n. [19th C. (sense 2): from Gk. *tupos* 'type' + -LOGY.]

Tyr /ti(ə)r/ Scand. Mythol. the god of battle, identified with Mars, after whom Tuesday is named.

ty·ra·mine /'tīrə,mēn/ ▶ n. Biochem. a compound, $C_6H_4(OH)CH_2CH_2NH_2$, that occurs naturally in cheese and other foods and can cause dangerously high blood pressure in people taking a monoamine oxidase inhibitor. [20th C.: from *tyr(osine)* + AMINE.]

ty·ran·ni·cal /tə'ranikəl/ ▶ adj. exercising power in a cruel or arbitrary way. ■ characteristic of tyranny; oppressive and controlling. — **ty·ran·ni·cal·ly** /-ik(ə)lē/ adv. [16th C.: from OFr. *tyrannique*, via L. from Gk. *turannikos*, from *turannos* (see TYRANT).]

ty·ran·ni·cide /tə'rani,sīd/ ▶ n. the killing of a tyrant. ■ the killer of a tyrant. — **ty·ran·ni·cid·al** /tə,rani'sīdl/ adj. [17th C.: from Fr., from L. *tyrannicida* 'killer of a tyrant,' *tyrannicidium* 'killing of a tyrant' (see TYRANT, -CIDE).]

tyr·an·nize /'tirə,nīz/ ▶ v. [trans.] rule or treat (someone) despotically or cruelly: *she tyrannized her family* | [intrans.] *he tyrannizes over the servants.*

ty·ran·no·saur /tə'ranə,sôr/ (also **ty·ran·no·sau·rus** /tə,ranə'sôrəs/) ▶ n. a very large bipedal carnivorous dinosaur (family Tyrannosauridae, infraorder Carnosauria, suborder Theopoda) of the late Cretaceous period, with powerful jaws and small clawlike front legs. See illustration at DINOSAUR. [mod. L., from Gk. *turannos* 'tyrant' + *sauros* 'lizard.']

tyr·an·ny /'tirənē/ ▶ n. (pl. **-nies**) cruel and oppressive government or rule. ■ a nation under such cruel and oppressive government. ■ cruel, unreasonable, or arbitrary use of power or control. ■ (esp. in ancient Greece) rule by one who has absolute power without legal right. — **tyr·an·nous** /-nəs/ adj. **tyr·an·nous·ly** /-nəslē/ adv. [ME: from OFr. *tyrannie*, from late L. *tyrannia*, from L. *turannus* (see TYRANT).]

ty·rant /'tīrənt/ ▶ n. **1** a cruel and oppressive ruler. ■ a person exercising power or control in a cruel, unreasonable, or arbitrary way. ■ (esp. in ancient Greece) a ruler who seized power without legal right. **2** a tyrant flycatcher. [ME: from OFr., via L. from Gk. *turannos*.]

ty·rant fly·catch·er ▶ n. a New World perching bird (family Tyrannidae) that resembles the Old World flycatchers in behavior, typically with brightly colored plumage. [18th C.: so named because of its aggressive behavior toward other birds approaching its nest.]

Tyre /tī(ə)r/ a port in southern Lebanon; pop. 14,000. Founded in the 2nd millennium BC, it was for centuries a Phoenician port. — **Tyr·i·an** /'tirēən/ adj. & n.

tyre ▶ n. British spelling of TIRE[2].

Tyr·i·an pur·ple /'tirēən/ ▶ n. see PURPLE.

ty·ro /'tīrō/ (also **ti·ro**) ▶ n. (pl. **-ros**) a beginner or novice. [ME: from L. *tiro*, med. L. *tyro* 'recruit.']

Ty·rol /tə'rōl; tī'rōl; 'tī,rōl/ an Alpine state in western Austria; capital, Innsbruck. German name TIROL. — **Ty·ro·le·an** /tə'rōlēən; tī-/ adj. & n. **Tyr·o·lese** /,tirə'lēz; ,tirə-; -'lēs/ adj. & n.

Ty·rone /tī'rōn/ one of the Six Counties of Northern Ireland; pop. 144,000; chief town, Omagh.

ty·ro·si·nase /tī'räsə,nās; -,nāz/ ▶ n. Biochem. a copper-containing enzyme that catalyzes the formation of quinones from phenols and polyphenols (e.g., melanin from tyrosine).

ty·ro·sine /'tīrə,sēn/ ▶ n. Biochem. a hydrophilic amino acid, $C_6H_4(OH)CH_2CH(NH_2)COOH$, that is a constituent of most proteins and is important in the synthesis of some hormones. [19th C.: formed irregularly from Gk. *turos* 'cheese' + -INE[4].]

Tyr·rhe·ni·an /tə'rēnēən/ ▶ adj. of, relating to, or denoting the Tyrrhenian Sea or the surrounding region. ■ archaic Etruscan. ▶ n. archaic an Etruscan.

Tyr·rhe·ni·an Sea a part of the Mediterranean Sea between mainland Italy and Sicily and Sardinia.

Tyu·men /tyoo'men/ a city in west Siberian Russia, in the eastern foothills of the Ural Mountains; pop. 487,000. Founded in 1586, it is thought to be one of the oldest cities in Siberia.

tyu·ya·mu·nite /,tyooyə'moonīt/ ▶ n. a yellowish earthy mineral that is an ore of uranium. It consists of a hydrated vanadate of calcium and uranium. [20th C.: from *Tyuya Muyun*, the name of a Kyrgyz village, + -ITE[1].]

tzar, etc. ▶ n. var. of CZAR, etc.

tza·ri·na ▶ n. var. of CZARINA.

tze·da·kah /tsi'dôkə; tsədä'kä/ ▶ n. (among the Jews) charitable giving, typically seen as a moral obligation. [from Heb. *ṣĕdāqāh* 'righteousness.']

tzi·gane /(t)si'gän/ ▶ n. (pl. same or **-ganes**) a Hungarian gypsy. [18th C.: from Fr., from Hungarian *c(z)igány*.]

tzim·mes (also **tzim·mis**) ▶ n. var. of TSIMMES.

T-zone ▶ n. the central part of a person's face, including the forehead, nose, and chin, esp. as having oilier skin than the rest of the face. [*T* designating the shape of the area defined.]

Tzu-po variant of ZIBO.

PRONUNCIATION KEY ə *ago, up*; ər *over, fur*; a *hat*; ā *ate*; ä *car*; e *let*; ē *see*; i *fit*; ī *by*; NG *sing*; ō *go*; ô *law, for*; oi *toy*; oo *good*; oo *goo*; ou *out*; TH *thin*; TH *then*; ZH *vision*

Uu

U[1] /yoo/ (also **u**) ▸ **n.** (pl. **Us** or **U's**) **1** the twenty-first letter of the alphabet. ▪ denoting the next after T in a set of items, categories, etc. **2** (**U**) a shape like that of a capital U, esp. a cross section: [in comb.] *U-shaped glaciated valleys.*

U[2] ▸ **symb.** the chemical element uranium.

U[3] ▸ **adj.** informal, esp. Brit. (of language or social behavior) characteristic of or appropriate to the upper social classes: *U manners.* [abbr. of UPPER CLASS; coined in 1954 by Alan S. C. Ross, professor of linguistics, the term was popularized by its use in Nancy Mitford's *Noblesse Oblige* (1956).]

U[4] /oo/ ▸ **n.** a Burmese title of respect before a man's name, equivalent to Mr.: *U Thien San.*

u ▸ **abbr.** Physics denoting quantum states or wave functions that change sign on inversion through the origin. The opposite of G. [from Ger. *ungerade* 'odd.']

UAE ▸ **abbr.** United Arab Emirates.

U·ban·ghi Sha·ri /(y)oo'banggē 'shärē; -'bäng-/ former name (until 1958) of CENTRAL AFRICAN REPUBLIC.

U·ban·gi Riv·er /(y)oo'banggē/ (French spelling **Oubangui**) a river that flows for 660 miles (1,060 km) from the border of the Central African Republic and the Democratic Republic of the Congo (formerly Zaire), to join the Congo River.

uber- /'oobər/ (also **über-** /'ybər/) ▸ **prefix** denoting an outstanding or supreme example of a particular kind of person or thing: *the uberstudent.* [Ger. *über* 'super.']

Ü·ber·mensch /'oobər,mench; 'ybər-/ ▸ **n.** (pl. **-mensch·en** /-,menchən/) the ideal superior man of the future who could rise above conventional Christian morality to create and impose his own values, originally described by Nietzsche in *Thus Spake Zarathustra* (1883–85). Also called SUPERMAN and OVERMAN. [Ger., lit. 'superhuman person.']

-ubility ▸ **suffix** forming nouns from or corresponding to adjectives ending in *-uble* (such as *solubility* from *soluble*).

u·bi·qui·none /yoo'bikwə,nōn/ ▸ **n.** Biochem. any of a class of compounds that occur in all living cells and that act as electron-transfer agents in cell respiration. They are substituted quinones. [1950s: blend of UBIQUITOUS and QUINONE.]

u·bi·qui·tin /yoo'bikwitin/ ▸ **n.** Biochem. a compound found in living cells that plays a role in the degradation of defective and superfluous proteins. It is a single-chain polypeptide. [1970s: from UBIQUITOUS + -IN[1].]

u·biq·ui·tous /yoo'bikwətəs/ ▸ **adj.** present, appearing, or found everywhere: *his ubiquitous influence.* — **u·biq·ui·tous·ly** **adv.** **u·biq·ui·tous·ness** **n.** **u·biq·ui·ty** /-wətē/ **n.** [19th C.: from mod. L. *ubiquitas* (from L. *ubique* 'everywhere,' from *ubi* 'where') + -OUS.]

-uble ▸ **suffix** (forming adjectives) able to: *voluble.* ▪ able to be: *soluble.* Compare with -ABLE. [from Fr., from L. *-ubilis.*]

-ubly ▸ **suffix** forming adverbs corresponding to adjectives ending in *-uble* (such as *volubly* corresponding to *voluble*).

U-boat ▸ **n.** a German submarine used in World War I or World War II. [from Ger. *U-Boot*, abbr. of *Unterseeboot* 'undersea boat.']

u.c. ▸ **abbr.** uppercase.

Uca·ya·li River /,ookə'yälē/ a river that flows for 1,000 miles (1,600 km) through Peru to join the Marañón River to form the Amazon River.

UCC ▸ **abbr.** Uniform Commercial Code.

ud·der /'ədər/ ▸ **n.** the mammary gland of female cattle, sheep, goats, horses, and related ungulates, hanging near the hind legs as a baglike organ with two or more teats. [OE *ūder*, of West Gmc. origin; rel. to Du. *uier* and Ger. *Euter.*]

u·don /'oo,dän/ ▸ **n.** (in Japanese cooking) wheat pasta made in thick strips.

UEFA /yoo'efə/ ▸ **abbr.** Union of European Football Associations, the governing body of soccer in Europe.

U·fa /oo'fä/ the capital of Bashkiria, in southwestern Russia; pop. 1,094,000.

UFO ▸ **n.** (pl. **UFOs**) a mysterious object seen in the sky for which, it is claimed, no orthodox scientific explanation can be found. [1950s: acronym from *unidentified flying object.*]

u·fol·o·gy /yoo'fäləjē/ ▸ **n.** the study of UFOs. — **u·fo·log·i·cal** /,yoofə'läjikəl/ **adj.** **u·fol·o·gist** /-jist/ **n.**

U·gan·da /yoo'gandə/ a country in East Africa. *See box.* — **U·gan·dan** **adj.** & **n.**

U·ga·rit /'(y)oogərit; (y)oo'gärit/ an ancient port and Bronze Age trading city in northern Syria. — **U·ga·rit·ic** /,(y)oogə'ritik/ **adj.** & **n.**

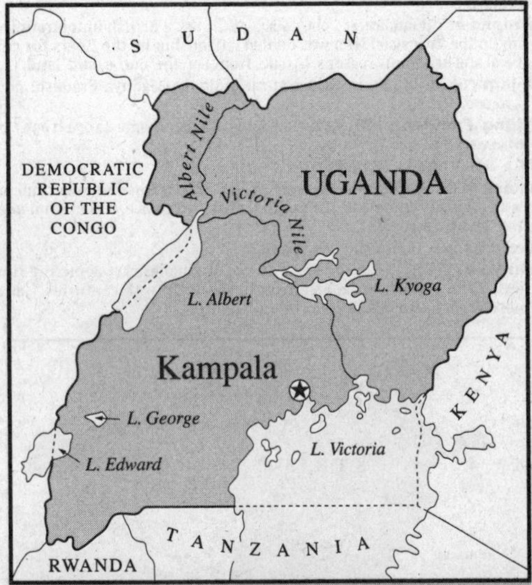

Uganda

Official name: Republic of Uganda
Location: East Africa, west of Kenya
Area: 91,200 square miles (236,000 sq km)
Population: 26,404,000
Capital: Kampala
Languages: English (official), Arabic, Swahili, and other languages
Currency: Ugandan shilling

ugh /əg; əKH; ooKH/ ▸ **exclam.** informal used to express disgust or horror: *Ugh—what's this disgusting object?* [18th C.: imitative.]

Ug·li fruit /'əglē/ ▸ **n.** (pl. same) trademark a mottled green and yellow citrus fruit that is a hybrid of grapefruit and tangerine, obtained from the tree *Citrus × tangelo.*

ug·ly /'əglē/ ▸ **adj.** (**-li·er**, **-li·est**) unpleasant or repulsive, esp. in appearance: *she thought she was ugly and fat.* ▪ (of a situation or mood) involving or likely to involve violence or other unpleasantness: *the mood in the room turned ugly.* ▪ unpleasantly suggestive; causing disquiet: *ugly rumors persisted.* ▪ morally repugnant: *racism and its ugly manifestations.* — **ug·li·fi·ca·tion** /,əgləfi'kāshən/ **n.** **ug·li·fy** /'əglə,fī/ **v.** **ug·li·ly** /-ləlē/ **adv.** **ug·li·ness** **n.** [ME: from ON *uggligr* 'to be dreaded,' from *ugga* 'to dread.']

ug·ly A·mer·i·can ▸ **n.** informal an American who behaves offensively when abroad.

ug·ly duck·ling ▸ **n.** a person, esp. a child, who turns out to be beautiful or talented against all expectations. [from the title of one of Hans Christian Andersen's fairy tales, in which the "ugly duckling" becomes a swan.]

U·gri·an /'(y)oogrēən/ ▸ **adj.** another term for UGRIC.

U·gric /'(y)oogrik/ ▸ **adj.** of, relating to, or denoting a branch of the Finno-Ugric language family comprising Hungarian and the Ob-Ugric languages. [from Russ. *Ugry* (the name of a people dwelling east of the Urals) + -IC.]

uh /ə; əN/ ▸ **exclam.** **1** used to express hesitation: *"I was just, uh, passing by."* **2** another way of saying HUH. [1960s: imitative.]

UHF ▸ **abbr.** ultrahigh frequency.

uh-huh /ə 'hə; əN 'hən/ ▸ **exclam.** used to express assent or as a noncommittal response to a question or remark: *"Do you understand?" "Uh-huh."* [1920s: imitative.]

uh·lan /o͞o'län; '(y)o͞olən/ ▶**n.** hist. a cavalryman armed with a lance as a member of various European armies. [18th C.: via Fr. and Ger. from Pol. *(h)ulan*, from Turk. *oğ lan* 'youth, servant.']

uh-oh /'ə ,ō/ ▶**exclam.** used to express alarm, dismay, or realization of a difficulty: *"Uh-oh! Take cover!"*

uh-uh /'ən ,ən; 'ən 'ən/ ▶**exclam.** used to express a negative response to a question or remark. [1920s: imitative.]

Ui·ghur /'wē,go͝or/ (also **Ui·gur, Uy·gur**) ▶**n. 1** a member of a people of northwestern China, particularly the Xinjiang region, and adjoining areas. **2** the Turkic language of this people. ▶**adj.** of or relating to this people or their language. [the name in Uighur.]

u·in·ta·ite /yo͞o'intə,īt/ ▶**n** a pure form of asphalt mined in the Uinta Mountains and used to soften petroleum products, as well as in manufacturing paints and inks.

Uin·ta Moun·tains /yo͞o'intə/ a range of the Rocky Mountains in northeastern Utah.

Uit·land·er /'īt,landər; 'āt-; 'out-/ ▶**n.** S. African, hist. a British immigrant living in the Transvaal who was denied citizenship by the Boers for cultural and economic reasons. [Afrik., from Du. *uit* 'out' + *land* 'land.']

Uj·jain /'o͞o,jīn/ a city in west central India, in Madhya Pradesh; pop. 376,000.

U·jung Pan·dang /'o͞o,jo͝ong 'pän,däng/ former name (1971-1999) of **Makassar.**

UK ▶**abbr.** United Kingdom.

u·kase /yo͞o'kās; -'kāz/ ▶**n.** an edict of the Czarist Russian government. ■ an arbitrary command. [from Russ. *ukaz* 'ordinance, edict,' from *ukazat'* 'show, decree.']

uke /yo͞ok/ ▶**n.** informal short for **ukulele.**

u·ki·yo-e /,o͞okē(y)ō'ā; 'yo͞o-/ ▶**n.** a school of Japanese art depicting subjects from everyday life, dominant in the 17th–19th centuries. [Japanese, from *ukiyo* 'fleeting world' + *e* 'picture.']

Ukraine

Location: eastern Europe, north of the Black Sea
Area: 233,100 square miles (603,700 sq km)
Population: 47,732,000
Capital: Kiev
Languages: Ukrainian (official), Russian, Romanian, Polish, Hungarian
Currency: hryvnia

U·kraine /yo͞o'krān; 'yo͞o,krān/ (also **the U·kraine**) a country in eastern Europe. *See box.*

U·krain·i·an /yo͞o'krānēən/ ▶**n. 1** a native or national of Ukraine, or a person of Ukrainian descent. **2** the East Slavic language of Ukraine. ▶**adj.** of or relating to Ukraine, its people, or their language.

u·ku·le·le /,yo͞okə'lālē/ ▶**n.** a small four-stringed guitar of Hawaiian origin. [19th C.: from Hawaiian, lit. 'jumping flea.']

u·la·ma ▶**n.** var. of **ulema.**

U·laan·baa·tar /o͞o'län 'bä,tär/ (also **Ulan Bator** /o͞o'län 'bä,tôr; 'o͞o,län/) the capital of Mongolia; pop. 575,000. Former name (until 1924) **Urga.**

U·lan-U·de /o͞o'län o͞o'dā/ al city in southern Russia, capital of the republic of Buryatia; pop. 359,000. Former name (until 1934) **Verkhneudinsk.**

-ular ▶**suffix** forming adjectives, sometimes corresponding to nouns ending in *-ule* (such as *pustular* corresponding to *pustule*), but often without diminutive force (as in *angular, granular*). — **-ularity suffix** forming corresponding nouns. [from L. *-ularis.*]

ul·cer /'əlsər/ ▶**n.** an open sore on an external or internal surface of the body, caused by a break in the skin or mucous membrane that fails to heal. ■ fig. a moral blemish or corrupting influence. — **ul·cered adj. ul·cer·ous** /'əls(ə)rəs/ **adj.** [ME: from L. *ulcus, ulcer-.*]

ul·cer·ate /'əlsə,rāt/ ▶**v.** [intrans.] develop into or become affected by an ulcer. — **ul·cer·a·tion** /,əlsə'rāshən/ **n. ul·cer·a·tive** /-rətiv; -,rātiv/ **adj.**

-ule ▶**suffix** forming diminutive nouns such as *capsule* and *pustule.* [from L. *-ulus, -ula, -ulum.*]

u·le·ma /'o͞olə,mä/ (also **u·la·ma**) ▶**n.** [treated as sing. or pl.] a body of Muslim scholars recognized as having specialist knowledge of Islamic sacred law and theology. ■ a member of such a body. [from Arab. *'ulamā'*, pl. of *'ālim* 'learned,' from *'alima* 'know.']

-ulent ▶**suffix** (forming adjectives) abounding in; full of: *fraudulent* | *purulent* | *virulent.* Compare with **-lent.** — **-ulence suffix** forming corresponding nouns. [from L. *-ulentus.*]

u·lex·ite /'yo͞olək,sīt/ ▶**n.** a mineral occurring on alkali flats as rounded masses of small white crystals. It is a hydrated borate of sodium and calcium. [19th C.: from George L. *Ulex* (died 1883), German chemist, + **-ite**[1].]

Ul·has·na·gar /,o͞olhəs'nəgər; -'nägər/ a city in western India, in the state of Maharashtra; pop. 369,000.

Uli·thi /o͞o'lēthē/ an atoll in the western Caroline Islands, in the Federated States of Micronesia.

ul·lage /'əlij/ ▶**n.** the amount by which a container falls short of being full. ■ loss of liquid by evaporation or leakage. [ME: from Anglo-Norman Fr. *ulliage*, from OFr. *euillier* 'fill up,' based on L. *oculus* 'eye.']

ul·lage rock·et ▶**n.** an auxiliary rocket engine used in weightless conditions to provide sufficient acceleration to maintain the flow of liquid propellant from the fuel tank.

Ulm /o͞olm/ an industrial city in southern Germany; pop. 112,000.

ul·na /'əlnə/ ▶**n.** (pl. **-nae** /-,nē; -,nī/ or **-nas**) the thinner and longer of the two bones in the human forearm, on the side opposite to the thumb. Compare with **radius** (sense 2). ■ the corresponding bone in a quadruped's foreleg or a bird's wing. — **ul·nar adj.** [ME (denoting the humerus): from L.; rel. to **ell**[1].]

U-lock ▶**n.** a mechanism used to secure a bicycle when parked, consisting of a U-shaped bar and a crosspiece.

-ulous ▶**suffix** forming adjectives such as *incredulous, garrulous.* [from L. *-ulosus, -ulus.*]

Ul·san /'o͞ol'sän/ a city on the southern coast of South Korea; pop. 683,000.

Ul·ster /'əlstər/ a former province of Ireland. ■ (in general use) Northern Ireland. — **Ul·ster·man** /-mən/ **n.** (pl. **-men**) **Ul·ster·wom·an** /-,wo͝omən/ **n.** (pl. **-wom·en**).

ul·ster /'əlstər/ ▶**n.** a man's long, loose overcoat of rough cloth, typically with a belt at the back. [19th C.: from **Ulster.**]

ult. ▶**abbr.** ■ ultimate. ■ ultimo.

ul·te·ri·or /,əl'ti(ə)rēər/ ▶**adj.** existing beyond what is obvious or admitted; intentionally hidden: *an ulterior motive behind his request.* ■ beyond what is immediate or present; coming in the future: *ulterior pay promised to the mariners.* [17th C.: from L., lit. 'further, more distant.']

ul·ti·ma·ta /,əltə'mātə; -'mätə/ plural form of **ultimatum.**

ul·ti·mate /'əltəmit/ ▶**adj.** being or happening at the end of a process; final: *their ultimate aim was to force his resignation.* ■ being the best or most extreme example of its kind. ■ basic or fundamental: *the ultimate constituents of atoms.* ■ Physics denoting the maximum possible strength or resistance beyond which an object breaks. ▶**n. 1** (**the ultimate**) the best achievable or imaginable of its kind: *the ultimate in decorative luxury.* **2** a final or fundamental fact or principle. — **ul·ti·ma·cy** /-məsē/ **n.** (pl. **-cies**) **ul·ti·mate·ly adv.** [17th C.: from late L. *ultimatus*, past part. of *ultimare* 'come to an end.']

ul·ti·ma Thu·le /'əltəmə 'tho͞olē; 'tho͞ol/ ▶**n.** a distant unknown region; the extreme limit of travel and discovery. [L., lit. 'furthest Thule' (see **Thule**).]

ul·ti·ma·tum /,əltə'mātəm; -'mät-/ ▶**n.** (pl. **-ma·tums** or **-ma·ta** /-'mātə; -'mätə/) a final demand or statement of terms, the rejection of which will result in retaliation or a breakdown in relations: *a UN Security Council ultimatum/* [18th C.: from L., neut. past part. of *ultimare* 'come to an end.']

ul·ti·mo /'əltə,mō/ (abbr.: **ult.** or **ulto**) ▶**adj.** [postpositive] dated of last month: *the 3rd ultimo.* [from L. *ultimo mense* 'in the last month.']

ul·ti·mo·bran·chi·al /,əltəmō'brangkēəl/ ▶**adj.** Zool. relating to or denoting a gland in the neck that in many lower vertebrates regulates the calcium level in the body.

ul·ti·mo·gen·i·ture /,əltəmō'jenichər; -,cho͝or/ ▶**n.** Law a principle of inheritance in which the right of succession belongs to the youngest son. Compare with **primogeniture.**

ul·ti·sol /'əltə,säl; -,sôl/ ▶**n.** Soil Science a leached red or reddish-yellow acid soil with a clay subsoil, occurring in warm, humid climates. [1960s: from **ultimate** + L. *solum* 'soil.']

ul·tra /'əltrə/ informal ▶**n.** an extremist. ▶**adv.** [as submodifier] very; extremely: *the play was not just boring, it was ultra boring.* [19th C.: from **ultra-.**]

ultra- ▶**prefix 1** beyond; on the other side of: *ultramontane.* Often contrasted with **cis-. 2** extreme; to an extreme degree: *ultramicroscopic* | *ultraradical.* [from L. *ultra* 'beyond.']

ul·tra·ba·sic /,əltrə'bāsik/ ▶**adj.** Geol. relating to or denoting igneous rocks having a silica content less than 45 percent by weight.

ul·tra·cen·tri·fuge /,əltrə'sentrə,fyo͞oj/ ▶**n.** a very fast centrifuge used to precipitate large biological molecules. ▶**v.** [trans.] subject to the action of an ultracentrifuge. — **ul·tra·cen·tri·fu·ga·tion** /-,sentrəfyo͞o'gāshən; -sen,trif(y)ə-/ **n.**

ul·tra·con·serv·a·tive /,əltrəkən'sərvətiv/ ▶**adj.** extremely conservative in politics or in the observance of religion. ▶**n.** a person who is extremely conservative in politics or religion. — **ul·tra·con·serv·a·tism** /-və,tizəm/ **n.**

ul·tra·di·an /əl'trādēən/ ▶**adj.** Physiol. (of a rhythm or cycle) having a period of recurrence shorter than a day but longer than an hour. [1960s: from **ultra-** 'beyond' + **-ian.**]

ul·tra·fil·tra·tion /ˌəltrəfilˈtrāsʜən/ ▶ n. filtration using a medium fine enough to retain colloidal particles, viruses, or large molecules. — **ul·tra·fil·ter** /ˈəltrəˌfiltər/ n. & v.

ul·tra·high fre·quen·cy /ˈəltrəˌhī; ˌəltrəˈhī/ (abbr.: **UHF**) ▶ n. a radio frequency in the range 300 to 3,000 MHz.

ul·tra·ism /ˈəltrəˌizəm/ ▶ n. the holding of extreme opinions. — **ul·tra·ist** n.

ul·tra·light /ˌəltrəˈlīt; ˈəltrəˌlīt/ ▶ adj. extremely lightweight. ▶ n. /ˈəltrəˌlīt/ a small, light, single-seater aircraft.

ul·tra·maf·ic /ˌəltrəˈmafik/ ▶ adj. Geol. relating to or denoting igneous rocks composed chiefly of mafic minerals.

ul·tra·ma·rine /ˌəltrəməˈrēn/ ▶ n. a brilliant deep blue pigment originally obtained from lapis lazuli. ■ an imitation of such a pigment, made from powdered fired clay, sodium carbonate, sulfur, and resin. ■ a brilliant deep blue color. [16th C.: from med. L. *ultramarinus* 'beyond the sea.']

ul·tra·mi·cro·scope /ˌəltrəˈmīkrəˌskōp/ ▶ n. an optical microscope used to detect particles smaller than the wavelength of light.

ul·tra·mi·cro·scop·ic /ˌəltrəˌmīkrəˈskäpik/ ▶ adj. too small to be seen by an ordinary optical microscope. ■ of or relating to an ultramicroscope.

ul·tra·mod·ern /ˌəltrəˈmädərn/ ▶ adj incorporating ideas, styles, or techniques only recently developed or available: *ultramodern architecture.*

ul·tra·mon·tane /ˌəltrəˌmänˈtān; -ˈmänˌtān/ ▶ adj. **1** advocating supreme papal authority in matters of faith and discipline. Compare with **Gallican**. **2** situated on the other side of the Alps from the point of view of the speaker. ▶ n. a person advocating supreme papal authority. — **ul·tra·mon·ta·nism** /-ˈmäntəˌnizəm/ n. [16th C.: from med. L. *ultramontanus*, from L. *ultra* 'beyond' + *mons, mont-* 'mountain.']

ul·tra·mun·dane /ˌəltrəˈmənˌdān; -ˌmənˈdān/ ▶ adj. literary existing outside the known world, the solar system, or the universe. [17th C.: from late L. *ultramundanus*, from *ultra* 'beyond' + *mundanus* (from *mundus* 'world').]

ul·tra·nat·ion·al·ism /ˌəltrəˈnasʜənəˌlizəm/ ▶ n extreme nationalism that promotes the interest of one state or people above all others. — **ul·tra·nat·ion·al·ist** n. & adj. **ul·tra·nat·ion·al·ist·ic** /-ˌnasʜənəˈlistik/ adj.

ul·tra·sau·rus /ˈəltrəˌsôrəs; ˌəltrəˈsôrəs/ ▶ n. a late Jurassic dinosaur (genus *Ultrasaurus*, infraorder Sauropoda) related to the brachiosaurus, known from only a few bones but probably the tallest animal ever, and possibly the heaviest at up to 130 tons. [mod. L., from L. *ultra* 'beyond' + Gk. *sauros* 'lizard.']

ul·tra·short /ˌəltrəˈsʜôrt/ ▶ adj. (of radio waves) having a wavelength significantly shorter than that of the usual shortwaves, in particular shorter than 10 meters.

ul·tra·son·ic /ˌəltrəˈsänik/ ▶ adj. of or involving sound waves with a frequency above the upper limit of human hearing. — **ul·tra·son·i·cal·ly** /-ik(ə)lē/ adv.

ul·tra·son·ics /ˌəltrəˈsäniks/ ▶ plural n. [treated as sing.] the science and application of ultrasonic waves. ■ [treated as sing. or pl.] ultrasonic waves; ultrasound.

ul·tra·so·nog·ra·phy /ˌəltrəsəˈnägrəfē/ ▶ n. Med. a technique using echoes of ultrasound pulses to delineate objects or areas of different density in the body. — **ul·tra·son·o·graph·ic** /əltrəˌsänəˈgrafik; -ˌsōnə-/ adj.

ul·tra·sound /ˈəltrəˌsound/ ▶ n. sound or other vibrations having an ultrasonic frequency, particularly as used in medical imaging. ■ an ultrasound scan, esp. one of a pregnant woman to examine the fetus.

ul·tra·struc·ture /ˈəltrəˌstrəkcʜər/ ▶ n. Biol. a fine structure, esp. within a cell, that can be seen only with the high magnification obtainable with an electron microscope. — **ul·tra·struc·tur·al** /-cʜərəl/ adj.

ul·tra·vi·o·let /ˌəltrəˈvī(ə)lət/ Physics ▶ adj. (of electromagnetic radiation) having a wavelength shorter than that of the violet end of the visible spectrum but longer than that of X-rays. ■ (of equipment or techniques) using or concerned with this radiation: *an ultraviolet telescope.* ▶ n. the ultraviolet part of the spectrum; ultraviolet radiation.

ul·tra·vi·o·let lamp ▶ n. a lamp with a bulb that produces ultraviolet light.

ul·tra vi·res /ˌəltrə ˈvīrēz/ ▶ adj. & adv. Law beyond one's legal power or authority. [L., lit. 'beyond the powers.']

ul·u·late /ˈəlyəˌlāt; ˈyo͞ol-/ ▶ v. [intrans.] howl or wail as an expression of strong emotion, typically grief. — **ul·u·lant** /-lənt/ adj. **ul·u·la·tion** /ˌəlyəˈlāsʜən; ˌyo͞ol-/ n. [17th C.: from L. *ululat-* 'howled, shrieked,' from the verb *ululare*, of imitative origin.]

Ul·u·ru /ˌo͞oləˈro͞o/ Aboriginal name for **Ayers Rock**.

U·lys·ses /yo͞oˈlisēz/ Rom. Mythol. Roman name for **Odysseus**.

um /(ə)m/ ▶ exclam. expressing hesitation or a pause in speech: *anyway, um, where was I?* [natural utterance: early 17th C.]

-um ▶ suffix var. of **-ium** (sense 1).

U·may·yad /o͞oˈmī(y)əd; -ˌ(y)ad/ (also **O·may·yad** /ōˈmī-/) ▶ n. a member of a Muslim dynasty that ruled the Islamic world from AD 660 to 750 and Moorish Spain from 756 to 1031. ▶ adj. of or relating to this dynasty.

Um·ban·da /o͞omˈbändə/ ▶ n. a Brazilian folk religion combining elements of macumba, Roman Catholicism, and South American Indian practices. [Port.]

um·bel /ˈəmbəl/ ▶ n. Bot. a flower cluster in which stalks of nearly equal length spring from a common center and form a flat or curved surface, characteristic of the parsley family. — **um·bel·late** /ˈəmbəlit; -ˌlāt; ˌəmˈbelit/ adj. [16th C.: from obs. Fr. *umbelle* or L. *umbella* 'sunshade.']

um·bel·lif·er /ˌəmˈbeləfər/ ▶ n. Bot. a plant of the parsley family (Umbelliferae). — **um·bel·lif·er·ous** /-bəˈlif(ə)rəs/ adj. [18th C.: from obs. Fr. *umbellifère*, from L. *umbella* 'parasol' + *-fer* 'bearing.']

um·ber /ˈəmbər/ ▶ n. a natural pigment darker than ocher, normally dark yellowish-brown in color (**raw umber**) or dark brown when roasted (**burnt umber**). ■ the color of this pigment. [16th C.: from Fr. *(terre d')ombre* or Ital. *(terra di) ombra*, lit. '(earth of) shadow.']

um·bil·i·cal /ˌəmˈbilikəl/ ▶ adj. relating to or affecting the navel or umbilical cord: *the umbilical artery.* ■ fig. extremely close; inseparable: *their umbilical attachment to the state.* ■ (of a pipe, cable, etc.) connecting someone or something to a source of essential supplies. ▶ n. short for **umbilical cord**. — **um·bil·i·cal·ly** /-ik(ə)lē/ adv.

um·bil·i·cal cord ▶ n. a flexible cordlike structure containing blood vessels and attaching a human or other mammalian fetus to the placenta during gestation. ■ a flexible cable, pipe, or other line carrying essential services or supplies.

um·bil·i·cate /ˌəmˈbilikit; -ˌkāt/ ▶ adj. Bot. & Zool. (esp. of the cap of a fungus) having a central depression. ■ (of a shell) having an umbilicus.

um·bil·i·cus /ˌəmˈbilikəs/ ▶ n. (pl. **-ci** /-ˌkī; -ˌsī; -ˌkē/ or **-cus·es**) Anat. the navel. ■ Zool. a depression or hole at the center of the shell whorls of some gastropod mollusks. ■ Zool. a hole at each end of the hollow shaft of a feather. [17th C.: from L.: rel. to Gk. *omphalos*, also to **navel**.]

um·bo /ˈəmbō/ ▶ n. (pl. **um·bo·nes** /ˌəmˈbōnēz/ or **um·bos**) **1** hist. the central boss of a shield. **2** Biol. a rounded knob or protuberance. ■ Zool. the highest point of each valve of a bivalve shell. ■ Bot. a central swelling on the cap of a mushroom or toadstool. — **um·bo·nal** /ˈəmbənəl; əmˈbōnəl/ adj. **um·bo·nate** /ˈəmbənit; -ˌnāt/ adj. [18th C.: from L., 'shield boss.']

um·bra /ˈəmbrə/ ▶ n. (pl. **-bras** or **-brae** /-ˌbrē; -ˌbrī/) the fully shaded inner region of a shadow cast by an opaque object, esp. the area on the earth or moon experiencing the total phase of an eclipse. Compare with **penumbra**. ■ Astron. the dark central part of a sunspot. ■ esp. literary shadow or darkness. — **um·bral** adj. [16th C.: from L., lit. 'shade.']

um·brage /ˈəmbrij/ ▶ n. **1** offense or annoyance: *she took umbrage at his remarks.* **2** archaic shade or shadow, esp. as cast by trees. — **um·bra·geous** /ˌəmˈbrājəs/ adj. [ME (sense 2): from OFr., from L. *umbra* 'shadow.']

um·brel·la /ˌəmˈbrelə/ ▶ n. **1** a device consisting of a circular canopy of cloth on a folding metal frame supported by a central rod, used as protection against rain or sometimes sun. ■ fig. a protecting force or influence: *the American nuclear umbrella over the west.* ■ [usu. as adj.] a thing that includes or contains many different elements or parts: *an umbrella organization.* **2** Zool. the gelatinous disk of a jellyfish, which it contracts and expands to move through the water. — **um·brel·laed** adj. **um·brel·la·like** /-ˌlīk/ adj. [17th C.: from Ital. *ombrella*, dimin. of *ombra* 'shade,' from L. *umbra* (see **umbra**).]

um·brel·la bird (also **um·brel·la·bird**) ▶ n. a large tropical American passerine bird (genus *Cephalopterus*, family Cotingidae) with black plumage, a radiating crest, and typically long wattles.

um·brel·la plant ▶ n. a tropical Old World sedge (*Cyperus alternifolius*) that has stiff green stems, each terminating in a whorl of arching green leaflike bracts. It is commonly grown as a houseplant.

um·brel·la tree ▶ n. either of two small trees or shrubs with leaves or leaflets arranged in umbrellalike whorls: ■ a North American magnolia (*Magnolia tripetala*). ■ an Australian plant that is widely grown elsewhere as a houseplant (*Schefflera actinophylla*, family Araliaceae).

Um·bri·a /ˈəmbrēə/ a region in central Italy, in the valley of the Tiber River; capital, Perugia.

Um·bri·an /ˈəmbrēən/ ▶ adj. of or relating to Umbria, its people, or their languages. ▶ n. **1** a native or inhabitant of Umbria, esp. in pre-Roman times. **2** an extinct Italic language of central Italy, related to Oscan and surviving in inscriptions mainly of the 2nd and 1st centuries BC.

Um·bun·du /əmˈbo͝onˌdo͞o/ see **Mbundu**.

um·laut /ˈo͝omˌlout/ Ling. ▶ n. a mark (¨) used over a vowel to indicate a different vowel quality, usually fronting or rounding. ▶ v. [trans.] modify (a form or a sound) by using an umlaut. [19th C.: from Ger. *Umlaut*, from *um* 'about' + *Laut* 'sound.']

um·ma /ˈo͝omə/ (also **um·mah**) ▶ n. the whole community of Muslims bound together by ties of religion. [Arab., lit. 'people, community.']

Umm al Qai·wain /ˈo͝om äl kīˈwīn; al/ one of the member states of the United Arab Emirates; pop. 35,000.

ump /əmp/ ▶ n. & v. informal short for **umpire**.

umph ▶ n. var. of **oomph**.

um·pire /ˈəmˌpī(ə)r/ ▶ n. (in some sports) an official who watches a game or match closely to enforce the rules and arbitrate on matters arising from the play. ■ a person chosen to arbitrate between contending parties. ▶ v. [intrans.] act as an umpire. ■ [trans.] act as umpire in (a game or match). — **um·pire·ship** /-ˌsʜip/ n. [ME (orig. as *noumpere*): from OFr. *nonper* 'not equal.']

ump·teen /ˈəm(p)ˌtēn/ informal ▶ cardinal number indefinitely many; a lot of: *umpteen pieces of identification.* — **ump·teenth** /-ˌtēnᴛʜ/ ordinal number. [20th C.: from **-teen**.]

PRONUNCIATION KEY ə *ago, up*; ər *over, fur*; a *hat*; ā *ate*; ä *car*; e *let*; ē *see*; i *fit*; ī *by*; NG *sing*; ō *go*; ô *law, for*; oi *toy*; o͝o *good*; o͞o *goo*; ou *out*; TH *thin*; T͟H *then*; ZH *vision*

Um·welt /ˈo͝om,velt/ ▸ **n.** (pl. **-welt·en** /-,velt(ə)n/) (in ethology) the world as it is experienced by a particular organism. [Ger., lit. 'environment.']

UN ▸ **abbr.** United Nations.

un-¹ ▸ **prefix** **1** (added to adjectives, participles, and their derivatives) denoting the absence of a quality or state; not: *unabashed.* ■ the reverse of (usually with an implication of approval or disapproval, or with another special connotation): *unselfish.* **2** (added to nouns) a lack of: *unrest.* [OE, of Gmc. origin; from an Indo-Eur. root shared by L. *in-* and Gk. *a-*.]

un-² ▸ **prefix** added to verbs: **1** denoting the reversal or cancellation of an action or state: *untie* | *unsettle.* **2** denoting deprivation, separation, or reduction to a lesser state: *unmask* | *unman.* ■ denoting release: *unburden* | *unhand.* [OE *un-*, *on-*, of Gmc. origin; rel. to Du. *ont-* and Ger. *ent-*.]

'un /ən/ informal ▸ **contr.** one: *a good 'un* | *a wild 'un.*

un·a·bashed /,ənəˈbasHt/ ▸ **adj.** not embarrassed, disconcerted, or ashamed. — **un·a·bash·ed·ly** /-ˈbasHədlē/ **adv.**

un·a·bat·ed /,ənəˈbātid/ ▸ **adj.** without any reduction in intensity or strength: *the storm was raging unabated.* — **un·a·bat·ed·ly adv.**

un·a·ble /,ənˈābəl/ ▸ **adj.** [with infin.] lacking the skill, means, or opportunity to do something.

U·na·bomb·er /ˈyo͞onə,bämər/ the name given by the FBI to Ted Kaczynski (1942–), the elusive perpetrator of a series of bombings 1975–1995 in the US that killed 3 and wounded 23. The victims were mainly academics and business executives.

un·a·bridged /,ənəˈbrijd/ ▸ **adj.** (of a text) not cut or shortened; complete: *an unabridged edition.*

un·ac·cept·a·ble /,ənəkˈseptəbəl/ ▸ **adj.** not satisfactory or allowable: *unacceptable behavior.* — **un·ac·cept·a·bil·i·ty** /-,septəˈbilətē/ **n.** **un·ac·cept·a·bly** /-blē/ **adv.**

un·ac·com·pa·nied /,ənəˈkəmp(ə)nēd/ ▸ **adj.** having no companion or escort: *no unaccompanied children allowed.* ■ (of a piece of music) sung or played without instrumental accompaniment. ■ (of a state, condition, or event) taking place without something specified taking place at the same time: *the political change was unaccompanied by social change.*

un·ac·count·a·ble /,ənəˈkountəbəl/ ▸ **adj.** **1** unable to be explained: *a strange and unaccountable fact.* ■ (of a person or their behavior) unpredictable and strange. **2** (of a person, organization, or institution) not required or expected to justify actions or decisions; not responsible for results or consequences. — **un·ac·count·a·bil·i·ty** /-,kountəˈbilətē/ **n.** **un·ac·count·a·bly** /-blē/ **adv.**

un·ac·count·ed /,ənəˈkountid/ ▸ **adj.** (**unaccounted for**) not included in (an account or calculation) through being lost or disregarded.

un·ac·cus·tomed /,ənəˈkəstəmd/ ▸ **adj.** not familiar or usual; out of the ordinary: *unaccustomed speed.* ■ [predic.] (**unaccustomed to**) not familiar with or used to: *the visitors were unaccustomed to country roads.* — **un·ac·cus·tomed·ly adv.**

u·na cor·da /ˈo͞onə ˈkôrdə/ Music ▸ **adv. & adj.** (esp. as a direction) using the soft pedal on a piano. [Ital., lit. 'one string.']

un·a·dul·ter·at·ed /,ənəˈdəltə,rātid/ ▸ **adj.** not mixed or diluted with any different or extra elements; complete and absolute: *pure, unadulterated jealousy.* ■ (of food or drink) having no inferior added substances; pure: *unadulterated whole-milk yogurt.*

un·ad·vis·a·ble /,ənədˈvīzəbəl/ ▸ **adj.** another term for **INADVISABLE**.

un·ad·vis·ed·ly /,ənədˈvīzidlē/ ▸ **adv.** in an unwise or rash manner.

un·aes·thet·ic /,ənesˈTHetik/ ▸ **adj.** not visually pleasing; unattractive. ■ not motivated by aesthetic principles.

un·af·fect·ed /,ənəˈfektid/ ▸ **adj.** **1** feeling or showing no effects or changes: *people who are unaffected by vertigo.* **2** (of a person) without artificiality or insincerity: *his manner was natural and unaffected.* — **un·af·fect·ed·ly adv.** **un·af·fect·ed·ness n.**

Un·a·las·ka /,ənəˈlaskə/ an island in the eastern Aleutian Islands of Alaska.

un·al·le·vi·at·ed /,ənəˈlēvē,ātid/ ▸ **adj.** not alleviated; relentless: *a time of unalleviated misery.*

un·al·loyed /,ənəˈloid/ ▸ **adj.** (of metal) not alloyed; pure: *unalloyed copper.* ■ (chiefly of emotions) complete and unreserved.

un·am·big·u·ous /,ənamˈbigyo͞oəs/ ▸ **adj.** not open to more than one interpretation. — **un·am·bi·gu·i·ty** /-,ambəˈgyo͞oətē/ **n.** **un·am·big·u·ous·ly adv.**

un-A·mer·i·can /,ənəˈmerikən/ ▸ **adj.** not in accordance with American characteristics: *such un-American concepts as subsidized medicine.* ■ esp. hist. contrary to the interests of the US and therefore treasonable. — **un-A·mer·i·can·ism** /-kə,nizəm/ **n.**

U·na·mi /o͞oˈnämē/ ▸ **n.** see **DELAWARE**² (sense 2).

un·a·mused /,ənəˈmyo͞ozd/ ▸ **adj.** not responding in a positive way to something intended to be amusing; feeling somewhat annoyed or disapproving: *she was unamused by some of the things written about her.*

un·a·neled /,ənəˈnēld/ ▸ **adj.** archaic having died without receiving extreme unction; unanointed.

U·na·ni /yo͞oˈnänē/ ▸ **n.** [usu. as adj.] a system of medicine practiced in parts of India, thought to be derived via medieval Muslim physicians from Byzantine Greece. It is sometimes contrasted with the Ayurvedic system. [from Arab. *Yūnānī* 'Greek.']

u·nan·i·mous /yo͞oˈnanəməs/ ▸ **adj.** (of two or more people) fully in agreement. ■ (of an opinion, decision, or vote) held or carried by everyone involved. — **u·na·nim·i·ty** /,yo͞onəˈnimətē/ **n.** **u·nan·i·mous·ly adv.** [17th C.: from L. *unanimus* (from *unus* 'one' + *animus* 'mind') + **-OUS**.]

un·an·nounced /,ənəˈnounst/ ▸ **adj.** not made known; not publicized. ■ without previous notice or arrangement and therefore unexpected.

un·an·swer·a·ble /,ənˈans(ə)rəbəl/ ▸ **adj.** unable to be answered: *unanswerable questions.* ■ unable to be disclaimed or proven wrong: *the case for abolishing the fee is unanswerable.* — **un·an·swer·a·bly** /-blē/ **adv.**

un·an·swered /,ənˈansərd/ ▸ **adj.** not answered or responded to: *unanswered letters.* ■ without any scoring in return by the opposition: *the Hornets scored 34 unanswered points in the second half.*

un·ap·peal·a·ble /,ənəˈpēləbəl/ ▸ **adj.** Law (of a case or ruling) not able to be referred to a higher court.

un·ap·pe·tiz·ing /,ənˈapə,tīziNG/ ▸ **adj.** not inviting or attractive; unwholesome. — **un·ap·pe·tiz·ing·ly adv.**

un·ap·proach·a·ble /,ənəˈprōCHəbəl/ ▸ **adj.** (of a person or institution) not welcoming or friendly. ■ archaic (of a place) remote and inaccessible. — **un·ap·proach·a·bil·i·ty** /-,prōCHəˈbilətē/ **n.** **un·ap·proach·a·bly** /-blē/ **adv.**

un·ar·gu·a·ble /,ənˈärgyo͞oəbəl/ ▸ **adj.** not open to disagreement; indisputable: *unarguable proof of conspiracy.* ■ not able to be discussed or asserted. — **un·ar·gu·a·bly** /-blē/ **adv.**

un·armed /,ənˈärmd/ ▸ **adj.** not equipped with or carrying weapons: *he was shooting unarmed civilians.*

un·ar·tic·u·lat·ed /,ənärˈtikyə,lātid/ ▸ **adj.** not mentioned or coherently expressed: *repressed hurt and previously unarticulated anger are explored.*

u·na·ry /ˈyo͞onərē/ ▸ **adj.** (esp. of a mathematical operation) consisting of or involving a single component or element.

un·a·shamed /,ənəˈSHāmd/ ▸ **adj.** expressed or acting openly and without guilt or embarrassment: *an unashamed emotionalism.* — **un·a·sham·ed·ly** /-ˈSHāmidlē/ **adv.** **un·a·sham·ed·ness** /-ˈSHām(i)dnis/ **n.**

un·asked /,ənˈas(k)t/ ▸ **adj.** (of a question) not asked. ■ (of an action) not invited or requested: *the memories he had poured unasked into her head.* ■ (**unasked for**) not sought or requested: *unasked-for advice.*

un·as·sail·a·ble /,ənəˈsāləbəl/ ▸ **adj.** unable to be attacked, questioned, or defeated: *an unassailable lead.* — **un·as·sail·a·bil·i·ty** /-,sāləˈbilətē/ **n.** **un·as·sail·a·bly** /-blē/ **adv.**

un·as·signed /,ənəˈsīnd/ ▸ **adj.** not allocated or set aside for a specific purpose: *the number of unassigned numbers is being exhausted.*

un·as·sist·ed /,ənəˈsistid/ ▸ **adj.** not helped by anyone or anything: *medically unassisted births.* ■ (of a play in a team sport) done by one player, without an assist from another player.

un·as·suaged /,ənəˈswājd/ ▸ **adj.** not soothed or relieved: *her unassuaged grief.* — **un·as·suage·a·ble** /-əˈswājəbəl/ **adj.**

un·as·sum·ing /,ənəˈso͞omiNG/ ▸ **adj.** not pretentious or arrogant; modest: *an unassuming and kindly man.* — **un·as·sum·ing·ly adv.** **un·as·sum·ing·ness n.**

un·at·tached /,ənəˈtaCHt/ ▸ **adj.** not working for or belonging to a particular body or organization. ■ not fastened to anything; loose. ■ not married or having an established partner; single.

un·at·tain·a·ble /,ənəˈtānəbəl/ ▸ **adj.** not able to be reached or achieved: *an unattainable goal.* — **un·at·tain·a·ble·ness n.** **un·at·tain·a·bly** /-blē/ **adv.**

un·at·tend·ed /,ənəˈtendid/ ▸ **adj.** not noticed or dealt with: *her behavior went unnoticed and **unattended to**.* ■ not supervised or looked after: *it is not acceptable for parents to leave children unattended at that age.*

un·at·test·ed /,ənəˈtestid/ ▸ **adj** not existing in any documented form: *if a will contains unattested changes, the changes will be disregarded.* ■ Ling. a form or usage or pronunciation of a word for which there is no evidence: *logically possible but unattested word-formation.*

un·at·trib·ut·ed /,ənəˈtribyətid/ ▸ **adj.** (of a quotation, story, or work of art) not ascribed to any source; of unknown or unpublished provenance. — **un·at·trib·ut·a·ble** /-yətəbəl/ **adj.** **un·at·trib·ut·a·bly** /-yətəblē/ **adv.**

un·au·then·tic /,ənôˈTHentik/ ▸ **adj.** not made or done in a way that reflects tradition or faithfully resembles an original. — **un·au·then·ti·cal·ly** /-ik(ə)lē/ **adv.**

un·a·vail·ing /,ənəˈvāliNG/ ▸ **adj.** achieving little or nothing; ineffective: *their efforts were unavailing.* — **un·a·vail·ing·ly adv.**

un·a·void·a·ble /,ənəˈvoidəbəl/ ▸ **adj.** not able to be avoided, prevented, or ignored; inevitable: *the natural and unavoidable consequences of growing old.* — **un·a·void·a·bil·i·ty** /-,voidəˈbilətē/ **n.** **un·a·void·a·bly** /-blē/ **adv.**

un·a·ware /,ənəˈwe(ə)r/ ▸ **adj.** [predic.] having no knowledge of a situation or fact: *they were **unaware of** his absence.* ▸ **adv.** variant of **UNAWARES**. — **un·a·ware·ness n.**

un·a·wares /,ənəˈwe(ə)rz/ (also **un·a·ware**) ▸ **adv.** without being aware of a situation: *it will be flagged so that people don't stumble on it unawares.*

– PHRASES **catch** (or **take**) **someone unawares** take someone by surprise. [16th C.: from **UNAWARE** + **-S**³.]

un·backed /,ənˈbakt/ ▸ **adj.** **1** having no financial, material, or moral support. **2** (of a horse) having no backers in a race. **3** having no backing layer: *unbacked burlap.*

un·bal·ance /,ənˈbaləns/ ▸ **v.** [trans.] make (someone or something) unsteady so that they tip or fall. ■ upset or disturb the equilibrium of (a state of affairs or someone's state of mind). ▶ n. a lack of symmetry, balance, or stability.

un·bal·anced /ˌənˈbalənst/ ▶ adj. not keeping or showing an even balance; not evenly distributed. ■ (of a person) emotionally or mentally disturbed. ■ (of an account) not giving accurate, fair, or equal coverage to all aspects; partial.

un·ban /ˌənˈban/ ▶ v. (**-banned**, **-ban·ning**) [trans.] remove a ban on (a person, group, or activity).

un·bar /ˌənˈbär/ ▶ v. (**-barred**, **-bar·ring**) [trans.] remove the bars from (a gate or door); unlock.

un·bear·a·ble /ˌənˈbe(ə)rəbəl/ ▶ adj. not able to be endured or tolerated: *the heat was getting unbearable.* — **un·bear·a·ble·ness** n. **un·bear·a·bly** /-blē/ adv. [as submodifier] *it was unbearably hot.*

un·beat·a·ble /ˌənˈbētəbəl/ ▶ adj. not able to be defeated or exceeded in a contest or commercial market: *the shop sells bikes at unbeatable prices.* ■ extremely good; outstanding: *unbeatable views.* — **un·beat·a·bly** /-blē/ adv.

un·beat·en /ˌənˈbētn/ ▶ adj. not defeated or surpassed: *they were the only team to remain unbeaten.* ■ not stirred or whipped: *the white of an unbeaten egg.*

un·be·com·ing /ˌənbiˈkəmiNG/ ▶ adj. (esp. of clothing or a color) not flattering. ■ (of a person's attitude or behavior) not fitting or appropriate; unseemly. — **un·be·com·ing·ly** adv. **un·be·com·ing·ness** n.

un·be·got·ten /ˌənbəˈgätn/ ▶ adj. archaic not brought into existence by the process of reproduction.

un·be·known /ˌənbiˈnōn/ (also **un·be·knownst** /-ˈnōnst/) ▶ adj. [predic.] (**unbeknown to**) without the knowledge of (someone): *unbeknown to me, she made some inquiries.* [17th C.: from UN-[1] 'not' + archaic *beknown* 'known.']

un·be·lief /ˌənbəˈlēf/ ▶ n. lack of religious belief; an absence of faith. ■ another term for DISBELIEF. — **un·be·liev·er** /-ˈlēvər/ n. **un·be·liev·ing** /-ˈlēviNG/ adj. **un·be·liev·ing·ly** /-ˈlēviNGlē/ adv.

un·be·liev·a·ble /ˌənbəˈlēvəbəl/ ▶ adj. not able to be believed; unlikely to be true: *unbelievable or not, it happened.* ■ so great or extreme as to be difficult to believe; extraordinary: *your audacity is unbelievable.* — **un·be·liev·a·bil·i·ty** /-ˌlēvəˈbilətē/ n. **un·be·liev·a·bly** /-ˈlēvəblē/ adv. [as submodifier] *he worked unbelievably long hours.*

un·belt /ˌənˈbelt/ ▶ v. [trans.] remove or undo the belt of (a garment): *he unbelted his kimono.*

un·belt·ed /ˌənˈbeltid/ ▶ adj. (of a garment) without a belt. ■ (of a person) not wearing a belt, in particular a vehicle seat belt.

un·bend /ˌənˈbend/ ▶ v. (past and past part. **-bent**) **1** make or become straight from a bent or twisted form or position. ■ [intrans.] become less reserved, formal, or strict. **2** [trans.] Sailing unfasten (sails) from yards and stays. ■ cast (a cable) loose. ■ untie (a rope).

un·bend·ing /ˌənˈbendiNG/ ▶ adj. stiff; inflexible. ■ strict and austere in one's behavior or attitudes: *they were unbending in their demands.* — **un·bend·ing·ly** adv. **un·bend·ing·ness** n.

un·bi·ased /ˌənˈbīəst/ (also esp. Brit. **un·bi·assed**) ▶ adj. showing no prejudice for or against something; impartial.

un·bib·li·cal /ˌənˈbiblikəl/ ▶ adj. not found in, authorized by, or based on the Bible.

un·bid·den /ˌənˈbidn/ ▶ adj. without having been commanded or invited: *unbidden guests.* ■ (esp. of a thought or feeling) arising without conscious effort: *unbidden tears came to his eyes.*

un·bind /ˌənˈbīnd/ ▶ v. (past and past part. **-bound**) [trans.] release from bonds or restraints.

un·birth·day /ˌənˈbərTHˌdā/ ▶ n. humorous any day except one's birthday: [as adj.] *an unbirthday present.*

un·blessed /ˌənˈblest/ (also **un·blest**) ▶ adj. not made holy; not consecrated: *unblessed food.* ■ unfortunate; wretched: *a desolate and unblest extent of buffalo grass.* ■ (**unblessed with**) not endowed with (a particular quality or attribute): *to us, unblessed by our own children, he was almost a son.*

un·blind /ˌənˈblīnd/ ▶ v. [trans.] conduct (a test or experiment) in such a way that it is not blind.

un·blink·ing /ˌənˈbliNGkiNG/ ▶ adj. (of a person or their gaze or eyes) not blinking. ■ (of a portrayal or scrutiny) direct, thorough, and honest: *an unblinking portrait of the man.* — **un·blink·ing·ly** adv.

un·block /ˌənˈbläk/ ▶ v. [trans.] remove an obstruction from (something, esp. a pipe or drain).

un·blush·ing /ˌənˈbləSHiNG/ ▶ adj. not feeling or showing embarrassment or shame. — **un·blush·ing·ly** adv.

un·bolt /ˌənˈbōlt/ ▶ v. [trans.] open (a door or window) by drawing back a bolt.

un·bolt·ed /ˌənˈbōltid/ ▶ adj. **1** (of a door or window) not bolted. **2** (of flour, etc.) not sifted.

un·born /ˌənˈbôrn/ ▶ adj. (of a baby) not yet born: fig. *without training, your full talent remains unborn* | [as pl. n.] *the side with the most power will determine how America treats its unborn.*

un·bos·om /ˌənˈbo͝ozəm/ ▶ v. [trans.] archaic disclose (one's thoughts or secrets).

un·both·ered /ˌənˈbäT͟Hərd/ ▶ adj. showing or feeling a lack of concern about or interest in something.

un·bound[1] /ˌənˈbound/ ▶ adj. not bound or tied up: fig. *they were unbound by convention.* ■ (of printed sheets) not bound together. ■ (of a book) not provided with a proper or permanent cover. ■ Chem. & Physics not held by a chemical bond, gravity, or other physical force: *unbound electrons.*

un·bound[2] past and past participle of UNBIND.

un·bound·ed /ˌənˈboundid/ ▶ adj. having or appearing to have no limits: *the possibilities are unbounded.* — **un·bound·ed·ly** adv. **un·bound·ed·ness** n.

un·bowed /ˌənˈboud/ ▶ adj. not having submitted to pressure or demands: *they are unbowed by centuries of colonial rule.*

un·brace /ˌənˈbrās/ ▶ v. [trans.] remove a support from.

un·bri·dle /ənˈbrīdl/ ▶ v. [trans.] remove the bridle from (a horse or mule). ■ release from restraint: [as adj.] *unbridled market forces.*

un·bri·dled /ˌənˈbrīdld/ ▶ adj. uncontrolled; unconstrained: *unbridled lust.*

un·bro·ken /ˌənˈbrōkən/ ▶ adj. not broken, fractured, or damaged: *an unbroken glass.* ■ not interrupted or disturbed; continuous: *a night of unbroken sleep.* ■ (of a record) not surpassed: *an unbroken record of increasing profits.* ■ (of a horse) not tamed or accustomed to being ridden. ■ (of land) not cultivated. — **un·bro·ken·ly** adv. **un·bro·ken·ness** n.

un·build /ˌənˈbild/ ▶ v. (past and past part. **-built**) [trans.] demolish or destroy (something, esp. a building or system). ■ [as adj.] (**unbuilt**) (of buildings or land) not yet built or built on: *a slope of unbuilt land.*

un·bun·dle /ˌənˈbəndl/ ▶ v. [trans.] **1** market or charge for (items or services) separately rather than as part of a package. **2** split (a company or conglomerate) into its constituent businesses, esp. before selling them off. — **un·bun·dler** n. (in sense 2).

un·bur·den /ˌənˈbərdn/ ▶ v. [trans.] relieve (someone) of something that is causing anxiety or distress: *the need to* ***unburden yourself to someone*** *who will listen.*

un·but·ton /ˌənˈbətn/ ▶ v. [trans.] unfasten the buttons of (a garment). ■ [intrans.] informal relax and become less inhibited.

un·called /ˌənˈkôld/ ▶ adj. not summoned or invited. ■ (**uncalled for**) (esp. of a person's behavior) undesirable and unnecessary: *uncalled-for remarks.*

un·can·ny /ˌənˈkanē/ ▶ adj. (**-ni·er**, **-ni·est**) strange or mysterious, esp. in an unsettling way: *an uncanny feeling that she was being watched.* — **un·can·ni·ly** /-ˈkanəl-ē/ adv. **un·can·ni·ness** n. [16th C.: from UN-[1] 'not' + CANNY.]

un·cared /ˌənˈke(ə)rd/ ▶ adj. (**uncared for**) not taken care of properly: *it was sad to see the old place uncared for and neglected* | *uncared-for teeth.*

un·car·ing /ˌənˈke(ə)riNG/ ▶ adj. not displaying sympathy or concern for others: *an uncaring father.* ■ not feeling interest in or attaching importance to something. — **un·car·ing·ly** adv.

Un·cas /ˈəNGkəs/ (c.1588–1683) Mohegan Indian chief. He fought on the side of the British in the Pequot War 1637 and King Philip's War 1675–76.

un·ceas·ing /ˌənˈsēsiNG/ ▶ adj. not coming to an end; continuous: *the unceasing efforts of the staff.* — **un·ceas·ing·ly** adv.

un·cel·e·brat·ed /ˌənˈseləˌbrātid/ ▶ adj. not publicly acclaimed: *an uncelebrated but indispensable role.*

un·cer·e·mo·ni·ous /ˌənserəˈmōnēəs/ ▶ adj. having or showing a lack of formality: *her entertaining was gracious but unceremonious.* ■ abrupt or discourteous: *they make their unceremonious exit from the window.* — **un·cer·e·mo·ni·ous·ly** adv. **un·cer·e·mo·ni·ous·ness** n.

un·cer·tain /ˌənˈsərtn/ ▶ adj. not able to be relied on; not known or definite: *an uncertain future.* ■ (of a person) not completely confident or sure of something: *I was uncertain how to proceed.*

– PHRASES **in no uncertain terms** clearly and forcefully. — **un·cer·tain·ly** adv.

un·cer·tain·ty /ˌənˈsərtntē/ ▶ n. (pl. **-ties**) the state of being uncertain: *times of uncertainty and danger.* ■ (usu. **uncertainties**) something that is uncertain or that causes one to feel uncertain: *financial uncertainties.*

un·cer·tain·ty prin·ci·ple ▶ n. Physics the principle that the momentum and position of a particle cannot both be precisely determined at the same time.

un·chal·lenged /ˌənˈCHalənjd/ ▶ adj. not disputed or questioned: *the report's findings* ***did not go unchallenged.*** ■ (esp. of a person in power) not opposed or defeated. ■ not called on to prove one's identity or allegiance: *they walked unchallenged into a hospital and stole a baby.*

un·charged /ˌənˈCHärjd/ ▶ adj. not charged, in particular: ■ not accused of an offense under the law. ■ not carrying an electric charge. ■ not charged to a particular account.

un·char·i·ta·ble /ˌənˈCHaritəbəl/ ▶ adj. (of a person's behavior or attitude toward others) unkind; unsympathetic. — **un·char·i·ta·ble·ness** n. **un·char·i·ta·bly** /-blē/ adv.

un·chart·ed /ˌənˈCHärtid/ ▶ adj. (of an area of land or sea) not mapped or surveyed.

un·chaste /ˌənˈCHāst/ ▶ adj. relating to or engaging in sexual activity, esp. of an illicit or extramarital nature. — **un·chaste·ly** adv. **un·chas·ti·ty** /-ˈCHastətē/ n.

un·chas·tened /,ən'CHāsənd/ ▶ **adj.** (of a person) not restrained or subdued.

un·chris·tian /,ən'krisCHən/ ▶ **adj.** not professing Christianity or its teachings. ■ (of a person or behavior) unkind, unfair, or morally wrong. — **un·chris·tian·ly adv.**

un·church /,ən'CHərCH/ ▶ **v.** [trans.] officially exclude (someone) from participation in the Christian sacraments; excommunicate. ■ deprive (a building) of its status as a church.

un·churched /,ən'CHərCHt/ ▶ **adj.** [attrib.] not belonging to or connected with a church.

uncial

uncial

un·ci·al /'ənsHəl; -sēəl/ ▶ **adj.** of or written in a majuscule script with rounded unjoined letters that is found in European manuscripts of the 4th–8th centuries and from which modern capital letters are derived. ▶ **n.** an uncial letter or script. ■ a manuscript in uncial script. [17th C.: from L. *uncialis*, from *uncia* 'inch.' Sense 1 is in the late L. sense of *unciales litterae* 'uncial letters.']

un·ci·form /'ənsə,fôrm/ ▶ **adj.** another term for UNCINATE. ■ dated denoting the hamate bone of the wrist.

un·ci·na·ri·a·sis /,ənsənə'rīəsis/ ▶ **n.** another term for ANCYLOSTOMIASIS. [20th C.: from mod. L. *Uncinaria* (the name of a genus of hookworms) + -IASIS.]

un·ci·nate /'ənsənit; -,nāt/ ▶ **adj.** esp. Anat. having a hooked shape. [18th C.: from L. *uncinatus*, from *uncinus* 'hook.']

un·cir·cum·cised /,ən'sərkəm,sīzd/ ▶ **adj.** (of a boy or man) not circumcised. ■ archaic irreligious or heathen. — **un·cir·cum·ci·sion** /-,sərkəm'siZHən/ **n.**

un·civ·il /,ən'sivəl/ ▶ **adj.** discourteous; impolite. — **un·civ·il·ly adv.**

un·civ·i·lized /,ən'sivə,līzd/ ▶ **adj.** (of a place or people) not considered to be socially, culturally, or morally advanced. ■ impolite; badmannered.

un·clad /,ən'klad/ ▶ **adj. 1** unclothed; naked. **2** not provided with cladding: *unclad girders.*

un·clasp /,ən'klasp/ ▶ **v.** [trans.] unfasten (a clasp or similar device): *they unclasped their seat belts.* ■ release the grip of: *I unclasped her fingers from my hair.*

un·clas·si·fied /,ən'klasə,fīd/ ▶ **adj.** not arranged in or assigned to classes or categories: *many texts remain unclassified or uncatalogued.* ■ (of information or documents) not designated as secret.

un·cle /'əNGkəl/ ▶ **n.** the brother of one's father or mother or the husband of one's aunt. ■ informal an unrelated older male friend, esp. of a child. ■ archaic informal a pawnbroker.
– PHRASES **cry** (or **say**) **uncle** informal surrender or admit defeat. [ME: from OFr. *oncle*, from late L. *aunculus*, alt. of L. *avunculus* 'maternal uncle' (see AVUNCULAR).]

-uncle ▶ **suffix** forming chiefly diminutive nouns: *carbuncle* | *peduncle.* [from OFr. *-oncle*, *-uncle*, or from L. *-unculus*, a special form of *-ulus.*]

un·clean /,ən'klēn/ ▶ **adj.** dirty: *the company was fined for operating in unclean premises.* ■ morally wrong: *unclean thoughts.* ■ (of food) regarded in a particular religion as impure and unfit to be eaten. ■ (in biblical use) ritually impure; (of a spirit) evil. — **un·clean·ness n.**

un·clean·li·ness /,ən'klenlēnis/ ▶ **n.** the state of being dirty: *head lice and general uncleanliness in schools.*

un·clean·ly /,ən'klenlē/ ▶ **adj.** archaic term for UNCLEAN.

un·clear /,ən'kli(ə)r/ ▶ **adj.** not easy to see, hear, or understand: *the motive for this killing is unclear.* ■ not obvious or definite; ambiguous. ■ having or feeling doubt or confusion. — **un·clear·ly adv. un·clear·ness n.**

un·cleared /,ən'kli(ə)rd/ ▶ **adj.** not having been cleared or cleared up, in particular: ■ (of a check) not having passed through a clearinghouse and been paid into the payee's account. ■ (of land) not cleared of vegetation before cultivation.

Un·cle Sam /sam/ a personification of the federal government or citizens of the US, typically portrayed as a tall, thin, bearded man wearing a suit of red, white, and blue. [19th C.: said to be an expansion of *US.*]

Un·cle Tom /täm/ ▶ **n.** derog. a black man considered to be excessively obedient or servile. — **Un·cle Tom·ism** /'täm,izəm/ **n.** [1920s: from the name of the hero of H. B. Stowe's *Uncle Tom's Cabin* (1852).]

un·climbed /,ən'klīmd/ ▶ **adj.** (of a mountain or rock face) not previously climbed: *the unclimbed south ridge.* — **un·climb·a·ble** /-'klīməbəl/ **adj.**

un·cloak /,ən'klōk/ ▶ **v.** [trans.] literary uncover; reveal.

un·clog /,ən'klôg; -'kläg/ ▶ **v.** (**-clogged, -clog·ging**) [trans.] remove accumulated glutinous matter from: *exfoliation unclogs pores and prevents blackheads.*

un·clothe /,ən'klōTH/ ▶ **v.** [trans.] remove the clothes from (oneself or someone).

un·co /'əNGkō; -kə/ Scot. ▶ **adj.** unusual or remarkable. ▶ **adv.** [as submodifier] remarkably; very: *it's got an unco fine taste.* ▶ **n.** (pl. **-cos**) a stranger. ■ (**uncos**) news. [ME: alt. of UNCOUTH.]

un·coil /,ən'koil/ ▶ **v.** straighten or cause to straighten from a coiled or curled position.

un·col·lect·ed /,ənkə'lektid/ ▶ **adj.** (esp. of money) not collected or claimed: *the reward remained uncollected.* ■ left awaiting collection: *bursting sacks of uncollected trash.* ■ (of literary works) not previously published.

un·col·ored /,ən'kələrd/ (Brit. **un·col·oured**) ▶ **adj.** having no color; neutral in color. ■ not influenced, esp. in a negative way: *explanations that are uncolored by the observer's feelings.*

un·com·fort·a·ble /,ən'kəmfərtəbəl; -'kəmftərbəl/ ▶ **adj.** causing or feeling slight pain or physical discomfort: *athlete's foot is a painful and uncomfortable condition.* ■ causing or feeling unease or awkwardness. *an uncomfortable silence.* — **un·com·fort·a·ble·ness n. un·com·fort·a·bly** /-blē/ **adv.** [as submodifier] *the house was dark and uncomfortably cold.*

un·com·ment /,ən'käm,ent/ ▶ **v.** [trans.] Comput. change (a piece of text within a program) from being a comment to being part of the program that is run by the computer.

un·com·mer·cial /,ənkə'mərsHəl/ ▶ **adj.** not making, intended to make, or allowing a profit. ■ not having profit as a primary aim.

un·com·mit·ted /,ənkə'mitid/ ▶ **adj.** not committed to a particular course or policy: *uncommitted voters.* ■ (of resources) not pledged or set aside for future use. ■ (of a person) not pledged to remain in a long-term emotional relationship with someone.

un·com·mon /,ən'kämən/ ▶ **adj.** out of the ordinary; unusual: *an uncommon name.* ■ [attrib.] remarkably great (used for emphasis): *an uncommon amount of noise.* ▶ **adv.** [as submodifier] archaic remarkably: *he was uncommon afraid.* — **un·com·mon·ly adv.** [as submodifier] *an uncommonly large crowd.* **un·com·mon·ness n.**

un·com·mu·ni·ca·tive /,ənkə'myōōnəkətiv; -,kātiv/ ▶ **adj.** unwilling to talk or impart information. ■ (of something such as writing or art) not conveying much or any meaning or sense. — **un·com·mu·ni·ca·tive·ly adv. un·com·mu·ni·ca·tive·ness n.**

un·com·pen·sat·ed /,ən'kämpən,sātid/ ▶ **adj.** (of a person or expense) not compensated or reimbursed. ■ (of an action) not compensated for: *uncompensated exploitation of the Third World.* ■ (of work) unpaid.

un·com·pet·i·tive /,ənkəm'petətiv/ ▶ **adj.** (with reference to business or commerce) not competitive. ■ characterized by a desire to avoid fair competition: *uncompetitive practices.* — **un·com·pet·i·tive·ly adv. un·com·pet·i·tive·ness n.**

un·com·plain·ing /,ənkəm'plāniNG/ ▶ **adj.** not complaining; resigned. — **un·com·plain·ing·ly adv.**

un·com·pli·cat·ed /,ən'kämplə,kātid/ ▶ **adj.** simple or straightforward.

un·com·pre·hend·ing /,ən,kämpri'hendiNG/ ▶ **adj.** showing or having an inability to comprehend something: *an uncomprehending silence.* — **un·com·pre·hend·ing·ly adv.**

un·com·pro·mis·ing /,ən'kämprə,mīziNG/ ▶ **adj.** showing an unwillingness to make concessions to others, esp. by changing one's ways or opinions. ■ harsh or relentless: *the uncompromising ugliness of her home.* — **un·com·pro·mis·ing·ly adv. un·com·pro·mis·ing·ness n.**

un·con·cern /,ənkən'sərn/ ▶ **n.** a lack of worry or interest, esp. when surprising or callous.

un·con·cerned /,ənkən'sərnd/ ▶ **adj.** showing a lack of worry or interest, esp. when this is surprising or callous: *Scott seemed unconcerned by his companion's problem.* — **un·con·cern·ed·ly** /-'sərnədlē/ **adv.**

un·con·di·tion·al /,ənkən'disHənl; -'disHnəl/ ▶ **adj.** not subject to any conditions: *unconditional surrender.* — **un·con·di·tion·al·i·ty** /-,disHə'nalətē/ **n. un·con·di·tion·al·ly adv.**

un·con·di·tioned /,ənkən'disHənd/ ▶ **adj. 1** not subject to conditions or to an antecedent condition; unconditional: *pure and unconditioned love.* **2** relating to or denoting instinctive reflexes or other behavior not formed or influenced by conditioning or learning: *an unconditioned response.* **3** not subjected to a conditioning process: *waste in its raw, unconditioned form.*

un·con·form·a·ble /,ənkən'fôrməbəl/ ▶ **adj.** Geol. (of rock strata in contact) marking a discontinuity in the geological record, and typically not having the same direction of stratification. — **un·com·form·a·bly** /-blē/ **adv.**

un·con·form·i·ty /,ənkən'fôrmətē/ ▶ **n.** Geol. a surface of contact between two groups of unconformable strata. ■ the condition of being unconformable.

un·con·nect·ed /,ənkə'nektid/ ▶ **adj.** not joined together or to something else: *the ground wire was left unconnected.* ■ not associated or linked in a sequence: *two unconnected events.* ■ not having relatives in important or influential positions. — **un·con·nect·ed·ly adv. un·con·nect·ed·ness n.**

un·con·quer·a·ble /,ən'käNGk(ə)rəbəl/ ▶ **adj.** (esp. of a place, people, or emotion) not conquerable: *an unconquerable pride.* — **un·con·quer·a·bly** /-blē/ **adv.**

un·con·scion·a·ble /,ən'känsH(ə)nəbəl/ ▶ **adj.** not right or reasonable: *the unconscionable conduct of his son.* ■ unreasonably excessive: *shareholders have had to wait an unconscionable time for the facts to be established.* — **un·con·scion·a·bly** /-blē/ **adv.** [16th C.: from UN-[1] 'not' + obs. *conscionable*, from CONSCIENCE + -ABLE.]

un·con·scious /,ən'känsHəs/ ▶ **adj.** not conscious. ■ done or existing without one realizing: *an unconscious gesture of annoyance.* ■ [predic.] (**unconscious of**) unaware of: *"What is it?" he said again, unconscious of the repetition.* ▶ **n.** (**the unconscious**) the part of the mind that is inaccessible to the conscious mind but that affects behavior and emotions. — **un·con·scious·ly adv. un·con·scious·ness n.**

un·con·sid·ered /ˌənkənˈsidərd/ ▶ **adj.** disregarded and unappreciated: *a penchant for picking up unconsidered trifles.* ■ (of a statement or action) not thought about in advance, and therefore rash or harsh.

un·con·sol·a·ble /ˌənkənˈsōləbəl/ ▶ **adj.** inconsolable. — **un·con·sol·a·bly** /-blē/ **adv.**

un·con·sti·tu·tion·al /ˌənˌkänstəˈt(y)o͞oshənl/ ▶ **adj.** not in accordance with a political constitution, esp. the US Constitution, or with procedural rules. — **un·con·sti·tu·tion·al·i·ty** /-ˌt(y)o͞oshəˈnalətē/ **n.** **un·con·sti·tu·tion·al·ly adv.**

un·con·straint /ˌənkənˈstrānt/ ▶ **n.** freedom from constraint.

un·con·struct·ed /ˌənkənˈstrəktid/ ▶ **adj.** (of a garment) unstructured.

un·con·tro·vert·ed /ˌənˌkäntrəˈvərtid/ ▶ **adj.** of which the truth or validity is not disputed.

un·con·ven·tion·al /ˌənkənˈvenshənl/ ▶ **adj.** not based on or conforming to what is generally done or believed: *his unconventional approach to life.* — **un·con·ven·tion·al·i·ty** /-ˌvenshəˈnalətē/ **n.** **un·con·ven·tion·al·ly adv.**

un·con·vert·ed /ˌənkənˈvərtid/ ▶ **adj.** not converted, in particular: ■ (of a building) not adapted to a different use. ■ not having adopted a different religion, belief, or practice: *unconverted pagans.*

un·con·vinced /ˌənkənˈvinst/ ▶ **adj.** not certain that something is true or can be relied on or trusted: *Parisians remain* ***unconvinced that*** *the project will be approved.*

un·con·vinc·ing /ˌənkənˈvinsiNG/ ▶ **adj.** failing to make someone believe that something is true or valid. ■ failing to impress: *an unconvincing fusion of forces.* — **un·con·vinc·ing·ly adv.**

un·cool /ˌənˈko͞ol/ ▶ **adj.** informal not fashionable or impressive: *an uncool haircut.*

un·cork /ˌənˈkôrk/ ▶ **v.** [trans.] pull the cork out of (a bottle or other container). ■ fig. allow (feelings) to be vented. ■ informal (in a game or sport) deliver (a kick, throw, or punch): *he uncorked the best throw of his career.*

un·count·a·ble /ˌənˈkountəbəl/ ▶ **adj.** too many to be counted (usually in hyperbolic use): *she'd spent uncountable nights in this very bed.* — **un·count·a·bil·i·ty** /-ˌkountəˈbilətē/ **n.** **un·count·a·bly** /-blē/ **adv.**

un·count·ed /ˌənˈkountid/ ▶ **adj.** not counted. ■ very numerous: *uncounted millions of dollars.*

un·cou·ple /ˌənˈkəpəl/ ▶ **v.** [trans.] disconnect (something, esp. a railroad vehicle that has been coupled to another). ■ [intrans.] become disconnected: *the groups of cells commonly uncouple from surrounding tissue.* ■ release (hunting dogs) from being fastened together in couples.

un·court·ly /ˌənˈkôrtlē/ ▶ **adj.** not courteous or refined.

un·couth /ˌənˈko͞oTH/ ▶ **adj.** (of a person or their appearance or behavior) lacking good manners, refinement, or grace: *he is unwashed, uncouth, and drunk most of the time.* ■ (esp. of art or language) lacking sophistication or delicacy. ■ archaic (of a place) uncomfortable, esp. because of remoteness or poor conditions. — **un·couth·ly adv.** **un·couth·ness n.** [OE *uncūth* 'unknown,' from **UN-¹** 'not' + *cūth* (past part. of *cunnan* 'know, be able').]

un·cov·e·nant·ed /ˌənˈkəv(ə)nəntid/ ▶ **adj.** not bound by or in accordance with a covenant or agreement. ■ not promised by or based on a covenant, esp. a covenant with God.

un·cov·er /ˌənˈkəvər/ ▶ **v.** [trans.] remove a cover or covering from: *he uncovered the face of the dead man.* ■ discover (something previously secret or unknown): *further evidence has been uncovered.* ■ [intrans.] archaic remove one's hat, esp. as a mark of respect.

un·cov·ered /ˌənˈkəvərd/ ▶ **adj.** **1** without a lid or cover: *bake uncovered until cheese begins to brown.* ■ having had the cover removed. ■ without a hat or other covering for the head. **2** not covered by insurance. ■ (of loans) not secured by collateral. **3** not treated or dealt with along with other subjects: *he left the most important topic uncovered.*

un·cre·ate /ˌənkrēˈāt/ ▶ **v.** [trans.] literary destroy.

un·cre·at·ed /ˌənkrēˈātid/ ▶ **adj.** (esp. of a divine being) existing without having been created. ■ not yet created.

un·crit·i·cal /ˌənˈkritikəl/ ▶ **adj.** not expressing criticism; complacently accepting: *uncritical acclaim in the media.* ■ not using one's critical faculties: *uncritical apologists for the country.* ■ not in accordance with the principles of critical analysis: *uncritical reasoning.* — **un·crit·i·cal·ly** /-ik(ə)lē/ **adv.**

un·cross /ˌənˈkrôs; -ˈkräs/ ▶ **v.** [trans.] move (something) back from a crossed position: *the reporter uncrossed his legs.*

un·crown /ˌənˈkroun/ ▶ **v.** [trans.] deprive (a monarch) of their ruling position.

un·crowned /ˌənˈkround/ ▶ **adj.** not formally crowned as a monarch.

UNCSTD ▶ **abbr.** United Nations Conference on Science and Technology for Development.

UNCTAD /ˈəNGkˌtad/ ▶ **abbr.** United Nations Conference on Trade and Development.

unc·tion /ˈəNG(k)shən/ ▶ **n.** **1** formal the action of anointing someone with oil or ointment as a religious rite or as a symbol of investiture as a monarch. ■ the oil or ointment so used. ■ short for **EXTREME UNCTION**. **2** archaic treatment with a medicinal oil or ointment. ■ an ointment: *mercury in the form of unctions.* **3** a manner of expression arising or apparently arising from deep emotion, esp. as intended to flatter: *he spoke the last two words with exaggerated unction.* [ME: from L. *unctio(n-)*, from *unguere* 'anoint.']

unc·tu·ous /ˈəNG(k)CHo͞oəs/ ▶ **adj.** **1** (of a person) excessively or ingratiatingly flattering; oily: *anxious to please in an unctuous way.* **2** (chiefly of minerals) having a greasy or soapy feel. — **unc·tu·ous·ly adv.** **unc·tu·ous·ness n.** [ME (in the sense 'greasy'): from med. L. *unctuosus*, from L. *unctus* 'anointing,' from *unguere* 'anoint.']

un·cul·ti·vat·ed /ˌənˈkəltəˌvātid/ ▶ **adj.** (of land) not used for growing crops. ■ (of a person) not highly educated.

un·curl /ˌənˈkərl/ ▶ **v.** straighten or cause to straighten from a curled position.

un·cut /ˌənˈkət/ ▶ **adj.** not cut: *her hair was left uncut.* ■ (of a text, movie, or performance) complete; unabridged. ■ (of a stone, esp. a diamond) not shaped by cutting. ■ (of alcohol or a drug) not diluted or adulterated: *large amounts of uncut heroin.* ■ esp. hist. (of a book) with the edges of its pages not slit open or trimmed off. ■ (of fabric) having its pile loops intact.

un·daunt·ed /ˌənˈdôntid; -ˈdän-/ ▶ **adj.** not intimidated or discouraged by difficulty, danger, or disappointment. — **un·daunt·ed·ly adv.** **un·daunt·ed·ness n.**

un·dead /ˌənˈded/ ▶ **adj.** (of a fictional being, esp. a vampire) technically dead but still animate.

un·dec·a·gon /ˌənˈdekəˌgän/ ▶ **n.** another term for **HENDECAGON**. [18th C.: from L. *undecim* 'eleven.']

un·de·ceive /ˌəndiˈsēv/ ▶ **v.** [trans.] tell (someone) that an idea or belief is mistaken: *they took her for a nun, and Mary said nothing to undeceive them.*

un·de·cid·a·ble /ˌəndiˈsīdəbəl/ ▶ **adj.** not able to be firmly established or refuted. ■ Logic (of a proposition or theorem) not able to be proved or disproved. — **un·de·cid·a·bil·i·ty** /-ˌsīdəˈbilətē/ **n.**

un·de·clared /ˌəndiˈkle(ə)rd/ ▶ **adj.** not publicly announced, admitted, or acknowledged: *his undeclared candidacy, which surged in the polls last spring.* ■ (esp. of taxable income or dutiable goods) not declared.

un·de·lete /ˌəndiˈlēt/ ▶ **v.** [trans.] Comput. cancel the deletion of (text or a file).

un·de·mon·stra·tive /ˌəndiˈmänstrətiv/ ▶ **adj.** (of a person) not tending to express feelings, esp. of affection, openly: *John is silent and undemonstrative, like Dad.* — **un·de·mon·stra·tive·ly adv.** **un·de·mon·stra·tive·ness n.**

un·de·ni·a·ble /ˌəndiˈnīəbəl/ ▶ **adj.** unable to be denied or disputed: *an undeniable fact | ornate fireplaces give the place undeniable class.* — **un·de·ni·a·bly** /-blē/ **adv.** [sentence adverb] *the topic is undeniably an important one.*

un·der /ˈəndər/ ▶ **prep.** **1** extending or directly below: *the streams that ran under the melting glaciers.* ■ below (something covering or protecting): *a hot plate under an insulated lid.* **2** at a lower level or layer than: *the room under his study.* ■ behind (a physical surface): *it was written on the new canvas under a gluey coating.* ■ behind or hidden behind (an appearance or disguise): *he had a deep sense of fun under his quiet exterior.* ■ lower in grade or rank than: *under him in the hierarchy.* **3** used to express dominance or control: *under his spell.* ■ during (a specified time period, reign, or administration): *under the pontificate of Paul II.* ■ as a reaction to or undergoing the pressure of (something): *certain institutions may be under threat.* ■ as provided for by the rules of; in accordance with: *flowers supplied under contract by a local florist.* ■ used to express grouping or classification: *published under his own name.* ■ Comput. within the environment of (a particular operating system): *the program runs under DOS.* **4** lower than (a specified amount, rate, or norm): *they averaged just under 2.8 percent.* **5** undergoing (a process): *under construction.* ■ in an existent state of: *children living under difficult circumstances.* ■ planted with: *fields under wheat.* ▶ **adv.** **1** extending or directly below something: *weaving the body through the crossbars, over and under.* **2** under water: *he was floating but suddenly went under.* ▶ **adj.** **1** denoting the lowest part or surface of something; on the underside: *the under part of the shell is concave.* **2** unconscious, typically as a result of general anesthesia: *she was only under for 15 minutes.* — **un·der·most** /-ˌmōst/ **adj.** [OE, of Gmc. origin; rel. to Du. *onder* and Ger. *unter.*]

under- ▶ **prefix** **1** below; beneath: *underclothes | undercover.* ■ lower in status; subordinate: *undersecretary.* **2** insufficiently; incompletely: *undernourished.*

un·der·a·chieve /ˌəndərəˈCHēv/ ▶ **v.** [intrans.] do less well than is expected, esp. in schoolwork. — **un·der·a·chieve·ment n.** **un·der·a·chiev·er n.**

un·der·act /ˌəndərˈakt/ ▶ **v.** [intrans.] act a part in a play or film in an overly restrained or unemotional way.

un·der·age /ˌəndərˈāj/ ▶ **adj.** (of a person) too young to engage legally in a particular activity, esp. drinking alcohol or having sex. ■ [attrib.] (of an activity) engaged in by people who are underage: *underage drinking.*

un·der·arm /ˈəndərˌärm/ ▶ **adj.** & **adv.** another term for **UNDERHAND** (sense 2). ▶ **n.** a person's armpit: [as adj.] *use an underarm deodorant.*

un·der·bel·ly /ˈəndərˌbelē/ ▶ **n.** (pl. **-lies**) the soft underside or abdomen of an animal. ■ fig. an area vulnerable to attack: *these multinationals have a soft underbelly.* ■ fig. a hidden unpleasant or criminal part of society.

un·der·bid ▶ **v.** /ˌəndərˈbid/ (**-bid·ding**; past and past part. **-bid**) [trans.] (in an auction or when seeking a contract) make a lower bid than (someone). ■ Bridge make a lower bid on (one's hand) than its strength warrants.

▶**n.** /ˈəndər,bid/ a bid that is lower than another or than is justified. — **un·der·bid·der** /,əndərˈbidər/ **n.**

un·der·bite /ˈəndər,bīt/ ▶**n.** (in nontechnical use) the projection of the lower teeth beyond the upper.

un·der·bod·y /ˈəndər,bädē/ ▶**n.** (pl. **-bod·ies**) the underside of a road vehicle, ship, or animal's body.

un·der·boss /ˈəndər,bôs; -,bäs/ ▶**n.** a boss's deputy, esp. in a criminal organization.

un·der·bred /,əndərˈbred/ ▶**adj.** dated ill-mannered; rude.

un·der·brush /ˈəndər,brəsн/ ▶**n.** shrubs and small trees forming the undergrowth in a forest.

un·der·cap·i·tal·ize /,əndərˈkapətl,īz/ ▶**v.** [trans.] provide (a company) with insufficient capital to achieve desired results. — **un·der·cap·i·tal·i·za·tion** /-,kapətl-əˈzāsнən/ **n.**

un·der·card /ˈəndər,kärd/ ▶**n.** the list of less important bouts on the same bill as a main boxing match.

un·der·car·riage /ˈəndər,karij/ ▶**n.** a wheeled structure beneath an aircraft, typically retracted when not in use, that receives the impact on landing and supports the aircraft on the ground. ■ the supporting frame under the body of a vehicle.

un·der·cast /,əndərˈkast/ ▶**v.** (past and past part. **-cast**) [trans.] (usu. **be undercast**) allocate the parts in (a play or movie) to insufficiently skilled actors.

un·der·charge /,əndərˈcнärj/ ▶**v.** [trans.] **1** charge (someone) a price or amount that is too low. **2** give less than the proper charge to (an electric battery). ▶**n.** /ˈəndər,cнärj/ a charge that is insufficient.

un·der·class /ˈəndər,klas/ ▶**n.** the lowest social stratum in a country or community, consisting of the poor and unemployed.

un·der·class·man /,əndərˈklasmən/ ▶**n.** (pl. **underclassmen**) a student in high school or college who is not a senior.

un·der·cling /ˈəndər,kliNG/ Climbing ▶**n.** a handhold that faces down the rock face. ▶**v.** [intrans.] climb using such handholds.

un·der·clothes /ˈəndər,klō(TH)z/ ▶**plural n.** clothes worn under others, typically next to the skin.

un·der·cloth·ing /ˈəndər,klōTHiNG/ ▶**n.** underclothes.

un·der·coat /ˈəndər,kōt/ ▶**n.** **1** a layer of paint applied after the primer and before the topcoat. **2** an animal's underfur or down. ▶**v.** [trans.] apply a coat of undercoat to (something).

un·der·con·sump·tion /,əndərkənˈsəm(p)sнən/ ▶**n.** Econ. purchase of goods and services at a level lower than that of their supply.

un·der·cook /,əndərˈko͝ok; ˈəndər,ko͝ok/ ▶**v.** [trans.] [usu. as adj.] (**undercooked**) cook (something) insufficiently: *undercooked meats.*

un·der·cool /,əndərˈko͞ol/ ▶**v.** another term for SUPERCOOL.

un·der·count ▶**v.** /,əndərˈkount/ [trans.] enumerate (something, esp. a sector of a population in a census) at a lower figure than the actual figure. ▶**n.** /ˈəndər,kount/ a count or figure that is inaccurately low. ■ the amount by which such a count or figure falls short of the actual figure.

un·der·cov·er /,əndərˈkəvər/ ▶**adj.** (of a person or their activities) involved in or involving secret work within a community or organization, esp. for the purposes of police investigation or espionage: *an undercover police operation.* ▶**adv.** as an undercover agent: *a special unit of the police that operates undercover.*

un·der·croft /ˈəndər,krôft; -,kräft/ ▶**n.** the crypt of a church. [ME: from UNDER- + the rare term *croft* 'crypt,' from MDu. *crofte* 'cave,' from L. *crypta.*]

un·der·cur·rent /ˈəndər,kərənt/ ▶**n.** a current of water below the surface, moving in a different direction from any surface current. ■ fig. an underlying feeling or influence, esp. one that is contrary to the prevailing atmosphere and is not expressed openly: *an undercurrent of anger.*

un·der·cut ▶**v.** /,əndərˈkət/ (**-cut·ting**; past and past part. **-cut**) [trans.] **1** offer goods or services at a lower price than (a competitor): *these industries have been undercut by more efficient foreign producers.* **2** cut or wear away the part below or under (something, esp. a cliff). ■ fig. weaken; undermine: *the chairman denied his authority was being undercut.* ■ cut away material to leave (a carved design) in relief. **3** (in sports such as tennis or golf) strike (a ball) with a chopping motion so as to give it backspin. ▶**n.** /ˈəndər,kət/ **1** a space formed by the removal or absence of material from the lower part of something, such as a cliff, a coal seam, or part of a carving in relief. ■ a notch cut in a tree trunk to guide its fall when felled. **2** Brit. the underside of a sirloin of beef.

un·der·damp /,əndərˈdamp/ ▶**v.** [trans.] Physics damp (a system) incompletely, so as to allow a few oscillations after a single disturbance.

un·der·de·ter·mine /,əndərdiˈtərmən/ ▶**v.** [trans.] (usu. **be underdetermined**) account for (a theory or phenomenon) with less than the amount of evidence needed for proof or certainty. — **un·der·de·ter·mi·na·tion** /-,tərməˈnāsнən/ **n.**

un·der·de·vel·oped /,əndərdiˈveləpt/ ▶**adj.** not fully developed: *underdeveloped kidneys.* ■ (of a country or region) not advanced economically. ■ (of photographic film) not developed sufficiently to give a normal image. — **un·der·de·vel·op·ment** /-əpmənt/ **n.**

un·der·dog /ˈəndər,dôg; -,däg/ ▶**n.** a competitor thought to have little chance of winning a fight or contest. ■ a person who has little status in society.

un·der·done /,əndərˈdən/ ▶**adj.** (of food) insufficiently cooked.

un·der·draw·ing /ˈəndər,drôiNG/ ▶**n.** sketched lines made by a painter as a preliminary guide, and subsequently covered with layers of paint.

un·der·dress /,əndərˈdres/ ▶**v.** [intrans.] (also **be underdressed**) dress too plainly or too informally.

un·der·ed·u·cat·ed /,əndərˈejə,kātid/ ▶**adj.** poorly educated.

un·der·em·pha·size /,əndərˈemfə,sīz/ ▶**v.** [trans.] (usu. **be underemphasized**) place insufficient emphasis on: *history is underemphasized in the curriculum.* — **un·der·em·pha·sis** /-sis/ **n.**

un·der·em·ployed /,əndərimˈploid/ ▶**adj.** (of a person) not doing work that makes full use of their skills and abilities. ■ (of a person) not having enough paid work. — **un·der·em·ploy·ment** /-ˈploimənt/ **n.**

un·der·es·ti·mate ▶**v.** /,əndərˈestə,māt/ [trans.] estimate (something) to be smaller or less important than it actually is. ■ regard (someone) as less capable than they really are: *he had underestimated the new president.* ▶**n.** /-mit/ [usu. in sing.] an estimate that is too low. — **un·der·es·ti·ma·tion** /-,estəˈmāsнən/ **n.**

un·der·ex·pose /,əndərikˈspōz/ ▶**v.** [trans.] Photog. expose (film or an image) for too short a time. — **un·der·ex·po·sure** /-ˈspōzнər/ **n.**

un·der·fed /,əndərˈfed/ ▶**adj.** insufficiently fed or nourished.

un·der·floor /,əndərˈflôr/ ▶**adj.** situated or operating beneath the floor.

un·der·flow /ˈəndər,flō/ ▶**n.** **1** an undercurrent. ■ a horizontal flow of water through the ground, esp. one underneath a riverbed. **2** Comput. the generation of a number that is too small to be represented in the device meant to store it.

un·der·foot /,əndərˈfo͝ot/ ▶**adv.** under one's feet; on the ground: *it was very muddy underfoot.* ■ constantly present and in one's way: *the last thing my mother wanted was a child underfoot.*

un·der·fund /,əndərˈfənd/ ▶**v.** [trans.] (usu. **be underfunded**) provide with insufficient funding. — **un·der·fund·ing** **n.**

un·der·fur /ˈəndər,fər/ ▶**n.** an inner layer of short, fine fur or down underlying an animal's outer fur, providing warmth and waterproofing.

un·der·gar·ment /ˈəndər,gärmənt/ ▶**n.** an article of underclothing.

un·der·gird /,əndərˈgərd/ ▶**v.** [trans.] secure or fasten from the underside, esp. by a rope or chain passed underneath. ■ formal provide support or a firm basis for.

un·der·glaze /ˈəndər,glāz/ ▶**adj.** (of decoration on pottery) done before the glaze is applied. ■ (of colors) used in such decoration. ▶**n.** a color or design applied in this way.

un·der·go /,əndərˈgō/ ▶**v.** (**-goes**; past **-went**; past part. **-gone**) [trans.] experience or be subjected to (something, typically something unpleasant, painful, or arduous): *the baby underwent a life-saving brain operation.*

un·der·grad /ˈəndər,grad/ ▶**n.** informal an undergraduate.

un·der·grad·u·ate /,əndərˈgrajo͞oit/ ▶**n.** a student at a college or university who has not yet earned a bachelor's or equivalent degree. ▶**adj.** designed for or typical of undergraduates: *I'm taking undergraduate classes.*

un·der·ground ▶**adv.** /,əndərˈground/ beneath the surface of the ground: *miners working underground.* ■ in or into secrecy or hiding, esp. as a result of carrying out subversive political activities: *many were forced to go underground by the government.* ▶**adj.** /ˈəndər,ground/ situated beneath the surface of the ground: *underground parking garages.* ■ of or relating to the secret activities of people working to subvert an established order: *Czech underground literature.* ■ of or denoting a group or movement seeking to explore alternative forms of lifestyle or artistic expression; radical and experimental: *the New York underground art scene.* ▶**n.** /ˈəndər,ground/ **1** a group or movement organized secretly to work against an existing regime: *I got involved with the French underground.* ■ a group or movement seeking to explore alternative forms of lifestyle or artistic expression. **2** (**the Underground**) Brit. a subway, esp. the one in London: *travel chaos on the Underground.*

un·der·ground e·con·o·my ▶**n.** the part of a country's economic activity that is unrecorded and untaxed by its government.

Un·der·ground Rail·road a secret network for helping slaves escape from the South to the North and Canada in the years before the American Civil War.

un·der·growth /ˈəndər,grōTH/ ▶**n.** a dense growth of shrubs and other plants, esp. under trees in woodland.

un·der·hand ▶**adj.** /ˈəndər,hand/ **1** (of a throw or stroke in sports) made with the arm or hand below shoulder level: *he has a surprisingly good motion, more sidearm than underhand* | [as adv.] *I served underhand.* ■ with the palm of the hand upward or outward: *an underhand grip.* **2** another term for UNDERHANDED: *Laura would never agree to anything that smacked of underhand snooping.*

un·der·hand·ed /,əndərˈhandəd/ ▶**adj.** acting or done in a secret or dishonest way: *an underhanded method of snatching clients from rivals.* — **un·der·hand·ed·ly** **adv.**

un·der·hung /,əndərˈhəNG/ ▶**adj.** another term for UNDERSHOT (sense 2).

un·der·in·sured /,əndərinˈsнo͝ord/ ▶**adj.** (of a person) having inadequate insurance coverage. — **un·der·in·sur·ance** /ˈəndərin,sнo͝orəns/ **n.**

un·der·in·vest /,əndərinˈvest/ ▶**v.** [intrans.] fail to invest sufficient money or resources in a project or enterprise: *we persistently underinvest in historic buildings.* — **un·der·in·vest·ment** **n.**

un·der·lay[1] ▶**v.** /,əndərˈlā/ (past and past part. **-laid**) [trans.] (usu. **be underlaid**) place something under (something else), esp. to support or raise it: *the green fields are underlaid with limestone.* ▶**n.** /ˈəndər,lā/ something placed under or behind something else, esp. material laid under a carpet for protection or support. ■ Music the manner in which the words are set to the notes in a piece of vocal music.

un·der·lay[2] past tense of UNDERLIE.

un·der·lay·ment /ˌəndərˈlāmənt/ ▶n. a layer between a subfloor and a finished floor of linoleum or tile that facilitates leveling and adhesion.

un·der·let /ˌəndərˈlet/ ▶v. (**-let·ting**; past and past part. **-let**) another term for SUBLET. ■ lease (land or property) at less than the true value.

un·der·lie /ˌəndərˈlī/ ▶v. (**-ly·ing**; past **-lay**; past part. **-lain**) [trans.] (esp. of a layer of rock or soil) lie or be situated under (something). ■ be the cause or basis of (something): *the fundamental issue that underlies the conflict* | [as adj.] (**underlying**) *the underlying causes of poverty and drug addiction.*

un·der·life /ˈəndərˌlīf/ ▶n. a way of living that the general public does not normally encounter.

un·der·line ▶v. /ˈəndərˌlīn/ [trans.] draw a line under (a word or phrase) to give emphasis or indicate special type. ■ emphasize (something): *the improvement in retail sales was underlined by these figures.* ▶n. **1** a line drawn under a word or phrase, esp. for emphasis. **2** the line of the lower part of an animal's body.

un·der·lin·en /ˈəndərˌlinin/ ▶n. archaic underclothes, esp. those made of linen.

un·der·ling /ˈəndərliNG/ ▶n. (usu. **underlings**) esp. derog. a person lower in status or rank.

un·der·lip /ˈəndərˌlip/ ▶n. the lower lip of a person or animal.

un·der·ly·ing /ˌəndərˈlī-iNG/ present participle of UNDERLIE.

un·der·man /ˌəndərˈman/ ▶v. (**-manned**, **-man·ning**) [trans.] (usu. **be undermanned**) fail to provide with enough workers or crew: *the public prosecutor's offices are hopelessly undermanned.*

un·der·men·tioned /ˌəndərˈmenCHənd/ ▶adj. Brit. mentioned at a later place in a book or document.

un·der·mine /ˌəndərˈmīn; ˈəndərˌmīn/ ▶v. [trans.] erode the base or foundation of (a rock formation). ■ dig or excavate beneath (a building or fortification) so as to make it collapse. ■ fig. damage or weaken (someone or something), esp. gradually or insidiously: *this could undermine years of hard work.* — **un·der·min·er** n.

un·der·neath /ˌəndərˈnēTH/ ▶prep. & adv. **1** situated directly below (something else): [as prep.] *our bedroom is right underneath theirs* | [as adv.] *his eyes had black bags underneath* | [as adj.] *on longer hair, the underneath layers can be permed to give extra body.* ■ situated on a page directly below (a picture or another piece of writing): [as prep.] *four names written neatly underneath one another* | [as adv.] *there was writing underneath.* **2** so as to be concealed by (something else): [as prep.] *money changed hands underneath the table* | fig. *underneath his aloof air, Nicky was a warm and open young man* | [as adv.] *paint peeling off in flakes to reveal grayish plaster underneath.* ■ partly or wholly concealed by (a garment): [as prep.] *she could easily see the broadness of his shoulders underneath a tailored white shirt* | [as adv.] *I wear button-downs, and my T-shirts show underneath.* ▶n. [in sing.] the part or side of something facing toward the ground; the underside. [OE *underneothan*; cf. BENEATH.]

un·der·nour·ished /ˌəndərˈnərisHt; -ˈnə-risht/ ▶adj. having insufficient food or other substances for good health and condition: *undernourished children.* — **un·der·nour·ish·ment** /-ˈnərisHmənt/ n.

un·der·paid /ˌəndərˈpād/ past and past participle of UNDERPAY.

un·der·paint·ing /ˈəndərˌpāntiNG/ ▶n. paint subsequently overlaid with another layer or with a finishing coat.

un·der·pants /ˈəndərˌpan(t)s/ ▶plural n. an undergarment covering the lower part of the torso and having two holes for the legs.

un·der·part /ˈəndərˌpärt/ ▶n. a lower part or portion of something. ■ (**underparts**) the underside of an animal's body, esp. when of a specified color or pattern.

un·der·pass /ˈəndərˌpas/ ▶n. a road or pedestrian tunnel passing under another road or a railroad.

un·der·pay /ˌəndərˈpā/ ▶v. (past and past part. **-paid**) [trans.] pay too little to (someone). ■ pay less than is due for (something): [as adj.] (**underpaid**) *late or underpaid tax.* — **un·der·pay·ment** /ˌəndərˈpāmənt; ˈəndərˌpā-/ n.

un·der·per·form /ˌəndərpərˈfôrm/ ▶v. [intrans.] perform less well than expected. ■ [trans.] increase in value less than: *the shares have underperformed the market.* — **un·der·per·for·mance** /-ˈfôrməns/ n.

un·der·pin /ˌəndərˈpin/ ▶v. (**-pinned**, **-pin·ning**) [trans.] support (a building or other structure) from below by laying a solid foundation below ground level or by substituting stronger for weaker materials. ■ support, justify, or form the basis for: *the theme of honor underpinning the two books.*

un·der·pin·ning /ˈəndərˌpiniNG/ ▶n. a solid foundation laid below ground level to support or strengthen a building. ■ a set of ideas, motives, or devices that justify or form the basis for something: *the theoretical underpinning for free-market economics.*

un·der·plant /ˌəndərˈplant/ ▶v. [trans.] plant or cultivate the ground around (a tall plant) with smaller plants.

un·der·play /ˌəndərˈplā; ˈəndərˌplā/ ▶v. [trans.] perform (something) in a restrained way: *the violins underplayed the romantic element in the music.* ■ represent (something) as being less important than it actually is.

un·der·plot /ˈəndərˌplät/ ▶n. a subordinate plot in a play, novel, or similar work.

un·der·pop·u·lat·ed /ˌəndərˈpäpyəˌlātid/ ▶adj. having an insufficient or very small population. — **un·der·pop·u·la·tion** /-ˌpäpyəˈlāsHən/ n.

un·der·pow·ered /ˌəndərˈpouərd/ ▶adj. lacking sufficient mechanical, electrical, or other power.

un·der·pre·pared /ˌəndərpriˈpe(ə)rd/ ▶adj. not having prepared sufficiently to carry out a task.

un·der·price /ˌəndərˈprīs/ ▶v. [trans.] sell or offer something at a lower price than (the competition). ■ sell or offer (something) at too low a price: *we try not to underprice our books.*

un·der·priv·i·leged /ˌəndərˈpriv(ə)lijd/ ▶adj. (of a person) not enjoying the same standard of living or rights as the majority of people in a society.

un·der·pro·duce /ˌəndərprəˈd(y)o͞os/ ▶v. [trans.] **1** produce less of (a commodity) than is wanted or needed. **2** [often as adj.] (**underproduced**) record or produce (a song or movie) in such a basic way that it appears rough or unfinished: *many of the album's best tracks are relatively underproduced.* — **un·der·pro·duc·tion** /-prəˈdəksHən/ n.

un·der·proof /ˌəndərˈpro͞of/ ▶adj. containing less alcohol than proof spirit does.

un·der·prop /ˌəndərˈpräp/ ▶v. (**-propped**, **-prop·ping**) [trans.] archaic support, esp. with a prop.

un·der·rate /ˌəndə(r)ˈrāt/ ▶v. [trans.] [often as adj.] (**underrated**) underestimate the extent, value, or importance of (someone or something): *a very underrated film.*

un·der·re·hearsed /ˌəndə(r)riˈhərst/ ▶adj. (of a performance or performer) having had insufficient rehearsals.

un·der·re·port /ˌəndə(r)riˈpôrt/ ▶v. [trans.] fail to report (something) fully: *athletes are inclined to underreport their use of drugs* | [as adj.] (**underreported**) *underreported domestic violence.*

un·der·rep·re·sent /ˌəndə(r)ˌrepriˈzent/ ▶v. [trans.] provide with insufficient or inadequate representation: *women are underrepresented at high levels.* — **un·der·rep·re·sen·ta·tion** /-zenˈtāsHən; -zən-/ n.

un·der·rep·re·sent·ed /ˌəndərˌrepriˈzentid/ ▶adj. not represented in adequate numbers or amounts: *women are underrepresented as senior scientists at the research center.*

un·der·re·sourced /ˌəndə(r)ˈrēˌsôrst; -riˈsôrst/ ▶adj. provided with insufficient resources. — **un·der·re·sourc·ing** /-ˈrēˌsôrsiNG; -riˈsôrs-/ n.

un·der·sat·u·rat·ed /ˌəndərˈsacHəˌrātid/ ▶adj. tech. falling short of being saturated with a particular constituent. — **un·der·sat·u·ra·tion** /-ˌsacHəˈrāsHən/ n.

un·der·score ▶v. /ˈəndərˌskôr; ˌəndərˈskôr/ another term for UNDERLINE. ▶n. /ˈəndərˌskôr/ another term for UNDERLINE (sense 1).

un·der·sea /ˌəndərˈsē/ ▶adj. below the sea or the surface of the sea: *undersea cables.*

un·der·sec·re·tar·y /ˌəndərˈsekriˌterē/ ▶n. (pl. **-tar·ies**) a subordinate official, in particular (in the US) the principal assistant to a member of the cabinet, or (in the UK) a junior minister or senior civil servant.

un·der·sell /ˌəndərˈsel/ ▶v. (past and past part. **-sold**) [trans.] sell something at a lower price than (a competitor): *we can equal or undersell mail order.* ■ promote or rate (something) insufficiently; undervalue: *don't undersell yourself.*

un·der·set ▶v. /ˌəndərˈset/ (**-set·ting**; past and past part. **-set**) [trans.] rare place (something) under something else, esp. for support. ▶n. another term for UNDERCURRENT.

un·der·sexed /ˌəndərˈsekst/ ▶adj. having unusually weak sexual desires.

un·der·sher·iff /ˈəndərˌsherif/ ▶n. a deputy sheriff.

un·der·shirt /ˈəndərˌsHərt/ ▶n. an undergarment worn under a shirt.

un·der·shoot ▶v. /ˌəndərˈsHo͞ot/ (past and past part. **-shot**) [trans.] fall short of (a point or target): *the figure undershot the government's original estimate.* ■ (of an aircraft) land short of (the runway). ▶n. an act of undershooting.

un·der·shorts /ˈəndərˌsHôrts/ ▶plural n. underpants, esp. those worn by men or boys.

un·der·shot /ˈəndərˌsHät/ past and past participle of UNDERSHOOT. ▶adj. **1** (of a waterwheel) turned by water flowing under it. **2** denoting or having a lower jaw that projects beyond the upper jaw.

un·der·side /ˈəndərˌsīd/ ▶n. the bottom or lower side or surface of something: *the butterfly's wings have a mottled brown pattern on the underside.* ■ fig. the less favorable aspect of something: *the sordid underside of the glamorous 1980s.*

un·der·signed /ˈəndərˌsīnd/ ▶adj. [usu. as pl. n.] (**the undersigned**) formal whose signature is appended: *we, the undersigned, wish to protest the activities of the company.*

un·der·sized /ˌəndərˈsīzd/ (also **un·der·size**) ▶adj. of less than the usual size.

un·der·skirt /ˈəndərˌskərt/ ▶n. a skirt worn under another; a petticoat.

un·der·slung /ˌəndərˈsləNG/ ▶adj. suspended from the underside of something: *helicopters hover to lift underslung loads.* ■ (of a vehicle chassis) hanging lower than the axles.

un·der·soil /ˈəndərˌsoil/ ▶n. subsoil.

un·der·sold /ˌəndərˈsōld/ past and past participle of UNDERSELL.

un·der·spend ▶v. /ˌəndərˈspend/ (past and past part. **-spent**) [intrans.] spend too little. ■ [trans.] spend less than (a specified or allocated amount): *schools have underspent their training budgets.*

un·der·staff /ˌəndərˈstaf/ ▶v. [trans.] provide (an organization) with too few staff members to operate effectively: [as adj.] (**understaffed**) *the department is understaffed and overworked.* — **un·der·staff·ing** n.

un·der·stand /ˌəndərˈstand/ ▶ **v.** (past and past part. **-stood**) **1** [trans.] perceive the intended meaning of (words, a language, or speaker): *he could usually **make himself understood*** | [with clause] *she understood what he was saying.* ■ perceive the significance, explanation, or cause of (something): *she didn't really understand the situation* | [intrans.] *you don't understand—she has left me.* ■ be sympathetically or knowledgeably aware of the character or nature of: *Picasso understood color.* ■ interpret or view (something) in a particular way: *as the term is usually understood, legislation refers to regulations and directives.* **2** infer something from information received (often used as a polite formula in conversation): *as I understood it, she was flying back to New Zealand tomorrow.* ■ [trans.] (often **be understood**) regard (a missing word, phrase, or idea) as present; supply mentally: *"present company excepted" is always understood when sweeping generalizations are being made.* ■ [trans.] (often **be understood**) assume to be the case; take for granted: *he liked to play the field—that was understood.* — **un·der·stand·er n.** [OE *understandan* (see UNDER-, STAND).]

un·der·stand·a·ble /ˌəndərˈstandəbəl/ ▶ **adj.** able to be understood: *though his accent was strange, the words were perfectly understandable.* ■ to be expected; natural, reasonable, or forgivable: *such fears are understandable.* — **un·der·stand·a·bil·i·ty** /-ˌstandəˈbilətē/ **n.** **un·der·stand·a·bly** /-blē/ **adv.**

un·der·stand·ing /ˌəndərˈstandiNG/ ▶ **n.** the ability to understand something; comprehension: *foreign visitors with little understanding of English.* ■ the power of abstract thought; intellect: *a child of sufficient understanding.* ■ an individual's perception or judgment of a situation: *my understanding was that he would try to find a new supplier.* ■ sympathetic awareness or tolerance: *a problem that needs to be handled with understanding.* ■ an informal or unspoken agreement or arrangement: *he had only been allowed to come **on the understanding that** he would be on his best behavior.* ▶ **adj.** **1** sympathetically aware of other people's feelings; tolerant and forgiving: *people expect us to be understanding.* **2** archaic having insight or good judgment. — **un·der·stand·ing·ly adv.**

un·der·state /ˌəndərˈstāt/ ▶ **v.** [trans.] describe or represent (something) as being smaller or less good or important than it actually is: *the press has understated the extent of the problem.* — **un·der·stat·er** /ˈəndərˌstātər/ **n.**

un·der·stat·ed /ˌəndərˈstātid/ ▶ **adj.** presented or expressed in a subtle and effective way: *understated elegance.* — **un·der·stat·ed·ly adv.**

un·der·state·ment /ˈəndərˌstātmənt/ ▶ **n.** the presentation of something as being smaller or less good or important than it actually is: *to say I am delighted is an understatement.*

un·der·steer /ˌəndərˈsti(ə)r/ ▶ **v.** [intrans.] (of a motor vehicle) have a tendency to turn less sharply than is intended: *the car understeers on very fast bends.* ▶ **n.** /ˈəndərˌstir/ the tendency of a vehicle to turn in such a way.

un·der·stood /ˌəndərˈstŏŏd/ past and past participle of UNDERSTAND.

un·der·sto·ry /ˈəndərˌstôrē/ (Brit. **un·der·sto·rey**) ▶ **n.** (pl. **-ries**) Ecol. a layer of vegetation beneath the main canopy of a forest.

un·der·strap·per /ˈəndərˌstrapər/ ▶ **n.** informal, dated an assistant or junior official.

un·der·stud·y /ˈəndərˌstədē/ ▶ **n.** (pl. **-stud·ies**) (in the theater) a person who learns another's role in order to be able to act as a replacement at short notice. ▶ **v.** (**-stud·ies, -stud·ied**) [trans.] learn (a role) or the role played by (an actor): *he had to understudy Prospero.*

un·der·sub·scribed /ˌəndərsəbˈskrībd/ ▶ **adj.** (of a course or event) having more places available than applications.

un·der·sur·face /ˈəndərˌsərfəs/ ▶ **n.** the lower or under surface of something.

un·der·take /ˌəndərˈtāk/ ▶ **v.** (past **-took**; past part. **-tak·en**) [trans.] commit oneself to and begin (an enterprise or responsibility); take on: *a firm of builders undertook the construction work.* ■ [usu. with infin.] promise to do a particular thing: *the firm undertook to keep price increases to a minimum.* ■ [with clause] guarantee or affirm something; give as a formal pledge: *a truck driver implicitly **undertakes that** he is reasonably skilled as a driver.*

un·der·tak·er /ˈəndərˌtākər/ ▶ **n.** a person whose business is preparing dead bodies for burial or cremation and making arrangements for funerals.

un·der·tak·ing /ˈəndərˌtākiNG; ˌəndərˈtā-/ ▶ **n.** **1** a formal pledge or promise to do something: *I give **an undertaking that** we shall proceed with the legislation.* ■ a task that is taken on; an enterprise: *a mammoth undertaking that involved digging into a cliff face.* ■ the action of undertaking to do something: *the undertaking of an obligation.* **2** /ˈəndərˌtākiNG/ the management of funerals as a profession.

un·der·things /ˈəndərˌTHiNGz/ ▶ **plural n.** underclothes, esp. those worn by a woman or girl.

un·der·thrust /ˌəndərˈTHrəst/ Geol. ▶ **v.** (past and past part. **-thrust**) [trans.] force (a crustal plate or other body of rock) beneath another formation. ■ be forced underneath (another formation). ▶ **n.** an instance of such forced movement.

un·der·tint /ˈəndərˌtint/ ▶ **n.** a subdued or delicate tint.

un·der·tone /ˈəndərˌtōn/ ▶ **n.** a subdued or muted tone of sound or color: *a pallid undertone to her tanned skin.* ■ an underlying quality or feeling: *the sexual undertones of most advertising.*

un·der·took /ˌəndərˈtŏŏk/ past participle of UNDERTAKE.

un·der·tow /ˈəndərˌtō/ ▶ **n.** a current below the surface of the sea moving in the opposite direction to the surface current, esp. away from the shore. ■ fig. an implicit quality, emotion, or influence underlying the superficial aspects of something and leaving a particular impression: *there's a dark undertow of loss that links the novel with earlier works.*

un·der·trained /ˌəndərˈtrānd/ ▶ **adj.** with insufficient training for a job, sport, etc.

un·der·trick /ˈəndərˌtrik/ ▶ **n.** Bridge a trick by which the declarer falls short of their contract.

un·der·use /ˌəndərˈyōōz/ ▶ **v.** [trans.] [usu. as adj.] (**underused**) use (something) below the optimum level: *a lot of underused space in that garage.* ▶ **n.** insufficient use: *underuse of existing services.*

un·der·u·ti·lize /ˌəndərˈyōōtlˌīz/ ▶ **v.** [trans.] underuse (something). — **un·der·u·ti·li·za·tion** /-ˌyōōtl-əˈzāSHən/ **n.**

un·der·val·ue /ˌəndərˈvalyōō/ ▶ **v.** (**-val·ues, -val·ued, -val·u·ing**) [trans.] [often as adj.] (**undervalued**) rate (something) insufficiently highly; fail to appreciate: *the skills of the housewife remain undervalued in society.* ■ underestimate the financial value of (something): *the company's assets were undervalued in its balance sheet.* — **un·der·val·u·a·tion** /-ˌvalyōōˈāSHən/ **n.**

un·der·vest /ˈəndərˌvest/ ▶ **n.** esp. Brit. an undershirt.

un·der·vote /ˈəndərˌvōt/ ▶ **n.** a ballot not counted because of unclear marking by the voter.

un·der·wa·ter /ˌəndərˈwôtər; -ˈwätər/ ▶ **adj. & adv.** situated, occurring, or done beneath the surface of the water: [as adj.] *underwater volcanoes* | [as adv.] *they learn to navigate underwater.*

un·der·wear /ˈəndərˌwe(ə)r/ ▶ **n.** clothing worn under other clothes, typically next to the skin.

un·der·weight /ˈəndərˌwāt; ˌəndərˈwāt/ ▶ **adj.** below a weight considered normal or desirable: *he was thirty pounds underweight.* ■ Finance (also **un·der·weight·ed**) having less investment in a particular area than is considered desirable or appropriate. ▶ **v.** [trans.] apply too little weight to (something): *we feared the hot-air balloon had been underweighted.* ▶ **n.** insufficient weight.

un·der·went /ˌəndərˈwent/ past of UNDERGO.

un·der·whelm /ˌəndərˈ(h)welm/ ▶ **v.** [trans.] (usu. **be underwhelmed**) humorous fail to impress or make a positive impact on (someone); disappoint: *American voters seem underwhelmed by the choices for president.* [1950s: suggested by OVERWHELM.]

un·der·wing /ˈəndərˌwiNG/ ▶ **n.** **1** the hind wing of an insect, esp. when it is normally hidden by a forewing. **2** the underside of a bird's wing. **3** (also **un·der·wing moth**) [usu. with adj.] a moth (family Noctuidae) with drab forewings and brightly colored hind wings, typically yellow or red with a black terminal band.

un·der·wire /ˈəndərˌwī(ə)r/ ▶ **n.** a semicircular wire support stitched under each cup of a bra. — **un·der·wired adj.**

un·der·wood /ˈəndərˌwŏŏd/ ▶ **n.** small trees and shrubs growing beneath taller timber trees.

un·der·work /ˌəndərˈwərk/ ▶ **v.** [trans.] (usu. **be underworked**) impose too little work on (someone): *its members are viewed by the public as overpaid and underworked.*

un·der·world /ˈəndərˌwərld/ ▶ **n.** **1** the world of criminals or of organized crime. **2** the mythical abode of the dead, imagined as being under the earth.

un·der·write /ˈəndə(r)ˌrīt; ˌəndə(r)ˈrīt/ ▶ **v.** (past **-wrote**; past part. **-writ·ten**) [trans.] **1** sign and accept liability under (an insurance policy), thus guaranteeing payment in case loss or damage occurs. ■ accept (a liability or risk) in this way. **2** (of a bank or other financial institution) engage to buy all the unsold shares in (an issue of new securities). ■ undertake to finance or otherwise support or guarantee (something): *underwrite the construction of a ship.* **3** archaic write (something) below something else, esp. other written matter. — **un·der·writ·er** /ˈəndə(r)ˌrītər/ **n.**

un·de·scend·ed /ˌəndiˈsendid/ ▶ **adj.** Med. (of a testicle) remaining in the abdomen instead of descending normally into the scrotum.

un·de·served /ˌəndiˈzərvd/ ▶ **adj.** not warranted, merited, or earned: *an undeserved term of imprisonment.* — **un·de·serv·ed·ly** /-ˈzərvədlē/ **adv.**

un·de·serv·ing /ˌəndiˈzərviNG/ ▶ **adj.** not deserving or worthy of something positive, esp. help or praise. — **un·de·serv·ing·ly adv.**

un·de·sir·a·ble /ˌəndiˈzīrəbəl/ ▶ **adj.** not wanted or desirable because harmful, objectionable, or unpleasant: *the drug's undesirable side effects.* ▶ **n.** a person considered to be objectionable in some way. — **un·de·sir·a·bil·i·ty n.** **un·de·sir·a·ble·ness n.** **un·de·sir·a·bly** /-blē/ **adv.**

un·de·ter·mined /ˌəndiˈtərmənd/ ▶ **adj.** not authoritatively decided or settled: *the acquisition will result in an as yet undetermined number of lay-offs.* ■ not known: *the bus was traveling with an undetermined number of passengers when it crashed.*

un·de·vel·oped /ˌəndiˈveləpt/ ▶ **adj.** not having been developed: *undeveloped coal reserves.* ■ not having developed: *undeveloped buds and shoots.*

un·did /ˌənˈdid/ past of UNDO.

un·dies /ˈəndēz/ ▶ **plural n.** informal articles of underwear, esp. those of a woman or girl. [20th C.: abbr.]

un·dif·fer·enced /ˌənˈdif(ə)rənst/ ▶ **adj.** Heraldry (of arms) not made distinct by a mark of difference.

un·dine /ˌənˈdēn; ˈənˌdēn/ ▶ **n.** a female spirit or nymph inhabiting water. [19th C.: from mod. L. *undina*, from L. *unda* 'a wave.']

un·dip·lo·mat·ic /ˌənˌdipləˈmatik/ ▶ **adj.** being or appearing insensitive and tactless. — **un·dip·lo·mat·i·cal·ly** /-ik(ə)lē/ adv.

un·di·rect·ed /ˌəndəˈrektəd; -ˌdī-/ ▶ adj. lacking direction; without a particular aim, purpose, or target.

un·dis·guised /ˌəndisˈgīzd/ ▶ adj. (of a feeling) not disguised or concealed; open: *undisguised contempt.* — **un·dis·guis·ed·ly** /-ˈgīzidlē/ adv.

un·dis·so·ci·at·ed /ˌəndiˈsōsHēˌātid; -ˈsōsē/ ▶ adj. Chem. (of a molecule) not dissociated into oppositely charged ions.

un·dis·tin·guish·a·ble /ˌəndiˈstiNGgwisHəbəl/ ▶ adj. indistinguishable.

un·dis·trib·ut·ed mid·dle ▶ n. Logic a fallacy arising from the failure of the middle term of a syllogism to refer to all the members of a class in at least one premise.

un·di·vid·ed /ˌəndəˈvīdid/ ▶ adj. not divided, separated, or broken into parts. ■ concentrated on or devoted completely to one object: *I can now give you my undivided attention.*

un·do /ˌənˈdo͞o/ ▶ v. (-does /-ˈdəz/; past -did; past part. -done) [trans.] **1** unfasten, untie, or loosen (something): *the knot was difficult to undo.* **2** cancel or reverse the effects or results of (a previous action or measure): *undo the damage.* ■ cancel (the last command executed by a computer). **3** formal cause the downfall or ruin of: *Iago's hatred of women undoes him.* ▶ n. Comput. a feature of a computer program that allows a user to cancel or reverse the last command executed.

un·dock /ˌənˈdäk/ ▶ v. [trans.] **1** separate (a spacecraft) from another in space: *Conrad undocked Gemini and backed slowly away* | [intrans.] *Atlantis will undock from Mir.* **2** take (a ship) out of or away from a dock.

un·do·ing /ˌənˈdo͞o-iNG/ ▶ n. [in sing.] a person's ruin or downfall: *he knew of his ex-partner's role in his undoing.* ■ the cause of such ruin or downfall: *that complacency was to be their undoing.*

un·done /ˌənˈdən/ past participle of UNDO. ▶ adj. **1** not tied or fastened. **2** not done or finished: *he had left his homework undone.* **3** formal or humorous (of a person) ruined by a disastrous or devastating setback or reverse: *I am undone!*

un·doubt·ed /ˌənˈdoutid/ ▶ adj. not questioned or doubted by anyone: *her undoubted ability.* — **un·doubt·ed·ly** adv.

UNDP ▶ abbr. United Nations Development Program.

un·draped /ˌənˈdrāpt/ ▶ adj. not covered with cloth or drapery. ■ (esp. of a model or subject in art) naked.

un·dreamed /ˌənˈdrēmd/ (Brit. also **un·dreamt** /-ˈdremt/) ▶ adj. (**undreamed of**) not thought to be possible (used to express pleasant surprise at the amount, extent, or level of something): *comfort undreamed of in earlier times* | *undreamed-of success.*

un·dress /ˌənˈdres/ ▶ v. [intrans.] take off one's clothes: *I went into the bathroom to get undressed.* ■ [trans.] take the clothes off (someone else). ▶ n. **1** the state of being naked or only partially clothed: *women in various states of undress.* **2** Mil. ordinary clothing or uniform, as opposed to that worn on ceremonial occasions. Compare with FULL DRESS.

un·dressed /ˌənˈdrest/ ▶ adj. **1** wearing no clothes: *he was undressed and ready for bed.* **2** not treated, processed, or prepared for use: *undressed deerskin* | *a rough, undressed stone slab.* **3** (of food) not having a dressing: *an undressed salad.*

UNDRO ▶ abbr. United Nations Disaster Relief Office.

un·due /ˌənˈd(y)o͞o/ ▶ adj. unwarranted or inappropriate because excessive or disproportionate: *this figure did not give rise to undue concern.* — **un·du·ly** /-ˈd(y)o͞olē/ adv.

un·due in·flu·ence ▶ n. Law influence by which a person is induced to act otherwise than by their own free will or without adequate attention to the consequences.

un·du·lant /ˈənjələnt; ˈəndyə-/ ▶ adj. having a rising and falling motion or appearance like that of waves; undulating. — **un·du·lance** n. [19th C.: from L. *undulant-* 'moving like a wave,' from the verb *undulare.*]

un·du·lant fe·ver ▶ n. brucellosis in humans.

un·du·late ▶ v. /ˈənjəˌlāt; ˈəndyə-/ [intrans.] move with a smooth wavelike motion: *her body undulated to the thumping rhythm of the music.* ■ [usu. adj.] (**undulating**) have a wavy form or outline: *delightful views over undulating countryside.* ▶ adj. /-lit; -ˌlāt/ Bot. & Zool. (esp. of a leaf) having a wavy surface or edge. — **un·du·late·ly** /-litlē/ adv. **un·du·la·tion** /ˌənjəˈlāsHən; ˌəndyə-/ n. **un·du·la·to·ry** /ˈənjələˌtôrē; ˈəndyə-/ adj. [17th C.: from late L. *undulatus*, from L. *unda* 'a wave.']

un·dy /ˈəndē/ ▶ adj. [usu. postpositive] Heraldry another term for WAVY.

un·dy·ing /ˌənˈdī-iNG/ ▶ adj. (esp. of an emotion) lasting forever: *promises of undying love.* — **un·dy·ing·ly** adv.

un·earned /ˌənˈərnd/ ▶ adj. not earned or deserved: *unearned privileges.* ■ Baseball (of a run) scored as the result of or following an error made by the fielding side (specifically when the fielder has failed to make the third out of the inning), and not recorded in the pitcher's statistics.

un·earned in·come ▶ n. income from investments rather than from work.

un·earned in·cre·ment ▶ n. an increase in the value of land or property without labor or expenditure on the part of the owner.

un·earth /ˌənˈərTH/ ▶ v. [trans.] find (something) in the ground by digging. ■ discover (something hidden, lost, or kept secret) by investigation or searching: *unearth the truth.*

un·earth·ly /ˌənˈərTHlē/ ▶ adj. **1** unnatural or mysterious, esp. in a disturbing way: *unearthly quiet.* **2** informal unreasonably early or inconvenient: *a job that involves getting up at an unearthly hour.* — **un·earth·li·ness** n.

un·ease /ˌənˈēz/ ▶ n. anxiety or discontent: *public unease about defense policy.*

un·eas·y /ˌənˈēzē/ ▶ adj. (-eas·i·er, -eas·i·est) causing or feeling anxiety; troubled or uncomfortable: *an uneasy silence.* — **un·eas·i·ly** /-zəlē/ adv. **un·eas·i·ness** n.

un·ec·o·nom·ic /ˌənˌekəˈnämik; -ˌēkə-/ ▶ adj. unprofitable: *costs for seven huge, uneconomic reactors.* ■ constituting an inefficient use of money or other resources: *it may be uneconomic to repair some goods.*

un·ec·o·nom·i·cal /ˌənˌekəˈnämikəl; -ˌēkə-/ ▶ adj. wasteful of money or other resources; not economical. — **un·ec·o·nom·i·cal·ly** /-ik(ə)lē/ adv.

un·e·mo·tion·al /ˌəniˈmōsHənl/ ▶ adj. not having or showing strong feelings: *a flat, unemotional voice.* — **un·e·mo·tion·al·ly** /-sHənl-ē/ adv.

un·em·ploy·a·ble /ˌənimˈploi-əbəl/ ▶ adj. (of a person) not able or likely to get paid employment, esp. because of a lack of skills or qualifications. ▶ n. an unemployable person. — **un·em·ploy·a·bil·i·ty** /-ˌploiəˈbilətē/ n.

un·em·ployed /ˌənimˈploid/ ▶ adj. (of a person) without a paid job but available to work: *I was unemployed for three years* | [as pl. n.] (**the unemployed**) *a training program for the long-term unemployed.* ■ (of a thing) not in use.

un·em·ploy·ment /ˌənimˈploimənt/ ▶ n. the state of being unemployed. ■ the number or proportion of unemployed people: *a time of high unemployment.*

un·em·ploy·ment com·pen·sa·tion ▶ n. money that substitutes for wages or salary, paid to recently unemployed workers under a government- or union-run program.

un·end·ing /ˌənˈendiNG/ ▶ adj. having or seeming to have no end. ■ countless or continual: *unending demands.* — **un·end·ing·ly** adv. **un·end·ing·ness** n.

un-Eng·lish /ˌənˈiNG(g)lisH/ ▶ adj. not considered characteristic of English people or the English language.

un·en·tan·gle /ˌəninˈtaNGgəl/ ▶ v. another term for DISENTANGLE.

un·en·vi·a·ble /ˌənˈenvēəbəl/ ▶ adj. difficult, undesirable, or unpleasant: *an unenviable reputation for drunkenness.* — **un·en·vi·a·bly** /-blē/ adv.

UNEP ▶ abbr. United Nations Environment Program.

un·e·qual /ˌənˈēkwəl/ ▶ adj. **1** not equal in quantity, size, or value: *two rooms of unequal size* | *unequal odds.* ■ not fair, evenly balanced, or having equal advantage: *the ownership of capital is unequal in this country.* **2** [predic.] not having the ability or resources to meet a challenge: *she felt* **unequal to** *the task before her.* ▶ n. a person or thing considered to be different from another in status or level. — **un·e·qual·ly** adv.

un·e·qualed /ˌənˈēkwəld/ (Brit. **un·e·qualled**) ▶ adj. superior to all others in performance or extent: *trout of unequaled quality.*

un·e·quiv·o·cal /ˌəniˈkwivəkəl/ ▶ adj. leaving no doubt; unambiguous: *an unequivocal answer.* — **un·e·quiv·o·cal·ly** /-ik(ə)lē/ adv. **un·e·quiv·o·cal·ness** n.

un·err·ing /ˌənˈəriNG; -ˈer-/ ▶ adj. always right or accurate: *an unerring sense of direction.* — **un·err·ing·ly** adv. **un·err·ing·ness** n.

un·es·cap·a·ble /ˌənəˈskāpəbəl/ ▶ adj. another term for INESCAPABLE.

UNESCO /yo͞oˈneskō/ (also **Unesco**) an agency of the United Nations established in 1945 to promote the exchange of information, ideas, and culture. In 1984 the US withdrew from the organization, but in 2003, after being satisfied with certain reforms, it rejoined.

un·es·cort·ed /ˌənəˈskôrtid; -ˈesˌkôrtid/ ▶ adj. not escorted, esp. for protection, security, or as a mark of rank: *unescorted enemy merchant ships.* ■ unaccompanied by a social partner.

un·es·sen·tial /ˌənəˈsencHəl/ ▶ adj. & n. another term for INESSENTIAL.

un·e·ven /ˌənˈēvən/ ▶ adj. not level or smooth: *the floors are cracked and uneven.* ■ not regular, consistent, or equal: *the uneven distribution of resources.* ■ (of a contest) not equally balanced: *Fran struggled briefly but soon gave up the uneven contest.* — **un·e·ven·ly** adv. **un·e·ven·ness** n.

un·e·ven bars (also **un·e·ven par·al·lel bars**) ▶ plural n. a pair of parallel bars set at different heights, used in women's gymnastics. ■ the set of exercises performed on such a piece of equipment.

un·ex·am·pled /ˌənigˈzampəld/ ▶ adj. formal having no precedent or parallel: *a regime that brought such unexampled disaster on its people.*

un·ex·cep·tion·a·ble /ˌənikˈsepsH(ə)nəbəl/ ▶ adj. not open to objection: *the unexceptionable belief that society should be governed by law.* — **un·ex·cep·tion·a·ble·ness** n. **un·ex·cep·tion·a·bly** /-blē/ adv.

un·ex·cep·tion·al /ˌənikˈsepsHənl/ ▶ adj. not out of the ordinary; usual: *an unexceptional movie.* — **un·ex·cep·tion·al·ly** adv.

un·ex·pect·ed /ˌənikˈspektid/ ▶ adj. not expected or regarded as likely to happen: *his death was totally unexpected* | [as n.] (**the unexpected**) *he seemed to have a knack for saying the unexpected.* — **un·ex·pect·ed·ly** adv. [as submodifier] *an unexpectedly high price* **un·ex·pect·ed·ness** n.

un·ex·plain·a·ble /ˌənikˈsplānəbəl/ ▶ adj. unable to be explained or accounted for: *unexplainable rages.* — **un·ex·plain·a·bly** /-blē/ adv.

un·ex·plained /ˌənikˈsplānd/ ▶ adj. not described or made clear; unknown. ■ not accounted for or attributable to an identified cause: *SIDS is still an unexplained phenomenon.*

un·ex·ploit·ed /ˌənikˈsploitid/ ▶ adj. (of resources) not used to maximum benefit.

un·ex·plored /ˌənikˈsplôrd/ ▶ adj. (of a country or area) not investigated or mapped. ■ not evaluated or discussed in detail: *the research focuses on an unexplored theme in European history.*

un·ex·posed /ˌənikˈspōzd/ ▶ **adj.** covered or protected; not vulnerable. ■ [predic.] not introduced to or acquainted with something: *a person unexposed to spiritualist traditions.* ■ [predic.] not made public; concealed. ■ (of photographic film) not subjected to light.

un·ex·pressed /ˌənikˈsprest/ ▶ **adj.** (of a thought or feeling) not communicated or made known. ■ Genet. (of a gene) not appearing in a phenotype.

un·face·a·ble /ˌənˈfāsəbəl/ ▶ **adj.** (of a situation or circumstance) not able to be confronted or dealt with.

un·fail·ing /ˌənˈfāliNG/ ▶ **adj.** without error or fault: *his unfailing memory for names.* ■ reliable or constant: *his mother had always been an unfailing source of reassurance.* — **un·fail·ing·ly adv. un·fail·ing·ness n.**

un·fair /ˌənˈfe(ə)r/ ▶ **adj.** not based on or behaving according to the principles of equality and justice: *at times like these the legal system appears inhumane and unfair.* ■ unkind, inconsiderate, or unreasonable: *you're unfair to criticize like that when she's never done you any harm.* ■ not following the rules of a game or sport. — **un·fair·ly adv. un·fair·ness n.**

un·faith·ful /ˌənˈfāTHfəl/ ▶ **adj.** not faithful, in particular: ■ engaging in sexual relations with a person other than one's regular partner in contravention of a previous promise or understanding: *you haven't been unfaithful to him, have you?* ■ disloyal, treacherous, or insincere: *unfaithful to her parents' memory.* — **un·faith·ful·ly adv. un·faith·ful·ness n.**

un·fa·mil·iar /ˌənfəˈmilyər/ ▶ **adj.** not known or recognized: *his voice was unfamiliar to her.* ■ unusual or uncharacteristic: *the yellow taxicab was an unfamiliar sight on these roads.* ■ [predic.] (**unfamiliar with**) not having knowledge or experience of: *people who might be unfamiliar with legal procedures.* — **un·fa·mil·i·ar·i·ty** /-ˌmilēˈe(ə)ritē; -fəmilˈyer-/ **n.**

un·fash·ioned /ˌənˈfasHənd/ ▶ **adj.** esp. literary not made into a specific shape; formless.

un·fas·ten /ˌənˈfasən/ ▶ **v.** [trans.] open the fastening of; undo (something): *unfastening her earrings* | [as adj.] (**unfastened**) *he had left the door unfastened.* ■ [intrans.] become loose or undone.

un·fa·thered /ˌənˈfäT͟Hərd/ ▶ **adj.** dated having no known or acknowledged father; illegitimate. ■ esp. literary of unknown or obscure origin: *unfathered rumors.*

un·fa·vor·a·ble /ˌənˈfāv(ə)rəbəl/ (Brit. **un·fa·vour·a·ble**) ▶ **adj. 1** expressing or showing a lack of approval or support: *unfavorable press attention.* **2** adverse; inauspicious: *it would be unwise to sell the company while the economic circumstances are so unfavorable.* — **un·fa·vor·a·ble·ness n. un·fa·vor·a·bly** /-blē/ **adv.**

un·feel·ing /ˌənˈfēliNG/ ▶ **adj.** unsympathetic, harsh, or callous. ■ lacking physical sensation or sensitivity. — **un·feel·ing·ly adv. un·feel·ing·ness n.**

un·feigned /ˌənˈfānd/ ▶ **adj.** genuine; sincere: *a broad smile of unfeigned delight.* — **un·feign·ed·ly** /-ˈfānidlē/ **adv.**

un·fet·ter /ˌənˈfetər/ ▶ **v.** [trans.] [usu. as adj.] (**unfettered**) release from restraint or inhibition: *his imagination is unfettered by the laws of logic.*

un·fil·i·al /ˌənˈfilēəl; -ˈfilyəl/ ▶ **adj.** not having or showing the qualities associated with a son or daughter. — **un·fil·i·al·ly adv.**

un·fil·tered /ˌənˈfiltərd/ ▶ **adj. 1** not having been filtered: *unfiltered tap water.* **2** (of a cigarette) not provided with a filter.

un·fin·ished /ˌənˈfinisHt/ ▶ **adj.** not finished or concluded; incomplete: *her last novel is unfinished.* ■ (of an object) not having been given an attractive surface appearance as the final stage of manufacture.

un·fit /ˌənˈfit/ ▶ **adj. 1** [predic.] (of a thing) not of the necessary quality or standard to meet a particular purpose: *the land is unfit for food crops.* ■ (of a person) not having the requisite qualities or skills to undertake something competently. ■ Biol. (of a species) not able to produce viable offspring or survive in a particular environment. **2** (of a person) not in good physical condition, typically as a result of failure to exercise regularly. ▶ **v.** (**-fit·ted, -fit·ting**) [trans.] archaic make (something or someone) unsuitable; disqualify. — **un·fit·ly adv. un·fit·ness n.**

un·fit·ted /ˌənˈfitid/ ▶ **adj.** [predic.] (of a person) not fitted or suited for a particular task or vocation.

un·fit·ting /ˌənˈfitiNG/ ▶ **adj.** not fitting or suitable; unbecoming. — **un·fit·ting·ly adv.**

un·fixed /ˌənˈfikst/ ▶ **adj.** not fixed, in particular: ■ not fixed in a definite place or position; unfastened; loose. ■ uncertain or variable: *a being of unfixed gender.* ■ informal (of a venture or situation) doubtful or unsuccessful; coming to nothing: *the deal came unfixed.* — **un·fix v.**

un·flag·ging /ˌənˈflagiNG/ ▶ **adj.** tireless; persistent: *his apparently unflagging enthusiasm impressed her.* — **un·flag·ging·ly adv.**

un·flap·pa·ble /ˌənˈflapəbəl/ ▶ **adj.** informal having or showing calmness in a crisis. — **un·flap·pa·bil·i·ty** /-ˌflapəˈbilətē/ **n. un·flap·pa·bly** /-blē/ **adv.**

un·fledged /ˌənˈflejd/ ▶ **adj.** (of a bird) not yet having wing feathers large enough for flight. ■ fig. (of a person) inexperienced; youthful.

un·fleshed /ˌənˈflesHt/ ▶ **adj.** esp. literary not covered with flesh.

un·flinch·ing /ˌənˈflinCHiNG/ ▶ **adj.** not showing fear or hesitation in the face of danger or difficulty: *unflinching determination.* — **un·flinch·ing·ly adv.**

un·fo·cused /ˌənˈfōkəst/ (also **un·fo·cussed**) ▶ **adj.** (of a person or their eyes) not seeing clearly; appearing glazed or expressionless. ■ (of an optical device) not adjusted to focus. ■ (of a lens) not making incident light rays meet at a single point. ■ (of an object of vision) not in focus; indistinct. ■ (of feelings or plans) without a specific aim or direction: *real but unfocused aspirations.*

un·fold /ˌənˈfōld/ ▶ **v.** open or spread out from a folded position. ■ [trans.] reveal or disclose (thoughts or information): *Miss Eva unfolded her secret exploits to Mattie.* ■ [intrans.] (of information or a sequence of events) be revealed or disclosed: *there was a fascinating scene unfolding before me.* — **un·fold·ment n.**

un·forced er·ror ▶ **n.** Sports a mistake made on an easy shot by a competitor in a nonpressure situation.

un·fore·told /ˌənfôrˈtōld; -fər-/ ▶ **adj.** literary not foretold; unpredicted.

un·for·get·ta·ble /ˌənfərˈgetəbəl/ ▶ **adj.** impossible to forget; very memorable: *that unforgettable first kiss.* — **un·for·get·ta·bly** /-blē/ **adv.**

un·for·giv·a·ble /ˌənfərˈgivəbəl/ ▶ **adj.** so bad as to be unable to be forgiven or excused: *losing your temper with him was unforgivable.* — **un·for·giv·a·bly** /-blē/ **adv.**

un·for·giv·ing /ˌənfərˈgiviNG/ ▶ **adj.** not willing to forgive or excuse people's faults or wrongdoings: *he was always a proud and unforgiving man.* ■ (of conditions) harsh; hostile: *the moor can be a wild and unforgiving place in bad weather.* — **un·for·giv·ing·ly adv. un·for·giv·ing·ness n.**

un·formed /ˌənˈfôrmd/ ▶ **adj.** without a definite form or shape: *she packed the unformed butter into the mold.* ■ not having developed or been developed fully: *he had an ambitious, albeit unformed, idea for a novel.*

un·for·tu·nate /ˌənˈfôrCHənət/ ▶ **adj.** having or marked by bad fortune; unlucky. ■ (of a circumstance) unfavorable or inauspicious: *the delay at the airport was an unfortunate start to our vacation.* ■ regrettable or inappropriate: *his unfortunate remark silenced the gathering.* ▶ **n.** (often **unfortunates**) a person who suffers bad fortune. ■ archaic a person who is considered immoral or lacking in religious faith or instruction, esp. a prostitute.

un·for·tu·nate·ly /ˌənˈfôrCHənətlē/ ▶ **adv.** [sentence adverb] it is unfortunate that: *unfortunately, we do not have the time to interview every applicant.*

un·found·ed /ˌənˈfoundid/ ▶ **adj.** having no foundation or basis in fact: *her persistent fear that she had cancer was unfounded.* — **un·found·ed·ly adv. un·found·ed·ness n.**

UNFPA ▶ **abbr.** United Nations Fund for Population Activities.

un·freeze /ˌənˈfrēz/ ▶ **v.** (past **-froze**; past part. **-fro·zen**) [trans.] cause (something) to thaw. ■ [intrans.] become thawed. ■ remove restrictions on the use or transfer of (an asset).

un·fre·quent·ed /ˌənˈfrēkwəntid; -frēˈkwen-/ ▶ **adj.** (of a place) visited only rarely: *an unfrequented dirt path off the road to the beach.*

un·friend·ed /ˌənˈfrendid/ ▶ **adj.** literary without friends: *murder left innocent people bereft and unfriended.*

un·friend·ly /ˌənˈfren(d)lē/ ▶ **adj.** (**-li·er, -li·est**) not friendly: *she shot him an unfriendly glance* | *environmentally unfriendly activities.* — **un·friend·li·ness n.**

un·frock /ˌənˈfräk/ ▶ **v.** another term for DEFROCK.

un·fro·zen /ˌənˈfrōzən/ past participle of UNFREEZE. ▶ **adj.** not or no longer frozen: *larvae remain unfrozen under the ice.*

un·fruit·ful /ˌənˈfro͞otfəl/ ▶ **adj. 1** not producing good or helpful results; unproductive: *the meeting was unfruitful.* **2** not producing fruit or crops; unfertile. — **un·fruit·ful·ly adv. un·fruit·ful·ness n.**

un·ful·filled /ˌənfo͝olˈfild/ ▶ **adj.** not carried out or brought to completion: *his unfulfilled ambition to write.* ■ not having fully utilized or exploited one's abilities or character. — **un·ful·fill·a·ble** /-ˈfiləbəl/ **adj. un·ful·fill·ing** /-ˈfiliNG/ **adj.**

un·furl /ˌənˈfərl/ ▶ **v.** make or become spread out from a rolled or folded state, esp. in order to be open to the wind: [trans.] *a man was unfurling a sail* | [intrans.] *the flags unfurl.*

un·fur·nished /ˌənˈfərnisHt/ ▶ **adj. 1** (of a house or apartment) without furniture, esp. available to be rented without furniture: *an unfurnished apartment.* **2** archaic not supplied: *he is unfurnished with the ideas of justice.*

un·gain·ly /ˌənˈgānlē/ ▶ **adj.** (of a person or movement) awkward; clumsy: *an ungainly walk.* — **un·gain·li·ness n.** [17th C.: from UN-[1] 'not' + obs. *gainly* 'graceful,' based on ON *gegn* 'straight.']

un·get·at·a·ble /ˌənˈgetˌatəbəl/ ▶ **adj.** informal inaccessible.

un·gird /ˌənˈgərd/ ▶ **v.** [trans.] archaic release or take off by undoing a belt or girth.

un·giv·ing /ˌənˈgiviNG/ ▶ **adj.** (of a person) cold or stubborn in relationships with other people. ■ (of a material) not bending or pliable; stiff.

un·gloved /ˌənˈgləvd/ ▶ **adj.** not wearing a glove or gloves.

un·glued /ˌənˈglo͞od/ ▶ **adj.** not or no longer stuck: *grease particles come unglued from the plate.* | fig. *the whole operation came unglued.* ■ informal (of a person or state of mind) confused and emotionally strained: *tempers were becoming unglued.*

un·god·ly /ˌənˈgädlē/ ▶ **adj.** irreligious or immoral: *ungodly lives of self-obsession, lust, and pleasure.* ■ informal unreasonably early or inconvenient: *I've been troubled by telephone calls at ungodly hours.* — **un·god·li·ness n.**

un·gra·cious /ˌənˈgrāsHəs/ ▶ **adj. 1** not polite or friendly: *after Anna's kindness I wouldn't want to seem ungracious.* **2** not graceful or elegant. — **un·gra·cious·ly adv. un·gra·cious·ness n.**

un·gram·mat·i·cal /ˌəngrəˈmatikəl/ ▶ **adj.** not conforming to grammatical rules; not well formed: *ungrammatical sentences.* — **un·gram·mat·i·cal·i·ty** /-,mati'kalətē/ **n.** (pl. **-ties**). **un·gram·mat·i·cal·ly** /-ik(ə)lē/ **adv.** **un·gram·mat·i·cal·ness n.**

un·grate·ful /,ən'grātfəl/ ▶ **adj.** not feeling or showing gratitude: *she's so ungrateful for everything we do.* ■ not pleasant or acceptable: *he turned to the ungrateful task of forming a police cordon.* — **un·grate·ful·ly adv.** **un·grate·ful·ness n.**

un·green /,ən'grēn/ ▶ **adj.** (of a product or practice) harmful to the environment; not ecologically acceptable: *an ungreen commercial development.* ■ (of a person or organization) not supporting protection of the environment. — **un·green·ly adv.**

un·ground·ed /,ən'groundid/ ▶ **adj. 1** having no basis or justification; unfounded: *ungrounded fears.* **2** not electrically grounded. **3** [predic.] (**ungrounded in**) not properly instructed or proficient in (a subject or activity).

un·group /,ən'groop/ ▶ **v.** [trans.] Comput. separate (items) from a group formed within a word-processing or graphics package.

un·gual /'əNGgwəl; -gyooəl/ ▶ **adj.** Zool. Med. of, relating to, or affecting a nail, hoof, or claw. [19th C.: from L. *unguis* 'nail' + **-AL.**]

un·guard·ed /,ən'gärdid/ ▶ **adj.** without protection or a guard: *the museum was unguarded at night.* ■ not well considered; careless: *an unguarded remark.* — **un·guard·ed·ly adv. un·guard·ed·ness n.**

un·guent /'əNGgwənt/ ▶ **n.** a soft greasy or viscous substance used as an ointment or for lubrication. [ME: from L. *unguentum*, from *unguere* 'anoint.']

un·guic·u·late /,əNG'gwikyə,lāt; -lət/ ▶ **adj.** Zool. having one or more nails or claws. ■ Bot. (of a petal) having a narrow stalklike base. [19th C.: from mod. L. *unguiculatus*, from L. *unguiculus* 'fingernail, toenail,' dimin. of *unguis* 'nail.']

un·guis /'əNGgwis/ ▶ **n.** (pl. **un·gues** /'əNGgwēz/) Zool. a nail, claw, or fang. [18th C.: from L.]

un·gu·late /'əNGgyələt; -,lāt/ ▶ **n.** Zool. a hoofed mammal of the former order Ungulata, now divided into two unrelated orders (see **ARTIODACTYLA** and **PERISSODACTYLA**). See also **EVEN-TOED UNGULATE, ODD-TOED UNGULATE.** [19th C.: from late L. *ungulatus*, from L. *ungula* 'hoof.']

un·guled /'əNG,gyoold/ ▶ **adj.** Heraldry (of an animal) having hoofs of a specified different tincture.

un·hal·lowed /,ən'halōd/ ▶ **adj.** not formally consecrated: *unhallowed ground.* ■ unholy; wicked: *unhallowed retribution.*

un·hand /,ən'hand/ ▶ **v.** [trans.] [usu. in imper.] archaic humorous release (someone) from one's grasp: *"Unhand me, sir!" she cried.*

un·hand·some /,ən'han(d)səm/ ▶ **adj.** [often with negative] not handsome: *Bobby was not unhandsome in his uniform.*

un·hand·y /,ən'handē/ ▶ **adj. 1** not easy to handle or manage; awkward. **2** not skillful in using the hands. — **un·hand·i·ly** /-dəlē/ **adv.** **un·hand·i·ness n.**

un·hang /,ən'haNG/ ▶ **v.** (past and past part. **-hung**) rare [trans.] take down from a hanging position.

un·hap·pen /,ən'hapən/ ▶ **v.** [intrans.] (of an occurrence) become as though never having happened; be reversed: *things had happened that could never unhappen.*

un·hap·pi·ly /,ən'hapəlē/ ▶ **adv.** in an unhappy manner. ■ [sentence adverb] unfortunately: *unhappily, such days do not come too often.*

un·hap·py /,ən'hapē/ ▶ **adj.** (**-pi·er, -pi·est**) not happy: *an unhappy marriage.* ■ [predic.] (**unhappy at/about/with**) not satisfied or pleased with (a situation): *many were unhappy about the scale of the cuts.* ■ unfortunate: *an unhappy coincidence.* — **un·hap·pi·ness n.**

un·har·ness /,ən'härnəs/ ▶ **v.** [trans.] remove a harness from (a horse or other animal).

un·hasp /,ən'hasp/ ▶ **v.** [trans.] archaic unfasten.

UNHCR an agency of the United Nations set up in 1951 to aid, protect, and monitor refugees.

un·health·ful /,ən'helTHfəl/ ▶ **adj.** harmful to health: *radon can build up to unhealthful levels.* — **un·health·ful·ness n.**

un·health·y /,ən'helTHē/ ▶ **adj.** (**-health·i·er, -health·i·est**) harmful to health: *an unhealthy diet.* ■ not having or showing good health: *his face looked pale and unhealthy.* ■ (of a person's attitude or behavior) not sensible or well balanced; abnormal and harmful: *an unhealthy obsession with fast cars.* — **un·health·i·ly** /-THəlē/ **adv. un·health·i·ness n.**

un·heard /,ən'hərd/ ▶ **adj.** not heard or listened to: *my protests went unheard.* ■ (**unheard of**) not previously known of or done: *sales tax was unheard of in Kansas up until 1937.*

un·hedged /,ən'hejd/ ▶ **adj. 1** not bounded by a hedge: *an unhedged field.* **2** (of an investment or investor) not protected against loss by balancing or compensating contracts or transactions: *the bank collapsed due to unhedged trading.*

un·heim·lich /,oon'hīmliKH; ,ən-/ ▶ **adj.** uncanny; weird. [Ger.]

un·her·ald·ed /,ən'herəldid/ ▶ **adj.** not previously announced, expected, or recognized.

un·hinge /,ən'hinj/ ▶ **v.** [trans.] **1** [usu. as adj.] (**unhinged**) make (someone) mentally unbalanced: *I thought she must be unhinged by grief.* ■ deprive of stability or fixity; throw into disorder. **2** take (a door) off its hinges.

un·his·tor·ic /,ənhi'stôrik; -'stär-/ ▶ **adj.** not historic or historical.

un·hitch /,ən'hiCH/ ▶ **v.** [trans.] unhook or unfasten (something tethered to or caught on something else).

un·ho·ly /,ən'hōlē/ ▶ **adj.** (**-li·er, -li·est**) sinful; wicked. ■ not holy; unconsecrated: *an unholy marriage.* ■ denoting an alliance with potentially harmful implications between two or more parties that are not natural allies: *an unholy alliance between economic and political power.* ■ informal awful; dreadful (used for emphasis): *she was making an unholy racket.* — **un·ho·li·ness n.**

un·hood /,ən'hood/ ▶ **v.** [trans.] remove the hood from (something, esp. a falcon or horse).

un·hoped /,ən'hōpt/ ▶ **adj.** (**unhoped for**) exceeding hope or expectation: *an unhoped-for piece of good luck.*

un·horse /,ən'hôrs/ ▶ **v.** [trans.] cause to fall from a horse: *having unhorsed each other, the two men finished the fight on foot* | fig. *her mission is to unhorse fashionable literary theories.*

un·hou·seled /,ən'houzəld/ ▶ **adj.** archaic (of a person) not having received the Eucharist. [16th C.: based on obs. *housel* 'Eucharist.']

un·hu·man /,ən'(h)yoomən/ ▶ **adj.** not resembling or having the qualities of a human being.

un·hung[1] /,ən'həNG/ ▶ **adj. 1** (esp. of a picture) not hanging or hung. **2** [predic.] (of a wicked person) still living when expected to be executed by hanging.

un·hung[2] past and past participle of **UNHANG.**

un·hur·ried /,ən'hərēd; -'hə-rēd/ ▶ **adj.** moving, acting, or taking place without haste or urgency. — **un·hur·ried·ly** /-'hərēdlē; -'hərəd-/ **adv.**

un·husk /,ən'həsk/ ▶ **v.** [trans.] remove a husk or shell from (a seed or fruit): [as adj.] (**unhusked**) *unhusked rice.*

uni- ▶ **comb. form** one; having or consisting of one: *unicellular* | *unicycle.* [from L. *unus* 'one.']

U·ni·ate /'yoonē,at; -it; -,āt/ (also **U·ni·at**) ▶ **adj.** denoting or relating to any community of Christians in eastern Europe or the Near East that acknowledges papal supremacy but retains its own liturgy. ▶ **n.** a member of such a community. [19th C.: from Russ. *uniat*, from *uniya*, from L. *unio* (see **UNION**).]

u·ni·ax·i·al /,yoonē'aksēəl/ ▶ **adj.** having or relating to a single axis. ■ (of crystals) having one optic axis, as in the hexagonal, trigonal, and tetragonal systems.

u·ni·bod·y /'yoonə,bädē/ ▶ **n.** (pl. **-bod·ies**) a single molded unit forming both the bodywork and chassis of a vehicle.

u·ni·cam·er·al /,yoonə'kam(ə)rəl/ ▶ **adj.** (of a legislative body) having a single legislative chamber. [19th C.: from **UNI-** 'one' + L. *camera* 'chamber' + **-AL.**]

UNICEF /'yoonə,sef/ an agency of the United Nations established in 1946 to help governments improve the health and education of children and their mothers.

u·ni·cel·lu·lar /,yoonə'selyələr/ ▶ **adj.** Biol. (of protozoans, certain algae and spores, etc.) consisting of a single cell. ■ (of an evolutionary or developmental stage) characterized by the formation or presence of a single cell or cells.

U·ni·code /'yooni,kōd/ ▶ **n.** Computing an international encoding standard for use with different languages and scripts, by which each letter, digit, or symbol is assigned a unique numeric value that applies across different platforms and programs.

u·ni·col·or /'yoonə,kələr/ (also **u·ni·col·ored**) (Brit. **-col·our** or **-col·oured**) ▶ **adj.** of one color.

u·ni·com /'yoonə,käm/ ▶ **n.** a radio communications system of a type used at small airports.

unicorn 1

u·ni·corn /'yoonə,kôrn/ ▶ **n. 1** a mythical animal typically represented as a horse with a single straight horn projecting from its forehead. ■ a heraldic representation of such an animal, with a twisted horn, a deer's feet, a goat's beard, and a lion's tail. **2** hist. a carriage drawn by three horses, two abreast and one leader. ■ a team of three horses arranged in such a way. [ME: via OFr. from L. *unicornis*, from *uni-* 'single' + *cornu* 'horn.']

u·ni·cum /'yoonəkəm/ ▶ **n.** (pl. **-ca** /-kə/) a unique example or specimen. [19th C.: from L., neut. of *unicus* 'unique.']

u·ni·cur·sal /,yoonə'kərsəl/ ▶ **adj.** Math. relating to or denoting a curve or surface that is closed and can be drawn or swept out in a single movement. [19th C.: from **uni-** 'one' + L. *cursus* 'course' + **-al**.]

u·ni·cus·pid /ˌyo͞onəˈkəspid/ ▶ **adj.** having one cusp or point. ▶ **n.** a tooth with a single cusp, esp. a canine tooth.

u·ni·cy·cle /ˈyo͞onəˌsīkəl/ ▶ **n.** a cycle with a single wheel, typically used by acrobats. — **u·ni·cy·clist** /-ˌsīklist/ **n.**

un·i·den·ti·fied fly·ing ob·ject ▶ **n.** see **UFO**.

u·ni·di·men·sion·al /ˌyo͞onədəˈmensʜənl/ ▶ **adj.** having one dimension: *a unidimensional model.*

u·ni·di·rec·tion·al /ˌyo͞onidiˈreksʜənl/ ▶ **adj.** moving or operating in a single direction. — **u·ni·di·rec·tion·al·i·ty** /-ˌreksʜəˈnalitē/ **n.** **u·ni·di·rec·tion·al·ly** **adv.**

UNIDO ▶ **abbr.** United Nations Industrial Development Organization.

u·ni·fi·ca·tion /ˌyo͞onəfiˈkāsʜən/ ▶ **n.** the process of being united or made into a whole. — **u·ni·fi·ca·to·ry** /-ˈkātərē/ **adj.**

u·ni·fied field the·o·ry ▶ **n.** Physics a theory that describes two or more of the four interactions (electromagnetic, gravitational, weak, and strong) previously described by separate theories.

u·ni·form /ˈyo͞onəˌfôrm/ ▶ **adj.** **1** not changing in form or character; remaining the same in all cases and at all times: *a uniform decline in fertility.* ■ of a similar form or character to another or others: *a uniform package of amenities at a choice of hotels.* **2** denoting a garment forming part of a person's uniform: *black uniform jackets.* ▶ **n.** **1** the distinctive clothing worn by members of the same organization or body or by children attending certain schools: *airline pilots in dark blue uniforms | an officer in uniform.* ■ informal a police officer wearing a uniform: *uniforms were already on the scene.* **2** a code word representing the letter U, used in radio communication. ▶ **v.** [trans.] **1** make uniform. **2** provide or dress (someone) in a uniform. — **u·ni·form·ly** /ˈyo͞onəˌfôrmlē; ˌyo͞onəˈfôrm-/ **adv.** [16th C.: from Fr. *uniforme* or L. *uniformis* (see **uni-**, **form**).]

U·ni·form Com·mer·ci·al Code (abbr.: **UCC**) ▶ **n.** the body of laws governing commercial transactions in the United States.

u·ni·formed /ˈyo͞onəˌfôrmd/ ▶ **adj.** (of a person) wearing a uniform: *uniformed police officers.*

u·ni·form·i·tar·i·an·ism /ˌyo͞onəˌfôrməˈte(ə)rēəˌnizəm/ ▶ **n.** Geol. the theory that changes in the earth's crust during geological history have resulted from the action of continuous and uniform processes. Often contrasted with **catastrophism**. — **u·ni·form·i·tar·i·an** **adj. & n.**

u·ni·form·i·ty /ˌyo͞onəˈfôrmətē/ ▶ **n.** (pl. **-ties**) the quality or state of being uniform: *an attempt to impose administrative and cultural uniformity.*

u·ni·form re·source lo·ca·tor (abbr.: **URL**) ▶ **n.** a location or address identifying where documents can be found on the Internet.

u·ni·fy /ˈyo͞onəˌfī/ ▶ **v.** (**-fies, -fied**) make or become united, uniform, or whole: [trans.] *the government hoped to centralize and unify the nation* | [intrans.] *opposition groups struggling to unify* | [as adj.] (**unified**) *a unified system of national education.* — **u·ni·fi·er** **n.** [16th C.: from Fr. *unifier* or late L. *unificare* 'make into a whole.']

u·ni·lat·er·al /ˌyo͞onəˈlat(ə)rəl/ ▶ **adj.** **1** (of an action or decision) performed by or affecting only one person, group, or country involved in a particular situation, without the agreement of another or the others: *unilateral nuclear disarmament.* **2** relating to, occurring on, or affecting only one side of an organ or structure, or of the body. — **u·ni·lat·er·al·ly** **adv.**

u·ni·lat·er·al·ism /ˌyo͞onəˈlat(ə)rəˌlizəm/ ▶ **n.** the process of acting, reaching a decision, or espousing a principle unilaterally. — **u·ni·lat·er·al·ist** **n. & adj.**

u·ni·lin·e·ar /ˌyo͞onəˈlinēər/ ▶ **adj.** developing or arranged serially and predictably, without deviation: *a unilinear path of language learning.* ■ (of Web sites) allowing or designed for controlled navigation, following a single path. — **u·ni·lin·e·ar·ly** **adv.**

u·ni·lin·gual /ˌyo͞onəˈlinɢgwəl; -gyo͞oəl/ ▶ **adj.** conducted in, concerned with, or speaking only one language. — **u·ni·lin·gual·ly** **adv.**

u·ni·loc·u·lar /ˌyo͞onəˈläkyələr/ ▶ **adj.** Bot. Zool. having, consisting of, or characterized by only one loculus or cavity; single-chambered.

un·im·ag·i·na·ble /ˌənəˈmaj(ə)nəbəl/ ▶ **adj.** difficult or impossible to imagine or comprehend: *lives of almost unimaginable deprivation.* — **un·im·ag·i·na·bly** /-blē/ **adv.**

u·ni·mod·al /ˌyo͞onəˈmōdl/ ▶ **adj.** having or involving one mode. ■ (of a statistical distribution) having one maximum.

u·ni·mo·lec·u·lar /ˌyo͞onəməˈlekyələr/ ▶ **adj.** Chem. consisting of or involving a single molecule.

un·im·peach·a·ble /ˌənimˈpēcʜəbəl/ ▶ **adj.** not able to be doubted, questioned, or criticized; entirely trustworthy: *an unimpeachable witness.* — **un·im·peach·a·bly** /-blē/ **adv.**

un·im·proved /ˌənimˈpro͞ovd/ ▶ **adj.** not made better. ■ (of land) not cleared or cultivated.

un·in·cor·po·rat·ed /ˌəninˈkôrpəˌrātid; ˌəninɢ-/ ▶ **adj.** **1** (of a company or other organization) not formed into a legal corporation: *an unincorporated business.* **2** not included as part of a whole. ■ (of territory) not designated as belonging to a particular country, town, or area.

un·in·flect·ed /ˌəninˈflektid/ ▶ **adj.** **1** Gram. (of a word or a language) not undergoing changes to express particular grammatical functions or attributes: *English is largely uninflected.* **2** not varying in intonation or pitch: *her voice was flat and uninflected.*

un·in·hib·it·ed /ˌəninˈhibitid/ ▶ **adj.** expressing one's feelings or thoughts unselfconsciously and without restraint: *fits of uninhibited laughter.* — **un·in·hib·it·ed·ly** **adv.** **un·in·hib·it·ed·ness** **n.**

un·in·i·ti·at·ed /ˌənəˈnisʜēˌātid/ ▶ **adj.** without special knowledge or experience: [as pl. n.] (**the uninitiated**) *the discussion wasn't easy to follow for the uninitiated.*

un·in·spired /ˌəninˈspī(ə)rd/ ▶ **adj.** **1** lacking in imagination or originality: *repetitive and uninspired poetry.* **2** (of a person) not filled with excitement.

un·in·stall /ˌəninˈstôl/ (Brit. also **un·in·stal**) ▶ **v.** [trans.] remove (an application or file) from a computer. ▶ **adj.** denoting a command, function, or capability to remove software. — **un·in·stal·la·tion** /ˌən-instəˈlāsʜən/ **n.** **un·in·stall·er** **n.**

un·in·struct·ed /ˌəninˈstrəktid/ ▶ **adj.** (of a person) not taught or having learned a subject or skill. ■ (of behavior) not acquired by teaching; natural or spontaneous: *her own instinctive, uninstructed response.*

un·in·sur·a·ble /ˌəninˈsʜo͝orəbəl/ ▶ **adj.** not eligible for insurance coverage: *uninsurable activities.*

un·in·tel·li·gent /ˌəninˈteləjənt/ ▶ **adj.** having or showing a low level of intelligence: *a good-natured but unintelligent boy.* — **un·in·tel·li·gence** **n.** **un·in·tel·li·gent·ly** **adv.**

un·in·tel·li·gi·ble /ˌəninˈteləjəbəl/ ▶ **adj.** impossible to understand: *dolphin sounds are unintelligible to humans.* — **un·in·tel·li·gi·bil·i·ty** /-ˌteləjəˈbilətē/ **n.** **un·in·tel·li·gi·bly** /-blē/ **adv.**

un·in·ter·est·ed /ˌənˈintristid; -ˈintəˌrestid/ ▶ **adj.** not interested in or concerned about something or someone: *I was totally* ***uninterested in*** *boys.* — **un·in·ter·est·ed·ly** **adv.** **un·in·ter·est·ed·ness** **n.**

un·in·ter·pret·a·ble /ˌəninˈtərprətəbəl/ ▶ **adj.** impossible to explain or understand in terms of meaning or significance.

un·in·ter·rupt·ed /ˌənˌintəˈrəptid/ ▶ **adj.** without a break in continuity: *an uninterrupted flow of traffic.* ■ (of a view) unobstructed. — **un·in·ter·rupt·ed·ly** **adv.**

un·in·ter·rupt·i·ble /ˌənˌintəˈrəptəbəl/ ▶ **adj.** not able to be broken in continuity: *an uninterruptible power supply.*

u·ni·nu·cle·ate /ˌyo͞onəˈn(y)o͞oklēit/ ▶ **adj.** Biol. having a single nucleus.

un·in·vit·ed /ˌəninˈvītid/ ▶ **adj.** (of a person) attending somewhere or doing something without having been asked: *a series of uninvited guests.* ■ (of a thought or act) involuntary, unwelcome, or unwarranted: *strange uninvited thoughts crossed her mind.* — **un·in·vit·ed·ly** **adv.**

Un·ion /ˈyo͞onyən/ a township in northeastern New Jersey; pop. 50,024.

un·ion /ˈyo͞onyən/ ▶ **n.** **1** the action or fact of joining together or being joined together, esp. in a political context: *closer political or economic union with Europe | a currency union.* ■ a state of harmony or agreement: *they live in perfect union.* ■ a marriage. **2** a labor union: *the National Farmers' Union.* ■ a club, society, or association formed by people with a common interest or purpose: *members of the Students' Union.* ■ Brit., hist. a number of parishes consolidated for the purposes of administering the Poor Laws. ■ (also **un·ion work·house** or **un·ion house**) a workhouse set up by such a group of parishes. **3** (also **Un·ion**) a political unit consisting of a number of states or provinces with the same central government, in particular: ■ the United States, esp. from its founding by the original thirteen states in 1787–90 to the secession of the Confederate states in 1860–61. ■ (also **the Fed·er·al Un·ion**) the northern states that opposed the seceding Confederate states in the Civil War. **4** a building at a college or university used by students for recreation and other nonacademic activities. **5** Math. the set that comprises all the elements (and no others) contained in any of two or more given sets. ■ the operation of forming such a set. **6** a joint or coupling for pipes. **7** a part of a flag with an emblem symbolizing national union, typically occupying the upper corner next to the staff. **8** a fabric made of two or more different yarns, typically cotton and linen or silk. [ME: from OFr., or from eccles. L. *unio(n-)* 'unity,' from L. *unus* 'one.']

un·ion-bash·ing ▶ **n.** informal active or vocal opposition to labor unions and their rights.

un·ion cat·a·log ▶ **n.** a list of the combined holdings of several libraries.

Un·ion Cit·y **1** a city in north central California; pop. 53,762. **2** a city in northeastern New Jersey, across from New York City; pop. 58,102.

un·ion·ist /ˈyo͞onyənist/ ▶ **n.** **1** a member of a labor union. ■ an advocate or supporter of labor unions. **2** (**Un·ion·ist**) a person who opposed secession during the Civil War. ■ a person in Northern Ireland supporting or advocating union with Great Britain. — **un·ion·ism** /-ˌnizəm/ **n.** **un·ion·is·tic** /ˌyo͞onyəˈnistik/ **adj.**

un·ion·ize /ˈyo͞onyəˌnīz/ ▶ **v.** become or cause to become members of a labor union. — **un·ion·i·za·tion** /ˌyo͞onyəniˈzāsʜən; -ˌnīˈzā-/ **n.**

un·ion·ized /ˈyo͞onyəˌnīzd/ ▶ **adj.** (of workers or their workplace) belonging to, or having workers belonging to, a labor union: *unionized factories.*

un·i·o·nized /ˌənˈīəˌnīzd/ ▶ **adj.** not ionized.

Un·ion Jack ▶ **n.** **1** the national flag of the United Kingdom, consisting of red and white crosses on a blue background. **2** (**un·ion jack**) (in the US) a small flag consisting of the union from the national flag, flown at the bows of vessels in harbor.

Un·ion of My·an·mar official name for **Myanmar**.

Un·ion of So·vi·et So·cial·ist Re·pub·lics (abbr.: **USSR**) full name of **Soviet Union**.

un·ion shop ▶ **n.** a place of work where employers may hire nonunion workers who must join a labor union within an agreed time. Compare with **closed shop**.

un·ion suit ▶ **n.** dated a single undergarment combining shirt and pants.

Un·ion Ter·ri·to·ry any of several territories of India that are administered by the central government.

u·nip·ar·ous /yo͞o'nip(ə)rəs/ ▶ **adj.** esp. Zool. producing a single offspring at a birth. [17th C.: from mod. L. *uniparus* (from L. *uni-* 'one' + *-parus* 'bearing') + **-ous**.]

u·ni·per·son·al /,yo͞onə'pərsənəl/ ▶ **adj.** rare comprising, or existing as, one person only.

u·ni·pla·nar /,yo͞onə'plānər/ ▶ **adj.** lying in one plane.

u·ni·po·lar /,yo͞onə'pōlər/ ▶ **adj.** having or relating to a single pole or kind of polarity: *a unipolar magnetic charge.* ■ (of psychiatric illness) characterized by either depressive or (more rarely) manic episodes but not both. ■ (of a nerve cell) having only one axon or process. ■ Electron. (of a transistor or other device) using charge carriers of a single polarity. — **u·ni·po·lar·i·ty** /-pə'laritē; -pō-/ **n.**

u·nip·o·tent /yo͞o'nipətənt/ ▶ **adj. 1** Math. (of a subgroup) having only one idempotent element. **2** Biol. (of an immature or stem cell) capable of giving rise to only one cell type.

u·nique /yo͞o'nēk/ ▶ **adj.** being the only one of its kind; unlike anything else: *the situation was unique in modern politics | original and unique designs.* ■ particularly remarkable, special, or unusual: *a unique opportunity to see the spectacular Bolshoi Ballet.* ■ [predic.] (**unique to**) belonging or connected to (one particular person, group, or place): *a style of architecture that is unique to Portugal.* ▶ **n.** archaic a unique person or thing. — **u·nique·ly adv. u·nique·ness n.** [17th C.: from Fr., from L. *unicus*, from *unus* 'one.']

u·ni·sex /'yo͞onə,seks/ ▶ **adj.** (esp. of clothing or hairstyles) designed to be suitable for both sexes. ▶ **n.** a style in which men and women look and dress in a similar way.

u·ni·sex·u·al /,yo͞onə'seksHo͞oəl/ ▶ **adj.** (of an organism) either male or female; not hermaphrodite. ■ Bot. (of a flower) having either stamens or pistils but not both. — **u·ni·sex·u·al·i·ty** /-,seksHo͞o'alitē/ **n. u·ni·sex·u·al·ly adv.**

u·ni·son /'yo͞onəsən; -zən/ ▶ **n. 1** simultaneous performance of action or utterance of speech: *"Yes, sir," said the girls* ***in unison.*** **2** Music coincidence in pitch of sounds or notes: *the flutes play* ***in unison with*** *the violas.* ■ a combination of notes, voices, or instruments at the same pitch or (esp. when singing) in octaves: *good unisons are formed by flutes, oboes, and clarinets.* ▶ **adj.** [attrib.] performed in unison. — **u·nis·o·nous** /yo͞o'nisənəs/ **adj.** [ME (sense 2): from OFr., or from late L. *unisonus*, from L. *uni-* 'one' + *sonus* 'sound.']

u·nit /'yo͞onit/ ▶ **n. 1** an individual thing or person regarded as single and complete, esp. for purposes of calculation: *the family unit.* ■ each of the individuals or collocations into which a complex whole may be divided: *large areas of land made up of smaller units.* ■ a device that has a specified function, esp. one forming part of a complex mechanism. ■ a piece of furniture or equipment for fitting with others like it or made of complementary parts: *a sink unit.* ■ a self-contained section of accommodations in a larger building or group of buildings: *two-bedroom units.* ■ a part of an institution such as a hospital having a special function. ■ a subdivision of a larger military grouping. ■ an amount of educational instruction, typically determined by the number of hours spent in class. ■ an item manufactured: [as adj.] *unit cost.* ■ a police car. **2** a quantity chosen as a standard in terms of which other quantities may be expressed: *40 units of serum.* **3** the number one. ■ (**units**) the digit before the decimal point in decimal notation, representing an integer less than ten. [16th C.: from L. *unus*.]

u·ni·tard /'yo͞onə,tärd/ ▶ **n.** a tight-fitting one-piece garment of stretchable fabric that covers the body from the neck to the knees or feet. [1960s: from **UNI-** 'single' + **LEOTARD**.]

U·ni·tar·i·an /,yo͞oni'te(ə)rēən/ ▶ **n.** Theol. a person, esp. a Christian, who asserts the unity of God and rejects the doctrine of the Trinity. ■ a member of a church or religious body maintaining this belief and typically rejecting formal dogma in favor of a rationalist and inclusivist approach to belief. ▶ **adj.** of or relating to the Unitarians. — **U·ni·tar·i·an·ism** /-,nizəm/ **n.**

U·ni·tar·i·an U·ni·ver·sal·ism /,yo͞onə'vərsə,lizəm/ ▶ **n.** the religious denomination formed in 1961 by the merger of the Unitarians and the Universalists. — **U·ni·tar·i·an U·ni·ver·sal·ist adj. & n.**

u·ni·tar·y /'yo͞oni,terē/ ▶ **adj. 1** single; uniform. ■ of or relating to a system of government or organization in which the powers of the separate constituent parts are vested in a central body. **2** unified; whole: *it was just this unitary beauty that the Ptolemaic cosmology lacked.* **3** of or relating to a unit or units. — **u·ni·tar·i·ly** /'yo͞onə,terəlē; ,yo͞onə'te(ə)r-/ **adv. u·ni·tar·i·ty** /,yo͞onə'te(ə)ritē/ **n.**

U·ni·tas /yo͞o'nītəs/, Johnny (1933–2002), US football player; full name *John Constantine Unitas.* He played quarterback with the Baltimore Colts 1956–72.

u·nit cell ▶ **n.** Crystallog. the smallest group of atoms that has the overall symmetry of a crystal, and from which the entire lattice can be built up by repetition in three dimensions.

u·nite /yo͞o'nīt/ ▶ **v.** come or bring together for a common purpose or action: [intrans.] *he called on the party to unite* | [trans.] *they are united by their love of cars.* ■ come or bring together to form a unit or whole, esp. in a political context: [intrans.] *the two Germanys officially united* | [trans.] *he aimed to unite Italy and Sicily.* ■ [trans.] archaic join in marriage. — **u·ni·tive** /'yo͞onətiv; yo͞o'nī-/ **adj.** [ME: from L. *unit-* 'joined together,' from the v. *unire*, from *unus* 'one.']

u·nit·ed /yo͞o'nītid/ ▶ **adj.** joined together politically, for a common purpose, or by common feelings. — **u·nit·ed·ly adv.**

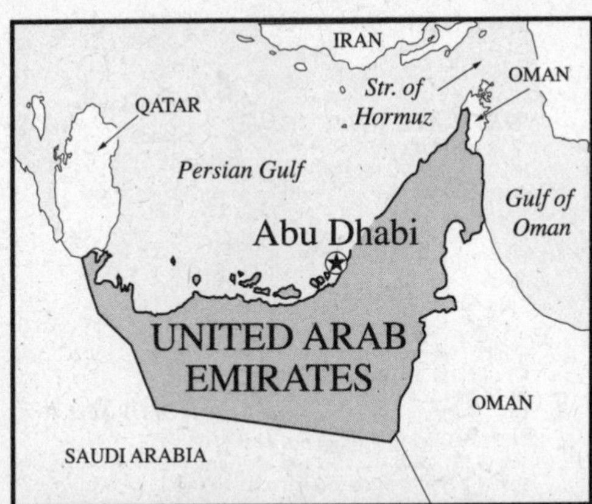

United Arab Emirates

Location: Middle East, on the Arabian peninsula, bordered to the north by the Persian Gulf
Area: 32,000 square miles (82,900 sq km)
Population: 2,523,000
Capital: Abu Dhabi
Languages: Arabic (official), Persian, English, Hindi, Urdu
Currency: Emirati dirham

U·nit·ed Ar·ab E·mir·ates (abbr.: **UAE**) a country in the Middle East, on the Persian Gulf. *See box.*

U·nit·ed Ar·ab Re·pub·lic (abbr.: **UAR**) a former political union established by Egypt and Syria in 1958. Yemen entered into loose association with it 1958–66 and Syria withdrew in 1961. Egypt retained the name United Arab Republic until 1971.

U·nit·ed King·dom (abbr.: **UK**) a country in western Europe. *See box on next page.*

U·nit·ed Na·tions (abbr.: **UN**) an international organization of countries set up in 1945, in succession to the League of Nations, to promote international peace, security, and cooperation.

U·nit·ed States (abbr.: **U.S.** or **US**) a country that occupies the southern half of North America. *See box on page 1505.*

u·nit·ize /'yo͞onə,tīz/ ▶ **v.** [trans.] [usu. as adj.] (**unitized**) form into a single unit by combining parts into a whole: *a unitized body with thousands of welds.* ■ package (cargo) into unit loads: *a unitized load.*

u·nit pric·ing ▶ **n.** identification of the retail price per unit of related products, allowing for easier price comparisons between products in different sized containers.

u·ni·ty /'yo͞onətē/ ▶ **n.** (pl. **-ties**) **1** the state of being united or joined as a whole, esp. in a political context. ■ harmony or agreement between people or groups. ■ the state of forming a complete and pleasing whole, esp. in an artistic context: *the repeated phrase gives the piece unity and cohesion.* ■ a thing forming a complex whole. ■ in Aristotle's *Poetics*, each of the three dramatic principles requiring limitation of the supposed time of a drama to that occupied in acting it or to a single day (**unity of time**), use of one scene throughout (**unity of place**), and concentration on the development of a single plot (**unity of action**). **2** Math. esp. Brit. the number one. [ME: from OFr. *unite*, from L. *unitas*, from *unus* 'one.']

Univ. ▶ **abbr.** University.

univ. ▶ **abbr.** universal.

u·ni·va·lent /,yo͞onə'vālənt; yo͞o'nivələnt/ ▶ **adj. 1** Biol. (of a chromosome) remaining unpaired during meiosis. **2** Chem. another term for **MONOVALENT**. ▶ **n.** Biol. a univalent chromosome.

u·ni·valve /'yo͞onə,valv/ Zool. ▶ **adj.** having one valve or shell. ▶ **n.** another term for **GASTROPOD** (see **GASTROPODA**).

u·ni·ver·sal /,yo͞onə'vərsəl/ ▶ **adj.** of, affecting, or done by all people or things in the world or in a particular group. ■ Logic denoting a proposition in which something is asserted of all of a class. Contrasted with **PARTICULAR**. ■ Ling. denoting or relating to a grammatical rule, set of rules, or other linguistic feature that is found in all languages. ■ (of a tool or machine) adjustable to or appropriate for all requirements; not restricted to a single purpose or position. ▶ **n.** a person or thing having universal effect, currency, or application, in particular: ■ Logic a universal proposition. ■ Philos. a term or concept of general application. ■ Philos. a nature or essence signified by a general term. ■ Ling. a universal grammatical rule or linguistic feature. — **u·ni·ver·sal·i·ty** /-vər'salətē/ **n.** [ME: from OFr., or from L. *universalis*, from *universus* (see **UNIVERSE**).]

United Kingdom

Official name: United Kingdom of Great Britain and Northern Ireland
Location: western Europe, consisting of England, Wales, Scotland, and Northern Ireland
Area: 94,500 square miles (244,800 sq km)
Population: 60,270,000
Capital: London
Languages: English, Welsh, Scottish Gaelic
Currency: British pound

u·ni·ver·sal do·nor ▶ n. a person of blood group O, who can in theory donate blood to recipients of any ABO blood group.

u·ni·ver·sal·ist /ˌyo͞onəˈvərsəlist/ ▶ n. **1** Christian Theol. a person who believes that all humankind will eventually be saved. ■ (usu. **Universalist**) a member of an organized body of Christians who hold such beliefs. **2** a person advocating loyalty to and concern for others without regard to national or other allegiances. ▶ adj. **1** Christian Theol. of or relating to universalists. **2** universal in scope or character. — **u·ni·ver·sal·ism** /-ˌlizəm/ n. **u·ni·ver·sal·is·tic** /-ˌvərsəˈlistik/ adj.

u·ni·ver·sal·ize /ˌyo͞onəˈvərsəˌlīz/ ▶ v. [trans.] give a universal character or application to (something, esp. something abstract): *theories that universalize experience.* ■ bring into universal use; make available for all. — **u·ni·ver·sal·iz·a·bil·i·ty** /-ˌvərsəˌlīzəˈbilətē/ n. **u·ni·ver·sal·i·za·tion** /-ˌvərsəliˈzāsʜən/ n.

u·ni·ver·sal joint (also **u·ni·ver·sal coup·ling**) ▶ n. a coupling or joint that can transmit rotary power by a shaft over a range of angles.

u·ni·ver·sal·ly /ˌyo͞onəˈvərsəlē/ ▶ adv. by everyone; in every case: *progress is not always universally welcomed.*

U·ni·ver·sal Prod·uct Code ▶ n. more formal term for BAR CODE.

u·ni·ver·sal re·cip·i·ent ▶ n. a person of blood group AB, who can in theory receive donated blood of any ABO blood group.

u·ni·ver·sal set ▶ n. Math. Logic the set containing all objects or elements and of which all other sets are subsets.

U·ni·ver·sal Time (also **U·ni·ver·sal Time Co·or·di·nat·ed**) another term for GREENWICH MEAN TIME.

u·ni·verse /ˈyo͞onəˌvərs/ ▶ n. (**the universe**) all existing matter and space considered as a whole; the cosmos. The universe is believed to be at least 10 billion light years in diameter and contains a vast number of galaxies; it has been expanding since its creation in the big bang about 13 billion years ago. ■ a particular sphere of activity, interest, or experience. ■ (Logic also **u·ni·verse of dis·course**) another term for UNIVERSAL SET. [ME: from OFr. *univers* or L. *universum*, neut. of *universus* 'combined into one, whole,' from *uni-* 'one' + *versus* 'turned' (past part. of *vertere*).]

u·ni·ver·si·ty /ˌyo͞onəˈvərsətē/ ▶ n. (pl. **-ties**) an educational institution designed for instruction, examination, or both, of students in many branches of advanced learning, conferring degrees in various faculties, and often embodying colleges and similar institutions. ■ the members of this collectively. ■ the grounds and buildings of such an institution. [ME: from OFr. *universite*, from L. *universitas* 'the whole,' in late L. 'society, guild,' from *universus* (see UNIVERSE).]

u·niv·o·cal /ˌyo͞onəˈvōkəl; yo͞oˈnivə-/ ▶ adj. Philos. Ling. (of a word or term) having only one possible meaning; unambiguous: *a univocal set of instructions.* — **u·niv·o·cal·i·ty** /ˌyo͞onəˌvōˈkalətē/ n. **u·niv·o·cal·ly** adv.

U·nix /ˈyo͞oniks/ (also **UNIX**) ▶ n. Comput., trademark a widely used multiuser operating system.

un·joint /ˌənˈjoint/ ▶ v. [trans.] rare separate or dislocate the joints of.

un·just /ˌənˈjəst/ ▶ adj. not based on or behaving according to what is morally right and fair. — **un·just·ly** adv. **un·just·ness** n.

un·kempt /ˌənˈkem(p)t/ ▶ adj. (esp. of a person) having an untidy or disheveled appearance. — **un·kempt·ly** adv. **un·kempt·ness** n. [ME: from UN-[1] 'not' + *kempt* 'combed' (past part. of archaic *kemb*, rel. to COMB).]

un·kept /ˌənˈkept/ ▶ adj. **1** (of a commitment or undertaking) not honored or fulfilled: *unkept appointments.* **2** not tidy or cared for.

un·kind /ˌənˈkīnd/ ▶ adj. inconsiderate and harsh to others: *you were terribly unkind to her.* — **un·kind·ly** adv. **un·kind·ness** n.

un·kink /ˌənˈkiɴɢk/ ▶ v. straighten or become straight.

un·knit /ˌənˈnit/ ▶ v. (**-knit·ted, -knit·ting**) [trans.] separate (things that are joined, knotted, or interlocked).

un·knot /ˌənˈnät/ ▶ v. (**-knot·ted, -knot·ting**) **1** [trans.] release or untie the knot or knots in. **2** [intrans.] (of a muscle) relax after being tense and hard: *his shoulders unknotted.*

un·know·a·ble /ˌənˈnōəbəl/ ▶ adj. not able to be known: *the total cost is unknowable.* — **un·know·a·bil·i·ty** /-ˌnōəˈbilətē/ n.

un·know·ing /ˌənˈnō-iɴɢ/ ▶ adj. not knowing or aware. ▶ n. lack of awareness or knowledge. — **un·know·ing·ly** adv. **un·know·ing·ness** n.

un·known /ˌənˈnōn/ ▶ adj. not known or familiar. ■ (of a performer or artist) not well known or famous. ▶ n. an unknown person or thing. ■ Math. an unknown quantity or variable. ■ (**the unknown**) that which is unknown.
– PHRASES **unknown to** without the knowledge of: *unknown to Miller, the police had taped their conversation.* — **un·known·ness** n.

un·known quan·ti·ty ▶ n. a person or thing whose nature, value, or significance cannot be determined or is not yet known.

Un·known Sol·dier ▶ n. an unidentified representative member of a country's armed forces killed in war, given burial with special honors in a national memorial.

un·lace /ˌənˈlās/ ▶ v. [trans.] undo the laces of (a shoe or garment).

un·lade /ˌənˈlād/ ▶ v. [trans.] archaic unload (a ship or cargo).

un·la·dy·like /ˌənˈlādēˌlīk/ ▶ adj. not behaving or dressing in a way considered appropriate for a well-bred woman or girl: *Sharon gave an unladylike snort.* ■ (of an activity or occupation) not considered suitable for a woman or girl.

un·laid[1] /ˌənˈlād/ past and past participle of UNLAY.

un·lash /ˌənˈlasʜ/ ▶ v. [trans.] unfasten (something securely tied with a cord or rope).

un·law·ful /ˌənˈlôfəl/ ▶ adj. not conforming to, permitted by, or recognized by law or rules. — **un·law·ful·ly** /-fəlē/ adv. **un·law·ful·ness** n.

un·lay /ˌənˈlā/ ▶ v. (past and past part. **-laid**) [trans.] Naut. untwist (a rope) into separate strands.

un·lead·ed /ˌənˈledid/ ▶ adj. **1** (esp. of gasoline) without added tetraethyl lead. **2** not covered, weighted, or framed with lead. **3** Print. (of type) with no space or leads added between lines. ▶ n. gasoline without added lead.

un·learn /ˌənˈlərn/ ▶ v. [trans.] discard (something learned, esp. a bad habit or false or outdated information) from one's memory.

un·learn·ed[1] /ˌənˈlərnid/ ▶ adj. (of a person) not well educated. — **un·learn·ed·ly** adv.

un·learned[2] /ˌənˈlərnd/ ▶ adj. not having been learned: *she found herself on the stage, lines unlearned.* ■ not needing to be learned because innate.

un·leash /ˌənˈlēsʜ/ ▶ v. [trans.] release from a leash or restraint.

un·less /ənˈles; ˌən-/ ▶ conj. except if (used to introduce the case in which a statement being made is not true or valid): *unless you have a photographic memory, repetition is vital.* [ME: from ON or IN (assimilated through lack of stress to UN-[1]) + LESS.]

United States

Official name: United States of America
Location: North America and islands in the Pacific Ocean
Area: 3,718,800 square miles (9,629,100 sq km)
Population: 293,027,000
Capital: Washington, DC
Languages: English (official), Spanish
Currency: US dollar

un·let·tered /,ən'letərd/ ▶ **adj.** (of a person) poorly educated or illiterate.

un·like /,ən'līk/ ▶ **prep.** different from; not similar to. ■ in contrast to; differently from. ■ uncharacteristic of (someone). ▶ **adj.** dissimilar or different from each other. ■ **(unlike to/from)** archaic not like; different from. — **un·like·ness** n. [ME: perh. alt. of ON *úlíkr*.]

un·like·ly /,ən'līklē/ ▶ **adj.** (**-li·er, -li·est**) not likely to happen, be done, or be true; improbable. — **un·like·li·hood** /-,ho͝od/ n. **un·like·li·ness** n.

un·lim·ber /,ən'limbər/ ▶ **v.** [trans.] detach (a gun) from its limber so that it can be used. ■ unpack or unfasten (something) ready for use.

un·lim·it·ed /,ən'limitid/ ▶ **adj.** not limited or restricted in terms of number, quantity, or extent. ■ Brit. (of a company) not limited. ■ Math. (of a problem) having an infinite number of solutions. — **un·lim·it·ed·ly** adv. **un·lim·it·ed·ness** n.

un·lined[1] /,ən'līnd/ ▶ **adj.** not marked or covered with lines: *her face was still unlined | unlined paper.*

un·lined[2] ▶ **adj.** (of a container or garment) without a lining: *unlined curtains.*

un·link /,ən'liNGk/ ▶ **v.** [trans.] make no longer connected: *cutting any one loop unlinks the other two.* ■ [as adj.] (**unlinked**) unconnected.

un·liq·ui·dat·ed /,ən'likwə,dātid/ ▶ **adj.** (of a debt) not cleared or paid off.

un·list·ed /,ən'listid/ ▶ **adj.** not included on a list. ■ (of a person or telephone number) not listed in a telephone directory or available through directory assistance, at the wish of the subscriber. ■ denoting or relating to a company whose shares are not listed on a stock exchange.

un·lis·ten·a·ble /,ən'lisənəbəl/ ▶ **adj.** (esp. of music) impossible or unbearable to listen to.

un·lit /,ən'lit/ ▶ **adj.** **1** not provided with lighting. **2** not having been set alight: *his unlit pipe.*

un·liv·a·ble /,ən'livəbəl/ ▶ **adj.** not able to be lived in; uninhabitable.

un·lived-in /,ən'livd/ ▶ **adj.** not appearing to be used or inhabited; not homey or comfortable.

un·load /,ən'lōd/ ▶ **v.** [trans.] **1** remove goods from (a vehicle, ship, container, etc.). ■ remove (goods) from a vehicle, ship, container, etc. ■ [intrans.] (of a vehicle, ship, container, etc.) have goods removed: *the street was jammed with trucks unloading.* ■ informal get rid of (something unwanted). ■ informal give expression to (oppressive thoughts or feelings). **2** remove (ammunition) from a gun or (film) from a camera. — **un·load·er** n.

un·lock /,ən'läk/ ▶ **v.** [trans.] undo the lock of (something) by using a key: *he unlocked the door to his room.* ■ make (something previously inaccessible or unexploited) available for use.

un·looked-for /,ən'lo͝okt ,fôr/ ▶ **adj.** unexpected; unforeseen: *in his family he found unlooked-for happiness.*

PRONUNCIATION KEY ə ago, up; ər over, fur; a hat; ā ate; ä car; e let; ē see; i fit; ī by; NG sing; ō go; ô law, for; oi toy; o͝o good; o͞o goo; ou out; TH thin; T͟H then; ZH vision

un·loose /ˌən'lo͞os/ (also **un·loos·en**) ▶ **v.** [trans.] undo; let free.

un·love·ly /ˌən'ləvlē/ ▶ **adj.** not attractive; ugly. — **un·love·li·ness n.**

un·luck·y /ˌən'ləkē/ ▶ **adj.** (**-luck·i·er, -luck·i·est**) having, bringing, or resulting from bad luck. — **un·luck·i·ly** /-'ləkəlē/ **adv. un·luck·i·ness n.**

un·made /ˌən'mād/ ▶ **adj.** (of a bed) not having the bedclothes arranged tidily ready for sleeping in.

un·maid·en·ly /ˌən'mādn-lē/ ▶ **adj.** not befitting or characteristic of a young, sexually inexperienced woman. — **un·maid·en·li·ness n.**

un·make /ˌən'māk/ ▶ **v.** (past and past part. **-made**) [trans.] reverse or undo the making of; annul. ■ ruin; destroy.

un·man /ˌən'man/ ▶ **v.** (**-manned, -man·ning**) [trans.] literary deprive of qualities traditionally associated with men, such as self-control or courage.

un·man·age·a·ble /ˌən'manijəbəl/ ▶ **adj.** difficult or impossible to manage, manipulate, or control. — **un·man·age·a·ble·ness n. un·man·age·a·bly** /-blē/ **adv.**

un·man·aged /ˌən'manijd/ ▶ **adj. 1** not controlled or regulated: *a critique of unmanaged capitalism.* **2** (of land) left wild; in a natural state.

un·man·ly /ˌən'manlē/ ▶ **adj.** not manly; weak or cowardly: *unmanly behavior.* — **un·man·li·ness n.**

un·manned /ˌən'mand/ ▶ **adj.** not having or needing a crew or staff: *an unmanned space flight.*

un·man·nered /ˌən'manərd/ ▶ **adj.** not affected or artificial in style.

un·man·ner·ly /ˌən'manərlē/ ▶ **adj.** not having or showing good manners: *uncouth, unmannerly fellows.* — **un·man·ner·li·ness n.**

un·mapped /ˌən'mapt/ ▶ **adj.** (of an area or feature) not represented on a geographical map. ■ unexplored: *unmapped corners of Africa.* ■ Biol. (of a gene or chromosome) not yet mapped.

un·marked /ˌən'märkt/ ▶ **adj. 1** not marked. ■ Ling. (of a word or other linguistic unit) having a more general meaning or use than a corresponding marked term: *"duck" is unmarked, whereas "drake" is marked.* **2** not noticed: *our unmarked efforts.*

un·mask /ˌən'mask/ ▶ **v.** [trans.] expose the true character of or hidden truth about. ■ [often as adj.] (**unmasked**) remove the mask from. — **un·mask·er n.**

un·match·a·ble /ˌən'macʜəbəl/ ▶ **adj.** incapable of being matched, equaled, or rivaled. — **un·match·a·bly** /-blē/ **adv.**

un·mean·ing /ˌən'mēniɴɢ/ ▶ **adj.** having no meaning or significance; meaningless: *a sweet, unmeaning smile.* — **un·mean·ing·ly adv.**

un·meas·ured /ˌən'meᴢʜərd/ ▶ **adj. 1** not having been measured: *unmeasured risk factors.* **2** esp. literary immense; limitless.

un·me·di·at·ed /ˌən'mēdēˌātid/ ▶ **adj.** without anyone or anything intervening or acting as an intermediate; direct.

un·men·tion·a·ble /ˌən'mencʜənəbəl/ ▶ **adj.** too embarrassing, offensive, or shocking to be spoken about. ▶ **n.** (**unmentionables**) informal undergarments. — **un·men·tion·a·bil·i·ty** /-ˌmencʜənə'bilətē/ **n. un·men·tion·a·ble·ness n. un·men·tion·a·bly** /-blē/ **adv.**

un·mer·ci·ful /ˌən'mərsəfəl/ ▶ **adj.** cruel or harsh; showing no mercy. — **un·mer·ci·ful·ly** /-f(ə)lē/ **adv. un·mer·ci·ful·ness n.**

un·met·ri·cal /ˌən'metrikəl/ ▶ **adj.** not composed in or using meter: *an unmetrical poet.*

un·mind·ful /ˌən'mīndfəl/ ▶ **adj.** not conscious or aware: *unmindful of her parents' plight.* — **un·mind·ful·ly adv. un·mind·ful·ness n.**

un·miss·a·ble /ˌən'misəbəl/ ▶ **adj. 1** so good that it should not be missed. **2** so clear or obvious that it cannot be missed.

un·mit·i·gat·ed /ˌən'mitəˌgātid/ ▶ **adj.** [attrib.] absolute; unqualified. — **un·mit·i·gat·ed·ly adv.**

un·moor /ˌən'mo͝or/ ▶ **v.** [trans.] release the moorings of (a vessel).

un·mor·al /ˌən'môrəl; -'mär-/ ▶ **adj.** not influenced by or concerned with morality. Compare with IMMORAL. — **un·mo·ral·i·ty** /-mə'ralətē; -mô-/ **n.**

un·moth·er·ly /ˌən'məᴛʜərlē/ ▶ **adj.** not having or showing the affectionate feelings associated with a mother.

un·mo·ti·vat·ed /ˌən'mōtəˌvātid/ ▶ **adj. 1** not having interest in or enthusiasm for something, esp. work or study. **2** without a reason or motive: *an unmotivated attack.*

un·moved /ˌən'mo͞ovd/ ▶ **adj.** [predic.] not affected by emotion or excitement: *he was unmoved by her outburst.* ■ not changed in one's purpose or intention. ■ not changed in position. — **un·mov·a·ble** /-vəbəl/ (also **un·move·a·ble**) **adj.**

un·muf·fle /ˌən'məfəl/ ▶ **v.** [trans.] free (something) from something that muffles or conceals.

un·mur·mur·ing /ˌən'mərməriɴɢ/ ▶ **adj.** literary not complaining. — **un·mur·mur·ing·ly adv.**

un·mu·si·cal /ˌən'myo͞ozikəl/ ▶ **adj.** not pleasing to the ear. ■ unskilled in or indifferent to music. — **un·mu·si·cal·i·ty** /-ˌmyo͞ozi'kalətē/ **n. un·mu·si·cal·ly** /-zik(ə)lē/ **adv. un·mu·si·cal·ness n.**

un·muz·zle /ˌən'məzəl/ ▶ **v.** [trans.] remove a muzzle from (an animal). ■ fig. allow (a person or the press) to express their views freely and without censorship.

un·muz·zled /ˌən'məzəld/ ▶ **adj.** (of an animal) not wearing a muzzle.

un·name·a·ble /ˌən'nāməbəl/ (also **un·nam·a·ble**) ▶ **adj.** not able to be named, esp. because too bad or horrific.

un·nat·u·ral /ˌən'nacʜ(ə)rəl/ ▶ **adj.** contrary to the ordinary course of nature; abnormal. ■ not existing in nature; artificial. ■ affected or stilted. ■ lacking feelings of kindness and sympathy that are considered to be natural. — **un·nat·u·ral·ly adv. un·nat·u·ral·ness n.**

un·nec·es·sar·y /ˌən'nesəˌserē/ ▶ **adj.** not needed. ■ more than is needed; excessive. ■ (of a remark) not appropriate and likely to be offensive or impertinent. ▶ **plural n.** (**unnecessaries**) unnecessary things. — **un·nec·es·sar·i·ly** /-ˌnesə'se(ə)rəlē/ **adv. un·nec·es·sar·i·ness n.**

un·nerve /ˌən'nərv/ ▶ **v.** [trans.] make (someone) lose courage or confidence. — **un·nerv·ing·ly adv.**

un·num·bered /ˌən'nəmbərd/ ▶ **adj. 1** not marked with or assigned a number. **2** not counted, typically because very great.

un·o·blig·ing /ˌənə'blījiɴɢ/ ▶ **adj.** not helpful or cooperative.

un·ob·tru·sive /ˌənəb'tro͞osiv/ ▶ **adj.** not conspicuous or attracting attention. — **un·ob·tru·sive·ly adv. un·ob·tru·sive·ness n.**

un·oc·cu·pied /ˌən'äkyəˌpīd/ ▶ **adj. 1** (of ground) not occupied by inhabitants. ■ (of premises) having fixtures and furniture but no inhabitants or occupants. Compare with VACANT. **2** not engaged in work or a pursuit; idle. **3** not occupied by enemy troops.

un·or·dained /ˌənôr'dānd/ ▶ **adj.** not having been ordained as a priest or minister.

un·or·gan·ized /ˌən'ôrgəˌnīzd/ ▶ **adj.** not organized. ■ not represented by or formed into a labor union.

un·or·tho·dox /ˌən'ôrᴛʜəˌdäks/ ▶ **adj.** contrary to what is usual, traditional, or accepted; not orthodox. — **un·or·tho·dox·ly adv. un·or·tho·dox·y** /-ˌdäksē/ **n.**

un·owned /ˌən'ōnd/ ▶ **adj. 1** not having an owner. **2** not admitted to; unacknowledged.

un·pack /ˌən'pak/ ▶ **v.** [trans.] open and remove the contents of (a suitcase, bag, or package). ■ remove (something) from a suitcase, bag, or package. ■ Comput. convert (data) from a compressed form to a usable form. — **un·pack·er n.**

un·paged /ˌən'pājd/ ▶ **adj.** (of a book) not having the pages numbered: *a rare unpaged leaf.*

un·paid /ˌən'pād/ ▶ **adj. 1** (of a debt) not yet discharged by payment. **2** (of work or a period of leave) undertaken without payment. ■ (of a person) not receiving payment for work done.

un·paired /ˌən'pe(ə)rd/ ▶ **adj. 1** not arranged in pairs. **2** not forming one of a pair.

un·pal·at·a·ble /ˌən'palətəbəl/ ▶ **adj.** not pleasant to taste. ■ difficult to put up with or accept. — **un·pal·at·a·bil·i·ty** /-ˌpalətə'bilitē/ **n. un·pal·at·a·bly** /-blē/ **adv.**

un·par·al·leled /ˌən'parəˌleld/ ▶ **adj.** having no parallel or equal; exceptional.

un·par·lia·men·ta·ry /ˌənˌpärlə'mentərē/ ▶ **adj.** (esp. of language) contrary to the rules or procedures of a parliament.

un·peg /ˌən'peg/ ▶ **v.** (**-pegged, -peg·ging**) [trans.] unfasten by the removal of pegs. ■ cease to maintain a fixed relationship between (a currency) and another currency.

un·peo·ple /ˌən'pēpəl/ ▶ **v.** [trans.] [usu. as adj.] (**unpeopled**) empty of people; depopulate.

un·per·son /'ənpərsən; -ˌpər-/ ▶ **n.** (pl. **-per·sons**) a person whose name or existence is denied or ignored, esp. because of a political misdemeanor.

un·per·turbed /ˌənpər'tərbd/ ▶ **adj.** not perturbed or concerned. — **un·per·turbed·ly** /-'tərbədlē/ **adv.**

un·phil·o·soph·i·cal /ˌənˌfilə'säfikəl/ ▶ **adj.** not following philosophical principles or methods. — **un·phil·o·soph·ic adj.** (archaic) **un·phil·o·soph·i·cal·ly** /-ik(ə)lē/ **adv.**

un·phys·i·cal /ˌən'fizikəl/ ▶ **adj.** not in accordance with the laws or principles of physics; not corresponding to a physically possible situation.

un·phys·i·o·log·i·cal /ˌənˌfizēə'läjikəl/ ▶ **adj.** not in accordance with normal physiological conditions. — **un·phys·i·o·log·ic adj. un·phys·i·o·log·i·cal·ly** /-ik(ə)lē/ **adv.**

un·picked /ˌən'pikt/ ▶ **adj. 1** (of a flower, fruit, or vegetable) not picked: *unpicked tomatoes.* **2** not selected.

un·pin /ˌən'pin/ ▶ **v.** (**-pinned, -pin·ning**) [trans.] unfasten or detach by removing a pin or pins. ■ Chess release (a pinned piece or pawn), e.g., by moving away the piece it is shielding.

un·pit·y·ing /ˌən'pitē-iɴɢ/ ▶ **adj.** not feeling or showing pity. — **un·pit·y·ing·ly adv.**

un·place·a·ble /ˌən'plāsəbəl/ ▶ **adj.** not able to be placed or classified: *an unplaceable accent.*

un·placed /ˌən'plāst/ ▶ **adj.** not having or assigned to a specific place. ■ esp. Horse Racing not one of the first three to finish in a race or competition. ■ not appropriate or correct in the circumstances: *a feeling of unplaced alarm.*

un·plant·ed /ˌən'plantid/ ▶ **adj.** (of land) uncultivated.

un·play·a·ble /ˌən'plāəbəl/ ▶ **adj.** not able to be played or played on. ■ (of music) too difficult or bad to perform. — **un·play·a·bly** /-blē/ **adv.**

un·pleas·ant /ˌən'plezənt/ ▶ **adj.** causing discomfort, unhappiness, or revulsion; disagreeable. ■ (of a person or their manner) unfriendly and inconsiderate; rude. — **un·pleas·ant·ly adv.**

un·pleas·ant·ness /ˌən'plezəntnəs/ ▶ **n.** the state or quality of being unpleasant. ■ bad feeling or quarreling between people.

un·pleas·ant·ry /ˌən'plezəntrē/ ▶ **n.** (pl. **-ries**) **1** (**unpleasantries**) disagreeable matters or comments. **2** dated quarreling or other disagreeable behavior.

un·pleas·ing /ˌən'plēziɴɢ/ ▶ **adj.** not giving satisfaction, esp. of an aesthetic kind. — **un·pleas·ing·ly adv.**

un·plea·sure /ˌənˈplezHər/ ▶ **n.** Psychoanal. the sense of inner pain, discomfort, or anxiety that results from the blocking of an instinctual impulse by the ego.

un·plug /ˌənˈpləg/ ▶ **v.** (**-plugged, -plug·ging**) [trans.] **1** disconnect (an electrical device) by removing its plug from a socket. **2** remove an obstacle or blockage from.

un·plugged /ˌənˈpləgd/ ▶ **adj.** trademark (of pop or rock music) performed or recorded with acoustic rather than electrically amplified instruments.

un·plumbed /ˌənˈpləmd/ ▶ **adj.** **1** unsounded; unfathomed: *like a stingray from unplumbed depths.* ■ not fully explored or understood. **2** (of a building or room) not having water and drainage pipes installed and connected. — **un·plumb·a·ble** /-ˈpləməbəl/ **adj.**

un·point·ed /ˌənˈpointid/ ▶ **adj.** **1** not having a sharpened or tapered tip. **2** (of a Semitic language) written without dots or small strokes to indicate vowels or distinguish consonants. **3** (of brickwork, a brick structure, or tiling) having joints that are not filled in or repaired.

un·pol·ished /ˌənˈpälisHt/ ▶ **adj.** not having a polished surface: *his shoes were unpolished.* ■ unrefined in style or behavior.

un·pol·i·tic /ˌənˈpäliˌtik/ ▶ **adj.** rare term for IMPOLITIC.

un·po·lit·i·cal /ˌənpəˈlitikəl/ ▶ **adj.** not concerned with politics; apolitical.

un·polled /ˌənˈpōld/ ▶ **adj.** **1** (of a voter) not having voted, or registered to vote, at an election. ■ (of a vote) not cast at or registered for an election. **2** (of a person) not included in an opinion poll.

un·pop·u·lar /ˌənˈpäpyələr/ ▶ **adj.** not liked or popular. — **un·pop·u·lar·i·ty** /-ˌpäpyəˈlaritē/ **n.**

un·pop·u·lat·ed /ˌənˈpäpyəˌlātid/ ▶ **adj.** (of a place) having no inhabitants. ■ (of a printed circuit board) having no components fitted.

un·pos·sessed /ˌənpəˈzest/ ▶ **adj.** not owned. ■ not having (an ability, quality, or characteristic): *unpossessed of the social graces.*

un·pow·ered /ˌənˈpouərd/ ▶ **adj.** having no fuel-burning source of power for propulsion.

un·prac·ti·cal /ˌənˈpraktikəl/ ▶ **adj.** another term for IMPRACTICAL (sense 1). — **un·prac·ti·cal·i·ty** /-ˌpraktiˈkalətē/ **n.**

un·prac·ticed /ˌənˈpraktist/ (Brit. **un·prac·tised**) ▶ **adj.** (of a person or faculty) not trained or experienced. ■ (of an action or performance) not often done before.

un·prec·e·dent·ed /ˌənˈpresəˌdəntid/ ▶ **adj.** never done or known before. — **un·prec·e·dent·ed·ly** **adv.**

un·pre·dict·a·ble /ˌənpriˈdiktəbəl/ ▶ **adj.** not able to be predicted. ■ (of a person) behaving in a way that is not easily predicted. — **un·pre·dict·a·bil·i·ty** /-ˌdiktəˈbilətē/ **n.** **un·pre·dict·a·bly** /-blē/ **adv.**

un·pre·med·i·tat·ed /ˌənpriˈmedəˌtātid; -prē-/ ▶ **adj.** (of an act, remark, or state) not thought out or planned beforehand. — **un·pre·med·i·tat·ed·ly** **adv.**

un·pre·pared /ˌənpriˈpe(ə)rd/ ▶ **adj.** [predic.] not ready or able to deal with something. ■ not willing to do something: *unprepared to accept what was proposed.* ■ (of a thing) not made ready for use. — **un·pre·par·ed·ness** /-ˈpe(ə)r(i)dnis/ **n.**

un·pre·pos·ses·sing /ˌənˌprēpəˈzesiNG/ ▶ **adj.** not attractive or appealing to the eye.

un·pre·sent·a·ble /ˌənpriˈzentəbəl/ ▶ **adj.** not clean, smart, or decent enough to be seen in public.

un·pres·sur·ized /ˌənˈpresHəˌrīzd/ ▶ **adj.** (of a gas or its container) not having raised pressure that is produced or maintained artificially. ■ (of an aircraft cabin) not having normal atmospheric pressure maintained at a high altitude.

un·pre·tend·ing /ˌənpriˈtendiNG/ ▶ **adj.** archaic not pretentious or false; genuine.

un·pre·ten·tious /ˌənpriˈtencHəs/ ▶ **adj.** not attempting to impress others with an appearance of greater importance, talent, or culture than is actually possessed. ■ (of a place) pleasantly simple and functional; modest. — **un·pre·ten·tious·ly** **adv.** **un·pre·ten·tious·ness** **n.**

un·primed /ˌənˈprīmd/ ▶ **adj.** not made ready for use or action, in particular: ■ (of wood, canvas, or metal) not covered with primer or undercoat. ■ Biol. Med. (of a cell) not having an induced susceptibility or proclivity.

un·prin·ci·pled /ˌənˈprinsəpəld/ ▶ **adj.** (of a person or their behavior) not acting in accordance with moral principles.

un·print·a·ble /ˌənˈprintəbəl/ ▶ **adj.** (of words, comments, or thoughts) too offensive or shocking to be published. — **un·print·a·bly** /-blē/ **adv.**

un·print·ed /ˌənˈprintid/ ▶ **adj.** (of a book or piece of writing) not published.

un·pro·fes·sion·al /ˌənprəˈfesHənl/ ▶ **adj.** below or contrary to the standards expected in a particular profession. — **un·pro·fes·sion·al·ism** /-ˌizəm/ **n.** **un·pro·fes·sion·al·ly** **adv.**

un·prof·it·a·ble /ˌənˈpräfitəbəl/ ▶ **adj.** (of a business or activity) not yielding profit or financial gain. ■ (of an activity) not beneficial or useful. — **un·prof·it·a·bil·i·ty** /-ˌpräfitəˈbilitē/ **n.** **un·prof·it·a·bly** /-blē/ **adv.**

un·prom·is·ing /ˌənˈprämәsiNG/ ▶ **adj.** not giving hope of future success or good results. — **un·prom·is·ing·ly** **adv.**

un·prompt·ed /ˌənˈpräm(p)tid/ ▶ **adv.** without being encouraged or assisted to say or do something. ▶ **adj.** said, done, or acting without being encouraged or assisted: *unprompted remarks.*

un·pro·nounce·a·ble /ˌənprəˈnounsəbəl/ ▶ **adj.** (of a word or name) too difficult to say. — **un·pro·nounce·a·bly** /-blē/ **adv.**

un·pro·tect·ed /ˌənprəˈtektid/ ▶ **adj.** not protected or kept safe from harm or injury. ■ (of a dangerous machine or mechanism) not fitted with safety guards. ■ (of sexual intercourse) performed without a condom. ■ Comput. (of data or a memory location) able to be accessed or used without restriction.

un·prov·a·ble /ˌənˈprōōvəbəl/ ▶ **adj.** unable to be demonstrated by evidence or argument as true or existing. — **un·prov·a·bil·i·ty** /-ˌprōōvəˈbilətē/ **n.**

un·prov·en /ˌənˈprōōvən/ (also **un·proved** /-ˈprōōvd/) ▶ **adj.** not demonstrated by evidence or argument as true or existing. ■ (of a new or alternative product, system, or treatment) not tried and tested.

un·pro·vid·ed /ˌənprəˈvīdid/ ▶ **adj.** [predic.] not provided. ■ (**unprovided with**) not equipped with (something useful or necessary). ■ (**unprovided for**) (of a dependent) not supplied with sufficient money to cover the cost of living.

un·punc·tu·at·ed /ˌənˈpəNGkcHōōˌātid/ ▶ **adj.** (of a continuing event) not interrupted or marked by something occurring at intervals. ■ (of text) not containing punctuation marks.

un·pun·ished /ˌənˈpənisHt/ ▶ **adj.** [as complement] (of an offense or offender) not receiving a penalty or sanction as retribution for transgression.

un·put·down·a·ble /ˌənˌpōōtˈdounəbəl/ ▶ **adj.** informal (of a book) so engrossing that one cannot stop reading it.

un·qual·i·fied /ˌənˈkwäləˌfīd/ ▶ **adj.** **1** (of a person) not officially recognized as a practitioner of a particular profession or activity through having satisfied the relevant conditions or requirements. ■ not competent or sufficiently knowledgeable to do something. **2** without reservation or limitation; total. — **un·qual·i·fied·ly** /-ˌfī(i)dlē/ **adv.**

un·ques·tion·a·ble /ˌənˈkwesCHənəbəl/ ▶ **adj.** not able to be disputed or doubted. — **un·ques·tion·a·bil·i·ty** /-ˈkwesCHənəˈbilətē/ **n.** **un·ques·tion·a·bly** /-blē/ **adv.**

un·ques·tioned /ˌənˈkwesCHənd/ ▶ **adj.** not disputed or doubted; certain. ■ not examined or inquired into. ■ not subjected to questioning.

un·ques·tion·ing /ˌənˈkwesCHəniNG/ ▶ **adj.** accepting something without dissent or doubt. — **un·ques·tion·ing·ly** **adv.**

un·qui·et /ˌənˈkwīət/ ▶ **adj.** not inclined to be quiet or inactive; restless. ■ uneasy; anxious. — **un·qui·et·ly** **adv.** **un·qui·et·ness** **n.**

un·quot·ed /ˌənˈkwōtid/ ▶ **adj.** not quoted or listed on a stock exchange: *an unquoted company.*

un·rat·ed /ˌənˈrātid/ ▶ **adj.** not having received a rating or assessment. ■ (of a film) not allocated an official classification, typically because regarded as unsuitable for general release. ■ informal not highly regarded.

un·rav·el /ˌənˈravəl/ ▶ **v.** (**-rav·eled, -rav·el·ing** ; Brit. **-rav·elled, -rav·el·ling**) [trans.] **1** undo (twisted, knitted, or woven threads). ■ [intrans.] (of twisted, knitted, or woven threads) become undone. ■ unwind (something wrapped around another object). **2** investigate and solve or explain (something complicated or puzzling). ■ [intrans.] begin to fail or collapse.

un·read /ˌənˈred/ ▶ **adj.** (of a book or document) not read. ■ archaic (of a person) not well read.

un·read·a·ble /ˌənˈrēdəbəl/ ▶ **adj.** (of writing) not clear enough to read; illegible. ■ too dull or difficult to be worth reading. ■ (of a facial expression) unable to be interpreted. — **un·read·a·bil·i·ty** /-ˌrēdəˈbilətē/ **n.** **un·read·a·bly** /-blē/ **adv.**

un·re·al /ˌənˈrē(ə)l/ ▶ **adj.** so strange as to appear imaginary; not seeming real. ■ unrealistic: *unreal expectations.* ■ informal incredible; amazing. — **un·re·al·i·ty** /-rēˈalətē/ **n.** **un·re·al·ly** **adv.**

un·re·al·iz·a·ble /ˌənˈrēəˌlīzəbəl; -ˌrēəˈlī-/ ▶ **adj.** not able to be achieved or made to happen.

un·rea·son /ˌənˈrēzən/ ▶ **n.** inability to act or think reasonably.

un·rea·son·a·ble /ˌənˈrēz(ə)nəbəl/ ▶ **adj.** not guided by or based on good sense. ■ beyond the limits of acceptability or fairness. — **un·rea·son·a·ble·ness** **n.** **un·rea·son·a·bly** /-blē/ **adv.**

un·rea·son·ing /ˌənˈrēz(ə)niNG/ ▶ **adj.** not guided by or based on good sense; illogical. — **un·rea·son·ing·ly** **adv.**

un·re·cip·ro·cat·ed /ˌənriˈsiprəˌkātid/ ▶ **adj.** not reciprocated.

un·reck·oned /ˌənˈrekənd/ ▶ **adj.** not calculated or taken into account.

un·re·con·struct·ed /ˌənˌrēkənˈstrəktid/ ▶ **adj.** not reconciled or converted to the current political theory or movement.

un·re·cov·er·a·ble /ˌənriˈkəvərəbəl/ ▶ **adj.** not able to be recovered or corrected.

un·reel /ˌənˈrēl/ ▶ **v.** [trans.] unwind (something wrapped around another object). ■ [intrans.] (of a film) wind from one reel to another during projection.

un·reeve /ˌənˈrēv/ ▶ **v.** (past **-rove** /-ˈrōv/) [trans.] Naut. withdraw (a rope) from a pulley block or other object.

un·re·flect·ing /ˌənriˈflektiNG/ ▶ **adj.** **1** not engaging in reflection or thought. **2** not reflecting light. — **un·re·flect·ing·ly** **adv.** **un·re·flect·ing·ness** **n.** **un·re·flec·tive** /-tiv/ **adj.**

un·re·gard·ed /ˌənriˈgärdid/ ▶ **adj.** not respected or considered; ignored.

un·re·gen·er·ate /ˌənriˈjenərət/ ▶ **adj.** not reforming or showing repentance; obstinately wrong or bad. — **un·re·gen·er·a·cy** /-rəsē/ **n.** **un·re·gen·er·ate·ly** **adv.**

un·re·lent·ing /ˌənriˈlentiNG/ ▶ **adj.** not yielding in strength, severity, or determination: *the heat was unrelenting.* ■ (of a person or their behavior) not giving way to kindness or compassion. — **un·re·lent·ing·ly adv. un·re·lent·ing·ness n.**

un·re·lieved /ˌənriˈlēvd/ ▶ **adj.** lacking variation or change; monotonous. ■ not provided with relief; not aided or assisted. — **un·re·liev·ed·ly** /-ˈlēvidlē/ **adv.**

un·re·li·gious /ˌənriˈlijəs/ ▶ **adj.** indifferent or hostile to religion. ■ not connected with religion.

un·re·mark·a·ble /ˌənriˈmärkəbəl/ ▶ **adj.** not particularly interesting or surprising. — **un·re·mark·a·bly** /-blē/ **adv.**

un·re·marked /ˌənriˈmärkt/ ▶ **adj.** not mentioned or remarked upon; unnoticed.

un·re·mit·ting /ˌənriˈmitiNG/ ▶ **adj.** never relaxing or slackening; incessant. — **un·re·mit·ting·ly adv. un·re·mit·ting·ness n.**

un·re·peat·a·ble /ˌənriˈpētəbəl/ ▶ **adj.** not able to be done or made again. ■ too offensive or shocking to be said again. — **un·re·peat·a·bil·i·ty** /-ˌpētəˈbilətē/ **n.**

un·re·quit·ed /ˌənriˈkwītid/ ▶ **adj.** (of a feeling, esp. love) not returned or rewarded. — **un·re·quit·ed·ly adv. un·re·quit·ed·ness n.**

un·re·serve /ˌənriˈzərv/ ▶ **n.** archaic lack of reserve; frankness.

un·re·served /ˌənriˈzərvd/ ▶ **adj. 1** without reservations; complete: *he has had their unreserved support.* ■ frank and open: *a tall, unreserved young man.* **2** not set apart for a particular purpose or booked in advance: *unreserved grandstand seats.* — **un·re·serv·ed·ly** /-ˈzərvidlē/ **adv. un·re·serv·ed·ness** /-ˈzərvədnəs/ **n.**

un·re·solved /ˌənriˈzälvd; -ˈzôlvd/ ▶ **adj.** (of a problem, question, or dispute) not resolved. ■ archaic (of a person) uncertain of what to think or do. — **un·re·solv·ed·ly** /-ˈzälvidlē; -ˈzôl-/ **adv. un·re·solv·ed·ness** /-ˈzälvidnəs; -ˈzôl-/ **n.**

un·rest /ˌənˈrest/ ▶ **n.** a state of dissatisfaction, disturbance, and agitation in a group of people, typically involving public demonstrations or disorder. ■ a feeling of disturbance and dissatisfaction in a person: *the frenzy and unrest of her own life.*

un·rest·ing /ˌənˈrestiNG/ ▶ **adj.** ceaselessly active. — **un·rest·ing·ly adv.**

un·re·strained /ˌənriˈstrānd/ ▶ **adj.** not restrained or restricted: *a display of unrestrained delight.* — **un·re·strain·ed·ly** /-ˈstrānidlē/ **adv. un·re·strain·ed·ness** /-ˈstrānidnis/ **n.**

un·re·straint /ˌənriˈstrānt/ ▶ **n.** lack of restraint, or freedom from it; wildness: *they enjoyed the unrestraint of drunkenness.*

un·re·turned /ˌənriˈtərnd/ ▶ **adj.** not reciprocated or responded to: *phone calls go unreturned.*

un·rid·den /ˌənˈridn/ ▶ **adj.** not ridden or never having been ridden or broken in.

un·rid·dle /ˌənˈridl/ ▶ **v.** [trans.] rare solve; explain.

un·ride·a·ble /ˌənˈrīdəbəl/ (also **un·rid·a·ble**) ▶ **adj.** not able to be ridden.

un·rig /ˌənˈrig/ ▶ **v.** (**-rigged, -rig·ging**) [trans.] remove the rigging from (a ship).

un·right·eous /ˌənˈrīCHəs/ ▶ **adj.** formal not righteous; wicked. — **un·right·eous·ly adv. un·right·eous·ness n.** [OE *unrihtwīs* (see UN-[1], RIGHTEOUS).]

un·rip /ˌənˈrip/ ▶ **v.** (**-ripped, -rip·ping**) [trans.] rare open by ripping: *he carefully unripped one of the seams.*

un·ri·valed /ˌənˈrīvəld/ (Brit. **un·ri·valled**) ▶ **adj.** better than everyone or everything of the same type.

un·riv·et /ˌənˈrivit/ ▶ **v.** (**-riv·et·ed, -riv·et·ing**) [trans.] rare undo, unfasten, or detach by the removal of rivets.

un·road·wor·thy /ˌənˈrōdˌwərT͟Hē/ ▶ **adj.** (of a vehicle) not roadworthy.

un·robe /ˌənˈrōb/ ▶ **v.** less common term for DISROBE.

un·roll /ˌənˈrōl/ ▶ **v.** open or cause to open out from a rolled-up state: [intrans.] *the blanket unrolled as he tugged it* | [trans.] *two carpets had been unrolled.*

un·roof /ˌənˈro͞of; -ˈro͝of/ ▶ **v.** [trans.] rare remove the roof of.

un·root /ˌənˈro͞ot; -ˈro͝ot/ ▶ **v.** [trans.] uproot (something).

un·rope /ˌənˈrōp/ ▶ **v.** [intrans.] Climbing detach oneself from a rope.

un·round·ed /ˌənˈroundid/ ▶ **adj.** not rounded. ■ Phonet. (of a vowel) pronounced with the lips not rounded.

un·rove /ˌənˈrōv/ past of UNREEVE.

un·ruf·fled /ˌənˈrəfəld/ ▶ **adj.** not disordered or disarranged: *the unruffled waters of the lake.* ■ (of a person) not agitated or disturbed; calm.

un·ruled /ˌənˈro͞old/ ▶ **adj. 1** literary not ruled, governed, or under control: *men with passions unruled.* **2** (of paper) not having ruled lines.

un·ru·ly /ˌənˈro͞olē/ ▶ **adj.** (**-li·er, -li·est**) disorderly and disruptive and not amenable to discipline or control: *complaints about unruly behavior.* ■ (of hair) difficult to keep neat and tidy. — **un·ru·li·ness n.** [ME: from UN-[1] 'not' + archaic *ruly* 'amenable to discipline or order' (from RULE).]

UNRWA /ˈənrə/ ▶ **abbr.** United Nations Relief and Works Agency.

un·sad·dle /ˌənˈsadl/ ▶ **v.** [trans.] remove the saddle from (a horse or other ridden animal). ■ dislodge from a saddle.

un·safe sex ▶ **n.** sexual activity in which precautions are not taken to reduce the risk of spreading sexually transmitted diseases, esp. AIDS.

un·said /ˌənˈsed/ past and past participle of UNSAY. ▶ **adj.** not said or uttered.

un·sal·a·ble /ˌənˈsāləbəl/ (also **un·sale·a·ble**) ▶ **adj.** not able to be sold: *the house proved unsalable.* — **un·sal·a·bil·i·ty** /-ˌsāləˈbilətē/ **n.**

un·sat·is·fac·to·ry /ˌənˌsatəsˈfakt(ə)rē/ ▶ **adj.** unacceptable because poor or not good enough. — **un·sat·is·fac·to·ri·ly** /-ˈfakt(ə)rəlē/ **adv. un·sat·is·fac·to·ri·ness n.**

un·sat·u·rat·ed /ˌənˈsaCHəˌrātid/ ▶ **adj.** Chem. (of organic molecules) having carbon–carbon double or triple bonds and therefore not containing the greatest possible number of hydrogen atoms. — **un·sat·u·ra·tion** /-ˌsaCHəˈrāSHən/ **n.**

un·saved /ˌənˈsāvd/ ▶ **adj.** not saved, in particular (in Christian use) not having had one's soul saved from damnation.

un·sa·vor·y /ˌənˈsāv(ə)rē/ (Brit. **un·sa·vour·y**) ▶ **adj.** disagreeable to taste, smell, or look at. ■ disagreeable and unpleasant because morally disreputable: *an unsavory reputation.* — **un·sa·vor·i·ly** /-rəlē/ **adv. un·sa·vor·i·ness n.**

un·say /ˌənˈsā/ ▶ **v.** (past and past part. **-said**) [trans.] withdraw or retract (a statement).

un·say·a·ble /ˌənˈsāəbəl/ ▶ **adj.** not able to be said, esp. because considered too controversial or offensive to mention.

un·scathed /ˌənˈskāT͟Hd/ ▶ **adj.** [predic.] without suffering any injury, damage, or harm: *I came through all those perils unscathed.*

un·schooled /ˌənˈsko͞old/ ▶ **adj.** not educated at or made to attend school: *unschooled children.* ■ lacking knowledge or training in a particular field. ■ not affected or artificial; natural and spontaneous.

un·sci·en·tif·ic /ˌənˌsīənˈtifik/ ▶ **adj. 1** not in accordance with scientific principles or methodology. **2** lacking knowledge of or interest in science. — **un·sci·en·tif·i·cal·ly** /-ik(ə)lē/ **adv.**

un·scram·ble /ˌənˈskrambəl/ ▶ **v.** [trans.] restore (something that has been scrambled) to an intelligible, readable, or viewable state. — **un·scram·bler** /-b(ə)lər/ **n.**

un·screened /ˌənˈskrēnd/ ▶ **adj. 1** not subjected to testing or investigation by screening. ■ not filtered or sorted using a screen. **2** (of a movie or television program) not shown or broadcast: *copies of the unscreened episodes.* **3** not provided with or hidden by a screen.

un·screw /ˌənˈskro͞o/ ▶ **v.** (with reference to a lid or other object held in place by a spiral thread) unfasten or be unfastened by twisting: [trans.] *Will unscrewed the cap* | [intrans.] *the spout usually unscrews easily.* ■ [trans.] detach, open, or slacken (something) by removing or loosening the screws holding it in place.

un·script·ed /ˌənˈskriptid/ ▶ **adj.** said or delivered without a prepared script; impromptu.

un·scru·pu·lous /ˌənˈskro͞opyələs/ ▶ **adj.** having or showing no moral principles; not honest or fair. — **un·scru·pu·lous·ly adv. un·scru·pu·lous·ness n.**

un·seal /ˌənˈsēl/ ▶ **v.** [trans.] remove or break the seal of.

un·search·a·ble /ˌənˈsərCHəbəl/ ▶ **adj.** literary unable to be clearly understood; inscrutable. — **un·search·a·ble·ness n. un·search·a·bly** /-blē/ **adv.**

un·sea·son·a·ble /ˌənˈsēzənəbəl/ ▶ **adj.** (of weather) unusual for the time of year: *an unseasonable warm spell.* ■ untimely; inopportune. — **un·sea·son·a·ble·ness n. un·sea·son·a·bly** /-blē/ **adv.**

un·sea·son·al /ˌənˈsēzənəl/ ▶ **adj.** (esp. of weather) unusual or inappropriate for the time of year.

un·sea·soned /ˌənˈsēzənd/ ▶ **adj. 1** (of food) not flavored with salt, pepper, or other spices or seasonings. **2** (of timber) not treated or matured. ■ (of a person) inexperienced.

un·seat /ˌənˈsēt/ ▶ **v.** [trans.] cause (someone) to fall from a horse or bicycle. ■ remove from a position of power or authority.

un·se·cured /ˌənsiˈkyo͝ord/ ▶ **adj. 1** (of a loan) made without an asset given as security. ■ (of a creditor) having made such a loan. **2** not made secure or safe.

un·see·a·ble /ˌənˈsēəbəl/ ▶ **adj.** not able to be seen; invisible.

un·see·ing /ˌənˈsēiNG/ ▶ **adj.** with one's eyes open but without noticing or seeing anything. — **un·see·ing·ly adv.**

un·seem·ly /ˌənˈsēmlē/ ▶ **adj.** (of behavior or actions) not proper or appropriate: *an unseemly squabble.* — **un·seem·li·ness n.**

un·seen /ˌənˈsēn/ ▶ **adj.** not seen or noticed. ■ not foreseen or predicted: *unseen problems.* ■ esp. Brit. (of a passage for translation in a test or examination) not previously read or prepared.

un·self·con·scious /ˌənˌselfˈkänsHəs/ ▶ **adj.** not suffering from or exhibiting self-consciousness; not shy or embarrassed. — **un·self·con·scious·ly adv. un·self·con·scious·ness n.**

un·self·ish /ˌənˈselfiSH/ ▶ **adj.** willing to put the needs or wishes of others before one's own: *unselfish devotion.* — **un·self·ish·ly adv. un·self·ish·ness n.**

Un·ser /ˈənsər/ a family of US race car drivers. Bobby (1934–), full name *Robert William Unser,* won three Indy 500 races during 1968–81. His brother Al (1939–), full name *Alfred Unser,* won four Indy 500 races during 1970–87. Al's son Al, Jr. (1962–), full name *Alfred Unser, Jr.,* won two Indy 500 races 1992, 1994.

un·served /ˌənˈsərvd/ ▶ **adj. 1** (of a person or section of society) not attended to: *unserved audiences.* **2** Law (of a writ or summons) not officially delivered to a person: *there is no point in leaving a writ unserved.*

un·set /ˌənˈset/ ▶ **adj. 1** (of a jewel) not yet placed in a setting; unmounted: *ten unset sapphires.* **2** (of cement) not yet hardened.

un·set·tle /ˌənˈsetl/ ▶ **v.** [trans.] cause to feel anxious or uneasy; disturb. — **un·set·tle·ment n. un·set·tling·ly adv.**

un·set·tled /ˌənˈsetld/ ▶ **adj. 1** lacking stability: *an unsettled child-*

hood. ■ worried and uneasy. ■ liable to change; unpredictable: *a spell of unsettled weather.* ■ not yet resolved. ■ (of a bill) not yet paid. **2** (of an area) having no settlers or inhabitants. — **un·set·tled·ness** n.

un·sex /,ən'seks/ ▶ v. [trans.] deprive of gender, sexuality, or the characteristic attributes or qualities of one or other sex.

un·sexed /,ən'sekst/ ▶ adj. having no sexual characteristics.

un·sex·y /,ən'seksē/ ▶ adj. (**-sex·i·er, -sex·i·est**) not sexually attractive or exciting.

un·shack·le /,ən'SHakəl/ ▶ v. [trans.] (usu. **be unshackled**) release from shackles, chains, or other physical restraints: *his feet were unshackled.* ■ fig. liberate; set free.

un·shad·ed /,ən'SHādid/ ▶ adj. **1** (of a light bulb or lamp) not having a shade or cover. ■ not screened from direct light. **2** (of an area of a diagram) not shaded with pencil lines or a block of color.

un·shad·owed /,ən'SHadōd/ ▶ adj. not covered or darkened by a shadow or shadows.

un·shak·a·ble /,ən'SHākəbəl/ (also **un·shake·a·ble**) ▶ adj. (of a belief, feeling, or opinion) strongly felt and unable to be changed: *an unshakable faith in God.* ■ unable to be disputed or questioned. — **un·shak·a·bil·i·ty** /-,SHākə'bilətē/ n. **un·shak·a·bly** /-blē/ adv.

un·shak·en /,ən'SHākən/ ▶ adj. not disturbed from a firm position or state; steadfast and unwavering. — **un·sha·ken·ly** adv.

un·shaped /,ən'SHāpt/ ▶ adj. having a vague, ill-formed, or unfinished shape.

un·shav·en /,ən'SHāvən/ ▶ adj. not having recently shaved or been shaved.

un·sheathe /,ən'SHēTH/ ▶ v. [trans.] draw or pull out (a knife, sword, or similar weapon) from its sheath or covering.

un·shed /,ən'SHed/ ▶ adj. (of tears) welling in a person's eyes but not falling on their cheeks.

un·ship /,ən'SHip/ ▶ v. (**-shipped, -ship·ping**) [trans.] esp. Naut. remove (an oar, mast, or other object) from its fixed or regular position. ■ unload (a cargo) from a ship or boat.

un·shrink·a·ble /,ən'SHriNGkəbəl/ ▶ adj. (of fabric, etc.) not liable to shrink. — **un·shrink·a·bil·i·ty** /-,SHriNGkə'bilətē/ n.

un·shrink·ing /,ən'SHriNGkiNG/ ▶ adj. unhesitating; fearless. — **un·shrink·ing·ly** adv.

un·sight·ed /,ən'sītid/ ▶ adj. lacking the power of sight. ■ not seen: *a distant unsighted object.* ■ (esp. in sports) prevented from having a clear view of something.

un·sight·ly /,ən'sītlē/ ▶ adj. unpleasant to look at; ugly. — **un·sight·li·ness** n.

un·signed /,ən'sīnd/ ▶ adj. **1** not identified or authorized by a person's signature: *an unsigned check.* ■ (of a musician or sports player) not having signed a contract of employment. **2** Math. Comput. not having a plus or minus sign, or a bit representing this.

un·sis·ter·ly /,ən'sistərlē/ ▶ adj. not showing the support and affection that is thought to be characteristic of a sister.

un·sized /,ən'sīzd/ ▶ adj. (of fabric, paper, or a wall) not treated with size.

un·skilled /,ən'skild/ ▶ adj. not having or requiring special skill or training: *unskilled manual workers.*

un·skill·ful /,ən'skilfəl/ ▶ adj. not having or showing skill. — **un·skill·ful·ly** adv. **un·skill·ful·ness** n.

un·sleep·ing /,ən'slēpiNG/ ▶ adj. not or never sleeping. — **un·sleep·ing·ly** adv.

un·sling /,ən'sliNG/ ▶ v. (past and past part. **-slung**) [trans.] remove (something) from the place where it has been slung or suspended.

un·smil·ing /,ən'smīliNG/ ▶ adj. (of a person or their manner or expression) serious or unfriendly; not smiling. — **un·smil·ing·ly** adv. **un·smil·ing·ness** n.

un·smoked /,ən'smōkt/ ▶ adj. **1** (of meat or fish) not cured by exposure to smoke. **2** (of tobacco or a cigarette) not having been smoked.

un·snap /,ən'snap/ ▶ v. (**-snapped, -snap·ping**) [trans.] unfasten or open with a brisk movement and a sharp sound: *he unsnapped the clasps.*

un·snarl /,ən'snärl/ ▶ v. [trans.] disentangle; sort out.

un·so·cia·ble /,ən'sōSHəbəl/ ▶ adj. not enjoying or making an effort to behave sociably in the company of others. ■ not conducive to friendly social relations. — **un·so·cia·bil·i·ty** /-,sōSHə'bilətē/ n. **un·so·cia·ble·ness** n. **un·so·cia·bly** /-blē/ adv.

un·so·cial /,ən'sōSHəl/ ▶ adj. not seeking the company of others: *woodchucks lead a relatively unsocial life.* ■ causing annoyance and disapproval in others; antisocial: *the unsocial behavior of young teenagers.* — **un·so·cial·ly** adv.

un·sold /,ən'sōld/ ▶ adj. (of an item) not sold.

un·sol·der /,ən'sädər; -'sôdər/ ▶ v. [trans.] undo the soldering of.

un·so·lic·it·ed /,ənsə'lisitid/ ▶ adj. not asked for; given or done voluntarily: *unsolicited junk mail.* — **un·so·lic·it·ed·ly** adv.

un·so·phis·ti·cat·ed /,ənsə'fistə,kātid/ ▶ adj. lacking refined worldly knowledge or tastes. ■ not complicated or highly developed; basic: *unsophisticated computer software.* ■ not artificial. — **un·so·phis·ti·cat·ed·ly** adv. **un·so·phis·ti·cat·ed·ness** n. **un·so·phis·ti·ca·tion** /-,fisti'kāSHən/ n.

un·sound /,ən'sound/ ▶ adj. not safe or robust; in poor condition: *the tower is structurally unsound.* ■ not based on sound evidence or reasoning and therefore unreliable or unacceptable. ■ (of a person) not competent, reliable, or holding acceptable views. ■ injured, ill, or diseased, esp. (of a horse) lame. — **un·sound·ly** adv. **un·sound·ness** n.

un·sound·ed[1] /,ən'soundid/ ▶ adj. not uttered, pronounced, or made to sound.

un·sound·ed[2] ▶ adj. unfathomed.

un·spar·ing /,ən'spe(ə)riNG/ ▶ adj. **1** merciless; severe. **2** given freely and generously: *unsparing approval.* — **un·spar·ing·ly** adv. **un·spar·ing·ness** n.

un·speak·a·ble /,ən'spēkəbəl/ ▶ adj. not able to be expressed in words: *an unspeakable tenderness.* ■ too bad or horrific to express in words. — **un·speak·a·ble·ness** n. **un·speak·a·bly** /-blē/ adv.

un·speak·ing /,ən'spēkiNG/ ▶ adj. not speaking; silent.

un·spec·tac·u·lar /,ənspek'takyələr; -spək-/ ▶ adj. not spectacular; unremarkable. — **un·spec·tac·u·lar·ly** adv.

un·spent /,ən'spent/ ▶ adj. not spent. ■ not exhausted or used up: *he shook with unspent rage.*

un·spilled /,ən'spild/ (also **un·spilt** /-'spilt/) ▶ adj. not spilt.

un·spir·i·tu·al /,ən'spiriCHōōəl/ ▶ adj. not spiritual; worldly: *the clergymen were deplorably unspiritual.* — **un·spir·i·tu·al·i·ty** /-,spiriCHōō'alitē/ n. **un·spir·i·tu·al·ly** adv.

un·spoiled /,ən'spoild/ (Brit. also **un·spoilt** /,ən'spoilt/) ▶ adj. not spoiled, in particular (of a place) not marred by development: *unspoiled countryside.*

un·spool /,ən'spōōl/ ▶ v. [intrans.] unwind from or as if from a spool. ■ (of a film) be screened. ■ [trans.] show (a film).

un·sports·man·like /,ən'spôrtsmən,līk/ ▶ adj. not fair, generous, or sportsmanlike.

un·sprung /,ən'sprəNG/ ▶ adj. not provided with springs.

un·sta·ble /,ən'stābəl/ ▶ adj. (**-bler, -blest**) prone to change, fail, or give way; not stable. ■ prone to psychiatric problems or sudden changes of mood: *he was mentally unstable.* — **un·sta·ble·ness** n. **un·sta·bly** /-blē/ adv.

un·stage·a·ble /,ən'stājəbəl/ ▶ adj. (of a play) impossible or very difficult to present to an audience.

un·states·man·like /,ən'stātsmən,līk/ ▶ adj. not suitable for or befitting a statesman.

un·stead·y /,ən'stedē/ ▶ adj. (**-stead·i·er, -stead·i·est**) **1** liable to fall or shake; not firm. **2** not uniform or regular: *a soft unsteady voice.* — **un·stead·i·ly** /-'stedl-ē/ adv. **un·stead·i·ness** n.

un·step /,ən'step/ ▶ v. (**-stepped, -step·ping**) [trans.] remove (a mast) from its step.

un·stick /,ən'stik/ ▶ v. (past and past part. **-stuck**) [trans.] cause to become no longer stuck together.

– PHRASES **come** (or **get**) **unstuck** become separated or unfastened. ■ informal fail completely: *all their clever ideas came unstuck.*

un·stint·ing /,ən'stintiNG/ ▶ adj. given or giving without restraint; unsparing: *he was unstinting in his praise.* — **un·stint·ing·ly** adv.

un·stirred /,ən'stərd/ ▶ adj. not moved, agitated, or stirred.

un·stop /,ən'stäp/ ▶ v. (**-stopped, -stop·ping**) [trans.] free (something) from obstruction. ■ remove the stopper from (a bottle or other container).

un·stop·pa·ble /,ən'stäpəbəl/ ▶ adj. impossible to stop or prevent: *an unstoppable army.* — **un·stop·pa·bil·i·ty** /-,stäpə'bilətē/ n. **un·stop·pa·bly** /-blē/ adv.

un·strap /,ən'strap/ ▶ v. (**-strapped, -strap·ping**) [trans.] undo the strap or straps of. ■ release (someone or something) by undoing straps.

un·stressed /,ən'strest/ ▶ adj. **1** Phonet. (of a syllable) not pronounced with stress: *an unstressed syllable.* **2** not subjected to stress: *an unstressed person.*

un·string /,ən'striNG/ ▶ v. (past and past part. **-strung**) [trans.] **1** [usu. as adj.] (**unstrung**) unnerve. **2** remove or relax the string or strings of (a bow or musical instrument). **3** remove from a string: *unstring the beads.*

un·struc·tured /,ən'strəkCHərd/ ▶ adj. without formal organization or structure: *an unstructured interview.*

un·stuck /,ən'stək/ past and past participle of UNSTICK.

un·stud·ied /,ən'stədēd/ ▶ adj. not labored or artificial; natural: *she had an unstudied grace in every step.* — **un·stud·ied·ly** adv.

un·sub·scribe /,ənsəb'skrīb/ ▶ v. [intrans.] cancel a subscription, esp. to an Internet newsletter, newsgroup, or electronic mailing list.

un·sub·stan·tial /,ənsəb'stanCHəl/ ▶ adj. having little or no solidity, reality, or factual basis. — **un·sub·stan·ti·al·i·ty** /-,stanCHē'alitē/ n. **un·sub·stan·tial·ly** adv.

un·sug·ared /,ən'SHōōgərd/ ▶ adj. not sweetened or sprinkled with sugar.

un·suit·ed /,ən'sōōtid/ ▶ adj. [predic.] not right or appropriate: *he was totally unsuited for the job.*

un·sung /,ən'səNG/ ▶ adj. not celebrated or praised.

un·su·per·vised /,ən'sōōpər,vīzd/ ▶ adj. not done or acting under supervision: *unsupervised visits.* ■ (of a person) not watched over in the interest of their or others' security: *unsupervised youths pose a threat.*

un·sup·port·ed /,ənsə'pôrtid/ ▶ adj. (of a structure, object, or person) not supported physically. ■ not borne out by evidence or facts. ■ (of a person or activity) not given financial or other assistance. ■ Comput. (of a program, language, or device) not having assistance for the user available from a manufacturer or system manager.

un·sup·port·ive /ˌənsəˈpôrtiv/ ▶ **adj.** not providing encouragement or emotional help.

un·sure /ˌənˈSHo͝or/ ▶ **adj.** not feeling, showing, or done with confidence and certainty: *she was **unsure of** herself | she was unsure how to reply.* ■ (of a fact) not fixed or certain: *the date is unsure.* — **un·sure·ly adv. un·sure·ness n.**

un·sur·faced /ˌənˈsərfist/ ▶ **adj.** (of a road or path) not provided with a durable upper layer.

un·sur·mount·a·ble /ˌənsərˈmoun(t)əbəl/ ▶ **adj.** not able to be overcome; insurmountable.

un·sus·cep·ti·ble /ˌənsəˈseptəbəl/ ▶ **adj. 1** not likely or liable to be influenced or harmed by a particular thing: *infants are relatively **unsusceptible** to infections.* **2** [predic.] (**unsusceptible of**) not capable or admitting of: *their meaning is unsusceptible of analysis.* — **un·sus·cep·ti·bil·i·ty** /-ˌseptəˈbilitē/ **n.**

un·sus·pect·ed /ˌənsəˈspektid/ ▶ **adj.** not known or thought to exist or be present; not imagined possible. ■ (of a person) not regarded with suspicion. — **un·sus·pect·ed·ly adv.**

un·sus·pect·ing /ˌənsəˈspektiNG/ ▶ **adj.** (of a person or animal) not aware of the presence of danger; feeling no suspicion: *mines lie in wait for their unsuspecting victims.* — **un·sus·pect·ing·ly adv. un·sus·pect·ing·ness n.**

un·sus·pi·cious /ˌənsəˈspiSHəs/ ▶ **adj.** not having or showing suspicion. — **un·sus·pi·cious·ly** /ˌənsəˈspiSHəslē/ **adv. un·sus·pi·cious·ness** /ˌənsəˈspiSHəsnəs/ **n.**

un·sus·tain·a·ble /ˌənsəˈstānəbəl/ ▶ **adj.** not able to be maintained at the current rate or level. ■ Ecol. upsetting the ecological balance by depleting natural resources: *unsustainable fishing practices.* ■ not able to be upheld or defended. — **un·sus·tain·a·bly** /-blē/ **adv.**

un·swayed /ˌənˈswād/ ▶ **adj.** (of a person) not influenced or affected.

un·swept /ˌənˈswept/ ▶ **adj.** (of an area) not cleaned by having the dirt or litter on it swept up.

un·swerv·ing /ˌənˈswərviNG/ ▶ **adj.** not changing or becoming weaker; steady or constant: *unswerving loyalty.* — **un·swerv·ing·ly adv.**

un·sworn /ˌənˈswôrn/ ▶ **adj.** Law (of testimony or evidence) not given under oath.

un·sym·pa·thet·ic /ˌənˌsimpəˈTHetik/ ▶ **adj.** not feeling, showing, or expressing sympathy. ■ not showing approval or favor toward an idea or action: *they were **unsympathetic toward** the cause.* ■ (of a person) not friendly or cooperative; unlikeable. — **un·sym·pa·thet·i·cal·ly** /-ik(ə)lē/ **adv.**

un·sys·tem·at·ic /ˌənˌsistəˈmatik/ ▶ **adj.** not done or acting according to a fixed plan or system; unmethodical: *they were unsystematic in their use of the data.* — **un·sys·tem·at·i·cal·ly** /-ik(ə)lē/ **adv.**

un·tack[1] /ˌənˈtak/ ▶ **v.** [trans.] detach (something) by the removal of tacks.

un·tack[2] ▶ **v.** [trans.] remove the saddle and bridle from (a horse).

un·tak·en /ˌənˈtākən/ ▶ **adj. 1** (of a region or person) not taken by force; uncaptured. **2** (of an action) not put into effect.

un·tan·gle /ˌənˈtaNGgəl/ ▶ **v.** [trans.] free from a tangled or twisted state: *fishermen untangle their nets.* ■ make (something complicated or confusing) easier to understand or deal with.

un·tapped /ˌənˈtapt/ ▶ **adj. 1** (of a resource) not yet exploited or used: *a huge, untapped market for bagels.* **2** (of a telephone, etc.) free from listening devices.

un·tast·ed /ˌənˈtāstid/ ▶ **adj.** (of food or drink) not sampled or tested for flavor.

un·taught /ˌənˈtôt/ ▶ **adj.** (of a person) not trained by teaching: *she is totally untaught and will not listen.* ■ not acquired by teaching; natural or spontaneous.

un·teach /ˌənˈtēCH/ ▶ **v.** (past and past part. **-taught**) **1** cause (someone) to forget or discard previous knowledge. **2** remove from the mind (something known or taught) by different teaching.

un·tem·pered /ˌənˈtempərd/ ▶ **adj.** not moderated or lessened by anything: *untempered by political imagination.* ■ (of a material) not brought to the proper hardness or consistency.

un·ten·a·ble /ˌənˈtenəbəl/ ▶ **adj.** (esp. of a position or view) not able to be maintained or defended against attack or objection: *this argument is clearly untenable.* — **un·ten·a·bil·i·ty** /-ˌtenəˈbilitē/ **n. un·ten·a·bly** /-blē/ **adv.**

un·tend·ed /ˌənˈtendid/ ▶ **adj.** not cared for or looked after; neglected: *untended gravestones.*

un·ten·ured /ˌənˈtenyərd/ ▶ **adj.** (of a teacher, lecturer, or other professional) not having a permanent post. ■ (of an academic or other post) not permanent.

Un·ter·mensch /ˈo͝ontərˌmenCH/ ▶ **n.** (pl. **-mensch·en** /-ˌmenCHən/) a person considered racially or socially inferior. [Ger., lit. 'underperson.']

Un·ter·mey·er /ˈəntərˌmīər/, Louis (1885–1977), US writer and poet. He published critical anthologies, as well as his own poetry, such as "Long Feud" (1962).

un·teth·er /ˌənˈteT͟Hər/ ▶ **v.** [trans.] release or free from a tether: *I reached the horses and untethered them.*

un·thanked /ˌənˈTHaNGkt/ ▶ **adj.** without receiving thanks: *the women's kind gesture did not go **unthanked**.*

un·thaw /ˌənˈTHô/ ▶ **v. 1** melt or thaw: [trans.] *the warm weather helped unthaw the rail lines.* **2** [as adj.] (**unthawed**) still frozen; unmelted.

un·think·a·ble /ˌənˈTHiNGkəbəl/ ▶ **adj.** (of a situation or event) too unlikely or undesirable to be considered a possibility: *it was unthinkable that John could be dead* | [as n.] (**the unthinkable**) *the unthinkable happened.* — **un·think·a·bil·i·ty** /-ˌTHiNGkəˈbilitē/ **n. un·think·a·bly** /-blē/ **adv.** *unthinkably vast spaces.*

un·think·ing /ˌənˈTHiNGkiNG/ ▶ **adj.** expressed, done, or acting without proper consideration of the consequences: *she was at pains to correct unthinking prejudices.* — **un·think·ing·ly adv. un·think·ing·ness n.**

un·thought /ˌənˈTHôt/ ▶ **adj.** not formed by the process of thinking. ■ (**unthought of**) not imagined or dreamed of: *the old develop interests unthought of in earlier years.*

un·thread /ˌənˈTHred/ ▶ **v.** [trans.] take (a thread) out of a needle. ■ remove (an object) from a thread.

un·threat·en·ing /ˌənˈTHretniNG/ ▶ **adj.** not having a hostile or frightening quality or manner; not causing someone to feel vulnerable or at risk. — **un·threat·ened** /ˌənˈTHretnd/ **adj.**

un·thrift·y /ˌənˈTHriftē/ ▶ **adj. 1** not using money and other resources carefully; wasteful. **2** esp. archaic dialect (of livestock or plants) not strong and healthy. — **un·thrift·i·ly** /-tl-ē/ **adv. un·thrift·i·ness n.**

un·throne /ˌənˈTHrōn/ ▶ **v.** archaic term for DETHRONE.

un·ti·dy /ˌənˈtīdē/ ▶ **adj.** (**-ti·di·er, -ti·di·est**) not arranged neatly and in order. ■ (of a person) not inclined to keep one's possessions or appearance neat and in order. — **un·ti·di·ly** /-ˈtīdl-ē/ **adv. un·ti·di·ness n.**

un·tie /ˌənˈtī/ ▶ **v.** (**-tied, -ty·ing**) [trans.] undo or unfasten (a cord or knot): *she knelt to untie her laces.* ■ undo a cord or similar fastening that binds (someone or something): *Morton untied the parcel.*

un·tied /ˌənˈtīd/ ▶ **adj.** not fastened or knotted.

un·til /ˌənˈtil; ən-/ ▶ **prep. & conj.** up to (the point in time or the event mentioned): [as prep.] *we have until October 11th to deliver.* [ME: from ON *und* 'as far as' + TILL[1].]

un·time·ly /ˌənˈtīmlē/ ▶ **adj.** (of an event or act) happening or done at an unsuitable time. ■ (of a death or end) happening too soon or sooner than normal: *his untimely death in military action.* ▶ **adv.** archaic at a time that is unsuitable or premature. — **un·time·li·ness n.**

un·tinged /ˌənˈtinjd/ ▶ **adj.** [predic.] (**untinged by/with**) not in the slightest affected by.

un·ti·tled /ˌənˈtītld/ ▶ **adj. 1** (of a book, composition, or other artistic work) having no name. **2** (of a person) not having a title indicating high social or official rank: *lesser untitled officials.*

un·to /ˈəntoo͞/ ▶ **prep. 1** archaic term for TO: *do unto others | I say unto you, be gone.* **2** archaic term for UNTIL: *marriage unto death.* [ME: from UNTIL.]

un·told /ˌənˈtōld/ ▶ **adj. 1** too much or too many to be counted or measured: *untold damage.* **2** (of a story or event) not narrated.

un·toned /ˌənˈtōnd/ ▶ **adj. 1** (of a person's body) lacking in tone or muscular definition. **2** (esp. of music) lacking in variation of tone or subtlety.

un·touch·a·ble /ˌənˈtəCHəbəl/ ▶ **adj. 1** not able to be touched or affected. ■ unable to be matched or rivaled. **2** of or belonging to the lowest-caste Hindu group or the people outside the caste system. ▶ **n.** a member of the lowest-caste Hindu group or a person outside the caste system. Contact with untouchables is traditionally held to defile members of higher castes. — **un·touch·a·bil·i·ty** /-ˌtəCHəˈbilitē/ **n.**

– USAGE The use of the term **untouchable** to refer to a member of the lowest caste in Hindu society is now illegal in India and Pakistan. The official term today is **scheduled caste**.

un·touched /ˌənˈtəCHt/ ▶ **adj. 1** not handled, used, or tasted: *Annabel pushed aside her untouched plate.* ■ (of a subject) not treated in writing or speech; not discussed: *no detail is left untouched.* **2** not affected, changed, or damaged in any way.

un·to·ward /ˌənˈtôrd; -t(ə)ˈwôrd/ ▶ **adj.** unexpected and inappropriate or inconvenient: *untoward jokes.* — **un·to·ward·ly adv. un·to·ward·ness n.**

un·traced /ˌənˈtrāst/ ▶ **adj.** not found or discovered by investigation.

un·tracked /ˌənˈtrakt/ ▶ **adj. 1** (of land) not previously explored or traversed; without a path or tracks. ■ (of snow or a snowy slope) not marked by skis, vehicles, people, or animals. **2** not found after attempts at detection, esp. by means of radar or satellite: *the previously untracked object.*

– PHRASES **get untracked** get into one's stride or find good form, esp. in sporting contexts.

un·trained /ˌənˈtrānd/ ▶ **adj.** not having been trained in a particular skill: *untrained in diagnosis | to **the untrained eye**, the two products look the same.* — **un·train·a·ble** /-ˈtrānəbəl/ **adj.**

un·tram·meled /ˌənˈtraməld/ (Brit. also **un·tram·melled**) ▶ **adj.** not deprived of freedom of action or expression; not restricted or hampered.

un·trans·lat·ed /ˌənˈtranzˌlātid; -ˈtrans-/ ▶ **adj.** (of words or text) not having their sense expressed in another language. ■ (of a sequence of nucleotides in messenger RNA) not converted to the amino acid sequence of a protein or polypeptide during synthesis.

un·treat·a·ble /ˌənˈtrētəbəl/ ▶ **adj.** (of a patient, a disease, or other condition) for whom or which no medical care is available or possible.

un·treat·ed /ˌənˈtrētid/ ▶ **adj. 1** (of a patient, disease, or other condition) not given medical care. **2** not preserved, improved, or altered by the use of a chemical, physical, or biological agent.

un·tried /ˌənˈtrīd/ ▶ **adj. 1** not yet tested to discover quality or reliability; inexperienced: *untried actors.* **2** Law (of an accused person) not yet subjected to a trial in court.

un·trod·den /ˌənˈträdn/ ▶ **adj.** (of a surface) not having been walked on: *untrodden snow.*

un·trou·bled /ˌənˈtrəbəld/ ▶ **adj.** not feeling, showing, or affected by anxiety or problems.

un·true /ˌənˈtro͞o/ ▶ **adj. 1** not in accordance with fact or reality; false or incorrect. **2** not faithful or loyal. **3** incorrectly positioned or balanced; not upright or level. — **un·tru·ly** /-ˈtro͞olē/ **adv.**

un·truss /ˌənˈtrəs/ ▶ **v.** [trans.] unfasten (esp. a trussed fowl).

un·trussed /ˌənˈtrəst/ ▶ **adj.** (of a chicken or other bird prepared for eating) having had its wings and legs unfastened before cooking: *an untrussed chicken.*

un·trust·wor·thy /ˌənˈtrəstˌwərT͟Hē/ ▶ **adj.** not able to be relied on as honest or truthful. — **un·trust·wor·thi·ness n.**

un·truth /ˌənˈtro͞oTH/ ▶ **n.** (pl. **-truths** /-ˈtro͞oT͟Hz; -ˈtro͞oTHs/) a lie or false statement (often used euphemistically). ■ the quality of being false.

un·truth·ful /ˌənˈtro͞oTHfəl/ ▶ **adj.** saying or consisting of something that is false or incorrect. — **un·truth·ful·ly adv. un·truth·ful·ness n.**

un·tucked /ˌənˈtəkt/ ▶ **adj.** with the edges or ends hanging loose; not tucked in: *an untucked shirt.*

un·tun·a·ble /ˌənˈt(y)o͞onəbəl/ ▶ **adj.** (of a piano, etc.) that cannot be tuned.

un·tuned /ˌənˈt(y)o͞ond/ ▶ **adj.** not tuned or properly adjusted.

un·tune·ful /ˌənˈt(y)o͞onfəl/ ▶ **adj.** not having a pleasing melody; unmusical: *an untuneful hymn.* — **un·tune·ful·ly adv.**

un·turned /ˌənˈtərnd/ ▶ **adj. 1** not turned: *unturned soil.* **2** (of a wooden object) not shaped on a lathe.

un·tu·tored /ˌənˈt(y)o͞otərd/ ▶ **adj.** not formally taught or trained.

un·twist /ˌənˈtwist/ ▶ **v.** open or cause to open from a twisted position.

un·ty·ing /ˌənˈtī-iNG/ present participle of **UNTIE.**

un·typ·i·cal /ˌənˈtipikəl/ ▶ **adj.** not having the distinctive qualities of a particular type of person or thing; unusual or uncharacteristic. — **un·typ·i·cal·ly** /-ik(ə)lē/ **adv.**

un·used /ˌənˈyo͞ozd;/ ▶ **adj. 1** not being, or never having been, used: *return the unused equipment.* **2** /-ˈyo͞ost/ (**unused to**) not familiar with or accustomed to something: *unused to spicy food.*

un·u·su·al /ˌənˈyo͞oZHo͞oəl/ ▶ **adj.** not habitually or commonly occurring or done. ■ remarkable or interesting because different from or better than others: *a man of unusual talent.* — **un·u·su·al·ly adv. un·u·su·al·ness n.**

un·ut·ter·a·ble /ˌənˈətərəbəl/ ▶ **adj.** too great, intense, or awful to describe: *unutterable grief.* — **un·ut·ter·a·bly** /-blē/ **adv.**

un·ut·tered /ˌənˈətərd/ ▶ **adj.** (of words or thoughts) not spoken or expressed: *her lips mouthed unuttered thanks.*

un·val·ued /ˌənˈvalyo͞od/ ▶ **adj. 1** not considered to be important or beneficial: *he felt unvalued.* **2** archaic not valued or appraised with regard to monetary worth.

un·van·quished /ˌənˈvaNGkwisHt/ ▶ **adj.** (of an opponent or obstacle) not conquered or overcome: *the idea of humbling the hitherto unvanquished islanders.*

un·var·nished /ˌənˈvärnisHt/ ▶ **adj.** not covered with varnish. ■ (of a statement or manner) plain and straightforward: *please tell me the unvarnished truth.*

un·var·y·ing /ˌənˈve(ə)rē-iNG/ ▶ **adj.** not changing; constant or uniform: *the unvarying routine of parsonage life.* — **un·var·y·ing·ly adv.** [as submodifier] *they found her to be unvaryingly polite.* **un·var·y·ing·ness n.**

un·veil /ˌənˈvāl/ ▶ **v.** [trans.] remove a veil or covering from, esp. uncover (a new monument or work of art) as part of a public ceremony: *the mayor unveiled a plaque* | [as n.] (**unveiling**) *the unveiling of the memorial.* ■ show or announce publicly for the first time: *the manufacturer unveiled plans for expanding into aviation.*

un·vi·o·lat·ed /ˌənˈvīəˌlātid/ ▶ **adj.** not violated or desecrated: *the ground above the stone was undisturbed, the stone unviolated.* ■ (of a woman) virginal.

un·vi·ti·at·ed /ˌənˈvisHēˌātid/ ▶ **adj.** archaic pure and uncorrupted.

un·voiced /ˌənˈvoist/ ▶ **adj. 1** not expressed in words; unuttered: *a person's unvoiced thoughts.* **2** Phonet. (of a speech sound) uttered without vibration of the vocal cords.

un·walled /ˌənˈwôld/ ▶ **adj.** (of a place) without enclosing or defensive walls.

un·war·rant·a·ble /ˌənˈwôrəntəbəl; -ˈwär-/ ▶ **adj.** not able to be authorized or sanctioned; unjustifiable: *an unwarrantable intrusion into personal matters.* — **un·war·rant·a·bly** /-blē/ **adv.**

un·war·rant·ed /ˌənˈwôrəntid; -ˈwär-/ ▶ **adj.** not justified or authorized: *I am sure your fears are unwarranted.*

un·war·y /ˌənˈwe(ə)rē/ ▶ **adj.** not cautious of possible dangers or problems: *accidents can happen to the unwary traveler* | [as pl. n.] (**the unwary**) *hidden traps for the unwary.* — **un·war·i·ly** /-ˈwe(ə)rəlē/ **adv. un·war·i·ness n.**

un·washed /ˌənˈwôsHt; -ˈwäsHt/ ▶ **adj.** not having been washed.
– PHRASES **the (great) unwashed** derog. the mass or multitude of ordinary people.

un·watch·a·ble /ˌənˈwäCHəbəl/ ▶ **adj.** (of a film or television program) too poor, tedious, or disturbing to be viewed.

un·wa·ver·ing /ˌənˈwāvəriNG/ ▶ **adj.** steady or resolute; not wavering: *she fixed him with an unwavering stare.* — **un·wa·ver·ing·ly adv.**

un·wea·ried /ˌənˈwi(ə)rēd/ ▶ **adj.** not tired or becoming tired. — **un·wea·ried·ly adv.**

un·wea·ry·ing /ˌənˈwi(ə)rē-iNG/ ▶ **adj.** never tiring or slackening. — **un·wea·ry·ing·ly adv.**

un·wed /ˌənˈwed/ (also **un·wed·ded**) ▶ **adj.** not married: *an unwed teenage mother.* — **un·wed·ded·ness n.**

un·weighed /ˌənˈwād/ ▶ **adj. 1** not considered; hasty. **2** (of goods) not weighed.

un·weight /ˌənˈwāt/ ▶ **v.** [trans.] momentarily stop pressing heavily on (a ski or skateboard) in order to make a turn more easily. [1930s: back-form. from **UNWEIGHTED.**]

un·weight·ed /ˌənˈwātid/ ▶ **adj. 1** without a weight attached. **2** Stat. (of a figure or sample) not adjusted or biased to reflect importance or value.

un·wel·come /ˌənˈwelkəm/ ▶ **adj.** (of a guest or new arrival) not gladly received: *guards kept out unwelcome visitors.* ■ not much needed or desired: *unwelcome attentions from men.* — **un·wel·come·ly adv. un·wel·come·ness n.**

un·wel·com·ing /ˌənˈwelkəmiNG/ ▶ **adj.** having an inhospitable or uninviting atmosphere or appearance: *Jean crept into her cold and unwelcoming bed.* ■ (of a person or their manner) not friendly toward someone arriving or approaching.

un·well /ˌənˈwel/ ▶ **adj.** [predic.] sick: *consult a doctor if you feel unwell.*

un·wept /ˌənˈwept/ ▶ **adj.** esp. literary (of a person) not mourned or lamented.

un·whole·some /ˌənˈhōlsəm/ ▶ **adj.** not characterized by or conducive to health or moral well-being: *the use of the living room as sleeping quarters led to unwholesome crowding.* — **un·whole·some·ly adv. un·whole·some·ness n.**

un·wield·y /ˌənˈwēldē/ ▶ **adj.** (**-wield·i·er, -wield·i·est**) difficult to carry or move because of its size, shape, or weight: *the first mechanical clocks were large and unwieldy.* ■ (of a system or bureaucracy) too big or badly organized to function efficiently. — **un·wield·i·ly** /-ˈwēldəlē/ **adv. un·wield·i·ness n.**

un·will·ing /ˌənˈwiliNG/ ▶ **adj.** [often with infin.] not ready, eager, or prepared to do something: *he was unwilling to take on that responsibility* | *unwilling conscripts.* — **un·will·ing·ly adv. un·will·ing·ness n.**

un·wind /ˌənˈwīnd/ ▶ **v.** (past and past part. **-wound** /-ˈwound/) undo or be undone after winding or being wound: [trans.] *Ella unwound the long woolen scarf from her neck* | [intrans.] *the net unwinds from the reel.* ■ [intrans.] relax after a period of work or tension: *the Grand Hotel is a superb place to unwind.*

un·wink·ing /ˌənˈwiNGkiNG/ ▶ **adj.** (of a stare or a shining light) steady; unwavering: *the lights shone unwinking in the still air* | *unwinking blue eyes.* — **un·wink·ing·ly adv.**

un·wis·dom /ˌənˈwizdəm/ ▶ **n.** folly; lack of wisdom: *it stresses the unwisdom of fathers leaving their children.*

un·wise /ˌənˈwīz/ ▶ **adj.** (of a person or action) not wise or sensible; foolish: *it is unwise to rely on hearsay evidence* | *unwise policy decisions.* — **un·wise·ly adv.** [sentence adverb] *unwisely, she repeated the remark to her mother.*

un·wished /ˌənˈwisHt/ ▶ **adj.** (usu. **unwished-for**) not wanted or desired: *an unwished-for child.*

un·wit·nessed /ˌənˈwitnist/ ▶ **adj.** (esp. of an event) not witnessed.

un·wit·ting /ˌənˈwitiNG/ ▶ **adj.** (of a person) not aware of the full facts: *an unwitting accomplice.* ■ not done on purpose; unintentional: *we are anxious to rectify the unwitting mistakes made in the past.* — **un·wit·ting·ly adv.** [sentence adverb] *quite unwittingly, you played right into my hands that night.* **un·wit·ting·ness n.** [OE *unwitende* 'not knowing or realizing' (see **UN-**[1], **WIT**[2]).]

un·wom·an·ly /ˌənˈwo͝omənlē/ ▶ **adj.** not having or showing qualities traditionally associated with women: *initiative of any overt sort was considered unwomanly.* — **un·wom·an·li·ness n.**

un·wont·ed /ˌənˈwôntid/ ▶ **adj.** [attrib.] unaccustomed or unusual: *there was an unwonted gaiety in her manner.* — **un·wont·ed·ly adv. un·wont·ed·ness n.**

un·wood·ed /ˌənˈwo͝odid/ ▶ **adj. 1** not having many trees. **2** (of a wine) not stored in a wooden cask.

un·work·a·ble /ˌənˈwərkəbəl/ ▶ **adj.** not able to function or be carried out successfully; impractical: *complex, unworkable theories.* ■ (of a material) not able to be worked: *the alloy becomes brittle and almost unworkable.* — **un·work·a·bil·i·ty** /-ˌwərkəˈbilitē/ **n. un·work·a·bly** /-blē/ **adv.**

un·work·man·like /ˌənˈwərkmənˌlīk/ ▶ **adj.** badly done or made.

un·world·ly /ˌənˈwərldlē/ ▶ **adj.** (of a person) not having much awareness of the realities of life, in particular, not motivated by material or practical considerations: *she was so shrewd in some ways, but hopelessly unworldly in others.* ■ not seeming to belong to this planet; strange: *the unworldly monolith loomed four stories high.* — **un·world·li·ness n.**

un·wor·thy /ˌənˈwərT͟Hē/ ▶ **adj.** (**-thi·er, -thi·est**) not deserving effort, attention, or respect: *he was unworthy of trust and unfit to hold office.* ■ (of a person's action or behavior) not acceptable, esp. from someone with a good reputation or social position: *the expression of anger was* *frowned upon as being unworthy.* ■ having little value or merit: *many pieces are unworthy and ungrammatical.* — **un·wor·thi·ly** /-T͟Həlē/ **adv.** **un·wor·thi·ness** **n.**

un·wound /,ən'wound/ past and past participle of UNWIND. ▶ **adj.** (of a clock or watch) not wound or wound up.

un·wrap /,ən'rap/ ▶ **v.** (**-wrapped, -wrap·ping**) [trans.] remove the wrapping from a package: *children excitedly unwrapping and playing with their new presents.*

un·wrin·kled /,ən'riNGkəld/ ▶ **adj.** (esp. of fabric or a person's skin) free from wrinkles.

un·writ·ten /,ən'ritn/ ▶ **adj.** not recorded in writing: *documenting unwritten languages.* ■ (esp. of a law) resting originally on custom or judicial decision rather than on statute: *an unwritten constitution.* ■ (of a convention) understood and accepted by everyone, although not formally established: *the unwritten rules of social life.*

un·wrought /,ən'rôt/ ▶ **adj.** (of metals or other materials) not worked into a finished condition. ■ (of a mine or ore deposit) not worked or mined.

un·yield·ing /,ən'yēldiNG/ ▶ **adj.** (of a mass or structure) not giving way to pressure; hard or solid: *the Atlantic hurled its waves at the unyielding rocks.* ■ (of a person or their behavior) unlikely to be swayed; resolute: *his unyielding faith.* — **un·yield·ing·ly** **adv.** **un·yield·ing·ness** **n.**

un·yoke /,ən'yōk/ ▶ **v.** [trans.] release (a pair of animals) from a yoke. ■ [intrans.] archaic cease work.

un·zip /,ən'zip/ ▶ **v.** (**-zipped, -zip·ping**) [trans.] unfasten the zipper of (an item of clothing). ■ Comput. decompress (a file) that has previously been compressed.

up /əp/ ▶ **adv.** **1** toward the sky or a higher position. ■ upstairs. ■ out of bed. ■ (of the sun) visible in the sky after daybreak. ■ expressing movement toward or position in the north: *I drove up to Detroit.* ■ to or at a place perceived as higher: *going for a walk up to the stores.* ■ Brit. toward or in the capital or a major city: *when you're up in London.* ■ (of food that has been eaten) regurgitated from the stomach. ■ [as exclam.] used as a command to a soldier or an animal to stand up and be ready to move or attack. **2** to the place where someone is: *Dot didn't hear Mrs. Parvis come creeping up behind her.* **3** at or to a higher level of intensity, volume, or activity: *she turned the volume up.* ■ at or to a higher price, value, or rank: *unemployment is up.* ■ winning or at an advantage by a specified margin: *up by 11 points.* **4** into the desired or a proper condition: *the mayor agreed to set up a committee.* ■ so as to be finished or closed: *I zipped up my sweater.* **5** into a happy mood: *you can't cheer me up.* **6** displayed on a bulletin board or other publicly visible site: *he put up posters around the city.* **7** (of sailing) against the current or the wind. ■ (of a ship's helm) moved around to windward so that the rudder is to leeward. **8** Baseball at bat. ▶ **prep.** from a lower to a higher point on (something); upward along: *I climbed up a flight of steps.* ■ from one end to another of (a street or other area), not necessarily with any noticeable change in altitude: *bicycling up Pleasant Avenue.* ■ to a higher part of (a river or stream), away from the sea: *a cruise up the Rhine.* ▶ **adj.** **1** [attrib.] directed or moving toward a higher place or position: *the up escalator.* ■ Physics denoting a flavor of quark having a charge of +2⁄3. Protons and neutrons are thought to be composed of combinations of up and down quarks. **2** in a cheerful mood; ebullient: *the mood here is up.* **3** (of a computer system) functioning properly. **4** at an end: *his contract was up in three weeks.* **5** (of a jockey) in the saddle. ▶ **n.** informal a period of good fortune. ▶ **v.** (**upped, up·ping**) **1** [intrans.] informal do something abruptly or boldly: *she upped and left him.* **2** [trans.] cause (a level or amount) to be increased. **3** [trans.] lift (something) up. ■ [intrans.] (**up with**) informal raise or pick up (something): *this woman ups with a stone.*

– PHRASES **get it up** vulgar slang have a penile erection. **it is all up with** informal it is the end of or there is no hope for (someone or something). **on the up and up** informal **1** honest or sincere. **2** Brit. steadily improving or becoming more successful. **something is up** informal something unusual or undesirable is happening or afoot. **up against** close to or in contact with. ■ informal confronted with or opposed by: *think of what teachers are up against today.* ■ (**up against it**) informal facing some serious but unspecified difficulty. **up and running** in operation; functioning. **up for** **1** available for: *the house next door is up for sale.* **2** being considered for: *up for promotion.* **3** due for: *his contract is up for renewal.* **up for it** informal ready to take part in a particular activity. **up on** well informed about. **up to** **1** as far as: *up to his waist.* ■ (also **up until**) until: *up to now.* **2** indicating a maximum amount: *it can take up to two years.* **3** [with negative or in questions] as good as; good enough for: *I was not up to her standards.* ■ capable of or fit for: *not up to the job.* **4** the duty, responsibility, or choice of (someone). **5** informal occupied or busy with. **up with ——** an exclamation expressing support for a stated person or thing. **up yours** vulgar slang an exclamation expressing contemptuous defiance or rejection of someone. **what's up?** informal **1** what is going on? **2** what is the matter? [OE *up(p), uppe,* of Gmc. origin; rel. to Du. *op* and Ger. *auf.*]

up- ▶ **prefix** **1** (added to verbs and their derivatives) upward: *upturned* | *upthrow.* ■ to a more recent time; to a newer or better state: *upbeat* | *update.* **2** (added to nouns) denoting (direction of) motion up: *upriver* | *uphill.* **3** (added to nouns) higher: *upland* | *upstroke* ■ increased: *up-tempo.*

up·an·chor ▶ **v.** [intrans.] (of a ship) weigh anchor.

up-and-com·ing ▶ **adj.** (of a person beginning a particular activity or occupation) making good progress and likely to become successful. — **up-and-com·er** **n.**

U·pan·i·shad /(y)o͝o'panə,SHad; o͞o'pəni,SHəd/ ▶ **n.** each of a series of Hindu sacred treatises written in Sanskrit *c.*800–200 BC, expounding the Vedas in predominantly mystical and monistic terms. [from Sanskrit, lit. 'sitting near (i.e., at the feet of a master),' from *upa* 'near' + *ni-ṣad* 'sit down.']

u·pas /'yo͞opəs/ (also **u·pas tree**) ▶ **n.** a tropical Asian tree (*Antiaris toxicaria*) of the mulberry family, the milky sap of which has been used as arrow poison and for ritual purposes. ■ (in folklore) a Javanese tree alleged to poison its surroundings and said to be fatal to approach. [18th C.: from Malay *(pohun) upas* 'poison.']

up·beat /'əp,bēt/ ▶ **n.** (in music) an unaccented beat preceding an accented beat. ▶ **adj.** informal cheerful; optimistic.

up·bow /bō/ ▶ **n.** (on a stringed instrument) a stroke begun with the tip of the bow and proceeding toward the base.

up·braid /,əp'brād/ ▶ **v.** [trans.] find fault with (someone); scold: *he was upbraided for his slovenly appearance.* [OE *upbrēdan* 'allege (something) as a basis for censure,' based on BRAID in the obs. sense 'brandish.']

up·bring·ing /'əp,briNGiNG/ ▶ **n.** the treatment and instruction received by a child from its parents throughout its childhood. [15th C.: from obs. *upbring* 'to rear' (see UP-, BRING).]

up·build /,əp'bild/ ▶ **v.** (past and past part. **-built**) [trans.] esp. literary construct or develop (something).

UPC ▶ **abbr.** Universal Product Code.

up·cast /'əp,kast/ ▶ **n.** (also **up·cast shaft**) a shaft through which air leaves a mine. ▶ **v.** (past and past part. **-cast**) [trans.] cast (something) upward: [as adj.] (**upcast**) *upcast light.*

up·chuck /'əp,CHək/ ▶ **v.** informal vomit.

up·close /,əp'klōs/ ▶ **adv.** at very close range. ▶ **adj.** showing or allowing considerable detail.

up·coast /,əp'kōst/ ▶ **adv. & adj.** further up the coast.

up·com·ing /'əp,kəmiNG/ ▶ **adj.** forthcoming; about to happen: *the upcoming election.*

up·coun·try /,əp'kəntrē; 'əp,kəntrē/ ▶ **adv. & adj.** in or toward the interior of a country; inland: [as adv.] *she comes from somewhere upcountry* | [as adj.] *a little upcountry town.*

up·date /,əp'dāt; 'əp,dāt/ ▶ **v.** [trans.] make (something) more modern or up to date. ■ give (someone) the latest information about something: *the reporter promised to keep the viewers updated.* ▶ **n.** /'əp,dāt/ an act of bringing something or someone up to date, or an updated version of something. — **up·dat·a·ble** **adj.** (Comput.).

Up·dike /'əp,dīk/, John Hoyer (1932–), US writer. His novels include *Rabbit, Run* (1960), *Rabbit Redux* (1971), and *The Witches of Eastwick* (1984).

up·do /'əp,do͞o/ ▶ **n.** informal a hairstyle in which the hair is swept up and fastened away from the face and neck.

up·dom·ing /'əp,dōmiNG/ ▶ **n.** Geol. the upward deformation of a rock mass into a dome shape.

up·draft /'əp,draft/ (Brit. **up·draught**) ▶ **n.** an upward current or draft of air.

up·end /,əp'end/ ▶ **v.** [trans.] set or turn (something) on its end or upside down. ■ [intrans.] (of a swimming duck or other waterbird) submerge the head and foreparts in order to feed, so that the tail is raised in the air.

up·field /,əp'fēld/ ▶ **adv., adj.** Football another term for DOWNFIELD.

up·flung /'əp,fləNG/ ▶ **adj.** esp. literary (esp. of limbs) flung upward, esp. in a gesture of helplessness or alarm.

up·front /,əp'frənt/ informal ▶ **adv.** (usu. **up front**) **1** at the front; in front: *I was sitting up front.* **2** (of a payment) in advance. ▶ **adj.** **1** bold, honest, and frank. **2** [attrib.] (of a payment) made in advance. **3** at the front or the most prominent position.

up·grade /'əp,grād; ,əp'grād/ ▶ **v.** [trans.] raise (something) to a higher standard, in particular improve (equipment or machinery) by adding or replacing components. ■ raise (an employee) to a higher grade or rank. ▶ **n.** /'əp,grād/ an act of upgrading something. ■ an improved or more modern version of something, esp. a piece of computing equipment. — **up·grad·a·bil·i·ty** /,əp,grādə'bilitē/ (also **up·grade·a·bil·i·ty**) **n.** **up·grad·a·ble** /,əp'grādəbəl/ (also **up·grade·a·ble**) **adj.**

up·growth /'əp,grōTH/ ▶ **n.** the process or result of growing upward. ■ an upward growth.

up·heav·al /,əp'hēvəl/ ▶ **n.** a violent or sudden change or disruption to something. ■ an upward displacement of part of the earth's crust.

up·heave /,əp'hēv/ ▶ **v.** [trans.] literary heave or lift up (something, esp. part of the earth's surface).

up·hill ▶ **adv.** /,əp'hil/ in an ascending direction up a hill or slope: *follow the track uphill.* ▶ **adj.** /'əp,hil/ sloping upward; ascending. ■ fig. requiring great effort; difficult. ▶ **n.** /'əp,hil/ an upward slope.

up·hold /,əp'hōld/ ▶ **v.** (past and past part. **-held**) [trans.] confirm or support (something that has been questioned): *the court upheld his claim for damages.* ■ maintain (a custom or practice). — **up·hold·er** **n.**

up·hol·ster /əp'hōlstər; ə'pōl-/ ▶ **v.** [trans.] provide (furniture) with a soft, padded covering. ■ cover the walls or furniture in (a room) with textiles. [19th C.: back-form. from UPHOLSTERER.]

up·hol·ster·er /əp'hōlstərər; ə'pōl-/ ▶ **n.** a person who upholsters furniture, esp. professionally. [17th C.: from the obsolete n. *upholster* (from UPHOLD in the obs. sense 'keep in repair') + -STER.]

up·hol·ster·y /əp'hōlst(ə)rē; ə'pōl-/ ▶ **n.** soft, padded textile covering that is fixed to furniture such as armchairs and sofas. ■ the art or practice of fitting such a covering.

UPI ▶ abbr. United Press International.

up·keep /'əp,kēp/ ▶ n. the process of keeping something in good condition. ■ financial or material support of a person or animal.

Up·land /'əplənd/ a city in southwestern California; pop. 63,374.

up·land /'əplənd; -,land/ ▶ n. (also **up·lands**) an area of high or hilly land: *conservation of areas of upland.*

up·land cot·ton ▶ n. a type of cotton (*Gossypium hirsutum* var. *latifolium*) grown in the US that typically yields medium- and short-staple forms of cotton.

up·land sand·pip·er ▶ n. a North American sandpiper (*Bartramia longicauda*) that breeds on upland fields. Also called UPLAND PLOVER.

up·lift ▶ v. /,əp'lift/ [trans.] **1** [usu. as adj.] (**uplifted**) lift (something) up; raise: *her uplifted face.* ■ (**be uplifted**) (of an island, mountain, etc.) be created by an upward movement of the earth's surface. **2** elevate or stimulate (someone) morally or spiritually. ▶ n. /'əp,lift/ **1** an act of raising something. ■ Geol. the upward movement of part of the earth's surface. ■ [often as adj.] support, esp. for a woman's bust, from a garment: *an uplift bra.* **2** a morally or spiritually elevating influence. — **up·lift·er** /,əp'liftər/ n.

up·light /'əp,līt/ (also **up·light·er**) /-,lītər/ ▶ n. a light placed or designed to throw illumination upward. — **up·light·ing** n.

up·link /'əp,liNGk/ ▶ n. a communications link to a satellite. ▶ v. [trans.] provide (someone) with or send (something) by such a link.

up·load /'əp,lōd; ,əp'lōd/ Comput. ▶ v. [trans.] transfer (data) to a larger computer system. ▶ n. /'əp,lōd/ the action or process of transferring data in such a way.

up·mar·ket /,əp'märkit; 'əp,mär-/ (also **up-mar·ket**) ▶ adj. & adv. upscale.

up·most /'əp,mōst/ ▶ adj. another term for UPPERMOST.

up·on /ə'pän; ə'pôn/ ▶ prep. more formal term for ON, esp. in abstract senses: *it was based upon two principles.* [ME: from UP + ON.]

up·per[1] /'əpər/ ▶ adj. **1** situated above another part. ■ higher in position or status. **2** situated on higher ground. ■ situated to the north: *Upper California.* **3** Geol. Archaeol. denoting a younger (and hence usually shallower) part of a stratigraphic division or archaeological deposit or the period in which it was formed or deposited: *the Upper Paleolithic age.* ▶ n. **1** the part of a boot or shoe above the sole. **2** upper dentures or teeth.

– PHRASES **have** (or **gain**) **the upper hand** have or gain advantage or control over someone or something. **on one's uppers** esp. Brit., informal extremely short of money. [ME: from the adj. UP + -ER[2].]

up·per[2] ▶ n. (usu. **uppers**) informal a stimulating drug, esp. amphetamine. [1960s: from the v. UP + -ER[1].]

Up·per Can·a·da the mainly English-speaking region of Canada north of the Great Lakes.

up·per·case /'əpər'kās/ (also **up·per case**) ▶ n. capital letters as opposed to small letters (lowercase). [referring orig. to two type cases positioned on an angled stand, the case containing the capital letters being higher and further away from the compositor.]

up·per cham·ber ▶ n. another term for UPPER HOUSE.

up·per class ▶ n. [treated as sing. or pl.] the social group that has the highest status in society, esp. the aristocracy. ▶ adj. of, relating to, or characteristic of such a group.

up·per·class·man /,əpər'klasmən/ ▶ n. (pl. **-men**) a junior or senior in high school or college.

up·per crust ▶ n. (**the upper crust**) informal the upper classes.

up·per·cut /'əpər,kət/ ▶ n. a punch delivered with an upward motion and the arm bent. ▶ v. [trans.] hit with an uppercut.

up·per house ▶ n. the higher house in a bicameral parliament or similar legislature, such as the Senate in the US Congress. ■ (**the Upper House**) (in the UK) the House of Lords.

up·per·most /'əpər,mōst/ ▶ adj. (also **up·most**) highest in place, rank, or importance. ▶ adv. at or to the highest or most important position.

Up·per Peninsula (abbr.: **UP**) the northern section of Michigan that is separated from the southern part of the state by Lake Michigan, the Straits of Mackinac, and Lake Huron.

up·per re·gions ▶ plural n. archaic literary the sky or heavens.

Up·per Vol·ta former name (until 1984) for BURKINA FASO.

up·pish /'əpisH/ ▶ adj. informal arrogantly self-assertive. — **up·pish·ly** adv. **up·pish·ness** n.

up·pi·ty /'əpətē/ ▶ adj. informal self-important; arrogant. [19th C.: a fanciful formation from UP.]

Upp·sa·la /'o͝op,sälə/ a city in eastern Sweden; pop. 167,000.

up·raise /,əp'rāz/ ▶ v. [trans.] raise (something) to a higher level: *concentration upraises things.*

up·right /'əp,rīt/ ▶ adj. **1** vertical; erect. ■ (of a piano) having vertical strings. ■ greater in height than breadth: *an upright freezer.* ■ denoting a device designed to be used in a vertical position. **2** (of a person or their behavior) strictly honorable or honest: *an upright member of the community.* ▶ adv. in or into a vertical position. ▶ n. **1** a post or rod fixed vertically, esp. as a structural support: *the stone uprights of the parapet.* ■ (**uprights**) Football the vertical posts extending up from the goal post, between which a field goal must pass to score. **2** an upright piano. — **up·right·ly** adv. **up·right·ness** n. [OE *upriht*, (see UP, RIGHT).]

up·rise /,əp'rīz/ ▶ v. (past **-rose**; past part. **-ris·en**) [intrans.] archaic literary rise to a standing or elevated position: *bright and red uprose the sun.*

up·ris·ing /'əp,rīziNG/ ▶ n. an act of resistance or rebellion; a revolt: *an armed uprising.*

up·riv·er /'əp'rivər/ ▶ adv. & adj. toward or situated at a point nearer the source of a river: [as adv.] *the salmon head upriver to spawn* | [as adj.] *the upriver side.*

up·roar /'əp,rôr/ ▶ n. a loud and impassioned noise or disturbance: *the room was in an uproar.* ■ a public expression of protest or outrage. [16th C.: from MDu. *uproer*, from *op* 'up' + *roer* 'confusion,' associated with ROAR.]

up·roar·i·ous /,əp'rôrēəs/ ▶ adj. characterized by or provoking loud noise or uproar: *an uproarious party.* ■ provoking loud laughter; very funny. — **up·roar·i·ous·ly** adv. **up·roar·i·ous·ness** n.

up·root /,əp'ro͞ot; -'ro͝ot/ ▶ v. [trans.] pull (something, esp. a tree or plant) out of the ground. ■ move (someone) from their home or a familiar location. ■ fig. eradicate; destroy. — **up·root·er** n.

up·rose /,əp'rōz/ past of UPRISE.

up·rush /'əp,rəsH/ ▶ n. a sudden upward surge or flow, esp. of a feeling: *an uprush of joy.*

UPS ▶ abbr. uninterruptible power supply.

ups-a-dai·sy /'əpsə'dāzē/ (also **up·sa-dai·sy**) ▶ exclam. var. of UPSY-DAISY.

ups and downs ▶ plural n. a succession of both good and bad experiences: *I have my ups and downs.* ■ rises and falls, esp. in the value or success of something: *the ups and downs of the market.*

up·scale /,əp'skāl; 'əp,skāl/ ▶ adj. & adv. toward or relating to the more expensive or affluent sector of the market: [as adj.] *Hawaii's upscale hotels* | [as adv.] *fish dishes have moved upscale.*

up·set ▶ v. /,əp'set/ (**-set·ting**; past and past part. **-set**) [trans.] **1** make (someone) unhappy, disappointed, or worried. **2** knock (something) over: *he upset a tureen of soup.* ■ cause disorder in (something); disrupt. ■ disturb the digestion of (a person's stomach); cause (someone) to feel nauseous or unwell. **3** [often as n.] (**upsetting**) shorten and thicken the end or edge of (a metal bar, wheel rim, or other object), esp. by hammering or pressure when heated. ▶ n. /'əp,set/ **1** a state of being unhappy, disappointed, or worried: *domestic upsets.* **2** an unexpected result or situation, esp. in a sports competition. **3** a disturbance of a person's digestive system. ▶ adj. /,əp'set/ **1** unhappy, disappointed, or worried. **2** (of a person's stomach) having disturbed digestion, esp. because of something eaten. — **up·set·ter** /,əp'setər/ n. **up·set·ting·ly** adv.

up·set price /'əp,set/ ▶ n. the lowest acceptable selling price for a property in an auction; a reserve price.

up·shift /'əp,sHift/ ▶ v. [intrans.] change to a higher gear in a motor vehicle. ■ [trans.] increase: *laws that upshifted the penalties.* ▶ n. a change to a higher gear.

up·shot /'əp,sHät/ ▶ n. [in sing.] the final or eventual outcome or conclusion of a discussion, action, or series of events.

up·side /'əp,sīd/ ▶ n. [in sing.] **1** the positive aspect of something. **2** an upward movement of stock prices.

– PHRASES **upside the head** on the side of head.

up·side down ▶ adv. & adj. with the upper part where the lower part should be; in an inverted position. ■ in or into total disorder or confusion. [ME: orig. *up so down*, perh. in the sense 'up as if down.']

up·side-down cake ▶ n. a cake that is baked over a layer of fruit in syrup and inverted for serving.

up·si·lon /'əpsə,län; '(y)o͞op-/ ▶ n. the twentieth letter of the Greek alphabet (Υ, υ), transliterated in the traditional Latin style as 'y' (as in *cycle*) or in the modern style as 'u' (as in the etymologies of this dictionary). ■ (also **up·si·lon par·ti·cle**) Physics a meson thought to contain a *b* quark bound to its antiparticle, produced in particle accelerators. [17th C.: Gk., lit. 'plain or simple U,' from *psilos* 'plain.']

up·size /'əp,sīz/ ▶ v. increase or cause to increase in size or complexity.

up·slope /'əp,slōp/ ▶ n. an upward slope. ▶ adv. & adj. /,əp'slōp/ at or toward a higher point on a slope.

up·stage /,əp'stāj/ ▶ adv. & adj. at or toward the back of a theater stage. ■ [as adj.] informal, dated superior; aloof. ▶ v. [trans.] divert attention from (someone) toward oneself; outshine: *they were totally upstaged by their costar.* ■ (of an actor) move toward the back of a stage to make (another actor) face away from the audience.

up·stairs ▶ adv. /,əp'ste(ə)rz/ on or to an upper floor of a building: *I tiptoed upstairs.* ■ used to refer to someone's mental health: *is he, uh, all right upstairs?* ▶ adj. /'əp'ste(ə)rz/ [attrib.] situated on an upper floor. ▶ n. /,əp'ste(ə)rz; 'əp,ste(ə)rz/ an upper floor.

– PHRASES **the man upstairs** a humorous name for God.

up·stand·ing /,əp'standiNG; 'əp,stan-/ ▶ adj. **1** honest; respectable: *an upstanding member of the community.* **2** standing up; erect: *upstanding feathered plumes.*

up·start /'əp,stärt/ ▶ n. derog. a person who has risen suddenly to wealth or high position, esp. one who behaves arrogantly.

up·state /'əp'stāt/ ▶ adj. & adv. of, in, or to a part of a state remote from its large cities, esp. the northern part. ▶ n. such an area: *visiting farmers from upstate.* ■ (also **Upstate**) in New York, parts of the state north of New York City, thought of as distinct culturally and politically. — **up·stat·er** n.

up·stream /ˌəpˈstrēm/ ▶ **adv. & adj.** moving or situated in the opposite direction from that in which a stream or river flows; nearer to the source. ■ Biol. situated in or toward the part of a sequence of genetic material where transcription takes place earlier than at a given point. ■ at a stage in the process of gas or oil extraction and production before the raw material is ready for refining.

up·stroke /ˈəpˌstrōk/ ▶ **n.** a stroke made upward.

up·surge /ˈəpˌsərj/ ▶ **n.** an upward surge in the strength or quantity of something; an increase.

up·sweep ▶ **v.** /ˌəpˈswēp/ [intrans.] be arranged in an upswept fashion. ■ [trans.] sweep upward. ▶ **n.** /ˈəpˌswēp/ **1** an upward rise or sweep. ■ a marked rise in activity. **2** an upswept hairdo.

up·swell /ˈəpˌswel/ ▶ **n.** rare an increase or upsurge.

up·swept /ˈəpˌswept/ ▶ **adj.** curved, sloping, or directed upward: *an upswept mustache.* ■ (of the hair) brushed or held upward and off the face.

up·swing /ˈəpˌswiNG/ ▶ **n.** an increase in strength or quantity; an upward trend.

up·sy-dai·sy /ˈəpsē ˌdāzē/ (also **ups-a-dai·sy**, **up·sa-daisy** /ˈəpsə ˈdāzē/) ▶ **exclam.** used to express encouragement to a child who has fallen or is being lifted. [19th C.: alt. of earlier *up-a-daisy*.]

up·take /ˈəpˌtāk/ ▶ **n. 1** the action of taking up or making use of something that is available. ■ the taking in or absorption of a substance by a living organism or bodily organ. **2** a pipe or flue leading air, smoke, or gases up to a chimney.
– PHRASES **be quick** (or **slow**) **on the uptake** informal be quick (or slow) to understand something.

up·tem·po /ˈəpˌtempō/ ▶ **adj. & adv.** Music played with a fast or increased tempo: [as adj.] *uptempo guitar work.*

up·throw /ˈəpˌTHrō/ Geol. ▶ **v.** [trans.] [usu. as adj.] (**upthrown**) displace (a rock formation) upward. ▶ **n.** an upward displacement of rock strata.

up·thrust /ˈəpˌTHrəst/ ▶ **n.** Physics the upward force that a liquid or gas exerts on a body floating in it. ■ Geol. another term for UPLIFT. ■ an upward thrust. ▶ **v.** [trans.] [usu. as adj.] (**upthrust**) thrust (something) upward: *Turco's upthrust beard.*

up·tick /ˈəpˌtik/ ▶ **n.** a small increase.

up·tight /ˌəpˈtīt/ ▶ **adj.** informal anxious or angry in a tense and overly controlled way.

up·time /ˈəpˌtīm/ ▶ **n.** time during which a machine, esp. a computer, is in operation.

up to date ▶ **adj.** incorporating the latest developments and trends: *a modern, up-to-date hospital.* ■ incorporating or aware of the latest information: *the book will keep you up to date.*

up-to-the-min·ute ▶ **adj.** incorporating the very latest information or developments.

up·town /ˌəpˈtoun/ ▶ **adj.** of, in, or characteristic of the residential area of a city or town. ■ of or characteristic of an affluent area or people. ▶ **adv.** /ˌəpˈtoun/ in or into such an area. ▶ **n.** /ˈəpˌtoun/ a residential area in a town or city. — **up·town·er** /ˌəpˈtounər/ **n.**

up·trend /ˈəpˌtrend/ ▶ **n.** an upward tendency.

up·turn /ˈəpˌtərn/ ▶ **n.** an improvement or upward trend, esp. in economic conditions or someone's fortunes: *an upturn in the economy.* ▶ **v.** /ˈəpˌtərn; ˌəpˈtərn/ [trans.] turn (something) upward or upside down.

uPVC ▶ **abbr.** unplasticized polyvinyl chloride, a rigid, chemically resistant form of PVC used for piping, window frames, and other structures.

up·ward /ˈəpwərd/ ▶ **adv.** (also **up·wards**) toward a higher place, point, or level: *she peered upward at the sky.* ▶ **adj.** moving, pointing, or leading to a higher place, point, or level: *an upward trend in sales.*
– PHRASES **upwards** (or **upward**) **of** more than. — **up·ward·ly adv.**

up·ward·ly mo·bile /ˈəpwərdlē/ ▶ **adj.** moving to a higher social class; acquiring wealth and status. — **upward mobility n.**

up·well·ing /ˌəpˈweliNG/ ▶ **n.** a rising up of seawater, magma, or other liquid. ▶ **adj.** (esp. of emotion) building up or gathering strength: *upwelling grief.*

up·wind /ˌəpˈwind/ ▶ **adv. & adj.** against the direction of the wind.

Ur /ər; o͝or/ an ancient Sumerian city, formerly on the Euphrates River, in southern Iraq.

ur- ▶ **comb. form** primitive; original; earliest: *urtext.* [from Ger.]

u·ra·cil /ˈyo͝orəˌsil/ ▶ **n.** Biochem. a compound, $C_4H_4N_2O_2$, found in living tissue as a constituent base of RNA. In DNA it is replaced by thymine. [19th C.: from *ur(ea)* + *ac(etic)* + -IL.]

u·rae·mi·a ▶ **n.** British spelling of UREMIA.

u·rae·us /yo͝oˈrēəs/ ▶ **n.** (pl. **u·rae·i** /yo͝oˈrēˌī; -ˈrēˌē/) a representation of a sacred serpent as an emblem of supreme power, worn on the headdresses of ancient Egyptian deities and sovereigns. [19th C.: mod. L., from Gk. *ouraios*, representing the Egyptian word for 'cobra.']

U·ral-Al·ta·ic /ˈyo͝orəl alˈtāik/ ▶ **adj.** of, relating to, or denoting a hypothetical language group formerly proposed to include both the Uralic and the Altaic languages.

U·ral·ic /yo͝oˈralik/ ▶ **adj. 1** of, relating to, or denoting a family of languages spoken from northern Scandinavia to western Siberia, comprising the Finno-Ugric and Samoyedic groups. **2** of or relating to the Ural Mountains or the surrounding areas. ▶ **n.** the Uralic languages collectively.

U·ral Moun·tains /ˈyo͝orəl/ (also **the U·rals**) a mountain range in northern Russia that extends from the Arctic Ocean to the Aral Sea.

U·ral Riv·er /ˈyo͝orəl/ a river that rises at the southern end of the Ural Mountains and flows to the Caspian Sea.

U·ra·ni·a /yo͝oˈrānēə/ Greek & Rom. Mythol. the Muse of astronomy.

u·ran·i·nite /yo͝oˈrānəˌnīt; -ˈranə-/ ▶ **n.** a black, gray, or brown mineral that consists mainly of uranium dioxide and is the chief ore of uranium. [19th C.: from URANO-[2] + -ITE[1].]

u·ra·ni·um /yo͝oˈrānēəm/ ▶ **n.** the chemical element of atomic number 92, a gray, dense radioactive metal used as a fuel in nuclear reactors. (Symbol: **U**) [18th C.: mod. L., from URANUS + -IUM.]

urano-[1] ▶ **comb. form** relating to the heavens: *uranography.* [from Gk. *ouranos* 'heavens, sky.']

urano-[2] ▶ **comb. form** representing URANIUM.

u·ra·nog·ra·phy /ˌyo͝orəˈnägrəfē/ ▶ **n.** archaic the branch of astronomy concerned with describing and mapping the stars. — **u·ra·nog·ra·pher** /-fər/ **n.** **u·ra·no·graph·ic** /-nəˈgrafik/ **adj.**

U·ran·us /ˈyo͝orənəs; yo͝oˈrā-/ **1** Gk. Mythol. a personification of heaven or the sky, the most ancient of the Greek gods and first ruler of the universe. He was overthrown and castrated by his son Cronus. **2** Astron. a distant planet of the solar system, seventh in order from the sun, discovered by William Herschel in 1781.

u·ra·nyl /ˈyo͝orəˌnil/ ▶ **n.** [as adj.] Chem. the cation $UO_2$2+, present in some compounds of uranium. [19th C.: from URANIUM + -YL.]

u·rate /ˈyo͝orˌāt/ ▶ **n.** a salt or ester of uric acid.

ur·ban /ˈərbən/ ▶ **adj. 1** in, relating to, or characteristic of a city or town: *the urban population.* **2** (also **urban contemporary**) denoting or relating to popular dance music of black origin: *a party that features the best in urban music.* ■ denoting popular black culture in general. [17th C.: from L. *urbanus*, from *urbs*, *urb-* 'city.']

Ur·bana /ərˈbanə/ a city in east central Illinois; pop. 36,344.

ur·bane /ˌərˈbān/ ▶ **adj.** (of a person, esp. a man) suave, courteous, and refined in manner. — **ur·bane·ly adv.** [16th C. (in the sense 'urban'): from Fr. *urbain* or L. *urbanus* (see URBAN).]

ur·ban for·est ▶ **n.** a densely wooded area located in a city.

ur·ban·ism /ˈərbəˌnizəm/ ▶ **n. 1** the lifestyle of city dwellers. **2** urbanization.

ur·ban·ist /ˈərbənist/ ▶ **n.** an advocate of or expert in city planning.

ur·ban·ite /ˈərbəˌnīt/ ▶ **n.** informal a person who lives in a city or town.

ur·ban·i·ty /ˌərˈbanitē/ ▶ **n. 1** suavity, courteousness, and refinement of manner. **2** urban life.

ur·ban·ize /ˈərbəˌnīz/ ▶ **v.** [trans.] make or become urban in character. — **ur·ban·i·za·tion** /ˌərbənəˈzāSHən/ **n.**

ur·ban leg·end (also esp. Brit. **ur·ban myth**) ▶ **n.** an entertaining story or piece of information of uncertain origin that is circulated as though true.

ur·ban re·new·al ▶ **n.** the redevelopment of areas within a large city, typically involving the clearance of slums.

ur·ban sprawl ▶ **n.** the uncontrolled expansion of urban areas.

urbs /ərbz/ ▶ **n.** esp. literary the city, esp. as a symbol of harsh or busy modern life. [L.]

ur·chin /ˈərCHin/ ▶ **n. 1** a mischievous young child, esp. one who is poorly or raggedly dressed. ■ archaic a goblin. **2** short for SEA URCHIN. ■ Brit., esp. dialect a hedgehog. [ME *hirchon*, *urchon* 'hedgehog,' from Old North. Fr. *herichon*, based on L. *hericius* 'hedgehog.']

Ur·du /ˈo͝ordo͞o; ˈər-/ ▶ **n.** a form of Hindustani written in Persian script, with many loanwords from Persian and Arabic. It is an official language of Pakistan and is widely used in India and elsewhere. [from Pers. *(zabān-i-)urdū* '(language of the) camp.']

-ure ▶ **suffix** forming nouns: **1** denoting an action, process, or result: *censure* | *closure* | *scripture.* **2** denoting an office or function: *judicature.* **3** denoting a collective: *legislature.* [from OFr. *-ure*, from L. *-ura.*]

u·re·a /yo͝oˈrēə/ ▶ **n.** Biochem. a colorless crystalline compound, $CO(NH_2)_2$, that is the main nitrogenous breakdown product of protein metabolism in mammals and is excreted in urine. [19th C.: mod. L., from Fr. *urée*, from Gk. *ouron* 'urine.']

u·re·ase /ˈyo͝orēˌās; -ˌāz/ ▶ **n.** a naturally occurring enzyme that hydrolyzes urea into ammonium carbonate.

u·re·ide /ˈyo͝orēˌīd; -id/ ▶ **n.** Chem. any of a group of compounds that are acyl derivatives of urea.

u·re·mi·a /yo͝oˈrēmēə/ (Brit. **u·rae·mi·a**) ▶ **n.** Med. a raised level in the blood of urea and other nitrogenous waste compounds that are normally eliminated by the kidneys. — **u·re·mic** /yo͝oˈrēmik/ **adj.** [19th C.: mod. L., from Gk. *ouron* 'urine' + *haima* 'blood.']

u·re·ter /ˈyo͝oritər; yo͝oˈrētər/ ▶ **n.** Anat. & Zool. the duct by which urine passes from the kidney to the bladder or cloaca. — **u·re·ter·al** /yo͝oˈrētərəl/ **adj.** **u·re·ter·ic** /ˌyo͝oriˈterik/ **adj.** [16th C.: from Fr. *uretère* or mod. L. *ureter*, from Gk. *ourētēr*, from *ourein* 'urinate.']

u·re·thane /ˈyo͝orəˌTHān/ ▶ **n.** Chem. a synthetic crystalline compound, $CO(NH_2)OC_2H_5$, used in making pesticides and fungicides, and formerly as an anesthetic. ■ short for POLYURETHANE. [19th C.: from Fr. *uréthane* (see UREA, ETHANE).]

u·re·thra /yo͝oˈrēTHrə/ ▶ **n.** Anat. Zool. the duct by which urine is conveyed out of the body from the bladder, and which in male vertebrates also conveys semen. — **u·re·thral adj.** [17th C.: from late L., from Gk. *ourēthra*, from *ourein* 'urinate.']

u·re·thri·tis /ˌyo͝orəˈTHrītis/ ▶ **n.** Med. inflammation of the urethra.

U·rey /ˈyŏŏrē/, Harold Clayton (1893–1981), US chemist. He was director of the Manhattan Project at Columbia University. Nobel Prize for Chemistry (1934).

Ur·ga /ˈŏŏrgə/ former name (until 1924) of ULAANBAATAR.

urge /ərj/ ▶v. [trans.] try earnestly or persistently to persuade (someone) to do something. ■ recommend or advocate (something) strongly. ■ encourage (a person or animal) to move more quickly or in a particular direction. ■ (**urge someone on**) encourage someone to continue or succeed in something. ▶n. a strong desire or impulse: *the urge for revenge.* [16th C.: from L. *urgere* 'press, drive.']

ur·gent /ˈərjənt/ ▶adj. (of a state or situation) requiring immediate action or attention. ■ (of an action or event) done or arranged in response to such a situation. ■ (of a person or their manner) earnest and persistent in response to such a situation. —**ur·gen·cy** n. **ur·gent·ly** adv. [15th C.: from OFr., from L. *urgent-* 'pressing, driving,' from the v. *urgere* (see URGE).]

-uria ▶comb. form in nouns denoting that a substance is present in the urine, esp. in excess: *glycosuria.* [mod. L., from Gk. *-ouria*, from *ouron* 'urine.']

U·ri·ah /yŏŏˈrīə/ (in the Bible) a Hittite officer in David's army, whom David, desiring his wife Bathsheba, caused to be killed in battle.

u·ric ac·id /ˈyŏŏrik/ ▶n. Biochem. an almost insoluble compound, $C_5H_4N_4O_3$, which is a breakdown product of nitrogenous metabolism. It is the main excretory product in birds, reptiles, and insects. —**u·rate** /ˈyŏŏrˌāt/ n. [19th C.: *uric* from Fr. *urique*, from *urine* (see URINE).]

u·ri·dine /ˈyŏŏrəˌdēn; -dn/ ▶n. Biochem. a compound formed by partial hydrolysis of RNA. It is a nucleoside containing uracil linked to ribose. [20th C.: from *ur(acil)* + -IDE + -INE[4].]

U·rim and Thum·mim /ˈ(y)ŏŏrim; ŏŏˈrēm and ˈTHəmim; tŏŏˈmēm/ ▶plural n. hist. two objects of a now unknown nature, possibly used for divination, worn on the breastplate of a Jewish high priest. [from Heb.]

u·ri·nal /ˈyŏŏrənl/ ▶n. a bowl or other receptacle, typically attached to a wall in a public toilet, into which men may urinate.

u·ri·nal·y·sis /ˌyŏŏrəˈnaləsis/ ▶n. (pl. **-ses** /-ˌsēz/) Med. analysis of urine by physical, chemical, and microscopical means to test for the presence of disease, drugs, etc.

u·ri·nar·y /ˈyŏŏrəˌnerē/ ▶adj. of or relating to urine. ■ of, relating to, or denoting the system of organs, structures, and ducts by which urine is produced and discharged, in mammals comprising the kidneys, ureters, bladder, and urethra.

u·ri·nate /ˈyŏŏrəˌnāt/ ▶v. [intrans.] discharge urine; pass water. —**u·ri·na·tion** /ˌyŏŏrəˈnāSHən/ n.

u·rine /ˈyŏŏrən/ ▶n. a yellowish fluid stored in the bladder and discharged through the urethra, consisting of excess water and waste substances removed from the blood by the kidneys. [ME: via OFr. from L. *urina.*]

Ur·is /ˈyŏŏrəs/, Leon Marcus (1924–2003), US writer. His works include *Exodus* (1958) and *Trinity* (1976).

URL ▶abbr. Comput. uniform (or universal) resource locator, the address of a World Wide Web page.

urn /ərn/ ▶n. **1** a tall, rounded vase with a base, and often a stem, esp. one used for storing the ashes of a cremated person. **2** a large metal container with a tap, in which tea or coffee is made and kept hot, or water for making such drinks is boiled: *a tea urn.* ▶v. [trans.] archaic place (something) in an urn. [ME: from L. *urna*; rel. to *urceus* 'pitcher.']

urn 1

uro-[1] ▶comb. form of or relating to urine or the urinary organs: *urogenital.* [from Gk. *ouron* 'urine.']

uro-[2] ▶comb. form Zool. relating to a tail or the caudal region: *urodele.* [from Gk. *oura* 'tail.']

u·ro·bo·ros /ˌ(y)ŏŏrəˈbôrəs/ (also **ou·ro·bo·ros**) ▶n. a circular symbol depicting a snake, or less commonly a dragon, swallowing its tail, as an emblem of wholeness or infinity. —**u·ro·bo·ric** /-ˈbôrik/ adj. [1940s: from Gk. *(drakōn) ouroboros* '(snake) devouring its tail.']

Ur·o·chor·da·ta /ˌyŏŏrəkôrˈdätə; -ˈdātə/ Zool. a group of chordate animals (subphylum Urochordata, phylum Chordata) that comprises the tunicates. —**u·ro·chor·date** /-ˈkôrdət; -ˌdāt/ n. & adj.

Ur·o·de·la /ˌyŏŏrəˈdēlə/ Zool. an order of amphibians that comprises the newts and salamanders, which retain the tail as adults. —**u·ro·dele** /ˈyŏŏrəˌdēl/ n. & adj. [mod. L. (pl.), from URO-[2] 'tail' + Gk. *dēlos* 'evident.']

ur·o·dy·nam·ics /ˌyŏŏrədīˈnamiks/ ▶plural n. [treated as sing.] Med. the diagnostic study of pressure in the bladder, in treating incontinence. —**u·ro·dy·nam·ic** adj.

u·ro·gen·i·tal /ˌyŏŏrōˈjenətl; ˌyŏŏrə-/ ▶adj. of, relating to, or denoting both the urinary and genital organs.

u·rog·ra·phy /yŏŏˈrägrəfē/ ▶n. another term for PYELOGRAPHY. —**u·ro·gram** /ˈyŏŏrəˌgram/ n.

u·ro·ki·nase /ˌyŏŏrōˈkīˌnās; -ˌnāz/ ▶n. Biochem. an enzyme produced in the kidneys that promotes the conversion of plasminogen to plasmin and can be used to dissolve blood clots.

u·ro·li·thi·a·sis /ˌyŏŏrələˈTHīəsis/ ▶n. Med. the formation of stony concretions in the bladder or urinary tract.

u·rol·o·gy /yŏŏˈräləjē/ ▶n. the branch of medicine and physiology concerned with the function and disorders of the urinary system. —**u·ro·log·ic** /ˌyŏŏrəˈläjik/ adj. **u·ro·log·i·cal** /ˌyŏŏrəˈläjikəl/ adj. **u·rol·o·gist** /-jist/ n.

u·ron·ic ac·id /yŏŏˈränik/ ▶n. Biochem. any of a class of compounds that are derived from sugars by oxidizing a $-CH_2OH$ group to an acid group ($-COOH$). [1920s: *uronic* from URO-[1] 'urine' + -IC, with the insertion of *-n-*.]

u·ro·pod /ˈyŏŏrəˌpäd/ ▶n. Zool. the sixth and last pair of abdominal appendages of lobsters and related crustaceans, forming part of the tail fan. [19th C.: from URO-[2] 'tail' + Gk. *pous, pod-* 'pod.']

u·ro·pyg·i·um /ˌyŏŏrəˈpijēəm/ ▶n. Zool. the rump of a bird, supporting the tail feathers. —**u·ro·pyg·i·al** /-ˈpijēəl/ adj. [18th C.: via med. L. from Gk. *ouropugion.*]

u·ros·co·py /yŏŏˈräskəpē/ ▶n. Med., hist. the diagnostic examination of urine by simple inspection.

u·ro·style /ˈyŏŏrəˌstīl/ ▶n. Zool. a long bone formed from fused vertebrae at the base of the vertebral column in some lower vertebrates, esp. frogs and toads.

Ur·sa Ma·jor /ˈərsə ˈmājər/ Astron. one of the largest and most prominent northern constellations (the Great Bear). The seven brightest stars form a familiar formation known by various names (esp. the Big Dipper and the Plow) and include the Pointers.

Ur·sa Mi·nor /ˈərsə ˈmīnər/ Astron. a northern constellation (the Little Bear) that contains the north celestial pole and the star Polaris. The brightest stars form a shape that is also known as the Little Dipper.

ur·sine /ˈərˌsin; -ˌsēn/ ▶adj. of, relating to, or resembling bears. [16th C.: from L. *ursinus*, from *ursus* 'bear.']

Ur·su·la, St. /ˈərs(y)ələ/ a legendary British saint and martyr, said to have been put to death with 11,000 virgins after being captured by Huns.

Ur·su·line /ˈərs(y)əlin; -ˌlīn; -ˌlēn/ ▶n. a nun of an order founded by St. Angela Merici (1470–1540) at Brescia in 1535 for nursing the sick and teaching girls. ▶adj. of or relating to this order. [from St. *Ursula*, the founder's patron saint.]

ur·text /ˈŏŏrˌtekst/ ▶n. (pl. **-tex·te** /-ˌtekstə/) an original or the earliest version of a text, to which later versions can be compared.

ur·ti·car·i·a /ˌərtiˈke(ə)rēə/ ▶n. Med. a rash of round, red welts on the skin that itch intensely, sometimes with dangerous swelling, caused by an allergic reaction, typically to specific foods. Also called NETTLERASH or HIVES. [18th C.: mod. L., from L. *urtica* 'nettle,' from *urere* 'to burn.']

ur·ti·cate /ˈərtiˌkāt/ ▶v. [intrans.] cause a stinging or prickling sensation like that given by a nettle. —**ur·ti·ca·tion** /ˌərtiˈkāSHən/ n. [19th C.: from med. L. *urticat-* 'stung,' from the v. *urticare*, from L. *urtica* (see URTICARIA).]

Uruguay

Official name: Oriental Republic of Uruguay
Location: eastern South America, on the Atlantic coast south of Brazil
Area: 68,000 square miles (176,200 sq km)
Population: 3,399,000
Capital: Montevideo
Language: Spanish
Currency: Uruguayan peso

U·ru·guay /ˈ(y)ŏŏrəˌgwī; -ˌgwā/ a country in eastern South America. *See box.* —**U·ru·guay·an** /ˌ(y)ŏŏrəˈgwīən; -ˈgwā-/ adj. & n.

U·rum·qi /ˈŏŏˈrŏŏmˈCHē/ (also **U·rum·chi**) the capital of Xinjiang autonomous region in northwestern China; pop. 1,110,000. Former name (until 1954) TIHWA.

PRONUNCIATION KEY ə *ago, up*; ər *over, fur*; a *hat*; ā *ate*; ä *car*; e *let*; ē *see*; i *fit*; ī *by*; NG *sing*; ō *go*; ô *law, for*; oi *toy*; ŏŏ *good*; ōō *goo*; ou *out*; TH *thin*; T͟H *then*; ZH *vision*

u·rus /ˈyo͝orəs/ ▶ n. another term for AUROCHS. [17th C.: from L., from Gk. *ouros.*]

u·ru·shi·ol /(y)o͞oˈro͞oshē,ôl; -,ōl; -,äl/ ▶ n. Biochem. an oily liquid that is the main constituent of Japanese lacquer and is responsible for the irritant properties of poison ivy and other plants. It consists of a mixture of catechol derivatives. [20th C.: from Japanese *urushi* 'Japanese lacquer' + -OL.]

US ▶ abbr. ■ United States.

us /əs/ ▶ pron. [first person pl.] **1** used by a speaker to refer to himself or herself and one or more other people as the object of a verb or preposition: *let us know.* Compare with WE. ■ used after the verb "to be" and after "than" or "as": *it's us or them | they are richer than us.* ■ informal to or for ourselves: *we got us some good hunting.* **2** informal me: *give us a kiss.*
– PHRASES **us and them** (or **them and us**) expressing a sense of division within a group of people. [OE ūs, accusative and dative of WE, of Gmc. origin; rel. to Du. *ons* and Ger. *uns.*]

USA ▶ abbr. ■ United States of America. ■ United States Army.

us·a·ble /ˈyo͞ozəbəl/ (also **use·a·ble**) ▶ adj. able or fit to be used: *usable information.* — **us·a·bil·i·ty** /,yo͞ozəˈbilətē/ n.

USAF ▶ abbr. United States Air Force.

us·age /ˈyo͞osij; -zij/ ▶ n. the action of using something or the fact of being used. ■ the way in which a word or phrase is normally and correctly used. ■ habitual or customary practice, esp. as creating a right, obligation, or standard. [ME (in the sense 'customary practice'): from OFr., from *us* 'a use' (see USE).]

us·ance /ˈyo͞ozəns/ ▶ n. archaic **1** another term for USAGE. **2** the time allowed for the payment of foreign bills of exchange, according to law or commercial practice.

USB ▶ abbr. Computing universal serial bus, a connection technology for attaching peripheral devices to a computer, providing fast data exchange.

USC ▶ abbr. Law United States Code.

USCG ▶ abbr. United States Coast Guard.

USD ▶ abbr. United States dollar.

USDA ▶ abbr. United States Department of Agriculture.

use ▶ v. **1** /yo͞oz/ [trans.] take, hold, or deploy (something) as a means of accomplishing a purpose or achieving a result; employ. ■ take or consume (an amount) from a limited supply of something. ■ exploit (a person or situation) for one's own advantage. ■ treat (someone) in a particular way: *use your troops well.* ■ apply (a name or title) to oneself: *she still used her maiden name.* ■ (**one could use**) informal one would like or benefit from: *I could use another cup of coffee.* ■ informal take (an illegal drug). **2** /yo͞ost/ (**used to**) describing an action or state of affairs that was done repeatedly or existed for a period in the past: *I used to give him lifts home.* **3** /yo͞ost/ (**be/get used to**) be or become familiar with someone or something through experience: *you just have to get used to him.* ▶ n. /yo͞os/ the action of using something or the state of being used for some purpose. ■ the ability or power to exercise or manipulate something, esp. one's mind or body. ■ a purpose for or way in which something can be used: *culinary uses.* ■ the value or advantage of something: *what's the use of crying?* ■ Law, hist. the benefit or profit of lands, esp. lands that are in the possession of another who holds them solely for the beneficiary. ■ the characteristic ritual and liturgy of a church or diocese. ■ the action of taking or habitual consumption of a drug.
– PHRASES **have no use for** be unable to find a purpose for; have no need for. ■ informal dislike or be impatient with. **make use of** use for a purpose. ■ benefit from. **use and wont** formal established custom.
– PHRASAL VERBS **use something up** consume or expend the whole of something. ■ find a purpose for something that is left over. ■ (**be used up**) informal (of a person) be worn out, esp. with overwork. [ME: the n. from OFr. *us*, from L. *usus*, from *uti* 'to use.']

use·a·ble ▶ adj. var. of USABLE.

used /yo͞ozd/ ▶ adj. **1** having already been used: *scrawling on the back of a used envelope.* **2** secondhand: *a used car.*

use·ful /ˈyo͞osfəl/ ▶ adj. able to be used for a practical purpose or in several ways.
– PHRASES **make oneself useful** do something that is of some value or benefit to someone. — **use·ful·ly** adv. **use·ful·ness** n.

use·ful load ▶ n. the load able to be carried by an aircraft in addition to its own weight.

use·less /ˈyo͞osləs/ ▶ adj. not fulfilling or not expected to achieve the intended purpose or desired outcome. ■ informal having no ability or skill in a specified activity or area: *he was useless at football.* — **use·less·ly** adv. **use·less·ness** n.

Use·net /ˈyo͞oz,net/ (also **USENET**) Comput. an Internet service consisting of thousands of newsgroups.

us·er /ˈyo͞ozər/ ▶ n. **1** a person who uses or operates something, esp. a computer or other machine. ■ a person who takes illegal drugs; a drug user. ■ a person who manipulates others for their own gain: *he was a gifted user of other people.* **2** Law the continued use or enjoyment of a right.

us·er-de·fin·a·ble ▶ adj. Comput. having a function or meaning that can be specified and varied by a user.

us·er-friend·ly ▶ adj. (of a machine or system) easy to use or understand: *the search software is user-friendly.* — **us·er-friend·li·ness** n.

us·er-hos·tile ▶ adj. (of a machine or system) difficult to use or understand.

us·er in·ter·face ▶ n. Comput. the means by which the user and a computer system interact, in particular the use of input devices and software.

us·er·name /ˈyo͞ozər,nām/ ▶ n. Comput. an identification used by a person with access to a computer network.

us·er-o·ri·ent·ed ▶ adj. (of a machine or system) designed with the user's convenience given priority.

ush·er /ˈəshər/ ▶ n. **1** a person who shows people to their seats, esp. in a theater or at a wedding. ■ Brit. a person employed to walk before a person of high rank on special occasions. **2** Brit., archaic an assistant teacher. ▶ v. [trans.] show or guide (someone) somewhere. ■ fig. cause or mark the start of (something new). [ME (denoting a doorkeeper): from Anglo-Norman Fr. *usser*, from med. L. *ustiarius*, from L. *ostiarius*, from *ostium* 'door.']

ush·er·ette /,əshəˈret/ ▶ n. a woman who shows people to their seats in a theater.

USIA ▶ abbr. United States Information Agency.

Üs·kü·dar /,o͞oskəˈdär/ a city in northwestern Turkey; pop. 396,000. Former name SCUTARI.

USMC ▶ abbr. United States Marine Corps.

USN ▶ abbr. United States Navy.

USO ▶ abbr. ■ United Service Organizations.

U·so·ni·an /yo͞oˈsōnēən/ ▶ adj. of or relating to the United States: *the Usonian city.* [20th C.: an acronym from *United States* + *-onian* after *Amazonian, Devonian*, etc.] ■ relating to or denoting the style of buildings designed in the 1930s by Frank Lloyd Wright, characterized by inexpensive construction and flat roofs. ▶ n. a native or inhabitant of the United States. ■ a house built in the 1930s by Frank Lloyd Wright.

Us·pa·lla·ta Pass /,o͞ospäˈyätə/ a pass over the Andes in South America that links Argentina with Chile.

USPS ▶ abbr. United States Postal Service.

us·que·baugh /ˈəskwə,bô; -,bä/ ▶ n. esp. Irish Scot. whiskey. [16th C.: from Irish and Scot. Gael. *uisge beatha* 'water of life'; cf. WHISKEY.]

USS ▶ abbr. United States Ship, used in the names of ships in the US Navy: *the USS* Maine.

USSR hist. ▶ abbr. Union of Soviet Socialist Republics.

U·sti·nov /ˈyo͞ostə,nôf; -,nôv; o͞oˈstēnəf/ former name (1984–87) of IZHEVSK.

usu. ▶ abbr. usual; usually.

u·su·al /ˈyo͞ozho͞oəl/ ▶ adj. habitually or typically occurring or done; customary. ▶ n. (**the/one's usual**) informal the drink someone habitually orders or prefers. ■ the thing that is typically done or present. — **u·su·al·ly** adv. **u·su·al·ness** n. [ME: from OFr., or from late L. *usualis*, from L. *usus* 'a use' (see USE).]

u·su·fruct /ˈyo͞ozə,frəkt; -sə-/ ▶ n. Roman Law the right to enjoy the use and advantages of another's property short of the destruction or waste of its substance. — **u·su·fruc·tu·ar·y** /,yo͞ozəˈfrəkcho͞o,erē; -sə-/ adj. & n. [17th C.: from med. L. *usufructus*, from L. *usus (et) fructus* 'use (and) enjoyment,' from *usus* 'a use' + *fructus* 'fruit.']

u·su·rer /ˈyo͞ozhərər/ ▶ n. a person who lends money at unreasonably high rates of interest.

u·su·ri·ous /yo͞oˈzho͞orēəs/ ▶ adj. of or relating to the practice of usury: *they lend money at usurious rates.* — **u·su·ri·ous·ly** adv.

u·surp /yo͞oˈsərp/ ▶ v. [trans.] take (a position of power or importance) illegally or by force. ■ take the place of (someone in a position of power) illegally; supplant. ■ [intrans.] (**usurp on/upon**) archaic encroach or infringe upon (someone's rights). — **u·sur·pa·tion** /,yo͞osərˈpāshən/ n. **u·surp·er** n. [ME: from OFr. *usurper*, from L. *usurpare* 'seize for use.']

u·su·ry /ˈyo͞ozh(ə)rē/ ▶ n. the illegal action or practice of lending money at unreasonably high rates of interest. ■ archaic interest at such rates. [ME: from Anglo-Norman Fr. *usurie*, or from med. L. *usuria*, from L. *usura*, from *usus* 'a use' (see USE).]

UT ▶ abbr. ■ Universal Time. ■ Utah (in official postal use).

U·tah /ˈyo͞o,tô; -,tä/ a state in the western US; pop. 2,233,169; capital, Salt Lake City; statehood, Jan. 4, 1896 (45). The region, a part of Mexico from 1821, was ceded to the US in 1848. The first permanent settlers, who arrived in 1847, were Mormons fleeing persecution. — **U·tah·an** /-tô(ə)n; -ˈtä(ə)n/ adj. & n.

U·tah Beach a name given to the westernmost of the beaches in Normandy where US troops landed on D-day in June 1944.

u·tah·rap·tor /ˈyo͞o,tô,raptər; -,tä-/ ▶ n. a large dromaeosaurid dinosaur (genus *Utahraptor*, suborder Theropoda), the remains of which were discovered in Utah in 1992. It was twice the size of deinonychus. [mod. L., from UTAH + RAPTOR.]

UTC ▶ abbr. Universal Time Coordinated. Also expanded as COORDINATED UNIVERSAL TIME.

Ute /yo͞ot/ ▶ n. (pl. same or **Utes**) **1** a member of an American Indian people living chiefly in Colorado and Utah. **2** the Uto-Aztecan language of this people. ▶ adj. of or relating to the Ute or their language. [from earlier *Utah*, from Sp. *Yuta*; cf. PAIUTE.]

ute /yo͞ot/ ▶ n. informal a utility vehicle. [1940s: abbrev.]

u·ten·sil /yo͞oˈtensəl/ ▶ n. an implement, container, or other article, esp. for household use. [ME: from OFr. *utensile*, from med. L., neut. of L. *utensilis* 'usable,' from *uti* 'to use' (see USE).]

u·ter·i /ˈyo͞otə,rī; -,rē/ plural form of UTERUS.

u·ter·ine /ˈyo͞otərin; -,rīn/ ▶ adj. of or relating to the uterus or womb: *uterine contractions.* ■ [attrib.] born of the same mother but not having the same father: *a uterine sister.* [ME: from UTERUS + -INE[1], or, in the sense 'born of the same mother,' from late L. *uterinus*.]

u·ter·us /'yo͞otərəs/ ▶ **n.** (pl. **u·ter·i** /'yo͞otə,rī; -,rē/) the organ in the lower body of a woman or female mammal where offspring are conceived and in which they gestate before birth; the womb. [L.]

U·ther Pen·drag·on /'(y)o͞oTHər pen'dragən/ (in Arthurian legend) king of the Britons and father of Arthur.

U·ti·ca /'yo͞otikə/ a city in central New York; pop. 60,651.

u·tile[1] /'yo͞otl; 'yo͞o,tīl/ ▶ **adj.** rare advantageous. [15th C.: via OFr. from L. *utilis*, from *uti* 'to use.']

u·ti·le[2] /'yo͞otl-ē/ ▶ **n.** a large tropical African hardwood tree (*Entandrophragma utile*, family Meliaceae) with timber that is widely used as a substitute for mahogany. [1950s: mod. L., specific epithet (see above).]

u·til·i·tar·i·an /yo͞o,tili'te(ə)rēən/ ▶ **adj. 1** designed to be useful or practical rather than attractive. **2** Philos. of, relating to, or adhering to the doctrine of utilitarianism: *a utilitarian theorist*. ▶ **n.** Philos. an adherent of utilitarianism.

u·til·i·tar·i·an·ism /yo͞o,tilə'te(ə)rēə,nizəm/ ▶ **n.** the doctrine that actions are right if they are useful or for the benefit of a majority. ■ the doctrine that an action is right insofar as it promotes happiness, and that the greatest happiness of the greatest number should be the guiding principle of conduct.

u·til·i·ty /yo͞o'tilətē/ ▶ **n.** (pl. **-ties**) **1** the state of being useful, profitable, or beneficial. ■ (in game theory or economics) a measure of that which is sought to be maximized in any situation involving a choice. **2** a public utility. ■ stocks and bonds in public utilities. **3** Comput. a utility program. ▶ **adj.** [attrib.] **1** useful, esp. through being able to perform several functions: *a utility truck*. ■ denoting a player capable of playing in several different positions in a sport. **2** functional rather than attractive: *utility clothing*. **3** of or relating to the lowest US government grade of beef. **4** (of domestic animals) raised for potential profit and not for show or as pets. [ME: from OFr. *utilite*, from L. *utilitas*, from *utilis* 'useful.']

u·til·i·ty knife ▶ **n.** a knife with a small sharp blade, often retractable, designed to cut wood, cardboard, and other materials.

u·til·i·ty pole ▶ **n.** another term for TELEPHONE POLE.

u·til·i·ty pro·gram ▶ **n.** Comput. a program for carrying out a routine function.

u·til·i·ty room ▶ **n.** a room equipped with appliances for washing and other domestic work.

u·til·i·ty ve·hi·cle (also **u·til·i·ty truck**) ▶ **n.** a truck with low sides designed for carrying small loads.

u·ti·lize /'yo͞otl,īz/ ▶ **v.** [trans.] make practical and effective use of: *vitamin C helps your body utilize iron*. — **u·ti·liz·a·ble** /,yo͞otl'īzəbəl; 'yo͞otl,ī-/ **adj.** **u·ti·li·za·tion** /,yo͞otl-ə'zāSHən/ **n.** **u·ti·liz·er n.** [19th C.: from Fr. *utiliser*, from Ital. *utilizzare*, from *utile* (see UTILE[1]).]

-ution ▶ **suffix** (forming nouns) equivalent to -ATION (as in *solution*). [via Fr. from L. *-utio(n-)*.]

ut·most /'ət,mōst/ ▶ **adj.** [attrib.] most extreme; greatest. ▶ **n.** (**the utmost**) the greatest or most extreme extent or amount: *a plot that stretches credulity to the utmost*. [OE *ūt(e)mest* 'outermost' (see OUT, -MOST).]

U·to-Az·tec·an /'yo͞otō'az,tekən/ ▶ **n.** a language family of Central America and western North America including Comanche, Hopi, Nahuatl (the language of the Aztecs), Paiute, Pima, and Shoshone. ▶ **adj.** of, relating to, or denoting this language family.

U·to·pi·a /yo͞o'tōpēə/ (also **u·to·pi·a**) ▶ **n.** an imagined place or state of things in which everything is perfect. The word was first used in the book *Utopia* (1516) by Sir Thomas More. The opposite of DYSTOPIA. [based on Gk. *ou* 'not' + *topos* 'place.']

U·to·pi·an /yo͞o'tōpēən/ (also **u·to·pi·an**) ▶ **adj.** modeled on or aiming for a state in which everything is perfect; idealistic. ▶ **n.** an idealistic reformer. — **U·to·pi·an·ism** /-ə,nizəm/ **n.**

u·to·pi·an so·cial·ism ▶ **n.** socialism achieved by the moral persuasion of capitalists to surrender the means of production peacefully to the people.

U·trecht /'yo͞o,trekt; 'Y,treKHt/ a city in the central Netherlands; pop. 231,000.

u·tri·cle /'yo͞otrəkəl/ ▶ **n.** a small cell, sac, or bladderlike protuberance in an animal or plant. ■ (also **u·tric·u·lus** /yo͞o'trikyələs/) the larger of the two fluid-filled cavities forming part of the labyrinth of the inner ear. Compare with SACCULE. — **u·tric·u·lar** /yo͞o'trikyələr/ **adj.** [18th C.: from Fr. *utricule* or L. *utriculus*, dimin. of *uter* 'leather bag.']

U·tril·lo /o͝o'trēō; yo͞o'trilō/, Maurice (1883–1955), French painter, chiefly known for his depictions of the Montmartre district.

Ut·tar Pra·desh /'o͝otər prə'dāSH; -'deSH/ a state in northern India that borders on Tibet and Nepal; capital, Lucknow.

ut·ter[1] /'ətər/ ▶ **adj.** complete; absolute. — **ut·ter·ly adv.** [OE *ūtera, ūttra* 'outer,' compar. of *ūt* 'out'; cf. OUTER.]

ut·ter[2] ▶ **v.** [trans.] **1** make (a sound) with one's voice. ■ say (something) aloud. **2** Law put (forged money) into circulation. — **ut·ter·a·ble adj.** **ut·ter·er n.** [ME: from MDu. *ūteren* 'speak.']

ut·ter·ance /'ətərəns/ ▶ **n.** a spoken word, statement, or vocal sound. ■ the action of saying or expressing something aloud: *the simple utterance of a few platitudes*. ■ Ling. an uninterrupted chain of spoken or written language.

ut·ter·most /'ətər,mōst/ ▶ **adj. & n.** another term for UTMOST.

U-turn ▶ **n.** the turning of a vehicle in a U-shaped course so as to face in the opposite direction. ■ fig. a change of plan, esp. a reversal of political policy: *another U-turn by the government*.

UV ▶ **abbr.** ultraviolet.

UVA ▶ **abbr.** ultraviolet radiation of relatively long wavelengths.

u·va·rov·ite /(y)o͞o'värə,vīt/ ▶ **n.** an emerald green variety of garnet, containing chromium. [19th C.: from the name of Count Sergei S. *Uvarov* (1785–1855), Russ. statesman, + -ITE[1].]

UVB ▶ **abbr.** ultraviolet radiation of relatively short wavelengths.

u·ve·a /'yo͞ovēə/ ▶ **n.** the pigmented layer of the eye, lying beneath the sclera and cornea, and comprising the iris, choroid, and ciliary body. — **u·ve·al adj.** [ME (denoting the choroid layer of the eye): from med. L., from L. *uva* 'grape.']

u·ve·i·tis /,yo͞ovē'ītis/ ▶ **n.** Med. inflammation of the uvea.

u·vu·la /'yo͞ovyələ/ ▶ **n.** (pl. **-lae** /-,lē; -,lī/) Anat. (also **pal·a·tine u·vu·la**) a fleshy extension at the back of the soft palate that hangs above the throat. ■ a similar fleshy hanging structure in any organ of the body, particularly one at the opening of the bladder. [ME: from late L., dimin. of L. *uva* 'grape.']

u·vu·lar /'yo͞ovyələr/ ▶ **adj. 1** Phonet. (of a sound) articulated with the back of the tongue and the uvula, as *r* in French and *q* in Arabic. **2** Anat. of or relating to the uvula. ▶ **n.** Phonet. a uvular consonant.

ux·o·ri·al /,ək'sôrēəl; əg'zôr-/ ▶ **adj.** of or relating to a wife. [19th C.: from L. *uxor* 'wife' + -IAL.]

ux·o·ri·cide /,ək'sôrə,sīd; ,əg'zôr-/ ▶ **n.** the killing of one's wife. ■ a man who kills his wife. — **ux·o·ri·cid·al** /ək,sôrə'sīdl; əg,zôr-/ **adj.** [19th C.: from L. *uxor* 'wife' + -CIDE.]

ux·o·ri·ous /,ək'sôrēəs; ,əg'zôr-/ ▶ **adj.** having or showing an excessive or submissive fondness for one's wife. — **ux·o·ri·ous·ly adv.** **ux·o·ri·ous·ness n.** [16th C.: from L. *uxoriosus*, from *uxor* 'wife.']

Uy·gur ▶ **n. & adj.** var. of UIGHUR.

Uz·bek /'o͝oz,bek; 'əz-; o͝oz'bek/ ▶ **n. 1** a member of a Turkic people living mainly in the republic of Uzbekistan and elsewhere in southwestern Asia. ■ a native or national of Uzbekistan. **2** the Turkic language of Uzbekistan. ▶ **adj.** of or relating to Uzbekistan, the Uzbeks, or their language. [the name in Uzbek.]

Uzbekistan

Official name: Republic of Uzbekistan
Location: central Asia, south of Kazakhstan
Area: 172,800 square miles (447,400 sq km)
Population: 26,410,000
Capital: Tashkent
Languages: Uzbek (official), Russian
Currency: Uzbekistani sum

Uz·bek·i·stan /o͝oz'bekə,stan; əz-; -,stän/ a republic in central Asia. *See box.*

U·zi /'o͞ozē/ ▶ **n.** a type of submachine gun of Israeli design. [1950s: from *Uziel* Gal, the Israeli army officer who designed it.]

Vv

V[1] /vē/ (also **v**) ▶**n.** (pl. **Vs** or **V's**) **1** the twenty-second letter of the alphabet. ▪ denoting the next after U in a set of items, categories, etc. **2** (also **vee**) a shape like that of a letter V: [in comb.] *deep, V-shaped valleys.* ▪ [as adj.] denoting an internal combustion engine with a number of cylinders arranged in two rows at an angle to each other in a V-shape: *a V-engine.* **3** the Roman numeral for five.

V[2] ▶**abbr.** ▪ volt(s). ▶**symb.** ▪ the chemical element vanadium. ▪ voltage or potential difference: $V = IR$. ▪ (in mathematical formulae) volume: $pV = nRT$.

v. ▶**abbr.** ▪ Gram. verb. ▪ (in textual references) verse. ▪ verso. ▪ versus. ▪ very. ▪ (in textual references) *vide.* ▶**symb.** velocity.

V-1 ▶**n.** a small flying bomb powered by a simple jet engine, used by the Germans in World War II. [abbrev. of Ger. *Vergeltungswaffe* 'reprisal weapon.']

V-2 ▶**n.** a rocket-powered flying bomb, which was the first ballistic missile, used by the Germans in World War II. [see **V-1**.]

VA ▶**abbr.** ▪ (in the US) Veterans Affairs (formerly Veterans Administration). ▪ Vicar Apostolic. ▪ Vice Admiral. ▪ Virginia (in official postal use).

Va. ▶**abbr.** Virginia.

Vaal /väl/ a river in South Africa that rises in the Drakensberg Mountains and flows to the Orange River.

vac /vak/ ▶**n.** **1** informal term for **VACUUM CLEANER**. **2** Brit. informal term for **VACATION**.

va·can·cy /'vākənsē/ ▶**n.** (pl. **-cies**) **1** an unoccupied position or job: *a vacancy for a shorthand typist.* ▪ an available room in a hotel or other establishment providing accommodations. **2** empty space: *Cathy stared into vacancy, seeing nothing.* ▪ emptiness of mind; lack of intelligence or understanding. ▪ Crystallog. a defect in a crystal lattice, consisting of the absence of an atom or an ion from a position where there should be one.

va·cant /'vākənt/ ▶**adj.** (of premises) having no fixtures, furniture, or inhabitants; empty. Compare with **UNOCCUPIED** (sense 1). ▪ (of a position or employment) not filled. ▪ (of a person or their expression) having or showing no intelligence or interest: *a vacant stare.* — **va·cant·ly** **adv.** [ME: from OFr., or from L. *vacant-* 'remaining empty,' from the v. *vacare.*]

va·cate /'vā,kāt/ ▶**v.** [trans.] **1** leave (a place that one previously occupied): *rooms must be vacated by noon.* ▪ give up (a position or employment). **2** Law cancel or annul (a judgment, contract, or charge). [17th C.: from L. *vacat-* 'left empty,' from the v. *vacare.*]

va·ca·tion /vā'kāsHən; və-/ ▶**n.** **1** an extended period of recreation, esp. one spent away from home or in traveling. ▪ a fixed holiday period between terms in schools and courts of law. **2** the action of leaving something one previously occupied: *his marriage led to the vacation of his fellowship.* ▶**v.** [intrans.] take a vacation: *I was vacationing in Europe with my family.* — **va·ca·tion·er** **n.** **va·ca·tion·ist** /-ist/ **n.** [ME: from OFr., or from L. *vacatio(n-)*, from *vacare* 'be unoccupied' (see **VACATE**).]

va·ca·tion·land /vā'kāsHən,land; və-/ ▶**n.** an area providing attractions for people on vacation.

vac·ci·nate /'vaksə,nāt/ ▶**v.** [trans.] treat with a vaccine to produce immunity against a disease; inoculate. — **vac·ci·na·tion** /,vaksə'nāsHən/ **n.** **vac·ci·na·tor** /-,nātər/ **n.**

vac·cine /vak'sēn/ ▶**n.** Med. a substance used to stimulate the production of antibodies and provide immunity against one or several diseases, prepared from the causative agent of a disease, its products, or a synthetic substitute, treated to act as an antigen without inducing the disease. ▪ Comput. a program designed to detect computer viruses and prevent them from operating. [18th C.: from L. *vaccinus*, from *vacca* 'cow' (because of the early use of the cowpox virus against smallpox).]

vac·cin·i·a /vak'sinēə/ ▶**n.** Med. cowpox, or the virus that causes it. [19th C.: mod. L., from L. *vaccinus* (see **VACCINE**).]

vac·il·late /'vasə,lāt/ ▶**v.** [intrans.] alternate or waver between different opinions or actions; be indecisive. — **vac·il·la·tion** /,vasə'lāsHən/ **n.** **vac·il·la·tor** /-,lātər/ **n.** [16th C. (in the sense 'sway unsteadily'): from L. *vacillat-* 'swayed,' from the v. *vacillare.*]

vac·u·a /'vakyəwə/ plural form of **VACUUM**.

vac·u·ole /'vakyōō,ōl/ ▶**n.** Biol. a space or vesicle within the cytoplasm of a cell, enclosed by a membrane and typically containing fluid. ▪ a small cavity or space in tissue, esp. in nervous tissue as the result of disease. — **vac·u·o·lar** /,vakyōō'ōlər; 'vakyōōələr/ **adj.** **vac·u·o·la·tion** /,vakyōōə'lāsHən/ **n.** [19th C.: from Fr., dimin. of L. *vacuus* 'empty.']

vac·u·ous /'vakyōōəs/ ▶**adj.** having or showing a lack of thought or intelligence; mindless: *a vacuous smile.* ▪ archaic empty. — **va·cu·i·ty** /va'kyōōətē; və-/ **n.** **vac·u·ous·ly** **adv.** **vac·u·ous·ness** **n.** [17th C. (in the sense 'empty of matter'): from L. *vacuus* 'empty' + **-OUS**.]

vac·u·um /'vak,yōō(ə)m; -yəm/ ▶**n.** (pl. **-u·ums** or **-u·a** /-yōōə/) **1** a space entirely devoid of matter. ▪ a space or container from which the air has been completely or partly removed. ▪ [usu. in sing.] a gap left by the loss, death, or departure of someone or something formerly playing a significant part in a situation or activity. **2** (pl. **-u·ums**) informal a vacuum cleaner. ▶**v.** [trans.] informal clean with a vacuum cleaner.
– PHRASES **in a vacuum** (of an activity or a problem to be considered) isolated from the context normal to it and in which it can best be understood or assessed. [16th C.: mod. L., neut. of L. *vacuus* 'empty.']

vac·uum bot·tle ▶**n.** another term for **THERMOS**.

vac·u·um brake ▶**n.** a railroad vehicle brake operated by changes in pressure in a continuous pipe that is generally kept exhausted of air by a pump and controls similar brakes throughout the train.

vac·u·um clean·er ▶**n.** an electrical apparatus that by means of suction collects dust and small particles from floors and other surfaces. — **vac·uum-clean** **v.**

vac·u·um dis·til·la·tion ▶**n.** Chem. distillation of a liquid under reduced pressure, enabling it to boil at a lower temperature than normal.

vac·u·um ex·trac·tion ▶**n.** the application of reduced pressure to extract something, particularly to assist childbirth or as a method of abortion, or as a technique for removing components of a chemical mixture.

vac·u·um ex·trac·tor ▶**n.** a cup-shaped appliance for performing vacuum extraction in childbirth.

vac·u·um flask ▶**n.** another term for **THERMOS**.

vac·u·um gauge ▶**n.** a gauge for testing pressure after the production of a vacuum.

vac·u·um-pack ▶**v.** [trans.] seal (a product) in packaging after any air has been removed so that the packaging is tight and firm.

vac·u·um pump ▶**n.** a pump used for creating a vacuum.

vac·u·um tube ▶**n.** a sealed glass tube containing a near-vacuum that allows the free passage of electric current.

va·de me·cum /,vädē 'mākəm; ,vādē 'mē-/ ▶**n.** a handbook or guide that is kept constantly at hand for consultation. [17th C.: mod. L., lit. 'go with me.']

Va·do·da·ra /və'dōdərə; -,rä/ a city in western India; pop. 1,021,000.

va·dose /'vā,dōs/ ▶**adj.** relating to or denoting underground water above the water table. Compare with **PHREATIC**. [19th C.: from L. *vadosus*, from *vadum* 'shallow expanse of water.']

Va·duz /vä'dōōts; fä-/ the capital of Liechtenstein; pop. 5,000.

vag·a·bond /'vagə,bänd/ ▶**n.** a person who wanders from place to place without a home or job. ▪ informal, dated a rascal; a rogue. ▶**adj.** [attrib.] having no settled home. ▶**v.** [intrans.] archaic wander about as or like a vagabond. — **vag·a·bond·age** /-,bändij/ **n.** [ME: from OFr., or from L. *vagabundus*, from *vagari* 'wander.']

va·gal /'vāgəl/ ▶**adj.** of or relating to the vagus nerve.

va·gar·i·ous /və'ge(ə)rēəs; vā-/ ▶**adj.** rare erratic and unpredictable in behavior or direction.

va·gar·y /'vāgərē/ ▶**n.** (pl. **-gar·ies**) (usu. **vagaries**) an unexpected and inexplicable change in a situation or in someone's behavior: *the vagaries of the weather.* [16th C.: from L. *vagari* 'wander.']

va·gi /'vā,gī; -jī; -,gē; -jē/ plural form of **VAGUS**.

va·gi·na /və'jīnə/ ▶**n.** (pl. **-nas** or **-nae** /-nē; -nī/) the muscular tube leading from the external genitals to the cervix of the uterus in women and most female mammals. ▪ Bot. Zool. any sheathlike structure, esp. a sheath formed around a stem by the base of a leaf. — **vag·i·nal** /'vajənl/ **adj.** [17th C.: from L., lit. 'sheath, scabbard.']

va·gi·na den·ta·ta /den'tätə/ ▶**n.** the motif of a vagina with teeth, occurring in folklore and fantasy and said to symbolize male fears of the dangers of sexual intercourse, esp. of castration. [20th C.: *dentata*, fem. of L. *dentatus* 'having teeth.']

vag·i·nal plug ▶**n.** Zool. a secretion that blocks the vagina of some rodents and insectivores after mating.

vag·i·nis·mus /,vajə'nizməs/ ▶**n.** painful spasmodic contraction of the vagina in response to physical contact or pressure (esp. in sexual intercourse). [19th C.: mod. L., from L. *vagina* (see **VAGINA**).]

vag·i·ni·tis /,vajə'nītis/ ▶**n.** inflammation of the vagina.

va·got·o·my /vā'gätəmē/ ▶ **n.** (pl. **-mies**) a surgical operation in which one or more branches of the vagus nerve are cut, typically to reduce the rate of gastric secretion (e.g., in treating peptic ulcers). — **va·got·o·mized** /-,mīzd/ **adj.**

va·go·to·ni·a /,vagə'tōnēə/ ▶ **n.** the condition in which there is increased influence of the parasympathetic nervous system and increased excitability of the vagus nerve, producing bradycardia and faintness.

va·grant /'vāgrənt/ ▶ **n.** a person without a settled home or regular work who wanders from place to place and lives by begging. ■ archaic a wanderer. ■ Ornithol. a bird that has strayed or been blown from its usual range or migratory route. Also called ACCIDENTAL. ▶ **adj.** characteristic of, relating to, or living the life of a vagrant: *vagrant beggars.* ■ moving from place to place; wandering: *vagrant whales.* ■ literary moving or occurring unpredictably; inconstant: *the vagrant heart of my mother.* — **va·gran·cy** /-grənsē/ **n.** **va·grant·ly** **adv.** [ME: from Anglo-Norman Fr. *vagarant* 'wandering around,' from the v. *vagrer*.]

vague /vāg/ ▶ **adj.** of uncertain, indefinite, or unclear character or meaning: *patients with vague symptoms.* ■ thinking or communicating in an unfocused or imprecise way: *he had been vague about his activities.* — **vague·ly** **adv.** **vague·ness** **n.** **vagu·ish** **adj.** [16th C.: from Fr., or from L. *vagus* 'wandering, uncertain.']

va·gus /'vāgəs/ ▶ **n.** (pl. **va·gi** /-gī; -jī; -gē; -jē/) (also **va·gus nerve**) Anat. each of the tenth pair of cranial nerves, supplying the heart, lungs, upper digestive tract, and other organs of the chest and abdomen. [19th C.: from L. (see VAGUE).]

vail /vāl/ ▶ **v.** [trans.] archaic take off or lower (one's hat or crown) as a token of respect or submission. ■ [intrans.] take off one's hat or otherwise show respect or submission to someone. [ME: shortening of obs. *avale*, from OFr. *avaler* 'to lower,' from *a val* 'down' (lit. 'in the valley').]

vain /vān/ ▶ **adj.** **1** having or showing an excessively high opinion of one's appearance, abilities, or worth. **2** producing no result; useless: *a vain attempt to sleep.* ■ having no meaning or likelihood of fulfillment.
– PHRASES **in vain** without success or a result. **take someone's name in vain** use someone's name in a way that shows a lack of respect. — **vain·ly** **adv.** [ME: via OFr. from L. *vanus* 'empty.']

vain·glo·ry /'vān,glôrē; ,vān'glôrē/ ▶ **n.** literary inordinate pride in oneself or one's achievements; excessive vanity. — **vain·glo·ri·ous** /,vān'glôrēəs/ **adj.** **vain·glo·ri·ous·ly** /,vān'glôrēəslē/ **adv.** **vain·glo·ri·ous·ness** /,vān'glôrēəsnəs/ **n.**

vair /ve(ə)r/ ▶ **n.** **1** fur, typically bluish-gray, obtained from a variety of squirrel, used in the 13th and 14th centuries as a trimming or lining for garments. **2** Heraldry fur, represented by interlocking rows of shield-shaped or bell-shaped figures that are typically alternately blue and white, as a tincture. [ME: via OFr. from L. *varius* (see VARIOUS).]

Vaish·na·va /'vīshnəvə/ ▶ **n.** a member of one of the main branches of modern Hinduism, devoted to the worship of the god Vishnu as the supreme being, esp. in his incarnation as Krishna. [from Sanskrit *vaiṣṇava*.]

Vaish·ya /'vīshyə; 'vīs-/ (also **Vais·ya**) ▶ **n.** a member of the third of the four Hindu castes, comprising the merchants and farmers. [from Sanskrit *vaiśya* 'peasant, laborer.']

val·ance /'valəns; 'vāləns/ ▶ **n.** a length of decorative drapery attached to the canopy or frame of a bed in order to screen the structure or the space beneath it. ■ a length of decorative drapery hung above a window to screen the curtain fittings. ■ a dust ruffle. — **val·anced** **adj.** [ME: perh. Anglo-Norman Fr., from a shortened form of OFr. *avaler* 'descend' (see VAIL).]

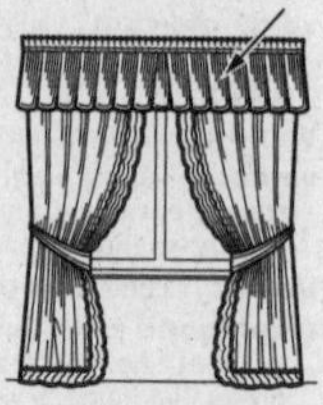

valance

vale[1] /vāl/ ▶ **n.** a valley (used in place names or as a poetic term): *the Vale of Glamorgan.*
– PHRASES **vale of tears** literary the world regarded as a scene of trouble or sorrow. [ME: from OFr. *val*, from L. *vallis, valles*.]

vale[2] /'välā/ archaic ▶ **exclam.** farewell. ▶ **n.** a written or spoken farewell. [L., lit. 'be well!, be strong!,' imper. of *valere*.]

val·e·dic·tion /,valə'diksHən/ ▶ **n.** the action of saying farewell: *he spread his palm in valediction.* ■ a statement or address made at or as a farewell. [17th C.: based on L. *vale* 'goodbye' + *dicere* 'to say,' on the pattern of *benediction*.]

val·e·dic·to·ri·an /,valə,dik'tôrēən/ ▶ **n.** a student, typically having the highest academic achievements of the class, who delivers the valedictory at a graduation ceremony.

val·e·dic·to·ry /,valə'dikt(ə)rē/ ▶ **adj.** serving as a farewell: *a valedictory wave.* ▶ **n.** (pl. **-ries**) a farewell address.

va·lence /'vāləns/ ▶ **n.** Chem. the combining power of an element, esp. as measured by the number of hydrogen atoms it can displace or combine with. ■ [as adj.] relating to or denoting electrons involved in or available for chemical bond formation: *molecules with unpaired valence electrons.* ■ Ling. the number of grammatical elements with which a particular word, esp. a verb, combines in a sentence. [ME: from late L. *valentia* 'power, competence,' from *valere* 'be well or strong.']

Va·len·ci·a /və'lensēə; -'lenTHēə/ **1** an autonomous region of eastern Spain. ■ its capital, on the Mediterranean coast; pop. 777,000. **2** a city in northern Venezuela; pop. 903,000.

Va·len·ci·ennes /və,lensē'en; ,valən-/ ▶ **n.** a type of bobbin lace. [after a town in France.]

va·len·cy /'vālənsē/ ▶ **n.** (pl. **-cies**) Chem. Ling., esp. Brit. another term for VALENCE. [17th C.: from late L. *valentia* 'power' (see VALENCE).]

-val·ent ▶ **comb. form** **1** having a valency of the specified number: *trivalent.* **2** Genet. (denoting a meiotic structure) composed of the specified number of chromosomes: *univalent.*

val·en·tine /'valən,tīn/ ▶ **n.** a card sent on St. Valentine's Day, February 14, to a person one loves or is attracted to. ■ a person to whom one sends such a card or whom one asks to be one's sweetheart.

Val·en·tine, St. /'valən,tīn/ either of two early Italian saints (who may have been the same person) traditionally commemorated on February 14—a Roman priest martyred *c.*269 and a bishop of Terni martyred at Rome.

Val·en·ti·no /,valən'tēnō/, Rudolph (1895–1926), US actor; born in Italy; born *Rodolfo Guglielmi di Valentina d'Antonguolla.* He played the romantic hero in silent movies such as *The Sheik* (1921).

Va·le·ra, Eamon de, see DE VALERA.

Va·le·ri·an /və'li(ə)rēən/ (died 260), Roman emperor 253–260; Latin name *Publius Licinius Valerianus.*

va·le·ri·an /və'li(ə)rēən/ ▶ **n.** a plant (family Valerianaceae) that typically bears clusters of small pink or white flowers. Native to Eurasia, several species have been introduced to North America. Its several species include the **red valerian** (*Centranthus ruber*), whose flowers attract butterflies. ■ a drug obtained from the root of common valerian, used as a sedative and antispasmodic. [ME: from OFr. *valeriane*, from med. L. *valeriana (herba)*, appar. the fem. of *Valerianus* 'of Valerius' (a personal name).]

va·ler·ic ac·id /və'le(ə)rik; -'li(ə)r-/ ▶ **n.** Chem. another term for PENTANOIC ACID. [19th C.: *valeric* from VALERIAN + -IC.]

Va·lé·ry /,välā'rē/, Ambroise Paul Toussaint Jules (1871–1945), French poet, essayist, and critic. His poetry includes *La Jeune parque* (1917).

val·et /va'lā; 'valā; 'valit/ ▶ **n.** **1** a man's personal male attendant, responsible for his clothes and appearance. ■ a hotel employee performing such duties for guests. ■ a rack or stand on which to hang clothing. **2** a person employed to park cars. ▶ **v.** (**-eted, -et·ing**) [trans.] act as a valet to (a particular man). ■ [intrans.] work as a valet. [15th C.: from Fr.; rel. to VASSAL.]

val·et park·ing ▶ **n.** a service provided at a restaurant, club, or airport whereby an attendant parks and retrieves patrons' vehicles.

val·e·tu·di·nar·i·an /,valə,t(y)ōōdn'e(ə)rēən/ ▶ **n.** a person who is unduly anxious about their health. ■ a person suffering from poor health. ▶ **adj.** showing undue concern about one's health. ■ suffering from poor health. — **val·e·tu·di·nar·i·an·ism** /-ə,nizəm/ **n.** [18th C.: from L. *valetudinarius* 'in ill health' (from *valetudo* 'health,' from *valere* 'be well') + -AN.]

val·e·tu·di·nar·y /,valə't(y)ōōdn,erē/ ▶ **adj.** & **n.** (pl. **-nar·ies**) another term for VALETUDINARIAN.

val·gus /'valgəs/ ▶ **n.** Med. a deformity involving oblique displacement of part of a limb away from the midline. The opposite of VARUS. [19th C.: from L., lit. 'knock-kneed.']

Val·hal·la /val'halə; väl'hälə/ Scand. Mythol. a hall in which heroes killed in battle were believed to feast with Odin for eternity. [mod. L., from ON *Valhǫll*, from *valr* 'the slain' + *hǫll* 'hall.']

val·iant /'valyənt/ ▶ **adj.** possessing or showing courage or determination: *a valiant warrior.* — **val·iant·ly** **adv.** [ME (also in the sense 'robust, well-built'): from OFr. *vailant*, based on L. *valere* 'be strong.']

val·id /'valid/ ▶ **adj.** actually supporting the intended point or claim; acceptable as cogent: *a valid criticism.* ■ legally binding due to having been executed in compliance with the law. ■ legally acceptable. — **va·lid·i·ty** /və'lidətē/ **n.** **val·id·ly** **adv.** [16th C.: from Fr. *valide* or L. *validus* 'strong,' from *valere* 'be strong.']

val·i·date /'valə,dāt/ ▶ **v.** [trans.] check or prove the validity or accuracy of (something). ■ demonstrate or support the truth or value of: *her feelings are validated.* ■ make or declare legally valid. — **val·i·da·tion** /,valə'dāsHən/ **n.**

val·ine /'val,ēn; 'vā,lēn/ ▶ **n.** Biochem. an amino acid, $(CH_3)_2CHCH(NH_2)COOH$, that is a constituent of most proteins. It is an essential nutrient in the diet of vertebrates. [20th C.: from *val(eric acid)* + -INE[4].]

va·lise /və'lēs/ ▶ **n.** a small traveling bag or suitcase. [17th C.: from Fr., from Ital. *valigia*.]

Val·i·um /'valēəm/ ▶ **n.** trademark for DIAZEPAM.

Val·kyr·ie /val'ki(ə)rē; 'valkərē/ ▶ **n.** Scand. Mythol. each of Odin's twelve handmaidens who conducted the slain warriors of their choice from the battlefield to Valhalla. [from ON *Valkyrja*, lit. 'chooser of the slain,' from *valr* 'the slain' + *kyrja* 'chooser.']

Val·la·do·lid /,valədə'lid; ,bäyədə'lēd/ **1** a city in northern Spain; pop. 345,000. **2** former name (until 1828) of MORELIA.

val·lec·u·la /və'lekyələ/ ▶ **n.** (pl. **-lae** /-,lē; -,lī/) Anat. Bot. a groove or furrow. — **val·lec·u·lar** /-lər/ **adj.** [19th C.: from a late L. var. of L. *vallicula*, dimin. of L. *vallis* 'valley.']

Val·le·jo /və'lāō; -,hō/ a city in north central California; pop. 109,199.

Val·let·ta /və'letə/ the capital and chief port of Malta; pop. 9,000.

val·ley /'valē/ ▶ **n.** (pl. **-leys**) **1** a low area of land between hills or mountains, typically with a river or stream flowing through it. **2** Archit. an internal angle formed by the intersecting planes of a roof, or by the slope of a roof and a wall. [ME: from OFr. *valee*, based on L. *vallis, valles*; cf. VALE[1].]

val·ley fe·ver (also **San Joa·quin Val·ley fe·ver**) ▶n. informal term for COCCIDIOIDOMYCOSIS.

Val·ley Forge the site on the Schuylkill River in Pennsylvania where George Washington's Continental Army spent the winter of 1777–78 in conditions of extreme hardship.

Val·ley of the Kings a valley near ancient Thebes in Egypt where pharaohs were buried.

Va·lois /val'wä; 'val,wä/ the French royal house from the accession of Philip VI, successor to the last Capetian king, in 1328 to the death of Henry III in 1589, when the throne passed to the Bourbons.

va·lo·ni·a /və'lōnēə/ ▶n. (also **va·lo·ni·a oak**) an evergreen oak tree (*Quercus macrolepis*) native to southern Europe and western Asia. Its acorn cups yield a black dye used in tanning. [18th C.: from Ital. *vallonia*, based on Gk. *balanos* 'acorn.']

val·or /'valər/ (Brit. **val·our**) ▶n. great courage in the face of danger, esp. in battle: *acts of valor.* — **val·or·ous** /-ərəs/ adj. [ME: via OFr. from late L. *valor*, from *valere* 'be strong.']

val·or·ize /'valə,rīz/ ▶v. [trans.] give or ascribe value or validity to (something): *the culture valorizes the man.* ■ raise or fix the price or value of (a commodity or currency) by artificial means, esp. by government action. — **val·or·i·za·tion** /,valərə'zāsHən/ n.

Val·pa·raí·so /,valpə'rīzō; ,bälpärä'ēsō/ the principal port of Chile, near Santiago; pop. 277,000.

Val·po·li·cel·la /,val,pōlə'cHelə; ,väl-/ ▶n. red Italian wine made in the Val Policella district.

val·pro·ic ac·id /val'prō-ik/ ▶n. Chem. a synthetic crystalline compound, $C_7H_{15}COOH$, with anticonvulsant properties, used (generally as salts) in the treatment of epilepsy. — **val·pro·ate** /-'prō,āt; -ət/ n. [1970s: *valproic* from *valeric* (see VALERIC ACID) + *pro(pyl)* + -IC.]

Val·sal·va ma·neu·ver /val'salvə/ ▶n. Med. the action of attempting to exhale with the nostrils and mouth, or the glottis, closed. This increases pressure in the middle ear and the chest, as when bracing to lift heavy objects, and is used as a means of equalizing pressure in the ears. [19th C.: named after Antonio M. *Valsalva* (1666–1723), Italian anatomist.]

valse /väls/ ▶n. (pl. same) French term for WALTZ (esp. as used in the titles of pieces of music). [18th C.: via Fr. from Ger. *Walzer*.]

val·u·a·ble /'valy(o͝o)əbəl/ ▶adj. worth a great deal of money: *a valuable antique.* ■ extremely useful or important: *my time is valuable.* ▶n. (usu. **valuables**) a thing that is of great worth, esp. a small item of personal property. — **val·u·a·bly** /-blē/ adv.

val·u·a·tion /,valyo͞o'āsHən/ ▶n. an estimation of something's worth, esp. one carried out by a professional appraiser. ■ the monetary worth of something, esp. as estimated by an appraiser. — **val·u·ate** /'valyo͞o,āt/ v.

val·u·a·tor /'valyə,wātər/ ▶n. archaic a person who makes valuations.

val·ue /'valyo͞o/ ▶n. **1** the regard that something is held to deserve; the importance or preciousness of something: *your support is of great value.* ■ the material or monetary worth of something: *a total value of $500.* ■ the worth of something compared to the price paid or asked for it: *at $12.50 the book is a good value.* ■ the usefulness of something considered in respect of a particular purpose: *some new drugs are of great value in treating cancer.* ■ the relative rank, importance, or power of a playing card, chess piece, etc., according to the rules of the game. **2** (**values**) a person's principles or standards of behavior; one's judgment of what is important in life. **3** the numerical amount denoted by an algebraic term; a magnitude, quantity, or number: *the mean value of x.* **4** Music the relative duration of the sound signified by a note. **5** Ling. the meaning of a word or other linguistic unit. ■ the quality or tone of a spoken sound; the sound represented by a letter. **6** Art the relative degree of lightness or darkness of a particular color: *the artist has used adjacent color values.* ▶v. (**-ues, -ued, -u·ing**) [trans.] **1** (often **be valued**) estimate the monetary worth of (something): *his estate was valued at $45,000.* **2** consider (someone or something) to be important or beneficial; have a high opinion of. [ME: from OFr., fem. past part. of *valoir* 'be worth,' from L. *valere*.]

val·ue add·ed ▶n. Econ. the amount by which the value of an article is increased at each stage of its production, exclusive of initial costs. ▶adj. (**value-added**) (of goods) having features added to a basic line or model for which the buyer is prepared to pay extra. ■ (of a company) offering specialized or extended services in a commercial area.

val·ue-add·ed tax (abbr.: **VAT**) ▶n. a tax on the amount by which the value of an article has been increased at each stage of its production or distribution.

val·ue-free ▶adj. free from criteria imposed by subjective values or standards; purely objective.

val·ue judg·ment /'valyo͞o ,jəjmənt/ ▶n. an assessment of something as good or bad in terms of one's standards or priorities.

val·ue·less /'valyo͞oləs/ ▶adj. having no value; worthless: *cherished but valueless heirlooms.* — **val·ue·less·ness** n.

va·lu·ta /və'lo͞otə/ ▶n. the value of one currency with respect to its exchange rate with another. ■ foreign currency. [19th C.: from Ital., lit. 'value.']

val·vate /'val,vāt/ ▶adj. Bot. (of sepals or other parts) having adjacent edges abutting rather than overlapping. Compare with IMBRICATE. [19th C.: fom L. *valvatus* 'having folding doors,' from *valva* 'valve.']

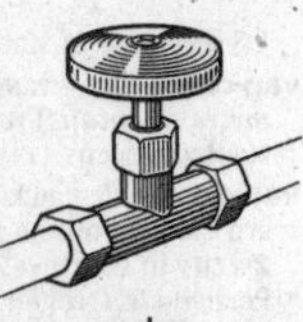
valve

valve /valv/ ▶n. a device for controlling the passage of fluid through a pipe or duct, esp. an automatic device allowing movement in one direction only. ■ (in full **ther·mi·on·ic valve**) Electron. British term for THERMIONIC TUBE. ■ Music a cylindrical mechanism in a brass instrument that, when depressed or turned, admits air into different sections of tubing and so extends the range of available notes. ■ Anat. Zool. a membranous fold in a hollow organ or tubular structure, such as a blood vessel or the digestive tract, that maintains the flow of the contents in one direction by closing in response to any pressure from reverse flow. ■ Zool. each of the halves of the hinged shell of a bivalve mollusk or brachiopod, or of the parts of the compound shell of a barnacle. ■ Bot. each of the halves or sections into which a dry fruit (esp. a pod or capsule) dehisces. — **valved** adj. [in comb.] *a two-valved outer covering* **valve·less** adj. [ME: from L. *valva*.]

val·vu·lar /'valvyələr/ ▶adj. relating to, having, or acting as a valve or valves: *valvular heart disease.*

val·vu·li·tis /,valvyə'lītis/ ▶n. Med. inflammation of the valves of the heart.

vam·brace /'vam,brās/ ▶n. hist. a piece of armor for the arm, esp. the forearm. [ME: from an Anglo-Norman Fr. shortening of OFr. *avantbras*, from *avant* 'before' + *bras* 'arm.']

va·moose /va'mo͞os; və-/ ▶v. [intrans.] informal depart hurriedly: *we'd better vamoose before we're caught.* [19th C.: from Sp. *vamos* 'let us go.']

vamp[1] /vamp/ ▶n. **1** the upper front part of a boot or shoe. **2** (in jazz and popular music) a short, simple introductory passage, usually repeated several times until otherwise instructed. ▶v. **1** [trans.] attach a new upper to (a boot or shoe). ■ (**vamp something up**) informal repair or improve something: *the production values have been vamped up.* **2** [intrans.] repeat a short, simple passage of music. [ME: shortening of OFr. *avantpie*, from *avant* 'before' + *pie* 'foot.']

vamp[2] informal ▶n. a woman who uses sexual attraction to exploit men. [20th C.: abbrev. of VAMPIRE.] ▶v. [trans.] blatantly set out to attract. — **vamp·ish** adj. **vamp·ish·ly** adv. **vamp·y** adj.

vam·pire /'vam,pī(ə)r/ ▶n. **1** a corpse supposed, in European folklore, to leave its grave at night to drink the blood of the living by biting their necks with long pointed canine teeth. ■ fig. a person who preys ruthlessly on others. **2** (also **vam·pire bat**) a small bat that feeds on the blood of mammals or birds using its two sharp incisor teeth and anticoagulant saliva, found mainly in tropical America. It belongs to the family Desmodontidae (or Phyllostomidae) and includes three species, esp. the **common vampire** (*Desmodus rotundus*). — **vam·pir·ic** /vam'pirik/ adj. [18th C.: from Fr., from Hungarian *vampir*, perh. from Turk. *uber* 'witch.']

vam·pir·ism /'vampī,rizəm/ ▶n. the action or practices of a vampire.

vam·plate /'vam,plāt/ ▶n. hist. a circular plate on a spear or lance designed to protect the hand. [ME: from Anglo-Norman Fr. *vauntplate*, from *avant* 'before' + *plate* 'thin plate.' Cf. VAMBRACE.]

van[1] /van/ ▶n. a covered boxlike motor vehicle, typically having a rear door and sliding doors on the side panels, used for transporting goods or people. ■ a covered truck used for moving goods, esp. furniture. ■ Brit. an enclosed railroad car for conveying something other than passengers. ■ Brit. a caravan. [19th C.: shortening of CARAVAN.]

van[2] ▶n. (**the van**) the foremost part of a company of people moving or preparing to move forward, esp. the foremost division of an advancing military force. ■ fig. the forefront: *in the van of the movement.* [17th C.: abbrev. of VANGUARD.]

van[3] ▶n. **1** archaic a winnowing fan. **2** archaic literary a bird's wing. [ME: dial. var. of FAN[1].]

van·a·date /'vanə,dāt/ ▶n. Chem. a salt in which the anion contains both vanadium and oxygen, esp. one of the anion VO_4^{3-}. [19th C.: from VANADIUM + -ATE[1].]

va·nad·i·nite /və'nădn,īt; -'nadn-/ ▶n. a rare reddish-brown mineral consisting of a vanadate and chloride of lead, typically occurring as an oxidation product of lead ores. [19th C.: from VANADIUM + -ITE[1].]

va·na·di·um /və'nādēəm/ ▶n. the chemical element of atomic number 23, a hard gray metal of the transition series, used to make alloy steels. (Symbol: **V**) [19th C.: mod. L., from ON *Vanadis* (a name of the Scand. goddess Freya).]

va·na·di·um steel ▶n. a strong alloy of steel containing vanadium.

Van Al·len /van'alən/, James Alfred (1914–2006), US physicist. He studied cosmic radiation in the upper atmosphere.

Van Al·len belt ▶n. each of two regions of intense radiation partly surrounding the earth at heights of several thousand kilometers.

Van·brugh /'vanbrə/, Sir John (1664–1726), English architect and playwright. His comedies include *The Relapse* (1696). As an architect, he collaborated with Nicholas Hawksmoor (1661–1736) on Blenheim Palace (1705).

Van Bu·ren /van 'byo͞orən/, Martin (1782–1862), 8th president of the US 1837–41; known as **Old Kinderhook**. A New Yorker noted for his development of the two-party system, he was a US Senator 1821–28,

US secretary of state 1829–31, and US vice president 1833–37.

van·co·my·cin /ˌvaNGkəˈmīsin/ ▶ **n.** Med. a bacterial antibiotic (*Streptomyces orientalis*) used against resistant strains of streptococcus and staphylococcus. [1950s: from *vanco-* (of unknown origin) + -MYCIN.]

Van·cou·ver¹ /vanˈko͞ovər/ **1** a city in British Columbia, in southwestern Canada, on the mainland opposite Vancouver Island; pop. 471,844. **2** a city in southwestern Washington, on the Columbia River, north of Portland in Oregon; pop. 143,560.

Van·cou·ver², George (1757–98), English explorer. He charted much of the west coast of North America between southern Alaska and California.

Van·cou·ver Is·land a large island off the Pacific coast of Canada, in southwestern British Columbia.

van·dal /ˈvandl/ ▶ **n.** **1** a person who deliberately destroys or damages public or private property. **2** (**Vandal**) a member of a Germanic people that ravaged Gaul, Spain, and North Africa in the 4th–5th centuries and sacked Rome in AD 455. [from L. *Vandalus*, of Gmc. origin.]

van·dal·ism /ˈvandlˌizəm/ ▶ **n.** action involving deliberate destruction of or damage to public or private property. — **van·dal·is·tic** /ˌvandlˈistik/ **adj.** **van·dal·is·ti·cal·ly** /ˌvandlˈistik(ə)lē/ **adv.**

van·dal·ize /ˈvandlˌīz/ ▶ **v.** [trans.] deliberately destroy or damage (public or private property): *stations have been wrecked and vandalized beyond recognition.*

Van de Graaff gen·er·a·tor /ˈvan də ˌgraf/ ▶ **n.** Physics a machine devised to generate electrostatic charge by means of a vertical endless belt collecting charge from a voltage source and transferring it to a large insulated metal dome, where a high voltage is produced. [20th C.: named after Robert Jemison *Van de Graaff* (1901–67), American physicist.]

Van·der·bijl·park /ˈvandərˌbīlˌpärk/ a city in South Africa, south of Johannesburg; pop. 540,000.

Van·der·bilt /ˈvandərˌbilt/, Cornelius (1794–1877), US businessman and philanthropist. He amassed a fortune from shipping and railroads.

van der Waals forc·es /ˈvan dər ˌwôlz; -ˌvälz/ ▶ **plural n.** Chem. weak, short-range electrostatic attractive forces between uncharged molecules, arising from the interaction of permanent or transient electric dipole moments. [19th C.: named after Johannes *van der Waals* (1837–1923), Dutch physicist.]

Van De·van·ter /van dəˈvantər/, Willis (1859–1941), US Supreme Court associate justice 1910–37.

van de Vel·de /ˌvän də ˈveldə/ a family of Dutch painters. Willem (1611–93), known as **Willem van de Velde the Elder**, and his son, Willem (1633–1707), known as **Willem van de Velde the Younger**, painted marine subjects. Another son, Adriaen (1636–72), painted landscapes, portraits, and biblical and genre scenes.

Van Die·men's Land /van ˈdēmənz/ former name (until 1855) of TASMANIA.

Van Dor·en /van ˈdôrən/ a family of US writers and poets. Carl Clinton (1885–1950) wrote *Benjamin Franklin* (1938). His brother Mark Albert (1894–1972) was a poet whose work appears in *Collected Poems* (1939). Mark's son, Charles Lincoln (1926–), wrote *The Idea of Progress* (1967). In 1959, he was involved in a quiz show scandal because he had been given the answers for television's "Twenty One."

Van Dyck /van ˈdīk/ (also **Van·dyke**), Sir Anthony (1599–1641), Flemish painter.

Van·dyke (also **van·dyke**) ▶ **n.** **1** a broad lace or linen collar with an edge deeply cut into large points (in imitation of a style frequently depicted in portraits by Sir Anthony Van Dyck), fashionable in the 18th century. ■ each of a number of large deep-cut points on the border or fringe of a garment or piece of material. **2** (also **Van·dyke beard**) a neat, pointed beard. ▶ **adj.** denoting a style of garment or decorative design associated with the portraits of Van Dyck.

Van·dyke brown ▶ **n.** a deep rich brown.

vane /vān/ ▶ **n.** a broad blade attached to a rotating axis or wheel that pushes or is pushed by wind or water and forms part of a machine or device such as a windmill, propeller, or turbine. ■ short for WEATHERVANE. ■ the flat part on either side of the shaft of a feather. ■ a broad, flat projecting surface designed to guide the motion of a projectile, such as a feather on an arrow or a fin on a torpedo. — **vaned** **adj.** [usu. in comb.] *a three-vaned windmill.* [ME: dial. var. of obs. *fane* 'banner,' of Gmc. origin.]

Vä·nern /ˈvenə(r)n/ a lake in southwestern Sweden, the largest lake in the country.

Van Eyck /van ˈīk/, Jan (*c.*1370–1441), Flemish painter. His works include *The Adoration of the Lamb* (1432).

vang /vaNG/ ▶ **n.** Sailing each of two guy ropes running from the end of a gaff to opposite sides of the deck. [18th C.: var. of obs. *fang*, denoting a gripping device, from ON *fang* 'grasp,' of Gmc. origin.]

Van Gogh /van ˈgō; ˈgäKH/, Vincent Willem (1853–90), Dutch post-Impressionist painter. His works include *The Potato Eaters* (1885) and *Starry Night* (1889).

van·guard /ˈvanˌgärd/ ▶ **n.** a group of people leading the way in new developments or ideas. ■ a position at the forefront of new developments or ideas: ***in the vanguard of*** *technical development.* ■ the foremost part of an advancing army or naval force. — **van·guard·ism** /-ˌizəm/ **n.** **van·guard·ist** **n.** [ME: shortening of OFr. *avan(t)garde*, from *avant* 'before' + *garde* 'guard.']

va·nil·la /vəˈnilə/ ▶ **n.** **1** a substance obtained from vanilla beans or produced artificially and used to flavor sweet foods or to impart a fragrant scent to cosmetic preparations: [as adj.] *vanilla ice cream.* ■ ice cream flavored with vanilla: *a scoop of vanilla.* **2** a tropical climbing orchid (genus *Vanilla*) that has fragrant flowers and long podlike fruit. Its many species include *V. planifolia*, the chief commercial source of vanilla beans. ■ (also **va·nil·la bean** or **va·nil·la pod**) the fruit of this plant, which is cured and then either used in cooking or processed to extract an essence that is used for flavor and fragrance. ▶ **adj.** having no special or extra features; ordinary: *vanilla sex.* [17th C.: from Sp. *vainilla* 'pod,' dimin. of *vaina* 'sheath, pod,' from L. *vagina* 'sheath.']

va·nil·lin /vəˈnilin; ˈvanl-/ ▶ **n.** Chem. a fragrant compound, $CH_3OC_6H_3(OH)CHO$, that is the essential constituent of vanilla. [19th C.: from VANILLA + -IN¹.]

Va·nir /ˈväni(ə)r/ ▶ **n.** Scand. Mythol. a race of Norse gods, allies of the Aesir, that function as fertility divinities.

van·ish /ˈvanisH/ ▶ **v.** [intrans.] **1** disappear suddenly and completely: *Mary vanished without trace.* ■ gradually cease to exist: *those days are vanishing.* **2** Math. become zero. [ME: shortening of OFr. *e(s)vaniss-*, lengthened stem of *e(s)vanir*, from L. *evanescere* 'die away.']

van·ish·ing cream ▶ **n.** dated a cream or ointment that leaves no visible trace when rubbed into the skin.

van·ish·ing·ly /ˈvanisHiNGlē/ ▶ **adv.** in such a manner or to such a degree as almost to become invisible, nonexistent, or negligible: ***vanishingly small probability.***

van·ish·ing point ▶ **n.** **1** the point at which receding parallel lines viewed in perspective appear to converge. **2** [in sing.] the point at which something that has been growing smaller or increasingly faint disappears altogether: *fees have dropped close to the vanishing point.*

van·i·tas /ˈvanəˌtäs/ ▶ **n.** a still-life painting of a 17th-century Dutch genre containing symbols of death or change as a reminder of their inevitability. [L., lit. 'vanity.']

van·i·ty /ˈvanətē/ ▶ **n.** (pl. **-ties**) **1** excessive pride in or admiration of one's own appearance or achievements. ■ [as adj.] denoting a person or company that publishes works at the author's expense: *a vanity press.* **2** the quality of being worthless or futile. **3** a dressing table. ■ a bathroom unit consisting of a washbasin typically set into a counter with a cabinet beneath. [ME: from OFr. *vanite*, from L. *vanitas*, from *vanus* 'empty' (see VAIN).]

van·i·ty case ▶ **n.** a small case fitted with a mirror and compartments for makeup.

Van·i·ty Fair the world regarded as a place of frivolity and idle amusement (originally with reference to Bunyan's *Pilgrim's Progress*).

van·i·ty mir·ror ▶ **n.** a small mirror used for applying makeup, esp. one fitted in a visor of a motor vehicle.

van·i·ty plate ▶ **n.** a vehicle license plate bearing a distinctive or personalized combination of letters, numbers, or both.

van·i·ty ta·ble ▶ **n.** a dressing table.

van·quish /ˈvaNGkwisH/ ▶ **v.** [trans.] defeat thoroughly. — **van·quish·a·ble** **adj.** **van·quish·er** **n.** [ME: from OFr. *vencus, venquis* (past part. and past tense of *veintre*), *vainquiss-* (lengthened stem of *vainquir*), from L. *vincere* 'conquer.']

Van Rens·se·laer /ˌvan ˌrensəˈli(ə)r; ˈrensələr/, Stephen (1764–1839), US army officer and politician. A Federalist who served in the US House of Representatives 1822–29, he founded the school (1824) that became Rensselaer Polytechnic Institute in Troy, New York.

van·tage /ˈvantij/ (usu. **van·tage point**) ▶ **n.** a place or position affording a good view of something. [ME: from Anglo-Norman Fr., shortening of OFr. *avantage* 'advantage.']

Va·nu·a·tu /ˌvänoo͝ˈätoo͞; ˌvanoo͞-/ a country in the southwestern Pacific Ocean. *See box on next page.* — **Va·nu·a·tu·an** /-ˈätoo͞ən/ **adj.** & **n.**

Van·zet·ti /vanˈzetē/, Bartolomeo (1888–1927), US political radical; born in Italy. In 1921, along with Nicola Sacco, he was accused and convicted of murder, and, in 1927, executed. In 1977, their names were cleared, but the case remains controversial.

vap·id /ˈvapid/ ▶ **adj.** offering nothing that is stimulating or challenging: *tuneful but vapid musical comedies.* — **va·pid·i·ty** /vaˈpidətē/ **n.** **vap·id·ly** **adv.** [17th C.: from L. *vapidus*.]

va·por /ˈvāpər/ (Brit. **va·pour**) ▶ **n.** a substance diffused or suspended in the air, esp. one normally liquid or solid: *dense clouds of smoke and toxic vapor.* ■ Physics a gaseous substance that is below its critical temperature, and can therefore be liquefied by pressure alone. Compare with GAS. ■ (**the vapors**) dated a sudden feeling of faintness or nervousness or a state of depression. ▶ **v.** [intrans.] talk in a vacuous, boasting, or pompous way. — **va·por·ous** /ˈvāpərəs/ **adj.** **va·por·ous·ness** /ˈvāpərəsnəs/ **n.** **va·por·ish** **adj.** (archaic) **va·por·y** /ˈvāpərē/ **adj.** [ME: from OFr. *vapour*, or from L. *vapor* 'steam, heat.']

va·por den·si·ty ▶ **n.** Chem. the density of a particular gas or vapor relative to that of hydrogen at the same pressure and temperature.

va·po·ret·to /ˌväpəˈretō; ˌvapə-/ ▶ **n.** (pl. **-ret·ti** /-ˈretē/ or **-ret·tos**) (in Venice) a canal boat (originally a steamboat, now a motorboat) used for public transportation. [Ital., dimin. of *vapore* 'steam,' from L. *vapor*.]

va·por·ize /ˈvāpəˌrīz/ ▶ **v.** convert or be converted into vapor: [trans.] *a large current which is sufficient to vaporize carbon* | [intrans.] *cold gasoline does not vaporize readily.* — **va·por·iz·a·ble** **adj.** **va·por·i·za·tion** /ˌvāpərəˈzāsHən; -ˌrīˈzā-/ **n.**

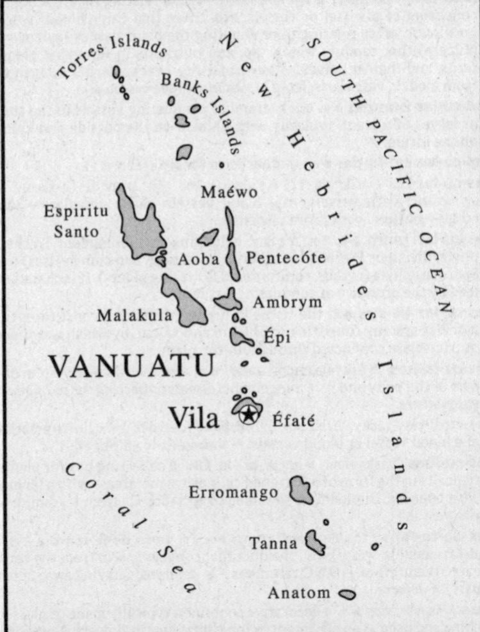

Vanuatu

Official name: Republic of Vanuatu
Location: southwestern Pacific Ocean, a group of chiefly volcanic islands
Area: 4,700 square miles (12,200 sq km)
Population: 202,000
Capital: Vila
Languages: Bislama, English, and French (all official)
Currency: vatu

va·por·iz·er /'vāpə,rīzər/ ▶ **n.** a device that generates a particular substance in the form of vapor, esp. for medicinal inhalation.

va·por lock ▶ **n.** an interruption in the flow of a liquid through a fuel line or other pipe as a result of vaporization of the liquid.

va·por pres·sure ▶ **n.** Chem. the pressure of a vapor in contact with its liquid or solid form.

va·por trail ▶ **n.** another term for CONTRAIL.

va·por·ware /'vāpər,we(ə)r/ (Brit. **va·pour·ware**) ▶ **n.** Comput., informal software or hardware that has been advertised but is not yet available to buy, either because it is only a concept or because it is still being written or designed.

va·pour ▶ **n.** British spelling of VAPOR.

va·que·ro /vä'kerō/ ▶ **n.** (pl. **-ros**) (in Spanish-speaking parts of the US) a cowboy; a cattle driver. [Sp., from *vaca* 'cow.']

VAR ▶ **abbr.** value-added reseller, a company that adds extra features to products it has bought before selling them on. ■ value at risk, a method of quantifying the risk of holding a financial asset.

var. ▶ **abbr.** variety.

va·ra /'värə/ ▶ **n.** **1** a unit of linear measure, formerly used in Latin America and Texas, equal to about 33 inches (84 cm). **2** a long spiked lance used by a picador.

va·rac·tor /'ve(ə)r,aktər; və'raktər/ ▶ **n.** Electron. a semiconductor diode with a capacitance dependent on the applied voltage. [1950s: from elements of *variable reactor*.]

Va·ra·na·si /və'ränəsē/ a city on the Ganges River, in Uttar Pradesh, in northern India; pop. 926,000.

Va·ran·gi·an /və'ranjēən/ ▶ **n.** any of the Scandinavian voyagers who traveled by land and up rivers into Russia in the 9th and 10th centuries AD, establishing the Rurik dynasty and gaining great influence in the Byzantine Empire. [from med. L. *Varangus* (a name ult. from ON, prob. based on *vár* 'pledge') + -IAN.]

Var·gas /'värgəs/, Getúlio Dornelles (1883–1954); president of Brazil 1930–45 and 1951–54.

Var·gas Llo·sa /'värgəs 'yōsə/, Jorge Mario Pedro (1936–), Peruvian writer. His novels include *The War of the End of the World* (1982).

var·i·a·ble /'ve(ə)rēəbəl/ ▶ **adj.** **1** not consistent or having a fixed pattern; liable to change. ■ (of a wind) tending to change direction. ■ Math. (of a quantity) able to assume different numerical values. ■ Bot. Zool. (of a species) liable to deviate from the typical color or form, or to occur in different colors or forms. **2** able to be changed or adapted. ■ (of a gear) designed to give varying ratios or speeds. ▶ **n.** an element, feature, or factor that is liable to vary or change. ■ Math. a quantity that during a calculation is assumed to vary or be capable of varying in value. ■ Comput. a data item that may take on more than one value during or between programs. ■ Astron. short for VARIABLE STAR. ■ (**variables**) the region of light, variable winds to the north of the northeast trade winds or (in the southern hemisphere) between the southeast trade winds and the westerlies. — **var·i·a·bil·i·ty** /,ve(ə)rēə'bilitē/ **n.** **var·i·a·ble·ness** **n.** **var·i·a·bly** /-blē/ **adv.** [ME: via OFr. from L. *variabilis*, from *variare* (see VARY).]

var·i·a·ble-rate mort·gage ▶ **n.** a mortgage whose rate of interest is readjusted periodically to reflect market conditions.

var·i·a·ble star ▶ **n.** Astron. a star whose brightness changes, either irregularly or regularly.

var·i·ance /'ve(ə)rēəns/ ▶ **n.** the fact or quality of being different, divergent, or inconsistent: *her light tone was at variance with her sudden trembling.* ■ the state or fact of disagreeing or quarreling: *they were at variance with all their previous allies.* ■ esp. Law a discrepancy between two statements or documents. ■ Law an official dispensation from a rule or regulation, typically a building regulation. ■ Stat. a quantity equal to the square of the standard deviation. ■ (in accounting) the difference between expected and actual costs, profits, output, etc., in a statistical analysis.

var·i·ant /'ve(ə)rēənt/ ▶ **n.** a form or version of something that differs in some respect from other forms of the same thing or from a standard: *variants of malaria.*

var·i·ate /'ve(ə)rē-it; -,āt/ ▶ **n.** another term for RANDOM VARIABLE.

var·i·a·tion /,ve(ə)rē'āshən/ ▶ **n.** **1** a change or slight difference in condition, amount, or level, typically with certain limits: *regional variations in house prices.* ■ Astron. a deviation of a celestial body from its mean orbit or motion. ■ Math. a change in the value of a function due to small changes in the values of its argument or arguments. ■ (also **mag·net·ic var·i·a·tion**) the angular difference between true north and magnetic north at a particular place. ■ Biol. the occurrence of an organism in more than one distinct color or form. **2** a different or distinct form or version of something. ■ Music a version of a theme, modified in melody, rhythm, harmony, or ornamentation, so as to present it in a new but still recognizable form. ■ Ballet a solo dance as part of a performance. — **var·i·a·tion·al** /-shənl/ **adj.**

var·i·a·tion·ist /,ve(ə)rē'āshənist/ ▶ **n.** a person who studies variations in usage among different speakers of the same language.

var·i·ce·al /,varə'sēəl/ ▶ **adj.** Zool. Med. of, relating to, or involving a varix. [1960s: from L. *varix, varic-*.]

var·i·cel·la /,varə'selə/ ▶ **n.** Med. technical term for CHICKEN POX. ■ (also **var·i·cel·la-zos·ter**) a herpesvirus that causes chicken pox and shingles; herpes zoster. [18th C.: mod. L., irregular dimin. of VARIOLA.]

var·i·ces /'varə,sēz/ plural form of VARIX.

var·i·co·cele /'varikō,sēl/ ▶ **n.** Med. a mass of varicose veins in the spermatic cord. [18th C.: from L. *varix, varic-* 'dilated vein' + -CELE.]

var·i·col·ored /'ve(ə)ri,kələrd/ (Brit. **var·i·col·oured**) ▶ **adj.** consisting of several different colors. [17th C.: from L. *varius* 'diverse' + COLORED.]

var·i·cose /'varə,kōs/ ▶ **adj.** [attrib.] affected by a condition causing the swelling and tortuous lengthening of veins, most often in the legs: *varicose veins.* — **var·i·cosed** **adj.** **var·i·cos·i·ty** /,vari'käsitē/ **n.** [ME: from L. *varicosus*, from *varix* (see VARIX).]

var·ied /'ve(ə)rēd/ ▶ **adj.** incorporating a number of different types or elements; showing variation or variety. — **var·ied·ly** **adv.**

var·i·e·gat·ed /'ver(ē)ə,gātid/ ▶ **adj.** exhibiting different colors, esp. as irregular patches or streaks. ■ Bot. (of a plant or foliage) having or consisting of leaves that are edged or patterned in a second color, esp. white as well as green. ■ marked by variety. — **var·i·e·gate** /'ve(ə)r(ē)i,gāt/ **var·i·e·ga·tion** /,ver(ē)i'gāshən/ **n.** [17th C.: from L. *variegat-* 'made varied' (from the v. *variegare*, from *varius* 'diverse') + -ED².]

va·ri·e·tal /və'rīətl/ ▶ **adj.** **1** (of a wine or grape) made from or belonging to a single specified variety of grape. **2** esp. Bot. Zool. of, relating to, characteristic of, or forming a variety: *varietal names.* ▶ **n.** a varietal wine. — **va·ri·e·tal·ly** **adv.**

va·ri·e·ty /və'rīətē/ ▶ **n.** (pl. **-ties**) **1** the quality or state of being different or diverse; the absence of uniformity, sameness, or monotony. ■ (**a variety of**) a number or range of things of the same general class that are different or distinct in character or quality: *a variety of leisure activities.* ■ a thing that differs in some way from others of the same general class or sort; a type: *fifty varieties of pasta.* ■ a form of television or theater entertainment consisting of a series of different types of acts, such as singing, dancing, and comedy. **2** Biol. a taxonomic category that ranks below subspecies (where present) or species, its members differing from others of the same subspecies or species in minor but permanent or heritable characteristics. Compare with FORM (sense 3) and SUBSPECIES. ■ a cultivated form of a plant. See CULTIVAR. ■ a plant or animal that varies in some trivial respect from its immediate parent or type. [15th C.: from Fr. *variété* or L. *varietas*, from *varius* (see VARIOUS).]

va•ri•e•ty meats ▶ plural n. meat consisting of the entrails and internal organs of an animal.

va•ri•e•ty store ▶ n. a small store selling a wide range of inexpensive items.

var•i•form /'ve(ə)rə,fôrm/ ▶ adj. (of a group of things) differing from one another in form: *variform languages.* ■ (of a single thing or a mass) consisting of a variety of forms or things: *a variform education.* [17th C.: from L. *varius* 'diverse' + -FORM.]

va•ri•o•la /və'rīələ; ,ve(ə)rē'ōlə/ ▶ n. Med. technical term for SMALLPOX. — **va•ri•o•lar** /-lər/ adj. **va•ri•o•lous** /-ləs/ adj. (archaic) [18th C.: from med. L., lit. 'pustule, pock,' from L. *varius* 'diverse.']

var•i•o•loid /'ve(ə)rēə,loid/ Med. ▶ adj. resembling smallpox. ▶ n. a mild form of smallpox affecting people who have already had the disease or have been vaccinated against it.

var•i•om•e•ter /,ve(ə)rē'ämitər/ ▶ n. **1** a device for indicating an aircraft's rate of climb or descent. **2** an inductor whose total inductance can be varied by altering the relative position of two coaxial coils connected in series, or by permeability tuning, and so can be used to tune an electric circuit. **3** an instrument for measuring variations in the intensity of the earth's magnetic field.

var•i•o•rum /,ve(ə)rē'ôrəm/ ▶ adj. (of an edition of an author's works) having notes by various editors or commentators. ■ including variant readings from manuscripts or earlier editions. ▶ n. a variorum edition. [18th C.: genitive pl. of *varius* 'diverse,' from L. *editio cum notis variorum* 'edition with notes by various (commentators).']

var•i•ous /'ve(ə)rēəs/ ▶ adj. different from one another; of different kinds or sorts: *dresses of various colors.* ■ having or showing different properties or qualities. ▶ adj. & pron. more than one; individual and separate: [as adj.] *various people* | [as pron.] *various of her friends.* — **var•i•ous•ness** n. [ME: from L. *varius* 'changing, diverse' + -OUS.]

var•i•ous•ly /'ve(ə)rēəslē/ ▶ adv. in several or different ways: *his early successes can be variously accounted for.*

var•is•tor /və'ristər/ ▶ n. a semiconductor diode with resistance dependent on the applied voltage. [1930s: contr. of *varying resistor.*]

var•ix /'ve(ə)riks/ ▶ n. (pl. **var•i•ces** /'ve(ə)ri,sēz/) **1** Med. a varicose vein. **2** Zool. each of the ridges on the shell of a gastropod mollusk, marking a former position of the aperture. [ME: from L.]

var•let /'värlət/ ▶ n. hist. a man or boy acting as an attendant or servant. ■ a knight's page. ■ archaic an unprincipled rogue or rascal. — **var•let•ry** /-lətrē/ n. [ME: from OFr., var. of *valet* 'attendant' (see VALET).]

var•mint /'värmənt/ ▶ n. dialect, informal a troublesome wild animal, esp. a fox. ■ a troublesome and mischievous person, esp. a child. [16th C.: alt. of VERMIN.]

Var•na /'värnə/ a city in eastern Bulgaria, on the Black Sea; pop. 321,000.

var•na /'vərnə; 'vär-/ ▶ n. each of the four Hindu castes, Brahman, Kshatriya, Vaishya, and Shudra. [Sanskrit, lit. 'color, class.']

var•nish /'värnisʜ/ ▶ n. resin dissolved in a liquid for applying on wood, metal, or other materials to form a hard, clear, shiny surface when dry. ■ [in sing.] archaic an external or superficially attractive appearance of a specific quality. ▶ v. [trans.] apply varnish to. ■ disguise or gloss over (a fact): *the White House is varnishing over the defeat of the president's proposal.* — **var•nish•er** n. [ME: from OFr. *vernis*, from med. L. *veronix* 'fragrant resin, sandarac' or med. Gk. *berenikē*, prob. from *Berenice*, a town in Cyrenaica.]

var•nish tree ▶ n. another term for LACQUER TREE.

Var•ro /'varō/, Marcus Terentius (116–27 BC), Roman scholar and satirist. His works covered many subjects.

var•si•ty /'värsətē/ ▶ n. (pl. **-ties**) a sports team representing a school or college. ■ Brit., dated university: *he had his hair cut as soon as he got back from varsity.* ■ [as adj.] Brit. (esp. of a sporting event or team) of or relating to a university, esp. Oxford or Cambridge: *a varsity match.* [17th C.: shortening of UNIVERSITY.]

Var•u•na /'vərŏŏnə; 'vär-/ Hinduism one of the gods in the Rig Veda. Originally the sovereign lord of the universe and guardian of cosmic law, he is known in later Hinduism as god of the waters.

var•us /'ve(ə)rəs/ ▶ n. Med. a deformity involving oblique displacement of part of a limb toward the midline. The opposite of VALGUS. [19th C.: from L., lit. 'bent, crooked.']

varve /'värv/ ▶ n. Geol. a pair of thin layers of clay and silt of contrasting color and texture that represent the deposit of a single year (summer and winter) in a lake. Such layers can be measured to determine the chronology of glacial sediments. — **varved** adj. [20th C.: from Swed. *varv* 'layer.']

var•y /'ve(ə)rē/ ▶ v. (**var•ies, var•ied**) [intrans.] differ in size, amount, degree, or nature from something else of the same general class: *the properties vary in price.* ■ change from one condition, form, or state to another. ■ [trans.] introduce modifications or changes into (something) so as to make it different or less uniform: *he tried to vary his diet.* — **var•y•ing•ly** adv. [ME: from OFr. *varier* or L. *variare*, from *varius* 'diverse'.]

vas /vas/ ▶ n. (pl. **va•sa** /'vāsə; -zə/) Anat. a vessel or duct. — **va•sal** /'vāsəl; -zəl/ adj. [16th C.: from L. 'vessel.']

Va•sa•ri /və'särē/, Giorgio (1511–74), Italian painter and biographer. His *Lives of the Artists* (1550, enlarged 1568) formed the basis for the later study of art history in the West.

Vas•co da Ga•ma /,väskō də 'gämə/ see DA GAMA.

vas•cu•lar /'vaskyələr/ ▶ adj. Anat., Zool., Med. of, relating to, affecting, or consisting of a vessel or vessels, esp. those that carry blood: *vascular disease.* ■ Bot. relating to or denoting the plant tissues (xylem and phloem) that conduct water, sap, and nutrients in flowering plants, ferns, and their relatives. — **vas•cu•lar•i•ty** /,vaskyə'laritē/ n. [17th C.: from mod. L. *vascularis*, from L. *vasculum* (see VASCULUM).]

vas•cu•lar bun•dle ▶ n. Bot. a strand of conducting vessels in the stem or leaves of a plant, typically with phloem on the outside and xylem on the inside.

vas•cu•lar cyl•in•der ▶ n. another term for STELE (sense 1).

vas•cu•lar•ize /'vaskyələ,rīz/ ▶ v. [trans.] Biol. Anat. provide (a tissue or structure) with vessels, esp. blood vessels; make vascular. — **vas•cu•lar•i•za•tion** /,vaskyələrə'zāsʜən/ n.

vas•cu•lar plant ▶ n. Bot. a plant belonging to subkingdom Tracheophyta, divisions Pteridophyta (ferns, horsetails, and club mosses) and Spermatophyta (cycads, conifers, and flowering plants). It is characterized by the presence of conducting tissue.

vas•cu•lar tis•sue ▶ n. the tissue in higher plants that constitutes the vascular system, consisting of phloem and xylem, by which water and nutrients are conducted throughout the plant.

vas•cu•la•ture /'vaskyələ,cʜŏŏr; -cʜər/ ▶ n. Anat. the vascular system of a part of the body and its arrangement: *diseases affecting the pulmonary vasculature.*

vas•cu•li•tis /,vaskyə'lītis/ ▶ n. (pl. **-lit•i•des** /-'liti,dēz/) Med. inflammation of a blood vessel or blood vessels. — **vas•cu•lit•ic** /-'litik/ adj.

vas•cu•lum /'vaskyələm/ ▶ n. (pl. **-la** /-lə/) Bot. a collecting box for plants, typically in the form of a flattened cylindrical metal case with a lengthwise opening, carried by a shoulder strap. [18th C.: from L., dimin. of *vas* 'vessel.']

vas de•fe•rens /,vas 'defərənz; -,renz/ ▶ n. (pl. **va•sa de•fe•ren•ti•a** /,vāsə ,defə'rensʜ(ē)ə; ,vāzə/) Anat. the duct that conveys sperm from the testicle to the urethra. [16th C.: from VAS + L. *deferens* 'carrying away,' pres. part. of *deferre.*]

vase /vās; vāz; väz/ ▶ n. a decorative container, typically made of glass or china and used as an ornament or for displaying cut flowers. — **vase•ful** /-,fŏŏl/ n. (pl. **-fuls**). [ME: from Fr., from L. *vas* 'vessel.']

vas•ec•to•my /və'sektəmē; va-/ ▶ n. (pl. **-mies**) the surgical cutting and sealing of part of each vas deferens, typically as a means of sterilization. — **va•sec•to•mize** /-,mīz/ v.

Vas•e•line /,vasə'lēn; 'vasə,lēn/ ▶ n. trademark a type of petroleum jelly used as an ointment and lubricant. ▶ v. [trans.] cover or smear with this.

vaso- ▶ comb. form of or relating to a vessel or vessels, esp. blood vessels: *vasoconstriction.* [from L. *vas* 'vessel.']

vas•o•ac•tive /,vāzō'aktiv; ,vasō-/ ▶ adj. Physiol. affecting the diameter of blood vessels (and hence blood pressure).

vas•o•con•stric•tion /,vāzōkən'striksʜən; ,vasō-/ ▶ n. the constriction of blood vessels, which increases blood pressure. — **vas•o•con•stric•tive** /-'striktiv/ adj. **vas•o•con•stric•tor** /-'striktər/ n.

vas•o•di•la•tion /,vāzōdī'lāsʜən; ,vasō-/ (also **vas•o•di•la•ta•tion** /-,dilə'tāsʜən/) ▶ n. the dilatation of blood vessels, which decreases blood pressure. — **vas•o•di•la•tor** /-'dī,lātər/ n. **vas•o•dil•a•to•ry** /-'dilə,tôrē/ adj.

vas•o•mo•tor /,vāzō'mōtər; ,vaso-/ ▶ adj. [attrib.] causing or relating to the constriction or dilatation of blood vessels. ■ denoting a region in the medulla of the brain (the **vasomotor center**) that regulates blood pressure by controlling reflex alterations in the heart rate and the diameter of the blood vessels, in response to stimuli from receptors in the circulatory system or from other parts of the brain.

vas•o•pres•sin /,vāzō'presən; ,vasō-/ ▶ n. Biochem. a pituitary hormone that acts to promote the retention of water by the kidneys and increase blood pressure. [1920s: from *vasopressor* 'causing constriction in blood vessels' + -IN[1].]

va•so•pres•sor /'vasō,presər; 'vāzō-/ ▶ adj. causing the constriction of blood vessels. ▶ n. a drug with this effect.

va•so•spasm /'vasō,spazəm; 'vāzō-/ ▶ n. sudden constriction of a blood vessel, reducing its diameter and flow rate. — **va•so•spas•tic** /,vasō'spastik; ,vāzō-/ adj.

va•so•va•gal /,vāzō'vāgəl; ,vasō-/ ▶ adj. [attrib.] Med. relating to or denoting a temporary fall in blood pressure, with pallor, fainting, sweating, and nausea, caused by overactivity of the vagus nerve, esp. as a result of stress.

vas•sal /'vasəl/ ▶ n. hist. a holder of land by feudal tenure on conditions of homage and allegiance. ■ a person or country in a subordinate position to another: [as adj.] *a vassal state of the Chinese empire.* — **vas•sal•age** /-əlij/ n. [ME: via OFr. from med. L. *vassallus* 'retainer,' of Celtic origin.]

vast /vast/ ▶ adj. of very great extent or quantity; immense: *a vast plain of buffalo grass.* ▶ n. archaic an immense space. — **vast•ly** adv. **vast•ness** n. **vast•y** adj. [ME: from L. *vastus* 'void, immense.']

vas•ti•tude /'vasti,t(y)ōōd/ ▶ n. **1** the quality of being vast; immensity. **2** a vast extent or space.

VAT /vat/ ▶ abbr. value added tax.

vat /vat/ ▶ n. **1** a large tank or tub used to hold liquid, esp. in industry: *a vat of hot tar.* **2** short for VAT DYE. ▶ v. (**vat•ted, vat•ting**) [trans.] (often **be vatted**) place or treat in a vat. [ME: dial. var. of obs. *fat* 'container,' of Gmc. origin; rel. to Ger. *Fass.*]

vat dye ▶ n. a water-insoluble dye that is applied as an alkaline solution of a soluble leuco form, the color being obtained through oxidation. — **vat-dyed** adj.

vat·ic /ˈvatik/ ▶ **adj.** literary describing or predicting what will happen in the future: *vatic utterances.* [17th C.: from L. *vates* 'prophet' + -IC.]

Vat·i·can /ˈvatikən/ ▶ **n.** (usu. **the Vatican**) the palace and official residence of the pope in Rome. ■ [treated as sing. or pl.] the administrative center of the Roman Catholic Church.

Vat·i·can Cit·y an independent papal state in the city of Rome, the seat of government of the Roman Catholic Church; pop. 1,000.

va·tic·i·nate /vəˈtisəˌnāt/ ▶ **v.** [intrans.] rare foretell the future. — **va·tic·i·nal** /-ənl/ **adj.** **va·tic·i·na·tion** /-ˌtisəˈnāsʜən/ **n.** **va·tic·i·na·tor** /-ˌnātər/ **n.** **va·tic·i·na·to·ry** /-ənəˌtôrē/ **adj.** [17th C.: from L. *vaticinat-* 'prophesied,' from the v. *vaticinari*, from *vates* 'prophet.']

Vät·tern /ˈvetə(r)n/ a lake in southern Sweden.

va·tu /ˈväˌto͞o/ ▶ **n.** (pl. same) the basic monetary unit of Vanuatu.

Vaud /vō/ a canton on Lake Geneva in western Switzerland; capital, Lausanne. German name **WAADT**.

vaude·ville /ˈvôd(ə)ˌvil; -vəl/ ▶ **n.** a type of entertainment popular chiefly in the US in the early 20th century, featuring a mixture of specialty acts such as burlesque comedy and song and dance. ■ a stage play on a trivial theme with interspersed songs. ■ archaic a satirical or topical song with a refrain. — **vaude·vil·lian** /ˌvôd(ə)ˈvilyən; -ˈvilēən/ **adj. & n.** [18th C.: from Fr., said to be a name given orig. to songs by a composer from *Vau de Vire* in Normandy.]

Vaughan Wil·liams, Ralph (1872–1958), English composer. His works include *A London Symphony* (1914) and the *Mass in G minor* (1922).

vault¹ /vôlt/ ▶ **n.** **1** a roof in the form of an arch or a series of arches, typical of churches and other large, formal buildings. ■ literary a thing resembling an arched roof, esp. the sky: *the vault of heaven.* ■ Anat. the arched roof of a cavity, esp. that of the skull: *the cranial vault.* **2** a large room or chamber used for storage, esp. an underground one. ■ a secure room in a bank in which valuables are stored. ■ a chamber beneath a church or in a graveyard used for burials. ▶ **v.** [trans.] [usu. as adj.] (**vaulted**) provide (a building or room) with an arched roof or roofs: *a vaulted arcade.* ■ make (a roof) in the form of a vault: *there was a high ceiling, vaulted with cut slate.* [ME: from OFr. *voute*, based on L. *volvere* 'to roll.']

vault² ▶ **v.** [no obj., with adverbial of direction] leap or spring while supporting or propelling oneself with one or both hands or with the help of a pole. ■ [trans.] jump over (an obstacle) in such a way. ▶ **n.** an act of vaulting. — **vault·er** **n.** [16th C.: from OFr. *volter* 'to turn (a horse), gambol,' based on L. *volvere* 'to roll.']

vault·ing /ˈvôltiɴɢ/ ▶ **n.** **1** ornamental work in a vaulted roof or ceiling. **2** the action of vaulting over obstacles as a gymnastic or athletic exercise.

vault·ing horse ▶ **n.** a padded wooden block used for vaulting over by gymnasts and athletes.

vaunt /vônt; vänt/ ▶ **v.** [trans.] [usu. as adj.] (**vaunted**) boast about or praise (something), esp. excessively: *something has gone awry with the government's much vaunted fight against crime.* ▶ **n.** archaic a boast. — **vaunt·er** **n.** **vaunt·ing·ly** **adv.** [ME: the n. a shortening of obs. *avaunt* 'boasting, a boast'; the v. from OFr. *vanter*, from late L. *vantare*, based on L. *vanus* 'vain, empty.']

vav /väv; vôv/ ▶ **n.** the sixth letter of the Hebrew alphabet.

vav·a·so·ry /ˈvavəˌsôrē/ ▶ **n.** (pl. **-ries**) hist. the estate of a vavasor.

vav·a·sor /ˈvavəˌsôr/ (also **vavasour**) ▶ **n.** hist. a vassal owing allegiance to a powerful lord and having other vassals under him. [ME: from OFr. *vavas(s)our*, from med. L. *vavassor*, perh. from *vassus vassorum* 'vassal of vassals.']

va-va-voom /ˌvä vä ˈvo͞om/ informal ▶ **n.** the quality of being exciting, vigorous, or sexually attractive: *she's lost none of her va-va-voom since giving birth to her daughter.* ▶ **adj.** sexually attractive: *her va-va-voom figure.* [1950s: representing the sound of a car engine being revved.]

VC ▶ **abbr.** ■ Vice-Chairman. ■ Vice-Chancellor. ■ Vice-Consul. ■ Victoria Cross. ■ Vietcong.

V-chip ▶ **n.** a computer chip installed in a television receiver that can be programmed by the user to block or scramble material containing a special code in its signal indicating that it is deemed violent or sexually explicit.

VCR ▶ **abbr.** videocassette recorder.

VD ▶ **abbr.** venereal disease.

V-day ▶ **n.** Victory Day, esp. with reference to the Allied victories in World War II.

VDT ▶ **abbr.** video display terminal.

've informal ▶ **abbr.** have (usually after the pronouns *I*, *you*, *we*, and *they*): *we've tried our best.*

veal /vēl/ ▶ **n.** the flesh of a calf, used as food. [ME: from Anglo-Norman Fr. *ve(e)l*, from L. *vitellus*, dimin. of *vitulus* 'calf.']

veal·er /ˈvēlər/ ▶ **n.** a calf raised to become veal.

Veb·len /ˈveblən/, Thorstein Bunde (1857–1929), US economist and sociologist. He coined the phrase "conspicuous consumption."

vec·tor /ˈvektər/ ▶ **n.** **1** Math. Physics a quantity having direction as well as magnitude, esp. as determining the position of one point in space relative to another. Compare with **SCALAR**. ■ Math. a matrix with one row or one column. ■ a course to be taken by an aircraft. ■ [as adj.] Comput. denoting a type of graphical representation using straight lines to construct the outlines of objects. **2** an organism, typically a biting insect or tick, that transmits a disease or parasite from one animal or plant to another. ■ Genet. a bacteriophage or plasmid that transfers genetic material into a cell, or from one bacterium to another. ▶ **v.** [with obj. and adverbial of direction] (often **be vectored**) direct (an aircraft in flight) to a desired point. — **vec·to·ri·al** /vekˈtôrēəl/ **adj.** (in sense 1 of the **noun**). **vec·to·ri·al·ly** /vekˈtôrēəlē/ **adv.** (in sense 1 of the **noun**) **vec·tor·i·za·tion** /ˌvektərəˈzāsʜən/ **n.** **vec·tor·ize** /-ˌrīz/ **v.** (in sense 1 of the **noun**). [19th C.: from L., lit. 'carrier,' from *vehere* 'convey.']

x y z y x y x z

vector 1

vec·tor prod·uct ▶ **n.** Math. the product of two vectors that is itself a vector at right angles to both the original vectors and equal to the product of the magnitudes of the original vectors and the sine of the angle between them (written as **a** × **b**).

Ve·da /ˈvādə; ˈvēdə/ ▶ **n.** [treated as sing. or pl.] the most ancient Hindu scriptures, in particular the Rig Veda, Sama Veda, Yajur Veda, and Atharva Veda. [Sanskrit, lit. '(sacred) knowledge.']

Ve·dan·ta /vāˈdäntə; və-/ ▶ **n.** a Hindu philosophy based on the doctrine of the Upanishads, esp. in its monistic form. — **Ve·dan·tic** /-tik/ **adj.** **Ve·dan·tist** /-tist/ **n.** [from Sanskrit *vedānta*, from *veda* (see **VEDA**) + *anta* 'end.']

V-E Day ▶ **n.** Victory in Europe Day: the day (May 8, 1945) marking the Allied victory in Europe in World War II. [*V-E*, abbrev. of *Victory in Europe*.]

Ved·da /ˈvedə/ ▶ **n.** a member of an aboriginal people inhabiting the forests of Sri Lanka. [from Sinhalese *vaddā* 'hunter.']

ve·dette /viˈdet/ (also **vi·dette**) ▶ **n.** **1** hist. a mounted sentry positioned beyond an army's outposts to observe the movements of the enemy. **2** a leading star of stage, screen, or television. [17th C.: from Fr., lit. 'scout,' from an alt. of southern Ital. *veletta*, perh. based on Sp. *velar* 'keep watch.']

Ve·dic /ˈvādik; ˈvēdik/ ▶ **adj.** of or relating to the Veda or Vedas. ▶ **n.** the language of the Vedas, an early form of Sanskrit.

vee /vē/ ▶ **n.** the letter V. ■ a thing shaped like a V: *a broken vee of birds.*

vee·jay /ˈvēˌjā/ ▶ **n.** informal a person who introduces and plays popular music videos. [1980s: from *VJ*, short for *video jockey*.]

vee·na /ˈvēnə/ (also **vi·na**) ▶ **n.** an Indian stringed instrument, with four main and three auxiliary strings. The southern type has a lutelike body; the older northern type has a tubular body and a gourd fitted to each end as a resonator. [from Sanskrit *vīṇā*.]

veep /vēp/ ▶ **n.** informal a vice president. [1940s: from the initials *VP*.]

veer¹ /vi(ə)r/ ▶ **v.** [no obj., with adverbial of direction] change direction suddenly: *an oil tanker that had veered off course.* ■ fig. suddenly change an opinion, subject, type of behavior, etc.: *the conversation veered away from theatrical things.* ■ (of the wind) change direction clockwise around the points of the compass. The opposite of **BACK**. ▶ **n.** a sudden change of direction. [16th C.: from Fr. *virer*, perh. from an alt. of L. *gyrare* (see **GYRATE**).]

veer² ▶ **v.** [trans.] Naut. dated slacken or let out (a rope or cable) in a controlled way. [ME: from MDu. *vieren*.]

veer·y /ˈvi(ə)rē/ ▶ **n.** a North American woodland thrush (*Catharus fuscescens*) with a brown back and speckled breast. [19th C.: perh. imitative.]

veg¹ /vej/ ▶ **v.** (**veg·ges**, **veg·ging**, **vegged**) [intrans.] informal relax to the point of complete inertia: *they were vegging out in front of the TV.* [1920s: abbrev. of **VEGETATE**.]

veg² ▶ **n.** (pl. same) Brit. informal a vegetable or vegetables: *meat and two veg.*

Ve·ga¹ /ˈvāgə/, Lope de (1562–1635), Spanish playwright and poet; full name *Lope Felix de Vega Carpio*. He is regarded as the founder of Spanish drama.

Ve·ga² Astron. the fifth brightest star in the sky, and the brightest in the constellation Lyra, overhead in summer to observers in the northern hemisphere.

ve·ga /ˈvāgə/ ▶ **n.** (in Spain and Spanish America) a large plain or valley, typically a fertile and grassy one. [Sp. and Catalan.]

veg·an /ˈvēgən; ˈvejən/ ▶ **n.** a person who does not eat or use animal products. [1940s: from **VEGETARIAN** + **-AN**.]

veg·e·ta·ble /ˈvejtəbəl; ˈvejətə-/ ▶ **n.** **1** a plant or part of a plant used as food, typically as accompaniment to meat or fish, such as a cabbage, potato, carrot, or bean. **2** informal, offens. a person who is incapable of normal mental or physical activity, esp. through brain damage. ■ informal a person with a dull or inactive life. ▶ **adj.** of or relating to vegetables as food: *vegetable soup.* ■ of or relating to plants or plant life, esp. as distinct from animal life or mineral substances. [ME: from OFr., or from late L. *vegetabilis* 'animating,' from L. *vegetare* (see **VEGETATE**).]

veg·e·ta·ble but·ter ▶ **n.** vegetable fat with the consistency of butter.

veg·e·ta·ble i·vo·ry ▶ **n.** a hard white material obtained from the endosperm of the ivory nut.

veg·e·ta·ble mar·row ▶ **n.** see MARROW (sense 1).

veg·e·ta·ble oil ▶ **n.** an oil derived from plants, e.g., canola oil, sunflower oil.

veg·e·ta·ble spa·ghet·ti ▶ **n.** another term for SPAGHETTI SQUASH.

veg·e·ta·ble sponge ▶ **n.** another term for LOOFAH.

veg·e·ta·ble tal·low ▶ **n.** vegetable fat used as tallow.

veg·e·tal /ˈvejətl/ ▶ **adj.** **1** formal of or relating to plants. **2** Embryol. of or relating to that pole of the ovum or embryo that contains the less active cytoplasm, and frequently most of the yolk, in the early stages of development: *vegetal cells* | *the vegetal region.* [ME: from med. L. *vegetalis*, from L. *vegetare* 'animate.']

veg·e·tar·i·an /ˌvejiˈte(ə)rēən/ ▶ **n.** a person who does not eat meat, and sometimes other animal products, esp. for moral, religious, or health reasons. ▶ **adj.** of or relating to the exclusion of meat or other animal products from the diet: *a vegetarian restaurant.* — **veg·e·tar·i·an·ism** /-əˌnizəm/ **n.** [19th C.: formed irregularly from VEGETABLE + -ARIAN.]

veg·e·tate /ˈvejəˌtāt/ ▶ **v.** [intrans.] **1** live or spend a period of time in a dull, inactive, unchallenging way. **2** dated (of a plant or seed) grow; sprout. ■ [trans.] cause plants to grow in or cover (a place). **3** Med. (of an abnormal growth) increase in size. [17th C.: from L. *vegetat-* 'enlivened,' from the v. *vegetare*, from *vegetus* 'active,' from *vegere* 'be active.']

veg·e·tat·ed /ˈvejəˌtātid/ ▶ **adj.** covered with vegetation or plant life: *densely vegetated wetlands.*

veg·e·ta·tion /ˌvejəˈtāsʜən/ ▶ **n.** **1** plants considered collectively, esp. those found in a particular area or habitat: *the chalk cliffs are mainly sheer with little vegetation.* **2** the action or process of vegetating. **3** Med. an abnormal growth on or in the body. — **veg·e·ta·tion·al** /-sʜənl/ **adj.**

veg·e·ta·tive /ˈvejəˌtātiv/ ▶ **adj.** **1** Biol. of, relating to, or denoting reproduction or propagation achieved by asexual means, either naturally (budding, rhizomes, runners, bulbs, etc.) or artificially (grafting, layering, or taking cuttings): *vegetative spores.* ■ of, relating to, or concerned with growth rather than sexual reproduction: *vegetative development.* **2** of or relating to vegetation or plant life. **3** Med. (of a person) alive but comatose and without apparent brain activity or responsiveness. — **veg·e·ta·tive·ly** **adv.** **veg·e·ta·tive·ness** **n.**

veg·gie /ˈvejē/ (also **veg·ie**) ▶ **n. & adj.** informal **1** another term for VEGETABLE. **2** another term for VEGETARIAN. [1970s: abbrev.]

veg·gie burg·er ▶ **n.** a patty resembling a hamburger but made with vegetable protein, soybeans, etc., instead of meat.

ve·he·ment /ˈvēəmənt/ ▶ **adj.** showing strong feeling; forceful, passionate, or intense: *vehement criticism.* — **ve·he·mence** **n.** **ve·he·ment·ly** **adv.** [ME: from Fr. *véhément* or L. *vehement-* 'impetuous, violent.']

ve·hi·cle /ˈvēəkəl; ˈvēˌhikəl/ ▶ **n.** **1** a thing used for transporting people or goods, esp. on land, such as a car, truck, or cart. **2** a thing used to express, embody, or fulfill something: *I use paint as a vehicle for my ideas.* ■ a substance that facilitates the use of a drug, pigment, or other material mixed with it. ■ the figurative language used in a metaphor, as distinct from the metaphor's subject. Often contrasted with TENOR² (sense 1). ■ a film, television program, song, etc., that is intended to display the leading performer to the best advantage. — **ve·hic·u·lar** /vēˈhikyələr/ **adj.** (in sense 1). [17th C.: from Fr. *véhicule* or L. *vehiculum*, from *vehere* 'carry.']

veil /vāl/ ▶ **n.** a piece of fine material worn by women to protect or conceal the face: *a white bridal veil.* ■ a piece of linen or other fabric forming part of a nun's headdress, resting on the head and shoulders. ■ a thing that conceals, disguises, or obscures something: *shrouded in an eerie veil of mist.* ■ Bot. a membrane that is attached to the immature fruiting body of some toadstools and ruptures in the course of development, either (**universal veil**) enclosing the whole fruiting body or (**partial veil**) joining the edges of the cap to the stalk. ■ (in Jewish antiquity) the piece of precious cloth separating the sanctuary from the body of the Temple or the Tabernacle. ▶ **v.** [trans.] cover with or as though with a veil. ■ [usu. as adj.] (**veiled**) partially conceal, disguise, or obscure: *a thinly veiled threat.*
– PHRASES **beyond the veil** in a mysterious or hidden place or state, esp. the unknown state of life after death. **draw a veil over** avoid discussing or calling attention to (something), esp. because it is embarrassing or unpleasant. **take the veil** become a nun. — **veil·less** **adj.** [ME: from Anglo-Norman Fr. *veil(e)*, from L. *vela*, pl. of *velum* (see VELUM).]

veil·ing /ˈvāliNG/ ▶ **n.** **1** the action of wearing or covering someone or something with a veil. **2** a light gauzy fabric or fine lace used for veils.

vein /vān/ ▶ **n.** **1** any of the tubes forming part of the blood circulation system of the body, carrying mainly oxygen-depleted blood toward the heart. Compare with ARTERY. ■ (in general and figurative use) a blood vessel. ■ (in plants) a slender rib running through a leaf or bract, typically dividing or branching, and containing a vascular bundle. ■ (in insects) a hardened branching rib that forms part of the supporting framework of a wing, consisting of an extension of the tracheal system; a nervure. ■ a streak or stripe of a different color in wood, marble, cheese, etc. ■ a fracture in rock containing a deposit of minerals or ore and typically having an extensive course underground. ■ fig. a source of a specified quality or other abstract resource: *the thick vein of discontent.* **2** [in sing.] a distinctive quality, style, or tendency. — **vein·less** **adj.** **vein·let** /-lit/ **n.** **vein·like** /-ˌlīk/ **adj. & adv.** **vein·y** **adj.** (**vein·i·er**, **vein·i·est**). [ME: from OFr. *veine*, from L. *vena*.]

veined /vānd/ ▶ **adj.** marked with or as if with veins.

vein·ing /ˈvāniNG/ ▶ **n.** a pattern of lines, streaks, or veins: *the marble's characteristic surface veining.*

vein·ous /ˈvānəs/ ▶ **adj.** having prominent or noticeable veins. Compare with VENOUS.

vein·stone /ˈvānˌstōn/ ▶ **n.** another term for GANGUE.

Ve·la /ˈvēlə; ˈvā-/ Astron. a southern constellation (the Sails), lying partly in the Milky Way between Carina and Pyxis and originally part of Argo.

ve·la /ˈvēlə/ plural form of VELUM.

ve·la·men /vəˈlāmən/ ▶ **n.** (pl. **-lam·i·na** /-ˈlamənə/) Bot. an outer layer of empty cells in the aerial roots of epiphytic orchids and aroids. [19th C.: from L., from *velare* 'to cover.']

ve·lar /ˈvēlər/ ▶ **adj.** **1** of or relating to a veil or velum. **2** Phonet. (of a speech sound) pronounced with the back of the tongue near the soft palate, as in *k* and *g* in English. ▶ **n.** a velar sound. [18th C.: from L. *velaris*, from *velum* (see VELUM).]

ve·lar·i·um /viˈle(ə)rēəm/ ▶ **n.** (pl. **-lar·i·a** /-ˈle(ə)rēə/) a large awning of a type used in ancient Rome to cover a theater or amphitheater as a protection against the weather, now more commonly used as an inner ceiling to improve acoustics. [L.]

ve·lar·i·za·tion /ˌvēlərəˈzāsʜən/ ▶ **n.** Phonet. a secondary articulation involving movement of the back of the tongue toward the velum.

ve·lar·ize /ˈvēləˌrīz/ ▶ **v.** [trans.] make velar; articulate or supplement the articulation of (a sound, esp. a consonant) by raising the tongue to or toward the soft palate: *a velarized /l/.*

Ve·láz·quez /vəˈläsˌk(w)ez; -kəs/, Diego Rodríguez de Silva y (1599–1660), Spanish painter. His works include *Pope Innocent X* (1650) and *Las Meninas* (*c.*1656).

Ve·láz·quez de Cué·llar /vəˈläsˌk(w)ez dā ˈkwāyär/, Diego (*c.*1465–1524), Spanish conquistador. He began the conquest of Cuba in 1511.

Vel·cro /ˈvelkrō/ ▶ **n.** trademark a fastener consisting of two strips of thin plastic sheet, one covered with tiny loops and the other with tiny flexible hooks, which adhere when pressed together. ▶ **v.** [with obj. and adverbial] fasten, join, or fix with such a fastener. — **Vel·croed** **adj.**

veld /velt/ (also **veldt**) ▶ **n.** open, uncultivated country or grassland in southern Africa. It is conventionally divided by altitude into highveld, middleveld, and lowveld. [Afrik., from Du., lit. 'field.']

Vel·de, van de, Willem and sons, see VAN DE VELDE.

ve·li·ger /ˈveləjər; ˈvēlə-/ ▶ **n.** Zool. the final larval stage of certain mollusks, having two ciliated flaps for swimming and feeding. [19th C.: from VELUM + L. *-ger* 'bearing.']

vel·le·i·ty /vəˈlēətē; ve-/ ▶ **n.** (pl. **-ties**) formal a wish or inclination not strong enough to lead to action. [17th C.: from med. L. *velleitas*, from L. *velle* 'to wish.']

vel·lum /ˈveləm/ ▶ **n.** **1** fine parchment made originally from the skin of a calf. **2** smooth writing paper imitating vellum. [ME: from OFr. *velin*, from *veel* (see VEAL).]

ve·lo·cim·e·ter /ˌveləˈsimitər; ˌvēlə-/ ▶ **n.** an instrument for measuring velocity. — **ve·lo·cim·e·try** /-itrē/ **n.**

ve·loc·i·pede /vəˈläsəˌpēd/ ▶ **n.** hist. an early form of bicycle propelled by working pedals on cranks fitted to the front axle. ■ a child's tricycle. — **ve·loc·i·ped·ist** /-dist/ **n.** [19th C.: from Fr. *vélocipède*, from L. *velox, veloc-* 'swift' + *pes, ped-* 'foot.']

ve·loc·i·rap·tor /vəˈläsəˌraptər/ ▶ **n.** a small dromaeosaurid dinosaur (genus *Velociraptor*) of the late Cretaceous period. See illustration at DINOSAUR. [mod. L., from L. *velox, veloc-* 'swift' + RAPTOR.]

ve·loc·i·ty /vəˈläsətē/ ▶ **n.** (pl. **-ties**) the speed of something in a given direction. ■ (in general use) speed. [ME: from Fr. *vélocité* or L. *velocitas*, from *velox, veloc-* 'swift.']

ve·lo·drome /ˈveləˌdrōm; ˈvēlə-/ ▶ **n.** a cycle-racing track, typically with steeply banked curves. ■ a stadium containing such a track. [19th C.: from Fr. *vélodrome*, from *vélo* 'bicycle' + *-drome* (see -DROME).]

ve·lour /vəˈlo͝or/ (also **ve·lours**) ▶ **n.** a plush woven fabric resembling velvet, chiefly used for soft furnishings, clothing, and hats. ■ dated a hat made of such fabric. [18th C.: from Fr. *velours* 'velvet,' from OFr. *velour*, from L. *villosus* 'hairy,' from *villus* (see VELVET).]

ve·lou·té /vəlo͞oˈtā/ ▶ **n.** a rich white sauce made with chicken, veal, pork, or fish stock, thickened with cream and egg yolks. [Fr., lit. 'velvety.']

ve·lum /ˈvēləm/ ▶ **n.** (pl. **ve·la** /-lə/) esp. Anat., Zool., Bot. a membrane or membranous structure, typically covering another structure or partly obscuring an opening, in particular: ■ Anat. the soft palate. ■ Zool. a membrane, typically bordering a cavity, esp. in certain mollusks, medusae, and other invertebrates. ■ Bot. the veil of a toadstool. [18th C.: from L., lit. 'sail, curtain, covering, veil.']

ve·lure /vəˈlo͝or/ ▶ **n.** VELVET or VELOUR.

vel·vet /ˈvelvət/ ▶ **n.** a closely woven fabric of silk, cotton, or nylon that has a thick short pile on one side. ■ soft downy skin that covers a deer's antler while it is growing.
– PHRASES **on velvet** informal, dated in an advantageous or prosperous position. — **vel·vet·ed** **adj.** **vel·vet·y** **adj.** [ME: from OFr. *veluotte*, from *velu* 'velvety,' from med. L. *villutus*, from L. *villus* 'tuft, down.']

vel·vet ant ▶ **n.** an antlike velvety-bodied insect (family Mutillidae, superfamily Scolioidea) related to the wasps. The female is wingless, and the larvae parasitize the young of bees and wasps in the nest.

vel·vet·een /ˈvelvəˌtēn; ˌvelvəˈtēn/ ▶ **n.** a cotton fabric with a pile resembling velvet.

vel·vet rev·o·lu·tion ▶ n. a nonviolent political revolution, esp. the relatively smooth change from communism to a Western-style democracy in Czechoslovakia at the end of 1989.

Ven. ▶ abbr. Venerable (as the title of an archdeacon).

ve·na /ˈvēnə/ ▶ n. Anat. & Zool. a vein.

ve·na ca·va /ˌvēnə ˈkävə; ˈkāvə/ ▶ n. (pl. **ve·nae ca·vae** /ˈvēnē ˈkävē; ˈkāvē; ˈvēnī ˈkävī; ˈkāvī/) a large vein carrying deoxygenated blood into the heart. There are two in humans, the **inferior vena cava** (carrying blood from the lower body) and the **superior vena cava** (carrying blood from the head, arms, and upper body). [16th C.: from L., lit. 'hollow vein.']

ve·nal /ˈvēnl/ ▶ adj. showing or motivated by susceptibility to bribery: *venal politicians*. — **ve·nal·i·ty** /vēˈnalətē; və-/ n. **ve·nal·ly** adv. [17th C.: from L. *venalis*, from *venum* 'thing for sale.']

ve·na·tion /vēˈnāsнən/ ▶ n. Biol. the arrangement of veins in a leaf or in an insect's wing. ■ the system of venous blood vessels in an animal. — **ve·na·tion·al** /-sнənl/ adj. [17th C.: from L. *vena* 'vein' + -ATION.]

vend /vend/ ▶ v. [trans.] offer (small items, esp. food) for sale, esp. either from a stall or from a vending machine. ■ Law or formal sell (something). — **vend·i·ble** (also **vend·a·ble**) adj. [17th C. (in the sense 'be sold'): from Fr. *vendre* or L. *vendere* 'sell,' from *venum* 'something for sale' + a var. of *dare* 'give.']

Ven·da[1] /ˈvendə/ a former homeland established in South Africa for the Venda people, now part of Limpopo province.

Ven·da[2] ▶ n. (pl. same or **-das**) **1** a member of a people living in Limpopo province, South Africa, and southern Zimbabwe. **2** the Bantu language of this people. ▶ adj. of or relating to this people or their language. [the stem of Venda *Muvenda* (in sense 1), *Tshivenda* (in sense 2).]

vend·er /ˈvendər/ ▶ n. var. of VENDOR.

ven·det·ta /venˈdetə/ ▶ n. a blood feud in which the family of a murdered person seeks vengeance on the murderer or the murderer's family. ■ a prolonged bitter quarrel with or campaign against someone. [19th C.: from Ital., from L. *vindicta* 'vengeance.']

vend·ing ma·chine ▶ n. a machine that dispenses small articles such as food, drinks, or cigarettes when a coin, bill, or token is inserted.

ven·dor /ˈvendər; -ˌdôr/ (also **vend·er**) ▶ n. a person or company offering something for sale, esp. a trader in the street: *an Italian ice cream vendor*. ■ a person or company whose principal product lines are office supplies and equipment. ■ Law the seller in a sale, esp. of property. [16th C.: from Anglo-Norman Fr. *vendour* (see VEND).]

ven·due /venˈd(y)o͞o; vän-/ ▶ n. a public auction. [17th C.: via Du. from Fr. dial. *vendue* 'sale,' from *vendre* 'sell.']

ve·neer /vəˈni(ə)r/ ▶ n. a thin decorative covering of fine wood applied to a coarser wood or other material. ■ a layer of wood used to make plywood. ■ [in sing.] an attractive appearance that covers or disguises someone or something's true nature or feelings. ▶ v. [trans.] cover (something) with a decorative layer of fine wood. ■ cover or disguise (someone or something's true nature) with an attractive appearance. [18th C. (earlier as *fineer*): from Ger. *furni(e)ren*, from OFr. *fournir* 'furnish.']

ve·neer·ing /vəˈni(ə)rɪɴɢ/ ▶ n. **1** material used as veneer. **2** the action of covering something with a veneer.

ven·e·punc·ture ▶ n. esp. Brit. var. of VENIPUNCTURE.

ven·er·a·ble /ˈven(ə)rəbəl/ ▶ adj. accorded a great deal of respect, esp. because of age, wisdom, or character: *a venerable statesman*. ■ (in the Roman Catholic Church) a title given to a deceased person who has attained a certain degree of sanctity but has not been fully beatified or canonized. ■ (in the Anglican Church) a title given to an archdeacon. — **ven·er·a·bil·i·ty** /ˌven(ə)rəˈbilətē/ n. **ven·er·a·ble·ness** n. **ven·er·a·bly** /-blē/ adv.

ven·er·ate /ˈvenəˌrāt/ ▶ v. [trans.] (often **be venerated**) regard with great respect; revere. — **ven·er·a·tion** /ˌvenəˈrāsнən/ n. **ven·er·a·tor** /-ˌrātər/ n. [17th C.: from L. *venerat-* 'adored, revered,' from the v. *venerari*.]

ve·ne·re·al /vəˈni(ə)rēəl/ ▶ adj. of or relating to sexual desire or sexual intercourse. ■ of or relating to venereal disease. — **ve·ne·re·al·ly** adv. [ME: from L. *venereus* (from *venus, vener-* 'sexual love') + -AL.]

ve·ne·re·al dis·ease ▶ n. a disease typically contracted by sexual contact with a person already infected; a sexually transmitted disease.

ve·ne·re·ol·o·gy /vəˌni(ə)rēˈäləjē/ ▶ n. the branch of medicine concerned with venereal diseases. — **ve·ne·re·o·log·i·cal** /-əˈläjikəl/ adj. **ve·ne·re·ol·o·gist** /-jist/ n.

ven·er·y[1] /ˈvenərē/ ▶ n. archaic sexual indulgence. [ME: from med. L. *veneria*, from *venus, vener-* 'sexual love.']

ven·er·y[2] ▶ n. archaic hunting. [ME: from OFr. *venerie*, from *vener* 'to hunt,' from L. *venari*.]

ven·e·sec·tion /ˈvēnəˌseksнən; ˈvenə-/ ▶ n. another term for PHLEBOTOMY. [17th C.: from med. L. *venae sectio(n-)* 'cutting of a vein.']

Ve·ne·ti·a /vəˈnēsнə/ a region in northeastern Italy; capital, Venice. Italian name VENETO.

Ve·ne·tian /vəˈnēsнən/ ▶ adj. of or relating to Venice or its people. ▶ n. a native or citizen of Venice. ■ the dialect of Italian spoken in Venice.

ve·ne·tian blind ▶ n. a window blind consisting of horizontal slats that can be pivoted to control the amount of light that passes through it.

Ve·ne·tian glass ▶ n. decorative glassware of a type associated with Venice, esp. the nearby island of Murano.

Ve·ne·tian red ▶ n. a reddish-brown pigment consisting of ferric oxide. ■ a strong reddish-brown color.

Ve·ne·tian win·dow ▶ n. a large window consisting of a central arched section flanked by two narrow rectangular sections.

Ve·ne·zia /vəˈnetsēə/ Italian name for VENICE.

Ven·e·zue·la /ˌvenəzˈwālə/ a republic on the north coast of South America. *See box.* — **Ven·e·zue·lan** adj. & n.

Venezuela

Official name: Bolivarian Republic of Venezuela
Location: South America, on the northern coast
Area: 352,200 square miles (912,100 sq km)
Population: 25,017,000
Capital: Caracas
Languages: Spanish (official), many Amerindian languages
Currency: bolivar

venge·ance /ˈvenjəns/ ▶ n. punishment inflicted or retribution exacted for an injury or wrong.
– PHRASES **with a vengeance** used to emphasize the degree to which something occurs or is true: *her headache was back with a vengeance*. [ME: from OFr., from *venger* 'avenge.']

venge·ful /ˈvenjfəl/ ▶ adj. seeking to harm someone in return for a perceived injury: *a vengeful ex-con*. — **venge·ful·ly** adv. **venge·ful·ness** n. [16th C.: from obs. *venge* 'avenge' (see VENGEANCE).]

ve·ni·al /ˈvēnēəl; ˈvēnyəl/ ▶ adj. Christian Theol. denoting a sin that is not regarded as depriving the soul of divine grace. Often contrasted with MORTAL. ■ (of a fault or offense) slight and pardonable. — **ve·ni·al·i·ty** /ˌvēnēˈalətē/ n. **ve·ni·al·ly** adv. [ME: via OFr. from late L. *venialis*, from *venia* 'forgiveness.']

ve·ni·al sin ▶ n. (in Roman Catholicism) a relatively slight sin that does not entail damnation of the soul.

Ven·ice /ˈvenis/ **1** a city in northeastern Italy; pop. 318,000. Italian name VENEZIA. **2** a beachfront section of Los Angeles in California, west of downtown.

ven·i·punc·ture /ˈvēnəˌpəɴɢkcнər; ˈvenə-/ (esp. Brit. also **ven·e·punc·ture**) ▶ n. the puncture of a vein as part of a medical procedure, typically to withdraw a blood sample or for an intravenous injection. [1920s: from L. *vena* 'vein' + PUNCTURE.]

ven·i·son /ˈvenəsən; -zən/ ▶ n. meat from a deer. [ME: from OFr. *veneso(u)n*, from L. *venatio(n-)* 'hunting,' from *venari* 'to hunt.']

Ve·ni·te /vəˈnītē; -ˈnētē; -ˈnēˌtā/ ▶ n. Psalm 95 used as a canticle in Christian liturgy, chiefly at matins.

Venn di·a·gram /ven/ ▶ n. a diagram representing mathematical or logical sets pictorially as circles or closed curves within an enclosing rectangle (the universal set), common elements of the sets being represented by intersections of the circles. [20th C.: named after John Venn (1834–1923), English logician.]

ve·no·gram /ˈvēnəˌgram/ ▶ n. Med. an image produced by venography.

ve·nog·ra·phy /viˈnägrəfē/ ▶ n. Med. radiography of a vein after injection of a radiopaque fluid. — **ve·no·graph·ic** /ˌvēnəˈgrafik/ adj. **ve·no·graph·i·cal·ly** /ˌvēnəˈgrafik(ə)lē/ adv. [1930s: from L. *vena* 'vein' + -GRAPHY.]

ven·om /ˈvenəm/ ▶ n. poisonous fluid secreted by animals such as snakes and scorpions and typically injected into prey or aggressors by biting or stinging. ■ fig. extreme malice and bitterness shown in someone's attitudes, speech, or actions. [ME: from OFr. *venim*, var. of *venin*, from an alt. of L. *venenum* 'poison.']

ven·om·ous /ˈvenəməs/ ▶ adj. (of animals, esp. snakes, or their parts) secreting venom; capable of injecting venom by means of a bite or sting. ■ fig. (of a person or their behavior) full of malice or spite: *she replied with a venomous glance.* — **ven·om·ous·ly** adv. **ven·om·ous·ness** n.

ve·nous /ˈvēnəs/ ▶ adj. of or relating to a vein or the veins. ■ of or relating to the dark red, oxygen-poor blood in the veins and pulmonary artery. — **ve·nos·i·ty** /viˈnäsətē/ n. **ve·nous·ly** adv. [17th C.: from L. *venosus* 'venous,' from *vena* 'vein.']

vent[1] /vent/ ▶ n. an opening that allows air, gas, or liquid to pass out of or into a confined space. ■ fig. release or expression of a strong emotion, energy, etc.: ***children give vent to their anger.*** ■ the opening of a volcano, through which lava and other materials are emitted. ■ hist. the touch hole of a gun. ■ the anus, esp. one in a lower animal such as a fish that serves for both excretion and reproduction. ▶ v. [trans.] **1** give free expression to (a strong emotion). **2** provide with an outlet for air, gas, or liquid. ■ discharge or expel (air, gas, or liquid) through an outlet. ■ permit air to enter (a beer cask). — **vent·less** adj. [ME: partly from Fr. *vent* 'wind,' from L. *ventus,* reinforced by Fr. *évent,* from *éventer* 'expose to air,' based on L. *ventus* 'wind.']

vent[2] ▶ n. a slit in a garment, esp. in the lower edge of the back of a coat through the seam. [ME: alt. of dial. *fent,* from OFr. *fente* 'slit,' based on L. *findere* 'cleave.']

ven·tail /ˈvenˌtāl/ ▶ n. hist. the lower movable front of a medieval helmet. ■ the whole movable front of such a helmet, including the visor.

ven·ter /ˈventər/ ▶ n. Zool. the underside or abdomen of an animal. [18th C.: from L., 'belly.']

ven·ti·fact /ˈventəˌfakt/ ▶ n. Geol. a stone shaped by the erosive action of windblown sand. [20th C.: from L. *ventus* 'wind' + *factum,* neut. past part. of *facere* 'make.']

ven·ti·late /ˈventəˌlāt/ ▶ v. [trans.] **1** cause air to enter and circulate freely in (a room, building, etc.). ■ (of air) purify or freshen (something) by blowing on or through it: *a colossus ventilated by the dawn breeze.* ■ Med. subject to artificial respiration. ■ archaic oxygenate (the blood). **2** discuss or examine (an opinion, issue, complaint, etc.) in public. [ME: from L. *ventilat-* 'blown, winnowed,' from the v. *ventilare,* from *ventus* 'wind.']

ven·ti·la·tion /ˌventəˈlāshən/ ▶ n. **1** the provision of fresh air to a room, building, etc. ■ Med. the supply of air to the lungs, esp. by artificial means. **2** public discussion or examination of an opinion, issue, complaint, etc.

ven·ti·la·tor /ˈventəˌlātər/ ▶ n. **1** an appliance or aperture for ventilating a room or other space. **2** Med. an appliance for artificial respiration; a respirator.

ven·ti·la·to·ry /ˈventələˌtôrē/ ▶ adj. Physiol. of, relating to, or serving for the provision of air to the lungs or respiratory system.

ven·tral /ˈventrəl/ ▶ adj. Anat., Zool., & Bot. of, on, or relating to the underside of an animal or plant; abdominal. Compare with DORSAL. — **ven·tral·ly** adv. [ME: from L. *venter, ventr-* 'belly' + -AL.]

ven·tral fin ▶ n. Zool. another term for PELVIC FIN. ■ an unpaired fin on the underside of certain fishes. ■ a single vertical fin under the fuselage or tail of an aircraft.

ven·tri·cle /ˈventrəkəl/ ▶ n. Anat. a hollow part or cavity in an organ, in particular: ■ each of the two main chambers of the heart, left and right. ■ each of the four connected fluid-filled cavities in the center of the brain. — **ven·tric·u·lar** /venˈtrikyələr/ adj. [ME: from L. *ventriculus,* dimin. of *venter* 'belly.']

ven·tri·cose /ˈventrəˌkōs/ ▶ adj. **1** having a protruding belly. **2** Bot. distended, inflated. [18th C.: formed irregularly from VENTRICLE + -OSE[1].]

ven·tric·u·lus /venˈtrikyələs/ ▶ n. technical term for GIZZARD.

ven·tril·o·quist /venˈtriləˌkwist/ ▶ n. a person who can speak or utter sounds so that they seem to come from somewhere else, esp. an entertainer who makes their voice appear to come from a dummy of a person or animal. — **ven·tri·lo·qui·al** /ˌventrəˈlōkwēəl/ adj. **ven·tril·o·quism** /-ˌkwizəm/ n. **ven·tril·o·quize** /-ˌkwīz/ v. **ven·tril·o·quy** /-kwē/ n. [17th C.: from mod. L. *ventriloquium* (from L. *venter* 'belly' + *loqui* 'speak') + -IST.]

ven·tro·lat·er·al /ˌventrōˈlat(ə)rəl/ ▶ adj. Biol. situated toward the junction of the ventral and lateral sides. — **ven·tro·lat·er·al·ly** adv.

ven·tro·me·di·al /ˌventrōˈmēdēəl/ ▶ adj. Biol. situated toward the middle of the ventral side. — **ven·tro·me·di·al·ly** adv.

Ven·tu·ra /venˈchŏŏrə/ (official name **San Buenaventura**) a city in southern California; pop. 92,575.

ven·ture /ˈvenchər/ ▶ n. a risky or daring journey or undertaking: *pioneering ventures into little-known waters.* ■ a business enterprise involving considerable risk. ▶ v. [no obj., with infin. or adverbial] dare to do something or go somewhere that may be dangerous or unpleasant: ***she ventured out into the blizzard.*** ■ dare to do or say something that may be considered audacious (often used as a polite expression of hesitation or apology): *I ventured to write to her* | [trans.] *he ventured an opinion.* ■ [trans.] expose (something) to the risk of loss. [ME: shortening of ADVENTURE.]

ven·ture cap·i·tal ▶ n. capital invested in a project in which there is a substantial element of risk, typically a new or expanding business. — **ven·ture cap·i·tal·ist** n.

ven·tur·er /ˈvenchərər/ ▶ n. archaic a person who undertakes or shares in a trading venture.

ven·ture·some /ˈvenchərsəm/ ▶ adj. willing to take risks or embark on difficult or unusual courses of action. — **ven·ture·some·ly** adv. **ven·ture·some·ness** n.

ven·tu·ri /venˈto͝orē/ ▶ n. (pl. **-ris**) a short piece of narrow tube between wider sections for measuring flow rate or exerting suction. [19th C.: named after Giovanni B. *Venturi* (1746–1822), Italian physicist.]

ven·ue /ˈvenˌyo͞o/ ▶ n. the place where something happens, esp. an organized event such as a concert, conference, or sports event. ■ Law the county or district within which a criminal or civil case must be heard. [16th C.: from OFr., lit. 'a coming,' fem. past part. of *venir* 'come,' from L. *venire.*]

ven·ule /ˈvenˌyo͞ol/ ▶ n. Anat. a very small vein, esp. one collecting blood from the capillaries. [19th C.: from L. *venula,* dimin. of *vena* 'vein.']

Ve·nus /ˈvēnəs/ **1** Rom. Mythol. a goddess, worshiped as the goddess of love in classical Rome though apparently a spirit of kitchen gardens in earlier times. Greek equivalent APHRODITE. ■ [as n.] **(a Venus)** esp. literary a beautiful woman. **2** Astron. the second planet from the sun in the solar system, the brightest celestial object after the sun and moon and frequently appearing in the twilight sky as the evening or morning star. — **Ve·nu·si·an** /vəˈn(y)o͞osh(ē)ən; -zhən; -sēən/ adj. & n.

Ve·nus·berg /ˈvēnəsˌbərg/ ▶ n. (in German legend) the court of Venus.

Ve·nus de Mi·lo /də ˈmēlō; ˈmī-/ a classical sculpture of Aphrodite dated to c.100 BC.

Ve·nus fly·trap (also **Ve·nus's fly·trap**) ▶ n. a small carnivorous bog plant (*Dionaea muscipula,* family Droseraceae) with hinged leaves that spring shut on and digest insects that land on them. Native to the southeastern US, it is also kept as an indoor plant.

Ve·nus's hair ▶ n. the maidenhair fern *Adiantum capillus-veneris.*

Ve·nus's look·ing glass ▶ n. a blue-flowered plant of the bellflower family, whose shiny brown seeds inside their open capsule supposedly resemble mirrors. Two species: the North American *Triodanis perfoliata* and the European *Legousia hybrida.*

ve·ra·cious /vəˈrāshəs/ ▶ adj. formal speaking or representing the truth. — **ve·ra·cious·ly** adv. **ve·ra·cious·ness** n. [17th C.: from L. *verax, verac-* (from *verus* 'true') + -IOUS.]

ve·rac·i·ty /vəˈrasətē/ ▶ n. conformity to facts; accuracy: *the veracity of the story.* ■ habitual truthfulness: *his veracity and character.*

Ve·ra·cruz /ˌverəˈkro͞oz; -ˈkro͞os/ **1** a state in east central Mexico. **2** a city in eastern Mexico; pop. 328,000.

ve·ran·da /vəˈrandə/ (also **ve·ran·dah**) ▶ n. a roofed platform along the outside of a house, level with the ground floor. — **ve·ran·daed** adj. [18th C.: from Hindi *varaṇḍā,* from Port. *varanda* 'railing, balustrade.']

ve·ra·pa·mil /vəˈrapəməl/ ▶ n. Med. a synthetic compound that acts as a calcium antagonist and is used to treat angina pectoris and cardiac arrhythmias. [1960s: from *v(al)er(onitr)il(e)* (from VALERIC ACID + NITRILE), with the insertion of *-apam-* (of unknown origin).]

ver·a·trine /ˈverəˌtrēn; -trin/ ▶ n. Chem. a poisonous substance consisting of a mixture of alkaloids that occurs in the seeds of sabadilla and related plants, used, esp. formerly, to relieve neuralgia and rheumatism. [19th C.: from Fr. *vératrine,* from L. *veratrum* 'hellebore.']

ve·ra·trum /vəˈrātrəm/ ▶ n. (pl. **-trums**) a plant of the lily family belonging to a genus (*Veratrum*) that includes the false hellebores. [mod. L., from L., 'hellebore.']

verb /vərb/ ▶ n. Gram. a word used to describe an action, state, or occurrence, and forming the main part of the predicate of a sentence, such as *hear, become, happen.* — **verb·less** adj. [ME: from OFr. *verbe* or L. *verbum* 'word, verb.']

ver·bal /ˈvərbəl/ ▶ adj. **1** relating to or in the form of words: *verbal abuse.* ■ spoken rather than written; oral: *a verbal agreement.* ■ tending to talk a lot: *he's very verbal.* **2** Gram. of, relating to, or derived from a verb. ▶ n. Gram. a word or words functioning as a verb. ■ a verbal noun. — **ver·bal·ly** adv.

ver·bal·ism /ˈvərbəˌlizəm/ ▶ n. concentration on forms of expression rather than content. ■ a verbal expression. ■ excessive or empty use of language. — **ver·bal·ist** n. **ver·bal·is·tic** /ˌvərbəˈlistik/ adj.

ver·bal·ize /ˈvərbəˌlīz/ ▶ v. **1** [trans.] express (ideas or feelings) in words, esp. by speaking out loud. **2** [intrans.] speak, esp. at excessive length and with little real content: *the dangers of verbalizing about art.* **3** [trans.] make (a word, esp. a noun) into a verb. — **ver·bal·iz·a·ble** adj. **ver·bal·i·za·tion** /ˌvərbələˈzāshən; -ˌlīˈzā-/ n. **ver·bal·iz·er** n.

ver·bal noun ▶ n. Gram. a noun formed as an inflection of a verb and partly sharing its constructions, such as *smoking* in *smoking is forbidden.* See -ING[1].

ver·ba·tim /vərˈbātəm/ ▶ adv. & adj. in exactly the same words as were used originally: [as adv.] *recite the passage verbatim* | [as adj.] *verbatim quotes.* [15th C.: from med. L., from L. *verbum* 'word.']

ver·be·na /vərˈbēnə/ ▶ n. a chiefly American herbaceous plant (genus *Verbena,* family Verbenaceae) that bears heads of bright showy flowers, widely cultivated as a garden ornamental. Its many species include a group of complex cultivars. [mod. L., from L., lit. 'sacred bough,' in med. L. 'vervain.']

ver·bi·age /ˈvərbē-ij/ ▶ n. speech or writing that uses too many words or excessively technical expressions. [18th C.: from Fr., from obs. *verbeier* 'to chatter,' from *verbe* 'word' (see VERB).]

ver·bose /vərˈbōs/ ▶ adj. using or expressed in more words than are needed. — **ver·bose·ly** adv. **ver·bos·i·ty** /-ˈbäsətē/ n. [17th C.: from L. *verbosus,* from *verbum* 'word.']

ver·bo·ten /fərˈbōtn; vər-/ ▶ adj. forbidden, esp. by an authority. [Ger.]

verb phrase ▶ n. Gram. the part of a sentence containing the verb and any direct or indirect object, but not the subject.

ver·dant /ˈvərdnt/ ▶ adj. (of countryside) green with grass or other rich vegetation. ■ of the bright green color of lush grass. — **ver·dan·cy** /ˈvərdn-sē/ n. **ver·dant·ly** adv. [16th C.: perh. from OFr. *verdeant*, pres. part. of *verdoier* 'be green,' based on L. *viridis* 'green.']

verd an·tique /ˈvərd anˈtēk/ ▶ n. a green ornamental marble consisting of serpentine with calcite and dolomite veins. ■ verdigris on ancient bronze or copper. ■ a green form of porphyry. [18th C.: from obs. Fr., lit. 'antique green.']

Ver·de·lho /vərˈdelyōō/ ▶ n. (pl. **-lhos**) a white grape originally grown in Madeira, now also in Portugal, Sicily, Australia, and South Africa. ■ a medium Madeira made from this grape.

Ver·di /ˈve(ə)rdē/, Giuseppe Fortunino Francesco (1813–1901), Italian composer. His operas include *La Traviata* (1853), *Aida* (1871), and *Otello* (1887).

Ver·dic·chi·o /vərˈdēkē,ō/ ▶ n. a variety of white wine grape grown in the Marche region of Italy. ■ a dry white wine made from this grape.

ver·dict /ˈvərdikt/ ▶ n. a decision on a disputed issue in a civil or criminal case or an inquest. ■ an opinion or judgment. [ME: from Anglo-Norman Fr. *verdit*, from OFr. *veir* 'true' (from L. *verus*) + *dit* (from L. *dictum* 'saying').]

ver·di·gris /ˈvərdə,grēs; -,gris; -,grē/ ▶ n. a bright bluish-green encrustation or patina formed on copper or brass by atmospheric oxidation, consisting of basic copper carbonate. [ME: from OFr. *verte-gres*, earlier *vert de Grece* 'green of Greece.']

ver·din /ˈvərdn/ ▶ n. a small songbird (*Auriparus flaviceps*, family Remizidae) with a gray body and yellowish head, found in the semideserts of southwestern North America. [19th C.: from Fr., lit. 'yellowhammer.']

ver·di·ter /ˈvərdətər/ ▶ n. a light blue or bluish-green pigment, typically prepared by adding chalk or whiting to a solution of copper nitrate, used in making crayons and as a watercolor. ▶ adj. of this color. [16th C.: from OFr. *verd de terre*, lit. 'earth green.']

Ver·dun, Bat·tle of /vərˈdən/ a long and severe battle in 1916, during World War I, at the fortified town of Verdun in northeastern France.

ver·dure /ˈvərjər/ ▶ n. lush green vegetation. ■ the fresh green color of such vegetation. ■ literary a condition of freshness. — **ver·dured** adj. **ver·dur·ous** /-jərəs/ adj. [ME: via Fr. from OFr. *verd* 'green,' from L. *viridis*.]

verge[1] /vərj/ ▶ n. an edge or border. ■ an extreme limit beyond which something specified will happen: *I was **on the verge of** tears.* ■ Brit. a grass edging such as that by the side of a road or path. ■ Archit. an edge of tiles projecting over a gable. ▶ v. [intrans.] approach (something) closely; be close or similar to (something): *despair **verging on** the suicidal.* [ME: via OFr. from L. *virga* 'rod.']

verge[2] ▶ n. a wand or rod carried before a bishop or dean as an emblem of office. [ME: from L. *virga* 'rod.']

verge[3] ▶ v. [no obj., with adverbial of direction] incline in a certain direction or toward a particular state: *his style verged into the art nouveau school.* [17th C.: from L. *vergere* 'to bend, incline.']

ver·gence /ˈvərjəns/ ▶ n. **1** Physiol. the simultaneous movement of the pupils of the eyes toward or away from one another during focusing. **2** Geol. the direction in which a fold is inclined or overturned: *a zone of opposing fold vergence.*

verg·er /ˈvərjər/ ▶ n. **1** an official in a church who acts as a caretaker and attendant. **2** an officer who carries a rod before a bishop or dean as a symbol of office. — **verg·er·ship** /-,SHip/ n.

Ver·gil var. of VIRGIL.

ver·glas /verˈglä/ ▶ n. a thin coating of ice or frozen rain on an exposed surface. [19th C.: Fr., from *verre* 'glass' + *glas* (now *glace*) 'ice.']

ve·rid·i·cal /vəˈridikəl/ ▶ adj. formal truthful. ■ coinciding with reality: *is his recall veridical?* — **ve·rid·i·cal·i·ty** /-,ridəˈkalətē/ n. **ve·rid·i·cal·ly** /-ik(ə)lē/ adv. [17th C.: from L. *veridicus* (from *verus* 'true' + *dicere* 'say') + -AL.]

ver·i·est /ˈverēist/ ▶ adj. (**the veriest**) esp. archaic used to emphasize the degree to which a description applies to someone or something: *everyone but the veriest greenhorn knows by now.* [16th C.: superlative of VERY.]

ver·i·fi·ca·tion /,verəfiˈkāSHən/ ▶ n. the process of establishing the truth, accuracy, or validity of something: *the verification of official documents.* ■ [often as adj.] Philos. the establishment by empirical means of the validity of a proposition. ■ the process of ensuring that procedures laid down in weapons limitation agreements are followed.

ver·i·fy /ˈverə,fī/ ▶ v. (**-fies, -fied**) [trans.] (often **be verified**) make sure or demonstrate that (something) is true, accurate, or justified. ■ Law swear to or support (a statement) by affidavit. — **ver·i·fi·a·ble** /ˈverə,fīəbəl; ,verəˈfī-/ adj. **ver·i·fi·a·bly** /ˈverə,fīəblē; ,verəˈfī-/ adv. **ver·i·fi·er** n. [ME (as a legal term): from OFr. *verifier*, from med. L. *verificare*, from *verus* 'true.']

ver·i·ly /ˈverəlē/ ▶ adv. archaic truly; certainly. [ME: from VERY.]

ver·i·si·mil·i·tude /,verəsəˈmili,t(y)ōōd/ ▶ n. the appearance of being true or real. — **ver·i·sim·i·lar** /-ˈsimələr/ adj. [17th C.: from L. *verisimilitudo*, from *verisimilis* 'probable,' from *veri* (genitive of *verus* 'true') + *similis* 'like.']

ve·ris·mo /vəˈrizmō; ve-/ ▶ n. realism in the arts, esp. late 19th-century Italian opera. ■ this genre of opera, as composed principally by Puccini, Mascagni, and Leoncavallo.

ve·ris·tic /vəˈristik/ ▶ adj. (of art or literature) extremely or strictly naturalistic. — **ver·ism** /ˈver,izəm/ n. **ver·ist** /ˈverist/ n. & adj. [19th C.: from L. *verum* (neut.) 'true' or Ital. *vero* 'true' + -IST + -IC.]

ver·i·ta·ble /ˈveritəbəl/ ▶ adj. used as an intensifier, often to qualify a metaphor: *a veritable price explosion.* — **ver·i·ta·bly** /-blē/ adv. [ME: from OFr., from *verite* 'truth' (see VERITY).]

vé·ri·té /,veriˈtā/ ▶ n. a genre of film, television, and radio programs emphasizing realism and naturalism. [Fr., lit. 'truth.']

ver·i·ty /ˈveritē/ ▶ n. (pl. **-ties**) a true principle or belief, esp. one of fundamental importance. ■ truth: *irrefutable, objective verity.* [ME: from OFr. *verite*, from L. *veritas*, from *verus* 'true.']

ver·juice /ˈvər,jōōs/ ▶ n. a sour juice obtained from crab apples, unripe grapes, or other fruit, used in cooking and formerly in medicine. [ME: from OFr. *vertjus*, from *vert* 'green' + *jus* 'juice.']

Ver·khne·u·dinsk /,verknəˈōōdinsk/ former name (until 1934) of ULAN-UDE.

Ver·laine /vərˈlān; verˈlen/, Paul (1844–96), French symbolist poet. Collections of his poetry include *Poèmes saturniens* (1867).

Ver·meer /vərˈmi(ə)r/, Jan (1632–75), Dutch painter. He generally painted domestic genre scenes, including *The Kitchen Maid* (c.1658).

ver·meil /ˈvərməl; -,māl; vərˈmā(l)/ ▶ n. [often as adj.] **1** gilded silver or bronze. **2** literary vermilion. [ME (sense 2): from OFr. (see VERMILION).]

vermi- ▶ comb. form of or relating to a worm or worms, esp. parasitic ones: *vermiform.* [from L. *vermis* 'worm.']

ver·mi·an /ˈvərmēən/ ▶ adj. **1** literary relating to or resembling a worm; wormlike. **2** Anat. of or relating to the vermis of the brain. [19th C.: from L. *vermis* 'worm' + -IAN.]

ver·mi·cel·li /,vərməˈCHelē; -ˈselē/ ▶ n. pasta made in long slender threads. [Ital., pl. of *vermicello*, dimin. of *verme* 'worm,' from L. *vermis*.]

ver·mi·cide /ˈvərmə,sīd/ ▶ n. a substance that is poisonous to worms.

ver·mic·u·lar /vərˈmikyələr/ ▶ adj. **1** like a worm in form or movement; vermiform. **2** of, denoting, or caused by intestinal worms. **3** marked with close wavy lines. [17th C.: from med. L. *vermicularis*, from L. *vermiculus*, dimin. of *vermis* 'worm.']

ver·mic·u·late /vərˈmikyə,lāt; -lət/ ▶ adj. **1** another term for VERMICULAR. **2** another term for VERMICULATED.

ver·mic·u·lat·ed /vərˈmikyə,lātid/ ▶ adj. **1** (esp. of the plumage of a bird) marked with sinuous or wavy lines. **2** archaic worm-eaten. **3** Archit. carved or molded with shallow wavy grooves resembling the tracks of worms. — **ver·mic·u·la·tion** /vər,mikyəˈlāSHən/ n.

ver·mic·u·lite /vərˈmikyə,līt/ ▶ n. a yellow or brown mineral found as an alteration product of mica and other minerals, and used for insulation or as a moisture-retentive medium for growing plants. [19th C.: from L. *vermiculari* 'be full of worms.']

ver·mi·form /ˈvərmə,fôrm/ ▶ adj. esp. Zool. or Anat. resembling or having the form of a worm.

ver·mi·form ap·pen·dix ▶ n. technical term for APPENDIX (sense 1).

ver·mi·fuge /ˈvərmə,fyōōj/ ▶ n. Med. an anthelmintic medicine.

ver·mil·ion /vərˈmilyən/ (also **ver·mil·lion**) ▶ n. a brilliant red pigment made from mercury sulfide (cinnabar). ■ a brilliant red color. [ME: from OFr. *vermeillon*, from *vermeil*, from L. *vermiculus*, dimin. of *vermis* 'worm.']

ver·min /ˈvərmən/ ▶ n. [treated as pl.] wild mammals and birds that are believed to be harmful to crops, farm animals, or game, or that carry disease, e.g., foxes, rodents, and insect pests. ■ parasitic worms or insects. ■ fig. people perceived as despicable and as causing problems for the rest of society. — **ver·min·ous** /-mənəs/ adj. [ME: from OFr., based on L. *vermis* 'worm.']

ver·mis /ˈvərməs/ ▶ n. Anat. the rounded and elongated central part of the cerebellum, between the two hemispheres. [19th C.: from L., 'worm.']

Ver·mont /vərˈmänt/ a state in the northeastern US, on the border with Canada, one of the six New England States; pop. 608,827; capital, Montpelier; statehood, Mar. 4, 1791 (14). Explored and settled by the French 1600s–1700s, it became an independent republic in 1777 until it was admitted as a US state. — **Ver·mont·er** n.

ver·mouth /vərˈmōōTH/ ▶ n. a red or white wine flavored with aromatic herbs, chiefly made in France and Italy and drunk mixed with gin. [from Fr. *vermout*, from Ger. *Wermut* 'wormwood.']

ver·nac·u·lar /vərˈnakyələr/ ▶ n. **1** (usu. **the vernacular**) the language or dialect spoken by the ordinary people in a particular country or region. ■ [with adj.] informal the terminology used by people belonging to a specified group or engaging in a specialized activity: *gardening vernacular.* **2** architecture concerned with domestic and functional rather than monumental buildings: *buildings in which Gothic merged into farmhouse vernacular.* ▶ adj. **1** (of language) spoken as one's mother tongue; not learned or imposed as a second language. ■ (of speech or written works) using such a language. **2** (of architecture) concerned with domestic and functional rather than monumental buildings. — **ver·nac·u·lar·ism** /-lə,rizəm/ n. **ver·nac·u·lar·i·ty** /-,nakyəˈlaritē/ n. **ver·nac·u·lar·ize** /-lə,rīz/ v. **ver·nac·u·lar·ly** adv. [17th C.: from L. *vernaculus* 'domestic, native' (from *verna* 'home-born slave') + -AR[1].]

ver·nal /ˈvərnl/ ▶ adj. of, in, or appropriate to spring. — **ver·nal·ly**

adv. [16th C.: from L. *vernalis*, from *vernus* 'of the spring,' from *ver* 'spring.']·

ver·nal e·qui·nox ▶ n. the equinox in spring, on about March 20 in the northern hemisphere and September 22 in the southern hemisphere. ■ Astron. the equinox in March. Also called SPRING EQUINOX. ■ Astron. another term for *FIRST POINT OF ARIES* (see ARIES).

ver·nal·i·za·tion /ˌvərnl-əˈzāsHən/ ▶ n. the cooling of seed during germination in order to accelerate flowering when it is planted. — **ver·nal·ize** /ˈvərnlˌīz/ v.

ver·na·tion /vərˈnāsHən/ ▶ n. Bot. the arrangement of young leaves in a leaf bud before it opens. Compare with ESTIVATION. [18th C.: from mod. L. *vernatio(n-)*, from L. *vernare* 'to grow (as in the spring),' from *vernus* (see VERNAL).]

Verne /vərn/, Jules (1828–1905), French witer. One of the first writers of science fiction, his novels include *Journey to the Center of the Earth* (1864).

Ver·ner's Law /ˈvernərz; ˈvər-/ Ling. the observation that voiceless fricatives in Germanic predicted by Grimm's Law became voiced if the preceding syllable in the corresponding Indo-European word was unstressed. [19th C.: named after Karl A. *Verner* (1846–96), Danish philologist.]

ver·ni·cle /ˈvərnəkəl/ ▶ n. another term for VERONICA (sense 2). [ME: from OFr., alt. of *vernique*, from med. L. *veronica*.]

ver·nier /ˈvərnēər/ (also **vernier scale**) ▶ n. a small movable graduated scale for obtaining fractional parts of subdivisions on a fixed main scale of a barometer, sextant, or other measuring instrument. [18th C.: named after Pierre *Vernier* (1580–1637), French mathematician.]

ver·nis·sage /ˌvernəˈsäzH/ ▶ n. (pl. same) a private viewing of paintings before public exhibition. [Fr., lit. 'varnishing.']

ver·nix /ˈvərniks/ ▶ n. (in full **ver·nix ca·se·o·sa**) /ˌkāsēˈōsə/ a greasy deposit covering the skin of a baby at birth. [16th C.: from med. L., var. of *veronix* 'fragrant resin' (see VARNISH).]

Ve·ro·na /vəˈrōnə/ a city on the Adige River, in northeastern Italy; pop. 259,000.

Ve·ro·ne·se /ˌverəˈnāzā/, Paolo (*c.*1528–88), Italian painter; born *Paolo Caliari*. His works include *The Marriage at Cana* (1562).

ve·ron·i·ca /vəˈränəkə/ ▶ n. **1** a herbaceous plant (genus *Veronica*) of the figwort family, typically with upright stems bearing narrow pointed leaves and spikes of blue or purple flowers, found in north temperate regions. **2** a cloth supposedly impressed with an image of Jesus' face. ■ a picture of Jesus' face similar to this. **3** (in bullfighting) a slow movement of the cape away from a charging bull by the matador, who stands in place. [16th C.: from med. L., from the given name *Veronica*.]

Ve·ron·i·ca, St. /vəˈränəkə/ (in Christian tradition) a woman of Jerusalem who offered her veil, or handkerchief, to Jesus on the way to Calvary, to wipe the blood and sweat from his face.

ve·ron·ique /ˌverəˈnēk; ˌvārô-/ ▶ adj. [postpositive] denoting a dish, typically of fish or chicken, prepared or garnished with grapes. [from the Fr. given name *Véronique*.]

Ver·ra·za·no /ˌverätˈsänō/, Giovanni da (c.1480–1527), Italian explorer. He was the first European to enter New York Bay 1524.

ver·ru·ca /vəˈro͞okə/ ▶ n. (pl. **-cae** /-kē; -kī/ or **-cas**) a contagious and usually painful wart on the sole of the foot; a plantar wart. ■ (in medical use) a wart of any kind. — **ver·ru·cose** /ˈverəˌkōs; vəˈro͞o-/ adj. **ver·ru·cous** /vəˈro͞okəs/ adj. [ME: from L.]

Ver·sa·ce /vərˈsächē/, Gianni (1946–97), Italian fashion designer; full name *Giovanni Versace*.

Ver·sailles /vərˈsī; ver-/ a palace built for Louis XIV near Versailles, southwest of Paris.

Ver·sailles, Trea·ty of **1** a treaty that terminated the American Revolution in 1783. **2** a treaty signed in 1919 that brought a formal end to World War I.

ver·sal /ˈvərsəl/ ▶ adj. of or relating to a style of ornate capital letter used to start a verse, paragraph, etc., in a manuscript, typically built up by inking between pen strokes and with long, rather flat serifs. ▶ n. a versal letter. [19th C.: from L. *vers-* 'turned' + -AL, influenced by VERSE.]

ver·sant /ˈvərsənt/ ▶ n. a region of land sloping in one general direction. [19th C.: from Fr., pres. part. (used as a n.) of *verser* 'tilt over,' from L. *versare*.]

ver·sa·tile /ˈvərsətl/ ▶ adj. **1** able to adapt or be adapted to many different functions or activities: *a versatile saw.* **2** archaic changeable; inconstant. — **ver·sa·tile·ly** adv. **ver·sa·til·i·ty** /ˌvərsəˈtilətē/ n. [17th C.: from Fr., or from L. *versatilis*, from *versat-* 'turned around, revolved,' from the v. *versare*, frequentative of *vertere* 'to turn.']

verse /vərs/ ▶ n. writing arranged with a metrical rhythm, typically having a rhyme. ■ a group of lines that form a unit in a poem or song; a stanza. ■ each of the short numbered divisions of a chapter in the Bible or other scripture. ■ a versicle. ■ archaic a line of poetry. ■ a passage in an anthem for a soloist or a small group of voices. ▶ v. [intrans.] archaic speak in or compose verse; versify. — **verse·let** /-lət/ n. [OE *fers*, from L. *versus* 'a turn of the plow, a furrow, a line of writing,' from *vertere* 'to turn.']

versed /vərst/ ▶ adj. (**versed in**) experienced or skilled in; knowledgeable about: *well versed in art.* [17th C.: from Fr. *versé* or L. *versatus*, past part. of *versari* 'be engaged in.']

versed sine ▶ n. Math. one minus cosine. ■ Archit. the rise of an arch of a bridge.

ver·si·cle /ˈvərsikəl/ ▶ n. (usu. **versicles**) a short sentence said or sung by the minister in a church service, to which the congregation gives a response. [ME: from OFr. *versicule* or L. *versiculus*, dimin. of *versus* (see VERSE).]

ver·si·col·ored /ˈvərsiˌkələrd/ (Brit. **ver·si·col·oured**) ▶ adj. archaic **1** changing from one color to another in different lights. **2** variegated. [18th C.: from L. *versicolor* (from *versus* 'turned' + *color* 'color') + -ED².]

ver·si·fy /ˈvərsəˌfī/ ▶ v. (**-fies, -fied**) [trans.] turn into or express in verse. — **ver·si·fi·ca·tion** /ˌvərsəfiˈkāsHən/ n. **ver·si·fi·er** n.

ver·sine /ˈvərˌsīn/ (also **ver·sin**) ▶ n. Math. another term for VERSED SINE. [19th C.: abbrev.]

ver·sion /ˈvərzHən/ ▶ n. **1** a particular form of something differing in certain respects from an earlier form or other forms of the same type of thing. ■ a particular edition or translation of a book or other work: *the English version will be published next year.* ■ an adaptation of a novel, piece of music, etc., into another medium or style: *a film version of a funny cult novel.* ■ a particular updated edition of a piece of computer software. ■ an account of a matter from a particular person's point of view. **2** Med. the manual turning of a fetus in the uterus to make delivery easier. ■ an abnormal displacement of the uterus. ▶ v. [trans.] [often as n.] (**versioning**) create a new version of: *it's the software for you if you need versioning and group editing.* — **ver·sion·al** /-zHənl/ adj. [ME (in the sense 'translation'): from Fr., or from med. L. *versio(n-)*, from L. *vertere* 'to turn.']

ver·sion con·trol ▶ n. Comput. the task of keeping a software system consisting of many versions and configurations well organized.

vers li·bre /ˌver ˈlēbrə/ ▶ n. another term for FREE VERSE. [Fr.]

ver·so /ˈvərsō/ ▶ n. (pl. **-sos**) **1** a left-hand page of an open book, or the back of a loose document. Contrasted with RECTO. **2** the reverse of something such as a coin or painting. [19th C.: from L. *verso (folio)* 'on the turned (leaf).']

verst /vərst/ ▶ n. a Russian measure of length, about 0.66 mile (1.1 km). [from Russ. *versta*.]

ver·sus /ˈvərsəs; -səz/ (abbr.: **v.** or **vs.**) ▶ prep. against (esp. in sports and legal use): *Penn versus Princeton.* ■ as opposed to; in contrast to. [ME: from a med. L. use of L. *versus* 'toward.']

vert /vərt/ ▶ n. green, as a heraldic tincture: [postpositive] *three piles vert.* [ME (as an adj.): via OFr. from L. *viridis* 'green.']

ver·te·bra /ˈvərtəbrə/ ▶ n. (pl. **-brae** /-ˌbrē; -ˌbrā/) each of the series of small bones forming the backbone, having several projections for articulation and muscle attachment, and a hole through which the spinal cord passes. — **ver·te·bral** /-brəl; vərˈtē-/ adj. [17th C.: from L., from *vertere* 'to turn.']

ver·te·bral col·umn ▶ n. another term for SPINAL COLUMN.

ver·te·brate /ˈvərtəbrət; -ˌbrāt/ ▶ n. an animal of a large group distinguished by the possession of a backbone or spinal column, including mammals, birds, reptiles, amphibians, and fishes. Compare with INVERTEBRATE. ▶ adj. of or relating to the vertebrates.

ver·tex /ˈvərˌteks/ ▶ n. (pl. **-ti·ces** /-təˌsēz/ or **-tex·es**) **1** the highest point; the top or apex. ■ Anat. the crown of the head. **2** Geom. each angular point of a polygon, polyhedron, or other figure. ■ a meeting point of two lines that form an angle. ■ the point at which an axis meets a curve or surface. [ME: from L., 'whirlpool, crown of a head, vertex,' from *vertere* 'to turn.']

ver·ti·cal /ˈvərtikəl/ ▶ adj. **1** at right angles to a horizontal plane; in a direction, or having an alignment, such that the top is directly above the bottom. **2** archaic denoting a point at the zenith or the highest point of something. **3** Anat. of or relating to the crown of the head. **4** involving different levels of a hierarchy or progression, in particular: ■ involving all the stages from the production to the sale of a class of goods. ■ (esp. of the transmission of disease or genetic traits) passed from one generation to the next. ▶ n. **1** (usu. **the vertical**) a vertical line or plane. **2** an upright structure: *unadorned verticals.* **3** the distance between the highest and lowest points of a ski area: *the resort claims a vertical of 2100 meters.* — **ver·ti·cal·i·ty** /ˌvərtiˈkalətē/ n. **ver·ti·cal·ize** /-kəˌlīz/ v. **ver·ti·cal·ly** /-ik(ə)lē/ adv. [16th C. (in the sense 'directly overhead'): from Fr., or from late L. *verticalis*, from *vertex* (see VERTEX).]

ver·ti·cal an·gles ▶ plural n. Math. each of the pairs of opposite angles made by two intersecting lines.

ver·ti·cal cir·cle ▶ n. a great circle of the celestial sphere whose diameter runs from zenith to nadir.

ver·ti·cal in·te·gra·tion ▶ n. the combination in one company of two or more stages of production normally operated by separate companies.

ver·ti·cal sta·bi·liz·er ▶ n. Aeron. a small, flattened projecting surface or attachment on an aircraft or rocket for providing aerodynamic stability.

ver·ti·cal un·ion ▶ n. another term for INDUSTRIAL UNION.

ver·ti·cil·li·um /ˌvərtəˈsilēəm/ ▶ n. a fungus (genus *Verticillium*, subdivision Deuteromycotina) of a genus that includes a number of species that cause wilt in plants. ■ wilt caused by such fungi. [mod. L., from L. *verticillus* 'spindle whorl.']

ver·tig·i·nous /vərˈtijənəs/ ▶ adj. causing vertigo, esp. by being extremely high or steep. ■ relating to or affected by vertigo. — **ver·tig·i·nous·ly** adv. [17th C.: from L. *vertiginosus*, from *vertigo* 'whirling around' (see VERTIGO).]

ver·ti·go /ˈvərtəgō/ ▶ n. a sensation of whirling and loss of balance, associated particularly with looking down from a great height, or caused by disease affecting the inner ear or the vestibular nerve; giddiness. [ME: from L., 'whirling,' from *vertere* 'to turn.']

ver·ti·sol /'vərtə,säl; -,sôl/ ▶ **n.** Soil Science a clayey soil with little organic matter that occurs in regions having distinct wet and dry seasons. [1960s: from VERTICAL + L. *solum* 'soil.']

ver·tu ▶ **n.** var. of VIRTU.

ver·vain /'vər,vān/ ▶ **n.** a widely distributed herbaceous plant (*Verbena officinalis*) of the verbena family, with small blue, white, or purple flowers and a long history of use as a medicinal herb. [ME: from OFr. *verveine*, from L. *verbena* (see VERBENA).]

verve /vərv/ ▶ **n.** vigor and spirit or enthusiasm. [17th C.: from Fr., 'vigor,' from L. *verba* 'words.']

ver·vet /'vərvət/ (also **ver·vet mon·key**) ▶ **n.** a common African guenon (*Cercopithecus aethiops*) with greenish-brown upper parts and a black face, esp. the race *C. a. pygerythrus* of southern and eastern Africa. Compare with GREEN MONKEY, GRIVET. [19th C.: from Fr., of unknown origin.]

Ver·woerd /fər'vōōrt/, Hendrik Frensch (1901–66), prime minister of South Africa 1958–66. As minister of Bantu affairs (1950–58), he developed the segregation policy of apartheid. He declared South Africa a republic in 1961.

ver·y /'verē/ ▶ **adv.** used for emphasis: ■ in a high degree: *very large.* ■ used to emphasize that the following description applies without qualification: *the very best quality* | *his very own car.* ▶ **adj.** actual; precise (used to emphasize the exact identity of a particular person or thing): *his very words.* ■ emphasizing an extreme point in time or space: *from the very beginning.* ■ with no addition of or contribution from anything else; mere: *the very thought of him.* ■ archaic real; genuine.

– PHRASES **not very 1** in a low degree: *"Bad news?" "Not very."* **2** far from being: *I'm not very impressed.* **very good** (or **well**) an expression of consent. [ME: from OFr. *verai*, based on L. *verus* 'true.']

very high fre·quen·cy ▶ **n.** (abbr.: **VHF**) the band of frequencies between 30 and 300 megahertz, typically used for broadcasting television signals.

Very Large Ar·ray (abbr.: **VLA**) ▶ **n.** the world's largest radio telescope, consisting of 27 dish antennas in Socorro, New Mexico.

Ver·y light /'verē; 'vi(ə)rē/ ▶ **n.** a flare fired into the air from a pistol for signaling or for temporary illumination. [20th C.: named after Edward W. *Very* (1847–1910), American naval officer.]

very low fre·quen·cy ▶ **n.** (abbr.: **VLF**) the band of frequencies between 3 and 30 kilohertz.

Ver·y pis·tol ▶ **n.** a hand-held gun used for firing a Very light.

VESA ▶ **abbr.** Video Electronics Standards Association, a US-based organization that defines formats for displays and buses used in computers.

Ve·sak /'vā,säk/ (also **We·sak** or **Vi·sā·kha** /vi'säkə/) ▶ **n.** the most important Buddhist festival, commemorating the birth, enlightenment, and death of the Buddha, and celebrated at the full moon in the Indian month of Vaishaka (April–May). [Sinhalese *vesak*, via Pali from Sanskrit *vaiśākha*, denoting the month April–May.]

Ve·sa·li·us /və'sālēəs/, Andreas (1514–64), Flemish anatomist; the founder of modern anatomy.

ve·si·cal /'vesəkəl/ ▶ **adj.** Anat. Med. of, relating to, or affecting the urinary bladder. [18th C.: from L. *vesica* 'bladder' + -AL.]

ves·i·cant /'vesəkənt/ ▶ **adj.** tending to cause blistering. ▶ **n.** an agent that causes blistering.

ve·si·ca pis·cis /'vesikə 'pis(k)is; 'pīsis; və'sēkə; və'sīkə/ ▶ **n.** (pl. **ve·si·cae pis·cis** /-,kī; -,kē/) another term for MANDORLA. [L., lit. 'fish's bladder.']

ves·i·cate /'vesi,kāt/ ▶ **v.** [trans.] esp. Med. raise blisters on. ■ [intrans.] form blisters. — **ves·i·ca·tion** /,vesi'kāsʜən/ **n.** **ves·i·ca·to·ry** /'vesəkə,tôrē; və'sikə-/ **adj. & n.**

ve·si·cle /'vesikəl/ ▶ **n.** a fluid- or air-filled cavity or sac, in particular: ■ Anat. Zool. a small fluid-filled bladder, sac, cyst, or vacuole within the body. ■ Bot. an air-filled swelling in a plant, esp. a seaweed. ■ Geol. a small cavity in volcanic rock, produced by gas bubbles. ■ Med. a small blister full of clear fluid. — **ve·sic·u·lar** /və'sikyələr/ **adj.** **ve·sic·u·lat·ed** /və'sikyə,lātid/ **adj.** **ve·sic·u·la·tion** /və,sikyə'lāsʜən/ **n.** [16th C.: from Fr. *vésicule* or L. *vesicula*, dimin. of *vesica* 'bladder.']

ve·sic·u·late ▶ **v.** /və'sikyə,lāt/ make or become vesicular. ▶ **adj.** /və'sikyəlit; -,lāt/ containing or covered with vesicles or small cavities.

Ves·pa·sian /ves'pāzʜən/ (AD 9–79), Roman emperor 69–79 and founder of the Flavian dynasty; Latin name *Titus Flavius Vespasianus.*

ves·per /'vespər/ ▶ **n.** evening prayer. See also VESPERS. ■ archaic evening. ■ (**Vesper**) literary Venus as the evening star. [ME: from L. *vesper* 'evening (star).']

ves·per·al /'vespərəl/ ▶ **adj.** **1** of or pertaining to evening. **2** of or pertaining to vespers. ▶ **n.** a book containing the psalms, canticles, anthems, and the like with their musical settings that are used at vespers.

ves·pers /'vespərz/ ▶ **n.** a service of evening prayer in the Divine Office of the Western Christian Church (sometimes said earlier in the day). ■ a service of evening prayer in other churches. [15th C.: from OFr. *vespres* 'evensong,' from L. *vesperas* (accusative pl.).]

ves·per spar·row ▶ **n.** a small North American songbird (*Pooecetes gramineus*) of the bunting family, having streaked brown plumage and known for its evening song.

ves·per·til·i·o·nid /,vespər'tilēə,nid/ ▶ **n.** Zool. a bat of a large family (Vespertilionidae) that includes most of the typical insectivorous bats of north temperate regions. [19th C.: from mod. L. *Vespertilionidae* (pl.), from L. *vespertilio* 'bat.']

ves·per·tine /'vespər,tīn; -,tēn/ ▶ **adj.** **1** tech. literary of, relating to, occurring, or active in the evening. **2** Bot. (of a flower) opening in the evening. **3** Zool. active in the evening. [ME: from L. *vespertinus*, from *vesper* 'evening.']

ves·pi·ar·y /'vespē,erē/ ▶ **n.** (pl. **-ar·ies**) a nest of wasps. [19th C.: from L. *vespa* 'wasp.']

ves·pine /'ves,pīn; -pin/ ▶ **adj.** of or relating to wasps. [19th C.: from L. *vespa* 'wasp' + -INE[1].]

Ves·puc·ci /ves'p(y)ōōcʜē/, Amerigo (1451–1512), Italian explorer. The Latin form of his first name is believed to have given rise to the name of America.

ves·sel /'vesəl/ ▶ **n.** **1** a ship or large boat. **2** a hollow container, esp. one used to hold liquid, such as a bowl or cask. ■ (chiefly in or alluding to biblical use) a person, esp. regarded as holding or embodying a particular quality: *as unto the weaker vessel.* **3** Anat. Zool. a duct or canal holding or conveying blood or other fluid. See also BLOOD VESSEL. ■ Bot. any of the tubular structures in the vascular system of a plant, serving to conduct water and mineral nutrients from the root. [ME: from Anglo-Norman Fr. *vessel(e)*, from late L. *vascellum*, dimin. of *vas* 'vessel.']

vest /vest/ ▶ **n.** a close-fitting waist-length garment, typically having no sleeves or collar and buttoning down the front. ■ a similar garment worn on the upper part of the body for a particular purpose or activity: *a bulletproof vest.* ■ a piece of material showing at the neck of a woman's dress. ■ Brit. an undershirt. ▶ **v.** **1** [trans.] (usu. **be vested in**) confer or bestow (power, authority, property, etc.) on someone. ■ (usu. **be vested with**) give (someone) the legal right to power, property, etc. ■ [intrans.] (**vest in**) (of power, property, etc.) come into the possession of: *the bankrupt's property vests in his trustee.* **2** [intrans.] (of a chorister or member of the clergy) put on vestments. ■ [trans.] literary dress (someone). [ME (as a v.): from OFr. *vestu* 'clothed,' past part. of *vestir*, from L. *vestire* from *vestis* 'garment.']

Ves·ta /'vestə/ Rom. Mythol. the goddess of the hearth and household. Her temple in Rome contained no image but a fire that was kept constantly burning and was tended by the Vestal Virgins.

ves·ta /'vestə/ ▶ **n.** esp. hist. a short wooden or wax match. [19th C.: from VESTA.]

ves·tal /'vestl/ ▶ **adj.** of or relating to the Roman goddess Vesta: *a vestal temple.* ■ literary chaste; pure. ▶ **n.** a Vestal Virgin. ■ literary a chaste woman, esp. a nun.

Ves·tal Vir·gin (also **ves·tal vir·gin**) ▶ **n.** (in ancient Rome) a virgin consecrated to Vesta and vowed to chastity, sharing the charge of maintaining the sacred fire burning on the goddess's altar.

vest·ed /'vestid/ ▶ **adj.** **1** secured in the possession of or assigned to a person: *a state law vested the ownership of all wild birds to the individual counties.* ■ protected or established by law or contract. ■ (of a person) legally entitled to a future benefit, as from a pension: *he was vested after five years with the company.* **2** supplied or worn with a vest. **3** wearing vestments.

vest·ed in·ter·est ▶ **n.** [usu. in sing.] a personal stake or involvement in an undertaking or state of affairs, esp. one with an expectation of financial gain. ■ a person or group having such a personal stake or involvement. ■ Law an interest (usually in land or money held in trust) recognized as belonging to a particular person.

vest·ee /,ve'stē/ ▶ **n.** a vestlike piece of material showing at the neck of a woman's dress.

ves·ti·ar·y /'vestē,erē/ ▶ **adj.** literary of or relating to clothes or dress. ▶ **n.** (pl. **-ar·ies**) a room or building in a monastery or other large establishment in which clothes are kept. [ME (denoting a vestry): from OFr. *vestiarie*, from L. *vestiarium* (see VESTRY).]

ves·tib·u·lar /ve'stibyələr; və-/ ▶ **adj.** esp. Anat. of or relating to a vestibule, particularly that of the inner ear, or more generally to the sense of balance.

ves·ti·bule /'vestə,byōōl/ ▶ **n.** **1** an antechamber, hall, or lobby next to the outer door of a building. ■ an enclosed entrance compartment in a railroad car. **2** Anat. a chamber or channel communicating with or opening into another, in particular: ■ the central cavity of the labyrinth of the inner ear. ■ the part of the mouth outside the teeth. ■ the space in the vulva into which both the urethra and vagina open. — **ves·ti·buled** **adj.** [17th C.: from Fr., or from L. *vestibulum* 'entrance court.']

ves·tige /'vestij/ ▶ **n.** a trace of something that is disappearing or no longer exists. ■ [usu. with negative] the smallest amount (used to emphasize the absence of something): *without a vestige of sympathy.* ■ Biol. a part or organ of an organism that has become reduced or functionless in the course of evolution. [ME: from Fr., from L. *vestigium* 'footprint.']

ves·tig·i·al /ve'stij(ē)əl/ ▶ **adj.** forming a very small remnant of something that was once much larger or more noticeable: *he felt a vestigial flicker of anger.* ■ Biol. (of an organ or part of the body) degenerate, rudimentary, or atrophied, having become functionless in the course of evolution: *vestigial wings.* — **ves·tig·i·al·ly** **adv.**

PRONUNCIATION KEY ə *ago, up;* ər *over, fur;* a *hat;* ā *ate;* ä *car;* e *let;* ē *see;* i *fit;* ī *by;* NG *sing;* ō *go;* ô *law, for;* oi *toy;* ŏŏ *good;* ōō *goo;* ou *out;* TH *thin;* T̲H̲ *then;* ZH *vision*

ves·ti·men·ta·ry /ˌvestəˈment(ə)rē/ ▶ **adj.** formal of or relating to clothing or dress: *lack of vestimentary rigor.* [19th C.: from L. *vestimentum* 'clothing' + -ARY¹.]

vest·ing /ˈvestiNG/ ▶ **n.** **1** the conveying to an employee of unconditional entitlement to a share in a pension fund. **2** medium- to heavy-weight cloth with a decorated or raised pattern, used for vests and other garments.

ves·ti·ture /ˈvestiCHər; -ˌCHo͝or/ ▶ **n.** archaic clothing. [19th C.: based on L. *vestire* 'clothe.']

Vest·man·na·ey·jar /ˈvestˌmänəˈāˌyär/ Icelandic name for WESTMANN ISLANDS.

vest·ment /ˈves(t)mənt/ ▶ **n.** (usu. **vestments**) a chasuble or other robe worn by the clergy or choristers during services. ■ archaic a garment, esp. a ceremonial or official robe. [ME: from OFr. *vestiment,* from L. *vestimentum,* from *vestire* 'clothe' (see VEST).]

vest-pock·et ▶ **adj.** (esp. of a reference book) small enough to fit into a pocket. ■ very small in size or scale: *a vest-pocket park.*

ves·try /ˈvestrē/ ▶ **n.** (pl. **-tries**) a room or building attached to a church, used as an office and for changing into vestments. ■ a meeting of parishioners, originally in a vestry, for the conduct of parochial business. ■ a body of parishioners meeting in such a way. [ME: prob. from an Anglo-Norman Fr. alt. of OFr. *vestiarie,* from L. *vestiarium.*]

ves·try·man /ˈvestrēmən/ ▶ **n.** (pl. **-men**) a member of a parochial vestry.

ves·ture /ˈvesCHər/ ▶ **n.** literary clothing; dress. [ME: from OFr., based on L. *vestire* 'clothe.']

ve·su·vi·an·ite /vəˈso͞ovēəˌnīt/ ▶ **n.** another term for IDOCRASE. [19th C.: from VESUVIUS + -AN + -ITE¹.]

Ve·su·vi·us /vəˈso͞ovēəs/ an active volcano near Naples, in southern Italy. A violent eruption in AD 79 buried the towns of Pompeii and Herculaneum.

vet¹ /vet/ ▶ **n.** informal a veterinary surgeon. ▶ **v.** (**vet·ted, vet·ting**) [trans.] make a careful and critical examination of (something). ■ (often **be vetted**) esp. Brit. investigate (someone) thoroughly, esp. in order to ensure that they are suitable for a job requiring secrecy, loyalty, or trustworthiness: *each applicant will be vetted by police.* [19th C.: abbrev. of VETERINARY or VETERINARIAN.]

vet² ▶ **n.** informal a veteran.

vetch /veCH/ ▶ **n.** a widely distributed scrambling herbaceous plant (genus *Vicia*) of the pea family that is cultivated as a silage or fodder crop. [ME: from Anglo-Norman Fr. *veche,* from L. *vicia.*]

vetch·ling /ˈveCHliNG/ ▶ **n.** a widely distributed scrambling plant (genus *Lathyrus*) of the pea family, related to the vetches but typically having fewer leaflets.

vet·er·an /ˈvet(ə)rən/ ▶ **n.** a person who has had long experience in a particular field, esp. military service: *a veteran of two world wars.* [16th C.: from Fr. *vétéran* or L. *veteranus,* from *vetus* 'old.']

Vet·er·ans Day ▶ **n.** a public holiday held on the anniversary of the end of World War I (November 11) to honor US veterans and victims of all wars. It replaced Armistice Day in 1954.

vet·er·i·nar·i·an /ˌvet(ə)rəˈne(ə)rēən/ ▶ **n.** a person qualified to treat diseased or injured animals.

vet·er·i·nar·y /ˈvet(ə)rəˌnerē/ ▶ **adj.** of or relating to the diseases, injuries, and treatment of farm and domestic animals: *veterinary medicine.* ▶ **n.** (pl. **-nar·ies**) dated a veterinarian. [18th C.: from L. *veterinarius,* from *veterinae* 'cattle.']

vet·i·ver /ˈvetəvər/ (also **vet·i·vert** /-vərt/) ▶ **n.** a fragrant extract or essential oil obtained from the root of an Indian grass (*Vetiveria zizanioides*), used in perfumery and aromatherapy. [19th C.: from Fr. *vétiver,* from Tamil *veṭṭivēr,* from *vēr* 'root.']

ve·to /ˈvētō/ ▶ **n.** (pl. **-toes**) a constitutional right to reject a decision or proposal made by a law-making body: *a veto over appointments to key posts.* ■ such a rejection. ■ a prohibition: *his veto on drinking.* ▶ **v.** (**-toes, -toed**) [trans.] exercise a veto against (a decision or proposal made by a law-making body). ■ refuse to accept or allow. — **ve·to·er n.** [17th C.: from L., 'I forbid.']

vex /veks/ ▶ **v.** [trans.] make (someone) feel annoyed, frustrated, or worried, esp. with trivial matters. ■ archaic cause distress to: *thou shalt not vex a stranger.* — **vex·er n. vex·ing·ly adv.** [ME: from OFr. *vexer,* from L. *vexare* 'shake, disturb.']

vex·a·tion /vekˈsāSHən/ ▶ **n.** the state of being annoyed, frustrated, or worried: *Jenny bit her lip in vexation.* ■ something that causes annoyance, frustration, or worry: *the cares and vexations of life.*

vex·a·tious /vekˈsāSHəs/ ▶ **adj.** causing or tending to cause annoyance, frustration, or worry. ■ Law denoting an action or the bringer of an action that is brought without sufficient grounds for winning, purely to cause annoyance to the defendant. — **vex·a·tious·ly adv. vex·a·tious·ness n.**

vexed /vekst/ ▶ **adj.** **1** [attrib.] (of a problem or issue) difficult and much debated; problematic. **2** annoyed, frustrated, or worried. — **vex·ed·ly** /ˈveksədlē/ **adv.**

vex·il·lol·o·gy /ˌveksəˈläləjē/ ▶ **n.** the study of flags. — **vex·il·lo·log·i·cal** /-ləˈläjikəl/ **adj. vex·il·lol·o·gist** /-jist/ **n.** [1950s: from L. *vexillum* 'flag' + -LOGY.]

vex·il·lum /vekˈsiləm/ ▶ **n.** (pl. **vex·il·la** /vekˈsilə/) **1** a Roman military standard or banner, esp. one of a maniple. ■ a body of troops under such a standard. **2** Bot. the standard of a papilionaceous flower. **3** Ornithol. the vane of a feather. [L., from *vehere* 'carry.']

VF ▶ **abbr.** ■ video frequency. ■ visual field.

VFR ▶ **abbr.** visual flight rules, used under conditions of good visibility.

VG ▶ **abbr.** ■ very good. ■ vicar-general.

VGA ▶ **abbr.** video graphics array, a standard for defining color display screens for computers.

VHF ▶ **abbr.** very high frequency (denoting radio waves of a frequency of *c.*30–300 MHz and a wavelength of *c.*1–10 meters).

VHS trademark ▶ **abbr.** video home system, denoting the video system and tape used by domestic video recorders and some camcorders.

VI ▶ **abbr.** Virgin Islands.

vi·a /ˈvīə; ˈvēə/ ▶ **prep.** traveling through (a place) en route to a destination: *they came to Europe via Turkey.* ■ by way of; through: *they can see the artists' works via a camera hookup.* ■ by means of: *a file sent via e-mail.* [18th C.: from L., ablative of *via* 'way, road.']

Vi·a Ap·pi·a /ˈvēə ˈäpēə; ˈvīə/ Latin name for APPIAN WAY.

vi·a·ble /ˈvīəbəl/ ▶ **adj.** capable of working successfully; feasible: *the proposed investment was economically viable.* ■ Bot. (of a seed or spore) able to germinate. ■ Biol. (of a plant, animal, or cell) capable of surviving or living successfully, esp. under particular environmental conditions. ■ Med. (of a fetus or unborn child) able to live after birth. — **vi·a·bil·i·ty** /ˌvīəˈbilətē/ **n. vi·a·bly** /-blē/ **adv.** [19th C.: from Fr., from *vie* 'life,' from L. *vita.*]

Vi·a Cru·cis /ˈvēə ˈkro͞oCHis/ ▶ **n.** another term for THE WAY OF THE CROSS (see WAY). ■ fig. a lengthy and distressing or painful procedure. [L.]

vi·a dol·o·ro·sa /ˈvēə ˌdäləˈrōsə; ˌdōlə-/ ▶ **n.** (**the Via Dolorosa**) the route believed to have been taken by Jesus through Jerusalem to Calvary. ■ fig. a distressing or painful journey or process. [L., lit. 'painful path.']

vi·a·duct /ˈvīəˌdəkt/ ▶ **n.** a long bridgelike structure, typically a series of arches, carrying a road or railroad across a valley or other low ground. [19th C.: from L. *via* 'way,' on the pattern of *aqueduct.*]

Vi·ag·ra /vīˈagrə/ ▶ **n.** trademark a synthetic compound used to enhance male potency.

vi·al /ˈvī(ə)l/ ▶ **n.** a small container, typically cylindrical and made of glass, used esp. for holding liquid medicines. [ME: alt. of PHIAL.]

vi·a me·di·a /ˈvēə ˈmädēə; ˈvīə ˈmēdēə/ ▶ **n.** formal a middle way or compromise between extremes. [L.]

vi·and /ˈvīənd/ ▶ **n.** (usu. **viands**) literary an item of food: *an unlimited assortment of viands.* [ME: from OFr. *viande* 'food,' from an alt. of L. *vivenda,* neut. pl. gerundive of *vivere* 'to live.']

vi·a ne·ga·ti·va /ˈvēə ˌnegəˈtēvə; ˈvīə/ ▶ **n.** Theol. a way of describing something by saying what it is not, esp. denying that any finite concept of attribute can be identified with or used of God or ultimate reality. [L., lit. 'negative path.']

vi·at·i·cal set·tle·ment /vīˈatikəl; vē-/ ▶ **n.** an arrangement whereby a person with a terminal illness sells their life insurance policy to a third party for less than its mature value, in order to benefit from the proceeds while alive. [1990s: *viatical* from L. *viaticus* 'relating to a journey or departing' + -AL.]

vi·at·i·cum /vīˈatikəm; vē-/ ▶ **n.** (pl. **-ca** /-kə/) **1** the Eucharist as given to a person near or in danger of death. **2** archaic a supply of provisions or an official allowance of money for a journey. [16th C.: from L., neut. of *viaticus,* from *via* 'road.']

vibe /vīb/ ▶ **n.** informal **1** (usu. **vibes**) a person's emotional state or the atmosphere of a place as communicated to and felt by others: *a lot of moody people giving off* **bad vibes**. [abbrev. of *vibrations.*] **2** (**vibes**) another term for VIBRAPHONE.

vib·ist /ˈvībist/ ▶ **n.** a musician who plays the vibraphone.

vi·brac·u·lum /vīˈbrakyələm/ ▶ **n.** (pl. **-la** /-lə/) Zool. (in some bryozoans) any of a number of modified zooids that bear a long whiplike seta, serving to prevent other organisms from settling on the colony. — **vi·brac·u·lar** /-lər/ **adj.** [19th C.: mod. L., from L. *vibrare* (see VIBRATE).]

vi·bra·harp /ˈvībrəˌhärp/ ▶ **n.** another term for VIBRAPHONE.

vi·brant /ˈvībrənt/ ▶ **adj.** full of energy and enthusiasm. ■ quivering; pulsating: *Rose was vibrant with anger.* ■ (of color) bright and striking. ■ (of sound) strong or resonating: *a vibrant male voice.* — **vi·bran·cy** /-brənsē/ **n. vi·brant·ly adv.**

vibraphone

vi·bra·phone /ˈvībrəˌfōn/ ▶ **n.** a musical percussion instrument with a double row of tuned metal bars, each above a tubular resonator containing a motor-driven rotating vane, giving a vibrato effect. — **vi·bra·**

phon·ist /-ˌfōnist/ n. [1920s: from VIBRATO + -PHONE.]

vi·brate /ˈvīˌbrāt/ ▶v. move or cause to move continuously and rapidly to and fro: [intrans.] *the cabin started to vibrate* | [trans.] *the bumblebee vibrated its wings.* ■ [intrans.] (**vibrate with**) quiver with (a quality or emotion). ■ [intrans.] (of a sound) resonate; continue to be heard. ■ [intrans.] (of a pendulum) swing to and fro. [ME: from L. *vibrat-* 'moved to and fro,' from the v. *vibrare.*]

vi·bra·tile /ˈvībrətl; -ˌtīl/ ▶adj. Biol. (of cilia, flagella, or other small appendages) capable of or characterized by oscillatory motion.

vi·bra·tion /vīˈbrāsHən/ ▶n. an instance of vibrating. ■ Physics an oscillation of the parts of a fluid or an elastic solid whose equilibrium has been disturbed or of an electromagnetic wave. ■ (**vibrations**) informal a person's emotional state, the atmosphere of a place, or the associations of an object, as communicated to and felt by others. — **vi·bra·tion·al** /-sHənl/ adj.

vi·bra·to /vəˈbrätō; vī-/ ▶n. Music a rapid, slight variation in pitch in singing or playing some musical instruments, producing a stronger or richer tone. Compare with TREMOLO. [19th C.: Ital., past part. of *vibrare* 'vibrate.']

vi·bra·tor /ˈvīˌbrātər/ ▶n. a device that vibrates or causes vibration, in particular: ■ a device used for massage or sexual stimulation. ■ Music a reed in a reed organ.

vi·bra·to·ry /ˈvībrəˌtôrē/ ▶adj. of, relating to, or causing vibration.

vib·ri·o /ˈvibrēˌō/ ▶n. (pl. **-os**) Med. a waterborne bacterium (*Vibrio* and related genera) of a group that includes some pathogenic kinds that cause cholera, gastroenteritis, and septicemia. [mod. L., from L. *vibrare* 'vibrate.']

vi·bris·sa /vīˈbrisə/ ▶n. (pl. **-bris·sae** /-brisē; -ˈbrisˌī/) Zool. any of the long stiff hairs growing around the mouth or elsewhere on the face of many mammals, used as organs of touch; whiskers. ■ Ornithol. each of the coarse bristlelike feathers growing around the gape of certain insectivorous birds that catch insects in flight. [17th C.: from L., 'nostril hair.']

vi·bur·num /vīˈbərnəm/ ▶n. a shrub or small tree (genus *Viburnum*) of the honeysuckle family, typically bearing flat or rounded clusters of small white flowers. Its many species and ornamental hybrids include the guelder rose and wayfaring tree. [mod. L., from L., 'wayfaring tree.']

vic·ar /ˈvikər/ ▶n. (in the Roman Catholic Church) a representative or deputy of a bishop. ■ (in the Episcopal Church) a clergyman in charge of a chapel. ■ (in the Church of England) an incumbent of a parish where tithes formerly passed to a chapter or religious house or layman. ■ (in other Anglican Churches) a member of the clergy deputizing for another. ■ a cleric or choir member appointed to sing certain parts of a cathedral service. — **vic·ar·ship** /-ˌsHip/ n. [ME: via Anglo-Norman Fr. from OFr. *vicaire*, from L. *vicarius* 'substitute,' from *vic-* 'change, turn, place' (cf. VICE[3]).]

vic·ar·age /ˈvikərij/ ▶n. the residence of a vicar. ■ hist. the benefice or living of a vicar.

vic·ar ap·os·tol·ic ▶n. a Roman Catholic missionary. ■ a titular bishop.

vic·ar-gen·er·al ▶n. (pl. **vic·ars-gen·er·al**) an Anglican official serving as a deputy or assistant to a bishop or archbishop. ■ (in the Roman Catholic Church) a bishop's representative in matters of jurisdiction or administration.

vi·car·i·al /vīˈke(ə)rēəl; vi-/ ▶adj. archaic of, relating to, or serving as a vicar.

vi·car·i·ate /viˈke(ə)rēit; vī-; -ˌāt/ ▶n. the office or authority of a vicar. ■ a church or parish ministered to by a vicar.

vi·car·i·ous /vīˈkerēəs; vi-/ ▶adj. experienced in the imagination through the feelings or actions of another person: *vicarious pleasure.* ■ acting or done for another: *a vicarious atonement.* ■ Physiol. of or pertaining to the performance by one organ of the functions normally discharged by another. — **vi·car·i·ous·ly** adv. **vi·car·i·ous·ness** n. [17th C.: from L. *vicarius* 'substitute' (see VICAR) + -OUS.]

Vic·ar of Christ ▶n. (in the Roman Catholic Church) a title of the pope.

vice[1] /vīs/ ▶n. immoral or wicked behavior. ■ criminal activities involving prostitution, pornography, or drugs. ■ an immoral or wicked personal characteristic. ■ a weakness of character or behavior; a bad habit: *cigars happen to be my father's vice.* — **vice·less** adj. [ME: via OFr. from L. *vitium.*]

vice[2] ▶n. British spelling of VISE.

vice[3] /vīs; ˈvīsē; ˈvīsə/ ▶prep. as a substitute for: *the letter was drafted by David Hunt, vice Bevin who was ill.* [L., ablative of *vic-* 'change.']

vice[4] /vīs/ (also **vice-**) ▶comb. form acting as deputy or substitute for; next in rank: *vice regent* | *vice-consul.* [from L. *vice* 'in place of' (cf. VICE[3]).]

vice ad·mi·ral /vīs/ ▶n. a naval officer of very high rank, in particular an officer in the US Navy or Coast Guard ranking above rear admiral and below admiral.

vice chan·cel·lor /vīs/ ▶n. **1** a deputy chancellor, esp. one of a British university who discharges most of its administrative duties. **2** Law a judge appointed to assist a chancellor, esp. in chancery court or court of equity.

vice·ge·rent /ˌvīsˈji(ə)rənt/ ▶n. formal a person exercising delegated power on behalf of a sovereign or ruler. ■ a person regarded as an earthly representative of God or a god, esp. the pope. — **vice·ge·ren·cy** n. (pl. **-cies**). [16th C.: from med. L. *vicegerent-* '(person) holding office,' from L. *vic-* 'office, place, turn' + *gerere* 'carry on, hold.']

vice pres·i·dent /vīs/ ▶n. an official or executive ranking below and deputizing for a president. — **vice pres·i·den·cy** n. (pl. **-cies**) **vice pres·i·den·tial** /ˌpreziˈdencHəl/ adj.

vice·re·gal /ˌvīsˈrēgəl/ ▶adj. of or relating to a viceroy.

vice·reine /ˈvīsˌrān/ ▶n. the wife of a viceroy. ■ a female viceroy. [19th C.: from Fr., from *vice-* 'in place of' + *reine* 'queen.']

vice·roy /ˈvīsˌroi/ ▶n. **1** a ruler exercising authority in a colony on behalf of a sovereign. **2** a migratory orange and black butterfly (*Limenitis archippus*) that closely resembles the monarch but is typically somewhat smaller. The caterpillar feeds on willow leaves, and the adult mimics the unpalatable monarch. — **vice·roy·al** /ˌvīsˈroi-əl/ adj. **vice·roy·ship** /-ˌsHip/ n. [16th C.: from archaic Fr., from *vice-* 'in place of' + *roi* 'king.']

vice·roy·al·ty /ˌvīsˈroi-əltē; ˈvīsˌroi-/ (also **Vice·roy·al·ty**) ▶n. (pl. **-ties**) the office, position, or authority of a viceroy. ■ a territory governed by a viceroy.

vice squad /vīs/ ▶n. a department or division of a police force that enforces laws against prostitution, drug abuse, illegal gambling, etc.

vice ver·sa /ˈvīs ˈvərsə; ˈvīsə/ ▶adv. with the main items in the preceding statement the other way around. [17th C.: from L., lit. 'in-turned position.']

Vi·chy /ˈvēsHē; ˈvisHē/ a town in south central France; pop. 28,000. A spa town, it is the source of an effervescent mineral water. During World War II, it was the headquarters of the regime set up after the German occupation of northern France.

vi·chys·soise /ˌvēsHēˈswäz; ˌvisHē-; ˈvēsHēˌswäz; ˈvisHē-/ ▶n. a soup made with potatoes, leeks, and cream and typically served chilled. [Fr. (fem.), 'of *Vichy*' (see VICHY).]

vic·i·nage /ˈvisənij/ ▶n. another term for VICINITY.

vic·i·nal /ˈvisənl/ ▶adj. rare neighboring; adjacent. ■ Chem. relating to or denoting substituents attached to adjacent atoms in a ring or chain. [17th C.: from Fr., or from L. *vicinalis*, from *vicinus* 'neighbor.']

vi·cin·i·ty /vəˈsinətē/ ▶n. (pl. **-ties**) the area near or surrounding a particular place. [16th C. (in the sense 'proximity'): from L. *vicinitas*, from *vicinus* 'neighbor.']

vi·cious /ˈvisHəs/ ▶adj. **1** deliberately cruel or violent. ■ (of an animal) wild and dangerous to people. ■ fig. serious or dangerous: *a vicious flu bug.* ■ literary immoral: *every soul on earth shall perish.* **2** archaic (of language or a line of reasoning) imperfect; defective. — **vi·cious·ly** adv. **vi·cious·ness** n. [ME: from OFr. *vicious* or L. *vitiosus*, from *vitium* 'vice.']

vi·cious cir·cle (also **vi·cious cy·cle**) ▶n. **1** a sequence of reciprocal cause and effect in which two or more elements intensify and aggravate each other, leading inexorably to a worsening of the situation. **2** Logic a definition or statement that begs the question.

vi·cis·si·tude /vəˈsisəˌt(y)o͞od/ ▶n. (usu. **vicissitudes**) a change of circumstances or fortune, typically one that is unwelcome or unpleasant. ■ literary alternation between opposite or contrasting things: *the vicissitude of the seasons.* — **vi·cis·si·tu·di·nous** /-ˌsisəˈt(y)o͞odn-əs; -ˈt(y)o͞odnəs/ adj. [17th C. (in the sense 'alternation'): from Fr., or from L. *vicissitudo*, from *vicissim* 'by turns,' from *vic-* 'turn, change.']

Vicks·burg /ˈviksˌbərg/ a city on the Mississippi River, in western Mississippi; pop. 26,407. In 1863, during the Civil War, it was successfully besieged by Union forces.

vi·comte /vēˈkôNt/ ▶n. (pl. same) a French nobleman corresponding in rank to a viscount.

vi·com·tesse /ˌvēkôNˈtes/ ▶n. (pl. same) a French noblewoman corresponding in rank to a viscountess.

vic·tim /ˈviktəm/ ▶n. a person harmed, injured, or killed as a result of a crime, accident, or other event or action. ■ a person who is tricked or duped: *the victim of a hoax.* ■ a living creature killed as a religious sacrifice.

– PHRASES **fall victim to** be hurt, killed, damaged, or destroyed by: *streams have fallen victim to the drought.* [15th C.: from L. *victima.*]

vic·tim·ize /ˈviktəˌmīz/ ▶v. [trans.] single (someone) out for cruel or unjust treatment. — **vic·tim·i·za·tion** /ˌviktəməˈzāsHən/ n. **vic·tim·iz·er** n.

vic·tim·less /ˈviktəmləs/ ▶adj. denoting a crime in which there is no injured party.

vic·tim·less crime ▶n. a legal offense to which all parties consent and no party is injured.

vic·tim·ol·o·gy /ˌviktəˈmäləjē/ ▶n. (pl. **-gies**) the study of the victims of crime and the psychological effects on them of their experience. ■ the possession of an outlook, arising from real or imagined victimization, that seems to glorify and indulge the state of being a victim.

vic·tor /ˈviktər/ ▶n. **1** a person who defeats an enemy or opponent in a battle, game, or other competition. **2** a code word representing the letter V, used in radio communication. [ME: from Anglo-Norman Fr. *victo(u)r* or L. *victor*, from *vincere* 'conquer.']

Victor Em·man·u·el II /ˈviktər iˈmanyo͞oəl/ (1820–78), ruler of the kingdom of Sardinia 1849–61 and first king of united Italy 1861–78.

Victor Em·man·u·el III (1869–1947), king of Italy 1900–46. He invited Mussolini to form a government in 1922 and lost all political power.

Vic·to·ri·a[1] /vik'tôrēə/ **1** a state in southeastern Australia; pop. 4,394,000; capital, Melbourne. **2** a city at the southern tip of Vancouver Island, capital of British Columbia; pop. 71,228. **3** the capital of the Seychelles, on the island of Mahé; pop. 24,000. **4** the administrative center of Hong Kong; pop. 591,000.

Vic·to·ri·a[2] (1819–1901), queen of Great Britain and Ireland 1837–1901 and empress of India 1876–1901. Her reign was the longest in British history.

Vic·to·ri·a[3] (also **vic·to·ri·a**) ▶ **n.** hist. a light four-wheeled horse-drawn carriage with a collapsible hood, seats for two passengers, and an elevated driver's seat in front.

Vic·to·ri·a, Lake the largest lake in Africa, in Uganda and Tanzania.

Vic·to·ri·a Cross (abbr.: **VC**) ▶ **n.** a decoration awarded for conspicuous bravery in the British Commonwealth armed services, instituted by Queen Victoria in 1856.

Vic·to·ri·a Day n. (in Canada) the Monday preceding May 24, observed as a national holiday to commemorate the birthday of Queen Victoria.

Vic·to·ri·a de Du·ran·go /vik'tôrēə dā do͞o'rängɡō; d(y)o͞o'raNG-/ full name for DURANGO.

Vic·to·ri·a Falls a waterfall 355 feet (109 m) high, on the Zambezi River, on the Zimbabwe–Zambia border.

Vic·to·ri·an /vik'tôrēən/ ▶ **adj.** of or relating to the reign of Queen Victoria: *a Victorian house.* ■ of or relating to the attitudes and values of this period, regarded as characterized esp. by a stifling and prudish moral earnestness. ▶ **n.** a person who lived during the Victorian period. — **Vic·to·ri·an·ism** /-ə,nizəm/ **n.**

Vic·to·ri·an·a /vik,tôrē'anə; -'änə/ ▶ **plural n.** articles, esp. collectors' items, from the Victorian period. ■ matters or attitudes relating to or characteristic of this period.

Vic·to·ri·a Nile the upper part of the White Nile River.

vic·to·ri·ous /vik'tôrēəs/ ▶ **adj.** having won a victory; triumphant: *a victorious army.* ■ of or characterized by victory: *victorious campaigns.* — **vic·to·ri·ous·ly adv. vic·to·ri·ous·ness n.**

vic·to·ry /'vikt(ə)rē/ ▶ **n.** (pl. **-ies**) an act of defeating an enemy or opponent in a battle, game, or other competition: *an election victory.* [ME: from Anglo-Norman Fr. *victorie*, from L. *victoria*.]

vic·to·ry gar·den ▶ **n.** a vegetable garden, esp. a home garden, planted to increase food production during a war.

vic·to·ry lap ▶ **n.** a celebratory circuit of a sports field, track, or court by the person or team that has won a contest.

vic·to·ry roll ▶ **n.** a roll performed by an aircraft as a sign of triumph, typically after a successful mission.

vict·ual /'vitl/ dated ▶ **n.** (**victuals**) food or provisions, typically as prepared for consumption. ▶ **v.** (**-ualed, -ual·ing**; Brit. **-ualled, -ual·ling**) [trans.] provide with food or other stores. ■ [intrans.] archaic obtain or lay in food or other stores. ■ [intrans.] archaic eat: *victual with me next Saturday.* [ME: from OFr. *vitaille*, from late L. *victualia*, neut. pl. of L. *victualis*, from *victus* 'food'; rel. to *vivere* 'to live.']

vict·ual·er /'vitl-ər/ (Brit. **vic·tu·al·ler**) ▶ **n. 1** dated a person providing or selling food or other provisions. ■ a ship providing supplies for troops or other ships. **2** (also **li·censed vic·tu·al·er**) Brit. a person who is licensed to sell alcoholic liquor.

vi·cu·ña /vī'k(y)o͞onə və-; 'ko͞onyə/ ▶ **n.** a mammal (*Vicugna vicugna*) of the camel family, a wild relative of the llama, inhabiting mountainous regions of South America and valued for its fine silky wool. ■ cloth made from this wool, or an imitation of it. [17th C.: from Sp., from Quechua.]

vid /vid/ ▶ **n.** informal short for VIDEO.

Vi·dal /vi'däl/, Gore (1925–), US writer; born *Eugene Luther Vidal*. His novels include *Myra Breckenridge* (1968) and *Lincoln* (1984).

vi·de /'vēdē; 'vē,dā; 'vīdē/ ▶ **v.** [with obj., in imper.] see; consult (used as an instruction in a text to refer the reader to a specified passage, book, author, etc., for fuller or further information): *vide the chart on page 10.* [L., 'see!,' imper. of *videre*.]

vi·de·li·cet /və'delə,set; -sət; -'dālə,ket/ ▶ **adv.** more formal term for VIZ. [L., from *videre* 'to see' + *licet* 'it is permissible.']

vid·e·o /'vidē,ō/ ▶ **n.** (pl. **-os**) the system of recording, reproducing, or broadcasting moving visual images on or from videotape. ■ a movie or other piece of material recorded on videotape. ■ a videocassette. ■ a short movie made by a pop or rock group to accompany a song when broadcast on television. ■ Brit. a videocassette recorder. [1930s: from L. *videre* 'to see,' on the pattern of *audio*.]

vid·e·o ar·cade ▶ **n.** an indoor area containing coin-operated video games.

vid·e·o cam·er·a ▶ **n.** a camera for recording images on videotape or for transmitting them to a monitor screen.

vid·e·o·cas·sette /,vidēōkə'set/ ▶ **n.** a cassette of videotape.

vid·e·o·cas·sette re·cord·er (abbr.: **VCR**) ▶ **n.** a device that, when linked to a television set, can be used for recording on and playing videotapes.

vid·e·o·con·fer·ence /'vidēō,känf(ə)rəns/ ▶ **n.** an arrangement in which television sets linked to telephone lines are used to enable a group of people in several different locations to communicate with each other in sound and vision. — **vid·e·o·con·fer·enc·ing n.**

vid·e·o·disc /'vidēō,disk/ (also **vid·e·o·disk**) ▶ **n.** a CD-ROM or other disk used to store visual images and sound.

vid·e·o dis·play ter·min·al (abbr.: **VDT**) ▶ **n.** Comput. a device for displaying input signals as characters on a screen, typically a monitor.

vid·e·o game ▶ **n.** a game played by electronically manipulating images produced by a computer program on a television screen or display.

vid·e·o·graph·ics /,vidēō'grafiks/ ▶ **plural n.** visual images produced using computer technology. ■ [treated as sing.] the manipulation of video images using a computer.

vid·e·og·ra·phy /,vidē'ägrəfē/ ▶ **n.** the process or art of making video films. — **vid·e·og·ra·pher** /-fər/ **n.**

vid·e·o jock·ey ▶ **n.** a person who introduces and plays music videos for a broadcast, party, or other entertainment.

vid·e·o mail ▶ **n.** an e-mail message with a video clip attached.

vid·e·o·phile /'vidēə,fīl/ ▶ **n.** an enthusiast for or devotee of video recordings or video technology.

vid·e·o·phone /'vidēō,fōn/ ▶ **n.** a telephone device transmitting and receiving a visual image as well as sound.

vid·e·o·play /'vidēō,plā/ ▶ **n.** another term for TELEPLAY.

vid·e·o re·cord·er ▶ **n.** another term for VIDEOCASSETTE RECORDER. — **video recording n.**

vid·e·o·scope /'vidēə,skōp/ ▶ **n.** a fiber-optic rod attached to a camera that transmits images from within the body to a television monitor, used in diagnosis and surgery.

vid·e·o·tape /'vidēō,tāp/ ▶ **n.** magnetic tape for recording and reproducing visual images and sound. ■ a videocassette. ■ a film or other piece of material recorded on videotape. ▶ **v.** [trans.] make a video recording of (an event or broadcast): *his arrest was videotaped.*

vid·e·o·tex /'vidēō,teks/ (also **vid·e·o·text** /-,tekst/) ▶ **n.** an electronic information system such as teletext. [1970s: from VIDEO + TEXT.]

vi·dette ▶ **n.** var. of VEDETTE.

vid·i·con /'vidi,kän/ ▶ **n.** Electron. a small television camera tube in which the image is formed on a transparent electrode coated with photoconductive material, the current from which varies as it is scanned by a beam of low-speed electrons. [1950s: from VIDEO and *iconoscope*.]

vid·i·ot /'vidēət/ ▶ **n.** informal a habitual, undiscriminating watcher of television or videotapes. [1960s: blend of VIDEO and IDIOT.]

vie /vī/ ▶ **v.** (**vy·ing**) [intrans.] compete eagerly with someone in order to do or achieve something. [16th C.: prob. a shortening of obs. *envy*, via OFr. from L. *invitare* 'challenge.']

Vi·en·na /vē'enə/ the capital of Austria, in the northeastern part of the country on the Danube River; pop. 1,533,000. German name WIEN. — **Vi·en·nese** /,vēə'nēz; -'nēs/ **adj. & n.**

Vi·en·na sau·sage ▶ **n.** a small frankfurter made of pork, beef, or veal.

Vi·en·nese waltz ▶ **n.** a waltz characterized by a slight anticipation of the second beat of the bar and having a romantic quality. ■ a piece of music written in this style.

Vien·tiane /,vyen'tyän; vē,entē'än/ the capital of Laos, on the Mekong River; pop. 377,000.

Vier·wald·stät·ter·see /fir'vält,SHtetər,zā/ German name for Lake Lucerne (see LUCERNE, LAKE).

Vi·et·cong /vē,et'kôNG; ,vyet-; ,vēət-; -'käNG/ (also **Vi·et Cong**) ▶ **n.** (pl. same) a member of the communist guerrilla movement in Vietnam that fought the South Vietnamese government forces 1954–75 with the support of the North Vietnamese army and opposed the South Vietnamese and US forces in the Vietnam War. [Vietnamese, lit. 'Vietnamese Communist.']

Vi·et·minh /vē,et'min; ,vyet-; ,vēət-/ ▶ **n.** (pl. same) a member of a communist-dominated nationalist movement, formed in 1941, that fought for Vietnamese independence from French rule. Members of the Vietminh later joined with the Vietcong. [from Vietnamese *Viet*-Nam Dôc-Lâp Dông-*Minh* 'Vietnamese Independence League.']

Vi·et·nam /vē,et'näm; ,vyet-; ,vēət-; -'nam/ a country in Southeast Asia. *See box on next page.*

Vi·et·nam·ese /vē,etnə'mēz; ,vyet-; ,vēət-; -'mēs/ ▶ **adj.** of or relating to Vietnam, its people, or their language. ▶ **n.** (pl. same) **1** a native or national of Vietnam, or a person of Vietnamese descent. **2** the language of Vietnam, which is probably a Mon-Khmer language although much of its vocabulary is derived from Chinese.

Vi·et·nam·i·za·tion /vē,etnəmə'zāSHən; ,vyet-; ,vēət-/ ▶ **n.** (in the Vietnam War) the US policy of withdrawing its troops and transferring the responsibility and direction of the war effort to the government of South Vietnam.

Vi·et·nam War a war between communist North Vietnam and US-backed South Vietnam. Since the partition of Vietnam in 1954, the communist North had attempted to unite the country as a communist state. In 1964, US Army forces were sent to Vietnam, supported by contingents from South Korea, Australia, New Zealand, and Thailand. The Tet Offensive of 1968 damaged US confidence and US forces began to be withdrawn, finally leaving in 1973. The North Vietnamese captured Saigon to end the war in 1975.

view /vyo͞o/ ▶ **n. 1** the ability to see something or to be seen from a particular place. ■ a sight or prospect, typically of attractive natural scenery, that can be taken in by the eye from a particular place: *a view of the castle.* ■ a work of art depicting such a sight. ■ the visual appearance or an image of something when looked at in a particular way: *an aerial view of the lake.* ■ an inspection of things for sale by prospective purchasers, esp. of works of art at an exhibition. ■ Law (in court proceedings) a formal inspection by the judge and jury of the scene of a crime or property mentioned in evidence. **2** a particular way of considering or regarding something; an attitude or opinion: *strong political views.* ▶**v. 1** [trans.] look at or inspect (something). ■ watch (something) on television. ■ Hunting see (a fox) break cover. **2** [with obj. and adverbial] regard in a particular light or with a particular attitude: *viewing the rise in rabbit numbers.*

– PHRASES **in full view** clearly visible. **in view** visible to someone. ■ as one's aim or objective. ■ in one's mind when forming a judgment. **in view of** because or as a result of. **on view** (esp. of a work of art) being shown or exhibited to the public. **with a view to** with the hope, aim, or intention of. — **view·a·ble** adj. [ME: from Anglo-Norman Fr. *vieue*, fem. past part. of *veoir* 'see,' from L. *videre*.]

Vietnam

Official name: Socialist Republic of Vietnam
Location: Southeast Asia, on the South China Sea
Area: 127,300 square miles (329,600 sq km)
Population: 82,689,000
Capital: Hanoi
Languages: Vietnamese (official), English, French, Chinese, and Khmer mountain area languages
Currency: dong

view·da·ta /'vyōō,datə; -,dātə/ esp. Brit. ▶**n.** a news and information service in which computer data is sent by a telephone link and displayed on a television screen.

view·er /'vyōōər/ ▶**n. 1** a person who looks at or inspects something. ■ a person watching television or a movie. **2** a device for looking at slides or similar photographic images.

view·er·ship /'vyōōər,SHip/ ▶**n.** [treated as sing. or pl.] the audience for a particular television program or channel.

view·find·er /'vyōō,fīndər/ ▶**n.** a device on a camera showing the field of view of the lens, used in framing and focusing the picture.

view·graph /'vyōō,graf/ ▶**n.** a graph or other data produced as a transparency for projection onto a screen or for transmission during a teleconference.

view hal·loo ▶**n.** a shout given by a hunter on seeing a fox break cover.

view·ing /'vyōōiNG/ ▶**n.** the action of inspecting or looking at something: *viewing by appointment.* ■ the action of watching something on television. ■ an opportunity to see something, esp. a work of art.

view·less /'vyōōləs/ ▶**adj. 1** not having or affording a pleasant sight or prospect. **2** literary unable to be seen; invisible.

view·point /'vyōō,point/ ▶**n.** another term for POINT OF VIEW.

view·port /'vyōō,pôrt/ ▶**n.** a window in a spacecraft or in the conning tower of an oil rig. ■ Comput. a framed area on a display screen for viewing information.

view·screen /'vyōō,skrēn/ ▶**n.** the screen on a television, VDT, or similar device on which images and data are displayed.

viff /vif/ (also **VIFF**) Aeron., informal ▶**n.** a technique used by a vertical takeoff aircraft to change direction abruptly by altering the direction of thrust of the aircraft's jet engines. ▶**v.** [intrans.] (of a vertical takeoff aircraft) change direction in such a way. [1970s: acronym from *vectoring in forward flight*.]

vig /vig/ ▶**n.** short for VIGORISH.

vi·ga /'vēgə/ ▶**n.** a rough-hewn roof timber or rafter, esp. in an adobe building. [Sp.]

vi·ges·i·mal /vī'jesəməl/ ▶**adj.** rare relating to or based on the number twenty. [17th C.: from L. *vigesimus* (from *viginti* 'twenty') + -AL.]

vig·il /'vijəl/ ▶**n. 1** a period of keeping awake during the time usually spent asleep, esp. to keep watch or pray. ■ a stationary, peaceful demonstration in support of a particular cause, typically without speeches. **2** (in the Christian Church) the eve of a festival or holy day as an occasion of religious observance. ■ (**vigils**) nocturnal devotions. [ME (sense 2): via OFr. from L. *vigilia*, from *vigil* 'awake.']

vig·i·lance /'vijələns/ ▶**n.** the action or state of keeping careful watch for possible danger or difficulties.

vig·i·lance com·mit·tee ▶**n.** a body of vigilantes.

vig·i·lant /'vijələnt/ ▶**adj.** keeping careful watch for possible danger or difficulties: *the burglar was spotted by vigilant neighbors.* — **vig·i·lant·ly** adv.

vig·i·lan·te /,vijə'lantē/ ▶**n.** a member of a self-appointed group of citizens who undertake law enforcement in their community without legal authority, typically because the legal agencies are thought to be inadequate. — **vig·i·lan·tism** /-,tizəm/ n. [19th C.: from Sp., lit. 'vigilant.']

vig·il light ▶**n.** a candle lighted and placed on a shrine as an act of devotion.

vig·ne·ron /,vēnyə'rôn; -'rōn/ ▶**n.** a person who cultivates grapes for winemaking. [Fr., from *vigne* 'vine.']

vi·gnette /vin'yet/ ▶**n. 1** a brief evocative description, account, or episode. **2** a small illustration or portrait photograph that fades into its background without a definite border. ■ a small ornamental design filling a space in a book or carving, typically based on foliage. ▶**v.** [trans.] portray (someone) in the style of a vignette. ■ produce (a photograph) in the style of a vignette by softening or shading away the edges of the subject. — **vi·gnet·tist** /-'yetist/ n. [ME: from Fr., dimin. of *vigne* 'vine.']

Vi·gny /vēn'yē/, Alfred Victor, Comte de (1797–1863), French poet, playwright, and novelist.

Vi·go /'vēgō/ a city in northwestern Spain; pop. 277,000.

vig·or /'vigər/ (Brit. **vig·our**) ▶**n. 1** physical strength and good health. ■ effort, energy, and enthusiasm: *they set about the new task with vigor.* ■ strong, healthy growth of a plant. **2** Law legal or binding force; validity. — **vig·or·less** /'vigərləs/ adj. [ME: from OFr. *vigour*, from L. *vigor*, from *vigere* 'be lively.']

vig·or·ish /'vigəriSH/ ▶**n.** informal **1** [in sing.] an excessive rate of interest on a loan, typically one from an illegal moneylender. **2** the percentage deducted from a gambler's winnings by the organizers of a game. [20th C.: prob. from Yiddish, from Russ. *vyigrysh* 'gain, winnings.']

vig·or·ous /'vig(ə)rəs/ ▶**adj.** (of a person) strong, healthy, and full of energy. ■ characterized by or involving physical strength, effort, or energy: *vigorous aerobic exercise.* ■ (of language) forceful: *a vigorous denial.* ■ (of a plant) growing strongly. — **vig·or·ous·ly** adv. **vig·or·ous·ness** n.

vi·hue·la /vē'(h)wālə/ ▶**n.** a type of early Spanish stringed musical instrument, in particular a type of guitar or a type of viol.

Vi·king[1] /'vīkiNG/ ▶**n.** any of the Scandinavian seafaring pirates and traders who raided and settled in many parts of northwestern Europe in the 8th–11th centuries. ▶**adj.** of or relating to the Vikings or the period in which they lived. [from ON *víkingr*, from *vík* 'creek' or OE *wīc* 'camp, dwelling place.']

Vi·king[2] either of two American space probes sent to Mars in 1975, each of which consisted of a lander that conducted experiments on the surface and an orbiter.

Vi·la /'vēlə/ (also **Port Vi·la**) the capital of Vanuatu, on the island of Efate; pop. 20,000.

vile /vīl/ ▶**adj.** extremely unpleasant. ■ morally bad; wicked: *as vile a rogue as ever lived.* ■ archaic of little worth or value. — **vile·ly** adv. **vile·ness** n. [ME: via OFr. from L. *vilis* 'cheap, base.']

vil·i·fy /ˈviləˌfī/ ▶ v. (-fies, -fied) [trans.] speak or write about in an abusively disparaging manner. — **vil·i·fi·ca·tion** /ˌviləfiˈkāsʜən/ n. **vil·i·fi·er** n. [ME (in the sense 'lower in value'): from late L. *vilificare*, from L. *vilis* 'of low value' (see VILE).]

vil·i·pend /ˈviləˌpend/ ▶ v. [trans.] archaic **1** regard as worthless or of little value; despise. **2** speak slightingly or abusively of; vilify. — **vil·i·pend·er** n. **vil·i·pens·ive** adj.

Vil·la /ˈvēyə/, Francisco (1878–1923), Mexican revolutionary; born *Doroteo Arango*, known as **Pancho Villa**.

vil·la /ˈvilə/ ▶ n. (esp. in continental Europe) a large and luxurious country residence. ■ a large country house of Roman times, having an estate and consisting of farm and residential buildings arranged around a courtyard. ■ Brit. a detached or semidetached house in a residential district, typically one that is Victorian or Edwardian in style. [17th C.: from Ital., from L.]

Vil·la·fran·chi·an /ˌviləˈfrаɴɢkēən/ ▶ adj. of, relating to, or denoting an age (or stage) in Europe crossing the boundary of the Upper Pliocene and Lower Pleistocene, lasting from about 3 to 1 million years ago. ■ [as n.] (**the Villafranchian**) the Villafranchian age or stage, or the system of deposits laid down during it. [19th C.: from Fr. *villafranchien*, from *Villafranca* d'Asti, village in Italy.]

vil·lage /ˈvilij/ ▶ n. a group of houses and associated buildings, larger than a hamlet and smaller than a town, situated in a rural area. ■ a self-contained district or community within a town or city, regarded as having features characteristic of village life: *the Olympic village.* ■ (in the US) a small municipality with limited corporate powers. — **vil·lag·er** n. [ME: from OFr., from L. *villa* 'country house.']

vil·lage id·i·ot ▶ n. esp. archaic a person of very low intelligence resident and well known in a village.

vil·lain /ˈvilən/ ▶ n. **1** a person guilty or capable of a crime or wickedness. ■ the person or thing responsible for specified trouble, harm, or damage: *the industrialized nations are the real villains.* ■ (in a play or novel) a character whose evil actions or motives are important to the plot. **2** archaic var. of VILLEIN. — **vil·lain·ess** /ˈvilənəs/ n. [ME (in the sense 'a rustic, boor'): from OFr. *vilein*, based on L. *villa* (see VILLA).]

vil·lain·ous /ˈvilənəs/ ▶ adj. relating to, constituting, or guilty of wicked or criminal behavior. ■ informal extremely bad or unpleasant. — **vil·lain·ous·ly** adv. **vil·lain·ous·ness** n.

vil·lain·y /ˈvilənē/ ▶ n. (pl. -lain·ies) wicked or criminal behavior: *the villainy of professional racketeers.*

vil·la·nel·la /ˌviləˈnelə/ ▶ n. (pl. **-nel·le** /-ˈnelē/ or **-nel·las**) a form of Italian part-song originating in Naples in the 16th century, in rustic style with a vigorous rhythm. [Ital., fem. of *villanello* 'rural,' dimin. of *villano* 'peasant.']

vil·la·nelle /ˌviləˈnel/ ▶ n. a nineteen-line poem with two rhymes throughout, consisting of five tercets and a quatrain, with the first and third lines of the opening tercet recurring alternately at the end of the other tercets and with both repeated at the close of the concluding quatrain. [19th C.: from Fr., from Ital. *villanella* (see VILLANELLA).]

-ville ▶ comb. form informal used in fictitious place names with reference to a particular quality: *dullsville.* [from Fr. *ville* 'town.']

vil·lein /ˈvilən; -ˌān/ ▶ n. (in medieval England) a feudal tenant entirely subject to a lord or manor to whom he paid dues and services in return for land. [ME: var. of VILLAIN.]

vil·lein·age /ˈvilənij; -ˌānij/ ▶ n. hist. the tenure or status of a villein.

vil·lous /ˈviləs/ ▶ adj. Anat. (of a structure, esp. the epithelium) covered with villi. ■ Med. (of a condition) affecting the villi: *villous atrophy.* ■ Bot. shaggy.

vil·lus /ˈviləs/ (pl. **vil·li** /ˈvilī; ˈvilē/) ▶ n. **1** Anat. any of numerous minute elongated projections set closely together on a surface, typically increasing its surface area for the absorption of substances, in particular: ■ a fingerlike projection of the lining of the small intestine. ■ a fold of the chorion. **2** [(usu. in pl.)] Bot. a long slender hair. [18th C.: from L., lit. 'shaggy hair.']

Vil·ni·us /ˈvilnēəs/ the capital of Lithuania, in the southeastern part of the country; pop. 593,000.

vim /vim/ ▶ n. informal energy; enthusiasm. [19th C. (orig. US): perh. from L., accusative of *vis* 'energy.']

Vi·my Ridge, Bat·tle of /ˈvēmē; ˈvimē; vēˈmē/ an Allied attack on the German position of Vimy Ridge, near the town of Arras, France, during World War I. A key point on the Western Front, it was taken on April 9, 1917, by Canadian troops.

VIN /vin/ ▶ abbr. vehicle identification number.

vin /vаɴ; van/ ▶ n. [usu. with adj.] French wine: *vin blanc.* [Fr., lit. 'wine.']

vi·na ▶ n. var. of VEENA.

vi·na·ceous /vīˈnāsʜəs; və-/ ▶ adj. of the color of red wine. [17th C.: from L. *vinaceus* (from *vinum* 'wine') + -OUS.]

vin·ai·grette /ˌvinəˈgret/ ▶ n. **1** (also **vin·ai·grette dress·ing**) salad dressing of oil, wine vinegar, and seasoning. **2** hist. a small ornamental bottle for holding smelling salts. [Fr., dimin. of *vinaigre* 'vinegar.']

vin·blas·tine /vinˈblasˌtēn/ ▶ n. Med. a cytotoxic compound of the alkaloid class obtained from the Madagascar periwinkle and used to treat Hodgkin's disease and other cancers of the lymphatic system. [1960s: from mod. L. *Vinca* (see VINCA) + *(leuco)blast*.]

vin·ca /ˈviɴɢkə/ ▶ n. another term for PERIWINKLE[1]. [1930s: from mod. L. *Vinca* (genus name), from late L. *pervinca* (see PERIWINKLE[1]).]

Vin·cent de Paul, St. /ˈvinsənt də ˈpôl/ (1581–1660), French priest. He established the Daughters of Charity (Sisters of Charity of St. Vincent de Paul) 1633.

Vin·cent's an·gi·na ▶ n. a painful ulcerative condition of the inside of the mouth or of the gums, associated with trench mouth.

Vin·ci, Leonardo da, see LEONARDO DA VINCI.

vin·ci·ble /ˈvinsəbəl/ ▶ adj. literary (of an opponent or obstacle) able to be overcome or conquered. — **vin·ci·bil·i·ty** /ˌvinsəˈbilətē/ n. [16th C.: from L. *vincibilis*, from *vincere* 'to overcome.']

vin·cris·tine /vinˈkrisˌtēn/ ▶ n. Med. a cytotoxic compound of the alkaloid class obtained from the Madagascar periwinkle and used to treat acute leukemia and other cancers. [1960s: from mod. L. *Vinca* (see VINCA) + a second element perh. based on CRISTA + -INE[4].]

vin·cu·lum /ˈviɴɢkyələm/ ▶ n. (pl. **-la** /-lə/) **1** Anat. a connecting band of tissue, such as that attaching a flexor tendon to the bone of a finger or toe. **2** Math. a horizontal line drawn over a group of terms in a mathematical expression to indicate that they are to be operated on as a single entity by the preceding or following operator. — **vin·cu·lar** /-lər/ adj. [17th C.: from L., lit. 'bond,' from *vincire* 'bind.']

vin·da·loo /ˈvindəˌlo͞o; ˌvindəˈlo͞o/ ▶ n. a highly spiced hot Indian curry made with meat or fish. [prob. from Port. *vin d'alho* 'wine and garlic (sauce),' from *vinho* 'wine' + *alho* 'garlic.']

vin de ta·ble /ˌvаɴ də ˈtābl(ə); ˌvan/ ▶ n. (pl. **vins de ta·ble** pronunc. same) French table wine of reasonable quality, suitable for accompanying a meal. [Fr., lit. 'table wine.']

vin·di·cate /ˈvindəˌkāt/ ▶ v. [trans.] clear (someone) of blame or suspicion. ■ show or prove to be right, reasonable, or justified. — **vin·di·ca·ble** /-kəbəl/ adj. **vin·di·ca·tion** /ˌvindəˈkāsʜən/ n. **vin·di·ca·tor** /-ˌkātər/ n. **vin·di·ca·to·ry** /-kəˌtôrē/ adj. [16th C.: from L. *vindicat-* 'claimed, avenged,' from the v. *vindicare*, from *vindex*, *vindic-* 'claimant, avenger.']

vin·dic·tive /vinˈdiktiv/ ▶ adj. having or showing a strong or unreasoning desire for revenge. — **vin·dic·tive·ly** adv. **vin·dic·tive·ness** n. [17th C.: from L. *vindicta* 'vengeance' + -IVE.]

vine /vīn/ ▶ n. a climbing or trailing woody-stemmed plant (*Vitis* and other genera) of the grape family. ■ used in names of climbing or trailing plants of other families, e.g., **trumpet vine**. ■ the slender stem of a trailing or climbing plant. — **vin·y** adj. [ME: from OFr., from L. *vinea* 'vineyard, vine,' from *vinum* 'wine.']

vine dress·er ▶ n. a person who prunes, trains, and cultivates vines.

vin·e·gar /ˈvinəgər/ ▶ n. a sour-tasting liquid containing acetic acid, obtained by fermenting dilute alcoholic liquids, typically wine, cider, or beer, and used as a condiment or for pickling. ■ fig. sourness or peevishness of behavior, character, or speech: *her aggrieved tone held a touch of vinegar.* — **vin·e·gar·ish** adj. **vin·e·gar·y** adj. [ME: from OFr. *vyn egre*, based on L. *vinum* 'wine' + *acer* 'sour.']

Vin·e·gar Joe see STILWELL.

vin·er·y /ˈvīn(ə)rē/ ▶ n. (pl. **-er·ies**) a greenhouse for grapevines. ■ a vineyard.

vine·yard /ˈvinyərd/ ▶ n. a plantation of grapevines, typically producing grapes used in winemaking.

vingt-et-un /ˌvant ā ˈən; ˌvаɴ tā ˈœɴ/ ▶ n. the card game blackjack. [Fr., lit. 'twenty-one.']

vini- ▶ comb. form of or relating to wine: *viniculture.* [from L. *vinum* 'wine.']

vin·i·cul·ture /ˈvinəˌkəlcʜər/ ▶ n. the cultivation of grapevines for winemaking. — **vin·i·cul·tur·al** /ˌvinəˈkəlcʜərəl/ adj. **vin·i·cul·tur·ist** /ˌvinəˈkəlcʜərist/ n. [19th C.: from L. *vinum* 'wine.']

vin·i·fi·ca·tion /ˌvinəfiˈkāsʜən/ ▶ n. the conversion of grape juice or other vegetable extract into wine by fermentation. — **vin·i·fy** /ˈvinəˌfī/ v. (**-fies, -fied**).

vin·ing /ˈvīniɴɢ/ ▶ adj. (of a plant) growing as a vine with climbing or trailing woody stems.

Vin·land /ˈvinlənd/ the region of the northeastern coast of North America that was visited in the 11th century by Norsemen led by Leif Ericsson. It was so named from the report that grapevines were found growing there. The exact location is uncertain.

vi·no /ˈvēnō/ ▶ n. (pl. **-nos**) Spanish or Italian wine. [Sp. and Ital., 'wine.']

vin or·di·naire /ˌvаɴn ˌôrdēˈne(ə)r; ˈvan/ ▶ n. (pl. **vins or·di·naires** /ˌvаɴz ˌôrdēˈne(ə)r; ˈvanz/) cheap table wine for everyday use. [Fr., lit. 'ordinary wine.']

vi·nous /ˈvīnəs/ ▶ adj. of, resembling, or associated with wine: *a vinous smell.* ■ fond of or influenced by drinking wine: *his vinous companion.* ■ of the reddish color of wine. — **vi·nos·i·ty** /vīˈnäsətē/ n. **vi·nous·ly** adv. [ME: from L. *vinum* 'wine' + -OUS.]

Vin·son /ˈvinsən/, Frederick Moore (1890–1953), Chief Justice of the US 1946–53. A Kentucky Democrat, he served in the US House of Representatives 1924–29 and 1931–38, and was secretary of the US Treasury 1945–46.

Vin·son Mas·sif /ˈvinsən maˈsēf/ the highest mountain range in Antarctica, rising to 16,863 feet (5,140 m).

vin·tage /ˈvintij/ ▶ n. the year or place in which wine, esp. wine of high quality, was produced. ■ a wine of high quality made from the crop of a single identified district in a good year. ■ literary wine. ■ the harvesting of grapes for winemaking. ■ the grapes or wine produced in a particular season. ■ the time that something of quality was produced. ▶ adj. of, relating to, or denoting wine of high quality: *vintage claret.* ■ denoting something of high quality, esp. something from the past or characteristic of the best period of a person's work: *a vintage Sherlock Holmes adventure.* [ME: alt. of earlier *vendage*, from OFr. *vendange*, from L. *vindemia* (from *vinum* 'wine' + *demere* 'remove').]

vin·tag·er /'vintijər/ ▶ n. a person who harvests grapes.

vin·tage year ▶ n. the year that a particular wine was produced. ■ a particularly successful year for some pursuit or product: *it was a vintage year for home-run hitters.*

vint·ner /'vintnər/ ▶ n. **1** a wine merchant. **2** a wine maker. [ME: via Anglo-Latin from OFr. *vinetier*, from med. L. *vinetarius*, from L. *vinetum* 'vineyard,' from *vinum* 'wine.']

vi·nyl /'vīnl/ ▶ n. **1** synthetic resin or plastic consisting of polyvinyl chloride or a related polymer, used esp. for wallpapers and other covering materials and formerly as the standard material for phonograph records before the introduction of compact discs. **2** [as adj.] Chem. of or denoting the unsaturated hydrocarbon radical $-CH{=}CH_2$, derived from ethylene by removal of a hydrogen atom: *a vinyl group.* [19th C.: from L. *vinum* 'wine' + -YL.]

vi·nyl chlo·ride ▶ n. Chem. a colorless toxic gas, CH_2CHCl, used in the production of polyvinyl chloride and other commercially important polymers.

vi·ol /'vīəl/ ▶ n. a musical instrument of the Renaissance and baroque periods, typically six-stringed, held vertically and played with a bow. [15th C.: from OFr. *viele*, from Provençal *viola.*]

vi·o·la[1] /vī'ōlə; vē-; 'vīələ/ ▶ n. an instrument of the violin family, larger than the violin and tuned a fifth lower. [18th C.: from Ital. and Sp.; cf. VIOL.]

vi·o·la[2] /vē'ōlə/ ▶ n. a plant of a genus (*Viola*) that includes the pansies and violets. [mod. L., from L., lit. 'violet.']

vi·o·la·ceous /,vīə'lāsHəs/ ▶ adj. **1** of a violet color. **2** Bot. of, relating to, or denoting plants of the violet family (Violaceae).

vi·o·la da brac·cio /vē'ōlə də 'brächō/ ▶ n. an early musical instrument of the violin family (as distinct from a viol), specifically one corresponding to the modern viola. [Ital., lit. 'viol for the arm.']

vi·o·la da gam·ba /vē'ōlə də 'gämbə; 'gam-/ (also **vi·ol da gam·ba**) ▶ n. a viol, specifically a bass viol (corresponding to the modern cello). [Ital., lit. 'viol for the leg.']

vi·o·la d'a·mo·re /vē'ōlə dä'môrā; də-; -'môrē/ ▶ n. a sweet-toned 18th-century musical instrument similar to a viola, but with six or seven strings, and additional sympathetic strings below the fingerboard. [Ital., lit. 'viol of love.']

vi·o·late /'vīə,lāt/ ▶ v. [trans.] break or fail to comply with (a rule or formal agreement). ■ fail to respect (someone's peace, privacy, or rights). ■ treat (something sacred) with irreverence or disrespect. ■ rape or sexually assault (someone). — **vi·o·la·tor** /-,lātər/ n. **vi·o·la·ble** /-ləbəl/ adj. (rare). **vi·o·la·tive** adj. [ME: from L. *violat-* 'treated violently,' from the v. *violare.*]

vi·o·la·tion /,vīə'lāsHən/ ▶ n. the action of violating someone or something.

vi·o·lence /'vī(ə)ləns/ ▶ n. behavior involving physical force intended to hurt, damage, or kill someone or something. ■ strength of emotion or an unpleasant or destructive natural force. ■ Law the unlawful exercise of physical force or intimidation by the exhibition of such force.
– PHRASES **do violence to** damage or adversely affect.

vi·o·lent /'vī(ə)lənt/ ▶ adj. using or involving physical force intended to hurt, damage, or kill someone or something: *a violent confrontation with riot police.* ■ (esp. of an emotion or unpleasant or destructive natural force) very strong or powerful: *violent dislike.* ■ (of a color) vivid. ■ Law involving an unlawful exercise or exhibition of force. — **vi·o·lent·ly** adv. [ME: via OFr. from L. *violent-* 'vehement, violent.']

vi·o·let /'vī(ə)lət/ ▶ n. **1** a herbaceous plant (genus *Viola*, family Violaceae) of temperate regions, typically having purple, blue, or white five-petaled flowers, one of the petals forming a landing pad for pollinating insects. ■ used in names of similar-flowered plants of other families, e.g., **African violet**. **2** a bluish-purple color seen at the end of the spectrum opposite red. ▶ adj. of a bluish-purple color. [ME: from OFr. *violette*, dimin. of *viole*, from L. *viola* 'violet.']

vi·o·lin /,vīə'lin/ ▶ n. a stringed musical instrument of treble pitch, played with a horsehair bow. The classical European violin was developed in the 16th century. It has four strings and a body of characteristic rounded shape, narrowed at the middle and with two f-shaped sound holes. — **vi·o·lin·ist** /-ist/ n. **vi·o·lin·is·tic** /-li'nistik/ adj. [16th C.: from Ital. *violino*, dimin. of *viola* (see VIOLA[1]).]

violin

vi·o·lin spi·der ▶ n. another term for BROWN RECLUSE.

vi·o·list ▶ n. **1** /vē'ōlist/ a viola player. **2** /'vīəlist/ a viol player.

vi·o·lon·cel·lo /,vīələn'cHelō; ,vē-/ ▶ n. formal term for CELLO. — **vi·o·lon·cel·list** /-'cHelist/ n. [18th C.: Ital., dimin. of *violone* (see VIOLONE).]

vi·o·lo·ne /,vēə'lōnā/ ▶ n. an early form of double bass, esp. a large bass viol. [Ital., augmentative of *viola* (see VIOLA[1]).]

VIP ▶ abbr. ■ very important person. ■ Biochem. vasoactive intestinal polypeptide (or peptide), a substance that acts as a neurotransmitter, esp. in the brain and gastrointestinal tract.

vi·pas·sa·na /vi'päsənə/ (also **Vi·pas·sa·na**) ▶ n. (in Theravada Buddhism) meditation involving concentration on the body, or the insight that this provides. [Pali, lit. 'inward vision.']

vi·per /'vīpər/ ▶ n. a venomous snake (family Viperidae) with large hinged fangs, typically having a broad head and stout body, with dark patterns on a lighter background. ■ a spiteful or treacherous person. — **vi·per·ine** /'vīpə,rīn; -rin/ adj. **vi·per·ish** adj. **vi·per·ous** /'vīp(ə)rəs/ adj. [16th C.: from Fr. *vipère* or L. *vipera*, from *vivus* 'alive' + *parere* 'bring forth.']

vi·per's bu·gloss ▶ n. a bristly plant (*Echium vulgare*) of the borage family, with pink buds that open to blue flowers. Formerly used in the treatment of snake bites and native to Eurasia, it is now widespread throughout North America.

vi·rae·mia ▶ n. British spelling of VIREMIA.

vi·ra·go /və'rägō; -'rā-/ ▶ n. (pl. **-gos** or **-goes**) a domineering, violent, or bad-tempered woman. ■ archaic a woman of masculine strength or spirit; a female warrior. [OE, from L., 'heroic woman, female warrior,' from *vir* 'man.']

vi·ral /'vīrəl/ ▶ adj. **1** of the nature of, caused by, or relating to a virus or viruses. **2** of or involving the rapid spread of information about a product or service by viral marketing techniques: *a viral video ad.* — **vi·ral·ly** adv.

vi·ral load ▶ n. a measurement of the amount of a virus in an organism, typically in the bloodstream, usu. stated in virus particles per milliliter.

vi·ral mar·ket·ing ▶ n. a method of product promotion that relies on getting customers to market an idea, product, or service on their own by telling their friends about it, usually by e-mail.

vir·e·lay /'virə,lā/ (also **vir·e·lai**) ▶ n. a lyric poem of a type originating in medieval France, featuring short and long lines with an interlaced rhyme scheme. [ME: from OFr. *virelai.*]

vi·re·mi·a /vī'rēmēə/ (Brit. also **vi·rae·mi·a**) ▶ n. Med. the presence of viruses in the blood. — **vi·re·mic** /-mik/ adj. [1940s: from VIRUS + -EMIA.]

vir·e·o /'virē,ō/ ▶ n. (pl. **-os**) a small American songbird (genus *Vireo*, family Vireonidae), typically having a green or gray back and yellow or white underparts. [19th C.: from L., perh. denoting a greenfinch.]

vi·res·cent /və'resənt; vī-/ ▶ adj. literary greenish. — **vi·res·cence** n. **vi·res·cent·ly** adv. [19th C.: from L. *virescent-* 'turning green,' inceptive of *virere* 'be green.']

vir·ga /'vərgə/ ▶ n. (pl. **-gae** /-gē; -gī/) Meteorol. a mass of streaks of rain appearing to hang under a cloud and evaporating before reaching the ground. [1940s: from L., 'rod, stripe.']

vir·gate /'vərgət; -,gāt/ ▶ n. Brit., hist. a varying measure of land, typically 30 acres.

Vir·gil /'vərjəl/ (also **Ver·gil**) (70–19 BC), Roman poet; Latin name *Publius Vergilius Maro.* His major works include the *Eclogues*, the *Georgics*, and the *Aeneid* (see AENEID). — **Vir·gil·i·an** /vər'jilēən/ adj.

vir·gin /'vərjən/ ▶ n. a person, typically a woman, who has never had sexual intercourse. ■ a naive or inexperienced person, esp. in a particular context: *a political virgin.* ■ (**the Virgin**) the mother of Jesus; the Virgin Mary. ■ a woman who has taken a vow to remain a virgin. ■ (**the Virgin**) the zodiacal sign or constellation Virgo. ■ Entomol. a female insect that produces eggs without being fertilized. ▶ adj. **1** [attrib.] being, relating to, or appropriate for a virgin: *his virgin bride.* **2** not yet touched, used, or exploited: *virgin snow.* ■ (of clay) not yet fired. ■ (of wool) not yet, or only once, spun or woven. ■ (of olive oil) obtained from the first pressing of olives. ■ (of metal) made from ore by smelting. [ME: from OFr. *virgine*, from L. *virgo, virgin-.*]

vir·gin·al /'vərjənl/ ▶ adj. being, relating to, or appropriate for a virgin: *virginal shyness.* ▶ n. (usu. **virginals**) an early spinet with the strings parallel to the keyboard, typically rectangular, and popular in 16th and 17th century houses. [perh. because usually played by young women.] — **vir·gin·al·ist** /-jənl-ist/ n. **vir·gin·al·ly** adv.

vir·gin birth ▶ n. **1** (**the Virgin Birth**) the doctrine of Christ's birth from a mother, Mary, who was a virgin. **2** Zool. parthenogenesis.

Vir·gin·ia /vər'jinyə/ a state in the eastern US, on the Atlantic coast; pop. 7,078,515; capital, Richmond; statehood, June 25, 1788 (10). It was the site of the first permanent European settlement in North America, at Jamestown in 1607, and was one of the original thirteen states. — **Vir·gin·ian** n. & adj.

Vir·gin·ia Beach a city in southeastern Virginia; pop. 425,257.

Vir·gin·ia blue·bell ▶ n. a North American woodland plant (*Mertensia virginica*) of the borage family, bearing nodding, trumpet-shaped blue flowers. Also called **Virginia cowslip**.

Vir·gin·ia Cit·y a historic settlement in western Nevada, site of the 1850s–60s Comstock Lode gold and silver boom.

Vir·gin·ia creep·er ▶ n. a North American vine (genus *Parthenocissus*) of the grape family, chiefly cultivated for its red autumn foliage.

Vir·gin·ia ham ▶ n. a smoke-cured ham from a hog fed on peanuts and corn.

Vir·gin·ia reel ▶ n. a lively American country dance performed by a number of couples facing each other in parallel lines.

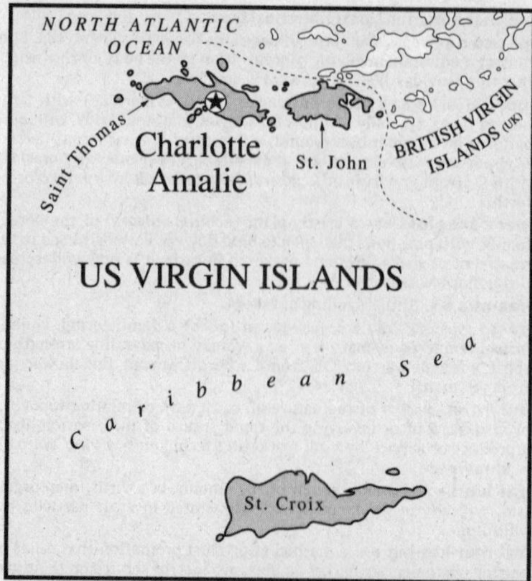

Vir·gin Is·lands /'vərjən/ a group of Caribbean islands at the eastern end of the Greater Antilles, divided between US and British administration. The US islands include about 50 islands; pop. 102,000; capital, Charlotte Amalie (on St. Thomas). The British islands consist of about 40 islands in the northeastern part of the group; pop. 17,000; capital, Road Town (on Tortola).

vir·gin·i·ty /vər'jinətē/ ▶**n.** the state of never having had sexual intercourse: *he lost his virginity in college.* ■ the state of being naive, innocent, or inexperienced in a particular context: *his political virginity.*

Vir·gin Mar·y the mother of Jesus (see **Mary**[1]).

vir·gin queen ▶**n.** **1** an unfertilized queen bee. **2** (**the Virgin Queen**) Queen Elizabeth I of England, who died unmarried.

vir·gin's bow·er ▶**n.** a North American clematis (*Clematis virginiana*) with white flowers.

Vir·go /'vərgō/ **1** Astron. a large constellation (the Virgin), said to represent a maiden or goddess associated with the harvest. It contains several bright stars, the brightest of which is Spica, and a dense cluster of galaxies. **2** Astrol. the sixth sign of the zodiac, which the sun enters about August 23. ■ (**a Virgo**) (pl. **-gos**) a person born when the sun is in this sign. — **Vir·go·an** /-gōən/ **n. & adj.** (in sense 2).

vir·go in·tac·ta /'vərgō in'taktə/ ▶**n.** esp. Law a girl or woman who has never had sexual intercourse, originally a virgin whose hymen is intact. [L., lit. 'untouched virgin.']

vir·gule /'vər,gyo͞ol/ ▶**n.** another term for **slash**[1] (sense 2). [19th C.: from Fr., lit. 'comma,' from L. *virgula*, dimin. of *virga* 'rod.']

vir·i·des·cent /,virə'desənt/ ▶**adj.** greenish or becoming green. — **vir·i·des·cence n.** [19th C.: from late L. *viridescent-* 'becoming green,' from the v. *viridescere*, from L. *viridis* 'green.']

vi·rid·i·an /və'ridēən/ ▶**n.** a bluish-green pigment consisting of hydrated chromium hydroxide. ■ the bluish-green color of this. [19th C.: from L. *viridis* 'green' (from *virere* 'be green') + **-ian**.]

vir·ile /'virəl/ ▶**adj.** (of a man) having strength, energy, and a strong sex drive. ■ having or characterized by strength and energy. — **vi·ril·i·ty** /və'rilitē/ **n.** [15th C.: from Fr. *viril* or L. *virilis*, from *vir* 'man.']

vir·il·ism /'virə,lizəm/ ▶**n.** Med. the condition that results from virilization.

vir·il·i·za·tion /,virələ'zāshən/ ▶**n.** Med. the development of male physical characteristics (such as muscle bulk, body hair, and deep voice) in a female or precociously in a boy, typically as a result of excess androgen production.

vi·ri·on /'virē,än; 'vī-/ ▶**n.** Microbiol. the complete, infective form of a virus outside a host cell, with a core of RNA or DNA and a capsid. [1950s: from **virus** + **-on**.]

vi·roid /'vī,roid/ ▶**n.** Microbiol. an infectious entity affecting plants, smaller than a virus and consisting only of nucleic acid without a protein coat.

vi·rol·o·gy /vī'räləjē/ ▶**n.** the branch of science that deals with the study of viruses. — **vi·ro·log·i·cal** /,vīrə'läjikəl/ **adj.** **vi·ro·log·i·cal·ly** /,vīrə'läjik(ə)lē/ **adv.** **vi·rol·o·gist** /-jist/ **n.**

vir·tu /,vər'to͞o/ (also **ver·tu**) ▶**n.** **1** knowledge of or expertise in the fine arts. ■ curios or objets d'art collectively. **2** literary the good qualities inherent in a person or thing.
– PHRASES **article** (or **object**) **of virtu** an article that is interesting because of its antiquity, beauty, quality of workmanship, etc. [18th C.: from Ital. *virtù* 'virtue'; the var. *vertu* is an alt., as if from Fr.]

vir·tu·al /'vərcho͞oəl/ ▶**adj.** almost or nearly as described, but not completely or according to strict definition: *the virtual absence of border controls.* ■ Comput. not physically existing as such but made by software to appear to do so: *a virtual computer.* See also **virtual reality**. ■ Optics relating to the points at which rays would meet if produced backward. ■ Physics denoting particles or interactions with extremely short lifetimes and (owing to the uncertainty principle) indefinitely great energies, postulated as intermediates in some processes. — **vir·tu·al·i·ty** /,vərcho͞o'alitē/ **n.** [ME: from med. L. *virtualis*, from L. *virtus* 'virtue.']

vir·tu·al im·age ▶**n.** Optics an optical image formed from the apparent divergence of light rays from a point, as opposed to an image formed from their actual divergence.

vir·tu·al·ly /'vərcho͞oəlē/ ▶**adv.** nearly; almost. ■ Comput. by means of virtual reality techniques.

vir·tu·al mem·o·ry (also **vir·tu·al stor·age**) ▶**n.** Comput. memory that appears to exist as main storage although most of it is supported by data held in secondary storage, transfer between the two being made automatically as required.

vir·tu·al re·al·i·ty ▶**n.** Comput. the computer-generated simulation of a three-dimensional image or environment that can be interacted with in a seemingly real or physical way by a person using special electronic equipment, such as a helmet with a screen inside or gloves fitted with sensors.

vir·tue /'vərcho͞o/ ▶**n.** **1** behavior showing high moral standards: *paragons of virtue.* ■ a quality considered morally good or desirable in a person. ■ a good or useful quality of a thing: *there's no virtue in suffering in silence.* ■ archaic virginity or chastity, esp. of a woman. **2** (**virtues**) (in traditional Christian angelology) the seventh highest order of the ninefold celestial hierarchy.
– PHRASES **by** (or **in**) **virtue of** because or as a result of. **make a virtue of** derive benefit or advantage from submitting to (an unwelcome obligation or unavoidable circumstance). — **vir·tue·less adj.** [ME: from OFr. *vertu*, from L. *virtus* 'valor, merit, moral perfection,' from *vir* 'man.']

vir·tu·o·so /,vərcho͞o'ōsō/ ▶**n.** (pl. **-si** /-sē/ or **-sos**) a person highly skilled in music or another artistic pursuit. ■ a person with a special knowledge of or interest in works of art or curios. — **vir·tu·os·ic** /-'äsik; -'ōsik/ **adj.** **vir·tu·os·i·ty** /-'äsitē/ **n.** [17th C.: from Ital., lit. 'learned, skillful,' from late L. *virtuosus* (see **virtuous**).]

vir·tu·ous /'vərcho͞oəs/ ▶**adj.** having or showing high moral standards. ■ archaic (esp. of a woman) chaste. — **vir·tu·ous·ly adv.** **vir·tu·ous·ness n.**

vir·u·lent /'vir(y)ələnt/ ▶**adj.** **1** (of a disease or poison) extremely severe or harmful in its effects. ■ (of a pathogen, esp. a virus) highly infective. **2** bitterly hostile: *a virulent attack on liberalism.* — **vir·u·lence n.** **vir·u·lent·ly adv.** [ME: from L. *virulentus*, from *virus* 'poison' (see **virus**).]

vi·rus /'vīrəs/ ▶**n.** an infective agent that typically consists of a nucleic acid molecule in a protein coat, is too small to be seen by light microscopy, and is able to multiply only within the living cells of a host. ■ informal an infection or disease caused by such an agent. ■ fig. a harmful or corrupting influence. ■ (also **com·pu·ter vi·rus**) a piece of code that is capable of copying itself and typically has a detrimental effect, such as corrupting the system or destroying data. [ME (denoting the venom of a snake): from L., 'slimy liquid, poison.']

Vis. ▶**abbr.** Viscount.

vi·sa /'vēzə/ ▶**n.** an endorsement on a passport indicating that the holder is allowed to enter, leave, or stay for a specified period of time in a country. [19th C.: via Fr. from L. *visa*, past part. (neut. pl.) of *videre* 'to see.']

vis·age /'vizij/ ▶**n.** [usu. in sing.] literary a person's face, with reference to the form or proportions of the features: *an elegant, angular visage.* ■ a person's facial expression: *his visage of cheerfulness.* ■ fig. the surface of an object presented to view: *the moonlit visage of the buildings.* — **vis·aged adj.** [in comb.] *a stern-visaged old man.* [ME: via OFr. from L. *visus* 'sight,' from *videre* 'to see.']

Vi·sā·kha /vi'säkə/ ▶**n.** var. of **Vesak**.

vis-à-vis /'vēz ə 'vē/ ▶**prep.** in relation to; with regard to: *women's needs vis-à-vis employment.* ■ as compared with; as opposed to. ▶**adv.** archaic in a position facing a specified or implied subject: *he was there vis-à-vis with Miss Arundel.* ▶**n.** (pl. same) **1** a person or group occupying a corresponding position to that of another person or group in a different area or domain; a counterpart. **2** a face-to-face meeting. [18th C.: Fr., lit. 'face to face,' from OFr. *vis* 'face.']

Visc. ▶**abbr.** Viscount.

vis·ca·cha /vi'skächə/ ▶**n.** a large South American burrowing rodent (genera *Lagidium* and *Lagostomus*) of the chinchilla family, sometimes hunted for its fur and flesh. [17th C.: via Sp. from Quechua *(h)uiscacha*.]

vis·cer·a /'visərə/ ▶**plural n.** (sing. **vis·cus** /'viskəs/) the internal organs in the main cavities of the body, esp. those in the abdomen, e.g., the intestines. [17th C.: from L., pl. of *viscus* (see **viscus**).]

vis·cer·al /'vis(ə)rəl/ ▶**adj.** of or relating to the viscera. ■ relating to deep inward feelings rather than to the intellect: *the voters' visceral fear of change.* — **vis·cer·al·ly adv.**

vis·cid /'visid/ ▶**adj.** glutinous; sticky. — **vis·cid·i·ty** /və'sidətē/ **n.** [17th C.: from late L. *viscidus*, from L. *viscum* 'birdlime.']

vis·co·e·las·tic·i·ty /,viskō-i,las'tisitē; -,ēla-/ ▶**n.** Physics the property of a substance of exhibiting both elastic and viscous behavior, the application of stress causing temporary deformation if the stress is quickly removed but permanent deformation if it is maintained. — **vis·co·e·las·tic** /ˌ-iˈlastik/ **adj.**

vis·com·e·ter /viˈskämətər/ ▶ **n.** an instrument for measuring the viscosity of liquids. — **vis·co·met·ric** /ˌviskəˈmetrik/ **adj.** **vis·co·met·ri·cal·ly** /ˌviskəˈmetrik(ə)lē/ **adv.** **vis·com·e·try** /-ətrē/ **n.** [19th C.: from late L. *viscosus* 'viscous' + -METER.]

vis·cose /ˈvisˌkōs; -ˌkōz/ ▶ **n.** a viscous orange-brown solution obtained by treating cellulose with sodium hydroxide and carbon disulfide, used as the basis of manufacturing rayon fiber and transparent cellulose film. ■ rayon fabric or fiber made from this. [19th C.: from late L. *viscosus*, from L. *viscus* 'birdlime.']

vis·co·sim·e·ter /ˌviskəˈsimitər/ ▶ **n.** another term for VISCOMETER.

vis·cos·i·ty /ˌviˈskäsitē/ ▶ **n.** (pl. **-ties**) the state of being thick, sticky, and semifluid in consistency, due to internal friction. ■ a quantity expressing the magnitude of such friction, as measured by the force per unit area resisting a flow in which parallel layers unit distance apart have unit speed relative to one another. [ME: from OFr. *viscosite* or med. L. *viscositas*, from late L. *viscosus* (see VISCOUS).]

vis·count /ˈvīˌkount/ ▶ **n.** a British nobleman ranking above a baron and below an earl. — **vis·count·cy** /-ˌkountsē/ **n.** [ME: from OFr. *visconte*, from med. L. *vicecomes, vicecomit-* (see VICE-, COUNT[2]).]

vis·count·ess /ˈvīˌkountəs/ ▶ **n.** the wife or widow of a viscount. ■ a woman holding the rank of viscount in her own right.

vis·count·y /ˈvīˌkountē/ ▶ **n.** the land under the authority of a particular viscount.

vis·cous /ˈviskəs/ ▶ **adj.** having a thick, sticky consistency between solid and liquid; having a high viscosity. — **vis·cous·ly adv.** **vis·cous·ness n.** [ME: from Anglo-Norman Fr. *viscous* or late L. *viscosus*, from L. *viscum* 'birdlime.']

vis·cus /ˈviskəs/ singular form of VISCERA. [L.]

vise /vīs/ (Brit. **vice**) ▶ **n.** a metal tool with movable jaws that are used to hold an object firmly in place while work is done on it, typically attached to a workbench. — **vise·like adj.** [ME (denoting a screw or winch): from OFr. *vis*, from L. *vitis* 'vine.']

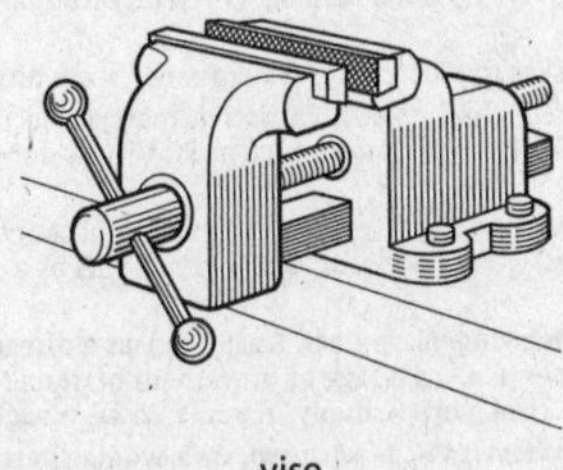

vise

Vish·nu /ˈvishno͞o/ Hinduism a god, regarded by his worshipers as the supreme deity and savior, by others as the preserver of the cosmos in a triad with Brahma and Shiva. Vishnu is considered by Hindus to have had nine earthly incarnations, including Rama, Krishna, and the historical Buddha. — **Vish·nu·ism** /-ˌizəm/ **n.** **Vish·nu·ite** /-ˌīt/ **n. & adj.**

vis·i·bil·i·ty /ˌvizəˈbilitē/ ▶ **n.** the state of being able to see or be seen. ■ the distance one can see as determined by light and weather conditions. ■ the degree to which something has attracted general attention; prominence.

vis·i·ble /ˈvizəbəl/ ▶ **adj.** **1** able to be seen. ■ Physics (of light) within the range of wavelengths to which the eye is sensitive. ■ able to be perceived or noticed easily: *a visible improvement.* ■ in a position of public prominence: *a highly visible senator.* **2** of or relating to imports or exports of tangible commodities: *the visible trade gap.* — **vis·i·ble·ness n.** **vis·i·bly** /-blē/ **adv.** [ME: from OFr., or from L. *visibilis*, from *videre* 'to see.']

Vis·i·goth /ˈvizəˌgäTH/ ▶ **n.** a member of the branch of the Goths who invaded the Roman Empire between the 3rd and 5th centuries AD and ruled much of Spain until overthrown by the Moors in 711. — **Vis·i·goth·ic** /ˌvizəˈgäTHik/ **adj.** [from late L. *Visigothus*, the first element possibly meaning 'west.']

vi·sion /ˈviZHən/ ▶ **n.** **1** the faculty or state of being able to see: *she had defective vision.* ■ the ability to think about or plan the future with imagination or wisdom. ■ a mental image of what the future will or could be like: *a socialist vision of society.* ■ the images seen on a television screen. **2** an experience of seeing someone or something in a dream or trance, or as a supernatural apparition. ■ (often **visions**) a vivid mental image, esp. a fanciful one of the future: *he had visions of stardom.* ■ a person or sight of unusual beauty. ▶ **v.** [trans.] rare imagine. — **vi·sion·al** /-ZHənl/ **adj.** **vi·sion·less adj.** [ME (denoting a supernatural apparition): via OFr. from L. *visio(n-)*, from *videre* 'to see.']

vi·sion·ar·y /ˈviZHəˌnerē/ ▶ **adj.** **1** (esp. of a person) thinking about or planning the future with imagination or wisdom: *a visionary leader.* ■ archaic (of a scheme or idea) not practical. **2** of, relating to, or able to see visions in a dream or trance, or as a supernatural apparition. ■ archaic existing only in a vision or in the imagination. ▶ **n.** (pl. **-ar·ies**) a person with original ideas about what the future will or could be like. — **vi·sion·ar·i·ness n.**

vi·sion·ing /ˈviZHəniNG/ ▶ **n.** **1** the development of a plan, goal, or vision for the future: *months of visioning and dedicated effort have culminated in the building of a cultural center.* **2** the action or fact of seeing visions.

vis·it /ˈvizit/ ▶ **v.** (**-it·ed, -it·ing**) [trans.] **1** go to see and spend time with (someone) socially. ■ go to see and spend time in (a place) as a tourist. ■ stay temporarily with (someone) or at (a place) as a guest: *visit us again* | [intrans.] *I'm only visiting.* ■ go to see (someone or something) for a specific purpose, such as to make an inspection or to receive or give professional advice or help. ■ [intrans.] (**visit with**) go to see (someone) socially. ■ [intrans.] informal chat: *visit with one another.* ■ access and view (a Web site or Web page). ■ (chiefly in biblical use) (of God) come to (a person or place) in order to bring comfort or salvation. **2** (often **be visited**) inflict (something harmful or unpleasant) on someone: *the mockery visited upon him.* ■ (of something harmful or unpleasant) afflict (someone): *they were visited with epidemics of a strange disease.* ■ archaic punish (a person or a wrongful act). ▶ **n.** an act of going or coming to see a person or place socially, as a tourist, or for some other purpose. ■ a temporary stay with a person or at a place. ■ an informal conversation. — **vis·it·a·ble adj.** [ME: from OFr. *visiter* or L. *visitare* 'go to see,' from *visare* 'to view,' from *videre* 'to see.']

vis·it·ant /ˈvizətənt/ ▶ **n.** chiefly literary a supernatural being or agency; an apparition: *in the poem, the angels of death appeared as spectral visitants.* ■ archaic a visitor or guest. ■ Ornithol. a visitor. ▶ **adj.** archaic literary paying a visit: *the visitant niece.*

vis·it·a·tion /ˌvizəˈtāSHən/ ▶ **n.** **1** an official or formal visit, in particular: ■ (in church use) an official visit of inspection, esp. one by a bishop to a church in his diocese. ■ the appearance of a divine or supernatural being. ■ a gathering with the family of a deceased person before the funeral. ■ Law a divorced person's right to spend time with their children in the custody of a former spouse. **2** a disaster or difficulty regarded as a divine punishment: *a visitation of the plague.* **3** (**the Visitation**) the visit of the Virgin Mary to Elizabeth related in Luke 1:39–56. ■ the festival commemorating this on May 31 (formerly July 2).

vis·it·a·to·ri·al /ˌvizətəˈtôrēəl/ ▶ **adj.** another term for VISITORIAL.

vis·it·ing /ˈviziting/ ▶ **adj.** [attrib.] (of a person) on a visit to a person or place: *a visiting speaker.* ■ (of an academic) working for a fixed period of time at another institution: *a visiting professor.*

vis·it·ing card ▶ **n.** Brit. a calling card.

vis·it·ing fire·man ▶ **n.** informal an important visitor to a city or organization who is given an official welcome and especially cordial treatment. ■ a visitor or tourist who is accorded special attention because they are expected to spend extravagantly.

vis·it·ing nurse ▶ **n.** a nurse who visits and treats patients in their homes, operating as part of a social service agency.

vis·it·ing pro·fes·sor ▶ **n.** a professor on a short-term contract to teach at a college or university other than the one that mainly employs them.

vis·i·tor /ˈvizitər/ ▶ **n.** a person visiting a person or place, esp. socially or as a tourist. ■ (usu. **visitors**) a member of a sports team on tour or playing away from home. ■ Ornithol. a migratory bird present in a locality for only part of the year.

vis·i·to·ri·al /ˌvizəˈtôrēəl/ ▶ **adj.** of or relating to an official visitor or visitation: *visitorial jurisdiction.*

vis me·di·ca·trix na·tu·rae /ˈvis ˌmediˈkātriks nəˈto͝orē; ˈwēs ˌmediˈkātriks näˈto͝orˌī/ ▶ **n.** the body's natural ability to heal itself. [L., 'the healing power of nature.']

vi·sor /ˈvīzər/ (also **vi·zor**) ▶ **n.** a stiff bill at the front of a cap. ■ a movable part of a helmet that can be pulled down to cover the face. ■ a screen for protecting the eyes from unwanted light, esp. one at the top of a vehicle windshield. ■ hist. a mask. — **vi·sored adj.** [ME: from Anglo-Norman Fr. *viser*, from OFr. *vis* 'face,' from L. *visus* (see VISAGE).]

VISTA /ˈvistə/ ▶ **abbr.** ■ Volunteers in Service to America.

vis·ta /ˈvistə/ ▶ **n.** a pleasing view, esp. one seen through a long, narrow opening: *a vista of church spires.* ■ a mental view of a succession of remembered or anticipated events: *vistas of freedom.* [17th C.: from Ital., lit. 'view,' from *visto* 'seen,' past part. of *vedere* 'see,' from L. *videre*.]

Vis·tu·la /ˈvisCHələ/ a river in Poland that rises in the Carpathian Mountains and flows north to the Baltic Sea. Polish name WISŁA.

vis·u·al /ˈviZHo͞oəl/ ▶ **adj.** of or relating to seeing or sight: *visual perception.* ▶ **n.** (usu. **visuals**) a picture, piece of film, or display used to illustrate or accompany something. — **vis·u·al·i·ty** /ˌviZHo͞oˈalitē/ **n.** **vis·u·al·ly adv.** [ME: from late L. *visualis*, from L. *visus* 'sight,' from *videre* 'to see.']

vis·ual acu·ity ▶ **n.** sharpness of vision, measured by the ability to discern letters or numbers at a given distance according to a fixed standard.

vis·u·al aid ▶ **n.** (usu. **visual aids**) an item of illustrative matter, such as a film, slide, or model, designed to supplement written or spoken information so that it can be understood more easily.

vis·u·al an·gle ▶ **n.** Optics the angle formed at the eye by rays from the extremities of an object viewed.

vis·u·al bi·na·ry ▶ n. Astron. a binary star of which the components are sufficiently far apart to be resolved by an optical telescope.

vis·u·al cor·tex ▶ n. Anat. the part of the cerebral cortex that receives and processes sensory nerve impulses from the eyes.

vis·u·al field ▶ n. another term for FIELD OF VISION.

vis·u·al·ize /'vizhōōə,līz/ ▶ v. [trans.] **1** form a mental image of; imagine. **2** make (something) visible to the eye: *the cells were better visualized by staining.* — **vis·u·al·iz·a·ble** adj. **vis·u·al·i·za·tion** /,vizhōōələ'zāshən/ n.

vis·u·al pur·ple ▶ n. another term for RHODOPSIN.

vis·u·o·spa·tial /,vizhōō'spāshəl/ ▶ adj. [attrib.] Psychol. relating to or denoting the visual perception of the spatial relationships of objects.

vi·tal /'vītl/ ▶ adj. **1** absolutely necessary or important; essential: *secrecy is of vital importance.* ■ indispensable to the continuance of life: *vital organs.* **2** full of energy; lively: *a beautiful, vital girl.* **3** archaic fatal: *the wound is vital.* ▶ n. (**vitals**) the body's important internal organs, esp. the gut or the genitalia. ■ short for VITAL SIGNS. — **vi·tal·ly** adv. [ME: via OFr. from L. *vitalis*, from *vita* 'life.']

vi·tal ca·pac·i·ty ▶ n. the greatest volume of air that can be expelled from the lungs after taking the deepest possible breath.

vi·tal force ▶ n. the energy or spirit that animates living creatures; the soul. ■ Philos. (in some theories, particularly that of Bergson) a hypothetical force, independent of physical and chemical forces, regarded as being the causative factor in the evolution and development of living organisms. ■ a person or thing that gives something vitality and strength: *he was a vital force in British music.*

vi·tal·ism /'vītl,izəm/ ▶ n. the theory that the origin and phenomena of life are dependent on a force or principle distinct from purely chemical or physical forces. — **vi·tal·ist** n. & adj. **vi·tal·is·tic** /,vītl'istik/ adj.

vi·tal·i·ty /vī'talitē/ ▶ n. the state of being strong and active; energy. ■ the power giving continuance of life, present in all living things: *the vitality of seeds.*

vi·tal·ize /'vītl,īz/ ▶ v. [trans.] give strength and energy to: *yoga calms and vitalizes body and mind.* — **vi·tal·i·za·tion** /,vītl-ə'zāshən/ n.

vi·tal signs /'vītl 'sīnz/ ▶ plural n. clinical measurements, specifically pulse rate, temperature, respiration rate, and blood pressure, that indicate the state of a patient's essential body functions.

vi·tal sta·tis·tics /'vītl stə'tistiks/ ▶ plural n. **1** quantitative data concerning a population, such as the number of births, marriages, and deaths. **2** informal the measurements of a woman's bust, waist, and hips.

vi·ta·min /'vītəmən/ ▶ n. any of a group of organic compounds that are essential for normal growth and nutrition and are required in small quantities in the diet because they cannot be synthesized by the body. [20th C.: from L. *vita* 'life' + AMINE.]

vi·ta·min A ▶ n. another term for RETINOL.

vi·ta·min B ▶ n. any of a group of substances (the **vitamin B complex**) that are essential for the working of certain enzymes in the body, including thiamine (**vitamin B_1**), riboflavin (**vitamin B_2**), pyridoxine (**vitamin B_6**), and cyanocobalamin (**vitamin B_{12}**).

vi·ta·min C ▶ n. another term for ASCORBIC ACID.

vi·ta·min D ▶ n. any of a group of vitamins found in liver and fish oils, essential for the absorption of calcium and the prevention of rickets in children and osteomalacia in adults. They include calciferol (**vitamin D_2**) and cholecalciferol (**vitamin D_3**).

vi·ta·min E ▶ n. another term for TOCOPHEROL.

vi·ta·min H ▶ n. another term for BIOTIN.

vi·ta·min K ▶ n. any of a group of vitamins found mainly in green leaves and essential for the blood-clotting process. They include phylloquinone (**vitamin K_1**), menaquinone (**vitamin K_2**), and menadione (**vitamin K_3**).

vi·ta·min M ▶ n. another term for FOLIC ACID.

vi·ta·min P ▶ n. the bioflavonoids, regarded collectively as a vitamin.

vi·tel·li /və'tel,ī; vī-; -'telē/ plural form of VITELLUS.

vi·tel·lin /və'telən; vī-/ ▶ n. Biochem. the chief protein constituent of egg yolk. [19th C.: from VITELLUS + -IN[1].]

vi·tel·line /və'telən; vī-; -,ēn; -,īn/ ▶ adj. Zool. Embryol. of or relating to the yolk (or yolk sac) of an egg or embryo, or to yolk-producing organs. [ME: from med. L. *vitellinus*, from *vitellus* (see VITELLUS).]

vi·tel·line mem·brane ▶ n. Embryol. a transparent membrane surrounding and secreted by the fertilized ovum, preventing the entry of further spermatozoa.

vi·tel·lus /və'teləs; vī-/ ▶ n. Embryol. the yolk of an egg or ovum. [18th C.: from L., 'yolk.']

vi·ti·ate /'vishē,āt/ ▶ v. [trans.] formal spoil or impair the quality or efficiency of: *programs vitiated by red tape.* ■ destroy or impair the legal validity of. — **vi·ti·a·tion** /,vishē'āshən/ n. **vi·ti·a·tor** /-,ātər/ n. [16th C.: from L. *vitiat-* 'impaired,' from the v. *vitiare*, from *vitium* (see VICE[1]).]

vit·i·cul·ture /'viti,kəlchər/ ▶ n. the cultivation of grapevines. ■ the study of grape cultivation. — **vit·i·cul·tur·al** /,viti'kəlchərəl/ adj. **vit·i·cul·tur·ist** /-chərist/ n. [19th C.: from L. *vitis* 'vine.']

Vi·ti Le·vu /'vētē 'lā,vōō; 'lev,ōō/ the largest of the Fiji islands. Its chief settlement is Suva.

vit·i·li·go /,vitl'īgō; -'ēgō/ ▶ n. Med. a condition in which the pigment is lost from areas of the skin, causing whitish patches, often with no clear cause. Also called LEUCODERMA. [16th C.: from L., 'tetter.']

Vi·to·ria /vi'tôrēə/ a city in northeastern Spain, capital of the Basque Provinces; pop. 209,000.

Vi·tó·ri·a /vi'tôrēə/ a city in eastern Brazil; pop. 276,000.

vit·re·ous /'vitrēəs/ ▶ adj. like glass in appearance or physical properties. ■ (of a substance) derived from or containing glass. — **vit·re·ous·ness** n. [ME: from L. *vitreus* (from *vitrum* 'glass') + -OUS.]

vit·re·ous hu·mor ▶ n. the transparent jellylike tissue filling the eyeball behind the lens. Compare with AQUEOUS HUMOR.

vi·tres·cent /və'tresənt/ ▶ adj. rare capable of or susceptible to being turned into glass. — **vi·tres·cence** n. [18th C.: from L. *vitrum* 'glass' + -ESCENT.]

vit·ri·form /'vitrə,fôrm/ ▶ adj. having the form or appearance of glass.

vit·ri·fy /'vitrə,fī/ ▶ v. (**-fies, -fied**) [trans.] (often **be vitrified**) convert (something) into glass or a glasslike substance, typically by exposure to heat. — **vit·ri·fac·tion** /,vitrə'fakshən/ n. **vit·ri·fi·a·ble** /'vitrə,fīəbəl; ,vitrə'fī-/ adj. **vit·ri·fi·ca·tion** /,vitrəfi'kāshən/ n. [ME: from Fr. *vitrifier*, or based on L. *vitrum* 'glass.']

vi·trine /və'trēn/ ▶ n. a glass display case. [Fr., from *vitre* 'glass pane.']

vit·ri·ol /'vitrēəl; -,ôl/ ▶ n. archaic literary sulfuric acid. ■ fig. cruel and bitter criticism. — **vit·ri·ol·ic** /,vitrē'älik/ adj. [ME (denoting the sulfate of various metals): from OFr., or from med. L. *vitriolum*, from L. *vitrum* 'glass.']

Vi·tru·vi·us /və'trōōvēəs/ (*fl.* 1st century BC), Roman architect; full name *Marcus Vitruvius Pollio.* He wrote a 10-volume treatise on architecture.

vit·ta /'vitə/ ▶ n. (pl. **vit·tae** /'vitē; 'vitī/) **1** Bot. an oil tube in the fruit of some plants. **2** Zool. a band or stripe of color. [19th C.: from L., 'band, chaplet.']

vit·tle ▶ n. archaic var. of VICTUAL.

vi·tu·per·ate /və't(y)ōōpə,rāt; vī-/ ▶ v. [trans.] archaic blame or insult (someone) in strong or violent language. — **vi·tu·per·a·tor** /-pə,rātər/ n. [16th C.: from L. *vituperat-* 'censured, disparaged,' from the v. *vituperare*, from *vitium* 'fault' + *parare* 'prepare.']

vi·tu·per·a·tion /və,t(y)ōōpə'rāshən; vī-/ ▶ n. bitter and abusive language.

vi·tu·per·a·tive /və't(y)ōōpə,rātiv; vī-; -p(ə)rətiv/ ▶ adj. bitter and abusive.

Vi·tus, St. /'vītəs/ (died *c.*300), Christian martyr. He is the patron of those who suffer from disorders such as St. Vitus's dance (Sydenham's chorea).

vi·va /'vēvə/ ▶ exclam. long live (used to express acclaim for a specified person or thing): *"Viva Mexico!"* ▶ n. a cry of this as a salute or cheer. [Ital. and Sp.]

vi·va·ce /vē'vä,chā; -chē/ Music ▶ adv. & adj. (esp. as a direction) in a lively and brisk manner. ▶ n. a passage or movement marked to be performed in this manner. [Ital., 'brisk, lively,' from L. *vivax, vivac-*.]

vi·va·cious /və'vāshəs; vī-/ ▶ adj. (esp. of a woman) attractively lively and animated. — **vi·va·cious·ly** adv. **vi·va·cious·ness** n. **vi·vac·i·ty** /və'vasitē; vī-/ n. [17th C.: from L. *vivax, vivac-* 'lively, vigorous' (from *vivere* 'to live') + -IOUS.]

Vi·val·di /vi'väldē; -'vôldē/, Antonio Lucio (1678–1741), Italian composer. His works include the concerto *The Four Seasons* (1725).

vi·var·i·um /vī've(ə)rēəm/ ▶ n. (pl. **-var·i·a** /-'ve(ə)rēə/) an enclosure, container, or structure adapted or prepared for keeping animals under seminatural conditions for observation or study or as pets; an aquarium or terrarium. [17th C.: from L., 'warren, fishpond,' from *vivus* 'living,' from *vivere* 'to live.']

vi·vat /'vē,vat; -,vät; 'vī,vat/ ▶ exclam. & n. Latin term for VIVA.

vi·va vo·ce /,vēvə 'vōchā; ,vīvə 'vōsē/ ▶ adj. (esp. of an examination) oral rather than written. ▶ adv. orally rather than in writing. ▶ n. (also **vi·va**) Brit. an oral examination, typically for an academic qualification. [16th C.: from med. L., lit. 'with the living voice.']

vive la dif·fé·rence /'vēv(ə) lä ,difə'räns/ ▶ exclam. esp. humorous an expression of approval of difference, esp. that between the sexes. [from Fr., lit. 'long live the difference.']

vi·ver·id /vī'verid; vi-/ ▶ n. Zool. a mammal of the civet family (Viverridae). [20th C.: from mod. L. *Viverridae*, from L. *viverra* 'ferret.']

viv·i·an·ite /'vivēə,nīt/ ▶ n. a mineral consisting of a phosphate of iron that occurs as a secondary mineral in ore deposits. It is colorless when fresh but becomes blue or green with oxidization. [19th C.: named after John H. *Vivian* (1785–1855), British mineralogist, + -ITE[1].]

viv·id /'vivid/ ▶ adj. **1** producing powerful feelings or strong, clear images in the mind: *vivid memories.* ■ (of a color) intensely deep or bright. **2** archaic (of a person or animal) lively and vigorous. — **viv·id·ly** adv. **viv·id·ness** n. [17th C.: from L. *vividus*, from *vivere* 'to live.']

viv·i·fy /'vivə,fī/ ▶ v. (**-fies, -fied**) [trans.] enliven or animate: *outings vivify learning for children.* — **viv·i·fi·ca·tion** /,vivəfi'kāshən/ n. [ME: from Fr. *vivifier*, from late L. *vivificare*, from L. *vivus* 'living,' from *vivere* 'to live.']

vi·vip·a·rous /vī'vip(ə)rəs; vi-/ ▶ adj. Zool. (of an animal) bringing forth live young that have developed inside the body of the parent. Compare with OVIPAROUS and OVOVIVIPAROUS. ■ Bot. (of a plant) reproducing from buds that form plantlets while still attached to the parent plant, or from seeds that germinate within the fruit. — **viv·i·par·i·ty** /,vivə'paritē; ,vīvə-/ n. **vi·vip·a·rous·ly** adv. [17th C.: from L. *viviparus* (from *vivus* 'alive' + *-parus* 'bearing') + -OUS.]

viv·i·sect /ˈvivəˌsekt; ˌvivəˈsekt/ ▶v. [trans.] perform vivisection on (an animal) (used only by people who are opposed to the practice). — **viv·i·sec·tor** /-tər/ n. [19th C.: back-form. from VIVISECTION.]

viv·i·sec·tion /ˌvivəˈsekshən/ ▶n. the practice of performing operations on live animals for the purpose of experimentation or scientific research (used only by people who are opposed to such work). ■ fig. ruthlessly sharp and detailed criticism or analysis: *the vivisection of America's seamy underbelly.* — **viv·i·sec·tion·ist** /-ist/ n. & adj. [18th C.: from L. *vivus* 'living,' on the pattern of *dissection*.]

vix·en /ˈviksən/ ▶n. a female fox. ■ a spiteful or quarrelsome woman. — **vix·en·ish** adj. [ME *fixen*, perh. from the OE adj. *fyxen* 'of a fox.' The *v-* is from dial.]

Vi·yel·la /vīˈelə/ ▶n. trademark a fabric made from a twilled mixture of cotton and wool.

viz. /viz/ ▶adv. namely; in other words (used esp. to introduce a gloss or explanation): *the first music-reproducing media, viz., the music box and the player piano.* [abbrev. of VIDELICET, z being a med. L. symbol for *-et.*]

viz·ard /ˈvizərd/ ▶n. archaic a mask or disguise. [16th C.: alt. of VISOR.]

vi·zier /vəˈzi(ə)r/ ▶n. hist. a high official in some Muslim countries, esp. in Turkey under Ottoman rule. — **vi·zier·ate** /-ˈzi(ə)rit; -ˈzi(ə)rˌāt/ n. **vi·zier·i·al** /-ˈzi(ə)rēəl/ adj. **vi·zier·ship** /-ˌship/ n. [16th C.: via Turk. from Arab. *wazīr* 'caliph's chief counselor.']

vi·zor ▶n. var. of VISOR.

vizs·la /ˈvizhlə; ˈvēzlə/ ▶n. a dog of a breed of golden-brown pointer with large drooping ears. [1940s: from the name of a town in Hungary.]

VJ ▶abbr. video jockey.

V-J Day ▶n. Victory over Japan Day: the day (August 15, 1945) on which Japan ceased fighting in World War II, or the day (September 2, 1945) on which Japan formally surrendered. [*V-J*, abbrev. of *Victory over Japan*.]

VLA ▶abbr. Very Large Array (telescope).

Vlach /vläk; vlak/ ▶n. a member of the indigenous population of Romania and Moldova, claiming descent from the inhabitants of the Roman province of Dacia. ▶adj. of or relating to this people. [from a Slavic word meaning 'foreigner,' from Gmc.]

Vla·di·kav·kaz /ˌvladəˌkäfˈkäz; -ˈkäs/ a city in southwestern Russia; pop. 306,000. Former names ORDZHONIKIDZE (1931–44 and 1954–93) and DZAUDZHIKAU (1944–54).

Vlad·i·mir /ˈvladəˌmi(ə)r; vləˈd(y)ēmir/ a city in western Russia, east of Moscow; pop. 353,000.

Vlad·i·mir I (956–1015), grand prince of Kiev 980–1015; known as **Vladimir the Great**; canonized as **St. Vladimir**.

Vla·di·vos·tok /ˌvladəˈväsˌtäk; -vəˈstäk/ a city in southeastern Russia; pop. 643,000.

Vla·minck /vləˈmaNGk; -ˈmaNk/, Maurice de (1876–1958), French painter. He was a leading exponent of fauvism.

VLF ▶abbr. very low frequency (denoting radio waves of frequency 3–30 kHz and wavelength 10–100 km).

VLSI Electron. ▶abbr. very large-scale integration, the process of integrating hundreds of thousands of components on a single silicon chip.

Vl·ta·va /ˈvəltəvə/ a river in the Czech Republic that rises on the German–Czech border and flows north to the Elbe River north of Prague. German name MOLDAU.

V-mail ▶n. **1** a method of microfilming US soldiers' mail to and from home to cut down on shipping costs during World War II, with "V" standing for "victory." **2** short for VOICE MAIL. **3** short for VIDEO MAIL.

VMD ▶abbr. ■ Doctor of Veterinary Medicine. [from L., *Veterinariae Medicinae Doctor*.]

V-neck ▶n. a neckline of a garment, having straight sides meeting at a point to form a V-shape. ■ a garment with a neckline of this type. — **V-necked** adj.

voc. ▶abbr. ■ vocational. ■ Gram. vocative.

vocab. ▶abbr. ■ vocabulary.

vo·ca·ble /ˈvōkəbəl/ ▶n. a word, esp. with reference to form rather than meaning. [ME (denoting a name): from Fr., or from L. *vocabulum*, from *vocare* 'call.']

vo·cab·u·lar·y /vōˈkabyəˌlerē/ ▶n. (pl. **-lar·ies**) the body of words used in a particular language. ■ a part of such a body of words used on a particular occasion or in a particular sphere: *the vocabulary of law.* ■ the body of words known to an individual person: *he had a wide vocabulary.* ■ a list of difficult or unfamiliar words with an explanation of their meanings, accompanying a piece of specialist or foreign-language text. ■ a range of artistic or stylistic forms, techniques, or movements: *dance companies have their own vocabularies of movement.* [16th C.: from med. L. *vocabularius*, from L. *vocabulum* (see VOCABLE).]

vo·cal /ˈvōkəl/ ▶adj. **1** of or relating to the human voice. ■ Anat. used in the production of speech sounds. ■ Phonet. (of a sound in speech) made with the voice rather than the breath alone; voiced. **2** expressing opinions or feelings freely or loudly: *he was vocal in condemning the action.* **3** (of music) consisting of or incorporating singing. ▶n. (often **vocals**) a part of a piece of music that is sung. ■ a musical performance involving singing. — **vo·cal·i·ty** /vōˈkalətē/ n. **vo·cal·ly** adv. [ME: from L. *vocalis*, from *vox, voc-* (see VOICE).]

vo·cal cords (also **vo·cal folds**) ▶plural n. folds of membranous tissue that project inward from the sides of the larynx to form a slit across the glottis in the throat, and whose edges vibrate in the airstream to produce the voice.

vo·cal·ese /ˌvōkəˈlēz/ ▶n. a style of singing in which singers put words to jazz tunes, esp. to previously improvised instrumental solos. See SCAT[2].

vo·cal·ic /vōˈkalik; və-/ ▶adj. Phonet. of, relating to, or consisting of a vowel or vowels.

vo·ca·lise /ˈvōkəˌlēz; ˌvōkəˈlēz/ ▶n. Music a singing exercise using individual syllables or vowel sounds to develop flexibility and control of pitch and tone. ■ a vocal passage consisting of a melody without words: *the second movement is in the spirit of a vocalise.*

vo·cal·ism /ˈvōkəˌlizəm/ ▶n. **1** the use of the voice or vocal organs in speech. ■ the skill or art of exercising the voice in singing. **2** Phonet. a vowel sound or articulation. ■ a system of vowels used in a given language.

vo·cal·ist /ˈvōkəlist/ ▶n. a singer, typically one who regularly performs with a jazz or pop group.

vo·cal·ize /ˈvōkəˌlīz/ ▶v. [trans.] **1** utter (a sound or word): *the child vocalizes a number of distinct sounds* | [intrans.] *a warbler vocalized from a reed bed.* ■ express (something) with words. ■ [intrans.] Music sing with several notes to one vowel. **2** Phonet. change (a consonant) to a semivowel or vowel. **3** write (a language such as Hebrew) with vowel points. — **vo·cal·i·za·tion** /ˌvōkələˈzāshən/ n. **vo·cal·iz·er** n.

vo·cal sac ▶n. Zool. (in many male frogs) a loose fold of skin on each side of the mouth, which can be inflated to produce sound.

vo·cal score ▶n. a musical score showing the voice parts in full, but with the accompaniment reduced or omitted.

vo·ca·tion /vōˈkāshən/ ▶n. a strong feeling of suitability for a particular career or occupation. ■ a person's employment or main occupation, esp. regarded as particularly worthy and requiring great dedication. ■ a trade or profession. [ME: from OFr., or from L. *vocatio(n-)*, from *vocare* 'to call.']

vo·ca·tion·al /vōˈkāshənl/ ▶adj. of or relating to an occupation or employment. ■ (of education or training) directed at a particular occupation and its skills: *vocational school.* — **vo·ca·tion·al·ism** /-ˌizəm/ n. **vo·ca·tion·al·ize** /-ˌīz/ v. **vo·ca·tion·al·ly** adv.

voc·a·tive /ˈväkətiv/ Gram. ▶adj. relating to or denoting a case of nouns, pronouns, and adjectives in Latin and other languages, used in addressing or invoking a person or thing. ▶n. a word in the vocative case. ■ (**the vocative**) the vocative case. [ME: from OFr. *vocatif, -ive* or L. *vocativus*, from *vocare* 'to call.']

vo·cif·er·ate /vəˈsifəˌrāt; vō-/ ▶v. [intrans.] shout, complain, or argue loudly or vehemently: *he then began to vociferate pretty loudly* | [trans.] *he entered, vociferating curses.* — **vo·cif·er·ant** /-ərənt/ adj. **vo·cif·er·a·tion** /-ˌsifəˈrāshən/ n. [16th C.: from L. *vociferat-* 'exclaimed,' from the v. *vociferari*, from *vox* 'voice' + *ferre* 'carry.']

vo·cif·er·ous /vəˈsifərəs; vō-/ ▶adj. (esp. of a person or speech) vehement or clamorous. — **vo·cif·er·ous·ly** adv. **vo·cif·er·ous·ness** n.

vo·cod·er /ˈvōˌkōdər/ ▶n. a synthesizer that produces sounds from an analysis of speech input. [1930s: from VOICE + CODE + -ER[1].]

VOD ▶abbr. video-on-demand.

vod·ka /ˈvädkə/ ▶n. an alcoholic spirit of Russian origin made by distillation of rye, wheat, or potatoes. [Russ., dimin. of *voda* 'water.']

vo·dun /vōˈdo͞on/ ▶n. another term for VOODOO. [Fon, 'fetish.']

vogue /vōg/ ▶n. [usu. in sing.] the prevailing fashion or style at a particular time: *the vogue is realism.* ■ general acceptance or favor; popularity: *art deco was much in vogue.* ▶adj. [attrib.] popular; fashionable. — **vogu·ish** adj. [16th C.: from Fr., from Ital. *voga* 'rowing, fashion,' from *vogare* 'row, go well.']

voice /vois/ ▶n. **1** the sound produced in a person's larynx and uttered through the mouth, as speech or song. ■ an agency by which a particular point of view is expressed or represented: *the proud voice of middle-class conservatism.* ■ [in sing.] the right to express an opinion: *it gives minority parties a voice.* ■ a particular opinion expressed: *a dissenting voice.* ■ the ability to speak or sing: *she'd lost her voice.* ■ (usu. **voices**) the supposed utterance of a guiding spirit, typically giving instructions or advice. ■ the distinctive tone or style of a literary work or author. **2** Music the range of pitch or type of tone with which a person sings, such as soprano or tenor. ■ a vocal part in a composition. ■ a constituent part in a fugue. ■ each of the notes or sounds able to be produced simultaneously by a musical instrument (esp. an electronic one) or a computer. ■ (in an electronic musical instrument) each of a number of preset or programmable tones. **3** Phonet. sound uttered with resonance of the vocal cords (used in the pronunciation of vowels and certain consonants). **4** Gram. a form or set of forms of a verb showing the relation of the subject to the action: *the passive voice.* ▶v. [trans.] **1** express (something) in words: *get teachers to voice their opinions on important subjects.* **2** [usu. as adj.] (**voiced**) Phonet. utter (a speech sound) with resonance of the vocal cords (e.g., *b, d, g, v, z*). **3** Music regulate the tone quality of (organ pipes).
– PHRASES **give voice to** allow (a particular emotion, opinion, or point of view) to be expressed. ■ allow (a person or group) to express their emotions, opinion, or point of view. **in voice** in proper vocal condition for singing or speaking: *the soprano is in marvelous voice.* **with one voice** in complete agreement. — **voiced** adj. [in comb.] *deep-voiced.* **voic·er** n. (in sense 3 of the **verb**). [ME: from OFr. *vois*, from L. *vox, voc-*.]

voice box ▶ n. the larynx.

voice·less /'voislis/ ▶ adj. mute; speechless. ■ not expressed. ■ (of a person or group) lacking the power or right to express an opinion or exert control over affairs. ■ Phonet. (of a speech sound) uttered without resonance of the vocal cords, e.g., *f* as opposed to *v*, *p* as opposed to *b*, and *s* as opposed to *z*. — **voice·less·ly** adv. **voice·less·ness** n.

voice mail (also **voice·mail**) ▶ n. a centralized electronic system that can store messages from telephone callers.

voice-o·ver ▶ n. a piece of narration in a movie or broadcast, not accompanied by an image of the speaker.

voice·print /'vois,print/ ▶ n. a visual record of speech, analyzed with respect to frequency, duration, and amplitude. [1960s: on the pattern of *fingerprint*.]

voice re·cog·ni·tion tech·nol·o·gy ▶ n. the technology that enables a machine or computer program to receive and interpret dictation or to understand and carry out spoken commands.

void /void/ ▶ adj. **1** not valid or legally binding. ■ (of speech or action) ineffectual; useless. **2** completely empty: *void spaces surround the tanks.* ■ (**void of**) free from; lacking: *void of meaning.* ■ formal (of an office or position) vacant. **3** (in bridge and whist) having been dealt no cards in a particular suit. ▶ n. **1** a completely empty space: *the black void of space.* ■ an emptiness caused by the loss of something. ■ an unfilled space in a wall, building, or structure. **2** (in bridge and whist) a suit in which a player is dealt no cards. ▶ v. [trans.] **1** declare that (something) is not valid or legally binding: *the Supreme Court voided the statute.* **2** discharge or drain away (water, gases, etc.). ■ esp. Med. excrete (waste matter). ■ empty or evacuate (a container or space). — **void·a·ble** adj. **void·ness** n. [ME: from a dial. var. of Old Fr. *vuide*; rel. to L. *vacare* 'vacate'; the v. partly a shortening of AVOID, reinforced by OFr. *voider*.]

void·ance /'voidns/ ▶ n. the action of voiding something or the state of being voided. ■ esp. Law an annulment of a contract. ■ Christian Church a vacancy in a benefice.

void·ed /'voidid/ ▶ adj. Heraldry (of a bearing) having the central area cut away so as to show the field.

voi·là /vwä'lä/ (also **voi·la**) ▶ exclam. there it is; there you are: *"Voilà!" she said, producing a pair of white sandals.* [Fr.]

voile /voil/ ▶ n. a thin, plain-weave, semitransparent fabric of cotton, wool, or silk. [19th C.: Fr., lit. 'veil.']

VOIP ▶ abbr. voice over Internet protocol, a technology for making telephone calls over the Internet in which speech sounds are converted into binary data.

voir dire /'vwär 'di(ə)r/ ▶ n. Law a preliminary examination of a witness or a juror by a judge or counsel. ■ an oath taken by such a witness. [Law Fr., from OFr. *voir* 'true' + *dire* 'say.']

Voj·vo·di·na /'voivə,dēnə/ a province in northern Serbia; capital, Novi Sad.

vol. ▶ abbr. volume.

Vo·lans /'vōlənz/ Astron. an inconspicuous southern constellation (the Flying Fish), between Carina and the south celestial pole.

vo·lant /'vōlənt/ ▶ adj. Zool. (of an animal) able to fly or glide: *newly volant young.* ■ of, relating to, or characterized by flight. ■ [usu. postpositive] Heraldry represented as flying: *a falcon volant.* ■ literary moving rapidly or lightly. [16th C.: from Fr., lit. 'flying,' pres. part. of *voler*, from L. *volare* 'to fly.']

Vo·la·pük /'vōlə,po͝ok; 'vôlə-; 'välə-/ ▶ n. an artificial language devised in 1879 and proposed for international use by a German cleric, Johann M. Schleyer, and based on extremely modified forms of words from English and Romance languages. [from *vol* representing Engl. *world* + *-a-* + *pük* representing Engl. *speak* or *speech*.]

vo·lar /'vōlər/ ▶ adj. Anat. relating to the palm of the hand or the sole of the foot. [19th C.: from L. *vola* 'hollow of hand or foot' + -AR[1].]

vol·a·tile /'välətl/ ▶ adj. **1** (of a substance) easily evaporated at normal temperatures. **2** liable to change rapidly and unpredictably, esp. for the worse: *the situation was becoming more volatile.* ■ (of a person) liable to display rapid changes of emotion. ■ (of a computer's memory) retaining data only as long as there is a power supply connected. ▶ n. (usu. **volatiles**) a volatile substance. — **vol·a·til·i·ty** /,välə'tilitē/ n. [ME: from OFr. *volatil* or L. *volatilis*, from *volare* 'to fly.']

vol·a·tile oil ▶ n. another term for ESSENTIAL OIL.

vol·a·til·ize /'välətl,īz/ ▶ v. [trans.] cause (a substance) to evaporate or disperse in vapor. ■ [intrans.] become volatile; evaporate. — **vol·a·til·iz·a·ble** adj. **vol·a·til·i·za·tion** /,välətl-ə'zāsʜən/ n.

vol-au-vent /,vôl ō'vän/ ▶ n. a small round case of puff pastry filled with a savory mixture, typically of meat or fish in a richly flavored sauce. [Fr., lit. 'flight in the wind.']

vol·can·ic /väl'kanik; vôl-/ ▶ adj. of, relating to, or produced by a volcano or volcanoes. ■ fig. (esp. of a feeling or emotion) bursting out or liable to burst out violently. — **vol·can·i·cal·ly** /-ik(ə)lē/ adv.

vol·can·ic bomb ▶ n. see BOMB (sense 2).

vol·can·ic glass ▶ n. another term for OBSIDIAN.

vol·can·ic·i·ty /,välkə'nisitē; ,vôl-/ ▶ n. another term for VOLCANISM.

vol·can·ic neck ▶ n. see NECK (sense 2).

vol·can·ism /'välkə,nizəm; 'vôl-/ (also **vul·can·ism**) ▶ n. Geol. volcanic activity or phenomena.

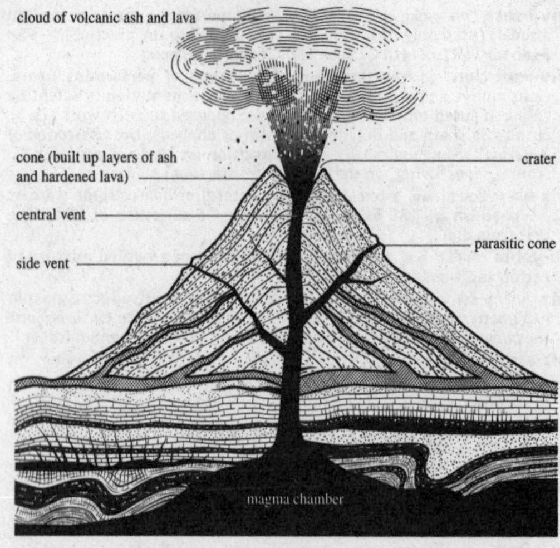

volcano

vol·ca·no /väl'kānō; vôl-/ ▶ n. (pl. **-noes** or **-nos**) a mountain or hill, typically conical, having a crater or vent through which lava, rock fragments, hot vapor, and gas are or have been erupted from the earth's crust. ■ fig. an intense suppressed emotion or situation liable to burst out suddenly. [17th C.: from Ital., from L. *Volcanus* 'Vulcan.']

vol·can·ol·o·gy /,välkə'näləjē; ,vôl-/ (also **vul·can·ol·o·gy**) ▶ n. the scientific study of volcanoes. — **vol·can·o·log·i·cal** /,välkanl'äjikəl; ,vôl-/ adj. **vol·can·ol·o·gist** /-jist/ n.

vole /vōl/ ▶ n. a small, typically burrowing, mouselike rodent (*Microtus* and other genera, subfamily Microtinae) with a rounded muzzle, found in both Eurasia and North America. [19th C. (orig. *vole-mouse*): from Norw. *voll(mus)* 'field (mouse).']

Vol·ga /'vōlgə; 'väl-; 'vôl-/ the longest river in Europe, rising in northwestern Russia and flowing east for 2,292 miles (3,688 km) to the Caspian Sea.

Vol·go·grad /'vōlgə,grad; 'väl-; 'vôl-/ a city in southwestern Russia; pop. 1,005,000. Former names TSARITSYN (until 1925) and STALINGRAD (1925–61).

vo·li·tion /və'lisʜən; vō-/ ▶ n. the faculty or power of using one's will.
– PHRASES **of** (or **by** or **on**) **one's own volition** voluntarily: *they choose to leave early of their own volition.* — **vo·li·tion·al** /-sʜənl/ adj. **vo·li·tion·al·ly** /-sʜənl-ē/ adv. **vol·i·tive** /'välətiv/ adj. (formal tech.). [17th C.: from Fr., or from med. L. *volitio(n-)*, from *volo* 'I wish.']

volks·lied /'fōks,lēt; 'fôlks-/ ▶ n. a German folk song, or a song in the style of one. ■ a national anthem, esp. that of the 19th-century Transvaal Republic.

vol·ley /'välē/ ▶ n. (pl. **-leys**) **1** a number of bullets, arrows, or other projectiles discharged at one time. ■ a series of utterances directed at someone in quick succession: *he unleashed a volley of angry questions.* ■ Tennis an exchange of shots. **2** (in sports, esp. tennis or soccer) a strike or kick of the ball made before it touches the ground. ▶ v. (**-leys, -leyed**) [trans.] (in sports, esp. tennis or soccer) strike or kick (the ball) before it touches the ground. ■ score (a goal) with such a shot. ■ (in tennis and similar games) play a pregame point, sometimes in order to determine who will serve first. ■ utter or discharge in quick succession: *dog volleying joyful barks.* — **vol·ley·er** n. [16th C.: from Fr. *volée*, based on L. *volare* 'to fly.']

vol·ley·ball /'välē,bôl/ ▶ n. a game for two teams, usually of six players, in which a large ball is hit by hand over a high net, the aim being to score points by making the ball reach the ground on the opponent's side of the court. ■ the inflated ball used in this game.

vol·plane /'väl,plān; 'vôl-/ Aeron. ▶ n. a controlled dive or downward flight at a steep angle, esp. by an airplane with the engine shut off. ▶ v. [no obj., with adverbial of direction] (of an airplane) make such a dive or downward flight. [20th C.: from Fr. *vol plané*, lit. 'glided flight.']

vols ▶ abbr. volumes.

Vol·scian /'välsʜən; 'vôlskēən/ ▶ n. **1** a member of an ancient Italic people who fought the Romans in Latium in the 5th and 4th centuries BC until absorbed into Rome after their final defeat in 304 BC. **2** the Italic language of the Volscians. ▶ adj. of or relating to the Volscians. [from L. *Volsci* (the name of the people) + -AN.]

Vol·stead Act /'väl,sted; 'vôl-; 'vōl-/ a law that enforced alcohol prohibition in the US from 1920–33. [named after Andrew J. *Volstead* (1860–1947), American legislator.]

volt[1] /vōlt/ (abbr.: **V**) ▶ n. the SI unit of electromotive force, the difference of potential that would carry one ampere of current against one ohm resistance. [19th C.: named after A. *Volta* (see VOLTA[2]).]

volt[2] /vōlt; vôlt; vält/ (also **volte**) ▶ n. Fencing a sudden quick jump or other movement to escape a thrust. ▶ v. [intrans.] Fencing make a quick movement to avoid a thrust. [17th C.: from Fr. *volter* (see VOLTE).]

Vol·ta[1] /ˈvōltə; ˈväl-; ˈvôl-/ a river in West Africa that is formed in central Ghana by the junction of its headwaters, the Black Volta, the White Volta, and the Red Volta rivers. It flows south to the Gulf of Guinea.

Vol·ta[2] /ˈvōltə/, Alessandro Giuseppe Antonio Anastasio, Count (1745–1827), Italian physicist. He developed the voltaic pile or electrochemical battery in 1800.

volt·age /ˈvōltij/ ▶ n. Physics an electromotive force or potential difference expressed in volts.

volt·age di·vid·er ▶ n. a series of resistors or capacitors that can be tapped at any intermediate point to produce a specific fraction of the voltage applied between its ends.

Vol·ta·ic /välˈtā-ik; vōl-; vôl-/ ▶ adj. & n. another term for GUR.

vol·ta·ic /välˈtā-ik; vōl-; vôl-/ ▶ adj. of or relating to electricity produced by chemical action in a primary battery; galvanic. [19th C.: from the name of A. *Volta* (see VOLTA[2]) + -IC.]

Vol·taire /vōlˈte(ə)r; vôl-/ (1694–1778), French writer; pen name of *François-Marie Arouet*. A leading figure of the Enlightenment, his works include *Candide* (1759).

volt-am·pere ▶ n. a unit of electrical power equal to the product of one volt and one ampere and equivalent to one watt of direct current.

volte ▶ n. **1** var. of VOLT[2]. **2** a movement performed in dressage and classical riding, in which a horse describes a circle of 6 yards diameter. [17th C.: from Fr., from Ital. *volta* 'a turn,' from *volgere* 'to turn.']

volte-face /ˌvält(ə) ˈfäs; ˌvōlt(ə); ˌvôlt(ə)/ ▶ n. (pl. same) an act of turning around so as to face in the opposite direction. ■ an abrupt and complete reversal of attitude, opinion, or position: *a remarkable volte-face on taxes.* [19th C.: from Fr., from Ital. *voltafaccia*, based on L. *volvere* 'to roll' + *facies* 'appearance, face.']

volt·me·ter /ˈvōltˌmētər/ ▶ n. an instrument for measuring electric potential in volts.

vol·u·ble /ˈvälyəbəl/ ▶ adj. speaking or spoken incessantly and fluently. — **vol·u·bil·i·ty** /ˌvälyəˈbilətē/ n. **vol·u·ble·ness** n. **vol·u·bly** /-blē/ adv. [16th C.: from Fr., or from L. *volubilis*, from *volvere* 'to roll.']

vol·ume /ˈvälyəm; -ˌyo͞om/ ▶ n. **1** a book forming part of a work or series. ■ a single book or a bound collection of printed sheets. ■ a consecutive sequence of issues of a periodical. ■ hist. a scroll of parchment or papyrus containing written matter. **2** the amount of space that a substance or object occupies, or that is enclosed within a container, esp. when great. ■ the amount or quantity of something, esp. when great: *the volume of consumer spending.* ■ **(a volume of/volumes of)** a certain, typically large, amount of something: *volumes of data.* ■ fullness or expansive thickness of something, esp. of a person's hair. **3** quantity or power of sound; degree of loudness. [ME: from OFr. *volum(e)*, from L. *volumen* 'a roll,' from *volvere* 'to roll.']

vol·u·met·ric /ˌvälyəˈmetrik/ ▶ adj. of or relating to the measurement of volume. ■ (of chemical analysis) based on measuring the volumes of reagents, esp. by titration. — **vol·u·met·ri·cal·ly** /-ˈmetrik(ə)lē/ adv. [19th C.: from VOLUME + METRIC[1].]

vol·u·met·ric ef·fi·cien·cy ▶ n. the ratio of the volume of fluid actually displaced by a piston or plunger to its swept volume.

vo·lu·mi·nous /vəˈlo͞omənəs/ ▶ adj. occupying or containing much space; large in volume, in particular: ■ (of clothing or drapery) loose and ample. ■ (of writing) very lengthy and full. ■ (of a writer) producing many books. — **vo·lu·mi·nous·ly** adv. **vo·lu·mi·nous·ness** n. [17th C.: partly from late L. *voluminosus* 'having many coils,' partly from L. *volumen, volumin-* (see VOLUME).]

vol·u·mize /ˈvälyəˌmīz; -yo͞o-/ ▶ v. [trans.] (of a product or styling technique) give body to (hair). — **vol·um·iz·er** n.

vol·un·ta·rism /ˈvälәntəˌrizəm/ ▶ n. **1** the principle of relying on voluntary action (used esp. with reference to the involvement of voluntary organizations in social welfare). ■ hist. (esp. in the 19th century) the principle that churches or schools should be independent of the state and supported by voluntary contributions. **2** Philos. the doctrine that the will is a fundamental or dominant factor in the individual or the universe. — **vol·un·ta·rist** n. & adj. **vol·un·ta·ris·tic** /ˌväləntəˈristik/ adj.

vol·un·tar·y /ˈvälənˌterē/ ▶ adj. done, given, or acting of one's own free will: *voluntary contributions.* ■ working, done, or maintained without payment. ■ supported by contributions rather than taxes or fees. ■ Physiol. under the conscious control of the brain. ■ Law (of a conveyance or disposition) made without return in money or other consideration. ▶ n. (pl. **-tar·ies**) an organ solo played before, during, or after a church service. ■ hist. a piece of music performed extempore, esp. as a prelude to other music, or composed in a free style. — **vol·un·tar·i·ly** /ˌvälənˈte(ə)rəlē; ˈvälənˌter-/ adv. **vol·un·tar·i·ness** n. [ME: from OFr. *volontaire* or L. *voluntarius*, from *voluntas* 'will.']

vol·un·tar·y·ism /ˈvälənˌterēˌizəm/ ▶ n. less common term for VOLUNTARISM (sense 1). — **vol·un·tar·y·ist** n.

vol·un·teer /ˌvälənˈti(ə)r/ ▶ n. a person who freely offers to take part in an enterprise or undertake a task. ■ a person who works for an organization without being paid. ■ a person who freely enrolls for military service rather than being conscripted, esp. a member of a force formed by voluntary enrollment and distinct from the regular army. ■ a plant that has not been deliberately planted. ■ Law a person to whom a voluntary conveyance or deposition is made. ▶ v. [intrans.] freely offer to do something. ■ [trans.] offer (help) in such a way: *he volunteered his services as a driver for the convoy.* ■ say or suggest something without being asked: [trans.] *never volunteer information* | [with direct speech] *"Her name's Louise," Christina volunteered.* ■ work for an organization without being paid. ■ [trans.] commit (someone) to a particular undertaking, typically without consulting them. [16th C.: from Fr. *volontaire* 'voluntary.']

vol·un·teer·ism /ˌvälənˈti(ə)rˌizəm/ ▶ n. the use or involvement of volunteer labor, esp. in community services.

vo·lup·tu·ar·y /vəˈləpcho͞oˌerē/ ▶ n. (pl. **-ar·ies**) a person devoted to luxury and sensual pleasure. ▶ adj. concerned with luxury and sensual pleasure.

vo·lup·tu·ous /vəˈləpcho͞oəs/ ▶ adj. of, relating to, or characterized by luxury or sensual pleasure. ■ (of a woman) curvaceous and sexually attractive. — **vo·lup·tu·ous·ly** adv. **vo·lup·tu·ous·ness** n. [ME: from OFr. *voluptueux* or L. *voluptuosus*, from *voluptas* 'pleasure.']

vo·lute /vəˈlo͞ot/ ▶ n. **1** Archit. a spiral scroll characteristic of Ionic capitals and also used in Corinthian and composite capitals. **2** a deep-water marine mollusk (*Voluta* and other genera, family Volutidae) with a thick spiral shell that is colorful and prized by collectors. ▶ adj. forming a spiral curve or curves: *volute springs.* — **vo·lut·ed** adj. [16th C.: from Fr., or from L. *voluta*, fem. past part. of *volvere* 'to roll.']

volute 1

vo·lu·tion /vəˈlo͞oshən/ ▶ n. **1** literary a rolling or revolving motion. **2** a single turn of a spiral or coil.

vol·va /ˈvälvə; ˈvôl-/ ▶ n. Bot. (in certain fungi) a veil that encloses the fruiting body, often persisting after rupture as a sheath at the base of the stalk. [18th C.: mod. L., from L. *volvere* 'to roll, wrap around.']

vol·vox /ˈvälˌväks; ˈvôl-/ ▶ n. Biol. a green, single-celled aquatic organism (genus *Volvox*, division Chlorophyta) that forms minute, free-swimming spherical colonies. [mod. L., from L. *volvere* 'to roll.']

vol·vu·lus /ˈvälvyələs; ˈvôl-/ ▶ n. (pl. **-li** /-ˌlī; -ˌlē/ or **-lus·es**) Med. an obstruction caused by twisting of the stomach or intestine. [17th C.: mod. or med. L., from L. *volvere* 'to roll.']

vo·mer /ˈvōmər/ ▶ n. Anat. the small thin bone separating the left and right nasal cavities in humans and most vertebrates. [18th C.: from L., 'plowshare.']

vom·it /ˈvämət/ ▶ v. (**-it·ed, -it·ing**) [intrans.] eject matter from the stomach through the mouth: *it made him want to vomit* | [trans.] *she used to vomit up her food.* ■ [trans.] emit (something) in an uncontrolled stream or flow: *the machine vomited fold after fold of paper.* ▶ n. **1** matter vomited from the stomach. **2** archaic an emetic. — **vom·it·er** n. [ME: from OFr. *vomite* (n.) or L. *vomitus*, from *vomere* 'to vomit.']

vom·i·to·ri·um /ˌväməˈtôrēəm/ ▶ n. (pl. **-tor·i·a** /-ˈtôrēə/) **1** each of a series of entrance or exit passages in an ancient Roman amphitheater or theater. **2** a place in which, according to popular misconception, the ancient Romans are supposed to have vomited during feasts to make room for more food.

vom·i·to·ry /ˈväməˌtôrē/ ▶ adj. **1** denoting the entrance or exit passages in a theater or amphitheater. **2** rare relating to or inducing vomiting. ▶ n. (pl. **-ries**) another term for VOMITORIUM (sense 1).

vom·i·tous /ˈvämətəs/ ▶ adj. nauseating.

vom·i·tus /ˈvämətəs/ ▶ n. esp. Med. matter that has been vomited. [20th C.: from L.]

von Braun /vän ˈbrôn; fôn ˈbroun/ see BRAUN[3].

Von·ne·gut /ˈvänigət/, Kurt, Jr. (1922–2007), US writer. His novels include *Cat's Cradle* (1963) and *Slaughterhouse-Five* (1969).

von Neu·mann /vän ˈnoiˌmän; -mən/ see NEUMANN.

voo·doo /ˈvo͞oˌdo͞o/ ▶ n. a black religious cult practiced in the Caribbean and the southern US, combining elements of Roman Catholic ritual with traditional African magical and religious rites, and characterized by sorcery and spirit possession. ■ a person skilled in such practice. ▶ v. (**-doos, -dooed**) [trans.] affect (someone) by the practice of such witchcraft. — **voo·doo·ism** /-ˌizəm/ n. **voo·doo·ist** /-ist/ n. [19th C.: from Louisiana Fr., from Kwa *vodū*.]

VOR ▶ abbr. visual omnirange, denoting a type of navigation system using a series of radio beacons.

vo·ra·cious /vəˈrāshəs/ ▶ adj. wanting or devouring great quantities of food: *he had a voracious appetite.* ■ having a very eager approach to an activity. — **vo·ra·cious·ly** adv. **vo·ra·cious·ness** n. **vo·rac·i·ty** /-ˈrasitē/ n. [17th C.: from L. *vorax, vorac-* (from *vorare* 'devour') + -IOUS.]

Vo·ro·nezh /vəˈrônish; -ˈrō-/ a city in Russia, south of Moscow; pop. 895,000.

-vorous ▶ comb. form feeding on a specified food: *carnivorous* | *herbivorous.* — **-vora** comb. form in corresponding names of groups **-vore** comb. form in corresponding names of individuals within such groups. [from L. *-vorus* (from *vorare* 'devour') + -OUS.]

vor·tex /ˈvôrˌteks/ ▶ n. (pl. **-tex·es** or **-ti·ces** /-təˌsēz/) a mass of whirling fluid or air, esp. a whirlpool or whirlwind. ■ fig. something regarded as a whirling mass. — **vor·ti·cal** /ˈvôrtikəl/ adj. **vor·ti·cal·ly** /ˈvôrtik(ə)lē/ adv. **vor·tic·i·ty** /vôrˈtisitē/ n. **vor·ti·cose** /ˈvôrtəˌkōs/ adj. **vor·tic·u·lar**

/vôr'tikyələr/ **adj.** [17th C.: from L. *vortex, vortic-*, 'eddy,' var. of VERTEX.]

vor·ti·cel·la /,vôrtə'selə/ ▶**n.** Zool. a sedentary, single-celled aquatic animal (genus *Vorticella*, phylum Ciliophora) with a contractile stalk and a bell-shaped body bearing a ring of cilia. [18th C.: mod. L., dimin. of L. *vortex, vortic-* 'eddy.']

Vor·ti·cist /'vôrtəsist/ ▶**n.** hist. a member of a British artistic movement of 1914–15 influenced by cubism and futurism and favoring machinelike forms. — **Vor·ti·cism** /-,sizəm/ **n.** [from L. *vortex, vortic-* 'eddy' + -IST.]

Vosges /vōzH/ a mountain range in eastern France.

Vos·tok /'väs,täk; ,və'stôk/ a series of six manned Soviet orbiting spacecraft, the first of which, launched in April 1961, carried the first man in space (Yuri Gagarin).

vo·ta·ry /'vōtərē/ ▶**n.** (pl. **-ries**) a person, such as a monk or nun, who has made vows of dedication to religious service. ■ a devoted follower, adherent, or advocate of someone or something: *he was a votary of John Keats.* — **vo·ta·rist** /-rist/ **n.** [16th C.: from L. *vot-* 'vowed' (from the v. *vovere*) + -ARY[1].]

vote /vōt/ ▶**n.** a formal indication of a choice between two or more candidates or courses of action, expressed typically through a ballot or a show of hands. ■ an act of expressing such an indication of choice. ■ **(the vote)** the choice expressed collectively by a body of electors or by a specified group. ■ **(the vote)** the right to indicate a choice in an election. ▶**v.** [intrans.] give or register a vote. ■ [with obj. and adverbial or complement] cause (someone) to gain or lose a particular post or honor by means of a vote: *incompetent judges are voted out of office.* ■ informal used to express a wish to follow a particular course of action: *I vote we have one more game.* ■ [trans.] (of a legislature) grant or confer by vote. ■ [trans.] **(vote something down)** reject (something) by means of a vote.

– PHRASES **vote of confidence** a vote showing that a majority continues to support the policy of a leader or governing body. **vote of no confidence** (or **vote of censure**) a vote showing that a majority does not support the policy of a leader or governing body. — **vote·less adj.** [ME: from L. *votum* 'a vow, wish,' from *vovere* 'to vow.']

vot·er /'vōtər/ ▶**n.** a person who votes or has the right to vote at an election.

vot·ing booth ▶**n.** a compartment with one open side in which one voter at a time stands to mark their ballot paper.

vot·ing ma·chine ▶**n.** a machine for the automatic registering of votes.

vo·tive /'vōtiv/ ▶**adj.** offered or consecrated in fulfillment of a vow: *votive offerings.* ▶**n.** an object offered in this way, such as a candle used as a vigil light. [16th C.: from L. *votivus*, from *votum* (see VOTE).]

vo·tive Mass ▶**n.** (in the Roman Catholic Church) a Mass celebrated for a special purpose or occasion.

vouch /voucH/ ▶**v.** [intrans.] **(vouch for)** assert or confirm as a result of one's own experience that something is true or accurately so described. ■ confirm that someone is who they say they are or that they are of good character: *someone could vouch for him.* [ME: from OFr. *voucher* 'summon,' based on L. *vocare* 'to call.']

vouch·er /'voucHər/ ▶**n.** a small printed piece of paper that entitles the holder to a discount or that may be exchanged for goods or services. ■ a receipt.

vouch·safe /,voucH'sāf; 'voucH,sāf/ ▶**v.** [trans.] (often **be vouchsafed**) give or grant (something) to (someone) in a gracious or condescending manner: *it is a blessing vouchsafed him by heaven.* ■ reveal or disclose (information). [ME: orig. as the phr. *vouch* something *safe* on someone, i.e., 'warrant the secure conferment of (something on someone).']

vous·soir /voo'swär/ ▶**n.** Archit. a wedge-shaped or tapered stone used to construct an arch. [18th C.: via Fr. from pop. L. *volsorium*, based on L. *volvere* 'to roll.']

Vou·vray /voo'vrā/ ▶**n.** dry white wine, either still or sparkling, produced in the Vouvray district of the Loire valley.

vow /vou/ ▶**n.** a solemn promise. ■ **(vows)** a set of such promises committing one to a prescribed role, calling, or course of action, typically to marriage or a monastic career. ▶**v. 1** [reporting verb] solemnly promise to do a specified thing: [with direct speech] *one fan vowed, "I'll picket every home game."* **2** [trans.] archaic dedicate to someone or something, esp. a deity: *I vowed myself to this enterprise.* [ME: from Old Fr. *vou*, from L. *votum* (see VOTE); the v. from OFr. *vouer*.]

vow·el /'vouəl/ ▶**n.** a speech sound that is produced by comparatively open configuration of the vocal tract, with vibration of the vocal cords but without audible friction and is a unit of the sound system of a language that forms the nucleus of a syllable. Contrasted with CONSONANT. ■ a letter representing such a sound, such as *a, e, i, o, u.* — **vow·eled** /'vouəld/ (Brit. **vow·elled**) **adj. vow·el·less adj.** [ME: from OFr. *vouel*, from L. *vocalis (littera)* 'vocal (letter).']

vow·el·ize /'vouə,līz/ ▶**v.** [trans.] supply (something such as a Hebrew or shorthand text) with vowel points or signs representing vowels.

vow·el point ▶**n.** each of a set of marks indicating vowels in writing phonetically explicit text in Semitic languages such as Hebrew and Arabic.

vow·el shift ▶**n.** Phonet. a phonetic change in a vowel or vowels. ■ **(the Great Vowel Shift)** a series of changes between medieval and modern English affecting the long vowels of the standard language.

vox an·gel·i·ca /'väks an'jelikə/ ▶**n.** a soft stop on an organ or harmonium that is tuned slightly sharp to produce a tremolo effect. [19th C.: from late L., lit. 'angelic voice.']

vox·el /'väksəl/ ▶**n.** (in computer-based modeling or graphic simulation) each of an array of elements of volume that constitute a notional three-dimensional space, esp. each of an array of discrete elements into which a representation of a three-dimensional object is divided. [1970s: from the initial letters of VOLUME and ELEMENT, with the insertion of *-x-* for ease of pronunc.]

vox hu·ma·na /'väks (h)yoo'mänə; -'manə; -'mānə/ ▶**n.** an organ stop with a tone supposedly resembling the human voice. [18th C.: from L., 'human voice.']

vox po·pu·li /'väks 'päpyə,lī; -,lē/ ▶**n.** [in sing.] the opinions or beliefs of the majority. [16th C.: from L., 'the people's voice.']

voy·age /'voi-ij/ ▶**n.** a long journey involving travel by sea or in space. ▶**v.** [no obj., with adverbial of direction] go on a long journey, typically by sea or in space. ■ [trans.] archaic sail over or along (a sea or river). — **voy·age·a·ble adj.** (archaic) **voy·ag·er n.** [ME (as a n. denoting a journey): from OFr. *voiage*, from L. *viaticum* 'provisions for a journey' (in late L. 'journey').]

Voy·ag·er /'voi-ijər/ either of two American space probes launched in 1977 to investigate the outer planets. Voyager 1 encountered Jupiter and Saturn, while Voyager 2 reached Jupiter, Saturn, Uranus, and finally Neptune (1989).

vo·ya·geur /,vwäyə'zHər; ,voi-ə-/ ▶**n.** hist. (in Canada) a boatman employed by the fur companies in transporting goods and passengers to and from the trading posts on the lakes and rivers. [Fr., lit. 'voyager,' from *voyager* 'to travel.']

vo·yeur /voi'yər; vwä-/ ▶**n.** a person who gains sexual pleasure from watching others when they are naked or engaged in sexual activity. ■ a person who enjoys seeing the pain or distress of others. — **vo·yeur·ism** /'voiyə,rizəm; voi'yər,izəm; vwä'yər-/ **n. voy·eur·is·tic** /,voiyə'ristik; ,vwäyə-/ **adj. voy·eur·is·ti·cal·ly** /,voiyə'ristik(ə)lē; ,vwäyə-/ **adv.** [20th C.: from Fr., from *voir* 'see.']

VP ▶**abbr.** vice president.

VPL informal ▶**abbr.** visible panty line.

VR ▶**abbr.** ■ Queen Victoria. [abbrev. of L. *Victoria Regina.*] ■ virtual reality.

VRAM /'vē,ram/ ▶**n.** Electron. a type of RAM used in computer display cards. [1990s: acronym from *video random access memory.*]

VRML Comput. ▶**abbr.** virtual reality modeling language.

vroom /vroom; vroom/ informal ▶**v.** [intrans.] (of an engine in a vehicle) make a roaring sound by being run at very high speed. ■ [trans.] cause (an engine in a vehicle) to make such a sound in this way. ■ [no obj., with adverbial of direction] (of a vehicle or its driver) travel at great speed. ▶**n.** the roaring sound of an engine or motor vehicle. ▶**exclam.** used to express or imitate such a sound to suggest speed or acceleration: *press the button and vroom!* [1960s: imitative.]

VS ▶**abbr.** veterinary surgeon.

vs ▶**abbr.** versus.

V-sign ▶**n. 1** a sign resembling the letter V made with the palm of the hand facing outward, used as a symbol or gesture of victory. **2** Brit. a similar sign made with the first two fingers pointing up and the back of the hand facing outward, used as a gesture of abuse or contempt.

VSO ▶**abbr.** Voluntary Service Overseas.

VSOP ▶**abbr.** Very Special Old Pale, a kind of brandy.

VT ▶**abbr.** Vermont (in official postal use).

Vt. ▶**abbr.** Vermont.

VTO ▶**abbr.** vertical takeoff.

VTOL /'vē,täl; -,tôl/ ▶**abbr.** vertical takeoff and landing.

VTR ▶**abbr.** videotape recorder.

vug /vəg/ ▶**n.** Geol. a cavity in rock, lined with mineral crystals. — **vug·gy** /'vəgē/ **adj. vug·u·lar** /'vəgyələr/ **adj.** [19th C.: from Cornish *vooga.*]

Vul·can /'vəlkən/ Rom. Mythol. the god of fire. Greek equivalent HEPHAESTUS.

Vul·ca·ni·an /,vəl'kānēən/ ▶**adj. 1** associated with the god Vulcan. ■ (also **vulcanian**) associated with metalworking or metallurgy. **2** (also **vulcanian**) Geol. relating to or denoting a type of volcanic eruption marked by periodic explosive events. [20th C.: from *Vulcano*, the name of a volcano in the Lipari Islands, Italy, + -IAN.]

vul·can·ism /'vəlkə,nizəm/ ▶**n.** var. of VOLCANISM.

vul·can·ite /'vəlkə,nīt/ ▶**n.** hard black vulcanized rubber. [19th C.: from VULCAN + -ITE[1].]

vul·can·ize /'vəlkə,nīz/ ▶**v.** [trans.] harden (rubber or rubberlike material) by treating it with sulfur at a high temperature. — **vul·can·iz·a·ble adj. vul·can·i·za·tion** /,vəlkənə'zāsHən/ **n. vul·can·iz·er n.** [19th C. (in the sense 'throw into a fire'): from VULCAN + -IZE.]

vul·can·ol·o·gy /,vəlkə'näləjē/ ▶**n.** var. of VOLCANOLOGY.

Vulg. ▶**abbr.** ■ Vulgate.

vul·gar /'vəlgər/ ▶**adj.** lacking sophistication or good taste; unrefined: *the vulgar trappings of wealth.* ■ making explicit and offensive reference to sex or bodily functions; coarse and rude: *a vulgar joke.* ■ dated characteristic of or belonging to the masses. — **vul·gar·i·ty** /,vəl'garitē/ **n.** (pl. **-ties**) **vul·gar·ly adv.** [ME: from L. *vulgaris*, from *vulgus* 'common people.']

vul·gar frac·tion ▶**n.** British term for COMMON FRACTION.

vul·gar·i·an /,vəl'ge(ə)rēən/ ▶**n.** an unrefined person, esp. one with newly acquired power or wealth.

vul·gar·ism /'vəlgə,rizəm/ ▶**n.** a word or expression that is considered inelegant, esp. one that makes explicit and offensive reference to sex or bodily functions. ■ archaic an instance of rude or offensive behavior.

vul·gar·ize /ˈvəlgə,rīz/ ▶ **v.** [trans.] make less refined. ■ make commonplace or less subtle or complex. — **vul·gar·i·za·tion** /,vəlgərəˈzāsʜən/ **n.**

vul·gar Lat·in ▶ **n.** informal Latin of classical times.

vul·gar tongue ▶ **n.** (**the vulgar tongue**) dated the national or vernacular language of a people (used typically to contrast such a language with Latin).

Vul·gate /ˈvəl,gāt; -gət/ ▶ **n. 1** the principal Latin version of the Bible, prepared mainly by St. Jerome in the late 4th century, and (as revised in 1592) adopted as the official text for the Roman Catholic Church. **2** (**vul·gate**) [in sing.] formal common or colloquial speech: *I required a formal language, not the vulgate.* **3** (**vul·gate**) the traditionally accepted text of any author. [from L. *vulgata (editio(n-))* '(edition) prepared for the public,' fem. past part. of *vulgare*, from *vulgus* 'common people.']

vuln /vəln/ ▶ **v.** [trans.] Heraldry wound. [16th C.: formed irregularly from L. *vulnerare* 'to wound.']

vul·ner·a·ble /ˈvəln(ə)rəbəl/ ▶ **adj.** exposed to the possibility of being attacked or harmed, either physically or emotionally: *we were in a vulnerable position.* ■ Bridge (of a partnership) liable to higher penalties, either by convention or through having won one game toward a rubber. — **vul·ner·a·bil·i·ty** /,vəln(ə)rəˈbilitē/ **n.** (pl. **-ties**) **vul·ner·a·ble·ness n. vul·ner·a·bly** /-blē/ **adv.** [17th C.: from late L. *vulnerabilis*, from L. *vulnerare* 'to wound,' from *vulnus* 'wound.']

vul·ner·ar·y /ˈvəlnə,rerē/ archaic ▶ **adj.** (of a drug, plant, etc.) of use in the healing of wounds. ▶ **n.** (pl. **-ar·ies**) a medicine of this kind. [16th C.: from L. *vulnerarius*, from *vulnus* 'wound.']

Vul·pec·u·la /,vəlˈpekyələ/ Astron. an inconspicuous northern constellation (the Fox), lying in the Milky Way between Cygnus and Aquila.

vul·pine /ˈvəl,pīn/ ▶ **adj.** of or relating to a fox or foxes. ■ crafty; cunning: *Karl gave a vulpine smile.* [17th C.: from L. *vulpinus*, from *vulpes* 'fox.']

vul·ture /ˈvəlcʜər/ ▶ **n. 1** a large bird of prey (order Accipitriformes) with the head and neck more or less bare of feathers, feeding chiefly on carrion. They are classified as **Old World vultures** (family Accipitridae) and **New World vultures** (family Cathartidae). **2** a contemptible person who preys on or exploits others. — **vul·tur·ine** /-,rīn/ **adj. vul·tur·ish adj. vul·tur·ous** /-cʜərəs/ **adj.** [ME: from Anglo-Norman Fr. *vultur*, from L. *vulturius*.]

vul·va /ˈvəlvə/ ▶ **n.** Anat. the female external genitals. ■ Zool. the external opening of the vagina or reproductive tract in a female mammal or nematode. — **vul·val adj. vul·var adj.** [ME: from L., 'womb.']

vul·vi·tis /,vəlˈvītis/ ▶ **n.** Med. inflammation of the vulva.

vul·vo·vag·in·i·tis /,vəlvō,vajəˈnītis/ ▶ **n.** inflammation of the vulva and vagina.

vv. ▶ **abbr.** ■ verses. ■ volumes.

vy·ing /ˈvī-iɴɢ/ present participle of **VIE**.

Ww

W¹ /ˈdəbəl,yo͞o/ (also **w**) ▸ **n.** (pl. **Ws** or **W's**) **1** the twenty-third letter of the alphabet. ■ denoting the next after V in a set of items, categories, etc. **2** a shape like that of a letter W.

W² ▸ **abbr.** ■ Wales. ■ warden. ■ (in tables of sports results) games won. ■ watt(s). ■ Wednesday. ■ week. ■ (**w**) weight. ■ Welsh. ■ West or Western: *104° W* | *W Europe.* ■ (in personal ads) White. ■ width: *23 in. H x 20.5 in. W x 16 in. D.* ■ (in personal ads) widowed. ■ (in genealogies) wife. ■ women's (clothes size). ■ Physics work. ▸ **symb.** ■ the chemical element tungsten. [from mod. L. *wolframium.*]

WA ▸ **abbr.** ■ Washington (State) (in official postal use). ■ Western Australia.

Waac /wak/ ▸ **n.** a member of the Women's Army Auxiliary Corps (later the WAC) formed in 1942, now no longer a separate branch. [acronym.]

Waadt /vät/ German name for **VAUD.**

Waal /väl/ a river in the south central Netherlands. A major distributary of the Rhine River, it flows for 52 miles (84 km) to the estuary of the Meuse (Maas) River on the North Sea.

Wa·bash Riv·er /ˈwôˌbasʜ/ a river that flows for 475 miles (765 km) from western Ohio to the Ohio River.

WAC /wak/ ▸ **abbr.** Women's Army Corps. See **WAAC.** ■ (also **Wac**) a member of the Women's Army Corps.

wack /wak/ informal ▸ **adj.** bad; inferior: *a wack radio station.* ▸ **n. 1** a crazy or eccentric person. **2** worthless or stupid ideas, work, or talk; rubbish: *this track is a load of wack.* [1930s: prob. a back-form. from **WACKY.**]

wacked ▸ **adj.** var. of **WHACKED.**

wack·o /ˈwakō/ (also **whack·o**) informal ▸ **adj.** mad; insane: *wacko fundamentalists.* ▸ **n.** (pl. **-os**) a crazy person. [1970s: from **WACKY** + **-O.**]

wack·y /ˈwakē/ (also **whack·y**) ▸ **adj.** (**wack·i·er, wack·i·est**) informal funny or amusing in a slightly odd or peculiar way: *a wacky chase movie.* — **wack·i·ly** /ˈwakəlē/ **adv. wack·i·ness n.** [19th C. (orig. dial.): from the n. **WHACK** + **-Y¹.**]

Wa·co /ˈwākō/ a city in east central Texas; pop. 103,590.

wad /wäd/ ▸ **n. 1** a lump or bundle of a soft material, used for padding, stuffing, or wiping: *a **wad** of cotton.* ■ esp. hist. a disk of felt or another material used to keep powder or shot in place in a gun barrel. ■ a portion of chewing gum, tobacco, or another material when used for chewing. **2** a bundle of paper, banknotes, or documents: *a thick **wad** of index cards.* ■ informal a large amount of something, esp. money: *she was working on TV and had **wads** of money.* ▸ **v.** (**wad·ded, wad·ding**) [trans.] [usu. as adj.] (**wadded**) **1** compress (a soft material) into a lump or bundle: *a wadded handkerchief.* **2** stop up (an aperture or a gun barrel) with a bundle or lump of soft material. ■ line or stuff (a garment or piece of furniture) with wadding. [16th C.: perh. rel. to Du. *watten,* Fr. *ouate* 'padding, absorbent cotton.']

wad·ding /ˈwädiɴɢ/ ▸ **n.** soft, thick material used to line garments or pack fragile items, esp. absorbent cotton. ■ a material from which wads for guns are made.

wad·dle /ˈwädl/ ▸ **v.** [no obj., with adverbial of direction] walk with short steps and a clumsy swaying motion. ▸ **n.** [in sing.] a waddling gait: *I walk with a waddle.* — **wad·dler** /ˈwädlər; ˈwädl-ər/ **n.** [16th C.: perh. a frequentative of **WADE.**]

wade /wād/ ▸ **v.** [no obj., with adverbial] walk through water or another liquid or soft substance: *we waded ashore.* ■ [trans.] walk through (something filled with water): *firefighters waded the waist-deep flood water.* ■ (**wade through**) read laboriously through (a long piece of writing). ■ (**wade into**) informal get involved in (something) vigorously or forcefully: *he waded into the crowd.* ■ (**wade in**) informal make a vigorous attack or intervention: *Nicola waded in and grabbed him.* ▸ **n.** [in sing.] an act of wading. — **wad·a·ble** (also **wade·a·ble**) **adj.** [OE *wadan* 'move onward,' also 'penetrate,' from a Gmc. word meaning 'go (through),' from an Indo-Eur. root shared by L. *vadere* 'go.']

Wade–Giles /ˈwād ˈjīlz/ ▸ **n.** a system of romanized spelling for transliterating Chinese, devised by Sir Thomas Francis Wade (1818–95) and Herbert Allen Giles (1845–1935). It has been largely superseded by Pinyin.

wad·er /ˈwādər/ ▸ **n. 1** a person or animal, esp. a bird, that wades, in particular: ■ a wading bird of the order Ciconiiformes, which comprises the herons, storks, and their allies. **2** (**waders**) high waterproof boots, or a waterproof garment for the legs and body, used esp. by anglers when fishing.

wa·di /ˈwädē/ ▸ **n.** (pl. **-dis** /-dēz/ or **-dies** /-dēz/) (in certain Arabic-speaking countries) a valley, ravine, or channel that is dry except in the rainy season. [17th C.: from Arab. *wādī.*]

WAF /waf/ ▸ **abbr.** Women in the Air Force. ▸ **n.** a member of the WAF.

wa·fer /ˈwāfər/ ▸ **n.** a very thin, light, crisp, sweet cookie or cracker, esp. one of a kind eaten with ice cream. ■ a thin disk of unleavened bread used in the Eucharist. ■ Electron. a very thin slice of a semiconductor crystal used as the substrate for solid-state circuitry. ■ hist. a small disk of dried paste formerly used for fastening letters or holding papers together. ■ a round, thin piece of something: *a wafer of ice.* — **wa·fer·y adj.** [ME: from an Anglo-Norman Fr. var. of OFr. *gaufre* (see **GOFFER**), from Mid. Low Ger. *wāfel* 'waffle'; cf. **WAFFLE².**]

wa·fer-thin ▸ **adj. & adv.** very thin or thinly: [as adj.] *plates of wafer-thin metal* | [as adv.] *slicing meats wafer-thin.*

Waf·fen SS /ˈväfən/ ▸ **n.** (**the Waffen SS**) the combat units of the SS in Nazi Germany during World War II. [Ger. *Waffen* 'arms, weapons.']

waf·fle¹ /ˈwäfəl; ˈwô-/ informal ▸ **v.** [intrans.] **1** fail to make up one's mind: *Joseph had been waffling over where to go.* **2** esp. Brit. speak or write, esp. at great length, without saying anything important or useful. ▸ **n. 1** a failure to make up one's mind. **2** esp. Brit. lengthy but trivial or useless talk or writing. — **waf·fler** /ˈwäf(ə)lər; ˈwôf-/ **n. waf·fly** /ˈwäf(ə)lē; ˈwôf-/ **adj.** [17th C. (orig. in the sense 'yap, yelp'): frequentative of dial. *waff* 'yelp,' of imitative origin.]

waf·fle² ▸ **n.** a small crisp batter cake, baked in a waffle iron and eaten hot with butter or syrup. ▸ **adj.** denoting a style of fine honeycomb weaving or a fabric woven to give a honeycomb effect. [18th C.: from Du. *wafel*; cf. **WAFER** and **GOFFER.**]

waf·fle i·ron ▸ **n.** a utensil, typically consisting of two shallow metal pans hinged together, used for baking waffles.

waft /wäft; waft/ ▸ **v.** pass or cause to pass easily or gently through or as if through the air: [no obj., with adverbial of direction] *the smell of stale fat wafted out from the restaurant* | [with obj. and adverbial of direction] *each breeze would waft pollen around the house.* ▸ **n.** a gentle movement of air. ■ a scent or odor carried on such a movement of air. [16th C.: back-form. from obs. *wafter* 'armed convoy vessel,' from Low Ger., Du. *wachter,* from *wachten* 'to guard.']

wag¹ /wag/ ▸ **v.** (**wagged, wag·ging**) (with reference to an animal's tail) move or cause to move rapidly to and fro: [intrans.] *his tail began to wag* | [trans.] *the dog went out, wagging its tail.* ■ [trans.] move (an upward-pointing finger) from side to side to signify a warning or reprimand: *she wagged a finger at Elinor.* ■ [intrans.] (used of a tongue, jaw, or chin, as representing a person) talk, esp. in order to gossip or spread rumors: *tongues are beginning to wag.* ▸ **n.** a single rapid movement from side to side: *a chirpy wag of the head.* [ME: from the Gmc. base of OE *wagian* 'to sway.']

wag² ▸ **n.** dated a person who makes facetious jokes. [16th C.: prob. from obs. *waghalter* 'person likely to be hanged' (see **WAG¹, HALTER**).]

wage /wāj/ ▸ **n.** (usu. **wages**) a fixed regular payment, typically paid on a daily or weekly basis, made by an employer to an employee, esp. to a manual or unskilled worker: *struggling to get better wages.* Compare with **SALARY.** ■ (**wages**) Econ. the part of total production that is the return to labor as earned income as distinct from the remuneration received by capital as unearned income. ■ fig. the result or effect of doing something considered wrong or unwise: *the wages of sin.* ▸ **v.** [trans.] carry on (a war or campaign): *their capacity to wage war.* [ME: from Anglo-Norman Fr. and Old North. Fr., of Gmc. origin; rel. to **GAGE¹** and **WED.**]

wa·ger /ˈwājər/ ▸ **n. & v.** more formal term for **BET.** [ME (also in the sense 'solemn pledge'): from Anglo-Norman Fr. *wageure,* from *wager* 'to wage.']

wag·gish /ˈwagisʜ/ ▸ **adj.** dated humorous in a playful, mischievous, or facetious manner: *a waggish riposte.* — **wag·gish·ly adv. wag·gish·ness n.**

wag·gle /ˈwagəl/ ▸ **v.** informal move or cause to move with short quick movements from side to side or up and down. ■ [trans.] swing (a golf club) loosely to and fro over the ball before playing a shot. ▸ **n.** an act of waggling. [16th C.: frequentative of **WAG¹.**]

wag·gle dance ▸ **n.** a waggling movement performed by a honeybee at the hive or nest, to indicate to other bees the direction and distance of a source of food.

wag·gly /ˈwag(ə)lē/ ▸ **adj.** moving with quick short movements from side to side or up and down: *a waggly tail.*

Wag·ner¹ /ˈwagnər/, Honus (1874–1955), US baseball player and manager; full name *John Peter Wagner;* known as the **Flying Dutchman.** He played shortstop for the Pittsburgh Pirates 1900–1917.

Wag·ner² /ˈvägnər/, Wilhelm Richard (1813–83), German composer. His works include *The Flying Dutchman* (1841) and *Der Ring des Nibelungen* (1847–74).

Wag·ne·ri·an /vägˈne(ə)rēən/ ▶adj. of, relating to, or characteristic of the operas of Richard Wagner. ■ fig. having the enormous dramatic scale and intensity of a Wagner opera. ▶n. an admirer of Wagner or his music.

wag·on /ˈwagən/ (Brit. also **wag·gon**) ▶n. a vehicle used for transporting goods or another specified purpose. ■ a four-wheeled trailer for agricultural use, or a small version of this for use as a child's toy. ■ a light horse-drawn vehicle, esp. a covered wagon used by early settlers in North America and elsewhere. ■ a wheeled cart or hut used as a food stall. ■ a small cart or wheeled table used for serving drinks or food. ■ a vehicle like a camper used by gypsies or circus performers. ■ informal short for STATION WAGON. ■ Brit. a railroad freight vehicle.
– PHRASES **fix someone's wagon** bring about a person's downfall or spoil their chances of success. **off the wagon** informal drinking alcohol after a period of abstinence. **on the wagon** informal abstaining from drinking alcohol. [15th C.: from Du. *wagen*.]

wag·on·er /ˈwagənər/ (Brit. also **wag·goner**) ▶n. the driver of a horse-drawn wagon. [16th C.: from Du. *wagenaar*, from *wagen* (see WAGON).]

wag·on train ▶n. hist. a convoy or train of covered horse-drawn wagons, as used by pioneers or settlers in North America.

wag·tail /ˈwag,tāl/ ▶n. a slender Eurasian and African songbird (genera *Motacilla* and *Dendronanthus*, family Motacillidae) with a long tail that is frequently wagged up and down, typically living by water.

Wah·ha·bi /wəˈhäbē; wä-/ (also **Wa·ha·bi**) ▶n. (pl. **-bis** /-bēz/) a member of a strictly orthodox Sunni Muslim sect founded by Muhammad ibn Abd al-Wahhab (1703–92). — **Wah·ha·bism** /-bizəm/ n. **Wah·ha·bite** n. & adj.

wa·hi·ne /wäˈhēnē/ ▶n. **1** a Polynesian woman or wife, esp. in Hawaii or New Zealand. **2** a young woman surfer. [Hawaiian or Maori.]

wa·hoo¹ /ˈwä,hoo; ,wäˈhoo/ ▶n. **1** (also **wa·hoo elm**) another term for WINGED ELM. [perh. from Creek *ahá·hwa* 'walnut.'] **2** a North American burning bush (*Euonymus atropurpurea*, family Celastraceae). [from Dakota.] **3** a large predatory tropical marine fish (*Acanthocybium solanderi*) of the mackerel family, prized as a game fish. [20th C.: of unknown origin.]

wa·hoo² ▶exclam. another term for YAHOO². [1940s: prob. a natural exclamation.]

wah-wah /ˈwä ˈwä/ (also **wa-wa**) ▶n. a musical effect achieved on brass instruments by alternately applying and removing a mute and on an electric guitar by controlling the output from the amplifier with a pedal. ■ a pedal for producing such an effect on an electric guitar.

waif /wāf/ ▶n. **1** a homeless and helpless person, esp. a neglected or abandoned child: *various waifs and strays*. ■ an abandoned pet animal. **2** Law a piece of property thrown away by a fleeing thief and held by the state in trust for the owner to claim. — **waif·ish** adj. [ME: from an Anglo-Norman Fr. var. of Old North. Fr. *gaif*, prob. of Scand. origin.]

Wai·ka·to /wīˈkätō; -ˈkatō/ a river in New Zealand, on North Island, that flows northwest to the Tasman Sea.

Wai·ki·ki /,wīkiˈkē/ a resort in Hawaii, on Oahu.

wail /wāl/ ▶n. a prolonged high-pitched cry of pain, grief, or anger: *Christopher let out a wail.* ■ a sound resembling this: *the wail of an air-raid siren.* ▶v. [intrans.] give such a cry of pain, grief, or anger. ■ make a sound resembling such a cry: *the wind wailed.* ■ [trans.] literary manifest or feel deep sorrow for; lament. — **wail·er** n. **wail·ing·ly** adv. [ME: from ON; rel. to WOE.]

Wail·ing Wall /ˈwāliNG/ a high wall in Jerusalem said to stand on the site of Herod's temple, where Jews traditionally pray and lament on Fridays.

wain·scot /ˈwān,skōt; -skət; -,skät/ ▶n. [in sing.] an area of wooden paneling on the lower part of the walls of a room. ▶v. (**-scot·ed**, **-scot·ing** or **-scot·ted**, **-scot·ting**) [trans.] line (a room or wall) with wooden paneling. [ME: from Mid. Low Ger. *wagenschot*, appar. from *wagen* 'wagon' + *schot*, prob. meaning 'partition.']

wain·scot·ing /ˈwān,skōtiNG; -,skä-/ (also **wain·scot·ting**) ▶n. wooden paneling that lines the lower part of the walls of a room. ■ material for such paneling.

wain·wright /ˈwān,rīt/ ▶n. hist. a wagon-builder.

WAIS /wās/ ▶abbr. Comput. wide area information service, designed to provide access to information across a computer network.

waist /wāst/ ▶n. the part of the human body below the ribs and above the hips. ■ the circumference of this: *her waist is 28 inches.* ■ a narrowing of the trunk of the body at this point: *the last time you had a waist was around 1978.* ■ the part of a garment encircling or covering the waist. ■ the point at which a garment is shaped so as to narrow between the rib cage and the hips: *a high waist.* ■ a blouse or bodice. ■ a narrow part in the middle of anything, such as a violin, an hourglass, the body of wasp, etc. ■ the middle part of a ship, between the forecastle and the quarterdeck. — **waist·ed** adj. [in comb.] *high-waisted.* **waist·less** adj. [ME: appar. representing an OE word from the Gmc. root of WAX².]

waist·band /ˈwāst,band/ ▶n. a strip of cloth forming the waist of a garment such as a skirt or a pair of trousers.

waist·coat /ˈwāst,kōt; ˈweskət/ ▶n. Brit. a vest, esp. one worn by men over a shirt and under a jacket. ■ hist. a man's quilted long-sleeved garment worn under a doublet in the 16th and 17th centuries.

waist·line /ˈwāst,līn/ ▶n. an imaginary line around a person's body at the waist, esp. with respect to its size. ■ the shaping and position of the waist of a garment.

wait /wāt/ ▶v. [intrans.] **1** stay where one is or delay action until a particular time or until something else happens. ■ remain in readiness for some purpose: *the car was waiting on the platform.* ■ be left until a later time before being dealt with: *that will have to wait.* ■ [trans.] informal defer (a meal) until a person's arrival: *he will wait supper for me.* ■ (**wait on/upon**) esp. Brit. await the convenience of. **2** (**cannot wait**) used to indicate that one is eagerly impatient to do something or for something to happen: *I can't wait for tomorrow.* **3** act as a waiter or waitress, serving food and drink. ▶n. [in sing.] a period of waiting.
– PHRASAL VERBS **wait on** (or **upon**) act as an attendant to (someone): *a maid was appointed to wait on her.* ■ serve (a customer) in a store. ■ archaic pay a respectful visit to. [ME: from Old North. Fr. *waitier*, of Gmc. origin; rel. to WAKE¹.]

Waite /wāt/, Morrison Remick (1816–88), Chief Justice of the US 1874–88.

wait·er /ˈwātər/ ▶n. **1** a man whose job is to serve customers at their tables in a restaurant. **2** a person who waits for a time, event, or opportunity. **3** a small tray; a salver.

wait·ing /ˈwātiNG/ ▶n. **1** the action of staying where one is or delaying action until a particular time or until something else happens. **2** official attendance at court. See also LADY-IN-WAITING.

wait·ing game ▶n. a tactic in which one refrains from action for a time in order to act more effectively at a later date or stage: *playing a waiting game.*

wait·ing list ▶n. a list of people waiting for something, esp. housing or admission to a school.

wait·ing room ▶n. a room provided for the use of people who are waiting.

wait list ▶n. another term for WAITING LIST. ▶v. (**wait-list**) [trans.] put (someone) on a waiting list.

wait·per·son /ˈwāt,pərsən/ ▶n. a waiter or waitress (used as a neutral alternative).

wait·ress /ˈwātris/ ▶n. a woman whose job is to serve customers at their tables in a restaurant.

wait·ress·ing /ˈwātrisiNG/ ▶n. the action or occupation of working as a waitress.

wait·ron /ˈwāträn; -trən/ ▶n. a waiter or waitress (used as a neutral alternative).

wait·staff /ˈwāt,staf/ ▶n. [treated as sing. or pl.] waiters and waitresses collectively.

waive /wāv/ ▶v. [trans.] refrain from insisting on or using (a right or claim): *waive all rights to the money.* ■ refrain from applying or enforcing (a rule, restriction, or fee): *her tuition fees would be waived.* [ME: from an Anglo-Norman Fr. var. of OFr. *gaiver* 'allow to become a waif, abandon.']

waiv·er /ˈwāvər/ ▶n. an act or instance of waiving a right or claim. ■ a document recording such waiving of a right or claim.

Wa·kam·ba /wäˈkämbə/ plural form of KAMBA.

wa·ka·me /ˈwäkə,mā; wäˈkämā/ ▶n. an edible brown seaweed (*Undaria pinnatifida*, class Phaeophyceae) used, typically in dried form, in Chinese and Japanese cooking. [Japanese.]

Wa·kash·an /wäˈkasHən/ ▶adj. of, relating to, or denoting a small family of almost extinct American Indian languages of the northern Pacific coast, including Kwakiutl and Nootka. ▶n. this family of languages. [from Nootka *waukash* 'good' (said to have been applied to the people by Captain Cook) + -AN.]

wake¹ /wāk/ ▶v. (past **woke** /wōk/ or **waked**; past part. **wok·en** /ˈwōkən/ or **waked**) **1** emerge or cause to emerge from a state of sleep; stop sleeping. ■ [intrans.] (**wake up to**) become alert to or aware of: *wake up to reality.* ■ [trans.] fig. cause (something) to stir or come to life. **2** [trans.] dialect hold a vigil beside (someone who has died): *we waked Jim last night.* ▶n. a watch or vigil held beside the body of someone who has died, sometimes accompanied by ritual observances including eating and drinking. — **wak·er** n. [OE (recorded only in the past tense *wōc*), also partly from the weak verb *wacian* 'remain awake, hold a vigil,' of Gmc. origin.]

wake² ▶n. a trail of disturbed water or air left by the passage of a ship or aircraft. ■ fig. used to refer to the aftermath or consequences of something: *in the wake of the inquiry.* [15th C.: prob. via Mid. Low Ger. from ON *vǫk*, *vaka* 'hole or opening in ice.']

wake·board /ˈwāk,bôrd/ ▶n. a board towed behind a motor boat, shaped like a broad waterski and ridden like a surfboard. ▶v. ride a wakeboard: *I have wakeboarded for three years.* — **wake·board·ing** n.

wake·ful /ˈwākfəl/ ▶adj. (of a person) unable or not needing to sleep: *he had been wakeful all night.* ■ alert and vigilant. ■ (of a period of time) passed with little or no sleep: *wakeful nights.* — **wake·ful·ly** adv. **wake·ful·ness** n.

Wake Is·land /wāk/ a coral atoll in the Pacific Ocean, north of the Marshall Islands. It was the scene of World War II fighting.

wake-rob·in ▶n. another term for TRILLIUM.

wake-up ▶n. [in sing.] an instance of a person waking up or being woken up.

wake-up call ▶n. a telephone call made according to a prior arrangement to wake the person called. ■ fig. a person or thing that causes people to become fully alert to an unsatisfactory situation and to take action to remedy it: *a wake-up call for the administration.*

wak·ing /ˈwākiNG/ ▶ n. the state of being awake.

Waks·man /ˈwäksmən; ˈwak-/, Selman Abraham (1888–1973), US microbiologist; born in Russia. He discovered the antibiotic streptomycin. Nobel Prize for Physiology or Medicine (1952).

Wa·la·chi·a var. of WALLACHIA.

Wal·den Pond /ˈwôldən/ a pond in Concord, Massachusetts, that is associated with Henry David Thoreau.

Wald·heim /ˈvôld,hīm; ˈwôld-; ˈvält-/, Kurt (1918–); president of Austria 1986–92. He was secretary-general of the UN 1972–81. His later career was blemished by revelations about his service as a German officer in World War II.

Wal·dorf sal·ad /ˈwôl,dôrf/ ▶ n. a salad made from apples, walnuts, celery, and mayonnaise. [named after the *Waldorf*-Astoria Hotel in New York, where it was first served.]

wale /wāl/ ▶ n. **1** a ridge on a textured woven fabric such as corduroy. **2** Naut. a plank running along the side of a wooden ship, thicker than the usual planking, and strengthening and protecting the hull. **3** a horizontal band around a woven basket. [OE *walu* 'stripe, weal.']

Wales /wālz/ a principality of the United Kingdom, west of central England; pop. 2,798,000; capital, Cardiff. Welsh name CYMRU. See map at UNITED KINGDOM.

Wales, Prince of see PRINCE OF WALES; CHARLES, PRINCE.

Wa·łę·sa /vəˈlensə; vəˈwensə/, Lech (1943–), labor leader and president of Poland 1990–95. He founded the labor union Solidarity in 1980. Nobel Peace Prize (1983).

wa·li /ˈwälē/ ▶ n. the governor of a province in an Arab country. [from Arab. *(al-)wālī*.]

walk /wôk/ ▶ v. **1** [no obj., usu. with adverbial] move at a regular and fairly slow pace by lifting and setting down each foot in turn, never having both feet off the ground at once: *I walked across the lawn.* ■ use similar movements but of a different part of one's body or a support: *he could walk on his hands.* ■ go on foot for recreation and exercise: *you can walk in the mountain.* ■ [trans.] travel along or over (a route or area) on foot: *walk a beat.* ■ (of a quadruped) proceed with the slowest gait, always having at least two feet on the ground at once. ■ [trans.] ride (a horse) at this pace. ■ informal abandon or suddenly withdraw from a job, commitment, or situation: *they can walk away from the deal.* ■ informal be released from suspicion or from a charge. ■ used to suggest that someone has achieved a state or position easily or undeservedly: *walk straight into a well-paid job.* ■ (of a ghost) be present and visible. ■ archaic used to describe the way in which someone lives or behaves. ■ Baseball be awarded first base after not swinging at four balls pitched outside the strike zone. ■ [trans.] Baseball allow or enable (a batter) to do this. ■ Baseball (of a pitcher) give a walk with the bases loaded so as to force in (a run). ■ Basketball another term for TRAVEL (sense 2). **2** [with obj. and adverbial of direction] cause or enable (someone or something) to walk or move as though walking: *she walked her fingers over the dresses.* ■ guide, accompany, or escort (someone) on foot. ■ [trans.] take (a domestic animal, typically a dog) out for exercise. ■ push (a bicycle or motorcycle) while walking alongside it. ▶ n. **1** an act of traveling or an excursion on foot: *he went out for a walk.* ■ [in sing.] used to indicate the time that it will take someone to reach a place on foot or the distance that they must travel: *a five minutes' walk.* ■ a route recommended or marked out for recreational walking. ■ a sidewalk or path. ■ a part of a forest under one keeper. **2** [in sing.] an unhurried rate of movement on foot: *a leisurely walk.* ■ the slowest gait of an animal. ■ a person's manner of walking. **3** Baseball an instance of being awarded (or allowing a batter to reach) first base after not swinging at four balls pitched outside the strike zone.
– PHRASES **walk all over** informal treat in a thoughtless, disrespectful, and exploitative manner. ■ defeat easily. **walk someone off their feet** walk with someone until they are exhausted. **walk of life** the position within society that someone holds or the part of society to which they belong as a result of their job or social status. **walk on eggshells** be extremely cautious about one's words or actions. **walk one's talk** (also **walk the walk**) suit one's actions to one's words. **walk the streets 1** walk freely in a town or city. **2** work as a prostitute. **win in a walk** win without effort or competition.
– PHRASAL VERBS **walk away** easily, casually, or irresponsibly abandon a situation in which one is involved or for which one is responsible. **walk in on** enter suddenly or unexpectedly. ■ intrude on: *he'd clearly not expected her to walk in on him.* **walk into** informal encounter or become involved in through ignorance or carelessness. **walk off with** informal **1** steal. **2** win. **walk out** depart suddenly or angrily. ■ leave one's job suddenly. ■ go on strike. ■ abandon someone or something toward which one has responsibilities: *he walked out on his wife.* **walk through** rehearse (a play or other piece), reading the lines aloud from a script and performing the actions of the characters. ■ act or perform in a perfunctory or lackluster manner. **walk someone through** guide (someone) carefully through a process. —**walk·a·ble** /ˈwôkəbəl/ adj. [OE *wealcan* 'roll, toss,' also 'wander,' of Gmc. origin.]

walk·a·bout /ˈwôkə,bout/ ▶ n. Austral. a journey on foot undertaken by an Australian Aboriginal in order to live in the traditional manner.
– PHRASES **go walkabout** (of an Australian Aboriginal) wander into the bush away from white society in order to live in the traditional manner. ■ wander around from place to place in a protracted or leisurely way.

walk·a·thon /ˈwôkə,THän/ ▶ n. informal a long-distance walk organized as a fund-raising event. [1930s: from WALK, on the pattern of *marathon*.]

Walk·er[1] /ˈwôkər/, Alice Malsenior (1944–), US writer. Her novels include *The Color Purple* (1982).

Walk·er[2], Jimmy (1881–1946), US politician; full name *James John Walker*. He was mayor of New York City 1926–32.

Walk·er[3], Sarah Breedlove (1867–1919), US entrepreneur and philanthropist; known as **Madame C. J. Walker**. In 1905, she invented and marketed a preparation to straighten kinky hair.

walk·er /ˈwôkər/ ▶ n. a person who walks, esp. for exercise or enjoyment. ■ a device for helping a baby learn to walk, consisting of a harness set into a frame on wheels. ■ a frame used by disabled or infirm people for support while walking.

walk·ie-talk·ie /ˈwôkē ˈtôkē/ ▶ n. a portable two-way radio.

walk-in ▶ adj. **1** (esp. of a storage area) large enough to walk into: *a walk-in closet.* **2** (of a service) available for customers or clients without the need for an appointment: *a walk-in clinic.* ▶ n. a walk-in customer or a walk-in storage-area.

walk·ing fern ▶ n. a North American fern (*Asplenium rhizophyllus*, family Aspleniaceae) with long slender tapering fronds that form new plantlets where the tips touch the ground, typically growing on limestone.

walk·ing pa·pers ▶ plural n. informal notice of dismissal from a job: *the reporter has been given his walking papers.*

walk·ing pneu·mo·ni·a ▶ n. a type of pneumonia caused by mycoplasmas, with symptoms similar to but milder than those associated with bacterial or viral pneumonia.

walk·ing shoe ▶ n. a sturdy, practical shoe with good treads, suitable for regular or extensive walking.

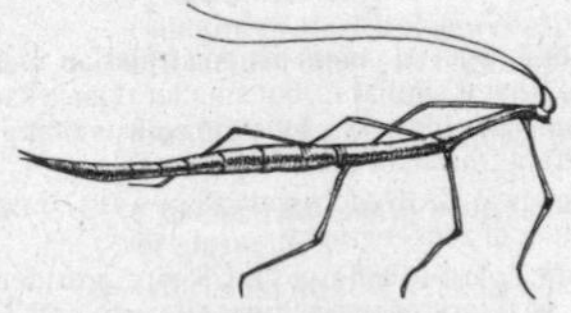

walking stick 2

walk·ing stick ▶ n. **1** a stick, typically with a curved handle, used for support when walking. **2** (also **walk·ing·stick**) a long, slender, slow-moving insect (family Phasmatidae, order Phasmida) that resembles a twig.

walk·ing tour ▶ n. a sightseeing tour made on foot.

walk·ing wound·ed /ˈwo͞ondid/ ▶ plural n. (usu. **the walking wounded**) people who have been injured in a battle or major accident but who are still able to walk. ■ people who have suffered emotional wounds.

Walk·man /ˈwôkmən; -,man/ ▶ n. (pl. **-mans** or **-men**) trademark a type of personal stereo.

walk-on ▶ adj. denoting a small nonspeaking part in a play or film. ▶ n. a person who plays such a part, or the part itself. ■ a sports player with no regular status in a team.

walk·out /ˈwôk,out/ ▶ n. a sudden angry departure, esp. as a protest or strike.

walk·o·ver /ˈwôk,ōvər/ ▶ n. **1** an easy victory. ■ a win by forfeit. **2** a somersault in which a gymnast performs a handstand and then slowly moves the feet backward and down to the floor, or first arches back into a handstand and then slowly moves the feet forward and down to the floor.

walk-through ▶ n. **1** a careful demonstration or explanation of the details of a process or procedure. ■ a rough rehearsal of a play, film, or other performance, without an audience or cameras. ■ Comput. a product review of software carried out before release. **2** an undemanding task. ■ an unchallenging role in a play or other performance. ■ a perfunctory or lackluster performance. **3** Comput. a software model of a building or other object in which the user can simulate walking around or through. ▶ adj. [attrib.] designed to be walked through.

walk-up ▶ adj. (of a building) allowing access to the upper floors by stairs only; having no elevator. ■ (of a room or apartment) accessed in this way. ■ (of a building or service) easily accessible to pedestrians: *a walk-up food stand.* ■ (of a travel fare) at the price charged for immediate use rather than at the lower level provided when a customer makes a reservation in advance. ▶ n. a building allowing access to the upper floors by stairs only.

walk·way /ˈwôk,wā/ ▶ n. a passage or path for walking along, esp. a raised passageway connecting different sections of a building or a path in a park or garden.

wall /wôl/ ▶ n. a continuous vertical brick or stone structure that encloses or divides an area of land. ■ a side of a building or room, typically forming part of the building's structure. ■ any high vertical surface or facade, esp. one that is imposing in scale: fig. *a wall of sound.* ■ a thing perceived as a protective or restrictive barrier. ■ Soccer a line of defenders forming a barrier against a free kick taken near the penalty area. ■ Mining the rock enclosing a lode or seam. ■ Anat. Zool. the

membranous outer layer or lining of an organ or cavity. ▶v. [trans.] enclose (an area) within walls, esp. to protect it or lend it some privacy. ■ (**wall something up**) block or seal a place by building a wall around or across it. ■ (**wall someone/something in/up**) confine or imprison someone or something in a restricted or sealed place.
– PHRASES **drive someone up the wall** informal make someone very irritated or angry. **go to the wall** informal **1** (of a business) fail; go out of business. **2** support someone or something, no matter what the cost to oneself. **hit the wall** (of an athlete) experience a sudden loss of energy in a long race. **off the wall** informal **1** eccentric or unconventional. **2** (of a person) angry. **3** (of an accusation) without basis or foundation. **walls have ears** proverb be careful what you say as people may be eavesdropping. **wall-to-wall** (of a carpet or other floor covering) fitted to cover an entire floor. ■ informal denoting great extent or number: *wall-to-wall customers.* — **wall-less** adj. [OE, from L. *vallum* 'rampart,' from *vallus* 'stake.']

agile wallaby

wal·la·by /'wäləbē/ ▶n. (pl. **-bies**) an Australasian marsupial (family Macropodidae) that is similar to, but smaller than, a kangaroo. Several genera and numerous species include the **agile wallaby** (*Macropus agilis*). [19th C.: from Dharuk *walabi* or *waliba*.]

Wal·lace[1] /'wôləs; 'wäl-/, Alfred Russel (1823–1913), English naturalist. He was a founder of zoogeography.

Wall·ace[2], Henry Agard (1888–1965), US vice president 1941–45. He served as US secretary of agriculture 1933–40 and US secretary of commerce 1945–46.

Wall·ace[3], George Corley (1919–98), US politician. He was governor of Alabama 1963–67, 1971–79, and 1983–87. In the early 1960s, he defied the law to integrate public schools. While campaigning for the 1972 Democratic presidential nomination, he was shot and paralyzed.

Wal·lace[4], Sir William (*c.*1270–1305), Scottish national hero. He defeated the English army at Stirling in 1297 but was defeated in 1298 and subsequently executed.

Wal·lace's line Zool. a hypothetical line, proposed by Alfred Russel Wallace, marking the boundary between the Oriental and Australian zoogeographical regions. Wallace's line is now placed along the continental shelf of Southeast Asia.

Wal·la·chi·a /wä'lākēə; wə-/ (also **Wa·la·chi·a**) a former principality in southeastern Europe. In 1861, it was united with Moldavia to form Romania. — **Wal·la·chi·an** adj. & n.

wal·lah /'wälə/ ▶n. [in comb. or with adj.] Indian or informal a person concerned or involved with a specified thing or business: *ice cream wallahs.* ■ a native or inhabitant of a specified place: *Bombay wallahs.* [from the Hindi suffix *-vālā* 'doer' (commonly interpreted in the sense 'fellow'), from Sanskrit *pālaka* 'keeper.']

wal·la·roo /,wôlə'ro͞o/ ▶n. a large Australian kangaroo (genus *Macropus*), the female of which is paler than the male. [19th C.: from Dharuk *walaru*.]

wall·board /'wôl,bôrd/ ▶n. a type of board made from wood pulp, plaster, or other material, used for covering walls and ceilings. ■ a piece of such board.

wall chart ▶n. a chart or poster designed for display on a wall as a teaching aid or source of information.

wall cov·er·ing ▶n. material such as wallpaper or fabric used as a decorative covering for interior walls.

wall·creep·er /'wôl,krēpər/ ▶n. a Eurasian songbird (*Tichodroma muraria*, family Sittidae) related to the nuthatches, having mainly gray plumage with broad bright red wings, and living among rocks in mountainous country.

Wal·len·berg /'wôlən,bərg; 'välən,ber(yə)/, Raoul (1912–?), Swedish diplomat in Budapest. In 1944, he helped many thousands of Jews escape death by issuing them Swedish passports. Arrested by the Soviets in 1945, his fate remains uncertain.

Wal·ler /'wälər/, Fats (1904–43), US jazz pianist and songwriter; born *Thomas Wright Waller.* He wrote "Ain't Misbehavin'" (1928) and "Honeysuckle Rose" (1929).

wal·let /'wälit; 'wô-/ ▶n. a pocket-sized, flat, folding holder for money and plastic cards. [ME: prob. via Anglo-Norman Fr. from a Gmc. word rel. to WELL[2].]

wall·eye /'wôl,ī/ ▶n. **1** an eye with a streaked or opaque white iris. ■ an eye squinting outward. **2** a North American pikeperch (*Stizostedion vitreum*) with large, opaque silvery eyes. It is a commercially valuable food fish and a popular sporting fish. — **wall·eyed** adj. [16th C.: back-form. from earlier *wall-eyed*, from ON *vagleygr*; rel. to Icelandic *vagl* 'film over the eye.']

wall·flow·er /'wôl,flouər/ ▶n. **1** a southern European plant (*Cheiranthus cheiri*) of the cabbage family, with fragrant yellow, orange-red, dark red, or brown flowers, cultivated for its early spring blooming. **2** informal a person who has no one to dance with or who feels shy, awkward, or excluded at a party.

wall hang·ing ▶n. a large decorative piece of fabric or other material to be hung on the wall of a room.

Wal·lis and Fu·tu·na Is·lands /'wäləs and fo͞o'to͞onə; 'wôləs/ an overseas territory of France that consists of two groups of islands in the central Pacific Ocean; pop. 15,000; capital, Mata-Utu.

wall-mount·ed ▶adj. fixed to a wall.

Wal·loon /wä'lo͞on/ ▶n. **1** a member of a people who speak a French dialect and live in southern and eastern Belgium and neighboring parts of France. Compare with FLEMING[3]. **2** the French dialect spoken by this people. ▶adj. of or concerning the Walloons or their language. [from Fr. *Wallon*, from med. L. *Wallon-*, from the same Gmc. origin as WELSH.]

wal·lop /'wäləp/ informal ▶v. (**-loped, -lop·ing**) [trans.] strike or hit (someone or something) very hard: *they walloped the back of his head.* ■ heavily defeat (an opponent). ▶n. **1** a heavy blow or punch. ■ [in sing.] fig. a potent effect: ***packs a wallop.*** **2** Brit. alcoholic drink, esp. beer. — **wal·lop·er** n. [ME: from Old North. Fr. *walop* (n.), *waloper* (v.), perh. from a Gmc. phr. meaning 'run well.']

wal·lop·ing /'wäləpiNG/ informal ▶n. [in sing.] a beating. ▶adj. [attrib.] large and powerful: *a walloping shock.*

wal·low /'wälō/ ▶v. [intrans.] **1** (chiefly of large mammals) roll about or lie relaxed in mud or water, esp. to keep cool, avoid biting insects, or spread scent. ■ (of a boat or aircraft) roll from side to side. **2** (**wallow in**) (of a person) indulge in an unrestrained way in (something that creates a pleasurable sensation): *wallowing in self-pity.* ▶n. **1** an act of wallowing: ***a wallow in nostalgia.*** **2** an area of mud or shallow water where mammals go to wallow, typically developing into a depression in the ground over long use. — **wal·low·er** n. [OE *walwian* 'to roll around,' of Gmc. origin, from an Indo-Eur. root shared by L. *volvere* 'to roll.']

wall·pa·per /'wôl,pāpər/ ▶n. paper that is pasted in vertical strips over the walls of a room to provide a decorative or textured surface. ■ Comput. an optional background pattern or picture on a computer screen. ▶v. [trans.] apply wallpaper to (a wall or room).

wall plate ▶n. **1** a timber laid horizontally in or on a wall as a support for a girder, rafter, or joist. **2** a metal plate fixed to a wall, for attaching a bracket or other device.

wall rock·et ▶n. a yellow-flowered European plant (*Diplotaxis muralis*) of the cabbage family that resembles mustard and emits a foul smell when crushed.

wall rue ▶n. a small delicate spleenwort (*Asplenium ruta-muraria*) that resembles rue, growing on walls and rocks in Europe and North America and sensitive to atmospheric pollution.

Wall Street a street in lower Manhattan, the financial center of New York City. ■ used allusively to refer to the US money market or financial interests.

wall tent ▶n. a tent with nearly perpendicular sides.

wal·nut /'wôl,nət/ ▶n. **1** the large wrinkled edible seed of a deciduous tree, consisting of two halves contained within a hard shell that is enclosed in a green fruit. **2** (also **wal·nut tree**) the tall tree (genus *Juglans*, family Juglandaceae) that produces this nut, with compound leaves and valuable ornamental timber. Its several species include the **common** (or **English**) **walnut** (*J. regia*) and the **black walnut** (*J. nigra*). [OE *walh-hnutu*, from a Gmc. compound meaning 'foreign nut.' See also WELSH.]

Wal·pole[1] /'wôl,pōl/, Horace, 4th Earl of Orford (1717–97), English writer and politician; son of Sir Robert Walpole. He wrote *The Castle of Otranto* (1764).

Wal·pole[2], Sir Hugh Seymour (1884–1941), British writer, born in New Zealand. He is noted for *The Herries Chronicle* (1930–33), a historical sequence.

Wal·pole[3], Sir Robert, 1st Earl of Orford (1676–1745), British statesman; first lord of the treasury and chancellor of the exchequer 1715–17 and 1721–42; father of Horace Walpole.

walrus

wal·rus /'wôlrəs; 'wäl-/ ▶n. a large gregarious marine mammal (*Odobenus rosmarus*) related to the eared seals, having two large downward-pointing tusks and found in the Arctic Ocean. [18th C.: prob. from Du. *walrus*, (influenced by *walvis* 'whale-fish') of ON *hrosshvalr* 'horse-whale.']

wal·rus mus·tache ▶n. a long, thick, drooping mustache.

Wal·sall /'wôl,sôl; 'wäl,säl/ a town in western central England; pop. 256,000.

Wal·ter Mit·ty /ˈwôltər ˈmitē/ the hero of a story (by James Thurber) who indulged in extravagant daydreams of his own triumphs. ■ [as n.] [often as adj.] used to refer to a person who fantasizes about a life much more exciting and glamorous than their own life.

Wal·tham /ˈwôl,THam; -,THam/ a city in eastern Massachusetts, west of Boston; pop. 59,226.

Wal·ton[1] /ˈwôltn/, Ernest Thomas Sinton (1903–95), Irish physicist. In 1932 he succeeded, with Sir John Cockcroft, in splitting the atom. Nobel Prize for Physics (1951, shared with Cockcroft).

Wal·ton[2], Izaak (1593–1683), English writer. He is chiefly known for *The Compleat Angler* (1653; rewritten 1655).

Wal·ton[3], Sam (1918–92), US businessman; full name *Samuel Moore Walton*. He founded Wal-Mart discount stores in 1962.

waltz /wôlts/ ▸ **n.** a dance in triple time performed by a couple who as a pair turn rhythmically around and around as they progress around the dance floor. ■ a piece of music written for or in the style of this dance. ▸ **v.** [intrans.] dance a waltz. ■ [with obj. and adverbial of direction] guide (someone) in or as if in a waltz. ■ [no obj., with adverbial of direction] move or act lightly, casually, or inconsiderately: *you can't just* **waltz in** *and expect to make a mark.* — **waltz·er n.** [18th C.: from Ger. *Walzer*, from *walzen* 'revolve.']

Wam·pa·no·ag /,wämpəˈnō-ag/ ▸ **n.** (pl. same or **-ags**) a member of a confederacy of native peoples of southeastern Massachusetts who spoke various dialects of the extinct Algonquian language Massachusett. ▸ **adj.** of, relating to, or denoting these people. [from an Algonquian name, lit. 'easterners.']

wam·pum /ˈwämpəm/ ▸ **n.** hist. a quantity of small cylindrical beads made by North American Indians from quahog shells, strung together and worn as a decorative belt or other decoration or used as money. [from Algonquian *wampumpeag*, from *wap* 'white' + *umpe* 'string' + the pl. suffix *-ag*.]

WAN /wan/ ▸ **abbr.** ■ Comput. wide area network.

wan /wän/ ▸ **adj.** (of a person's complexion or appearance) pale and giving the impression of illness or exhaustion. ■ (of light) pale; weak: *the wan dawn light.* ■ (of a smile) weak; strained. ■ literary (of the sea) without luster; dark and gloomy. — **wan·ly adv. wan·ness n.** [OE *wann* 'dark, black,' of unknown origin.]

Wan·a·mak·er /ˈwänə,mākər/, John (1838–1922), US businessman. He turned a men's clothing store in Philadelphia into a department store in 1877 and opened another in New York City 1896.

wand /wänd/ ▸ **n.** a long, thin stick or rod, in particular: ■ a stick or rod thought to have magic properties, held by a magician, fairy, or conjuror and used in casting spells or performing tricks: *the fairy godmother waves her magic wand.* ■ a staff or rod held as a symbol of office. ■ informal a conductor's baton. ■ a hand-held electronic device that can be passed over a bar code to read the encoded data. ■ a device emitting a laser beam, used esp. to create a pointer on a projected image or text. ■ a small stick with a brush at one end used for the application of mascara. ■ Archery a target 6 feet (1.83 m) high and 2 inches (5.8 cm) wide, set at 100 yards (91.44 m) for men and 60 yards (54.86 m) for women. ■ (**wands**) one of the suits in some tarot packs, corresponding to batons in others. [ME: from ON *vǫndr*, prob. of Gmc. origin and rel. to WEND and WIND[2].]

wan·der /ˈwändər/ ▸ **v.** [no obj., with adverbial of direction] walk or move in a leisurely, casual, or aimless way. ■ [intrans.] move slowly away from a fixed point or place: *please don't* **wander off** *again.* ■ (of a road or river) wind with gentle twists and turns in a particular direction; meander. ■ [trans.] move or travel slowly through or over (a place or area). ■ [intrans.] be unfaithful to one's spouse or regular sexual partner. ▸ **n.** an act or instance of wandering. — **wan·der·er n.** [OE *wandrian*, of West Gmc. origin.]

wan·der·ing al·ba·tross ▸ **n.** a very large albatross (*Diomedea exulans*) of southern oceans, having white plumage with black wings and a wingspan of up to 11 feet (3.3 m).

Wan·der·ing Jew (also **wan·der·ing Jew**) ▸ **n. 1** a legendary person said to have been condemned by Christ to wander the earth until the Second Coming. ■ a person who never settles down. **2** a tender trailing tradescantia, typically having striped leaves that are suffused with purple.

wan·der·lust /ˈwändər,ləst/ ▸ **n.** a strong desire to travel: *a man consumed by wanderlust.* [20th C.: from Ger. *Wanderlust*.]

wane[1] /wān/ ▸ **v.** [intrans.] (of the moon) have a progressively smaller part of its visible surface illuminated, so that it appears to decrease in size. ■ (esp. of a condition or feeling) decrease in vigor, power, or extent; become weaker: *confidence waned.*

– PHRASES **on the wane** becoming weaker, less vigorous, or less extensive: *the epidemic was on the wane.* [OE *wanian* 'lessen,' of Gmc. origin; rel. to L. *vanus* 'vain.']

wane[2] ▸ **n.** the amount by which a plank or log is beveled or falls short of a squared shape. — **wane·y adj.** [17th C.: from WANE[1].]

Wang /wäNG/, An (1920–90), US inventor; born in China. In 1948, he invented a magnetic core memory for computers.

wan·gle /ˈwaNGgəl/ informal ▸ **v.** [trans.] obtain (something that is desired) by persuading others to comply or by manipulating events. ▸ **n.** an act or an instance of obtaining something in such a way. — **wan·gler** /ˈwaNG(ə)lər/ **n.** [19th C.: of unknown origin.]

Wan·kel en·gine /ˈwäNGkəl; ˈwaNG-/ ▸ **n.** a rotary internal combustion engine in which a curvilinear, triangular, eccentrically pivoted piston rotates in an elliptical chamber. [1960s: named after Felix Wankel (1902–88), German engineer.]

wan·na /ˈwônə; ˈwä-/ informal ▸ **contr.** want to; want a.

wan·na·be /ˈwänəbē; ˈwô-/ ▸ **n.** informal, derog. a person who tries to be like someone else or to fit in with a particular group of people: *a star-struck wannabe.* [1980s: representing a pronunc. of *want to be*.]

want /wänt; wônt/ ▸ **v. 1** [trans.] have a desire to possess or do (something); wish for. ■ wish to consult or speak to (someone). ■ (usu. **be wanted**) (of the police) desire to question or apprehend (a suspected criminal). ■ desire (someone) sexually. ■ [with infin.] informal ought, should, or need to do something: *you don't want to believe everything you hear.* ■ [intrans.] (**want in/into/out/away**) informal desire to be in or out of a particular place or situation. **2** [intrans.] esp. archaic lack or be short of something desirable or essential: *you shall* **want for nothing**. ■ [trans.] (chiefly used in expressions of time) be short of or lack (a specified amount or thing): *it wanted twenty minutes to midnight.* ▸ **n. 1** esp. archaic a lack or deficiency of something: *houses* **in want of** *repair.* ■ the state of being poor and in need of essentials; poverty. **2** a desire for something.

– PHRASES **for want of** because of a lack of (something): *for want of a better location.* [ME: the n. from Old Norse *vant*, neut. of *vanr* 'lacking'; the v. from ON *vanta* 'be lacking.']

want ad ▸ **n.** informal a classified advertisement in a newspaper or magazine; a small ad.

want·ing /ˈwäntiNG; wôn-/ ▸ **adj.** [predic.] lacking in a certain required or necessary quality: *their products would be* **found wanting** *in a direct comparison.* ■ not existing or supplied; absent.

wan·ton /ˈwäntn/ ▸ **adj. 1** (of a cruel or violent action) deliberate and unprovoked. **2** (esp. of a woman) sexually immodest or promiscuous. ■ literary growing profusely; luxuriant: *wanton ivy.* ■ literary lively; playful. ▸ **n.** archaic a sexually immodest or promiscuous woman. ▸ **v.** [intrans.] archaic or literary **1** play; frolic. **2** behave in a sexually immodest or promiscuous way. — **wan·ton·ly adv. wan·ton·ness n.** [ME *wantowen* 'rebellious, lacking discipline,' from *wan-* 'badly' + OE *togen* 'trained.']

WAP /wap/ ▸ **abbr.** Wireless Application Protocol, a set of protocols for connecting cellular phones and other radio devices to the Internet.

wap·i·ti /ˈwäpitē/ ▸ **n.** (pl. **-tis**) another term for ELK. [19th C.: from Shawnee, lit. 'white rump.']

Wap·si·pin·i·con Riv·er /,wäpsəˈpinikən/ a river that flows for 225 miles (360 km) across eastern Iowa to the Mississippi River.

war /wôr/ ▸ **n.** a state of armed conflict between different nations or states or different groups within a nation or state. ■ a particular armed conflict: *after the war, they emigrated to America.* ■ a state of competition, conflict, or hostility between different people or groups: *a price war.* ■ a sustained effort to deal with or end a particular unpleasant or undesirable situation or condition: *a war on drugs.* ▸ **v.** (**warred, warring**) [intrans.] engage in a war.

– PHRASES **go to war** declare, begin, or see active service in a war. **war clouds** a threatening situation of instability in international relations. **war of attrition** a prolonged war or period of conflict during which each side seeks to gradually wear out the other by a series of small-scale actions. **war of words** a prolonged debate conducted by means of the spoken or printed word. **war to end all wars** a war, esp. World War I, regarded as making subsequent wars unnecessary. [OE *werre*, from an Anglo-Norman Fr. var. of OFr. *guerre*, from a Gmc. base shared by WORSE.]

war·bird /ˈwôr,bərd/ ▸ **n.** a vintage military aircraft.

war·ble[1] /ˈwôrbəl/ ▸ **v.** [intrans.] (of a bird) sing softly and with a succession of constantly changing notes. ■ (of a person) sing in a trilling or quavering voice. ▸ **n.** a warbling sound or utterance. [ME: from Old North. Fr. *werble* (n.), *werbler* (v.), of Gmc. origin.]

war·ble[2] ▸ **n.** a swelling or abscess beneath the skin on the back of cattle, horses, and other mammals, caused by the presence of the larva of a warble fly. ■ the larva causing this. [ME: of uncert. origin.]

war·ble fly ▸ **n.** a large fly (genus *Hypoderma*, family Oestridae) that lays its eggs on the legs of mammals such as cattle and horses. The larvae migrate internally to the host's back, where they form a small lump with a breathing hole, dropping to the ground later when fully grown.

war·bler /ˈwôrb(ə)lər/ ▸ **n. 1** any of a number of small insectivorous songbirds that typically have a warbling song, in particular: ■ a New World bird (subfamily Parulinae) of the bunting family. ■ an Old World bird of the family Sylviidae, which includes the blackcap, whitethroat, and chiffchaff. **2** informal a person who sings in a trilling or quavering voice.

war bon·net ▸ **n.** see BONNET (sense 1).

war bride ▸ **n.** a woman who marries a man whom she met while he was on active service.

War·burg /ˈwôr,bərg/, Otto Heinrich (1883–1970), German biochemist. He pioneered the use of the techniques of chemistry for biochemical investigations. Nobel Prize for Physiology or Medicine (1931).

war chest ▸ **n.** a reserve of funds used for fighting a war. ■ a sum of money used for conducting a campaign or business.

war cor·re·spond·ent ▸ **n.** a journalist reporting from a scene of war.

war crime ▸ **n.** an action carried out during the conduct of a war that violates accepted international rules of war. — **war crim·i·nal n.**

Ward[1] /wôrd/, Artemas (1727–1800), American general and politician. During the American Revolution, he was second in command to

George Washington.

Ward[2], Aaron Montgomery (1843–1913), US businessman. In 1872, he founded a dry-goods business, which became Montgomery Ward & Co., the first mail-order firm in the US.

ward /wôrd/ ▶n. **1** a separate room in a hospital, typically one allocated to a particular type of patient: *a children's ward.* ■ one of the divisions of a prison. **2** an administrative division of a city or borough that typically elects and is represented by a councilor or councilors. ■ a territorial division of the Mormon Church presided over by a bishop. **3** a person, usually a minor, under the care and control of a guardian appointed by their parents or a court. ■ archaic guardianship or the state of being subject to a guardian. **4** (usu. **wards**) any of the internal ridges or bars in a lock that prevent the turning of any key that does not have grooves of corresponding form or size. ■ the corresponding grooves in the bit of a key. **5** archaic the action of keeping a lookout for danger: *keeping ward at the gates.* **6** hist. an area of ground enclosed by the encircling walls of a fortress or castle. **7** Fencing a defensive position or motion. ▶v. [trans.] **1** archaic guard; protect. **2** admit (a patient) to a hospital ward.

– PHRASES **ward of the court** a person, usually a minor or of unsound mind, for whom a guardian has been appointed by a court or who has become directly subject to the authority of that court.

– PHRASAL VERBS **ward someone/something off** prevent from harming or affecting one. — **ward•ship** /-ˌSHip/ n. [OE *weard* (in sense 5, also 'body of guards'), *weardian* 'keep safe, guard,' of Gmc. origin; reinforced in ME by Old North. Fr. *warde* (n.), *warder* (v.) 'guard.']

-ward (also **-wards**) ▶suffix added to nouns of place or destination and to adverbs of direction: **1** (usu. **-wards**) (forming adverbs) toward the specified place or direction: *eastward.* **2** (usu. **-ward**) (forming adjectives) turned or tending toward: *onward.* [OE *-weard*, from a Gmc. base meaning 'turn.']

war dance ▶n. a ceremonial dance performed before a battle or to celebrate victory.

war•den /ˈwôrdn/ ▶n. a person responsible for the supervision of a particular place or thing or for ensuring that regulations associated with it are obeyed: *an air-raid warden.* ■ the head official in charge of a prison. ■ a churchwarden. — **war•den•ship** /-ˌSHip/ n. [ME: from Anglo-Norman Fr. and Old North. Fr. *wardein*, var. of OFr. *guarden* 'guardian.']

ward•robe /ˈwôrˌdrōb/ ▶n. a large, tall cabinet in which clothes may be hung or stored. ■ a person's entire collection of clothes: *her wardrobe is extensive.* ■ the costume department or costumes of a theater or film company. [ME: from Old North. Fr. *warderobe*, var. of OFr. *garderobe*.]

ward•room /ˈwôrdˌro͝om; -ˌro͞om/ ▶n. a commissioned officers' mess on board a warship.

war drum ▶n. a drum beaten as a summons or an accompaniment to battle.

-wards ▶suffix var. of -WARD.

ware[1] /we(ə)r/ ▶n. [usu. with adj.] pottery, typically that of a specified type: *majolica ware.* ■ manufactured articles of a specified type: *crystal ware.* ■ (**wares**) articles offered for sale: *traders displayed their wares.* [OE *waru* 'commodities,' of Gmc. origin, perh. the same word as Scots *ware* 'cautiousness,' and having the primary sense 'object of care'.]

ware[2] ▶adj. [predic.] archaic aware: *thou speak'st wiser than thou art ware of.* [OE *wær*.]

ware[3] (also **'ware**) ▶v. [in imper.] beware (used as a warning cry, typically in a hunting context). [OE *warian* 'be on one's guard,' from a Gmc. base meaning 'observe, take care.']

ware•house /ˈwe(ə)rˌhous/ ▶n. a large building where raw materials or manufactured goods may be stored before their export or distribution for sale. ■ a large wholesale or retail store: *a discount warehouse.* ▶v. /-ˌhous; -ˌhouz/ [trans.] store (goods) in a warehouse. ■ place (imported goods) in a bonded warehouse pending the payment of import duty. ■ informal place (someone, typically a prisoner or a psychiatric patient) in a large, impersonal institution.

ware•hous•ing /ˈwe(ə)rˌhouziNG/ ▶n. the practice or process of storing goods in a warehouse. ■ warehouses considered collectively. ■ informal the practice of placing people, typically prisoners or psychiatric patients, in large, impersonal institutions.

war•fare /ˈwôrˌfe(ə)r/ ▶n. engagement in or the activities involved in war or conflict: *guerrilla warfare.*

war•fa•rin /ˈwôrfərin/ ▶n. a water-soluble compound, $C_{19}H_{16}O_4$, with anticoagulant properties, used as a rat poison and in the treatment of thrombosis. [1950s: from the initial letters of *Wisconsin Alumni Research Foundation* + *-arin* on the pattern of *coumarin*.]

war game ▶n. a military exercise carried out to test or improve tactical expertise. ■ a simulated military conflict carried out as a game, leisure activity, or exercise in personal development. ▶v. [trans.] (**war-game**) engage in (a campaign or course of action) using the strategies of such a military exercise. — **war-gam•er** n. **war•gam•ing** (also **war gam•ing**) n.

war•head /ˈwôrˌhed/ ▶n. the explosive head of a missile, torpedo, or similar weapon.

War•hol /ˈwôrˌhôl; -ˌhōl/, Andy (c.1928–87), US painter and graphic artist; born *Andrew Warhola.* A major exponent of pop art, he created silkscreen prints and acrylic paintings of familiar objects (such as Campbell's soup cans) and famous people (such as Marilyn Monroe).

war•horse /ˈwôrˌhôrs/ ▶n. (in historical contexts) a large, powerful horse ridden in a battle. ■ informal an elderly person such as a soldier, politician, or sports player who has fought many campaigns or contests. ■ a musical, theatrical, or literary work that has been heard or performed repeatedly.

war•like /ˈwôrˌlīk/ ▶adj. disposed toward or threatening war; hostile: *a warlike clan.* ■ (of plans, preparations, or munitions) directed toward or prepared for war.

war•lock /ˈwôrˌläk/ ▶n. a man who practices witchcraft; a sorcerer. [OE *wǣrloga* 'traitor, scoundrel, monster,' also 'the Devil,' from *wǣr* 'covenant' + an element rel. to *lēogan* 'belie, deny.']

war•lord /ˈwôrˌlôrd/ ▶n. a military commander, esp. an aggressive regional commander with individual autonomy.

warm /wôrm/ ▶adj. **1** of or at a fairly or comfortably high temperature: *a warm evening* | [as complement] *I walked quickly to keep warm.* ■ (of clothes or coverings) made of a material that helps the body to retain heat; suitable for cold weather. ■ (of a color) containing red, yellow, or orange tones. ■ Hunting (of a scent or trail) fresh; strong. ■ (of a soil) quick to absorb heat or retaining heat. **2** having, showing, or expressive of enthusiasm, affection, or kindness: *a warm welcome.* ■ archaic characterized by lively or heated disagreement. ■ archaic sexually explicit or titillating. **3** [predic.] informal (esp. in children's games) close to discovering something or guessing the correct answer: *you're getting warmer.* ▶v. make or become warm: [trans.] *I stamped my feet to warm them up* | | [intrans.] *it'll soon warm up.*

– PHRASES **keep something warm for someone** hold or occupy a place or post until another person is ready to do so.

– PHRASAL VERBS **warm down** recover from strenuous physical exertion by doing gentle stretches and exercises. **warm to/toward** (or **warm up to/toward**) begin to like (someone). ■ become more interested in or enthusiastic about (something). **warm up** prepare for physical exertion or a performance by exercising or practicing gently beforehand. ■ (of an engine or electrical appliance) reach a temperature high enough to allow it to operate efficiently. ■ become livelier or more animated. **warm something up** (or **over**) reheat previously cooked food. ■ amuse or entertain an audience or crowd so as to make them more receptive to the main act. — **warm•er** n. [usu. in comb.] *a towel-warmer.* **warm•ish** adj. **warm•ly** adv. **warm•ness** n. [OE *wearm* (adj.), *werman, wearmian* (v.), of Gmc. origin; rel. to Du. and Ger. *warm*, from an Indo-Eur. root.]

war ma•chine ▶n. **1** the military resources of a country organized for waging war. **2** an instrument or weapon of war.

warm-blood•ed ▶adj. **1** relating to or denoting animals (chiefly mammals and birds) that maintain a constant body temperature, typically above that of the surroundings, by metabolic means; homeothermic. **2** ardent; passionate. — **warm-blood•ed•ness** n.

warmed-o•ver ▶adj. **1** (also **warmed-up**) (of food or drink) reheated: *warmed-over chicken and pasta.* **2** (of an idea or product) secondhand; stale.

war me•mo•ri•al ▶n. a monument commemorating those killed in a war.

warm front ▶n. Meteorol. the boundary of an advancing mass of warm air, in particular the leading edge of the warm sector of a low-pressure system.

warm•heart•ed /ˈwôrm ˈhärtəd/ ▶adj. (of a person or their actions) sympathetic and kind. — **warm•heart•ed•ly** adv. **warm•heart•ed•ness** n.

warm•ing pan ▶n. hist. a wide, flat brass pan on a long handle, filled with hot coals and used for warming a bed.

war•mon•ger /ˈwôrˌməNGgər; -ˌmäNG-/ ▶n. a sovereign or political leader or activist who encourages or advocates aggression or warfare toward other nations or groups. — **war•mon•ger•ing** n. & adj.

Warm Springs a resort in northwestern Georgia. It is associated with Franklin D. Roosevelt and his "Little White House," where he died; pop. 407.

warmth /wôrmTH/ ▶n. the quality, state, or sensation of being warm; moderate and comfortable heat. ■ enthusiasm, affection, or kindness. ■ vehemence or intensity of emotion.

warm-up (also **warm•up**) ▶n. a period or act of preparation for a game, performance, or exercise session, involving gentle exercise or practice. ■ (**warm-ups**) a garment worn during light exercise or training; a sweatsuit. ■ a period before a stage performance in which the audience is amused or entertained in order to make it more receptive to the main act.

warn /wôrn/ ▶v. [reporting verb] inform someone in advance of an impending or possible danger, problem, or other unpleasant situation: [trans.] *his father had warned him of what might happen.* ■ give someone forceful or cautionary advice about their actions or conduct: [trans.] *friends warned her against the marriage.*

– PHRASAL VERBS **warn someone off** tell someone forcefully or threateningly to go or keep away from somewhere. ■ advise someone forcefully against (a particular thing or course of action). — **warn•er** n. [OE *war(e)nian, wearnian*, from a West Gmc. base meaning 'be cautious.']

War•ner /ˈwôrnər/, Pop (1871–1954), US football coach; full name *Glenn Scobey Warner.* A football league for youths is named for him.

War•ner Broth•ers /ˈwôrnər/ a movie production company founded in 1923 by brothers Harry, Jack, Sam, and Albert Warner. The company produced the first full-length sound movie, *The Jazz Singer*, in 1927.

warn•ing /ˈwôrniNG/ ▶n. a statement or event that indicates a possible or impending danger, problem, or other unpleasant situation: *a warning* *about heavy thunderstorms.* ■ cautionary advice. ■ advance notice of something: *four days' warning.* ■ an experience or sight that serves as a cautionary example to others. — **warn·ing·ly adv.** [OE *war(e)nung.*]

warn·ing col·or·a·tion ▶ **n.** Zool. conspicuous coloring that warns a predator that an animal is unpalatable or poisonous.

War of 1812 a conflict between the US and the UK (1812–14).

warp /wôrp/ ▶ **v. 1** become or cause to become bent or twisted out of shape, typically as a result of the effects of heat or dampness. ■ [trans.] cause to become abnormal or strange; have a distorting effect on: *judgment warped by your dislike of him.* **2** [with obj. and adverbial of direction] move (a ship) along by hauling on a rope attached to a stationary object on shore. ■ [no obj., with adverbial of direction] (of a ship) move in such a way. **3** [trans.] (in weaving) arrange (yarn) so as to form the warp of a piece of cloth. **4** [trans.] cover (land) with a deposit of alluvial soil by natural or artificial flooding. ▶ **n. 1** a twist or distortion in the shape or form of something. ■ fig. an abnormality or perversion in a person's character. ■ [as adj.] relating to or denoting (fictional or hypothetical) space travel by means of distorting space-time: *warp drive.* **2** [in sing.] (in weaving) the threads on a loom over and under which other threads (the weft) are passed to make cloth: *the warp and weft.* **3** a rope attached at one end to a fixed point and used for moving or mooring a ship. — **warp·age** /'wôrpij/ **n.** (in sense 1 of the **verb**). **warp·er n.** (in sense 3 of the **verb**). [OE *weorpan* (v.), *wearp* (n.), of Gmc. origin; rel. to Du. *werpen* and Ger. *werfen* 'to throw.']

war·paint /'wôr,pānt/ ▶ **n.** a pigment or paint traditionally used in some societies, esp. those of North American Indians, to decorate the face and body before battle. ■ informal elaborate or excessively applied makeup.

war·path /'wôr,paTH/ ▶ **n.** (in phrase **on the warpath**) in an angry and aggressive state about a conflict of dispute: *he intends to go on the warpath.* [with ref. to Amer. Indians heading toward a battle with an enemy.]

war·plane /'wôr,plān/ ▶ **n.** an airplane designed and equipped to engage in air combat or to drop bombs.

war·rant /'wôrənt; 'wär-/ ▶ **n. 1** a document issued by a legal or government official authorizing the police or some other body to make an arrest, search premises, or carry out some other action relating to the administration of justice: *an extradition warrant.* ■ a document that entitles the holder to receive goods, money, or services. ■ Finance a negotiable security allowing the holder to buy shares at a specified price at or before some future date. ■ [usu. with negative] justification or authority for an action, belief, or feeling: *there is no warrant for this assumption.* **2** an official certificate of appointment issued to an officer of lower rank than a commissioned officer. ▶ **v.** [trans.] justify or necessitate (a certain course of action). ■ officially affirm or guarantee. — **war·rant·er n.** [ME: from vars. of OFr. *guarant* (n.), *guarantir* (v.), of Gmc. origin.]

war·rant·a·ble /'wôrəntəbəl; 'wär-/ ▶ **adj.** (of an action or statement) able to be authorized or sanctioned; justifiable. — **war·rant·a·ble·ness n. war·rant·a·bly** /-blē/ **adv.**

war·ran·tee /,wôrən'tē; ,wär-/ ▶ **n.** Law a person to whom a warranty is given.

war·rant of·fi·cer ▶ **n.** an officer in the US armed forces ranking below the commissioned officers and above the noncommissioned officers.

war·ran·tor /'wôrəntər; 'wär-/ ▶ **n.** a person or company that provides a warranty.

war·ran·ty /'wôrəntē; 'wär-/ ▶ **n.** (pl. **-ties**) a written guarantee, issued to the purchaser of an article by its manufacturer, promising to repair or replace it if necessary within a specified period of time. ■ (in contract law) a promise that something in furtherance of the contract is guaranteed by one of the contractors, esp. the seller's promise that the thing being sold is as promised or represented. ■ (in an insurance contract) an engagement by the insured party that certain statements are true or that certain conditions shall be fulfilled, the breach of it invalidating the policy. ■ (in property law) a covenant by which the seller binds themselves and their heirs to secure to the buyer the estate conveyed in the deed. ■ (in contract law) a term or promise in a contract, breach of which entitles the innocent party to damages but not to treat the contract as discharged by breach. ■ [usu. with negative] archaic justification or grounds for an action or belief: *you have no warranty for such an audacious doctrine.* [ME: from Anglo-Norman Fr. *warantie*, var. of *garantie* (see **GUARANTY**).]

War·ren[1] /'wôrən; 'wär-/ , a family of American physicians. Joseph (1741–75), a Revolutionary War patriot, is remembered for having sent Paul Revere on his famous ride in 1775. His brother, John (1753–1815), founded Harvard Medical School in 1783. John's son, John Collins (1778–1856), helped to found Massachusetts General Hospital in 1811.

War·ren[2], Earl (1891–1974), Chief Justice of the US 1953–69. He extended civil liberties, including the prohibition of segregation in schools. He also headed the Warren Commission in 1964 that looked into the assassination of President Kennedy.

War·ren[3], Mercy Otis (1728–1814), American writer; the sister of James Otis. She wrote the satirical play *The Adulateur* (1773).

War·ren[4], Robert Penn (1905–89), US poet, novelist, and critic. He became the first US poet laureate in 1986. He wrote *All the King's Men* (1946).

war·ren /'wôrən; 'wär-/ ▶ **n.** (also **rabbit warren**) a network of interconnecting rabbit burrows. ■ a densely populated or labyrinthine building or district. ■ Brit., hist. an enclosed piece of land set aside for breeding game, esp. rabbits. [ME: from an Anglo-Norman Fr. and Old North. Fr. var. of OFr. *garenne* 'game park,' of Gaulish origin.]

war·ren·er /'wôrənər; 'wär-/ ▶ **n.** hist. a gamekeeper. ■ a person in charge of a rabbit warren, either as owner or on behalf of its owner. [ME: from Anglo-Norman Fr. *warener*, from *warenne* 'game park.']

war·ring /'wôriNG/ ▶ **adj.** [attrib.] (of two or more people or groups) in conflict with each other: *warring factions.*

war·ri·or /'wôrēər/ ▶ **n.** (esp. in former times) a brave or experienced soldier or fighter. [ME: from Old North. Fr. *werreior*, var. of OFr. *guerreior*, from *guerreier* 'make war,' from *guerre* 'war.']

war room ▶ **n.** a room from which a war is directed. ■ a room from which business or political strategy is planned.

War·saw /'wôr,sô/ the capital of Poland, on the Vistula River; pop. 1,656,000. Polish name **WARSZAWA**.

War·saw Pact a treaty of mutual defense and military aid signed at Warsaw on May 14, 1955, by communist states of Europe under Soviet influence, in response to the admission of West Germany to NATO. The pact was dissolved in 1991.

war·ship /'wôr,SHip/ ▶ **n.** a ship equipped with weapons and designed to take part in warfare at sea.

Wars of the Ros·es the 15th-century English civil wars between the Houses of York and Lancaster, represented by white and red roses respectively, during the reigns of Henry VI, Edward IV, and Richard III.

wart /wôrt/ ▶ **n.** a small, hard, benign growth on the skin, caused by a virus. ■ any rounded excrescence on the skin of an animal or the surface of a plant. ■ informal an obnoxious or objectionable person. ■ an undesirable or disfiguring feature: *few products are without their warts.*

– PHRASES **warts and all** informal including features or qualities that are not appealing or attractive. — **wart·y** /'wôrtē/ **adj.** [OE *wearte*, of Gmc. origin; rel. to Du. *wrat* and Ger. *Warze.*]

wart·hog /'wôrt,häg/ ▶ **n.** an African wild pig (*Phacochoerus aethiopicus*) with bristly gray skin, a large head, warty lumps on the face, and curved tusks.

war·time /'wôr,tīm/ ▶ **n.** a period during which a war is taking place.

war-torn ▶ **adj.** (of a place) racked or devastated by war.

War·wick[1] /'wôrwik; wär-/ a city in east central Rhode Island, south of Providence; pop. 85,808.

War·wick[2] /'wôrik; 'wär-/, Richard Neville, Earl of (1428–71), English statesman; known as **Warwick the Kingmaker**. During the Wars of the Roses he fought first on the Yorkist side and then on the Lancastrian side.

war·y /'we(ə)rē/ ▶ **adj.** (**war·i·er, war·i·est**) feeling or showing caution about possible dangers or problems: *dogs are often wary of strangers.* — **war·i·ly** /-rəlē/ **adv. war·i·ness n.**

was /wəz; wäz/ first and third person singular past of **BE**.

wa·sa·bi /wə'säbē/ ▶ **n.** a Japanese plant (*Eutrema wasabi*) of the cabbage family with a thick green root that tastes like strong horseradish and is used in cooking. [20th C.: from Japanese.]

Wa·satch Range /'wô,sacH/ a range of the Rocky Mountains that extends south from Idaho into central Utah.

Wash. ▶ **abbr.** Washington.

wash /wäsH; wôsH/ ▶ **v. 1** [trans.] clean with water and, typically, soap or detergent. ■ [intrans.] clean oneself, esp. one's hands and face with soap and water. ■ (of an animal) clean (itself or another) by licking. ■ [with obj. and adverbial] remove (a stain or dirt) from something by cleaning with water and detergent: *keep washing the mold off the walls.* ■ [no obj., with adverbial] (of dirt or a stain) be removed in such a way. ■ [no obj., with adverbial] (of fabric, a garment, or dye) withstand cleaning to a specified degree without shrinking or fading. ■ [intrans.] do one's laundry. ■ (usu. **be washed**) literary wet or moisten (something) thoroughly. **2** [with obj. and adverbial of direction] (of flowing water) carry (someone or something) in a particular direction: *floods washed away the bridges.* ■ [no obj., with adverbial of direction] be carried by flowing water. ■ [no obj., with adverbial of direction] (esp. of waves) sweep, move, or splash in a particular direction. ■ [trans.] (usu. **be washed**) (of a river, sea, or lake) flow through or lap against (a country, coast, etc.): *warm blue seas.* ■ [intrans.] (**wash over**) (of a feeling) affect (someone) suddenly: *sadness washed over her.* ■ [intrans.] (**wash over**) occur all around without greatly affecting (someone): *conversation washed over her.* ■ [trans.] sift metallic particles from (earth or gravel) by running water through it. **3** [trans.] (usu. **be washed**) brush with a thin coat of diluted paint or ink: *walls washed with shades of umber.* ■ (**wash something with**) coat inferior metal with (a film of gold or silver from a solution). **4** [no obj., with negative] informal seem convincing or genuine. ▶ **n. 1** [usu. in sing.] an act of washing something or an instance of being washed. ■ a quantity of clothes needing to be or just having been washed: *she hung out her wash.* ■ a medicinal or cleansing solution: *mouth wash.* **2** [in sing.] the disturbed water or air behind a moving boat or aircraft or the sound made by this. ■ the surging of water or breaking of waves or the sound made by this. **3** a layer of paint or metal spread thinly on a surface: *a pale lemon wash.* **4** silt or gravel carried by a stream or river and deposited as sediment. ■ a sandbank exposed only at low tide. ■ (in the western US) a dry bed of a stream, typically in a ravine, that flows only seasonally. **5** kitchen slops and other food waste fed to pigs. **6** malt fermenting in preparation for distillation. **7** [in sing.] informal a situation or result that is of no benefit to either of two opposing sides: *the plan's impact on jobs would be a wash, creating as many as it costs.*

– PHRASES **come out in the wash** informal be resolved eventually with no lasting harm: *he assures me it'll all come out in the wash.* **in the wash** (of clothes, bed linen, or similar) put aside for washing or in the process of being washed. **one hand washes the other** mutual favors are exchanged. **wash one's dirty linen** (or **laundry**) **in public** informal discuss or argue about one's personal affairs in public. **wash one's hands** go to the toilet (used euphemistically). **wash one's hands of** disclaim responsibility for. [orig. with biblical allusion to Matt. 27:24.]

– PHRASAL VERBS **wash something down 1** wash or clean something thoroughly: *wash down the walls.* **2** accompany or follow food with a drink. **wash out** (or **wash someone out**) be excluded (or exclude someone) from a course or position after a failure to meet the required standards: *they had washed out of pilot training.* **wash something out 1** clean the inside of something with water. **2** wash something, esp. a garment, quickly or briefly. **3** (usu. **be washed out**) cause an event to be postponed or canceled because of rain. **4** (of a flood or downpour) make a breach in a road. [OE *wæscan* (v.), of Gmc. origin; rel. to Du. *wassen*, Ger. *waschen*.]

wash·a·ble /ˈwäsHəbəl; ˈwô-/ ▶ **adj.** (esp. of fabric or clothes) able to be washed without shrinkage or other damage: *washable curtains.* — **wash·a·bil·i·ty** /ˌwäsHəˈbilitē; ˌwôsH-/ **n.**

wash-and-wear ▶ **adj.** (of a garment or fabric) easily washed, drying quickly, and not needing to be ironed.

wash·ba·sin /ˈwäsH,bāsən; ˈwôsH-/ ▶ **n.** a basin, typically fixed to a wall or on a pedestal, used for washing one's hands and face.

wash·board /ˈwäsH,bôrd; ˈwôsH-/ ▶ **n. 1** a board made of ridged wood or a sheet of corrugated zinc, used when washing clothes as a surface against which to scrub them. ■ a similar board played as a percussion instrument by scraping. ■ the surface of a worn, uneven road. ■ [as adj.] denoting a man's stomach that is lean and has well-defined muscles. **2** a board fixed along the side of a boat to prevent water from spilling in over the edge. ▶ **v.** [trans.] [usu. as adj.] (**washboarded**) cause ridges to develop in (a road or road surface).

wash·cloth /ˈwäsH,klôTH; ˈwôsH-/ ▶ **n.** a cloth for washing one's face and body, typically made of terrycloth or other absorbent material.

wash·day /ˈwäsH,dā; ˈwôsH-/ ▶ **n.** a day on which a household's clothes, bed linens, etc., are washed, esp. when the same day each week.

washed-out ▶ **adj.** faded by or as if by sunlight or repeated washing. ■ (of a person) pale and tired.

washed-up ▶ **adj.** deposited by the tide on a shore. ■ informal no longer effective or successful.

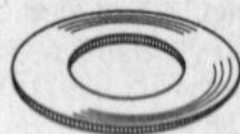

flat washer

split-ring lock washer

internal tooth washer

external tooth washer

washers 2

wash·er /ˈwäsHər; ˈwô-/ ▶ **n. 1** [usu. with adj.] a person or device that washes something. ■ a washing machine. **2** a small flat ring made of metal, rubber, or plastic fixed under a nut or the head of a bolt to spread the pressure when tightened or between two joining surfaces as a spacer or seal.

wash·er·wom·an /ˈwäsHər,wo͝omən; ˈwô-/ ▶ **n.** (pl. **-wom·en**) a woman whose occupation is washing clothes.

wash·ing /ˈwäsHiNG; ˈwô-/ ▶ **n.** the action of washing oneself or laundering clothes, bed linen, etc. ■ a quantity of clothes, bed linen, etc., that is to be washed or has just been washed.

wash·ing ma·chine ▶ **n.** a machine for washing clothes, bed linens, etc.

Wash·ing·ton[1] /ˈwôsHiNGtən; ˈwä-/ **1** a state in the northwestern US, on the Pacific coast, bordered by Canada; pop. 5,894,121; capital, Olympia; statehood, Nov. 11, 1889 (42). **2** the capital of the US; pop. 572,059. It is coextensive with the District of Columbia, a federal district on the Potomac River. Founded in 1790, during the presidency of George Washington, the city was planned by engineer Pierre-Charles L'Enfant (1754–1825). Full name **WASHINGTON, DC.** — **Wash·ing·to·ni·an** /ˌwôsHiNGˈtōnēən; ˌwäsH-/ **n. & adj.**

Wash·ing·ton[2], Booker T. (1856–1915), US educator; full name *Booker Taliaferro Washington.* He established the Tuskegee Institute in Alabama (1881).

Wash·ing·ton[3], Bushrod (1762–1829), US Supreme Court associate justice 1798–1829, He was a nephew of George Washington.

Wash·ing·ton[4], George (1732–99), 1st president of the US 1789–97. Commander in chief of the Continental Army, he helped to win the American Revolution by keeping his army together through the winter of 1777–78 and by winning a decisive battle at Yorktown in 1781. In 1787, he chaired the convention at Philadelphia that drew up the US Constitution. In his two terms as president, he followed a policy of neutrality in international affairs and of expansion on the domestic front.

Wash·ing·ton Mon·u·ment a colossal obelisk erected in honor of George Washington as a national memorial in Washington, DC.

Wash·ing·ton, Mount a peak in north central New Hampshire, the highest in the northeastern US at 6,288 feet (1,918 m).

Wash·i·ta Riv·er /ˈwôsHi,tô; ˈwä-/ a river that flows from the Texas Panhandle across southern Oklahoma to the Red River at Lake Texoma.

wash·out /ˈwäsH,out; ˈwôsH-/ ▶ **n. 1** [usu. in sing.] informal an event that is spoiled by constant or heavy rain. ■ a disappointing failure: *the film was a washout.* **2** a breach in a road or railroad track caused by flooding. ■ Geol. a channel cut into a sedimentary deposit by rushing water and filled with younger material. **3** Med. the removal of material or a substance from the body or a part of it, either by washing with a fluid, or by allowing it to be eliminated over a period.

wash·rag /ˈwäsH,rag; ˈwôsH-/ ▶ **n.** another term for **WASHCLOTH.**

wash·room /ˈwäsH,ro͞om; ˈwôsH-; -,ro͝om/ ▶ **n.** a room with washing and toilet facilities.

wash·stand /ˈwäsH,stand; ˈwôsH-/ ▶ **n.** esp. hist. a piece of furniture designed to hold a jug, bowl, or basin for the purpose of washing one's hands and face.

wash·tub /ˈwäsH,təb; ˈwôsH-/ ▶ **n.** a large metal tub used for washing clothes and linen.

was·n't /ˈwəzənt; ˈwäz-/ ▶ **contr.** was not.

Wasp /wäsp/ (also **WASP**) ▶ **n.** an upper- or middle-class American white Protestant, considered to be a member of the most powerful group in society. [1950s: acronym from *white Anglo-Saxon Protestant.*] — **Wasp·ish adj. Wasp·y adj.**

wasp /wäsp/ ▶ **n. 1** a social winged insect (*Vespula, Polistes,* and other genera, family Vespidae) that has a narrow waist and a sting. It constructs a paper nest from wood pulp and raises the larvae on a diet of insects. See illustrations at **PAPER WASP, MUD DAUBER. 2** a solitary winged insect (several superfamilies) with a narrow waist, mostly distantly related to the social wasps and including many parasitic kinds. [OE *wæfs, wæps, wæsp*, of West Gmc. origin, from an Indo-Eur. root shared by L. *vespa*.]

wasp·ish /ˈwäspisH/ ▶ **adj.** readily expressing anger or irritation: *a waspish tongue.* — **wasp·ish·ly adv. wasp·ish·ness n.**

wasp waist ▶ **n.** a very narrow or tightly corseted waist. — **wasp-waist·ed adj.**

was·sail /ˈwäsəl; -,sāl/ archaic ▶ **n.** spiced ale or mulled wine drunk during celebrations for Twelfth Night and Christmas Eve. ■ lively and noisy festivities involving the drinking of plentiful amounts of alcohol; revelry. ▶ **v. 1** [intrans.] drink plentiful amounts of alcohol and enjoy oneself with others in a noisy, lively way. **2** go from house to house at Christmas singing carols: *here we go a-wassailing.* — **was·sail·er n.** [ME *wæs hæil* 'be in (good) health!': from ON *ves heill* (cf. **HAIL[2]**).]

Was·ser·mann test /ˈwäsərmən; ˈvä-/ ▶ **n.** Med. a diagnostic test for syphilis using a specific antibody reaction (the **Wassermann reaction**) of the patient's blood serum. [20th C.: named after August P. *Wassermann* (1866–1925), German pathologist.]

Was·ser·stein /ˈwäsər,stīn; -,stēn/, Wendy (1950–2006), US playwright. Her plays include *The Heidi Chronicles* (1988) and *Third* (2005).

wast·age /ˈwāstij/ ▶ **n. 1** the action or process of losing or destroying something by using it carelessly or extravagantly: *the wastage of natural resources.* ■ the amount of something lost or destroyed in such a way: *wastage was cut by 50 percent.* **2** the weakening or deterioration of a part of the body, typically as a result of illness or lack of use.

waste /wāst/ ▶ **v. 1** [trans.] use or expend carelessly, extravagantly, or to no purpose. ■ (usu. **be wasted on**) bestow or expend on an unappreciative recipient. ■ (usu. **be wasted**) fail to make full or good use of: *we're wasted in this job.* **2** [intrans.] (of a person or a part of the body) become progressively weaker and more emaciated. ■ [trans.] archaic cause to do this. **3** [trans.] literary devastate or ruin (a place): *he wasted their country.* ■ informal kill or severely injure (someone). **4** [intrans.] literary (of time) pass away; be spent. ▶ **adj.** [attrib.] **1** (of a material, substance, or by-product) eliminated or discarded as no longer useful or required after the completion of a process: *waste materials.* **2** (of an area of land, typically in a city or town) not used, cultivated, or built on. ▶ **n. 1** an act or instance of using or expending something carelessly, extravagantly, or to no purpose: *it's a waste of time.* ■ archaic the gradual loss or diminution of something. **2** material that is not wanted; the unusable remains or byproducts of something: (**wastes**) *hazardous industrial wastes.* **3** (usu. **wastes**) a large area of barren, typically uninhabited land. **4** Law damage to an estate caused by an act or by neglect, esp. by a life-tenant.

– PHRASES **go to waste** be unused or expended to no purpose. **lay waste to** (or **lay something (to) waste**) completely destroy. **waste not, want not** proverb if you use a commodity or resource carefully and without extravagance, you will never be in need. [ME: from Old North. Fr. *wast(e)* (n.), *waster* (v.), based on L. *vastus* 'unoccupied, uncultivated.']

waste·bas·ket /ˈwāst,baskit/ ▶ **n.** a receptacle for small quantities of rubbish.

wast·ed /ˈwāstid/ ▶ **adj. 1** used or expended carelessly, extravagantly, or to no purpose: *wasted fuel.* ■ (of an action) not producing the desired result: *a wasted journey.* **2** (of a person or a part of the body) weak and emaciated. ■ informal under the influence of alcohol or illegal drugs.

waste·ful /ˈwāstfəl/ ▶ **adj.** (of a person, action, or process) using or expending something of value carelessly, extravagantly, or to no purpose: *wasteful energy consumption.* — **waste·ful·ly** adv. **waste·ful·ness** n.

waste·gate /ˈwāst,gāt/ ▶ **n.** a device in a turbocharger that regulates the pressure at which exhaust gases pass to the turbine by opening or closing a vent to the exterior.

waste·land /ˈwāst,land/ ▶ **n.** an unused area of land that has become barren or overgrown. ■ a bleak, unattractive, and unused or neglected urban or industrial area: *industrial wasteland* | fig. *a cultural wasteland.*

waste·pa·per bas·ket ▶ **n.** a wastebasket.

waste pipe ▶ **n.** a pipe carrying waste water, such as that from a sink, bathtub, or shower, to a drain.

wast·er /ˈwāstər/ ▶ **n.** a wasteful person or thing. ■ informal a person who does little or nothing of value. ■ a discarded piece of defective pottery.

wast·rel /ˈwāstrəl/ ▶ **n.** **1** literary a wasteful or good-for-nothing person. **2** archaic a waif; a neglected child. [16th C. (denoting a strip of wasteland): from the V. WASTE + -REL.]

watch /wäCH/ ▶ **v.** [trans.] look at or observe attentively, typically over a period of time. ■ keep under careful or protective observation: *he was watched over by a single guard.* ■ secretly follow or spy on. ■ follow closely or maintain an interest in. ■ exercise care, caution, or restraint about: [with clause] *you should watch what you say!* ■ [intrans.] (**watch for**) look out or be on the alert for. ■ [intrans.] [usu. in imper.] (**watch out**) be careful. ■ (**watch it/yourself**) [usu. in imper.] informal be careful (used as a warning or threat). ▶ **n.** **1** a small timepiece worn typically on a strap on one's wrist. **2** [usu. in sing.] an act or instance of carefully observing someone or something over a period of time: *keeping a close watch on our activities.* ■ a period of vigil during which a person is stationed to look out for danger or trouble, typically during the night. ■ a fixed period of duty on a ship, usually lasting four hours. ■ (also **star·board** or **port watch**) the officers and crew on duty during one such period. ■ fig. the period someone spends in a particular role or job. ■ (usu. **the watch**) hist. a watchman or group of watchmen who patrolled and guarded the streets of a town before the introduction of the police force. ■ a body of soldiers making up a guard.
– PHRASES **be on the watch** be carefully looking out for something, esp. a possible danger. **keep watch** stay on the lookout for danger or trouble. **the watches of the night** literary the hours of night, portrayed as a time when one cannot sleep. **watch one's step** used as a warning to someone to walk or act carefully. **watch the time** ensure that one is aware of the time in order to avoid being late. — **watch·er** n. [often in comb.] *a bird-watcher.* [OE *wæcce* 'watchfulness,' *wæccende* 'remaining awake'.]

watch·a·ble /ˈwäCHəbəl/ ▶ **adj.** (of a film or television program) moderately enjoyable to watch. — **watch·a·bil·i·ty** /,wäCHəˈbilitē/ **n.**

watch cap ▶ **n.** a close-fitting knitted cap of a kind worn by members of the US Navy in cold weather.

watch·case /ˈwäCH,kās/ ▶ **n.** a metal case enclosing the works of a watch.

watch chain ▶ **n.** a metal chain securing a pocket watch.

watch·dog /ˈwäCH,dôg/ ▶ **n.** a dog kept to guard private property. ■ a person or group whose function is to monitor the practices of companies providing a particular service or utility. ▶ **v.** (**-dogged, -dog·ging**) [trans.] maintain surveillance over (a person, activity, or situation).

watch·fire /ˈwäCH,fī(ə)r/ ▶ **n.** a fire maintained during the night as a signal or for the use of someone who is on watch.

watch·ful /ˈwäCHfəl/ ▶ **adj.** watching or observing someone or something closely; alert and vigilant: *the watchful eye of their father.* ■ archaic wakeful; sleepless. — **watch·ful·ly** adv. **watch·ful·ness** n.

watch list ▶ **n.** a list of individuals, groups, or items that require close surveillance, typically for legal or political reasons.

watch·mak·er /ˈwäCH,mākər/ ▶ **n.** a person who makes and repairs watches and clocks. — **watch·mak·ing** /-,mākiNG/ **n.**

watch·man /ˈwäCHmən/ ▶ **n.** (pl. **-men**) a man employed to look after an empty building, esp. at night. ■ hist. a member of a body of people employed to keep watch in a town at night.

watch spring ▶ **n.** a mainspring in a watch.

watch·tow·er /ˈwäCH,touər/ ▶ **n.** a tower built to create an elevated observation point.

watch·word /ˈwäCH,wərd/ ▶ **n.** a word or phrase expressing a person's or group's core aim or belief. ■ archaic a military password.

wa·ter /ˈwôtər; ˈwät-/ ▶ **n.** **1** a colorless, transparent, odorless, tasteless liquid that forms the seas, lakes, rivers, and rain and is the basis of the fluids of living organisms: chemical formula H_2O. ■ this as supplied to houses or commercial establishments through pipes and taps. ■ one of the four elements in ancient and medieval philosophy and in astrology (considered essential to the nature of the signs Cancer, Scorpio, and Pisces). ■ (usu. **the waters**) the water of a mineral spring, typically as used medicinally for bathing in or drinking. ■ [with adj.] a solution of a specified substance in water: *ammonia water.* **2** (**the water**) a stretch or area of water, such as a river, sea, or lake. ■ the surface of such an area of water. ■ [as adj.] found in, on, or near such areas of water. ■ (**waters**) the water of a particular sea, river, or lake: *the waters of Hudson Bay.* ■ (**waters**) an area of sea regarded as under the jurisdiction of a particular country. **3** the quality of transparency and brilliance shown by a diamond or other gem. **4** Finance capital stock that represents a book value greater than the true assets of a company. ▶ **v.** **1** [trans.] pour or sprinkle water over (a plant or an area of ground), typically in order to encourage plant growth. ■ give a drink of water to (an animal). ■ (usu. **be watered**) (of a river) flow through (an area of land). ■ Finance increase (a company's debt, or nominal capital) by the issue of new shares without a corresponding addition to assets. **2** [intrans.] (of the eyes) become full of moisture or tears. ■ (of the mouth) produce saliva, typically in response to the sight or smell of appetizing food. **3** [trans.] dilute or adulterate (a drink, typically an alcoholic one) with water: ***watering down** the drinks.* ■ (**water something down**) make a statement or proposal less forceful or controversial by changing or leaving out certain details: *the report was watered down.*
– PHRASES **by water** using a ship or boat for travel or transport. **like water** in great quantities: *spending money like water.* **make water** **1** urinate. **2** (of a ship or boat) take in water through a leak. **under water** submerged; flooded. **water on the brain** informal hydrocephalus. **water under the bridge** (or **water over the dam**) used to refer to events or situations that are in the past and consequently no longer to be regarded as important or as a source of concern. — **wa·ter·er** n. **wa·ter·less** adj. [OE *wæter* (n.), *wæterian* (v.), of Gmc. origin.]

wa·ter ar·um /ˈe(ə)rəm/ ▶ **n.** a plant (*Calla palustris*) of the arum family, with heart-shaped leaves, a white spathe, and a green spadix. It grows in swamps and boggy ground in north temperate regions. Also called WILD CALLA.

water arum

wa·ter bag ▶ **n.** a bag made of leather, canvas, or other material, used for carrying water.

wa·ter-based ▶ **adj.** (of a substance or solution) using or having water as a medium or main ingredient: *a water-based paint.*

wa·ter bath ▶ **n.** Chem. a container of water heated to a given temperature, used for heating substances placed in smaller containers.

wa·ter bear ▶ **n.** a minute invertebrate (phylum Tardigrada) with a short plump body and four pairs of stubby legs, living in water or in the film of water on plants such as mosses.

Wa·ter Bear·er (**the Water Bearer**) the zodiacal sign or constellation Aquarius.

wa·ter·bed /ˈwôtər,bed; ˈwät-/ ▶ **n.** a bed with a water-filled rubber or plastic mattress.

wa·ter bee·tle ▶ **n.** any of a large number of beetles (Dytiscidae, Hydrophilidae, and other families) that live in fresh water.

wa·ter·bird /ˈwôtər,bərd; ˈwät-/ ▶ **n.** a bird that frequents water, esp. one that habitually wades or swims in fresh water.

wa·ter birth ▶ **n.** a birth in which the mother spends the final stages of labor in a birthing pool, with delivery taking place either in or out of the water.

wa·ter bloom ▶ **n.** another term for ALGAL BLOOM (see BLOOM[1]).

wa·ter boat·man ▶ **n.** an aquatic bug (*Corixa, Sigara,* and other genera, family Corixidae) that spends much of its time on the bottom, using its front legs to sieve food from the water and its hair-fringed rear legs for swimming. ■ another term for BACKSWIMMER.

wa·ter·bod·y /ˈwôtər,bädē; ˈwät-/ ▶ **n.** (pl. **-bod·ies**) a body of water forming a physiographical feature, for example a sea or a reservoir.

wa·ter-bomb·er ▶ **n.** Canadian an aircraft used for extinguishing forest fires by dropping water.

wa·ter·borne ▶ **adj.** (of a vehicle or goods) conveyed by, traveling on, or involving travel or transportation on water. ■ (of a disease) communicated or propagated by contaminated water.

wa·ter·buck /ˈwôtər,bək; ˈwät-/ ▶ **n.** a large African antelope (*Kobus ellipsiprymnus*) occurring near rivers and lakes in the savanna.

wa·ter buf·fa·lo ▶ **n.** a large black domesticated buffalo (*Bubalus bubalis*) with heavy swept-back horns, used as a beast of burden throughout the tropics. It is the descendant of the wild *B. arnee*, which is confined to remote parts of India and Southeast Asia.

wa·ter can·non ▶ **n.** a device that ejects a powerful jet of water, typically used to disperse a crowd.

wa·ter chest·nut ▶ **n.** **1** (also **Chi·nese wa·ter chest·nut**) the tuber of a tropical sedge that is widely used in Asian cooking, its white flesh remaining crisp after cooking. **2** the sedge (*Eleocharis tuberosa*) that yields this tuber, which is cultivated in flooded fields in Southeast Asia. **3** (also **wa·ter cal·trop**) an aquatic plant (*Trapa natans*, family Trapaceae) with small white flowers, producing an edible rounded seed with two large projecting horns.

wa·ter clock ▶ **n.** hist. a clock that used the flow of water to measure time.

wa·ter clos·et ▶n. dated a flush toilet. ■ a room containing such a toilet.

wa·ter·cock /ˈwôtər,käk; ˈwät-/ ▶n. a brown and gray aquatic Asian rail (*Gallicrex cinerea*), the male of which develops black plumage and a red frontal shield in the breeding season.

wa·ter·col·or /ˈwôtər,kələr; ˈwät-/ (Brit. **wa·ter·col·our**) ▶n. (also **watercolors**) artists' paint made with a water-soluble binder such as gum arabic, and thinned with water rather than oil, giving a transparent color. ■ a picture painted with watercolors. ■ the art of painting with watercolors, esp. using a technique of producing paler colors by diluting rather than by adding white. — **wa·ter·col·or·ist** n.

wa·ter cool·er ▶n. a dispenser of cooled drinking water, typically used in office workplaces. ■ [as adj.] informal denoting the type of informal conversation or socializing among office workers that takes place in the communal area in which such a dispenser is located: *water-cooler gossip*.

wa·ter·course /ˈwôtər,kôrs; ˈwät-/ ▶n. a brook, stream, or artificially constructed water channel. ■ the bed along which this flows.

wa·ter·craft /ˈwôtər,kraft; ˈwät-/ ▶n. (pl. same) **1** a boat or other vessel that travels on water. **2** skill in sailing and other activities that take place on water.

wa·ter·cress /ˈwôtər,kres; ˈwät-/ ▶n. a cress (*Nasturtium officinale*) that grows in running water and whose pungent leaves are used in salad.

wa·ter crow·foot ▶n. see CROWFOOT.

wa·ter cure ▶n. esp. hist. a session of treatment by hydropathy.

wa·ter cy·cle ▶n. the cycle of processes by which water circulates between the earth's oceans, atmosphere, and land, involving precipitation as rain and snow, drainage in streams and rivers, and return to the atmosphere by evaporation and transpiration.

wa·ter·dog /ˈwôtər,dôg; ˈwät-/ ▶n. an aquatic North American salamander (genus *Necturus*, family Proteidae) that is a smaller relative of the mudpuppy, typically living in flowing water.

wa·tered silk ▶n. silk that has been treated in such a way as to give it a wavy lustrous finish.

wa·ter·fall /ˈwôtər,fôl; ˈwät-/ ▶n. a cascade of water falling from a height, formed when a river or stream flows over a precipice or steep incline.

wa·ter fern ▶n. **1** a small aquatic or semiaquatic fern (families Azollaceae, Marsileaceae and Salviniaceae) that is either free-floating or anchored by the roots, found chiefly in tropical and warm countries. **2** an Australian fern (genus *Blechnum*, family Blechnaceae) with large coarse fronds, typically growing in marshy areas and rain forests.

wa·ter flea ▶n. another term for DAPHNIA.

Wa·ter·ford /ˈwôtərfərd; ˈwätər-/ a county in southeastern Republic of Ireland, in Munster; main administrative center, Dungarvan. ■ its county town; pop. 40,000.

Wa·ter·ford glass ▶n. fine clear, colorless flint glassware first manufactured in Waterford, Ireland, in the 18th and 19th centuries.

wa·ter·fowl /ˈwôtər,foul; ˈwät-/ ▶plural n. ducks, geese, or other large aquatic birds, esp. when regarded as game.

wa·ter·front /ˈwôtər,frənt; ˈwät-/ ▶n. a part of a town that borders a body of water.

wa·ter gap ▶n. a transverse gap in a mountain ridge through which a stream or river flows.

wa·ter gar·den ▶n. a garden with pools or a stream, for growing aquatic plants.

wa·ter gas ▶n. a fuel gas consisting mainly of carbon monoxide and hydrogen, made by passing steam over incandescent coke.

Wa·ter·gate /ˈwôtər,gāt; ˈwät-/ a political scandal in which an attempt to bug the national headquarters of the Democratic Party (in the Watergate building in Washington, DC) led to the resignation of President Nixon (1974).

wa·ter·gate /ˈwôtər,gāt; ˈwät-/ ▶n. a gate of a town or castle opening on to a lake, river, or sea. ■ archaic a sluice; a floodgate.

wa·ter glass ▶n. **1** a solution of sodium or potassium silicate. It solidifies on exposure to air and is used to make silica gel and for preserving eggs and hardening artificial stone. **2** an instrument for making observations beneath the surface of water, consisting of a bucket with a glass bottom. **3** a glass for holding drinking water.

wa·ter ham·mer ▶n. a knocking noise in a water pipe that occurs when a tap is turned off briskly.

wa·ter hem·lock ▶n. a highly poisonous plant (genus *Cicuta*) of the parsley family that grows in ditches and marshy ground.

wa·ter·hen /ˈwôtər,hen; ˈwät-/ ▶n. an aquatic rail (genera *Gallinula* and *Amaurornis*), esp. a moorhen or related bird.

wa·ter·hole /ˈwôtər,hōl; ˈwät-/ ▶n. a depression in which water collects, esp. one from which animals regularly drink.

wa·ter hy·a·cinth ▶n. a free-floating tropical American water plant (*Eichhornia crassipes*, family Pontederiaceae) that has been introduced elsewhere as an ornamental and in some warmer regions has become a serious weed of waterways.

wa·ter·ing can ▶n. a portable water container with a long spout and a detachable perforated cap, used for watering plants.

wa·ter·ing hole ▶n. a waterhole from which animals regularly drink. ■ informal a tavern or bar.

wa·ter jack·et ▶n. a casing containing water surrounding and protecting something from extremes of temperature. — **wa·ter-jack·et·ed** adj.

wa·ter jump ▶n. an obstacle in a jumping competition or steeplechase, where a horse must jump over or into water.

wa·ter·leaf /ˈwôtər,lēf; ˈwät-/ ▶n. a North American woodland plant (genus *Hydrophyllum*, family Hydrophyllaceae) with bell-shaped flowers and leaves that appear to be stained with water.

wa·ter let·tuce ▶n. a tropical aquatic plant (*Pistia stratiotes*) of the arum family that forms a floating rosette of leaves.

wa·ter lev·el ▶n. **1** the height reached by the water in a reservoir, river, storage tank, etc. ■ another term for WATER TABLE. **2** an implement that uses water to indicate the horizontal.

wa·ter li·ly ▶n. an aquatic plant (family Nymphaeaceae) with large round floating leaves and large, typically cup-shaped, floating flowers. Several genera and many species include the white-flowered **fragrant water lily** (*Nymphaea odorata*) of eastern North America.

fragrant water lily

wa·ter·line /ˈwôtər,līn; ˈwät-/ ▶n. **1** the line to which a vessel's hull is immersed when loaded in a specified way. ■ the level reached by the sea or a river visible as a line on a rock face, beach, or riverbank. ■ any of various structural lines of a ship, parallel with the surface of the water, representing the contour of the hull at various heights above the keel. **2** a vertical watermark made in laid paper.

wa·ter·logged /ˈwôtər,lôgd; ˈwät-/ ▶adj. saturated with or full of water. [18th C.: past part. of the verb *waterlog* 'make (a ship) unmanageable by flooding,' from WATER + the v. LOG[1].]

Wa·ter·loo, Battle of /ˈwôtər,loo; ˈwät-/ a battle fought on June 18, 1815, near the village of Waterloo (in what is now Belgium), in which Napoleon's army was defeated by the British (under the Duke of Wellington) and Prussians. ■ [as n.] (**a Waterloo**) a decisive defeat or failure: *the team met their Waterloo*.

wa·ter main ▶n. the main pipe in a water supply system.

wa·ter·man /ˈwôtərmən; ˈwät-/ ▶n. (pl. **-men**) a boatman. ■ an oarsman who has attained a particular level of knowledge or skill.

wa·ter·mark /ˈwôtər,märk; ˈwät-/ ▶n. a faint design made in some paper during manufacture, that is visible when held against the light and typically identifies the maker. ▶v. [trans.] mark with such a design.

wa·ter mass ▶n. a large body of seawater that is distinguishable by its characteristic temperature and salinity range.

wa·ter meas·ur·er ▶n. a long, thin aquatic bug (genus *Hydrometra*, family Hydrometridae) that walks slowly on the surface film of water and spears small prey with its beak.

wa·ter·mel·on /ˈwôtər,melən; ˈwät-/ ▶n. **1** the large melonlike fruit of a plant of the gourd family, with smooth green skin, red pulp, and watery juice. **2** the widely cultivated African plant (*Citrullus lanatus*) that yields this fruit.

wa·ter mil·foil ▶n. see MILFOIL (sense 2).

wa·ter mill /ˈwôtər,mil; ˈwät-/ ▶n. a mill worked by a waterwheel.

wa·ter moc·ca·sin ▶n. another term for COTTONMOUTH.

wa·ter nymph ▶n. (in folklore and classical mythology) a nymph inhabiting or presiding over water, esp. a Naiad or Nereid.

wa·ter of crys·tal·li·za·tion ▶n. Chem. water molecules forming an essential part of the crystal structure of some compounds.

wa·ter o·pos·sum (also **wa·ter pos·sum**) ▶n. another term for YAPOK.

wa·ter ou·zel ▶n. another term for DIPPER (sense 1).

wa·ter pep·per ▶n. a widely distributed plant (genus *Polygonum*) of the dock family that grows in wet ground, with peppery-tasting leaves and sap that is a skin irritant.

wa·ter pipe ▶n. **1** a pipe for conveying water. **2** a pipe for smoking tobacco, cannabis, etc., that draws the smoke through water to cool it.

wa·ter pis·tol ▶n. a toy pistol that shoots a jet of water.

wa·ter plan·tain ▶n. an aquatic or marshland plant (genus *Alisma*, family Alismataceae) of north temperate regions, with leaves that resemble those of plantains and a tall stem bearing numerous white or pink flowers.

wa·ter po·lo ▶n. a seven-a-side game played by swimmers in a pool, with a ball like a volleyball that is thrown into the opponent's net.

wa·ter pow·er ▶n. power that is derived from the weight or motion of water, used as a force to drive machinery. — **wa·ter-pow·ered** adj.

wa·ter·proof /ˈwôtər,proof; ˈwät-/ ▶adj. impervious to water. ■ not liable to be washed away by water. ▶v. [trans.] make impervious to water. — **wa·ter·proof·er** n. **wa·ter·proof·ness** n.

wa·ter rat ▶n. a large, semiaquatic, ratlike rodent.

wa·ter-re·pel·lent ▶adj. not easily penetrated by water, esp. as a result of being treated for such a purpose with a surface coating.

wa·ter-re·sis·tant ▶adj. able to resist the penetration of water to some degree but not entirely. — **wa·ter-re·sis·tance** n.

wa·ter right ▶n. **1** [usu. pl.] the right to make use of the water from a stream, lake, or irrigation canal. **2** Naut. the right to navigate on particular waters.

Wa·ters[1] /ˈwôtərz; ˈwät-/, Ethel (1896–1977), US blues and jazz singer.

Wa·ters[2], Muddy (1915–83), US blues singer and guitarist; born *McKinley Morganfield*. He became well known for his song "Rollin' Stone" (1950).

wa·ter·scape /ˈwôtər,skāp; ˈwät-/ ▶n. a landscape in which an expanse of water is a dominant feature.

wa·ter scor·pi·on ▶ **n.** a mainly tropical predatory water bug (*Nepa, Ranatra,* and other genera, family Nepidae) with grasping forelegs, breathing from the surface via a bristlelike "tail."

wa·ter·shed /ˈwôtər,sнed; ˈwät-/ ▶ **n.** an area or ridge of land that separates waters flowing to different rivers, basins, or seas. ■ an area or region drained by a river, river system, or other body of water. ■ an event or period marking a turning point in a course of action or state of affairs: *a watershed in the history of music.*

wa·ter shrew ▶ **n.** a large semiaquatic shrew (*Sorex, Neomys,* and other genera) that preys on aquatic invertebrates.

wa·ter·side /ˈwôtər,sīd; ˈwät-/ ▶ **n.** the edge of or area adjoining a sea, lake, or river.

wa·ter·ski /ˈwôtər,skē; ˈwät-/ ▶ **n.** (pl. **-skis**) each of a pair of skis enabling the wearer to skim the surface of the water when towed by a motorboat. ▶ **v.** [intrans.] skim the surface of water on waterskis. — **wa·ter·ski·er n.**

wa·ter slide ▶ **n.** a slide into a swimming pool, typically flowing with water and incorporating a number of twists and turns.

wa·ter snake ▶ **n.** a harmless snake (*Natrix* and other genera, family Colubridae) that is a powerful swimmer and spends part of its time in fresh water hunting for prey. Water snakes are found in Africa, Asia, and America.

wa·ter sof·ten·er ▶ **n.** a device or substance that softens hard water by removing certain minerals.

wa·ter sol·dier ▶ **n.** an aquatic European plant (*Stratiotes aloides,* family Hydrocharitaceae) with slender, spiny-toothed leaves in submerged rosettes that rise to the surface at flowering time.

wa·ter spi·der ▶ **n.** a semiaquatic spider, including the European *Argyroneta aquatica* (family Argyronetidae), which lives in an underwater dome of silk filled with air.

wa·ter sports ▶ **plural n.** sports that are carried out on water, such as waterskiing and windsurfing. ■ informal sexual activity involving urination.

wa·ter·spout /ˈwôtər,spout; ˈwät-/ ▶ **n.** a rotating column of water and spray formed by a whirlwind occurring over the sea or other body of water.

wa·ter strid·er ▶ **n.** a slender predatory bug (*Gerris* and other genera, family Gerridae) that moves quickly across the surface film of water, using its front legs for catching prey.

wa·ter ta·ble ▶ **n.** the level below which the ground is saturated with water.

wa·ter·thrush /ˈwôtər,тнrəsн; ˈwät-/ ▶ **n.** a thrushlike North American warbler (genus *Seiurus*) related to the ovenbird, found near woodland streams and swamps.

wa·ter·tight /ˈwôtər,tīt; ˈwät-/ ▶ **adj.** closely sealed, fastened, or fitted so that no water enters or passes through. ■ (of an argument or account) unable to be disputed or questioned.

wa·ter·tight com·part·ment ▶ **n.** any of the sections with intervening watertight partitions into which the interior of a large ship is now usually divided for safety.

wa·ter tor·ture ▶ **n.** a form of torture in which the victim is exposed to the incessant dripping of water on the head or to the sound of dripping.

wa·ter tow·er ▶ **n.** a tower supporting an elevated water tank, whose height creates the pressure required to distribute the water through a piped system. ■ a firefighting apparatus for lifting hoses to great heights.

wa·ter·vas·cu·lar sys·tem ▶ **n.** Zool. (in an echinoderm) a network of water vessels in the body, the tube feet being operated by hydraulic pressure within the vessels.

wa·ter·way /ˈwôtər,wā; ˈwät-/ ▶ **n.** **1** a river, canal, or other route for travel by water. **2** a thick plank or angle iron at the outer edge of the deck of a vessel, which joins the vessel's side to its deck and directs water overboard via the scuppers.

wa·ter·weed /ˈwôtər,wēd; ˈwät-/ ▶ **n.** **1** any aquatic plant with inconspicuous flowers, esp. a pondweed. **2** a submerged aquatic American plant (genus *Elodea,* family Hydrocharitaceae) that is grown in aquariums and ornamental ponds.

waterwheel

wa·ter·wheel /ˈwôtər,(h)wēl; ˈwät-/ ▶ **n.** a large wheel driven by flowing water, used to work machinery or to raise water to a higher level.

wa·ter wings ▶ **plural n.** inflated floats that may be fixed to the arms of someone learning to swim to give increased buoyancy.

wa·ter witch (also **wa·ter witch·er**) ▶ **n.** a person who searches for underground water by using a dowsing rod. — **wa·ter witch·ing n.**

wa·ter·works /ˈwôtər,wərks; ˈwät-/ ▶ **plural n.** **1** [treated as sing.] an establishment for managing a water supply. **2** informal used to refer to the shedding of tears.

wa·ter·y /ˈwôtərē; ˈwät-/ ▶ **adj.** consisting of, containing, or resembling water: *a watery fluid.* ■ thin or tasteless as a result of containing too much water. ■ weak; pale. ■ (of a person's eyes) full of or running with tears. — **wa·ter·i·ness n.** [OE *wæterig.*]

WATS /wäts/ ▶ **abbr.** Wide Area Telecommunications Service.

Wat·son[1] /ˈwätsən/, James Dewey (1928–), US biologist. Together with Francis Crick, he proposed a model for the structure of the DNA molecule. Nobel Prize for Physiology or Medicine (1962, shared with Crick and Wilkins).

Wat·son[2], John Broadus (1878–1958), US psychologist. He founded the school of behaviorism.

Wat·son-Watt /ˈwätsən ˈwät/, Sir Robert Alexander (1892–1973), Scottish physicist. He led a team that developed a practical system for locating aircraft by using radar.

Watt /wät/, James (1736–1819), Scottish engineer. He greatly improved the efficiency of the Newcomen steam engine. He also introduced the term *horsepower.*

watt /wät/ (abbr.: **W**) ▶ **n.** the SI unit of power, equivalent to one joule per second, corresponding to the rate of energy in an electric circuit where the potential difference is one volt and the current one ampere. [19th C.: named after J. **Watt**.]

watt·age /ˈwätij/ ▶ **n.** an amount of electrical power expressed in watts. ■ the operating power of a lamp or other electrical appliance expressed in watts.

Wat·teau /wäˈtō/, Jean Antoine (1684–1721), French painter. He initiated the rococo style.

watt-hour ▶ **n.** a measure of electrical energy equivalent to a power consumption of one watt for one hour.

wat·tle[1] /ˈwätl/ ▶ **n.** **1** a material for making fences, walls, etc., consisting of rods or stakes interlaced with twigs or branches. **2** esp. Austral. an acacia. ▶ **v.** [trans.] make, enclose, or fill up with wattle. [OE *watul,* of unknown origin.]

wat·tle[2] ▶ **n.** a colored fleshy lobe hanging from the head or neck of domestic chickens, turkeys, and some other birds. — **wat·tled adj.** [16th C.: of unknown origin.]

wattle[2]

wat·tle and daub ▶ **n.** a material formerly or traditionally used in building walls, consisting of a network of interwoven sticks and twigs covered with mud or clay.

wat·tle·bird /ˈwätl,bərd/ ▶ **n.** the largest of the honeyeaters (genera *Anthochaera* and *Melidectes*) found in Australia, with a wattle hanging from each cheek.

watt·me·ter /ˈwät,mētər/ ▶ **n.** a meter for measuring electric power in watts.

Watts /wäts/ a district in southern Los Angeles in California.

Wa·tu·si /wäˈto͞osē/ ▶ **n.** **1** (also **Wa·tut·si** /-ˈto͞otsē/) dated [treated as pl.] the Tutsi people collectively. **2** an energetic dance popular in the 1960s. ▶ **v.** [intrans.] dance the Watusi. [from the Kinyarwanda language of the Bantu family, from the pl. prefix *wa-* + **Tutsi**.]

Waugh /wô/, Evelyn Arthur St. John (1903–66), English writer. His works include *Brideshead Revisited* (1945).

waul /wôl/ ▶ **v.** [intrans.] give a loud plaintive cry like that of a cat. [16th C.: imitative.]

wave /wāv/ ▶ **v.** **1** [intrans.] move one's hand to and fro in greeting or as a signal. ■ [trans.] move (one's hand or arm, or something held in one's hand) to and fro: *he waved a sheaf of papers.* ■ move to and fro with a swaying or undulating motion while remaining fixed to one point. ■ [trans.] convey (a greeting or other message) by moving one's hand or something held in it to and fro: *we waved our farewells.* ■ [with obj. and adverbial of direction] instruct (someone) to move in a particular direction by moving one's hand: *he waved her back.* **2** [trans.] style (hair) so that it curls slightly. ■ [intrans.] (of hair) grow with a slight curl: [as adj.] (**waving**) *thick, waving gray hair.* ▶ **n.** **1** a long body of water curling into an arched form and breaking on the shore. ■ a ridge of water between two depressions in open water: *gulls and cormorants bobbed on the waves.* ■ a shape seen as comparable to a breaking wave. ■ (usu. **the wave**) an effect resembling a moving wave produced by successive sections of the crowd in a stadium standing up, raising their arms, lowering them, and sitting down again. ■ (**the waves**) literary the sea. ■ an intense burst of a particular feeling or emotion: *a wave of apprehension.* ■ a sudden

WZ

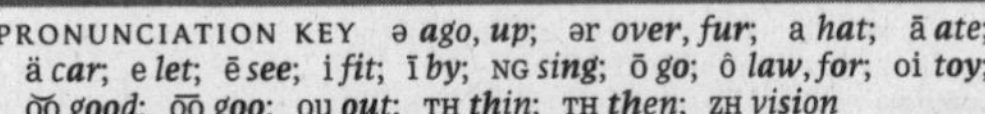

PRONUNCIATION KEY ə *ago, up;* ər *over, fur;* a *hat;* ā *ate;* ä *car;* e *let;* ē *see;* i *fit;* ī *by;* NG *sing;* ō *go;* ô *law, for;* oi *toy;* o͝o *good;* o͞o *goo;* ou *out;* TH *thin;* T̲H̲ *then;* ZH *vision*

occurrence of or increase in a specified phenomenon: *a wave of strikes.* **2** a gesture or signal made by moving one's hand to and fro. **3** a slightly curling lock of hair. ■ a tendency to curl in a person's hair. **4** Physics a periodic disturbance of the particles of a substance that may be propagated without net movement of the particles, such as in the passage of undulating motion, heat, or sound. See also STANDING WAVE and TRAVELING WAVE. ■ a single curve in the course of this motion. ■ a similar variation of an electromagnetic field in the propagation of light or other radiation through a medium or vacuum.

– PHRASES **make waves** informal create a significant impression. ■ cause trouble.

– PHRASAL VERBS **wave something aside** dismiss something as unnecessary or irrelevant. **wave someone/something down** use one's hand to give a signal to stop to a driver or vehicle. — **wave·less** adj. **wave·like** adj. & adv. [OE *wafian* (verb), from the Gmc. base of WAVER; the n. by alt. (influenced by the v.) of ME *wawe* '(sea) wave.']

wave·band /ˈwāvˌband/ ▶ n. a range of wavelengths falling between two given limits, used in radio transmission.

wave·form /ˈwāvˌfôrm/ ▶ n. Physics a curve showing the shape of a wave at a given time.

wave·front /ˈwāvˌfrənt/ ▶ n. Physics a surface containing points affected in the same way by a wave at a given time.

wave func·tion ▶ n. Physics a function that satisfies a wave equation and describes the properties of a wave.

wave·guide /ˈwāvˌgīd/ ▶ n. a metal tube or other device confining and conveying microwaves.

wave·length /ˈwāvˌleNG(k)TH/ ▶ n. Physics the distance between successive crests of a wave, esp. points in a sound wave or electromagnetic wave. (Symbol: λ) ■ this distance as a distinctive feature of radio waves from a transmitter. ■ fig. a person's ideas and way of thinking, esp. as it affects their ability to communicate with others: *we're on the same wavelength.*

wave·let /ˈwāvlit/ ▶ n. a small wave of water; a ripple.

wave me·chan·ics ▶ plural n. [treated as sing.] Physics a method of analysis of the behavior of atomic phenomena with particles represented by wave equations.

wave pack·et ▶ n. Physics a group of superposed waves that together form a traveling localized disturbance, esp. one described by Schrödinger's equation and regarded as representing a particle.

wa·ver /ˈwāvər/ ▶ v. [intrans.] shake with a quivering motion. ■ become unsteady or unreliable. ■ be undecided between two opinions or courses of action; be irresolute. — **wa·ver·er** n. **wa·ver·ing·ly** adv. **wa·ver·y** adj. [ME: from ON *vafra* 'flicker,' of Gmc. origin.]

WAVES /wāvz/ ▶ plural n. the women's section of the US Naval Reserve, established in 1942, or, since 1948, of the US Navy. [acronym from *Women Appointed* (later *Accepted*) *for Volunteer Emergency Service.*]

wave the·o·ry n. Physics, hist. the theory that light is propagated through the ether by a wave motion imparted to the ether by the molecular vibrations of the radiant body.

wav·i·cle /ˈwāvikəl/ ▶ n. Physics an entity having characteristic properties of both waves and particles.

wav·y /ˈwāvē/ ▶ adj. (**wav·i·er, wav·i·est**) (of a line or surface) having or consisting of a series of undulating and wavelike curves: *wavy hair.* ■ [usu. postpositive] Heraldry divided or edged with a line formed of alternating shallow curves. — **wav·i·ly** /ˈwāvəlē/ adv. **wav·i·ness** n.

wa-wa ▶ n. var. of WAH-WAH.

wax[1] /waks/ ▶ n. a sticky yellowish moldable substance secreted by honeybees as the material of honeycomb; beeswax. ■ a white translucent material obtained by bleaching and purifying this substance and used for such purposes as making candles, modeling, and as a basis of polishes. ■ a similar viscous substance, typically a lipid or hydrocarbon. ■ earwax. ■ informal used in reference to phonograph records: *he didn't get on wax until 1959.* ▶ v. [trans.] **1** cover or treat (something) with wax or a similar substance, typically to polish or protect it. ■ remove unwanted hair from (a part of the body) by applying wax and then peeling off the wax and hairs together. **2** informal make a recording of: *he waxed a series of track.* — **wax·er** n. [OE *wæx, weax*, of Gmc. origin; rel. to Du. *was* and Ger. *Wachs.*]

wax[2] ▶ v. [intrans.] (of the moon between new and full) have a progressively larger part of its visible surface illuminated, increasing its apparent size. ■ literary become larger or stronger: *his anger waxed.* ■ [with complement] begin to speak or write about something in the specified manner: *they waxed lyrical about the old days.*

– PHRASES **wax and wane** undergo alternate increases and decreases. [OE *weaxan*, of Gmc. origin; rel. to Du. *wassen* and Ger. *wachsen*, from an Indo-Eur. root shared by Gk. *auxanein* and L. *augere* 'to increase.']

wax bean ▶ n. a dwarf bean of a variety with yellow, stringless pods.

wax·ber·ry /ˈwaksˌberē/ ▶ n. a shrub with berries that have a waxy coating, in particular a bayberry or wax myrtle.

wax·bill /ˈwaksˌbil/ ▶ n. a small, finchlike Old World songbird (*Estrilda* and other genera), typically brightly colored and with a red bill that resembles sealing wax in color. The **waxbill family** (Estrildidae) also includes the avadavats, mannikins, Java sparrow, zebra finch, etc., many popular as cage birds.

waxed pa·per (also **wax pa·per**) ▶ n. paper that has been impregnated with wax to make it waterproof or greaseproof, used esp. in cooking and the wrapping of foodstuffs.

wax·en /ˈwaksən/ ▶ adj. having a smooth, pale, translucent surface or appearance like that of wax: *a canopy of waxen, creamy blooms.* ■ archaic or literary made of wax.

wax moth ▶ n. a brownish moth (genera *Galleria* and *Achroea*, family Pyralidae) that lays its eggs in beehives. The caterpillars cover the combs with silken tunnels and feed on beeswax.

wax mu·se·um ▶ n. an exhibition of wax dummies, typically representing famous people and fictional characters.

wax myr·tle ▶ n. an evergreen bayberry, esp. the common *Myrica cerifera* of the southern US. The wax covering its nutlets is used for making scented candles.

wax palm ▶ n. either of two South American palm trees from which wax is obtained: ■ an Andean palm (*Ceroxylon alpinum*) with a stem coated in a mixture of resin and wax. ■ a carnauba.

wax re·sist ▶ n. a process similar to batik used in pottery and printing.

wax·wing /ˈwaksˌwiNG/ ▶ n. a crested Eurasian and American songbird (genus *Bombycilla*, family Bombycillidae) with mainly pinkish-brown plumage, having small tips like red sealing wax on some wing feathers. See illustration at CEDAR WAXWING.

wax·work /ˈwaksˌwərk/ ▶ n. a lifelike dummy modeled in wax. ■ (**waxworks**) [treated as sing.] an exhibition of wax dummies.

wax·y /ˈwaksē/ ▶ adj. (**wax·i·er, wax·i·est**) resembling wax in consistency or appearance. — **wax·i·ly** /ˈwaksəlē/ adv. **wax·i·ness** n.

way /wā/ ▶ n. **1** a method, style, or manner of doing something: *two ways of approaching the problem.* ■ a person's characteristic or habitual manner of behavior or expression. ■ (**ways**) the customary modes of behavior or practices of a group: *French ways.* ■ [in sing.] the typical manner in which something happens or in which someone or something behaves: *that's the way with adolescent boys.* **2** a road, track, path, or street for traveling along. ■ [usu. in sing.] a course of travel or route taken in order to reach a place. ■ a means of entry or exit from somewhere, such as a door or gate: *the back way.* ■ [in sing.] (also informal **ways**) a distance traveled or to be traveled; the distance from one place to another: *a long way to go.* ■ [in sing.] a period between one point in time and another: *June is a long way off.* ■ [in sing.] travel or motion along a particular route; the route along which someone or something would travel if unobstructed: *he blocked her way.* ■ [in sing.] a specified direction: *a car coming the other way.* ■ (often **ways**) parts into which something divides or is divided: [in comb.] *a five-way bidding war.* ■ (**one's way**) used with a verb and adverbial phrase to intensify the force of an action or to denote movement or progress: *I shouldered my way to the bar.* ■ forward or backward motion of a ship or boat through water. **3** [in sing.] [with adj. or possessive] informal a particular area or locality: *over Fayetteville way.* **4** a particular aspect of something; a respect: *in every way.* **5** [in sing.] [with adj.] a specified condition or state: *in a bad way.* **6** (**ways**) a sloping structure down which a new ship is launched. ▶ adv. informal at or to a considerable distance or extent; far (used before an adverb or preposition for emphasis): *way off target.* ■ [as submodifier] much: *way too fast.* ■ [usu. as submodifier] extremely; really (used for emphasis): *way cool.* [shortening of AWAY.]

– PHRASES **across the way** nearby, esp. on the opposite side of the street. **be on one's way** have started one's journey. ■ [in imper.] (**(be) on your way**) informal go away: *on your way, and stop wasting my time!* **by a long way** by a great amount; by far. **by the way 1** incidentally (used to introduce a minor topic not connected with what was being spoken about previously): *by the way, pay in advance.* **2** during the course of a journey. **by way of 1** so as to pass through or across; via: *we went to Nice by way of Paris.* **2** constituting; as a form of: *by way of apology.* **3** by means of: *noncompliance is punishable by way of a fine.* **come one's way** happen or become available to one. **find a way** discover a means of obtaining one's object. **get** (or **have**) **one's** (**own**) **way** get or do what one wants in spite of opposition. **give way 1** yield to someone or something: *not one to give way to pressure.* ■ (of a support or structure) be unable to carry a load or withstand a force; collapse or break. ■ (**give way to**) allow oneself to be overcome by or to succumb to (an emotion or impulse): *she gave way to weeping.* **2** allow someone or something to be or go first. ■ (**give way to**) be replaced or superseded by. **go all the** (or **go the whole**) **way** continue a course of action to its conclusion. ■ informal have full sexual intercourse with someone. **go out of one's way** [usu. with infin.] make a special effort to do something. **go one's own way** act independently or as one wishes, esp. against contrary advice. **go one's way 1** (of events, circumstances, etc.) be favorable to one. **2** leave: *each went his way singing.* **go someone's way** travel in the same direction as someone. **have it your** (**own**) **way** [in imper.] informal used to indicate angrily that although one disagrees with something someone has said or proposed, one is not going to argue further. **have a way with** have a particular talent for dealing with or ability in. **have one's way with** humorous have sexual intercourse with (someone) (typically implying that it is against their wishes or better judgment). **in more ways than one** used to indicate that a statement has more than one meaning. **in a way** (or **in some ways** or **in one way**) to a certain extent, but not altogether or completely (used to reduce the effect of a statement). **in the** (or **one's**) **way** forming an obstacle or hindrance to movement or action. **in someone/something's** (**own**) **way** if regarded from a particular standpoint appropriate to that person or thing. **in no way** not at all. **keep** (or **stay**) **out of someone's way** avoid someone. **lead the way** go first along a route to show someone the way. ■ be a pioneer in a particular activity. **look the other way** deliberately avoid seeing or noticing someone or something. **one way and another** taking most aspects or considerations into account. **one way or another** (or **one way or the other**) used to indicate that something is the case for any of various unspecified reasons. ■ by some means: *they'll get rid of me one way or another.* ■ whichever of two given alternatives is the case. **on the** (or **one's**) **way** in the course of a journey. **on the** (or **its**) **way** about to arrive or happen. ■ informal (of a child) conceived but not yet born. **on the** (or **one's**) **way out** in the process of leaving. ■ informal going out of fashion or favor. **the other way around** in the opposite position or direction. ■ the opposite of what is expected or supposed. **out of one's way** not on one's intended route. **put someone in the way of** dated give someone the opportunity of. **that way** dated used euphemistically to indicate that someone is homosexual. **to someone's** (or **one's**) **way of thinking** in someone's (or one's) opinion. **way back** (also **way back when**) informal long ago. **the way of the Cross 1** the journey of Jesus to the place of his crucifixion. **2** a set of images representing the Stations of the Cross. **3** fig. the suffering and self-sacrifice of a Christian. **way of life** the typical pattern of behavior of a person or group. **the way of the world** the manner in which people typically behave or things typically happen (used to express one's resignation to it). **ways and means** the methods and resources at someone's disposal for achieving something. **way to go** informal used to express pleasure, approval, or excitement. [OE *weg*, of Gmc. origin; rel. to Du. *weg* and Ger. *Weg*, from a base meaning 'move, carry.']

-way ▶ **suffix** equivalent to **-WAYS**.

wa·yang /'wäyäNG/ ▶ **n.** (in Indonesia and Malaysia) a theatrical performance employing puppets or human dancers. ■ (also **wa·yang ku·lit**) a Javanese and Balinese shadow puppet play. [Javanese.]

way·bill /'wā,bil/ ▶ **n.** a list of passengers or goods being carried on a vehicle.

way·far·er /'wā,fe(ə)rər/ ▶ **n.** literary a person who travels on foot. — **way·far·ing n.**

way·far·ing tree /'wā,fe(ə)riNG/ ▶ **n.** a white-flowered Eurasian shrub (*Viburnum lantana*) of the honeysuckle family that has berries at different stages of ripening (green, red, and black) occurring together, growing chiefly on calcareous soils.

way·lay /'wā,lā/ ▶ **v.** (past and past part. **-laid**) [trans.] stop or interrupt (someone) and detain them in conversation or trouble them in some other way. — **way·lay·er n.**

Wayne[1] /wān/, Anthony (1745–96), American general; known as **Mad Anthony**. He is credited with saving West Point from British occupation following Benedict Arnold's betrayal. He defeated the Indians at the Battle of Fallen Timbers in Ohio in 1794.

Wayne[2], James Moore (c.1790–1867), US Supreme Court associate justice 1835–67.

way-out ▶ **adj.** informal regarded as extremely unconventional, unusual, or avant-garde.

way·point /'wā,point/ ▶ **n.** a stopping place on a journey. ■ an endpoint of the leg of a course, esp. one whose coordinates have been generated by a computer.

-ways ▶ **suffix** forming adjectives and adverbs of direction or manner: *edgeways* | *lengthways*. Compare with **-WISE**.

way·side /'wā,sīd/ ▶ **n.** the edge of a road.

– PHRASES **fall by the wayside** fail to persist in an endeavor or undertaking. [with biblical allusion to Luke 8:5.]

way sta·tion ▶ **n.** a stopping point on a journey. ■ a minor station on a railroad.

way·ward /'wāwərd/ ▶ **adj.** difficult to control or predict because of unusual or perverse behavior: *her wayward, difficult sister.* — **way·ward·ly adv. way·ward·ness n.** [ME: shortening of obs. *awayward* 'turned away.']

way·worn /'wā,wôrn/ (also **way-worn**) ▶ **adj.** archaic weary with traveling.

wa·zoo /wä'zo͞o/ ▶ **n.** informal the anus.

– PHRASES **up** (or **out**) **the wazoo** very much; in great quantity; to a great degree: *he's insured out the wazoo.*

Wb ▶ **abbr.** weber(s).

WBA ▶ **abbr.** World Boxing Association.

WBC ▶ **abbr.** World Boxing Council.

W bo·son /'bō,sän/ ▶ **n.** another term for **W PARTICLE**.

WC ▶ **abbr.** ■ Brit. water closet. ■ (of a region) west central.

WCC ▶ **abbr.** World Council of Churches.

we /wē/ ▶ **pron.** [first person pl.] **1** used by a speaker to refer to himself or herself and one or more other people considered together: *shall we have a drink?* ■ used to refer to the speaker together with other people regarded in the same category: *we teachers.* ■ people in general: *we should eat a varied diet.* **2** used in formal contexts for or by a royal person, or by a writer or editor, to refer to himself or herself. **3** used condescendingly to refer to the person being addressed: *how are we today?* [OE, of Gmc. origin; rel. to Du. *wij* and Ger. *wir*.]

weak /wēk/ ▶ **adj.** **1** lacking the power to perform physically demanding tasks; lacking physical strength and energy. ■ lacking political or social power or influence: *a government too weak to impose order* ■ (of a crew, team, or army) containing too few members or members of insufficient quality. ■ (of a faculty or part of the body) not able to fulfill its functions properly: *a weak stomach.* ■ of a low standard; performing or performed badly: *a weak cast.* ■ not convincing or logically forceful. ■ exerting only a small force: *a weak magnetic field.* **2** liable to break or give way under pressure; easily damaged. ■ lacking the force of character to hold to one's own decisions, beliefs, or principles; irresolute. ■ (of a belief, emotion, or attitude) not held or felt with such conviction or intensity as to prevent its being abandoned or dispelled. ■ not in a secure financial position: *people have no faith in weak banks.* ■ (of prices or a market) having a downward tendency. **3** lacking intensity or brightness: *a weak light.* ■ (of a liquid or solution) lacking flavor or effectiveness because of being heavily diluted: *weak coffee.* ■ displaying or characterized by a lack of enthusiasm or energy. ■ (of features) not striking or strongly marked: *a weak chin.* ■ (of a syllable) unstressed. **4** Gram. denoting a class of verbs in Germanic languages that form the past tense and past participle by addition of a suffix (in English, typically *-ed*). **5** Physics of, relating to, or denoting the weakest of the known kinds of force between particles, which acts only at distances less than about 10–15 cm, is very much weaker than the electromagnetic and the strong interactions, and conserves neither strangeness, parity, nor isospin.

– PHRASES **the weaker sex** [treated as sing. or pl.] dated, derog. women regarded collectively. **weak in the knees** helpless with emotion. **the weak link** the point at which a system, sequence, or organization is most vulnerable; the least dependable element or member. — **weak·ish adj.** [OE *wāc* 'pliant,' 'of little worth,' 'not steadfast,' reinforced in ME by ON *veikr*, from a Gmc. base meaning 'yield, give way.']

weak·en /'wēkən/ ▶ **v.** make or become weaker in power, resolve, or physical strength: [trans.] *fault lines had weakened the rocks* | [intrans.] *his resistance had weakened.* — **weak·en·er n.**

weak end·ing ▶ **n.** Pros. an unstressed syllable in a place at the end of a line of verse that normally receives a stress.

weak·fish /'wēk,fisH/ ▶ **n.** (pl. same or **-fish·es**) a large, slender-bodied marine fish (*Cynoscion regalis*) of the drum family, living along the east coast of North America, popular as a food fish and for sport. [18th C.: from obs. Du. *weekvisch*, from *week* 'soft' + *visch* 'fish.']

weak in·ter·ac·tion ▶ **n.** Physics interaction at short distances between subatomic particles mediated by the weak force.

weak-kneed ▶ **adj.** weak and shaky as a result of fear or excitement. ■ lacking in resolve or courage; cowardly.

weak·ling /'wēkliNG/ ▶ **n.** a person or animal that is physically weak and frail. ■ an ineffectual or cowardly person.

weak·ly /'wēklē/ ▶ **adv.** in a way that lacks strength or force. ▶ **adj.** (**-li·er, -li·est**) sickly; not robust. — **weak·li·ness n.**

weak-mind·ed ▶ **adj.** lacking determination, emotional strength, or intellectual capacity. — **weak-mind·ed·ness n.**

weak·ness /'wēknis/ ▶ **n.** the state or condition of lacking strength. ■ a quality or feature regarded as a disadvantage or fault: *the product's strengths and weaknesses.* ■ a person or thing that one is unable to resist or likes excessively: *you're his one weakness.* ■ [in sing.] (**weakness for**) a self-indulgent liking for: *a weakness for Scotch whisky.*

weak side ▶ **n.** Sports (on teams with an odd number of players) the half of an offensive or defensive alignment that has one player fewer.

weak sis·ter ▶ **n.** informal a weak, ineffectual, or unreliable member of a group.

weal[1] /wēl/ (also esp. Med. **wheal**) ▶ **n.** a red, swollen mark left on flesh by a blow or pressure. ■ Med. an area of the skin that is temporarily raised, typically reddened, and usually accompanied by itching. [19th C.: var. of **WALE**, influenced by obs. *wheal* 'suppurate.']

weal[2] ▶ **n.** formal that which is best for someone or something: *in the public weal.* [OE *wela* 'wealth, well-being,' of West Gmc. origin.]

Weald /wēld/ a region of southeastern England that included parts of Kent, Surrey, and East Sussex.

wealth /welTH/ ▶ **n.** an abundance of valuable possessions or money. ■ the state of being rich; material prosperity. ■ plentiful supplies of a particular resource: *mineral wealth.* ■ [in sing.] a plentiful supply of a particular desirable thing: *a wealth of information.* ■ archaic well-being; prosperity. [ME *welthe*, from **WELL**[1] or **WEAL**[2], on the pattern of *health*.]

wealth·y /'welTHē/ ▶ **adj.** (**wealth·i·er, wealth·i·est**) having a great deal of money, resources, or assets; rich: [as pl. n.] (**the wealthy**) *the burden of taxation on the wealthy.* — **wealth·i·ly** /-THəlē/ **adv.**

wean /wēn/ ▶ **v.** [trans.] accustom (an infant or other young mammal) to food other than its mother's milk. ■ accustom (someone) to managing without something on which they have become dependent or of which they have become excessively fond: *wean her off the sleeping pills.* ■ (**be weaned on**) be strongly influenced by (something), esp. from an early age: *I was weaned on a diet of fantasy.* [OE *wenian*, of Gmc. origin; rel. to Du. *wennen* and Ger. *entwöhnen*.]

wean·ling /'wēnliNG/ ▶ **n.** a newly weaned animal.

weap·on /'wepən/ ▶ **n.** a thing designed or used for inflicting bodily harm or physical damage. ■ fig. a means of gaining an advantage or defending oneself in a conflict or contest: *resignation threats are a weapon in his armory.* — **weap·oned adj. weap·on·less adj.** [OE *wǣp(e)n*, of Gmc. origin; rel. to Du. *wapen* and Ger. *Waffe*.]

weap·on of mass de·struc·tion ▶ **n.** a chemical, biological, or radioactive weapon capable of causing widespread death and destruction.

weap·on·ry /'wepənrē/ ▶ **n.** [treated as sing. or pl.] weapons regarded collectively.

wear[1] /we(ə)r/ ▶ **v.** (past **wore** /wôr/; past part. **worn** /wôrn/) **1** [trans.] have on one's body or a part of one's body as clothing, decoration, protection, or for some other purpose. ■ habitually have on one's body or be dressed in: *she didn't wear black.* ■ exhibit or present (a particular facial expression or appearance): *wear a frozen smile.* ■ [with obj. and complement or adverbial] have (one's hair or beard) at a specified length or arranged in a specified style. ■ (of a ship) fly (a flag). **2** [with obj. and adverbial or complement] damage, erode, or destroy by friction or use: *worn down in part to bare rock.* ■ [no obj., with adverbial or complement] undergo such damage, erosion, or destruction: *mountains are wearing down.* ■ [trans.] form (a hole, path, etc.) by constant friction or use. ■ [intrans.] (**wear on**) cause weariness or fatigue to. **3** [no obj., with adverbial] withstand continued use or life in a specified way: *laminate seems to wear well.* **4** [intrans.] (**wear on**) (of a period of time) pass, esp. slowly or tediously: *the afternoon wore on.* ■ [trans.] literary pass (a period of time) in some activity: *spinning long stories, wearing half the day.* ▶ **n. 1** the wearing of something or the state of being worn as clothing. **2** [with adj.] clothing suitable for a particular purpose or of a particular type: *evening wear.* **3** damage or deterioration sustained from continuous use: *a deduction for wear and tear.* ■ the capacity for withstanding continuous use without such damage: *plenty of wear left in those clothes.*

– PHRASES **wear thin** be gradually used up or become less convincing or acceptable: *his patience was wearing thin.*

– PHRASAL VERBS **wear someone/something down** overcome or exhaust someone or something by persistence. **wear off** lose effectiveness or intensity. **wear something out** (or **wear out**) **1** use or be used until no longer in good condition or working order. **2** (**wear someone/something out**) exhaust or tire someone or something. — **wear·a·bil·i·ty** /ˌwerəˈbilitē/ **n. wear·a·ble adj. wear·er n.** [OE *werian*, of Gmc. origin, from an Indo-Eur. root shared by L. *vestis* 'clothing.']

wear[2] ▶ **v.** (past and past part. **wore**) [trans.] Sailing bring (a ship) about by turning its head away from the wind: *Shannon gives the order to wear ship.* [17th C.: of unknown origin.]

wear·ing /ˈwe(ə)riNG/ ▶ **adj.** mentally or physically tiring. — **wear·ing·ly adv.**

wear·i·some /ˈwi(ə)rēsəm/ ▶ **adj.** causing one to feel tired or bored. — **wea·ri·some·ly adv. wea·ri·some·ness n.**

wear·y /ˈwi(ə)rē/ ▶ **adj.** (**wear·i·er, wear·i·est**) feeling or showing tiredness, esp. as a result of excessive exertion or lack of sleep. ■ reluctant to see or experience any more of; tired of: [in comb.] *war-weary Americans.* ■ calling for a great amount of energy or endurance; tiring and tedious. ▶ **v.** (**wear·i·es, wear·i·ed**) [trans.] cause to become tired: *she was wearied by her cough.* ■ [intrans.] (**weary of**) grow tired of or bored with: *she wearied of her life.*

– PHRASES **no rest** (or **peace**) **for the weary** humorous one's heavy workload or lack of tranquility is due to one's own choices, or to one's sinful life. [with biblical allusion to Isa. 48:22, 57:21.] — **wea·ri·less adj. wea·ri·ly** /ˈwi(ə)rəlē/ **adv. wea·ri·ness n. wea·ry·ing·ly adv.** [OE *wērig, wǣrig*, of West Gmc. origin.]

wea·sel /ˈwēzəl/ ▶ **n.** a small, slender, carnivorous mammal (genus *Mustela*), esp. *M. nivalis* of northern Eurasia and northern North America, related to, but generally smaller than, the stoat. The **weasel family** (Mustelidae) also includes the polecats, minks, martens, skunks, wolverine, otters, and badgers. ■ fig., informal a deceitful or treacherous person. ▶ **v.** (**-seled, -sel·ing**; Brit. **-selled, -sel·ling**) [intrans.] achieve something by use of cunning or deceit: *trying to weasel my way into his affections.* ■ behave or talk evasively. — **wea·sel·ly adj.** [OE *wesle, wesule*, of West Gmc. origin.]

wea·sel words ▶ **plural n.** words or statements that are intentionally ambiguous or misleading.

weath·er /ˈweTHər/ ▶ **n.** the state of the atmosphere at a place and time as regards heat, cloudiness, dryness, sunshine, wind, rain, etc. ■ a report on such conditions as broadcast on radio or television. ■ cold, wet, and unpleasant or unpredictable atmospheric conditions; the elements: *shelter from wind and weather.* ■ [as adj.] denoting the side from which the wind is blowing, esp. on board a ship; windward: *the weather side of the yacht.* Contrasted with LEE. ▶ **v.** [trans.] **1** wear away or change the appearance or texture of (something) by long exposure to the atmosphere: [with obj. and complement] *his skin was weathered almost black.* ■ [intrans.] (of rock or other material) be worn away or altered by such processes: *specimens that weather away quickly.* ■ [usu. as n.] (**weathering**) Falconry allow (a hawk) to spend a period perched on a block in the open air. **2** come safely through (a storm). ■ withstand (a difficulty or danger): *the ability to weather recession.* ■ Sailing (of a ship) get to the windward of (a cape or other obstacle). **3** make (boards or tiles) overlap downward to keep out rain. ■ (in building) slope or bevel (a surface) to throw off rain.

– PHRASES **in all weathers** in every kind of weather, both good and bad. **keep a weather eye on** observe very carefully, esp. for changes or developments. **under the weather** informal slightly unwell or in low spirits. [OE *weder*, of Gmc. origin; rel. to Du. *weer* and Ger. *Wetter*.]

weath·er bal·loon ▶ **n.** a balloon equipped with meteorological apparatus that is sent into the atmosphere to provide information about the weather.

weath·er-beat·en ▶ **adj.** damaged or worn by exposure to the weather: *a tiny weather-beaten church.* ■ (of a person or a person's face) having skin that is lined and tanned or reddened through prolonged time spent outdoors.

weath·er·board /ˈweTHərˌbôrd/ ▶ **n.** each of a series of horizontal boards nailed to outside walls with edges overlapping to keep out the rain; clapboard. ▶ **v.** [trans.] fit or supply with weatherboards.

weath·er·board·ing /ˈweTHərˌbôrdiNG/ ▶ **n.** weatherboards collectively.

weath·er·cock /ˈweTHərˌkäk/ ▶ **n.** a weathervane in the form of a rooster. ▶ **v.** [intrans.] (of a boat or aircraft) tend to turn its head into the wind.

weath·er·ize /ˈweTHəˌrīz/ ▶ **v.** [with obj.] to make a house or building resistant to cold weather by adding insulation, siding, storm windows, etc.

weath·er·ly /ˈweTHərlē/ ▶ **adj.** Sailing (of a boat) able to sail close to the wind without drifting much to leeward. — **weath·er·li·ness n.**

weath·er·man /ˈweTHərˌman/ ▶ **n.** (pl. **-men**) a man who broadcasts a description and forecast of weather conditions.

weath·er·proof /ˈweTHərˌpro͞of/ ▶ **adj.** resistant to the effects of bad weather, esp. rain. ▶ **v.** [trans.] make (something) resistant to the effects of bad weather, esp. rain.

weath·er sta·tion ▶ **n.** an observation post where weather conditions and meteorological data are observed and recorded.

weath·er·strip /ˈweTHərˌstrip/ ▶ **n.** a strip of rubber, metal, or other material used to seal the edges of a door or window against rain and wind. ▶ **v.** (**-stripped, -strip·ping**) [trans.] apply such a strip to (a door or window). — **weath·er·strip·ping n.**

weath·er·tight /ˈweTHərˌtīt/ ▶ **adj.** (of a building) sealed against rain and wind.

weath·er·vane /ˈweTHərˌvān/ ▶ **n.** a revolving pointer to show the direction of the wind, typically mounted on top of a building.

weathervane

weath·er·worn /ˈweTHərˌwôrn/ ▶ **adj.** eroded or altered by being exposed to the weather.

weave[1] /wēv/ ▶ **v.** (past **wove** /wōv/; past part. **woven** /ˈwōvən/ or **wove**) [trans.] form (fabric or a fabric item) by interlacing long threads passing in one direction with others at a right angle to them: *linen was woven in the district.* ■ form (thread) into fabric in this way: *mohairs can be difficult to weave.* ■ [intrans.] [usu. as n.] (**weaving**) make fabric in this way typically by working at a loom. ■ (**weave something into**) include something as an integral part or element of (a woven fabric). ■ make (basketwork or a wreath) by interlacing rods or flowers. ■ make (a complex story or pattern) from a number of interconnected elements. ■ (**weave something into**) include an element in (such a story or pattern): *interpretative comments are woven into the narrative.* ▶ **n.** [usu. with adj.] a particular style or manner in which something is woven: *a very fine weave.* [OE *wefan*, of Gmc. origin.]

weave[2] ▶ **v.** [intrans.] twist and turn from side to side while moving somewhere in order to avoid obstructions: *he had to weave his way through the crowds.* ■ take evasive action in an aircraft, typically by moving it from side to side. ■ (of a horse) repeatedly swing the head and forepart of the body from side to side (considered to be a vice). [16th C.: prob. from ON *veifa* 'to wave, brandish.']

weav·er /ˈwēvər/ ▶ **n. 1** a person who weaves fabric. **2** (also **weav·er·bird**) a finchlike songbird (*Ploceus* and other genera, family Ploceidae) of tropical Africa and Asia, related to the sparrows. They build elaborately woven nests.

weav·er's knot (also **weav·er's hitch**) ▶ **n.** a sheet bend used for joining threads in weaving.

web /web/ ▶ **n. 1** a network of fine threads constructed by a spider from fluid secreted by its spinnerets, used to catch its prey. ■ a similar filmy network spun by some insect larvae, esp. communal caterpillars. ■ fig. a complex system of interconnected elements, esp. one perceived as a trap or danger: ***a web of bureaucracy.*** ■ (**the Web**) short for WORLD WIDE WEB. **2** a membrane between the toes of a swimming bird or other aquatic animal. ■ a thin flat part connecting thicker or more solid parts in machinery. **3** a roll of paper used in a continuous printing process. ■ the endless wire mesh in a papermaking machine on which such paper is made. **4** a piece of woven fabric. ▶ **v.** (**webbed, web·bing**) [no obj., with adverbial] move or hang so as to form a weblike shape: *an intricate transportation network webs from coast to coast.* ■ [trans.] (usu. **be webbed**) cover with or as though with a web: *his skin was webbed with fine creases.* — **web·like** /-ˌlīk/ **adj.** [OE *web(b)* 'woven fabric,' of Gmc. origin; rel. to Du. *web*, also to WEAVE[1].]

webbed /webd/ ▶ **adj. 1** (of the feet of a swimming bird or other aquatic animal) having the toes connected by a membrane. ■ Med. (of fingers or toes) abnormally united for all or part of their length by a fold of skin. **2** (of a band or strip of tough material) made from webbing or similar fabric.

web·bing /ˈwebiNG/ ▶ **n. 1** strong, closely woven fabric used for making items such as straps and belts, and for supporting the seats of upholstered chairs. **2** the part of a baseball glove between the thumb and forefinger.

web·cam /ˈwebˌkam/ (also trademark **Webcam**) ▶ **n.** a video camera that inputs to a computer connected to the Internet, so that its images can be seen by Internet users.

web·cast /ˈwebˌkast/ (also **Web·cast**) ▶ **n.** a live video broadcast of an event transmitted across the Internet. — **web·cast·ing n.**

We·ber[1] /ˈvābər/, Carl Maria Friedrich Ernst von (1786–1826), German composer. He is regarded as the founder of the German romantic school of opera.

We·ber[2], Max (1864–1920), German economist and sociologist, regarded as one of the founders of modern sociology.

We·ber[3], Wilhelm Eduard (1804–91), German physicist. He proposed a unified system for electrical units.

we·ber /ˈwebər/ (abbr.: **Wb**) ▶ **n.** the SI unit of magnetic flux, causing the electromotive force of one volt in a circuit of one turn when generated or removed in one second. [19th C.: named after W. E. *Weber* (see **Weber**[3]).]

We·bern /ˈvābərn/, Anton Friedrich Ernst von (1883–1945), Austrian composer. A leading exponent of serialism, his music is marked by its brevity.

web-foot·ed ▶ **adj.** (of a swimming bird or other aquatic animal) having webbed feet.

web·log /ˈwebˌlôg; -ˌläg/ ▶ **n.** fuller form of **blog.** — **web·log·ger n. web·log·ging n.**

Web·mas·ter /ˈwebˌmastər/ (also **web·mas·ter**) ▶ **n.** Comput. a person who designs and develops Web sites.

web off·set ▶ **n.** offset printing on continuous paper fed from a reel.

Web page (also **web page**) ▶ **n.** Comput. a document connected to the World Wide Web and viewable by anyone with an Internet connection and a browser.

Web site (also **web site** or **web·site**) ▶ **n.** Comput. a location connected to the Internet that maintains one or more pages on the World Wide Web.

web-spin·ner ▶ **n.** a slender mainly tropical insect (order Embioptera) with a soft brownish body, living under stones or logs in a tunnel of silk produced by glands on the front legs.

Web·ster[1] /ˈwebstər/, Daniel (1782–1852), US statesman and lawyer. A noted orator, he served in Congress 1813–17, 1823–41, and 1845–50. As secretary of state 1841–43, he negotiated the Webster-Ashburton Treaty, which settled boundary disputes with Canada.

Web·ster[2], John (*c.*1580–*c.*1625), English playwright. His works include *The Duchess of Malfi* (1623).

Web·ster[3], Noah (1758–1843), US lexicographer. His *American Dictionary of the English Language* (1828) was the first dictionary to give comprehensive coverage of usage in the US.

web·work /ˈwebˌwərk/ ▶ **n.** a mesh or network of links or connecting pieces.

web·worm /ˈwebˌwərm/ ▶ **n.** a caterpillar (*Loxostega* and other genera, family Pyralidae) that spins a web in which to rest or feed. When present in large numbers, it can become a serious pest.

web·zine /ˈwebˌzēn/ ▶ **n.** a magazine published on the Internet.

Wed. ▶ **abbr.** Wednesday.

wed /wed/ ▶ **v.** (**wed·ding** ; past and past part. **wed·ded** or **wed**) [trans.] esp. formal or archaic get married to. ■ [intrans.] get married: *they wed a week after meeting.* ■ give or join in marriage. ■ [as adj.] (**wedded**) of or concerning marriage: *25 years of wedded bliss.* ■ combine (two factors or qualities, esp. desirable ones): *this recording weds jazz and blues.* ■ (**be wedded to**) be obstinately attached or devoted to (an activity, belief, or system). [OE *weddian*, from the Gmc. base of Scots *wed* 'a pledge.']

we'd /wēd/ ▶ **contr.** we had: *we'd already been on board.* ■ we should or we would: *we'd like to make you an offer.*

Wed·dell Sea /ˈwedl; wəˈdel/ an arm of the Atlantic Ocean, off the coast of Antarctica.

wed·ding /ˈwediNG/ ▶ **n.** a marriage ceremony, esp. considered as including the associated celebrations. [OE *weddung*.]

wed·ding band ▶ **n.** a wedding ring.

wed·ding bells ▶ **plural n.** bells rung to celebrate a wedding (used to allude to the likelihood of marriage between two people): *all her friends could hear wedding bells.*

wed·ding cake ▶ **n.** a rich iced cake, typically in two or more tiers, served at a wedding reception. ■ [as adj.] denoting a building or architectural style that is very decorative or ornate: *a wedding-cake mansion.*

wed·ding night ▶ **n.** the night after a wedding (esp. with reference to its consummation).

wedge /wej/ ▶ **n.** a piece of wood, metal, or some other material having one thick end and tapering to a thin edge, that is driven between two objects or parts of an object to secure or separate them. ■ an object or piece of something having such a shape: *a wedge of cheese.* ■ a formation of people or animals with such a shape. ■ a golf club with a low, angled face for maximum loft. ■ a shot made with such a club. ■ a shoe, typically having a fairly high heel, of which the heel and sole form a solid block, with no gap under the instep. ■ a heel of this kind. ■ Music another term for **dash.** ▶ **v. 1** [trans.] fix in position using a wedge: [with obj. and complement] *the door was wedged open.* **2** [with obj. and adverbial] force into a narrow space.

– PHRASES **drive a wedge between** separate. ■ cause disagreement or hostility between. **thin end of the wedge** informal an action or procedure of little importance in itself, but likely to lead to more serious developments. [OE *wecg* (n.), of Gmc. origin; rel. to Du. *wig*.]

wedg·ie /ˈwejē/ ▶ **n.** informal **1** a shoe with a wedged heel. **2** an uncomfortable tightening of the underpants between the buttocks, typically produced when someone pulls the underpants up from the back as a practical joke.

Wedg·wood /ˈwejˌwo͝od/ ▶ **n.** trademark ceramic ware made by the English potter Josiah Wedgwood (1730–95) and his successors. ■ a powder-blue color characteristic of this stoneware.

wed·lock /ˈwedˌläk/ ▶ **n.** the state of being married.

– PHRASES **born in** (or **out of**) **wedlock** born of married (or unmarried) parents. [OE *wedlāc* 'marriage vow,' from *wed* 'pledge' + the suffix *-lāc* (denoting action).]

Wednes·day /ˈwenzdā; -dē/ ▶ **n.** the day of the week before Thursday and following Tuesday: *a report goes before the councilors on Wednesday.* ▶ **adv.** on Wednesday. ■ (**Wednesdays**) on Wednesdays; each Wednesday: *Wednesdays, the jazz DJ hosts a jam session.* [OE *Wōdnesdæg*, named after the Gmc. god **Odin**; translation of late L. *Mercurii dies*; cf. Du. *woensdag*.]

Weds. ▶ **abbr.** Wednesday.

wee /wē/ ▶ **adj.** (**we·er, we·est**) esp. Scot. little: *a wee bairn.*

– PHRASES **the wee hours** the early hours of the morning after midnight. [ME: from OE *wēg(e)*.]

weed /wēd/ ▶ **n.** a wild plant growing where it is not wanted and in competition with cultivated plants. ■ any wild plant growing in salt or fresh water. ■ informal marijuana. ■ (**the weed**) informal tobacco. ■ informal a leggy, loosely built horse. ▶ **v.** [trans.] remove unwanted plants from (an area of ground or the plants cultivated in it). ■ (**weed something out**) remove something, esp. inferior or unwanted items or members from a group or collection. — **weed·er n. weed·less adj.** [OE *wēod* (n.), *wēodian* (verb), of unknown origin; rel. to Du. *wieden* (v.).]

weed whack·er ▶ **n.** an electrically powered grass trimmer with a nylon cutting cord that rotates rapidly on a spindle.

weed·y /ˈwēdē/ ▶ **adj.** (**weed·i·er, weed·i·est**) **1** containing or covered with many weeds: *a weedy path.* ■ of the nature of or resembling a weed. **2** informal (of a person) thin and physically weak in appearance. — **weed·i·ness n.**

wee·juns /ˈwējənz/ (also **Wee·juns**) trademark ▶ **plural n.** moccasin-style shoes for casual wear. [1950s: a fanciful formation.]

week /wēk/ ▶ **n.** a period of seven days. ■ the period of seven days generally reckoned from and to midnight on Saturday night: *she has class twice a week.* ■ workdays as opposed to the weekend; the five days from Monday to Friday: *I work during the week.* ■ the time spent working in this period: *a 48-hour week.* ■ a period of five or seven days devoted to a specified purpose or beginning on a specified day: *Super Bowl week.* ■ informal, esp. Brit. used after the name of a day to indicate that something will happen seven days after that day: *a dance on Sunday week.*

– PHRASES **week after week** during each successive week, esp. over a long period. **week by week** gradually and steadily over the weeks. **a week from ——** used to state that something is due to happen seven days after the specified day or date: *a week from Friday.* **week in, week out** every week without exception. [OE *wice*, of Gmc. origin; rel. to Du. *week* and Ger. *Woche*, from a base prob. meaning 'sequence, series.']

week·day /ˈwēkˌdā/ ▶ **n.** a day of the week other than Sunday or Saturday.

week·end /ˈwēkˌend/ ▶ **n.** the period from Friday evening through Sunday evening, esp. regarded as a time for leisure: *she spent the weekend camping.* ■ (also **long week·end**) this period plus one or two days immediately before or after: *the long holiday weekend.* ▶ **v.** [no obj., with adverbial] informal spend a weekend somewhere: *weekending in the country.*

week·end·er /ˈwēkˌendər/ ▶ **n.** a person who spends time in a particular place only on weekends. ■ a bag or suitcase suitable for weekend travel. ■ a small pleasure boat.

week-long (also **weeklong**) ▶ **adj.** [attrib.] lasting for a week.

week·ly /ˈwēklē/ ▶ **adj.** [attrib.] done, produced, or occurring once a week: *a weekly dance.* ■ relating to or calculated in terms of a week: *weekly income.* ▶ **adv.** once a week. ▶ **n.** (pl. **-lies**) a newspaper or periodical issued every week.

week·night /ˈwēkˌnīt/ ▶ **n.** a night of the week other than Sunday or Saturday.

ween /wēn/ ▶ **v.** [intrans.] archaic be of the opinion; think or suppose: *he, I ween, is no sacred personage.* [OE *wēnan*, of Gmc. origin; rel. to Du. *wanen* 'imagine,' Ger. *wähnen* 'suppose wrongly.']

wee·nie /ˈwēnē/ ▶ **n. 1** another term for **wiener** (sense 1). **2** vulgar slang a man's penis. ■ (also **wie·ner**) informal a weak, socially inept, or boringly studious person: *the tech weenies.*

wee·ny /ˈwēnē/ ▶ **adj.** (**-ni·er, -ni·est**) informal tiny. [18th C.: from **wee**, on the pattern of *tiny*.]

weep /wēp/ ▶ **v.** (past and past part. **wept** /wept/) [intrans.] **1** shed tears. ■ utter or express with tears: [with direct speech] *"No!" she wept.* ■ [trans.] archaic mourn for; shed tears over. **2** exude liquid: *she rubbed one of the sores, making it weep.* ▶ **n.** [in sing.] a fit or spell of shedding tears. [OE *wēpan* (v.), of Gmc. origin, prob. imitative.]

weep·er /ˈwēpər/ ▶ **n. 1** a person who weeps. ■ hist. a hired mourner at a funeral. ■ a small image of a mourner on a monument. ■ another term for **weepie. 2** (**weepers**) hist. funeral garments, in particular: ■ a man's crepe hatband worn at funerals. ■ a widow's black crepe veil and white cuffs.

weep·ie /ˈwēpē/ ▶ **n.** (pl. **-ies**) informal a sentimental or emotional film, novel, or song.

weep·ing /ˈwēpiNG/ ▶ **adj.** [attrib.] **1** shedding tears. ■ exuding liquid. **2** used in names of tree and shrub varieties with drooping branches, e.g., **weeping cherry.** — **weep·ing·ly adv.**

weep·ing wid·ow ▶ **n.** a mushroom (*Lacrymaria velutina*, family Coprinaceae) that has a buff cap with purplish-black gills that appear to secrete drops of fluid when damp, found commonly in Eurasia and North America.

weep·ing wil·low ▶ n. a willow (esp. *Salix babylonica*) with trailing branches and foliage reaching down to the ground, widely grown as an ornamental in waterside settings.

weep·y /ˈwēpē/ ▶ adj. (**weep·i·er, weep·i·est**) informal tearful; inclined to weep. ■ sentimental: *a weepy made-for-TV movie.* — **weep·i·ly** /-əlē/ adv. **weep·i·ness** n.

wee·ver /ˈwēvər/ (also **wee·ver fish**) ▶ n. a small, long-bodied fish (family Trachinidae) with eyes at the top of the head and venomous dorsal spines. It occurs along eastern Atlantic coasts, typically buried in the sand with just the eyes and spines protruding. [17th C.: perh. a transferred use of OFr. *wivre* 'serpent, dragon,' from L. *vipera* 'viper.']

wee·vil /ˈwēvəl/ ▶ n. a small beetle (Curculionidae and other families, superfamily Curculionoidea) with an elongated snout, the larvae of which typically develop inside seeds, stems, or other plant parts. Many are pests of crops or stored foodstuffs. ■ informal any small insect that damages stored grain. — **wee·vil·y** adj. [OE *wifel* 'beetle,' from a Gmc. base meaning 'move briskly.']

wee-wee informal ▶ n. a child's word for urine. ▶ v. [intrans.] urinate. [1930s: imitative.]

weft /weft/ ▶ n. [in sing.] (in weaving) the crosswise threads on a loom over and under which other threads (the warp) are passed to make cloth. [OE *weft(a)*, of Gmc. origin.]

Wehr·macht /ˈver,mäkt; -,mäKHt/ the German armed forces, esp. the army, from 1921 to 1945. [Ger., 'defensive force.']

Wei /wā/ the name of several dynasties that ruled in China, esp. that of AD 386–535.

Weich·sel /ˈvīksəl/ ▶ n. [usu. as adj.] Geol. the final Pleistocene glaciation in northern Europe. ■ the system of deposits laid down at this time. — **Weich·sel·i·an** /vīkˈsilēən/ adj. & n. [1930s: from the German name of the Vistula River in Poland.]

wei·ge·la /wīˈjēlə/ ▶ n. an Asian flowering shrub (genus *Weigela*) of the honeysuckle family, that has pink, red, or yellow flowers and is a popular ornamental. [mod. L., named after Christian E. *Weigel* (1748–1831), German physician.]

weigh[1] /wā/ ▶ v. [trans.] **1** find out how heavy (someone or something) is, typically using scales. ■ have a specified weight: *it weighed ten pounds.* ■ balance in the hands to guess or as if to guess the weight of: *weighed the brick in her right hand.* ■ (**weigh something out**) measure and take from a larger quantity of a substance a portion of a particular weight: *she weighed out two ounces of loose tobacco.* ■ [intrans.] (**weigh on**) be depressing or burdensome to. **2** assess the nature or importance of, esp. with a view to a decision or action: *the consequences must be carefully weighed.* ■ (**weigh something against**) compare the importance of one factor with that of (another): *weigh benefit against risk.* ■ [intrans.] influence a decision or action; be considered important: *the evidence weighed heavily against him.*
– PHRASES **weigh one's words** carefully choose the way one expresses something.
– PHRASAL VERBS **weigh someone down** be heavy and cumbersome to someone. ■ be oppressive or burdensome to someone: *weighed down by responsibility.* **weigh in** (chiefly of a boxer or jockey) be officially weighed before or after a contest. **weigh in at** informal be of (a specified weight). ■ informal cost (a specified amount). **weigh in with** informal make a forceful contribution to a competition or argument by means of: *Baker weighed in with a three-pointer.* **weigh into** informal join in forcefully or enthusiastically. ■ attack physically or verbally: *he weighed into the companies for their high costs.* **weigh out** (of a jockey) be weighed before a race. — **weigh·a·ble** adj. **weigh·er** n. [OE *wegan*, of Gmc. origin; from an Indo-Eur. root shared by L. *vehere* 'convey.']

weigh[2] ▶ n. (in phrase **under weigh**) Naut. another way of saying UNDER WAY (see UNDER). [18th C.: from an erroneous association with *weigh anchor* (see ANCHOR).]

weigh-in ▶ n. an official or regular weighing of something or someone, e.g., of boxers before a fight.

weigh sta·tion ▶ n. a roadside station where commercial vehicles are required to stop and be inspected, thus protecting the road from travel by overweight or unsafe vehicles.

weight /wāt/ ▶ n. **1** a body's relative mass or the quantity of matter contained by it, giving rise to a downward force; the heaviness of a person or thing: *175 pounds in weight.* ■ Physics the force exerted on the mass of a body by a gravitational field. Compare with MASS. ■ the quality of being heavy: *the boards creaked under his weight.* ■ a unit or system of units used for expressing how much an object or quantity of matter weighs. ■ a piece of metal known to weigh a definite amount and used on scales to determine how heavy an object or quantity of a substance is. ■ the amount that a jockey is expected or required to weigh, or the amount that a horse can easily carry. ■ any of several divisions based on relative lightness and heaviness into which boxers and wrestlers are classified for competition. ■ the surface density of cloth, used as a measure of its quality. ■ Print. the degree of blackness of a type font. **2** a heavy object, esp. one being lifted or carried. ■ a heavy object used to give an impulse or act as a counterpoise in a mechanism. ■ a heavy object thrown by a shot-putter. ■ (**weights**) blocks or discs of metal or other heavy material used in weightlifting or weight training. ■ a burden or responsibility. **3** the ability of someone or something to influence decisions or actions: *a recommendation will carry great weight.* ■ the importance attached to something. ■ Stat. a factor associated with one of a set of numerical quantities, used to represent its importance relative to the other members of the set. ▶ v. [trans.] **1** hold (something) down by placing a heavy object on top of it: *a mug weighted down a stack of papers.* ■ make (something) heavier by attaching a heavy object to it, esp. so as to make it stay in place: *muslin veils weighted with colored beads.* **2** attach importance or value to: *speaking, reading, and writing should be weighted equally in the assessment.* ■ (**be weighted**) be planned or arranged so as to put a specified person, group, or factor in a position of advantage or disadvantage. ■ Stat. multiply the components of (an average) by factors to take account of their importance. **3** assign a handicap weight to (a horse). **4** treat (a fabric) with a mineral to make it seem thicker and heavier.
– PHRASES **put on** (or **lose**) **weight** become fatter (or thinner). **throw one's weight around** informal be unpleasantly self-assertive. **throw one's weight behind** informal use one's influence to help support. **the weight of the world** used in reference to a very heavy burden of worry or responsibility. **be a weight off one's mind** come as a great relief after one has been worried. **worth one's weight in gold** (of a person) exceedingly useful or helpful. [OE *(ge)wiht*, of Gmc. origin; rel. to Du. *wicht* and Ger. *Gewicht*.]

weight belt ▶ n. a belt to which weights are attached, designed to help divers stay submerged.

weight·ed av·er·age ▶ n. Stat. an average resulting from the multiplication of each component by a factor reflecting its importance.

weight·ing /ˈwātiNG/ ▶ n. allowance or adjustment made in order to take account of special circumstances or compensate for a distorting factor. ■ an allocated proportion of something, esp. an investment: *the company recommends a 35% weighting in bonds.* ■ emphasis or priority.

weight·less /ˈwātlis/ ▶ adj. (of a body, esp. in an orbiting spacecraft) not apparently acted on by gravity. — **weight·less·ly** adv. **weight·less·ness** n.

weight·lift·ing /ˈwāt,liftiNG/ ▶ n. the sport or activity of lifting barbells or other heavy weights. — **weight·lift·er** n.

weight-watch·er ▶ n. a person who is concerned about their weight, esp. one who diets. — **weight-watch·ing** n. & adj. [from the proprietary name *Weight Watchers*, an organization promoting dietary control as a means of losing weight.]

weight·y /ˈwātē/ ▶ adj. (**weight·i·er, weight·i·est**) weighing a great deal; heavy. ■ of great seriousness and importance: *weighty considerations of state.* ■ having a great deal of influence on events or decisions. — **weight·i·ly** /-təlē/ adv. **weight·i·ness** n.

Weil /vīl; vā/, Simone (1909–43), French writer. She joined the resistance movement in England during World War II.

Weill /vīl/, Kurt (1900–50), German composer, resident in the US from 1935. He wrote operas with Bertolt Brecht, including *The Threepenny Opera* (1928).

Wei·mar /ˈvī,mär/ a city in Thuringia, in central Germany; pop. 59,000.

Wei·mar·an·er /ˈwīmə,ränər; ˈvī-/ ▶ n. a dog of a thin-coated, typically gray breed of pointer used as a gun dog. [1940s: from Ger., from WEIMAR in Germany, where the breed was developed.]

Wei·mar Re·pub·lic the German republic of 1919–33, so called because its constitution was drawn up at Weimar. It was overthrown by the Nazi Party of Adolf Hitler.

Wein·berg /ˈwīn,bərg/, Steven (1933–), US theoretical physicist. He devised a theory to unify electromagnetic interactions and the weak forces within the nucleus of an atom. Nobel Prize for Physics (1979, shared with Sheldon Glashow 1932– and Abduis Salam 1926–96).

weir /wi(ə)r/ ▶ n. a low dam built across a river to raise the level of water upstream or regulate its flow. ■ an enclosure of stakes set in a stream as a trap for fish. [OE *wer*, from *werian* 'dam up.']

weird /wi(ə)rd/ ▶ adj. suggesting something supernatural; uncanny: *the weird crying of a seal.* ■ informal very strange; bizarre: *a weird coincidence.* ■ archaic connected with fate. ▶ n. archaic, esp. Scot. a person's destiny. ▶ v. [trans.] (**weird someone out**) informal induce a sense of disbelief or alienation in someone. — **weird·ly** adv. **weird·ness** n. [OE *wyrd* 'destiny,' of Gmc. origin.]

weird·o /ˈwi(ə)rdō/ ▶ n. (pl. **-dos**) informal a person whose dress or behavior seems strange or eccentric.

weird sis·ters ▶ plural n. (usu. **the weird sisters**) the Fates. ■ witches, esp. those in Shakespeare's *Macbeth*.

Weis·mann /ˈvīsmən/, August Friedrich Leopold (1834–1914), German biologist. He was one of the founders of modern genetics. — **Weis·mann·ism** /-mə,nizəm/ n. **Weis·mann·ist** /-mənist/ n. & adj.

weiss·wurst /ˈvīs,wərst; -,wŏŏrst/ ▶ n. whitish German sausage made chiefly of veal. [Ger., 'white sausage.']

Weiz·mann /ˈvītsmən/, Chaim Azriel (1874–1952), president of Israel 1949–52; born in Russia. He helped to persuade the US government to recognize the new state of Israel in 1948.

we·ka /ˈwekə/ ▶ n. a large flightless New Zealand rail (*Gallirallus australis*) with heavily built legs and feet. [19th C.: from Maori, imitative of its cry.]

welch /welCH/ ▶ v. var. of WELSH.

wel·come /ˈwelkəm/ ▶ n. an instance or manner of greeting someone: *we received a warm welcome.* ▶ exclam. used to greet someone in a glad or friendly way. ▶ v. [trans.] greet (someone arriving) in a glad, polite, or friendly way: *welcome guests in their own language.* ■ be glad to entertain (someone) or receive (something). ■ react with pleasure or approval to (an event or development). ▶ adj. (of a guest or new arrival) gladly received. ■ very pleasing because much needed or desired: *a welcome pot of coffee.* ■ [predic., with infin.] allowed or invited to do a specified thing: *anyone is welcome to join them.* ■ [predic.] (**welcome to**) used to indicate that one is relieved to be relinquishing the control or possession of something to another: *the job is all yours and you're welcome to it!*

– PHRASES **make someone welcome** receive and treat someone hospitably. **wear out** (or **overstay** or **outstay**) **one's welcome** stay as a visitor longer than one is wanted. **you're welcome** used as a polite response to thanks. — **wel•come•ly** adv. **wel•come•ness** n. **wel•com•er** n. **wel•com•ing•ly** adv. [OE *wilcuma* 'a person whose coming is pleasing,' *wilcumian* (v.), from *wil-* 'desire, pleasure' + *cuman* 'come.']

weld[1] /weld/ ▶ v. [trans.] join together (metal pieces or parts) by heating the surfaces to the point of melting with a blowpipe, electric arc, or other means, and uniting them by pressing, hammering, etc. ■ forge (an article) by such means. ■ unite (pieces of plastic or other material) by melting or softening of surfaces in contact. ■ fig. cause to combine and form a harmonious or effective whole: *an effort to **weld together** the religious parties.* ▶ n. a welded joint. — **weld•a•bil•i•ty** /ˌweldəˈbilitē/ n. **weld•a•ble** adj. **weld•er** n. [16th C.: alt. (prob. influenced by the past part.) of WELL[2] in the obs. sense 'melt or weld (heated metal).']

weld[2] ▶ n. a widely distributed plant (*Reseda luteola*, family Resedaceae) related to mignonette, yielding a yellow dye. ■ the yellow dye made from this plant, which has been used since Neolithic times and was a popular color for Roman wedding garments. [ME: rel. to Du. *wouw*.]

wel•fare /ˈwelˌfe(ə)r/ ▶ n. the health, happiness, and fortunes of a person or group. ■ statutory procedure or social effort designed to promote the basic physical and material well-being of people in need: *rights to education, housing, and welfare.* ■ financial support given for this purpose.

– PHRASES **on welfare** receiving government financial assistance for basic material needs. [ME: from the adv. WELL[1] + the v. FARE.]

wel•fare state ▶ n. a system whereby the government undertakes to protect the health and well-being of its citizens, esp. those in financial or social need, by means of grants, pensions, and other benefits. ■ a country practicing such a system.

wel•fare-to-work ▶ adj. denoting government policies that encourage those receiving welfare benefits to find a job, for example by providing job training.

wel•fare work ▶ n. organized effort to promote the basic physical and material well-being of people in need. — **wel•fare work•er** n.

wel•far•ism /ˈwelfe(ə)ˌrizəm/ ▶ n. the principles or policies associated with a welfare state. — **wel•far•ist** n. & adj.

wel•kin /ˈwelkin/ ▶ n. literary the sky. ■ heaven.

– PHRASES **make the welkin ring** make a very loud sound. [OE *wolcen* 'cloud, sky,' of West Gmc. origin; rel. to Du. *wolk* and Ger. *Wolke*.]

well[1] /wel/ ▶ adv. (**bet•ter, best**) **1** in a good or satisfactory way: *the whole team played well.* ■ in a way that is appropriate to the facts or circumstances: *you did well to come and tell me.* ■ so as to have a fortunate outcome. ■ in a kind way: *treat the animals well.* ■ with praise or approval: *people spoke well of him.* ■ with equanimity: *she took it very well.* ■ profitably; advantageously: *she would marry well or not at all.* ■ in a condition of prosperity or comfort: *they lived well.* ■ archaic luckily; opportunely: *hail fellow, well met.* **2** in a thorough manner: *mix well.* ■ to a great extent or degree (often used for emphasis): [as submodifier, in comb.] *a well-loved mother.* ■ intimately; closely. ■ [with submodifier] used as an intensifier: *I should bloody well hope so.* **3** [with modal] very probably; in all likelihood: *that may well be the first sign.* ■ without difficulty: *she could well afford to pay.* ■ with good reason: *"What are we doing here?" "You may well ask."* ▶ adj. (**bet•ter, best**) [predic.] **1** in good health; free or recovered from illness. ■ in a satisfactory state or position: *all is not well in post-Soviet Russia.* **2** sensible; advisable: *it would be well to know.* ▶ exclam. used to express a range of emotions including surprise, anger, resignation, or relief: *Well, really! The manners of some people!* ■ used when pausing to consider one's next words. ■ used to express agreement or acceptance, often in a qualified or slightly reluctant way: *well, all right, but be quick.* ■ used to introduce the resumption of a narrative or a change of subject. ■ used to mark the end of a conversation or activity: *well, cheers, Tom—I must run.* ■ used to indicate that one is waiting for an answer or explanation from someone: *Well? You promised to tell me all about it.*

– PHRASES **as well 1** in addition; too: *the museum provides hours of fun and a few surprises as well* | *a shop that sold books **as well as** newspapers.* **2** (**as well** or **just as well**) with equal reason or an equally good result: *I **may as well** have a look.* ■ sensible, appropriate, or desirable: *it would be as well to let him go.* **as well he** (or **she**, etc.) **might** (or **may**) used to convey the speaker's opinion that a reaction is appropriate or unsurprising: *she sounded rather chipper, as well she might, given her bright prospects.* **be well out of** Brit., informal be fortunate to be no longer involved in (a situation). **be well in with** informal have a good relationship with (someone in a position of influence or authority): *you're well in with O'Brien aren't you.* **be well up on** (or **in**) know a great deal about (a particular thing). **do well for oneself** be successful, typically in material or financial terms. **leave** (or **let**) **well enough alone** refrain from interfering with or trying to improve something that is satisfactory or adequate as it is. **very well** used to express agreement or understanding: *oh very well then, come in.* (**all**) **well and good** used to express acceptance of a first statement before introducing a contradictory or confirming second statement: *well, that's all well and good, but why didn't he phone her to say so?* **well and truly** completely: *Leith was well and truly rattled.* **well enough** to a reasonable degree: *he liked Isobel well enough, but wouldn't want to make a close friend of her.* **well worth** certainly worth: *Salzburg is well worth a visit.* [OE *wel(l)*, of Gmc. origin; rel. to Du. *wel* and Ger. *wohl*; prob. also to the v. WILL[1].]

well[2] ▶ n. **1** a shaft sunk into the ground to obtain water, oil, or gas. ■ a plentiful source or supply: *she could feel a deep well of sympathy and compassion.* ■ archaic a water spring or fountain. ■ short for INKWELL. ■ a depression made to hold liquid: *put the flour on a flat surface and make a well to hold the eggs.* ■ (**Wells**) [in place names] esp. Brit. a place where there are mineral springs: *Tunbridge Wells.* **2** an enclosed space in the middle of a building, giving room for stairs or an elevator, or to allow light or ventilation. ■ Brit. the place in a law court where the clerks and ushers sit. **3** Physics a region of minimum potential: *a gravity well.* ▶ v. [no obj., with adverbial] (of a liquid) rise up to the surface and spill or be about to spill: *tears were beginning to well in her eyes.* ■ (of an emotion) arise and become more intense: *all the old bitterness began to **well up** inside her again.* [OE *wella*, of Gmc. origin; rel. to Du. *wel* and Ger. *Welle* 'a wave.']

we'll /wēl/ ▶ contr. we shall; we will.

well-ad•just•ed ▶ adj. successfully altered or moved so as to achieve a desired fit, appearance, or result: *her eyes were well adjusted to the darkness.* ■ (of a person) mentally and emotionally stable: *a well-adjusted, happy child is less likely to be physically ill.*

well-ad•vised ▶ adj. [with infin.] sensible; wise: *you would be well advised to obtain legal advice.*

Wel•land Ca•nal /ˈwelənd/ (also **Wel•land Ship Ca•nal**) a canal in southern Canada, 26 mi. (42 km.) long, that links Lake Erie with Lake Ontario. It bypasses Niagara Falls and forms part of the St. Lawrence Seaway.

well-ap•point•ed ▶ adj. (of a building or room) having a high standard of equipment or furnishing.

well-a•ware ▶ adj. having full knowledge of a situation or fact: *we are well aware of the dangerous side effects that some herbs can have.*

well-be•haved ▶ adj. conducting oneself in an appropriate manner: *the crowd was very well behaved.* ■ (of a computer program) communicating with hardware via standard operating system calls rather than directly and therefore able to be used on different machines.

well-be•ing ▶ n. the state of being comfortable, healthy, or happy: *an improvement in the patient's well-being.*

well-born ▶ adj. from a noble or wealthy family.

well-bred ▶ adj. having or showing good breeding or manners.

well-built ▶ adj. (of a person) large and strong. ■ of strong, solid construction.

well-con•duct•ed ▶ adj. properly organized or carried out. ■ archaic well behaved.

well-con•nect•ed ▶ adj. acquainted with or related to people with prestige or influence.

well deck ▶ n. an open space on the main deck of a ship, lying at a lower level between the forecastle and poop.

well-dis•posed ▶ adj. having a positive, sympathetic, or friendly attitude toward someone or something: ***well-disposed to** the idea.*

well-done ▶ adj. **1** (of a task or undertaking) carried out successfully or satisfactorily: *the decoration is very well done.* **2** (of meat) thoroughly cooked. ▶ exclam. used to express congratulation or approval.

well-dressed ▶ adj. wearing smart or fashionable clothes.

well-earned ▶ adj. fully merited or deserved.

well-en•dowed ▶ adj. having plentiful supplies of a resource. ■ well provided with money; wealthy. ■ informal, humorous (of a man) having large genitals. ■ informal, humorous (of a woman) large-breasted.

Welles /welz/, Orson (1915–85), US director, writer, and actor; full name *George Orson Welles.* His radio dramatization in 1938 of H. G. Wells's *The War of the Worlds* persuaded many listeners that a Martian invasion was really happening. His movies include *Citizen Kane* (1941).

well-fa•vored ▶ adj. having special advantages, esp. good looks.

well-fed ▶ adj. having good meals regularly.

well-formed ▶ adj. correctly or attractively proportioned or shaped. ■ (esp. of a sentence or phrase) constructed according to grammatical rules. ■ conforming to the formation rules of a logical system.

well-found ▶ adj. (chiefly of a boat) well equipped and maintained.

well-found•ed ▶ adj. (esp. of a suspicion or belief) based on good evidence or reasons.

well-groomed ▶ adj. (esp. of a person) clean, tidy, and well dressed.

well-ground•ed ▶ adj. based on good evidence or reasons. ■ having a good training in or knowledge of a subject: ***well grounded in** traditional academic subjects.*

well•head /ˈwelˌhed/ ▶ n. **1** the place where a spring comes out of the ground. **2** the structure over a well, typically an oil or gas well.

well-heeled ▶ adj. informal wealthy.

well house ▶ n. a small building or room enclosing a well and its apparatus.

well-hung ▶ adj. **1** informal (of a man) having large genitals. **2** (of meat or game) hung until sufficiently dry, tender, or high before cooking.

well-in•formed ▶ adj. having or showing much knowledge about a wide range of subjects, or about one particular subject.

Wel·ling·ton[1] /ˈweliNGtən/ the capital of New Zealand, on North Island; pop. 150,000.

Wel·ling·ton[2], Arthur Wellesley, 1st Duke of (1769–1852), British soldier and statesman; prime minister 1828–30 and 1834; known as **the Iron Duke**. He commanded the British forces against Napoleon 1808–14 and defeated him at the Battle of Waterloo 1815.

wel·ling·ton /ˈweliNGtən/ (also **wel·ling·ton boot**) ▶ **n.** esp. Brit. a knee-length waterproof rubber or plastic boot. [19th C.: named after the 1st Duke of *Wellington* (see **Wellington**[2]).]

wel·ling·to·nia /ˌweliNGˈtōnēə/ ▶ **n.** Brit. another term for giant redwood (see **redwood**). [19th C.: mod. L., from the former binomial *Wellingtonia gigantea* (from **Wellington**[2]).]

well-in·ten·tioned ▶ **adj.** having or showing good intentions despite a lack of success or fortunate results.

well-kept ▶ **adj.** (esp. of property) kept clean, tidy, and in good condition. ■ (of a secret) not told to anyone or made widely known.

well-knit ▶ **adj.** (of a person or animal) strongly and compactly built.

well-known ▶ **adj.** known widely or thoroughly.

well-made ▶ **adj.** strongly or skillfully constructed.

well-man·nered ▶ **adj.** having or showing good manners; polite.

well-matched ▶ **adj.** (of two or more people or items) appropriate for or very similar to each other.

well-mean·ing (also **well-meant**) ▶ **adj.** well intentioned.

well·ness /ˈwelnis/ ▶ **n.** the state or condition of being in good physical and mental health: *stress affects every aspect of wellness.*

well-nigh ▶ **adv.** esp. literary almost.

well-off ▶ **adj.** wealthy. ■ in a favorable situation or circumstances.

well-oiled ▶ **adj. 1** [predic.] informal drunk. **2** (esp. of an organization) operating smoothly.

well-pleased ▶ **adj.** [predic.] highly gratified or satisfied.

well-pre·served ▶ **adj.** (of something old) having remained in good condition. ■ (of an old person) showing little sign of aging.

well-round·ed ▶ **adj.** having a curved shape. ■ (of a person) plump. ■ pleasingly varied or balanced: *a well-rounded wine.* ■ (of a person) having a personality that is fully developed in all aspects. ■ (of a phrase or sentence) carefully composed and balanced.

Wells[1] /welz/, H. G. (1866–1946), English writer; full name *Herbert George Wells.* He wrote some of the earliest science-fiction novels, including *The War of the Worlds* (1898).

Wells[2], Henry, see **Wells, Fargo & Co.**.

well-set ▶ **adj.** (of a construction) firmly established; solidly fixed or arranged. ■ (also **well-set-up**) (of a person) strongly built.

Wells, Far·go & Co. /ˌwelz ˈfärgō/ a US transportation company founded in 1852 by the businessmen Henry Wells (1805–78), William Fargo (1818–81), and others. It carried mail to and from the newly developed West and founded a San Francisco bank.

well-spent ▶ **adj.** (of money or time) usefully or profitably expended.

well-spo·ken ▶ **adj.** (of a person) speaking in an educated and refined manner.

well·spring /ˈwelˌspriNG/ ▶ **n.** literary an original and bountiful source of something: *sadness is the wellspring of creativity.*

well-tak·en ▶ **adj.** (of a comment, argument, etc.) shrewd and accurate.

well-tem·pered ▶ **adj.** (of a person or animal) having a cheerful or emotionally stable disposition. ■ (of a process or activity) properly regulated, controlled, or moderated.

well-thumbed ▶ **adj.** (of a book, magazine, etc.) having been read often and bearing marks of frequent handling.

well-to-do ▶ **adj.** wealthy; prosperous.

well-trav·eled ▶ **adj. 1** (of a person) having traveled widely. **2** (of a route) much frequented by travelers.

well-trod·den ▶ **adj.** much frequented by travelers.

well-turned ▶ **adj. 1** (of a compliment, phrase, or verse) elegantly expressed. **2** (esp. of an ankle or leg) having an elegant and attractive shape.

well-up·hol·stered ▶ **adj.** (of a chair or sofa) having plenty of padding. ■ humorous (of a person) fat.

well-used ▶ **adj.** much used. ■ worn or shabby through much use, handling, or wear.

well-wish·er ▶ **n.** a person who desires happiness or success for another, or who expresses such a desire.

well-worn ▶ **adj.** showing the signs of extensive use or wear. ■ (of a phrase, idea, or joke) used or repeated so often that it no longer has interest or significance.

well-wrought ▶ **adj.** skillfully constructed or put together.

welly /ˈwelē/ (also **wel·lie**) ▶ **n.** (pl. **-lies**) Brit., informal **1** short for **wellington**. **2** power or vigor: *big voices with plenty of welly.*

Welsh /welsH/ ▶ **adj.** of or relating to Wales, its people, or their Celtic language. ▶ **n. 1** the Celtic language of Wales, spoken by about 500,000 people (mainly bilingual in English). **2** [as pl. n.] (**the Welsh**) the people of Wales collectively. — **Welsh·ness n.** [OE *Welisc, Wælisc*, from a Gmc. word meaning 'foreigner;' cf. L. *Volcae*, the name of a Celtic people in southern Gaul.]

welsh /welsH/ (also **welch**) ▶ **v.** [intrans.] (**welsh on**) fail to honor (a debt or obligation incurred through a promise or agreement). — **welsh·er n.** [19th C.: of unknown origin.]

Welsh cor·gi ▶ **n.** (pl. **Welsh cor·gis**) a dog of a short-legged breed with a foxlike head. [1920s: from Welsh, from *cor* 'dwarf' + *ci* 'dog.']

Welsh corgi

Welsh·man /ˈwelsHmən/ ▶ **n.** (pl. **-men**) a male native or national of Wales, or a man of Welsh descent.

Welsh rare·bit (also **Welsh rab·bit**) ▶ **n.** another term for **rarebit**.

Welsh spring·er ▶ **n.** (usu. **Welsh spring·er span·iel**) see **springer** (sense 1).

Welsh ter·ri·er ▶ **n.** a stocky, rough-coated, typically black-and-tan terrier of a breed with a square muzzle and drop ears.

Welsh·wom·an /ˈwelsHˌwo͝omən/ ▶ **n.** (pl. **-wom·en**) a female native or national of Wales, or a woman of Welsh descent.

welt /welt/ ▶ **n. 1** a leather rim sewn around the edge of a shoe upper to which the sole is attached. ■ a ribbed, reinforced, or decorative border of a garment or pocket. **2** a red, swollen mark left on flesh by a blow or pressure. ■ a heavy blow. ▶ **v.** [trans.] **1** provide with a welt. **2** strike (someone or something) hard and heavily. ■ [intrans.] develop a raised scar: *his lip was beginning to welt.* [ME: of unknown origin.]

Welt·an·schau·ung /ˈveltˌänˌsHouəNG/ ▶ **n.** (pl. **-schau·ung·en** /-ˌsHouəNGən/) a particular philosophy or view of life; the worldview of an individual or group. [Ger., from *Welt* 'world' + *Anschauung* 'perception.']

wel·ter /ˈweltər/ ▶ **v.** [intrans.] literary move in a turbulent fashion. ■ lie steeped in blood with no help or care. ▶ **n.** a large number of items in no order; a confused mass. ■ a state of general disorder: *a welter of bloody, confused fighting.* [ME (in the sense 'writhe, wallow'): from MDu., Mid. Low Ger. *welteren.*]

wel·ter·weight /ˈweltərˌwāt/ ▶ **n.** a weight in boxing and other sports intermediate between lightweight and middleweight. In the amateur boxing scale it ranges from 140 to 147 pounds (63.5–67 kg). ■ a boxer or other competitor of this weight. [19th C.: *welter* of unknown origin.]

Welt·schmerz /ˈveltˌsHmerts/ ▶ **n.** a feeling of melancholy and world-weariness. [Ger., from *Welt* 'world' + *Schmerz* 'pain.']

Wel·ty /ˈweltē/, Eudora (1909–2001), US writer. Her novels include *Delta Wedding* (1946) and *The Optimist's Daughter* (Pulitzer Prize, 1972).

wen[1] /wen/ ▶ **n.** a boil or other swelling or growth on the skin, esp. a sebaceous cyst. ■ archaic a very large or overcrowded city. [OE *wen(n).*]

wen[2] (also **wyn** /win/) ▶ **n.** a runic letter, used in Old and Middle English, later replaced by *w*. [OE, lit. 'joy'; so named because it is the first letter of this word.]

Wen·ce·slas /ˈwensəsˌläs; -ˌlôs/ (also **Wen·ces·laus**) (1361–1419), Holy Roman emperor 1378–1400 and king of Bohemia (as Wenceslas IV) 1378–1419.

Wen·ce·slas, St. (also **Wenceslaus**) (*c.*907–29), duke of Bohemia and patron saint of the Czech Republic; also known as **Good King Wenceslas**. He worked to Christianize the people of Bohemia.

wench /wencH/ ▶ **n.** archaic or humorous a girl or young woman. ■ archaic a prostitute. ▶ **v.** [intrans.] archaic (of a man) consort with prostitutes. [ME: abbrev. of obs. *wenchel* 'child, servant, prostitute.']

Wen-Chou /ˈwen ˈCHō/ variant of **Wenzhou**.

Wend /wend/ ▶ **n.** another term for **Sorb**. [from Ger. *Wende*, of unknown origin.]

wend /wend/ ▶ **v.** [no obj., with adverbial] (**wend one's way**) go in a specified direction, typically slowly or by an indirect route. [OE *wendan* 'to turn, depart,' of Gmc. origin.]

wen·di·go ▶ **n.** var. of **windigo**.

Wend·ish /ˈwendisH/ ▶ **adj. & n.** another term for **Sorbian**.

went /went/ past of **go**[1].

wen·tle·trap /ˈwentlˌtrap/ ▶ **n.** a marine mollusk (family Epitoniidae) that has a tall spiral shell with many whorls that are ringed with oblique ridges. [18th C.: from Du. *wenteltrap*, lit. 'winding stair.']

Wen·zhou /ˈwənˈjō; ˈwen-/ (also **Wen-Chou** /ˈwen ˈCHō/) a city in eastern China; pop. 1,650,400.

wept /wept/ past and past participle of **weep**.

were /wər/ second person singular past, plural past, and past subjunctive of **be**.

we're /wi(ə)r/ ▶ **contr.** we are.

were·n't /wər(ə)nt/ ▶ **contr.** were not.

were·wolf /ˈwe(ə)rˌwo͝olf/ ▶ **n.** (pl. **-wolves**) (in myth or fiction) a person who changes for periods of time into a wolf, typically when there is a full moon. [OE *werewulf*; the first element has usually been identified with OE *wer* 'man.']

Wer·ner /ˈvernər/, Alfred (1866–1919), Swiss chemist, born in France. He was a pioneer in the study of coordination compounds. Nobel Prize for Chemistry (1913).

Wer·ner's syn·drome /ˈwərnərz/ ▶ **n.** Med. a rare hereditary syndrome causing rapid premature aging, susceptibility to cancer, and other disorders. [1930s: named after Carl O. *Werner* (1879–1936), German physician.]

Wer·nick·e's ar·e·a /ˈve(ə)rnikēz; -kəz/ ▶ **n.** Anat. a region of the brain concerned with the comprehension of language. Damage in this area causes **Wernicke's aphasia**, characterized by superficially fluent speech but an inability to use or understand more than the most basic nouns and verbs. [19th C.: named after Karl *Wernicke* (1848–1905), German neuropsychiatrist.]

Wer·nick·e's en·ceph·a·lop·a·thy (also **Wer·nick·e's syn·drome**) ▶ **n.** Med. a neurological disorder caused by thiamine deficiency, typically from chronic alcoholism or persistent vomiting, and marked by mental confusion, abnormal eye movements, and unsteady gait. [19th C.: named after K. *Wernicke* (see **WERNICKE'S AREA**).]

wert /wərt/ archaic second person singular past of **BE**.

We·sak ▶ **n.** var. of **VESAK**.

We·ser /ˈvāzər/ a river in northwestern Germany that flows north to the North Sea near Bremerhaven.

Wes·ley /ˈweslē; ˈwezlē/, John (1703–91), English preacher. He was a cofounder of Methodism, which formed a separate denomination in 1791. His brother Charles (1707–88) was also a founding Methodist.

Wes·ley·an /ˈweslēən; ˈwez-/ ▶ **adj.** of, relating to, or denoting the teachings of John Wesley or the main branch of the Methodist Church that he founded. ▶ **n.** a follower of Wesley or adherent of the main Methodist tradition. — **Wes·ley·an·ism** /-əˌnizəm/ **n.**

Wes·sex /ˈwesiks/ the kingdom of the West Saxons, established in the early 6th century and extended by conquest to include much of southern England.

Wes·si /ˈwesē; ˈvesē/ informal ▶ **n.** a citizen of West Germany.

West[1] /west/, Benjamin (1738–1820), US painter, resident in Britain from 1763. He became the second president of the Royal Academy in 1792.

West[2], Dorothy (1907–98), US writer. She was a spokesman for the Harlem Renaissance in the 1920s. Her novels include *The Wedding* (1995).

West[3], Nathanael (1903–40), US writer; born *Nathan Wallenstein Weinstein.* His works included *Miss Lonelyhearts* (1933) and *The Day of the Locust* (1939).

West[4], Dame Rebecca (1892–1983), British writer and feminist, born in Ireland; born *Cicily Isabel Fairfield*. Her works include *The Meaning of Treason* (1949) and *The Fountain Overflows* (1957).

west /west/ ▶ **n.** (usu. **the west**) **1** the direction toward the point of the horizon where the sun sets at the equinoxes, on the left-hand side of a person facing north, or the part of the horizon lying in this direction. ■ the compass point corresponding to this. **2** the western part of the world or of a specified country, region, or town. ■ (usu. **the West**) Europe and its culture seen in contrast to other civilizations. ■ (usu. **the West**) hist. the noncommunist states of Europe and North America, contrasted with the former communist states of eastern Europe. ■ (usu. **the West**) the western part of the United States, esp. the states west of the Mississippi. **3** [as name] (**West**) Bridge the player sitting to the right of North and partnering East. ▶ **adj. 1** [attrib.] lying toward, near, or facing the west: *the west coast.* ■ (of a wind) blowing from the west. **2** of or denoting the western part of a specified area, city, or country or its inhabitants. ▶ **adv.** to or toward the west: *the accident happened a mile west of Bowes.* [OE, of Gmc. origin; rel. to Du. and Ger. *west*, from an Indo-Eur. root shared by Gk. *hesperos*, L. *vesper* 'evening.']

West Af·ri·ca the western part of the African continent, esp. the countries bounded by and including Mauritania, Mali, and Niger in the north and Gabon in the south.

West Bank a region west of the Jordan River and northwest of the Dead Sea. It became part of Jordan in 1948 and was occupied by Israel following the Six Day War of 1967. An agreement was signed in 1993 that granted limited autonomy to the Palestinians, who comprise 97 percent of its inhabitants; withdrawal of Israeli troops began in 1994.

West Ben·gal a state in eastern India; capital, Calcutta.

West Ber·lin see **BERLIN**[1].

west·bound /ˈwestˌbound/ ▶ **adj.** leading or traveling toward the west.

West·ches·ter Coun·ty /ˈwestˌCHestər/ a suburban county in southeastern New York, northeast of New York City; pop. 923,459.

West Coast ▶ **n.** the western seaboard of the US from Washington to California.

West Coun·try the southwestern counties of England.

West End the entertainment and shopping area of London to the west of the City.

west·er·ing /ˈwestəriNG/ ▶ **adj.** literary (esp. of the sun) nearing the west. [17th C.: from the literary v. *wester*, from **WEST**.]

west·er·ly /ˈwestərlē/ ▶ **adj. & adv.** in a westward position or direction. ■ (of a wind) blowing from the west. ▶ **n.** (often **westerlies**) a wind blowing from the west. ■ (**westerlies**) the belt of prevailing westerly winds in medium latitudes in the southern hemisphere. [15th C.: from obs. *wester* 'western' + **-LY**[1].]

west·ern /ˈwestərn/ ▶ **adj. 1** [attrib.] situated in the west, or directed toward or facing the west. ■ (of a wind) blowing from the west. **2** (usu. **West·ern**) living in or originating from the west, in particular Europe or the United States. ■ of, relating to, or characteristic of the west or its inhabitants: *western art.* ■ hist. of or originating from the noncommunist states of Europe and North America in contrast to the Eastern bloc. ▶ **n.** (also **West·ern**) a film, television drama, or novel about cowboys in western North America, esp. in the late 19th and early 20th centuries. — **west·ern·most** /-ˌmōst/ **adj.**

West·ern Aus·tra·lia a state in western Australia; pop. 1,643,000; capital, Perth.

West·ern blot ▶ **n.** Biochem. an adaptation of the Southern blot procedure, used to identify specific amino-acid sequences in proteins. [suggested by **SOUTHERN BLOT**.]

West·ern Cape a province in southwestern South Africa, formerly part of Cape Province; capital, Cape Town.

West·ern Church the part of the Christian Church historically originating in the Latin Church of the Western Roman Empire, including the Roman Catholic Church and the Anglican, Lutheran, and Reformed Churches, esp. as distinct from the Eastern Orthodox Church.

West·ern Em·pire the western part of the Roman Empire, after its division in AD 395.

West·ern·er /ˈwestərnər/ (also **west·ern·er**) ▶ **n.** a native or inhabitant of the west, esp. of western Europe or North America.

West·ern Front the zone of fighting in western Europe in World War I. For most of the war the front line stretched from eastern France through Belgium.

west·ern hem·i·sphere the half of the earth that contains the Americas.

West·ern Isles another name for **HEBRIDES**.

west·ern·ize /ˈwestərˌnīz/ ▶ **v.** [trans.] (usu. **be westernized**) cause (a country, person, or system) to adopt or be influenced by the cultural, economic, or political systems of Europe and North America. ■ [intrans.] be in the process of adopting or being influenced by the systems of the West. — **west·ern·i·za·tion** /ˌwestərniˈzāSHən/ **n.** **west·ern·iz·er n.**

west·ern om·e·let ▶ **n.** an omelet containing a filling of onion, green pepper, and ham.

West·ern Ro·man Em·pire see **ROMAN EMPIRE**.

West·ern sad·dle ▶ **n.** a saddle with a deep seat, high pommel and cantle, and broad stirrups. See illustration at **SADDLE**.

West·ern Sa·har·a a region in northwestern Africa, on the Atlantic coast between Morocco and Mauritania; pop. 187,000; capital, La'youn. Formerly an overseas Spanish province called Spanish Sahara, it was renamed and annexed by Morocco and Mauritania in 1976. Mauritania withdrew in 1979 and Morocco extended its control over the entire region. A liberation movement, the Polisario Front, struggled against Morocco in an attempt to establish an independent Saharawi Arab Democratic Republic; a cease-fire came into effect in 1991.

West·ern Sa·mo·a see **SAMOA**.

West·ern Wall another name for **WAILING WALL**.

West·ern Zhou see **ZHOU**.

West·fa·len /vestˈfälən/ German name for **WESTPHALIA**.

West Flan·ders a province of northwestern Belgium; capital, Bruges.

West Fri·sian Is·lands see **FRISIAN ISLANDS**.

West Ger·man·ic ▶ **n.** the western group of Germanic languages, comprising High and Low German, Dutch, Frisian, and English. ▶ **adj.** of or relating to West Germanic.

West Ger·ma·ny see **GERMANY**.

West High·land ter·ri·er (also **West High·land white ter·ri·er**) ▶ **n.** a dog of a small, short-legged breed of terrier with a white coat and erect ears and tail, developed in the West Highlands.

West In·di·an ▶ **n.** a native or national of any of the islands of the West Indies. ■ a person of West Indian descent. ▶ **adj.** of or relating to the West Indies or its people.

West In·di·an sat·in·wood ▶ **n.** see **SATINWOOD**.

West In·dies a chain of islands that extends from the Florida peninsula to the coast of Venezuela and lies between the Caribbean Sea and the Atlantic Ocean. They consist of three main island groups: the Greater and Lesser Antilles and the Bahamas. Originally inhabited by Arawak and Carib Indians, the islands were visited by Columbus in 1492 and named by him in the belief that he had reached the coast of India.

west·ing /ˈwestiNG/ ▶ **n.** distance traveled or measured westward, esp. at sea. ■ a figure or line representing westward distance on a map.

West·ing·house /ˈwestiNGˌhous/, George (1846–1914), US engineer. He developed vacuum-operated safety brakes and electrically controlled signals for railways. He built up a huge company to manufacture his products.

West·mann Is·lands /ˈwes(t)mən; ˈves(t)-/ a group of fifteen volcanic islands off the southern coast of Iceland. Icelandic name **VESTMANNAEYJAR**.

West·meath /ˌwes(t)ˈmēTH; -ˈmēTH/ a county of the Republic of Ireland, in the province of Leinster; county town, Mullingar.

West·min·ster /ˈwes(t)ˌminstər; ˌwes(t)ˈmin-/ **1** a city in north central Colorado, northwest of Denver; pop. 100,940. **2** an inner London borough that contains the Houses of Parliament and many government offices. ■ used in reference to the British Parliament: *Westminster enforced successive cuts in pay.*

West·min·ster Ab·bey the collegiate church of St. Peter in Westminster,

PRONUNCIATION KEY ə *ago, up*; ər *over, fur*; a *hat*; ā *ate*; ä *car*; e *let*; ē *see*; i *fit*; ī *by*; NG *sing*; ō *go*; ô *law, for*; oi *toy*; o͝o *good*; o͞o *goo*; ou *out*; TH *thin*; T̲H̲ *then*; ZH *vision*

London. Nearly all the kings and queens of England have been crowned in Westminster Abbey; it is also the burial place of many of England's monarchs and other leading figures.

West Nile vi·rus ▶ n. a flavivirus of African origin that can be spread to humans and other mammals via mosquitoes, causing encephalitis and flulike symptoms, with some fatalities.

west-north·west ▶ n. the direction or compass point midway between west and northwest.

West·pha·lia /wes(t)'fālyə; -'fālēə/ a former province of northwestern Germany. German name WESTFALEN. — **West·pha·lian** adj. & n.

West·pha·li·a, Trea·ty of the peace accord (1648) that ended the Thirty Years War, signed simultaneously in Osnabrück and Münster.

West Point the US Military Academy, founded in 1802, located on the site of a former strategic fort on the west bank of the Hudson River in New York.

West Quod·dy Head /'kwädē/ the easternmost (66° 57' W) point in the US, in Lubec in Maine, south of Passamaquoddy Bay.

West Rox·bury a southwestern district of Boston, Massachusetts. It was a separate town until 1874 and was the site of the experimental Brook Farm.

West Sax·on ▶ n. **1** a native or inhabitant of the Anglo-Saxon kingdom of Wessex. **2** the dialect of Old English used by the West Saxons, the chief literary dialect of Old English. ▶ adj. of or relating to the West Saxons or their dialect.

West Side the residential and commercial districts west of Fifth Avenue in Manhattan in New York City.

west-south·west ▶ n. the direction or compass point midway between west and southwest.

West Val·ley Cit·y a city in north central Utah, south of Salt Lake City; pop. 108,896.

West Vir·gin·ia a state in the eastern US; pop. 1,808,344; capital, Charleston; statehood, June 20, 1863 (35). It separated from Virginia in 1861, at the beginning of the Civil War, because the two areas were at odds over the questions of secession and of slavery. — **West Vir·gin·ian** n. & adj.

west·ward /'westwərd/ ▶ adj. toward the west. ▶ adv. (also **west·wards**) in a westerly direction. ▶ n. (**the westward**) a direction or region toward the west. — **west·ward·ly** adv.

West·wood /'west,wo͝od/ a section in western Los Angeles in California, home to the University of California at Los Angeles (UCLA).

wet /wet/ ▶ adj. (**wet·ter, wet·test**) **1** covered or saturated with water or another liquid. ■ (of the weather) rainy. ■ (of paint, ink, plaster, or a similar substance) not yet having dried or hardened. ■ (of a baby or young child) having urinated in its diaper or underwear. ■ involving the use of water or liquid: *wet methods of photography.* **2** informal (of a country or region or of its legislation) allowing the sale of alcoholic beverages. ■ (of a person) addicted to alcohol. ▶ v. (**wet·ting**; past and past part. **wet** or **wet·ted**) [trans.] cover or touch with liquid; moisten: *he wet a finger.* ■ (esp. of a baby or young child) urinate in or on. ■ (**wet oneself**) urinate involuntarily. ▶ n. **1** liquid that makes something damp: *the wet of his tears.* ■ (**the wet**) rainy weather. ■ a person opposed to the prohibition of alcoholic beverages. **2** Brit., informal a person lacking forcefulness or strength of character.
– PHRASES **all wet** completely wrong. **wet behind the ears** informal lacking experience; immature. **wet through** (or **to the skin**) with one's clothes soaked; completely drenched. **wet one's whistle** informal have a drink. — **wet·ly** adv. **wet·ness** n. **wet·ta·ble** adj. **wet·tish** adj. [OE *wǣt* (adj. and n.), *wǣtan* (v.).]

we·ta /'wetə/ ▶ n. a large brown wingless insect (family Stenopelmatidae) related to the grasshoppers, with long spiny legs and wood-boring larvae, found only in New Zealand. Its several genera include *Deinacrida* (the **giant wetas**). [19th C.: from Maori.]

wet·back /'wet,bak/ ▶ n. informal, derog. a Mexican living in the US, esp. one who is an illegal immigrant. [1920s: so named from the practice of swimming the Rio Grande to reach the US.]

wet bar ▶ n. a bar or counter equipped with running water and a sink, for serving alcoholic drinks at home.

wet blan·ket ▶ n. informal a person who spoils other people's fun by failing to join in with or by disapproving of their activities.

wet bulb ▶ n. one of the two thermometers of a psychrometer, the bulb of which is enclosed in wetted material so that water is constantly evaporating from it and cooling the bulb.

wet cell ▶ n. a primary electric cell in which the electrolyte is a liquid. Compare with DRY CELL.

wet dock ▶ n. a dock in which water is maintained at a level that keeps a vessel afloat.

wet dream ▶ n. an erotic dream associated with involuntary ejaculation of semen.

wet fly ▶ n. an artificial fishing fly designed to sink below the surface of the water.

weth·er /'weT͟Hər/ ▶ n. a castrated ram. [OE, of Gmc. origin; rel. to Du. *weer* and Ger. *Widder*.]

wet·land /'wet,land; -lənd/ ▶ n. (also **wetlands**) land consisting of marshes or swamps; saturated land.

wet look ▶ n. [in sing.] an artificially wet or shiny appearance, in particular one possessed by a clothing fabric or achieved by applying a type of gel to the hair.

wet nurse ▶ n. esp. hist. a woman employed to suckle another woman's child. ▶ v. (**wet-nurse**) [trans.] act as a wet nurse to. ■ informal look after (someone) as though they were a helpless infant.

wet plate ▶ n. Photog. a sensitized collodion plate exposed in the camera while the collodion is moist.

wet·suit /'wet,so͞ot/ ▶ n. a close-fitting rubber garment typically covering the entire body, worn for warmth in water sports or diving.

wet·ting a·gent ▶ n. a chemical that can be added to a liquid to reduce its surface tension and make it more effective in spreading over and penetrating surfaces.

wet·ware /'wet,we(ə)r/ ▶ n. human brain cells or thought processes regarded as analogous to, or in contrast with, computer systems. ■ (chiefly in science fiction) computer technology in which the brain is linked to artificial systems, or used as a model for artificial systems based on biochemical processes.

we've /wēv/ ▶ contr. we have.

Wex·ford /'weksfərd/ a county in southeastern Republic of Ireland, in the province of Leinster.

w.f. Print. ▶ abbr. wrong font (used as a proofreading mark).

whack /(h)wak/ informal ▶ v. [trans.] strike forcefully with a sharp blow: *he whacked him on the head.* ■ murder: *he was whacked while sitting in his car.* ▶ n. **1** a sharp or resounding blow. **2** a try or attempt: ***take a whack** at spotting the trends.*
– PHRASES **at a** (or **one**) **whack** at one time. **out of whack** out of order; not working.
– PHRASAL VERBS **whack off** vulgar slang masturbate. — **whack·er** n. [18th C.: imitative, or perh. an alt. of THWACK.]

whacked /(h)wakt/ (also **whacked out**) ▶ adj. informal completely exhausted: *I'm not staying long—I'm whacked.* ■ under the influence of drugs.

whack·o ▶ adj. & n. (pl. **-os**) var. of WACKO.

whack·y ▶ adj. var. of WACKY.

whale[1] /(h)wāl/ ▶ n. (pl. same or **whales**) a very large marine mammal (order Cetacea) with a streamlined hairless body, a horizontal tail fin, and a blowhole on top of the head for breathing. See BALEEN WHALE and TOOTHED WHALE. ■ a gambler who makes very large bets: *casinos meet the whales at the airport with limousines.* [OE *hwæl*, of Gmc. origin.]

whale[2] ▶ v. [trans.] informal beat; hit: *Dad came upstairs and whaled me.* [18th C.: var. of WALE.]

whale·back /'(h)wāl,bak/ ▶ n. a thing that is shaped like a whale's back, esp. an arched structure over the bow or stern part of the deck of a steamer, or a large elongated hill.

whale·boat /'(h)wāl,bōt/ ▶ n. a long rowboat with a bow at either end for easy maneuverability, formerly used in whaling. ■ a similar boat used as a ship's lifeboat and utility boat.

whale·bone /'(h)wāl,bōn/ ▶ n. an elastic horny substance that grows in a series of thin parallel plates in the upper jaw of some whales and is used by them to strain plankton from the seawater. Also called BALEEN. ■ strips of this substance, much used formerly as stays in corsets and dresses. ■ bone or ivory from a whale or walrus.

whale·bone whale ▶ n. another term for BALEEN WHALE.

whale oil ▶ n. oil obtained from the blubber of a whale, formerly used in oil lamps or for making soap.

whal·er /'(h)wālər/ ▶ n. a whaling ship. ■ a seaman engaged in whaling.

whale shark ▶ n. a very large tropical shark, *Rhincodon typus*, family Rhincodontidae, that typically swims close to the surface, where it feeds chiefly on plankton. It is the largest known fish.

whal·ing /'(h)wāliNG/ ▶ n. the practice or industry of hunting and killing whales for their oil, meat, or whalebone.

wham /(h)wam/ informal ▶ exclam. used to express the sound of a forcible impact: *the bombs landed—wham!—right on target.* ■ used to express the idea of a sudden, dramatic, and decisive occurrence. ▶ v. (**whammed, wham·ming**) [no obj., with adverbial] strike something forcefully. ■ make a loud sound as of a forceful impact. [1920s: imitative.]

wham bam informal ▶ exclam. used to express the idea of a sudden or dramatic occurrence or change of events.
– PHRASES **wham-bam-thank-you-ma'am** used in reference to sexual activity conducted roughly and quickly, without tenderness. [1950s (as *wham-bang*): from WHAM + BAM or the v. BANG[1].]

wham·mo /'(h)wamō/ ▶ exclam. another term for WHAM.

wham·my /'(h)wamē/ ▶ n. (pl. **-mies**) informal an event with a powerful and unpleasant effect; a blow. See also DOUBLE WHAMMY. ■ an evil or unlucky influence: ***put the whammy on** them.* [1940s: from the n. WHAM + -Y[1].]

whang /(h)waNG/ informal ▶ v. [no obj., with adverbial] make or produce a resonant noise. ■ [trans.] strike or throw heavily and loudly. ▶ n. a noisy blow. [17th C.: var. of THONG; senses describing noise are imitative.]

whap /(h)wap/ ▶ v. (**whapped, whap·ping**) & n. var. of WHOP.

wharf /(h)wôrf/ ▶ n. (pl. **wharves** /(h)wôrvz/ or **wharfs**) a level area to which a ship may be moored to load and unload. [OE *hwearf*, of Gmc. origin.]

wharf·age /'(h)wôrfij/ ▶ n. accommodations provided at a wharf for the loading, unloading, or storage of goods. ■ payment made for such accommodations.

wharf·in·ger /'(h)wôrfinjər/ ▶ n. an owner or keeper of a wharf. [ME: from WHARFAGE + -ER[1].]

Whar·ton /'(h)wôrtn/, Edith Newbold (1862–1937), US writer, resident in France from 1907. Her novels include *Ethan Frome* (1911) and *The Age of Innocence* (Pulitzer Prize, 1920).

wharves /(h)wôrvz/ plural form of WHARF.

what /(h)wət; (h)wät/ ▶ **pron. 1** [interrog. pron.] asking for information specifying something: *what is your name?* ■ asking for repetition of something not heard or confirmation of something not understood: *what? I can't hear you.* **2** [relative pron.] the thing or things that (used in specifying something): *what we need is a commitment.* ■ (referring to the whole of an amount) whatever: *I want to do what I can.* ■ dialect who or that: *the one what got to my house.* **3** (in exclamations) emphasizing something surprising or remarkable: *what some people do for attention!* ▶ **adj. 1** [interrog. adj.] asking for information specifying something: *what time is it?* **2** [relative adj.] (referring to the whole of an amount) whatever: *what little money he had.* **3** (in exclamations) how great or remarkable: [as adj.] *what luck!* ▶ **interrog. adv. 1** to what extent?: *what does it matter?* **2** used to indicate an estimate or approximation: *see you, what, about four?* **3** informal, dated used for emphasis or to invite agreement: *pretty poor show, what?*
– PHRASES **and** (or **or**) **what have you** informal and/or anything else similar: *soup, gravy, cream, or what have you.* **and what not** informal and other similar things. **what about ——? 1** used when asking for information or an opinion on something: *what about the practical angle?* **2** used to make a suggestion: *what about a walk?* **what ever** used for emphasis in questions, typically expressing surprise or confusion: *what ever did I do?* See usage at WHATEVER. **what for?** informal for what reason? **what if ——? 1** what would result if ——?: *what if nobody shows up?* **2** what does it matter if ——?: *what if our house is a mess?* **what is more** and as an additional point; moreover. **what of ——?** what is the news concerning ——? **what of it?** why should that be considered significant? **what's-his** (or **-its**) **-name** another term for WHATSHISNAME. **what say ——?** used to make a suggestion: *what say we take a break?* **what's what** informal what is useful or important: *I'll teach her what's what.* **what with** because of (used usually to introduce several causes of something): *what with the drought and the neglect, the garden is in a sad condition.* [OE *hwæt*, of Gmc. origin; rel. to Du. *wat* and Ger. *was*, from an Indo-Eur. root shared by L. *quod*.]

what·cha /'(h)wəCHə; '(h)wä-/ (also **wat·cha** /'wəCHə; 'wä-/) ▶ **exclam.** nonstandard contraction of: ■ what are you: *hey, whatcha gonna do?* ■ what have you: *whatcha got this hammer for?* ■ what do you: *whatcha want to make a mess like that for?*

what·cha·ma·call·it /'(h)wəCHəmə,kôlit; '(h)wä-/ ▶ **n.** informal used to refer to a person or thing whose name one cannot recall, does not know, or does not wish to specify: *get the whatchamacallit from her bureau.*

what·e'er /,(h)wət'e(ə)r; ,(h)wät-/ literary ▶ **contr.** whatever.

what·ev·er /,(h)wət'evər; ,(h)wät-/ ▶ **rel. pron. & adj.** used to emphasize a lack of restriction in referring to any thing or amount, no matter what: [as pron.] *do whatever you like* | [as adj.] *take whatever action is needed.* ■ regardless of what: [as pron.] *whatever you decide* | [as adj.] *whatever decision he made.* ▶ **interrog. pron.** used for emphasis instead of "what" in questions, typically expressing surprise or confusion: *whatever is the matter?* ▶ **adv. 1** [with negative] at all; of any kind (used for emphasis): *they received no help whatever.* **2** informal no matter what happens: *we'd back him whatever.* ▶ **exclam.** used to express skepticism or exasperation: *Joseph's commentary was "Yeah, well. Whatever."*
– PHRASES **or whatever** informal or anything similar.

what·not /'(h)wət,nät; '(h)wät-/ ▶ **n. 1** informal used to refer to an item or items that are not identified but are felt to have something in common with items already named: *pictures and books and manuscripts and whatnot.* **2** a stand with shelves for small objects.

whats·his·name /'(h)wətsiz,nām; '(h)wät-/ (also **whats·his·name, whats·his·face** /-,fās/, or **what's·her·name** /-sər,nām/) ▶ **n.** informal used to refer to a person whose name one cannot recall, does not know, or does not wish to specify: *poor Mr. Whatsisname just blew a fuse.*

whats·is /'(h)wətsəs; '(h)wät-/ ▶ **n.** informal used to refer to a thing whose name one cannot recall, does not know, or does not wish to specify: *I am up to my whatsis in snow.*

whats·it /'(h)wətsit; '(h)wät-/ ▶ **n.** another term for WHATCHAMACALLIT.

what·so /'(h)wət,sō; '(h)wät-/ ▶ **pron. & adj.** archaic whatever: [as pron.] *whatso goes into their brain comes out as prose.* [ME: reduced form of OE *swā hwæt swā* 'so what so.']

what·so·e'er /,(h)wətsō'e(ə)r; ,(h)wät-/ literary ▶ **contr.** whatsoever.

what·so·ev·er /,(h)wətsō'evər; ,(h)wät-/ ▶ **adv.** [with negative] at all (used for emphasis): *no doubt whatsoever.* ▶ **adj. & pron.** archaic whatever.

wheal /(h)wēl/ ▶ **n.** var. of WEAL[1].

wheat /(h)wēt/ ▶ **n.** a cereal plant (genus *Triticum*) that is the most important kind grown in temperate countries, the grain of which is ground to make flour for bread, pasta, pastry, etc. ■ the grain of this plant. [OE *hwǣte*, of Gmc. origin; rel. to Du. *weit*, Ger. *Weizen*.]

wheat·ear /'(h)wēt,i(ə)r/ ▶ **n.** a mainly Eurasian and African songbird (genus *Oenanthe*) of the thrush family, related to the chats, with black and buff or black and white plumage and a white rump, in particular the gray-backed **northern wheatear** (*O. oenanthe*), found in the arctic barrens of Eurasia and northeastern Canada. [16th C.: appar. from WHITE (assimilated to WHEAT) + ARSE (assimilated to EAR[2]).]

wheat·en /'(h)wētn/ ▶ **adj.** (esp. of bread) made of wheat. ■ of a color resembling that of wheat; a pale yellow-beige.

wheat·en ter·ri·er ▶ **n.** a terrier of a breed with a pale golden soft wavy coat.

wheat germ ▶ **n.** a nutritious foodstuff of a dry floury consistency consisting of the extracted embryos of grains of wheat.

wheat·grass /'(h)wēt,gras/ ▶ **n.** another term for COUCH GRASS.

Wheat·ley /'(h)wētlē/, Phillis (c.1752–84), American poet; born in Africa. Sold as a slave at age eight to the John Wheatley family of Boston, she was educated by them. Her first volume of poetry, *Poems on Various Subjects, Religious and Moral* (1773), was published in London.

wheat·meal /'(h)wēt,mēl/ ▶ **n.** flour made from wheat from which some of the bran and germ has been removed.

Wheat·stone /'(h)wēt,stōn/, Sir Charles (1802–75), English physicist and inventor. He is best known for his electrical inventions.

Wheat·stone bridge ▶ **n.** a simple circuit for measuring an unknown resistance by connecting it so as to form a quadrilateral with three known resistances and applying a voltage between a pair of opposite corners.

whee /(h)wē/ ▶ **exclam.** used to express delight, excitement, or exhilaration. [natural exclamation: first recorded in English in the 1920s.]

whee·dle /'(h)wēdl/ ▶ **v.** [intrans.] employ endearments or flattery to persuade someone to do something or give one something: *you can wheedle your way onto a court.* ■ [trans.] **(wheedle someone into doing something)** coax or persuade someone to do something. ■ [trans.] **(wheedle something out of)** coax or persuade (someone) to say or give something. — **whee·dler n. whee·dling·ly adv.** [17th C.: perh. from Ger. *wedeln* 'cringe, fawn,' from *Wedel* 'tail, fan.']

wheel /(h)wēl/ ▶ **n. 1** a circular object that revolves on an axle and is fixed below a vehicle or other object to enable it to move over the ground. ■ a circular object that revolves on an axle and forms part of a machine. ■ **(the wheel)** used in reference to the cycle of a specified condition or set of events: *the wheel of life.* ■ **(the wheel)** hist. a large wheel used as an instrument of punishment or torture, esp. by binding someone to it and breaking their limbs: *sentenced to be broken on the wheel.* **2** a machine or structure having a wheel as its essential part. ■ **(the wheel)** a steering wheel (used in reference to driving or steering a vehicle or vessel). ■ a vessel's propeller or paddle-wheel. ■ a device with a revolving disk or drum used in various games of chance. ■ a system, or a part of a system, regarded as a relentlessly moving machine: *the wheels of justice.* **3 (wheels)** informal a car. ■ a bicycle. **4** a thing resembling a wheel in form or function, in particular a cheese made in the form of a shallow disk. **5** an instance of wheeling; a turn or rotation. ▶ **v. 1** [trans.] push or pull (a vehicle with wheels): *the sea sled was **wheeled out** to the flight deck.* ■ [with obj. and adverbial of direction] carry (someone or something) in or on a vehicle with wheels: *she was wheeled into the operating room.* ■ **(wheel something in/on/out)** informal produce something that is unimpressive because it has been frequently seen or heard before: *old arguments have to be wheeled out.* **2** [intrans.] (of a bird or aircraft) fly in a wide circle or curve. ■ turn around quickly so as to face another way: *Robert **wheeled around**.* ■ turn or seem to turn on an axis or pivot: *the stars wheeled through the sky.*
– PHRASES **on wheels 1** by, or traveling by, car or bicycle. ■ (of a service) brought to one's home or district; mobile. **2** informal used to emphasize one's distaste or dislike of the person or thing mentioned: *she was a bitch on wheels.* **wheel and deal** engage in commercial or political scheming, esp. unscrupulously. **the wheel of Fortune** the wheel that the deity Fortune is fabled to turn as a symbol of random luck or change. **wheels within wheels** used to indicate that a situation is complicated and affected by secret or indirect influences. — **wheeled adj.** [in comb.] *a four-wheeled cart.* **wheel·less adj.** [OE *hwēol* (n.), of Gmc. origin, from an Indo-Eur. root shared by Sanskrit *cakra* 'wheel, circle' and Gk. *kuklos* 'circle.']

wheel and ax·le ▶ **n.** a simple lifting machine consisting of a rope that unwinds from a wheel onto a cylindrical drum or shaft joined to the wheel to provide mechanical advantage.

wheel arch ▶ **n.** an arch-shaped cavity in the body of a vehicle, which houses a wheel.

wheel·bar·row /'(h)wēl,barō/ ▶ **n.** a small cart with a single wheel at the front and two supporting legs and two handles at the rear, used typically for carrying loads in building work or gardening. ▶ **v.** [trans.] carry (a load) in a wheelbarrow.

wheelbarrow

wheel·base /'(h)wēl,bās/ ▶ **n.** the distance between the front and rear axles of a vehicle.

wheel·chair /'(h)wēl,CHe(ə)r/ ▶ **n.** a chair built on wheels for an invalid or disabled person, either pushed by another person or propelled by the occupant.

wheel dog ▶ **n.** the dog harnessed nearest to the sleigh in a dog team.

Whee·ler /'(h)wēlər/, John Archibald (1911–), US physicist. He coined the term **black hole** in 1968.

wheel·er /'(h)wēlər/ ▶ **n. 1** [in comb.] a vehicle having a specified number of wheels: *a huge eighteen-wheeler truck.* **2** a wheelwright. **3** a horse harnessed next to the wheels of a cart and behind a leading horse.

wheel·er-deal·er (also **wheel·er and deal·er**) ▶ **n.** a person who engages in commercial or political scheming. — **wheel·er-deal·ing n.**

Whee·ler Peak /'(h)wēlər/ a peak in the Sangre de Cristo Mountains in New Mexico.

wheel horse ▶ **n.** a horse harnessed nearest the wheels of a vehicle.

■ fig. a responsible and hardworking person, esp. an experienced and conscientious member of a political party.

wheel·house /'(h)wēl,hous/ ▶ **n.** a part of a boat or ship serving as a shelter for the person at the wheel.

wheel·ie /'(h)wēlē/ ▶ **n.** informal a trick or maneuver whereby a bicycle or motorcycle is ridden for a short distance with the front wheel raised off the ground.

Whee·ling /'(h)wēliNG/ a city in northern West Virginia, on the Ohio River; pop. 31,419.

wheel·man /'(h)wēl,mən/ ▶ **n.** (pl. **-men**) a person who drives a car or takes the wheel of a boat. ■ a cyclist.

wheels·man /'(h)wēlzmən/ ▶ **n.** (pl. **-men**) a person who steers a ship or boat.

wheel·spin /'(h)wēl,spin/ ▶ **n.** rotation of a vehicle's wheels without traction.

wheel well ▶ **n.** a recess in a vehicle in which a wheel is located.

wheel·wright /'(h)wēl,rīt/ ▶ **n.** esp. hist. a person who makes or repairs wooden wheels.

wheeze /(h)wēz/ ▶ **v.** [intrans.] (of a person) breathe with a whistling or rattling sound in the chest, as a result of obstruction in the air passages. ■ [trans.] utter with such a sound: *he could barely wheeze out his pleas.* ■ [no obj., with adverbial of direction] walk or move slowly with such a sound: *she wheezed up the hill.* ■ (of a device) make an irregular rattling or spluttering sound: *the engine wheezed.* ▶ **n.** [usu. in sing.] **1** a sound of or as of a person wheezing. **2** an old joke, story, aphorism, act, or routine. — **wheez·er n. wheez·ing·ly adv.** [ME: prob. from ON *hvæsa* 'to hiss.']

wheez·y /'(h)wēzē/ ▶ **adj.** making the sound of a person wheezing. — **wheez·i·ly** /-əlē/ **adv. wheez·i·ness n.**

whelk[1] /(h)welk/ ▶ **n.** a predatory marine mollusk (family Buccinidae) with a heavy, pointed spiral shell, some kinds of which are edible. [OE *wioloc, weoloc*, of unknown origin.]

whelk[1]

whelk[2] ▶ **n.** archaic a pimple. [OE *hwylca*, rel. to *hwelian* 'suppurate.']

whelm /(h)welm/ archaic literary ▶ **v.** [trans.] engulf, submerge, or bury (someone or something): *a swimmer whelmed in a raging storm.* ■ [no obj., with adverbial of direction] flow or heap up abundantly. ▶ **n.** an act or instance of flowing or heaping up abundantly; a surge. [ME: representing an OE form parallel to *hwelfan* 'overturn (a vessel).']

whelp /(h)welp/ ▶ **n.** a puppy. ■ a cub. ■ a boy or young man (often as a disparaging form of address). ■ (**whelps**) a set of projections on the barrel of a capstan or windlass, designed to reduce the slippage of a rope. ▶ **v.** [trans.] (of a female dog) give birth to (a puppy).
– PHRASES **in whelp** (of a female dog) pregnant. [OE *hwelp* (n.), of Gmc. origin; rel. to Du. *welp* and Ger. *Welf*.]

when /(h)wen/ ▶ **interrog. adv.** at what time: *when did you last see him?* ■ how soon: *when can I see you?* ■ in what circumstances: *when would such a rule be justifiable?* ▶ **rel. adv.** at or on which (referring to a time or circumstance): *the day when I get my hair done.* ▶ **conj. 1** at or during the time that: *when I was in school.* ■ after: *call me when you're finished.* ■ at any time that; whenever: *can you spare five minutes when it's convenient?* **2** after which; and just then (implying suddenness): *he had just gone to sleep when the phone rang.* **3** in view of the fact that; considering that: *why bother to paint it when you can photograph it?* **4** although; whereas: *I'm saying it now when I should have told you long ago.* [OE *hwanne, hwenne*, of Gmc. origin; rel. to Ger. *wenn* 'if,' *wann* 'when.']

whence /(h)wens/ (also **from whence**) formal or archaic ▶ **interrog. adv.** from what place or source. ▶ **rel. adv.** from which; from where. ■ to the place from which: *he will be sent back whence he came.* ■ as a consequence of which: *whence it followed that the strategies were obsolete.* [ME *whennes*, from earlier *whenne* (from OE *hwanon*, of Gmc. origin) + *-s*[3] (later respelled *-ce* to denote the unvoiced sound).]

whence·so·ev·er /,(h)wensō'evər/ ▶ **rel. adv.** formal or archaic from whatever place or source.

when·e'er /,(h)wen'e(ə)r/ literary ▶ **contr.** whenever.

when·ev·er /,(h)wen'evər/ ▶ **conj.** at whatever time; on whatever occasion (emphasizing a lack of restriction): *ask for help whenever you need it.* ■ every time that: *the springs creak whenever I change position.* ▶ **interrog. adv.** used for emphasis instead of "when" in questions, typically expressing surprise or confusion: *whenever shall we get there?*
– PHRASES **or whenever** informal or at any time: *tonight or tomorrow or whenever.*

when-is·sued ▶ **adj.** Finance of or relating to trading in securities that have not yet been issued.

when·so·e'er /,(h)wensō'e(ə)r/ literary ▶ **contr.** whensoever.

when·so·ev·er /,(h)wensō'evər/ ▶ **conj. & adv.** formal term for WHENEVER.

where /(h)we(ə)r/ ▶ **interrog. adv.** in or to what place or position: *where do you live?* ■ in what direction or respect: *where does the argument lead?* ■ in or from what source: *where did you read that?* ■ in or to what situation or condition: *where is all this leading us?* ▶ **rel. adv. 1** at, in, or to which (used after reference to a place or situation): *Paris, where I lived in the early sixties.* **2** the place or situation in which: *this is where I live.* ■ in or to a place or situation in which: *sit where I can see you.* ■ in or to any place in which; wherever: *go where you like.* ▶ **conj.** informal **1** that: *I see where the hotel has changed hands again.* **2** whereas: *where some care-givers burn out, others become too involved.* ▶ **n.** [(prec. by the)] the place; the scene of something. [OE *hwǣr*, of Gmc. origin; rel. to Du. *waar* and Ger. *wo*.]

where·a·bouts ▶ **interrog. adv.** /'(h)we(ə)rə,bouts/ where or approximately where: *whereabouts do you come from?* ▶ **n.** [treated as sing. or pl.] the place where someone or something is: *his whereabouts remain secret.*

where·af·ter /,(h)we(ə)r'aftər/ ▶ **rel. adv.** formal after which: *dinner was delicious, whereafter we sipped liqueurs by the fire.*

where·as /,(h)we(ə)r'az/ ▶ **conj.** in contrast or comparison with the fact that. ■ (esp. in legal preambles) taking into consideration the fact that.

where·at /,(h)we(ə)r'at/ ▶ **rel. adv. & conj.** archaic or formal at which: *they made new demands, whereat negotiations broke down.*

where·by /,(h)we(ə)r'bī/ ▶ **rel. adv.** by which.

wher·e'er /,(h)we(ə)r'e(ə)r/ literary ▶ **contr.** wherever.

where·fore /'(h)we(ə)r,fôr/ archaic ▶ **interrog. adv.** for what reason: *she took an ill turn, but wherefore I cannot say.* ▶ **rel. adv. & conj.** as a result of which: [as conj.] *truly he cared for me, wherefore I title him with all respect.*
– PHRASES **whys and wherefores** see WHY.

where·from /,(h)we(ə)r'frəm/ ▶ **rel. adv.** archaic from which or from where: *one day you may lose this pride of place wherefrom you now dominate.*

where·in /,(h)we(ə)r'in/ formal ▶ **adv. 1** [relative adv.] in which. **2** [interrog. adv.] in what place or respect?: *so wherein lies the difference?*

where·of /,(h)we'räv; -'əv/ ▶ **rel. adv.** formal of what or which: *I know whereof I speak.*

where·on /,(h)we(ə)r'än; -'ôn/ ▶ **rel. adv.** archaic on which.

where·so·e'er /,(h)we(ə)rsō'e(ə)r/ literary ▶ **contr.** wheresoever.

where·so·ev·er /,(h)we(ə)rsō'evər/ ▶ **adv. & conj.** formal word for WHEREVER.

where·to /,(h)we(ə)r'tōō/ ▶ **rel. adv.** archaic formal to which: *young ambition's ladder, whereto the climber-upward turns his face.*

where·up·on /,(h)we(ə)rə'pän/ ▶ **conj.** immediately after which: *he qualified in February, whereupon he was promoted.*

wher·ev·er /,(h)we(ə)r'evər/ ▶ **rel. adv.** in or to whatever place (emphasizing a lack of restriction): *meet me wherever you like.* ■ in all places; regardless of where: *wherever you go to shop.* ▶ **interrog. adv.** used for emphasis instead of "where" in questions, typically expressing surprise or confusion: *wherever can he have gone to?* ▶ **conj.** in every case when: *use whole grain cereals wherever possible.*
– PHRASES **or wherever** informal or any similar place.

where·with /,(h)we(ə)r'wiTH; -'wiTH/ ▶ **rel. adv.** formal or archaic with or by which: *the instrumental means wherewith the action is performed.*

where·with·al /'(h)we(ə)rwiTH,ôl; -wiTH-/ ▶ **n.** [usu. with infin.] (**the wherewithal**) the money or other means needed for a particular purpose.

wher·ry /'(h)werē/ ▶ **n.** (pl. **-ries**) a light rowboat used chiefly for carrying passengers. — **wher·ry·man** /'(h)werēmən/ **n.** (pl. **-men**). [ME: of unknown origin.]

whet /(h)wet/ ▶ **v.** (**whet·ted, whet·ting**) [trans.] sharpen the blade of (a tool or weapon). ■ excite or stimulate (someone's desire, interest, or appetite). — **whet·ter n.** (rare). [OE *hwettan*, of Gmc. origin; rel. to Ger. *wetzen*, based on an adj. meaning 'sharp.']

wheth·er /'(h)weTHər/ ▶ **conj.** expressing a doubt or choice between alternatives: *he seemed undecided* **whether** *to go* **or** *stay.* ■ expressing an inquiry or investigation (often used in indirect questions): *I'll see whether she's at home.* ■ indicating that a statement applies whichever of the alternatives mentioned is the case: ***whether** you like it **or not**.*
– PHRASES **whether or no** whether or not. [OE *hwæther, hwether*, of Gmc. origin; rel. to Ger. *weder* 'neither.']

whet·stone /'(h)wet,stōn/ ▶ **n.** a fine-grained stone used for sharpening cutting tools.

whew /hyōō; hwyōō/ ▶ **exclam.** used to express surprise, relief, or a feeling of being very hot or tired. [ME: imitative.]

whey /(h)wā/ ▶ **n.** the watery part of milk that remains after the formation of curds. [OE *hwæg, hweg*, of Gmc. origin; rel. to Du. *wei*.]

whey-faced ▶ **adj.** (of a person) pale, esp. as a result of ill health, shock, or fear.

which /(h)wiCH/ ▶ **interrog. pron. & adj.** asking for information specifying one or more people or things from a definite set: [as pron.] *which are the best varieties of grapes?* | ***which** of the suspects escaped?* | [as adj.] *which way is south?* ▶ **rel. pron. & adj.** used referring to something previously mentioned when introducing a clause giving further information: [as pron.] *a conference in Vienna, which ended on Friday* | [after prep.] *it was a crisis for which he was totally unprepared.*
– PHRASES **which is which** used when two or more people or things are difficult to distinguish from each other. [OE *hwilc*, from the Gmc. bases of WHO and ALIKE.]

which·a·way /'(h)wiCHə,wā/ informal, dialect ▶ **interrog. adv. 1** in which direction? **2** how? in which way? ▶ **rel. adv.** however; in whatever way.
– PHRASES **every whichaway** in a disorderly fashion: *books are skewed and lounge against one another every whichaway.*

which·ev·er /,(h)wiCH'evər/ ▶ **rel. adj. & pron.** used to emphasize a lack of restriction in selecting one of a definite set of alternatives: [as adj.] *whichever brand you prefer* | [as pron.] *earnings or prices, whichever is the higher.* ■ regardless of which: [as adj.] *they could intercept him whichever way he ran* | [as pron.] *whichever they choose, we must accept it.*

which·so·ev·er /ˌ(h)wichsōˈevər/ ▶ **adj. & pron.** archaic whichever.

whick·er /ˈ(h)wikər/ ▶ **v.** [intrans.] **1** utter a half-suppressed laugh; snigger; titter: *she whickered her amusement.* ■ (of a horse) give a soft breathy whinny: *the palomino whickered when she saw him.* **2** move with a sound as of something hurtling through or beating the air: *the soft whicker of the wind.* ▶ **n.** **1** a snigger; a soft, breathy whinny. **2** the sound of something beating the air. [17th C. (in the sense 'to snigger, titter'): imitative.]

whid·ah ▶ **n.** archaic spelling of WHYDAH.

Whid·bey Is·land /ˈ(h)widbē/ an island in northwestern Washington, north of Puget Sound.

whiff /(h)wif/ ▶ **n.** **1** a smell that is only smelled briefly or faintly: *I caught a whiff of perfume.* ■ [in sing.] an act of sniffing or inhaling, typically so as to determine or savor a scent: *one whiff of clothing.* ■ [in sing.] a trace or hint of something bad, menacing, or exciting. **2** a puff or breath of air or smoke. **3** informal (chiefly in baseball or golf) an unsuccessful attempt to hit the ball. ▶ **v.** **1** [trans.] get a brief or faint smell of: *he whiffed Limburger.* **2** [intrans.] informal (chiefly in baseball or golf) try unsuccessfully to hit the ball. [16th C. (orig. in the senses 'gust of wind' and 'inhalation of tobacco smoke,' also, as a v., 'blow with a slight gust'): imitative.]

whif·fle /ˈ(h)wifəl/ ▶ **v.** [no obj., with adverbial of direction] (of the wind) blow lightly in a specified direction: *air began whiffling down off Bald Peak.* ■ move lightly as if blown by a puff of air: *geese came whiffling down onto the grass.* ■ [trans.] blow or move (something) with or as if with a puff of air: *the mouse whiffled its whiskers.* ▶ **n.** **1** a slight movement of air or the sound of such a movement. **2** (also **whif·fle cut**) informal a very short haircut worn by US soldiers in World War II. [16th C.: frequentative (v.), dimin. (n.) of WHIFF.]

whif·fle·tree /ˈ(h)wifəlˌtrē/ ▶ **n.** a singletree. [19th C.: var. of WHIPPLETREE.]

Whig /(h)wig/ hist. ▶ **n.** **1** a member of the British reforming and constitutional party that sought the supremacy of Parliament and was eventually succeeded in the 19th century by the Liberal Party. **2** an American colonist who supported the American Revolution. ■ a member of an American political party in the 19th century, succeeded by the Republicans. **3** a 17th-century Scottish Presbyterian. **4** [as adj.] denoting a historian who interprets history as the continuing and inevitable victory of progress over reaction. — **Whig·ger·y** /ˈ(h)wigərē/ **n.** **Whig·gish adj.** **Whig·gism** /ˈ(h)wigˌizəm/ **n.** [prob. a shortening of Scots *whiggamore*, the nickname of 17th-cent. Scot. rebels, from *whig* 'to drive' + MARE[1].]

while /(h)wīl/ ▶ **n.** **1** a period of time: *we chatted for a while.* ■ **(a while)** for some time: *can I keep it a while?* **2** **(the while)** at the same time; meanwhile: *he walked on, talking the while.* ■ literary during the time that: *beseeching him, the while his hand she wrung.* ▶ **conj.** **1** during the time that; at the same time as: *while he was away.* **2** whereas (indicating a contrast): *one wants out, while the other wants to continue.* ■ in spite of the fact that; although: *while I wouldn't recommend a nighttime visit, by day the area is full of interest.* ▶ **rel. adv.** during which: *the period while the animal remains alive.* ▶ **v.** [trans.] (often **while away the time**) pass time in a leisurely manner: *while away the long afternoons.*
– PHRASES **between whiles** archaic at intervals: *add salt, shaking vigorously between whiles.* **worth one's while** worth the time or effort spent. [OE *hwīl* 'period of time,' of Gmc. origin; rel. to Du. *wijl*, Ger. *Weile*; the conjunction is an abbrev. of OE *thā hwīle the* 'the while that.']

whiles /(h)wīlz/ ▶ **conj.** archaic form of WHILE. [ME: orig. in adverbs such as *somewhiles* 'formerly,' *otherwhiles* 'at times.']

while-you-wait ▶ **adj.** [attrib.] (of a service) performed immediately.

whi·lom /ˈ(h)wīləm/ archaic ▶ **adv.** formerly; in the past: *the wistful eyes which whilom glanced down upon the fields.* ▶ **adj.** former; erstwhile. [OE *hwīlum* 'at times,' dative pl. of *hwīl* (see WHILE).]

whilst /(h)wīlst/ ▶ **conj. & rel. adv.** esp. Brit. while. [ME: from WHILES + *-t* as in AGAINST.]

whim /(h)wim/ ▶ **n.** **1** a sudden desire or change of mind, esp. one that is unusual or unexplained. **2** archaic a windlass for raising ore or water from a mine. [17th C.: of unknown origin. Sense 2 (mid 18th C.) is a transferred use.]

whim·brel /ˈ(h)wimbrəl/ ▶ **n.** a small migratory curlew (*Numenius phaeopus*) of northern Eurasia and northern Canada, with a striped crown and a trilling call. [16th C.: from WHIMPER or synonymous dial. *whimp* (imitative of the bird's call) + -REL.]

whim·per /ˈ(h)wimpər/ ▶ **v.** [intrans.] (of a person or animal) make a series of low, feeble sounds expressive of fear, pain, or discontent. ■ [with direct speech] say something in a low, feeble voice expressive of such emotions: *"He's not dead, is he?" she whimpered.* ▶ **n.** a low, feeble sound expressive of such emotions. ■ **(a whimper)** a feeble or anticlimactic tone or ending: *ended with a whimper rather than a bang.* [with allusion to T. S. Eliot's "This is the way the world ends Not with a bang but a whimper" (*Hollow Men*, 1925).] — **whim·per·er n.** **whim·per·ing·ly adv.** [16th C.: from dial. *whimp* 'to whimper,' of imitative origin.]

whim·si·cal /ˈ(h)wimzikəl/ ▶ **adj.** **1** playfully quaint or fanciful, esp. in an appealing and amusing way. **2** acting or behaving in a capricious manner. — **whim·si·cal·i·ty** /ˌ(h)wimziˈkalitē/ **n.** **whim·si·cal·ly** /-zik(ə)lē/ **adv.**

whim·sy /ˈ(h)wimzē/ (also **whim·sey**) ▶ **n.** (pl. **-sies** or **-seys**) playfully quaint or fanciful behavior or humor. ■ a whim. ■ a thing that is fanciful or odd. [17th C.: prob. based on WHIM-WHAM.]

whim-wham ▶ **n.** archaic a quaint and decorative object; a trinket. ■ a whim. [16th C.: fanciful reduplication.]

whin·chat /ˈwinˌchat/ ▶ **n.** a small Eurasian and North African chat (*Saxicola rubetra*), with a brown back and orange-buff underparts. [17th C.]

whine /(h)wīn/ ▶ **n.** a long, high-pitched complaining cry. ■ a long, high-pitched unpleasant sound. ■ a complaining tone of voice. ■ a feeble or petulant complaint. ▶ **v.** [intrans.] give or make a long, high-pitched complaining cry or sound. ■ [reporting verb] complain in a feeble or petulant way. — **whin·er n.** **whin·ing·ly adv.** **whin·y adj.** [OE *hwīnan* 'whistle through the air.' The n. dates from the mid 17th C.]

whinge /(h)winj/ Brit. informal ▶ **v.** (**whinge·ing**) [intrans.] complain persistently and in a peevish or irritating way. ▶ **n.** an act of complaining in such a way. — **whinge·ing·ly adv.** **whing·er n.** **whing·y** /ˈ(h)winjē/ **adj.** [OE *hwinsian*, of Gmc. origin; rel. to Ger. *winseln*.]

whin·ny /ˈ(h)winē/ ▶ **n.** (pl. **-nies**) a gentle, high-pitched neigh. ▶ **v.** (**-nies, -nied**) [intrans.] (of a horse) make such a sound. [ME: imitative.]

whip /(h)wip/ ▶ **n.** **1** a strip of leather or length of cord fastened to a handle, used for flogging or beating a person or for urging on an animal. ■ fig. a thing causing mental or physical pain or acting as a stimulus to action. **2** a thing or person resembling a whip in form or function: *a licorice whip.* ■ a utensil such as a whisk or an eggbeater for beating cream, eggs, or other food. ■ a slender, unbranched shoot or plant. ■ short for WHIPPER-IN. ■ [with adj.] a scythe for cutting specified crops. ■ a rope-and-pulley hoisting apparatus. **3** an official of a political party appointed to maintain discipline among its members in Congress or Parliament, esp. so as to ensure attendance and voting in debates. ■ **(the whip)** Brit. party membership of a Member of Parliament or other elected body. **4** a dessert consisting of cream or eggs beaten into a light fluffy mass with fruit, chocolate, or other ingredients. **5** [in sing.] a violent striking or beating movement. ■ [in sing.] in metaphorical use referring to something that acts as a stimulus to work or action: *the governor cracked the whip.* ▶ **v.** (**whipped, whip·ping**) [trans.] **1** beat (a person or animal) with a whip or similar instrument, esp. as a punishment or to urge them on. ■ (of a flexible object or rain or wind) strike or beat violently. ■ beat (cream, eggs, or other food) into a froth. ■ **(whip someone into)** urge or rouse someone into (a specified state or position): *whipped them into a frenzy.* ■ informal (of a player or team) defeat (a person or team) heavily in a sporting contest. **2** [no obj., with adverbial of direction] move fast or suddenly in a specified direction: *I whipped around the corner.* ■ [with obj. and adverbial of direction] take out or move (something) fast or suddenly: *he whipped out his revolver.* **3** bind (something) with spirally wound twine. ■ sew or gather (something) with overcast stitches.
– PHRASES **the whip hand** a position of power or control over someone.
– PHRASAL VERBS **whip in** act as whipper-in. **whip something out** (or **off**) write something hurriedly. **whip someone up** deliberately excite someone into having a strong feeling or reaction. **whip something up** **1** cause water, sand, etc., to rise up and be flung about in a violent manner: *the sea was whipped up.* ■ stimulate a particular feeling in someone. **2** make or prepare something, typically something to eat, very quickly. — **whip·like** /-ˌlīk/ **adj.** **whip·per n.** [ME: prob. from Mid. Low Ger. and MDu. *wippen* 'swing, leap, dance,' from a Gmc. base meaning 'move quickly.']

whip·cord /ˈ(h)wipˌkôrd/ ▶ **n.** **1** thin, tough, tightly twisted cord used for making the flexible end part of whips. **2** a closely woven ribbed worsted fabric, used for making garments such as jodhpurs.

whip·lash /ˈ(h)wipˌlash/ ▶ **n.** **1** [usu. in sing.] the lashing action of a whip: fig. *he cringed before the icy whiplash of Curtis's tongue.* ■ the flexible part of a whip or something resembling it. **2** injury caused by a severe jerk to the head, typically in a motor accident. ▶ **v.** [trans.] jerk or jolt (someone or something) suddenly, typically so as to cause injury. ■ [no obj., with adverbial of direction] move suddenly and forcefully, like a whip being cracked.

whip pan ▶ **n.** a camera panning movement fast enough to give a blurred picture. ▶ **v.** (**whip-pan**) [intrans.] pan quickly to give a blurred picture.

whipped /(h)wipt/ ▶ **adj.** **1** [attrib.] having been flogged or beaten with a whip. ■ [predic.] informal worn out; exhausted. **2** (of cream, eggs, or other food) beaten into a froth.

whip·per-in ▶ **n.** (pl. **whip·pers-in**) a huntsman's assistant who brings straying hounds back into the pack.

whip·per·snap·per /ˈ(h)wipərˌsnapər/ ▶ **n.** informal a young and inexperienced person considered to be presumptuous or overconfident. [17th C.: perh. representing *whipsnapper*, expressing noise and unimportance.]

whip·pet /ˈ(h)wipit/ ▶ **n.** a dog of a small slender breed originally produced as a cross between the greyhound and the terrier or spaniel, bred for racing. [17th C.: partly from obs. *whippet* 'move briskly.']

whip·ping /ˈ(h)wiping/ ▶ **n.** **1** a thrashing or beating with a whip or similar implement. **2** cord or twine used to bind or cover a rope.

whip·ping boy ▶ **n.** a person who is blamed or punished for the faults or incompetence of others. [extended use of the original term (17th C.) denoting a boy educated with a young prince or other royal person and punished instead of him.]

whip·ping cream ▶ **n.** fairly thick cream containing enough butterfat to make it suitable for whipping.

whip·ping post ▶ n. hist. a post to which offenders were tied in order to be whipped as a public punishment.

whip·pit /'(h)wipit/ ▶ n. a small container of nitrous oxide intended for home use in whipped cream charging bottles but often used as an inhalant.

whip·ple·tree /'(h)wipəl,trē/ ▶ n. archaic term for SINGLETREE. [18th C.: appar. from WHIP + TREE.]

whip·poor·will /'(h)wipər,wil/ (also **whip-poor-will**) ▶ n. a North and Central American nightjar (*Caprimulgus vociferus*) with a distinctive call. [18th C.: imitative of its call.]

whip·py /'(h)wipē/ ▶ adj. flexible; springy. — **whip·pi·ness** n.

whip·saw /'(h)wip,sô/ ▶ n. a saw with a narrow blade and a handle at both ends, used typically by two people. ▶ v. (past part. **-sawn** or **-sawed**) [trans.] cut with a whipsaw. ■ informal subject to two difficult situations or opposing pressures at the same time: *the army has been whipsawed by a shrinking budget and a growing pool of recruits.* ■ informal compel to do something. ■ (usu. **be whipsawed**) Stock Market, informal subject to a double loss, as when buying a security before the price falls and selling before the price rises. ■ cheat or beat (someone) in two ways at once or by the collusion of two others.

whip scor·pi·on ▶ n. an arachnid (order Uropygi) that resembles a scorpion, with stout pincerlike mouthparts and a long, slender taillike appendage, living in leaf litter and under stones in tropical and semi-tropical regions.

whip snake ▶ n. any of a number of slender, fast-moving snakes that often feed on lizards and catch their prey by pursuing it, in particular: ■ a harmless snake (*Coluber* and other genera, family Colubridae) found in Eurasia, America, and Africa. ■ a venomous Australian snake (*Desmansia* and other genera, family Elapidae.

whip·stitch /'(h)wip,stich/ ▶ n. an overcast stitch. ▶ v. [trans.] sew (something) with such stitches.

whip·stock /'(h)wip,stäk/ ▶ n. the handle of a whip.

whip·tail /'(h)wip,tāl/ (also **whip·tail liz·ard**) ▶ n. a slender long-tailed American lizard (genus *Cnemidophorus*, family Teiidae) with an alert manner and a jerky gait.

whip·worm /'(h)wip,wərm/ ▶ n. a parasitic nematode (genus *Trichuris*, class Aphasmida) with a stout posterior and slender anterior part, esp. one that infests the intestines of domestic animals.

whir /(h)wər/ (also **whirr**) ▶ v. (**whirred**, **whir·ring**) [intrans.] (esp. of a machine or a bird's wings) make a low, continuous, regular sound. ▶ n. a sound of such a type: *the whir of the projector.* [ME (in the sense 'move with a whirring sound'): prob. of Scand. origin.]

whirl /(h)wərl/ ▶ v. move or cause to move rapidly around and around. ■ move or cause to move rapidly. ■ [intrans.] (of the head, mind, or senses) seem to spin around: *her mind whirled with the choices.* ■ [no obj., with adverbial of direction] (of thoughts or mental images) follow each other in bewildering succession: *a kaleidoscope of images whirled through her brain.* ▶ n. [in sing.] a rapid movement around and around. ■ frantic activity of a specified kind: *the mad social whirl.* ■ [with adj.] a specified kind of candy or cookie with a spiral shape: *a hazelnut whirl.*

– PHRASES **give something a whirl** informal give something a try. **in a whirl** in a state of confusion. — **whirl·er** n. **whirl·ing·ly** adv. [ME: the v. prob. from Old Norse *hvirfla* 'turn around'; the n. partly from Mid. Low Ger., MDu. *wervel* 'spindle,' or from ON *hvirfill* 'circle,' from a Gmc. base meaning 'rotate.']

whirl·i·gig /'(h)wərlē,gig/ ▶ n. **1** a toy that spins around, for example a top or windmill. ■ another term for MERRY-GO-ROUND. **2** [in sing.] a thing regarded as hectic or constantly changing. **3** (also **whirl·i·gig bee·tle**) a small black predatory beetle (*Gyrinus* and other genera, family Gyrinidae) that swims rapidly in circles on the surface of still or slow-moving water and dives when alarmed. [ME: from WHIRL + obs. *gig* 'a top.']

whirl·ing der·vish ▶ n. see DERVISH.

whirl·ing dis·ease ▶ n. a disease of juvenile trout and salmon caused by a parasitic protozoan (*Myxobolus cerebralis*), affecting the balance of the fish and causing it to swim with a whirling motion.

whirl·pool /'(h)wərl,po͞ol/ ▶ n. a rapidly rotating mass of water in a river or sea into which objects may be drawn, typically caused by the meeting of conflicting currents. ■ fig. a turbulent situation from which it is hard to escape. ■ (also **whirl·pool bath**) a heated pool in which hot, typically aerated water is continuously circulated.

whirl·wind /'(h)wərl,wind/ ▶ n. a column of air moving rapidly around and around in a cylindrical or funnel shape. ■ used in similes and metaphors to describe a very energetic or tumultuous person or process: [as adj.] *a whirlwind romance.*

– PHRASES **(sow the wind and) reap the whirlwind** suffer serious consequences as a result of one's actions. [with biblical allusion to Hos. 8:7.]

whirl·y·bird /'(h)wərlē,bərd/ ▶ n. informal a helicopter.

whirr ▶ n. & v. var. of WHIR.

whisht /(h)wisht/ (also **whist**) ▶ exclam. esp. Scot. & Irish hush (used to demand silence): *"Whisht, child. Away and do what you're told."* [natural exclamation: first recorded in English in the mid 16th C.]

whisk /(h)wisk/ ▶ v. **1** [with obj. and adverbial of direction] take or move (someone or something) in a particular direction suddenly and quickly. ■ move (something) through the air with a light, sweeping movement. **2** [trans.] beat or stir (a substance, esp. cream or eggs) with a light, rapid movement. **3** brush with a whisk broom. ▶ n. **1** a utensil for whipping eggs or cream. **2** short for WHISK BROOM. **3** (also **fly whisk**) a bunch of grass, twigs, or bristles for removing dust or flies. **4** [in sing.] a brief, rapid action or movement. [ME: of Scand. origin.]

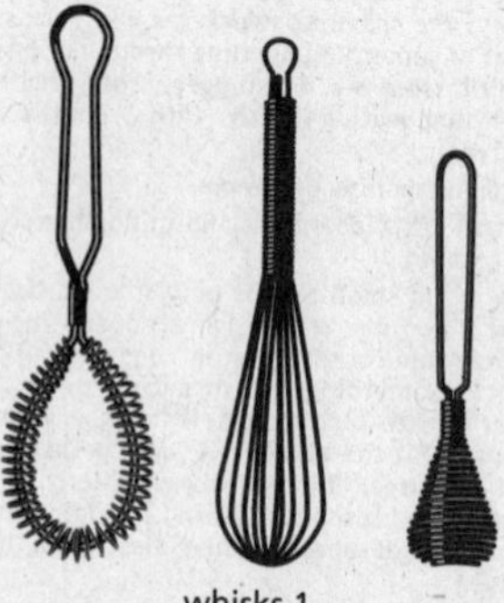

whisks 1

whisk broom ▶ n. a small, stiff, short-handled broom used esp. to brush clothing.

whisk·er /'(h)wiskər/ ▶ n. **1** a long projecting hair or bristle growing from the face or snout of many mammals. ■ (**whiskers**) the hair growing on a man's face, esp. on his cheeks. ■ a single crystal of a material in the form of a filament with no dislocations. **2** (a **whisker**) informal a very small amount: *they won by a whisker.* **3** a spar for extending the clews of a sail so that it can catch more wind.

– PHRASES **within a whisker of** informal extremely close or near to doing, achieving, or suffering something. — **whiskered** adj. **whiskery** adj. [ME (orig. denoting a bundle of feathers, twigs, etc., used for whisking): from the v. WHISK + -ER[1].]

whis·key /'(h)wiskē/ ▶ n. (pl. **-keys**) **1** (also **whis·ky** (pl. **-kies**)) a spirit distilled from malted grain, esp. barley or rye. **2** a code word representing the letter W, used in radio communication. [18th C.: abbrev. of obs. *whiskybae*, var. of USQUEBAUGH.]

whis·key jack ▶ n. informal another term for GRAY JAY.

whis·per /'(h)wispər/ ▶ v. [intrans.] speak very softly using one's breath rather than one's throat, esp. for the sake of secrecy. ■ literary (of leaves, wind, or water) rustle or murmur softly. ■ (**be whispered**) be rumored. ▶ n. a soft or confidential tone of voice; a whispered word or phrase. ■ literary a soft rustling or murmuring sound. ■ a rumor or piece of gossip. ■ [usu. in sing.] a slight trace; a hint. — **whis·per·er** n. **whis·per·y** adj. [OE *hwisprian*, of Gmc. origin; rel. to Ger. *wispeln*, from the imitative base of WHISTLE.]

whis·per·ing gal·ler·y ▶ n. a gallery or dome with acoustic properties such that a faint sound may be heard around its entire circumference.

whist[1] /(h)wist/ ▶ n. a card game, usually for two pairs of players, in which points are scored according to the number of tricks won. [17th C. (earlier as *whisk*): perhaps from WHISK (with ref. to whisking away the tricks); perh. associated with WHIST[2].]

whist[2] ▶ exclam. var. of WHISHT.

whis·tle /'(h)wisəl/ ▶ n. a clear, high-pitched sound made by forcing breath through a small hole between partly closed lips, or between one's teeth. ■ a similar sound, esp. one made by a bird, machine, or the wind. ■ an instrument used to produce such a sound, esp. for giving a signal. ▶ v. **1** [intrans.] emit a clear, high-pitched sound by forcing breath through a small hole between one's lips or teeth. ■ express surprise, admiration, or derision by making such a sound. ■ [trans.] produce (a tune) in such a way. ■ (esp. of a bird or machine) produce a similar sound. ■ [no obj., with adverbial] produce such a sound by moving rapidly through the air or a narrow opening: *the wind was whistling down the chimney.* ■ blow an instrument that makes such a sound, esp. as a signal. ■ [trans.] (**whistle someone/something up**) summon something or someone by making such a sound. **2** (**whistle for**) wish for or expect (something) in vain.

– PHRASES **blow the whistle on** informal bring an illicit activity to an end by informing on the person responsible. **(as) clean as a whistle** extremely clean or clear. ■ informal free of incriminating evidence. **whistle something down the wind** let something go; abandon something. ■ turn a trained hawk loose by casting it off with the wind. **whistle in the dark** pretend to be unafraid. **whistle in the wind** try unsuccessfully to influence something that cannot be changed. [OE *(h)wistlian* (v.), *(h)wistle* (n.), of Gmc. origin; imitative and rel. to Swed. *vissla* 'to whistle.']

whis·tle-blow·er (also **whis·tle·blow·er**) ▶ n. a person who informs on someone engaged in an illicit activity. — **whis·tle-blow·ing** n.

Whis·tler /'(h)wis(ə)lər/, James Abbott McNeill (1834–1903), US painter. His works include *Arrangement in Gray and Black: The Artist's Mother* (known as *Whistler's Mother*, 1872).

whis·tler /'(h)wis(ə)lər/ ▶ n. **1** a person who whistles. ■ an atmospheric radio disturbance heard as a whistle that falls in pitch, caused by lightning. **2** a robust Australasian and Indonesian songbird (*Pachycephala* and other genera, family Pachycephalidae) with a strong and typically hooked bill and a loud melodious call. **3** another term for HOARY MARMOT.

whis·tle-stop ▶ adj. [attrib.] very fast and with only brief pauses: *a whis-*

tle-stop tour. ▶ n. a small unimportant town on a railroad line. ■ a brief pause in a tour by a politician for an electioneering speech.

whis·tling duck ▶ n. a long-legged duck (genus *Dendrocygna*) with an upright stance and a whistling call, often perching on branches. Also called TREE DUCK.

whis·tling swan ▶ n. a bird of the North American race of the tundra swan (*Cygnus columbianus columbianus*), breeding in northern Canada and overwintering on the coasts of the US.

whit /(h)wit/ ▶ n. [in sing.] a very small part or amount.
– PHRASES **every whit** wholly. **not** (or **never**) **a whit** not at all. [ME: appar. an alt. of obs. *wight* 'small amount.']

White[1] /(h)wīt/, Byron Raymond (1917–2002), US Supreme Court associate justice 1962–93.

White[2], E. B. (1899–1985), US writer; full name *Elwyn Brooks White*. He wrote the children's classics *Stuart Little* (1945), *Charlotte's Web* (1952), and *The Trumpet of the Swan* (1970).

White[3], Edward Douglass, Jr. (1845–1921), Chief Justice of the US 1910–21, previously an associate justice 1894–1910.

White[4], Edward H., see GRISSOM.

White[5], Patrick Victor Martindale (1912–90), Australian writer; born in Britain. His novels include *The Tree of Man* (1955) and *Voss* (1957). Nobel Prize for Literature (1973).

White[6], T. H. (1906–64), British writer, born in India; full name *Terence Hanbury White*. He is best known for the tetralogy *The Once and Future King* (1938–77), his reworking of the Arthurian legend.

white /(h)wīt/ ▶ adj. **1** of the color of milk or fresh snow, due to the reflection of all visible rays of light; the opposite of black. ■ approaching such a color; very pale: *white with fear.* ■ fig. morally or spiritually pure; innocent and untainted: *as white as the driven snow.* ■ (of a plant) having white flowers or pale-colored fruit. ■ (of a tree) having light-colored bark. ■ (of wine) made from white grapes, or dark grapes with the skins removed, and having a yellowish color. ■ Brit. (of coffee or tea) served with milk or cream. ■ (of glass) transparent; colorless. ■ (of bread) made from a light-colored, sifted, or bleached flour. **2** (also **White**) belonging to or denoting a human group having light-colored skin (chiefly used of peoples of European extraction). ■ of or relating to such people. **3** hist. counter-revolutionary or reactionary. Contrasted with RED (sense 2). ▶ n. **1** white color or pigment: *woodwork of an immaculate white.* ■ white clothes or material. ■ (**whites**) white clothes, esp. as worn for playing tennis, or as naval uniform, or in the context of washing. ■ white wine. ■ (**White**) the player of the white pieces in chess or checkers. ■ the white pieces in chess. ■ a white thing, in particular the white ball (the cue ball) in billiards. ■ the outer part (white when cooked) that surrounds the yolk of an egg; the albumen. ■ white bread. **2** the visible pale part of the eyeball around the iris. **3** (also **White**) a member of a light-skinned people, esp. one of European extraction. **4** [with adj.] a white or cream butterfly (*Pieris* and other genera, family Pieridae) that has dark veins or spots on the wings. It can be a serious crop pest. ▶ v. [trans.] archaic paint or turn (something) white: *your passion hath whited your face.*
– PHRASES **bleed someone/something white** drain someone or something of wealth or resources. **whited sepulcher** literary a hypocrite. [with biblical allusion to Matt. 23:27.] **white man's burden** the task that white colonizers believed they had to impose their civilization on the black inhabitants of their colonies. [from Rudyard Kipling's *The White Man's Burden* (1899).] **whiter than white** extremely white. ■ morally beyond reproach.
– PHRASAL VERBS **white out** (of vision) become impaired by exposure to sudden bright light. ■ (of a person) lose color vision as a prelude to losing consciousness. **white something out 1** obliterate a mistake with white correction fluid. ■ cover one's face or facial blemishes completely with makeup. **2** impair someone's vision with a sudden bright light. — **white·ly** adv. **white·ness** n. **whit·ish** adj. [OE *hwit*, of Gmc. origin; rel. to Du. *wit* and Ger. *weiss*, also to WHEAT.]

white ad·mi·ral ▶ n. a North American butterfly (*Limenitis arthemis*, subfamily Limenitinae, family Nymphalidae) that has black wings bearing a broad white band and a marginal row of blue dashes.

white ant ▶ n. another term for TERMITE.

White Ar·my ▶ n. any of the armies that opposed the Bolsheviks during the Russian Civil War of 1918–21.

white ar·se·nic ▶ n. an extremely toxic soluble white solid, As_2O_3, made by burning arsenic.

white·bait /'(h)wīt,bāt/ ▶ n. the small silvery-white young of herrings, sprats, and similar marine fish, eaten in numbers as food.

white bal·ance ▶ n. the color balance on a video camera. ■ a control or system for adjusting this.

white bass /bas/ ▶ n. a North American freshwater bass (*Morone chrysops*) with dark horizontal stripes.

white birch ▶ n. a birch tree with white bark, esp. the paper birch or the European silver birch.

white blood cell ▶ n. less technical term for LEUKOCYTE.

white·board /'(h)wīt,bôrd/ ▶ n. a wipeable board with a white surface used for teaching or presentations. ■ Comput. an area common to several users or applications, where they can exchange information, in particular as handwriting or graphics.

white book ▶ n. a book of rules, standards, or records, esp. an official government report, bound in white.

white-bread ▶ adj. informal of, belonging to, or representative of the white middle classes; not progressive, radical, or innovative.

white bry·o·ny ▶ n. see BRYONY (sense 1).

white·cap /'(h)wīt,kap/ ▶ n. a small wave with a foamy crest.

white ce·dar ▶ n. a North American tree (*Thuja* and other genera) of the cypress family, in particular the **northern white cedar** (*T. occidentalis*).

white cell ▶ n. less technical term for LEUKOCYTE.

white clo·ver ▶ n. see CLOVER.

white-col·lar ▶ adj. of or relating to the work done or those who work in an office or other professional environment. ■ denoting nonviolent crime committed by white-collar workers, esp. fraud.

white cur·rant ▶ n. a cultivated variety of red currant with pale edible berries. The berries are insipid and generally used for jams and jellies, in combination with other fruits.

white dwarf ▶ n. Astron. a small very dense star that is typically the size of a planet. A white dwarf is formed when a low-mass star has exhausted all its central nuclear fuel and lost its outer layers as a planetary nebula.

white el·e·phant ▶ n. a possession that is useless or troublesome, esp. one that is expensive to maintain or difficult to dispose of. [from the story that the kings of Siam gave such animals as a gift to courtiers considered obnoxious, in order to ruin the recipient by the great expense incurred in maintaining the animal.]

white-eye ▶ n. a small Old World songbird (*Zosterops* and other genera, family Zosteropidae) with a ring of white feathers around the eye.

white·face /'(h)wīt,fās/ ▶ n. **1** white stage makeup. **2** a Hereford cow or bull.

White Fa·ther ▶ n. **1** a white man regarded by people of a nonwhite race as having authority over them. **2** a member of the Society of Missionaries of Africa, a Roman Catholic order founded in Algiers in 1868. [translating Fr. *Père Blanc*.]

white feath·er ▶ n. a white feather given to someone as a sign that the giver considers them a coward. [18th C.: with ref. to a white feather in the tail of a game bird being a mark of bad breeding.]

white fir ▶ n. a North American fir tree (*Abies concolor*) that has a whitish coloration on both sides of its flat needles. White firs are common in the mountainous coastal areas of California, the Sierra Nevada, and the southern Rockies.

white·fish /'(h)wīt,fisн/ ▶ n. (pl. same or **-fish·es**) a mainly freshwater fish (*Coregonus* and other genera) of the salmon family, widely used as food.

white fish ▶ n. fish with pale flesh, such as plaice, halibut, cod, and haddock.

white flag ▶ n. a white flag or cloth used as a symbol of surrender, truce, or a desire to parley.

white flight ▶ n. the move of native-born white city-dwellers to the suburbs to escape the influx of immigrants or migrants.

white flour ▶ n. fine wheat flour, typically bleached, from which most of the bran and germ have been removed.

white·fly /'(h)wīt,flī/ ▶ n. (pl. same or **-flies**) a minute winged bug (family Aleyrodidae, suborder Homoptera) covered with powdery white wax, damaging plants by feeding on the sap and coating them with honeydew.

white-foot·ed mouse ▶ n. a common deer mouse (*Peromyscus leucopus*) with white feet, found in the US and Mexico.

White Fri·ar ▶ n. a Carmelite monk. [ME: so named because of the white habits worn by the monks.]

white gold ▶ n. a silver-colored alloy of gold with nickel, platinum, or another metal.

white goods ▶ plural n. **1** large electrical goods used domestically, such as refrigerators and washing machines, typically white in color. **2** archaic domestic linen.

White·hall /'(h)wīt,hôl/ a street in Westminster, London, on which many government offices are located.

White·head /'(h)wīt,(h)ed/, Alfred North (1861–1947), English mathematician. He co-authored *Principia Mathematica* (1910–13) with his pupil Bertrand Russell.

white·head /'(h)wīt,hed/ ▶ n. informal a pale or white-topped pustule on the skin.

white heat ▶ n. the temperature or state of something that is so hot that it emits white light. ■ [in sing.] fig. a state of intense passion or activity.

white hole ▶ n. Astron. a hypothetical celestial object that expands outward from a space-time singularity and emits energy, in the manner of a time-reversed black hole.

white hope ▶ n. a person expected to bring much success to a group or organization: *he was the great white hope for many kids.* ■ formerly, a white boxer believed by fans to be able to beat a black champion.

White·horse /'(h)wīt,hôrs/ the capital of Yukon Territory in northwestern Canada; pop. 17,925.

white hors·es ▶ plural n. white-crested waves at sea.

white-hot ▶ adj. at white heat.

White House 1 the official residence of the US president in Washington,

DC. ■ the US president, presidency, or government. **2** the Russian parliament building.

white i·bis ▶ n. a white ibis (*Eudocimus albus*) with a red face and a long decurved red bill, found chiefly from the southern US to northern South America. See illustration at IBIS.

white knight ▶ n. a person or thing that comes to someone's aid. ■ a person or company making an acceptable counteroffer for a company facing a hostile takeover bid.

white-knuck·le ▶ adj. [attrib.] (esp. of a vehicle, boat, or airplane ride) causing excitement or tension. [1970s: with ref. to the effect caused by gripping tightly to steady oneself.]

white-knuck·led ▶ adj. informal (of a person) showing signs of extreme tension due to fear or anger.

white-la·bel ▶ adj. denoting a musical recording for which the fully printed commercial label is not yet available, and which has been supplied with a plain white label before general release for promotional purposes. ▶ n. (**white label**) a recording released in such a way.

white lead /led/ ▶ n. a white pigment consisting of a mixture of lead carbonate and lead hydroxide.

white lie ▶ n. a harmless or trivial lie, esp. one told to avoid hurting someone's feelings.

white light ▶ n. apparently colorless light, such as ordinary daylight. It contains all the wavelengths of the visible spectrum at equal intensity. ■ the light supposedly seen by people as they approach death.

white light·ning ▶ n. illicit homemade whiskey, typically colorless and distilled from corn.

white list ▶ n. informal a list of people or products viewed with approval.

white mag·ic ▶ n. magic used only for good purposes. — **white ma·gi·cian** n.

white mat·ter ▶ n. the paler tissue of the brain and spinal cord, consisting mainly of nerve fibers with their myelin sheaths. Compare with GRAY MATTER.

white meat ▶ n. pale meat such as poultry, veal, and rabbit. Often contrasted with RED MEAT.

white met·al ▶ n. a white or silvery alloy, esp. a tin-based alloy used for the surfaces of bearings.

White Moun·tains a range that rises to 6,288 feet (1,918 m) at Mount Washington, situated in northern New Hampshire.

white mouse ▶ n. an albino form of the house mouse, widely bred as a pet and laboratory animal.

whit·en /ˈ(h)wītn/ ▶ v. make or become white. — **whit·en·er** n.

white night ▶ n. **1** a sleepless night. [translating Fr. *nuit blanche*.] **2** a night when it is never properly dark, as in high latitudes in summer.

White Nile the name for the main, western branch of the Nile River that flows between the Uganda–Sudan border and its confluence with the Blue Nile at Khartoum.

white noise ▶ n. Physics noise containing many frequencies with equal intensities. ■ such noise as used to mask other noises: [as adj.] *a white-noise machine.*

white·out /ˈ(h)wītˌout/ ▶ n. **1** a dense blizzard, esp. in polar regions. ■ a weather condition in which the features and horizon of snow-covered country are indistinguishable due to uniform light diffusion. **2** white correction fluid for covering typing or writing mistakes. **3** a loss of color vision due to rapid acceleration, often before a loss of consciousness.

white pages ▶ n. the part of the telephone book that lists residential and business telephone numbers in alphabetical order by name, usually without any advertising copy.

white pa·per ▶ n. a government or other authoritative report giving information or proposals on an issue.

white pep·per ▶ n. the husked ripe or unripe berries of the pepper (see PEPPER sense 2), typically ground and used as a condiment.

white phos·pho·rus ▶ n. see PHOSPHORUS.

white pine ▶ n. any of a number of coniferous trees with whitish timber, in particular a North American pine tree (*Pinus strobus*) that yields high-quality timber.

white point·er ▶ n. another term for GREAT WHITE SHARK.

white pop·lar ▶ n. a Eurasian poplar (*Populus alba*) with lobed leaves that are white underneath and gray-green above.

white rhi·noc·er·os ▶ n. a very large two-horned African rhinoceros (*Ceratotherium simum*) with broad lips.

White Riv·er **1** a river that flows from northwestern Arkansas across the Ozark Plateau to the Mississippi River. **2** a river that flows in two main branches through Indiana to the Wabash River. **3** a river that flows from northwestern Nebraska into South Dakota to the Missouri River.

White Rus·sia former name for BELARUS.

White Rus·sian ▶ n. a Belorussian. ■ an opponent of the Bolsheviks during the Russian Civil War. ▶ adj. Belorussian. ■ of or relating to the opponents of the Bolsheviks.

white sage ▶ n. see SAGE[1] (sense 2).

white sale ▶ n. a store's sale of household linens.

white san·dal·wood ▶ n. see SANDALWOOD.

White Sands an area of white gypsum salt flats in central New Mexico, designated a national monument in 1933. It was the site of the detonation of the first nuclear weapon in 1945.

white sauce ▶ n. a sauce of flour, melted butter, and milk or cream.

White Sea an inlet of the Barents Sea off the coast of northwestern Russia.

white sea bass /bas/ ▶ n. see SEA BASS.

white shark ▶ n. see GREAT WHITE SHARK.

white-shoe ▶ adj. informal denoting a company, esp. a law firm, owned and run by members of the WASP elite, generally regarded as cautious and conservative. [with ref. to the white shoes fashionable among Ivy League college students in the 1950s.]

white slave ▶ n. a woman tricked or forced into prostitution, typically one taken to a foreign country for this purpose. — **white slav·er** n. **white slav·er·y** n.

white·smith /ˈ(h)wītˌsmiTH/ ▶ n. a person who makes articles out of metal, esp. tin. ■ a polisher or finisher of metal goods.

white snake·root ▶ n. see SNAKEROOT.

white spruce ▶ n. a North American spruce (*Picea glauca*) with yellow-green or blue-green needles and cylindrical cones, found principally in Canada.

White·stone /ˈ(h)wītˌstōn/ a largely residential section of northern Queens in New York City, to which it is joined by the Bronx-Whitestone Bridge.

white sug·ar ▶ n. purified sugar.

white su·pre·ma·cy ▶ n. the belief that white people are superior to those of all other races, esp. the black race, and should therefore dominate society.

whitetail deer

white·tail deer /(h)wītˌtāl/ (also **white-tailed deer** or **white·tail**) ▶ n. a reddish to grayish American deer (*Odocoileus virginianus*) with white on the belly and the underside of the tail.

white·thorn /ˈ(h)wītˌTHôrn/ ▶ n. the hawthorn.

white·throat /ˈ(h)wītˌTHrōt/ ▶ n. a migratory Eurasian and North African warbler (genus *Sylvia*, family Sylviidae) with a gray head and white throat.

white tie ▶ n. a white bow tie worn by men as part of full evening dress. ■ full evening dress with a white bow tie. ▶ adj. (of an event) requiring full evening dress to be worn, including a white bow tie.

white trash ▶ n. derog. poor white people, esp. those living in the southern US.

white truf·fle ▶ n. an underground fungus (*Tuber magnatum*, family Tuberaceae) eaten in Europe as a delicacy.

white vit·ri·ol /ˈvitrēəl/ ▶ n. archaic crystalline zinc sulfate.

white·wall /ˈ(h)wītˌwôl/ ▶ n. **1** (also **white·wall tire**) a tire with a white stripe round the outside, or a white sidewall. **2** [as adj.] denoting a haircut in which the sides of the head are shaved and the top and back are left longer.

white wal·nut ▶ n. another term for BUTTERNUT (sense 1).

white·wash /ˈ(h)wītˌwäSH; -ˌwôSH/ ▶ n. **1** a solution of lime and water or of whiting, size, and water, used for painting walls white. ■ [in sing.] a deliberate concealment of someone's mistakes or faults in order to clear their name. **2** a victory in a game in which the loser scores no points. ▶ v. [trans.] **1** [usu. as adj.] (**whitewashed**) paint (a wall, building, or room) with whitewash. ■ try to clear (someone or their name) by deliberately concealing their mistakes or faults. ■ deliberately conceal (someone's mistakes or faults). **2** defeat (an opponent), keeping them from scoring. — **white·wash·er** n.

white·wa·ter /(h)wītˈwôtər; ˈwä-/ (also **white wa·ter**) ▶ n. [often as adj.] (also **white-wa·ter**) fast shallow stretches of water in a river: *white-water rafting.*

white whale ▶ n. another term for BELUGA (sense 1).

white witch ▶ n. a person, typically a woman, who practices magic for altruistic purposes.

white·wood /ˈ(h)wītˌwo͝od/ ▶ n. **1** light-colored wood, esp. when made into furniture and ready for staining, varnishing, or painting. **2** any of a number of trees that yield pale timber, in particular a silver fir, a basswood, or the tulip tree.

white·work /ˈ(h)wītˌwərk/ ▶ n. embroidery worked in white thread on a white ground.

whit·ey /ˈ(h)wītē/ ▶ n. (pl. **-eys**) informal, derog. used by black people to refer to a white person. ■ [in sing.] white people collectively.

whith·er /'(h)wiT͟Hər/ archaic literary ▶ **interrog. adv.** to what place or state: *whither are we bound?* ■ what is the likely future of: *whither modern architecture?* ▶ **rel. adv.** to which (with reference to a place): *the lake, whither we were conducted.* ■ to whatever place; wherever: *we could drive whither we pleased.* [OE *hwider*, from the Gmc. base of WHICH.]

whith·er·so·ev·er /,(h)wiT͟Hərsō'evər/ ▶ **rel. adv.** archaic wherever: *whithersoever she chose.*

whit·ing[1] /'(h)wītiNG/ ▶ **n.** (pl. same) **1** a slender-bodied marine fish (*Merlangius merlangus*) of the cod family. It lives in shallow European waters and is a commercially important food fish. **2** [usu. with adj.] any of a number of similar marine fishes, in particular the northern kingfish of eastern North America. [ME: from MDu. *wijting*, from *wijt* 'white.']

whit·ing[2] ▶ **n.** ground chalk used for purposes such as whitewashing and cleaning metal plate.

Whit·lam /'(h)witləm/, Gough (1916–), prime minister of Australia 1972–75; full name *Edward Gough Whitlam.*

whit·leath·er /'(h)wit,leT͟Hər/ ▶ **n.** leather that has been prepared by dressing with alum and salt so as to retain its natural color. [ME: from WHITE + LEATHER.]

whit·low /'(h)wit,lō/ ▶ **n.** an abscess in the soft tissue near a fingernail or toenail. [ME (also as *whitflaw*, *-flow*), appar. from WHITE + FLAW[1] in the sense 'crack,' but perh. rel. to Du. *fijt* 'whitlow.']

Whit·man /'(h)witmən/, Walt (1819–92), US poet. In 1855, he published *Leaves of Grass*, a poetry collection that included "I Sing the Body Electric" and "Song of Myself."

Whit·ney[1] /'(h)witnē/, Eli (1765–1825), US inventor. He is best known for his invention of the cotton gin (patented 1794) to automate the removal of seeds from raw cotton.

Whit·ney[2], Gertrude Vanderbilt (1876–1942) US sculptor and philanthropist; the daughter of Cornelius Vanderbilt. She founded the Whitney Museum of American Art in New York City in 1931.

Whit·ney, Mount a mountain in the Sierra Nevada in California. Rising to 14,495 feet (4,418 m), it is the highest peak in the continental US outside of Alaska.

Whit·sun /'(h)witsən/ ▶ **n.** Whitsuntide. [ME: from WHITSUNDAY, reduced as if from *Whitsun Day.*]

Whit·sun·day /'(h)wit'sən,dā; -dē; '(h)witsən-/ **n.** another term for PENTECOST (sense 1). [OE *Hwīta Sunnandæg*, lit. 'white Sunday,' prob. with ref. to the white robes of those newly baptized at Pentecost.]

Whit·sun·tide /'(h)witsən,tīd/ ▶ **n.** the weekend or week including Whitsunday.

Whit·ta·ker /'(h)witikər/, Charles Evans (1901–73), US Supreme Court associate justice 1957–62.

Whit·ti·er, John Greenleaf (1807–92), US poet and abolitionist. His poems include "Snow-Bound" (1866).

Whit·ting·ton /'(h)witiNGtən/, Dick (d.1423), English merchant and lord mayor of London 1397–98, 1406–07, and 1419–20; full name *Sir Richard Whittington.*

whit·tle /'(h)witl/ ▶ **v.** [trans.] carve (wood) into an object by repeatedly cutting small slices from it. ■ carve (an object) from wood in this way. ■ (**whittle something away/down**) reduce something in size, amount, or extent by a gradual series of steps: *the short list was whittled down to five.* — **whit·tler n.** [16th C.: from dial. *whittle* 'knife.']

whiz /(h)wiz/ (also **whizz**) ▶ **v.** (**whizzed, whiz·zing**) **1** [no obj., with adverbial of direction] move quickly through the air with a whistling or whooshing sound: *the missiles whizzed past.* ■ (**whiz through**) do or deal with quickly. ■ [intrans.] cause to rotate in a machine, esp. a food processor. **2** [intrans.] informal urinate. ▶ **n. 1** a whistling or whooshing sound made by something moving fast through the air. **2** (also **wiz**) informal a person who is extremely clever at something: *a computer whiz.* [20th C.: influenced by WIZARD.] **3** informal an act of urinating. [16th C.: imitative.]

whiz-bang (also **whizz-bang**) informal ▶ **n.** (esp. during World War I) a low-velocity shell. ■ a resounding success: *a whiz-bang at mechanical things.* ▶ **adj.** lively or sensational; fast-paced.

whiz kid ▶ **n.** informal a young person who is outstandingly skillful or successful at something.

whiz·zy /'(h)wizē/ ▶ **adj.** technologically innovative or advanced.

WHO ▶ **abbr.** World Health Organization.

who /hōō/ ▶ **pron. 1** [interrog. pron.] what or which person or people: *who is that woman?* **2** [relative pron.] used to introduce a clause giving further information about a person or people previously mentioned: *the mouse who married the playboy.* ■ archaic the person that; whoever: *who holds the sea, perforce doth hold the land.*

– PHRASES **who am I** (or **are you, is he**, etc.) **to do something** what right or authority do I (or you, he, etc.) have to do something. [OE *hwā*, of Gmc. origin; rel. to Du. *wie* and Ger. *wer.*]

whoa /(h)wō/ ▶ **exclam.** used as a command to a horse to make it stop or slow down. ■ informal used as a greeting, to express surprise or interest, or to command attention. [ME: var. of HO[2].]

who'd /hōōd/ ▶ **contr.** ■ who had. ■ who would.

who·dun·it /hōō'dənit/ (Brit. **who·dun·nit**) ▶ **n.** informal a story or play about a murder in which the identity of the murderer is not revealed until the end. [1930s: from *who done it?*, nonstandard form of *who did it?*]

who·e'er /hōō'e(ə)r/ literary ▶ **contr.** whoever.

who·ev·er /hōō'evər/ ▶ **rel. pron.** the person or people who; any person who. ■ regardless of who: *come out, whoever you are.* ▶ **interrog. pron.** used for emphasis instead of "who" in questions, typically expressing surprise or confusion: *whoever would want to make up something like that?*

whole /hōl/ ▶ **adj. 1** [attrib.] all of; entire: *he spent the whole day walking.* ■ used to emphasize a large extent or number: *a whole lot of money.* **2** in an unbroken or undamaged state; in one piece: *owls usually swallow their prey whole.* ■ [attrib.] (of milk, blood, or other substances) with no part removed. ■ [predic.] healthy: *whole in body, mind, and spirit.* ▶ **n. 1** a thing that is complete in itself: *a coherent whole.* **2** (**the whole**) all of something: *the whole of his life.* ▶ **adv.** [as submodifier] informal used to emphasize the novelty or distinctness of something: *he's given a whole new meaning to the term "cowboy."*

– PHRASES **as a whole** as a single unit and not as separate parts; in general. **in whole** entirely or fully. **in the whole (wide) world** anywhere; of all. **on the whole** taking everything into account; in general. **the whole nine yards** informal everything possible or available. — **whole·ness n.** [OE *hāl*, of Gmc. origin; rel. to Du. *heel* and Ger. *heil*, also to HAIL[2].]

whole blood ▶ **n.** blood drawn directly from the body from which none of the components, such as plasma or platelets, has been removed.

whole cloth ▶ **n.** cloth of the full size as manufactured, as distinguished from a piece cut off for a garment or other item.

– PHRASES **out of (the) whole cloth** informal totally false: *allegations created out of whole cloth.*

whole food ▶ **n.** (also **whole foods**) food that has been processed or refined as little as possible and is free from additives or other artificial substances.

whole-grain ▶ **adj.** made with or containing whole unprocessed grains of something.

whole·heart·ed /'hōl'härtid/ ▶ **adj.** showing or characterized by complete sincerity and commitment. — **whole·heart·ed·ly adv. whole·heart·ed·ness n.**

whole-life ▶ **adj.** [attrib.] relating to or denoting a life insurance policy that pays a specified amount only on the death of the person insured.

whole note ▶ **n.** Music a note having the time value of two half notes or four quarter notes, represented by a ring with no stem. Also called SEMIBREVE.

whole num·ber ▶ **n.** a number without fractions; an integer.

whole·sale /'hōl,sāl/ ▶ **n.** the selling of goods in large quantities to be retailed by others. ▶ **adv.** being sold in such a way: *this wine sells wholesale for $72 a case.* ■ on a large scale. ▶ **adj.** done on a large scale; extensive: *wholesale destruction.* ▶ **v.** [trans.] sell (goods) in large quantities at low prices to be retailed by others. — **whole·sal·er n.** [ME: orig. as *by whole sale* 'in large quantities.']

whole·some /'hōlsəm/ ▶ **adj.** conducive to or suggestive of good health and physical well-being. ■ conducive to or promoting moral well-being. — **whole·some·ly adv. whole·some·ness n.** [ME: prob. already in OE (see WHOLE, -SOME[1]).]

whole step ▶ **n.** Music an interval of a (whole) tone.

whole-tone scale ▶ **n.** Music a scale consisting entirely of intervals of a tone, with no semitones.

whole-wheat ▶ **adj.** denoting flour or bread made from whole grains of wheat, including the husk or outer layer. ▶ **n.** whole-wheat bread or flour.

who·lism /'hōlizəm/ ▶ **n.** var. of HOLISM. — **who·lis·tic adj. who·lis·ti·cal·ly adv.**

whol·ly /'hōl(l)ē/ ▶ **adv.** entirely; fully. [ME: prob. already in OE (see WHOLE, -LY[2]).]

whol·ly-owned ▶ **adj.** denoting a company all of whose shares are owned by another company.

whom /hōōm/ ▶ **pron.** used instead of "who" as the object of a verb or preposition: [interrog. pron.] *whom did he marry?* | [relative pron.] *her mother, in whom she confided, said it wasn't easy for her.*

whom·ev·er /hōōm'evər/ ▶ **pron.** esp. formal or literary used instead of "whoever" as the object of a verb or preposition: *I'll talk to whomever I like.*

whomp /(h)wämp; (h)wômp/ informal ▶ **v.** [trans.] strike heavily; thump. ■ defeat decisively: *I whomped him good.* ▶ **n.** a dull heavy sound. [1920s: imitative.]

whom·so /'hōōmsō/ ▶ **pron.** archaic used instead of "whoso" as the object of a verb or preposition.

whom·so·ev·er /,hōōmsō'evər/ ▶ **rel. pron.** formal used instead of "whosoever" as the object of a verb or preposition.

whoomp /(h)wōōmp/ (also **whoomph** /(h)wōōmf/) ▶ **n.** a sudden loud sound, such as that made by a muffled or distant explosion. [1950s: imitative.]

whoop /(h)wōōp; hōōp/ ▶ **n.** a loud cry of joy or excitement. ■ a hooting cry or sound. ■ a long rasping indrawn breath, typically of someone with whooping cough. ▶ **v.** [intrans.] give or make a whoop: *whooping with laughter.*

– PHRASES **whoop it up** informal enjoy oneself or celebrate in a noisy way. ■ create or stir up excitement or enthusiasm. [ME: prob. imitative.]

whoop·ee /'(h)wōōpē; '(h)wōō'pē/ informal ▶ **exclam.** expressing wild excitement or joy. ▶ **n.** wild revelry: ■ dated a wild party.

– PHRASES **make whoopee 1** celebrate wildly. **2** have sexual intercourse.

whoop·ee cush·ion /'wōōpē/ (also **whoop·ie cush·ion**) ▶ **n.** a rubber cushion that makes a sound like the breaking of wind when someone sits on it.

whoop·er /'(h)wo͞opər; 'ho͞opər/ ▶ **n.** **1** (also **whoop·er swan**) a large migratory swan (*Cygnus cygnus*) with a black and yellow bill and a loud trumpeting call, breeding in northern Eurasia and Greenland. **2** short for WHOOPING CRANE.

whoop·ing cough ▶ **n.** a contagious bacterial disease chiefly affecting children, characterized by convulsive coughs followed by a whoop. The organism responsible is *Bordetella pertussis*, a Gram-negative bacterium intermediate between a coccus and a bacillus. Also called PERTUSSIS.

whoop·ing crane ▶ **n.** a large mainly white crane (*Grus americana*) with a trumpeting call, breeding in central Canada and now endangered.

whoops /wo͝ops; wo͞ops/ ▶ **exclam.** informal another term for OOPS. [1920s: prob. an alt. of UPSY-DAISY; cf. OOPS.]

whoosh /(h)wo͞osh; (h)wo͝osh/ (also **woosh**) ▶ **v.** [no obj., with adverbial of direction] move quickly or suddenly with a rushing sound: *a train whooshed by.* ■ [with obj. and adverbial or complement] move (something) in such a way. ▶ **n.** a sudden movement accompanied by a rushing sound: *a big whoosh of air.* ▶ **exclam.** used to imitate such a movement and sound. [19th C.: imitative.]

whop /(h)wäp/ (also **whap**) informal ▶ **v.** (**whopped, whop·ping**) [trans.] hit hard. ■ defeat, overcome. ▶ **n.** a heavy blow or the sound of such a blow. ■ the regular pulsing sound of a helicopter rotor. [ME: var. of dial. *wap* 'strike,' of unknown origin.]

whop·per /'(h)wäpər/ ▶ **n.** informal a thing that is extremely or unusually large. ■ a gross or blatant lie.

whop·ping /'(h)wäpiNG/ ▶ **adj.** informal very large: [as submodifier] *a whopping big party.*

whore /hôr/ ▶ **n.** derog. a prostitute. ■ a promiscuous woman. ▶ **v.** [intrans.] (of a woman) work as a prostitute. ■ [often as n.] (**whoring**) (of a man) use the services of prostitutes: *he indulged in whoring and eating.* ■ debase oneself by doing something for unworthy motives, typically to make money. [OE *hōre*, of Gmc. origin; rel. to Du. *hoer* and Ger. *Hure*, from an Indo-Eur. root shared by L. *carus* 'dear.']

whore·dom /'hôrdəm/ ▶ **n.** dated prostitution or other promiscuous sexual activity.

whore·house /'hôr,hous/ ▶ **n.** informal a brothel.

whore·mas·ter /'hôr,mastər/ ▶ **n.** archaic **1** a whoremonger. **2** a procurer or pimp.

whore·mon·ger /'hôr,mäNGgər; -,məNG-/ ▶ **n.** archaic a person who has dealings with prostitutes, esp. a sexually promiscuous man.

whore·son /'hôrsən/ ▶ **n.** archaic an unpleasant or greatly disliked person. [ME: from WHORE + SON, suggested by Anglo-Norman Fr. *fiz a putain.*]

whor·ish /'hôrisH/ ▶ **adj.** belonging to or characteristic of a prostitute. — **whor·ish·ly adv. whor·ish·ness n.**

whorl /(h)wôrl/ ▶ **n.** a coil or ring, in particular: ■ Zool. each of the turns or convolutions in a spiral shell. ■ Bot. a set of leaves, flowers, or branches springing from the stem at the same level and encircling it. ■ Bot. (in a flower) each of the sets of organs, esp. the petals and sepals, arranged concentrically around the receptacle. ■ a complete circle in a fingerprint. ■ esp. hist. a small wheel or pulley in a spinning wheel, spinning machine, or spindle. ▶ **v.** [intrans.] literary spiral or move in a twisted and convoluted fashion: *dance steps whorl into wildness.* — **whorled adj.** [ME (denoting a small flywheel): appar. a var. of WHIRL, influenced by OE *wharve* 'whorl of a spindle.']

whor·tle·ber·ry /'(h)wərtl,berē/ ▶ **n.** a bilberry. [16th C.: dial. var. of ME *hurtleberry*, of unknown origin.]

who's /ho͞oz/ ▶ **contr.** ■ who is: *who's that?* ■ who has: *who's done the reading?*

whose /ho͞oz/ ▶ **interrogative possessive adj. & pron.** belonging to or associated with which person: [as adj.] *whose round is it?* | [as pron.] *a minivan drove by and Juliet wondered whose it was.* ▶ **rel. possessive adj.** of whom or which (used to indicate that the following noun belongs to or is associated with the person or thing mentioned in the previous clause): *he's a man whose opinion I respect.* [OE *hwæs*, genitive of *hwā* 'who' and *hwæt* 'what.']

whose·so·ev·er /,ho͞ozsō'evər/ ▶ **rel. pron. & adj.** formal whoever's.

whos·ev·er /,ho͞oz'evər/ ▶ **rel. pron. & adj.** rare belonging to or associated with whichever person; whoever's: [as pron.] *the choice, whosever it was, is interesting* | [as adj.] *she dialed whosever number she could still remember.*

who·sis /'ho͞ozis/ (also **who·sit** /-zit/) ▶ **n.** informal (often in titles) a person whose name one cannot recall, does not know, or does not wish to specify: *lunch with Senator Whosis.* [1920s: contraction of *who is this?*]

who·so /'ho͞osō/ ▶ **pron.** archaic term for WHOEVER. [ME: shortening of OE *swā hwā swā* 'so who so.']

who·so·ev·er /,ho͞osō'evər/ ▶ **pron.** formal term for WHOEVER.

who's who ▶ **n.** a list or directory of facts about notable people.

whump /(h)wəmp/ ▶ **n.** [usu. in sing.] a dull thudding sound. ▶ **v.** [no obj., with adverbial] make such a sound. ■ [trans.] strike (something) heavily with such a sound: *she began whumping him on his lower back.* [19th C.: imitative.]

whup /(h)wo͞op/ ▶ **v.** (**whupped, whup·ping**) [trans.] informal beat; thrash. ■ defeat convincingly. [19th C.: var. of WHIP.]

wh-word ▶ **n.** Gram. any of a class of English words used to introduce questions and relative clauses. The main wh-words are *why, who, which, what, where, when,* and *how.*

why /(h)wī/ ▶ **interrog. adv.** for what reason or purpose. ■ [with negative] used to make or agree to a suggestion: *why don't I give you a lift?* ▶ **rel. adv.** (with reference to a reason) on account of which; for which. ■ the reason for which: *each has faced similar hardships, and that is why they are friends.* ▶ **exclam. 1** expressing surprise or indignation: *Why, that's absurd!* **2** used to add emphasis to a response: *"You think so?" "Why, yes."* ▶ **n.** (pl. **whys**) a reason or explanation: *the **whys and wherefores** of these procedures.*
– PHRASES **why so?** for what reason or purpose? [OE *hwī, hwȳ* 'by what cause,' instrumental case of *hwæt* 'what,' of Gmc. origin.]

whyd·ah /'(h)widə/ (also **why·da**) ▶ **n.** an African weaverbird (genus *Vidua*), the male of which has a black back and a very long black tail used in display flight. [18th C. (orig. *widow-bird*): alt. by association with *Whidah* (now Ouidah), a town in Benin.]

WI ▶ **abbr.** ■ West Indies. ■ Wisconsin (in official postal use).

WIC /wik/ ▶ **abbr.** Women, Infants, and Children (a government program to ensure proper nutrition for poor mothers and their children).

Wic·ca /'wikə/ ▶ **n.** the religious cult of modern witchcraft, esp. an initiatory tradition founded in England in the mid-20th century and claiming its origins in pre-Christian pagan religions. — **Wic·can adj. & n.** [representing OE *wicca* 'witch.']

Wich·i·ta /'wicHə,tô; -,tä/ a city in southern Kansas, on the Arkansas River, the largest city in the state; pop. 344,284.

wick[1] /wik/ ▶ **n.** a strip of porous material up which liquid fuel is drawn by capillary action to the flame in a candle, lamp, or lighter. ■ Med. a gauze strip inserted in a wound to drain it. ▶ **v.** [trans.] absorb or draw off (liquid) by capillary action: *these excellent socks will **wick away** the sweat.*
– PHRASES **dip one's wick** vulgar slang (of a man) have sexual intercourse. [OE *wēoce*, of West Gmc. origin; rel. to Du. *wiek* and Ger. *Wieche* 'wick yarn.']

wick[2] ▶ **n.** [in place names] a town, hamlet, or district: *Warwick.* [OE *wīc* 'dwelling place,' prob. based on L. *vicus* 'street, village.']

wick·ed /'wikid/ ▶ **adj.** (**-ed·er, -ed·est**) evil or morally wrong. ■ intended to or capable of harming someone or something: *his wicked driving.* ■ informal extremely unpleasant: *the wind outside was wicked.* ■ playfully mischievous: *a wicked sense of humor.* ■ informal excellent; wonderful. ■ informal [as submodifier] very; extremely: *he runs wicked fast.* — **wick·ed·ly adv. wick·ed·ness n.** [ME: prob. from OE *wicca* 'witch' + -ED[1].]

wick·er /'wikər/ ▶ **n.** pliable twigs, typically of willow, plaited or woven to make items such as furniture and baskets. [ME: of Scand. origin; cf. Swed. *viker* 'willow'; rel. to *vika* 'to bend.']

wick·er·work /'wikər,wərk/ ▶ **n.** wicker. ■ furniture or other items made of wicker.

wick·et /'wikit/ ▶ **n. 1** (also **wick·et door** or **wick·et gate**) a small door or gate, esp. one beside or in a larger one. ■ an opening in a door or wall, often fitted with glass or a grille and used for selling tickets or a similar purpose. ■ one of the wire hoops on a croquet course. **2** Cricket each of the sets of three stumps with two bails across the top at either end of the pitch, defended by a batsman. ■ the prepared strip of ground between these two sets of stumps. ■ the dismissal of a batsman; each of ten dismissals regarded as marking a division of a side's innings.
– PHRASES **a sticky wicket** Cricket a pitch that has been drying after rain and is difficult to bat on. ■ [in sing.] informal a tricky or awkward situation: *the problem of who sits where can create a sticky wicket.* [ME: from Anglo-Norman Fr. and Old North. Fr. *wiket*; origin uncert., usually referred to the Gmc. root of ON *víkja* 'to turn, move.']

wick·i·up /'wikē,əp/ ▶ **n.** an American Indian hut consisting of an oval frame covered with brushwood or grass. [Algonquian.]

Wick·low /'wiklō/ a county in eastern Republic of Ireland, in the province of Leinster.

wid·der·shins /'widər,sHinz/ (also **with·er·shins**) ▶ **adv.** esp. Scot. in a direction contrary to the sun's course, considered as unlucky; counterclockwise. [16th C.: from Mid. Low Ger. *weddersins*, from Mid. High Ger. *widersinnes*, from *wider* 'against' + *sin* 'direction'; the second element was associated with Scots *sin* 'sun.']

wide /wīd/ ▶ **adj.** (**wid·er, wid·est**) **1** of great or more than average width. ■ (after a measurement and in questions) from side to side: *how wide do you think this house is?* ■ open to the full extent: *wide eyes.* ■ considerable: *a wide margin.* **2** including a great variety of people or things. ■ spread among a large number of people or over a large area: *wider acceptance.* ■ [in comb.] extending over the whole of: *an industry-wide trend.* **3** at a considerable or specified distance from a point or mark: *Bodie's shot was inches wide.* ■ Baseball (of a pitch) outside. ■ Baseball (of a throw) to either side of a base. ■ (in field sports) at or near the side of the field: *he played in a wide left position.* **4** Phonet. another term for LAX. ▶ **adv. 1** to the full extent: *his eyes opened wide.* **2** far from a particular point or mark. ■ at or near the side of the field; toward the sideline. ▶ **n.** Cricket
– PHRASES **wide awake** fully awake. **wide of the mark** a long way away from an intended target. ■ inaccurate: *the accusation was a little wide of the mark.* **wide open 1** stretching over an outdoor expanse: *wide open spaces.* **2** offering a great variety of opportunities. **3** (of a contest) of which the outcome is not predictable. **4** vulnerable, esp. to attack. — **wide·ness n. wid·ish adj.** [OE *wīd* 'spacious, extensive,' *wīde* 'over a large area,' of Gmc. origin.]

wide-an·gle ▶ **adj.** (of a lens) having a short focal length and hence a field covering a wide angle.

wide ar·e·a net·work (abbr.: **WAN**) ▶ n. a computer network in which the computers connected may be far apart, generally having a radius of half a mile or more.

wide-a·wake ▶ n. a soft felt hat with a low crown and wide brim. [19th C.: punningly so named, because the hat does not have a nap.]

wide-band ▶ adj. (of a radio, or other device or activity involving broadcasting) having or using a wide band of frequencies or wavelengths.

wide-bod·y /'wīd,bädē/ ▶ adj. [attrib.] (also **wide-bod·ied**) having a wide body, in particular: ■ (of a large jet airplane) having a wide fuselage. ■ (of a tennis racket) having a wide head. ▶ n. (pl. **-bod·ies**) (also **wide·bod·y**) **1** a large jet airplane with a wide fuselage. **2** a tennis racket with a wide head. **3** informal a large, heavily built person, esp. one who plays a team sport.

wide-eyed ▶ adj. having one's eyes wide open in amazement. ■ fig. innocent. ▶ adv. with one's eyes wide open in amazement.

wide·ly /'wīdlē/ ▶ adv. **1** over a wide area or at a wide interval: *he smiled widely.* ■ to a large degree in nature or character (used to describe considerable variation or difference): [as submodifier] *people in widely different circumstances.* **2** over a large area or range; extensively: *she's traveled widely.* ■ by many people or in many places: *credit cards are widely accepted.*

wid·en /'wīdn/ ▶ v. make or become wider. — **wid·en·er** n.

wide·out /'wīd,out/ ▶ n. a wide receiver.

wide-rang·ing ▶ adj. covering an extensive range.

wide re·ceiv·er ▶ n. Football an offensive player who is positioned at a distance from the end and is used primarily as a pass receiver.

wide-screen (also **wide·screen**) ▶ adj. [attrib.] designed with or for a screen presenting a wide field of vision in relation to its height: *a widescreen TV.* ▶ n. (**widescreen**) a movie or television screen presenting a wide field of vision in relation to its height. ■ a film format presenting a wide field of vision in relation to height.

wide·spread /'wīd'spred/ ▶ adj. found or distributed over a large area or number of people.

widg·eon ▶ n. var. of WIGEON.

widg·et /'wijit/ ▶ n. informal a small gadget or mechanical device, esp. one whose name is unknown or unspecified. ■ Comput. a component of a user interface that operates in a particular way. [1930s: perh. an alt. of GADGET.]

wid·ow /'widō/ ▶ n. **1** a woman who has lost her husband by death and has not remarried. ■ [with adj.] humorous a woman whose husband is often away participating in a specified sport or activity: *a golf widow.* **2** Print. a last word or short last line of a paragraph falling at the top of a page or column and considered undesirable. ▶ v. [trans.] make into a widow or widower: *she was widowed by the plane crash* | [as adj.] *cared for his widowed mother.* [OE *widewe*, from an Indo-Eur. root meaning 'be empty.']

wid·ow·er /'widōər/ ▶ n. a man who has lost his wife by death and has not remarried.

wid·ow·hood /'widō,ho͝od/ ▶ n. the state or period of being a widow or widower.

wid·ow-mak·er ▶ n. informal a thing with the potential to kill men. ■ a dead branch caught precariously high in a tree which may fall on a person below.

wid·ow's mite ▶ n. a small monetary contribution from someone who is poor. [with biblical allusion to Mark 12:43.]

wid·ow's peak ▶ n. a V-shaped growth of hair toward the center of the forehead. [19th C.: so called because it was formerly believed to be a predictor of widowhood for a woman.]

widow's walk

wid·ow's walk ▶ n. a railed or balustraded platform built on a roof, originally in early New England houses, typically for providing an unimpeded view of the sea. [1930s: with ref. to its use as a viewpoint for the hoped-for return of a seafaring husband.]

wid·ow's weeds ▶ plural n. black clothes worn by a widow in mourning. [18th C. (earlier as *mourning weeds*): *weeds* (obs. in the general sense 'garments') is from OE *wǣd(e)*, of Gmc. origin.]

width /width; witth/ ▶ n. the measurement or extent of something from side to side. ■ a piece of something at its full extent from side to side: *a single width of hardboard.* ■ the sideways extent of a swimming pool as a measure of the distance swum. ■ the quality of covering or accepting a broad range of things; scope. [17th C.: from WIDE + -TH[2], on the pattern of *breadth* (replacing *wideness*).]

width·wise /'width,wīz; 'witth-/ (also **width·ways** /-,wāz/) ▶ adv. in a direction parallel with a thing's width: *fold the pastry in half widthwise.*

wield /wēld/ ▶ v. [trans.] hold and use (a weapon or tool). ■ have and be able to use (power or influence). — **wield·er** n. [OE *wealdan, wieldan* 'govern, subdue, direct,' of Gmc. origin; rel. to Ger. *walten.*]

wield·y /'wēldē/ ▶ adj. (**wield·i·er, wield·i·est**) easily controlled or handled. [16th C.: back-form. from UNWIELDY.]

Wien /vēn/ German name for VIENNA.

Wie·ner /'wēnər/, Norbert (1894–1964), US mathematician. He established the science of cybernetics in the late 1940s.

wie·ner /'wēnər/ (also informal **wee·nie, wie·nie** /-nē/) ▶ n. **1** a frankfurter or similar sausage. [20th C.: abbrev. of Ger. *Wienerwurst* 'Vienna sausage.'] **2** another term for WEENIE.

Wie·ner schnit·zel /'vēnər ,shnitsəl/ ▶ n. a dish consisting of a thin slice of veal that is breaded, fried, and garnished. [from Ger., lit. 'Vienna cutlet.']

Wies·ba·den /'vēs,bädn/ a city in western Germany, on the Rhine River; pop. 264,000.

Wie·sel /vē'zəl; 'vēzəl; wi'zel/, Elie (1928–), US writer and human rights activist, born in Romania; full name *Eliezer Wiesel.* A survivor of the Auschwitz and Buchenwald concentration camps, he wrote numerous books about the Holocaust experience. Nobel Peace Prize (1986).

Wie·sen·thal /'vēzən,täl; -,thäl/, Simon (1908–2005), Austrian investigator of Nazi war crimes. He campaigned to bring Nazi war criminals to justice, tracing some 1,000 unprosecuted criminals, including Adolf Eichmann.

wife /wīf/ ▶ n. (pl. **wives** /wīvz/) a married woman considered in relation to her husband. ■ [with adj.] the wife of a man with a specified occupation: *a faculty wife.* ■ archaic or dialect a woman, esp. an old or uneducated one. — **wife·hood** /-,ho͝od/ n. **wife·less** adj. **wife·like** /-,līk/ adj. **wife·li·ness** /'wīflēnis/ n. **wife·ly** adj. [OE *wīf* 'woman,' of Gmc. origin; rel. to Du. *wijf* and Ger. *Weib.*]

wife-beat·er ▶ n. informal a man's sleeveless undershirt or T-shirt. [1990s: appar. by assoc. of such a garment with men who commit domestic violence.]

wife-swap·ping ▶ n. informal the practice within a group of married couples of exchanging sexual partners on a casual basis.

wif·ey /'wīfē/ ▶ n. (pl. **-eys**) informal a condescending way of referring to a man's wife.

Wif·fle ball /'wifəl/ ▶ n. trademark a light perforated ball used in a type of baseball. ■ a game played with such a ball. [1950s: *Wiffle*, var. of WHIFFLE.]

Wi-Fi /'wī 'fī/ ▶ abbr. Wireless Fidelity, a group of technical standards enabling the transmission of data over wireless networks.

wig[1] /wig/ ▶ n. a covering for the head made of real or artificial hair, typically worn by people for adornment or by people trying to conceal their baldness. — **wigged** adj. **wig·less** adj. [17th C.: shortening of PERIWIG.]

wig[2] ▶ v. (**wigged, wig·ging**) [trans.] Brit., informal dated rebuke (someone) severely.
– PHRASAL VERBS **wig out** informal, esp. US become deliriously excited; go completely wild. [19th C.: appar. from WIG[1], perh. from BIGWIG and associated with a rebuke given by a person in authority.]

wig·eon /'wijən/ (also **widg·eon**) ▶ n. a dabbling duck (genus *Anas*) with mainly reddish-brown and gray plumage, the male having a whistling call. [16th C.: perh. of imitative origin and suggested by PIGEON[1].]

wig·ger informal ▶ n. **1** a white person who tries to emulate or acquire African-American cultural behavior and tastes. **2** an unreliable or flaky person.

wig·gle /'wigəl/ ▶ v. move or cause to move up and down or from side to side with small rapid movements: [trans.] *Stasia wiggled her toes* | [intrans.] *my tooth was wiggling around.* ■ (**wiggle out of**) avoid (something), esp. by devious means. ▶ n. a wiggling movement. ■ a deviation in a line.
– PHRASES **get a wiggle on** informal get moving; hurry. — **wig·gly** /'wig(ə)lē/ adj. (**-gli·er, -gli·est**). [ME: from Mid. Low Ger. and MDu. *wiggelen* (frequentative).]

wig·gler /'wig(ə)lər/ ▶ n. a person or thing that wiggles or causes something to wiggle. ■ Physics a magnet designed to make a beam of particles in an accelerator follow a sinusoidal path, in order to increase the amount of radiation they produce. ■ dialect an earthworm. ■ informal a mosquito larva.

wig·gle room ▶ n. informal room to maneuver; flexibility, esp. in one's options or interpretation.

wig·gy /'wigē/ ▶ adj. (**-gi·er, -gi·est**) informal emotionally uncontrolled or weird. [1960s: from US slang *wig out* (see WIG[2]).]

wight /wīt/ ▶ n. [usu. with adj.] archaic or dialect a person of a specified kind, esp. one regarded as unfortunate: *he was an unlucky wight.* ■ literary a spirit, ghost, or other supernatural being. [OE *wiht* 'thing, creature,' of Gmc. origin; rel. to Du. *wicht* 'little child' and Ger. *Wicht* 'creature.']

Wight, Isle of /wīt/ an island off the southern coast of England; pop. 127,000; administrative center, Newport.

wig·wag /'wig,wag/ ▶ v. (**-wagged, -wag·ging**) [intrans.] informal move to and fro. ■ signal by waving an arm, flag, light, or other object: *Ned furiously wigwagged at her.* [16th C.: reduplication of WAG[1].]

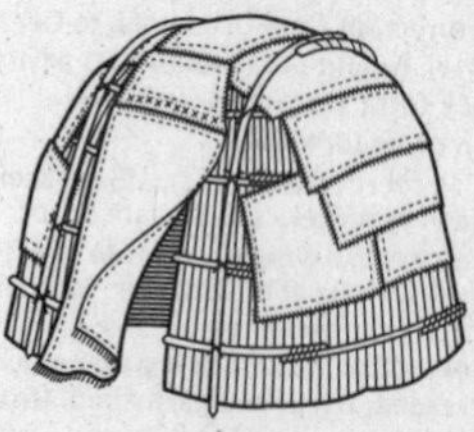
wigwam

wig·wam /ˈwig,wäm/ ▶ **n.** a dome-shaped hut or tent made by fastening mats, skins, or bark over a framework of poles, used by some North American Indian peoples. [17th C.: from Abnaki, 'their house,' from an Algonquian base meaning 'dwell,' shared with WICKIUP.]

wi·ki /ˈwikē/ ▶ **n.** a Web site developed collaboratively by a community of users, allowing any user to add and edit content. [from *WikiWikiWeb* (1995), coined by US programmer Ward Cunningham (1949–), from Hawaiian *wiki wiki* 'very quick,' emphatic form of *wiki* 'quick.']

wil·co /ˈwilkō/ ▶ **exclam.** expressing compliance or agreement, esp. acceptance of instructions received by radio. [1940s (orig. in military use): abbrev. of *will comply*.]

wild /wīld/ ▶ **adj. 1** (of an animal or plant) living or growing in the natural environment; not domesticated or cultivated. ■ (of people) not civilized; barbarous. ■ (of scenery or a region) desolate-looking: *the wild coastline.* **2** uncontrolled or unrestrained, esp. in pursuit of pleasure. ■ haphazard, esp. rashly so: *a wild guess.* ■ extravagant or unreasonable; fanciful: *who in their wildest dreams could have anticipated such a victory?* ■ stormy. ■ informal very enthusiastic or excited. ■ informal very angry. ■ (of looks, appearance, etc.) indicating distraction. ■ (of a playing card) deemed to have any value, suit, color, or other property in a game at the discretion of the player holding it. See also WILD CARD. ▶ **adv.** in an uncontrolled manner: *the bad guys shot wild.* ■ in a very excited or angry state: *wild with enthusiasm.* ▶ **n.** (**the wild**) a natural state or uncultivated or uninhabited region: *kiwis are virtually extinct in the wild.* ■ (**the wilds**) a remote uninhabited or sparsely inhabited area.
– PHRASES **run wild** (of an animal, plant, or person) grow or develop without restraint or discipline: fig. *her imagination had run wild.* **wild and woolly** uncouth in appearance or behavior. — **wild·ish adj. wild·ly adv. wild·ness n.** [OE *wilde*, of Gmc. origin; rel. to Du. and Ger. *wild*.]

wild ar·um ▶ **n.** another term for CUCKOOPINT.

wild boar ▶ **n.** see BOAR (sense 1).

wild cal·la /ˈkalə/ ▶ **n.** another term for WATER ARUM.

wild card ▶ **n.** a playing card that can have any value, suit, color, or other property in a game at the discretion of the player holding it. ■ a person or thing whose influence is unpredictable or whose qualities are uncertain. ■ Comput. a character that will match any character or sequence of characters in a search. ■ an opportunity to enter a sports competition without having to take part in qualifying matches or be ranked at a particular level. ■ a player or team given such an opportunity.

wild car·rot ▶ **n.** another term for QUEEN ANNE'S LACE.

wild·cat /ˈwīld,kat/ ▶ **n. 1** a small native Eurasian and African cat (*Felis silvestris*) that is typically gray with black markings and a bushy tail, noted for its ferocity. Its African race is believed to be the ancestor of the domestic cat. ■ any of the smaller members of the cat family, esp. the bobcat. ■ a hot-tempered or ferocious person, typically a woman. **2** an exploratory oil well. ▶ **adj.** [attrib.] (of a strike) sudden and unofficial. ■ commercially unsound or risky. ▶ **v.** [intrans.] prospect for oil.

wild·cat·ter /ˈwīld,katər/ ▶ **n.** a prospector who sinks exploratory oil wells. ■ a risky investor.

wild-caught ▶ **adj.** (of an animal) taken from the wild rather than bred from captive stock.

wild·craft /ˈwīld,kraft/ ▶ **v.** gather herbs, plants, and fungi from the wild. ▶ **n.** the action or practice of wildcrafting.

wild dog ▶ **n.** a wild member of the dog family, esp. the hunting dog of Africa, the dhole of India, or the dingo of Australia.

Wilde /wīld/, Oscar Fingal O'Flahertie Wills (1854–1900), Irish writer. He wrote the novel *The Picture of Dorian Gray* (1890) and the plays *Lady Windermere's Fan* (1892) and *The Importance of Being Earnest* (1895).

wil·de·beest /ˈwildə,bēst/ ▶ **n.** (pl. same or **-beests**) another term for GNU. [19th C.: from Afrik., lit. 'wild beast.']

Wil·der[1] /ˈwīldər/, Billy (1906–2002), US director and screenwriter, born in Austria; born *Samuel Wilder*. His movies include *Sunset Boulevard* (1950) and *Some Like It Hot* (1959).

Wil·der[2], Laura Ingalls (1867–1957), US writer. She wrote a series of children's books, including *Little House on the Prairie* (1935), about her experiences growing up on the US frontier during the late 1800s.

Wil·der[3], Thornton Niven (1897–1975), US writer. He wrote the novel *The Bridge of San Luis Rey* (1927) and the play *Our Town* (1938).

wil·der /ˈwildər/ ▶ **v.** [trans.] archaic cause to lose one's way; lead or drive astray: *unknowne Lands, where we have wildered ourselves.* ■ perplex; bewilder: *the sad Queen, wildered of thought.* [17th C.: origin uncert.; perh. based on WILDERNESS.]

wil·der·ness /ˈwildərnis/ ▶ **n.** [usu. in sing.] an uncultivated, uninhabited, and inhospitable region. ■ a neglected or abandoned area of a garden or town. ■ fig. a position of disfavor, esp. in a political context.
– PHRASES **a voice in the wilderness** an unheeded advocate of reform (see Matt. 3:3, etc.). [OE *wildēornes* 'land inhabited only by wild animals,' from *wild dēor* 'wild deer' + -NESS.]

Wil·der·ness Road a historic route, opened by Daniel Boone in the 1770s and used until the 1840s, that allowed western migration through the Allegheny Mountains by way of the Cumberland Gap.

wild-eyed ▶ **adj.** (of a person or animal) with an expression of panic or desperation in their eyes. ■ fig. emotionally volatile, typically fearful or desperate. ■ senseless or impractical.

wild·fire /ˈwīld,fī(ə)r/ ▶ **n. 1** a large, destructive fire that spreads quickly. **2** hist. a combustible liquid such as Greek fire that was readily ignited and difficult to extinguish, used esp. in warfare. **3** less common term for WILL-O'-THE-WISP.
– PHRASES **spread like wildfire** spread with great speed.

wild·flow·er /ˈwīld,flouər/ (also **wild flow·er**) ▶ **n.** a flower of an uncultivated variety or a flower growing freely without human intervention.

wild·fowl /ˈwīld,foul/ ▶ **plural n.** game birds, esp. aquatic ones; waterfowl.

wild gin·ger ▶ **n.** a North American plant (*Asarum canadense*, family Aristolochiaceae) with large heart-shaped leaves and hairy leafstalks. Its aromatic root is used as a ginger substitute.

wild-goose chase ▶ **n.** a foolish and hopeless pursuit of something unattainable.

wild horse ▶ **n.** a domestic horse that has returned to the wild, or that is allowed to live under natural conditions; a feral horse. ■ a horse that has not been broken in. ■ a wild animal of the horse family.
– PHRASES **wild horses wouldn't ——** used to convey that nothing could persuade or force someone to do something.

wild·ing[1] /ˈwīlding/ ▶ **n.** informal the activity by a gang of youths of going on a protracted and violent rampage in a public place, attacking or mugging people at random. [1980s: from the adj. WILD + -ING[1].]

wild·ing[2] (also **wild·ling** /-ling/) ▶ **n.** a wild plant, esp. an apple tree descended from cultivated varieties, or its fruit. [16th C.: from the adj. WILD + -ING[3].]

wild·life /ˈwīld,līf/ ▶ **n.** wild animals collectively; the native fauna (and sometimes flora) of a region.

wild·life park ▶ **n.** see PARK (sense 1).

wild man ▶ **n.** a man with a fierce or wildly unruly nature. ■ the image of a primitive or uncivilized man as a symbol of the wild side of human nature. ■ a supposed manlike animal such as a yeti.

wild mus·tard ▶ **n.** charlock.

wild oat ▶ **n.** an Old World grass (*Avena fatua*) that is related to the cultivated oat and is commonly found as a weed of other cereal plants.

wild pitch Baseball ▶ **n.** an errant pitch that is not hit by the batter and cannot be stopped by the catcher, enabling a base runner to advance. ▶ **v.** (**wild-pitch**) [trans.] enable (a base runner) to advance by making such a pitch: *Reed was wild-pitched to second.*

wild rice ▶ **n.** a tall aquatic North American grass (*Zizania aquatica*) related to rice, with edible grains. ■ the grain of this plant used as food.

wild silk ▶ **n.** coarse silk produced by wild silkworms, esp. tussore.

wild type ▶ **n.** Genet. a strain, gene, or characteristic that prevails among individuals in natural conditions, as distinct from an atypical mutant type.

Wild West the western US in a time of lawlessness in its early history.

wild·wood /ˈwīld,wo͝od/ ▶ **n.** esp. literary an uncultivated wood or forest that has been allowed to grow naturally.

wile /wīl/ ▶ **n.** (**wiles**) devious or cunning stratagems employed in manipulating or persuading someone to do what one wants. ▶ **v.** [trans.] **1** archaic lure; entice. **2** (**wile away the time**) another way of saying *WHILE AWAY THE TIME*. See WHILE. [ME: perh. from an ON word rel. to *vél* 'craft.']

wil·ful ▶ **adj.** var. of WILLFUL.

Wil·helm I /ˈvil,helm; ˈwil-/ (1797–1888), king of Prussia 1861–88 and emperor of Germany 1871–88. His reign saw the rise of German socialism, to which he responded with repressive measures.

Wil·helm II (1859–1941), emperor of Germany 1888–1918; grandson of Wilhelm I and of Queen Victoria; known as **Kaiser Wilhelm**. Vilified by Allied propaganda as the instigator of World War I, he abdicated and went into exile in 1918.

Wil·hel·mi·na /,vilhelˈmēnə; ,wiləˈmēnə/, (1880–1962), queen of the Netherlands 1890–1948. During World War II, she maintained a government in exile in London and through radio broadcasts was a symbol of resistance to the Dutch people.

Wilkes /wilks/, Charles (1798–1877), US naval officer and explorer. He determined that Antarctica is a continent during an 1838–42 expedition. Antarctica's Wilkes Land was named in his honor.

Wilkes Land /wilks/ a region of Antarctica that has a coast on the Indian Ocean. It is claimed by Australia.

Wil·kins[1] /ˈwilkinz/, Maurice Hugh Frederick (1916– 2004), British biologist, born in New Zealand. From X-ray diffraction analysis of DNA, he and Rosalind Franklin (1920–58) confirmed the double helix structure proposed by Francis Crick and James Watson in 1953. Nobel Prize for Physiology or Medicine (1962, shared with Crick and Watson).

Wil·kins[2], Roy (1901–81), US civil rights leader. He served as executive secretary of the NAACP 1955–77.

will[1] /wil/ ▶ **modal verb** (3rd sing. pres. **will**; past **would** /wo͝od; wəd/) **1** expressing the future tense: *you will regret it later.* ■ expressing a strong intention or assertion about the future: *I will succeed.* **2** expressing inevitable events: *accidents will happen.* **3** expressing a request: *will you stop here, please.* ■ expressing desire, consent, or willingness: *will you have a cognac?* **4** expressing facts about ability or capacity: *a rock so light that it will float on water.* **5** expressing habitual behavior: *she will dance for hours.* ■ (pronounced stressing "will") indicating annoyance about the habitual behavior described: *he will keep intruding.* **6** expressing probability or expectation about something in the present: *they will be miles away by now.*

– PHRASES **will do** informal expressing willingness to carry out a request or suggestion. [OE *wyllan*, of Gmc. origin; rel. to Du. *willen*, Ger. *wollen*, from an Indo-Eur. root shared by L. *velle* 'will, wish.']

will² ▶ n. **1** [usu. in sing.] the faculty by which a person decides on and initiates action: *she has an iron will.* ■ (also **will·pow·er**) control deliberately exerted to do something or to restrain one's own impulses: *a stupendous effort of will.* ■ a deliberate or fixed desire or intention: [with infin.] *the will to live.* ■ the thing that one desires or ordains: *the disaster was God's will.* **2** a legal document containing instructions as to what should be done with one's money and property after one's death. ▶ v. [trans.] **1** chiefly formal or literary intend, desire, or wish (something) to happen: *he was doing what the saint willed.* ■ [with obj. and infin.] make or try to make (someone) do something or (something) happen by the exercise of mental powers: *reluctantly he willed himself to turn and go back.* **2** (**will something to**) bequeath something to (someone) by the terms of one's will: *his father willed the farm to Sam.* ■ [with clause] leave specified instructions in one's will: *he willed that his body be given to the hospital.*

– PHRASES **at will** at whatever time or in whatever way one pleases. **have a will of one's own** have a willful character. **have one's will** archaic obtain what one wants. **if you will** said when politely inviting a listener or reader to do something or when using an unusual or fanciful term: *imagine, if you will, a typical silversmith's shop.* **where there's a will there's a way** proverb determination will overcome any obstacle. **with the best will in the world** however good one's intentions (used to imply that success in a particular undertaking is unlikely although desired). **with a will** energetically and resolutely. — **willed** adj. [in comb.] *I'm strong-willed.* **will·less·ness** n. **will·er** n. [OE *willa* (n.), *willian* (v.), of Gmc. origin; rel. to Du. *wil*, Ger. *Wille* (nouns).]

Wil·lam·ette Riv·er /wə'lamit/ a river that flows through western Oregon to the Columbia River.

Wil·lard¹ /'wilərd/, Emma (1787–1870), US educator. She founded a boarding school in Vermont in 1814 to teach subjects, such as mathematics and philosophy, not then available to women.

Wil·lard², Frances Elizabeth Caroline (1839–98), US women's rights and temperance activist. She was an organizer of the Prohibition Party in 1882 and president of the National Council of Women 1890.

wil·lem·ite /'wilə,mīt/ ▶ n. a mineral, typically greenish-yellow and fluorescent, consisting of a silicate of zinc. [19th C.: from the name of *Willem* I (1772–1843), king of the Netherlands, + -ITE¹.]

Wil·lem·stad /'viləm,stät; 'wil-/ the capital of the Netherlands Antilles, on the island of Curaçao; pop. 50,000.

wil·let /'wilit/ ▶ n. (pl. same or **-lets**) a large North American sandpiper (*Catoptrophorus semipalmatus*). [19th C.: imitative of its call, *pill-will-willet*.]

will·ful /'wilfəl/ (also **wil·ful**) ▶ adj. (of an immoral or illegal act or omission) intentional; deliberate. ■ having or showing a stubborn and determined intention to do as one wants, regardless of the consequences or effects. — **will·ful·ly** /'wilfəlē/ adv. **will·ful·ness** /'wilfəlnəs/ n. [ME: from the n. WILL² + -FUL.]

Wil·liam /'wilyəm/ the name of two kings of England and two of Great Britain and Ireland: ■ William I (c.1027–87), reigned 1066–87; the first Norman king of England; known as **William the Conqueror**. He invaded England and defeated Harold II at the Battle of Hastings (1066). ■ William II (c.1060–1100), reigned 1087–1100; son of William I; known as **William Rufus**. ■ William III (1650–1702), reigned 1689–1702; grandson of Charles I; husband of Mary II; known as **William of Orange**. In 1688, he deposed James II at the invitation of disaffected politicians and was crowned along with his wife Mary. ■ William IV (1765–1837), reigned 1830–7; known as **the Sailor King**; son of George III.

Will·iam I¹ (1143–1214), king of Scotland 1165–1214; known as **William the Lion**; grandson of David I.

Will·iam I² (1533–84), prince of the House of Orange; first stadtholder (chief magistrate) of the United Provinces of the Netherlands 1572–84; known as **William the Silent**.

Will·iam of Oc·cam /'äkəm/ (also **Ock·ham**) (c.1285–1349), English philosopher and Franciscan monk. He is known for the maxim called "Occam's razor."

Will·iams¹ /'wilyəmz/, Hank (1923–53), US country singer and songwriter; born *Hiram King Williams*. "Your Cheatin' Heart," recorded in 1952, was released after his death.

Wil·liams², Roger (c.1603–83), American clergyman; born in England. Banished from Massachusetts, he founded the colony of Rhode Island in 1636 as a refuge from political and religious persecution.

Wil·liams³, Ted (1918–2002), US baseball player; full name *Theodore Samuel Williams*; known as one the greatest hitters of all time. His outfielding for the Boston Red Sox 1939–1960 was interrupted by his service as a Marine pilot in World War II and the Korean War.

Will·iams⁴, Tennessee (1911–83), US playwright; born *Thomas Lanier Williams*. His plays include *A Streetcar Named Desire* (1947) and *Cat on a Hot Tin Roof* (1955).

Will·iams⁵, William Carlos (1883–1963), US poet. His poetry is collected in *Spring and All* (1923) and *Pictures from Brueghel* (1963).

Wil·liams·burg /'wilyəmz,bərg/ a city in southeastern Virginia, between the James and York rivers; pop. 11,530. A large part of the town has been restored and reconstructed so that it appears as it was during the colonial era.

Will·iam the Con·quer·or, William I of England (see WILLIAM).

wil·lies /'wilēz/ ▶ plural n. (**the willies**) informal a strong feeling of nervous discomfort. [19th C. (orig. US): of unknown origin.]

will·ing /'wiliNG/ ▶ adj. [often with infin.] ready, eager, or prepared to do something. ■ given or done readily: *willing obedience.* — **will·ing·ly** adv. **will·ing·ness** n.

wil·li·waw /'wilē,wô/ ▶ n. a sudden violent squall blowing offshore from a mountainous coast. [19th C.: of unknown origin.]

will-o'-the-wisp /'wil ə T͟Hə 'wisp/ ▶ n. an ignis fatuus. ■ fig. a person or thing that is difficult or impossible to find, reach, or catch. [17th C.: orig. as *Will with the wisp*, the sense of *wisp* being 'handful of (lighted) hay.']

wil·low /'wilō/ ▶ n. **1** (also **wil·low tree**) a tree or shrub (genus *Salix*, family Salicaceae) of temperate climates that typically has narrow leaves, bears catkins, and grows near water. Its pliant branches yield osiers for basketry. **2** a machine with revolving spikes used for cleaning cotton, wool, or other fibers. [OE *welig*, of Gmc. origin; rel. to Du. *wilg*.]

wil·low grouse ▶ n. another term for WILLOW PTARMIGAN.

wil·low herb (also **wil·low-herb**) ▶ n. a plant (*Epilobium* and related genera, family Onagraceae) of temperate regions that typically has willowlike leaves and pink or pale purple flowers.

wil·low pat·tern ▶ n. a conventional design representing a Chinese scene in blue on white pottery, typically showing three figures on a bridge, with a willow tree and two birds above.

wil·low ptar·mi·gan ▶ n. a common Eurasian and North American grouse (*Lagopus lagopus*) with reddish-brown and white plumage, turning mainly white in winter.

wil·low·ware /'wilō,we(ə)r/ ▶ n. pottery with a willow-pattern design.

wil·low·y /'wilōē/ ▶ adj. **1** bordered, shaded, or covered by willows. **2** (of a person) tall, slim, and lithe.

will·pow·er /'wil,pou(ə)r/ ▶ n. see WILL² (sense 1).

Wills Mood·y /wilz/, Helen (1905–98), US tennis player; born *Helen Newington Wills*. Between 1923 and 1938, she won the Wimbledon women's singles championship eight times, the US Open seven times, and the French Open four times.

wil·ly /'wilē/ (also **wil·lie**) ▶ n. (pl. **-lies**) informal a penis. [20th C.: nickname for the given name *William*.]

wil·ly-nil·ly /'wilē 'nilē/ ▶ adv. **1** whether one likes it or not: *he would be forced to collaborate willy-nilly.* **2** without direction or planning; haphazardly. [17th C.: later spelling of *will I, nill I* 'I am willing, I am unwilling.']

Wil·ming·ton /'wilmiNGtən/ **1** the largest city in Delaware, on the Delaware River; pop. 72,664. **2** a city in southeastern North Carolina, on the Cape Fear River and the Atlantic Ocean; pop. 75,838.

Wilms' tu·mor /wilmz/ ▶ n. a malignant tumor of the kidney, of a type that occurs in young children. [20th C.: named after Max *Wilms* (1867–1918), German surgeon.]

Wil·son¹ /'wilsən/, Charles Thomson Rees (1869–1959), Scottish physicist. He invented the cloud chamber, which became a major tool of particle physicists. Nobel Prize for Physics (1927, shared with Arthur Compton).

Wil·son², Edmund (1895–1972), US writer and critic. He was a friend of F. Scott Fitzgerald and edited the latter's unfinished novel *The Last Tycoon* (1941).

Wil·son³, Harold, Baron Wilson of Rievaulx (1916–95), prime minister of Great Britain 1964–70 and 1974–76; full name *James Harold Wilson*. His government introduced comprehensive schooling and renegotiated Britain's terms of entry into the European Economic Community.

Wil·son⁴, James (1742–98), US Supreme Court associate justice 1789–98; born in Scotland. He was a signer of the Declaration of Independence 1776.

Wil·son⁵, John Tuzo (1908–93), Canadian geophysicist. A pioneer in the study of plate tectonics, he introduced the term *plate* in this context in the early 1960s.

Wil·son⁶, Woodrow (1856–1924), 28th president of the US 1913–21; full name *Thomas Woodrow Wilson*. A Democrat, he eventually took the US into World War I in 1917 and later played a leading role in the peace negotiations and the formation of the League of Nations. Nobel Peace Prize (1920).

Wil·son, Mount a peak in the San Gabriel Mountains of southwestern California, near Pasadena, site of a major astronomical observatory.

wilt¹ /wilt/ ▶ v. [intrans.] (of a plant, leaf, or flower) become limp through heat, loss of water, or disease; droop. ■ (of a person) lose one's energy or vigor. ▶ n. [usu. with adj.] any of a number of fungal or bacterial diseases of plants characterized by wilting of the foliage. [17th C. (orig. dialect): perh. an alt. of dial. *welk* 'lose freshness,' of Low Ger. origin.]

wilt[2] archaic second person singular of **WILL**[1].

Wil·ton /'wiltn/ ▶ **n.** a woven carpet resembling a Brussels carpet but with a velvet pile. [18th C.: from *Wilton*, a town in southern England, noted for the manufacture of carpets.]

Wilts. ▶ **abbr.** Wiltshire.

Wilt·shire /'wilt,SHi(ə)r; -SHər/ a county of southern England; county town, Trowbridge.

wil·y /'wīlē/ ▶ **adj.** (**wil·i·er, wil·i·est**) skilled at gaining an advantage, esp. deceitfully. — **wil·i·ly** /'wīlәlē/ **adv. wil·i·ness n.**

Wim·ble·don /'wimbəldən/ an annual international tennis championship played on grass for individual players and pairs, held at the headquarters of the All England Lawn Tennis and Croquet Club in the London suburb of Wimbledon. It has been played since 1877.

wim·min /'wimin/ ▶ **plural n.** nonstandard spelling of "women" adopted by some feminists to avoid the word ending *-men*.

WIMP ▶ **n.** Physics a hypothetical subatomic particle of large mass that interacts only weakly with ordinary matter, postulated as a constituent of the dark matter of the universe. [1980s: acronym from *weakly interacting massive particle*.]

wimp /wimp/ informal ▶ **n.** a weak and cowardly or unadventurous person. ▶ **v.** [intrans.] (**wimp out**) withdraw from a course of action or a stated position in a way that is seen as feeble or cowardly. — **wimp·ish adj. wimp·ish·ly adv. wimp·ish·ness n. wimp·y adj.** [1920s: origin uncert., perh. from **WHIMPER**.]

wim·ple /'wimpəl/ ▶ **n.** a cloth headdress covering the head, the neck, and the sides of the face, formerly worn by women and still worn by some nuns. — **wim·pled adj.** [OE *wimpel*, of Gmc. origin; rel. to Ger. *Wimpel* 'pennon, streamer.']

wimple

win /win/ ▶ **v.** (**win·ning** ; past and past part. **won** /wən/) [trans.] **1** be successful or victorious in (a contest or conflict). **2** acquire or secure as a result of a contest, conflict, bet, or other endeavor: *prizes to be won.* ■ gain (a person's attention, support, or love), typically gradually or by effort. ■ (**win someone over**) gain the support or favor of someone by action or persuasion. ■ [intrans.] (**win out**) manage to succeed or achieve something by effort: *talent won out over bureaucracy.* ■ archaic manage to reach (a place) by effort. ■ obtain (ore) from a mine. ▶ **n.** a successful result in a contest, conflict, bet, or other endeavor; a victory.

– PHRASES **one can't win** informal said when someone feels that no course of action open to them will bring success or please people. **win the day** be victorious in battle, sport, or argument. **win or lose** whether one succeeds or fails. **win** (or **earn**) **one's spurs** hist. gain a knighthood by an act of bravery. ■ informal gain one's first distinction or honors. **you can't win them all** (or **win some, lose some**) informal said to express consolation or resignation after failure in a contest. — **win·less n. win·na·ble adj.** [OE *winnan* 'strive, contend,' also 'subdue and take possession of, acquire,' of Gmc. origin.]

wince[1] /wins/ ▶ **v.** [intrans.] give a slight involuntary grimace or shrinking movement of the body out of pain or distress. ▶ **n.** [in sing.] a slight grimace or shrinking movement caused by pain or distress. — **winc·er n. winc·ing·ly adv.** [ME (orig. in the sense 'kick restlessly from pain or impatience'): from an Anglo-Norman Fr. var. of OFr. *guenchir* 'turn aside.']

wince[2] ▶ **n.** Brit. a roller for moving textile fabric through a dyeing vat. [17th C. (in the sense 'winch'): var. of **WINCH**.]

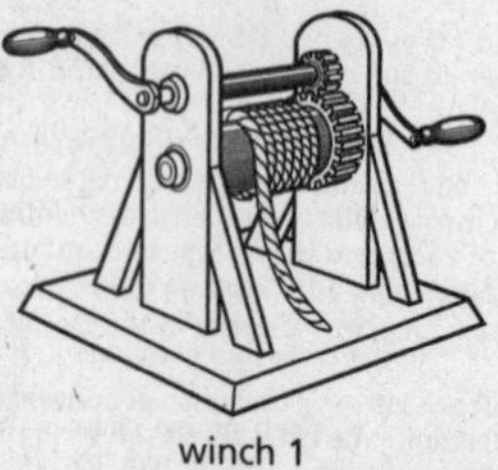
winch 1

winch /winCH/ ▶ **n. 1** a hauling or lifting device consisting of a rope or chain winding around a horizontal rotating drum, turned by a crank or by motor or other power source; a windlass. **2** the crank of a wheel or axle. ▶ **v.** [trans.] hoist or haul with a winch. — **winch·er n.** [OE *wince* 'reel, pulley,' of Gmc. origin; rel. to the verb **WINK**. The v. dates from the early 16th C.]

Win·ches·ter /'win,CHestər; -CHəstər/ ▶ **n. 1** (also **Win·ches·ter ri·fle**) trademark a breech-loading side-action repeating rifle. [named after Oliver F. *Winchester* (1810–80), the American manufacturer of the rifle.] **2** (in full **Win·ches·ter disk** or **drive**) Comput. a disk drive in a sealed unit containing a high-capacity hard disk and the read-write heads. [so named because its original numerical designation corresponded to the caliber of the rifle (see sense 1).]

wind[1] /wind/ ▶ **n. 1** the perceptible natural movement of the air, esp. in the form of a current of air blowing from a particular direction: *an easterly wind.* ■ [as adj.] relating to or denoting energy obtained from harnessing the wind with windmills or wind turbines. ■ used to suggest something very fast, unrestrained, or changeable: *run like the wind.* ■ used in reference to an influence or tendency that cannot be resisted: *a wind of change.* ■ used in reference to an impending situation: *he saw which way the wind was blowing.* ■ the rush of air caused by a fast-moving body. ■ a scent carried by the wind, indicating the presence or proximity of an animal or person. **2** breath as needed in physical exertion or in speech. ■ the power of breathing without difficulty while running or making a similar continuous effort. **3** empty, pompous, or boastful talk; meaningless rhetoric. ■ air swallowed while eating or gas generated in the stomach and intestines by digestion. **4** air or breath used for sounding an organ or a wind instrument. ■ (also **winds**) [treated as sing. or pl.] wind instruments, or specifically woodwind instruments, forming a band or a section of an orchestra: *concerto for piano, violin, and thirteen winds.* ▶ **v.** [trans.] **1** (often **be winded**) cause (someone) to have difficulty breathing because of exertion or a blow to the stomach: *the fall nearly winded him.* **2** detect the presence of (a person or animal) by scent. **3** (past and past part. **wind·ed** /'windid; 'wīn-/ or **wound** /wound/) literary sound (a bugle or call) by blowing: *but scarce again his horn he wound.*

– PHRASES **before the wind** Sailing with the wind blowing more or less from astern. **get wind of** informal begin to suspect that (something) is happening; hear a rumor of. [referring orig. to the scent of game in hunting.] **it's an ill wind that blows no good** proverb few things are so bad that no one profits from them. **off the wind** Sailing with the wind on the quarter. **on a wind** Sailing against a wind on either bow. **sail close to** (or **near**) **the wind 1** Sailing sail as nearly against the wind as possible while still making headway. **2** informal verge on indecency, dishonesty, or disaster. **take the wind out of someone's sails** frustrate someone by unexpectedly anticipating an action or remark. **to the wind (s)** (or **the four winds**) in all directions. ■ so as to be abandoned or neglected: *I threw my friends' advice to the winds.* [from 'And fear of death deliver to the winds' (Milton's *Paradise Lost*).] — **wind·less adj.** [OE, of Gmc. origin; rel. to Du. *wind* and Ger. *Wind*, from an Indo-Eur. root shared by L. *ventus*.]

wind[2] /wīnd/ ▶ **v.** (past **wound** /wound/) **1** [no obj., with adverbial of direction] move in or take a twisting or spiral course: *the path wound among olive trees.* **2** [with obj. and adverbial] pass (something) around a thing or person so as to encircle or enfold. ■ repeatedly twist or coil (a length of something) around itself or a core: *Anne wound the wool into a ball.* ■ [no obj., with adverbial] be twisted or coiled in such a way. ■ wrap or surround (a core) with a coiled length of something: *devices wound with copper wire.* **3** [trans.] make (a clock or other device, typically one operated by clockwork) operate by turning a key or handle: *he wound up the clock every Saturday night.* ■ turn (a key or handle) repeatedly around and around. ■ [with obj. and adverbial of direction] cause (an audio or videotape or a film) to move back or forward to a desired point: *wind your tape back and listen.* ■ [with obj. and adverbial of direction] hoist or draw (something) with a windlass, winch, or similar device. ▶ **n. 1** a twist or turn in a course. **2** a single turn made when winding.

– PHRASAL VERBS **wind down** (of a mechanism, esp. one operated by clockwork) gradually lose power. ■ informal (of a person) relax after stress or excitement. ■ (also **wind something down**) draw or bring gradually to a close: *business began to wind down.* **wind up** informal **1** arrive or end up in a specified state, situation, or place. **2** another way of saying **WIND SOMETHING UP** (sense 2): *he wound up by attacking Nonconformists.* **3** Baseball (of a pitcher) use the windup delivery. **wind someone up** (usu. **be wound up**) make tense or angry. **wind something up 1** arrange the affairs of and dissolve a company. **2** gradually or finally bring an activity to a conclusion. **3** informal increase the tension, intensity, or power of something: *he wound up the engine.* [OE *windan* 'go rapidly,' 'twine,' of Gmc. origin; rel. to **WANDER** and **WEND**.]

wind·age /'windij/ ▶ **n.** the air resistance of a moving object, such as a vessel or a rotating machine part, or the force of the wind on a stationary object. ■ the effect of the wind in deflecting a missile such as a bullet.

Win·daus /'vin,dous/, Adolf (1876–1959), German organic chemist. He did pioneering work on the chemistry of steroids and cholesterol, investigated the D vitamins and vitamin B_1, and discovered histamine. Nobel Prize for Chemistry (1928).

wind·bag /'wind,bag/ ▶ **n.** informal, derog. a person who talks at length but says little of any value. — **wind·bag·ger·y** /-ərē/ **n.**

wind-borne ▶ **adj.** carried by the wind: *wind-borne paper bags.*

wind·bound /'wind,bound/ ▶ **adj.** (of a sailing ship) unable to sail because of extreme or contrary winds.

wind·break /'wind,brāk/ ▶ **n.** a thing, such as a row of trees or a fence, wall, or screen, that provides shelter or protection from the wind.

wind·break·er /'wind,brākər/ ▶ **n.** trademark a wind-resistant jacket with a close-fitting neck, waistband, and cuffs.

wind·burn /'wind,bərn/ ▶ **n.** reddening and soreness of the skin caused by prolonged exposure to the wind. — **wind·burned** (also esp. Brit. **wind·burnt**) **adj.**

wind·chill /'win(d),CHil/ (also **wind·chill fac·tor** or **chill fac·tor**) ▶ **n.** a quantity expressing the perceived lowering of the air temperature caused by the wind.

wind chimes /wind/ ▶ **plural n.** a decorative arrangement of small pieces of glass, metal, or shell suspended from a frame, typically hung near a door or window so as make a tinkling sound in the breeze.

wind·er /ˈwīndər/ ▶ n. a device or mechanism used to wind something, esp. something such as a watch or clock or the film in a camera.

Win·der·mere /ˈwindər,mi(ə)r/ a lake in northwestern England, in the Lake District. About 10 miles (17 km) in length, it is the largest lake in England.

wind·fall /ˈwind,fôl/ ▶ n. an apple or other fruit blown down from a tree or bush by the wind. ■ a piece of unexpected good fortune, typically one that involves receiving a large amount of money.

wind farm /wind/ ▶ n. an area of land with a group of energy-producing windmills or wind turbines.

wind·flow·er /ˈwind,flouər/ ▶ n. an anemone.

wind·gall /ˈwind,gôl/ ▶ n. a small painless swelling just above the fetlock of a horse, caused by inflammation of the tendon sheath.

wind gap /wind/ ▶ n. a valley cut through a ridge by erosion by a river that no longer follows a course through the valley.

wind gauge /wind/ ▶ n. an anemometer. ■ an apparatus attached to the sights of a gun enabling allowance to be made for the wind in shooting.

wind harp /wind/ ▶ n. another term for AEOLIAN HARP.

Wind·hoek /ˈvint,ho͝ok; ˈwind-/ the capital of Namibia, in the center of the country; pop. 59,000.

win·di·go /ˈwindi,gō/ (also **wen·di·go**) ▶ n. (pl. **-gos** or **-goes**) (in the folklore of the northern Algonquian Indians) a cannibalistic giant; a person who has been transformed into a monster by the consumption of human flesh. [from Ojibwa.]

wind·ing /ˈwīndiNG/ ▶ n. **1** the action of winding something or of moving in a twisting or spiral course. ■ (**windings**) twisting movements: *the windings of the stream.* ■ an electrical conductor that is wound around a magnetic material, esp. one encircling part of the stator or rotor of an electric motor or generator or forming part of a transformer. ■ (**windings**) things that wind or are wound around something. **2** [in sing.] (**winding up**) the process of arranging and closing someone's business affairs. ■ the process of closing down a company or a financial institution: *the return of capital on a winding up.* **3** [in sing.] (**winding down**) the action of gradually drawing or being drawn to a close: *the winding down of the investigation.* ▶ adj. following a twisting or spiral course: *a winding staircase.*

wind·ing sheet /ˈwīndiNG/ ▶ n. a sheet in which a corpse is wrapped for burial; a shroud.

wind in·stru·ment /wind/ ▶ n. a musical instrument in which sound is produced by the vibration of air, typically by the player blowing into the instrument. ■ a woodwind instrument as distinct from a brass instrument.

wind·jam·mer /ˈwind,jamər/ ▶ n. hist. a merchant sailing ship.

wind·lass /ˈwindləs/ ▶ n. a type of winch used esp. on ships to hoist anchors and haul on mooring lines and, esp. formerly, to lower buckets into and hoist them up from wells. ▶ v. [trans.] haul or lift (something) with a windlass. [ME: prob. an alt. of obs. *windas*, via Anglo-Norman Fr. from ON *vindáss*, 'winding pole.']

windlass

wind load /wind/ (also **wind load·ing**) ▶ n. Engin. the force on a structure arising from the impact of wind on it.

wind ma·chine /wind/ ▶ n. a machine used in the theater or in filmmaking for producing a blast of air or imitating the sound of wind. ■ a wind-driven turbine for producing electricity.

wind·mill /ˈwind,mil/ ▶ n. a building with sails or vanes that turn in the wind and generate power to grind grain into flour. ■ a similar structure used to generate electricity or draw water. ■ a propeller, esp. one used formerly on an autogiro. ▶ v. [trans.] move (one's arms) around in a circle in a manner suggestive of the rotating sails or vanes of a windmill. ■ [intrans.] (of one's arms) move in such a way. ■ [intrans.] (of the propeller or rotor of an aircraft, or the aircraft itself) spin unpowered.

windmill

win·dow /ˈwindō/ ▶ n. **1** an opening in the wall or roof of a building or vehicle that is fitted with glass in a frame to admit light or air and allow people to see out. ■ a pane of glass filling such an opening. ■ an opening in a wall or screen through which customers are served in a bank, ticket office, or similar building. ■ a space behind the window of a shop where goods are displayed for sale. **2** a thing resembling such an opening in form or function, in particular: ■ a transparent panel on an envelope to show an address. ■ Comput. a framed area on a display screen for viewing information. ■ (**window on/into/to**) a means of observing and learning about. ■ Physics a range of electromagnetic wavelengths for which a medium (esp. the atmosphere) is transparent. **3** an interval or opportunity for action. ■ an interval during which atmospheric and astronomical circumstances are suitable for the launch of a spacecraft. **4** strips of metal foil or metal filings dispersed in the air to obstruct radar detection. [military code word.]

– PHRASES **go out the window** informal (of a plan or pattern or behavior) no longer exist; disappear. **window of opportunity** a favorable opportunity for doing something that must be seized immediately if it is not to be missed. **windows of the soul** organs of sense, esp. the eyes. — **win·dow·less** adj. (in sense 1). [ME: from ON *vindauga*, from *vindr* 'wind' + *auga* 'eye.']

win·dow box ▶ n. a long narrow box in which flowers and other plants are grown, placed on an outside window sill.

win·dow clean·er ▶ n. a person employed to clean windows. ■ a substance used for cleaning windows.

win·dow dress·ing ▶ n. the arrangement of an attractive display in a shop window. ■ an adroit but superficial or actually misleading presentation of something, designed to create a favorable impression.

win·dowed /ˈwindōd/ ▶ adj. **1** having a window or windows for admitting light or air: [in comb.] *a row of bay-windowed houses.* **2** Comput. having or using framed areas on a display screen for viewing information.

win·dow frame ▶ n. a supporting frame for the glass of a window.

win·dow·ing /ˈwindōiNG/ ▶ n. Comput. the use of windows for the simultaneous display of more than one item on a screen.

win·dow ledge ▶ n. another term for WINDOWSILL.

win·dow·pane /ˈwindō,pān/ ▶ n. **1** a pane of glass in a window. **2** a broad flatfish (*Scophthalmus aquosus*, family Scophthalmidae) with numerous dark spots, found in the western Atlantic. Also called SAND DAB. **3** (in full **win·dow·pane ac·id**) Informal a gelatin chip containing LSD.

Win·dow Rock a community in northeastern Arizona, capital of the Navajo reservation, named for a limestone formation; pop. 3,306.

Win·dows /ˈwindōz/ ▶ plural n. [treated as sing.] trademark a computer operating system with a graphical user interface.

win·dow seat ▶ n. a seat below a window, esp. one in a bay or alcove. ■ a seat next to a window in an aircraft, train, or other vehicle.

win·dow-shop ▶ v. [intrans.] look at the goods displayed in shop windows, esp. without intending to buy anything. — **win·dow-shop·per** n.

win·dow·sill /ˈwindō,sil/ (also **win·dow sill**) ▶ n. a ledge or sill forming the bottom part of a window.

wind·pack /ˈwind,pak/ ▶ n. snow that has been compacted by the wind.

wind·pipe /ˈwind,pīp/ ▶ n. the air passage from the throat to the lungs; the trachea.

Wind Riv·er Range /wind/ a range of the Rocky Mountains in western Wyoming that rises to 13,804 feet (4,207 m) at Gannett Peak, the highest in the state.

wind rose /wind/ ▶ n. a diagram showing the relative frequency of wind directions at a place.

wind·row /ˈwind,rō/ ▶ n. a long line of raked hay or sheaves of grain laid out to dry in the wind. ■ a long line of material heaped up by the wind.

wind·sail /ˈwind,sāl/ ▶ n. hist. a long wide tube or funnel of sailcloth used to convey air to the lower parts of a ship.

wind shear /wind/ ▶ n. variation in wind velocity occurring along a direction at right angles to the wind's direction and tending to exert a turning force.

wind·shield /ˈwin(d),SHēld/ ▶ n. a glass shield at the front of a motor vehicle.

wind·shield wip·er ▶ n. a motor-driven device for keeping a windshield clear of rain, typically one with a rubber blade on an arm that moves in an arc.

wind·slab /ˈwind,slab/ ▶ n. a thick crust formed on the surface of soft snow by the wind, of a kind liable to slip and create an avalanche.

wind·sock /ˈwind,säk/ ▶ n. a light, flexible cylinder or cone mounted on a mast to show the direction and strength of the wind, esp. at an airfield.

Wind·sor[1] /ˈwinzər/ a city in Ontario, southern Canada, on Lake Erie, opposite the US city of Detroit; pop. 191,435.

Wind·sor[2] the name of the British royal family since 1917. Previously Saxe-Coburg-Gotha, it was changed in response to anti-German feeling in World War I.

Wind·sor, Duke of the title conferred on Britain's Edward VIII upon his abdication in 1936.

Wind·sor Cas·tle a royal residence at Windsor, founded by William the Conqueror on the site of an earlier fortress and extended by his successors.

Wind·sor chair ▶ n. a wooden dining chair with a semicircular back supported by upright rods.

Windsor chair

Wind·sor knot ▶ n. a large, loose triangular knot in a necktie, produced by making extra turns when tying.

Wind·sor tie ▶ n. dated a wide silk bias-cut necktie, tied in a loose double knot.

wind sprint /wind/ ▶ n. Track & Field a form of exercise involving moving from a walk or slow run to a faster run and repeatedly reversing the process.

wind·storm /ˈwind,stôrm/ ▶n. a storm with very strong wind but little or no rain or snow; a gale.

wind·suck·ing /wind/ ▶n. (in a horse) habitual behavior involving repeated arching of the neck and sucking in and swallowing air, often accompanied by a grunting sound. — **wind-suck·er** n.

wind·surf·er /ˈwind,sərfər/ ▶n. a person who takes part in windsurfing. ■ (trademark in the US) a sailboard.

wind·surf·ing /ˈwind,sərfiNG/ ▶n. the sport or pastime of riding on water on a sailboard. — **wind·surf** v.

wind·swept /ˈwind,swept/ ▶adj. 1 (of a place) exposed to strong winds. 2 (of a person or their appearance) untidy after being exposed to the wind: *windswept hair.*

wind tun·nel /wind/ ▶n. a tunnellike apparatus for producing an airstream of known velocity past models of aircraft, buildings, etc., in order to investigate flow or the effect of wind on the full-size object. ■ an open space through which strong winds are channelled by surrounding tall buildings.

wind tur·bine /wind/ ▶n. a turbine having a large vaned wheel rotated by the wind to generate electricity.

wind·up /ˈwīnd,əp/ ▶n. 1 an act of concluding or finishing something. 2 Baseball the motions of a pitcher immediately before delivering the ball, in which they take a step back, lift the hands over the head, and step forward. ▶adj. (of a toy or other device) functioning by means of winding a key or handle: *a windup clock.*

wind·ward /ˈwindwərd/ ▶adj. & adv. facing the wind or on the side facing the wind: [as adj.] *the windward side of the boat.* Contrasted with LEEWARD. ▶n. the side or direction from which the wind is blowing.

Wind·ward Is·lands 1 a group of islands in the eastern Caribbean Sea that constitute the southern part of the Lesser Antilles. They include Martinique, Dominica, St. Lucia, Barbados, St. Vincent and the Grenadines, and Grenada. 2 an island group in the eastern Society Islands in French Polynesia that include Moorea and Tahiti. French name ÎLES DU VENT.

Wind·ward Passage an ocean channel between Cuba on the west and Haiti on the east that connects the Caribbean Sea with the Atlantic Ocean.

wind·y[1] /ˈwindē/ ▶adj. (**wind·i·er, wind·i·est**) 1 (of weather, a period of time, or a place) marked by or exposed to strong winds. ■ resembling the wind in sound or force. 2 Brit. suffering from, marked by, or causing an accumulation of gas in the alimentary canal. ■ informal using or expressed in many words that sound impressive but mean little: *windy speeches.* — **wind·i·ly** /-əlē/ adv. **wind·i·ness** n. [OE *windig* (see WIND[1], -Y[1]).]

wind·y[2] /ˈwīndē/ ▶adj. (of a road or river) following a curving or twisting course.

wine /wīn/ ▶n. an alcoholic drink made from fermented grape juice. ■ [with adj.] an alcoholic drink made from the fermented juice of specified other fruits or plants: *a glass of dandelion wine.* ■ (also **wine red**) a dark red color. ▶v. [trans.] (**wine and dine someone**) entertain someone by offering them drinks or a meal: *lavishly wined and dined.* ■ [intrans.] (of a person) take part in such entertainment. — **wine·y** (also **win·y**) adj. [OE *wīn*, of Gmc. origin; rel. to Du. *wijn*, Ger. *Wein*, based on L. *vinum.*]

wine bar ▶n. a bar or small restaurant where wine is the main drink available.

wine·ber·ry /ˈwīn,berē/ ▶n. a bristly deciduous shrub (*Rubus phoenicolasius*) of the rose family native to China and Japan, producing scarlet berries used in cooking. ■ the fruit of this bush.

wine·bib·ber /ˈwīn,bibər/ ▶n. archaic or literary a habitual drinker of alcohol. — **wine·bib·bing** /-,bibiNG/ n. & adj.

wine bot·tle ▶n. a glass bottle for wine, the standard size holding 75 cl or 26 23 fl. oz.

wine cel·lar ▶n. a cellar in which wine is stored. ■ a stock of wine.

wine cool·er ▶n. a container for chilling a bottle of wine. ■ a bottled drink made from wine, fruit juice, and carbonated water.

wine·glass /ˈwīn,glas/ ▶n. a glass with a stem and foot, used for drinking wine. — **wine·glass·ful** /ˈwīnglas,fo͝ol/ n. (pl. **-fuls**).

wine·grow·er /ˈwīn,grōər/ ▶n. a cultivator of grapes for wine.

wine list ▶n. a list of the wines available in a restaurant: ■ a restaurant's selection or stock or wines.

wine·mak·er /ˈwīn,mākər/ ▶n. a producer of wine; a winegrower.

wine·mak·ing /ˈwīn,mākiNG/ ▶n. the production of wine.

wine·press /ˈwīn,pres/ ▶n. a press in which grapes are squeezed in making wine.

win·er·y /ˈwīnərē/ ▶n. (pl. **-er·ies**) a place where wine is made.

Wine·sap /ˈwīn,sap/ ▶n. a large red apple, used for cooking and as a dessert apple.

wine·skin /ˈwīn,skin/ ▶n. an animal skin sewn up and used to hold wine.

wine stew·ard ▶n. a waiter responsible for serving wine.

wine tast·ing ▶n. an event at which people taste and compare a number of wines. ■ the action of judging the quality of wine by tasting it. — **wine tast·er** n.

wine vin·e·gar ▶n. vinegar made from wine rather than malt.

wing /wiNG/ ▶n. 1 any of a number of specialized paired appendages that enable some animals to fly, in particular: ■ (in a bird) a modified forelimb that bears large feathers. ■ (in a bat or pterosaur) a modified forelimb with skin stretched between or behind the fingers. ■ (in most insects) each of two or four flat extensions of the thoracic cuticle, either transparent or covered in scales. ■ the meat on the wing bone of a bird used as food. ■ (usu. **wings**) fig. power or means of flight or rapid motion: *time flies by on wings.* 2 a rigid horizontal structure that projects from both sides of an aircraft and supports it in the air. ■ (**wings**) a pilot's certificate of ability to fly a plane, indicated by a badge representing a pair of wings. 3 a part that projects, in particular: ■ Brit. a raised part of the body of a car or other vehicle above the wheel. ■ [usu. with adj.] a part of a large building, esp. one that projects from the main part: *the maternity wing.* ■ either end (port or starboard) of a ship's navigational bridge. ■ Anat. a lateral part or projection of an organ or structure. ■ Bot. a thin membranous appendage of a fruit or seed that is dispersed by the wind. 4 a group within a political party or other organization that holds particular views or has a particular function: *Sinn Fein, the political wing of the IRA.* 5 a side area, or a person or activity associated with that area, in particular: ■ (**the wings**) the sides of a theater stage out of view of the audience. ■ (in soccer, rugby, and other games) the part of the field close to the sidelines. ■ a flank of a battle array. 6 an air force unit of several squadrons or groups. ▶v. 1 [no obj., with adverbial of direction] travel on wings or by aircraft; fly: *a bird came winging around the corner.* ■ move, travel, or be sent quickly, as if flying: *the prize will be winging its way to you soon.* ■ [with obj. and adverbial of direction] throw with the arm: *he winged the ball toward Freddie.* ■ [with obj. and adverbial of direction] send or convey (something) quickly, as if by air: *just put it on a postcard and wing it to us.* 2 [trans.] shoot (a bird) in the wing, so as to prevent flight without causing death. ■ wound (someone) superficially, esp. in the arm or shoulder. 3 (**wing it**) informal speak or act without preparation; improvise. [from theatrical slang, orig. meaning 'to play a role without properly knowing the text' (either by relying on a prompter in the wings or by studying the part in the wings between scenes).]

— PHRASES **in the wings** ready to do something or to be used at the appropriate time. **on the wing** (of a bird) in flight. **on a wing and a prayer** with only the slightest chance of success. **spread** (or **stretch** or **try**) **one's wings** extend one's activities and interests or start new ones. **take wing** (of a bird, insect, or other winged creature) fly away. **under one's wing** in or into one's protective care. — **wing·less** adj. **wing·like** /-,līk/ adj. [ME (orig. in the plural): from ON *vængir*, pl. of *vængr*.]

wing·back ▶n. 1 Football an offensive back who lines up outside an end. 2 Soccer a player who plays in a wide position on the field, taking part both in attack and defense.

wing·beat /ˈwiNG,bēt/ ▶n. one complete set of motions of a wing in flying.

wing case ▶n. each of a pair of modified toughened forewings that cover the functional wings in certain insects, esp. an elytron of a beetle.

wing chair ▶n. a high-backed armchair with side pieces projecting from the back, originally in order to protect the sitter from drafts.

wing chair

wing col·lar ▶n. a high stiff shirt collar with turned-down corners.

wing cov·ert ▶n. (in a bird's wing) each of the smaller feathers covering the bases of the flight feathers.

wing dam ▶n. a dam or barrier built into a stream to deflect the current.

wing·ding /ˈwiNG,diNG/ ▶n. informal a lively event or party. [1920s (in the sense 'spasm, seizure,' esp. one associated with drug-taking): of unknown origin.]

winged /wiNGd/ ▶adj. 1 having wings for flight. ■ /usu. ˈwiNGid/ fig., literary gracefully swift; able to move as if with wings: *the entire evening had gone by on winged feet.* 2 having one or more lateral parts, appendages, or projections.

winged elm ▶n. a North American elm (*Ulmus alata*) that has extremely short leafstalks and flat corky projections on its branchlets.

Winged Vic·to·ry ▶n. a winged statue of Nike, the Greek goddess of victory, esp. the Nike of Samothrace (*c.*200 BC) preserved in the Louvre in Paris.

wing·er /ˈwiNGər/ ▶n. 1 an attacking player on the wing in soccer, hockey, and other sports. 2 [in comb.] a member of a specified political wing: *a left-winger.*

wing for·ward ▶n. Soccer see WING (sense 5 of the **noun**).

wing·let /ˈwiNGlit/ ▶n. a little wing. ■ a vertical projection on the tip of an aircraft wing for reducing drag.

wing·man /ˈwiNGmən/ ▶n. (pl. **-men**) 1 a pilot whose aircraft is positioned behind and outside the leading aircraft in a formation. ■ informal a man who supports another in approaching a desirable woman, typically in a public place such as a bar. 2 another term for WINGER (sense 1).

wing nut (also **wing·nut**) ▶n. a nut with a pair of projections for the fingers to turn it on a screw. See illustration at NUT.

wing·o·ver /ˈwiNG,ōvər/ ▶n. a maneuver in which an aircraft turns at the top of a steep climb and flies back along its original path.

wing oys·ter ▶n. an edible marine bivalve mollusk (*Pteria* and other genera, family Pteridae) with a flattened fragile shell, the hinge of which bears winglike projections.

wing sail ▶ **n.** a rigid or semirigid structure similar to an aircraft wing fixed vertically on a boat to provide thrust from the action of the wind.

wing shoot·ing ▶ **n.** the shooting of birds in flight.

wing·span /ˈwiNG,span/ (also **wing·spread** /-ˌspred/) ▶ **n.** the maximum extent across the wings of an aircraft, bird, or other flying animal, measured from tip to tip.

wing·stroke /ˈwiNG,strōk/ ▶ **n.** another term for WINGBEAT.

wing tip 2

wing tip (also **wing·tip**) ▶ **n. 1** the tip of the wing of an aircraft, bird, or other animal. **2** a shoe with a toe cap having a backward extending point and curving sides, resembling the shape of a wing. ■

wing walk·ing ▶ **n.** acrobatic stunts performed on the wings of an airborne aircraft as a public entertainment.

wink /wiNGk/ ▶ **v.** [intrans.] close and open one eye quickly, typically to indicate that something is a joke or a secret or as a signal of affection or greeting. ■ (**wink at**) pretend not to notice (something bad or illegal). ■ (of a bright object or a light) shine or flash intermittently. ▶ **n.** an act of closing and opening one eye quickly, typically as a signal.
– PHRASES **as easy as winking** informal very easy or easily. **in the wink of an eye** (or **in a wink**) very quickly. **not sleep** (or **get**) **a wink** (or **not get a wink of sleep**) not sleep at all. [OE *wincian* 'close the eyes,' of Gmc. origin; rel. to Ger. *winken* 'to wave,' also to WINCE[1].]

win·kle /ˈwiNGkəl/ ▶ **n.** a small herbivorous shore-dwelling mollusk (family Littorinidae) with a spiral shell. ▶ **v.** [trans.] (**winkle something out**) esp. Brit. extract or obtain something with difficulty: *she winkled it all out of me.* — **win·kler** /ˈwiNGk(ə)lər/ **n.** [16th C.: shortening of PERIWINKLE[2].]

Win·ne·ba·go /ˌwinəˈbāgō/ ▶ **n.** (pl. same or **-gos**) **1** a member of an American Indian people formerly living in eastern Wisconsin and now mainly in southern Wisconsin and Nebraska. **2** the Siouan language of this people. **3** (pl. **-gos**) trademark a motor vehicle with living accommodations used when traveling long distances or camping. ▶ **adj.** of or relating to the Winnebago people or their language. [Algonquian, lit. 'person of the dirty water,' referring to the muddy Fox River.]

Win·ne·ba·go, Lake the largest lake in Wisconsin, in the east central part of the state.

win·ner /ˈwinər/ ▶ **n.** a person or thing that wins something. ■ a goal or shot that wins a winner or point. ■ Bridge a card that can be relied on to win a trick. ■ informal a thing that is a success or is likely to be successful.

win·ner's cir·cle ▶ **n.** a small circular area or enclosure at a racetrack where the winning horse and jockey are brought to receive their awards and have photographs taken.

win·ning /ˈwiniNG/ ▶ **adj. 1** [attrib.] gaining, resulting in, or relating to victory in a contest or competition. **2** attractive; endearing. ▶ **n. 1** (**winnings**) money won, esp. by gambling. **2** Mining a shaft or pit together with the apparatus for extracting coal or other mineral. — **win·ning·ly adv.** (in sense 2 of the **adjective**).

win·ning·est /ˈwiniNGist/ ▶ **adj.** informal having achieved the most success in competition: *the winningest coach in pro-football history.*

win·ning post ▶ **n.** a post marking the end of a race.

Win·ni·peg /ˈwinə,peg/ a city in southern central Canada, the capital of the province of Manitoba, south of Lake Winnipeg; pop. 616,790.

Win·ni·peg, Lake a large lake in central Canada, in southern central Manitoba, north of the city of Winnipeg.

Win·ni·pe·sau·kee, Lake /ˌwinəpəˈsôkē; -ˈsäkē/ the largest lake in New Hampshire, in the east central part of the state.

win·now /ˈwinō/ ▶ **v. 1** [trans.] blow a current of air through (grain) in order to remove the chaff. ■ remove (chaff) from grain. ■ reduce the number in a set of (people or things) gradually until only the best ones are left. ■ find or identify (a valuable or useful part of something): *it's difficult to winnow out the truth.* ■ identify and remove (the least valuable or useful people or things). **2** [intrans.] literary (of the wind) blow: *the autumn wind winnowing its way through the grass.* ■ [trans.] (of a bird) fan (the air) with wings. — **win·now·er n.** [OE *windwian*, from *wind* (see WIND[1]).]

win·o /ˈwīnō/ ▶ **n.** (pl. **-os**) informal a person who drinks excessive amounts of cheap wine or other alcohol, esp. one who is homeless.

win·some /ˈwinsəm/ ▶ **adj.** attractive or appealing in appearance or character. — **win·some·ly adv. win·some·ness n.** [OE *wynsum*, from *wyn* 'joy' + -SOME[1].]

Wins·ton-Sa·lem /ˌwinstən ˈsāləm/ a city in north central North Carolina, a tobacco-processing center; pop. 185,776.

win·ter /ˈwintər/ ▶ **n.** the coldest season of the year, in the northern hemisphere from December to February and in the southern hemisphere from June to August: [as adj.] *the winter months.* ■ Astron. the period from the winter solstice to the vernal equinox. ■ (**winters**) literary years: *he seemed a hundred winters old.* ▶ **adj.** [attrib.] (of fruit and vegetables) ripening late in the growing season and suitable for storage over the winter. ■ (of wheat or other crops) sown in autumn for harvesting the following year. ▶ **v.** [no obj., with adverbial of place] (esp. of a bird) spend the winter in a particular place: *birds wintering in the south.* ■ [trans.] keep or feed (plants or cattle) during winter. — **win·ter·er n. win·ter·less adj. win·ter·ly adj.** [OE, of Gmc. origin; rel. to Du. *winter* and Ger. *Winter*, prob. also to WET.]

win·ter ac·o·nite ▶ **n.** see ACONITE.

win·ter·ber·ry /ˈwintər,berē/ (also **win·ter·ber·ry hol·ly**) ▶ **n.** (pl. **-ries**) a North American holly with toothed, nonprickly leaves and berries that persist through the winter.

win·ter cress ▶ **n.** a bitter-tasting cress (genus *Barbarea*) of north temperate regions.

win·ter floun·der ▶ **n.** a common flatfish (*Pseudopleuronectes americanus*, family Pleuronectidae) of the western Atlantic, having cryptic gray-brown coloration and popular as food in winter in North America.

win·ter gar·den ▶ **n.** a garden of plants, such as evergreens, that flourish in winter. ■ a conservatory in which flowers and other plants are grown in winter.

win·ter·green /ˈwintər,grēn/ ▶ **n. 1** a North American plant from which a pungent oil is obtained, in particular the checkerberry or related shrubs. ■ (also **oil of win·ter·green**) a pungent oil containing methyl salicylate, now obtained chiefly from the sweet birch or made synthetically, used medicinally and as a flavoring. **2** a low-growing plant (*Chimaphila*, *Pyrola* and other genera, family Pyrolaceae or Monotropaceae) of acid soils in north temperate regions, with spikes of white bell-shaped flowers. [16th C.: the plants so named because of remaining green in winter, suggested by Du. *wintergroen*, Ger. *Wintergrün*.]

win·ter·ize /ˈwintə,rīz/ ▶ **v.** [trans.] (usu. **be winterized**) adapt or prepare (something, esp. a house or an automobile) for use in cold weather. — **win·ter·i·za·tion** /ˌwintəriˈzāSHən/ **n.**

win·ter mel·on ▶ **n.** a variety of muskmelon with a sweet, edible flesh that requires a long growing season and ripens in late autumn, making it available in many supermarkets during the winter.

win·ter moth ▶ **n.** a moth (family Geometridae) that emerges in the winter, the female of which has only vestigial wings. It was formerly a major pest of fruit trees.

Win·ter Pal·ace the former Russian imperial residence in St. Petersburg, stormed in the Revolution of 1917 and later used as a museum and art gallery.

win·ter quar·ters ▶ **plural n.** accommodations for the winter, esp. for soldiers.

win·ter sleep ▶ **n.** hibernation.

win·ter sol·stice ▶ **n.** the solstice that marks the onset of winter, at the time of the shortest day, about December 22 in the northern hemisphere and June 21 in the southern hemisphere. ■ Astron. the solstice in December.

win·ter sports ▶ **plural n.** sports performed on snow or ice, such as skiing and ice skating.

win·ter squash ▶ **n.** a squash (*Cucurbita moschata* and *C. maxima*) that has a hard rind and may be stored.

win·ter·sweet /ˈwintər,swēt/ ▶ **n.** a deciduous Chinese shrub (*Chimonanthus praecox*, family Calycanthaceae) that produces heavily scented yellow flowers in winter before the leaves appear, grown in North America as an ornamental.

win·ter·tide /ˈwintər,tīd/ ▶ **n.** poetic/literary term for WINTERTIME.

win·ter·time /ˈwintər,tīm/ ▶ **n.** the season or period of winter.

Win·throp[1] /ˈwinTHrəp/, John (1588–1649), American colonial leader; born in England. He was the first governor 1630–49 of the Massachusetts Bay Colony.

Win·throp[2], John (1714–79), American astronomer and physicist. He practiced experimental science, gave laboratory demonstrations of electricity in 1746, and predicted the return of Halley's Comet in 1759.

win·try /ˈwintrē/ (also **win·ter·y** /ˈwint(ə)rē/) ▶ **adj.** (**-tri·er**, **-tri·est**) characteristic of winter, esp. in feeling or looking very cold and bleak: *a wintry landscape.* — **win·tri·ly** /-trəlē/ **adv. win·tri·ness n.** [OE *wintrig* (see WINTER, -Y[1]).]

win-win ▶ **adj.** [attrib.] of or denoting a situation in which each party benefits in some way.

WIP ▶ **abbr.** work in progress (chiefly in business and financial contexts).

wipe /wīp/ ▶ **v.** [trans.] clean or dry (something) by rubbing its surface with a cloth, a piece of paper, or one's hand: *he wiped down the kitchen wall.* ■ [with obj. and adverbial] remove (dirt or moisture) from something by rubbing its surface with a cloth, a piece of paper, or one's hand: *she wiped away a tear.* ■ clean (something) by rubbing it against a surface. ■ [with obj. and adverbial] spread (a liquid) over a surface by rubbing: *gently wipe the lotion over the eyelids.* ■ [with obj. and adverbial] fig. remove or eliminate (something) completely: *events wiped the smile off Kate's face.* ■ erase (data) from a magnetic medium. ▶ **n. 1** an act of wiping. **2** a piece of disposable absorbent cloth, esp. one treated with a cleansing agent, for wiping something clean. **3** a cinematographic effect in which an existing picture seems to be wiped out by a new one as the boundary between them moves across the screen.

– PHRASES **wipe the floor with** informal inflict a humiliating defeat on. **wipe the slate clean** forgive or forget past faults or offenses; make a fresh start.

– PHRASAL VERBS **wipe something off** subtract an amount from a value or debt: *the crash wiped 24 percent off stock prices.* **wipe out** informal fall over or off a vehicle. ■ be capsized by a wave while surfing. **wipe someone out 1** kill a large number of people. **2** (usu. **be wiped out**) ruin someone financially. **3** informal exhaust or intoxicate someone. **wipe something out** eliminate something completely. — **wipe·a·ble** adj. [OE *wīpian*, of Gmc. origin; rel. to WHIP.]

wipe·out /ˈwīpˌout/ ▶ n. informal an instance of complete destruction. ■ a complete failure. ■ the obliteration of one radio signal by another. ■ a fall from a surfboard.

wip·er /ˈwīpər/ ▶ n. **1** a windshield wiper. **2** an electrical contact that moves across a surface.

WIPO ▶ abbr. World Intellectual Property Organization.

wire /wī(ə)r/ ▶ n. **1** metal drawn out into the form of a thin flexible thread or rod. ■ a piece of such metal. ■ a length or quantity of wire used, for example, for fencing or to carry an electric current. ■ Horse Racing a wire stretched across and above the track at the finish of a racetrack. ■ an electronic listening device that can be concealed on a person. **2** informal a telegram or cablegram. ▶ v. [trans.] **1** install electric circuits or wires in: *they wired the place themselves.* ■ connect (someone or something) to a piece of electronic equipment. **2** provide, fasten, or reinforce with wires: *they wired his jaw.* **3** informal send a telegram or cablegram to. ■ [with two objs.] send (money) to (someone) by means of a telegram or cablegram: *he was expecting a friend to wire him $1,500.* **4** snare (an animal) with wire. **5** (usu. **be wired**) Croquet obstruct (a ball, shot, or player) by a wicket.

– PHRASES **by wire** by telegraph. **down to the wire** informal used to denote a situation whose outcome is not decided until the very last minute. **under the wire** informal at the last possible opportunity; just in time. — **wir·er** n. [OE *wīr*, of Gmc. origin, prob. from the base of L. *viere* 'plait, weave.']

wire cloth ▶ n. cloth woven from wire.

wire cut·ter ▶ n. (usu. **wire cutters**) a tool for cutting wire.

wired /wī(ə)rd/ ▶ adj. informal **1** making use of computers and information technology to transfer or receive information, esp. by means of the Internet: *the economic arguments for getting your business wired.* **2** [predic.] in a nervous, tense, or edgy state. ■ under the influence of drugs or alcohol.

wire-draw ▶ v. (past **-drew**; past part. **-drawn**) [trans.] [often as n.] (**wire-drawing**) draw out (metal) into wire by passing it through a series of holes of diminishing diameter in a steel plate. — **wire-draw·er** n.

wire·frame /ˈwī(ə)rˌfrām/ ▶ n. Comput. a skeletal three-dimensional model in which only lines and vertices are represented.

wire fraud ▶ n. financial fraud involving the use of telecommunications or information technology.

wire gauge ▶ n. a gauge for measuring the diameter of wire. ■ the diameter of wire; any of a series of standard sizes in which wire is made.

wire gauze ▶ n. See GAUZE.

wire grass ▶ n. a grass (genera *Aristida* and *Poa*) with tough wiry stems.

wire-guid·ed ▶ adj. (of a missile) directed by means of electrical signals transmitted along fine connecting wires that uncoil during the missile's flight.

wire-haired ▶ adj. (esp. of a dog breed) having stiff or wiry hair: *a wire-haired terrier.*

wire·less /ˈwī(ə)rlis/ ▶ adj. using radio, microwaves, etc. (as opposed to wires) to transmit signals. ▶ n. **1** computer networking, broadcasting, telephony, or telegraphy using radio signals. **2** (also **wire·less set**) dated, chiefly Brit. a radio receiving set. — **wire·less·ly** adv.

wire·line /ˈwī(ə)rˌlīn/ ▶ n. **1** a telegraph or telephone wire. **2** (in the oil industry) a cable for lowering and raising tools and other equipment in a well shaft. ■ an electric cable used to connect measuring devices in an oil well with indicating or recording instruments at the surface. **3** a horizontal watermark in laid paper.

wire·man /ˈwī(ə)rˌmən/ ▶ n. (pl. **-men**) **1** an installer or repairer of electric wiring. **2** a journalist working for a news agency. **3** Informal a professional wiretapper.

wire·pull·er /ˈwīrˌpo͝olər/ ▶ n. informal a person, esp. a politician, who exerts control or influence from behind the scenes. — **wire·pull·ing** /-ˌpo͝oliNG/ n.

wire rope ▶ n. a length of rope made from wires twisted together as strands.

wire serv·ice ▶ n. a news agency that supplies syndicated news by wire to newspapers, radio, and television stations.

wire·tap·ping /ˈwī(ə)rˌtapiNG/ ▶ n. the practice of connecting a listening device to a telephone line to secretly monitor a conversation. — **wire·tap** n. & v. **wire·tap·per** /-ˌtapər/ n.

wire wheel ▶ n. a wheel on a car, esp. a sports car, having narrow metal spokes.

wire·worm /ˈwī(ə)rˌwərm/ ▶ n. a wormlike hard-skinned larva, esp. of a click beetle. Many wireworms feed on the underground parts of plants and can cause damage to arable and other crops. ■ a myriapod, esp. of the millipede genus *Iulus*, which damages plant roots.

wir·ing /ˈwī(ə)riNG/ ▶ n. a system of wires providing electric circuits for a device or building. ■ the installation of this. ■ informal the structure of the nervous system or brain perceived as determining a basic or innate pattern of behavior.

Wirt·schafts·wun·der /ˈvirtsHäftsˌvo͝ondər/ ▶ n. an economic miracle, esp. the economic recovery of the Federal Republic of West Germany after World War II. [Ger.]

wir·y /ˈwī(ə)rē/ ▶ adj. (**wir·i·er**, **wir·i·est**) resembling wire in form and texture: *his wiry black hair.* ■ (of a person) lean, tough, and sinewy. — **wir·i·ly** /ˈwī(ə)rəlē/ adv. **wir·i·ness** n.

Wis. ▶ abbr. Wisconsin.

Wis·con·sin[1] /wisˈkänsən/ a state in the northern US that borders on lakes Superior (in the northwest) and Michigan (in the east); pop. 5,363,675; capital, Madison; statehood, May 29, 1848 (30). — **Wis·con·sin·ite** /-səˌnīt/ n.

Wis·con·sin[2] ▶ n. [usu. as adj.] Geol. the last (or last two) of the Pleistocene glaciations of North America, approximating to the Weichsel of northern Europe. ■ the system of deposits laid down at this time.

Wis·con·sin Riv·er a river that flows through central Wisconsin to the Mississippi River at Prairie du Chien.

Wisd. ▶ abbr. (in biblical references) Wisdom of Solomon (Apocrypha).

wis·dom /ˈwizdəm/ ▶ n. the quality of having experience, knowledge, and good judgment; the quality of being wise. ■ the soundness of an action or decision with regard to the application of such experience, knowledge, and good judgment: *some questioned the wisdom of building the dam so close to an active volcano.* ■ the body of knowledge and principles that develops within a specified society or period: *oriental wisdom.*

– PHRASES **in someone's wisdom** used ironically to suggest that an action is not well judged: *in their wisdom they decided to dispense with him.* [OE *wīsdōm* (see WISE[1], -DOM).]

wis·dom lit·er·a·ture ▶ n. the biblical books of Job, Proverbs, Ecclesiastes, Song of Songs, Wisdom of Solomon, and Ecclesiasticus collectively. ■ similar works, esp. from the ancient Near East, containing proverbial sayings and practical maxims.

Wis·dom of Sol·o·mon a book of the Apocrypha ascribed to Solomon and containing a meditation on wisdom. The book is thought actually to date from about the 1st century BC to the 1st century AD.

wis·dom tooth ▶ n. each of the four hindmost molars in humans, which usually appear at about the age of twenty.

wise[1] /wīz/ ▶ adj. having or showing experience, knowledge, and good judgment: *a wise precaution.* ■ responding sensibly or shrewdly to a particular situation: *it would be wise to discuss the matter.* ■ [predic.] having knowledge in a specified subject: *families wise in the way of hurricane survival.* ■ [predic.] (**wise to**) informal alert to or aware of.

– PHRASES **be wise after the event** understand and assess an event or situation only after its implications have become obvious. **be none** (or **not any**) **the wiser** know no more than before. **get wise** become alert or aware.

– PHRASAL VERBS **wise off** Informal make wisecracks. **wise up** [often in imper.] informal become alert to or aware of something: *wise up before it's too late.* — **wise·ly** adv. [OE *wīs*, of Gmc. origin; rel. to Du. *wijs* and Ger. *weise*, also to WIT[2].]

wise[2] ▶ n. archaic the manner or extent of something.

– PHRASES **in no wise** not at all. [OE *wīse*, of Gmc. origin; rel. to WIT[2].]

-wise ▶ suffix forming adjectives and adverbs of manner or respect such as *clockwise*, *otherwise*. Compare with -WAYS. ■ informal with respect to; concerning: *security-wise, there are few problems.* [from WISE[2].]

wise·a·cre /ˈwīzˌākər/ ▶ n. a person with an affectation of wisdom or knowledge, regarded with scorn or irritation by others; a know-it-all. [16th C.: from MDu. *wijssegghe*r 'soothsayer,' prob. from the Gmc. base of WIT[2]. The assimilation to ACRE remains unexplained.]

wise·ass /ˈwīzˌas/ ▶ n. & adj. Informal another term for SMART ALECK.

wise·crack /ˈwīzˌkrak/ informal ▶ n. a clever and pithy spoken witticism. ▶ v. [intrans.] make a wisecrack: [as n.] (**wisecracking**) *his warmth, boisterousness, and constant wisecracking.* — **wise·crack·er** n.

wise guy informal ▶ n. **1** a person who speaks and behaves as if they know more than others. **2** a member of the Mafia.

wise man ▶ n. a man versed in magic, witchcraft, or astrology. See also THREE WISE MEN.

wis·en·heim·er /ˈwīzənˌhīmər/ ▶ n. informal a person who behaves in an irritatingly smug or arrogant fashion, typically by making clever remarks and displaying their knowledge. [20th C.: from WISE[1] + the suffix *-(n)heimer* found in surnames such as *Oppenheimer*.]

wi·sent /ˈvēzent/ ▶ n. the European bison (*Bison bonasus*), now found only in Poland. [19th C.: from Ger.; rel. to BISON.]

wise saw ▶ n. a proverbial saying.

wise wom·an ▶ n. esp. hist. a woman considered to be knowledgeable in matters such as herbal healing, magic charms, or other traditional lore.

wish /wisH/ ▶ v. [intrans.] feel or express a strong desire or hope for something that is not easily attainable; want something that cannot or probably will not happen: *we wished for peace.* ■ silently invoke such a hope or desire, esp. in a ritualized way. ■ [with infin.] feel or express a desire to do something. ■ [with obj. and infin.] ask (someone) to do something or that (something) be done: *I wish it to be clearly understood.* ■ [with two objs.] express a desire for (the success or good fortune) of (someone):

they wish her every success. ■ [trans.] (**wish something on**) hope that something unpleasant will happen to: *I would not wish it on the vilest soul.* ▶ n. a desire or hope for something to happen. ■ (usu. **wishes**) an expression of such a desire, typically in the form of a request or instruction. ■ an invocation or recitation of a hope or desire: *he makes a wish.* ■ (usu. **wishes**) an expression of a desire for someone's success or good fortune: *they had received good wishes from total strangers.* ■ a thing or event that is or has been desired; an object of desire.
– PHRASES **if wishes were horses, beggars would ride** proverb if you could achieve your aims simply by wishing for them, life would be very easy. **wish someone well** feel or express a desire for someone's well-being. **the wish is father to the thought** proverb we believe a thing because we wish it to be true. — **wish·er** n. [in comb.] *an ill-wisher.* [OE *wȳscan*, of Gmc. origin; rel. to Ger. *wünschen*, also to **WEEN** and **WONT**.]

wish·bone /ˈwisʜˌbōn/ ▶ n. **1** a forked bone (the furcula) between the neck and breast of a bird. According to a popular custom, this bone from a cooked bird is broken by two people, with the holder of the longer portion being entitled to make a wish. **2** an object of similar shape, in particular: ■ Football an offensive formation in which the fullback lines up immediately behind the quarterback with the two halfbacks behind and on either side of the fullback. ■ a forked element in the suspension of a motor vehicle or aircraft, typically attached to a wheel at one end with the two arms hinged to the chassis. ■ Sailing a boom in two halves that curve outward around a sail and meet aft of it.

wish book ▶ n. informal a mail-order catalog.

wish·ful /ˈwisʜfəl/ ▶ adj. having or expressing a desire or hope for something to happen. ■ expressing or containing a desire or hope for something impractical or unfeasible: *the proposed measures were merely wishful thinking.* — **wish·ful·ly** adv. **wish·ful·ness** n.

wish ful·fil·ment ▶ n. the satisfying of unconscious desires in dreams or fantasies.

wish·ing well ▶ n. a well into which one drops a coin and makes a wish.

wish list ▶ n. a list of desired things or occurrences.

wish-wash ▶ n. informal a weak or watery drink: *one pot of wish-wash called "tea."* ■ insipid or excessively sentimental talk or writing. [18th C.: reduplication of **WASH**.]

wish·y-wash·y /ˈwisʜē ˈwäsʜē; -ˈwôsʜē/ ▶ adj. (of drink or liquid food such as soup) weak; watery. ■ feeble or insipid in quality or character; lacking strength or boldness. [18th C.]

Wis·ła /ˈvēswä/ Polish name for **VISTULA**.

wisp /wisp/ ▶ n. a small thin or twisted bunch, piece, or amount of something: *wisps of smoke.* ■ a small bunch of hay or straw used for drying or grooming a horse. ■ a small thin person, typically a child. — **wisp·i·ly** /ˈwispilē/ adv. **wisp·i·ness** /ˈwispēnis/ n. **wisp·y** adj. (**wisp·i·er, wisp·i·est**). [ME: origin uncert.; perh. rel. to **WHISK**.]

Wis·sen·schaft /ˈvisənˌsʜäft/ ▶ n. the systematic pursuit of knowledge, learning, and scholarship (esp. as contrasted with its application). [Ger., lit. 'knowledge.']

wist /wist/ past and past participle of **WIT**².

Wis·tar rat /ˈwistər/ ▶ n. Biol. Med. a rat of a strain developed for laboratory purposes. [1930s: named after the *Wistar* Institute of Anatomy and Biology, Philadelphia, Pennsylvania.]

wis·te·ri·a /wiˈsti(ə)rēə/ (also **wis·ta·ri·a** /-ˈste(ə)rēə/) ▶ n. a climbing shrub (genus *Wisteria*) of the pea family, with hanging clusters of pale bluish-lilac flowers. [mod. L., named after Caspar *Wistar* (or *Wister*) (1761–1818), American anatomist.]

wist·ful /ˈwistfəl/ ▶ adj. having or showing a feeling of vague or regretful longing. — **wist·ful·ly** adv. **wist·ful·ness** n. [17th C.: appar. from obs. *wistly* 'intently,' influenced by **WISHFUL**.]

wit[1] /wit/ ▶ n. **1** mental sharpness and inventiveness; keen intelligence. ■ (**wits**) the intelligence required for normal activity; basic human intelligence. **2** a natural aptitude for using words and ideas in a quick and inventive way to create humor. ■ a person who has such an aptitude: *she is such a wit.*
– PHRASES **be at one's wits' end** be overwhelmed with difficulties and at a loss as to what to do next. **be frightened** (or **scared**) **out of one's wits** be extremely frightened; be immobilized by fear. **gather** (or **collect**) **one's wits** allow oneself to think calmly and clearly in a demanding situation. **have** (or **keep**) **one's wits about one** be constantly alert and vigilant. **live by one's wits** earn money by clever and sometimes dishonest means, having no regular employment. **pit one's wits against** compete with (someone or something). — **wit·ted** adj. [in comb.] *slow-witted.* [OE *wit(t)*, *gewit(t)*, denoting the mind as the seat of consciousness, of Gmc. origin; rel. to Du. *weet* and Ger. *Witz*, also to **WIT**².]

wit[2] ▶ v. (**wot** /wät/, **wit·ting** ; past and past part. **wist** /wist/) [intrans.] **1** archaic have knowledge: [trans.] *I wot that but too well.* **2** (**to wit**) that is to say (used to make clearer or more specific something already said or referred to). [OE *witan*, of Gmc. origin; rel. to Du. *weten* and Ger. *wissen*, from an Indo-Eur. root shared by Sanskrit *veda* 'knowledge' and L. *videre* 'see.']

witch /wicʜ/ ▶ n. **1** a woman thought to have evil magic powers. Witches are popularly depicted as wearing a black cloak and pointed hat, and flying on a broomstick. ■ a follower or practitioner of modern witchcraft; a Wiccan priest or priestess. ■ informal an ugly or unpleasant old woman; a hag. ■ a girl or woman capable of enchanting or bewitching a man. **2** an edible North Atlantic flatfish (*Glyptocephalus cynoglossus*, family Pleuronectidae) that is of some commercial value. ▶ v. [trans.] (of a witch) cast an evil spell on. ■ (of a girl or woman) enchant (a man).
– PHRASES **as cold as** (or **colder than**) **a witch's tit** informal very cold. — **witch·like** /-ˌlīk/ adj. **witch·y** adj. [OE *wicca* (masc.), *wicce* (fem.), *wiccian* (verb); current senses of the v. are prob. a shortening of **BEWITCH**.]

witch·craft /ˈwicʜˌkraft/ ▶ n. the practice of magic, esp. black magic; the use of spells and the invocation of spirits. See also **WICCA**.

witch doc·tor ▶ n. (among tribal peoples) a magician credited with powers of healing, divination, and protection against the magic of others.

witch elm ▶ n. var. of **WYCH ELM**.

witch·er·y /ˈwicʜərē/ ▶ n. the practice of magic. ■ compelling power exercised by beauty, eloquence, or other attractive or fascinating qualities.

witch·es' broom ▶ n. dense twiggy growth in a tree caused by infection with fungus (esp. rusts), mites, or viruses.

witch·es' sab·bath ▶ n. see **SABBATH** (sense 2).

witch·grass /ˈwicʜˌgras/ (also **witch grass**) ▶ n. a tough creeping grass that can become an invasive weed, esp. couch grass or the North American grass *Panicum capillare*.

witch ha·zel ▶ n. a shrub (genus *Hamamelis*, family Hamamelidaceae) with fragrant yellow flowers that is widely grown as an ornamental. ■ an astringent lotion made from the bark and leaves of this plant, esp. *H. virginiana*. [16th C.: *witch*, var. of *wych* (see **WYCH ELM**).]

witch-hunt ▶ n. hist. a search for and subsequent persecution of a supposed witch. ■ informal a campaign directed against a person or group holding unorthodox or unpopular views. — **witch-hunt·ing** n.

witch·ing /ˈwicʜiɴɢ/ ▶ n. the practice of witchcraft.
– PHRASES **the witching hour** midnight (with reference to the belief that witches are active and magic takes place at that time). [with allusion to *the witching time of night* from Shakespeare's *Hamlet* (III. ii. 377).]

with /wit͟h; witʜ/ ▶ prep. **1** accompanied by (another person or thing): *steak with a bottle of red wine.* ■ in the same direction as: *swim with the current.* ■ along with (with reference to time): *wisdom comes with age.* ■ in proportion to: *the form changes with period in a systematic way.* **2** possessing (something) as a feature or accompaniment: *a blouse with a white collar.* ■ marked by or wearing: *a small man with thick glasses.* **3** indicating the instrument used to perform an action: *cut it with a knife.* ■ indicating the material used for some purpose: *fill the bowl with water.* **4** in opposition to: *fighting with each other.* **5** indicating the manner or attitude of the person doing something: *with great reluctance.* **6** indicating responsibility: *leave it with me.* **7** in relation to: *he will be angry with me.* **8** employed by: *she's with IBM now.* ■ as a member or employee of. ■ using the services of: *I bank with the TSB.* **9** affected by (a particular fact or condition): *in bed with lumbago.* ■ indicating the cause of an action or condition: *trembling with fear.* **10** indicating separation or removal from something: *to part with one's dearest possessions.*
– PHRASES **away** (or **off** or **out**, etc.) **with** used in exhortations to take or send someone or something away, in, out, etc.: *off with his head.* **be with someone 1** agree with or support someone. **2** informal follow someone's meaning: *I'm not with you.* **with it 1** knowledgeable about and following modern ideas and fashions. **2** [usu. with negative] alert and comprehending: *I'm not really with it today.* **with that** at that point; immediately after saying or doing something dramatic: *with that, she flounced out.* [OE, prob. a shortening of a Gmc. prep. rel. to obs. Engl. *wither* 'adverse, opposite.']

with·al /wit͟hˈôl; witʜ-/ archaic ▶ adv. in addition; as a further factor or consideration: *useful but ornamental withal.* ■ all the same; nevertheless (used when adding something that contrasts with a previous comment). ▶ prep. with (used at the end of a clause): *we sat with little to nourish ourselves withal but vile water.* [ME: orig. as *with all*.]

with·draw /wit͟hˈdrô; witʜ-/ ▶ v. (past **-drew**; past part. **-drawn**) **1** [trans.] remove or take away (something) from a particular place or position: *Ruth withdrew her hand from his.* ■ take (money) out of an account: *you can withdraw up to $50.* ■ take back or away (something bestowed, proposed, or used). ■ (in parliamentary procedure) remove or recall a motion, amendment, etc., from consideration. ■ say that (a statement one has made) is untrue or unjustified: *withdraw his remarks.* ■ [intrans.] (of a man) practice coitus interruptus. **2** [intrans.] leave or come back from a place, esp. a war zone: *Iraqi forces withdrew from Kuwait.* ■ [trans.] cause (someone) to leave or come back from a place, esp. a war zone. ■ no longer participate in an activity or be a member of a team or organization. ■ depart to another room or place, esp. in search of quiet or privacy. ■ retreat from contact or communication with other people: *he withdrew into himself.* **3** [intrans.] cease to take an addictive drug: *a cocaine user who wanted to withdraw without medication.* [ME: from the prefix *with-* 'away' + the v. **DRAW**.]

with·draw·al /wit͟hˈdrô(ə)l; witʜ-/ ▶ n. the action of withdrawing something. ■ an act of taking money out of an account. ■ a sum of money withdrawn from an account. ■ the action of ceasing to participate in an activity. ■ the process of ceasing to take an addictive drug. ■ coitus interruptus.
– PHRASES **withdrawal symptoms** the unpleasant physical reaction that accompanies the process of ceasing to take an addictive drug.

with·drawn /wit͟hˈdrôn; witʜ-/ past participle of **WITHDRAW**. ▶ adj. not

PRONUNCIATION KEY ə *ago, up*; ər *over, fur*; a *hat*; ā *ate*; ä *car*; e *let*; ē *see*; i *fit*; ī *by*; ɴɢ *sing*; ō *go*; ô *law, for*; oi *toy*; o͝o *good*; o͞o *goo*; ou *out*; ᴛʜ *thin*; ᴛ͟ʜ *then*; ᴢʜ *vision* wanting to communicate with other people: *a disorder characterized by withdrawn behavior.*

withe /wiᴛʜ; wiᴛʜ/ ▶ **n.** var. of WITHY.

with·er /ˈwiᴛʜər/ ▶ **v.** **1** [intrans.] (of a plant) become dry and shriveled. ■ (of a person, limb, or the skin) become shrunken or wrinkled from age or disease. ■ cease to flourish; fall into decay or decline. **2** [trans.] cause harm or damage to: *a business that withers the hardiest ego.* ■ mortify (someone) with a scornful look or manner.
– PHRASES **wither on the vine** fail to be implemented or dealt with because of neglect or inaction. [ME: appar. a var. of WEATHER, ult. differentiated for certain senses.]

with·er·ing /ˈwiᴛʜəriɴɢ/ ▶ **adj.** **1** intended to make someone feel mortified or humiliated. **2** (of heat) intense; scorching. ▶ **n.** the action of becoming dry and shriveled. ■ the action of declining or decaying. — **with·er·ing·ly** **adv.** (in sense 1 of the **adjective**).

with·er·ite /ˈwiᴛʜə,rīt/ ▶ **n.** a rare white mineral consisting of barium carbonate, occurring esp. in veins of galena. [18th C.: from the name of William *Withering* (1741–99), the English physician and scientist who first described it, + -ITE[1].]

with·ers /ˈwiᴛʜərz/ ▶ **plural n.** the highest part of a horse's back, lying at the base of the neck above the shoulders. The height of a horse is measured to the withers. [16th C.: appar. a reduced form of *widersome*, from obs. *wither-* 'against, contrary' (as the part that resists the strain of the collar) + a second element of obscure origin.]

with·er·shins /ˈwiᴛʜər,sʜinz/ ▶ **adv.** var. of WIDDERSHINS.

with·hold /wiᴛʜˈhōld; wiᴛʜ-/ ▶ **v.** (past and past part. **-held**) [trans.] refuse to give (something that is due to or is desired by another): [as n.] (**withholding**) *the withholding of consent to treatment.* ■ suppress or hold back (an emotion or reaction). ■ (of an employer) deduct (tax) from an employee's paycheck and send it directly to the government. — **with·hold·er** **n.** [ME: from the prefix *with-* 'away' + the v. HOLD[1].]

with·hold·ing tax ▶ **n.** the amount of an employee's pay withheld by the employer and sent directly to the government as partial payment of income tax.

with·in /wiᴛʜˈin; wiᴛʜ-/ ▶ **prep.** inside (something): *within the building.* ■ inside the range of (an area or boundary). ■ inside the range of (a specified action or perception): *within reach.* ■ not further off than (used with distances): *within a few miles of Honesdale.* ■ occurring inside (a particular period of time): *sold out within two hours.* ■ inside the bounds set by (a concept, argument, etc.): *within the terms of the treaty.* ▶ **adv.** inside; indoors: *inquire within.* ■ internally or inwardly: *beauty from within.*
– PHRASES **within doors** indoors. [OE *withinnan* 'on the inside.']

with·out /wiᴛʜˈout; wiᴛʜ-/ ▶ **prep.** **1** in the absence of: *he went without her.* ■ not having the use or benefit of: *he made the ascent without oxygen.* ■ [often with verbal n.] in circumstances in which the action mentioned does not happen: *they looked at each other without speaking.* **2** archaic or literary outside: *the barbarians without the gates.* ▶ **adv.** archaic or literary outside: *the enemy without.* ▶ **conj.** archaic or dialect without it being the case that. ■ unless. [OE *withūtan* 'on the outside.']

with·stand /wiᴛʜˈstand; wiᴛʜ-/ ▶ **v.** (past and past part. **-stood**) [trans.] remain undamaged or unaffected by; resist: *designed to withstand winds of 100 mph.* ■ offer strong resistance or opposition to (someone or something). — **with·stand·er** **n.** [OE *withstandan*, from the prefix *with-* 'against' + the v. STAND.]

with·y /ˈwiᴛʜē; ˈwiᴛʜē/ (also **withe** /wiᴛʜ; wiᴛʜ; wīᴛʜ/) ▶ **n.** (pl. **with·ies** or **withes** /wiᴛʜs; wiᴛʜz/) a tough flexible branch of an osier or other willow, used for tying, binding, or basketry. ■ another term for OSIER. [OE *wīthig*, of Gmc. origin; rel. to Ger. *Weide*.]

wit·less /ˈwitlis/ ▶ **adj.** foolish; stupid. ■ [as complement] to such an extent that one cannot think clearly or rationally: *I was scared witless.* — **wit·less·ly** **adv.** **wit·less·ness** **n.** [OE *witlēas* 'crazy, dazed' (see WIT[1], -LESS).]

wit·ling /ˈwitliɴɢ/ ▶ **n.** archaic, usu. derog. a person who considers themselves to be witty.

wit·loof /ˈwit,lōf/ ▶ **n.** chicory of a broad-leaved variety grown for blanching. [19th C.: from Du., lit. 'white leaf.']

wit·ness /ˈwitnis/ ▶ **n.** **1** a person who sees an event, typically a crime or accident, take place. ■ a person giving sworn testimony to a court of law or the police. ■ a person who is present at the signing of a document and signs it themselves to confirm this. **2** evidence; proof: *his presence was witness to his interest.* ■ used to refer to confirmation or evidence given by signature, under oath, or otherwise: *in witness thereof, the parties sign this document.* ■ open profession of one's religious faith through words or actions. **3** a member of the Jehovah's Witnesses. ▶ **v.** **1** [trans.] see (an event, typically a crime or accident) take place. ■ have knowledge of (an event or change) from personal observation or experience. ■ (of a time, place, or other context) be the setting in which (a particular event) takes place: *the 1960s witnessed stirring social changes.* ■ be present as someone signs (a document) or gives (their signature) to a document and sign it oneself to confirm this. ■ [in imper.] look at (used to introduce a fact illustrating a preceding statement). **2** [intrans.] (**witness to**) give or serve as evidence of; testify to: *his writings are witness to an inner toughness.* ■ (of a person) openly profess one's religious faith in.
– PHRASES **as God is my witness** (or **God be my witness**) an invocation of God as confirmation of the truth of a statement. **call someone or something to witness** archaic appeal or refer to someone or something for confirmation or evidence of something. [OE *witnes* (see WIT[1], -NESS).]

wit·ness stand (Brit. **wit·ness box**) ▶ **n.** Law the place in a court where a witness stands to give evidence.

Wit·ten·berg /ˈwitn,bərg; ˈvitn,berk/ a town in eastern Germany, on the Elbe River; pop. 87,000. It was the scene in 1517 of Martin Luther's campaign against the Roman Catholic Church that was a major factor in the rise of the Reformation.

Witt·gen·stein /ˈvitgən,stīn; -,sʜtīn/, Ludwig Josef Johann (1889–1951), British philosopher, born in Austria. His major works examine language and its relationship to the world.

wit·ti·cism /ˈwiti,sizəm/ ▶ **n.** a witty remark. [1677: coined by Dryden from WITTY, on the pattern of *criticism*.]

wit·ting /ˈwitiɴɢ/ ▶ **adj.** done in full awareness or consciousness; deliberate. ■ (of a person) conscious or aware of the full facts of a situation: *witting accomplices.* — **wit·ting·ly** **adv.** [ME: from WIT[2] + -ING[2].]

wit·tol /ˈwitl/ ▶ **n.** archaic a man who is aware and tolerant of his wife's infidelity; an acquiescent cuckold. [ME: appar. from WIT[2] + the last syllable (with the loss of *-d*) of CUCKOLD.]

wit·ty /ˈwitē/ ▶ **adj.** (**-ti·er**, **-ti·est**) showing or characterized by quick and inventive verbal humor: *a witty remark.* — **wit·ti·ly** /ˈwitl-ē/ **adv.** **wit·ti·ness** **n.** [OE *wit(t)ig* 'having wisdom' (see WIT[1], -Y[1]).]

Wit·wa·ters·rand /ˈwit,wôtərz,rand; -,wätərz-; -,ränd/ (**the Witwatersrand**) a region in South Africa, around the city of Johannesburg. The region contains rich gold deposits that were first discovered in 1886. Also called *THE RAND* (see RAND[1]).

wives /wīvz/ plural form of WIFE.

wiz /wiz/ ▶ **n.** var. of WHIZ (sense 2).

wiz·ard /ˈwizərd/ ▶ **n.** **1** a man who has magical powers, esp. in legends and fairy tales. ■ a person who is very skilled in a particular field or activity. **2** Comput. a help feature of a software package that automates complex tasks by asking the user a series of easy-to-answer questions. ▶ **adj.** informal, dated, esp. Brit. wonderful; excellent. — **wiz·ard·ly** **adj.** (in sense 1 of the **noun**). [ME (in the sense 'philosopher, sage'): from WISE[1] + -ARD.]

wiz·ard·ry /ˈwizərdrē/ ▶ **n.** the art or practice of magic. ■ great skill in a particular area of activity. ■ the product of such skill: *hi-tech wizardry.*

wiz·en /ˈwizən; ˈwē-/ ▶ **adj.** archaic variant of WIZENED.

wiz·ened /ˈwizənd; ˈwē-/ ▶ **adj.** shriveled or wrinkled with age. [16th C.: past part. of archaic *wizen* 'shrivel,' of Gmc. origin.]

wk ▶ **abbr.** week.

Wła·dys·ław II /vläˈdis,läf; -,wäf/ see LADISLAUS II.

WLTM ▶ **abbr.** would like to meet (used in lonely hearts advertisements).

Wm. ▶ **abbr.** William.

WMD ▶ **abbr.** weapon(s) of mass destruction.

WMO ▶ **abbr.** World Meteorological Organization.

WNW ▶ **abbr.** west-northwest.

WO ▶ **abbr.** Warrant Officer.

w/o ▶ **abbr.** ■ without.

woad /wōd/ ▶ **n.** a yellow-flowered European plant (*Isatis tinctoria*) of the cabbage family. ■ a blue dye obtained from this plant, now superseded by synthetic products. [OE *wād*, of Gmc. origin; rel. to Du. *wede* and Ger. *Waid*.]

wob·ble /ˈwäbəl/ ▶ **v.** [intrans.] move unsteadily from side to side. ■ [trans.] cause to move in such a way. ■ [with adverbial of direction] move in such a way in a particular direction: *they wobble around on their bikes.* ■ (of the voice) tremble; quaver: *her voice wobbled.* ■ fig. hesitate or waver between different courses of action; vacillate. ▶ **n.** an unsteady movement from side to side. ■ a tremble or quaver in the voice. ■ a moment of hesitation or vacillation. [17th C. (earlier as *wabble*): of Gmc. origin; cf. ON *vafla* 'waver'; rel. to the v. WAVE.]

wob·bler /ˈwäb(ə)lər/ ▶ **n.** a person or thing that wobbles. ■ (in angling) a lure that wobbles and does not spin.

Wob·blies /ˈwäb(ə)lēz/ ▶ **plural n.** popular name for members of INDUSTRIAL WORKERS OF THE WORLD. [20th C.: of unknown origin.]

wob·bly /ˈwäb(ə)lē/ ▶ **adj.** (**-bli·er**, **-bli·est**) tending to move unsteadily from side to side. ■ (of a person or their legs) weak and unsteady from illness, tiredness, or anxiety. ■ (of a person, action or state) uncertain, wavering, or insecure. ■ (of a speaker, singer, or voice) having a tendency to move out of tone or slightly vary in pitch. ■ (of a line or handwriting) not straight or regular; shaky. — **wob·bli·ness** **n.**

Wode·house /ˈwŏŏd,hous/, Sir P. G. (1881–1975), English writer; full name *Pelham Grenville Wodehouse*. His best-known works are humorous stories of Bertie Wooster and his valet Jeeves.

Wo·den /ˈwōdn/ another name for ODIN.

woe /wō/ ▶ **n.** often humorous great sorrow or distress. ■ (**woes**) things that cause sorrow or distress; troubles.
– PHRASES **woe betide someone** (or **woe to someone**) used humorously to warn someone that they will be in trouble if they do a specified thing. **woe is me!** an ironical or humorous exclamation of sorrow or distress. [natural exclamation of lament: recorded as *wā* in OE and found in several Gmc. languages.]

woe·be·gone /ˈwōbi,gôn; -,gän/ ▶ **adj.** sad or miserable in appearance. [ME (in the sense 'afflicted with grief'): from WOE + *begone* 'surrounded' (past part. of obs. *bego* 'go around, beset').]

woe·ful /ˈwōfəl/ ▶ **adj.** characterized by, expressive of, or causing sorrow or misery. ■ very bad; deplorable: *woeful ignorance.* — **woe·ful·ly** **adv.** [as submodifier] *the police response was woefully inadequate.* **woe·ful·ness** **n.**

Wöh·ler /ˈvœlər/, Friedrich (1800–82), German chemist. His synthesis of urea from ammonium cyanate in 1828 demonstrated that organic compounds could be made from inorganic compounds.

wok

wok /wäk/ ▸ **n.** a bowl-shaped frying pan used typically in Chinese cooking. [Chin. (Cantonese dial.).]

woke /wōk/ past of WAKE[1].

wok·en /ˈwōkən/ past participle of WAKE[1].

wold /wōld/ ▸ **n.** [often in place names] (usu. **wolds**) (in Britain) a piece of high, open, uncultivated land or moor: *the Lincolnshire Wolds.* [OE *wald* 'wooded upland,' of Gmc. origin; perh. rel. to WILD. Cf. WEALD.]

wolf /wo͝olf/ ▸ **n.** (pl. **wolves** /wo͝olvz/) **1** a wild carnivorous mammal (*Corvus frugilegus*) that is the largest member of the dog family, living and hunting in packs. It is native to both Eurasia and North America, but has been widely exterminated. ■ used in names of similar or related mammals, e.g., **maned wolf. 2** used in similes and metaphors to refer to a rapacious, ferocious, or voracious person or thing. ■ informal a man who habitually seduces women. **3** a harsh or out-of-tune effect produced when playing particular notes or intervals on a musical instrument, caused either by the instrument's construction or by divergence from equal temperament. ▸ **v.** [trans.] devour (food) greedily: *he wolfed down his breakfast.*

– PHRASES **cry wolf** call for help when it is not needed, with the effect that one is not believed when one really does need help. [with allusion to Aesop's fable of the shepherd boy who deluded people with false cries of "Wolf!"] **hold** (or **have**) **a wolf by the ears** be in a precarious position. **keep the wolf from the door** have enough money to avert hunger or starvation (used hyperbolically). **throw someone to the wolves** leave someone to be roughly treated or criticized without trying to help or defend them. **a wolf in sheep's clothing** a person or thing that appears friendly or harmless but is really hostile. [with biblical allusion to Matt. 7:15.] — **wolf·ish adj. wolf·ish·ly adv. wolf·like** /-ˌlīk/ **adj.** [OE *wulf*, of Gmc. origin; rel. to Du. *wolf* and Ger. *Wolf*, from an Indo-Eur. root shared by L. *lupus* and Gk. *lukos*. The v. dates from the mid 19th C.]

Wolfe[1] /wo͝olf/, James (1727–59), British general. He commanded the attack on Quebec, Canada's French capital, in 1759. He was fatally wounded while leading his troops to victory on the Plains of Abraham.

Wolfe[2], Thomas Clayton (1900–38), US writer. His novels include *Look Homeward Angel* (1929) and *You Can't Go Home Again* (1940).

Wolfe[3], Tom (1931–), US writer; born *Thomas Kennerley Wolfe, Jr.* He examined contemporary culture in the US in *The Electric Kool-Aid Acid Test* (1968) and *The Bonfire of the Vanities* (1988).

wolf·fish /ˈwo͝olfˌfisн/ ▸ **n.** a large long-bodied marine fish (family Anarhichadidae) with a long-based dorsal fin and sharp doglike teeth, inhabiting the deep waters of the northern hemisphere. Its several species include the edible *Anarhichas lupus*.

wolf·hound /ˈwo͝olfˌhound/ ▸ **n.** a dog of a large breed originally used to hunt wolves.

wolf pack ▸ **n.** a group of people or things that operate as a hunting and attacking pack, in particular a group of attacking submarines or aircraft.

wolf·ram /ˈwo͝olfrəm/ ▸ **n.** tungsten or its ore, esp. as a commercial commodity. [18th C.: from Ger., assumed to be a miners' term, perh. from *Wolf* 'wolf' + Mid. High Ger. *rām* 'soot.']

wolf·ram·ite /ˈwo͝olfrəˌmīt/ ▸ **n.** a black or brown mineral that is the chief ore of tungsten. It consists of a tungstate of iron and manganese.

Wolf Riv·er a river that flows through central Wisconsin.

wolfs·bane /ˈwo͝olfsˌbān/ ▸ **n.** a northern European aconite.

Wolfs·burg /ˈwo͝olfsˌbərg; ˈvôlfsˌbo͝ork/ a city in Lower Saxony, in northwestern Germany; pop. 129,000.

wolf·skin /ˈwo͝olfˌskin/ ▸ **n.** the skin or pelt of a wolf.

wolf spi·der ▸ **n.** a fast-moving ground spider (family Lycosidae, order Araneae) that runs after and springs on its prey.

wolf whis·tle ▸ **n.** a whistle with a rising and falling pitch, directed toward someone to express sexual attraction or admiration. ▸ **v.** (**wolf-whis·tle**) [trans.] whistle in such a way at: *fans wolf-whistled her as she took off her jacket.*

Wol·las·ton /ˈwo͝oləstən/, William Hyde (1766–1828), English chemist and physicist. He pioneered techniques in powder metallurgy.

wol·las·ton·ite /ˈwo͝oləstəˌnīt/ ▸ **n.** a white or grayish mineral typically occurring in tabular masses in metamorphosed limestone. It is a silicate of calcium and is used as a source of rock wool. [19th C.: from the name of W. H. *Wollaston* (see WOLLASTON) + -ITE[1].]

Wol·lon·gong /ˈwo͝olənˌgôɴg; -ˌgäɴg/ a city in southeastern Australia; pop. 211,000.

Woll·stone·craft /ˈwo͝olstənˌkraft/, Mary (1759–97), English writer and feminist. She wrote *A Vindication of the Rights of Woman* (1792). In 1797 she married William Godwin and died shortly after giving birth to their daughter, Mary Shelley.

Wo·lof /ˈwōˌläf/ ▸ **n.** (pl. same or **-lofs**) **1** a member of a people living in Senegal and Gambia. **2** the Niger–Congo language of this people. ▸ **adj.** of or relating to the Wolof or their language. [the name in Wolof.]

Wol·sey /ˈwo͝olzē/, Thomas (*c.*1474–1530), English clergyman; known as **Cardinal Wolsey**. He incurred royal displeasure through his failure to secure the papal dispensation necessary for Henry VIII's divorce from Catherine of Aragon.

Wol·ver·hamp·ton /ˈwo͝olvərˌham(p)tən; ˌwo͝olvərˈham(p)-/ a city in western central England; pop. 240,000.

European wolverine

wol·ver·ine /ˌwo͝olvəˈrēn/ ▸ **n.** a heavily built short-legged carnivorous mammal of the weasel family, with a shaggy dark coat and a bushy tail, native to the tundra and forests of arctic and subarctic regions. Two species: *Gulo luscus* of North America and *G. gulo* of Europe. [16th C. (earlier as *wolvering*): from *wolv-*, pl. stem of WOLF.]

wolves /wo͝olvz/ plural form of WOLF.

wom·an /ˈwo͝omən/ ▸ **n.** (pl. **wom·en** /ˈwimin/) an adult human female. ■ a female worker or employee. ■ a wife, girlfriend, or lover: *Billy had his woman with him.* ■ [with adj.] a female person associated with a particular place, activity, or occupation: *a young American woman.* ■ [in sing.] female adults in general. ■ a female paid to clean someone's house and carry out general domestic duties. ■ a peremptory form of address to a woman: *don't be daft, woman.*

– PHRASES **the little woman** a condescending way of referring to a man's wife. **woman of letters** a female scholar or author. **woman of the streets** dated used euphemistically to refer to a prostitute. **woman to woman** in a direct and frank way between two women. — **wom·an·less adj. wom·an·like** /-ˌlīk/ **adj.** [OE *wifmon, -man* (see WIFE, MAN), a formation peculiar to Engl., the ancient word being WIFE.]

-woman ▸ **comb. form** in nouns denoting: ■ a female of a specified nationality: *Frenchwoman.* ■ a woman of specified origin or place of abode: *Yorkshirewoman.* ■ a woman belonging to a distinct specified group: *laywoman.* ■ a woman having a specified occupation or professional status: *saleswoman.* ■ a woman skilled in or associated with a specified activity, esp. a craft or sport: *needlewoman.*

wom·an·hood /ˈwo͝omənˌho͝od/ ▸ **n.** the state or condition of being a woman: *on the brink of womanhood.* ■ the qualities considered to be natural to or characteristic of a woman. ■ women considered collectively: *African-American womanhood.*

wom·an·ish /ˈwo͝omənisн/ ▸ **adj.** derog. suitable to or characteristic of a woman. ■ (of a man) effeminate; unmanly. — **wom·an·ish·ly adv. wom·an·ish·ness n.**

wom·an·ize /ˈwo͝oməˌnīz/ ▸ **v.** [intrans.] (of a man) engage in numerous casual sexual affairs with women (used to express disapproval): [as n.] (**womanizing**) *his womanizing had now become intolerable.* — **wom·an·iz·er n.**

wom·an·kind /ˈwo͝omənˌkīnd/ ▸ **n.** women considered collectively.

wom·an·ly /ˈwo͝omənlē/ ▸ **adj.** relating to or having the characteristics of a woman or women. ■ (of a girl's or woman's body) fully developed and curvaceous. — **wom·an·li·ness n.**

womb /wo͞om/ ▸ **n.** the uterus. ■ a place of origination and development: *the womb of evil.* — **womb·like** /-ˌlīk/ **adj.** [OE *wamb, womb*, of Gmc. origin.]

common wombat

wom·bat /ˈwämˌbat/ ▸ **n.** a burrowing plant-eating Australian marsupial (family Vombatidae) that resembles a small bear with short legs. Two genera and three species include the **common wombat** (*Vombatus ursinus*). [18th C.: from Dharuk.]

wom·en /ˈwimin/ plural form of WOMAN.

wom·en·folk /ˈwimin,fōk/ ▶ plural n. the women of a particular family or community considered collectively.

wom·en's lib ▶ n. informal short for WOMEN'S LIBERATION. — **wom·en's lib·ber** n.

wom·en's lib·er·a·tion ▶ n. the advocacy of the liberation of women from inequalities and subservient status in relation to men, and from attitudes causing these (now generally replaced by the term *feminism*).

wom·en's move·ment ▶ n. a broad movement campaigning for women's liberation and rights.

wom·en's rights ▶ plural n. rights that promote a position of legal and social equality of women with men.

wom·en's room ▶ n. another term for LADIES' ROOM.

wom·en's stud·ies ▶ plural n. [usu. treated as sing.] academic courses in sociology, history, literature, and psychology that focus on the roles, experiences, and achievements of women in society.

wom·en's suf·frage ▶ n. the right of women to vote.

wom·ens·wear /ˈwiminz,we(ə)r/ (also **wom·en's wear**) ▶ n. clothing for women.

wom·en's work ▶ n. work traditionally and historically undertaken by women, esp. tasks of a domestic nature such as cooking, needlework, and child rearing.

wom·yn /ˈwimin/ ▶ plural n. nonstandard spelling of "women" adopted by some feminists in order to avoid the word ending *-men*.

won[1] /wən/ past and past participle of WIN.

won[2] /wän/ ▶ n. (pl. same) the basic monetary unit of North and South Korea, equal to 100 jun in North Korea and 100 jeon in South Korea. [from Kor. *wŏn*.]

won·der /ˈwəndər/ ▶ n. a feeling of surprise mingled with admiration, caused by something beautiful, unexpected, unfamiliar, or inexplicable. ■ the quality of a person or thing that causes such a feeling: *Athens was a place of wonder.* ■ a strange or remarkable person, thing, or event. ■ [as adj.] having remarkable properties or abilities: *a wonder drug.* ■ [in sing.] a surprising event or situation. ▶ v. [intrans.] **1** desire or be curious to know something. ■ [with clause] used to express a polite question or request: *I wonder whether you have thought more about it?* ■ feel doubt. **2** feel admiration and amazement; marvel: *people wondered at such bravery.* ■ be surprised: *it is not to be wondered at.*

– PHRASES **I shouldn't wonder** informal, esp. Brit. I think it likely. **no** (or **little** or **small**) **wonder** it is not surprising. **ninety-day** (or **thirty-day** or **one-day**) **wonder** something that attracts enthusiastic interest for a short while but is then ignored or forgotten. ■ (usu. **ninety-day** (or **thirty-day**) **wonder**) a person who has had intensive military training for the specified time. **wonders will never cease** an exclamation of great surprise at something pleasing. **work** (or **do**) **wonders** have a very beneficial effect on someone or something. — **won·der·er** n. **won·der·ing·ly** adv. [OE *wundor* (n.), *wundrian* (v.), of Gmc. origin; rel. to Du. *wonder* and Ger. *Wunder*, of unknown ultimate origin.]

won·der·ful /ˈwəndərfəl/ ▶ adj. inspiring delight, pleasure, or admiration; extremely good; marvelous. — **won·der·ful·ly** /-f(ə)lē/ adv. [as submodifier] *the bed was wonderfully comfortable.* **won·der·ful·ness** n. [OE *wunderfull* (see WONDER, -FUL).]

won·der·land /ˈwəndər,land/ ▶ n. a land or place full of wonderful things.

won·der·ment /ˈwəndərmənt/ ▶ n. a state of awed admiration or respect: *shook his head in wonderment.*

won·der·struck /ˈwəndər,strək/ ▶ adj. (of a person) experiencing a sudden feeling of awed delight or wonder.

won·der·work·er /ˈwəndər,wərkər/ ▶ n. a person who performs miracles or wonders. — **won·der·work·ing** adj.

won·drous /ˈwəndrəs/ ▶ adj. literary inspiring a feeling of wonder or delight; marvelous. ▶ adv. [as submodifier] archaic marvelously; wonderfully. — **won·drous·ly** adv. **won·drous·ness** n. [15th C.: alt. of obs. *wonders* (adj. and adv.), genitive of WONDER, on the pattern of *marvelous*.]

wonk /wängk/ ▶ n. informal, derog. a studious or hardworking person: *any kid interested in science was a wonk.* ■ a person who takes an excessive interest in minor details of political policy: *a policy wonk.* [1920s: of unknown origin.]

won·ky /ˈwängkē/ ▶ adj. (**-ki·er, -ki·est**) informal crooked; off-center; askew. ■ (of a thing) unsteady; shaky: *sitting on wonky stools.* ■ faulty. — **won·ki·ly** /ˈwängkəlē/ adv. **won·ki·ness** n. [20th C.: fanciful formation.]

wont /wônt; wōnt/ ▶ adj. [predic., with infin.] literary (of a person) in the habit of doing something; accustomed. ▶ n. (**one's wont**) formal or humorous one's customary behavior in a particular situation: *Constance, as was her wont, left early.* ▶ v. (3rd sing. pres. **wonts** or **wont** ; past **wont** or **wonted**) archaic make or be or become accustomed. [OE *gewunod*, past part. of *wunian*, 'dwell, be accustomed' of Gmc. origin.]

won't /wōnt/ ▶ contr. will not.

wont·ed /ˈwôntid; ˈwōn-/ ▶ adj. literary habitual; usual. [ME: from WONT.]

won·ton (also **won ton**) /ˈwän,tän/ ▶ n. (in Chinese cooking) a small round dumpling or roll with a savory filling, usually eaten boiled in soup. [from Chin. (Cantonese dial.) *wān t ān*.]

woo /wo͞o/ ▶ v. (**woos, wooed**) [trans.] try to gain the love of (someone, typically a woman), esp. with a view to marriage. ■ seek the favor, support, or custom of: *pop stars are wooed by film companies.* — **woo·a·ble** adj. **woo·er** n. [OE *wōgian* (intransitive), *āwōgian* (transitive), of unknown origin.]

Wood /wo͝od/, Grant De Volsen (1892–1942), US artist. He is most noted for his scenes of his native Iowa in paintings such as *American Gothic* (1930).

wood /wo͝od/ ▶ n. **1** the hard fibrous material that forms the main substance of the trunk or branches of a tree or shrub. ■ such material when cut and used as timber or fuel. ■ a golf club with a wooden or other head that is relatively broad from face to back (often with a numeral indicating the degree to which the face is angled to loft the ball). ■ a shot made with such a club. **2** (also **woods**) an area of land, smaller than a forest, that is covered with growing trees: *a long walk in the woods.*

– PHRASES **get wood** vulgar slang have an erection. **knock on wood** said in order to prevent a confident statement from bringing bad luck. [with ref. to the custom of touching something wooden to ward off bad luck.] **out of the wood** (or **woods**) out of danger or difficulty. — **wood·less** adj. [OE *wudu*, from a Gmc. word rel. to Welsh *gwŷdd* 'trees.']

wood al·co·hol ▶ n. crude methanol made by distillation from wood.

wood a·nem·o·ne ▶ n. see ANEMONE.

wood bet·o·ny ▶ n. a North American lousewort *Pedicularis canadensis*.

wood·bine /ˈwo͝od,bīn/ ▶ n. either of two climbing plants: ■ Virginia creeper. ■ Brit. the common honeysuckle.

wood·block /ˈwo͝od,bläk/ ▶ n. a block of wood, esp. one from which woodcut prints are made. ■ a print made in such a way. ■ a hollow wooden block used as a percussion instrument.

Wood·bur·y /ˈwo͝od,berē; -bərē/, Levi (1789–1851), US Supreme Court associate justice 1846–51.

wood·carv·ing /ˈwo͝od,kärviNG/ ▶ n. the action or skill of carving wood to make functional or ornamental objects. ■ an object made in this way. — **wood·carv·er** n.

wood·chat /ˈwo͝od,CHat/ (also **wood·chat shrike**) ▶ n. a shrike (*Lanius senator*) of southern Europe, North Africa, and the Middle East, having black and white plumage with a chestnut head.

wood·chuck /ˈwo͝od,CHək/ ▶ n. a North American marmot (*Marmota monax*) with a heavy body and short legs. [17th C.: alt. (by association with WOOD) of an Amer. Ind. name; cf. Cree *wuchak, otchock*.]

wood·cock /ˈwo͝od,käk/ ▶ n. (pl. same) a woodland bird (genus *Scolopax*) of the sandpiper family, with a long bill, brown camouflaged plumage, and a distinctive display flight.

wood·craft /ˈwo͝od,kraft/ ▶ n. **1** skill in woodwork. **2** knowledge of the woods, esp. with reference to camping and other outdoor pursuits.

wood·cut /ˈwo͝od,kət/ ▶ n. a print of a type made from a design cut in a block of wood, formerly widely used for illustrations in books. Compare with WOOD ENGRAVING. ■ the technique of making such prints.

wood·cut·ter /ˈwo͝od,kətər/ ▶ n. **1** a person who cuts down trees or branches, esp. for fuel. **2** a person who makes woodcuts. — **wood·cut·ting** n.

wood duck ▶ n. a tree-nesting North American duck (*Aix sponsa*), the male of which has brightly colored plumage. Also called CAROLINA DUCK.

wood·ed /ˈwo͝odid/ ▶ adj. (of an area of land) covered with woods or many trees.

wood·en /ˈwo͝odn/ ▶ adj. **1** made of wood. **2** like or characteristic of wood: *a dull wooden sound.* ■ stiff and awkward in movement or manner. — **wood·en·ly** adv. (in sense 2) **wood·en·ness** n. (in sense 2).

wood en·grav·ing ▶ n. a print made from a finely detailed design cut into the end grain of a block of wood. Compare with WOODCUT. ■ the technique of making such prints. — **wood en·grav·er** n.

wood·en·head ▶ n. informal a stupid person. — **wood·en·head·ed** adj. **wood·en·head·ed·ness** n.

wood·fern /ˈwo͝od,fərn/ ▶ n. an evergreen fern (genus *Dryopteris*, family Polypodiaceae) with leathery dark-green fronds. Numerous species include the common **evergreen** (or **marginal**) **woodfern** (*D. marginalis*).

evergreen woodfern

wood fi·ber /ˈwo͝od ,fībər/ ▶ n. fiber obtained from wood and used esp. in the manufacture of paper.

wood·grain /ˈwo͝od,grān/ ▶ n. a pattern of fibers seen in a cut surface of wood. ■ [as adj.] denoting a surface or finish imitating such a pattern.

wood·grouse /ˈwo͝od,grous/ ▶ n. a grouse that frequents woodlands, esp. a capercaillie, spruce grouse, or willow grouse.

wood·hoo·poe /ˈho͞o,pō; -po͞o/ ▶ n. a long-tailed African bird (genus *Phoeniculus*, family Phoeniculidae) with a long, slender, down-curved bill and blackish plumage with a blue or green gloss.

wood i·bis ▶ n. a stork (genus *Mycteria*) with a slightly down-curved bill and a bare face or head, found in America and Africa.

wood·ie /ˈwo͝odē/ ▶ n. **1** vulgar slang (also **wood·y**) (of a man) a penile erection. **2** a station wagon with wood exterior paneling.

wood·land /ˈwo͝odlənd; -,land/ ▶ n. (also **woodlands**) land covered with trees: [as adj.] *woodland birds are often drably colored.*

wood·land·er /ˈwŏŏdləndər; -ˌlandər/ ▶ n. an inhabitant of woodland.

wood·lark /ˈwŏŏdˌlärk/ ▶ n. a small European and North African lark (*Lullula arborea*) with a short tail and melodious song, frequenting open ground with scattered trees.

wood louse ▶ n. (pl. **wood lice**) a small terrestrial crustacean (*Oniscus* and other genera, order Isopoda) with a grayish segmented body and seven pairs of legs, living in damp habitats.

wood·man /ˈwŏŏdmən/ ▶ n. (pl. **-men**) esp. hist. a person working in woodland, esp. a forester or woodcutter.

wood mouse ▶ n. a dark brown Eurasian mouse (genus *Apodemus*) with a long tail and large eyes, in particular the widespread *A. sylvaticus.* Also called FIELD MOUSE.

wood mush·room ▶ n. an edible mushroom (*Agaricus silvicola*, family Agaricaceae) with a white cap and brown gills, smelling strongly of aniseed and found in woodland in both Eurasia and North America.

wood·note /ˈwŏŏdˌnōt/ ▶ n. literary a natural and untrained musical note resembling the song of a bird.

wood nymph 2

wood nymph (also **wood·nymph**) ▶ n. **1** (in folklore and classical mythology) a nymph inhabiting woodland, esp. a Dryad or Hamadryad. **2** a brown American butterfly of grassy habitats and light woodlands, with large eyespots on the forewings and smaller ones on the hind wings. Genus *Cercyonis*, subfamily Satyrinae: includes several species, in particular the widespread *C. pegala.*

wood·peck·er /ˈwŏŏdˌpekər/ ▶ n. a strong-billed, stiff-tailed bird that climbs tree trunks to find insects and drums on dead wood to mark territory. The **woodpecker family** (Picidae) also includes the wrynecks, flickers, and sapsuckers. See illustration at DOWNY WOODPECKER.

wood pi·geon ▶ n. a large Eurasian and African pigeon (genus *Columba*) with mainly gray plumage, using wing claps in display flight.

wood·pile /ˈwŏŏdˌpīl/ ▶ n. a stack of wood stored for fuel.

wood pulp ▶ n. wood fiber reduced chemically or mechanically to pulp and used in the manufacture of paper.

wood rat ▶ n. another term for PACK RAT.

wood·ruff /ˈwŏŏdˌrəf/ ▶ n. a white-flowered plant (genera *Galium* and *Asperula*) of the bedstraw family with whorled leaves, smelling of new-mown hay when dried or crushed, esp. **sweet woodruff** (*G. odoratum*). [OE *wudurofe*, from *wudu* 'wood' + an element of unknown meaning.]

wood·rush /ˈwŏŏdˌrəsн/ ▶ n. a grasslike plant (genus *Luzula*, family Juncaceae) that typically has long flat leaves fringed with long hairs.

Woods[1] /wŏŏdz/, Tiger (1975–), US golfer; full name *Eldrick Woods.* During 1997–2006, he won 12 major championships.

Woods[2], William Burnham (1824–87), US Supreme Court associate justice 1880–87.

wood screw ▶ n. a tapering metal screw with a sharp point. See illustration at SCREW.

wood·shed /ˈwŏŏdˌsнed/ ▶ n. a shed where wood for fuel is stored. ▶ v. [intrans.] practice a musical instrument.

– PHRASES **take someone to the woodshed** informal reprove or punish someone, esp. discreetly.

wood·si·a /ˈwŏŏdzēə/ ▶ n. a small tufted fern (genus *Woodsia*, family Woodsiaceae) that grows among rocks in mountains in temperate and cool regions. [mod. L., named after Joseph *Woods* (1776–1864), English architect and botanist.]

woods·man /ˈwŏŏdzmən/ ▶ n. (pl. **-men**) a person living or working in the woods, esp. a forester, hunter, or woodcutter.

wood·smoke /ˈwŏŏdˌsmōk/ ▶ n. the smoke from a wood fire.

wood sor·rel ▶ n. a small woodland plant (genus *Oxalis*, family Oxalidaceae) with cloverlike leaves and five-petaled flowers. Several species include the yellow-flowered creeping **yellow wood sorrel** (*O. stricta*) and the purple-flowered **violet wood sorrel** (*O. violacea*).

wood spir·it ▶ n. another term for WOOD ALCOHOL.

Wood·stock /ˈwŏŏdˌstäk/ a small town in upstate New York, near Albany. It gave its name in the summer of 1969 to a huge rock music festival, actually held about 60 miles (96 km) to the southwest in Bethel, New York.

wood stork ▶ n. another term for WOOD IBIS.

woods·y /ˈwŏŏdzē/ ▶ adj. of, relating to, or characteristic of wood or woodlands: *the woodsy smells of cedar and pine.* [19th C.: formed irregularly from WOOD (differentiated from *woody*).]

wood thrush ▶ n. a thrush (*Hylocichla mustelina*) of eastern North America, with a brown back, rufous head, and dark-spotted white breast, and a loud liquid song.

wood tick ▶ n. a North American tick (genus *Dermacentor*, family Ixodidae, esp. *D. andersoni*) that infests wild and domestic animals and is responsible for transmitting spotted fever.

wood tick

wood·turn·ing /ˈwŏŏdˌtərniɴɢ/ ▶ n. the action of shaping wood with a lathe. — **wood·turn·er** /-ˌtərnər/ n.

Wood·ward[1] /ˈwŏŏdwərd/, Robert Burns (1917–79), US organic chemist. With Roald Hoffmann (1937–), a US chemist, born in Poland, he discovered symmetry-based rules governing the course of rearrangement reactions involving cyclic intermediates. Nobel Prize for Chemistry (1965).

Wood·ward[2], Robert Upshur (1943–), US journalist. He was the Washington Post reporter who, with Carl Bernstein, broke the story of the Watergate burglary and traced the financial payoffs to President Nixon. With Bernstein, he wrote *All the President's Men* (1974) and *The Final Days* (1976).

wood·wasp /ˈwŏŏdˌwäsp/ ▶ n. another term for HORNTAIL.

wood·wind /ˈwŏŏdˌwind/ ▶ n. [treated as sing. or pl.] wind instruments other than brass instruments forming a section of an orchestra, including flutes, oboes, clarinets, and bassoons.

wood wool·ly foot ▶ n. see WOOLLY FOOT.

wood·work /ˈwŏŏdˌwərk/ ▶ n. the wooden parts of a room or building, such as window frames or doors.

– PHRASES **come out of the woodwork** (of an unpleasant person or thing) emerge from obscurity; be revealed. — **wood·work·er** n.

wood·work·ing /ˈwŏŏdˌwərkiɴɢ/ ▶ n. the activity or skill of making things from wood.

wood·worm /ˈwŏŏdˌwərm/ ▶ n. the worm or larva of a beetle that bores into wood. ■ the damaged condition of wood resulting from infestation with this larva.

wood·y /ˈwŏŏdē/ ▶ adj. (**wood·i·er**, **wood·i·est**) (of an area of land) covered with trees. ■ made of, resembling, or suggestive of wood. ■ Bot. (of a plant or its stem) of the nature of or consisting of wood; lignified. — **wood·i·ness** n.

wood·yard /ˈwŏŏdˌyärd/ ▶ n. a yard where wood is chopped or stored.

wood·y night·shade ▶ n. see NIGHTSHADE.

woof[1] /wŏŏf/ ▶ n. the barking sound made by a dog. ▶ v. [intrans.] (of a dog) bark. ■ black slang say something in an ostentatious or aggressive manner but with no intention to act. [19th C.: imitative.]

woof[2] ▶ n. another term for WEFT. [OE *ōwef*, a compound from the base of WEAVE[1]; ME *oof* later became *woof* by association with WARP in the phr. *warp and woof.*]

woof·er /ˈwŏŏfər/ ▶ n. a loudspeaker designed to reproduce low frequencies. [1930s: from the v. WOOF[1] + -ER[1].]

wool /wŏŏl/ ▶ n. **1** the fine soft curly or wavy hair forming the coat of a sheep, goat, or similar animal, esp. when shorn and prepared for use in making cloth or yarn. ■ yarn or textile fiber made from such hair: *a sampler in colored wools.* **2** a thing resembling such hair in form or texture, in particular: ■ [with adj.] the soft underfur or down of some other mammals. ■ [with adj.] a metal or mineral made into a mass of fine fibers.

– PHRASES **pull the wool over someone's eyes** deceive someone by telling untruths. — **wool·like** /-ˌlīk/ adj. [OE *wull*, of Gmc. origin; rel. to Du. *wol* and Ger. *Wolle*, from an Indo-Eur. root shared by L. *lana* 'wool,' *vellus* 'fleece.']

wool clip ▶ n. the total quantity of wool shorn from a particular flock or in a particular area in the course of a year.

wool·en /ˈwŏŏlən/ (Brit. **wool·len**) ▶ adj. [attrib.] of or relating to the production of wool: *a woolen mill.* ■ made wholly or partly of wool. ▶ n. (usu. **woolens**) an article of clothing made of wool. [OE *wullen* (see WOOL, -EN[2]).]

Woolf /wŏŏlf/, Virginia (1882–1941), English writer; born *Adeline Virginia Stephen.* She was a member of the Bloomsbury Group. Her novels include *Mrs. Dalloway* (1925) and *To the Lighthouse* (1927).

wool·gath·er·ing /ˈwŏŏlˌgaтн(ə)riɴɢ/ ▶ n. indulgence in aimless thought or dreamy imagining; absentmindedness. — **wool·gath·er** /-ˌgaтнər/ v.

wool·grow·er /ˈwŏŏlˌgrō(ə)r/ ▶ n. a breeder of sheep for wool.

Woll·cott /ˈwŏŏlkət/, Alexander Humpreys (1887–1943), US critic. He was the drama critic for *The New York Times* 1914–22 and the *New York World* 1925–28.

Wool·ley /ˈwŏŏlē/, Sir Charles Leonard (1880–1960), English archaeologist. He directed an excavation of the Sumerian city of Ur 1922–34 that uncovered rich royal tombs and thousands of clay tablets.

wool·ly /ˈwŏŏlē/ (also **wool·y**) ▶ adj. (**-li·er**, **-li·est**) **1** made of wool. ■ (of an animal, plant, or part) bearing or naturally covered with wool or hair resembling wool. ■ resembling wool in texture or appearance. **2** vague or confused in expression or character: *woolly thinking.* ■ (of a sound) indistinct or distorted. ▶ n. (pl. **-lies**) **1** (usu. **woollies**) informal, esp. Brit. a garment made of wool, esp. a pullover. **2** a sheep. — **wool·li·ness** n. (in sense 2 of the adjective).

wool·ly a·del·gid /əˈdeljid/ ▶ n. any of several small aphidlike insects (superfamily Aphidoidea, family Adelgidae) that feeds on conifers, esp. hemlocks, spruces, and firs. By sucking the sap from young twigs, the insect retards or prevents tree growth and causes needles to discolor and drop prematurely.

wool·ly bear ▶ n. a large hairy caterpillar, esp. that of a tiger moth.

wool·ly foot (also **wood wool·ly foot**) ▶ n. a yellowish-brown toadstool (*Collybia peronata*, family Tricholomataceae) with a slender stem, the base of which bears long woolly hairs, found commonly in woodlands in both Eurasia and North America.

wool·ly mam·moth ▶ n. a mammoth (*Mammuthus primigenius*) that was adapted to the cold periods of the Pleistocene, with a long shaggy coat, small ears, and a thick layer of fat. Individuals are sometimes found frozen in the permafrost of Siberia.

woolly mammoth

wool·ly rhi·noc·er·os ▶ n. an extinct two-horned Eurasian rhinoceros (genus *Coelodonta*) that was adapted to the cold periods of the Pleistocene, with a long woolly coat.

wool·ly spi·der mon·key ▶ n. a large spider monkey (*Brachyteles arachnoides*) with long thin limbs and tail, dense woolly fur, and a large protruding belly, native to the rain forests of southeastern Brazil.

wool-sort·ers' dis·ease ▶ n. see ANTHRAX.

wool-sta·pler ▶ n. archaic a person who buys wool from a producer, grades it, and sells it to a manufacturer.

wool work ▶ n. needlework executed in wool on a canvas foundation.

Wool·worth /ˈwo͝ol,wərTH/, Frank Winfield (1852–1919), US businessman. He pioneered the concept of low-priced retailing in 1878 and from this built a large international chain of stores.

wool·y ▶ adj. var. of WOOLLY.

Woo·me·ra /ˈwo͝omərə; ˈwo͞omə-/ a town in central South Australia, a site used since the 1960s for tracking space satellites.

woo·mer·a /ˈwo͝omərə/ ▶ n. Austral. an Aboriginal stick used to throw a dart or spear more forcibly. [from Dharuk *wamara*.]

woo·nerf /ˈvo͞onərf/ ▶ n. a road in which devices for reducing or slowing the flow of traffic have been installed. [1970s: from Du., from *wonen* 'reside' + *erf* 'premises, ground.']

woop·ie /ˈwo͝opē/ (also **woop·y**) ▶ n. (pl. **-ies**) informal an affluent retired person able to pursue an active lifestyle. [1980s: elaboration of the acronym from *well-off older person*.]

woosh ▶ v., n., exclam., & adv. var. of WHOOSH.

wooz·y /ˈwo͞ozē/ ▶ adj. (**wooz·i·er, wooz·i·est**) informal unsteady, dizzy, or dazed. — **wooz·i·ly** /ˈwo͞ozəlē/ adv. **wooz·i·ness** n. [19th C.: of unknown origin.]

wop /wäp/ ▶ n. derog. an Italian or other southern European. [20th C. (orig. US): origin uncert., perh. from Ital. *guappo* 'bold, showy,' from Sp. *guapo* 'dandy.']

Worces·ter[1] /ˈwo͝ostər/ a city in central Massachusetts, on the Blackstone River; pop. 172,648.

Worces·ter[2] (also **Roy·al Worces·ter**) ▶ n. trademark porcelain made at Worcester, England, in a factory founded in 1751.

Worces·ter·shire sauce /ˈwo͝ostər,SHi(ə)r; -SHər/ ▶ n. a pungent sauce containing soy sauce and vinegar, first made in Worcester, England.

Worcs. ▶ abbr. Worcestershire.

word /wərd/ ▶ n. a single distinct meaningful element of speech or writing, used with others (or sometimes alone) to form a sentence and typically shown with a space on either side when written or printed. ■ a single distinct conceptual unit of language, comprising inflected and variant forms. ■ (usu. **words**) something that someone says or writes; a remark or piece of information: *a word of warning*. ■ speech as distinct from action. ■ [with negative] (**a word**) even the smallest amount of something spoken or written: *don't believe a word of it*. ■ (**one's word**) a person's account of the truth, esp. when it differs from that of another person: *his word against mine*. ■ (**one's word**) a promise or assurance. ■ (**words**) the text or spoken part of a play, opera, or other performed piece; a script. ■ (**words**) angry talk: *her father had words with her*. ■ a message; news. ■ a command, password, or motto: *someone gave me the word to start playing*. ■ a basic unit of data in a computer, typically 16 or 32 bits long. ▶ v. [trans.] choose and use particular words in order to say or write (something). ▶ exclam. black slang used to express agreement: *"That Jay is one dangerous character." "Word."*

– PHRASES **at a word** as soon as requested. **be as good as one's word** do what one has promised to do. **break one's word** fail to do what one has promised. **have a word** speak briefly to someone. **in other words** expressed in a different way; that is to say. **in so many words** [often with negative] in the way mentioned: *I haven't told him in so many words, but he'd understand*. **in a word** briefly. **keep one's word** do what one has promised. **a man/woman of his/her word** a person who keeps their promises. **(on/upon) my word** an exclamation of surprise or emphasis. **of few words** taciturn. **put something into words** express something in speech or writing. **put words into someone's mouth** falsely or inaccurately report what someone has said. ■ prompt or encourage someone to say something that they may not otherwise have said. **take someone at their word** interpret a person's words literally or exactly, esp. by believing them or doing as they suggest. **take the words out of someone's mouth** say what someone else was about to say. **take someone's word (for it)** believe what someone says or writes without checking for oneself. **waste words 1** talk in vain. **2** talk at length. **the Word (of God) 1** the Bible, or a part of it. **2** Jesus Christ (see LOGOS). **word for word** in exactly the same or, when translated, exactly equivalent words. **word of honor** a solemn promise. **word of mouth** spoken language; informal or unofficial discourse. **the word on the street** informal a rumor or piece of information currently being circulated. **words fail me** used to express one's disbelief or dismay. **a word to the wise** a hint or brief explanation given, that being all that is required.

– PHRASAL VERBS **word up** [as imper.] black English listen. — **word·age** /ˈwərdij/ n. **word·less** adj. **word·less·ly** adv. **word·less·ness** n. [OE, of Gmc. origin; rel. to Du. *woord* and Ger. *Wort*, from an Indo-Eur. root shared by L. *verbum* 'word.']

-word ▶ comb. form denoting a slang word, or one that may be offensive or have a negative connotation, specified by the word's first letter: *the F-word*.

word as·so·ci·a·tion ▶ n. the spontaneous and unreflective production of other words in response to a given word, as a game, a prompt to creative thought or memory, or a technique in psychiatric evaluation.

word blind·ness ▶ n. less technical (and less accurate) term for DYSLEXIA.

word·book /ˈwərd,bo͝ok/ ▶ n. a reference book containing lists of words and meanings or other related information.

word break (also **word di·vi·sion**) ▶ n. Print. a point at which a word is split between two lines of text by means of a hyphen.

word class ▶ n. a category of words of similar form or function; a part of speech.

word deaf·ness ▶ n. an inability to identify spoken words, resulting from a brain defect such as Wernicke's aphasia.

word game ▶ n. a game involving the making, guessing, or selection of words.

word·ing /ˈwərdiNG/ ▶ n. the words used to express something; the way in which something is expressed.

word length ▶ n. Comput. the number of bits in a word.

word or·der ▶ n. the sequence of words in a sentence, esp. as governed by grammatical rules and as affecting meaning.

word-per·fect /ˈpərfəkt/ ▶ adj. another term for LETTER-PERFECT.

word pic·ture ▶ n. a vivid description in writing.

word·play /ˈwərd,plā/ ▶ n. the witty exploitation of the meanings and ambiguities of words, esp. in puns.

word prob·lem ▶ n. a mathematics exercise presented in the form of a hypothetical situation that requires an equation to be solved.

word proc·ess·ing ▶ n. the production, storage, and manipulation of text on a word processor. — **word-proc·ess** v.

word proc·es·sor ▶ n. a dedicated computer or program for storing, manipulating, and formatting text entered from a keyboard and providing a printout.

word sal·ad ▶ n. a confused or unintelligible mixture of seemingly random words and phrases, specifically (in psychiatry) as a form of speech indicative of advanced schizophrenia.

word·smith /ˈwərd,smiTH/ ▶ n. a skilled user of words.

Words·worth[1] /ˈwərdz,wərTH/, Dorothy (1771–1855), English writer, sister of William Wordsworth. Her *Grasmere Journal* (1800–03) documents her intense response to nature.

Words·worth[2], William (1770–1850), English poet. *Lyrical Ballads* (1798), which was composed with Coleridge and included "Tintern Abbey," was a landmark in romanticism. He was appointed British poet laureate in 1843.

word wrap ▶ n. a feature on a word processor that automatically moves a word that is too long to fit on a line to the beginning of the next line.

word·y /ˈwərdē/ ▶ adj. (**word·i·er, word·i·est**) using or expressed in too many words. ■ archaic consisting of words. — **word·i·ly** /-dl-ē/ adv. **word·i·ness** n. [OE *wordig* (see WORD, -Y[1]).]

wore[1] /wôr/ past of WEAR[1].

wore[2] past and past participle of WEAR[2].

work /wərk/ ▶ n. **1** activity involving mental or physical effort done in order to achieve a purpose or result. ■ (**works**) [in comb.] a place or premises for industrial activity, typically manufacturing: *a job in the ironworks*. **2** such activity as a means of earning income; employment. ■ the place where one engages in such activity: *returning home from work*. ■ the period of time spent during the day engaged in such activity. **3** a task or tasks to be undertaken; something a person or thing has to do: *the work was progressing smoothly*. ■ the materials for this: *took work home with her*. ■ (**works**) Theol. good or moral deeds. **4** something done or made: *her work hangs in several galleries*. ■ the result of the action of a specified person or thing: *the work of three scientists*. ■ a literary or musical composition or other piece of fine art. ■ (**works**) all such pieces by a particular author, composer, or artist, regarded collectively: *the works of Schubert*. ■ a piece of embroidery, sewing, or knitting, typically made using a specified stitch or method. ■ (usu. **works**) Mil. a defensive structure. ■ (**works**) an architectural or engineering structure such as a bridge or dam. ■ the record of the successive calculations made in solving a mathematical problem: *show your work on a separate sheet of paper.* **5** (**works**) the operative part of a clock or other machine. **6** Physics the exertion of force overcoming resistance or producing molecular change. **7** (**the works**) informal everything needed, desired, or expected: *pizza with the works.* ▶**v.** (past **worked** or archaic **wrought** /rôt/) [intrans.] **1** be engaged in physical or mental activity in order to achieve a purpose or result, esp. in one's job; do work. ■ be employed, typically in a specified occupation or field. ■ (**work in**) (of an artist) produce articles or pictures using (a particular material or medium): *he works in clay.* ■ [trans.] produce (an article or design) using a specified material or sewing stitch. ■ [trans.] set to or keep at work. ■ [trans.] cultivate (land) or extract materials from (a mine or quarry). ■ [trans.] solve (a puzzle or mathematical problem). ■ [trans.] practice one's occupation or operate in or at (a particular place): *I worked a few clubs.* ■ make efforts to achieve something; campaign: *working for the lacto-vegetarian cause.* **2** (of a machine or system) operate or function, esp. properly or effectively. ■ (of a machine or a part of it) run; go through regular motions. ■ (esp. of a person's features) move violently or convulsively. ■ [trans.] cause (a device or machine) to operate: *how to work a VCR.* ■ (of a plan or method) have the desired result or effect. ■ [trans.] bring about; produce as a result: *you can work miracles.* ■ [trans.] informal arrange or contrive. ■ (**work on/upon**) exert influence or use one's persuasive power on (someone or their feelings). ■ [trans.] use one's persuasive power to stir the emotions of (a person or group of people): *working a crowd.* **3** [with obj. and adverbial or complement] bring (a material or mixture) to a desired shape or consistency by hammering, kneading, or some other method: *work the mixture into a paste with your hands.* ■ bring into a specified state, esp. an emotional state: *worked himself into a rage.* **4** move or cause to move gradually or with difficulty into another position, typically by means of constant movement or pressure. ■ (of joints, such as those in a wooden ship) loosen and flex under repeated stress. ■ [with adverbial] Sailing make progress to windward, with repeated tacking.

– PHRASES **at work** engaged in work. ■ in action: *an infectious agent was at work.* **give someone the works** informal treat someone harshly. ■ kill someone. **have one's work cut out** be faced with a hard or lengthy task. **in the works** being planned, worked on, or produced. **out of work** unemployed. **set to work** (or **set someone to work**) begin or cause to begin work. **the work of ——** a task occupying a specified amount of time. **work one's ass** (**butt**, etc.) **off** vulgar slang work extremely hard. **work one's will on/upon** accomplish one's purpose on.

– PHRASAL VERBS **work something in** include or incorporate something, typically in something spoken or written. **work something off 1** discharge a debt by working. **2** reduce or get rid of something by work or activity. **work out 1** (of an equation) be capable of being solved. ■ (**work out at**) be calculated at. **2** have a good or specified result. **3** engage in vigorous physical exercise or training, typically at a gym. **work someone out** understand someone's character. **work something out 1** solve a sum or determine an amount by calculation. ■ solve or find the answer to something. **2** plan or devise something in detail: *work out a seating plan.* **3** literary accomplish or attain something with difficulty. **4** (usu. **be worked out**) work a mine until it is exhausted of minerals. **5** another way of saying WORK SOMETHING OFF above. **work someone over** informal treat someone with violence; beat someone severely. **work through** go through a process of understanding and accepting (a painful or difficult situation). **work to** follow or operate within the constraints of (a plan or system): *working to tight deadlines.* **work up to** proceed gradually toward (something more advanced or intense). **work someone up** (often **get worked up**) gradually bring someone, esp. oneself, to a state of intense excitement, anger, or anxiety. **work something up 1** bring something gradually to a more complete or satisfactory state. **2** develop or produce by activity or effort: *worked up a fair sweat.* —**work•less adj.** [OE *weorc* (n.), *wyrcan* (v.), of Gmc. origin; rel. to Du. *werk* and Ger. *Werk*, from an Indo-Eur. root shared by Gk. *ergon.*]

-work ▶**comb. form** denoting things or parts made of a specified material or with specified tools: *silverwork.* ■ denoting a mechanism or structure of a specified kind: *clockwork.* ■ denoting ornamentation of a specified kind, or articles having such ornamentation: *knotwork.*

work•a•ble /'wərkəbəl/ ▶**adj. 1** able to be worked, fashioned, or manipulated: *a workable dough.* **2** capable of producing the desired effect or result; practicable; feasible. —**work•a•bil•i•ty** /ˌwərkə'bilitē/ **n. work•a•bly** /-blē/ **adv.**

work•a•day /'wərkəˌdā/ ▶**adj.** of or relating to work or one's job. ■ not special, unusual, or interesting in any way; ordinary.

work•a•hol•ic /ˌwərkə'hôlik; -'hälik/ ▶**n.** informal a person who compulsively works hard and long hours. —**work•a•hol•ism** /'wərkəˌhôlizəm; -ˌhäl-/ **n.**

work•a•like /'wərkəˌlīk/ ▶**n.** Comput. a computer that is able to use the software of another specified machine without special modification. ■ a piece of software identical in function to another software package.

work•a•round /'wərkəˌround/ ▶**n.** Comput. a method for overcoming a problem or limitation in a program or system.

work•bas•ket /'wərkˌbaskət/ (also **work•bag**) ▶**n.** a basket (or bag) used for storing sewing materials.

work•bench /'wərkˌbench/ ▶**n.** a bench at which carpentry or other mechanical or practical work is done.

work•boat /'wərkˌbōt/ ▶**n.** a boat used for work such as commercial fishing or transporting freight, rather than leisure or naval service.

work•book /'wərkˌbo͝ok/ ▶**n.** a student's book containing instruction and exercises relating to a particular subject.

work•box /'wərkˌbäks/ ▶**n.** a portable box used for storing or holding tools and materials for activities such as sewing.

work camp ▶**n.** a camp at which community work is done, esp. by young volunteers. ■ another term for LABOR CAMP.

work•day /'wərkˌdā/ ▶**n.** a day on which one works. ■ the part of the day devoted or allotted to work: *18-hour workdays.*

work•er /'wərkər/ ▶**n. 1** a person or animal that works, in particular: ■ [with adj.] a person who does a specified type of work: *a farm worker.* ■ an employee, esp. one who does manual or nonexecutive work. ■ (**workers**) used in Marxist or leftist contexts to refer to the working class. ■ [with adj.] a person who works in a specified way. ■ informal a person who works hard. ■ (in social insects such as bees, wasps, ants, and termites) a neuter or undeveloped female that is usually the most numerous caste and does the basic work of the colony. See illustration at HONEYBEE. **2** a creator or producer of a specified thing.

work eth•ic ▶**n.** [in sing.] the principle that hard work is intrinsically virtuous or worthy of reward. See also PROTESTANT ETHIC.

work•fare /'wərkˌfe(ə)r/ ▶**n.** a welfare system that requires those receiving benefits to perform some work or to participate in job training. [1960s: from WORK + a shortened form of WELFARE.]

work•flow /'wərkˌflō/ ▶**n.** the sequence of industrial, administrative, or other processes through which a piece of work passes from initiation to completion.

work force (also **work•force**) ▶**n.** [treated as sing. or pl.] the people engaged in or available for work, either in a country or area or in a particular company or industry.

work func•tion ▶**n.** Physics the minimum quantity of energy that is required to remove an electron to infinity from the surface of a given solid, usually a metal. (Symbol: φ.)

work•group /'wərkˌgro͞op/ ▶**n.** a group within a workforce that normally works together. ■ Comput. a group of this type who share data via a local network.

work-hard•en ▶**v.** [trans.] [often as n.] (**work-hardening**) Metallurgy toughen (a metal) as a result of cold-working.

work•horse /'wərkˌhôrs/ ▶**n.** a horse used for work on a farm. ■ a person or machine that dependably performs hard work over a long period of time.

work•house /'wərkˌhous/ ▶**n. 1** hist. (in the UK) a public institution in which the destitute of a parish received board and lodging in return for work. **2** a prison in which petty offenders are expected to work.

work•ing /'wərkiNG/ ▶**adj.** [attrib.] **1** having paid employment. ■ engaged in manual labor. ■ relating to, suitable for, or for the purpose of work. ■ (of a meal) during which business is discussed. ■ (of an animal) used in farming, hunting, or for guard duties; not kept as a pet or for show. ■ (of something possessed) sufficient to work with: *a working knowledge of contract law.* ■ (of a theory, definition, or title) used as the basis for work or argument and likely to be developed, adapted, or improved later. **2** functioning or able to function. ■ (of parts of a machine) moving and causing a machine to operate. ■ (of the face or features) moving convulsively. ▶**n. 1** the action of doing work. ■ the action of extracting minerals from a mine. ■ (usu. **workings**) a mine or a part of a mine from which minerals are being extracted. **2** (**workings**) the way in which a machine, organization, or system operates: *the workings of government.*

work•ing cap•i•tal ▶**n.** Finance the capital of a business that is used in its day-to-day trading operations, calculated as the current assets minus the current liabilities.

work•ing class ▶**n.** [treated as sing. or pl.] the social group consisting of people who are employed for wages, esp. in manual or industrial work. ▶**adj.** (**working-class**) of, relating to, or characteristic of people belonging to such a group.

work•ing day ▶**n.** another term for WORKDAY.

work•ing girl ▶**n.** informal, esp. dated a woman who goes out to work rather than remaining at home. ■ a prostitute.

work•ing group ▶**n.** a committee or group appointed to study and report on a particular question and make recommendations based on its findings.

work•ing load ▶**n.** the maximum load that a machine or other structure is designed to bear.

work•ing mem•o•ry ▶**n.** Psychol. the part of short-term memory that is concerned with immediate conscious perceptual and linguistic processing. ■ Comput. an area of high-speed memory used to store programs or data currently in use.

work•ing stor•age ▶**n.** Comput. a part of a computer's memory that is used by a program for the storage of intermediate results or other temporary items.

work•load /'wərkˌlōd/ ▶**n.** the amount of work to be done by someone or something.

work•man /'wərkmən/ ▶**n.** (pl. **-men**) a man employed to do manual labor. ■ [with adj.] a person with specified skill in a job or craft.

work•man•like /'wərkmənˌlīk/ ▶**adj.** showing efficient competence.

work·man·ship /ˈwərkmən,SHip/ ▶ **n.** the degree of skill with which a product is made or a job done.

work·out /ˈwərk,out/ ▶ **n.** a session of vigorous physical exercise or training.

work per·mit ▶ **n.** an official document giving a foreigner permission to take a job in a country.

work·piece /ˈwərk,pēs/ ▶ **n.** an object being worked on with a tool or machine.

work·place /ˈwərk,plās/ ▶ **n.** a place where people work, such as an office or factory.

work re·lease ▶ **n.** leave of absence from prison by day enabling a prisoner to continue in normal employment.

work·room /ˈwərk,ro͞om; -,ro͝om/ ▶ **n.** a room for working in, esp. one equipped for a particular kind of work.

work·sheet /ˈwərk,SHēt/ ▶ **n.** **1** a paper listing questions or tasks for students. **2** a paper for recording work done or in progress. ■ Comput. a data file created and used by a spreadsheet program, which takes the form of a matrix of cells when displayed.

work·shop /ˈwərk,SHäp/ ▶ **n.** **1** a room or building in which goods are manufactured or repaired. **2** a meeting at which a group of people engage in intensive discussion and activity on a particular subject or project. ▶ **v.** [trans.] present a performance of (a dramatic work), using intensive group discussion and improvisation in order to explore aspects of the production before formal staging.

work-shy ▶ **adj.** (of a person) lazy and disinclined to work.

work·site /ˈwərk,sīt/ ▶ **n.** an area where an industry is located or where work takes place.

work·space /ˈwərk,spās/ ▶ **n.** space in which to work. ■ an area rented or sold for commercial purposes. ■ Comput. a memory storage facility for temporary use.

work·sta·tion /ˈwərk,stāSHən/ ▶ **n.** **1** a general-purpose computer with a higher performance level than a personal computer. **2** an area where work of a particular nature is carried out, such as a specific location on a manufacturing assembly line. **3** a desk with a computer or a computer terminal and keyboard.

work-stud·y ▶ **adj.** [attrib.] of or relating to a college program that enables students to work part-time while attending school.

work sur·face ▶ **n.** another term for **countertop**.

work·wear /ˈwərk,we(ə)r/ ▶ **n.** heavy-duty clothes for physical or manual work.

work·week /ˈwərk,wēk/ ▶ **n.** the total number of hours or days worked in a week.

world /wərld/ ▶ **n.** **1** (usu. **the world**) the earth, together with all of its countries, peoples, and natural features. ■ (**the world**) all of the people, societies, and institutions on the earth. ■ [as adj.] denoting one of the most important or influential people or things of its class: *a world power.* ■ another planet like the earth: *life on other worlds.* ■ the material universe or all that exists; everything. **2** a part or aspect of human life or of the natural features of the earth, in particular: ■ a region or group of countries: *the English-speaking world.* ■ a period of history: *the ancient world.* ■ a group of living things: *the animal world.* ■ the people, places, and activities to do with a particular thing. ■ human and social interaction: *the ways of the world.* ■ average, respectable, or fashionable people or their customs or opinions. ■ (**one's world**) a person's life and activities. ■ everything that exists outside oneself. ■ [in sing.] a stage of human life, either mortal or after death: *in this world and the next.* ■ secular interests and affairs.
– PHRASES **be not long for this world** have only a short time to live. **the best of both** (or **all possible**) **worlds** the benefits of widely differing situations, enjoyed at the same time. **bring someone into the world** give birth to or assist at the birth of someone. **come into the world** be born. **come up** (or **go down**) **in the world** rise (or drop) in status, esp. by becoming richer (or poorer). **in the world** used for emphasis in questions, esp. to express astonishment or disbelief. **look for all the world like** look precisely like (used for emphasis). **man** (or **woman**) **of the world** a person who is experienced in the ways of sophisticated society. **not do something for the world** not do something whatever the inducement. **out of this world** informal extremely enjoyable or impressive. **see the world** travel widely and gain wide experience. **think the world of** have a very high regard for (someone). **the world, the flesh, and the devil** all forms of temptation to sin. **a** (or **the**) **world of** a very great deal of: *a world of difference.* (**all**) **the world over** everywhere on the earth. **worlds apart** very different or distant. [OE *w(e)oruld*, from a Gmc. compound meaning 'age of man'; rel. to Du. *wereld* and Ger. *Welt*.]

World Bank an international banking organization established to control the distribution of economic aid between member nations, and to make loans to them in times of financial crisis.

world beat ▶ **n.** Western music incorporating elements of traditional music from any part of the world, esp. from developing nations.

world-beat·er ▶ **n.** a person or thing that is better than all others in its field. — **world-beat·ing adj.**

world ci·ty ▶ **n.** a cosmopolitan city, with foreigners visiting and residing.

world-class ▶ **adj.** (of a person, thing, or activity) of or among the best in the world.

World Coun·cil of Church·es (abbr.: **WCC**) an association established in 1948 to promote unity among the many different Christian Churches. Its member Churches include virtually all Christian traditions except Roman Catholicism and Unitarianism.

World Cup ▶ **n.** a sports competition between teams from several countries, in particular an international soccer tournament held every four years. ■ a trophy awarded for such a competition.

world fair ▶ **n.** see **world's fair**.

world-fa·mous ▶ **adj.** known throughout the world.

World Health Or·gan·i·za·tion (abbr.: **WHO**) an agency of the United Nations, established in 1948 to promote health and control communicable diseases.

World Her·it·age Site ▶ **n.** a natural or man-made site, area, or structure recognized as being of outstanding international importance and therefore as deserving special protection. Sites are nominated to and designated by the World Heritage Convention (an organization of UNESCO).

World In·tel·lec·tu·al Pro·per·ty Or·gan·i·za·tion (abbr.: **WIPO**) an organization, established in 1967 and an agency of the United Nations from 1974, for cooperation between governments in matters concerning patents, trademarks, and copyright, and the transfer of technology between countries.

world lan·guage ▶ **n.** a language known or spoken in many countries: *English is now the world language.* ■ an artificial language for international use.

world line ▶ **n.** Physics a curve in space-time joining the positions of a particle throughout its existence.

world·ling /ˈwərldliNG/ ▶ **n.** a cosmopolitan and sophisticated person.

world·ly /ˈwərldlē/ ▶ **adj.** (**-li·er**, **-li·est**) of or concerned with material values or ordinary life rather than a spiritual existence. ■ (of a person) experienced and sophisticated.
– PHRASES **worldly goods** (or **possessions** or **wealth**) everything that someone owns. — **world·li·ness n.** [OE *woruldlic* (see **world**, **-ly**[1]).]

world·ly-mind·ed ▶ **adj.** intent on worldly things.

world·ly-wise ▶ **adj.** prepared by experience for life's difficulties; not easily shocked or deceived. — **world·ly wis·dom n.**

World Me·te·or·o·log·i·cal Or·gan·i·za·tion (abbr.: **WMO**) an agency of the United Nations, established in 1950 with the aim of facilitating worldwide cooperation in meteorological observations, research, and services.

world mu·sic ▶ **n.** traditional music from the developing world. ■ Western popular music incorporating elements of such music.

world or·der ▶ **n.** a system controlling events in the world, esp. a set of arrangements established internationally for preserving global political stability.

World Se·ries the professional championship for North American major league baseball, played at the end of the season between the champions of the American League and the National League.

world's fair (also **world fair**) ▶ **n.** an international exhibition of the industrial, scientific, technological, and artistic achievements of the participating nations.

world-shak·ing ▶ **adj.** (in hyperbolic use) of supreme importance or having a momentous effect.

world soul ▶ **n.** Philos. the immanent cause or principle of life, order, consciousness, and self-awareness in the physical world. [19th C.: translating Ger. *Weltgeist*.]

World Trade Cen·ter a complex of buildings in New York City featuring twin towers 110 stories high. The towers were destroyed in a terrorist attack on September 11, 2001, with the loss of about 2,700 lives.

World Trade Or·gan·i·za·tion (abbr.: **WTO**) an international body founded in 1995 to promote international trade and economic development by reducing tariffs and other restrictions.

world·view /ˈwərld,vyo͞o/ (also **world view**) ▶ **n.** a particular philosophy of life or conception of the world.

world war ▶ **n.** a war involving many large nations in all different parts of the world. The name is commonly given to the wars of 1914–18 and 1939–45. See **World War I**, **World War II**.

World War I a war (1914–18) in which the Central Powers (Germany and Austria-Hungary, joined later by Turkey and Bulgaria) were defeated by an alliance of Britain and its dominions, France, Russia, and others, joined later by Italy and the US.

World War II a war (1939–45) in which the Axis Powers (Germany, Italy, and Japan) were defeated by an alliance eventually including the United Kingdom and its dominions, the Soviet Union, and the United States.

world-wea·ry ▶ **adj.** feeling or indicating feelings of weariness, boredom, or cynicism as a result of long experience of life. — **world-wea·ri·ness n.**

world·wide /ˈwərldˈwīd/ ▶ **adj.** extending or reaching throughout the world. ▶ **adv.** throughout the world.

World Wide Web Comput. a widely used information system on the Internet that provides facilities for documents to be connected to other documents by hypertext links, enabling the user to search for information by moving from one document to another.

WORM /wərm/ ▶ **abbr.** write-once read-many, denoting a type of computer memory device.

worm /wərm/ ▶ **n.** **1** any of a number of creeping or burrowing invertebrate animals with long, slender, soft bodies and no limbs. The numerous phyla include Annelida (segmented worms), Nematoda (roundworms), and Platyhelminthes (flatworms). ■ short for EARTHWORM. ■ (**worms**) intestinal or other internal parasites. ■ used in names of long, slender insect larvae, esp. those in fruit or wood, e.g., **army worm, woodworm.** ■ used in names of other animals that resemble worms in some way, e.g., **shipworm.** ■ a maggot supposed to eat dead bodies buried in the ground. ■ Comput. a self-replicating program able to propagate itself across a network, typically having a detrimental effect. **2** informal a weak or despicable person (used as a general term of contempt). **3** a helical device or component, in particular: ■ the threaded cylinder in a worm gear. ■ the coiled pipe of a still in which the vapor is cooled and condensed. ▶ **v. 1** [intrans.] move with difficulty by crawling or wriggling. ■ (**worm one's way into**) insinuate one's way into. ■ [trans.] move (something) into a confined space by wriggling it. ■ (**worm something out of**) obtain information from (someone) by cunning persistence. **2** [trans.] treat (an animal) with a preparation designed to expel parasitic worms. **3** [trans.] Naut., archaic make (a rope) smooth by winding small cordage between the strands.

– PHRASES (**even**) **a worm will turn** proverb (even) a meek person will resist or retaliate if pushed too far. [OE *wyrm* (n.), of Gmc. origin; rel. to L. *vermis* 'worm' and Gk. *rhomox* 'woodworm.']

worm cast (also **worm cast·ing**) ▶ **n.** a convoluted mass of soil, mud, or sand thrown up by an earthworm or lugworm on the surface after passing through the worm's body.

worm-eat·en ▶ **adj.** (of organic tissue) eaten into by worms. ■ (of wood or a wooden object) full of holes made by woodworm.

worm·er /'wərmər/ ▶ **n.** a substance administered to animals or birds to expel parasitic worms.

worm-fish·ing ▶ **n.** the activity or practice of angling with worms for bait.

worm gear ▶ **n.** a mechanical arrangement consisting of a toothed wheel worked by a short revolving cylinder (worm) bearing a screw thread.

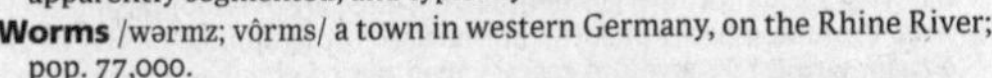

worm gear

worm·hole /'wərm,hōl/ ▶ **n.** a hole made by a burrowing insect larva or worm in wood, fruit, books, or other materials. ■ Physics a hypothetical connection between widely separated regions of space-time.

worm liz·ard ▶ **n.** a subterranean burrowing reptile (suborder Amphisbaenia, order Squamata) that resembles an earthworm, being blind, apparently segmented, and typically without limbs.

Worms /wərmz; vôrms/ a town in western Germany, on the Rhine River; pop. 77,000.

worm·seed /'wərm,sēd/ ▶ **n.** a plant whose seeds have anthelmintic properties, in particular: ■ (also **Levant wormseed**) santonica. ■ (also **American wormseed**) an American plant (*Chenopodium ambrosioides*) of the goosefoot family.

worm's-eye view ▶ **n.** a view as seen from below or from a humble position.

worm snake ▶ **n. 1** a small harmless North American snake (*Carphophis amoena*, family Colubridae) that resembles an earthworm. **2** another term for BLIND SNAKE.

worm wheel ▶ **n.** the wheel of a worm gear.

worm·wood /'wərm,wo͝od/ ▶ **n. 1** a woody shrub (genus *Artemisia*) of the daisy family with a bitter aromatic taste, used, esp. formerly, as an ingredient of vermouth and absinthe and in medicine. **2** fig. a state or source of bitterness or grief. [OE *wermōd*. The change in spelling in ME was due to association with WORM and WOOD. Cf. VERMOUTH.]

worm·y /'wərmē/ ▶ **adj.** (**worm·i·er, worm·i·est**) **1** (of organic tissue) infested with or eaten into by worms. ■ (of wood or a wooden object) full of holes made by woodworm. **2** informal (of a person) weak, abject, or revolting. — **worm·i·ness n.**

worn /wôrn/ past participle of WEAR[1]. ▶ **adj.** damaged and shabby as a result of much use. ■ very tired.

worn out ▶ **adj. 1** (of a person or animal) extremely tired; exhausted. **2** damaged or shabby to the point of being no longer usable. ■ (of an idea, method, or system) used so often or existing for so long as to be considered valueless.

wor·ri·ment /'wərēmənt; 'wə-rē-/ ▶ **n.** archaic or humorous term for WORRY.

wor·ri·some /'wərē,səm; 'wə-rē-/ ▶ **adj.** causing anxiety or concern. — **wor·ri·some·ly adv.**

wor·ry /'wərē; 'wə-rē-/ ▶ **v.** (**-ries, -ried**) **1** [intrans.] give way to anxiety or unease; allow one's mind to dwell on difficulty or troubles. ■ [trans.] cause to feel anxiety or concern: *I've been worrying myself sick over my mother.* ■ [as adj.] (**worried**) expressing anxiety: *a worried frown.* ■ [trans.] cause annoyance to: *the noise never stops, but it doesn't worry me.* **2** [trans.] (of a dog or other carnivorous animal) tear at or pull about with the teeth: *worrying a bone.* ■ (of a dog) chase and attack (livestock, esp. sheep). ■ [intrans.] (**worry at**) pull at or fiddle with repeatedly. ▶ **n.** (pl. **-ries**) a state of anxiety and uncertainty over actual or potential problems. ■ a source of anxiety: *people whose greatest worry is fear of attack.*

– PHRASES **not to worry** informal used to reassure someone by telling them that a situation is not serious. — **wor·ried·ly adv. wor·ri·er n. wor·ry·ing·ly adv.** [OE *wyrgan* 'strangle,' of West Gmc. origin.]

wor·ry beads ▶ **plural n.** a string of beads that one fingers and moves in order to calm oneself.

wor·ry·wart /'wərē,wôrt; 'wə-rē-/ ▶ **n.** informal a person who tends to dwell unduly on difficulty or troubles.

worse /wərs/ ▶ **adj.** comparative of BAD, ILL. of poorer quality or lower standard; less good or desirable: *the accommodations were awful, and the food was worse.* ■ more serious or severe. ■ more reprehensible or evil. ■ [predic. or as complement] in a less satisfactory or pleasant condition; more ill or unhappy: *he felt worse.* ▶ **adv.** comparative of BADLY, ILL. less well or skillfully. ■ more seriously or severely. ■ [sentence adverb] used to introduce a statement of circumstances felt by the speaker to be more serious or undesirable than others already mentioned: *My shoes were wet. Even worse, I began to develop blisters from walking.* ▶ **n.** a more serious or unpleasant event or circumstance: *worse was to follow.* ■ (**the worse**) a less good, favorable, or pleasant condition.

– PHRASES **none the worse for** not adversely affected by. **or worse** used to suggest a possibility that is still more serious or unpleasant than one already considered, but that the speaker does not wish or need to specify. **so much the worse for ——** used to suggest that a problem, failure, or other unfortunate event or situation is the fault of the person specified and that the speaker does not feel any great concern about it. **the worse for wear** informal **1** damaged by use or weather over time; battered and shabby. **2** (of a person) feeling rather unwell, esp. as a result of drinking too much alcohol. **worse off** in a less advantageous position; less fortunate or prosperous. [OE *wyrsa, wiersa* (adj.), *wiers* (adv.), of Gmc. origin; rel. to WAR.]

wors·en /'wərsən/ ▶ **v.** make or become worse.

wor·ship /'wərsнip/ ▶ **n.** the feeling or expression of reverence and adoration for a deity: *ancestor worship.* ■ the acts or rites that make up a formal expression of reverence for a deity; a religious ceremony or ceremonies. ■ adoration or devotion comparable to religious homage, shown toward a person or principle. ■ archaic honor given to someone in recognition of their merit. ■ [as title] (**His/Your Worship**) esp. Brit. used in addressing or referring to an important or high-ranking person, esp. a magistrate or mayor: *His Worship the Mayor.* ▶ **v.** (**-shiped, -ship·ing**; also **-shipped, -ship·ping**) [trans.] show reverence and adoration for (a deity); honor with religious rites. ■ treat (someone or something) with the reverence and adoration appropriate to a deity. ■ [intrans.] take part in a religious ceremony. — **wor·ship·er** (also **wor·ship·per**) **n.** [OE *weorthscipe* 'worthiness, acknowledgment of worth' (see WORTH, -SHIP).]

wor·ship·ful /'wərsнipfəl/ ▶ **adj.** feeling or showing reverence and adoration. ■ archaic entitled to honor or respect. — **wor·ship·ful·ly adv. wor·ship·ful·ness n.**

worst /wərst/ ▶ **adj.** superlative of BAD, ILL. ■ of the poorest quality or the lowest standard. ■ least pleasant, desirable, or tolerable: *the worst conditions imaginable.* ■ most severe, serious, or dangerous: *Australia's worst bus accident.* ■ least suitable or advantageous. ▶ **adv.** superlative of BADLY, ILL. most severely or seriously: *the industries worst affected by falling employment.* ■ least well, skillfully, or pleasingly. ■ [sentence adverb] used to introduce the fact or circumstance that the speaker considers most serious or unpleasant. ▶ **n.** the most serious or unpleasant thing that could happen. ■ the most serious, dangerous, or unpleasant part or stage of something. ▶ **v.** [trans.] (usu. **be worsted**) get the better of; defeat.

– PHRASES **at its** (or **someone's**) **worst** in the most unpleasant, unimpressive, or unattractive state of which someone or something is capable. ■ at the most severe or serious point or level. **at worst** (or **the worst**) in the most serious case. ■ under the most unfavorable interpretation. **do one's worst** do as much damage as one can (often used to express defiance in the face of threats). **get** (or **have**) **the worst of it** be in the least advantageous or successful position; suffer the most. **if worst comes to worst** if the most serious or difficult circumstances arise. **in the worst way** informal very much. [OE *wierresta, wyrresta* (adj.), *wierst, wyrst* (adv.), of Gmc. origin; rel. to WORSE.]

worst-case ▶ **adj.** (of a projected development) characterized by the worst of the possible foreseeable circumstances.

wor·sted /'wo͝ostid; 'wərstid/ ▶ **n.** a fine smooth yarn spun from combed long-staple wool. ■ fabric made from such yarn, having a close-textured surface with no nap. [ME: from *Worstead*, the name of a parish in Norfolk, England.]

wort /wərt; wôrt/ ▶ **n. 1** [in comb.] used in names of plants and herbs, esp. those used, esp. formerly, as food or medicinally, e.g., **butterwort, woundwort.** ■ archaic such a plant or herb. **2** the sweet infusion of ground malt or other grain before fermentation, used to produce beer and distilled malt liquors. [OE *wyrt*, of Gmc. origin; rel. to ROOT[1].]

Worth /wərтн/, Charles Frederick (1825–95), English couturier, resident in France from 1845. He was regarded as the founder of Parisian *haute couture.*

worth /wərтн/ ▶ **adj.** [predic.] equivalent in value to the sum or item specified. ■ sufficiently good, important, or interesting to justify a specified action; deserving to be treated or regarded in the way specified: *the museums are well worth a visit.* ■ used to suggest that the specified course of action may be advisable: *worth checking out.* ■ having income or property amounting to a specified sum: *worth $10 million.* ▶ **n.** the value equivalent to that of someone or something under consideration; the level at which someone or something deserves to be valued or rated. ■ an amount of a commodity equivalent to a specified sum of money. ■ the amount that could be achieved or produced in a specified time. ■ high value or merit: *his inner worth.*

– PHRASES **for all someone is worth** informal **1** as energetically or enthusiastically as someone can. **2** so as to obtain everything one can from someone. **for what it is worth** used to present a comment, suggestion, or opinion without making a claim as to its importance or validity. **worth it** informal sufficiently good, enjoyable, or successful to repay any effort, trouble, or expense. [OE *w(e)orth* (adj. and n.), of Gmc. origin; rel. to Du. *waard* and Ger. *wert*.]

worth·less /'wərTHlis/ ▶ **adj.** having no real value or use. ■ (of a person) having no good qualities; deserving contempt. — **worth·less·ly** **adv.** **worth·less·ness** **n.**

worth·while /'wərTH'(h)wīl/ ▶ **adj.** worth the time, money, or effort spent; of value or importance. — **worth·while·ness** **n.**

wor·thy /'wərTHē/ ▶ **adj.** (**-thi·er**, **-thi·est**) deserving effort, attention, or respect. ■ having or showing the qualities or abilities that merit recognition in a specified way. ■ good enough; suitable. ▶ **n.** (pl. **-thies**) often derog. or humorous a person notable or important in a particular sphere: *schools governed by local worthies.* — **wor·thi·ly** /-THəlē/ **adv.** **wor·thi·ness** **n.** [ME: from WORTH + -Y[1].]

-worthy ▶ **comb. form** deserving of a specified thing: *newsworthy.* ■ suitable or fit for a specified thing: *roadworthy.* [from WORTHY.]

wot[1] /wät/ ▶ **pron., adj., & interrog. adv.** nonstandard spelling of WHAT, chiefly representing informal or humorous use.

wot[2] singular present of WIT[2].

Wo·tan /'vō,tän/ another name for ODIN.

Wouk /wōk; wo͝ok/, Herman (1915–), US writer. His novels include *The Caine Mutiny* (1951) and *The Winds of War* (1971).

would /wo͝od/ ▶ **modal verb** (3rd sing. pres. **would**) **1** past of WILL[1], in various senses: *he said he would be away for a couple of days | the windows would not close.* **2** (expressing the conditional mood) indicating the consequence of an imagined event or situation: *he would lose his job.* ■ (**I would**) used to give advice. **3** expressing a desire or inclination: *would you like some water?* **4** expressing a polite request. ■ expressing willingness or consent. **5** expressing a conjecture, opinion, or hope. **6** used to make a comment about behavior that is typical: derog. *they would say that, wouldn't they?* **7** [with clause] literary expressing a wish or regret: *would that he had lived to finish it.* [OE *wolde*, past of *wyllan* (see WILL[1]).]

would-be often derog. ▶ **adj.** [attrib.] desiring or aspiring to be a specified type of person.

would·n't /'wo͝odnt/ ▶ **contr.** would not.
– PHRASES **I wouldn't know** informal used to indicate that one can't be expected to know the answer to someone's question or to comment on a matter.

wouldst /wo͝odst/ (also **would·est** /'wo͝odist/) archaic second person singular of WOULD.

wound[1] /wo͞ond/ ▶ **n.** an injury to living tissue caused by a cut, blow, or other impact, typically one in which the skin is cut or broken. ■ an injury to a person's feelings or reputation. ▶ **v.** [trans.] (often **be wounded**) inflict an injury on (someone): *the sergeant was seriously wounded.* ■ injure (a person's feelings). — **wound·ing·ly** **adv.** **wound·less** **adj.** [OE *wund* (n.), *wundian* (v.), of Gmc. origin; rel. to Du. *wond* and Ger. *Wunde*, of unknown ultimate origin.]

wound[2] /wound/ alternate past and past participle of WIND[1].

wound[3] /wound/ past and past participle of WIND[2].

Wound·ed Knee a village in southwestern South Dakota, in the Pine Ridge Indian reservation, the site of an 1890 massacre and 1973 demonstrations.

Wound·ed Knee, Bat·tle of /'wo͞ondid 'nē/ the last major confrontation (1890) between the US Army and American Indians, at the village of Wounded Knee in South Dakota. More than 150 largely unarmed Sioux were massacred.

wound·wort /'wo͞ond,wərt; -,wôrt/ ▶ **n.** a hairy Eurasian plant (genus *Stachys*) of the mint family, resembling a dead-nettle and formerly used in the treatment of wounds.

wove /wōv/ past of WEAVE[1].

wo·ven /'wōvən/ past participle of WEAVE[1]. ▶ **adj.** (of fabric) formed by interlacing long threads passing in one direction with others at a right angle to them. ■ (of basketwork or a wreath) made by interlacing items such as cane, stems, flowers, or leaves. ■ [with submodifier] (of a complex story or pattern) made in a specified way from a number of interconnected elements: *a neatly woven tale of intrigue.*

wove pa·per ▶ **n.** paper made on a wire-gauze mesh so as to have a uniform unlined surface. Compare with LAID PAPER. [19th C.: *wove*, var. of WOVEN.]

wow[1] /wou/ informal ▶ **exclam.** (also **wow·ee** /'wouē; 'wou'ē/) expressing astonishment or admiration. ▶ **n.** a sensational success. ▶ **v.** [trans.] impress and excite (someone) greatly. [natural exclamation: first recorded in Scots in the early 16th C.]

wow[2] ▶ **n.** slow pitch fluctuation in sound reproduction, perceptible in long notes. Compare with FLUTTER (sense 1). [20th C.: imitative.]

Woz·ni·ak /'wäznē,ak/, Steve (1950–), US computer entrepreneur. He cofounded the Apple computer company in 1976 with Steve Jobs.

WP ▶ **abbr.** word processing or word processor.

w.p. ▶ **abbr.** weather permitting.

W par·ti·cle ▶ **n.** Physics a heavy charged elementary particle considered to transmit the weak interaction between other elementary particles. [*W*, the initial letter of *weak*.]

wpb ▶ **abbr.** wastepaper basket.

wpm ▶ **abbr.** words per minute (used after a number to indicate typing speed).

wrack[1] ▶ **v.** var. of RACK[1] (sense 1).

wrack[2] /rak/ ▶ **n.** any of a number of coarse brown seaweeds of the genera *Fucus*, *Ascophyllum*, and *Pelvetia*, class Phaeophyceae, that grow on the shoreline and frequently form a distinct band in relation to high- and low-water marks. Many have air bladders for buoyancy. [16th C.: appar. from WRACK[4].]

wrack[3] ▶ **n.** var. of RACK[5]. [ME: var. of RACK[5].]

wrack[4] ▶ **n.** archaic or dialect a wrecked ship; a shipwreck. ■ wreckage. [ME: from MDu. *wrak*; rel. to WREAK and WRECK.]

wraith /rāTH/ ▶ **n.** a ghost or ghostlike image of someone, esp. one seen shortly before or after their death. ■ used in similes and metaphors to describe a pale, thin, or insubstantial person or thing: *heart attacks had reduced his mother to a wraith.* ■ literary a wisp or faint trace of something. — **wraith·like** /-,līk/ **adj.** [16th C. (orig. Scots): of unknown origin.]

Wran·gel Is·land /'raNGgəl/ an island in the East Siberian Sea, off the coast of northeastern Russia.

Wran·gell Moun·tains /'raNGgəl/ a range in southeastern Alaska, along the Pacific coast and the border of the Yukon Territory.

wran·gle /'raNGgəl/ ▶ **n.** a dispute or argument, typically one that is long and complicated. ▶ **v.** **1** [intrans.] have such a dispute or argument. **2** [trans.] round up, herd, or take charge of (livestock): *the horses were wrangled early.* **3** another term for WANGLE. [ME: cf. Low Ger. *wrangeln*, frequentative of *wrangen* 'to struggle'; rel. to WRING.]

wran·gler /'raNGg(ə)lər/ ▶ **n.** **1** a person in charge of horses or other livestock on a ranch. **2** a person engaging in a lengthy and complicated quarrel or dispute.

wrap /rap/ ▶ **v.** (**wrapped**, **wrap·ping**) **1** [trans.] cover or enclose (someone or something) in paper or soft material. ■ clasp; embrace: *she wrapped him in her arms.* ■ cover (the body) with a body wrap. ■ cover (the fingernails) with a nail wrap. **2** [trans.] (**wrap something around**) arrange paper or soft material around (someone or something), typically as a covering or for warmth or protection. ■ place an arm, finger, or leg around (someone or something). ■ informal crash a vehicle into (a stationary object). **3** [trans.] Comput. cause (a word or unit of text) to be carried over to a new line automatically as the margin is reached, or to fit around embedded features such as pictures. ■ [intrans.] (of a word or unit or text) be carried over in such a way. **4** [intrans.] informal finish filming or recording. ▶ **n.** **1** a loose outer garment or piece of material. ■ [as adj.] denoting a garment having one part overlapping another; wrap-around. ■ paper or soft material used for wrapping: *plastic wrap.* ■ (usu. **wraps**) fig. a veil of secrecy maintained about something, esp. a new project. **2** [usu. in sing.] informal the end of a session of filming or recording. **3** a sandwich in which the filling is rolled in a soft tortilla. **4** short for BODY WRAP. ■ short for NAIL WRAP.
– PHRASES **be wrapped up in** be so engrossed or absorbed in (something) that one does not notice other people or things.
– PHRASAL VERBS **wrap up** (also **wrap someone up**) put on (or dress someone in) warm clothes. **wrap something up** complete or conclude a discussion or agreement. ■ win a game or competition: *Boston wrapped up the series 4–0.* [ME: of unknown origin.]

wrap·a·round /'rapə,round/ ▶ **adj.** [attrib.] curving or extending around at the edges or sides. ■ (of a garment) having one part overlapping another and fastened loosely. ▶ **n.** **1** a wraparound garment. **2** Comput. a facility by which a linear sequence of memory locations or screen positions is treated as a continuous circular series.

wrap·per /'rapər/ ▶ **n.** **1** a piece of paper, plastic, or foil covering and protecting something sold. ■ a cover enclosing a newspaper or magazine for posting. ■ the dust jacket of a book. ■ a tobacco leaf of superior quality enclosing a cigar. **2** a loose robe or gown.

wrap·ping /'rapiNG/ ▶ **n.** paper or soft material used to cover or enclose someone or something.

wrap·ping pa·per ▶ **n.** strong or decorative paper for wrapping parcels or presents.

wrapt /rapt/ ▶ **adj.** archaic or poetic form of **wrapped**: *wrapt in her music no birdsong shall ever equal.*

wrap-up ▶ **n.** a summary or résumé, in particular: ■ a review of a sporting event. ■ an overview of the products of one company or in one field. ▶ **adj.** serving to summarize, complete, or conclude something.

wrasse /ras/ ▶ **n.** (pl. same or **wrass·es**) a marine fish (family Labridae) with thick lips and strong teeth, typically brightly colored with marked differences between the male and female. [17th C.: from Cornish *wrah*; rel. to Welsh *gwrach*, lit. 'old woman.']

wrath /raTH/ ▶ **n.** extreme anger (chiefly used for humorous or rhetorical effect). [OE *wrǣththu*, from *wrāth* (see WROTH).]

wrath·ful /'raTHfəl/ ▶ **adj.** literary full of or characterized by intense anger. — **wrath·ful·ly** **adv.** **wrath·ful·ness** **n.**

wrath·y /'raTHē/ ▶ **adj.** informal, dated another term for WRATHFUL.

wreak /rēk/ ▶ **v.** [trans.] cause (a large amount of damage or harm): *torrential rainstorms **wreaked havoc** yesterday.* ■ inflict (vengeance): *he was determined to **wreak** his revenge **on** them.* ■ archaic avenge (someone who has been wronged). — **wreak·er** **n.** [OE *wrecan* 'drive (out), avenge,' of Gmc. origin; rel. to Du. *wreken* and Ger. *rächen*; cf. WRACK[4], WRECK, and WRETCH.]

wreath /rēTH/ ▶ **n.** (pl. **wreaths** /rēTHz; rēTHs/) an arrangement of flowers, leaves, or stems fastened in a ring and used for decoration or for laying on a grave. ■ a carved representation of such a wreath. ■ a similar ring made of or resembling soft, twisted material. ■ Heraldry a representation of such a ring below a crest (esp. where it joins a helmet). ■ a curl or ring of smoke or cloud: *wreaths of mist.* [OE *writha*, rel. to WRITHE.]

wreathe /rēTH/ ▶ v. [trans.] (usu. **be wreathed**) cover, surround, or encircle (something): *his face was wreathed in smiles.* ■ [with obj. and adverbial of direction] literary twist or entwine (something flexible) around or over something. ■ form (flowers, leaves, or stems) into a wreath. ■ [no obj., with adverbial of direction] (esp. of smoke) move with a curling motion: *he watched the smoke wreathe into the night air.* [16th C.: partly a back-form. from archaic *wrethen*, past part. of WRITHE, reinforced by WREATH.]

wreck /rek/ ▶ n. the destruction of a ship at sea; a shipwreck. ■ a ship destroyed in such a way. ■ Law goods brought ashore by the sea from a wreck and not claimed by the owner within a specified period (usually a year). ■ something, esp. a vehicle or building, that has been badly damaged or destroyed. ■ the disorganized remains of something that has suffered damage or destruction. ■ a road or rail crash. ■ a person whose physical or mental health or strength has failed. ▶ v. [trans.] (usu. **be wrecked**) cause the destruction of (a ship) by sinking or breaking up. ■ involve (someone) in such a wreck: *sailors who were wrecked on these coasts.* ■ [intrans.] [usu. as n.] (**wrecking**) esp. hist. cause the destruction of a ship in order to steal the cargo. ■ [intrans.] archaic suffer or undergo shipwreck. ■ destroy or severely damage (a structure or vehicle). ■ spoil completely. ■ [intrans.] [usu. as n.] (**wrecking**) engage in breaking up badly damaged vehicles, demolishing old buildings, or similar activities to obtain usable spares or scrap. [ME (as a legal term denoting wreckage washed ashore): from Anglo-Norman Fr. *wrec*, from the base of ON *reka* 'to drive'; rel. to WREAK.]

wreck·age /ˈrekij/ ▶ n. the remains of something that has been badly damaged or destroyed.

wrecked /rekt/ ▶ adj. **1** having been wrecked: *a wrecked marriage.* **2** informal under the influence of or suffering the effects of drugs or alcohol.

wreck·er /ˈrekər/ ▶ n. **1** a person or thing that wrecks, damages, or destroys something. ■ a person who breaks up damaged vehicles, demolishes old buildings, salvages wrecked ships, etc., to obtain usable spares or scrap. ■ esp. hist. a person on the shore who tries to bring about a shipwreck in order to profit from the wreckage. **2** a tow truck.

wreck·ing ball (also **wreck·er's ball**) ▶ n. a heavy metal ball swung from a crane into a building to demolish it.

Wren[1] /ren/, Sir Christopher (1632–1723), English architect. Following the Fire of London in 1666, he was responsible for the design of the new St. Paul's Cathedral 1675–1711.

Wren[2], P. C. (1885–1941), English novelist; full name *Percival Christopher Wren.* His works include *Beau Geste* (1924).

Wren[3] ▶ n. (in the UK) a member of the former Women's Royal Naval Service. [20th C.: orig. in the pl., from the abbrev. *WRNS.*]

wren /ren/ ▶ n. **1** a small short-winged songbird (numerous genera, family Troglodytidae) found chiefly in the New World. **2** [usu. with adj.] any of a number of small songbirds that resemble the true wrens in size or appearance. [OE *wrenna*, of Gmc. origin.]

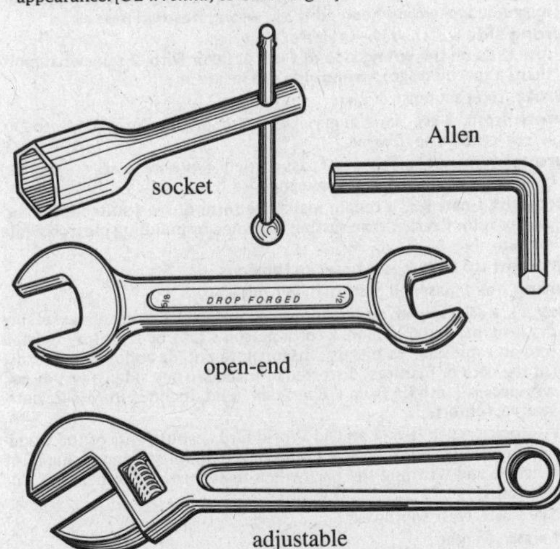

wrenches 2

wrench /renCH/ ▶ n. **1** [usu. in sing.] a sudden violent twist or pull. ■ fig. an act of leaving someone or something that causes sadness or distress. **2** a tool used for gripping and turning nuts or bolts. **3** Mech. a combination of a couple with a force along its axis. ▶ v. [trans.] pull or twist (someone or something) suddenly and violently. ■ injure (a part of the body) as a result of a sudden twisting movement. ■ turn (something, esp. a nut or bolt) with a wrench. ■ archaic distort to fit a particular theory or interpretation.
– PHRASES **a wrench in the works** another way of saying *A MONKEY WRENCH IN THE WORKS* (see MONKEY WRENCH). [OE *wrencan* 'twist,' of unknown origin.]

wrench fault ▶ n. another term for STRIKE-SLIP FAULT.

wren·tit /ˈrenˌtit/ ▶ n. a long-tailed North American songbird (*Chamaea fasciata*) that is the only American member of the babbler family (Timaliidae).

wrest /rest/ ▶ v. [trans.] forcibly pull (something) from a person's grasp. ■ take (something, esp. power or control) from someone or something else after considerable effort or difficulty: *they tied to wrest control of their lives from impersonal bureaucracies.* ■ archaic distort the meaning or interpretation of (something) to suit one's own interests or views. ▶ n. archaic a key for tuning a harp or piano. [OE *wrǣstan* 'twist, tighten,' of Gmc. origin; rel. to Dan. *vriste*, also to WRIST.]

wres·tle /ˈresəl/ ▶ v. [intrans.] take part in a fight, either as a sport or in earnest, that involves grappling with one's opponent and trying to throw or force them to the ground. ■ [with obj. and adverbial] force (someone) into a particular position or place by fighting in such a way: *the security guards wrestled them to the ground.* ■ fig. struggle with a difficulty or problem. ■ [with obj. and adverbial] move or manipulate (something) in a specified way with difficulty and some physical effort. ▶ n. [in sing.] a wrestling bout or contest. ■ a hard struggle. — **wres·tler** /ˈres(ə)lər/ n. [OE, frequentative of *wrǣstan* 'wrest.']

wres·tling /ˈres(ə)liNG/ ▶ n. the sport or activity of grappling with an opponent and trying to throw or hold them down on the ground, typically according to a code of rules.

wretch /reCH/ ▶ n. an unfortunate or unhappy person. ■ informal a despicable or contemptible person. [OE *wrecca* (also in the sense 'banished person'), of West Gmc. origin; rel. to Ger. *Recke* 'warrior, hero,' also to the v. WREAK.]

wretch·ed /ˈreCHid/ ▶ adj. (**-ed·er**, **-ed·est**) (of a person) in a very unhappy or unfortunate state. ■ of poor quality; very bad. ■ used to express anger or annoyance: *she disliked the wretched man intensely.* — **wretch·ed·ly** adv. [as submodifier] *a wretchedly poor country.* **wretch·ed·ness** n. [ME: formed irregularly from WRETCH + -ED[1].]

wrig·gle /ˈrigəl/ ▶ v. [intrans.] twist and turn with quick writhing movements. ■ [trans.] cause to move in such a way: *she wriggled her toes.* ■ [no obj., with adverbial of direction] move in a particular direction with wriggling movements: *Susie wriggled out of her clothes.* ■ (**wriggle out of**) avoid (something), esp. by devious means. ▶ n. [in sing.] a wriggling movement. — **wrig·gly** /ˈrig(ə)lē/ adj. [15th C.: from Mid. Low Ger. *wriggelen*, frequentative of *wriggen* 'twist, turn.']

wrig·gler /ˈrig(ə)lər/ ▶ n. a person or thing that wriggles. ■ a wriggling animalcule or the larva of a mosquito. Also called WIGGLER.

Wright[1] /rīt/, Frank Lloyd (1869–1959), US architect. His "prairie-style" houses are characterized by a close relationship among building, landscape, and materials used. His buildings include the Kaufmann House, which incorporated a waterfall, in Pennsylvania 1935–39 and the Guggenheim Museum of Art in New York 1956–59.

Wright[2] US aviation pioneers. Wilbur (1867–1912) and his brother Orville (1871–1948) were the first to make brief powered sustained and controlled flights in an airplane (1903), which was designed and built by them.

wright /rīt/ ▶ n. archaic a maker or builder. [OE *wryhta*, *wyrhta*, of West Gmc. origin; rel. to WORK.]

wring /riNG/ ▶ v. (past **wrung** /rəNG/) [trans.] squeeze and twist (something) to force liquid from it: *she wrung the cloth out in the sink.* ■ [with obj. and adverbial] extract (liquid) by squeezing and twisting something. ■ break (an animal's neck) by twisting it forcibly. ■ squeeze (someone's hand) tightly, esp. with sincere emotion. ■ [with obj. and adverbial] obtain (something) with difficulty or effort. ■ cause pain or distress to. ▶ n. [in sing.] an act of squeezing or twisting something.
– PHRASES **wring one's hands** clasp and twist one's hands together as a gesture of great distress, esp. when one is powerless to change the situation. [OE *wringan* (v.), of West Gmc. origin; rel. to Du. *wringen*, also to WRONG.]

wring·er /ˈriNGər/ ▶ n. a device for wringing water from wet clothes, mops, or other objects.
– PHRASES **put someone through the wringer** informal subject someone to a very stressful experience, esp. a severe interrogation.

wrin·kle /ˈriNGkəl/ ▶ n. **1** a slight line or fold in something, esp. fabric or the skin of the face. ■ informal a minor difficulty; a snag. **2** informal a clever innovation, or useful piece of information or advice. ▶ v. [trans.] [often as adj.] (**wrinkled**) make or cause lines or folds in (something, esp. fabric or the skin). ■ grimace and cause wrinkles on (a part of the face). ■ [intrans.] form or become marked with lines or folds. [ME: origin obscure, possibly a back-form. from the OE past part. *gewrinclod* 'sinuous' (of which no infinitive is recorded).]

wrin·kly /ˈriNGk(ə)lē/ ▶ adj. (**-kli·er**, **-kli·est**) having many lines or folds.

wrist /rist/ ▶ n. **1** the joint connecting the hand with the forearm. See also CARPUS. ■ the equivalent joint (the carpal joint) in the foreleg of a quadruped or the wing of a bird. ■ the part of a garment covering the wrist; a cuff. **2** (also **wrist pin**) (in a machine) a stud projecting from a crank as an attachment for a connecting rod. [OE, of Gmc. origin, prob. from the base of WRITHE.]

wrist·band /ˈristˌband/ ▶ n. a strip of material worn around the wrist, in particular: ■ a small strap or bracelet, esp. one used for identification or as a fashion item. ■ a strip of absorbent material worn during sports or strenuous exercise to soak up sweat. ■ the cuff of a shirt or blouse.

wrist-drop ▶ n. paralysis of the muscles that normally raise the hand at the wrist and extend the fingers, typically caused by nerve damage.

wrist·guard /ˈrist,gärd/ ▶ n. a band of leather or leatherlike material worn around the wrist for support and protection, esp. for athletic activities such as archery and fencing.

wrist·let /ˈristlit/ ▶ n. a band or bracelet worn on the wrist, typically as an ornament.

wrist pin ▶ n. another term for WRIST (sense 2).

wrist·watch /ˈrist,wäCH/ ▶ n. a watch worn on a strap around the wrist.

wrist·work /ˈrist,wərk/ ▶ n. the action of working the hand without moving the arm, esp. in fencing and ball games.

wrist·y /ˈristē/ ▶ adj. Tennis (of a stroke) performed using a pronounced movement of the wrist.

writ[1] /rit/ ▶ n. a form of written command in the name of a court or other legal authority to act, or abstain from acting, in some way. ■ (**one's writ**) one's power to enforce compliance or submission; one's authority. [OE, as a general term denoting written matter, from the Gmc. base of WRITE.]

writ[2] ▶ v. archaic past participle of WRITE.

– PHRASES **writ large** clear and obvious. ■ in a stark or exaggerated form.

write /rīt/ ▶ v. (past **wrote** /rōt/; past part. **writ·ten** /ˈritn/) [trans.] **1** mark (letters, words, or other symbols) on a surface, typically paper, with a pen, pencil, or similar implement. ■ [intrans.] have the ability to mark coherent letters or words in this way: *he couldn't read or write.* ■ fill out or complete (a sheet, check, or similar) in this way. ■ [intrans.] write in a cursive hand, as opposed to printing individual letters. **2** compose, write, and send (a letter) to someone. ■ write and send a letter to (someone). ■ [trans.] (**write in**) write to an organization, esp. a broadcasting station, with a question, suggestion, or opinion. **3** compose (a text or work) for written or printed reproduction or publication; put into literary form and set down in writing: *I didn't know you wrote poetry.* ■ compose (a musical work). ■ (**write someone into/out of**) add or remove a character to or from (a long-running story or series). ■ archaic describe in writing: *if I could write the beauty of your eyes.* **4** [with obj. and adverbial] Comput. enter (data) into a specified storage medium or location in store. **5** underwrite (an insurance policy).

– PHRASES **be nothing to write home about** informal be very mediocre or unexceptional. **be** (or **have something**) **written all over one** (or **one's face**) informal used to convey that the presence of a particular quality or feeling is clearly revealed by a person's expression. (**and**) **that's all she wrote** informal used to convey that there is or was nothing more to be said about a matter.

– PHRASAL VERBS **write something down 1** reduce the nominal value of stock or goods. **2** write as if for those considered inferior. **write someone in** (when voting) add the name of someone not on the original list of candidates and vote for them. **write something off 1** (**write someone/something off**) dismiss someone or something as insignificant. **2** cancel the record of a bad debt; acknowledge the loss of or failure to recover an asset. **write something up 1** write a full or formal account of something. ■ make entries to bring a diary or similar record up to date. **2** reduce the nominal value of stock or goods. — **writ·a·ble** adj. [OE *wrītan* 'score, form (letters) by carving, write,' of Gmc. origin; rel. to Ger. *reissen* 'sketch, drag.']

write-down ▶ n. Finance a reduction in the estimated or nominal value of an asset.

write-in ▶ n. a vote cast for an unlisted candidate by writing their name on a ballot paper. ■ a candidate for whom votes are cast in such a way.

write-off ▶ n. **1** Finance a cancellation from an account of a bad debt or worthless asset. **2** a worthless or ineffectual person or thing.

write-once ▶ adj. Comput. denoting a memory or storage device, typically an optical one, on which data, once written, cannot be modified.

write-pro·tect ▶ v. [trans.] Comput. protect (a disk) from accidental writing or erasure, as by removing the cover from a notch in casing. ▶ adj. denoting a notch or other device that fulfills this function.

writ·er /ˈrītər/ ▶ n. a person who has written a particular text. ■ a person who writes books, stories, or articles as a job or regular occupation. ■ [with adj.] a person who writes in a specified way: *Dickens was a prolific writer.* ■ a composer of musical works. ■ Comput. a device that writes data to a storage medium. ■ Stock market a broker who makes an option available for purchase or sells options. ■ [with adj.] a person who has a specified kind of handwriting: *neat writers.*

– PHRASES **writer's block** the condition of being unable to think of what to write or how to proceed with writing. **writer's cramp** pain or stiffness in the hand caused by excessive writing. [OE *wrītere* (see WRITE).]

writ·er-in-res·i·dence ▶ n. (pl. **writ·ers-in-res·i·dence**) a writer holding a temporary residential post in an academic establishment, in order to share his or her professional insights.

writ·er·ly /ˈrītərlē/ ▶ adj. of or characteristic of a professional author. ■ consciously literary.

write-up ▶ n. **1** a full written account. ■ a newspaper or magazine article giving the author's opinion of a recent event, performance, or product. **2** Finance an increase in the estimated or nominal value of an asset.

writhe /rī*TH*/ ▶ v. [intrans.] make continual twisting, squirming movements or contortions of the body. ■ [trans.] cause to move in such a way: *a snake writhing its body in a sinuous movement.* ■ (**writhe in/with/at**) respond with great emotional or physical discomfort to (a violent or unpleasant feeling or thought): *writhing in suppressed fury.* ▶ n. rare a twisting, squirming movement. [OE *wrīthan* 'make into coils, plait, fasten with a cord,' of Gmc. origin; rel. to WREATHE.]

writh·en /ˈri*TH*ən/ ▶ adj. **1** literary twisted or contorted out of normal shape or form. **2** (of antique glass or silver) having spirally twisted ornamentation. [OE in the sense 'plaited, entwined,' archaic past part. of WRITHE.]

writ·ing /ˈrītiNG/ ▶ n. **1** the activity or skill of marking coherent words on paper and composing text. ■ the activity or occupation of composing text for publication: *she made a decent living from writing.* **2** written work, esp. with regard to its style or quality. ■ (**writings**) books, stories, articles, or other written works. ■ (**the Writings**) the Hagiographa. **3** a sequence of letters, words, or symbols marked on paper or some other surface. ■ handwriting: *his writing looked crabbed.*

– PHRASES **in writing** in written form, esp. as proof of an agreement or grievance. **the writing** (or **handwriting**) **is on the wall** there are clear signs that something unpleasant or unwelcome is going to happen. [with biblical allusion to Dan. 5:5, 25–8.]

writ of ex·e·cu·tion ▶ n. Law a judicial order that a judgment be enforced.

writ·ten /ˈritn/ past participle of WRITE.

Wro·cław /ˈvrôt,swäf; -,släf/ a city on the Oder River, in western Poland; pop. 643,000. German name BRESLAU.

wrong /rôNG/ ▶ adj. **1** not correct or true. ■ [predic.] mistaken: *I was wrong about him.* ■ unsuitable or undesirable. ■ [predic.] in a bad or abnormal condition; amiss: *something was wrong with the pump.* **2** unjust, dishonest, or immoral: *they were wrong to take the law into their own hands.* ▶ adv. in an unsuitable or undesirable manner or direction: *what am I doing wrong?* ■ with an incorrect result. ▶ n. an unjust, dishonest, or immoral action. ■ Law a breach, by commission or omission, of one's legal duty. ■ Law an invasion of right to the damage or prejudice of another. ▶ v. [trans.] act unjustly or dishonestly toward (someone): *the people I have wronged.* ■ mistakenly attribute bad motives to; misrepresent.

– PHRASES **get someone wrong** misunderstand someone, esp. by falsely imputing malice. **go down the wrong way** (of food) enter the windpipe instead of the gullet. **go wrong** develop in an undesirable way. **in the wrong** responsible for a quarrel, mistake, or offense. **two wrongs don't make a right** proverb the fact that someone has done something unjust or dishonest is no justification for acting in a similar way. — **wrong·er** n. **wrong·ly** adv. **wrong·ness** n. [OE *wrang*, from ON *rangr* 'awry, unjust'; rel. to WRING.]

wrong·do·ing /ˈrôNG,do͞oiNG/ ▶ n. illegal or dishonest behavior. — **wrong·do·er** n.

wrong·ful /ˈrôNGfəl/ ▶ adj. (of an act) not fair, just, or legal. — **wrong·ful·ly** adv. **wrong·ful·ness** n.

wrong·ful death ▶ adj. denoting a civil action in which damages are sought against a party for causing a death, typically when criminal action has failed or is not attempted

wrong·head·ed /ˈrôNG,hedid/ ▶ adj. having or showing bad judgment; misguided. — **wrong·head·ed·ly** adv. **wrong·head·ed·ness** n.

wrong side ▶ n. the reverse side of a fabric.

– PHRASES **on the wrong side of 1** out of favor with. **2** somewhat more than (a specified age). **wrong side out** inside out.

wrote /rōt/ past tense of WRITE.

wroth /rôTH/ ▶ adj. archaic angry. [OE *wrāth*, of Gmc. origin; rel. to Du. *wreed* 'cruel,' also to WRITHE.]

wrought /rôt/ archaic past and past participle of WORK. ▶ adj. (of metals) beaten out or shaped by hammering.

wrought i·ron ▶ n. a tough, malleable form of iron suitable for forging or rolling rather than casting, obtained by puddling pig iron while molten.

wrought up ▶ adj. [predic.] upset and anxious.

wrung /rəNG/ past and past participle of WRING.

wry /rī/ ▶ adj. (**wry·er**, **wry·est** or **wri·er**, **wri·est**) **1** using or expressing dry, esp. mocking, humor. **2** (of a person's face or features) twisted into an expression of disgust, disappointment, or annoyance. ■ archaic (of the neck or features) distorted or turned to one side. — **wry·ly** adv. **wry·ness** n. [16th C.: from OE *wrīgian* 'tend, incline,' in ME 'deviate, swerve, contort.']

wry·neck /ˈrī,nek/ ▶ n. **1** an Old World bird (genus *Jynx*) of the woodpecker family, with brown camouflaged plumage and a habit of twisting and writhing the neck when disturbed. **2** another term for TORTICOLLIS.

WSW ▶ abbr. west-southwest.

wt ▶ abbr. weight.

WTO ▶ abbr. World Trade Organization.

Wu /wo͞o/ ▶ n. a dialect of Chinese spoken in Jiangsu and Zhejiang provinces and the city of Shanghai. [the name in Chin.]

Wu·han /ˈwo͞oˈhän/ a port in east central China, the capital of Hubei province; pop. 3,710,000. It is situated at the confluence of the Han and the Yangtze rivers.

wul·fen·ite /ˈwo͝olfə,nīt/ ▶ n. an orange-yellow mineral consisting of a molybdate of lead, typically occurring as tabular crystals. [19th C.: from the name of F. X. von *Wulfen* (1728–1805), Austrian scientist, + -ITE[1].]

Wun·der·kam·mer /ˈvo͝ondər,kämər/ ▶ n. (pl. **-kam·mern**) a place where a collection of curiosities and rarities is exhibited. [Ger., lit. 'wonder chamber.']

wun·der·kind /'wŏŏndər,kind,/ ▸ **n.** (pl. **-kinds** or **-kind·er** /-,kindər/) a person who achieves great success when relatively young. [19th C.: from Ger., from *Wunder* 'wonder' + *Kind* 'child.']

Wundt /vŏŏnt/, Wilhelm (1832–1920), German psychologist. He founded psychology as a separate discipline and established a laboratory devoted to its study.

wun·ner·ful /'wənərfəl/ ▸ **adj.** nonstandard spelling of **WONDERFUL**, representing dialect pronunciation.

Wup·per·tal /'vŏŏpər,täl; 'wŏŏp-/ a city in western Germany, northeast of Düsseldorf; pop. 385,000.

Wur·litz·er /'wərlitsər/ ▸ **n.** trademark a large pipe organ or electric organ, esp. one used in the movie theaters of the 1930s. [named after Rudolf *Wurlitzer* (1831–1914), the German-born American instrument-maker who founded the manufacturing company.]

Würm /vŏŏrm/ ▸ **n.** [usu. as adj.] Geol. the final Pleistocene glaciation in the Alps, possibly corresponding to the Weichsel of northern Europe. ■ the system of deposits laid down at this time. [20th C.: the former name of the Starnberger See, a lake in Bavaria.]

wurst /wərst; wŏŏrst/ ▸ **n.** German or Austrian sausage. [from Ger. *Wurst.*]

wurtz·ite /'wərt,sīt/ ▸ **n.** a mineral consisting of zinc sulfide, typically occurring as brownish-black pyramidal crystals. [19th C.: from the name of Charles A. *Wurtz* (1817–84), French chemist, + **-ITE**[1].]

Würz·burg /'vərts,bərg; 'wərts-; 'vʏrts,bŏŏrk/ a city on the Main River in Bavaria, in southern Germany; pop. 128,000.

wu·shu /'wōō'shōō/ ▸ **n.** the Chinese martial arts. [from Chin. *wǔ shù*, from *wǔ* 'military' + *shù* 'art.']

wuss /wŏŏs/ ▸ **n.** informal a weak or ineffectual person (often used as a general term of abuse). — **wuss·y** /'wŏŏsē/ **n.** (pl. **-ies**) & **adj.** [20th C.: of unknown origin.]

Wu·xi /'wōō'shē/ (also **Wu-hsi**) a city on the Grand Canal in Jiangsu province, in eastern China; pop. 930,000.

wuz /wəz/ ▸ **v.** nonstandard spelling of **WAS**, representing dialect or informal pronunciation.

WV ▸ **abbr.** West Virginia (in official postal use).

W.Va. ▸ **abbr.** West Virginia.

WWF ▸ **abbr.** ■ World Wrestling Federation.

WWI ▸ **abbr.** World War I.

WWII ▸ **abbr.** World War II.

WWW ▸ **abbr.** World Wide Web.

WY ▸ **abbr.** Wyoming (in official postal use).

Wy·an·dot /'wīən,dät/ (also **Wy·an·dotte**) ▸ **n.** **1** a member of an American Indian community formed by Huron-speaking peoples, originally in Ontario, now living mainly in Oklahoma and Quebec. **2** the Iroquoian language of this people. **3** (usu. **Wyandotte**) a domestic chicken of a medium-sized breed. ▸ **adj.** of or relating to the Wyandot people or their language. [18th C.: from Fr. *Ouendat*, from Huron *Wendat.*]

wych elm /wich/ (also **witch elm**) ▸ **n.** a European elm (*Ulmus glabra*) with large rough leaves, chiefly growing in woodland or near flowing water. [17th C.: *wych*, used in names of trees with pliant branches, from OE *wic(e)*, appar. from a Gmc. root meaning 'bend'; rel. to **WEAK**.]

Wych·er·ley /'wichərlē/, William (*c.*1640–1716), English playwright. His Restoration comedies are characterized by their acute examination of sexual morality and marriage conventions.

Wyc·lif /'wiklif/ (also **Wyc·liffe**), John (*c.*1330–84), English religious reformer. He instituted the first English translation of the complete Bible. His followers were known as Lollards.

Wye /wī/ a river that rises in the mountains of western Wales and flows southeast before entering the Severn estuary at Chepstow. It forms part of the border between Wales and England.

wye /wī/ ▸ **n.** a support or other structure shaped like a Y, in particular: ■ a triangle of railroad track, used for turning locomotives or trains. ■ (in plumbing) a short pipe with a branch joining it at an acute angle. [19th C.: the letter *Y* represented as a word.]

Wyeth /'wīəth/, a family of US painters. N. C. (1882–1945); full name *Newell Convers Wyeth*, was noted for his magazine and book illustrations. His son, Andrew Newell (1917–), painted *Christina's World* (1948) and the Helga series (1971–85). Andrew's son Jamie (1946–), full name *James Browning Wyeth*, painted *Portrait of J.F.K.* (1965) and a series of portraits of Orca Bates.

Wy·ler /'wīlər/, William (1902–81), US director; born in Germany. He directed *Mrs. Miniver* (1941), *The Best Years of Our Lives* (1946), and *Funny Girl* (1968).

wyn /win/ ▸ **n.** var. of **WEN**[2].

Wynd·ham /'windəm/, John (1903–69), English writer; pen name of *John Wyndham Parkes Lucas Beynon Harris*. His science fiction novels include *The Day of the Triffids* (1951) and *The Chrysalids* (1955).

Wyo. ▸ **abbr.** Wyoming.

Wy·o·ming /wī'ōming/ a state in the western central US; pop. 493,782; capital, Cheyenne; statehood, July 10, 1890 (44). Acquired, in part, by the Louisiana Purchase in 1803, it gave the vote to women in 1869, the first state to do so. — **Wy·o·ming·ite** /-ming,īt/ **n.**

Wy·o·ming Val·ley a valley in northeastern Pennsylvania, along the Susquehanna River.

WYSIWYG /'wizē,wig/ (also **wysiwyg**) ▸ **adj.** Comput. denoting the representation of text on screen in a form exactly corresponding to its appearance on a printout. [1980s: acronym from *what you see is what you get.*]

wyvern

wy·vern /'wīvərn/ ▸ **n.** Heraldry a winged two-legged dragon with a barbed tail. [ME (denoting a viper): from OFr. *wivre*, from L. *vipera.*]

X[1] /eks/ (also **x**) ▶ n. (pl. **Xs** or **X's**) **1** the twenty-fourth letter of the alphabet. ■ denoting the next after W in a set of items, categories, etc. ■ denoting an unknown or unspecified person or thing. ■ **(x)** (used in describing play in bridge) denoting an unspecified card other than an honor. ■ (usu. *x*) the first unknown quantity in an algebraic expression, usually the independent variable. [the introduction of *x*, *y*, and *z* as symbols of unknown quantities is due to Descartes (*Géométrie*, 1637), who took *z* as the first unknown and then proceeded backward in the alphabet.] ■ (usu. *x*) denoting the principal or horizontal axis in a system of coordinates: [in comb.] *the x-axis.* **2** a cross-shaped written symbol, in particular: ■ used to indicate a position on a map or diagram. ■ used to indicate a mistake or incorrect answer. ■ used in a letter or message to symbolize a kiss. ■ used to indicate one's vote on a ballot paper. ■ used in place of the signature of a person who cannot write. **3** a shape like that of a letter X. **4** the Roman numeral for ten. ▶ v. **(X's, X'd, X'ing)** [trans.] mark or make a sign with an X. ■ overwrite or obliterate with an X or series of X's. ■ make void or annul; invalidate.

X[2] ▶ symb. films classified as suitable for adults only (replaced in 1990 by *NC-17*).

-x ▶ suffix forming the plural of many nouns ending in *-u* taken from French: *tableaux.* [from Fr.]

X-act·o knife /ig'zaktō/ ▶ n. trademark a utility knife with a very sharp replaceable blade. [1940s: respelling of the adj. EXACT + -O.]

Xan·a·du /'zanə,do͞o/ ▶ n. (pl. **-dus**) used to convey an impression of a place as almost unattainably luxurious or beautiful. [alt. of *Shang-tu*, the name of an ancient city in southeastern Mongolia, as portrayed in Coleridge's poem *Kubla Khan* (1816).]

Xan·ax /'zan,aks/ ▶ n. trademark for ALPRAZOLAM.

xan·than gum /'zanTHən; -,THan/ ▶ n. Chem. a substance produced by bacterial fermentation or synthetically and used in foods as a gelling agent and thickener. [1960s: from the mod. L. name of the bacterium *Xanthomonas campestris* + -AN.]

xan·thene /'zan,THēn/ ▶ n. Chem. a yellowish crystalline compound, $C_{13}H_{10}O$, whose molecule contains two benzene rings joined by a methylene group and an oxygen atom, and whose derivatives include brilliant, often fluorescent dyes such as fluorescein and rhodamines. [19th C.: from Gk. *xanthos* 'yellow' + -ENE.]

xan·thic ac·id /'zanTHik/ ▶ n. Chem. an organic acid containing the group $-OCS_2H$, examples of which are typically reactive solids. — **xanthate** /'zan,THāt/ n. [19th C.: *xanthic* from Gk. *xanthos* 'yellow' + -IC.]

xan·thine /'zan,THēn; -THin/ ▶ n. Biochem. a crystalline compound, $C_5H_4N_4O_2$, that is found in blood and urine and is an intermediate in the metabolic breakdown of nucleic acids to uric acid. ■ any of the derivatives of this, including caffeine and related alkaloids. [19th C.: from *xanthic* (from Gk. *xanthos* 'yellow' + -IC) + -INE[4].]

Xan·thip·pe /zan'tipē; -'THipē/ (also **Xan·tip·pe** /-'tipē/) (5th century BC), wife of Socrates. She had a reputation as a shrew.

xan·tho·ma /zan'THōmə/ ▶ n. (pl. **-mas** or **-ma·ta** /-mətə/) Med. an irregular yellow patch or nodule on the skin, caused by deposition of lipids. [19th C.: from Gk. *xanthos* 'yellow' + -OMA.]

xan·tho·phyll /'zanTHə,fil/ ▶ n. Biochem. a yellow or brown carotenoid plant pigment that causes the autumn colors of leaves. [19th C.: from Gk. *xanthos* 'yellow' + *phullon* 'leaf.']

Xa·vi·er, St. Fran·cis /(ig)'zāvēər/ (1506–52), Spanish Catholic missionary; known as **the Apostle of the Indies.** He was one of the original seven Jesuits.

X chro·mo·some ▶ n. Genet. (in humans and other mammals) a sex chromosome, two of which are normally present in female cells (designated XX) and only one in male cells (designated XY). Compare with **Y CHROMOSOME.**

xd ▶ abbr. ex dividend.

Xe ▶ symb. the chemical element xenon.

xe·bec /'zē,bek/ (also **ze·bec**) ▶ n. hist. a small three-masted Mediterranean sailing ship with lateen and sometimes square sails. [18th C.: alt. (influenced by Sp. *xabeque*) of Fr. *chebec*, via Ital. from Arab. *šabbāk*.]

Xe·nar·thra /zə'närTHrə/ Zool. an order of mammals that comprises the edentates. Also called **EDENTATA.** — **xe·nar·thran** n. & adj. [mod. L. (pl.), from XENO- 'strange' + Gk. *arthron* 'joint' (because of the peculiar accessory articulations in the vertebrae).]

xe·ni·a /'zēnēə; -nyə/ ▶ n. Bot. the influence or effect of pollen on the endosperm or embryo, resulting in hybrid characteristics in form, color, etc., of the derived seed.

xeno- ▶ comb. form relating to a foreigner or foreigners: *xenophobia.* ■ other; different in origin: *xenograft.* [from Gk. *xenos* 'stranger, foreigner,' (adj.) 'strange.']

xen·o·bi·ot·ic /,zenəbī'ätik; ,zēnə-/ ▶ adj. relating to or denoting a substance, typically a synthetic chemical, that is foreign to the body or to an ecological system. ▶ n. (usu. **xenobiotics**) a substance of this kind.

xe·nog·a·my /zə'nägəmē/ ▶ n. Bot. fertilization of a flower by pollen from a flower on a genetically different plant. — **xe·nog·a·mous** /-məs/ adj.

xen·o·ge·ne·ic /,zenōjə'nē-ik; ,zēnō-/ ▶ adj. Immunol. denoting, relating to, or involving tissues or cells belonging to individuals of different species. Compare with **ALLOGENEIC.**

xen·o·graft /'zenə,graft; 'zēnə-/ ▶ n. a tissue graft or organ transplant from a donor of a different species from the recipient.

xen·o·lith /'zenə,liTH; 'zēnə-/ ▶ n. Geol. a piece of rock within an igneous mass that is not derived from the original magma but has been introduced from elsewhere, esp. the surrounding country rock.

xe·non /'zē,nän; 'zen,än/ ▶ n. the chemical element of atomic number 54, a member of the noble gas series. It is obtained by distillation of liquid air and is used in some specialized electric lamps. (Symbol: **Xe**) [19th C.: from Gk., neut. of *xenos* 'strange.']

Xe·noph·a·nes /zə'näfə,nēz/ (*c.*570–*c.*480 BC), Greek philosopher. He argued for a form of pantheism.

xen·o·phile /'zenə,fil; 'zē-/ ▶ n. an individual who is attracted to foreign peoples, manners, or cultures.

xen·o·pho·bi·a /,zēnə'fōbēə; ,zenə-/ ▶ n. intense or irrational dislike or fear of people from other countries. — **xen·o·phobe** /'zēnə,fōb; 'zenə-/ n. **xen·o·pho·bic** /-'fōbik/ adj.

Xen·o·phon /'zenəfən; -,fän/ (*c.*435–*c.*354 BC), Greek historian and military leader. He wrote the *Anabasis* and the *Hellenica*, a history of Greece.

xen·o·time /'zenə,tīm; 'zēnə-/ ▶ n. a yellowish-brown mineral that occurs in some igneous rocks and consists of a phosphate of yttrium and other rare-earth elements. [19th C.: from XENO-, appar. erroneously for Gk. *kenos* 'vain, empty,' + *timē* 'honor' (because it was wrongly supposed to contain a new metal).]

xen·o·trans·plan·ta·tion /,zenə,transplan'tāSHən; ,zēnə-/ ▶ n. the process of grafting or transplanting organs or tissues between members of different species. — **xen·o·trans·plant** /-'trans,plant/ n.

xe·ric /'zi(ə)rik; 'zer-/ ▶ adj. Ecol. (of an environment or habitat) containing little moisture; very dry. Compare with **HYDRIC** and **MESIC**[1]. [1920s: from XERO- 'dry' + -IC.]

xe·ri·scape /'zi(ə)rə,skāp; 'zerə-/ ▶ n. a style of landscape design requiring little or no irrigation or other maintenance, used in arid regions. ■ a garden or landscape created in such a style. ▶ v. [trans.] landscape (an area) in such a style. [1980s: from XERIC + -SCAPE.]

xero- ▶ comb. form dry: *xeroderma* | *xerophyte.* [from Gk. *xēros* 'dry.']

xe·ro·der·ma /,zi(ə)rə'dərmə/ ▶ n. any of various diseases characterized by extreme dryness of the skin, esp. a mild form of ichthyosis. [19th C.: mod. L., from XERO- 'dry' + Gk. *derma* 'skin.']

xe·rog·ra·phy /zi'rägrəfē/ ▶ n. a dry copying process in which black or colored powder adheres to parts of a surface remaining electrically charged after being exposed to light from an image of the document to be copied. — **xe·ro·graph·ic** /,zi(ə)rə'grafik/ adj. **xe·ro·graph·i·cal·ly** /,zi(ə)rə'grafik(ə)lē/ adv.

xe·roph·i·lous /zi'räfələs/ ▶ adj. Bot. Zool. (of a plant or animal) adapted to a very dry climate or habitat, or to conditions where moisture is scarce. — **xer·o·phile** /'zi(ə)rə,fīl/ n.

xe·roph·thal·mi·a /,zi(ə)räf'THalmēə; ,zi(ə)räp-/ ▶ n. Med. abnormal dryness of the conjunctiva and cornea of the eye, with inflammation and ridge formation, typically associated with vitamin A deficiency.

xe·ro·phyte /'zi(ə)rə,fīt/ ▶ n. Bot. a plant that needs very little water. — **xe·ro·phyt·ic** /,zi(ə)rə'fitik/ adj.

Xe·rox /'zi(ə)r,äks/ ▶ n. trademark a xerographic copying process. ■ a copy made using such a process. ■ a machine for copying by xerography. ▶ v. **(xerox)** [trans.] copy (a document) by such a process. [1950s: an invented name, based on XEROGRAPHY.]

Xerx·es I /'zərk,sēz/ (*c.*519–465 BC), king of Persia 486–465; son of Darius I. He attacked the Greeks but was defeated at Salamis in 480 and Plataea in 479.

x-height ▶ n. the height of a lower-case x, considered characteristic of a given typeface or script.

Xho·sa /'kōsə; 'kô-; 'KHō-; 'KHô-/ ▶ n. (pl. same or **-sas**) **1** a member of a South African people traditionally living in the Eastern Cape Province.

They form the second largest ethnic group in South Africa after the Zulus. **2** the Nguni language of this people. ▶ **adj.** of or relating to this people or their language. [from the stem of Xhosa *umXhosa* (pl. *amaXhosa*).]

xi /zī; sī; ksē/ ▶ **n.** the fourteenth letter of the Greek alphabet (Ξ, ξ), transliterated as 'x.'

Xia·men /'sн(y)ä'mən/ (also **Hsia·men**) a city in Fujian province, in southeastern China; pop. 639,000. Also called **Amoy**.

Xi·an /'shē'än/ (also **Hsi·an**) a city in central China, capital of Shaanxi province; pop. 2,710,000. The city has been inhabited since the 11th century BC, having previously been the capital of the Han, Sui, and Tang dynasties. Former names **Changan, Siking**.

Xi·ang /shy'äng/ (also **Hsi·ang**) ▶ **n.** a dialect of Chinese spoken by about 36 million people, mainly in Hunan province.

Xing·tai /'shing'tī/ a city in northeastern China, south of Shijiazhuang; pop. 1,167,000.

Xin·gú /shing'gōō/ a South American river that rises in western Brazil and flows north for about 1,230 miles (1,979 km) to the Amazon delta.

Xi·ning /'shē'ning/ (also **Hsi·ning**) a city in northern central China; pop. 698,000.

Xin·jiang /'shin'jy'äng; -jē'äng/ an autonomous region in northwestern China, on the border with Mongolia and Kazakhstan; pop. 15,170,000; capital, Urumqi.

-xion ▶ **suffix** forming nouns such as *fluxion*. [from L. participial stems (see also **-ion**).]

xiph·i·ster·num /,zifə'stərnəm/ ▶ **n.** Anat. the lowest part of the sternum; the xiphoid process. [19th C.: from Gk. *xiphos* 'sword' + **sternum**.]

xiph·oid proc·ess /'zifoid/ (also **xiph·oid car·ti·lage**) ▶ **n.** Anat. the cartilaginous section at the lower end of the sternum, which is not attached to any ribs and gradually ossifies during adult life. [18th C. (as *xiphoid cartilage*): *xiphoid* from Gk. *xiphoeidēs*, from *xiphos* 'sword.']

Xi·zang /'shē'zäng/ Chinese name for **Tibet**.

XL ▶ **abbr.** extra large (as a clothes size).

Xmas /'krisməs; 'eksməs/ ▶ **n.** informal term for **Christmas**. [*X* representing the initial chi of Gk. *Khristos* 'Christ.']

XML ▶ **abbr.** Comput. ■ Extensible Markup Language, a metalanguage that allows users to define their own customized markup languages, especially in order to display documents on the World Wide Web.

XMS ▶ **abbr.** extended memory system, a system for increasing the amount of memory available to a personal computer.

x-ra·di·a·tion ▶ **n.** treatment with or exposure to X-rays. ■ radiation in the form of X-rays.

X-rat·ed /'eks ,rātid/ ▶ **adj.** pornographic or indecent. ■ hist. (of a film) given an X classification (see **X²**).

X-ray /'eks ,rā/ (also **x-ray** or **X ray**) ▶ **n.** **1** an electromagnetic wave of high energy and very short wavelength (between ultraviolet light and gamma rays) that is able to pass through many materials opaque to light. ■ [as adj.] informal denoting an apparent or supposed faculty for seeing beyond an outward form: *you didn't need X-ray eyes to know what was going on behind those doors.* **2** a photographic or digital image of the internal composition of something, esp. a part of the body, produced by X-rays being passed through it and being absorbed to different degrees by different materials. ■ an act of photographing someone or something in this way: *he will have an X-ray today.* **3** a code word representing the letter X, used in radio communication. ▶ **v.** [trans.] photograph or examine with X-rays. [translation of Ger. *X-Strahlen* (pl.), from *X-* (because, when discovered in 1895, the nature of the rays was unknown) + *Strahl* 'ray.']

X-ray as·tron·o·my ▶ **n.** the branch of astronomy concerned with the detection and measurement of high-energy electromagnetic radiation emitted by celestial objects.

X-ray crys·tal·log·ra·phy ▶ **n.** the study of crystals and their structure by means of the diffraction of X-rays by the regularly spaced atoms of crystalline materials.

X-ray dif·frac·tion ▶ **n.** the scattering of X-rays by the regularly spaced atoms of a crystal, useful in obtaining information about the structure of the crystal.

X-ray fish ▶ **n.** a small almost transparent freshwater fish (*Pristella riddlei*, family Characidae) with an opaque body cavity. Native to South America, it is popular in aquariums.

X-ray ther·a·py ▶ **n.** medical treatment of a disease using controlled doses of X-rays.

X-ray tube ▶ **n.** Physics a device for generating X-rays by accelerating electrons to high energies and causing them to strike a metal target from which the X-rays are emitted.

xu /sōō/ ▶ **n.** (pl. same) a monetary unit of Vietnam, equal to one hundredth of a dong. [Vietnamese, from Fr. *sou*.]

Xu·zhou /'shōō'jō/ (also **Hsu-chou** /'shōō'jō/) a city in eastern China; pop. 910,000. Former name (1912–45) **Tongshan**.

XXL ▶ **abbr.** ■ extra extra large.

xy·lan /'zīlan; -lən/ ▶ **n.** a polysaccharide found in plant cell walls that hydrolyzes to xylose.

xy·lem /'zīləm/ ▶ **n.** Bot. the vascular tissue in plants that conducts water and dissolved nutrients upward from the root and also helps to form the woody element in the stem. Compare with **phloem**. [19th C.: from Gk. *xulon* 'wood' + the passive suffix *-ēma*.]

xy·lene /'zī,lēn/ ▶ **n.** Chem. a volatile liquid hydrocarbon, $C_6H_4(CH_3)_2$, obtained by distilling wood, coal tar, or petroleum, and used in fuels and solvents and in chemical synthesis. [19th C.: from **xylo-** 'of wood' + **-ene**.]

xy·li·dine /'zīli,dēn; -din; 'zili-/ ▶ **n.** any one of six isomeric compounds, $(CH_3)_2C_6H_3NH_2$, that are derived from xylene and used in the manufacture of dyes. ■ a mixture of xylidine isomers in the form of an oily liquid.

xy·li·tol /'zīlə,tôl; -,täl/ ▶ **n.** Chem. a sweet-tasting crystalline alcohol, $CH_2OH(CHOH)_3CH_2OH$, derived from xylose, present in some plant tissues and used as an artificial sweetener in foods. [19th C.: from **xylose** + **-ite¹** + **-ol**.]

xylo- ▶ **comb. form** of or relating to wood: *xylophagous*. [from Gk. *xulon* 'wood.']

xy·log·ra·phy /zī'lägrəfē/ ▶ **n.** rare the art of making woodcuts or wood engravings, esp. by a relatively primitive technique. — **xy·lo·graph·ic** /,zīlə'grafik/ **adj.**

xy·loph·a·gous /zī'läfəgəs/ ▶ **adj.** Zool. (esp. of an insect larva or mollusk) feeding on or boring into wood.

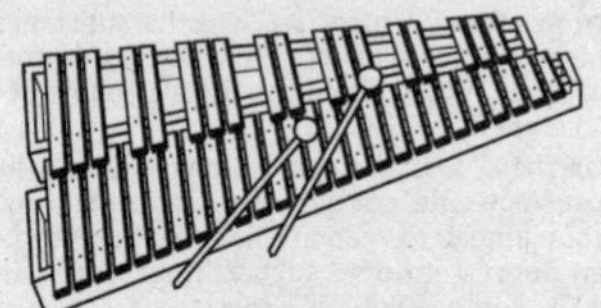

xylophone

xy·lo·phone /'zīlə,fōn/ ▶ **n.** a musical instrument played by striking a row of wooden bars of graduated length with one or more small wooden or plastic mallets. — **xy·lo·phon·ic** /,zīlə'fänik/ **adj.** **xy·lo·phon·ist** /'zīlə,fōnist/ **n.** [19th C.: from **xylo-** 'of wood' + **-phone**.]

xy·lose /'zī,lōs; -,lōz/ ▶ **n.** Chem. a sugar of the pentose class that occurs widely in plants, esp. as a component of hemicelluloses.

XYZ Af·fair an incident in Franco-American relations in which a bribery attempt perpetrated by French agents in 1797 led the US to the brink of formal war with France.

Yy

Y¹ /wī/ (also **y**) ▶ **n.** (pl. **Ys** or **Y's**) **1** the twenty-fifth letter of the alphabet. ■ denoting the next after X in a set of items, categories, etc. ■ denoting a second unknown or unspecified person or thing: *chemical X causes birth defect Y.* ■ (usu. *y*) the second unknown quantity in an algebraic expression, usually the dependent variable. [the introduction of *x, y,* and *z* as symbols of unknown quantities is due to Descartes (see **X¹**).] ■ (usu. *y*) denoting the secondary or vertical axis in a system of coordinates: [in comb.] *the y-axis.* **2** (**Y**) a shape like that of a capital Y.

Y² ▶ **abbr.** ■ yen: *Y140.* ■ informal a YMCA or YWCA hostel: *Scott was living at the Y.* ▶ **symb.** the chemical element yttrium.

y ▶ **abbr.** year(s): *orbital period (Pluto): 248.5y.*

-y¹ /ē/ ▶ **suffix** forming adjectives: **1** (from nouns) full of; having the quality of: *messy* | *milky.* ■ with depreciatory reference: *boozy* | *tinny.* **2** (from verbs) inclined to; apt to: *sticky.* [OE *-ig*, of Gmc. origin.]

-y² (also **-ey** or **-ie**) ▶ **suffix** forming diminutive nouns and adjectives, nicknames, hypocoristics, etc.: *aunty.* ■ forming verbs: *shinny.* [ME: orig. Scots.]

-y³ ▶ **suffix** forming nouns: **1** denoting a state, condition, or quality: *glory* | *jealousy.* **2** denoting an action or its result: *blasphemy* | *victory.* [from Fr. *-ie*, from L. *-ia*, *-ium*, or Gk. *-eia*, *-ia*.]

Y2K ▶ **abbr.** ■ year 2000.

ya /yə/ ▶ **pron. & possessive adj.** nonstandard spelling of **YOU** or **YOUR**, used to represent informal pronunciation: *see ya later.*

yab·ber /ˈyabər/ ▶ **v.** [intrans.] informal chatter. [prob. from Wuywurung (an Aboriginal language).]

YAC ▶ **abbr.** ■ Biol. yeast artificial chromosome.

yacht /yät/ ▶ **n.** a medium-sized sailboat equipped for cruising or racing. ■ [with adj.] a powered boat or small ship equipped for cruising, typically for private or official use: *a steam yacht.* ▶ **v.** [intrans.] race or cruise in a yacht. [16th C.: from early mod. Du. *jaghte*, from *jaghtschip* 'fast pirate ship,' from *jag(h)t* 'hunting' + *schip* 'ship.']

yacht·ing /ˈyätiNG/ ▶ **n.** the sport or pastime of racing or sailing in yachts.

yachts·man /ˈyätsmən/ ▶ **n.** (pl. **-men**) a man who sails yachts.

yachts·wom·an /ˈyätsˌwo͝omən/ ▶ **n.** (pl. **-wom·en**) a woman who sails yachts.

yack /yak/ ▶ **n. & v.** var. of **YAK²**.

yack·e·ty-yak /ˈyakətēˈyak/ (also **yack·et·y-yack**) ▶ **n. & v.** another term for **YAK²**. [1950s: imitative.]

yad·da yad·da yad·da /ˈyädə ˈyädə ˈyädə/ informal used as a substitute in written and spoken contexts for actual words where they are too lengthy or tedious to recite in full: *boy meets girl, yadda yadda yadda.*

Yad·kin Riv·er /ˈyadkin/ a river in western North Carolina that joins the Uwharrie River to form the Pee Dee River.

YAG /yag/ ▶ **n.** a synthetic crystal of yttrium aluminum garnet, used in certain lasers and as an imitation diamond in jewelry. [1960s: acronym from *yttrium aluminum garnet.*]

ya·gé /yäˈZHā ˈyäˌhā/ ▶ **n.** another term for **AYAHUASCA**. [1920s: from Amer. Sp.]

Ya·gi an·ten·na /ˈyägē; ˈyagē/ ▶ **n.** a highly directional radio antenna made of several short rods mounted across an insulating support and transmitting or receiving a narrow band of frequencies. [1940s: named after Hidetsugu *Yagi* (1886–1976), Japanese engineer.]

yah /yä; ya/ ▶ **exclam.** expressing derision: *yah, you missed!* [natural exclamation: first recorded in Engl. in the early 17th C.]

ya·hoo¹ /ˈyäˌho͞o; yäˈho͞o/ ▶ **n.** informal a rude, noisy, or violent person. [18th C.: from the name of an imaginary race of brutish creatures in Swift's *Gulliver's Travels* (1726).]

ya·hoo² /yäˈho͞o/ ▶ **exclam.** expressing great joy or excitement: *yahoo—my plan worked!* [natural exclamation: first recorded in Engl. in the 1970s.]

yahr·zeit /ˈyärˌtsīt; ˈyôr-/ ▶ **n.** (among Jews) the anniversary of someone's death, esp. a parent's. [19th C.: Yiddish, lit. 'anniversary time.']

Yah·weh /ˈyäˌwā; -ˌwe; -ˌvā/ (also **Yah·veh** /-ˌvā; -ˌve/) ▶ **n.** a form of the Hebrew name of God used in the Bible. The name came to be regarded by Jews (*c.*300 BC) as too sacred to be spoken, and the vowel sounds are uncertain. [from Heb. *YHWH* with added vowels; cf. **JEHOVAH**.]

Yah·wist /ˈyäwist; -vist/ (also **Yah·vist** /-vist/) ▶ **n.** the postulated author or authors of parts of the first six books of the Bible, in which God is regularly named *Yahweh.* Compare with **ELOHIST**.

Yaj·ur Ve·da /ˈyəjo͝or ˈvādə; ˈvēdə/ Hinduism one of the four Vedas, based on a collection of sacrificial formulae in early Sanskrit used in the Vedic religion by the priest in charge of sacrificial ritual. [from Sanskrit *yajus* 'sacrificial formula' and **VEDA**.]

yak¹ /yak/ ▶ **n.** a large domesticated wild ox (genus *Bos*) with shaggy hair, humped shoulders, and large horns, used in Tibet as a pack animal and for its milk, meat, and hide. The domesticated *B. grunniens* is descended from the wild *B. mutus*, which rarely is still found at high altitude. [18th C.: from Tibetan *gyag.*]

yak¹

yak² (also **yack** or **yack·et·y-yak**) informal ▶ **n.** [in sing.] a trivial or unduly persistent conversation. ▶ **v.** (**yakked, yak·king**) [intrans.] talk at length about trivial or boring subjects. [1950s: imitative.]

Yak·i·ma ▶ **n.** (pl. same or **-mas**) **1** a member of a North American Indian people of south central Washington. **2** the language of this people. ▶ **adj.** of or relating to this people or their language. [unknown, but possibly from a Salish language.]

ya·ki·to·ri /ˌyäkiˈtôrē/ ▶ **n.** a Japanese dish of chicken pieces grilled on a skewer. [Japanese, from *yaki* 'grilling, toasting' + *tori* 'bird.']

Ya·kut /yəˈko͞ot/ ▶ **n.** (pl. same or **-kuts**) **1** a member of an indigenous people living in scattered settlements in northern Siberia. **2** the Turkic language of this people. ▶ **adj.** of or relating to this people or their language. [via Russ. from Yakut.]

Ya·ku·tia /yəˈko͞oSH(ē)ə/ an autonomous republic in eastern Russia; pop. 1,081,000; capital, Yakutsk. Official name **SAKHA, REPUBLIC OF**.

ya·ku·za /yäˈko͞ozə; ˈyäko͞oˌzä/ ▶ **n.** (pl. same) a Japanese gangster or racketeer. ■ a Japanese organized crime syndicate similar to the Mafia. [Japanese, from *ya* 'eight' + *ku* 'nine' + *za* 'three,' referring to the worst hand in a gambling game.]

Yale¹ /yāl/, Elihu (1649–1721), English colonial administrator. He was a benefactor of the Collegiate School in Saybrook, Connecticut, which eventually became Yale University in New Haven.

Yale² (also **Yale lock**) ▶ **n.** [often as adj.] trademark a type of lock with a latch bolt and a flat key with a serrated edge. [19th C.: named after Linus *Yale*, Jr. (1821–68), the American locksmith who invented the mechanism.]

Yale U·ni·ver·si·ty an Ivy League university at New Haven, Connecticut, founded in 1701.

y'all /yôl/ ▶ **contr.** you-all.

Yal·ta Con·fer·ence /ˈyôltə; ˈyäl-/ a meeting between the Allied leaders Churchill, Roosevelt, and Stalin in February 1945 at Yalta, a Crimean port on the Black Sea. The leaders planned the final stages of World War II and agreed on the subsequent territorial division of Europe.

Ya·lu /ˈyäˌlo͞o/ a river in eastern Asia that rises in northeastern China and flows southwest to the Yellow Sea. It forms most of the border between China and North Korea.

yam /yam/ ▶ **n.** **1** the edible starchy tuber of a climbing plant, widely distributed in tropical and subtropical countries. **2** the plant (genus *Dioscorea*, family Dioscoreaceae) that yields this tuber. **3** a sweet potato. [16th C.: from Port. *inhame* or obs. Sp. *iñame*, prob. of West Afr. origin.]

Ya·ma·mo·to /ˌyäməˈmōtō/, Isoroku (1884–1943), Japanese admiral. He was responsible for planning the Japanese attack on Pearl Harbor in 1941.

Ya·ma·sa·ki /ˌyäməˈsäkē/, Minoru (1912–86), US architect. He designed the World Trade Center in New York City in 1972.

Ya·ma·to-e /yäˈmätōˌā/ ▶ **n.** a style of decorative painting in Japan during the 12th and early 13th centuries, characterized by strong color and flowing lines. [Japanese, from *Yamato* 'Japan' + *e* 'picture.']

ya·men /ˈyämən/ ▶ **n.** informal the office or residence of a public official in the Chinese Empire.

yam·mer /ˈyamər/ informal dialect ▶ **n.** loud and sustained or repetitive noise: *the yammer of enemy fire.* ▶ **v.** [intrans.] make a loud repetitive noise. ■ talk volubly. — **yam·mer·er n.** [ME (as a v. meaning 'lament, cry out'): alt. of earlier *yomer*, from OE *geōmrian* 'to lament,' suggested by MDu. *jammeren*.]

Ya·mous·sou·kro /,yämə'sōōkrō/ the capital of the Ivory Coast; pop. 120,000. It replaced Abidjan as the capital in 1983.

Ya·mu·na /'yəmōōnə/ Hindi name for JUMNA.

yang /yaNG; yäNG/ ▶ **n.** (in Chinese philosophy) the active male principle of the universe, characterized as male and creative and associated with heaven, heat, and light. Contrasted with YIN. See illustration at YIN. [from Chin. *yáng* 'male genitals,' 'sun,' 'positive.']

Yan·gon /,yäNG'gōn/ Burmese name for RANGOON.

Yang·tze /'yaNG'(t)sē/ the principal river in China. It rises as the Jinsha in the Tibetan highlands and flows through central China to the East China Sea at Shanghai. Also called CHANG JIANG.

Yank /yaNGk/ ▶ **n.** another term for YANKEE (senses 1 and 2).

yank /yaNGk/ informal ▶ **v.** [trans.] pull with a jerk: *her hair was yanked* | [intrans.] *Liz* ***yanked at her arm.*** ▶ **n.** [in sing.] a sudden hard pull. [18th C. (as a Scots word in the sense 'sudden sharp blow'): of unknown origin.]

Yan·kee /'yaNGkē/ ▶ **n.** informal **1** often derog. a person who lives in, or is from, the US. **2** an inhabitant of New England or one of the northern states. ■ hist. a Union soldier in the Civil War. **3** a code word representing the letter Y, used in radio communication. **4** (also **Yan·kee jib**) Sailing a large jib set forward of a staysail in light winds. **5** a bet on four or more horses to win (or be placed) in different races. [18th C.: origin uncert.; recorded in the late 17th C. as a nickname; perh. from Du. *Janke*, dimin. of *Jan* 'John.']

Yan·kee Doo·dle /'dōōdl/ ▶ **n. 1** (also **Yan·kee Doo·dle Dan·dy**) a song popular during the American Revolution. Informally regarded as a national song, it is the official state song of Connecticut. **2** Brit. another term for YANKEE (senses 1 and 2).

Yank·ton /'yaNGktən/ ▶ **n.** (pl. same or **-tons**) **1** a member of an American Indian people of the Great Plains of North and South Dakota. **2** the Siouan language of this people. ▶ **adj.** of or related to this people or their language. [from Sioux *ihą̄kthų́wą̄*, lit. 'those dwelling at the end.']

Yank·to·nai /,yaNGktə'nī/ ▶ **n.** a Sioux people now living in the Dakotas and eastern Montana, formerly living in northern Minnesota. ■ a member of this people.

Yan·qui ▶ **n.** var. of YANKEE, typically used in Latin American contexts.

Yan·tai /'yan'tī/ (also **Yen·tai** /'yen-/) a city in eastern China, on the Yellow Sea; pop. 3,204,600. Former name (3rd century BC–15th century) CHEFOO.

yan·tra /'yəntrə; 'yan-; 'yän-/ ▶ **n.** a geometric diagram, or any object, used as an aid to meditation in tantric worship. [Sanskrit, lit. 'device for holding or fastening.']

Yao /you/ ▶ **n.** (pl. same) **1** a member of a mountain-dwelling people of southern China. **2** the language of this people. ▶ **adj.** of or relating to this people or their language. [from Chin. *Yáo*, lit. 'precious jade.']

Ya·oun·dé /,youn'dā/ the capital of Cameroon, in the southern part of the country; pop. 800,000.

yap /yap/ ▶ **v.** (**yapped, yap·ping**) [intrans.] give a sharp, shrill bark: *the dachshunds yapped at his heels.* ■ informal talk at length in an irritating manner. ▶ **n. 1** a sharp, shrill bark. **2** informal a person's mouth (used in expressions to do with speaking): *shut your yap.* ■ loud, irritating talk: *she'll give you a lot of yap.* — **yap·per n.** [17th C. (denoting a dog that yaps): imitative.]

ya·pok /yə'päk/ (also **ya·pock**) ▶ **n.** a semiaquatic carnivorous opossum (*Chironectes minimus*) with dark-banded gray fur and webbed hind feet, native to tropical America. Also called WATER OPOSSUM. [19th C.: from *Oyapock*, the name of a northern Brazilian river.]

yap·py /'yapē/ ▶ **adj.** (**-pi·er, -pi·est**) informal (of a dog) inclined to bark in a sharp, shrill way. ■ inclined to talk foolishly or at length.

Ya·qui /'yäkē/ ▶ **n.** (pl. same or **-quis**) **1** a member of an American Indian people of northwestern Mexico and Arizona. **2** the Uto-Aztecan language of this people. ▶ **adj.** of or relating to this people or their language. [Sp., from earlier *Hiaquis*, from Yaqui *Hiaki*.]

yar·ak /'yar,ak/ ▶ **n.** (in phrase **in yarak**) (of a trained hawk) fit and in a proper condition for hunting. [19th C.: perh. from Pers. *yārakī* 'strength, ability' or from Turk. *yarağ* 'readiness.']

yar·bor·ough /'yär,bərō; -,bə-rō/ ▶ **n.** (in bridge or whist) a hand with no card above a nine. [20th C.: named after the Earl of *Yarborough* (died 1897), said to have bet 1000 to 1 against its occurrence.]

yard[1] /yärd/ ▶ **n. 1** (abbr.: **yd.**) a unit of linear measure equal to 3 feet (0.9144 meter). ■ (**yards of**) informal a great length. ■ a square or cubic yard, esp. of sand or other building materials. **2** a cylindrical spar, tapering to each end, slung across a ship's mast for a sail to hang from. **3** informal one hundred dollars; a one hundred dollar bill. [OE *gerd* (in sense 2), of West Gmc. origin; rel. to Du. *gard* 'twig, rod' and Ger. *Gerte*.]

yard[2] ▶ **n.** a piece of ground adjoining a building or house. ■ an area of ground surrounded by walls or buildings. ■ an area of land used for a particular purpose or business: *a storage yard.* ■ an area where deer or moose gather as a herd for the winter. ▶ **v. 1** [trans.] store or transport (wood) in or to a lumberyard. **2** [intrans.] (of deer or moose) gather as a herd for the winter.

– PHRASES **the Yard** Brit. informal term for SCOTLAND YARD. [OE *geard* 'building, home, region,' from a Gmc. base rel. to Russ. *gorod* 'town.' Cf. GARDEN and ORCHARD.]

yard·age /'yärdij/ ▶ **n. 1** a distance or length measured in yards: *the caddie was working out yardages from tee to green.* ■ Football the distance covered in advancing the ball. **2** archaic the use of a yard for storage or the keeping of animals or payment for such use.

yard·arm /'yärd,ärm/ ▶ **n.** the outer extremity of a ship's yard.

yard·bird /'yärd,bərd/ ▶ **n.** informal **1** a new military recruit, esp. one assigned to menial tasks. **2** a convict. [1940s: perh. suggested by JAILBIRD.]

yard·man /'yärd,man/ ▶ **n.** (pl. **-men**) **1** a person working in a railroad or lumberyard. **2** a person who does various outdoor jobs.

yard·mas·ter /'yärd,mastər/ ▶ **n.** a person who is in charge of a railroad yard.

yard of ale ▶ **n.** esp. Brit. the amount of beer (typically two to three pints) held by a narrow glass about a yard high. ■ a glass of this kind.

yard sale ▶ **n.** a garage sale.

yard·stick /'yärd,stik/ ▶ **n.** a measuring rod a yard long, typically divided into inches. ■ a standard used for comparison.

yare /yär; ye(ə)r/ ▶ **adj.** (of a ship) moving lightly and easily; easily manageable. [OE *gearu* 'prepared, ready,' of Gmc. origin; rel. to Du. *gaar* 'done, dressed' and Ger. *gar* 'ready.']

yar·mul·ke /'yämə(l)kə/ (also **yar·mul·ka**) ▶ **n.** a skullcap worn in public by Orthodox Jewish men or during prayer by other Jewish men. [20th C.: from Yiddish *yarmolke*.]

yarn /yärn/ ▶ **n. 1** spun thread used for knitting, weaving, or sewing. **2** informal a long or rambling story, esp. one that is implausible. ▶ **v.** [intrans.] informal tell a long or implausible story.

– PHRASES **spin a yarn** see SPIN. [OE *gearn*, of Gmc. origin; rel. to Du. *garen*.]

yarn-dyed ▶ **adj.** (of fabric) dyed as yarn, before being woven.

Ya·ro·slavl /,yärə'slävəl/ a city in western Russia, on the Volga River; pop. 636,000.

yar·row /'yarō/ ▶ **n.** a Eurasian plant (*Achillea millefolium*) of the daisy family, with feathery leaves and heads of small white, yellow, or pink aromatic flowers. [OE *gearwe*, of West Gmc. origin; rel. to Du. *gerwe*.]

yarrow

yash·mak /yäsH'mäk; 'yasH,mak/ ▶ **n.** a veil concealing all of the face except the eyes, worn by some Muslim women in public. [19th C.: via Arab. from Turk.]

yat·a·ghan /'yatəgən; -,gan/ ▶ **n.** esp. hist. a sword without a guard and typically with a double-curved blade, used in Muslim countries. [from Turk. *yatağan*.]

yat·ter /'yatər/ informal ▶ **v.** [intrans.] talk incessantly; chatter. ▶ **n.** incessant talk. [19th C.: imitative, perh. suggested by YAMMER and CHATTER.]

yau·pon /'yô,pän; 'yōō-/ (also **yau·pon hol·ly**) ▶ **n.** a holly (*Ilex vomitoria*) of the southern US. Sometimes dried and brewed as a tea, its bitter leaves contain caffeine and have emetic properties. [18th C.: from Catawba (a Siouan language spoken in South Carolina) *yopún*, dimin. of *yop* 'tree, shrub.']

yau·ti·a /you'tēə/ ▶ **n.** a tropical American plant (genus *Xanthosoma*) of the arum family, cultivated for its edible tubers and sometimes its leaves. Its several species include the fleshy-leaved **malanga** (*X. atrovirens*) of Latin America. [19th C.: Amer. Sp., from Maya *yaaj* 'wound, poison' + *té* 'mouth' with ref. to its caustic properties.]

yaw /yô/ ▶ **v.** [intrans.] (of a moving ship or aircraft) twist or oscillate about a vertical axis. ▶ **n.** a twisting or oscillation of a moving ship or aircraft around a vertical axis. [16th C.: of unknown origin.]

yawl /yôl/ ▶ **n.** a two-masted fore-and-aft-rigged sailboat with the mizzenmast stepped far aft so that the mizzen boom overhangs the stern. ■ hist. a ship's jolly boat with four or six oars. [16th C.: from Mid. Low Ger. *jolle* or Du. *jol*, of unknown origin; cf. JOLLY[2].]

yawn /yôn/ ▶ **v.** [intrans.] involuntarily open one's mouth wide and inhale deeply due to tiredness or boredom. ■ [usu. as adj.] (**yawning**) be wide open. ▶ **n.** a reflex act of opening one's mouth wide and inhaling deeply due to tiredness or boredom. ■ informal a thing that is considered boring or tedious. — **yawn·ing·ly adv.** [OE *geonian*, of Gmc. origin, from an Indo-Eur. root shared by L. *hiare* and Gk. *khainein*.]

yawn·er /'yônər/ ▶ **n.** informal a thing that is considered extremely boring: *the game was a real yawner.*

yawp /yôp/ ▶ **n.** a harsh or hoarse cry or yelp. ■ foolish or noisy talk. ▶ **v.** [intrans.] shout or exclaim hoarsely. ■ talk foolishly or noisily. — **yawp·er n.** [ME (as a v.): imitative. The n. dates from the early 19th C.]

yaws /yôz/ ▶ **plural n.** [treated as sing.] a contagious disease of tropical countries, caused by a bacterium (*Treponema pallidum* subsp. *pertenue*) that enters skin abrasions and gives rise to small crusted lesions that may develop into deep ulcers. Also called FRAMBESIA. [17th C.: prob. from Carib *yaya*, from a South Amer. Ind. language.]

yay[1] /yā/ ▶ **exclam.** informal expressing triumph, approval, or encouragement: *Yay! Great, Julie!* [1960s: perh. an alt. of YEAH.]

yay[2] (also **yea**) ▶ **adv.** informal (with adjectives of measure) so; to this extent: *I knew him when he was yay big.* [1960s: prob. a var. of the adv. YEA[1].]

Yaz·oo Riv·er /'yazōō; ya'zōō/ a river that flows from northern Mississippi to join the Mississippi River at Vicksburg. The fertile land between the rivers is the **Mississippi Delta,** or **Yazoo Delta.**

Yb ▶ **symb.** the chemical element ytterbium.

Y chro·mo·some ▶ **n.** Genet. (in humans and other mammals) a sex chromosome that is normally present only in male cells, which are designated XY. Compare with **X CHROMOSOME**.

y·clept /iˈklept/ ▶ **adj.** archaic humorous by the name of: *a lady yclept Eleanora.* [OE *gecleopod*, past part. of *cleopian* 'call,' of Gmc. origin.]

yd. ▶ **abbr.** yard (measure).

ye[1] /yē/ ▶ **pron.** [second person pl.] archaic dialect plural form of **THOU**[1]: *gather ye rosebuds, while ye may.*
– PHRASES **ye gods!** an exclamation of astonishment. [OE *gē*, of Gmc. origin; rel. to Du. *gij* and Ger. *ihr*.]

ye[2] /yē; T͟Hē/ ▶ **adj.** pseudo-archaic term for **THE**: *Ye Olde Bookshoppe.* [graphic var.; in ME t (see **THORN**) came to be written identically with y, so that *the* could be written *ye*. This spelling (usually ye) was kept as a convenient abbrev. in handwriting until the 19th C., but it was never pronounced as "ye."]

yea[1] /yā/ archaic formal ▶ **adv.** yes: *say yea or nay.* ■ used for emphasis, esp. to introduce a stronger or more accurate word than one just used: *he was full, yea, crammed with anxieties.* ▶ **n.** an affirmative answer: *they would give the final yea.* ■ (in the US Congress) an affirmative vote. [OE *gēa, gē*, of Gmc. origin; rel. to Du. and Ger. *ja*.]

yea[2] ▶ **adv.** var. of **YAY**[2].

Yea·ger /ˈyāgər/, Chuck (1923–), US aviator; full name *Charles Elwood Yeager*. In 1947, he became the first person to break the sound barrier.

yeah /ˈye(ə)/ (also **yeh**) ▶ **exclam. & n.** nonstandard spelling of **YES**, representing informal pronunciation.

yean /yēn/ ▶ **v.** [trans.] archaic (of a sheep or goat) give birth to (a lamb or kid). [ME: perh. representing an OE v. rel. to *ēanian* 'to lamb.']

year /yi(ə)r/ ▶ **n.** **1** the time taken by a planet to make one revolution around the sun. The length of the earth's year depends on the manner of calculation, but for ordinary purposes is taken to be the **solar year** (also called **astronomical year, equinoctial year,** or **tropical year**), which is the time between successive spring or autumnal equinoxes, or winter or summer solstices, roughly 365 days, 5 hours, 48 minutes, and 46 seconds in length. **2** (or dated **in the year of grace**) the period of 365 days (or 366 days in leap years) starting from the first of January, used for reckoning time in ordinary affairs. ■ a period of the same length as this starting at any point: *the year starting July 1.* ■ [with adj.] such a period regarded in terms of the quality of produce, typically wine: *single-vineyard wine of a good year.* ■ a similar period used for reckoning time according to other calendars: *the Muslim year.* **3** (**one's years**) one's age or time of life. **4** (**years**) informal a very long time; ages. **5** a set of students grouped together as being of roughly similar ages, mostly entering a school or college in the same academic year: *the girls in my year.*
– PHRASES **in the year of our Lord ——** in the year AD ——: *I was born in the year of our Lord 1786.* **—— of the year** a person or thing chosen as outstanding in a specified field or of a specified kind in a particular year: *man of the year.* **year in and year out** continuously or repeatedly over a period of years. [OE *gē(a)r*, of Gmc. origin; rel. to Du. *jaar* and Ger. *Jahr*, from an Indo-Eur. root shared by Gk. *hōra* 'season.']

year·book /ˈyi(ə)rˌbo͝ok/ ▶ **n.** an annual publication giving current information and listing events or aspects of the previous year, esp. in a particular field. ■ a book containing photographs of the senior class in a school or college and details of school activities in the previous year.

year end (also **year's end**) ▶ **n.** the end of the fiscal year.

year·ling /ˈyi(ə)rliNG/ ▶ **n.** an animal (esp. a sheep, calf, or foal) a year old, or in its second year. ■ a racehorse in the calendar year after its year of foaling. ▶ **adj.** having lived or existed for a year; a year old. ■ of or relating to something that is a year old.

year·long /ˈyi(ə)rˈlôNG; -ˈläNG/ (also **year-long**) ▶ **adj.** lasting for or throughout a year: *his yearlong battle with lung cancer.*

year·ly /ˈyi(ə)rlē/ ▶ **adj. & adv.** happening or produced once a year or every year: [as adj.] *yearly visits to Africa* | [as adv.] *rent was paid yearly.* [OE *gēarlic* (see **YEAR, -LY**[1]).]

yearn /yərn/ ▶ **v.** [intrans.] have an intense feeling of loss or lack and longing for something. ■ archaic be filled with compassion or warm feeling. — **yearn·er n. yearn·ing n. yearn·ing·ly adv.** [OE *giernan*, from a Gmc. base meaning 'eager.']

year-round ▶ **adj. & adv.** happening or continuing throughout the year: [as adj.] *a pool for year-round use* | [as adv.] (also **year round**) *the center is open year round.*

yea·say·er /ˈyāˌsāər/ ▶ **n.** **1** a person with a positive, confident outlook. **2** a person who always agrees with or is submissive to others.

yeast /yēst/ ▶ **n.** a microscopic fungus (genus *Saccharomyces*, subdivision Ascomycotina) consisting of single oval cells that reproduce by budding, and are capable of converting sugar into alcohol and carbon dioxide. ■ a grayish-yellow preparation of this obtained chiefly from fermented beer, used as a fermenting agent, to raise bread dough, and as a food supplement. ■ Biol. any unicellular fungus that reproduces vegetatively by budding or fission, including forms such as candida that can cause disease. — **yeast·like** /-ˌlīk/ **adj.** [OE, of Gmc. origin; rel. to Du. *gist* and Ger. *Gischt* 'froth, yeast,' from an Indo-Eur. root shared by Gk. *zein* 'to boil.']

yeast·y /ˈyēstē/ ▶ **adj.** (**yeast·i·er, yeast·i·est**) of, resembling, or containing yeast: *the yeasty smell of rising dough.* ■ fig. characterized by or producing upheaval or agitation; in a state of turbulence, typically a creative or productive one: *the yeasty days of yesterday's revolution.* — **yeast·i·ly** /ˈyēstl-ē/ **adv. yeast·i·ness n.**

Yeats /yāts/, William Butler (1865–1939), Irish poet and playwright. His poetry includes "Sailing to Byzantium" and "Leda and the Swan." Nobel Prize for Literature (1923).

yech /yəKH; yək; yeKH; yek/ (also **yecch**) ▶ **exclam.** informal expressing aversion or disgust. — **yech·y adj.** [1960s: imitative; cf. **YUCK**.]

yee-haw /ˈyēˌhô/ (also **yee-hah** /ˈyēˌhä/) ▶ **exclam.** an expression of enthusiasm or exuberance, typically associated with cowboys or rural inhabitants of the southern US. [natural exclamation: first recorded in Amer. Engl. in the 1970s.]

yegg /yeg/ ▶ **n.** informal a burglar or safecracker. [20th C.: of unknown origin.]

yeh /ye(ə)/ ▶ **exclam.** var. of **YEAH**. ▶ **pron.** nonstandard spelling of **YOU**, used to represent various accents or dialects: *are yeh all right, lads?*

Ye·ka·te·rin·burg /yiˈkatərinˌbərg; yikətyərinˈbo͝ork/ another name for **EKATERINBURG**.

yell /yel/ ▶ **n.** a loud, sharp cry, esp. of pain, surprise, or delight; a shout. ■ an organized cheer, esp. one used to support a sports team. ▶ **v.** [intrans.] give a loud, sharp cry: *you heard me **yelling at** her.* [OE *g(i)ellan* (v.), of Gmc. origin; rel. to Du. *gillen* and Ger. *gellen*.]

yel·low /ˈyelō/ ▶ **adj.** **1** of the color between green and orange in the spectrum, a primary subtractive color complementary to blue; colored like ripe lemons or egg yolks: *curly yellow hair.* ■ offens. having a naturally yellowish or olive skin (as used to describe Chinese or Japanese people). ■ denoting a warning of danger that is thought to be near but not actually imminent: *yellow alert.* **2** informal cowardly. **3** (of a book or newspaper) unscrupulously sensational: *the yellow press.* ▶ **n.** **1** yellow color or pigment. ■ yellow clothes or material: *everyone dresses in yellow.* **2** the yolk of an egg. **3** (**yellows**) any of a number of plant diseases in which the leaves turn yellow, typically caused by viruses and transmitted by insects. ▶ **v.** [intrans.] become a yellow color, esp. with age. — **yel·low·ish adj. yel·low·ly adv. yel·low·ness n. yel·low·y adj.** [OE *geolu, geolo*, of West Gmc. origin; rel. to Du. *geel* and Ger. *gelb*, also to **GOLD**.]

yel·low·back /ˈyelōˌbak/ ▶ **n.** hist. a cheap and typically sensational novel, with a yellow board or cloth binding.

yel·low-bel·lied sap·suck·er ▶ **n.** a woodpecker (*Sphyrapicus varius*) of eastern North America with black-and-white plumage, a pale yellow belly, and, in the male, a scarlet crown and throat.

yel·low-bel·ly ▶ **n.** informal **1** a coward. **2** any of number of animals with yellow underparts. — **yel·low-bel·lied adj.**

yel·low bile ▶ **n.** hist. another term for **CHOLER**.

yel·low birch ▶ **n.** a tall North American birch (*Betula alleghaniensis*) with silvery or yellowish gray bark that peels in thin curls. Its broken twigs smell of wintergreen.

yel·low·cake /ˈyelōˌkāk/ ▶ **n.** impure uranium oxide obtained during processing of uranium ore. [1950s: so named because it is obtained as a yellow precipitate.]

yel·low dog informal ▶ **n.** a contemptible or cowardly person or thing.

yel·low-dog con·tract ▶ **n.** a contract between a worker and an employer in which the worker agrees not to remain in or join a union.

yel·low-dog Dem·o·crat (also **Yellow Dog Democrat**) ▶ **n.** informal a diehard Democrat, who will vote for any Democratic candidate, regardless of the candidate's personal qualities. See also **BLUE DOG DEMOCRAT**.

yel·low earth ▶ **n.** a yellowish loess occurring in northern China.

yel·low fe·ver ▶ **n.** a tropical viral disease affecting the liver and kidneys, causing fever and jaundice and often fatal. It is transmitted by mosquitoes.

yel·low·fin /ˈyelōˌfin/ (also **yel·low·fin tu·na**) ▶ **n.** a widely distributed, commercially important tuna (*Thunnus albacares*) that has yellow anal and dorsal fins.

yel·low flag ▶ **n.** **1** a ship's yellow flag, denoting the letter Q for 'quarantine.' When flown with another flag, it indicates disease on board; when flown alone, it indicates the absence of disease and signifies a request for customs clearance. Also called **QUARANTINE FLAG**. ■ Auto Racing a yellow flag used to signal to drivers that there is a hazard such as oil or a crashed car on the track. **2** a yellow-flowered iris (*Iris pseudacorus*) that grows by water and in marshy places, native to Europe and naturalized in North America.

yel·low·ham·mer /ˈyelōˌhamər/ ▶ **n.** **1** another term for ***YELLOW-SHAFTED FLICKER*** (see **FLICKER**[2]). **2** a common Eurasian bunting (*Emberiza citrinella*), the male of which has a yellow head, neck, and breast. [16th C.: *-hammer* is perh. from OE *amore* (a kind of bird), possibly conflated with *hama* 'feathers.']

yel·low jack ▶ **n.** **1** another term for **YELLOW FLAG** (sense 1). **2** archaic term for **YELLOW FEVER**. **3** an edible marine fish (*Caranx bartholomaei*) of the jack family, with yellowish underparts, found primarily in the Gulf of Mexico and the Caribbean Sea.

yel·low jack·et ▶ **n.** informal a wasp or hornet with bright yellow markings. *See illustration on next page.*

yellow jacket

yel·low jas·mine (also **yel·low jes·sa·mine**) ▶ n. an ornamental climbing shrub (*Gelsemium sempervirens*, family Loganiaceae) with fragrant yellow flowers, native to the southeastern US. Its rhizome yields gelsemium.

yel·low jer·sey ▶ n. (in a cycling race involving stages) a yellow jersey worn by the overall leader in a cycle race, at the end of any one day, and ultimately presented to the winner.

yel·low jour·nal·ism ▶ n. journalism that is based upon sensationalism and crude exaggeration. — **yellow journalist** n. [1895: from the appearance in an issue of the *New York World* of a cartoon in which a child in a yellow dress ('The Yellow Kid') was the central figure.]

Yel·low·knife /ˈyelō,nīf/ the capital, since 1967, of the Northwest Territories in Canada; pop. 15,179.

yel·low·legs /ˈyelō,legz/ ▶ n. a migratory sandpiper (genus *Tringa*) with bright yellow legs, breeding in Alaska and Canada.

yel·low o·cher ▶ n. a yellow pigment that usually contains limonite, a yellowish-brown oxide of iron. ■ a moderate orange color with yellow overtones.

Yel·low Pag·es (also **yel·low pag·es**) ▶ plural n. a telephone directory, or a section of one, printed on yellow paper and listing businesses and other organizations according to the goods or services they offer. ■ a similar directory available online through the Internet.

yel·low per·il ▶ n. offens. the political or military threat regarded as being posed by the Chinese or by the peoples of Southeast Asia.

yel·low pine ▶ n. any of several North American pines having a strong yellowish wood. ■ the wood of such a tree.

yel·low pop·lar ▶ n. another term for TULIP TREE.

yel·low rain ▶ n. a toxic yellow substance reported as falling in Southeast Asia, alleged to be a chemical warfare agent but now believed to consist of contaminated bee droppings.

Yel·low Riv·er a river in China. It rises in the mountains of western central China and flows in a huge semicircle before it enters Bo Hai, an inlet of the Yellow Sea. Chinese name HUANG HO.

Yel·low Sea an arm of the East China Sea that separates the Korean peninsula from the eastern coast of China. Chinese name HUANG HAI.

yel·low spot ▶ n. the region of greatest visual acuity around the fovea of the eye; the macula lutea (see MACULA).

Yel·low·stone Na·tion·al Park /ˈyelō,stōn/ a national park in northwestern Wyoming and Montana. It contains the geyser Old Faithful.

yel·low·tail /ˈyelō,tāl/ ▶ n. (pl. same or **-tails**) a marine fish that has yellow coloration on the fins, esp. a number of species prized as food fish, in particular the large sport fish *Seriola lalandi* of the jack family of southern California and the flounder *Limanda ferruginea* of the Atlantic coast from Labrador to Virginia.

yel·low·throat /ˈyelō,THrōt/ ▶ n. a small American warbler (genus *Geothlypis*, family Parulidae) with a bright yellow throat.

yel·low un·der·wing ▶ n. an underwing moth that has yellow hind wings with a black terminal band. *Noctua* and other genera, family Noctuidae, and several species include the **large yellow underwing** (*N. pronuba*), the larva of which is a destructive cutworm.

yel·low·wood /ˈyelō,wŏŏd/ ▶ n. any of a number of trees that have yellowish timber or yield a yellow dye, in particular *Cladrastis lutea*, a North American tree of the pea family.

yelp /yelp/ ▶ n. a short sharp cry, esp. of pain or alarm. ▶ v. [intrans.] utter such a cry: *my dogs were yelping at Linus.* — **yelp·er** n. [OE *g(i)elpan* (v.) 'to boast,' from a Gmc. imitative base.]

Yel·tsin /ˈyeltsən/, Boris Nikolaevich (1931–2007), president of the Russian Federation 1991–99.

Yem·en /ˈyemən/ a country in the Middle East, on the Arabian peninsula. *See box.* — **Yem·e·ni** /ˈyemənē/ adj. & n.

Yem·en·ite /ˈyemə,nīt/ ▶ n. another term for YEMENI (see YEMEN). ■ a Jew who was, or whose ancestors were, formerly resident in Yemen. ▶ adj. of or relating to Yemeni Arabs or Jews. [from Arab. *yamanī* 'Yemeni' + -ITE[1].]

yen[1] /yen/ ▶ n. (pl. same) the basic monetary unit of Japan. [from Japanese *en* 'round.']

yen[2] informal ▶ n. [in sing.] a longing or yearning. ▶ v. (**yenned, yen·ning**) [intrans.] feel a longing or yearning: *it's no use yenning for the old simplicities.* [19th C. (in the sense 'craving (of a drug addict) for a drug'): from Chin. *yăn*.]

Yen·i·sei /,yenəˈsā/ a river in Russia, in Siberia, that rises on the Mongolian border and flows north to the Arctic coast, where it empties into the Kara Sea.

yen·ta /ˈyentə/ ▶ n. a woman who is a gossip or busybody. [1920s: Yiddish, orig. a given name.]

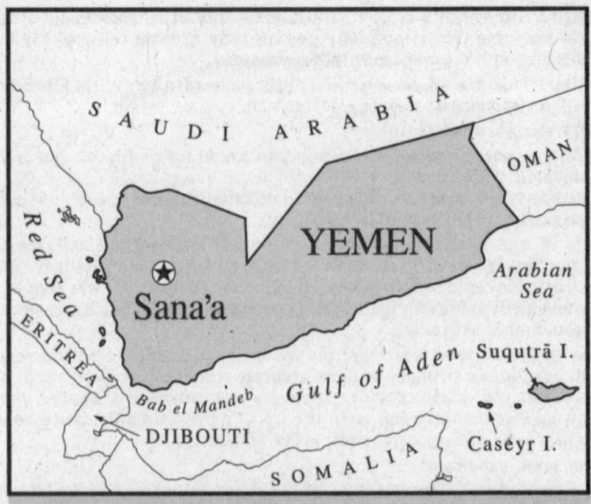

Yemen

Official name: Republic of Yemen
Location: Middle East, the southwestern part of the Arabian peninsula
Area: 203,900 square miles (528,000 sq km)
Population: 20,024,000
Capital: Sana'a
Language: Arabic
Currency: Yemeni rial

yeo·man /ˈyōmən/ ▶ n. (pl. **-men**) **1** hist. a man holding and cultivating a small landed estate; a freeholder. ■ a person qualified for certain duties and rights, such as to serve on juries and vote for the knight of the shire, by virtue of possessing free land of an annual value of 40 shillings. **2** hist. a servant in a royal or noble household, ranking between a sergeant and a groom or a squire and a page. **3** Brit. a member of the yeomanry force. **4** a petty officer in the US Navy or Coast Guard performing clerical duties on board ship.
– PHRASES **yeoman service** efficient or useful help in need. — **yeo·man·ly** adj. [ME: prob. from YOUNG + MAN.]

Yeo·man of the Guard ▶ n. a member of the British sovereign's bodyguard, now having only ceremonial duties. Also called BEEFEATER. ■ used erroneously to refer to a Yeoman Warder.

yeo·man·ry /ˈyōmənrē/ ▶ n. [treated as sing. or pl.] hist. a group of men who held and cultivated small landed estates. ■ (in Britain) a volunteer cavalry force raised from such a group (1794–1908).

Yeo·man Ward·er ▶ n. a warder at the Tower of London. Also called BEEFEATER.

yeow /you; yēˈou/ ▶ exclam. another word for YOW. [natural exclamation: first recorded in Amer. Engl. in the 1920s.]

yep /yep/ (also **yup**) ▶ exclam. & n. nonstandard spelling of YES, representing informal pronunciation.

yer /yər/ ▶ possessive adj. nonstandard spelling of YOUR, used in representing dialectal speech: *eat yer dinner.* ▶ contr. you are, used in representing dialectal speech: *yer a dang fool.* ▶ pron. nonstandard spelling of YOU, used in representing dialectal speech: *well, are yer comin'?*

-yer ▶ suffix var. of -IER esp. after *w* (as in *lawyer, sawyer*).

yer·ba /ˈyerbə; ˈyər-/ (also **yer·ba ma·té** /ˈmätā; mäˈtā/) ▶ n. another term for MATÉ. [19th C.: from Sp., lit. 'herb.']

yer·ba bue·na /ˈbwānə/ ▶ n. a trailing aromatic herb (*Satureja douglasii*) of the mint family, with whitish or lilac flowers, related to savory. Native to the western US, it has been used medicinally and as a local tea. [19th C.: from Sp., lit. 'good herb.']

Ye·re·van /,yeriˈvän/ (also **E·re·van**) the capital of Armenia, in the western part of the country; pop. 1,202,000.

yes /yes/ ▶ exclam. **1** used to give an affirmative response: *"Do you understand?" "Yes."* ■ expressing agreement with a positive statement just made: *"That was a grand evening." "Yes, it was."* ■ expressing contradiction of a negative statement: *"You don't want to go." "Yes, I do."* **2** used as a response to someone addressing one or otherwise trying to attract one's attention: *"Oh, Bob." "Yes?"* **3** used to question a remark or ask for more detail about it: *"It should be easy to check." "Oh yes? How?"* ■ asked at the end of a statement to indicate the expectation of agreement: *you think I lied, yes?* **4** encouraging someone to continue speaking: *"When you bought those photographs ..." "Yes?"* **5** expressing delight: *plenty to eat, including pie (yes!).* ▶ n. (pl. **yes·es** or **yes·ses**) an affirmative answer or decision, esp. in voting. [OE *gēse, gīse*, prob. from an unrecorded phr. meaning 'may it be so.']

ye·shi·va /yəˈSHēvə/ ▶ n. an Orthodox Jewish college or seminary. ■ an Orthodox Jewish elementary or secondary school. [from Heb. *yĕšīḇāh*.]

yes-man ▶ n. (pl. **-men**) informal a weak person who always agrees with their political leader or their superior at work.

yes·sir /'yesər; 'yes'sər/ (also **yes·sir·ee** /-sə'rē/) informal ▶ **exclam.** used to express assent: *"Do you understand me?" "Yessir!"* ■ used to express emphatic affirmation: *yessir, the food was cheap.* [20th C.: alt. of *yes sir.*]

yes·sum /'yesəm/ ▶ **exclam.** dated, esp. black English used as a polite form of assent addressed to a woman: *"You feel all right?" she asked. "Yessum."* [20th C.: alt. of *yes ma'am.*]

yester- ▶ **comb. form** literary archaic of yesterday: *yestereve | yesteryear.* [OE *geostran,* of Gmc. origin; rel. to Du. *gisteren* and Ger. *gestern* 'yesterday,' from an Indo-Eur. root shared by L. *heri* and Gk. *khthes.*]

yes·ter·day /'yestər,dā; -dē/ ▶ **adv.** on the day before today: *he returned to a hero's welcome yesterday.* ■ in the recent past. ▶ **n.** the day before today: *yesterday was Tuesday.* ■ the recent past: *yesterday's best sellers.* [OE *giestran dæg* (see YESTER-, DAY).]

yes·ter·night /'yestər,nīt/ ▶ **n.** archaic last night. ▶ **adv.** during last night.

yes·ter·year /'yestər,yi(ə)r/ ▶ **n.** literary last year or the recent past, esp. as nostalgically recalled.

yet /yet/ ▶ **adv. 1** up until the present or an unspecified or implied time; by now or then: *I haven't left yet.* ■ [with negative] as soon as the present or a specified or implied time: *wait, don't go yet.* ■ from now into the future for a specified length of time: *I hope to continue for some time yet.* ■ referring to something that will or may happen in the future: *further research may yet explain the enigma.* ■ up to and including the present or time mentioned; still: *is it raining yet?* **2** still; even (used to emphasize increase or repetition): *yet another diet book.* **3** nevertheless; in spite of that. ▶ **conj.** but at the same time; but nevertheless.
– PHRASES **as yet** see AS[1]. **nor yet** and also not. [OE *gīet(a),* of unknown origin.]

yet·i /'yetē; 'yātē/ ▶ **n.** a large hairy creature resembling a human or bear, said to live in the highest part of the Himalayas. [1930s: from Tibetan *yeh-teh* 'little manlike animal.']

Yev·tu·shen·ko /,yevtə'SHENGkō/, Yevgeni Aleksandrovich (1933–), Russian poet. His poetry encapsuled the feelings and aspirations of the post-Stalin generation and included *Babi Yar* (1961).

yew /yōō/ ▶ **n.** (also **yew tree**) a coniferous tree (genus *Taxus,* family Taxaceae) that has poisonous red berrylike fruits and dense, springy wood. [OE *īw, ēow,* of Gmc. origin.]

yez /yəz/ ▶ **pron.** nonstandard spelling of YOUSE, used in representing dialectal speech.

Ygg·dra·sil /'igdrəsil/ Scand. Mythol. a huge ash tree located at the center of the earth, with three roots, one extending to Niflheim (the underworld), one to Jotunheim (land of the giants), and one to Asgard (land of the gods). [from ON *yg(g)drasill,* appar. from *Yggr* 'Odin' + *drasill* 'horse.']

YHVH (also **YHWH**) ▶ **abbr.** the Hebrew Tetragrammaton representing the name of God. See also TETRAGRAMMATON.

Yid /yid/ ▶ **n.** informal, offens. a Jew. [19th C.: back-form. from YIDDISH.]

Yid·dish /'yidiSH/ ▶ **n.** a language used by Jews in central and eastern Europe before the Holocaust. It was originally a German dialect with words from Hebrew and several modern languages and is still spoken mainly in the US, Israel, and Russia. ▶ **adj.** of or relating to this language. [19th C.: from Yiddish *yidish (daytsh)* 'Jewish Ger.']

Yid·dish·ism /'yidə,SHizəm/ ▶ **n. 1** a Yiddish word or idiom, esp. one adopted into another language. **2** advocacy of Yiddish culture. — **Yid·dish·ist n.** (in sense 2).

Yid·dish·keit /'yidiSH,kīt/ ▶ **n.** the quality of being Jewish; the Jewish way of life or its customs and practices. [19th C.: from Yiddish *yidishkeyt.*]

yield /yēld/ ▶ **v. 1** [trans.] produce or provide (a natural, agricultural, or industrial product). ■ (of an action or process) produce or deliver (a result or gain). ■ (of a financial or commercial process or transaction) generate (a specified financial return). **2** [intrans.] give way to arguments, demands, or pressure: *he yielded to the demands of his partners.* ■ [trans.] relinquish possession of (something); give (something) up: *they are forced to yield ground.* ■ [trans.] cease to argue about: *I yielded the point.* ■ (esp. in a legislature) allow another the right to speak in a debate: *I yield to the gentleman from Kentucky.* ■ give right of way to other traffic. ■ (of a mass or structure) give way under force or pressure. ▶ **n.** the full amount of an agricultural or industrial product: *the milk yield was poor.* ■ Finance the amount of money brought in, e.g., interest from an investment, revenue from a tax; return. ■ Chem. the amount obtained from a process or reaction relative to the theoretical maximum amount obtainable. ■ (of a nuclear weapon) the force in tons or kilotons of TNT required to produce an equivalent explosion. — **yield·er n.** [OE *g(i)eldan* 'pay, repay,' of Gmc. origin. The senses 'produce, bear' and 'surrender' arose in ME.]

yield·ing /'yēldiNG/ ▶ **adj. 1** (of a substance or object) giving way under pressure; not hard or rigid. ■ (of a person) complying with the requests or desires of others: *a gentle, yielding person.* **2** [in comb.] giving a product or generating a financial return of a specified amount: *higher-yielding wheat.* — **yield·ing·ly adv.**

yield point ▶ **n.** Physics the stress beyond which a material becomes plastic.

yield strength ▶ **n.** Physics (in materials that do not exhibit a well-defined yield point) the stress at which a specific amount of plastic deformation is produced, usually taken as 0.2 percent of the unstressed length.

yikes /yīks/ ▶ **exclam.** informal expressing shock and alarm, often for humorous effect: *Yikes! It is cold!.* [1970s: of unknown origin; cf. YOICKS.]

yin /yin/ ▶ **n.** (in Chinese philosophy) the passive female principle of the universe, characterized as female and sustaining and associated with earth, dark, and cold. Contrasted with YANG. [from Chin. *yīn* 'feminine,' 'moon,' 'shade.']

Yin·chuan /'yin'CHwän/ a city in northern central China, on the Yellow River; pop. 658,000.

symbol for yin and yang

yip /yip/ ▶ **n.** a short, sharp cry or yelp, esp. of excitement or delight. ▶ **v.** (**yipped, yip·ping**) [intrans.] give such a cry or yelp. [20th C. (orig. US): imitative.]

yipe /yīp/ ▶ **exclam.** an expression of surprise, fear, pain, etc.

yip·pee /'yipē; ,yip'ē/ ▶ **exclam.** expressing wild excitement or delight.

yip·pie /'yipē/ ▶ **n.** (pl. **-pies**) a member of a group of politically active hippies, originally in the US. [1960s: acronym from *Youth International Party* + the suffix *-ie,* suggested by HIPPIE.]

yips /yips/ ▶ **plural n.** (**the yips**) informal extreme nervousness causing a golfer to miss easy putts. [20th C.: of unknown origin.]

Yi·shuv /yi'SHōōv/ the Jewish community or settlement in Palestine during the 19th century and until the formation of the state of Israel in 1948. [from Heb. *yiššūḇ* 'settlement.']

Yiz·kor /'yiskər; 'yiz-; yēz'kôr/ ▶ **n.** (pl. same or **-kors**) a memorial service held by Jews on certain holy days for deceased relatives or martyrs. [from Heb. *yizkōr,* lit. 'may (God) remember.']

-yl ▶ **suffix** Chem. forming names of radicals: *hydroxyl | phenyl.* [from Gk. *hulē* 'wood, material.']

y·lang-y·lang /'ē,läNG 'ē,läNG/ (also **i·lang-i·lang**) ▶ **n. 1** a sweet-scented essential oil obtained from the flowers of a tropical tree, used in perfumery and aromatherapy. **2** the yellow-flowered tree (*Cananga odorata*) of the custard apple family, native to the Malay peninsula and the Philippines, from which this oil is obtained. [19th C.: from Tagalog *ilang-ilang.*]

y·lem /'īləm/ ▶ **n.** Astron. (in the big bang theory) the primordial matter of the universe, originally conceived as composed of neutrons at high temperature and density. [1940s: from late L. *hylem* (accusative) 'matter.']

YMCA ▶ **n.** Young Men's Christian Association, a welfare movement that began in London in 1844 and now has branches all over the world. ■ a hostel or recreational facility run by this association.

YMHA ▶ **abbr.** Young Men's Hebrew Association.

Y·mir /'ē,mi(ə)r/ Scand. Mythol. the primeval giant from whose body the gods created the world.

-yne ▶ **suffix** Chem. forming names of unsaturated compounds containing a triple bond: *ethyne.* [alt. of -INE[4].]

yo[1] /yō/ ▶ **exclam.** informal used to greet someone, attract their attention, or express excitement. [natural exclamation: first recorded in ME.]

yo[2] ▶ **pron.** nonstandard spelling of YOU, used to represent black English. ▶ **possessive adj.** nonstandard spelling of YOUR, used to represent black English.

yob /yäb/ ▶ **n.** Brit., informal a rude, noisy, and aggressive young man. — **yob·bish adj. yob·bish·ly adv. yob·bish·ness n. yob·by adj.** [19th C.: backward spelling of BOY.]

yob·bo /'yäbō/ ▶ **n.** (pl. **-bos** or **-boes**) Brit., informal another term for YOB.

yock /yäk/ ▶ **n.** var. of YUK.

yocto- ▶ **comb. form** (used in units of measurement) denoting a factor of 10^{-24}: *yoctojoule.* [adapted from OCTO-, on the pattern of combining forms such as *peta-* and *exa-.*]

yod /yôd; yōōd/ ▶ **n. 1** the tenth and smallest letter of the Hebrew alphabet. **2** Phonet. the semivowel or glide. [from Heb. *yōḏ;* rel. to *yaḏ* 'hand.']

yo·del /'yōdl/ ▶ **v.** (**-deled, -del·ing;** Brit. **-delled, -del·ling**) [intrans.] practice a form of singing or calling marked by rapid alternation between the normal voice and falsetto. ▶ **n.** a song, melody, or call delivered in such a way. — **yo·del·er n.** [19th C.: from Ger. *jodeln.*]

yo·ga /'yōgə/ ▶ **n.** a Hindu spiritual and ascetic discipline, a part of which, including breath control, simple meditation, and the adoption of specific bodily postures, is widely practiced for health and relaxation. — **yo·gic** /-gik/ **adj.** [Sanskrit, lit. 'union.']

yogh /yōg; yōKH/ ▶ **n.** a Middle English letter (ȝ) used mainly where modern English has *gh* and *y.* [ME: of unknown origin.]

yo·gi /'yōgē/ ▶ **n.** (pl. **-gis**) a person who is proficient in yoga. [from Sanskrit *yogī,* from *yoga* (see YOGA).]

yo·gic fly·ing ▶ **n.** a technique used chiefly by Transcendental Meditation practitioners that involves thrusting oneself off the ground while in the lotus position.

yo·gurt /'yōgərt/ (also **yo·ghurt** or **yo·ghourt**) ▶ **n.** a semisolid sourish food prepared from milk fermented by added bacteria, often sweetened and flavored. [17th C.: from Turk. *yoğurt.*]

Yog·ya·kar·ta /,yägyə'kärtə/ (also **Jog·ja·kar·ta** /,jägyə-; ,jägjə-/) a city in Indonesia, on the southern coast of Java; pop. 412,000. It was the capital of Indonesia 1945–49.

yo-heave-ho /'yō,hēv 'hō/ ▶ **exclam. & n.** another term for HEAVE-HO.

yo·him·be /yō'himbā; -bē/ ▶ **n.** a tropical West African tree (*Pausinystalia johimbe*) of the bedstraw family, from which the drug yohimbine is obtained. [19th C.: a local word.]

yo·him·bine /yō'him,bēn/ ▶**n.** Chem. a toxic crystalline compound, $C_{21}H_{26}O_3N_2$, obtained from the bark of the yohimbe tree, used as an adrenergic blocking agent and also in the treatment of impotence. [19th C.: from YOHIMBE + -INE[4].]

yo-ho-ho /'yō,hō'hō/ (also **yo-ho**) ▶**exclam. 1** dated used to attract attention. **2** Naut., archaic a seaman's chant used while hauling ropes or performing other strenuous work.

yoicks /yoiks/ ▶**exclam.** used by fox hunters to urge on the hounds. [18th C.: of unknown origin.]

yoke /yōk/ ▶**n. 1** a wooden crosspiece that is fastened over the necks of two animals and attached to the plow or cart that they are to pull. ■ (pl. same or **yokes**) a pair of animals coupled together in such a way: *a yoke of oxen.* ■ a frame fitting over the neck and shoulders of a person, used for carrying pails or baskets. ■ used of something that is regarded as oppressive or burdensome: *the yoke of imperialism.* ■ used of something that represents a bond between two parties: *the yoke of marriage.* **2** something resembling or likened to such a crosspiece, in particular: ■ a part of a garment that fits over the shoulders and to which the main part of the garment is attached, typically in gathers or pleats. ■ the crossbar of a rudder, to whose ends ropes are fastened. ■ a bar of soft iron between the poles of an electromagnet. ■ (in ancient Rome) an arch of three spears under which a defeated army was made to march. ■ a control lever in an aircraft. ▶**v.** [trans.] put a yoke on (a pair of animals); couple or attach with or to a yoke. [OE *geoc* (n.), *geocian* (v.), of Gmc. origin; rel. to Du. *juk*, Ger. *Joch*, from an Indo-Eur. root shared by L. *jugum* and Gk. *zugon*, also by L. *jungere* 'to join.']

yoke 1

yo·kel /'yōkəl/ ▶**n.** an uneducated and unsophisticated person from the countryside. [19th C.: perh. figuratively from dial. *yokel* 'green woodpecker.']

Yo·ko·ha·ma /,yōkə'hämə/ a city in central Japan, on Honshu; pop. 3,220,000.

yo·ko·zu·na /,yōkə'zōōnə/ ▶**n.** (pl. same) a grand champion sumo wrestler. [Japanese, from *yoko* 'crosswise' + *tsuna* 'rope' (orig. denoting a kind of belt presented to the champion).]

yolk /yōk/ ▶**n.** the yellow internal part of a bird's egg, which is surrounded by the white, is rich in protein and fat, and nourishes the developing embryo. ■ Zool. the corresponding part in the ovum or larva of all egg-laying vertebrates and many invertebrates. — **yolked adj.** [also in comb.] **yolk·less adj. yolk·y adj.** [OE *geol(o)ca*, from *geolu* 'yellow.']

yolk sac ▶**n.** Zool. a membranous sac containing yolk attached to the embryos of reptiles and birds and the larvae of some fishes. ■ a sac lacking yolk in the early embryo of a mammal.

yolk stalk ▶**n.** a tubular connection between the yolk sac and the digestive tract of a developing embryo.

Yom Kip·pur /'yôm ki'pōōr; 'yōm; 'yäm; 'kipər/ ▶**n.** the most solemn religious fast of the Jewish year, the last of the ten days of penitence that begin with Rosh Hashanah (the Jewish New Year). Also called DAY OF ATONEMENT. [Heb.]

Yom Kip·pur War the Israeli name for the Arab–Israeli conflict in 1973. Arab name OCTOBER WAR.

yon /yän/ literary dialect ▶**adj. & adv.** yonder; that: [as adj.] *there's some big ranches yon side of the Sierra.* ▶**pron.** yonder person or thing: *what do you make of yon?*
– PHRASES **hither and yon** see HITHER. [OE *geon*, of Gmc. origin; rel. to Ger. *jener* 'that one.']

yond /yänd/ archaic ▶**adv. & adj.** yonder.

yon·der /'yändər/ ▶**adv.** archaic dialect at some distance in the direction indicated; over there. ▶**adj.** archaic dialect that or those (used to refer to something situated at a distance). ▶**n.** (**the yonder**) the far distance. [ME: of Gmc. origin; rel. to Du. *ginder* 'over there,' also to YON.]

yo·ni /'yōnē/ ▶**n.** (pl. **-nis**) Hinduism the vulva, esp. as a symbol of divine procreative energy conventionally represented by a circular stone. Compare with LINGAM. [Sanskrit, lit. 'source, womb, female genitals.']

Yon·kers /'yängkərz/ a city in southeastern New York, north of the Bronx in New York City; pop. 196,086.

yonks /yängks/ ▶**plural n.** Brit., informal a very long time: *I haven't seen him for yonks.* [1960s: of unknown origin; perh. rel. to *donkey's years* (see DONKEY).]

yoo-hoo /'yōō ,hōō/ ▶**exclam.** a call used to attract attention to one's arrival or presence: *Yoo-hoo!—I'm home!* ▶**v.** [intrans.] (of a person) make such a call. [natural exclamation: first recorded in Engl. in the 1920s.]

yore /yôr/ ▶**n.** (in phrase **of yore**) literary of long ago or former times (used in nostalgic or mock-nostalgic recollection): *a great empire in days of yore.* [OE *geāra, geāre*, of unknown origin.]

York /yôrk/ a city in northern England, on the Ouse River; pop. 101,000.

York, Cape a cape at the northeastern tip of Australia, in Queensland.

York, House of the English royal house that ruled England from 1461 (Edward IV) until the defeat and death of Richard III in 1485, with a short break in 1470–71 (the restoration of Henry VI).

York·ie /'yôrkē/ ▶**n.** (pl. **-ies**) informal YORKSHIRE TERRIER.

York·ist /'yôrkist/ hist. ▶**n.** an adherent or a supporter of the House of York, esp. in the Wars of the Roses. ▶**adj.** of or relating to the House of York.

York·shire /'yôrk,shi(ə)r; -shər/ a former county in northern England, traditionally divided into East, West, and North Ridings. — **York·shire·man** /-mən/ **n.** (pl. **-men**) **York·shire·wom·an** /-,wōōmən/ **n.** (pl. **-wom·en**).

York·shire pud·ding ▶**n.** a popover made of baked unsweetened egg batter, typically eaten with roast beef.

York·shire ter·ri·er ▶**n.** a dog of a small, long-haired blue-gray and tan breed of terrier.

York·town /'yôrk,toun/ a historic site in southeastern Virginia, site of both the last (October 1781) battle of the American Revolution and a Civil War battle (1862).

Yo·ru·ba /'yôrəbə/ ▶**n.** (pl. same or **-bas**) **1** a member of a people of southwestern Nigeria and Benin. **2** the Kwa language of this people and an official language of Nigeria. ▶**adj.** of or relating to the Yoruba or their language. [the name in Yoruba.]

Yo·sem·i·te Na·tion·al Park /yō'semətē/ a national park in the Sierra Nevada, in central California. It includes Yosemite Falls, the highest waterfall in the US.

yotta- ▶**comb. form** (used in units of measurement) denoting a factor of 10^{24}: *yottameter.* [appar. adapted from Ital. *otto* 'eight' (see also VOCTO-).]

you /yōō/ ▶**pron.** [second person sing. or pl.] **1** used to refer to the person or people that the speaker is addressing: *are you listening?* | *I love you.* ■ used to refer to the person being addressed together with other people regarded in the same class: *you Australians.* ■ used in exclamations to address one or more people: *you fools* | *hey, you!* **2** used to refer to any person in general: *after a while, you get used to it.* [OE *ēow*, accusative and dative of *gē* (see YE[1]), of West Gmc. origin; rel. to Du. *u* and Ger. *euch*.]

you-all /,yōō 'ôl; yôl/ (also **y'all**) ▶**pron.** dialect (in the southern US) you (used to refer to more than one person): *how are you-all?*

you'd /yōōd/ ▶**contr.** ■ you had: *you'd better remember it.* ■ you would: *I was afraid you'd ask me that.*

you'll /yōōl/ ▶**contr.** you will; you shall.

Young[1] /yəng/, Brigham (1801–77), US Mormon leader. He succeeded Joseph Smith in 1844 and established Mormon headquarters at Salt Lake City, Utah.

Young[2], Cy (1867–1955), US baseball player; born *Denton True Young*; also known as the **Cyclone**. Baseball's Cy Young Award for outstanding pitchers is named for him.

Young[3], Thomas (1773–1829), English physicist, physician, and Egyptologist. He helped establish the wave theory of light and played a major part in the deciphering of the Rosetta Stone.

young /yəng/ ▶**adj.** (**young·er** /'yənggər/, **young·est** /'yənggəst/) having lived or existed for only a short time: *a young girl* | [as pl. n.] (**the young**) *the young are amazingly resilient.* ■ not as old as the norm or as would be expected: *dying young.* ■ relating to, characteristic of, or consisting of young people: *young love.* ■ immature or inexperienced: *she's very young for her age.* ■ having the qualities popularly associated with young people, such as enthusiasm and optimism. ■ (**the Younger**) used to denote the younger of two people of the same name: *Pitt the Younger.* ■ (**younger**) [postpositive] Scot. denoting the heir of a landed commoner: *Hugh Magnus Macleod, younger of Macleod.* ▶**n.** [treated as pl.] offspring, esp. of an animal before or soon after birth: *this species carries its young.*
– PHRASES **with young** (of an animal) pregnant. — **young·ish** /'yəngish/ **adj.** [OE *g(e)ong*, of Gmc. origin; rel. to Du. *jong* and Ger. *jung*, also to YOUTH; from an Indo-Eur. root shared by L. *juvenis*.]

young·ber·ry /'yəng,berē/ ▶**n.** (pl. **-ries**) a bramble of a variety that bears large, edible reddish-black fruit, believed to be a hybrid of a dewberry. [1920s: named after B. M. *Young* (*fl.* 1905), the American horticulturalist who first raised it.]

young gun ▶**n.** informal a young man perceived as assertive and aggressively self-confident.

young la·dy ▶**n.** a woman who is not far advanced in life; a girl. ■ a form of address used by an adult to a girl, often in anger. ■ dated a girlfriend.

young·ling /'yəngling/ ▶**n.** literary a young person or animal.

young man ▶**n.** a man who is not far advanced in life; a boy. ■ a form of address used by an adult to a boy, often in anger. ■ dated a boyfriend.

Young Pre·tend·er see STUART[1].

Young's mod·u·lus /yəngz/ ▶**n.** Physics a measure of elasticity, equal to the ratio of the stress acting on a substance to the strain produced. [19th C.: named after T. *Young* (see YOUNG[3]).]

young·ster /'yəngstər/ ▶**n.** a child, young person, or young animal.

Youngs·town /'yəngz,toun/ a city in northeastern Ohio; pop. 82,026.

Young Turk ▶**n.** a member of a revolutionary party in the Ottoman Empire that carried out the revolution of 1908 and deposed the sultan Abdul Hamid II. ■ a young person eager for radical change to the established order.

young 'un ▶ **n.** informal a youngster.

youn·ker /'yəNGkər/ ▶ **n.** dated a youngster. [16th C. (denoting a young nobleman): from MDu. *jonckher*, from *jonc* 'young' + *hēre* 'lord.' Cf. JUNKER.]

your /yôr; yŏŏr/ ▶ **possessive adj. 1** belonging to or associated with the person or people that the speaker is addressing: *what is your name?* **2** belonging to or associated with any person in general: *the sight is enough to break your heart.* ■ informal used to denote someone or something that is familiar or typical of its kind: *one of your chatty types.* **3** (**Your**) used when addressing the holder of certain titles: *Your Majesty* | *Your Eminence.* [OE *ēower*, genitive of *gē* (see YE[1]), of Gmc. origin; rel. to Ger. *euer*.]

you're /yŏŏr; yôr/ ▶ **contr.** you are.

yours /yôrz; yŏŏrz/ ▶ **possessive pron. 1** used to refer to a thing or things belonging to or associated with the person or people that the speaker is addressing. ■ dated (chiefly in commercial use) your letter. **2** used in formulas ending a letter: *Yours sincerely, John.*
– PHRASES **up yours** see UP. **you and yours** see YOU. **yours truly** see TRULY.

your·self /yər'self; yôr-; yŏŏr-/ ▶ **pron.** [second person sing.] (pl. **-selves** /-'selvz/) **1** [reflexive] used to refer to the person being addressed as the object of a verb or preposition when they are also the subject of the clause: *help yourselves, boys* | *see for yourself.* **2** [emphatic] you personally (used to emphasize the person being addressed): *you're going to have to do it yourself.*

youse /yōōz/ ▶ **pron.** dialect you (usually more than one person).

youth /yōōTH/ ▶ **n.** (pl. **youths** /yōōTHs; yōōTHz/) **1** [in sing.] the period between childhood and adult age. ■ the state or quality of being young, esp. as associated with vigor, freshness, or immaturity. ■ an early stage in the development of something. **2** [treated as sing. or pl.] young people considered as a group: *middle-class youth* | [as adj.] *youth culture.* ■ a young man: *he was attacked by a gang of youths.* [OE *geoguth*, of Gmc. origin; rel. to Du. *jeugd*, Ger. *Jugend*, also to YOUNG.]

youth·ful /'yōōTHfəl/ ▶ **adj.** young or seeming young. ■ typical or characteristic of young people. — **youth·ful·ly adv. youth·ful·ness n.**

youth hos·tel ▶ **n.** a place providing cheap accommodations aimed mainly at young people on walking or cycling tours.

you've /yōōv/ ▶ **contr.** you have.

yow /you/ (also **yeow**) ▶ **exclam.** used to express pain or shock. [ME: imitative. The word was not recorded again until the 19th C., when it was used to express the cry of a dog or cat.]

yowl /youl/ ▶ **n.** a loud wailing cry, esp. one of pain or distress. ▶ **v.** [intrans.] make such a cry. [ME: imitative.]

yo-yo /'yō,yō/ ▶ **n.** (pl. **-yos**) a toy consisting of a pair of joined discs with a deep groove between them in which string is attached and wound, which can be spun alternately downward and upward by its weight and momentum as the string unwinds and rewinds. ■ [often as adj.] a thing that repeatedly falls and rises again: *the yo-yo syndrome of losing and gaining weight.* ■ informal a stupid, insane, or unpredictable person. ▶ **v.** (**-yoes, -yoed**) [no obj., usu. with adverbial of direction] move up and down; fluctuate. ■ [trans.] manipulate or maneuver (someone or something): *he gets to yo-yo me around.* [20th C.: of unknown origin.]

Y·pres, Bat·tle of each of three battles on the Western Front near Ypres, Belgium, during World War I in 1914, 1915, and 1917. See also PASSCHENDAELE, BATTLE OF.

yr. ▶ **abbr.** ■ year or years. ■ younger. ■ your.

yrs. ▶ **abbr.** ■ years. ■ yours (as a formula ending a letter).

YT ▶ **abbr.** Yukon Territory (in official postal use).

yt·ter·bi·um /i'tərbēəm/ ▶ **n.** the chemical element of atomic number 70, a silvery-white metal of the lanthanide series. (Symbol: **Yb**) [19th C.: mod. L., from *Ytterby*, the name of a Swedish quarry where it was first found.]

yt·tri·um /'itrēəm/ ▶ **n.** the chemical element of atomic number 39, a grayish-white metal generally included among the rare-earth elements. (Symbol: **Y**) [19th C.: mod. L., from *Ytterby* (see YTTERBIUM).]

Yu·an /yōō'än/ a dynasty that ruled China AD 1259–1368, established by the Mongols under Kublai Khan. It preceded the Ming dynasty.

yu·an /yōō'än/ ▶ **n.** (pl. same) the basic monetary unit of China, equal to 10 jiao or 100 fen. [Chin., lit. 'round'; cf. YEN[1].]

Yuan Jiang /yōō'än 'jyäNG; jē'äNG/ Chinese name for RED RIVER (sense 1).

yuc·a /'yōōkə/ ▶ **n.** another term for CASSAVA. [Carib.]

Yu·ca·tán /,yōōkə'tan; -'tän; 'yōōkə,tan; -,tän/ a state in southeastern Mexico; capital, Mérida.

Yu·ca·tán Pen·in·su·la a peninsula in southern Mexico that lies between the Gulf of Mexico and the Caribbean Sea.

Yu·ca·tec /'yōōkə,tek/ ▶ **n.** (pl. same or **-tecs**) **1** a member of a native people of the Yucatán peninsula. ■ informal a native or inhabitant of the peninsula or the state of Yucatán. **2** the Mayan language of the Yucatec people. ▶ **adj.** of or relating to the Yucatec or their language. — **Yu·ca·tec·an** /,yōōkə'tekən/ **adj.** [from Sp. *yucateco*.]

yuc·ca /'yəkə/ ▶ **n.** a plant (genus *Yucca*) of the agave family with stiff swordlike leaves and spikes of white bell-shaped flowers that are dependent upon the yucca moth for fertilization, found esp. in warm regions of North America and Mexico. Many species include the Spanish bayonet and Adam's-needle. [16th C. (denoting cassava): from Carib.]

yuck /yək/ informal ▶ **exclam.** (also **yuk**) used to express strong distaste or disgust: *"Raw herring! Yuck!"* ▶ **n.** something messy or disgusting: *blood and yuck.* [1960s (orig. US): imitative.]

yuck·y /'yəkē/ (also **yuk·ky**) ▶ **adj.** (**yuck·i·er, yuck·i·est**) informal messy or disgusting: *yucky green-gray slushy cabbage.*

Yu·e /yōō'ā/ ▶ **n.** another term for CANTONESE (the language).

yu·ga /'yōōgə/ ▶ **n.** Hinduism any of the four ages of the life of the world. [Sanskrit.]

Yu·go·slav /'yōōgō,släv; ,yōōgō'släv; -gə-/ ▶ **n.** a native or national of the former federal republic of Yugoslavia, or a person of Yugoslav descent. ▶ **adj.** of or relating to Yugoslavia or its people. [from Austrian Ger. *Jugoslav*, from Serbo-Croat *jug* 'south' + SLAV.]

Yu·go·sla·vi·a /,yōōgō'slävēə; ,yōōgə-/ a former federal republic in SE Europe. — **Yu·go·sla·vi·an adj. & n.**

yuk ▶ **exclam.** var. of YUCK. ▶ **n.** informal a laugh, esp. a loud hearty one. [1930s (theatrical slang): prob. imitative.]

yu·ka·ta /yōō'kätə/ ▶ **n.** (pl. same or **-tas**) a light cotton kimono. [Japanese, from *yu* 'hot water' (because orig. worn indoors after a bath) + *kata(bira)* 'light kimono.']

yuk·ky ▶ **adj.** var. of YUCKY.

Yu·kon /'yōō,kän/ a river in northwestern North America that rises in northwestern Canada and flows west for 1,870 miles (3,020 km) through central Alaska to the Bering Sea.

Yu·kon Ter·ri·to·ry a territory in northwestern Canada, on the border with Alaska; pop. 27,797; capital, Whitehorse.

yu·lan /'yōō,lan; -lən/ ▶ **n.** a Chinese magnolia (*Magnolia heptapeta*) with showy white flowers. [19th C.: from Chin. *yùlán*, from *yù* 'gem' + *lán* 'plant.']

Yule /yōōl/ ▶ **n.** archaic term for CHRISTMAS. [OE *gēol(a)* 'Christmas Day'; cf. ON *jól*, orig. applied to a heathen festival lasting twelve days, later to Christmas.]

yule log ▶ **n.** a large log traditionally burned in the fireplace on Christmas Eve. ■ a log-shaped chocolate cake eaten at Christmas.

Yule·tide /'yōōl,tīd/ ▶ **n.** archaic term for CHRISTMAS.

yum /yəm/ (also **yum-yum**) informal ▶ **exclam.** used to express pleasure at eating, or at the prospect of eating, a particular food. ▶ **adj.** (of food) delicious. [19th C.: imitative.]

Yu·ma[1] /'yōōmə/ a city in southwestern Arizona, near the Mexican border; pop. 77,515.

Yu·ma[2] ▶ **n. 1** (pl. same or **-mas**) a member of an American Indian people living mainly in southwestern Arizona. **2** the Yuman language of this people. ▶ **adj.** of or relating to this people. [from Pima *yumǐ*.]

Yu·man /'yōōmən/ ▶ **n.** a family of American Indian languages including Yuma. ▶ **adj.** of or relating to the Yuman languages or their speakers. [from YUMA + -AN.]

yum·my /'yəmē/ ▶ **adj.** (**-mi·er, -mi·est**) informal (of food) delicious: *yummy pumpkin cakes.* ■ highly attractive and desirable: *I scooped up this yummy young man.* [19th C.: from YUM + -Y[1].]

Yun·nan /yōō'nän/ a province in southwestern China; capital, Kunming.

yup /yəp/ ▶ **exclam. & n.** var. of YEP.

Yu·pik /'yōōpik/ ▶ **n.** (pl. same or **-piks**) **1** a member of an Eskimo people of Siberia, the Aleutian Islands, and southwestern Alaska. **2** any of the Eskimo languages of this people. ▶ **adj.** of or relating to this people or their languages. [from Alaskan Yupik *Yup'ik* 'real person.']

yup·pie /'yəpē/ (also **yup·py**) ▶ **n.** (pl. **-pies**) informal, derog. a well-paid young middle-class professional who works in a city job and has a luxurious lifestyle. — **yup·pie·dom** /-dəm/ **n.** [1980s: elaboration of the acronym from *young urban professional*.]

yup·pie flu (also **yup·pie dis·ease**) ▶ **n.** informal derogatory term for CHRONIC FATIGUE SYNDROME.

yup·pi·fy /'yəpə,fī/ ▶ **v.** (**-fies, -fied**) [trans.] informal, derog. make more affluent and upmarket in keeping with the taste and lifestyle of yuppies. — **yup·pi·fi·ca·tion** /,yəpəfi'kāSHən/ **n.**

Yu·rok /'yōōr,äk; -ək/ ▶ **n.** (pl. same or **-roks**) **1** a member of an American Indian people of northern California. **2** the language of this people, distantly related to Algonquian. ▶ **adj.** of or relating to this people or their language. [from Karok *yúruk*, lit. 'downstream.']

yurt /yŏŏrt; yərt/ ▶ **n.** a circular tent of felt or skins on a collapsible framework, used by nomads in Mongolia, Siberia, and Turkey. [from Russ. *yurta*, via Fr. or Ger. from Turkic *jurt*.]

YWCA ▶ **n.** Young Women's Christian Association, a welfare movement with branches in many countries that began in Britain in 1855. ■ a hostel or recreational facility run by this association.

YWHA ▶ **abbr.** Young Women's Hebrew Association.

Zz

Z¹ /zē/ (also **z**) ▶ **n.** (pl. **Zs** or **Z's**) **1** the twenty-sixth letter of the alphabet. ■ denoting the next after Y in a set of items, categories, etc. ■ denoting a third unknown or unspecified person or thing: *X sold a car to Y (a car dealer) who in turn sold it to Z (a finance company).* ■ (usu. z) the third unknown quantity in an algebraic expression. [the introduction of *x*, *y*, and *z* as symbols of unknown quantities is due to Descartes (see **X¹**).] ■ (usu. z) denoting the third axis in a three-dimensional system of coordinates: [in comb.] *the z-axis.* **2** a shape like that of a capital Z. **3** used in repeated form to represent the sound of buzzing or snoring.
– PHRASES **catch some** (or **a few**) **Zs** informal get some sleep: *I'll go back to the hotel and catch some Zs.*

Z² ▶ **symb.** Chem. atomic number.

za·ba·glio·ne /ˌzäbəlˈyōnē/ ▶ **n.** an Italian dessert made of whipped and heated egg yolks, sugar, and Marsala wine, served either hot or cold. [Ital.]

Zab·rze /ˈzäbzhə/ a city in southern Poland; pop. 205,000. A German city until 1945, from 1915 to 1945 it was called Hindenburg.

Za·ca·te·cas /ˌzäkəˈtākəs; ˌsäkə-/ a state in northern central Mexico. ■ its capital; pop. 165,000.

zaf·fer /ˈzafər/ (also **zaf·fre**) ▶ **n.** impure cobalt oxide, formerly used to make smalt and blue enamels. [17th C.: from Ital. *zaffera* or Fr. *safre*.]

zaf·tig /ˈzäftig; -tik/ (also **zof·tig**) ▶ **adj.** informal (of a woman) having a full, rounded figure; plump. [1930s: Yiddish, from Ger. *saftig* 'juicy.']

zag /zag/ ▶ **n.** a sharp change of direction in a zigzag course: *we traveled in a series of zigs and zags.* ▶ **v.** (**zagged, zag·ging**) [intrans.] make a sharp change of direction. [18th C.: shortening of **zigzag**.]

Za·greb /ˈzäˌgreb/ the capital of Croatia, in the north central part of the country; pop. 707,000.

Zag·ros Moun·tains /ˈzagrəs; -ˌrōs/ a mountain range in western Iran that rises to 14,921 feet (4,548 m) at Zard Kuh.

Za·har·i·as /zəˈharēəs/, Babe (1914–56), US track and field athlete and golfer; full name *Mildred Ella Didrikson Zaharias*. After winning Olympic gold medals in the javelin throw and 80-meter hurdle events in 1932, she turned to golf and won many major professional titles between 1936 and 1954.

zai·ba·tsu /zīˈbätˌso͞o; -ˈbat-/ ▶ **n.** (pl. same) a large Japanese business conglomerate. [Japanese, from *zai* 'wealth' + *batsu* 'clique.']

Za·ire /zäˈi(ə)r/ Former name of (until 1997) **Congo, Democratic Republic of the.** — **Za·ir·e·an** /-ˈi(ə)rēən/ (also **Za·ir·i·an**) **adj. & n.**

za·ire /zäˈi(ə)r/ ▶ **n.** (pl. same) the basic monetary unit of Zaire (now the Democratic Republic of the Congo), equal to 100 makuta. [from *Zaire*, a local name for the Congo River in central Africa.]

Za·ire Riv·er see **Congo**.

za·kat /zəˈkät; -ˈkat/ ▶ **n.** obligatory payment made annually under Islamic law on certain kinds of property and used for charitable and religious purposes. [via Pers. and Urdu from Arab. *zakā(t)* 'almsgiving.']

Za·kin·thos /ˈzäkinˌthôs/ (also **Za·kyn·thos**) a Greek island in the Ionian Sea; pop. 33,000. Also called **Zante**.

Zam·be·zi /zamˈbēzē/ a river in East Africa that rises in northwestern Zambia and flows through Angola and Zambia to Victoria Falls where it turns to form the border between Zambia and Zimbabwe before crossing Mozambique and entering the Indian Ocean.

Zam·bi·a /ˈzambēə/ a country in central Africa. *See box.* — **Zam·bi·an adj. & n.**

Zam·bo·an·ga /ˌzambōˈänggə/ a city in southern Philippines, on Mindanao; pop. 442,000.

Zam·bo·ni /zamˈbōnē/ ▶ **n.** trademark for a machine used to resurface ice for skating.

za·mi·a /ˈzāmēə/ (Austral. also **za·mi·a palm**) ▶ **n.** an American or Australian cycad (family Zamiaceae), some kinds of which produce roots or seeds that are edible after careful preparation. Genera include *Zamia* (of America) and *Macrozamia* (of Australia). [19th C.: mod. L., from *zamiae*, misreading (in Pliny) of *azaniae* 'pine cones.']

za·min·dar /ˈzamənˌdär; zəˌmēnˈdär/ ▶ **n.** Indian a landowner, esp. one who leases his land to tenant farmers. [via Urdu from Pers. *zamīndār*, from *zamīn* 'land' + *-dār* 'holder.']

zam·in·dar·i /ˌzamənˈdärē; zəˌmēn-/ ▶ **n.** Indian, hist. the system under which zamindars held land. [Urdu.]

Zan·de /ˈzandē/ (also **A·zan·de** /əˈzandē/) ▶ **n.** (pl. same or **A·zan·de**) **1** a member of a central African people of mixed ethnic origin. **2** the Niger-Congo language of this people, spoken mainly in northern Democratic Republic of the Congo (formerly Zaire) and Sudan. ▶ **adj.** of or relating to this people or their language. [the name in Zande.]

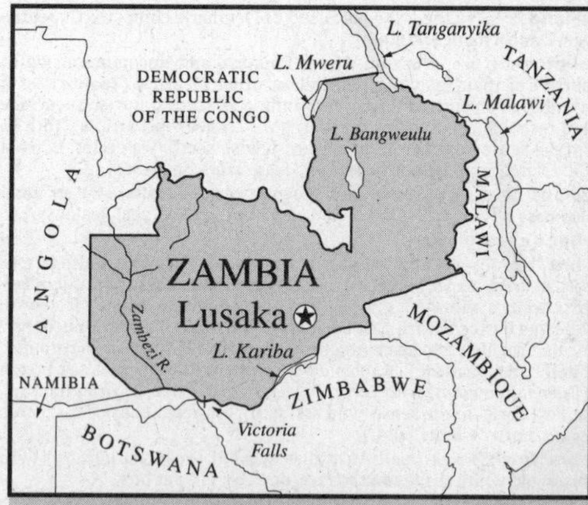

Zambia

Official name: Republic of Zambia
Location: central Africa, separated from Zimbabwe by the Zambezi River
Area: 290,700 square miles (752,600 sq km)
Population: 10,462,000
Capital: Lusaka
Languages: English (official), many Bantu languages
Currency: Zambian kwacha

Zan·te /ˈzantē/ another name for **Zakinthos**.

Zan·uck /ˈzanək/, Darryl Francis (1902–79), US movie producer. He was an executive at Twentieth Century Fox and its president from 1965 to 1971.

za·ny /ˈzānē/ ▶ **adj.** (**-ni·er, -ni·est**) amusingly unconventional and idiosyncratic: *zany humor.* ▶ **n.** an erratic or eccentric person. ■ hist. a comic performer partnering a clown, whom he imitated in an amusing way. — **za·ni·ly** /-nl-ē/ **adv.** **za·ni·ness n.** [16th C.: from Fr. *zani* or Ital. *zan(n)i*, Venetian form of *Gianni, Giovanni* 'John,' stock name of the servants acting as clowns in the *commedia dell'arte*.]

Zan·zi·bar /ˈzanzəˌbär/ an island off the coast of East Africa, part of Tanzania; pop. 641,000. — **Zan·zi·ba·ri** /ˌzanzəˈbärē/ **adj. & n.**

Zao·zhuang /ˈdzouˈjwäng; -jəˈwäng/ (also **Tsao-chuang**) a city in eastern China; pop. 3,192,000.

zap /zap/ informal ▶ **v.** (**zapped, zap·ping**) [trans.] **1** destroy or obliterate: *zap the enemy's artillery.* **2** cause to move suddenly and rapidly in a specified direction: *the boat zapped us up river.* ■ [no obj., with adverbial of direction] move suddenly and rapidly, esp. between television channels or sections of videotape by use of a remote control. **3** cook or warm (food or a hot drink) in a microwave oven. ▶ **n.** a sudden effect or event that makes a dramatic impact, esp. a sudden burst of energy or sound. [1920s (orig. US): imitative.]

Za·pa·ta /zəˈpätə/, Emiliano (1879–1919), Mexican revolutionary. He attempted to implement his program of agrarian reform by means of guerrilla warfare.

za·pa·te·a·do /ˌzäpətēˈädō; -tā-/ ▶ **n.** (pl. **-dos**) a flamenco dance with rhythmic stamping of the feet. [19th C.: Sp., from *zapato* 'shoe.']

Za·po·tec /ˈzäpəˌtek/ ▶ **n.** (pl. same or **-tecs**) **1** a member of a native people living in and around Oaxaca in southern Mexico. **2** the Otomanguean language of this people. ▶ **adj.** of or relating to the Zapotec or their language. [from Sp. *zapoteco*, from Nahuatl *tzapoteca*, pl. of *tzapotecatl*, lit. 'person of the place of the sapodilla.']

zap·per /ˈzapər/ ▶ **n.** informal **1** a remote control for a television, video, or other piece of electronic equipment. **2** an electronic device used for killing insects.

zap·py /ˈzapē/ ▶ **adj.** (**-pi·er, -pi·est**) informal lively; energetic: *a zappy musical tapestry.*

Za·ra·go·za /ˌsärəˈgōsə; ˌTHärəˈgōTHə/ Spanish name for SARAGOSSA.

Zar·a·thus·tra /ˌzarəˈTHōōstrə/ the Avestan name for the Persian prophet Zoroaster. —**Zar·a·thus·tri·an** /-ˈTHōōstrēən/ **adj. & n.**

za·re·ba /zəˈrēbə/ (also **za·ree·ba**) ▶**n.** a protective enclosure of thorn bushes or stakes surrounding a campsite or village in northeastern Africa.

zar·zue·la /zärˈzwālə/ ▶**n.** **1** a Spanish traditional form of musical comedy. **2** a Spanish dish of various kinds of seafood cooked in a rich sauce. [Sp., appar. from a place name.]

za·yin /ˈzäyin/ ▶**n.** the seventh letter of the Hebrew alphabet.

za·zen /ˌzäˈzen/ ▶**n.** Zen meditation, usually performed in the lotus position. [Japanese, from *za* 'sitting' + *zen* (see ZEN).]

Z bo·son ▶**n.** another term for Z PARTICLE.

zeal /zēl/ ▶**n.** great energy or enthusiasm in pursuit of a cause or an objective: *his **zeal** for privatization.* [ME: via eccles. L. from Gk. *zēlos*.]

Zea·land /ˈzēlənd/ the principal island of Denmark; chief city, Copenhagen. Danish name SJÆLLAND.

zeal·ot /ˈzelət/ ▶**n.** a person who is fanatical and uncompromising in pursuit of their religious, political, or other ideals. ■ (**Zeal·ot**) hist. a member of an ancient Jewish sect aiming at a world Jewish theocracy and resisting the Romans until AD 70. —**zeal·ot·ry** /-ətrē/ **n.** [16th C. (in the sense 'member of an ancient Jewish sect'): via eccles. L. from Gk. *zēlōtēs*, from *zēloun* 'be jealous,' from *zēlos* (see ZEAL).]

zeal·ous /ˈzeləs/ ▶**adj.** having or showing zeal. —**zeal·ous·ly adv. zeal·ous·ness n.** [16th C.: from a med. L. deriv. of L. *zelus* 'zeal, jealousy.']

ze·bec ▶**n.** var. of XEBEC.

ze·bra /ˈzēbrə/ ▶**n.** **1** an African wild horse with black-and-white stripes and an erect mane. Three species: the **common zebra** (*Equus burchellii*), **Grevy's zebra** (*E. grevyi*), and the **mountain zebra** (*E. zebra*). **2** a large butterfly with pale bold stripes on a dark background, in particular: a yellow and black American butterfly (*Heliconius charitonius*, family Nymphalidae). **3** (also **ze·bra fish**) a silvery-gold sea bream (*Diplodus cervinus*) with vertical black stripes. [17th C.: from Ital., Sp., or Port., orig. in the sense 'wild ass,' perh. ult. from L. *equiferus*, from *equus* 'horse' + *ferus* 'wild.']

ze·bra finch ▶**n.** a small Australian waxbill (*Poephila guttata*) with black and white stripes on the face, popular as a pet bird.

ze·bra mus·sel ▶**n.** a small freshwater bivalve mollusk (*Dreissena polymorpha*, family Dreissenidae) with zigzag markings on the shell, sometimes becoming a pest because it blocks water pipes.

ze·bra·wood /ˈzēbrəˌwŏŏd/ ▶**n.** any of a number of tropical trees that produce ornamental striped timber that is used chiefly in cabinetmaking. Species are in several families, such as *Connarus guianensis* (family Connaraceae) of Guyana and *Diospyros marmorata* (family Ebenaceae) of the Andaman Islands.

ze·bu /ˈzēˌb(y)ōō/ ▶**n.** another term for BRAHMAN (sense 3). [18th C.: from Fr. *zébu*, of unknown origin.]

Zeb·u·lun /ˈzebyələn/ (also **Zeb·u·lon**) (in the Bible) a Hebrew patriarch. ■ the tribe of Israel traditionally descended from him.

Zech. ▶**abbr.** Bible Zechariah.

Zech·a·ri·ah /ˌzekəˈrīə/ a Hebrew minor prophet of the 6th century BC. ■ a book of the Bible including his prophecies.

zed /zed/ ▶**n.** Brit. the letter Z. [ME: from Fr. *zède*, via late L. from Gk. *zēta* (see ZETA).]

Zed·e·ki·ah /ˌzedəˈkīə/ (in the Bible) the last king of Judea, who was carried off to Babylon into captivity.

zed·o·a·ry /ˈzedōˌerē/ ▶**n.** an Indian plant (*Curcuma zedoaria*, family Zingiberaceae) related to turmeric, with an aromatic rhizome. ■ a gingerlike substance made from this rhizome, used in medicine, perfumery, and dyeing. [ME: from med. L. *zedoarium*, from Pers. *zadwār*.]

zee /zē/ ▶**n.** the letter Z. [17th C.: var. of ZED.]

Zee·man ef·fect /ˈzēmən; ˈzā-/ ▶**n.** Physics the splitting of the spectrum line into several components by the application of a magnetic field. [19th C.: named after Pieter *Zeeman* (1865–1943), Dutch physicist.]

Zef·fi·rel·li /ˌzefəˈrelē/, Franco (1923–), Italian director; born *Gianfranco Corsi*. His movies include *Romeo and Juliet* (1968) and *Tea with Mussolini* (1999).

ze·in /ˈzē-in/ ▶**n.** Biochem. the principal protein of corn. [19th C.: from mod. L. *Zea* (genus name of corn) + -IN[1].]

zeit·ge·ber /ˈtsītˌgābər; ˈzīt-/ ▶**n.** Physiol. a cue given by the environment, such as a change in light or temperature, to reset the internal body clock. [20th C.: from Ger. *Zeitgeber*, from *Zeit* 'time' + *Geber* 'giver.']

zeit·geist /ˈtsītˌgīst; ˈzīt-/ ▶**n.** [in sing.] the defining spirit or mood of a particular period of history as shown by the ideas and beliefs of the time: *the story captured the zeitgeist of the late 1960s.* [19th C.: from Ger. *Zeitgeist*, from *Zeit* 'time' + *Geist* 'spirit.']

zel·ko·va /zelˈkōvə/ ▶**n.** an Asian tree (genus *Zelkova*) of the elm family, often cultivated as an ornamental, for its timber, or as a bonsai tree.

zem·stvo /ˈzemst-vō/ ▶**n.** one of a system of elected councils established in czarist Russia to administer local affairs after the abolition of serfdom.

Zen /zen/ (also **Zen Bud·dhism**) ▶**n.** a Japanese school of Mahayana Buddhism emphasizing the value of meditation and intuition rather than ritual worship or study of scriptures. —**Zen Bud·dhist n.** [Japanese, lit. 'meditation,' from Chin. *chán* 'quietude,' from Sanskrit *dhyāna* 'meditation.']

ze·na·na /zəˈnänə/ ▶**n.** (in India and Iran) the part of a house for the seclusion of women. [from Pers. and Urdu *zanānah*, from *zan* 'woman.']

Zend /zend/ ▶**n.** an interpretation of the Avesta, each Zend being part of the Zend-Avesta. [from Pers. *zand* 'interpretation.']

Zend-A·ves·ta ▶**n.** the Zoroastrian sacred writings, comprising the Avesta (the text) and Zend (the commentary).

Ze·ner /ˈzēnər/ (in full **Ze·ner di·ode**) ▶**n.** Electron. a form of semiconductor diode in which at a critical reverse voltage a large reverse current can flow. [1950s: named after Clarence M. *Zener* (1905–93), American physicist.]

ze·nith /ˈzēniTH/ ▶**n.** [in sing.] the highest point reached by a celestial or other object. ■ the point in the sky or celestial sphere directly above an observer. The opposite of NADIR. ■ the time at which something is most powerful or successful. —**ze·nith·al** /-nəTHəl/ **adj.** [ME: from OFr. or med. L. *cenit*, based on Arab. *samt (ar-ra's)* 'path (over the head).']

Ze·no[1] /ˈzēnō/ (*fl.* 5th century BC), Greek philosopher. He formulated paradoxes that appeared to demonstrate the impossibility of motion.

Ze·no[2] (*c.*335–*c.*263 BC), Greek philosopher; known as **Zeno of Citium**. He founded Stoic philosophy *c.*300 (see STOICISM).

Ze·no·bi·a /zəˈnōbēə/ (3rd century AD), queen of Palmyra *c.*267–272. She conquered Egypt and much of Asia Minor.

ze·o·lite /ˈzēəˌlīt/ ▶**n.** any of a large group of minerals consisting of hydrated aluminosilicates of sodium, potassium, calcium, and barium. —**ze·o·lit·ic** /ˌzēəˈlitik/ **adj.** [18th C.: from Swed. and Ger. *zeolit*, from Gk. *zein* 'to boil' + -LITE (from their characteristic swelling when heated in the laboratory).]

Zeph. ▶**abbr.** Bible Zephaniah.

Zeph·a·ni·ah /ˌzefəˈnīə/ a Hebrew minor prophet of the 7th century BC. ■ a book of the Bible containing his prophecies.

zeph·yr /ˈzefər/ ▶**n.** **1** literary a soft gentle breeze. **2** hist. a fine cotton gingham. ■ a very light article of clothing. [OE *zefferus*, denoting a personification of the west wind, via L. from Gk. *zephuros* '(god of the) west wind.']

Zep·pe·lin[1] /ˈzep(ə)lən/, Ferdinand Adolf August Heinrich, Count von (1838–1917), German aviation pioneer. He developed the dirigible airship.

Zep·pe·lin[2] ▶**n.** hist. a large German dirigible airship of the early 20th century, long and cylindrical in shape and with a rigid framework. Zeppelins were used during World War I for reconnaissance and bombing, and after the war as passenger transports until the 1930s.

zepto- ▶**comb. form** (used in units of measurement) denoting a factor of 10^{-21}: *zeptosecond.* [adapted from SEPTI-, on the pattern of combining forms such as *peta-* and *exa-*.]

ze·ro /ˈzi(ə)rō/ ▶**cardinal number** (pl. **-ros**) no quantity or number; naught; the figure 0. ■ a point on a scale or instrument from which a positive or negative quantity is reckoned. ■ the temperature corresponding to 0° on the Celsius scale (32° Fahrenheit), marking the freezing point of water. ■ [usu. as adj.] Ling. the absence of an actual word or morpheme to realize a syntactic or morphological phenomenon: *the zero plural in "three sheep."* ■ the lowest possible amount or level; nothing at all. ■ short for ZERO HOUR. ■ informal a worthless or contemptibly undistinguished person. ▶**v.** (**-roes, -roed**) [trans.] **1** adjust (an instrument) to zero. **2** set the sights of (a gun) for firing.
– PHRASAL VERBS **zero in** take aim with a gun or missile: *jet fighters zeroed in on the rebel positions.* ■ focus one's attention: *they zeroed in on the clues he gave away.* **zero out** phase out or reduce to zero. [17th C.: from Fr. *zéro* or Ital. *zero*, via Old Sp. from Arab. *ṣifr* 'cipher.']

ze·ro-based ▶**adj.** Finance (of a budget or budgeting) having each item costed anew, rather than in relation to its size or status in the previous budget.

ze·ro-cou·pon ▶**adj.** of or pertaining to a debt obligation that pays no interest to the holder until it reaches maturity or is sold.

ze·ro-cou·pon bond ▶**n.** a bond that is issued at a deep discount to its face value but pays no interest.

ze·ro-e·mis·sion ▶**adj.** denoting a road vehicle that emits no pollutants from its exhaust.

ze·ro G ▶**abbr.** zero gravity.

ze·ro grav·i·ty ▶**n.** Physics the state or condition in which there is no apparent force of gravity acting on a body, either because the force is locally weak, or because both the body and its surroundings are freely and equally accelerating under the force.

ze·ro hour ▶**n.** the time at which a planned operation, typically a military one, is set to begin.

ze·ro op·tion ▶**n.** a disarmament proposal for the total removal of certain types of weapons on both sides.

ze·ro pop·u·la·tion growth ▶**n.** maintaining a population at a constant level by limiting the number of live births to only what is needed to replace the existing population.

ze·ro-sum ▶**adj.** (of a game or situation) in which whatever is gained by one side is lost by the other.

ze·roth /ˈzi(ə)rōTH/ ▶**adj.** immediately preceding what is regarded as first in a series. [19th C.: from ZERO + -TH[1].]

ze·ro tol·er·ance ▶**n.** refusal to accept antisocial behavior, typically by strict and uncompromising application of the law.

zest /zest/ ▶**n.** **1** great enthusiasm and energy. ■ a quality of excitement and piquancy. **2** the outer colored part of the peel of citrus fruit, used as flavoring. — **zest·ful** /-fəl/ **adj.** **zest·ful·ly** /-fəlē/ **adv.** **zest·ful·ness** /-fəlnəs/ **n.** **zest·y** **adj.** [15th C.: from Fr. *zeste* 'orange or lemon peel,' of unknown origin.]

zest·er /'zestər/ ▶ **n.** a kitchen utensil for removing fine shreds of zest from citrus fruit.

ze·ta /'zātə; 'zē-/ ▶ **n.** the sixth letter of the Greek alphabet (Z, ζ), transliterated as 'z.'

ze·tet·ic /zə'tetik/ ▶ **adj.** rare proceeding by inquiry. [17th C.: from Gk. *zētētikos*, from *zētein* 'seek.']

zetta- ▶ **comb. form** (used in units of measurement) denoting a factor of 10^{21}: *zettahertz*. [appar. adapted from Ital. *sette* 'seven' (see also ZEPTO-).]

zeug·ma /'zōōgmə/ ▶ **n.** a figure of speech in which a word applies to two others in different senses (e.g., *John and his license expired last week*) or to two others of which it semantically suits only one (e.g., *with weeping eyes and hearts*). Compare with SYLLEPSIS. — **zeug·mat·ic** /zōōg'matik/ **adj.** [ME: via L. from Gk., from *zeugnunai* 'to yoke'; rel. to *zugon* 'yoke.']

Zeus /zōōs/ Gk. Mythol. the supreme god, the son of Cronus (whom he dethroned) and Rhea, and brother and husband of Hera. Zeus was the protector and ruler of humankind, the dispenser of good and evil, and the god of weather and atmospheric phenomena (such as rain and thunder). Roman equivalent JUPITER. [Gk.: rel. to Sanskrit *dyauḥ* 'sky.']

ZEV ▶ **abbr.** zero-emission vehicle.

Zhang·jia·kou /'jäNG'jyä'kō; -jē'ä'kō/ (also **Chang-chia·kow**) a city in northestern China, near the Great Wall; pop. 720,000. Mongolian name KALGAN.

Zhan·jiang /'jän'jyäNG; -jē'äNG/ (also **Chan-chiang**) a city in southern China; pop. 1,049,000.

Zhda·nov /'ZHdänəf/ former name (1948–89) of MARIUPOL.

Zhe·jiang /'jə'jyäNG; -jē'äNG/ (also **Che·kiang**) a province in eastern China; capital, Hangzhou.

Zheng·zhou /'jəNG'jō/ (also **Cheng·chow**) a city in northeastern central China; pop. 1,660,000.

Zhen·jiang /'jən'jyäNG; -jē'äNG/ (also **Chen-chiang, Chin·kiang**) a city in eastern China, on the Yangtze River; pop. 1,280,000.

Zhong·shan /'jōōNG'SHän/ (also **Chung-shan**) a city in southeastern China; pop. 1,073,000.

Zhou /jō/ (also **Chou**) a dynasty that ruled in China from the 11th century BC to 256 BC.

Zhou En·lai /'jō'en'lī/ (also **Chou En-lai**) (1898–1976), prime minister of China 1949–76. He was a founder of the Chinese Communist Party. He presided over the moves toward détente with the US in 1972–73.

Zhu·kov /'ZHōō,kôf; -,kôv; -kəf/, Georgi Konstantinovich (1896–1974), Soviet military leader; born in Russia. During World War II, he defeated the Germans at Stalingrad in 1943, and led the final assault on Germany and the capture of Berlin in 1945.

Z·ia ul-Haq /'zēə ŏŏl 'häk/, Muhammad (1924–88); president of Pakistan 1978–88.

zib·e·line /'zibə,līn; -,lēn; -lin/ ▶ **n.** **1** a thick soft fabric made of wool and other animal hair, such as mohair, with a flattened silky nap. **2** the fur of the sable. ▶ **adj.** of or pertaining to the sable.

Zi·bo /'zə'bō/ (also **Tzu-po**) a city in eastern China; pop. 2,484,000.

zi·do·vu·dine /zī'dävyə,dēn; zə-; -'dō-/ ▶ **n.** Med. an antiviral drug, $C_{10}H_{13}N_5O_4$, used in the treatment of AIDS. It slows the growth of HIV infection in the body, but is not curative. [1980s: arbitrary alt. of AZIDOTHYMIDINE.]

Zieg·feld /'zig,feld; -,fēld/, Florenz (1869–1932), US theater manager. His *Ziegfeld Follies* revues first appeared in 1907.

ZIF sock·et /zif/ ▶ **n.** a type of socket for mounting electronic devices that is designed not to stress or damage them during insertion. [20th C.: acronym from *zero insertion force*.]

zig /zig/ ▶ **n.** a sharp change of direction in a zigzag course: *he went round and round in zigs and zags*. ▶ **v.** (**zigged, zig·ging**) [intrans.] make a sharp change of direction: *we zigged to the right*. [1960s: by abbrev. of ZIGZAG.]

zig·gu·rat /'zigə,rat/ ▶ **n.** (in ancient Mesopotamia) a rectangular stepped tower, sometimes surmounted by a temple. Ziggurats are first attested in the late 3rd millennium BC and probably inspired the biblical story of the Tower of Babel (Gen. 11:1–9). [from Akkadian *ziqqurratu*.]

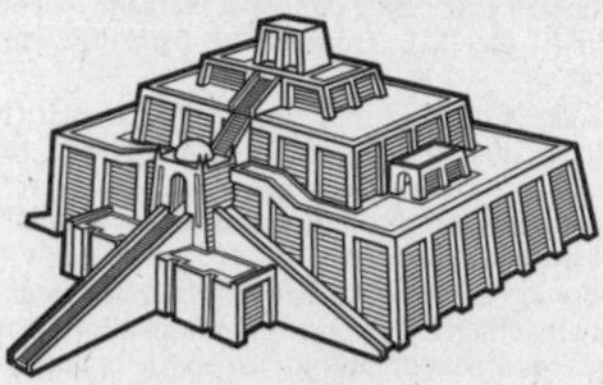

ziggurat

zig·zag /'zig,zag/ ▶ **n.** a line or course having abrupt alternate right and left turns. ■ a turn on such a course: *a series of sharp zigzags*. ▶ **adj.** having the form of a zigzag; veering to right and left alternately: *a zigzag course*. ▶ **adv.** so as to move right and left alternately. ▶ **v.** (**-zagged, -zag·ging**) [intrans.] have or move along in a zigzag course: *the path zigzagged*. — **zig·zag·ged·ly** /-,zagədlē/ **adv.** [18th C.: from Fr., from Ger. *Zickzack*, symbolic of alternation of direction, first applied to fortifications.]

zilch /zilCH/ informal ▶ **pron.** nothing: *I did absolutely zilch*. ▶ **adj.** not any; no: *the character has zilch class*. [1960s: of unknown origin.]

zil·lion /'zilyən/ ▶ **cardinal number** informal an extremely large number of people or things: ***zillions of bugs***. — **zil·lionth** /-yənTH/ **adj.** [1940s: from *Z* (perh. as a symbol of an unknown quantity) + MILLION.]

zil·lion·aire /,zilyə'ne(ə)r/ ▶ **n.** informal an extremely rich person.

Zim·bab·we /zim'bäbwā; -wē/ a country in southeastern Africa. *See box*. — **Zim·bab·we·an** /-wāən; -wēən/ **adj. & n.**

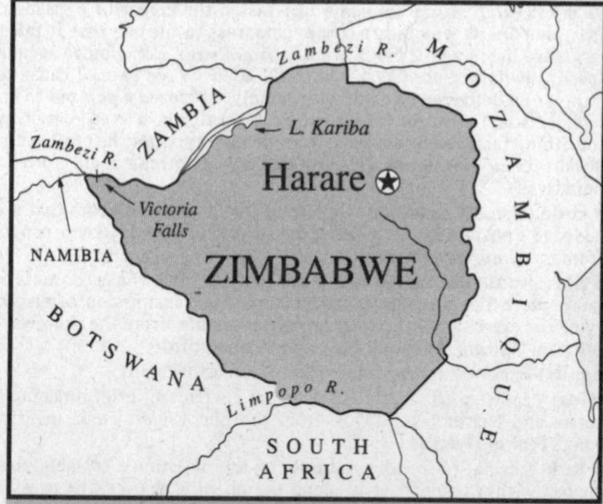

Zimbabwe

Official name: Republic of Zimbabwe
Location: southeastern Africa, west of Mozambique
Area: 150,800 square miles (390,600 sq km)
Population: 12,671,000
Capital: Harare
Languages: English (official), Shona, Ndebele, and others
Currency: Zimbabwean dollar

zinc /ziNGk/ ▶ **n.** the chemical element of atomic number 30, a silvery-white metal that is a constituent of brass and is used for coating (galvanizing) iron and steel to protect against corrosion. (Symbol: **Zn**) ■ [usu. as adj.] galvanized iron or steel, esp. as the material of domestic utensils or corrugated roofs. ▶ **v.** [trans.] [usu. as adj.] (**zinced**) coat (iron) with zinc or a zinc compound to prevent rust. [17th C.: from Ger. *Zink*, of unknown origin.]

zinc blende ▶ **n.** another term for SPHALERITE.

zinc·ite /'ziNG,kīt/ ▶ **n.** a rare deep red or orange-yellow mineral consisting chiefly of zinc oxide, occurring typically as granular or foliated masses. [19th C.: from ZINC + -ITE[1].]

zin·co /'ziNGkō/ ▶ **n.** (pl. **-cos**) an etched letterpress printing plate made of zinc.

zinc oint·ment (in full **zinc ox·ide oint·ment**) ▶ **n.** ointment containing zinc oxide, used for various skin conditions.

zinc ox·ide ▶ **n.** an insoluble white solid, ZnO, used as a pigment and in medicinal ointments.

zinc white ▶ **n.** a white pigment consisting of zinc oxide.

'zine /zēn/ (also **'zine**) ▶ **n.** informal a magazine, esp. a fanzine.

zin·eb /'zin,eb/ ▶ **n.** a white compound, $C_4H_6N_2S_4Zn$, used as a fungicidal powder on vegetables and fruit. [1950s: from *zin(c)* + *e(thylene)* + *b(is-)*, from the systematic name.]

Zin·fan·del /'zinfən,del/ ▶ **n.** a variety of wine grape grown in California. ■ a red or blush dry wine made from this grape. [of unknown origin.]

zing /ziNG/ informal ▶ **n.** energy, enthusiasm, or liveliness. ■ strong or piquant flavor. ▶ **v.** [no obj., with adverbial of direction] move swiftly: *an arrow zinging through the air*. ■ [trans.] attack or criticize sharply: *he zinged the mayor*. — **zing·y** **adj.** [20th C.: imitative.]

zing·er /'ziNGər/ ▶ **n.** informal a striking or amusing remark: *open a speech with a zinger*. ■ an outstanding person or thing: *a zinger of a shot*.

Zin·jan·thro·pus /,zin'janTHrəpəs; ,zinjan'THrō-/ ▶ **n.** a genus name sometimes applied to AUSTRALOPITHECUS. [1950s: mod. L., from Arab. *Zinj*, the early med. name for East Africa, + Gk. *anthrōpos* 'man.']

Zinne·mann /'zinəmən/, Fred (1907–97), US movie director; born in Austria. He won Academy Awards for *From Here to Eternity* (1953) and *A Man For All Seasons* (1966).

zin·ni·a /'zinēə/ ▶ **n.** an American plant (genus *Zinnia*) of the daisy family, widely cultivated for its bright showy flowers. [mod. L., named after Johann G. *Zinn* (1727–59), German physician and botanist.]

Zi·on /ˈzīən/ (also **Si·on**) ▶ **n.** the hill of Jerusalem on which the city of David was built. ■ the citadel of ancient Jerusalem. ■ Jerusalem. ■ (in Christian thought) the heavenly city or kingdom of heaven. ■ the Jewish people or religion. ■ the Christian Church. [OE, from eccles. L. *Sion*, from Heb. *ṣiyōn*.]

Zi·on·ism /ˈzīəˌnizəm/ ▶ **n.** a movement for (originally) the reestablishment and (now) the development and protection of a Jewish nation in Israel. It was established as a political organization in 1897 under Theodor Herzl, and was later led by Chaim Weizmann. — **Zi·on·ist n. & adj.**

zip /zip/ ▶ **v.** (**zipped, zip·ping**) **1** [trans.] fasten with a zipper: *I zipped up my sweater.* ■ (**zip someone up**) fasten the zipper of a garment that someone is wearing. ■ Comput. compress (a file) so that it takes less space in storage. **2** [no obj., with adverbial of direction] informal move at high speed: *swallows zipped back and forth.* ■ [with obj. and adverbial] cause to move or be delivered or dealt with rapidly: *he zipped a pass out to his receiver.* ▶ **n. 1** (also **zip fas·ten·er**) esp. Brit. a zipper. ■ [as adj.] denoting something fastened by a zipper. **2** informal energy; vigor: *he's full of zip.* **3** short for ZIP CODE. ▶ **pron.** (also **zip·po**) informal nothing at all. [19th C.: imitative.]

zip code (also **ZIP code**) ▶ **n.** a group of five or nine numbers that are added to a postal address to assist the sorting of mail. [1960s: acronym from *zone improvement plan*.]

zip file (also **ZIP file, zipped file**) ▶ **n.** a computer file whose contents of one or more files are compressed for storage or transmission, often carrying the extension .ZIP: *a self-extracting zip file.* [from the shareware program *WinZip*, a popular file compression utility.]

zip gun ▶ **n.** informal a cheap homemade or makeshift gun.

zip·less /ˈziplis/ ▶ **adj.** informal (of a sexual encounter) brief, uncomplicated, and passionless. [1970s: from the phr. *Zipless Fuck*, in Erica Jong's *Fear of Flying*.]

zip·lock /ˈzipˌläk/ (also trademark **Zip·loc**) ▶ **adj.** denoting a sealable plastic bag with a two-part strip along the opening that can be pressed together and readily reopened.

zip·per /ˈzipər/ ▶ **n. 1** a device consisting of two flexible strips of metal or plastic with interlocking projections closed or opened by pulling a slide along them, used to fasten garments, bags, and other items. **2** a display of news or advertisements that scrolls across an illuminated screen fixed to the upper part of a building. ▶ **v.** [trans.] fasten or provide (something) with a zipper.

zip·per·head /ˈzipərˌhed/ ▶ **n.** offens. an Asian person.

Zip·po /ˈzipō/ ▶ **n.** (pl. **-pos**) trademark a type of cigarette lighter with a hinged lid, using lighter fluid as fuel. [1930s: of unknown origin.]

zip·po /ˈzipō/ ▶ **pron.** another term for ZIP.

zip·py /ˈzipē/ ▶ **adj.** (**-pi·er, -pi·est**) informal bright, fresh, or lively: *a zippy, zingy, almost citrusy tang.* ■ fast or speedy: *zippy new sedans.* — **zip·pi·ly** /ˈzipəlē/ **adv. zip·pi·ness n.**

zip-up ▶ **adj.** [attrib.] esp. Brit. (of a garment, pocket, bag, etc.) able to be fastened with a zipper: *a zip-up jacket.*

zir·ca·loy /ˈzərkəˌloi/ ▶ **n.** an alloy of zirconium, tin, and other metals, used chiefly as cladding for nuclear reactor fuel. [1950s: from ZIRCONIUM + ALLOY.]

zir·con /ˈzərˌkän/ ▶ **n.** a mineral occurring as prismatic crystals, typically brown but sometimes in translucent forms of gem quality. It consists of zirconium silicate and is the chief ore of zirconium. [18th C.: from Ger. *Zirkon*.]

zir·co·ni·a /ˌzərˈkōnēə/ ▶ **n.** zirconium dioxide, ZrO_2, a white solid used in ceramic glazes and refractory coatings and as a synthetic substitute for diamonds in jewelry. Compare with CUBIC ZIRCONIA. [18th C.: from ZIRCON + -IA[1].]

zir·co·ni·um /ˌzərˈkōnēəm/ ▶ **n.** the chemical element of atomic number 40, a hard silver-gray metal of the transition series. (Symbol: **Zr**) [19th C.: mod. L., from ZIRCON.]

zit /zit/ ▶ **n.** informal a pimple on the skin. [1960s: of unknown origin; appar. orig. American teenagers' slang.]

zith·er /ˈziT͟Hər; ˈziTH-/ ▶ **n.** a musical instrument consisting of a flat wooden sound box with numerous strings stretched across it, placed horizontally and played with the fingers and a plectrum. It is used esp. in central European folk music. — **zith·er·ist** /-ərist/ **n.** [19th C.: from Ger., from L. *cithara* (see CITTERN).]

zi·ti /ˈzētē/ ▶ **n.** pasta in the form of tubes resembling large macaroni. [Ital.]

zi·zith /tsēˈtsēt/ ▶ **plural n.** Judaism the 613 fringes of thread, symbolizing the 613 commandments in the Hebrew Scriptures, formerly worn at the corners of the shawllike garment known as the tallith.

zlo·ty /ˈzlôtē; ˈzlät-/ ▶ **n.** (pl. same or **-tys**) the basic monetary unit of Poland, equal to 100 groszy. [Pol., lit. 'golden.']

Zn ▶ **symb.** the chemical element zinc.

zo- ▶ **comb.form** var. of **zoo-**, shortened before a vowel (as in *Zoantharia*)

Zo·an·thar·i·a /ˌzōənˈTHe(ə)rēə/ Zool. a group of coelenterates (subclass Zoantharia, class Anthozoa) with polyps that bear more than eight tentacles, including the sea anemones and stony corals. — **zo·an·thar·i·an n. & adj.** [mod. L. (pl.), from Gk. *zōion* 'animal' + *anthos* 'flower.']

zo·ca·lo /ˈsōkəˌlō; sôˈkäˌlō/ ▶ **n.** (in Mexico) a public square or plaza.

zo·di·ac /ˈzōdēˌak/ ▶ **n.** Astrol. a belt of the heavens within about 8° either side of the ecliptic, including all apparent positions of the sun, moon, and planets, and divided by astrologers into twelve equal divisions or signs. ■ a representation of the signs of the zodiac or of a similar astrological system. — **zo·di·a·cal** /zōˈdīəkəl/ **adj.** [ME: from OFr. *zodiaque*, via L. from Gk. *zōidiakos*, from *zōidion* 'sculptured animal figure,' dimin. of *zōion* 'animal.']

zo·di·a·cal light ▶ **n.** Astron. a faint elongated cone of light sometimes seen in the night sky, extending from the horizon along the ecliptic. It is thought to be due to the reflection of sunlight from particles of ice and dust within the plane of the solar system.

zo·di·a·cal sign ▶ **n.** see SIGN (sense 3).

zo·e·a /zōˈēə/ ▶ **n.** (pl. **zo·e·ae** /zōˈēˌē/ or **zo·e·as**) a larval form of certain crustaceans, such as the crab, having a spiny carapace and rudimentary limbs on the abdomen and thorax.

zo·e·trope /ˈzō-ēˌtrōp/ ▶ **n.** a 19th-century optical toy consisting of a cylinder with a series of pictures on the inner surface that, when viewed through slits with the cylinder rotating, give an impression of continuous motion. [19th C.: formed irregularly from Gk. *zōē* 'life' + *-tropos* 'turning.']

zof·tig ▶ **adj.** var. of ZAFTIG.

Zog I /zôg/ (1895–1961), king of Albania 1928–39; full name *Ahmed Bey Zogu*.

Zo·har /ˈzōˌhär/ ▶ **n.** the chief text of the Jewish Kabbalah, presented as an allegorical or mystical interpretation of the Pentateuch. [from Heb. *zōhar*, lit. 'light, splendor.']

-zo·ic ▶ **suffix 1** forming adjectives relating to a particular manner of animal existence (such as *cryptozoic*). **2** of or relating to a particular geologic era (such as *Paleozoic*).

zois·ite /ˈzoiˌsīt/ ▶ **n.** a grayish-white or grayish-green crystalline mineral of the epidote group consisting of a hydroxyl silicate of calcium and aluminum. [19th C.: from the name of Baron S. von Edelstein *Zois* (1747–1819), Austrian scholar, + -ITE[1].]

Zo·la /ˌzōˈlä; ˈzōˌlä/, Émile Édouard Charles Antoine (1840–1902), French writer. His 20 novels collectively entitled *Les Rougon-Macquart* (1871–93) include *Nana* (1880) and *Germinal* (1885).

zom·bie /ˈzämbē/ ▶ **n. 1** originally, a snake-deity of or deriving from West Africa and Haiti. **2** a soulless corpse said to be revived by witchcraft, esp. in certain African and Caribbean religions. ■ informal a person who is or appears lifeless, apathetic, or completely unresponsive to their surroundings. **3** a tall mixed drink consisting of several kinds of rum, liqueur, and fruit juice. — **zom·bie·like** /-ˌlīk/ **adj.** [19th C.: of West Afr. origin; cf. Kikongo *zumbi* 'fetish.']

zom·bi·fy /ˈzämbəˌfī/ ▶ **v.** [trans.] [usu. as adj.] (**zombified**) informal deprive of energy or vitality.

zo·na pel·lu·ci·da /ˈzōnə pəˈlo͞osədə/ ▶ **n.** (pl. **zo·nae pel·lu·ci·dae** /ˈzōˌnē pəˈlo͞osəˌdē; ˈzōˌnī pəˈlo͞osəˌdī/) Anat. Zool. the thick transparent membrane surrounding a mammalian ovum before implantation. [19th C.: from L., lit. 'pellucid girdle.']

zo·na·tion /zōˈnāSHən/ ▶ **n.** distribution in zones or regions of definite character. ■ Ecol. the distribution of plants or animals into specific zones according to such parameters as altitude or depth, each characterized by its dominant species.

zone /zōn/ ▶ **n. 1** [usu. with adj.] an area or stretch of land having a particular characteristic, purpose, or use, or subject to particular restrictions: *a pedestrian zone.* ■ Geog. a well-defined region extending around the earth between definite limits, esp. between two parallels of latitude: *a zone of easterly winds.* ■ (also **time zone**) a range of longitudes where a common standard time is used. ■ a specific region or area within which uniform rates are charged for transportation, parcel post delivery, or other service. ■ esp. Bot. Zool. an encircling band or stripe of distinctive color, texture, or character. **2** archaic a belt or girdle worn around a person's body. **3** Math. an area between two exact or approximate concentric circles. ■ a part of the surface of a sphere enclosed between two parallel planes, or of a cone or cylinder, etc., between such planes cutting it perpendicularly to the axis. **4** Geol. Paleontol. a range between specified limits of depth, height, etc., esp. a section of strata distinguished by characteristic fossils. ▶ **v.** [trans.] **1** divide into or assign to zones, in particular: ■ [often as n.] (**zoning**) divide (a town or stretch of land) into areas subject to particular planning restrictions. ■ designate (a specific area) for use or development in such a manner: *the land is zoned for housing.* **2** archaic encircle as or with a band or stripe.

– PHRASAL VERBS **zone out** informal fall asleep or lose concentration or consciousness: *I just zoned out for a moment.* — **zon·al** /ˈzōnl/ **adj.** **zon·al·ly** /ˈzōnl-ē/ **adv.** [ME: from Fr., or from L. *zona* 'girdle,' from Gk. *zōnē*.]

zoned /zōnd/ ▶ **adj. 1** divided into zones, in particular (of land) designated for a particular type of use or development: *zoned industrial land.* **2** esp. Bot. Zool. marked with circles or bands of color: *strongly zoned leaves.* **3** informal under the influence of drugs or alcohol. [1970s: blend of ZONKED and STONED.]

zone de·fense ▶ **n.** Sports in basketball, football, and hockey, a system of defensive play in which each player guards an allotted area of the field of play and guards an opponent only when the opponent is in his area.

zone plate ▶ **n.** a plate of glass marked out into concentric zones or rings alternately transparent and opaque, used like a lens to bring light to a focus.

zonk /zäNGk; zôNGk/ informal ▶ **v. 1** [trans.] hit or strike. **2** fall or cause to fall suddenly and heavily asleep or lose consciousness: [intrans.] *I always just zonk out* | [trans.] *rowing zonks me out.* [1940s: imitative.]

zonked /zäNGkt; zôNGkt/ ▶ **adj.** informal under the influence of drugs or alcohol: ***a zonked-out beach bum.*** ■ exhausted; tired out.

zon·ule /ˈzōn,yo͞ol/ ▶ **n.** tech., esp. Anat. a small zone, band, or belt.

zoo /zo͞o/ ▶ **n.** an establishment that maintains a collection of wild animals, typically in a park or gardens, for study, conservation, or display to the public. [19th C.: abbrev. of ZOOLOGICAL GARDEN, orig. applied specifically to that of Regent's Park, London.] ■ informal a situation characterized by confusion and disorder: ***it's a zoo in the lobby.*** — **zoo·ey adj.** (informal).

zoo- ▶ **comb. form** of animals; relating to animal life: *zoogeography.* [from Gk. *zōion* 'animal.']

zo·o·gen·ic /,zōəˈjenik/ ▶ **adj. 1** produced by or originating in animals. **2** related or pertaining to animal development or evolution.

zoo·ge·og·ra·phy /,zōəjēˈägrəfē/ ▶ **n.** the branch of zoology that deals with the geographical distribution of animals. — **zo·o·ge·og·ra·pher** /-fər/ **n.** **zo·o·ge·o·graph·ic** /-,jēəˈgrafik/ **adj.** **zo·o·ge·o·graph·i·cal** /-,jēəˈgrafikəl/ **adj.** **zo·o·ge·o·graph·i·cal·ly** /-jēəˈgrafik(ə)lē/ **adv.**

zo·oid /ˈzō,oid/ ▶ **n.** Zool. an animal arising from another by budding or division, esp. each of the individuals that make up a colonial organism and typically have different forms and functions. — **zo·oi·dal** /,zōˈoidl/ **adj.** [19th C.: from ZOO- 'relating to animals' + -OID.]

zoo·keep·er /ˈzo͞o,kēpər/ ▶ **n.** an animal attendant employed in a zoo.

zool. ▶ **abbr.** ■ zoological. ■ zoologist. ■ zoology.

zo·ol·a·try /zōˈälətrē; zo͞o-/ ▶ **n.** rare the worship of animals.

zo·o·log·i·cal /,zōəˈläjikəl; ,zo͞oə-/ ▶ **adj.** of or relating to zoology: *zoological classification.* ■ of or relating to animals: *eighty zoological woodcuts.* — **zo·o·log·i·cal·ly** /-ik(ə)lē/ **adv.**

zo·o·log·i·cal gar·den ▶ **n.** dated a zoo.

zo·ol·o·gy /zōˈäləjē; zo͞o-/ ▶ **n.** the scientific study of the behavior, structure, physiology, classification, and distribution of animals. ■ the animal life of a particular area or time. — **zo·ol·o·gist** /-jist/ **n.** [17th C.: from mod. L. *zoologia* (see ZOO-, -LOGY).]

zoom /zo͞om/ ▶ **v.** [no obj., with adverbial of direction] **1** (esp. of a car or aircraft) move or travel very quickly. ■ [intrans.] (of prices) rise sharply. **2** (of a camera) change smoothly from a long shot to a close-up or vice versa. ■ [trans.] cause (a lens or camera) to do this. ▶ **n.** a camera shot that changes smoothly from a long shot to a close-up or vice versa. ■ short for ZOOM LENS. ▶ **exclam.** used to express sudden fast movement. [19th C.: imitative.]

zoom lens ▶ **n.** a lens allowing a camera to change smoothly from a long shot to a close-up or vice versa by varying the focal length.

zo·o·mor·phic /,zōəˈmôrfik/ ▶ **adj.** having or representing animal forms or gods of animal form. — **zo·o·mor·phism** /-ˈmôr,fizəm/ **n.** [19th C.: from ZOO- 'of animals' + Gk. *morphē* 'form' + -IC.]

zo·on·o·sis /zōəˈnōsəs; zōˈänə-/ ▶ **n.** (pl. **-ses** /-,sēz/) a disease that can be transmitted to humans from animals. — **zo·o·not·ic** /,zōəˈnätik/ **adj.** [19th C.: from ZOO- 'of animals' + Gk. *nosos* 'disease.']

zo·o·phyte /ˈzōə,fīt/ ▶ **n.** Zool., dated a plantlike animal, esp. a coral, sea anemone, sponge, or sea lily. [17th C.: from Gk. *zōiophuton* (see ZOO-, -PHYTE).]

zo·o·plank·ton /ˈzōə,plaNGktən/ ▶ **n.** Biol. plankton consisting of small animals and the immature stages of larger animals.

zo·o·spo·ran·gi·um /,zōəspəˈranjēəm/ ▶ **n.** Bot. (pl. **-gi·a** /-jēə/) a sporangium or spore case in which zoospores develop.

zo·o·spore /ˈzōə,spôr/ ▶ **n.** Biol. a spore of certain algae, fungi, and protozoans, capable of swimming by means of a flagellum. Also called SWARMER.

zoot suit /zo͞ot/ ▶ **n.** a man's suit of an exaggerated style, characterized by a long loose jacket with padded shoulders and high-waisted tapering trousers, popular in the 1940s. [1940s: rhyming formation on SUIT.]

zo·ri /ˈzôrē/ ▶ **n.** (pl. **zo·ris**) a traditional Japanese style of flip-flop, originally made with a straw sole. [Japanese.]

zo·ril·la /zəˈrilə/ (also **zo·ril** or **zo·rille** /ˈzôril; ˈzär-/) ▶ **n.** a black and white carnivorous mammal (*Ictonyx striatus*) of the weasel family that resembles a skunk, inhabiting arid regions of southern Africa. [18th C.: via Fr. from Sp. *zorrilla*, dimin. of *zorro* 'fox.']

Zo·ro·as·ter /ˈzôrō,astər/ (*c.*628–*c.*551 BC), Persian prophet; Avestan name *Zarathustra.* He founded Zoroastrianism.

Zo·ro·as·tri·an·ism /,zôrōˈastrēə,nizəm/ ▶ **n.** a monotheistic pre-Islamic religion of ancient Persia founded by Zoroaster in the 6th century BC. — **Zo·ro·as·tri·an adj. & n.**

zos·ter /ˈzästər/ ▶ **n. 1** short for HERPES ZOSTER. **2** (in ancient Greece) a belt or girdle.

Zou·ave /zo͞oˈäv; zwäv/ ▶ **n. 1** a member of a light-infantry corps in the French army, originally formed of Algerians and long retaining their oriental uniform. ■ a member of such an infantry unit patterned on the French Zouaves, esp. in the Union Army in the Civil War. **2** (**zouaves**) dated women's trousers with wide tops, tapering to a narrow ankle. [19th C.: from Fr., from Kabyle *Zouaoua*, the name of a tribe.]

Zoug /zo͞og/ French name for ZUG.

zouk /zo͞ok/ ▶ **n.** an exuberant style of popular music combining Caribbean and Western elements and having a fast heavy beat. [1970s: Guadeloupian Creole, lit. 'to party.']

zounds /zoundz/ ▶ **exclam.** archaic humorous expressing surprise or indignation. [16th C.: contr. from *(God)'s wounds* (i.e., those of Christ on the Cross).]

Zo·vi·rax /zōˈvī,raks/ ▶ **n.** trademark for ACYCLOVIR.

zow·ie /ˈzou-ē; zouˈē/ ▶ **exclam.** informal expressing astonishment or admiration. [natural exclamation: first recorded in Amer. Engl. in the early 20th C.]

zoy·si·a /ˈzoisēə; -zēə; -SHə; -ZHə/ ▶ **n.** a low-growing grass of the genus *Zoysia*, native to tropical Asia and New Zealand and widely used for lawns.

Z par·ti·cle ▶ **n.** Physics a heavy, uncharged elementary particle considered to transmit the weak interaction between other elementary particles.

ZPG ▶ **abbr.** zero population growth.

Z-plas·ty /ˈzē,plastē/ ▶ **n.** a technique in orthopedic and cosmetic surgery in which one or more Z-shaped incisions are made, the diagonals forming one straight line, and the two triangular sections so formed are drawn across the diagonal before being stitched.

Zr ▶ **symb.** the chemical element zirconium.

zuc·chet·to /(t)so͞oˈketō; zo͞o-/ ▶ **n.** (pl. **-tos**) a Roman Catholic cleric's skullcap: black for a priest, purple for a bishop, red for a cardinal, and white for the pope. [19th C.: from Ital. *zucchetta*, dimin. of *zucca* 'gourd, head.']

zuc·chi·ni /zo͞oˈkēnē/ ▶ **n.** (pl. same or **-nis**) a green variety of smooth-skinned summer squash. [Ital., pl. of *zucchino*, dimin. of *zucca* 'gourd.']

Zug /tso͞ok; zo͞og/ a canton in central Switzerland. ■ its capital; pop. 21,000. French name ZOUG.

zug·zwang /ˈzəg,zwaNG; ˈtso͞og,tsvaNG/ ▶ **n.** Chess a situation in which the obligation to make a move in one's turn is a serious, often decisive, disadvantage: *black is in zugzwang.* [20th C.: from Ger. *Zug* 'move' + *Zwang* 'compulsion.']

Zui·der Zee /,zīdər ˈzē; ˈzā/ a former shallow inlet of the North Sea, in the Netherlands. Large parts of it have been drained and reclaimed as polders.

Zu·kor /ˈzo͞okər/, Adolph (1873–1973), US movie producer and executive; born in Hungary. He created the Famous Players Co. in 1912; it eventually became Paramount Pictures with Zukor at the head.

Zu·lu /ˈzo͞olo͞o/ ▶ **n. 1** a member of a South African people living mainly in KwaZulu-Natal province. ■ the Nguni language of this people. **2** a code word representing the letter Z, used in radio communication. ▶ **adj.** of or relating to the Zulu people or language. [from the stem of Zulu *umZulu* (pl. *amaZulu*).]

Zu·ni /ˈzo͞onē/ (also **Zu·ñi** /ˈzo͞onyē/) ▶ **n.** (pl. same or **Zu·nis**) **1** a member of a Pueblo Indian people of western New Mexico. **2** the language of this people. ▶ **adj.** of or relating to this people or their language. [from Sp. *Zuñi*, prob. from Keresan.]

zup·pa in·gle·se /ˈtso͞opə iNGˈglāzā; ˈzo͞opə; -zē/ ▶ **n.** a rich Italian dessert resembling trifle. [Ital., lit. 'English soup.']

Zu·rich /ˈzo͞orik/ a city in northern central Switzerland, on Lake Zurich; pop. 343,000.

zwie·back /ˈswē,bak; ˈzwē-; ˈswī-; ˈzwī-/ ▶ **n.** a rusk or cracker made by baking a small loaf and then toasting slices until they are dry and crisp. [Ger., lit. 'twice-bake.']

Zwing·li /ˈzwiNG(g)lē; ˈswiNG-; ˈtsfiNG-/, Ulrich (1484–1531), Swiss reformer. He was the principal figure of the Swiss Reformation. — **Zwing·li·an** /-lēən/ **adj. & n.**

zwit·ter·i·on /ˈ(t)switər,īən/ ▶ **n.** Chem. a molecule or ion having separate positively and negatively charged groups. — **zwit·ter·i·on·ic** /,(t)switər-īˈänik/ **adj.** [20th C.: from Ger., from *Zwitter* 'a hybrid' + *Ion* 'ion.']

Zwor·y·kin /ˈzwôrikən; ˈzvôr-/, Vladimir Kuzmich (1889–1982), US physicist; born in Russia. He pioneered in the development of the television camera.

zy·de·co /ˈzīdə,kō/ ▶ **n.** a kind of black American dance music originally from southern Louisiana, typically featuring accordion and guitar. [1960s: Louisiana Creole, possibly from a pronunc. of Fr. *les haricots* in a dance-tune title.]

zyg·a·poph·y·sis /,zigəˈpäfəsis; ,zīgə-/ ▶ **n.** one of the two paired processes of a vertebra that interlock it with the adjacent vertebrae.

zygo- ▶ **comb. form** relating to joining or pairing: *zygodactyl.* [from Gk. *zugon* 'yoke.']

zy·go·dac·tyl /,zīgōˈdaktl/ ▶ **adj.** (of a bird's feet) having two toes pointing forward and two backward. ▶ **n.** a bird with zygodactyl feet. — **zy·go·dac·ty·lous** /-ˈdaktl-əs/ **adj.**

zy·go·ma /zīˈgōmə/ ▶ **n.** (pl. **-ma·ta** /-mətə/) Anat. the bony arch of the cheek formed by connection of the zygomatic and temporal bones. — **zy·go·mat·ic** /,zīgəˈmatik/ **adj.** [17th C.: from Gk. *zugōma*, from *zugon* 'yoke.']

zy·go·mat·ic arch ▶ **n.** Anat. the zygoma.

zy·go·mat·ic bone ▶ **n.** Anat. the bone that forms the prominent part of the cheek and the outer side of the eye socket.

zy·go·mat·ic proc·ess ▶ **n.** Anat. a projection of the temporal bone that forms part of the zygoma.

zy·go·mor·phic /,zīgəˈmôrfik/ ▶ **adj.** Bot. (of a flower) having only one plane of symmetry, as in a pea or snapdragon; bilaterally symmetrical. Compare with ACTINOMORPHIC. — **zy·go·mor·phy** /ˈzīgə,môrfē/ **n.**

zy·go·spore /ˈzīgə,spôr/ ▶ **n.** Biol. the thick-walled resting cell of certain fungi and algae, arising from the fusion of two similar gametes. Compare with OOSPORE.

zy·gote /ˈzīˌgōt/ ▶**n.** Biol. a diploid cell resulting from the fusion of two haploid gametes; a fertilized ovum. — **zy·got·ic** /zīˈgätik/ **adj.** [19th C.: from Gk. *zugōtos* 'yoked,' from *zugoun* 'to yoke.']

zy·go·tene /ˈzīgəˌtēn/ ▶**n.** Biol. the second stage of the prophase of meiosis, following leptotene, during which homologous chromosomes begin to pair.

zy·mase /ˈzīˌmās; -ˌmāz/ ▶**n.** Biochem. a mixture of enzymes obtained from yeast that catalyze the breakdown of sugars in alcoholic fermentation. [19th C.: from Fr., from Gk. *zumē* 'leaven.']

zymo- (also **zym-** before a vowel) ▶**comb. form** relating to enzymes or fermentation: *zymogen* | *zymase.* [from Gk. *zumē* 'leaven.']

zy·mo·gen /ˈzīməjən/ ▶**n.** Biochem. an inactive substance that is converted into an enzyme when activated by another enzyme.

zy·mur·gy /ˈzīˌmərjē/ ▶**n.** the study or practice of fermentation in brewing, winemaking, or distilling. [19th C.: from Gk. *zumē* 'leaven,' on the pattern of *metallurgy.*]